C++

HOW TO PROGRAM

FIFTH EDITION

Pearson International Edition

D1455843

How To Program Series

Advanced Java™ 2 Platform How to Program
C How to Program, 4/E
C++ How to Program, 5/E
C# How to Program
e-Business and e-Commerce How to Program
Internet and World Wide Web How to Program, 3/E
Java How to Program, 6/E
Small C++ How to Program, 5/E
Small Java™ How to Program, 6/E
Perl How to Program
Python How to Program
Visual C++® .NET How to Program
Visual Basic® 6 How to Program
Visual Basic® .NET How to Program, 2/E
Wireless Internet & Mobile Business How to Program
XML How to Program

Simply Series

Simply C++: An Application-Driven
  Tutorial Approach
Simply C#: An Application-Driven
  Tutorial Approach
Simply Java™ Programming: An
  Application-Driven Tutorial Approach
Simply Visual Basic® .NET: An
  Application Driven Tutorial Approach
  (Visual Studio .NET 2002 Edition)
Simply Visual Basic® .NET: An
  Application Driven Tutorial Approach
  (Visual Studio .NET 2003 Edition)

For Managers Series

e-Business and e-Commerce for
  Managers

.NET How to Program Series

C# How to Program
Visual Basic® .NET How to Program, 2/E
Visual C++® .NET How to Program

Visual Studio® Series

C# How to Program
Visual Basic® .NET How to Program, 2/E
Getting Started with Microsoft® Visual
  C++® 6 with an Introduction to MFC
Visual Basic® 6 How to Program

Also Available

e-books
CourseCompass, WebCT and
  Blackboard support
Pearson Choices: SafariX

Multimedia Cyber Classroom and Web-Based Training Series

C++ Multimedia Cyber Classroom, 5/E

C# Multimedia Cyber Classroom

e-Business and e-Commerce Multimedia Cyber Classroom

Internet and World Wide Web Multimedia Cyber Classroom, 2/E

Java™ Multimedia Cyber Classroom, 6/E

Perl Multimedia Cyber Classroom

Python Multimedia Cyber Classroom

Visual Basic® 6 Multimedia Cyber Classroom

Visual Basic® .NET Multimedia Cyber Classroom, 2/E

Wireless Internet & Mobile Business Programming Multimedia Cyber Classroom

XML Multimedia Cyber Classroom

The Complete Training Course Series

The Complete C++ Training Course, 4/E

The Complete C# Training Course

The Complete e-Business and e-Commerce Programming Training Course

The Complete Internet and World Wide Web Programming Training Course, 2/E

The Complete Java™ 2 Training Course, 5/E

The Complete Perl Training Course

The Complete Python Training Course

The Complete Visual Basic® 6 Training Course

The Complete Visual Basic® .NET Training Course, 2/E

The Complete Wireless Internet & Mobile Business Programming Training Course

The Complete XML Programming Training Course

To follow the Deitel publishing program, please register at:

    `www.deitel.com/newsletter/subscribe.html`

for the free *DEITEL® BUZZ ONLINE* e-mail newsletter.

To communicate with the authors, send e-mail to:

    `deitel@deitel.com`

For information on corporate on-site seminars offered by Deitel & Associates, Inc. worldwide, visit:

    `www.deitel.com or write to deitel@deitel.com`

For continuing updates on Prentice Hall/Deitel publications visit:

    `www.deitel.com,`
    `www.prenhall.com/deitel or`
    `www.InformIT.com/deitel`

Vice President and Editorial Director, ECS: **Marcia J. Horton**
Senior Acquisitions Editor: **Kate Hargett**
Associate Editor: **Jennifer Cappello**
Assistant Editor: **Sarah Parker**
Editorial Assistant: **Michael Giacobbe**
Executive Managing Editor: **Vince O'Brien**
Managing Editor: **Tom Manshreck**
Production Editor: **John F. Lovell**
Production Editor, Media: **Bob Engelhardt**
Production Assistant: **Asha Rohra**
Director of Creative Services: **Paul Belfanti**
A/V Production Editor: **Xiaohong Zhu**
Art Studio: **Artworks, York, PA**
Art Director: **Kristine Carney**
Cover Design: **Abbey S. Deitel, Harvey M. Deitel, Francesco Santalucia, Geoffrey Cassar**
Interior Design: **Harvey M. Deitel, Geoffrey Cassar**
Assistant Manufacturing Manager: **Michael Bell**
Manufacturing Buyer: **Lisa McDowell**
Marketing Manager: **Pamela Hersperger**
Marketing Assistant: **Barrie Reinhold**

Printed in the People's Republic of China

10 9 8 7 6 5 4 3 2 1

ISBN 0-13-197109-3

Pearson Education Ltd., *London*
Pearson Education Australia Pty. Ltd., *Sydney*
Pearson Education Singapore, Pte. Ltd.
Pearson Education North Asia Ltd., *Hong Kong*
Pearson Education Canada, Inc., *Toronto*
Pearson Educacion de Mexico, S.A. de C.V.
Pearson Education–Japan, *Tokyo*
Pearson Education Malaysia, Pte. Ltd.
Pearson Education, Inc., *Upper Saddle River, New Jersey*

C++

HOW TO PROGRAM

FIFTH EDITION

Pearson International Edition

H. M. Deitel

Deitel & Associates, Inc.

P. J. Deitel

Deitel & Associates, Inc.

Pearson Education International

Trademarks

Borland and C++ Builder are trademarks or registered trademarks of Borland.

Cygwin is a trademark and copyrighted work of Red Hat, Inc. in the United States and other countries.

Dive Into is a registered trademark of Deitel & Associates, Inc.

GNU is a trademark of the Free Software Foundation.

Java and all Java-based marks are trademarks or registered trademarks of Sun Microsystems, Inc. in the United States and other countries. Pearson Education is independent of Sun Microsystems, Inc.

Linux is a registered trademark of Linus Torvalds.

Microsoft, Microsoft® Internet Explorer and the Windows logo are either registered trademarks or trademarks of Microsoft Corporation in the United States and/or other countries.

Netscape browser window © 2004 Netscape Communications Corporation. Used with permission. Netscape Communications has not authorized, sponsored, endorsed, or approved this publication and is not responsible for its content.

Object Management Group, OMG, Unified Modeling Language and UML are trademarks of Object Management Group, Inc.

To:

Stephen Clamage

Chairman of the J16 committee, "Programming Language
C++" that is responsible for the C++ standard; Senior Staff
Engineer, Sun Microsystems, Inc., Software Division.

Don Kostuch

Independent Consultant

and Mike Miller

Former Vice Chairman and Core Language Working Group
Chairman of the J16 committee, "Programming Language
C++;" Software Design Engineer, Edison Design Group, Inc.

For your mentorship, friendship, and tireless devotion
to insisting that we "get it right" and helping us do so.

It is a privilege to work with such consummate
C++ professionals.

Harvey M. Deitel and Paul J. Deitel

Contents

18   Class string and String Stream Processing   877

19   Web Programming   905

20   Searching and Sorting   969

F   Preprocessor   1212

G   ATM Case Study Code   1225

H   UML 2: Additional Diagram Types   1257

Preface

"The chief merit of language is clearness ... "
—Galen

Welcome to C++ and *C++ How to Program, Fifth Edition*! C++ is a world-class programming language for developing industrial-strength, high-performance computer applications. We believe that this book and its support materials have everything instructors and students need for an informative, interesting, challenging and entertaining C++ educational experience. In this Preface, we overview the many new features of *C++ How to Program, 5/e*. The *Tour of the Book* section of the Preface gives instructors, students and professionals a sense of *C++ How to Program, 5/e's* coverage of C++ and object-oriented programming. We also overview various conventions used in the book, such as syntax coloring the code examples, "code washing" and code highlighting. We provide information about free compilers that you can find on the Web. We also discuss the comprehensive suite of educational materials that help instructors maximize their students' learning experience, including the Instructor's Resource material contained on the Instructor's version of the *Deitel Cyber Classroom*, PowerPoint® Slide lecture notes, course management systems, SafariX (Pearson Education's WebBook publications) and more. (Instructors who wish to know more about the *Deitel Cyber Classroom* should e-mail asia@pearsoned.com.hk, or telephone 852-31810884 or fax 852-27592391.)

Features of C++ How to Program, 5/e

At Deitel & Associates, we write college-level computer science textbooks and professional books. To create *C++ How to Program, 5/e*, we put the previous edition of *C++ How to Program* under the microscope. The new edition has many compelling features:

- **Major Content Revisions.** All the chapters have been significantly updated and upgraded. We tuned the writing for clarity and precision. We also adjusted our use of C++ terminology in accordance with the ANSI/ISO C++ standard document that defines the language.

- **Smaller Chapters.** Larger chapters have been divided into smaller, more manageable chapters (e.g., Chapter 1 of the Fourth Edition has been split into Chapters 1–2; Chapter 2 of the Fourth Edition is now Chapters 4–5).

- **Early Classes and Objects Approach.** We changed to an early classes and objects pedagogy. Students are introduced to the basic concepts and terminology of object technology in Chapter 1. In the previous edition, students began developing customized, reusable classes and objects in Chapter 6, but in this edition, they do so in our completely new Chapter 3. Chapters 4–7 have been carefully rewritten from an "early classes and objects" perspective. This new edition is object oriented, where appropriate, from the start and throughout the text. Moving the discussion of objects and classes to earlier chapters gets students "thinking about objects" immediately and mastering these concepts more completely. Object-oriented programming is not trivial by any means, but it's fun to write object-oriented programs, and students can see immediate results.

- **Integrated Case Studies.** We have added several case studies spanning multiple sections and chapters that often build on a class introduced earlier in the book to demonstrate new programming concepts later in the book. These case studies include the development of the GradeBook class in Chapters 3–7, the Time class in several sections of Chapters 9–10, the Employee class in Chapters 12–13, and the optional OOD/UML ATM case study in Chapters 1-7, 9, 13 and Appendix G.

- **Integrated GradeBook Case Study.** We added a new GradeBook case study to reinforce our early classes presentation. It uses classes and objects in Chapters 3–7 to incrementally build a GradeBook class that represents an instructor's grade book and performs various calculations based on a set of student grades, such as calculating the average grade, finding the maximum and minimum and printing a bar chart.

- **Unified Modeling Language™ 2.0 (UML 2.0)—Introducing the UML 2.0.** The Unified Modeling Language (UML) has become the preferred graphical modeling language for designers of object-oriented systems. All the UML diagrams in the book comply with the new UML 2.0 specification. We use UML class diagrams to visually represent classes and their inheritance relationships, and we use UML activity diagrams to demonstrate the flow of control in each of C++'s control statements. We make especially heavy use of the UML in the optional OOD/UML ATM case study

- **Optional OOD/UML ATM Case Study.** We replaced the optional elevator simulator case study from the previous edition with a new optional OOD/UML automated teller machine (ATM) case study in the Software Engineering Case Study sections of Chapters 1–7, 9 and 13. The new case study is simpler, smaller, more "real world" and more appropriate for first and second programming courses. The nine case study sections present a carefully paced introduction to object-oriented design using the UML. We introduce a concise, simplified subset of the UML 2.0, then guide the reader through a first design experience intended for the novice object-oriented designer/programmer. Our goal in this case study is to help students develop an object-oriented design to complement the object-oriented programming concepts they begin learning in Chapter 1 and implementing in Chapter 3. The case study was reviewed by a distinguished team of OOD/UML academic and industry professionals. The case study is not an exercise; rather, it is a fully developed end-to-end learning experience that concludes with a detailed walkthrough of the complete 877-line C++ code implementation. We take a detailed tour of the nine sections of this case study later in the Preface.

- **Compilation and Linking Process for Multiple-Source-File Programs.** Chapter 3 includes a detailed diagram and discussion of the compilation and linking process that produces an executable application.

- **Function Call Stack Explanation.** In Chapter 6, we provide a detailed discussion (with illustrations) of the function call stack and activation records to explain how C++ is able to keep track of which function is currently executing, how automatic variables of functions are maintained in memory and how a function knows where to return after it completes execution.

- **Early Introduction of C++ Standard Library `string` and `vector` Objects.** The `string` and `vector` classes are used to make earlier examples more object-oriented.

- **Class `string`.** We use class `string` instead of C-like pointer-based char * strings for most string manipulations throughout the book. We continue to include discussions of char * strings in Chapter 8, 10, 11 and 22 to give students practice with pointer manipulations, to illustrate dynamic memory allocation with new and delete, to build our own String class, and to prepare students for assignments in industry where they will work with char * strings in C and C++ legacy code.

- **Class Template `vector`.** We use class template `vector` instead of C-like pointer-based array manipulations throughout the book. However, we begin by discussing C-like pointer-based arrays in Chapter 7 to prepare students for working with C and C++ legacy code in industry and to use as a basis for building our own customized Array class in Chapter 11, Operating Overloading.

- **Tuned Treatment of Inheritance and Polymorphism.** Chapters 12–13 have been carefully tuned, making the treatment of inheritance and polymorphism clearer and more accessible for students who are new to OOP. An Employee hierarchy replaces the Point/Circle/Cylinder hierarchy used in prior editions to introduce inheritance and polymorphism. The new hierarchy is more natural.

- **Discussion and Illustration of How Polymorphism Works "Under the Hood."** Chapter 13 contains a detailed diagram and explanation of how C++ can implement polymorphism, virtual functions and dynamic binding internally. This gives students a solid understanding of how these capabilities really work. More importantly, it helps students appreciate the overhead of polymorphism—in terms of additional memory consumption and processor time. This helps students determine when to use polymorphism and when to avoid it.

- **Web Programming.** Chapter 19, Web Programming, has everything readers need to begin developing their own Web-based applications that will run on the Internet! Students will learn how to build so-called *n*-tier applications, in which the functionality provided by each tier can be distributed to separate computers across the Internet or executed on the same computer. Using the popular Apache HTTP server (which is available free for download from www.apache.org) we present the CGI (common Gateway Interface) protocol and discuss how CGI allows a Web server to communicate with the top tier (e.g., a Web browser running on the user's computer) and CGI scripts (i.e., our C++ programs) executing on a remote system. The chapter examples conclude with an e-business case study of an online bookstore that allows users to add books to an electronic shopping cart.

- **Standard Template Library (STL).** This might be one of the most important topics in the book in terms of your appreciation of software reuse. The STL defines powerful, template-based, reusable components that implement many common data structures and algorithms used to process those data structures. Chapter 22 introduces the STL and discusses its three key components—containers, iterators and algorithms. We show that using STL components provides tremendous expressive power and can reduce many lines of code to a single statement.

- **XHTML.** The World Wide Web Consortium (W3C) has declared HyperText Markup Language (HTML) to be a legacy technology that will undergo no further development. HTML is being replaced by the Extensible HyperText Markup Language (XHTML)—an XML-based technology that rapidly is becoming the standard for describing Web content. We use XHTML in Chapter 19, Web Programming; Appendix J and Appendix K introduce XHTML.

- **ANSI/ISO C++ Standard Compliance.** We have audited our presentation against the most recent ANSI/ISO C++ standard document for completeness and accuracy. [*Note:* If you need additional technical details on C++, you may want to read the C++ standard document. An electronic PDF copy of the C++ standard document, number INCITS/ISO/IEC 14882-2003, is available for $18 at webstore.ansi.org/ansidocstore/default.asp.]

- **New Debugger Appendices.** We include two new Using the Debugger appendices—Appendix L, Using the Visual Studio .NET Debugger, and Appendix M, Using the GNU C++ Debugger.

- **New Interior Design.** Working with the creative services team at Prentice Hall, we redesigned the interior styles for our *How to Program* Series. The new fonts are easier on the eyes and the new art package is more appropriate for the more detailed illustrations. We now place the defining occurrence of each key term both in the text and in the index in blue, bold style text for easier reference. We emphasize on-screen components in the bold **Helvetica** font (e.g., the **File** menu) and emphasize C++ program text in the Lucida font (e.g., int x = 5).

- **Syntax Coloring.** We syntax color all the C++ code, which is consistent with most C++ integrated development environments and code editors. This greatly improves code readability—an especially important goal, given that this book contains 16,423 lines of code. Our syntax-coloring conventions are as follows:

```
comments appear in green
keywords appear in dark blue
constants and literal values appear in light blue
errors appear in red
all other code appears in black
```

- **Code Highlighting.** Extensive code highlighting makes it easy for readers to locate each program's new features and helps students review the material rapidly when preparing for exams or labs.

- **"Code washing."** This is our term for using extensive and meaningful comments, using meaningful identifiers, applying uniform indentation conventions, aligning curly braces vertically, using a // end... comment on every line with a right curly brace and using vertical spacing to highlight significant program units such as control statements and functions. This process results in programs that are easy to read and self-documenting. We have extensively "code washed" all of the source-code programs in both the text and the book's ancillaries. We have worked hard to make our code exemplary.

- **Code Testing on Multiple Platforms.** We tested the code examples on various popular C++ platforms. For the most part, all of the book's examples port easily to all popular ANSI/ISO standard-compliant compilers. We will post any problems at www.deitel.com/books/cpphtp5/index.html.

- **Errors and Warnings Shown for Multiple Platforms.** For programs that intentionally contain errors to illustrate a key concept, we show the error messages that result on several popular platforms.

- **Large Review Team.** The book has been carefully scrutinized by a team of 30 distinguished academic and industry reviewers (listed later in the Preface).

As you read this book, if you have questions, send an e-mail to deitel@deitel.com; we will respond promptly. Please visit our Web site, www.deitel.com and be sure to sign up for the free *DEITEL® Buzz Online* e-mail newsletter at www.deitel.com/newsletter/subscribe.html for updates to this book and the latest information on C++. We also use the Web site and the newsletter to keep our readers and industry clients informed of the latest news on Deitel publications and services. Please check the following Web site regularly for errata, updates regarding the C++ software, free downloads and other resources:

> www.deitel.com/books/cpphtp5/index.html

Teaching Approach

C++ How to Program, 5/e contains an abundant collection of examples, exercises and projects drawn from many fields to provide the student with a chance to solve interesting real-world problems. The book concentrates on the principles of good software engineering and stresses program clarity. We avoid arcane terminology and syntax specifications in favor of teaching by example. We are educators who teach programming languages courses in industry classrooms worldwide. Dr. Harvey M. Deitel has 20 years of college teaching experience, including serving as chairman of the Computer Science Department at Boston College, and 15 years of industry teaching experience. Paul Deitel has 12 years of industry teaching experience. The Deitels have taught C++ courses at all levels to the government, industry, military and academic clients of Deitel & Associates.

Learning C++ using the LIVE-CODE Approach

C++ How to Program, 5/e, is loaded with C++ programs—each new concept is presented in the context of a complete working C++ program that is immediately followed by one or more sample executions showing the program's inputs and outputs. This style exemplifies the way we teach and write about programming. We call this method of teaching and writing the LIVE-CODE Approach. *We use programming languages to teach programming languages.* Reading the examples in the text is much like typing and running them on a computer. We provide all the source code for the book's examples on the accompanying CD and at www.deitel.com—making it easy for students to run each example as they study it.

World Wide Web Access

All the source-code examples for *C++ How to Program, 5/e* (and our other publications) are available on the Internet as downloads from

    www.deitel.com

Registration is quick and easy, and the downloads are free. We suggest downloading all the examples (or copying them from the CD included in the back of this book), then running each program as you read the corresponding text. Making changes to the examples and immediately seeing the effects of those changes is a great way to enhance your C++ learning experience.

Objectives

Each chapter begins with a statement of objectives. This lets students know what to expect and gives them an opportunity, after reading the chapter, to determine if they have met these objectives. This is a confidence builder and a source of positive reinforcement.

Quotations

The learning objectives are followed by quotations. Some are humorous, some philosophical and some offer interesting insights. We hope that you will enjoy relating the quotations to the chapter material. Many of the quotations are worth a second look after reading the chapter.

Outline

The chapter outline helps students approach the material in a top-down fashion, so they can anticipate what is to come, and set a comfortable and effective learning pace.

16,423 Lines of Syntax-Colored Code in 235 Example Programs with Program Inputs and Outputs)

Our LIVE-CODE programs range in size from just a few lines of code to more substantial examples. Each program is followed by a window containing the input/output dialogue produced when the program is run, so students can confirm that the programs run as expected. Relating outputs to the program statements that produce them is an excellent way to learn and to reinforce concepts. Our programs demonstrate the diverse features of C++. The code is line-numbered and syntax colored—with C++ keywords, comments and other program text each appearing in different colors. This facilitates reading the code—students will especially appreciate the syntax coloring when they read the larger programs.

695 Illustrations/Figures

An abundance of charts, tables, line drawings, programs and program outputs is included. We model the flow of control in control statements with UML activity diagrams. UML class diagrams model the data members, constructors and member functions of classes. We use additional types of UML diagrams throughout our optional OOD/UML ATM Software Engineering Case Study.

552 *Programming Tips*

We include programming tips to help students focus on important aspects of program development. We highlight these tips in the form of *Good Programming Practices, Common Programming Errors, Performance Tips, Portability Tips, Software Engineering Observations* and *Error-Prevention Tips.* These tips and practices represent the best we have gleaned from a combined six decades of programming and teaching experience. One of our students, a mathematics major, told us that she feels this approach is like the highlighting of axioms, theorems, lemmas and corollaries in mathematics books—it provides a basis on which to build good software.

Good Programming Practices

Good Programming Practices *are tips for writing clear programs. These techniques help students produce programs that are more readable, self-documenting and easier to maintain.*

Common Programming Errors

Students who are new to programming (or a programming language) tend to make certain errors frequently. Focusing on these Common Programming Errors *reduces the likelihood that students will make the same mistakes and shortens long lines outside instructors' offices during office hours!*

Performance Tips

In our experience, teaching students to write clear and understandable programs is by far the most important goal for a first programming course. But students want to write the programs that run the fastest, use the least memory, require the smallest number of keystrokes or dazzle in other nifty ways. Students really care about performance. They want to know what they can do to "turbo charge" their programs. So we highlight opportunities for improving program performance—making programs run faster or minimizing the amount of memory that they occupy.

Portability Tips

Software development is a complex and expensive activity. Organizations that develop software must often produce versions customized to a variety of computers and operating systems. So there is a strong emphasis today on portability, i.e., on producing software that will run on a variety of computer systems with few, if any, changes. Some programmers assume that if they implement an application in standard C++, the application will be portable. This simply is not the case. Achieving portability requires careful and cautious design. There are many pitfalls. We include Portability Tips *to help students write portable code and to provide insights on how C++ achieves its high degree of portability.*

Software Engineering Observations

The object-oriented programming paradigm necessitates a complete rethinking of the way we build software systems. C++ is an effective language for achieving good software engineering. The Software Engineering Observations *highlight architectural and design issues that affect the construction of software systems, especially large-scale systems. Much of what the student learns here will be useful in upper-level courses and in industry as the student begins to work with large, complex real-world systems.*

 Error-Prevention Tips

When we first designed this "tip type," we thought we would use it strictly to tell people how to test and debug C++ programs. In fact, many of the tips describe aspects of C++ that reduce the likelihood of "bugs" and thus simplify the testing and debugging processes.

Summary (1067 Summary bullets)

We present a thorough, bullet-list-style summary at the end of every chapter. On average, there are 40 summary bullets per chapter. This focuses the student's review and reinforces key concepts.

Terminology (1611 Terms)

We include an alphabetized list of the important terms defined in each chapter—again, for further reinforcement. There is an average of 82 terms per chapter. Each term also appears in the index, and the defining occurrence of each term is highlighted in the index with a blue, bold page number so the student can locate the definitions of key terms quickly.

604 Self-Review Exercises and Answers (Count Includes Separate Parts)

Extensive self-review exercises and answers are included in each chapter. This gives the student a chance to build confidence with the material and prepare for the regular exercises. We encourage students to do all the self-review exercises and check their answers.

818 Exercises (Solutions in Instructor's Manual; Count Includes Separate Parts)

Each chapter concludes with a substantial set of exercises including simple recall of important terminology and concepts; writing individual C++ statements; writing small portions of C++ functions and classes; writing complete C++ functions, classes and programs; and writing major term projects. The large number of exercises enables instructors to tailor their courses to the unique needs of their audiences and to vary course assignments each semester. Instructors can use these exercises to form homework assignments, short quizzes and major examinations. The solutions for the vast majority of the exercises are included on the Instructor version of the free, Web-based *Cyber Classroom,* which is *available only to instructors* through their Prentice Hall representatives. [**NOTE: Please do not write to us requesting access to the Instructor's Cyber Classroom. Distribution of this ancillary is limited strictly to college instructors teaching from the book. Instructors may obtain the solutions manual only from their Prentice Hall representatives.**] For more information about the *Cyber Classroom,* please visit www.deitel.com or sign up for the free *DEITEL® Buzz Online* e-mail newsletter at www.deitel.com/newsletter/subscribe.html.

Approximately 6,000 Index Entries

We have included an extensive index. This helps students find terms or concepts by keyword. The index is useful to people reading the book for the first time and is especially useful to practicing programmers who use the book as a reference.

"Double Indexing" of All C++ LIVE-CODE Examples

C++ How to Program, 5/e has 235 live-code examples and 818 exercises (including separate parts). We have double indexed each of the live-code examples and most of the more substantial exercises. For every source-code program in the book, we indexed the figure caption both alphabetically and as a subindex item under "Examples." This makes it easier to find examples using particular features. The more substantial exercises are also indexed both alphabetically and as subindex items under "Exercises."

Tour of the Book

In this section, we take a tour of the many capabilities of C++ you will study in *C++ How to Program, 5/e*. Figure 1 illustrates the dependencies among the chapters. We recommend studying these topics in the order indicated by the arrows, though other orders are possible. This book is widely used in all levels of C++ programming courses. Search the Web for "syllabus," "C++" and "Deitel" to find syllabi used with recent editions of this book.

Chapter 1—Introduction to Computers, the Internet and World Wide Web—discusses what computers are, how they work and how they are programmed. The chapter gives a brief history of the development of programming languages from machine languages to assembly languages and high-level languages. The origin of the C++ programming language is discussed. Our free *Dive Into™* Series publications for other platforms are available at www.deitel.com/books/downloads.html. The chapter includes an introduction to a typical C++ programming environment. We walk readers through a "test drive" of a typical C++ application on Windows and Linux platforms. This chapter also introduces basic object technology concepts and terminology and the Unified Modeling Language.

Chapter 2—Introduction to C++ Programming—provides a lightweight introduction to programming applications in the C++ programming language. The chapter introduces nonprogrammers to basic programming concepts and constructs. The programs in this chapter illustrate how to display data on the screen and how to obtain data from the user at the keyboard. Chapter 2 ends with detailed treatments of decision making and arithmetic operations.

Chapter 3—Introduction to Classes and Objects—is the "featured" chapter for the new edition. It provides a friendly early introduction to classes and objects. Carefully developed and completely new in this edition, Chapter 3 gets students working with object orientation comfortably from the start. It was developed with the guidance of a distinguished team of industry and academic reviewers. We introduce classes, objects, member functions, constructors and data members using a series of simple real-world examples. We develop a well-engineered framework for organizing object-oriented programs in C++. First, we motivate the notion of classes with a simple example. Then we present a carefully paced sequence of seven complete working programs to demonstrate creating and using your own classes. These examples begin our **integrated case study on developing a grade-book class** that instructors can use to maintain student test scores.

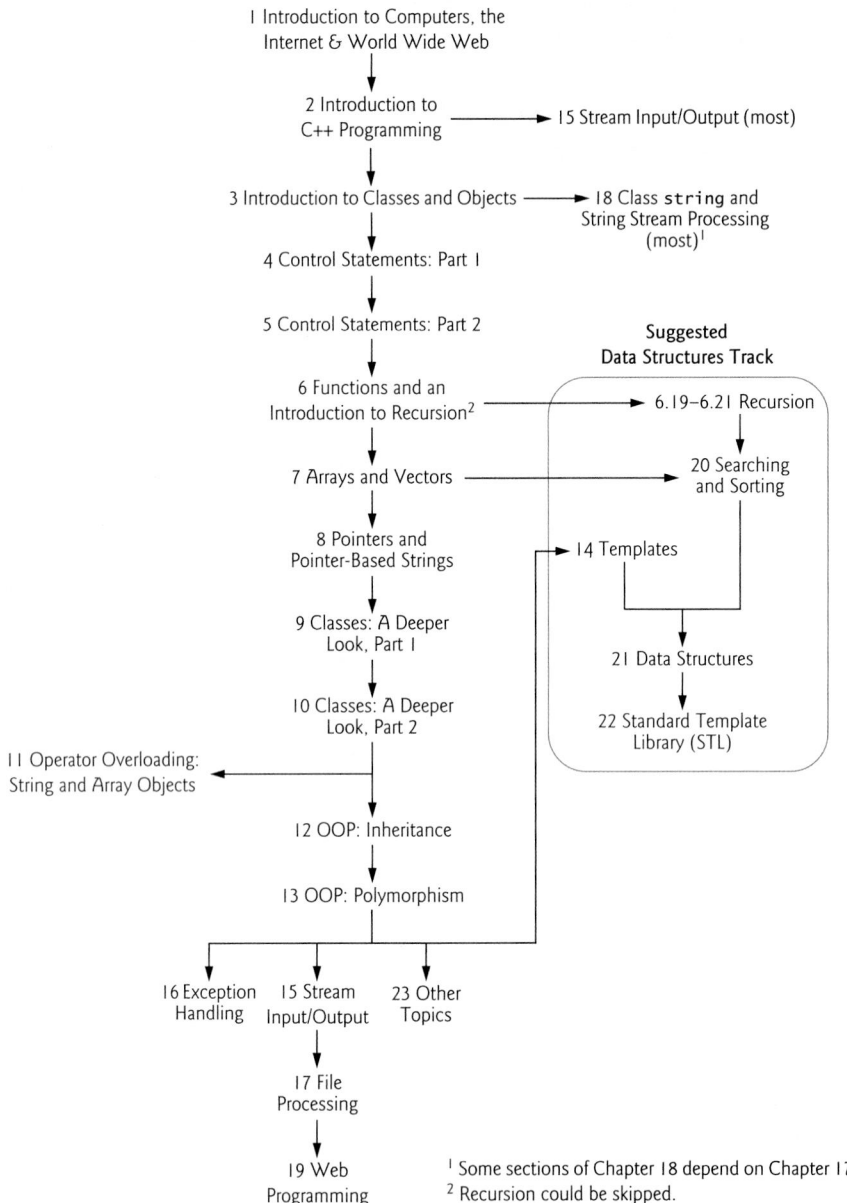

Fig. 1 | Flowchart illustrating the dependencies among chapters in C++ *How to Program, 5/e.*

This case study is enhanced over the next several chapters, culminating with the version presented in Chapter 7, Arrays and Vectors. The GradeBook class case study describes how to define a class and how to use it to create an object. The case study discusses how to declare and define member functions to implement the class's behaviors, how to declare data members to implement the class's attributes and how to call an object's member functions to make them perform their tasks. We introduce C++ Standard Library class string and create string objects to store the name of the course that a GradeBook object represents. Chapter 3 explains the differences between data members of a class and local variables of a function and how to use a constructor to ensure that an object's data is initialized when the object is created. We show how to promote software reusability by separating a class definition from the client code (e.g., function main) that uses the class. We also introduce another fundamental principle of good software engineering—separating interface from implementation. The chapter includes a detailed diagram and discussion explaining the compilation and linking process that produces an executable application.

Chapter 4—Control Statements: Part 1—focuses on the program-development process involved in creating useful classes. The chapter discusses how to take a problem statement and develop a working C++ program from it, including performing intermediate steps in pseudocode. The chapter introduces some simple control statements for decision making (if and if...else) and repetition (while). We examine counter-controlled and sentinel-controlled repetition using the **GradeBook class** from Chapter 3, and introduce C++'s increment, decrement and assignment operators. The chapter includes **two enhanced versions of the GradeBook class**, each based on Chapter 3's final version. These versions each include a member function that uses control statements to calculate the average of a set of student grades. In the first version, the member function uses counter-controlled repetition to input 10 student grades from the user, then determines the average grade. In the second version, the member function uses sentinel-controlled repetition to input an arbitrary number of grades from the user, then calculates the average of the grades that were entered. The chapter uses simple UML activity diagrams to show the flow of control through each of the control statements.

Chapter 5—Control Statements: Part 2—continues the discussion of C++ control statements with examples of the for repetition statement, the do...while repetition statement, the switch selection statement, the break statement and the continue statement. We create an **enhanced version of class GradeBook** that uses a switch statement to count the number of A, B, C, D and F grades entered by the user. This version uses sentinel-controlled repetition to input the grades. While reading the grades from the user, a member function modifies data members that keep track of the count of grades in each letter grade category. Another member function of the class then uses these data members to display a summary report based on the grades entered. The chapter includes a discussion of logical operators.

Chapter 6—Functions and an Introduction to Recursion—takes a deeper look inside objects and their member functions. We discuss C++ Standard-Library functions and examine more closely how students can build their own functions. The techniques presented in Chapter 6 are essential to the production of properly organized programs, especially the kinds of larger programs and software that system programmers and application programmers are likely to develop in real-world applications. The "divide and conquer" strategy is presented as an effective means for solving complex problems by dividing them into simpler interacting components. The chapter's first example continues the **GradeBook class case study** with an example of a function with multiple parameters. Students will enjoy the chapter's treatment of random numbers and simulation, and the discussion of the dice game of craps, which makes elegant use of control statements. The chapter discusses the so-called "C++ enhancements to C," including inline functions, ref-

erence parameters, default arguments, the unary scope resolution operator, function overloading and function templates. We also present C++'s call-by-value and call-by-reference
capabilities. The header files table introduces many of the header files that the reader will
use throughout the book. In this new edition, we provide a detailed discussion (with illustrations) of the function call stack and activation records to explain how C++ is able to
keep track of which function is currently executing, how automatic variables of functions
are maintained in memory and how a function knows where to return after it completes
execution. The chapter then offers a solid introduction to recursion and includes a table
summarizing the recursion examples and exercises distributed throughout the remainder
of the book. Some texts leave recursion for a chapter late in the book; we feel this topic is
best covered gradually throughout the text. The extensive collection of exercises at the end
of the chapter includes several classic recursion problems, including the Towers of Hanoi.

Chapter 7—Arrays and Vectors—explains how to process lists and tables of values.
We discuss the structuring of data in arrays of data items of the same type and demonstrate
how arrays facilitate the tasks performed by objects. The early parts of this chapter use C-
style, pointer-based arrays, which, as you will see in Chapter 8, are really pointers to the
array contents in memory. We then present arrays as full-fledged objects in the last section
of the chapter, where we introduce the C++ Standard Library vector class template—a
robust array data structure. The chapter presents numerous examples of both one-dimensional arrays and two-dimensional arrays. Examples in the chapter investigate various
common array manipulations, printing bar charts, sorting data and passing arrays to functions. The chapter includes the **final two GradeBook case study sections**, in which we use
arrays to store student grades for the duration of a program's execution. Previous versions
of the class process a set of grades entered by the user, but do not maintain the individual
grade values in data members of the class. In this chapter, we use arrays to enable an object
of the GradeBook class to maintain a set of grades in memory, thus eliminating the need to
repeatedly input the same set of grades. The first version of the class stores the grades in a
one-dimensional array and can produce a report containing the average of the grades, the
minimum and maximum grades and a bar chart representing the grade distribution. The
second version (i.e., the final version in the case study) uses a two-dimensional array to store
the grades of a number of students on multiple exams in a semester. This version can calculate each student's semester average, as well as the minimum and maximum grades across
all grades received for the semester. The class also produces a bar chart displaying the overall
grade distribution for the semester. Another key feature of this chapter is the discussion of
elementary sorting and searching techniques. The end-of-chapter exercises include a
variety of interesting and challenging problems, such as improved sorting techniques, the
design of a simple airline reservations system, an introduction to the concept of turtle
graphics (made famous in the LOGO language) and the Knight's Tour and Eight Queens
problems that introduce the notion of heuristic programming widely employed in the field
of artificial intelligence. The exercises conclude with many recursion problems including
selection sort, palindromes, linear search, the Eight Queens, printing an array, printing a
string backwards and finding the minimum value in an array.

Chapter 8—Pointers and Pointer-Based Strings—presents one of the most powerful features of the C++ language—pointers. The chapter provides detailed explanations
of pointer operators, call by reference, pointer expressions, pointer arithmetic, the relationship between pointers and arrays, arrays of pointers and pointers to functions. We

demonstrate how to use `const` with pointers to enforce the principle of least privilege to build more robust software. We also introduce and using the `sizeof` operator to determine the size of a data type or data items in bytes during program compilation. There is an intimate relationship between pointers, arrays and C-style strings in C++, so we introduce basic C-style string-manipulation concepts and discuss some of the most popular C-style string-handling functions, such as `getline` (input a line of text), `strcpy` and `strncpy` (copy a string), `strcat` and `strncat` (concatenate two strings), `strcmp` and `strncmp` (compare two strings), `strtok` ("tokenize" a string into its pieces) and `strlen` (return the length of a string). In this new edition, we use `string` objects (introduced in Chapter 3) in place of C-style, `char *` pointer-based strings wherever possible. However, we include `char *` strings in Chapter 8 to help the reader master pointers and prepare for the professional world in which the reader will see a great deal of C legacy code that has been implemented over the last three decades. Thus, the reader will become familiar with the two most prevalent methods of creating and manipulating strings in C++. Many people find that the topic of pointers is, by far, the most difficult part of an introductory programming course. In C and "raw C++" arrays and strings are pointers to array and string contents in memory (even function names are pointers). Studying this chapter carefully should reward you with a deep understanding of pointers. The chapter is loaded with challenging exercises. The chapter exercises include a simulation of the classic race between the tortoise and the hare, card-shuffling and dealing algorithms, recursive quicksort and recursive maze traversals. A special section entitled Building Your Own Computer also is included. This section explains machine-language programming and proceeds with a project involving the design and implementation of a computer simulator that leads the student to write and run machine-language programs. This unique feature of the text will be especially useful to the reader who wants to understand how computers really work. Our students enjoy this project and often implement substantial enhancements, many of which are suggested in the exercises. A second special section includes challenging string-manipulation exercises related to text analysis, word processing, printing dates in various formats, check protection, writing the word equivalent of a check amount, Morse Code and metric-to-English conversions.

Chapter 9—Classes: A Deeper Look, Part 1—continues our discussion of object-oriented programming. This chapter uses a rich `Time` class case study to illustrate accessing class members, separating interface from implementation, using access functions and utility functions, initializing objects with constructors, destroying objects with destructors, assignment by default memberwise copy and software reusability. Students learn the order in which constructors and destructors are called during the lifetime of an object. A modification of the `Time` case study demonstrates the problems that can occur when a member function returns a reference to a `private` data member, which breaks the encapsulation of the class. The chapter exercises challenge the student to develop classes for times, dates, rectangles and playing tic-tac-toe. Students generally enjoy game-playing programs. Mathematically inclined readers will enjoy the exercises on creating class `Complex` (for complex numbers), class `Rational` (for rational numbers) and class `HugeInteger` (for arbitrarily large integers).

Chapter 10—Classes: A Deeper Look, Part 2—continues the study of classes and presents additional object-oriented programming concepts. The chapter discusses declaring and using constant objects, constant member functions, composition—the process of building classes that have objects of other classes as members, `friend` functions and `friend` classes that have special access rights to the `private` and `protected` members of classes, the `this` pointer, which enables an object to know its own address, dynamic memory allocation, `static` class members for containing and manipulating class-wide data, examples of popular abstract data types (arrays, strings and queues), container classes and iterators. In our discussion of `const` objects, we mention keyword `mutable` which is used in a subtle manner to enable modification of "non-visible" implementation in `const` objects. We discuss dynamic memory allocation using `new` and `delete`. When `new` fails, the program terminates by default because `new` "throws an exception" in standard C++. We motivate the discussion of `static` class members with a video-game-based example. We emphasize how important it is to hide implementation details from clients of a class; then, we discuss proxy classes, which provide a means of hiding implementation (including the `private` data in class headers) from clients of a class. The chapter exercises include developing a savings-account class and a class for holding sets of integers.

Chapter 11—Operator Overloading; String and Array Objects—presents one of the most popular topics in our C++ courses. Students really enjoy this material. They find it a perfect match with the detailed discussion of crafting valuable classes in Chapters 9 and 10. Operator overloading enables the programmer to tell the compiler how to use existing operators with objects of new types. C++ already knows how to use these operators with objects of built-in types, such as integers, floats and characters. But suppose that we create a new `String` class—what would the plus sign mean when used between `String` objects? Many programmers use plus (+) with strings to mean concatenation. In Chapter 11, the programmer will learn how to "overload" the plus sign, so when it is written between two `String` objects in an expression, the compiler will generate a function call to an "operator function" that will concatenate the two `String`s. The chapter discusses the fundamentals of operator overloading, restrictions in operator overloading, overloading with class member functions vs. with nonmember functions, overloading unary and binary operators and converting between types. Chapter 11 features the collection of substantial case studies including an array class, a `String` class, a date class, a huge integer class and a complex numbers class (the last two appear with full source code in the exercises). Mathematically inclined students will enjoy creating the `polynomial` class in the exercises. This material is different from most programming languages and courses. Operator overloading is a complex topic, but an enriching one. Using operator overloading wisely helps you add extra "polish" to your classes. The discussions of class `Array` and class `String` are particularly valuable to students who have already used the C++ Standard Library `string` class and `vector` class template that provide similar capabilities. The exercises encourage the student to add operator overloading to classes `Complex`, `Rational` and `HugeInteger` to enable convenient manipulation of objects of these classes with operator symbols—as in mathematics—rather than with function calls as the student did in the Chapter 10 exercises.

Chapter 12—Object-Oriented Programming: Inheritance—introduces one of the most fundamental capabilities of object-oriented programming languages—inheritance: a form of software reusability in which new classes are developed quickly and easily by absorbing the capabilities of existing classes and adding appropriate new capabilities. In the context of an **Employee hierarchy** case study, this substantially revised chapter presents a five-example sequence demonstrating `private` data, `protected` data and good software engineering with inheritance. We begin by demonstrating a class with `private` data members and `public` member functions to manipulate that data. Next, we implement a second class with additional capabilities, intentionally and tediously duplicating much of the first example's code. The third example begins our discussion of inheritance and software reuse—we use the class from the first example as a base class and quickly and simply inherit its data and functionality into a new derived class. This example introduces the inheritance mechanism and demonstrates that a derived class cannot access its base class's `private` members directly. This motivates our fourth example, in which we introduce `protected` data in the base class and demonstrate that the derived class can indeed access the `protected` data inherited from the base class. The last example in the sequence demonstrates proper software engineering by defining the base class's data as `private` and using the base class's `public` member functions (that were inherited by the derived class) to manipulate the base class's `private` data in the derived class. The chapter discusses the notions of base classes and derived classes, `protected` members, `public` inheritance, `protected` inheritance, `private` inheritance, direct base classes, indirect base classes, constructors and destructors in base classes and derived classes, and software engineering with inheritance. The chapter also compares inheritance (the "*is-a*" relationship) with composition (the "*has-a*" relationship) and introduces the "*uses-a*" and "*knows-a*" relationships.

Chapter 13—Object-Oriented Programming: Polymorphism—deals with another fundamental capability of object-oriented programming: polymorphic behavior. The completely revised Chapter 13 builds on the inheritance concepts presented in Chapter 12 and focuses on the relationships among classes in a class hierarchy and the powerful processing capabilities that these relationships enable. When many classes are related to a common base class through inheritance, each derived-class object may be treated as a base-class object. This enables programs to be written in a simple and general manner independent of the specific types of the derived-class objects. New kinds of objects can be handled by the same program, thus making systems more extensible. Polymorphism enables programs to eliminate complex `switch` logic in favor of simpler "straight-line" logic. A screen manager of a video game, for example, can send a `draw` message to every object in a linked list of objects to be drawn. Each object knows how to draw itself. An object of a new class can be added to the program without modifying that program (as long as that new object also knows how to draw itself). The chapter discusses the mechanics of achieving polymorphic behavior via `virtual` functions. It distinguishes between abstract classes (from which objects cannot be instantiated) and concrete classes (from which objects can be instantiated). Abstract classes are useful for providing an inheritable interface to classes throughout the hierarchy. We demonstrate abstract classes and polymorphic behavior by revisiting the **Employee hierarchy** of Chapter 12. We introduce an abstract `Employee` base class, from which classes `CommissionEmployee`, `HourlyEmployee` and `SalariedEmployee` inherit directly and class `BasePlusCommissionEmployee` inherits indirectly. In the past, our professional clients have insisted that we provide a deeper explanation that shows precisely how polymorphism is implemented in C++, and hence, precisely what execution time and memory "costs" are incurred when programming with this powerful capability. We responded by developing an illustration and a precise explanation of the *vtables* (`virtual` function tables) that the C++ compiler builds automatically to support polymorphism. To conclude, we introduce run-time type information (RTTI) and dynamic casting, which enable a program to determine an object's type at execution time, then act on that object accordingly. Using RTTI and dynamic casting, we give a 10% pay increase to employees of a specific type, then calculate the earnings for such employees. For all other employee types, we calculate their earnings polymorphically.

Chapter 14—Templates—discusses one of C++'s more powerful software reuse features, namely templates. Function templates and class templates enable programmers to specify, with a single code segment, an entire range of related overloaded functions (called function template specializations) or an entire range of related classes (called class-template specializations). This technique is called generic programming. Function templates were introduced in Chapter 6. This chapter presents additional discussions and examples on function template. We might write a single class template for a stack class, then have C++ generate separate class-template specializations, such as a "stack-of-`int`" class, a "stack-of-`float`" class, a "stack-of-`string`" class and so on. The chapter discusses using type parameters, nontype parameters and default types for class templates. We also discuss the relationships between templates and other C++ features, such as overloading, inheritance, friends and `static` members. The exercises challenge the student to write a variety of function templates and class templates and to employ these in complete programs. We greatly enhance the treatment of templates in our discussion of the Standard Template Library (STL) containers, iterators and algorithms in Chapter 22.

Chapter 15—C++ Stream Input/Output—contains a comprehensive treatment of standard C++ input/output capabilities. This chapter discusses a range of capabilities sufficient for performing most common I/O operations and overviews the remaining capabilities. Many of the I/O features are object oriented. This style of I/O makes use of other C++ features, such as references, function overloading and operator overloading. The various I/O capabilities of C++, including output with the stream insertion operator, input with the stream extraction operator, type-safe I/O, formatted I/O, unformatted I/O (for performance). Users can specify how to perform I/O for objects of user-defined types by overloading the stream insertion operator (`<<`) and the stream extraction operator (`>>`). This extensibility is one of C++'s most valuable features. C++ provides various stream manipulators that perform formatting tasks. This chapter discusses stream manipulators that provide capabilities such as displaying integers in various bases, controlling floating-point precision, setting field widths, displaying decimal point and trailing zeros, justifying output, setting and unsetting format state, setting the fill character in fields. We also present an example that creates user-defined output stream manipulators.

Chapter 16—Exception Handling—discusses how exception handling enables programmers to write programs that are robust, fault tolerant and appropriate for business-critical and mission-critical environments. The chapter discusses when exception handling is appropriate; introduces the basic capabilities of exception handling with `try` blocks, `throw` statements and `catch` handlers; indicates how and when to rethrow an exception; explains how to write an exception specification and process unexpected exceptions; and discusses the important ties between exceptions and constructors, destructors and inheritance. The exercises in this chapter show the student the diversity and power of C++'s exception-handling capabilities. We discuss rethrowing an exception, and we illustrate how `new` can fail when memory is exhausted. Many older C++ compilers return 0 by default when `new` fails. We show the new style of `new` failing by throwing a `bad_alloc` (bad allocation) exception. We illustrate how to use function `set_new_handler` to specify a custom function to be called to deal with memory-exhaustion situations. We discuss how to use the `auto_ptr` class template to `delete` dynamically allocated memory implicitly, thus avoiding memory leaks. To conclude this chapter, we present the Standard Library exception hierarchy.

Chapter 17—File Processing—discusses techniques for creating and processing both sequential files and random-access files. The chapter begins with an introduction to the data hierarchy from bits, to bytes, to fields, to records and to files. Next, we present the C++ view of files and streams. We discuss sequential files and build programs that show how to open and close files, how to store data sequentially in a file and how to read data sequentially from a file. We then discuss random-access files and build programs that show how to create a file for random access, how to read and write data to a file with random access and how to read data sequentially from a randomly accessed file. The case study combines the techniques of accessing files both sequentially and randomly into a complete transaction-processing program. Students in our industry seminars have mentioned that, after studying the material on file processing, they were able to produce substantial file-processing programs that were immediately useful in their organizations. The exercises ask the student to implement a variety of programs that build and process both sequential files and random-access files.

Chapter 18—Class `string` and String Stream Processing—The chapter discusses C++'s capabilities for inputting data from strings in memory and outputting data to strings in memory; these capabilities often are referred to as in-core formatting or stringstream processing. Class `string` is a required component of the Standard Library. We preserved the treatment of C-like, pointer-based strings in Chapter 8 and later for several reasons. First, it strengthens the reader's understanding of pointers. Second, for the next decade or so, C++ programmers will need to be able to read and modify the enormous amounts of C legacy code that has accumulated over the last quarter of a century—this code processes strings as pointers, as does a large portion of the C++ code that has been written in industry over the last many years. In Chapter 18 we discuss `string` assignment, concatenation and comparison. We show how to determine various `string` characteristics such as a `string`'s size, capacity and whether or not it is empty. We discuss how to resize a `string`. We consider the various "find" functions that enable us to find a substring in a `string` (searching the `string` either forwards or backwards), and we show how to find either the first occurrence or last occurrence of a character selected from a `string` of characters, and how to find the first occurrence or last occurrence of a character that is not in a selected `string` of characters. We show how to replace, erase and insert characters in a `string` and how to convert a `string` object to a C-style `char *` string.

Chapter 19—Web Programming—This optional chapter has everything you need to begin developing your own Web-based applications that will really run on the Internet! You will learn how to build so-called *n*-tier applications, in which the functionality provided by each tier can be distributed to separate computers across the Internet or executed on the same computer. In particular, we build a three-tier online bookstore application. The bookstore's information is stored in the application's bottom tier, also called the data tier. In industrial-strength applications, the data tier is typically a database such as Oracle, Microsoft® SQL Server or MySQL. For simplicity, we use text files and employ the file-processing techniques of Chapter 17 to access and modify these files. The user enters requests and receives responses at the application's top tier, also called the user-interface tier or the client tier, which is typically a computer running a popular Web browser such as Microsoft Internet Explorer, Mac® OS X Safari™, Mozilla Firefox, Opera or

Netscape®. Web browsers, of course, know how to communicate with Web sites throughout the Internet. The middle tier, also called the business-logic tier, contains both a Web server and an application-specific C++ program (e.g., our bookstore application). The Web server communicates with the C++ program (and vice versa) via the CGI (Common Gateway Interface) protocol. This program is referred to as a CGI script. We use the popular Apache HTTP server, which is available free for download from the Apache Web site, `www.apache.org`. Apache installation instructions for many popular platforms, including Linux and Windows systems, are available at that site and at `www.deitel.com` and `www.prenhall.com/deitel`. The Web server knows how to talk to the client tier across the Internet using a protocol called HTTP (Hypertext Transfer Protocol). We discuss the two most popular HTTP methods for sending data to a Web server—GET and POST. We then discuss the crucial role of the Web server in Web programming and provide a simple example that requests an Extensible HyperText Markup Language (XHTML)[1] document from a Web server. We discuss CGI and how it allows a Web server to communicate with the top tier and CGI applications. We provide a simple example that gets the server's time and renders it in a browser. Other examples demonstrate how to process form-based user input via the string processing techniques introduced in Chapter 18. In our forms-based examples we use buttons, password fields, check boxes and text fields. We present an example of an interactive portal for a travel company that displays airfares to various cities. Travel-club members can log in and view discounted airfares. We also discuss various methods of storing client-specific data, which include hidden fields (i.e., information stored in a Web page but not rendered by the Web browser) and cookies—small text files that the browser stores on the client's machine. The chapter examples conclude with a case study of an online book store that allows users to add books to a shopping cart. This case study contains several CGI scripts that interact to form a complete application. The online book store is password protected, so users first must log in to gain access. The chapter's Web resources include information about the CGI specification, C++ CGI libraries and Web sites related to the Apache HTTP server.

Chapter 20—Searching and Sorting—discusses two of the most important classes of algorithms in computer science. We consider a variety of specific algorithms for each and compare them with regard to their memory consumption and processor consumption (introducing Big O notation, which indicates how hard an algorithm may have to work to solve a problem). Searching data involves determining whether a value (referred to as the search key) is present in the data and, if so, finding the value's location. In the examples and exercises of this chapter, we discuss a variety of searching algorithms, including: binary search and recursive versions of linear search and binary search. Through examples and exercises, Chapter 20 discusses the recursive merge sort, bubble sort, bucket sort and the recursive quicksort.

Chapter 21—Data Structures—discusses the techniques used to create and manipulate dynamic data structures. The chapter begins with discussions of self-referential classes and dynamic memory allocation, then proceeds with a discussion of how to create and

---

1.   XHTML is a markup language for identifying the elements of an XHTML document (Web page) so that a browser can render (i.e., display) that page on your computer screen. XHTML is a new technology designed by the World Wide Web Consortium to replace the HyperText Markup Language (HTML) as the primary means of specifying Web content. In Appendices J and K, we introduce XHTML.

maintain various dynamic data structures, including linked lists, queues (or waiting lines), stacks and trees. For each type of data structure, we present complete, working programs and show sample outputs. The chapter also helps the student master pointers. The chapter includes abundant examples that use indirection and double indirection—a particularly difficult concept. One problem when working with pointers is that students have trouble visualizing the data structures and how their nodes are linked together. We have included illustrations that show the links and the sequence in which they are created. The binary-tree example is a superb capstone for the study of pointers and dynamic data structures. This example creates a binary tree, enforces duplicate elimination and introduces recursive preorder, inorder and postorder tree traversals. Students have a genuine sense of accomplishment when they study and implement this example. They particularly appreciate seeing that the inorder traversal prints the node values in sorted order. We include a substantial collection of exercises. A highlight of the exercises is the special section Building Your Own Compiler. The exercises walk the student through the development of an infix-to-postfix-conversion program and a postfix-expression-evaluation program. We then modify the postfix-evaluation algorithm to generate machine-language code. The compiler places this code in a file (using the techniques of Chapter 17. Students then run the machine language produced by their compilers on the software simulators they built in the exercises of Chapter 8! The 35 exercises include recursively searching a list, recursively printing a list backwards, binary-tree node deletion, level-order traversal of a binary tree, printing trees, writing a portion of an optimizing compiler, writing an interpreter, inserting/deleting anywhere in a linked list, implementing lists and queues without tail pointers, analyzing the performance of binary-tree searching and sorting, implementing an indexed-list class and a supermarket simulation that uses queueing. After studying Chapter 21, the reader is prepared for the treatment of STL containers, iterators and algorithms in Chapter 22. The STL containers are prepackaged, templatized data structures that most programmers will find sufficient for the vast majority of applications they will need to implement. The STL is a giant leap forward in achieving the vision of reuse.

Chapter 22—Standard Template Library (STL)—Throughout this book, we discuss the importance of software reuse. Recognizing that many data structures and algorithms are commonly used by C++ programmers, the C++ standard committee added the Standard Template Library (STL) to the C++ Standard Library. The STL defines powerful, template-based, reusable components that implement many common data structures and algorithms used to process those data structures. The STL offers proof of concept for generic programming with templates—introduced in Chapter 14 and demonstrated in detail in Chapter 21. This chapter introduces the STL and discusses its three key components—containers (popular templatized data structures), iterators and algorithms. The STL containers are data structures capable of storing objects of any data type. We will see that there are three container categories—first-class containers, adapters and near containers. STL iterators, which have similar properties to those of pointers, are used by programs to manipulate the STL-container elements. In fact, standard arrays can be manipulated as STL containers, using standard pointers as iterators. We will see that manipulating containers with iterators is convenient and provides tremendous expressive power when combined with STL algorithms—in some cases, reducing many lines of code to a single statement. STL algorithms are functions that perform common data manipulations such as searching, sorting and comparing elements (or entire containers). There are approximately 70 algorithms implemented in the STL. Most of these use iterators to access container elements. We will see that each first-class container supports specific iterator types, some of which are more powerful than others. A container's supported iterator type determines whether the container can be used with a specific algorithm. Iterators encapsulate the mechanism used to access container elements. This encapsulation enables many of the STL algorithms to be applied to several containers without regard for the underlying container implementation. As long as a container's iterators support the minimum requirements of the algorithm, then the algorithm can process that container's elements. This also enables programmers to create algorithms that can process the elements of multiple different container types. Chapter 21 discusses how to implement data structures with pointers, classes and dynamic memory. Pointer-based code is complex, and the slightest omission or oversight can lead to serious memory-access violations and memory-leak errors with no compiler complaints. Implementing additional data structures such as deques, priority queues, sets, maps, etc. requires substantial additional work. In addition, if many programmers on a large project implement similar containers and algorithms for different tasks, the code becomes difficult to modify, maintain and debug. An advantage of the STL is that programmers can reuse the STL containers, iterators and algorithms to implement common data representations and manipulations. This reuse results in substantial development-time and resource savings. This is a friendly, accessible chapter that should convince you of the value of the STL and encourage further study.

Chapter 23—Other Topics—is a collection of miscellaneous C++ topics. This chapter discusses one additional cast operator—`const_cast`. This operator, along with `static_cast` (Chapter 5), `dynamic_cast` (Chapter 13) and `reinterpret_cast` (Chapter 17), provide a more robust mechanism for converting between types than do the original cast operators C++ inherited from C (which are now deprecated). We discuss namespaces, a feature particularly crucial for software developers who build substantial systems, especially for those who build systems from class libraries. Namespaces prevent naming collisions, which can hinder such large software efforts. The chapter discusses the operator keywords, which are useful for programmers who have keyboards that do not support certain characters used in operator symbols, such as !, &, ^, ~ and |. These operators can also be used by programmers who do not like cryptic operator symbols. We discuss keyword `mutable`, which allows a member of a `const` object to be changed. Previously, this was accomplished by "casting away `const`-ness", which is considered a dangerous practice. We also discuss pointer-to-member operators `.*` and `->*`, multiple inheritance (including the problem of "diamond inheritance") and `virtual` base classes.

Appendix A—Operator Precedence and Associativity Chart—presents the complete set of C++ operator symbols, in which each operator appears on a line by itself with its operator symbol, its name and its associativity.

Appendix B—ASCII Character Set—All the programs in this book use the ASCII character set, which is presented in this appendix.

Appendix C—Fundamental Types—lists all fundamental types defined in the *C++ Standard*.

Appendix D—Number Systems—discusses the binary, octal, decimal and hexadecimal number systems. It considers how to convert numbers between bases and explains the one's complement and two's complement binary representations.

Appendix E—C Legacy-Code Topics—presents additional topics including several advanced topics not ordinarily covered in introductory courses. We show how to redirect program input to come from a file, redirect program output to be placed in a file, redirect the output of one program to be the input of another program (piping) and append the output of a program to an existing file. We develop functions that use variable-length argument lists and show how to pass command-line arguments to function `main` and use them in a program. We discuss how to compile programs whose components are spread across multiple files, register functions with `atexit` to be executed at program termination and terminate program execution with function `exit`. We also discuss the `const` and `volatile` type qualifiers, specifying the type of a numeric constant using the integer and floating-point suffixes, using the signal-handling library to trap unexpected events, creating and using dynamic arrays with `calloc` and `realloc`, using `unions` as a space-saving technique and using linkage specifications when C++ programs are to be linked with legacy C code. As the title suggests, this appendix is intended primarily for C++ programmers who will be working with C legacy code as most C++ programmers are almost certain to do at one point in their careers.

Appendix F—Preprocessor—provides detailed discussions of the preprocessor directives. The appendix includes more complete information on the `#include` directive, which causes a copy of a specified file to be included in place of the directive before the file is compiled and the `#define` directive that creates symbolic constants and macros. The appendix explains conditional compilation for enabling the programmer to control the execution of preprocessor directives and the compilation of program code. The `#` operator that converts its operand to a string and the `##` operator that concatenates two tokens are discussed. The various predefined preprocessor symbolic constants (`__LINE__`, `__FILE__`, `__DATE__`, `__STDC__`, `__TIME__` and `__TIMESTAMP__`) are presented. Finally, macro `assert` of the header file `<cassert>` is discussed, which is valuable in program testing, debugging, verification and validation.

Appendix G—ATM Case Study Code—contains the implementation of our case study on object-oriented design with the UML. This appendix is discussed in the overview of the case study (presented shortly).

Appendix H—UML 2 Diagrams—Overviews the UML 2 diagram types that are not found in the OOD/UML Case Study.

Appendix I—C++ Internet and Web Resources—contains a listing of valuable C++ resources, such as demos, information about popular compilers (including "freebies"), books, articles, conferences, job banks, journals, magazines, help, tutorials, FAQs (frequently asked questions), newsgroups, Web-based courses, product news and C++ development tools.

Appendix J—Introduction to XHTML—provides an introduction to XHTML—a markup language for describing the elements of a Web page so that a browser, such as Microsoft Internet Explorer or Netscape, can render that page. The reader should be familiar with the contents of this appendix before studying Chapter 16, Web Programming with CGI. This appendix does not contain any C++ programming. Some key topics covered include incorporating text and images into an XHTML document, linking to other XHTML documents, incorporating special characters (such as copyright and trademark symbols) into an XHTML document, separating parts of an XHTML document with horizontal lines (called horizontal rules), presenting information in lists and tables, and collecting information from users browsing a site.

Appendix K—XHTML Special Characters—lists many commonly used XHTML special characters, called character entity references.

Appendix L—Using the Visual C++ .NET Debugger—demonstrates key features of the Visual Studio .NET Debugger, which allows a programmer to monitor the execution of applications to locate and remove logic errors. The appendix presents step-by-step instructions, so students learn how to use the debugger in a hands-on manner.

Appendix M—Using the GNU C++ Debugger—demonstrates key features of the GNU C++ Debugger, which allows a programmer to monitor the execution of applications to locate and remove logic errors. The appendix presents step-by-step instructions, so students learn how to use the debugger in a hands-on manner.

Bibliography—lists over 100 books and articles to encourage the student to do further reading on C++ and OOP.

Index—The comprehensive index enables the reader to locate by keyword any term or concept throughout the text.

Object-Oriented Design of an ATM with the UML: A Tour of the Optional Software Engineering Case Study

In this section we tour the book's optional case study of object-oriented design with the UML. This tour previews the contents of the nine Software Engineering Case Study sections (in Chapters 1–7, 9 and 13). After completing this case study, the reader will be thoroughly familiar with a carefully reviewed object-oriented design and implementation for a significant C++ application.

The design presented in the ATM case study was developed at Deitel & Associates, Inc. and scrutinized by a distinguished developmental review team of industry professionals and academics. We crafted this design to meet the requirements of introductory course sequences. Real ATM systems used by banks and their customers worldwide are based on more sophisticated designs that take into consideration many more issues than we have addressed here. Our primary goal throughout the design process was to create a simple design that would be clear to OOD and UML novices, while still demonstrating key OOD concepts and the related UML modeling techniques. We worked hard to keep the design and the code relatively small so that it would work well in the introductory course sequence.

Section 1.17—Software Engineering Case Study: Introduction to Object Technology and the UML—introduces the object-oriented design case study with the UML. The section introduces the basic concepts and terminology of object technology, including classes, objects, encapsulation, inheritance and polymorphism. We discuss the history of the UML. This is the only required section of the case study.

Section 2.8—(Optional) Software Engineering Case Study: Examining the ATM Requirements Document—discusses a *requirements document* that specifies the requirements for a system that we will design and implement—the software for a simple automated teller machine (ATM). We investigate the structure and behavior of object-oriented systems in general. We discuss how the UML will facilitate the design process in subsequent Software Engineering Case Study sections by providing several additional types of diagrams to model our system. We include a list of URLs and book references on object-oriented design with the UML. We discuss the interaction between the ATM system specified by the requirements document and its user. Specifically, we investigate the scenarios that may occur between the user and the system itself—these are called *use cases*. We model these interactions, using *use case diagrams* of the UML.

Section 3.11—(Optional) Software Engineering Case Study: Identifying the Classes in the ATM Requirements Documents—begins to design the ATM system. We identify its classes, or "building blocks," by extracting the nouns and noun phrases from the requirements document. We arrange these classes into a UML class diagram that describes the class structure of our simulation. The class diagram also describes relationships, known as *associations*, among classes.

Section 4.13—(Optional) Software Engineering Case Study: Identifying Class Attributes in the ATM System—focuses on the attributes of the classes discussed in Section 3.11. A class contains both *attributes* (data) and *operations* (behaviors). As we will see in later sections, changes in an object's attributes often affect the object's behavior. To determine the attributes for the classes in our case study, we extract the adjectives describing the nouns and noun phrases (which defined our classes) from the requirements document, then place the attributes in the class diagram we created in Section 3.11.

Section 5.11—(Optional) Software Engineering Case Study: Identifying Objects' States and Activities in the ATM System—discusses how an object, at any given time, occupies a specific condition called a *state*. A *state transition* occurs when that object receives a message to change state. The UML provides the *state machine diagram*, which identifies the set of possible states that an object may occupy and models that object's state transitions. An object also has an *activity*—the work it performs in its lifetime. The UML provides the *activity diagram*—a flowchart that models an object's activity. In this section, we use both types of diagrams to begin modeling specific behavioral aspects of our ATM system, such as how the ATM carries out a withdrawal transaction and how the ATM responds when the user is authenticated.

Section 6.22—(Optional) Software Engineering Case Study: Identifying Class Operations in the ATM System—identifies the operations, or services, of our classes. We extract from the requirements document the verbs and verb phrases that specify the operations for each class. We then modify the class diagram of Section 3.11 to include each operation with its associated class. At this point in the case study, we will have gathered all information possible from the requirements document. However, as future chapters introduce such topics as inheritance, we will modify our classes and diagrams.

Section 7.12—(Optional) Software Engineering Case Study: Collaboration Among Objects in the ATM System—provides a "rough sketch" of the model for our ATM system. In this section, we see how it works. We investigate the behavior of the simulation by discussing *collaborations*—messages that objects send to each other to communicate. The class operations that we discovered in Section 6.22 turn out to be the collaborations among the objects in our system. We determine the collaborations, then collect them into a *communication diagram*—the UML diagram for modeling collaborations. This diagram reveals which objects collaborate and when. We present a communication diagram of the collaborations among objects to perform an ATM balance inquiry. We then present the UML *sequence diagram* for modeling interactions in a system. This diagram emphasizes the chronological ordering of messages. A sequence diagram models how objects in the system interact to carry out withdrawal and deposit transactions.

Section 9.12—(Optional) Software Engineering Case Study: Starting to Program the Classes of the ATM System—takes a break from designing the behavior of our system. We begin the implementation process to emphasize the material discussed in Chapter 9. Using the UML class diagram of Section 3.11 and the attributes and operations discussed in Section 4.13 and Section 6.22, we show how to implement a class in C++ from a design. We do not implement all classes—because we have not completed the design process. Working from our UML diagrams, we create code for the `Withdrawal` class.

Section 13.10—(Optional) Software Engineering Case Study: Incorporating Inheritance into the ATM System—continues our discussion of object-oriented programming. We consider inheritance—classes sharing common characteristics may inherit attributes and operations from a "base" class. In this section, we investigate how our ATM system can benefit from using inheritance. We document our discoveries in a class diagram that models inheritance relationships—the UML refers to these relationships as *generalizations*. We modify the class diagram of Section 3.11 by using inheritance to group classes with similar characteristics. This section concludes the design of the model portion of our simulation. We fully implement this model in 877 lines of C++ code in Appendix G.

Appendix G—ATM Case Study Code—The majority of the case study involves designing the model (i.e., the data and logic) of the ATM system. In this appendix, we implement that model in C++. Using all the UML diagrams we created, we present the C++ classes necessary to implement the model. We apply the concepts of object-oriented design with the UML and object-oriented programming in C++ that you learned in the chapters. By the end of this appendix, students will have completed the design and implementation of a real-world system, and should feel confident tackling larger systems, such as those that professional software engineers build.

Appendix H—UML 2 Additional Diagrams—Overviews the UML 2 diagram types that are not found in the OOD/UML Case Study.

Software Bundled with C++ *How to Program, 5/e*

For the academic educational market only, this textbook is available in a value pack with Microsoft® Visual C++ .NET 2003 Standard Edition integrated development environment as a free supplement. There is no time limit for using the software. [*Note:* If you are a professional using this publication, you will have to either purchase the necessary software to build and run the applications in this textbook or download one of the many free compilers available online.][*Note:* If you are a student in a course for which this book is the required textbook, you must purchase your book from your college bookstore to ensure that you get the value pack with the software. College bookstores will need to order the books directly from Prentice Hall to get the value pack with the software. A caution—used books may not include the software.]

Free C++ Compilers and Trial-Edition C++ Compilers on the Web

Many C++ compilers are available for download from the Web. We discuss several that are available for free or as free-trial versions. Please keep in mind that in many cases, the trial-edition software cannot be used after the (often brief) trial period has expired.

One popular organization that develops free software is the GNU Project (`www.gnu.org`), originally created to develop a free operating system similar to UNIX.

GNU offers developer resources, including editors, debuggers and compilers. Many developers use the GCC (GNU Compiler Collection) compilers, available for download from gcc.gnu.org. The GCC contains compilers for C, C++, Java and other languages. The GCC compiler is a command-line compiler (i.e., it does not provide a graphical user interface). Many Linux and UNIX systems come with the GCC compiler installed. Red Hat has developed Cygwin (www.cygwin.com), an emulator that allows developers to use UNIX commands on Windows. Cygwin includes the GCC compiler.

Borland provides a Windows-based C++ developer product called C++Builder (www.borland.com/cbuilder/cppcomp/index.html). The basic C++Builder compiler (a command-line compiler) is free for download. Borland also provides several versions of C++Builder that contain graphical user interfaces (GUIs). These GUIs are formally called integrated development environments (IDEs) and enable the developer to edit, debug and test programs quickly and conveniently. Using an IDE, many of the tasks that involved tedious commands can now be executed via menus and buttons. Some of these products are available on a free-trial basis. For more information on C++Builder, visit

> www.borland.com/products/downloads/download_cbuilder.html

For Linux developers, Borland provides the Borland Kylix development environment. The Borland Kylix Open Edition, which includes an IDE, can be downloaded from

> www.borland.com/products/downloads/download_kylix.html

Borland also provides C++BuilderX—a cross-platform integrated C++ development environment. The free Personal Edition is available from

> www.borland.com/products/downloads/download_cbuilderx.html

The command-line compiler (version 5.6.4) that comes with C++BuilderX was one of several compilers we used to test the programs in this book. Many of the downloads available from Borland require users to register.

The Digital Mars C++ Compiler (www.digitalmars.com), is available for Windows and DOS, and includes tutorials and documentation. Readers can download a command-line or IDE version of the compiler. The DJGPP C/C++ development system is available for computers running DOS. DJGPP stands for DJ's GNU Programming Platform, where DJ is for DJ Delorie, the creator of DJGPP. Information on DJGPP can be found at www.delorie.com/djgpp. Locations where the compiler can be downloaded at are provided at www.delorie.com/djgpp/getting.html.

For a list of other compilers that are available free for download, visit the following sites:

> www.thefreecountry.com/developercity/ccompilers.shtml
> www.compilers.net

Warnings and Error Messages on Older C++ Compilers

The programs in this book are designed to be used with compilers that support standard C++. However, there are variations among compilers that may cause occasional warnings or errors. In addition, though the standard specifies various situations that require errors to be generated, it does not specify the messages that compilers should issue. Warnings and error messages vary among compilers—this is normal.

Some older C++ compilers, such as Microsoft Visual C++ 6, Borland C++ 5.5 and various earlier versions of GNU C++ generate error or warning messages in places where newer compilers do not. Although most of the examples in this book will work with these older compilers, there are a few examples that need minor modifications to work with older compilers. The Web site for this book (www.deitel.com/books/cpphtp5/index.html) lists the warnings and error messages that are produced by several older compilers and what, if anything, you can do to fix the warnings and errors.

Notes Regarding *using* Declarations and C Standard Library Functions

The C++ Standard Library includes the functions from the C Standard Library. According to the C++ standard document, the contents of the header files that come from the C Standard Library are part of the "std" namespace. Some compilers (old and new) generate error messages when using declarations are encountered for C functions. We will post a list of these issues at www.deitel.com/books/cpphtp5/index.html.

Dive Into™ Series Tutorials for Popular C++ Environments

Our free *Dive Into™* Series publications, which are available with the resources for *C++ How to Program, 5/e* at www.deitel.com/books/downloads.html, help students and instructors familiarize themselves with various C++ development tools. These publications include:

- *Dive Into Microsoft® Visual C++® 6*
- *Dive Into Microsoft® Visual C++® .NET*
- *Dive Into Borland™ C++Builder™ Compiler* (command-line version)
- *Dive Into Borland™ C++Builder™ Personal* (IDE version)
- *Dive Into GNU C++ on Linux* and *Dive Into GNU C++ via Cygwin on Windows* (Cygwin is a UNIX emulator for Windows. It includes the GNU C++ compiler)

Each of these tutorials shows how to compile, execute and debug C++ applications in that particular compiler product. Many of these documents also provide step-by-step instructions with screenshots to help readers install the software. Each document overviews the compiler and its online documentation.

Teaching Resources for *C++ How to Program, 5/e*

C++ How to Program, 5/e, has extensive resources for instructors. The Instructor version of the *Cyber Classroom* contains the *Solutions Manual* with solutions to the vast majority of the end-of-chapter exercises, a *Test Item File* of multiple-choice questions (approximately two per book section) and PowerPoint slides containing all the code and figures in the text, plus bulleted items that summarize the key points in the text. Instructors can customize the slides. [*Note:* The Instructor version of the Cyber Classroom is *available only to instructors* through their Prentice Hall representatives. Instructors who wish to know more about the *Deitel Cyber Classroom* should e-mail asia@pearsoned.com.hk, or telephone 852-31810884 or fax 852-27592391.

If you need additional help or if you have any questions about the IRCD, please e-mail us at `deitel@deitel.com`. We will respond promptly.]

C++ in the Lab

C++ in the Lab: Lab Manual to Accompany C++ How to Program, 5/e, our free online lab manual, complements *C++ How to Program, 5/e*, and *Small C++ How to Program, 5/e*, with hands-on lab assignments designed to reinforce students' comprehension of lecture material. *C++ in the Lab* will be available with the purchase of new books. This lab manual is designed for closed laboratories—regularly scheduled classes supervised by an instructor. Closed laboratories provide an excellent learning environment, because students can use concepts presented in class to solve carefully designed lab problems. Instructors are better able to measure the students' understanding of the material by monitoring the students' progress in lab. This lab manual also can be used for open laboratories, homework and for self-study.

The lab manual chapters are divided into *Prelab Activities*, *Lab Exercises* and *Postlab Activities*. Each chapter contains objectives that introduce the lab's key topics and an assignment checklist for students to mark which exercises the instructor has assigned.

Solutions to the lab manual's *Prelab Activities*, *Lab Exercises* and *Postlab Activities* are available in electronic form. Instructors can obtain these materials from their regular Prentice Hall representatives; the solutions are not available to students.

Prelab Activities

Prelab Activities are intended to be completed by students after studying each chapter of *Small C++ How to Program, 5/e*. *Prelab Activities* test students' understanding of the textbook material and prepare students for the programming exercises in the lab session. The exercises focus on important terminology and programming concepts and are effective for self-review. *Prelab Activities* include *Matching Exercises*, *Fill-in-the-Blank Exercises*, *Short-Answer Questions*, *Programming-Output Exercises* (determine what short code segments do without actually running the program) and *Correct-the-Code Exercises* (identify and correct all errors in short code segments).

Lab Exercises

The most important section in each chapter is the *Lab Exercises*. These teach students how to apply the material learned in *C++ How to Program, 5/e*, and prepare them for writing C++ programs. Each lab contains one or more lab exercises and a debugging problem. The *Lab Exercises* contain the following:

- *Lab Objectives* highlight specific concepts on which the lab exercise focuses.
- *Problem Descriptions* provide the details of the exercise and hints to help students implement the program.
- *Sample Outputs* illustrate the desired program behavior, which further clarifies the problem descriptions and aids the students with writing programs.
- *Program Templates* take complete C++ programs and replace key lines of code with comments describing the missing code.

- *Problem-Solving Tips* highlight key issues that students need to consider when solving the lab exercises.

- *Follow-Up Questions and Activities* ask students to modify solutions to the lab exercises, write new programs that are similar to their lab-exercise solutions or explain the implementation choices that were made when solving lab exercises.

- *Debugging Problems* consist of blocks of code that contain syntax errors and/or logic errors. These alert students to the types of errors they are likely to encounter while programming.

Postlab Activities

Professors typically assign *Postlab Activities* to reinforce key concepts or to provide students with more programming experience outside the lab. *Postlab Activities* test the students' understanding of the *Prelab* and *Lab Exercise* material, and ask students to apply their knowledge to creating programs from scratch. The section provides two types of programming activities: coding exercises and programming challenges. Coding exercises are short and serve as review after the *Prelab Activities* and *Lab Exercises* have been completed. The coding exercises ask students to write programs or program segments using key concepts from the textbook. *Programming Challenges* allow students to apply their knowledge to substantial programming exercises. Hints, sample outputs and pseudocode are provided to aid students with these problems. Students who successfully complete the *Programming Challenges* for a chapter have mastered the chapter material. Answers to the programming challenges are available at `www.deitel.com/books/downloads.html`.

PearsonChoices

Today's students have increasing demands on their time and money, and they need to be resourceful about how, when and where they study. Pearson/Prentice Hall, a division of Pearson Education, has responded to that need by creating PearsonChoices to allow faculty and students to choose from a variety of textbook formats and prices.

Small C++ How to Program, 5/e is our alternative print edition to *C++ How to Program, 5/e*. *Small C++ How to Program, 5/e* is a smaller text that is focused on Computer Science 1 (CS1) programming courses and is priced lower than our 23-chapter *C++ How to Program, 5/e* and other competing texts in the CS1 market.

Chapters in Both Small C++ How to Program, 5/e *and* C++ How to Program, 5/e

Chapter 1—Introduction to Computers, the Internet and World Wide Web
Chapter 2—Introduction to C++ Programming
Chapter 3—Introduction to Classes and Objects
Chapter 4—Control Statements: Part 1
Chapter 5—Control Statements: Part 2
Chapter 6—Functions and an Introduction to Recursion
Chapter 7—Arrays and Vectors
Chapter 8—Pointers and Pointer-Based Strings
Chapter 9—Classes: A Deeper Look, Part 1
Chapter 10—Classes: A Deeper Look, Part 2
Chapter 11—Operator Overloading: String and Array Objects

Chapter 12—Object-Oriented Programming: Inheritance
Chapter 13—Object-Oriented Programming: Polymorphism

Appendices in Both Small C++ How to Program, 5/e *and* C++ How to Program, 5/e

Operator Precedence and Associativity Chart
ASCII Character Set
Fundamental Types
Number Systems
C++ Internet and Web Resources
Using the Visual C++ .NET Debugger
Using the GNU C++ Debugger

Chapters in Only C++ How to Program, 5/e

Chapter 14—Templates
Chapter 15—Stream Input/Output
Chapter 16—Exception Handling
Chapter 17—File Processing
Chapter 18—Class `string` and String Stream Processing
Chapter 19—Web Programming
Chapter 20—Searching and Sorting
Chapter 21—Data Structures
Chapter 22—Standard Template Library
Chapter 23—Other Topics

Appendices in Only C++ How to Program, 5/e

C Legacy-Code Topics
Preprocessor
ATM Case Study Code
UML 2 Diagrams
Introduction to XHTML
XHTML Special Characters

SafariX WebBooks

SafariX Textbooks Online is a new service for college students looking to save money on required or recommended textbooks for academic courses. This secure WebBooks platform creates a new option in the higher education market; an additional choice for students alongside conventional textbooks and online learning services. Pearson provides students with a WebBook at 50% of the cost of its conventional print equivalent.

SafariX WebBooks are viewed through a Web browser connected to the Internet. No special plug-ins are required and no applications need to be downloaded. Students simply log in, purchase access and begin studying. With SafariX Textbooks Online students can search the text, make notes online, print out reading assignments that incorporate their professors' lecture notes and bookmark important passages they want to review later. They can navigate easily to a page number, reading assignment, or chapter. The Table of Contents of each WebBook appears in the left-hand column alongside the text.

We are pleased to offer students the *C++ How to Program, 5/e* SafariX WebBook available soon. Visit www.pearsonchoices.com for more information. Other Deitel titles available as SafariX WebBooks include *Java How to Program, 6/e, Small Java How to Program, 6/e, Small C++ How to Program, 5/e* and *Simply C++: An Application-Driven Tutorial Approach*. Visit www.safarix.com/tour.html for more information.

THE DEITEL® *Buzz Online* Free E-mail Newsletter

Our free e-mail newsletter, the DEITEL® *Buzz Online* is sent to approximately 38,000 opt-in, registered subscribers and includes commentary on industry trends and developments, links to free articles and resources from our published books and upcoming publications, product-release schedules, errata, challenges, anecdotes, information on our corporate instructor-led training courses and more. It's also our way to notify our readers rapidly about issues related to *C++ How to Program, 5/e*. To subscribe, visit

> www.deitel.com/newsletter/subscribe.html

Acknowledgments

One of the great pleasures of writing a textbook is acknowledging the efforts of many people whose names may not appear on the cover, but whose hard work, cooperation, friendship and understanding were crucial to the production of the book. Many people at Deitel & Associates, Inc. devoted long hours to working with us on this project.

- Andrew B. Goldberg is a graduate of Amherst College, where he earned a bachelor's degree in Computer Science. Andrew updated Chapters 1–13 based on the book's new early-classes presentation and other content revisions. He co-designed and co-authored the new, optional OOD/UML ATM case study that appears in Chapters 1–7, 9 and 13. He also contributed to Chapter 19 and co-authored Appendices G and H.

- Jeff Listfield is a Computer Science graduate of Harvard College. Jeff contributed to Chapters 18, 20, Appendices A–F and co-authored Appendices L and M.

- Su Zhang holds B.Sc. and a M.Sc. degrees in Computer Science from McGill University. Su contributed to Chapters 14–23.

- Cheryl Yaeger graduated from Boston University in three years with a bachelor's degree in Computer Science. Cheryl contributed to Chapters 4, 6, 8, 9 and 13.

- Barbara Deitel, Chief Financial Officer at Deitel & Associates, Inc. researched the quotes at the beginning of each chapter and applied copyedits to the book.

- Abbey Deitel, President of Deitel & Associates, Inc., is an Industrial Management graduate of Carnegie Mellon University. She contributed to the Preface and Chapter 1. She applied copyedits to several chapters in the book, managed the review process and suggested the theme and bug names for the cover of the book.

- Christi Kelsey is a graduate of Purdue University with a bachelor's degree in Management and a minor in Information Systems. Christi contributed to the Preface and Chapter 1. She edited the Index, paged the manuscript and coordinated many aspects of our publishing relationship with Prentice Hall.

We are fortunate to have worked on this project with the talented and dedicated team of publishing professionals at Prentice Hall. We especially appreciate the extraordinary efforts of our Computer Science Editor, Kate Hargett and her boss and our mentor in publishing—Marcia Horton, Editorial Director of Prentice Hall's Engineering and Computer Science Division. Jennifer Cappello did an extraordinary job recruiting the review team and managing the review process from the Prentice Hall side. Vince O'Brien, Tom Manshreck and John Lovell did a marvelous job managing the production of the book. The talents of Paul Belfanti, Carole Anson, Xiaohong Zhu and Geoffrey Cassar are evident in the redesign of the book's interior and the new cover art, and Sarah Parker managed the publication of the book's extensive ancillary package.

We sincerely appreciate the efforts of our fourth-edition post-publication reviewers and our fifth-edition reviewers:

Academic Reviewers
Richard Albright, Goldey Beacom College
Karen Arlien, Bismarck State College
David Branigan, DeVry University, Illinois
Jimmy Chen, Salt Lake Community College
Martin Dulberg, North Carolina State University
Ric Heishman, Northern Virginia Community College
Richard Holladay, San Diego Mesa College
William Honig, Loyola University
Earl LaBatt, OPNET Technologies, Inc./ University of New Hampshire
Brian Larson, Modesto Junior College
Robert Myers, Florida State University
Gavin Osborne, Saskatchewan Institute of Applied Science and Technology
Wolfgang Pelz, The University of Akron
Donna Reese, Mississippi State University

Industry Reviewers
Curtis Green, Boeing Integrated Defense Systems
Mahesh Hariharan, Microsoft
James Huddleston, Independent Consultant
Ed James-Beckham, Borland Software Corporation
Don Kostuch, Independent Consultant
Meng Lee, Hewlett-Packard
Kriang Lerdsuwanakij, Siemens Limited
William Mike Miller, Edison Design Group, Inc.
Mark Schimmel, Borland International
Vicki Scott, Metrowerks
James Snell, Boeing Integrated Defense Systems
Raymond Stephenson, Microsoft

OOD/UML Optional Software Engineering Case Study Reviewers
Sinan Si Alhir, Independent Consultant
Karen Arlien, Bismarck State College
David Branigan, DeVry University, Illinois
Martin Dulberg, North Carolina State University

Ric Heishman, Northern Virginia Community College
Richard Holladay, San Diego Mesa College
Earl LaBatt, OPNET Technologies, Inc./ University of New Hampshire
Brian Larson, Modesto Junior College
Gavin Osborne, Saskatchewan Institute of Applied Science and Technology
Praveen Sadhu, Infodat International, Inc.
Cameron Skinner, Embarcadero Technologies, Inc. / OMG
Steve Tockey, Construx Software

C++ 4/e Post-Publication Reviewers
Butch Anton, Wi-Tech Consulting
Karen Arlien, Bismarck State College
Jimmy Chen, Salt Lake Community College
Martin Dulberg, North Carolina State University
William Honig, Loyola University
Don Kostuch, Independent Consultant
Earl LaBatt, OPNET Technologies, Inc./ University of New Hampshire
Brian Larson, Modesto Junior College
Kriang Lerdsuwanakij, Siemens Limited
Robert Myers, Florida State University
Gavin Osborne, Saskatchewan Institute of Applied Science and Technology
Wolfgang Pelz, The University of Akron
David Papurt, Independent Consultant
Donna Reese, Mississippi State University
Catherine Wyman, DeVry University, Phoenix
Salih Yurttas, Texas A&M University

Under tight deadline pressure, they scrutinized every aspect of the text and made countless suggestions for improving the accuracy and completeness of the presentation.

Well, there you have it! Welcome to the exciting world of C++ and object-oriented programming. We hope you enjoy this look at contemporary computer programming. Good luck! As you read the book, we would sincerely appreciate your comments, criticisms, corrections and suggestions for improving the text. Please address all correspondence to:

deitel@deitel.com

We will respond promptly, and we will post corrections and clarifications on:

www.deitel.com/books/cpphtp5/index.html

We hope you enjoy learning with *C++ How to Program, Fifth Edition* as much as we enjoyed writing it!

Dr. Harvey M. Deitel
Paul J. Deitel

About the Authors

Dr. Harvey M. Deitel, Chairman and Chief Strategy Officer of Deitel & Associates, Inc., has 43 years experience in the computing field, including extensive industry and academic experience. Dr. Deitel earned B.S. and M.S. degrees from the Massachusetts Institute of Technology and a Ph.D. from Boston University. He worked on the pioneering virtual-memory operating-systems projects at IBM and MIT that developed techniques now widely implemented in systems such as UNIX, Linux and Windows XP. He has 20 years of college teaching experience, including earning tenure and serving as the Chairman of the Computer Science Department at Boston College before founding Deitel & Associates, Inc., with his son, Paul J. Deitel. Dr. Deitel has delivered hundreds of professional seminars to major corporations, academic institutions, government organizations and the military. He and Paul are the co-authors of several dozen books and multimedia packages and they are writing many more. With translations published in Japanese, German, Russian, Spanish, Traditional Chinese, Simplified Chinese, Korean, French, Polish, Italian, Portuguese, Greek, Urdu and Turkish, the Deitels' texts have earned international recognition.

Paul J. Deitel, CEO and Chief Technical Officer of Deitel & Associates, Inc., is a graduate of MIT's Sloan School of Management, where he studied Information Technology. Through Deitel & Associates, Inc., he has delivered C++, Java, C, Internet and World Wide Web courses to industry clients including IBM, Sun Microsystems, Dell, Lucent Technologies, Fidelity, NASA at the Kennedy Space Center, the National Severe Storm Laboratory, PalmSource, White Sands Missile Range, Rogue Wave Software, Boeing, Stratus, Cambridge Technology Partners, TJX, One Wave, Hyperion Software, Adra Systems, Entergy, CableData Systems and many other organizations. Paul is one of the world's most experienced Java and C++ corporate trainers having taught over 100 professional Java and C++ training courses. He has also lectured on C++ and Java for the Boston Chapter of the Association for Computing Machinery. He and his father, Dr. Harvey M. Deitel, are the world's best-selling Computer Science textbook authors.

About Deitel & Associates, Inc.

Deitel & Associates, Inc., is an internationally recognized corporate training and content-creation organization specializing in computer programming languages, Internet/World Wide Web software technology and object technology education. The company provides instructor-led courses on major programming languages and platforms such as Java, Advanced Java, C, C++, .NET programming languages, XML, Perl, Python; object technology; and Internet and World Wide Web programming. The founders of Deitel & Associates, Inc., are Dr. Harvey M. Deitel and Paul J. Deitel. The company's clients include many of the world's largest computer companies, government agencies, branches of the military and business organizations. Through its 29-year publishing partnership with Prentice Hall, Deitel & Associates, Inc. publishes leading-edge programming textbooks, professional books, interactive multimedia *Cyber Classrooms*, *Complete Training Courses*, Web-based training courses and course management systems e-content for popular CMSs such as WebCT, Blackboard and Pearson's CourseCompass. Deitel & Associates, Inc., and the authors can be reached via e-mail at:

    deitel@deitel.com

To learn more about Deitel & Associates, Inc., its publications and its worldwide *Dive Into*™ Series Corporate Training curriculum, see the last few pages of this book or visit:

```
www.deitel.com
```

and subscribe to the free DEITEL® *Buzz Online* e-mail newsletter at:

```
www.deitel.com/newsletter/subscribe.html
```

Individuals wishing to purchase Deitel books, Cyber Classrooms, Complete Training Courses and Web-based training courses can do so through:

```
www.deitel.com/books/index.html
```

Bulk orders by corporations and academic institutions should be placed directly with Prentice Hall. See the last few pages of this book for worldwide ordering details.

Before You Begin

Please follow the instructions in this section to ensure that the book's examples are copied properly to your computer before you begin using this book.

Font and Naming Conventions

We use fonts to distinguish between on-screen components (such as menu names and menu items) and C++ code or commands. Our convention is to emphasize on-screen components in a sans-serif bold **Helvetica** font (for example, **File** menu) and to emphasize C++ code and commands in a sans-serif Lucida font (for example, cout << "Hello";).

Resources on the CD That Accompanies C++ *How to Program, Fifth Edition*

The CD that accompanies this book includes:

- Hundreds of C++ LIVE-CODE examples
- Links to free C++ compilers and integrated development environments (IDEs)
- Hundreds of Web resources, including general references, tutorials, FAQs, newsgroups and STL information.

If you have any questions, please feel free to email us at deitel@deitel.com. We will respond promptly.

Copying and Organizing Files

All of the examples for *C++ How To Program, Fifth Edition* are included on the CD that accompanies this book. Follow the steps in the next section, *Copying the Book Examples from the CD*, to copy the examples directory from the CD onto your hard drive. We suggest that you work from your hard drive rather than your CD drive for two reasons: The CD is read-only, so you cannot save your applications to the book's CD, and files can be accessed faster from a hard drive than from a CD. The examples from the book are also available for download from:

```
www.deitel.com/books/cpphtp5/index.html
www.prenhall.com/deitel
```

We assume for the purpose of this Before You Begin section that you are using a computer running Microsoft Windows. Screen shots in the following section might differ slightly from what you see on your computer, depending on whether you are using Windows 2000 or Windows XP. If you are running a different operating system and have questions about copying the example files to your computer, please see your instructor.

Copying the Book Examples from the CD

1. *Inserting the CD.* Insert the CD that accompanies *C++ How To Program, Fifth Edition* into your computer's CD drive. The window displayed in Fig. 1 should appear. If the page appears, proceed to *Step 3* of this section. If the page does not appear, proceed to *Step 2.*

2. *Opening the CD directory using My Computer.* If the page shown in Fig. 1 does not appear, double click the **My Computer** icon on your desktop. In the **My Computer** window, double click your CD-ROM drive (Fig. 2) to load the CD (Fig. 1).

3. *Opening the CD-ROM directory.* If the page in Fig. 1 does appear, click the **Browse CD Contents** link (Fig. 1) to access the CD's contents.

4. *Copying the examples directory.* Right click the examples directory (Fig. 3), then select **Copy**. Next, go to **My Computer** and double click the **C:** drive. Select the **Edit** menu's **Paste** option to copy the directory and its contents from the CD to your **C:** drive. [*Note*: We save the examples to the **C:** drive and refer to this drive throughout the text. You may choose to save your files to a different drive based on your computer's setup, the setup in your school's lab or your personal preferences. If you are working in a computer lab, please see your instructor for more information to confirm where the examples should be saved.]

The example files you copied onto your computer from the CD are read-only. Next, you will remove the read-only property so you can modify and run the examples.

Changing the Read-Only Property of Files

1. *Opening the Properties dialog.* Right click the examples directory and select **Properties** from the menu. The **examples Properties** dialog appears (Fig. 4).

2. *Changing the read-only property.* In the **Attributes** section of this dialog, click the box next to **Read-only** to remove the check mark (Fig. 5). Click **Apply** to apply the changes.

3. *Changing the property for all files.* Clicking **Apply** will display the **Confirm Attribute Changes** window (Fig. 6). In this window, click the radio button next to **Apply changes to this folder, subfolders and files** and click **OK** to remove the read-only property for all of the files and directories in the examples directory.

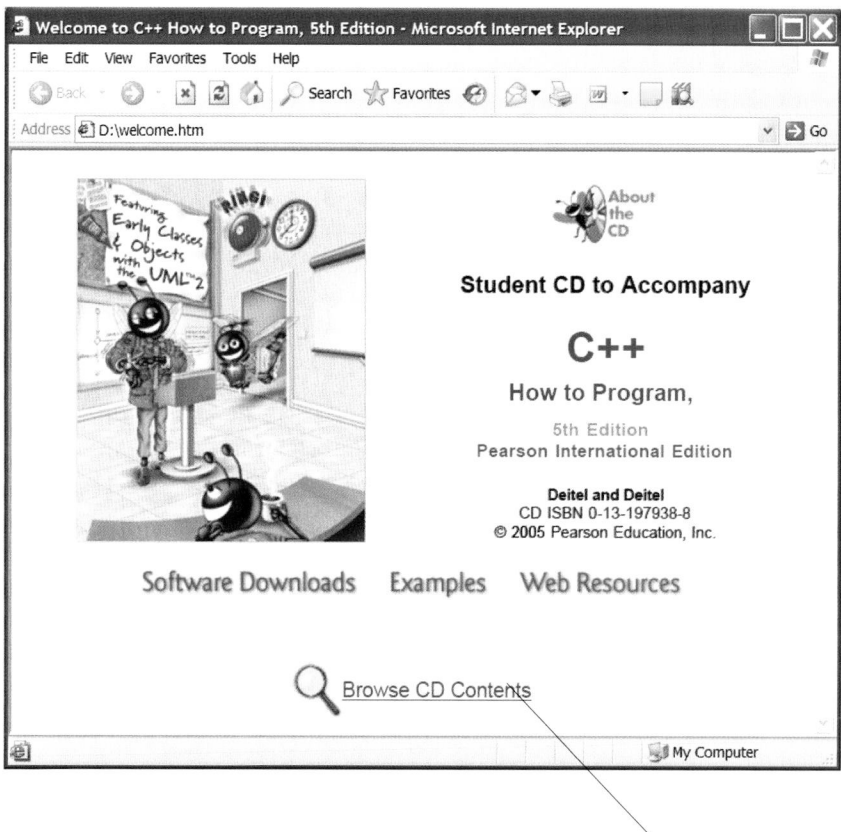

Click the **Browse CD Contents**
link to access the CD's contents

Fig. 1 | Welcome page for C++ *How to Program* CD.

Selected CD-ROM drive

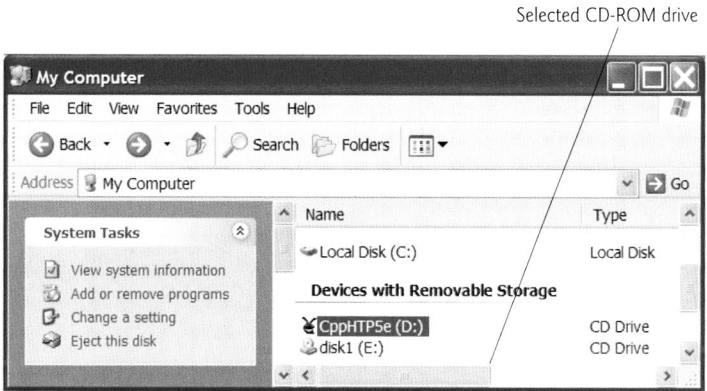

Fig. 2 | Locating the CD-ROM drive.

Right click the
`examples` directory

Select **Copy**

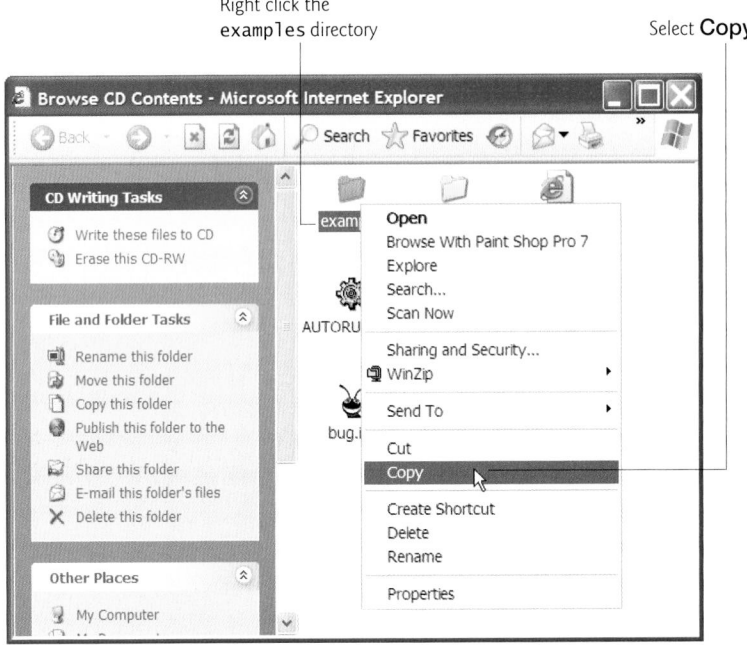

Fig. 3 | Copying the `examples` directory.

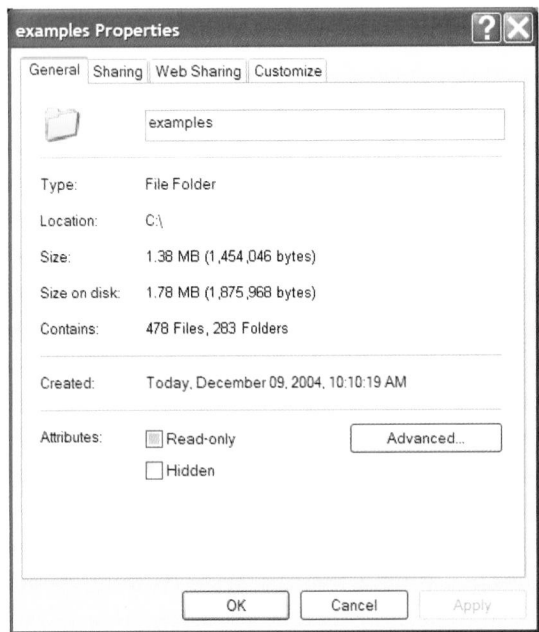

Fig. 4 | **examples Properties** dialog.

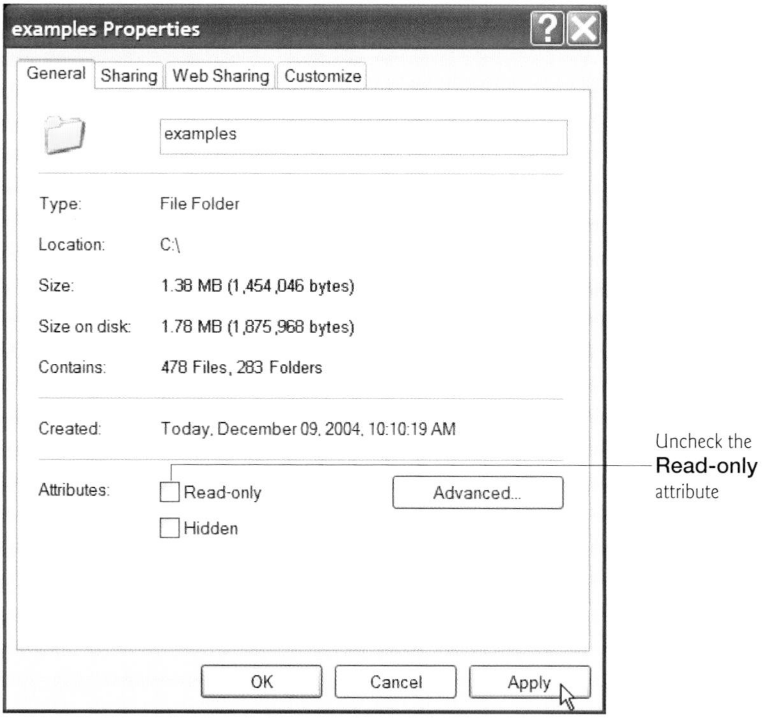

Fig. 5 | Unchecking the **Read-only** check box.

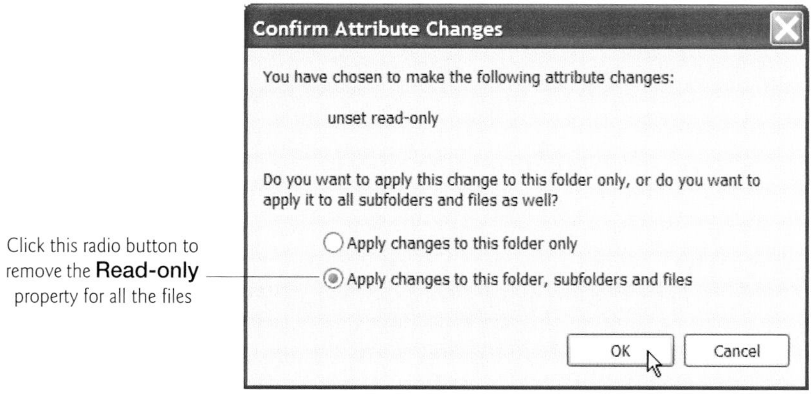

Fig. 6 | Removing read-only for all the files in the `examples` directory.

You are now ready to begin your C++ studies with *C++ How to Program*. We hope you enjoy the book! You can reach us easily at deitel@deitel.com. We will respond promptly.

Introduction to Computers, the Internet and World Wide Web

1

OBJECTIVES

In this chapter you will learn:

■ Basic hardware and software concepts.

■ Basic object-technology concepts, such as classes, objects, attributes, behaviors, encapsulation and inheritance.

■ The different types of programming languages.

■ A typical C++ program development environment.

■ The history of the industry-standard object-oriented system modeling language, the UML.

■ The history of the Internet and the World Wide Web.

■ To test-drive C++ applications in two popular C++ environments—GNU C++ running on Linux and Microsoft's Visual C++® .NET running on Windows® XP.

1.1   Introduction

Welcome to C++! We have worked hard to create what we hope you will find to be an informative, entertaining and challenging learning experience. C++ is a powerful computer programming language that is appropriate for technically oriented people with little or no programming experience and for experienced programmers to use in building substantial information systems. *C++ How to Program, Fifth Edition*, is an effective learning tool for each of these audiences.

The core of the book emphasizes achieving program *clarity* through the proven techniques of object-oriented programming—this is an "early classes and objects" book—nonprogrammers will learn programming the right way from the beginning. The presentation is clear, straightforward and abundantly illustrated. We teach C++ features in the context of complete working C++ programs and show the outputs produced when those programs are run on a computer—we call this the live-code approach. The example programs are included on the CD that accompanies this book, or you may download them from www.deitel.com or www.prenhall.com/deitel.

The early chapters introduce the fundamentals of computers, computer programming and the C++ computer programming language, providing a solid foundation for the deeper treatment of C++ in the later chapters. Experienced programmers tend to read the early chapters quickly, then find the treatment of C++ in the remainder of the book both rigorous and challenging.

Most people are at least somewhat familiar with the exciting things computers do. Using this textbook, you will learn how to command computers to do those things. Computers (often referred to as hardware) are controlled by software (i.e., the instructions you write to command the computer to perform actions and make decisions). C++ is one of today's most popular software development languages. This text provides an introduction to programming in the version of C++ standardized in the United States through the

American National Standards Institute (ANSI) and worldwide through the efforts of the International Organization for Standardization (ISO).

Computer use is increasing in almost every field of endeavor. Computing costs have been decreasing dramatically due to rapid developments in both hardware and software technologies. Computers that might have filled large rooms and cost millions of dollars a few decades ago can now be inscribed on silicon chips smaller than a fingernail, costing a few dollars each. (Those large computers were called mainframes and are widely used today in business, government and industry.) Fortunately, silicon is one of the most abundant materials on earth—it's an ingredient in common sand. Silicon chip technology has made computing so economical that about a billion general-purpose computers are in use worldwide, helping people in business, industry and government, and in their personal lives.

Over the years, many programmers learned the programming methodology called structured programming. You will learn structured programming and an exciting newer methodology, object-oriented programming. Why do we teach both? Object orientation is the key programming methodology used by programmers today. You will create and work with many software objects in this text. You will discover however, that their internal structure is often built using structured-programming techniques. Also, the logic of manipulating objects is occasionally expressed with structured programming.

You are embarking on a challenging and rewarding path. As you proceed, if you have any questions, please send e-mail to

        deitel@deitel.com

We will respond promptly. To keep up to date with C++ developments at Deitel & Associates, please register for our free e-mail newsletter, the *Deitel® Buzz Online,* at

        www.deitel.com/newsletter/subscribe.html

We hope that you will enjoy learning with C++ *How to Program, Fifth Edition.*

1.2   What Is a Computer?

A computer is a device capable of performing computations and making logical decisions at speeds millions (even billions) of times faster than human beings can. For example, many of today's personal computers can perform a billion additions per second. A person operating a desk calculator could spend an entire lifetime performing calculations and still not complete as many calculations as a powerful personal computer can perform in one second! (Points to ponder: How would you know whether the person added the numbers correctly? How would you know whether the computer added the numbers correctly?) Today's fastest supercomputers can perform trillions of additions per second!

Computers process data under the control of sets of instructions called computer programs. These programs guide the computer through orderly sets of actions specified by people called computer programmers.

A computer consists of various devices referred to as hardware (e.g., the keyboard, screen, mouse, hard disk, memory, DVDs and processing units). The programs that run on a computer are referred to as software. Hardware costs have been declining dramatically in recent years, to the point that personal computers have become a commodity. In this book, you will learn proven methods that are reducing software development costs—object-oriented programming and (in our optional Software Engineering Case Study in Chapters 2–7, 9 and 13) object-oriented design.

1.3 Computer Organization

Regardless of differences in physical appearance, virtually every computer may be envisioned as divided into six logical units or sections:

1. Input unit. This is the "receiving" section of the computer. It obtains information (data and computer programs) from input devices and places this information at the disposal of the other units for processing. Most information is entered into computers through keyboards and mouse devices. Information also can be entered in many other ways, including by speaking to your computer, scanning images and having your computer receive information from a network, such as the Internet.

2. Output unit. This is the "shipping" section of the computer. It takes information that the computer has processed and places it on various output devices to make the information available for use outside the computer. Most information output from computers today is displayed on screens, printed on paper or used to control other devices. Computers also can output their information to networks, such as the Internet.

3. Memory unit. This is the rapid-access, relatively low-capacity "warehouse" section of the computer. It stores computer programs while they are being executed. It retains information that has been entered through the input unit, so that it will be immediately available for processing when needed. The memory unit also retains processed information until it can be placed on output devices by the output unit. Information in the memory unit is typically lost when the computer's power is turned off. The memory unit is often called either memory or primary memory. [Historically, this unit has been called "core memory," but that term is fading from use today.]

4. Arithmetic and logic unit (ALU). This is the "manufacturing" section of the computer. It is responsible for performing calculations, such as addition, subtraction, multiplication and division. It contains the decision mechanisms that allow the computer, for example, to compare two items from the memory unit to determine whether they are equal.

5. Central processing unit (CPU). This is the "administrative" section of the computer. It coordinates and supervises the operation of the other sections. The CPU tells the input unit when information should be read into the memory unit, tells the ALU when information from the memory unit should be used in calculations and tells the output unit when to send information from the memory unit to certain output devices. Many of today's computers have multiple CPUs and, hence, can perform many operations simultaneously—such computers are called multiprocessors.

6. Secondary storage unit. This is the long-term, high-capacity "warehousing" section of the computer. Programs or data not actively being used by the other units normally are placed on secondary storage devices, such as your hard drive, until they are again needed, possibly hours, days, months or even years later. Information in secondary storage takes much longer to access than information in primary memory, but the cost per unit of secondary storage is much less than that of primary memory. Other secondary storage devices include CDs and DVDs, which can hold hundreds of millions of characters and billions of characters, respectively.

1.4 Early Operating Systems

Early computers could perform only one job or task at a time. This is often called single-user batch processing. The computer runs a single program at a time while processing data in groups or batches. In these early systems, users generally submitted their jobs to a computer center on decks of punched cards and often had to wait hours or even days before printouts were returned to their desks.

Software systems called operating systems were developed to make using computers more convenient. Early operating systems smoothed and speeded up the transition between jobs, and hence increased the amount of work, or throughput, computers could process.

As computers became more powerful, it became evident that single-user batch processing was inefficient, because so much time was spent waiting for slow input/output devices to complete their tasks. It was thought that many jobs or tasks could *share* the resources of the computer to achieve better utilization. This is achieved by multiprogramming. Multiprogramming involves the simultaneous operation of many jobs that are competing to share the computer's resources. With early multiprogramming operating systems, users still submitted jobs on decks of punched cards and waited hours or days for results.

In the 1960s, several groups in industry and the universities pioneered timesharing operating systems. Timesharing is a special case of multiprogramming in which users access the computer through terminals, typically devices with keyboards and screens. Dozens or even hundreds of users share the computer at once. The computer actually does not run them all simultaneously. Rather, it runs a small portion of one user's job, then moves on to service the next user, perhaps providing service to each user several times per second. Thus, the users' programs *appear* to be running simultaneously. An advantage of timesharing is that user requests receive almost immediate responses.

1.5 Personal, Distributed and Client/Server Computing

In 1977, Apple Computer popularized personal computing. Computers became so economical that people could buy them for their own personal or business use. In 1981, IBM, the world's largest computer vendor, introduced the IBM Personal Computer. This quickly legitimized personal computing in business, industry and government organizations, as IBM mainframes were heavily used.

These computers were "stand-alone" units—people transported disks back and forth between them to share information (often called "sneakernet"). Although early personal computers were not powerful enough to timeshare several users, these machines could be linked together in computer networks, sometimes over telephone lines and sometimes in local area networks (LANs) within an organization. This led to the phenomenon of distributed computing, in which an organization's computing, instead of being performed only at some central computer installation, is distributed over networks to the sites where the organization's work is performed. Personal computers were powerful enough to handle the computing requirements of individual users as well as the basic communications tasks of passing information between computers electronically.

Today's personal computers are as powerful as the million-dollar machines of just a few decades ago. The most powerful desktop machines—called workstations—provide individual users with enormous capabilities. Information is shared easily across computer networks, where computers called file servers offer a common data store that may be used by client computers distributed throughout the network, hence the term client/server computing. C++ has become widely used for writing software for operating systems, for computer networking and for distributed client/server applications. Today's popular operating systems such as UNIX, Linux, Mac OS X and Microsoft's Windows-based systems provide the kinds of capabilities discussed in this section.

1.6 The Internet and the World Wide Web

The Internet—a global network of computers—was initiated almost four decades ago with funding supplied by the U.S. Department of Defense. Originally designed to connect the main computer systems of about a dozen universities and research organizations, the Internet today is accessible by computers worldwide.

With the introduction of the World Wide Web—which allows computer users to locate and view multimedia-based documents on almost any subject over the Internet—the Internet has exploded into one of the world's premier communication mechanisms.

The Internet and the World Wide Web are surely among humankind's most important and profound creations. In the past, most computer applications ran on computers that were not connected to one another. Today's applications can be written to communicate among the world's computers. The Internet mixes computing and communications technologies. It makes our work easier. It makes information instantly and conveniently accessible worldwide. It enables individuals and local small businesses to get worldwide exposure. It is changing the way business is done. People can search for the best prices on virtually any product or service. Special-interest communities can stay in touch with one another. Researchers can be made instantly aware of the latest breakthroughs. After you master Chapter 19, Web Programming, you will be able to develop Internet-based computer applications.

1.7 Machine Languages, Assembly Languages and High-Level Languages

Programmers write instructions in various programming languages, some directly understandable by computers and others requiring intermediate translation steps. Hundreds of computer languages are in use today. These may be divided into three general types:

1. Machine languages

2. Assembly languages

3. High-level languages

Any computer can directly understand only its own machine language. Machine language is the "natural language" of a computer and as such is defined by its hardware design. [*Note:* Machine language is often referred to as object code. This term predates "object-oriented programming." These two uses of "object" are unrelated.] Machine languages generally consist of strings of numbers (ultimately reduced to 1s and 0s) that instruct computers to perform their most elementary operations one at a time. Machine languages are machine dependent (i.e., a particular machine language can be used on only one type of computer). Such languages are cumbersome for humans, as illustrated by the following section of an early machine-language program that adds overtime pay to base pay and stores the result in gross pay:

```
+1300042774
+1400593419
+1200274027
```

Machine-language programming was simply too slow, tedious and error-prone for most programmers. Instead of using the strings of numbers that computers could directly understand, programmers began using English-like abbreviations to represent elementary operations. These abbreviations formed the basis of assembly languages. Translator programs called assemblers were developed to convert early assembly-language programs to machine language at computer speeds. The following section of an assembly-language program also adds overtime pay to base pay and stores the result in gross pay:

```
load    basepay
add     overpay
store   grosspay
```

Although such code is clearer to humans, it is incomprehensible to computers until translated to machine language.

Computer usage increased rapidly with the advent of assembly languages, but programmers still had to use many instructions to accomplish even the simplest tasks. To speed the programming process, high-level languages were developed in which single statements could be written to accomplish substantial tasks. Translator programs called compilers convert high-level language programs into machine language. High-level languages allow programmers to write instructions that look almost like everyday English and contain commonly used mathematical notations. A payroll program written in a high-level language might contain a statement such as

```
grossPay = basePay + overTimePay;
```

From the programmer's standpoint, obviously, high-level languages are preferable to machine and assembly language. C, C++, Microsoft's .NET languages (e.g., Visual Basic .NET, Visual C++ .NET and C#) and Java are among the most widely used high-level programming languages.

The process of compiling a high-level language program into machine language can take a considerable amount of computer time. Interpreter programs were developed to execute high-level language programs directly, although much more slowly. Interpreters are popular in program development environments in which new features are being added and errors corrected. Once a program is fully developed, a compiled version can be produced to run most efficiently.

1.8 History of C and C++

C++ evolved from C, which evolved from two previous programming languages, BCPL and B. BCPL was developed in 1967 by Martin Richards as a language for writing operating-systems software and compilers for operating systems. Ken Thompson modeled many features in his language B after their counterparts in BCPL and used B to create early versions of the UNIX operating system at Bell Laboratories in 1970.

The C language was evolved from B by Dennis Ritchie at Bell Laboratories. C uses many important concepts of BCPL and B. C initially became widely known as the development language of the UNIX operating system. Today, most operating systems are written in C and/or C++. C is now available for most computers and is hardware independent. With careful design, it is possible to write C programs that are portable to most computers.

The widespread use of C with various kinds of computers (sometimes called hardware platforms) unfortunately led to many variations. This was a serious problem for program developers, who needed to write portable programs that would run on several platforms. A standard version of C was needed. The American National Standards Institute (ANSI) cooperated with the International Organization for Standardization (ISO) to standardize C worldwide; the joint standard document was published in 1990 and is referred to as *ANSI/ISO 9899: 1990*.

Portability Tip 1.1

Because C is a standardized, hardware-independent, widely available language, applications written in C often can be run with little or no modification on a wide range of computer systems.

C++, an extension of C, was developed by Bjarne Stroustrup in the early 1980s at Bell Laboratories. C++ provides a number of features that "spruce up" the C language, but more importantly, it provides capabilities for object-oriented programming.

A revolution is brewing in the software community. Building software quickly, correctly and economically remains an elusive goal, and this at a time when the demand for new and more powerful software is soaring. Objects are essentially reusable software components that model items in the real world. Software developers are discovering that using a modular, object-oriented design and implementation approach can make them much more productive than they can be with previous popular programming techniques. Object-oriented programs are easier to understand, correct and modify.

1.9 C++ Standard Library

C++ programs consist of pieces called classes and functions. You can program each piece that you may need to form a C++ program. However, most C++ programmers take advantage of the rich collections of existing classes and functions in the C++ Standard Library. Thus, there are really two parts to learning the C++ "world." The first is learning the C++ language itself; the second is learning how to use the classes and functions in the C++ Standard Library. Throughout the book, we discuss many of these classes and functions. P J. Plauger's book, *The Standard C Library* (Upper Saddle River, NJ: Prentice Hall PTR, 1992), is a must read for programmers who need a deep understanding of the ANSI C library functions that are included in C++, how to implement them and how to use them to write portable code. The standard class libraries generally are provided by compiler vendors. Many special-purpose class libraries are supplied by independent software vendors.

Software Engineering Observation 1.1

Use a "building-block" approach to create programs. Avoid reinventing the wheel. Use existing pieces wherever possible. Called software reuse, this practice is central to object-oriented programming.

> **Software Engineering Observation 1.2**
>
> *When programming in C++, you typically will use the following building blocks: Classes and functions from the C++ Standard Library, classes and functions you and your colleagues create and classes and functions from various popular third-party libraries.*

We include many Software Engineering Observations throughout the book to explain concepts that affect and improve the overall architecture and quality of software systems. We also highlight other kinds of tips, including Good Programming Practices (to help you write programs that are clearer, more understandable, more maintainable and easier to test and debug—or remove programming errors), Common Programming Errors (problems to watch out for and avoid), Performance Tips (techniques for writing programs that run faster and use less memory), Portability Tips (techniques to help you write programs that can run, with little or no modification, on a variety of computers— these tips also include general observations about how C++ achieves its high degree of portability) and Error-Prevention Tips (techniques for removing bugs from your programs and, more important, techniques for writing bug-free programs in the first place). Many of these are only guidelines. You will, no doubt, develop your own preferred programming style.

The advantage of creating your own functions and classes is that you will know exactly how they work. You will be able to examine the C++ code. The disadvantage is the time-consuming and complex effort that goes into designing, developing and maintaining new functions and classes that are correct and that operate efficiently.

> **Performance Tip 1.1**
>
> *Using C++ Standard Library functions and classes instead of writing your own versions can improve program performance, because they are written carefully to perform efficiently. This technique also shortens program development time.*

> **Portability Tip 1.2**
>
> *Using C++ Standard Library functions and classes instead of writing your own improves program portability, because they are included in every C++ implementation.*

1.10 Typical C++ Development Environment

Let's consider the steps in creating and executing a C++ application using a C++ development environment (illustrated in Fig. 1.1). C++ systems generally consist of three parts: a program development environment, the language and the C++ Standard Library. C++ programs typically go through six phases: edit, preprocess, compile, link, load and execute. The following discussion explains a typical C++ program development environment. [*Note:* On our Web site at www.deitel.com/books/downloads.html, we provide *DEITEL®️ DIVE INTO™ Series* publications to help you begin using several popular C++ development tools, including Borland® C++Builder™, Microsoft® Visual C++® 6, Microsoft® Visual C++® .NET, GNU C++ on Linux and GNU C++ on the Cygwin™ UNIX® environment for Windows®. We will make other *DIVE INTO™ Series* publications available as instructors request them.]

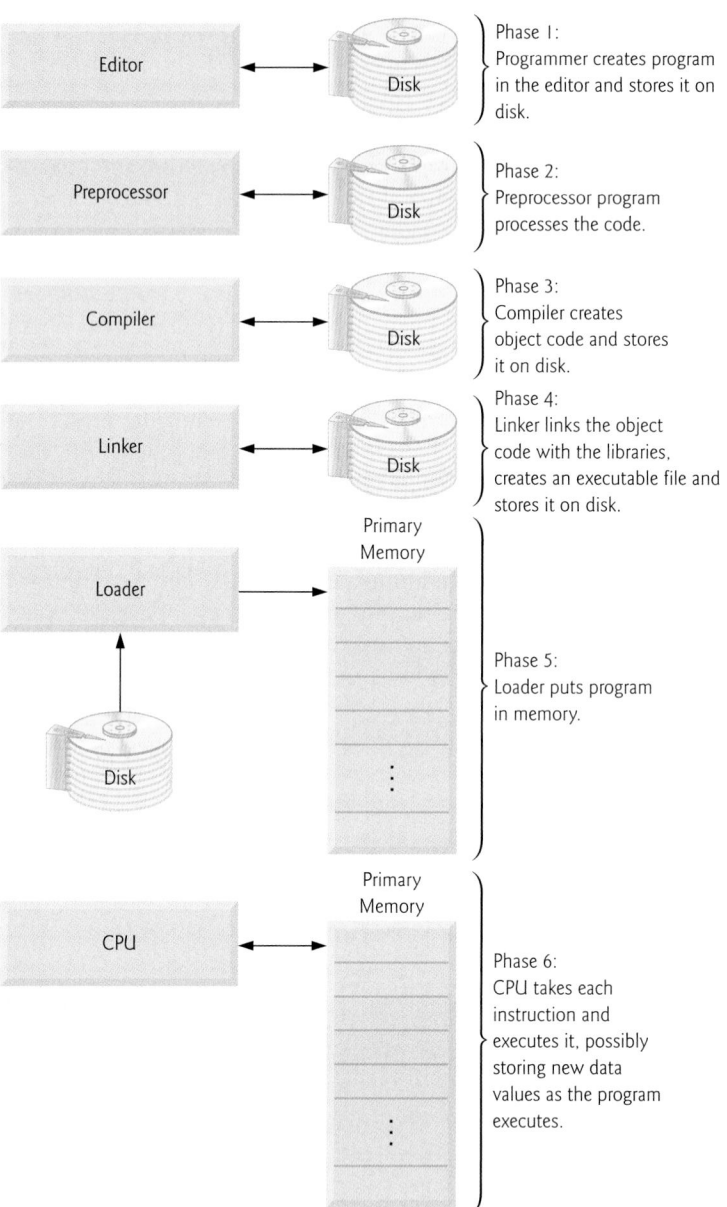

Fig. 1.1 | Typical C++ environment.

Phase 1: Creating a Program

Phase 1 consists of editing a file with an editor program (normally known simply as an editor). You type a C++ program (typically referred to as source code) using the editor, make any necessary corrections and save the program on a secondary storage device, such as your hard drive. C++ source code file names often end with the `.cpp`, `.cxx`, `.cc` or `.C` extensions (note that `C` is in uppercase) which indicate that a file contains C++ source code. See the documentation for your C++ environment for more information on file-name extensions.

Two editors widely used on UNIX systems are `vi` and `emacs`. C++ software packages for Microsoft Windows such as Borland C++ (`www.borland.com`), Metrowerks CodeWarrior (`www.metrowerks.com`) and Microsoft Visual C++ (`www.msdn.microsoft.com/visualc/`) have editors integrated into the programming environment. You can also use a simple text editor, such as Notepad in Windows, to write your C++ code. We assume the reader knows how to edit a program.

Phases 2 and 3: Preprocessing and Compiling a C++ Program

In phase 2, the programmer gives the command to compile the program. In a C++ system, a preprocessor program executes automatically before the compiler's translation phase begins (so we call preprocessing phase 2 and compiling phase 3). The C++ preprocessor obeys commands called preprocessor directives, which indicate that certain manipulations are to be performed on the program before compilation. These manipulations usually include other text files to be compiled and perform various text replacements. The most common preprocessor directives are discussed in the early chapters; a detailed discussion of all the preprocessor features appears in Appendix F, Preprocessor. In phase 3, the compiler translates the C++ program into machine-language code (also referred to as object code).

Phase 4: Linking

Phase 4 is called linking. C++ programs typically contain references to functions and data defined elsewhere, such as in the standard libraries or in the private libraries of groups of programmers working on a particular project. The object code produced by the C++ compiler typically contains "holes" due to these missing parts. A linker links the object code with the code for the missing functions to produce an executable image (with no missing pieces). If the program compiles and links correctly, an executable image is produced.

Phase 5: Loading

Phase 5 is called loading. Before a program can be executed, it must first be placed in memory. This is done by the loader, which takes the executable image from disk and transfers it to memory. Additional components from shared libraries that support the program are also loaded.

Phase 6: Execution

Finally, the computer, under the control of its CPU, executes the program one instruction at a time.

Problems That May Occur at Execution Time

Programs do not always work on the first try. Each of the preceding phases can fail because of various errors that we discuss throughout the book. For example, an executing program might attempt to divide by zero (an illegal operation for whole-number arithmetic in C++). This would cause the C++ program to display an error message. If this occurs, you would have to return to the edit phase, make the necessary corrections and proceed through the remaining phases again to determine that the corrections fix the problem(s).

Most programs in C++ input and/or output data. Certain C++ functions take their input from `cin` (the standard input stream; pronounced "see-in"), which is normally the keyboard, but `cin` can be redirected to another device. Data is often output to `cout` (the standard output stream; pronounced "see-out"), which is normally the computer screen, but `cout` can be redirected to another device. When we say that a program prints a result, we normally mean that the result is displayed on a screen. Data may be output to other devices, such as disks and hardcopy printers. There is also a standard error stream referred to as `cerr`. The `cerr` stream (normally connected to the screen) is used for displaying error messages. It is common for users to assign `cout` to a device other than the screen while keeping `cerr` assigned to the screen, so that normal outputs are separated from errors.

Common Programming Error 1.1

Errors like division by zero occur as a program runs, so they are called runtime errors or execution-time errors. Fatal runtime errors cause programs to terminate immediately without having successfully performed their jobs. Nonfatal runtime errors allow programs to run to completion, often producing incorrect results. [Note: On some systems, divide-by-zero is not a fatal error. Please see your system documentation.]

1.11 Notes About C++ and *C++ How to Program, 5/e*

Experienced C++ programmers sometimes take pride in being able to create some weird, contorted, convoluted usage of the language. This is a poor programming practice. It makes programs more difficult to read, more likely to behave strangely, more difficult to test and debug, and more difficult to adapt to changing requirements. This book is geared for novice programmers, so we stress program *clarity*. The following is our first "good programming practice."

Good Programming Practice 1.1

Write your C++ programs in a simple and straightforward manner. This is sometimes referred to as KIS ("keep it simple"). Do not "stretch" the language by trying bizarre usages.

You have heard that C and C++ are portable languages, and that programs written in C and C++ can run on many different computers. *Portability is an elusive goal.* The ANSI C standard document contains a lengthy list of portability issues, and complete books have been written that discuss portability.

Portability Tip 1.3

Although it is possible to write portable programs, there are many problems among different C and C++ compilers and different computers that can make portability difficult to achieve. Writing programs in C and C++ does not guarantee portability. The programmer often will need to deal directly with compiler and computer variations. As a group, these are sometimes called platform variations.

We have audited our presentation against the ANSI/ISO C++ standard document for completeness and accuracy. However, C++ is a rich language, and there are some features we have not covered. If you need additional technical details on C++, you may want to read the C++ standard document, which can be ordered from the ANSI Web site at

```
webstore.ansi.org/ansidocstore/default.asp
```

The title of the document is "Information Technology – Programming Languages – C++" and its document number is INCITS/ISO/IEC 14882-2003.

We have included an extensive bibliography of books and papers on C++ and object-oriented programming. We also have included a C++ Resources appendix containing many Internet and Web sites relating to C++ and object-oriented programming. We have listed several Web sites in Section 1.14 including links to free C++ compilers, resource sites and some fun C++ games and game programming tutorials.

Good Programming Practice 1.2

Read the manuals for the version of C++ you are using. Refer to these manuals frequently to be sure you are aware of the rich collection of C++ features and that you are using them correctly.

Good Programming Practice 1.3

Your computer and compiler are good teachers. If after reading your C++ language manual, you still are not sure how a feature of C++ works, experiment using a small "test program" and see what happens. Set your compiler options for "maximum warnings." Study each message that the compiler generates and correct the programs to eliminate the messages.

1.12 Test-Driving a C++ Application

In this section, you will run and interact with your first C++ application. You will begin by running an entertaining guess-the-number game, which picks a number from 1 to 1000 and prompts you to guess the number. If your guess is correct, the game ends. If your guess is not correct, the application indicates whether your guess is higher or lower than the correct number. There is no limit on the number of guesses you can make. [*Note:* For this test drive only, we have modified this application from the exercise you will be asked to create in Chapter 6, Functions and an Introduction to Recursion. Typically this application selects different numbers for you to guess each time you run it, because it chooses the numbers to guess at random. Our modified application chooses the same "correct" guesses every time you execute the program. This allows you to use the same guesses and see the same results that we show as we walk you through interacting with your first C++ application.]

We will demonstrate running a C++ application in two ways—using the Windows XP **Command Prompt** and using a shell on Linux (similar to a Windows **Command Prompt**). The application runs similarly on both platforms. Many development environments are available in which readers can compile, build and run C++ applications, such as Borland's C++Builder, Metrowerks, GNU C++, Microsoft Visual C++ .NET, etc. While we don't test-drive each of these environments, we do provide information in Section 1.14 regarding free C++ compilers available for download on the Internet. Please see your instructor for information on your specific development environment. Also, we provide several *Dive-Into™ Series* publications to help you get started with various C++ compliers. These are available free for download at `www.deitel.com/books/cpphtp5/index.html`.

In the following steps, you will run the application and enter various numbers to guess the correct number. The elements and functionality that you see in this application are typical of those you will learn to program in this book. Throughout the book, we use fonts to distinguish between features you see on the screen (e.g., the **Command Prompt**) and elements that are not directly related to the screen. Our convention is to emphasize screen features like titles and menus (e.g., the **File** menu) in a semibold **sans-serif Helvetica** font and to emphasize file names, text displayed by an application and values you should enter into an application (e.g., `GuessNumber` or `500`), in a `sans-serif Lucida` font. As you have noticed, the defining occurrence of each term is set in blue, heavy bold. For the figures in this section, we highlight the user input required by each step and point out significant parts of the application. To make these features more visible, we have modified the background color of the **Command Prompt** window (for the Windows test-drive only). To modify the colors of the **Command Prompt** on your system, open a **Command Prompt**, then right click the title bar and select **Properties**. In the "**Command Prompt**" **Properties** dialog box that appears, click the **Colors** tab, and select your preferred text and background colors.]

Running a C++ application from the Windows XP Command Prompt

1. *Checking your setup.* Read the *Before You Begin* section at the beginning of this textbook to make sure that you have copied the book's examples to your hard drive correctly.

2. *Locating the completed application.* Open a **Command Prompt** window. For readers using Windows 95, 98 or 2000, select **Start > Programs > Accessories > Command Prompt**. For Windows XP users, select **Start > All Programs > Accessories > Command Prompt**. To change to your completed **GuessNumber** application directory, type **cd C:\examples\ch01\GuessNumber\Windows**, then press *Enter* (Fig. 1.2). The command cd is used to change directories.

3. *Running the GuessNumber application.* Now that you are in the directory that contains the **GuessNumber** application, type the command **GuessNumber** (Fig. 1.3) and press *Enter*. [*Note:* GuessNumber.exe is the actual name of the application; however, Windows assumes the .exe extension by default.]

4. *Entering your first guess.* The application displays "Please type your first guess.", then displays a question mark (?) as a prompt on the next line (Fig. 1.3). At the prompt, enter **500** (Fig. 1.4).

5. *Entering another guess.* The application displays "Too high. Try again.", meaning that the value you entered is greater than the number the application chose as the correct guess. So, you should enter a lower number for your next guess. At the prompt, enter **250** (Fig. 1.5). The application again displays "Too high. Try again.", because the value you entered is still greater than the number that the correct guess.

```
C:\>cd C:\examples\ch01\GuessNumber\Windows
C:\examples\ch01\GuessNumber\Windows>
```

Fig. 1.2 | Opening a **Command Prompt** window and changing the directory.

```
C:\examples\ch01\GuessNumber\Windows>GuessNumber
I have a number between 1 and 1000.
Can you guess my number?
Please type your first guess.
?
```

Fig. 1.3 | Running the **GuessNumber** application.

```
Command Prompt - GuessNumber                                    _ □ x
C:\examples\ch01\GuessNumber\Windows>GuessNumber
I have a number between 1 and 1000.
Can you guess my number?
Please type your first guess.
? 500
Too high. Try again.
?
```

Fig. 1.4 | Entering your first guess.

```
Command Prompt - GuessNumber                                    _ □ x
C:\examples\ch01\GuessNumber\Windows>GuessNumber
I have a number between 1 and 1000.
Can you guess my number?
Please type your first guess.
? 500
Too high. Try again.
? 250
Too high. Try again.
? _
```

Fig. 1.5 | Entering a second guess and receiving feedback.

6. ***Entering additional guesses.*** Continue to play the game by entering values until you guess the correct number. Once you guess the answer, the application will display "Excellent! You guessed the number!" (Fig. 1.6).

7. ***Playing the game again or exiting the application.*** After guessing the correct number, the application asks if you would like to play another game (Fig. 1.6). At the "Would you like to play again (y or n)?" prompt, entering the one character **y** causes the application to choose a new number and displays the message "Please enter your first guess." followed by a question mark prompt (Fig. 1.7) so you can make your first guess in the new game. Entering the character **n** ends the application and returns you to the application's directory at the **Command Prompt** (Fig. 1.8). Each time you execute this application from the beginning (i.e., *Step 3*), it will choose the same numbers for you to guess.

8. *Close the* **Command Prompt** *window.*

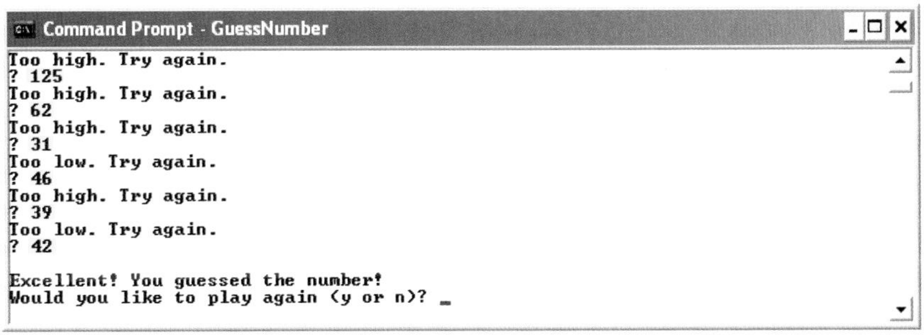

```
Command Prompt - GuessNumber                                    _ □ x
Too high. Try again.
? 125
Too high. Try again.
? 62
Too high. Try again.
? 31
Too low. Try again.
? 46
Too high. Try again.
? 39
Too low. Try again.
? 42

Excellent! You guessed the number!
Would you like to play again (y or n)? _
```

Fig. 1.6 | Entering additional guesses and guessing the correct number.

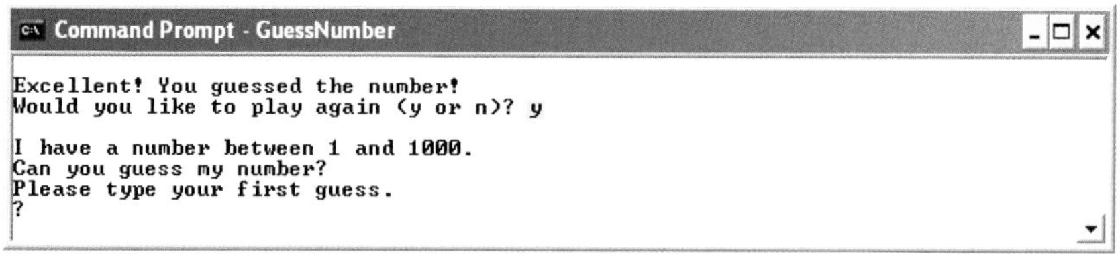

```
Command Prompt - GuessNumber                              _ □ ×
Excellent! You guessed the number!
Would you like to play again (y or n)? y

I have a number between 1 and 1000.
Can you guess my number?
Please type your first guess.
?
```

Fig. 1.7 | Playing the game again.

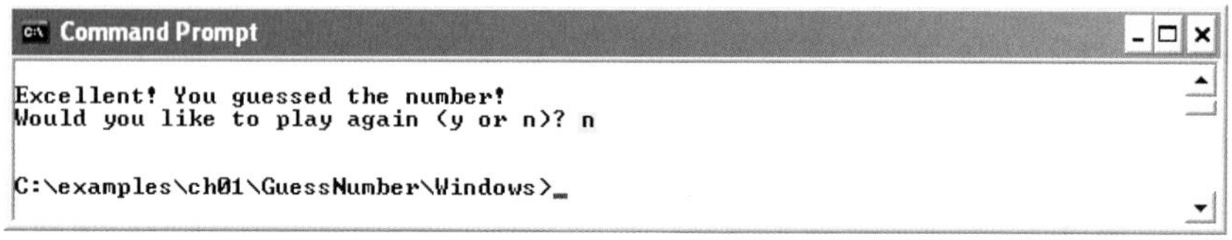

```
Command Prompt                                            _ □ ×
Excellent! You guessed the number!
Would you like to play again (y or n)? n

C:\examples\ch01\GuessNumber\Windows>_
```

Fig. 1.8 | Exiting the game.

Running a C++ Application Using GNU C++ with Linux

For this test drive, we assume that you know how to copy the examples into your home directory. Please see your instructor if you have any questions regarding copying the files to your Linux system. Also, for the figures in this section, we use a bold highlight to point out the user input required by each step. The prompt in the shell on our system uses the tilde (~) character to represent the home directory and each prompt ends with the dollar sign ($) character. The prompt will vary among Linux systems.

1. **Locating the completed application.** From a Linux shell, change to the completed **GuessNumber** application directory (Fig. 1.9) by typing

   `cd Examples\ch01\GuessNumber\GNU_Linux`

   then pressing *Enter*. The command cd is used to change directories.

2. *Compiling the GuessNumber application.* To run an application on the GNU C++ compiler, it must first be compiled by typing

   `g++ GuessNumber.cpp -o GuessNumber`

   as in Fig. 1.10. The preceding command compiles the application and produces an executable file called GuessNumber.

3. *Running the GuessNumber application.* To run the executable file GuessNumber, type ./GuessNumber at the next prompt, then press *Enter* (Fig. 1.11).

```
~$ cd examples/ch01/GuessNumber/GNU_Linux
~/examples/ch01/GuessNumber/GNU_Linux$
```

Fig. 1.9 | Changing to the **GuessNumber** application's directory after logging in to your Linux account.

```
~/examples/ch01/GuessNumber/GNU_Linux$ g++ GuessNumber.cpp -o GuessNumber
~/examples/ch01/GuessNumber/GNU_Linux$
```

Fig. 1.10 | Compiling the **GuessNumber** application using the g++ command.

```
~/examples/ch01/GuessNumber/GNU_Linux$ ./GuessNumber
I have a number between 1 and 1000.
Can you guess my number?
Please type your first guess.
?
```

Fig. 1.11 | Running the **GuessNumber** application.

4. *Entering your first guess.* The application displays "Please type your first guess.", then displays a question mark (?) as a prompt on the next line (Fig. 1.11). At the prompt, enter **500** (Fig. 1.12). [*Note:* This is the same application that we modified and test-drove for Windows, but the outputs could vary, based on the compiler being used.]

5. *Entering another guess.* The application displays "Too high. Try again.", meaning that the value you entered is greater than the number the application chose as the correct guess (Fig. 1.12). At the next prompt, enter **250** (Fig. 1.13). This time the application displays "Too low. Try again.", because the value you entered is less than the correct guess.

6. *Entering additional guesses.* Continue to play the game (Fig. 1.14) by entering values until you guess the correct number. When you guess the answer, the application displays "Excellent! You guessed the number!" (Fig. 1.14).

```
~/examples/ch01/GuessNumber/GNU_Linux$ ./GuessNumber
I have a number between 1 and 1000.
Can you guess my number?
Please type your first guess.
? 500
Too high. Try again.
?
```

Fig. 1.12 | Entering an initial guess.

```
~/examples/ch01/GuessNumber/GNU_Linux$ ./GuessNumber
I have a number between 1 and 1000.
Can you guess my number?
Please type your first guess.
? 500
Too high. Try again.
? 250
Too low. Try again.
?
```

Fig. 1.13 | Entering a second guess and receiving feedback.

```
Too low. Try again.
? 375
Too low. Try again.
? 437
Too high. Try again.
? 406
Too high. Try again.
? 391
Too high. Try again.
? 383
Too low. Try again.
? 387
Too high. Try again.
? 385
Too high. Try again.
? 384

Excellent! You guessed the number.
Would you like to play again (y or n)?
```

Fig. 1.14 | Entering additional guesses and guessing the correct number.

7. ***Playing the game again or exiting the application.*** After guessing the correct number, the application asks if you would like to play another game. At the "Would you like to play again (y or n)?" prompt, entering the one character **y** causes the application to choose a new number and displays the message "Please enter your first guess." followed by a question mark prompt (Fig. 1.15) so you can make your first guess in the new game. Entering the character **n** ends the application and returns you to the application's directory in the shell (Fig. 1.16). Each time you execute this application from the beginning (i.e., *Step 3*), it will choose the same numbers for you to guess.

```
Excellent! You guessed the number.
Would you like to play again (y or n)? y

I have a number between 1 and 1000.
Can you guess my number?
Please type your first guess.
?
```

Fig. 1.15 | Playing the game again.

```
Excellent! You guessed the number.
Would you like to play again (y or n)? n

~/examples/ch01/GuessNumber/GNU_Linux$
```

Fig. 1.16 | Exiting the game.

1.13 Software Engineering Case Study: Introduction to Object Technology and the UML (Required)

Now we begin our early introduction to object orientation, a natural way of thinking about the world and writing computer programs. Chapters 1–7, 9 and 13 all end with a brief "Software Engineering Case Study" section in which we present a carefully paced introduction to object orientation. Our goal here is to help you develop an object-oriented way of thinking and to introduce you to the Unified Modeling Language™ (UML™)—a graphical language that allows people who design object-oriented software systems to use an industry-standard notation to represent them.

In this required section, we introduce basic object-oriented concepts and terminology. The optional sections in Chapters 2–7, 9 and 13 present an object-oriented design and implementation of the software for a simple automated teller machine (ATM) system. The "Software Engineering Case Study" sections at the ends of Chapters 2–7

- analyze a typical requirements document that describes a software system (the ATM) to be built
- determine the objects required to implement that system
- determine the attributes the objects will have
- determine the behaviors these objects will exhibit
- specify how the objects interact with one another to meet the system requirements

The "Software Engineering Case Study" sections at the ends of Chapters 9 and 13 modify and enhance the design presented in Chapters 2–7. Appendix G contains a complete, working C++ implementation of the object-oriented ATM system.

Although our case study is a scaled-down version of an industry-level problem, we nevertheless cover many common industry practices. You will experience a solid introduction to object-oriented design with the UML. Also, you will sharpen your code-reading skills by touring the complete, carefully written and well-documented C++ implementation of the ATM.

Basic Object Technology Concepts

We begin our introduction to object orientation with some key terminology. Everywhere you look in the real world you see objects—people, animals, plants, cars, planes, buildings, computers and so on. Humans think in terms of objects. Telephones, houses, traffic lights, microwave ovens and water coolers are just a few more objects we see around us every day.

We sometimes divide objects into two categories: animate and inanimate. Animate objects are "alive" in some sense—they move around and do things. Inanimate objects, on the other hand, do not move on their own. Objects of both types, however, have some things in common. They all have attributes (e.g., size, shape, color and weight), and they all exhibit behaviors (e.g., a ball rolls, bounces, inflates and deflates; a baby cries, sleeps, crawls, walks and blinks; a car accelerates, brakes and turns; a towel absorbs water). We will study the kinds of attributes and behaviors that software objects have.

Humans learn about existing objects by studying their attributes and observing their behaviors. Different objects can have similar attributes and can exhibit similar behaviors. Comparisons can be made, for example, between babies and adults and between humans and chimpanzees.

Object-oriented design (OOD) models software in terms similar to those that people use to describe real-world objects. It takes advantage of class relationships, where objects of a certain class, such as a class of vehicles, have the same characteristics—cars, trucks, little red wagons and roller skates have much in common. OOD takes advantage of inheritance relationships, where new classes of objects are derived by absorbing characteristics of existing classes and adding unique characteristics of their own. An object of class "convertible" certainly has the characteristics of the more general class "automobile," but more specifically, the roof goes up and down.

Object-oriented design provides a natural and intuitive way to view the software design process—namely, modeling objects by their attributes, behaviors and interrelationships just as we describe real-world objects. OOD also models communication between objects. Just as people send messages to one another (e.g., a sergeant commands a soldier to stand at attention), objects also communicate via messages. A bank account object may receive a message to decrease its balance by a certain amount because the customer has withdrawn that amount of money.

OOD encapsulates (i.e., wraps) attributes and operations (behaviors) into objects—an object's attributes and operations are intimately tied together. Objects have the property of information hiding. This means that objects may know how to communicate with one another across well-defined interfaces, but normally they are not allowed to know how other objects are implemented—implementation details are hidden within the objects themselves. We can drive a car effectively, for instance, without knowing the details of how engines, transmissions, brakes and exhaust systems work internally—as long as we know how to use the accelerator pedal, the brake pedal, the steering wheel and so on. Information hiding, as we will see, is crucial to good software engineering.

Languages like C++ are object oriented. Programming in such a language is called object-oriented programming (OOP), and it allows computer programmers to implement an object-oriented design as a working software system. Languages like C, on the other hand, are procedural, so programming tends to be action oriented. In C, the unit of programming is the function. In C++, the unit of programming is the class from which objects are eventually instantiated (an OOP term for "created"). C++ classes contain functions that implement operations and data that implements attributes.

C programmers concentrate on writing functions. Programmers group actions that perform some common task into functions, and group functions to form programs. Data is certainly important in C, but the view is that data exists primarily in support of the actions that functions perform. The verbs in a system specification help the C programmer determine the set of functions that will work together to implement the system.

Classes, Data Members and Member Functions

C++ programmers concentrate on creating their own user-defined types called classes. Each class contains data as well as the set of functions that manipulate that data and provide services to clients (i.e., other classes or functions that use the class). The data components of a class are called data members. For example, a bank account class might include an account number and a balance. The function components of a class are called member functions (typically called methods in other object-oriented programming languages such as Java). For example, a bank account class might include member functions to make a deposit (increasing the balance), make a withdrawal (decreasing the balance) and inquire what the current balance is. The programmer uses built-in types (and other user-defined types) as the "building blocks" for constructing new user-defined types (classes). The nouns in a system specification help the C++ programmer determine the set of classes from which objects are created that work together to implement the system.

Classes are to objects as blueprints are to houses—a class is a "plan" for building an object of the class. Just as we can build many houses from one blueprint, we can instantiate (create) many objects from one class. You cannot cook meals in the kitchen of a blueprint; you can cook meals in the kitchen of a house. You cannot sleep in the bedroom of a blueprint; you can sleep in the bedroom of a house.

Classes can have relationships with other classes. For example, in an object-oriented design of a bank, the "bank teller" class needs to relate to other classes, such as the "customer" class, the "cash drawer" class, the "safe" class, and so on. These relationships are called associations.

Packaging software as classes makes it possible for future software systems to reuse the classes. Groups of related classes are often packaged as reusable components. Just as realtors often say that the three most important factors affecting the price of real estate are "location, location and location," people in the software development community often say that the three most important factors affecting the future of software development are "reuse, reuse and reuse."

Software Engineering Observation 1.3

Reuse of existing classes when building new classes and programs saves time, money and effort. Reuse also helps programmers build more reliable and effective systems, because existing classes and components often have gone through extensive testing, debugging and performance tuning.

Indeed, with object technology, you can build much of the new software you will need by combining existing classes, just as automobile manufacturers combine interchangeable parts. Each new class you create will have the potential to become a valuable software asset that you and other programmers can reuse to speed and enhance the quality of future software development efforts.

Introduction to Object-Oriented Analysis and Design (OOAD)

Soon you will be writing programs in C++. How will you create the code for your programs? Perhaps, like many beginning programmers, you will simply turn on your computer and start typing. This approach may work for small programs (like the ones we present in the early chapters of the book), but what if you were asked to create a software system to control thousands of automated teller machines for a major bank? Or what if you were asked to work on a team of 1,000 software developers building the next generation of the U.S. air traffic control system? For projects so large and complex, you could not simply sit down and start writing programs.

To create the best solutions, you should follow a detailed process for analyzing your project's requirements (i.e., determining *what* the system is supposed to do) and developing a design that satisfies them (i.e., deciding *how* the system should do it). Ideally, you would go through this process and carefully review the design (or have your design reviewed by other software professionals) before writing any code. If this process involves analyzing and designing your system from an object-oriented point of view, it is called object-oriented analysis and design (OOAD). Experienced programmers know that analysis and design can save many hours by helping avoid an ill-planned system development approach that has to be abandoned partway through its implementation, possibly wasting considerable time, money and effort.

OOAD is the generic term for the process of analyzing a problem and developing an approach for solving it. Small problems like the ones discussed in these first few chapters do not require an exhaustive OOAD process. It may be sufficient, before we begin writing C++ code, to write pseudocode—an informal text-based means of expressing program logic. It is not actually a programming language, but we can use it as a kind of outline to guide us as we write our code. We introduce pseudocode in Chapter 4.

As problems and the groups of people solving them increase in size, the methods of OOAD quickly become more appropriate than pseudocode. Ideally, a group should agree on a strictly defined process for solving its problem and a uniform way of communicating the results of that process to one another. Although many different OOAD processes exist, a single graphical language for communicating the results of *any* OOAD process has come into wide use. This language, known as the Unified Modeling Language (UML), was developed in the mid-1990s under the initial direction of three software methodologists: Grady Booch, James Rumbaugh and Ivar Jacobson.

History of the UML

In the 1980s, increasing numbers of organizations began using OOP to build their applications, and a need developed for a standard OOAD process. Many methodologists—including Booch, Rumbaugh and Jacobson—individually produced and promoted separate processes to satisfy this need. Each process had its own notation, or "language" (in the form of graphical diagrams), to convey the results of analysis and design.

By the early 1990s, different organizations, and even divisions within the same organization, were using their own unique processes and notations. At the same time, these organizations also wanted to use software tools that would support their particular processes. Software vendors found it difficult to provide tools for so many processes. Clearly, a standard notation and standard processes were needed.

In 1994, James Rumbaugh joined Grady Booch at Rational Software Corporation (now a division of IBM), and the two began working to unify their popular processes. They soon were joined by Ivar Jacobson. In 1996, the group released early versions of the UML to the software engineering community and requested feedback. Around the same time, an organization known as the Object Management Group™ (OMG™) invited submissions for a common modeling language. The OMG (www.omg.org) is a nonprofit organization that promotes the standardization of object-oriented technologies by issuing guidelines and specifications, such as the UML. Several corporations—among them HP, IBM, Microsoft, Oracle and Rational Software—had already recognized the need for a common modeling language. In response to the OMG's request for proposals, these companies formed UML Partners—the consortium that developed the UML version 1.1 and submitted it to the OMG. The OMG accepted the proposal and, in 1997, assumed responsibility for the continuing maintenance and revision of the UML. In March 2003, the OMG released UML version 1.5. The UML version 2—which had been adopted and was in the process of being finalized at the time of this publication—marks the first major revision since the 1997 version 1.1 standard. Many books, modeling tools and industry experts are already using the UML version 2, so we present UML version 2 terminology and notation throughout this book.

What Is the UML?

The Unified Modeling Language is now the most widely used graphical representation scheme for modeling object-oriented systems. It has indeed unified the various popular notational schemes. Those who design systems use the language (in the form of diagrams) to model their systems, as we do throughout this book.

An attractive feature of the UML is its flexibility. The UML is extensible (i.e., capable of being enhanced with new features) and is independent of any particular OOAD process. UML modelers are free to use various processes in designing systems, but all developers can now express their designs with one standard set of graphical notations.

The UML is a complex, feature-rich graphical language. In our "Software Engineering Case Study" sections on developing the software for an automated teller machine (ATM), we present a simple, concise subset of these features. We then use this subset to guide you through a first design experience with the UML, intended for novice object-oriented programmers in a first- or second-semester programming course.

This case study was carefully developed under the guidance of distinguished academic and professional reviewers. We sincerely hope you enjoy working through it. If you have the slightest question, please communicate with us at `deitel@deitel.com`. We will respond promptly.

Internet and Web UML Resources

For more information about the UML, refer to the following Web sites. For additional UML sites, please refer to the Internet and Web resources listed at the end of Section 2.8.

`www.uml.org`
This UML resource page from the Object Management Group (OMG) provides specification documents for the UML and other object-oriented technologies.

`www.ibm.com/software/rational/uml`
This is the UML resource page for IBM Rational—the successor to the Rational Software Corporation (the company that created the UML).

Recommended Readings

Many books on the UML have been published. The following recommended books provide information about object-oriented design with the UML.

- Arlow, J., and I. Neustadt. *UML and the Unified Process: Practical Object-Oriented Analysis and Design*. London: Pearson Education Ltd., 2002.

- Fowler, M. *UML Distilled, Third Edition: A Brief Guide to the Standard Object Modeling Language*. Boston: Addison-Wesley, 2004.

- Rumbaugh, J., I. Jacobson and G. Booch. *The Unified Modeling Language User Guide*. Reading, MA: Addison-Wesley, 1999.

For additional books on the UML, please refer to the recommended readings listed at the end of Section 2.8, or visit `www.amazon.com` or `www.bn.com`. IBM Rational, formerly Rational Software Corporation, also provides a recommended-reading list for UML books at `www.ibm.com/software/rational/info/technical/books.jsp`.

Section 1.13 Self-Review Exercises

1.1   List three examples of real-world objects that we did not mention. For each object, list several attributes and behaviors.

1.2   Pseudocode is _____.
   a)   another term for OOAD
   b)   a programming language used to display UML diagrams
   c)   an informal means of expressing program logic
   d)   a graphical representation scheme for modeling object-oriented systems

1.3   The UML is used primarily to _____.
   a)   test object-oriented systems
   b)   design object-oriented systems
   c)   implement object-oriented systems
   d)   Both a and b

Answers to Section 1.13 Self-Review Exercises

1.1   [*Note:* Answers may vary.] a) A television's attributes include the size of the screen, the number of colors it can display, its current channel and its current volume. A television turns on and off, changes channels, displays video and plays sounds. b) A coffee maker's attributes include the maximum volume of water it can hold, the time required to brew a pot of coffee and the temperature of the heating plate under the coffee pot. A coffee maker turns on and off, brews coffee and heats coffee. c) A turtle's attributes include its age, the size of its shell and its weight. A turtle walks, retreats into its shell, emerges from its shell and eats vegetation.

1.2   c.

1.3   b.

1.14 Web Resources

This section provides many Web resources that will be useful to you as you learn C++. The sites include C++ resources, C++ development tools for students and professionals and some links to fun games built with C++. This section also lists our own Web sites where you can find downloads and resources associated with this book. You will find additional Web Resources in Appendix I.

Deitel & Associates Web Sites

www.deitel.com/books/cppHTP5/index.html
The Deitel & Associates *C++ How to Program, Fifth Edition* site. Here you will find links to the book's examples (also included on the CD that accompanies the book) and other resources, such as our free *Dive Into*™ guides that help you get started with several C++ integrated development environments (IDEs).

www.deitel.com
Please check the Deitel & Associates site for updates, corrections and additional resources for all Deitel publications.

www.deitel.com/newsletter/subscribe.html
Please visit this site to subscribe for the *Deitel*® *Buzz Online* e-mail newsletter to follow the Deitel & Associates publishing program.

www.prenhall.com/deitel
Prentice Hall's site for Deitel publications. Here you will find detailed product information, sample chapters and *Companion Web Sites* containing book- and chapter-specific resources for students and instructors.

Compilers and Development Tools

www.thefreecountry.com/developercity/ccompilers.shtml
This site lists free C and C++ compilers for a variety of operating systems.

msdn.microsoft.com/visualc
The *Microsoft Visual C++* site provides product information, overviews, supplemental materials and ordering information for the Visual C++ compiler.

www.borland.com/bcppbuilder
This is a link to the *Borland C++Builder.* A free command-line version is available for download.

www.compilers.net
Compilers.net is designed to help users locate compilers.

developer.intel.com/software/products/compilers/cwin/index.htm
An evaluation download of the *Intel C++ compiler* is available at this site.

www.kai.com/C_plus_plus
This site offers the *Kai C++ compiler* for a 30-day free trial.

www.symbian.com/developer/development/cppdev.html
Symbian provides a C++ Developer's Pack and links to various resources, including code and development tools for C++ programmers implementing mobile applications for the Symbian operating system, which is popular on devices such as mobile phones.

Resources

www.hal9k.com/cug
The *C/C++ Users Group (CUG)* site contains C++ resources, journals, shareware and freeware.

www.devx.com
DevX is a comprehensive resource for programmers that provides the latest news, tools and techniques for various programming languages. The *C++ Zone* offers tips, discussion forums, technical help and online newsletters.

www.acm.org/crossroads/xrds3-2/ovp32.html
The Association for Computing Machinery (ACM) site offers a comprehensive listing of C++ resources, including recommended texts, journals and magazines, published standards, newsletters, FAQs and newsgroups.

www.accu.informika.ru/resources/public/terse/cpp.htm
The Association of C & C++ Users (ACCU) site contains links to C++ tutorials, articles, developer information, discussions and book reviews.

www.cuj.com
The *C/C++ User's Journal* is an online magazine that contains articles, tutorials and downloads. The site features news about C++, forums and links to information about development tools.

www.research.att.com/~bs/homepage.html
This is the site for Bjarne Stroustrup, designer of the C++ programming language. This site provides a list of C++ resources, FAQs and other useful C++ information.

Games

www.codearchive.com/list.php?go=0708
This site has several C++ games available for download.

www.mathtools.net/C_C__/Games/
This site includes links to numerous games built with C++. The source code for most of the games is available for download.

`www.gametutorials.com`
This site has tutorials on game programming in C++. Each tutorial includes a description of the game and a list of the methods and functions used in the tutorial.

`www.forum.nokia.com/main/0,6566,050_20,00.html`
Visit this Nokia site to learn how to use C++ to program games for some Nokia wireless devices.

Summary

- The various devices that comprise a computer system are referred to as hardware.

- The computer programs that run on a computer are referred to as software.

- A computer is capable of performing computations and making logical decisions at speeds millions (even billions) of times faster than human beings can.

- Computers process data under the control of sets of instructions called computer programs, which guide the computer through orderly sets of actions specified by computer programmers.

- The input unit is the "receiving" section of the computer. It obtains information from input devices and places it at the disposal of the other units for processing.

- The output unit is the "shipping" section of the computer. It takes information processed by the computer and places it on output devices to make it available for use outside the computer.

- The memory unit is the rapid-access, relatively low-capacity "warehouse" section of the computer. It retains information that has been entered through the input unit, making it immediately available for processing when needed, and retains information that has already been processed until it can be placed on output devices by the output unit.

- The arithmetic and logic unit (ALU) is the "manufacturing" section of the computer. It is responsible for performing calculations and making decisions.

- The central processing unit (CPU) is the "administrative" section of the computer. It coordinates and supervises the operation of the other sections.

- The secondary storage unit is the long-term, high-capacity "warehousing" section of the computer. Programs or data not being used by the other units are normally placed on secondary storage devices (e.g., disks) until they are needed, possibly hours, days, months or even years later.

- Operating systems were developed to help make it more convenient to use computers.

- Multiprogramming involves the sharing of a computer's resources among the jobs competing for its attention, so that the jobs appear to run simultaneously.

- With distributed computing, an organization's computing is distributed over networks to the sites where the work of the organization is performed.

- Any computer can directly understand only its own machine language, which generally consist of strings of numbers that instruct computers to perform their most elementary operations.

- English-like abbreviations form the basis of assembly languages. Translator programs called assemblers convert assembly-language programs to machine language.

- Compilers translate high-level language programs into machine-language programs. High-level languages (like C++) contain English words and conventional mathematical notations.

- Interpreter programs directly execute high-level language programs, eliminating the need to compile them into machine language.

- C++ evolved from C, which evolved from two previous programming languages, BCPL and B.

- C++ is an extension of C developed by Bjarne Stroustrup in the early 1980s at Bell Laboratories. C++ enhances the C language and provides capabilities for object-oriented programming.

- Objects are reusable software components that model items in the real world. Using a modular, object-oriented design and implementation approach can make software development groups more productive than with previous programming techniques.

- C++ programs consist of pieces called classes and functions. You can program each piece you may need to form a C++ program. However, most C++ programmers take advantage of the rich collections of existing classes and functions in the C++ Standard Library.

- The .NET platform's three primary programming languages are Visual Basic .NET (based on the original BASIC), Visual C++ .NET (based on C++) and C# (a new language based on C++ and Java that was developed expressly for the .NET platform).

- C++ systems generally consist of three parts: a program development environment, the language and the C++ Standard Library.

- C++ programs typically go through six phases: *edit, preprocess, compile, link, load* and *execute.*

- C++ source code file names often end with the .cpp, .cxx, .cc or .C extensions.

- A preprocessor program executes automatically before the compiler's translation phase begins. The C++ preprocessor obeys commands called preprocessor directives, which indicate that certain manipulations are to be performed on the program before compilation.

- The object code produced by the C++ compiler typically contains "holes" due to references to functions and data defined elsewhere. A linker links the object code with the code for the missing functions to produce an executable image (with no missing pieces).

- The loader takes the executable image from disk and transfers it to memory for execution.

- Most programs in C++ input and/or output data. Data is often input from cin (the standard input stream) which is normally the keyboard, but cin can be redirected from another device. Data is often output to cout (the standard output stream), which is normally the computer screen, but cout can be redirected to another device. The cerr stream is used to display error messages.

- The Unified Modeling Language (UML) is a graphical language that allows people who build systems to represent their object-oriented designs in a common notation.

- Object-oriented design (OOD) models software components in terms of real-world objects. It takes advantage of class relationships, where objects of a certain class have the same characteristics. It also takes advantage of inheritance relationships, where newly created classes of objects are derived by absorbing characteristics of existing classes and adding unique characteristics of their own. OOD encapsulates data (attributes) and functions (behavior) into objects—the data and functions of an object are intimately tied together.

- Objects have the property of information hiding—objects normally are not allowed to know how other objects are implemented.

- Object-oriented programming (OOP) allows programmers to implement object-oriented designs as working systems.

- C++ programmers create their own user-defined types called classes. Each class contains data (known as data members) and the set of functions (known as member functions) that manipulate that data and provide services to clients.

- Classes can have relationships with other classes. These relationships are called associations.

- Packaging software as classes makes it possible for future software systems to reuse the classes. Groups of related classes are often packaged as reusable components.

- An instance of a class is called an object.

- With object technology, programmers can build much of the software they will need by combining standardized, interchangeable parts called classes.
- The process of analyzing and designing a system from an object-oriented point of view is called object-oriented analysis and design (OOAD).

Terminology

action
American National Standards Institute (ANSI)
analysis
ANSI/ISO standard C
ANSI/ISO standard C++
arithmetic and logic unit (ALU)
assembler
assembly language
association
attribute of an object
batch processing
behavior of an object
Booch, Grady
C
C++
C++ Standard Library
C#
central processing unit (CPU)
class
client
client/server computing
compile phase
compiler
component
computer
computer program
computer programmer
core memory
data
data member
debug
decision
design
distributed computing
edit phase
editor
encapsulate
executable image
execute phase
extensible
file server
function
hardware

hardware platform
high-level language
information hiding
inheritance
input device
input unit
input/output (I/O)
instantiate
interface
International Organization for
    Standardization (ISO)
Internet
interpreter
Jacobson, Ivar
Java
link phase
linker
live-code approach
load phase
loader
local area networks (LANs)
logical unit
machine dependent
machine independent
machine language
member function
memory
memory unit
method
multiprocessor
multiprogramming
.NET languages
object
object code
Object Management Group (OMG)
object-oriented analysis and design (OOAD)
object-oriented design (OOD)
object-oriented programming (OOP)
operating system
operation
output device
output unit
personal computing

platform	software reuse
portable	source code
preprocess phase	supercomputer
preprocessor directives	task
primary memory	throughput
procedural programming	timesharing
pseudocode	translation
Rational Software Corporation	translator program
requirements document	Unified Modeling Language (UML)
Rumbaugh, James	user-defined type
runtime errors or execution-time errors	Visual C++ .NET
secondary storage unit	workstation
software	World Wide Web

Self-Review Exercises

1.1   Fill in the blanks in each of the following:
  a) The company that popularized personal computing was _____.
  b) The computer that made personal computing legitimate in business and industry was the _____.
  c) Computers process data under the control of sets of instructions called computer _____.
  d) The six key logical units of the computer are the _____, _____, _____, _____, _____ and the _____.
  e) The three classes of languages discussed in the chapter are _____, _____, and _____.
  f) The programs that translate high-level language programs into machine language are called _____.
  g) C is widely known as the development language of the _____ operating system.

1.2   Fill in the blanks in each of the following sentences about the C++ environment.
  a) C++ programs are normally typed into a computer using a(n) _____ program.
  b) In a C++ system, a(n) _____ program executes before the compiler's translation phase begins.
  c) The _____ program combines the output of the compiler with various library functions to produce an executable image.
  d) The _____ program transfers the executable image of a C++ program from disk to memory.

1.3   Fill in the blanks in each of the following statements (based on Section 1.13):
  a) Objects have the property of _____—although objects may know how to communicate with one another across well-defined interfaces, they normally are not allowed to know how other objects are implemented.
  b) C++ programmers concentrate on creating _____, which contain data members and the member functions that manipulate those data members and provide services to clients.
  c) Classes can have relationships with other classes. These relationships are called _____.
  d) The process of analyzing and designing a system from an object-oriented point of view is called _____.

e) OOD also takes advantage of _____ relationships, where new classes of objects are derived by absorbing characteristics of existing classes, then adding unique characteristics of their own.

f) _____ is a graphical language that allows people who design software systems to use an industry-standard notation to represent them.

g) The size, shape, color and weight of an object are considered _____ of the object.

Answers to Self-Review Exercises

1.1   a) Apple. b) IBM Personal Computer. c) programs. d) input unit, output unit, memory unit, arithmetic and logic unit, central processing unit, secondary storage unit. e) machine languages, assembly languages and high-level languages. f) compilers. g) UNIX. h) Pascal. i) multitasking.

1.2   a) editor. b) preprocessor. c) linker. d) loader.

1.3   a) information hiding. b) classes. c) associations. d) object-oriented analysis and design (OOAD). e) inheritance. f) The Unified Modeling Language (UML). g) attributes.

Exercises

1.4   Categorize each of the following items as either hardware or software:
a) CPU
b) C++ compiler
c) ALU
d) C++ preprocessor
e) input unit
f) an editor program

1.5   Why might you want to write a program in a machine-independent language instead of a machine-dependent language? Why might a machine-dependent language be more appropriate for writing certain types of programs?

1.6   Fill in the blanks in each of the following statements:
a) Which logical unit of the computer receives information from outside the computer for use by the computer? _____.
b) The process of instructing the computer to solve specific problems is called _____.
c) What type of computer language uses English-like abbreviations for machine-language instructions? _____.
d) Which logical unit of the computer sends information that has already been processed by the computer to various devices so that the information may be used outside the computer? _____.
e) Which logical unit of the computer retains information? _____.
f) Which logical unit of the computer performs calculations? _____.
g) Which logical unit of the computer makes logical decisions? _____.
h) The level of computer language most convenient to the programmer for writing programs quickly and easily is _____.
i) The only language that a computer directly understands is called that computer's _____.
j) Which logical unit of the computer coordinates the activities of all the other logical units? _____.

1.7   Why is so much attention today focused on object-oriented programming in general and C++ in particular?

1.8   Distinguish between the terms fatal error and nonfatal error. Why might you prefer to experience a fatal error rather than a nonfatal error?

1.9   Give a brief answer to each of the following questions:
   a)   What are the typical steps (mentioned in the text) of an object-oriented design process?
   b)   What kinds of messages do people send to one another?
   c)   Objects send messages to one another across well-defined interfaces. What interfaces does a car radio (object) present to its user (a person object)?

1.10   You are probably wearing on your wrist one of the world's most common types of objects—a watch. Discuss how each of the following terms and concepts applies to the notion of a watch: object, attributes, behaviors, class, inheritance (consider, for example, an alarm clock), abstraction, modeling, messages, encapsulation, interface, information hiding, data members and member functions.

2

Introduction to C++ Programming

OBJECTIVES

In this chapter you will learn:

- To write simple computer programs in C++.
- To write simple input and output statements.
- To use fundamental types.
- Basic computer memory concepts.
- To use arithmetic operators.
- The precedence of arithmetic operators.
- To write simple decision-making statements.

2.1 Introduction

We now introduce C++ programming, which facilitates a disciplined approach to program design. Most of the C++ programs you will study in this book process information and display results. In this chapter, we present five examples that demonstrate how your programs can display messages and obtain information from the user for processing. The first three examples simply display messages on the screen. The next is a program that obtains two numbers from a user, calculates their sum and displays the result. The accompanying discussion shows you how to perform various arithmetic calculations and save their results for later use. The fifth example demonstrates decision-making fundamentals by showing you how to compare two numbers, then display messages based on the comparison results. We analyze each program one line at a time to help you ease your way into C++ programming. To help you apply the skills you learn here, we provide many programming problems in the chapter's exercises.

2.2 First Program in C++: Printing a Line of Text

C++ uses notations that may appear strange to nonprogrammers. We now consider a simple program that prints a line of text (Fig. 2.1). This program illustrates several important features of the C++ language. We consider each line in detail.

Lines 1 and 2

```
// Fig. 2.1: fig02_01.cpp
// Text-printing program.
```

each begin with //, indicating that the remainder of each line is a comment. Programmers insert comments to document programs and also help people read and understand them. Comments do not cause the computer to perform any action when the program is run—they are ignored by the C++ compiler and do not cause any machine-language object code to be generated. The comment Text-printing program describes the purpose of the program. A comment beginning with // is called a single-line comment because it terminates at the end of the current line. [*Note:* C++ programmers also may use C's style in which a comment—possibly containing many lines—begins with the pair of characters /* and ends with */.]

```
 1   // Fig. 2.1: fig02_01.cpp
 2   // Text-printing program.
 3   #include <iostream> // allows program to output data to the screen
 4
 5   // function main begins program execution
 6   int main()
 7   {
 8      std::cout << "Welcome to C++!\n"; // display message
 9
10      return 0; // indicate that program ended successfully
11
12   } // end function main
```

```
Welcome to C++!
```

Fig. 2.1 | Text-printing program.

Good Programming Practice 2.1

Every program should begin with a comment that describes the purpose of the program, author, date and time. (We are not showing the author, date and time in this book's programs because this information would be redundant.)

Line 3

```
#include <iostream> // allows program to output data to the screen
```

is a preprocessor directive, which is a message to the C++ preprocessor (introduced in Section 1.14). Lines that begin with # are processed by the preprocessor before the program is compiled. This line notifies the preprocessor to include in the program the contents of the input/output stream header file <iostream>. This file must be included for any program that outputs data to the screen or inputs data from the keyboard using C++-style stream input/output. The program in Fig. 2.1 outputs data to the screen, as we will soon see. We discuss header files in more detail in Chapter 6 and explain the contents of iostream in Chapter 15.

Common Programming Error 2.1

Forgetting to include the <iostream> header file in a program that inputs data from the keyboard or outputs data to the screen causes the compiler to issue an error message, because the compiler cannot recognize references to the stream components (e.g., cout).

Line 4 is simply a blank line. Programmers use blank lines, space characters and tab characters (i.e., "tabs") to make programs easier to read. Together, these characters are known as white space. White-space characters are normally ignored by the compiler. In this chapter and several that follow, we discuss conventions for using white-space characters to enhance program readability.

Good Programming Practice 2.2

Use blank lines and space characters to enhance program readability.

Line 5

```
// function main begins program execution
```

is another single-line comment indicating that program execution begins at the next line.
Line 6

```
int main()
```

is a part of every C++ program. The parentheses after `main` indicate that `main` is a program
building block called a function. C++ programs typically consist of one or more functions
and classes (as you will learn in Chapter 3). Exactly one function in every program must
be `main`. Figure 2.1 contains only one function. C++ programs begin executing at function
`main`, even if `main` is not the first function in the program. The keyword `int` to the left of
`main` indicates that `main` "returns" an integer (whole number) value. A keyword is a word
in code that is reserved by C++ for a specific use. The complete list of C++ keywords can
be found in Fig. 4.3. We will explain what it means for a function to "return a value" when
we demonstrate how to create your own functions in Section 3.5 and when we study functions in greater depth in Chapter 6. For now, simply include the keyword `int` to the left
of `main` in each of your programs.

The left brace, {, (line 7) must begin the body of every function. A corresponding
right brace, }, (line 12) must end each function's body. Line 8

```
std::cout << "Welcome to C++!\n"; // display message
```

instructs the computer to perform an action—namely, to print the string of characters
contained between the double quotation marks. A string is sometimes called a character
string, a message or a string literal. We refer to characters between double quotation
marks simply as strings. White-space characters in strings are not ignored by the compiler.

The entire line 8, including `std::cout`, the << operator, the string `"Welcome to
C++!\n"` and the semicolon (;), is called a statement. Every C++ statement must end with
a semicolon (also known as the statement terminator). Preprocessor directives (like
`#include`) do not end with a semicolon. Output and input in C++ are accomplished with
streams of characters. Thus, when the preceding statement is executed, it sends the stream
of characters `Welcome to C++!\n` to the standard output stream object—`std::cout`—
which is normally "connected" to the screen. We discuss `std::cout`'s many features in
detail in Chapter 15, Stream Input/Output.

Notice that we placed `std::` before `cout`. This is required when we use names that
we've brought into the program by the preprocessor directive `#include <iostream>`. The
notation `std::cout` specifies that we are using a name, in this case `cout`, that belongs to
"namespace" `std`. The names `cin` (the standard input stream) and `cerr` (the standard error
stream)—introduced in Chapter 1—also belong to namespace `std`. Namespaces are an
advanced C++ feature that we discuss in depth in Chapter 24, Other Topics. For now, you
should simply remember to include `std::` before each mention of `cout`, `cin` and `cerr` in
a program. This can be cumbersome—in Fig. 2.13, we introduce the `using` declaration,
which will enable us to omit `std::` before each use of a name in the `std` namespace.

The << operator is referred to as the stream insertion operator. When this program
executes, the value to the right of the operator, the right operand, is inserted in the output
stream. Notice that the operator points in the direction of where the data goes. The characters of the right operand normally print exactly as they appear between the double

quotes. Notice, however, that the characters \n are not printed on the screen. The backslash (\) is called an escape character. It indicates that a "special" character is to be output. When a backslash is encountered in a string of characters, the next character is combined with the backslash to form an escape sequence. The escape sequence \n means newline. It causes the cursor (i.e., the current screen-position indicator) to move to the beginning of the next line on the screen. Some other common escape sequences are listed in Fig. 2.2.

Common Programming Error 2.2

Omitting the semicolon at the end of a C++ statement is a syntax error. (Again, preprocessor directives do not end in a semicolon.) The syntax of a programming language specifies the rules for creating a proper program in that language. A syntax error occurs when the compiler encounters code that violates C++'s language rules (i.e., its syntax). The compiler normally issues an error message to help the programmer locate and fix the incorrect code. Syntax errors are also called compiler errors, compile-time errors or compilation errors, because the compiler detects them during the compilation phase. You will be unable to execute your program until you correct all the syntax errors in it. As you will see, some compilation errors are not syntax errors.

Line 10

```
return 0; // indicate that program ended successfully
```

is one of several means we will use to exit a function. When the `return` statement is used at the end of `main`, as shown here, the value 0 indicates that the program has terminated successfully. In Chapter 6 we discuss functions in detail, and the reasons for including this statement will become clear. For now, simply include this statement in each program, or the compiler may produce a warning on some systems. The right brace, }, (line 12) indicates the end of function `main`.

Good Programming Practice 2.3

Many programmers make the last character printed by a function a newline (\n). This ensures that the function will leave the screen cursor positioned at the beginning of a new line. Conventions of this nature encourage software reusability—a key goal in software development.

Escape sequence	Description
\n	Newline. Position the screen cursor to the beginning of the next line.
\t	Horizontal tab. Move the screen cursor to the next tab stop.
\r	Carriage return. Position the screen cursor to the beginning of the current line; do not advance to the next line.
\a	Alert. Sound the system bell.
\\	Backslash. Used to print a backslash character.
\'	Single quote. Use to print a single quote character.
\"	Double quote. Used to print a double quote character.

Fig. 2.2 | Escape sequences.

Good Programming Practice 2.4

Indent the entire body of each function one level within the braces that delimit the body of the function. This makes a program's functional structure stand out and helps make the program easier to read.

Good Programming Practice 2.5

Set a convention for the size of indent you prefer, then apply it uniformly. The tab key may be used to create indents, but tab stops may vary. We recommend using either 1/4-inch tab stops or (preferably) three spaces to form a level of indent.

2.3 Modifying Our First C++ Program

This section continues our introduction to C++ programming with two examples, showing how to modify the program in Fig. 2.1 to print text on one line by using multiple statements and to print text on several lines by using a single statement.

Printing a Single Line of Text with Multiple Statements

Welcome to C++! can be printed several ways. For example, Fig. 2.3 performs stream insertion in multiple statements (lines 8–9), yet produces the same output as the program of Fig. 2.1. [*Note:* From this point forward, we use a darker shade of gray than the code table background to highlight the key features each program introduces.] Each stream insertion resumes printing where the previous one stopped. The first stream insertion (line 8) prints Welcome followed by a space, and the second stream insertion (line 9) begins printing on the same line immediately following the space. In general, C++ allows the programmer to express statements in a variety of ways.

Printing Multiple Lines of Text with a Single Statement

A single statement can print multiple lines by using newline characters, as in line 8 of Fig. 2.4. Each time the \n (newline) escape sequence is encountered in the output stream, the screen cursor is positioned to the beginning of the next line. To get a blank line in your output, place two newline characters back to back, as in line 8.

```
1   // Fig. 2.3: fig02_03.cpp
2   // Printing a line of text with multiple statements.
3   #include <iostream> // allows program to output data to the screen
4
5   // function main begins program execution
6   int main()
7   {
8      std::cout << "Welcome ";
9      std::cout << "to C++!\n";
10
11     return 0; // indicate that program ended successfully
12
13  } // end function main
```

```
Welcome to C++!
```

Fig. 2.3 | Printing a line of text with multiple statements.

```
 1   // Fig. 2.4: fig02_04.cpp
 2   // Printing multiple lines of text with a single statement.
 3   #include <iostream> // allows program to output data to the screen
 4
 5   // function main begins program execution
 6   int main()
 7   {
 8      std::cout << "Welcome\nto\n\n C++!\n";
 9
10      return 0; // indicate that program ended successfully
11
12   } // end function main
```

```
Welcome
to

C++!
```

Fig. 2.4 | Printing multiple lines of text with a single statement.

2.4 Another C++ Program: Adding Integers

Our next program uses the input stream object std::cin and the stream extraction operator, >>, to obtain two integers typed by a user at the keyboard, computes the sum of these values and outputs the result using std::cout. Figure 2.5 shows the program and sample inputs and outputs. Note that we highlight the user's input in bold.

The comments in lines 1 and 2

```
// Fig. 2.5: fig02_05.cpp
// Addition program that displays the sum of two numbers.
```

state the name of the file and the purpose of the program. The C++ preprocessor directive

```
#include <iostream> // allows program to perform input and output
```

in line 3 includes the contents of the iostream header file in the program.

The program begins execution with function main (line 6). The left brace (line 7) marks the beginning of main's body and the corresponding right brace (line 25) marks the end of main.

Lines 9–11

```
int number1; // first integer to add
int number2; // second integer to add
int sum; // sum of number1 and number2
```

are declarations. The identifiers number1, number2 and sum are the names of variables. A variable is a location in the computer's memory where a value can be stored for use by a program. These declarations specify that the variables number1, number2 and sum are data of type int, meaning that these variables will hold integer values, i.e., whole numbers such as 7, –11, 0 and 31914. All variables must be declared with a name and a data type before they can be used in a program. Several variables of the same type may be declared in one

```
 1   // Fig. 2.5: fig02_05.cpp
 2   // Addition program that displays the sum of two numbers.
 3   #include <iostream> // allows program to perform input and output
 4
 5   // function main begins program execution
 6   int main()
 7   {
 8      // variable declarations
 9      int number1; // first integer to add
10      int number2; // second integer to add
11      int sum; // sum of number1 and number2
12
13      std::cout << "Enter first integer: "; // prompt user for data
14      std::cin >> number1; // read first integer from user into number1
15
16      std::cout << "Enter second integer: "; // prompt user for data
17      std::cin >> number2; // read second integer from user into number2
18
19      sum = number1 + number2; // add the numbers; store result in sum
20
21      std::cout << "Sum is " << sum << std::endl; // display sum; end line
22
23      return 0; // indicate that program ended successfully
24
25   } // end function main
```

```
Enter first integer: 45
Enter second integer: 72
Sum is 117
```

Fig. 2.5 | Addition program that displays the sum of two integers entered at the keyboard.

declaration or in multiple declarations. We could have declared all three variables in one declaration as follows:

```
int number1, number2, sum;
```

This makes the program less readable and prevents us from providing comments that describe each variable's purpose. If more than one name is declared in a declaration (as shown here), the names are separated by commas (,). This is referred to as a comma-separated list.

Good Programming Practice 2.6

Place a space after each comma (,) to make programs more readable.

Good Programming Practice 2.7

Some programmers prefer to declare each variable on a separate line. This format allows for easy insertion of a descriptive comment next to each declaration.

We will soon discuss the data type `double` for specifying real numbers, and the data type `char` for specifying character data. Real numbers are numbers with decimal points, such as 3.4, 0.0 and –11.19. A `char` variable may hold only a single lowercase letter, a single uppercase letter, a single digit or a single special character (e.g., $ or *). Types such as int, double and char are often called fundamental types, primitive types or built-in types. Fundamental-type names are keywords and therefore must appear in all lowercase letters. Appendix C contains the complete list of fundamental types.

A variable name (such as number1) is any valid identifier that is not a keyword. An identifier is a series of characters consisting of letters, digits and underscores (_) that does not begin with a digit. C++ is case sensitive—uppercase and lowercase letters are different, so a1 and A1 are different identifiers.

Portability Tip 2.1

C++ allows identifiers of any length, but your C++ implementation may impose some restrictions on the length of identifiers. Use identifiers of 31 characters or fewer to ensure portability.

Good Programming Practice 2.8

Choosing meaningful identifiers helps make a program self-documenting—a person can understand the program simply by reading it rather than having to refer to manuals or comments.

Good Programming Practice 2.9

Avoid using abbreviations in identifiers. This promotes program readability.

Good Programming Practice 2.10

Avoid identifiers that begin with underscores and double underscores, because C++ compilers may use names like that for their own purposes internally. This will prevent names you choose from being confused with names the compilers choose.

Error-Prevention Tip 2.1

Languages like C++ are "moving targets." As they evolve, more keywords could be added to the language. Avoid using "loaded" words like "object" as identifiers. Even though "object" is not currently a keyword in C++, it could become one; therefore, future compiling with new compilers could break existing code.

Declarations of variables can be placed almost anywhere in a program, but they must appear before their corresponding variables are used in the program. For example, in the program of Fig. 2.5, the declaration in line 9

```
int number1; // first integer to add
```
could have been placed immediately before line 14
```
std::cin >> number1; // read first integer from user into number1
```
the declaration in line 10
```
int number2; // second integer to add
```
could have been placed immediately before line 17
```
std::cin >> number2; // read second integer from user into number2
```
and the declaration in line 11
```
int sum; // sum of number1 and number2
```
could have been placed immediately before line 19
```
sum = number1 + number2; // add the numbers; store result in sum
```

Good Programming Practice 2.11

Always place a blank line between a declaration and adjacent executable statements. This makes the declarations stand out in the program and contributes to program clarity.

Good Programming Practice 2.12

If you prefer to place declarations at the beginning of a function, separate them from the executable statements in that function with one blank line to highlight where the declarations end and the executable statements begin.

Line 13

```
std::cout << "Enter first integer: "; // prompt user for data
```

prints the string Enter first integer: (also known as a string literal or a literal) on the screen. This message is called a prompt because it directs the user to take a specific action. We like to pronounce the preceding statement as "std::cout *gets* the character string "Enter first integer: "." Line 14

```
std::cin >> number1; // read first integer from user into number1
```

uses the input stream object cin (of namespace std) and the stream extraction operator, >>, to obtain a value from the keyboard. Using the stream extraction operator with std::cin takes character input from the standard input stream, which is usually the keyboard. We like to pronounce the preceding statement as, "std::cin *gives* a value to number1" or simply "std::cin *gives* number1."

Error-Prevention Tip 2.2

Programs should validate the correctness of all input values to prevent erroneous information from affecting a program's calculations.

When the computer executes the preceding statement, it waits for the user to enter a value for variable number1. The user responds by typing an integer (as characters), then pressing the *Enter* key (sometimes called the *Return* key) to send the characters to the computer. The computer converts the character representation of the number to an integer and assigns (copies) this number (or value) to the variable number1. Any subsequent references to number1 in this program will use this same value.

The std::cout and std::cin stream objects facilitate interaction between the user and the computer. Because this interaction resembles a dialog, it is often called conversational computing or interactive computing.

Line 16

```
std::cout << "Enter second integer: "; // prompt user for data
```

prints Enter second integer: on the screen, prompting the user to take action. Line 17

```
std::cin >> number2; // read second integer from user into number2
```

obtains a value for variable number2 from the user.

The assignment statement in line 19

```
sum = number1 + number2; // add the numbers; store result in sum
```

calculates the sum of the variables `number1` and `number2` and assigns the result to variable `sum` using the assignment operator `=`. The statement is read as, "`sum` *gets* the value of `number1 + number2`." Most calculations are performed in assignment statements. The `=` operator and the `+` operator are called binary operators because each has two operands. In the case of the `+` operator, the two operands are `number1` and `number2`. In the case of the preceding `=` operator, the two operands are `sum` and the value of the expression `number1 + number2`.

Good Programming Practice 2.13

Place spaces on either side of a binary operator. This makes the operator stand out and makes the program more readable.

Line 21

```
std::cout << "Sum is " << sum << std::endl; // display sum; end line
```

displays the character string `Sum is` followed by the numerical value of variable `sum` followed by `std::endl`—a so-called stream manipulator. The name `endl` is an abbreviation for "end line" and belongs to namespace `std`. The `std::endl` stream manipulator outputs a newline, then "flushes the output buffer." This simply means that, on some systems where outputs accumulate in the machine until there are enough to "make it worthwhile" to display on the screen, `std::endl` forces any accumulated outputs to be displayed at that moment. This can be important when the outputs are prompting the user for an action, such as entering data.

Note that the preceding statement outputs multiple values of different types. The stream insertion operator "knows" how to output each type of data. Using multiple stream insertion operators (`<<`) in a single statement is referred to as concatenating, chaining or cascading stream insertion operations. It is unnecessary to have multiple statements to output multiple pieces of data.

Calculations can also be performed in output statements. We could have combined the statements in lines 19 and 21 into the statement

```
std::cout << "Sum is " << number1 + number2 << std::endl;
```

thus eliminating the need for the variable `sum`.

A powerful feature of C++ is that users can create their own data types called classes (we introduce this capability in Chapter 3 and explore it in depth in Chapters 9 and 10). Users can then "teach" C++ how to input and output values of these new data types using the `>>` and `<<` operators (this is called operator overloading—a topic we explore in Chapter 11).

2.5 Memory Concepts

Variable names such as `number1`, `number2` and `sum` actually correspond to locations in the computer's memory. Every variable has a name, a type, a size and a value.

In the addition program of Fig. 2.5, when the statement

```
std::cin >> number1; // read first integer from user into number1
```

in line 14 is executed, the characters typed by the user are converted to an integer that is placed into a memory location to which the name `number1` has been assigned by the C++

compiler. Suppose the user enters the number 45 as the value for number1. The computer will place 45 into location number1, as shown in Fig. 2.6.

Whenever a value is placed in a memory location, the value overwrites the previous value in that location; thus, placing a new value into a memory location is said to be destructive.

Returning to our addition program, when the statement

```
std::cin >> number2; // read second integer from user into number2
```

in line 17 is executed, suppose the user enters the value 72. This value is placed into location number2, and memory appears as in Fig. 2.7. Note that these locations are not necessarily adjacent in memory.

Once the program has obtained values for number1 and number2, it adds these values and places the sum into variable sum. The statement

```
sum = number1 + number2; // add the numbers; store result in sum
```

that performs the addition also replaces whatever value was stored in sum. This occurs when the calculated sum of number1 and number2 is placed into location sum (without regard to what value may already be in sum; that value is lost). After sum is calculated, memory appears as in Fig. 2.8. Note that the values of number1 and number2 appear exactly as they did before they were used in the calculation of sum. These values were used, but not destroyed, as the computer performed the calculation. Thus, when a value is read out of a memory location, the process is nondestructive.

number1	45

Fig. 2.6 | Memory location showing the name and value of variable number1.

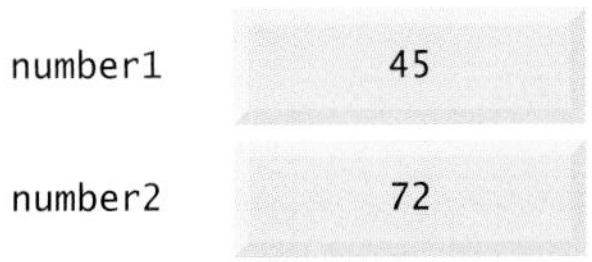

number1	45
number2	72

Fig. 2.7 | Memory locations after storing values for number1 and number2.

number1	45
number2	72
sum	117

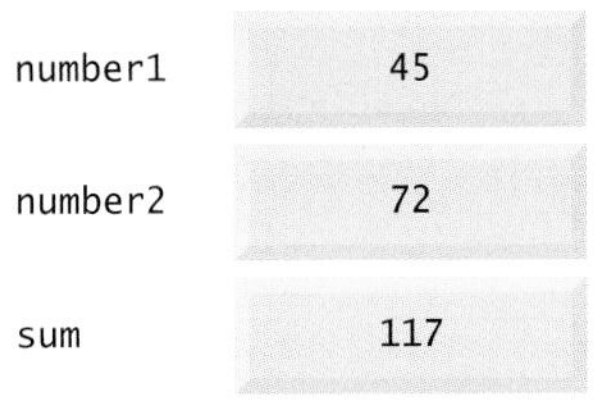

Fig. 2.8 | Memory locations after calculating and storing the sum of number1 and number2.

2.6 Arithmetic

Most programs perform arithmetic calculations. Figure 2.9 summarizes the C++ arithmetic operators. Note the use of various special symbols not used in algebra. The asterisk (*) indicates multiplication and the percent sign (%) is the modulus operator that will be discussed shortly. The arithmetic operators in Fig. 2.9 are all binary operators, i.e., operators that take two operands. For example, the expression number1 + number2 contains the binary operator + and the two operands number1 and number2.

Integer division (i.e., where both the numerator and the denominator are integers) yields an integer quotient; for example, the expression 7 / 4 evaluates to 1 and the expression 17 / 5 evaluates to 3. Note that any fractional part in integer division is discarded (i.e., truncated)—no rounding occurs.

C++ provides the modulus operator, %, that yields the remainder after integer division. The modulus operator can be used only with integer operands. The expression x % y yields the remainder after x is divided by y. Thus, 7 % 4 yields 3 and 17 % 5 yields 2. In later chapters, we discuss many interesting applications of the modulus operator, such as determining whether one number is a multiple of another (a special case of this is determining whether a number is odd or even).

Common Programming Error 2.3

Attempting to use the modulus operator (%) with noninteger operands is a compilation error.

Arithmetic Expressions in Straight-Line Form

Arithmetic expressions in C++ must be entered into the computer in straight-line form. Thus, expressions such as "a divided by b" must be written as a / b, so that all constants, variables and operators appear in a straight line. The algebraic notation

$$\frac{a}{b}$$

is generally not acceptable to compilers, although some special-purpose software packages do exist that support more natural notation for complex mathematical expressions.

Parentheses for Grouping Subexpressions

Parentheses are used in C++ expressions in the same manner as in algebraic expressions. For example, to multiply a times the quantity b + c we write a * (b + c).

C++ operation	C++ arithmetic operator	Algebraic expression	C++ expression
Addition	+	$f + 7$	f + 7
Subtraction	–	$p - c$	p - c
Multiplication	*	bm or $b \cdot m$	b * m
Division	/	x / y or $\frac{x}{y}$ or $x \div y$	x / y
Modulus	%	$r \bmod s$	r % s

Fig. 2.9 | Arithmetic operators.

Rules of Operator Precedence

C++ applies the operators in arithmetic expressions in a precise sequence determined by the following rules of operator precedence, which are generally the same as those followed in algebra:

1. Operators in expressions contained within pairs of parentheses are evaluated first. Thus, *parentheses may be used to force the order of evaluation to occur in any sequence desired by the programmer.* Parentheses are said to be at the "highest level of precedence." In cases of nested, or embedded, parentheses, such as

   ((a + b) + c)

   the operators in the innermost pair of parentheses are applied first.

2. Multiplication, division and modulus operations are applied next. If an expression contains several multiplication, division and modulus operations, operators are applied from left to right. Multiplication, division and modulus are said to be on the same level of precedence.

3. Addition and subtraction operations are applied last. If an expression contains several addition and subtraction operations, operators are applied from left to right. Addition and subtraction also have the same level of precedence.

The set of rules of operator precedence defines the order in which C++ applies operators. When we say that certain operators are applied from left to right, we are referring to the associativity of the operators. For example, in the expression

    a + b + c

the addition operators (+) associate from left to right, so a + b is calculated first, then c is added to that sum to determine the value of the whole expression. We will see that some operators associate from right to left. Figure 2.10 summarizes these rules of operator precedence. This table will be expanded as additional C++ operators are introduced. A complete precedence chart is included in Appendix A.

Operator(s)	Operation(s)	Order of evaluation (precedence)
( )	Parentheses	Evaluated first. If the parentheses are nested, the expression in the innermost pair is evaluated first. If there are several pairs of parentheses "on the same level" (i.e., not nested), they are evaluated left to right.
* / %	Multiplication Division Modulus	Evaluated second. If there are several, they are evaluated left to right.
+ –	Addition Subtraction	Evaluated last. If there are several, they are evaluated left to right.

Fig. 2.10 | Precedence of arithmetic operators.

Sample Algebraic and C++ Expressions

Now consider several expressions in light of the rules of operator precedence. Each example lists an algebraic expression and its C++ equivalent. The following is an example of an arithmetic mean (average) of five terms:

Algebra: $m = \dfrac{a + b + c + d + e}{5}$

C++:   `m = ( a + b + c + d + e ) / 5;`

The parentheses are required because division has higher precedence than addition. The entire quantity (a + b + c + d + e) is to be divided by 5. If the parentheses are erroneously omitted, we obtain a + b + c + d + e / 5, which evaluates incorrectly as

$$\iota + b + c + d + \frac{e}{5}$$

The following is an example of the equation of a straight line:

Algebra: $y = mx + b$

C++:   `y = m * x + b;`

No parentheses are required. The multiplication is applied first because multiplication has a higher precedence than addition.

The following example contains modulus (%), multiplication, division, addition, subtraction and assignment operations:

Algebra: $z = pr\,\%q + w/x - y$

C++:   `z = p * r % q + w / x - y;`
          ⑥   ①   ②   ④   ③   ⑤

The circled numbers under the statement indicate the order in which C++ applies the operators. The multiplication, modulus and division are evaluated first in left-to-right order (i.e., they associate from left to right) because they have higher precedence than addition and subtraction. The addition and subtraction are applied next. These are also applied left to right. Then the assignment operator is applied.

Evaluation of a Second-Degree Polynomial

To develop a better understanding of the rules of operator precedence, consider the evaluation of a second-degree polynomial ($y = ax^2 + bx + c$):

`y = a * x * x + b * x + c;`
      ⑥   ①   ②   ④   ③   ⑤

The circled numbers under the statement indicate the order in which C++ applies the operators. There is no arithmetic operator for exponentiation in C++, so we have represented x^2 as x * x. We will soon discuss the standard library function pow ("power") that performs exponentiation. Because of some subtle issues related to the data types required by pow, we defer a detailed explanation of pow until Chapter 6.

Common Programming Error 2.4

Some programming languages use operators ** or ∧ to represent exponentiation. C++ does not support these exponentiation operators; using them for exponentiation results in errors.

Suppose variables a, b, c and x in the preceding second-degree polynomial are initialized as follows: a = 2, b = 3, c = 7 and x = 5. Figure 2.11 illustrates the order in which the operators are applied.

As in algebra, it is acceptable to place unnecessary parentheses in an expression to make the expression clearer. These are called redundant parentheses. For example, the preceding assignment statement could be parenthesized as follows:

```
y = ( a * x * x ) + ( b * x ) + c;
```

Good Programming Practice 2.14

Using redundant parentheses in complex arithmetic expressions can make the expressions clearer.

2.7 Decision Making: Equality and Relational Operators

This section introduces a simple version of C++'s if statement that allows a program to make a decision based on the truth or falsity of some condition. If the condition is met, i.e., the condition is true, the statement in the body of the if statement is executed. If the condition is not met, i.e., the condition is false, the body statement is not executed. We will see an example shortly.

Step 1. y = 2 * 5 * 5 + 3 * 5 + 7;   (Leftmost multiplication)

2 * 5 is 10

Step 2. y = 10 * 5 + 3 * 5 + 7;   (Leftmost multiplication)

10 * 5 is 50

Step 3. y = 50 + 3 * 5 + 7;   (Multiplication before addition)

3 * 5 is 15

Step 4. y = 50 + 15 + 7;   (Leftmost addition)

50 + 15 is 65

Step 5. y = 65 + 7;   (Last addition)

65 + 7 is 72

Step 6. y = 72   (Last operation—place 72 in y)

Fig. 2.11 | Order in which a second-degree polynomial is evaluated.

Conditions in if statements can be formed by using the equality operators and relational operators summarized in Fig. 2.12. The relational operators all have the same level of precedence and associate left to right. The equality operators both have the same level of precedence, which is lower than that of the relational operators, and associate left to right.

Common Programming Error 2.5

A syntax error will occur if any of the operators ==, !=, >= and <= appears with spaces between its pair of symbols.

Common Programming Error 2.6

Reversing the order of the pair of symbols in any of the operators !=, >= and <= (by writing them as =!, => and =<, respectively) is normally a syntax error. In some cases, writing != as =! will not be a syntax error, but almost certainly will be a logic error that has an effect at execution time. You will understand why when you learn about logical operators in Chapter 5. A fatal logic error causes a program to fail and terminate prematurely. A nonfatal logic error allows a program to continue executing, but usually produces incorrect results.

Common Programming Error 2.7

Confusing the equality operator == with the assignment operator = results in logic errors. The equality operator should be read "is equal to," and the assignment operator should be read "gets" or "gets the value of" or "is assigned the value of." Some people prefer to read the equality operator as "double equals." As we discuss in Section 5.9, confusing these operators may not necessarily cause an easy-to-recognize syntax error, but may cause extremely subtle logic errors.

The following example uses six if statements to compare two numbers input by the user. If the condition in any of these if statements is satisfied, the output statement associated with that if statement is executed. Figure 2.13 shows the program and the input/output dialogs of three sample executions.

Standard algebraic equality or relational operator	C++ equality or relational operator	Sample C++ condition	Meaning of C++ condition
Relational operators			
>	>	x > y	x is greater than y
<	<	x < y	x is less than y
≥	>=	x >= y	x is greater than or equal to y
≤	<=	x <= y	x is less than or equal to y
Equality operators			
=	==	x == y	x is equal to y
≠	!=	x != y	x is not equal to y

Fig. 2.12 | Equality and relational operators.

Lines 6–8

```
using std::cout; // program uses cout
using std::cin;  // program uses cin
using std::endl; // program uses endl
```

are using declarations that eliminate the need to repeat the std:: prefix as we did in earlier programs. Once we insert these using declarations, we can write cout instead of std::cout, cin instead of std::cin and endl instead of std::endl, respectively, in the remainder of the program. [*Note:* From this point forward in the book, each example contains one or more using declarations.]

```
 1   // Fig. 2.13: fig02_13.cpp
 2   // Comparing integers using if statements, relational operators
 3   // and equality operators.
 4   #include <iostream> // allows program to perform input and output
 5
 6   using std::cout; // program uses cout
 7   using std::cin;  // program uses cin
 8   using std::endl; // program uses endl
 9
10   // function main begins program execution
11   int main()
12   {
13      int number1; // first integer to compare
14      int number2; // second integer to compare
15
16      cout << "Enter two integers to compare: "; // prompt user for data
17      cin >> number1 >> number2; // read two integers from user
18
19      if ( number1 == number2 )
20         cout << number1 << " == " << number2 << endl;
21
22      if ( number1 != number2 )
23         cout << number1 << " != " << number2 << endl;
24
25      if ( number1 < number2 )
26         cout << number1 << " < " << number2 << endl;
27
28      if ( number1 > number2 )
29         cout << number1 << " > " << number2 << endl;
30
31      if ( number1 <= number2 )
32         cout << number1 << " <= " << number2 << endl;
33
34      if ( number1 >= number2 )
35         cout << number1 << " >= " << number2 << endl;
36
37      return 0; // indicate that program ended successfully
38
39   } // end function main
```

Fig. 2.13 | Equality and relational operators. (Part 1 of 2.)

```
Enter two integers to compare: 3 7
3 != 7
3 < 7
3 <= 7
```

```
Enter two integers to compare: 22 12
22 != 12
22 > 12
22 >= 12
```

```
Enter two integers to compare: 7 7
7 == 7
7 <= 7
7 >= 7
```

Fig. 2.13 | Equality and relational operators. (Part 2 of 2.)

Good Programming Practice 2.15

Place using declarations immediately after the #include to which they refer.

Lines 13–14

```
int number1; // first integer to compare
int number2; // second integer to compare
```

declare the variables used in the program. Remember that variables may be declared in one declaration or in multiple declarations.

The program uses cascaded stream extraction operations (line 17) to input two integers. Remember that we are allowed to write cin (instead of std::cin) because of line 7. First a value is read into variable number1, then a value is read into variable number2.

The if statement at lines 19–20

```
if ( number1 == number2 )
    cout << number1 << " == " << number2 << endl;
```

compares the values of variables number1 and number2 to test for equality. If the values are equal, the statement at line 20 displays a line of text indicating that the numbers are equal. If the conditions are true in one or more of the if statements starting at lines 22, 25, 28, 31 and 34, the corresponding body statement displays an appropriate line of text.

Notice that each if statement in Fig. 2.13 has a single statement in its body and that each body statement is indented. In Chapter 4 we show how to specify if statements with multiple-statement bodies (by enclosing the body statements in a pair of braces, { }, creating what is called a compound statement or a block).

Good Programming Practice 2.16

Indent the statement(s) in the body of an if statement to enhance readability.

Good Programming Practice 2.17

For readability, there should be no more than one statement per line in a program.

Common Programming Error 2.8

Placing a semicolon immediately after the right parenthesis after the condition in an if state-ment is often a logic error (although not a syntax error). The semicolon causes the body of the if statement to be empty, so the if statement performs no action, regardless of whether or not its condition is true. Worse yet, the original body statement of the if statement now would become a statement in sequence with the if statement and would always execute, often causing the pro-gram to produce incorrect results.

Note the use of white space in Fig. 2.13. Recall that white-space characters, such as tabs, newlines and spaces, are normally ignored by the compiler. So, statements may be split over several lines and may be spaced according to the programmer's preferences. It is a syntax error to split identifiers, strings (such as `"hello"`) and constants (such as the number 1000) over several lines.

Common Programming Error 2.9

It is a syntax error to split an identifier by inserting white-space characters (e.g., writing main as ma in).

Good Programming Practice 2.18

A lengthy statement may be spread over several lines. If a single statement must be split across lines, choose meaningful breaking points, such as after a comma in a comma-separated list, or after an operator in a lengthy expression. If a statement is split across two or more lines, indent all subsequent lines and left-align the group.

Figure 2.14 shows the precedence and associativity of the operators introduced in this chapter. The operators are shown top to bottom in decreasing order of precedence. Notice that all these operators, with the exception of the assignment operator =, associate from left to right. Addition is left-associative, so an expression like x + y + z is evaluated as if it had been written (x + y) + z. The assignment operator = associates from right to left, so an expression such as x = y = 0 is evaluated as if it had been written x = (y = 0), which, as we will soon see, first assigns 0 to y then assigns the result of that assignment—0—to x.

Operators				Associativity	Type
()				left to right	parentheses
*	/	%		left to right	multiplicative
+	−			left to right	additive
<<	>>			left to right	stream insertion/extraction
<	<=	>	>=	left to right	relational
==	!=			left to right	equality
=				right to left	assignment

Fig. 2.14 | Precedence and associativity of the operators discussed so far.

Good Programming Practice 2.19

Refer to the operator precedence and associativity chart when writing expressions containing many operators. Confirm that the operators in the expression are performed in the order you expect. If you are uncertain about the order of evaluation in a complex expression, break the expression into smaller statements or use parentheses to force the order of evaluation, exactly as you would do in an algebraic expression. Be sure to observe that some operators such as assignment (=) associate right to left rather than left to right.

2.8 (Optional) Software Engineering Case Study: Examining the ATM Requirements Document

Now we begin our optional object-oriented design and implementation case study. The "Software Engineering Case Study" sections at the ends of this and the next several chapters will ease you into object orientation. We will develop software for a simple automated teller machine (ATM) system, providing you with a concise, carefully paced, complete design and implementation experience. In Chapters 3–7, 9 and 13, we will perform the various steps of an object-oriented design (OOD) process using the UML, while relating these steps to the object-oriented concepts discussed in the chapters. Appendix G implements the ATM using the techniques of object-oriented programming (OOP) in C++. We present the complete case study solution. This is not an exercise; rather, it is an end-to-end learning experience that concludes with a detailed walkthrough of the C++ code that implements our design. It will acquaint you with the kinds of substantial problems encountered in industry and their potential solutions.

We begin our design process by presenting a requirements document that specifies the overall purpose of the ATM system and *what* it must do. Throughout the case study, we refer to the requirements document to determine precisely what functionality the system must include.

Requirements Document

A local bank intends to install a new automated teller machine (ATM) to allow users (i.e., bank customers) to perform basic financial transactions (Fig. 2.15). Each user can have only one account at the bank. ATM users should be able to view their account balance, withdraw cash (i.e., take money out of an account) and deposit funds (i.e., place money into an account).

The user interface of the automated teller machine contains the following hardware components:

- a screen that displays messages to the user
- a keypad that receives numeric input from the user
- a cash dispenser that dispenses cash to the user and
- a deposit slot that receives deposit envelopes from the user.

The cash dispenser begins each day loaded with 500 $20 bills. [*Note:* Owing to the limited scope of this case study, certain elements of the ATM described here do not accurately mimic those of a real ATM. For example, a real ATM typically contains a device that reads a user's account number from an ATM card, whereas this ATM asks the user to type an account number on the keypad. A real ATM also usually prints a receipt at the end of a session, but all output from this ATM appears on the screen.]

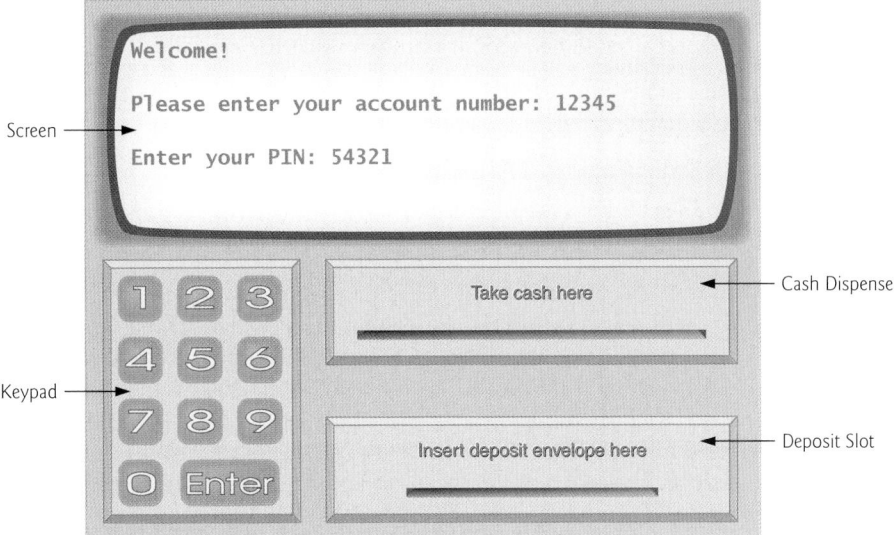

Screen

```
Welcome!

Please enter your account number: 12345

Enter your PIN: 54321
```

Take cash here — Cash Dispenser

Keypad

```
1 2 3
4 5 6
7 8 9
0 Enter
```

Insert deposit envelope here — Deposit Slot

Fig. 2.15 | Automated teller machine user interface.

The bank wants you to develop software to perform the financial transactions initiated by bank customers through the ATM. The bank will integrate the software with the ATM's hardware at a later time. The software should encapsulate the functionality of the hardware devices (e.g., cash dispenser, deposit slot) within software components, but it need not concern itself with how these devices perform their duties. The ATM hardware has not been developed yet, so instead of writing your software to run on the ATM, you should develop a first version of the software to run on a personal computer. This version should use the computer's monitor to simulate the ATM's screen, and the computer's keyboard to simulate the ATM's keypad.

An ATM session consists of authenticating a user (i.e., proving the user's identity) based on an account number and personal identification number (PIN), followed by creating and executing financial transactions. To authenticate a user and perform transactions, the ATM must interact with the bank's account information database. [*Note:* A database is an organized collection of data stored on a computer.] For each bank account, the database stores an account number, a PIN and a balance indicating the amount of money in the account. [*Note:* For simplicity, we assume that the bank plans to build only one ATM, so we do not need to worry about multiple ATMs accessing this database at the same time. Furthermore, we assume that the bank does not make any changes to the information in the database while a user is accessing the ATM. Also, any business system like an ATM faces reasonably complicated security issues that go well beyond the scope of a first- or second-semester computer science course. We make the simplifying assumption, however, that the bank trusts the ATM to access and manipulate the information in the database without significant security measures.]

Upon first approaching the ATM, the user should experience the following sequence of events (shown in Fig. 2.15):

1. The screen displays a welcome message and prompts the user to enter an account number.

2. The user enters a five-digit account number, using the keypad.

3. The screen prompts the user to enter the PIN (personal identification number) associated with the specified account number.

4. The user enters a five-digit PIN, using the keypad.

5. If the user enters a valid account number and the correct PIN for that account, the screen displays the main menu (Fig. 2.16). If the user enters an invalid account number or an incorrect PIN, the screen displays an appropriate message, then the ATM returns to *Step 1* to restart the authentication process.

After the ATM authenticates the user, the main menu (Fig. 2.16) displays a numbered option for each of the three types of transactions: balance inquiry (option 1), withdrawal (option 2) and deposit (option 3). The main menu also displays an option that allows the user to exit the system (option 4). The user then chooses either to perform a transaction (by entering 1, 2 or 3) or to exit the system (by entering 4). If the user enters an invalid option, the screen displays an error message, then redisplays to the main menu.

If the user enters 1 to make a balance inquiry, the screen displays the user's account balance. To do so, the ATM must retrieve the balance from the bank's database.

The following actions occur when the user enters 2 to make a withdrawal:

6. The screen displays a menu (shown in Fig. 2.17) containing standard withdrawal amounts: $20 (option 1), $40 (option 2), $60 (option 3), $100 (option 4) and $200 (option 5). The menu also contains an option to allow the user to cancel the transaction (option 6).

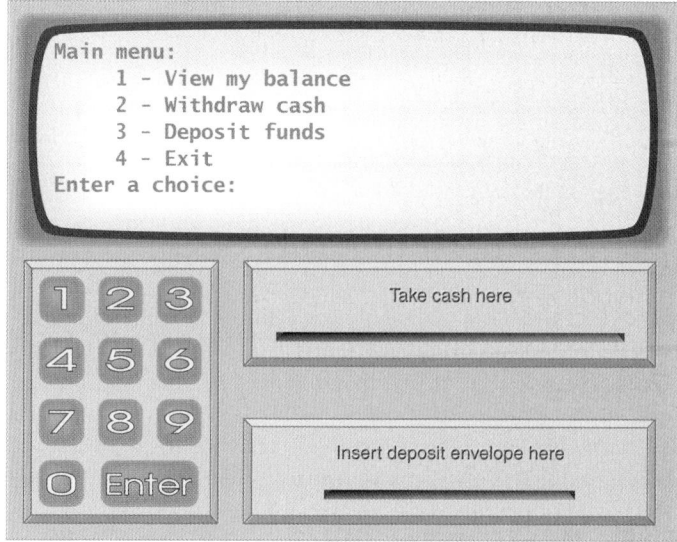

Fig. 2.16 | ATM main menu.

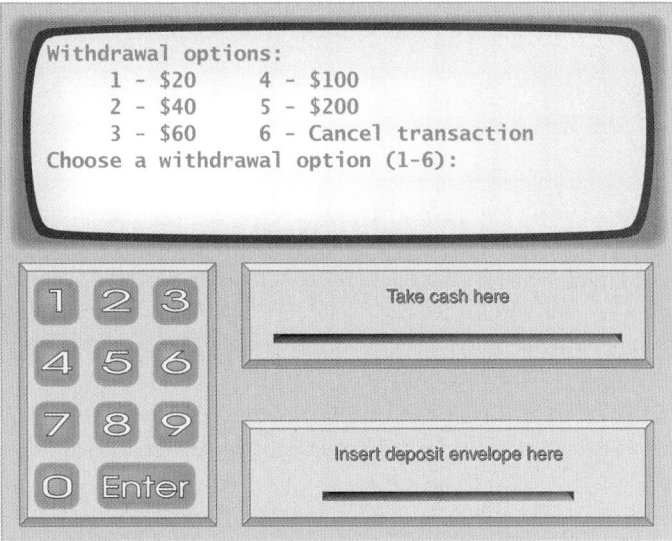

Fig. 2.17 | ATM withdrawal menu.

7. The user enters a menu selection (1–6) using the keypad.

8. If the withdrawal amount chosen is greater than the user's account balance, the screen displays a message stating this and telling the user to choose a smaller amount. The ATM then returns to *Step 1*. If the withdrawal amount chosen is less than or equal to the user's account balance (i.e., an acceptable withdrawal amount), the ATM proceeds to *Step 4*. If the user chooses to cancel the transaction (option 6), the ATM displays the main menu (Fig. 2.16) and waits for user input.

9. If the cash dispenser contains enough cash to satisfy the request, the ATM proceeds to *Step 5*. Otherwise, the screen displays a message indicating the problem and telling the user to choose a smaller withdrawal amount. The ATM then returns to *Step 1*.

10. The ATM debits (i.e., subtracts) the withdrawal amount from the user's account balance in the bank's database.

11. The cash dispenser dispenses the desired amount of money to the user.

12. The screen displays a message reminding the user to take the money.

The following actions occur when the user enters 3 (while the main menu is displayed) to make a deposit:

13. The screen prompts the user to enter a deposit amount or to type 0 (zero) to cancel the transaction.

14. The user enters a deposit amount or 0, using the keypad. [*Note:* The keypad does not contain a decimal point or a dollar sign, so the user cannot type a real dollar amount (e.g., $1.25). Instead, the user must enter a deposit amount as a number of cents (e.g., 125). The ATM then divides this number by 100 to obtain a number representing a dollar amount (e.g., 125 ÷ 100 = 1.25).]

15. If the user specifies a deposit amount, the ATM proceeds to *Step 4*. If the user chooses to cancel the transaction (by entering 0), the ATM displays the main menu (Fig. 2.16) and waits for user input.

16. The screen displays a message telling the user to insert a deposit envelope into the deposit slot.

17. If the deposit slot receives a deposit envelope within two minutes, the ATM credits (i.e., adds) the deposit amount to the user's account balance in the bank's database. [*Note:* This money is not immediately available for withdrawal. The bank first must physically verify the amount of cash in the deposit envelope, and any checks in the envelope must clear (i.e., money must be transferred from the check writer's account to the check recipient's account). When either of these events occurs, the bank appropriately updates the user's balance stored in its database. This occurs independently of the ATM system.] If the deposit slot does not receive a deposit envelope within this time period, the screen displays a message that the system has canceled the transaction due to inactivity. The ATM then displays the main menu and waits for user input.

After the system successfully executes a transaction, the system should redisplay the main menu (Fig. 2.16) so that the user can perform additional transactions. If the user chooses to exit the system (option 4), the screen should display a thank you message, then display the welcome message for the next user.

Analyzing the ATM System

The preceding statement is a simplified example of a requirements document. Typically, such a document is the result of a detailed process of requirements gathering that might include interviews with potential users of the system and specialists in fields related to the system. For example, a systems analyst who is hired to prepare a requirements document for banking software (e.g., the ATM system described here) might interview financial experts to gain a better understanding of *what* the software must do. The analyst would use the information gained to compile a list of system requirements to guide systems designers.

The process of requirements gathering is a key task of the first stage of the software life cycle. The software life cycle specifies the stages through which software evolves from the time it is first conceived to the time it is retired from use. These stages typically include: analysis, design, implementation, testing and debugging, deployment, maintenance and retirement. Several software life cycle models exist, each with its own preferences and specifications for when and how often software engineers should perform each of these stages. Waterfall models perform each stage once in succession, whereas iterative models may repeat one or more stages several times throughout a product's life cycle.

The analysis stage of the software life cycle focuses on defining the problem to be solved. When designing any system, one must certainly *solve the problem right*, but of equal importance, one must *solve the right problem*. Systems analysts collect the requirements that indicate the specific problem to solve. Our requirements document describes our ATM system in sufficient detail that you do not need to go through an extensive analysis stage—it has been done for you.

To capture what a proposed system should do, developers often employ a technique known as use case modeling. This process identifies the use cases of the system, each of which represents a different capability that the system provides to its clients. For example,

ATMs typically have several use cases, such as "View Account Balance," "Withdraw Cash," "Deposit Funds," "Transfer Funds Between Accounts" and "Buy Postage Stamps." The simplified ATM system we build in this case study allows only the first three use cases (Fig. 2.18).

Each use case describes a typical scenario in which the user uses the system. You have already read descriptions of the ATM system's use cases in the requirements document; the lists of steps required to perform each type of transaction (i.e., balance inquiry, withdrawal and deposit) actually described the three use cases of our ATM—"View Account Balance," "Withdraw Cash" and "Deposit Funds."

Use Case Diagrams

We now introduce the first of several UML diagrams in our ATM case study. We create a use case diagram to model the interactions between a system's clients (in this case study, bank customers) and the system. The goal is to show the kinds of interactions users have with a system without providing the details—these are provided in other UML diagrams (which we present throughout the case study). Use case diagrams are often accompanied by informal text that describes the use cases in more detail—like the text that appears in the requirements document. Use case diagrams are produced during the analysis stage of the software life cycle. In larger systems, use case diagrams are simple but indispensable tools that help system designers remain focused on satisfying the users' needs.

Figure 2.18 shows the use case diagram for our ATM system. The stick figure represents an actor, which defines the roles that an external entity—such as a person or another system—plays when interacting with the system. For our automated teller machine, the actor is a User who can view an account balance, withdraw cash and deposit funds from the ATM. The User is not an actual person, but instead comprises the roles that a real person—when playing the part of a User—can play while interacting with the ATM. Note that a use case diagram can include multiple actors. For example, the use case diagram for a real bank's ATM system might also include an actor named Administrator who refills the cash dispenser each day.

We identify the actor in our system by examining the requirements document, which states, "ATM users should be able to view their account balance, withdraw cash and deposit funds." Therefore, the actor in each of the three use cases is the User who interacts with the ATM. An external entity—a real person—plays the part of the User to perform financial

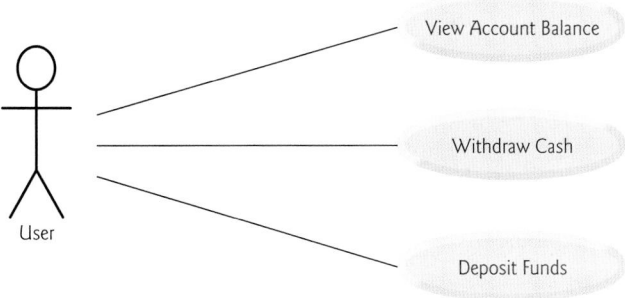

Fig. 2.18 | Use case diagram for the ATM system from the user's perspective.

transactions. Figure 2.18 shows one actor, whose name, User, appears below the actor in the diagram. The UML models each use case as an oval connected to an actor with a solid line.

Software engineers (more precisely, systems designers) must analyze the requirements document or a set of use cases and design the system before programmers implement it in a particular programming language. During the analysis stage, systems designers focus on understanding the requirements document to produce a high-level specification that describes *what* the system is supposed to do. The output of the design stage—a design specification—should specify clearly *how* the system should be constructed to satisfy these requirements. In the next several "Software Engineering Case Study" sections, we perform the steps of a simple object-oriented design (OOD) process on the ATM system to produce a design specification containing a collection of UML diagrams and supporting text. Recall that the UML is designed for use with any OOD process. Many such processes exist, the best known of which is the Rational Unified Process™ (RUP) developed by Rational Software Corporation (now a division of IBM). RUP is a rich process intended for designing "industrial strength" applications. For this case study, we present our own simplified design process.

Designing the ATM System

We now begin the design stage of our ATM system. A system is a set of components that interact to solve a problem. For example, to perform the ATM system's designated tasks, our ATM system has a user interface (Fig. 2.15), contains software that executes financial transactions and interacts with a database of bank account information. System structure describes the system's objects and their interrelationships. System behavior describes how the system changes as its objects interact with one another. Every system has both structure and behavior—designers must specify both. There are several distinct types of system structures and behaviors. For example, the interactions among objects in the system differ from those between the user and the system, yet both constitute a portion of the system behavior.

The UML 2 specifies 13 diagram types for documenting the models of systems. Each models a distinct characteristic of a system's structure or behavior—six diagrams relate to system structure; the remaining seven relate to system behavior. We list here only the six types of diagrams used in our case study—one of these (class diagrams) models system structure—the remaining five model system behavior. We overview the remaining seven UML diagram types in Appendix H, UML 2: Additional Diagram Types.

1. Use case diagrams, such as the one in Fig. 2.18, model the interactions between a system and its external entities (actors) in terms of use cases (system capabilities, such as "View Account Balance," "Withdraw Cash" and "Deposit Funds").

2. Class diagrams, which you will study in Section 3.11, model the classes, or "building blocks," used in a system. Each noun or "thing" described in the requirements document is a candidate to be a class in the system (e.g., "account," "keypad"). Class diagrams help us specify the structural relationships between parts of the system. For example, the ATM system class diagram will specify that the ATM is physically composed of a screen, a keypad, a cash dispenser and a deposit slot.

3. State machine diagrams, which you will study in Section 3.11, model the ways in which an object changes state. An object's state is indicated by the values of all the object's attributes at a given time. When an object changes state, that object may behave differently in the system. For example, after validating a user's PIN,

the ATM transitions from the "user not authenticated" state to the "user authenticated" state, at which point the ATM allows the user to perform financial transactions (e.g., view account balance, withdraw cash, deposit funds).

4. **Activity diagrams**, which you will also study in Section 5.11, model an object's activity—the object's workflow (sequence of events) during program execution. An activity diagram models the actions the object performs and specifies the order in which it performs these actions. For example, an activity diagram shows that the ATM must obtain the balance of the user's account (from the bank's account information database) before the screen can display the balance to the user.

5. **Communication diagrams** (called **collaboration diagrams** in earlier versions of the UML) model the interactions among objects in a system, with an emphasis on *what* interactions occur. You will learn in Section 7.12 that these diagrams show which objects must interact to perform an ATM transaction. For example, the ATM must communicate with the bank's account information database to retrieve an account balance.

6. **Sequence diagrams** also model the interactions among the objects in a system, but unlike communication diagrams, they emphasize *when* interactions occur. You will learn in Section 7.12 that these diagrams help show the order in which interactions occur in executing a financial transaction. For example, the screen prompts the user to enter a withdrawal amount before cash is dispensed.

In Section 3.11, we continue designing our ATM system by identifying the classes from the requirements document. We accomplish this by extracting key nouns and noun phrases from the requirements document. Using these classes, we develop our first draft of the class diagram that models the structure of our ATM system.

Internet and Web Resources
The following URLs provide information on object-oriented design with the UML.

`www-306.ibm.com/software/rational/uml/`
Lists frequently asked questions about the UML, provided by IBM Rational.

`www.softdocwiz.com/Dictionary.htm`
Hosts the Unified Modeling Language Dictionary, which lists and defines all terms used in the UML.

`www-306.ibm.com/software/rational/offerings/design.html`
Provides information about IBM Rational software available for designing systems. Provides downloads of 30-day trial versions of several products, such as IBM Rational Rose® XDE Developer.

`www.embarcadero.com/products/describe/index.html`
Provides a 15-day trial license for the Embarcadero Technologies® UML modeling tool Describe.™

`www.borland.com/together/index.html`
Provides a free 30-day license to download a trial version of Borland® Together® Control-Center™—a software development tool that supports the UML.

`www.ilogix.com/rhapsody/rhapsody.cfm`
Provides a free 30-day license to download a trial version of I-Logix Rhapsody®—a UML 2-based model-driven development environment.

`argouml.tigris.org`
Contains information and downloads for ArgoUML, a free open-source UML tool.

`www.objectsbydesign.com/books/booklist.html`
Lists books on the UML and object-oriented design.

`www.objectsbydesign.com/tools/umltools_byCompany.html`
Lists software tools that use the UML, such as IBM Rational Rose, Embarcadero Describe, Sparx Systems Enterprise Architect, I-Logix Rhapsody and Gentleware Poseidon for UML.
`www.ootips.org/ood-principles.html`
Provides answers to the question, "What Makes a Good Object-Oriented Design?"
`www.cetus-links.org/oo_uml.html`
Introduces the UML and provides links to numerous UML resources.
`www.agilemodeling.com/essays/umlDiagrams.htm`
Provides in-depth descriptions and tutorials on each of the 13 UML 2 diagram types.

Recommended Readings

The following books provide information on object-oriented design with the UML.

Booch, G. *Object-Oriented Analysis and Design with Applications*, Third Edition. Boston: Addison-Wesley, 2004.

Eriksson, H., et al. *UML 2 Toolkit*. New York: John Wiley, 2003.

Kruchten, P. *The Rational Unified Process: An Introduction*. Boston: Addison-Wesley, 2004.

Larman, C. *Applying UML and Patterns: An Introduction to Object-Oriented Analysis and Design*, Second Edition. Upper Saddle River, NJ: Prentice Hall, 2002.

Roques, P. *UML in Practice: The Art of Modeling Software Systems Demonstrated Through Worked Examples and Solutions*. New York: John Wiley, 2004.

Rosenberg, D., and K. Scott. *Applying Use Case Driven Object Modeling with UML: An Annotated e-Commerce Example*. Reading, MA: Addison-Wesley, 2001.

Rumbaugh, J., I. Jacobson and G. Booch. *The Complete UML Training Course*. Upper Saddle River, NJ: Prentice Hall, 2000.

Rumbaugh, J., I. Jacobson and G. Booch. *The Unified Modeling Language Reference Manual*. Reading, MA: Addison-Wesley, 1999.

Rumbaugh, J., I. Jacobson and G. Booch. *The Unified Software Development Process*. Reading, MA: Addison-Wesley, 1999.

Software Engineering Case Study Self-Review Exercises

2.1   Suppose we enabled a user of our ATM system to transfer money between two bank accounts. Modify the use case diagram of Fig. 2.18 to reflect this change.

2.2   _____ model the interactions among objects in a system with an emphasis on *when* these interactions occur.
   a) Class diagrams
   b) Sequence diagrams
   c) Communication diagrams
   d) Activity diagrams

2.3   Which of the following choices lists stages of a typical software life cycle in sequential order?
   a) design, analysis, implementation, testing
   b) design, analysis, testing, implementation
   c) analysis, design, testing, implementation
   d) analysis, design, implementation, testing

Answers to Software Engineering Case Study Self-Review Exercises

2.1   Figure 2.19 contains a use case diagram for a modified version of our ATM system that also allows users to transfer money between accounts.

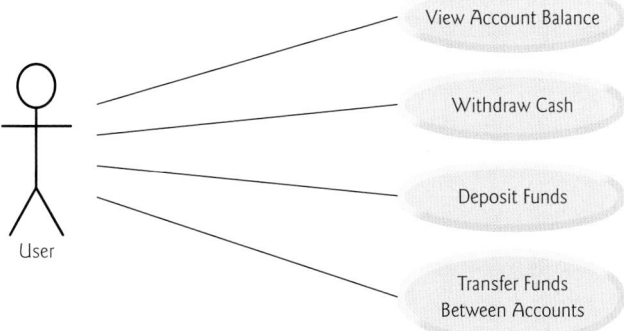

Fig. 2.19 | Use case diagram for a modified version of our ATM system that also allows users to transfer money between accounts.

2.2   b.

2.3   d.

Summary

- Single-line comments begin with //. Programmers insert comments to document programs and improve their readability.
- Comments do not cause the computer to perform any action when the program is run—they are ignored by the C++ compiler and do not cause any machine-language object code to be generated.
- A preprocessor directive begins with # and is a message to the C++ preprocessor. Preprocessor directives are processed by the preprocessor before the program is compiled and don't end with a semicolon as C++ statements do.
- The line #include <iostream> tells the C++ preprocessor to include the contents of the input/output stream header file in the program. This file contains information necessary to compile programs that use std::cin and std::cout and operators << and >>.
- Programmers use white space (i.e., blank lines, space characters and tab characters) to make programs easier to read. White-space characters are ignored by the compiler.
- C++ programs begin executing at the function main, even if main does not appear first in the program.
- The keyword int to the left of main indicates that main "returns" an integer value.
- A left brace, {, must begin the body of every function. A corresponding right brace, }, must end each function's body.
- A string in double quotes is sometimes referred to as a character string, message or string literal. White-space characters in strings are not ignored by the compiler.
- Every statement must end with a semicolon (also known as the statement terminator).
- Output and input in C++ are accomplished with streams of characters.
- The output stream object std::cout—normally connected to the screen—is used to output data. Multiple data items can be output by concatenating stream insertion (<<) operators.

- The input stream object std::cin—normally connected to the keyboard—is used to input data. Multiple data items can be input by concatenating stream extraction (>>) operators.

- The std::cout and std::cin stream objects facilitate interaction between the user and the computer. Because this interaction resembles a dialog, it is often called conversational computing or interactive computing.

- The notation std::cout specifies that we are using a name, in this case cout, that belongs to "namespace" std.

- When a backslash (i.e., an escape character) is encountered in a string of characters, the next character is combined with the backslash to form an escape sequence.

- The escape sequence \n means newline. It causes the cursor (i.e., the current screen-position indicator) to move to the beginning of the next line on the screen.

- A message that directs the user to take a specific action is known as a prompt.

- C++ keyword return is one of several means to exit a function.

- All variables in a C++ program must be declared before they can be used.

- A variable name in C++ is any valid identifier that is not a keyword. An identifier is a series of characters consisting of letters, digits and underscores (_). Identifiers cannot start with a digit. C++ identifiers can be any length; however, some systems and/or C++ implementations may impose some restrictions on the length of identifiers.

- C++ is case sensitive.

- Most calculations are performed in assignment statements.

- A variable is a location in the computer's memory where a value can be stored for use by a program.

- Variables of type int hold integer values, i.e., whole numbers such as 7, –11, 0, 31914.

- Every variable stored in the computer's memory has a name, a value, a type and a size.

- Whenever a new value is placed in a memory location, the process is destructive; i.e., the new value replaces the previous value in that location. The previous value is lost.

- When a value is read from memory, the process is nondestructive; i.e., a copy of the value is read, leaving the original value undisturbed in the memory location.

- The std::endl stream manipulator outputs a newline, then "flushes the output buffer."

- C++ evaluates arithmetic expressions in a precise sequence determined by the rules of operator precedence and associativity.

- Parentheses may be used to force the order of evaluation to occur in any sequence desired by the programmer.

- Integer division (i.e., both the numerator and the denominator are integers) yields an integer quotient. Any fractional part in integer division is truncated—no rounding occurs.

- The modulus operator, %, yields the remainder after integer division. The modulus operator can be used only with integer operands.

- The if statement allows a program to make a decision when a certain condition is met. The format for an if statement is

      if (*condition*)
          statement;

  If the condition is true, the statement in the body of the if is executed. If the condition is not met, i.e., the condition is false, the body statement is skipped.

- Conditions in if statements are commonly formed by using equality operators and relational operators. The result of using these operators is always the value true or false.

- The declaration

  ```
  using std::cout;
  ```

  is a `using` declaration that eliminates the need to repeat the `std::` prefix. Once we include this `using` declaration, we can write `cout` instead of `std::cout` in the remainder of a program.

Terminology

/* ... */ comment (C-style comment)
// comment
arithmetic operator
assignment operator (=)
associativity of operators
binary operator
block
body of a function
cascading stream insertion operations
case sensitive
chaining stream insertion operations
character string
`cin` object
comma-separated list
comment (//)
compilation error
compiler error
compile-time error
compound statement
concatenating stream insertion operations
condition
`cout` object
cursor
data type
decision
declaration
destructive write
equality operators
   == "is equal to"
   != "is not equal to"
escape character (\)
escape sequence
exit a function
fatal error
function
identifier
`if` statement
input/output stream header file <iostream>
`int` data type
integer (`int`)
integer division
left-to-right associativity
literal

logic error
`main` function
memory
memory location
message
modulus operator (%)
multiplication operator (*)
nested parentheses
newline character (\n)
nondestructive read
nonfatal logic error
operand
operator
operator associativity
parentheses ()
perform an action
precedence
preprocessor directive
prompt
redundant parentheses
relational operators
   < "is less than"
   <= "is less than or equal to"
   > "is greater than"
   >= "is greater than or equal to"
`return` statement
rules of operator precedence
self-documenting program
semicolon (;) statement terminator
standard input stream object (`cin`)
standard output stream object (`cout`)
statement
statement terminator (;)
stream
stream insertion operator (<<)
stream extraction operator (>>)
stream manipulator
string
string literal
syntax error
`using` declaration
variable
white space

Self-Review Exercises

2.1   Fill in the blanks in each of the following.
   a) Every C++ program begins execution at the function _____.
   b) The _____ begins the body of every function and the _____ ends the body of every function.
   c) Every C++ statement ends with a(n) _____.
   d) The escape sequence \n represents the _____ character, which causes the cursor to position to the beginning of the next line on the screen.
   e) The _____ statement is used to make decisions.

2.2   State whether each of the following is *true* or *false*. If *false*, explain why. Assume the statement using std::cout; is used.
   a) Comments cause the computer to print the text after the // on the screen when the program is executed.
   b) The escape sequence \n, when output with cout and the stream insertion operator, causes the cursor to position to the beginning of the next line on the screen.
   c) All variables must be declared before they are used.
   d) All variables must be given a type when they are declared.
   e) C++ considers the variables number and NuMbEr to be identical.
   f) Declarations can appear almost anywhere in the body of a C++ function.
   g) The modulus operator (%) can be used only with integer operands.
   h) The arithmetic operators *, /, %, + and – all have the same level of precedence.
   i) A C++ program that prints three lines of output must contain three statements using cout and the stream insertion operator.

2.3   Write a single C++ statement to accomplish each of the following (assume that using declarations have not been used):
   a) Declare the variables c, thisIsAVariable, q76354 and number to be of type int.
   b) Prompt the user to enter an integer. End your prompting message with a colon (:) followed by a space and leave the cursor positioned after the space.
   c) Read an integer from the user at the keyboard and store the value entered in integer variable age.
   d) If the variable number is not equal to 7, print "The variable number is not equal to 7".
   e) Print the message "This is a C++ program" on one line.
   f) Print the message "This is a C++ program" on two lines. End the first line with C++.
   g) Print the message "This is a C++ program" with each word on a separate line.
   h) Print the message "This is a C++ program" with each word separated from the next by a tab.

2.4   Write a statement (or comment) to accomplish each of the following (assume that using declarations have been used):
   a) State that a program calculates the product of three integers.
   b) Declare the variables x, y, z and result to be of type int (in separate statements).
   c) Prompt the user to enter three integers.
   d) Read three integers from the keyboard and store them in the variables x, y and z.
   e) Compute the product of the three integers contained in variables x, y and z, and assign the result to the variable result.
   f) Print "The product is " followed by the value of the variable result.
   g) Return a value from main indicating that the program terminated successfully.

2.5   Using the statements you wrote in Exercise 2.4, write a complete program that calculates and displays the product of three integers. Add comments to the code where appropriate. [*Note:* You will need to write the necessary using declarations.]

2.6 Identify and correct the errors in each of the following statements (assume that the statement `using std::cout;` is used):

a) `if ( c < 7 );`
   `cout << "c is less than 7\n";`

b) `if ( c => 7 )`
   `cout << "c is equal to or greater than 7\n";`

Answers to Self-Review Exercises

2.1 a) `main`. b) left brace ({), right brace (}). c) semicolon. d) newline. e) `if`.

2.2 a) False. Comments do not cause any action to be performed when the program is executed. They are used to document programs and improve their readability.
   b) True.
   c) True.
   d) True.
   e) False. C++ is case sensitive, so these variables are unique.
   f) True.
   g) True.
   h) False. The operators `*`, `/` and `%` have the same precedence, and the operators `+` and `-` have a lower precedence.
   i) False. A single cout statement with multiple \n escape sequences can print several lines.

2.3 a) `int c, thisIsAVariable, q76354, number;`
   b) `std::cout << "Enter an integer: ";`
   c) `std::cin >> age;`
   d) `if ( number != 7 )`
      `std::cout << "The variable number is not equal to 7\n";`
   e) `std::cout << "This is a C++ program\n";`
   f) `std::cout << "This is a C++\nprogram\n";`
   g) `std::cout << "This\nis\na\nC++\nprogram\n";`
   h) `std::cout << "This\tis\ta\tC++\tprogram\n";`

2.4 a) `// Calculate the product of three integers`
   b) `int x;`
      `int y;`
      `int z;`
      `int result;`
   c) `cout << "Enter three integers: ";`
   d) `cin >> x >> y >> z;`
   e) `result = x * y * z;`
   f) `cout << "The product is " << result << endl;`
   g) `return 0;`

2.5 (See program below)

```
1   // Calculate the product of three integers
2   #include <iostream> // allows program to perform input and output
3
4   using std::cout; // program uses cout
5   using std::cin; // program uses cin
```

```
 6   using std::endl; // program uses endl
 7
 8   // function main begins program execution
 9   int main()
10   {
11      int x; // first integer to multiply
12      int y; // second integer to multiply
13      int z; // third integer to multiply
14      int result; // the product of the three integers
15
16      cout << "Enter three integers: "; // prompt user for data
17      cin >> x >> y >> z; // read three integers from user
18      result = x * y * z; // multiply the three integers; store result
19      cout << "The product is " << result << endl; // print result; end line
20
21      return 0; // indicate program executed successfully
22   } // end function main
```

2.6   a) Error: Semicolon after the right parenthesis of the condition in the if statement.
   Correction: Remove the semicolon after the right parenthesis. [*Note:* The result of this
   error is that the output statement will be executed whether or not the condition in the
   if statement is true.] The semicolon after the right parenthesis is a null (or empty) statement—a statement that does nothing. We will learn more about the null statement in
   the next chapter.

   b) Error: The relational operator =>.
   Correction: Change => to >=, and you may want to change "equal to or greater than" to
   "greater than or equal to" as well.

Exercises

2.7   Discuss the meaning of each of the following objects:
   a) std::cin
   b) std::cout

2.8   Fill in the blanks in each of the following:
   a) _____ are used to document a program and improve its readability.
   b) The object used to print information on the screen is _____.
   c) A C++ statement that makes a decision is _____.
   d) Most calculations are normally performed by _____ statements.
   e) The _____ object inputs values from the keyboard.

2.9   Write a single C++ statement or line that accomplishes each of the following:
   a) Print the message "Enter two numbers".
   b) Assign the product of variables b and c to variable a.
   c) State that a program performs a payroll calculation (i.e., use text that helps to document
      a program).
   d) Input three integer values from the keyboard into integer variables a, b and c.

2.10   State which of the following are *true* and which are *false*. If *false*, explain your answers.
   a) C++ operators are evaluated from left to right.
   b) The following are all valid variable names: _under_bar_, m928134, t5, j7, her_sales,
      his_account_total, a, b, c, z, z2.
   c) The statement cout << "a = 5;"; is a typical example of an assignment statement.
   d) A valid C++ arithmetic expression with no parentheses is evaluated from left to right.

e) The following are all invalid variable names: 3g, 87, 67h2, h22, 2h.

2.11 Fill in the blanks in each of the following:

a) What arithmetic operations are on the same level of precedence as multiplication?
_____.

b) When parentheses are nested, which set of parentheses is evaluated first in an arithmetic expression? _____.

c) A location in the computer's memory that may contain different values at various times throughout the execution of a program is called a _____.

2.12 What, if anything, prints when each of the following C++ statements is performed? If nothing prints, then answer "nothing." Assume x = 2 and y = 3.

a) `cout << x;`
b) `cout << x + x;`
c) `cout << "x=";`
d) `cout << "x = " << x;`
e) `cout << x + y << " = " << y + x;`
f) `z = x + y;`
g) `cin >> x >> y;`
h) `// cout << "x + y = " << x + y;`
i) `cout << "\n";`

2.13 Which of the following C++ statements contain variables whose values are replaced?

a) `cin >> b >> c >> d >> e >> f;`
b) `p = i + j + k + 7;`
c) `cout << "variables whose values are replaced";`
d) `cout << "a = 5";`

2.14 Given the algebraic equation $y = ax^3 + 7$, which of the following, if any, are correct C++ statements for this equation?

a) `y = a * x * x * x + 7;`
b) `y = a * x * x * ( x + 7 );`
c) `y = ( a * x ) * x * ( x + 7 );`
d) `y = (a * x) * x * x + 7;`
e) `y = a * ( x * x * x ) + 7;`
f) `y = a * x * ( x * x + 7 );`

2.15 State the order of evaluation of the operators in each of the following C++ statements and show the value of x after each statement is performed.

a) `x = 7 + 3 * 6 / 2 - 1;`
b) `x = 2 % 2 + 2 * 2 - 2 / 2;`
c) `x = ( 3 * 9 * ( 3 + ( 9 * 3 / ( 3 ) ) ) );`

2.16 Write a program that asks the user to enter two numbers, obtains the two numbers from the user and prints the sum, product, difference, and quotient of the two numbers.

2.17 Write a program that prints the numbers 1 to 4 on the same line with each pair of adjacent numbers separated by one space. Do this several ways:

a) Using one statement with one stream insertion operator.
b) Using one statement with four stream insertion operators.
c) Using four statements.

2.18 Write a program that asks the user to enter two integers, obtains the numbers from the user, then prints the larger number followed by the words "is larger." If the numbers are equal, print the message "These numbers are equal."

2.19   Write a program that inputs three integers from the keyboard and prints the sum, average, product, smallest and largest of these numbers. The screen dialog should appear as follows:

```
Input three different integers: 13 27 14
Sum is 54
Average is 18
Product is 4914
Smallest is 13
Largest is 27
```

2.20   Write a program that reads in the radius of a circle as an integer and prints the circle's diameter, circumference and area. Use the constant value 3.14159 for π. Do all calculations in output statements. [*Note:* In this chapter, we have discussed only integer constants and variables. In Chapter 4 we discuss floating-point numbers, i.e., values that can have decimal points.]

2.21   Write a program that prints a box, an oval, an arrow and a diamond as follows:

```
*********        ***              *                *
*       *      *     *           ***             *   *
*       *     *       *         *****           *     *
*       *     *       *           *            *       *
*       *     *       *           *           *         *
*       *     *       *           *           *         *
*       *     *       *           *            *       *
*       *      *     *            *             *   *
*********        ***              *                *
```

2.22   What does the following code print?

```
cout << "*\n**\n***\n****\n*****" << endl;
```

2.23   Write a program that reads in five integers and determines and prints the largest and the smallest integers in the group. Use only the programming techniques you learned in this chapter.

2.24   Write a program that reads an integer and determines and prints whether it is odd or even. [*Hint:* Use the modulus operator. An even number is a multiple of two. Any multiple of two leaves a remainder of zero when divided by 2.]

2.25   Write a program that reads in two integers and determines and prints if the first is a multiple of the second. [*Hint:* Use the modulus operator.]

2.26   Display the following checkerboard pattern with eight output statements, then display the same pattern using as few statements as possible.

```
* * * * * * * *
 * * * * * * * *
* * * * * * * *
 * * * * * * * *
* * * * * * * *
 * * * * * * * *
* * * * * * * *
 * * * * * * * *
```

2.27 Here is a peek ahead. In this chapter you learned about integers and the type int. C++ can also represent uppercase letters, lowercase letters and a considerable variety of special symbols. C++ uses small integers internally to represent each different character. The set of characters a computer uses and the corresponding integer representations for those characters is called that computer's character set. You can print a character by enclosing that character in single quotes, as with

```
cout << 'A'; // print an uppercase A
```

You can print the integer equivalent of a character using static_cast as follows:

```
cout << static_cast< int >( 'A' ); // print 'A' as an integer
```

This is called a cast operation (we formally introduce casts in Chapter 4). When the preceding statement executes, it prints the value 65 (on systems that use the ASCII character set). Write a program that prints the integer equivalent of a character typed at the keyboard. Test your program several times using uppercase letters, lowercase letters, digits and special characters (like $).

2.28 Write a program that inputs a five-digit integer, separates the integer into its individual digits and prints the digits separated from one another by three spaces each. [*Hint:* Use the integer division and modulus operators.] For example, if the user types in 42339, the program should print:

```
4   2   3   3   9
```

2.29 Using only the techniques you learned in this chapter, write a program that calculates the squares and cubes of the integers from 0 to 10 and uses tabs to print the following neatly formatted table of values:

```
integer square   cube
0        0        0
1        1        1
2        4        8
3        9        27
4        16       64
5        25       125
6        36       216
7        49       343
8        64       512
9        81       729
10       100      1000
```

3

Introduction to Classes and Objects

OBJECTIVES

In this chapter you will learn:

- What classes, objects, member functions and data members are.
- How to define a class and use it to create an object.
- How to define member functions in a class to implement the class's behaviors.
- How to declare data members in a class to implement the class's attributes.
- How to call a member function of an object to make that member function perform its task.
- The differences between data members of a class and local variables of a function.
- How to use a constructor to ensure that an object's data is initialized when the object is created.
- How to engineer a class to separate its interface from its implementation and encourage reuse.

3.1 Introduction

In Chapter 2, you created simple programs that displayed messages to the user, obtained information from the user, performed calculations and made decisions. In this chapter, you will begin writing programs that employ the basic concepts of object-oriented programming that we introduced in Section 1.17. One common feature of every program in Chapter 2 was that all the statements that performed tasks were located in function main. Typically, the programs you develop in this book will consist of function main and one or more classes, each containing data members and member functions. If you become part of a development team in industry, you might work on software systems that contain hundreds, or even thousands, of classes. In this chapter, we develop a simple, well-engineered framework for organizing object-oriented programs in C++.

First, we motivate the notion of classes with a real-world example. Then we present a carefully paced sequence of seven complete working programs to demonstrate creating and using your own classes. These examples begin our integrated case study on developing a grade-book class that instructors can use to maintain student test scores. This case study is enhanced over the next several chapters, culminating with the version presented in Chapter 7, Arrays and Vectors.

3.2 Classes, Objects, Member Functions and Data Members

Let's begin with a simple analogy to help you reinforce your understanding from Section 1.17 of classes and their contents. Suppose you want to drive a car and make it go faster by pressing down on its accelerator pedal. What must happen before you can do this? Well, before you can drive a car, someone has to design it and build it. A car typically begins as engineering drawings, similar to the blueprints used to design a house. These drawings include the design for an accelerator pedal that the driver will use to make the car go faster. In a sense, the pedal "hides" the complex mechanisms that actually make the car go faster, just as the brake pedal "hides" the mechanisms that slow the car, the steering wheel "hides" the mechanisms that turn the car and so on. This enables people with little or no knowledge of how cars are engineered to drive a car easily, simply by using the accelerator pedal, the brake pedal, the steering wheel, the transmission shifting mechanism and other such simple and user-friendly "interfaces" to the car's complex internal mechanisms.

Unfortunately, you cannot drive the engineering drawings of a car—before you can drive a car, it must be built from the engineering drawings that describe it. A completed car will have an actual accelerator pedal to make the car go faster. But even that's not enough—the car will not accelerate on its own, so the driver must press the accelerator pedal to tell the car to go faster.

Now let's use our car example to introduce the key object-oriented programming concepts of this section. Performing a task in a program requires a function (such as main, as described in Chapter 2). The function describes the mechanisms that actually perform its tasks. The function hides from its user the complex tasks that it performs, just as the accelerator pedal of a car hides from the driver the complex mechanisms of making the car go faster. In C++, we begin by creating a program unit called a class to house a function, just as a car's engineering drawings house the design of an accelerator pedal. Recall from Section 1.17 that a function belonging to a class is called a member function. In a class, you provide one or more member functions that are designed to perform the class's tasks. For example, a class that represents a bank account might contain one member function to deposit money into the account, another to withdraw money from the account and a third to inquire what the current account balance is.

Just as you cannot drive an engineering drawing of a car, you cannot "drive" a class. Just as someone has to build a car from its engineering drawings before you can actually drive the car, you must create an object of a class before you can get a program to perform the tasks the class describes. That is one reason C++ is known as an object-oriented programming language. Note also that just as *many* cars can be built from the same engineering drawing, *many* objects can be built from the same class.

When you drive a car, pressing its gas pedal sends a message to the car to perform a task—that is, make the car go faster. Similarly, you send messages to an object—each message is known as a member-function call and tells a member function of the object to perform its task. This is often called requesting a service from an object.

Thus far, we have used the car analogy to introduce classes, objects and member functions. In addition to the capabilities a car provides, it also has many attributes, such as its color, the number of doors, the amount of gas in its tank, its current speed and its total miles driven (i.e., its odometer reading). Like the car's capabilities, these attributes are represented as part of a car's design in its engineering diagrams. As you drive a car, these attributes are always associated with the car. Every car maintains its own attributes. For example, each car knows how much gas is in its own gas tank, but not how much is in the tanks of other cars. Similarly, an object has attributes that are carried with the object as it is used in a program. These attributes are specified as part of the object's class. For example, a bank account object has a balance attribute that represents the amount of money in the account. Each bank account object knows the balance in the account it represents, but not the balances of the other accounts in the bank. Attributes are specified by the class's data members.

3.3 Overview of the Chapter Examples

The remainder of this chapter presents seven simple examples that demonstrate the concepts we introduced in the context of the car analogy. These examples, summarized below, incrementally build a GradeBook class to demonstrate these concepts:

1. The first example presents a GradeBook class with one member function that simply displays a welcome message when it is called. We then show how to create an object of that class and call the member function so that it displays the welcome message.

2. The second example modifies the first by allowing the member function to receive a course name as a so-called argument. Then, the member function displays the course name as part of the welcome message.

3. The third example shows how to store the course name in a GradeBook object. For this version of the class, we also show how to use member functions to set the course name in the object and get the course name from the object.

4. The fourth example demonstrates how the data in a GradeBook object can be initialized when the object is created—the initialization is performed by a special member function called the class's constructor. This example also demonstrates that each GradeBook object maintains its own course name data member.

5. The fifth example modifies the fourth by demonstrating how to place class GradeBook into a separate file to enable software reusability.

6. The sixth example modifies the fifth by demonstrating the good software-engineering principle of separating the interface of the class from its implementation. This makes the class easier to modify without affecting any clients of the class's objects—that is, any classes or functions that call the member functions of the class's objects from outside the objects.

7. The last example enhances class GradeBook by introducing data validation, which ensures that data in an object adheres to a particular format or is in a proper value range. For example, a Date object would require a month value in the range 1–12. In this GradeBook example, the member function that sets the course name for a GradeBook object ensures that the course name is 25 characters or fewer. If not, the member function uses only the first 25 characters of the course name and displays a warning message.

Note that the GradeBook examples in this chapter do not actually process or store grades. We begin processing grades with class GradeBook in Chapter 4 and we store grades in a GradeBook object in Chapter 7, Arrays and Vectors.

3.4 Defining a Class with a Member Function

We begin with an example (Fig. 3.1) that consists of class GradeBook, which represents a grade book that an instructor can use to maintain student test scores, and a main function (lines 20–25) that creates a GradeBook object. This is the first in a series of graduated examples leading up to a fully functional GradeBook class in Chapter 7, Arrays and Vectors. Function main uses this object and its member function to display a message on the screen welcoming the instructor to the grade-book program.

```
 1   // Fig. 3.1: fig03_01.cpp
 2   // Define class GradeBook with a member function displayMessage;
 3   // Create a GradeBook object and call its displayMessage function.
 4   #include <iostream>
 5   using std::cout;
 6   using std::endl;
 7
 8   // GradeBook class definition
 9   class GradeBook
10   {
11   public:
12      // function that displays a welcome message to the GradeBook user
13      void displayMessage()
14      {
15         cout << "Welcome to the Grade Book!" << endl;
16      } // end function displayMessage
17   }; // end class GradeBook
18
19   // function main begins program execution
20   int main()
21   {
22      GradeBook myGradeBook; // create a GradeBook object named myGradeBook
23      myGradeBook.displayMessage(); // call object's displayMessage function
24      return 0; // indicate successful termination
25   } // end main
```

```
Welcome to the Grade Book!
```

Fig. 3.1 | Defining class GradeBook with a member function, creating a GradeBook object and calling its member function.

First we describe how to define a class and a member function. Then we explain how an object is created and how to call a member function of an object. The first few examples contain function main and the GradeBook class it uses in the same file. Later in the chapter, we introduce more sophisticated ways to structure your programs to achieve better software engineering.

Class GradeBook
Before function main (lines 20–25) can create an object of class GradeBook, we must tell the compiler what member functions and data members belong to the class. This is known as defining a class. The GradeBook class definition (lines 9–17) contains a member function called displayMessage (lines 13–16) that displays a message on the screen (line 15). Recall that a class is like a blueprint—so we need to make an object of class GradeBook (line 22) and call its displayMessage member function (line 23) to get line 15 to execute and display the welcome message. We'll soon explain lines 22–23 in detail.

The class definition begins at line 9 with the keyword class followed by the class name GradeBook. By convention, the name of a user-defined class begins with a capital letter, and for readability, each subsequent word in the class name begins with a capital letter. This capitalization style is often referred to as camel case, because the pattern of uppercase and lowercase letters resembles the silhouette of a camel.

Every class's body is enclosed in a pair of left and right braces ({ and }), as in lines 10 and 17. The class definition terminates with a semicolon (line 17).

Common Programming Error 3.1

Forgetting the semicolon at the end of a class definition is a syntax error.

Recall that the function main is always called automatically when you execute a program. Most functions do not get called automatically. As you will soon see, you must call member function displayMessage explicitly to tell it to perform its task.

Line 11 contains the access-specifier label public:. The keyword public is called an access specifier. Lines 13–16 define member function displayMessage. This member function appears after access specifier public: to indicate that the function is "available to the public"—that is, it can be called by other functions in the program and by member functions of other classes. Access specifiers are always followed by a colon (:). For the remainder of the text, when we refer to the access specifier public, we will omit the colon as we did in this sentence. Section 3.6 introduces a second access specifier, private (again, we omit the colon in our discussions, but include it in our programs).

Each function in a program performs a task and may return a value when it completes its task—for example, a function might perform a calculation, then return the result of that calculation. When you define a function, you must specify a return type to indicate the type of the value returned by the function when it completes its task. In line 13, keyword void to the left of the function name displayMessage is the function's return type. Return type void indicates that displayMessage will perform a task but will not return (i.e., give back) any data to its calling function (in this example, main, as we'll see in a moment) when it completes its task. (In Fig. 3.5, you will see an example of a function that returns a value.)

The name of the member function, displayMessage, follows the return type. By convention, function names begin with a lowercase first letter and all subsequent words in the name begin with a capital letter. The parentheses after the member function name indicate that this is a function. An empty set of parentheses, as shown in line 13, indicates that this member function does not require additional data to perform its task. You will see an example of a member function that does require additional data in Section 3.5. Line 13 is commonly referred to as the function header. Every function's body is delimited by left and right braces ({ and }), as in lines 14 and 16.

The body of a function contains statements that perform the function's task. In this case, member function displayMessage contains one statement (line 15) that displays the message "Welcome to the Grade Book!". After this statement executes, the function has completed its task.

Common Programming Error 3.2

Returning a value from a function whose return type has been declared void is a compilation error.

Common Programming Error 3.3

Defining a function inside another function is a syntax error.

*Testing Class **GradeBook***

Next, we'd like to use class GradeBook in a program. As you learned in Chapter 2, function main begins the execution of every program. Lines 20–25 of Fig. 3.1 contain the main function that will control our program's execution.

In this program, we'd like to call class GradeBook's displayMessage member function to display the welcome message. Typically, you cannot call a member function of a class until you create an object of that class. (As you will learn in Section 10.7, static member functions are an exception.) Line 22 creates an object of class GradeBook called myGrade-Book. Note that the variable's type is GradeBook—the class we defined in lines 9–17. When we declare variables of type int, as we did in Chapter 2, the compiler knows what int is— it's a fundamental type. When we write line 22, however, the compiler does not automatically know what type GradeBook is—it's a user-defined type. Thus, we must tell the compiler what GradeBook is by including the class definition, as we did in lines 9–17. If we omitted these lines, the compiler would issue an error message (such as "'GradeBook': undeclared identifier" in Microsoft Visual C++ .NET or "'GradeBook': undeclared" in GNU C++). Each new class you create becomes a new type that can be used to create objects. Programmers can define new class types as needed; this is one reason why C++ is known as an extensible language.

Line 23 calls the member function displayMessage (defined in lines 13–16) using variable myGradeBook followed by the dot operator (.), the function name displayMessage and an empty set of parentheses. This call causes the displayMessage function to perform its task. At the beginning of line 23, "myGradeBook." indicates that main should use the GradeBook object that was created in line 22. The empty parentheses in line 13 indicate that member function displayMessage does not require additional data to perform its task. (In Section 3.5, you'll see how to pass data to a function.) When displayMessage completes its task, function main continues executing at line 24, which indicates that main performed its tasks successfully. This is the end of main, so the program terminates.

*UML Class Diagram for Class **GradeBook***

Recall from Section 1.17 that the UML is a graphical language used by programmers to represent their object-oriented systems in a standardized manner. In the UML, each class is modeled in a class diagram as a rectangle with three compartments. Figure 3.2 presents a UML class diagram for class GradeBook of Fig. 3.1. The top compartment contains the name of the class, centered horizontally and in boldface type. The middle compartment contains the class's attributes, which correspond to data members in C++. In Fig. 3.2 the middle compartment is empty, because the version of class GradeBook in Fig. 3.1 does not have any attributes. (Section 3.6 presents a version of the GradeBook class that does have an attribute.) The bottom compartment contains the class's operations, which correspond

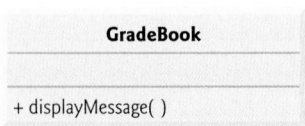

Fig. 3.2 | UML class diagram indicating that class GradeBook has a public displayMessage operation.

to member functions in C++. The UML models operations by listing the operation name followed by a set of parentheses. The class GradeBook has only one member function, displayMessage, so the bottom compartment of Fig. 3.2 lists one operation with this name. Member function displayMessage does not require additional information to perform its tasks, so the parentheses following displayMessage in the class diagram are empty, just as they are in the member function's header in line 13 of Fig. 3.1. The plus sign (+) in front of the operation name indicates that displayMessage is a public operation in the UML (i.e., a public member function in C++). We frequently use UML class diagrams to summarize class attributes and operations.

3.5 Defining a Member Function with a Parameter

In our car analogy from Section 3.2, we mentioned that pressing a car's gas pedal sends a message to the car to perform a task—make the car go faster. But how fast should the car accelerate? As you know, the farther down you press the pedal, the faster the car accelerates. So the message to the car includes both the task to perform and additional information that helps the car perform the task. This additional information is known as a parameter—the value of the parameter helps the car determine how fast to accelerate. Similarly, a member function can require one or more parameters that represent additional data it needs to perform its task. A function call supplies values—called arguments—for each of the function's parameters. For example, to make a deposit into a bank account, suppose a deposit member function of an Account class specifies a parameter that represents the deposit amount. When the deposit member function is called, an argument value representing the deposit amount is copied to the member function's parameter. The member function then adds that amount to the account balance.

Defining and Testing Class *GradeBook*

Our next example (Fig. 3.3) redefines class GradeBook (lines 14–23) with a displayMessage member function (lines 18–22) that displays the course name as part of the welcome message. The new displayMessage member function requires a parameter (courseName in line 18) that represents the course name to output.

Before discussing the new features of class GradeBook, let's see how the new class is used in main (lines 26–40). Line 28 creates a variable of type string called nameOfCourse that will be used to store the course name entered by the user. A variable of type string represents a string of characters such as "CS101 Introduction to C++ Programming". A string is actually an object of the C++ Standard Library class string. This class is defined in header file <string>, and the name string, like cout, belongs to namespace std. To enable line 28 to compile, line 9 includes the <string> header file. Note that the using declaration in line 10 allows us to simply write string in line 28 rather than std::string. For now, you can think of string variables like variables of other types such as int. You will learn about additional string capabilities in Section 3.10.

Line 29 creates an object of class GradeBook named myGradeBook. Line 32 prompts the user to enter a course name. Line 33 reads the name from the user and assigns it to the nameOfCourse variable, using the library function getline to perform the input. Before we explain this line of code, let's explain why we cannot simply write

```
cin >> nameOfCourse;
```

```
1   // Fig. 3.3: fig03_03.cpp
2   // Define class GradeBook with a member function that takes a parameter;
3   // Create a GradeBook object and call its displayMessage function.
4   #include <iostream>
5   using std::cout;
6   using std::cin;
7   using std::endl;
8
9   #include <string> // program uses C++ standard string class
10  using std::string;
11  using std::getline;
12
13  // GradeBook class definition
14  class GradeBook
15  {
16  public:
17     // function that displays a welcome message to the GradeBook user
18     void displayMessage( string courseName )
19     {
20        cout << "Welcome to the grade book for\n" << courseName << "!"
21           << endl;
22     } // end function displayMessage
23  }; // end class GradeBook
24
25  // function main begins program execution
26  int main()
27  {
28     string nameOfCourse; // string of characters to store the course name
29     GradeBook myGradeBook; // create a GradeBook object named myGradeBook
30
31     // prompt for and input course name
32     cout << "Please enter the course name:" << endl;
33     getline( cin, nameOfCourse ); // read a course name with blanks
34     cout << endl; // output a blank line
35
36     // call myGradeBook's displayMessage function
37     // and pass nameOfCourse as an argument
38     myGradeBook.displayMessage( nameOfCourse );
39     return 0; // indicate successful termination
40  } // end main
```

```
Please enter the course name:
CS101 Introduction to C++ Programming

Welcome to the grade book for
CS101 Introduction to C++ Programming!
```

Fig. 3.3 | Defining class GradeBook with a member function that takes a parameter.

to obtain the course name. In our sample program execution, we use the course name "CS101 Introduction to C++ Programming," which contains multiple words. (Recall that we highlight user-supplied input in bold.) When cin is used with the stream extraction operator, it reads characters until the first white-space character is reached. Thus, only

"CS101" would be read by the preceding statement. The rest of the course name would have to be read by subsequent input operations.

In this example, we'd like the user to type the complete course name and press *Enter* to submit it to the program, and we'd like to store the entire course name in the string variable nameOfCourse. The function call getline(cin, nameOfCourse) in line 33 reads characters (including the space characters that separate the words in the input) from the standard input stream object cin (i.e., the keyboard) until the newline character is encountered, places the characters in the string variable nameOfCourse and discards the newline character. Note that when you press *Enter* while typing program input, a newline is inserted in the input stream. Also note that the <string> header file must be included in the program to use function getline and that the name getline belongs to namespace std.

Line 38 calls myGradeBook's displayMessage member function. The nameOfCourse variable in parentheses is the argument that is passed to member function displayMessage so that it can perform its task. The value of variable nameOfCourse in main becomes the value of member function displayMessage's parameter courseName in line 18. When you execute this program, notice that member function displayMessage outputs as part of the welcome message the course name you type (in our sample execution, CS101 Introduction to C++ Programming).

More on Arguments and Parameters

To specify that a function requires data to perform its task, you place additional information in the function's parameter list, which is located in the parentheses following the function name. The parameter list may contain any number of parameters, including none at all (represented by empty parentheses as in Fig. 3.1, line 13) to indicate that a function does not require any parameters. Member function displayMessage's parameter list (Fig. 3.3, line 18) declares that the function requires one parameter. Each parameter should specify a type and an identifier. In this case, the type string and the identifier courseName indicate that member function displayMessage requires a string to perform its task. The member function body uses the parameter courseName to access the value that is passed to the function in the function call (line 38 in main). Lines 20–21 display parameter courseName's value as part of the welcome message. Note that the parameter variable's name (line 18) can be the same as or different from the argument variable's name (line 38)—you'll learn why in Chapter 6, Functions and an Introduction to Recursion.

A function can specify multiple parameters by separating each parameter from the next with a comma (we'll see an example in Figs. 6.4–6.5). The number and order of arguments in a function call must match the number and order of parameters in the parameter list of the called member function's header. Also, the argument types in the function call must match the types of the corresponding parameters in the function header. (As you will learn in subsequent chapters, an argument's type and its corresponding parameter's type need not always be identical, but they must be "consistent.") In our example, the one string argument in the function call (i.e., nameOfCourse) exactly matches the one string parameter in the member-function definition (i.e., courseName).

Common Programming Error 3.4

Placing a semicolon after the right parenthesis enclosing the parameter list of a function definition is a syntax error.

Common Programming Error 3.5

Defining a function parameter again as a local variable in the function is a compilation error.

Good Programming Practice 3.1

To avoid ambiguity, do not use the same names for the arguments passed to a function and the corresponding parameters in the function definition.

Good Programming Practice 3.2

Choosing meaningful function names and meaningful parameter names makes programs more readable and helps avoid excessive use of comments.

Updated UML Class Diagram for Class GradeBook

The UML class diagram of Fig. 3.4 models class GradeBook of Fig. 3.3. Like the class GradeBook defined in Fig. 3.1, this GradeBook class contains public member function displayMessage. However, this version of displayMessage has a parameter. The UML models a parameter by listing the parameter name, followed by a colon and the parameter type in the parentheses following the operation name. The UML has its own data types similar to those of C++. The UML is language-independent—it is used with many different programming languages—so its terminology does not exactly match that of C++. For example, the UML type String corresponds to the C++ type string. Member function displayMessage of class GradeBook (Fig. 3.3; lines 18–22) has a string parameter named courseName, so Fig. 3.4 lists courseName : String between the parentheses following the operation name displayMessage. Note that this version of the GradeBook class still does not have any data members.

3.6 Data Members, *set* Functions and *get* Functions

In Chapter 2, we declared all of a program's variables in its main function. Variables declared in a function definition's body are known as local variables and can be used only from the line of their declaration in the function to the immediately following closing right brace (}) of the function definition. A local variable must be declared before it can be used in a function. A local variable cannot be accessed outside the function in which it is declared. When a function terminates, the values of its local variables are lost. (You will see an exception to this in Chapter 6 when we discuss static local variables.) Recall from Section 3.2 that an object has attributes that are carried with it as it is used in a program. Such attributes exist throughout the life of the object.

GradeBook
+ displayMessage(courseName : String)

Fig. 3.4 | UML class diagram indicating that class GradeBook has a displayMessage operation with a courseName parameter of UML type String.

A class normally consists of one or more member functions that manipulate the attributes that belong to a particular object of the class. Attributes are represented as variables in a class definition. Such variables are called data members and are declared inside a class definition but outside the bodies of the class's member-function definitions. Each object of a class maintains its own copy of its attributes in memory. The example in this section demonstrates a GradeBook class that contains a courseName data member to represent a particular GradeBook object's course name.

GradeBook *Class with a Data Member, a* set *Function and a* get *Function*

In our next example, class GradeBook (Fig. 3.5) maintains the course name as a data member so that it can be used or modified at any time during a program's execution. The class contains member functions setCourseName, getCourseName and displayMessage. Member function setCourseName stores a course name in a GradeBook data member—member function getCourseName obtains a GradeBook's course name from that data member. Member function displayMessage—which now specifies no parameters—still displays a welcome message that includes the course name. However, as you will see, the function now obtains the course name by calling another function in the same class—getCourseName.

```cpp
1   // Fig. 3.5: fig03_05.cpp
2   // Define class GradeBook that contains a courseName data member
3   // and member functions to set and get its value;
4   // Create and manipulate a GradeBook object with these functions.
5   #include <iostream>
6   using std::cout;
7   using std::cin;
8   using std::endl;
9
10  #include <string> // program uses C++ standard string class
11  using std::string;
12  using std::getline;
13
14  // GradeBook class definition
15  class GradeBook
16  {
17  public:
18     // function that sets the course name
19     void setCourseName( string name )
20     {
21        courseName = name; // store the course name in the object
22     } // end function setCourseName
23
24     // function that gets the course name
25     string getCourseName()
26     {
27        return courseName; // return the object's courseName
28     } // end function getCourseName
29
```

Fig. 3.5 | Defining and testing class GradeBook with a data member and *set* and *get* functions. (Part 1 of 2.)

```
30     // function that displays a welcome message
31     void displayMessage()
32     {
33        // this statement calls getCourseName to get the
34        // name of the course this GradeBook represents
35        cout << "Welcome to the grade book for\n" << getCourseName() << "!"
36           << endl;
37     } // end function displayMessage
38  private:
39     string courseName; // course name for this GradeBook
40  }; // end class GradeBook
41
42  // function main begins program execution
43  int main()
44  {
45     string nameOfCourse; // string of characters to store the course name
46     GradeBook myGradeBook; // create a GradeBook object named myGradeBook
47
48     // display initial value of courseName
49     cout << "Initial course name is: " << myGradeBook.getCourseName()
50        << endl;
51
52     // prompt for, input and set course name
53     cout << "\nPlease enter the course name:" << endl;
54     getline( cin, nameOfCourse ); // read a course name with blanks
55     myGradeBook.setCourseName( nameOfCourse ); // set the course name
56
57     cout << endl; // outputs a blank line
58     myGradeBook.displayMessage(); // display message with new course name
59     return 0; // indicate successful termination
60  } // end main
```

```
Initial course name is:

Please enter the course name:
CS101 Introduction to C++ Programming

Welcome to the grade book for
CS101 Introduction to C++ Programming!
```

Fig. 3.5 | Defining and testing class GradeBook with a data member and *set* and *get* functions. (Part 2 of 2.)

 Good Programming Practice 3.3

Place a blank line between member-function definitions to enhance program readability.

A typical instructor teaches more than one course, each with its own course name. Line 39 declares that courseName is a variable of type string. Because the variable is declared in the class definition (lines 15–40) but outside the bodies of the class's member-function definitions (lines 19–22, 25–28 and 31–37), line 39 is a declaration for a data member. Every instance (i.e., object) of class GradeBook contains one copy of each of the class's data members. For example, if there are two GradeBook objects, each object has its own copy of courseName (one per object), as we'll see in the example of Fig. 3.7. A benefit of making courseName a data member is that all the member functions of the class (in this case, GradeBook) can manipulate any data members that appear in the class definition (in this case, courseName).

Access Specifiers *public and private*

Most data member declarations appear after the access-specifier label private: (line 38). Like public, keyword private is an access specifier. Variables or functions declared after access specifier private (and before the next access specifier) are accessible only to member functions of the class for which they are declared. Thus, data member courseName can be used only in member functions setCourseName, getCourseName and displayMessage of (every object of) class GradeBook. Data member courseName, because it is private, cannot be accessed by functions outside the class (such as main) or by member functions of other classes in the program. Attempting to access data member courseName in one of these program locations with an expression such as myGradeBook.courseName would result in a compilation error containing a message similar to

```
cannot access private member declared in class 'GradeBook'
```

Software Engineering Observation 3.1

As a rule of thumb, data members should be declared private and member functions should be declared public. (We will see that it is appropriate to declare certain member functions private, if they are to be accessed only by other member functions of the class.)

Common Programming Error 3.6

An attempt by a function, which is not a member of a particular class (or a friend of that class, as we will see in Chapter 10), to access a private member of that class is a compilation error.

The default access for class members is private so all members after the class header and before the first access specifier are private. The access specifiers public and private may be repeated, but this is unnecessary and can be confusing.

Good Programming Practice 3.4

Despite the fact that the public and private access specifiers may be repeated and intermixed, list all the public members of a class first in one group and then list all the private members in another group. This focuses the client's attention on the class's public interface, rather than on the class's implementation.

Good Programming Practice 3.5

If you choose to list the private members first in a class definition, explicitly use the private access specifier despite the fact that private is assumed by default. This improves program clarity.

Declaring data members with access specifier private is known as data hiding. When a program creates (instantiates) an object of class GradeBook, data member courseName is encapsulated (hidden) in the object and can be accessed only by member functions of the object's class. In class GradeBook, member functions setCourseName and getCourseName manipulate the data member courseName directly (and displayMessage could do so if necessary).

Software Engineering Observation 3.2

We will learn in Chapter 10, Classes: A Deeper Look, Part 2, that functions and classes declared by a class to be friends can access the private members of the class.

Error-Prevention Tip 3.1

Making the data members of a class private and the member functions of the class public facilitates debugging because problems with data manipulations are localized to either the class's member functions or the friends of the class.

Member Functions *setCourseName* and *getCourseName*

Member function setCourseName (defined in lines 19–22) does not return any data when it completes its task, so its return type is void. The member function receives one parameter—name—which represents the course name that will be passed to it as an argument (as we will see in line 55 of main). Line 21 assigns name to data member courseName. In this example, setCourseName does not attempt to validate the course name—i.e., the function does not check that the course name adheres to any particular format or follows any other rules regarding what a "valid" course name looks like. Suppose, for instance, that a university can print student transcripts containing course names of only 25 characters or fewer. In this case, we might want class GradeBook to ensure that its data member courseName never contains more than 25 characters. We discuss basic validation techniques in Section 3.10.

Member function getCourseName (defined in lines 25–28) returns a particular GradeBook object's courseName. The member function has an empty parameter list, so it does not require additional data to perform its task. The function specifies that it returns a string. When a function that specifies a return type other than void is called and completes its task, the function returns a result to its calling function. For example, when you go to an automated teller machine (ATM) and request your account balance, you expect the ATM to give you back a value that represents your balance. Similarly, when a statement calls member function getCourseName on a GradeBook object, the statement expects to receive the GradeBook's course name (in this case, a string, as specified by the function's return type). If you have a function square that returns the square of its argument, the statement

```
int result = square( 2 );
```

returns 4 from function square and initializes the variable result with the value 4. If you have a function maximum that returns the largest of three integer arguments, the statement

```
int biggest = maximum( 27, 114, 51 );
```

returns 114 from function maximum and initializes variable biggest with the value 114.

Common Programming Error 3.7

Forgetting to return a value from a function that is supposed to return a value is a compilation error.

Note that the statements at lines 21 and 27 each use variable courseName (line 39) even though it was not declared in any of the member functions. We can use courseName in the member functions of class GradeBook because courseName is a data member of the class. Also note that the order in which member functions are defined does not determine when they are called at execution time. So member function getCourseName could be defined before member function setCourseName.

Member Function *displayMessage*

Member function displayMessage (lines 31–37) does not return any data when it completes its task, so its return type is void. The function does not receive parameters, so its parameter list is empty. Lines 35–36 output a welcome message that includes the value of data member courseName. Line 35 calls member function getCourseName to obtain the value of courseName. Note that member function displayMessage could also access data member courseName directly, just as member functions setCourseName and getCourse-Name do. We explain shortly why we choose to call member function getCourseName to obtain the value of courseName.

Testing Class *GradeBook*

The main function (lines 43–60) creates one object of class GradeBook and uses each of its member functions. Line 46 creates a GradeBook object named myGradeBook. Lines 49–50 display the initial course name by calling the object's getCourseName member function. Note that the first line of the output does not show a course name, because the object's courseName data member (i.e., a string) is initially empty—by default, the initial value of a string is the so-called empty string, i.e., a string that does not contain any characters. Nothing appears on the screen when an empty string is displayed.

Line 53 prompts the user to enter a course name. Local string variable nameOfCourse (declared in line 45) is set to the course name entered by the user, which is obtained by the call to the getline function (line 54). Line 55 calls object myGradeBook's setCourse-Name member function and supplies nameOfCourse as the function's argument. When the function is called, the argument's value is copied to parameter name (line 19) of member function setCourseName (lines 19–22). Then the parameter's value is assigned to data member courseName (line 21). Line 57 skips a line in the output; then line 58 calls object myGradeBook's displayMessage member function to display the welcome message containing the course name.

Software Engineering with Set *and* Get *Functions*

A class's private data members can be manipulated only by member functions of that class (and by "friends" of the class, as we will see in Chapter 10, Classes: A Deeper Look, Part 2). So a client of an object—that is, any class or function that calls the object's member functions from outside the object—calls the class's public member functions to request the class's services for particular objects of the class. This is why the statements in function main (Fig. 3.5, lines 43–60) call member functions setCourseName, getCourse-Name and displayMessage on a GradeBook object. Classes often provide public member functions to allow clients of the class to *set* (i.e., assign values to) or *get* (i.e., obtain the values of) private data members. The names of these member functions need not begin with *set* or *get*, but this naming convention is common. In this example, the member function that *sets* the courseName data member is called setCourseName, and the member function that *gets* the value of the courseName data member is called getCourseName. Note that *set* functions are also sometimes called mutators (because they mutate, or change, values), and *get* functions are also sometimes called accessors (because they access values).

Recall that declaring data members with access specifier private enforces data hiding. Providing public *set* and *get* functions allows clients of a class to access the hidden data, but only *indirectly*. The client knows that it is attempting to modify or obtain an object's data, but the client does not know how the object performs these operations. In some cases, a class may internally represent a piece of data one way, but expose that data to clients in a different way. For example, suppose a Clock class represents the time of day as a private int data member time that stores the number of seconds since midnight. However, when a client calls a Clock object's getTime member function, the object could return the time with hours, minutes and seconds in a string in the format "HH:MM:SS". Similarly, suppose the Clock class provides a *set* function named setTime that takes a string parameter in the "HH:MM:SS" format. Using string capabilities presented in Chapter 18, the setTime function could convert this string to a number of seconds, which the function stores in its private data member. The *set* function could also check that the value it receives represents a valid time (e.g., "12:30:45" is valid but "42:85:70" is not). The *set* and *get* functions allow a client to interact with an object, but the object's private data remains safely encapsulated (i.e., hidden) in the object itself.

The *set* and *get* functions of a class also should be used by other member functions within the class to manipulate the class's private data, although these member functions *can* access the private data directly. In Fig. 3.5, member functions setCourseName and getCourseName are public member functions, so they are accessible to clients of the class, as well as to the class itself. Member function displayMessage calls member function getCourseName to obtain the value of data member courseName for display purposes, even though displayMessage can access courseName directly—accessing a data member via its *get* function creates a better, more robust class (i.e., a class that is easier to maintain and less likely to stop working). If we decide to change the data member courseName in some way, the displayMessage definition will not require modification—only the bodies of the *get* and *set* functions that directly manipulate the data member will need to change. For example, suppose we decide that we want to represent the course name as two separate data members—courseNumber (e.g., "CS101") and courseTitle (e.g., "Introduction to C++ Programming"). Member function displayMessage can still issue a single call to member function getCourseName to obtain the full course to display as part of the welcome message. In this case, getCourseName would need to build and return a string containing the courseNumber followed by the courseTitle. Member function displayMessage would continue to display the complete course title "CS101 Introduction to C++ Programming," because it is unaffected by the change to the class's data members. The benefits of calling a *set* function from another member function of a class will become clear when we discuss validation in Section 3.10.

Good Programming Practice 3.6

Always try to localize the effects of changes to a class's data members by accessing and manipulating the data members through their get *and* set *functions. Changes to the name of a data member or the data type used to store a data member then affect only the corresponding* get *and* set *functions, but not the callers of those functions.*

Software Engineering Observation 3.3

It is important to write programs that are understandable and easy to maintain. Change is the rule rather than the exception. Programmers should anticipate that their code will be modified.

Software Engineering Observation 3.4

The class designer need not provide set *or* get *functions for each* private *data item; these capabilities should be provided only when appropriate. If a service is useful to the client code, that service should typically be provided in the class's* public *interface.*

GradeBook's UML Class Diagram with a Data Member and* set *and* get *Functions
Figure 3.6 contains an updated UML class diagram for the version of class GradeBook in
Fig. 3.5. This diagram models class GradeBook's data member courseName as an attribute
in the middle compartment of the class. The UML represents data members as attributes
by listing the attribute name, followed by a colon and the attribute type. The UML type
of attribute courseName is String, which corresponds to string in C++. Data member
courseName is private in C++, so the class diagram lists a minus sign (–) in front of the
corresponding attribute's name. The minus sign in the UML is equivalent to the private
access specifier in C++. Class GradeBook contains three public member functions, so the
class diagram lists three operations in the third compartment. Recall that the plus (+) sign
before each operation name indicates that the operation is public in C++. Operation set-
CourseName has a String parameter called name. The UML indicates the return type of an
operation by placing a colon and the return type after the parentheses following the operation name. Member function getCourseName of class GradeBook (Fig. 3.5) has a string
return type in C++, so the class diagram shows a String return type in the UML. Note
that operations setCourseName and displayMessage do not return values (i.e., they return
void), so the UML class diagram does not specify a return type after the parentheses of
these operations. The UML does not use void as C++ does when a function does not return a value.

3.7 Initializing Objects with Constructors

As mentioned in Section 3.6, when an object of class GradeBook (Fig. 3.5) is created, its
data member courseName is initialized to the empty string by default. What if you want
to provide a course name when you create a GradeBook object? Each class you declare can
provide a constructor that can be used to initialize an object of the class when the object
is created. A constructor is a special member function that must be defined with the same
name as the class, so that the compiler can distinguish it from the class's other member
functions. An important difference between constructors and other functions is that constructors cannot return values, so they cannot specify a return type (not even void). Normally, constructors are declared public. The term "constructor" is often abbreviated as
"ctor" in the literature—we prefer not to use this abbreviation.

C++ requires a constructor call for each object that is created, which helps ensure that
the object is initialized properly before it is used in a program—the constructor call occurs
implicitly when the object is created. In any class that does not explicitly include a constructor, the compiler provides a default constructor—that is, a constructor with no

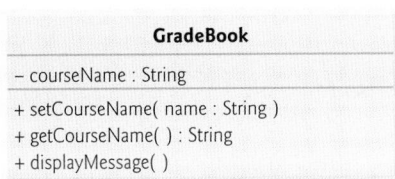

Fig. 3.6 | UML class diagram for class GradeBook with a private courseName attribute and
public operations setCourseName, getCourseName and displayMessage.

parameters. For example, when line 46 of Fig. 3.5 creates a GradeBook object, the default constructor is called, because the declaration of myGradeBook does not specify any constructor arguments. The default constructor provided by the compiler creates a GradeBook object without giving any initial values to the object's data members. [*Note:* For data members that are objects of other classes, the default constructor implicitly calls each data member's default constructor to ensure that the data member is initialized properly. In fact, this is why the string data member courseName (in Fig. 3.5) was initialized to the empty string—the default constructor for class string sets the string's value to the empty string. In Section 10.3, you will learn more about initializing data members that are objects of other classes.]

In the example of Fig. 3.7, we specify a course name for a GradeBook object when the object is created (line 49). In this case, the argument "CS101 Introduction to C++ Programming" is passed to the GradeBook object's constructor (lines 17–20) and used to initialize the courseName. Figure 3.7 defines a modified GradeBook class containing a constructor with a string parameter that receives the initial course name.

```cpp
 1  // Fig. 3.7: fig03_07.cpp
 2  // Instantiating multiple objects of the GradeBook class and using
 3  // the GradeBook constructor to specify the course name
 4  // when each GradeBook object is created.
 5  #include <iostream>
 6  using std::cout;
 7  using std::endl;
 8
 9  #include <string> // program uses C++ standard string class
10  using std::string;
11
12  // GradeBook class definition
13  class GradeBook
14  {
15  public:
16     // constructor initializes courseName with string supplied as argument
17     GradeBook( string name )
18     {
19        setCourseName( name ); // call set function to initialize courseName
20     } // end GradeBook constructor
21
22     // function to set the course name
23     void setCourseName( string name )
24     {
25        courseName = name; // store the course name in the object
26     } // end function setCourseName
27
28     // function to get the course name
29     string getCourseName()
30     {
31        return courseName; // return object's courseName
32     } // end function getCourseName
```

Fig. 3.7 | Instantiating multiple objects of the GradeBook class and using the GradeBook constructor to specify the course name when each GradeBook object is created. (Part 1 of 2.)

```
33
34      // display a welcome message to the GradeBook user
35      void displayMessage()
36      {
37         // call getCourseName to get the courseName
38         cout << "Welcome to the grade book for\n" << getCourseName()
39            << "!" << endl;
40      } // end function displayMessage
41   private:
42      string courseName; // course name for this GradeBook
43   }; // end class GradeBook
44
45   // function main begins program execution
46   int main()
47   {
48      // create two GradeBook objects
49      GradeBook gradeBook1( "CS101 Introduction to C++ Programming" );
50      GradeBook gradeBook2( "CS102 Data Structures in C++" );
51
52      // display initial value of courseName for each GradeBook
53      cout << "gradeBook1 created for course: " << gradeBook1.getCourseName()
54         << "\ngradeBook2 created for course: " << gradeBook2.getCourseName()
55         << endl;
56      return 0; // indicate successful termination
57   } // end main
```

```
gradeBook1 created for course: CS101 Introduction to C++ Programming
gradeBook2 created for course: CS102 Data Structures in C++
```

Fig. 3.7 | Instantiating multiple objects of the GradeBook class and using the GradeBook constructor to specify the course name when each GradeBook object is created. (Part 2 of 2.)

Defining a Constructor

Lines 17–20 of Fig. 3.7 define a constructor for class GradeBook. Notice that the constructor has the same name as its class, GradeBook. A constructor specifies in its parameter list the data it requires to perform its task. When you create a new object, you place this data in the parentheses that follow the object name (as we did in lines 49–50). Line 17 indicates that class GradeBook's constructor has a string parameter called name. Note that line 17 does not specify a return type, because constructors cannot return values (or even void).

Line 19 in the constructor's body passes the constructor's parameter name to member function setCourseName, which assigns a value to data member courseName. The setCourseName member function (lines 23–26) simply assigns its parameter name to the data member courseName, so you might be wondering why we bother making the call to setCourseName in line 19—the constructor certainly could perform the assignment courseName = name. In Section 3.10, we modify setCourseName to perform validation (ensuring that, in this case, the courseName is 25 or fewer characters in length). At that point the benefits of calling setCourseName from the constructor will become clear. Note that both the constructor (line 17) and the setCourseName function (line 23) use a parameter called name. You can use the same parameter names in different functions because the parameters are local to each function; they do not interfere with one another.

*Testing Class **GradeBook***

Lines 46–57 of Fig. 3.7 define the `main` function that tests class `GradeBook` and demonstrates initializing `GradeBook` objects using a constructor. Line 49 in function `main` creates and initializes a `GradeBook` object called `gradeBook1`. When this line executes, the Grade-Book constructor (lines 17–20) is called (implicitly by C++) with the argument `"CS101 Introduction to C++ Programming"` to initialize `gradeBook1`'s course name. Line 50 repeats this process for the `GradeBook` object called `gradeBook2`, this time passing the argument `"CS102 Data Structures in C++"` to initialize `gradeBook2`'s course name. Lines 53–54 use each object's `getCourseName` member function to obtain the course names and show that they were indeed initialized when the objects were created. The output confirms that each `GradeBook` object maintains its own copy of data member `courseName`.

Two Ways to Provide a Default Constructor for a Class

Any constructor that takes no arguments is called a default constructor. A class gets a default constructor in one of two ways:

1. The compiler implicitly creates a default constructor in a class that does not define a constructor. Such a default constructor does not initialize the class's data members, but does call the default constructor for each data member that is an object of another class. [*Note:* An uninitialized variable typically contains a "garbage" value (e.g., an uninitialized `int` variable might contain `-858993460`, which is likely to be an incorrect value for that variable in most programs).]

2. The programmer explicitly defines a constructor that takes no arguments. Such a default constructor will perform the initialization specified by the programmer and will call the default constructor for each data member that is an object of another class.

If the programmer defines a constructor with arguments, C++ will not implicitly create a default constructor for that class. Note that for each version of class `GradeBook` in Fig. 3.1, Fig. 3.3 and Fig. 3.5 the compiler implicitly defined a default constructor.

Error-Prevention Tip 3.2

Unless no initialization of your class's data members is necessary (almost never), provide a constructor to ensure that your class's data members are initialized with meaningful values when each new object of your class is created.

Software Engineering Observation 3.5

Data members can be initialized in a constructor of the class or their values may be set later after the object is created. However, it is a good software engineering practice to ensure that an object is fully initialized before the client code invokes the object's member functions. In general, you should not rely on the client code to ensure that an object gets initialized properly.

*Adding the Constructor to Class **GradeBook**'s UML Class Diagram*

The UML class diagram of Fig. 3.8 models class `GradeBook` of Fig. 3.7, which has a constructor with a `name` parameter of type `string` (represented by type `String` in the UML). Like operations, the UML models constructors in the third compartment of a class in a class diagram. To distinguish a constructor from a class's operations, the UML places the word "constructor" between guillemets (« and ») before the constructor's name. It is customary to list the class's constructor before other operations in the third compartment.

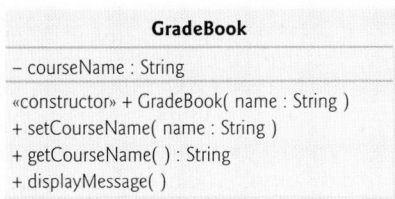

Fig. 3.8 | UML class diagram indicating that class GradeBook has a constructor with a name parameter of UML type String.

3.8 Placing a Class in a Separate File for Reusability

We have developed class GradeBook as far as we need to for now from a programming perspective, so let's consider some software engineering issues. One of the benefits of creating class definitions is that, when packaged properly, our classes can be reused by programmers—potentially worldwide. For example, we can reuse C++ Standard Library type string in any C++ program by including the header file <string> in the program (and, as we will see, by being able to link to the library's object code).

Unfortunately, programmers who wish to use our GradeBook class cannot simply include the file from Fig. 3.7 in another program. As you learned in Chapter 2, function main begins the execution of every program, and every program must have exactly one main function. If other programmers include the code from Fig. 3.7, they get extra baggage—our main function—and their programs will then have two main functions. When they attempt to compile their programs, the compiler will indicate an error because, again, each program can have only one main function. For example, attempting to compile a program with two main functions in Microsoft Visual C++ .NET produces the error

```
error C2084: function 'int main(void)' already has a body
```

when the compiler tries to compile the second main function it encounters. Similarly, the GNU C++ compiler produces the error

```
redefinition of 'int main()'
```

These errors indicate that a program already has a main function. So, placing main in the same file with a class definition prevents that class from being reused by other programs. In this section, we demonstrate how to make class GradeBook reusable by separating it into another file from the main function.

Header Files

Each of the previous examples in the chapter consists of a single .cpp file, also known as a source-code file, that contains a GradeBook class definition and a main function. When building an object-oriented C++ program, it is customary to define reusable source code (such as a class) in a file that by convention has a .h filename extension—known as a header file. Programs use #include preprocessor directives to include header files and take advantage of reusable software components, such as type string provided in the C++ Standard Library and user-defined types like class GradeBook.

In our next example, we separate the code from Fig. 3.7 into two files—GradeBook.h (Fig. 3.9) and fig03_10.cpp (Fig. 3.10). As you look at the header file in Fig. 3.9, notice that it contains only the GradeBook class definition (lines 11–41) and lines 3–8, which allow class GradeBook to use cout, endl and type string. The main function that uses class GradeBook is defined in the source-code file fig03_10.cpp (Fig. 3.10) at lines 10–21. To help you prepare for the larger programs you will encounter later in this book and in industry, we often use a separate source-code file containing function main to test our classes (this is called a *driver program*). You will soon learn how a source-code file with main can use the class definition found in a header file to create objects of a class.

Including a Header File That Contains a User-Defined Class
A header file such as GradeBook.h (Fig. 3.9) cannot be used to begin program execution, because it does not contain a main function. If you try to compile and link GradeBook.h by itself to create an executable application, Microsoft Visual C++ .NET will produce the linker error message:

```
error LNK2019: unresolved external symbol _main referenced in
function _mainCRTStartup
```

```
1   // Fig. 3.9: GradeBook.h
2   // GradeBook class definition in a separate file from main.
3   #include <iostream>
4   using std::cout;
5   using std::endl;
6
7   #include <string> // class GradeBook uses C++ standard string class
8   using std::string;
9
10  // GradeBook class definition
11  class GradeBook
12  {
13  public:
14     // constructor initializes courseName with string supplied as argument
15     GradeBook( string name )
16     {
17        setCourseName( name ); // call set function to initialize courseName
18     } // end GradeBook constructor
19
20     // function to set the course name
21     void setCourseName( string name )
22     {
23        courseName = name; // store the course name in the object
24     } // end function setCourseName
25
26     // function to get the course name
27     string getCourseName()
28     {
29        return courseName; // return object's courseName
30     } // end function getCourseName
31
```

Fig. 3.9 | GradeBook class definition. (Part 1 of 2.)

```
32     // display a welcome message to the GradeBook user
33     void displayMessage()
34     {
35        // call getCourseName to get the courseName
36        cout << "Welcome to the grade book for\n" << getCourseName()
37           << "!" << endl;
38     } // end function displayMessage
39  private:
40     string courseName; // course name for this GradeBook
41  }; // end class GradeBook
```

Fig. 3.9 | GradeBook class definition. (Part 2 of 2.)

Running GNU C++ on Linux produces a linker error message containing:

```
undefined reference to 'main'
```

This error indicates that the linker could not locate the program's main function. To test class GradeBook (defined in Fig. 3.9), you must write a separate source-code file containing a main function (such as Fig. 3.10) that instantiates and uses objects of the class.

Recall from Section 3.4 that, while the compiler knows what fundamental data types like int are, the compiler does not know what a GradeBook is because it is a user-defined type. In fact, the compiler does not even know the classes in the C++ Standard Library. To help it understand how to use a class, we must explicitly provide the compiler with the class's definition—that's why, for example, to use type string, a program must include

```
1   // Fig. 3.10: fig03_10.cpp
2   // Including class GradeBook from file GradeBook.h for use in main.
3   #include <iostream>
4   using std::cout;
5   using std::endl;
6
7   #include "GradeBook.h" // include definition of class GradeBook
8
9   // function main begins program execution
10  int main()
11  {
12     // create two GradeBook objects
13     GradeBook gradeBook1( "CS101 Introduction to C++ Programming" );
14     GradeBook gradeBook2( "CS102 Data Structures in C++" );
15
16     // display initial value of courseName for each GradeBook
17     cout << "gradeBook1 created for course: " << gradeBook1.getCourseName()
18        << "\ngradeBook2 created for course: " << gradeBook2.getCourseName()
19        << endl;
20     return 0; // indicate successful termination
21  } // end main
```

```
gradeBook1 created for course: CS101 Introduction to C++ Programming
gradeBook2 created for course: CS102 Data Structures in C++
```

Fig. 3.10 | Including class GradeBook from file GradeBook.h for use in main.

the <string> header file. This enables the compiler to determine the amount of memory that it must reserve for each object of the class and ensure that a program calls the class's member functions correctly.

To create GradeBook objects gradeBook1 and gradeBook2 in lines 13–14 of Fig. 3.10, the compiler must know the size of a GradeBook object. While objects conceptually contain data members and member functions, C++ objects typically contain only data. The compiler creates only one copy of the class's member functions and shares that copy among all the class's objects. Each object, of course, needs its own copy of the class's data members, because their contents can vary among objects (such as two different BankAccount objects having two different balance data members). The member function code, however, is not modifiable, so it can be shared among all objects of the class. Therefore, the size of an object depends on the amount of memory required to store the class's data members. By including GradeBook.h in line 7, we give the compiler access to the information it needs (Fig. 3.9, line 40) to determine the size of a GradeBook object and to determine whether objects of the class are used correctly (in lines 13–14 and 17–18 of Fig. 3.10).

Line 7 instructs the C++ preprocessor to replace the directive with a copy of the contents of GradeBook.h (i.e., the GradeBook class definition) *before* the program is compiled. When the source-code file fig03_10.cpp is compiled, it now contains the GradeBook class definition (because of the #include), and the compiler is able to determine how to create GradeBook objects and see that their member functions are called correctly. Now that the class definition is in a header file (without a main function), we can include that header in *any* program that needs to reuse our GradeBook class.

How Header Files Are Located

Notice that the name of the GradeBook.h header file in line 7 of Fig. 3.10 is enclosed in quotes (" ") rather than angle brackets (< >). Normally, a program's source-code files and user-defined header files are placed in the same directory. When the preprocessor encounters a header file name in quotes (e.g., "GradeBook.h"), the preprocessor attempts to locate the header file in the same directory as the file in which the #include directive appears. If the preprocessor cannot find the header file in that directory, it searches for it in the same location(s) as the C++ Standard Library header files. When the preprocessor encounters a header file name in angle brackets (e.g., <iostream>), it assumes that the header is part of the C++ Standard Library and does not look in the directory of the program that is being preprocessed.

Error-Prevention Tip 3.3

To ensure that the preprocessor can locate header files correctly, #include preprocessor directives should place the names of user-defined header files in quotes (e.g., "GradeBook.h") and place the names of C++ Standard Library header files in angle brackets (e.g., <iostream>).

Additional Software Engineering Issues

Now that class GradeBook is defined in a header file, the class is reusable. Unfortunately, placing a class definition in a header file as in Fig. 3.9 still reveals the entire implementation of the class to the class's clients—GradeBook.h is simply a text file that anyone can open and read. Conventional software engineering wisdom says that to use an object of a class, the client code needs to know only what member functions to call, what arguments to provide to each member function and what return type to expect from each member function. The client code does not need to know how those functions are implemented.

If client code does know how a class is implemented, the client code programmer might write client code based on the class's implementation details. Ideally, if that implementation changes, the class's clients should not have to change. Hiding the class's implementation details makes it easier to change the class's implementation while minimizing, and hopefully eliminating, changes to client code.

In Section 3.9, we show how to break up the GradeBook class into two files so that

1. the class is reusable

2. the clients of the class know what member functions the class provides, how to call them and what return types to expect

3. the clients do not know how the class's member functions are implemented.

3.9 Separating Interface from Implementation

In the preceding section, we showed how to promote software reusability by separating a class definition from the client code (e.g., function main) that uses the class. We now introduce another fundamental principle of good software engineering—separating interface from implementation.

Interface of a Class

Interfaces define and standardize the ways in which things such as people and systems interact with one another. For example, a radio's controls serve as an interface between the radio's users and its internal components. The controls allow users to perform a limited set of operations (such as changing the station, adjusting the volume, and choosing between AM and FM stations). Various radios may implement these operations differently—some provide push buttons, some provide dials and some support voice commands. The interface specifies *what* operations a radio permits users to perform but does not specify *how* the operations are implemented inside the radio.

Similarly, the interface of a class describes *what* services a class's clients can use and how to *request* those services, but not *how* the class carries out the services. A class's interface consists of the class's public member functions (also known as the class's public services). For example, class GradeBook's interface (Fig. 3.9) contains a constructor and member functions setCourseName, getCourseName and displayMessage. GradeBook's clients (e.g., main in Fig. 3.10) use these functions to request the class's services. As you will soon see, you can specify a class's interface by writing a class definition that lists only the member function names, return types and parameter types.

Separating the Interface from the Implementation

In our prior examples, each class definition contained the complete definitions of the class's public member functions and the declarations of its private data members. However, it is better software engineering to define member functions outside the class definition, so that their implementation details can be hidden from the client code. This practice ensures that programmers do not write client code that depends on the class's implementation details. If they were to do so, the client code would be more likely to "break" if the class's implementation changed.

The program of Figs. 3.11–3.13 separates class GradeBook's interface from its implementation by splitting the class definition of Fig. 3.9 into two files—the header file

GradeBook.h (Fig. 3.11) in which class GradeBook is defined, and the source-code file GradeBook.cpp (Fig. 3.12) in which GradeBook's member functions are defined. By convention, member-function definitions are placed in a source-code file of the same base name (e.g., GradeBook) as the class's header file but with a .cpp filename extension. The source-code file fig03_13.cpp (Fig. 3.13) defines function main (the client code). The code and output of Fig. 3.13 are identical to that of Fig. 3.10. Figure 3.14 shows how this three-file program is compiled from the perspectives of the GradeBook class programmer and the client-code programmer—we will explain this figure in detail.

GradeBook.h: Defining a Class's Interface with Function Prototypes

Header file GradeBook.h (Fig. 3.11) contains another version of GradeBook's class definition (lines 9–18). This version is similar to the one in Fig. 3.9, but the function definitions in Fig. 3.9 are replaced here with function prototypes (lines 12–15) that describe the class's public interface without revealing the class's member function implementations. A function prototype is a declaration of a function that tells the compiler the function's name, its return type and the types of its parameters. Note that the header file still specifies the class's private data member (line 17) as well. Again, the compiler must know the data members of the class to determine how much memory to reserve for each object of the class. Including the header file GradeBook.h in the client code (line 8 of Fig. 3.13) provides the compiler with the information it needs to ensure that the client code calls the member functions of class GradeBook correctly.

The function prototype in line 12 (Fig. 3.12) indicates that the constructor requires one string parameter. Recall that constructors do not have return types, so no return type appears in the function prototype. Member function setCourseName's function prototype (line 13) indicates that setCourseName requires a string parameter and does not return a value (i.e., its return type is void). Member function getCourseName's function prototype (line 14) indicates that the function does not require parameters and returns a string.

```
 1   // Fig. 3.11: GradeBook.h
 2   // GradeBook class definition. This file presents GradeBook's public
 3   // interface without revealing the implementations of GradeBook's member
 4   // functions, which are defined in GradeBook.cpp.
 5   #include <string> // class GradeBook uses C++ standard string class
 6   using std::string;
 7
 8   // GradeBook class definition
 9   class GradeBook
10   {
11   public:
12      GradeBook( string ); // constructor that initializes courseName
13      void setCourseName( string ); // function that sets the course name
14      string getCourseName(); // function that gets the course name
15      void displayMessage(); // function that displays a welcome message
16   private:
17      string courseName; // course name for this GradeBook
18   }; // end class GradeBook
```

Fig. 3.11 | GradeBook class definition containing function prototypes that specify the interface of the class.

Finally, member function `displayMessage`'s function prototype (line 15) specifies that `displayMessage` does not require parameters and does not return a value. These function prototypes are the same as the corresponding function headers in Fig. 3.9, except that the parameter names (which are optional in prototypes) are not included and each function prototype must end with a semicolon.

Common Programming Error 3.8

Forgetting the semicolon at the end of a function prototype is a syntax error.

Good Programming Practice 3.7

Although parameter names in function prototypes are optional (they are ignored by the compiler), many programmers use these names for documentation purposes.

Error-Prevention Tip 3.4

Parameter names in a function prototype (which, again, are ignored by the compiler) can be misleading if wrong or confusing names are used. For this reason, many programmers create function prototypes by copying the first line of the corresponding function definitions (when the source code for the functions is available), then appending a semicolon to the end of each prototype.

GradeBook.cpp: Defining Member Functions in a Separate Source-Code File

Source-code file `GradeBook.cpp` (Fig. 3.12) defines class `GradeBook`'s member functions, which were declared in lines 12–15 of Fig. 3.11. The member-function definitions appear in lines 11–34 and are nearly identical to the member-function definitions in lines 15–38 of Fig. 3.9.

Notice that each member function name in the function headers (lines 11, 17, 23 and 29) is preceded by the class name and ::, which is known as the binary scope resolution operator. This "ties" each member function to the (now separate) `GradeBook` class definition, which declares the class's member functions and data members. Without "Grade-Book::" preceding each function name, these functions would not be recognized by the compiler as member functions of class `GradeBook`—the compiler would consider them "free" or "loose" functions, like `main`. Such functions cannot access `GradeBook`'s `private` data or call the class's member functions, without specifying an object. So, the compiler would not be able to compile these functions. For example, lines 19 and 25 that access variable `courseName` would cause compilation errors because `courseName` is not declared as a local variable in each function—the compiler would not know that `courseName` is already declared as a data member of class `GradeBook`.

Common Programming Error 3.9

When defining a class's member functions outside that class, omitting the class name and binary scope resolution operator (::) preceding the function names causes compilation errors.

To indicate that the member functions in `GradeBook.cpp` are part of class `GradeBook`, we must first include the `GradeBook.h` header file (line 8 of Fig. 3.12). This allows us to access the class name `GradeBook` in the `GradeBook.cpp` file. When compiling Grade-Book.cpp, the compiler uses the information in `GradeBook.h` to ensure that

```
 1   // Fig. 3.12: GradeBook.cpp
 2   // GradeBook member-function definitions. This file contains
 3   // implementations of the member functions prototyped in GradeBook.h.
 4   #include <iostream>
 5   using std::cout;
 6   using std::endl;
 7
 8   #include "GradeBook.h" // include definition of class GradeBook
 9
10   // constructor initializes courseName with string supplied as argument
11   GradeBook::GradeBook( string name )
12   {
13      setCourseName( name ); // call set function to initialize courseName
14   } // end GradeBook constructor
15
16   // function to set the course name
17   void GradeBook::setCourseName( string name )
18   {
19      courseName = name; // store the course name in the object
20   } // end function setCourseName
21
22   // function to get the course name
23   string GradeBook::getCourseName()
24   {
25      return courseName; // return object's courseName
26   } // end function getCourseName
27
28   // display a welcome message to the GradeBook user
29   void GradeBook::displayMessage()
30   {
31      // call getCourseName to get the courseName
32      cout << "Welcome to the grade book for\n" << getCourseName()
33         << "!" << endl;
34   } // end function displayMessage
```

Fig. 3.12 | GradeBook member-function definitions represent the implementation of class GradeBook.

1. the first line of each member function (lines 11, 17, 23 and 29) matches its prototype in the GradeBook.h file—for example, the compiler ensures that get-CourseName accepts no parameters and returns a string.

2. each member function knows about the class's data members and other member functions—for example, lines 19 and 25 can access variable courseName because it is declared in GradeBook.h as a data member of class GradeBook, and lines 13 and 32 can call functions setCourseName and getCourseName, respectively, because each is declared as a member function of the class in GradeBook.h (and because these calls conform with the corresponding prototypes).

Testing Class **GradeBook**

Figure 3.13 performs the same GradeBook object manipulations as Fig. 3.10. Separating GradeBook's interface from the implementation of its member functions does not affect

```
1   // Fig. 3.13: fig03_13.cpp
2   // GradeBook class demonstration after separating
3   // its interface from its implementation.
4   #include <iostream>
5   using std::cout;
6   using std::endl;
7
8   #include "GradeBook.h" // include definition of class GradeBook
9
10  // function main begins program execution
11  int main()
12  {
13     // create two GradeBook objects
14     GradeBook gradeBook1( "CS101 Introduction to C++ Programming" );
15     GradeBook gradeBook2( "CS102 Data Structures in C++" );
16
17     // display initial value of courseName for each GradeBook
18     cout << "gradeBook1 created for course: " << gradeBook1.getCourseName()
19        << "\ngradeBook2 created for course: " << gradeBook2.getCourseName()
20        << endl;
21     return 0; // indicate successful termination
22  } // end main
```

```
gradeBook1 created for course: CS101 Introduction to C++ Programming
gradeBook2 created for course: CS102 Data Structures in C++
```

Fig. 3.13 | GradeBook class demonstration after separating its interface from its implementation.

the way that this client code uses the class. It affects only how the program is compiled and linked, which we discuss in detail shortly.

As in Fig. 3.10, line 8 of Fig. 3.13 includes the GradeBook.h header file so that the compiler can ensure that GradeBook objects are created and manipulated correctly in the client code. Before executing this program, the source-code files in Fig. 3.12 and Fig. 3.13 must both be compiled, then linked together—that is, the member-function calls in the client code need to be tied to the implementations of the class's member functions—a job performed by the linker.

The Compilation and Linking Process
The diagram in Fig. 3.14 shows the compilation and linking process that results in an executable GradeBook application that can be used by instructors. Often a class's interface and implementation will be created and compiled by one programmer and used by a separate programmer who implements the class's client code. So, the diagram shows what is required by both the class-implementation programmer and the client-code programmer. The dashed lines in the diagram show the pieces required by the class-implementation programmer, the client-code programmer and the GradeBook application user, respectively. [*Note:* Figure 3.14 is not a UML diagram.]

A class-implementation programmer responsible for creating a reusable GradeBook class creates the header file GradeBook.h and source-code file GradeBook.cpp that #includes the

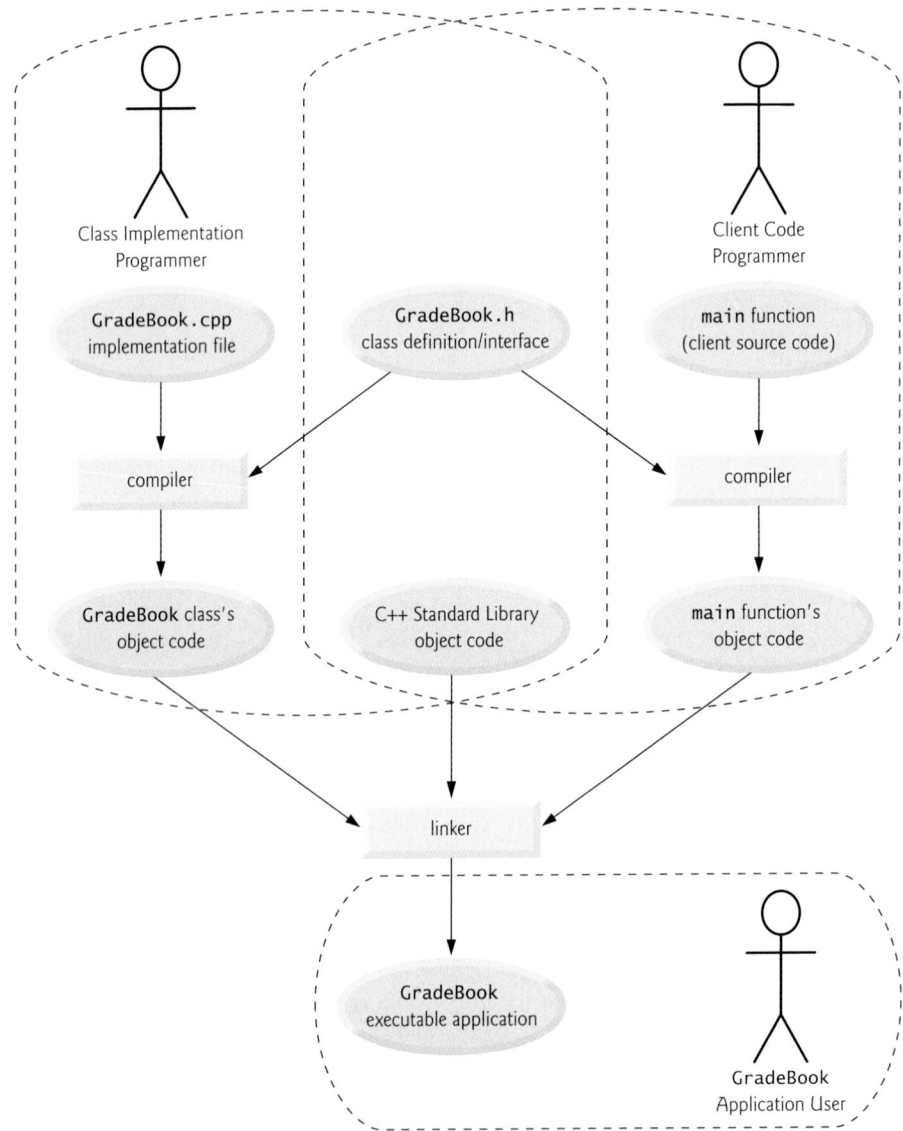

Fig. 3.14 | Compilation and linking process that produces an executable application.

header file, then compiles the source-code file to create GradeBook's object code. To hide the implementation details of GradeBook's member functions, the class-implementation programmer would provide the client-code programmer with the header file GradeBook.h (which specifies the class's interface and data members) and the object code for class Grade-Book which contains the machine-language instructions that represent GradeBook's member functions. The client-code programmer is not given GradeBook's source-code file, so the client remains unaware of how GradeBook's member functions are implemented.

The client code needs to know only GradeBook's interface to use the class and must be able to link its object code. Since the interface of the class is part of the class definition in the GradeBook.h header file, the client-code programmer must have access to this file and #include it in the client's source-code file. When the client code is compiled, the compiler uses the class definition in GradeBook.h to ensure that the main function creates and manipulates objects of class GradeBook correctly.

To create the executable GradeBook application to be used by instructors, the last step is to link

1. the object code for the main function (i.e., the client code)

2. the object code for class GradeBook's member function implementations

3. the C++ Standard Library object code for the C++ classes (e.g., string) used by the class implementation programmer and the client-code programmer.

The linker's output is the executable GradeBook application that instructors can use to manage their students' grades.

For further information on compiling multiple-source-file programs, see your compiler's documentation or study the Dive-Into™ publications that we provide for various C++ compilers at www.deitel.com/books/cpphtp5.

3.10 Validating Data with *set* Functions

In Section 3.6, we introduced *set* functions for allowing clients of a class to modify the value of a private data member. In Fig. 3.5, class GradeBook defines member function set-CourseName to simply assign a value received in its parameter name to data member courseName. This member function does not ensure that the course name adheres to any particular format or follows any other rules regarding what a "valid" course name looks like. As we stated earlier, suppose that a university can print student transcripts containing course names of only 25 characters or less. If the university uses a system containing GradeBook objects to generate the transcripts, we might want class GradeBook to ensure that its data member courseName never contains more than 25 characters. The program of Figs. 3.15–3.17 enhances class GradeBook's member function setCourseName to perform this validation (also known as validity checking).

GradeBook *Class Definition*

Notice that GradeBook's class definition (Fig. 3.15)—and hence, its interface—is identical to that of Fig. 3.11. Since the interface remains unchanged, clients of this class need not be changed when the definition of member function setCourseName is modified. This enables clients to take advantage of the improved GradeBook class simply by linking the client code to the updated GradeBook's object code.

Validating the Course Name with *GradeBook Member Function* **setCourseName**

The enhancement to class GradeBook is in the definition of setCourseName (Fig. 3.16, lines 18–31). The if statement in lines 20–21 determines whether parameter name contains a valid course name (i.e., a string of 25 or fewer characters). If the course name is valid, line 21 stores the course name in data member courseName. Note the expression name.length() in line 20. This is a member-function call just like myGradeBook.display-Message(). The C++ Standard Library's string class defines a member function length

```
1   // Fig. 3.15: GradeBook.h
2   // GradeBook class definition presents the public interface of
3   // the class. Member-function definitions appear in GradeBook.cpp.
4   #include <string> // program uses C++ standard string class
5   using std::string;
6
7   // GradeBook class definition
8   class GradeBook
9   {
10  public:
11     GradeBook( string ); // constructor that initializes a GradeBook object
12     void setCourseName( string ); // function that sets the course name
13     string getCourseName(); // function that gets the course name
14     void displayMessage(); // function that displays a welcome message
15  private:
16     string courseName; // course name for this GradeBook
17  }; // end class GradeBook
```

Fig. 3.15 | GradeBook class definition.

```
1   // Fig. 3.16: GradeBook.cpp
2   // Implementations of the GradeBook member-function definitions.
3   // The setCourseName function performs validation.
4   #include <iostream>
5   using std::cout;
6   using std::endl;
7
8   #include "GradeBook.h" // include definition of class GradeBook
9
10  // constructor initializes courseName with string supplied as argument
11  GradeBook::GradeBook( string name )
12  {
13     setCourseName( name ); // validate and store courseName
14  } // end GradeBook constructor
15
16  // function that sets the course name;
17  // ensures that the course name has at most 25 characters
18  void GradeBook::setCourseName( string name )
19  {
20     if ( name.length() <= 25 ) // if name has 25 or fewer characters
21        courseName = name; // store the course name in the object
22
23     if ( name.length() > 25 ) // if name has more than 25 characters
24     {
25        // set courseName to first 25 characters of parameter name
26        courseName = name.substr( 0, 25 ); // start at 0, length of 25
27
28        cout << "Name \"" << name << "\" exceeds maximum length (25).\n"
29           << "Limiting courseName to first 25 characters.\n" << endl;
30     } // end if
31  } // end function setCourseName
```

Fig. 3.16 | Member-function definitions for class GradeBook with a *set* function that validates the length of data member courseName. (Part 1 of 2.)

```
32
33   // function to get the course name
34   string GradeBook::getCourseName()
35   {
36      return courseName; // return object's courseName
37   } // end function getCourseName
38
39   // display a welcome message to the GradeBook user
40   void GradeBook::displayMessage()
41   {
42      // call getCourseName to get the courseName
43      cout << "Welcome to the grade book for\n" << getCourseName()
44         << "!" << endl;
45   } // end function displayMessage
```

Fig. 3.16 | Member-function definitions for class GradeBook with a *set* function that validates the length of data member courseName. (Part 2 of 2.)

that returns the number of characters in a string object. Parameter name is a string object, so the call name.length() returns the number of characters in name. If this value is less than or equal to 25, name is valid and line 21 executes.

The if statement in lines 23–30 handles the case in which setCourseName receives an invalid course name (i.e., a name that is more than 25 characters long). Even if parameter name is too long, we still want to leave the GradeBook object in a consistent state—that is, a state in which the object's data member courseName contains a valid value (i.e., a string of 25 characters or less). Thus, we truncate (i.e., shorten) the specified course name and assign the first 25 characters of name to the courseName data member (unfortunately, this could truncate the course name awkwardly). Standard class string provides member function substr (short for "substring") that returns a new string object created by copying part of an existing string object. The call in line 26 (i.e., name.substr(0, 25)) passes two integers (0 and 25) to name's member function substr. These arguments indicate the portion of the string name that substr should return. The first argument specifies the starting position in the original string from which characters are copied—the first character in every string is considered to be at position 0. The second argument specifies the number of characters to copy. Therefore, the call in line 26 returns a 25-character substring of name starting at position 0 (i.e., the first 25 characters in name). For example, if name holds the value "CS101 Introduction to Programming in C++", substr returns "CS101 Introduction to Pro". After the call to substr, line 26 assigns the substring returned by substr to data member courseName. In this way, member function set-CourseName ensures that courseName is always assigned a string containing 25 or fewer characters. If the member function has to truncate the course name to make it valid, lines 28–29 display a warning message.

Note that the if statement in lines 23–30 contains two body statements—one to set the courseName to the first 25 characters of parameter name and one to print an accompanying message to the user. We want both of these statements to execute when name is too long, so we place them in a pair of braces, { }. Recall from Chapter 2 that this creates a block. You will learn more about placing multiple statements in the body of a control statement in Chapter 4.

Note that the cout statement in lines 28–29 could also appear without a stream insertion operator at the start of the second line of the statement, as in:

```
cout << "Name \"" << name << "\" exceeds maximum length (25).\n"
      "Limiting courseName to first 25 characters.\n" << endl;
```

The C++ compiler combines adjacent string literals, even if they appear on separate lines of a program. Thus, in the statement above, the C++ compiler would combine the string literals "\" exceeds maximum length (25).\n" and "Limiting courseName to first 25 characters.\n" into a single string literal that produces output identical to that of lines 28–29 in Fig. 3.16. This behavior allows you to print lengthy strings by breaking them across lines in your program without including additional stream insertion operations.

Testing Class *GradeBook*

Figure 3.17 demonstrates the modified version of class GradeBook (Figs. 3.15–3.16) featuring validation. Line 14 creates a GradeBook object named gradeBook1. Recall that the

```cpp
 1  // Fig. 3.17: fig03_17.cpp
 2  // Create and manipulate a GradeBook object; illustrate validation.
 3  #include <iostream>
 4  using std::cout;
 5  using std::endl;
 6
 7  #include "GradeBook.h" // include definition of class GradeBook
 8
 9  // function main begins program execution
10  int main()
11  {
12     // create two GradeBook objects;
13     // initial course name of gradeBook1 is too long
14     GradeBook gradeBook1( "CS101 Introduction to Programming in C++" );
15     GradeBook gradeBook2( "CS102 C++ Data Structures" );
16
17     // display each GradeBook's courseName
18     cout << "gradeBook1's initial course name is: "
19        << gradeBook1.getCourseName()
20        << "\ngradeBook2's initial course name is: "
21        << gradeBook2.getCourseName() << endl;
22
23     // modify myGradeBook's courseName (with a valid-length string)
24     gradeBook1.setCourseName( "CS101 C++ Programming" );
25
26     // display each GradeBook's courseName
27     cout << "\ngradeBook1's course name is: "
28        << gradeBook1.getCourseName()
29        << "\ngradeBook2's course name is: "
30        << gradeBook2.getCourseName() << endl;
31     return 0; // indicate successful termination
32  } // end main
```

Fig. 3.17 | Creating and manipulating a GradeBook object in which the course name is limited to 25 characters in length. (Part 1 of 2.)

```
Name "CS101 Introduction to Programming in C++" exceeds maximum length (25).
Limiting courseName to first 25 characters.

gradeBook1's initial course name is: CS101 Introduction to Pro
gradeBook2's initial course name is: CS102 C++ Data Structures

gradeBook1's course name is: CS101 C++ Programming
gradeBook2's course name is: CS102 C++ Data Structures
```

Fig. 3.17 | Creating and manipulating a GradeBook object in which the course name is limited to 25 characters in length. (Part 2 of 2.)

GradeBook constructor calls member function setCourseName to initialize data member courseName. In previous versions of the class, the benefit of calling setCourseName in the constructor was not evident. Now, however, the constructor takes advantage of the validation provided by setCourseName. The constructor simply calls setCourseName, rather than duplicating its validation code. When line 14 of Fig. 3.17 passes an initial course name of "CS101 Introduction to Programming in C++" to the GradeBook constructor, the constructor passes this value to setCourseName, where the actual initialization occurs. Because this course name contains more than 25 characters, the body of the second if statement executes, causing courseName to be initialized to the truncated 25-character course name "CS101 Introduction to Pro" (the truncated part is highlighted in red in line 14). Notice that the output in Fig. 3.17 contains the warning message output by lines 28–29 of Fig. 3.16 in member function setCourseName. Line 15 creates another GradeBook object called gradeBook2—the valid course name passed to the constructor is exactly 25 characters.

Lines 18–21 of Fig. 3.17 display the truncated course name for gradeBook1 (we highlight this in red in the program output) and the course name for gradeBook2. Line 24 calls gradeBook1's setCourseName member function directly, to change the course name in the GradeBook object to a shorter name that does not need to be truncated. Then, lines 27–30 output the course names for the GradeBook objects again.

Additional Notes on Set Functions
A public *set* function such as setCourseName should carefully scrutinize any attempt to modify the value of a data member (e.g., courseName) to ensure that the new value is appropriate for that data item. For example, an attempt to *set* the day of the month to 37 should be rejected, an attempt to *set* a person's weight to zero or a negative value should be rejected, an attempt to *set* a grade on an exam to 185 (when the proper range is zero to 100) should be rejected, etc.

Software Engineering Observation 3.6

Making data members private and controlling access, especially write access, to those data members through public member functions helps ensure data integrity.

Error-Prevention Tip 3.5

The benefits of data integrity are not automatic simply because data members are made private—the programmer must provide appropriate validity checking and report the errors.

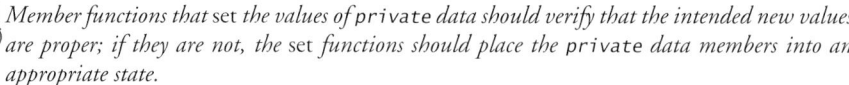

Software Engineering Observation 3.7

Member functions that set *the values of* private *data should verify that the intended new values are proper; if they are not, the* set *functions should place the* private *data members into an appropriate state.*

A class's *set* functions can return values to the class's clients indicating that attempts were made to assign invalid data to objects of the class. A client of the class can test the return value of a *set* function to determine whether the client's attempt to modify the object was successful and to take appropriate action. In Chapter 16, we demonstrate how clients of a class can be notified via the exception-handling mechanism when an attempt is made to modify an object with an inappropriate value. To keep the program of Figs. 3.15–3.17 simple at this early point in the book, setCourseName in Fig. 3.16 just prints an appropriate message on the screen.

3.11 (Optional) Software Engineering Case Study: Identifying the Classes in the ATM Requirements Document

Now we begin designing the ATM system that we introduced in Chapter 2. In this section, we identify the classes that are needed to build the ATM system by analyzing the nouns and noun phrases that appear in the requirements document. We introduce UML class diagrams to model the relationships between these classes. This is an important first step in defining the structure of our system.

Identifying the Classes in a System

We begin our OOD process by identifying the classes required to build the ATM system. We will eventually describe these classes using UML class diagrams and implement these classes in C++. First, we review the requirements document of Section 2.8 and find key nouns and noun phrases to help us identify classes that comprise the ATM system. We may decide that some of these nouns and noun phrases are attributes of other classes in the system. We may also conclude that some of the nouns do not correspond to parts of the system and thus should not be modeled at all. Additional classes may become apparent to us as we proceed through the design process.

Figure 3.18 lists the nouns and noun phrases in the requirements document. We list them from left to right in the order in which they appear in the requirements document. We list only the singular form of each noun or noun phrase.

We create classes only for the nouns and noun phrases that have significance in the ATM system. We do not need to model "bank" as a class, because the bank is not a part of the ATM system—the bank simply wants us to build the ATM. "Customer" and "user" also represent entities outside of the system—they are important because they interact with our ATM system, but we do not need to model them as classes in the ATM software. Recall that we modeled an ATM user (i.e., a bank customer) as the actor in the use case diagram of Fig. 2.18.

We do not model "$20 bill" or "deposit envelope" as classes. These are physical objects in the real world, but they are not part of what is being automated. We can adequately represent the presence of bills in the system using an attribute of the class that models the cash dispenser. (We assign attributes to classes in Section 4.13.) For example, the cash dispenser maintains a count of the number of bills it contains. The requirements document does not

Nouns and noun phrases in the requirements document		
bank	money / fund	account number
ATM	screen	PIN
user	keypad	bank database
customer	cash dispenser	balance inquiry
transaction	$20 bill / cash	withdrawal
account	deposit slot	deposit
balance	deposit envelope	

Fig. 3.18 | Nouns and noun phrases in the requirements document.

say anything about what the system should do with deposit envelopes after it receives them. We can assume that simply acknowledging the receipt of an envelope—an operation performed by the class that models the deposit slot—is sufficient to represent the presence of an envelope in the system. (We assign operations to classes in Section 6.22.)

In our simplified ATM system, representing various amounts of "money," including the "balance" of an account, as attributes of other classes seems most appropriate. Likewise, the nouns "account number" and "PIN" represent significant pieces of information in the ATM system. They are important attributes of a bank account. They do not, however, exhibit behaviors. Thus, we can most appropriately model them as attributes of an account class.

Though the requirements document frequently describes a "transaction" in a general sense, we do not model the broad notion of a financial transaction at this time. Instead, we model the three types of transactions (i.e., "balance inquiry," "withdrawal" and "deposit") as individual classes. These classes possess specific attributes needed for executing the transactions they represent. For example, a withdrawal needs to know the amount of money the user wants to withdraw. A balance inquiry, however, does not require any additional data. Furthermore, the three transaction classes exhibit unique behaviors. A withdrawal includes dispensing cash to the user, whereas a deposit involves receiving deposit envelopes from the user. [*Note:* In Section 13.10, we "factor out" common features of all transactions into a general "transaction" class using the object-oriented concepts of abstract classes and inheritance.]

We determine the classes for our system based on the remaining nouns and noun phrases from Fig. 3.18. Each of these refers to one or more of the following:

- ATM
- screen
- keypad
- cash dispenser
- deposit slot
- account
- bank database
- balance inquiry

- withdrawal

- deposit

The elements of this list are likely to be classes we will need to implement our system.

We can now model the classes in our system based on the list we have created. We capitalize class names in the design process—a UML convention—as we will do when we write the actual C++ code that implements our design. If the name of a class contains more than one word, we run the words together and capitalize each word (e.g., `MultipleWordName`). Using this convention, we create classes ATM, `Screen`, `Keypad`, `CashDispenser`, `DepositSlot`, `Account`, `BankDatabase`, `BalanceInquiry`, `Withdrawal` and `Deposit`. We construct our system using all of these classes as building blocks. Before we begin building the system, however, we must gain a better understanding of how the classes relate to one another.

Modeling Classes

The UML enables us to model, via class diagrams, the classes in the ATM system and their interrelationships. Figure 3.19 represents class ATM. In the UML, each class is modeled as a rectangle with three compartments. The top compartment contains the name of the class, centered horizontally and in boldface. The middle compartment contains the class's attributes. (We discuss attributes in Section 4.13 and Section 5.11.) The bottom compartment contains the class's operations (discussed in Section 6.22). In Fig. 3.19 the middle and bottom compartments are empty, because we have not yet determined this class's attributes and operations.

Class diagrams also show the relationships between the classes of the system. Figure 3.20 shows how our classes ATM and `Withdrawal` relate to one another. For the moment, we choose to model only this subset of classes for simplicity. We present a more complete class diagram later in this section. Notice that the rectangles representing classes in this diagram are not subdivided into compartments. The UML allows the suppression of class attributes and operations in this manner, when appropriate, to create more readable diagrams. Such a diagram is said to be an elided diagram—one in which some information, such as the contents of the second and third compartments, is not modeled. We will place information in these compartments in Section 4.13 and Section 6.22

In Fig. 3.20, the solid line that connects the two classes represents an association—a relationship between classes. The numbers near each end of the line are multiplicity values, which indicate how many objects of each class participate in the association. In this. case, following the line from one end to the other reveals that, at any given moment,

ATM

Fig. 3.19 | Representing a class in the UML using a class diagram.

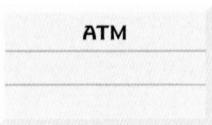

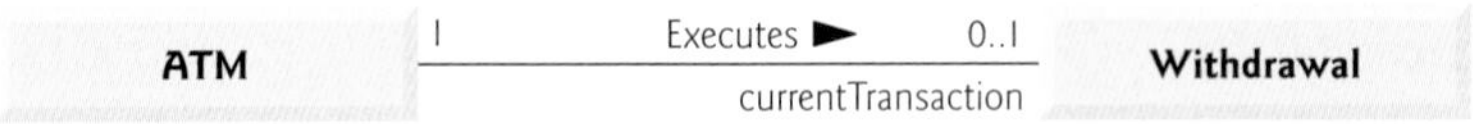

Fig. 3.20 | Class diagram showing an association among classes.

one ATM object participates in an association with either zero or one Withdrawal objects—zero if the current user is not currently performing a transaction or has requested a different type of transaction, and one if the user has requested a withdrawal. The UML can model many types of multiplicity. Figure 3.21 lists and explains the multiplicity types.

An association can be named. For example, the word Executes above the line connecting classes ATM and Withdrawal in Fig. 3.20 indicates the name of that association. This part of the diagram reads "one object of class ATM executes zero or one objects of class Withdrawal." Note that association names are directional, as indicated by the filled arrowhead—so it would be improper, for example, to read the preceding association from right to left as "zero or one objects of class Withdrawal execute one object of class ATM."

The word currentTransaction at the Withdrawal end of the association line in Fig. 3.20 is a role name, which identifies the role the Withdrawal object plays in its relationship with the ATM. A role name adds meaning to an association between classes by identifying the role a class plays in the context of an association. A class can play several roles in the same system. For example, in a school personnel system, a person may play the role of "professor" when relating to students. The same person may take on the role of "colleague" when participating in a relationship with another professor, and "coach" when coaching student athletes. In Fig. 3.20, the role name currentTransaction indicates that the Withdrawal object participating in the Executes association with an object of class ATM represents the transaction currently being processed by the ATM. In other contexts, a Withdrawal object may take on other roles (e.g., the previous transaction). Notice that we do not specify a role name for the ATM end of the Executes association. Role names in class diagrams are often omitted when the meaning of an association is clear without them.

In addition to indicating simple relationships, associations can specify more complex relationships, such as objects of one class being composed of objects of other classes. Consider a real-world automated teller machine. What "pieces" does a manufacturer put together to build a working ATM? Our requirements document tells us that the ATM is composed of a screen, a keypad, a cash dispenser and a deposit slot.

Symbol	Meaning
0	None
1	One
m	An integer value
0..1	Zero or one
m, n	m or n
$m..n$	At least m, but not more than n
*	Any nonnegative integer (zero or more)
0..*	Zero or more (identical to *)
1..*	One or more

Fig. 3.21 | Multiplicity types.

In Fig. 3.22, the solid diamonds attached to the association lines of class ATM indicate that class ATM has a composition relationship with classes Screen, Keypad, CashDispenser and DepositSlot. Composition implies a whole/part relationship. The class that has the composition symbol (the solid diamond) on its end of the association line is the whole (in this case, ATM), and the classes on the other end of the association lines are the parts—in this case, classes Screen, Keypad, CashDispenser and DepositSlot. The compositions in Fig. 3.22 indicate that an object of class ATM is formed from one object of class Screen, one object of class CashDispenser, one object of class Keypad and one object of class DepositSlot. The ATM "has a" screen, a keypad, a cash dispenser and a deposit slot. The "has-a" relationship defines composition. (We will see in the "Software Engineering Case Study" section in Chapter 13 that the "is-a" relationship defines inheritance.)

According to the UML specification, composition relationships have the following properties:

1. Only one class in the relationship can represent the whole (i.e., the diamond can be placed on only one end of the association line). For example, either the screen is part of the ATM or the ATM is part of the screen, but the screen and the ATM cannot both represent the whole in the relationship.

2. The parts in the composition relationship exist only as long as the whole, and the whole is responsible for the creation and destruction of its parts. For example, the act of constructing an ATM includes manufacturing its parts. Furthermore, if the ATM is destroyed, its screen, keypad, cash dispenser and deposit slot are also destroyed.

3. A part may belong to only one whole at a time, although the part may be removed and attached to another whole, which then assumes responsibility for the part.

The solid diamonds in our class diagrams indicate composition relationships that fulfill these three properties. If a "has-a" relationship does not satisfy one or more of these criteria, the UML specifies that hollow diamonds be attached to the ends of association lines to indicate aggregation—a weaker form of composition. For example, a personal computer and a computer monitor participate in an aggregation relationship—the computer "has a" monitor, but

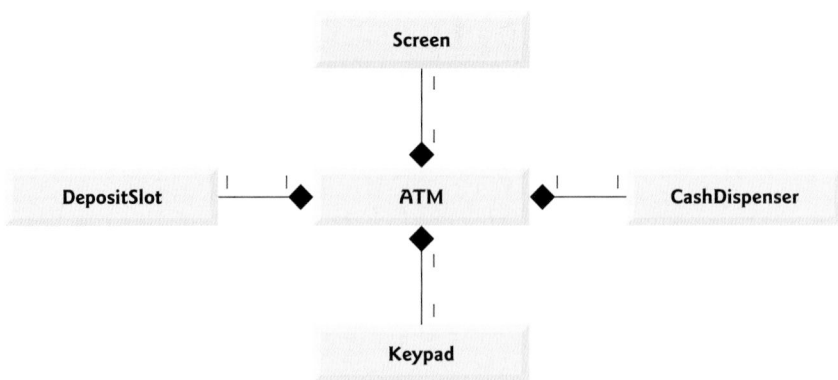

Fig. 3.22 | Class diagram showing composition relationships.

the two parts can exist independently, and the same monitor can be attached to multiple computers at once, thus violating the second and third properties of composition.

Figure 3.23 shows a class diagram for the ATM system. This diagram models most of the classes that we identified earlier in this section, as well as the associations between them that we can infer from the requirements document. [*Note:* Classes BalanceInquiry and Deposit participate in associations similar to those of class Withdrawal, so we have chosen to omit them from this diagram to keep it simple. In Chapter 13, we expand our class diagram to include all the classes in the ATM system.]

Figure 3.23 presents a graphical model of the structure of the ATM system. This class diagram includes classes BankDatabase and Account, and several associations that were not present in either Fig. 3.20 or Fig. 3.22. The class diagram shows that class ATM has a one-to-one relationship with class BankDatabase—one ATM object authenticates users against one BankDatabase object. In Fig. 3.23, we also model the fact that the bank's database contains information about many accounts—one object of class BankDatabase participates in a composition relationship with zero or more objects of class Account. Recall from Fig. 3.21 that the multiplicity value 0..* at the Account end of the association between class BankDatabase and class Account indicates that zero or more objects of class Account take part in the association. Class BankDatabase has a one-to-many relationship with class Account—the BankDatabase stores many Accounts. Similarly, class Account has a many-to-one relationship with class BankDatabase—there can be many Accounts stored in the BankDatabase. [*Note:* Recall from Fig. 3.21 that the multiplicity value * is identical to 0..*. We include 0..* in our class diagrams for clarity.]

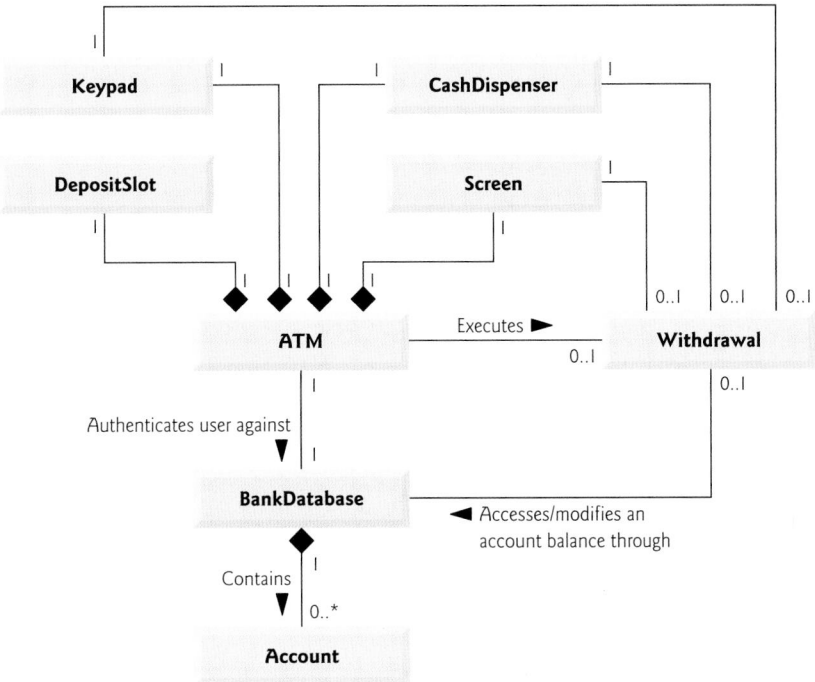

Fig. 3.23 | Class diagram for the ATM system model.

Figure 3.23 also indicates that if the user is performing a withdrawal, "one object of class `Withdrawal` accesses/modifies an account balance through one object of class `Bank-Database`." We could have created an association directly between class `Withdrawal` and class `Account`. The requirements document, however, states that the "ATM must interact with the bank's account information database" to perform transactions. A bank account contains sensitive information, and systems engineers must always consider the security of personal data when designing a system. Thus, only the `BankDatabase` can access and manipulate an account directly. All other parts of the system must interact with the database to retrieve or update account information (e.g., an account balance).

The class diagram in Fig. 3.23 also models associations between class `Withdrawal` and classes `Screen`, `CashDispenser` and `Keypad`. A withdrawal transaction includes prompting the user to choose a withdrawal amount and receiving numeric input. These actions require the use of the screen and the keypad, respectively. Furthermore, dispensing cash to the user requires access to the cash dispenser.

Classes `BalanceInquiry` and `Deposit`, though not shown in Fig. 3.23, take part in several associations with the other classes of the ATM system. Like class `Withdrawal`, each of these classes associates with classes `ATM` and `BankDatabase`. An object of class `Balance-Inquiry` also associates with an object of class `Screen` to display the balance of an account to the user. Class `Deposit` associates with classes `Screen`, `Keypad` and `DepositSlot`. Like withdrawals, deposit transactions require use of the screen and the keypad to display prompts and receive input, respectively. To receive deposit envelopes, an object of class `Deposit` accesses the deposit slot.

We have now identified the classes in our ATM system (although we may discover others as we proceed with the design and implementation). In Section 4.13, we determine the attributes for each of these classes, and in Section 5.11, we use these attributes to examine how the system changes over time. In Section 6.22, we determine the operations of the classes in our system.

Software Engineering Case Study Self-Review Exercises

3.1 Suppose we have a class `Car` that represents a car. Think of some of the different pieces that a manufacturer would put together to produce a whole car. Create a class diagram (similar to Fig. 3.22) that models some of the composition relationships of class `Car`.

3.2 Suppose we have a class `File` that represents an electronic document in a stand-alone, non-networked computer represented by class `Computer`. What sort of association exists between class `Computer` and class `File`?
   a) Class `Computer` has a one-to-one relationship with class `File`.
   b) Class `Computer` has a many-to-one relationship with class `File`.
   c) Class `Computer` has a one-to-many relationship with class `File`.
   d) Class `Computer` has a many-to-many relationship with class `File`.

3.3 State whether the following statement is *true* or *false*, and if *false*, explain why: A UML diagram in which a class's second and third compartments are not modeled is said to be an elided diagram.

3.4 Modify the class diagram of Fig. 3.23 to include class `Deposit` instead of class `Withdrawal`.

Answers to Software Engineering Case Study Self-Review Exercises

3.1 [*Note:* Student answers may vary.] Figure 3.24 presents a class diagram that shows some of the composition relationships of a class `Car`.

3.2 c. [*Note:* In a computer network, this relationship could be many-to-many.]

3.3 True.

3.4 Figure 3.25 presents a class diagram for the ATM including class Deposit instead of class Withdrawal (as in Fig. 3.23). Note that Deposit does not access CashDispenser, but does access DepositSlot.

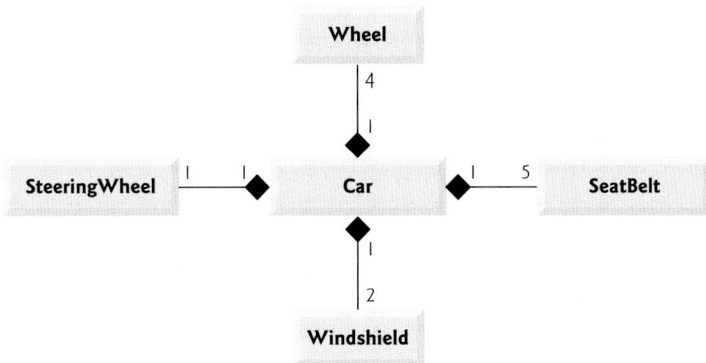

Fig. 3.24 | Class diagram showing composition relationships of a class Car.

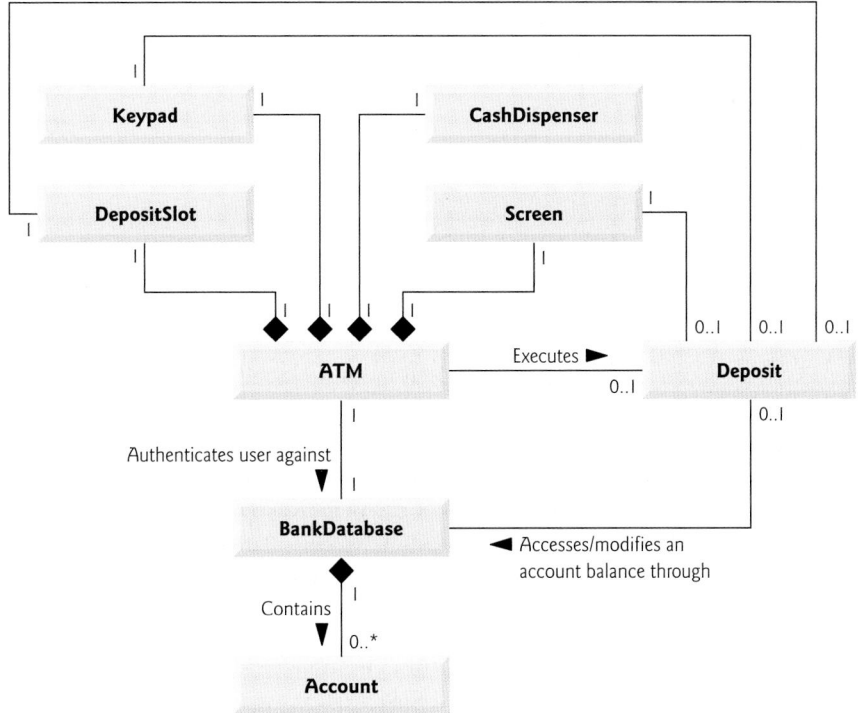

Fig. 3.25 | Class diagram for the ATM system model including class Deposit.

Summary

- Performing a task in a program requires a function. The function hides from its user the complex tasks that it performs.
- A function in a class is known as a member function and performs one of the class's tasks.
- You must create an object of a class before a program can perform the tasks the class describes. That is one reason C++ is known as an object-oriented programming language.
- Each message sent to an object is a member-function call that tells the object to perform a task.
- An object has attributes that are carried with the object as it is used in a program. These attributes are specified as data members in the object's class.
- A class definition contains the data members and member functions that define the class's attributes and behaviors, respectively.
- A class definition begins with the keyword class followed immediately by the class name.
- By convention, the name of a user-defined class begins with a capital letter and, for readability, each subsequent word in the class name begins with a capital letter.
- Every class's body is enclosed in a pair of braces ({ and }) and ends with a semicolon.
- Member functions that appear after access specifier public can be called by other functions in a program and by member functions of other classes.
- Access specifiers are always followed by a colon (:).
- Keyword void is a special return type which indicates that a function will perform a task but will not return any data to its calling function when it completes its task.
- By convention, function names begin with a lowercase first letter and all subsequent words in the name begin with a capital letter.
- An empty set of parentheses after a function name indicates that the function does not require additional data to perform its task.
- Every function's body is delimited by left and right braces ({ and }).
- Typically, you cannot call a member function until you create an object of its class.
- Each new class you create becomes a new type in C++ that can be used to declare variables and create objects. This is one reason why C++ is known as an extensible language.
- A member function can require one or more parameters that represent additional data it needs to perform its task. A function call supplies arguments for each of the function's parameters.
- A member function is called by following the object name with a dot operator (.), the function name and a set of parentheses containing the function's arguments.
- A variable of C++ Standard Library class string represents a string of characters. This class is defined in header file <string>, and the name string belongs to namespace std.
- Function getline (from header <string>) reads characters from its first argument until a newline character is encountered, then places the characters (not including the newline) in the string variable specified as its second argument. The newline character is discarded.
- A parameter list may contain any number of parameters, including none at all (represented by empty parentheses) to indicate that a function does not require any parameters.
- The number of arguments in a function call must match the number of parameters in the parameter list of the called member function's header. Also, the argument types in the function call must be consistent with the types of the corresponding parameters in the function header.
- Variables declared in a function's body are local variables and can be used only from the point of their declaration in the function to the immediately following closing right brace (}). When a function terminates, the values of its local variables are lost.

- A local variable must be declared before it can be used in a function. A local variable cannot be accessed outside the function in which it is declared.
- Data members normally are `private`. Variables or functions declared `private` are accessible only to member functions of the class in which they are declared.
- When a program creates (instantiates) an object of a class, its `private` data members are encapsulated (hidden) in the object and can be accessed only by member functions of the object's class.
- When a function that specifies a return type other than `void` is called and completes its task, the function returns a result to its calling function.
- By default, the initial value of a `string` is the empty string—i.e., a string that does not contain any characters. Nothing appears on the screen when an empty string is displayed.
- Classes often provide `public` member functions to allow clients of the class to *set* or *get* `private` data members. The names of these member functions normally begin with *set* or *get*.
- Providing `public` *set* and *get* functions allows clients of a class to indirectly access the hidden data. The client knows that it is attempting to modify or obtain an object's data, but the client does not know how the object performs these operations.
- The *set* and *get* functions of a class also should be used by other member functions within the class to manipulate the class's `private` data, although these member functions *can* access the `private` data directly. If the class's data representation is changed, member functions that access the data only via the *set* and *get* functions will not require modification—only the bodies of the *set* and *get* functions that directly manipulate the data member will need to change.
- A `public` *set* function should carefully scrutinize any attempt to modify the value of a data member to ensure that the new value is appropriate for that data item.
- Each class you declare should provide a constructor to initialize an object of the class when the object is created. A constructor is a special member function that must be defined with the same name as the class, so that the compiler can distinguish it from the class's other member functions.
- A difference between constructors and functions is that constructors cannot return values, so they cannot specify a return type (not even `void`). Normally, constructors are declared `public`.
- C++ requires a constructor call at the time each object is created, which helps ensure that every object is initialized before it is used in a program.
- A constructor that takes no arguments is a default constructor. In any class that does not include a constructor, the compiler provides a default constructor. The class programmer can also define a default constructor explicitly. If the programmer defines a constructor for a class, C++ will not create a default constructor.
- Class definitions, when packaged properly, can be reused by programmers worldwide.
- It is customary to define a class in a header file that has a `.h` filename extension.
- If the class's implementation changes, the class's clients should not be required to change.
- Interfaces define and standardize the ways in which things such as people and systems interact.
- The interface of a class describes the `public` member functions (also known as `public` services) that are made available to the class's clients. The interface describes *what* services clients can use and how to *request* those services, but does not specify *how* the class carries out the services.
- A fundamental principle of good software engineering is to separate interface from implementation. This makes programs easier to modify. Changes in the class's implementation do not affect the client as long as the class's interface originally provided to the client remains unchanged.
- A function prototype contains a function's name, its return type and the number, types and order of the parameters the function expects to receive.

- Once a class is defined and its member functions are declared (via function prototypes), the member functions should be defined in a separate source-code file
- For each member function defined outside of its corresponding class definition, the function name must be preceded by the class name and the binary scope resolution operator (::).
- Class string's length member function returns the number of characters in a string object.
- Class string's member function substr (short for "substring") returns a new string object created by copying part of an existing string object. The function's first argument specifies the starting position in the original string from which characters are copied. Its second argument specifies the number of characters to copy.
- In the UML, each class is modeled in a class diagram as a rectangle with three compartments. The top compartment contains the class name, centered horizontally in boldface. The middle compartment contains the class's attributes (data members in C++). The bottom compartment contains the class's operations (member functions and constructors in C++).
- The UML models operations by listing the operation name followed by a set of parentheses. A plus sign (+) preceding the operation name indicates a public operation in the UML (i.e., a public member function in C++).
- The UML models a parameter of an operation by listing the parameter name, followed by a colon and the parameter type between the parentheses following the operation name.
- The UML has its own data types. Not all the UML data types have the same names as the corresponding C++ types. The UML type String corresponds to the C++ type string.
- The UML represents data members as attributes by listing the attribute name, followed by a colon and the attribute type. Private attributes are preceded by a minus sign (–) in the UML.
- The UML indicates the return type of an operation by placing a colon and the return type after the parentheses following the operation name.
- UML class diagrams do not specify return types for operations that do not return values.
- The UML models constructors as operations in a class diagram's third compartment. To distinguish a constructor from a class's operations, the UML places the word "constructor" between guillemets (« and ») before the constructor's name.

Terminology

access specifier	data member
accessor	default constructor
argument	default precision
attribute (UML)	defining a class
binary scope resolution operator (::)	dot operator (.)
body of a class definition	empty string
calling function (caller)	extensible language
camel case	function call
class definition	function header
class diagram (UML)	function prototype
class-implementation programmer	*get* function
client-code programmer	getline function of <string> library
client of an object or class	guillemets, « and » (UML)
compartment in a class diagram (UML)	header file
consistent state	implementation of a class
constructor	instance of a class
data hiding	interface of a class

invoke a member function
length member function of class string
local variable
member function
member-function call
message (send to an object)
minus (-) sign (UML)
mutator
object code
operation (UML)
operation parameter (UML)
parameter
parameter list
plus (+) sign (UML)
precision

private access specifier
public access specifier
public services of a class
return type
separate interface from implementation
set function
software engineering
source-code file
string class
<string> header file
substr member function of class string
UML class diagram
validation
validity checking
void return type

Self-Review Exercises

3.1 Fill in the blanks in each of the following:
   a) A house is to a blueprint as a(n) _____ is to a class.
   b) Every class definition contains keyword _____ followed immediately by the class's name.
   c) A class definition is typically stored in a file with the _____ filename extension.
   d) Each parameter in a function header should specify both a(n) _____ and a(n) _____.
   e) When each object of a class maintains its own copy of an attribute, the variable that represents the attribute is also known as a(n) _____.
   f) Keyword public is a(n) _____.
   g) Return type _____ indicates that a function will perform a task but will not return any information when it completes its task.
   h) Function _____ from the <string> library reads characters until a newline character is encountered, then copies those characters into the specified string.
   i) When a member function is defined outside the class definition, the function header must include the class name and the _____, followed by the function name to "tie" the member function to the class definition.
   j) The source-code file and any other files that use a class can include the class's header file via an _____ preprocessor directive.

3.2 State whether each of the following is *true* or *false*. If *false*, explain why.
   a) By convention, function names begin with a capital letter and all subsequent words in the name begin with a capital letter.
   b) Empty parentheses following a function name in a function prototype indicate that the function does not require any parameters to perform its task.
   c) Data members or member functions declared with access specifier private are accessible to member functions of the class in which they are declared.
   d) Variables declared in the body of a particular member function are known as data members and can be used in all member functions of the class.
   e) Every function's body is delimited by left and right braces ({ and }).
   f) Any source-code file that contains int main() can be used to execute a program.
   g) The types of arguments in a function call must match the types of the corresponding parameters in the function prototype's parameter list.

3.3   What is the difference between a local variable and a data member?

3.4   Explain the purpose of a function parameter. What is the difference between a parameter and an argument?

Answers to Self-Review Exercises

3.1   a) object. b) class. c) .h d) type, name. e) data member. f) access specifier. g) void. h) getline. i) binary scope resolution operator (::). j) #include.

3.2   a) False. By convention, function names begin with a lowercase letter and all subsequent words in the name begin with a capital letter. b) True. c) True. d) False. Such variables are called local variables and can be used only in the member function in which they are declared. e) True. f) True. g) True.

3.3   A local variable is declared in the body of a function and can be used only from the point at which it is declared to the immediately following closing brace. A data member is declared in a class definition, but not in the body of any of the class's member functions. Every object (instance) of a class has a separate copy of the class's data members. Also, data members are accessible to all member functions of the class.

3.4   A parameter represents additional information that a function requires to perform its task. Each parameter required by a function is specified in the function header. An argument is the value supplied in the function call. When the function is called, the argument value is passed into the function parameter so that the function can perform its task.

Exercises

3.5   Explain the difference between a function prototype and a function definition.

3.6   What is a default constructor? How are an object's data members initialized if a class has only an implicitly defined default constructor?

3.7   Explain the purpose of a data member.

3.8   What is a header file? What is a source-code file? Discuss the purpose of each.

3.9   Explain how a program could use class string without inserting a using declaration.

3.10   Explain why a class might provide a *set* function and a *get* function for a data member.

3.11   *(Modifying Class GradeBook)* Modify class GradeBook (Figs. 3.11–3.12) as follows:
   a) Include a second string data member that represents the course instructor's name.
   b) Provide a *set* function to change the instructor's name and a *get* function to retrieve it.
   c) Modify the constructor to specify two parameters—one for the course name and one for the instructor's name.
   d) Modify member function displayMessage such that it first outputs the welcome message and course name, then outputs "This course is presented by: " followed by the instructor's name.
Use your modified class in a test program that demonstrates the class's new capabilities.

3.12   *(Account Class)* Create a class called Account that a bank might use to represent customers' bank accounts. Your class should include one data member of type int to represent the account balance. [*Note:* In subsequent chapters, we'll use numbers that contain decimal points (e.g., 2.75)—called floating-point values—to represent dollar amounts.] Your class should provide a constructor that receives an initial balance and uses it to initialize the data member. The constructor should validate the initial balance to ensure that it is greater than or equal to 0. If not, the balance should be set to 0 and the constructor should display an error message, indicating that the initial balance was invalid. The class should provide three member functions. Member function credit should add an amount to the current balance. Member function debit should withdraw money from the Account and should ensure that the debit amount does not exceed the Account's balance. If it does, the balance should be left unchanged and the function should print a message indicating "Debit amount exceeded account balance." Member function getBalance should return the current balance. Create a program that creates two Account objects and tests the member functions of class Account.

3.13   *(Invoice Class)* Create a class called Invoice that a hardware store might use to represent an invoice for an item sold at the store. An Invoice should include four pieces of information as data members—a part number (type string), a part description (type string), a quantity of the item being purchased (type int) and a price per item (type int). [*Note:* In subsequent chapters, we'll use numbers that contain decimal points (e.g., 2.75)—called floating-point values—to represent dollar amounts.] Your class should have a constructor that initializes the four data members. Provide a *set* and a *get* function for each data member. In addition, provide a member function named get-InvoiceAmount that calculates the invoice amount (i.e., multiplies the quantity by the price per item), then returns the amount as an int value. If the quantity is not positive, it should be set to 0. If the price per item is not positive, it should be set to 0. Write a test program that demonstrates class Invoice's capabilities.

3.14   *(Employee Class)* Create a class called Employee that includes three pieces of information as data members—a first name (type string), a last name (type string) and a monthly salary (type int). [*Note:* In subsequent chapters, we'll use numbers that contain decimal points (e.g., 2.75)—called floating-point values—to represent dollar amounts.] Your class should have a constructor that initializes the three data members. Provide a *set* and a *get* function for each data member. If the monthly salary is not positive, set it to 0. Write a test program that demonstrates class Employee's capabilities. Create two Employee objects and display each object's *yearly* salary. Then give each Employee a 10 percent raise and display each Employee's yearly salary again.

3.15   *(Date Class)* Create a class called Date that includes three pieces of information as data members—a month (type int), a day (type int) and a year (type int). Your class should have a constructor with three parameters that uses the parameters to initialize the three data members. For the purpose of this exercise, assume that the values provided for the year and day are correct, but ensure that the month value is in the range 1–12; if it is not, set the month to 1. Provide a *set* and a *get* function for each data member. Provide a member function displayDate that displays the month, day and year separated by forward slashes (/). Write a test program that demonstrates class Date's capabilities

4

Control Statements: Part 1

OBJECTIVES

In this chapter you will learn:

- Basic problem-solving techniques.
- To develop algorithms through the process of top-down, stepwise refinement.
- To use the `if` and `if...else` selection statements to choose among alternative actions.
- To use the `while` repetition statement to execute statements in a program repeatedly.
- Counter-controlled repetition and sentinel-controlled repetition.
- To use the increment, decrement and assignment operators.

4.1 Introduction

Before writing a program to solve a problem, we must have a thorough understanding of the problem and a carefully planned approach to solving it. When writing a program, we must also understand the types of building blocks that are available and employ proven program construction techniques. In this chapter and in Chapter 5, Control Statements: Part 2, we discuss these issues in presenting of the theory and principles of structured programming. The concepts presented here are crucial to building effective classes and manipulating objects.

In this chapter, we introduce C++'s if, if...else and while statements, three of the building blocks that allow programmers to specify the logic required for member functions to perform their tasks. We devote a portion of this chapter (and Chapters 5 and 7) to further developing the GradeBook class introduced in Chapter 3. In particular, we add a member function to the GradeBook class that uses control statements to calculate the average of a set of student grades. Another example demonstrates additional ways to combine control statements to solve a similar problem. We introduce C++'s assignment operators and explore C++'s increment and decrement operators. These additional operators abbreviate and simplify many program statements.

4.2 Algorithms

Any solvable computing problem can be solved by the execution of a series of actions in a specific order. A procedure for solving a problem in terms of

1. the actions to execute and

2. the order in which these actions execute

is called an algorithm. The following example demonstrates that correctly specifying the order in which the actions execute is important.

Consider the "rise-and-shine algorithm" followed by one junior executive for getting out of bed and going to work: (1) Get out of bed, (2) take off pajamas, (3) take a shower, (4) get dressed, (5) eat breakfast, (6) carpool to work. This routine gets the executive to work well prepared to make critical decisions. Suppose that the same steps are performed in a slightly different order: (1) Get out of bed, (2) take off pajamas, (3) get dressed, (4) take a shower, (5) eat breakfast, (6) carpool to work. In this case, our junior executive shows up for work soaking wet. Specifying the order in which statements (actions) execute in a computer program is called program control. This chapter investigates program control using C++'s control statements.

4.3 Pseudocode

Pseudocode (or "fake" code) is an artificial and informal language that helps programmers develop algorithms without having to worry about the strict details of C++ language syntax. The pseudocode we present here is particularly useful for developing algorithms that will be converted to structured portions of C++ programs. Pseudocode is similar to everyday English; it is convenient and user friendly, although it is not an actual computer programming language.

Pseudocode does not execute on computers. Rather, it helps the programmer "think out" a program before attempting to write it in a programming language, such as C++. This chapter provides several examples of how to use pseudocode to develop C++ programs.

The style of pseudocode we present consists purely of characters, so programmers can type pseudocode conveniently, using any editor program. The computer can produce a freshly printed copy of a pseudocode program on demand. A carefully prepared pseudocode program can easily be converted to a corresponding C++ program. In many cases, this simply requires replacing pseudocode statements with C++ equivalents.

Pseudocode normally describes only executable statements, which cause specific actions to occur after a programmer converts a program from pseudocode to C++ and the program is run on a computer. Declarations (that do not have initializers or do not involve constructor calls) are not executable statements. For example, the declaration

```
int i;
```

tells the compiler variable i's type and instructs the compiler to reserve space in memory for the variable. This declaration does not cause any action—such as input, output or a calculation—to occur when the program executes. We typically do not include variable declarations in our pseudocode. However, some programmers choose to list variables and mention their purposes at the beginning of pseudocode programs.

We now look at an example of pseudocode that may be written to help a programmer create the addition program of Fig. 2.5. This pseudocode (Fig. 4.1) corresponds to the algorithm that inputs two integers from the user, adds these integers and displays their sum. Although we show the complete pseudocode listing here, we will show how to create pseudocode from a problem statement later in the chapter.

Lines 1–2 correspond to the statements in lines 13–14 of Fig. 2.5. Notice that the pseudocode statements are simply English statements that convey what task is to be performed in C++. Likewise, lines 4–5 correspond to the statements in lines 16–17 of Fig. 2.5 and lines 7–8 correspond to the statements in lines 19 and 21 of Fig. 2.5.

1   *Prompt the user to enter the first integer*
2   *Input the first integer*
3
4   *Prompt the user to enter the second integer*
5   *Input the second integer*
6
7   *Add first integer and second integer, store result*
8   *Display result*

Fig. 4.1 | Pseudocode for the addition program of Fig. 2.5.

There are a few important aspects of the pseudocode in Fig. 4.1. Notice that the pseudocode corresponds to code only in function `main`. This occurs because pseudocode is normally used for algorithms, not complete programs. In this case, the pseudocode is used to represent the algorithm. The function in which this code is placed is not important to the algorithm itself. For the same reason, line 23 of Fig. 2.5 (the `return` statement) is not included in the pseudocode—this `return` statement is placed at the end of every `main` function and is not important to the algorithm. Finally, lines 9–11 of Fig. 2.5 are not included in the pseudocode because these variable declarations are not executable statements.

4.4 Control Structures

Normally, statements in a program execute one after the other in the order in which they are written. This is called *sequential execution*. Various C++ statements we will soon discuss enable the programmer to specify that the next statement to execute may be other than the next one in sequence. This is called *transfer of control*.

During the 1960s, it became clear that the indiscriminate use of transfers of control was the root of much difficulty experienced by software development groups. The finger of blame was pointed at the *goto statement*, which allows the programmer to specify a transfer of control to one of a wide range of possible destinations in a program (creating what is often called "spaghetti code"). The notion of so-called *structured programming* became almost synonymous with "*goto elimination*."

The research of Böhm and Jacopini[1] demonstrated that programs could be written without any `goto` statements. It became the challenge of the era for programmers to shift their styles to "goto-less programming." It was not until the 1970s that programmers started taking structured programming seriously. The results have been impressive, as software development groups have reported reduced development times, more frequent on-time delivery of systems and more frequent within-budget completion of software projects. The key to these successes is that structured programs are clearer, are easier to debug, test and modify and are more likely to be bug-free in the first place.

Böhm and Jacopini's work demonstrated that all programs could be written in terms of only three *control structures*, namely, the *sequence structure*, the *selection structure* and the *repetition structure*. The term "control structures" comes from the field of com-

---

1.   Böhm, C., and G. Jacopini, "Flow Diagrams, Turing Machines, and Languages with Only Two Formation Rules," *Communications of the ACM*, Vol. 9, No. 5, May 1966, pp. 366–371.

puter science. When we introduce C++'s implementations of control structures, we will refer to them in the terminology of the C++ standard document[2] as "control statements."

Sequence Structure in C++

The sequence structure is built into C++. Unless directed otherwise, the computer executes C++ statements one after the other in the order in which they are written—that is, in sequence. The Unified Modeling Language (UML) activity diagram of Fig. 4.2 illustrates a typical sequence structure in which two calculations are performed in order. C++ allows us to have as many actions as we want in a sequence structure. As we will soon see, anywhere a single action may be placed, we may place several actions in sequence.

In this figure, the two statements involve adding a grade to a `total` variable and adding the value 1 to a `counter` variable. Such statements might appear in a program that takes the average of several student grades. To calculate an average, the total of the grades being averaged is divided by the number of grades. A counter variable would be used to keep track of the number of values being averaged. You will see similar statements in the program of Section 4.8.

Activity diagrams are part of the UML. An activity diagram models the workflow (also called the activity) of a portion of a software system. Such workflows may include a portion of an algorithm, such as the sequence structure in Fig. 4.2. Activity diagrams are composed of special-purpose symbols, such as action state symbols (a rectangle with its left and right sides replaced with arcs curving outward), diamonds and small circles; these symbols are connected by transition arrows, which represent the flow of the activity.

Like pseudocode, activity diagrams help programmers develop and represent algorithms, although many programmers prefer pseudocode. Activity diagrams clearly show how control structures operate.

Consider the sequence-structure activity diagram of Fig. 4.2. It contains two action states that represent actions to perform. Each action state contains an action expression—e.g., "add grade to total" or "add 1 to counter"—that specifies a particular action to perform. Other actions might include calculations or input/output operations. The arrows

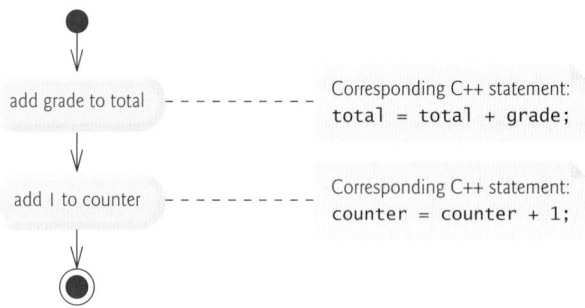

Fig. 4.2 | Sequence-structure activity diagram.

---

2. This document is more specifically known as *NCITS/ISO/IEC 14882-2003 Programming languages—C++* and is available for download (for a fee) at: `webstore.ansi.org/ansidocstore/product.asp?sku=INCITS%2FISO%2FIEC+14882%2D2003`.

in the activity diagram are called transition arrows. These arrows represent transitions, which indicate the order in which the actions represented by the action states occur—the program that implements the activities illustrated by the activity diagram in Fig. 4.2 first adds grade to total, then adds 1 to counter.

The solid circle located at the top of the activity diagram represents the activity's initial state—the beginning of the workflow before the program performs the modeled activities. The solid circle surrounded by a hollow circle that appears at the bottom of the activity diagram represents the final state—the end of the workflow after the program performs its activities.

Figure 4.2 also includes rectangles with the upper-right corners folded over. These are called notes in the UML. Notes are explanatory remarks that describe the purpose of symbols in the diagram. Notes can be used in any UML diagram—not just activity diagrams. Figure 4.2 uses UML notes to show the C++ code associated with each action state in the activity diagram. A dotted line connects each note with the element that the note describes. Activity diagrams normally do not show the C++ code that implements the activity. We use notes for this purpose here to illustrate how the diagram relates to C++ code. For more information on the UML, see our optional case study, which appears in the Software Engineering Case Study sections at the ends of Chapters 1–7, 9, 10, 12 and 13, or visit www.uml.org.

Selection Statements in C++

C++ provides three types of selection statements (discussed in this chapter and Chapter 5). The if selection statement either performs (selects) an action if a condition (predicate) is true or skips the action if the condition is false. The if...else selection statement performs an action if a condition is true or performs a different action if the condition is false. The switch selection statement (Chapter 5) performs one of many different actions, depending on the value of an integer expression.

The if selection statement is a single-selection statement because it selects or ignores a single action (or, as we will soon see, a single group of actions). The if...else statement is called a double-selection statement because it selects between two different actions (or groups of actions). The switch selection statement is called a multiple-selection statement because it selects among many different actions (or groups of actions).

Repetition Statements in C++

C++ provides three types of repetition statements (also called looping statements or loops) that enable programs to perform statements repeatedly as long as a condition (called the loop-continuation condition) remains true. The repetition statements are the while, do...while and for statements. (Chapter 5 presents the do...while and for statements.) The while and for statements perform the action (or group of actions) in their bodies zero or more times—if the loop-continuation condition is initially false, the action (or group of actions) will not execute. The do...while statement performs the action (or group of actions) in its body at least once.

Each of the words if, else, switch, while, do and for is a C++ keyword. These words are reserved by the C++ programming language to implement various features, such as C++'s control statements. Keywords must not be used as identifiers, such as variable names. Figure 4.3 contains a complete list of C++ keywords.

C++ Keywords

Keywords common to the C and C++ programming languages

auto	break	case	char	const
continue	default	do	double	else
enum	extern	float	for	goto
if	int	long	register	return
short	signed	sizeof	static	struct
switch	typedef	union	unsigned	void
volatile	while			

C++-only keywords

and	and_eq	asm	bitand	bitor
bool	catch	class	compl	const_cast
delete	dynamic_cast	explicit	export	false
friend	inline	mutable	namespace	new
not	not_eq	operator	or	or_eq
private	protected	public	reinterpret_cast	static_cast
template	this	throw	true	try
typeid	typename	using	virtual	wchar_t
xor	xor_eq			

Fig. 4.3 | C++ keywords.

Common Programming Error 4.1

Using a keyword as an identifier is a syntax error.

Common Programming Error 4.2

Spelling a keyword with any uppercase letters is a syntax error. All of C++'s keywords contain only lowercase letters.

Summary of Control Statements in C++

C++ has only three kinds of control structures, which from this point forward we refer to as control statements: the sequence statement, selection statements (three types—if, if...else and switch) and repetition statements (three types—while, for and do...while). Each C++ program combines as many of these control statements as is appropriate for the algorithm the program implements. As with the sequence statement of Fig. 4.2, we can model each control statement as an activity diagram. Each diagram contains an initial state and a final state, which represent a control statement's entry point and exit point, respectively. These single-entry/single-exit control statements make it easy to build programs—the control statements are attached to one another by connecting the exit point of one to the entry point of the next. This is similar to the way a child stacks building blocks, so we call this control-statement stacking. We will learn shortly that there is only one other way to connect control statements—called control-statement nesting, in which one control statement is contained inside another. Thus, algorithms in C++ programs are constructed from only three kinds of control statements, combined in only two ways. This is the essence of simplicity.

Software Engineering Observation 4.1

Any C++ program we will ever build can be constructed from only seven different types of control statements (sequence, if, if...else, switch, while, do...while and for) combined in only two ways (control-statement stacking and control-statement nesting).

4.5 if Selection Statement

Programs use selection statements to choose among alternative courses of action. For example, suppose the passing grade on an exam is 60. The pseudocode statement

> *If student's grade is greater than or equal to 60*
>   *Print "Passed"*

determines whether the condition "student's grade is greater than or equal to 60" is true or false. If the condition is true, then "Passed" is printed and the next pseudocode statement in order is "performed" (remember that pseudocode is not a real programming language). If the condition is false, the print statement is ignored and the next pseudocode statement in order is performed. Note that the second line of this selection statement is indented. Such indentation is optional, but it is recommended because it emphasizes the inherent structure of structured programs. When you convert your pseudocode into C++ code, the C++ compiler ignores white-space characters (like blanks, tabs and newlines) used for indentation and vertical spacing.

Good Programming Practice 4.1

Consistently applying reasonable indentation conventions throughout your programs greatly improves program readability. We suggest three blanks per indent. Some people prefer using tabs but these can vary across editors, causing a program written on one editor to align differently when used with another.

The preceding pseudocode *If* statement can be written in C++ as

```
if ( grade >= 60 )
   cout << "Passed";
```

Notice that the C++ code corresponds closely to the pseudocode. This is one of the properties of pseudocode that makes it such a useful program development tool.

Figure 4.4 illustrates the single-selection if statement. It contains what is perhaps the most important symbol in an activity diagram—the diamond or decision symbol, which indicates that a decision is to be made. A decision symbol indicates that the workflow will continue along a path determined by the symbol's associated guard conditions, which can be true or false. Each transition arrow emerging from a decision symbol has a guard condition (specified in square brackets above or next to the transition arrow). If a particular guard condition is true, the workflow enters the action state to which that transition arrow points. In Fig. 4.4, if the grade is greater than or equal to 60, the program prints "Passed" to the screen, then transitions to the final state of this activity. If the grade is less than 60, the program immediately transitions to the final state without displaying a message.

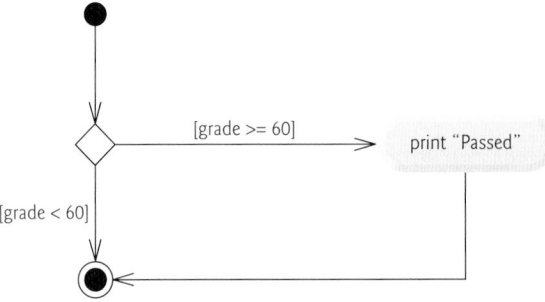

Fig. 4.4 | `if` single-selection statement activity diagram.

We learned in Chapter 1 that decisions can be based on conditions containing relational or equality operators. Actually, in C++, a decision can be based on any expression—if the expression evaluates to zero, it is treated as false; if the expression evaluates to nonzero, it is treated as true. C++ provides the data type `bool` for variables that can hold only the values `true` and `false`—each of these is a C++ keyword.

> ### Portability Tip 4.1
> *For compatibility with earlier versions of C, which used integers for Boolean values, the `bool` value `true` also can be represented by any nonzero value (compilers typically use 1) and the `bool` value `false` also can be represented as the value zero.*

Note that the `if` statement is a single-entry/single-exit statement. We will see that the activity diagrams for the remaining control statements also contain initial states, transition arrows, action states that indicate actions to perform, decision symbols (with associated guard conditions) that indicate decisions to be made and final states. This is consistent with the action/decision model of programming we have been emphasizing.

We can envision seven bins, each containing only empty UML activity diagrams of one of the seven types of control statements. The programmer's task, then, is assembling a program from the activity diagrams of as many of each type of control statement as the algorithm demands, combining the activity diagrams in only two possible ways (stacking or nesting), then filling in the action states and decisions with action expressions and guard conditions in a manner appropriate to form a structured implementation for the algorithm. We will discuss the variety of ways in which actions and decisions may be written.

4.6 `if...else` Double-Selection Statement

The `if` single-selection statement performs an indicated action only when the condition is `true`; otherwise the action is skipped. The `if...else` double-selection statement allows the programmer to specify an action to perform when the condition is true and a different action to perform when the condition is `false`. For example, the pseudocode statement

> *If student's grade is greater than or equal to 60*
> *   Print "Passed"*
> *Else*
> *   Print "Failed"*

prints "Passed" if the student's grade is greater than or equal to 60, but prints "Failed" if the student's grade is less than 60. In either case, after printing occurs, the next pseudocode statement in sequence is "performed."

The preceding pseudocode *If...Else* statement can be written in C++ as

```
if ( grade >= 60 )
   cout << "Passed";
else
   cout << "Failed";
```

Note that the body of the else is also indented. Whatever indentation convention you choose should be applied consistently throughout your programs. It is difficult to read programs that do not obey uniform spacing conventions.

Good Programming Practice 4.2

Indent both body statements of an if...else statement.

Good Programming Practice 4.3

If there are several levels of indentation, each level should be indented the same additional amount of space.

Figure 4.5 illustrates the flow of control in the if...else statement. Once again, note that (besides the initial state, transition arrows and final state) the only other symbols in the activity diagram represent action states and decisions. We continue to emphasize this action/decision model of computing. Imagine again a deep bin of empty UML activity diagrams of double-selection statements—as many as the programmer might need to stack and nest with the activity diagrams of other control statements to form a structured implementation of an algorithm. The programmer fills in the action states and decision symbols with action expressions and guard conditions appropriate to the algorithm.

Conditional Operator (?:)

C++ provides the conditional operator (?:), which is closely related to the if...else statement. The conditional operator is C++'s only ternary operator—it takes three operands. The operands, together with the conditional operator, form a conditional expression. The

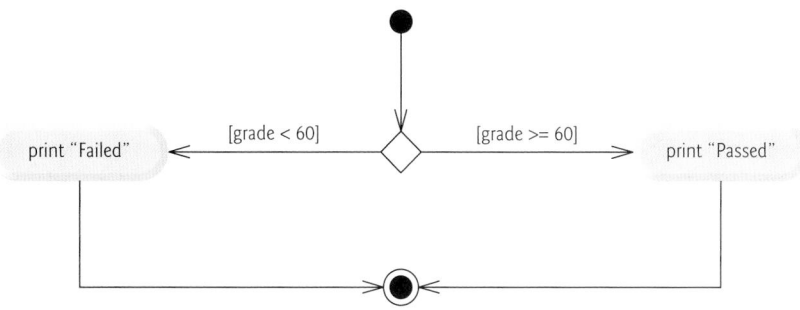

Fig. 4.5 | if...else double-selection statement activity diagram.

first operand is a condition, the second operand is the value for the entire conditional expression if the condition is `true` and the third operand is the value for the entire conditional expression if the condition is `false`. For example, the output statement

```
cout << ( grade >= 60 ? "Passed" : "Failed" );
```

contains a conditional expression, `grade >= 60 ? "Passed" : "Failed"`, that evaluates to the string `"Passed"` if the condition `grade >= 60` is `true`, but evaluates to the string `"Failed"` if the condition is `false`. Thus, the statement with the conditional operator performs essentially the same as the preceding `if...else` statement. As we will see, the precedence of the conditional operator is low, so the parentheses in the preceding expression are required.

Error-Prevention Tip 4.1

To avoid precedence problems (and for clarity), place conditional expressions (that appear in larger expressions) in parentheses.

The values in a conditional expression also can be actions to execute. For example, the following conditional expression also prints `"Passed"` or `"Failed"`:

```
grade >= 60 ? cout << "Passed" : cout << "Failed";
```

The preceding conditional expression is read, "If `grade` is greater than or equal to 60, then `cout << "Passed"`; otherwise, `cout << "Failed"`." This, too, is comparable to the preceding `if...else` statement. Conditional expressions can appear in some program locations where `if...else` statements cannot.

Nested *if...else* Statements

Nested `if...else` statements test for multiple cases by placing `if...else` selection statements inside other `if...else` selection statements. For example, the following pseudocode `if...else` statement prints A for exam grades greater than or equal to 90, B for grades in the range 80 to 89, C for grades in the range 70 to 79, D for grades in the range 60 to 69 and F for all other grades:

> *If student's grade is greater than or equal to 90*
> > *Print "A"*
> *Else*
> > *If student's grade is greater than or equal to 80*
> > > *Print "B"*
> > *Else*
> > > *If student's grade is greater than or equal to 70*
> > > > *Print "C"*
> > > *Else*
> > > > *If student's grade is greater than or equal to 60*
> > > > > *Print "D"*
> > > > *Else*
> > > > > *Print "F"*

This pseudocode can be written in C++ as

```
if ( studentGrade >= 90 ) // 90 and above gets "A"
   cout << "A";
else
   if ( studentGrade >= 80 ) // 80-89 gets "B"
      cout << "B";
   else
      if ( studentGrade >= 70 ) // 70-79 gets "C"
         cout << "C";
      else
         if ( studentGrade >= 60 ) // 60-69 gets "D"
            cout << "D";
         else // less than 60 gets "F"
            cout << "F";
```

If studentGrade is greater than or equal to 90, the first four conditions will be true, but only the cout statement after the first test will execute. After that cout executes, the program skips the else-part of the "outermost" if...else statement. Most C++ programmers prefer to write the preceding if...else statement as

```
if ( studentGrade >= 90 ) // 90 and above gets "A"
   cout << "A";
else if ( studentGrade >= 80 ) // 80-89 gets "B"
   cout << "B";
else if ( studentGrade >= 70 ) // 70-79 gets "C"
   cout << "C";
else if ( studentGrade >= 60 ) // 60-69 gets "D"
   cout << "D";
else // less than 60 gets "F"
   cout << "F";
```

The two forms are identical except for the spacing and indentation, which the compiler ignores. The latter form is popular because it avoids deep indentation of the code to the right. Such indentation often leaves little room on a line, forcing lines to be split and decreasing program readability.

Performance Tip 4.1

A nested if...else statement can perform much faster than a series of single-selection if statements because of the possibility of early exit after one of the conditions is satisfied.

Performance Tip 4.2

In a nested if...else statement, test the conditions that are more likely to be true at the beginning of the nested if...else statement. This will enable the nested if...else statement to run faster and exit earlier than testing infrequently occurring cases first.

Dangling-else Problem

The C++ compiler always associates an else with the immediately preceding if unless told to do otherwise by the placement of braces ({ and }). This behavior can lead to what is referred to as the dangling-else problem. For example,

```
if ( x > 5 )
   if ( y > 5 )
      cout << "x and y are > 5";
else
   cout << "x is <= 5";
```

appears to indicate that if x is greater than 5, the nested if statement determines whether y is also greater than 5. If so, "x and y are > 5" is output. Otherwise, it appears that if x is not greater than 5, the else part of the if...else outputs "x is <= 5".

Beware! This nested if...else statement does not execute as it appears. The compiler actually interprets the statement as

```
if ( x > 5 )
   if ( y > 5 )
      cout << "x and y are > 5";
   else
      cout << "x is <= 5";
```

in which the body of the first if is a nested if...else. The outer if statement tests whether x is greater than 5. If so, execution continues by testing whether y is also greater than 5. If the second condition is true, the proper string—"x and y are > 5"—is displayed. However, if the second condition is false, the string "x is <= 5" is displayed, even though we know that x is greater than 5.

To force the nested if...else statement to execute as it was originally intended, we must write it as follows:

```
if ( x > 5 )
{
   if ( y > 5 )
      cout << "x and y are > 5";
}
else
   cout << "x is <= 5";
```

The braces ({}) indicate to the compiler that the second if statement is in the body of the first if and that the else is associated with the first if. Exercise 4.23 and Exercise 4.24 further investigate the dangling-else problem.

Blocks

The if selection statement normally expects only one statement in its body. Similarly, the if and else parts of an if...else statement each expect only one body statement. To include several statements in the body of an if or in either part of an if...else, enclose the statements in braces ({ and }). A set of statements contained within a pair of braces is called a compound statement or a block. We use the term "block" from this point forward.

Software Engineering Observation 4.2

A block can be placed anywhere in a program that a single statement can be placed.

The following example includes a block in the else part of an if...else statement.

```
if ( studentGrade >= 60 )
   cout << "Passed.\n";
else
{
   cout << "Failed.\n";
   cout << "You must take this course again.\n";
}
```

In this case, if studentGrade is less than 60, the program executes both statements in the body of the else and prints

```
Failed.
You must take this course again.
```

Notice the braces surrounding the two statements in the else clause. These braces are important. Without the braces, the statement

```
cout << "You must take this course again.\n";
```

would be outside the body of the else part of the if and would execute regardless of whether the grade is less than 60. This is an example of a logic error.

Common Programming Error 4.3

Forgetting one or both of the braces that delimit a block can lead to syntax errors or logic errors in a program.

Good Programming Practice 4.4

Always putting the braces in an if...else statement (or any control statement) helps prevent their accidental omission, especially when adding statements to an if or else clause at a later time. To avoid omitting one or both of the braces, some programmers prefer to type the beginning and ending braces of blocks even before typing the individual statements within the braces.

Just as a block can be placed anywhere a single statement can be placed, it is also possible to have no statement at all—called a null statement (or an empty statement). The null statement is represented by placing a semicolon (;) where a statement would normally be.

Common Programming Error 4.4

Placing a semicolon after the condition in an if statement leads to a logic error in single-selection if statements and a syntax error in double-selection if...else statements (when the if part contains an actual body statement).

4.7 while Repetition Statement

A repetition statement (also called a looping statement or a loop) allows the programmer to specify that a program should repeat an action while some condition remains true. The pseudocode statement

> *While there are more items on my shopping list*
> *Purchase next item and cross it off my list*

describes the repetition that occurs during a shopping trip. The condition, "there are more items on my shopping list" is either true or false. If it is true, then the action, "Purchase next item and cross it off my list" is performed. This action will be performed repeatedly while the condition remains true. The statement contained in the *While* repetition statement constitutes the body of the *While*, which can be a single statement or a block. Eventually, the condition will become false (when the last item on the shopping list has been purchased and crossed off the list). At this point, the repetition terminates, and the first pseudocode statement after the repetition statement executes.

As an example of C++'s `while` repetition statement, consider a program segment designed to find the first power of 3 larger than 100. Suppose the integer variable `product` has been initialized to 3. When the following `while` repetition statement finishes executing, `product` contains the result:

```
int product = 3;

while ( product <= 100 )
    product = 3 * product;
```

When the `while` statement begins execution, the value of `product` is 3. Each repetition of the `while` statement multiplies product by 3, so `product` takes on the values 9, 27, 81 and 243 successively. When `product` becomes 243, the `while` statement condition—`product <= 100`—becomes `false`. This terminates the repetition, so the final value of `product` is 243. At this point, program execution continues with the next statement after the `while` statement.

Common Programming Error 4.5

Not providing, in the body of a `while` statement, an action that eventually causes the condition in the `while` to become false normally results in a logic error called an infinite loop, *in which the repetition statement never terminates. This can make a program appear to "hang" or "freeze" if the loop body does not contain statements that interact with the user.*

The UML activity diagram of Fig. 4.6 illustrates the flow of control that corresponds to the preceding `while` statement. Once again, the symbols in the diagram (besides the initial state, transition arrows, a final state and three notes) represent an action state and a decision. This diagram also introduces the UML's merge symbol, which joins two flows of activity into one flow of activity. The UML represents both the merge symbol and the decision symbol as diamonds. In this diagram, the merge symbol joins the transitions from the initial state and from the action state, so they both flow into the decision that determines whether the loop should begin (or continue) executing. The decision and merge symbols can be distinguished by the number of "incoming" and "outgoing" transition arrows. A decision symbol has one transition arrow pointing to the diamond and two or more transition arrows pointing out from the diamond to indicate possible transitions from that point. In addition, each transition arrow pointing out of a decision symbol has a guard condition next to it. A merge symbol has two or more transition arrows pointing to the diamond and only one transition arrow pointing from the diamond, to indicate multiple activity flows merging to continue the activity. Note that, unlike the decision symbol, the merge symbol does not have a counterpart in C++ code. None of the transition arrows associated with a merge symbol have guard conditions.

The diagram of Fig. 4.6 clearly shows the repetition of the `while` statement discussed earlier in this section. The transition arrow emerging from the action state points to the merge, which transitions back to the decision that is tested each time through the loop until the guard condition `product > 100` becomes true. Then the `while` statement exits (reaches its final state) and control passes to the next statement in sequence in the program.

Imagine a deep bin of empty UML `while` repetition statement activity diagrams—as many as the programmer might need to stack and nest with the activity diagrams of other control statements to form a structured implementation of an algorithm. The programmer fills in the action states and decision symbols with action expressions and guard conditions appropriate to the algorithm.

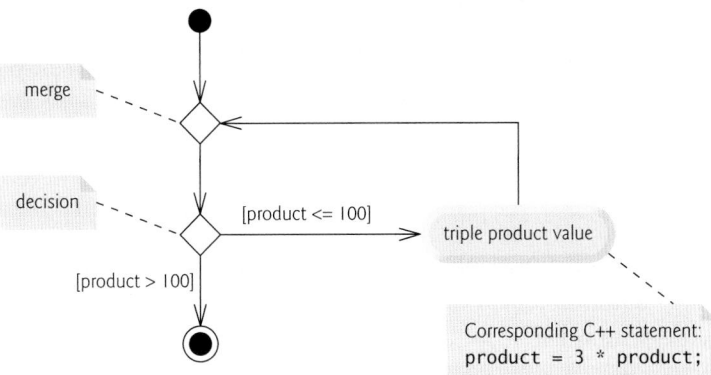

Fig. 4.6 | `while` repetition statement UML activity diagram.

> **Performance Tip 4.3**
>
> *Many of the performance tips we mention in this text result in only small improvements, so the reader might be tempted to ignore them. However, a small performance improvement for code that executes many times in a loop can result in substantial overall performance improvement.*

4.8 Formulating Algorithms: Counter-Controlled Repetition

To illustrate how programmers develop algorithms, this section and Section 4.9 solve two variations of a class average problem. Consider the following problem statement:

> *A class of ten students took a quiz. The grades (integers in the range 0 to 100) for this quiz are available to you. Calculate and display the total of all student grades and the class average on the quiz.*

The class average is equal to the sum of the grades divided by the number of students. The algorithm for solving this problem on a computer must input each of the grades, calculate the average and print the result.

Pseudocode Algorithm with Counter-Controlled Repetition

Let's use pseudocode to list the actions to execute and specify the order in which these actions should occur. We use counter-controlled repetition to input the grades one at a time. This technique uses a variable called a counter to control the number of times a group of statements will execute (also known as the number of iterations of the loop).

Counter-controlled repetition is often called definite repetition because the number of repetitions is known before the loop begins executing. In this example, repetition terminates when the counter exceeds 10. This section presents a fully developed pseudocode algorithm (Fig. 4.7) and a version of class GradeBook (Fig. 4.8–Fig. 4.9) that implements the algorithm in a C++ member function. The section then presents an application (Fig. 4.10) that demonstrates the algorithm in action. In Section 4.9 we demonstrate how to use pseudocode to develop such an algorithm from scratch.

> **Software Engineering Observation 4.3**
>
> *Experience has shown that the most difficult part of solving a problem on a computer is developing the algorithm for the solution. Once a correct algorithm has been specified, the process of producing a working C++ program from the algorithm is normally straightforward.*

Note the references in the pseudocode algorithm of Fig. 4.7 to a total and a counter. A total is a variable used to accumulate the sum of several values. A counter is a variable used to count—in this case, the grade counter indicates which of the 10 grades is about to be entered by the user. Variables used to store totals are normally initialized to zero before being used in a program; otherwise, the sum would include the previous value stored in the total's memory location.

```
 1   Set total to zero
 2   Set grade counter to one
 3
 4   While grade counter is less than or equal to ten
 5       Prompt the user to enter the next grade
 6       Input the next grade
 7       Add the grade into the total
 8       Add one to the grade counter
 9
10   Set the class average to the total divided by ten
11   Print the total of the grades for all students in the class
12   Print the class average
```

Fig. 4.7 | Pseudocode algorithm that uses counter-controlled repetition to solve the class average problem.

```cpp
 1   // Fig. 4.8: GradeBook.h
 2   // Definition of class GradeBook that determines a class average.
 3   // Member functions are defined in GradeBook.cpp
 4   #include <string> // program uses C++ standard string class
 5   using std::string;
 6
 7   // GradeBook class definition
 8   class GradeBook
 9   {
10   public:
11      GradeBook( string ); // constructor initializes course name
12      void setCourseName( string ); // function to set the course name
13      string getCourseName(); // function to retrieve the course name
14      void displayMessage(); // display a welcome message
15      void determineClassAverage(); // averages grades entered by the user
16   private:
17      string courseName; // course name for this GradeBook
18   }; // end class GradeBook
```

Fig. 4.8 | Class average problem using counter-controlled repetition: GradeBook header file.

```cpp
1   // Fig. 4.9: GradeBook.cpp
2   // Member-function definitions for class GradeBook that solves the
3   // class average program with counter-controlled repetition.
4   #include <iostream>
5   using std::cout;
6   using std::cin;
7   using std::endl;
8
9   #include "GradeBook.h" // include definition of class GradeBook
10
11  // constructor initializes courseName with string supplied as argument
12  GradeBook::GradeBook( string name )
13  {
14     setCourseName( name ); // validate and store courseName
15  } // end GradeBook constructor
16
17  // function to set the course name;
18  // ensures that the course name has at most 25 characters
19  void GradeBook::setCourseName( string name )
20  {
21     if ( name.length() <= 25 ) // if name has 25 or fewer characters
22        courseName = name; // store the course name in the object
23     else // if name is longer than 25 characters
24     { // set courseName to first 25 characters of parameter name
25        courseName = name.substr( 0, 25 ); // select first 25 characters
26        cout << "Name \"" << name << "\" exceeds maximum length (25).\n"
27           << "Limiting courseName to first 25 characters.\n" << endl;
28     } // end if...else
29  } // end function setCourseName
30
31  // function to retrieve the course name
32  string GradeBook::getCourseName()
33  {
34     return courseName;
35  } // end function getCourseName
36
37  // display a welcome message to the GradeBook user
38  void GradeBook::displayMessage()
39  {
40     cout << "Welcome to the grade book for\n" << getCourseName() << "!\n"
41        << endl;
42  } // end function displayMessage
43
44  // determine class average based on 10 grades entered by user
45  void GradeBook::determineClassAverage()
46  {
47     int total; // sum of grades entered by user
48     int gradeCounter; // number of the grade to be entered next
49     int grade; // grade value entered by user
50     int average; // average of grades
51
```

Fig. 4.9 | Class average problem using counter-controlled repetition: GradeBook source code file. (Part 1 of 2.)

```
52        // initialization phase
53        total = 0; // initialize total
54        gradeCounter = 1; // initialize loop counter
55
56        // processing phase
57        while ( gradeCounter <= 10 ) // loop 10 times
58        {
59           cout << "Enter grade: "; // prompt for input
60           cin >> grade; // input next grade
61           total = total + grade; // add grade to total
62           gradeCounter = gradeCounter + 1; // increment counter by 1
63        } // end while
64
65        // termination phase
66        average = total / 10; // integer division yields integer result
67
68        // display total and average of grades
69        cout << "\nTotal of all 10 grades is " << total << endl;
70        cout << "Class average is " << average << endl;
71     } // end function determineClassAverage
```

Fig. 4.9 | Class average problem using counter-controlled repetition: `GradeBook` source code file. (Part 2 of 2.)

Enhancing GradeBook Validation

Before we discuss the implementation of the class average algorithm, let's consider an enhancement we made to our GradeBook class. In Fig. 3.16, our setCourseName member function would validate the course name by first testing if the course name's length was less than or equal to 25 characters, using an if statement. If this was true, the course name would be set. This code was then followed by another if statement that tested if the course name's length was larger than 25 characters (in which case the course name would be shortened). Notice that the second if statement's condition is the exact opposite of the first if statement's condition. If one condition evaluates to true, the other must evaluate to false. Such a situation is ideal for an if...else statement, so we have modified our code, replacing the two if statements with one if...else statement (lines 21–28 of Fig. 4.9).

Implementing Counter-Controlled Repetition in Class GradeBook

Class GradeBook (Fig. 4.8–Fig. 4.9) contains a constructor (declared in line 11 of Fig. 4.8 and defined in lines 12–15 of Fig. 4.9) that assigns a value to the class's instance variable courseName (declared in line 17 of Fig. 4.8). Lines 19–29, 32–35 and 38–42 of Fig. 4.9 define member functions setCourseName, getCourseName and displayMessage, respectively. Lines 45–71 define member function determineClassAverage, which implements the class average algorithm described by the pseudocode in Fig. 4.7.

Lines 47–50 declare local variables total, gradeCounter, grade and average to be of type int. Variable grade stores the user input. Notice that the preceding declarations appear in the body of member function determineClassAverage.

In this chapter's versions of class GradeBook, we simply read and process a set of grades. The averaging calculation is performed in member function determineClassAverage using local variables—we do not preserve any information about student grades in the

```
1   // Fig. 4.10: fig04_10.cpp
2   // Create GradeBook object and invoke its determineClassAverage function.
3   #include "GradeBook.h" // include definition of class GradeBook
4
5   int main()
6   {
7      // create GradeBook object myGradeBook and
8      // pass course name to constructor
9      GradeBook myGradeBook( "CS101 C++ Programming" );
10
11     myGradeBook.displayMessage(); // display welcome message
12     myGradeBook.determineClassAverage(); // find average of 10 grades
13     return 0; // indicate successful termination
14  } // end main
```

```
Welcome to the grade book for
CS101 C++ Programming

Enter grade: 67
Enter grade: 78
Enter grade: 89
Enter grade: 67
Enter grade: 87
Enter grade: 98
Enter grade: 93
Enter grade: 85
Enter grade: 82
Enter grade: 100

Total of all 10 grades is 846
Class average is 84
```

Fig. 4.10 | Class average problem using counter-controlled repetition: Creating an object of class GradeBook (Fig. 4.8–Fig. 4.9) and invoking its determineClassAverage member function.

class's instance variables. In Chapter 7, Arrays and Vectors, we modify class GradeBook to maintain the grades in memory using an instance variable that refers to a data structure known as an array. This allows a GradeBook object to perform various calculations on the same set of grades without requiring the user to enter the grades multiple times.

 Good Programming Practice 4.5

Separate declarations from other statements in functions with a blank line for readability.

Lines 53–54 initialize total to 0 and gradeCounter to 1. Note that variables total and gradeCounter are initialized before they are used in a calculation. Counter variables normally are initialized to zero or one, depending on their use (we will present examples showing each possibility). An uninitialized variable contains a "garbage" value (also called an undefined value)—the value last stored in the memory location reserved for that variable. Variables grade and average (for the user input and calculated average, respectively) need not be initialized here—their values will be assigned as they are input or calculated later in the function.

Common Programming Error 4.6

Not initializing counters and totals can lead to logic errors.

Error-Prevention Tip 4.2

Initialize each counter and total, either in its declaration or in an assignment statement. Totals are normally initialized to 0. Counters are normally initialized to 0 or 1, depending on how they are used (we will show examples of when to use 0 and when to use 1).

Good Programming Practice 4.6

Declare each variable on a separate line with its own comment to make programs more readable.

Line 57 indicates that the while statement should continue looping (also called iterating) as long as gradeCounter's value is less than or equal to 10. While this condition remains true, the while statement repeatedly executes the statements between the braces that delimit its body (lines 58–63).

Line 59 displays the prompt "Enter grade: ". This line corresponds to the pseudocode statement *"Prompt the user to enter the next grade."* Line 60 reads the grade entered by the user and assigns it to variable grade. This line corresponds to the pseudocode statement *"Input the next grade."* Recall that variable grade was not initialized earlier in the program, because the program obtains the value for grade from the user during each iteration of the loop. Line 61 adds the new grade entered by the user to the total and assigns the result to total, which replaces its previous value.

Line 62 adds 1 to gradeCounter to indicate that the program has processed a grade and is ready to input the next grade from the user. Incrementing gradeCounter eventually causes gradeCounter to exceed 10. At that point the while loop terminates because its condition (line 57) becomes false.

When the loop terminates, line 66 performs the averaging calculation and assigns its result to the variable average. Line 69 displays the text "Total of all 10 grades is " followed by variable total's value. Line 70 then displays the text "Class average is " followed by variable average's value. Member function determineClassAverage, then returns control to the calling function (i.e., main in Fig. 4.10).

Demonstrating Class *GradeBook*

Figure 4.10 contains this application's main function, which creates an object of class GradeBook and demonstrates its capabilities. Line 9 of Fig. 4.10 creates a new GradeBook object called myGradeBook. The string in line 9 is passed to the GradeBook constructor (lines 12–15 of Fig. 4.9). Line 11 of Fig. 4.10 calls myGradeBook's displayMessage member function to display a welcome message to the user. Line 12 then calls myGradeBook's determineClassAverage member function to allow the user to enter 10 grades, for which the member function then calculates and prints the average—the member function performs the algorithm shown in the pseudocode of Fig. 4.7.

Notes on Integer Division and Truncation

The averaging calculation performed by member function determineClassAverage in response to the function call at line 12 in Fig. 4.10 produces an integer result. The program's output indicates that the sum of the grade values in the sample execution is 846, which, when divided by 10, should yield 84.6—a number with a decimal point. However, the result of the calculation `total / 10` (line 66 of Fig. 4.9) is the integer 84, because `total` and 10 are both integers. Dividing two integers results in integer division—any fractional part of the calculation is lost (i.e., *truncated*). We will see how to obtain a result that includes a decimal point from the averaging calculation in the next section.

Common Programming Error 4.7

Assuming that integer division rounds (rather than truncates) can lead to incorrect results. For example, 7 ÷ 4, which yields 1.75 in conventional arithmetic, truncates to 1 in integer arithmetic, rather than rounding to 2.

In Fig. 4.9, if line 66 used `gradeCounter` rather than 10 for the calculation, the output for this program would display an incorrect value, 76. This occurs because in the final iteration of the `while` statement, `gradeCounter` was incremented to the value 11 in line 62.

Common Programming Error 4.8

Using a loop's counter-control variable in a calculation after the loop often causes a common logic error called an off-by-one-error. *In a counter-controlled loop that counts up by one each time through the loop, the loop terminates when the counter's value is one higher than its last legitimate value (i.e., 11 in the case of counting from 1 to 10).*

4.9 Formulating Algorithms: Sentinel-Controlled Repetition

Let us generalize the class average problem. Consider the following problem:

> *Develop a class average program that processes grades for an arbitrary number of students each time it is run.*

In the previous class average example, the problem statement specified the number of students, so the number of grades (10) was known in advance. In this example, no indication is given of how many grades the user will enter during the program's execution. The program must process an arbitrary number of grades. How can the program determine when to stop the input of grades? How will it know when to calculate and print the class average?

One way to solve this problem is to use a special value called a sentinel value (also called a signal value, a dummy value or a flag value) to indicate "end of data entry." The user types grades in until all legitimate grades have been entered. The user then types the sentinel value to indicate that the last grade has been entered. Sentinel-controlled repetition is often called indefinite repetition because the number of repetitions is not known before the loop begins executing.

Clearly, the sentinel value must be chosen so that it cannot be confused with an acceptable input value. Grades on a quiz are normally nonnegative integers, so –1 is an acceptable sentinel value for this problem. Thus, a run of the class average program might process a stream of inputs such as 95, 96, 75, 74, 89 and –1. The program would then compute and print the class average for the grades 95, 96, 75, 74 and 89. Since –1 is the sentinel value, it should not enter into the averaging calculation.

Common Programming Error 4.9

Choosing a sentinel value that is also a legitimate data value is a logic error.

Developing the Pseudocode Algorithm with Top-Down, Stepwise Refinement: The Top and First Refinement

We approach the class average program with a technique called top-down, stepwise refinement, a technique that is essential to the development of well-structured programs. We begin with a pseudocode representation of the top—a single statement that conveys the overall function of the program:

> *Determine the class average for the quiz*

The top is, in effect, a *complete* representation of a program. Unfortunately, the top (as in this case) rarely conveys sufficient detail from which to write a program. So we now begin the refinement process. We divide the top into a series of smaller tasks and list these in the order in which they need to be performed. This results in the following first refinement.

> *Initialize variables*
> *Input, sum and count the quiz grades*
> *Calculate and print the total of all student grades and the class average*

This refinement uses only the sequence structure—the steps listed should execute in order, one after the other.

 Software Engineering Observation 4.4

Each refinement, as well as the top itself, is a complete specification of the algorithm; only the level of detail varies.

 Software Engineering Observation 4.5

Many programs can be divided logically into three phases: an initialization phase that initializes the program variables; a processing phase that inputs data values and adjusts program variables (such as counters and totals) accordingly; and a termination phase that calculates and outputs the final results.

Proceeding to the Second Refinement

The preceding *Software Engineering Observation* is often all you need for the first refinement in the top-down process. To proceed to the next level of refinement, i.e., the second refinement, we commit to specific variables. In this example, we need a running total of the numbers, a count of how many numbers have been processed, a variable to receive the value of each grade as it is input by the user and a variable to hold the calculated average. The pseudocode statement

> *Initialize variables*

can be refined as follows:

> *Initialize total to zero*
> *Initialize counter to zero*

Only the variables *total* and *counter* need to be initialized before they are used. The variables *average* and *grade* (for the calculated average and the user input, respectively) need not be initialized, because their values will be replaced as they are calculated or input.

The pseudocode statement

   Input, sum and count the quiz grades

requires a repetition statement (i.e., a loop) that successively inputs each grade. We do not know in advance how many grades are to be processed, so we will use sentinel-controlled repetition. The user enters legitimate grades one at a time. After entering the last legitimate grade, the user enters the sentinel value. The program tests for the sentinel value after each grade is input and terminates the loop when the user enters the sentinel value. The second refinement of the preceding pseudocode statement is then

   Prompt the user to enter the first grade
   Input the first grade (possibly the sentinel)

   While the user has not yet entered the sentinel
      Add this grade into the running total
      Add one to the grade counter
      Prompt the user to enter the next grade
      Input the next grade (possibly the sentinel)

In pseudocode, we do not use braces around the statements that form the body of the *While* structure. We simply indent the statements under the *While* to show that they belong to the *While*. Again, pseudocode is only an informal program development aid.

   The pseudocode statement

   Calculate and print the total of all student grades and the class average

can be refined as follows:

   If the counter is not equal to zero
      Set the average to the total divided by the counter
      Print the total of the grades for all students in the class
      Print the class average
   else
      Print "No grades were entered"

We are careful here to test for the possibility of division by zero—normally a fatal logic error that, if undetected, would cause the program to fail (often called "bombing" or "crashing"). The complete second refinement of the pseudocode for the class average problem is shown in Fig. 4.11.

Common Programming Error 4.10

An attempt to divide by zero normally causes a fatal runtime error.

Error-Prevention Tip 4.3

When performing division by an expression whose value could be zero, explicitly test for this possibility and handle it appropriately in your program (such as by printing an error message) rather than allowing the fatal error to occur.

   In Fig. 4.7 and Fig. 4.11, we include some blank lines and indentation in the pseudocode to make it more readable. The blank lines separate the pseudocode algorithms into their various phases, and the indentation emphasizes the control statement bodies.

1   *Initialize total to zero*
2   *Initialize counter to zero*
3
4   *Prompt the user to enter the first grade*
5   *Input the first grade (possibly the sentinel)*
6
7   *While the user has not yet entered the sentinel*
8   *Add this grade into the running total*
9   *Add one to the grade counter*
10   *Prompt the user to enter the next grade*
11   *Input the next grade (possibly the sentinel)*
12
13   *If the counter is not equal to zero*
14   *Set the average to the total divided by the counter*
15   *Print the total of the grades for all students in the class*
16   *Print the class average*
17   *else*
18   *Print "No grades were entered"*

Fig. 4.11 | Class average problem pseudocode algorithm with sentinel-controlled repetition.

The pseudocode algorithm in Fig. 4.11 solves the more general class average problem. This algorithm was developed after only two levels of refinement. Sometimes more levels are necessary.

Software Engineering Observation 4.6

Terminate the top-down, stepwise refinement process when the pseudocode algorithm is specified in sufficient detail for you to be able to convert the pseudocode to C++. Normally, implementing the C++ program is then straightforward.

Software Engineering Observation 4.7

Many experienced programmers write programs without ever using program development tools like pseudocode. These programmers feel that their ultimate goal is to solve the problem on a computer and that writing pseudocode merely delays the production of final outputs. Although this method might work for simple and familiar problems, it can lead to serious difficulties in large, complex projects.

Implementing Sentinel-Controlled Repetition in Class *GradeBook*

Figures 4.12 and 4.13 show the C++ class GradeBook containing member function determineClassAverage that implements the pseudocode algorithm of Fig. 4.11 (this class is demonstrated in Fig. 4.14). Although each grade entered is an integer, the averaging calculation is likely to produce a number with a decimal point—in other words, a real number or floating-point number (e.g., 7.33, 0.0975 or 1000.12345). The type int cannot represent such a number, so this class must use another type to do so. C++ provides several data types for storing floating-point numbers in memory, including float and double. The primary difference between these types is that, compared to float variables, double variables can store numbers with larger magnitude and finer detail (i.e., more digits to the right of the decimal point—also known as the number's precision). This program introduces a special operator called a cast operator to force the averaging calculation to produce a floating-point numeric result. These features are explained in detail as we discuss the program.

In this example, we see that control statements can be stacked on top of one another (in sequence) just as a child stacks building blocks. The while statement (lines 67–75 of Fig. 4.13) is immediately followed by an if...else statement (lines 78–90) in sequence. Much of the code in this program is identical to the code in Fig. 4.9, so we concentrate on the new features and issues.

```
1   // Fig. 4.12: GradeBook.h
2   // Definition of class GradeBook that determines a class average.
3   // Member functions are defined in GradeBook.cpp
4   #include <string> // program uses C++ standard string class
5   using std::string;
6
7   // GradeBook class definition
8   class GradeBook
9   {
10  public:
11     GradeBook( string ); // constructor initializes course name
12     void setCourseName( string ); // function to set the course name
13     string getCourseName(); // function to retrieve the course name
14     void displayMessage(); // display a welcome message
15     void determineClassAverage(); // averages grades entered by the user
16  private:
17     string courseName; // course name for this GradeBook
18  }; // end class GradeBook
```

Fig. 4.12 | Class average problem using sentinel-controlled repetition: GradeBook header file.

```
1   // Fig. 4.13: GradeBook.cpp
2   // Member-function definitions for class GradeBook that solves the
3   // class average program with sentinel-controlled repetition.
4   #include <iostream>
5   using std::cout;
6   using std::cin;
7   using std::endl;
8   using std::fixed; // ensures that decimal point is displayed
9
10  #include <iomanip> // parameterized stream manipulators
11  using std::setprecision; // sets numeric output precision
12
13  // include definition of class GradeBook from GradeBook.h
14  #include "GradeBook.h"
15
```

Fig. 4.13 | Class average problem using sentinel-controlled repetition: GradeBook source code file. (Part 1 of 3.)

```
16   // constructor initializes courseName with string supplied as argument
17   GradeBook::GradeBook( string name )
18   {
19      setCourseName( name ); // validate and store courseName
20   } // end GradeBook constructor
21
22   // function to set the course name;
23   // ensures that the course name has at most 25 characters
24   void GradeBook::setCourseName( string name )
25   {
26      if ( name.length() <= 25 ) // if name has 25 or fewer characters
27         courseName = name; // store the course name in the object
28      else // if name is longer than 25 characters
29      { // set courseName to first 25 characters of parameter name
30         courseName = name.substr( 0, 25 ); // select first 25 characters
31         cout << "Name \"" << name << "\" exceeds maximum length (25).\n"
32            << "Limiting courseName to first 25 characters.\n" << endl;
33      } // end if...else
34   } // end function setCourseName
35
36   // function to retrieve the course name
37   string GradeBook::getCourseName()
38   {
39      return courseName;
40   } // end function getCourseName
41
42   // display a welcome message to the GradeBook user
43   void GradeBook::displayMessage()
44   {
45      cout << "Welcome to the grade book for\n" << getCourseName() << "!\n"
46         << endl;
47   } // end function displayMessage
48
49   // determine class average based on 10 grades entered by user
50   void GradeBook::determineClassAverage()
51   {
52      int total; // sum of grades entered by user
53      int gradeCounter; // number of grades entered
54      int grade; // grade value
55      double average; // number with decimal point for average
56
57      // initialization phase
58      total = 0; // initialize total
59      gradeCounter = 0; // initialize loop counter
60
61      // processing phase
62      // prompt for input and read grade from user
63      cout << "Enter grade or -1 to quit: ";
64      cin >> grade; // input grade or sentinel value
65
```

Fig. 4.13 | Class average problem using sentinel-controlled repetition: GradeBook source code file. (Part 2 of 3.)

```
66      // loop until sentinel value read from user
67      while ( grade != -1 ) // while grade is not -1
68      {
69         total = total + grade; // add grade to total
70         gradeCounter = gradeCounter + 1; // increment counter
71
72         // prompt for input and read next grade from user
73         cout << "Enter grade or -1 to quit: ";
74         cin >> grade; // input grade or sentinel value
75      } // end while
76
77      // termination phase
78      if ( gradeCounter != 0 ) // if user entered at least one grade...
79      {
80         // calculate average of all grades entered
81         average = static_cast< double >( total ) / gradeCounter;
82
83         // display total and average (with two digits of precision)
84         cout << "\nTotal of all " << gradeCounter << " grades entered is "
85            << total << endl;
86         cout << "Class average is " << setprecision( 2 ) << fixed << average
87            << endl;
88      } // end if
89      else // no grades were entered, so output appropriate message
90         cout << "No grades were entered" << endl;
91   } // end function determineClassAverage
```

Fig. 4.13 | Class average problem using sentinel-controlled repetition: GradeBook source code file. (Part 3 of 3.)

```
1    // Fig. 4.14: fig04_14.cpp
2    // Create GradeBook object and invoke its determineClassAverage function.
3
4    // include definition of class GradeBook from GradeBook.h
5    #include "GradeBook.h"
6
7    int main()
8    {
9       // create GradeBook object myGradeBook and
10      // pass course name to constructor
11      GradeBook myGradeBook( "CS101 C++ Programming" );
12
13      myGradeBook.displayMessage(); // display welcome message
14      myGradeBook.determineClassAverage(); // find average of 10 grades
15      return 0; // indicate successful termination
16   } // end main
```

Fig. 4.14 | Class average problem using sentinel-controlled repetition: Creating an object of class GradeBook (Fig. 4.12–Fig. 4.13) and invoking its determineClassAverage member function. (Part 1 of 2.)

```
Welcome to the grade book for
CS101 C++ Programming

Enter grade or -1 to quit: 97
Enter grade or -1 to quit: 88
Enter grade or -1 to quit: 72
Enter grade or -1 to quit: -1

Total of all 3 grades entered is 257
Class average is 85.67
```

Fig. 4.14 | Class average problem using sentinel-controlled repetition: Creating an object of class GradeBook (Fig. 4.12–Fig. 4.13) and invoking its determineClassAverage member function. (Part 2 of 2.)

Line 55 declares the double variable average. Recall that we used an int variable in the preceding example to store the class average. Using type double in the current example allows us to store the class average calculation's result as a floating-point number. Line 59 initializes the variable gradeCounter to 0, because no grades have been entered yet. Remember that this program uses sentinel-controlled repetition. To keep an accurate record of the number of grades entered, the program increments variable gradeCounter only when the user enters a valid grade value (i.e., not the sentinel value) and the program completes the processing of the grade. Finally, notice that both input statements (lines 64 and 74) are preceded by an output statement that prompts the user for input.

 Good Programming Practice 4.7

Prompt the user for each keyboard input. The prompt should indicate the form of the input and any special input values. For example, in a sentinel-controlled loop, the prompts requesting data entry should explicitly remind the user what the sentinel value is.

Program Logic for Sentinel-Controlled Repetition vs. Counter-Controlled Repetition
Compare the program logic for sentinel-controlled repetition in this application with that for counter-controlled repetition in Fig. 4.9. In counter-controlled repetition, each iteration of the while statement (lines 57–63 of Fig. 4.9) reads a value from the user, for the specified number of iterations. In sentinel-controlled repetition, the program reads the first value (lines 63–64 of Fig. 4.13) before reaching the while. This value determines whether the program's flow of control should enter the body of the while. If the condition of the while is false, the user entered the sentinel value, so the body of the while does not execute (i.e., no grades were entered). If, on the other hand, the condition is true, the body begins execution, and the loop adds the grade value to the total (line 69). Then lines 73–74 in the loop's body input the next value from the user. Next, program control reaches the closing right brace (}) of the body at line 75, so execution continues with the test of the while's condition (line 67). The condition uses the most recent grade input by the user to determine whether the loop's body should execute again. Note that the value of variable grade is always input from the user immediately before the program tests the while condition. This allows the program to determine whether the value just input is the sentinel value *before* the program processes that value (i.e., adds it to the total and incre-

ments `gradeCounter`). If the sentinel value is input, the loop terminates, and the program does not add –1 to the `total`.

After the loop terminates, the `if...else` statement at lines 78–90 executes. The condition at line 78 determines whether any grades were entered. If none were, the `else` part (lines 89–90) of the `if...else` statement executes and displays the message "No grades were entered" and the member function returns control to the calling function.

Notice the block in the `while` loop in Fig. 4.13. Without the braces, the last three statements in the body of the loop would fall outside the loop, causing the computer to interpret this code incorrectly, as follows:

```
// loop until sentinel value read from user
while ( grade != -1 )
   total = total + grade; // add grade to total
gradeCounter = gradeCounter + 1; // increment counter

// prompt for input and read next grade from user
cout << "Enter grade or -1 to quit: ";
cin >> grade;
```

This would cause an infinite loop in the program if the user did not input –1 for the first grade (at line 64).

Common Programming Error 4.11

Omitting the braces that delimit a block can lead to logic errors, such as infinite loops. To prevent this problem, some programmers enclose the body of every control statement in braces, even if the body contains only a single statement.

Floating-Point Number Precision and Memory Requirements

Variables of type `float` represent single-precision floating-point numbers and have seven significant digits on most 32-bit systems today. Variables of type `double` represent double-precision floating-point numbers. These require twice as much memory as `float` variables and provide 15 significant digits on most 32-bit systems today—approximately double the precision of `float` variables. For the range of values required by most programs, variables of type `float` should suffice, but you can use `double` to "play it safe." In some programs, even variables of type `double` will be inadequate—such programs are beyond the scope of this book. Most programmers represent floating-point numbers with type `double`. In fact, C++ treats all floating-point numbers you type in a program's source code (such as 7.33 and 0.0975) as `double` values by default. Such values in the source code are known as floating-point constants. See Appendix C, Fundamental Types, for the ranges of values for `float`s and `double`s.

Floating-point numbers often arise as a result of division. In conventional arithmetic, when we divide 10 by 3, the result is 3.3333333…, with the sequence of 3s repeating infinitely. The computer allocates only a fixed amount of space to hold such a value, so clearly the stored floating-point value can be only an approximation.

Common Programming Error 4.12

Using floating-point numbers in a manner that assumes they are represented exactly (e.g., using them in comparisons for equality) can lead to incorrect results. Floating-point numbers are represented only approximately by most computers.

Although floating-point numbers are not always 100% precise, they have numerous applications. For example, when we speak of a "normal" body temperature of 98.6, we do not need to be precise to a large number of digits. When we read the temperature on a thermometer as 98.6, it may actually be 98.5999473210643. Calling this number simply 98.6 is fine for most applications involving body temperatures. Due to the imprecise nature of floating-point numbers, type `double` is preferred over type `float`, because `double` variables can represent floating-point numbers more accurately. For this reason, we use type `double` throughout the book.

Converting Between Fundamental Types Explicitly and Implicitly

The variable `average` is declared to be of type `double` (line 55 of Fig. 4.13) to capture the fractional result of our calculation. However, `total` and `gradeCounter` are both integer variables. Recall that dividing two integers results in integer division, in which any fractional part of the calculation is lost (i.e., *truncated*). In the following statement:

```
average = total / gradeCounter;
```

the division calculation is performed first, so the fractional part of the result is lost before it is assigned to `average`. To perform a floating-point calculation with integer values, we must create temporary values that are floating-point numbers for the calculation. C++ provides the unary cast operator to accomplish this task. Line 81 uses the cast operator `static_cast< double >( total )` to create a *temporary* floating-point copy of its operand in parentheses—`total`. Using a cast operator in this manner is called explicit conversion. The value stored in `total` is still an integer.

The calculation now consists of a floating-point value (the temporary `double` version of `total`) divided by the integer `gradeCounter`. The C++ compiler knows how to evaluate only expressions in which the data types of the operands are identical. To ensure that the operands are of the same type, the compiler performs an operation called promotion (also called implicit conversion) on selected operands. For example, in an expression containing values of data types `int` and `double`, C++ promotes `int` operands to `double` values. In our example, we are treating `total` as a `double` (by using the unary cast operator), so the compiler promotes `gradeCounter` to `double`, allowing the calculation to be performed—the result of the floating-point division is assigned to `average`. In Chapter 6, Functions and an Introduction to Recursion, we discuss all the fundamental data types and their order of promotion.

 Common Programming Error 4.13

The cast operator can be used to convert between fundamental numeric types, such as `int` and `double`, and between related class types (as we discuss in Chapter 13, Object-Oriented Programming: Polymorphism). Casting to the wrong type may cause compilation errors or runtime errors.

Cast operators are available for use with every data type and with class types as well. The `static_cast` operator is formed by following keyword `static_cast` with angle brackets (< and >) around a data type name. The cast operator is a unary operator—an operator that takes only one operand. In Chapter 2, we studied the binary arithmetic operators. C++ also supports unary versions of the plus (+) and minus (-) operators, so that the programmer can write such expressions as -7 or +5. Cast operators have higher precedence than other unary operators, such as unary + and unary -. This precedence is higher than that of the multiplicative operators *, / and %, and lower than that of parentheses. We indicate the cast operator with the notation `static_cast< type >()` in our precedence charts (see, for example, Fig. 4.22).

Formatting for Floating-Point Numbers

The formatting capabilities in Fig. 4.13 are discussed here briefly and explained in depth in Chapter 15, Stream Input/Output. The call to `setprecision` in line 86 (with an argument of 2) indicates that `double` variable `average` should be printed with two digits of precision to the right of the decimal point (e.g., 92.37). This call is referred to as a parameterized stream manipulator (because of the 2 in parentheses). Programs that use these calls must contain the preprocessor directive (line 10)

```
#include <iomanip>
```

Line 11 specifies the names from the `<iomanip>` header file that are used in this program. Note that `endl` is a nonparameterized stream manipulator (because it is not followed by a value or expression in parentheses) and does not require the `<iomanip>` header file. If the precision is not specified, floating-point values are normally output with six digits of precision (i.e., the default precision on most 32-bit systems today), although we will see an exception to this in a moment.

The stream manipulator `fixed` (line 86) indicates that floating-point values should be output in so-called fixed-point format, as opposed to scientific notation. Scientific notation is a way of displaying a number as a floating-point number between the values of 1 and 10, multiplied by a power of 10. For instance, the value 3,100 would be displayed in scientific notation as 3.1×10^3. Scientific notation is useful when displaying values that are very large or very small. Formatting using scientific notation is discussed further in Chapter 15. Fixed-point formatting, on the other hand, is used to force a floating-point number to display a specific number of digits. Specifying fixed-point formatting also forces the decimal point and trailing zeros to print, even if the value is a whole number amount, such as 88.00. Without the fixed-point formatting option, such a value prints in C++ as 88 without the trailing zeros and without the decimal point. When the stream manipulators `fixed` and `setprecision` are used in a program, the printed value is rounded to the number of decimal positions indicated by the value passed to `setprecision` (e.g., the value 2 in line 86), although the value in memory remains unaltered. For example, the values 87.946 and 67.543 are output as 87.95 and 67.54, respectively. Note that it also is possible to force a decimal point to appear by using stream manipulator `showpoint`. If `showpoint` is specified without `fixed`, then trailing zeros will not print. Like `endl`, stream manipulators `fixed` and `showpoint` are nonparameterized and do not require the `<iomanip>` header file. Both can be found in header `<iostream>`.

Lines 86 and 87 of Fig. 4.13 output the class average. In this example, we display the class average rounded to the nearest hundredth and output it with exactly two digits to the right of the decimal point. The parameterized stream manipulator (line 86) indicates that variable `average`'s value should be displayed with two digits of precision to the right of the decimal point—indicated by `setprecision( 2 )`. The three grades entered during the sample execution of the program in Fig. 4.14 total 257, which yields the average 85.666666.... The parameterized stream manipulator `setprecision` causes the value to be rounded to the specified number of digits. In this program, the average is rounded to the hundredths position and displayed as `85.67`.

4.10 Formulating Algorithms: Nested Control Statements

For the next example, we once again formulate an algorithm by using pseudocode and top-down, stepwise refinement, and write a corresponding C++ program. We have seen that control statements can be stacked on top of one another (in sequence) just as a child stacks building blocks. In this case study, we examine the only other structured way control statements can be connected, namely, by **nesting** one control statement within another.

Consider the following problem statement:

> *A college offers a course that prepares students for the state licensing exam for real estate brokers. Last year, ten of the students who completed this course took the exam. The college wants to know how well its students did on the exam. You have been asked to write a program to summarize the results. You have been given a list of these 10 students. Next to each name is written a 1 if the student passed the exam or a 2 if the student failed.*
>
> *Your program should analyze the results of the exam as follows:*
>
> > *1. Input each test result (i.e., a 1 or a 2). Display the prompting message "Enter result" each time the program requests another test result.*
> >
> > *2. Count the number of test results of each type.*
> >
> > *3. Display a summary of the test results indicating the number of students who passed and the number who failed.*
> >
> > *4. If more than eight students passed the exam, print the message "Raise tuition."*

After reading the problem statement carefully, we make the following observations:

1. The program must process test results for 10 students. A counter-controlled loop can be used because the number of test results is known in advance.

2. Each test result is a number—either a 1 or a 2. Each time the program reads a test result, the program must determine whether the number is a 1 or a 2. We test for a 1 in our algorithm. If the number is not a 1, we assume that it is a 2. (Exercise 4.20 considers the consequences of this assumption.)

3. Two counters are used to keep track of the exam results—one to count the number of students who passed the exam and one to count the number of students who failed the exam.

4. After the program has processed all the results, it must decide whether more than eight students passed the exam.

Let us proceed with top-down, stepwise refinement. We begin with a pseudocode representation of the top:

> *Analyze exam results and decide whether tuition should be raised*

Once again, it is important to emphasize that the top is a *complete* representation of the program, but several refinements are likely to be needed before the pseudocode evolves naturally into a C++ program.

Our first refinement is

> *Initialize variables*
> *Input the 10 exam results, and count passes and failures*
> *Print a summary of the exam results and decide if tuition should be raised*

Here, too, even though we have a complete representation of the entire program, further refinement is necessary. We now commit to specific variables. Counters are needed to record the passes and failures, a counter will be used to control the looping process and a variable is needed to store the user input. The last variable is not initialized, because its value is read from the user during each iteration of the loop.

The pseudocode statement

Initialize variables

can be refined as follows:

Initialize passes to zero
Initialize failures to zero
Initialize student counter to one

Notice that only the counters are initialized at the start of the algorithm.

The pseudocode statement

Input the 10 exam results, and count passes and failures

requires a loop that successively inputs the result of each exam. Here it is known in advance that there are precisely 10 exam results, so counter-controlled looping is appropriate. Inside the loop (i.e., **nested** within the loop), an if...else statement will determine whether each exam result is a pass or a failure and will increment the appropriate counter. The refinement of the preceding pseudocode statement is then

While student counter is less than or equal to 10
   Prompt the user to enter the next exam result
   Input the next exam result

   If the student passed
      Add one to passes
   Else
      Add one to failures

   Add one to student counter

We use blank lines to isolate the *If…Else* control structure, which improves readability.

The pseudocode statement

Print a summary of the exam results and decide whether tuition should be raised

can be refined as follows:

Print the number of passes
Print the number of failures

If more than eight students passed
   Print "Raise tuition"

The complete second refinement appears in Fig. 4.15. Notice that blank lines are also used to set off the *While* structure for program readability. This pseudocode is now sufficiently refined for conversion to C++.

Conversion to Class Analysis

The C++ class that implements the pseudocode algorithm is shown in Fig. 4.16–Fig. 4.17, and two sample executions appear in Fig. 4.18.

```
1    Initialize passes to zero
2    Initialize failures to zero
3    Initialize student counter to one
4
5    While student counter is less than or equal to 10
6        Prompt the user to enter the next exam result
7        Input the next exam result
8
9        If the student passed
10            Add one to passes
11        Else
12            Add one to failures
13
14        Add one to student counter
15
16    Print the number of passes
17    Print the number of failures
18
19    If more than eight students passed
20        Print "Raise tuition"
```

Fig. 4.15 | Pseudocode for examination-results problem.

```
1    // Fig. 4.16: Analysis.h
2    // Definition of class Analysis that analyzes examination results.
3    // Member function is defined in Analysis.cpp
4
5    // Analysis class definition
6    class Analysis
7    {
8    public:
9       void processExamResults(); // process 10 students' examination results
10   }; // end class Analysis
```

Fig. 4.16 | Examination-results problem: Analysis header file.

```
1    // Fig. 4.17: Analysis.cpp
2    // Member-function definitions for class Analysis that
3    // analyzes examination results.
4    #include <iostream>
5    using std::cout;
6    using std::cin;
7    using std::endl;
```

Fig. 4.17 | Examination-results problem: Nested control statements in Analysis source code file. (Part 1 of 2.)

```
8
9   // include definition of class Analysis from Analysis.h
10  #include "Analysis.h"
11
12  // process the examination results of 10 students
13  void Analysis::processExamResults()
14  {
15     // initializing variables in declarations
16     int passes = 0; // number of passes
17     int failures = 0; // number of failures
18     int studentCounter = 1; // student counter
19     int result; // one exam result (1 = pass, 2 = fail)
20
21     // process 10 students using counter-controlled loop
22     while ( studentCounter <= 10 )
23     {
24        // prompt user for input and obtain value from user
25        cout << "Enter result (1 = pass, 2 = fail): ";
26        cin >> result; // input result
27
28        // if...else nested in while
29        if ( result == 1 )           // if result is 1,
30           passes = passes + 1;      // increment passes;
31        else                         // else result is not 1, so
32           failures = failures + 1; // increment failures
33
34        // increment studentCounter so loop eventually terminates
35        studentCounter = studentCounter + 1;
36     } // end while
37
38     // termination phase; display number of passes and failures
39     cout << "Passed " << passes << "\nFailed " << failures << endl;
40
41     // determine whether more than eight students passed
42     if ( passes > 8 )
43        cout << "Raise tuition " << endl;
44  } // end function processExamResults
```

Fig. 4.17 | Examination-results problem: Nested control statements in `Analysis` source code file. (Part 2 of 2.)

```
1   // Fig. 4.18: fig04_18.cpp
2   // Test program for class Analysis.
3   #include "Analysis.h" // include definition of class Analysis
4
5   int main()
6   {
7      Analysis application; // create Analysis object
8      application.processExamResults(); // call function to process results
9      return 0; // indicate successful termination
10  } // end main
```

Fig. 4.18 | Test program for class `Analysis`. (Part 1 of 2.)

```
Enter result (1 = pass, 2 = fail): 1
Enter result (1 = pass, 2 = fail): 1
Enter result (1 = pass, 2 = fail): 1
Enter result (1 = pass, 2 = fail): 1
Enter result (1 = pass, 2 = fail): 2
Enter result (1 = pass, 2 = fail): 1
Enter result (1 = pass, 2 = fail): 1
Enter result (1 = pass, 2 = fail): 1
Enter result (1 = pass, 2 = fail): 1
Enter result (1 = pass, 2 = fail): 1
Passed 9
Failed 1
Raise tuition
```

```
Enter result (1 = pass, 2 = fail): 1
Enter result (1 = pass, 2 = fail): 2
Enter result (1 = pass, 2 = fail): 2
Enter result (1 = pass, 2 = fail): 1
Enter result (1 = pass, 2 = fail): 1
Enter result (1 = pass, 2 = fail): 1
Enter result (1 = pass, 2 = fail): 2
Enter result (1 = pass, 2 = fail): 1
Enter result (1 = pass, 2 = fail): 1
Enter result (1 = pass, 2 = fail): 2
Passed 6
Failed 4
```

Fig. 4.18 | Test program for class Analysis. (Part 2 of 2.)

Lines 16–18 of Fig. 4.17 declare the variables that member function processExamResults of class Analysis uses to process the examination results. Note that we have taken advantage of a feature of C++ that allows variable initialization to be incorporated into declarations (passes is initialized to 0, failures is initialized to 0 and studentCounter is initialized to 1). Looping programs may require initialization at the beginning of each repetition; such reinitialization normally would be performed by assignment statements rather than in declarations or by moving the declarations inside the loop bodies.

The while statement (lines 22–36) loops 10 times. During each iteration, the loop inputs and processes one exam result. Notice that the if...else statement (lines 29–32) for processing each result is nested in the while statement. If the result is 1, the if...else statement increments passes; otherwise, it assumes the result is 2 and increments failures. Line 35 increments studentCounter before the loop condition is tested again at line 22. After 10 values have been input, the loop terminates and line 39 displays the number of passes and the number of failures. The if statement at lines 42–43 determines whether more than eight students passed the exam and, if so, outputs the message "Raise Tuition".

Demonstrating Class Analysis
Figure 4.18 creates an Analysis object (line 7) and invokes the object's processExamResults member function (line 8) to process a set of exam results entered by the user. Figure 4.18 shows the input and output from two sample executions of the program. At

the end of the first sample execution, the condition at line 42 of member function pro-cessExamResults in Fig. 4.17 is true—more than eight students passed the exam, so the program outputs a message indicating that the tuition should be raised.

4.11 Assignment Operators

C++ provides several assignment operators for abbreviating assignment expressions. For example, the statement

        c = c + 3;

can be abbreviated with the addition assignment operator += as

        c += 3;

The += operator adds the value of the expression on the right of the operator to the value of the variable on the left of the operator and stores the result in the variable on the left of the operator. Any statement of the form

        variable = variable operator expression;

in which the same *variable* appears on both sides of the assignment operator and *operator* is one of the binary operators +, -, *, /, or % (or others we'll discuss later in the text), can be written in the form

        variable operator= expression;

Thus the assignment c += 3 adds 3 to c. Figure 4.19 shows the arithmetic assignment operators, sample expressions using these operators and explanations.

4.12 Increment and Decrement Operators

In addition to the arithmetic assignment operators, C++ also provides two unary operators for adding 1 to or subtracting 1 from the value of a numeric variable. These are the unary increment operator, ++, and the unary decrement operator, --, which are summarized in Fig. 4.20. A program can increment by 1 the value of a variable called c using the increment operator, ++, rather than the expression c = c + 1 or c += 1. An increment or decrement operator that is prefixed to (placed before) a variable is referred to as the prefix

Assignment operator	Sample expression	Explanation	Assigns
Assume: int c = 3, d = 5, e = 4, f = 6, g = 12;			
+=	c += 7	c = c + 7	10 to c
-=	d -= 4	d = d - 4	1 to d
*=	e *= 5	e = e * 5	20 to e
/=	f /= 3	f = f / 3	2 to f
%=	g %= 9	g = g % 9	3 to g

Fig. 4.19 | Arithmetic assignment operators.

Operator	Called	Sample expression	Explanation
++	preincrement	++a	Increment a by 1, then use the new value of a in the expression in which a resides.
++	postincrement	a++	Use the current value of a in the expression in which a resides, then increment a by 1.
--	predecrement	--b	Decrement b by 1, then use the new value of b in the expression in which b resides.
--	postdecrement	b--	Use the current value of b in the expression in which b resides, then decrement b by 1.

Fig. 4.20 | Increment and decrement operators.

increment or prefix decrement operator, respectively. An increment or decrement operator that is postfixed to (placed after) a variable is referred to as the postfix increment or postfix decrement operator, respectively.

Using the prefix increment (or decrement) operator to add (or subtract) 1 from a variable is known as preincrementing (or predecrementing) the variable. Preincrementing (or predecrementing) causes the variable to be incremented (decremented) by 1, and then the new value of the variable is used in the expression in which it appears. Using the postfix increment (or decrement) operator to add (or subtract) 1 from a variable is known as postincrementing (or postdecrementing) the variable. Postincrementing (or postdecrementing) causes the current value of the variable to be used in the expression in which it appears, and then the variable's value is incremented (decremented) by 1.

Good Programming Practice 4.8

Unlike binary operators, the unary increment and decrement operators should be placed next to their operands, with no intervening spaces.

Figure 4.21 demonstrates the difference between the prefix increment and postfix increment versions of the ++ increment operator. The decrement operator (--) works similarly. Note that this example does not contain a class, but just a source code file with function main performing all the application's work. In this chapter and in Chapter 3, you have seen examples consisting of one class (including the header and source code files for this class), as well as another source code file testing the class. This source code file contained function main, which created an object of the class and called its member functions. In this example, we simply want to show the mechanics of the ++ operator, so we use only one source code file with function main. Occasionally, when it does not make sense to try to create a reusable class to demonstrate a simple concept, we will use a mechanical example contained entirely within the main function of a single source code file.

Line 12 initializes the variable c to 5, and line 13 outputs c's initial value. Line 14 outputs the value of the expression c++. This expression postincrements the variable c, so c's original value (5) is output, then c's value is incremented. Thus, line 14 outputs c's initial value (5) again. Line 15 outputs c's new value (6) to prove that the variable's value was indeed incremented in line 14.

```
 1   // Fig. 4.21: fig04_21.cpp
 2   // Preincrementing and postincrementing.
 3   #include <iostream>
 4   using std::cout;
 5   using std::endl;
 6
 7   int main()
 8   {
 9      int c;
10
11      // demonstrate postincrement
12      c = 5; // assign 5 to c
13      cout << c << endl; // print 5
14      cout << c++ << endl; // print 5 then postincrement
15      cout << c << endl; // print 6
16
17      cout << endl; // skip a line
18
19      // demonstrate preincrement
20      c = 5; // assign 5 to c
21      cout << c << endl; // print 5
22      cout << ++c << endl; // preincrement then print 6
23      cout << c << endl; // print 6
24      return 0; // indicate successful termination
25   } // end main
```

```
5
5
6

5
6
6
```

Fig. 4.21 | Preincrementing and postincrementing.

Line 20 resets c's value to 5, and line 21 outputs c's value. Line 22 outputs the value of the expression ++c. This expression preincrements c, so its value is incremented, then the new value (6) is output. Line 23 outputs c's value again to show that the value of c is still 6 after line 22 executes.

The arithmetic assignment operators and the increment and decrement operators can be used to simplify program statements. The three assignment statements in Fig. 4.17

```
passes = passes + 1;
failures = failures + 1;
studentCounter = studentCounter + 1;
```

can be written more concisely with assignment operators as

```
passes += 1;
failures += 1;
studentCounter += 1;
```

with prefix increment operators as

```
++passes;
++failures;
++studentCounter;
```

or with postfix increment operators as

```
passes++;
failures++;
studentCounter++;
```

Note that, when incrementing (++) or decrementing (--) of a variable occurs in a statement by itself, the preincrement and postincrement forms have the same effect, and the predecrement and postdecrement forms have the same effect. It is only when a variable appears in the context of a larger expression that preincrementing the variable and postincrementing the variable have different effects (and similarly for predecrementing and postdecrementing).

Common Programming Error 4.14

Attempting to use the increment or decrement operator on an expression other than a modifiable variable name or reference, e.g., writing ++(x + 1), is a syntax error.

Figure 4.22 shows the precedence and associativity of the operators introduced to this point. The operators are shown top-to-bottom in decreasing order of precedence. The second column indicates the associativity of the operators at each level of precedence. Notice that the conditional operator (?:), the unary operators preincrement (++), predecrement (--), plus (+) and minus (-), and the assignment operators =, +=, -=, *=, /= and %= associate from right to left. All other operators in the operator precedence chart of Fig. 4.22 associate from left to right. The third column names the various groups of operators.

Operators						Associativity	Type
()						left to right	parentheses
++	--	static_cast< *type* >()				left to right	unary (postfix)
++	--	+	-			right to left	unary (prefix)
*	/	%				left to right	multiplicative
+	-					left to right	additive
<<	>>					left to right	insertion/extraction
<	<=	>	>=			left to right	relational
==	!=					left to right	equality
?:						right to left	conditional
=	+=	-=	*=	/=	%=	right to left	assignment

Fig. 4.22 | Operator precedence for the operators encountered so far in the text.

4.13 (Optional) Software Engineering Case Study: Identifying Class Attributes in the ATM System

In Section 3.11, we began the first stage of an object-oriented design (OOD) for our ATM system—analyzing the requirements document and identifying the classes needed to implement the system. We listed the nouns and noun phrases in the requirements document and identified a separate class for each one that plays a significant role in the ATM system. We then modeled the classes and their relationships in a UML class diagram (Fig. 3.23). Classes have attributes (data) and operations (behaviors). Class attributes are implemented in C++ programs as data members, and class operations are implemented as member functions. In this section, we determine many of the attributes needed in the ATM system. In Chapter 5, we examine how these attributes represent an object's state. In Chapter 6, we determine class operations.

Identifying Attributes

Consider the attributes of some real-world objects: A person's attributes include height, weight and whether the person is left-handed, right-handed or ambidextrous. A radio's attributes include its station setting, its volume setting and its AM or FM setting. A car's attributes include its speedometer and odometer readings, the amount of gas in its tank and what gear it is in. A personal computer's attributes include its manufacturer (e.g., Dell, Sun, Apple or IBM), type of screen (e.g., LCD or CRT), main memory size and hard disk size.

We can identify many attributes of the classes in our system by looking for descriptive words and phrases in the requirements document. For each one we find that plays a significant role in the ATM system, we create an attribute and assign it to one or more of the classes identified in Section 3.11. We also create attributes to represent any additional data that a class may need, as such needs become clear throughout the design process.

Figure 4.23 lists the words or phrases from the requirements document that describe each class. We formed this list by reading the requirements document and identifying any words or phrases that refer to characteristics of the classes in the system. For example, the requirements document describes the steps taken to obtain a "withdrawal amount," so we list "amount" next to class `Withdrawal`.

Class	Descriptive words and phrases
`ATM`	user is authenticated
`BalanceInquiry`	account number
`Withdrawal`	account number amount
`Deposit`	account number amount
`BankDatabase`	[no descriptive words or phrases]

Fig. 4.23 | Descriptive words and phrases from the ATM requirements. (Part 1 of 2.)

Class	Descriptive words and phrases
Account	account number PIN balance
Screen	[no descriptive words or phrases]
Keypad	[no descriptive words or phrases]
CashDispenser	begins each day loaded with 500 $20 bills
DepositSlot	[no descriptive words or phrases]

Fig. 4.23 | Descriptive words and phrases from the
ATM requirements. (Part 2 of 2.)

Figure 4.23 leads us to create one attribute of class ATM. Class ATM maintains information about the state of the ATM. The phrase "user is authenticated" describes a state of the ATM (we introduce states in Section 5.11), so we include userAuthenticated as a Boolean attribute (i.e., an attribute that has a value of either true or false). The UML Boolean type is equivalent to the bool type in C++. This attribute indicates whether the ATM has successfully authenticated the current user—userAuthenticated must be true for the system to allow the user to perform transactions and access account information. This attribute helps ensure the security of the data in the system.

Classes BalanceInquiry, Withdrawal and Deposit share one attribute. Each transaction involves an "account number" that corresponds to the account of the user making the transaction. We assign an integer attribute accountNumber to each transaction class to identify the account to which an object of the class applies.

Descriptive words and phrases in the requirements document also suggest some differences in the attributes required by each transaction class. The requirements document indicates that to withdraw cash or deposit funds, users must enter a specific "amount" of money to be withdrawn or deposited, respectively. Thus, we assign to classes Withdrawal and Deposit an attribute amount to store the value supplied by the user. The amounts of money related to a withdrawal and a deposit are defining characteristics of these transactions that the system requires for them to take place. Class BalanceInquiry, however, needs no additional data to perform its task—it requires only an account number to indicate the account whose balance should be retrieved.

Class Account has several attributes. The requirements document states that each bank account has an "account number" and "PIN," which the system uses for identifying accounts and authenticating users. We assign to class Account two integer attributes: accountNumber and pin. The requirements document also specifies that an account maintains a "balance" of the amount of money in the account and that money the user deposits does not become available for a withdrawal until the bank verifies the amount of cash in the deposit envelope, and any checks in the envelope clear. An account must still record the amount of money that a user deposits, however. Therefore, we decide that an account should represent a balance using two attributes of UML type Double: availableBalance and totalBalance. Attribute availableBalance tracks the amount of money that a user can withdraw from the account. Attribute `totalBalance` refers to the total amount of money that the user has "on deposit" (i.e., the amount of money available, plus the amount waiting to be verified or cleared). For example, suppose an ATM user deposits $50.00 into an empty account. The `totalBalance` attribute would increase to $50.00 to record the deposit, but the `availableBalance` would remain at $0. [*Note:* We assume that the bank updates the `availableBalance` attribute of an `Account` soon after the ATM transaction occurs, in response to confirming that $50 worth of cash or checks was found in the deposit envelope. We assume that this update occurs through a transaction that a bank employee performs using some piece of bank software other than the ATM. Thus, we do not discuss this transaction in our case study.]

Class `CashDispenser` has one attribute. The requirements document states that the cash dispenser "begins each day loaded with 500 $20 bills." The cash dispenser must keep track of the number of bills it contains to determine whether enough cash is on hand to satisfy withdrawal requests. We assign to class `CashDispenser` an integer attribute `count`, which is initially set to 500.

For real problems in industry, there is no guarantee that requirements documents will be rich enough and precise enough for the object-oriented systems designer to determine all the attributes or even all the classes. The need for additional classes, attributes and behaviors may become clear as the design process proceeds. As we progress through this case study, we too will continue to add, modify and delete information about the classes in our system.

Modeling Attributes

The class diagram in Fig. 4.24 lists some of the attributes for the classes in our system— the descriptive words and phrases in Fig. 4.23 helped us identify these attributes. For simplicity, Fig. 4.24 does not show the associations among classes—we showed these in Fig. 3.23. This is a common practice of systems designers when designs are being developed. Recall from Section 5.11 that in the UML, a class's attributes are placed in the middle compartment of the class's rectangle. We list each attribute's name and type separated by a colon (`:`), followed in some cases by an equal sign (`=`) and an initial value.

Consider the `userAuthenticated` attribute of class `ATM`:

```
userAuthenticated : Boolean = false
```

This attribute declaration contains three pieces of information about the attribute. The attribute name is `userAuthenticated`. The attribute type is `Boolean`. In C++, an attribute can be represented by a fundamental type, such as `bool`, `int` or `double`, or a class type— as discussed in Chapter 3. We have chosen to model only primitive-type attributes in Fig. 4.24—we discuss the reasoning behind this decision shortly. [*Note:* Figure 4.24 lists UML data types for the attributes. When we implement the system, we will associate the UML types `Boolean`, `Integer` and `Double` with the C++ fundamental types `bool`, `int` and `double`, respectively.]

We can also indicate an initial value for an attribute. The `userAuthenticated` attribute in class `ATM` has an initial value of `false`. This indicates that the system initially does not consider the user to be authenticated. If an attribute has no initial value specified, only its name and type (separated by a colon) are shown. For example, the `accountNumber` attribute of class `BalanceInquiry` is an `Integer`. Here we show no initial value, because

Fig. 4.24 | Classes with attributes.

the value of this attribute is a number that we do not yet know. This number will be determined at execution time based on the account number entered by the current ATM user.

Figure 4.24 does not include any attributes for classes `Screen`, `Keypad` and `DepositSlot`. These are important components of our system, for which our design process simply has not yet revealed any attributes. We may still discover some, however, in the remaining phases of design or when we implement these classes in C++. This is perfectly normal for the iterative process of software engineering.

Software Engineering Observation 4.8

At early stages in the design process, classes often lack attributes (and operations). Such classes should not be eliminated, however, because attributes (and operations) may become evident in the later phases of design and implementation.

Note that Fig. 4.24 also does not include attributes for class `BankDatabase`. Recall from Chapter 3 that in C++, attributes can be represented by either fundamental types or class types. We have chosen to include only fundamental-type attributes in the class diagram in Fig. 4.24 (and in similar class diagrams throughout the case study). A class-type attribute is modeled more clearly as an association (in particular, a composition) between the class with the attribute and the class of the object of which the attribute is an instance. For example, the class diagram in Fig. 3.23 indicates that class `BankDatabase` participates in a composition relationship with zero or more Account objects. From this composition, we can determine that when we implement the ATM system in C++, we will be required to create an attribute of class BankDatabase to hold zero or more Account objects. Similarly, we will assign attributes to class ATM that correspond to its composition relationships with classes Screen, Keypad, CashDispenser and DepositSlot. These composition-based attributes would be redundant if modeled in Fig. 4.24, because the compositions modeled in Fig. 3.23 already convey the fact that the database contains information about zero or more accounts and that an ATM is composed of a screen, keypad, cash dispenser and deposit slot. Software developers typically model these whole/part relationships as compositions rather than as attributes required to implement the relationships.

The class diagram in Fig. 4.24 provides a solid basis for the structure of our model, but the diagram is not complete. In Section 5.11, we identify the states and activities of the objects in the model, and in Section 6.22 we identify the operations that the objects perform. As we present more of the UML and object-oriented design, we will continue to strengthen the structure of our model.

Software Engineering Case Study Self-Review Exercises

4.1   We typically identify the attributes of the classes in our system by analyzing the _____ in the requirements document.
  a) nouns and noun phrases
  b) descriptive words and phrases
  c) verbs and verb phrases
  d) All of the above.

4.2   Which of the following is not an attribute of an airplane?
  a) length
  b) wingspan
  c) fly
  d) number of seats

4.3   Describe the meaning of the following attribute declaration of class CashDispenser in the class diagram in Fig. 4.24:

```
count : Integer = 500
```

Answers to Software Engineering Case Study Self-Review Exercises

4.1   b.

4.2   c. Fly is an operation or behavior of an airplane, not an attribute.

4.3   This indicates that count is an Integer with an initial value of 500. This attribute keeps track of the number of bills available in the CashDispenser at any given time.

Summary

- An algorithm is a procedure for solving a problem in terms of the actions to execute and the order in which to execute them.
- Specifying the order in which statements (actions) execute in a program is called program control.
- Pseudocode helps a programmer think out a program before attempting to write it in a programming language.

- Activity diagrams are part of the Unified Modeling Language (UML)—an industry standard for modeling software systems.
- An activity diagram models the workflow (also called the activity) of a software system.
- Activity diagrams are composed of special-purpose symbols, such as action state symbols, diamonds and small circles. These symbols are connected by transition arrows that represent the flow of the activity.
- Like pseudocode, activity diagrams help programmers develop and represent algorithms.
- An action state is represented as a rectangle with its left and right sides replaced with arcs curving outward. The action expression appears inside the action state.
- The arrows in an activity diagram represent transitions, which indicate the order in which the actions represented by action states occur.
- The solid circle located at the top of an activity diagram represents the initial state—the beginning of the workflow before the program performs the modeled actions.
- The solid circle surrounded by a hollow circle that appears at the bottom of the activity diagram represents the final state—the end of the workflow after the program performs its actions.
- Rectangles with the upper-right corners folded over are called notes in the UML. Notes are explanatory remarks that describe the purpose of symbols in the diagram. A dotted line connects each note with the element that the note describes.
- A diamond or decision symbol in an activity diagram indicates that a decision is to be made. The workflow will continue along a path determined by the symbol's associated guard conditions, which can be true or false. Each transition arrow emerging from a decision symbol has a guard condition (specified in square brackets next to the transition arrow). If a guard condition is true, the workflow enters the action state to which the transition arrow points.
- A diamond in an activity diagram also represents the merge symbol, which joins two flows of activity into one. A merge symbol has two or more transition arrows pointing to the diamond and only one transition arrow pointing from the diamond, to indicate multiple activity flows merging to continue the activity.
- Top-down, stepwise refinement is a process for refining pseudocode by maintaining a complete representation of the program during each refinement.
- There are three types of control structures—sequence, selection and repetition.
- The sequence structure is built into C++—by default, statements execute in the order they appear.
- A selection structure chooses among alternative courses of action.
- The `if` single-selection statement either performs (selects) an action if a condition is true, or skips the action if the condition is false.
- The `if...else` double-selection statement performs (selects) an action if a condition is true and performs a different action if the condition is false.
- To include several statements in an `if`'s body (or the body of an `else` for an `if...else` statement), enclose the statements in braces (`{` and `}`). A set of statements contained within a pair of braces is called a block. A block can be placed anywhere in a program that a single statement can be placed.
- A null statement, indicating that no action is to be taken, is indicated by a semicolon (`;`).
- A repetition statement specifies that an action is to be repeated while some condition remains true.
- A value that contains a fractional part is referred to as a floating-point number and is represented approximately by data types such as `float` and `double`.
- Counter-controlled repetition is used when the number of repetitions is known before a loop begins executing, i.e., when there is definite repetition.

- The unary cast operator static_cast can be used to create a temporary floating-point copy of its operand.
- Unary operators take only one operand; binary operators take two.
- The parameterized stream manipulator setprecision indicates the number of digits of precision that should be displayed to the right of the decimal point.
- The stream manipulator fixed indicates that floating-point values should be output in so-called fixed-point format, as opposed to scientific notation.
- Sentinel-controlled repetition is used when the number of repetitions is not known before a loop begins executing, i.e., when there is indefinite repetition.
- A nested control statement appears in the body of another control statement.
- C++ provides the arithmetic assignment operators +=, -=, *=, /= and %= for abbreviating assignment expressions.
- The increment operator, ++, and the decrement operator, --, increment or decrement a variable by 1, respectively. If the operator is prefixed to the variable, the variable is incremented or decremented by 1 first, and then its new value is used in the expression in which it appears. If the operator is postfixed to the variable, the variable is first used in the expression in which it appears, and then the variable's value is incremented or decremented by 1.

Terminology

action
action expression
action state
action state symbol
action/decision model of programming
activity diagram
addition assignment operator (+=)
algorithm
approximation of floating-point numbers
arithmetic assignment operators
arrow symbol
assignment operators
associate from left to right
associate from right to left
averaging calculation
binary arithmetic operator
block
"bombing"
bool
cast operator
compound statement
conditional expression
conditional operator (?:)
control statement
control-statement nesting
control-statement stacking
counter
counter-controlled repetition
"crashing"

dangling-else problem
decision symbol
decrement operator (--)
default precision
definite repetition
diamond symbol
dotted line
double data type
double-precision floating-point number
double-selection statement
dummy value
empty statement
executable statement
explicit conversion
fatal logic error
final state
first refinement
fixed-point format
fixed stream manipulator
flag value
float data type
floating-point constant
floating-point number
"garbage" value
goto elimination
goto statement
if...else double-selection statement
implicit conversion
increment operator (++)

indefinite repetition	pseudocode
initial state	repetition statement
integer division	rounding
integer promotion	scientific notation
iterating	second refinement
iterations of a loop	selection statement
keywords	sentinel-controlled repetition
loop	sentinel value
loop-continuation condition	sequence statement
loop iterations	sequence-statement activity diagram
loop nested within a loop	sequential execution
looping statement	`setprecision` stream manipulator
merge symbol	`showpoint` stream manipulator
multiple-selection statement	signal value
nested control statement	single-entry/single-exit control statement
nonparameterized stream manipulator	single-selection `if` statement
note	single-precision floating-point number
null statement	small circle symbol
object-oriented design (OOD)	solid circle symbol
off-by-one error	stream manipulator
operand	structured programming
operator precedence	ternary operator
order in which actions should execute	top
parameterized stream manipulator	top-down, stepwise refinement
postdecrement	total
postfix decrement operator	transfer of control
postfix increment operator	transition
postincrement	transition arrow symbol
precision	truncate
predecrement	unary cast operator
prefix decrement operator	unary minus (-) operator
prefix increment operator	unary operator
preincrement	unary plus (+) operator
procedure	undefined value
program control	`while` repetition statement
promotion	workflow of a portion of a software system

Self-Review Exercises

4.1   Answer each of the following questions.
   a) All programs can be written in terms of three types of control structures: _____, _____ and _____.
   b) The _____ selection statement is used to execute one action when a condition is `true` or a different action when that condition is `false`.
   c) Repeating a set of instructions a specific number of times is called _____ repetition.
   d) When it is not known in advance how many times a set of statements will be repeated, a(n) _____ value can be used to terminate the repetition.

4.2   Write four different C++ statements that each add 1 to integer variable x.

4.3   Write C++ statements to accomplish each of the following:

a) In one statement, assign the sum of the current value of x and y to z and postincrement the value of x.

b) Determine whether the value of the variable count is greater than 10. If it is, print "Count is greater than 10."

c) Predecrement the variable x by 1, then subtract it from the variable total.

d) Calculate the remainder after q is divided by divisor and assign the result to q. Write this statement two different ways.

4.4   Write C++ statements to accomplish each of the following tasks.

a) Declare variables sum and x to be of type int.

b) Set variable x to 1.

c) Set variable sum to 0.

d) Add variable x to variable sum and assign the result to variable sum.

e) Print "The sum is: " followed by the value of variable sum.

4.5   Combine the statements that you wrote in Exercise 4.4 into a program that calculates and prints the sum of the integers from 1 to 10. Use the while statement to loop through the calculation and increment statements. The loop should terminate when the value of x becomes 11.

4.6   State the values of eachm variable after the calculation is performed. Assume that, when each statement begins executing, all variables have the integer value 5.

a) product *= x++;

b) quotient /= ++x;

4.7   Write single C++ statements that do the following:

a) Input integer variable x with cin and >>.

b) Input integer variable y with cin and >>.

c) Set integer variable i to 1.

d) Set integer variable power to 1.

e) Multiply variable power by x and assign the result to power.

f) Postincrement variable i by 1.

g) Determine whether i is less than or equal to y.

h) Output integer variable power with cout and <<.

4.8   Write ma C++ program that uses the statements in Exercise 4.7 to calculate x raised to the y power. The program should have a while repetition statement.

4.9   Identify and correct the errors in each of the following:

a) while (c <= 5)
   {
      product *= c;
      c++;

b) cin << value;

c) if (gender == 1)
      cout << "Woman" << endl;
   else;
      cout << "Man" << endl;

4.10   What is wrong with the following while repetition statement?

```
while ( z >= 0 )
   sum += z;
```

Answers to Self-Review Exercises

4.1   a) Sequence, selection and repetition. b) if...else. c) Counter-controlled or definite.
d) Sentinel, signal, flag or dummy.

4.2   x = x + 1;

x += 1;

++x;

x++;

4.3   a) z = x++ + y;
       b) if (count > 10)
               cout << "Count is greater than 10" << endl;
       c) total -= --x;
       d) q %= divisor;
           q = q % divisor;

4.4   a) int sum;
           int x;
       b) x = 1;
       c) sum = 0;
       d) sum += x;
           or
           sum = sum + x;
       e) cout << "The sum is: " << sum << endl;

4.5   See the following code:

```
1   // Exercise 4.5 Solution: ex04_05.cpp
2   // Calculate the sum of the integers from 1 to 10.
3   #include <iostream>
4   using std::cout;
5   using std::endl;
6
7   int main()
8   {
9      int sum; // stores sum of integers 1 to 10
10      int x; // counter
11
12      x = 1; // count from 1
13      sum = 0; // initialize sum
14
15      while ( x <= 10 ) // loop 10 times
16      {
17         sum += x; // add x to sum
18         x++; // increment x
19      } // end while
20
21      cout << "The sum is: " << sum << endl;
22      return 0; // indicate successful termination
23   } // end main
```

```
The sum is: 55
```

4.6   a) product = 25, x = 6;
       b) quotient = 0, x = 6;

```
1   // Exercise 4.6 Solution: ex04_06.cpp
2   // Calculate the value of product and quotient.
3   #include <iostream>
4   using std::cout;
5   using std::endl;
6
7   int main()
8   {
9      int x = 5;
10     int product = 5;
11     int quotient = 5;
12
13     // part a
14     product *= x++; // part a statement
15     cout << "Value of product after calculation: " << product << endl;
16     cout << "Value of x after calculation: " << x << endl << endl;
17
18     // part b
19     x = 5; // reset value of x
20     quotient /= ++x; // part b statement
21     cout << "Value of quotient after calculation: " << quotient << endl;
22     cout << "Value of x after calculation: " << x << endl << endl;
23     return 0; // indicate successful termination
24  } // end main
```

```
Value of product after calculation: 25
Value of x after calculation: 6

Value of quotient after calculation: 0
Value of x after calculation: 6
```

4.7   a) cin >> x;
       b) cin >> y;
       c) i = 1;
       d) power = 1;
       e) power *= x; *or* power = power * x;
       f) i++;
       g) if (i <= y)
       h) cout << power << endl;

4.8   See the following code:

```
1   // Exercise 4.8 Solution: ex04_08.cpp
2   // Raise x to the y power.
3   #include <iostream>
4   using std::cout;
5   using std::cin;
6   using std::endl;
7
8   int main()
```

```
 9   {
10       int x; // base
11       int y; // exponent
12       int i; // counts from 1 to y
13       int power; // used to calculate x raised to power y
14
15       i = 1; // initialize i to begin counting from 1
16       power = 1; // initialize power
17
18       cout << "Enter base as an integer: ";  // prompt for base
19       cin >> x; // input base
20
21       cout << "Enter exponent as an integer: "; // prompt for exponent
22       cin >> y; // input exponent
23
24       // count from 1 to y and multiply power by x each time
25       while ( i <= y )
26       {
27          power *= x;
28          i++;
29       } // end while
30
31       cout << power << endl; // display result
32       return 0; // indicate successful termination
33   } // end main
```

```
Enter base as an integer: 2
Enter exponent as an integer: 3
8
```

4.9   a) Error: Missing the closing right brace of the while body.
            Correction: Add closing right brace after the statement c++;.
         b) Error: Used stream insertion instead of stream extraction.
            Correction: Change << to >>.
         c) Error: Semicolon after else results in a logic error. The second output statement will
            always be executed.
            Correction: Remove the semicolon after else.

4.10   The value of the variable z is never changed in the while statement. Therefore, if the loop-
continuation condition (z >= 0) is initially true, an infinite loop is created. To prevent the infinite
loop, z must be decremented so that it eventually becomes less than 0.

Exercises

4.11   Identify and correct the error(s) in each of the following:
         a) if (age >= 65);
                cout << "Age is greater than or equal to 65" << endl;
            else
                cout << "Age is less than 65 << endl";
         b) if (age >= 65)
                cout << "Age is greater than or equal to 65" << endl;
            else;
                cout << "Age is less than 65 << endl";

c)
```
int x = 1, total;

while ( x <= 10 )
{
   total += x;
   x++;
}
```
d)
```
While ( x <= 100 )
   total += x;
   x++;
```
e)
```
while ( y > 0 )
{
   cout << y << endl;
   y++;
}
```

4.12 What does the following program print?

```
 1   // Exercise 4.12: ex04_12.cpp
 2   // What does this program print?
 3   #include <iostream>
 4   using std::cout;
 5   using std::endl;
 6
 7   int main()
 8   {
 9      int y; // declare y
10      int x = 1; // initialize x
11      int total = 0; // initialize total
12
13      while ( x <= 10 ) // loop 10 times
14      {
15         y = x * x; // perform calculation
16         cout << y << endl; // output result
17         total += y; // add y to total
18         x++; // increment counter x
19      } // end while
20
21      cout << "Total is " << total << endl; // display result
22      return 0; // indicate successful termination
23   } // end main
```

For Exercise 4.13 to Exercise 4.16, perform each of these steps:
a) Read the problem statement.
b) Formulate the algorithm using pseudocode and top-down, stepwise refinement.
c) Write a C++ program.
d) Test, debug and execute the C++ program.

4.13 Drivers are concerned with the mileage obtained by their automobiles. One driver has kept track of several tankfuls of gasoline by recording miles driven and gallons used for each tankful. Develop a C++ program that uses a while statement to input the miles driven and gallons used for each tankful. The program should calculate and display the miles per gallon obtained for each tankful and print the combined miles per gallon obtained for all tankfuls up to this point.

```
Enter the miles used (-1 to quit): 287
Enter gallons: 13
MPG this tankful: 22.076923
Total MPG: 22.076923

Enter the miles used (-1 to quit): 200
Enter gallons: 10
MPG this tankful: 20.000000
Total MPG: 21.173913

Enter the miles used (-1 to quit): 120
Enter gallons: 5
MPG this tankful: 24.000000
Total MPG: 21.678571

Enter miles (-1 to quit): -1
```

4.14   Develop a C++ program that will determine whether a department-store customer has exceeded the credit limit on a charge account. For each customer, the following facts are available:

     a) Account number (an integer)
     b) Balance at the beginning of the month
     c) Total of all items charged by this customer this month
     d) Total of all credits applied to this customer's account this month
     e) Allowed credit limit

     The program should use a `while` statement to input each of these facts, calculate the new balance (= beginning balance + charges − credits) and determine whether the new balance exceeds the customer's credit limit. For those customers whose credit limit is exceeded, the program should display the customer's account number, credit limit, new balance and the message "Credit Limit Exceeded."

```
Enter account number (-1 to end): 100
Enter beginning balance: 5394.78
Enter total charges: 1000.00
Enter total credits: 500.00
Enter credit limit: 5500.00
New balance is 5894.78
Account:      100
Credit limit: 5500.00
Balance:      5894.78
Credit Limit Exceeded.

Enter Account Number (or -1 to quit): 200
Enter beginning balance: 1000.00
Enter total charges: 123.45
Enter total credits: 321.00
Enter credit limit: 1500.00
New balance is 802.45

Enter Account Number (or -1 to quit): 300
Enter beginning balance: 500.00
Enter total charges: 274.73
Enter total credits: 100.00
Enter credit limit: 800.00
New balance is 674.73

Enter Account Number (or -1 to quit): -1
```

4.15 One large chemical company pays its salespeople on a commission basis. The salespeople each receive $200 per week plus 9 percent of their gross sales for that week. For example, a salesperson who sells $5000 worth of chemicals in a week receives $200 plus 9 percent of $5000, or a total of $650. Develop a C++ program that uses a while statement to input each salesperson's gross sales for last week and calculates and displays that salesperson's earnings. Process one salesperson's figures at a time.

```
Enter sales in dollars (-1 to end): 5000.00
Salary is: $650.00

Enter sales in dollars (-1 to end): 6000.00
Salary is: $740.00

Enter sales in dollars (-1 to end): 7000.00
Salary is: $830.00

Enter sales in dollars (-1 to end): -1
```

4.16 Develop a C++ program that uses a while statement to determine the gross pay for each of several employees. The company pays "straight time" for the first 40 hours worked by each employee and pays "time-and-a-half" for all hours worked in excess of 40 hours. You are given a list of the employees of the company, the number of hours each employee worked last week and the hourly rate of each employee. Your program should input this information for each employee and should determine and display the employee's gross pay.

```
Enter hours worked (-1 to end): 39
Enter hourly rate of the worker ($00.00): 10.00
Salary is $390.00

Enter hours worked (-1 to end): 40
Enter hourly rate of the worker ($00.00): 10.00
Salary is $400.00

Enter hours worked (-1 to end): 41
Enter hourly rate of the worker ($00.00): 10.00
Salary is $415.00

Enter hours worked (-1 to end): -1
```

4.17 The process of finding the largest number (i.e., the maximum of a group of numbers) is used frequently in computer applications. For example, a program that determines the winner of a sales contest inputs the number of units sold by each salesperson. The salesperson who sells the most units wins the contest. Write a pseudocode program, then a C++ program that uses a while statement to determine and print the largest number of 10 numbers input by the user. Your program should use three variables, as follows:

counter:	A counter to count to 10 (i.e., to keep track of how many numbers have been input and to determine when all 10 numbers have been processed).
number:	The current number input to the program.
largest:	The largest number found so far.

4.18 Write a C++ program that uses a `while` statement and the tab escape sequence `\t` to print the following table of values:

N	10*N	100*N	1000*N
1	10	100	1000
2	20	200	2000
3	30	300	3000
4	40	400	4000
5	50	500	5000

4.19 Using an approach similar to that in Exercise 4.17, find the *two* largest values among the 10 numbers. [*Note:* You must input each number only once.]

4.20 The examination-results program of Fig. 4.16–Fig. 4.18 assumes that any value input by the user that is not a 1 must be a 2. Modify the application to validate its inputs. On any input, if the value entered is other than 1 or 2, keep looping until the user enters a correct value.

4.21 What does the following program print?

```
1   // Exercise 4.21: ex04_21.cpp
2   // What does this program print?
3   #include <iostream>
4   using std::cout;
5   using std::endl;
6
7   int main()
8   {
9      int count = 1; // initialize count
10
11     while ( count <= 10 ) // loop 10 times
12     {
13        // output line of text
14        cout << ( count % 2 ? "****" : "++++++++" ) << endl;
15        count++; // increment count
16     } // end while
17
18     return 0; // indicate successful termination
19  } // end main
```

4.22 What does the following program print?

```
1   // Exercise 4.22: ex04_22.cpp
2   // What does this program print?
3   #include <iostream>
4   using std::cout;
5   using std::endl;
6
7   int main()
```

```
8   {
9       int row = 10; // initialize row
10      int column; // declare column
11
12      while ( row >= 1 ) // loop until row < 1
13      {
14          column = 1; // set column to 1 as iteration begins
15
16          while ( column <= 10 ) // loop 10 times
17          {
18              cout << ( row % 2 ? "<" : ">" ); // output
19              column++; // increment column
20          } // end inner while
21
22          row--; // decrement row
23          cout << endl; // begin new output line
24      } // end outer while
25
26      return 0; // indicate successful termination
27  } // end main
```

4.23   *(Dangling-Else Problem)* State the output for each of the following when x is 9 and y is 11 and when x is 11 and y is 9. Note that the compiler ignores the indentation in a C++ program. The C++ compiler always associates an else with the previous if unless told to do otherwise by the placement of braces {}. On first glance, the programmer may not be sure which if and else match, so this is referred to as the "dangling-else" problem. We eliminated the indentation from the following code to make the problem more challenging. [*Hint:* Apply indentation conventions you have learned.]

a)
```
if ( x < 10 )
if ( y > 10 )
cout << "*****" << endl;
else
cout << "#####" << endl;
cout << "$$$$$" << endl;
```

b)
```
if ( x < 10 )
{
if ( y > 10 )
cout << "*****" << endl;
}
else
{
cout << "#####" << endl;
cout << "$$$$$" << endl;
}
```

4.24   *(Another Dangling-Else Problem)* Modify the following code to produce the output shown. Use proper indentation techniques. You must not make any changes other than inserting braces. The compiler ignores indentation in a C++ program. We eliminated the indentation from the following code to make the problem more challenging. [*Note:* It is possible that no modification is necessary.]

```
if ( y == 8 )
if ( x == 5 )
cout << "@@@@@" << endl;
```

```
      else
      cout << "#####" << endl;
      cout << "$$$$$" << endl;
      cout << "&&&&&" << endl;
```

a) Assuming x = 5 and y = 8, the following output is produced.

```
@@@@@
$$$$$
&&&&&
```

b) Assuming x = 5 and y = 8, the following output is produced.

```
@@@@@
```

c) Assuming x = 5 and y = 8, the following output is produced.

```
@@@@@
&&&&&
```

d) Assuming x = 5 and y = 7, the following output is produced. [*Note:* The last three output statements after the else are all part of a block.]

```
#####
$$$$$
&&&&&
```

4.25   Write a program that reads in the size of the side of a square and then prints a hollow square of that size out of asterisks and blanks. Your program should work for squares of all side sizes between 1 and 20. For example, if your program reads a size of 5, it should print

```
*****
*   *
*   *
*   *
*****
```

4.26   A palindrome is a number or a text phrase that reads the same backwards as forwards. For example, each of the following five-digit integers is a palindrome: 12321, 55555, 45554 and 11611. Write a program that reads in a five-digit integer and determines whether it is a palindrome. [*Hint:* Use the division and modulus operators to separate the number into its individual digits.]

4.27   Input an integer containing only 0s and 1s (i.e., a "binary" integer) and print its decimal equivalent. Use the modulus and division operators to pick off the "binary" number's digits one at a time from right to left. Much as in the decimal number system, where the rightmost digit has a positional value of 1, the next digit left has a positional value of 10, then 100, then 1000, and so on, in the binary number system the rightmost digit has a positional value of 1, the next digit left has a positional value of 2, then 4, then 8, and so on. Thus the decimal number 234 can be interpreted as 2 * 100 + 3 * 10 + 4 * 1. The decimal equivalent of binary 1101 is 1 * 1 + 0 * 2 + 1 * 4 + 1 * 8 or 1 + 0 + 4 + 8, or 13. [*Note:* The reader not familiar with binary numbers might wish to refer to Appendix D.]

4.28 Write a program that displays the checkerboard pattern shown below. Your program must use only three output statements, one of each of the following forms:

```
cout << "* ";
cout << ' ';
cout << endl;
```

```
* * * * * * * *
 * * * * * * * *
* * * * * * * *
 * * * * * * * *
* * * * * * * *
 * * * * * * * *
* * * * * * * *
 * * * * * * * *
```

4.29 Write a program that prints the powers of the integer 2, namely 2, 4, 8, 16, 32, 64, etc. Your `while` loop should not terminate (i.e., you should create an infinite loop). To do this, simply use the keyword `true` as the expression for the `while` statement. What happens when you run this program?

4.30 Write a program that reads the radius of a circle (as a `double` value) and computes and prints the diameter, the circumference and the area. Use the value 3.14159 for π.

4.31 What is wrong with the following statement? Provide the correct statement to accomplish what the programmer was probably trying to do.

```
cout << ++( x + y );
```

4.32 Write a program that reads three nonzero `double` values and determines and prints whether they could represent the sides of a triangle.

4.33 Write a program that reads three nonzero integers and determines and prints whether they could be the sides of a right triangle.

4.34 *(Cryptography)* A company wants to transmit data over the telephone, but is concerned that its phones could be tapped. All of the data are transmitted as four-digit integers. The company has asked you to write a program that encrypts the data so that it can be transmitted more securely. Your program should read a four-digit integer and encrypt it as follows: Replace each digit by *(the sum of that digit plus 7) modulus 10*. Then, swap the first digit with the third, swap the second digit with the fourth and print the encrypted integer. Write a separate program that inputs an encrypted four-digit integer and decrypts it to form the original number.

4.35 The factorial of a nonnegative integer n is written $n!$ (pronounced "n factorial") and is defined as follows:

$$n! = n \cdot (n-1) \cdot (n-2) \cdot \ldots \cdot 1 \quad \text{(for values of } n \text{ greater than to 1)}$$

and

$$n! = 1 \quad \text{(for } n = 0 \text{ or } n = 1).$$

For example, $5! = 5 \cdot 4 \cdot 3 \cdot 2 \cdot 1$, which is 120. Use `while` statements in each of the following:

a) Write a program that reads a nonnegative integer and computes and prints its factorial.
b) Write a program that estimates the value of the mathematical constant e by using the formula:

$$e = 1 + \frac{1}{1!} + \frac{1}{2!} + \frac{1}{3!} + \dots$$

Prompt the user for the desired accuracy of e (i.e., the number of terms in the summation).

c) Write a program that computes the value of e^x by using the formula

$$e^x = 1 + \frac{x}{1!} + \frac{x^2}{2!} + \frac{x^3}{3!} + \dots$$

Prompt the user for the desired accuracy of e (i.e., the number of terms in the summation).

4.36 [*Note:* This exercise corresponds to Section 4.13, a portion of our software engineering case study.] Describe in 200 words or fewer what an automobile is and does. List the nouns and verbs separately. In the text, we stated that each noun might correspond to an object that will need to be built to implement a system, in this case a car. Pick five of the objects you listed, and, for each, list several attributes and several behaviors. Describe briefly how these objects interact with one another and other objects in your description. You have just performed several of the key steps in a typical object-oriented design.

5

Control Statements: Part 2

OBJECTIVES

In this chapter you will learn:

- The essentials of counter-controlled repetition.
- To use the **for** and **do...while** repetition statements to execute statements in a program repeatedly.
- To understand multiple selection using the **switch** selection statement.
- To use the **break** and **continue** program control statements to alter the flow of control.
- To use the logical operators to form complex conditional expressions in control statements.
- To avoid the consequences of confusing the equality and assignment operators.

5.1 Introduction

Chapter 4 began our introduction to the types of building blocks that are available for problem solving. We used those building blocks to employ proven program construction techniques. In this chapter, we continue our presentation of the theory and principles of structured programming by introducing C++'s remaining control statements. The control statements we study here and in Chapter 4 will help us in building and manipulating objects. We continue our early emphasis on object-oriented programming that began with a discussion of basic concepts in Chapter 1 and extensive object-oriented code examples and exercises in Chapters 3–4.

In this chapter, we demonstrate the `for`, `do...while` and `switch` statements. Through a series of short examples using `while` and `for`, we explore the essentials of counter-controlled repetition. We devote a portion of the chapter to expanding the `GradeBook` class presented in Chapters 3–4. In particular, we create a version of class `GradeBook` that uses a `switch` statement to count the number of A, B, C, D and F grades in a set of letter grades entered by the user. We introduce the `break` and `continue` program control statements. We discuss the logical operators, which enable programmers to use more powerful conditional expressions in control statements. We also examine the common error of confusing the equality (==) and assignment (=) operators, and how to avoid it. Finally, we summarize C++'s control statements and the proven problem-solving techniques presented in this chapter and Chapter 4.

5.2 Essentials of Counter-Controlled Repetition

This section uses the `while` repetition statement introduced in Chapter 4 to formalize the elements required to perform counter-controlled repetition. Counter-controlled repetition requires

1. the name of a control variable (or loop counter)
2. the initial value of the control variable

3. the loop-continuation condition that tests for the final value of the control variable (i.e., whether looping should continue)

4. the increment (or decrement) by which the control variable is modified each time through the loop.

Consider the simple program in Fig. 5.1, which prints the numbers from 1 to 10. The declaration at line 9 *names* the control variable (counter), declares it to be an integer, reserves space for it in memory and sets it to an *initial value* of 1. Declarations that require initialization are, in effect, executable statements. In C++, it is more precise to call a declaration that also reserves memory—as the preceding declaration does—a definition. Because definitions are declarations, too, we will use the term "declaration" except when the distinction is important.

The declaration and initialization of counter (line 9) also could have been accomplished with the statements

```
int counter; // declare control variable
counter = 1; // initialize control variable to 1
```

We use both methods of initializing variables.

Line 14 *increments* the loop counter by 1 each time the loop's body is performed. The loop-continuation condition (line 11) in the while statement determines whether the value of the control variable is less than or equal to 10 (the final value for which the condition is true). Note that the body of this while executes even when the control variable is 10. The loop terminates when the control variable is greater than 10 (i.e., when counter becomes 11).

```
1   // Fig. 5.1: fig05_01.cpp
2   // Counter-controlled repetition.
3   #include <iostream>
4   using std::cout;
5   using std::endl;
6
7   int main()
8   {
9      int counter = 1; // declare and initialize control variable
10
11     while ( counter <= 10 ) // loop-continuation condition
12     {
13        cout << counter << " ";
14        counter++; // increment control variable by 1
15     } // end while
16
17     cout << endl; // output a newline
18     return 0; // successful termination
19  } // end main
```

```
1 2 3 4 5 6 7 8 9 10
```

Fig. 5.1 | Counter-controlled repetition.

Figure 5.1 can be made more concise by initializing `counter` to 0 and by replacing the `while` statement with

```
while ( ++counter <= 10 ) // loop-continuation condition
   cout << counter << " ";
```

This code saves a statement, because the incrementing is done directly in the `while` condition before the condition is tested. Also, the code eliminates the braces around the body of the `while`, because the `while` now contains only one statement. Coding in such a condensed fashion takes some practice and can lead to programs that are more difficult to read, debug, modify and maintain.

Common Programming Error 5.1

Floating-point values are approximate, so controlling counting loops with floating-point variables can result in imprecise counter values and inaccurate tests for termination.

Error-Prevention Tip 5.1

Control counting loops with integer values.

Good Programming Practice 5.1

Put a blank line before and after each control statement to make it stand out in the program.

Good Programming Practice 5.2

Too many levels of nesting can make a program difficult to understand. As a rule, try to avoid using more than three levels of indentation.

Good Programming Practice 5.3

Vertical spacing above and below control statements and indentation of the bodies of control statements within the control statement headers give programs a two-dimensional appearance that greatly improves readability.

5.3 for Repetition Statement

Section 5.2 presented the essentials of counter-controlled repetition. The `while` statement can be used to implement any counter-controlled loop. C++ also provides the **for repetition statement**, which specifies the counter-controlled repetition details in a single line of code. To illustrate the power of `for`, let us rewrite the program of Fig. 5.1. The result is shown in Fig. 5.2.

When the `for` statement (lines 11–12) begins executing, the control variable `counter` is declared and initialized to 1. Then, the loop-continuation condition `counter <= 10` is checked. The initial value of `counter` is 1, so the condition is satisfied and the body statement (line 12) prints the value of `counter`, namely 1. Then, the expression `counter++` increments control variable `counter` and the loop begins again with the loop-continuation test. The control variable is now equal to 2, so the final value is not exceeded and the program performs the body statement again. This process continues until the loop body has executed 10 times and the control variable `counter` is incremented to 11—this causes the loop-continuation test (line 11 between the semicolons) to fail and repetition to terminate. The program continues by performing the first statement after the `for` statement (in this case, the output statement at line 14).

```
 1   // Fig. 5.2: fig05_02.cpp
 2   // Counter-controlled repetition with the for statement.
 3   #include <iostream>
 4   using std::cout;
 5   using std::endl;
 6
 7   int main()
 8   {
 9      // for statement header includes initialization,
10      // loop-continuation condition and increment.
11      for ( int counter = 1; counter <= 10; counter++ )
12         cout << counter << " ";
13
14      cout << endl; // output a newline
15      return 0; // indicate successful termination
16   } // end main
```

```
1 2 3 4 5 6 7 8 9 10
```

Fig. 5.2 | Counter-controlled repetition with the **for** statement.

for *Statement Header Components*

Figure 5.3 takes a closer look at the **for** statement header (line 11) of Fig. 5.2. Notice that the **for** statement header "does it all"—it specifies each of the items needed for counter-controlled repetition with a control variable. If there is more than one statement in the body of the **for**, braces are required to enclose the body of the loop.

Notice that Fig. 5.2 uses the loop-continuation condition counter <= 10. If the programmer incorrectly wrote counter < 10, then the loop would execute only 9 times. This is a common off-by-one error.

Common Programming Error 5.2

Using an incorrect relational operator or using an incorrect final value of a loop counter in the condition of a while *or* for *statement can cause off-by-one errors.*

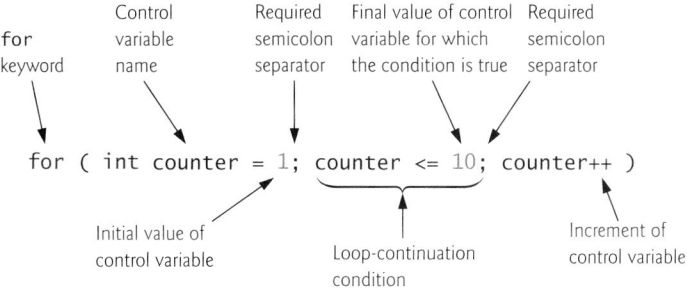

Fig. 5.3 | **for** statement header components.

Good Programming Practice 5.4

Using the final value in the condition of a while *or* for *statement and using the* <= *relational operator will help avoid off-by-one errors. For a loop used to print the values 1 to 10, for example, the loop-continuation condition should be* counter <= 10 *rather than* counter < 10 *(which is an off-by-one error) or* counter < 11 *(which is nevertheless correct). Many programmers prefer so-called* zero-based counting, *in which, to count 10 times through the loop,* counter *would be initialized to zero and the loop-continuation test would be* counter < 10.

The general form of the for statement is

```
for ( initialization; loopContinuationCondition; increment )
    statement
```

where the *initialization* expression initializes the loop's control variable, *loopContinuation-Condition* determines whether the loop should continue executing (this condition typically contains the final value of the control variable for which the condition is true) and *increment* increments the control variable. In most cases, the for statement can be represented by an equivalent while statement, as follows:

```
initialization;

while ( loopContinuationCondition )
{
    statement
    increment;
}
```

There is an exception to this rule, which we will discuss in Section 5.7.

If the *initialization* expression in the for statement header declares the control variable (i.e., the control variable's type is specified before the variable name), the control variable can be used only in the body of the for statement—the control variable will be unknown outside the for statement. This restricted use of the control variable name is known as the variable's scope. The scope of a variable specifies where it can be used in a program. Scope is discussed in detail in Chapter 6, Functions and an Introduction to Recursion.

Common Programming Error 5.3

When the control variable of a for *statement is declared in the initialization section of the* for *statement header, using the control variable after the body of the statement is a compilation error.*

Portability Tip 5.1

In the C++ standard, the scope of the control variable declared in the initialization section of a for *statement differs from the scope in older C++ compilers. In pre-standard compilers, the scope of the control variable does not terminate at the end of the block defining the body of the* for *statement; rather, the scope terminates at the end of the block that encloses the* for *statement. C++ code created with prestandard C++ compilers can break when compiled on standard-compliant compilers. If you are working with prestandard compilers and you want to be sure your code will work with standard-compliant compilers, there are two defensive programming strategies you can use: either declare control variables with different names in every* for *statement, or, if you prefer to use the same name for the control variable in several* for *statements, declare the control variable before the first* for *statement.*

As we will see, the *initialization* and *increment* expressions can be comma-separated lists of expressions. The commas, as used in these expressions, are comma operators, which guarantee that lists of expressions evaluate from left to right. The comma operator has the lowest precedence of all C++ operators. The value and type of a comma-separated list of expressions is the value and type of the rightmost expression in the list. The comma operator most often is used in for statements. Its primary application is to enable the programmer to use multiple initialization expressions and/or multiple increment expressions. For example, there may be several control variables in a single for statement that must be initialized and incremented.

Good Programming Practice 5.5

Place only expressions involving the control variables in the initialization and increment sections of a for statement. Manipulations of other variables should appear either before the loop (if they should execute only once, like initialization statements) or in the loop body (if they should execute once per repetition, like incrementing or decrementing statements).

The three expressions in the for statement header are optional (but the two semicolon separators are required). If the *loopContinuationCondition* is omitted, C++ assumes that the condition is true, thus creating an infinite loop. One might omit the *initialization* expression if the control variable is initialized earlier in the program. One might omit the *increment* expression if the increment is calculated by statements in the body of the for or if no increment is needed. The increment expression in the for statement acts as a stand-alone statement at the end of the body of the for. Therefore, the expressions

```
counter = counter + 1
counter += 1
++counter
counter++
```

are all equivalent in the incrementing portion of the for statement (when no other code appears there). Many programmers prefer the form counter++, because for loops evaluate the increment expression after the loop body executes. The postincrementing form therefore seems more natural. The variable being incremented here does not appear in a larger expression, so both preincrementing and postincrementing actually have the same effect.

Common Programming Error 5.4

Using commas instead of the two required semicolons in a for header is a syntax error.

Common Programming Error 5.5

Placing a semicolon immediately to the right of the right parenthesis of a for header makes the body of that for statement an empty statement. This is usually a logic error.

Software Engineering Observation 5.1

Placing a semicolon immediately after a for header is sometimes used to create a so-called delay loop. Such a for loop with an empty body still loops the indicated number of times, doing nothing other than the counting. For example, you might use a delay loop to slow down a program that is producing outputs on the screen too quickly for you to read them. Be careful though, because such a time delay will vary among systems with different processor speeds.

The initialization, loop-continuation condition and increment expressions of a for statement can contain arithmetic expressions. For example, if x = 2 and y = 10, and x and y are not modified in the loop body, the for header

```
for ( int j = x; j <= 4 * x * y; j += y / x )
```

is equivalent to

```
for ( int j = 2; j <= 80; j += 5 )
```

The "increment" of a for statement can be negative, in which case it is really a decrement and the loop actually counts downward (as shown in Section 5.4).

If the loop-continuation condition is initially false, the body of the for statement is not performed. Instead, execution proceeds with the statement following the for.

Frequently, the control variable is printed or used in calculations in the body of a for statement, but this is not required. It is common to use the control variable for controlling repetition while never mentioning it in the body of the for statement.

 Error-Prevention Tip 5.2

Although the value of the control variable can be changed in the body of a for statement, avoid doing so, because this practice can lead to subtle logic errors.

for Statement UML Activity Diagram

The for statement's UML activity diagram is similar to that of the while statement (Fig. 4.6). Figure 5.4 shows the activity diagram of the for statement in Fig. 5.2. The diagram makes it clear that initialization occurs once before the loop-continuation test is

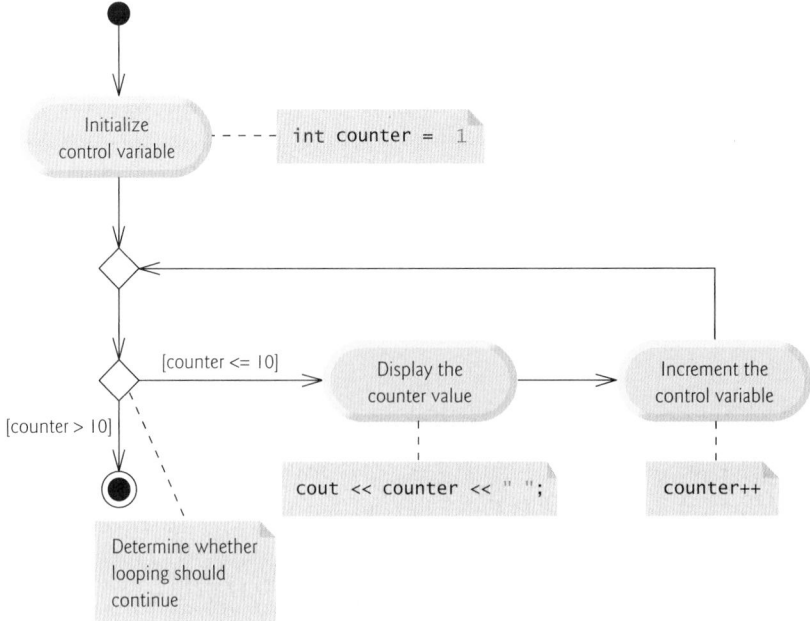

Fig. 5.4 | UML activity diagram for the for statement in Fig. 5.2.

evaluated the first time, and that incrementing occurs each time through the loop *after* the body statement executes. Note that (besides an initial state, transition arrows, a merge, a final state and several notes) the diagram contains only action states and a decision. Imagine, again, that the programmer has a bin of empty for statement UML activity diagrams—as many as the programmer might need to stack and nest with the activity diagrams of other control statements to form a structured implementation of an algorithm. The programmer fills in the action states and decision symbols with action expressions and guard conditions appropriate to the algorithm.

5.4 Examples Using the for Statement

The following examples show methods of varying the control variable in a for statement. In each case, we write the appropriate for statement header. Note the change in the relational operator for loops that decrement the control variable.

a) Vary the control variable from 1 to 100 in increments of 1.

```
for ( int i = 1; i <= 100; i++ )
```

b) Vary the control variable from 100 down to 1 in increments of -1 (that is, decrements of 1).

```
for ( int i = 100; i >= 1; i-- )
```

c) Vary the control variable from 7 to 77 in steps of 7.

```
for ( int i = 7; i <= 77; i += 7 )
```

d) Vary the control variable from 20 down to 2 in steps of -2.

```
for ( int i = 20; i >= 2; i -= 2 )
```

e) Vary the control variable over the following sequence of values: 2, 5, 8, 11, 14, 17, 20.

```
for ( int i = 2; i <= 20; i += 3 )
```

f) Vary the control variable over the following sequence of values: 99, 88, 77, 66, 55, 44, 33, 22, 11, 0.

```
for ( int i = 99; i >= 0; i -= 11 )
```

Common Programming Error 5.6

Not using the proper relational operator in the loop-continuation condition of a loop that counts downward (such as incorrectly using i <= 1 instead of i >= 1 in a loop counting down to 1) is usually a logic error that yields incorrect results when the program runs.

Application: Summing the Even Integers from 2 to 20

The next two examples provide simple applications of the for statement. The program of Fig. 5.5 uses a for statement to sum the even integers from 2 to 20. Each iteration of the loop (lines 12–13) adds the current value of the control variable number to variable total.

```
1   // Fig. 5.5: fig05_05.cpp
2   // Summing integers with the for statement.
3   #include <iostream>
4   using std::cout;
5   using std::endl;
6
7   int main()
8   {
9      int total = 0; // initialize total
10
11     // total even integers from 2 through 20
12     for ( int number = 2; number <= 20; number += 2 )
13        total += number;
14
15     cout << "Sum is " << total << endl; // display results
16     return 0; // successful termination
17  } // end main
```

```
Sum is 110
```

Fig. 5.5 | Summing integers with the for statement.

Note that the body of the for statement in Fig. 5.5 actually could be merged into the increment portion of the for header by using the comma operator as follows:

```
for ( int number = 2; // initialization
        number <= 20; // loop continuation condition
        total += number, number += 2 ) // total and increment
   ; // empty body
```

Good Programming Practice 5.6

Although statements preceding a for and statements in the body of a for often can be merged into the for header, doing so can make the program more difficult to read, maintain, modify and debug.

Good Programming Practice 5.7

Limit the size of control statement headers to a single line, if possible.

Application: Compound Interest Calculations

The next example computes compound interest using a for statement. Consider the following problem statement:

> *A person invests $1000.00 in a savings account yielding 5 percent interest. Assuming that all interest is left on deposit in the account, calculate and print the amount of money in the account at the end of each year for 10 years. Use the following formula for determining these amounts:*
> $$a = p (1 + r)^{\, n}$$
> *where*
> > *p is the original amount invested (i.e., the principal),*
> > *r is the annual interest rate,*
> > *n is the number of years and*
> > *a is the amount on deposit at the end of the nth year.*

This problem involves a loop that performs the indicated calculation for each of the 10 years the money remains on deposit. The solution is shown in Fig. 5.6.

The for statement (lines 28–35) executes its body 10 times, varying a control variable from 1 to 10 in increments of 1. C++ does not include an exponentiation operator, so we use the standard library function pow (line 31) for this purpose. The function pow(x, y) calculates the value of x raised to the yth power. In this example, the algebraic expression $(1 + r)^n$ is written as pow(1.0 + rate, year), where variable rate represents r and variable year represents n. Function pow takes two arguments of type double and returns a double value.

This program will not compile without including header file <cmath> (line 12). Function pow requires two double arguments. Note that year is an integer. Header <cmath>

```
1   // Fig. 5.6: fig05_06.cpp
2   // Compound interest calculations with for.
3   #include <iostream>
4   using std::cout;
5   using std::endl;
6   using std::fixed;
7
8   #include <iomanip>
9   using std::setw; // enables program to set a field width
10  using std::setprecision;
11
12  #include <cmath> // standard C++ math library
13  using std::pow; // enables program to use function pow
14
15  int main()
16  {
17     double amount; // amount on deposit at end of each year
18     double principal = 1000.0; // initial amount before interest
19     double rate = .05; // interest rate
20
21     // display headers
22     cout << "Year" << setw( 21 ) << "Amount on deposit" << endl;
23
24     // set floating-point number format
25     cout << fixed << setprecision( 2 );
26
27     // calculate amount on deposit for each of ten years
28     for ( int year = 1; year <= 10; year++ )
29     {
30        // calculate new amount for specified year
31        amount = principal * pow( 1.0 + rate, year );
32
33        // display the year and the amount
34        cout << setw( 4 ) << year << setw( 21 ) << amount << endl;
35     } // end for
36
37     return 0; // indicate successful termination
38  } // end main
```

Fig. 5.6 | Compound interest calculations with for. (Part 1 of 2.)

```
Year      Amount on deposit
  1              1050.00
  2              1102.50
  3              1157.63
  4              1215.51
  5              1276.28
  6              1340.10
  7              1407.10
  8              1477.46
  9              1551.33
 10              1628.89
```

Fig. 5.6 | Compound interest calculations with `for`. (Part 2 of 2.)

includes information that tells the compiler to convert the value of `year` to a temporary `double` representation before calling the function. This information is contained in `pow`'s function prototype. Chapter 6 provides a summary of other math library functions.

Common Programming Error 5.7

In general, forgetting to include the appropriate header file when using standard library functions (e.g., `<cmath>` in a program that uses math library functions) is a compilation error.

A Caution about Using Type *double* for Monetary Amounts

Notice that lines 17–19 declare the variables `amount`, `principal` and `rate` to be of type `double`. We have done this for simplicity because we are dealing with fractional parts of dollars, and we need a type that allows decimal points in its values. Unfortunately, this can cause trouble. Here is a simple explanation of what can go wrong when using `float` or `double` to represent dollar amounts (assuming `setprecision( 2 )` is used to specify two digits of precision when printing): Two dollar amounts stored in the machine could be 14.234 (which prints as 14.23) and 18.673 (which prints as 18.67). When these amounts are added, they produce the internal sum 32.907, which prints as 32.91. Thus your printout could appear as

```
   14.23
+ 18.67
 -------
   32.91
```

but a person adding the individual numbers as printed would expect the sum 32.90! You have been warned!

Good Programming Practice 5.8

Do not use variables of type `float` or `double` to perform monetary calculations. The imprecision of floating-point numbers can cause errors that result in incorrect monetary values. In the Exercises, we explore the use of integers to perform monetary calculations. [Note: Some third-party vendors sell C++ class libraries that perform precise monetary calculations. We include several URLs in Appendix I.]

Using Stream Manipulators to Format Numeric Output

The output statement at line 25 before the `for` loop and the output statement at line 34 in the `for` loop combine to print the values of the variables `year` and `amount` with the formatting specified by the parameterized stream manipulators `setprecision` and `setw` and the nonparameterized stream manipulator `fixed`. The stream manipulator `setw( 4 )` specifies that the next value output should appear in a *field width* of 4—i.e., cout prints the value with at least 4 character positions. If the value to be output is less than 4 character positions wide, the value is *right justified* in the field by default. If the value to be output is more than 4 character positions wide, the field width is extended to accommodate the entire value. To indicate that values should be output *left justified*, simply output nonparameterized stream manipulator `left` (found in header `<iostream>`). Right justification can be restored by outputting nonparameterized stream manipulator `right`.

The other formatting in the output statements indicates that variable `amount` is printed as a fixed-point value with a decimal point (specified in line 25 with the stream manipulator `fixed`) right justified in a field of 21 character positions (specified in line 34 with `setw( 21 )`) and two digits of precision to the right of the decimal point (specified in line 25 with manipulator `setprecision( 2 )`). We applied the stream manipulators `fixed` and `setprecision` to the output stream (i.e., cout) before the for loop because these format settings remain in effect until they are changed—such settings are called *sticky settings*. Thus, they do not need to be applied during each iteration of the loop. However, the field width specified with `setw` applies only to the next value output. We discuss C++'s powerful input/output formatting capabilities in detail in Chapter 15.

Note that the calculation `1.0 + rate`, which appears as an argument to the pow function, is contained in the body of the for statement. In fact, this calculation produces the same result during each iteration of the loop, so repeating it is wasteful—it should be performed once before the loop.

Performance Tip 5.1

Avoid placing expressions whose values do not change inside loops—but, even if you do, many of today's sophisticated optimizing compilers will automatically place such expressions outside the loops in the generated machine-language code.

Performance Tip 5.2

Many compilers contain optimization features that improve the performance of the code you write, but it is still better to write good code from the start.

For fun, be sure to try our Peter Minuit problem in Exercise 5.29. This problem demonstrates the wonders of compound interest.

5.5 do...while Repetition Statement

The do...while repetition statement is similar to the while statement. In the while statement, the loop-continuation condition test occurs at the beginning of the loop before the body of the loop executes. The do...while statement tests the loop-continuation condition *after* the loop body executes; therefore, the loop body always executes at least once. When a do...while terminates, execution continues with the statement after the while clause. Note that it is not necessary to use braces in the do...while statement if there is only one statement in the body; however, most programmers include the braces to avoid confusion between the while and do...while statements. For example,

```
while ( condition )
```

normally is regarded as the header of a while statement. A do...while with no braces around the single statement body appears as

```
do
    statement
while ( condition );
```

which can be confusing. The last line—while(*condition*);—might be misinterpreted by the reader as a while statement containing as its body an empty statement. Thus, the do...while with one statement is often written as follows to avoid confusion:

```
do
{
    statement
} while ( condition );
```

Good Programming Practice 5.9

Always including braces in a do...while statement helps eliminate ambiguity between the while *statement and the do...while statement containing one statement.*

Figure 5.7 uses a do...while statement to print the numbers 1–10. Upon entering the do...while statement, line 13 outputs counter's value and line 14 increments counter. Then the program evaluates the loop-continuation test at the bottom of the loop (line 15). If the condition is true, the loop continues from the first body statement in the do...while (line 13). If the condition is false, the loop terminates and the program continues with the next statement after the loop (line 17).

do...while Statement UML Activity Diagram

Figure 5.8 contains the UML activity diagram for the do...while statement. This diagram makes it clear that the loop-continuation condition is not evaluated until after the loop performs the loop-body action states at least once. Compare this activity diagram with that

```
1    // Fig. 5.7: fig05_07.cpp
2    // do...while repetition statement.
3    #include <iostream>
4    using std::cout;
5    using std::endl;
6
7    int main()
8    {
9       int counter = 1; // initialize counter
10
11      do
12      {
13         cout << counter << " "; // display counter
14         counter++; // increment counter
15      } while ( counter <= 10 ); // end do...while
16
17      cout << endl; // output a newline
18      return 0; // indicate successful termination
19   } // end main
```

Fig. 5.7 | do...while repetition statement. (Part 1 of 2.)

```
1 2 3 4 5 6 7 8 9 10
```

Fig. 5.7 | do...while repetition statement. (Part 2 of 2.)

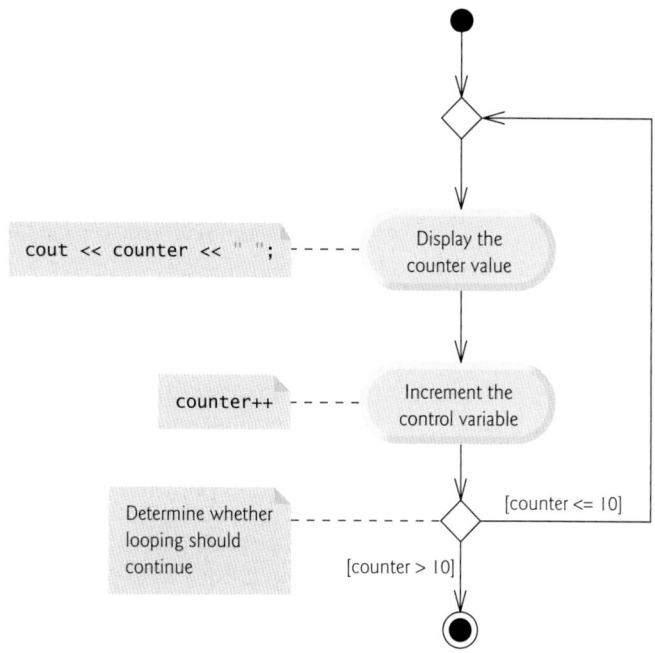

Fig. 5.8 | UML activity diagram for the do...while repetition statement of Fig. 5.7.

of the while statement (Fig. 4.6). Again, note that (besides an initial state, transition arrows, a merge, a final state and several notes) the diagram contains only action states and a decision. Imagine, again, that the programmer has access to a bin of empty do...while statement UML activity diagrams—as many as the programmer might need to stack and nest with the activity diagrams of other control statements to form a structured implementation of an algorithm. The programmer fills in the action states and decision symbols with action expressions and guard conditions appropriate to the algorithm.

5.6 switch Multiple-Selection Statement

We discussed the if single-selection statement and the if...else double-selection statement in Chapter 4. C++ provides the switch multiple-selection statement to perform many different actions based on the possible values of a variable or expression. Each action is associated with the value of a constant integral expression (i.e., any combination of character constants and integer constants that evaluates to a constant integer value) that the variable or expression on which the switch is based may assume.

*GradeBook Class with **switch** Statement to Count A, B, C, D and F Grades*

In the next example, we present an enhanced version of the GradeBook class introduced in Chapter 3 and further developed in Chapter 4. The new version of the class asks the user to enter a set of letter grades, then displays a summary of the number of students who received each grade. The class uses a switch to determine whether each grade entered is an A, B, C, D or F and to increment the appropriate grade counter. Class GradeBook is defined in Fig. 5.9, and its member-function definitions appear in Fig. 5.10. Figure 5.11 shows sample inputs and outputs of the main program that uses class GradeBook to process a set of grades.

Like earlier versions of the class definition, the GradeBook class definition (Fig. 5.9) contains function prototypes for member functions setCourseName (line 13), getCourse-Name (line 14) and displayMessage (line 15), as well as the class's constructor (line 12). The class definition also declares private data member courseName (line 19).

Class GradeBook (Fig. 5.9) now contains five additional private data members (lines 20–24)—counter variables for each grade category (i.e., A, B, C, D and F). The class also contains two additional public member functions—inputGrades and displayGradeReport. Member function inputGrades (declared in line 16) reads an arbitrary number of letter grades from the user using sentinel-controlled repetition and updates the appropriate grade counter for each grade entered. Member function displayGradeReport (declared in line 17) outputs a report containing the number of students who received each letter grade.

Source-code file GradeBook.cpp (Fig. 5.10) contains the member-function definitions for class GradeBook. Notice that lines 16–20 in the constructor initialize the five

```
 1   // Fig. 5.9: GradeBook.h
 2   // Definition of class GradeBook that counts A, B, C, D and F grades.
 3   // Member functions are defined in GradeBook.cpp
 4
 5   #include <string> // program uses C++ standard string class
 6   using std::string;
 7
 8   // GradeBook class definition
 9   class GradeBook
10   {
11   public:
12      GradeBook( string ); // constructor initializes course name
13      void setCourseName( string ); // function to set the course name
14      string getCourseName(); // function to retrieve the course name
15      void displayMessage(); // display a welcome message
16      void inputGrades(); // input arbitrary number of grades from user
17      void displayGradeReport(); // display a report based on the grades
18   private:
19      string courseName; // course name for this GradeBook
20      int aCount; // count of A grades
21      int bCount; // count of B grades
22      int cCount; // count of C grades
23      int dCount; // count of D grades
24      int fCount; // count of F grades
25   }; // end class GradeBook
```

Fig. 5.9 | GradeBook class definition.

```
 1   // Fig. 5.10: GradeBook.cpp
 2   // Member-function definitions for class GradeBook that
 3   // uses a switch statement to count A, B, C, D and F grades.
 4   #include <iostream>
 5   using std::cout;
 6   using std::cin;
 7   using std::endl;
 8
 9   #include "GradeBook.h" // include definition of class GradeBook
10
11   // constructor initializes courseName with string supplied as argument;
12   // initializes counter data members to 0
13   GradeBook::GradeBook( string name )
14   {
15      setCourseName( name ); // validate and store courseName
16      aCount = 0; // initialize count of A grades to 0
17      bCount = 0; // initialize count of B grades to 0
18      cCount = 0; // initialize count of C grades to 0
19      dCount = 0; // initialize count of D grades to 0
20      fCount = 0; // initialize count of F grades to 0
21   } // end GradeBook constructor
22
23   // function to set the course name; limits name to 25 or fewer characters
24   void GradeBook::setCourseName( string name )
25   {
26      if ( name.length() <= 25 ) // if name has 25 or fewer characters
27         courseName = name; // store the course name in the object
28      else // if name is longer than 25 characters
29      { // set courseName to first 25 characters of parameter name
30         courseName = name.substr( 0, 25 ); // select first 25 characters
31         cout << "Name \"" << name << "\" exceeds maximum length (25).\n"
32            << "Limiting courseName to first 25 characters.\n" << endl;
33      } // end if...else
34   } // end function setCourseName
35
36   // function to retrieve the course name
37   string GradeBook::getCourseName()
38   {
39      return courseName;
40   } // end function getCourseName
41
42   // display a welcome message to the GradeBook user
43   void GradeBook::displayMessage()
44   {
45      // this statement calls getCourseName to get the
46      // name of the course this GradeBook represents
47      cout << "Welcome to the grade book for\n" << getCourseName() << "!\n"
48         << endl;
49   } // end function displayMessage
50
```

Fig. 5.10 | GradeBook class uses switch statement to count letter grades A, B, C, D and F. (Part 1 of 3.)

```
51    // input arbitrary number of grades from user; update grade counter
52    void GradeBook::inputGrades()
53    {
54       int grade; // grade entered by user
55
56       cout << "Enter the letter grades." << endl
57          << "Enter the EOF character to end input." << endl;
58
59       // loop until user types end-of-file key sequence
60       while ( ( grade = cin.get() ) != EOF )
61       {
62          // determine which grade was entered
63          switch ( grade ) // switch statement nested in while
64          {
65             case 'A': // grade was uppercase A
66             case 'a': // or lowercase a
67                aCount++; // increment aCount
68                break; // necessary to exit switch
69
70             case 'B': // grade was uppercase B
71             case 'b': // or lowercase b
72                bCount++; // increment bCount
73                break; // exit switch
74
75             case 'C': // grade was uppercase C
76             case 'c': // or lowercase c
77                cCount++; // increment cCount
78                break; // exit switch
79
80             case 'D': // grade was uppercase D
81             case 'd': // or lowercase d
82                dCount++; // increment dCount
83                break; // exit switch
84
85             case 'F': // grade was uppercase F
86             case 'f': // or lowercase f
87                fCount++; // increment fCount
88                break; // exit switch
89
90             case '\n': // ignore newlines,
91             case '\t': // tabs,
92             case ' ': // and spaces in input
93                break; // exit switch
94
95             default: // catch all other characters
96                cout << "Incorrect letter grade entered."
97                   << " Enter a new grade." << endl;
98                break; // optional; will exit switch anyway
99          } // end switch
100      } // end while
101   } // end function inputGrades
```

Fig. 5.10 | GradeBook class uses switch statement to count letter grades A, B, C, D and F. (Part 2 of 3.)

```
102
103  // display a report based on the grades entered by user
104  void GradeBook::displayGradeReport()
105  {
106     // output summary of results
107     cout << "\n\nNumber of students who received each letter grade:"
108        << "\nA: " << aCount // display number of A grades
109        << "\nB: " << bCount // display number of B grades
110        << "\nC: " << cCount // display number of C grades
111        << "\nD: " << dCount // display number of D grades
112        << "\nF: " << fCount // display number of F grades
113        << endl;
114  } // end function displayGradeReport
```

Fig. 5.10 | GradeBook class uses switch statement to count letter grades A, B, C, D and F. (Part 3 of 3.)

grade counters to 0—when a GradeBook object is first created, no grades have been entered yet. As you will soon see, these counters are incremented in member function input-Grades as the user enters grades. The definitions of member functions setCourseName, getCourseName and displayMessage are identical to those found in the earlier versions of class GradeBook. Let's consider the new GradeBook member functions in detail.

Reading Character Input
The user enters letter grades for a course in member function inputGrades (lines 52–101). Inside the while header, at line 60, the parenthesized assignment (grade = cin.get()) executes first. The cin.get() function reads one character from the keyboard and stores that character in integer variable grade (declared in line 54). Characters normally are stored in variables of type **char**; however, characters can be stored in any integer data type, because they are represented as 1-byte integers in the computer. Thus, we can treat a character either as an integer or as a character, depending on its use. For example, the statement

```
cout << "The character (" << 'a' << ") has the value "
   << static_cast< int > ( 'a' ) << endl;
```

prints the character a and its integer value as follows:

```
The character (a) has the value 97
```

The integer 97 is the character's numerical representation in the computer. Most computers today use the ASCII (American Standard Code for Information Interchange) character set, in which 97 represents the lowercase letter 'a'. A table of the ASCII characters and their decimal equivalents is presented in Appendix B.

Assignment statements as a whole have the value that is assigned to the variable on the left side of the =. Thus, the value of the assignment expression grade = cin.get() is the same as the value returned by cin.get() and assigned to the variable grade.

The fact that assignment statements have values can be useful for assigning the same value to several variables. For example,

```
a = b = c = 0;
```

first evaluates the assignment c = 0 (because the = operator associates from right to left). The variable b is then assigned the value of the assignment c = 0 (which is 0). Then, the variable a is assigned the value of the assignment b = (c = 0) (which is also 0). In the program, the value of the assignment grade = cin.get() is compared with the value of EOF (a symbol whose acronym stands for "end-of-file"). We use EOF (which normally has the value –1) as the sentinel value. *However, you do not type the value –1, nor do you type the letters EOF as the sentinel value.* Rather, you type a system-dependent keystroke combination that means "end-of-file" to indicate that you have no more data to enter. EOF is a symbolic integer constant defined in the <iostream> header file. If the value assigned to grade is equal to EOF, the while loop (lines 60–100) terminates. We have chosen to represent the characters entered into this program as ints, because EOF has an integer value.

On UNIX/Linux systems and many others, end-of-file is entered by typing

    <ctrl> d

on a line by itself. This notation means to press and hold down the *Ctrl* key, then press the *d* key. On other systems such as Microsoft Windows, end-of-file can be entered by typing

    <ctrl> z

[*Note:* In some cases, you must press *Enter* after the preceding key sequence. Also, the characters ^Z sometimes appear on the screen to represent end-of-file, as is shown in Fig. 5.11.]

Portability Tip 5.2

The keystroke combinations for entering end-of-file are system dependent.

Portability Tip 5.3

Testing for the symbolic constant EOF rather than –1 makes programs more portable. The ANSI/ISO C standard, from which C++ adopts the definition of EOF, states that EOF is a negative integral value (but not necessarily –1), so EOF could have different values on different systems.

In this program, the user enters grades at the keyboard. When the user presses the *Enter* (or *Return*) key, the characters are read by the cin.get() function, one character at a time. If the character entered is not end-of-file, the flow of control enters the switch statement (lines 63–99), which increments the appropriate letter-grade counter based on the grade entered.

switch *Statement Details*
The switch statement consists of a series of case labels and an optional default case. These are used in this example to determine which counter to increment, based on a grade. When the flow of control reaches the switch, the program evaluates the expression in the parentheses (i.e., grade) following keyword switch (line 63). This is called the controlling expression. The switch statement compares the value of the controlling expression with each case label. Assume the user enters the letter C as a grade. The program compares C to each case in the switch. If a match occurs (case 'C': at line 75), the program executes the statements for that case. For the letter C, line 77 increments cCount by 1. The break statement (line 78) causes program control to proceed with the first statement after the

switch—in this program, control transfers to line 100. This line marks the end of the body of the while loop that inputs grades (lines 60–100), so control flows to the while's condition (line 60) to determine whether the loop should continue executing.

The cases in our switch explicitly test for the lowercase and uppercase versions of the letters A, B, C, D and F. Note the cases at lines 65–66 that test for the values 'A' and 'a' (both of which represent the grade A). Listing cases consecutively in this manner with no statements between them enables the cases to perform the same set of statements—when the controlling expression evaluates to either 'A' or 'a', the statements at lines 67–68 will execute. Note that each case can have multiple statements. The switch selection statement differs from other control statements in that it does not require braces around multiple statements in each case.

Without break statements, each time a match occurs in the switch, the statements for that case and subsequent cases execute until a break statement or the end of the switch is encountered. This is often referred to as "falling through" to the statements in subsequent cases. (This feature is perfect for writing a concise program that displays the iterative song "The Twelve Days of Christmas" in Exercise 5.28.)

Common Programming Error 5.8

Forgetting a break statement when one is needed in a switch statement is a logic error.

Common Programming Error 5.9

Omitting the space between the word case and the integral value being tested in a switch statement can cause a logic error. For example, writing case3: instead of writing case 3: simply creates an unused label. We will say more about this in Appendix E, C Legacy Code Topics. In this situation, the switch statement will not perform the appropriate actions when the switch's controlling expression has a value of 3.

Providing a default Case

If no match occurs between the controlling expression's value and a case label, the default case (lines 95–98) executes. We use the default case in this example to process all controlling-expression values that are neither valid grades nor newline, tab or space characters (we discuss how the program handles these white-space characters shortly). If no match occurs, the default case executes, and lines 96–97 print an error message indicating that an incorrect letter grade was entered. If no match occurs in a switch statement that does not contain a default case, program control simply continues with the first statement after the switch.

Good Programming Practice 5.10

Provide a default case in switch statements. Cases not explicitly tested in a switch statement without a default case are ignored. Including a default case focuses the programmer on the need to process exceptional conditions. There are situations in which no default processing is needed. Although the case clauses and the default case clause in a switch statement can occur in any order, it is common practice to place the default clause last.

Good Programming Practice 5.11

In a switch statement that lists the default clause last, the default clause does not require a break statement. Some programmers include this break for clarity and for symmetry with other cases.

Ignoring Newline, Tab and Blank Characters in Input

Note that lines 90–93 in the switch statement of Fig. 5.10 cause the program to skip newline, tab and blank characters. Reading characters one at a time can cause some problems. To have the program read the characters, we must send them to the computer by pressing the *Enter* key on the keyboard. This places a newline character in the input after the character we wish to process. Often, this newline character must be specially processed to make the program work correctly. By including the preceding cases in our switch statement, we prevent the error message in the default case from being printed each time a newline, tab or space is encountered in the input.

 Common Programming Error 5.10

Not processing newline and other white-space characters in the input when reading characters one at a time can cause logic errors.

*Testing Class **GradeBook***

Figure 5.11 creates a GradeBook object (line 9). Line 11 invokes the object's display-Message member function to output a welcome message to the user. Line 12 invokes the object's inputGrades member function to read a set of grades from the user and keep track of the number of students who received each grade. Note that the input/output window in Fig. 5.11 shows an error message displayed in response to entering an invalid grade (i.e., E). Line 13 invokes GradeBook member function displayGradeReport (defined in lines 104–114 of Fig. 5.10), which outputs a report based on the grades entered (as in the output in Fig. 5.11).

switch Statement UML Activity Diagram

Figure 5.12 shows the UML activity diagram for the general switch multiple-selection statement. Most switch statements use a break in each case to terminate the switch statement after processing the case. Figure 5.12 emphasizes this by including break statements in the activity diagram. Without the break statement, control would not transfer to the first statement after the switch statement after a case is processed. Instead, control would transfer to the next case's actions.

```
1   // Fig. 5.11: fig05_11.cpp
2   // Create GradeBook object, input grades and display grade report.
3
4   #include "GradeBook.h" // include definition of class GradeBook
5
6   int main()
7   {
8      // create GradeBook object
9      GradeBook myGradeBook( "CS101 C++ Programming" );
10
11     myGradeBook.displayMessage(); // display welcome message
12     myGradeBook.inputGrades(); // read grades from user
13     myGradeBook.displayGradeReport(); // display report based on grades
14     return 0; // indicate successful termination
15  } // end main
```

Fig. 5.11 | Creating a GradeBook object and calling its member functions. (Part 1 of 2.)

```
Welcome to the grade book for
CS101 C++ Programming!

Enter the letter grades.
Enter the EOF character to end input.
a
B
c
C
A
d
f
C
E
Incorrect letter grade entered. Enter a new grade.
D
A
b
^Z


Number of students who received each letter grade:
A: 3
B: 2
C: 3
D: 2
F: 1
```

Fig. 5.11 | Creating a GradeBook object and calling its member functions. (Part 2 of 2.)

The diagram makes it clear that the break statement at the end of a case causes control to exit the switch statement immediately. Again, note that (besides an initial state, transition arrows, a final state and several notes) the diagram contains action states and decisions. Also, note that the diagram uses merge symbols to merge the transitions from the break statements to the final state.

Imagine, again, that the programmer has a bin of empty switch statement UML activity diagrams—as many as the programmer might need to stack and nest with the activity diagrams of other control statements to form a structured implementation of an algorithm. The programmer fills in the action states and decision symbols with action expressions and guard conditions appropriate to the algorithm. Note that, although nested control statements are common, it is rare to find nested switch statements in a program.

When using the switch statement, remember that it can be used only for testing a *constant* integral expression—any combination of character constants and integer constants that evaluates to a constant integer value. A character constant is represented as the specific character in single quotes, such as 'A'. An integer constant is simply an integer value. Also, each case label can specify only one constant integral expression.

 Common Programming Error 5.11

Specifying an expression including variables (e.g., a + b) in a switch statement's case label is a syntax error.

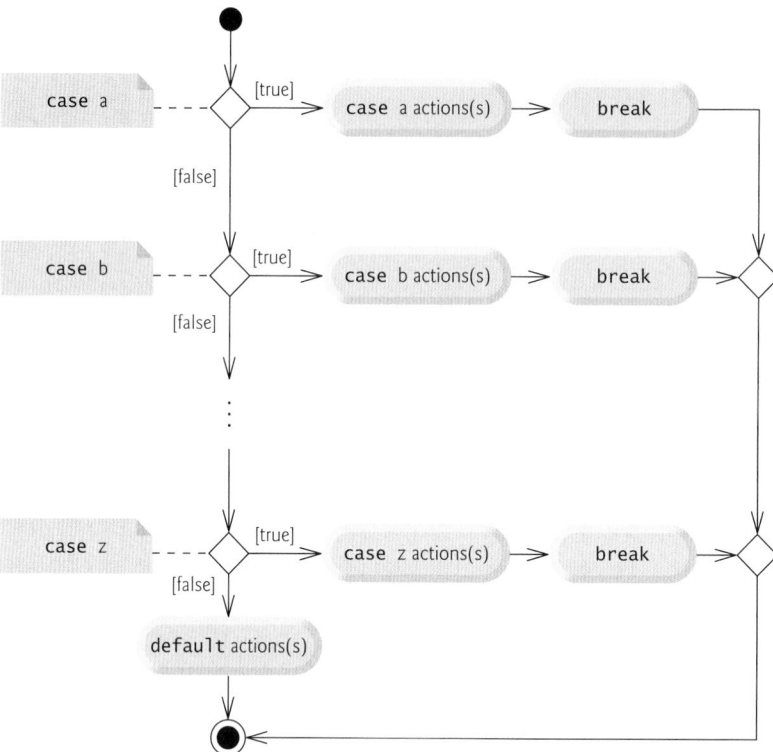

Fig. 5.12 | `switch` multiple-selection statement UML activity diagram with `break` statements.

Common Programming Error 5.12

Providing identical case labels in a `switch` statement is a compilation error. Providing case labels containing different expressions that evaluate to the same value also is a compilation error. For example, placing case 4 + 1: and case 3 + 2: in the same `switch` statement is a compilation error, because these are both equivalent to case 5:.

In Chapter 13, we present a more elegant way to implement `switch` logic. We will use a technique called polymorphism to create programs that are often clearer, more concise, easier to maintain and easier to extend than programs that use `switch` logic.

Notes on Data Types
C++ has flexible data type sizes (see Appendix C, Fundamental Types). Different applications, for example, might need integers of different sizes. C++ provides several data types to represent integers. The range of integer values for each type depends on the particular computer's hardware. In addition to the types `int` and `char`, C++ provides the types `short` (an abbreviation of `short int`) and `long` (an abbreviation of `long int`). The minimum range of values for `short` integers is –32,768 to 32,767. For the vast majority of integer calculations, `long` integers are sufficient. The minimum range of values for `long` integers is -2,147,483,648 to –2,147,483,647. On most computers, `int`s are equiv-

alent either to short or to long. The range of values for an int is at least the same as that for short integers and no larger than that for long integers. The data type char can be used to represent any of the characters in the computer's character set. It also can be used to represent small integers.

Portability Tip 5.4

Because ints can vary in size between systems, use long integers if you expect to process integers outside the range −32,768 to 32,767 and you would like to run the program on several different computer systems.

Performance Tip 5.3

If memory is at a premium, it might be desirable to use smaller integer sizes.

Performance Tip 5.4

Using smaller integer sizes can result in a slower program if the machine's instructions for manipulating them are not as efficient as those for the natural-size integers, i.e., integers whose size equals the machine's word size (e.g., 32 bits on a 32-bit machine, 64 bits on a 64-bit machine). Always test proposed efficiency "upgrades" to be sure they really improve performance.

5.7 break and continue Statements

In addition to the selection and repetition statements, C++ provides statements break and continue to alter the flow of control. The preceding section showed how break can be used to terminate a switch statement's execution. This section discusses how to use break in a repetition statement.

break *Statement*

The break statement, when executed in a while, for, do...while or switch statement, causes immediate exit from that statement. Program execution continues with the next statement. Common uses of the break statement are to escape early from a loop or to skip the remainder of a switch statement (as in Fig. 5.10). Figure 5.13 demonstrates the break statement (line 14) exiting a for repetition statement.

```cpp
1   // Fig. 5.13: fig05_13.cpp
2   // break statement exiting a for statement.
3   #include <iostream>
4   using std::cout;
5   using std::endl;
6
7   int main()
8   {
9      int count; // control variable also used after loop terminates
10
11     for ( count = 1; count <= 10; count++ ) // loop 10 times
12     {
13        if ( count == 5 )
14           break; // break loop only if x is 5
15
16        cout << count << " ";
17     } // end for
```

Fig. 5.13 | break statement exiting a for statement. (Part 1 of 2.)

```
18
19      cout << "\nBroke out of loop at count = " << count << endl;
20      return 0; // indicate successful termination
21   } // end main
```

```
1 2 3 4
Broke out of loop at count = 5
```

Fig. 5.13 | break statement exiting a for statement. (Part 2 of 2.)

When the if statement detects that count is 5, the break statement executes. This terminates the for statement, and the program proceeds to line 19 (immediately after the for statement), which displays a message indicating the value of the control variable that terminated the loop. The for statement fully executes its body only four times instead of 10. Note that the control variable count is defined outside the for statement header, so that we can use the control variable both in the body of the loop and after the loop completes its execution.

continue *Statement*

The continue statement, when executed in a while, for or do...while statement, skips the remaining statements in the body of that statement and proceeds with the next iteration of the loop. In while and do...while statements, the loop-continuation test evaluates immediately after the continue statement executes. In the for statement, the increment expression executes, then the loop-continuation test evaluates.

Figure 5.14 uses the continue statement (line 12) in a for statement to skip the output statement (line 14) when the nested if (lines 11–12) determines that the value of count is 5. When the continue statement executes, program control continues with the increment of the control variable in the for header (line 9) and loops five more times.

```
1   // Fig. 5.14: fig05_14.cpp
2   // continue statement terminating an iteration of a for statement.
3   #include <iostream>
4   using std::cout;
5   using std::endl;
6
7   int main()
8   {
9      for ( int count = 1; count <= 10; count++ ) // loop 10 times
10     {
11        if ( count == 5 ) // if count is 5,
12           continue;      // skip remaining code in loop
13
14        cout << count << " ";
15     } // end for
16
17     cout << "\nUsed continue to skip printing 5" << endl;
18     return 0; // indicate successful termination
19  } // end main
```

Fig. 5.14 | continue statement terminating a single iteration of a for statement. (Part 1 of 2.)

```
1 2 3 4 6 7 8 9 10
Used continue to skip printing 5
```

Fig. 5.14 | `continue` statement terminating a single iteration of a `for` statement. (Part 2 of 2.)

In Section 5.3, we stated that the `while` statement could be used in most cases to represent the `for` statement. The one exception occurs when the increment expression in the `while` statement follows the `continue` statement. In this case, the increment does not execute before the program tests the loop-continuation condition, and the `while` does not execute in the same manner as the `for`.

Good Programming Practice 5.12

Some programmers feel that `break` *and* `continue` *violate structured programming. The effects of these statements can be achieved by structured programming techniques we soon will learn, so these programmers do not use* `break` *and* `continue`. *Most programmers consider the use of* `break` *in* `switch` *statements acceptable.*

Performance Tip 5.5

The `break` *and* `continue` *statements, when used properly, perform faster than do the corresponding structured techniques.*

Software Engineering Observation 5.2

There is a tension between achieving quality software engineering and achieving the best-performing software. Often, one of these goals is achieved at the expense of the other. For all but the most performance-intensive situations, apply the following rule of thumb: First, make your code simple and correct; then make it fast and small, but only if necessary.

5.8 Logical Operators

So far we have studied only simple conditions, such as `counter <= 10`, `total > 1000` and `number != sentinelValue`. We expressed these conditions in terms of the relational operators `>`, `<`, `>=` and `<=`, and the equality operators `==` and `!=`. Each decision tested precisely one condition. To test multiple conditions while making a decision, we performed these tests in separate statements or in nested `if` or `if...else` statements.

C++ provides logical operators that are used to form more complex conditions by combining simple conditions. The logical operators are `&&` (logical AND), `||` (logical OR) and `!` (logical NOT, also called logical negation).

Logical AND (&&) Operator

Suppose that we wish to ensure that two conditions are *both* `true` before we choose a certain path of execution. In this case, we can use the `&&` (logical AND) operator, as follows:

```
if ( gender == 1 && age >= 65 )
    seniorFemales++;
```

This `if` statement contains two simple conditions. The condition `gender == 1` is used here to determine whether a person is a female. The condition `age >= 65` determines whether a person is a senior citizen. The simple condition to the left of the `&&` operator evaluates first, because the precedence of `==` is higher than the precedence of `&&`. If necessary, the simple condition to the right of the && operator evaluates next, because the precedence of >= is higher than the precedence of &&. As we will discuss shortly, the right side of a logical AND expression is evaluated only if the left side is true. The if statement then considers the combined condition

```
gender == 1 && age >= 65
```

This condition is true if and only if both of the simple conditions are true. Finally, if this combined condition is indeed true, the statement in the if statement's body increments the count of seniorFemales. If either of the simple conditions is false (or both are), then the program skips the incrementing and proceeds to the statement following the if. The preceding combined condition can be made more readable by adding redundant parentheses:

```
( gender == 1 ) && ( age >= 65 )
```

 Common Programming Error 5.13

Although 3 < x < 7 is a mathematically correct condition, it does not evaluate as you might expect in C++. Use (3 < x && x < 7) to get the proper evaluation in C++.

Figure 5.15 summarizes the && operator. The table shows all four possible combinations of false and true values for *expression1* and *expression2*. Such tables are often called truth tables. C++ evaluates to false or true all expressions that include relational operators, equality operators and/or logical operators.

Logical OR (||) Operator

Now let us consider the || (logical OR) operator. Suppose we wish to ensure at some point in a program that either *or* both of two conditions are true before we choose a certain path of execution. In this case, we use the || operator, as in the following program segment:

```
if ( ( semesterAverage >= 90 ) || ( finalExam >= 90 ) )
   cout << "Student grade is A" << endl;
```

This preceding condition also contains two simple conditions. The simple condition semesterAverage >= 90 evaluates to determine whether the student deserves an "A" in the course because of a solid performance throughout the semester. The simple condition finalExam >= 90 evaluates to determine whether the student deserves an "A" in the course because of an outstanding performance on the final exam. The if statement then considers the combined condition

```
( semesterAverage >= 90 ) || ( finalExam >= 90 )
```

expression1	expression2	expression1 && expression2
false	false	false
false	true	false
true	false	false
true	true	true

Fig. 5.15 | && (logical AND) operator truth table.

and awards the student an "A" if either or both of the simple conditions are `true`. Note that the message "`Student grade is A`" prints unless both of the simple conditions are `false`. Figure 5.16 is a truth table for the logical OR operator (`||`).

The `&&` operator has a higher precedence than the `||` operator. Both operators associate from left to right. An expression containing `&&` or `||` operators evaluates only until the truth or falsehood of the expression is known. Thus, evaluation of the expression

```
( gender == 1 ) && ( age >= 65 )
```

stops immediately if `gender` is not equal to 1 (i.e., the entire expression is `false`) and continues if `gender` is equal to 1 (i.e., the entire expression could still be `true` if the condition `age >= 65` is `true`). This performance feature for the evaluation of logical AND and logical OR expressions is called short-circuit evaluation.

Performance Tip 5.6

In expressions using operator &&, if the separate conditions are independent of one another, make the condition most likely to be `false` the leftmost condition. In expressions using operator ||, make the condition most likely to be `true` the leftmost condition. This use of short-circuit evaluation can reduce a program's execution time.

Logical Negation (!) Operator

C++ provides the `!` (logical NOT, also called logical negation) operator to enable a programmer to "reverse" the meaning of a condition. Unlike the `&&` and `||` binary operators, which combine two conditions, the unary logical negation operator has only a single condition as an operand. The unary logical negation operator is placed before a condition when we are interested in choosing a path of execution if the original condition (without the logical negation operator) is `false`, such as in the following program segment:

```
if ( !( grade == sentinelValue ) )
    cout << "The next grade is " << grade << endl;
```

The parentheses around the condition `grade == sentinelValue` are needed because the logical negation operator has a higher precedence than the equality operator.

In most cases, the programmer can avoid using logical negation by expressing the condition with an appropriate relational or equality operator. For example, the preceding `if` statement also can be written as follows:

```
if ( grade != sentinelValue )
    cout << "The next grade is " << grade << endl;
```

expression1	expression2	expression1 || expression2
false	false	false
false	true	true
true	false	true
true	true	true

Fig. 5.16 | || (logical OR) operator truth table.

This flexibility often can help a programmer express a condition in a more "natural" or convenient manner. Figure 5.17 is a truth table for the logical negation operator (!).

Logical Operators Example
Figure 5.18 demonstrates the logical operators by producing their truth tables. The output shows each expression that is evaluated and its `bool` result. By default, `bool` values `true` and `false` are displayed by `cout` and the stream insertion operator as 1 and 0, respectively. However, we use stream manipulator `boolalpha` in line 11 to specify that the value of

expression	!expression
false	true
true	false

Fig. 5.17 | ! (logical negation) operator truth table.

```
 1   // Fig. 5.18: fig05_18.cpp
 2   // Logical operators.
 3   #include <iostream>
 4   using std::cout;
 5   using std::endl;
 6   using std::boolalpha; // causes bool values to print as "true" or "false"
 7
 8   int main()
 9   {
10      // create truth table for && (logical AND) operator
11      cout << boolalpha << "Logical AND (&&)"
12         << "\nfalse && false: " << ( false && false )
13         << "\nfalse && true: " << ( false && true )
14         << "\ntrue && false: " << ( true && false )
15         << "\ntrue && true: " << ( true && true ) << "\n\n";
16
17      // create truth table for || (logical OR) operator
18      cout << "Logical OR (||)"
19         << "\nfalse || false: " << ( false || false )
20         << "\nfalse || true: " << ( false || true )
21         << "\ntrue || false: " << ( true || false )
22         << "\ntrue || true: " << ( true || true ) << "\n\n";
23
24      // create truth table for ! (logical negation) operator
25      cout << "Logical NOT (!)"
26         << "\n!false: " << ( !false )
27         << "\n!true: " << ( !true ) << endl;
28      return 0; // indicate successful termination
29   } // end main
```

Fig. 5.18 | Logical operators. (Part 1 of 2.)

```
Logical AND (&&)
false && false: false
false && true: false
true && false: false
true && true: true

Logical OR (||)
false || false: false
false || true: true
true || false: true
true || true: true

Logical NOT (!)
!false: true
!true: false
```

Fig. 5.18 | Logical operators. (Part 2 of 2.)

each bool expression should be displayed either as the word "true" or the word "false." For example, the result of the expression false && false in line 12 is false, so the second line of output includes the word "false." Lines 11–15 produce the truth table for &&. Lines 18–22 produce the truth table for ||. Lines 25–27 produce the truth table for !.

Summary of Operator Precedence and Associativity
Figure 5.19 adds the logical operators to the operator precedence and associativity chart. The operators are shown from top to bottom, in decreasing order of precedence.

Operators						Associativity	Type
()						left to right	parentheses
++	--	static_cast< *type* >()				left to right	unary (postfix)
++	--	+	-	!		right to left	unary (prefix)
*	/	%				left to right	multiplicative
+	-					left to right	additive
<<	>>					left to right	insertion/extraction
<	<=	>	>=			left to right	relational
==	!=					left to right	equality
&&						left to right	logical AND
||						left to right	logical OR
?:						right to left	conditional
=	+=	-=	*=	/=	%=	right to left	assignment
,						left to right	comma

Fig. 5.19 | Operator precedence and associativity.

5.9 Confusing Equality (==) and Assignment (=) Operators

There is one type of error that C++ programmers, no matter how experienced, tend to make so frequently that we feel it requires a separate section. That error is accidentally swapping the operators == (equality) and = (assignment). What makes these swaps so damaging is the fact that they ordinarily do not cause syntax errors. Rather, statements with these errors tend to compile correctly and the programs run to completion, often generating incorrect results through runtime logic errors. [*Note:* Some compilers issue a warning when = is used in a context where == normally is expected.]

There are two aspects of C++ that contribute to these problems. One is that any expression that produces a value can be used in the decision portion of any control statement. If the value of the expression is zero, it is treated as false, and if the value is nonzero, it is treated as true. The second is that assignments produce a value—namely, the value assigned to the variable on the left side of the assignment operator. For example, suppose we intend to write

```
if ( payCode == 4 )
    cout << "You get a bonus!" << endl;
```

but we accidentally write

```
if ( payCode = 4 )
    cout << "You get a bonus!" << endl;
```

The first if statement properly awards a bonus to the person whose payCode is equal to 4. The second if statement—the one with the error—evaluates the assignment expression in the if condition to the constant 4. Any nonzero value is interpreted as true, so the condition in this if statement is always true and the person always receives a bonus regardless of what the actual paycode is! Even worse, the paycode has been modified when it was only supposed to be examined!

Common Programming Error 5.14

Using operator == for assignment and using operator = for equality are logic errors.

Error-Prevention Tip 5.3

Programmers normally write conditions such as x == 7 with the variable name on the left and the constant on the right. By reversing these so that the constant is on the left and the variable name is on the right, as in 7 == x, the programmer who accidentally replaces the == operator with = will be protected by the compiler. The compiler treats this as a compilation error, because you can't change the value of a constant. This will prevent the potential devastation of a runtime logic error.

Variable names are said to be *lvalues* (for "left values") because they can be used on the left side of an assignment operator. Constants are said to be *rvalues* (for "right values") because they can be used on only the right side of an assignment operator. Note that *lvalues* can also be used as *rvalues*, but not vice versa.

There is another equally unpleasant situation. Suppose the programmer wants to assign a value to a variable with a simple statement like

```
x = 1;
```

but instead writes

```
x == 1;
```

Here, too, this is not a syntax error. Rather, the compiler simply evaluates the conditional expression. If x is equal to 1, the condition is true and the expression evaluates to the value true. If x is not equal to 1, the condition is false and the expression evaluates to the value false. Regardless of the expression's value, there is no assignment operator, so the value simply is lost. The value of x remains unaltered, probably causing an execution-time logic error. Unfortunately, we do not have a handy trick available to help you with this problem!

Error-Prevention Tip 5.4

Use your text editor to search for all occurrences of = in your program and check that you have the correct assignment operator or logical operator in each place.

5.10 **Structured Programming Summary**

Just as architects design buildings by employing the collective wisdom of their profession, so should programmers design programs. Our field is younger than architecture is, and our collective wisdom is considerably sparser. We have learned that structured programming produces programs that are easier than unstructured programs to understand, test, debug, modify, and even prove correct in a mathematical sense.

Figure 5.20 uses activity diagrams to summarize C++'s control statements. The initial and final states indicate the single entry point and the single exit point of each control statement. Arbitrarily connecting individual symbols in an activity diagram can lead to unstructured programs. Therefore, the programming profession uses only a limited set of control statements that can be combined in only two simple ways to build structured programs.

For simplicity, only single-entry/single-exit control statements are used—there is only one way to enter and only one way to exit each control statement. Connecting control statements in sequence to form structured programs is simple—the final state of one control statement is connected to the initial state of the next control statement—that is, the control statements are placed one after another in a program. We have called this "control-statement stacking." The rules for forming structured programs also allow for control statements to be nested.

Figure 5.21 shows the rules for forming structured programs. The rules assume that action states may be used to indicate any action. The rules also assume that we begin with the so-called simplest activity diagram (Fig. 5.22), consisting of only an initial state, an action state, a final state and transition arrows.

Applying the rules of Fig. 5.21 always results in an activity diagram with a neat, building-block appearance. For example, repeatedly applying Rule 2 to the simplest activity diagram results in an activity diagram containing many action states in sequence (Fig. 5.23). Rule 2 generates a stack of control statements, so let us call Rule 2 the stacking rule. [*Note:* The vertical dashed lines in Fig. 5.23 are not part of the UML. We use them to separate the four activity diagrams that demonstrate Rule 2 of Fig. 5.21 being applied.]

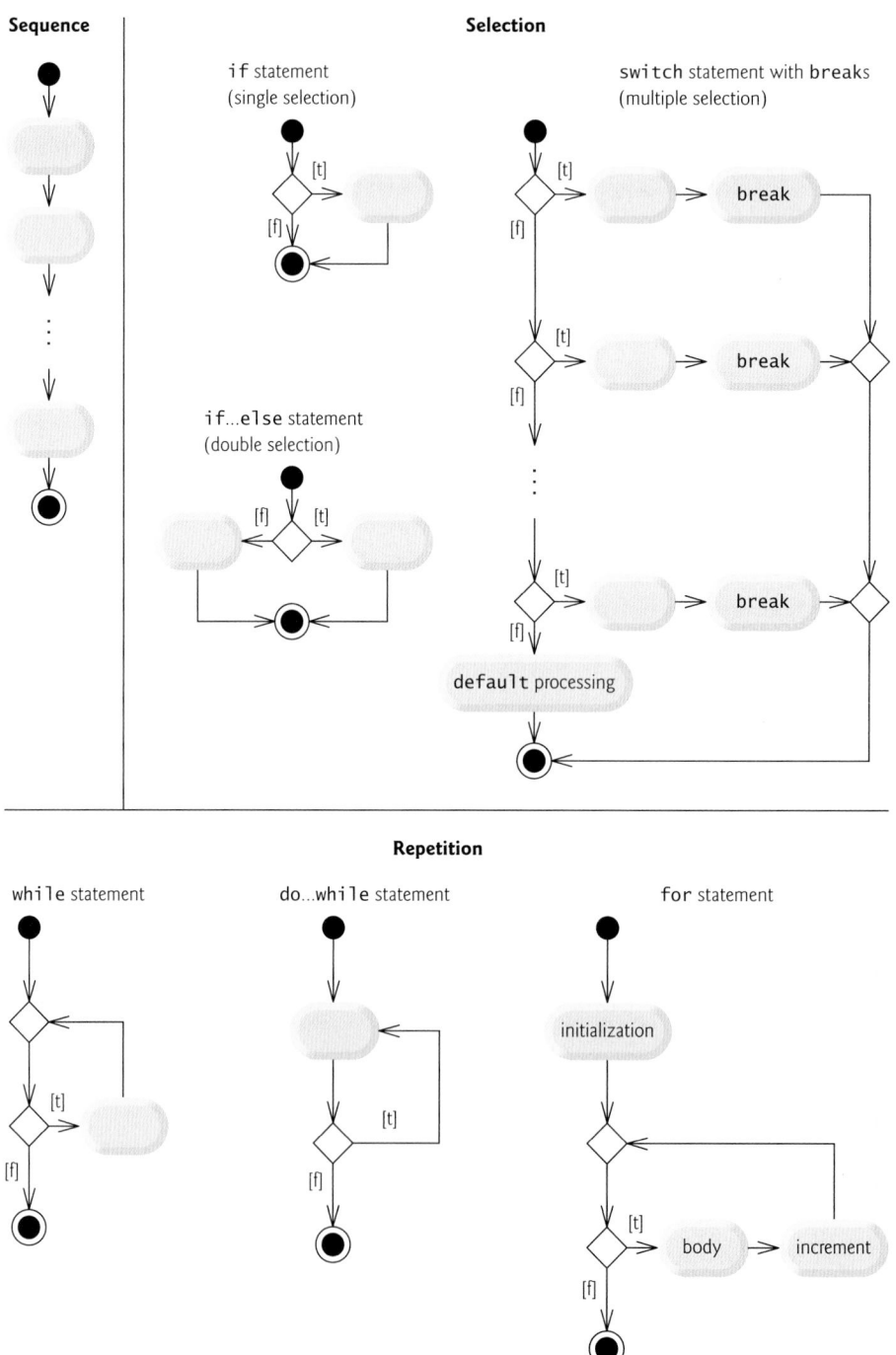

Fig. 5.20 | C++'s single-entry/single-exit sequence, selection and repetition statements.

Rules for Forming Structured Programs

1)   Begin with the "simplest activity diagram" (Fig. 5.22).

2)   Any action state can be replaced by two action states in sequence.

3)   Any action state can be replaced by any control statement (sequence, `if`, `if...else`, `switch`, `while`, `do...while` or `for`).

4)   Rules 2 and 3 can be applied as often as you like and in any order.

Fig. 5.21 | Rules for forming structured programs.

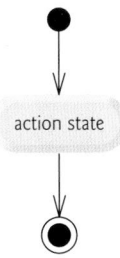

Fig. 5.22 | Simplest activity diagram.

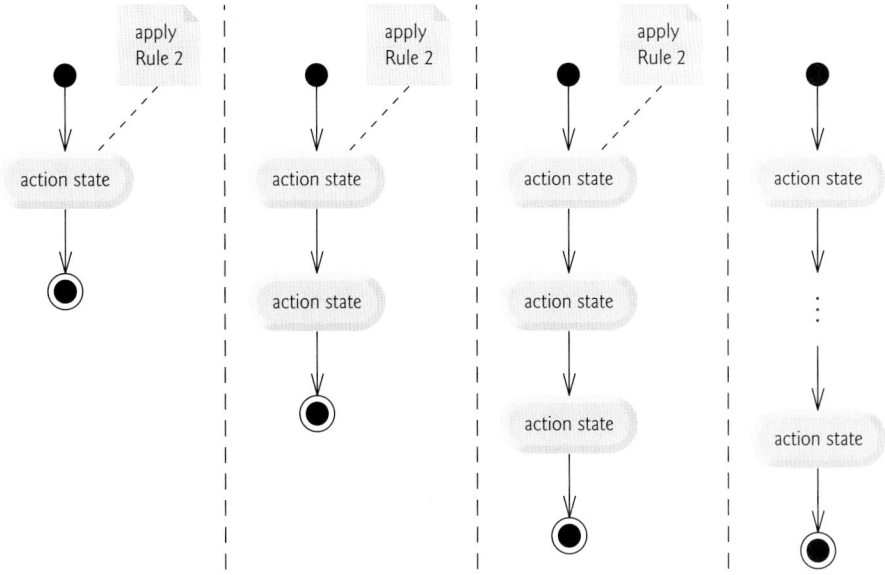

Fig. 5.23 | Repeatedly applying Rule 2 of Fig. 5.21 to the simplest activity diagram.

Rule 3 is called the nesting rule. Repeatedly applying Rule 3 to the simplest activity diagram results in an activity diagram with neatly nested control statements. For example, in Fig. 5.24, the action state in the simplest activity diagram is replaced with a double-selection (if…else) statement. Then Rule 3 is applied again to the action states in the double-selection statement, replacing each of these action states with a double-selection statement. The dashed action-state symbols around each of the double-selection statements represent an action state that was replaced in the preceding activity diagram. [*Note:* The dashed arrows and dashed action state symbols shown in Fig. 5.24 are not part of the UML.]

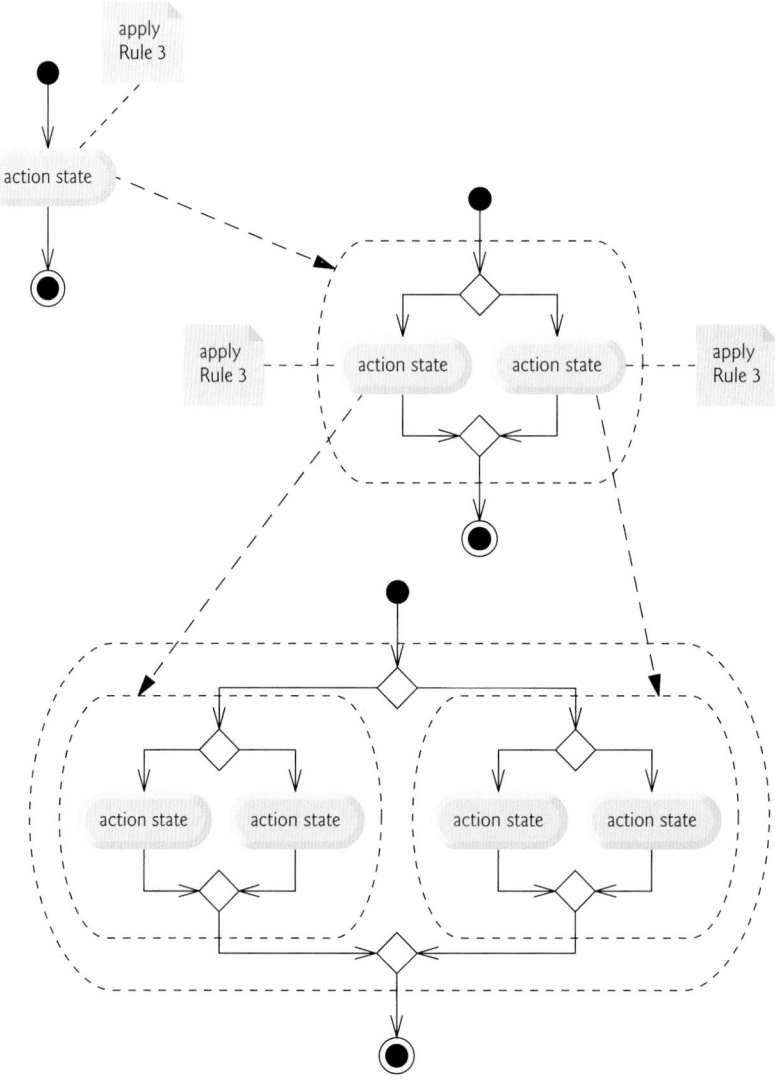

Fig. 5.24 | Applying Rule 3 of Fig. 5.21 to the simplest activity diagram several times.

They are used here as pedagogic devices to illustrate that any action state may be replaced with a control statement.]

Rule 4 generates larger, more involved and more deeply nested statements. The diagrams that emerge from applying the rules in Fig. 5.21 constitute the set of all possible activity diagrams and hence the set of all possible structured programs. The beauty of the structured approach is that we use only seven simple single-entry/single-exit control statements and assemble them in only two simple ways.

If the rules in Fig. 5.21 are followed, an activity diagram with illegal syntax (such as that in Fig. 5.25) cannot be created. If you are uncertain about whether a particular diagram is legal, apply the rules of Fig. 5.21 in reverse to reduce the diagram to the simplest activity diagram. If it is reducible to the simplest activity diagram, the original diagram is structured; otherwise, it is not.

Structured programming promotes simplicity. Böhm and Jacopini have given us the result that only three forms of control are needed:

- Sequence
- Selection
- Repetition

The sequence structure is trivial. Simply list the statements to execute in the order in which they should execute.

Selection is implemented in one of three ways:

- `if` statement (single selection)
- `if...else` statement (double selection)
- `switch` statement (multiple selection)

It is straightforward to prove that the simple `if` statement is sufficient to provide any form of selection—everything that can be done with the `if...else` statement and the `switch` statement can be implemented (although perhaps not as clearly and efficiently) by combining `if` statements.

Repetition is implemented in one of three ways:

- `while` statement
- `do...while` statement
- `for` statement

It is straightforward to prove that the `while` statement is sufficient to provide any form of repetition. Everything that can be done with the `do...while` statement and the `for` statement can be done (although perhaps not as smoothly) with the `while` statement.

Combining these results illustrates that any form of control ever needed in a C++ program can be expressed in terms of the following:

- sequence
- `if` statement (selection)
- `while` statement (repetition)

and that these control statements can be combined in only two ways—stacking and nesting. Indeed, structured programming promotes simplicity.

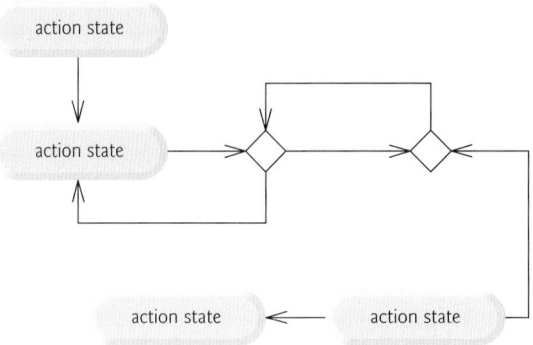

Fig. 5.25 | Activity diagram with illegal syntax.

5.11 (Optional) Software Engineering Case Study: Identifying Objects' States and Activities in the ATM System

In Section 4.13, we identified many of the class attributes needed to implement the ATM system and added them to the class diagram in Fig. 4.24. In this section, we show how these attributes represent an object's state. We identify some key states that our objects may occupy and discuss how objects change state in response to various events occurring in the system. We also discuss the workflow, or activities, that objects perform in the ATM system. We present the activities of BalanceInquiry and Withdrawal transaction objects in this section, as they represent two of the key activities in the ATM system.

State Machine Diagrams

Each object in a system goes through a series of discrete states. An object's current state is indicated by the values of the object's attributes at a given time. State machine diagrams (commonly called state diagrams) model key states of an object and show under what circumstances the object changes state. Unlike the class diagrams presented in earlier case study sections, which focused primarily on the structure of the system, state diagrams model some of the behavior of the system.

Figure 5.26 is a simple state diagram that models some of the states of an object of class ATM. The UML represents each state in a state diagram as a rounded rectangle with the name of the state placed inside it. A solid circle with an attached stick arrowhead designates the initial state. Recall that we modeled this state information as the Boolean attribute userAuthenticated in the class diagram of Fig. 4.24. This attribute is initialized to false, or the "User not authenticated" state, according to the state diagram.

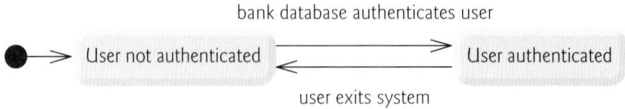

Fig. 5.26 | State diagram for the ATM object.

The arrows with stick arrowheads indicate transitions between states. An object can transition from one state to another in response to various events that occur in the system. The name or description of the event that causes a transition is written near the line that corresponds to the transition. For example, the ATM object changes from the "User not authenticated" state to the "User authenticated" state after the database authenticates the user. Recall from the requirements document that the database authenticates a user by comparing the account number and PIN entered by the user with those of the corresponding account in the database. If the database indicates that the user has entered a valid account number and the correct PIN, the ATM object transitions to the "User authenticated" state and changes its userAuthenticated attribute to a value of true. When the user exits the system by choosing the "exit" option from the main menu, the ATM object returns to the "User not authenticated" state in preparation for the next ATM user.

Software Engineering Observation 5.3

Software designers do not generally create state diagrams showing every possible state and state transition for all attributes—there are simply too many of them. State diagrams typically show only the most important or complex states and state transitions.

Activity Diagrams

Like a state diagram, an activity diagram models aspects of system behavior. Unlike a state diagram, an activity diagram models an object's workflow (sequence of events) during program execution. An activity diagram models the actions the object will perform and in what order. Recall that we used UML activity diagrams to illustrate the flow of control for the control statements presented in Chapter 4 and Chapter 5.

The activity diagram in Fig. 5.27 models the actions involved in executing a Balance-Inquiry transaction. We assume that a BalanceInquiry object has already been initialized and assigned a valid account number (that of the current user), so the object knows which balance to retrieve. The diagram includes the actions that occur after the user selects a balance inquiry from the main menu and before the ATM returns the user to the main menu—a BalanceInquiry object does not perform or initiate these actions, so we do not

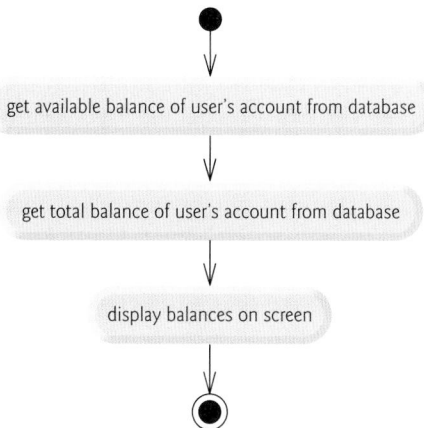

Fig. 5.27 | Activity diagram for a BalanceInquiry transaction.

model them here. The diagram begins with retrieving the available balance of the user's account from the database. Next, the `BalanceInquiry` retrieves the total balance of the account. Finally, the transaction displays the balances on the screen. This action completes the execution of the transaction.

The UML represents an action in an activity diagram as an action state modeled by a rectangle with its left and right sides replaced by arcs curving outward. Each action state contains an action expression—for example, "get available balance of user's account from database"—that specifies an action to be performed. An arrow with a stick arrowhead connects two action states, indicating the order in which the actions represented by the action states occur. The solid circle (at the top of Fig. 5.27) represents the activity's initial state—the beginning of the workflow before the object performs the modeled actions. In this case, the transaction first executes the "get available balance of user's account from database" action expression. Second, the transaction retrieves the total balance. Finally, the transaction displays both balances on the screen. The solid circle enclosed in an open circle (at the bottom of Fig. 5.27) represents the final state—the end of the workflow after the object performs the modeled actions.

Figure 5.28 shows an activity diagram for a `Withdrawal` transaction. We assume that a `Withdrawal` object has been assigned a valid account number. We do not model the user selecting a withdrawal from the main menu or the ATM returning the user to the main menu because these are not actions performed by a `Withdrawal` object. The transaction first displays a menu of standard withdrawal amounts (Fig. 2.17) and an option to cancel the transaction. The transaction then inputs a menu selection from the user. The activity flow now arrives at a decision symbol. This point determines the next action based on the associated guard conditions. If the user cancels the transaction, the system displays an appropriate message. Next, the cancellation flow reaches a merge symbol, where this activity flow joins the transaction's other possible activity flows (which we discuss shortly). Note that a merge can have any number of incoming transition arrows, but only one outgoing transition arrow. The decision at the bottom of the diagram determines whether the transaction should repeat from the beginning. When the user has canceled the transaction, the guard condition "cash dispensed or user canceled transaction" is true, so control transitions to the activity's final state.

If the user selects a withdrawal amount from the menu, the transaction sets `amount` (an attribute of class `Withdrawal` originally modeled in Fig. 4.24) to the value chosen by the user. The transaction next gets the available balance of the user's account (i.e., the `availableBalance` attribute of the user's `Account` object) from the database. The activity flow then arrives at another decision. If the requested withdrawal amount exceeds the user's available balance, the system displays an appropriate error message informing the user of the problem. Control then merges with the other activity flows before reaching the decision at the bottom of the diagram. The guard decision "cash not dispensed and user did not cancel" is true, so the activity flow returns to the top of the diagram, and the transaction prompts the user to input a new amount.

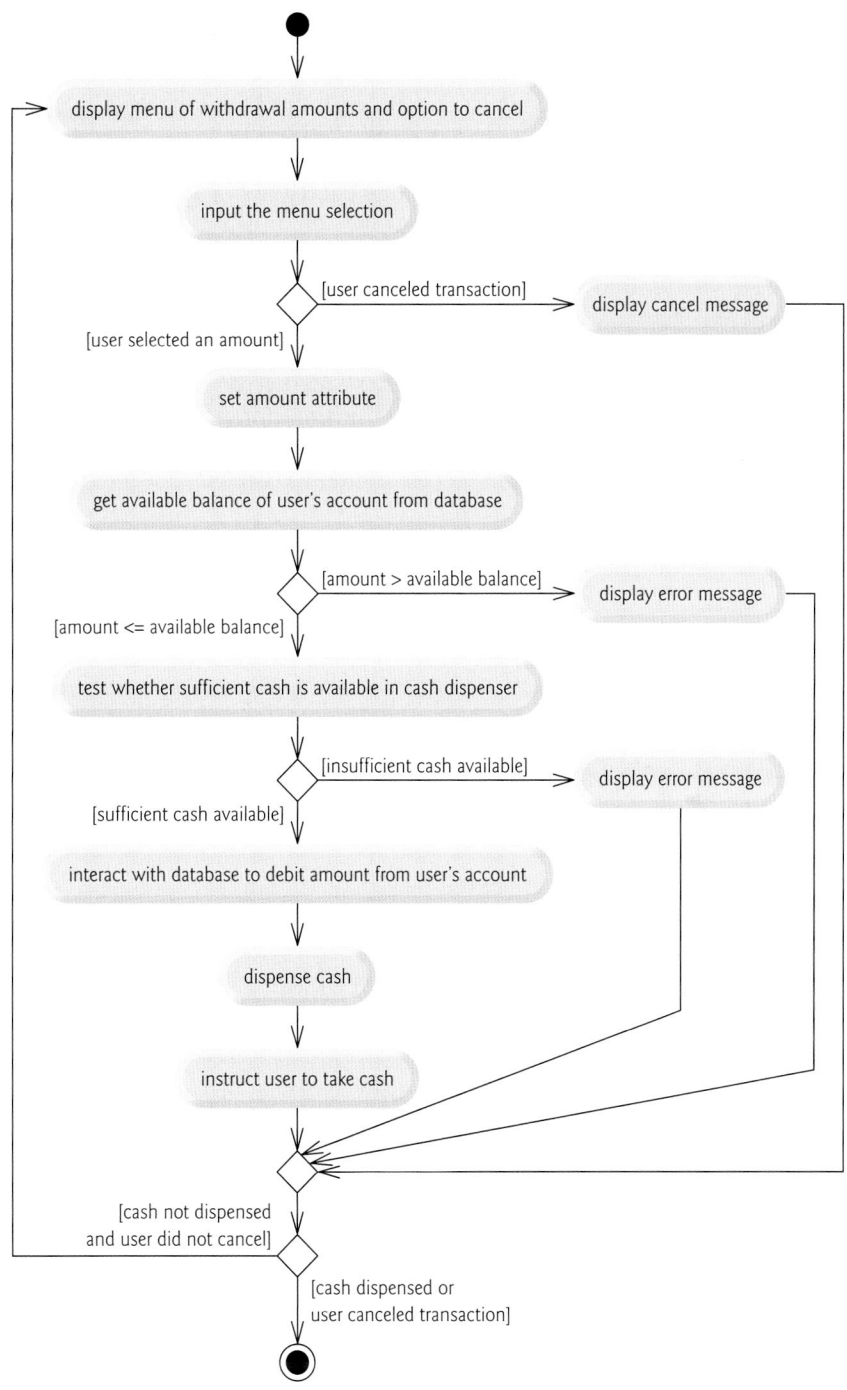

Fig. 5.28 | Activity diagram for a `Withdrawal` transaction.

If the requested withdrawal amount is less than or equal to the user's available balance, the transaction tests whether the cash dispenser has enough cash to satisfy the withdrawal request. If it does not, the transaction displays an appropriate error message and passes through the merge before reaching the final decision. Cash was not dispensed, so the activity flow returns to the beginning of the activity diagram, and the transaction prompts the user to choose a new amount. If sufficient cash is available, the transaction interacts with the database to debit the withdrawal amount from the user's account (i.e., subtract the amount from both the `available-Balance` and `totalBalance` attributes of the user's `Account` object). The transaction then dispenses the desired amount of cash and instructs the user to take the cash that is dispensed. The main flow of activity next merges with the two error flows and the cancellation flow. In this case, cash was dispensed, so the activity flow reaches the final state.

We have taken the first steps in modeling the behavior of the ATM system and have shown how an object's attributes participate in the object's activities. In Section 6.22, we investigate the operations of our classes to create a more complete model of the system's behavior.

Software Engineering Case Study Self-Review Exercises

5.1   State whether the following statement is *true* or *false*, and if *false*, explain why: State diagrams model structural aspects of a system.

5.2   An activity diagram models the _____ that an object performs and the order in which it performs them.
- a) actions
- b) attributes
- c) states
- d) state transitions

5.3   Based on the requirements document, create an activity diagram for a deposit transaction.

Answers to Software Engineering Case Study Self-Review Exercises

5.1   False. State diagrams model some of the behavior of a system.

5.2   a.

5.3   Figure 5.29 presents an activity diagram for a deposit transaction. The diagram models the actions that occur after the user chooses the deposit option from the main menu and before the ATM returns the user to the main menu. Recall that part of receiving a deposit amount from the user involves converting an integer number of cents to a dollar amount. Also recall that crediting a deposit amount to an account involves increasing only the `totalBalance` attribute of the user's `Account` object. The bank updates the `availableBalance` attribute of the user's `Account` object only after confirming the amount of cash in the deposit envelope and after the enclosed checks clear—this occurs independently of the ATM system.

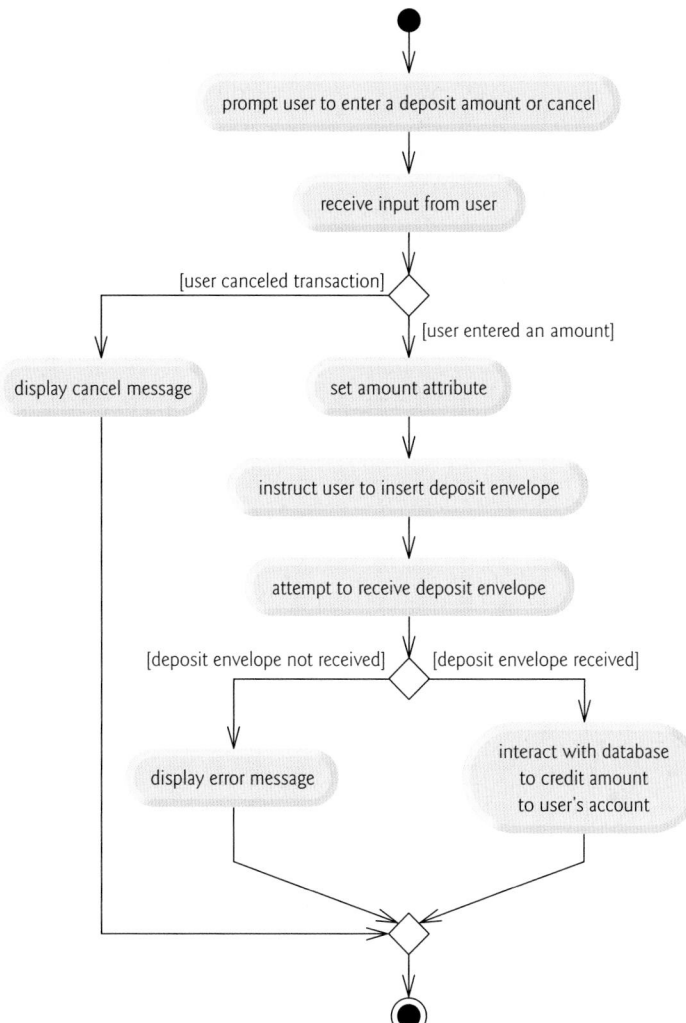

Summary

- In C++, it is more precise to call a declaration that also reserves memory a definition.
- The for repetition statement handles all the details of counter-controlled repetition. The general format of the for statement is

```
for ( initialization; loopContinuationCondition; increment )
    statement
```

where *initialization* initializes the loop's control variable, *loopContinuationCondition* is the condition that determines whether the loop should continue executing and *increment* increments the control variable.

- Typically, `for` statements are used for counter-controlled repetition and `while` statements are used for sentinel-controlled repetition.

- The scope of a variable specifies where it can be used in a program. For example, a control variable declared in the header of a `for` statement can be used only in the body of the `for` statement—the control variable will be unknown outside the `for` statement.

- The initialization and increment expressions in a `for` statement header can be comma-separated lists of expressions. The commas, as used in these expressions, are comma operators, which guarantee that lists of expressions evaluate from left to right. The comma operator has the lowest precedence of all C++ operators. The value and type of a comma-separated list of expressions is the value and type of the rightmost expression in the list.

- The initialization, loop-continuation condition and increment expressions of a `for` statement can contain arithmetic expressions. Also, the increment of a `for` statement can be negative, in which case it is really a decrement and the loop counts downward.

- If the loop-continuation condition in a `for` header is initially `false`, the body of the `for` statement is not performed. Instead, execution proceeds with the statement following the `for`.

- Standard library function `pow( x, y )` calculates the value of x raised to the yth power. Function `pow` takes two arguments of type `double` and returns a `double` value.

- Parameterized stream manipulator `setw` specifies the field width in which the next value output should appear. The value is right justified in the field by default. If the value to be output is larger than the field width, the field width is extended to accommodate the entire value. Nonparameterized stream manipulator `left` (found in header `<iostream>`) can be used to cause a value to be left justified in a field and `right` can be used to restore right justification.

- Sticky settings are those output-formatting settings that remain in effect until they are changed.

- The `do…while` repetition statement tests the loop-continuation condition at the end of the loop, so the body of the loop will be executed at least once. The format for the `do…while` statement is

```
do
{
    statement
} while ( condition );
```

- The `switch` multiple-selection statement performs different actions based on the possible values of a variable or expression. Each action is associated with the value of a constant integral expression (i.e., any combination of character constants and integer constants that evaluates to a constant integer value) that the variable or expression on which the `switch` is based may assume.

- The `switch` statement consists of a series of `case` labels and an optional `default` case.

- The `cin.get()` function reads one character from the keyboard. Characters normally are stored in variables of type `char`; however, characters can be stored in any integer data type, because they are represented as 1-byte integers in the computer. Thus, a character can be treated either as an integer or as a character, depending on its use.

- The end-of-file indicator is a system-dependent keystroke combination that specifies that there is no more data to input. `EOF` is a symbolic integer constant defined in the `<iostream>` header file that indicates "end-of-file."

- The expression in the parentheses following keyword `switch` is called the controlling expression of the `switch`. The `switch` statement compares the value of the controlling expression with each `case` label.

- Listing cases consecutively with no statements between them enables the cases to perform the same set of statements.

- Each case can have multiple statements. The switch selection statement differs from other control statements in that it does not require braces around multiple statements in each case.

- The switch statement can be used only for testing a constant integral expression. A character constant is represented as the specific character in single quotes, such as 'A'. An integer constant is simply an integer value. Also, each case label can specify only one constant integral expression.

- C++ provides several data types to represent integers—int, char, short and long. The range of integer values for each type depends on the particular computer's hardware.

- The break statement, when executed in one of the repetition statements (for, while and do...while), causes immediate exit from the statement.

- The continue statement, when executed in one of the repetition statements (for, while and do...while), skips any remaining statements in the body of the repetition statement and proceeds with the next iteration of the loop. In a while or do...while statement, execution continues with the next evaluation of the condition. In a for statement, execution continues with the increment expression in the for statement header.

- Logical operators enable programmers to form complex conditions by combining simple conditions. The logical operators are && (logical AND), || (logical OR) and ! (logical NOT, also called logical negation).

- The && (logical AND) operator ensures that two conditions are *both* true before choosing a certain path of execution.

- The || (logical OR) operator ensures that either *or* both of two conditions are true before choosing a certain path of execution.

- An expression containing && or || operators evaluates only until the truth or falsehood of the expression is known. This performance feature for the evaluation of logical AND and logical OR expressions is called short-circuit evaluation.

- The ! (logical NOT, also called logical negation) operator enables a programmer to "reverse" the meaning of a condition. The unary logical negation operator is placed before a condition to choose a path of execution if the original condition (without the logical negation operator) is false. In most cases, the programmer can avoid using logical negation by expressing the condition with an appropriate relational or equality operator.

- When used as a condition, any nonzero value implicitly converts to true; 0 (zero) implicitly converts to false.

- By default, bool values true and false are displayed by cout as 1 and 0, respectively. Stream manipulator boolalpha specifies that the value of each bool expression should be displayed as either the word "true" or the word "false."

- Any form of control ever needed in a C++ program can be expressed in terms of sequence, selection and repetition statements, and these can be combined in only two ways—stacking and nesting.

Terminology

!, logical NOT operator
&&, logical AND operator
||, logical OR operator
ASCII character set
boolalpha stream manipulator
break statement

case label
char fundamental type
comma operator
constant integral expression
continue statement
controlling expression of a switch

decrement a control variable
default case in switch
definition
delay loop
field width
final value of a control variable
for repetition statement
for header
increment a control variable
initial value of a control variable
left justification
left stream manipulator
logical AND (&&)
logical negation (!)
logical NOT (!)
logical operator
logical OR (||)
loop-continuation condition

lvalue ("left value")
name of a control variable
nesting rule
off-by-one error
right justification
right stream manipulator
rvalue ("right value")
scope of a variable
setw stream manipulator
short-circuit evaluation
simple condition
stacking rule
standard library function pow
sticky setting
switch multiple-selection statement
truth table
zero-based counting

Self-Review Exercises

5.1 State whether the following are *true* or *false*. If the answer is *false*, explain why.
   a) The default case is required in the switch selection statement.
   b) The break statement is required in the default case of a switch selection statement to exit the switch properly.
   c) The expression (x > y && a < b) is true if either the expression x > y is true or the expression a < b is true.
   d) An expression containing the || operator is true if either or both of its operands are true.

5.2 Write a C++ statement or a set of C++ statements to accomplish each of the following:
   a) Sum the odd integers between 1 and 99 using a for statement. Assume the integer variables sum and count have been declared.
   b) Print the value 333.546372 in a field width of 15 characters with precisions of 1, 2 and 3. Print each number on the same line. Left-justify each number in its field. What three values print?
   c) Calculate the value of 2.5 raised to the power 3 using function pow. Print the result with a precision of 2 in a field width of 10 positions. What prints?
   d) Print the integers from 1 to 20 using a while loop and the counter variable x. Assume that the variable x has been declared, but not initialized. Print only 5 integers per line. [*Hint:* Use the calculation x % 5. When the value of this is 0, print a newline character; otherwise, print a tab character.]
   e) Repeat Exercise 5.2 (d) using a for statement.

5.3 Find the error(s) in each of the following code segments and explain how to correct it (them).
```
a) x = 1;
   while ( x <= 10 );
      x++;
   }
b) for ( y = .1; y != 1.0; y += .1 )
      cout << y << endl;
```

c)
```
switch ( n )
{
    case 1:
        cout << "The number is 1" << endl;
    case 2:
        cout << "The number is 2" << endl;
        break;
    default:
        cout << "The number is not 1 or 2" << endl;
        break;
}
```

d) The following code should print the values 1 to 10.
```
n = 1;
while ( n < 10 )
    cout << n++ << endl;
```

Answers to Self-Review Exercises

5.1 a) False. The `default` case is optional. If no default action is needed, then there is no need for a `default` case. Nevertheless, it is considered good software engineering to always provide a `default` case.

b) False. The `break` statement is used to exit the `switch` statement. The `break` statement is not required when the `default` case is the last case. Nor will the `break` statement be required if having control proceed with the next case makes sense.

c) False. When using the `&&` operator, both of the relational expressions must be `true` for the entire expression to be `true`.

d) True.

5.2 a)
```
sum = 0;
for ( count = 1; count <= 99; count += 2 )
    sum += count;
```

b)
```
cout << fixed << left
    << setprecision( 1 ) << setw( 15 ) << 333.546372
    << setprecision( 2 ) << setw( 15 ) << 333.546372
    << setprecision( 3 ) << setw( 15 ) << 333.546372
    << endl;
```
Output is:
```
333.5          333.55         333.546
```

c)
```
cout << fixed << setprecision( 2 )
    << setw( 10 ) << pow( 2.5, 3 )
    << endl;
```
Output is:
```
     15.63
```

d)
```
x = 1;

while ( x <= 20 )
{
    cout << x;

    if ( x % 5 == 0 )
        cout << endl;
```

```
        else
            cout << '\t';

        x++;
    }
```

e)
```
for ( x = 1; x <= 20; x++ )
{
    cout << x;

    if ( x % 5 == 0 )
        cout << endl;
    else
        cout << '\t';
}
```

or

```
for ( x = 1; x <= 20; x++ )
{
    if ( x % 5 == 0 )
        cout << x << endl;
    else
        cout << x << '\t';
}
```

5.3   a) Error: The semicolon after the while header causes an infinite loop.
            Correction: Replace the semicolon by a {, or remove both the ; and the }.
       b) Error: Using a floating-point number to control a for repetition statement.
            Correction: Use an integer and perform the proper calculation in order to get the values
            you desire.

```
for ( y = 1; y != 10; y++ )
    cout << ( static_cast< double >( y ) / 10 ) << endl;
```

       c) Error: Missing break statement in the first case.
            Correction: Add a break statement at the end of the statements for the first case. Note
            that this is not an error if the programmer wants the statement of case 2: to execute
            every time the case 1: statement executes.
       d) Error: Improper relational operator used in the while repetition-continuation condi-
            tion.
            Correction: Use <= rather than <, or change 10 to 11.

Exercises

5.4   Find the error(s) in each of the following:
       a)
```
For ( x = 100, x >= 1, x++ )
    cout << x << endl;
```
       b) The following code should print whether integer value is odd or even:

```
switch ( value % 2 )
{
    case 0:
        cout << "Even integer" << endl;
    case 1:
        cout << "Odd integer" << endl;
}
```

c) The following code should output the odd integers from 19 to 1:

```
for ( x = 19; x >= 1; x += 2 )
    cout << x << endl;
```

d) The following code should output the even integers from 2 to 100:

```
counter = 2;

do
{
    cout << counter << endl;
    counter += 2;
} While ( counter < 100 );
```

5.5   Write a program that uses a for statement to sum a sequence of integers. Assume that the first integer read specifies the number of values remaining to be entered. Your program should read only one value per input statement. A typical input sequence might be

    5 100 200 300 400 500

where the 5 indicates that the subsequent 5 values are to be summed.

5.6   Write a program that uses a for statement to calculate and print the average of several integers. Assume the last value read is the sentinel 9999. A typical input sequence might be

    10 8 11 7 9 9999

indicating that the program should calculate the average of all the values preceding 9999.

5.7   What does the following program do?

```
1   // Exercise 5.7: ex05_07.cpp
2   // What does this program print?
3   #include <iostream>
4   using std::cout;
5   using std::cin;
6   using std::endl;
7
8   int main()
9   {
10      int x; // declare x
11      int y; // declare y
12
13      // prompt user for input
14      cout << "Enter two integers in the range 1-20: ";
15      cin >> x >> y;   // read values for x and y
16
17      for ( int i = 1; i <= y; i++ ) // count from 1 to y
18      {
19          for ( int j = 1; j <= x; j++ ) // count from 1 to x
```

```
20          cout << '@'; // output @
21
22      cout << endl; // begin new line
23   } // end outer for
24
25   return 0; // indicate successful termination
26 } // end main
```

5.8 Write a program that uses a for statement to find the smallest of several integers. Assume that the first value read specifies the number of values remaining and that the first number is not one of the integers to compare.

5.9 Write a program that uses a for statement to calculate and print the product of the odd integers from 1 to 15.

5.10 The factorial function is used frequently in probability problems. Using the definition of factorial in Exercise 4.35, write a program that uses a for statement to evaluate the factorials of the integers from 1 to 5. Print the results in tabular format. What difficulty might prevent you from calculating the factorial of 20?

5.11 Modify the compound interest program of Section 5.4 to repeat its steps for the interest rates 5 percent, 6 percent, 7 percent, 8 percent, 9 percent and 10 percent. Use a for statement to vary the interest rate.

5.12 Write a program that uses for statements to print the following patterns separately, one below the other. Use for loops to generate the patterns. All asterisks (*) should be printed by a single statement of the form cout << '*'; (this causes the asterisks to print side by side). [*Hint:* The last two patterns require that each line begin with an appropriate number of blanks. *Extra credit:* Combine your code from the four separate problems into a single program that prints all four patterns side by side by making clever use of nested for loops.]

```
(a)              (b)              (c)              (d)
*                **********       **********                *
**               *********         *********               **
***              ********           ********               ***
****             *******             *******               ****
*****            ******               ******               *****
******           *****                 *****               ******
*******          ****                   ****               *******
********         ***                     ***               ********
*********        **                       **               *********
**********       *                         *               **********
```

5.13 One interesting application of computers is the drawing of graphs and bar charts. Write a program that reads five numbers (each between 1 and 30). Assume that the user enters only valid values. For each number that is read, your program should print a line containing that number of adjacent asterisks. For example, if your program reads the number 7, it should print *******.

5.14 A mail order house sells five different products whose retail prices are: product 1 — $2.98, product 2—$4.50, product 3—$9.98, product 4—$4.49 and product 5—$6.87. Write a program that reads a series of pairs of numbers as follows:
  a) product number
  b) quantity sold

Your program should use a `switch` statement to determine the retail price for each product. Your program should calculate and display the total retail value of all products sold. Use a sentinel-controlled loop to determine when the program should stop looping and display the final results.

5.15   Modify the `GradeBook` program of Fig. 5.9–Fig. 5.11 so that it calculates the grade-point average for the set of grades. A grade of A is worth 4 points, B is worth 3 points, etc.

5.16   Modify the program in Fig. 5.6 so it uses only integers to calculate the compound interest. [*Hint:* Treat all monetary amounts as integral numbers of pennies. Then "break" the result into its dollar portion and cents portion by using the division and modulus operations. Insert a period.]

5.17   Assume `i = 1, j = 2, k = 3` and `m = 2`. What does each of the following statements print? Are the parentheses necessary in each case?

```
a)  cout << ( i == 1 ) << endl;
b)  cout << ( j == 3 ) << endl;
c)  cout << ( i >= 1 && j < 4 ) << endl;
d)  cout << ( m <= 99 && k < m ) << endl;
e)  cout << ( j >= i || k == m ) << endl;
f)  cout << ( k + m < j || 3 - j >= k ) << endl;
g)  cout << ( !m ) << endl;
h)  cout << ( !( j - m ) ) << endl;
i)  cout << ( !( k > m ) ) << endl;
```

5.18   Write a program that prints a table of the binary, octal and hexadecimal equivalents of the decimal numbers in the range 1 through 256. If you are not familiar with these number systems, read Appendix D, Number Systems, first.

5.19   Calculate the value of π from the infinite series

$$\pi = 4 - \frac{4}{3} + \frac{4}{5} - \frac{4}{7} + \frac{4}{9} - \frac{4}{11} + \cdots$$

Print a table that shows the approximate value of π after each of the first 1,000 terms of this series.

5.20   *(Pythagorean Triples)* A right triangle can have sides that are all integers. A set of three integer values for the sides of a right triangle is called a Pythagorean triple. These three sides must satisfy the relationship that the sum of the squares of two of the sides is equal to the square of the hypotenuse. Find all Pythagorean triples for `side1`, `side2` and `hypotenuse` all no larger than 500. Use a triple-nested `for` loop that tries all possibilities. This is an example of brute force computing. You will learn in more advanced computer-science courses that there are many interesting problems for which there is no known algorithmic approach other than sheer brute force.

5.21   A company pays its employees as managers (who receive a fixed weekly salary), hourly workers (who receive a fixed hourly wage for up to the first 40 hours they work and "time-and-a-half"—1.5 times their hourly wage—for overtime hours worked), commission workers (who receive $250 plus 5.7 percent of their gross weekly sales), or pieceworkers (who receive a fixed amount of money per item for each of the items they produce—each pieceworker in this company works on only one type of item). Write a program to compute the weekly pay for each employee. You do not know the number of employees in advance. Each type of employee has its own pay code: Managers have code 1, hourly workers have code 2, commission workers have code 3 and pieceworkers have code 4. Use a `switch` to compute each employee's pay according to that employee's paycode. Within the `switch`, prompt the user (i.e., the payroll clerk) to enter the appropriate facts your program needs to calculate each employee's pay according to that employee's paycode.

5.22   *(De Morgan's Laws)* In this chapter, we discussed the logical operators `&&`, `||` and `!`. De Morgan's laws can sometimes make it more convenient for us to express a logical expression. These laws state that the expression `!( condition1 && condition2 )` is logically equivalent to the expression

(!*condition1* || !*condition2*). Also, the expression !(*condition1* || *condition2*) is logically equivalent to the expression (!*condition1* && !*condition2*). Use De Morgan's laws to write equivalent expressions for each of the following, then write a program to show that the original expression and the new expression in each case are equivalent:

a) !(x < 5) && !(y >= 7)
b) !(a == b) || !(g != 5)
c) !((x <= 8) && (y > 4))
d) !((i > 4) || (j <= 6))

5.23 Write a program that prints the following diamond shape. You may use output statements that print either a single asterisk (*) or a single blank. Maximize your use of repetition (with nested for statements) and minimize the number of output statements.

```
        *
       ***
      *****
     *******
    *********
     *******
      *****
       ***
        *
```

5.24 Modify the program you wrote in Exercise 5.23 to read an odd number in the range 1 to 19 to specify the number of rows in the diamond, then display a diamond of the appropriate size.

5.25 A criticism of the break and continue statements is that each is unstructured. Actually they statements can always be replaced by structured statements, although doing so can be awkward. Describe in general how you would remove any break statement from a loop in a program and replace it with some structured equivalent. [*Hint:* The break statement leaves a loop from within the body of the loop. Another way to leave is by failing the loop-continuation test. Consider using in the loop-continuation test a second test that indicates "early exit because of a 'break' condition."] Use the technique you developed here to remove the break statement from the program of Fig. 5.13.

5.26 What does the following program segment do?

```
 1   for ( int i = 1; i <= 5; i++ )
 2   {
 3      for ( int j = 1; j <= 3; j++ )
 4      {
 5         for ( int k = 1; k <= 4; k++ )
 6            cout << '*';
 7
 8         cout << endl;
 9      } // end inner for
10
11      cout << endl;
12   } // end outer for
```

5.27 Describe in general how you would remove any continue statement from a loop in a program and replace it with some structured equivalent. Use the technique you developed here to remove the continue statement from the program of Fig. 5.14.

5.28 *("The Twelve Days of Christmas" Song)* Write a program that uses repetition and `switch` statements to print the song "The Twelve Days of Christmas." One `switch` statement should be used to print the day (i.e., "First," "Second," etc.). A separate `switch` statement should be used to print the remainder of each verse. Visit the Web site `www.12days.com/library/carols/12daysofxmas.htm` for the complete lyrics to the song.

5.29 *(Peter Minuit Problem)* Legend has it that, in 1626, Peter Minuit purchased Manhattan Island for $24.00 in barter. Did he make a good investment? To answer this question, modify the compound interest program of Fig. 5.6 to begin with a principal of $24.00 and to calculate the amount of interest on deposit if that money had been kept on deposit until this year (e.g., 379 years through 2005). Place the `for` loop that performs the compound interest calculation in an outer `for` loop that varies the interest rate from 5 percent to 10 percent to observe the wonders of compound interest.

6

Functions and an Introduction to Recursion

Form ever follows function.
—Louis Henri Sullivan

E pluribus unum.
(One composed of many.)
—Virgil

O! call back yesterday, bid time return.
—William Shakespeare

Call me Ishmael.
—Herman Melville

When you call me that, smile!
—Owen Wister

Answer me in one word.
—William Shakespeare

There is a point at which methods devour themselves.
—Frantz Fanon

Life can only be understood backwards; but it must be lived forwards.
—Soren Kierkegaard

OBJECTIVES

In this chapter you will learn:

- To construct programs modularly from functions.
- To use common math functions available in the C++ Standard Library.
- To create functions with multiple parameters.
- The mechanisms for passing information between functions and returning results.
- How the function call/return mechanism is supported by the function call stack and activation records.
- To use random number generation to implement game-playing applications.
- How the visibility of identifiers is limited to specific regions of programs.
- To write and use recursive functions, i.e., functions that call themselves.

6.1 Introduction

Most computer programs that solve real-world problems are much larger than the programs presented in the first few chapters of this book. Experience has shown that the best way to develop and maintain a large program is to construct it from small, simple pieces, or components. This technique is called divide and conquer. We introduced functions (as program pieces) in Chapter 3. In this chapter, we study functions in more depth. We emphasize how to declare and use functions to facilitate the design, implementation, operation and maintenance of large programs.

We will overview a portion of the C++ Standard Library's math functions, showing several that require more than one parameter. Next, you will learn how to declare a function with more than one parameter. We will also present additional information about function prototypes and how the compiler uses them to convert the type of an argument in a function call to the type specified in a function's parameter list, if necessary.

Next, we'll take a brief diversion into simulation techniques with random number generation and develop a version of the casino dice game called craps that uses most of the programming techniques you have learned to this point in the book.

We then present C++'s storage classes and scope rules. These determine the period during which an object exists in memory and where its identifier can be referenced in a program. You will also learn how C++ is able to keep track of which function is currently executing, how parameters and other local variables of functions are maintained in memory and how a function knows where to return after it completes execution. We discuss two topics that help improve program performance—inline functions that can eliminate the overhead of a function call and reference parameters that can be used to pass large data items to functions efficiently.

Many of the applications you develop will have more than one function of the same name. This technique, called function overloading, is used by programmers to implement functions that perform similar tasks for arguments of different types or possibly for different numbers of arguments. We consider function templates—a mechanism for defining a family of overloaded functions. The chapter concludes with a discussion of functions that call themselves, either directly, or indirectly (through another function)—a topic called recursion that is discussed at length in upper-level computer science courses.

6.2 Program Components in C++

C++ programs are typically written by combining new functions and classes the programmer writes with "prepackaged" functions and classes available in the C++ Standard Library. In this chapter, we concentrate on functions.

The C++ Standard Library provides a rich collection of functions for performing common mathematical calculations, string manipulations, character manipulations, input/output, error checking and many other useful operations. This makes the programmer's job easier, because these functions provide many of the capabilities programmers need. The C++ Standard Library functions are provided as part of the C++ programming environment.

Software Engineering Observation 6.1

Read the documentation for your compiler to familiarize yourself with the functions and classes in the C++ Standard Library.

Functions (called **methods** or **procedures** in other programming languages) allow the programmer to modularize a program by separating its tasks into self-contained units. You have used functions in every program you have written. These functions are sometimes referred to as **user-defined functions** or **programmer-defined functions**. The statements in the function bodies are written only once, are reused from perhaps several locations in a program and are hidden from other functions.

There are several motivations for modularizing a program with functions. One is the divide-and-conquer approach, which makes program development more manageable by constructing programs from small, simple pieces. Another is software reusability—using existing functions as building blocks to create new programs. For example, in earlier programs, we did not have to define how to read a line of text from the keyboard—C++ provides this capability via the `getline` function of the `<string>` header file. A third motivation is to avoid repeating code. Also, dividing a program into meaningful functions makes the program easier to debug and maintain.

Software Engineering Observation 6.2

To promote software reusability, every function should be limited to performing a single, well-defined task, and the name of the function should express that task effectively. Such functions make programs easier to write, test, debug and maintain.

Error-Prevention Tip 6.1

A small function that performs one task is easier to test and debug than a larger function that performs many tasks.

Software Engineering Observation 6.3

If you cannot choose a concise name that expresses a function's task, your function might be attempting to perform too many diverse tasks. It is usually best to break such a function into several smaller functions.

As you know, a function is invoked by a function call, and when the called function completes its task, it either returns a result or simply returns control to the caller. An analogy to this program structure is the hierarchical form of management (Figure 6.1). A boss (similar to the calling function) asks a worker (similar to the called function) to perform a task and report back (i.e., return) the results after completing the task. The boss function does not know how the worker function performs its designated tasks. The worker may also call other worker functions, unbeknownst to the boss. This hiding of implementation details promotes good software engineering. Figure 6.1 shows the boss function communicating with several worker functions in a hierarchical manner. The boss function divides the responsibilities among the various worker functions. Note that worker1 acts as a "boss function" to worker4 and worker5.

6.3 Math Library Functions

As you know, a class can provide member functions that perform the services of the class. For example, in Chapters 3–5, you have called the member functions of various versions of a GradeBook object to display the GradeBook's welcome message, to set its course name, to obtain a set of grades and to calculate the average of those grades.

Sometimes functions are not members of a class. Such functions are called global functions. Like a class's member functions, the function prototypes for global functions

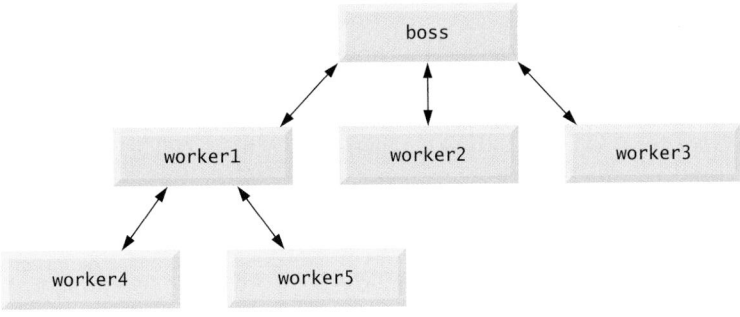

Fig. 6.1 | Hierarchical boss function/worker function relationship.

are placed in header files, so that the global functions can be reused in any program that includes the header file and that can link to the function's object code. For example, recall that we used function pow of the <cmath> header file to raise a value to a power in Figure 5.6. We introduce various functions from the <cmath> header file here to present the concept of global functions that do not belong to a particular class. In this chapter and in subsequent chapters, we use a combination of global functions (such as main) and classes with member functions to implement our example programs.

The <cmath> header file provides a collection of functions that enable you to perform common mathematical calculations. For example, you can calculate the square root of 900.0 with the function call

        sqrt(900.0)

The preceding expression evaluates to 30.0. Function sqrt takes an argument of type double and returns a double result. Note that there is no need to create any objects before calling function sqrt. Also note that *all* functions in the <cmath> header file are global functions—therefore, each is called simply by specifying the name of the function followed by parentheses containing the function's arguments.

Function arguments may be constants, variables or more complex expressions. If c = 13.0, d = 3.0 and f = 4.0, then the statement

        cout << sqrt(c + d * f) << endl;

calculates and prints the square root of 13.0 + 3.0 * 4.0 = 25.0—namely, 5.0. Some math library functions are summarized in Fig. 6.2. In the figure, the variables x and y are of type double.

Function	Description	Example
ceil(x)	rounds x to the smallest integer not less than x	ceil(9.2) is 10.0 ceil(-9.8) is -9.0
cos(x)	trigonometric cosine of x (x in radians)	cos(0.0) is 1.0
exp(x)	exponential function e^x	exp(1.0) is 2.71828 exp(2.0) is 7.38906
fabs(x)	absolute value of x	fabs(5.1) is 5.1 fabs(0.0) is 0.0 fabs(-8.76) is 8.76
floor(x)	rounds x to the largest integer not greater than x	floor(9.2) is 9.0 floor(-9.8) is -10.0
fmod(x, y)	remainder of x/y as a floating-point number	fmod(2.6, 1.2) is 0.2
log(x)	natural logarithm of x (base e)	log(2.718282) is 1.0 log(7.389056) is 2.0

Fig. 6.2 | Math library functions. (Part I of 2.)

Function	Description	Example
log10(x)	logarithm of x (base 10)	log10(10.0) is 1.0 log10(100.0) is 2.0
pow(x, y)	x raised to power y (x^y)	pow(2, 7) is 128 pow(9, .5) is 3
sin(x)	trigonometric sine of x (x in radians)	sin(0.0) is 0
sqrt(x)	square root of x (where x is a nonnegative value)	sqrt(9.0) is 3.0
tan(x)	trigonometric tangent of x (x in radians)	tan(0.0) is 0

Fig. 6.2 | Math library functions. (Part 2 of 2.)

6.4 Function Definitions with Multiple Parameters

Chapters 3–5 presented classes containing simple functions that had at most one parameter. Functions often require more than one piece of information to perform their tasks. We now consider functions with multiple parameters.

The program in Figs. 6.3–6.5 modifies our GradeBook class by including a user-defined function called maximum that determines and returns the largest of three int values. When the application begins execution, the main function (lines 5–14 of Fig. 6.5) creates one object of class GradeBook (line 8) and calls the object's inputGrades member function (line 11) to read three integer grades from the user. In class GradeBook's implementation file (Fig. 6.4), lines 54–55 of member function inputGrades prompt the user to enter three integer values and read them from the user. Line 58 calls member function maximum (defined in lines 62–75). Function maximum determines the largest value, then the return statement (line 74) returns that value to the point at which function inputGrades invoked maximum (line 58). Member function inputGrades then stores maximum's return value in data member maximumGrade. This value is then output by calling function displayGradeReport (line 12 of Fig. 6.5). [*Note:* We named this function displayGradeReport because subsequent versions of class GradeBook will use this function to display a complete grade report, including the maximum and minimum grades.] In Chapter 7, Arrays and Vectors, we'll enhance the GradeBook to process an arbitrary number of grades.

```
1   // Fig. 6.3: GradeBook.h
2   // Definition of class GradeBook that finds the maximum of three grades.
3   // Member functions are defined in GradeBook.cpp
4   #include <string> // program uses C++ standard string class
5   using std::string;
6
```

Fig. 6.3 | GradeBook header file. (Part 1 of 2.)

```
 7   // GradeBook class definition
 8   class GradeBook
 9   {
10   public:
11      GradeBook( string ); // constructor initializes course name
12      void setCourseName( string ); // function to set the course name
13      string getCourseName(); // function to retrieve the course name
14      void displayMessage(); // display a welcome message
15      void inputGrades(); // input three grades from user
16      void displayGradeReport(); // display a report based on the grades
17      int maximum( int, int, int ); // determine max of 3 values
18   private:
19      string courseName; // course name for this GradeBook
20      int maximumGrade; // maximum of three grades
21   }; // end class GradeBook
```

Fig. 6.3 | GradeBook header file. (Part 2 of 2.)

```
 1   // Fig. 6.4: GradeBook.cpp
 2   // Member-function definitions for class GradeBook that
 3   // determines the maximum of three grades.
 4   #include <iostream>
 5   using std::cout;
 6   using std::cin;
 7   using std::endl;
 8
 9   #include "GradeBook.h" // include definition of class GradeBook
10
11   // constructor initializes courseName with string supplied as argument;
12   // initializes studentMaximum to 0
13   GradeBook::GradeBook( string name )
14   {
15      setCourseName( name ); // validate and store courseName
16      maximumGrade = 0; // this value will be replaced by the maximum grade
17   } // end GradeBook constructor
18
19   // function to set the course name; limits name to 25 or fewer characters
20   void GradeBook::setCourseName( string name )
21   {
22      if ( name.length() <= 25 ) // if name has 25 or fewer characters
23         courseName = name; // store the course name in the object
24      else // if name is longer than 25 characters
25      { // set courseName to first 25 characters of parameter name
26         courseName = name.substr( 0, 25 ); // select first 25 characters
27         cout << "Name \"" << name << "\" exceeds maximum length (25).\n"
28            << "Limiting courseName to first 25 characters.\n" << endl;
29      } // end if...else
30   } // end function setCourseName
31
```

Fig. 6.4 | GradeBook class defines function maximum. (Part 1 of 2.)

```
32   // function to retrieve the course name
33   string GradeBook::getCourseName()
34   {
35      return courseName;
36   } // end function getCourseName
37
38   // display a welcome message to the GradeBook user
39   void GradeBook::displayMessage()
40   {
41      // this statement calls getCourseName to get the
42      // name of the course this GradeBook represents
43      cout << "Welcome to the grade book for\n" << getCourseName() << "!\n"
44         << endl;
45   } // end function displayMessage
46
47   // input three grades from user; determine maximum
48   void GradeBook::inputGrades()
49   {
50      int grade1; // first grade entered by user
51      int grade2; // second grade entered by user
52      int grade3; // third grade entered by user
53
54      cout << "Enter three integer grades: ";
55      cin >> grade1 >> grade2 >> grade3;
56
57      // store maximum in member studentMaximum
58      maximumGrade = maximum( grade1, grade2, grade3 );
59   } // end function inputGrades
60
61   // returns the maximum of its three integer parameters
62   int GradeBook::maximum( int x, int y, int z )
63   {
64      int maximumValue = x; // assume x is the largest to start
65
66      // determine whether y is greater than maximumValue
67      if ( y > maximumValue )
68         maximumValue = y; // make y the new maximumValue
69
70      // determine whether z is greater than maximumValue
71      if ( z > maximumValue )
72         maximumValue = z; // make z the new maximumValue
73
74      return maximumValue;
75   } // end function maximum
76
77   // display a report based on the grades entered by user
78   void GradeBook::displayGradeReport()
79   {
80      // output maximum of grades entered
81      cout << "Maximum of grades entered: " << maximumGrade << endl;
82   } // end function displayGradeReport
```

Fig. 6.4 | GradeBook class defines function maximum. (Part 2 of 2.)

```
1   // Fig. 6.5: fig06_05.cpp
2   // Create GradeBook object, input grades and display grade report.
3   #include "GradeBook.h" // include definition of class GradeBook
4
5   int main()
6   {
7      // create GradeBook object
8      GradeBook myGradeBook( "CS101 C++ Programming" );
9
10     myGradeBook.displayMessage(); // display welcome message
11     myGradeBook.inputGrades(); // read grades from user
12     myGradeBook.displayGradeReport(); // display report based on grades
13     return 0; // indicate successful termination
14  } // end main
```

```
Welcome to the grade book for
CS101 C++ Programming!

Enter three integer grades: 86 67 75
Maximum of grades entered: 86
```

```
Welcome to the grade book for
CS101 C++ Programming!

Enter three integer grades: 67 86 75
Maximum of grades entered: 86
```

```
Welcome to the grade book for
CS101 C++ Programming!

Enter three integer grades: 67 75 86
Maximum of grades entered: 86
```

Fig. 6.5 | Demonstrating function maximum.

Software Engineering Observation 6.4

The commas used in line 58 of Fig. 6.4 to separate the arguments to function maximum are not comma operators as discussed in Section 5.3. The comma operator guarantees that its operands are evaluated left to right. The order of evaluation of a function's arguments, however, is not specified by the C++ standard. Thus, different compilers can evaluate function arguments in different orders. The C++ standard does guarantee that all arguments in a function call are evaluated before the called function executes.

Portability Tip 6.1

Sometimes when a function's arguments are more involved expressions, such as those with calls to other functions, the order in which the compiler evaluates the arguments could affect the values of one or more of the arguments. If the evaluation order changes between compilers, the argument values passed to the function could vary, causing subtle logic errors.

Error-Prevention Tip 6.2

If you have doubts about the order of evaluation of a function's arguments and whether the order would affect the values passed to the function, evaluate the arguments in separate assignment statements before the function call, assign the result of each expression to a local variable, then pass those variables as arguments to the function.

The prototype of member function `maximum` (Fig. 6.3, line 17) indicates that the function returns an integer value, that the function's name is `maximum` and that the function requires three integer parameters to accomplish its task. Function `maximum`'s header (Fig. 6.4, line 62) matches the function prototype and indicates that the parameter names are `x`, `y` and `z`. When `maximum` is called (Fig. 6.4, line 58), the parameter `x` is initialized with the value of the argument `grade1`, the parameter `y` is initialized with the value of the argument `grade2` and the parameter `z` is initialized with the value of the argument `grade3`. There must be one argument in the function call for each parameter (also called a **formal parameter**) in the function definition.

Notice that multiple parameters are specified in both the function prototype and the function header as a comma-separated list. The compiler refers to the function prototype to check that calls to `maximum` contain the correct number and types of arguments and that the types of the arguments are in the correct order. In addition, the compiler uses the prototype to ensure that the value returned by the function can be used correctly in the expression that called the function (e.g., a function call that returns `void` cannot be used as the right side of an assignment statement). Each argument must be consistent with the type of the corresponding parameter. For example, a parameter of type `double` can receive values like 7.35, 22 or –0.03456, but not a string like `"hello"`. If the arguments passed to a function do not match the types specified in the function's prototype, the compiler attempts to convert the arguments to those types. Section 6.5 discusses this conversion.

Common Programming Error 6.1

Declaring method parameters of the same type as `double x, y` instead of `double x, double y` is a syntax error—an explicit type is required for each parameter in the parameter list.

Common Programming Error 6.2

Compilation errors occur if the function prototype, function header and function calls do not all agree in the number, type and order of arguments and parameters, and in the return type.

Software Engineering Observation 6.5

A function that has many parameters may be performing too many tasks. Consider dividing the function into smaller functions that perform the separate tasks. Limit the function header to one line if possible.

To determine the maximum value (lines 62–75 of Fig. 6.4), we begin with the assumption that parameter `x` contains the largest value, so line 64 of function `maximum` declares local variable `maximumValue` and initializes it with the value of parameter `x`. Of course, it is possible that parameter `y` or `z` contains the actual largest value, so we must compare each of these values with `maximumValue`. The `if` statement at lines 67–68 determines whether `y` is greater than `maximumValue` and, if so, assigns `y` to `maximumValue`. The `if` statement at lines 71–72 determines whether `z` is greater than `maximumValue` and, if so, assigns z to maximumValue. At this point the largest of the three values is in maximumValue, so line 74 returns that value to the call in line 58. When program control returns to the point in the program where maximum was called, maximum's parameters x, y and z are no longer accessible to the program. We'll see why in the next section.

There are three ways to return control to the point at which a function was invoked. If the function does not return a result (i.e., the function has a void return type), control returns when the program reaches the function-ending right brace, or by execution of the statement

```
return;
```

If the function does return a result, the statement

```
return expression;
```

evaluates *expression* and returns the value of *expression* to the caller.

6.5 Function Prototypes and Argument Coercion

A function prototype (also called a function declaration) tells the compiler the name of a function, the type of data returned by the function, the number of parameters the function expects to receive, the types of those parameters and the order in which the parameters of those types are expected.

Software Engineering Observation 6.6

Function prototypes are required in C++. Use #include preprocessor directives to obtain function prototypes for the C++ Standard Library functions from the header files for the appropriate libraries (e.g., the prototype for math function sqrt is in header file <cmath>; a partial list of C++ Standard Library header files appears in Section 6.6). Also use #include to obtain header files containing function prototypes written by you or your group members.

Common Programming Error 6.3

If a function is defined before it is invoked, then the function's definition also serves as the function's prototype, so a separate prototype is unnecessary. If a function is invoked before it is defined, and that function does not have a function prototype, a compilation error occurs.

Software Engineering Observation 6.7

Always provide function prototypes, even though it is possible to omit them when functions are defined before they are used (in which case the function header acts as the function prototype as well). Providing the prototypes avoids tying the code to the order in which functions are defined (which can easily change as a program evolves).

Function Signatures

The portion of a function prototype that includes the name of the function and the types of its arguments is called the function signature or simply the signature. The function signature does not specify the function's return type. Function in the same scope must have unique signatures. The scope of a function is the region of a program in which the function is known and accessible. We'll say more about scope in Section 6.10.

> **Common Programming Error 6.4**
> *It is a compilation error if two functions in the same scope have the same signature but different return types.*

In Fig. 6.3, if the function prototype in line 17 had been written

```
void maximum( int, int, int );
```

the compiler would report an error, because the `void` return type in the function prototype would differ from the `int` return type in the function header. Similarly, such a prototype would cause the statement

```
cout << maximum( 6, 9, 0 );
```

to generate a compilation error, because that statement depends on `maximum` to return a value to be displayed.

Argument Coercion

An important feature of function prototypes is argument coercion—i.e., forcing arguments to the appropriate types specified by the parameter declarations. For example, a program can call a function with an integer argument, even though the function prototype specifies a `double` argument—the function will still work correctly.

Argument Promotion Rules

Sometimes, argument values that do not correspond precisely to the parameter types in the function prototype can be converted by the compiler to the proper type before the function is called. These conversions occur as specified by C++'s promotion rules. The promotion rules indicate how to convert between types without losing data. An `int` can be converted to a `double` without changing its value. However, a `double` converted to an `int` truncates the fractional part of the `double` value. Keep in mind that `double` variables can hold numbers of much greater magnitude than `int` variables, so the loss of data may be considerable. Values may also be modified when converting large integer types to small integer types (e.g., `long` to `short`), signed to unsigned or unsigned to signed.

The promotion rules apply to expressions containing values of two or more data types; such expressions are also referred to as mixed-type expressions. The type of each value in a mixed-type expression is promoted to the "highest" type in the expression (actually a temporary version of each value is created and used for the expression—the original values remain unchanged). Promotion also occurs when the type of a function argument does not match the parameter type specified in the function definition or prototype. Figure 6.6 lists the fundamental data types in order from "highest type" to "lowest type."

Converting values to lower fundamental types can result in incorrect values. Therefore, a value can be converted to a lower fundamental type only by explicitly assigning the value to a variable of lower type (some compilers will issue a warning in this case) or by using a cast operator (see Section 4.9). Function argument values are converted to the parameter types in a function prototype as if they were being assigned directly to variables of those types. If a `square` function that uses an integer parameter is called with a floating-

Data types
long double
double
float
unsigned long int (synonymous with unsigned long)
long int (synonymous with long)
unsigned int (synonymous with unsigned)
int
unsigned short int (synonymous with unsigned short)
short int (synonymous with short)
unsigned char
char
bool

Fig. 6.6 | Promotion hierarchy for fundamental data types.

point argument, the argument is converted to int (a lower type), and square could return an incorrect value. For example, square(4.5) returns 16, not 20.25.

Common Programming Error 6.5

Converting from a higher data type in the promotion hierarchy to a lower type, or between signed and unsigned, can corrupt the data value, causing a loss of information.

Common Programming Error 6.6

It is a compilation error if the arguments in a function call do not match the number and types of the parameters declared in the corresponding function prototype. It is also an error if the number of arguments in the call matches, but the arguments cannot be implicitly converted to the expected types.

6.6 C++ Standard Library Header Files

The C++ Standard Library is divided into many portions, each with its own header file. The header files contain the function prototypes for the related functions that form each portion of the library. The header files also contain definitions of various class types and functions, as well as constants needed by those functions. A header file "instructs" the compiler on how to interface with library and user-written components.

Figure 6.7 lists some common C++ Standard Library header files, most of which are discussed later in the book. The term "macro" that is used several times in Fig. 6.7 is discussed in detail in Appendix F, Preprocessor. Header file names ending in .h are "old-style" header files that have been superseded by the C++ Standard Library header files. We use only the C++ Standard Library versions of each header file in this book to ensure that our examples will work on most standard C++ compilers.

C++ Standard Library header file	Explanation
`<iostream>`	Contains function prototypes for the C++ standard input and standard output functions, introduced in Chapter 2, and is covered in more detail in Chapter 15, Stream Input/Output. This header file replaces header file `<iostream.h>`.
`<iomanip>`	Contains function prototypes for stream manipulators that format streams of data. This header file is first used in Section 4.9 and is discussed in more detail in Chapter 15, Stream Input/Output. This header file replaces header file `<iomanip.h>`.
`<cmath>`	Contains function prototypes for math library functions (discussed in Section 6.3). This header file replaces header file `<math.h>`.
`<cstdlib>`	Contains function prototypes for conversions of numbers to text, text to numbers, memory allocation, random numbers and various other utility functions. Portions of the header file are covered in Section 6.7; Chapter 11, Operator Overloading; String and Array Objects; Chapter 16, Exception Handling; Chapter 19, Web Programming; Chapter 22, Bits, Characters, C-Strings and `structs`; and Appendix E, C Legacy Code Topics. This header file replaces header file `<stdlib.h>`.
`<ctime>`	Contains function prototypes and types for manipulating the time and date. This header file replaces header file `<time.h>`. This header file is used in Section 6.7.
`<vector>`, `<list>`, `<deque>`, `<queue>`, `<stack>`, `<map>`, `<set>`, `<bitset>`	These header files contain classes that implement the C++ Standard Library containers. Containers store data during a program's execution. The `<vector>` header is first introduced in Chapter 7, Arrays and Vectors. We discuss all these header files in Chapter 23, Standard Template Library (STL).
`<cctype>`	Contains function prototypes for functions that test characters for certain properties (such as whether the character is a digit or a punctuation), and function prototypes for functions that can be used to convert lowercase letters to uppercase letters and vice versa. This header file replaces header file `<ctype.h>`. These topics are discussed in Chapter 8, Pointers and Pointer-Based Strings, and Chapter 22, Bits, Characters, C-Strings and `structs`.
`<cstring>`	Contains function prototypes for C-style string-processing functions. This header file replaces header file `<string.h>`. This header file is used in Chapter 11, Operator Overloading; String and Array Objects.
`<typeinfo>`	Contains classes for runtime type identification (determining data types at execution time). This header file is discussed in Section 13.8.
`<exception>`, `<stdexcept>`	These header files contain classes that are used for exception handling (discussed in Chapter 16).

Fig. 6.7 | C++ Standard Library header files. (Part 1 of 2.)

C++ Standard Library header file	Explanation
`<memory>`	Contains classes and functions used by the C++ Standard Library to allocate memory to the C++ Standard Library containers. This header is used in Chapter 16, Exception Handling.
`<fstream>`	Contains function prototypes for functions that perform input from files on disk and output to files on disk (discussed in Chapter 17, File Processing). This header file replaces header file `<fstream.h>`.
`<string>`	Contains the definition of class `string` from the C++ Standard Library (discussed in Chapter 18).
`<sstream>`	Contains function prototypes for functions that perform input from strings in memory and output to strings in memory (discussed in Chapter 18, Class `string` and String Stream Processing).
`<functional>`	Contains classes and functions used by C++ Standard Library algorithms. This header file is used in Chapter 23.
`<iterator>`	Contains classes for accessing data in the C++ Standard Library containers. This header file is used in Chapter 23, Standard Template Library (STL).
`<algorithm>`	Contains functions for manipulating data in C++ Standard Library containers. This header file is used in Chapter 23.
`<cassert>`	Contains macros for adding diagnostics that aid program debugging. This replaces header file `<assert.h>` from pre-standard C++. This header file is used in Appendix F, Preprocessor.
`<cfloat>`	Contains the floating-point size limits of the system. This header file replaces header file `<float.h>`.
`<climits>`	Contains the integral size limits of the system. This header file replaces header file `<limits.h>`.
`<cstdio>`	Contains function prototypes for the C-style standard input/output library functions and information used by them. This header file replaces header file `<stdio.h>`.
`<locale>`	Contains classes and functions normally used by stream processing to process data in the natural form for different languages (e.g., monetary formats, sorting strings, character presentation, etc.).
`<limits>`	Contains classes for defining the numerical data type limits on each computer platform.
`<utility>`	Contains classes and functions that are used by many C++ Standard Library header files.

Fig. 6.7 | C++ Standard Library header files. (Part 2 of 2.)

6.7 Case Study: Random Number Generation

We now take a brief and hopefully entertaining diversion into a popular programming application, namely simulation and game playing. In this and the next section, we develop a game-playing program that includes multiple functions. The program uses many of the control statements and concepts discussed to this point.

The element of chance can be introduced into computer applications by using the C++ Standard Library function rand.

Consider the following statement:

```
i = rand();
```

The function rand generates an unsigned integer between 0 and RAND_MAX (a symbolic constant defined in the <cstdlib> header file). The value of RAND_MAX must be at least 32767—the maximum positive value for a two-byte (16-bit) integer. For GNU C++, the value of RAND_MAX is 214748647; for Visual Studio, the value of RAND_MAX is 32767. If rand truly produces integers at random, every number between 0 and RAND_MAX has an equal *chance* (or **probability**) of being chosen each time rand is called.

The range of values produced directly by the function rand often is different than what a specific application requires. For example, a program that simulates coin tossing might require only 0 for "heads" and 1 for "tails." A program that simulates rolling a six-sided die would require random integers in the range 1 to 6. A program that randomly predicts the next type of spaceship (out of four possibilities) that will fly across the horizon in a video game might require random integers in the range 1 through 4.

Rolling a Six-Sided Die

To demonstrate rand, let us develop a program (Fig. 6.8) to simulate 20 rolls of a six-sided die and print the value of each roll. The function prototype for the rand function is in <cstdlib>. To produce integers in the range 0 to 5, we use the modulus operator (%) with rand as follows:

```
rand() % 6
```

This is called **scaling**. The number 6 is called the **scaling factor**. We then **shift** the range of numbers produced by adding 1 to our previous result. Figure 6.8 confirms that the results are in the range 1 to 6.

```cpp
// Fig. 6.8: fig06_08.cpp
// Shifted and scaled random integers.
#include <iostream>
using std::cout;
using std::endl;

#include <iomanip>
using std::setw;

#include <cstdlib> // contains function prototype for rand
using std::rand;

int main()
{
```

Fig. 6.8 | Shifted, scaled integers produced by `1 + rand() % 6`. (Part 1 of 2.)

```
15      // loop 20 times
16      for ( int counter = 1; counter <= 20; counter++ )
17      {
18         // pick random number from 1 to 6 and output it
19         cout << setw( 10 ) << ( 1 + rand() % 6 );
20
21         // if counter is divisible by 5, start a new line of output
22         if ( counter % 5 == 0 )
23            cout << endl;
24      } // end for
25
26      return 0; // indicates successful termination
27   } // end main
```

6	6	5	5	6
5	1	1	5	3
6	6	2	4	2
6	2	3	4	1

Fig. 6.8 | Shifted, scaled integers produced by `1 + rand() % 6`. (Part 2 of 2.)

Rolling a Six-Sided Die 6,000,000 Times
To show that the numbers produced by function rand occur with approximately equal likelihood, Fig. 6.9 simulates 6,000,000 rolls of a die. Each integer in the range 1 to 6 should appear approximately 1,000,000 times. This is confirmed by the output window at the end of Fig. 6.9.

```
1   // Fig. 6.9: fig06_09.cpp
2   // Roll a six-sided die 6,000,000 times.
3   #include <iostream>
4   using std::cout;
5   using std::endl;
6
7   #include <iomanip>
8   using std::setw;
9
10  #include <cstdlib> // contains function prototype for rand
11  using std::rand;
12
13  int main()
14  {
15     int frequency1 = 0; // count of 1s rolled
16     int frequency2 = 0; // count of 2s rolled
17     int frequency3 = 0; // count of 3s rolled
18     int frequency4 = 0; // count of 4s rolled
19     int frequency5 = 0; // count of 5s rolled
20     int frequency6 = 0; // count of 6s rolled
21
22     int face; // stores most recently rolled value
23
```

Fig. 6.9 | Rolling a six-sided die 6,000,000 times. (Part 1 of 2.)

```
24      // summarize results of 6,000,000 rolls of a die
25      for ( int roll = 1; roll <= 6000000; roll++ )
26      {
27         face = 1 + rand() % 6; // random number from 1 to 6
28
29         // determine roll value 1-6 and increment appropriate counter
30         switch ( face )
31         {
32            case 1:
33               ++frequency1; // increment the 1s counter
34               break;
35            case 2:
36               ++frequency2; // increment the 2s counter
37               break;
38            case 3:
39               ++frequency3; // increment the 3s counter
40               break;
41            case 4:
42               ++frequency4; // increment the 4s counter
43               break;
44            case 5:
45               ++frequency5; // increment the 5s counter
46               break;
47            case 6:
48               ++frequency6; // increment the 6s counter
49               break;
50            default: // invalid value
51               cout << "Program should never get here!";
52         } // end switch
53      } // end for
54
55      cout << "Face" << setw( 13 ) << "Frequency" << endl; // output headers
56      cout << "    1" << setw( 13 ) << frequency1
57         << "\n    2" << setw( 13 ) << frequency2
58         << "\n    3" << setw( 13 ) << frequency3
59         << "\n    4" << setw( 13 ) << frequency4
60         << "\n    5" << setw( 13 ) << frequency5
61         << "\n    6" << setw( 13 ) << frequency6 << endl;
62      return 0; // indicates successful termination
63   } // end main
```

Face	Frequency
1	999702
2	1000823
3	999378
4	998898
5	1000777
6	1000422

Fig. 6.9 | Rolling a six-sided die 6,000,000 times. (Part 2 of 2.)

As the program output shows, we can simulate the rolling of a six-sided die by scaling and shifting the values produced by rand. Note that the program should never get to the default case (lines 50–51) provided in the switch structure, because the switch's controlling expression (face) always has values in the range 1–6; however, we provide the default case as a matter of good practice. After we study arrays in Chapter 7, we show how to replace the entire switch structure in Fig. 6.9 elegantly with a single-line statement.

 Error-Prevention Tip 6.3

Provide a default case in a switch to catch errors even if you are absolutely, positively certain that you have no bugs!

Randomizing the Random Number Generator
Executing the program of Fig. 6.8 again produces

6	6	5	5	6
5	1	1	5	3
6	6	2	4	2
6	2	3	4	1

Notice that the program prints exactly the same sequence of values shown in Fig. 6.8. How can these be random numbers? Ironically, this repeatability is an important characteristic of function rand. When debugging a simulation program, this repeatability is essential for proving that corrections to the program work properly.

Function rand actually generates **pseudorandom numbers**. Repeatedly calling rand produces a sequence of numbers that appears to be random. However, the sequence repeats itself each time the program executes. Once a program has been thoroughly debugged, it can be conditioned to produce a different sequence of random numbers for each execution. This is called **randomizing** and is accomplished with the C++ Standard Library function **srand**. Function srand takes an unsigned integer argument and **seeds** the rand function to produce a different sequence of random numbers for each execution of the program.

Figure 6.10 demonstrates function srand. The program uses the data type unsigned, which is short for unsigned int. An int is stored in at least two bytes of memory (typically four bytes of memory on today's popular 32-bit systems) and can have positive and negative values. A variable of type unsigned int is also stored in at least two bytes of memory. A two-byte unsigned int can have only nonnegative values in the range 0–65535. A four-byte unsigned int can have only nonnegative values in the range 0–4294967295. Function srand takes an unsigned int value as an argument. The function prototype for the srand function is in header file <cstdlib>.

```cpp
// Fig. 6.10: fig06_10.cpp
// Randomizing die-rolling program.
#include <iostream>
using std::cout;
using std::cin;
using std::endl;

```

Fig. 6.10 | Randomizing the die-rolling program. (Part 1 of 2.)

```
 8   #include <iomanip>
 9   using std::setw;
10
11   #include <cstdlib> // contains prototypes for functions srand and rand
12   using std::rand;
13   using std::srand;
14
15   int main()
16   {
17      unsigned seed; // stores the seed entered by the user
18
19      cout << "Enter seed: ";
20      cin >> seed;
21      srand( seed ); // seed random number generator
22
23      // loop 10 times
24      for ( int counter = 1; counter <= 10; counter++ )
25      {
26         // pick random number from 1 to 6 and output it
27         cout << setw( 10 ) << ( 1 + rand() % 6 );
28
29         // if counter is divisible by 5, start a new line of output
30         if ( counter % 5 == 0 )
31            cout << endl;
32      } // end for
33
34      return 0; // indicates successful termination
35   } // end main
```

```
Enter seed: 67
         6         1         4         6         2
         1         6         1         6         4
```

```
Enter seed: 432
         4         6         3         1         6
         3         1         5         4         2
```

```
Enter seed: 67
         6         1         4         6         2
         1         6         1         6         4
```

Fig. 6.10 | Randomizing the die-rolling program. (Part 2 of 2.)

Let us run the program several times and observe the results. Notice that the program produces a *different* sequence of random numbers each time it executes, provided that the user enters a different seed. We used the same seed in the first and third sample outputs, so the same series of 10 numbers is displayed in each of those outputs.

To randomize without having to enter a seed each time, we may use a statement like

```
srand( time( 0 ) );
```

This causes the computer to read its clock to obtain the value for the seed. Function time (with the argument 0 as written in the preceding statement) returns the current time as the number of seconds since January 1, 1970 at midnight Greenwich Mean Time (GMT). This value is converted to an unsigned integer and used as the seed to the random number generator. The function prototype for time is in <ctime>.

Common Programming Error 6.7

Calling function srand more than once in a program restarts the pseudorandom number sequence and can affect the randomness of the numbers produced by rand.

Generalized Scaling and Shifting of Random Numbers

Previously, we demonstrated how to write a single statement to simulate the rolling of a six-sided die with the statement

```
face = 1 + rand() % 6;
```

which always assigns an integer (at random) to variable face in the range $1 \le \text{face} \le 6$. Note that the width of this range (i.e., the number of consecutive integers in the range) is 6 and the starting number in the range is 1. Referring to the preceding statement, we see that the width of the range is determined by the number used to scale rand with the modulus operator (i.e., 6), and the starting number of the range is equal to the number (i.e., 1) that is added to the expression rand % 6. We can generalize this result as

number = *shiftingValue* + rand() % *scalingFactor*;

where *shiftingValue* is equal to the first number in the desired range of consecutive integers and *scalingFactor* is equal to the width of the desired range of consecutive integers. The exercises show that it is possible to choose integers at random from sets of values other than ranges of consecutive integers.

Common Programming Error 6.8

Using srand in place of rand to attempt to generate random numbers is a compilation error—function srand does not return a value.

6.8 Case Study: Game of Chance and Introducing enum

One of the most popular games of chance is a dice game known as "craps," which is played in casinos and back alleys worldwide. The rules of the game are straightforward:

> *A player rolls two dice. Each die has six faces. These faces contain 1, 2, 3, 4, 5 and 6 spots. After the dice have come to rest, the sum of the spots on the two upward faces is calculated. If the sum is 7 or 11 on the first roll, the player wins. If the sum is 2, 3 or 12 on the first roll (called "craps"), the player loses (i.e., the "house" wins). If the sum is 4, 5, 6, 8, 9 or 10 on the first roll, then that sum becomes the player's "point." To win, you must continue rolling the dice until you "make your point." The player loses by rolling a 7 before making the point.*

The program in Fig. 6.11 simulates the game of craps.

In the rules of the game, notice that the player must roll two dice on the first roll and on all subsequent rolls. We define function rollDice (lines 71–83) to roll the dice and compute and print their sum. Function rollDice is defined once, but it is called from two places (lines 27 and 51) in the program. Interestingly, rollDice takes no arguments, so we have indicated an empty parameter list in the prototype (line 14) and in the function header (line 71). Function rollDice does return the sum of the two dice, so return type int is indicated in the function prototype and function header.

```cpp
1   // Fig. 6.11: fig06_11.cpp
2   // Craps simulation.
3   #include <iostream>
4   using std::cout;
5   using std::endl;
6
7   #include <cstdlib> // contains prototypes for functions srand and rand
8   using std::rand;
9   using std::srand;
10
11  #include <ctime> // contains prototype for function time
12  using std::time;
13
14  int rollDice(); // rolls dice, calculates amd displays sum
15
16  int main()
17  {
18     // enumeration with constants that represent the game status
19     enum Status { CONTINUE, WON, LOST }; // all caps in constants
20
21     int myPoint; // point if no win or loss on first roll
22     Status gameStatus; // can contain CONTINUE, WON or LOST
23
24     // randomize random number generator using current time
25     srand( time( 0 ) );
26
27     int sumOfDice = rollDice(); // first roll of the dice
28
29     // determine game status and point (if needed) based on first roll
30     switch ( sumOfDice )
31     {
32        case 7: // win with 7 on first roll
33        case 11: // win with 11 on first roll
34           gameStatus = WON;
35           break;
36        case 2: // lose with 2 on first roll
37        case 3: // lose with 3 on first roll
38        case 12: // lose with 12 on first roll
39           gameStatus = LOST;
40           break;
41        default: // did not win or lose, so remember point
42           gameStatus = CONTINUE; // game is not over
43           myPoint = sumOfDice; // remember the point
44           cout << "Point is " << myPoint << endl;
45           break; // optional at end of switch
46     } // end switch
47
```

Fig. 6.11 | Craps simulation. (Part 1 of 3.)

```
48        // while game is not complete
49        while ( gameStatus == CONTINUE ) // not WON or LOST
50        {
51           sumOfDice = rollDice(); // roll dice again
52
53           // determine game status
54           if ( sumOfDice == myPoint ) // win by making point
55              gameStatus = WON;
56           else
57              if ( sumOfDice == 7 ) // lose by rolling 7 before point
58                 gameStatus = LOST;
59        } // end while
60
61        // display won or lost message
62        if ( gameStatus == WON )
63           cout << "Player wins" << endl;
64        else
65           cout << "Player loses" << endl;
66
67        return 0; // indicates successful termination
68     } // end main
69
70     // roll dice, calculate sum and display results
71     int rollDice()
72     {
73        // pick random die values
74        int die1 = 1 + rand() % 6; // first die roll
75        int die2 = 1 + rand() % 6; // second die roll
76
77        int sum = die1 + die2; // compute sum of die values
78
79        // display results of this roll
80        cout << "Player rolled " << die1 << " + " << die2
81           << " = " << sum << endl;
82        return sum; // end function rollDice
83     } // end function rollDice
```

```
Player rolled 2 + 5 = 7
Player wins
```

```
Player rolled 6 + 6 = 12
Player loses
```

```
Player rolled 3 + 3 = 6
Point is 6
Player rolled 5 + 3 = 8
Player rolled 4 + 5 = 9
Player rolled 2 + 1 = 3
Player rolled 1 + 5 = 6
Player wins
```

Fig. 6.11 | Craps simulation. (Part 2 of 3.)

```
Player rolled 1 + 3 = 4
Point is 4
Player rolled 4 + 6 = 10
Player rolled 2 + 4 = 6
Player rolled 6 + 4 = 10
Player rolled 2 + 3 = 5
Player rolled 2 + 4 = 6
Player rolled 1 + 1 = 2
Player rolled 4 + 4 = 8
Player rolled 4 + 3 = 7
Player loses
```

Fig. 6.11 | Craps simulation. (Part 3 of 3.)

The game is reasonably involved. The player may win or lose on the first roll or on any subsequent roll. The program uses variable gameStatus to keep track of this. Variable gameStatus is declared to be of new type Status. Line 19 declares a user-defined type called an **enumeration**. An enumeration, introduced by the keyword **enum** and followed by a type name (in this case, Status), is a set of integer constants represented by identifiers. The values of these **enumeration constants** start at 0, unless specified otherwise, and increment by 1. In the preceding enumeration, the constant CONTINUE has the value 0, WON has the value 1 and LOST has the value 2. The identifiers in an enum must be unique, but separate enumeration constants can have the same integer value (we show how to accomplish this momentarily).

Good Programming Practice 6.1

Capitalize the first letter of an identifier used as a user-defined type name.

Good Programming Practice 6.2

Use only uppercase letters in the names of enumeration constants. This makes these constants stand out in a program and reminds the programmer that enumeration constants are not variables.

Variables of user-defined type Status can be assigned only one of the three values declared in the enumeration. When the game is won, the program sets variable gameStatus to WON (lines 34 and 55). When the game is lost, the program sets variable gameStatus to LOST (lines 39 and 58). Otherwise, the program sets variable gameStatus to CONTINUE (line 42) to indicate that the dice must be rolled again.

Another popular enumeration is

```
enum Months { JAN = 1, FEB, MAR, APR, MAY, JUN, JUL, AUG,
   SEP, OCT, NOV, DEC };
```

which creates user-defined type Months with enumeration constants representing the months of the year. The first value in the preceding enumeration is explicitly set to 1, so the remaining values increment from 1, resulting in the values 1 through 12. Any enumeration constant can be assigned an integer value in the enumeration definition, and subsequent enumeration constants each have a value 1 higher than the preceding constant in the list until the next explicit setting.

After the first roll, if the game is won or lost, the program skips the body of the `while` statement (lines 49–59) because `gameStatus` is not equal to `CONTINUE`. The program proceeds to the `if...else` statement at lines 62–65, which prints `"Player wins"` if `gameStatus` is equal to `WON` and `"Player loses"` if `gameStatus` is equal to `LOST`.

After the first roll, if the game is not over, the program saves the sum in `myPoint` (line 43). Execution proceeds with the `while` statement, because `gameStatus` is equal to `CON-TINUE`. During each iteration of the `while`, the program calls `rollDice` to produce a new sum. If sum matches `myPoint`, the program sets `gameStatus` to `WON` (line 55), the `while`-test fails, the `if...else` statement prints `"Player wins"` and execution terminates. If sum is equal to 7, the program sets `gameStatus` to `LOST` (line 58), the `while`-test fails, the `if...else` statement prints `"Player loses"` and execution terminates.

Note the interesting use of the various program control mechanisms we have discussed. The craps program uses two functions—main and `rollDice`—and the `switch`, `while`, `if...else`, nested `if...else` and nested `if` statements. In the exercises, we investigate various interesting characteristics of the game of craps.

Good Programming Practice 6.3

Using enumerations rather than integer constants can make programs clearer and more maintainable. You can set the value of an enumeration constant once in the enumeration declaration.

Common Programming Error 6.9

Assigning the integer equivalent of an enumeration constant to a variable of the enumeration type is a compilation error.

Common Programming Error 6.10

After an enumeration constant has been defined, attempting to assign another value to the enumeration constant is a compilation error.

6.9 Storage Classes

The programs you have seen so far use identifiers for variable names. The attributes of variables include name, type, size and value. This chapter also uses identifiers as names for user-defined functions. Actually, each identifier in a program has other attributes, including storage class, scope and linkage.

C++ provides five **storage-class specifiers**: `auto`, `register`, `extern`, `mutable` and `static`. This section discusses storage-class specifiers `auto`, `register`, `extern` and `static`. Storage-class specifier `mutable` (discussed in detail in Chapter 24) is used exclusively with classes.

Storage Class, Scope and Linkage

An identifier's **storage class** determines the period during which that identifier exists in memory. Some identifiers exist briefly, some are repeatedly created and destroyed and others exist for the entire execution of a program. This section discusses two storage classes: static and automatic.

An identifier's **scope** is where the identifier can be referenced in a program. Some identifiers can be referenced throughout a program; others can be referenced from only limited portions of a program. Section 6.10 discusses the scope of identifiers.

An identifier's linkage determines whether an identifier is known only in the source file where it is declared or across multiple files that are compiled, then linked together. An identifier's storage-class specifier helps determine its storage class and linkage.

Storage Class Categories

The storage-class specifiers can be split into two storage classes: automatic storage class and static storage class. Keywords `auto` and `register` are used to declare variables of the automatic storage class. Such variables are created when program execution enters the block in which they are defined, they exist while the block is active and they are destroyed when the program exits the block.

Local Variables

Only local variables of a function can be of automatic storage class. A function's local variables and parameters normally are of automatic storage class. The storage class specifier `auto` explicitly declares variables of automatic storage class. For example, the following declaration indicates that `double` variables x and y are local variables of automatic storage class—they exist only in the nearest enclosing pair of curly braces within the body of the function in which the definition appears:

```
auto double x, y;
```

Local variables are of automatic storage class by default, so keyword `auto` rarely is used. For the remainder of the text, we refer to variables of automatic storage class simply as automatic variables.

 Performance Tip 6.1

Automatic storage is a means of conserving memory, because automatic storage class variables exist in memory only when the block in which they are defined is executing.

 Software Engineering Observation 6.8

Automatic storage is an example of the principle of least privilege, which is fundamental to good software engineering. In the context of an application, the principle states that code should be granted only the amount of privilege and access that it needs to accomplish its designated task, but no more. Why should we have variables stored in memory and accessible when they are not needed?

Register Variables

Data in the machine-language version of a program is normally loaded into registers for calculations and other processing.

 Performance Tip 6.2

The storage-class specifier `register` can be placed before an automatic variable declaration to suggest that the compiler maintain the variable in one of the computer's high-speed hardware registers rather than in memory. If intensely used variables such as counters or totals are maintained in hardware registers, the overhead of repeatedly loading the variables from memory into the registers and storing the results back into memory is eliminated.

Common Programming Error 6.11

Using multiple storage-class specifiers for an identifier is a syntax error. Only one storage class specifier can be applied to an identifier. For example, if you include register*, do not also include* auto.

The compiler might ignore register declarations. For example, there might not be a sufficient number of registers available for the compiler to use. The following definition *suggests* that the integer variable counter be placed in one of the computer's registers; regardless of whether the compiler does this, counter is initialized to 1:

```
register int counter = 1;
```

The register keyword can be used only with local variables and function parameters.

Performance Tip 6.3

Often, register *is unnecessary. Today's optimizing compilers are capable of recognizing frequently used variables and can decide to place them in registers without needing a* register *declaration from the programmer.*

Static Storage Class

Keywords extern and static declare identifiers for variables of the static storage class and for functions. Static-storage-class variables exist from the point at which the program begins execution and last for the duration of the program. A static-storage-class variable's storage is allocated when the program begins execution. Such a variable is initialized once when its declaration is encountered. For functions, the name of the function exists when the program begins execution, just as for all other functions. However, even though the variables and the function names exist from the start of program execution, this does not mean that these identifiers can be used throughout the program. Storage class and scope (where a name can be used) are separate issues, as we will see in Section 6.10.

Identifiers with Static Storage Class

There are two types of identifiers with static storage class—external identifiers (such as global variables and global function names) and local variables declared with the storage class specifier static. Global variables are created by placing variable declarations outside any class or function definition. Global variables retain their values throughout the execution of the program. Global variables and global functions can be referenced by any function that follows their declarations or definitions in the source file.

Software Engineering Observation 6.9

Declaring a variable as global rather than local allows unintended side effects to occur when a function that does not need access to the variable accidentally or maliciously modifies it. This is another example of the principle of least privilege. In general, except for truly global resources such as cin *and* cout*, the use of global variables should be avoided except in certain situations with unique performance requirements.*

Software Engineering Observation 6.10

Variables used only in a particular function should be declared as local variables in that function rather than as global variables.

Local variables declared with the keyword `static` are still known only in the function in which they are declared, but, unlike automatic variables, `static` local variables retain their values when the function returns to its caller. The next time the function is called, the `static` local variables contain the values they had when the function last completed execution. The following statement declares local variable `count` to be `static` and to be initialized to 1:

```
static int count = 1;
```

All numeric variables of the static storage class are initialized to zero if they are not explicitly initialized by the programmer, but it is nevertheless a good practice to explicitly initialize all variables.

Storage-class specifiers `extern` and `static` have special meaning when they are applied explicitly to external identifiers such as global variables and global function names. In Appendix E, C Legacy Code Topics, we discuss using `extern` and `static` with external identifiers and multiple-source-file programs.

6.10 Scope Rules

The portion of the program where an identifier can be used is known as its scope. For example, when we declare a local variable in a block, it can be referenced only in that block and in blocks nested within that block. This section discusses four scopes for an identifier—function scope, file scope, block scope and function-prototype scope. Later we will see two other scopes—class scope (Chapter 9) and namespace scope (Chapter 24).

An identifier declared outside any function or class has file scope. Such an identifier is "known" in all functions from the point at which it is declared until the end of the file. Global variables, function definitions and function prototypes placed outside a function all have file scope.

Labels (identifiers followed by a colon such as `start:`) are the only identifiers with function scope. Labels can be used anywhere in the function in which they appear, but cannot be referenced outside the function body. Labels are used in `goto` statements (Appendix E). Labels are implementation details that functions hide from one another.

Identifiers declared inside a block have block scope. Block scope begins at the identifier's declaration and ends at the terminating right brace (}) of the block in which the identifier is declared. Local variables have block scope, as do function parameters, which are also local variables of the function. Any block can contain variable declarations. When blocks are nested and an identifier in an outer block has the same name as an identifier in an inner block, the identifier in the outer block is "hidden" until the inner block terminates. While executing in the inner block, the inner block sees the value of its own local identifier and not the value of the identically named identifier in the enclosing block. Local variables declared `static` still have block scope, even though they exist from the time the program begins execution. Storage duration does not affect the scope of an identifier.

The only identifiers with function prototype scope are those used in the parameter list of a function prototype. As mentioned previously, function prototypes do not require names in the parameter list—only types are required. Names appearing in the parameter list of a function prototype are ignored by the compiler. Identifiers used in a function prototype can be reused elsewhere in the program without ambiguity. In a single prototype, a particular identifier can be used only once.

Common Programming Error 6.12

Accidentally using the same name for an identifier in an inner block that is used for an identifier in an outer block, when in fact the programmer wants the identifier in the outer block to be active for the duration of the inner block, is normally a logic error.

Good Programming Practice 6.4

Avoid variable names that hide names in outer scopes. This can be accomplished by avoiding the use of duplicate identifiers in a program.

The program of Fig. 6.12 demonstrates scoping issues with global variables, automatic local variables and static local variables.

```
1   // Fig. 6.12: fig06_12.cpp
2   // A scoping example.
3   #include <iostream>
4   using std::cout;
5   using std::endl;
6
7   void useLocal( void ); // function prototype
8   void useStaticLocal( void ); // function prototype
9   void useGlobal( void ); // function prototype
10
11  int x = 1; // global variable
12
13  int main()
14  {
15     int x = 5; // local variable to main
16
17     cout << "local x in main's outer scope is " << x << endl;
18
19     { // start new scope
20        int x = 7; // hides x in outer scope
21
22        cout << "local x in main's inner scope is " << x << endl;
23     } // end new scope
24
25     cout << "local x in main's outer scope is " << x << endl;
26
27     useLocal(); // useLocal has local x
28     useStaticLocal(); // useStaticLocal has static local x
29     useGlobal(); // useGlobal uses global x
30     useLocal(); // useLocal reinitializes its local x
31     useStaticLocal(); // static local x retains its prior value
32     useGlobal(); // global x also retains its value
33
34     cout << "\nlocal x in main is " << x << endl;
35     return 0; // indicates successful termination
36  } // end main
37
```

Fig. 6.12 | Scoping example. (Part 1 of 2.)

```
38   // useLocal reinitializes local variable x during each call
39   void useLocal( void )
40   {
41      int x = 25; // initialized each time useLocal is called
42
43      cout << "\nlocal x is " << x << " on entering useLocal" << endl;
44      x++;
45      cout << "local x is " << x << " on exiting useLocal" << endl;
46   } // end function useLocal
47
48   // useStaticLocal initializes static local variable x only the
49   // first time the function is called; value of x is saved
50   // between calls to this function
51   void useStaticLocal( void )
52   {
53      static int x = 50; // initialized first time useStaticLocal is called
54
55      cout << "\nlocal static x is " << x << " on entering useStaticLocal"
56         << endl;
57      x++;
58      cout << "local static x is " << x << " on exiting useStaticLocal"
59         << endl;
60   } // end function useStaticLocal
61
62   // useGlobal modifies global variable x during each call
63   void useGlobal( void )
64   {
65      cout << "\nglobal x is " << x << " on entering useGlobal" << endl;
66      x *= 10;
67      cout << "global x is " << x << " on exiting useGlobal" << endl;
68   } // end function useGlobal
```

```
local x in main's outer scope is 5
local x in main's inner scope is 7
local x in main's outer scope is 5

local x is 25 on entering useLocal
local x is 26 on exiting useLocal

local static x is 50 on entering useStaticLocal
local static x is 51 on exiting useStaticLocal

global x is 1 on entering useGlobal
global x is 10 on exiting useGlobal

local x is 25 on entering useLocal
local x is 26 on exiting useLocal

local static x is 51 on entering useStaticLocal
local static x is 52 on exiting useStaticLocal

global x is 10 on entering useGlobal
global x is 100 on exiting useGlobal

local x in main is 5
```

Fig. 6.12 | Scoping example. (Part 2 of 2.)

Line 11 declares and initializes global variable x to 1. This global variable is hidden in any block (or function) that declares a variable named x. In main, line 15 declares a local variable x and initializes it to 5. Line 17 outputs this variable to show that the global x is hidden in main. Next, lines 19–23 define a new block in main in which another local variable x is initialized to 7 (line 20). Line 22 outputs this variable to show that it hides x in the outer block of main. When the block exits, the variable x with value 7 is destroyed automatically. Next, line 25 outputs the local variable x in the outer block of main to show that it is no longer hidden.

To demonstrate other scopes, the program defines three functions, each of which takes no arguments and returns nothing. Function useLocal (lines 39–46) declares automatic variable x (line 41) and initializes it to 25. When the program calls useLocal, the function prints the variable, increments it and prints it again before the function returns program control to its caller. Each time the program calls this function, the function recreates automatic variable x and reinitializes it to 25.

Function useStaticLocal (lines 51–60) declares static variable x and initializes it to 50. Local variables declared as static retain their values even when they are out of scope (i.e., the function in which they are declared is not executing). When the program calls useStaticLocal, the function prints x, increments it and prints it again before the function returns program control to its caller. In the next call to this function, static local variable x contains the value 51. The initialization in line 53 occurs only once—the first time useStaticLocal is called.

Function useGlobal (lines 63–68) does not declare any variables. Therefore, when it refers to variable x, the global x (preceding main) is used. When the program calls useGlobal, the function prints the global variable x, multiplies it by 10 and prints again before the function returns program control to its caller. The next time the program calls useGlobal, the global variable has its modified value, 10. After executing functions useLocal, useStaticLocal and useGlobal twice each, the program prints the local variable x in main again to show that none of the function calls modified the value of x in main, because the functions all referred to variables in other scopes.

6.11 Function Call Stack and Activation Records

To understand how C++ performs function calls, we first need to consider a data structure (i.e., collection of related data items) known as a stack. Think of a stack as analogous to a pile of dishes. When a dish is placed on the pile, it is normally placed at the top (referred to as pushing the dish onto the stack). Similarly, when a dish is removed from the pile, it is normally removed from the top (referred to as popping the dish off the stack). Stacks are known as last-in, first-out (LIFO) data structures—the last item pushed (inserted) on the stack is the first item popped (removed) from the stack.

One of the most important mechanisms for computer science students to understand is the function call stack (sometimes referred to as the program execution stack). This data structure—working "behind the scenes"—supports the function call/return mechanism. It also supports the creation, maintenance and destruction of each called function's automatic variables. We explained the last-in, first-out (LIFO) behavior of stacks with our dish-stacking example. As we'll see in Figs. 6.14–6.16, this LIFO behavior is exactly what a function does when returning to the function that called it.

As each function is called, it may, in turn, call other functions, which may, in turn, call other functions—all before any of the functions returns. Each function eventually must return control to the function that called it. So, somehow, we must keep track of the return addresses that each function needs to return control to the function that called it. The function call stack is the perfect data structure for handling this information. Each time a function calls another function, an entry is pushed onto the stack. This entry, called a stack frame or an activation record, contains the return address that the called function needs to return to the calling function. It also contains some additional information we will soon discuss. If the called function returns, instead of calling another function before returning, the stack frame for the function call is popped, and control transfers to the return address in the popped stack frame.

The beauty of the call stack is that each called function always finds the information it needs to return to its caller at the top of the call stack. And, if a function makes a call to another function, a stack frame for the new function call is simply pushed onto the call stack. Thus, the return address required by the newly called function to return to its caller is now located at the top of the stack.

The stack frames have another important responsibility. Most functions have automatic variables—parameters and any local variables the function declares. Automatic variables need to exist while a function is executing. They need to remain active if the function makes calls to other functions. But when a called function returns to its caller, the called function's automatic variables need to "go away." The called function's stack frame is a perfect place to reserve the memory for the called function's automatic variables. That stack frame exists as long as the called function is active. When the called function returns—and no longer needs its local automatic variables—its stack frame is popped from the stack, and those local automatic variables are no longer known to the program.

Of course, the amount of memory in a computer is finite, so only a certain amount of memory can be used to store activation records on the function call stack. If more function calls occur than can have their activation records stored on the function call stack, an error known as stack overflow occurs.

Function Call Stack in Action

So, as we have seen, the call stack and activation records support the function call/return mechanism and the creation and destruction of automatic variables. Now let's consider how the call stack supports the operation of a square function called by main (lines 11–17 of Fig. 6.13). First the operating system calls main—this pushes an activation record onto the stack (shown in Fig. 6.14). The activation record tells main how to return to the

```
1   // Fig. 6.13: fig06_13.cpp
2   // square function used to demonstrate the function
3   // call stack and activation records.
4   #include <iostream>
5   using std::cin;
6   using std::cout;
7   using std::endl;
8
```

Fig. 6.13 | square function used to demonstrate the function call stack and activation records. (Part 1 of 2.)

```
9   int square( int ); // prototype for function square
10
11  int main()
12  {
13     int a = 10; // value to square (local automatic variable in main)
14
15     cout << a << " squared: " << square( a ) << endl; // display a squared
16     return 0; // indicate successful termination
17  } // end main
18
19  // returns the square of an integer
20  int square( int x ) // x is a local variable
21  {
22     return x * x; // calculate square and return result
23  } // end function square
```

```
10 squared: 100
```

Fig. 6.13 | square function used to demonstrate the function call stack and activation records. (Part 2 of 2.)

Step 1: Operating system invokes main to execute application.

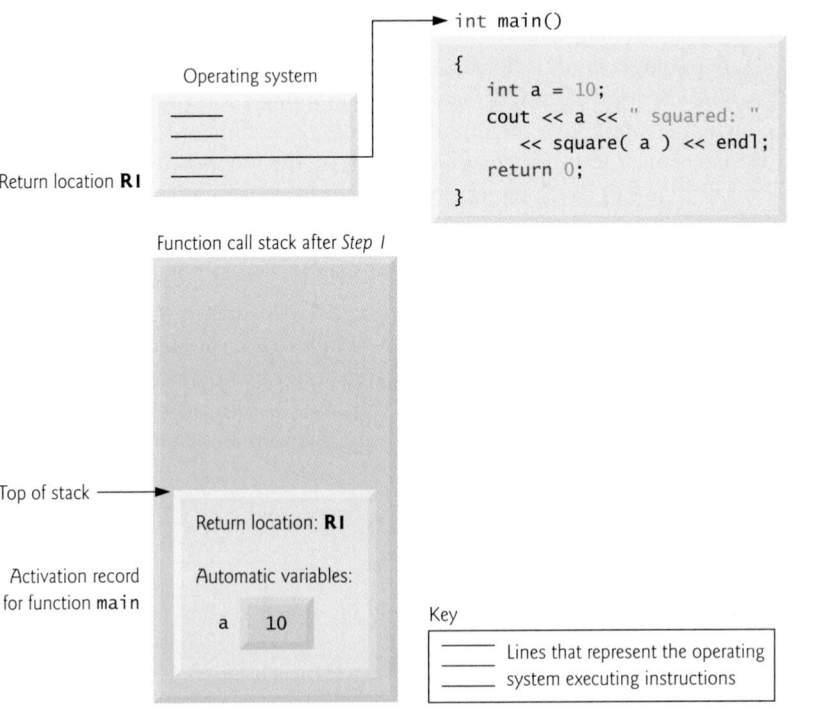

Fig. 6.14 | Function call stack after the operating system invokes main to execute the application.

operating system (i.e., transfer to return address R1) and contains the space for main's automatic variable (i.e., a, which is initialized to 10).

Function main—before returning to the operating system—now calls function square in line 15 of Fig. 6.13. This causes a stack frame for square (lines 20–23) to be pushed onto the function call stack (Fig. 6.15). This stack frame contains the return address that square needs to return to main (i.e., R2) and the memory for square's automatic variable (i.e., x).

After square calculates the square of its argument, it needs to return to main—and no longer needs the memory for its automatic variable x. So the stack is popped—giving square the return location in main (i.e., R2) and losing square's automatic variable. Figure 6.16 shows the function call stack after square's activation record has been popped.

Function main now displays the result of calling square (line 15), then executes the return statement (line 16). This causes the activation record for main to be popped from the stack. This gives main the address it needs to return to the operating system (i.e., R1 in Fig. 6.14) and causes the memory for main's automatic variable (i.e., a) to become unavailable.

You have now seen how valuable the notion of the stack data structure is in implementing a key mechanism that supports program execution. Data structures have many

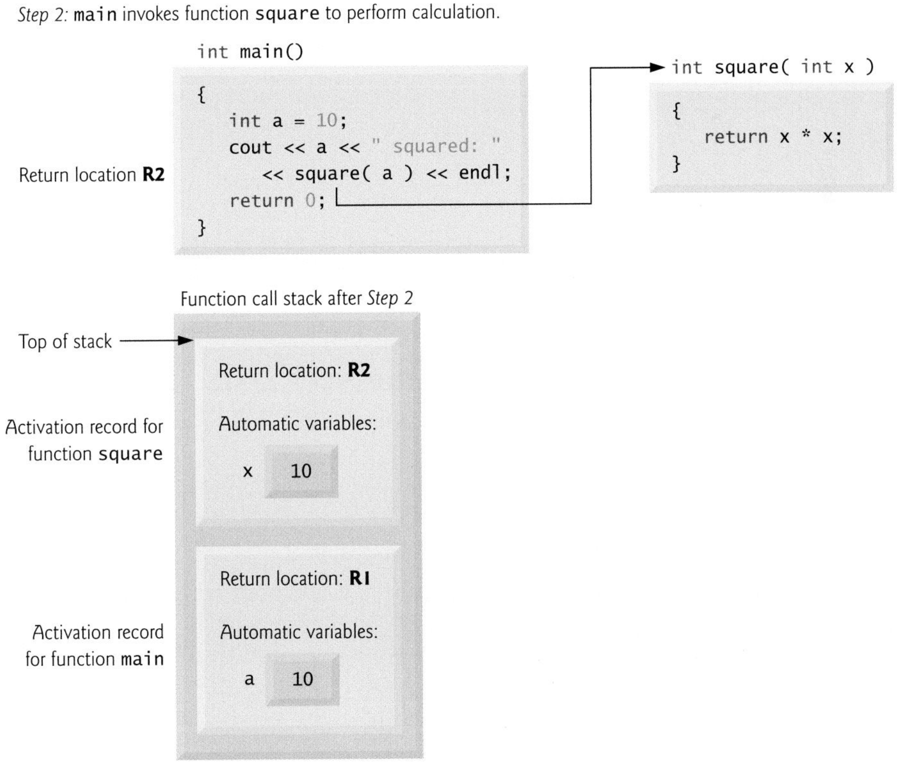

Fig. 6.15 | Function call stack after main invokes function square to perform the calculation.

Step 3: square returns its result to main.

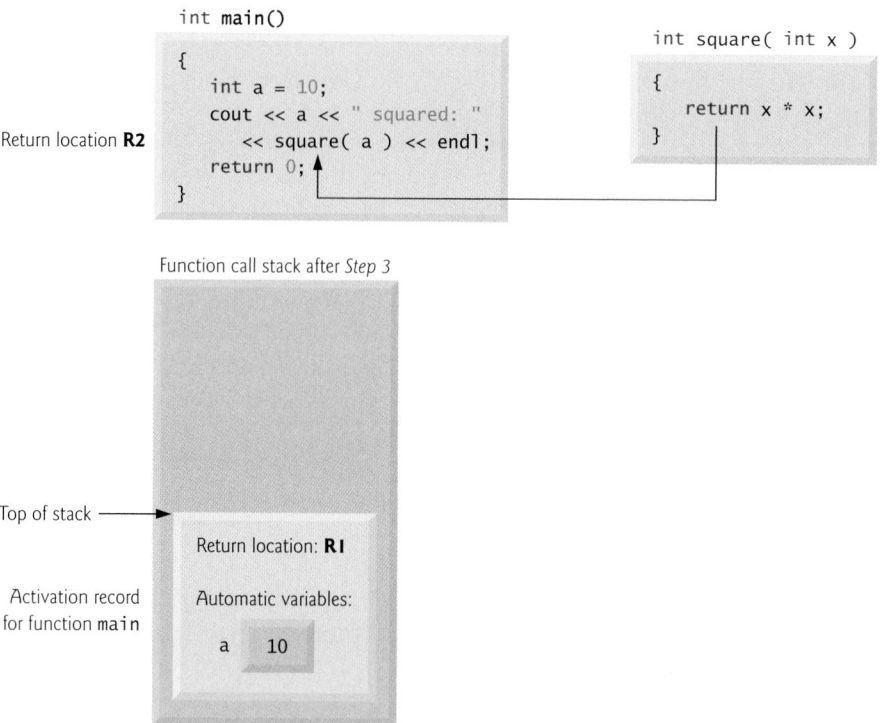

Fig. 6.16 | Function call stack after function square returns to main.

important applications in computer science. We discuss stacks, queues, lists, trees and other data structures in Chapter 21, Data Structures, and Chapter 23, Standard Template Library (STL).

6.12 Functions with Empty Parameter Lists

In C++, an empty parameter list is specified by writing either void or nothing at all in parentheses. The prototype

```
void print();
```

specifies that function print does not take arguments and does not return a value. Figure 6.17 demonstrates both ways to declare and use functions with empty parameter lists.

Portability Tip 6.2

The meaning of an empty function parameter list in C++ is dramatically different than in C. In C, it means all argument checking is disabled (i.e., the function call can pass any arguments it wants). In C++, it means that the function explicitly takes no arguments. Thus, C programs using this feature might cause compilation errors when compiled in C++.

```
1   // Fig. 6.17: fig06_17.cpp
2   // Functions that take no arguments.
3   #include <iostream>
4   using std::cout;
5   using std::endl;
6
7   void function1(); // function that takes no arguments
8   void function2( void ); // function that takes no arguments
9
10  int main()
11  {
12     function1(); // call function1 with no arguments
13     function2(); // call function2 with no arguments
14     return 0; // indicates successful termination
15  } // end main
16
17  // function1 uses an empty parameter list to specify that
18  // the function receives no arguments
19  void function1()
20  {
21     cout << "function1 takes no arguments" << endl;
22  } // end function1
23
24  // function2 uses a void parameter list to specify that
25  // the function receives no arguments
26  void function2( void )
27  {
28     cout << "function2 also takes no arguments" << endl;
29  } // end function2
```

```
function1 takes no arguments
function2 also takes no arguments
```

Fig. 6.17 | Functions that take no arguments.

Common Programming Error 6.13

C++ programs do not compile unless function prototypes are provided for every function or each function is defined before it is called.

6.13 Inline Functions

Implementing a program as a set of functions is good from a software engineering stand-point, but function calls involve execution-time overhead. C++ provides inline functions to help reduce function call overhead—especially for small functions. Placing the qualifier inline before a function's return type in the function definition "advises" the compiler to generate a copy of the function's code in place (when appropriate) to avoid a function call. The trade-off is that multiple copies of the function code are inserted in the program (of-ten making the program larger) rather than there being a single copy of the function to which control is passed each time the function is called. The compiler can ignore the inline qualifier and typically does so for all but the smallest functions.

Software Engineering Observation 6.11

Any change to an inline function could require all clients of the function to be recompiled. This can be significant in some program development and maintenance situations.

Good Programming Practice 6.5

The inline qualifier should be used only with small, frequently used functions.

Performance Tip 6.4

Using inline functions can reduce execution time but may increase program size.

Figure 6.18 uses inline function cube (lines 11–14) to calculate the volume of a cube of side side. Keyword const in the parameter list of function cube (line 11) tells the compiler that the function does not modify variable side. This ensures that the value of side is not changed by the function when the calculation is performed. (Keyword const is discussed in detail in Chapter 7, Chapter 8 and Chapter 10.) Notice that the complete definition of function cube appears before it is used in the program. This is required so that the compiler knows how to expand a cube function call into its inlined code. For this reason, reusable inline functions are typically placed in header files, so that their definitions can be included in each source file that uses them.

Software Engineering Observation 6.12

The const qualifier should be used to enforce the principle of least privilege. Using the principle of least privilege to properly design software can greatly reduce debugging time and improper side effects and can make a program easier to modify and maintain.

```
1   // Fig. 6.18: fig06_18.cpp
2   // Using an inline function to calculate the volume of a cube.
3   #include <iostream>
4   using std::cout;
5   using std::cin;
6   using std::endl;
7
8   // Definition of inline function cube. Definition of function appears
9   // before function is called, so a function prototype is not required.
10  // First line of function definition acts as the prototype.
11  inline double cube( const double side )
12  {
13     return side * side * side; // calculate cube
14  } // end function cube
15
16  int main()
17  {
18     double sideValue; // stores value entered by user
19     cout << "Enter the side length of your cube: ";
20     cin >> sideValue; // read value from user
21
```

Fig. 6.18 | inline function that calculates the volume of a cube. (Part 1 of 2.)

```
22        // calculate cube of sideValue and display result
23        cout << "Volume of cube with side "
24           << sideValue << " is " << cube( sideValue ) << endl;
25        return 0; // indicates successful termination
26     } // end main
```

```
Enter the side length of your cube: 3.5
Volume of cube with side 3.5 is 42.875
```

Fig. 6.18 | `inline` function that calculates the volume of a cube. (Part 2 of 2.)

6.14 References and Reference Parameters

Two ways to pass arguments to functions in many programming languages are pass-by-value and pass-by-reference. When an argument is passed by value, a *copy* of the argument's value is made and passed (on the function call stack) to the called function. Changes to the copy do not affect the original variable's value in the caller. This prevents the accidental side effects that so greatly hinder the development of correct and reliable software systems. Each argument that has been passed in the programs in this chapter so far has been passed by value.

Performance Tip 6.5

One disadvantage of pass-by-value is that, if a large data item is being passed, copying that data can take a considerable amount of execution time and memory space.

Reference Parameters

This section introduces reference parameters—the first of two means C++ provides for performing pass-by-reference. With pass-by-reference, the caller gives the called function the ability to access the caller's data directly, and to modify that data if the called function chooses to do so.

Performance Tip 6.6

Pass-by-reference is good for performance reasons, because it can eliminate the pass-by-value overhead of copying large amounts of data.

Software Engineering Observation 6.13

Pass-by-reference can weaken security, because the called function can corrupt the caller's data.

Later, we will show how to achieve the performance advantage of pass-by-reference while simultaneously achieving the software engineering advantage of protecting the caller's data from corruption.

A reference parameter is an alias for its corresponding argument in a function call. To indicate that a function parameter is passed by reference, simply follow the parameter's type in the function prototype by an ampersand (&); use the same convention when listing the parameter's type in the function header. For example, the following declaration in a function header

```
int &count
```

when read from right to left is pronounced "count is a reference to an int." In the function call, simply mention the variable by name to pass it by reference. Then, mentioning the variable by its parameter name in the body of the called function actually refers to the original variable in the calling function, and the original variable can be modified directly by the called function. As always, the function prototype and header must agree.

Passing Arguments by Value and by Reference

Figure 6.19 compares pass-by-value and pass-by-reference with reference parameters. The "styles" of the arguments in the calls to function squareByValue and function squareByReference are identical—both variables are simply mentioned by name in the function calls. Without checking the function prototypes or function definitions, it is not possible to tell from the calls alone whether either function can modify its arguments. Because function prototypes are mandatory, however, the compiler has no trouble resolving the ambiguity.

```cpp
1  // Fig. 6.19: fig06_19.cpp
2  // Comparing pass-by-value and pass-by-reference with references.
3  #include <iostream>
4  using std::cout;
5  using std::endl;
6
7  int squareByValue( int ); // function prototype (value pass)
8  void squareByReference( int & ); // function prototype (reference pass)
9
10 int main()
11 {
12    int x = 2; // value to square using squareByValue
13    int z = 4; // value to square using squareByReference
14
15    // demonstrate squareByValue
16    cout << "x = " << x << " before squareByValue\n";
17    cout << "Value returned by squareByValue: "
18       << squareByValue( x ) << endl;
19    cout << "x = " << x << " after squareByValue\n" << endl;
20
21    // demonstrate squareByReference
22    cout << "z = " << z << " before squareByReference" << endl;
23    squareByReference( z );
24    cout << "z = " << z << " after squareByReference" << endl;
25    return 0; // indicates successful termination
26 } // end main
27
28 // squareByValue multiplies number by itself, stores the
29 // result in number and returns the new value of number
30 int squareByValue( int number )
31 {
32    return number *= number; // caller's argument not modified
33 } // end function squareByValue
34
```

Fig. 6.19 | Passing arguments by value and by reference. (Part 1 of 2.)

```
35    // squareByReference multiplies numberRef by itself and stores the result
36    // in the variable to which numberRef refers in function main
37    void squareByReference( int &numberRef )
38    {
39       numberRef *= numberRef; // caller's argument modified
40    } // end function squareByReference
```

```
x = 2 before squareByValue
Value returned by squareByValue: 4
x = 2 after squareByValue

z = 4 before squareByReference
z = 16 after squareByReference
```

Fig. 6.19 | Passing arguments by value and by reference. (Part 2 of 2.)

Common Programming Error 6.14

Because reference parameters are mentioned only by name in the body of the called function, the programmer might inadvertently treat reference parameters as pass-by-value parameters. This can cause unexpected side effects if the original copies of the variables are changed by the function.

Chapter 8 discusses pointers; pointers enable an alternate form of pass-by-reference in which the style of the call clearly indicates pass-by-reference (and the potential for modifying the caller's arguments).

Performance Tip 6.7

For passing large objects, use a constant reference parameter to simulate the appearance and security of pass-by-value and avoid the overhead of passing a copy of the large object.

Software Engineering Observation 6.14

Many programmers do not bother to declare parameters passed by value as const, *even though the called function should not be modifying the passed argument. Keyword* const *in this context would protect only a copy of the original argument, not the original argument itself, which when passed by value is safe from modification by the called function.*

To specify a reference to a constant, place the const qualifier before the type specifier in the parameter declaration.

Note in line 37 of Fig. 6.19 the placement of & in the parameter list of function squareByReference. Some C++ programmers prefer to write int& numberRef.

Software Engineering Observation 6.15

For the combined reasons of clarity and performance, many C++ programmers prefer that modifiable arguments be passed to functions by using pointers (which we study in Chapter 8), small nonmodifiable arguments be passed by value and large nonmodifiable arguments be passed to functions by using references to constants.

References as Aliases within a Function

References can also be used as aliases for other variables within a function (although they typically are used with functions as shown in Fig. 6.19). For example, the code

```
int count = 1; // declare integer variable count
int &cRef = count; // create cRef as an alias for count
cRef++; // increment count (using its alias cRef)
```

increments variable count by using its alias cRef. Reference variables must be initialized in their declarations (see Fig. 6.20 and Fig. 6.21) and cannot be reassigned as aliases to other variables. Once a reference is declared as an alias for another variable, all operations supposedly performed on the alias (i.e., the reference) are actually performed on the original variable. The alias is simply another name for the original variable. Taking the address of a reference and comparing references do not cause syntax errors; rather, each operation actually occurs on the variable for which the reference is an alias. Unless it is a reference to a constant, a reference argument must be an *lvalue* (e.g., a variable name), not a constant or expression that returns an *rvalue* (e.g., the result of a calculation). See Section 5.9 for definitions of the terms *lvalue* and *rvalue*.

```
1   // Fig. 6.20: fig06_20.cpp
2   // References must be initialized.
3   #include <iostream>
4   using std::cout;
5   using std::endl;
6
7   int main()
8   {
9      int x = 3;
10     int &y = x; // y refers to (is an alias for) x
11
12     cout << "x = " << x << endl << "y = " << y << endl;
13     y = 7; // actually modifies x
14     cout << "x = " << x << endl << "y = " << y << endl;
15     return 0; // indicates successful termination
16  } // end main
```

```
x = 3
y = 3
x = 7
y = 7
```

Fig. 6.20 | Initializing and using a reference.

```
1   // Fig. 6.21: fig06_21.cpp
2   // References must be initialized.
3   #include <iostream>
4   using std::cout;
5   using std::endl;
6
7   int main()
8   {
9      int x = 3;
10     int &y; // Error: y must be initialized
```

Fig. 6.21 | Uninitialized reference causes a syntax error. (Part 1 of 2.)

```
11
12      cout << "x = " << x << endl << "y = " << y << endl;
13      y = 7;
14      cout << "x = " << x << endl << "y = " << y << endl;
15      return 0; // indicates successful termination
16   } // end main
```

Borland C++ command-line compiler error message:

```
Error E2304 C:\cpphtp5_examples\ch06\Fig06_21\fig06_21.cpp 10:
   Reference variable 'y' must be initialized in function main()
```

Microsoft Visual C++ compiler error message:

```
C:\cpphtp5_examples\ch06\Fig06_21\fig06_21.cpp(10) : error C2530: 'y' :
   references must be initialized
```

GNU C++ compiler error message:

```
fig06_21.cpp:10: error: 'y' declared as a reference but not initialized
```

Fig. 6.21 | Uninitialized reference causes a syntax error. (Part 2 of 2.)

Returning a Reference from a Function

Functions can return references, but this can be dangerous. When returning a reference to a variable declared in the called function, the variable should be declared static within that function. Otherwise, the reference refers to an automatic variable that is discarded when the function terminates; such a variable is said to be "undefined," and the program's behavior is unpredictable. References to undefined variables are called dangling references.

Common Programming Error 6.15

Not initializing a reference variable when it is declared is a compilation error, unless the declaration is part of a function's parameter list. Reference parameters are initialized when the function in which they are declared is called.

Common Programming Error 6.16

Attempting to reassign a previously declared reference to be an alias to another variable is a logic error. The value of the other variable is simply assigned to the variable for which the reference is already an alias.

Common Programming Error 6.17

Returning a reference to an automatic variable in a called function is a logic error. Some compilers issue a warning when this occurs.

Error Messages for Uninitialized References

Note that the C++ standard does not specify the error messages that compilers use to indicate particular errors. For this reason, Fig. 6.21 shows the error messages produced by the Borland C++ 5.5 command-line compiler, Microsoft Visual C++.NET compiler and GNU C++ compiler when a reference is not initialized.

6.15 Default Arguments

It is not uncommon for a program to invoke a function repeatedly with the same argument value for a particular parameter. In such cases, the programmer can specify that such a parameter has a *default argument*, i.e., a default value to be passed to that parameter. When a program omits an argument for a parameter with a default argument in a function call, the compiler rewrites the function call and inserts the default value of that argument to be passed as an argument to the function call.

Default arguments must be the rightmost (trailing) arguments in a function's parameter list. When calling a function with two or more default arguments, if an omitted argument is not the rightmost argument in the argument list, then all arguments to the right of that argument also must be omitted. Default arguments should be specified with the first occurrence of the function name—typically, in the function prototype. If the function prototype is omitted because the function definition also serves as the prototype, then the default arguments should be specified in the function header. Default values can be any expression, including constants, global variables or function calls. Default arguments also can be used with `inline` functions.

Figure 6.22 demonstrates using default arguments in calculating the volume of a box. The function prototype for `boxVolume` (line 8) specifies that all three parameters have been given default values of 1. Note that we provided variable names in the function prototype for readability. As always, variable names are not required in function prototypes.

Common Programming Error 6.18

It is a compilation error to specify default arguments in both a function's prototype and header.

```
1    // Fig. 6.22: fig06_22.cpp
2    // Using default arguments.
3    #include <iostream>
4    using std::cout;
5    using std::endl;
6
7    // function prototype that specifies default arguments
8    int boxVolume( int length = 1, int width = 1, int height = 1 );
9
10   int main()
11   {
12      // no arguments--use default values for all dimensions
13      cout << "The default box volume is: " << boxVolume();
14
15      // specify length; default width and height
16      cout << "\n\nThe volume of a box with length 10,\n"
17         << "width 1 and height 1 is: " << boxVolume( 10 );
18
19      // specify length and width; default height
20      cout << "\n\nThe volume of a box with length 10,\n"
21         << "width 5 and height 1 is: " << boxVolume( 10, 5 );
22
```

Fig. 6.22 | Default arguments to a function. (Part 1 of 2.)

```
23      // specify all arguments
24      cout << "\n\nThe volume of a box with length 10,\n"
25          << "width 5 and height 2 is: " << boxVolume( 10, 5, 2 )
26          << endl;
27      return 0; // indicates successful termination
28   } // end main
29
30   // function boxVolume calculates the volume of a box
31   int boxVolume( int length, int width, int height )
32   {
33      return length * width * height;
34   } // end function boxVolume
```

```
The default box volume is: 1

The volume of a box with length 10,
width 1 and height 1 is: 10

The volume of a box with length 10,
width 5 and height 1 is: 50

The volume of a box with length 10,
width 5 and height 2 is: 100
```

Fig. 6.22 | Default arguments to a function. (Part 2 of 2.)

The first call to boxVolume (line 13) specifies no arguments, thus using all three default values of 1. The second call (line 17) passes a length argument, thus using default values of 1 for the width and height arguments. The third call (line 21) passes arguments for length and width, thus using a default value of 1 for the height argument. The last call (line 25) passes arguments for length, width and height, thus using no default values. Note that any arguments passed to the function explicitly are assigned to the function's parameters from left to right. Therefore, when boxVolume receives one argument, the function assigns the value of that argument to its length parameter (i.e., the leftmost parameter in the parameter list). When boxVolume receives two arguments, the function assigns the values of those arguments to its length and width parameters in that order. Finally, when boxVolume receives all three arguments, the function assigns the values of those arguments to its length, width and height parameters, respectively.

Good Programming Practice 6.6

Using default arguments can simplify writing function calls. However, some programmers feel that explicitly specifying all arguments is clearer.

Software Engineering Observation 6.16

If the default values for a function change, all client code using the function must be recompiled.

Common Programming Error 6.19

Specifying and attempting to use a default argument that is not a rightmost (trailing) argument (while not simultaneously defaulting all the rightmost arguments) is a syntax error.

6.16 Unary Scope Resolution Operator

It is possible to declare local and global variables of the same name. C++ provides the unary scope resolution operator (::) to access a global variable when a local variable of the same name is in scope. The unary scope resolution operator cannot be used to access a local variable of the same name in an outer block. A global variable can be accessed directly without the unary scope resolution operator if the name of the global variable is not the same as that of a local variable in scope.

Figure 6.23 demonstrates the unary scope resolution operator with local and global variables of the same name (lines 7 and 11). To emphasize that the local and global versions of variable number are distinct, the program declares one variable of type int and the other double.

Using the unary scope resolution operator (::) with a given variable name is optional when the only variable with that name is a global variable.

Common Programming Error 6.20

It is an error to attempt to use the unary scope resolution operator (::) to access a nonglobal variable in an outer block. If no global variable with that name exists, a compilation error occurs. If a global variable with that name exists, this is a logic error, because the program will refer to the global variable when you intended to access the nonglobal variable in the outer block.

Good Programming Practice 6.7

Always using the unary scope resolution operator (::) to refer to global variables makes programs easier to read and understand, because it makes it clear that you are intending to access a global variable rather than a nonglobal variable.

```cpp
1   // Fig. 6.23: fig06_23.cpp
2   // Using the unary scope resolution operator.
3   #include <iostream>
4   using std::cout;
5   using std::endl;
6
7   int number = 7; // global variable named number
8
9   int main()
10  {
11     double number = 10.5; // local variable named number
12
13     // display values of local and global variables
14     cout << "Local double value of number = " << number
15        << "\nGlobal int value of number = " << ::number << endl;
16     return 0; // indicates successful termination
17  } // end main
```

```
Local double value of number = 10.5
Global int value of number = 7
```

Fig. 6.23 | Unary scope resolution operator.

Software Engineering Observation 6.17

Always using the unary scope resolution operator (::) to refer to global variables makes programs easier to modify by reducing the risk of name collisions with nonglobal variables.

Error-Prevention Tip 6.4

Always using the unary scope resolution operator (::) to refer to a global variable eliminates possible logic errors that might occur if a nonglobal variable hides the global variable.

Error-Prevention Tip 6.5

Avoid using variables of the same name for different purposes in a program. Although this is allowed in various circumstances, it can lead to errors.

6.17 Function Overloading

C++ enables several functions of the same name to be defined, as long as these functions have different sets of parameters (at least as far as the parameter types or the number of parameters or the order of the parameter types are concerned). This capability is called function overloading. When an overloaded function is called, the C++ compiler selects the proper function by examining the number, types and order of the arguments in the call. Function overloading is commonly used to create several functions of the same name that perform similar tasks, but on different data types. For example, many functions in the math library are overloaded for different numeric data types.[1]

Good Programming Practice 6.8

Overloading functions that perform closely related tasks can make programs more readable and understandable.

Overloaded *square* Functions

Figure 6.24 uses overloaded `square` functions to calculate the square of an `int` (lines 8–12) and the square of a `double` (lines 15–19). Line 23 invokes the `int` version of function `square` by passing the literal value 7. C++ treats whole number literal values as type `int` by default. Similarly, line 25 invokes the `double` version of function `square` by passing the literal value 7.5, which C++ treats as a `double` value by default. In each case the compiler chooses the proper function to call, based on the type of the argument. The last two lines of the output window confirm that the proper function was called in each case.

```
1   // Fig. 6.24: fig06_24.cpp
2   // Overloaded functions.
3   #include <iostream>
4   using std::cout;
5   using std::endl;
6
```

Fig. 6.24 | Overloaded `square` functions. (Part 1 of 2.)

---

1. The C++ standard requires `float`, `double` and `long double` overloaded versions of the math library functions discussed in Section 6.3.

```
 7   // function square for int values
 8   int square( int x )
 9   {
10      cout << "square of integer " << x << " is ";
11      return x * x;
12   } // end function square with int argument
13
14   // function square for double values
15   double square( double y )
16   {
17      cout << "square of double " << y << " is ";
18      return y * y;
19   } // end function square with double argument
20
21   int main()
22   {
23      cout << square( 7 ); // calls int version
24      cout << endl;
25      cout << square( 7.5 ); // calls double version
26      cout << endl;
27      return 0; // indicates successful termination
28   } // end main
```

```
square of integer 7 is 49
square of double 7.5 is 56.25
```

Fig. 6.24 | Overloaded square functions. (Part 2 of 2.)

How the Compiler Differentiates Overloaded Functions

Overloaded functions are distinguished by their signatures. A signature is a combination of a function's name and its parameter types (in order). The compiler encodes each function identifier with the number and types of its parameters (sometimes referred to as name mangling or name decoration) to enable type-safe linkage. Type-safe linkage ensures that the proper overloaded function is called and that the types of the arguments conform to the types of the parameters.

Figure 6.25 was compiled with the Borland C++ 5.6.4 command-line compiler. Rather than showing the execution output of the program (as we normally would), we show the mangled function names produced in assembly language by Borland C++. Each mangled name begins with @ followed by the function name. The function name is then separated from the mangled parameter list by $q. In the parameter list for function nothing2 (line 25; see the fourth output line), c represents a char, i represents an int, rf represents a float & (i.e., a reference to a float) and rd represents a double & (i.e., a reference to a double). In the parameter list for function nothing1, i represents an int, f represents a float, c represents a char and ri represents an int &. The two square functions are distinguished by their parameter lists; one specifies d for double and the other specifies i for int. The return types of the functions are not specified in the mangled names. Overloaded functions can have different return types, but if they do, they must also have different parameter lists. Again, you cannot have two functions with the same signa-

```
1    // Fig. 6.25: fig06_25.cpp
2    // Name mangling.
3
4    // function square for int values
5    int square( int x )
6    {
7       return x * x;
8    } // end function square
9
10   // function square for double values
11   double square( double y )
12   {
13      return y * y;
14   } // end function square
15
16   // function that receives arguments of types
17   // int, float, char and int &
18   void nothing1( int a, float b, char c, int &d )
19   {
20      // empty function body
21   } // end function nothing1
22
23   // function that receives arguments of types
24   // char, int, float & and double &
25   int nothing2( char a, int b, float &c, double &d )
26   {
27      return 0;
28   } // end function nothing2
29
30   int main()
31   {
32      return 0; // indicates successful termination
33   } // end main
```

```
@square$qi
@square$qd
@nothing1$qifcri
@nothing2$qcirfrd
_main
```

Fig. 6.25 | Name mangling to enable type-safe linkage.

ture and different return types. Note that function name mangling is compiler specific. Also note that function main is not mangled, because it cannot be overloaded.

 Common Programming Error 6.21

Creating overloaded functions with identical parameter lists and different return types is a compilation error.

The compiler uses only the parameter lists to distinguish between functions of the same name. Overloaded functions need not have the same number of parameters. Programmers should use caution when overloading functions with default parameters, because this may cause ambiguity.

Common Programming Error 6.22

A function with default arguments omitted might be called identically to another overloaded function; this is a compilation error. For example, having in a program both a function that explicitly takes no arguments and a function of the same name that contains all default arguments results in a compilation error when an attempt is made to use that function name in a call passing no arguments. The compiler does not know which version of the function to choose.

Overloaded Operators

In Chapter 11, we discuss how to overload operators to define how they should operate on objects of user-defined data types. (In fact, we have been using many overloaded operators to this point, including the stream insertion operator << and the stream extraction operator >>, each of which is overloaded to be able to display data of all the fundamental types. We say more about overloading << and >> to be able to handle objects of user-defined types in Chapter 11.) Section 6.18 introduces function templates for automatically generating overloaded functions that perform identical tasks on different data types.

6.18 Function Templates

Overloaded functions are normally used to perform similar operations that involve different program logic on different data types. If the program logic and operations are identical for each data type, overloading may be performed more compactly and conveniently by using function templates. The programmer writes a single function template definition. Given the argument types provided in calls to this function, C++ automatically generates separate function template specializations to handle each type of call appropriately. Thus, defining a single function template essentially defines a whole family of overloaded functions.

Figure 6.26 contains the definition of a function template (lines 4–18) for a maximum function that determines the largest of three values. All function template definitions begin with the template keyword (line 4) followed by a template parameter list to the function template enclosed in angle brackets (< and >). Every parameter in the template

```
1   // Fig. 6.26: maximum.h
2   // Definition of function template maximum.
3
4   template < class T >  // or template< typename T >
5   T maximum( T value1, T value2, T value3 )
6   {
7      T maximumValue = value1; // assume value1 is maximum
8
9      // determine whether value2 is greater than maximumValue
10     if ( value2 > maximumValue )
11        maximumValue = value2;
12
13     // determine whether value3 is greater than maximumValue
14     if ( value3 > maximumValue )
15        maximumValue = value3;
16
17     return maximumValue;
18  } // end function template maximum
```

Fig. 6.26 | Function template maximum header file.

parameter list (often referred to as a formal type parameter) is preceded by keyword type-name or keyword class (which are synonyms). The formal type parameters are placeholders for fundamental types or user-defined types. These placeholders are used to specify the types of the function's parameters (line 5), to specify the function's return type (line 5) and to declare variables within the body of the function definition (line 7). A function template is defined like any other function, but uses the formal type parameters as placeholders for actual data types.

The function template in Fig. 6.26 declares a single formal type parameter T (line 4) as a placeholder for the type of the data to be tested by function maximum. The name of a type parameter must be unique in the template parameter list for a particular template definition. When the compiler detects a maximum invocation in the program source code, the type of the data passed to maximum is substituted for T throughout the template definition, and C++ creates a complete function for determining the maximum of three values of the specified data type. Then the newly created function is compiled. Thus, templates are a means of code generation.

Common Programming Error 6.23

Not placing keyword class or keyword typename before every formal type parameter of a function template (e.g., writing < class S, T > instead of < class S, class T >) is a syntax error.

Figure 6.27 uses the maximum function template (lines 20, 30 and 40) to determine the largest of three int values, three double values and three char values.

```cpp
1   // Fig. 6.27: fig06_27.cpp
2   // Function template maximum test program.
3   #include <iostream>
4   using std::cout;
5   using std::cin;
6   using std::endl;
7
8   #include "maximum.h" // include definition of function template maximum
9
10  int main()
11  {
12     // demonstrate maximum with int values
13     int int1, int2, int3;
14
15     cout << "Input three integer values: ";
16     cin >> int1 >> int2 >> int3;
17
18     // invoke int version of maximum
19     cout << "The maximum integer value is: "
20        << maximum( int1, int2, int3 );
21
22     // demonstrate maximum with double values
23     double double1, double2, double3;
24
25     cout << "\n\nInput three double values: ";
26     cin >> double1 >> double2 >> double3;
```

Fig. 6.27 | Demonstrating function template maximum. (Part 1 of 2.)

```
27
28      // invoke double version of maximum
29      cout << "The maximum double value is: "
30         << maximum( double1, double2, double3 );
31
32      // demonstrate maximum with char values
33      char char1, char2, char3;
34
35      cout << "\n\nInput three characters: ";
36      cin >> char1 >> char2 >> char3;
37
38      // invoke char version of maximum
39      cout << "The maximum character value is: "
40         << maximum( char1, char2, char3 ) << endl;
41      return 0; // indicates successful termination
42   } // end main
```

```
Input three integer values: 1 2 3
The maximum integer value is: 3

Input three double values: 3.3 2.2 1.1
The maximum double value is: 3.3

Input three characters: A C B
The maximum character value is: C
```

Fig. 6.27 | Demonstrating function template `maximum`. (Part 2 of 2.)

In Fig. 6.27, three functions are created as a result of the calls in lines 20, 30 and 40—expecting three int values, three double values and three char values, respectively. The function template specialization created for type int replaces each occurrence of T with int as follows:

```
int maximum( int value1, int value2, int value3 )
{
   int maximumValue = value1;

   // determine whether value2 is greater than maximumValue
   if ( value2 > maximumValue )
      maximumValue = value2;

   // determine whether value3 is greater than maximumValue
   if ( value3 > maximumValue )
      maximumValue = value3;

   return maximumValue;
} // end function template maximum
```

6.19 Recursion

The programs we have discussed are generally structured as functions that call one another in a disciplined, hierarchical manner. For some problems, it is useful to have functions call themselves. A recursive function is a function that calls itself, either directly, or indirectly (through another function).[2] Recursion is an important topic discussed at length in upper-level computer science courses. This section and the next present simple examples of recursion. This book contains an extensive treatment of recursion. Figure 6.33 (at the end of Section 6.21) summarizes the recursion examples and exercises in the book.

We first consider recursion conceptually, then examine two programs containing recursive functions. Recursive problem-solving approaches have a number of elements in common. A recursive function is called to solve a problem. The function actually knows how to solve only the simplest case(s), or so-called base case(s). If the function is called with a base case, the function simply returns a result. If the function is called with a more complex problem, it typically divides the problem into two conceptual pieces—a piece that the function knows how to do and a piece that it does not know how to do. To make recursion feasible, the latter piece must resemble the original problem, but be a slightly simpler or slightly smaller version. This new problem looks like the original problem, so the function launches (calls) a fresh copy of itself to work on the smaller problem—this is referred to as a recursive call and is also called the recursion step. The recursion step often includes the keyword return, because its result will be combined with the portion of the problem the function knew how to solve to form a result that will be passed back to the original caller, possibly main.

The recursion step executes while the original call to the function is still open, i.e., it has not yet finished executing. The recursion step can result in many more such recursive calls, as the function keeps dividing each new subproblem with which the function is called into two conceptual pieces. In order for the recursion to eventually terminate, each time the function calls itself with a slightly simpler version of the original problem, this sequence of smaller and smaller problems must eventually converge on the base case. At that point, the function recognizes the base case and returns a result to the previous copy of the function, and a sequence of returns ensues all the way up the line until the original function call eventually returns the final result to main. All of this sounds quite exotic compared to the kind of "conventional" problem solving we have been using to this point. As an example of these concepts at work, let us write a recursive program to perform a popular mathematical calculation.

The factorial of a nonnegative integer n, written $n!$ (and pronounced "n factorial"), is the product

$$n \cdot (n-1) \cdot (n-2) \cdot \ldots \cdot 1$$

with 1! equal to 1, and 0! defined to be 1. For example, 5! is the product $5 \cdot 4 \cdot 3 \cdot 2 \cdot 1$, which is equal to 120.

The factorial of an integer, number, greater than or equal to 0, can be calculated iteratively (nonrecursively) by using a for statement as follows:

```
factorial = 1;

for ( int counter = number; counter >= 1; counter-- )
   factorial *= counter;
```

---

2. Although many compilers allow function main to call itself, Section 3.6.1, paragraph 3, of the C++ standard document indicates that main should not be called within a program. Its sole purpose is to be the starting point for program execution.

A recursive definition of the factorial function is arrived at by observing the following relationship:

$$n! = n \cdot (n-1)!$$

For example, 5! is clearly equal to 5 * 4! as is shown by the following:

$$5! = 5 \cdot 4 \cdot 3 \cdot 2 \cdot 1$$
$$5! = 5 \cdot (4 \cdot 3 \cdot 2 \cdot 1)$$
$$5! = 5 \cdot (4!)$$

The evaluation of 5! would proceed as shown in Fig. 6.28. Figure 6.28(a) shows how the succession of recursive calls proceeds until 1! is evaluated to be 1, which terminates the recursion. Figure 6.28(b) shows the values returned from each recursive call to its caller until the final value is calculated and returned.

The program of Fig. 6.29 uses recursion to calculate and print the factorials of the integers 0–10. (The choice of the data type unsigned long is explained momentarily.) The recursive function factorial (lines 23–29) first determines whether the terminating condition number <= 1 (line 25) is true. If number is indeed less than or equal to 1, function factorial returns 1 (line 26), no further recursion is necessary and the function terminates. If number is greater than 1, line 28 expresses the problem as the product of number and a recursive call to factorial evaluating the factorial of number - 1. Note that factorial(number - 1) is a slightly simpler problem than the original calculation factorial(number).

Function factorial has been declared to receive a parameter of type unsigned long and return a result of type unsigned long. This is shorthand notation for unsigned long

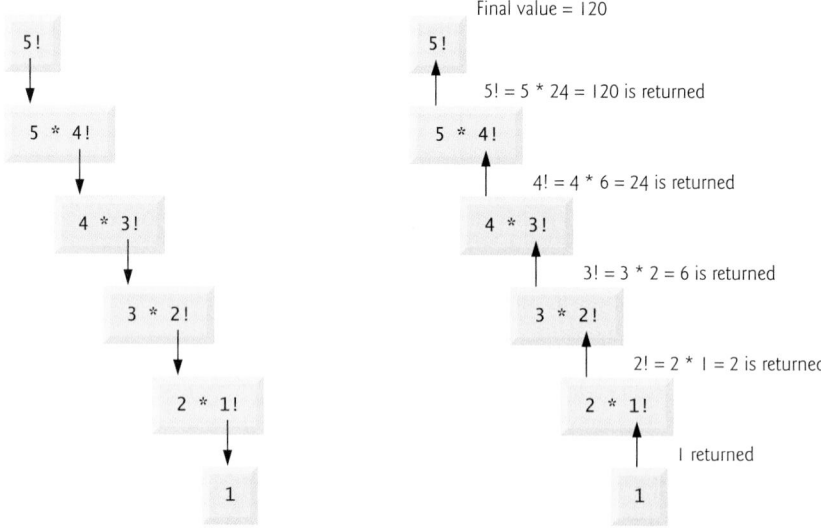

(a) Procession of recursive calls.   (b) Values returned from each recursive call.

Fig. 6.28 | Recursive evaluation of 5!.

```
 1  // Fig. 6.29: fig06_29.cpp
 2  // Testing the recursive factorial function.
 3  #include <iostream>
 4  using std::cout;
 5  using std::endl;
 6
 7  #include <iomanip>
 8  using std::setw;
 9
10  unsigned long factorial( unsigned long ); // function prototype
11
12  int main()
13  {
14     // calculate the factorials of 0 through 10
15     for ( int counter = 0; counter <= 10; counter++ )
16        cout << setw( 2 ) << counter << "! = " << factorial( counter )
17           << endl;
18
19     return 0; // indicates successful termination
20  } // end main
21
22  // recursive definition of function factorial
23  unsigned long factorial( unsigned long number )
24  {
25     if ( number <= 1 ) // test for base case
26        return 1; // base cases: 0! = 1 and 1! = 1
27     else // recursion step
28        return number * factorial( number - 1 );
29  } // end function factorial
```

```
 0! = 1
 1! = 1
 2! = 2
 3! = 6
 4! = 24
 5! = 120
 6! = 720
 7! = 5040
 8! = 40320
 9! = 362880
10! = 3628800
```

Fig. 6.29 | Demonstrating function `factorial`.

int. The C++ standard document requires that a variable of type unsigned long int be stored in at least four bytes (32 bits); thus, it can hold a value in the range 0 to at least 4294967295. (The data type long int is also stored in at least four bytes and can hold a value at least in the range −2147483648 to 2147483647.) As can be seen in Fig. 6.29, factorial values become large quickly. We chose the data type unsigned long so that the program can calculate factorials greater than 7! on computers with small (such as two-byte) integers. Unfortunately, function factorial produces large values so quickly that even unsigned long does not help us compute many factorial values before even the size of an unsigned long variable is exceeded.

The exercises explore using variables of data type `double` to calculate factorials of larger numbers. This points to a weakness in most programming languages, namely, that the languages are not easily extended to handle the unique requirements of various applications. As we will see when we discuss object-oriented programming in more depth, C++ is an extensible language that allows us to create classes that can represent arbitrarily large integers if we wish. Such classes already are available in popular class libraries,[3] and we work on similar classes of our own in Exercise 9.14 and Exercise 11.5.

 Common Programming Error 6.24

Either omitting the base case, or writing the recursion step incorrectly so that it does not converge on the base case, causes "infinite" recursion, eventually exhausting memory. This is analogous to the problem of an infinite loop in an iterative (nonrecursive) solution.

6.20 Example Using Recursion: Fibonacci Series

The Fibonacci series

> 0, 1, 1, 2, 3, 5, 8, 13, 21, …

begins with 0 and 1 and has the property that each subsequent Fibonacci number is the sum of the previous two Fibonacci numbers.

The series occurs in nature and, in particular, describes a form of spiral. The ratio of successive Fibonacci numbers converges on a constant value of 1.618…. This number, too, frequently occurs in nature and has been called the golden ratio or the golden mean. Humans tend to find the golden mean aesthetically pleasing. Architects often design windows, rooms and buildings whose length and width are in the ratio of the golden mean. Postcards are often designed with a golden mean length/width ratio.

The Fibonacci series can be defined recursively as follows:

> fibonacci(0) = 0
> fibonacci(1) = 1
> fibonacci(n) = fibonacci(n – 1) + fibonacci(n – 2)

The program of Fig. 6.30 calculates the nth Fibonacci number recursively by using function `fibonacci`. Notice that Fibonacci numbers also tend to become large quickly, although slower than factorials do. Therefore, we chose the data type `unsigned long` for the parameter type and the return type in function `fibonacci`. Figure 6.30 shows the execution of the program, which displays the Fibonacci values for several numbers.

The application begins with a `for` statement that calculates and displays the Fibonacci values for the integers 0–10 and is followed by three calls to calculate the Fibonacci values of the integers 20, 30 and 35 (lines 18–20). The calls to `fibonacci` (lines 15, 18, 19 and 20) from `main` are not recursive calls, but the calls from line 30 of `fibonacci` are recursive. Each time the program invokes `fibonacci` (lines 25–31), the function immediately tests the base case to determine whether `number` is equal to 0 or 1 (line 27). If this is true, line 28 returns `number`. Interestingly, if `number` is greater than 1, the recursion step (line 30) generates *two* recursive calls, each for a slightly smaller problem than the original call to `fibonacci`. Figure 6.31 shows how function `fibonacci` would evaluate `fibonacci( 3 )`.

---

3. Such classes can be found at `shoup.net/ntl`, `cliodhna.cop.uop.edu/~hetrick/c-sources.html` and `www.trumphurst.com/cpplibs/datapage.phtml?category='intro'`.

```cpp
 1   // Fig. 6.30: fig06_30.cpp
 2   // Testing the recursive fibonacci function.
 3   #include <iostream>
 4   using std::cout;
 5   using std::cin;
 6   using std::endl;
 7
 8   unsigned long fibonacci( unsigned long ); // function prototype
 9
10   int main()
11   {
12      // calculate the fibonacci values of 0 through 10
13      for ( int counter = 0; counter <= 10; counter++ )
14         cout << "fibonacci( " << counter << " ) = "
15            << fibonacci( counter ) << endl;
16
17      // display higher fibonacci values
18      cout << "fibonacci( 20 ) = " << fibonacci( 20 ) << endl;
19      cout << "fibonacci( 30 ) = " << fibonacci( 30 ) << endl;
20      cout << "fibonacci( 35 ) = " << fibonacci( 35 ) << endl;
21      return 0; // indicates successful termination
22   } // end main
23
24   // recursive method fibonacci
25   unsigned long fibonacci( unsigned long number )
26   {
27      if ( ( number == 0 ) || ( number == 1 ) ) // base cases
28         return number;
29      else // recursion step
30         return fibonacci( number - 1 ) + fibonacci( number - 2 );
31   } // end function fibonacci
```

```
fibonacci( 0 ) = 0
fibonacci( 1 ) = 1
fibonacci( 2 ) = 1
fibonacci( 3 ) = 2
fibonacci( 4 ) = 3
fibonacci( 5 ) = 5
fibonacci( 6 ) = 8
fibonacci( 7 ) = 13
fibonacci( 8 ) = 21
fibonacci( 9 ) = 34
fibonacci( 10 ) = 55
fibonacci( 20 ) = 6765
fibonacci( 30 ) = 832040
fibonacci( 35 ) = 9227465
```

Fig. 6.30 | Demonstrating function `fibonacci`.

This figure raises some interesting issues about the order in which C++ compilers will evaluate the operands of operators. This is a separate issue from the order in which operators are applied to their operands, namely, the order dictated by the rules of operator precedence and associativity. Figure 6.31 shows that evaluating `fibonacci( 3 )` causes two

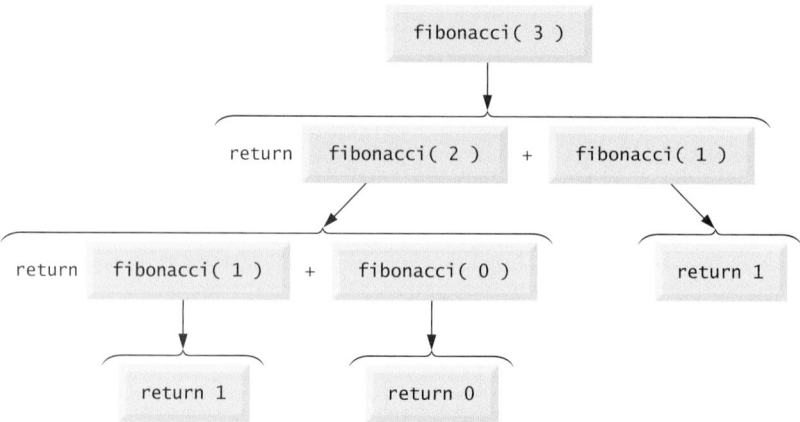

Fig. 6.31 | Set of recursive calls to function `fibonacci`.

recursive calls, namely, `fibonacci( 2 )` and `fibonacci( 1 )`. But in what order are these calls made?

Most programmers simply assume that the operands are evaluated left to right. The C++ language does not specify the order in which the operands of most operators (including +) are to be evaluated. Therefore, the programmer must make no assumption about the order in which these calls execute. The calls could in fact execute `fibonacci( 2 )` first, then `fibonacci( 1 )`, or they could execute in the reverse order: `fibonacci( 1 )`, then `fibonacci( 2 )`. In this program and in most others, it turns out that the final result would be the same. However, in some programs the evaluation of an operand can have side effects (changes to data values) that could affect the final result of the expression.

The C++ language specifies the order of evaluation of the operands of only four operators—namely, &&, ||, the comma (,) operator and ?:. The first three are binary operators whose two operands are guaranteed to be evaluated left to right. The last operator is C++'s only ternary operator. Its leftmost operand is always evaluated first; if it evaluates to non-zero (true), the middle operand evaluates next and the last operand is ignored; if the leftmost operand evaluates to zero (false), the third operand evaluates next and the middle operand is ignored.

Common Programming Error 6.25

Writing programs that depend on the order of evaluation of the operands of operators other than &&, ||, ?: and the comma (,) operator can lead to logic errors.

Portability Tip 6.3

Programs that depend on the order of evaluation of the operands of operators other than &&, ||, ?: and the comma (,) operator can function differently on systems with different compilers.

A word of caution is in order about recursive programs like the one we use here to generate Fibonacci numbers. Each level of recursion in function `fibonacci` has a doubling effect on the number of function calls; i.e., the number of recursive calls that are required to calculate the nth Fibonacci number is on the order of 2^n. This rapidly gets out of hand. Calculating only the 20th Fibonacci number would require on the order of 2^{20} or about a million calls, calculating the 30th Fibonacci number would require on the order of 2^{30} or about a billion calls, and so on. Computer scientists refer to this as exponential complexity. Problems of this nature humble even the world's most powerful computers! Complexity issues in general, and exponential complexity in particular, are discussed in detail in the upper-level computer science course generally called "Algorithms."

Performance Tip 6.8

Avoid Fibonacci-style recursive programs that result in an exponential "explosion" of calls.

6.21 Recursion vs. Iteration

In the two previous sections, we studied two functions that easily can be implemented recursively or iteratively. This section compares the two approaches and discusses why the programmer might choose one approach over the other in a particular situation.

Both iteration and recursion are based on a control statement: Iteration uses a repetition structure; recursion uses a selection structure. Both iteration and recursion involve repetition: Iteration explicitly uses a repetition structure; recursion achieves repetition through repeated function calls. Iteration and recursion both involve a termination test: Iteration terminates when the loop-continuation condition fails; recursion terminates when a base case is recognized. Iteration with counter-controlled repetition and recursion both gradually approach termination: Iteration modifies a counter until the counter assumes a value that makes the loop-continuation condition fail; recursion produces simpler versions of the original problem until the base case is reached. Both iteration and recursion can occur infinitely: An infinite loop occurs with iteration if the loop-continuation test never becomes false; infinite recursion occurs if the recursion step does not reduce the problem during each recursive call in a manner that converges on the base case.

To illustrate the differences between iteration and recursion, let us examine an iterative solution to the factorial problem (Fig. 6.32). Note that a repetition statement is used (lines 28–29 of Fig. 6.32) rather than the selection statement of the recursive solution (lines 24–27 of Fig. 6.29). Note that both solutions use a termination test. In the recursive solution, line 24 tests for the base case. In the iterative solution, line 28 tests the loop-continuation condition—if the test fails, the loop terminates. Finally, note that instead of producing simpler versions of the original problem, the iterative solution uses a counter that is modified until the loop-continuation condition becomes false.

```
1    // Fig. 6.32: fig06_32.cpp
2    // Testing the iterative factorial function.
3    #include <iostream>
4    using std::cout;
5    using std::endl;
6
7    #include <iomanip>
8    using std::setw;
```

Fig. 6.32 | Iterative factorial solution. (Part 1 of 2.)

```
 9
10   unsigned long factorial( unsigned long ); // function prototype
11
12   int main()
13   {
14      // calculate the factorials of 0 through 10
15      for ( int counter = 0; counter <= 10; counter++ )
16         cout << setw( 2 ) << counter << "! = " << factorial( counter )
17            << endl;
18
19      return 0;
20   } // end main
21
22   // iterative function factorial
23   unsigned long factorial( unsigned long number )
24   {
25      unsigned long result = 1;
26
27      // iterative declaration of function factorial
28      for ( unsigned long i = number; i >= 1; i-- )
29         result *= i;
30
31      return result;
32   } // end function factorial
```

```
 0! = 1
 1! = 1
 2! = 2
 3! = 6
 4! = 24
 5! = 120
 6! = 720
 7! = 5040
 8! = 40320
 9! = 362880
10! = 3628800
```

Fig. 6.32 | Iterative factorial solution. (Part 2 of 2.)

Recursion has many negatives. It repeatedly invokes the mechanism, and consequently the overhead, of function calls. This can be expensive in both processor time and memory space. Each recursive call causes another copy of the function (actually only the function's variables) to be created; this can consume considerable memory. Iteration normally occurs within a function, so the overhead of repeated function calls and extra memory assignment is omitted. So why choose recursion?

Software Engineering Observation 6.18

Any problem that can be solved recursively can also be solved iteratively (nonrecursively). A recursive approach is normally chosen in preference to an iterative approach when the recursive approach more naturally mirrors the problem and results in a program that is easier to understand and debug. Another reason to choose a recursive solution is that an iterative solution is not apparent.

Performance Tip 6.9

Avoid using recursion in performance situations. Recursive calls take time and consume additional memory.

Common Programming Error 6.26

Accidentally having a nonrecursive function call itself, either directly or indirectly (through another function), is a logic error.

Most programming textbooks introduce recursion much later than we have done here. We feel that recursion is a sufficiently rich and complex topic that it is better to introduce it earlier and spread the examples over the remainder of the text. Figure 6.33 summarizes the recursion examples and exercises in the text.

Location in Text	Recursion Examples and Exercises
Chapter 6	
Section 6.19, Fig. 6.29	Factorial function
Section 6.19, Fig. 6.30	Fibonacci function
Exercise 6.7	Sum of two integers
Exercise 6.40	Raising an integer to an integer power
Exercise 6.42	Towers of Hanoi
Exercise 6.44	Visualizing recursion
Exercise 6.45	Greatest common divisor
Exercise 6.50, Exercise 6.51	Mystery "What does this program do?" exercise
Chapter 7	
Exercise 7.18	Mystery "What does this program do?" exercise
Exercise 7.21	Mystery "What does this program do?" exercise
Exercise 7.31	Selection sort
Exercise 7.32	Determine whether a string is a palindrome
Exercise 7.33	Linear search
Exercise 7.34	Binary search
Exercise 7.35	Eight Queens
Exercise 7.36	Print an array
Exercise 7.37	Print a string backward
Exercise 7.38	Minimum value in an array
Chapter 8	
Exercise 8.24	Quicksort
Exercise 8.25	Maze traversal

Fig. 6.33 | Summary of recursion examples and exercises in the text. (Part 1 of 2.)

Location in Text	Recursion Examples and Exercises
Exercise 8.26	Generating Mazes Randomly
Exercise 8.27	Mazes of Any Size
Chapter 20	
Section 20.3.3, Figs. 20.5–20.7	Mergesort
Exercise 20.8	Linear search
Exercise 20.9	Binary search
Exercise 20.10	Quicksort
Chapter 21	
Section 21.7, Figs. 21.20–21.22	Binary tree insert
Section 21.7, Figs. 21.20–21.22	Preorder traversal of a binary tree
Section 21.7, Figs. 21.20–21.22	Inorder traversal of a binary tree
Section 21.7, Figs. 21.20–21.22	Postorder traversal of a binary tree
Exercise 21.20	Print a linked list backward
Exercise 21.21	Search a linked list
Exercise 21.22	Binary tree delete
Exercise 21.25	Printing tree

Fig. 6.33 | Summary of recursion examples and exercises in the text. (Part 2 of 2.)

6.22 (Optional) Software Engineering Case Study: Identifying Class Operations in the ATM System

In the "Software Engineering Case Study" sections at the ends of Chapters 3, 4 and 5, we performed the first few steps in the object-oriented design of our ATM system. In Chapter 3, we identified the classes that we will need to implement and we created our first class diagram. In Chapter 4, we described some attributes of our classes. In Chapter 5, we examined objects' states and modeled objects' state transitions and activities. In this section, we determine some of the class operations (or behaviors) needed to implement the ATM system.

Identifying Operations

An operation is a service that objects of a class provide to clients of the class. Consider the operations of some real-world objects. A radio's operations include setting its station and volume (typically invoked by a person adjusting the radio's controls). A car's operations include accelerating (invoked by the driver pressing the accelerator pedal), decelerating (invoked by the driver pressing the brake pedal or releasing the gas pedal), turning and shifting gears. Software objects can offer operations as well—for example, a software graphics object might offer operations for drawing a circle, drawing a line, drawing a square and the like. A spreadsheet software object might offer operations like printing the spreadsheet, totaling the elements in a row or column and graphing information in the spreadsheet as a bar chart or pie chart.

We can derive many of the operations of each class by examining the key verbs and verb phrases in the requirements document. We then relate each of these to particular classes in our system (Fig. 6.34). The verb phrases in Fig. 6.34 help us determine the operations of each class.

Modeling Operations

To identify operations, we examine the verb phrases listed for each class in Fig. 6.34. The "executes financial transactions" phrase associated with class ATM implies that class ATM instructs transactions to execute. Therefore, classes `BalanceInquiry`, `Withdrawal` and `Deposit` each need an operation to provide this service to the ATM. We place this operation (which we have named `execute`) in the third compartment of the three transaction classes in the updated class diagram of Fig. 6.35. During an ATM session, the ATM object will invoke the `execute` operation of each transaction object to tell it to execute.

The UML represents operations (which are implemented as member functions in C++) by listing the operation name, followed by a comma-separated list of parameters in parentheses, a colon and the return type:

operationName (*parameter1*, *parameter2*, …, *parameterN*) : *return type*

Each parameter in the comma-separated parameter list consists of a parameter name, followed by a colon and the parameter type:

parameterName : *parameterType*

For the moment, we do not list the parameters of our operations—we will identify and model the parameters of some of the operations shortly. For some of the operations, we do not yet know the return types, so we also omit them from the diagram. These omissions are perfectly normal at this point. As our design and implementation proceed, we will add the remaining return types.

Class	Verbs and verb phrases
ATM	executes financial transactions
BalanceInquiry	[none in the requirements document]
Withdrawal	[none in the requirements document]
Deposit	[none in the requirements document]
BankDatabase	authenticates a user, retrieves an account balance, credits a deposit amount to an account, debits a withdrawal amount from an account
Account	retrieves an account balance, credits a deposit amount to an account, debits a withdrawal amount from an account
Screen	displays a message to the user
Keypad	receives numeric input from the user
CashDispenser	dispenses cash, indicates whether it contains enough cash to satisfy a withdrawal request
DepositSlot	receives a deposit envelope

Fig. 6.34 | Verbs and verb phrases for each class in the ATM system.

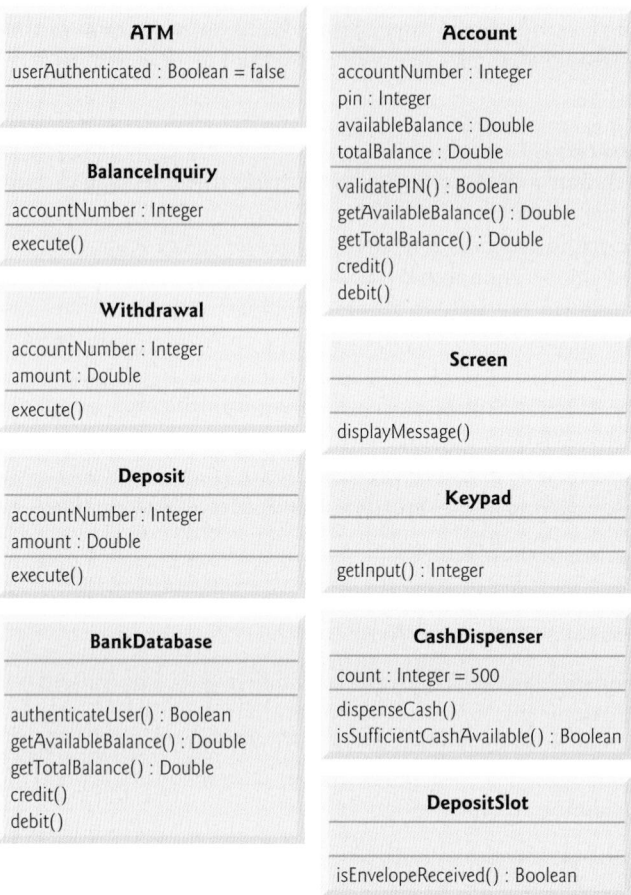

Fig. 6.35 | Classes in the ATM system with attributes and operations.

*Operations of Class **BankDatabase** and Class **Account***

Figure 6.34 lists the phrase "authenticates a user" next to class BankDatabase—the database is the object that contains the account information necessary to determine whether the account number and PIN entered by a user match those of an account held at the bank. Therefore, class BankDatabase needs an operation that provides an authentication service to the ATM. We place the operation authenticateUser in the third compartment of class BankDatabase (Fig. 6.35). However, an object of class Account, not class BankDatabase, stores the account number and PIN that must be accessed to authenticate a user, so class Account must provide a service to validate a PIN obtained through user input against a PIN stored in an Account object. Therefore, we add a validatePIN operation to class Account. Note that we specify a return type of Boolean for the authenticateUser and validatePIN operations. Each operation returns a value indicating either that the operation was successful in performing its task (i.e., a return value of true) or that it was not (i.e., a return value of false).

Figure 6.34 lists several additional verb phrases for class `BankDatabase`: "retrieves an account balance," "credits a deposit amount to an account" and "debits a withdrawal amount from an account." Like "authenticates a user," these remaining phrases refer to services that the database must provide to the ATM, because the database holds all the account data used to authenticate a user and perform ATM transactions. However, objects of class `Account` actually perform the operations to which these phrases refer. Thus, we assign an operation to both class `BankDatabase` and class `Account` to correspond to each of these phrases. Recall from Section 3.11 that, because a bank account contains sensitive information, we do not allow the ATM to access accounts directly. The database acts as an intermediary between the ATM and the account data, thus preventing unauthorized access. As we will see in Section 7.12, class `ATM` invokes the operations of class `BankDatabase`, each of which in turn invokes the operation with the same name in class `Account`.

The phrase "retrieves an account balance" suggests that classes `BankDatabase` and `Account` each need a `getBalance` operation. However, recall that we created two attributes in class `Account` to represent a balance—`availableBalance` and `totalBalance`. A balance inquiry requires access to both balance attributes so that it can display them to the user, but a withdrawal needs to check only the value of `availableBalance`. To allow objects in the system to obtain each balance attribute individually, we add operations `getAvailableBalance` and `getTotalBalance` to the third compartment of classes `Bank-Database` and `Account` (Fig. 6.35). We specify a return type of `Double` for each of these operations, because the balance attributes which they retrieve are of type `Double`.

The phrases "credits a deposit amount to an account" and "debits a withdrawal amount from an account" indicate that classes `BankDatabase` and `Account` must perform operations to update an account during a deposit and withdrawal, respectively. We therefore assign `credit` and `debit` operations to classes `BankDatabase` and `Account`. You may recall that crediting an account (as in a deposit) adds an amount only to the `totalBalance` attribute. Debiting an account (as in a withdrawal), on the other hand, subtracts the amount from both balance attributes. We hide these implementation details inside class `Account`. This is a good example of encapsulation and information hiding.

If this were a real ATM system, classes `BankDatabase` and `Account` would also provide a set of operations to allow another banking system to update a user's account balance after either confirming or rejecting all or part of a deposit. Operation `confirmDepositAmount`, for example, would add an amount to the `availableBalance` attribute, thus making deposited funds available for withdrawal. Operation `rejectDepositAmount` would subtract an amount from the `totalBalance` attribute to indicate that a specified amount, which had recently been deposited through the ATM and added to the `totalBalance`, was not found in the deposit envelope. The bank would invoke this operation after determining either that the user failed to include the correct amount of cash or that any checks did not clear (i.e, they "bounced"). While adding these operations would make our system more complete, we do not include them in our class diagrams or our implementation because they are beyond the scope of the case study.

Operations of Class *Screen*

Class `Screen` "displays a message to the user" at various times in an ATM session. All visual output occurs through the screen of the ATM. The requirements document describes many types of messages (e.g., a welcome message, an error message, a thank-you message) that the screen displays to the user. The requirements document also indicates that the screen displays prompts and menus to the user. However, a prompt is really just a message describing what the user should input next, and a menu is essentially a type of prompt consisting of a series of messages (i.e., menu options) displayed consecutively. Therefore, rather than assign class Screen an individual operation to display each type of message, prompt and menu, we simply create one operation that can display any message specified by a parameter. We place this operation (displayMessage) in the third compartment of class Screen in our class diagram (Fig. 6.35). Note that we do not worry about the parameter of this operation at this time—we model the parameter later in this section.

Operations of Class Keypad

From the phrase "receives numeric input from the user" listed by class Keypad in Fig. 6.34, we conclude that class Keypad should perform a getInput operation. Because the ATM's keypad, unlike a computer keyboard, contains only the numbers 0–9, we specify that this operation returns an integer value. Recall from the requirements document that in different situations the user may be required to enter a different type of number (e.g., an account number, a PIN, the number of a menu option, a deposit amount as a number of cents). Class Keypad simply obtains a numeric value for a client of the class—it does not determine whether the value meets any specific criteria. Any class that uses this operation must verify that the user enters appropriate numbers, and if not, display error messages via class Screen). [*Note:* When we implement the system, we simulate the ATM's keypad with a computer keyboard, and for simplicity we assume that the user does not enter nonnumeric input using keys on the computer keyboard that do not appear on the ATM's keypad. Later in the book, you will learn how to examine inputs to determine if they are of particular types.]

Operations of Class CashDispenser and Class DepositSlot

Figure 6.34 lists "dispenses cash" for class CashDispenser. Therefore, we create operation dispenseCash and list it under class CashDispenser in Fig. 6.35. Class CashDispenser also "indicates whether it contains enough cash to satisfy a withdrawal request." Thus, we include isSufficientCashAvailable, an operation that returns a value of UML type Boolean, in class CashDispenser. Figure 6.34 also lists "receives a deposit envelope" for class DepositSlot. The deposit slot must indicate whether it received an envelope, so we place an operation isEnvelopeReceived, which returns a Boolean value, in the third compartment of class DepositSlot. [*Note:* A real hardware deposit slot would most likely send the ATM a signal to indicate that an envelope was received. We simulate this behavior, however, with an operation in class DepositSlot that class ATM can invoke to find out whether the deposit slot received an envelope.]

Operations of Class ATM

We do not list any operations for class ATM at this time. We are not yet aware of any services that class ATM provides to other classes in the system. When we implement the system with C++ code, however, operations of this class, and additional operations of the other classes in the system, may emerge.

Identifying and Modeling Operation Parameters

So far, we have not been concerned with the parameters of our operations—we have attempted to gain only a basic understanding of the operations of each class. Let's now take a closer look at some operation parameters. We identify an operation's parameters by examining what data the operation requires to perform its assigned task.

Consider the authenticateUser operation of class BankDatabase. To authenticate a user, this operation must know the account number and PIN supplied by the user. Thus we specify that operation authenticateUser takes integer parameters userAccountNumber and userPIN, which the operation must compare to the account number and PIN of an Account object in the database. We prefix these parameter names with "user" to avoid confusion between the operation's parameter names and the attribute names that belong to class Account. We list these parameters in the class diagram in Fig. 6.36 that models only class BankDatabase. [*Note:* It is perfectly normal to model only one class in a class diagram. In this case, we are most concerned with examining the parameters of this one class in particular, so we omit the other classes. In class diagrams later in the case study, in which parameters are no longer the focus of our attention, we omit these parameters to save space. Remember, however, that the operations listed in these diagrams still have parameters.]

Recall that the UML models each parameter in an operation's comma-separated parameter list by listing the parameter name, followed by a colon and the parameter type (in UML notation). Figure 6.36 thus specifies that operation authenticateUser takes two parameters—userAccountNumber and userPIN, both of type Integer. When we implement the system in C++, we will represent these parameters with int values.

Class BankDatabase operations getAvailableBalance, getTotalBalance, credit and debit also each require a userAccountNumber parameter to identify the account to which the database must apply the operations, so we include these parameters in the class

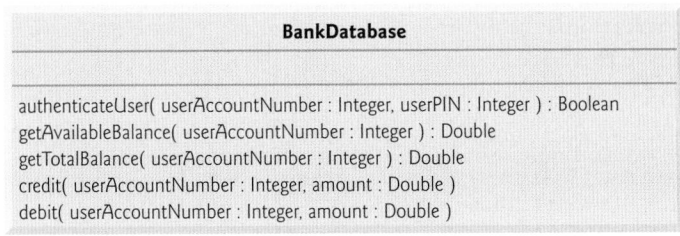

BankDatabase

authenticateUser(userAccountNumber : Integer, userPIN : Integer) : Boolean
getAvailableBalance(userAccountNumber : Integer) : Double
getTotalBalance(userAccountNumber : Integer) : Double
credit(userAccountNumber : Integer, amount : Double)
debit(userAccountNumber : Integer, amount : Double)

Fig. 6.36 | Class BankDatabase with operation parameters.

Account

accountNumber : Integer
pin : Integer
availableBalance : Double
totalBalance : Double

validatePIN(userPIN: Integer) : Boolean
getAvailableBalance() : Double
getTotalBalance() : Double
credit(amount : Double)
debit(amount : Double)

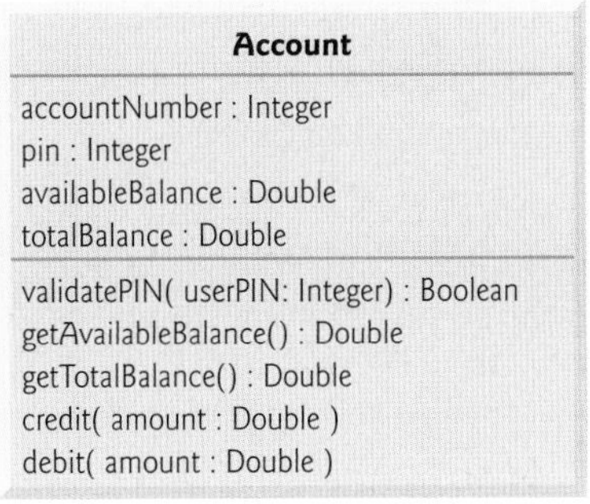

Fig. 6.37 | Class Account with operation parameters.

diagram of Fig. 6.36. In addition, operations `credit` and `debit` each require a `Double` parameter amount to specify the amount of money to be credited or debited, respectively.

The class diagram in Fig. 6.37 models the parameters of class `Account`'s operations. Operation `validatePIN` requires only a `userPIN` parameter, which contains the user-specified PIN to be compared with the PIN associated with the account. Like their counterparts in class `BankDatabase`, operations `credit` and `debit` in class `Account` each require a `Double` parameter amount that indicates the amount of money involved in the operation. Operations `getAvailableBalance` and `getTotalBalance` in class `Account` require no additional data to perform their tasks. Note that class `Account`'s operations do not require an account number parameter—each of these operations can be invoked only on a specific `Account` object, so including a parameter to specify an `Account` is unnecessary.

Figure 6.38 models class `Screen` with a parameter specified for operation `displayMessage`. This operation requires only a `String` parameter `message` that indicates the text to be displayed. Recall that the parameter types listed in our class diagrams are in UML notation, so the `String` type listed in Fig. 6.38 refers to the UML type. When we implement the system in C++, we will in fact use a C++ `string` object to represent this parameter.

The class diagram in Fig. 6.39 specifies that operation `dispenseCash` of class `CashDispenser` takes a `Double` parameter amount to indicate the amount of cash (in dollars) to be dispensed. Operation `isSufficientCashAvailable` also takes a `Double` parameter amount to indicate the amount of cash in question.

Note that we do not discuss parameters for operation `execute` of classes `BalanceInquiry`, `Withdrawal` and `Deposit`, operation `getInput` of class `Keypad` and operation `isEnvelopeReceived` of class `DepositSlot`. At this point in our design process, we cannot determine whether these operations require additional data to perform their tasks, so we leave their parameter lists empty. As we progress through the case study, we may decide to add parameters to these operations.

In this section, we have determined many of the operations performed by the classes in the ATM system. We have identified the parameters and return types of some of the operations. As we continue our design process, the number of operations belonging to each class may vary—we might find that new operations are needed or that some current

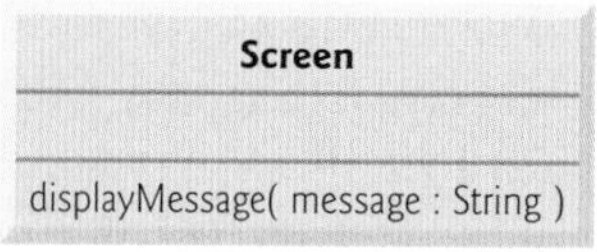

Fig. 6.38 | Class `Screen` with operation parameters.

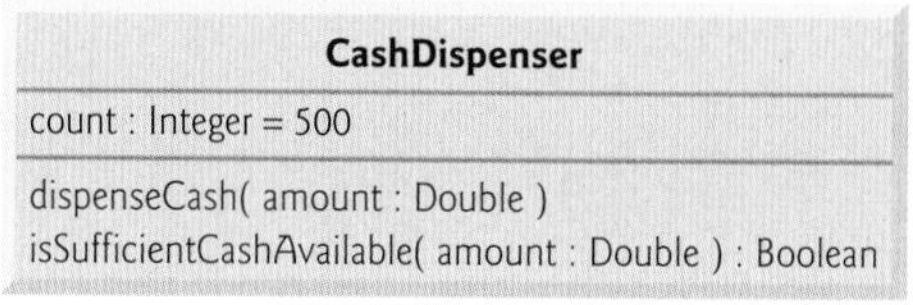

Fig. 6.39 | Class `CashDispenser` with operation parameters.

operations are unnecessary—and we might determine that some of our class operations need additional parameters and different return types.

Software Engineering Case Study Self-Review Exercises

6.1 Which of the following is not a behavior?
a) reading data from a file
b) printing output
c) text output
d) obtaining input from the user

6.2 If you were to add to the ATM system an operation that returns the amount attribute of class Withdrawal, how and where would you specify this operation in the class diagram of Fig. 6.35?

6.3 Describe the meaning of the following operation listing that might appear in a class diagram for an object-oriented design of a calculator:

```
add( x : Integer, y : Integer ) : Integer
```

Answers to Software Engineering Case Study Self-Review Exercises

6.1 c.

6.2 To specify an operation that retrieves the amount attribute of class Withdrawal, the following operation would be placed in the operation (i.e., third) compartment of class Withdrawal:

```
getAmount( ) : Double
```

6.3 This is an operation named add that takes integers x and y as parameters and returns an integer value.

Summary

- Experience has shown that the best way to develop and maintain a large program is to construct it from small, simple pieces, or components. This technique is called divide and conquer.
- C++ programs are typically written by combining new functions and classes the programmer writes with "prepackaged" functions and classes available in the C++ Standard Library.
- Functions allow the programmer to modularize a program by separating its tasks into self-contained units.
- The statements in the function bodies are written only once, are reused from perhaps several locations in a program and are hidden from other functions.
- The compiler refers to the function prototype to check that calls to a method contain the correct number and types of arguments, that the types of the arguments are in the correct order and that the value returned by the function can be used correctly in the expression that called the function.
- There are three ways to return control to the point at which a function was invoked. If the function does not return a result, control returns when the program reaches the function-ending right brace, or by execution of the statement

```
return;
```

  If the function does return a result, the statement

```
return expression;
```

  evaluates *expression* and returns the value of *expression* to the caller.

- A function prototype tells the compiler the name of a function, the type of data returned by that function, the number of parameters the function expects to receive, the types of those parameters and the order in which the parameters of those types are expected.

- The portion of a function prototype that includes the name of the function and the types of its arguments is called the function signature or simply the signature.

- An important feature of function prototypes is argument coercion—i.e., forcing arguments to the appropriate types specified by the parameter declarations.

- Argument values that do not correspond precisely to the parameter types in the function prototype can be converted by the compiler to the proper type as specified by C++'s promotion rules. The promotion rules indicate how to convert between types without losing data.

- The element of chance can be introduced into computer applications by using the C++ Standard Library function rand.

- Function rand actually generates pseudorandom numbers. Calling rand repeatedly produces a sequence of numbers that appears to be random. However, the sequence repeats itself each time the program executes.

- Once a program has been thoroughly debugged, it can be conditioned to produce a different sequence of random numbers for each execution. This is called randomizing and is accomplished with the C++ Standard Library function srand.

- Function srand takes an unsigned integer argument and seeds the rand function to produce a different sequence of random numbers for each execution of the program.

- Random numbers in a range can be generated with

    number = *shiftingValue* + rand() % *scalingFactor*;

where *shiftingValue* is equal to the first number in the desired range of consecutive integers and *scalingFactor* is equal to the width of the desired range of consecutive integers.

- An enumeration, introduced by the keyword enum and followed by a type name, is a set of integer constants represented by identifiers. The values of these enumeration constants start at 0, unless specified otherwise, and increment by 1.

- An identifier's storage class determines the period during which that identifier exists in memory.

- An identifier's scope is where the identifier can be referenced in a program.

- An identifier's linkage determines whether an identifier is known only in the source file where it is declared or across multiple files that are compiled, then linked together.

- Keywords auto and register are used to declare variables of the automatic storage class. Such variables are created when program execution enters the block in which they are defined, they exist while the block is active and they are destroyed when the program exits the block.

- Only local variables of a function can be of automatic storage class.

- The storage class specifier auto explicitly declares variables of automatic storage class. Local variables are of automatic storage class by default, so keyword auto rarely is used.

- Keywords extern and static declare identifiers for variables of the static storage class and for functions. Static-storage-class variables exist from the point at which the program begins execution and last for the duration of the program.

- A static-storage-class variable's storage is allocated when the program begins execution. Such a variable is initialized once when its declaration is encountered. For functions, the name of the function exists when the program begins execution, just as for all other functions.

- There are two types of identifiers with static storage class—external identifiers (such as global variables and global function names) and local variables declared with the storage class specifier static.
- Global variables are created by placing variable declarations outside any class or function definition. Global variables retain their values throughout the execution of the program. Global variables and global functions can be referenced by any function that follows their declarations or definitions in the source file.
- Local variables declared with the keyword static are still known only in the function in which they are declared, but, unlike automatic variables, static local variables retain their values when the function returns to its caller. The next time the function is called, the static local variables contain the values they had when the function last completed execution.
- An identifier declared outside any function or class has file scope.
- Labels are the only identifiers with function scope. Labels can be used anywhere in the function in which they appear, but cannot be referenced outside the function body.
- Identifiers declared inside a block have block scope. Block scope begins at the identifier's declaration and ends at the terminating right brace (}) of the block in which the identifier is declared.
- The only identifiers with function-prototype scope are those used in the parameter list of a function prototype.
- Stacks are known as last-in, first-out (LIFO) data structures—the last item pushed (inserted) on the stack is the first item popped (removed) from the stack.
- One of the most important mechanisms for computer science students to understand is the function call stack (sometimes referred to as the program execution stack). This data structure supports the function call/return mechanism.
- The function call stack also supports the creation, maintenance and destruction of each called function's automatic variables.
- Each time a function calls another function, an entry is pushed onto the stack. This entry, called a stack frame or an activation record, contains the return address that the called function needs to return to the calling function, as well as the automatic variables for the function call.
- The stack frame exists as long as the called function is active. When the called function returns—and no longer needs its local automatic variables—its stack frame is popped from the stack, and those local automatic variables are no longer known to the program.
- In C++, an empty parameter list is specified by writing either void or nothing in parentheses.
- C++ provides inline functions to help reduce function call overhead—especially for small functions. Placing the qualifier inline before a function's return type in the function definition "advises" the compiler to generate a copy of the function's code in place to avoid a function call.
- Two ways to pass arguments to functions in many programming languages are pass-by-value and pass-by-reference.
- When an argument is passed by value, a *copy* of the argument's value is made and passed (on the function call stack) to the called function. Changes to the copy do not affect the original variable's value in the caller.
- With pass-by-reference, the caller gives the called function the ability to access the caller's data directly and to modify it if the called function chooses to do so.
- A reference parameter is an alias for its corresponding argument in a function call.
- To indicate that a function parameter is passed by reference, simply follow the parameter's type in the function prototype by an ampersand (&); use the same convention when listing the parameter's type in the function header.

- Once a reference is declared as an alias for another variable, all operations supposedly performed on the alias (i.e., the reference) are actually performed on the original variable. The alias is simply another name for the original variable.

- It is not uncommon for a program to invoke a function repeatedly with the same argument value for a particular parameter. In such cases, the programmer can specify that such a parameter has a default argument, i.e., a default value to be passed to that parameter.

- When a program omits an argument for a parameter with a default argument, the compiler rewrites the function call and inserts the default value of that argument to be passed as an argument to the function call.

- Default arguments must be the rightmost (trailing) arguments in a function's parameter list.

- Default arguments should be specified with the first occurrence of the function name—typically, in the function prototype.

- C++ provides the unary scope resolution operator (::) to access a global variable when a local variable of the same name is in scope.

- C++ enables several functions of the same name to be defined, as long as these functions have different sets of parameters. This capability is called function overloading.

- When an overloaded function is called, the C++ compiler selects the proper function by examining the number, types and order of the arguments in the call.

- Overloaded functions are distinguished by their signatures.

- The compiler encodes each function identifier with the number and types of its parameters to enable type-safe linkage. Type-safe linkage ensures that the proper overloaded function is called and that the types of the arguments conform to the types of the parameters.

- Overloaded functions are normally used to perform similar operations that involve different program logic on different data types. If the program logic and operations are identical for each data type, overloading may be performed more compactly and conveniently using function templates.

- The programmer writes a single function template definition. Given the argument types provided in calls to this function, C++ automatically generates separate function template specializations to handle each type of call appropriately. Thus, defining a single function template essentially defines a family of overloaded functions.

- All function template definitions begin with the `template` keyword followed by a template parameter list to the function template enclosed in angle brackets (< and >).

- The formal type parameters are placeholders for fundamental types or user-defined types. These placeholders are used to specify the types of the function's parameters, to specify the function's return type and to declare variables within the body of the function definition.

- A recursive function is a function that calls itself, either directly or indirectly.

- A recursive function knows how to solve only the simplest case(s), or so-called base case(s). If the function is called with a base case, the function simply returns a result.

- If the function is called with a more complex problem, the function typically divides the problem into two conceptual pieces—a piece that the function knows how to do and a piece that it does not know how to do. To make recursion feasible, the latter piece must resemble the original problem, but be a slightly simpler or slightly smaller version of it.

- In order for the recursion to eventually terminate, each time the function calls itself with a slightly simpler version of the original problem, this sequence of smaller and smaller problems must eventually converge on the base case.

- The ratio of successive Fibonacci numbers converges on a constant value of 1.618.... This number frequently occurs in nature and has been called the golden ratio or the golden mean.
- Iteration and recursion have many similarities: both are based on a control statement, involve repetition, involve a termination test, gradually approach termination and can occur infinitely.
- Recursion has many negatives. It repeatedly invokes the mechanism, and consequently the overhead, of function calls. This can be expensive in both processor time and memory space. Each recursive call causes another copy of the function (actually only the function's variables) to be created; this can consume considerable memory.

Terminology

& to declare reference
activation record
alias
argument coercion
auto storage-class specifier
automatic local variable
automatic storage class
base case(s)
block scope
class scope
converge on a base case
dangling reference
default argument
divide-and-conquer approach
enum keyword
enumeration
enumeration constant
exponential complexity
extern storage-class specifier
factorial
Fibonacci series
file scope
formal parameter
formal type parameter
function call stack
function declaration
function definition
function name
function overloading
function prototype
function-prototype scope
function scope
function signature
function template
function template specialization
function call overhead
global function
global variable
golden mean
golden ratio

"highest" type
infinite loop
infinite recursion
initializing a reference
inline function
inline keyword
inner block
integral size limits
invoke a method
iteration
iterative solution
label
LIFO (last-in, first-out)
linkage
"lowest type"
mandatory function prototypes
mangled function name
methods
mixed-type expression
modularizing a program with functions
mutable storage-class specifier
name decoration
name mangling
name of a variable
namespace scope
nested blocks
numerical data type limits
optimizing compiler
out of scope
outer block
overloading
parameter
pass-by-reference
pass-by-value
pop off a stack
"prepackaged" functions
principle of least privilege
procedure
program execution stack
programmer-defined function

promotion rules
pseudorandom numbers
push onto a stack
rand function
RAND_MAX symbolic constant
random number
randomizing
recursion
recursion overhead
recursion step
recursive call
recursive evaluation
recursive function
recursive solution
reference parameter
reference to a constant
reference to an automatic variable
register storage-class specifier
repeatability of function rand
returning a reference from a function
rightmost (trailing) arguments
scaling
scaling factor
scope of an identifier
seed
seed function rand
sequence of random numbers
shift a range of numbers
shifted, scaled integers
shifting value
side effect of an expression

signature
software reuse
srand function
stack
stack frame
stack overflow
static keyword
static local variable
static storage class
static storage-class specifier
storage class
storage-class specifiers
template definition
template function
template keyword
template parameter list
terminating condition
terminating right brace (}) of a block
termination test
truncate fractional part of a double
type name (enumerations)
type of a variable
type parameter
type-safe linkage
unary scope resolution operator (::)
user-defined function
user-defined type
validate a function call
void return type
width of random number range

Self-Review Exercises

6.1   Answer each of the following:
  a) Program components in C++ are called _____ and_____.
  b) A function is invoked with a(n) _____.
  c) A variable that is known only within the function in which it is defined is called a(n)
      _____.
  d) The _____ statement in a called function passes the value of an expression back
      to the calling function.
  e) The keyword _____ is used in a function header to indicate that a function does
      not return a value or to indicate that a function contains no parameters.
  f) The _____ of an identifier is the portion of the program in which the identifier
      can be used.
  g) The three ways to return control from a called function to a caller are _____,
      _____ and _____.
  h) A(n) _____ allows the compiler to check the number, types and order of the argu-
      ments passed to a function.
  i) Function _____ is used to produce random numbers.
  j) Function _____ is used to set the random number seed to randomize a program.

k) The storage-class specifiers are mutable, _____, _____, _____ and _____.

l) Variables declared in a block or in the parameter list of a function are assumed to be of storage class _____ unless specified otherwise.

m) Storage-class specifier _____ is a recommendation to the compiler to store a variable in one of the computer's registers.

n) A variable declared outside any block or function is a(n) _____ variable.

o) For a local variable in a function to retain its value between calls to the function, it must be declared with the _____ storage-class specifier.

p) The six possible scopes of an identifier are _____, _____, _____, _____, _____ and _____.

q) A function that calls itself either directly or indirectly (i.e., through another function) is a(n) _____ function.

r) A recursive function typically has two components: One that provides a means for the recursion to terminate by testing for a(n) _____ case and one that expresses the problem as a recursive call for a slightly simpler problem than the original call.

s) In C++, it is possible to have various functions with the same name that operate on different types or numbers of arguments. This is called function _____.

t) The _____ enables access to a global variable with the same name as a variable in the current scope.

u) The _____ qualifier is used to declare read-only variables.

v) A function _____ enables a single function to be defined to perform a task on many different data types.

6.2 For the program in Fig. 6.40, state the scope (either function scope, file scope, block scope or function-prototype scope) of each of the following elements:

a) The variable x in main.

b) The variable y in cube.

c) The function cube.

d) The function main.

e) The function prototype for cube.

f) The identifier y in the function prototype for cube.

```cpp
1   // Exercise 6.2: Ex06_02.cpp
2   #include <iostream>
3   using std::cout;
4   using std::endl;
5
6   int cube( int y ); // function prototype
7
8   int main()
9   {
10      int x;
11
12      for ( x = 1; x <= 10; x++ ) // loop 10 times
13         cout << cube( x ) << endl; // calculate cube of x and output results
14
15      return 0; // indicates successful termination
16   } // end main
17
18   // definition of function cube
```

Fig. 6.40 | Program for Exercise 6.2

308 Chapter 6 Functions and an Introduction to Recursion

```
19   int cube( int y )
20   {
21       return y * y * y;
22   } // end function cube
```

Fig. 6.40 | Program for Exercise 6.2

6.3 Write a program that tests whether the examples of the math library function calls shown in Fig. 6.2 actually produce the indicated results.

6.4 Give the function header for each of the following functions:
  a) Function hypotenuse that takes two double-precision, floating-point arguments, side1 and side2, and returns a double-precision, floating-point result.
  b) Function smallest that takes three integers, x, y and z, and returns an integer.
  c) Function instructions that does not receive any arguments and does not return a value. [*Note:* Such functions are commonly used to display instructions to a user.]
  d) Function intToDouble that takes an integer argument, number, and returns a double-precision, floating-point result.

6.5 Give the function prototype for each of the following:
  a) The function described in Exercise 6.4(a).
  b) The function described in Exercise 6.4(b).
  c) The function described in Exercise 6.4(c).
  d) The function described in Exercise 6.4(d).

6.6 Write a declaration for each of the following:
  a) Integer count that should be maintained in a register. Initialize count to 0.
  b) Double-precision, floating-point variable lastVal that is to retain its value between calls to the function in which it is defined.

6.7 Find the error in each of the following program segments, and explain how the error can be corrected (see also Exercise 6.53):
  a)
```
int g( void )
{
   cout << "Inside function g" << endl;
   int h( void )
   {
      cout << "Inside function h" << endl;
   }
}
```
  b)
```
int sum( int x, int y )
{
   int result;

   result = x + y;
}
```
  c)
```
int sum( int n )
{
   if ( n == 0 )
      return 0;
   else
      n + sum( n - 1 );
}
```

d) `void f( double a );`
```
{
    float a;
    cout << a << endl;
}
```

e) `void product( void )`
```
{
    int a;
    int b;
    int c;
    int result;
    cout << "Enter three integers: ";
    cin >> a >> b >> c;
    result = a * b * c;
    cout << "Result is " << result;
    return result;
}
```

6.8   Why would a function prototype contain a parameter type declaration such as `double &`?

6.9   (True/False) All arguments to function calls in C++ are passed by value.

6.10   Write a complete program that prompts the user for the radius of a sphere, and calculates and prints the volume of that sphere. Use an `inline` function `sphereVolume` that returns the result of the following expression: `( 4.0 / 3.0 ) * 3.14159 * pow( radius, 3 )`.

Answers to Self-Review Exercises

6.1   a) functions, classes. b) function call. c) local variable. d) `return`. e) `void`. f) scope. g) `return;`, `return` *expression*; or encounter the closing right brace of a function. h) function prototype. i) `rand`. j) `srand`. k) `auto`, `register`, `extern`, `static`. l) `auto`. m) `register`. n) global. o) `static`. p) function scope, file scope, block scope, function-prototype scope, class scope, namespace scope. q) recursive. r) base. s) overloading. t) unary scope resolution operator (`::`). u) `const`. v) template.

6.2   a) block scope. b) block scope. c) file scope. d) file scope. e) file scope. f) function-prototype scope.

6.3   See the following program:

```
// Exercise 6.3: Ex06_03.cpp
// Testing the math library functions.
#include <iostream>
using std::cout;
using std::endl;
using std::fixed;

#include <iomanip>
using std::setprecision;

#include <cmath>
using namespace std;

int main()
{
    cout << fixed << setprecision( 1 );
```

```
17
18      cout << "sqrt(" << 900.0 << ") = " << sqrt( 900.0 )
19         << "\nsqrt(" << 9.0 << ") = " << sqrt( 9.0 );
20      cout << "\nexp(" << 1.0 << ") = " << setprecision( 6 )
21         << exp( 1.0 ) << "\nexp(" << setprecision( 1 ) << 2.0
22         << ") = " << setprecision( 6 ) << exp( 2.0 );
23      cout << "\nlog(" << 2.718282 << ") = " << setprecision( 1 )
24         << log( 2.718282 )
25         << "\nlog(" << setprecision( 6 ) << 7.389056 << ") = "
26         << setprecision( 1 ) << log( 7.389056 );
27      cout << "\nlog10(" << 1.0 << ") = " << log10( 1.0 )
28         << "\nlog10(" << 10.0 << ") = " << log10( 10.0 )
29         << "\nlog10(" << 100.0 << ") = " << log10( 100.0 ) ;
30      cout << "\nfabs(" << 13.5 << ") = " << fabs( 13.5 )
31         << "\nfabs(" << 0.0 << ") = " << fabs( 0.0 )
32         << "\nfabs(" << -13.5 << ") = " << fabs( -13.5 );
33      cout << "\nceil(" << 9.2 << ") = " << ceil( 9.2 )
34         << "\nceil(" << -9.8 << ") = " << ceil( -9.8 );
35      cout << "\nfloor(" << 9.2 << ") = " << floor( 9.2 )
36         << "\nfloor(" << -9.8 << ") = " << floor( -9.8 );
37      cout << "\npow(" << 2.0 << ", " << 7.0 << ") = "
38         << pow( 2.0, 7.0 ) << "\npow(" << 9.0 << ", "
39         << 0.5 << ") = " << pow( 9.0, 0.5 );
40      cout << setprecision(3) << "\nfmod("
41         << 13.675 << ", " << 2.333 << ") = "
42         << fmod( 13.675, 2.333 ) << setprecision( 1 );
43      cout << "\nsin(" << 0.0 << ") = " << sin( 0.0 );
44      cout << "\ncos(" << 0.0 << ") = " << cos( 0.0 );
45      cout << "\ntan(" << 0.0 << ") = " << tan( 0.0 ) << endl;
46      return 0; // indicates successful termination
47   } // end main
```

```
sqrt(900.0) = 30.0
sqrt(9.0) = 3.0
exp(1.0) = 2.718282
exp(2.0) = 7.389056
log(2.718282) = 1.0
log(7.389056) = 2.0
log10(1.0) = 0.0
log10(10.0) = 1.0
log10(100.0) = 2.0
fabs(13.5) = 13.5
fabs(0.0) = 0.0
fabs(-13.5) = 13.5
ceil(9.2) = 10.0
ceil(-9.8) = -9.0
floor(9.2) = 9.0
floor(-9.8) = -10.0
pow(2.0, 7.0) = 128.0
pow(9.0, 0.5) = 3.0
fmod(13.675, 2.333) = 2.010
sin(0.0) = 0.0
cos(0.0) = 1.0
tan(0.0) = 0.0
```

6.4 a) `double hypotenuse( double side1, double side2 )`
b) `int smallest( int x, int y, int z )`
c) `void instructions( void ) // in C++ (void) can be written ()`
d) `double intToDouble( int number )`

6.5 a) `double hypotenuse( double, double );`
b) `int smallest( int, int, int );`
c) `void instructions( void ); // in C++ (void) can be written ()`
d) `double intToDouble( int );`

6.6 a) `register int count = 0;`
b) `static double lastVal;`

6.7 a) Error: Function h is defined in function g.
Correction: Move the definition of h out of the definition of g.
b) Error: The function is supposed to return an integer, but does not.
Correction: Delete variable `result` and place the following statement in the function:

   `return x + y;`

c) Error: The result of n + sum(n - 1) is not returned; sum returns an improper result.
Correction: Rewrite the statement in the else clause as

   `return n + sum( n - 1 );`

d) Errors: Semicolon after the right parenthesis that encloses the parameter list, and re-defining the parameter a in the function definition.
Corrections: Delete the semicolon after the right parenthesis of the parameter list, and delete the declaration `float a;`.
e) Error: The function returns a value when it is not supposed to.
Correction: Eliminate the `return` statement.

6.8 This creates a reference parameter of type "reference to `double`" that enables the function to modify the original variable in the calling function.

6.9 False. C++ enables pass-by-reference using reference parameters (and pointers, as we discuss in Chapter 8).

6.10 See the following program:

```
1   // Exercise 6.10 Solution: Ex06_10.cpp
2   // Inline function that calculates the volume of a sphere.
3   #include <iostream>
4   using std::cin;
5   using std::cout;
6   using std::endl;
7
8   #include <cmath>
9   using std::pow;
10
11  const double PI = 3.14159; // define global constant PI
12
13  // calculates volume of a sphere
14  inline double sphereVolume( const double radius )
15  {
16     return 4.0 / 3.0 * PI * pow( radius, 3 );
17  } // end inline function sphereVolume
```

```
18
19   int main()
20   {
21       double radiusValue;
22
23       // prompt user for radius
24       cout << "Enter the length of the radius of your sphere: ";
25       cin >> radiusValue; // input radius
26
27       // use radiusValue to calculate volume of sphere and display result
28       cout << "Volume of sphere with radius " << radiusValue
29           << " is " << sphereVolume( radiusValue ) << endl;
30       return 0; // indicates successful termination
31   } // end main
```

Exercises

6.11 Show the value of x after each of the following statements is performed:
  a) x = fabs(7.5)
  b) x = floor(7.5)
  c) x = fabs(0.0)
  d) x = ceil(0.0)
  e) x = fabs(-6.4)
  f) x = ceil(-6.4)
  g) x = ceil(-fabs(-8 + floor(-5.5)))

6.12 A parking garage charges a $2.00 minimum fee to park for up to three hours. The garage charges an additional $0.50 per hour for each hour *or part thereof* in excess of three hours. The maximum charge for any given 24-hour period is $10.00. Assume that no car parks for longer than 24 hours at a time. Write a program that calculates and prints the parking charges for each of three customers who parked their cars in this garage yesterday. You should enter the hours parked for each customer. Your program should print the results in a neat tabular format and should calculate and print the total of yesterday's receipts. The program should use the function calculateCharges to determine the charge for each customer. Your outputs should appear in the following format:

```
Car       Hours         Charge
1           1.5           2.00
2           4.0           2.50
3          24.0          10.00
TOTAL      29.5          14.50
```

6.13 An application of function floor is rounding a value to the nearest integer. The statement

    y = floor(x + .5);

rounds the number x to the nearest integer and assigns the result to y. Write a program that reads several numbers and uses the preceding statement to round each of these numbers to the nearest integer. For each number processed, print both the original number and the rounded number.

6.14 Function floor can be used to round a number to a specific decimal place. The statement

    y = floor(x * 10 + .5) / 10;

rounds x to the tenths position (the first position to the right of the decimal point). The statement

```
y = floor( x * 100 + .5 ) / 100;
```

rounds x to the hundredths position (the second position to the right of the decimal point). Write a program that defines four functions to round a number x in various ways:

    a) `roundToInteger( number )`
    b) `roundToTenths( number )`
    c) `roundToHundredths( number )`
    d) `roundToThousandths( number )`

    For each value read, your program should print the original value, the number rounded to the nearest integer, the number rounded to the nearest tenth, the number rounded to the nearest hundredth and the number rounded to the nearest thousandth.

6.15   Answer each of the following questions:
    a) What does it mean to choose numbers "at random?"
    b) Why is the rand function useful for simulating games of chance?
    c) Why would you randomize a program by using srand? Under what circumstances is it desirable not to randomize?
    d) Why is it often necessary to scale or shift the values produced by rand?
    e) Why is computerized simulation of real-world situations a useful technique?

6.16   Write statements that assign random integers to the variable n in the following ranges:
    a) $1 \leq n \leq 2$
    b) $1 \leq n \leq 100$
    c) $0 \leq n \leq 9$
    d) $1000 \leq n \leq 1112$
    e) $-1 \leq n \leq 1$
    f) $-3 \leq n \leq 11$

6.17   For each of the following sets of integers, write a single statement that prints a number at random from the set:
    a) 2, 4, 6, 8, 10.
    b) 3, 5, 7, 9, 11.
    c) 6, 10, 14, 18, 22.

6.18   Write a function `integerPower( base, exponent )` that returns the value of

$$base^{\ exponent}$$

For example, `integerPower( 3, 4 )` = 3 * 3 * 3 * 3. Assume that *exponent* is a positive, non-zero integer and that *base* is an integer. The function `integerPower` should use for or while to control the calculation. Do not use any math library functions.

6.19   *(Hypotenuse)* Define a function hypotenuse that calculates the length of the hypotenuse of a right triangle when the other two sides are given. Use this function in a program to determine the length of the hypotenuse for each of the triangles shown below. The function should take two double arguments and return the hypotenuse as a double.

Triangle	Side 1	Side 2
1	3.0	4.0
2	5.0	12.0
3	8.0	15.0

6.20   Write a function `multiple` that determines for a pair of integers whether the second is a multiple of the first. The function should take two integer arguments and return `true` if the second is a multiple of the first, `false` otherwise. Use this function in a program that inputs a series of pairs of integers.

6.21   Write a program that inputs a series of integers and passes them one at a time to function `even`, which uses the modulus operator to determine whether an integer is even. The function should take an integer argument and return `true` if the integer is even and `false` otherwise.

6.22   Write a function that displays at the left margin of the screen a solid square of asterisks whose side is specified in integer parameter `side`. For example, if `side` is 4, the function displays the following:

```
****
****
****
****
```

6.23   Modify the function created in Exercise 6.22 to form the square out of whatever character is contained in character parameter `fillCharacter`. Thus, if `side` is 5 and `fillCharacter` is #, then this function should print the following:

```
#####
#####
#####
#####
#####
```

6.24   Use techniques similar to those developed in Exercise 6.22 and Exercise 6.23 to produce a program that graphs a wide range of shapes.

6.25   Write program segments that accomplish each of the following:
  a) Calculate the integer part of the quotient when integer a is divided by integer b.
  b) Calculate the integer remainder when integer a is divided by integer b.
  c) Use the program pieces developed in (a) and (b) to write a function that inputs an integer between 1 and 32767 and prints it as a series of digits, each pair of which is separated by two spaces. For example, the integer 4562 should print as follows:

```
4  5  6  2
```

6.26   Write a function that takes the time as three integer arguments (hours, minutes and seconds) and returns the number of seconds since the last time the clock "struck 12." Use this function to calculate the amount of time in seconds between two times, both of which are within one 12-hour cycle of the clock.

6.27   *(Celsius and Fahrenheit Temperatures)* Implement the following integer functions:
  a) Function `celsius` returns the Celsius equivalent of a Fahrenheit temperature.
  b) Function `fahrenheit` returns the Fahrenheit equivalent of a Celsius temperature.

c) Use these functions to write a program that prints charts showing the Fahrenheit equivalents of all Celsius temperatures from 0 to 100 degrees, and the Celsius equivalents of all Fahrenheit temperatures from 32 to 212 degrees. Print the outputs in a neat tabular format that minimizes the number of lines of output while remaining readable.

6.28 Write a program that inputs three double-precision, floating-point numbers and passes them to a function that returns the smallest number.

6.29 *(Perfect Numbers)* An integer is said to be a *perfect number* if the sum of its factors, including 1 (but not the number itself), is equal to the number. For example, 6 is a perfect number, because 6 = 1 + 2 + 3. Write a function perfect that determines whether parameter number is a perfect number. Use this function in a program that determines and prints all the perfect numbers between 1 and 1000. Print the factors of each perfect number to confirm that the number is indeed perfect. Challenge the power of your computer by testing numbers much larger than 1000.

6.30 *(PrimeNumbers)* An integer is said to be *prime* if it is divisible by only 1 and itself. For example, 2, 3, 5 and 7 are prime, but 4, 6, 8 and 9 are not.
a) Write a function that determines whether a number is prime.
b) Use this function in a program that determines and prints all the prime numbers between 2 and 10,000. How many of these numbers do you really have to test before being sure that you have found all the primes?
c) Initially, you might think that $n/2$ is the upper limit for which you must test to see whether a number is prime, but you need only go as high as the square root of n. Why? Rewrite the program, and run it both ways. Estimate the performance improvement.

6.31 *(Reverse Digits)* Write a function that takes an integer value and returns the number with its digits reversed. For example, given the number 7631, the function should return 1367.

6.32 The *greatest common divisor (GCD)* of two integers is the largest integer that evenly divides each of the numbers. Write a function gcd that returns the greatest common divisor of two integers.

6.33 Write a function qualityPoints that inputs a student's average and returns 4 if a student's average is 90–100, 3 if the average is 80–89, 2 if the average is 70–79, 1 if the average is 60–69 and 0 if the average is lower than 60.

6.34 Write a program that simulates coin tossing. For each toss of the coin, the program should print Heads or Tails. Let the program toss the coin 100 times and count the number of times each side of the coin appears. Print the results. The program should call a separate function flip that takes no arguments and returns 0 for tails and 1 for heads. [*Note:* If the program realistically simulates the coin tossing, then each side of the coin should appear approximately half the time.]

6.35 *(Computers in Education)* Computers are playing an increasing role in education. Write a program that helps an elementary school student learn multiplication. Use rand to produce two positive one-digit integers. It should then type a question such as

    How much is 6 times 7?

The student then types the answer. Your program checks the student's answer. If it is correct, print "Very good!", then ask another multiplication question. If the answer is wrong, print "No. Please try again.", then let the student try the same question repeatedly until the student finally gets it right.

6.36 *(Computer Assisted Instruction)* The use of computers in education is referred to as *computer-assisted instruction* (CAI). One problem that develops in CAI environments is student fatigue. This can be eliminated by varying the computer's dialogue to hold the student's attention. Modify the program of Exercise 6.35 so the various comments are printed for each correct answer and each incorrect answer as follows:

Responses to a correct answer

```
Very good!
Excellent!
Nice work!
Keep up the good work!
```

Responses to an incorrect answer

```
No. Please try again.
Wrong. Try once more.
Don't give up!
No. Keep trying.
```

Use the random number generator to choose a number from 1 to 4 to select an appropriate response to each answer. Use a switch statement to issue the responses.

6.37   More sophisticated computer-aided instruction systems monitor the student's performance over a period of time. The decision to begin a new topic often is based on the student's success with previous topics. Modify the program of Exercise 6.36 to count the number of correct and incorrect responses typed by the student. After the student types 10 answers, your program should calculate the percentage of correct responses. If the percentage is lower than 75 percent, your program should print "Please ask your instructor for extra help" and terminate.

6.38   (*Guess the Number Game*) Write a program that plays the game of "guess the number" as follows: Your program chooses the number to be guessed by selecting an integer at random in the range 1 to 1000. The program then displays the following:

```
I have a number between 1 and 1000.
Can you guess my number?
Please type your first guess.
```

The player then types a first guess. The program responds with one of the following:

```
1. Excellent! You guessed the number!
   Would you like to play again (y or n)?
2. Too low. Try again.
3. Too high. Try again.
```

If the player's guess is incorrect, your program should loop until the player finally gets the number right. Your program should keep telling the player Too high or Too low to help the player "zero in" on the correct answer.

6.39   Modify the program of Exercise 6.38 to count the number of guesses the player makes. If the number is 10 or fewer, print "Either you know the secret or you got lucky!" If the player guesses the number in 10 tries, then print "Ahah! You know the secret!" If the player makes more than 10 guesses, then print "You should be able to do better!" Why should it take no more than 10 guesses? Well, with each "good guess" the player should be able to eliminate half of the numbers. Now show why any number from 1 to 1000 can be guessed in 10 or fewer tries.

6.40   Write a recursive function power(base, exponent) that, when invoked, returns

$$base^{\,exponent}$$

For example, power(3, 4) = 3 * 3 * 3 * 3. Assume that exponent is an integer greater than or equal to 1. *Hint:* The recursion step would use the relationship

$$base^{\,exponent} = base \cdot base^{\,exponent\,-\,1}$$

and the terminating condition occurs when $exponent$ is equal to 1, because

$$base^1 = base$$

6.41   *(Fibonacci Series)* The Fibonacci series

0, 1, 1, 2, 3, 5, 8, 13, 21, …

begins with the terms 0 and 1 and has the property that each succeeding term is the sum of the two preceding terms. (a) Write a *nonrecursive* function `fibonacci( n )` that calculates the *n*th Fibonacci number. (b) Determine the largest `int` Fibonacci number that can be printed on your system. Modify the program of part (a) to use `double` instead of `int` to calculate and return Fibonacci numbers, and use this modified program to repeat part (b).

6.42   *(Towers of Hanoi)* In this chapter, you studied functions that can be easily implemented both recursively and iteratively. In this exercise, we present a problem whose recursive solution demonstrates the elegance of recursion, and whose iterative solution may not be as apparent.

The Towers of Hanoi is one of the most famous classic problems every budding computer scientist must grapple with. Legend has it that in a temple in the Far East, priests are attempting to move a stack of golden disks from one diamond peg to another (Fig. 6.41). The initial stack has 64 disks threaded onto one peg and arranged from bottom to top by decreasing size. The priests are attempting to move the stack from one peg to another under the constraints that exactly one disk is moved at a time and at no time may a larger disk be placed above a smaller disk. Three pegs are provided, one being used for temporarily holding disks. Supposedly, the world will end when the priests complete their task, so there is little incentive for us to facilitate their efforts.

Let us assume that the priests are attempting to move the disks from peg 1 to peg 3. We wish to develop an algorithm that prints the precise sequence of peg-to-peg disk transfers.

If we were to approach this problem with conventional methods, we would rapidly find ourselves hopelessly knotted up in managing the disks. Instead, attacking this problem with recursion in mind allows the steps to be simple. Moving *n* disks can be viewed in terms of moving only *n* – 1 disks (hence, the recursion), as follows:

a)   Move *n* – 1 disks from peg 1 to peg 2, using peg 3 as a temporary holding area.
b)   Move the last disk (the largest) from peg 1 to peg 3.
c)   Move the *n* – 1 disks from peg 2 to peg 3, using peg 1 as a temporary holding area.

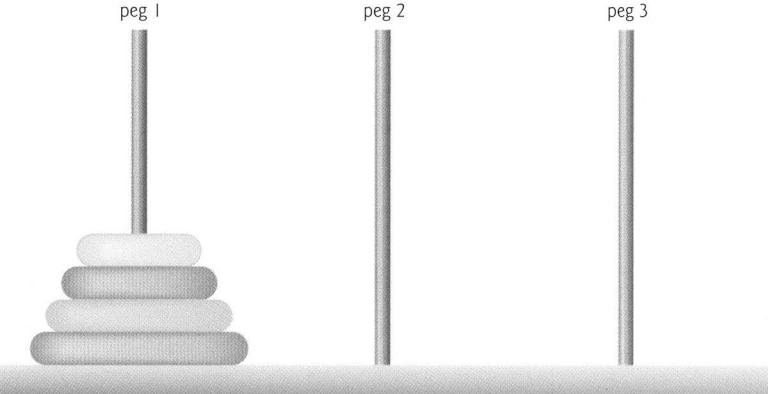

Fig. 6.41 | Towers of Hanoi for the case with four disks.

The process ends when the last task involves moving $n = 1$ disk (i.e., the base case). This task is accomplished by simply moving the disk, without the need for a temporary holding area.

Write a program to solve the Towers of Hanoi problem. Use a recursive function with four parameters:

a) The number of disks to be moved
b) The peg on which these disks are initially threaded
c) The peg to which this stack of disks is to be moved
d) The peg to be used as a temporary holding area

Your program should print the precise instructions it will take to move the disks from the starting peg to the destination peg. For example, to move a stack of three disks from peg 1 to peg 3, your program should print the following series of moves:

1 → 3 (This means move one disk from peg 1 to peg 3.)
1 → 2
3 → 2
1 → 3
2 → 1
2 → 3
1 → 3

6.43   Any program that can be implemented recursively can be implemented iteratively, although sometimes with more difficulty and less clarity. Try writing an iterative version of the Towers of Hanoi. If you succeed, compare your iterative version with the recursive version developed in Exercise 6.42. Investigate issues of performance, clarity and your ability to demonstrate the correctness of the programs.

6.44   *(Visualizing Recursion)* It is interesting to watch recursion "in action." Modify the factorial function of Fig. 6.29 to print its local variable and recursive call parameter. For each recursive call, display the outputs on a separate line and add a level of indentation. Do your utmost to make the outputs clear, interesting and meaningful. Your goal here is to design and implement an output format that helps a person understand recursion better. You may want to add such display capabilities to the many other recursion examples and exercises throughout the text.

6.45   *(Recursive Greatest Common Divisor)* The greatest common divisor of integers x and y is the largest integer that evenly divides both x and y. Write a recursive function gcd that returns the greatest common divisor of x and y, defined recursively as follows: If y is equal to 0, then gcd(x, y) is x; otherwise, gcd(x, y) is gcd(y, x % y), where % is the modulus operator. [*Note:* For this algorithm, x must be larger than y.]

6.46   Can main be called recursively on your system? Write a program containing a function main. Include static local variable count and initialize it to 1. Postincrement and print the value of count each time main is called. Compile your program. What happens?

6.47   Exercises 6.35–6.37 developed a computer-assisted instruction program to teach an elementary school student multiplication. This exercise suggests enhancements to that program.

a) Modify the program to allow the user to enter a grade-level capability. A grade level of 1 means to use only single-digit numbers in the problems, a grade level of 2 means to use numbers as large as two digits, etc.
b) Modify the program to allow the user to pick the type of arithmetic problems he or she wishes to study. An option of 1 means addition problems only, 2 means subtraction problems only, 3 means multiplication problems only, 4 means division problems only and 5 means a random mix of problems of all these types.

6.48   Write function distance that calculates the distance between two points *(x1, y1)* and *(x2, y2)*. All numbers and return values should be of type double.

6.49   What is wrong with the following program?

```
1   // Exercise 6.49: ex06_49.cpp
2   // What is wrong with this program?
3   #include <iostream>
4   using std::cin;
5   using std::cout;
6
7   int main()
8   {
9      int c;
10
11     if ( ( c = cin.get() ) != EOF )
12     {
13        main();
14        cout << c;
15     } // end if
16
17     return 0; // indicates successful termination
18  } // end main
```

6.50   What does the following program do?

```
1   // Exercise 6.50: ex06_50.cpp
2   // What does this program do?
3   #include <iostream>
4   using std::cout;
5   using std::cin;
6   using std::endl;
7
8   int mystery( int, int ); // function prototype
9
10  int main()
11  {
12     int x, y;
13
14     cout << "Enter two integers: ";
15     cin >> x >> y;
16     cout << "The result is " << mystery( x, y ) << endl;
17
18     return 0; // indicates successful termination
19  } // end main
20
21  // Parameter b must be a positive integer to prevent infinite recursion
22  int mystery( int a, int b )
23  {
24     if ( b == 1 ) // base case
25        return a;
26     else // recursion step
27        return a + mystery( a, b - 1 );
28  } // end function mystery
```

6.51 After you determine what the program of Exercise 6.50 does, modify the program to function properly after removing the restriction that the second argument be nonnegative.

6.52 Write a program that tests as many of the math library functions in Fig. 6.2 as you can. Exercise each of these functions by having your program print out tables of return values for a diversity of argument values.

6.53 Find the error in each of the following program segments and explain how to correct it:

a) `float cube( float ); // function prototype`

```
double cube( float number ) // function definition
{
    return number * number * number;
}
```

b) `register auto int x = 7;`

c) `int randomNumber = srand();`

d) `float y = 123.45678;`
```
int x;

x = y;
cout << static_cast< float >( x ) << endl;
```

e)
```
double square( double number )
{
    double number;
    return number * number;
}
```

f)
```
int sum( int n )
{
    if ( n == 0 )
        return 0;
    else
        return n + sum( n );
}
```

6.54 Modify the craps program of Fig. 6.11 to allow wagering. Package as a function the portion of the program that runs one game of craps. Initialize variable bankBalance to 1000 dollars. Prompt the player to enter a wager. Use a while loop to check that wager is less than or equal to bankBalance and, if not, prompt the user to reenter wager until a valid wager is entered. After a correct wager is entered, run one game of craps. If the player wins, increase bankBalance by wager and print the new bankBalance. If the player loses, decrease bankBalance by wager, print the new bankBalance, check on whether bankBalance has become zero and, if so, print the message "Sorry. You busted!" As the game progresses, print various messages to create some "chatter" such as "Oh, you're going for broke, huh?", "Aw cmon, take a chance!" or "You're up big. Now's the time to cash in your chips!".

6.55 Write a C++ program that prompts the user for the radius of a circle then calls inline function circleArea to calculate the area of that circle.

6.56 Write a complete C++ program with the two alternate functions specified below, of which each simply triples the variable count defined in main. Then compare and contrast the two approaches. These two functions are

a) function tripleByValue that passes a copy of count by value, triples the copy and returns the new value and

    a) function `tripleByReference` that passes count by reference via a reference parameter and triples the original value of count through its alias (i.e., the reference parameter).

6.57   What is the purpose of the unary scope resolution operator?

6.58   Write a program that uses a function template called `min` to determine the smaller of two arguments. Test the program using integer, character and floating-point number arguments.

6.59   Write a program that uses a function template called `max` to determine the largest of three arguments. Test the program using integer, character and floating-point number arguments.

6.60   Determine whether the following program segments contain errors. For each error, explain how it can be corrected. [*Note:* For a particular program segment, it is possible that no errors are present in the segment.]

a)
```
template < class A >
int sum( int num1, int num2, int num3 )
{
   return num1 + num2 + num3;
}
```
b)
```
void printResults( int x, int y )
{
   cout << "The sum is " << x + y << '\n';
   return x + y;
}
```
c)
```
template < A >
A product( A num1, A num2, A num3 )
{
   return num1 * num2 * num3;
}
```
d)
```
double cube( int );
int cube( int );
```

7

Arrays and Vectors

OBJECTIVES

In this chapter you will learn:

- To use the array data structure to represent a set of related data items.
- To use arrays to store, sort and search lists and tables of values.
- To declare arrays, initialize arrays and refer to the individual elements of arrays.
- To pass arrays to functions.
- Basic searching and sorting techniques.
- To declare and manipulate multidimensional arrays.
- To use C++ Standard Library class template `vector`.

7.1   Introduction

This chapter introduces the important topic of data structures—collections of related data items. Arrays are data structures consisting of related data items of the same type. You learned about classes in Chapter 3. In Chapter 9, we discuss the notion of structures. Structures and classes are each capable of holding related data items of possibly different types. Arrays, structures and classes are "static" entities in that they remain the same size throughout program execution. (They may, of course, be of automatic storage class and hence be created and destroyed each time the blocks in which they are defined are entered and exited.)

After discussing how arrays are declared, created and initialized, this chapter presents a series of practical examples that demonstrate several common array manipulations. We then explain how character strings (represented until now by `string` objects) can also be represented by character arrays. We present an example of searching arrays to find particular elements. The chapter also introduces one of the most important computing applications—sorting data (i.e., putting the data in some particular order). Two sections of the chapter enhance the case study of class `GradeBook` in Chapters 3–6. In particular, we use arrays to enable the class to maintain a set of grades in memory and analyze student grades from multiple exams in a semester—two capabilities that were absent from previous versions of the `GradeBook` class. These and other chapter examples demonstrate the ways in which arrays allow programmers to organize and manipulate data.

The style of arrays we use throughout most of this chapter are C-style pointer-based arrays. (We will study pointers in Chapter 8.) In the final section of this chapter, and in Chapter 22, Standard Template Library (STL), we will cover arrays as full-fledged objects called vectors. We will discover that these object-based arrays are safer and more versatile than the C-like, pointer-based arrays we discuss in the early part of this chapter.

7.2 Arrays

An array is a consecutive group of memory locations that all have the same type. To refer to a particular location or element in the array, we specify the name of the array and the **position number** of the particular element in the array.

Figure 7.1 shows an integer array called c. This array contains 12 **elements**. A program refers to any one of these elements by giving the name of the array followed by the position number of the particular element in square brackets ([]). The position number is more formally called a **subscript** or **index** (this number specifies the number of elements from the beginning of the array). The first element in every array has **subscript 0** (zero) and is sometimes called the **zeroth element**. Thus, the elements of array c are c[0] (pronounced "c sub zero"), c[1], c[2] and so on. The highest subscript in array c is 11, which is 1 less than 12—the number of elements in the array. Array names follow the same conventions as other variable names, i.e., they must be identifiers.

A subscript must be an integer or integer expression (using any integral type). If a program uses an expression as a subscript, then the program evaluates the expression to determine the subscript. For example, if we assume that variable a is equal to 5 and that variable b is equal to 6, then the statement

    c[a + b] += 2;

adds 2 to array element c[11]. Note that a subscripted array name is an *lvalue*—it can be used on the left side of an assignment, just as non-array variable names can.

Let us examine array c in Fig. 7.1 more closely. The **name** of the entire array is c. The 12 elements of array c are referred to as c[0], c[1], c[2], ..., c[11]. The **value** of c[0] is -45, the value of c[1] is 6, the value of c[2] is 0, the value of c[7] is 62, and

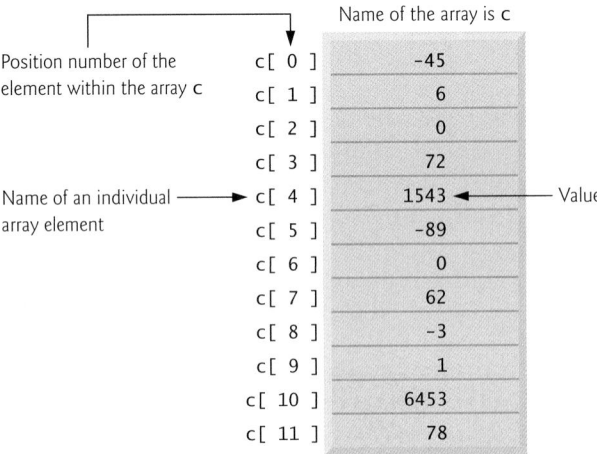

Fig. 7.1 | Array of 12 elements

the value of c[11] is 78. To print the sum of the values contained in the first three elements of array c, we would write

```
cout << c[ 0 ] + c[ 1 ] + c[ 2 ] << endl;
```

To divide the value of c[6] by 2 and assign the result to the variable x, we would write

```
x = c[ 6 ] / 2;
```

Common Programming Error 7.1

It is important to note the difference between the "seventh element of the array" and "array element 7." Array subscripts begin at 0, so the "seventh element of the array" has a subscript of 6, while "array element 7" has a subscript of 7 and is actually the eighth element of the array. Unfortunately, this distinction frequently is a source of off-by-one errors. To avoid such errors, we refer to specific array elements explicitly by their array name and subscript number (e.g., c[6] or c[7]).

The brackets used to enclose the subscript of an array are actually an operator in C++. Brackets have the same level of precedence as parentheses. Figure 7.2 shows the precedence and associativity of the operators introduced so far. Note that brackets ([]) have been added to the first row of Fig. 7.2. The operators are shown top to bottom in decreasing order of precedence with their associativity and type.

7.3   Declaring Arrays

Arrays occupy space in memory. The programmer specifies the type of the elements and the number of elements required by an array as follows:

type arrayName[*arraySize*];

Operators	Associativity	Type
() []	left to right	highest
++ -- static_cast< *type* >(*operand*)	left to right	unary (postfix)
++ -- + - !	right to left	unary (prefix)
* / %	left to right	multiplicative
+ -	left to right	additive
<< >>	left to right	insertion/extraction
< <= > >=	left to right	relational
== !=	left to right	equality
&&	left to right	logical AND
||	left to right	logical OR
?:	right to left	conditional
= += -= *= /= %=	right to left	assignment
,	left to right	comma

Fig. 7.2 | Operator precedence and associativity.

and the compiler reserves the appropriate amount of memory. The *arraySize* must be an integer constant greater than zero. For example, to tell the compiler to reserve 12 elements for integer array c, use the declaration

```
int c[ 12 ]; // c is an array of 12 integers
```

Memory can be reserved for several arrays with a single declaration. The following declaration reserves 100 elements for the integer array b and 27 elements for the integer array x.

```
int b[ 100 ], // b is an array of 100 integers
    x[ 27 ]; // x is an array of 27 integers
```

Good Programming Practice 7.1

We prefer to declare one array per declaration for readability, modifiability and ease of commenting.

Arrays can be declared to contain values of any non-reference data type. For example, an array of type char can be used to store a character string. Until now, we have used string objects to store character strings. Section 7.4 introduces using character arrays to store strings. Character strings and their similarity to arrays (a relationship C++ inherited from C), and the relationship between pointers and arrays, are discussed in Chapter 8.

7.4 Examples Using Arrays

This section presents many examples that demonstrate how to declare arrays, how to initialize arrays and how to perform many common array manipulations.

Declaring an Array and Using a Loop to Initialize the Array's Elements
The program in Fig. 7.3 declares 10-element integer array n (line 12). Lines 15–16 use a for statement to initialize the array elements to zeros. The first output statement (line 18) displays the column headings for the columns printed in the subsequent for statement (lines 21–22), which prints the array in tabular format. Remember that setw specifies the field width in which only the *next* value is to be output.

Initializing an Array in a Declaration with an Initializer List
The elements of an array also can be initialized in the array declaration by following the array name with an equals sign and a comma-separated list (enclosed in braces) of initializers. The program in Fig. 7.4 uses an initializer list to initialize an integer array with 10 values (line 13) and prints the array in tabular format (lines 15–19).

If there are fewer initializers than elements in the array, the remaining array elements are initialized to zero. For example, the elements of array n in Fig. 7.3 could have been initialized to zero with the declaration

```
int n[ 10 ] = { 0 }; // initialize elements of array n to 0
```

The declaration explicitly initializes the first element to zero and implicitly initializes the remaining nine elements to zero, because there are fewer initializers than elements in the array. Automatic arrays are not implicitly initialized to zero although static arrays are. The programmer must at least initialize the first element to zero with an initializer list for the remaining elements to be implicitly set to zero. The initialization method shown in Fig. 7.3 can be performed repeatedly as a program executes.

```
1   // Fig. 7.3: fig07_03.cpp
2   // Initializing an array.
3   #include <iostream>
4   using std::cout;
5   using std::endl;
6
7   #include <iomanip>
8   using std::setw;
9
10  int main()
11  {
12     int n[ 10 ]; // n is an array of 10 integers
13
14     // initialize elements of array n to 0
15     for ( int i = 0; i < 10; i++ )
16        n[ i ] = 0; // set element at location i to 0
17
18     cout << "Element" << setw( 13 ) << "Value" << endl;
19
20     // output each array element's value
21     for ( int j = 0; j < 10; j++ )
22        cout << setw( 7 ) << j << setw( 13 ) << n[ j ] << endl;
23
24     return 0; // indicates successful termination
25  } // end main
```

```
Element        Value
      0            0
      1            0
      2            0
      3            0
      4            0
      5            0
      6            0
      7            0
      8            0
      9            0
```

Fig. 7.3 | Initializing an array's elements to zeros and printing the array.

```
1   // Fig. 7.4: fig07_04.cpp
2   // Initializing an array in a declaration.
3   #include <iostream>
4   using std::cout;
5   using std::endl;
6
7   #include <iomanip>
8   using std::setw;
9
10  int main()
11  {
```

Fig. 7.4 | Initializing the elements of an array in its declaration. (Part 1 of 2.)

```
12      // use initializer list to initialize array n
13      int n[ 10 ] = { 32, 27, 64, 18, 95, 14, 90, 70, 60, 37 };
14
15      cout << "Element" << setw( 13 ) << "Value" << endl;
16
17      // output each array element's value
18      for ( int i = 0; i < 10; i++ )
19         cout << setw( 7 ) << i << setw( 13 ) << n[ i ] << endl;
20
21      return 0; // indicates successful termination
22   } // end main
```

```
Element        Value
      0           32
      1           27
      2           64
      3           18
      4           95
      5           14
      6           90
      7           70
      8           60
      9           37
```

Fig. 7.4 | Initializing the elements of an array in its declaration. (Part 2 of 2.)

If the array size is omitted from a declaration with an initializer list, the compiler determines the number of elements in the array by counting the number of elements in the initializer list. For example,

```
int n[] = { 1, 2, 3, 4, 5 };
```

creates a five-element array.

If the array size and an initializer list are specified in an array declaration, the number of initializers must be less than or equal to the array size. The array declaration

```
int n[ 5 ] = { 32, 27, 64, 18, 95, 14 };
```

causes a compilation error, because there are six initializers and only five array elements.

Common Programming Error 7.2

Providing more initializers in an array initializer list than there are elements in the array is a compilation error.

Common Programming Error 7.3

Forgetting to initialize the elements of an array whose elements should be initialized is a logic error.

Specifying an Array's Size with a Constant Variable and Setting Array Elements with Calculations

Figure 7.5 sets the elements of a 10-element array s to the even integers 2, 4, 6, …, 20 (lines 17–18) and prints the array in tabular format (lines 20–24). These numbers are generated (line 18) by multiplying each successive value of the loop counter by 2 and adding 2.

```
1   // Fig. 7.5: fig07_05.cpp
2   // Set array s to the even integers from 2 to 20.
3   #include <iostream>
4   using std::cout;
5   using std::endl;
6
7   #include <iomanip>
8   using std::setw;
9
10  int main()
11  {
12     // constant variable can be used to specify array size
13     const int arraySize = 10;
14
15     int s[ arraySize ]; // array s has 10 elements
16
17     for ( int i = 0; i < arraySize; i++ ) // set the values
18        s[ i ] = 2 + 2 * i;
19
20     cout << "Element" << setw( 13 ) << "Value" << endl;
21
22     // output contents of array s in tabular format
23     for ( int j = 0; j < arraySize; j++ )
24        cout << setw( 7 ) << j << setw( 13 ) << s[ j ] << endl;
25
26     return 0; // indicates successful termination
27  } // end main
```

Element	Value
0	2
1	4
2	6
3	8
4	10
5	12
6	14
7	16
8	18
9	20

Fig. 7.5 | Generating values to be placed into elements of an array.

Line 13 uses the **const qualifier** to declare a so-called constant variable arraySize with the value 10. Constant variables must be initialized with a constant expression when they are declared and cannot be modified thereafter (as shown in Fig. 7.6 and Fig. 7.7). Constant variables are also called named constants or read-only variables.

Common Programming Error 7.4

Not assigning a value to a constant variable when it is declared is a compilation error.

Common Programming Error 7.5

Assigning a value to a constant variable in an executable statement is a compilation error.

```
 1   // Fig. 7.6: fig07_06.cpp
 2   // Using a properly initialized constant variable.
 3   #include <iostream>
 4   using std::cout;
 5   using std::endl;
 6
 7   int main()
 8   {
 9      const int x = 7; // initialized constant variable
10
11      cout << "The value of constant variable x is: " << x << endl;
12
13      return 0; // indicates successful termination
14   } // end main
```

```
The value of constant variable x is: 7
```

Fig. 7.6 | Initializing and using a constant variable.

```
 1   // Fig. 7.7: fig07_07.cpp
 2   // A const variable must be initialized.
 3
 4   int main()
 5   {
 6      const int x; // Error: x must be initialized
 7
 8      x = 7; // Error: cannot modify a const variable
 9
10      return 0; // indicates successful termination
11   } // end main
```

Borland C++ command-line compiler error message:

```
Error E2304 fig07_07.cpp 6: Constant variable 'x' must be initialized
   in function main()
Error E2024 fig07_07.cpp 8: Cannot modify a const object in function main()
```

Microsoft Visual C++.NET compiler error message:

```
C:\cpphtp5_examples\ch07\fig07_07.cpp(6) : error C2734: 'x' : const object
   must be initialized if not extern
C:\cpphtp5_examples\ch07\fig07_07.cpp(8) : error C2166: l-value specifies
   const object
```

GNU C++ compiler error message:

```
fig07_07.cpp:6: error: uninitialized const `x'
fig07_07.cpp:8: error: assignment of read-only variable `x'
```

Fig. 7.7 | const variables must be initialized.

Constant variables can be placed anywhere a constant expression is expected. In Fig. 7.5, constant variable arraySize specifies the size of array s in line 15.

Common Programming Error 7.6

Only constants can be used to declare the size of automatic and static arrays. Not using a constant for this purpose is a compilation error.

Using constant variables to specify array sizes makes programs more scalable. In Fig. 7.5, the first for statement could fill a 1000-element array by simply changing the value of arraySize in its declaration from 10 to 1000. If the constant variable arraySize had not been used, we would have to change lines 15, 17 and 23 of the program to scale the program to handle 1000 array elements. As programs get larger, this technique becomes more useful for writing clearer, easier-to-modify programs.

Software Engineering Observation 7.1

Defining the size of each array as a constant variable instead of a literal constant can make programs more scalable.

Good Programming Practice 7.2

Defining the size of an array as a constant variable instead of a literal constant makes programs clearer. This technique eliminates so-called magic numbers. For example, repeatedly mentioning the size 10 in array-processing code for a 10-element array gives the number 10 an artificial significance and can unfortunately confuse the reader when the program includes other 10s that have nothing to do with the array size.

Summing the Elements of an Array
Often, the elements of an array represent a series of values to be used in a calculation. For example, if the elements of an array represent exam grades, a professor may wish to total the elements of the array and use that sum to calculate the class average for the exam. The examples using class GradeBook later in the chapter, namely Figs. 7.16–7.17 and Figs. 7.23–7.24, use this technique.

The program in Fig. 7.8 sums the values contained in the 10-element integer array a. The program declares, creates and initializes the array at line 10. The for statement (lines 14–15) performs the calculations. The values being supplied as initializers for array a also could be read into the program from the user at the keyboard, or from a file on disk (see Chapter 17, File Processing). For example, the for statement

```
for ( int j = 0; j < arraySize; j++ )
   cin >> a[ j ];
```

reads one value at a time from the keyboard and stores the value in element a[j].

```
1   // Fig. 7.8: fig07_08.cpp
2   // Compute the sum of the elements of the array.
3   #include <iostream>
4   using std::cout;
5   using std::endl;
6
```

Fig. 7.8 | Computing the sum of the elements of an array. (Part 1 of 2.)

```
 7   int main()
 8   {
 9      const int arraySize = 10; // constant variable indicating size of array
10      int a[ arraySize ] = { 87, 68, 94, 100, 83, 78, 85, 91, 76, 87 };
11      int total = 0;
12
13      // sum contents of array a
14      for ( int i = 0; i < arraySize; i++ )
15         total += a[ i ];
16
17      cout << "Total of array elements: " << total << endl;
18
19      return 0; // indicates successful termination
20   } // end main
```

```
Total of array elements: 849
```

Fig. 7.8 | Computing the sum of the elements of an array. (Part 2 of 2.)

Using Bar Charts to Display Array Data Graphically

Many programs present data to users in a graphical manner. For example, numeric values are often displayed as bars in a bar chart. In such a chart, longer bars represent proportionally larger numeric values. One simple way to display numeric data graphically is with a bar chart that shows each numeric value as a bar of asterisks (*).

Professors often like to examine the distribution of grades on an exam. A professor might graph the number of grades in each of several categories to visualize the grade distribution. Suppose the grades were 87, 68, 94, 100, 83, 78, 85, 91, 76 and 87. Note that there was one grade of 100, two grades in the 90s, four grades in the 80s, two grades in the 70s, one grade in the 60s and no grades below 60. Our next program (Fig. 7.9) stores this grade distribution data in an array of 11 elements, each corresponding to a category of grades. For example, n[0] indicates the number of grades in the range 0–9, n[7] indicates the number of grades in the range 70–79 and n[10] indicates the number of grades of 100. The two versions of class GradeBook later in the chapter (Figs. 7.16–7.17 and Figs. 7.23–7.24) contain code that calculates these grade frequencies based on a set of grades. For now, we manually create the array by looking at the set of grades.

```
 1   // Fig. 7.9: fig07_09.cpp
 2   // Bar chart printing program.
 3   #include <iostream>
 4   using std::cout;
 5   using std::endl;
 6
 7   #include <iomanip>
 8   using std::setw;
 9
10   int main()
11   {
12      const int arraySize = 11;
```

Fig. 7.9 | Bar chart printing program. (Part 1 of 2.)

```
13        int n[ arraySize ] = { 0, 0, 0, 0, 0, 0, 1, 2, 4, 2, 1 };
14
15        cout << "Grade distribution:" << endl;
16
17        // for each element of array n, output a bar of the chart
18        for ( int i = 0; i < arraySize; i++ )
19        {
20           // output bar labels ("0-9:", ..., "90-99:", "100:" )
21           if ( i == 0 )
22              cout << "  0-9: ";
23           else if ( i == 10 )
24              cout << "  100: ";
25           else
26              cout << i * 10 << "-" << ( i * 10 ) + 9 << ": ";
27
28           // print bar of asterisks
29           for ( int stars = 0; stars < n[ i ]; stars++ )
30              cout << '*';
31
32           cout << endl; // start a new line of output
33        } // end outer for
34
35        return 0; // indicates successful termination
36     } // end main
```

```
Grade distribution:
  0-9:
10-19:
20-29:
30-39:
40-49:
50-59:
60-69: *
70-79: **
80-89: ****
90-99: **
  100: *
```

Fig. 7.9 | Bar chart printing program. (Part 2 of 2.)

The program reads the numbers from the array and graphs the information as a bar chart. The program displays each grade range followed by a bar of asterisks indicating the number of grades in that range. To label each bar, lines 21–26 output a grade range (e.g., "70-79: ") based on the current value of counter variable i. The nested for statement (lines 29–30) outputs the bars. Note the loop-continuation condition at line 29 (stars < n[i]). Each time the program reaches the inner for, the loop counts from 0 up to n[i], thus using a value in array n to determine the number of asterisks to display. In this example, n[0]–n[5] contain zeros because no students received a grade below 60. Thus, the program displays no asterisks next to the first six grade ranges.

Common Programming Error 7.7

Although it is possible to use the same control variable in a for statement and a second for statement nested inside, this is confusing and can lead to logic errors.

Using the Elements of an Array as Counters

Sometimes, programs use counter variables to summarize data, such as the results of a survey. In Fig. 6.9, we used separate counters in our die-rolling program to track the number of occurrences of each side of a die as the program rolled the die 6,000,000 times. An array version of this program is shown in Fig. 7.10.

```cpp
1   // Fig. 7.10: fig07_10.cpp
2   // Roll a six-sided die 6,000,000 times.
3   #include <iostream>
4   using std::cout;
5   using std::endl;
6
7   #include <iomanip>
8   using std::setw;
9
10  #include <cstdlib>
11  using std::rand;
12  using std::srand;
13
14  #include <ctime>
15  using std::time;
16
17  int main()
18  {
19     const int arraySize = 7; // ignore element zero
20     int frequency[ arraySize ] = { 0 };
21
22     srand( time( 0 ) ); // seed random number generator
23
24     // roll die 6,000,000 times; use die value as frequency index
25     for ( int roll = 1; roll <= 6000000; roll++ )
26        frequency[ 1 + rand() % 6 ]++;
27
28     cout << "Face" << setw( 13 ) << "Frequency" << endl;
29
30     // output each array element's value
31     for ( int face = 1; face < arraySize; face++ )
32        cout << setw( 4 ) << face << setw( 13 ) << frequency[ face ]
33           << endl;
34
35     return 0; // indicates successful termination
36  } // end main
```

```
Face    Frequency
   1     1000167
   2     1000149
   3     1000152
   4      998748
   5      999626
   6     1001158
```

Fig. 7.10 | Die-rolling program using an array instead of `switch`.

Figure 7.10 uses the array `frequency` (line 20) to count the occurrences of each side of the die. *The single statement in line 26 of this program replaces the `switch` statement in lines 30–52 of Fig. 6.9.* Line 26 uses a random value to determine which `frequency` element to increment during each iteration of the loop. The calculation in line 26 produces a random subscript from 1 to 6, so array `frequency` must be large enough to store six counters. However, we use a seven-element array in which we ignore `frequency[ 0 ]`—it is more logical to have the die face value 1 increment `frequency[ 1 ]` than `frequency[ 0 ]`. Thus, each face value is used as a subscript for array `frequency`. We also replace lines 56–61 of Fig. 6.9 by looping through array `frequency` to output the results (lines 31–33).

Using Arrays to Summarize Survey Results

Our next example (Fig. 7.11) uses arrays to summarize the results of data collected in a survey. Consider the following problem statement:

> *Forty students were asked to rate the quality of the food in the student cafeteria on a scale of 1 to 10 (1 meaning awful and 10 meaning excellent). Place the 40 responses in an integer array and summarize the results of the poll.*

This is a typical array-processing application. We wish to summarize the number of responses of each type (i.e., 1 through 10). The array `responses` (lines 17–19) is a 40-element integer array of the students' responses to the survey. Note that array `responses` is declared `const`, as its values do not (and should not) change. We use an 11-element array `frequency` (line 22) to count the number of occurrences of each response. Each element of the array is used as a counter for one of the survey responses and is initialized to zero. As in Fig. 7.10, we ignore `frequency[ 0 ]`.

```cpp
1   // Fig. 7.11: fig07_11.cpp
2   // Student poll program.
3   #include <iostream>
4   using std::cout;
5   using std::endl;
6
7   #include <iomanip>
8   using std::setw;
9
10  int main()
11  {
12     // define array sizes
13     const int responseSize = 40; // size of array responses
14     const int frequencySize = 11; // size of array frequency
15
16     // place survey responses in array responses
17     const int responses[ responseSize ] = { 1, 2, 6, 4, 8, 5, 9, 7, 8,
18        10, 1, 6, 3, 8, 6, 10, 3, 8, 2, 7, 6, 5, 7, 6, 8, 6, 7,
19        5, 6, 6, 5, 6, 7, 5, 6, 4, 8, 6, 8, 10 };
20
21     // initialize frequency counters to 0
22     int frequency[ frequencySize ] = { 0 };
23
```

Fig. 7.11 | Poll analysis program. (Part 1 of 2.)

```
24      // for each answer, select responses element and use that value
25      // as frequency subscript to determine element to increment
26      for ( int answer = 0; answer < responseSize; answer++ )
27         frequency[ responses[ answer ] ]++;
28
29      cout << "Rating" << setw( 17 ) << "Frequency" << endl;
30
31      // output each array element's value
32      for ( int rating = 1; rating < frequencySize; rating++ )
33         cout << setw( 6 ) << rating << setw( 17 ) << frequency[ rating ]
34            << endl;
35
36      return 0; // indicates successful termination
37   } // end main
```

```
Rating          Frequency
    1                2
    2                2
    3                2
    4                2
    5                5
    6               11
    7                5
    8                7
    9                1
   10                3
```

Fig. 7.11 | Poll analysis program. (Part 2 of 2.)

Software Engineering Observation 7.2

The const *qualifier should be used to enforce the principle of least privilege. Using the principle of least privilege to properly design software can greatly reduce debugging time and improper side effects and can make a program easier to modify and maintain.*

Good Programming Practice 7.3

Strive for program clarity. It is sometimes worthwhile to trade off the most efficient use of memory or processor time in favor of writing clearer programs.

Performance Tip 7.1

Sometimes performance considerations far outweigh clarity considerations.

The first for statement (lines 26–27) takes the responses one at a time from the array responses and increments one of the 10 counters in the frequency array (frequency[1] to frequency[10]). The key statement in the loop is line 27, which increments the appropriate frequency counter, depending on the value of responses[answer].

Let's consider several iterations of the for loop. When control variable answer is 0, the value of responses[answer] is the value of responses[0] (i.e., 1 in line 17), so the program interprets frequency[responses[answer]]++ as

```
frequency[ 1 ]++
```

which increments the value in array element 1. To evaluate the expression, start with the value in the innermost set of square brackets (`answer`). Once you know `answer`'s value (which is the value of the loop control variable in line 26), plug it into the expression and evaluate the next outer set of square brackets (i.e., `responses[ answer ]`, which is a value selected from the `responses` array in lines 17–19). Then use the resulting value as the subscript for the `frequency` array to specify which counter to increment.

When `answer` is 1, `responses[ answer ]` is the value of `responses[ 1 ]`, which is 2, so the program interprets `frequency[ responses[ answer ] ]++` as

    frequency[2]++

which increments array element 2.

When `answer` is 2, `responses[ answer ]` is the value of `responses[ 2 ]`, which is 6, so the program interprets `frequency[ responses[ answer ] ]++` as

    frequency[6]++

which increments array element 6, and so on. Regardless of the number of responses processed in the survey, the program requires only an 11-element array (ignoring element zero) to summarize the results, because all the response values are between 1 and 10 and the subscript values for an 11-element array are 0 through 10.

If the data in the `responses` array had contained an invalid value, such as 13, the program would have attempted to add 1 to `frequency[ 13 ]`, which is outside the bounds of the array. *C++ has no array bounds checking to prevent the computer from referring to an element that does not exist.* Thus, an executing program can "walk off" either end of an array without warning. The programmer should ensure that all array references remain within the bounds of the array.

Common Programming Error 7.8

Referring to an element outside the array bounds is an execution-time logic error. It is not a syntax error.

Error-Prevention Tip 7.1

When looping through an array, the array subscript should never go below 0 and should always be less than the total number of elements in the array (one less than the size of the array). Make sure that the loop-termination condition prevents accessing elements outside this range.

Portability Tip 7.1

The (normally serious) effects of referencing elements outside the array bounds are system dependent. Often this results in changes to the value of an unrelated variable or a fatal error that terminates program execution.

C++ is an extensible language. Section 7.11 presents C++ Standard Library class template `vector`, which enables programmers to perform many operations that are not available for C++'s built-in arrays. For example, we will be able to compare `vector`s directly and assign one `vector` to another. In Chapter 11, we extend C++ further by implementing an array as a user-defined class of our own. This new array definition will enable us to input and output entire arrays with `cin` and `cout`, initialize arrays when they are created, prevent access to out-of-range array elements and change the range of subscripts (and even their subscript type) so that the first element of an array is not required to be element 0. We will even be able to use noninteger subscripts.

 Error-Prevention Tip 7.2

In Chapter 11, we will see how to develop a class representing a "smart array," which checks that all subscript references are in bounds at runtime. Using such smart data types helps eliminate bugs.

Using Character Arrays to Store and Manipulate Strings

To this point, we have discussed only integer arrays. However, arrays may be of any type. We now introduce storing character strings in character arrays. Recall that, starting in Chapter 3, we have been using `string` objects to store character strings, such as the course name in our `GradeBook` class. A string such as "hello" is actually an array of characters. While `string` objects are convenient to use and reduce the potential for errors, character arrays that represent strings have several unique features, which we discuss in this section. As you continue your study of C++, you may encounter C++ capabilities that require you to use character arrays in preference to `string` objects. You may also be asked to update existing code using character arrays.

A character array can be initialized using a string literal. For example, the declaration

```
char string1[] = "first";
```

initializes the elements of array `string1` to the individual characters in the string literal "first". The size of array `string1` in the preceding declaration is determined by the compiler based on the length of the string. It is important to note that the string "first" contains five characters *plus* a special string-termination character called the null character. Thus, array `string1` actually contains six elements. The character constant representation of the null character is '\0' (backslash followed by zero). All strings represented by character arrays end with this character. A character array representing a string should always be declared large enough to hold the number of characters in the string and the terminating null character.

Character arrays also can be initialized with individual character constants in an initializer list. The preceding declaration is equivalent to the more tedious form

```
char string1[] = { 'f', 'i', 'r', 's', 't', '\0' };
```

Note the use of single quotes to delineate each character constant. Also, note that we explicitly provided the terminating null character as the last initializer value. Without it, this array would simply represent an array of characters, not a string. As we discuss in Chapter 8, not providing a terminating null character for a string can cause logic errors.

Because a string is an array of characters, we can access individual characters in a string directly with array subscript notation. For example, `string1[ 0 ]` is the character 'f', `string1[ 3 ]` is the character 's' and `string1[ 5 ]` is the null character.

We also can input a string directly into a character array from the keyboard using `cin` and `>>`. For example, the declaration

```
char string2[ 20 ];
```

creates a character array capable of storing a string of 19 characters and a terminating null character. The statement

```
cin >> string2;
```

reads a string from the keyboard into `string2` and appends the null character to the end of the string input by the user. Note that the preceding statement provides only the name of the array and no information about the size of the array. It is the programmer's responsibility to ensure that the array into which the string is read is capable of holding any string the user types at the keyboard. By default, `cin` reads characters from the keyboard until the first white-space character is encountered—regardless of the array size. Thus, inputting data with `cin` and `>>` can insert data beyond the end of the array (see Section 8.13 for information on preventing insertion beyond the end of a `char` array).

 Common Programming Error 7.9

Not providing `cin >>` with a character array large enough to store a string typed at the keyboard can result in loss of data in a program and other serious runtime errors.

A character array representing a null-terminated string can be output with `cout` and `<<`. The statement

```
cout << string2;
```

prints the array `string2`. Note that `cout <<`, like `cin >>`, does not care how large the character array is. The characters of the string are output until a terminating null character is encountered. [*Note:* `cin` and `cout` assume that character arrays should be processed as strings terminated by null characters; `cin` and `cout` do not provide similar input and output processing capabilities for other array types.]

Figure 7.12 demonstrates initializing a character array with a string literal, reading a string into a character array, printing a character array as a string and accessing individual characters of a string.

```cpp
1   // Fig. 7.12: fig07_12.cpp
2   // Treating character arrays as strings.
3   #include <iostream>
4   using std::cout;
5   using std::cin;
6   using std::endl;
7
8   int main()
9   {
10      char string1[ 20 ]; // reserves 20 characters
11      char string2[] = "string literal"; // reserves 15 characters
12
13      // read string from user into array string1
14      cout << "Enter the string \"hello there\": ";
15      cin >> string1; // reads "hello" [space terminates input]
16
17      // output strings
18      cout << "string1 is: " << string1 << "\nstring2 is: " << string2;
19
20      cout << "\nstring1 with spaces between characters is:\n";
```

Fig. 7.12 | Character arrays processed as strings. (Part 1 of 2.)

```
21
22       // output characters until null character is reached
23       for ( int i = 0; string1[ i ] != '\0'; i++ )
24          cout << string1[ i ] << ' ';
25
26       cin >> string1; // reads "there"
27       cout << "\nstring1 is: " << string1 << endl;
28
29       return 0; // indicates successful termination
30    } // end main
```

```
Enter the string "hello there": hello there
string1 is: hello
string2 is: string literal
string1 with spaces between characters is:
h e l l o
string1 is: there
```

Fig. 7.12 | Character arrays processed as strings. (Part 2 of 2.)

Lines 23–24 of Fig. 7.12 use a for statement to loop through the string1 array and print the individual characters separated by spaces. The condition in the for statement, string1[i] != '\0', is true until the loop encounters the terminating null character of the string.

Static Local Arrays and Automatic Local Arrays
Chapter 6 discussed the storage class specifier static. A static local variable in a function definition exists for the duration of the program, but is visible only in the function body.

Performance Tip 7.2

We can apply static to a local array declaration so that the array is not created and initialized each time the program calls the function and is not destroyed each time the function terminates in the program. This can improve performance, especially when using large arrays.

A program initializes static local arrays when their declarations are first encountered. If a static array is not initialized explicitly by the programmer, each element of that array is initialized to zero by the compiler when the array is created. Recall that C++ does not perform such default initialization for automatic variables.

Figure 7.13 demonstrates function staticArrayInit (lines 25–41) with a static local array (line 28) and function automaticArrayInit (lines 44–60) with an automatic local array (line 47).

```
1    // Fig. 7.13: fig07_13.cpp
2    // Static arrays are initialized to zero.
3    #include <iostream>
4    using std::cout;
5    using std::endl;
6
7    void staticArrayInit( void ); // function prototype
```

Fig. 7.13 | static array initialization and automatic array initialization. (Part 1 of 3.)

```
 8  void automaticArrayInit( void ); // function prototype
 9
10  int main()
11  {
12     cout << "First call to each function:\n";
13     staticArrayInit();
14     automaticArrayInit();
15
16     cout << "\n\nSecond call to each function:\n";
17     staticArrayInit();
18     automaticArrayInit();
19     cout << endl;
20
21     return 0; // indicates successful termination
22  } // end main
23
24  // function to demonstrate a static local array
25  void staticArrayInit( void )
26  {
27     // initializes elements to 0 first time function is called
28     static int array1[ 3 ]; // static local array
29
30     cout << "\nValues on entering staticArrayInit:\n";
31
32     // output contents of array1
33     for ( int i = 0; i < 3; i++ )
34        cout << "array1[" << i << "] = " << array1[ i ] << "   ";
35
36     cout << "\nValues on exiting staticArrayInit:\n";
37
38     // modify and output contents of array1
39     for ( int j = 0; j < 3; j++ )
40        cout << "array1[" << j << "] = " << ( array1[ j ] += 5 ) << "   ";
41  } // end function staticArrayInit
42
43  // function to demonstrate an automatic local array
44  void automaticArrayInit( void )
45  {
46     // initializes elements each time function is called
47     int array2[ 3 ] = { 1, 2, 3 }; // automatic local array
48
49     cout << "\n\nValues on entering automaticArrayInit:\n";
50
51     // output contents of array2
52     for ( int i = 0; i < 3; i++ )
53        cout << "array2[" << i << "] = " << array2[ i ] << "   ";
54
55     cout << "\nValues on exiting automaticArrayInit:\n";
56
57     // modify and output contents of array2
58     for ( int j = 0; j < 3; j++ )
59        cout << "array2[" << j << "] = " << ( array2[ j ] += 5 ) << "   ";
60  } // end function automaticArrayInit
```

Fig. 7.13 | static array initialization and automatic array initialization. (Part 2 of 3.)

```
First call to each function:

Values on entering staticArrayInit:
array1[0] = 0   array1[1] = 0   array1[2] = 0
Values on exiting staticArrayInit:
array1[0] = 5   array1[1] = 5   array1[2] = 5

Values on entering automaticArrayInit:
array2[0] = 1   array2[1] = 2   array2[2] = 3
Values on exiting automaticArrayInit:
array2[0] = 6   array2[1] = 7   array2[2] = 8

Second call to each function:

Values on entering staticArrayInit:
array1[0] = 5   array1[1] = 5   array1[2] = 5
Values on exiting staticArrayInit:
array1[0] = 10   array1[1] = 10   array1[2] = 10

Values on entering automaticArrayInit:
array2[0] = 1   array2[1] = 2   array2[2] = 3
Values on exiting automaticArrayInit:
array2[0] = 6   array2[1] = 7   array2[2] = 8
```

Fig. 7.13 | `static` array initialization and automatic array initialization. (Part 3 of 3.)

Function `staticArrayInit` is called twice (lines 13 and 17). The `static` local array is initialized to zero by the compiler the first time the function is called. The function prints the array, adds 5 to each element and prints the array again. The second time the function is called, the `static` array contains the modified values stored during the first function call. Function `automaticArrayInit` also is called twice (lines 14 and 18). The elements of the automatic local array are initialized (line 47) with the values 1, 2 and 3. The function prints the array, adds 5 to each element and prints the array again. The second time the function is called, the array elements are reinitialized to 1, 2 and 3. The array has automatic storage class, so the array is recreated during each call to `automaticArrayInit`.

 Common Programming Error 7.10

Assuming that elements of a function's local `static` array are initialized every time the function is called can lead to logic errors in a program.

7.5 Passing Arrays to Functions

To pass an array argument to a function, specify the name of the array without any brackets. For example, if array `hourlyTemperatures` has been declared as

```
int hourlyTemperatures[ 24 ];
```

the function call

```
modifyArray( hourlyTemperatures, 24 );
```

passes array `hourlyTemperatures` and its size to function `modifyArray`. When passing an array to a function, the array size is normally passed as well, so the function can process the specific number of elements in the array. (Otherwise, we would need to build this knowledge into the called function itself or, worse yet, place the array size in a global variable.) In Section 7.11, when we present C++ Standard Library class template vector to represent a more robust type of array, you will see that the size of a vector is built in—every vector object "knows" its own size, which can be obtained by invoking the vector object's size member function. Thus, when we pass a vector *object* into a function, we will not have to pass the size of the vector as an argument.

C++ passes arrays to functions by reference—the called functions can modify the element values in the callers' original arrays. The value of the name of the array is the address in the computer's memory of the first element of the array. Because the starting address of the array is passed, the called function knows precisely where the array is stored in memory. Therefore, when the called function modifies array elements in its function body, it is modifying the actual elements of the array in their original memory locations.

Performance Tip 7.3

Passing arrays by reference makes sense for performance reasons. If arrays were passed by value, a copy of each element would be passed. For large, frequently passed arrays, this would be time consuming and would require considerable storage for the copies of the array elements.

Although entire arrays are passed by reference, individual array elements are passed by value exactly as simple variables are. Such simple single pieces of data are called scalars or scalar quantities. To pass an element of an array to a function, use the subscripted name of the array element as an argument in the function call. In Chapter 6, we showed how to pass scalars (i.e., individual variables and array elements) by reference with references. In Chapter 8, we show how to pass scalars by reference with pointers.

For a function to receive an array through a function call, the function's parameter list must specify that the function expects to receive an array. For example, the function header for function modifyArray might be written as

```
void modifyArray( int b[], int arraySize )
```

indicating that modifyArray expects to receive the address of an array of integers in parameter b and the number of array elements in parameter arraySize. The size of the array is not required between the array brackets. If it is included, the compiler ignores it. Because C++ passes arrays to functions by reference, when the called function uses the array name b, it will in fact be referring to the actual array in the caller (i.e., array hourlyTemperatures discussed at the beginning of this section).

Note the strange appearance of the function prototype for modifyArray

```
void modifyArray( int [], int );
```

This prototype could have been written

```
void modifyArray( int anyArrayName[], int anyVariableName );
```

but, as we learned in Chapter 3, C++ compilers ignore variable names in prototypes. Remember, the prototype tells the compiler the number of arguments and the type of each argument (in the order in which the arguments are expected to appear).

The program in Fig. 7.14 demonstrates the difference between passing an entire array and passing an array element. Lines 22–23 print the five original elements of integer array a. Line 28 passes a and its size to function modifyArray (lines 45–50), which multiplies each of a's elements by 2 (through parameter b). Then, lines 32–33 print array a again in main. As the output shows, the elements of a are indeed modified by modifyArray. Next, line 36 prints the value of scalar a[3], then line 38 passes element a[3] to function modifyElement (lines 54–58), which multiplies its parameter by 2 and prints the new value. Note that when line 39 again prints a[3] in main, the value has not been modified, because individual array elements are passed by value.

```cpp
1   // Fig. 7.14: fig07_14.cpp
2   // Passing arrays and individual array elements to functions.
3   #include <iostream>
4   using std::cout;
5   using std::endl;
6
7   #include <iomanip>
8   using std::setw;
9
10  void modifyArray( int [], int ); // appears strange
11  void modifyElement( int );
12
13  int main()
14  {
15     const int arraySize = 5; // size of array a
16     int a[ arraySize ] = { 0, 1, 2, 3, 4 }; // initialize array a
17
18     cout << "Effects of passing entire array by reference:"
19        << "\n\nThe values of the original array are:\n";
20
21     // output original array elements
22     for ( int i = 0; i < arraySize; i++ )
23        cout << setw( 3 ) << a[ i ];
24
25     cout << endl;
26
27     // pass array a to modifyArray by reference
28     modifyArray( a, arraySize );
29     cout << "The values of the modified array are:\n";
30
31     // output modified array elements
32     for ( int j = 0; j < arraySize; j++ )
33        cout << setw( 3 ) << a[ j ];
34
35     cout << "\n\n\nEffects of passing array element by value:"
36        << "\n\na[3] before modifyElement: " << a[ 3 ] << endl;
37
```

Fig. 7.14 | Passing arrays and individual array elements to functions. (Part I of 2.)

```
38        modifyElement( a[ 3 ] ); // pass array element a[ 3 ] by value
39        cout << "a[3] after modifyElement: " << a[ 3 ] << endl;
40
41        return 0; // indicates successful termination
42    } // end main
43
44    // in function modifyArray, "b" points to the original array "a" in memory
45    void modifyArray( int b[], int sizeOfArray )
46    {
47        // multiply each array element by 2
48        for ( int k = 0; k < sizeOfArray; k++ )
49            b[ k ] *= 2;
50    } // end function modifyArray
51
52    // in function modifyElement, "e" is a local copy of
53    // array element a[ 3 ] passed from main
54    void modifyElement( int e )
55    {
56        // multiply parameter by 2
57        cout << "Value of element in modifyElement: " << ( e *= 2 ) << endl;
58    } // end function modifyElement
```

```
Effects of passing entire array by reference:

The values of the original array are:
   0   1   2   3   4
The values of the modified array are:
   0   2   4   6   8


Effects of passing array element by value:

a[3] before modifyElement: 6
Value of element in modifyElement: 12
a[3] after modifyElement: 6
```

Fig. 7.14 | Passing arrays and individual array elements to functions. (Part 2 of 2.)

There may be situations in your programs in which a function should not be allowed to modify array elements. C++ provides the type qualifier const that can be used to prevent modification of array values in the caller by code in a called function. When a function specifies an array parameter that is preceded by the const qualifier, the elements of the array become constant in the function body, and any attempt to modify an element of the array in the function body results in a compilation error. This enables the programmer to prevent accidental modification of array elements in the function's body.

Figure 7.15 demonstrates the const qualifier. Function tryToModifyArray (lines 21–26) is defined with parameter const int b[], which specifies that array b is constant and cannot be modified. Each of the three attempts by the function to modify array b's elements (lines 23–25) results in a compilation error. The Microsoft Visual C++.NET compiler, for example, produces the error "l-value specifies const object." [*Note:* The C++ standard defines an "object" as any "region of storage," thus including variables or array elements of fundamental data types as well as instances of classes (what we've been

```
 1   // Fig. 7.15: fig07_15.cpp
 2   // Demonstrating the const type qualifier.
 3   #include <iostream>
 4   using std::cout;
 5   using std::endl;
 6
 7   void tryToModifyArray( const int [] ); // function prototype
 8
 9   int main()
10   {
11      int a[] = { 10, 20, 30 };
12
13      tryToModifyArray( a );
14      cout << a[ 0 ] << ' ' << a[ 1 ] << ' ' << a[ 2 ] << '\n';
15
16      return 0; // indicates successful termination
17   } // end main
18
19   // In function tryToModifyArray, "b" cannot be used
20   // to modify the original array "a" in main.
21   void tryToModifyArray( const int b[] )
22   {
23      b[ 0 ] /= 2; // error
24      b[ 1 ] /= 2; // error
25      b[ 2 ] /= 2; // error
26   } // end function tryToModifyArray
```

Borland C++ command-line compiler error message:

```
Error E2024 fig07_15.cpp 23: Cannot modify a const object
   in function tryToModifyArray(const int * const)
Error E2024 fig07_15.cpp 24: Cannot modify a const object
   in function tryToModifyArray(const int * const)
Error E2024 fig07_15.cpp 25: Cannot modify a const object
   in function tryToModifyArray(const int * const)
```

Microsoft Visual C++.NET compiler error message:

```
C:\cpphtp5_examples\ch07\fig07_15.cpp(23) : error C2166: l-value specifies
   const object
C:\cpphtp5_examples\ch07\fig07_15.cpp(24) : error C2166: l-value specifies
   const object
C:\cpphtp5_examples\ch07\fig07_15.cpp(25) : error C2166: l-value specifies
   const object
```

GNU C++ compiler error message:

```
fig07_15.cpp:23: error: assignment of read-only location
fig07_15.cpp:24: error: assignment of read-only location
fig07_15.cpp:25: error: assignment of read-only location
```

Fig. 7.15 | const type qualifier applied to an array parameter.

calling objects).] This message indicates that using a const object (e.g., b[0]) as an *lvalue* is an error—you cannot assign a new value to a const object by placing it on the left of an assignment operator. Note that compiler error messages vary between compilers (as shown in Fig. 7.15). The const qualifier will be discussed again in Chapter 10.

Common Programming Error 7.11

Forgetting that arrays in the caller are passed by reference, and hence can be modified in called functions, may result in logic errors.

Software Engineering Observation 7.3

Applying the const type qualifier to an array parameter in a function definition to prevent the original array from being modified in the function body is another example of the principle of least privilege. Functions should not be given the capability to modify an array unless it is absolutely necessary.

7.6 Case Study: Class GradeBook Using an Array to Store Grades

This section further evolves class GradeBook, introduced in Chapter 3 and expanded in Chapters 4–6. Recall that this class represents a grade book used by a professor to store and analyze a set of student grades. Previous versions of the class process a set of grades entered by the user, but do not maintain the individual grade values in data members of the class. Thus, repeat calculations require the user to reenter the same grades. One way to solve this problem would be to store each grade entered in an individual data member of the class. For example, we could create data members grade1, grade2, …, grade10 in class GradeBook to store 10 student grades. However, the code to total the grades and determine the class average would be cumbersome. In this section, we solve this problem by storing grades in an array.

Storing Student Grades in an Array in Class *GradeBook*

The version of class GradeBook (Figs. 7.16–7.17) presented here uses an array of integers to store the grades of several students on a single exam. This eliminates the need to repeatedly input the same set of grades. Array grades is declared as a data member in line 29 of Fig. 7.16—therefore, each GradeBook object maintains its own set of grades.

```
1   // Fig. 7.16: GradeBook.h
2   // Definition of class GradeBook that uses an array to store test grades.
3   // Member functions are defined in GradeBook.cpp
4
5   #include <string> // program uses C++ Standard Library string class
6   using std::string;
7
8   // GradeBook class definition
9   class GradeBook
10  {
11  public:
12      // constant -- number of students who took the test
13      const static int students = 10; // note public data
```

Fig. 7.16 | Definition of class GradeBook using an array to store test grades. (Part 1 of 2.)

```
14
15      // constructor initializes course name and array of grades
16      GradeBook( string, const int [] );
17
18      void setCourseName( string ); // function to set the course name
19      string getCourseName(); // function to retrieve the course name
20      void displayMessage(); // display a welcome message
21      void processGrades(); // perform various operations on the grade data
22      int getMinimum(); // find the minimum grade for the test
23      int getMaximum(); // find the maximum grade for the test
24      double getAverage(); // determine the average grade for the test
25      void outputBarChart(); // output bar chart of grade distribution
26      void outputGrades(); // output the contents of the grades array
27   private:
28      string courseName; // course name for this grade book
29      int grades[ students ]; // array of student grades
30   }; // end class GradeBook
```

Fig. 7.16 | Definition of class **GradeBook** using an array to store test grades. (Part 2 of 2.)

```
1    // Fig. 7.17: GradeBook.cpp
2    // Member-function definitions for class GradeBook that
3    // uses an array to store test grades.
4    #include <iostream>
5    using std::cout;
6    using std::cin;
7    using std::endl;
8    using std::fixed;
9
10   #include <iomanip>
11   using std::setprecision;
12   using std::setw;
13
14   #include "GradeBook.h" // GradeBook class definition
15
16   // constructor initializes courseName and grades array
17   GradeBook::GradeBook( string name, const int gradesArray[] )
18   {
19      setCourseName( name ); // initialize courseName
20
21      // copy grades from gradeArray to grades data member
22      for ( int grade = 0; grade < students; grade++ )
23         grades[ grade ] = gradesArray[ grade ];
24   } // end GradeBook constructor
25
26   // function to set the course name
27   void GradeBook::setCourseName( string name )
28   {
29      courseName = name; // store the course name
30   } // end function setCourseName
31
```

Fig. 7.17 | GradeBook class member functions manipulating an array of grades. (Part 1 of 4.)

```
32   // function to retrieve the course name
33   string GradeBook::getCourseName()
34   {
35      return courseName;
36   } // end function getCourseName
37
38   // display a welcome message to the GradeBook user
39   void GradeBook::displayMessage()
40   {
41      // this statement calls getCourseName to get the
42      // name of the course this GradeBook represents
43      cout << "Welcome to the grade book for\n" << getCourseName() << "!"
44         << endl;
45   } // end function displayMessage
46
47   // perform various operations on the data
48   void GradeBook::processGrades()
49   {
50      // output grades array
51      outputGrades();
52
53      // call function getAverage to calculate the average grade
54      cout << "\nClass average is " << setprecision( 2 ) << fixed <<
55         getAverage() << endl;
56
57      // call functions getMinimum and getMaximum
58      cout << "Lowest grade is " << getMinimum() << "\nHighest grade is "
59         << getMaximum() << endl;
60
61      // call function outputBarChart to print grade distribution chart
62      outputBarChart();
63   } // end function processGrades
64
65   // find minimum grade
66   int GradeBook::getMinimum()
67   {
68      int lowGrade = 100; // assume lowest grade is 100
69
70      // loop through grades array
71      for ( int grade = 0; grade < students; grade++ )
72      {
73         // if current grade lower than lowGrade, assign it to lowGrade
74         if ( grades[ grade ] < lowGrade )
75            lowGrade = grades[ grade ]; // new lowest grade
76      } // end for
77
78      return lowGrade; // return lowest grade
79   } // end function getMinimum
80
81   // find maximum grade
82   int GradeBook::getMaximum()
83   {
84      int highGrade = 0; // assume highest grade is 0
```

Fig. 7.17 | GradeBook class member functions manipulating an array of grades. (Part 2 of 4.)

```
85
86      // loop through grades array
87      for ( int grade = 0; grade < students; grade++ )
88      {
89         // if current grade higher than highGrade, assign it to highGrade
90         if ( grades[ grade ] > highGrade )
91            highGrade = grades[ grade ]; // new highest grade
92      } // end for
93
94      return highGrade; // return highest grade
95   } // end function getMaximum
96
97   // determine average grade for test
98   double GradeBook::getAverage()
99   {
100     int total = 0; // initialize total
101
102     // sum grades in array
103     for ( int grade = 0; grade < students; grade++ )
104        total += grades[ grade ];
105
106     // return average of grades
107     return static_cast< double >( total ) / students;
108  } // end function getAverage
109
110  // output bar chart displaying grade distribution
111  void GradeBook::outputBarChart()
112  {
113     cout << "\nGrade distribution:" << endl;
114
115     // stores frequency of grades in each range of 10 grades
116     const int frequencySize = 11;
117     int frequency[ frequencySize ] = { 0 };
118
119     // for each grade, increment the appropriate frequency
120     for ( int grade = 0; grade < students; grade++ )
121        frequency[ grades[ grade ] / 10 ]++;
122
123     // for each grade frequency, print bar in chart
124     for ( int count = 0; count < frequencySize; count++ )
125     {
126        // output bar labels ("0-9:", ..., "90-99:", "100:" )
127        if ( count == 0 )
128           cout << "  0-9: ";
129        else if ( count == 10 )
130           cout << "  100: ";
131        else
132           cout << count * 10 << "-" << ( count * 10 ) + 9 << ": ";
133
134        // print bar of asterisks
135        for ( int stars = 0; stars < frequency[ count ]; stars++ )
136           cout << '*';
```

Fig. 7.17 | GradeBook class member functions manipulating an array of grades. (Part 3 of 4.)

```
137
138        cout << endl; // start a new line of output
139     } // end outer for
140 } // end function outputBarChart
141
142 // output the contents of the grades array
143 void GradeBook::outputGrades()
144 {
145    cout << "\nThe grades are:\n\n";
146
147    // output each student's grade
148    for ( int student = 0; student < students; student++ )
149       cout << "Student " << setw( 2 ) << student + 1 << ": " << setw( 3 )
150          << grades[ student ] << endl;
151 } // end function outputGrades
```

Fig. 7.17 | GradeBook class member functions manipulating an array of grades. (Part 4 of 4.)

Note that the size of the array in line 29 of Fig. 7.16 is specified by public const static data member students (declared in line 13). This data member is public so that it is accessible to the clients of the class. We will soon see an example of a client program using this constant. Declaring students with the const qualifier indicates that this data member is constant—its value cannot be changed after being initialized. Keyword static in this variable declaration indicates that the data member is shared by all objects of the class—all GradeBook objects store grades for the same number of students. Recall from Section 3.6 that when each object of a class maintains its own copy of an attribute, the variable that represents the attribute is also known as a data member—each object (instance) of the class has a separate copy of the variable in memory. There are variables for which each object of a class does not have a separate copy. That is the case with static data members, which are also known as class variables. When objects of a class containing static data members are created, all the objects of that class share one copy of the class's static data members. A static data member can be accessed within the class definition and the member-function definitions just like any other data member. As you will soon see, a public static data member can also be accessed outside of the class, even when no objects of the class exist, using the class name followed by the binary scope resolution operator (::) and the name of the data member. You will learn more about static data members in Chapter 10.

The class's constructor (declared in line 16 of Fig. 7.16 and defined in lines 17–24 of Fig. 7.17) has two parameters—the name of the course and an array of grades. When a program creates a GradeBook object (e.g., line 13 of fig07_18.cpp), the program passes an existing int array to the constructor, which copies the values in the passed array to the data member grades (lines 22–23 of Fig. 7.17). The grade values in the passed array could have been input from a user or read from a file on disk (as discussed in Chapter 17, File Processing). In our test program, we simply initialize an array with a set of grade values (Fig. 7.18, lines 10–11). Once the grades are stored in data member grades of class GradeBook, all the class's member functions can access the grades array as needed to perform various calculations.

```
1    // Fig. 7.18: fig07_18.cpp
2    // Creates GradeBook object using an array of grades.
3
4    #include "GradeBook.h" // GradeBook class definition
5
6    // function main begins program execution
7    int main()
8    {
9       // array of student grades
10      int gradesArray[ GradeBook::students ] =
11         { 87, 68, 94, 100, 83, 78, 85, 91, 76, 87 };
12
13      GradeBook myGradeBook(
14         "CS101 Introduction to C++ Programming", gradesArray );
15      myGradeBook.displayMessage();
16      myGradeBook.processGrades();
17      return 0;
18   } // end main
```

```
Welcome to the grade book for
CS101 Introduction to C++ Programming!

The grades are:

Student  1:  87
Student  2:  68
Student  3:  94
Student  4: 100
Student  5:  83
Student  6:  78
Student  7:  85
Student  8:  91
Student  9:  76
Student 10:  87

Class average is 84.90
Lowest grade is 68
Highest grade is 100

Grade distribution:
  0-9:
 10-19:
 20-29:
 30-39:
 40-49:
 50-59:
 60-69: *
 70-79: **
 80-89: ****
 90-99: **
   100: *
```

Fig. 7.18 | Creates a GradeBook object using an array of grades, then invokes member function processGrades to analyze them.

Member function processGrades (declared in line 21 of Fig. 7.16 and defined in lines 48–63 of Fig. 7.17) contains a series of member function calls that output a report summarizing the grades. Line 51 calls member function outputGrades to print the contents of the array grades. Lines 148–150 in member function outputGrades use a for statement to output each student's grade. Although array indices start at 0, a professor would typically number students starting at 1. Thus, lines 149–150 output student + 1 as the student number to produce grade labels "Student 1: ", "Student 2: ", and so on.

Member function processGrades next calls member function getAverage (lines 54–55) to obtain the average of the grades in the array. Member function getAverage (declared in line 24 of Fig. 7.16 and defined in lines 98–108) uses a for statement to total the values in array grades before calculating the average. Note that the averaging calculation in line 107 uses const static data member students to determine the number of grades being averaged.

Lines 58–59 in member function processGrades call member functions getMinimum and getMaximum to determine the lowest and highest grades of any student on the exam, respectively. Let us examine how member function getMinimum finds the lowest grade. Because the highest grade allowed is 100, we begin by assuming that 100 is the lowest grade (line 68). Then, we compare each of the elements in the array to the lowest grade, looking for smaller values. Lines 71–76 in member function getMinimum loop through the array, and lines 74–75 compare each grade to lowGrade. If a grade is less than lowGrade, lowGrade is set to that grade. When line 78 executes, lowGrade contains the lowest grade in the array. Member function getMaximum (lines 82–95) works similarly to member function getMinimum.

Finally, line 62 in member function processGrades calls member function output-BarChart to print a distribution chart of the grade data using a technique similar to that in Fig. 7.9. In that example, we manually calculated the number of grades in each category (i.e., 0–9, 10–19, ..., 90–99 and 100) by simply looking at a set of grades. In this example, lines 120–121 use a technique similar to that in Fig. 7.10 and Fig. 7.11 to calculate the frequency of grades in each category. Line 117 declares and creates array frequency of 11 ints to store the frequency of grades in each grade category. For each grade in array grades, lines 120–121 increment the appropriate element of the frequency array. To determine which element to increment, line 121 divides the current grade by 10 using integer division. For example, if grade is 85, line 121 increments frequency[8] to update the count of grades in the range 80–89. Lines 124–139 next print the bar chart (see Fig. 7.18) based on the values in array frequency. Like lines 29–30 of Fig. 7.9, lines 135–136 of Fig. 7.17 use a value in array frequency to determine the number of asterisks to display in each bar.

Testing Class *GradeBook*

The program of Fig. 7.18 creates an object of class GradeBook (Figs. 7.16–7.17) using the int array gradesArray (declared and initialized in lines 10–11). Note that we use the binary scope resolution operator (::) in the expression "GradeBook::students" (line 10) to access class GradeBook's static constant students. We use this constant here to create an array that is the same size as array grades stored as a data member in class GradeBook. Lines 13–14 pass a course name and gradesArray to the GradeBook constructor. Line 15 displays a welcome message, and line 16 invokes the GradeBook object's processGrades member function. The output reveals the summary of the 10 grades in myGradeBook.

7.7 Searching Arrays with Linear Search

Often a programmer will be working with large amounts of data stored in arrays. It may be necessary to determine whether an array contains a value that matches a certain key value. The process of finding a particular element of an array is called searching. In this section we discuss the simple linear search. Exercise 7.33 at the end of this chapter asks you to implement a recursive version of the linear search. In Chapter 20, Searching and Sorting, we present the more complex, yet more efficient, binary search.

Linear Search

The linear search (Fig. 7.19, lines 37–44) compares each element of an array with a search key (line 40). Because the array is not in any particular order, it is just as likely that the value will be found in the first element as the last. On average, therefore, the program must compare the search key with half the elements of the array. To determine that a value is not in the array, the program must compare the search key to every element in the array.

The linear searching method works well for small arrays or for unsorted arrays (i.e., arrays whose elements are in no particular order). However, for large arrays, linear searching is inefficient. If the array is sorted (e.g., its elements are in ascending order), you can use the high-speed binary search technique that you will learn about in Chapter 20, Searching and Sorting.

```cpp
1  // Fig. 7.19: fig07_19.cpp
2  // Linear search of an array.
3  #include <iostream>
4  using std::cout;
5  using std::cin;
6  using std::endl;
7
8  int linearSearch( const int [], int, int ); // prototype
9
10 int main()
11 {
12    const int arraySize = 100; // size of array
13    int a[ arraySize ]; // create array a
14    int searchKey; // value to locate in array a
15
16    for ( int i = 0; i < arraySize; i++ )
17       a[ i ] = 2 * i; // create some data
18
19    cout << "Enter integer search key: ";
20    cin >> searchKey;
21
22    // attempt to locate searchKey in array a
23    int element = linearSearch( a, searchKey, arraySize );
24
25    // display results
26    if ( element != -1 )
27       cout << "Found value in element " << element << endl;
28    else
29       cout << "Value not found" << endl;
```

Fig. 7.19 | Linear search of an array. (Part 1 of 2.)

```
30
31      return 0; // indicates successful termination
32   } // end main
33
34   // compare key to every element of array until location is
35   // found or until end of array is reached; return subscript of
36   // element if key or -1 if key not found
37   int linearSearch( const int array[], int key, int sizeOfArray )
38   {
39      for ( int j = 0; j < sizeOfArray; j++ )
40         if ( array[ j ] == key ) // if found,
41            return j; // return location of key
42
43      return -1; // key not found
44   } // end function linearSearch
```

```
Enter integer search key: 36
Found value in element 18
```

```
Enter integer search key: 37
Value not found
```

Fig. 7.19 | Linear search of an array. (Part 2 of 2.)

7.8 Sorting Arrays with Insertion Sort

Sorting data (i.e., placing the data into some particular order such as ascending or descending) is one of the most important computing applications. A bank sorts all checks by account number so that it can prepare individual bank statements at the end of each month. Telephone companies sort their phone directories by last name and, within that, by first name to make it easy to find phone numbers. Virtually every organization must sort some data and, in many cases, massive amounts of data. Sorting data is an intriguing problem that has attracted some of the most intense research efforts in the field of computer science. In this chapter, we discuss a simple sorting scheme. In the exercises and Chapter 20, Searching and Sorting, we investigate more complex schemes that yield superior performance, and we introduce Big O (pronounced "Big Oh") notation for characterizing how hard each scheme must work to accomplish its task.

 Performance Tip 7.4

Sometimes, simple algorithms perform poorly. Their virtue is that they are easy to write, test and debug. More complex algorithms are sometimes needed to realize optimal performance.

Insertion Sort

The program in Fig. 7.20 sorts the values of the 10-element array `data` into ascending order. The technique we use is called insertion sort—a simple, but inefficient, sorting algorithm. The first iteration of this algorithm takes the second element and, if it is less than the first element, swaps it with the first element (i.e., the program *inserts* the second element in front of the first element). The second iteration looks at the third element and inserts it into the correct position with respect to the first two elements, so all three elements are in order. At the ith iteration of this algorithm, the first i elements in the original array will be sorted.

Line 13 of Fig. 7.20 declares and initializes array data with the following values:

34	56	4	10	77	51	93	30	5	52

The program first looks at data[0] and data[1], whose values are 34 and 56, respectively. These two elements are already in order, so the program continues—if they were out of order, the program would swap them.

```cpp
 1   // Fig. 7.20: fig07_20.cpp
 2   // This program sorts an array's values into ascending order.
 3   #include <iostream>
 4   using std::cout;
 5   using std::endl;
 6
 7   #include <iomanip>
 8   using std::setw;
 9
10   int main()
11   {
12      const int arraySize = 10; // size of array a
13      int data[ arraySize ] = { 34, 56, 4, 10, 77, 51, 93, 30, 5, 52 };
14      int insert; // temporary variable to hold element to insert
15
16      cout << "Unsorted array:\n";
17
18      // output original array
19      for ( int i = 0; i < arraySize; i++ )
20         cout << setw( 4 ) << data[ i ];
21
22      // insertion sort
23      // loop over the elements of the array
24      for ( int next = 1; next < arraySize; next++ )
25      {
26         insert = data[ next ]; // store the value in the current element
27
28         int moveItem = next; // initialize location to place element
29
30         // search for the location in which to put the current element
31         while ( ( moveItem > 0 ) && ( data[ moveItem - 1 ] > insert ) )
32         {
33            // shift element one slot to the right
34            data[ moveItem ] = data[ moveItem - 1 ];
35            moveItem--;
36         } // end while
37
38         data[ moveItem ] = insert; // place inserted element into the array
39      } // end for
40
41      cout << "\nSorted array:\n";
```

Fig. 7.20 | Sorting an array with insertion sort. (Part 1 of 2.)

```
42
43      // output sorted array
44      for ( int i = 0; i < arraySize; i++ )
45         cout << setw( 4 ) << data[ i ];
46
47      cout << endl;
48      return 0; // indicates successful termination
49   } // end main
```

```
Unsorted array:
  34  56   4  10  77  51  93  30   5  52
Sorted array:
   4   5  10  30  34  51  52  56  77  93
```

Fig. 7.20 | Sorting an array with insertion sort. (Part 2 of 2.)

In the second iteration, the program looks at the value of data[2], 4. This value is less than 56, so the program stores 4 in a temporary variable and moves 56 one element to the right. The program then checks and determines that 4 is less than 34, so it moves 34 one element to the right. The program has now reached the beginning of the array, so it places 4 in data[0]. The array now is

    4   34   56   10   77   51   93   30   5   52

In the third iteration, the program stores the value of data[3], 10, in a temporary variable. Then the program compares 10 to 56 and moves 56 one element to the right because it is larger than 10. The program then compares 10 to 34, moving 34 right one element. When the program compares 10 to 4, it observes that 10 is larger than 4 and places 10 in data[1]. The array now is

    4   10   34   56   77   51   93   30   5   52

Using this algorithm, at the ith iteration, the first i elements of the original array are sorted. They may not be in their final locations, however, because smaller values may be located later in the array.

The sorting is performed by the for statement in lines 24–39 that loops over the elements of the array. In each iteration, line 26 temporarily stores in variable insert (declared in line 14) the value of the element that will be inserted into the sorted portion of the array. Line 28 declares and initializes the variable moveItem, which keeps track of where to insert the element. Lines 31–36 loop to locate the correct position where the element should be inserted. The loop terminates either when the program reaches the front of the array or when it reaches an element that is less than the value to be inserted. Line 34 moves an element to the right, and line 35 decrements the position at which to insert the next element. After the while loop ends, line 38 inserts the element into place. When the for statement in lines 24–39 terminates, the elements of the array are sorted.

The chief virtue of the insertion sort is that it is easy to program; however, it runs slowly. This becomes apparent when sorting large arrays. In the exercises, we will investigate some alternate algorithms for sorting an array. We investigate sorting and searching in greater depth in Chapter 20.

7.9 Multidimensional Arrays

Multidimensional arrays with two dimensions are often used to represent tables of values consisting of information arranged in rows and columns. To identify a particular table element, we must specify two subscripts. By convention, the first identifies the element's row and the second identifies the element's column. Arrays that require two subscripts to identify a particular element are called two-dimensional arrays or 2-D arrays. Note that multidimensional arrays can have more than two dimensions (i.e., subscripts). Figure 7.21 illustrates a two-dimensional array, a. The array contains three rows and four columns, so it is said to be a 3-by-4 array. In general, an array with m rows and n columns is called an m-by-n array.

Every element in array a is identified in Fig. 7.21 by an element name of the form a[i][j], where a is the name of the array, and i and j are the subscripts that uniquely identify each element in a. Notice that the names of the elements in row 0 all have a first subscript of 0; the names of the elements in column 3 all have a second subscript of 3.

Common Programming Error 7.12

Referencing a two-dimensional array element a[x][y] incorrectly as a[x, y] is an error. Actually, a[x, y] is treated as a[y], because C++ evaluates the expression x, y (containing a comma operator) simply as y (the last of the comma-separated expressions).

A multidimensional array can be initialized in its declaration much like a one-dimensional array. For example, a two-dimensional array b with values 1 and 2 in its row 0 elements and values 3 and 4 in its row 1 elements could be declared and initialized with

```
int b[ 2 ][ 2 ] = { { 1, 2 }, { 3, 4 } };
```

The values are grouped by row in braces. So, 1 and 2 initialize b[0][0] and b[0][1], respectfully, and 3 and 4 initialize b[1][0] and b[1][1], respectfully. If there are not enough initializers for a given row, the remaining elements of that row are initialized to 0. Thus, the declaration

```
int b[ 2 ][ 2 ] = { { 1 }, { 3, 4 } };
```

initializes b[0][0] to 1, b[0][1] to 0, b[1][0] to 3 and b[1][1] to 4.

Figure 7.22 demonstrates initializing two-dimensional arrays in declarations. Lines 11–13 declare three arrays, each with two rows and three columns.

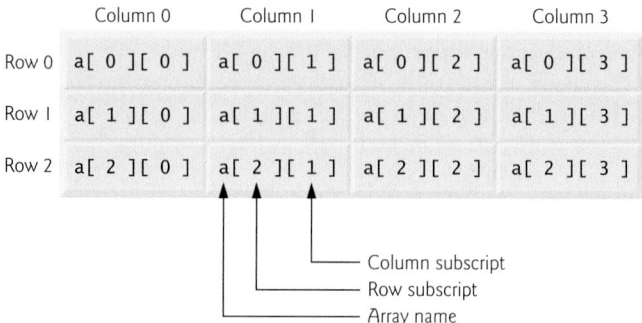

Fig. 7.21 | Two-dimensional array with three rows and four columns.

```
 1  // Fig. 7.22: fig07_22.cpp
 2  // Initializing multidimensional arrays.
 3  #include <iostream>
 4  using std::cout;
 5  using std::endl;
 6
 7  void printArray( const int [][ 3 ] ); // prototype
 8
 9  int main()
10  {
11     int array1[ 2 ][ 3 ] = { { 1, 2, 3 }, { 4, 5, 6 } };
12     int array2[ 2 ][ 3 ] = { 1, 2, 3, 4, 5 };
13     int array3[ 2 ][ 3 ] = { { 1, 2 }, { 4 } };
14
15     cout << "Values in array1 by row are:" << endl;
16     printArray( array1 );
17
18     cout << "\nValues in array2 by row are:" << endl;
19     printArray( array2 );
20
21     cout << "\nValues in array3 by row are:" << endl;
22     printArray( array3 );
23     return 0; // indicates successful termination
24  } // end main
25
26  // output array with two rows and three columns
27  void printArray( const int a[][ 3 ] )
28  {
29     // loop through array's rows
30     for ( int i = 0; i < 2; i++ )
31     {
32        // loop through columns of current row
33        for ( int j = 0; j < 3; j++ )
34           cout << a[ i ][ j ] << ' ';
35
36        cout << endl; // start new line of output
37     } // end outer for
38  } // end function printArray
```

```
Values in array1 by row are:
1 2 3
4 5 6

Values in array2 by row are:
1 2 3
4 5 0

Values in array3 by row are:
1 2 0
4 0 0
```

Fig. 7.22 | Initializing multidimensional arrays.

The declaration of array1 (line 11) provides six initializers in two sublists. The first sublist initializes row 0 of the array to the values 1, 2 and 3; and the second sublist initializes row 1 of the array to the values 4, 5 and 6. If the braces around each sublist are removed from the array1 initializer list, the compiler initializes the elements of row 0 followed by the elements of row 1, yielding the same result.

The declaration of array2 (line 12) provides only five initializers. The initializers are assigned to row 0, then row 1. Any elements that do not have an explicit initializer are initialized to zero, so array2[1][2] is initialized to zero.

The declaration of array3 (line 13) provides three initializers in two sublists. The sublist for row 0 explicitly initializes the first two elements of row 0 to 1 and 2; the third element is implicitly initialized to zero. The sublist for row 1 explicitly initializes the first element to 4 and implicitly initializes the last two elements to zero.

The program calls function printArray to output each array's elements. Notice that the function definition (lines 27–38) specifies the parameter const int a[][3]. When a function receives a one-dimensional array as an argument, the array brackets are empty in the function's parameter list. The size of the first dimension (i.e., the number of rows) of a two-dimensional array is not required either, but all subsequent dimension sizes are required. The compiler uses these sizes to determine the locations in memory of elements in multidimensional arrays. All array elements are stored consecutively in memory, regardless of the number of dimensions. In a two-dimensional array, row 0 is stored in memory followed by row 1. In a two-dimensional array, each row is a one-dimensional array. To locate an element in a particular row, the function must know exactly how many elements are in each row so it can skip the proper number of memory locations when accessing the array. Thus, when accessing a[1][2], the function knows to skip row 0's three elements in memory to get to row 1. Then, the function accesses element 2 of that row.

Many common array manipulations use for repetition statements. For example, the following for statement sets all the elements in row 2 of array a in Fig. 7.21 to zero:

```
for ( column = 0; column < 4; column++ )
   a[ 2 ][ column ] = 0;
```

The for statement varies only the second subscript (i.e., the column subscript). The preceding for statement is equivalent to the following assignment statements:

```
a[ 2 ][ 0 ] = 0;
a[ 2 ][ 1 ] = 0;
a[ 2 ][ 2 ] = 0;
a[ 2 ][ 3 ] = 0;
```

The following nested for statement determines the total of all the elements in array a:

```
total = 0;

for ( row = 0; row < 3; row++ )

   for ( column = 0; column < 4; column++ )
      total += a[ row ][ column ];
```

The for statement totals the elements of the array one row at a time. The outer for statement begins by setting row (i.e., the row subscript) to 0, so the elements of row 0 may be totaled by the inner for statement. The outer for statement then increments row to 1, so the elements of row 1 can be totaled. Then, the outer for statement increments row to 2, so the elements of row 2 can be totaled. When the nested for statement terminates, total contains the sum of all the array elements.

7.10 Case Study: Class GradeBook Using a Two-Dimensional Array

In Section 7.6, we presented class GradeBook (Figs. 7.16–7.17), which used a one-dimensional array to store student grades on a single exam. In most semesters, students take several exams. Professors are likely to want to analyze grades across the entire semester, both for a single student and for the class as a whole.

Storing Student Grades in a Two-Dimensional Array in Class GradeBook

Figures 7.23–7.24 contain a version of class GradeBook that uses a two-dimensional array grades to store the grades of a number of students on multiple exams. Each row of the array represents a single student's grades for the entire course, and each column represents all the grades the students earned for one particular exam. A client program, such as fig07_25.cpp, passes the array as an argument to the GradeBook constructor. In this example, we use a ten-by-three array containing ten students' grades on three exams.

Five member functions (declared in lines 23–27 of Fig. 7.23) perform array manipulations to process the grades. Each of these member functions is similar to its counterpart in the earlier one-dimensional array version of class GradeBook (Figs. 7.16–7.17). Member function getMinimum (defined in lines 65–82 of Fig. 7.24) determines the lowest grade of any student for the semester. Member function getMaximum (defined in lines 85–102 of Fig. 7.24) determines the highest grade of any student for the semester. Member function getAverage (lines 105–115 of Fig. 7.24) determines a particular student's semester average. Member function outputBarChart (lines 118–149 of Fig. 7.24) outputs a bar chart of the distribution of all student grades for the semester. Member function output-Grades (lines 152–177 of Fig. 7.24) outputs the two-dimensional array in a tabular format, along with each student's semester average.

```
1   // Fig. 7.23: GradeBook.h
2   // Definition of class GradeBook that uses a
3   // two-dimensional array to store test grades.
4   // Member functions are defined in GradeBook.cpp
5   #include <string> // program uses C++ Standard Library string class
6   using std::string;
7
8   // GradeBook class definition
9   class GradeBook
10  {
11  public:
12     // constants
13     const static int students = 10; // number of students
14     const static int tests = 3; // number of tests
15
16     // constructor initializes course name and array of grades
17     GradeBook( string, const int [][ tests ] );
18
19     void setCourseName( string ); // function to set the course name
20     string getCourseName(); // function to retrieve the course name
```

Fig. 7.23 | Definition of class GradeBook with a two-dimensional array to store grades. (Part 1 of 2.)

```
21       void displayMessage(); // display a welcome message
22       void processGrades(); // perform various operations on the grade data
23       int getMinimum(); // find the minimum grade in the grade book
24       int getMaximum(); // find the maximum grade in the grade book
25       double getAverage( const int [], const int ); // find average of grades
26       void outputBarChart(); // output bar chart of grade distribution
27       void outputGrades(); // output the contents of the grades array
28    private:
29       string courseName; // course name for this grade book
30       int grades[ students ][ tests ]; // two-dimensional array of grades
31    }; // end class GradeBook
```

Fig. 7.23 | Definition of class GradeBook with a two-dimensional array to store grades. (Part 2 of 2.)

```
1    // Fig. 7.24: GradeBook.cpp
2    // Member-function definitions for class GradeBook that
3    // uses a two-dimensional array to store grades.
4    #include <iostream>
5    using std::cout;
6    using std::cin;
7    using std::endl;
8    using std::fixed;
9
10   #include <iomanip> // parameterized stream manipulators
11   using std::setprecision; // sets numeric output precision
12   using std::setw; // sets field width
13
14   // include definition of class GradeBook from GradeBook.h
15   #include "GradeBook.h"
16
17   // two-argument constructor initializes courseName and grades array
18   GradeBook::GradeBook( string name, const int gradesArray[][ tests ] )
19   {
20      setCourseName( name ); // initialize courseName
21
22      // copy grades from gradeArray to grades
23      for ( int student = 0; student < students; student++ )
24
25         for ( int test = 0; test < tests; test++ )
26            grades[ student ][ test ] = gradesArray[ student ][ test ];
27   } // end two-argument GradeBook constructor
28
29   // function to set the course name
30   void GradeBook::setCourseName( string name )
31   {
32      courseName = name; // store the course name
33   } // end function setCourseName
```

Fig. 7.24 | GradeBook class member-function definitions manipulating a two-dimensional array of grades. (Part 1 of 4.)

```
34
35   // function to retrieve the course name
36   string GradeBook::getCourseName()
37   {
38      return courseName;
39   } // end function getCourseName
40
41   // display a welcome message to the GradeBook user
42   void GradeBook::displayMessage()
43   {
44      // this statement calls getCourseName to get the
45      // name of the course this GradeBook represents
46      cout << "Welcome to the grade book for\n" << getCourseName() << "!"
47         << endl;
48   } // end function displayMessage
49
50   // perform various operations on the data
51   void GradeBook::processGrades()
52   {
53      // output grades array
54      outputGrades();
55
56      // call functions getMinimum and getMaximum
57      cout << "\nLowest grade in the grade book is " << getMinimum()
58         << "\nHighest grade in the grade book is " << getMaximum() << endl;
59
60      // output grade distribution chart of all grades on all tests
61      outputBarChart();
62   } // end function processGrades
63
64   // find minimum grade
65   int GradeBook::getMinimum()
66   {
67      int lowGrade = 100; // assume lowest grade is 100
68
69      // loop through rows of grades array
70      for ( int student = 0; student < students; student++ )
71      {
72         // loop through columns of current row
73         for ( int test = 0; test < tests; test++ )
74         {
75            // if current grade less than lowGrade, assign it to lowGrade
76            if ( grades[ student ][ test ] < lowGrade )
77               lowGrade = grades[ student ][ test ]; // new lowest grade
78         } // end inner for
79      } // end outer for
80
81      return lowGrade; // return lowest grade
82   } // end function getMinimum
83
```

Fig. 7.24 | GradeBook class member-function definitions manipulating a two-dimensional array of grades. (Part 2 of 4.)

```
84   // find maximum grade
85   int GradeBook::getMaximum()
86   {
87      int highGrade = 0; // assume highest grade is 0
88
89      // loop through rows of grades array
90      for ( int student = 0; student < students; student++ )
91      {
92         // loop through columns of current row
93         for ( int test = 0; test < tests; test++ )
94         {
95            // if current grade greater than lowGrade, assign it to highGrade
96            if ( grades[ student ][ test ] > highGrade )
97               highGrade = grades[ student ][ test ]; // new highest grade
98         } // end inner for
99      } // end outer for
100
101     return highGrade; // return highest grade
102  } // end function getMaximum
103
104  // determine average grade for particular set of grades
105  double GradeBook::getAverage( const int setOfGrades[], const int grades )
106  {
107     int total = 0; // initialize total
108
109     // sum grades in array
110     for ( int grade = 0; grade < grades; grade++ )
111        total += setOfGrades[ grade ];
112
113     // return average of grades
114     return static_cast< double >( total ) / grades;
115  } // end function getAverage
116
117  // output bar chart displaying grade distribution
118  void GradeBook::outputBarChart()
119  {
120     cout << "\nOverall grade distribution:" << endl;
121
122     // stores frequency of grades in each range of 10 grades
123     const int frequencySize = 11;
124     int frequency[ frequencySize ] = { 0 };
125
126     // for each grade, increment the appropriate frequency
127     for ( int student = 0; student < students; student++ )
128
129        for ( int test = 0; test < tests; test++ )
130           ++frequency[ grades[ student ][ test ] / 10 ];
131
132     // for each grade frequency, print bar in chart
133     for ( int count = 0; count < frequencySize; count++ )
134     {
```

Fig. 7.24 | GradeBook class member-function definitions manipulating a two-dimensional array of grades. (Part 3 of 4.)

```
135             // output bar label ("0-9:", ..., "90-99:", "100:" )
136          if ( count == 0 )
137             cout << "  0-9: ";
138          else if ( count == 10 )
139             cout << "  100: ";
140          else
141             cout << count * 10 << "-" << ( count * 10 ) + 9 << ": ";
142
143             // print bar of asterisks
144          for ( int stars = 0; stars < frequency[ count ]; stars++ )
145             cout << '*';
146
147          cout << endl; // start a new line of output
148       } // end outer for
149 } // end function outputBarChart
150
151 // output the contents of the grades array
152 void GradeBook::outputGrades()
153 {
154    cout << "\nThe grades are:\n\n";
155    cout << "               "; // align column heads
156
157    // create a column heading for each of the tests
158    for ( int test = 0; test < tests; test++ )
159       cout << "Test " << test + 1 << "  ";
160
161    cout << "Average" << endl; // student average column heading
162
163    // create rows/columns of text representing array grades
164    for ( int student = 0; student < students; student++ )
165    {
166       cout << "Student " << setw( 2 ) << student + 1;
167
168          // output student's grades
169       for ( int test = 0; test < tests; test++ )
170          cout << setw( 8 ) << grades[ student ][ test ];
171
172          // call member function getAverage to calculate student's average;
173          // pass row of grades and the value of tests as the arguments
174       double average = getAverage( grades[ student ], tests );
175       cout << setw( 9 ) << setprecision( 2 ) << fixed << average << endl;
176    } // end outer for
177 } // end function outputGrades
```

Fig. 7.24 | GradeBook class member-function definitions manipulating a two-dimensional array of grades. (Part 4 of 4.)

Member functions getMinimum, getMaximum, outputBarChart and outputGrades each loop through array grades by using nested for statements For example, consider the nested for statement in member function getMinimum (lines 70–79). The outer for statement begins by setting student (i.e., the row subscript) to 0, so the elements of row 0 can be compared with variable lowGrade in the body of the inner for statement. The inner for statement loops through the grades of a particular row and compares each grade with lowGrade. If a grade is less than lowGrade, lowGrade is set to that grade. The outer for statement then increments the row subscript to 1. The elements of row 1 are compared with variable lowGrade. The outer for statement then increments the row subscript to 2, and the elements of row 2 are compared with variable lowGrade. This repeats until all rows of grades have been traversed. When execution of the nested statement is complete, low-Grade contains the smallest grade in the two-dimensional array. Member function get-Maximum works similarly to member function getMinimum.

Member function outputBarChart in Fig. 7.24 is nearly identical to the one in Fig. 7.17. However, to output the overall grade distribution for a whole semester, the member function uses a nested for statement (lines 127–130) to create the one-dimensional array frequency based on all the grades in the two-dimensional array. The rest of the code in each of the two outputBarChart member functions that displays the chart is identical.

Member function outputGrades (lines 152–177) also uses nested for statements to output values of the array grades, in addition to each student's semester average. The output in Fig. 7.25 shows the result, which resembles the tabular format of a professor's physical grade book. Lines 158–159 print the column headings for each test. We use a counter-controlled for statement so that we can identify each test with a number. Similarly, the for statement in lines 164–176 first outputs a row label using a counter variable to identify each student (line 166). Although array indices start at 0, note that lines 159 and 166 output

```cpp
1   // Fig. 7.25: fig07_25.cpp
2   // Creates GradeBook object using a two-dimensional array of grades.
3
4   #include "GradeBook.h" // GradeBook class definition
5
6   // function main begins program execution
7   int main()
8   {
9      // two-dimensional array of student grades
10     int gradesArray[ GradeBook::students ][ GradeBook::tests ] =
11        { { 87, 96, 70 },
12          { 68, 87, 90 },
13          { 94, 100, 90 },
14          { 100, 81, 82 },
15          { 83, 65, 85 },
16          { 78, 87, 65 },
17          { 85, 75, 83 },
18          { 91, 94, 100 },
19          { 76, 72, 84 },
20          { 87, 93, 73 } };
21
22     GradeBook myGradeBook(
23        "CS101 Introduction to C++ Programming", gradesArray );
24     myGradeBook.displayMessage();
25     myGradeBook.processGrades();
26     return 0; // indicates successful termination
27  } // end main
```

Fig. 7.25 | Creates a GradeBook object using a two-dimensional array of grades, then invokes member function processGrades to analyze them. (Part 1 of 2.)

```
Welcome to the grade book for
CS101 Introduction to C++ Programming!

The grades are:

            Test 1  Test 2  Test 3  Average
Student  1      87      96      70    84.33
Student  2      68      87      90    81.67
Student  3      94     100      90    94.67
Student  4     100      81      82    87.67
Student  5      83      65      85    77.67
Student  6      78      87      65    76.67
Student  7      85      75      83    81.00
Student  8      91      94     100    95.00
Student  9      76      72      84    77.33
Student 10      87      93      73    84.33

Lowest grade in the grade book is 65
Highest grade in the grade book is 100

Overall grade distribution:
   0-9:
  10-19:
  20-29:
  30-39:
  40-49:
  50-59:
  60-69: ***
  70-79: ******
  80-89: ************
  90-99: *******
    100: ***
```

Fig. 7.25 | Creates a GradeBook object using a two-dimensional array of grades, then invokes member function processGrades to analyze them. (Part 2 of 2.)

test + 1 and student + 1, respectively, to produce test and student numbers starting at 1 (see Fig. 7.25). The inner for statement in lines 169–170 uses the outer for statement's counter variable student to loop through a specific row of array grades and output each student's test grade. Finally, line 174 obtains each student's semester average by passing the current row of grades (i.e., grades[student]) to member function getAverage.

Member function getAverage (lines 105–115) takes two arguments—a one-dimensional array of test results for a particular student and the number of test results in the array. When line 174 calls getAverage, the first argument is grades[student], which specifies that a particular row of the two-dimensional array grades should be passed to getAverage. For example, based on the array created in Fig. 7.25, the argument grades[1] represents the three values (a one-dimensional array of grades) stored in row 1 of the two-dimensional array grades. A two-dimensional array can be considered an array whose elements are one-dimensional arrays. Member function getAverage calculates the sum of the array elements, divides the total by the number of test results and returns the floating-point result as a double value (line 114).

Testing Class GradeBook

The program in Fig. 7.25 creates an object of class GradeBook (Figs. 7.23–7.24) using the two-dimensional array of ints named gradesArray (declared and initialized in lines 10–20). Note that line 10 accesses class GradeBook's static constants students and tests to indicate the size of each dimension of array gradesArray. Lines 22–23 pass a course name and gradesArray to the GradeBook constructor. Lines 24–25 then invoke myGradeBook's displayMessage and processGrades member functions to display a welcome message and obtain a report summarizing the students' grades for the semester, respectively.

7.11 Introduction to C++ Standard Library Class Template vector

We now introduce C++ Standard Library class template vector, which represents a more robust type of array featuring many additional capabilities. As you will see in later chapters and in more advanced C++ courses, C-style pointer-based arrays (i.e., the type of arrays presented thus far) have great potential for errors. For example, as mentioned earlier, a program can easily "walk off" either end of an array, because C++ does not check whether subscripts fall outside the range of an array. Two arrays cannot be meaningfully compared with equality operators or relational operators. As you will learn in Chapter 8, pointer variables (known more commonly as pointers) contain memory addresses as their values. Array names are simply pointers to where the arrays begin in memory, and, of course, two arrays will always be at different memory locations. When an array is passed to a general-purpose function designed to handle arrays of any size, the size of the array must be passed as an additional argument. Furthermore, one array cannot be assigned to another with the assignment operator(s)—array names are const pointers, and, as you will learn in Chapter 8, a constant pointer cannot be used on the left side of an assignment operator. These and other capabilities certainly seem like "naturals" for dealing with arrays, but C++ does not provide such capabilities. However, the C++ Standard Library provides class template vector to allow programmers to create a more powerful and less error-prone alternative to arrays. In Chapter 11, Operator Overloading; String and Array Objects, we present the means to implement such array capabilities as those provided by vector. You will learn how to customize operators for use with your own classes (a technique known as operator overloading).

The vector class template is available to anyone building applications with C++. The notations that the vector example uses might be unfamiliar to you, because vectors use template notation. Recall that Section 6.18 discussed function templates. In Chapter 14, we discuss class templates. For now, you should feel comfortable using class template vector by mimicking the syntax in the example we show in this section. You will deepen your understanding as we study class templates in Chapter 14. Chapter 22 presents class template vector (and several other standard C++ container classes) in detail.

The program of Fig. 7.26 demonstrates capabilities provided by C++ Standard Library class template vector that are not available for C-style pointer-based arrays. Standard class template vector provides many of the same features as the Array class that we construct in Chapter 11, Operator Overloading; String and Array Objects. Standard class template vector is defined in header <vector> (line 11) and belongs to namespace std (line 12). Chapter 22 discusses the full functionality of standard class template vector.

Lines 19–20 create two vector objects that store values of type int—integers1 contains seven elements, and integers2 contains 10 elements. By default, all the elements of each `vector` object are set to 0. Note that `vectors` can be defined to store any data type, by replacing `int` in `vector< int >` with the appropriate data type. This notation, which specifies the type stored in the `vector`, is similar to the template notation that Section 6.18 introduced with function templates. Again, Chapter 14 discusses this syntax in detail.

```cpp
// Fig. 7.26: fig07_26.cpp
// Demonstrating C++ Standard Library class template vector.
#include <iostream>
using std::cout;
using std::cin;
using std::endl;

#include <iomanip>
using std::setw;

#include <vector>
using std::vector;

void outputVector( const vector< int > & ); // display the vector
void inputVector( vector< int > & ); // input values into the vector

int main()
{
   vector< int > integers1( 7 ); // 7-element vector< int >
   vector< int > integers2( 10 ); // 10-element vector< int >

   // print integers1 size and contents
   cout << "Size of vector integers1 is " << integers1.size()
      << "\nvector after initialization:" << endl;
   outputVector( integers1 );

   // print integers2 size and contents
   cout << "\nSize of vector integers2 is " << integers2.size()
      << "\nvector after initialization:" << endl;
   outputVector( integers2 );

   // input and print integers1 and integers2
   cout << "\nEnter 17 integers:" << endl;
   inputVector( integers1 );
   inputVector( integers2 );

   cout << "\nAfter input, the vectors contain:\n"
      << "integers1:" << endl;
   outputVector( integers1 );
   cout << "integers2:" << endl;
   outputVector( integers2 );

   // use inequality (!=) operator with vector objects
   cout << "\nEvaluating: integers1 != integers2" << endl;

   if ( integers1 != integers2 )
      cout << "integers1 and integers2 are not equal" << endl;
```

Fig. 7.26 | C++ Standard Library class template `vector`. (Part 1 of 4.)

```
48
49      // create vector integers3 using integers1 as an
50      // initializer; print size and contents
51      vector< int > integers3( integers1 ); // copy constructor
52
53      cout << "\nSize of vector integers3 is " << integers3.size()
54         << "\nvector after initialization:" << endl;
55      outputVector( integers3 );
56
57      // use overloaded assignment (=) operator
58      cout << "\nAssigning integers2 to integers1:" << endl;
59      integers1 = integers2; // integers1 is larger than integers2
60
61      cout << "integers1:" << endl;
62      outputVector( integers1 );
63      cout << "integers2:" << endl;
64      outputVector( integers2 );
65
66      // use equality (==) operator with vector objects
67      cout << "\nEvaluating: integers1 == integers2" << endl;
68
69      if ( integers1 == integers2 )
70         cout << "integers1 and integers2 are equal" << endl;
71
72      // use square brackets to create rvalue
73      cout << "\nintegers1[5] is " << integers1[ 5 ];
74
75      // use square brackets to create lvalue
76      cout << "\n\nAssigning 1000 to integers1[5]" << endl;
77      integers1[ 5 ] = 1000;
78      cout << "integers1:" << endl;
79      outputVector( integers1 );
80
81      // attempt to use out-of-range subscript
82      cout << "\nAttempt to assign 1000 to integers1.at( 15 )" << endl;
83      integers1.at( 15 ) = 1000; // ERROR: out of range
84      return 0;
85   } // end main
86
87   // output vector contents
88   void outputVector( const vector< int > &array )
89   {
90      size_t i; // declare control variable
91
92      for ( i = 0; i < array.size(); i++ )
93      {
94         cout << setw( 12 ) << array[ i ];
95
96         if ( ( i + 1 ) % 4 == 0 ) // 4 numbers per row of output
97            cout << endl;
98      } // end for
99
```

Fig. 7.26 | C++ Standard Library class template vector. (Part 2 of 4.)

```
100     if ( i % 4 != 0 )
101         cout << endl;
102  } // end function outputVector
103
104  // input vector contents
105  void inputVector( vector< int > &array )
106  {
107     for ( size_t i = 0; i < array.size(); i++ )
108         cin >> array[ i ];
109  } // end function inputVector
```

```
Size of vector integers1 is 7
vector after initialization:
            0           0           0           0
            0           0           0

Size of vector integers2 is 10
vector after initialization:
            0           0           0           0
            0           0           0           0
            0           0

Enter 17 integers:
1 2 3 4 5 6 7 8 9 10 11 12 13 14 15 16 17

After input, the vectors contain:
integers1:
            1           2           3           4
            5           6           7
integers2:
            8           9          10          11
           12          13          14          15
           16          17

Evaluating: integers1 != integers2
integers1 and integers2 are not equal

Size of vector integers3 is 7
vector after initialization:
            1           2           3           4
            5           6           7

Assigning integers2 to integers1:
integers1:
            8           9          10          11
           12          13          14          15
           16          17
integers2:
            8           9          10          11
           12          13          14          15
           16          17

Evaluating: integers1 == integers2
integers1 and integers2 are equal
```

(continued at top of next page…)

Fig. 7.26 | C++ Standard Library class template `vector`. (Part 3 of 4.)

```
                                        (...continued from bottom of previous page)
integers1[5] is 13

Assigning 1000 to integers1[5]
integers1:
          8          9         10         11
         12       1000         14         15
         16         17

Attempt to assign 1000 to integers1.at( 15 )

abnormal program termination
```

Fig. 7.26 | C++ Standard Library class template `vector`. (Part 4 of 4.)

Line 23 uses `vector` member function `size` to obtain the size (i.e., the number of elements) of `integers1`. Line 25 passes `integers1` to function `outputVector` (lines 88–102), which uses square brackets (`[]`) to obtain the value in each element of the `vector` as a value that can be used for output. Note the resemblance of this notation to the notation used to access the value of an array element. Lines 28 and 30 perform the same tasks for `integers2`.

Member function `size` of class template `vector` returns the number of elements in a `vector` as a value of type `size_t` (which represents the type `unsigned int` on many systems). As a result, line 90 declares the control variable `i` to be of type `size_t`, too. On some compilers, declaring `i` as an `int` causes the compiler to issue a warning message, since the loop-continuation condition (line 92) would compare a `signed` value (i.e., `int i`) and an `unsigned` value (i.e., a value of type `size_t` returned by function `size`).

Lines 34–35 pass `integers1` and `integers2` to function `inputVector` (lines 105–109) to read values for each `vector`'s elements from the user. Function `inputVector` uses square brackets (`[]`) to obtain *lvalues* that can be used to store the input values in each element of the `vector`.

Line 46 demonstrates that `vector` objects can be compared directly with the `!=` operator. If the contents of two `vector`s are not equal, the operator returns `true`; otherwise, the operator returns `false`.

C++ Standard Library class template `vector` allows programmers to create a new `vector` object that is initialized with the contents of an existing `vector`. Line 51 creates a `vector` object (`integers3`) and initializes it with a copy of `integers1`. This invokes `vector`'s so-called copy constructor to perform the copy operation. You will learn about copy constructors in detail in Chapter 11. Lines 53 and 55 output the size and contents of `integers3` to demonstrate that it was initialized correctly.

Line 59 assigns `integers2` to `integers1`, demonstrating that the assignment (`=`) operator can be used with `vector` objects. Lines 62 and 64 output the contents of both objects to show that they now contain identical values. Line 69 then compares `integers1` to `integers2` with the equality (`==`) operator to determine whether the contents of the two objects are equal after the assignment in line 59 (which they are).

Lines 73 and 77 demonstrate that a program can use square brackets (`[]`) to obtain a `vector` element as an *unmodifiable lvalue* and as a a *modifiable lvalue*, respectively. An unmodifiable *lvalue* is an expression that identifies an object in memory (such as an element in a `vector`), but cannot be used to modify that object. A modifiable *lvalue* also identifies an object in memory, but can be used to modify the object. As is the case with C-style pointer-based arrays, C++ does not perform any bounds checking when vector elements are accessed with square brackets. Therefore, the programmer must ensure that operations using [] do not accidentally attempt to manipulate elements outside the bounds of the vector. Standard class template vector does, however, provide bounds checking in its member function **at**, which "throws an exception" (see Chapter 16, Exception Handling) if its argument is an invalid subscript. By default, this causes a C++ program to terminate. If the subscript is valid, function at returns the element at the specified location as a modifiable *lvalue* or an unmodifiable *lvalue*, depending on the context (non-const or const) in which the call appears. Line 83 demonstrates a call to function at with an invalid subscript.

In this section, we demonstrated the C++ Standard Library class template vector, a robust, reusable class that can replace C-style pointer-based arrays. In Chapter 11, you will see that vector achieves many of its capabilities by "overloading" C++'s built-in operators, and you will learn how to customize operators for use with your own classes in similar ways. For example, we create an Array class that, like class template vector, improves upon basic array capabilities. Our Array class also provides additional features, such as the ability to input and output entire arrays with operators >> and <<, respectively.

7.12 (Optional) Software Engineering Case Study: Collaboration Among Objects in the ATM System

In this section, we concentrate on the collaborations (interactions) among objects in our ATM system. When two objects communicate with each other to accomplish a task, they are said to collaborate—they do this by invoking one another's operations. A collaboration consists of an object of one class sending a message to an object of another class. Messages are sent in C++ via member-function calls.

In Section 6.18, we determined many of the operations of the classes in our system. In this section, we concentrate on the messages that invoke these operations. To identify the collaborations in the system, we return to the requirements document in Section 2.8. Recall that this document specifies the range of activities that occur during an ATM session (e.g., authenticating a user, performing transactions). The steps used to describe how the system must perform each of these tasks are our first indication of the collaborations in our system. As we proceed through this and the remaining "Software Engineering Case Study" sections, we may discover additional collaborations.

Identifying the Collaborations in a System
We identify the collaborations in the system by carefully reading the sections of the requirements document that specify what the ATM should do to authenticate a user and to perform each transaction type. For each action or step described in the requirements document, we decide which objects in our system must interact to achieve the desired result. We identify one object as the sending object (i.e., the object that sends the message) and another as the receiving object (i.e., the object that offers that operation to clients of the class). We then select one of the receiving object's operations (identified in Section 6.18) that must be invoked by the sending object to produce the proper behavior. For example, the ATM displays a welcome message when idle. We know that an object of class Screen displays a message to the user via its displayMessage operation. Thus, we decide that the system can display a welcome message by employing a collaboration between the ATM and the Screen in which the ATM sends a displayMessage message to the Screen by invoking

the `displayMessage` operation of class `Screen`. [*Note:* To avoid repeating the phrase "an object of class…," we refer to each object simply by using its class name preceded by an article ("a," "an" or "the")—for example, "the `ATM`" refers to an object of class `ATM`.]

Figure 7.27 lists the collaborations that can be derived from the requirements document. For each sending object, we list the collaborations in the order in which they are discussed in the requirements document. We list each collaboration involving a unique sender, message and recipient only once, even though the collaboration may occur several times during an ATM session. For example, the first row in Fig. 7.27 indicates that the `ATM` collaborates with the `Screen` whenever the `ATM` needs to display a message to the user.

Let's consider the collaborations in Fig. 7.27. Before allowing a user to perform any transactions, the ATM must prompt the user to enter an account number, then to enter a PIN. It accomplishes each of these tasks by sending a `displayMessage` message to the `Screen`. Both of these actions refer to the same collaboration between the `ATM` and the `Screen`, which is already listed in Fig. 7.27. The `ATM` obtains input in response to a prompt by sending a `getInput` message to the `Keypad`. Next, the ATM must determine whether the user-specified account number and PIN match those of an account in the database. It

An object of class...	sends the message...	to an object of class...
ATM	displayMessage	Screen
	getInput	Keypad
	authenticateUser	BankDatabase
	execute	BalanceInquiry
	execute	Withdrawal
	execute	Deposit
BalanceInquiry	getAvailableBalance	BankDatabase
	getTotalBalance	BankDatabase
	displayMessage	Screen
Withdrawal	displayMessage	Screen
	getInput	Keypad
	getAvailableBalance	BankDatabase
	isSufficientCashAvailable	CashDispenser
	debit	BankDatabase
	dispenseCash	CashDispenser
Deposit	displayMessage	Screen
	getInput	Keypad
	isEnvelopeReceived	DepositSlot
	credit	BankDatabase
BankDatabase	validatePIN	Account
	getAvailableBalance	Account
	getTotalBalance	Account
	debit	Account
	credit	Account

Fig. 7.27 | Collaborations in the ATM system.

does so by sending an `authenticateUser` message to the `BankDatabase`. Recall that the `BankDatabase` cannot authenticate a user directly—only the user's `Account` (i.e., the `Account` that contains the account number specified by the user) can access the user's PIN to authenticate the user. Figure 7.27 therefore lists a collaboration in which the `BankDatabase` sends a `validatePIN` message to an `Account`.

After the user is authenticated, the `ATM` displays the main menu by sending a series of `displayMessage` messages to the `Screen` and obtains input containing a menu selection by sending a `getInput` message to the `Keypad`. We have already accounted for these collaborations. After the user chooses a type of transaction to perform, the `ATM` executes the transaction by sending an `execute` message to an object of the appropriate transaction class (i.e., a `BalanceInquiry`, a `Withdrawal` or a `Deposit`). For example, if the user chooses to perform a balance inquiry, the `ATM` sends an `execute` message to a `BalanceInquiry`.

Further examination of the requirements document reveals the collaborations involved in executing each transaction type. A `BalanceInquiry` retrieves the amount of money available in the user's account by sending a `getAvailableBalance` message to the `BankDatabase`, which responds by sending a `getAvailableBalance` message to the user's `Account`. Similarly, the `BalanceInquiry` retrieves the amount of money on deposit by sending a `getTotalBalance` message to the `BankDatabase`, which sends the same message to the user's `Account`. To display both measures of the user's balance at the same time, the `BalanceInquiry` sends a `displayMessage` message to the `Screen`.

A `Withdrawal` sends a series of `displayMessage` messages to the `Screen` to display a menu of standard withdrawal amounts (i.e., $20, $40, $60, $100, $200). The `Withdrawal` sends a `getInput` message to the `Keypad` to obtain the user's menu selection. Next, the `Withdrawal` determines whether the requested withdrawal amount is less than or equal to the user's account balance. The `Withdrawal` can obtain the amount of money available in the user's account by sending a `getAvailableBalance` message to the `BankDatabase`. The `Withdrawal` then tests whether the cash dispenser contains enough cash by sending an `isSufficientCashAvailable` message to the `CashDispenser`. A `Withdrawal` sends a `debit` message to the `BankDatabase` to decrease the user's account balance. The `BankDatabase` in turn sends the same message to the appropriate `Account`. Recall that debiting funds from an `Account` decreases both the `totalBalance` and the `availableBalance`. To dispense the requested amount of cash, the `Withdrawal` sends a `dispenseCash` message to the `CashDispenser`. Finally, the `Withdrawal` sends a `displayMessage` message to the `Screen`, instructing the user to take the cash.

A `Deposit` responds to an `execute` message first by sending a `displayMessage` message to the `Screen` to prompt the user for a deposit amount. The `Deposit` sends a `getInput` message to the `Keypad` to obtain the user's input. The `Deposit` then sends a `displayMessage` message to the `Screen` to tell the user to insert a deposit envelope. To determine whether the deposit slot received an incoming deposit envelope, the `Deposit` sends an `isEnvelopeReceived` message to the `DepositSlot`. The `Deposit` updates the user's account by sending a `credit` message to the `BankDatabase`, which subsequently sends a `credit` message to the user's `Account`. Recall that crediting funds to an `Account` increases the `totalBalance` but not the `availableBalance`.

Interaction Diagrams

Now that we have identified a set of possible collaborations between the objects in our ATM system, let us graphically model these interactions using the UML. The UML provides several types of interaction diagrams that model the behavior of a system by modeling how objects interact with one another. The communication diagram emphasizes which objects participate in collaborations. [*Note:* Communication diagrams were called collaboration diagrams in earlier versions of the UML.] Like the communication diagram, the sequence diagram shows collaborations among objects, but it emphasizes *when* messages are sent between objects *over time*.

Communication Diagrams

Figure 7.28 shows a communication diagram that models the ATM executing a BalanceInquiry. Objects are modeled in the UML as rectangles containing names in the form objectName : ClassName. In this example, which involves only one object of each type, we disregard the object name and list only a colon followed by the class name. [*Note:* Specifying the name of each object in a communication diagram is recommended when modeling multiple objects of the same type.] Communicating objects are connected with solid lines, and messages are passed between objects along these lines in the direction shown by arrows. The name of the message, which appears next to the arrow, is the name of an operation (i.e., a member function) belonging to the receiving object—think of the name as a service that the receiving object provides to sending objects (its "clients").

The solid filled arrow in Fig. 7.28 represents a message—or synchronous call—in the UML and a function call in C++. This arrow indicates that the flow of control is from the sending object (the ATM) to the receiving object (a BalanceInquiry). Since this is a synchronous call, the sending object may not send another message, or do anything at all, until the receiving object processes the message and returns control to the sending object. The sender just waits. For example, in Fig. 7.28, the ATM calls member function execute of a BalanceInquiry and may not send another message until execute has finished and returns control to the ATM. [*Note:* If this were an asynchronous call, represented by a stick arrowhead, the sending object would not have to wait for the receiving object to return control—it would continue sending additional messages immediately following the asynchronous call. Asynchronous calls often can be implemented in C++ using platform-specific libraries provided with your compiler. Such techniques are beyond the scope of this book.]

Sequence of Messages in a Communication Diagram

Figure 7.29 shows a communication diagram that models the interactions among objects in the system when an object of class BalanceInquiry executes. We assume that the object's accountNumber attribute contains the account number of the current user. The collaborations in Fig. 7.29 begin after the ATM sends an execute message to a BalanceInquiry (i.e., the interaction modeled in Fig. 7.28). The number to the left of a message name indicates the order in which the message is passed. The sequence of messages in a communication diagram progresses in numerical order from least to greatest. In this diagram, the numbering starts with message 1 and ends with message 3. The BalanceInquiry first sends a getAvailableBalance message to the BankDatabase (message 1), then sends a getTotal-

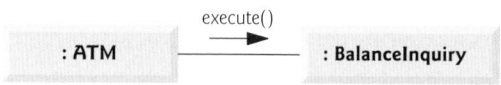

Fig. 7.28 | Communication diagram of the ATM executing a balance inquiry.

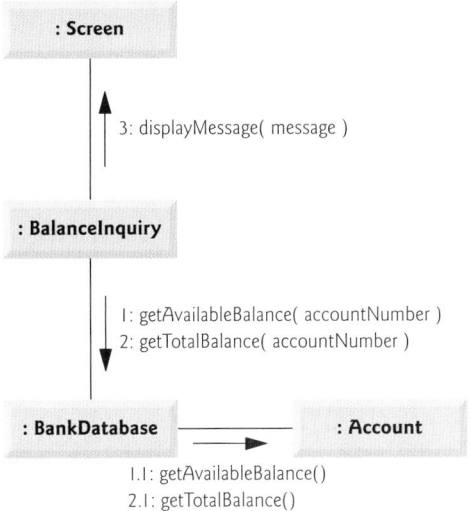

Fig. 7.29 | Communication diagram for executing a balance inquiry.

Balance message to the BankDatabase (message 2). Within the parentheses following a message name, we can specify a comma-separated list of the names of the parameters sent with the message (i.e., arguments in a C++ function call)—the BalanceInquiry passes attribute accountNumber with its messages to the BankDatabase to indicate which Account's balance information to retrieve. Recall from Fig. 6.33 that operations getAvailableBalance and getTotalBalance of class BankDatabase each require a parameter to identify an account. The BalanceInquiry next displays the availableBalance and the totalBalance to the user by passing a displayMessage message to the Screen (message 3) that includes a parameter indicating the message to be displayed.

Note, however, that Fig. 7.29 models two additional messages passing from the BankDatabase to an Account (message 1.1 and message 2.1). To provide the ATM with the two balances of the user's Account (as requested by messages 1 and 2), the BankDatabase must pass a getAvailableBalance and a getTotalBalance message to the user's Account. Such messages passed within the handling of another message are called nested messages. The UML recommends using a decimal numbering scheme to indicate nested messages. For example, message 1.1 is the first message nested in message 1—the BankDatabase passes a getAvailableBalance message during BankDatabase's processing of a message by the same name. [*Note:* If the BankDatabase needed to pass a second nested message while processing message 1, the second message would be numbered 1.2.] A message may be passed only when all the nested messages from the previous message have been passed. For example, the BalanceInquiry passes message 3 only after messages 2 and 2.1 have been passed, in that order.

The nested numbering scheme used in communication diagrams helps clarify precisely when and in what context each message is passed. For example, if we numbered the messages in Fig. 7.29 using a flat numbering scheme (i.e., 1, 2, 3, 4, 5), someone looking at the diagram might not be able to determine that BankDatabase passes the getAvailableBalance message (message 1.1) to an Account *during* the BankDatabase's processing of message 1, as opposed to *after* completing the processing of message 1. The nested decimal numbers make it clear that the second `getAvailableBalance` message (message `1.1`) is passed to an `Account` within the handling of the first `getAvailableBalance` message (message 1) by the `BankDatabase`.

Sequence Diagrams

Communication diagrams emphasize the participants in collaborations but model their timing a bit awkwardly. A sequence diagram helps model the timing of collaborations more clearly. Figure 7.30 shows a sequence diagram modeling the sequence of interactions that occur when a `Withdrawal` executes. The dotted line extending down from an object's rectangle is that object's lifeline, which represents the progression of time. Actions typi-

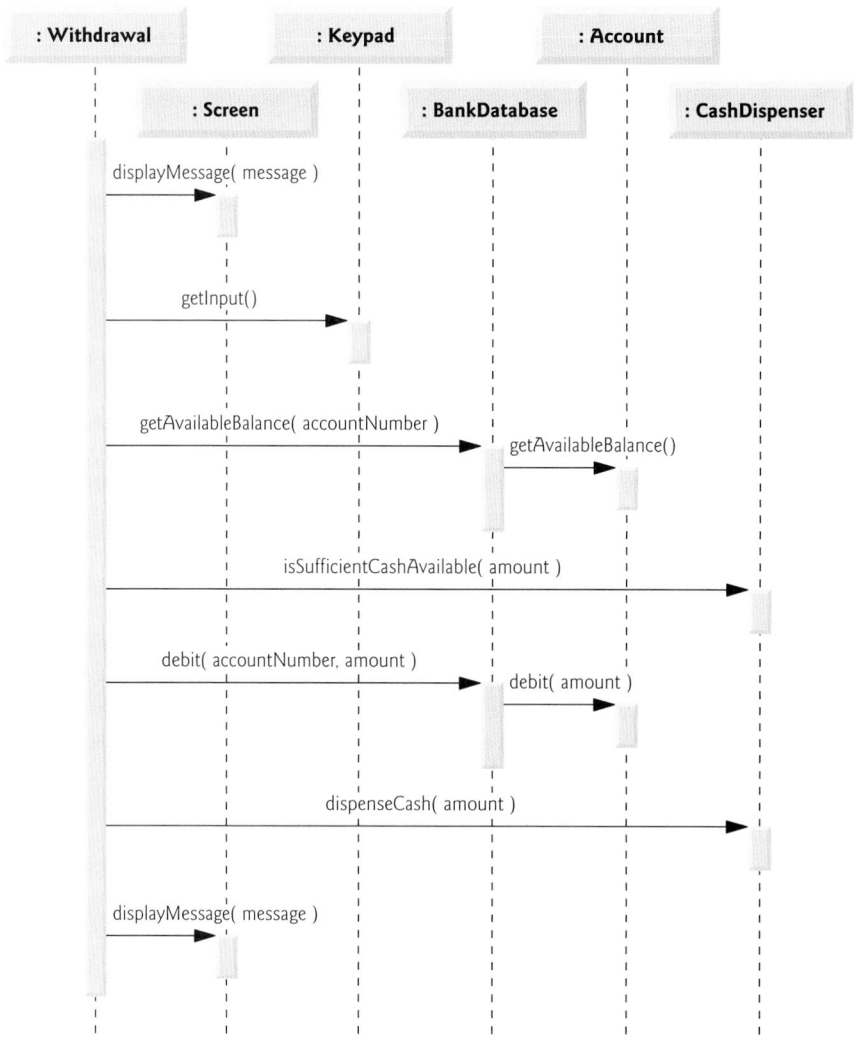

Fig. 7.30 | Sequence diagram that models a `Withdrawal` executing.

cally occur along an object's lifeline in chronological order from top to bottom—an action near the top typically happens before one near the bottom.

Message passing in sequence diagrams is similar to message passing in communication diagrams. A solid arrow with a filled arrowhead extending from the sending object to the receiving object represents a message between two objects. The arrowhead points to an activation on the receiving object's lifeline. An activation, shown as a thin vertical rectangle, indicates that an object is executing. When an object returns control, a return message, represented as a dashed line with a stick arrowhead, extends from the activation of the object returning control to the activation of the object that initially sent the message. To eliminate clutter, we omit the return-message arrows—the UML allows this practice to make diagrams more readable. Like communication diagrams, sequence diagrams can indicate message parameters between the parentheses following a message name.

The sequence of messages in Fig. 7.30 begins when a Withdrawal prompts the user to choose a withdrawal amount by sending a displayMessage message to the Screen. The Withdrawal then sends a getInput message to the Keypad, which obtains input from the user. We have already modeled the control logic involved in a Withdrawal in the activity diagram of Fig. 5.28, so we do not show this logic in the sequence diagram of Fig. 7.30. Instead, we model the best-case scenario in which the balance of the user's account is greater than or equal to the chosen withdrawal amount, and the cash dispenser contains a sufficient amount of cash to satisfy the request. For information on how to model control logic in a sequence diagram, please refer to the Web resources and recommended readings listed at the end of Section 2.8.

After obtaining a withdrawal amount, the Withdrawal sends a getAvailableBalance message to the BankDatabase, which in turn sends a getAvailableBalance message to the user's Account. Assuming that the user's account has enough money available to permit the transaction, the Withdrawal next sends an isSufficientCashAvailable message to the CashDispenser. Assuming that there is enough cash available, the Withdrawal decreases the balance of the user's account (i.e., both the totalBalance and the availableBalance) by sending a debit message to the BankDatabase. The BankDatabase responds by sending a debit message to the user's Account. Finally, the Withdrawal sends a dispenseCash message to the CashDispenser and a displayMessage message to the Screen, telling the user to remove the cash from the machine.

We have identified the collaborations among objects in the ATM system and modeled some of these collaborations using UML interaction diagrams—both communication diagrams and sequence diagrams. In the next "Software Engineering Case Study" section (Section 9.12), we enhance the structure of our model to complete a preliminary object-oriented design, then we begin implementing the ATM system.

Software Engineering Case Study Self-Review Exercises

7.1   A(n) _____ consists of an object of one class sending a message to an object of another class.
   a) association
   b) aggregation
   c) collaboration
   d) composition

7.2   Which form of interaction diagram emphasizes *what* collaborations occur? Which form emphasizes *when* collaborations occur?

7.3 Create a sequence diagram that models the interactions among objects in the ATM system that occur when a Deposit executes successfully, and explain the sequence of messages modeled by the diagram.

Answers to Software Engineering Case Study Self-Review Exercises

7.1 c.

7.2 Communication diagrams emphasize *what* collaborations occur. Sequence diagrams emphasize *when* collaborations occur.

7.3 Figure 7.31 presents a sequence diagram that models the interactions between objects in the ATM system that occur when a Deposit executes successfully. Figure 7.31 indicates that a Deposit first sends a displayMessage message to the Screen to ask the user to enter a deposit amount. Next the Deposit sends a getInput message to the Keypad to receive input from the user. The Deposit then instructs the user to enter a deposit envelope by sending a displayMessage message to the Screen. The Deposit next sends an isEnvelopeReceived message to the DepositSlot to confirm that the deposit envelope has been received by the ATM. Finally, the Deposit increases the totalBalance attribute (but not the availableBalance attribute) of the user's Account by sending a credit message to the BankDatabase. The BankDatabase responds by sending the same message to the user's Account.

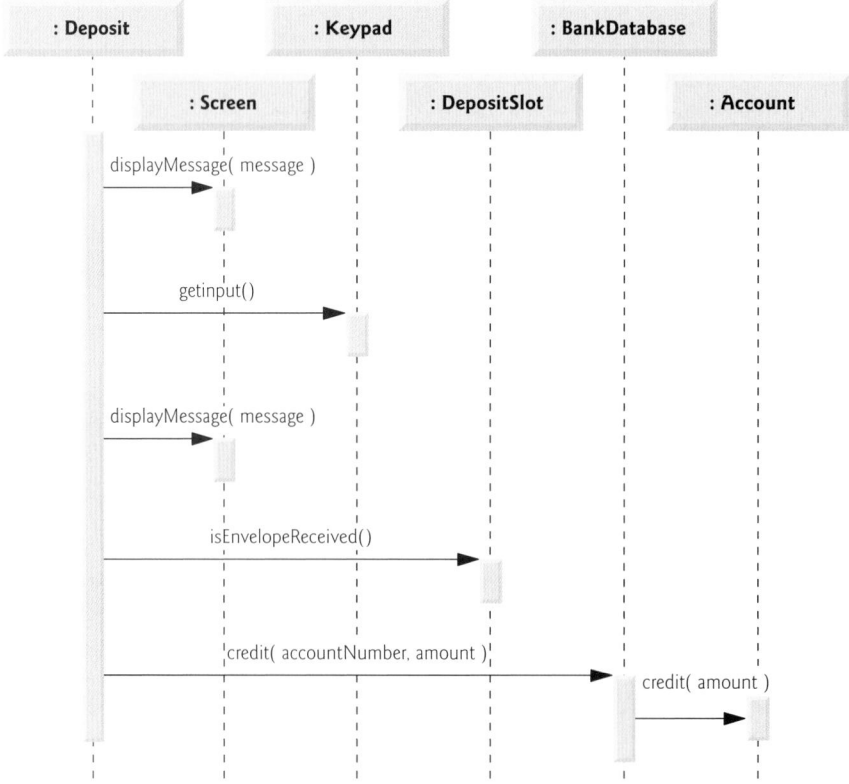

Fig. 7.31 | Sequence diagram that models a Deposit executing.

Summary

- Data structures are collections of related data items. Arrays are data structures consisting of related data items of the same type. Arrays are "static" entities in that they remain the same size throughout program execution. (They may, of course, be of automatic storage class and hence be created and destroyed each time the blocks in which they are defined are entered and exited.)
- An array is a consecutive group of memory locations that share the same type.
- To refer to a particular location or element in an array, we specify the name of the array and the position number of the particular element in the array.
- A program refers to any one of an array's elements by giving the name of the array followed by the position number of the particular element in square brackets ([ ]). The position number is more formally called a subscript or index (this number specifies the number of elements from the beginning of the array).
- The first element in every array has subscript zero and is sometimes called the zeroth element.
- A subscript must be an integer or integer expression (using any integral type).
- It is important to note the difference between the "seventh element of the array" and "array element 7." Array subscripts begin at 0, so the "seventh element of the array" has a subscript of 6, while "array element 7" has a subscript of 7 and is actually the eighth element of the array. This distinction frequently is a source of off-by-one errors.
- The brackets used to enclose the subscript of an array are an operator in C++. Brackets have the same level of precedence as parentheses.
- Arrays occupy space in memory. The programmer specifies the type of each element and the number of elements required by an array as follows:

  type arrayName[*arraySize*] ;

  and the compiler reserves the appropriate amount of memory.
- Arrays can be declared to contain any data type. For example, an array of type char can be used to store a character string.
- The elements of an array can be initialized in the array declaration by following the array name with an equals sign and an initializer list—a comma-separated list (enclosed in braces) of constant initializers. When initializing an array with an initializer list, if there are fewer initializers than elements in the array, the remaining elements are initialized to zero.
- If the array size is omitted from a declaration with an initializer list, the compiler determines the number of elements in the array by counting the number of elements in the initializer list.
- If the array size and an initializer list are specified in an array declaration, the number of initializers must be less than or equal to the array size. Providing more initializers in an array initializer list than there are elements in the array is a compilation error.
- Constants must be initialized with a constant expression when they are declared and cannot be modified thereafter. Constants can be placed anywhere a constant expression is expected.
- C++ has no array bounds checking to prevent the computer from referring to an element that does not exist. Thus, an executing program can "walk off" either end of an array without warning. Programmers should ensure that all array references remain within the bounds of the array.
- A character array can be initialized using a string literal. The size of a character array is determined by the compiler based on the length of the string *plus* a special string-termination character called the null character (represented by the character constant '\0').
- All strings represented by character arrays end with the null character. A character array representing a string should always be declared large enough to hold the number of characters in the string and the terminating null character.

- Character arrays also can be initialized with individual character constants in an initializer list.
- Individual characters in a string can be accessed directly with array subscript notation.
- A string can be input directly into a character array from the keyboard using `cin` and `>>`.
- A character array representing a null-terminated string can be output with `cout` and `<<`.
- A `static` local variable in a function definition exists for the duration of the program but is visible only in the function body.
- A program initializes `static` local arrays when their declarations are first encountered. If a `static` array is not initialized explicitly by the programmer, each element of that array is initialized to zero by the compiler when the array is created.
- To pass an array argument to a function, specify the name of the array without any brackets. To pass an element of an array to a function, use the subscripted name of the array element as an argument in the function call.
- Arrays are passed to functions by reference—the called functions can modify the element values in the callers' original arrays. The value of the name of the array is the address in the computer's memory of the first element of the array. Because the starting address of the array is passed, the called function knows precisely where the array is stored in memory.
- Individual array elements are passed by value exactly as simple variables are. Such simple single pieces of data are called scalars or scalar quantities.
- To receive an array argument, a function's parameter list must specify that the function expects to receive an array. The size of the array is not required between the array brackets.
- C++ provides the type qualifier `const` that can be used to prevent modification of array values in the caller by code in a called function. When an array parameter is preceded by the `const` qualifier, the elements of the array become constant in the function body, and any attempt to modify an element of the array in the function body results in a compilation error.
- The linear search compares each element of an array with a search key. Because the array is not in any particular order, it is just as likely that the value will be found in the first element as the last. On average, therefore, a program must compare the search key with half the elements of the array. To determine that a value is not in the array, the program must compare the search key to every element in the array. The linear searching method works well for small arrays and is acceptable for unsorted arrays.
- An array can be sorted using insertion sort. The first iteration of this algorithm takes the second element and, if it is less than the first element, swaps it with the first element (i.e., the program *inserts* the second element in front of the first element). The second iteration looks at the third element and inserts it into the correct position with respect to the first two elements, so all three elements are in order. At the ith iteration of this algorithm, the first i elements in the original array will be sorted. For small arrays, the insertion sort is acceptable, but for larger arrays it is inefficient compared to other more sophisticated sorting algorithms.
- Multidimensional arrays with two dimensions are often used to represent tables of values consisting of information arranged in rows and columns.
- Arrays that require two subscripts to identify a particular element are called two-dimensional arrays. An array with m rows and n columns is called an m-by-n array.
- C++ Standard Library class template `vector` represents a more robust alternative to arrays featuring many capabilities that are not provided for C-style pointer-based arrays.
- By default, all the elements of an integer `vector` object are set to 0.
- A `vector` can be defined to store any data type using a declaration of the form

        vector< *type* > *name*(*size*);

- Member function `size` of class template `vector` returns the number of elements in the `vector` on which it is invoked.
- The value of an element of a `vector` can be accessed or modified using square brackets (`[]`).
- Objects of standard class template `vector` can be compared directly with the equality (`==`) and inequality (`!=`) operators. The assignment (`=`) operator can also be used with `vector` objects.
- An unmodifiable *lvalue* is an expression that identifies an object in memory (such as an element in a `vector`), but cannot be used to modify that object. A modifiable *lvalue* also identifies an object in memory, but can be used to modify the object.
- Standard class template `vector` provides bounds checking in its member function `at`, which "throws an exception" if its argument is an invalid subscript. By default, this causes a C++ program to terminate.

Terminology

2-D array	null character (`'\0'`)
`a[ i ]`	off-by-one error
`a[ i ][ j ]`	one-dimensional array
array	pass-by-reference
array initializer list	passing arrays to functions
`at` member function of `vector`	position number
bounds checking	read-only variables
column of a two-dimensional array	row of a two-dimensional array
column subscript	row subscript
`const` type qualifier	scalability
constant variable	scalar
data structure	scalar quantity
declare an array	search an array
element of an array	search key
index	`size` member function of `vector`
index zero	sort an array
initialize an array	square brackets `[]`
initializer	`static` data member
initializer list	string represented by a character array
insertion sort	subscript
key value	table of values
linear search of an array	tabular format
magic number	two-dimensional array
m-by-*n* array	unmodifiable *lvalue*
modifiable *lvalue*	value of an element
multidimensional array	vector (C++ Standard Library class template)
name of an array	"walk off" an array
named constant	zeroth element

Self-Review Exercises

7.1   Answer each of the following:
   a)   Lists and tables of values can be stored in _____ or _____.
   b)   The elements of an array are related by the fact that they have the same _____ and _____.

c) The number used to refer to a particular element of an array is called its _____.

d) A(n) _____ should be used to declare the size of an array, because it makes the program more scalable.

e) The process of placing the elements of an array in order is called _____ the array.

f) The process of determining if an array contains a particular key value is called _____ the array.

g) An array that uses two subscripts is referred to as a(n) _____ array.

7.2 State whether the following are *true* or *false*. If the answer is *false*, explain why.

a) An array can store many different types of values.

b) An array subscript should normally be of data type float.

c) If there are fewer initializers in an initializer list than the number of elements in the array, the remaining elements are initialized to the last value in the initializer list.

d) It is an error if an initializer list contains more initializers than there are elements in the array.

e) An individual array element that is passed to a function and modified in that function will contain the modified value when the called function completes execution.

7.3 Write one or more statements that perform the following tasks for and array called fractions:

a) Define a constant variable arraySize initialized to 10.

b) Declare an array with arraySize elements of type double, and initialize the elements to 0.

c) Name the fourth element of the array.

d) Refer to array element 4.

e) Assign the value 1.667 to array element 9.

f) Assign the value 3.333 to the seventh element of the array.

g) Print array elements 6 and 9 with two digits of precision to the right of the decimal point, and show the output that is actually displayed on the screen.

h) Print all the array elements using a for statement. Define the integer variable i as a control variable for the loop. Show the output.

7.4 Answer the following questions regarding an array called table:

a) Declare the array to be an integer array and to have 3 rows and 3 columns. Assume that the constant variable arraySize has been defined to be 3.

b) How many elements does the array contain?

c) Use a for repetition statement to initialize each element of the array to the sum of its subscripts. Assume that the integer variables i and j are declared as control variables.

d) Write a program segment to print the values of each element of array table in tabular format with 3 rows and 3 columns. Assume that the array was initialized with the declaration

```
int table[ arraySize ][ arraySize ] = { { 1, 8 }, { 2, 4, 6 }, { 5 } };
```

and the integer variables i and j are declared as control variables. Show the output.

7.5 Find the error in each of the following program segments and correct the error:

a) #include <iostream>;

b) arraySize = 10; // arraySize was declared const

c) Assume that int b[10] = { 0 };
```
for ( int i = 0; i <= 10; i++ )
    b[ i ] = 1;
```

d) Assume that int a[2][2] = { { 1, 2 }, { 3, 4 } };
```
a[ 1, 1 ] = 5;
```

Answers to Self-Review Exercises

7.1   a) arrays, vectors. b) name, type. c) subscript (or index). d) constant variable. e) sorting. f) searching. g) two-dimensional.

7.2   a) False. An array can store only values of the same type.
b) False. An array subscript should be an integer or an integer expression.
c) False. The remaining elements are initialized to zero.
d) True.
e) False. Individual elements of an array are passed by value. If the entire array is passed to a function, then any modifications will be reflected in the original.

7.3   a) `const int arraySize = 10;`
b) `double fractions[ arraySize ] = { 0.0 };`
c) `fractions[ 3 ]`
d) `fractions[ 4 ]`
e) `fractions[ 9 ] = 1.667;`
f) `fractions[ 6 ] = 3.333;`
g) `cout << fixed << setprecision( 2 );`
`cout << fractions[ 6 ] << ' ' << fractions[ 9 ] << endl;`
Output: 3.33 1.67.
h) `for ( int i = 0; i < arraySize; i++ )`
`    cout << "fractions[" << i << "] = " << fractions[ i ] << endl;`
Output:
```
fractions[ 0 ] = 0.0
fractions[ 1 ] = 0.0
fractions[ 2 ] = 0.0
fractions[ 3 ] = 0.0
fractions[ 4 ] = 0.0
fractions[ 5 ] = 0.0
fractions[ 6 ] = 3.333
fractions[ 7 ] = 0.0
fractions[ 8 ] = 0.0
fractions[ 9 ] = 1.667
```

7.4   a) `int table[ arraySize ][ arraySize ];`
b) Nine.
c) `for ( i = 0; i < arraySize; i++ )`

```
    for ( j = 0; j < arraySize; j++ )
        table[ i ][ j ] = i + j;
```
d) `cout << "      [0]  [1]  [2]" << endl;`

```
for ( int i = 0; i < arraySize; i++ ) {
    cout << '[' << i << "] ";

    for ( int j = 0; j < arraySize; j++ )
       cout << setw( 3 ) << table[ i ][ j ] << "  ";

    cout << endl;
```

Output:
```
    [0]  [1]  [2]
```

```
[0]   1   8   0
[1]   2   4   6
[2]   5   0   0
```

7.5   a) Error: Semicolon at end of #include preprocessor directive.
           Correction: Eliminate semicolon.
       b) Error: Assigning a value to a constant variable using an assignment statement.
           Correction: Initialize the constant variable in a const int arraySize declaration.
       c) Error: Referencing an array element outside the bounds of the array (b[10]).
           Correction: Change the final value of the control variable to 9.
       d) Error: Array subscripting done incorrectly.
           Correction: Change the statement to a[1][1] = 5;

Exercises

7.6   Fill in the blanks in each of the following:
       a) The names of the four elements of array p (int p[4];) are _____, _____,
           _____ and _____.
       b) Naming an array, stating its type and specifying the number of elements in the array is
           called _____ the array.
       c) By convention, the first subscript in a two-dimensional array identifies an element's
           _____ and the second subscript identifies an element's _____.
       d) An *m*-by-*n* array contains _____ rows, _____ columns and _____ el-
           ements.
       e) The name of the element in row 3 and column 5 of array d is _____.

7.7   Determine whether each of the following is *true* or *false*. If *false*, explain why.
       a) To refer to a particular location or element within an array, we specify the name of the
           array and the value of the particular element.
       b) An array declaration reserves space for the array.
       c) To indicate that 100 locations should be reserved for integer array p, the programmer
           writes the declaration

               p[100];

       d) A for statement must be used to initialize the elements of a 15-element array to zero.
       e) Nested for statements must be used to total the elements of a two-dimensional array.

7.8   Write C++ statements to accomplish each of the following:
       a) Display the value of element 6 of character array f.
       b) Input a value into element 4 of one-dimensional floating-point array b.
       c) Initialize each of the 5 elements of one-dimensional integer array g to 8.
       d) Total and print the elements of floating-point array c of 100 elements.
       e) Copy array a into the first portion of array b. Assume double a[11], b[34];
       f) Determine and print the smallest and largest values contained in 99-element floating-
           point array w.

7.9   Consider a 2-by-3 integer array t.
       a) Write a declaration for t.
       b) How many rows does t have?
       c) How many columns does t have?
       d) How many elements does t have?
       e) Write the names of all the elements in row 1 of t.
       f) Write the names of all the elements in column 2 of t.

g) Write a single statement that sets the element of t in row 1 and column 2 to zero.
h) Write a series of statements that initialize each element of t to zero. Do not use a loop.
i) Write a nested `for` statement that initializes each element of t to zero.
j) Write a statement that inputs the values for the elements of t from the terminal.
k) Write a series of statements that determine and print the smallest value in array t.
l) Write a statement that displays the elements in row 0 of t.
m) Write a statement that totals the elements in column 3 of t.
n) Write a series of statements that prints the array t in neat, tabular format. List the column subscripts as headings across the top and list the row subscripts at the left of each row.

7.10 Use a one-dimensional array to solve the following problem. A company pays its salespeople on a commission basis. The salespeople each receive $200 per week plus 9 percent of their gross sales for that week. For example, a salesperson who grosses $5000 in sales in a week receives $200 plus 9 percent of $5000, or a total of $650. Write a program (using an array of counters) that determines how many of the salespeople earned salaries in each of the following ranges (assume that each salesperson's salary is truncated to an integer amount):

a) $200–$299
b) $300–$399
c) $400–$499
d) $500–$599
e) $600–$699
f) $700–$799
g) $800–$899
h) $900–$999
i) $1000 and over

7.11 *(Bubble Sort)* In the bubble sort algorithm, smaller values gradually "bubble" their way upward to the top of the array like air bubbles rising in water, while the larger values sink to the bottom. The bubble sort makes several passes through the array. On each pass, successive pairs of elements are compared. If a pair is in increasing order (or the values are identical), we leave the values as they are. If a pair is in decreasing order, their values are swapped in the array. Write a program that sorts an array of 10 integers using bubble sort.

7.12 The bubble sort described in Exercise 7.11 is inefficient for large arrays. Make the following simple modifications to improve the performance of the bubble sort:

a) After the first pass, the largest number is guaranteed to be in the highest-numbered element of the array; after the second pass, the two highest numbers are "in place," and so on. Instead of making nine comparisons on every pass, modify the bubble sort to make eight comparisons on the second pass, seven on the third pass, and so on.
b) The data in the array may already be in the proper order or near-proper order, so why make nine passes if fewer will suffice? Modify the sort to check at the end of each pass if any swaps have been made. If none have been made, then the data must already be in the proper order, so the program should terminate. If swaps have been made, then at least one more pass is needed.

7.13 Write single statements that perform the following one-dimensional array operations:

a) Initialize the 10 elements of integer array `counts` to zero.
b) Add 1 to each of the 15 elements of integer array `bonus`.
c) Read 12 values for `double` array `monthlyTemperatures` from the keyboard.
d) Print the 5 values of integer array `bestScores` in column format.

7.14 Find the error(s) in each of the following statements:

a) Assume that: `char str[ 5 ];`

```
cin >> str; // user types "hello"
```

b) Assume that: `int a[ 3 ];`

```
cout << a[ 1 ] << " " << a[ 2 ] << " " << a[ 3 ] << endl;
```

c) `double f[ 3 ] = { 1.1, 10.01, 100.001, 1000.0001 };`

d) Assume that: `double d[ 2 ][ 10 ];`

```
d[ 1, 9 ] = 2.345;
```

7.15   Use a one-dimensional array to solve the following problem. Read in 20 numbers, each of which is between 10 and 100, inclusive. As each number is read, validate it and store it in the array only if it is not a duplicate of a number already read. After reading all the values, display only the unique values that the user entered. Provide for the "worst case" in which all 20 numbers are different. Use the smallest possible array to solve this problem.

7.16   Label the elements of a 3-by-5 one-dimensional array `sales` to indicate the order in which they are set to zero by the following program segment:

```
for ( row = 0; row < 3; row++ )

   for ( column = 0; column < 5; column++ )
      sales[ row ][ column ] = 0;
```

7.17   Write a program that simulates the rolling of two dice. The program should use `rand` to roll the first die and should use `rand` again to roll the second die. The sum of the two values should then be calculated. [*Note:* Each die can show an integer value from 1 to 6, so the sum of the two values will vary from 2 to 12, with 7 being the most frequent sum and 2 and 12 being the least frequent sums.] Figure 7.32 shows the 36 possible combinations of the two dice. Your program should roll the two dice 36,000 times. Use a one-dimensional array to tally the numbers of times each possible sum appears. Print the results in a tabular format. Also, determine if the totals are reasonable (i.e., there are six ways to roll a 7, so approximately one-sixth of all the rolls should be 7).

	1	2	3	4	5	6
1	2	3	4	5	6	7
2	3	4	5	6	7	8
3	4	5	6	7	8	9
4	5	6	7	8	9	10
5	6	7	8	9	10	11
6	7	8	9	10	11	12

Fig. 7.32 | The 36 possible outcomes of rolling two dice.

7.18   What does the following program do?

```
1   // Ex. 7.18: Ex07_18.cpp
2   // What does this program do?
3   #include <iostream>
4   using std::cout;
5   using std::endl;
6
7   int whatIsThis( int [], int ); // function prototype
8
9   int main()
```

```
10  {
11      const int arraySize = 10;
12      int a[ arraySize ] = { 1, 2, 3, 4, 5, 6, 7, 8, 9, 10 };
13
14      int result = whatIsThis( a, arraySize );
15
16      cout << "Result is " << result << endl;
17      return 0; // indicates successful termination
18  } // end main
19
20  // What does this function do?
21  int whatIsThis( int b[], int size )
22  {
23      if ( size == 1 ) // base case
24          return b[ 0 ];
25      else // recursive step
26          return b[ size - 1 ] + whatIsThis( b, size - 1 );
27  } // end function whatIsThis
```

7.19 Modify the program of Fig. 6.11 to play 1000 games of craps. The program should keep track of the statistics and answer the following questions:

    a) How many games are won on the 1st roll, 2nd roll, ..., 20th roll, and after the 20th roll?

    b) How many games are lost on the 1st roll, 2nd roll, ..., 20th roll, and after the 20th roll?

    c) What are the chances of winning at craps? [*Note:* You should discover that craps is one of the fairest casino games. What do you suppose this means?]

    d) What is the average length of a game of craps?

    e) Do the chances of winning improve with the length of the game?

7.20 (*Airline Reservations System*) A small airline has just purchased a computer for its new automated reservations system. You have been asked to program the new system. You are to write a program to assign seats on each flight of the airline's only plane (capacity: 10 seats).

Your program should display the following menu of alternatives—Please type 1 for "First Class" and Please type 2 for "Economy". If the person types 1, your program should assign a seat in the first class section (seats 1-5). If the person types 2, your program should assign a seat in the economy section (seats 6-10). Your program should print a boarding pass indicating the person's seat number and whether it is in the first class or economy section of the plane.

Use a one-dimensional array to represent the seating chart of the plane. Initialize all the elements of the array to 0 to indicate that all seats are empty. As each seat is assigned, set the corresponding elements of the array to 1 to indicate that the seat is no longer available.

Your program should, of course, never assign a seat that has already been assigned. When the first class section is full, your program should ask the person if it is acceptable to be placed in the economy section (and vice versa). If yes, then make the appropriate seat assignment. If no, then print the message "Next flight leaves in 3 hours."

7.21 What does the following program do?

```
1  // Ex. 7.21: Ex07_21.cpp
2  // What does this program do?
3  #include <iostream>
4  using std::cout;
5  using std::endl;
6
7  void someFunction( int [], int, int ); // function prototype
8
```

```
 9   int main()
10   {
11      const int arraySize = 10;
12      int a[ arraySize ] = { 1, 2, 3, 4, 5, 6, 7, 8, 9, 10 };
13
14      cout << "The values in the array are:" << endl;
15      someFunction( a, 0, arraySize );
16      cout << endl;
17      return 0; // indicates successful termination
18   } // end main
19
20   // What does this function do?
21   void someFunction( int b[], int current, int size )
22   {
23      if ( current < size )
24      {
25         someFunction( b, current + 1, size );
26         cout << b[ current ] << "   ";
27      } // end if
28   } // end function someFunction
```

7.22   Use a two-dimensional array to solve the following problem. A company has four salespeople (1 to 4) who sell five different products (1 to 5). Once a day, each salesperson passes in a slip for each different type of product sold. Each slip contains the following:

a) The salesperson number
b) The product number
c) The total dollar value of that product sold that day

Thus, each salesperson passes in between 0 and 5 sales slips per day. Assume that the information from all of the slips for last month is available. Write a program that will read all this information for last month's sales and summarize the total sales by salesperson by product. All totals should be stored in the two-dimensional array sales. After processing all the information for last month, print the results in tabular format with each of the columns representing a particular salesperson and each of the rows representing a particular product. Cross total each row to get the total sales of each product for last month; cross total each column to get the total sales by salesperson for last month. Your tabular printout should include these cross totals to the right of the totaled rows and to the bottom of the totaled columns.

7.23   (*Turtle Graphics*) The Logo language, which is popular among elementary school children, made the concept of *turtle graphics* famous. Imagine a mechanical turtle that walks around the room under the control of a C++ program. The turtle holds a pen in one of two positions, up or down. While the pen is down, the turtle traces out shapes as it moves; while the pen is up, the turtle moves about freely without writing anything. In this problem, you will simulate the operation of the turtle and create a computerized sketchpad as well.

Use a 20-by-20 array floor that is initialized to zeros. Read commands from an array that contains them. Keep track of the current position of the turtle at all times and whether the pen is currently up or down. Assume that the turtle always starts at position (0, 0) of the floor with its pen up. The set of turtle commands your program must process are shown in Fig. 7.33.

Suppose that the turtle is somewhere near the center of the floor. The following "program" would draw and print a 12-by-12 square and end with the pen in the up position:

```
2
5,12
3
5,12
3
```

```
5,12
3
5,12
1
6
9
```

As the turtle moves with the pen down, set the appropriate elements of array floor to 1's. When the 6 command (print) is given, wherever there is a 1 in the array, display an asterisk or some other character you choose. Wherever there is a zero, display a blank. Write a program to implement the turtle graphics capabilities discussed here. Write several turtle graphics programs to draw interesting shapes. Add other commands to increase the power of your turtle graphics language.

7.24   (*Knight's Tour*) One of the more interesting puzzlers for chess buffs is the Knight's Tour problem. The question is this: Can the chess piece called the knight move around an empty chessboard and touch each of the 64 squares once and only once? We study this intriguing problem in depth in this exercise.

The knight makes L-shaped moves (over two in one direction and then over one in a perpendicular direction). Thus, from a square in the middle of an empty chessboard, the knight can make eight different moves (numbered 0 through 7) as shown in Fig. 7.34.

Command	Meaning
1	Pen up
2	Pen down
3	Turn right
4	Turn left
5,10	Move forward 10 spaces (or a number other than 10)
6	Print the 20-by-20 array
9	End of data (sentinel)

Fig. 7.33 | Turtle graphics commands.

Fig. 7.34 | The eight possible moves of the knight.

a) Draw an 8-by-8 chessboard on a sheet of paper and attempt a Knight's Tour by hand. Put a 1 in the first square you move to, a 2 in the second square, a 3 in the third, etc. Before starting the tour, estimate how far you think you will get, remembering that a full tour consists of 64 moves. How far did you get? Was this close to your estimate?

b) Now let us develop a program that will move the knight around a chessboard. The board is represented by an 8-by-8 two-dimensional array board. Each of the squares is initialized to zero. We describe each of the eight possible moves in terms of both their horizontal and vertical components. For example, a move of type 0, as shown in Fig. 7.34, consists of moving two squares horizontally to the right and one square vertically upward. Move 2 consists of moving one square horizontally to the left and two squares vertically upward. Horizontal moves to the left and vertical moves upward are indicated with negative numbers. The eight moves may be described by two one-dimensional arrays, horizontal and vertical, as follows:

```
horizontal[ 0 ] = 2
horizontal[ 1 ] = 1
horizontal[ 2 ] = -1
horizontal[ 3 ] = -2
horizontal[ 4 ] = -2
horizontal[ 5 ] = -1
horizontal[ 6 ] = 1
horizontal[ 7 ] = 2

vertical[ 0 ] = -1
vertical[ 1 ] = -2
vertical[ 2 ] = -2
vertical[ 3 ] = -1
vertical[ 4 ] = 1
vertical[ 5 ] = 2
vertical[ 6 ] = 2
vertical[ 7 ] = 1
```

Let the variables currentRow and currentColumn indicate the row and column of the knight's current position. To make a move of type moveNumber, where moveNumber is between 0 and 7, your program uses the statements

```
currentRow += vertical[ moveNumber ];
currentColumn += horizontal[ moveNumber ];
```

Keep a counter that varies from 1 to 64. Record the latest count in each square the knight moves to. Remember to test each potential move to see if the knight has already visited that square, and, of course, test every potential move to make sure that the knight does not land off the chessboard. Now write a program to move the knight around the chessboard. Run the program. How many moves did the knight make?

c) After attempting to write and run a Knight's Tour program, you have probably developed some valuable insights. We will use these to develop a heuristic (or strategy) for moving the knight. Heuristics do not guarantee success, but a carefully developed heuristic greatly improves the chance of success. You may have observed that the outer squares are more troublesome than the squares nearer the center of the board. In fact, the most troublesome, or inaccessible, squares are the four corners.

Intuition may suggest that you should attempt to move the knight to the most troublesome squares first and leave open those that are easiest to get to, so when the board gets congested near the end of the tour, there will be a greater chance of success.

We may develop an "accessibility heuristic" by classifying each square according to how accessible it is and then always moving the knight to the square (within the knight's L-shaped moves, of course) that is most inaccessible. We label a two-dimensional array `accessibility` with numbers indicating from how many squares each particular square is accessible. On a blank chessboard, each center square is rated as 8, each corner square is rated as 2 and the other squares have accessibility numbers of 3, 4 or 6 as follows:

```
2  3  4  4  4  4  3  2
3  4  6  6  6  6  4  3
4  6  8  8  8  8  6  4
4  6  8  8  8  8  6  4
4  6  8  8  8  8  6  4
4  6  8  8  8  8  6  4
3  4  6  6  6  6  4  3
2  3  4  4  4  4  3  2
```

Now write a version of the Knight's Tour program using the accessibility heuristic. At any time, the knight should move to the square with the lowest accessibility number. In case of a tie, the knight may move to any of the tied squares. Therefore, the tour may begin in any of the four corners. [*Note:* As the knight moves around the chessboard, your program should reduce the accessibility numbers as more and more squares become occupied. In this way, at any given time during the tour, each available square's accessibility number will remain equal to precisely the number of squares from which that square may be reached.] Run this version of your program. Did you get a full tour? Now modify the program to run 64 tours, one starting from each square of the chessboard. How many full tours did you get?

d) Write a version of the Knight's Tour program which, when encountering a tie between two or more squares, decides what square to choose by looking ahead to those squares reachable from the "tied" squares. Your program should move to the square for which the next move would arrive at a square with the lowest accessibility number.

7.25 (*Knight's Tour: Brute Force Approaches*) In Exercise 7.24, we developed a solution to the Knight's Tour problem. The approach used, called the "accessibility heuristic," generates many solutions and executes efficiently.

As computers continue increasing in power, we will be able to solve more problems with sheer computer power and relatively unsophisticated algorithms. This is the "brute force" approach to problem solving.

a) Use random number generation to enable the knight to walk around the chessboard (in its legitimate L-shaped moves, of course) at random. Your program should run one tour and print the final chessboard. How far did the knight get?

b) Most likely, the preceding program produced a relatively short tour. Now modify your program to attempt 1000 tours. Use a one-dimensional array to keep track of the number of tours of each length. When your program finishes attempting the 1000 tours, it should print this information in neat tabular format. What was the best result?

c) Most likely, the preceding program gave you some "respectable" tours, but no full tours. Now "pull all the stops out" and simply let your program run until it produces a full tour. [*Caution:* This version of the program could run for hours on a powerful computer.] Once again, keep a table of the number of tours of each length, and print this table when the first full tour is found. How many tours did your program attempt before producing a full tour? How much time did it take?

d) Compare the brute force version of the Knight's Tour with the accessibility heuristic version. Which required a more careful study of the problem? Which algorithm was more difficult to develop? Which required more computer power? Could we be certain (in advance) of obtaining a full tour with the accessibility heuristic approach? Could we be certain (in advance) of obtaining a full tour with the brute force approach? Argue the pros and cons of brute force problem solving in general.

7.26 (*Eight Queens*) Another puzzler for chess buffs is the Eight Queens problem. Simply stated: Is it possible to place eight queens on an empty chessboard so that no queen is "attacking" any other, i.e., no two queens are in the same row, the same column, or along the same diagonal? Use the thinking developed in Exercise 7.24 to formulate a heuristic for solving the Eight Queens problem. Run your program. [*Hint:* It is possible to assign a value to each square of the chessboard indicating how many squares of an empty chessboard are "eliminated" if a queen is placed in that square. Each of the corners would be assigned the value 22, as in Fig. 7.35.] Once these "elimination numbers" are placed in all 64 squares, an appropriate heuristic might be: Place the next queen in the square with the smallest elimination number. Why is this strategy intuitively appealing?

7.27 (*Eight Queens: Brute Force Approaches*) In this exercise, you will develop several brute-force approaches to solving the Eight Queens problem introduced in Exercise 7.26.
   a) Solve the Eight Queens exercise, using the random brute force technique developed in Exercise 7.25.
   b) Use an exhaustive technique, i.e., try all possible combinations of eight queens on the chessboard.

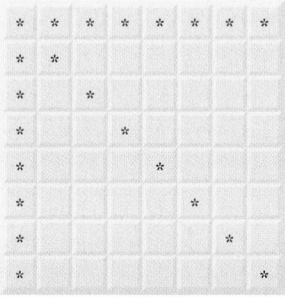

Fig. 7.35 | The 22 squares eliminated by placing a queen in the upper-left corner.

   c) Why do you suppose the exhaustive brute force approach may not be appropriate for solving the Knight's Tour problem?
   d) Compare and contrast the random brute force and exhaustive brute force approaches in general.

7.28 (*Knight's Tour: Closed-Tour Test*) In the Knight's Tour, a full tour occurs when the knight makes 64 moves touching each square of the chess board once and only once. A closed tour occurs when the 64th move is one move away from the location in which the knight started the tour. Modify the Knight's Tour program you wrote in Exercise 7.24 to test for a closed tour if a full tour has occurred.

7.29 (*The Sieve of Eratosthenes*) A prime integer is any integer that is evenly divisible only by itself and 1. The Sieve of Eratosthenes is a method of finding prime numbers. It operates as follows:

    a) Create an array with all elements initialized to 1 (true). Array elements with prime subscripts will remain 1. All other array elements will eventually be set to zero. You will ignore elements 0 and 1 in this exercise.

    b) Starting with array subscript 2, every time an array element is found whose value is 1, loop through the remainder of the array and set to zero every element whose subscript is a multiple of the subscript for the element with value 1. For array subscript 2, all elements beyond 2 in the array that are multiples of 2 will be set to zero (subscripts 4, 6, 8, 10, etc.); for array subscript 3, all elements beyond 3 in the array that are multiples of 3 will be set to zero (subscripts 6, 9, 12, 15, etc.); and so on.

When this process is complete, the array elements that are still set to one indicate that the subscript is a prime number. These subscripts can then be printed. Write a program that uses an array of 1000 elements to determine and print the prime numbers between 2 and 999. Ignore element 0 of the array.

7.30   (*Bucket Sort*) A bucket sort begins with a one-dimensional array of positive integers to be sorted and a two-dimensional array of integers with rows subscripted from 0 to 9 and columns subscripted from 0 to $n - 1$, where n is the number of values in the array to be sorted. Each row of the two-dimensional array is referred to as a bucket. Write a function `bucketSort` that takes an integer array and the array size as arguments and performs as follows:

    a) Place each value of the one-dimensional array into a row of the bucket array based on the value's ones digit. For example, 97 is placed in row 7, 3 is placed in row 3 and 100 is placed in row 0. This is called a "distribution pass."

    b) Loop through the bucket array row by row, and copy the values back to the original array. This is called a "gathering pass." The new order of the preceding values in the one-dimensional array is 100, 3 and 97.

    c) Repeat this process for each subsequent digit position (tens, hundreds, thousands, etc.).

On the second pass, 100 is placed in row 0, 3 is placed in row 0 (because 3 has no tens digit) and 97 is placed in row 9. After the gathering pass, the order of the values in the one-dimensional array is 100, 3 and 97. On the third pass, 100 is placed in row 1, 3 is placed in row zero and 97 is placed in row zero (after the 3). After the last gathering pass, the original array is now in sorted order.

    Note that the two-dimensional array of buckets is 10 times the size of the integer array being sorted. This sorting technique provides better performance than a insertion sort, but requires much more memory. The insertion sort requires space for only one additional element of data. This is an example of the space–time trade-off: The bucket sort uses more memory than the insertion sort, but performs better. This version of the bucket sort requires copying all the data back to the original array on each pass. Another possibility is to create a second two-dimensional bucket array and repeatedly swap the data between the two bucket arrays.

Recursion Exercises

7.31   (*Selection Sort*) A selection sort searches an array looking for the smallest element. Then, the smallest element is swapped with the first element of the array. The process is repeated for the subarray beginning with the second element of the array. Each pass of the array results in one element being placed in its proper location. This sort performs comparably to the insertion sort—for an array of n elements, $n - 1$ passes must be made, and for each subarray, $n - 1$ comparisons must be made to find the smallest value. When the subarray being processed contains one element, the array is sorted. Write recursive function `selectionSort` to perform this algorithm.

7.32   (*Palindromes*) A palindrome is a string that is spelled the same way forward and backward. Some examples of palindromes are "radar," "able was i ere i saw elba" and (if blanks are ignored) "a man a plan a canal panama." Write a recursive function `testPalindrome` that returns `true` if the string stored in the array is a palindrome, and `false` otherwise. The function should ignore spaces and punctuation in the string.

7.33 (*Linear Search*) Modify the program in Fig. 7.19 to use recursive function `linearSearch` to perform a linear search of the array. The function should receive an integer array and the size of the array as arguments. If the search key is found, return the array subscript; otherwise, return −1.

7.34 (*Eight Queens*) Modify the Eight Queens program you created in Exercise 7.26 to solve the problem recursively.

7.35 (*Print an array*) Write a recursive function `printArray` that takes an array, a starting subscript and an ending subscript as arguments and returns nothing. The function should stop processing and return when the starting subscript equals the ending subscript.

7.36 (*Print a string backward*) Write a recursive function `stringReverse` that takes a character array containing a string and a starting subscript as arguments, prints the string backward and returns nothing. The function should stop processing and return when the terminating null character is encountered.

7.37 (*Find the minimum value in an array*) Write a recursive function `recursiveMinimum` that takes an integer array, a starting subscript and an ending subscript as arguments, and returns the smallest element of the array. The function should stop processing and return when the starting subscript equals the ending subscript.

vector Exercises

7.38 Use a vector of integers to solve the problem described in Exercise 7.10.

7.39 Modify the dice-rolling program you created in Exercise 7.17 to use a vector to store the numbers of times each possible sum of the two dice appears.

7.40 (*Find the minimum value in a vector*) Modify your solution to Exercise 7.37 to find the minimum value in a vector instead of an array.

Pointers and Pointer-Based Strings

OBJECTIVES

In this chapter you will learn:

- What pointers are.
- The similarities and differences between pointers and references and when to use each.
- To use pointers to pass arguments to functions by reference.
- To use pointer-based C-style strings.
- The close relationships among pointers, arrays and C-style strings.
- To use pointers to functions.
- To declare and use arrays of C-style strings.

8.1 Introduction

This chapter discusses one of the most powerful features of the C++ programming language, the pointer. In Chapter 6, we saw that references can be used to perform pass-by-reference. Pointers also enable pass-by-reference and can be used to create and manipulate dynamic data structures (i.e., data structures that can grow and shrink), such as linked lists, queues, stacks and trees. This chapter explains basic pointer concepts and reinforces the intimate relationship among arrays and pointers. The view of arrays as pointers derives from the C programming language. As we saw in Chapter 7, C++ Standard Library class vector provides an implementation of arrays as full-fledged objects.

Similarly, C++ actually offers two types of strings—string class objects (which we have been using since Chapter 3) and C-style, char * pointer-based strings. This chapter on pointers discusses char * strings to deepen your knowledge of pointers. In fact, the null-terminated strings that we introduced in Section 7.4 and used in Fig. 7.12 are char * pointer-based strings. This chapter also includes a substantial collection of string-processing exercises that use char *strings. C-style, char * pointer-based strings are widely used in legacy C and C++ systems. So, if you work with legacy C or C++ systems, you may be required to manipulate these char * pointer-based strings.

We will examine the use of pointers with classes in Chapter 13, Object-Oriented Programming: Polymorphism, where we will see that the so-called "polymorphic processing" of object-oriented programming is performed with pointers and references. Chapter 21, Data Structures, presents examples of creating and using dynamic data structures that are implemented with pointers.

8.2 **Pointer Variable Declarations and Initialization**

Pointer variables contain memory addresses as their values. Normally, a variable directly contains a specific value. However, a pointer contains the memory address of a variable that, in turn, contains a specific value. In this sense, a variable name directly references a value, and a pointer indirectly references a value (Fig. 8.1). Referencing a value through a pointer is often called indirection. Note that diagrams typically represent a pointer as an arrow from the variable that contains an address to the variable located at that address in memory.

Pointers, like any other variables, must be declared before they can be used. For example, for the pointer in Fig. 8.1, the declaration

```
int *countPtr, count;
```

declares the variable `countPtr` to be of type `int *` (i.e., a pointer to an `int` value) and is read, "`countPtr` is a pointer to `int`" or "`countPtr` points to an object of type `int`." Also, variable `count` in the preceding declaration is declared to be an `int`, not a pointer to an `int`. The `*` in the declaration applies only to `countPtr`. Each variable being declared as a pointer must be preceded by an asterisk (`*`). For example, the declaration

```
double *xPtr, *yPtr;
```

indicates that both `xPtr` and `yPtr` are pointers to `double` values. When `*` appears in a declaration, it is not an operator; rather, it indicates that the variable being declared is a pointer. Pointers can be declared to point to objects of any data type.

 ### Common Programming Error 8.1

*Assuming that the * used to declare a pointer distributes to all variable names in a declaration's comma-separated list of variables can lead to errors. Each pointer must be declared with the * prefixed to the name (either with or without a space in between—the compiler ignores the space). Declaring only one variable per declaration helps avoid these types of errors and improves program readability.*

 ### Good Programming Practice 8.1

Although it is not a requirement, including the letters Ptr in pointer variable names makes it clear that these variables are pointers and that they must be handled appropriately.

Pointers should be initialized either when they are declared or in an assignment. A pointer may be initialized to 0, NULL or an address. A pointer with the value 0 or NULL

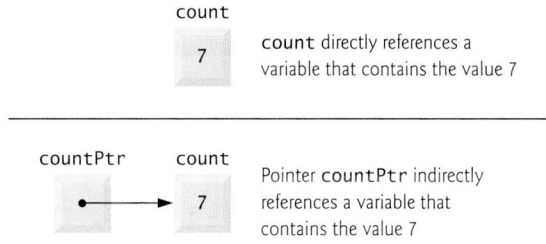

Fig. 8.1 | Directly and indirectly referencing a variable.

points to nothing and is known as a null pointer. Symbolic constant NULL is defined in header file `<iostream>` (and in several other standard library header files) to represent the value 0. Initializing a pointer to NULL is equivalent to initializing a pointer to 0, but in C++, 0 is used by convention. When 0 is assigned, it is converted to a pointer of the appropriate type. The value 0 is the only integer value that can be assigned directly to a pointer variable without casting the integer to a pointer type first. Assigning a variable's numeric address to a pointer is discussed in Section 8.3.

Error-Prevention Tip 8.1

Initialize pointers to prevent pointing to unknown or uninitialized areas of memory.

8.3 Pointer Operators

The address operator (&) is a unary operator that returns the memory address of its operand. For example, assuming the declarations

```
int y = 5; // declare variable y
int *yPtr; // declare pointer variable yPtr
```

the statement

```
yPtr = &y; // assign address of y to yPtr
```

assigns the address of the variable y to pointer variable yPtr. Then variable yPtr is said to "point to" y. Now, yPtr indirectly references variable y's value. Note that the use of the & in the preceding assignment statement is not the same as the use of the & in a reference variable declaration, which is always preceded by a data-type name.

Figure 8.2 shows a schematic representation of memory after the preceding assignment. The "pointing relationship" is indicated by drawing an arrow from the box that represents the pointer yPtr in memory to the box that represents the variable y in memory.

Figure 8.3 shows another representation of the pointer in memory, assuming that integer variable y is stored at memory location 600000 and that pointer variable yPtr is stored at memory location 500000. The operand of the address operator must be an *lvalue* (i.e., something to which a value can be assigned, such as a variable name or a reference); the address operator cannot be applied to constants or to expressions that do not result in references.

The * operator, commonly referred to as the indirection operator or dereferencing operator, returns a synonym (i.e., an alias or a nickname) for the object to which its pointer operand points. For example (referring again to Fig. 8.2), the statement

```
cout << *yPtr << endl;
```

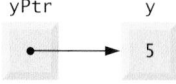

Fig. 8.2 | Graphical representation of a pointer pointing to a variable in memory.

Fig. 8.3 | Representation of y and yPtr in memory.

prints the value of variable y, namely, 5, just as the statement

```
cout << y << endl;
```

would. Using * in this manner is called **dereferencing a pointer**. Note that a dereferenced pointer may also be used on the left side of an assignment statement, as in

```
*yPtr = 9;
```

which would assign 9 to y in Fig. 8.3. The dereferenced pointer may also be used to receive an input value as in

```
cin >> *yPtr;
```

which places the input value in y. The dereferenced pointer is an *lvalue*.

Common Programming Error 8.2

Dereferencing a pointer that has not been properly initialized or that has not been assigned to point to a specific location in memory could cause a fatal execution-time error, or it could accidentally modify important data and allow the program to run to completion, possibly with incorrect results.

Common Programming Error 8.3

An attempt to dereference a variable that is not a pointer is a compilation error.

Common Programming Error 8.4

Dereferencing a null pointer is normally a fatal execution-time error.

The program in Fig. 8.4 demonstrates the & and * pointer operators. Memory locations are output by << in this example as hexadecimal (i.e., base-16) integers. (See Appendix D, Number Systems, for more information on hexadecimal integers.) Note that the hexadecimal memory addresses output by this program are compiler and operating-system dependent, so you may get different results when you run the program.

Portability Tip 8.1

The format in which a pointer is output is compiler dependent. Some systems output pointer values as hexadecimal integers, while others use decimal integers.

Notice that the address of a (line 15) and the value of aPtr (line 16) are identical in the output, confirming that the address of a is indeed assigned to the pointer variable aPtr. The & and * operators are inverses of one another—when they are both applied consecutively to aPtr in either order, they "cancel one another out" and the same result (the value in aPtr) is printed.

```
1   // Fig. 8.4: fig08_04.cpp
2   // Using the & and * operators.
3   #include <iostream>
4   using std::cout;
5   using std::endl;
6
7   int main()
8   {
9      int a; // a is an integer
10     int *aPtr; // aPtr is an int * -- pointer to an integer
11
12     a = 7; // assigned 7 to a
13     aPtr = &a; // assign the address of a to aPtr
14
15     cout << "The address of a is " << &a
16        << "\nThe value of aPtr is " << aPtr;
17     cout << "\n\nThe value of a is " << a
18        << "\nThe value of *aPtr is " << *aPtr;
19     cout << "\n\nShowing that * and & are inverses of "
20        << "each other.\n&*aPtr = " << &*aPtr
21        << "\n*&aPtr = " << *&aPtr << endl;
22     return 0; // indicates successful termination
23  } // end main
```

```
The address of a is 0012F580
The value of aPtr is 0012F580

The value of a is 7
The value of *aPtr is 7

Showing that * and & are inverses of each other.
&*aPtr = 0012F580
*&aPtr = 0012F580
```

Fig. 8.4 | Pointer operators & and *.

Figure 8.5 lists the precedence and associativity of the operators introduced to this point. Note that the address operator (&) and the dereferencing operator (*) are unary operators on the third level of precedence in the chart.

Operators	Associativity	Type
() []	left to right	highest
++ -- static_cast< *type* >(*operand*)	left to right	unary (postfix)
++ -- + - ! & *	right to left	unary (prefix)
* / %	left to right	multiplicative
+ -	left to right	additive

Fig. 8.5 | Operator precedence and associativity. (Part 1 of 2.)

Operators						Associativity	Type
<<	>>					left to right	insertion/extraction
<	<=	>	>=			left to right	relational
==	!=					left to right	equality
&&						left to right	logical AND
||						left to right	logical OR
?:						right to left	conditional
=	+=	-=	*=	/=	%=	right to left	assignment
,						left to right	comma

Fig. 8.5 | Operator precedence and associativity. (Part 2 of 2.)

8.4 Passing Arguments to Functions by Reference with Pointers

There are three ways in C++ to pass arguments to a function—pass-by-value, pass-by-reference with reference arguments and pass-by-reference with pointer arguments. Chapter 6 compared and contrasted pass-by-value and pass-by-reference with reference arguments. In this section, we explain pass-by-reference with pointer arguments.

As we saw in Chapter 6, return can be used to return one value from a called function to a caller (or to return control from a called function without passing back a value). We also saw that arguments can be passed to a function using reference arguments. Such arguments enable the called function to modify the original values of the arguments in the caller. Reference arguments also enable programs to pass large data objects to a function and avoid the overhead of passing the objects by value (which, of course, requires making a copy of the object). Pointers, like references, also can be used to modify one or more variables in the caller or to pass pointers to large data objects to avoid the overhead of passing the objects by value.

In C++, programmers can use pointers and the indirection operator (*) to accomplish pass-by-reference (exactly as pass-by-reference is done in C programs, because C does not have references). When calling a function with an argument that should be modified, the address of the argument is passed. This is normally accomplished by applying the address operator (&) to the name of the variable whose value will be modified.

As we saw in Chapter 7, arrays are not passed using operator &, because the name of the array is the starting location in memory of the array (i.e., an array name is already a pointer). The name of an array, arrayName, is equivalent to &arrayName[0]. When the address of a variable is passed to a function, the indirection operator (*) can be used in the function to form a synonym for the name of the variable—this in turn can be used to modify the value of the variable at that location in the caller's memory.

Figure 8.6 and Fig. 8.7 present two versions of a function that cubes an integer—cubeByValue and cubeByReference. Figure 8.6 passes variable number by value to function cubeByValue (line 15). Function cubeByValue (lines 21–24) cubes its argument and passes the new value back to main using a return statement (line 23). The new value is

```
 1   // Fig. 8.6: fig08_06.cpp
 2   // Cube a variable using pass-by-value.
 3   #include <iostream>
 4   using std::cout;
 5   using std::endl;
 6
 7   int cubeByValue( int ); // prototype
 8
 9   int main()
10   {
11      int number = 5;
12
13      cout << "The original value of number is " << number;
14
15      number = cubeByValue( number ); // pass number by value to cubeByValue
16      cout << "\nThe new value of number is " << number << endl;
17      return 0; // indicates successful termination
18   } // end main
19
20   // calculate and return cube of integer argument
21   int cubeByValue( int n )
22   {
23      return n * n * n; // cube local variable n and return result
24   } // end function cubeByValue
```

```
The original value of number is 5
The new value of number is 125
```

Fig. 8.6 | Pass-by-value used to cube a variable's value.

assigned to number (line 15) in main. Note that the calling function has the opportunity to examine the result of the function call before modifying variable number's value. For example, in this program, we could have stored the result of cubeByValue in another variable, examined its value and assigned the result to number only after determining that the returned value was reasonable.

Figure 8.7 passes the variable number to function cubeByReference using pass-by-reference with a pointer argument (line 15)—the address of number is passed to the function. Function cubeByReference (lines 22–25) specifies parameter nPtr (a pointer to int) to receive its argument. The function dereferences the pointer and cubes the value to which nPtr points (line 24). This directly changes the value of number in main.

 Common Programming Error 8.5

Not dereferencing a pointer when it is necessary to do so to obtain the value to which the pointer points is an error.

A function receiving an address as an argument must define a pointer parameter to receive the address. For example, the header for function cubeByReference (line 22) specifies that cubeByReference receives the address of an int variable (i.e., a pointer to an int) as an argument, stores the address locally in nPtr and does not return a value.

The function prototype for cubeByReference (line 7) contains int * in parentheses. As with other variable types, it is not necessary to include names of pointer parameters in

```
1    // Fig. 8.7: fig08_07.cpp
2    // Cube a variable using pass-by-reference with a pointer argument.
3    #include <iostream>
4    using std::cout;
5    using std::endl;
6
7    void cubeByReference( int * ); // prototype
8
9    int main()
10   {
11      int number = 5;
12
13      cout << "The original value of number is " << number;
14
15      cubeByReference( &number ); // pass number address to cubeByReference
16
17      cout << "\nThe new value of number is " << number << endl;
18      return 0; // indicates successful termination
19   } // end main
20
21   // calculate cube of *nPtr; modifies variable number in main
22   void cubeByReference( int *nPtr )
23   {
24      *nPtr = *nPtr * *nPtr * *nPtr; // cube *nPtr
25   } // end function cubeByReference
```

```
The original value of number is 5
The new value of number is 125
```

Fig. 8.7 | Pass-by-reference with a pointer argument used to cube a variable's value.

function prototypes. Parameter names included for documentation purposes are ignored by the compiler.

Figures 8.8–8.9 analyze graphically the execution of the programs in Fig. 8.6 and Fig. 8.7, respectively.

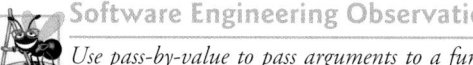

Software Engineering Observation 8.1

Use pass-by-value to pass arguments to a function unless the caller explicitly requires that the called function directly modify the value of the argument variable in the caller. This is another example of the principle of least privilege.

In the function header and in the prototype for a function that expects a one-dimensional array as an argument, the pointer notation in the parameter list of cubeByReference may be used. The compiler does not differentiate between a function that receives a pointer and a function that receives a one-dimensional array. This, of course, means that the function must "know" when it is receiving an array or simply a single variable for which it is to perform pass-by-reference. When the compiler encounters a function parameter for a one-dimensional array of the form int b[], the compiler converts the parameter to the pointer notation int *b (pronounced "b is a pointer to an integer"). Both forms of declaring a function parameter as a one-dimensional array are interchangeable.

Step 1: Before `main` calls `cubeByValue`:

```
int main()                              number
{
    int number = 5;                        5

    number = cubeByValue( number );
}
```

```
int cubeByValue( int n )
{
    return n * n * n;
}
                                            n

                                      undefined
```

Step 2: After `cubeByValue` receives the call:

```
int main()                              number
{
    int number = 5;                        5

    number = cubeByValue( number );
}
```

```
int cubeByValue( int n )
{
    return n * n * n;
}
                                            n

                                            5
```

Step 3: After `cubeByValue` cubes parameter `n` and before `cubeByValue` returns to `main`:

```
int main()                              number
{
    int number = 5;                        5

    number = cubeByValue( number );
}
```

```
int cubeByValue( int n )
{                             125
    return n * n * n;
}
                                            n

                                            5
```

Step 4: After `cubeByValue` returns to `main` and before assigning the result to `number`:

```
int main()                              number
{
    int number = 5;                        5
                         125
    number = cubeByValue( number );
}
```

```
int cubeByValue( int n )
{
    return n * n * n;
}
                                            n

                                      undefined
```

Step 5: After `main` completes the assignment to `number`:

```
int main()                              number
{
    int number = 5;                       125
         125            125
    number = cubeByValue( number );
}
```

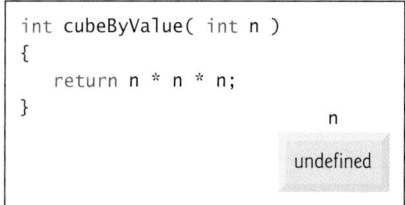

```
int cubeByValue( int n )
{
    return n * n * n;
}
                                            n

                                      undefined
```

Fig. 8.8 | Pass-by-value analysis of the program of Fig. 8.6.

Step 1: Before main calls cubeByReference:

```
int main()
{                                    number
   int number = 5;                      5
   cubeByReference( &number );
}
```

```
void cubeByReference( int *nPtr )
{
   *nPtr = *nPtr * *nPtr * *nPtr;
}
                                       nPtr

                                    undefined
```

Step 2: After cubeByReference receives the call and before *nPtr is cubed:

```
int main()
{                                    number
   int number = 5;                      5
   cubeByReference( &number );
}
```

```
void cubeByReference( int *nPtr )
{
   *nPtr = *nPtr * *nPtr * *nPtr;
}
                                       nPtr
call establishes this pointer
```

Step 3: After *nPtr is cubed and before program control returns to main:

```
int main()
{                                    number
   int number = 5;                     125
   cubeByReference( &number );
}
```

```
void cubeByReference( int *nPtr )
{                                 125
   *nPtr = *nPtr * *nPtr * *nPtr;
}
called function modifies caller's    nPtr
variable
```

Fig. 8.9 | Pass-by-reference analysis (with a pointer argument) of the program of Fig. 8.7.

8.5 Using const with Pointers

Recall that the const qualifier enables the programmer to inform the compiler that the value of a particular variable should not be modified.

Portability Tip 8.2

Although const is well defined in ANSI C and C++, some compilers do not enforce it properly. So a good rule is, "Know your compiler."

Over the years, a large base of legacy code was written in early versions of C that did not use const, because it was not available. For this reason, there are great opportunities for improvement in the software engineering of old (also called "legacy") C code. Also, many programmers currently using ANSI C and C++ do not use const in their programs, because they began programming in early versions of C. These programmers are missing many opportunities for good software engineering.

Many possibilities exist for using (or not using) const with function parameters. How do you choose the most appropriate of these possibilities? Let the principle of least privilege be your guide. Always award a function enough access to the data in its parameters to accomplish its specified task, but no more. This section discusses how to combine `const` with pointer declarations to enforce the principle of least privilege.

Chapter 6 explained that when a function is called using pass-by-value, a copy of the argument (or arguments) in the function call is made and passed to the function. If the copy is modified in the function, the original value is maintained in the caller without change. In many cases, a value passed to a function is modified so the function can accomplish its task. However, in some instances, the value should not be altered in the called function, even though the called function manipulates only a copy of the original value.

For example, consider a function that takes a one-dimensional array and its size as arguments and subsequently prints the array. Such a function should loop through the array and output each array element individually. The size of the array is used in the function body to determine the highest subscript of the array so the loop can terminate when the printing completes. The size of the array does not change in the function body, so it should be declared `const`. Of course, because the array is only being printed, it, too, should be declared `const`. This is especially important because an entire array is *always* passed by reference and could easily be changed in the called function.

Software Engineering Observation 8.2

If a value does not (or should not) change in the body of a function to which it is passed, the parameter should be declared `const` to ensure that it is not accidentally modified.

If an attempt is made to modify a `const` value, a warning or an error is issued, depending on the particular compiler.

Error-Prevention Tip 8.2

Before using a function, check its function prototype to determine the parameters that it can modify.

There are four ways to pass a pointer to a function: a nonconstant pointer to nonconstant data (Fig. 8.10), a nonconstant pointer to constant data (Fig. 8.11 and Fig. 8.12), a constant pointer to nonconstant data (Fig. 8.13) and a constant pointer to constant data (Fig. 8.14). Each combination provides a different level of access privileges.

Nonconstant Pointer to Nonconstant Data

The highest access is granted by a nonconstant pointer to nonconstant data—the data can be modified through the dereferenced pointer, and the pointer can be modified to point to other data. The declaration for a nonconstant pointer to nonconstant data does not include `const`. Such a pointer can be used to receive a null-terminated string in a function that changes the pointer value to process (and possibly modify) each character in the string. Recall from Section 7.4 that a null-terminated string can be placed in a character array that contains the characters of the string and a null character indicating where the string ends.

In Fig. 8.10, function `convertToUppercase` (lines 25–34) declares parameter `sPtr` (line 25) to be a nonconstant pointer to nonconstant data (again, `const` is not used). The function processes one character at a time from the null-terminated string stored in character array `phrase` (lines 27–33). Keep in mind that a character array's name is really equivalent to a pointer to the first character of the array, so passing `phrase` as an argument to `convertToUppercase` is possible. Function `islower` (line 29) takes a character argument and returns true if the character is a lowercase letter and false otherwise. Char-

```
1   // Fig. 8.10: fig08_10.cpp
2   // Converting lowercase letters to uppercase letters
3   // using a non-constant pointer to non-constant data.
4   #include <iostream>
5   using std::cout;
6   using std::endl;
7
8   #include <cctype> // prototypes for islower and toupper
9   using std::islower;
10  using std::toupper;
11
12  void convertToUppercase( char * );
13
14  int main()
15  {
16     char phrase[] = "characters and $32.98";
17
18     cout << "The phrase before conversion is: " << phrase;
19     convertToUppercase( phrase );
20     cout << "\nThe phrase after conversion is:  " << phrase << endl;
21     return 0; // indicates successful termination
22  } // end main
23
24  // convert string to uppercase letters
25  void convertToUppercase( char *sPtr )
26  {
27     while ( *sPtr != '\0' ) // loop while current character is not '\0'
28     {
29        if ( islower( *sPtr ) ) // if character is lowercase,
30           *sPtr = toupper( *sPtr ); // convert to uppercase
31
32        sPtr++; // move sPtr to next character in string
33     } // end while
34  } // end function convertToUppercase
```

```
The phrase before conversion is: characters and $32.98
The phrase after conversion is:  CHARACTERS AND $32.98
```

Fig. 8.10 | Converting a string to uppercase.

acters in the range 'a' through 'z' are converted to their corresponding uppercase letters by function toupper (line 30); others remain unchanged—function toupper takes one character as an argument. If the character is a lowercase letter, the corresponding uppercase letter is returned; otherwise, the original character is returned. Function toupper and function islower are part of the character-handling library <cctype>. After processing one character, line 32 increments sPtr by 1 (this would not be possible if sPtr were declared const). When operator ++ is applied to a pointer that points to an array, the memory address stored in the pointer is modified to point to the next element of the array (in this case, the next character in the string). Adding one to a pointer is one valid operation in **pointer arithmetic**, which is covered in detail in Section 8.8 and Section 8.9.

Nonconstant Pointer to Constant Data

A nonconstant pointer to constant data is a pointer that can be modified to point to any data item of the appropriate type, but the data to which it points cannot be modified through that pointer. Such a pointer might be used to receive an array argument to a function that will process each element of the array, but should not be allowed to modify the data. For example, function printCharacters (lines 22–26 of Fig. 8.11) declares parameter sPtr (line 22) to be of type const char *, so that it can receive a null-terminated pointer-based string. The declaration is read from right to left as "sPtr is a pointer to a character constant." The body of the function uses a for statement (lines 24–25) to output each character in the string until the null character is encountered. After each character is printed, pointer sPtr is incremented to point to the next character in the string (this works because the pointer is not const). Function main creates char array phrase to be passed to printCharacters. Again, we can pass the array phrase to printCharacters because the name of the array is really a pointer to the first character in the array.

Figure 8.12 demonstrates the compilation error messages produced when attempting to compile a function that receives a nonconstant pointer to constant data, then tries to use that pointer to modify the data. [*Note:* Remember that compiler error messages vary among compilers.]

```
1   // Fig. 8.11: fig08_11.cpp
2   // Printing a string one character at a time using
3   // a non-constant pointer to constant data.
4   #include <iostream>
5   using std::cout;
6   using std::endl;
7
8   void printCharacters( const char * ); // print using pointer to const data
9
10  int main()
11  {
12     const char phrase[] = "print characters of a string";
13
14     cout << "The string is:\n";
15     printCharacters( phrase ); // print characters in phrase
16     cout << endl;
17     return 0; // indicates successful termination
18  } // end main
19
20  // sPtr can be modified, but it cannot modify the character to which
21  // it points, i.e., sPtr is a "read-only" pointer
22  void printCharacters( const char *sPtr )
23  {
24     for ( ; *sPtr != '\0'; sPtr++ ) // no initialization
25        cout << *sPtr; // display character without modification
26  } // end function printCharacters
```

```
The string is:
print characters of a string
```

Fig. 8.11 | Printing a string one character at a time using a nonconstant pointer to constant data.

```
 1  // Fig. 8.12: fig08_12.cpp
 2  // Attempting to modify data through a
 3  // non-constant pointer to constant data.
 4
 5  void f( const int * ); // prototype
 6
 7  int main()
 8  {
 9     int y;
10
11     f( &y ); // f attempts illegal modification
12     return 0; // indicates successful termination
13  } // end main
14
15  // xPtr cannot modify the value of constant variable to which it points
16  void f( const int *xPtr )
17  {
18     *xPtr = 100; // error: cannot modify a const object
19  } // end function f
```

Borland C++ command-line compiler error message:

```
Error E2024 fig08_12.cpp 18:
   Cannot modify a const object in function f(const int *)
```

Microsoft Visual C++ compiler error message:

```
c:\cpphtp5_examples\ch08\Fig08_12\fig08_12.cpp(18) :
   error C2166: l-value specifies const object
```

GNU C++ compiler error message:

```
fig08_12.cpp: In function `void f(const int*)':
fig08_12.cpp:18: error: assignment of read-only location
```

Fig. 8.12 | Attempting to modify data through a nonconstant pointer to constant data.

As we know, arrays are aggregate data types that store related data items of the same type under one name. When a function is called with an array as an argument, the array is passed to the function by reference. However, objects are always passed by value—a copy of the entire object is passed. This requires the execution-time overhead of making a copy of each data item in the object and storing it on the function call stack. When an object must be passed to a function, we can use a pointer to constant data (or a reference to constant data) to get the performance of pass-by-reference and the protection of pass-by-value. When a pointer to an object is passed, only a copy of the address of the object must be made; the object itself is not copied. On a machine with four-byte addresses, a copy of four bytes of memory is made rather than a copy of a possibly large object.

Performance Tip 8.1

If they do not need to be modified by the called function, pass large objects using pointers to constant data or references to constant data, to obtain the performance benefits of pass-by-reference.

Software Engineering Observation 8.3

Pass large objects using pointers to constant data, or references to constant data, to obtain the security of pass-by-value.

Constant Pointer to Nonconstant Data

A constant pointer to nonconstant data is a pointer that always points to the same memory location; the data at that location can be modified through the pointer. This is the default for an array name. An array name is a constant pointer to the beginning of the array. All data in the array can be accessed and changed by using the array name and array subscripting. A constant pointer to nonconstant data can be used to receive an array as an argument to a function that accesses array elements using array subscript notation. Pointers that are declared const must be initialized when they are declared. (If the pointer is a function parameter, it is initialized with a pointer that is passed to the function.) The program of Fig. 8.13 attempts to modify a constant pointer. Line 11 declares pointer ptr to be of type int * const. The declaration in the figure is read from right to left as "ptr is a constant pointer to a nonconstant integer." The pointer is initialized with the address of integer variable x. Line 14 attempts to assign the address of y to ptr, but the compiler generates an error message. Note that no error occurs when line 13 assigns the value 7 to

```
 1   // Fig. 8.13: fig08_13.cpp
 2   // Attempting to modify a constant pointer to non-constant data.
 3
 4   int main()
 5   {
 6      int x, y;
 7
 8      // ptr is a constant pointer to an integer that can
 9      // be modified through ptr, but ptr always points to the
10      // same memory location.
11      int * const ptr = &; // const pointer must be initialized
12
13      *ptr = 7; // allowed: *ptr is not const
14      ptr = &y; // error: ptr is const; cannot assign to it a new address
15      return 0; // indicates successful termination
16   } // end main
```

Borland C++ command-line compiler error message:

```
Error E2024 fig08_13.cpp 14: Cannot modify a const object in function main()s
```

Microsoft Visual C++ compiler error message:

```
c:\cpphtp5e_examples\ch08\Fig08_13\fig08_13.cpp(14) : error C2166:
    l-value specifies const object
```

GNU C++ compiler error message:

```
fig08_13.cpp: In function `int main()':
fig08_13.cpp:14: error: assignment of read-only variable `ptr'
```

Fig. 8.13 | Attempting to modify a constant pointer to nonconstant data.

*ptr—the nonconstant value to which ptr points can be modified using the dereferenced ptr, even though ptr itself has been declared const.

 Common Programming Error 8.6

Not initializing a pointer that is declared const is a compilation error.

Constant Pointer to Constant Data

The least amount of access privilege is granted by a constant pointer to constant data. Such a pointer always points to the same memory location, and the data at that memory location cannot be modified using the pointer. This is how an array should be passed to a function that only reads the array, using array subscript notation, and does not modify the array. The program of Fig. 8.14 declares pointer variable ptr to be of type const int * const (line 14). This declaration is read from right to left as "ptr is a constant pointer to an integer constant." The figure shows the error messages generated when an attempt is

```
1   // Fig. 8.14: fig08_14.cpp
2   // Attempting to modify a constant pointer to constant data.
3   #include <iostream>
4   using std::cout;
5   using std::endl;
6
7   int main()
8   {
9      int x = 5, y;
10
11     // ptr is a constant pointer to a constant integer.
12     // ptr always points to the same location; the integer
13     // at that location cannot be modified.
14     const int *const ptr = &x;
15
16     cout << *ptr << endl;
17
18     *ptr = 7; // error: *ptr is const; cannot assign new value
19     ptr = &y; // error: ptr is const; cannot assign new address
20     return 0; // indicates successful termination
21  } // end main
```

Borland C++ command-line compiler error message:

```
Error E2024 fig08_14.cpp 18: Cannot modify a const object in function main()
Error E2024 fig08_14.cpp 19: Cannot modify a const object in function main()
```

Microsoft Visual C++ compiler error message:

```
c:\cpphtp5e_examples\ch08\Fig08_14\fig08_14.cpp(18) : error C2166:
   l-value specifies const object
c:\cpphtp5e_examples\ch08\Fig08_14\fig08_14.cpp(19) : error C2166:
   l-value specifies const object
```

Fig. 8.14 | Attempting to modify a constant pointer to constant data. (Part 1 of 2.)

GNU C++ compiler error message:

```
fig08_14.cpp: In function `int main()':
fig08_14.cpp:18: error: assignment of read-only location
fig08_14.cpp:19: error: assignment of read-only variable `ptr'
```

Fig. 8.14 | Attempting to modify a constant pointer to constant data. (Part 2 of 2.)

made to modify the data to which ptr points (line 18) and when an attempt is made to modify the address stored in the pointer variable (line 19). Note that no errors occur when the program attempts to dereference ptr, or when the program attempts to output the value to which ptr points (line 16), because neither the pointer nor the data it points to is being modified in this statement.

8.6 Selection Sort Using Pass-by-Reference

In this section, we define a sorting program to demonstrate passing arrays and individual array elements by reference. We use the selection sort algorithm, which is an easy-to-program, but unfortunately inefficient, sorting algorithm. The first iteration of the algorithm selects the smallest element in the array and swaps it with the first element. The second iteration selects the second-smallest element (which is the smallest element of the remaining elements) and swaps it with the second element. The algorithm continues until the last iteration selects the second-largest element and swaps it with the second-to-last index, leaving the largest element in the last index. After the ith iteration, the smallest i items of the array will be sorted into increasing order in the first i elements of the array.

As an example, consider the array

34   56   4   10   77   51   93   30   5   52

A program that implements selection sort first determines the smallest element (4) of this array, which is contained in element 2. The program swaps the 4 with the element 0 (34), resulting in

4   56   **34**   10   77   51   93   30   5   52

[*Note:* We use bold to highlight the values that were swapped.] The program then determines the smallest value of the remaining elements (all elements except 4), which is 5, contained in element 8. The program swaps the 5 with the element 1 (56), resulting in

4   **5**   34   10   77   51   93   30   **56**   52

On the third iteration, the program determines the next smallest value (10) and swaps it with the element 2 (34).

4   5   **10**   **34**   77   51   93   30   56   52

The process continues until the array is fully sorted.

4   5   10   30   34   51   52   56   77   93

Note that after the first iteration, the smallest element is in the first position. After the second iteration, the two smallest elements are in order in the first two positions. After the third iteration, the three smallest elements are in order in the first three positions.

Figure 8.15 implements selection sort using two functions—selectionSort and swap. Function selectionSort (lines 36–53) sorts the array. Line 38 declares the variable smallest, which will store the index of the smallest element in the remaining array. Lines 41–52 loop size - 1 times. Line 43 sets the index of the smallest element to the current index. Lines 46–49 loop over the remaining elements in the array. For each of these elements, line 48 compares its value to the value of the smallest element. If the current element is smaller than the smallest element, line 49 assigns the current element's index to smallest. When this loop finishes, smallest will contain the index of the smallest element in the remaining array. Line 51 calls function swap (lines 57–62) to place the smallest remaining element in the next spot in the array (i.e., exchange the array elements array[i] and array[smallest]).

Let us now look more closely at function swap. Remember that C++ enforces information hiding between functions, so swap does not have access to individual array elements in selectionSort. Because selectionSort *wants* swap to have access to the array elements to be swapped, selectionSort passes each of these elements to swap by refer-

```
1    // Fig. 8.15: fig08_15.cpp
2    // This program puts values into an array, sorts the values into
3    // ascending order and prints the resulting array.
4    #include <iostream>
5    using std::cout;
6    using std::endl;
7
8    #include <iomanip>
9    using std::setw;
10
11   void selectionSort( int * const, const int ); // prototype
12   void swap( int * const, int * const ); // prototype
13
14   int main()
15   {
16      const int arraySize = 10;
17      int a[ arraySize ] = { 2, 6, 4, 8, 10, 12, 89, 68, 45, 37 };
18
19      cout << "Data items in original order\n";
20
21      for ( int i = 0; i < arraySize; i++ )
22         cout << setw( 4 ) << a[ i ];
23
24      selectionSort( a, arraySize ); // sort the array
25
26      cout << "\nData items in ascending order\n";
27
28      for ( int j = 0; j < arraySize; j++ )
29         cout << setw( 4 ) << a[ j ];
30
31      cout << endl;
32      return 0; // indicates successful termination
33   } // end main
```

Fig. 8.15 | Selection sort with pass-by-reference. (Part 1 of 2.)

```
34
35   // function to sort an array
36   void selectionSort( int * const array, const int size )
37   {
38      int smallest; // index of smallest element
39
40      // loop over size - 1 elements
41      for ( int i = 0; i < size - 1; i++ )
42      {
43         smallest = i; // first index of remaining array
44
45         // loop to find index of smallest element
46         for ( int index = i + 1; index < size; index++ )
47
48            if ( array[ index ] < array[ smallest ] )
49               smallest = index;
50
51         swap( &array[ i ], &array[ smallest ] );
52      } // end if
53   } // end function selectionSort
54
55   // swap values at memory locations to which
56   // element1Ptr and element2Ptr point
57   void swap( int * const element1Ptr, int * const element2Ptr )
58   {
59      int hold = *element1Ptr;
60      *element1Ptr = *element2Ptr;
61      *element2Ptr = hold;
62   } // end function swap
```

```
Data items in original order
   2    6    4    8   10   12   89   68   45   37
Data items in ascending order
   2    4    6    8   10   12   37   45   68   89
```

Fig. 8.15 | Selection sort with pass-by-reference. (Part 2 of 2.)

ence—the address of each array element is passed explicitly. Although entire arrays are passed by reference, individual array elements are scalars and are ordinarily passed by value. Therefore, selectionSort uses the address operator (&) on each array element in the swap call (line 51) to effect pass-by-reference. Function swap (lines 57–62) receives &array[i] in pointer variable element1Ptr. Information hiding prevents swap from "knowing" the name array[i], but swap can use *element1Ptr as a synonym for array[i]. Thus, when swap references *element1Ptr, it is actually referencing array[i] in selectionSort. Similarly, when swap references *element2Ptr, it is actually referencing array[smallest] in selectionSort.

Even though swap is not allowed to use the statements

```
hold = array[ i ];
array[ i ] = array[ smallest ];
array[ smallest ] = hold;
```

precisely the same effect is achieved by

```
int hold = *element1Ptr;
*element1Ptr = *element2Ptr;
*element2Ptr = hold;
```

in the swap function of Fig. 8.15.

Several features of function selectionSort should be noted. The function header (line 36) declares array as int * const array, rather than int array[], to indicate that function selectionSort receives a one-dimensional array as an argument. Both parameter array's pointer and parameter size are declared const to enforce the principle of least privilege. Although parameter size receives a copy of a value in main and modifying the copy cannot change the value in main, selectionSort does not need to alter size to accomplish its task—the array size remains fixed during the execution of selectionSort. Therefore, size is declared const to ensure that it is not modified. If the size of the array were to be modified during the sorting process, the sorting algorithm would not run correctly.

Note that function selectionSort receives the size of the array as a parameter, because the function must have that information to sort the array. When a pointer-based array is passed to a function, only the memory address of the first element of the array is received by the function; the array size must be passed separately to the function.

By defining function selectionSort to receive the array size as a parameter, we enable the function to be used by any program that sorts one-dimensional int arrays of arbitrary size. The size of the array could have been programmed directly into the function, but this would restrict the function to processing an array of a specific size and reduce the function's reusability—only programs processing one-dimensional int arrays of the specific size "hard coded" into the function could use the function.

Software Engineering Observation 8.4

When passing an array to a function, also pass the size of the array (rather than building into the function knowledge of the array size). This makes the function more reusable.

8.7 *sizeof* Operators

C++ provides the unary operator sizeof to determine the size of an array (or of any other data type, variable or constant) in bytes during program compilation. When applied to the name of an array, as in Fig. 8.16 (line 14), the sizeof operator returns the total number of bytes in the array as a value of type size_t (an alias for unsigned int on most compilers). Note that this is different from the size of a vector< int >, for example, which is the number of integer elements in the vector. The computer we used to compile this program stores variables of type double in 8 bytes of memory, and array is declared to have 20 elements (line 12), so array uses 160 bytes in memory. When applied to a pointer parameter (line 24) in a function that receives an array as an argument, the sizeof operator returns the size of the pointer in bytes (4), not the size of the array.

Common Programming Error 8.7

Using the sizeof operator in a function to find the size in bytes of an array parameter results in the size in bytes of a pointer, not the size in bytes of the array.

```
1   // Fig. 8.16: fig08_16.cpp
2   // Sizeof operator when used on an array name
3   // returns the number of bytes in the array.
4   #include <iostream>
5   using std::cout;
6   using std::endl;
7
8   size_t getSize( double * ); // prototype
9
10  int main()
11  {
12     double array[ 20 ]; // 20 doubles; occupies 160 bytes on our system
13
14     cout << "The number of bytes in the array is " << sizeof( array );
15
16     cout << "\nThe number of bytes returned by getSize is "
17        << getSize( array ) << endl;
18     return 0; // indicates successful termination
19  } // end main
20
21  // return size of ptr
22  size_t getSize( double *ptr )
23  {
24     return sizeof( ptr );
25  } // end function getSize
```

```
The number of bytes in the array is 160
The number of bytes returned by getSize is 4
```

Fig. 8.16 | `sizeof` operator when applied to an array name returns the number of bytes in the array.

[*Note:* When the Borland C++ compiler is used to compile Fig. 8.16, the compiler generates the warning message "Parameter 'ptr' is never used in function get-Size(double *)." This warning occurs because `sizeof` is actually a compile-time operator; thus, variable `ptr` is not used in the function's body at execution time. Many compilers issue warnings like this to let you know that a variable is not being used so that you can either remove it from your code or modify your code to use the variable properly. Similar messages occur in Fig. 8.17 with various compilers.]

The number of elements in an array also can be determined using the results of two `sizeof` operations. For example, consider the following array declaration:

```
double realArray[ 22 ];
```

If variables of data type `double` are stored in eight bytes of memory, array `realArray` contains a total of 176 bytes. To determine the number of elements in the array, the following expression can be used:

```
sizeof realArray / sizeof( double ) // calculate number of elements
```

The expression determines the number of bytes in array `realArray` (176) and divides that value by the number of bytes used in memory to store a `double` value (8); the result is the number of elements in `realArray` (22).

Determining the Sizes of the Fundamental Types, an Array and a Pointer
The program of Fig. 8.17 uses the sizeof operator to calculate the number of bytes used to store most of the standard data types. Notice that, in the output, the types double and long double have the same size. Types may have different sizes based on the system the

```cpp
1   // Fig. 8.17: fig08_17.cpp
2   // Demonstrating the sizeof operator.
3   #include <iostream>
4   using std::cout;
5   using std::endl;
6
7   int main()
8   {
9      char c; // variable of type char
10     short s; // variable of type short
11     int i; // variable of type int
12     long l; // variable of type long
13     float f; // variable of type float
14     double d; // variable of type double
15     long double ld; // variable of type long double
16     int array[ 20 ]; // array of int
17     int *ptr = array; // variable of type int *
18
19     cout << "sizeof c = " << sizeof c
20        << "\tsizeof(char) = " << sizeof( char )
21        << "\nsizeof s = " << sizeof s
22        << "\tsizeof(short) = " << sizeof( short )
23        << "\nsizeof i = " << sizeof i
24        << "\tsizeof(int) = " << sizeof( int )
25        << "\nsizeof l = " << sizeof l
26        << "\tsizeof(long) = " << sizeof( long )
27        << "\nsizeof f = " << sizeof f
28        << "\tsizeof(float) = " << sizeof( float )
29        << "\nsizeof d = " << sizeof d
30        << "\tsizeof(double) = " << sizeof( double )
31        << "\nsizeof ld = " << sizeof ld
32        << "\tsizeof(long double) = " << sizeof( long double )
33        << "\nsizeof array = " << sizeof array
34        << "\nsizeof ptr = " << sizeof ptr << endl;
35     return 0; // indicates successful termination
36  } // end main
```

```
sizeof c = 1     sizeof(char) = 1
sizeof s = 2     sizeof(short) = 2
sizeof i = 4     sizeof(int) = 4
sizeof l = 4     sizeof(long) = 4
sizeof f = 4     sizeof(float) = 4
sizeof d = 8     sizeof(double) = 8
sizeof ld = 8    sizeof(long double) = 8
sizeof array = 80
sizeof ptr = 4
```

Fig. 8.17 | sizeof operator used to determine standard data type sizes.

program is run on. On another system, for example, `double` and `long double` may be defined to be of different sizes.

Portability Tip 8.3

The number of bytes used to store a particular data type may vary between systems. When writing programs that depend on data type sizes, and that will run on several computer systems, use `sizeof` *to determine the number of bytes used to store the data types.*

Operator `sizeof` can be applied to any variable name, type name or constant value. When `sizeof` is applied to a variable name (which is not an array name) or a constant value, the number of bytes used to store the specific type of variable or constant is returned. Note that the parentheses used with `sizeof` are required only if a type name (e.g., `int`) is supplied as its operand. The parentheses used with `sizeof` are not required when `sizeof`'s operand is a variable name or constant. Remember that `sizeof` is an operator, not a function, and that it has its effect at compile time, not execution time.

Common Programming Error 8.8

Omitting the parentheses in a `sizeof` *operation when the operand is a type name is a compilation error.*

Performance Tip 8.2

Because `sizeof` *is a compile-time unary operator, not an execution-time operator, using* `sizeof` *does not negatively impact execution performance.*

Error-Prevention Tip 8.3

To avoid errors associated with omitting the parentheses around the operand of operator `sizeof`, *many programmers include parentheses around every* `sizeof` *operand.*

8.8 Pointer Expressions and Pointer Arithmetic

Pointers are valid operands in arithmetic expressions, assignment expressions and comparison expressions. However, not all the operators normally used in these expressions are valid with pointer variables. This section describes the operators that can have pointers as operands and how these operators are used with pointers.

Several arithmetic operations may be performed on pointers. A pointer may be incremented (++) or decremented (--), an integer may be added to a pointer (+ or +=), an integer may be subtracted from a pointer (- or -=) or one pointer may be subtracted from another.

Assume that array `int v[ 5 ]` has been declared and that its first element is at memory location 3000. Assume that pointer `vPtr` has been initialized to point to `v[ 0 ]` (i.e., the value of `vPtr` is 3000). Figure 8.18 diagrams this situation for a machine with four-byte integers. Note that `vPtr` can be initialized to point to array `v` with either of the following statements (because the name of an array is equivalent to the address of its first element):

```
int *vPtr = v;
int *vPtr = &v[ 0 ];
```

Portability Tip 8.4

Most computers today have two-byte or four-byte integers. Some of the newer machines use eight-byte integers. Because the results of pointer arithmetic depend on the size of the objects a pointer points to, pointer arithmetic is machine dependent.

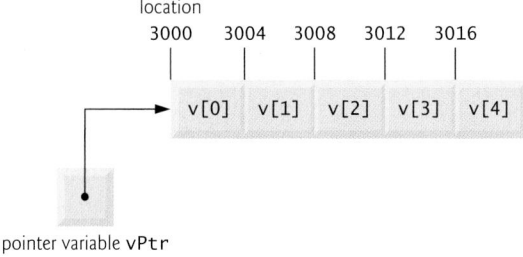

Fig. 8.18 | Array v and a pointer variable vPtr that points to v.

In conventional arithmetic, the addition 3000 + 2 yields the value 3002. This is normally not the case with pointer arithmetic. When an integer is added to, or subtracted from, a pointer, the pointer is not simply incremented or decremented by that integer, but by that integer times the size of the object to which the pointer refers. The number of bytes depends on the object's data type. For example, the statement

```
vPtr += 2;
```

would produce 3008 (3000 + 2 * 4), assuming that an int is stored in four bytes of memory. In the array v, vPtr would now point to v[2] (Fig. 8.19). If an integer is stored in two bytes of memory, then the preceding calculation would result in memory location 3004 (3000 + 2 * 2). If the array were of a different data type, the preceding statement would increment the pointer by twice the number of bytes it takes to store an object of that data type. When performing pointer arithmetic on a character array, the results will be consistent with regular arithmetic, because each character is one byte long.

If vPtr had been incremented to 3016, which points to v[4], the statement

```
vPtr -= 4;
```

would set vPtr back to 3000—the beginning of the array. If a pointer is being incremented or decremented by one, the increment (++) and decrement (--) operators can be used. Each of the statements

```
++vPtr;
vPtr++;
```

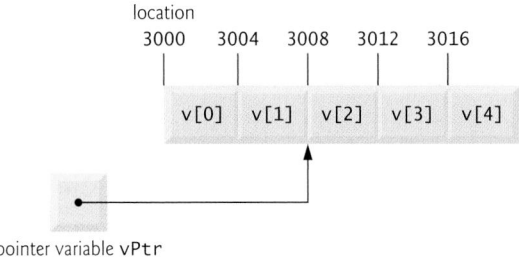

pointer variable vPtr

Fig. 8.19 | Pointer vPtr after pointer arithmetic.

increments the pointer to point to the next element of the array. Each of the statements

```
--vPtr;
vPtr--;
```

decrements the pointer to point to the previous element of the array.

Pointer variables pointing to the same array may be subtracted from one another. For example, if vPtr contains the location 3000 and v2Ptr contains the address 3008, the statement

```
x = v2Ptr - vPtr;
```

would assign to x the number of array elements from vPtr to v2Ptr—in this case, 2. Pointer arithmetic is meaningless unless performed on a pointer that points to an array. We cannot assume that two variables of the same type are stored contiguously in memory unless they are adjacent elements of an array.

Common Programming Error 8.9

Using pointer arithmetic on a pointer that does not refer to an array of values is a logic error.

Common Programming Error 8.10

Subtracting or comparing two pointers that do not refer to elements of the same array is a logic error.

Common Programming Error 8.11

Using pointer arithmetic to increment or decrement a pointer such that the pointer refers to an element past the end of the array or before the beginning of the array is normally a logic error.

A pointer can be assigned to another pointer if both pointers are of the same type. Otherwise, a cast operator must be used to convert the value of the pointer on the right of the assignment to the pointer type on the left of the assignment. The exception to this rule is the pointer to void (i.e., void *), which is a generic pointer capable of representing any pointer type. All pointer types can be assigned to a pointer of type void * without casting. However, a pointer of type void * cannot be assigned directly to a pointer of another type—the pointer of type void * must first be cast to the proper pointer type.

Software Engineering Observation 8.5

Nonconstant pointer arguments can be passed to constant pointer parameters. This is helpful when the body of a program uses a nonconstant pointer to access data, but does not want that data to be modified by a function called in the body of the program.

A void * pointer cannot be dereferenced. For example, the compiler "knows" that a pointer to int refers to four bytes of memory on a machine with four-byte integers, but a pointer to void simply contains a memory address for an unknown data type—the precise number of bytes to which the pointer refers and the type of the data are not known by the compiler. The compiler must know the data type to determine the number of bytes to be dereferenced for a particular pointer—for a pointer to void, this number of bytes cannot be determined from the type.

Common Programming Error 8.12

Assigning a pointer of one type to a pointer of another (other than void *) *without casting the first pointer to the type of the second pointer is a compilation error.*

Common Programming Error 8.13

All operations on a void * *pointer are compilation errors, except comparing* void * *pointers with other pointers, casting* void * *pointers to valid pointer types and assigning addresses to* void * *pointers.*

Pointers can be compared using equality and relational operators. Comparisons using relational operators are meaningless unless the pointers point to members of the same array. Pointer comparisons compare the addresses stored in the pointers. A comparison of two pointers pointing to the same array could show, for example, that one pointer points to a higher numbered element of the array than the other pointer does. A common use of pointer comparison is determining whether a pointer is 0 (i.e., the pointer is a null pointer—it does not point to anything).

8.9 Relationship Between Pointers and Arrays

Arrays and pointers are intimately related in C++ and may be used *almost* interchangeably. An array name can be thought of as a constant pointer. Pointers can be used to do any operation involving array subscripting.

Assume the following declarations:

```
int b[ 5 ]; // create 5-element int array b
int *bPtr; // create int pointer bPtr
```

Because the array name (without a subscript) is a (constant) pointer to the first element of the array, we can set bPtr to the address of the first element in array b with the statement

```
bPtr = b; // assign address of array b to bPtr
```

This is equivalent to taking the address of the first element of the array as follows:

```
bPtr = &b[ 0 ]; // also assigns address of array b to bPtr
```

Array element b[3] can alternatively be referenced with the pointer expression

```
*( bPtr + 3 )
```

The 3 in the preceding expression is the offset to the pointer. When the pointer points to the beginning of an array, the offset indicates which element of the array should be referenced, and the offset value is identical to the array subscript. The preceding notation is referred to as pointer/offset notation. The parentheses are necessary, because the precedence of * is higher than the precedence of +. Without the parentheses, the above expression would add 3 to the value of *bPtr (i.e., 3 would be added to b[0], assuming that bPtr points to the beginning of the array). Just as the array element can be referenced with a pointer expression, the address

```
&b[ 3 ]
```

can be written with the pointer expression

```
bPtr + 3
```

The array name can be treated as a pointer and used in pointer arithmetic. For example, the expression

```
*( b + 3 )
```

also refers to the array element b[3]. In general, all subscripted array expressions can be written with a pointer and an offset. In this case, pointer/offset notation was used with the name of the array as a pointer. Note that the preceding expression does not modify the array name in any way; b still points to the first element in the array.

Pointers can be subscripted exactly as arrays can. For example, the expression

```
bPtr[ 1 ]
```

refers to the array element b[1]; this expression uses pointer/subscript notation.

Remember that an array name is a constant pointer; it always points to the beginning of the array. Thus, the expression

```
b += 3
```

causes a compilation error, because it attempts to modify the value of the array name (a constant) with pointer arithmetic.

Common Programming Error 8.14

Although array names are pointers to the beginning of the array and pointers can be modified in arithmetic expressions, array names cannot be modified in arithmetic expressions, because array names are constant pointers.

Good Programming Practice 8.2

For clarity, use array notation instead of pointer notation when manipulating arrays.

Figure 8.20 uses the four notations discussed in this section for referring to array elements—array subscript notation, pointer/offset notation with the array name as a pointer, pointer subscript notation and pointer/offset notation with a pointer—to accomplish the same task, namely printing the four elements of the integer array b.

```cpp
1   // Fig. 8.20: fig08_20.cpp
2   // Using subscripting and pointer notations with arrays.
3   #include <iostream>
4   using std::cout;
5   using std::endl;
6
7   int main()
8   {
9       int b[] = { 10, 20, 30, 40 }; // create 4-element array b
10      int *bPtr = b; // set bPtr to point to array b
11
12      // output array b using array subscript notation
13      cout << "Array b printed with:\n\nArray subscript notation\n";
```

Fig. 8.20 | Referencing array elements with the array name and with pointers. (Part 1 of 2.)

```
14
15      for ( int i = 0; i < 4; i++ )
16         cout << "b[" << i << "] = " << b[ i ] << '\n';
17
18      // output array b using the array name and pointer/offset notation
19      cout << "\nPointer/offset notation where "
20         << "the pointer is the array name\n";
21
22      for ( int offset1 = 0; offset1 < 4; offset1++ )
23         cout << "*(b + " << offset1 << ") = " << *( b + offset1 ) << '\n';
24
25      // output array b using bPtr and array subscript notation
26      cout << "\nPointer subscript notation\n";
27
28      for ( int j = 0; j < 4; j++ )
29         cout << "bPtr[" << j << "] = " << bPtr[ j ] << '\n';
30
31      cout << "\nPointer/offset notation\n";
32
33      // output array b using bPtr and pointer/offset notation
34      for ( int offset2 = 0; offset2 < 4; offset2++ )
35         cout << "*(bPtr + " << offset2 << ") = "
36            << *( bPtr + offset2 ) << '\n';
37
38      return 0; // indicates successful termination
39   } // end main
```

```
Array b printed with:

Array subscript notation
b[0] = 10
b[1] = 20
b[2] = 30
b[3] = 40

Pointer/offset notation where the pointer is the array name
*(b + 0) = 10
*(b + 1) = 20
*(b + 2) = 30
*(b + 3) = 40

Pointer subscript notation
bPtr[0] = 10
bPtr[1] = 20
bPtr[2] = 30
bPtr[3] = 40

Pointer/offset notation
*(bPtr + 0) = 10
*(bPtr + 1) = 20
*(bPtr + 2) = 30
*(bPtr + 3) = 40
```

Fig. 8.20 | Referencing array elements with the array name and with pointers. (Part 2 of 2.)

To further illustrate the interchangeability of arrays and pointers, let us look at the two string-copying functions—copy1 and copy2—in the program of Fig. 8.21. Both functions copy a string into a character array. After a comparison of the function prototypes for copy1 and copy2, the functions appear identical (because of the interchangeability of arrays and pointers). These functions accomplish the same task, but they are implemented differently.

```cpp
1   // Fig. 8.21: fig08_21.cpp
2   // Copying a string using array notation and pointer notation.
3   #include <iostream>
4   using std::cout;
5   using std::endl;
6
7   void copy1( char *, const char * ); // prototype
8   void copy2( char *, const char * ); // prototype
9
10  int main()
11  {
12     char string1[ 10 ];
13     char *string2 = "Hello";
14     char string3[ 10 ];
15     char string4[] = "Good Bye";
16
17     copy1( string1, string2 ); // copy string2 into string1
18     cout << "string1 = " << string1 << endl;
19
20     copy2( string3, string4 ); // copy string4 into string3
21     cout << "string3 = " << string3 << endl;
22     return 0; // indicates successful termination
23  } // end main
24
25  // copy s2 to s1 using array notation
26  void copy1( char * s1, const char * s2 )
27  {
28     // copying occurs in the for header
29     for ( int i = 0; ( s1[ i ] = s2[ i ] ) != '\0'; i++ )
30        ; // do nothing in body
31  } // end function copy1
32
33  // copy s2 to s1 using pointer notation
34  void copy2( char *s1, const char *s2 )
35  {
36     // copying occurs in the for header
37     for ( ; ( *s1 = *s2 ) != '\0'; s1++, s2++ )
38        ; // do nothing in body
39  } // end function copy2
```

```
string1 = Hello
string3 = Good Bye
```

Fig. 8.21 | String copying using array notation and pointer notation.

Function copy1 (lines 26–31) uses array subscript notation to copy the string in s2 to the character array s1. The function declares an integer counter variable i to use as the array subscript. The for statement header (line 29) performs the entire copy operation— its body is the empty statement. The header specifies that i is initialized to zero and incremented by one on each iteration of the loop. The condition in the for, (s1[i] = s2[i]) != '\0', performs the copy operation character by character from s2 to s1. When the null character is encountered in s2, it is assigned to s1, and the loop terminates, because the null character is equal to '\0'. Remember that the value of an assignment statement is the value assigned to its left operand.

Function copy2 (lines 34–39) uses pointers and pointer arithmetic to copy the string in s2 to the character array s1. Again, the for statement header (line 37) performs the entire copy operation. The header does not include any variable initialization. As in function copy1, the condition (*s1 = *s2) != '\0' performs the copy operation. Pointer s2 is dereferenced, and the resulting character is assigned to the dereferenced pointer s1. After the assignment in the condition, the loop increments both pointers, so they point to the next element of array s1 and the next character of string s2, respectively. When the loop encounters the null character in s2, the null character is assigned to the dereferenced pointer s1 and the loop terminates. Note that the "increment portion" of this for statement has two increment expressions separated by a comma operator.

The first argument to both copy1 and copy2 must be an array large enough to hold the string in the second argument. Otherwise, an error may occur when an attempt is made to write into a memory location beyond the bounds of the array (recall that when using pointer-based arrays, there is no "built-in" bounds checking). Also, note that the second parameter of each function is declared as const char * (a pointer to a character constant—i.e., a constant string). In both functions, the second argument is copied into the first argument—characters are copied from the second argument one at a time, but the characters are never modified. Therefore, the second parameter is declared to point to a constant value to enforce the principle of least privilege—neither function needs to modify the second argument, so neither function is allowed to modify the second argument.

8.10 Arrays of Pointers

Arrays may contain pointers. A common use of such a data structure is to form an array of pointer-based strings, referred to simply as a **string array**. Each entry in the array is a string, but in C++ a string is essentially a pointer to its first character, so each entry in an array of strings is simply a pointer to the first character of a string. Consider the declaration of string array suit that might be useful in representing a deck of cards:

```
const char *suit[ 4 ] =
    { "Hearts", "Diamonds", "Clubs", "Spades" };
```

The suit[4] portion of the declaration indicates an array of four elements. The const char * portion of the declaration indicates that each element of array suit is of type "pointer to char constant data." The four values to be placed in the array are "Hearts", "Diamonds", "Clubs" and "Spades". Each is stored in memory as a null-terminated character string that is one character longer than the number of characters between quotes. The four strings are seven, nine, six and seven characters long (including their terminating null characters), respectively. Although it appears as though these strings are being placed in the `suit` array, only pointers are actually stored in the array, as shown in Fig. 8.22. Each pointer points to the first character of its corresponding string. Thus, even though the `suit` array is fixed in size, it provides access to character strings of any length. This flexibility is one example of C++'s powerful data-structuring capabilities.

The suit strings could be placed into a two-dimensional array, in which each row represents one suit and each column represents one of the letters of a suit name. Such a data structure must have a fixed number of columns per row, and that number must be as large as the largest string. Therefore, considerable memory is wasted when we store a large number of strings, of which most are shorter than the longest string. We use arrays of strings to help represent a deck of cards in the next section.

String arrays are commonly used with command-line arguments that are passed to function `main` when a program begins execution. Such arguments follow the program name when a program is executed from the command line. A typical use of command-line arguments is to pass options to a program. For example, from the command line on a Windows computer, the user can type

```
dir /P
```

to list the contents of the current directory and pause after each screen of information. When the `dir` command executes, the option `/P` is passed to `dir` as a command-line argument. Such arguments are placed in a string array that `main` receives as an argument. We discuss command-line arguments in Appendix E, C Legacy Code Topics.

8.11 Case Study: Card Shuffling and Dealing Simulation

This section uses random-number generation to develop a card shuffling and dealing simulation program. This program can then be used as a basis for implementing programs that play specific card games. To reveal some subtle performance problems, we have intentionally used suboptimal shuffling and dealing algorithms. In the exercises, we develop more efficient algorithms.

Using the top-down, stepwise-refinement approach, we develop a program that will shuffle a deck of 52 playing cards and then deal each of the 52 cards. The top-down approach is particularly useful in attacking larger, more complex problems than we have seen in the early chapters.

We use a 4-by-13 two-dimensional array `deck` to represent the deck of playing cards (Fig. 8.23). The rows correspond to the suits—row 0 corresponds to hearts, row 1 to diamonds, row 2 to clubs and row 3 to spades. The columns correspond to the face values of

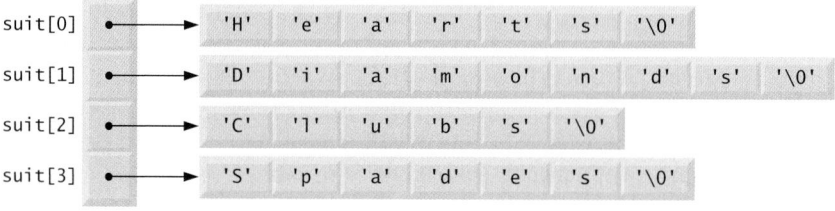

Fig. 8.22 | Graphical representation of the suit array.

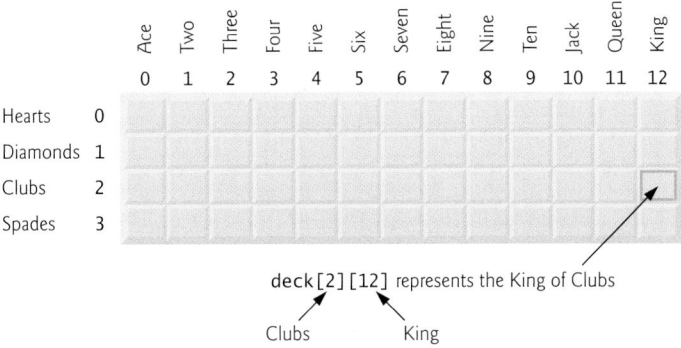

deck[2][12] represents the King of Clubs

Clubs   King

Fig. 8.23 | Two-dimensional array representation of a deck of cards.

the cards—columns 0 through 9 correspond to faces ace through 10, respectively, and columns 10 through 12 correspond to jack, queen and king, respectively. We shall load the string array suit with character strings representing the four suits (as in Fig. 8.22) and the string array face with character strings representing the 13 face values.

This simulated deck of cards may be shuffled as follows. First the array deck is initialized to zeros. Then, a row (0–3) and a column (0–12) are each chosen at random. The number 1 is inserted in array element deck[row][column] to indicate that this card is going to be the first one dealt from the shuffled deck. This process continues with the numbers 2, 3, …, 52 being randomly inserted in the deck array to indicate which cards are to be placed second, third, …, and 52nd in the shuffled deck. As the deck array begins to fill with card numbers, it is possible that a card will be selected twice (i.e., deck[row][column] will be nonzero when it is selected). This selection is simply ignored, and other rows and columns are repeatedly chosen at random until an unselected card is found. Eventually, the numbers 1 through 52 will occupy the 52 slots of the deck array. At this point, the deck of cards is fully shuffled.

This shuffling algorithm could execute for an indefinitely long period if cards that have already been shuffled are repeatedly selected at random. This phenomenon is known as indefinite postponement (also called starvation). In the exercises, we discuss a better shuffling algorithm that eliminates the possibility of indefinite postponement.

Performance Tip 8.3

Sometimes algorithms that emerge in a "natural" way can contain subtle performance problems such as indefinite postponement. Seek algorithms that avoid indefinite postponement.

To deal the first card, we search the array for the element deck[row][column] that matches 1. This is accomplished with a nested for statement that varies row from 0 to 3 and column from 0 to 12. What card does that slot of the array correspond to? The suit array has been preloaded with the four suits, so to get the suit, we print the character string suit[row]. Similarly, to get the face value of the card, we print the character string face[column]. We also print the character string " of ". Printing this information in the proper order enables us to print each card in the form "King of Clubs", "Ace of Diamonds" and so on.

Let us proceed with the top-down, stepwise-refinement process. The top is simply

Shuffle and deal 52 cards

Our first refinement yields

Initialize the suit array
Initialize the face array
Initialize the deck array
Shuffle the deck
Deal 52 cards

"Shuffle the deck" may be expanded as follows:

For each of the 52 cards
    Place card number in randomly selected unoccupied slot of deck

"Deal 52 cards" may be expanded as follows:

For each of the 52 cards
    Find card number in deck array and print face and suit of card

Incorporating these expansions yields our complete second refinement:

Initialize the suit array
Initialize the face array
Initialize the deck array

For each of the 52 cards
    Place card number in randomly selected unoccupied slot of deck

For each of the 52 cards
    Find card number in deck array and print face and suit of card

"Place card number in randomly selected unoccupied slot of deck" may be expanded as follows:

Choose slot of deck randomly

While chosen slot of deck has been previously chosen
    Choose slot of deck randomly

Place card number in chosen slot of deck

"Find card number in deck array and print face and suit of card" may be expanded as follows:

For each slot of the deck array
    If slot contains card number
        Print the face and suit of the card

Incorporating these expansions yields our third refinement (Fig. 8.24):

This completes the refinement process. Figures 8.25–8.27 contain the card shuffling and dealing program and a sample execution. Lines 61–67 of function `deal` (Fig. 8.26) implement lines 1–2 of Fig. 8.24. The constructor (lines 22–35 of Fig. 8.26) implements lines 1–3 of Fig. 8.24. Function `shuffle` (lines 38–55 of Fig. 8.26) implements lines 5–11 of Fig. 8.24. Function `deal` (lines 58–88 of Fig. 8.26) implements lines 13–16 of Fig. 8.24. Note the output formatting used in function `deal` (lines 81–83 of Fig. 8.26).

```
1   Initialize the suit array
2   Initialize the face array
3   Initialize the deck array
4
5   For each of the 52 cards
6       Choose slot of deck randomly
7
8       While slot of deck has been previously chosen
9           Choose slot of deck randomly
10
11      Place card number in chosen slot of deck
12
13  For each of the 52 cards
14      For each slot of deck array
15          If slot contains desired card number
16              Print the face and suit of the card
```

Fig. 8.24 | Pseudocode algorithm for card shuffling and dealing program.

```
1   // Fig. 8.25: DeckOfCards.h
2   // Definition of class DeckOfCards that
3   // represents a deck of playing cards.
4
5   // DeckOfCards class definition
6   class DeckOfCards
7   {
8   public:
9      DeckOfCards(); // constructor initializes deck
10     void shuffle(); // shuffles cards in deck
11     void deal(); // deals cards in deck
12  private:
13     int deck[ 4 ][ 13 ]; // represents deck of cards
14  }; // end class DeckOfCards
```

Fig. 8.25 | DeckOfCards header file.

```
1   // Fig. 8.26: DeckOfCards.cpp
2   // Member-function definitions for class DeckOfCards that simulates
3   // the shuffling and dealing of a deck of playing cards.
4   #include <iostream>
5   using std::cout;
6   using std::left;
7   using std::right;
8
9   #include <iomanip>
10  using std::setw;
11
```

Fig. 8.26 | Definitions of member functions for shuffling and dealing. (Part 1 of 3.)

```
12  #include <cstdlib> // prototypes for rand and srand
13  using std::rand;
14  using std::srand;
15
16  #include <ctime> // prototype for time
17  using std::time;
18
19  #include "DeckOfCards.h" // DeckOfCards class definition
20
21  // DeckOfCards default constructor initializes deck
22  DeckOfCards::DeckOfCards()
23  {
24     // loop through rows of deck
25     for ( int row = 0; row <= 3; row++ )
26     {
27        // loop through columns of deck for current row
28        for ( int column = 0; column <= 12; column++ )
29        {
30           deck[ row ][ column ] = 0; // initialize slot of deck to 0
31        } // end inner for
32     } // end outer for
33
34     srand( time( 0 ) ); // seed random number generator
35  } // end DeckOfCards default constructor
36
37  // shuffle cards in deck
38  void DeckOfCards::shuffle()
39  {
40     int row; // represents suit value of card
41     int column; // represents face value of card
42
43     // for each of the 52 cards, choose a slot of the deck randomly
44     for ( int card = 1; card <= 52; card++ )
45     {
46        do // choose a new random location until unoccupied slot is found
47        {
48           row = rand() % 4; // randomly select the row
49           column = rand() % 13; // randomly select the column
50        } while( deck[ row ][ column ] != 0 ); // end do...while
51
52        // place card number in chosen slot of deck
53        deck[ row ][ column ] = card;
54     } // end for
55  } // end function shuffle
56
57  // deal cards in deck
58  void DeckOfCards::deal()
59  {
60     // initialize suit array
61     static const char *suit[ 4 ] =
62        { "Hearts", "Diamonds", "Clubs", "Spades" };
63
```

Fig. 8.26 | Definitions of member functions for shuffling and dealing. (Part 2 of 3.)

```
64      // initialize face array
65      static const char *face[ 13 ] =
66         { "Ace", "Deuce", "Three", "Four", "Five", "Six", "Seven",
67         "Eight", "Nine", "Ten", "Jack", "Queen", "King" };
68
69      // for each of the 52 cards
70      for ( int card = 1; card <= 52; card++ )
71      {
72         // loop through rows of deck
73         for ( int row = 0; row <= 3; row++ )
74         {
75            // loop through columns of deck for current row
76            for ( int column = 0; column <= 12; column++ )
77            {
78               // if slot contains current card, display card
79               if ( deck[ row ][ column ] == card )
80               {
81                  cout << setw( 5 ) << right << face[ column ]
82                     << " of " << setw( 8 ) << left << suit[ row ]
83                     << ( card % 2 == 0 ? '\n' : '\t' );
84               } // end if
85            } // end innermost for
86         } // end inner for
87      } // end outer for
88   } // end function deal
```

Fig. 8.26 | Definitions of member functions for shuffling and dealing. (Part 3 of 3.)

The output statement outputs the face right justified in a field of five characters and outputs the suit left justified in a field of eight characters (Fig. 8.27). The output is printed in two-column format—if the card being output is in the first column, a tab is output after the card to move to the second column (line 83); otherwise, a newline is output.

There is also a weakness in the dealing algorithm. Once a match is found, even if it is found on the first try, the two inner for statements continue searching the remaining elements of deck for a match. In the exercises, we correct this deficiency.

```
1    // Fig. 8.27: fig08_27.cpp
2    // Card shuffling and dealing program.
3    #include "DeckOfCards.h" // DeckOfCards class definition
4
5    int main()
6    {
7       DeckOfCards deckOfCards; // create DeckOfCards object
8
9       deckOfCards.shuffle(); // shuffle the cards in the deck
10      deckOfCards.deal(); // deal the cards in the deck
11      return 0; // indicates successful termination
12   } // end main
```

Fig. 8.27 | Card shuffling and dealing program. (Part 1 of 2.)

```
  Nine of Spades           Seven of Clubs
  Five of Spades           Eight of Clubs
Queen of Diamonds          Three of Hearts
 Jack of Spades             Five of Diamonds
 Jack of Diamonds          Three of Diamonds
Three of Clubs               Six of Clubs
  Ten of Clubs             Nine of Diamonds
  Ace of Hearts           Queen of Hearts
Seven of Spades           Deuce of Spades
  Six of Hearts           Deuce of Clubs
  Ace of Clubs            Deuce of Diamonds
 Nine of Hearts           Seven of Diamonds
  Six of Spades           Eight of Diamonds
  Ten of Spades            King of Hearts
 Four of Clubs             Ace of Spades
  Ten of Hearts           Four of Spades
Eight of Hearts           Eight of Spades
 Jack of Hearts            Ten of Diamonds
 Four of Diamonds         King of Diamonds
Seven of Hearts           King of Spades
Queen of Spades           Four of Hearts
 Nine of Clubs             Six of Diamonds
Deuce of Hearts           Jack of Clubs
 King of Clubs            Three of Spades
Queen of Clubs             Five of Clubs
 Five of Hearts            Ace of Diamonds
```

Fig. 8.27 | Card shuffling and dealing program. (Part 2 of 2.)

8.12 Function Pointers

A pointer to a function contains the address of the function in memory. In Chapter 7, we saw that the name of an array is actually the address in memory of the first element of the array. Similarly, the name of a function is actually the starting address in memory of the code that performs the function's task. Pointers to functions can be passed to functions, returned from functions, stored in arrays and assigned to other function pointers.

Multipurpose Selection Sort Using Function Pointers
To illustrate the use of pointers to functions, Fig. 8.28 modifies the selection sort program of Fig. 8.15. Figure 8.28 consists of main (lines 17–55) and the functions selectionSort (lines 59–76), swap (lines 80–85), ascending (lines 89–92) and descending (lines 96–99). Function selectionSort receives a pointer to a function—either function ascending or function descending—as an argument in addition to the integer array to sort and the size of the array. Functions ascending and descending determine the sorting order. The program prompts the user to choose whether the array should be sorted in ascending order or in descending order (lines 24–26). If the user enters 1, a pointer to function ascending is passed to function selectionSort (line 37), causing the array to be sorted into increasing order. If the user enters 2, a pointer to function descending is passed to function selectionSort (line 45), causing the array to be sorted into decreasing order.

The following parameter appears in line 60 of selectionSort's function header:

```
bool ( *compare )( int, int )
```

This parameter specifies a pointer to a function. The keyword bool indicates that the function being pointed to returns a bool value. The text (*compare) indicates the name of the pointer to the function (the * indicates that parameter compare is a pointer). The text (int, int) indicates that the function pointed to by compare takes two integer arguments. Parentheses are needed around *compare to indicate that compare is a pointer to a function. If we had not included the parentheses, the declaration would have been

```
bool *compare( int, int )
```

which declares a function that receives two integers as parameters and returns a pointer to a bool value.

```
1   // Fig. 8.28: fig08_28.cpp
2   // Multipurpose sorting program using function pointers.
3   #include <iostream>
4   using std::cout;
5   using std::cin;
6   using std::endl;
7
8   #include <iomanip>
9   using std::setw;
10
11  // prototypes
12  void selectionSort( int [], const int, bool (*)( int, int ) );
13  void swap( int * const, int * const );
14  bool ascending( int, int ); // implements ascending order
15  bool descending( int, int ); // implements descending order
16
17  int main()
18  {
19     const int arraySize = 10;
20     int order; // 1 = ascending, 2 = descending
21     int counter; // array index
22     int a[ arraySize ] = { 2, 6, 4, 8, 10, 12, 89, 68, 45, 37 };
23
24     cout << "Enter 1 to sort in ascending order,\n"
25        << "Enter 2 to sort in descending order: ";
26     cin >> order;
27     cout << "\nData items in original order\n";
28
29     // output original array
30     for ( counter = 0; counter < arraySize; counter++ )
31        cout << setw( 4 ) << a[ counter ];
32
33     // sort array in ascending order; pass function ascending
34     // as an argument to specify ascending sorting order
35     if ( order == 1 )
36     {
37        selectionSort( a, arraySize, ascending );
38        cout << "\nData items in ascending order\n";
39     } // end if
40
```

Fig. 8.28 | Multipurpose sorting program using function pointers. (Part 1 of 3.)

```
41      // sort array in descending order; pass function descending
42      // as an argument to specify descending sorting order
43      else
44      {
45         selectionSort( a, arraySize, descending );
46         cout << "\nData items in descending order\n";
47      } // end else part of if...else
48
49      // output sorted array
50      for ( counter = 0; counter < arraySize; counter++ )
51         cout << setw( 4 ) << a[ counter ];
52
53      cout << endl;
54      return 0; // indicates successful termination
55   } // end main
56
57   // multipurpose selection sort; the parameter compare is a pointer to
58   // the comparison function that determines the sorting order
59   void selectionSort( int work[], const int size,
60                       bool (*compare)( int, int ) )
61   {
62      int smallestOrLargest; // index of smallest (or largest) element
63
64      // loop over size - 1 elements
65      for ( int i = 0; i < size - 1; i++ )
66      {
67         smallestOrLargest = i; // first index of remaining vector
68
69         // loop to find index of smallest (or largest) element
70         for ( int index = i + 1; index < size; index++ )
71            if ( !(*compare)( work[ smallestOrLargest ], work[ index ] ) )
72               smallestOrLargest = index;
73
74         swap( &work[ smallestOrLargest ], &work[ i ] );
75      } // end if
76   } // end function selectionSort
77
78   // swap values at memory locations to which
79   // element1Ptr and element2Ptr point
80   void swap( int * const element1Ptr, int * const element2Ptr )
81   {
82      int hold = *element1Ptr;
83      *element1Ptr = *element2Ptr;
84      *element2Ptr = hold;
85   } // end function swap
86
87   // determine whether element a is less than
88   // element b for an ascending order sort
89   bool ascending( int a, int b )
90   {
91      return a < b; // returns true if a is less than b
92   } // end function ascending
93
```

Fig. 8.28 | Multipurpose sorting program using function pointers. (Part 2 of 3.)

```
94    // determine whether element a is greater than
95    // element b for a descending order sort
96    bool descending( int a, int b )
97    {
98       return a > b; // returns true if a is greater than b
99    } // end function descending
```

```
Enter 1 to sort in ascending order,
Enter 2 to sort in descending order: 1

Data items in original order
   2   6   4   8  10  12  89  68  45  37
Data items in ascending order
   2   4   6   8  10  12  37  45  68  89
```

```
Enter 1 to sort in ascending order,
Enter 2 to sort in descending order: 2

Data items in original order
   2   6   4   8  10  12  89  68  45  37
Data items in descending order
  89  68  45  37  12  10   8   6   4   2
```

Fig. 8.28 | Multipurpose sorting program using function pointers. (Part 3 of 3.)

The corresponding parameter in the function prototype of selectionSort is

```
bool (*)( int, int )
```

Note that only types have been included. As always, for documentation purposes, the programmer can include names that the compiler will ignore.

The function passed to selectionSort is called in line 71 as follows:

```
( *compare )( work[ smallestOrLargest ], work[ index ] )
```

Just as a pointer to a variable is dereferenced to access the value of the variable, a pointer to a function is dereferenced to execute the function. The parentheses around *compare are again necessary—if they were left out, the * operator would attempt to dereference the value returned from the function call. The call to the function could have been made without dereferencing the pointer, as in

```
compare( work[ smallestOrLargest ], work[ index ] )
```

which uses the pointer directly as the function name. We prefer the first method of calling a function through a pointer, because it explicitly illustrates that compare is a pointer to a function that is dereferenced to call the function. The second method of calling a function through a pointer makes it appear as though compare is the name of an actual function in the program. This may be confusing to a user of the program who would like to see the definition of function compare and finds that it is not defined in the file.

Arrays of Pointers to Functions

One use of function pointers is in menu-driven systems. For example, a program might prompt a user to select an option from a menu by entering an integer values. The user's choice can be used as a subscript into an array of function pointers, and the pointer in the array can be used to call the function.

Figure 8.29 provides a mechanical example that demonstrates declaring and using an array of pointers to functions. The program defines three functions—function0, function1 and function2—that each take an integer argument and do not return a value. Line 17 stores pointers to these three functions in array f. In this case, all the functions to which the array points must have the same return type and same parameter types. The declaration in line 17 is read beginning in the leftmost set of parentheses as, "f is an array of three pointers to functions that each take an int as an argument and return void." The

```cpp
1   // Fig. 8.29: fig08_29.cpp
2   // Demonstrating an array of pointers to functions.
3   #include <iostream>
4   using std::cout;
5   using std::cin;
6   using std::endl;
7
8   // function prototypes -- each function performs similar actions
9   void function0( int );
10  void function1( int );
11  void function2( int );
12
13  int main()
14  {
15     // initialize array of 3 pointers to functions that each
16     // take an int argument and return void
17     void (*f[ 3 ])( int ) = { function0, function1, function2 };
18
19     int choice;
20
21     cout << "Enter a number between 0 and 2, 3 to end: ";
22     cin >> choice;
23
24     // process user's choice
25     while ( ( choice >= 0 ) && ( choice < 3 ) )
26     {
27        // invoke the function at location choice in
28        // the array f and pass choice as an argument
29        (*f[ choice ])( choice );
30
31        cout << "Enter a number between 0 and 2, 3 to end: ";
32        cin >> choice;
33     } // end while
34
35     cout << "Program execution completed." << endl;
36     return 0; // indicates successful termination
37  } // end main
```

Fig. 8.29 | Array of pointers to functions. (Part 1 of 2.)

```
38
39   void function0( int a )
40   {
41      cout << "You entered " << a << " so function0 was called\n\n";
42   } // end function function0
43
44   void function1( int b )
45   {
46      cout << "You entered " << b << " so function1 was called\n\n";
47   } // end function function1
48
49   void function2( int c )
50   {
51      cout << "You entered " << c << " so function2 was called\n\n";
52   } // end function function2
```

```
Enter a number between 0 and 2, 3 to end: 0
You entered 0 so function0 was called

Enter a number between 0 and 2, 3 to end: 1
You entered 1 so function1 was called

Enter a number between 0 and 2, 3 to end: 2
You entered 2 so function2 was called

Enter a number between 0 and 2, 3 to end: 3
Program execution completed.
```

Fig. 8.29 | Array of pointers to functions. (Part 2 of 2.)

array is initialized with the names of the three functions (which, again, are pointers). The program prompts the user to enter a number between 0 and 2, or 3 to terminate. When the user enters a value between 0 and 2, the value is used as the subscript into the array of pointers to functions. Line 29 invokes one of the functions in array f. In the call, f[choice] selects the pointer at location choice in the array. The pointer is dereferenced to call the function, and choice is passed as the argument to the function. Each function prints its argument's value and its function name to indicate that the function is called correctly. In the exercises, you will develop a menu-driven system. We will see in Chapter 13, Object-Oriented Programming: Polymorphism, that arrays of pointers to functions are used by compiler developers to implement the mechanisms that support virtual functions—the key technology behind polymorphism.

8.13 Introduction to Pointer-Based String Processing

In this section, we introduce some common C++ Standard Library functions that facilitate string processing. The techniques discussed here are appropriate for developing text editors, word processors, page layout software, computerized typesetting systems and other kinds of text-processing software. We have already used the C++ Standard Library string class in several examples to represent strings as full-fledged objects. For example, the GradeBook class case study in Chapters 3–7 represents a course name using a string object. In Chapter 18 we present class string in detail. Although using string objects is usually straightforward, we use null-terminated, pointer-based strings in this section. Many C++ Standard Library functions operate only on null-terminated, pointer-based strings, which are more complicated to use than `string` objects. Also, if you work with legacy C++ programs, you may be required to manipulate these pointer-based strings.

8.13.1 Fundamentals of Characters and Pointer-Based Strings

Characters are the fundamental building blocks of C++ source programs. Every program is composed of a sequence of characters that—when grouped together meaningfully—is interpreted by the compiler as a series of instructions used to accomplish a task. A program may contain character constants. A character constant is an integer value represented as a character in single quotes. The value of a character constant is the integer value of the character in the machine's character set. For example, `'z'` represents the integer value of z (122 in the ASCII character set; see Appendix B), and `'\n'` represents the integer value of newline (10 in the ASCII character set).

A string is a series of characters treated as a single unit. A string may include letters, digits and various special characters such as +, -, *, /and $. String literals, or string constants, in C++ are written in double quotation marks as follows:

```
"John Q. Doe"            (a name)
"9999 Main Street"       (a street address)
"Maynard, Massachusetts" (a city and state)
"(201) 555-1212"         (a telephone number)
```

A pointer-based string in C++ is an array of characters ending in the null character (`'\0'`), which marks where the string terminates in memory. A string is accessed via a pointer to its first character. The value of a string is the address of its first character. Thus, in C++, it is appropriate to say that *a string is a constant pointer*—in fact, a pointer to the string's first character. In this sense, strings are like arrays, because an array name is also a pointer to its first element.

A string literal may be used as an initializer in the declaration of either a character array or a variable of type `char *`. The declarations

```
char color[] = "blue";
const char *colorPtr = "blue";
```

each initialize a variable to the string `"blue"`. The first declaration creates a five-element array `color` containing the characters `'b'`, `'l'`, `'u'`, `'e'` and `'\0'`. The second declaration creates pointer variable `colorPtr` that points to the letter b in the string `"blue"` (which ends in `'\0'`) somewhere in memory. String literals have `static` storage class (they exist for the duration of the program) and may or may not be shared if the same string literal is referenced from multiple locations in a program. Also, string literals in C++ are constant—their characters cannot be modified.

The declaration `char color[] = "blue";` could also be written

```
char color[] = { 'b', 'l', 'u', 'e', '\0' };
```

When declaring a character array to contain a string, the array must be large enough to store the string and its terminating null character. The preceding declaration determines the size of the array, based on the number of initializers provided in the initializer list.

Common Programming Error 8.15

Not allocating sufficient space in a character array to store the null character that terminates a string is an error.

Common Programming Error 8.16

Creating or using a C-style string that does not contain a terminating null character can lead to logic errors.

Error-Prevention Tip 8.4

When storing a string of characters in a character array, be sure that the array is large enough to hold the largest string that will be stored. C++ allows strings of any length to be stored. If a string is longer than the character array in which it is to be stored, characters beyond the end of the array will overwrite data in memory following the array, leading to logic errors.

A string can be read into a character array using stream extraction with `cin`. For example, the following statement can be used to read a string into character array word[20]:

```
cin >> word;
```

The string entered by the user is stored in word. The preceding statement reads characters until a white-space character or end-of-file indicator is encountered. Note that the string should be no longer than 19 characters to leave room for the terminating null character. The `setw` stream manipulator can be used to ensure that the string read into word does not exceed the size of the array. For example, the statement

```
cin >> setw( 20 ) >> word;
```

specifies that `cin` should read a maximum of 19 characters into array word and save the 20th location in the array to store the terminating null character for the string. The `setw` stream manipulator applies only to the next value being input. If more than 19 characters are entered, the remaining characters are not saved in word, but will be read in and can be stored in another variable.

In some cases, it is desirable to input an entire line of text into an array. For this purpose, C++ provides the function **cin.getline** in header file <iostream>. In Chapter 3 you were introduced to the similar function getline from header file <string>, which read input until a newline character was entered, and stored the input (without the newline character) into a string specified as an argument. The cin.getline function takes three arguments—a character array in which the line of text will be stored, a length and a delimiter character. For example, the program segment

```
char sentence[ 80 ];
cin.getline( sentence, 80, '\n' );
```

declares array sentence of 80 characters and reads a line of text from the keyboard into the array. The function stops reading characters when the delimiter character '\n' is encountered, when the end-of-file indicator is entered or when the number of characters read so far is one less than the length specified in the second argument. (The last character in the array is reserved for the terminating null character.) If the delimiter character is encountered, it is read and discarded. The third argument to cin.getline has '\n' as a default value, so the preceding function call could have been written as follows:

```
cin.getline( sentence, 80 );
```

Chapter 15, Stream Input/Output, provides a detailed discussion of `cin.getline` and other input/output functions.

Common Programming Error 8.17

Processing a single character as a `char *` string can lead to a fatal runtime error. A `char *` string is a pointer—probably a respectably large integer. However, a character is a small integer (ASCII values range 0–255). On many systems, dereferencing a `char` value causes an error, because low memory addresses are reserved for special purposes such as operating system interrupt handlers—so "memory access violations" occur.

Common Programming Error 8.18

Passing a string as an argument to a function when a character is expected is a compilation error.

8.13.2 String Manipulation Functions of the String-Handling Library

The string-handling library provides many useful functions for manipulating string data, comparing strings, searching strings for characters and other strings, tokenizing strings (separating strings into logical pieces such as the separate words in a sentence) and determining the length of strings. This section presents some common string-manipulation functions of the string-handling library (from the C++ standard library). The functions are summarized in Fig. 8.30; then each is used in a live-code example. The prototypes for these functions are located in header file `<cstring>`.

Function prototype	Function description
`char *strcpy( char *s1, const char *s2 );`	
	Copies the string s2 into the character array s1. The value of s1 is returned.
`char *strncpy( char *s1, const char *s2, size_t n );`	
	Copies at most n characters of the string s2 into the character array s1. The value of s1 is returned.
`char *strcat( char *s1, const char *s2 );`	
	Appends the string s2 to s1. The first character of s2 overwrites the terminating null character of s1. The value of s1 is returned.
`char *strncat( char *s1, const char *s2, size_t n );`	
	Appends at most n characters of string s2 to string s1. The first character of s2 overwrites the terminating null character of s1. The value of s1 is returned.
`int strcmp( const char *s1, const char *s2 );`	
	Compares the string s1 with the string s2. The function returns a value of zero, less than zero (usually –1) or greater than zero (usually 1) if s1 is equal to, less than or greater than s2, respectively.

Fig. 8.30 | String-manipulation functions of the string-handling library. (Part 1 of 2.)

Function prototype	Function description
int strncmp(const char *s1, const char *s2, size_t n);	
	Compares up to n characters of the string s1 with the string s2. The function returns zero, less than zero or greater than zero if the n-character portion of s1 is equal to, less than or greater than the corresponding n-character portion of s2, respectively.
char *strtok(char *s1, const char *s2);	
	A sequence of calls to strtok breaks string s1 into "tokens"—logical pieces such as words in a line of text. The string is broken up based on the characters contained in string s2. For instance, if we were to break the string "this:is:a:string" into tokens based on the character ':', the resulting tokens would be "this", "is", "a" and "string". Function strtok returns only one token at a time, however. The first call contains s1 as the first argument, and subsequent calls to continue tokenizing the same string contain NULL as the first argument. A pointer to the current token is returned by each call. If there are no more tokens when the function is called, NULL is returned.
size_t strlen(const char *s);	
	Determines the length of string s. The number of characters preceding the terminating null character is returned.

Fig. 8.30 | String-manipulation functions of the string-handling library. (Part 2 of 2.)

Note that several functions in Fig. 8.30 contain parameters with data type size_t. This type is defined in the header file <cstring> to be an unsigned integral type such as unsigned int or unsigned long.

Common Programming Error 8.19

Forgetting to include the <cstring> header file when using functions from the string-handling library causes compilation errors.

Copying Strings with strcpy and strncpy

Function strcpy copies its second argument—a string—into its first argument—a character array that must be large enough to store the string and its terminating null character, (which is also copied). Function strncpy is equivalent to strcpy, except that strncpy specifies the number of characters to be copied from the string into the array. Note that function strncpy does not necessarily copy the terminating null character of its second argument—a terminating null character is written only if the number of characters to be copied is at least one more than the length of the string. For example, if "test" is the second argument, a terminating null character is written only if the third argument to strncpy is at least 5 (four characters in "test" plus one terminating null character). If the third argument is larger than 5, null characters are appended to the array until the total number of characters specified by the third argument is written.

Common Programming Error 8.20

*When using strcpy, the terminating null character of the second argument (a char * string)
will not be copied if the number of characters specified by strncpy's third argument is not greater
than the second argument's length. In that case, a fatal error may occur if the programmer does
not manually terminate the resulting char * string with a null character.*

Figure 8.31 uses strcpy (line 17) to copy the entire string in array x into array y and
uses strncpy (line 23) to copy the first 14 characters of array x into array z. Line 24
appends a null character ('\0') to array z, because the call to strncpy in the program does
not write a terminating null character. (The third argument is less than the string length
of the second argument plus one.)

Concatenating Strings with *strcat* and *strncat*

Function strcat appends its second argument (a string) to its first argument (a character
array containing a string). The first character of the second argument replaces the null character ('\0') that terminates the string in the first argument. The programmer must ensure
that the array used to store the first string is large enough to store the combination of the

```
1   // Fig. 8.31: fig08_31.cpp
2   // Using strcpy and strncpy.
3   #include <iostream>
4   using std::cout;
5   using std::endl;
6
7   #include <cstring> // prototypes for strcpy and strncpy
8   using std::strcpy;
9   using std::strncpy;
10
11  int main()
12  {
13     char x[] = "Happy Birthday to You"; // string length 21
14     char y[ 25 ];
15     char z[ 15 ];
16
17     strcpy( y, x ); // copy contents of x into y
18
19     cout << "The string in array x is: " << x
20        << "\nThe string in array y is: " << y << '\n';
21
22     // copy first 14 characters of x into z
23     strncpy( z, x, 14 ); // does not copy null character
24     z[ 14 ] = '\0'; // append '\0' to z's contents
25
26     cout << "The string in array z is: " << z << endl;
27     return 0; // indicates successful termination
28  } // end main
```

```
The string in array x is: Happy Birthday to You
The string in array y is: Happy Birthday to You
The string in array z is: Happy Birthday
```

Fig. 8.31 | strcpy and strncpy.

first string, the second string and the terminating null character (copied from the second string). Function `strncat` appends a specified number of characters from the second string to the first string and appends a terminating null character to the result. The program of Fig. 8.32 demonstrates function `strcat` (lines 19 and 29) and function `strncat` (line 24).

```cpp
1   // Fig. 8.32: fig08_32.cpp
2   // Using strcat and strncat.
3   #include <iostream>
4   using std::cout;
5   using std::endl;
6
7   #include <cstring> // prototypes for strcat and strncat
8   using std::strcat;
9   using std::strncat;
10
11  int main()
12  {
13     char s1[ 20 ] = "Happy "; // length 6
14     char s2[] = "New Year "; // length 9
15     char s3[ 40 ] = "";
16
17     cout << "s1 = " << s1 << "\ns2 = " << s2;
18
19     strcat( s1, s2 ); // concatenate s2 to s1 (length 15)
20
21     cout << "\n\nAfter strcat(s1, s2):\ns1 = " << s1 << "\ns2 = " << s2;
22
23     // concatenate first 6 characters of s1 to s3
24     strncat( s3, s1, 6 ); // places '\0' after last character
25
26     cout << "\n\nAfter strncat(s3, s1, 6):\ns1 = " << s1
27        << "\ns3 = " << s3;
28
29     strcat( s3, s1 ); // concatenate s1 to s3
30     cout << "\n\nAfter strcat(s3, s1):\ns1 = " << s1
31        << "\ns3 = " << s3 << endl;
32     return 0; // indicates successful termination
33  } // end main
```

```
s1 = Happy
s2 = New Year

After strcat(s1, s2):
s1 = Happy New Year
s2 = New Year

After strncat(s3, s1, 6):
s1 = Happy New Year
s3 = Happy

After strcat(s3, s1):
s1 = Happy New Year
s3 = Happy Happy New Year
```

Fig. 8.32 | `strcat` and `strncat`.

Comparing Strings with **strcmp** *and* **strncmp**

Figure 8.33 compares three strings using strcmp (lines 21, 22 and 23) and strncmp (lines 26, 27 and 28). Function strcmp compares its first string argument with its second string argument character by character. The function returns zero if the strings are equal, a negative value if the first string is less than the second string and a positive value if the first string is greater than the second string. Function strncmp is equivalent to strcmp, except that strncmp compares up to a specified number of characters. Function strncmp stops comparing characters if it reaches the null character in one of its string arguments. The program prints the integer value returned by each function call.

 Common Programming Error 8.21

Assuming that strcmp *and* strncmp *return one (a true value) when their arguments are equal is a logic error. Both functions return zero (C++'s false value) for equality. Therefore, when testing two strings for equality, the result of the* strcmp *or* strncmp *function should be compared with zero to determine whether the strings are equal.*

To understand just what it means for one string to be "greater than" or "less than" another string, consider the process of alphabetizing a series of last names. The reader would, no doubt, place "Jones" before "Smith," because the first letter of "Jones" comes

```cpp
 1   // Fig. 8.33: fig08_33.cpp
 2   // Using strcmp and strncmp.
 3   #include <iostream>
 4   using std::cout;
 5   using std::endl;
 6
 7   #include <iomanip>
 8   using std::setw;
 9
10   #include <cstring> // prototypes for strcmp and strncmp
11   using std::strcmp;
12   using std::strncmp;
13
14   int main()
15   {
16      char *s1 = "Happy New Year";
17      char *s2 = "Happy New Year";
18      char *s3 = "Happy Holidays";
19
20      cout << "s1 = " << s1 << "\ns2 = " << s2 << "\ns3 = " << s3
21         << "\n\nstrcmp(s1, s2) = " << setw( 2 ) << strcmp( s1, s2 )
22         << "\nstrcmp(s1, s3) = " << setw( 2 ) << strcmp( s1, s3 )
23         << "\nstrcmp(s3, s1) = " << setw( 2 ) << strcmp( s3, s1 );
24
25      cout << "\n\nstrncmp(s1, s3, 6) = " << setw( 2 )
26         << strncmp( s1, s3, 6 ) << "\nstrncmp(s1, s3, 7) = " << setw( 2 )
27         << strncmp( s1, s3, 7 ) << "\nstrncmp(s3, s1, 7) = " << setw( 2 )
28         << strncmp( s3, s1, 7 ) << endl;
29      return 0; // indicates successful termination
30   } // end main
```

Fig. 8.33 | strcmp and strncmp. (Part 1 of 2.)

```
s1 = Happy New Year
s2 = Happy New Year
s3 = Happy Holidays

strcmp(s1, s2) =  0
strcmp(s1, s3) =  1
strcmp(s3, s1) = -1

strncmp(s1, s3, 6) =  0
strncmp(s1, s3, 7) =  1
strncmp(s3, s1, 7) = -1
```

Fig. 8.33 | `strcmp` and `strncmp`. (Part 2 of 2.)

before the first letter of "Smith" in the alphabet. But the alphabet is more than just a list of 26 letters—it is an ordered list of characters. Each letter occurs in a specific position within the list. "Z" is more than just a letter of the alphabet; "Z" is specifically the 26th letter of the alphabet.

How does the computer know that one letter comes before another? All characters are represented inside the computer as numeric codes; when the computer compares two strings, it actually compares the numeric codes of the characters in the strings.

In an effort to standardize character representations, most computer manufacturers have designed their machines to utilize one of two popular coding schemes—ASCII or EBCDIC. Recall that ASCII stands for "American Standard Code for Information Interchange." EBCDIC stands for "Extended Binary Coded Decimal Interchange Code." There are other coding schemes, but these two are the most popular.

ASCII and EBCDIC are called character codes, or character sets. Most readers of this book will be using desktop or notebook computers that use the ASCII character set. IBM mainframe computers use the EBCDIC character set. As Internet and World Wide Web usage becomes pervasive, the newer Unicode character set is growing rapidly in popularity. For more information on Unicode, visit www.unicode.org. String and character manipulations actually involve the manipulation of the appropriate numeric codes and not the characters themselves. This explains the interchangeability of characters and small integers in C++. Since it is meaningful to say that one numeric code is greater than, less than or equal to another numeric code, it becomes possible to relate various characters or strings to one another by referring to the character codes. Appendix B contains the ASCII character codes.

 Portability Tip 8.5

The internal numeric codes used to represent characters may be different on different computers, because these computers may use different character sets.

 Portability Tip 8.6

Do not explicitly test for ASCII codes, as in if (rating == 65); *rather, use the corresponding character constant, as in* if (rating == 'A').

[*Note:* With some compilers, functions `strcmp` and `strncmp` always return -1, 0 or 1, as in the sample output of Fig. 8.33. With other compilers, these functions return 0 or the difference between the numeric codes of the first characters that differ in the strings being compared. For example, when s1 and s3 are compared, the first characters that differ between them are the first character of the second word in each string—N (numeric code 78) in s1 and H (numeric code 72) in s3, respectively. In this case, the return value will be 6 (or -6 if s3 is compared to s1).]

Tokenizing a String with strtok

Function strtok breaks a string into a series of tokens. A token is a sequence of characters separated by delimiting characters (usually spaces or punctuation marks). For example, in a line of text, each word can be considered a token, and the spaces separating the words can be considered delimiters.

Multiple calls to strtok are required to break a string into tokens (assuming that the string contains more than one token). The first call to strtok contains two arguments, a string to be tokenized and a string containing characters that separate the tokens (i.e., delimiters). Line 19 in Fig. 8.34 assigns to tokenPtr a pointer to the first token in sentence. The second argument, " ", indicates that tokens in sentence are separated by spaces. Function strtok searches for the first character in sentence that is not a delimiting character (space). This begins the first token. The function then finds the next delimiting character in the string and replaces it with a null ('\0') character. This terminates the cur-

```
1   // Fig. 8.34: fig08_34.cpp
2   // Using strtok.
3   #include <iostream>
4   using std::cout;
5   using std::endl;
6
7   #include <cstring> // prototype for strtok
8   using std::strtok;
9
10  int main()
11  {
12     char sentence[] = "This is a sentence with 7 tokens";
13     char *tokenPtr;
14
15     cout << "The string to be tokenized is:\n" << sentence
16        << "\n\nThe tokens are:\n\n";
17
18     // begin tokenization of sentence
19     tokenPtr = strtok( sentence, " " );
20
21     // continue tokenizing sentence until tokenPtr becomes NULL
22     while ( tokenPtr != NULL )
23     {
24        cout << tokenPtr << '\n';
25        tokenPtr = strtok( NULL, " " ); // get next token
26     } // end while
27
28     cout << "\nAfter strtok, sentence = " << sentence << endl;
29     return 0; // indicates successful termination
30  } // end main
```

Fig. 8.34 | strtok. (Part 1 of 2.)

```
The string to be tokenized is:
This is a sentence with 7 tokens

The tokens are:

This
is
a
sentence
with
7
tokens

After strtok, sentence = This
```

Fig. 8.34 | `strtok`. (Part 2 of 2.)

rent token. Function `strtok` saves (in a `static` variable) a pointer to the next character following the token in `sentence` and returns a pointer to the current token.

Subsequent calls to `strtok` to continue tokenizing `sentence` contain `NULL` as the first argument (line 25). The `NULL` argument indicates that the call to `strtok` should continue tokenizing from the location in `sentence` saved by the last call to `strtok`. Note that `strtok` maintains this saved information in a manner that is not visible to the programmer. If no tokens remain when `strtok` is called, `strtok` returns `NULL`. The program of Fig. 8.34 uses `strtok` to tokenize the string `"This is a sentence with 7 tokens"`. The program prints each token on a separate line. Line 28 outputs `sentence` after tokenization. Note that *strtok modifies the input string*; therefore, a copy of the string should be made if the program requires the original after the calls to `strtok`. When `sentence` is output after tokenization, note that only the word "`This`" prints, because `strtok` replaced each blank in `sentence` with a null character (`'\0'`) during the tokenization process.

Common Programming Error 8.22

Not realizing that `strtok` modifies the string being tokenized and then attempting to use that string as if it were the original unmodified string is a logic error.

Determining String Lengths

Function `strlen` takes a string as an argument and returns the number of characters in the string—the terminating null character is not included in the length. The length is also the index of the null character. The program of Fig. 8.35 demonstrates function `strlen`.

```
1  // Fig. 8.35: fig08_35.cpp
2  // Using strlen.
3  #include <iostream>
4  using std::cout;
5  using std::endl;
6
```

Fig. 8.35 | `strlen` returns the length of a `char *` string. (Part 1 of 2.)

```
7   #include <cstring> // prototype for strlen
8   using std::strlen;
9
10  int main()
11  {
12     char *string1 = "abcdefghijklmnopqrstuvwxyz";
13     char *string2 = "four";
14     char *string3 = "Boston";
15
16     cout << "The length of \"" << string1 << "\" is " << strlen( string1 )
17        << "\nThe length of \"" << string2 << "\" is " << strlen( string2 )
18        << "\nThe length of \"" << string3 << "\" is " << strlen( string3 )
19        << endl;
20     return 0; // indicates successful termination
21  } // end main
```

```
The length of "abcdefghijklmnopqrstuvwxyz" is 26
The length of "four" is 4
The length of "Boston" is 6
```

Fig. 8.35 | strlen returns the length of a char * string. (Part 2 of 2.)

Summary

- Pointers are variables that contain as their values memory addresses of other variables.
- The declaration

      int *ptr;

  declares ptr to be a pointer to a variable of type int and is read, "ptr is a pointer to int." The * as used here in a declaration indicates that the variable is a pointer.
- There are three values that can be used to initialize a pointer: 0, NULL or an address of an object of the same type. Initializing a pointer to 0 and initializing that same pointer to NULL are identical—0 is the convention in C++.
- The only integer that can be assigned to a pointer without casting is zero.
- The & (address) operator returns the memory address of its operand.
- The operand of the address operator must be a variable name (or another *lvalue*); the address operator cannot be applied to constants or to expressions that do not return a reference.
- The * operator, referred to as the indirection (or dereferencing) operator, returns a synonym, alias or nickname for the name of the object that its operand points to in memory. This is called dereferencing the pointer.
- When calling a function with an argument that the caller wants the called function to modify, the address of the argument may be passed. The called function then uses the indirection operator (*) to dereference the pointer and modify the value of the argument in the calling function.
- A function receiving an address as an argument must have a pointer as its corresponding parameter.
- The const qualifier enables the programmer to inform the compiler that the value of a particular variable cannot be modified through the specified identifier. If an attempt is made to modify a const value, the compiler issues either a warning or an error, depending on the particular compiler.

- There are four ways to pass a pointer to a function—a nonconstant pointer to nonconstant data, a nonconstant pointer to constant data, a constant pointer to nonconstant data and a constant pointer to constant data.
- The value of the array name is the address of (a pointer to) the array's first element.
- To pass a single element of an array by reference using pointers, pass the address of the specific array element.
- C++ provides unary operator `sizeof` to determine the size of an array (or of any other data type, variable or constant) in bytes at compile time.
- When applied to the name of an array, the `sizeof` operator returns the total number of bytes in the array as an integer.
- The arithmetic operations that may be performed on pointers are incrementing (++) a pointer, decrementing (--) a pointer, adding (+ or +=) an integer to a pointer, subtracting (- or -=) an integer from a pointer and subtracting one pointer from another.
- When an integer is added or subtracted from a pointer, the pointer is incremented or decremented by that integer times the size of the object to which the pointer refers.
- Pointers can be assigned to one another if both pointers are of the same type. Otherwise, a cast must be used. The exception to this is a `void *` pointer, which is a generic pointer type that can hold pointer values of any type. Pointers to `void` can be assigned pointers of other types. A `void *` pointer can be assigned to a pointer of another type only with an explicit type cast.
- The only valid operations on a `void *` pointer are comparing `void *` pointers with other pointers, assigning addresses to `void *` pointers and casting `void *` pointers to valid pointer types.
- Pointers can be compared using the equality and relational operators. Comparisons using relational operators are meaningful only if the pointers point to members of the same array.
- Pointers that point to arrays can be subscripted exactly as array names can.
- In pointer/offset notation, if the pointer points to the first element of the array, the offset is the same as an array subscript.
- All subscripted array expressions can be written with a pointer and an offset, using either the name of the array as a pointer or using a separate pointer that points to the array.
- Arrays may contain pointers.
- A pointer to a function is the address where the code for the function resides.
- Pointers to functions can be passed to functions, returned from functions, stored in arrays and assigned to other pointers.
- A common use of function pointers is in so-called menu-driven systems. The function pointers are used to select which function to call for a particular menu item.
- Function `strcpy` copies its second argument—a string—into its first argument—a character array. The programmer must ensure that the target array is large enough to store the string and its terminating null character.
- Function `strncpy` is equivalent to `strcpy`, except that a call to `strncpy` specifies the number of characters to be copied from the string into the array. The terminating null character will be copied only if the number of characters to be copied is at least one more than the length of the string.
- Function `strcat` appends its second string argument—including the terminating null character—to its first string argument. The first character of the second string replaces the null (`'\0'`) character of the first string. The programmer must ensure that the target array used to store the first string is large enough to store both the first string and the second string.
- Function `strncat` is equivalent to `strcat`, except that a call to `strncat` appends a specified number of characters from the second string to the first string. A terminating null character is appended to the result.

- Function `strcmp` compares its first string argument with its second string argument character by character. The function returns zero if the strings are equal, a negative value if the first string is less than the second string and a positive value if the first string is greater than the second string.

- Function `strncmp` is equivalent to `strcmp`, except that `strncmp` compares a specified number of characters. If the number of characters in one of the strings is less than the number of characters specified, `strncmp` compares characters until the null character in the shorter string is encountered.

- A sequence of calls to `strtok` breaks a string into tokens that are separated by characters contained in a second string argument. The first call specifies the string to be tokenized as the first argument, and subsequent calls to continue tokenizing the same string specify NULL as the first argument. The function returns a pointer to the current token from each call. If there are no more tokens when `strtok` is called, NULL is returned.

- Function `strlen` takes a string as an argument and returns the number of characters in the string—the terminating null character is not included in the length of the string.

Terminology

& (address operator)
* (pointer dereference or indirection operator)
'\0' (null character)
address operator (&)
array of pointers to functions
ASCII (American Standard Code for Information Interchange)
calling functions by reference
character code
character constant
command-line arguments
comparing strings
concatenating strings
const with function parameters
constant pointer
constant pointer to constant data
constant pointer to nonconstant data
copying strings
decrement a pointer
delimiter character
dereference a 0 pointer
dereference a pointer
dereferencing operator (*)
directly reference a value
EBCDIC (Extended Binary Coded Decimal Interchange Code)
function pointer
`getline` function of `cin`
increment a pointer
indefinite postponement
indirection
indirection (*) operator

indirectly reference a value
interchangeability of arrays and pointers
`islower` function (<cctype>)
modify a constant pointer
modify address stored in pointer variable
nonconstant pointer to constant data
nonconstant pointer to nonconstant data
null character ('\0')
null pointer
null-terminated string
offset to a pointer
pass-by-reference with pointer arguments
pass-by-reference with reference arguments
pointer arithmetic
pointer-based strings
pointer dereference (*) operator
pointer subtraction
pointer to a function
reference to constant data
referencing array elements
selection sort algorithm
`size_t` type
`sizeof` operator
special characters
starvation
`strcat` function of header file <cstring>
`strcmp` function of header file <cstring>
`strcpy` function of header file <cstring>
string array
string being tokenized
string constant
string copying

strlen function of header file <cstring>
strncat function of header file <cstring>
strncmp function of header file <cstring>
strncpy function of header file <cstring>
strtok function of header file <cstring>

terminating null character
token
tokenizing strings
toupper function (<cctype>)

Self-Review Exercises

8.1 Answer each of the following:
   a) A pointer is a variable that contains as its value the _____ of another variable.
   b) The three values that can be used to initialize a pointer are _____, _____ and _____.
   c) The only integer that can be assigned directly to a pointer is _____.

8.2 State whether the following are *true* or *false*. If the answer is *false*, explain why.
   a) The address operator & can be applied only to constants and to expressions.
   b) A pointer that is declared to be of type void * can be dereferenced.
   c) Pointers of different types can never be assigned to one another without a cast operation.

8.3 For each of the following, write C++ statements that perform the specified task. Assume that double-precision, floating-point numbers are stored in eight bytes and that the starting address of the array is at location 1002500 in memory. Each part of the exercise should use the results of previous parts where appropriate.
   a) Declare an array of type double called numbers with 10 elements, and initialize the elements to the values 0.0, 1.1, 2.2, ..., 9.9. Assume that the symbolic constant SIZE has been defined as 10.
   b) Declare a pointer nPtr that points to a variable of type double.
   c) Use a for statement to print the elements of array numbers using array subscript notation. Print each number with one position of precision to the right of the decimal point.
   d) Write two separate statements that each assign the starting address of array numbers to the pointer variable nPtr.
   e) Use a for statement to print the elements of array numbers using pointer/offset notation with pointer nPtr.
   f) Use a for statement to print the elements of array numbers using pointer/offset notation with the array name as the pointer.
   g) Use a for statement to print the elements of array numbers using pointer/subscript notation with pointer nPtr.
   h) Refer to the fourth element of array numbers using array subscript notation, pointer/offset notation with the array name as the pointer, pointer subscript notation with nPtr and pointer/offset notation with nPtr.
   i) Assuming that nPtr points to the beginning of array numbers, what address is referenced by nPtr + 8? What value is stored at that location?
   j) Assuming that nPtr points to numbers[5], what address is referenced by nPtr after nPtr -= 4 is executed? What is the value stored at that location?

8.4 For each of the following, write a single statement that performs the specified task. Assume that floating-point variables number1 and number2 have been declared and that number1 has been initialized to 7.3. Assume that variable ptr is of type char *. Assume that arrays s1 and s2 are each 100-element char arrays that are initialized with string literals.

a) Declare the variable `fPtr` to be a pointer to an object of type `double`.
b) Assign the address of variable `number1` to pointer variable `fPtr`.
c) Print the value of the object pointed to by `fPtr`.
d) Assign the value of the object pointed to by `fPtr` to variable `number2`.
e) Print the value of `number2`.
f) Print the address of `number1`.
g) Print the address stored in `fPtr`. Is the value printed the same as the address of `number1`?
h) Copy the string stored in array `s2` into array `s1`.
i) Compare the string in `s1` with the string in `s2`, and print the result.
j) Append the first 10 characters from the string in `s2` to the string in `s1`.
k) Determine the length of the string in `s1`, and print the result.
l) Assign to `ptr` the location of the first token in `s2`. The tokens delimiters are commas (`,`).

8.5   Perform the task specified by each of the following statements:
a) Write the function header for a function called `exchange` that takes two pointers to double-precision, floating-point numbers x and y as parameters and does not return a value.
b) Write the function prototype for the function in part (a).
c) Write the function header for a function called `evaluate` that returns an integer and that takes as parameters integer x and a pointer to function `poly`. Function `poly` takes an integer parameter and returns an integer.
d) Write the function prototype for the function in part (c).
e) Write two statements that each initialize character array `vowel` with the string of vowels, `"AEIOU"`.

8.6   Find the error in each of the following program segments. Assume the following declarations and statements:

```
int *zPtr;        // zPtr will reference array z
int *aPtr = 0;
void *sPtr = 0;
int number;
int z[ 5 ] = { 1, 2, 3, 4, 5 };
```

a) `++zPtr;`
b) `// use pointer to get first value of array`
    `number = zPtr;`
c) `// assign array element 2 (the value 3) to number`
    `number = *zPtr[ 2 ];`
d) `// print entire array z`
    `for ( int i = 0; i <= 5; i++ )`
    `   cout << zPtr[ i ] << endl;`
e) `// assign the value pointed to by sPtr to number`
    `number = *sPtr;`
f) `++z;`
g) `char s[ 10 ];`
    `cout << strncpy( s, "hello", 5 ) << endl;`
h) `char s[ 12 ];`
    `strcpy( s, "Welcome Home" );`

i) `if ( strcmp( string1, string2 ) )`
     `cout << "The strings are equal" << endl;`

8.7   What (if anything) prints when each of the following statements is performed? If the statement contains an error, describe the error and indicate how to correct it. Assume the following variable declarations:

```
char s1[ 50 ] = "jack";
char s2[ 50 ] = "jill";
char s3[ 50 ];
```

a) `cout << strcpy( s3, s2 ) << endl;`
b) `cout << strcat( strcat( strcpy( s3, s1 ), " and " ), s2 )`
     `<< endl;`
c) `cout << strlen( s1 ) + strlen( s2 ) << endl;`
d) `cout << strlen( s3 ) << endl;`

Answers to Self-Review Exercises

8.1   a) address. b) 0, `NULL`, an address. c) 0.

8.2   a) False. The operand of the address operator must be an *lvalue*; the address operator cannot be applied to constants or to expressions that do not result in references.
b) False. A pointer to void cannot be dereferenced. Such a pointer does not have a type that enables the compiler to determine the number of bytes of memory to dereference and the type of the data to which the pointer points.
c) False. Pointers of any type can be assigned to void pointers. Pointers of type void can be assigned to pointers of other types only with an explicit type cast.

8.3   a) `double numbers[ SIZE ] = { 0.0, 1.1, 2.2, 3.3, 4.4, 5.5, 6.6, 7.7, 8.8, 9.9 };`
b) `double *nPtr;`
c) `cout << fixed << showpoint << setprecision( 1 );`
     `for ( int i = 0; i < SIZE; i++ )`
         `cout << numbers[ i ] << ' ';`
d) `nPtr = numbers;`
     `nPtr = &numbers[ 0 ];`
e) `cout << fixed << showpoint << setprecision( 1 );`
     `for ( int j = 0; j < SIZE; j++ )`
         `cout << *( nPtr + j ) << ' ';`
f) `cout << fixed << showpoint << setprecision( 1 );`
     `for ( int k = 0; k < SIZE; k++ )`
         `cout << *( numbers + k ) << ' ';`
g) `cout << fixed << showpoint << setprecision( 1 );`
     `for ( int m = 0; m < SIZE; m++ )`
         `cout << nPtr[ m ] << ' ';`
h) `numbers[ 3 ]`
     `*( numbers + 3 )`
     `nPtr[ 3 ]`
     `*( nPtr + 3 )`
i) The address is `1002500 + 8 * 8 = 1002564`. The value is `8.8`.

j) The address of `numbers[ 5 ]` is 1002500 + 5 * 8 = 1002540.
The address of `nPtr -= 4` is 1002540 - 4 * 8 = 1002508.
The value at that location is 1.1.

8.4 a) `double *fPtr;`
  b) `fPtr = &number1;`
  c) `cout << "The value of *fPtr is " << *fPtr << endl;`
  d) `number2 = *fPtr;`
  e) `cout << "The value of number2 is " << number2 << endl;`
  f) `cout << "The address of number1 is " << &number1 << endl;`
  g) `cout << "The address stored in fPtr is " << fPtr << endl;`
   Yes, the value is the same.
  h) `strcpy( s1, s2 );`
  i) `cout << "strcmp(s1, s2) = " << strcmp( s1, s2 ) << endl;`
  j) `strncat( s1, s2, 10 );`
  k) `cout << "strlen(s1) = " << strlen( s1 ) << endl;`
  l) `ptr = strtok( s2, "," );`

8.5 a) `void exchange( double *x, double *y )`
  b) `void exchange( double *, double * );`
  c) `int evaluate( int x, int (*poly)( int ) )`
  d) `int evaluate( int, int (*)( int ) );`
  e) `char vowel[] = "AEIOU";`
   `char vowel[] = { 'A', 'E', 'I', 'O', 'U', '\0' };`

8.6 a) Error: `zPtr` has not been initialized.
   Correction: Initialize `zPtr` with `zPtr = z;`
  b) Error: The pointer is not dereferenced.
   Correction: Change the statement to `number = *zPtr;`
  c) Error: `zPtr[ 2 ]` is not a pointer and should not be dereferenced.
   Correction: Change `*zPtr[ 2 ]` to `zPtr[ 2 ]`.
  d) Error: Referring to an array element outside the array bounds with pointer subscripting.
   Correction: To prevent this, change the relational operator in the `for` statement to `<`.
  e) Error: Dereferencing a void pointer.
   Correction: To dereference the void pointer, it must first be cast to an integer pointer. Change the statement to `number = *static_cast< int * >( sPtr );`
  f) Error: Trying to modify an array name with pointer arithmetic.
   Correction: Use a pointer variable instead of the array name to accomplish pointer arithmetic, or subscript the array name to refer to a specific element.
  g) Error: Function `strncpy` does not write a terminating null character to array `s`, because its third argument is equal to the length of the string `"hello"`.
   Correction: Make 6 the third argument of `strncpy` or assign `'\0'` to `s[ 5 ]` to ensure that the terminating null character is added to the string.
  h) Error: Character array `s` is not large enough to store the terminating null character.
   Correction: Declare the array with more elements.
  i) Error: Function `strcmp` will return 0 if the strings are equal; therefore, the condition in the `if` statement will be false, and the output statement will not be executed.
   Correction: Explicitly compare the result of `strcmp` with 0 in the condition of the `if` statement.

8.7 a) jill
       b) jack and jill
       c) 8
       d) 13

Exercises

8.8 State whether the following are *true* or *false*. If *false*, explain why.
  a) Two pointers that point to different arrays cannot be compared meaningfully.
  b) Because the name of an array is a pointer to the first element of the array, array names can be manipulated in precisely the same manner as pointers.

8.9 For each of the following, write C++ statements that perform the specified task. Assume that unsigned integers are stored in two bytes and that the starting address of the array is at location 1002500 in memory.
  a) Declare an array of type unsigned int called values with five elements, and initialize the elements to the even integers from 2 to 10. Assume that the symbolic constant SIZE has been defined as 5.
  b) Declare a pointer vPtr that points to an object of type unsigned int.
  c) Use a for statement to print the elements of array values using array subscript notation.
  d) Write two separate statements that assign the starting address of array values to pointer variable vPtr.
  e) Use a for statement to print the elements of array values using pointer/offset notation.
  f) Use a for statement to print the elements of array values using pointer/offset notation with the array name as the pointer.
  g) Use a for statement to print the elements of array values by subscripting the pointer to the array.
  h) Refer to the fifth element of values using array subscript notation, pointer/offset notation with the array name as the pointer, pointer subscript notation and pointer/offset notation.
  i) What address is referenced by vPtr + 3? What value is stored at that location?
  j) Assuming that vPtr points to values[4], what address is referenced by vPtr -= 4? What value is stored at that location?

8.10 For each of the following, write a single statement that performs the specified task. Assume that long integer variables value1 and value2 have been declared and value1 has been initialized to 200000.
  a) Declare the variable longPtr to be a pointer to an object of type long.
  b) Assign the address of variable value1 to pointer variable longPtr.
  c) Print the value of the object pointed to by longPtr.
  d) Assign the value of the object pointed to by longPtr to variable value2.
  e) Print the value of value2.
  f) Print the address of value1.
  g) Print the address stored in longPtr. Is the value printed the same as value1's address?

8.11 Perform the task specified by each of the following statements:
  a) Write the function header for function zero that takes a long integer array parameter bigIntegers and does not return a value.
  b) Write the function prototype for the function in part (a).
  c) Write the function header for function add1AndSum that takes an integer array parameter oneTooSmall and returns an integer.
  d) Write the function prototype for the function described in part (c).

Note: Exercise 8.12 through Exercise 8.15 are reasonably challenging. Once you have solved these problems, you ought to be able to implement many popular card games.

8.12 Modify the program in Fig. 8.27 so that the card dealing function deals a five-card poker hand. Then write functions to accomplish each of the following:

a) Determine whether the hand contains a pair.
b) Determine whether the hand contains two pairs.
c) Determine whether the hand contains three of a kind (e.g., three jacks).
d) Determine whether the hand contains four of a kind (e.g., four aces).
e) Determine whether the hand contains a flush (i.e., all five cards of the same suit).
f) Determine whether the contains a straight (i.e., five cards of consecutive face values).

8.13 Use the functions developed in Exercise 8.12 to write a program that deals two five-card poker hands, evaluates each hand and determines which is the better hand.

8.14 Modify the program developed in Exercise 8.13 so that it can simulate the dealer. The dealer's five-card hand is dealt "face down" so the player cannot see it. The program should then evaluate the dealer's hand, and, based on the quality of the hand, the dealer should draw one, two or three more cards to replace the corresponding number of unneeded cards in the original hand. The program should then reevaluate the dealer's hand. [*Caution:* This is a difficult problem!]

8.15 Modify the program developed in Exercise 8.14 so that it handles the dealer's hand, but the player is allowed to decide which cards of the player's hand to replace. The program should evaluate both hands and determine who wins. Now use this new program to play 20 games against the computer. Who wins more games, you or the computer? Have one of your friends play 20 games against the computer. Who wins more games? Based on the results of these games, make appropriate modifications to refine your poker-playing program. [*Note:* This, too, is a difficult problem.] Play 20 more games. Does your modified program play a better game?

8.16 In the card shuffling and dealing program of Figs. 8.25–8.27, we intentionally used an inefficient shuffling algorithm that introduced the possibility of indefinite postponement. In this problem, you will create a high-performance shuffling algorithm that avoids indefinite postponement.

Modify Figs. 8.25–8.27 as follows. Initialize the `deck` array as shown in Fig. 8.36. Modify the `shuffle` function to loop row by row and column by column through the array, touching every element once. Each element should be swapped with a randomly selected element of the array. Print the resulting array to determine whether the deck is satisfactorily shuffled (as in Fig. 8.37, for example). You may want your program to call the `shuffle` function several times to ensure a satisfactory shuffle.

Note that, although the approach in this problem improves the shuffling algorithm, the dealing algorithm still requires searching the `deck` array for card 1, then card 2, then card 3 and so on. Worse yet, even after the dealing algorithm locates and deals the card, the algorithm continues searching through the remainder of the deck. Modify the program of Figs. 8.25–8.27 so that once a card is dealt, no further attempts are made to match that card number, and the program immediately proceeds with dealing the next card.

Unshuffled deck array												
	0	1	2	3	4	5	6	7	8	9	10	11	12
0	1	2	3	4	5	6	7	8	9	10	11	12	13
1	14	15	16	17	18	19	20	21	22	23	24	25	26
2	27	28	29	30	31	32	33	34	35	36	37	38	39
3	40	41	42	43	44	45	46	47	48	49	50	51	52

Fig. 8.36 | Unshuffled **deck** array.

Sample shuffled deck array												
	0	1	2	3	4	5	6	7	8	9	10	11	12
0	19	40	27	25	36	46	10	34	35	41	18	2	44
1	13	28	14	16	21	30	8	11	31	17	24	7	1
2	12	33	15	42	43	23	45	3	29	32	4	47	26
3	50	38	52	39	48	51	9	5	37	49	22	6	20

Fig. 8.37 | Sample shuffled **deck** array.

8.17 (*Simulation: The Tortoise and the Hare*) In this exercise, you will re-create the classic race of the tortoise and the hare. You will use random number generation to develop a simulation of this memorable event.

Our contenders begin the race at "square 1" of 70 squares. Each square represents a possible position along the race course. The finish line is at square 70. The first contender to reach or pass square 70 is rewarded with a pail of fresh carrots and lettuce. The course weaves its way up the side of a slippery mountain, so occasionally the contenders lose ground.

There is a clock that ticks once per second. With each tick of the clock, your program should adjust the position of the animals according to the rules in Fig. 8.38.

Use variables to keep track of the positions of the animals (i.e., position numbers are 1–70). Start each animal at position 1 (i.e., the "starting gate"). If an animal slips left before square 1, move the animal back to square 1.

Generate the percentages in the preceding table by producing a random integer i in the range $1 \le i \le 10$. For the tortoise, perform a "fast plod" when $1 \le i \le 5$, a "slip" when $6 \le i \le 7$ or a "slow plod" when $8 \le i \le 10$. Use a similar technique to move the hare.

Begin the race by printing

```
BANG !!!!!
AND THEY'RE OFF !!!!!
```

For each tick of the clock (i.e., each repetition of a loop), print a 70-position line showing the letter T in the tortoise's position and the letter H in the hare's position. Occasionally, the contenders land on the same square. In this case, the tortoise bites the hare and your program should print OUCH!!! beginning at that position. All print positions other than the T, the H or the OUCH!!! (in case of a tie) should be blank.

After printing each line, test if either animal has reached or passed square 70. If so, print the winner and terminate the simulation. If the tortoise wins, print TORTOISE WINS!!! YAY!!! If the

Animal	Move type	Percentage of the time	Actual move
Tortoise	Fast plod	50%	3 squares to the right
	Slip	20%	6 squares to the left
	Slow plod	30%	1 square to the right
Hare	Sleep	20%	No move at all
	Big hop	20%	9 squares to the right
	Big slip	10%	12 squares to the left
	Small hop	30%	1 square to the right
	Small slip	20%	2 squares to the left

Fig. 8.38 | Rules for moving the tortoise and the hare.

hare wins, print Hare wins. Yuch. If both animals win on the same clock tick, you may want to favor the tortoise (the "underdog"), or you may want to print It's a tie. If neither animal wins, perform the loop again to simulate the next tick of the clock. When you are ready to run your program, assemble a group of fans to watch the race. You'll be amazed how involved the audience gets!

Special Section: Building Your Own Computer

In the next several problems, we take a temporary diversion away from the world of high-level-language programming. We "peel open" a computer and look at its internal structure. We introduce machine-language programming and write several machine-language programs. To make this an especially valuable experience, we then build a computer (using software-based *simulation*) on which you can execute your machine-language programs!

8.18 (*Machine-Language Programming*) Let us create a computer we will call the Simpletron. As its name implies, it is a simple machine, but, as we will soon see, it is a powerful one as well. The Simpletron runs programs written in the only language it directly understands, that is, Simpletron Machine Language, or SML for short.

The Simpletron contains an *accumulator*—a "special register" in which information is put before the Simpletron uses that information in calculations or examines it in various ways. All information in the Simpletron is handled in terms of *words*. A word is a signed four-digit decimal number, such as +3364, -1293, +0007, -0001, etc. The Simpletron is equipped with a 100-word memory, and these words are referenced by their location numbers 00, 01, ..., 99.

Before running an SML program, we must *load*, or place, the program into memory. The first instruction (or statement) of every SML program is always placed in location 00. The simulator will start executing at this location.

Each instruction written in SML occupies one word of the Simpletron's memory; thus, instructions are signed four-digit decimal numbers. Assume that the sign of an SML instruction is always plus, but the sign of a data word may be either plus or minus. Each location in the Simpletron's memory may contain an instruction, a data value used by a program or an unused (and hence undefined) area of memory. The first two digits of each SML instruction are the *operation code* that specifies the operation to be performed. SML operation codes are shown in Fig. 8.39.

The last two digits of an SML instruction are the *operand*—the address of the memory location containing the word to which the operation applies.

Operation code	Meaning
Input/output operations	
`const int READ = 10;`	Read a word from the keyboard into a specific location in memory.
`const int WRITE = 11;`	Write a word from a specific location in memory to the screen.
Load and store operations	
`const int LOAD = 20;`	Load a word from a specific location in memory into the accumulator.
`const int STORE = 21;`	Store a word from the accumulator into a specific location in memory.
Arithmetic operations	
`const int ADD = 30;`	Add a word from a specific location in memory to the word in the accumulator (leave result in accumulator).
`const int SUBTRACT = 31;`	Subtract a word from a specific location in memory from the word in the accumulator (leave result in accumulator).
`const int DIVIDE = 32;`	Divide a word from a specific location in memory into the word in the accumulator (leave result in accumulator).
`const int MULTIPLY = 33;`	Multiply a word from a specific location in memory by the word in the accumulator (leave result in accumulator).
Transfer-of-control operations	
`const int BRANCH = 40;`	Branch to a specific location in memory.
`const int BRANCHNEG = 41;`	Branch to a specific location in memory if the accumulator is negative.
`const int BRANCHZERO = 42;`	Branch to a specific location in memory if the accumulator is zero.
`const int HALT = 43;`	Halt—the program has completed its task.

Fig. 8.39 | Simpletron Machine Language (SML) operation codes.

Now let us consider two simple SML programs. The first SML program (Fig. 8.40) reads two numbers from the keyboard and computes and prints their sum. The instruction +1007 reads the first number from the keyboard and places it into location 07 (which has been initialized to zero). Instruction +1008 reads the next number into location 08. The *load* instruction, +2007, places (copies) the first number into the accumulator, and the *add* instruction, +3008, adds the second number to the number in the accumulator. *All SML arithmetic instructions leave their results in the accumulator.* The *store* instruction, +2109, places (copies) the result back into memory location 09. Then the *write* instruction, +1109, takes the number and prints it (as a signed four-digit decimal number). The *halt* instruction, +4300, terminates execution.

Location	Number	Instruction
00	+1007	(Read A)
01	+1008	(Read B)
02	+2007	(Load A)
03	+3008	(Add B)
04	+2109	(Store C)
05	+1109	(Write C)
06	+4300	(Halt)
07	+0000	(Variable A)
08	+0000	(Variable B)
09	+0000	(Result C)

Fig. 8.40 | SML Example 1.

The SML program in Fig. 8.41 reads two numbers from the keyboard, then determines and prints the larger value. Note the use of the instruction +4107 as a conditional transfer of control, much the same as C++'s if statement.

Now write SML programs to accomplish each of the following tasks:

a) Use a sentinel-controlled loop to read positive numbers and compute and print their sum. Terminate input when a negative number is entered.

b) Use a counter-controlled loop to read seven numbers, some positive and some negative, and compute and print their average.

c) Read a series of numbers, and determine and print the largest number. The first number read indicates how many numbers should be processed.

Location	Number	Instruction
00	+1009	(Read A)
01	+1010	(Read B)
02	+2009	(Load A)
03	+3110	(Subtract B)
04	+4107	(Branch negative to 07)
05	+1109	(Write A)
06	+4300	(Halt)
07	+1110	(Write B)
08	+4300	(Halt)
09	+0000	(Variable A)
10	+0000	(Variable B)

Fig. 8.41 | SML Example 2.

8.19 (*Computer Simulator*) It may at first seem outrageous, but in this problem you are going to build your own computer. No, you will not be soldering components together. Rather, you will use the powerful technique of *software-based simulation* to create a *software model* of the Simpletron. You will not be disappointed. Your Simpletron simulator will turn the computer you are using into a Simpletron, and you actually will be able to run, test and debug the SML programs you wrote in Exercise 8.18.

When you run your Simpletron simulator, it should begin by printing

```
*** Welcome to Simpletron! ***

*** Please enter your program one instruction ***
*** (or data word) at a time. I will type the ***
*** location number and a question mark (?).  ***
*** You then type the word for that location. ***
*** Type the sentinel -99999 to stop entering ***
*** your program. ***
```

Your program should simulate the Simpletron's memory with a single-subscripted, 100-element array memory. Now assume that the simulator is running, and let us examine the dialog as we enter the program of Example 2 of Exercise 8.18:

```
00 ? +1009
01 ? +1010
02 ? +2009
03 ? +3110
04 ? +4107
05 ? +1109
06 ? +4300
07 ? +1110
08 ? +4300
09 ? +0000
10 ? +0000
11 ? -99999

*** Program loading completed ***
*** Program execution begins  ***
```

Note that the numbers to the right of each ? in the preceding dialog represent the SML program instructions input by the user.

The SML program has now been placed (or loaded) into array memory. Now the Simpletron executes your SML program. Execution begins with the instruction in location 00 and, like C++, continues sequentially, unless directed to some other part of the program by a transfer of control.

Use variable accumulator to represent the accumulator register. Use variable counter to keep track of the location in memory that contains the instruction being performed. Use variable operationCode to indicate the operation currently being performed (i.e., the left two digits of the instruction word). Use variable operand to indicate the memory location on which the current instruction operates. Thus, operand is the rightmost two digits of the instruction currently being performed. Do not execute instructions directly from memory. Rather, transfer the next instruction to be performed from memory to a variable called instructionRegister. Then "pick off" the left two digits and place them in operationCode, and "pick off" the right two digits and place them in operand. When Simpletron begins execution, the special registers are all initialized to zero.

Now let us "walk through" the execution of the first SML instruction, +1009 in memory location 00. This is called an *instruction execution cycle*.

The counter tells us the location of the next instruction to be performed. We *fetch* the contents of that location from memory by using the C++ statement

```
instructionRegister = memory[ counter ];
```

The operation code and operand are extracted from the instruction register by the statements

```
operationCode = instructionRegister / 100;
operand = instructionRegister % 100;
```

Now, the Simpletron must determine that the operation code is actually a *read* (versus a *write*, a *load*, etc.). A switch differentiates among the 12 operations of SML.

In the switch statement, the behavior of various SML instructions is simulated as shown in Fig. 8.42 (we leave the others to the reader).

The *halt* instruction also causes the Simpletron to print the name and contents of each register, as well as the complete contents of memory. Such a printout is often called a *computer dump* (and, no, a computer dump is not a place where old computers go). To help you program your dump function, a sample dump format is shown in Fig. 8.43. Note that a dump after executing a Simpletron program would show the actual values of instructions and data values at the moment execution terminated. To format numbers with their sign as shown in the dump, use stream manipulator showpos. To disable the display of the sign, use stream manipulator noshowpos. For numbers that have fewer than four digits, you can format numbers with leading zeros between the sign and the value by using the following statement before outputting the value:

```
cout << setfill( '0' ) << internal;
```

Parameterized stream manipulator setfill (from header <iomanip>) specifies the fill character that will appear between the sign and the value when a number is displayed with a field width of five characters but does not have four digits. (One position in the field width is reserved for the sign.) Stream manipulator internal indicates that the fill characters should appear between the sign and the numeric value .

read:	`cin >> memory[ operand ];`
load:	`accumulator = memory[ operand ];`
add:	`accumulator += memory[ operand ];`
branch:	We will discuss the branch instructions shortly.
halt:	This instruction prints the message `*** Simpletron execution terminated ***`

Fig. 8.42 | Behavior of SML instructions.

```
REGISTERS:
accumulator          +0000
counter                 00
instructionRegister  +0000
operationCode           00
operand                 00

MEMORY:
        0      1      2      3      4      5      6      7      8      9
 0  +0000  +0000  +0000  +0000  +0000  +0000  +0000  +0000  +0000  +0000
10  +0000  +0000  +0000  +0000  +0000  +0000  +0000  +0000  +0000  +0000
20  +0000  +0000  +0000  +0000  +0000  +0000  +0000  +0000  +0000  +0000
30  +0000  +0000  +0000  +0000  +0000  +0000  +0000  +0000  +0000  +0000
40  +0000  +0000  +0000  +0000  +0000  +0000  +0000  +0000  +0000  +0000
50  +0000  +0000  +0000  +0000  +0000  +0000  +0000  +0000  +0000  +0000
60  +0000  +0000  +0000  +0000  +0000  +0000  +0000  +0000  +0000  +0000
70  +0000  +0000  +0000  +0000  +0000  +0000  +0000  +0000  +0000  +0000
80  +0000  +0000  +0000  +0000  +0000  +0000  +0000  +0000  +0000  +0000
90  +0000  +0000  +0000  +0000  +0000  +0000  +0000  +0000  +0000  +0000
```

Fig. 8.43 | A sample dump.

Let us proceed with the execution of our program's first instruction—+1009 in location 00. As we have indicated, the switch statement simulates this by performing the C++ statement

```
cin >> memory[ operand ];
```

A question mark (?) should be displayed on the screen before the cin statement executes to prompt the user for input. The Simpletron waits for the user to type a value and press the *Enter* key. The value is then read into location 09.

At this point, simulation of the first instruction is complete. All that remains is to prepare the Simpletron to execute the next instruction. The instruction just performed was not a transfer of control, so we need merely increment the instruction counter register as follows:

```
++counter;
```

This completes the simulated execution of the first instruction. The entire process (i.e., the instruction execution cycle) begins anew with the fetch of the next instruction to execute.

Now let us consider how to simulate the branching instructions (i.e., the transfers of control). All we need to do is adjust the value in the instruction counter appropriately. Therefore, the unconditional branch instruction (40) is simulated in the switch as

```
counter = operand;
```

The conditional "branch if accumulator is zero" instruction is simulated as

```
if ( accumulator == 0 )
    counter = operand;
```

At this point, you should implement your Simpletron simulator and run each of the SML programs you wrote in Exercise 8.18. You may embellish SML with additional features and provide for these in your simulator.

Your simulator should check for various types of errors. During the program loading phase, for example, each number the user types into the Simpletron's memory must be in the range -9999 to +9999. Your simulator should use a while loop to test that each number entered is in this range and, if not, keep prompting the user to reenter the number until the user enters a correct number.

During the execution phase, your simulator should check for various serious errors, such as attempts to divide by zero, attempts to execute invalid operation codes, accumulator overflows (i.e., arithmetic operations resulting in values larger than +9999 or smaller than -9999) and the like. Such serious errors are called fatal errors. When a fatal error is detected, your simulator should print an error message such as

```
*** Attempt to divide by zero ***
*** Simpletron execution abnormally terminated ***
```

and should print a full computer dump in the format we have discussed previously. This will help the user locate the error in the program.

More Pointer Exercises

8.20   Modify the card shuffling and dealing program of Figs. 8.25–8.27 so the shuffling and dealing operations are performed by the same function (shuffleAndDeal). The function should contain one nested looping statement that is similar to function shuffle in Fig. 8.26.

8.21   What does this program do?

```
1   // Ex. 8.21: ex08_21.cpp
2   // What does this program do?
3   #include <iostream>
4   using std::cout;
5   using std::cin;
6   using std::endl;
7
8   void mystery1( char *, const char * ); // prototype
9
10  int main()
11  {
12     char string1[ 80 ];
13     char string2[ 80 ];
14
15     cout << "Enter two strings: ";
16     cin >> string1 >> string2;
17     mystery1( string1, string2 );
18     cout << string1 << endl;
19     return 0; // indicates successful termination
20  } // end main
21
22  // What does this function do?
23  void mystery1( char *s1, const char *s2 )
24  {
25     while ( *s1 != '\0' )
26        ++s1;
27
28     for ( ; *s1 = *s2; s1++, s2++ )
29        ; // empty statement
30  } // end function mystery1
```

8.22 What does this program do?

```
1   // Ex. 8.22: ex08_22.cpp
2   // What does this program do?
3   #include <iostream>
4   using std::cout;
5   using std::cin;
6   using std::endl;
7
8   int mystery2( const char * ); // prototype
9
10  int main()
11  {
12     char string1[ 80 ];
13
14     cout << "Enter a string: ";
15     cin >> string1;
16     cout << mystery2( string1 ) << endl;
17     return 0; // indicates successful termination
18  } // end main
19
```

```
20   // What does this function do?
21   int mystery2( const char *s )
22   {
23      int x;
24
25      for ( x = 0; *s != '\0'; s++ )
26         ++x;
27
28      return x;
29   } // end function mystery2
```

8.23 Find the error in each of the following segments. If the error can be corrected, explain how.

a) ```
int *number;
cout << number << endl;
```

b) ```
double *realPtr;
long *integerPtr;
integerPtr = realPtr;
```

c) ```
int * x, y;
x = y;
```

d) ```
char s[] = "this is a character array";
for ( ; *s != '\0'; s++)
   cout << *s << ' ';
```

e) ```
short *numPtr, result;
void *genericPtr = numPtr;
result = *genericPtr + 7;
```

f) ```
double x = 19.34;
double xPtr = &x;
cout << xPtr << endl;
```

g) ```
char *s;
cout << s << endl;
```

**8.24** (*Quicksort*) You have previously seen the sorting techniques of the bucket sort and selection sort. We now present the recursive sorting technique called Quicksort. The basic algorithm for a single-subscripted array of values is as follows:

a) *Partitioning Step:* Take the first element of the unsorted array and determine its final location in the sorted array (i.e., all values to the left of the element in the array are less than the element, and all values to the right of the element in the array are greater than the element). We now have one element in its proper location and two unsorted subarrays.

b) *Recursive Step:* Perform *Step 1* on each unsorted subarray.

Each time *Step 1* is performed on a subarray, another element is placed in its final location of the sorted array, and two unsorted subarrays are created. When a subarray consists of one element, that subarray must be sorted; therefore, that element is in its final location.

The basic algorithm seems simple enough, but how do we determine the final position of the first element of each subarray? As an example, consider the following set of values (the element in bold is the partitioning element—it will be placed in its final location in the sorted array):

**37** 2 6 4 89 8 10 12 68 45

a) Starting from the rightmost element of the array, compare each element with **37** until an element less than **37** is found. Then swap **37** and that element. The first element less than **37** is 12, so **37** and 12 are swapped. The values now reside in the array as follows:

*12* 2 6 4 89 8 10 **37** 68 45

Element 12 is in italics to indicate that it was just swapped with **37**.
```

b) Starting from the left of the array, but beginning with the element after 12, compare each element with **37** until an element greater than **37** is found. Then swap **37** and that element. The first element greater than **37** is 89, so **37** and 89 are swapped. The values now reside in the array as follows:

12   2   6   4   **37**   8   10   *89*   68   45

c) Starting from the right, but beginning with the element before 89, compare each element with **37** until an element less than **37** is found. Then swap **37** and that element. The first element less than **37** is 10, so **37** and 10 are swapped. The values now reside in the array as follows:

12   2   6   4   *10*   8   **37**   89   68   45

d) Starting from the left, but beginning with the element after 10, compare each element with **37** until an element greater than **37** is found. Then swap **37** and that element. There are no more elements greater than **37**, so when we compare **37** with itself, we know that **37** has been placed in its final location of the sorted array.

Once the partition has been applied to the array, there are two unsorted subarrays. The subarray with values less than 37 contains 12, 2, 6, 4, 10 and 8. The subarray with values greater than 37 contains 89, 68 and 45. The sort continues with both subarrays being partitioned in the same manner as the original array.

Based on the preceding discussion, write recursive function quickSort to sort a single-subscripted integer array. The function should receive as arguments an integer array, a starting subscript and an ending subscript. Function partition should be called by quickSort to perform the partitioning step.

8.25 (*Maze Traversal*) The grid of hashes (#) and dots (.) in Fig. 8.44 is a two-dimensional array representation of a maze. In the two-dimensional array, the hashes represent the walls of the maze and the dots represent squares in the possible paths through the maze. Moves can be made only to a location in the array that contains a dot.

There is a simple algorithm for walking through a maze that guarantees finding the exit (assuming that there is an exit). If there is not an exit, you will arrive at the starting location again. Place your right hand on the wall to your right and begin walking forward. Never remove your hand from the wall. If the maze turns to the right, you follow the wall to the right. As long as you do not remove your hand from the wall, eventually you will arrive at the exit of the maze. There may be a shorter path than the one you have taken, but you are guaranteed to get out of the maze if you follow the algorithm.

```
# # # # # # # # # # #
# . . . # . . . . . #
. . # . # . # # # # . #
# # # . # . . . . # . #
# . . . # # # . # . .
# # # # . # . # . # . #
# . . # . # . # . # . #
# # . # . # . # . # . #
# . . . . . . . # . #
# # # # # . # # # . #
# . . . . . # . . . #
# # # # # # # # # # #
```

Fig. 8.44 | Two-dimensional array representation of a maze.

Write recursive function `mazeTraverse` to walk through the maze. The function should receive arguments that include a 12-by-12 character array representing the maze and the starting location of the maze. As `mazeTraverse` attempts to locate the exit from the maze, it should place the character X in each square in the path. The function should display the maze after each move, so the user can watch as the maze is solved.

8.26   (*Generating Mazes Randomly*) Write a function `mazeGenerator` that takes as an argument a two-dimensional 12-by-12 character array and randomly produces a maze. The function should also provide the starting and ending locations of the maze. Try your function `mazeTraverse` from Exercise 8.25, using several randomly generated mazes.

8.27   (*Mazes of Any Size*) Generalize functions `mazeTraverse` and `mazeGenerator` of Exercise 8.25 and Exercise 8.26 to process mazes of any width and height.

8.28   (*Modifications to the Simpletron Simulator*) In Exercise 8.19, you wrote a software simulation of a computer that executes programs written in Simpletron Machine Language (SML). In this exercise, we propose several modifications and enhancements to the Simpletron Simulator. In Exercise 21.26 and Exercise 21.27, we propose building a compiler that converts programs written in a high-level programming language (a variation of BASIC) to SML. Some of the following modifications and enhancements may be required to execute the programs produced by the compiler. [*Note:* Some modifications may conflict with others and therefore must be done separately.]

a) Extend the Simpletron Simulator's memory to contain 1000 memory locations to enable the Simpletron to handle larger programs.

b) Allow the simulator to perform modulus calculations. This requires an additional Simpletron Machine Language instruction.

c) Allow the simulator to perform exponentiation calculations. This requires an additional Simpletron Machine Language instruction.

d) Modify the simulator to use hexadecimal values rather than integer values to represent Simpletron Machine Language instructions.

e) Modify the simulator to allow output of a newline. This requires an additional Simpletron Machine Language instruction.

f) Modify the simulator to process floating-point values in addition to integer values.

g) Modify the simulator to handle string input. [*Hint:* Each Simpletron word can be divided into two groups, each holding a two-digit integer. Each two-digit integer represents the ASCII decimal equivalent of a character. Add a machine-language instruction that will input a string and store the string beginning at a specific Simpletron memory location. The first half of the word at that location will be a count of the number of characters in the string (i.e., the length of the string). Each succeeding half-word contains one ASCII character expressed as two decimal digits. The machine-language instruction converts each character into its ASCII equivalent and assigns it to a half-word.]

h) Modify the simulator to handle output of strings stored in the format of part (g). [*Hint:* Add a machine-language instruction that will print a string beginning at a certain Simpletron memory location. The first half of the word at that location is a count of the number of characters in the string (i.e., the length of the string). Each succeeding half-word contains one ASCII character expressed as two decimal digits. The machine-language instruction checks the length and prints the string by translating each two-digit number into its equivalent character.]

i) Modify the simulator to include instruction `SML_DEBUG` that prints a memory dump after each instruction executes. Give `SML_DEBUG` an operation code of 44. The word +4401 turns on debug mode, and +4400 turns off debug mode.

8.29   What does this program do?

```
 1   // Ex. 8.30: ex08_30.cpp
 2   // What does this program do?
 3   #include <iostream>
 4   using std::cout;
 5   using std::cin;
 6   using std::endl;
 7
 8   bool mystery3( const char *, const char * ); // prototype
 9
10   int main()
11   {
12       char string1[ 80 ], string2[ 80 ];
13
14       cout << "Enter two strings: ";
15       cin >> string1 >> string2;
16       cout << "The result is " << mystery3( string1, string2 ) << endl;
17       return 0; // indicates successful termination
18   } // end main
19
20   // What does this function do?
21   bool mystery3( const char *s1, const char *s2 )
22   {
23       for ( ; *s1 != '\0' && *s2 != '\0'; s1++, s2++ )
24
25           if ( *s1 != *s2 )
26               return false;
27
28       return true;
29   } // end function mystery3
```

String-Manipulation Exercises

[*Note:* The following exercises should be implemented using C-style, pointer-based strings.]

8.30   Write a program that uses function strcmp to compare two strings input by the user. The program should state whether the first string is less than, equal to or greater than the second string.

8.31   Write a program that uses function strncmp to compare two strings input by the user. The program should input the number of characters to compare. The program should state whether the first string is less than, equal to or greater than the second string.

8.32   Write a program that uses random number generation to create sentences. The program should use four arrays of pointers to char called article, noun, verb and preposition. The program should create a sentence by selecting a word at random from each array in the following order: article, noun, verb, preposition, article and noun. As each word is picked, it should be concatenated to the previous words in an array that is large enough to hold the entire sentence. The words should be separated by spaces. When the final sentence is output, it should start with a capital letter and end with a period. The program should generate 20 such sentences.

The arrays should be filled as follows: The article array should contain the articles "the", "a", "one", "some" and "any"; the noun array should contain the nouns "boy", "girl", "dog", "town" and "car"; the verb array should contain the verbs "drove", "jumped", "ran", "walked" and "skipped"; the preposition array should contain the prepositions "to", "from", "over", "under" and "on".

After completing the program, modify it to produce a short story consisting of several of these sentences. (How about the possibility of a random term-paper writer!)

8.33   *(Limericks)* A limerick is a humorous five-line verse in which the first and second lines rhyme with the fifth, and the third line rhymes with the fourth. Using techniques similar to those developed in Exercise 8.32, write a C++ program that produces random limericks. Polishing this program to produce good limericks is a challenging problem, but the result will be worth the effort!

8.34   Write a program that encodes English language phrases into pig Latin. Pig Latin is a form of coded language often used for amusement. Many variations exist in the methods used to form pig Latin phrases. For simplicity, use the following algorithm: To form a pig-Latin phrase from an English-language phrase, tokenize the phrase into words with function strtok. To translate each English word into a pig-Latin word, place the first letter of the English word at the end of the English word and add the letters "ay." Thus, the word "jump" becomes "umpjay," the word "the" becomes "hetay" and the word "computer" becomes "omputercay." Blanks between words remain as blanks. Assume that the English phrase consists of words separated by blanks, there are no punctuation marks and all words have two or more letters. Function printLatinWord should display each word. [*Hint:* Each time a token is found in a call to strtok, pass the token pointer to function printLatinWord and print the pig-Latin word.]

8.35   Write a program that inputs a telephone number as a string in the form (555) 555-5555. The program should use function strtok to extract the area code as a token, the first three digits of the phone number as a token, and the last four digits of the phone number as a token. The seven digits of the phone number should be concatenated into one string. Both the area code and the phone number should be printed.

8.36   Write a program that inputs a line of text, tokenizes the line with function strtok and outputs the tokens in reverse order.

8.37   Use the string-comparison functions discussed in Section 8.13.2 and the techniques for sorting arrays developed in Chapter 7 to write a program that alphabetizes a list of strings. Use the names of 10 or 15 towns in your area as data for your program.

8.38   Write two versions of each string copy and string-concatenation function in Fig. 8.30. The first version should use array subscripting, and the second should use pointers and pointer arithmetic.

8.39   Write two versions of each string-comparison function in Fig. 8.30. The first version should use array subscripting, and the second should use pointers and pointer arithmetic.

8.40   Write two versions of function strlen in Fig. 8.30. The first version should use array subscripting, and the second should use pointers and pointer arithmetic.

Special Section: Advanced String-Manipulation Exercises

The preceding exercises are keyed to the text and designed to test the reader's understanding of fundamental string-manipulation concepts. This section includes a collection of intermediate and advanced string-manipulation exercises. The reader should find these problems challenging, yet enjoyable. The problems vary considerably in difficulty. Some require an hour or two of program writing and implementation. Others are useful for lab assignments that might require two or three weeks of study and implementation. Some are challenging term projects.

8.41   *(Text Analysis)* The availability of computers with string-manipulation capabilities has resulted in some rather interesting approaches to analyzing the writings of great authors. Much attention has been focused on whether William Shakespeare ever lived. Some scholars believe there is substantial evidence indicating that Christopher Marlowe or other authors actually penned the masterpieces attributed to Shakespeare. Researchers have used computers to find similarities in the writings of these two authors. This exercise examines three methods for analyzing texts with a computer. Note that thousands of texts, including Shakespeare, are available online at www.gutenberg.org.

a) Write a program that reads several lines of text from the keyboard and prints a table indicating the number of occurrences of each letter of the alphabet in the text. For example, the phrase

```
To be, or not to be: that is the question:
```

contains one "a," two "b's," no "c's," etc.

b) Write a program that reads several lines of text and prints a table indicating the number of one-letter words, two-letter words, three-letter words, etc., appearing in the text. For example, the phrase

```
Whether 'tis nobler in the mind to suffer
```

contains the following word lengths and occurrences:

Word length	Occurrences
1	0
2	2
3	1
4	2 (including 'tis)
5	0
6	2
7	1

c) Write a program that reads several lines of text and prints a table indicating the number of occurrences of each different word in the text. The first version of your program should include the words in the table in the same order in which they appear in the text. For example, the lines

```
To be, or not to be: that is the question:
Whether 'tis nobler in the mind to suffer
```

contain the words "to" three times, the word "be" two times, the word "or" once, etc. A more interesting (and useful) printout should then be attempted in which the words are sorted alphabetically.

8.42   *(Word Processing)* One important function in word-processing systems is *type justification*—the alignment of words to both the left and right margins of a page. This generates a professional-looking document that gives the appearance of being set in type rather than prepared on a typewriter. Type justification can be accomplished on computer systems by inserting blank characters between each of the words in a line so that the rightmost word aligns with the right margin.

Write a program that reads several lines of text and prints this text in type-justified format. Assume that the text is to be printed on paper 8 1/2 inches wide and that one-inch margins are to be allowed on both the left and right sides. Assume that the computer prints 10 characters to the horizontal inch. Therefore, your program should print 6-1/2 inches of text, or 65 characters per line.

8.43   *(Printing Dates in Various Formats)* Dates are commonly printed in several different formats in business correspondence. Two of the more common formats are

```
07/21/1955
July 21, 1955
```

Write a program that reads a date in the first format and prints that date in the second format.

8.44   *(Check Protection)* Computers are frequently employed in check-writing systems such as payroll and accounts-payable applications. Many strange stories circulate regarding weekly paychecks being printed (by mistake) for amounts in excess of $1 million. Weird amounts are printed by computerized check-writing systems, because of human error or machine failure. Systems designers build controls into their systems to prevent such erroneous checks from being issued.

Another serious problem is the intentional alteration of a check amount by someone who intends to cash a check fraudulently. To prevent a dollar amount from being altered, most computerized check-writing systems employ a technique called *check protection.*

Checks designed for imprinting by computer contain a fixed number of spaces in which the computer may print an amount. Suppose that a paycheck contains eight blank spaces in which the computer is supposed to print the amount of a weekly paycheck. If the amount is large, then all eight of those spaces will be filled, for example,

```
1,230.60    (check amount)
--------
12345678    (position numbers)
```

On the other hand, if the amount is less than $1000, then several of the spaces would ordinarily be left blank. For example,

```
   99.87
--------
12345678
```

contains three blank spaces. If a check is printed with blank spaces, it is easier for someone to alter the amount of the check. To prevent a check from being altered, many check-writing systems insert *leading asterisks* to protect the amount as follows:

```
***99.87
--------
12345678
```

Write a program that inputs a dollar amount to be printed on a check and then prints the amount in check-protected format with leading asterisks if necessary. Assume that nine spaces are available for printing an amount.

8.45   *(Writing the Word Equivalent of a Check Amount)* Continuing the discussion of the previous example, we reiterate the importance of designing check-writing systems to prevent alteration of check amounts. One common security method requires that the check amount be both written in numbers and "spelled out" in words. Even if someone is able to alter the numerical amount of the check, it is extremely difficult to change the amount in words.

Write a program that inputs a numeric check amount and writes the word equivalent of the amount. Your program should be able to handle check amounts as large as $99.99. For example, the amount 112.43 should be written as

```
ONE HUNDRED TWELVE and 43/100
```

8.46 *(Morse Code)* Perhaps the most famous of all coding schemes is the Morse code, developed by Samuel Morse in 1832 for use with the telegraph system. The Morse code assigns a series of dots and dashes to each letter of the alphabet, each digit and a few special characters (such as period, comma, colon and semicolon). In sound-oriented systems, the dot represents a short sound, and the dash represents a long sound. Other representations of dots and dashes are used with light-oriented systems and signal-flag systems.

Separation between words is indicated by a space, or, quite simply, the absence of a dot or dash. In a sound-oriented system, a space is indicated by a short period of time during which no sound is transmitted. The international version of the Morse code appears in Fig. 8.45.

Write a program that reads an English-language phrase and encodes it into Morse code. Also write a program that reads a phrase in Morse code and converts it into the English-language equivalent. Use one blank between each Morse-coded letter and three blanks between each Morse-coded word.

Character	Code	Character	Code
A	.-	N	-.
B	-...	O	---
C	-.-.	P	.--.
D	-..	Q	--.-
E	.	R	.-.
F	..-.	S	...
G	--.	T	-
H	....	U	..-
I	..	V	...-
J	.---	W	.--
K	-.-	X	-..-
L	.-..	Y	-.--
M	--	Z	--..
Digits			
1	.----	6	-....
2	..---	7	--...
3	...--	8	---..
4	....-	9	----.
5	.....	0	-----

Fig. 8.45 | Morse code alphabet.

8.47 *(A Metric Conversion Program)* Write a program that will assist the user with metric conversions. Your program should allow the user to specify the names of the units as strings (i.e., centimeters, liters, grams, etc., for the metric system and inches, quarts, pounds, etc., for the English system) and should respond to simple questions such as

```
"How many inches are in 2 meters?"
"How many liters are in 10 quarts?"
```

Your program should recognize invalid conversions. For example, the question

```
"How many feet are in 5 kilograms?"
```

is not meaningful, because "feet" are units of length, while "kilograms" are units of weight.

A Challenging String-Manipulation Project

8.48 *(A Crossword Puzzle Generator)* Most people have worked a crossword puzzle, but few have ever attempted to generate one. Generating a crossword puzzle is a difficult problem. It is suggested here as a string-manipulation project requiring substantial sophistication and effort. There are many issues that the programmer must resolve to get even the simplest crossword puzzle generator program working. For example, how does one represent the grid of a crossword puzzle inside the computer? Should one use a series of strings, or should two-dimensional arrays be used? The programmer needs a source of words (i.e., a computerized dictionary) that can be directly referenced by the program. In what form should these words be stored to facilitate the complex manipulations required by the program? The really ambitious reader will want to generate the "clues" portion of the puzzle, in which the brief hints for each "across" word and each "down" word are printed for the puzzle worker. Merely printing a version of the blank puzzle itself is not a simple problem.

9

Classes:
A Deeper Look,
Part I

OBJECTIVES

In this chapter you will learn:

- How to use a preprocessor wrapper to prevent multiple definition errors caused by including more than one copy of a header file in a source-code file.

- To understand class scope and accessing class members via the name of an object, a reference to an object or a pointer to an object.

- To define constructors with default arguments.

- How destructors are used to perform "termination housekeeping" on an object before it is destroyed.

- When constructors and destructors are called and the order in which they are called.

- The logic errors that may occur when a **public** member function of a class returns a reference to **private** data.

- To assign the data members of one object to those of another object by default memberwise assignment.

9.1   Introduction

In the preceding chapters, we introduced many basic terms and concepts of C++ object-oriented programming. We also discussed our program development methodology: We selected appropriate attributes and behaviors for each class and specified the manner in which objects of our classes collaborated with objects of C++ Standard Library classes to accomplish each program's overall goals.

In this chapter, we take a deeper look at classes. We use an integrated Time class case study in this chapter (three examples) and Chapter 10 (two examples) to demonstrate several class construction features. We begin with a Time class that reviews several of the features presented in the preceding chapters. The example also demonstrates an important C++ software engineering concept—using a "preprocessor wrapper" in header files to prevent the code in the header from being included into the same source code file more than once. Since a class can be defined only once, using such preprocessor directives prevents multiple definition errors.

Next, we discuss class scope and the relationships among members of a class. We also demonstrate how client code can access a class's public members via three types of "handles"—the name of an object, a reference to an object or a pointer to an object. As you will see, object names and references can be used with the dot (.) member selection operator to access a public member, and pointers can be used with the arrow (->) member selection operator.

We discuss access functions that can read or display data in an object. A common use of access functions is to test the truth or falsity of conditions—such functions are known as predicate functions. We also demonstrate the notion of a utility function (also called a helper function)—a private member function that supports the operation of the class's public member functions, but is not intended for use by clients of the class.

In the second example of the Time class case study, we demonstrate how to pass arguments to constructors and show how default arguments can be used in a constructor to enable client code to initialize objects of a class using a variety of arguments. Next, we discuss a special member function called a destructor that is part of every class and is used to perform "termination housekeeping" on an object before the object is destroyed. We then demonstrate the order in which constructors and destructors are called, because your programs' correctness depends on using properly initialized objects that have not yet been destroyed.

Our last example of the Time class case study in this chapter shows a dangerous programming practice in which a member function returns a reference to private data. We discuss how this breaks the encapsulation of a class and allows client code to directly access an object's data. This last example shows that objects of the same class can be assigned to one another using default memberwise assignment, which copies the data members in the object on the right side of the assignment into the corresponding data members of the object on the left side of the assignment. The chapter concludes with a discussion of software reusability.

9.2 Time Class Case Study

Our first example (Figs. 9.1–9.3) creates class Time and a driver program that tests the class. You have already created several classes in this book. In this section, we review many of the concepts covered in Chapter 3 and demonstrate an important C++ software engineering concept—using a "preprocessor wrapper" in header files to prevent the code in the header from being included into the same source code file more than once. Since a class can be defined only once, using such preprocessor directives prevents multiple-definition errors.

```
1   // Fig. 9.1: Time.h
2   // Declaration of class Time.
3   // Member functions are defined in Time.cpp
4
5   // prevent multiple inclusions of header file
6   #ifndef TIME_H
7   #define TIME_H
8
9   // Time class definition
10  class Time
11  {
12  public:
13     Time(); // constructor
14     void setTime( int, int, int ); // set hour, minute and second
15     void printUniversal(); // print time in universal-time format
16     void printStandard(); // print time in standard-time format
17  private:
18     int hour; // 0 - 23 (24-hour clock format)
19     int minute; // 0 - 59
20     int second; // 0 - 59
21  }; // end class Time
22
23  #endif
```

Fig. 9.1 | Time class definition.

Time Class Definition

The class definition (Fig. 9.1) contains prototypes (lines 13–16) for member functions Time, setTime, printUniversal and printStandard. The class includes private integer members hour, minute and second (lines 18–20). Class Time's private data members can be accessed only by its four member functions. Chapter 12 introduces a third access specifier, protected, as we study inheritance and the part it plays in object-oriented programming.

Good Programming Practice 9.1

For clarity and readability, use each access specifier only once in a class definition. Place public members first, where they are easy to locate.

Software Engineering Observation 9.1

Each element of a class should have private visibility unless it can be proven that the element needs public visibility. This is another example of the principle of least privilege.

In Fig. 9.1, note that the class definition is enclosed in the following preprocessor wrapper (lines 5–7 and 23):

```
// prevent multiple inclusions of header file
#ifndef TIME_H
#define TIME_H
   ...
#endif
```

When we build larger programs, other definitions and declarations will also be placed in header files. The preceding preprocessor wrapper prevents the code between #ifndef (which means "if not defined") and #endif from being included if the name TIME_H has been defined. If the header has not been included previously in a file, the name TIME_H is defined by the #define directive and the header file statements are included. If the header has been included previously, TIME_H is defined already and the header file is not included again. Attempts to include a header file multiple times (inadvertently) typically occur in large programs with many header files that may themselves include other header files. [*Note:* The commonly used convention for the symbolic constant name in the preprocessor directives is simply the header file name in upper case with the underscore character replacing the period.]

Error-Prevention Tip 9.1

Use #ifndef, #define and #endif preprocessor directives to form a preprocessor wrapper that prevents header files from being included more than once in a program.

Good Programming Practice 9.2

Use the name of the header file in upper case with the period replaced by an underscore in the #ifndef and #define preprocessor directives of a header file.

Time Class Member Functions

In Fig. 9.2, the Time constructor (lines 14–17) initializes the data members to 0 (i.e., the universal-time equivalent of 12 AM). This ensures that the object begins in a consistent state. Invalid values cannot be stored in the data members of a Time object, because the constructor is called when the Time object is created, and all subsequent attempts by a client to modify

```cpp
1   // Fig. 9.2: Time.cpp
2   // Member-function definitions for class Time.
3   #include <iostream>
4   using std::cout;
5
6   #include <iomanip>
7   using std::setfill;
8   using std::setw;
9
10  #include "Time.h" // include definition of class Time from Time.h
11
12  // Time constructor initializes each data member to zero.
13  // Ensures all Time objects start in a consistent state.
14  Time::Time()
15  {
16     hour = minute = second = 0;
17  } // end Time constructor
18
19  // set new Time value using universal time; ensure that
20  // the data remains consistent by setting invalid values to zero
21  void Time::setTime( int h, int m, int s )
22  {
23     hour = ( h >= 0 && h < 24 ) ? h : 0; // validate hour
24     minute = ( m >= 0 && m < 60 ) ? m : 0; // validate minute
25     second = ( s >= 0 && s < 60 ) ? s : 0; // validate second
26  } // end function setTime
27
28  // print Time in universal-time format (HH:MM:SS)
29  void Time::printUniversal()
30  {
31     cout << setfill( '0' ) << setw( 2 ) << hour << ":"
32        << setw( 2 ) << minute << ":" << setw( 2 ) << second;
33  } // end function printUniversal
34
35  // print Time in standard-time format (HH:MM:SS AM or PM)
36  void Time::printStandard()
37  {
38     cout << ( ( hour == 0 || hour == 12 ) ? 12 : hour % 12 ) << ":"
39        << setfill( '0' ) << setw( 2 ) << minute << ":" << setw( 2 )
40        << second << ( hour < 12 ? " AM" : " PM" );
41  } // end function printStandard
```

Fig. 9.2 | Time class member-function definitions.

the data members are scrutinized by function setTime (discussed shortly). Finally, it is important to note that the programmer can define several overloaded constructors for a class.

The data members of a class cannot be initialized where they are declared in the class body. It is strongly recommended that these data members be initialized by the class's constructor (as there is no default initialization for fundamental-type data members). Data members can also be assigned values by Time's *set* functions. [*Note:* Chapter 10 demonstrates that only a class's static const data members of integral or enum types can be initialized in the class's body.]

Common Programming Error 9.1

Attempting to initialize a non-static data member of a class explicitly in the class definition is a syntax error.

Function setTime (lines 21–26) is a public function that declares three int parameters and uses them to set the time. A conditional expression tests each argument to determine whether the value is in a specified range. For example, the hour value (line 23) must be greater than or equal to 0 and less than 24, because the universal-time format represents hours as integers from 0 to 23 (e.g., 1 PM is hour 13 and 11 PM is hour 23; midnight is hour 0 and noon is hour 12). Similarly, both minute and second values (lines 24 and 25) must be greater than or equal to 0 and less than 60. Any values outside these ranges are set to zero to ensure that a Time object always contains consistent data—that is, the object's data values are always kept in range, even if the values provided as arguments to function setTime were incorrect. In this example, zero is a consistent value for hour, minute and second.

A value passed to setTime is a correct value if it is in the allowed range for the member it is initializing. So, any number in the range 0–23 would be a correct value for the hour. A correct value is always a consistent value. However, a consistent value is not necessarily a correct value. If setTime sets hour to 0 because the argument received was out of range, then hour is correct only if the current time is coincidentally midnight.

Function printUniversal (lines 29–33 of Fig. 9.2) takes no arguments and outputs the date in universal-time format, consisting of three colon-separated pairs of digits—for the hour, minute and second, respectively. For example, if the time were 1:30:07 PM, function printUniversal would return 13:30:07. Note that line 31 uses parameterized stream manipulator setfill to specify the fill character that is displayed when an integer is output in a field wider than the number of digits in the value. By default, the fill characters appear to the left of the digits in the number. In this example, if the minute value is 2, it will be displayed as 02, because the fill character is set to zero ('0'). If the number being output fills the specified field, the fill character will not be displayed. Note that, once the fill character is specified with setfill, it applies for all subsequent values that are displayed in fields wider than the value being displayed (i.e., setfill is a "sticky" setting). This is in contrast to setw, which applies only to the next value displayed (setw is a "nonsticky" setting).

Error-Prevention Tip 9.2

Each sticky setting (such as a fill character or floating-point precision) should be restored to its previous setting when it is no longer needed. Failure to do so may result in incorrectly formatted output later in a program. Chapter 15, Stream Input/Output, discusses how to reset the fill character and precision.

Function printStandard (lines 36–41) takes no arguments and outputs the date in standard-time format, consisting of the hour, minute and second values separated by colons and followed by an AM or PM indicator (e.g., 1:27:06 PM). Like function print-Universal, function printStandard uses setfill('0') to format the minute and second as two digit values with leading zeros if necessary. Line 38 uses a conditional operator (?:) to determine the value of hour to be displayed—if the hour is 0 or 12 (AM or PM), it appears as 12; otherwise, the hour appears as a value from 1 to 11. The conditional operator in line 40 determines whether AM or PM will be displayed.

Defining Member Functions Outside the Class Definition; Class Scope
Even though a member function declared in a class definition may be defined outside that class definition (and "tied" to the class via the binary scope resolution operator), that member function is still within that class's **scope**; i.e., its name is known only to other members of the class unless referred to via an object of the class, a reference to an object of the class, a pointer to an object of the class or the binary scope resolution operator. We will say more about class scope shortly.

If a member function is defined in the body of a class definition, the C++ compiler attempts to inline calls to the member function. Member functions defined outside a class definition can be inlined by explicitly using keyword `inline`. Remember that the compiler reserves the right not to inline any function.

Performance Tip 9.1

Defining a member function inside the class definition inlines the member function (if the compiler chooses to do so). This can improve performance.

Software Engineering Observation 9.2

Defining a small member function inside the class definition does not promote the best software engineering, because clients of the class will be able to see the implementation of the function, and the client code must be recompiled if the function definition changes.

Software Engineering Observation 9.3

Only the simplest and most stable member functions (i.e., whose implementations are unlikely to change) should be defined in the class header.

Member Functions vs. Global Functions
It is interesting that the `printUniversal` and `printStandard` member functions take no arguments. This is because these member functions implicitly know that they are to print the data members of the particular `Time` object for which they are invoked. This can make member function calls more concise than conventional function calls in procedural programming.

Software Engineering Observation 9.4

Using an object-oriented programming approach can often simplify function calls by reducing the number of parameters to be passed. This benefit of object-oriented programming derives from the fact that encapsulating data members and member functions within an object gives the member functions the right to access the data members.

Software Engineering Observation 9.5

Member functions are usually shorter than functions in non-object-oriented programs, because the data stored in data members have ideally been validated by a constructor or by member functions that store new data. Because the data is already in the object, the member-function calls often have no arguments or at least have fewer arguments than typical function calls in non-object-oriented languages. Thus, the calls are shorter, the function definitions are shorter and the function prototypes are shorter. This facilitates many aspects of program development.

Error-Prevention Tip 9.3

The fact that member function calls generally take either no arguments or substantially fewer arguments than conventional function calls in non-object-oriented languages reduces the likelihood of passing the wrong arguments, the wrong types of arguments or the wrong number of arguments.

Using Class **Time**

Once class Time has been defined, it can be used as a type in object, array, pointer and reference declarations as follows:

```
Time sunset; // object of type Time
Time arrayOfTimes[ 5 ], // array of 5 Time objects
Time &dinnerTime = sunset; // reference to a Time object
Time *timePtr = &dinnerTime, // pointer to a Time object
```

Figure 9.3 uses class Time. Line 12 instantiates a single object of class Time called t. When the object is instantiated, the Time constructor is called to initialize each private data member to 0. Then, lines 16 and 18 print the time in universal and standard formats to confirm that the members were initialized properly. Line 20 sets a new time by calling member function setTime, and lines 24 and 26 print the time again in both formats. Line 28 attempts to use setTime to set the data members to invalid values—function setTime recognizes this and sets the invalid values to 0 to maintain the object in a consistent state. Finally, lines 33 and 35 print the time again in both formats.

Looking Ahead to Composition and Inheritance

Often, classes do not have to be created "from scratch." Rather, they can include objects of other classes as members or they may be **derived** from other classes that provide attributes and behaviors the new classes can use. Such software reuse can greatly enhance programmer productivity and simplify code maintenance. Including class objects as members of other classes is called **composition** (or **aggregation**) and is discussed in Chapter 10. Deriving new classes from existing classes is called **inheritance** and is discussed in Chapter 12.

Object Size

People new to object-oriented programming often suppose that objects must be quite large because they contain data members and member functions. Logically, this is true—the programmer may think of objects as containing data and functions (and our discussion has certainly encouraged this view); physically, however, this is not true.

 Performance Tip 9.2

Objects contain only data, so objects are much smaller than if they also contained member functions. Applying operator sizeof to a class name or to an object of that class will report only the size of the class's data members. The compiler creates one copy (only) of the member functions separate from all objects of the class. All objects of the class share this one copy. Each object, of course, needs its own copy of the class's data, because the data can vary among the objects. The function code is nonmodifiable (also called reentrant code or pure procedure) and, hence, can be shared among all objects of one class.

9.3 Class Scope and Accessing Class Members

A class's data members (variables declared in the class definition) and member functions (functions declared in the class definition) belong to that class's scope. Nonmember functions are defined at **file scope**.

Within a class's scope, class members are immediately accessible by all of that class's member functions and can be referenced by name. Outside a class's scope, public class members are referenced through one of the **handles** on an object—an object name, a reference to an object or a pointer to an object. The type of the object, reference or pointer

```
 1   // Fig. 9.3: fig09_03.cpp
 2   // Program to test class Time.
 3   // NOTE: This file must be compiled with Time.cpp.
 4   #include <iostream>
 5   using std::cout;
 6   using std::endl;
 7
 8   #include "Time.h" // include definition of class Time from Time.h
 9
10   int main()
11   {
12      Time t; // instantiate object t of class Time
13
14      // output Time object t's initial values
15      cout << "The initial universal time is ";
16      t.printUniversal(); // 00:00:00
17      cout << "\nThe initial standard time is ";
18      t.printStandard(); // 12:00:00 AM
19
20      t.setTime( 13, 27, 6 ); // change time
21
22      // output Time object t's new values
23      cout << "\n\nUniversal time after setTime is ";
24      t.printUniversal(); // 13:27:06
25      cout << "\nStandard time after setTime is ";
26      t.printStandard(); // 1:27:06 PM
27
28      t.setTime( 99, 99, 99 ); // attempt invalid settings
29
30      // output t's values after specifying invalid values
31      cout << "\n\nAfter attempting invalid settings:"
32         << "\nUniversal time: ";
33      t.printUniversal(); // 00:00:00
34      cout << "\nStandard time: ";
35      t.printStandard(); // 12:00:00 AM
36      cout << endl;
37      return 0;
38   } // end main
```

```
The initial universal time is 00:00:00
The initial standard time is 12:00:00 AM

Universal time after setTime is 13:27:06
Standard time after setTime is 1:27:06 PM

After attempting invalid settings:
Universal time: 00:00:00
Standard time: 12:00:00 AM
```

Fig. 9.3 | Program to test class Time.

specifies the interface (i.e., the member functions) accessible to the client. [We will see in Chapter 10 that an implicit handle is inserted by the compiler on every reference to a data member or member function from within an object.]

Member functions of a class can be overloaded, but only by other member functions of that class. To overload a member function, simply provide in the class definition a prototype for each version of the overloaded function, and provide a separate function definition for each version of the function.

Variables declared in a member function have block scope and are known only to that function. If a member function defines a variable with the same name as a variable with class scope, the class-scope variable is hidden by the block-scope variable in the block scope. Such a hidden variable can be accessed by preceding the variable name with the class name followed by the scope resolution operator (::). Hidden global variables can be accessed with the unary scope resolution operator (see Chapter 6).

The dot member selection operator (.) is preceded by an object's name or with a reference to an object to access the object's members. The arrow member selection operator (->) is preceded by a pointer to an object to access the object's members.

Figure 9.4 uses a simple class called Count (lines 8–25) with private data member x of type int (line 24), public member function setX (lines 12–15) and public member function print (lines 18–21) to illustrate accessing the members of a class with the member selection operators. For simplicity, we have included this small class in the same file as the main function that uses it. Lines 29–31 create three variables related to type Count—counter (a Count object), counterPtr (a pointer to a Count object) and counterRef (a reference to a Count object). Variable counterRef refers to counter, and variable counterPtr points to counter. In lines 34–35 and 38–39, note that the program can invoke member functions setX and print by using the dot (.) member selection operator preceded by either the name of the object (counter) or a reference to the object (counterRef, which is an alias for counter). Similarly, lines 42–43 demonstrate that the program can invoke member functions setX and print by using a pointer (countPtr) and the arrow (->) member selection operator.

9.4 Separating Interface from Implementation

In Chapter 3, we began by including a class's definition and member-function definitions in one file. We then demonstrated separating this code into two files—a header file for the class definition (i.e., the class's interface) and a source code file for the class's member-function definitions (i.e., the class's implementation). Recall that this makes it easier to modify programs—as far as clients of a class are concerned, changes in the class's implementation do not affect the client as long as the class's interface originally provided to the client remains unchanged.

Software Engineering Observation 9.6

Clients of a class do not need access to the class's source code in order to use the class. The clients do, however, need to be able to link to the class's object code (i.e., the compiled version of the class). This encourages independent software vendors (ISVs) to provide class libraries for sale or license. The ISVs provide in their products only the header files and the object modules. No proprietary information is revealed—as would be the case if source code were provided. The C++ user community benefits by having more ISV-produced class libraries available.

Actually, things are not quite this rosy. Header files do contain some portions of the implementation and hints about others. Inline member functions, for example, need to be in a header file, so that when the compiler compiles a client, the client can include the

```
1    // Fig. 9.4: fig09_04.cpp
2    // Demonstrating the class member access operators . and ->
3    #include <iostream>
4    using std::cout;
5    using std::endl;
6
7    // class Count definition
8    class Count
9    {
10   public: // public data is dangerous
11      // sets the value of private data member x
12      void setX( int value )
13      {
14         x = value;
15      } // end function setX
16
17      // prints the value of private data member x
18      void print()
19      {
20         cout << x << endl;
21      } // end function print
22
23   private:
24      int x;
25   }; // end class Count
26
27   int main()
28   {
29      Count counter; // create counter object
30      Count *counterPtr = &counter; // create pointer to counter
31      Count &counterRef = counter; // create reference to counter
32
33      cout << "Set x to 1 and print using the object's name: ";
34      counter.setX( 1 ); // set data member x to 1
35      counter.print(); // call member function print
36
37      cout << "Set x to 2 and print using a reference to an object: ";
38      counterRef.setX( 2 ); // set data member x to 2
39      counterRef.print(); // call member function print
40
41      cout << "Set x to 3 and print using a pointer to an object: ";
42      counterPtr->setX( 3 ); // set data member x to 3
43      counterPtr->print(); // call member function print
44      return 0;
45   } // end main
```

```
Set x to 1 and print using the object's name: 1
Set x to 2 and print using a reference to an object: 2
Set x to 3 and print using a pointer to an object: 3
```

Fig. 9.4 | Accessing an object's member functions through each type of object handle—the object's name, a reference to the object and a pointer to the object.

inline function definition in place. A class's `private` members are listed in the class definition in the header file, so these members are visible to clients even though the clients may not access the `private` members. In Chapter 10, we show how to use a "proxy class" to hide even the `private` data of a class from clients of the class.

 Software Engineering Observation 9.7

Information important to the interface to a class should be included in the header file. Information that will be used only internally in the class and will not be needed by clients of the class should be included in the unpublished source file. This is yet another example of the principle of least privilege.

9.5 Access Functions and Utility Functions

Access functions can read or display data. Another common use for access functions is to test the truth or falsity of conditions—such functions are often called predicate functions. An example of a predicate function would be an `isEmpty` function for any container class—a class capable of holding many objects—such as a linked list, a stack or a queue. A program might test `isEmpty` before attempting to read another item from the container object. An `isFull` predicate function might test a container-class object to determine whether it has no additional room. Useful predicate functions for our `Time` class might be `isAM` and `isPM`.

The program of Figs. 9.5–9.7 demonstrates the notion of a utility function (also called a helper function). A utility function is not part of a class's `public` interface; rather, it is a `private` member function that supports the operation of the class's `public` member functions. Utility functions are not intended to be used by clients of a class (but can be used by `friend`s of a class, as we will see in Chapter 10).

Class `SalesPerson` (Fig. 9.5) declares an array of 12 monthly sales figures (line 16) and the prototypes for the class's constructor and member functions that manipulate the array.

In Fig. 9.6, the `SalesPerson` constructor (lines 15–19) initializes array `sales` to zero. The `public` member function `setSales` (lines 36–43) sets the sales figure for one month

```
1   // Fig. 9.5: SalesPerson.h
2   // SalesPerson class definition.
3   // Member functions defined in SalesPerson.cpp.
4   #ifndef SALESP_H
5   #define SALESP_H
6
7   class SalesPerson
8   {
9   public:
10     SalesPerson(); // constructor
11     void getSalesFromUser(); // input sales from keyboard
12     void setSales( int, double ); // set sales for a specific month
13     void printAnnualSales(); // summarize and print sales
14   private:
15     double totalAnnualSales(); // prototype for utility function
16     double sales[ 12 ]; // 12 monthly sales figures
17   }; // end class SalesPerson
18
19   #endif
```

Fig. 9.5 | `SalesPerson` class definition.

```cpp
1   // Fig. 9.6: SalesPerson.cpp
2   // Member functions for class SalesPerson.
3   #include <iostream>
4   using std::cout;
5   using std::cin;
6   using std::endl;
7   using std::fixed;
8
9   #include <iomanip>
10  using std::setprecision;
11
12  #include "SalesPerson.h" // include SalesPerson class definition
13
14  // initialize elements of array sales to 0.0
15  SalesPerson::SalesPerson()
16  {
17     for ( int i = 0; i < 12; i++ )
18        sales[ i ] = 0.0;
19  } // end SalesPerson constructor
20
21  // get 12 sales figures from the user at the keyboard
22  void SalesPerson::getSalesFromUser()
23  {
24     double salesFigure;
25
26     for ( int i = 1; i <= 12; i++ )
27     {
28        cout << "Enter sales amount for month " << i << ": ";
29        cin >> salesFigure;
30        setSales( i, salesFigure );
31     } // end for
32  } // end function getSalesFromUser
33
34  // set one of the 12 monthly sales figures; function subtracts
35  // one from month value for proper subscript in sales array
36  void SalesPerson::setSales( int month, double amount )
37  {
38     // test for valid month and amount values
39     if ( month >= 1 && month <= 12 && amount > 0 )
40        sales[ month - 1 ] = amount; // adjust for subscripts 0-11
41     else // invalid month or amount value
42        cout << "Invalid month or sales figure" << endl;
43  } // end function setSales
44
45  // print total annual sales (with the help of utility function)
46  void SalesPerson::printAnnualSales()
47  {
48     cout << setprecision( 2 ) << fixed
49        << "\nThe total annual sales are: $"
50        << totalAnnualSales() << endl; // call utility function
51  } // end function printAnnualSales
52
```

Fig. 9.6 | SalesPerson class member-function definitions. (Part 1 of 2.)

```
53   // private utility function to total annual sales
54   double SalesPerson::totalAnnualSales()
55   {
56      double total = 0.0; // initialize total
57
58      for ( int i = 0; i < 12; i++ ) // summarize sales results
59         total += sales[ i ]; // add month i sales to total
60
61      return total;
62   } // end function totalAnnualSales
```

Fig. 9.6 | SalesPerson class member-function definitions. (Part 2 of 2.)

in array sales. The public member function printAnnualSales (lines 46–51) prints the total sales for the last 12 months. The private utility function totalAnnualSales (lines 54–62) totals the 12 monthly sales figures for the benefit of printAnnualSales. Member function printAnnualSales edits the sales figures into monetary format.

In Fig. 9.7, notice that the application's main function includes only a simple sequence of member-function calls—there are no control statements. The logic of manipulating the sales array is completely encapsulated in class SalesPerson's member functions.

> **Software Engineering Observation 9.8**
>
> *A phenomenon of object-oriented programming is that once a class is defined, creating and manipulating objects of that class often involve issuing only a simple sequence of member-function calls—few, if any, control statements are needed. By contrast, it is common to have control statements in the implementation of a class's member functions.*

9.6 Time Class Case Study: Constructors with Default Arguments

The program of Figs. 9.8–9.10 enhances class Time to demonstrate how arguments are implicitly passed to a constructor. The constructor defined in Fig. 9.2 initialized hour,

```
1    // Fig. 9.7: fig09_07.cpp
2    // Demonstrating a utility function.
3    // Compile this program with SalesPerson.cpp
4
5    // include SalesPerson class definition from SalesPerson.h
6    #include "SalesPerson.h"
7
8    int main()
9    {
10      SalesPerson s; // create SalesPerson object s
11
12      s.getSalesFromUser(); // note simple sequential code;
13      s.printAnnualSales(); // no control statements in main
14      return 0;
15   } // end main
```

Fig. 9.7 | Utility function demonstration. (Part I of 2.)

```
Enter sales amount for month 1: 5314.76
Enter sales amount for month 2: 4292.38
Enter sales amount for month 3: 4589.83
Enter sales amount for month 4: 5534.03
Enter sales amount for month 5: 4376.34
Enter sales amount for month 6: 5698.45
Enter sales amount for month 7: 4439.22
Enter sales amount for month 8: 5893.57
Enter sales amount for month 9: 4909.67
Enter sales amount for month 10: 5123.45
Enter sales amount for month 11: 4024.97
Enter sales amount for month 12: 5923.92

The total annual sales are: $60120.59
```

Fig. 9.7 | Utility function demonstration. (Part 2 of 2.)

```
1   // Fig. 9.8: Time.h
2   // Declaration of class Time.
3   // Member functions defined in Time.cpp.
4
5   // prevent multiple inclusions of header file
6   #ifndef TIME_H
7   #define TIME_H
8
9   // Time abstract data type definition
10  class Time
11  {
12  public:
13     Time( int = 0, int = 0, int = 0 ); // default constructor
14
15     // set functions
16     void setTime( int, int, int ); // set hour, minute, second
17     void setHour( int ); // set hour (after validation)
18     void setMinute( int ); // set minute (after validation)
19     void setSecond( int ); // set second (after validation)
20
21     // get functions
22     int getHour(); // return hour
23     int getMinute(); // return minute
24     int getSecond(); // return second
25
26     void printUniversal(); // output time in universal-time format
27     void printStandard(); // output time in standard-time format
28  private:
29     int hour; // 0 - 23 (24-hour clock format)
30     int minute; // 0 - 59
31     int second; // 0 - 59
32  }; // end class Time
33
34  #endif
```

Fig. 9.8 | Time class containing a constructor with default arguments.

minute and second to 0 (i.e., midnight in universal time). Like other functions, constructors can specify default arguments. Line 13 of Fig. 9.8 declares the Time constructor to include default arguments, specifying a default value of zero for each argument passed to the constructor. In Fig. 9.9, lines 14–17 define the new version of the Time constructor that

```cpp
 1   // Fig. 9.9: Time.cpp
 2   // Member-function definitions for class Time.
 3   #include <iostream>
 4   using std::cout;
 5
 6   #include <iomanip>
 7   using std::setfill;
 8   using std::setw;
 9
10   #include "Time.h" // include definition of class Time from Time.h
11
12   // Time constructor initializes each data member to zero;
13   // ensures that Time objects start in a consistent state
14   Time::Time( int hr, int min, int sec )
15   {
16      setTime( hr, min, sec ); // validate and set time
17   } // end Time constructor
18
19   // set new Time value using universal time; ensure that
20   // the data remains consistent by setting invalid values to zero
21   void Time::setTime( int h, int m, int s )
22   {
23      setHour( h ); // set private field hour
24      setMinute( m ); // set private field minute
25      setSecond( s ); // set private field second
26   } // end function setTime
27
28   // set hour value
29   void Time::setHour( int h )
30   {
31      hour = ( h >= 0 && h < 24 ) ? h : 0; // validate hour
32   } // end function setHour
33
34   // set minute value
35   void Time::setMinute( int m )
36   {
37      minute = ( m >= 0 && m < 60 ) ? m : 0; // validate minute
38   } // end function setMinute
39
40   // set second value
41   void Time::setSecond( int s )
42   {
43      second = ( s >= 0 && s < 60 ) ? s : 0; // validate second
44   } // end function setSecond
45
```

Fig. 9.9 | Time class member-function definitions including a constructor that takes arguments. (Part 1 of 2.)

```
46  // return hour value
47  int Time::getHour()
48  {
49     return hour;
50  } // end function getHour
51
52  // return minute value
53  int Time::getMinute()
54  {
55     return minute;
56  } // end function getMinute
57
58  // return second value
59  int Time::getSecond()
60  {
61     return second;
62  } // end function getSecond
63
64  // print Time in universal-time format (HH:MM:SS)
65  void Time::printUniversal()
66  {
67     cout << setfill( '0' ) << setw( 2 ) << getHour() << ":"
68        << setw( 2 ) << getMinute() << ":" << setw( 2 ) << getSecond();
69  } // end function printUniversal
70
71  // print Time in standard-time format (HH:MM:SS AM or PM)
72  void Time::printStandard()
73  {
74     cout << ( ( getHour() == 0 || getHour() == 12 ) ? 12 : getHour() % 12 )
75        << ":" << setfill( '0' ) << setw( 2 ) << getMinute()
76        << ":" << setw( 2 ) << getSecond() << ( hour < 12 ? " AM" : " PM" );
77  } // end function printStandard
```

Fig. 9.9 | Time class member-function definitions including a constructor that takes arguments. (Part 2 of 2.)

receives values for parameters hr, min and sec that will be used to initialize private data members hour, minute and second, respectively. Note that class Time provides *set* and *get* functions for each data member. The Time constructor now calls setTime, which calls the setHour, setMinute and setSecond functions to validate and assign values to the data members. The default arguments to the constructor ensure that, even if no values are provided in a constructor call, the constructor still initializes the data members to maintain the Time object in a consistent state. A constructor that defaults all its arguments is also a default constructor—i.e., a constructor that can be invoked with no arguments. There can be a maximum of one default constructor per class.

In Fig. 9.9, line 16 of the constructor calls member function setTime with the values passed to the constructor (or the default values). Function setTime calls setHour to ensure that the value supplied for hour is in the range 0–23, then calls setMinute and setSecond to ensure that the values for minute and second are each in the range 0–59. If a value is out of range, that value is set to zero (to ensure that each data member remains in a consistent state). In Chapter 16, Exception Handling, we throw exceptions to inform the user that a value is out of range, rather than simply assigning a default consistent value.

Note that the Time constructor could be written to include the same statements as member function setTime, or even the individual statements in the setHour, setMinute and setSecond functions. Calling setHour, setMinute and setSecond from the constructor may be slightly more efficient because the extra call to setTime would be eliminated. Similarly, copying the code from lines 31, 37 and 43 into constructor would eliminate the overhead of calling setTime, setHour, setMinute and setSecond. Coding the Time constructor or member function setTime as a copy of the code in lines 31, 37 and 43 would make maintenance of this class more difficult. If the implementations of setHour, setMinute and setSecond were to change, the implementation of any member function that duplicates lines 31, 37 and 43 would have to change accordingly. Having the Time constructor call setTime and having setTime call setHour, setMinute and set-Second enables us to limit the changes to code that validates the hour, minute or second to the corresponding *set* function. This reduces the likelihood of errors when altering the class's implementation. Also, the performance of the Time constructor and setTime can be enhanced by explicitly declaring them inline or by defining them in the class definition (which implicitly inlines the function definition).

Software Engineering Observation 9.9

If a member function of a class already provides all or part of the functionality required by a constructor (or other member function) of the class, call that member function from the constructor (or other member function). This simplifies the maintenance of the code and reduces the likelihood of an error if the implementation of the code is modified. As a general rule: Avoid repeating code.

Software Engineering Observation 9.10

Any change to the default argument values of a function requires the client code to be recompiled (to ensure that the program still functions correctly).

Function main in Fig. 9.10 initializes five Time objects—one with all three arguments defaulted in the implicit constructor call (line 11), one with one argument specified (line

```cpp
// Fig. 9.10: fig09_10.cpp
// Demonstrating a default constructor for class Time.
#include <iostream>
using std::cout;
using std::endl;

#include "Time.h" // include definition of class Time from Time.h

int main()
{
   Time t1; // all arguments defaulted
   Time t2( 2 ); // hour specified; minute and second defaulted
   Time t3( 21, 34 ); // hour and minute specified; second defaulted
   Time t4( 12, 25, 42 ); // hour, minute and second specified
   Time t5( 27, 74, 99 ); // all bad values specified
```

Fig. 9.10 | Constructor with default arguments. (Part 1 of 2.)

```
17      cout << "Constructed with:\n\nt1: all arguments defaulted\n   ";
18      t1.printUniversal(); // 00:00:00
19      cout << "\n   ";
20      t1.printStandard(); // 12:00:00 AM
21
22      cout << "\n\nt2: hour specified; minute and second defaulted\n   ";
23      t2.printUniversal(); // 02:00:00
24      cout << "\n   ";
25      t2.printStandard(); // 2:00:00 AM
26
27      cout << "\n\nt3: hour and minute specified; second defaulted\n   ";
28      t3.printUniversal(); // 21:34:00
29      cout << "\n   ";
30      t3.printStandard(); // 9:34:00 PM
31
32      cout << "\n\nt4: hour, minute and second specified\n   ";
33      t4.printUniversal(); // 12:25:42
34      cout << "\n   ";
35      t4.printStandard(); // 12:25:42 PM
36
37      cout << "\n\nt5: all invalid values specified\n   ";
38      t5.printUniversal(); // 00:00:00
39      cout << "\n   ";
40      t5.printStandard(); // 12:00:00 AM
41      cout << endl;
42      return 0;
43   } // end main
```

```
Constructed with:

t1: all arguments defaulted
   00:00:00
   12:00:00 AM

t2: hour specified; minute and second defaulted
   02:00:00
   2:00:00 AM

t3: hour and minute specified; second defaulted
   21:34:00
   9:34:00 PM

t4: hour, minute and second specified
   12:25:42
   12:25:42 PM

t5: all invalid values specified
   00:00:00
   12:00:00 AM
```

Fig. 9.10 | Constructor with default arguments. (Part 2 of 2.)

12), one with two arguments specified (line 13), one with three arguments specified (line 14) and one with three invalid arguments specified (line 15). Then the program displays each object in universal-time and standard-time formats.

Notes Regarding Class **Time***'s* Set *and* Get *Functions and Constructor*

Time's *set* and *get* functions are called throughout the body of the class. In particular, function setTime (lines 21–26 of Fig. 9.9) calls functions setHour, setMinute and setSecond, and functions printUniversal and printStandard call functions getHour, getMinute and get-Second in line 67–68 and lines 74–76, respectively. In each case, these functions could have accessed the class's private data directly without calling the *set* and *get* functions. However, consider changing the representation of the time from three int values (requiring 12 bytes of memory) to a single int value representing the total number of seconds that have elapsed since midnight (requiring only four bytes of memory). If we made such a change, only the bodies of the functions that access the private data directly would need to change—in particular, the individual *set* and *get* functions for the hour, minute and second. There would be no need to modify the bodies of functions setTime, printUniversal or printStandard, because they do not access the data directly. Designing the class in this manner reduces the likelihood of programming errors when altering the class's implementation.

Similarly, the Time constructor could be written to include a copy of the appropriate statements from function setTime. Doing so may be slightly more efficient, because the extra constructor call and call to setTime are eliminated. However, duplicating statements in multiple functions or constructors makes changing the class's internal data representation more difficult. Having the Time constructor call function setTime directly requires any changes to the implementation of setTime to be made only once.

Common Programming Error 9.2

A constructor can call other member functions of the class, such as set *or* get *functions, but because the constructor is initializing the object, the data members may not yet be in a consistent state. Using data members before they have been properly initialized can cause logic errors.*

9.7 Destructors

A destructor is another type of special member function. The name of the destructor for a class is the tilde character (~) followed by the class name. This naming convention has intuitive appeal, because as we will see in a later chapter, the tilde operator is the bitwise complement operator, and, in a sense, the destructor is the complement of the constructor. Note that a destructor is often referred to with the abbreviation "dtor" in the literature. We prefer not to use this abbreviation.

A class's destructor is called implicitly when an object is destroyed. This occurs, for example, as an automatic object is destroyed when program execution leaves the scope in which that object was instantiated. *The destructor itself does not actually release the object's memory*—it performs termination housekeeping before the system reclaims the object's memory, so the memory may be reused to hold new objects.

A destructor receives no parameters and returns no value. A destructor may not specify a return type—not even void. A class may have only one destructor—destructor overloading is not allowed.

Common Programming Error 9.3

It is a syntax error to attempt to pass arguments to a destructor, to specify a return type for a destructor (even void cannot be specified), to return values from a destructor or to overload a destructor.

Even though destructors have not been provided for the classes presented so far, every class has a destructor. If the programmer does not explicitly provide a destructor, the compiler creates an "empty" destructor. [*Note:* We will see that such an implicitly created destructor does, in fact, perform important operations on objects that are created through composition (Chapter 10) and inheritance (Chapter 12).] In Chapter 11, we will build destructors appropriate for classes whose objects contain dynamically allocated memory (e.g., for arrays and strings) or use other system resources (e.g., files on disk, which we study in Chapter 17). We discuss how to dynamically allocate and deallocate memory in Chapter 10.

Software Engineering Observation 9.11

As we will see in the remainder of the book, constructors and destructors have much greater prominence in C++ and object-oriented programming than is possible to convey after only our brief introduction here.

9.8 When Constructors and Destructors Are Called

Constructors and destructors are called implicitly by the compiler. The order in which these function calls occur depends on the order in which execution enters and leaves the scopes where the objects are instantiated. Generally, destructor calls are made in the reverse order of the corresponding constructor calls, but as we will see in Figs. 9.11–9.13, the storage classes of objects can alter the order in which destructors are called.

Constructors are called for objects defined in global scope before any other function (including `main`) in that file begins execution (although the order of execution of global object constructors between files is not guaranteed). The corresponding destructors are called when `main` terminates. Function `exit` forces a program to terminate immediately and does not execute the destructors of automatic objects. The function often is used to terminate a program when an error is detected in the input or if a file to be processed by the program cannot be opened. Function `abort` performs similarly to function `exit` but forces the program to terminate immediately, without allowing the destructors of any objects to be called. Function `abort` is usually used to indicate an abnormal termination of the program. (See Chapter 23, Other Topics, for more information on functions `exit` and `abort`.)

The constructor for an automatic local object is called when execution reaches the point where that object is defined—the corresponding destructor is called when execution leaves the object's scope (i.e., the block in which that object is defined has finished executing). Constructors and destructors for automatic objects are called each time execution enters and leaves the scope of the object. Destructors are not called for automatic objects if the program terminates with a call to function `exit` or function `abort`.

The constructor for a `static` local object is called only once, when execution first reaches the point where the object is defined—the corresponding destructor is called when `main` terminates or the program calls function `exit`. Global and `static` objects are destroyed in the reverse order of their creation. Destructors are not called for `static` objects if the program terminates with a call to function `abort`.

The program of Figs. 9.11–9.13 demonstrates the order in which constructors and destructors are called for objects of class `CreateAndDestroy` (Fig. 9.11 and Fig. 9.12) of various storage classes in several scopes. Each object of class `CreateAndDestroy` contains (lines 16–17) an integer (`objectID`) and a `string` (`message`) that are used in the program's output to identify the object. This mechanical example is purely for pedagogic purposes. For this reason, line 23 of the destructor in Fig. 9.12 determines whether the object being destroyed has an `objectID` value 1 or 6 and, if so, outputs a newline character. This line helps make the program's output easier to follow.

```
1   // Fig. 9.11: CreateAndDestroy.h
2   // Definition of class CreateAndDestroy.
3   // Member functions defined in CreateAndDestroy.cpp.
4   #include <string>
5   using std::string;
6
7   #ifndef CREATE_H
8   #define CREATE_H
9
10  class CreateAndDestroy
11  {
12  public:
13     CreateAndDestroy( int, string ); // constructor
14     ~CreateAndDestroy(); // destructor
15  private:
16     int objectID; // ID number for object
17     string message; // message describing object
18  }; // end class CreateAndDestroy
19
20  #endif
```

Fig. 9.11 | CreateAndDestroy class definition.

```
1   // Fig. 9.12: CreateAndDestroy.cpp
2   // Member-function definitions for class CreateAndDestroy.
3   #include <iostream>
4   using std::cout;
5   using std::endl;
6
7   #include "CreateAndDestroy.h"// include CreateAndDestroy class definition
8
9   // constructor
10  CreateAndDestroy::CreateAndDestroy( int ID, string messageString )
11  {
12     objectID = ID; // set object's ID number
13     message = messageString; // set object's descriptive message
14
15     cout << "Object " << objectID << "   constructor runs   "
16        << message << endl;
17  } // end CreateAndDestroy constructor
18
19  // destructor
20  CreateAndDestroy::~CreateAndDestroy()
21  {
22     // output newline for certain objects; helps readability
23     cout << ( objectID == 1 || objectID == 6 ? "\n" : "" );
24
25     cout << "Object " << objectID << "   destructor runs    "
26        << message << endl;
27  } // end ~CreateAndDestroy destructor
```

Fig. 9.12 | CreateAndDestroy class member-function definitions.

Figure 9.13 defines object `first` (line 12) in global scope. Its constructor is actually called before any statements in `main` execute and its destructor is called at program termination after the destructors for all other objects have run.

Function `main` (lines 14–26) declares three objects. Objects `second` (line 17) and `fourth` (line 23) are local automatic objects, and object `third` (line 18) is a `static` local object. The constructor for each of these objects is called when execution reaches the point where that object is declared. The destructors for objects `fourth` and then `second` are called (i.e., the reverse of the order in which their constructors were called) when execution reaches the end of `main`. Because object `third` is `static`, it exists until program termination. The destructor for object `third` is called before the destructor for global object `first`, but after all other objects are destroyed.

Function `create` (lines 29–36) declares three objects—`fifth` (line 32) and `seventh` (line 34) as local automatic objects, and `sixth` (line 33) as a `static` local object. The

```
 1   // Fig. 9.13: fig09_13.cpp
 2   // Demonstrating the order in which constructors and
 3   // destructors are called.
 4   #include <iostream>
 5   using std::cout;
 6   using std::endl;
 7
 8   #include "CreateAndDestroy.h" // include CreateAndDestroy class definition
 9
10   void create( void ); // prototype
11
12   CreateAndDestroy first( 1, "(global before main)" ); // global object
13
14   int main()
15   {
16      cout << "\nMAIN FUNCTION: EXECUTION BEGINS" << endl;
17      CreateAndDestroy second( 2, "(local automatic in main)" );
18      static CreateAndDestroy third( 3, "(local static in main)" );
19
20      create(); // call function to create objects
21
22      cout << "\nMAIN FUNCTION: EXECUTION RESUMES" << endl;
23      CreateAndDestroy fourth( 4, "(local automatic in main)" );
24      cout << "\nMAIN FUNCTION: EXECUTION ENDS" << endl;
25      return 0;
26   } // end main
27
28   // function to create objects
29   void create( void )
30   {
31      cout << "\nCREATE FUNCTION: EXECUTION BEGINS" << endl;
32      CreateAndDestroy fifth( 5, "(local automatic in create)" );
33      static CreateAndDestroy sixth( 6, "(local static in create)" );
34      CreateAndDestroy seventh( 7, "(local automatic in create)" );
35      cout << "\nCREATE FUNCTION: EXECUTION ENDS" << endl;
36   } // end function create
```

Fig. 9.13 | Order in which constructors and destructors are called. (Part 1 of 2.)

```
Object 1    constructor runs    (global before main)

MAIN FUNCTION: EXECUTION BEGINS
Object 2    constructor runs    (local automatic in main)
Object 3    constructor runs    (local static in main)

CREATE FUNCTION: EXECUTION BEGINS
Object 5    constructor runs    (local automatic in create)
Object 6    constructor runs    (local static in create)
Object 7    constructor runs    (local automatic in create)

CREATE FUNCTION: EXECUTION ENDS
Object 7    destructor runs     (local automatic in create)
Object 5    destructor runs     (local automatic in create)

MAIN FUNCTION: EXECUTION RESUMES
Object 4    constructor runs    (local automatic in main)

MAIN FUNCTION: EXECUTION ENDS
Object 4    destructor runs     (local automatic in main)
Object 2    destructor runs     (local automatic in main)

Object 6    destructor runs     (local static in create)
Object 3    destructor runs     (local static in main)

Object 1    destructor runs     (global before main)
```

Fig. 9.13 | Order in which constructors and destructors are called. (Part 2 of 2.)

destructors for objects `seventh` and then `fifth` are called (i.e., the reverse of the order in which their constructors were called) when `create` terminates. Because `sixth` is `static`, it exists until program termination. The destructor for `sixth` is called before the destructors for `third` and `first`, but after all other objects are destroyed.

9.9 Time Class Case Study: A Subtle Trap—Returning a Reference to a `private` Data Member

A reference to an object is an alias for the name of the object and, hence, may be used on the left side of an assignment statement. In this context, the reference makes a perfectly acceptable *lvalue* that can receive a value. One way to use this capability (unfortunately!) is to have a `public` member function of a class return a reference to a `private` data member of that class. Note that if a function returns a `const` reference, that reference cannot be used as a modifiable *lvalue*.

The program of Figs. 9.14–9.16 uses a simplified `Time` class (Fig. 9.14 and Fig. 9.15) to demonstrate returning a reference to a `private` data member with member function `badSetHour` (declared in Fig. 9.14 at line 15 and defined in Fig. 9.15 at lines 29–33). Such a reference return actually makes a call to member function `badSetHour` an alias for `private` data member `hour`! The function call can be used in any way that the `private` data member can be used, including as an *lvalue* in an assignment statement, thus enabling clients of the class to clobber the class's `private` data at will! Note that the same problem would occur if a pointer to the `private` data were to be returned by the function.

```
 1   // Fig. 9.14: Time.h
 2   // Declaration of class Time.
 3   // Member functions defined in Time.cpp
 4
 5   // prevent multiple inclusions of header file
 6   #ifndef TIME_H
 7   #define TIME_H
 8
 9   class Time
10   {
11   public:
12      Time( int = 0, int = 0, int = 0 );
13      void setTime( int, int, int );
14      int getHour();
15      int &badSetHour( int ); // DANGEROUS reference return
16   private:
17      int hour;
18      int minute;
19      int second;
20   }; // end class Time
21
22   #endif
```

Fig. 9.14 | Returning a reference to a private data member.

```
 1   // Fig. 9.15: Time.cpp
 2   // Member-function definitions for Time class.
 3   #include "Time.h" // include definition of class Time
 4
 5   // constructor function to initialize private data;
 6   // calls member function setTime to set variables;
 7   // default values are 0 (see class definition)
 8   Time::Time( int hr, int min, int sec )
 9   {
10      setTime( hr, min, sec );
11   } // end Time constructor
12
13   // set values of hour, minute and second
14   void Time::setTime( int h, int m, int s )
15   {
16      hour = ( h >= 0 && h < 24 ) ? h : 0; // validate hour
17      minute = ( m >= 0 && m < 60 ) ? m : 0; // validate minute
18      second = ( s >= 0 && s < 60 ) ? s : 0; // validate second
19   } // end function setTime
20
21   // return hour value
22   int Time::getHour()
23   {
24      return hour;
25   } // end function getHour
26
```

Fig. 9.15 | Returning a reference to a private data member. (Part 1 of 2.)

```
27    // POOR PROGRAMMING PRACTICE:
28    // Returning a reference to a private data member.
29    int &Time::badSetHour( int hh )
30    {
31       hour = ( hh >= 0 && hh < 24 ) ? hh : 0;
32       return hour; // DANGEROUS reference return
33    } // end function badSetHour
```

Fig. 9.15 | Returning a reference to a `private` data member. (Part 2 of 2.)

Figure 9.16 declares `Time` object `t` (line 12) and reference `hourRef` (line 15), which is initialized with the reference returned by the call `t.badSetHour(20)`. Line 17 displays the value of the alias `hourRef`. This shows how `hourRef` breaks the encapsulation of the class— statements in `main` should not have access to the `private` data of the class. Next, line 18 uses the alias to set the value of `hour` to 30 (an invalid value) and line 19 displays the value returned by function `getHour` to show that assigning a value to `hourRef` actually modifies the `private` data in the `Time` object `t`. Finally, line 23 uses the `badSetHour` function call itself as an *lvalue* and assigns 74 (another invalid value) to the reference returned by the function.

```
1     // Fig. 9.16: fig09_16.cpp
2     // Demonstrating a public member function that
3     // returns a reference to a private data member.
4     #include <iostream>
5     using std::cout;
6     using std::endl;
7
8     #include "Time.h" // include definition of class Time
9
10    int main()
11    {
12       Time t; // create Time object
13
14       // initialize hourRef with the reference returned by badSetHour
15       int &hourRef = t.badSetHour( 20 ); // 20 is a valid hour
16
17       cout << "Valid hour before modification: " << hourRef;
18       hourRef = 30; // use hourRef to set invalid value in Time object t
19       cout << "\nInvalid hour after modification: " << t.getHour();
20
21       // Dangerous: Function call that returns
22       // a reference can be used as an lvalue!
23       t.badSetHour( 12 ) = 74; // assign another invalid value to hour
24
25       cout << "\n\n***************************************************\n"
26          << "POOR PROGRAMMING PRACTICE!!!!!!!!\n"
27          << "t.badSetHour( 12 ) as an lvalue, invalid hour: "
28          << t.getHour()
29          << "\n***************************************************" << endl;
30       return 0;
31    } // end main
```

Fig. 9.16 | Returning a reference to a `private` data member. (Part 1 of 2.)

```
Valid hour before modification: 20
Invalid hour after modification: 30

**************************************************
POOR PROGRAMMING PRACTICE!!!!!!!!
t.badSetHour( 12 ) as an lvalue, invalid hour: 74
**************************************************
```

Fig. 9.16 | Returning a reference to a `private` data member. (Part 2 of 2.)

Line 28 again displays the value returned by function `getHour` to show that assigning a value to the result of the function call in line 23 modifies the `private` data in the `Time` object `t`.

Error-Prevention Tip 9.4

Returning a reference or a pointer to a private data member breaks the encapsulation of the class and makes the client code dependent on the representation of the class's data. So, returning pointers or references to private data is a dangerous practice that should be avoided.

9.10 Default Memberwise Assignment

The assignment operator (=) can be used to assign an object to another object of the same type. By default, such assignment is performed by memberwise assignment—each data member of the object on the right of the assignment operator is assigned individually to the same data member in the object on the left of the assignment operator. Figures 9.17–9.18 define class `Date` for use in this example. Line 20 of Fig. 9.19 uses default memberwise assignment to assign the data members of `Date` object `date1` to the

```
 1   // Fig. 9.17: Date.h
 2   // Declaration of class Date.
 3   // Member functions are defined in Date.cpp
 4
 5   // prevent multiple inclusions of header file
 6   #ifndef DATE_H
 7   #define DATE_H
 8
 9   // class Date definition
10   class Date
11   {
12   public:
13      Date( int = 1, int = 1, int = 2000 ); // default constructor
14      void print();
15   private:
16      int month;
17      int day;
18      int year;
19   }; // end class Date
20
21   #endif
```

Fig. 9.17 | `Date` class header file.

```
 1   // Fig. 9.18: Date.cpp
 2   // Member-function definitions for class Date.
 3   #include <iostream>
 4   using std::cout;
 5   using std::endl;
 6
 7   #include "Date.h" // include definition of class Date from Date.h
 8
 9   // Date constructor (should do range checking)
10   Date::Date( int m, int d, int y )
11   {
12      month = m;
13      day = d;
14      year = y;
15   } // end constructor Date
16
17   // print Date in the format mm/dd/yyyy
18   void Date::print()
19   {
20      cout << month << '/' << day << '/' << year;
21   } // end function print
```

Fig. 9.18 | Date class member-function definitions.

```
 1   // Fig. 9.19: fig09_19.cpp
 2   // Demonstrating that class objects can be assigned
 3   // to each other using default memberwise assignment.
 4   #include <iostream>
 5   using std::cout;
 6   using std::endl;
 7
 8   #include "Date.h" // include definition of class Date from Date.h
 9
10   int main()
11   {
12      Date date1( 7, 4, 2004 );
13      Date date2; // date2 defaults to 1/1/2000
14
15      cout << "date1 = ";
16      date1.print();
17      cout << "\ndate2 = ";
18      date2.print();
19
20      date2 = date1; // default memberwise assignment
21
22      cout << "\n\nAfter default memberwise assignment, date2 = ";
23      date2.print();
24      cout << endl;
25      return 0;
26   } // end main
```

Fig. 9.19 | Default memberwise assignment. (Part 1 of 2.)

```
date1 = 7/4/2004
date2 = 1/1/2000

After default memberwise assignment, date2 = 7/4/2004
```

Fig. 9.19 | Default memberwise assignment. (Part 2 of 2.)

corresponding data members of Date object date2. In this case, the month member of date1 is assigned to the month member of date2, the day member of date1 is assigned to the day member of date2 and the year member of date1 is assigned to the year member of date2. [*Caution:* Memberwise assignment can cause serious problems when used with a class whose data members contain pointers to dynamically allocated memory; we discuss these problems in Chapter 11 and show how to deal with them.] Notice that the Date constructor does not contain any error checking; we leave this to the exercises.

Objects may be passed as function arguments and may be returned from functions. Such passing and returning is performed using pass-by-value by default—a copy of the object is passed or returned. In such cases, C++ creates a new object and uses a copy constructor to copy the original object's values into the new object. For each class, the compiler provides a default copy constructor that copies each member of the original object into the corresponding member of the new object. Like memberwise assignment, copy constructors can cause serious problems when used with a class whose data members contain pointers to dynamically allocated memory. Chapter 11 discusses how programmers can define a customized copy constructor that properly copies objects containing pointers to dynamically allocated memory.

Performance Tip 9.3

Passing an object by value is good from a security standpoint, because the called function has no access to the original object in the caller, but pass-by-value can degrade performance when making a copy of a large object. An object can be passed by reference by passing either a pointer or a reference to the object. Pass-by-reference offers good performance but is weaker from a security standpoint, because the called function is given access to the original object. Pass-by-const-reference is a safe, good-performing alternative (this can be implemented with a const reference parameter or with a pointer-to-const-data parameter).

9.11 Software Reusability

People who write object-oriented programs concentrate on implementing useful classes. There is a tremendous motivation to capture and catalog classes so that they can be accessed by large segments of the programming community. Many substantial class libraries exist and others are being developed worldwide. Software is increasingly being constructed from existing, well-defined, carefully tested, well-documented, portable, high-performance, widely available components. This kind of software reusability speeds the development of powerful, high-quality software. Rapid applications development (RAD) through the mechanisms of reusable componentry has become an important field.

Significant problems must be solved, however, before the full potential of software reusability can be realized. We need cataloging schemes, licensing schemes, protection mechanisms to ensure that master copies of classes are not corrupted, description schemes so that designers of new systems can easily determine whether existing objects meet their needs, browsing mechanisms to determine what classes are available and how closely they meet software developer requirements and the like. Many interesting research and development problems need to be solved. There is great motivation to solve these problems, because the potential value of their solutions is enormous.

9.12 (Optional) Software Engineering Case Study: Starting to Program the Classes of the ATM System

In the "Software Engineering Case Study" sections in Chapters 1–7, we introduced the fundamentals of object orientation and developed an object-oriented design for our ATM system. Earlier in this chapter, we discussed many of the details of programming with C++ classes. We now begin implementing our object-oriented design in C++. At the end of this section, we show how to convert class diagrams to C++ header files. In the final "Software Engineering Case Study" section (Section 13.10), we modify the header files to incorporate the object-oriented concept of inheritance. We present the full C++ code implementation in Appendix G.

Visibility

We now apply access specifiers to the members of our classes. In Chapter 3, we introduced access specifiers `public` and `private`. Access specifiers determine the visibility or accessibility of an object's attributes and operations to other objects. Before we can begin implementing our design, we must consider which attributes and operations of our classes should be `public` and which should be `private`.

In Chapter 3, we observed that data members normally should be `private` and that member functions invoked by clients of a given class should be `public`. Member functions that are called only by other member functions of the class as "utility functions," however, normally should be `private`. The UML employs visibility markers for modeling the visibility of attributes and operations. Public visibility is indicated by placing a plus sign (+) before an operation or an attribute; a minus sign (–) indicates private visibility. Figure 9.20 shows our updated class diagram with visibility markers included. [*Note:* We do not include any operation parameters in Fig. 9.20. This is perfectly normal. Adding visibility markers does not affect the parameters already modeled in the class diagrams of Figs. 6.22–6.25.]

Navigability

Before we begin implementing our design in C++, we introduce an additional UML notation. The class diagram in Fig. 9.21 further refines the relationships among classes in the ATM system by adding navigability arrows to the association lines. Navigability arrows (represented as arrows with stick arrowheads in the class diagram) indicate in which direction an association can be traversed and are based on the collaborations modeled in communication and sequence diagrams (see Section 7.12). When implementing a system designed using the UML, programmers use navigability arrows to help determine which objects need references or pointers to other objects. For example, the navigability arrow pointing from class ATM to class BankDatabase indicates that we can navigate from the former to the latter, thereby enabling the ATM to invoke the BankDatabase's operations. However, since Fig. 9.21 does not contain a navigability arrow pointing from class BankDatabase to class ATM, the BankDatabase cannot access the ATM's operations. Note that associations in a class diagram that have

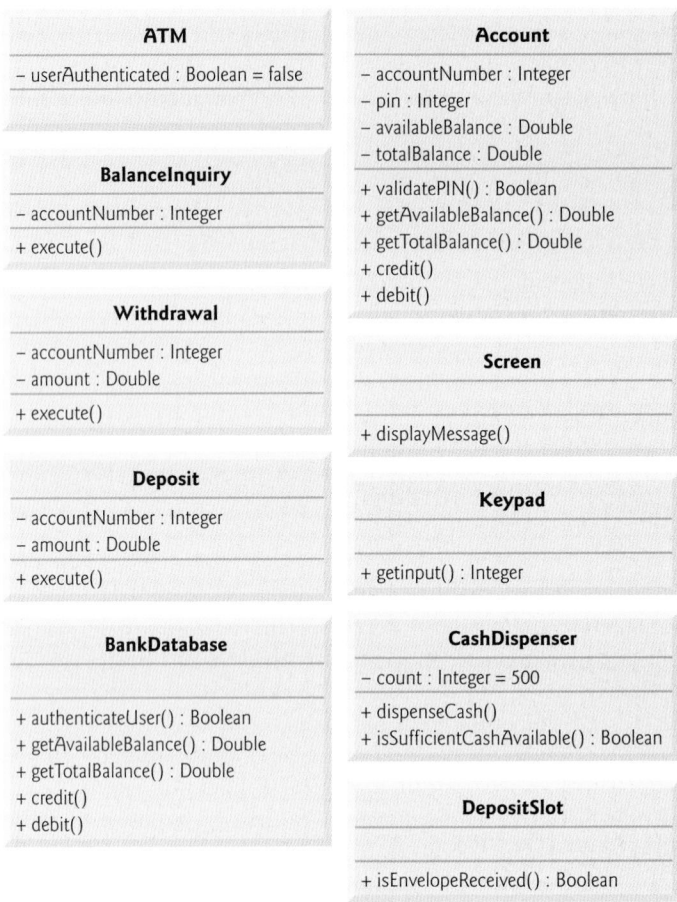

Fig. 9.20 | Class diagram with visibility markers.

navigability arrows at both ends or do not have navigability arrows at all indicate bidirectional navigability—navigation can proceed in either direction across the association.

Like the class diagram of Fig. 3.23 the class diagram of Fig. 9.21 omits classes BalanceInquiry and Deposit to keep the diagram simple. The navigability of the associations in which these classes participate closely parallels the navigability of class Withdrawal's associations. Recall from Section 3.11 that BalanceInquiry has an association with class Screen. We can navigate from class BalanceInquiry to class Screen along this association, but we cannot navigate from class Screen to class BalanceInquiry. Thus, if we were to model class BalanceInquiry in Fig. 9.21, we would place a navigability arrow at class Screen's end of this association. Also recall that class Deposit associates with classes Screen, Keypad and DepositSlot. We can navigate from class Deposit to each of these classes, but not vice versa. We therefore would place navigability arrows at the Screen, Keypad and DepositSlot ends of these associations. [*Note:* We model these additional classes and associations in our final class diagram in Section 13.10, after we have simplified the structure of our system by incorporating the object-oriented concept of inheritance.]

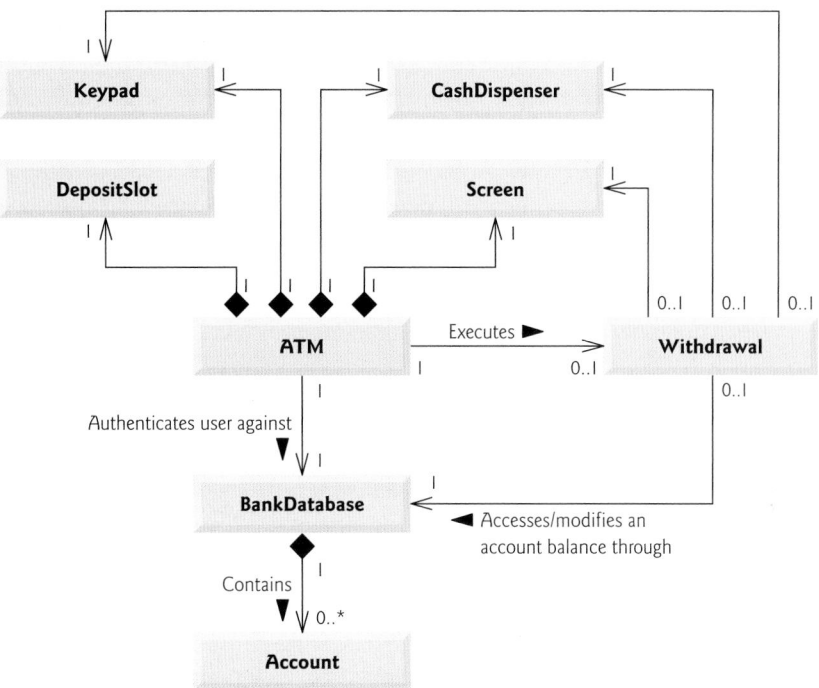

Fig. 9.21 | Class diagram with navigability arrows.

Implementing the ATM System from Its UML Design

We are now ready to begin implementing the ATM system. We first convert the classes in the diagrams of Fig. 9.20 and Fig. 9.21 into C++ header files. This code will represent the "skeleton" of the system. In Chapter 13, we modify the header files to incorporate the object-oriented concept of inheritance. In Appendix G, ATM Case Study Code, we present the complete working C++ code for our model.

As an example, we begin to develop the header file for class Withdrawal from our design of class Withdrawal in Fig. 9.20. We use this figure to determine the attributes and operations of the class. We use the UML model in Fig. 9.21 to determine the associations among classes. We follow the following five guidelines for each class:

1. Use the name located in the first compartment of a class in a class diagram to define the class in a header file (Fig. 9.22). Use #ifndef, #define and #endif preprocessor directives to prevent the header file from being included more than once in a program.

2. Use the attributes located in the class's second compartment to declare the data members. For example, the private attributes accountNumber and amount of class Withdrawal yield the code in Fig. 9.23.

3. Use the associations described in the class diagram to declare references (or pointers, where appropriate) to other objects. For example, according to Fig. 9.21, Withdrawal can access one object of class Screen, one object of class Keypad, one object of class CashDispenser and one object of class BankDatabase. Class Withdrawal

must maintain handles on these objects to send messages to them, so lines 19–22 of Fig. 9.24 declare four references as private data members. In the implementation of class Withdrawal in Appendix G, a constructor initializes these data members with references to actual objects. Note that lines 6–9 #include the header files containing the definitions of classes Screen, Keypad, CashDispenser and BankDatabase so that we can declare references to objects of these classes in lines 19–22.

4. It turns out that including the header files for classes Screen, Keypad, CashDispenser and BankDatabase in Fig. 9.24 does more than is necessary. Class Withdrawal contains *references* to objects of these classes—it does not contain actual objects—and the amount of information required by the compiler to create a reference differs from that which is required to create an object. Recall that creating an object requires that you provide the compiler with a definition of the class that introduces the name of the class as a new user-defined type and indicates the data members that determine how much memory is required to store the object. Declaring a *reference* (or pointer) to an object, however, requires only that the compiler knows that the object's class exists—it does not need to know the size of the object. Any reference (or pointer), regardless of the class of the object to which it refers, contains only the memory address of the actual object. The amount of memory required to store an address is a physical characteristic of the computer's hardware. The compiler thus knows the size of any reference (or pointer). As a result, including a class's full header file when declaring only a reference to an object of that class is unnecessary—we need to introduce the name of the class, but we do not need to provide the data layout of the object, because the compiler already knows the size of all references. C++ provides a statement called a forward declaration that signifies that a header file contains references or pointers to a class, but that the class definition lies outside the header file. We can replace the #includes in the Withdrawal class definition of Fig. 9.24 with forward declarations of classes Screen, Keypad, CashDispenser and BankDatabase (lines 6–9 in Fig. 9.25). Rather than #include the entire header file for each of these classes, we place only a forward declaration of each class in the header file for class Withdrawal. Note that if class Withdrawal contained actual objects instead of references (i.e., if the ampersands in lines 19–22 were omitted), then we would indeed need to #include the full header files.

```
 1   // Fig. 9.22: Withdrawal.h
 2   // Definition of class Withdrawal that represents a withdrawal transaction
 3   #ifndef WITHDRAWAL_H
 4   #define WITHDRAWAL_H
 5
 6   class Withdrawal
 7   {
 8   }; // end class Withdrawal
 9
10   #endif // WITHDRAWAL_H
```

Fig. 9.22 | Definition of class Withdrawal enclosed in preprocessor wrappers.

```
 1   // Fig. 9.23: Withdrawal.h
 2   // Definition of class Withdrawal that represents a withdrawal transaction
 3   #ifndef WITHDRAWAL_H
 4   #define WITHDRAWAL_H
 5
 6   class Withdrawal
 7   {
 8   private:
 9      // attributes
10      int accountNumber; // account to withdraw funds from
11      double amount; // amount to withdraw
12   }; // end class Withdrawal
13
14   #endif // WITHDRAWAL_H
```

Fig. 9.23 | Adding attributes to the Withdrawal class header file.

```
 1   // Fig. 9.24: Withdrawal.h
 2   // Definition of class Withdrawal that represents a withdrawal transaction
 3   #ifndef WITHDRAWAL_H
 4   #define WITHDRAWAL_H
 5
 6   #include "Screen.h" // include definition of class Screen
 7   #include "Keypad.h" // include definition of class Keypad
 8   #include "CashDispenser.h" // include definition of class CashDispenser
 9   #include "BankDatabase.h" // include definition of class BankDatabase
10
11   class Withdrawal
12   {
13   private:
14      // attributes
15      int accountNumber; // account to withdraw funds from
16      double amount; // amount to withdraw
17
18      // references to associated objects
19      Screen &screen; // reference to ATM's screen
20      Keypad &keypad; // reference to ATM's keypad
21      CashDispenser &cashDispenser; // reference to ATM's cash dispenser
22      BankDatabase &bankDatabase; // reference to the account info database
23   }; // end class Withdrawal
24
25   #endif // WITHDRAWAL_H
```

Fig. 9.24 | Declaring references to objects associated with class Withdrawal.

Note that using a forward declaration (where possible) instead of including a full header file helps avoid a preprocessor problem called a circular include. This problem occurs when the header file for a class A #includes the header file for a class B and vice versa. Some preprocessors are not be able to resolve such #include directives, causing a compilation error. If class A, for example, uses only a reference to an object of class B, then the #include in class A's header file can be replaced by a forward declaration of class B to prevent the circular include.

```
 1   // Fig. 9.25: Withdrawal.h
 2   // Definition of class Withdrawal that represents a withdrawal transaction
 3   #ifndef WITHDRAWAL_H
 4   #define WITHDRAWAL_H
 5
 6   class Screen; // forward declaration of class Screen
 7   class Keypad; // forward declaration of class Keypad
 8   class CashDispenser; // forward declaration of class CashDispenser
 9   class BankDatabase; // forward declaration of class BankDatabase
10
11   class Withdrawal
12   {
13   private:
14      // attributes
15      int accountNumber; // account to withdraw funds from
16      double amount; // amount to withdraw
17
18      // references to associated objects
19      Screen &screen; // reference to ATM's screen
20      Keypad &keypad; // reference to ATM's keypad
21      CashDispenser &cashDispenser; // reference to ATM's cash dispenser
22      BankDatabase &bankDatabase; // reference to the account info database
23   }; // end class Withdrawal
24
25   #endif // WITHDRAWAL_H
```

Fig. 9.25 | Using forward declarations in place of #include directives.

5. Use the operations located in the third compartment of Fig. 9.20 to write the function prototypes of the class's member functions. If we have not yet specified a return type for an operation, we declare the member function with return type void. Refer to the class diagrams of Figs. 6.22–6.25 to declare any necessary parameters. For example, adding the public operation execute in class Withdrawal, which has an empty parameter list, yields the prototype in line 15 of Fig. 9.26. [*Note:* We code the definitions of member functions in .cpp files when we implement the complete ATM system in Appendix G.]

```
 1   // Fig. 9.26: Withdrawal.h
 2   // Definition of class Withdrawal that represents a withdrawal transaction
 3   #ifndef WITHDRAWAL_H
 4   #define WITHDRAWAL_H
 5
 6   class Screen; // forward declaration of class Screen
 7   class Keypad; // forward declaration of class Keypad
 8   class CashDispenser; // forward declaration of class CashDispenser
 9   class BankDatabase; // forward declaration of class BankDatabase
10
```

Fig. 9.26 | Adding operations to the Withdrawal class header file. (Part 1 of 2.)

```
11   class Withdrawal
12   {
13   public:
14      // operations
15      void execute(); // perform the transaction
16   private:
17      // attributes
18      int accountNumber; // account to withdraw funds from
19      double amount; // amount to withdraw
20
21      // references to associated objects
22      Screen &screen; // reference to ATM's screen
23      Keypad &keypad; // reference to ATM's keypad
24      CashDispenser &cashDispenser; // reference to ATM's cash dispenser
25      BankDatabase &bankDatabase; // reference to the account info database
26   }; // end class Withdrawal
27
28   #endif // WITHDRAWAL_H
```

Fig. 9.26 | Adding operations to the `Withdrawal` class header file. (Part 2 of 2.)

Software Engineering Observation 9.12

Several UML modeling tools can convert UML-based designs into C++ code, considerably speeding the implementation process. For more information on these "automatic" code generators, refer to the Internet and Web resources listed at the end of Section 2.8.

This concludes our discussion of the basics of generating class header files from UML diagrams. In the final "Software Engineering Case Study" section (Section 3.11), we demonstrate how to modify the header files to incorporate the object-oriented concept of inheritance.

Software Engineering Case Study Self-Review Exercises

9.1   State whether the following statement is *true* or *false*, and if *false*, explain why: If an attribute of a class is marked with a minus sign (-) in a class diagram, the attribute is not directly accessible outside of the class.

9.2   In Fig. 9.21, the association between the ATM and the Screen indicates that:
   a) we can navigate from the Screen to the ATM
   b) we can navigate from the ATM to the Screen
   c) Both a and b; the association is bidirectional
   d) None of the above

9.3   Write C++ code to begin implementing the design for class Account.

Answers to Software Engineering Case Study Self-Review Exercises

9.1   True. The minus sign (–) indicates private visibility. We've mentioned "friendship" as an exception to private visibility. Friendship is discussed in Chapter 10.

9.2   b.

9.3   The design for class Account yields the header file in Fig. 9.27.

```
1   // Fig. 9.27: Account.h
2   // Account class definition. Represents a bank account.
3   #ifndef ACCOUNT_H
4   #define ACCOUNT_H
5
6   class Account
7   {
8   public:
9      bool validatePIN( int ); // is user-specified PIN correct?
10      double getAvailableBalance(); // returns available balance
11      double getTotalBalance(); // returns total balance
12      void credit( double ); // adds an amount to the Account
13      void debit( double ); // subtracts an amount from the Account
14   private:
15      int accountNumber; // account number
16      int pin; // PIN for authentication
17      double availableBalance; // funds available for withdrawal
18      double totalBalance; // funds available + funds waiting to clear
19   }; // end class Account
20
21   #endif // ACCOUNT_H
```

Fig. 9.27 | Account class header file based on Fig. 9.20 and Fig. 9.21.

Summary

- The preprocessor directives #ifndef (which means "if not defined") and #endif are used to prevent multiple inclusions of a header file. If the code between these directives has not previously been included in an application, #define defines a name that can be used to prevent future inclusions, and the code is included in the source code file.

- Data members of a class cannot be initialized where they are declared in the class body (except for a class's static const data members of integral or enum types as you'll see in Chapter 10). It is strongly recommended that these data members be initialized by the class's constructor (as there is no default initialization for data members of fundamental types).

- Stream manipulator setfill specifies the fill character that is displayed when an integer is output in a field that is wider than the number of digits in the value.

- By default, the fill characters appear before the digits in the number.

- Stream manipulator setfill is a "sticky" setting, meaning that once the fill character is set, it applies for all subsequent fields being printed.

- Even though a member function declared in a class definition may be defined outside that class definition (and "tied" to the class via the binary scope resolution operator), that member function is still within that class's scope; i.e., its name is known only to other members of the class unless referred to via an object of the class, a reference to an object of the class or a pointer to an object of the class.

- If a member function is defined in the body of a class definition, the C++ compiler attempts to inline calls to the member function.

- Classes do not have to be created "from scratch." Rather, they can include objects of other classes as members or they may be derived from other classes that provide attributes and behaviors the new classes can use. Including class objects as members of other classes is called composition.

- A class's data members and member functions belong to that class's scope.

- Nonmember functions are defined at file scope.

- Within a class's scope, class members are immediately accessible by all of that class's member functions and can be referenced by name.

- Outside a class's scope, class members are referenced through one of the handles on an object—an object name, a reference to an object or a pointer to an object.

- Member functions of a class can be overloaded, but only by other member functions of that class.

- To overload a member function, provide in the class definition a prototype for each version of the overloaded function, and provide a separate definition for each version of the function.

- Variables declared in a member function have block scope and are known only to that function.

- If a member function defines a variable with the same name as a variable with class scope, the class-scope variable is hidden by the block-scope variable in the block scope.

- The dot member selection operator (`.`) is preceded by an object's name or by a reference to an object to access the object's `public` members.

- The arrow member selection operator (`->`) is preceded by a pointer to an object to access that object's `public` members.

- Header files do contain some portions of the implementation and hints about others. Inline member functions, for example, need to be in a header file, so that when the compiler compiles a client, the client can include the `inline` function definition in place.

- A class's `private` members that are listed in the class definition in the header file are visible to clients, even though the clients may not access the `private` members.

- A utility function (also called a helper function) is a `private` member function that supports the operation of the class's `public` member functions. Utility functions are not intended to be used by clients of a class (but can be used by `friend`s of a class).

- Like other functions, constructors can specify default arguments.

- A class's destructor is called implicitly when an object of the class is destroyed.

- The name of the destructor for a class is the tilde (~) character followed by the class name.

- A destructor does not actually release an object's storage—it performs termination housekeeping before the system reclaims an object's memory, so the memory may be reused to hold new objects.

- A destructor receives no parameters and returns no value. A class may have only one destructor.

- If the programmer does not explicitly provide a destructor, the compiler creates an "empty" destructor, so every class has exactly one destructor.

- The order in which constructors and destructors are called depends on the order in which execution enters and leaves the scopes where the objects are instantiated.

- Generally, destructor calls are made in the reverse order of the corresponding constructor calls, but the storage classes of objects can alter the order in which destructors are called.

- A reference to an object is an alias for the name of the object and, hence, may be used on the left side of an assignment statement. In this context, the reference makes a perfectly acceptable *lvalue* that can receive a value. One way to use this capability (unfortunately!) is to have a `public` member function of a class return a reference to a `private` data member of that class. If the function returns a `const` reference, then the reference cannot be used as a modifiable *lvalue*.

- The assignment operator (=) can be used to assign an object to another object of the same type. By default, such assignment is performed by memberwise assignment—each member of the object on the right of the assignment operator is assigned individually to the same member in the object on the left of the assignment operator.

- Objects may be passed as function arguments and may be returned from functions. Such passing and returning is performed using pass-by-value by default—a copy of the object is passed or returned. In such cases, C++ creates a new object and uses a copy constructor to copy the original object's values into the new object. We explain these in detail in Chapter 11, Operator Overloading; String and Array Objects.

- For each class, the compiler provides a default copy constructor that copies each member of the original object into the corresponding member of the new object.

- Many substantial class libraries exist, and others are being developed worldwide.

- Software reusability speeds the development of powerful, high-quality software. Rapid applications development (RAD) through the mechanisms of reusable componentry has become an important field.

Terminology

abort function
access function
aggregation
arrow member selection operator (->)
assigning class objects
class libraries
class scope
composition
copy constructor
default arguments with constructors
default memberwise assignment
#define preprocessor directive
derive one class from another
destructor
#endif preprocessor directive
exit function
file scope
fill character
handle on an object
helper function
#ifndef preprocessor directive
implicit handle on an object
inheritance

initializer
memberwise assignment
name handle on an object
object handle
object leaves scope
order in which constructors and destructors are
    called
overloaded constructor
overloaded member function
pass an object by value
pointer handle on an object
predicate function
preprocessor wrapper
pure procedure
rapid application development (RAD)
reentrant code
reference handle on an object
reusable componentry
setfill parameterized stream manipulator
software asset
termination housekeeping
tilde character (~) in a destructor name

Self-Review Exercises

9.1 Fill in the blanks in each of the following:

a) Class members are accessed via the _____ operator in conjunction with the name of an object (or reference to an object) of the class or via the _____ operator in conjunction with a pointer to an object of the class.

b) Class members specified as _____ are accessible only to member functions of the class and friends of the class.

c) Class members specified as _____ are accessible anywhere an object of the class is in scope.

d) _____ can be used to assign an object of a class to another object of the same class.

9.2   Find the error(s) in each of the following and explain how to correct it (them):

a)   Assume the following prototype is declared in class `Time`:

```
void ~Time( int );
```

b)   The following is a partial definition of class `Time`:

```
class Time
{
public:
    // function prototypes

private:
    int hour = 0;
    int minute = 0;
    int second = 0;
}; // end class Time
```

c)   Assume the following prototype is declared in class `Employee`:

```
int Employee( const char *, const char * );
```

Answers to Self-Review Exercises

9.1   a) dot (.), arrow (->). b) `private`. c) `public`.   d) Default memberwise assignment (performed by the assignment operator).

9.2   a)   Error: Destructors are not allowed to return values (or even specify a return type) or take arguments.
Correction: Remove the return type `void` and the parameter `int` from the declaration.

b)   Error: Members cannot be explicitly initialized in the class definition.
Correction: Remove the explicit initialization from the class definition and initialize the data members in a constructor.

c)   Error: Constructors are not allowed to return values.
Correction: Remove the return type `int` from the declaration.

Exercises

9.3   What is the purpose of the scope resolution operator?

9.4   *(Enhancing Class `Time`)* Provide a constructor that is capable of using the current time from the `time()` function—declared in the C++ Standard Library header `<ctime>`—to initialize an object of the `Time` class.

9.5   *(Complex Class)* Create a class called `Complex` for performing arithmetic with complex numbers. Write a program to test your class.
Complex numbers have the form

```
realPart + imaginaryPart * i
```

where *i* is

$$\sqrt{-1}$$

Use `double` variables to represent the `private` data of the class. Provide a constructor that enables an object of this class to be initialized when it is declared. The constructor should contain default values in case no initializers are provided. Provide `public` member functions that perform the following tasks:

a)   Adding two `Complex` numbers: The real parts are added together and the imaginary parts are added together.

b) Subtracting two `Complex` numbers: The real part of the right operand is subtracted from the real part of the left operand, and the imaginary part of the right operand is subtracted from the imaginary part of the left operand.

c) Printing `Complex` numbers in the form `(a, b)`, where `a` is the real part and `b` is the imaginary part.

9.6   *(Rational Class)* Create a class called `Rational` for performing arithmetic with fractions. Write a program to test your class.

Use integer variables to represent the `private` data of the class—the `numerator` and the `denominator`. Provide a constructor that enables an object of this class to be initialized when it is declared. The constructor should contain default values in case no initializers are provided and should store the fraction in reduced form. For example, the fraction

$$\frac{2}{4}$$

would be stored in the object as 1 in the `numerator` and 2 in the `denominator`. Provide `public` member functions that perform each of the following tasks:

a) Adding two `Rational` numbers. The result should be stored in reduced form.

b) Subtracting two `Rational` numbers. The result should be stored in reduced form.

c) Multiplying two `Rational` numbers. The result should be stored in reduced form.

d) Dividing two `Rational` numbers. The result should be stored in reduced form.

e) Printing `Rational` numbers in the form a/b, where a is the numerator and b is the denominator.

f) Printing `Rational` numbers in floating-point format.

9.7   *(Enhancing Class Time)* Modify the `Time` class of Figs. 9.8–9.9 to include a `tick` member function that increments the time stored in a `Time` object by one second. The `Time` object should always remain in a consistent state. Write a program that tests the `tick` member function in a loop that prints the time in standard format during each iteration of the loop to illustrate that the `tick` member function works correctly. Be sure to test the following cases:

a) Incrementing into the next minute.

b) Incrementing into the next hour.

c) Incrementing into the next day (i.e., 11:59:59 PM to 12:00:00 AM).

9.8   *(Enhancing Class Date)* Modify the `Date` class of Figs. 9.17–9.18 to perform error checking on the initializer values for data members `month`, `day` and `year`. Also, provide a member function `nextDay` to increment the day by one. The `Date` object should always remain in a consistent state. Write a program that tests function `nextDay` in a loop that prints the date during each iteration to illustrate that `nextDay` works correctly. Be sure to test the following cases:

a) Incrementing into the next month.

b) Incrementing into the next year.

9.9   *(Combining Class Time and Class Date)* Combine the modified `Time` class of Exercise 9.7 and the modified `Date` class of Exercise 9.8 into one class called `DateAndTime`. (In Chapter 12, we will discuss inheritance, which will enable us to accomplish this task quickly without modifying the existing class definitions.) Modify the `tick` function to call the `nextDay` function if the time increments into the next day. Modify functions `printStandard` and `printUniversal` to output the date and time. Write a program to test the new class `DateAndTime`. Specifically, test incrementing the time into the next day.

9.10   *(Returning Error Indicators from Class Time's set Functions)* Modify the *set* functions in the `Time` class of Figs. 9.8–9.9 to return appropriate error values if an attempt is made to *set* a data member of an object of class `Time` to an invalid value. Write a program that tests your new version of class `Time`. Display error messages when *set* functions return error values.

9.11   *(Rectangle Class)* Create a class `Rectangle` with attributes `length` and `width`, each of which defaults to 1. Provide member functions that calculate the `perimeter` and the `area` of the rectangle. Also, provide *set* and *get* functions for the `length` and `width` attributes. The *set* functions should verify that `length` and `width` are each floating-point numbers larger than 0.0 and less than 20.0.

9.12   *(Enhancing Class Rectangle)* Create a more sophisticated `Rectangle` class than the one you created in Exercise 9.11. This class stores only the Cartesian coordinates of the four corners of the rectangle. The constructor calls a *set* function that accepts four sets of coordinates and verifies that each of these is in the first quadrant with no single *x*- or *y*-coordinate larger than 20.0. The *set* function also verifies that the supplied coordinates do, in fact, specify a rectangle. Provide member functions that calculate the `length`, `width`, `perimeter` and `area`. The length is the larger of the two dimensions. Include a predicate function `square` that determines whether the rectangle is a square.

9.13   *(Enhancing Class Rectangle)* Modify class `Rectangle` from Exercise 9.12 to include a `draw` function that displays the rectangle inside a 25-by-25 box enclosing the portion of the first quadrant in which the rectangle resides. Include a `setFillCharacter` function to specify the character out of which the body of the rectangle will be drawn. Include a `setPerimeterCharacter` function to specify the character that will be used to draw the border of the rectangle. If you feel ambitious, you might include functions to scale the size of the rectangle, rotate it, and move it around within the designated portion of the first quadrant.

9.14   *(HugeInteger Class)* Create a class `HugeInteger` that uses a 40-element array of digits to store integers as large as 40 digits each. Provide member functions `input`, `output`, `add` and `substract`. For comparing `HugeInteger` objects, provide functions `isEqualTo`, `isNotEqualTo`, `isGreaterThan`, `isLessThan`, `isGreaterThanOrEqualTo` and `isLessThanOrEqualTo`—each of these is a "predicate" function that simply returns `true` if the relationship holds between the two `HugeIntegers` and returns `false` if the relationship does not hold. Also, provide a predicate function `isZero`. If you feel ambitious, provide member functions `multiply`, `divide` and `modulus`.

9.15   *(TicTacToe Class)* Create a class `TicTacToe` that will enable you to write a complete program to play the game of tic-tac-toe. The class contains as `private` data a 3-by-3 two-dimensional array of integers. The constructor should initialize the empty board to all zeros. Allow two human players. Wherever the first player moves, place a 1 in the specified square. Place a 2 wherever the second player moves. Each move must be to an empty square. After each move, determine whether the game has been won or is a draw. If you feel ambitious, modify your program so that the computer makes the moves for one of the players. Also, allow the player to specify whether he or she wants to go first or second. If you feel exceptionally ambitious, develop a program that will play three-dimensional tic-tac-toe on a 4-by-4-by-4 board. [*Caution:* This is an extremely challenging project that could take many weeks of effort!]

10

Classes: A Deeper Look, Part 2

OBJECTIVES

In this chapter you will learn:

- To specify `const` (constant) objects and `const` member functions.

- To create objects composed of other objects.

- To use `friend` functions and `friend` classes.

- To use the `this` pointer.

- To create and destroy objects dynamically with operators `new` and `delete`, respectively.

- To use `static` data members and member functions.

- The concept of a container class.

- The notion of iterator classes that walk through the elements of container classes.

- To use proxy classes to hide implementation details from a class's clients.

10.1 Introduction

In this chapter, we continue our study of classes and data abstraction with several more advanced topics. We use const objects and const member functions to prevent modifications of objects and enforce the principle of least privilege. We discuss composition—a form of reuse in which a class can have objects of other classes as members. Next, we introduce friendship, which enables a class designer to specify non-member functions that can access class's non-public members—a technique that is often used in operator overloading (Chapter 11) for performance reasons. We discuss a special pointer (called this), which is an implicit argument to each of a class's non-static member functions that allows those member functions to access the correct object's data members and other non-static member functions. We then discuss dynamic memory management and show how to create and destroy objects dynamically with the new and delete operators. Next, we motivate the need for static class members and show how to use static data members and member functions in your own classes. Finally, we show how to create a proxy class to hide the implementation details of a class (including its private data members) from clients of the class.

Recall that Chapter 3 introduced C++ Standard Library class string to represent strings as full-fledged class objects. In this chapter, however, we use the pointer-based strings we introduced in Chapter 8 to help the reader master pointers and prepare for the professional world in which the reader will see a great deal of C legacy code implemented over the last two decades. Thus, the reader will become familiar with the two most prevalent methods of creating and manipulating strings in C++.

10.2 const (Constant) Objects and const Member Functions

We have emphasized the principle of least privilege as one of the most fundamental principles of good software engineering. Let us see how this principle applies to objects.

Some objects need to be modifiable and some do not. The programmer may use keyword `const` to specify that an object is not modifiable and that any attempt to modify the object should result in a compilation error. The statement

```
const Time noon( 12, 0, 0 );
```

declares a `const` object `noon` of class `Time` and initializes it to 12 noon.

Software Engineering Observation 10.1

Declaring an object as `const` helps enforce the principle of least privilege. Attempts to modify the object are caught at compile time rather than causing execution-time errors. Using `const` properly is crucial to proper class design, program design and coding.

Performance Tip 10.1

Declaring variables and objects `const` can improve performance—today's sophisticated optimizing compilers can perform certain optimizations on constants that cannot be performed on variables.

C++ compilers disallow member function calls for `const` objects unless the member functions themselves are also declared `const`. This is true even for *get* member functions that do not modify the object. In addition, the compiler does not allow member functions declared `const` to modify the object.

A function is specified as `const` *both* in its prototype (Fig. 10.1; lines 19–24) and in its definition (Fig. 10.2; lines 47, 53, 59 and 65) by inserting the keyword `const` after the function's parameter list and, in the case of the function definition, before the left brace that begins the function body.

Common Programming Error 10.1

Defining as `const` a member function that modifies a data member of an object is a compilation error.

Common Programming Error 10.2

Defining as `const` a member function that calls a non-`const` member function of the class on the same instance of the class is a compilation error.

Common Programming Error 10.3

Invoking a non-`const` member function on a `const` object is a compilation error.

Software Engineering Observation 10.2

A `const` member function can be overloaded with a non-`const` version. The compiler chooses which overloaded member function to use based on the object on which the function is invoked. If the object is `const`, the compiler uses the `const` version. If the object is not `const`, the compiler uses the non-`const` version.

An interesting problem arises for constructors and destructors, each of which typically modifies objects. The `const` declaration is not allowed for constructors and destructors. A constructor must be allowed to modify an object so that the object can be initialized properly. A destructor must be able to perform its termination housekeeping chores before an object's memory is reclaimed by the system.

Common Programming Error 10.4

Attempting to declare a constructor or destructor const is a compilation error.

Defining and Using const Member Functions

The program of Figs. 10.1–10.3 modifies class Time of Figs. 9.9–9.10 by making its *get* functions and printUniversal function const. In the header file Time.h (Fig. 10.1), lines 19–21 and 24 now include keyword const after each function's parameter list. The corresponding definition of each function in Fig. 10.2 (lines 47, 53, 59 and 65, respectively) also specifies keyword const after each function's parameter list.

Figure 10.3 instantiates two Time objects—non-const object wakeUp (line 7) and const object noon (line 8). The program attempts to invoke non-const member functions setHour (line 13) and printStandard (line 20) on the const object noon. In each case, the compiler generates an error message. The program also illustrates the three other member-function-call combinations on objects—a non-const member function on a non-const object (line 11), a const member function on a non-const object (line 15) and a const member function on a const object (lines 17–18). The error messages generated

```
 1    // Fig. 10.1: Time.h
 2    // Definition of class Time.
 3    // Member functions defined in Time.cpp.
 4    #ifndef TIME_H
 5    #define TIME_H
 6
 7    class Time
 8    {
 9    public:
10       Time( int = 0, int = 0, int = 0 ); // default constructor
11
12       // set functions
13       void setTime( int, int, int ); // set time
14       void setHour( int ); // set hour
15       void setMinute( int ); // set minute
16       void setSecond( int ); // set second
17
18       // get functions (normally declared const)
19       int getHour() const; // return hour
20       int getMinute() const; // return minute
21       int getSecond() const; // return second
22
23       // print functions (normally declared const)
24       void printUniversal() const; // print universal time
25       void printStandard(); // print standard time (should be const)
26    private:
27       int hour; // 0 - 23 (24-hour clock format)
28       int minute; // 0 - 59
29       int second; // 0 - 59
30    }; // end class Time
31
32    #endif
```

Fig. 10.1 | Time class definition with const member functions.

for non-const member functions called on a const object are shown in the output window. Notice that, although some current compilers issue only warning messages for lines 13 and 20 (thus allowing this program to be executed), we consider these warnings to be errors—the ANSI/ISO C++ standard disallows the invocation of a non-const member function on a const object.

```cpp
1   // Fig. 10.2: Time.cpp
2   // Member-function definitions for class Time.
3   #include <iostream>
4   using std::cout;
5
6   #include <iomanip>
7   using std::setfill;
8   using std::setw;
9
10  #include "Time.h" // include definition of class Time
11
12  // constructor function to initialize private data;
13  // calls member function setTime to set variables;
14  // default values are 0 (see class definition)
15  Time::Time( int hour, int minute, int second )
16  {
17     setTime( hour, minute, second );
18  } // end Time constructor
19
20  // set hour, minute and second values
21  void Time::setTime( int hour, int minute, int second )
22  {
23     setHour( hour );
24     setMinute( minute );
25     setSecond( second );
26  } // end function setTime
27
28  // set hour value
29  void Time::setHour( int h )
30  {
31     hour = ( h >= 0 && h < 24 ) ? h : 0; // validate hour
32  } // end function setHour
33
34  // set minute value
35  void Time::setMinute( int m )
36  {
37     minute = ( m >= 0 && m < 60 ) ? m : 0; // validate minute
38  } // end function setMinute
39
40  // set second value
41  void Time::setSecond( int s )
42  {
43     second = ( s >= 0 && s < 60 ) ? s : 0; // validate second
44  } // end function setSecond
45
```

Fig. 10.2 | Time class member-function definitions, including const member functions. (Part 1 of 2.)

```
46   // return hour value
47   int Time::getHour() const // get functions should be const
48   {
49      return hour;
50   } // end function getHour
51
52   // return minute value
53   int Time::getMinute() const
54   {
55      return minute;
56   } // end function getMinute
57
58   // return second value
59   int Time::getSecond() const
60   {
61      return second;
62   } // end function getSecond
63
64   // print Time in universal-time format (HH:MM:SS)
65   void Time::printUniversal() const
66   {
67      cout << setfill( '0' ) << setw( 2 ) << hour << ":"
68         << setw( 2 ) << minute << ":" << setw( 2 ) << second;
69   } // end function printUniversal
70
71   // print Time in standard-time format (HH:MM:SS AM or PM)
72   void Time::printStandard() // note lack of const declaration
73   {
74      cout << ( ( hour == 0 || hour == 12 ) ? 12 : hour % 12 )
75         << ":" << setfill( '0' ) << setw( 2 ) << minute
76         << ":" << setw( 2 ) << second << ( hour < 12 ? " AM" : " PM" );
77   } // end function printStandard
```

Fig. 10.2 | Time class member-function definitions, including const member functions. (Part 2 of 2.)

```
1    // Fig. 10.3: fig10_03.cpp
2    // Attempting to access a const object with non-const member functions.
3    #include "Time.h" // include Time class definition
4
5    int main()
6    {
7       Time wakeUp( 6, 45, 0 ); // non-constant object
8       const Time noon( 12, 0, 0 ); // constant object
9
10                           // OBJECT      MEMBER FUNCTION
11      wakeUp.setHour( 18 ); // non-const   non-const
12
13      noon.setHour( 12 );    // const       non-const
14
15      wakeUp.getHour();      // non-const   const
```

Fig. 10.3 | const objects and const member functions. (Part 1 of 2.)

```
16
17      noon.getMinute();       // const        const
18      noon.printUniversal(); // const        const
19
20      noon.printStandard();  // const        non-const
21      return 0;
22   } // end main
```

Borland C++ command-line compiler error messages:

```
Warning W8037 fig10_03.cpp 13: Non-const function Time::setHour(int)
   called for const object in function main()
Warning W8037 fig10_03.cpp 20: Non-const function Time::printStandard()
   called for const object in function main()
```

Microsoft Visual C++.NET compiler error messages:

```
C:\cpphtp5_examples\ch10\Fig10_01_03\fig10_03.cpp(13) : error C2662:
   'Time::setHour' : cannot convert 'this' pointer from 'const Time' to
   'Time &'
       Conversion loses qualifiers
C:\cpphtp5_examples\ch10\Fig10_01_03\fig10_03.cpp(20) : error C2662:
   'Time::printStandard' : cannot convert 'this' pointer from 'const Time' to
   'Time &'
       Conversion loses qualifiers
```

GNU C++ compiler error messages:

```
fig10_03.cpp:13: error: passing `const Time' as `this' argument of
   `void Time::setHour(int)' discards qualifiers
fig10_03.cpp:20: error: passing `const Time' as `this' argument of
   `void Time::printStandard()' discards qualifiers
```

Fig. 10.3 | const objects and const member functions. (Part 2 of 2.)

Notice that even though a constructor must be a non-const member function (Fig. 10.2, lines 15–18), it can still be used to initialize a const object (Fig. 10.3, line 8). The definition of the Time constructor (Fig. 10.2, lines 15–18) shows that the Time constructor calls another non-const member function—setTime (lines 21–26)—to perform the initialization of a Time object. Invoking a non-const member function from the constructor call as part of the initialization of a const object is allowed. The "constness" of a const object is enforced from the time the constructor completes initialization of the object until that object's destructor is called.

Also notice that line 20 in Fig. 10.3 generates a compilation error even though member function printStandard of class Time does not modify the object on which it is invoked. The fact that a member function does not modify an object is not sufficient to indicate that the function is constant function—the function must explicitly be declared const.

Initializing a **const** Data Member with a Member Initializer

The program of Figs. 10.4–10.6 introduces using member initializer syntax. All data members *can* be initialized using member initializer syntax, but const data members and

```
 1   // Fig. 10.4: Increment.h
 2   // Definition of class Increment.
 3   #ifndef INCREMENT_H
 4   #define INCREMENT_H
 5
 6   class Increment
 7   {
 8   public:
 9      Increment( int c = 0, int i = 1 ); // default constructor
10
11      // function addIncrement definition
12      void addIncrement()
13      {
14         count += increment;
15      } // end function addIncrement
16
17      void print() const; // prints count and increment
18   private:
19      int count;
20      const int increment; // const data member
21   }; // end class Increment
22
23   #endif
```

Fig. 10.4 | Increment class definition containing non-`const` data member `count` and `const` data member `increment`.

```
 1   // Fig. 10.5: Increment.cpp
 2   // Member-function definitions for class Increment demonstrate using a
 3   // member initializer to initialize a constant of a built-in data type.
 4   #include <iostream>
 5   using std::cout;
 6   using std::endl;
 7
 8   #include "Increment.h" // include definition of class Increment
 9
10   // constructor
11   Increment::Increment( int c, int i )
12      : count( c ), // initializer for non-const member
13        increment( i ) // required initializer for const member
14   {
15      // empty body
16   } // end constructor Increment
17
18   // print count and increment values
19   void Increment::print() const
20   {
21      cout << "count = " << count << ", increment = " << increment << endl;
22   } // end function print
```

Fig. 10.5 | Member initializer used to initialize a constant of a built-in data type.

```
 1   // Fig. 10.6: fig10_06.cpp
 2   // Program to test class Increment.
 3   #include <iostream>
 4   using std::cout;
 5
 6   #include "Increment.h" // include definition of class Increment
 7
 8   int main()
 9   {
10      Increment value( 10, 5 );
11
12      cout << "Before incrementing: ";
13      value.print();
14
15      for ( int j = 1; j <= 3; j++ )
16      {
17         value.addIncrement();
18         cout << "After increment " << j << ": ";
19         value.print();
20      } // end for
21
22      return 0;
23   } // end main
```

```
Before incrementing: count = 10, increment = 5
After increment 1: count = 15, increment = 5
After increment 2: count = 20, increment = 5
After increment 3: count = 25, increment = 5
```

Fig. 10.6 | Invoking an `Increment` object's `print` and `addIncrement` member functions.

data members that are references *must* be initialized using member initializers. Later in this chapter, we will see that member objects must be initialized this way as well. In Chapter 12 when we study inheritance, we will see that base-class portions of derived classes also must be initialized this way.

The constructor definition (Fig. 10.5, lines 11–16) uses a member initializer list to initialize class `Increment`'s data members—non-const integer `count` and `const` integer `increment` (declared in lines 19–20 of Fig. 10.4). Member initializers appear between a constructor's parameter list and the left brace that begins the constructor's body. The member initializer list (Fig. 10.5, lines 12–13) is separated from the parameter list with a colon (:). Each member initializer consists of the data member name followed by parentheses containing the member's initial value. In this example, `count` is initialized with the value of constructor parameter `c` and `increment` is initialized with the value of constructor parameter `i`. Note that multiple member initializers are separated by commas. Also, note that the member initializer list executes before the body of the constructor executes.

Software Engineering Observation 10.3

A `const` object cannot be modified by assignment, so it must be initialized. When a data member of a class is declared `const`, a member initializer must be used to provide the constructor with the initial value of the data member for an object of the class. The same is true for references.

*Erroneously Attempting to Initialize a **const** Data Member with an Assignment*
The program of Figs. 10.7–10.9 illustrates the compilation errors caused by attempting to initialize const data member increment with an assignment statement (Fig. 10.8, line 14) in the Increment constructor's body rather than with a member initializer. Note that line 13 of Fig. 10.8 does not generate a compilation error, because count is not declared const. Also note that the compilation errors produced by Microsoft Visual C++.NET refer to int data member increment as a "const object." The ANSI/ISO C++ standard defines an "object" as any "region of storage." Like instances of classes, fundamental-type variables also occupy space in memory, so they are often referred to as "objects."

Common Programming Error 10.5

Not providing a member initializer for a const data member is a compilation error.

Software Engineering Observation 10.4

Constant data members (const objects and const variables) and data members declared as references must be initialized with member initializer syntax; assignments for these types of data in the constructor body are not allowed.

Note that function print (Fig. 10.8, lines 18–21) is declared const. It might seem strange to label this function const, because a program probably will never have a const Increment object. However, it is possible that a program will have a const reference to an Increment object or a pointer to const that points to an Increment object. Typically, this occurs when objects of class Increment are passed to functions or returned from functions. In these cases, only the const member functions of class Increment can be called through the reference or pointer. Thus, it is reasonable to declare function print as const—doing so prevents errors in these situations where an Increment object is treated as a const object.

Error-Prevention Tip 10.1

Declare as const all of a class's member functions that do not modify the object in which they operate. Occasionally this may seem inappropriate, because you will have no intention of creating const objects of that class or accessing objects of that class through const references or pointers to const. Declaring such member functions const does offer a benefit, though. If the member function is inadvertently written to modify the object, the compiler will issue an error message.

```
 1   // Fig. 10.7: Increment.h
 2   // Definition of class Increment.
 3   #ifndef INCREMENT_H
 4   #define INCREMENT_H
 5
 6   class Increment
 7   {
 8   public:
 9      Increment( int c = 0, int i = 1 ); // default constructor
10
```

Fig. 10.7 | Increment class definition containing non-const data member count and const data member increment. (Part 1 of 2.)

```
11      // function addIncrement definition
12      void addIncrement()
13      {
14         count += increment;
15      } // end function addIncrement
16
17      void print() const; // prints count and increment
18   private:
19      int count;
20      const int increment; // const data member
21   }; // end class Increment
22
23   #endif
```

Fig. 10.7 | Increment class definition containing non-const data member count and const data member increment. (Part 2 of 2.)

```
1    // Fig. 10.8: Increment.cpp
2    // Attempting to initialize a constant of
3    // a built-in data type with an assignment.
4    #include <iostream>
5    using std::cout;
6    using std::endl;
7
8    #include "Increment.h" // include definition of class Increment
9
10   // constructor; constant member 'increment' is not initialized
11   Increment::Increment( int c, int i )
12   {
13      count = c; // allowed because count is not constant
14      increment = i; // ERROR: Cannot modify a const object
15   } // end constructor Increment
16
17   // print count and increment values
18   void Increment::print() const
19   {
20      cout << "count = " << count << ", increment = " << increment << endl;
21   } // end function print
```

Fig. 10.8 | Erroneous attempt to initialize a constant of a built-in data type by assignment.

```
1    // Fig. 10.9: fig10_09.cpp
2    // Program to test class Increment.
3    #include <iostream>
4    using std::cout;
5
6    #include "Increment.h" // include definition of class Increment
7
8    int main()
9    {
```

Fig. 10.9 | Program to test class Increment generates compilation errors. (Part 1 of 2.)

```
10        Increment value( 10, 5 );
11
12        cout << "Before incrementing: ";
13        value.print();
14
15        for ( int j = 1; j <= 3; j++ )
16        {
17           value.addIncrement();
18           cout << "After increment " << j << ": ";
19           value.print();
20        } // end for
21
22        return 0;
23     } // end main
```

Borland C++ command-line compiler error message:

```
Error E2024 Increment.cpp 14: Cannot modify a const object in function
   Increment::Increment(int,int)
```

Microsoft Visual C++.NET compiler error messages:

```
C:\cpphtp5_examples\ch10\Fig10_07_09\Increment.cpp(12) : error C2758:
   'Increment::increment' : must be initialized in constructor
   base/member initializer list
        C:\cpphtp5_examples\ch10\Fig10_07_09\Increment.h(20) :
           see declaration of 'Increment::increment'
C:\cpphtp5_examples\ch10\Fig10_07_09\Increment.cpp(14) : error C2166:
   l-value specifies const object
```

GNU C++ compiler error messages:

```
Increment.cpp:12: error: uninitialized member 'Increment::increment' with
   'const' type 'const int'
Increment.cpp:14: error: assignment of read-only data-member
   `Increment::increment'
```

Fig. 10.9 | Program to test class Increment generates compilation errors. (Part 2 of 2.)

10.3 Composition: Objects as Members of Classes

An AlarmClock object needs to know when it is supposed to sound its alarm, so why not include a Time object as a member of the AlarmClock class? Such a capability is called com-position and is sometimes referred to as a *has-a* relationship. A class can have objects of other classes as members.

 Software Engineering Observation 10.5

A common form of software reusability is composition, in which a class has objects of other classes as members.

When an object is created, its constructor is called automatically. Previously, we saw how to pass arguments to the constructor of an object we created in main. This section shows how an object's constructor can pass arguments to member-object constructors, which is accomplished via member initializers. Member objects are constructed in the order in which they are declared in the class definition (not in the order they are listed in the constructor's member initializer list) and before their enclosing class objects (sometimes called *host objects*) are constructed.

The program of Figs. 10.10–10.14 uses class `Date` (Figs. 10.10–10.11) and class `Employee` (Figs. 10.12–10.13) to demonstrate objects as members of other objects. The definition of class `Employee` (Fig. 10.12) contains `private` data members `firstName`, `lastName`, `birthDate` and `hireDate`. Members `birthDate` and `hireDate` are `const` objects of class `Date`, which contains `private` data members `month`, `day` and `year`. The `Employee` constructor's header (Fig. 10.13, lines 18–21) specifies that the constructor receives four parameters (`first`, `last`, `dateOfBirth` and `dateOfHire`). The first two parameters are used in the constructor's body to initialize the character arrays `firstName` and `lastName`. The last two parameters are passed via member initializers to the constructor for class `Date`. The colon (`:`) in the header separates the member initializers from the parameter list. The member initializers specify the `Employee` constructor parameters being passed to the constructors of the member `Date` objects. Parameter `dateOfBirth` is passed to object `birthDate`'s constructor (Fig. 10.13, line 20), and parameter `dateOfHire` is passed to object `hireDate`'s constructor (Fig. 10.13, line 21). Again, member initializers are separated by commas. As you study class `Date` (Fig. 10.10), notice that the class does not provide a constructor that receives a parameter of type `Date`. So, how is the member initializer list in class `Employee`'s constructor able to initialize the `birthDate` and `hireDate` objects by passing `Date` object's to their `Date` constructors? As we mentioned in Chapter 9, the compiler provides each class with a default copy constructor that copies each member of the constructor's argument object into the corresponding member of the object being initialized. Chapter 11 discusses how programmers can define customized copy constructors.

```cpp
1   // Fig. 10.10: Date.h
2   // Date class definition; Member functions defined in Date.cpp
3   #ifndef DATE_H
4   #define DATE_H
5
6   class Date
7   {
8   public:
9      Date( int = 1, int = 1, int = 1900 ); // default constructor
10     void print() const; // print date in month/day/year format
11     ~Date(); // provided to confirm destruction order
12   private:
13     int month; // 1-12 (January-December)
14     int day; // 1-31 based on month
15     int year; // any year
16
17     // utility function to check if day is proper for month and year
18     int checkDay( int ) const;
19  }; // end class Date
20
21  #endif
```

Fig. 10.10 | `Date` class definition.

Figure 10.14 creates two Date objects (lines 11–12) and passes them as arguments to the constructor of the Employee object created in line 13. Line 16 outputs the Employee object's data. When each Date object is created in lines 11–12, the Date constructor defined at lines 11–28 of Fig. 10.11 displays a line of output to show that the constructor was called (see the first two lines of the sample output). [*Note:* Line 13 of Fig. 10.14 causes two additional Date constructor calls that do not appear in the program's output. When each of the Employee's Date member object's is initialized in the Employee constructor's member initializer list, the default copy constructor for class Date is called. This constructor is defined implicitly by the compiler and does not contain any output statements to demonstrate when it is called. We discuss copy constructors and default copy constructors in detail in Chapter 11.]

```cpp
1   // Fig. 10.11: Date.cpp
2   // Member-function definitions for class Date.
3   #include <iostream>
4   using std::cout;
5   using std::endl;
6
7   #include "Date.h" // include Date class definition
8
9   // constructor confirms proper value for month; calls
10  // utility function checkDay to confirm proper value for day
11  Date::Date( int mn, int dy, int yr )
12  {
13     if ( mn > 0 && mn <= 12 ) // validate the month
14        month = mn;
15     else
16     {
17        month = 1; // invalid month set to 1
18        cout << "Invalid month (" << mn << ") set to 1.\n";
19     } // end else
20
21     year = yr; // could validate yr
22     day = checkDay( dy ); // validate the day
23
24     // output Date object to show when its constructor is called
25     cout << "Date object constructor for date ";
26     print();
27     cout << endl;
28  } // end Date constructor
29
30  // print Date object in form month/day/year
31  void Date::print() const
32  {
33     cout << month << '/' << day << '/' << year;
34  } // end function print
35
36  // output Date object to show when its destructor is called
37  Date::~Date()
38  {
```

Fig. 10.11 | Date class member-function definitions. (Part 1 of 2.)

```
39         cout << "Date object destructor for date ";
40         print();
41         cout << endl;
42    } // end ~Date destructor
43
44    // utility function to confirm proper day value based on
45    // month and year; handles leap years, too
46    int Date::checkDay( int testDay ) const
47    {
48        static const int daysPerMonth[ 13 ] =
49            { 0, 31, 28, 31, 30, 31, 30, 31, 31, 30, 31, 30, 31 };
50
51        // determine whether testDay is valid for specified month
52        if ( testDay > 0 && testDay <= daysPerMonth[ month ] )
53            return testDay;
54
55        // February 29 check for leap year
56        if ( month == 2 && testDay == 29 && ( year % 400 == 0 ||
57            ( year % 4 == 0 && year % 100 != 0 ) ) )
58            return testDay;
59
60        cout << "Invalid day (" << testDay << ") set to 1.\n";
61        return 1; // leave object in consistent state if bad value
62    } // end function checkDay
```

Fig. 10.11 | Date class member-function definitions. (Part 2 of 2.)

```
1    // Fig. 10.12: Employee.h
2    // Employee class definition.
3    // Member functions defined in Employee.cpp.
4    #ifndef EMPLOYEE_H
5    #define EMPLOYEE_H
6
7    #include "Date.h" // include Date class definition
8
9    class Employee
10   {
11   public:
12      Employee( const char * const, const char * const,
13         const Date &, const Date & );
14      void print() const;
15      ~Employee(); // provided to confirm destruction order
16   private:
17      char firstName[ 25 ];
18      char lastName[ 25 ];
19      const Date birthDate; // composition: member object
20      const Date hireDate; // composition: member object
21   }; // end class Employee
22
23   #endif
```

Fig. 10.12 | Employee class definition showing composition.

```cpp
1    // Fig. 10.13: Employee.cpp
2    // Member-function definitions for class Employee.
3    #include <iostream>
4    using std::cout;
5    using std::endl;
6
7    #include <cstring> // strlen and strncpy prototypes
8    using std::strlen;
9    using std::strncpy;
10
11   #include "Employee.h" // Employee class definition
12   #include "Date.h" // Date class definition
13
14   // constructor uses member initializer list to pass initializer
15   // values to constructors of member objects birthDate and hireDate
16   // [Note: This invokes the so-called "default copy constructor" which the
17   // C++ compiler provides implicitly.]
18   Employee::Employee( const char * const first, const char * const last,
19      const Date &dateOfBirth, const Date &dateOfHire )
20      : birthDate( dateOfBirth ), // initialize birthDate
21        hireDate( dateOfHire ) // initialize hireDate
22   {
23      // copy first into firstName and be sure that it fits
24      int length = strlen( first );
25      length = ( length < 25 ? length : 24 );
26      strncpy( firstName, first, length );
27      firstName[ length ] = '\0';
28
29      // copy last into lastName and be sure that it fits
30      length = strlen( last );
31      length = ( length < 25 ? length : 24 );
32      strncpy( lastName, last, length );
33      lastName[ length ] = '\0';
34
35      // output Employee object to show when constructor is called
36      cout << "Employee object constructor: "
37         << firstName << ' ' << lastName << endl;
38   } // end Employee constructor
39
40   // print Employee object
41   void Employee::print() const
42   {
43      cout << lastName << ", " << firstName << "  Hired: ";
44      hireDate.print();
45      cout << "  Birthday: ";
46      birthDate.print();
47      cout << endl;
48   } // end function print
49
50   // output Employee object to show when its destructor is called
51   Employee::~Employee()
52   {
```

Fig. 10.13 | Employee class member-function definitions, including constructor with a member initializer list. (Part I of 2.)

```
53      cout << "Employee object destructor: "
54         << lastName << ", " << firstName << endl;
55   } // end ~Employee destructor
```

Fig. 10.13 | Employee class member-function definitions, including constructor with a member initializer list. (Part 2 of 2.)

```
1   // Fig. 10.14: fig10_14.cpp
2   // Demonstrating composition--an object with member objects.
3   #include <iostream>
4   using std::cout;
5   using std::endl;
6
7   #include "Employee.h" // Employee class definition
8
9   int main()
10  {
11     Date birth( 7, 24, 1949 );
12     Date hire( 3, 12, 1988 );
13     Employee manager( "Bob", "Blue", birth, hire );
14
15     cout << endl;
16     manager.print();
17
18     cout << "\nTest Date constructor with invalid values:\n";
19     Date lastDayOff( 14, 35, 1994 ); // invalid month and day
20     cout << endl;
21     return 0;
22  } // end main
```

```
Date object constructor for date 7/24/1949
Date object constructor for date 3/12/1988
Employee object constructor: Bob Blue

Blue, Bob  Hired: 3/12/1988  Birthday: 7/24/1949

Test Date constructor with invalid values:
Invalid month (14) set to 1.
Invalid day (35) set to 1.
Date object constructor for date 1/1/1994

Date object destructor for date 1/1/1994
Employee object destructor: Blue, Bob
Date object destructor for date 3/12/1988
Date object destructor for date 7/24/1949
Date object destructor for date 3/12/1988
Date object destructor for date 7/24/1949
```

Fig. 10.14 | Member-object initializers.

Class Date and class Employee each include a destructor (lines 37–42 of Fig. 10.11 and lines 51–55 of Fig. 10.13, respectively) that prints a message when an object of its class is destroyed. This enables us to confirm in the program output that objects are constructed from the inside out and destroyed in the reverse order from the outside in (i.e., the Date member objects are destroyed after the Employee object that contains them). Notice the last four lines in the output of Fig. 10.14. The last two lines are the outputs of the Date destructor running on Date objects hire (line 12) and birth (line 11), respectively. These outputs confirm that the three objects created in main are destructed in the reverse of the order in which they were constructed. (The Employee destructor output is five lines from the bottom.) The fourth and third lines from the bottom of the output window show the destructors running for the Employee's member objects hireDate (Fig. 10.12, line 20) and birthDate (Fig. 10.12, line 19). These outputs confirm that the Employee object is destructed from the outside in—i.e., the Employee destructor runs first (output shown five lines from the bottom of the output window), then the member objects are destructed in the reverse order from which they were constructed. Again, the outputs in Fig. 10.14 did not show the constructors running for these objects, because these were the default copy constructors provided by the C++ compiler.

A member object does not need to be initialized explicitly through a member initializer. If a member initializer is not provided, the member object's default constructor will be called implicitly. Values, if any, established by the default constructor can be overridden by *set* functions. However, for complex initialization, this approach may require significant additional work and time.

Common Programming Error 10.6

A compilation error occurs if a member object is not initialized with a member initializer and the member object's class does not provide a default constructor (i.e., the member object's class defines one or more constructors, but none is a default constructor).

Performance Tip 10.2

Initialize member objects explicitly through member initializers. This eliminates the overhead of "doubly initializing" member objects—once when the member object's default constructor is called and again when set *functions are called in the constructor body (or later) to initialize the member object.*

Software Engineering Observation 10.6

If a class member is an object of another class, making that member object public *does not violate the encapsulation and hiding of that member object's* private *members. However, it does violate the encapsulation and hiding of the containing class's implementation, so member objects of class types should still be* private, *like all other data members.*

In line 26 of Fig. 10.11, notice the call to Date member function print. Many member functions of classes in C++ require no arguments. This is because each member function contains an implicit handle (in the form of a pointer) to the object on which it operates. We discuss the implicit pointer, which is represented by keyword this, in Section 10.5.

Class Employee uses two 25-character arrays (Fig. 10.12, lines 17–18) to represent the first name and last name of the Employee. These arrays may waste space for names shorter than 24 characters. (Remember, one character in each array is for the terminating null character, '\0', of the string.) Also, names longer than 24 characters must be truncated to fit in these fixed-size character arrays. Section 10.7 presents another version of class Employee that dynamically creates the exact amount of space required to hold the first and the last name.

Note that the simplest way to represent an `Employee`'s first and last name using the exact amount of space required is to use two `string` objects (C++ Standard Library class `string` was introduced in Chapter 3). If we did this, the `Employee` constructor would appear as follows

```
Employee::Employee( const string &first, const string &last,
   const Date &dateOfBirth, const Date &dateOfHire )
   : firstName( first), // initialize firstName
     lastName( last ), // initialize lastName
     birthDate( dateOfBirth ), // initialize birthDate
     hireDate( dateOfHire ) // initialize hireDate
{
   // output Employee object to show when constructor is called
   cout << "Employee object constructor: "
      << firstName << ' ' << lastName << endl;
} // end Employee constructor
```

Notice that data members `firstName` and `lastName` (now `string` objects) are initialized through member initializers. The `Employee` classes presented in Chapters 12–13 use `string` objects in this fashion. In this chapter, we use pointer-based strings to provide the reader with additional exposure to pointer manipulation.

10.4 `friend` Functions and `friend` Classes

A `friend function` of a class is defined outside that class's scope, yet has the right to access the non-`public` (and `public`) members of the class. Standalone functions or entire classes may be declared to be friends of another class.

Using `friend` functions can enhance performance. This section presents a mechanical example of how a `friend` function works. Later in the book, `friend` functions are used to overload operators for use with class objects (Chapter 11) and to create iterator classes (Chapter 21). Objects of an iterator class can successively select items or perform an operation on items in a container class object (see Section 10.9). Objects of container classes can store items. Using friends is often appropriate when a member function cannot be used for certain operations, as we will see in Chapter 11.

To declare a function as a friend of a class, precede the function prototype in the class definition with keyword `friend`. To declare all member functions of class `ClassTwo` as friends of class `ClassOne`, place a declaration of the form

```
friend class ClassTwo;
```

in the definition of class `ClassOne`.

Software Engineering Observation 10.7

Even though the prototypes for `friend` functions appear in the class definition, friends are not member functions.

Software Engineering Observation 10.8

Member access notions of `private`, `protected` and `public` are not relevant to `friend` declarations, so `friend` declarations can be placed anywhere in a class definition.

Good Programming Practice 10.1

Place all friendship declarations first inside the class definition's body and do not precede them with any access specifier.

Friendship is granted, not taken—i.e., for class B to be a friend of class A, class A must explicitly declare that class B is its friend. Also, the friendship relation is neither symmetric nor transitive; i.e., if class A is a friend of class B, and class B is a friend of class C, you cannot infer that class B is a friend of class A (again, friendship is not symmetric), that class C is a friend of class B (also because friendship is not symmetric), or that class A is a friend of class C (friendship is not transitive).

Software Engineering Observation 10.9

Some people in the OOP community feel that "friendship" corrupts information hiding and weakens the value of the object-oriented design approach. In this text, we identify several examples of the responsible use of friendship.

Modifying a Class's *private* Data With a Friend Function

Figure 10.15 is a mechanical example in which we define friend function setX to set the private data member x of class Count. Note that the friend declaration (line 10) appears first (by convention) in the class definition, even before public member functions are declared. Again, this friend declaration can appear anywhere in the class.

```
1   // Fig. 10.15: fig10_15.cpp
2   // Friends can access private members of a class.
3   #include <iostream>
4   using std::cout;
5   using std::endl;
6
7   // Count class definition
8   class Count
9   {
10     friend void setX( Count &, int ); // friend declaration
11  public:
12     // constructor
13     Count()
14        : x( 0 ) // initialize x to 0
15     {
16        // empty body
17     } // end constructor Count
18
19     // output x
20     void print() const
21     {
22        cout << x << endl;
23     } // end function print
24  private:
25     int x; // data member
26  }; // end class Count
27
```

Fig. 10.15 | Friends can access private members of a class. (Part 1 of 2.)

```
28    // function setX can modify private data of Count
29    // because setX is declared as a friend of Count (line 10)
30    void setX( Count &c, int val )
31    {
32       c.x = val; // allowed because setX is a friend of Count
33    } // end function setX
34
35    int main()
36    {
37       Count counter; // create Count object
38
39       cout << "counter.x after instantiation: ";
40       counter.print();
41
42       setX( counter, 8 ); // set x using a friend function
43       cout << "counter.x after call to setX friend function: ";
44       counter.print();
45       return 0;
46    } // end main
```

```
counter.x after instantiation: 0
counter.x after call to setX friend function: 8
```

Fig. 10.15 | Friends can access private members of a class. (Part 2 of 2.)

Function setX (lines 30–33) is a C-style, stand-alone function—it is not a member function of class Count. For this reason, when setX is invoked for object counter, line 42 passes counter as an argument to setX rather than using a handle (such as the name of the object) to call the function, as in

```
counter.setX( 8 );
```

As we mentioned, Fig. 10.15 is a mechanical example of using the friend construct. It would normally be appropriate to define function setX as a member function of class Count. It would also normally be appropriate to separate the program of Fig. 10.15 into three files:

1. A header file (e.g., Count.h) containing the Count class definition, which in turn contains the prototype of friend function setX

2. An implementation file (e.g., Count.cpp) containing the definitions of class Count's member functions and the definition of friend function setX

3. A test program (e.g., fig10_15.cpp) with main

Erroneously Attempting to Modify a private Member with a Non-friend Function
The program of Fig. 10.16 demonstrates the error messages produced by the compiler when non-friend function cannotSetX (lines 29–32) is called to modify private data member x.

It is possible to specify overloaded functions as friends of a class. Each overloaded function intended to be a friend must be explicitly declared in the class definition as a friend of the class.

```
 1    // Fig. 10.16: fig10_16.cpp
 2    // Non-friend/non-member functions cannot access private data of a class.
 3    #include <iostream>
 4    using std::cout;
 5    using std::endl;
 6
 7    // Count class definition (note that there is no friendship declaration)
 8    class Count
 9    {
10    public:
11       // constructor
12       Count()
13          : x( 0 ) // initialize x to 0
14       {
15          // empty body
16       } // end constructor Count
17
18       // output x
19       void print() const
20       {
21          cout << x << endl;
22       } // end function print
23    private:
24       int x; // data member
25    }; // end class Count
26
27    // function cannotSetX tries to modify private data of Count,
28    // but cannot because the function is not a friend of Count
29    void cannotSetX( Count &c, int val )
30    {
31       c.x = val; // ERROR: cannot access private member in Count
32    } // end function cannotSetX
33
34    int main()
35    {
36       Count counter; // create Count object
37
38       cannotSetX( counter, 3 ); // cannotSetX is not a friend
39       return 0;
40    } // end main
```

Borland C++ command-line compiler error message:

```
Error E2247 Fig10_16/fig10_16.cpp 31: 'Count::x' is not accessible in
   function cannotSetX(Count &,int)
```

Microsoft Visual C++.NET compiler error messages:

```
C:\cpphtp5_examples\ch10\Fig10_16\fig10_16.cpp(31) : error C2248: 'Count::x'
   : cannot access private member declared in class 'Count'
         C:\cpphtp5_examples\ch10\Fig10_16\fig10_16.cpp(24) : see declaration
            of 'Count::x'
         C:\cpphtp5_examples\ch10\Fig10_16\fig10_16.cpp(9) : see declaration
            of 'Count'
```

Fig. 10.16 | Non-friend/nonmember functions cannot access private members. (Part 1 of 2.)

GNU C++ compiler error messages:

```
fig10_16.cpp:24: error: `int Count::x' is private
fig10_16.cpp:31: error: within this context
```

Fig. 10.16 | Non-friend/nonmember functions cannot access `private` members. (Part 2 of 2.)

10.5 Using the this Pointer

We have seen that an object's member functions can manipulate the object's data. How do member functions know which object's data members to manipulate? Every object has access to its own address through a pointer called `this` (a C++ keyword). An object's `this` pointer is not part of the object itself—i.e., the size of the memory occupied by the `this` pointer is not reflected in the result of a `sizeof` operation on the object. Rather, the `this` pointer is passed (by the compiler) as an implicit argument to each of the object's non-static member functions. Section 10.7 introduces `static` class members and explains why the `this` pointer is *not* implicitly passed to `static` member functions.

Objects use the `this` pointer implicitly (as we have done to this point) or explicitly to reference their data members and member functions. The type of the `this` pointer depends on the type of the object and whether the member function in which `this` is used is declared `const`. For example, in a nonconstant member function of class `Employee`, the `this` pointer has type `Employee * const` (a constant pointer to a nonconstant `Employee` object). In a constant member function of the class `Employee`, the `this` pointer has the data type `const Employee * const` (a constant pointer to a constant `Employee` object).

Our first example in this section shows implicit and explicit use of the `this` pointer; later in this chapter and in Chapter 11, we show some substantial and subtle examples of using `this`.

Implicitly and Explicitly Using the* this *Pointer to Access an Object's Data Members
Figure 10.17 demonstrates the implicit and explicit use of the `this` pointer to enable a member function of class `Test` to print the `private` data x of a `Test` object.

For illustration purposes, member function `print` (lines 25–37) first prints x by using the `this` pointer implicitly (line 28)—only the name of the data member is specified. Then `print` uses two different notations to access x through the `this` pointer—the arrow

```
1   // Fig. 10.17: fig10_17.cpp
2   // Using the this pointer to refer to object members.
3   #include <iostream>
4   using std::cout;
5   using std::endl;
6
7   class Test
8   {
9   public:
10      Test( int = 0 ); // default constructor
11      void print() const;
```

Fig. 10.17 | `this` pointer implicitly and explicitly accessing an object's members. (Part 1 of 2.)

```
12    private:
13       int x;
14    }; // end class Test
15
16    // constructor
17    Test::Test( int value )
18       : x( value ) // initialize x to value
19    {
20       // empty body
21    } // end constructor Test
22
23    // print x using implicit and explicit this pointers;
24    // the parentheses around *this are required
25    void Test::print() const
26    {
27       // implicitly use the this pointer to access the member x
28       cout << "        x = " << x;
29
30       // explicitly use the this pointer and the arrow operator
31       // to access the member x
32       cout << "\n   this->x = " << this->x;
33
34       // explicitly use the dereferenced this pointer and
35       // the dot operator to access the member x
36       cout << "\n(*this).x = " << ( *this ).x << endl;
37    } // end function print
38
39    int main()
40    {
41       Test testObject( 12 ); // instantiate and initialize testObject
42
43       testObject.print();
44       return 0;
45    } // end main
```

```
        x = 12
   this->x = 12
(*this).x = 12
```

Fig. 10.17 | this pointer implicitly and explicitly accessing an object's members. (Part 2 of 2.)

operator (->) off the this pointer (line 32) and the dot operator (.) off the dereferenced this pointer (line 36).

Note the parentheses around *this (line 36) when used with the dot member selection operator (.). The parentheses are required because the dot operator has higher precedence than the * operator. Without the parentheses, the expression *this.x would be evaluated as if it were parenthesized as *(this.x), which is a compilation error, because the dot operator cannot be used with a pointer.

One interesting use of the this pointer is to prevent an object from being assigned to itself. As we will see in Chapter 11, self-assignment can cause serious errors when the object contains pointers to dynamically allocated storage.

Common Programming Error 10.7

Attempting to use the member selection operator (.) with a pointer to an object is a compilation error—the dot member selection operator may be used only with an lvalue *such as an object's name, a reference to an object or a dereferenced pointer to an object.*

Using the this Pointer to Enable Cascaded Function Calls

Another use of the this pointer is to enable cascaded member-function calls in which multiple functions are invoked in the same statement (as in line 14 of Fig. 10.20). The program of Figs. 10.18–10.20 modifies class Time's *set* functions setTime, setHour, setMinute and setSecond such that each returns a reference to a Time object to enable cascaded member-function calls. Notice in Fig. 10.19 that the last statement in the body of each of these member functions returns *this (lines 26, 33, 40 and 47) into a return type of Time &.

The program of Fig. 10.20 creates Time object t (line 11), then uses it in cascaded member-function calls (lines 14 and 26). Why does the technique of returning *this as a reference work? The dot operator (.) associates from left to right, so line 14 first evaluates t.setHour(18) then returns a reference to object t as the value of this function call. The remaining expression is then interpreted as

```
t.setMinute( 30 ).setSecond( 22 );
```

The t.setMinute(30) call executes and returns a reference to the object t. The remaining expression is interpreted as

```
t.setSecond( 22 );
```

Line 26 also uses cascading. The calls must appear in the order shown in line 26, because printStandard as defined in the class does not return a reference to t. Placing the call to printStandard before the call to setTime in line 26 results in a compilation error. Chapter 11 presents several practical examples of using cascaded function calls. One such example uses multiple << operators with cout to output multiple values in a single statement.

```
1   // Fig. 10.18: Time.h
2   // Cascading member function calls.
3
4   // Time class definition.
5   // Member functions defined in Time.cpp.
6   #ifndef TIME_H
7   #define TIME_H
8
9   class Time
10  {
11  public:
12     Time( int = 0, int = 0, int = 0 ); // default constructor
13
14     // set functions (the Time & return types enable cascading)
15     Time &setTime( int, int, int ); // set hour, minute, second
16     Time &setHour( int ); // set hour
17     Time &setMinute( int ); // set minute
18     Time &setSecond( int ); // set second
```

Fig. 10.18 | Time class definition modified to enable cascaded member-function calls. (Part 1 of 2.)

```
19
20     // get functions (normally declared const)
21     int getHour() const; // return hour
22     int getMinute() const; // return minute
23     int getSecond() const; // return second
24
25     // print functions (normally declared const)
26     void printUniversal() const; // print universal time
27     void printStandard() const; // print standard time
28   private:
29     int hour; // 0 - 23 (24-hour clock format)
30     int minute; // 0 - 59
31     int second; // 0 - 59
32   }; // end class Time
33
34   #endif
```

Fig. 10.18 | Time class definition modified to enable cascaded member-function calls. (Part 2 of 2.)

```
1    // Fig. 10.19: Time.cpp
2    // Member-function definitions for Time class.
3    #include <iostream>
4    using std::cout;
5
6    #include <iomanip>
7    using std::setfill;
8    using std::setw;
9
10   #include "Time.h" // Time class definition
11
12   // constructor function to initialize private data;
13   // calls member function setTime to set variables;
14   // default values are 0 (see class definition)
15   Time::Time( int hr, int min, int sec )
16   {
17      setTime( hr, min, sec );
18   } // end Time constructor
19
20   // set values of hour, minute, and second
21   Time &Time::setTime( int h, int m, int s ) // note Time & return
22   {
23      setHour( h );
24      setMinute( m );
25      setSecond( s );
26      return *this; // enables cascading
27   } // end function setTime
28
29   // set hour value
30   Time &Time::setHour( int h ) // note Time & return
31   {
```

Fig. 10.19 | Time class member-function definitions modified to enable cascaded member-function calls. (Part 1 of 2.)

```
32      hour = ( h >= 0 && h < 24 ) ? h : 0; // validate hour
33      return *this; // enables cascading
34  } // end function setHour
35
36  // set minute value
37  Time &Time::setMinute( int m ) // note Time & return
38  {
39      minute = ( m >= 0 && m < 60 ) ? m : 0; // validate minute
40      return *this; // enables cascading
41  } // end function setMinute
42
43  // set second value
44  Time &Time::setSecond( int s ) // note Time & return
45  {
46      second = ( s >= 0 && s < 60 ) ? s : 0; // validate second
47      return *this; // enables cascading
48  } // end function setSecond
49
50  // get hour value
51  int Time::getHour() const
52  {
53      return hour;
54  } // end function getHour
55
56  // get minute value
57  int Time::getMinute() const
58  {
59      return minute;
60  } // end function getMinute
61
62  // get second value
63  int Time::getSecond() const
64  {
65      return second;
66  } // end function getSecond
67
68  // print Time in universal-time format (HH:MM:SS)
69  void Time::printUniversal() const
70  {
71      cout << setfill( '0' ) << setw( 2 ) << hour << ":"
72          << setw( 2 ) << minute << ":" << setw( 2 ) << second;
73  } // end function printUniversal
74
75  // print Time in standard-time format (HH:MM:SS AM or PM)
76  void Time::printStandard() const
77  {
78      cout << ( ( hour == 0 || hour == 12 ) ? 12 : hour % 12 )
79          << ":" << setfill( '0' ) << setw( 2 ) << minute
80          << ":" << setw( 2 ) << second << ( hour < 12 ? " AM" : " PM" );
81  } // end function printStandard
```

Fig. 10.19 | Time class member-function definitions modified to enable cascaded member-function calls. (Part 2 of 2.)

```
1   // Fig. 10.20: fig10_20.cpp
2   // Cascading member function calls with the this pointer.
3   #include <iostream>
4   using std::cout;
5   using std::endl;
6
7   #include "Time.h" // Time class definition
8
9   int main()
10  {
11     Time t; // create Time object
12
13     // cascaded function calls
14     t.setHour( 18 ).setMinute( 30 ).setSecond( 22 );
15
16     // output time in universal and standard formats
17     cout << "Universal time: ";
18     t.printUniversal();
19
20     cout << "\nStandard time: ";
21     t.printStandard();
22
23     cout << "\n\nNew standard time: ";
24
25     // cascaded function calls
26     t.setTime( 20, 20, 20 ).printStandard();
27     cout << endl;
28     return 0;
29  } // end main
```

```
Universal time: 18:30:22
Standard time: 6:30:22 PM

New standard time: 8:20:20 PM
```

Fig. 10.20 | Cascading member-function calls.

10.6 Dynamic Memory Management with Operators new and delete

C++ enables programmers to control the allocation and deallocation of memory in a program for any built-in or user-defined type. This is known as dynamic memory management and is performed with operators new and delete. Recall that class Employee (Figs. 10.12–10.13) uses two 25-character arrays to represent the first and last name of an Employee. The Employee class definition (Fig. 10.12) must specify the number of elements in each of these arrays when it declares them as data members, because the size of the data members dictates the amount of memory required to store an Employee object. As we discussed earlier, these arrays may waste space for names shorter than 24 characters. Also, names longer than 24 characters must be truncated to fit in these fixed-size arrays.

Wouldn't it be nice if we could use arrays containing exactly the number of elements needed to store an Employee's first and last name? Dynamic memory management allows us to do exactly that. As you will see in the example of Section 10.7, if we replace array data members firstName and lastName with pointers to char, we can use the new operator to dynamically allocate (i.e., reserve) the exact amount of memory required to hold each name at execution time. Dynamically allocating memory in this fashion causes an array (or any other built-in or user-defined type) to be created in the free store (sometimes called the heap)—a region of memory assigned to each program for storing objects created at execution time. Once the memory for an array is allocated in the free store, we can gain access to it by aiming a pointer at the first element of the array. When we no longer need the array, we can return the memory to the free store by using the delete operator to deallocate (i.e., release) the memory, which can then be reused by future new operations.

Again, we present the modified Employee class as described here in the example of Section 10.7. First, we present the details of using the new and delete operators to dynamically allocate memory to store objects, fundamental types and arrays.

Consider the following declaration and statement:

```
Time *timePtr;
timePtr = new Time;
```

The new operator allocates storage of the proper size for an object of type Time, calls the default constructor to initialize the object and returns a pointer of the type specified to the right of the new operator (i.e., a Time *). Note that new can be used to dynamically allocate any fundamental type (such as int or double) or class type. If new is unable to find sufficient space in memory for the object, it indicates that an error occurred by "throwing an exception." Chapter 16, Exception Handling, discusses how to deal with new failures in the context of the ANSI/ISO C++ standard. In particular, we will show how to "catch" the exception thrown by new and deal with it. When a program does not "catch" an exception, the program terminates immediately. [*Note:* The new operator returns a 0 pointer in versions of C++ prior to the ANSI/ISO standard. We use the standard version of operator new throughout this book.]

To destroy a dynamically allocated object and free the space for the object, use the delete operator as follows:

```
delete timePtr;
```

This statement first calls the destructor for the object to which timePtr points, then deallocates the memory associated with the object. After the preceding statement, the memory can be reused by the system to allocate other objects.

 Common Programming Error 10.8

Not releasing dynamically allocated memory when it is no longer needed can cause the system to run out of memory prematurely. This is sometimes called a "memory leak."

C++ allows you to provide an initializer for a newly created fundamental-type variable, as in

```
double *ptr = new double( 3.14159 );
```

which initializes a newly created double to 3.14159 and assigns the resulting pointer to ptr. The same syntax can be used to specify a comma-separated list of arguments to the constructor of an object. For example,

```
     Time *timePtr = new Time( 12, 45, 0 );
```

initializes a newly created Time object to 12:45 PM and assigns the resulting pointer to timePtr.

As discussed earlier, the new operator can be used to allocate arrays dynamically. For example, a 10-element integer array can be allocated and assigned to gradesArray as follows:

```
     int *gradesArray = new int[ 10 ];
```

which declares pointer gradesArray and assigns it a pointer to the first element of a dynamically allocated 10-element array of integers. Recall that the size of an array created at compile time must be specified using a constant integral expression. However, the size of a dynamically allocated array can be specified using *any* integral expression that can be evaluated at execution time. Also note that, when allocating an array of objects dynamically, the programmer cannot pass arguments to each object's constructor. Instead, each object in the array is initialized by its default constructor. To delete the dynamically allocated array to which gradesArray points, use the statement

```
     delete [] gradesArray;
```

The preceding statement deallocates the array to which gradesArray points. If the pointer in the preceding statement points to an array of objects, the statement first calls the destructor for every object in the array, then deallocates the memory. If the preceding statement did not include the square brackets ([]) and gradesArray pointed to an array of objects, only the first object in the array would receive a destructor call.

Common Programming Error 10.9

Using delete instead of delete [] for arrays of objects can lead to runtime logic errors. To ensure that every object in the array receives a destructor call, always delete memory allocated as an array with operator delete []. Similarly, always delete memory allocated as an individual element with operator delete.

10.7 static Class Members

There is an important exception to the rule that each object of a class has its own copy of all the data members of the class. In certain cases, only one copy of a variable should be shared by all objects of a class. A **static data member** is used for these and other reasons. Such a variable represents "class-wide" information (i.e., a property of the class shared by all instances, not a property of a specific object of the class). The declaration of a static member begins with keyword static. Recall that the versions of class GradeBook in Chapter 7 use static data members to store constants representing the number of grades that all GradeBook objects can hold.

Let us further motivate the need for static class-wide data with an example. Suppose that we have a video game with Martians and other space creatures. Each Martian tends to be brave and willing to attack other space creatures when the Martian is aware that there are at least five Martians present. If fewer than five are present, each Martian becomes cowardly. So each Martian needs to know the martianCount. We could endow each instance of class `Martian` with `martianCount` as a data member. If we do, every `Martian` will have a separate copy of the data member. Every time we create a new `Martian`, we will have to update the data member `martianCount` in all `Martian` objects. Doing this would require every `Martian` object to have, or have access to, handles to all other `Martian` objects in memory. This wastes space with the redundant copies and wastes time in updating the separate copies. Instead, we declare `martianCount` to be `static`. This makes `martian-Count` class-wide data. Every `Martian` can access `martianCount` as if it were a data member of the `Martian`, but only one copy of the `static` variable `martianCount` is maintained by C++. This saves space. We save time by having the `Martian` constructor increment `static` variable `martianCount` and having the `Martian` destructor decrement `martianCount`. Because there is only one copy, we do not have to increment or decrement separate copies of `martianCount` for each `Martian` object.

Performance Tip 10.3

Use `static` data members to save storage when a single copy of the data for all objects of a class will suffice.

Although they may seem like global variables, a class's `static` data members have class scope. Also, `static` members can be declared `public`, `private` or `protected`. A fundamental-type `static` data member is initialized by default to 0. If you want a different initial value, a `static` data member can be initialized *once* (and only once). A `const static` data member of `int` or `enum` type can be initialized in its declaration in the class definition. However, all other `static` data members must be defined at file scope (i.e., outside the body of the class definition) and can be initialized only in those definitions. Note that `static` data members of class types (i.e., `static` member objects) that have default constructors need not be initialized because their default constructors will be called.

A class's `private` and `protected` `static` members are normally accessed through `public` member functions of the class or through `friend`s of the class. (In Chapter 12, we will see that a class's `private` and `protected` `static` members can also be accessed through `protected` member functions of the class.) A class's `static` members exist even when no objects of that class exist. To access a `public` `static` class member when no objects of the class exist, simply prefix the class name and the binary scope resolution operator (`::`) to the name of the data member. For example, if our preceding variable `martian-Count` is `public`, it can be accessed with the expression `Martian::martianCount` when there are no `Martian` objects. (Of course, using `public` data is discouraged.)

A class's `public` `static` class members can also be accessed through any object of that class using the object's name, the dot operator and the name of the member (e.g., `myMartian.martianCount`). To access a `private` or `protected` `static` class member when no objects of the class exist, provide a `public` `static` member function and call the function by prefixing its name with the class name and binary scope resolution operator. (As we will see in Chapter 12, a `protected` `static` member function can serve this purpose, too.) A `static` member function is a service of the *class*, not of a specific object of the class.

Software Engineering Observation 10.10

A class's `static` data members and `static` member functions exist and can be used even if no objects of that class have been instantiated.

The program of Figs. 10.21–10.23 demonstrates a private static data member called count (Fig. 10.21, line 21) and a public static member function called getCount (Fig. 10.21, line 15). In Fig. 10.22, line 14 defines and initializes the data member count to zero at file scope and lines 18–21 define static member function getCount. Notice that neither line 14 nor line 18 includes keyword static, yet both lines refer to static class members. When static is applied to an item at file scope, that item becomes known only in that file. The static members of the class need to be available from any client code that accesses the file, so we cannot declare them static in the .cpp file—we declare them static only in the .h file. Data member count maintains a count of the number of objects of class Employee that have been instantiated. When objects of class Employee exist, member count can be referenced through any member function of an Employee object—in Fig. 10.22, count is referenced by both line 33 in the constructor and line 48 in the destructor. Also, note that since count is an int, it could have been initialized in the header file at line 21 of Fig. 10.21.

Common Programming Error 10.10

It is a compilation error to include keyword static in the definition of a static data members at file scope.

In Fig. 10.22, note the use of the new operator (lines 27 and 30) in the Employee constructor to dynamically allocate the correct amount of memory for members firstName and lastName. If the new operator is unable to fulfill the request for memory for one or both of these character arrays, the program will terminate immediately. In Chapter 16, we will provide a better mechanism for dealing with cases in which new is unable to allocate memory.

```cpp
1   // Fig. 10.21: Employee.h
2   // Employee class definition.
3   #ifndef EMPLOYEE_H
4   #define EMPLOYEE_H
5
6   class Employee
7   {
8   public:
9      Employee( const char * const, const char * const ); // constructor
10     ~Employee(); // destructor
11     const char *getFirstName() const; // return first name
12     const char *getLastName() const; // return last name
13
14     // static member function
15     static int getCount(); // return number of objects instantiated
16   private:
17     char *firstName;
18     char *lastName;
19
20     // static data
21     static int count; // number of objects instantiated
22   }; // end class Employee
23
24   #endif
```

Fig. 10.21 | Employee class definition with a static data member to track the number of Employee objects in memory.

Also note in Fig. 10.22 that the implementations of functions getFirstName (lines 52–58) and getLastName (lines 61–67) return pointers to const character data. In this

```cpp
1   // Fig. 10.22: Employee.cpp
2   // Member-function definitions for class Employee.
3   #include <iostream>
4   using std::cout;
5   using std::endl;
6
7   #include <cstring> // strlen and strcpy prototypes
8   using std::strlen;
9   using std::strcpy;
10
11  #include "Employee.h" // Employee class definition
12
13  // define and initialize static data member at file scope
14  int Employee::count = 0;
15
16  // define static member function that returns number of
17  // Employee objects instantiated (declared static in Employee.h)
18  int Employee::getCount()
19  {
20     return count;
21  } // end static function getCount
22
23  // constructor dynamically allocates space for first and last name and
24  // uses strcpy to copy first and last names into the object
25  Employee::Employee( const char * const first, const char * const last )
26  {
27     firstName = new char[ strlen( first ) + 1 ];
28     strcpy( firstName, first );
29
30     lastName = new char[ strlen( last ) + 1 ];
31     strcpy( lastName, last );
32
33     count++; // increment static count of employees
34
35     cout << "Employee constructor for " << firstName
36        << ' ' << lastName << " called." << endl;
37  } // end Employee constructor
38
39  // destructor deallocates dynamically allocated memory
40  Employee::~Employee()
41  {
42     cout << "~Employee() called for " << firstName
43        << ' ' << lastName << endl;
44
45     delete [] firstName; // release memory
46     delete [] lastName; // release memory
47
48     count--; // decrement static count of employees
49  } // end ~Employee destructor
```

Fig. 10.22 | Employee class member-function definitions. (Part 1 of 2.)

```
50
51   // return first name of employee
52   const char *Employee::getFirstName() const
53   {
54      // const before return type prevents client from modifying
55      // private data; client should copy returned string before
56      // destructor deletes storage to prevent undefined pointer
57      return firstName;
58   } // end function getFirstName
59
60   // return last name of employee
61   const char *Employee::getLastName() const
62   {
63      // const before return type prevents client from modifying
64      // private data; client should copy returned string before
65      // destructor deletes storage to prevent undefined pointer
66      return lastName;
67   } // end function getLastName
```

Fig. 10.22 | Employee class member-function definitions. (Part 2 of 2.)

implementation, if the client wishes to retain a copy of the first name or last name, the client is responsible for copying the dynamically allocated memory in the Employee object after obtaining the pointer to const character data from the object. It is also possible to implement getFirstName and getLastName, so the client is required to pass a character array and the size of the array to each function. Then the functions could copy the first or last name into the character array provided by the client. Once again, note that we could have used class string here to return a copy of a string object to the caller rather than returning a pointer to the private data.

Figure 10.23 uses static member function getCount to determine the number of Employee objects currently instantiated. Note that when no objects are instantiated in the program, the Employee::getCount() function call is issued (lines 14 and 38). However, when objects are instantiated, function getCount can be called through either of the objects, as shown in the statement at lines 22–23, which uses pointer e1Ptr to invoke function getCount. Note that using e2Ptr->getCount() or Employee::getCount() in line 23 would produce the same result, because getCount always accesses the same static member count.

```
1    // Fig. 10.23: fig10_23.cpp
2    // Driver to test class Employee.
3    #include <iostream>
4    using std::cout;
5    using std::endl;
6
7    #include "Employee.h" // Employee class definition
8
9    int main()
10   {
```

Fig. 10.23 | static data member tracking the number of objects of a class. (Part 1 of 2.)

```
11      // use class name and binary scope resolution operator to
12      // access static number function getCount
13      cout << "Number of employees before instantiation of any objects is "
14         << Employee::getCount() << endl; // use class name
15
16      // use new to dynamically create two new Employees
17      // operator new also calls the object's constructor
18      Employee *e1Ptr = new Employee( "Susan", "Baker" );
19      Employee *e2Ptr = new Employee( "Robert", "Jones" );
20
21      // call getCount on first Employee object
22      cout << "Number of employees after objects are instantiated is "
23         << e1Ptr->getCount();
24
25      cout << "\n\nEmployee 1: "
26         << e1Ptr->getFirstName() << " " << e1Ptr->getLastName()
27         << "\nEmployee 2: "
28         << e2Ptr->getFirstName() << " " << e2Ptr->getLastName() << "\n\n";
29
30      delete e1Ptr; // deallocate memory
31      e1Ptr = 0; // disconnect pointer from free-store space
32      delete e2Ptr; // deallocate memory
33      e2Ptr = 0; // disconnect pointer from free-store space
34
35      // no objects exist, so call static member function getCount again
36      // using the class name and the binary scope resolution operator
37      cout << "Number of employees after objects are deleted is "
38         << Employee::getCount() << endl;
39      return 0;
40   } // end main
```

```
Number of employees before instantiation of any objects is 0
Employee constructor for Susan Baker called.
Employee constructor for Robert Jones called.
Number of employees after objects are instantiated is 2

Employee 1: Susan Baker
Employee 2: Robert Jones

~Employee() called for Susan Baker
~Employee() called for Robert Jones
Number of employees after objects are deleted is 0
```

Fig. 10.23 | static data member tracking the number of objects of a class. (Part 2 of 2.)

 Software Engineering Observation 10.11

Some organizations specify in their software engineering standards that all calls to static member functions be made using the class name and not an object handle.

A member function should be declared static if it does not access non-static data members or non-static member functions of the class. Unlike non-static member functions, a static member function does not have a this pointer, because static data members and static member functions exist independently of any objects of a class. The `this` pointer must refer to a specific object of the class, and when a `static` member function is called, there might not be any objects of its class in memory.

Common Programming Error 10.11

Using the `this` pointer in a `static` member function is a compilation error.

Common Programming Error 10.12

Declaring a `static` member function `const` is a compilation error. The `const` qualifier indicates that a function cannot modify the contents of the object in which it operates, but `static` member functions exist and operate independently of any objects of the class.

Lines 18–19 of Fig. 10.23 use operator `new` to dynamically allocate two `Employee` objects. Remember that the program will terminate immediately if it is unable to allocate one or both of these objects. When each `Employee` object is allocated, its constructor is called. When `delete` is used at lines 30 and 32 to deallocate the two `Employee` objects, each object's destructor is called.

Error-Prevention Tip 10.2

After deleting dynamically allocated memory, set the pointer that referred to that memory to 0. This disconnects the pointer from the previously allocated space on the free store. This space in memory could still contain information, despite having been deleted. By setting the pointer to 0, the program loses any access to that free-store space, which, in fact, could have already been reallocated for a different purpose. If you didn't set the pointer to 0, your code could inadvertently access this new information, causing extremely subtle, nonrepeatable logic errors.

10.8 Data Abstraction and Information Hiding

A class normally hides its implementation details from its clients. This is called information hiding. As an example of information hiding, let us consider the stack data structure introduced in Section 6.11.

Stacks can be implemented with arrays and with other data structures, such as linked lists. (We discuss stacks and linked lists in Chapter 14, Templates and Chapter 21, Data Structures.) A client of a stack class need not be concerned with the stack's implementation. The client knows only that when data items are placed in the stack, they will be recalled in last-in, first-out order. The client cares about *what* functionality a stack offers, not about *how* that functionality is implemented. This concept is referred to as **data abstraction**. Although programmers might know the details of a class's implementation, they should not write code that depends on these details. This enables a particular class (such as one that implements a stack and its operations, *push* and *pop*) to be replaced with another version without affecting the rest of the system. As long as the `public` services of the class do not change (i.e., every original `public` member function still has the same prototype in the new class definition), the rest of the system is not affected.

Many programming languages emphasize actions. In these languages, data exists to support the actions that programs must take. Data is "less interesting" than actions. Data is "crude." Only a few built-in data types exist, and it is difficult for programmers to create their own types. C++ and the object-oriented style of programming elevate the importance of data. The primary activities of object-oriented programming in C++ are the creation of types (i.e., classes) and the expression of the interactions among objects of those types. To create languages that emphasize data, the programming-languages community needed to formalize some notions about data. The formalization we consider here is the notion of abstract data types (ADTs), which improve the program development process.

What is an abstract data type? Consider the built-in type int, which most people would associate with an integer in mathematics. Rather, an int is an abstract representation of an integer. Unlike mathematical integers, computer ints are fixed in size. For example, type int on today's popular 32-bit machines is typically limited to the range –2,147,483,648 to +2,147,483,647. If the result of a calculation falls outside this range, an "overflow" error occurs and the computer responds in some machine-dependent manner. It might, for example, "quietly" produce an incorrect result, such as a value too large to fit in an int variable (commonly called arithmetic overflow). Mathematical integers do not have this problem. Therefore, the notion of a computer int is only an approximation of the notion of a real-world integer. The same is true with double.

Even char is an approximation; char values are normally eight-bit patterns of ones and zeros; these patterns look nothing like the characters they represent, such as a capital Z, a lowercase z, a dollar sign ($), a digit (5), and so on. Values of type char on most computers are quite limited compared with the range of real-world characters. The seven-bit ASCII character set (Appendix B) provides for 128 different character values. This is inadequate for representing languages such as Japanese and Chinese that require thousands of characters. As Internet and World Wide Web usage becomes pervasive, the newer Unicode character set is growing rapidly in popularity, owing to its ability to represent the characters of most languages. For more information on Unicode, visit www.unicode.org.

The point is that even the built-in data types provided with programming languages like C++ are really only approximations or imperfect models of real-world concepts and behaviors. We have taken int for granted until this point, but now you have a new perspective to consider. Types like int, double, char and others are all examples of abstract data types. They are essentially ways of representing real-world notions to some satisfactory level of precision within a computer system.

An abstract data type actually captures two notions: A data representation and the operations that can be performed on those data. For example, in C++, an int contains an integer value (data) and provides addition, subtraction, multiplication, division and modulus operations (among others)—division by zero is undefined. These allowed operations perform in a manner sensitive to machine parameters, such as the fixed word size of the underlying computer system. Another example is the notion of negative integers, whose operations and data representation are clear, but the operation of taking the square root of a negative integer is undefined. In C++, the programmer uses classes to implement abstract data types and their services. For example, to implement a stack ADT, we create our own stack classes in Chapter 14, Templates and Chapter 21, Data Structures, and we study the standard library stack class in Chapter 22, Standard Template Library (STL).

10.8.1 Example: Array Abstract Data Type

We discussed arrays in Chapter 7. As described there, an array is not much more than a pointer and some space in memory. This primitive capability is acceptable for performing array operations if the programmer is cautious and undemanding. There are many operations that would be nice to perform with arrays, but that are not built into C++. With C++

classes, the programmer can develop an array ADT that is preferable to "raw" arrays. The array class can provide many helpful new capabilities such as

- subscript range checking
- an arbitrary range of subscripts instead of having to start with 0
- array assignment
- array comparison
- array input/output
- arrays that know their sizes
- arrays that expand dynamically to accommodate more elements
- arrays that can print themselves in neat tabular format.

We create our own array class with many of these capabilities in Chapter 11, Operator Overloading; String and Array Objects. Recall that C++ Standard Library class template vector (introduced in Chapter 7) provides many of these capabilities as well. Chapter 22 explains class template vector in detail. C++ has a small set of built-in types. Classes extend the base programming language with new types.

> ### Software Engineering Observation 10.12
>
> *The programmer is able to create new types through the class mechanism. These new types can be designed to be used as conveniently as the built-in types. Thus, C++ is an extensible language. Although the language is easy to extend with these new types, the base language itself cannot be changed.*

New classes created in C++ environments can be proprietary to an individual, to small groups or to companies. Classes can also be placed in standard class libraries intended for wide distribution. ANSI (the American National Standards Institute) and ISO (the International Organization for Standardization) developed a standard version of C++ that includes a standard class library. The reader who learns C++ and object-oriented programming will be ready to take advantage of the new kinds of rapid, component-oriented software development made possible with increasingly abundant and rich libraries.

10.8.2 Example: String Abstract Data Type

C++ is an intentionally sparse language that provides programmers with only the raw capabilities needed to build a broad range of systems (consider it a tool for making tools). The language is designed to minimize performance burdens. C++ is appropriate for both applications programming and systems programming—the latter places extraordinary performance demands on programs. Certainly, it would have been possible to include a string data type among C++'s built-in data types. Instead, the language was designed to include mechanisms for creating and implementing string abstract data types through classes. We introduced the C++ Standard Library class string in Chapter 3, and in Chapter 11 we will develop our own String ADT. We discuss class string in detail in Chapter 18.

10.8.3 Example: Queue Abstract Data Type

Each of us stands in line from time to time. A waiting line is also called a queue. We wait in line at the supermarket checkout counter, we wait in line to get gasoline, we wait in line to board a bus, we wait in line to pay a highway toll, and students know all too well about waiting in line during registration to get the courses they want. Computer systems use many waiting lines internally, so we need to write programs that simulate what queues are and do.

A queue is a good example of an abstract data type. Queues offer well-understood behavior to their clients. Clients put things in a queue one at a time—invoking the queue's enqueue operation—and the clients get those things back one at a time on demand—invoking the queue's dequeue operation. Conceptually, a queue can become infinitely long. A real queue, of course, is finite. Items are returned from a queue in first-in, first-out (FIFO) order—the first item inserted in the queue is the first item removed from the queue.

The queue hides an internal data representation that somehow keeps track of the items currently waiting in line, and it offers a set of operations to its clients, namely, *enqueue* and *dequeue*. The clients are not concerned about the implementation of the queue. Clients merely want the queue to operate "as advertised." When a client enqueues a new item, the queue should accept that item and place it internally in some kind of first-in, first-out data structure. When the client wants the next item from the front of the queue, the queue should remove the item from its internal representation and deliver it to the outside world (i.e., to the client of the queue) in FIFO order (i.e., the item that has been in the queue the longest should be the next one returned by the next *dequeue* operation).

The queue ADT guarantees the integrity of its internal data structure. Clients may not manipulate this data structure directly. Only the queue member functions have access to its internal data. Clients may cause only allowable operations to be performed on the data representation; operations not provided in the ADT's public interface are rejected in some appropriate manner. This could mean issuing an error message, throwing an exception (see Chapter 16), terminating execution or simply ignoring the operation request.

We create our own queue class in Chapter 21, Data Structures, and we study the Standard Library queue class in Chapter 22, Standard Template Library (STL).

10.9 Container Classes and Iterators

Among the most popular types of classes are container classes (also called collection classes), i.e., classes designed to hold collections of objects. Container classes commonly provide services such as insertion, deletion, searching, sorting, and testing an item to determine whether it is a member of the collection. Arrays, stacks, queues, trees and linked lists are examples of container classes; we studied arrays in Chapter 7 and will study each of these other data structures in Chapter 21, Data Structures, and Chapter 22, Standard Template Library (STL).

It is common to associate iterator objects—or more simply iterators—with container classes. An iterator is an object that "walks through" a collection, returning the next item (or performing some action on the next item). Once an iterator for a class has been written, obtaining the next element from the class can be expressed simply. Just as a book being shared by several people could have several bookmarks in it at once, a container class can have several iterators operating on it at once. Each iterator maintains its own "position" information. We will discuss containers and iterators in detail in Chapter 22.

10.10 **Proxy Classes**

Recall that two of the fundamental principles of good software engineering are separating interface from implementation and hiding implementation details. We strive to achieve these goals by defining a class in a header file and implementing its member functions in a separate implementation file. However, as we pointed out in Chapter 9, header files *do* contain some portion of a class's implementation and hints about others. For example, a class's `private` members are listed in the class definition in a header file, so these members are visible to clients, even though the clients may not access the `private` members. Revealing a class's `private` data in this manner potentially exposes proprietary information to clients of the class. We now introduce the notion of a proxy class that allows you to hide even the `private` data of a class from clients of the class. Providing clients of your class with a proxy class that knows only the `public` interface to your class enables the clients to use your class's services without giving the client access to your class's implementation details.

Implementing a proxy class requires several steps, which we demonstrate in Figs. 10.24–10.27. First, we create the class definition for the class that contains the proprietary implementation we would like to hide. Our example class, called `Implementation`, is shown in Fig. 10.24. The proxy class `Interface` is shown in Figs. 10.25–10.26. The test program and sample output are shown in Fig. 10.27.

Class `Implementation` (Fig. 10.24) provides a single `private` data member called `value` (the data we would like to hide from the client), a constructor to initialize `value` and functions `setValue` and `getValue`.

We define a proxy class called `Interface` (Fig. 10.25) with an identical `public` interface (except for the constructor and destructor names) to that of class `Implementation`.

```
 1   // Fig. 10.24: Implementation.h
 2   // Header file for class Implementation
 3
 4   class Implementation
 5   {
 6   public:
 7      // constructor
 8      Implementation( int v )
 9         : value( v ) // initialize value with v
10      {
11         // empty body
12      } // end constructor Implementation
13
14      // set value to v
15      void setValue( int v )
16      {
17         value = v; // should validate v
18      } // end function setValue
19
20      // return value
21      int getValue() const
22      {
23         return value;
24      } // end function getValue
```

Fig. 10.24 | `Implementation` class definition. (Part 1 of 2.)

```
25    private:
26       int value; // data that we would like to hide from the client
27    }; // end class Implementation
```

Fig. 10.24 | Implementation class definition. (Part 2 of 2.)

```
 1    // Fig. 10.25: Interface.h
 2    // Header file for class Interface
 3    // Client sees this source code, but the source code does not reveal
 4    // the data layout of class Implementation.
 5
 6    class Implementation; // forward class declaration required by line 17
 7
 8    class Interface
 9    {
10    public:
11       Interface( int ); // constructor
12       void setValue( int ); // same public interface as
13       int getValue() const; // class Implementation has
14       ~Interface(); // destructor
15    private:
16       // requires previous forward declaration (line 6)
17       Implementation *ptr;
18    }; // end class Interface
```

Fig. 10.25 | Interface class definition.

The only private member of the proxy class is a pointer to an object of class Implementation. Using a pointer in this manner allows us to hide the implementation details of class Implementation from the client. Notice that the only mentions in class Interface of the proprietary Implementation class are in the pointer declaration (line 17) and in line 6, a forward class declaration. When a class definition (such as class Interface) uses only a pointer or reference to an object of another class (such as to an object of class Implementation), the class header file for that other class (which would ordinarily reveal the private data of that class) is not required to be included with #include. You can simply declare that other class as a data type with a forward class declaration (line 6) before the type is used in the file.

The member-function implementation file for proxy class Interface (Fig. 10.26) is the only file that includes the header file Implementation.h (line 5) containing class Implementation. The file Interface.cpp (Fig. 10.26) is provided to the client as a pre-compiled object code file along with the header file Interface.h that includes the function prototypes of the services provided by the proxy class. Because file Interface.cpp is made available to the client only as object code, the client is not able to see the interactions between the proxy class and the proprietary class (lines 9, 17, 23 and 29). Notice that the proxy class imposes an extra "layer" of function calls as the "price to pay" for hiding the private data of class Implementation. Given the speed of today's computers and the fact that many compilers can inline simple function calls automatically, the effect of these extra function calls on performance is often negligible.

```
1   // Fig. 10.26: Interface.cpp
2   // Implementation of class Interface--client receives this file only
3   // as precompiled object code, keeping the implementation hidden.
4   #include "Interface.h" // Interface class definition
5   #include "Implementation.h" // Implementation class definition
6
7   // constructor
8   Interface::Interface( int v )
9      : ptr ( new Implementation( v ) ) // initialize ptr to point to
10  {                                      // a new Implementation object
11     // empty body
12  } // end Interface constructor
13
14  // call Implementation's setValue function
15  void Interface::setValue( int v )
16  {
17     ptr->setValue( v );
18  } // end function setValue
19
20  // call Implementation's getValue function
21  int Interface::getValue() const
22  {
23     return ptr->getValue();
24  } // end function getValue
25
26  // destructor
27  Interface::~Interface()
28  {
29     delete ptr;
30  } // end ~Interface destructor
```

Fig. 10.26 | `Interface` class member-function definitions.

Figure 10.27 tests class `Interface`. Notice that only the header file for `Interface` is included in the client code (line 7)—there is no mention of the existence of a separate class called `Implementation`. Thus, the client never sees the `private` data of class `Implementation`, nor can the client code become dependent on the `Implementation` code.

Software Engineering Observation 10.13

A proxy class insulates client code from implementation changes.

```
1   // Fig. 10.27: fig10_27.cpp
2   // Hiding a class's private data with a proxy class.
3   #include <iostream>
4   using std::cout;
5   using std::endl;
6
7   #include "Interface.h" // Interface class definition
8
```

Fig. 10.27 | Implementing a proxy class. (Part 1 of 2.)

```
 9   int main()
10   {
11      Interface i( 5 ); // create Interface object
12
13      cout << "Interface contains: " << i.getValue()
14         << " before setValue" << endl;
15
16      i.setValue( 10 );
17
18      cout << "Interface contains: " << i.getValue()
19         << " after setValue" << endl;
20      return 0;
21   } // end main
```

```
Interface contains: 5 before setValue
Interface contains: 10 after setValue
```

Fig. 10.27 | Implementing a proxy class. (Part 2 of 2.)

Summary

- The keyword const can be used to specify that an object is not modifiable and that any attempt to modify the object should result in a compilation error.
- C++ compilers disallow non-const member function calls on const objects.
- An attempt by a const member function to modify an object of its class (*this) is a compilation error.
- A function is specified as const both in its prototype and in its definition.
- A const object must be initialized, not assigned to.
- Constructors and destructors cannot be declared const.
- const data member and data members that are references *must* be initialized using member initializers.
- A class can have objects of other classes as members—this concept is called composition.
- Member objects are constructed in the order in which they are declared in the class definition and before their enclosing class objects are constructed.
- If a member initializer is not provided for a member object, the member object's default constructor will be called implicitly.
- A friend function of a class is defined outside that class's scope, yet has the right to access the non-public (and public) members of the class. Stand-alone functions or entire classes may be declared to be friends of another class.
- A friend declaration can appear anywhere in the class. A friend is essentially a part of the public interface of the class.
- The friendship relation is neither symmetric nor transitive.
- Every object has access to its own address through the this pointer.
- An object's this pointer is not part of the object itself—i.e., the size of the memory occupied by the this pointer is not reflected in the result of a sizeof operation on the object.

- The this pointer is passed (by the compiler) as an implicit argument to each of the object's non-static member functions.

- Objects use the this pointer implicitly (as we have done to this point) or explicitly to reference their data members and member functions.

- The this pointer enables cascaded member-function calls in which multiple functions are invoked in the same statement.

- Dynamic memory management enables programmers to control the allocation and deallocation of memory in a program for any built-in or user-defined type.

- The free store (sometimes called the heap) is a region of memory assigned to each program for storing objects dynamically allocated at execution time.

- The new operator allocates storage of the proper size for an object, runs the object's constructor and returns a pointer of the correct type. The new operator can be used to dynamically allocate any fundamental type (such as int or double) or class type. If new is unable to find space in memory for the object, it indicates that an error occurred by "throwing" an "exception." This usually causes the program to terminate immediately.

- To destroy a dynamically allocated object and free the space for the object, use the delete operator.

- An array of objects can be allocated dynamically with new as in

```
int *ptr = new int[ 100 ];
```

which allocates an array of 100 integers and assigns the starting location of the array to ptr. The preceding array of integers is deleted with the statement

```
delete [] ptr;
```

- A static data member represents "class-wide" information (i.e., a property of the class shared by all instances, not a property of a specific object of the class).

- static data members have class scope and can be declared public, private or protected.

- A class's static members exist even when no objects of that class exist.

- To access a public static class member when no objects of the class exist, simply prefix the class name and the binary scope resolution operator (::) to the name of the data member.

- A class's public static class members can be accessed through any object of that class.

- A member function should be declared static if it does not access non-static data members or non-static member functions of the class. Unlike non-static member functions, a static member function does not have a this pointer, because static data members and static member functions exist independently of any objects of a class.

- Abstract data types are ways of representing real-world and conceptual notions to some satisfactory level of precision within a computer system.

- An abstract data type captures two notions: a data representation and the operations that can be performed on those data.

- C++ is an intentionally sparse language that provides programmers with only the raw capabilities needed to build a broad range of systems. C++ is designed to minimize performance burdens.

- Items are returned from a queue in first-in, first-out (FIFO) order—the first item inserted in the queue is the first item removed from the queue.

- Container classes (also called collection classes) are designed to hold collections of objects. Container classes commonly provide services such as insertion, deletion, searching, sorting, and testing an item to determine whether it is a member of the collection.

- It is common to associate iterators with container classes. An iterator is an object that "walks through" a collection, returning the next item (or performing some action on the next item).

- Providing clients of your class with a proxy class that knows only the public interface to your class enables the clients to use your class's services without giving the clients access to your class's implementation details, such as its private data.

- When a class definition uses only a pointer or reference to an object of another class, the class header file for that other class (which would ordinarily reveal the private data of that class) is not required to be included with #include. You can simply declare that other class as a data type with a forward class declaration before the type is used in the file.

- The implementation file containing the member functions for a proxy class is the only file that includes the header file for the class whose private data we would like to hide.

- The implementation file containing the member functions for the proxy class is provided to the client as a precompiled object code file along with the header file that includes the function prototypes of the services provided by the proxy class.

Terminology

abstract data type (ADT)	friend class
allocate memory	friend function
arithmetic overflow	*has-a* relationship
cascaded member-function calls	heap
collection class	host object
composition	information hiding
const member function	iterator
const object	last-in, first-out (LIFO)
container class	member initializer
data abstraction	member initializer list
data representation	member object
deallocate memory	member object constructor
delete operator	memory leak
delete[] operator	new [] operator
dequeue (queue operation)	new operator
dynamic memory management	operations in an ADT
dynamic objects	proxy class
enqueue (queue operation)	queue abstract data type
first-in, first-out (FIFO)	static data member
forward class declaration	static member function
free store	this pointer

Self-Review Exercises

10.1 Fill in the blanks in each of the following:
   a) _____ must be used to initialize constant members of a class.
   b) A nonmember function must be declared as a(n) _____ of a class to have access to that class's private data members.
   c) The _____ operator dynamically allocates memory for an object of a specified type and returns a _____ to that type.
   d) A constant object must be _____; it cannot be modified after it is created.
   e) A(n) _____ data member represents class-wide information.

f) An object's non-static member functions have access to a "self pointer" to the object called the _____ pointer.

g) The keyword _____ specifies that an object or variable is not modifiable after it is initialized.

h) If a member initializer is not provided for a member object of a class, the object's _____ is called.

i) A member function should be declared static if it does not access _____ class members.

j) Member objects are constructed _____ their enclosing class object.

k) The _____ operator reclaims memory previously allocated by new.

10.2   Find the errors in the following class and explain how to correct them:

```
class Example
{
public:
   Example( int y = 10 )
      : data( y )
   {
      // empty body
   } // end Example constructor

   int getIncrementedData() const
   {
      return data++;
   } // end function getIncrementedData

   static int getCount()
   {
      cout << "Data is " << data << endl;
      return count;
   } // end function getCount
private:
   int data;
   static int count;
}; // end class Example
```

Answers to Self-Review Exercises

10.1   a) member initializers. b) friend. c) new, pointer. d) initialized. e) static. f) this. g) const. h) default constructor. i) non-static. j) before. k) delete.

10.2   Error: The class definition for Example has two errors. The first occurs in function getIncrementedData. The function is declared const, but it modifies the object.
Correction: To correct the first error, remove the const keyword from the definition of getIncrementedData.
Error: The second error occurs in function getCount. This function is declared static, so it is not allowed to access any non-static member of the class.
Correction: To correct the second error, remove the output line from the getCount definition.

Exercises

10.3   Compare and contrast dynamic memory allocation and deallocation operators new, new [], delete and delete [].

10.4   Explain the notion of friendship in C++. Explain the negative aspects of friendship as described in the text.

10.5 Can a correct `Time` class definition include both of the following constructors? If not, explain why not.

```
Time( int h = 0, int m = 0, int s = 0 );
Time();
```

10.6 What happens when a return type, even `void`, is specified for a constructor or destructor?

10.7 Modify class `Date` in Fig. 10.10 to have the following capabilities:
a) Output the date in multiple formats such as

```
DDD YYYY
MM/DD/YY
June 14, 1992
```

b) Use overloaded constructors to create `Date` objects initialized with dates of the formats in part (a).
c) Create a `Date` constructor that reads the system date using the standard library functions of the `<ctime>` header and sets the `Date` members. (See your compiler's reference documentation or `www.cplusplus.com/ref/ctime/index.html` for information on the functions in header `<ctime>`.)

In Chapter 11, we will be able to create operators for testing the equality of two dates and for comparing dates to determine whether one date is prior to, or after, another.

10.8 Create a `SavingsAccount` class. Use a `static` data member `annualInterestRate` to store the annual interest rate for each of the savers. Each member of the class contains a `private` data member `savingsBalance` indicating the amount the saver currently has on deposit. Provide member function `calculateMonthlyInterest` that calculates the monthly interest by multiplying the `balance` by `annualInterestRate` divided by 12; this interest should be added to `savingsBalance`. Provide a `static` member function `modifyInterestRate` that sets the `static` `annualInterestRate` to a new value. Write a driver program to test class `SavingsAccount`. Instantiate two different objects of class `SavingsAccount`, `saver1` and `saver2`, with balances of $2000.00 and $3000.00, respectively. Set the `annualInterestRate` to 3 percent. Then calculate the monthly interest and print the new balances for each of the savers. Then set the `annualInterestRate` to 4 percent, calculate the next month's interest and print the new balances for each of the savers.

10.9 Create class `IntegerSet` for which each object can hold integers in the range 0 through 100. A set is represented internally as an array of ones and zeros. Array element a[i] is 1 if integer i is in the set. Array element a[j] is 0 if integer j is not in the set. The default constructor initializes a set to the so-called "empty set," i.e., a set whose array representation contains all zeros.

Provide member functions for the common set operations. For example, provide a `unionOfSets` member function that creates a third set that is the set-theoretic union of two existing sets (i.e., an element of the third set's array is set to 1 if that element is 1 in either or both of the existing sets, and an element of the third set's array is set to 0 if that element is 0 in each of the existing sets).

Provide an `intersectionOfSets` member function which creates a third set which is the set-theoretic intersection of two existing sets (i.e., an element of the third set's array is set to 0 if that element is 0 in either or both of the existing sets, and an element of the third set's array is set to 1 if that element is 1 in each of the existing sets).

Provide an `insertElement` member function that inserts a new integer k into a set (by setting a[k] to 1). Provide a `deleteElement` member function that deletes integer m (by setting a[m] to 0).

Provide a `printSet` member function that prints a set as a list of numbers separated by spaces. Print only those elements that are present in the set (i.e., their position in the array has a value of 1). Print `---` for an empty set.

Provide an isEqualTo member function that determines whether two sets are equal.

Provide an additional constructor that receives an array of integers and the size of that array and uses the array to initialize a set object.

Now write a driver program to test your IntegerSet class. Instantiate several IntegerSet objects. Test that all your member functions work properly.

10.10 It would be perfectly reasonable for the Time class of Figs. 10.18–10.19 to represent the time internally as the number of seconds since midnight rather than the three integer values hour, minute and second. Clients could use the same public methods and get the same results. Modify the Time class of Fig. 10.18 to implement the time as the number of seconds since midnight and show that there is no visible change in functionality to the clients of the class. [*Note:* This exercise nicely demonstrates the virtues of implementation hiding.]

11

Operator Overloading; String and Array Objects

OBJECTIVES

In this chapter you will learn:

- What operator overloading is and how it makes programs more readable and programming more convenient.

- To redefine (overload) operators to work with objects of user-defined classes.

- The differences between overloading unary and binary operators.

- To convert objects from one class to another class.

- When to, and when not to, overload operators.

- To create **PhoneNumber**, **Array**, **String** and **Date** classes that demonstrate operator overloading.

- To use overloaded operators and other member functions of standard library class **string**.

- To use keyword **explicit** to prevent the compiler from using single-argument constructors to perform implicit conversions.

11.1 **Introduction**

Chapters 9–10 introduced the basics of C++ classes. Services were obtained from objects by sending messages (in the form of member-function calls) to the objects. This function call notation is cumbersome for certain kinds of classes (such as mathematical classes). Also, many common manipulations are performed with operators (e.g., input and output). We can use C++'s rich set of built-in operators to specify common object manipulations. This chapter shows how to enable C++'s operators to work with objects—a process called operator overloading. It is straightforward and natural to extend C++ with these new capabilities, but it must be done cautiously.

One example of an overloaded operator built into C++ is <<, which is used both as the stream insertion operator and as the bitwise left-shift operator. Similarly, >> is also overloaded; it is used both as the stream extraction operator and as the bitwise right-shift operator. Both of these operators are overloaded in the C++ Standard Library.

Although operator overloading sounds like an exotic capability, most programmers implicitly use overloaded operators regularly. For example, the C++ language itself overloads the addition operator (+) and the subtraction operator (-). These operators perform differently, depending on their context in integer arithmetic, floating-point arithmetic and pointer arithmetic.

C++ enables the programmer to overload most operators to be sensitive to the context in which they are used—the compiler generates the appropriate code based on the context (in particular, the types of the operands). Some operators are overloaded frequently, especially the assignment operator and various arithmetic operators such as + and -. The jobs performed by overloaded operators can also be performed by explicit function calls, but operator notation is often clearer and more familiar to programmers.

We discuss when to, and when not to, use operator overloading. We implement user-defined classes `PhoneNumber`, `Array`, `String` and `Date` to demonstrate how to overload operators, including the stream insertion, stream extraction, assignment, equality, relational, subscript, logical negation, parentheses and increment operators. The chapter ends with an example of C++'s Standard Library class `string`, which provides many overloaded operators that are similar to our `String` class that we present earlier in the chapter. In the exercises, we ask you to implement several classes with overloaded operators. The exercises also use classes `Complex` (for complex numbers) and `HugeInt` (for integers larger than a computer can represent with type `long`) to demonstrate overloaded arithmetic operators + and – and ask you to enhance those classes by overloading other arithmetic operators.

11.2 Fundamentals of Operator Overloading

C++ programming is a type-sensitive and type-focused process. Programmers can use fundamental types and can define new types. The fundamental types can be used with C++'s rich collection of operators. Operators provide programmers with a concise notation for expressing manipulations of objects of fundamental types.

Programmers can use operators with user-defined types as well. Although C++ does not allow new operators to be created, it does allow most existing operators to be overloaded so that, when these operators are used with objects, the operators have meaning appropriate to those objects. This is a powerful capability.

 Software Engineering Observation 11.1

Operator overloading contributes to C++'s extensibility—one of the language's most appealing attributes.

 Good Programming Practice 11.1

Use operator overloading when it makes a program clearer than accomplishing the same operations with function calls.

 Good Programming Practice 11.2

Overloaded operators should mimic the functionality of their built-in counterparts—for example, the + operator should be overloaded to perform addition, not subtraction. Avoid excessive or inconsistent use of operator overloading, as this can make a program cryptic and difficult to read.

An operator is overloaded by writing a non-`static` member function definition or global function definition as you normally would, except that the function name now becomes the keyword `operator` followed by the symbol for the operator being overloaded. For example, the function name `operator+` would be used to overload the addition operator (+). When operators are overloaded as member functions, they must be non-`static`, because they must be called on an object of the class and operate on that object.

To use an operator on class objects, that operator *must* be overloaded—with three exceptions. The assignment operator (=) may be used with every class to perform memberwise assignment of the data members of the class—each data member is assigned from the "source" object to the "target" object of the assignment. We will soon see that such default memberwise assignment is dangerous for classes with pointer members; we will explicitly overload the assignment operator for such classes. The address (&) and comma (,) operators may also be used with objects of any class without overloading. The address operator returns the address of the object in memory. The comma operator evaluates the expression to its left then the expression to its right. Both of these operators can also be overloaded.

Overloading is especially appropriate for mathematical classes. These often require that a substantial set of operators be overloaded to ensure consistency with the way these mathematical classes are handled in the real world. For example, it would be unusual to overload only addition for a complex number class, because other arithmetic operators are also commonly used with complex numbers.

Operator overloading provides the same concise and familiar expressions for user-defined types that C++ provides with its rich collection of operators for fundamental types. Operator overloading is not automatic—you must write operator-overloading functions to perform the desired operations. Sometimes these functions are best made member functions; sometimes they are best as `friend` functions; occasionally they can be made global, non-`friend` functions. We discuss these issues throughout the chapter.

11.3 Restrictions on Operator Overloading

Most of C++'s operators can be overloaded. These are shown in Fig. 11.1. Figure 11.2 shows the operators that cannot be overloaded.

 Common Programming Error 11.1

Attempting to overload a nonoverloadable operator is a syntax error.

Precedence, Associativity and Number of Operands
The precedence of an operator cannot be changed by overloading. This can lead to awkward situations in which an operator is overloaded in a manner for which its fixed precedence is inappropriate. However, parentheses can be used to force the order of evaluation of overloaded operators in an expression.

Operators that can be overloaded							
+	-	*	/	%	^	&	|
~	!	=	<	>	+=	-=	*=
/=	%=	^=	&=	|=	<<	>>	>>=
<<=	==	!=	<=	>=	&&	||	++
--	->*	,	->	[]	()	new	delete
new[]	delete[]						

Fig. 11.1 | Operators that can be overloaded.

Operators that cannot be overloaded			
.	.*	::	?:

Fig. 11.2 | Operators that cannot be overloaded.

The associativity of an operator (i.e., whether the operator is applied right-to-left or left-to-right) cannot be changed by overloading.

It is not possible to change the "arity" of an operator (i.e., the number of operands an operator takes): Overloaded unary operators remain unary operators; overloaded binary operators remain binary operators. C++'s only ternary operator (?:) cannot be overloaded. Operators &, *, + and - all have both unary and binary versions; these unary and binary versions can each be overloaded.

Common Programming Error 11.2

Attempting to change the "arity" of an operator via operator overloading is a compilation error.

Creating New Operators

It is not possible to create new operators; only existing operators can be overloaded. Unfortunately, this prevents the programmer from using popular notations like the ** operator used in some other programming languages for exponentiation. [*Note:* You could overload the ∧ operator to perform exponentiation—as it does in some other languages.]

Common Programming Error 11.3

Attempting to create new operators via operator overloading is a syntax error.

Operators for Fundamental Types

The meaning of how an operator works on objects of fundamental types cannot be changed by operator overloading. The programmer cannot, for example, change the meaning of how + adds two integers. Operator overloading works only with objects of user-defined types or with a mixture of an object of a user-defined type and an object of a fundamental type.

Software Engineering Observation 11.2

At least one argument of an operator function must be an object or reference of a user-defined type. This prevents programmers from changing how operators work on fundamental types.

Common Programming Error 11.4

Attempting to modify how an operator works with objects of fundamental types is a compilation error.

Related Operators

Overloading an assignment operator and an addition operator to allow statements like

```
object2 = object2 + object1;
```

does not imply that the += operator is also overloaded to allow statements such as

```
object2 += object1;
```

Such behavior can be achieved only by explicitly overloading operator += for that class.

Common Programming Error 11.5

Assuming that overloading an operator such as + overloads related operators such as += or that overloading == overloads a related operator like != can lead to errors. Operators can be overloaded only explicitly; there is no implicit overloading.

11.4 Operator Functions as Class Members vs. Global Functions

Operator functions can be member functions or global functions; global functions are often made `friend`s for performance reasons. Member functions use the `this` pointer implicitly to obtain one of their class object arguments (the left operand for binary operators). Arguments for both operands of a binary operator must be explicitly listed in a global function call.

Operators That Must Be Overloaded as Member Functions

When overloading (), [], -> or any of the assignment operators, the operator overloading function must be declared as a class member. For the other operators, the operator overloading functions can be class members or global functions.

Operators as Member Functions and Global Functions

Whether an operator function is implemented as a member function or as a global function, the operator is still used the same way in expressions. So which implementation is best?

When an operator function is implemented as a member function, the leftmost (or only) operand must be an object (or a reference to an object) of the operator's class. If the left operand must be an object of a different class or a fundamental type, this operator function must be implemented as a global function (as we will do in Section 11.5 when overloading << and >> as the stream insertion and stream extraction operators, respectively). A global operator function can be made a `friend` of a class if that function must access `private` or `protected` members of that class directly.

Operator member functions of a specific class are called (implicitly by the compiler) only when the left operand of a binary operator is specifically an object of that class, or when the single operand of a unary operator is an object of that class.

Why Overloaded Stream Insertion and Stream Extraction Operators Are Overloaded as Global Functions

The overloaded stream insertion operator (<<) is used in an expression in which the left operand has type `ostream &`, as in `cout << classObject`. To use the operator in this manner where the right operand is an object of a user-defined class, it must be overloaded as a global function. To be a member function, operator << would have to be a member of the `ostream` class. This is not possible for user-defined classes, since we are not allowed to modify C++ Standard Library classes. Similarly, the overloaded stream extraction operator (>>) is used in an expression in which the left operand has type `istream &`, as in `cin >> classObject`, and the right operand is an object of a user-defined class, so it, too, must be a global function. Also, each of these overloaded operator functions may require access to the `private` data members of the class object being output or input, so these overloaded operator functions can be made `friend` functions of the class for performance reasons.

Performance Tip 11.1

It is possible to overload an operator as a global, non-`friend` function, but such a function requiring access to a class's `private` or `protected` data would need to use set or get functions provided in that class's `public` interface. The overhead of calling these functions could cause poor performance, so these functions can be inlined to improve performance.

Commutative Operators

Another reason why one might choose a global function to overload an operator is to enable the operator to be commutative. For example, suppose we have an object, `number`, of type `long int`, and an object `bigInteger1`, of class `HugeInteger` (a class in which integers may be arbitrarily large rather than being limited by the machine word size of the underlying hardware; class `HugeInteger` is developed in the chapter exercises). The addition operator (+) produces a temporary `HugeInteger` object as the sum of a `HugeInteger` and a `long int` (as in the expression `bigInteger1 + number`), or as the sum of a `long int` and a `HugeInteger` (as in the expression `number + bigInteger1`). Thus, we require the addition operator to be commutative (exactly as it is with two fundamental-type operands). The problem is that the class object must appear on the left of the addition operator if that operator is to be overloaded as a member function. So, we overload the operator as a global function to allow the `HugeInteger` to appear on the right of the addition. The `operator+` function, which deals with the `HugeInteger` on the left, can still be a member function.

11.5 Overloading Stream Insertion and Stream Extraction Operators

C++ is able to input and output the fundamental types using the stream extraction operator `>>` and the stream insertion operator `<<`. The class libraries provided with C++ compilers overload these operators to process each fundamental type, including pointers and C-like `char *` strings. The stream insertion and stream extraction operators also can be overloaded to perform input and output for user-defined types. The program of Figs. 11.3–11.5 demonstrates overloading these operators to handle data of a user-defined telephone number class called `PhoneNumber`. This program assumes telephone numbers are input correctly.

```
1   // Fig. 11.3: PhoneNumber.h
2   // PhoneNumber class definition
3   #ifndef PHONENUMBER_H
4   #define PHONENUMBER_H
5
6   #include <iostream>
7   using std::ostream;
8   using std::istream;
9
10  #include <string>
11  using std::string;
12
13  class PhoneNumber
14  {
15     friend ostream &operator<<( ostream &, const PhoneNumber & );
16     friend istream &operator>>( istream &, PhoneNumber & );
17  private:
18     string areaCode; // 3-digit area code
19     string exchange; // 3-digit exchange
```

Fig. 11.3 | `PhoneNumber` class with overloaded stream insertion and stream extraction operators as `friend` functions. (Part 1 of 2.)

```
20      string line; // 4-digit line
21    }; // end class PhoneNumber
22
23    #endif
```

Fig. 11.3 | PhoneNumber class with overloaded stream insertion and stream extraction operators as friend functions. (Part 2 of 2.)

```
 1    // Fig. 11.4: PhoneNumber.cpp
 2    // Overloaded stream insertion and stream extraction operators
 3    // for class PhoneNumber.
 4    #include <iomanip>
 5    using std::setw;
 6
 7    #include "PhoneNumber.h"
 8
 9    // overloaded stream insertion operator; cannot be
10    // a member function if we would like to invoke it with
11    // cout << somePhoneNumber;
12    ostream &operator<<( ostream &output, const PhoneNumber &number )
13    {
14       output << "(" << number.areaCode << ") "
15          << number.exchange << "-" << number.line;
16       return output; // enables cout << a << b << c;
17    } // end function operator<<
18
19    // overloaded stream extraction operator; cannot be
20    // a member function if we would like to invoke it with
21    // cin >> somePhoneNumber;
22    istream &operator>>( istream &input, PhoneNumber &number )
23    {
24       input.ignore(); // skip (
25       input >> setw( 3 ) >> number.areaCode; // input area code
26       input.ignore( 2 ); // skip ) and space
27       input >> setw( 3 ) >> number.exchange; // input exchange
28       input.ignore(); // skip dash (-)
29       input >> setw( 4 ) >> number.line; // input line
30       return input; // enables cin >> a >> b >> c;
31    } // end function operator>>
```

Fig. 11.4 | Overloaded stream insertion and stream extraction operators for class PhoneNumber.

```
 1    // Fig. 11.5: fig11_05.cpp
 2    // Demonstrating class PhoneNumber's overloaded stream insertion
 3    // and stream extraction operators.
 4    #include <iostream>
 5    using std::cout;
 6    using std::cin;
 7    using std::endl;
```

Fig. 11.5 | Overloaded stream insertion and stream extraction operators. (Part 1 of 2.)

```
 8
 9   #include "PhoneNumber.h"
10
11   int main()
12   {
13      PhoneNumber phone; // create object phone
14
15      cout << "Enter phone number in the form (123) 456-7890:" << endl;
16
17      // cin >> phone invokes operator>> by implicitly issuing
18      // the global function call operator>>( cin, phone )
19      cin >> phone;
20
21      cout << "The phone number entered was: ";
22
23      // cout << phone invokes operator<< by implicitly issuing
24      // the global function call operator<<( cout, phone )
25      cout << phone << endl;
26      return 0;
27   } // end main
```

```
Enter phone number in the form (123) 456-7890:
(800) 555-1212
The phone number entered was: (800) 555-1212
```

Fig. 11.5 | Overloaded stream insertion and stream extraction operators. (Part 2 of 2.)

The stream extraction operator function operator>> (Fig. 11.4, lines 22–31) takes istream reference input and PhoneNumber reference num as arguments and returns an istream reference. Operator function operator>> inputs phone numbers of the form

(800) 555-1212

into objects of class PhoneNumber. When the compiler sees the expression

cin >> phone

in line 19 of Fig. 11.5, the compiler generates the global function call

operator>>(cin, phone);

When this call executes, reference parameter input (Fig. 11.4, line 22) becomes an alias for cin and reference parameter number becomes an alias for phone. The operator function reads as strings the three parts of the telephone number into the areaCode (line 25), exchange (line 27) and line (line 29) members of the PhoneNumber object referenced by parameter number. Stream manipulator setw limits the number of characters read into each character array. When used with cin and strings, setw restricts the number of characters read to the number of characters specified by its argument (i.e., setw(3) allows three characters to be read). The parentheses, space and dash characters are skipped by calling istream member function ignore (Fig. 11.4, lines 24, 26 and 28), which discards the specified number of characters in the input stream (one character by default). Function operator>> returns istream reference input (i.e., cin). This enables input operations on

PhoneNumber objects to be cascaded with input operations on other PhoneNumber objects or on objects of other data types. For example, a program can input two PhoneNumber objects in one statement as follows:

```
cin >> phone1 >> phone2;
```

First, the expression `cin >> phone1` executes by making the global function call

```
operator>>( cin, phone1 );
```

This call then returns a reference to `cin` as the value of `cin >> phone1`, so the remaining portion of the expression is interpreted simply as `cin >> phone2`. This executes by making the global function call

```
operator>>( cin, phone2 );
```

The stream insertion operator function (Fig. 11.4, lines 12–17) takes an `ostream` reference (output) and a `const PhoneNumber` reference (number) as arguments and returns an `ostream` reference. Function `operator<<` displays objects of type `PhoneNumber`. When the compiler sees the expression

```
cout << phone
```

in line 25 of Fig. 11.5, the compiler generates the global function call

```
operator<<( cout, phone );
```

Function `operator<<` displays the parts of the telephone number as `string`s, because they are stored as `string` objects.

Error-Prevention Tip 11.1

Returning a reference from an overloaded << or >> operator function is typically successful because cout, cin *and most stream objects are global, or at least long-lived. Returning a reference to an automatic variable or other temporary object is dangerous—creating "dangling references" to nonexisting objects.*

Note that the functions `operator>>` and `operator<<` are declared in `PhoneNumber` as global, `friend` functions (Fig. 11.3, lines 15–16). They are global functions because the object of class `PhoneNumber` appears in each case as the right operand of the operator. Remember, overloaded operator functions for binary operators can be member functions only when the left operand is an object of the class in which the function is a member. Overloaded input and output operators are declared as `friend`s if they need to access nonpublic class members directly for performance reasons or because the class may not offer appropriate *get* functions. Also note that the `PhoneNumber` reference in function `operator<<`'s parameter list (Fig. 11.4, line 12) is `const`, because the `PhoneNumber` will simply be output, and the `PhoneNumber` reference in function `operator>>`'s parameter list (line 22) is non-`const`, because the `PhoneNumber` object must be modified to store the input telephone number in the object.

Software Engineering Observation 11.3

New input/output capabilities for user-defined types are added to C++ without modifying C++'s standard input/output library classes. This is another example of the extensibility of the C++ programming language.

11.6 Overloading Unary Operators

A unary operator for a class can be overloaded as a non-static member function with no arguments or as a global function with one argument; that argument must be either an object of the class or a reference to an object of the class. Member functions that implement overloaded operators must be non-static so that they can access the non-static data in each object of the class. Remember that static member functions can access only static data members of the class.

Later in this chapter, we will overload unary operator ! to test whether an object of the String class we create (Section 11.10) is empty and return a bool result. Consider the expression !s, in which s is an object of class String. When a unary operator such as ! is overloaded as a member function with no arguments and the compiler sees the expression !s, the compiler generates the call s.operator!(). The operand s is the class object for which the String class member function operator! is being invoked. The function is declared in the class definition as follows:

```
class String
{
public:
    bool operator!() const;
    ...
}; // end class String
```

A unary operator such as ! may be overloaded as a global function with one argument in two different ways—either with an argument that is an object (this requires a copy of the object, so the side effects of the function are not applied to the original object), or with an argument that is a reference to an object (no copy of the original object is made, so all side effects of this function are applied to the original object). If s is a String class object (or a reference to a String class object), then !s is treated as if the call operator!(s) had been written, invoking the global operator! function that is declared as follows:

```
bool operator!( const String & );
```

11.7 Overloading Binary Operators

A binary operator can be overloaded as a non-static member function with one argument or as a global function with two arguments (one of those arguments must be either a class object or a reference to a class object).

Later in this chapter, we will overload < to compare two String objects. When overloading binary operator < as a non-static member function of a String class with one argument, if y and z are String-class objects, then y < z is treated as if y.operator<(z) had been written, invoking the operator< member function declared below

```
class String

public:
    bool operator<( const String & ) const;
    ...
}; // end class String
```

If binary operator < is to be overloaded as a global function, it must take two arguments—one of which must be a class object or a reference to a class object. If y and z are

`String`-class objects or references to `String`-class objects, then y < z is treated as if the call `operator<( y, z )` had been written in the program, invoking global-function `operator<` declared as follows:

```
bool operator<( const String &, const String & );
```

11.8 Case Study: Array Class

Pointer-based arrays have a number of problems. For example, a program can easily "walk off" either end of an array, because C++ does not check whether subscripts fall outside the range of an array (the programmer can still do this explicitly though). Arrays of size n must number their elements 0, …, $n - 1$; alternate subscript ranges are not allowed. An entire non-`char` array cannot be input or output at once; each array element must be read or written individually. Two arrays cannot be meaningfully compared with equality operators or relational operators (because the array names are simply pointers to where the arrays begin in memory and, of course, two arrays will always be at different memory locations). When an array is passed to a general-purpose function designed to handle arrays of any size, the size of the array must be passed as an additional argument. One array cannot be assigned to another with the assignment operator(s) (because array names are `const` pointers and a constant pointer cannot be used on the left side of an assignment operator). These and other capabilities certainly seem like "naturals" for dealing with arrays, but pointer-based arrays do not provide such capabilities. However, C++ does provide the means to implement such array capabilities through the use of classes and operator overloading.

In this example, we create a powerful array class that performs range checking to ensure that subscripts remain within the bounds of the `Array`. The class allows one array object to be assigned to another with the assignment operator. Objects of the `Array` class know their size, so the size does not need to be passed separately as an argument when passing an `Array` to a function. Entire `Array`s can be input or output with the stream extraction and stream insertion operators, respectively. `Array` comparisons can be made with the equality operators `==` and `!=`.

This example will sharpen your appreciation of data abstraction. You will probably want to suggest other enhancements to this `Array` class. Class development is an interesting, creative and intellectually challenging activity—always with the goal of "crafting valuable classes."

The program of Figs. 11.6–11.8 demonstrates class `Array` and its overloaded operators. First we walk through `main` (Fig. 11.8). Then we consider the class definition (Fig. 11.6) and each of the class's member-function and `friend`-function definitions (Fig. 11.7).

```
1   // Fig. 11.6: Array.h
2   // Array class for storing arrays of integers.
3   #ifndef ARRAY_H
4   #define ARRAY_H
5
```

Fig. 11.6 | `Array` class definition with overloaded operators. (Part 1 of 2.)

```
 6   #include <iostream>
 7   using std::ostream;
 8   using std::istream;
 9
10   class Array
11   {
12      friend ostream &operator<<( ostream &, const Array & );
13      friend istream &operator>>( istream &, Array & );
14   public:
15      Array( int = 10 ); // default constructor
16      Array( const Array & ); // copy constructor
17      ~Array(); // destructor
18      int getSize() const; // return size
19
20      const Array &operator=( const Array & ); // assignment operator
21      bool operator==( const Array & ) const; // equality operator
22
23      // inequality operator; returns opposite of == operator
24      bool operator!=( const Array &right ) const
25      {
26         return ! ( *this == right ); // invokes Array::operator==
27      } // end function operator!=
28
29      // subscript operator for non-const objects returns modifiable lvalue
30      int &operator[]( int );
31
32      // subscript operator for const objects returns rvalue
33      int operator[]( int ) const;
34   private:
35      int size; // pointer-based array size
36      int *ptr; // pointer to first element of pointer-based array
37   }; // end class Array
38
39   #endif
```

Fig. 11.6 | Array class definition with overloaded operators. (Part 2 of 2.)

```
 1   // Fig 11.7: Array.cpp
 2   // Member-function definitions for class Array
 3   #include <iostream>
 4   using std::cerr;
 5   using std::cout;
 6   using std::cin;
 7   using std::endl;
 8
 9   #include <iomanip>
10   using std::setw;
11
12   #include <cstdlib> // exit function prototype
13   using std::exit;
```

Fig. 11.7 | Array class member- and friend-function definitions. (Part 1 of 4.)

```
14
15   #include "Array.h" // Array class definition
16
17   // default constructor for class Array (default size 10)
18   Array::Array( int arraySize )
19   {
20      size = ( arraySize > 0 ? arraySize : 10 ); // validate arraySize
21      ptr = new int[ size ]; // create space for pointer-based array
22
23      for ( int i = 0; i < size; i++ )
24         ptr[ i ] = 0; // set pointer-based array element
25   } // end Array default constructor
26
27   // copy constructor for class Array;
28   // must receive a reference to prevent infinite recursion
29   Array::Array( const Array &arrayToCopy )
30      : size( arrayToCopy.size )
31   {
32      ptr = new int[ size ]; // create space for pointer-based array
33
34      for ( int i = 0; i < size; i++ )
35         ptr[ i ] = arrayToCopy.ptr[ i ]; // copy into object
36   } // end Array copy constructor
37
38   // destructor for class Array
39   Array::~Array()
40   {
41      delete [] ptr; // release pointer-based array space
42   } // end destructor
43
44   // return number of elements of Array
45   int Array::getSize() const
46   {
47      return size; // number of elements in Array
48   } // end function getSize
49
50   // overloaded assignment operator;
51   // const return avoids: ( a1 = a2 ) = a3
52   const Array &Array::operator=( const Array &right )
53   {
54      if ( &right != this ) // avoid self-assignment
55      {
56         // for Arrays of different sizes, deallocate original
57         // left-side array, then allocate new left-side array
58         if ( size != right.size )
59         {
60            delete [] ptr; // release space
61            size = right.size; // resize this object
62            ptr = new int[ size ]; // create space for array copy
63         } // end inner if
64
```

Fig. 11.7 | Array class member- and friend-function definitions. (Part 2 of 4.)

```
65        for ( int i = 0; i < size; i++ )
66            ptr[ i ] = right.ptr[ i ]; // copy array into object
67     } // end outer if
68
69     return *this; // enables x = y = z, for example
70  } // end function operator=
71
72  // determine if two Arrays are equal and
73  // return true, otherwise return false
74  bool Array::operator==( const Array &right ) const
75  {
76     if ( size != right.size )
77        return false; // arrays of different number of elements
78
79     for ( int i = 0; i < size; i++ )
80        if ( ptr[ i ] != right.ptr[ i ] )
81            return false; // Array contents are not equal
82
83     return true; // Arrays are equal
84  } // end function operator==
85
86  // overloaded subscript operator for non-const Arrays;
87  // reference return creates a modifiable lvalue
88  int &Array::operator[]( int subscript )
89  {
90     // check for subscript out-of-range error
91     if ( subscript < 0 || subscript >= size )
92     {
93        cerr << "\nError: Subscript " << subscript
94           << " out of range" << endl;
95        exit( 1 ); // terminate program; subscript out of range
96     } // end if
97
98     return ptr[ subscript ]; // reference return
99  } // end function operator[]
100
101 // overloaded subscript operator for const Arrays
102 // const reference return creates an rvalue
103 int Array::operator[]( int subscript ) const
104 {
105    // check for subscript out-of-range error
106    if ( subscript < 0 || subscript >= size )
107    {
108       cerr << "\nError: Subscript " << subscript
109          << " out of range" << endl;
110       exit( 1 ); // terminate program; subscript out of range
111    } // end if
112
113    return ptr[ subscript ]; // returns copy of this element
114 } // end function operator[]
115
```

Fig. 11.7 | Array class member- and friend-function definitions. (Part 3 of 4.)

```
116   // overloaded input operator for class Array;
117   // inputs values for entire Array
118   istream &operator>>( istream &input, Array &a )
119   {
120      for ( int i = 0; i < a.size; i++ )
121         input >> a.ptr[ i ];
122
123      return input; // enables cin >> x >> y;
124   } // end function
125
126   // overloaded output operator for class Array
127   ostream &operator<<( ostream &output, const Array &a )
128   {
129      int i;
130
131      // output private ptr-based array
132      for ( i = 0; i < a.size; i++ )
133      {
134         output << setw( 12 ) << a.ptr[ i ];
135
136         if ( ( i + 1 ) % 4 == 0 ) // 4 numbers per row of output
137            output << endl;
138      } // end for
139
140      if ( i % 4 != 0 ) // end last line of output
141         output << endl;
142
143      return output; // enables cout << x << y;
144   } // end function operator<<
```

Fig. 11.7 | Array class member- and `friend`-function definitions. (Part 4 of 4.)

```
 1   // Fig. 11.8: fig11_08.cpp
 2   // Array class test program.
 3   #include <iostream>
 4   using std::cout;
 5   using std::cin;
 6   using std::endl;
 7
 8   #include "Array.h"
 9
10   int main()
11   {
12      Array integers1( 7 ); // seven-element Array
13      Array integers2; // 10-element Array by default
14
15      // print integers1 size and contents
16      cout << "Size of Array integers1 is "
17         << integers1.getSize()
18         << "\nArray after initialization:\n" << integers1;
19
```

Fig. 11.8 | Array class test program. (Part 1 of 3.)

```
20      // print integers2 size and contents
21      cout << "\nSize of Array integers2 is "
22         << integers2.getSize()
23         << "\nArray after initialization:\n" << integers2;
24
25      // input and print integers1 and integers2
26      cout << "\nEnter 17 integers:" << endl;
27      cin >> integers1 >> integers2;
28
29      cout << "\nAfter input, the Arrays contain:\n"
30         << "integers1:\n" << integers1
31         << "integers2:\n" << integers2;
32
33      // use overloaded inequality (!=) operator
34      cout << "\nEvaluating: integers1 != integers2" << endl;
35
36      if ( integers1 != integers2 )
37         cout << "integers1 and integers2 are not equal" << endl;
38
39      // create Array integers3 using integers1 as an
40      // initializer; print size and contents
41      Array integers3( integers1 ); // invokes copy constructor
42
43      cout << "\nSize of Array integers3 is "
44         << integers3.getSize()
45         << "\nArray after initialization:\n" << integers3;
46
47      // use overloaded assignment (=) operator
48      cout << "\nAssigning integers2 to integers1:" << endl;
49      integers1 = integers2; // note target Array is smaller
50
51      cout << "integers1:\n" << integers1
52         << "integers2:\n" << integers2;
53
54      // use overloaded equality (==) operator
55      cout << "\nEvaluating: integers1 == integers2" << endl;
56
57      if ( integers1 == integers2 )
58         cout << "integers1 and integers2 are equal" << endl;
59
60      // use overloaded subscript operator to create rvalue
61      cout << "\nintegers1[5] is " << integers1[ 5 ];
62
63      // use overloaded subscript operator to create lvalue
64      cout << "\n\nAssigning 1000 to integers1[5]" << endl;
65      integers1[ 5 ] = 1000;
66      cout << "integers1:\n" << integers1;
67
68      // attempt to use out-of-range subscript
69      cout << "\nAttempt to assign 1000 to integers1[15]" << endl;
70      integers1[ 15 ] = 1000; // ERROR: out of range
71      return 0;
72   } // end main
```

Fig. 11.8 | Array class test program. (Part 2 of 3.)

```
Size of Array integers1 is 7
Array after initialization:
          0             0             0             0
          0             0             0

Size of Array integers2 is 10
Array after initialization:
          0             0             0             0
          0             0             0             0
          0             0

Enter 17 integers:
1 2 3 4 5 6 7 8 9 10 11 12 13 14 15 16 17

After input, the Arrays contain:
integers1:
          1             2             3             4
          5             6             7
integers2:
          8             9            10            11
         12            13            14            15
         16            17

Evaluating: integers1 != integers2
integers1 and integers2 are not equal

Size of Array integers3 is 7
Array after initialization:
          1             2             3             4
          5             6             7

Assigning integers2 to integers1:
integers1:
          8             9            10            11
         12            13            14            15
         16            17
integers2:
          8             9            10            11
         12            13            14            15
         16            17

Evaluating: integers1 == integers2
integers1 and integers2 are equal

integers1[5] is 13

Assigning 1000 to integers1[5]
integers1:
          8             9            10            11
         12          1000            14            15
         16            17

Attempt to assign 1000 to integers1[15]

Error: Subscript 15 out of range
```

Fig. 11.8 | Array class test program. (Part 3 of 3.)

Creating *Arrays, Outputting Their Size and Displaying Their Contents*

The program begins by instantiating two objects of class `Array`—`integers1` (Fig. 11.8, line 12) with seven elements, and `integers2` (Fig. 11.8, line 13) with the default `Array` size—10 elements (specified by the `Array` default constructor's prototype in Fig. 11.6, line 15). Lines 16–18 use member function `getSize` to determine the size of `integers1` and output `integers1`, using the `Array` overloaded stream insertion operator. The sample output confirms that the `Array` elements were set correctly to zeros by the constructor. Next, lines 21–23 output the size of `Array` `integers2` and output `integers2`, using the `Array` overloaded stream insertion operator.

Using the Overloaded Stream Insertion Operator to Fill an *Array*

Line 26 prompts the user to input 17 integers. Line 27 uses the `Array` overloaded stream extraction operator to read these values into both arrays. The first seven values are stored in `integers1` and the remaining 10 values are stored in `integers2`. Lines 29–31 output the two arrays with the overloaded `Array` stream insertion operator to confirm that the input was performed correctly.

Using the Overloaded Inequality Operator

Line 36 tests the overloaded inequality operator by evaluating the condition

```
integers1 != integers2
```

The program output shows that the `Array`s indeed are not equal.

Initializing a New *Array* with a Copy of an Existing *Array*'s Contents

Line 41 instantiates a third `Array` called `integers3` and initializes it with a copy of `Array` `integers1`. This invokes the `Array` copy constructor to copy the elements of `integers1` into `integers3`. We discuss the details of the copy constructor shortly. Note that the copy constructor can also be invoked by writing line 41 as follows:

```
Array integers3 = integers1;
```

The equal sign in the preceding statement is *not* the assignment operator. When an equal sign appears in the declaration of an object, it invokes a constructor for that object. This form can be used to pass only a single argument to a constructor.

Lines 43–45 output the size of `integers3` and output `integers3`, using the `Array` overloaded stream insertion operator to confirm that the `Array` elements were set correctly by the copy constructor.

Using the Overloaded Assignment Operator

Next, line 49 tests the overloaded assignment operator (=) by assigning `integers2` to `integers1`. Lines 51–52 print both `Array` objects to confirm that the assignment was successful. Note that `integers1` originally held 7 integers and was resized to hold a copy of the 10 elements in `integers2`. As we will see, the overloaded assignment operator performs this resizing operation in a manner that is transparent to the client code.

Using the Overloaded Equality Operator

Next, line 57 uses the overloaded equality operator (==) to confirm that objects `integers1` and `integers2` are indeed identical after the assignment.

Using the Overloaded Subscript Operator

Line 61 uses the overloaded subscript operator to refer to integers1[5]—an in-range element of integers1. This subscripted name is used as an *rvalue* to print the value stored in integers1[5]. Line 65 uses integers1[5] as a modifiable *lvalue* on the left side of an assignment statement to assign a new value, 1000, to element 5 of integers1. We will see that operator[] returns a reference to use as the modifiable *lvalue* after the operator confirms that 5 is a valid subscript for integers1.

Line 70 attempts to assign the value 1000 to integers1[15]—an out-of-range element. In this example, operator[] determines that the subscript is out of range, prints a message and terminates the program. Note that we highlighted line 70 of the program in red to emphasize that it is an error to access an element that is out of range. This is a runtime logic error, not a compilation error.

Interestingly, the array subscript operator [] is not restricted for use only with arrays; it also can be used, for example, to select elements from other kinds of container classes, such as linked lists, strings and dictionaries. Also, when operator[] functions are defined, subscripts no longer have to be integers—characters, strings, floats or even objects of user-defined classes also could be used. In Chapter 22, Standard Template Library (STL), we discuss the STL map class that allows noninteger subscripts.

Array Class Definition

Now that we have seen how this program operates, let us walk through the class header (Fig. 11.6). As we refer to each member function in the header, we discuss that function's implementation in Fig. 11.7. In Fig. 11.6, lines 35–36 represent the private data members of class Array. Each Array object consists of a size member indicating the number of elements in the Array and an int pointer—ptr—that points to the dynamically allocated pointer-based array of integers managed by the Array object.

Overloading the Stream Insertion and Stream Extraction Operators as **friend***s*

Lines 12–13 of Fig. 11.6 declare the overloaded stream insertion operator and the overloaded stream extraction operator to be friends of class Array. When the compiler sees an expression like cout << arrayObject, it invokes global function operator<< with the call

```
operator<<( cout, arrayObject )
```

When the compiler sees an expression like cin >> arrayObject, it invokes global function operator>> with the call

```
operator>>( cin, arrayObject )
```

We note again that these stream insertion and stream extraction operator functions cannot be members of class Array, because the Array object is always mentioned on the right side of the stream insertion operator and the stream extraction operator. If these operator functions were to be members of class Array, the following awkward statements would have to be used to output and input an Array:

```
arrayObject << cout;
arrayObject >> cin;
```

Such statements would be confusing to most C++ programmers, who are familiar with cout and cin appearing as the left operands of << and >>, respectively.

Function operator<< (defined in Fig. 11.7, lines 127–144) prints the number of elements indicated by size from the integer array to which ptr points. Function operator>> (defined in Fig. 11.7, lines 118–124) inputs directly into the array to which ptr points. Each of these operator functions returns an appropriate reference to enable cascaded output or input statements, respectively. Note that each of these functions has access to an Array's private data because these functions are declared as friends of class Array. Also, note that class Array's getSize and operator[] functions could be used by operator<< and operator>>, in which case these operator functions would not need to be friends of class Array. However, the additional function calls might increase execution-time overhead.

Array Default Constructor

Line 15 of Fig. 11.6 declares the default constructor for the class and specifies a default size of 10 elements. When the compiler sees a declaration like line 13 in Fig. 11.8, it invokes class Array's default constructor (remember that the default constructor in this example actually receives a single int argument that has a default value of 10). The default constructor (defined in Fig. 11.7, lines 18–25) validates and assigns the argument to data member size, uses new to obtain the memory for the internal pointer-based representation of this array and assigns the pointer returned by new to data member ptr. Then the constructor uses a for statement to set all the elements of the array to zero. It is possible to have an Array class that does not initialize its members if, for example, these members are to be read at some later time; but this is considered to be a poor programming practice. Arrays, and objects in general, should be properly initialized and maintained in a consistent state.

Array Copy Constructor

Line 16 of Fig. 11.6 declares a copy constructor (defined in Fig. 11.7, lines 29–36) that initializes an Array by making a copy of an existing Array object. Such copying must be done carefully to avoid the pitfall of leaving both Array objects pointing to the same dynamically allocated memory. This is exactly the problem that would occur with default memberwise copying, if the compiler is allowed to define a default copy constructor for this class. Copy constructors are invoked whenever a copy of an object is needed, such as in passing an object by value to a function, returning an object by value from a function or initializing an object with a copy of another object of the same class. The copy constructor is called in a declaration when an object of class Array is instantiated and initialized with another object of class Array, as in the declaration in line 41 of Fig. 11.8.

Software Engineering Observation 11.4

The argument to a copy constructor should be a const reference to allow a const object to be copied.

Common Programming Error 11.6

Note that a copy constructor must receive its argument by reference, not by value. Otherwise, the copy constructor call results in infinite recursion (a fatal logic error) because receiving an object by value requires the copy constructor to make a copy of the argument object. Recall that any time a copy of an object is required, the class's copy constructor is called. If the copy constructor received its argument by value, the copy constructor would call itself recursively to make a copy of its argument!

The copy constructor for `Array` uses a member initializer (Fig. 11.7, line 30) to copy the `size` of the initializer `Array` into data member `size`, uses `new` (line 32) to obtain the memory for the internal pointer-based representation of this `Array` and assigns the pointer returned by `new` to data member `ptr`.[1] Then the copy constructor uses a `for` statement to copy all the elements of the initializer `Array` into the new `Array` object. Note that an object of a class can look at the `private` data of any other object of that class (using a handle that indicates which object to access).

 Common Programming Error 11.7

If the copy constructor simply copied the pointer in the source object to the target object's pointer, then both objects would point to the same dynamically allocated memory. The first destructor to execute would then delete the dynamically allocated memory, and the other object's `ptr` would be undefined, a situation called a dangling pointer—this would likely result in a serious run-time error (such as early program termination) when the pointer was used.

Array Destructor

Line 17 of Fig. 11.6 declares the destructor for the class (defined in Fig. 11.7, lines 39–42). The destructor is invoked when an object of class `Array` goes out of scope. The destructor uses `delete []` to release the memory allocated dynamically by `new` in the constructor.

getSize Member Function

Line 18 of Fig. 11.6 declares function `getSize` (defined in Fig. 11.7, lines 45–48) that returns the number of elements in the `Array`.

Overloaded Assignment Operator

Line 20 of Fig. 11.6 declares the overloaded assignment operator function for the class. When the compiler sees the expression `integers1 = integers2` in line 49 of Fig. 11.8, the compiler invokes member function `operator=` with the call

```
integers1.operator=( integers2 )
```

The implementation of member function `operator=` (Fig. 11.7, lines 52–70) tests for self assignment (line 54) in which an object of class `Array` is being assigned to itself. When `this` is equal to the address of the `right` operand, a self-assignment is being attempted, so the assignment is skipped (i.e., the object already is itself; in a moment we will see why self-assignment is dangerous). If it is not a self-assignment, then the member function determines whether the sizes of the two arrays are identical (line 58); in that case, the original array of integers in the left-side `Array` object is not reallocated. Otherwise, `operator=` uses `delete` (line 60) to release the memory originally allocated to the target array, copies the `size` of the source array to the `size` of the target array (line 61), uses `new` to allocate memory for the target array and places the pointer returned by `new` into the array's `ptr` member.[2] Then the `for` statement at lines 65–66 copies the array elements from the source array to the target array. Regardless of whether this is a self-assignment, the member function returns the current object (i.e., `*this` at line 69) as a constant reference; this enables cascaded `Array` assignments such as x = y = z. If self-assignment occurs, and function op-

---

1. Note that `new` could fail to obtain the needed memory. We deal with `new` failures in Chapter 16, Exception Handling.
2. Once again, `new` could fail. We discuss `new` failures in Chapter 16.

erator= did not test for this case, operator= would delete the dynamic memory associated with the Array object before the assignment was complete. This would leave ptr pointing to memory that had been deallocated, which could lead to fatal runtime errors.

 Software Engineering Observation 11.5

A copy constructor, a destructor and an overloaded assignment operator are usually provided as a group for any class that uses dynamically allocated memory.

 Common Programming Error 11.8

Not providing an overloaded assignment operator and a copy constructor for a class when objects of that class contain pointers to dynamically allocated memory is a logic error.

 Software Engineering Observation 11.6

It is possible to prevent one object of a class from being assigned to another. This is done by declaring the assignment operator as a private member of the class.

 Software Engineering Observation 11.7

It is possible to prevent class objects from being copied; to do this, simply make both the overloaded assignment operator and the copy constructor of that class private.

Overloaded Equality and Inequality Operators

Line 21 of Fig. 11.6 declares the overloaded equality operator (==) for the class. When the compiler sees the expression integers1 == integers2 in line 57 of Fig. 11.8, the compiler invokes member function operator== with the call

```
integers1.operator==( integers2 )
```

Member function operator== (defined in Fig. 11.7, lines 74–84) immediately returns false if the size members of the arrays are not equal. Otherwise, operator== compares each pair of elements. If they are all equal, the function returns true. The first pair of elements to differ causes the function to return false immediately.

Lines 24–27 of the header file define the overloaded inequality operator (!=) for the class. Member function operator!= uses the overloaded operator== function to determine whether one Array is equal to another, then returns the opposite of that result. Writing operator!= in this manner enables the programmer to reuse operator==, which reduces the amount of code that must be written in the class. Also, note that the full function definition for operator!= is in the Array header file. This allows the compiler to inline the definition of operator!= to eliminate the overhead of the extra function call.

Overloaded Subscript Operators

Lines 30 and 33 of Fig. 11.6 declare two overloaded subscript operators (defined in Fig. 11.7 at lines 88–99 and 103–114, respectively). When the compiler sees the expression integers1[5] (Fig. 11.8, line 61), the compiler invokes the appropriate overloaded operator[] member function by generating the call

```
integers1.operator[]( 5 )
```

The compiler creates a call to the const version of operator[] (Fig. 11.7, lines 103–114) when the subscript operator is used on a const Array object. For example, if const object z is instantiated with the statement

```
        const Array z( 5 );
```

then the `const` version of `operator[]` is required to execute a statement such as

```
        cout << z[ 3 ] << endl;
```

Remember, a program can invoke only the `const` member functions of a `const` object.

Each definition of `operator[]` determines whether the subscript it receives as an argument is in range. If it is not, each function prints an error message and terminates the program with a call to function `exit` (header `<cstdlib>`).[3] If the subscript is in range, the non-`const` version of `operator[]` returns the appropriate array element as a reference so that it may be used as a modifiable *lvalue* (e.g., on the left side of an assignment statement). If the subscript is in range, the `const` version of `operator[]` returns a copy of the appropriate element of the array. The returned character is an *rvalue*.

11.9 Converting between Types

Most programs process information of many types. Sometimes all the operations "stay within a type." For example, adding an `int` to an `int` produces an `int` (as long as the result is not too large to be represented as an `int`). It is often necessary, however, to convert data of one type to data of another type. This can happen in assignments, in calculations, in passing values to functions and in returning values from functions. The compiler knows how to perform certain conversions among fundamental types (as we discussed in Chapter 6). Programmers can use cast operators to force conversions among fundamental types.

But what about user-defined types? The compiler cannot know in advance how to convert among user-defined types, and between user-defined types and fundamental types, so the programmer must specify how to do this. Such conversions can be performed with conversion constructors—single-argument constructors that turn objects of other types (including fundamental types) into objects of a particular class. In Section 11.10, we use a conversion constructor to convert ordinary `char *` strings into `String` class objects.

A conversion operator (also called a cast operator) can be used to convert an object of one class into an object of another class or into an object of a fundamental type. Such a conversion operator must be a non-`static` member function. The function prototype

```
        A::operator char *() const;
```

declares an overloaded cast operator function for converting an object of user-defined type `A` into a temporary `char *` object. The operator function is declared `const` because it does not modify the original object. An overloaded cast operator function does not specify a return type—the return type is the type to which the object is being converted. If `s` is a class object, when the compiler sees the expression `static_cast< char * >( s )`, the compiler generates the call

```
        s.operator char *()
```

The operand `s` is the class object `s` for which the member function `operator char *` is being invoked.

---

3. Note that it is more appropriate when a subscript is out of range to "throw an exception" indicating the out-of-range subscript. Then the program can "catch" that exception, process it and possibly continue execution. See Chapter 16 for more information on exceptions.

Overloaded cast operator functions can be defined to convert objects of user-defined types into fundamental types or into objects of other user-defined types. The prototypes

```
A::operator int() const;
A::operator OtherClass() const;
```

declare overloaded cast operator functions that can convert an object of user-defined type A into an integer or into an object of user-defined type OtherClass, respectively.

One of the nice features of cast operators and conversion constructors is that, when necessary, the compiler can call these functions implicitly to create temporary objects. For example, if an object s of a user-defined String class appears in a program at a location where an ordinary char * is expected, such as

```
cout << s;
```

the compiler can call the overloaded cast-operator function operator char * to convert the object into a char * and use the resulting char * in the expression. With this cast operator provided for our String class, the stream insertion operator does not have to be overloaded to output a String using cout.

11.10 Case Study: String Class

As a capstone exercise to our study of overloading, we will build our own String class to handle the creation and manipulation of strings (Figs. 11.9–11.11). The C++ standard library provides a similar, more robust class string as well. We present an example of the standard class string in Section 11.13 and study class string in detail in Chapter 18. For now, we will make extensive use of operator overloading to craft our own class String.

First, we present the header file for class String. We discuss the private data used to represent String objects. Then we walk through the class's public interface, discussing each of the services the class provides. We discuss the member-function definitions for the class String. For each of the overloaded operator functions, we show the code in the program that invokes the overloaded operator function, and we provide an explanation of how the overloaded operator function works.

String Class Definition

Now let us walk through the String class header file in Fig. 11.9. We begin with the internal pointer-based representation of a String. Lines 55–56 declare the private data members of the class. Our String class has a length field, which represents the number of characters in the string, not including the null character at the end, and has a pointer sPtr that points to the dynamically allocated memory representing the character string.

```
 1  // Fig. 11.9: String.h
 2  // String class definition.
 3  #ifndef STRING_H
 4  #define STRING_H
 5
 6  #include <iostream>
 7  using std::ostream;
 8  using std::istream;
```

Fig. 11.9 | String class definition with operator overloading. (Part 1 of 2.)

```
9
10   class String
11   {
12      friend ostream &operator<<( ostream &, const String & );
13      friend istream &operator>>( istream &, String & );
14   public:
15      String( const char * = "" ); // conversion/default constructor
16      String( const String & ); // copy constructor
17      ~String(); // destructor
18
19      const String &operator=( const String & ); // assignment operator
20      const String &operator+=( const String & ); // concatenation operator
21
22      bool operator!() const; // is String empty?
23      bool operator==( const String & ) const; // test s1 == s2
24      bool operator<( const String & ) const; // test s1 < s2
25
26      // test s1 != s2
27      bool operator!=( const String &right ) const
28      {
29         return !( *this == right );
30      } // end function operator!=
31
32      // test s1 > s2
33      bool operator>( const String &right ) const
34      {
35         return right < *this;
36      } // end function operator>
37
38      // test s1 <= s2
39      bool operator<=( const String &right ) const
40      {
41         return !( right < *this );
42      } // end function operator <=
43
44      // test s1 >= s2
45      bool operator>=( const String &right ) const
46      {
47         return !( *this < right );
48      } // end function operator>=
49
50      char &operator[]( int ); // subscript operator (modifiable lvalue)
51      char operator[]( int ) const; // subscript operator (rvalue)
52      String operator()( int, int = 0 ) const; // return a substring
53      int getLength() const; // return string length
54   private:
55      int length; // string length (not counting null terminator)
56      char *sPtr; // pointer to start of pointer-based string
57
58      void setString( const char * ); // utility function
59   }; // end class String
60
61   #endif
```

Fig. 11.9 | String class definition with operator overloading. (Part 2 of 2.)

```
 1   // Fig. 11.10: String.cpp
 2   // Member-function definitions for class String.
 3   #include <iostream>
 4   using std::cerr;
 5   using std::cout;
 6   using std::endl;
 7
 8   #include <iomanip>
 9   using std::setw;
10
11   #include <cstring> // strcpy and strcat prototypes
12   using std::strcmp;
13   using std::strcpy;
14   using std::strcat;
15
16   #include <cstdlib> // exit prototype
17   using std::exit;
18
19   #include "String.h" // String class definition
20
21   // conversion (and default) constructor converts char * to String
22   String::String( const char *s )
23      : length( ( s != 0 ) ? strlen( s ) : 0 )
24   {
25      cout << "Conversion (and default) constructor: " << s << endl;
26      setString( s ); // call utility function
27   } // end String conversion constructor
28
29   // copy constructor
30   String::String( const String &copy )
31      : length( copy.length )
32   {
33      cout << "Copy constructor: " << copy.sPtr << endl;
34      setString( copy.sPtr ); // call utility function
35   } // end String copy constructor
36
37   // Destructor
38   String::~String()
39   {
40      cout << "Destructor: " << sPtr << endl;
41      delete [] sPtr; // release pointer-based string memory
42   } // end ~String destructor
43
44   // overloaded = operator; avoids self assignment
45   const String &String::operator=( const String &right )
46   {
47      cout << "operator= called" << endl;
48
49      if ( &right != this ) // avoid self assignment
50      {
51         delete [] sPtr; // prevents memory leak
52         length = right.length; // new String length
```

Fig. 11.10 | `String` class member-function and `friend`-function definitions. (Part 1 of 4.)

```
53          setString( right.sPtr ); // call utility function
54       } // end if
55       else
56          cout << "Attempted assignment of a String to itself" << endl;
57
58       return *this; // enables cascaded assignments
59    } // end function operator=
60
61    // concatenate right operand to this object and store in this object
62    const String &String::operator+=( const String &right )
63    {
64       size_t newLength = length + right.length; // new length
65       char *tempPtr = new char[ newLength + 1 ]; // create memory
66
67       strcpy( tempPtr, sPtr ); // copy sPtr
68       strcpy( tempPtr + length, right.sPtr ); // copy right.sPtr
69
70       delete [] sPtr; // reclaim old space
71       sPtr = tempPtr; // assign new array to sPtr
72       length = newLength; // assign new length to length
73       return *this; // enables cascaded calls
74    } // end function operator+=
75
76    // is this String empty?
77    bool String::operator!() const
78    {
79       return length == 0;
80    } // end function operator!
81
82    // Is this String equal to right String?
83    bool String::operator==( const String &right ) const
84    {
85       return strcmp( sPtr, right.sPtr ) == 0;
86    } // end function operator==
87
88    // Is this String less than right String?
89    bool String::operator<( const String &right ) const
90    {
91       return strcmp( sPtr, right.sPtr ) < 0;
92    } // end function operator<
93
94    // return reference to character in String as a modifiable lvalue
95    char &String::operator[]( int subscript )
96    {
97       // test for subscript out of range
98       if ( subscript < 0 || subscript >= length )
99       {
100         cerr << "Error: Subscript " << subscript
101            << " out of range" << endl;
102         exit( 1 ); // terminate program
103      } // end if
104
```

Fig. 11.10 | String class member-function and friend-function definitions. (Part 2 of 4.)

```
105         return sPtr[ subscript ]; // non-const return; modifiable lvalue
106      } // end function operator[]
107
108      // return reference to character in String as rvalue
109      char String::operator[]( int subscript ) const
110      {
111         // test for subscript out of range
112         if ( subscript < 0 || subscript >= length )
113         {
114            cerr << "Error: Subscript " << subscript
115                 << " out of range" << endl;
116            exit( 1 ); // terminate program
117         } // end if
118
119         return sPtr[ subscript ]; // returns copy of this element
120      } // end function operator[]
121
122      // return a substring beginning at index and of length subLength
123      String String::operator()( int index, int subLength ) const
124      {
125         // if index is out of range or substring length < 0,
126         // return an empty String object
127         if ( index < 0 || index >= length || subLength < 0 )
128            return ""; // converted to a String object automatically
129
130         // determine length of substring
131         int len;
132
133         if ( ( subLength == 0 ) || ( index + subLength > length ) )
134            len = length - index;
135         else
136            len = subLength;
137
138         // allocate temporary array for substring and
139         // terminating null character
140         char *tempPtr = new char[ len + 1 ];
141
142         // copy substring into char array and terminate string
143         strncpy( tempPtr, &sPtr[ index ], len );
144         tempPtr[ len ] = '\0';
145
146         // create temporary String object containing the substring
147         String tempString( tempPtr );
148         delete [] tempPtr; // delete temporary array
149         return tempString; // return copy of the temporary String
150      } // end function operator()
151
152      // return string length
153      int String::getLength() const
154      {
155         return length;
156      } // end function getLength
```

Fig. 11.10 | `String` class member-function and `friend`-function definitions. (Part 3 of 4.)

```
157
158   // utility function called by constructors and operator=
159   void String::setString( const char *string2 )
160   {
161      sPtr = new char[ length + 1 ]; // allocate memory
162
163      if ( string2 != 0 ) // if string2 is not null pointer, copy contents
164         strcpy( sPtr, string2 ); // copy literal to object
165      else // if string2 is a null pointer, make this an empty string
166         sPtr[ 0 ] = '\0'; // empty string
167   } // end function setString
168
169   // overloaded output operator
170   ostream &operator<<( ostream &output, const String &s )
171   {
172      output << s.sPtr;
173      return output; // enables cascading
174   } // end function operator<<
175
176   // overloaded input operator
177   istream &operator>>( istream &input, String &s )
178   {
179      char temp[ 100 ]; // buffer to store input
180      input >> setw( 100 ) >> temp;
181      s = temp; // use String class assignment operator
182      return input; // enables cascading
183   } // end function operator>>
```

Fig. 11.10 | String class member-function and friend-function definitions. (Part 4 of 4.)

```
 1   // Fig. 11.11: fig11_11.cpp
 2   // String class test program.
 3   #include <iostream>
 4   using std::cout;
 5   using std::endl;
 6   using std::boolalpha;
 7
 8   #include "String.h"
 9
10   int main()
11   {
12      String s1( "happy" );
13      String s2( " birthday" );
14      String s3;
15
16      // test overloaded equality and relational operators
17      cout << "s1 is \"" << s1 << "\"; s2 is \"" << s2
18         << "\"; s3 is \"" << s3 << '\"'
19         << boolalpha << "\n\nThe results of comparing s2 and s1:"
20         << "\ns2 == s1 yields " << ( s2 == s1 )
21         << "\ns2 != s1 yields " << ( s2 != s1 )
```

Fig. 11.11 | String class test program. (Part 1 of 4.)

```
22          << "\ns2 >  s1 yields " << ( s2 > s1 )
23          << "\ns2 <  s1 yields " << ( s2 < s1 )
24          << "\ns2 >= s1 yields " << ( s2 >= s1 )
25          << "\ns2 <= s1 yields " << ( s2 <= s1 );
26
27
28       // test overloaded String empty (!) operator
29       cout << "\n\nTesting !s3:" << endl;
30
31       if ( !s3 )
32       {
33          cout << "s3 is empty; assigning s1 to s3;" << endl;
34          s3 = s1; // test overloaded assignment
35          cout << "s3 is \"" << s3 << "\"";
36       } // end if
37
38       // test overloaded String concatenation operator
39       cout << "\n\ns1 += s2 yields s1 = ";
40       s1 += s2; // test overloaded concatenation
41       cout << s1;
42
43       // test conversion constructor
44       cout << "\n\ns1 += \" to you\" yields" << endl;
45       s1 += " to you"; // test conversion constructor
46       cout << "s1 = " << s1 << "\n\n";
47
48       // test overloaded function call operator () for substring
49       cout << "The substring of s1 starting at\n"
50          << "location 0 for 14 characters, s1(0, 14), is:\n"
51          << s1( 0, 14 ) << "\n\n";
52
53       // test substring "to-end-of-String" option
54       cout << "The substring of s1 starting at\n"
55          << "location 15, s1(15), is: "
56          << s1( 15 ) << "\n\n";
57
58       // test copy constructor
59       String *s4Ptr = new String( s1 );
60       cout << "\n*s4Ptr = " << *s4Ptr << "\n\n";
61
62       // test assignment (=) operator with self-assignment
63       cout << "assigning *s4Ptr to *s4Ptr" << endl;
64       *s4Ptr = *s4Ptr; // test overloaded assignment
65       cout << "*s4Ptr = " << *s4Ptr << endl;
66
67       // test destructor
68       delete s4Ptr;
69
70       // test using subscript operator to create a modifiable lvalue
71       s1[ 0 ] = 'H';
72       s1[ 6 ] = 'B';
73       cout << "\ns1 after s1[0] = 'H' and s1[6] = 'B' is: "
74          << s1 << "\n\n";
```

Fig. 11.11 | String class test program. (Part 2 of 4.)

```
75
76      // test subscript out of range
77      cout << "Attempt to assign 'd' to s1[30] yields:" << endl;
78      s1[ 30 ] = 'd'; // ERROR: subscript out of range
79      return 0;
80   } // end main
```

```
Conversion (and default) constructor: happy
Conversion (and default) constructor:  birthday
Conversion (and default) constructor:
s1 is "happy"; s2 is " birthday"; s3 is ""

The results of comparing s2 and s1:
s2 == s1 yields false
s2 != s1 yields true
s2 >  s1 yields false
s2 <  s1 yields true
s2 >= s1 yields false
s2 <= s1 yields true

Testing !s3:
s3 is empty; assigning s1 to s3;
operator= called
s3 is "happy"

s1 += s2 yields s1 = happy birthday

s1 += " to you" yields
Conversion (and default) constructor:  to you
Destructor:  to you
s1 = happy birthday to you

Conversion (and default) constructor: happy birthday
Copy constructor: happy birthday
Destructor: happy birthday
The substring of s1 starting at
location 0 for 14 characters, s1(0, 14), is:
happy birthday

Destructor: happy birthday
Conversion (and default) constructor: to you
Copy constructor: to you
Destructor: to you
The substring of s1 starting at
location 15, s1(15), is: to you

Destructor: to you
Copy constructor: happy birthday to you

*s4Ptr = happy birthday to you

assigning *s4Ptr to *s4Ptr
operator= called
Attempted assignment of a String to itself
```

(continued at top of next page...)

Fig. 11.11 | String class test program. (Part 3 of 4.)

```
                                              (...continued from bottom of previous page)
*s4Ptr = happy birthday to you
Destructor: happy birthday to you

s1 after s1[0] = 'H' and s1[6] = 'B' is: Happy Birthday to you

Attempt to assign 'd' to s1[30] yields:
Error: Subscript 30 out of range
```

Fig. 11.11 | String class test program. (Part 4 of 4.)

Overloading the Stream Insertion and Stream Extraction Operators as *friends*

Lines 12–13 (Fig. 11.9) declare the overloaded stream insertion operator function oper-
ator<< (defined in Fig. 11.10, lines 170–174) and the overloaded stream extraction operator function operator>> (defined in Fig. 11.10, lines 177–183) as friends of the class.
The implementation of operator<< is straightforward. Note that operator>> restricts the
total number of characters that can be read into array temp to 99 with setw (line 180); the
100th position is reserved for the string's terminating null character. [*Note:* We did not
have this restriction for operator>> in class Array (Figs. 11.6–11.7), because that class's
operator>> read one array element at a time and stopped reading values when the end of
the array was reached. Object cin does not know how to do this by default for input of
character arrays.] Also, note the use of operator= (line 181) to assign the C-style string
temp to the String object to which s refers. This statement invokes the conversion constructor to create a temporary String object containing the C-style string; the temporary
String is then assigned to s. We could eliminate the overhead of creating the temporary
String object here by providing another overloaded assignment operator that receives a
parameter of type const char *.

String Conversion Constructor

Line 15 (Fig. 11.9) declares a conversion constructor. This constructor (defined in
Fig. 11.10, lines 22–27) takes a const char * argument (that defaults to the empty string;
Fig. 11.9, line 15) and initializes a String object containing that same character string.
Any single-argument constructor can be thought of as a conversion constructor. As we
will see, such constructors are helpful when we are doing any String operation using char
* arguments. The conversion constructor can convert a char * string into a String object,
which can then be assigned to the target String object. The availability of this conversion
constructor means that it is not necessary to supply an overloaded assignment operator for
specifically assigning character strings to String objects. The compiler invokes the conversion constructor to create a temporary String object containing the character string;
then the overloaded assignment operator is invoked to assign the temporary String object
to another String object.

Software Engineering Observation 11.8

*When a conversion constructor is used to perform an implicit conversion, C++ can apply only
one implicit constructor call (i.e., a single user-defined conversion) to try to match the needs of
another overloaded operator. The compiler will not match an overloaded operator's needs by
performing a series of implicit, user-defined conversions.*

The String conversion constructor could be invoked in such a declaration as String s1("happy"). The conversion constructor calculates the length of its character-string argument and assigns it to data member length in the member-initializer list. Then, line 26 calls utility function setString (defined in Fig. 11.10, lines 159–167), which uses new to allocate a sufficient amount of memory to private data member sPtr and uses strcpy to copy the character string into the memory to which sPtr points.[4]

String Copy Constructor
Line 16 in Fig. 11.9 declares a copy constructor (defined in Fig. 11.10, lines 30–35) that initializes a String object by making a copy of an existing String object. As with our class Array (Figs. 11.6–11.7), such copying must be done carefully to avoid the pitfall in which both String objects point to the same dynamically allocated memory. The copy constructor operates similarly to the conversion constructor, except that it simply copies the length member from the source String object to the target String object. Note that the copy constructor calls setString to create new space for the target object's internal character string. If it simply copied the sPtr in the source object to the target object's sPtr, then both objects would point to the same dynamically allocated memory. The first destructor to execute would then delete the dynamically allocated memory, and the other object's sPtr would be undefined (i.e., sPtr would be a dangling pointer), a situation likely to cause a serious runtime error.

String Destructor
Line 17 of Fig. 11.9 declares the String destructor (defined in Fig. 11.10, lines 38–42). The destructor uses delete [] to release the dynamic memory to which sPtr points.

Overloaded Assignment Operator
Line 19 (Fig. 11.9) declares the overloaded assignment operator function operator= (defined in Fig. 11.10, lines 45–59). When the compiler sees an expression like string1 = string2, the compiler generates the function call

```
string1.operator=( string2 );
```

The overloaded assignment operator function operator= tests for self-assignment. If this is a self-assignment, the function does not need to change the object. If this test were omitted, the function would immediately delete the space in the target object and thus lose the character string, such that the pointer would no longer be pointing to valid data—a classic example of a dangling pointer. If there is no self-assignment, the function deletes the memory and copies the length field of the source object to the target object. Then operator= calls setString to create new space for the target object and copy the character

---

4. There is a subtle issue in the implementation of this conversion constructor. As implemented, if a null pointer (i.e., 0) is passed to the constructor, the program will fail. The proper way to implement this constructor would be to detect whether the constructor argument is a null pointer, then "throw an exception." Chapter 16 discusses how we can make classes more robust in this manner. Also, note that a null pointer (0) is not the same as the empty string (""). A null pointer is a pointer that does not point to anything. An empty string is an actual string that contains only a null character ('\0').

string from the source object to the target object. Whether or not this is a self-assignment, `operator=` returns `*this` to enable cascaded assignments.

Overloaded Addition Assignment Operator

Line 20 of Fig. 11.9 declares the overloaded string-concatenation operator += (defined in Fig. 11.10, lines 62–74). When the compiler sees the expression s1 += s2 (line 40 of Fig. 11.11), the compiler generates the member-function call

```
s1.operator+=( s2 )
```

Function `operator+=` calculates the combined length of the concatenated string and stores it in local variable `newLength`, then creates a temporary pointer (`tempPtr`) and allocates a new character array in which the concatenated string will be stored. Next, `operator+=` uses `strcpy` to copy the original character strings from `sPtr` and `right.sPtr` into the memory to which `tempPtr` points. Note that the location into which `strcpy` will copy the first character of `right.sPtr` is determined by the pointer-arithmetic calculation `tempPtr + length`. This calculation indicates that the first character of `right.sPtr` should be placed at location `length` in the array to which `tempPtr` points. Next, `operator+=` uses `delete []` to release the space occupied by this object's original character string, assigns `tempPtr` to `sPtr` so that this `String` object points to the new character string, assigns `newLength` to `length` so that this `String` object contains the new string length and returns `*this` as a `const String &` to enable cascading of += operators.

Do we need a second overloaded concatenation operator to allow concatenation of a `String` and a `char *`? No. The `const char *` conversion constructor converts a C-style string into a temporary `String` object, which then matches the existing overloaded concatenation operator. This is exactly what the compiler does when it encounters line 44 in Fig. 11.11. Again, C++ can perform such conversions only one level deep to facilitate a match. C++ can also perform an implicit compiler-defined conversion between fundamental types before it performs the conversion between a fundamental type and a class. Note that, when a temporary `String` object is created in this case, the conversion constructor and the destructor are called (see the output resulting from line 45, s1 += " to you", in Fig. 11.11). This is an example of function-call overhead that is hidden from the client of the class when temporary class objects are created and destroyed during implicit conversions. Similar overhead is generated by copy constructors in call-by-value parameter passing and in returning class objects by value.

> **Performance Tip 11.2**
>
> *Overloading the += concatenation operator with an additional version that takes a single argument of type* const char * *executes more efficiently than having only a version that takes a* String *argument. Without the* const char * *version of the += operator, a* const char * *argument would first be converted to a* String *object with class* String*'s conversion constructor, then the += operator that receives a* String *argument would be called to perform the concatenation.*

> **Software Engineering Observation 11.9**
>
> *Using implicit conversions with overloaded operators, rather than overloading operators for many different operand types, often requires less code, which makes a class easier to modify, maintain and debug.*

Overloaded Negation Operator

Line 22 of Fig. 11.9 declares the overloaded negation operator (defined in Fig. 11.10, lines 77–80). This operator determines whether an object of our String class is empty. For example, when the compiler sees the expression !string1, it generates the function call

```
string1.operator!()
```

This function simply returns the result of testing whether length is equal to zero.

Overloaded Equality and Relational Operators

Lines 23–24 of Fig. 11.9 declare the overloaded equality operator (defined in Fig. 11.10, lines 83–86) and the overloaded less-than operator (defined in Fig. 11.10, lines 89–92) for class String. These are similar, so let us discuss only one example, namely, overloading the == operator. When the compiler sees the expression string1 == string2, the compiler generates the member-function call

```
string1.operator==( string2 )
```

which returns true if string1 is equal to string2. Each of these operators uses function strcmp (from <cstring>) to compare the character strings in the String objects. Many C++ programmers advocate using some of the overloaded operator functions to implement others. So, the !=, >, <= and >= operators are implemented (Fig. 11.9, lines 27–48) in terms of operator== and operator<. For example, overloaded function operator>= (implemented at lines 45–48 in the header file) uses the overloaded < operator to determine whether one String object is greater than or equal to another. Note that the operator functions for !=, >, <= and >= are defined in the header file. The compiler inlines these definitions to eliminate the overhead of the extra function calls.

Software Engineering Observation 11.10

By implementing member functions using previously defined member functions, the programmer reuses code to reduce the amount of code that must be written and maintained.

Overloaded Subscript Operators

Lines 50–51 in the header file declare two overloaded subscript operators (defined in Fig. 11.10, lines 95–106 and 109–120, respectively)—one for non-const Strings and one for const Strings. When the compiler sees an expression like string1[0], the compiler generates the member-function call

```
string1.operator[]( 0 )
```

(using the appropriate version of operator[] based on whether the String is const). Each implementation of operator[] first validates the subscript to ensure that it is in range. If the subscript is out of range, each function prints an error message and terminates the program with a call to exit.[5] If the subscript is in range, the non-const version of operator[] returns a char & to the appropriate character of the String object; this char & may be used as an *lvalue* to modify the designated character of the String object. The const version of operator[] returns the appropriate character of the String object; this can be used only as an *rvalue* to read the value of the character.

---

5. Again, it is more appropriate when a subscript is out of range to "throw an exception" indicating the out-of-range subscript.

Error-Prevention Tip 11.2

*Returning a non-*const char *reference from an overloaded subscript operator in a* String *class is dangerous. For example, the client could use this reference to insert a null ('\0') anywhere in the string.*

Overloaded Function Call Operator

Line 52 of Fig. 11.9 declares the **overloaded function call operator** (defined in Fig. 11.10, lines 123–150). We overload this operator to select a substring from a String. The two integer parameters specify the start location and the length of the substring being selected from the String. If the start location is out of range or the substring length is negative, the operator simply returns an empty String. If the substring length is 0, then the substring is selected to the end of the String object. For example, suppose string1 is a String object containing the string "AEIOU". For the expression string1(2, 2), the compiler generates the member-function call

```
string1.operator()( 2, 2 )
```

When this call executes, it produces a String object containing the string "IO" and returns a copy of that object.

Overloading the function call operator () is powerful, because functions can take arbitrarily long and complex parameter lists. So we can use this capability for many interesting purposes. One such use of the function call operator is an alternate array-subscripting notation: Instead of using C's awkward double-square-bracket notation for pointer-based two-dimensional arrays, such as in a[b][c], some programmers prefer to overload the function call operator to enable the notation a(b, c). The overloaded function call operator must be a non-static member function. This operator is used only when the "function name" is an object of class String.

String Member Function **getLength**

Line 53 in Fig. 11.9 declares function getLength (defined in Fig. 11.10, lines 153–156), which returns the length of a String.

Notes on Our **String** *Class*

At this point, you should step through the code in main, examine the output window and check each use of an overloaded operator. As you study the output, pay special attention to the implicit constructor calls that are generated to create temporary String objects throughout the program. Many of these calls introduce additional overhead into the program that can be avoided if the class provides overloaded operators that take char * arguments. However, additional operator functions can make the class harder to maintain, modify and debug.

11.11 Overloading ++ and --

The prefix and postfix versions of the increment and decrement operators can all be overloaded. We will see how the compiler distinguishes between the prefix version and the postfix version of an increment or decrement operator.

To overload the increment operator to allow both prefix and postfix increment usage, each overloaded operator function must have a distinct signature, so that the compiler will be able to determine which version of ++ is intended. The prefix versions are overloaded exactly as any other prefix unary operator would be.

Overloading the Prefix Increment Operator

Suppose, for example, that we want to add 1 to the day in Date object d1. When the compiler sees the preincrementing expression ++d1, the compiler generates the member-function call

```
d1.operator++()
```

The prototype for this operator function would be

```
Date &operator++();
```

If the prefix increment operator is implemented as a global function, then, when the compiler sees the expression ++d1, the compiler generates the function call

```
operator++( d1 )
```

The prototype for this operator function would be declared in the Date class as

```
Date &operator++( Date & );
```

Overloading the Postfix Increment Operator

Overloading the postfix increment operator presents a challenge, because the compiler must be able to distinguish between the signatures of the overloaded prefix and postfix increment operator functions. The convention that has been adopted in C++ is that, when the compiler sees the postincrementing expression d1++, it generates the member-function call

```
d1.operator++( 0 )
```

The prototype for this function is

```
Date operator++( int )
```

The argument 0 is strictly a "dummy value" that enables the compiler to distinguish between the prefix and postfix increment operator functions.

If the postfix increment is implemented as a global function, then, when the compiler sees the expression d1++, the compiler generates the function call

```
operator++( d1, 0 )
```

The prototype for this function would be

```
Date operator++( Date &, int );
```

Once again, the 0 argument is used by the compiler to distinguish between the prefix and postfix increment operators implemented as global functions. Note that the postfix increment operator returns Date objects by value, whereas the prefix increment operator returns Date objects by reference, because the postfix increment operator typically returns a temporary object that contains the original value of the object before the increment occurred. C++ treats such objects as *rvalues*, which cannot be used on the left side of an assignment. The prefix increment operator returns the actual incremented object with its new value. Such an object can be used as an *lvalue* in a continuing expression.

Performance Tip 11.3

The extra object that is created by the postfix increment (or decrement) operator can result in a significant performance problem—especially when the operator is used in a loop. For this reason, you should use the postfix increment (or decrement) operator only when the logic of the program requires postincremnting (or postdecrementing).

Everything stated in this section for overloading prefix and postfix increment operators applies to overloading predecrement and postdecrement operators. Next, we examine a Date class with overloaded prefix and postfix increment operators.

11.12 Case Study: A Date Class

The program of Figs. 11.12–11.14 demonstrates a Date class. The class uses overloaded prefix and postfix increment operators to add 1 to the day in a Date object, while causing appropriate increments to the month and year if necessary. The Date header file (Fig. 11.12) specifies that Date's public interface includes an overloaded stream insertion operator (line 11), a default constructor (line 13), a setDate function (line 14), an overloaded prefix increment operator (line 15), an overloaded postfix increment operator (line 16), an overloaded += addition assignment operator (line 17), a function to test for leap years (line 18) and a function to determine whether a day is the last day of the month (line 19).

```cpp
1   // Fig. 11.12: Date.h
2   // Date class definition.
3   #ifndef DATE_H
4   #define DATE_H
5
6   #include <iostream>
7   using std::ostream;
8
9   class Date
10  {
11     friend ostream &operator<<( ostream &, const Date & );
12  public:
13     Date( int m = 1, int d = 1, int y = 1900 ); // default constructor
14     void setDate( int, int, int ); // set month, day, year
15     Date &operator++(); // prefix increment operator
16     Date operator++( int ); // postfix increment operator
17     const Date &operator+=( int ); // add days, modify object
18     bool leapYear( int ) const; // is date in a leap year?
19     bool endOfMonth( int ) const; // is date at the end of month?
20  private:
21     int month;
22     int day;
23     int year;
24
25     static const int days[]; // array of days per month
26     void helpIncrement(); // utility function for incrementing date
27  }; // end class Date
28
29  #endif
```

Fig. 11.12 | Date class definition with overloaded increment operators.

```
1   // Fig. 11.13: Date.cpp
2   // Date class member-function definitions.
3   #include <iostream>
4   #include "Date.h"
5
6   // initialize static member at file scope; one classwide copy
7   const int Date::days[] =
8      { 0, 31, 28, 31, 30, 31, 30, 31, 31, 30, 31, 30, 31 };
9
10  // Date constructor
11  Date::Date( int m, int d, int y )
12  {
13     setDate( m, d, y );
14  } // end Date constructor
15
16  // set month, day and year
17  void Date::setDate( int mm, int dd, int yy )
18  {
19     month = ( mm >= 1 && mm <= 12 ) ? mm : 1;
20     year = ( yy >= 1900 && yy <= 2100 ) ? yy : 1900;
21
22     // test for a leap year
23     if ( month == 2 && leapYear( year ) )
24        day = ( dd >= 1 && dd <= 29 ) ? dd : 1;
25     else
26        day = ( dd >= 1 && dd <= days[ month ] ) ? dd : 1;
27  } // end function setDate
28
29  // overloaded prefix increment operator
30  Date &Date::operator++()
31  {
32     helpIncrement(); // increment date
33     return *this; // reference return to create an lvalue
34  } // end function operator++
35
36  // overloaded postfix increment operator; note that the
37  // dummy integer parameter does not have a parameter name
38  Date Date::operator++( int )
39  {
40     Date temp = *this; // hold current state of object
41     helpIncrement();
42
43     // return unincremented, saved, temporary object
44     return temp; // value return; not a reference return
45  } // end function operator++
46
47  // add specified number of days to date
48  const Date &Date::operator+=( int additionalDays )
49  {
50     for ( int i = 0; i < additionalDays; i++ )
51        helpIncrement();
52
```

Fig. 11.13 | Date class member- and friend-function definitions. (Part 1 of 2.)

```
53        return *this; // enables cascading
54    } // end function operator+=
55
56    // if the year is a leap year, return true; otherwise, return false
57    bool Date::leapYear( int testYear ) const
58    {
59        if ( testYear % 400 == 0 ||
60           ( testYear % 100 != 0 && testYear % 4 == 0 ) )
61           return true; // a leap year
62        else
63           return false; // not a leap year
64    } // end function leapYear
65
66    // determine whether the day is the last day of the month
67    bool Date::endOfMonth( int testDay ) const
68    {
69        if ( month == 2 && leapYear( year ) )
70           return testDay == 29; // last day of Feb. in leap year
71        else
72           return testDay == days[ month ];
73    } // end function endOfMonth
74
75    // function to help increment the date
76    void Date::helpIncrement()
77    {
78        // day is not end of month
79        if ( !endOfMonth( day ) )
80           day++; // increment day
81        else
82           if ( month < 12 ) // day is end of month and month < 12
83           {
84              month++; // increment month
85              day = 1; // first day of new month
86           } // end if
87           else // last day of year
88           {
89              year++; // increment year
90              month = 1; // first month of new year
91              day = 1; // first day of new month
92           } // end else
93    } // end function helpIncrement
94
95    // overloaded output operator
96    ostream &operator<<( ostream &output, const Date &d )
97    {
98        static char *monthName[ 13 ] = { "", "January", "February",
99           "March", "April", "May", "June", "July", "August",
100          "September", "October", "November", "December" };
101       output << monthName[ d.month ] << ' ' << d.day << ", " << d.year;
102       return output; // enables cascading
103   } // end function operator<<
```

Fig. 11.13 | Date class member- and friend-function definitions. (Part 2 of 2.)

```cpp
1   // Fig. 11.14: fig11_14.cpp
2   // Date class test program.
3   #include <iostream>
4   using std::cout;
5   using std::endl;
6
7   #include "Date.h" // Date class definition
8
9   int main()
10  {
11     Date d1; // defaults to January 1, 1900
12     Date d2( 12, 27, 1992 ); // December 27, 1992
13     Date d3( 0, 99, 8045 ); // invalid date
14
15     cout << "d1 is " << d1 << "\nd2 is " << d2 << "\nd3 is " << d3;
16     cout << "\n\nd2 += 7 is " << ( d2 += 7 );
17
18     d3.setDate( 2, 28, 1992 );
19     cout << "\n\n  d3 is " << d3;
20     cout << "\n++d3 is " << ++d3 << " (leap year allows 29th)";
21
22     Date d4( 7, 13, 2002 );
23
24     cout << "\n\nTesting the prefix increment operator:\n"
25        << "  d4 is " << d4 << endl;
26     cout << "++d4 is " << ++d4 << endl;
27     cout << "  d4 is " << d4;
28
29     cout << "\n\nTesting the postfix increment operator:\n"
30        << "  d4 is " << d4 << endl;
31     cout << "d4++ is " << d4++ << endl;
32     cout << "  d4 is " << d4 << endl;
33     return 0;
34  } // end main
```

```
d1 is January 1, 1900
d2 is December 27, 1992
d3 is January 1, 1900

d2 += 7 is January 3, 1993

  d3 is February 28, 1992
++d3 is February 29, 1992 (leap year allows 29th)

Testing the prefix increment operator:
  d4 is July 13, 2002
++d4 is July 14, 2002
  d4 is July 14, 2002

Testing the postfix increment operator:
  d4 is July 14, 2002
d4++ is July 14, 2002
  d4 is July 15, 2002
```

Fig. 11.14 | Date class test program.

Function main (Fig. 11.14) creates three Date objects (lines 11–13)—d1 is initialized by default to January 1, 1900; d2 is initialized to December 27, 1992; and d3 is initialized to an invalid date. The Date constructor (defined in Fig. 11.13, lines 11–14) calls setDate to validate the month, day and year specified. An invalid month is set to 1, an invalid year is set to 1900 and an invalid day is set to 1.

Lines 15–16 of main output each of the constructed Date objects, using the overloaded stream insertion operator (defined in Fig. 11.13, lines 96–103). Line 16 of main uses the overloaded operator += to add seven days to d2. Line 18 uses function setDate to set d3 to February 28, 1992, which is a leap year. Then, line 20 preincrements d3 to show that the date increments properly to February 29. Next, line 22 creates a Date object, d4, which is initialized with the date July 13, 2002. Then line 26 increments d4 by 1 with the overloaded prefix increment operator. Lines 24–27 output d4 before and after the preincrement operation to confirm that it worked correctly. Finally, line 31 increments d4 with the overloaded postfix increment operator. Lines 29–32 output d4 before and after the postincrement operation to confirm that it worked correctly.

Overloading the prefix increment operator is straightforward. The prefix increment operator (defined in Fig. 11.13, lines 30–34) calls utility function helpIncrement (defined in Fig. 11.13, lines 76–93) to increment the date. This function deals with "wraparounds" or "carries" that occur when we increment the last day of the month. These carries require incrementing the month. If the month is already 12, then the year must also be incremented and the month must be set to 1. Function helpIncrement uses function endOfMonth to increment the day correctly.

The overloaded prefix increment operator returns a reference to the current Date object (i.e., the one that was just incremented). This occurs because the current object, *this, is returned as a Date &. This enables a preincremented Date object to be used as an *lvalue*, which is how the built-in prefix increment operator works for fundamental types.

Overloading the postfix increment operator (defined in Fig. 11.13, lines 38–45) is trickier. To emulate the effect of the postincrement, we must return an unincremented copy of the Date object. For example, that int variable x has the value 7, the statement

```
cout << x++ << endl;
```

outputs the original value of variable x. So we'd like our postfix increment operator to operate the same way on a Date object. On entry to operator++, we save the current object (*this) in temp (line 40). Next, we call helpIncrement to increment the current Date object. Then, line 44 returns the unincremented copy of the object previously stored in temp. Note that this function cannot return a reference to the local Date object temp, because a local variable is destroyed when the function in which it is declared exits. Thus, declaring the return type to this function as Date & would return a reference to an object that no longer exists. Returning a reference (or a pointer) to a local variable is a common error for which most compilers will issue a warning.

11.13 Standard Library Class string

In this chapter, you learned that you can build a String class (Figs. 11.9–11.11) that is better than the C-style, char * strings that C++ absorbed from C. You also learned that you can build an Array class (Figs. 11.6–11.8) that is better than the C-style, pointer-based arrays that C++ absorbed from C.

Building useful, reusable classes such as String and Array takes work. However, once such classes are tested and debugged, they can be reused by you, your colleagues, your company, many companies, an entire industry or even many industries (if they are placed in public or for-sale libraries). The designers of C++ did exactly that, building class string (which we have been using since Chapter 3) and class template vector (which we introduced in Chapter 7) into standard C++. These classes are available to anyone building applications with C++. As you will see in Chapter 22, Standard Template Library (STL), the C++ Standard Library provides several predefined class templates for use in your programs.

To close this chapter, we redo our String (Figs. 11.9–11.11) example, using the standard C++ string class. We rework our example to demonstrate similar functionality provided by standard class string. We also demonstrate three member functions of standard class string—empty, substr and at—that were not part of our String example. Function empty determines whether a string is empty, function substr returns a string that represents a portion of an existing string and function at returns the character at a specific index in a string (after checking that the index is in range). Chapter 18 presents class string in detail.

Standard Library Class *string*

The program of Fig. 11.15 reimplements the program of Fig. 11.11, using standard class string. As you will see in this example, class string provides all the functionality of our class String presented in Figs. 11.9–11.10. Class string is defined in header <string> (line 7) and belongs to namespace std (line 8).

```
 1   // Fig. 11.15: fig11_15.cpp
 2   // Standard Library string class test program.
 3   #include <iostream>
 4   using std::cout;
 5   using std::endl;
 6
 7   #include <string>
 8   using std::string;
 9
10   int main()
11   {
12      string s1( "happy" );
13      string s2( " birthday" );
14      string s3;
15
16      // test overloaded equality and relational operators
17      cout << "s1 is \"" << s1 << "\"; s2 is \"" << s2
18         << "\"; s3 is \"" << s3 << '\"'
19         << "\n\nThe results of comparing s2 and s1:"
20         << "\ns2 == s1 yields " << ( s2 == s1 ? "true" : "false" )
21         << "\ns2 != s1 yields " << ( s2 != s1 ? "true" : "false" )
22         << "\ns2 >  s1 yields " << ( s2 > s1 ? "true" : "false" )
23         << "\ns2 <  s1 yields " << ( s2 < s1 ? "true" : "false" )
24         << "\ns2 >= s1 yields " << ( s2 >= s1 ? "true" : "false" )
25         << "\ns2 <= s1 yields " << ( s2 <= s1 ? "true" : "false" );
26
```

Fig. 11.15 | Standard Library class string. (Part 1 of 3.)

```
27      // test string member-function empty
28      cout << "\n\nTesting s3.empty():" << endl;
29
30      if ( s3.empty() )
31      {
32         cout << "s3 is empty; assigning s1 to s3;" << endl;
33         s3 = s1; // assign s1 to s3
34         cout << "s3 is \"" << s3 << "\"";
35      } // end if
36
37      // test overloaded string concatenation operator
38      cout << "\n\ns1 += s2 yields s1 = ";
39      s1 += s2; // test overloaded concatenation
40      cout << s1;
41
42      // test overloaded string concatenation operator with C-style string
43      cout << "\n\ns1 += \" to you\" yields" << endl;
44      s1 += " to you";
45      cout << "s1 = " << s1 << "\n\n";
46
47      // test string member function substr
48      cout << "The substring of s1 starting at location 0 for\n"
49         << "14 characters, s1.substr(0, 14), is:\n"
50         << s1.substr( 0, 14 ) << "\n\n";
51
52      // test substr "to-end-of-string" option
53      cout << "The substring of s1 starting at\n"
54         << "location 15, s1.substr(15), is:\n"
55         << s1.substr( 15 ) << endl;
56
57      // test copy constructor
58      string *s4Ptr = new string( s1 );
59      cout << "\n*s4Ptr = " << *s4Ptr << "\n\n";
60
61      // test assignment (=) operator with self-assignment
62      cout << "assigning *s4Ptr to *s4Ptr" << endl;
63      *s4Ptr = *s4Ptr;
64      cout << "*s4Ptr = " << *s4Ptr << endl;
65
66      // test destructor
67      delete s4Ptr;
68
69      // test using subscript operator to create lvalue
70      s1[ 0 ] = 'H';
71      s1[ 6 ] = 'B';
72      cout << "\ns1 after s1[0] = 'H' and s1[6] = 'B' is: "
73         << s1 << "\n\n";
74
75      // test subscript out of range with string member function "at"
76      cout << "Attempt to assign 'd' to s1.at( 30 ) yields:" << endl;
77      s1.at( 30 ) = 'd'; // ERROR: subscript out of range
78      return 0;
79   } // end main
```

Fig. 11.15 | Standard Library class `string`. (Part 2 of 3.)

```
s1 is "happy"; s2 is " birthday"; s3 is ""

The results of comparing s2 and s1:
s2 == s1 yields false
s2 != s1 yields true
s2 >  s1 yields false
s2 <  s1 yields true
s2 >= s1 yields false
s2 <= s1 yields true

Testing s3.empty():
s3 is empty; assigning s1 to s3;
s3 is "happy"

s1 += s2 yields s1 = happy birthday

s1 += " to you" yields
s1 = happy birthday to you

The substring of s1 starting at location 0 for
14 characters, s1.substr(0, 14), is:
happy birthday

The substring of s1 starting at
location 15, s1.substr(15), is:
to you

*s4Ptr = happy birthday to you

assigning *s4Ptr to *s4Ptr
*s4Ptr = happy birthday to you

s1 after s1[0] = 'H' and s1[6] = 'B' is: Happy Birthday to you

Attempt to assign 'd' to s1.at( 30 ) yields:

abnormal program termination
```

Fig. 11.15 | Standard Library class string. (Part 3 of 3.)

Lines 12–14 create three string objects—s1 is initialized with the literal "happy", s2 is initialized with the literal " birthday" and s3 uses the default string constructor to create an empty string. Lines 17–18 output these three objects, using cout and operator <<, which the string class designers overloaded to handle string objects. Then lines 19–25 show the results of comparing s2 to s1 by using class string's overloaded equality and relational operators.

Our class String (Figs. 11.9–11.10) provided an overloaded operator! that tested a String to determine whether it was empty. Standard class string does not provide this functionality as an overloaded operator; instead, it provides member function *empty*, which we demonstrate on line 30. Member function empty returns true if the string is empty; otherwise, it returns false.

Line 33 demonstrates class string's overloaded assignment operator by assigning s1 to s3. Line 34 outputs s3 to demonstrate that the assignment worked correctly.

Line 39 demonstrates class `string`'s overloaded += operator for string concatenation. In this case, the contents of `s2` are appended to `s1`. Then line 40 outputs the resulting string that is stored in `s1`. Line 44 demonstrates that a C-style string literal can be appended to a `string` object by using operator +=. Line 45 displays the result.

Our class `String` (Figs. 11.9–11.10) provided overloaded `operator()` to obtain substrings. Standard class `string` does not provide this functionality as an overloaded operator; instead, it provides member function `substr` (lines 50 and 55). The call to `substr` in line 50 obtains a 14-character substring (specified by the second argument) of `s1` starting at position 0 (specified by the first argument). The call to `substr` in line 55 obtains a substring starting from position 15 of `s1`. When the second argument is not specified, `substr` returns the remainder of the `string` on which it is called.

Line 58 dynamically allocates a `string` object and initializes it with a copy of `s1`. This results in a call to class `string`'s copy constructor. Line 63 uses class `string`'s overloaded = operator to demonstrate that it handles self-assignment properly.

Lines 70–71 used class `string`'s overloaded [] operator to create *lvalues* that enable new characters to replace existing characters in `s1`. Line 73 outputs the new value of `s1`. In our class `String` (Figs. 11.9–11.10), the overloaded [] operator performed bounds checking to determine whether the subscript it received as an argument was a valid subscript in the string. If the subscript was invalid, the operator printed an error message and terminated the program. Standard class `string`'s overloaded [] operator does not perform any bounds checking. Therefore, the programmer must ensure that operations using standard class `string`'s overloaded [] operator do not accidentally manipulate elements outside the bounds of the `string`. Standard class `string` does provide bounds checking in its member function *at*, which "throws an exception" if its argument is an invalid subscript. By default, this causes a C++ program to terminate.[6] If the subscript is valid, function *at* returns the character at the specified location as a modifiable *lvalue* or an unmodifiable *lvalue* (i.e., a `const` reference), depending on the context in which the call appears. Line 77 demonstrates a call to function *at* with an invalid subscript.

11.14 explicit Constructors

In Section 11.8 and Section 11.9, we discussed that any single-argument constructor can be used by the compiler to perform an implicit conversion—the type received by the constructor is converted to an object of the class in which the constructor is defined. The conversion is automatic and the programmer need not use a cast operator. In some situations, implicit conversions are undesirable or error-prone. For example, our `Array` class in Fig. 11.6 defines a constructor that takes a single `int` argument. The intent of this constructor is to create an `Array` object containing the number of elements specified by the `int` argument. However, this constructor can be misused by the compiler to perform an implicit conversion.

 Common Programming Error 11.9

Unfortunately, the compiler might use implicit conversions in cases that you do not expect, resulting in ambiguous expressions that generate compilation errors or resulting in execution-time logic errors.

---

6. Again, Chapter 16, Exception Handling, demonstrates how to "catch" such exceptions.

Accidentally Using a Single-Argument Constructor as a Conversion Constructor
The program (Fig. 11.16) uses the Array class of Figs. 11.6–11.7 to demonstrate an improper implicit conversion.

Line 13 in main instantiates Array object integers1 and calls the single argument constructor with the int value 7 to specify the number of elements in the Array. Recall from Fig. 11.7 that the Array constructor that receives an int argument initializes all the array elements to 0. Line 14 calls function outputArray (defined in lines 20–24), which receives as its argument a const Array & to an Array. The function outputs the number of elements in its Array argument and the contents of the Array. In this case, the size of the Array is 7, so seven 0s are output.

Line 15 calls function outputArray with the int value 3 as an argument. However, this program does not contain a function called outputArray that takes an int argument. So, the compiler determines whether class Array provides a conversion constructor that can convert an int into an Array. Since any constructor that receives a single argument is considered to be a conversion constructor, the compiler assumes the Array constructor that receives a single int is a conversion constructor and uses it to convert the argument 3 into a temporary Array object that contains three elements. Then, the compiler passes the

```
1    // Fig. 11.16: Fig11_16.cpp
2    // Driver for simple class Array.
3    #include <iostream>
4    using std::cout;
5    using std::endl;
6
7    #include "Array.h"
8
9    void outputArray( const Array & ); // prototype
10
11   int main()
12   {
13      Array integers1( 7 ); // 7-element array
14      outputArray( integers1 ); // output Array integers1
15      outputArray( 3 ); // convert 3 to an Array and output Array's contents
16      return 0;
17   } // end main
18
19   // print Array contents
20   void outputArray( const Array &arrayToOutput )
21   {
22      cout << "The Array received has " << arrayToOutput.getSize()
23         << " elements. The contents are:\n" << arrayToOutput << endl;
24   } // end outputArray
```

```
The Array received has 7 elements. The contents are:
           0           0           0           0
           0           0           0

The Array received has 3 elements. The contents are:
           0           0           0
```

Fig. 11.16 | Single-argument constructors and implicit conversions.

temporary Array object to function `outputArray` to output the Array's contents. Thus, even though we do not explicitly provide an `outputArray` function that receives an `int` argument, the compiler is able to compile line 15. The output shows the contents of the three-element Array containing 0s.

Preventing Accidental Use of a Single-Argument Constructor as a Conversion Constructor

C++ provides the keyword `explicit` to suppress implicit conversions via conversion constructors when such conversions should not be allowed. A constructor that is declared `explicit` cannot be used in an implicit conversion. Figure 11.17 declares an `explicit` constructor in class Array. The only modification to `Array.h` was the addition of the key-

```cpp
1   // Fig. 11.17: Array.h
2   // Array class for storing arrays of integers.
3   #ifndef ARRAY_H
4   #define ARRAY_H
5
6   #include <iostream>
7   using std::ostream;
8   using std::istream;
9
10  class Array
11  {
12     friend ostream &operator<<( ostream &, const Array & );
13     friend istream &operator>>( istream &, Array & );
14  public:
15     explicit Array( int = 10 ); // default constructor
16     Array( const Array & ); // copy constructor
17     ~Array(); // destructor
18     int getSize() const; // return size
19
20     const Array &operator=( const Array & ); // assignment operator
21     bool operator==( const Array & ) const; // equality operator
22
23     // inequality operator; returns opposite of == operator
24     bool operator!=( const Array &right ) const
25     {
26        return ! ( *this == right ); // invokes Array::operator==
27     } // end function operator!=
28
29     // subscript operator for non-const objects returns lvalue
30     int &operator[]( int );
31
32     // subscript operator for const objects returns rvalue
33     const int &operator[]( int ) const;
34  private:
35     int size; // pointer-based array size
36     int *ptr; // pointer to first element of pointer-based array
37  }; // end class Array
38
39  #endif
```

Fig. 11.17 | Array class definition with `explicit` constructor.

word explicit to the declaration of the single-argument constructor at line 15. No modifications are required to the source-code file containing class Array's member-function definitions.

Figure 11.18 presents a slightly modified version of the program in Fig. 11.16. When this program is compiled, the compiler produces an error message indicating that the integer value passed to outputArray at line 15 cannot be converted to a const Array &. The compiler error message is shown in the output window. Line 16 demonstrates how the explicit constructor can be used to create a temporary Array of 3 elements and pass it to function outputArray.

Common Programming Error 11.10

Attempting to invoke an explicit constructor for an implicit conversion is a compilation error.

Common Programming Error 11.11

Using the explicit keyword on data members or member functions other than a single-argument constructor is a compilation error.

```
1   // Fig. 11.18: Fig11_18.cpp
2   // Driver for simple class Array.
3   #include <iostream>
4   using std::cout;
5   using std::endl;
6
7   #include "Array.h"
8
9   void outputArray( const Array & ); // prototype
10
11  int main()
12  {
13     Array integers1( 7 ); // 7-element array
14     outputArray( integers1 ); // output Array integers1
15     outputArray( 3 ); // convert 3 to an Array and output Array's contents
16     outputArray( Array( 3 ) ); // explicit single-argument constructor call
17     return 0;
18  } // end main
19
20  // print array contents
21  void outputArray( const Array &arrayToOutput )
22  {
23     cout << "The Array received has " << arrayToOutput.getSize()
24        << " elements. The contents are:\n" << arrayToOutput << endl;
25  } // end outputArray
```

```
c:\cpphtp5_examples\ch11\Fig11_17_18\Fig11_18.cpp(15) : error C2664:
   'outputArray' : cannot convert parameter 1 from 'int' to 'const Array &'
      Reason: cannot convert from 'int' to 'const Array'
      Constructor for class 'Array' is declared 'explicit'
```

Fig. 11.18 | Demonstrating an explicit constructor.

Error-Prevention Tip 11.3

Use the explicit *keyword on single-argument constructors that should not be used by the compiler to perform implicit conversions.*

Summary

- C++ enables the programmer to overload most operators to be sensitive to the context in which they are used—the compiler generates the appropriate code based on the context (in particular, the types of the operands).

- Many of C++'s operators can be overloaded to work with user-defined types.

- One example of an overloaded operator built into C++ is operator <<, which is used both as the stream insertion operator and as the bitwise left-shift operator. Similarly, >> is also overloaded; it is used both as the stream extraction operator and as the bitwise right-shift operator. Both of these operators are overloaded in the C++ Standard Library.

- The C++ language itself overloads + and -. These operators perform differently, depending on their context in integer arithmetic, floating-point arithmetic and pointer arithmetic.

- The jobs performed by overloaded operators can also be performed by function calls, but operator notation is often clearer and more familiar to programmers.

- An operator is overloaded by writing a non-static member-function definition or global function definition in which the function name is the keyword operator followed by the symbol for the operator being overloaded.

- When operators are overloaded as member functions, they must be non-static, because they must be called on an object of the class and operate on that object.

- To use an operator on class objects, that operator *must* be overloaded—with three exceptions: the assignment operator (=), the address operator (&) and the comma operator (,).

- You cannot change the precedence and associativity of an operator by overloading.

- You cannot change the "arity" of an operator (i.e., the number of operands an operator takes).

- You cannot create new operators; only existing operators can be overloaded.

- You cannot change the meaning of how an operator works on objects of fundamental types.

- Overloading an assignment operator and an addition operator for a class does not imply that the += operator is also overloaded. Such behavior can be achieved only by explicitly overloading operator += for that class.

- Operator functions can be member functions or global functions; global functions are often made friends for performance reasons. Member functions use the this pointer implicitly to obtain one of their class object arguments (the left operand for binary operators). Arguments for both operands of a binary operator must be explicitly listed in a global function call.

- When overloading (), [], -> or any of the assignment operators, the operator overloading function must be declared as a class member. For the other operators, the operator overloading functions can be class members or global functions.

- When an operator function is implemented as a member function, the leftmost (or only) operand must be an object (or a reference to an object) of the operator's class.

- If the left operand must be an object of a different class or a fundamental type, this operator function must be implemented as a global function.

- A global operator function can be made a `friend` of a class if that function must access `private` or `protected` members of that class directly.

- The overloaded stream insertion operator (`<<`) is used in an expression in which the left operand has type `ostream &`. For this reason, it must be overloaded as a global function. To be a member function, operator `<<` would have to be a member of the `ostream` class, but this is not possible, since we are not allowed to modify C++ Standard Library classes. Similarly, the overloaded stream extraction operator (`>>`) must be a global function.

- Another reason to choose a global function to overload an operator is to enable the operator to be commutative.

- When used with `cin` and `strings`, `setw` restricts the number of characters read to the number of characters specified by its argument.

- `istream` member function `ignore` discards the specified number of characters in the input stream (one character by default).

- Overloaded input and output operators are declared as `friends` if they need to access non-`public` class members directly for performance reasons.

- A unary operator for a class can be overloaded as a non-`static` member function with no arguments or as a global function with one argument; that argument must be either an object of the class or a reference to an object of the class.

- Member functions that implement overloaded operators must be non-`static` so that they can access the non-`static` data in each object of the class.

- A binary operator can be overloaded as a non-`static` member function with one argument or as a global function with two arguments (one of those arguments must be either a class object or a reference to a class object).

- A copy constructor initializes a new object of a class by copying the members of an existing object of that class. When objects of a class contain dynamically allocated memory, the class should provide a copy constructor to ensure that each copy of an object has its own separate copy of the dynamically allocated memory. Typically, such a class would also provide a destructor and an overloaded assignment operator.

- The implementation of member function `operator=` should test for self-assignment, in which an object is being assigned to itself.

- The compiler calls the `const` version of `operator[]` when the subscript operator is used on a `const` object and calls the non-`const` version of the operator when it is used on a non-`const` object.

- The array subscript operator (`[]`) is not restricted for use with arrays. It can be used to select elements from other types of container classes. Also, with overloading, the index values no longer need to be integers; characters or strings could be used, for example.

- The compiler cannot know in advance how to convert among user-defined types, and between user-defined types and fundamental types, so the programmer must specify how to do this. Such conversions can be performed with conversion constructors—single-argument constructors that turn objects of other types (including fundamental types) into objects of a particular class.

- A conversion operator (also called a cast operator) can be used to convert an object of one class into an object of another class or into an object of a fundamental type. Such a conversion operator must be a non-`static` member function. Overloaded cast-operator functions can be defined for converting objects of user-defined types into fundamental types or into objects of other user-defined types.

- An overloaded cast operator function does not specify a return type—the return type is the type to which the object is being converted.

- One of the nice features of cast operators and conversion constructors is that, when necessary, the compiler can call these functions implicitly to create temporary objects.

- Any single-argument constructor can be thought of as a conversion constructor.

- Overloading the function call operator () is powerful, because functions can take arbitrarily long and complex parameter lists.

- The prefix and postfix increment and decrement operator can all be overloaded.

- To overload the increment operator to allow both preincrement and postincrement usage, each overloaded operator function must have a distinct signature, so that the compiler will be able to determine which version of ++ is intended. The prefix versions are overloaded exactly as any other prefix unary operator would be. Providing a unique signature to the postfix increment operator is accomplished by providing a second argument, which must be of type int. This argument is not supplied in the client code. It is used implicitly by the compiler to distinguish between the prefix and postfix versions of the increment operator.

- Standard class string is defined in header <string> and belongs to namespace std.

- Class string provides many overloaded operators, including equality, relational, assignment, addition assignment (for concatenation) and subscript operators.

- Class string provides member function empty, which returns true if the string is empty; otherwise, it returns false.

- Standard class string member function substr obtains a substring of a length specified by the second argument, starting at the position specified by the first argument. When the second argument is not specified, substr returns the remainder of the string on which it is called.

- Class string's overloaded [] operator does not perform any bounds checking. Therefore, the programmer must ensure that operations using standard class string's overloaded [] operator do not accidentally manipulate elements outside the bounds of the string.

- Standard class string provides bounds checking with member function at, which "throws an exception" if its argument is an invalid subscript. By default, this causes a C++ program to terminate. If the subscript is valid, function at returns the character at the specified location as an *lvalue* or an *rvalue*, depending on the context in which the call appears.

- C++ provides the keyword explicit to suppress implicit conversions via conversion constructors when such conversions should not be allowed. A constructor that is declared explicit cannot be used in an implicit conversion.

Terminology

"arity" of an operator
Array class
assignment-operator functions
associativity not changed by overloading
cast operator function
commutative operation
const version of operator[]
conversion between fundamental and class types
conversion constructor
conversion operator
copy constructor

empty member function of string
explicit constructor
function call operator ()
global function to overload an operator
ignore member function of istream
implicit user-defined conversions
lvalue ("left value")
operator function
operator keyword
operator overloading
operator!

operator!=	overloaded < operator
operator()	overloaded << operator
operator+	overloaded <= operator
operator++	overloaded == operator
operator++(int)	overloaded > operator
operator<	overloaded >= operator
operator<<	overloaded >> operator
operator=	overloaded assignment (=) operator
operator==	overloaded [] operator
operator>=	overloaded stream insertion and stream extrac-
operator>>	tion operators
operator[]	overloading a binary operator
overloadable operators	overloading a unary operator
overloaded ! operator	self-assignment
overloaded != operator	string (standard C++ class)
overloaded () operator	string concatenation
overloaded + operator	substr member function of string
overloaded ++ operator	substring
overloaded ++(int) operator	user-defined conversion
overloaded += operator	user-defined type

Self-Review Exercises

11.1 Fill in the blanks in each of the following:

    a) Suppose a and b are integer variables and we form the sum a + b. Now suppose c and d are floating-point variables and we form the sum c + d. The two + operators here are clearly being used for different purposes. This is an example of _____.

    b) Keyword _____ introduces an overloaded-operator function definition.

    c) To use operators on class objects, they must be overloaded, with the exception of operators _____, _____ and _____.

    d) The _____, _____ and _____ of an operator cannot be changed by overloading the operator.

11.2 Explain the multiple meanings of the operators << and >> in C++.

11.3 In what context might the name operator/ be used in C++?

11.4 (True/False) In C++, only existing operators can be overloaded.

11.5 How does the precedence of an overloaded operator in C++ compare with the precedence of the original operator?

Answers to Self-Review Exercises

11.1 a) operator overloading. b) operator. c) assignment (=), address (&), comma (,). d) precedence, associativity, "arity."

11.2 Operator >> is both the right-shift operator and the stream extraction operator, depending on its context. Operator << is both the left-shift operator and the stream insertion operator, depending on its context.

11.3 For operator overloading: It would be the name of a function that would provide an overloaded version of the / operator for a specific class.

11.4 True.

11.5   The precedence is identical.

Exercises

11.6   Give as many examples as you can of operator overloading implicit in C++. Give a reasonable example of a situation in which you might want to overload an operator explicitly in C++.

11.7   The operators that cannot be overloaded are _____, _____, _____ and _____.

11.8   String concatenation requires two operands—the two strings that are to be concatenated. In the text, we showed how to implement an overloaded concatenation operator that concatenates the second `String` object to the right of the first `String` object, thus modifying the first `String` object. In some applications, it is desirable to produce a concatenated `String` object without modifying the `String` arguments. Implement `operator+` to allow operations such as

```
string1 = string2 + string3;
```

11.9   *(Ultimate operator overloading exercise)* To appreciate the care that should go into selecting operators for overloading, list each of C++'s overloadable operators, and for each, list a possible meaning (or several, if appropriate) for each of several classes you have studied in this text. We suggest you try:
   a)   Array
   b)   Stack
   c)   String

After doing this, comment on which operators seem to have meaning for a wide variety of classes. Which operators seem to be of little value for overloading? Which operators seem ambiguous?

11.10   Now work the process described in Exercise 11.9 in reverse. List each of C++'s overloadable operators. For each, list what you feel is perhaps the "ultimate operation" the operator should be used to represent. If there are several excellent operations, list them all.

11.11   One nice example of overloading the function call operator () is to allow another form of double-array subscripting popular in some programming languages. Instead of saying

```
chessBoard[ row ][ column ]
```

for an array of objects, overload the function call operator to allow the alternate form

```
chessBoard( row, column )
```

Create a class `DoubleSubscriptedArray` that has similar features to class `Array` in Figs. 11.6–11.7. At construction time, the class should be able to create an array of any number of rows and any number of columns. The class should supply `operator()` to perform double-subscripting operations. For example, in a 3-by-5 `DoubleSubscriptedArray` called a, the user could write a(1, 3) to access the element at row 1 and column 3. Remember that `operator()` can receive any number of arguments (see class `String` in Figs. 11.9–11.10 for an example of `operator()`). The underlying representation of the double-subscripted array should be a single-subscripted array of integers with *rows * columns* number of elements. Function `operator()` should perform the proper pointer arithmetic to access each element of the array. There should be two versions of `operator()`—one that returns `int &` (so that an element of a `DoubleSubscriptedArray` can be used as an *lvalue*) and one that returns `const int &` (so that an element of a `const DoubleSubscriptedArray` can be used only as an *rvalue*). The class should also provide the following operators: ==, !=, =, << (for outputting the array in row and column format) and >> (for inputting the entire array contents).

11.12   Overload the subscript operator to return the largest element of a collection, the second largest, the third largest, and so on.

11.13 Consider class `Complex` shown in Figs. 11.19–11.21. The class enables operations on so-called *complex numbers*. These are numbers of the form realPart + imaginaryPart $* i$, where i has the value $\sqrt{-1}$

a) Modify the class to enable input and output of complex numbers through the overloaded >> and << operators, respectively (you should remove the `print` function from the class).

b) Overload the multiplication operator to enable multiplication of two complex numbers as in algebra.

c) Overload the == and != operators to allow comparisons of complex numbers.

```cpp
// Fig. 11.19: Complex.h
// Complex class definition.
#ifndef COMPLEX_H
#define COMPLEX_H

class Complex
{
public:
   Complex( double = 0.0, double = 0.0 ); // constructor
   Complex operator+( const Complex & ) const; // addition
   Complex operator-( const Complex & ) const; // subtraction
   void print() const; // output
private:
   double real; // real part
   double imaginary; // imaginary part
}; // end class Complex

#endif
```

Fig. 11.19 | `Complex` class definition.

```cpp
// Fig. 11.20: Complex.cpp
// Complex class member-function definitions.
#include <iostream>
using std::cout;

#include "Complex.h" // Complex class definition

// Constructor
Complex::Complex( double realPart, double imaginaryPart )
   : real( realPart ),
     imaginary( imaginaryPart )
{
   // empty body
} // end Complex constructor

// addition operator
Complex Complex::operator+( const Complex &operand2 ) const
{
   return Complex( real + operand2.real,
```

Fig. 11.20 | `Complex` class member-function definitions. (Part 1 of 2.)

```
20          imaginary + operand2.imaginary );
21   } // end function operator+
22
23   // subtraction operator
24   Complex Complex::operator-( const Complex &operand2 ) const
25   {
26      return Complex( real - operand2.real,
27          imaginary - operand2.imaginary );
28   } // end function operator-
29
30   // display a Complex object in the form: (a, b)
31   void Complex::print() const
32   {
33      cout << '(' << real << ", " << imaginary << ')';
34   } // end function print
```

Fig. 11.20 | Complex class member-function definitions. (Part 2 of 2.)

```
1    // Fig. 11.21: fig11_21.cpp
2    // Complex class test program.
3    #include <iostream>
4    using std::cout;
5    using std::endl;
6
7    #include "Complex.h"
8
9    int main()
10   {
11      Complex x;
12      Complex y( 4.3, 8.2 );
13      Complex z( 3.3, 1.1 );
14
15      cout << "x: ";
16      x.print();
17      cout << "\ny: ";
18      y.print();
19      cout << "\nz: ";
20      z.print();
21
22      x = y + z;
23      cout << "\n\nx = y + z:" << endl;
24      x.print();
25      cout << " = ";
26      y.print();
27      cout << " + ";
28      z.print();
29
30      x = y - z;
31      cout << "\n\nx = y - z:" << endl;
32      x.print();
33      cout << " = ";
34      y.print();
35      cout << " - ";
```

Fig. 11.21 | Complex numbers. (Part 1 of 2.)

```
36        z.print();
37        cout << endl;
38        return 0;
39   } // end main
```

```
x: (0, 0)
y: (4.3, 8.2)
z: (3.3, 1.1)

x = y + z:
(7.6, 9.3) = (4.3, 8.2) + (3.3, 1.1)

x = y - z:
(1, 7.1) = (4.3, 8.2) - (3.3, 1.1)
```

Fig. 11.21 | Complex numbers. (Part 2 of 2.)

11.14 A machine with 32-bit integers can represent integers in the range of approximately −2 billion to +2 billion. This fixed-size restriction is rarely troublesome, but there are applications in which we would like to be able to use a much wider range of integers. This is what C++ was built to do, namely, create powerful new data types. Consider class HugeInt of Figs. 11.22–11.24. Study the class carefully, then answer the following:

    a) Describe precisely how it operates.
    b) What restrictions does the class have?
    c) Overload the * multiplication operator.
    d) Overload the / division operator.
    e) Overload all the relational and equality operators.

[*Note:* We do not show an assignment operator or copy constructor for class HugeInteger, because the assignment operator and copy constructor provided by the compiler are capable of copying the entire array data member properly.]

```
 1   // Fig. 11.22: Hugeint.h
 2   // HugeInt class definition.
 3   #ifndef HUGEINT_H
 4   #define HUGEINT_H
 5
 6   #include <iostream>
 7   using std::ostream;
 8
 9   class HugeInt
10   {
11      friend ostream &operator<<( ostream &, const HugeInt & );
12   public:
13      HugeInt( long = 0 ); // conversion/default constructor
14      HugeInt( const char * ); // conversion constructor
15
16      // addition operator; HugeInt + HugeInt
17      HugeInt operator+( const HugeInt & ) const;
18
19      // addition operator; HugeInt + int
```

Fig. 11.22 | HugeInt class definition. (Part 1 of 2.)

```
20      HugeInt operator+( int ) const;
21
22      // addition operator;
23      // HugeInt + string that represents large integer value
24      HugeInt operator+( const char * ) const;
25   private:
26      short integer[ 30 ];
27   }; // end class HugetInt
28
29   #endif
```

Fig. 11.22 | HugeInt class definition. (Part 2 of 2.)

11.15 Create a class RationalNumber (fractions) with the following capabilities:
a) Create a constructor that prevents a 0 denominator in a fraction, reduces or simplifies fractions that are not in reduced form and avoids negative denominators.
b) Overload the addition, subtraction, multiplication and division operators for this class.
c) Overload the relational and equality operators for this class.

11.16 Study the C string-handling library functions and implement each of the functions as part of class String (Figs. 11.9–11.10). Then, use these functions to perform text manipulations.

11.17 Develop class Polynomial. The internal representation of a Polynomial is an array of terms. Each term contains a coefficient and an exponent. The term

$$2x^4$$

has the coefficient 2 and the exponent 4. Develop a complete class containing proper constructor and destructor functions as well as *set* and *get* functions. The class should also provide the following overloaded operator capabilities:
a) Overload the addition operator (+) to add two Polynomials.
b) Overload the subtraction operator (-) to subtract two Polynomials.
c) Overload the assignment operator to assign one Polynomial to another.
d) Overload the multiplication operator (*) to multiply two Polynomials.
e) Overload the addition assignment operator (+=), subtraction assignment operator (-=), and multiplication assignment operator (*=).

```
1    // Fig. 11.23: Hugeint.cpp
2    // HugeInt member-function and friend-function definitions.
3    #include <cctype> // isdigit function prototype
4    #include <cstring> // strlen function prototype
5    #include "Hugeint.h" // HugeInt class definition
6
7    // default constructor; conversion constructor that converts
8    // a long integer into a HugeInt object
9    HugeInt::HugeInt( long value )
10   {
11      // initialize array to zero
12      for ( int i = 0; i <= 29; i++ )
13         integer[ i ] = 0;
14
15      // place digits of argument into array
16      for ( int j = 29; value != 0 && j >= 0; j-- )
```

Fig. 11.23 | HugeInt class member-function and friend-function definitions. (Part 1 of 3.)

```
17        {
18           integer[ j ] = value % 10;
19           value /= 10;
20        } // end for
21     } // end HugeInt default/conversion constructor
22
23     // conversion constructor that converts a character string
24     // representing a large integer into a HugeInt object
25     HugeInt::HugeInt( const char *string )
26     {
27        // initialize array to zero
28        for ( int i = 0; i <= 29; i++ )
29           integer[ i ] = 0;
30
31        // place digits of argument into array
32        int length = strlen( string );
33
34        for ( int j = 30 - length, k = 0; j <= 29; j++, k++ )
35
36           if ( isdigit( string[ k ] ) )
37              integer[ j ] = string[ k ] - '0';
38     } // end HugeInt conversion constructor
39
40     // addition operator; HugeInt + HugeInt
41     HugeInt HugeInt::operator+( const HugeInt &op2 ) const
42     {
43        HugeInt temp; // temporary result
44        int carry = 0;
45
46        for ( int i = 29; i >= 0; i-- )
47        {
48           temp.integer[ i ] =
49              integer[ i ] + op2.integer[ i ] + carry;
50
51           // determine whether to carry a 1
52           if ( temp.integer[ i ] > 9 )
53           {
54              temp.integer[ i ] %= 10;   // reduce to 0-9
55              carry = 1;
56           } // end if
57           else // no carry
58              carry = 0;
59        } // end for
60
61        return temp; // return copy of temporary object
62     } // end function operator+
63
64     // addition operator; HugeInt + int
65     HugeInt HugeInt::operator+( int op2 ) const
66     {
67        // convert op2 to a HugeInt, then invoke
68        // operator+ for two HugeInt objects
69        return *this + HugeInt( op2 );
70     } // end function operator+
```

Fig. 11.23 | HugeInt class member-function and friend-function definitions. (Part 2 of 3.)

```
71
72   // addition operator;
73   // HugeInt + string that represents large integer value
74   HugeInt HugeInt::operator+( const char *op2 ) const
75   {
76      // convert op2 to a HugeInt, then invoke
77      // operator+ for two HugeInt objects
78      return *this + HugeInt( op2 );
79   } // end operator+
80
81   // overloaded output operator
82   ostream& operator<<( ostream &output, const HugeInt &num )
83   {
84      int i;
85
86      for ( i = 0; ( num.integer[ i ] == 0 ) && ( i <= 29 ); i++ )
87         ; // skip leading zeros
88
89      if ( i == 30 )
90         output << 0;
91      else
92
93         for ( ; i <= 29; i++ )
94            output << num.integer[ i ];
95
96      return output;
97   } // end function operator<<
```

Fig. 11.23 | HugeInt class member-function and friend-function definitions. (Part 3 of 3.)

11.18 In the program of Figs. 11.3–11.5, Fig. 11.4 contains the comment "overloaded stream insertion operator; cannot be a member function if we would like to invoke it with cout << somePhoneNumber;." Actually, the stream insertion operator could be a PhoneNumber class member function if we were willing to invoke it either as somePhoneNumber.operator<<(cout); or as some-PhoneNumber << cout;. Rewrite the program of Fig. 11.5 with the overloaded stream insertion operator<< as a member function and try the two preceding statements in the program to demonstrate that they work.

```
1    // Fig. 11.24: fig11_24.cpp
2    // HugeInt test program.
3    #include <iostream>
4    using std::cout;
5    using std::endl;
6
7    #include "Hugeint.h"
8
9    int main()
10   {
11      HugeInt n1( 7654321 );
12      HugeInt n2( 7891234 );
13      HugeInt n3( "99999999999999999999999999999" );
14      HugeInt n4( "1" );
```

Fig. 11.24 | Huge integers. (Part 1 of 2.)

```
15        HugeInt n5;
16
17        cout << "n1 is " << n1 << "\nn2 is " << n2
18           << "\nn3 is " << n3 << "\nn4 is " << n4
19           << "\nn5 is " << n5 << "\n\n";
20
21        n5 = n1 + n2;
22        cout << n1 << " + " << n2 << " = " << n5 << "\n\n";
23
24        cout << n3 << " + " << n4 << "\n= " << ( n3 + n4 ) << "\n\n";
25
26        n5 = n1 + 9;
27        cout << n1 << " + " << 9 << " = " << n5 << "\n\n";
28
29        n5 = n2 + "10000";
30        cout << n2 << " + " << "10000" << " = " << n5 << endl;
31        return 0;
32    } // end main
```

```
n1 is 7654321
n2 is 7891234
n3 is 99999999999999999999999999999
n4 is 1
n5 is 0

7654321 + 7891234 = 15545555

99999999999999999999999999999 + 1
= 100000000000000000000000000000

7654321 + 9 = 7654330

7891234 + 10000 = 7901234
```

Fig. 11.24 | Huge integers. (Part 2 of 2.)

12

Object-Oriented Programming: Inheritance

OBJECTIVES

In this chapter you will learn:

- To create classes by inheriting from existing classes.
- How inheritance promotes software reuse.
- The notions of base classes and derived classes and the relationships between them.
- The **protected** member access specifier.
- The use of constructors and destructors in inheritance hierarchies.
- The differences between **public**, **protected** and **private** inheritance.
- The use of inheritance to customize existing software.

12.1 Introduction

This chapter continues our discussion of object-oriented programming (OOP) by introducing another of its key features—inheritance. Inheritance is a form of software reuse in which the programmer creates a class that absorbs an existing class's data and behaviors and enhances them with new capabilities. Software reusability saves time during program development. It also encourages the reuse of proven, debugged, high-quality software, which increases the likelihood that a system will be implemented effectively.

When creating a class, instead of writing completely new data members and member functions, the programmer can designate that the new class should inherit the members of an existing class. This existing class is called the base class, and the new class is referred to as the derived class. (Other programming languages, such as Java, refer to the base class as the superclass and the derived class as the subclass.) A derived class represents a more specialized group of objects. Typically, a derived class contains behaviors inherited from its base class plus additional behaviors. As we will see, a derived class can also customize behaviors inherited from the base class. A direct base class is the base class from which a derived class explicitly inherits. An indirect base class is inherited from two or more levels up in the class hierarchy. In the case of single inheritance, a class is derived from one base class. C++ also supports multiple inheritance, in which a derived class inherits from multiple (possibly unrelated) base classes. Single inheritance is straightforward—we show several examples that should enable the reader to become proficient quickly. Multiple inheritance can be complex and error prone. We cover multiple inheritance in Chapter 23, Other Topics

C++ offers three kinds of inheritance—`public`, `protected` and `private`. In this chapter, we concentrate on `public` inheritance and briefly explain the other two. In

Chapter 21, Data Structures, we show how `private` inheritance can be used as an alternative to composition. The third form, `protected` inheritance, is rarely used. With `public` inheritance, every object of a derived class is also an object of that derived class's base class. However, base-class objects are not objects of their derived classes. For example, if we have vehicle as a base class and car as a derived class, then all cars are vehicles, but not all vehicles are cars. As we continue our study of object-oriented programming in Chapter 12 and Chapter 13, we take advantage of this relationship to perform some interesting manipulations.

Experience in building software systems indicates that significant amounts of code deal with closely related special cases. When programmers are preoccupied with special cases, the details can obscure the big picture. With object-oriented programming, programmers focus on the commonalities among objects in the system rather than on the special cases.

We distinguish between the *is-a* relationship and the *has-a* relationship. The *is-a* relationship represents inheritance. In an *is-a* relationship, an object of a derived class also can be treated as an object of its base class—for example, a car *is a* vehicle, so any properties and behaviors of a vehicle are also properties of a car. By contrast, the *has-a* relationship represents composition. (Composition was discussed in Chapter 10.) In a *has-a* relationship, an object contains one or more objects of other classes as members. For example, a car includes many components—it *has a* steering wheel, *has a* brake pedal, *has a* transmission and *has* many other components.

Derived-class member functions might require access to base-class data members and member functions. A derived class can access the non-`private` members of its base class. Base-class members that should not be accessible to the member functions of derived classes should be declared `private` in the base class. A derived class can effect state changes in `private` base-class members, but only through non-`private` member functions provided in the base class and inherited into the derived class.

Software Engineering Observation 12.1
Member functions of a derived class cannot directly access `private` members of the base class.

Software Engineering Observation 12.2
If a derived class could access its base class's `private` members, classes that inherit from that derived class could access that data as well. This would propagate access to what should be `private` data, and the benefits of information hiding would be lost.

One problem with inheritance is that a derived class can inherit data members and member functions it does not need or should not have. It is the class designer's responsibility to ensure that the capabilities provided by a class are appropriate for future derived classes. Even when a base-class member function is appropriate for a derived class, the derived class often requires that member function to behave in a manner specific to the derived class. In such cases, the base-class member function can be redefined in the derived class with an appropriate implementation.

12.2 Base Classes and Derived Classes

Often, an object of one class *is an* object of another class, as well. For example, in geometry, a rectangle *is a* quadrilateral (as are squares, parallelograms and trapezoids). Thus, in C++, class `Rectangle` can be said to *inherit* from class `Quadrilateral`. In this context, class `Quadrilateral` is a base class, and class `Rectangle` is a derived class. A rectangle *is a* specific type of quadrilateral, but it is incorrect to claim that a quadrilateral *is a* rectangle—the quadrilateral could be a parallelogram or some other shape. Figure 12.1 lists several simple examples of base classes and derived classes.

Because every derived-class object *is an* object of its base class, and one base class can have many derived classes, the set of objects represented by a base class typically is larger than the set of objects represented by any of its derived classes. For example, the base class Vehicle represents all vehicles, including cars, trucks, boats, airplanes, bicycles and so on. By contrast, derived class Car represents a smaller, more specific subset of all vehicles.

Inheritance relationships form treelike hierarchical structures. A base class exists in a hierarchical relationship with its derived classes. Although classes can exist independently, once they are employed in inheritance relationships, they become affiliated with other classes. A class becomes either a base class—supplying members to other classes, a derived class—inheriting its members from other classes, or both.

Let us develop a simple inheritance hierarchy with five levels (represented by the UML class diagram in Fig. 12.2). A university community has thousands of members.

Base class	Derived classes
Student	GraduateStudent, UndergraduateStudent
Shape	Circle, Triangle, Rectangle, Sphere, Cube
Loan	CarLoan, HomeImprovementLoan, MortgageLoan
Employee	Faculty, Staff
Account	CheckingAccount, SavingsAccount

Fig. 12.1 | Inheritance examples.

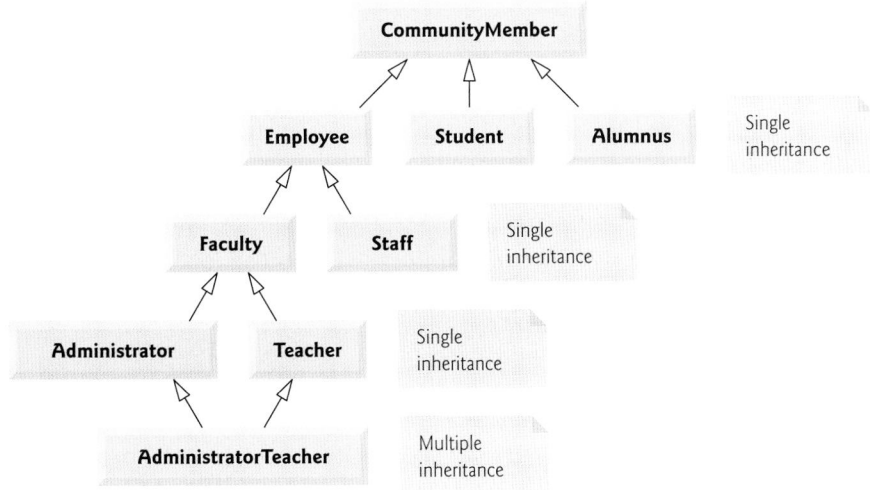

Fig. 12.2 | Inheritance hierarchy for university CommunityMembers.

These members consist of employees, students and alumni. Employees are either faculty members or staff members. Faculty members are either administrators (such as deans and department chairpersons) or teachers. Some administrators, however, also teach classes. Note that we have used multiple inheritance to form class AdministratorTeacher. Also note that this inheritance hierarchy could contain many other classes. For example, students can be graduate or undergraduate students. Undergraduate students can be freshmen, sophomores, juniors and seniors.

Each arrow in the hierarchy (Fig. 12.2) represents an *is-a* relationship. For example, as we follow the arrows in this class hierarchy, we can state "an Employee *is a* CommunityMember" and "a Teacher *is a* Faculty member." CommunityMember is the direct base class of Employee, Student and Alumnus. In addition, CommunityMember is an indirect base class of all the other classes in the diagram. Starting from the bottom of the diagram, the reader can follow the arrows and apply the *is-a* relationship to the topmost base class. For example, an AdministratorTeacher *is an* Administrator, *is a* Faculty member, *is an* Employee and *is a* CommunityMember.

Now consider the Shape inheritance hierarchy in Fig. 12.3. This hierarchy begins with base class Shape. Classes TwoDimensionalShape and ThreeDimensionalShape derive from base class Shape—Shapes are either TwoDimensionalShapes or ThreeDimensionalShapes. The third level of this hierarchy contains some more specific types of TwoDimensionalShapes and ThreeDimensionalShapes. As in Fig. 12.2, we can follow the arrows from the bottom of the diagram to the topmost base class in this class hierarchy to identify several *is-a* relationships. For instance, a Triangle *is a* TwoDimensionalShape and *is a* Shape, while a Sphere *is a* ThreeDimensionalShape and *is a* Shape. Note that this hierarchy could contain many other classes, such as Rectangles, Ellipses and Trapezoids, which are all TwoDimensionalShapes.

To specify that class TwoDimensionalShape (Fig. 12.3) is derived from (or inherits from) class Shape, class TwoDimensionalShape could be defined in C++ as follows:

```
class TwoDimensionalShape : public Shape
```

This is an example of **public inheritance**, the most commonly used form. We also will discuss **private inheritance** and **protected** inheritance (Section 12.6). With all forms of inheritance, private members of a base class are not accessible directly from that class's derived classes, but these private base-class members are still inherited (i.e., they are still considered parts of the derived classes). With public inheritance, all other base-class members retain

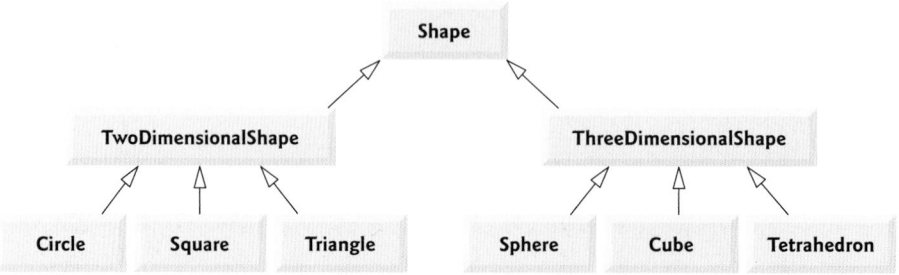

Fig. 12.3 | Inheritance hierarchy for Shapes.

their original member access when they become members of the derived class (e.g., public members of the base class become public members of the derived class, and, as we will soon see, protected members of the base class become protected members of the derived class). Through these inherited base-class members, the derived class can manipulate private members of the base class (if these inherited members provide such functionality in the base class). Note that friend functions are not inherited.

Inheritance is not appropriate for every class relationship. In Chapter 10, we discussed the *has-a* relationship, in which classes have members that are objects of other classes. Such relationships create classes by composition of existing classes. For example, given the classes Employee, BirthDate and TelephoneNumber, it is improper to say that an Employee *is a* BirthDate or that an Employee *is a* TelephoneNumber. However, it is appropriate to say that an Employee *has a* BirthDate and that an Employee *has a* TelephoneNumber.

It is possible to treat base-class objects and derived-class objects similarly; their commonalities are expressed in the members of the base class. Objects of all classes derived from a common base class can be treated as objects of that base class (i.e., such objects have an *is-a* relationship with the base class). In Chapter 13, Object-Oriented Programming: Polymorphism, we consider many examples that take advantage of this relationship.

12.3 protected Members

Chapter 3 introduced access specifiers public and private. A base class's public members are accessible within the body of that base class and anywhere that the program has a handle (i.e., a name, reference or pointer) to an object of that base class or one of its derived classes. A base class's private members are accessible only within the body of that base class and the friends of that base class. In this section, we introduce an additional access specifier: protected.

Using protected access offers an intermediate level of protection between public and private access. A base class's protected members can be accessed within the body of that base class, by members and friends of that base class, and by members and friends of any classes derived from that base class.

Derived-class member functions can refer to public and protected members of the base class simply by using the member names. When a derived-class member function redefines a base-class member function, the base-class member can be accessed from the derived class by preceding the base-class member name with the base-class name and the binary scope resolution operator (::). We discuss accessing redefined members of the base class in Section 12.4 and using protected data in Section 12.4.4.

12.4 Relationship between Base Classes and Derived Classes

In this section, we use an inheritance hierarchy containing types of employees in a company's payroll application to discuss the relationship between a base class and a derived class. Commission employees (who will be represented as objects of a base class) are paid a percentage of their sales, while base-salaried commission employees (who will be represented as objects of a derived class) receive a base salary plus a percentage of their sales. We divide our discussion of the relationship between commission employees and base-salaried commission employees into a carefully paced series of five examples:

1. In the first example, we create class CommissionEmployee, which contains as private data members a first name, last name, social security number, commission rate (percentage) and gross (i.e., total) sales amount.

2. The second example defines class BasePlusCommissionEmployee, which contains as private data members a first name, last name, social security number, commission rate, gross sales amount and base salary. We create the latter class by writing every line of code the class requires—we will soon see that it is much more efficient to create this class simply by inheriting from class CommissionEmployee.

3. The third example defines a new version of class BasePlusCommissionEmployee class that inherits directly from class CommissionEmployee (i.e., a BasePlusCommissionEmployee *is a* CommissionEmployee who also has a base salary) and attempts to access class CommissionEmployee's private members—this results in compilation errors, because the derived class does not have access to the base class's private data.

4. The fourth example shows that if CommissionEmployee's data is declared as protected, a new version of class BasePlusCommissionEmployee that inherits from class CommissionEmployee *can* access that data directly. For this purpose, we define a new version of class CommissionEmployee with protected data. Both the inherited and noninherited BasePlusCommissionEmployee classes contain identical functionality, but we show how the version of BasePlusCommissionEmployee that inherits from class CommissionEmployee is easier to create and manage.

5. After we discuss the convenience of using protected data, we create the fifth example, which sets the CommissionEmployee data members back to private to enforce good software engineering. This example demonstrates that derived class BasePlusCommissionEmployee can use base class CommissionEmployee's public member functions to manipulate CommissionEmployee's private data.

12.4.1 Creating and Using a CommissionEmployee Class

Let us first examine CommissionEmployee's class definition (Figs. 12.4–12.5). The CommissionEmployee header file (Fig. 12.4) specifies class CommissionEmployee's public services, which include a constructor (lines 12–13) and member functions earnings (line 30) and print (line 31). Lines 15–28 declare public *get* and *set* functions for manipulating the class's data members (declared in lines 33–37) firstName, lastName, socialSecurityNumber, grossSales and commissionRate. The CommissionEmployee header file specifies each of these data members as private, so objects of other classes cannot directly access this data. Declaring data members as private and providing non-private *get* and *set* functions to manipulate and validate the data members helps enforce good software engineering. Member functions setGrossSales (defined in lines 57–60 of Fig. 12.5) and setCommissionRate (defined in lines 69–72 of Fig. 12.5), for example, validate their arguments before assigning the values to data members grossSales and commissionRate, respectively.

The CommissionEmployee constructor definition purposely does not use member-initializer syntax in the first several examples of this section, so that we can demonstrate how private and protected specifiers affect member access in derived classes. As shown in Fig. 12.5, lines 13–15, we assign values to data members firstName, lastName and

```
1   // Fig. 12.4: CommissionEmployee.h
2   // CommissionEmployee class definition represents a commission employee.
3   #ifndef COMMISSION_H
4   #define COMMISSION_H
5
6   #include <string> // C++ standard string class
7   using std::string;
8
9   class CommissionEmployee
10  {
11  public:
12     CommissionEmployee( const string &, const string &, const string &,
13        double = 0.0, double = 0.0 );
14
15     void setFirstName( const string & ); // set first name
16     string getFirstName() const; // return first name
17
18     void setLastName( const string & ); // set last name
19     string getLastName() const; // return last name
20
21     void setSocialSecurityNumber( const string & ); // set SSN
22     string getSocialSecurityNumber() const; // return SSN
23
24     void setGrossSales( double ); // set gross sales amount
25     double getGrossSales() const; // return gross sales amount
26
27     void setCommissionRate( double ); // set commission rate (percentage)
28     double getCommissionRate() const; // return commission rate
29
30     double earnings() const; // calculate earnings
31     void print() const; // print CommissionEmployee object
32  private:
33     string firstName;
34     string lastName;
35     string socialSecurityNumber;
36     double grossSales; // gross weekly sales
37     double commissionRate; // commission percentage
38  }; // end class CommissionEmployee
39
40  #endif
```

Fig. 12.4 | CommissionEmployee class header file.

```
1   // Fig. 12.5: CommissionEmployee.cpp
2   // Class CommissionEmployee member-function definitions.
3   #include <iostream>
4   using std::cout;
5
6   #include "CommissionEmployee.h" // CommissionEmployee class definition
7
```

Fig. 12.5 | Implementation file for CommissionEmployee class that represents an employee who is paid a percentage of gross sales. (Part 1 of 3.)

```cpp
 8   // constructor
 9   CommissionEmployee::CommissionEmployee(
10      const string &first, const string &last, const string &ssn,
11      double sales, double rate )
12   {
13      firstName = first; // should validate
14      lastName = last;   // should validate
15      socialSecurityNumber = ssn; // should validate
16      setGrossSales( sales ); // validate and store gross sales
17      setCommissionRate( rate ); // validate and store commission rate
18   } // end CommissionEmployee constructor
19
20   // set first name
21   void CommissionEmployee::setFirstName( const string &first )
22   {
23      firstName = first; // should validate
24   } // end function setFirstName
25
26   // return first name
27   string CommissionEmployee::getFirstName() const
28   {
29      return firstName;
30   } // end function getFirstName
31
32   // set last name
33   void CommissionEmployee::setLastName( const string &last )
34   {
35      lastName = last; // should validate
36   } // end function setLastName
37
38   // return last name
39   string CommissionEmployee::getLastName() const
40   {
41      return lastName;
42   } // end function getLastName
43
44   // set social security number
45   void CommissionEmployee::setSocialSecurityNumber( const string &ssn )
46   {
47      socialSecurityNumber = ssn; // should validate
48   } // end function setSocialSecurityNumber
49
50   // return social security number
51   string CommissionEmployee::getSocialSecurityNumber() const
52   {
53      return socialSecurityNumber;
54   } // end function getSocialSecurityNumber
55
56   // set gross sales amount
57   void CommissionEmployee::setGrossSales( double sales )
58   {
```

Fig. 12.5 | Implementation file for `CommissionEmployee` class that represents an employee who is paid a percentage of gross sales. (Part 2 of 3.)

```
59        grossSales = ( sales < 0.0 ) ? 0.0 : sales;
60     } // end function setGrossSales
61
62     // return gross sales amount
63     double CommissionEmployee::getGrossSales() const
64     {
65        return grossSales;
66     } // end function getGrossSales
67
68     // set commission rate
69     void CommissionEmployee::setCommissionRate( double rate )
70     {
71        commissionRate = ( rate > 0.0 && rate < 1.0 ) ? rate : 0.0;
72     } // end function setCommissionRate
73
74     // return commission rate
75     double CommissionEmployee::getCommissionRate() const
76     {
77        return commissionRate;
78     } // end function getCommissionRate
79
80     // calculate earnings
81     double CommissionEmployee::earnings() const
82     {
83        return commissionRate * grossSales;
84     } // end function earnings
85
86     // print CommissionEmployee object
87     void CommissionEmployee::print() const
88     {
89        cout << "commission employee: " << firstName << ' ' << lastName
90           << "\nsocial security number: " << socialSecurityNumber
91           << "\ngross sales: " << grossSales
92           << "\ncommission rate: " << commissionRate;
93     } // end function print
```

Fig. 12.5 | Implementation file for CommissionEmployee class that represents an employee who is paid a percentage of gross sales. (Part 3 of 3.)

socialSecurityNumber in the constructor body. Later in this section, we will return to using member-initializer lists in the constructors.

Note that we do not validate the values of the constructor's arguments first, last and ssn before assigning them to the corresponding data members. We certainly could validate the first and last names—perhaps by ensuring that they are of a reasonable length. Similarly, a social security number could be validated to ensure that it contains nine digits, with or without dashes (e.g., 123-45-6789 or 123456789).

Member function earnings (lines 81–84) calculates a CommissionEmployee's earnings. Line 83 multiplies the commissionRate by the grossSales and returns the result. Member function print (lines 87–93) displays the values of a CommissionEmployee object's data members.

Figure 12.6 tests class CommissionEmployee. Lines 16–17 instantiate object employee of class CommissionEmployee and invoke CommissionEmployee's constructor to initialize the object with "Sue" as the first name, "Jones" as the last name, "222-22-2222" as the social security number, 10000 as the gross sales amount and .06 as the commission rate. Lines 23–29 use employee's *get* functions to display the values of its data members. Lines 31–32 invoke the object's member functions setGrossSales and setCommissionRate to change the values of data members grossSales and commissionRate, respectively. Line 36 then calls employee's print member function to output the updated CommissionEmployee information. Finally, line 39 displays the CommissionEmployee's earnings, calculated by the object's earnings member function using the updated values of data members gross-Sales and commissionRate.

```cpp
1   // Fig. 12.6: fig12_06.cpp
2   // Testing class CommissionEmployee.
3   #include <iostream>
4   using std::cout;
5   using std::endl;
6   using std::fixed;
7
8   #include <iomanip>
9   using std::setprecision;
10
11  #include "CommissionEmployee.h" // CommissionEmployee class definition
12
13  int main()
14  {
15     // instantiate a CommissionEmployee object
16     CommissionEmployee employee(
17        "Sue", "Jones", "222-22-2222", 10000, .06 );
18
19     // set floating-point output formatting
20     cout << fixed << setprecision( 2 );
21
22     // get commission employee data
23     cout << "Employee information obtained by get functions: \n"
24        << "\nFirst name is " << employee.getFirstName()
25        << "\nLast name is " << employee.getLastName()
26        << "\nSocial security number is "
27        << employee.getSocialSecurityNumber()
28        << "\nGross sales is " << employee.getGrossSales()
29        << "\nCommission rate is " << employee.getCommissionRate() << endl;
30
31     employee.setGrossSales( 8000 ); // set gross sales
32     employee.setCommissionRate( .1 ); // set commission rate
33
34     cout << "\nUpdated employee information output by print function: \n"
35        << endl;
36     employee.print(); // display the new employee information
37
38     // display the employee's earnings
39     cout << "\n\nEmployee's earnings: $" << employee.earnings() << endl;
40
41     return 0;
42  } // end main
```

Fig. 12.6 | CommissionEmployee class test program. (Part 1 of 2.)

```
Employee information obtained by get functions:

First name is Sue
Last name is Jones
Social security number is 222-22-2222
Gross sales is 10000.00
Commission rate is 0.06

Updated employee information output by print function:

commission employee: Sue Jones
social security number: 222-22-2222
gross sales: 8000.00
commission rate: 0.10

Employee's earnings: $800.00
```

Fig. 12.6 │ CommissionEmployee class test program. (Part 2 of 2.)

12.4.2 Creating a BasePlusCommissionEmployee Class Without Using Inheritance

We now discuss the second part of our introduction to inheritance by creating and testing (a completely new and independent) class BasePlusCommissionEmployee (Figs. 12.7–12.8), which contains a first name, last name, social security number, gross sales amount, commission rate and base salary.

Defining Class *BasePlusCommissionEmployee*

The BasePlusCommissionEmployee header file (Fig. 12.7) specifies class BasePlusCommissionEmployee's public services, which include the BasePlusCommissionEmployee constructor (lines 13–14) and member functions earnings (line 34) and print (line 35).

```
 1   // Fig. 12.7: BasePlusCommissionEmployee.h
 2   // BasePlusCommissionEmployee class definition represents an employee
 3   // that receives a base salary in addition to commission.
 4   #ifndef BASEPLUS_H
 5   #define BASEPLUS_H
 6
 7   #include <string> // C++ standard string class
 8   using std::string;
 9
10   class BasePlusCommissionEmployee
11   {
12   public:
13      BasePlusCommissionEmployee( const string &, const string &,
14         const string &, double = 0.0, double = 0.0, double = 0.0 );
15
16      void setFirstName( const string & ); // set first name
17      string getFirstName() const; // return first name
18
```

Fig. 12.7 │ BasePlusCommissionEmployee class header file. (Part 1 of 2.)

```
19       void setLastName( const string & ); // set last name
20       string getLastName() const; // return last name
21
22       void setSocialSecurityNumber( const string & ); // set SSN
23       string getSocialSecurityNumber() const; // return SSN
24
25       void setGrossSales( double ); // set gross sales amount
26       double getGrossSales() const; // return gross sales amount
27
28       void setCommissionRate( double ); // set commission rate
29       double getCommissionRate() const; // return commission rate
30
31       void setBaseSalary( double ); // set base salary
32       double getBaseSalary() const; // return base salary
33
34       double earnings() const; // calculate earnings
35       void print() const; // print BasePlusCommissionEmployee object
36    private:
37       string firstName;
38       string lastName;
39       string socialSecurityNumber;
40       double grossSales; // gross weekly sales
41       double commissionRate; // commission percentage
42       double baseSalary; // base salary
43    }; // end class BasePlusCommissionEmployee
44
45    #endif
```

Fig. 12.7 | BasePlusCommissionEmployee class header file. (Part 2 of 2.)

Lines 16–32 declare public *get* and *set* functions for the class's private data members (declared in lines 37–42) firstName, lastName, socialSecurityNumber, grossSales, commissionRate and baseSalary. These variables and member functions encapsulate all the necessary features of a base-salaried commission employee. Note the similarity between this class and class CommissionEmployee (Figs. 12.4–12.5)—in this example, we will not yet exploit that similarity.

Class BasePlusCommissionEmployee's earnings member function (defined in lines 96–99 of Fig. 12.8) computes the earnings of a base-salaried commission employee. Line 98 returns the result of adding the employee's base salary to the product of the commission rate and the employee's gross sales.

Testing Class *BasePlusCommissionEmployee*
Figure 12.9 tests class BasePlusCommissionEmployee. Lines 17–18 instantiate object employee of class BasePlusCommissionEmployee, passing "Bob", "Lewis", "333-33-3333", 5000, .04 and 300 to the constructor as the first name, last name, social security number, gross sales, commission rate and base salary, respectively. Lines 24–31 use BasePlusCommissionEmployee's *get* functions to retrieve the values of the object's data members for output. Line 33 invokes the object's setBaseSalary member function to change the base salary. Member function setBaseSalary (Fig. 12.8, lines 84–87) ensures that data member baseSalary is not assigned a negative value, because an employee's base salary cannot be negative. Line 37 of Fig. 12.9 invokes the object's print member function to output

the updated BasePlusCommissionEmployee's information, and line 40 calls member function earnings to display the BasePlusCommissionEmployee's earnings.

```cpp
1   // Fig. 12.8: BasePlusCommissionEmployee.cpp
2   // Class BasePlusCommissionEmployee member-function definitions.
3   #include <iostream>
4   using std::cout;
5
6   // BasePlusCommissionEmployee class definition
7   #include "BasePlusCommissionEmployee.h"
8
9   // constructor
10  BasePlusCommissionEmployee::BasePlusCommissionEmployee(
11     const string &first, const string &last, const string &ssn,
12     double sales, double rate, double salary )
13  {
14     firstName = first; // should validate
15     lastName = last; // should validate
16     socialSecurityNumber = ssn; // should validate
17     setGrossSales( sales ); // validate and store gross sales
18     setCommissionRate( rate ); // validate and store commission rate
19     setBaseSalary( salary ); // validate and store base salary
20  } // end BasePlusCommissionEmployee constructor
21
22  // set first name
23  void BasePlusCommissionEmployee::setFirstName( const string &first )
24  {
25     firstName = first; // should validate
26  } // end function setFirstName
27
28  // return first name
29  string BasePlusCommissionEmployee::getFirstName() const
30  {
31     return firstName;
32  } // end function getFirstName
33
34  // set last name
35  void BasePlusCommissionEmployee::setLastName( const string &last )
36  {
37     lastName = last; // should validate
38  } // end function setLastName
39
40  // return last name
41  string BasePlusCommissionEmployee::getLastName() const
42  {
43     return lastName;
44  } // end function getLastName
45
46  // set social security number
47  void BasePlusCommissionEmployee::setSocialSecurityNumber(
48     const string &ssn )
49  {
```

Fig. 12.8 | BasePlusCommissionEmployee class represents an employee who receives a base salary in addition to a commission. (Part 1 of 3.)

```
50        socialSecurityNumber = ssn; // should validate
51   } // end function setSocialSecurityNumber
52
53   // return social security number
54   string BasePlusCommissionEmployee::getSocialSecurityNumber() const
55   {
56      return socialSecurityNumber;
57   } // end function getSocialSecurityNumber
58
59   // set gross sales amount
60   void BasePlusCommissionEmployee::setGrossSales( double sales )
61   {
62      grossSales = ( sales < 0.0 ) ? 0.0 : sales;
63   } // end function setGrossSales
64
65   // return gross sales amount
66   double BasePlusCommissionEmployee::getGrossSales() const
67   {
68      return grossSales;
69   } // end function getGrossSales
70
71   // set commission rate
72   void BasePlusCommissionEmployee::setCommissionRate( double rate )
73   {
74      commissionRate = ( rate > 0.0 && rate < 1.0 ) ? rate : 0.0;
75   } // end function setCommissionRate
76
77   // return commission rate
78   double BasePlusCommissionEmployee::getCommissionRate() const
79   {
80      return commissionRate;
81   } // end function getCommissionRate
82
83   // set base salary
84   void BasePlusCommissionEmployee::setBaseSalary( double salary )
85   {
86      baseSalary = ( salary < 0.0 ) ? 0.0 : salary;
87   } // end function setBaseSalary
88
89   // return base salary
90   double BasePlusCommissionEmployee::getBaseSalary() const
91   {
92      return baseSalary;
93   } // end function getBaseSalary
94
95   // calculate earnings
96   double BasePlusCommissionEmployee::earnings() const
97   {
98      return baseSalary + ( commissionRate * grossSales );
99   } // end function earnings
100
```

Fig. 12.8 | BasePlusCommissionEmployee class represents an employee who receives a base salary in addition to a commission. (Part 2 of 3.)

```
101  // print BasePlusCommissionEmployee object
102  void BasePlusCommissionEmployee::print() const
103  {
104     cout << "base-salaried commission employee: " << firstName << ' '
105        << lastName << "\nsocial security number: " << socialSecurityNumber
106        << "\ngross sales: " << grossSales
107        << "\ncommission rate: " << commissionRate
108        << "\nbase salary: " << baseSalary;
109  } // end function print
```

Fig. 12.8 | BasePlusCommissionEmployee class represents an employee who receives a base salary in addition to a commission. (Part 3 of 3.)

```
1   // Fig. 12.9: fig12_09.cpp
2   // Testing class BasePlusCommissionEmployee.
3   #include <iostream>
4   using std::cout;
5   using std::endl;
6   using std::fixed;
7
8   #include <iomanip>
9   using std::setprecision;
10
11  // BasePlusCommissionEmployee class definition
12  #include "BasePlusCommissionEmployee.h"
13
14  int main()
15  {
16     // instantiate BasePlusCommissionEmployee object
17     BasePlusCommissionEmployee
18        employee( "Bob", "Lewis", "333-33-3333", 5000, .04, 300 );
19
20     // set floating-point output formatting
21     cout << fixed << setprecision( 2 );
22
23     // get commission employee data
24     cout << "Employee information obtained by get functions: \n"
25        << "\nFirst name is " << employee.getFirstName()
26        << "\nLast name is " << employee.getLastName()
27        << "\nSocial security number is "
28        << employee.getSocialSecurityNumber()
29        << "\nGross sales is " << employee.getGrossSales()
30        << "\nCommission rate is " << employee.getCommissionRate()
31        << "\nBase salary is " << employee.getBaseSalary() << endl;
32
33     employee.setBaseSalary( 1000 ); // set base salary
34
35     cout << "\nUpdated employee information output by print function: \n"
36        << endl;
37     employee.print(); // display the new employee information
38
```

Fig. 12.9 | BasePlusCommissionEmployee class test program. (Part 1 of 2.)

```
39        // display the employee's earnings
40        cout << "\n\nEmployee's earnings: $" << employee.earnings() << endl;
41
42        return 0;
43    } // end main
```

```
Employee information obtained by get functions:

First name is Bob
Last name is Lewis
Social security number is 333-33-3333
Gross sales is 5000.00
Commission rate is 0.04
Base salary is 300.00

Updated employee information output by print function:

base-salaried commission employee: Bob Lewis
social security number: 333-33-3333
gross sales: 5000.00
commission rate: 0.04
base salary: 1000.00

Employee's earnings: $1200.00
```

Fig. 12.9 | BasePlusCommissionEmployee class test program. (Part 2 of 2.)

Exploring the Similarities Between Class BasePlusCommissionEmployee and Class CommissionEmployee

Note that much of the code for class BasePlusCommissionEmployee (Figs. 12.7–12.8) is similar, if not identical, to the code for class CommissionEmployee (Figs. 12.4–12.5). For example, in class BasePlusCommissionEmployee, private data members firstName and lastName and member functions setFirstName, getFirstName, setLastName and getLastName are identical to those of class CommissionEmployee. Classes CommissionEmployee and BasePlusCommissionEmployee also both contain private data members socialSecurityNumber, commissionRate and grossSales, as well as *get* and *set* functions to manipulate these members. In addition, the BasePlusCommissionEmployee constructor is almost identical to that of class CommissionEmployee, except that BasePlusCommissionEmployee's constructor also sets the baseSalary. The other additions to class BasePlusCommissionEmployee are private data member baseSalary and member functions setBaseSalary and getBaseSalary. Class BasePlusCommissionEmployee's print member function is nearly identical to that of class CommissionEmployee, except that BasePlusCommissionEmployee's print also outputs the value of data member baseSalary.

We literally copied code from class CommissionEmployee and pasted it into class BasePlusCommissionEmployee, then modified class BasePlusCommissionEmployee to include a base salary and member functions that manipulate the base salary. This "copy-and-paste" approach is often error prone and time consuming. Worse yet, it can spread many physical copies of the same code throughout a system, creating a code-maintenance nightmare. Is there a way to "absorb" the data members and member functions of a class in a way that makes them part of other classes without duplicating code? In the next several examples, we do exactly this, using inheritance.

Software Engineering Observation 12.3

Copying and pasting code from one class to another can spread errors across multiple source code files. To avoid duplicating code (and possibly errors), use inheritance, rather than the "copy-and-paste" approach, in situations where you want one class to "absorb" the data members and member functions of another class.

Software Engineering Observation 12.4

With inheritance, the common data members and member functions of all the classes in the hierarchy are declared in a base class. When changes are required for these common features, software developers need to make the changes only in the base class—derived classes then inherit the changes. Without inheritance, changes would need to be made to all the source code files that contain a copy of the code in question.

12.4.3 Creating a CommissionEmployee-BasePlusCommissionEmployee Inheritance Hierarchy

Now we create and test a new version of class BasePlusCommissionEmployee (Figs. 12.10–12.11) that derives from class CommissionEmployee (Figs. 12.4–12.5). In this example, a BasePlusCommissionEmployee object *is a* CommissionEmployee (because inheritance passes on the capabilities of class CommissionEmployee), but class BasePlusCommissionEmployee

```
1   // Fig. 12.10: BasePlusCommissionEmployee.h
2   // BasePlusCommissionEmployee class derived from class
3   // CommissionEmployee.
4   #ifndef BASEPLUS_H
5   #define BASEPLUS_H
6
7   #include <string> // C++ standard string class
8   using std::string;
9
10  #include "CommissionEmployee.h" // CommissionEmployee class declaration
11
12  class BasePlusCommissionEmployee : public CommissionEmployee
13  {
14  public:
15     BasePlusCommissionEmployee( const string &, const string &,
16        const string &, double = 0.0, double = 0.0, double = 0.0 );
17
18     void setBaseSalary( double ); // set base salary
19     double getBaseSalary() const; // return base salary
20
21     double earnings() const; // calculate earnings
22     void print() const; // print BasePlusCommissionEmployee object
23  private:
24     double baseSalary; // base salary
25  }; // end class BasePlusCommissionEmployee
26
27  #endif
```

Fig. 12.10 | BasePlusCommissionEmployee class definition indicating inheritance relationship with class CommissionEmployee.

also has data member baseSalary (Fig. 12.10, line 24). The colon (:) in line 12 of the class definition indicates inheritance. Keyword public indicates the type of inheritance. As a derived class (formed with public inheritance), BasePlusCommissionEmployee inherits all the members of class CommissionEmployee, except for the constructor—each class provides its own constructors that are specific to the class. [Note that destructors, too, are not inherited.] Thus, the public services of BasePlusCommissionEmployee include its constructor (lines 15–16) and the public member functions inherited from class CommissionEmployee—although we cannot see these inherited member functions in BasePlusCommissionEmployee's source code, they are nevertheless a part of derived class BasePlusCommissionEmployee. The derived class's public services also include member functions setBaseSalary, getBaseSalary, earnings and print (lines 18–22).

Figure 12.11 shows BasePlusCommissionEmployee's member-function implementations. The constructor (lines 10–17) introduces base-class initializer syntax (line 14), which uses a member initializer to pass arguments to the base-class (CommissionEmployee) constructor. C++ requires a derived-class constructor to call its base-class constructor to initialize the base-class data members that are inherited into the derived class. Line 14 accomplishes this task by invoking the CommissionEmployee constructor by name, passing the constructor's parameters first, last, ssn, sales and rate as arguments to initialize base-class data members firstName, lastName, socialSecurityNumber, grossSales and commissionRate. If BasePlusCommissionEmployee's constructor did not invoke class CommissionEmployee's constructor explicitly, C++ would attempt to invoke class CommissionEmployee's default constructor—but the class does not have such a constructor, so the compiler would issue an error. Recall from Chapter 3 that the compiler provides a default constructor with no parameters in any class that does not explicitly include a constructor. However, CommissionEmployee *does* explicitly include a constructor, so a default constructor is not provided and any attempts to implicitly call CommissionEmployee's default constructor would result in compilation errors.

```cpp
1   // Fig. 12.11: BasePlusCommissionEmployee.cpp
2   // Class BasePlusCommissionEmployee member-function definitions.
3   #include <iostream>
4   using std::cout;
5
6   // BasePlusCommissionEmployee class definition
7   #include "BasePlusCommissionEmployee.h"
8
9   // constructor
10  BasePlusCommissionEmployee::BasePlusCommissionEmployee(
11     const string &first, const string &last, const string &ssn,
12     double sales, double rate, double salary )
13     // explicitly call base-class constructor
14     : CommissionEmployee( first, last, ssn, sales, rate )
15  {
16     setBaseSalary( salary ); // validate and store base salary
17  } // end BasePlusCommissionEmployee constructor
18
```

Fig. 12.11 | BasePlusCommissionEmployee implementation file: private base-class data cannot be accessed from derived class. (Part 1 of 3.)

```
19  // set base salary
20  void BasePlusCommissionEmployee::setBaseSalary( double salary )
21  {
22     baseSalary = ( salary < 0.0 ) ? 0.0 : salary;
23  } // end function setBaseSalary
24
25  // return base salary
26  double BasePlusCommissionEmployee::getBaseSalary() const
27  {
28     return baseSalary;
29  } // end function getBaseSalary
30
31  // calculate earnings
32  double BasePlusCommissionEmployee::earnings() const
33  {
34     // derived class cannot access the base class's private data
35     return baseSalary + ( commissionRate * grossSales );
36  } // end function earnings
37
38  // print BasePlusCommissionEmployee object
39  void BasePlusCommissionEmployee::print() const
40  {
41     // derived class cannot access the base class's private data
42     cout << "base-salaried commission employee: " << firstName << ' '
43        << lastName << "\nsocial security number: " << socialSecurityNumber
44        << "\ngross sales: " << grossSales
45        << "\ncommission rate: " << commissionRate
46        << "\nbase salary: " << baseSalary;
47  } // end function print
```

```
C:\cpphtp5_examples\ch12\Fig12_10_11\BasePlusCommission-Employee.cpp(35) :
   error C2248: 'CommissionEmployee::commissionRate' :
   cannot access private member declared in class 'CommissionEmployee'
      C:\cpphtp5_examples\ch12\Fig12_10_11\CommissionEmployee.h(37) :
         see declaration of 'CommissionEmployee::commissionRate'
      C:\cpphtp5e_examples\ch12\Fig12_10_11\CommissionEmployee.h(10) :
         see declaration of 'CommissionEmployee'

C:\cpphtp5_examples\ch12\Fig12_10_11\BasePlusCommission-Employee.cpp(35) :
   error C2248: 'CommissionEmployee::grossSales' :
   cannot access private member declared in class 'CommissionEmployee'
      C:\cpphtp5_examples\ch12\Fig12_10_11\CommissionEmployee.h(36) :
         see declaration of 'CommissionEmployee::grossSales'
      C:\cpphtp5_examples\ch12\Fig12_10_11\CommissionEmployee.h(10) :
         see declaration of 'CommissionEmployee'

C:\cpphtp5_examples\ch12\Fig12_10_11\BasePlusCommission-Employee.cpp(42) :
   error C2248: 'CommissionEmployee::firstName' :
   cannot access private member declared in class 'CommissionEmployee'
      C:\cpphtp5_examples\ch12\Fig12_10_11\CommissionEmployee.h(33) :
         see declaration of 'CommissionEmployee::firstName'
      C:\cpphtp5_examples\ch12\Fig12_10_11\CommissionEmployee.h(10) :
         see declaration of 'CommissionEmployee'
```

Fig. 12.11 | BasePlusCommissionEmployee implementation file: private base-class data cannot be accessed from derived class. (Part 2 of 3.)

```
C:\cpphtp5_examples\ch12\Fig12_10_11\BasePlusCommission-Employee.cpp(43) :
   error C2248: 'CommissionEmployee::lastName' :
   cannot access private member declared in class 'CommissionEmployee'
      C:\cpphtp5_examples\ch12\Fig12_10_11\CommissionEmployee.h(34) :
         see declaration of 'CommissionEmployee::lastName'
      C:\cpphtp5_examples\ch12\Fig12_10_11\CommissionEmployee.h(10) :
         see declaration of 'CommissionEmployee'

C:\cpphtp5_examples\ch12\Fig12_10_11\BasePlusCommission-Employee.cpp(43) :
   error C2248: 'CommissionEmployee::socialSecurity-Number' :
   cannot access private member declared in class 'CommissionEmployee'
      C:\cpphtp5_examples\ch12\Fig12_10_11\CommissionEmployee.h(35) :
         see declaration of 'CommissionEmployee::socialSecurityNumber'
      C:\cpphtp5_examples\ch12\Fig12_10_11\CommissionEmployee.h(10) :
         see declaration of 'CommissionEmployee'

C:\cpphtp5_examples\ch12\Fig12_10_11\BasePlusCommission-Employee.cpp(44) :
   error C2248: 'CommissionEmployee::grossSales' :
   cannot access private member declared in class 'CommissionEmployee'
      C:\cpphtp5_examples\ch12\Fig12_10_11\CommissionEmployee.h(36) :
         see declaration of 'CommissionEmployee::grossSales'
      C:\cpphtp5_examples\ch12\Fig12_10_11\CommissionEmployee.h(10) :
         see declaration of 'CommissionEmployee'

C:\cpphtp5_examples\ch12\Fig12_10_11\BasePlusCommission-Employee.cpp(45) :
   error C2248: 'CommissionEmployee::commissionRate' :
   cannot access private member declared in class 'CommissionEmployee'
      C:\cpphtp5_examples\ch12\Fig12_10_11\CommissionEmployee.h(37) :
         see declaration of 'CommissionEmployee::commissionRate'
      C:\cpphtp5_examples\ch12\Fig12_10_11\CommissionEmployee.h(10) :
         see declaration of 'CommissionEmployee'
```

Fig. 12.11 | BasePlusCommissionEmployee implementation file: `private` base-class data cannot be accessed from derived class. (Part 3 of 3.)

Common Programming Error 12.1

A compilation error occurs if a derived-class constructor calls one of its base-class constructors with arguments that are inconsistent with the number and types of parameters specified in one of the base-class constructor definitions.

Performance Tip 12.1

In a derived-class constructor, initializing member objects and invoking base-class constructors explicitly in the member initializer list prevents duplicate initialization in which a default constructor is called, then data members are modified again in the derived-class constructor's body.

The compiler generates errors for line 35 of Fig. 12.11 because base class CommissionEmployee's data members commissionRate and grossSales are private—derived class BasePlusCommissionEmployee's member functions are not allowed to access base class CommissionEmployee's private data. Note that we used red text in Fig. 12.11 to indicate erroneous code. The compiler issues additional errors at lines 42–45 of BasePlusCommissionEmployee's print member function for the same reason. As you can see, C++ rigidly enforces restrictions on accessing private data members, so that even a derived class (which is intimately related to its base class) cannot access the base class's private data. [*Note:* To save space, we show only the error messages from Visual C++ .NET in this example. The error messages produced by your compiler may differ from those shown here. Also notice that we highlight key portions of the lengthy error messages in bold.]

We purposely included the erroneous code in Fig. 12.11 to demonstrate that a derived class's member functions cannot access its base class's private data. The errors in BasePlusCommissionEmployee could have been prevented by using the *get* member functions inherited from class CommissionEmployee. For example, line 35 could have invoked getCommissionRate and getGrossSales to access CommissionEmployee's private data members commissionRate and grossSales, respectively. Similarly, lines 42–45 could have used appropriate *get* member functions to retrieve the values of the base class's data members. In the next example, we show how using protected data also allows us to avoid the errors encountered in this example.

Including the Base Class Header File in the Derived Class Header File with #include

Notice that we #include the base class's header file in the derived class's header file (line 10 of Fig. 12.10). This is necessary for three reasons. First, for the derived class to use the base class's name in line 12, we must tell the compiler that the base class exists—the class definition in CommissionEmployee.h does exactly that.

The second reason is that the compiler uses a class definition to determine the size of an object of that class (as we discussed in Section 3.8). A client program that creates an object of a class must #include the class definition to enable the compiler to reserve the proper amount of memory for the object. When using inheritance, a derived-class object's size depends on the data members declared explicitly in its class definition *and* the data members inherited from its direct and indirect base classes. Including the base class's definition in line 10 allows the compiler to determine the memory requirements for the base class's data members that become part of a derived-class object and thus contribute to the total size of the derived-class object.

The last reason for line 10 is to allow the compiler to determine whether the derived class uses the base class's inherited members properly. For example, in the program of Figs. 12.10–12.11, the compiler uses the base-class header file to determine that the data members being accessed by the derived class are private in the base class. Since these are inaccessible to the derived class, the compiler generates errors. The compiler also uses the base class's function prototypes to validate function calls made by the derived class to the inherited base-class functions—you will see an example of such a function call in Fig. 12.16.

Linking Process in an Inheritance Hierarchy

In Section 3.9, we discussed the linking process for creating an executable GradeBook application. In that example, you saw that the client's object code was linked with the object code for class GradeBook, as well as the object code for any C++ Standard Library classes used in either the client code or in class GradeBook.

The linking process is similar for a program that uses classes in an inheritance hierarchy. The process requires the object code for all classes used in the program and the object code for the direct and indirect base classes of any derived classes used by the program. Suppose a client wants to create an application that uses class BasePlusCommission-Employee, which is a derived class of CommissionEmployee (we will see an example of this in Section 12.4.4). When compiling the client application, the client's object code must be linked with the object code for classes BasePlusCommissionEmployee and Commission-

Employee, because BasePlusCommissionEmployee inherits member functions from its base class CommissionEmployee. The code is also linked with the object code for any C++ Standard Library classes used in class CommissionEmployee, class BasePlusCommission-Employee or the client code. This provides the program with access to the implementations of all of the functionality that the program may use.

12.4.4 CommissionEmployee–BasePlusCommissionEmployee Inheritance Hierarchy Using protected Data

To enable class BasePlusCommissionEmployee to directly access CommissionEmployee data members firstName, lastName, socialSecurityNumber, grossSales and commission-Rate, we can declare those members as protected in the base class. As we discussed in Section 12.3, a base class's protected members can be accessed by members and friends of the base class and by members and friends of any classes derived from that base class.

 Good Programming Practice 12.1

Declare public members first, protected members second and private members last.

Defining Base Class CommissionEmployee with protected Data
Class CommissionEmployee (Figs. 12.12–12.13) now declares data members firstName, lastName, socialSecurityNumber, grossSales and commissionRate as protected (Fig. 12.12, lines 33–37) rather than private. The member-function implementations in Fig. 12.13 are identical to those in Fig. 12.5.

```
1   // Fig. 12.12: CommissionEmployee.h
2   // CommissionEmployee class definition with protected data.
3   #ifndef COMMISSION_H
4   #define COMMISSION_H
5
6   #include <string> // C++ standard string class
7   using std::string;
8
9   class CommissionEmployee
10  {
11  public:
12     CommissionEmployee( const string &, const string &, const string &,
13        double = 0.0, double = 0.0 );
14
15     void setFirstName( const string & ); // set first name
16     string getFirstName() const; // return first name
17
18     void setLastName( const string & ); // set last name
19     string getLastName() const; // return last name
20
21     void setSocialSecurityNumber( const string & ); // set SSN
22     string getSocialSecurityNumber() const; // return SSN
23
```

Fig. 12.12 | CommissionEmployee class definition that declares protected data to allow access by derived classes. (Part 1 of 2.)

```
24      void setGrossSales( double ); // set gross sales amount
25      double getGrossSales() const; // return gross sales amount
26
27      void setCommissionRate( double ); // set commission rate
28      double getCommissionRate() const; // return commission rate
29
30      double earnings() const; // calculate earnings
31      void print() const; // print CommissionEmployee object
32   protected:
33      string firstName;
34      string lastName;
35      string socialSecurityNumber;
36      double grossSales; // gross weekly sales
37      double commissionRate; // commission percentage
38   }; // end class CommissionEmployee
39
40   #endif
```

Fig. 12.12 | CommissionEmployee class definition that declares protected data to allow access by derived classes. (Part 2 of 2.)

```
 1   // Fig. 12.13: CommissionEmployee.cpp
 2   // Class CommissionEmployee member-function definitions.
 3   #include <iostream>
 4   using std::cout;
 5
 6   #include "CommissionEmployee.h" // CommissionEmployee class definition
 7
 8   // constructor
 9   CommissionEmployee::CommissionEmployee(
10      const string &first, const string &last, const string &ssn,
11      double sales, double rate )
12   {
13      firstName = first; // should validate
14      lastName = last; // should validate
15      socialSecurityNumber = ssn; // should validate
16      setGrossSales( sales ); // validate and store gross sales
17      setCommissionRate( rate ); // validate and store commission rate
18   } // end CommissionEmployee constructor
19
20   // set first name
21   void CommissionEmployee::setFirstName( const string &first )
22   {
23      firstName = first; // should validate
24   } // end function setFirstName
25
26   // return first name
27   string CommissionEmployee::getFirstName() const
28   {
29      return firstName;
30   } // end function getFirstName
31
```

Fig. 12.13 | CommissionEmployee class with protected data. (Part 1 of 3.)

```
32    // set last name
33    void CommissionEmployee::setLastName( const string &last )
34    {
35       lastName = last; // should validate
36    } // end function setLastName
37
38    // return last name
39    string CommissionEmployee::getLastName() const
40    {
41       return lastName;
42    } // end function getLastName
43
44    // set social security number
45    void CommissionEmployee::setSocialSecurityNumber( const string &ssn )
46    {
47       socialSecurityNumber = ssn; // should validate
48    } // end function setSocialSecurityNumber
49
50    // return social security number
51    string CommissionEmployee::getSocialSecurityNumber() const
52    {
53       return socialSecurityNumber;
54    } // end function getSocialSecurityNumber
55
56    // set gross sales amount
57    void CommissionEmployee::setGrossSales( double sales )
58    {
59       grossSales = ( sales < 0.0 ) ? 0.0 : sales;
60    } // end function setGrossSales
61
62    // return gross sales amount
63    double CommissionEmployee::getGrossSales() const
64    {
65       return grossSales;
66    } // end function getGrossSales
67
68    // set commission rate
69    void CommissionEmployee::setCommissionRate( double rate )
70    {
71       commissionRate = ( rate > 0.0 && rate < 1.0 ) ? rate : 0.0;
72    } // end function setCommissionRate
73
74    // return commission rate
75    double CommissionEmployee::getCommissionRate() const
76    {
77       return commissionRate;
78    } // end function getCommissionRate
79
80    // calculate earnings
81    double CommissionEmployee::earnings() const
82    {
83       return commissionRate * grossSales;
84    } // end function earnings
```

Fig. 12.13 | CommissionEmployee class with protected data. (Part 2 of 3.)

```
85
86   // print CommissionEmployee object
87   void CommissionEmployee::print() const
88   {
89      cout << "commission employee: " << firstName << ' ' << lastName
90         << "\nsocial security number: " << socialSecurityNumber
91         << "\ngross sales: " << grossSales
92         << "\ncommission rate: " << commissionRate;
93   } // end function print
```

Fig. 12.13 | CommissionEmployee class with protected data. (Part 3 of 3.)

Modifying Derived Class *BasePlusCommissionEmployee*

We now modify class BasePlusCommissionEmployee (Figs. 12.14–12.15) so that it inherits from the version of class CommissionEmployee in Figs. 12.12–12.13. Because class BasePlusCommissionEmployee inherits from this version of class CommissionEmployee, objects of class BasePlusCommissionEmployee can access inherited data members that are declared protected in class CommissionEmployee (i.e., data members firstName, lastName, socialSecurityNumber, grossSales and commissionRate). As a result, the compiler does not generate errors when compiling the BasePlusCommissionEmployee earnings and print member-function definitions in Fig. 12.15 (lines 32–36 and 39–47, respectively).

```
1    // Fig. 12.14: BasePlusCommissionEmployee.h
2    // BasePlusCommissionEmployee class derived from class
3    // CommissionEmployee.
4    #ifndef BASEPLUS_H
5    #define BASEPLUS_H
6
7    #include <string> // C++ standard string class
8    using std::string;
9
10   #include "CommissionEmployee.h" // CommissionEmployee class declaration
11
12   class BasePlusCommissionEmployee : public CommissionEmployee
13   {
14   public:
15      BasePlusCommissionEmployee( const string &, const string &,
16         const string &, double = 0.0, double = 0.0, double = 0.0 );
17
18      void setBaseSalary( double ); // set base salary
19      double getBaseSalary() const; // return base salary
20
21      double earnings() const; // calculate earnings
22      void print() const; // print BasePlusCommissionEmployee object
23   private:
24      double baseSalary; // base salary
25   }; // end class BasePlusCommissionEmployee
26
27   #endif
```

Fig. 12.14 | BasePlusCommissionEmployee class header file.

```cpp
1   // Fig. 12.15: BasePlusCommissionEmployee.cpp
2   // Class BasePlusCommissionEmployee member-function definitions.
3   #include <iostream>
4   using std::cout;
5
6   // BasePlusCommissionEmployee class definition
7   #include "BasePlusCommissionEmployee.h"
8
9   // constructor
10  BasePlusCommissionEmployee::BasePlusCommissionEmployee(
11     const string &first, const string &last, const string &ssn,
12     double sales, double rate, double salary )
13     // explicitly call base-class constructor
14     : CommissionEmployee( first, last, ssn, sales, rate )
15  {
16     setBaseSalary( salary ); // validate and store base salary
17  } // end BasePlusCommissionEmployee constructor
18
19  // set base salary
20  void BasePlusCommissionEmployee::setBaseSalary( double salary )
21  {
22     baseSalary = ( salary < 0.0 ) ? 0.0 : salary;
23  } // end function setBaseSalary
24
25  // return base salary
26  double BasePlusCommissionEmployee::getBaseSalary() const
27  {
28     return baseSalary;
29  } // end function getBaseSalary
30
31  // calculate earnings
32  double BasePlusCommissionEmployee::earnings() const
33  {
34     // can access protected data of base class
35     return baseSalary + ( commissionRate * grossSales );
36  } // end function earnings
37
38  // print BasePlusCommissionEmployee object
39  void BasePlusCommissionEmployee::print() const
40  {
41     // can access protected data of base class
42     cout << "base-salaried commission employee: " << firstName << ' '
43        << lastName << "\nsocial security number: " << socialSecurityNumber
44        << "\ngross sales: " << grossSales
45        << "\ncommission rate: " << commissionRate
46        << "\nbase salary: " << baseSalary;
47  } // end function print
```

Fig. 12.15 | BasePlusCommissionEmployee implementation file for BasePlusCommissionEmployee class that inherits protected data from CommissionEmployee.

This shows the special privileges that a derived class is granted to access protected base-class data members. Objects of a derived class also can access protected members in any of that derived class's indirect base classes.

Class BasePlusCommissionEmployee does not inherit class CommissionEmployee's constructor. However, class BasePlusCommissionEmployee's constructor (Fig. 12.15, lines 10–17) calls class CommissionEmployee's constructor explicitly (line 14). Recall that BasePlusCommissionEmployee's constructor must explicitly call the constructor of class CommissionEmployee, because CommissionEmployee does not contain a default constructor that could be invoked implicitly.

Testing the Modified *BasePlusCommissionEmployee* Class

Figure 12.16 uses a BasePlusCommissionEmployee object to perform the same tasks that Fig. 12.9 performed on an object of the first version of class BasePlusCommissionEmployee (Figs. 12.7–12.8). Note that the outputs of the two programs are identical. We created the first class BasePlusCommissionEmployee without using inheritance and created this version of BasePlusCommissionEmployee using inheritance; however, both classes provide the same functionality. Note that the code for class BasePlusCommissionEmployee (i.e., the header and implementation files), which is 74 lines, is considerably shorter than the

```cpp
1   // Fig. 12.16: fig12_16.cpp
2   // Testing class BasePlusCommissionEmployee.
3   #include <iostream>
4   using std::cout;
5   using std::endl;
6   using std::fixed;
7
8   #include <iomanip>
9   using std::setprecision;
10
11  // BasePlusCommissionEmployee class definition
12  #include "BasePlusCommissionEmployee.h"
13
14  int main()
15  {
16     // instantiate BasePlusCommissionEmployee object
17     BasePlusCommissionEmployee
18        employee( "Bob", "Lewis", "333-33-3333", 5000, .04, 300 );
19
20     // set floating-point output formatting
21     cout << fixed << setprecision( 2 );
22
23     // get commission employee data
24     cout << "Employee information obtained by get functions: \n"
25        << "\nFirst name is " << employee.getFirstName()
26        << "\nLast name is " << employee.getLastName()
27        << "\nSocial security number is "
28        << employee.getSocialSecurityNumber()
29        << "\nGross sales is " << employee.getGrossSales()
30        << "\nCommission rate is " << employee.getCommissionRate()
31        << "\nBase salary is " << employee.getBaseSalary() << endl;
32
33     employee.setBaseSalary( 1000 ); // set base salary
34
```

Fig. 12.16 | protected base-class data can be accessed from derived class. (Part 1 of 2.)

```
35        cout << "\nUpdated employee information output by print function: \n"
36           << endl;
37        employee.print(); // display the new employee information
38
39        // display the employee's earnings
40        cout << "\n\nEmployee's earnings: $" << employee.earnings() << endl;
41
42        return 0;
43  } // end main
```

```
Employee information obtained by get functions:

First name is Bob
Last name is Lewis
Social security number is 333-33-3333
Gross sales is 5000.00
Commission rate is 0.04
Base salary is 300.00

Updated employee information output by print function:

base-salaried commission employee: Bob Lewis
social security number: 333-33-3333
gross sales: 5000.00
commission rate: 0.04
base salary: 1000.00

Employee's earnings: $1200.00
```

Fig. 12.16 | protected base-class data can be accessed from derived class. (Part 2 of 2.)

code for the noninherited version of the class, which is 154 lines, because the inherited version absorbs part of its functionality from CommissionEmployee, whereas the noninherited version does not absorb any functionality. Also, there is now only one copy of the CommissionEmployee functionality declared and defined in class CommissionEmployee. This makes the source code easier to maintain, modify and debug, because the source code related to a CommissionEmployee exists only in the files of Figs. 12.12–12.13.

Notes on Using *protected* Data

In this example, we declared base-class data members as protected, so that derived classes could modify the data directly. Inheriting protected data members slightly increases performance, because we can directly access the members without incurring the overhead of calls to *set* or *get* member functions. In most cases, however, it is better to use private data members to encourage proper software engineering, and leave code optimization issues to the compiler. Your code will be easier to maintain, modify and debug.

Using protected data members creates two major problems. First, the derived-class object does not have to use a member function to set the value of the base-class's protected data member. Therefore, a derived-class object easily can assign an invalid value to the protected data member, thus leaving the object in an inconsistent state. For example, with CommissionEmployee's data member grossSales declared as protected, a derived-class (e.g., `BasePlusCommissionEmployee`) object can assign a negative value to `grossSales`. The second problem with using `protected` data members is that derived-class member functions are more likely to be written so that they depend on the base-class implementation. In practice, derived classes should depend only on the base-class services (i.e., non-`private` member functions) and not on the base-class implementation. With `protected` data members in the base class, if the base-class implementation changes, we may need to modify all derived classes of that base class. For example, if for some reason we were to change the names of data members `firstName` and `lastName` to `first` and `last`, then we would have to do so for all occurrences in which a derived class references these base-class data members directly. In such a case, the software is said to be *fragile* or *brittle*, because a small change in the base class can "break" derived-class implementation. The programmer should be able to change the base-class implementation while still providing the same services to derived classes. (Of course, if the base-class services change, we must reimplement our derived classes—good object-oriented design attempts to prevent this.)

Software Engineering Observation 12.5

It is appropriate to use the `protected` access specifier when a base class should provide a service (i.e., a member function) only to its derived classes (and `friends`), not to other clients.

Software Engineering Observation 12.6

Declaring base-class data members `private` (as opposed to declaring them `protected`) enables programmers to change the base-class implementation without having to change derived-class implementations.

Error-Prevention Tip 12.1

When possible, avoid including `protected` data members in a base class. Rather, include non-private member functions that access `private` data members, ensuring that the object maintains a consistent state.

12.4.5 CommissionEmployee-BasePlusCommissionEmployee Inheritance Hierarchy Using private Data

We now reexamine our hierarchy once more, this time using the best software engineering practices. Class `CommissionEmployee` (Figs. 12.17–12.18) now declares data members `firstName`, `lastName`, `socialSecurityNumber`, `grossSales` and `commissionRate` as private (Fig. 12.17, lines 33–37) and provides `public` member functions `setFirstName`, `getFirstName`, `setLastName`, `getLastName`, `setSocialSecurityNumber`, `getSocialSecurityNumber`, `setGrossSales`, `getGrossSales`, `setCommissionRate`, `getCommissionRate`, `earnings` and `print` for manipulating these values. If we decide to change the data member names, the `earnings` and `print` definitions will not require modification—only the definitions of the *get* and *set* member functions that directly manipulate the data members will need to change. Note that these changes occur solely within the base class—no changes to the derived class are needed. Localizing the effects of changes like this is a good software engineering practice. Derived class `BasePlusCommissionEmployee` (Figs. 12.19–12.20) inherits `CommissionEmployee`'s non-`private` member functions and can access the `private` base-class members via those member functions.

```cpp
// Fig. 12.17: CommissionEmployee.h
// CommissionEmployee class definition with good software engineering.
#ifndef COMMISSION_H
#define COMMISSION_H

#include <string> // C++ standard string class
using std::string;

class CommissionEmployee
{
public:
   CommissionEmployee( const string &, const string &, const string &,
      double = 0.0, double = 0.0 );

   void setFirstName( const string & ); // set first name
   string getFirstName() const; // return first name

   void setLastName( const string & ); // set last name
   string getLastName() const; // return last name

   void setSocialSecurityNumber( const string & ); // set SSN
   string getSocialSecurityNumber() const; // return SSN

   void setGrossSales( double ); // set gross sales amount
   double getGrossSales() const; // return gross sales amount

   void setCommissionRate( double ); // set commission rate
   double getCommissionRate() const; // return commission rate

   double earnings() const; // calculate earnings
   void print() const; // print CommissionEmployee object
private:
   string firstName;
   string lastName;
   string socialSecurityNumber;
   double grossSales; // gross weekly sales
   double commissionRate; // commission percentage
}; // end class CommissionEmployee

#endif
```

Fig. 12.17 | CommissionEmployee class defined using good software engineering practices.

```cpp
// Fig. 12.18: CommissionEmployee.cpp
// Class CommissionEmployee member-function definitions.
#include <iostream>
using std::cout;

#include "CommissionEmployee.h" // CommissionEmployee class definition

```

Fig. 12.18 | CommissionEmployee class implementation file: CommissionEmployee class uses member functions to manipulate its private data. (Part 1 of 3.)

```
 8    // constructor
 9    CommissionEmployee::CommissionEmployee(
10       const string &first, const string &last, const string &ssn,
11       double sales, double rate )
12       : firstName( first ), lastName( last ), socialSecurityNumber( ssn )
13    {
14       setGrossSales( sales ); // validate and store gross sales
15       setCommissionRate( rate ); // validate and store commission rate
16    } // end CommissionEmployee constructor
17
18    // set first name
19    void CommissionEmployee::setFirstName( const string &first )
20    {
21       firstName = first; // should validate
22    } // end function setFirstName
23
24    // return first name
25    string CommissionEmployee::getFirstName() const
26    {
27       return firstName;
28    } // end function getFirstName
29
30    // set last name
31    void CommissionEmployee::setLastName( const string &last )
32    {
33       lastName = last; // should validate
34    } // end function setLastName
35
36    // return last name
37    string CommissionEmployee::getLastName() const
38    {
39       return lastName;
40    } // end function getLastName
41
42    // set social security number
43    void CommissionEmployee::setSocialSecurityNumber( const string &ssn )
44    {
45       socialSecurityNumber = ssn; // should validate
46    } // end function setSocialSecurityNumber
47
48    // return social security number
49    string CommissionEmployee::getSocialSecurityNumber() const
50    {
51       return socialSecurityNumber;
52    } // end function getSocialSecurityNumber
53
54    // set gross sales amount
55    void CommissionEmployee::setGrossSales( double sales )
56    {
57       grossSales = ( sales < 0.0 ) ? 0.0 : sales;
58    } // end function setGrossSales
```

Fig. 12.18 | CommissionEmployee class implementation file: CommissionEmployee class uses member functions to manipulate its private data. (Part 2 of 3.)

```
59
60    // return gross sales amount
61    double CommissionEmployee::getGrossSales() const
62    {
63       return grossSales;
64    } // end function getGrossSales
65
66    // set commission rate
67    void CommissionEmployee::setCommissionRate( double rate )
68    {
69       commissionRate = ( rate > 0.0 && rate < 1.0 ) ? rate : 0.0;
70    } // end function setCommissionRate
71
72    // return commission rate
73    double CommissionEmployee::getCommissionRate() const
74    {
75       return commissionRate;
76    } // end function getCommissionRate
77
78    // calculate earnings
79    double CommissionEmployee::earnings() const
80    {
81       return getCommissionRate() * getGrossSales();
82    } // end function earnings
83
84    // print CommissionEmployee object
85    void CommissionEmployee::print() const
86    {
87       cout << "commission employee: "
88          << getFirstName() << ' ' << getLastName()
89          << "\nsocial security number: " << getSocialSecurityNumber()
90          << "\ngross sales: " << getGrossSales()
91          << "\ncommission rate: " << getCommissionRate();
92    } // end function print
```

Fig. 12.18 | CommissionEmployee class implementation file: CommissionEmployee class uses member functions to manipulate its private data. (Part 3 of 3.)

In the CommissionEmployee constructor implementation (Fig. 12.18, lines 9–16), note that we use member initializers (line 12) to set the values of members firstName, lastName and socialSecurityNumber. We show how derived-class BasePlusCommissionEmployee (Figs. 12.19–12.20) can invoke non-private base-class member functions (setFirstName, getFirstName, setLastName, getLastName, setSocialSecurityNumber and getSocialSecurityNumber) to manipulate these data members.

Performance Tip 12.2

Using a member function to access a data member's value can be slightly slower than accessing the data directly. However, today's optimizing compilers are carefully designed to perform many optimizations implicitly (such as inlining set and get member-function calls). As a result, programmers should write code that adheres to proper software engineering principles, and leave optimization issues to the compiler. A good rule is, "Do not second-guess the compiler."

Class BasePlusCommissionEmployee (Figs. 12.19–12.20) has several changes to its member-function implementations (Fig. 12.20) that distinguish it from the previous version of the class (Figs. 12.14–12.15). Member functions earnings (Fig. 12.20, lines 32–35) and

```
1   // Fig. 12.19: BasePlusCommissionEmployee.h
2   // BasePlusCommissionEmployee class derived from class
3   // CommissionEmployee.
4   #ifndef BASEPLUS_H
5   #define BASEPLUS_H
6
7   #include <string> // C++ standard string class
8   using std::string;
9
10  #include "CommissionEmployee.h" // CommissionEmployee class declaration
11
12  class BasePlusCommissionEmployee : public CommissionEmployee
13  {
14  public:
15     BasePlusCommissionEmployee( const string &, const string &,
16        const string &, double = 0.0, double = 0.0, double = 0.0 );
17
18     void setBaseSalary( double ); // set base salary
19     double getBaseSalary() const; // return base salary
20
21     double earnings() const; // calculate earnings
22     void print() const; // print BasePlusCommissionEmployee object
23  private:
24     double baseSalary; // base salary
25  }; // end class BasePlusCommissionEmployee
26
27  #endif
```

Fig. 12.19 | BasePlusCommissionEmployee class header file.

```
1   // Fig. 12.20: BasePlusCommissionEmployee.cpp
2   // Class BasePlusCommissionEmployee member-function definitions.
3   #include <iostream>
4   using std::cout;
5
6   // BasePlusCommissionEmployee class definition
7   #include "BasePlusCommissionEmployee.h"
8
9   // constructor
10  BasePlusCommissionEmployee::BasePlusCommissionEmployee(
11     const string &first, const string &last, const string &ssn,
12     double sales, double rate, double salary )
13     // explicitly call base-class constructor
14     : CommissionEmployee( first, last, ssn, sales, rate )
15  {
```

Fig. 12.20 | BasePlusCommissionEmployee class that inherits from class CommissionEmployee but cannot directly access the class's private data. (Part 1 of 2.)

```
16        setBaseSalary( salary ); // validate and store base salary
17    } // end BasePlusCommissionEmployee constructor
18
19    // set base salary
20    void BasePlusCommissionEmployee::setBaseSalary( double salary )
21    {
22        baseSalary = ( salary < 0.0 ) ? 0.0 : salary;
23    } // end function setBaseSalary
24
25    // return base salary
26    double BasePlusCommissionEmployee::getBaseSalary() const
27    {
28        return baseSalary;
29    } // end function getBaseSalary
30
31    // calculate earnings
32    double BasePlusCommissionEmployee::earnings() const
33    {
34        return getBaseSalary() + CommissionEmployee::earnings();
35    } // end function earnings
36
37    // print BasePlusCommissionEmployee object
38    void BasePlusCommissionEmployee::print() const
39    {
40        cout << "base-salaried ";
41
42        // invoke CommissionEmployee's print function
43        CommissionEmployee::print();
44
45        cout << "\nbase salary: " << getBaseSalary();
46    } // end function print
```

Fig. 12.20 | `BasePlusCommissionEmployee` class that inherits from class `CommissionEmployee` but cannot directly access the class's `private` data. (Part 2 of 2.)

print (lines 38–46) each invoke member function getBaseSalary to obtain the base salary value, rather than accessing baseSalary directly. This insulates earnings and print from potential changes to the implementation of data member baseSalary. For example, if we decide to rename data member baseSalary or change its type, only member functions set-BaseSalary and getBaseSalary will need to change.

Class BasePlusCommissionEmployee's earnings function (Fig. 12.20, lines 32–35) redefines class CommissionEmployee's earnings member function (Fig. 12.18, lines 79–82) to calculate the earnings of a base-salaried commission employee. Class BasePlusCommissionEmployee's version of earnings obtains the portion of the employee's earnings based on commission alone by calling base-class CommissionEmployee's earnings function with the expression CommissionEmployee::earnings() (Fig. 12.20, line 34). BasePlusCommissionEmployee's earnings function then adds the base salary to this value to calculate the total earnings of the employee. Note the syntax used to invoke a redefined base-class member function from a derived class—place the base-class name and the binary scope resolution operator (::) before the base-class member-function name. This member-function invocation is a good software engineering practice: Recall from Software Engineering Observation 9.9 that, if an object's member function performs the actions needed by another object, we should call that member function rather than duplicating its code body. By having BasePlusCommissionEmployee's earnings function invoke Commission-Employee's earnings function to calculate part of a BasePlusCommissionEmployee object's earnings, we avoid duplicating the code and reduce code-maintenance problems.

Common Programming Error 12.2

When a base-class member function is redefined in a derived class, the derived-class version often calls the base-class version to do additional work. Failure to use the :: operator prefixed with the name of the base class when referencing the base class's member function causes infinite recursion, because the derived-class member function would then call itself.

Common Programming Error 12.3

Including a base-class member function with a different signature in the derived class hides the base-class version of the function. Attempts to call the base-class version through the public interface of a derived-class object result in compilation errors.

Similarly, BasePlusCommissionEmployee's print function (Fig. 12.20, lines 38–46) redefines class CommissionEmployee's print member function (Fig. 12.18, lines 85–92) to output information that is appropriate for a base-salaried commission employee. Class BasePlusCommissionEmployee's version displays part of a BasePlusCommissionEmployee object's information (i.e., the string "commission employee" and the values of class CommissionEmployee's private data members) by calling CommissionEmployee's print member function with the qualified name CommissionEmployee::print() (Fig. 12.20, line 43). BasePlusCommissionEmployee's print function then outputs the remainder of a BasePlusCommissionEmployee object's information (i.e., the value of class BasePlusCommissionEmployee's base salary).

Figure 12.21 performs the same manipulations on a BasePlusCommissionEmployee object as did Fig. 12.9 and Fig. 12.16 on objects of classes CommissionEmployee and BasePlusCommissionEmployee, respectively. Although each "base-salaried commission employee" class behaves identically, class BasePlusCommissionEmployee is the best engineered. By using inheritance and by calling member functions that hide the data and ensure consistency, we have efficiently and effectively constructed a well-engineered class.

```
1   // Fig. 12.21: fig12_21.cpp
2   // Testing class BasePlusCommissionEmployee.
3   #include <iostream>
4   using std::cout;
5   using std::endl;
6   using std::fixed;
7
8   #include <iomanip>
9   using std::setprecision;
10
11  // BasePlusCommissionEmployee class definition
12  #include "BasePlusCommissionEmployee.h"
```

Fig. 12.21 | Base-class private data is accessible to a derived class via public or protected member function inherited by the derived class. (Part 1 of 2.)

```
13
14  int main()
15  {
16      // instantiate BasePlusCommissionEmployee object
17      BasePlusCommissionEmployee
18          employee( "Bob", "Lewis", "333-33-3333", 5000, .04, 300 );
19
20      // set floating-point output formatting
21      cout << fixed << setprecision( 2 );
22
23      // get commission employee data
24      cout << "Employee information obtained by get functions: \n"
25          << "\nFirst name is " << employee.getFirstName()
26          << "\nLast name is " << employee.getLastName()
27          << "\nSocial security number is "
28          << employee.getSocialSecurityNumber()
29          << "\nGross sales is " << employee.getGrossSales()
30          << "\nCommission rate is " << employee.getCommissionRate()
31          << "\nBase salary is " << employee.getBaseSalary() << endl;
32
33      employee.setBaseSalary( 1000 ); // set base salary
34
35      cout << "\nUpdated employee information output by print function: \n"
36          << endl;
37      employee.print(); // display the new employee information
38
39      // display the employee's earnings
40      cout << "\n\nEmployee's earnings: $" << employee.earnings() << endl;
41
42      return 0;
43  } // end main
```

```
Employee information obtained by get functions:

First name is Bob
Last name is Lewis
Social security number is 333-33-3333
Gross sales is 5000.00
Commission rate is 0.04
Base salary is 300.00

Updated employee information output by print function:

base-salaried commission employee: Bob Lewis
social security number: 333-33-3333
gross sales: 5000.00
commission rate: 0.04
base salary: 1000.00

Employee's earnings: $1200.00
```

Fig. 12.21 | Base-class private data is accessible to a derived class via public or protected member function inherited by the derived class. (Part 2 of 2.)

In this section, you saw an evolutionary set of examples that was carefully designed to teach key capabilities for good software engineering with inheritance. You learned how to create a derived class using inheritance, how to use `protected` base-class members to enable a derived class to access inherited base-class data members and how to redefine base-class functions to provide versions that are more appropriate for derived-class objects. In addition, you learned how to apply software engineering techniques from Chapters 9–10 and this chapter to create classes that are easy to maintain, modify and debug.

12.5 Constructors and Destructors in Derived Classes

As we explained in the preceding section, instantiating a derived-class object begins a chain of constructor calls in which the derived-class constructor, before performing its own tasks, invokes its direct base class's constructor either explicitly (via a base-class member initializer) or implicitly (calling the base class's default constructor). Similarly, if the base class is derived from another class, the base-class constructor is required to invoke the constructor of the next class up in the hierarchy, and so on. The last constructor called in this chain is the constructor of the class at the base of the hierarchy, whose body actually finishes executing first. The original derived-class constructor's body finishes executing last. Each base-class constructor initializes the base-class data members that the derived-class object inherits. For example, consider the `CommissionEmployee/BasePlusCommissionEmployee` hierarchy from Figs. 12.17–12.20. When a program creates an object of class `BasePlusCommissionEmployee`, the `CommissionEmployee` constructor is called. Since class `CommissionEmployee` is at the base of the hierarchy, its constructor executes, initializing the `private` data members of `CommissionEmployee` that are part of the `BasePlusCommissionEmployee` object. When `CommissionEmployee`'s constructor completes execution, it returns control to `BasePlusCommissionEmployee`'s constructor, which initializes the `BasePlusCommissionEmployee` object's `baseSalary`.

Software Engineering Observation 12.7

When a program creates a derived-class object, the derived-class constructor immediately calls the base-class constructor, the base-class constructor's body executes, then the derived class's member initializers execute and finally the derived-class constructor's body executes. This process cascades up the hierarchy if the hierarchy contains more than two levels.

When a derived-class object is destroyed, the program calls that object's destructor. This begins a chain (or cascade) of destructor calls in which the derived-class destructor and the destructors of the direct and indirect base classes and the classes' members execute in reverse of the order in which the constructors executed. When a derived-class object's destructor is called, the destructor performs its task, then invokes the destructor of the next base class up the hierarchy. This process repeats until the destructor of the final base class at the top of the hierarchy is called. Then the object is removed from memory.

Software Engineering Observation 12.8

Suppose that we create an object of a derived class where both the base class and the derived class contain objects of other classes. When an object of that derived class is created, first the constructors for the base class's member objects execute, then the base-class constructor executes, then the constructors for the derived class's member objects execute, then the derived class's constructor executes. Destructors for derived-class objects are called in the reverse of the order in which their corresponding constructors are called.

Base-class constructors, destructors and overloaded assignment operators (see Chapter 11) are not inherited by derived classes. Derived-class constructors, destructors and overloaded assignment operators, however, can call base-class constructors, destructors and overloaded assignment operators.

Our next example revisits the commission employee hierarchy by defining class CommissionEmployee (Figs. 12.22–12.23) and class BasePlusCommissionEmployee (Figs. 12.24–12.25) that contain constructors and destructors, each of which prints a message when it is invoked. As you will see in the output in Fig. 12.26, these messages demonstrate the order in which the constructors and destructors are called for objects in an inheritance hierarchy.

```cpp
 1   // Fig. 12.22: CommissionEmployee.h
 2   // CommissionEmployee class definition represents a commission employee.
 3   #ifndef COMMISSION_H
 4   #define COMMISSION_H
 5
 6   #include <string> // C++ standard string class
 7   using std::string;
 8
 9   class CommissionEmployee
10   {
11   public:
12      CommissionEmployee( const string &, const string &, const string &,
13         double = 0.0, double = 0.0 );
14      ~CommissionEmployee(); // destructor
15
16      void setFirstName( const string & ); // set first name
17      string getFirstName() const; // return first name
18
19      void setLastName( const string & ); // set last name
20      string getLastName() const; // return last name
21
22      void setSocialSecurityNumber( const string & ); // set SSN
23      string getSocialSecurityNumber() const; // return SSN
24
25      void setGrossSales( double ); // set gross sales amount
26      double getGrossSales() const; // return gross sales amount
27
28      void setCommissionRate( double ); // set commission rate
29      double getCommissionRate() const; // return commission rate
30
31      double earnings() const; // calculate earnings
32      void print() const; // print CommissionEmployee object
33   private:
34      string firstName;
35      string lastName;
36      string socialSecurityNumber;
37      double grossSales; // gross weekly sales
38      double commissionRate; // commission percentage
39   }; // end class CommissionEmployee
40
41   #endif
```

Fig. 12.22 | CommissionEmployee class header file.

In this example, we modified the CommissionEmployee constructor (lines 10–21 of Fig. 12.23) and included a CommissionEmployee destructor (lines 24–29), each of which outputs a line of text upon its invocation. We also modified the BasePlusCommissionEmployee constructor (lines 11–22 of Fig. 12.25) and included a BasePlusCommissionEmployee destructor (lines 25–30), each of which outputs a line of text upon its invocation.

```cpp
1   // Fig. 12.23: CommissionEmployee.cpp
2   // Class CommissionEmployee member-function definitions.
3   #include <iostream>
4   using std::cout;
5   using std::endl;
6
7   #include "CommissionEmployee.h" // CommissionEmployee class definition
8
9   // constructor
10  CommissionEmployee::CommissionEmployee(
11     const string &first, const string &last, const string &ssn,
12     double sales, double rate )
13     : firstName( first ), lastName( last ), socialSecurityNumber( ssn )
14  {
15     setGrossSales( sales ); // validate and store gross sales
16     setCommissionRate( rate ); // validate and store commission rate
17
18     cout << "CommissionEmployee constructor: " << endl;
19     print();
20     cout << "\n\n";
21  } // end CommissionEmployee constructor
22
23  // destructor
24  CommissionEmployee::~CommissionEmployee()
25  {
26     cout << "CommissionEmployee destructor: " << endl;
27     print();
28     cout << "\n\n";
29  } // end CommissionEmployee destructor
30
31  // set first name
32  void CommissionEmployee::setFirstName( const string &first )
33  {
34     firstName = first; // should validate
35  } // end function setFirstName
36
37  // return first name
38  string CommissionEmployee::getFirstName() const
39  {
40     return firstName;
41  } // end function getFirstName
42
43  // set last name
44  void CommissionEmployee::setLastName( const string &last )
45  {
```

Fig. 12.23 | CommissionEmployee's constructor outputs text. (Part 1 of 3.)

```
46        lastName = last; // should validate
47   } // end function setLastName
48
49   // return last name
50   string CommissionEmployee::getLastName() const
51   {
52        return lastName;
53   } // end function getLastName
54
55   // set social security number
56   void CommissionEmployee::setSocialSecurityNumber( const string &ssn )
57   {
58        socialSecurityNumber = ssn; // should validate
59   } // end function setSocialSecurityNumber
60
61   // return social security number
62   string CommissionEmployee::getSocialSecurityNumber() const
63   {
64        return socialSecurityNumber;
65   } // end function getSocialSecurityNumber
66
67   // set gross sales amount
68   void CommissionEmployee::setGrossSales( double sales )
69   {
70        grossSales = ( sales < 0.0 ) ? 0.0 : sales;
71   } // end function setGrossSales
72
73   // return gross sales amount
74   double CommissionEmployee::getGrossSales() const
75   {
76        return grossSales;
77   } // end function getGrossSales
78
79   // set commission rate
80   void CommissionEmployee::setCommissionRate( double rate )
81   {
82        commissionRate = ( rate > 0.0 && rate < 1.0 ) ? rate : 0.0;
83   } // end function setCommissionRate
84
85   // return commission rate
86   double CommissionEmployee::getCommissionRate() const
87   {
88        return commissionRate;
89   } // end function getCommissionRate
90
91   // calculate earnings
92   double CommissionEmployee::earnings() const
93   {
94        return getCommissionRate() * getGrossSales();
95   } // end function earnings
96
```

Fig. 12.23 | CommissionEmployee's constructor outputs text. (Part 2 of 3.)

```
97   // print CommissionEmployee object
98   void CommissionEmployee::print() const
99   {
100     cout << "commission employee: "
101        << getFirstName() << ' ' << getLastName()
102        << "\nsocial security number: " << getSocialSecurityNumber()
103        << "\ngross sales: " << getGrossSales()
104        << "\ncommission rate: " << getCommissionRate();
105   } // end function print
```

Fig. 12.23 | CommissionEmployee's constructor outputs text. (Part 3 of 3.)

```
1    // Fig. 12.24: BasePlusCommissionEmployee.h
2    // BasePlusCommissionEmployee class derived from class
3    // CommissionEmployee.
4    #ifndef BASEPLUS_H
5    #define BASEPLUS_H
6
7    #include <string> // C++ standard string class
8    using std::string;
9
10   #include "CommissionEmployee.h" // CommissionEmployee class declaration
11
12   class BasePlusCommissionEmployee : public CommissionEmployee
13   {
14   public:
15      BasePlusCommissionEmployee( const string &, const string &,
16         const string &, double = 0.0, double = 0.0, double = 0.0 );
17      ~BasePlusCommissionEmployee(); // destructor
18
19      void setBaseSalary( double ); // set base salary
20      double getBaseSalary() const; // return base salary
21
22      double earnings() const; // calculate earnings
23      void print() const; // print BasePlusCommissionEmployee object
24   private:
25      double baseSalary; // base salary
26   }; // end class BasePlusCommissionEmployee
27
28   #endif
```

Fig. 12.24 | BasePlusCommissionEmployee class header file.

```
1    // Fig. 12.25: BasePlusCommissionEmployee.cpp
2    // Class BasePlusCommissionEmployee member-function definitions.
3    #include <iostream>
4    using std::cout;
5    using std::endl;
6
7    // BasePlusCommissionEmployee class definition
8    #include "BasePlusCommissionEmployee.h"
```

Fig. 12.25 | BasePlusCommissionEmployee's constructor outputs text. (Part 1 of 2.)

```
 9
10    // constructor
11    BasePlusCommissionEmployee::BasePlusCommissionEmployee(
12       const string &first, const string &last, const string &ssn,
13       double sales, double rate, double salary )
14       // explicitly call base-class constructor
15       : CommissionEmployee( first, last, ssn, sales, rate )
16    {
17       setBaseSalary( salary ); // validate and store base salary
18
19       cout << "BasePlusCommissionEmployee constructor: " << endl;
20       print();
21       cout << "\n\n";
22    } // end BasePlusCommissionEmployee constructor
23
24    // destructor
25    BasePlusCommissionEmployee::~BasePlusCommissionEmployee()
26    {
27       cout << "BasePlusCommissionEmployee destructor: " << endl;
28       print();
29       cout << "\n\n";
30    } // end BasePlusCommissionEmployee destructor
31
32    // set base salary
33    void BasePlusCommissionEmployee::setBaseSalary( double salary )
34    {
35       baseSalary = ( salary < 0.0 ) ? 0.0 : salary;
36    } // end function setBaseSalary
37
38    // return base salary
39    double BasePlusCommissionEmployee::getBaseSalary() const
40    {
41       return baseSalary;
42    } // end function getBaseSalary
43
44    // calculate earnings
45    double BasePlusCommissionEmployee::earnings() const
46    {
47       return getBaseSalary() + CommissionEmployee::earnings();
48    } // end function earnings
49
50    // print BasePlusCommissionEmployee object
51    void BasePlusCommissionEmployee::print() const
52    {
53       cout << "base-salaried ";
54
55       // invoke CommissionEmployee's print function
56       CommissionEmployee::print();
57
58       cout << "\nbase salary: " << getBaseSalary();
59    } // end function print
```

Fig. 12.25 | BasePlusCommissionEmployee's constructor outputs text. (Part 2 of 2.)

Figure 12.26 demonstrates the order in which constructors and destructors are called for objects of classes that are part of an inheritance hierarchy. Function main (lines 15–34) begins by instantiating CommissionEmployee object employee1 (lines 21–22) in a separate block inside main (lines 20–23). The object goes in and out of scope immediately (the end of the block is reached as soon as the object is created), so both the CommissionEmployee constructor and destructor are called. Next, lines 26–27 instantiate BasePlusCommissionEmployee object employee2. This invokes the CommissionEmployee constructor to display outputs with values passed from the BasePlusCommissionEmployee constructor, then the output specified in the BasePlusCommissionEmployee constructor is performed. Lines 30–31 then instantiate BasePlusCommissionEmployee object employee3. Again, the CommissionEmployee and BasePlusCommissionEmployee constructors are both called. Note that, in each case, the body of the CommissionEmployee constructor is executed before the body of the BasePlusCommissionEmployee constructor executes. When the end of main is reached, the destructors are called for objects employee2 and employee3. But, because destructors are called in the reverse order of their corresponding constructors, the BasePlusCommissionEmployee destructor and CommissionEmployee destructor are called (in that order) for object employee3, then the BasePlusCommissionEmployee and CommissionEmployee destructors are called (in that order) for object employee2.

```cpp
1   // Fig. 12.26: fig12_26.cpp
2   // Display order in which base-class and derived-class constructors
3   // and destructors are called.
4   #include <iostream>
5   using std::cout;
6   using std::endl;
7   using std::fixed;
8
9   #include <iomanip>
10  using std::setprecision;
11
12  // BasePlusCommissionEmployee class definition
13  #include "BasePlusCommissionEmployee.h"
14
15  int main()
16  {
17     // set floating-point output formatting
18     cout << fixed << setprecision( 2 );
19
20     { // begin new scope
21        CommissionEmployee employee1(
22           "Bob", "Lewis", "333-33-3333", 5000, .04 );
23     } // end scope
24
25     cout << endl;
26     BasePlusCommissionEmployee
27        employee2( "Lisa", "Jones", "555-55-5555", 2000, .06, 800 );
28
```

Fig. 12.26 | Constructor and destructor call order. (Part 1 of 3.)

```
29    cout << endl;
30    BasePlusCommissionEmployee
31        employee3( "Mark", "Sands", "888-88-8888", 8000, .15, 2000 );
32    cout << endl;
33    return 0;
34 } // end main
```

```
CommissionEmployee constructor:
commission employee: Bob Lewis
social security number: 333-33-3333
gross sales: 5000.00
commission rate: 0.04

CommissionEmployee destructor:
commission employee: Bob Lewis
social security number: 333-33-3333
gross sales: 5000.00
commission rate: 0.04


CommissionEmployee constructor:
base-salaried commission employee: Lisa Jones
social security number: 555-55-5555
gross sales: 2000.00
commission rate: 0.06

BasePlusCommissionEmployee constructor:
base-salaried commission employee: Lisa Jones
social security number: 555-55-5555
gross sales: 2000.00
commission rate: 0.06
base salary: 800.00


CommissionEmployee constructor:
commission employee: Mark Sands
social security number: 888-88-8888
gross sales: 8000.00
commission rate: 0.15

BasePlusCommissionEmployee constructor:
base-salaried commission employee: Mark Sands
social security number: 888-88-8888
gross sales: 8000.00
commission rate: 0.15
base salary: 2000.00

BasePlusCommissionEmployee destructor:
base-salaried commission employee: Mark Sands
social security number: 888-88-8888
gross sales: 8000.00
commission rate: 0.15
base salary: 2000.00
```

(continued at top of next page…)

Fig. 12.26 | Constructor and destructor call order. (Part 2 of 3.)

(…continued from bottom of previous page)

```
CommissionEmployee destructor:
commission employee: Mark Sands
social security number: 888-88-8888
gross sales: 8000.00
commission rate: 0.15

BasePlusCommissionEmployee destructor:
base-salaried commission employee: Lisa Jones
social security number: 555-55-5555
gross sales: 2000.00
commission rate: 0.06
base salary: 800.00

CommissionEmployee destructor:
commission employee: Lisa Jones
social security number: 555-55-5555
gross sales: 2000.00
commission rate: 0.06
```

Fig. 12.26 | Constructor and destructor call order. (Part 3 of 3.)

12.6 public, protected and private Inheritance

When deriving a class from a base class, the base class may be inherited through public, protected or private inheritance. Use of protected and private inheritance is rare, and each should be used only with great care; we normally use public inheritance in this book. (Chapter 21 demonstrates private inheritance as an alternative to composition.) Figure 12.27 summarizes for each type of inheritance the accessibility of base-class members in a derived class. The first column contains the base-class access specifiers.

When deriving a class from a public base class, public members of the base class become public members of the derived class and protected members of the base class become protected members of the derived class. A base class's private members are never accessible directly from a derived class, but can be accessed through calls to the public and protected members of the base class.

When deriving from a protected base class, public and protected members of the base class become protected members of the derived class. When deriving from a private base class, public and protected members of the base class become private members (e.g., the functions become utility functions) of the derived class. Private and protected inheritance are not *is-a* relationships.

12.7 Software Engineering with Inheritance

In this section, we discuss the use of inheritance to customize existing software. When we use inheritance to create a new class from an existing one, the new class inherits the data members and member functions of the existing class, as described in Fig. 12.27. We can customize the new class to meet our needs by including additional members and by redefining base-class members. The derived-class programmer does this in C++ without accessing the base class's source code. The derived class must be able to link to the base class's

Base-class member-access specifier	Type of inheritance		
	public inheritance	protected inheritance	private inheritance
public	public in derived class. Can be accessed directly by member functions, friend functions and nonmember functions.	protected in derived class. Can be accessed directly by member functions and friend functions.	private in derived class. Can be accessed directly by member functions and friend functions.
protected	protected in derived class. Can be accessed directly by member functions and friend functions.	protected in derived class. Can be accessed directly by member functions and friend functions.	private in derived class. Can be accessed directly by member functions and friend functions.
private	Hidden in derived class. Can be accessed by member functions and friend functions through public or protected member functions of the base class.	Hidden in derived class. Can be accessed by member functions and friend functions through public or protected member functions of the base class.	Hidden in derived class. Can be accessed by member functions and friend functions through public or protected member functions of the base class.

Fig. 12.27 | Summary of base-class member accessibility in a derived class.

object code. This powerful capability is attractive to independent software vendors (ISVs). ISVs can develop proprietary classes for sale or license and make these classes available to users in object-code format. Users then can derive new classes from these library classes rapidly and without accessing the ISVs' proprietary source code. All the ISVs need to supply with the object code are the header files.

Sometimes it is difficult for students to appreciate the scope of problems faced by designers who work on large-scale software projects in industry. People experienced with such projects say that effective software reuse improves the software development process. Object-oriented programming facilitates software reuse, thus shortening development times and enhancing software quality.

The availability of substantial and useful class libraries delivers the maximum benefits of software reuse through inheritance. Just as shrink-wrapped software produced by independent software vendors became an explosive-growth industry with the arrival of the personal computer, so, too, interest in the creation and sale of class libraries is growing exponentially. Application designers build their applications with these libraries, and library designers are being rewarded by having their libraries included with the applications. The standard C++ libraries that are shipped with C++ compilers tend to be rather general purpose and limited in scope. However, there is massive worldwide commitment to the development of class libraries for a huge variety of applications arenas.

Software Engineering Observation 12.9

At the design stage in an object-oriented system, the designer often determines that certain classes are closely related. The designer should "factor out" common attributes and behaviors and place these in a base class, then use inheritance to form derived classes, endowing them with capabilities beyond those inherited from the base class.

Software Engineering Observation 12.10

The creation of a derived class does not affect its base class's source code. Inheritance preserves the integrity of a base class.

Software Engineering Observation 12.11

Just as designers of non-object-oriented systems should avoid proliferation of functions, designers of object-oriented systems should avoid proliferation of classes. Proliferation of classes creates management problems and can hinder software reusability, because it becomes difficult for a client to locate the most appropriate class of a huge class library. The alternative is to create fewer classes that provide more substantial functionality, but such classes might provide too much functionality.

Performance Tip 12.3

If classes produced through inheritance are larger than they need to be (i.e., contain too much functionality), memory and processing resources might be wasted. Inherit from the class whose functionality is "closest" to what is needed.

Reading derived-class definitions can be confusing, because inherited members are not shown physically in the derived classes, but nevertheless are present. A similar problem exists when documenting derived-class members.

Summary

- Software reuse reduces program development time and cost.

- Inheritance is a form of software reuse in which the programmer creates a class that absorbs an existing class's data and behaviors and enhances them with new capabilities. The existing class is called the base class, and the new class is referred to as the derived class.

- A direct base class is the one from which a derived class explicitly inherits (specified by the class name to the right of the : in the first line of a class definition). An indirect base class is inherited from two or more levels up in the class hierarchy.

- With single inheritance, a class is derived from one base class. With multiple inheritance, a class inherits from multiple (possibly unrelated) base classes.

- A derived class represents a more specialized group of objects. Typically, a derived class contains behaviors inherited from its base class plus additional behaviors. A derived class can also customize behaviors inherited from the base class.

- Every object of a derived class is also an object of that class's base class. However, a base-class object is not an object of that class's derived classes.

- The *is-a* relationship represents inheritance. In an *is-a* relationship, an object of a derived class also can be treated as an object of its base class.

- The *has-a* relationship represents composition. In a *has-a* relationship, an object contains one or more objects of other classes as members, but does not disclose their behavior directly in its interface.

- A derived class cannot access the `private` members of its base class directly; allowing this would violate the encapsulation of the base class. A derived class can, however, access the `public` and `protected` members of its base class directly.

- A derived class can effect state changes in `private` base-class members, but only through non-`private` member functions provided in the base class and inherited into the derived class.

- When a base-class member function is inappropriate for a derived class, that member function can be redefined in the derived class with an appropriate implementation.

- Single-inheritance relationships form treelike hierarchical structures—a base class exists in a hierarchical relationship with its derived classes.

- It is possible to treat base-class objects and derived-class objects similarly; the commonality shared between the object types is expressed in the data members and member functions of the base class.

- A base class's `public` members are accessible anywhere that the program has a handle to an object of that base class or to an object of one of that base class's derived classes—or, when using the binary scope resolution operator, whenever the class's name is in scope.

- A base class's `private` members are accessible only within the definition of that base class or from friends of that class.

- A base class's `protected` members have an intermediate level of protection between `public` and `private` access. A base class's `protected` members can be accessed by members and friends of that base class and by members and friends of any classes derived from that base class.

- Unfortunately, `protected` data members often present two major problems. First, the derived-class object does not have to use a *set* function to change the value of the base-class's `protected` data. Second, derived-class member functions are more likely to depend on base-class implementation details.

- When a derived-class member function redefines a base-class member function, the base-class member function can be accessed from the derived class by qualifying the base-class member function name with the base-class name and the binary scope resolution operator (`::`).

- When an object of a derived class is instantiated, the base class's constructor is called immediately (either explicitly or implicitly) to initialize the base-class data members in the derived-class object (before the derived-class data members are initialized).

- Declaring data members `private`, while providing non-`private` member functions to manipulate and perform validation checking on this data, enforces good software engineering.

- When a derived-class object is destroyed, the destructors are called in the reverse order of the constructors—first the derived-class destructor is called, then the base-class destructor is called.

- When deriving a class from a base class, the base class may be declared as either `public`, `protected` or `private`.

- When deriving a class from a `public` base class, `public` members of the base class become `public` members of the derived class, and `protected` members of the base class become `protected` members of the derived class.

- When deriving a class from a `protected` base class, `public` and `protected` members of the base class become `protected` members of the derived class.

- When deriving a class from a `private` base class, `public` and `protected` members of the base class become `private` members of the derived class.

Terminology

base class	indirect base class
base-class constructor	inherit the members of an existing class
base-class default constructor	inheritance
base-class destructor	*is-a* relationship
base-class initializer	multiple inheritance
brittle software	`private` base class
class hierarchy	`private` inheritance
composition	`protected` base class
customize software	`protected` inheritance
derived class	`protected` keyword
derived-class constructor	`protected` member of a class
derived-class destructor	`public` base class
direct base class	`public` inheritance
fragile software	qualified name
`friend` of a base class	redefine a base-class member function
`friend` of a derived class	single inheritance
has-a relationship	subclass
hierarchical relationship	superclass

Self-Review Exercises

12.1 Fill in the blanks in each of the following statements:

a) _____ is a form of software reuse in which new classes absorb the data and behaviors of existing classes and embellish these classes with new capabilities.

b) A base class's _____ members can be accessed only in the base-class definition or in derived-class definitions.

c) In a(n) _____ relationship, an object of a derived class also can be treated as an object of its base class.

d) In a(n) _____ relationship, a class object has one or more objects of other classes as members.

e) In single inheritance, a class exists in a(n) _____ relationship with its derived classes.

f) A base class's _____ members are accessible within that base class and anywhere that the program has a handle to an object of that base class or to an object of one of its derived classes.

g) A base class's `protected` access members have a level of protection between those of `public` and _____ access.

h) C++ provides for _____, which allows a derived class to inherit from many base classes, even if these base classes are unrelated.

i) When an object of a derived class is instantiated, the base class's _____ is called implicitly or explicitly to do any necessary initialization of the base-class data members in the derived-class object.

j) When deriving a class from a base class with `public` inheritance, `public` members of the base class become _____ members of the derived class, and `protected` members of the base class become _____ members of the derived class.

k) When deriving a class from a base class with `protected` inheritance, `public` members of the base class become _____ members of the derived class, and `protected` members of the base class become _____ members of the derived class.

12.2 State whether each of the following is *true* or *false*. If *false*, explain why.

a) Base-class constructors are not inherited by derived classes.
b) A *has-a* relationship is implemented via inheritance.
c) A Car class has an *is-a* relationship with the SteeringWheel and Brakes classes.
d) Inheritance encourages the reuse of proven high-quality software.
e) When a derived-class object is destroyed, the destructors are called in the reverse order of the constructors.

Answers to Self-Review Exercises

12.1 a) Inheritance. b) protected. c) *is-a* or inheritance. d) *has-a* or composition or aggregation. e) hierarchical. f) public. g) private. h) multiple inheritance. i) constructor. j) public, protected. k) protected, protected.

12.2 a) True. b) False. A *has-a* relationship is implemented via composition. An *is-a* relationship is implemented via inheritance. c) False. This is an example of a *has-a* relationship. Class Car has an *is-a* relationship with class Vehicle. d) True. e) True.

Exercises

12.3 Many programs written with inheritance could be written with composition instead, and vice versa. Rewrite class BasePlusCommissionEmployee of the CommissionEmployee–BasePlusCommissionEmployee hierarchy to use composition rather than inheritance. After you do this, assess the relative merits of the two approaches for designing classes CommissionEmployee and BasePlusCommissionEmployee, as well as for object-oriented programs in general. Which approach is more natural? Why?

12.4 Discuss the ways in which inheritance promotes software reuse, saves time during program development and helps prevent errors.

12.5 Some programmers prefer not to use protected access because they believe it breaks the encapsulation of the base class. Discuss the relative merits of using protected access vs. using private access in base classes.

12.6 Draw an inheritance hierarchy for students at a university similar to the hierarchy shown in Fig. 12.2. Use Student as the base class of the hierarchy, then include classes UndergraduateStudent and GraduateStudent that derive from Student. Continue to extend the hierarchy as deep (i.e., as many levels) as possible. For example, Freshman, Sophomore, Junior and Senior might derive from UndergraduateStudent, and DoctoralStudent and MastersStudent might derive from GraduateStudent. After drawing the hierarchy, discuss the relationships that exist between the classes. [*Note:* You do not need to write any code for this exercise.]

12.7 The world of shapes is much richer than the shapes included in the inheritance hierarchy of Fig. 12.3. Write down all the shapes you can think of—both two-dimensional and three-dimensional—and form them into a more complete Shape hierarchy with as many levels as possible. Your hierarchy should have base class Shape from which class TwoDimensionalShape and class ThreeDimensionalShape are derived. [*Note:* You do not need to write any code for this exercise.] We will use this hierarchy in the exercises of Chapter 13 to process a set of distinct shapes as objects of base-class Shape. (This technique, called polymorphism, is the subject of Chapter 13.)

12.8 Draw an inheritance hierarchy for classes Quadrilateral, Trapezoid, Parallelogram, Rectangle and Square. Use Quadrilateral as the base class of the hierarchy. Make the hierarchy as deep as possible.

12.9 (*Package Inheritance Hierarchy*) Package-delivery services, such as FedEx®, DHL® and UPS®, offer a number of different shipping options, each with specific costs associated. Create an inheritance hierarchy to represent various types of packages. Use Package as the base class of the hierarchy, then include classes TwoDayPackage and OvernightPackage that derive from Package. Base class Package should include data members representing the name, address, city, state and ZIP code for both the sender and the recipient of the package, in addition to data members that store the weight (in ounces) and cost per ounce to ship the package. Package's constructor should initialize these data members. Ensure that the weight and cost per ounce contain positive values. Package should provide a public member function calculateCost that returns a double indicating the cost associated with shipping the package. Package's calculateCost function should determine the cost by multiplying the weight by the cost per ounce. Derived class TwoDayPackage should inherit the functionality of base class Package, but also include a data member that represents a flat fee that the shipping company charges for two-day-delivery service. TwoDayPackage's constructor should receive a value to initialize this data member. TwoDayPackage should redefine member function calculate-Cost so that it computes the shipping cost by adding the flat fee to the weight-based cost calculated by base class Package's calculateCost function. Class OvernightPackage should inherit directly from class Package and contain an additional data member representing an additional fee per ounce charged for overnight-delivery service. OvernightPackage should redefine member function calculateCost so that it adds the additional fee per ounce to the standard cost per ounce before calculating the shipping cost. Write a test program that creates objects of each type of Package and tests member function calculateCost.

12.10 *(Account Inheritance Hierarchy)* Create an inheritance hierarchy that a bank might use to represent customers' bank accounts. All customers at this bank can deposit (i.e., credit) money into their accounts and withdraw (i.e., debit) money from their accounts. More specific types of accounts also exist. Savings accounts, for instance, earn interest on the money they hold. Checking accounts, on the other hand, charge a fee per transaction (i.e., credit or debit).

Create an inheritance hierarchy containing base class Account and derived classes Savings-Account and CheckingAccount that inherit from class Account. Base class Account should include one data member of type double to represent the account balance. The class should provide a constructor that receives an initial balance and uses it to initialize the data member. The constructor should validate the initial balance to ensure that it is greater than or equal to 0.0. If not, the balance should be set to 0.0 and the constructor should display an error message, indicating that the initial balance was invalid. The class should provide three member functions. Member function credit should add an amount to the current balance. Member function debit should withdraw money from the Account and ensure that the debit amount does not exceed the Account's balance. If it does, the balance should be left unchanged and the function should print the message "Debit amount exceeded account balance." Member function getBalance should return the current balance.

Derived class SavingsAccount should inherit the functionality of an Account, but also include a data member of type double indicating the interest rate (percentage) assigned to the Account. SavingsAccount's constructor should receive the initial balance, as well as an initial value for the SavingsAccount's interest rate. SavingsAccount should provide a public member function calculateInterest that returns a double indicating the amount of interest earned by an account. Member function calculateInterest should determine this amount by multiplying the interest rate by the account balance. [*Note:* SavingsAccount should inherit member functions credit and debit as is without redefining them.]

Derived class CheckingAccount should inherit from base class Account and include an additional data member of type double that represents the fee charged per transaction. Checking-Account's constructor should receive the initial balance, as well as a parameter indicating a fee amount. Class CheckingAccount should redefine member functions credit and debit so that they subtract the fee from the account balance whenever either transaction is performed successfully. CheckingAccount's versions of these functions should invoke the base-class Account version to perform the updates to an account balance. CheckingAccount's debit function should charge a fee only if money is actually withdrawn (i.e., the debit amount does not exceed the account balance). [*Hint:* Define Account's debit function so that it returns a bool indicating whether money was withdrawn. Then use the return value to determine whether a fee should be charged.]

After defining the classes in this hierarchy, write a program that creates objects of each class and tests their member functions. Add interest to the SavingsAccount object by first invoking its calculateInterest function, then passing the returned interest amount to the object's credit function.

13

Object-Oriented Programming: Polymorphism

*One Ring to rule them all,
One Ring to find them,
One Ring to bring them all
and in the darkness bind
them.*
—John Ronald Reuel Tolkien

*The silence often of pure
innocence
Persuades when speaking
fails.*
—William Shakespeare

*General propositions do not
decide concrete cases.*
—Oliver Wendell Holmes

*A philosopher of imposing
stature doesn't think in a
vacuum. Even his most
abstract ideas are, to some
extent, conditioned by what
is or is not known in the time
when he lives.*
—Alfred North Whitehead

OBJECTIVES

In this chapter you will learn:

- What polymorphism is, how it makes programming more convenient, and how it makes systems more extensible and maintainable.

- To declare and use `virtual` functions to effect polymorphism.

- The distinction between abstract and concrete classes.

- To declare pure `virtual` functions to create abstract classes.

- How to use run-time type information (RTTI) with downcasting, `dynamic_cast`, `typeid` and `type_info`.

- How C++ implements `virtual` functions and dynamic binding "under the hood."

- How to use `virtual` destructors to ensure that all appropriate destructors run on an object.

13.1 Introduction

In Chapters 9–12, we discussed key object-oriented programming technologies including classes, objects, encapsulation, operator overloading and inheritance. We now continue our study of OOP by explaining and demonstrating polymorphism with inheritance hierarchies. Polymorphism enables us to "program in the general" rather than "program in the specific." In particular, polymorphism enables us to write programs that process objects of classes that are part of the same class hierarchy as if they are all objects of the hierarchy's base class. As we will soon see, polymorphism works off base-class pointer handles and base-class reference handles, but not off name handles.

Consider the following example of polymorphism. Suppose we create a program that simulates the movement of several types of animals for a biological study. Classes `Fish`, `Frog` and `Bird` represent the three types of animals under investigation. Imagine that each of these classes inherits from base class `Animal`, which contains a function move and maintains an animal's current location. Each derived class implements function move. Our program maintains a vector of pointers to objects of the various Animal derived classes. To simulate the animals' movements, the program sends each object the same message once per second—namely, move. However, each specific type of Animal responds to a move message in its own unique way—a Fish might swim two feet, a Frog might jump three feet and a Bird might fly ten feet. The program issues the same message (i.e., move) to each animal object generically, but each object knows how to modify its location appropriately for its specific type of movement. Relying on each object to know how to "do the right thing" (i.e., do what is appropriate for that type of object) in response to the same function call is the key concept of polymorphism. The same message (in this case, move) sent to a variety of objects has "many forms" of results—hence the term polymorphism.

With polymorphism, we can design and implement systems that are easily extensible—new classes can be added with little or no modification to the general portions of the program, as long as the new classes are part of the inheritance hierarchy that the program processes generically. The only parts of a program that must be altered to accommodate new classes are those that require direct knowledge of the new classes that the programmer adds to the hierarchy. For example, if we create class Tortoise that inherits from class Animal (which might respond to a move message by crawling one inch), we need to write only the Tortoise class and the part of the simulation that instantiates a Tortoise object. The portions of the simulation that process each Animal generically can remain the same.

We begin with a sequence of small, focused examples that lead up to an understanding of virtual functions and dynamic binding—polymorphism's two underlying technologies. We then present a case study that revisits Chapter 12's Employee hierarchy. In the case study, we define a common "interface" (i.e., set of functionality) for all the classes in the hierarchy. This common functionality among employees is defined in a so-called abstract base class, Employee, from which classes SalariedEmployee, HourlyEmployee and CommissionEmployee inherit directly and class BaseCommissionEmployee inherits indirectly. We will soon see what makes a class "abstract" or its opposite—"concrete."

In this hierarchy, every employee has an earnings function to calculate the employee's weekly pay. These earnings functions vary by employee type—for instance, SalariedEmployees are paid a fixed weekly salary regardless of the number of hours worked, while HourlyEmployees are paid by the hour and receive overtime pay. We show how to process each employee "in the general"—that is, using base-class pointers to call the earnings function of several derived-class objects. This way, the programmer needs to be concerned with only one type of function call, which can be used to execute several different functions based on the objects referred to by the base-class pointers.

A key feature of this chapter is its (optional) detailed discussion of polymorphism, virtual functions and dynamic binding "under the hood," which uses a detailed diagram to explain how polymorphism can be implemented in C++.

Occasionally, when performing polymorphic processing, we need to program "in the specific," meaning that operations need to be performed on a specific type of object in a hierarchy—the operation cannot be generally applied to several types of objects. We reuse our Employee hierarchy to demonstrate the powerful capabilities of run-time type information (RTTI) and dynamic casting, which enable a program to determine the type of an object at execution time and act on that object accordingly. We use these capabilities to determine whether a particular employee object is a BasePlusCommissionEmployee, then give that employee a 10 percent bonus on his or her base salary.

13.2 Polymorphism Examples

In this section, we discuss several polymorphism examples. With polymorphism, one function can cause different actions to occur, depending on the type of the object on which the function is invoked. This gives the programmer tremendous expressive capability. If class `Rectangle` is derived from class `Quadrilateral`, then a `Rectangle` object is a more specific version of a `Quadrilateral` object. Therefore, any operation (such as calculating the perimeter or the area) that can be performed on an object of class `Quadrilateral` also can be performed on an object of class `Rectangle`. Such operations also can be performed on other kinds of `Quadrilaterals`, such as `Squares`, `Parallelograms` and `Trapezoids`. The polymorphism occurs when a program invokes a `virtual` function through a base-class (i.e., `Quadrilateral`) pointer or reference—C++ dynamically (i.e., at execution time) chooses the correct function for the class from which the object was instantiated. You will see a code example that illustrates this process in Section 13.3.

As another example, suppose that we design a video game that manipulates objects of many different types, including objects of classes `Martian`, `Venutian`, `Plutonian`, `SpaceShip` and `LaserBeam`. Imagine that each of these classes inherits from the common base class `SpaceObject`, which contains member function `draw`. Each derived class implements this function in a manner appropriate for that class. A screen-manager program maintains a container (e.g., a `vector`) that holds `SpaceObject` pointers to objects of the various classes. To refresh the screen, the screen manager periodically sends each object the same message—namely, `draw`. Each type of object responds in a unique way. For example, a `Martian` object might draw itself in red with the appropriate number of antennae. A `SpaceShip` object might draw itself as a silver flying saucer. A `LaserBeam` object might draw itself as a bright red beam across the screen. Again, the same message (in this case, `draw`) sent to a variety of objects has "many forms" of results.

A polymorphic screen manager facilitates adding new classes to a system with minimal modifications to its code. Suppose that we want to add objects of class `Mercurian` to our video game. To do so, we must build a class `Mercurian` that inherits from `SpaceObject`, but provides its own definition of member function `draw`. Then, when pointers to objects of class `Mercurian` appear in the container, the programmer does not need to modify the code for the screen manager. The screen manager invokes member function `draw` on every object in the container, regardless of the object's type, so the new `Mercurian` objects simply "plug right in." Thus, without modifying the system (other than to build and include the classes themselves), programmers can use polymorphism to accommodate additional classes, including ones that were not even envisioned when the system was created.

Software Engineering Observation 13.1

With `virtual` functions and polymorphism, you can deal in generalities and let the execution-time environment concern itself with the specifics. You can direct a variety of objects to behave in manners appropriate to those objects without even knowing their types (as long as those objects belong to the same inheritance hierarchy and are being accessed off a common base-class pointer).

Software Engineering Observation 13.2

Polymorphism promotes extensibility: Software written to invoke polymorphic behavior is written independently of the types of the objects to which messages are sent. Thus, new types of objects that can respond to existing messages can be incorporated into such a system without modifying the base system. Only client code that instantiates new objects must be modified to accommodate new types.

13.3 Relationships Among Objects in an Inheritance Hierarchy

Section 12.4 created an employee class hierarchy, in which class `BasePlusCommission-Employee` inherited from class `CommissionEmployee`. The Chapter 12 examples manipulated `CommissionEmployee` and `BasePlusCommissionEmployee` objects by using the objects' names to invoke their member functions. We now examine the relationships among classes in a hierarchy more closely. The next several sections present a series of examples that demonstrate how base-class and derived-class pointers can be aimed at base-class and derived-class objects, and how those pointers can be used to invoke member functions that manipulate those objects. Toward the end of this section, we demonstrate how to get polymorphic behavior from base-class pointers aimed at derived-class objects.

In Section 13.3.1, we assign the address of a derived-class object to a base-class pointer, then show that invoking a function via the base-class pointer invokes the base-class functionality—i.e., the type of the handle determines which function is called. In Section 13.3.2, we assign the address of a base-class object to a derived-class pointer, which results in a compilation error. We discuss the error message and investigate why the compiler does not allow such an assignment. In Section 13.3.3, we assign the address of a derived-class object to a base-class pointer, then examine how the base-class pointer can be used to invoke only the base-class functionality—when we attempt to invoke derived-class member functions through the base-class pointer, compilation errors occur. Finally, in Section 13.3.4, we introduce `virtual` functions and polymorphism by declaring a base-class function as `virtual`. We then assign a derived-class object to the base-class pointer and use that pointer to invoke derived-class functionality—precisely the capability we need to achieve polymorphic behavior.

A key concept in these examples is to demonstrate that an object of a derived class can be treated as an object of its base class. This enables various interesting manipulations. For example, a program can create an array of base-class pointers that point to objects of many derived-class types. Despite the fact that the derived-class objects are of different types, the compiler allows this because each derived-class object *is an* object of its base class. However, we cannot treat a base-class object as an object of any of its derived classes. For example, a `CommissionEmployee` is not a `BasePlusCommissionEmployee` in the hierarchy defined in Chapter 12—a `CommissionEmployee` does not have a `baseSalary` data member and does not have member functions `setBaseSalary` and `getBaseSalary`. The *is-a* relationship applies only from a derived class to its direct and indirect base classes.

13.3.1 Invoking Base-Class Functions from Derived-Class Objects

The example in Figs. 13.1–13.5 demonstrates three ways to aim base-class pointers and derived-class pointers at base-class objects and derived-class objects. The first two are straightforward—we aim a base-class pointer at a base-class object (and invoke base-class functionality), and we aim a derived-class pointer at a derived-class object (and invoke derived-class functionality). Then, we demonstrate the relationship between derived classes and base classes (i.e., the *is-a* relationship of inheritance) by aiming a base-class pointer at a derived-class object (and showing that the base-class functionality is indeed available in the derived-class object).

Class `CommissionEmployee` (Figs. 13.1–13.2), which we discussed in Chapter 12, is used to represent employees who are paid a percentage of their sales. Class `BasePlusCom-`

```
1   // Fig. 13.1: CommissionEmployee.h
2   // CommissionEmployee class definition represents a commission employee.
3   #ifndef COMMISSION_H
4   #define COMMISSION_H
5
6   #include <string> // C++ standard string class
7   using std::string;
8
9   class CommissionEmployee
10  {
11  public:
12     CommissionEmployee( const string &, const string &, const string &,
13        double = 0.0, double = 0.0 );
14
15     void setFirstName( const string & ); // set first name
16     string getFirstName() const; // return first name
17
18     void setLastName( const string & ); // set last name
19     string getLastName() const; // return last name
20
21     void setSocialSecurityNumber( const string & ); // set SSN
22     string getSocialSecurityNumber() const; // return SSN
23
24     void setGrossSales( double ); // set gross sales amount
25     double getGrossSales() const; // return gross sales amount
26
27     void setCommissionRate( double ); // set commission rate
28     double getCommissionRate() const; // return commission rate
29
30     double earnings() const; // calculate earnings
31     void print() const; // print CommissionEmployee object
32  private:
33     string firstName;
34     string lastName;
35     string socialSecurityNumber;
36     double grossSales; // gross weekly sales
37     double commissionRate; // commission percentage
38  }; // end class CommissionEmployee
39
40  #endif
```

Fig. 13.1 | CommissionEmployee class header file.

missionEmployee (Figs. 13.3–13.4), which we also discussed in Chapter 12, is used to represent employees who receive a base salary plus a percentage of their sales. Each Base-PlusCommissionEmployee object *is a* CommissionEmployee that also has a base salary. Class BasePlusCommissionEmployee's earnings member function (lines 32–35 of Fig. 13.4) redefines class CommissionEmployee's earnings member function (lines 79–82 of Fig. 13.2) to include the object's base salary. Class BasePlusCommissionEmployee's print member function (lines 38–46 of Fig. 13.4) redefines class CommissionEmployee's print member function (lines 85–92 of Fig. 13.2) to display the same information as the print function in class CommissionEmployee, as well as the employee's base salary.

```cpp
1   // Fig. 13.2: CommissionEmployee.cpp
2   // Class CommissionEmployee member-function definitions.
3   #include <iostream>
4   using std::cout;
5
6   #include "CommissionEmployee.h" // CommissionEmployee class definition
7
8   // constructor
9   CommissionEmployee::CommissionEmployee(
10     const string &first, const string &last, const string &ssn,
11     double sales, double rate )
12     : firstName( first ), lastName( last ), socialSecurityNumber( ssn )
13  {
14     setGrossSales( sales ); // validate and store gross sales
15     setCommissionRate( rate ); // validate and store commission rate
16  } // end CommissionEmployee constructor
17
18  // set first name
19  void CommissionEmployee::setFirstName( const string &first )
20  {
21     firstName = first; // should validate
22  } // end function setFirstName
23
24  // return first name
25  string CommissionEmployee::getFirstName() const
26  {
27     return firstName;
28  } // end function getFirstName
29
30  // set last name
31  void CommissionEmployee::setLastName( const string &last )
32  {
33     lastName = last;   // should validate
34  } // end function setLastName
35
36  // return last name
37  string CommissionEmployee::getLastName() const
38  {
39     return lastName;
40  } // end function getLastName
41
42  // set social security number
43  void CommissionEmployee::setSocialSecurityNumber( const string &ssn )
44  {
45     socialSecurityNumber = ssn; // should validate
46  } // end function setSocialSecurityNumber
47
48  // return social security number
49  string CommissionEmployee::getSocialSecurityNumber() const
50  {
51     return socialSecurityNumber;
52  } // end function getSocialSecurityNumber
53
```

Fig. 13.2 | CommissionEmployee class implementation file. (Part 1 of 2.)

```
54   // set gross sales amount
55   void CommissionEmployee::setGrossSales( double sales )
56   {
57      grossSales = ( sales < 0.0 ) ? 0.0 : sales;
58   } // end function setGrossSales
59
60   // return gross sales amount
61   double CommissionEmployee::getGrossSales() const
62   {
63      return grossSales;
64   } // end function getGrossSales
65
66   // set commission rate
67   void CommissionEmployee::setCommissionRate( double rate )
68   {
69      commissionRate = ( rate > 0.0 && rate < 1.0 ) ? rate : 0.0;
70   } // end function setCommissionRate
71
72   // return commission rate
73   double CommissionEmployee::getCommissionRate() const
74   {
75      return commissionRate;
76   } // end function getCommissionRate
77
78   // calculate earnings
79   double CommissionEmployee::earnings() const
80   {
81      return getCommissionRate() * getGrossSales();
82   } // end function earnings
83
84   // print CommissionEmployee object
85   void CommissionEmployee::print() const
86   {
87      cout << "commission employee: "
88         << getFirstName() << ' ' << getLastName()
89         << "\nsocial security number: " << getSocialSecurityNumber()
90         << "\ngross sales: " << getGrossSales()
91         << "\ncommission rate: " << getCommissionRate();
92   } // end function print
```

Fig. 13.2 | CommissionEmployee class implementation file. (Part 2 of 2.)

```
1    // Fig. 13.3: BasePlusCommissionEmployee.h
2    // BasePlusCommissionEmployee class derived from class
3    // CommissionEmployee.
4    #ifndef BASEPLUS_H
5    #define BASEPLUS_H
6
7    #include <string> // C++ standard string class
8    using std::string;
9
```

Fig. 13.3 | BasePlusCommissionEmployee class header file. (Part 1 of 2.)

```
10   #include "CommissionEmployee.h" // CommissionEmployee class declaration
11
12   class BasePlusCommissionEmployee : public CommissionEmployee
13   {
14   public:
15      BasePlusCommissionEmployee( const string &, const string &,
16         const string &, double = 0.0, double = 0.0, double = 0.0 );
17
18      void setBaseSalary( double ); // set base salary
19      double getBaseSalary() const; // return base salary
20
21      double earnings() const; // calculate earnings
22      void print() const; // print BasePlusCommissionEmployee object
23   private:
24      double baseSalary; // base salary
25   }; // end class BasePlusCommissionEmployee
26
27   #endif
```

Fig. 13.3 | BasePlusCommissionEmployee class header file. (Part 2 of 2.)

```
1    // Fig. 13.4: BasePlusCommissionEmployee.cpp
2    // Class BasePlusCommissionEmployee member-function definitions.
3    #include <iostream>
4    using std::cout;
5
6    // BasePlusCommissionEmployee class definition
7    #include "BasePlusCommissionEmployee.h"
8
9    // constructor
10   BasePlusCommissionEmployee::BasePlusCommissionEmployee(
11      const string &first, const string &last, const string &ssn,
12      double sales, double rate, double salary )
13      // explicitly call base-class constructor
14      : CommissionEmployee( first, last, ssn, sales, rate )
15   {
16      setBaseSalary( salary ); // validate and store base salary
17   } // end BasePlusCommissionEmployee constructor
18
19   // set base salary
20   void BasePlusCommissionEmployee::setBaseSalary( double salary )
21   {
22      baseSalary = ( salary < 0.0 ) ? 0.0 : salary;
23   } // end function setBaseSalary
24
25   // return base salary
26   double BasePlusCommissionEmployee::getBaseSalary() const
27   {
28      return baseSalary;
29   } // end function getBaseSalary
30
```

Fig. 13.4 | BasePlusCommissionEmployee class implementation file. (Part 1 of 2.)

```
31   // calculate earnings
32   double BasePlusCommissionEmployee::earnings() const
33   {
34      return getBaseSalary() + CommissionEmployee::earnings();
35   } // end function earnings
36
37   // print BasePlusCommissionEmployee object
38   void BasePlusCommissionEmployee::print() const
39   {
40      cout << "base-salaried ";
41
42      // invoke CommissionEmployee's print function
43      CommissionEmployee::print();
44
45      cout << "\nbase salary: " << getBaseSalary();
46   } // end function print
```

Fig. 13.4 | BasePlusCommissionEmployee class implementation file. (Part 2 of 2.)

In Fig. 13.5, lines 19–20 create a CommissionEmployee object and line 23 creates a pointer to a CommissionEmployee object; lines 26–27 create a BasePlusCommission-Employee object and line 30 creates a pointer to a BasePlusCommissionEmployee object. Lines 37 and 39 use each object's name (commissionEmployee and basePlusCommis-sionEmployee, respectively) to invoke each object's print member function. Line 42 assigns the address of base-class object commissionEmployee to base-class pointer commissionEmployeePtr, which line 45 uses to invoke member function print on that CommissionEmployee object. This invokes the version of print defined in base class Com-missionEmployee. Similarly, line 48 assigns the address of derived-class object basePlus-CommissionEmployee to derived-class pointer basePlusCommissionEmployeePtr, which line 52 uses to invoke member function print on that BasePlusCommissionEmployee object. This invokes the version of print defined in derived class BasePlusCommission-Employee. Line 55 then assigns the address of derived-class object basePlusCommission-Employee to base-class pointer commissionEmployeePtr, which line 59 uses to invoke member function print. The C++ compiler allows this "crossover" because an object of a derived class *is an* object of its base class. Note that despite the fact that the base class

```
1    // Fig. 13.5: fig13_05.cpp
2    // Aiming base-class and derived-class pointers at base-class
3    // and derived-class objects, respectively.
4    #include <iostream>
5    using std::cout;
6    using std::endl;
7    using std::fixed;
8
9    #include <iomanip>
10   using std::setprecision;
11
```

Fig. 13.5 | Assigning addresses of base-class and derived-class objects to base-class and derived-class pointers. (Part 1 of 3.)

```
12   // include class definitions
13   #include "CommissionEmployee.h"
14   #include "BasePlusCommissionEmployee.h"
15
16   int main()
17   {
18      // create base-class object
19      CommissionEmployee commissionEmployee(
20         "Sue", "Jones", "222-22-2222", 10000, .06 );
21
22      // create base-class pointer
23      CommissionEmployee *commissionEmployeePtr = 0;
24
25      // create derived-class object
26      BasePlusCommissionEmployee basePlusCommissionEmployee(
27         "Bob", "Lewis", "333-33-3333", 5000, .04, 300 );
28
29      // create derived-class pointer
30      BasePlusCommissionEmployee *basePlusCommissionEmployeePtr = 0;
31
32      // set floating-point output formatting
33      cout << fixed << setprecision( 2 );
34
35      // output objects commissionEmployee and basePlusCommissionEmployee
36      cout << "Print base-class and derived-class objects:\n\n";
37      commissionEmployee.print(); // invokes base-class print
38      cout << "\n\n";
39      basePlusCommissionEmployee.print(); // invokes derived-class print
40
41      // aim base-class pointer at base-class object and print
42      commissionEmployeePtr = &commissionEmployee; // perfectly natural
43      cout << "\n\n\nCalling print with base-class pointer to "
44         << "\nbase-class object invokes base-class print function:\n\n";
45      commissionEmployeePtr->print(); // invokes base-class print
46
47      // aim derived-class pointer at derived-class object and print
48      basePlusCommissionEmployeePtr = &basePlusCommissionEmployee; // natural
49      cout << "\n\n\nCalling print with derived-class pointer to "
50         << "\nderived-class object invokes derived-class "
51         << "print function:\n\n";
52      basePlusCommissionEmployeePtr->print(); // invokes derived-class print
53
54      // aim base-class pointer at derived-class object and print
55      commissionEmployeePtr = &basePlusCommissionEmployee;
56      cout << "\n\n\nCalling print with base-class pointer to "
57         << "derived-class object\ninvokes base-class print "
58         << "function on that derived-class object:\n\n";
59      commissionEmployeePtr->print(); // invokes base-class print
60      cout << endl;
61      return 0;
62   } // end main
```

Fig. 13.5 | Assigning addresses of base-class and derived-class objects to base-class and derived-class pointers. (Part 2 of 3.)

```
Print base-class and derived-class objects:

commission employee: Sue Jones
social security number: 222-22-2222
gross sales: 10000.00
commission rate: 0.06

base-salaried commission employee: Bob Lewis
social security number: 333-33-3333
gross sales: 5000.00
commission rate: 0.04
base salary: 300.00


Calling print with base-class pointer to
base-class object invokes base-class print function:

commission employee: Sue Jones
social security number: 222-22-2222
gross sales: 10000.00
commission rate: 0.06


Calling print with derived-class pointer to
derived-class object invokes derived-class print function:

base-salaried commission employee: Bob Lewis
social security number: 333-33-3333
gross sales: 5000.00
commission rate: 0.04
base salary: 300.00


Calling print with base-class pointer to derived-class object
invokes base-class print function on that derived-class object:

commission employee: Bob Lewis
social security number: 333-33-3333
gross sales: 5000.00
commission rate: 0.04
```

Fig. 13.5 | Assigning addresses of base-class and derived-class objects to base-class and derived-class pointers. (Part 3 of 3.)

CommissionEmployee pointer points to a derived class BasePlusCommissionEmployee object, the base class CommissionEmployee's print member function is invoked (rather than BasePlusCommissionEmployee's print function). The output of each print member-function invocation in this program reveals that *the invoked functionality depends on the type of the handle (i.e., the pointer or reference type) used to invoke the function, not the type of the object to which the handle points*. In Section 13.3.4, when we introduce virtual functions, we demonstrate that it is possible to invoke the object type's functionality, rather than invoke the handle type's functionality. We will see that this is crucial to implementing polymorphic behavior—the key topic of this chapter.

13.3.2 Aiming Derived-Class Pointers at Base-Class Objects

In Section 13.3.1, we assigned the address of a derived-class object to a base-class pointer and explained that the C++ compiler allows this assignment, because a derived-class object *is a* base-class object. We take the opposite approach in Fig. 13.6, as we aim a derived-class pointer at a base-class object. [*Note*: This program uses classes CommissionEmployee and BasePlusCommissionEmployee of Figs. 13.1–13.4.] Lines 8–9 of Fig. 13.6 create a CommissionEmployee object, and line 10 creates a BasePlusCommissionEmployee pointer. Line 14 attempts to assign the address of base-class object commissionEmployee to derived-class pointer basePlusCommissionEmployeePtr, but the C++ compiler generates an error. The compiler prevents this assignment, because a CommissionEmployee is not a BasePlusCommissionEmployee. Consider the consequences if the compiler were to allow this assignment. Through a BasePlusCommissionEmployee pointer, we can invoke every BasePlusCommissionEmployee member function, including setBaseSalary, for the object to which the pointer points (i.e., the base-class object commissionEmployee). However, the CommissionEmployee object does not provide a setBaseSalary member function, nor does it provide a baseSalary data member to set. This could lead to problems, because member function setBaseSalary would assume that there is a baseSalary data member to set at its "usual location" in a BasePlusCommissionEmployee object. This memory does not belong to the CommissionEmployee object, so member function setBaseSalary might overwrite other important data in memory, possibly data that belongs to a different object.

```cpp
1   // Fig. 13.6: fig13_06.cpp
2   // Aiming a derived-class pointer at a base-class object.
3   #include "CommissionEmployee.h"
4   #include "BasePlusCommissionEmployee.h"
5
6   int main()
7   {
8      CommissionEmployee commissionEmployee(
9         "Sue", "Jones", "222-22-2222", 10000, .06 );
10     BasePlusCommissionEmployee *basePlusCommissionEmployeePtr = 0;
11
12     // aim derived-class pointer at base-class object
13     // Error: a CommissionEmployee is not a BasePlusCommissionEmployee
14     basePlusCommissionEmployeePtr = &commissionEmployee;
15     return 0;
16  } // end main
```

Borland C++ command-line compiler error messages:

```
Error E2034 Fig13_06\fig13_06.cpp 14: Cannot convert 'CommissionEmployee *'
   to 'BasePlusCommissionEmployee *' in function main()
```

GNU C++ compiler error messages:

```
fig13_06.cpp:14: error: invalid conversion from `CommissionEmployee*' to
   `BasePlusCommissionEmployee*'
```

Fig. 13.6 | Aiming a derived-class pointer at a base-class object. (Part 1 of 2.)

Microsoft Visual C++.NET compiler error messages:

```
C:\cpphtp5_examples\ch13\Fig13_06\fig13_06.cpp(14) : error C2440:
   '=' : cannot convert from 'CommissionEmployee *__w64 ' to
   'BasePlusCommissionEmployee *'
       Cast from base to derived requires dynamic_cast or static_cast
```

Fig. 13.6 | Aiming a derived-class pointer at a base-class object. (Part 2 of 2.)

13.3.3 Derived-Class Member-Function Calls via Base-Class Pointers

Off a base-class pointer, the compiler allows us to invoke only bases-class member functions. Thus, if a base-class pointer is aimed at a derived-class object, and an attempt is made to access a derived-class-only member function, a compilation error will occur.

Figure 13.7 shows the consequences of attempting to invoke a derived-class member function off a base-class pointer. [*Note:* We are again using classes CommissionEmployee and BasePlusCommissionEmployee of Figs. 13.1–13.4.] Line 9 creates commissionEmployeePtr—a pointer to a CommissionEmployee object—and lines 10–11 create a BasePlusCommissionEmployee object. Line 14 aims commissionEmployeePtr at derived-class object basePlusCommissionEmployee. Recall from Section 13.3.1 that the C++ compiler allows

```cpp
1   // Fig. 13.7: fig13_07.cpp
2   // Attempting to invoke derived-class-only member functions
3   // through a base-class pointer.
4   #include "CommissionEmployee.h"
5   #include "BasePlusCommissionEmployee.h"
6
7   int main()
8   {
9      CommissionEmployee *commissionEmployeePtr = 0; // base class
10     BasePlusCommissionEmployee basePlusCommissionEmployee(
11        "Bob", "Lewis", "333-33-3333", 5000, .04, 300 ); // derived class
12
13     // aim base-class pointer at derived-class object
14     commissionEmployeePtr = &basePlusCommissionEmployee;
15
16     // invoke base-class member functions on derived-class
17     // object through base-class pointer
18     string firstName = commissionEmployeePtr->getFirstName();
19     string lastName = commissionEmployeePtr->getLastName();
20     string ssn = commissionEmployeePtr->getSocialSecurityNumber();
21     double grossSales = commissionEmployeePtr->getGrossSales();
22     double commissionRate = commissionEmployeePtr->getCommissionRate();
23
24     // attempt to invoke derived-class-only member functions
25     // on derived-class object through base-class pointer
26     double baseSalary = commissionEmployeePtr->getBaseSalary();
27     commissionEmployeePtr->setBaseSalary( 500 );
28     return 0;
29  } // end main
```

Fig. 13.7 | Attempting to invoke derived-class-only functions via a base-class pointer. (Part 1 of 2.)

Borland C++ command-line compiler error messages:

```
Error E2316 Fig13_07\fig13_07.cpp 26: 'getBaseSalary' is not a member of
   'CommissionEmployee' in function main()
Error E2316 Fig13_07\fig13_07.cpp 27: 'setBaseSalary' is not a member of
   'CommissionEmployee' in function main()
```

Microsoft Visual C++.NET compiler error messages:

```
C:\cpphtp5_examples\ch13\Fig13_07\fig13_07.cpp(26) : error C2039:
   'getBaseSalary' : is not a member of 'CommissionEmployee'
      C:\cpphtp5_examples\ch13\Fig13_07\CommissionEmployee.h(10) :
         see declaration of 'CommissionEmployee'
C:\cpphtp5_examples\ch13\Fig13_07\fig13_07.cpp(27) : error C2039:
   'setBaseSalary' : is not a member of 'CommissionEmployee'
      C:\cpphtp5_examples\ch13\Fig13_07\CommissionEmployee.h(10) :
         see declaration of 'CommissionEmployee'
```

GNU C++ compiler error messages:

```
fig13_07.cpp:26: error: `getBaseSalary' undeclared (first use this function)
fig13_07.cpp:26: error: (Each undeclared identifier is reported only once for
   each function it appears in.)
fig13_07.cpp:27: error: `setBaseSalary' undeclared (first use this function)
```

Fig. 13.7 | Attempting to invoke derived-class-only functions via a base-class pointer. (Part 2 of 2.)

this, because a BasePlusCommissionEmployee *is a* CommissionEmployee (in the sense that a BasePlusCommissionEmployee object contains all the functionality of a CommissionEmployee object). Lines 18–22 invoke base-class member functions getFirstName, getLastName, getSocialSecurityNumber, getGrossSales and getCommissionRate off the base-class pointer. All of these calls are legitimate, because BasePlusCommissionEmployee inherits these member functions from CommissionEmployee. We know that commissionEmployeePtr is aimed at a BasePlusCommissionEmployee object, so in lines 26–27 we attempt to invoke BasePlusCommissionEmployee member functions getBaseSalary and setBaseSalary. The C++ compiler generates errors on both of these lines, because these are not member functions of base-class CommissionEmployee. The handle can invoke only those functions that are members of that handle's associated class type. (In this case, off a CommissionEmployee *, we can invoke only CommissionEmployee member functions setFirstName, getFirstName, setLastName, getLastName, setSocialSecurityNumber, getSocialSecurityNumber, setGrossSales, getGrossSales, setCommissionRate, getCommissionRate, earnings and print.)

It turns out that the C++ compiler does allow access to derived-class-only members from a base-class pointer that is aimed at a derived-class object if we explicitly cast the base-class pointer to a derived-class pointer—a technique known as downcasting. As you learned in Section 13.3.1, it is possible to aim a base-class pointer at a derived-class object. However, as we demonstrated in Fig. 13.7, a base-class pointer can be used to invoke only the functions declared in the base class. Downcasting allows a program to perform a derived-class-specific operation on a derived-class object pointed to by a base-class pointer.

After a downcast, the program can invoke derived-class functions that are not in the base class. We will show you a concrete example of downcasting in Section 13.8.

> **Software Engineering Observation 13.3**
>
> *If the address of a derived-class object has been assigned to a pointer of one of its direct or indirect base classes, it is acceptable to cast that base-class pointer back to a pointer of the derived-class type. In fact, this must be done to send that derived-class object messages that do not appear in the base class.*

13.3.4 Virtual Functions

In Section 13.3.1, we aimed a base-class `CommissionEmployee` pointer at a derived-class `BasePlusCommissionEmployee` object, then invoked member function `print` through that pointer. Recall that the type of the handle determines which class's functionality to invoke. In that case, the `CommissionEmployee` pointer invoked the `CommissionEmployee` member function `print` on the `BasePlusCommissionEmployee` object, even though the pointer was aimed at a `BasePlusCommissionEmployee` object that has its own customized `print` function. *With* `virtual` *functions, the type of the object being pointed to, not the type of the handle, determines which version of a* `virtual` *function to invoke.*

First, we consider why `virtual` functions are useful. Suppose that a set of shape classes such as `Circle`, `Triangle`, `Rectangle` and `Square` are all derived from base class `Shape`. Each of these classes might be endowed with the ability to draw itself via a member function `draw`. Although each class has its own `draw` function, the function for each shape is quite different. In a program that draws a set of shapes, it would be useful to be able to treat all the shapes generically as objects of the base class `Shape`. Then, to draw any shape, we could simply use a base-class `Shape` pointer to invoke function `draw` and let the program determine dynamically (i.e., at runtime) which derived-class `draw` function to use, based on the type of the object to which the base-class `Shape` pointer points at any given time.

To enable this kind of behavior, we declare `draw` in the base class as a `virtual function`, and we override `draw` in each of the derived classes to draw the appropriate shape. From an implementation perspective, overriding a function is no different than redefining one (which is the approach we have been using until now). An overridden function in a derived class has the same signature and return type (i.e., prototype) as the function it overrides in its base class. If we do not declare the base-class function as `virtual`, we can redefine that function. By contrast, if we declare the base-class function as `virtual`, we can override that function to enable polymorphic behavior. We declare a `virtual` function by preceding the function's prototype with the keyword `virtual` in the base class. For example,

```
virtual void draw() const;
```

would appear in base class `Shape`. The preceding prototype declares that function `draw` is a `virtual` function that takes no arguments and returns nothing. The function is declared `const` because a `draw` function typically would not make changes to the `Shape` object on which it is invoked. Virtual functions do not necessarily have to be `const` functions.

> **Software Engineering Observation 13.4**
>
> *Once a function is declared* `virtual`, *it remains* `virtual` *all the way down the inheritance hierarchy from that point, even if that function is not explicitly declared* `virtual` *when a class overrides it.*

Good Programming Practice 13.1

Even though certain functions are implicitly virtual because of a declaration made higher in the class hierarchy, explicitly declare these functions virtual at every level of the hierarchy to promote program clarity.

Error-Prevention Tip 13.1

When a programmer browses a class hierarchy to locate a class to reuse, it is possible that a function in that class will exhibit virtual function behavior even though it is not explicitly declared virtual. This happens when the class inherits a virtual function from its base class, and it can lead to subtle logic errors. Such errors can be avoided by explicitly declaring all virtual functions virtual throughout the inheritance hierarchy.

Software Engineering Observation 13.5

When a derived class chooses not to override a virtual function from its base class, the derived class simply inherits its base class's virtual function implementation.

If the program invokes a virtual function through a base-class pointer to a derived-class object (e.g., shapePtr->draw()), the program will choose the correct derived-class draw function dynamically (i.e., at execution time) based on the object type—not the pointer type. Choosing the appropriate function to call at execution time (rather than at compile time) is known as dynamic binding or late binding.

When a virtual function is called by referencing a specific object by name and using the dot member-selection operator (e.g., squareObject.draw()), the function invocation is resolved at compile time (this is called static binding) and the virtual function that is called is the one defined for (or inherited by) the class of that particular object—this is not polymorphic behavior. Thus, dynamic binding with virtual functions occurs only off pointer (and, as we will soon see, reference) handles.

Now let's see how virtual functions can enable polymorphic behavior in our employee hierarchy. Figures 13.8–13.9 are the header files for classes CommissionEmployee and BasePlusCommissionEmployee, respectively. Note that the only difference between these files and those of Fig. 13.1 and Fig. 13.3 is that we specify each class's earnings and print member functions as virtual (lines 30–31 of Fig. 13.8 and lines 21–22 of Fig. 13.9). Because functions earnings and print are virtual in class CommissionEmployee, class BasePlusCommissionEmployee's earnings and print functions override class CommissionEmployee's. Now, if we aim a base-class CommissionEmployee pointer at a derived-class BasePlusCommissionEmployee object, and the program uses that pointer to call either function earnings or print, the BasePlusCommissionEmployee object's corresponding function will be invoked. There were no changes to the member-function implementations of classes CommissionEmployee and BasePlusCommissionEmployee, so we reuse the versions of Fig. 13.2 and Fig. 13.4.

We modified Fig. 13.5 to create the program of Fig. 13.10. Lines 46–57 demonstrate again that a CommissionEmployee pointer aimed at a CommissionEmployee object can be used to invoke CommissionEmployee functionality, and a BasePlusCommissionEmployee pointer aimed at a BasePlusCommissionEmployee object can be used to invoke BasePlusCommissionEmployee functionality. Line 60 aims base-class pointer commissionEmployeePtr at derived-class object basePlusCommissionEmployee. Note that when line 67 invokes member function print off the base-class pointer, the derived-class BasePlusCommissionEmployee's print member function is invoked, so line 67 outputs different text than line 59 does in Fig. 13.5 (when member function print was not declared virtual).

```
1   // Fig. 13.8: CommissionEmployee.h
2   // CommissionEmployee class definition represents a commission employee.
3   #ifndef COMMISSION_H
4   #define COMMISSION_H
5
6   #include <string> // C++ standard string class
7   using std::string;
8
9   class CommissionEmployee
10  {
11  public:
12     CommissionEmployee( const string &, const string &, const string &,
13        double = 0.0, double = 0.0 );
14
15     void setFirstName( const string & ); // set first name
16     string getFirstName() const; // return first name
17
18     void setLastName( const string & ); // set last name
19     string getLastName() const; // return last name
20
21     void setSocialSecurityNumber( const string & ); // set SSN
22     string getSocialSecurityNumber() const; // return SSN
23
24     void setGrossSales( double ); // set gross sales amount
25     double getGrossSales() const; // return gross sales amount
26
27     void setCommissionRate( double ); // set commission rate
28     double getCommissionRate() const; // return commission rate
29
30     virtual double earnings() const; // calculate earnings
31     virtual void print() const; // print CommissionEmployee object
32  private:
33     string firstName;
34     string lastName;
35     string socialSecurityNumber;
36     double grossSales; // gross weekly sales
37     double commissionRate; // commission percentage
38  }; // end class CommissionEmployee
39
40  #endif
```

Fig. 13.8 | CommissionEmployee class header file declares earnings and print functions as virtual.

```
1   // Fig. 13.9: BasePlusCommissionEmployee.h
2   // BasePlusCommissionEmployee class derived from class
3   // CommissionEmployee.
4   #ifndef BASEPLUS_H
5   #define BASEPLUS_H
6
```

Fig. 13.9 | BasePlusCommissionEmployee class header file declares earnings and print functions as virtual. (Part 1 of 2.)

```
7   #include <string> // C++ standard string class
8   using std::string;
9
10  #include "CommissionEmployee.h" // CommissionEmployee class declaration
11
12  class BasePlusCommissionEmployee : public CommissionEmployee
13  {
14  public:
15     BasePlusCommissionEmployee( const string &, const string &,
16        const string &, double = 0.0, double = 0.0, double = 0.0 );
17
18     void setBaseSalary( double ); // set base salary
19     double getBaseSalary() const; // return base salary
20
21     virtual double earnings() const; // calculate earnings
22     virtual void print() const; // print BasePlusCommissionEmployee object
23  private:
24     double baseSalary; // base salary
25  }; // end class BasePlusCommissionEmployee
26
27  #endif
```

Fig. 13.9 | BasePlusCommissionEmployee class header file declares earnings and print functions as virtual. (Part 2 of 2.)

We see that declaring a member function virtual causes the program to dynamically determine which function to invoke based on the type of object to which the handle points, rather than on the type of the handle. The decision about which function to call is an example of polymorphism. Note again that when commissionEmployeePtr points to a CommissionEmployee object (line 46), class CommissionEmployee's print function is invoked, and when CommissionEmployeePtr points to a BasePlusCommissionEmployee object, class BasePlusCommissionEmployee's print function is invoked. Thus, the same message—print, in this case—sent (off a base-class pointer) to a variety of objects related by inheritance to that base class, takes on many forms—this is polymorphic behavior.

```
1   // Fig. 13.10: fig13_10.cpp
2   // Introducing polymorphism, virtual functions and dynamic binding.
3   #include <iostream>
4   using std::cout;
5   using std::endl;
6   using std::fixed;
7
8   #include <iomanip>
9   using std::setprecision;
10
11  // include class definitions
12  #include "CommissionEmployee.h"
13  #include "BasePlusCommissionEmployee.h"
```

Fig. 13.10 | Demonstrating polymorphism by invoking a derived-class virtual function via a base-class pointer to a derived-class object. (Part 1 of 3.)

```
14
15   int main()
16   {
17      // create base-class object
18      CommissionEmployee commissionEmployee(
19         "Sue", "Jones", "222-22-2222", 10000, .06 );
20
21      // create base-class pointer
22      CommissionEmployee *commissionEmployeePtr = 0;
23
24      // create derived-class object
25      BasePlusCommissionEmployee basePlusCommissionEmployee(
26         "Bob", "Lewis", "333-33-3333", 5000, .04, 300 );
27
28      // create derived-class pointer
29      BasePlusCommissionEmployee *basePlusCommissionEmployeePtr = 0;
30
31      // set floating-point output formatting
32      cout << fixed << setprecision( 2 );
33
34      // output objects using static binding
35      cout << "Invoking print function on base-class and derived-class "
36         << "\nobjects with static binding\n\n";
37      commissionEmployee.print(); // static binding
38      cout << "\n\n";
39      basePlusCommissionEmployee.print(); // static binding
40
41      // output objects using dynamic binding
42      cout << "\n\n\nInvoking print function on base-class and "
43         << "derived-class \nobjects with dynamic binding";
44
45      // aim base-class pointer at base-class object and print
46      commissionEmployeePtr = &commissionEmployee;
47      cout << "\n\nCalling virtual function print with base-class pointer"
48         << "\nto base-class object invokes base-class "
49         << "print function:\n\n";
50      commissionEmployeePtr->print(); // invokes base-class print
51
52      // aim derived-class pointer at derived-class object and print
53      basePlusCommissionEmployeePtr = &basePlusCommissionEmployee;
54      cout << "\n\nCalling virtual function print with derived-class "
55         << "pointer\nto derived-class object invokes derived-class "
56         << "print function:\n\n";
57      basePlusCommissionEmployeePtr->print(); // invokes derived-class print
58
59      // aim base-class pointer at derived-class object and print
60      commissionEmployeePtr = &basePlusCommissionEmployee;
61      cout << "\n\nCalling virtual function print with base-class pointer"
62         << "\nto derived-class object invokes derived-class "
63         << "print function:\n\n";
64
```

Fig. 13.10 | Demonstrating polymorphism by invoking a derived-class `virtual` function via a base-class pointer to a derived-class object. (Part 2 of 3.)

```
65      // polymorphism; invokes BasePlusCommissionEmployee's print;
66      // base-class pointer to derived-class object
67      commissionEmployeePtr->print();
68      cout << endl;
69      return 0;
70   } // end main
```

```
Invoking print function on base-class and derived-class
objects with static binding

commission employee: Sue Jones
social security number: 222-22-2222
gross sales: 10000.00
commission rate: 0.06

base-salaried commission employee: Bob Lewis
social security number: 333-33-3333
gross sales: 5000.00
commission rate: 0.04
base salary: 300.00


Invoking print function on base-class and derived-class
objects with dynamic binding

Calling virtual function print with base-class pointer
to base-class object invokes base-class print function:

commission employee: Sue Jones
social security number: 222-22-2222
gross sales: 10000.00
commission rate: 0.06

Calling virtual function print with derived-class pointer
to derived-class object invokes derived-class print function:

base-salaried commission employee: Bob Lewis
social security number: 333-33-3333
gross sales: 5000.00
commission rate: 0.04
base salary: 300.00

Calling virtual function print with base-class pointer
to derived-class object invokes derived-class print function:

base-salaried commission employee: Bob Lewis
social security number: 333-33-3333
gross sales: 5000.00
commission rate: 0.04
base salary: 300.00
```

Fig. 13.10 | Demonstrating polymorphism by invoking a derived-class `virtual` function via a base-class pointer to a derived-class object. (Part 3 of 3.)

13.3.5 Summary of the Allowed Assignments Between Base-Class and Derived-Class Objects and Pointers

Now that you have seen a complete application that processes diverse objects polymorphically, we summarize what you can and cannot do with base-class and derived-class objects and pointers. Although a derived-class object also *is a* base-class object, the two objects are nevertheless different. As discussed previously, derived-class objects can be treated as if they are base-class objects. This is a logical relationship, because the derived class contains all the members of the base class. However, base-class objects cannot be treated as if they are derived-class objects—the derived class can have additional derived-class-only members. For this reason, aiming a derived-class pointer at a base-class object is not allowed without an explicit cast—such an assignment would leave the derived-class-only members undefined on the base-class object. The cast relieves the compiler of the responsibility of issuing an error message. In a sense, by using the cast you are saying, "I know that what I'm doing is dangerous and I take full responsibility for my actions."

In the current section and in Chapter 12, we have discussed four ways to aim base-class pointers and derived-class pointers at base-class objects and derived-class objects:

1. Aiming a base-class pointer at a base-class object is straightforward—calls made off the base-class pointer simply invoke base-class functionality.

2. Aiming a derived-class pointer at a derived-class object is straightforward—calls made off the derived-class pointer simply invoke derived-class functionality.

3. Aiming a base-class pointer at a derived-class object is safe, because the derived-class object *is an* object of its base class. However, this pointer can be used to invoke only base-class member functions. If the programmer attempts to refer to a derived-class-only member through the base-class pointer, the compiler reports an error. To avoid this error, the programmer must cast the base-class pointer to a derived-class pointer. The derived-class pointer can then be used to invoke the derived-class object's complete functionality. However, this technique—called downcasting—is a potentially dangerous operation. Section 13.8 demonstrates how to safely use downcasting.

4. Aiming a derived-class pointer at a base-class object generates a compilation error. The *is-a* relationship applies only from a derived class to its direct and indirect base classes, and not vice versa. A base-class object does not contain the derived-class-only members that can be invoked off a derived-class pointer.

 Common Programming Error 13.1

After aiming a base-class pointer at a derived-class object, attempting to reference derived-class-only members with the base-class pointer is a compilation error.

 Common Programming Error 13.2

Treating a base-class object as a derived-class object can cause errors.

13.4 Type Fields and `switch` Statements

One way to determine the type of an object that is incorporated in a larger program is to use a `switch` statement. This allows us to distinguish among object types, then invoke an appropriate action for a particular object. For example, in a hierarchy of shapes in which each shape object has a shapeType attribute, a switch statement could check the object's shapeType to determine which print function to call.

However, using switch logic exposes programs to a variety of potential problems. For example, the programmer might forget to include a type test when one is warranted, or might forget to test all possible cases in a switch statement. When modifying a switch-based system by adding new types, the programmer might forget to insert the new cases in all relevant switch statements. Every addition or deletion of a class requires the modification of every switch statement in the system; tracking these statements down can be time consuming and error prone.

Software Engineering Observation 13.6

Polymorphic programming can eliminate the need for unnecessary switch logic. By using the C++ polymorphism mechanism to perform the equivalent logic, programmers can avoid the kinds of errors typically associated with switch logic.

Software Engineering Observation 13.7

An interesting consequence of using polymorphism is that programs take on a simplified appearance. They contain less branching logic and more simple, sequential code. This simplification facilitates testing, debugging and program maintenance.

13.5 Abstract Classes and Pure virtual Functions

When we think of a class as a type, we assume that programs will create objects of that type. However, there are cases in which it is useful to define classes from which the programmer never intends to instantiate any objects. Such classes are called abstract classes. Because these classes normally are used as base classes in inheritance hierarchies, we refer to them as abstract base classes. These classes cannot be used to instantiate objects, because, as we will soon see, abstract classes are incomplete—derived classes must define the "missing pieces." We build programs with abstract classes in Section 13.6.

The purpose of an abstract class is to provide an appropriate base class from which other classes can inherit. Classes that can be used to instantiate objects are called concrete classes. Such classes provide implementations of every member function they define. We could have an abstract base class TwoDimensionalShape and derive such concrete classes as Square, Circle and Triangle. We could also have an abstract base class ThreeDimensionalShape and derive such concrete classes as Cube, Sphere and Cylinder. Abstract base classes are too generic to define real objects; we need to be more specific before we can think of instantiating objects. For example, if someone tells you to "draw the two-dimensional shape," what shape would you draw? Concrete classes provide the specifics that make it reasonable to instantiate objects.

An inheritance hierarchy does not need to contain any abstract classes, but, as we will see, many good object-oriented systems have class hierarchies headed by abstract base classes. In some cases, abstract classes constitute the top few levels of the hierarchy. A good example of this is the shape hierarchy in Fig. 12.3, which begins with abstract base class Shape. On the next level of the hierarchy we have two more abstract base classes, namely, TwoDimensionalShape and ThreeDimensionalShape. The next level of the hierarchy defines concrete classes for two-dimensional shapes (namely, Circle, Square and Triangle) and for three-dimensional shapes (namely, Sphere, Cube and Tetrahedron).

A class is made abstract by declaring one or more of its `virtual` functions to be "pure." A pure `virtual` function is specified by placing "= 0" in its declaration, as in

```
virtual void draw() const = 0; // pure virtual function
```

The "= 0" is known as a pure specifier. Pure `virtual` functions do not provide implementations. Every concrete derived class must override all base-class pure `virtual` functions with concrete implementations of those functions. The difference between a `virtual` function and a pure `virtual` function is that a `virtual` function has an implementation and gives the derived class the *option* of overriding the function; by contrast, a pure `virtual` function does not provide an implementation and *requires* the derived class to override the function (for that derived class to be concrete; otherwise the derived class remains abstract).

Pure `virtual` functions are used when it does not make sense for the base class to have an implementation of a function, but the programmer wants all concrete derived classes to implement the function. Returning to our earlier example of space objects, it does not make sense for the base class `SpaceObject` to have an implementation for function `draw` (as there is no way to draw a generic space object without having more information about what type of space object is being drawn). An example of a function that would be defined as `virtual` (and not pure `virtual`) would be one that returns a name for the object. We can name a generic `SpaceObject` (for instance, as `"space object"`), so a default implementation for this function can be provided, and the function does not need to be pure `virtual`. The function is still declared `virtual`, however, because it is expected that derived classes will override this function to provide more specific names for the derived-class objects.

 Software Engineering Observation 13.8

An abstract class defines a common public interface for the various classes in a class hierarchy. An abstract class contains one or more pure `virtual` functions that concrete derived classes must override.

 Common Programming Error 13.3

Attempting to instantiate an object of an abstract class causes a compilation error.

 Common Programming Error 13.4

Failure to override a pure `virtual` function in a derived class, then attempting to instantiate objects of that class, is a compilation error.

 Software Engineering Observation 13.9

An abstract class has at least one pure `virtual` function. An abstract class also can have data members and concrete functions (including constructors and destructors), which are subject to the normal rules of inheritance by derived classes.

Although we cannot instantiate objects of an abstract base class, we *can* use the abstract base class to declare pointers and references that can refer to objects of any concrete classes derived from the abstract class. Programs typically use such pointers and references to manipulate derived-class objects polymorphically.

Let us consider another application of polymorphism. A screen manager needs to display a variety of objects, including new types of objects that the programmer will add to the system after writing the screen manager. The system might need to display various shapes, such as Circles, Triangles or Rectangles, which are derived from abstract base class Shape. The screen manager uses Shape pointers to manage the objects that are displayed. To draw any object (regardless of the level at which that object's class appears in the inheritance hierarchy), the screen manager uses a base-class pointer to the object to invoke the object's draw function, which is a pure virtual function in base class Shape; therefore, each concrete derived class must implement function draw. Each Shape object in the inheritance hierarchy knows how to draw itself. The screen manager does not have to worry about the type of each object or whether the screen manager has ever encountered objects of that type.

Polymorphism is particularly effective for implementing layered software systems. In operating systems, for example, each type of physical device could operate quite differently from the others. Even so, commands to *read* or *write* data from and to devices may have a certain uniformity. The *write* message sent to a device-driver object needs to be interpreted specifically in the context of that device driver and how that device driver manipulates devices of a specific type. However, the *write* call itself really is no different from the *write* to any other device in the system—place some number of bytes from memory onto that device. An object-oriented operating system might use an abstract base class to provide an interface appropriate for all device drivers. Then, through inheritance from that abstract base class, derived classes are formed that all operate similarly. The capabilities (i.e., the public functions) offered by the device drivers are provided as pure virtual functions in the abstract base class. The implementations of these pure virtual functions are provided in the derived classes that correspond to the specific types of device drivers. This architecture also allows new devices to be added to a system easily, even after the operating system has been defined. The user can just plug in the device and install its new device driver. The operating system "talks" to this new device through its device driver, which has the same public member functions as all other device drivers—those defined in the abstract base device driver class.

It is common in object-oriented programming to define an iterator class that can traverse all the objects in a container (such as an array). For example, a program can print a list of objects in a vector by creating an iterator object, then using the iterator to obtain the next element of the list each time the iterator is called. Iterators often are used in polymorphic programming to traverse an array or a linked list of pointers to objects from various levels of a hierarchy. The pointers in such a list are all base-class pointers. (Chapter 22, Standard Template Library (STL), presents a thorough treatment of iterators.) A list of pointers to objects of base class TwoDimensionalShape could contain pointers to objects of classes Square, Circle, Triangle and so on. Using polymorphism to send a draw message, off a TwoDimensionalShape * pointer, to each object in the list would draw each object correctly on the screen.

13.6 Case Study: Payroll System Using Polymorphism

This section reexamines the CommissionEmployee-BasePlusCommissionEmployee hierarchy that we explored throughout Section 12.4. In this example, we use an abstract class and polymorphism to perform payroll calculations based on the type of employee. We create an enhanced employee hierarchy to solve the following problem:

> *A company pays its employees weekly. The employees are of four types: Salaried employees are paid a fixed weekly salary regardless of the number of hours worked, hourly employees are paid by the hour and receive overtime pay for all hours worked in excess of 40 hours, commission employees are paid a percentage of their sales and base-salary-plus-commission employees receive a base salary plus a percentage of their sales. For the current pay period, the company has decided to reward base-salary-plus-commission employees by adding 10 percent to their base salaries. The company wants to implement a C++ program that performs its payroll calculations polymorphically.*

We use abstract class `Employee` to represent the general concept of an employee. The classes that derive directly from `Employee` are `SalariedEmployee`, `CommissionEmployee` and `HourlyEmployee`. Class `BasePlusCommissionEmployee`—derived from `Commission-Employee`—represents the last employee type. The UML class diagram in Fig. 13.11 shows the inheritance hierarchy for our polymorphic employee payroll application. Note that abstract class name `Employee` is italicized, as per the convention of the UML.

Abstract base class `Employee` declares the "interface" to the hierarchy—that is, the set of member functions that a program can invoke on all `Employee` objects. Each employee, regardless of the way his or her earnings are calculated, has a first name, a last name and a social security number, so `private` data members `firstName`, `lastName` and `socialSecurityNumber` appear in abstract base class `Employee`.

Software Engineering Observation 13.10

A derived class can inherit interface or implementation from a base class. Hierarchies designed for implementation inheritance tend to have their functionality high in the hierarchy—each new derived class inherits one or more member functions that were defined in a base class, and the derived class uses the base-class definitions. Hierarchies designed for interface inheritance tend to have their functionality lower in the hierarchy—a base class specifies one or more functions that should be defined for each class in the hierarchy (i.e., they have the same prototype), but the individual derived classes provide their own implementations of the function(s).

The following sections implement the `Employee` class hierarchy. The first five each implement one of the abstract or concrete classes. The last section implements a test program that builds objects of all these classes and processes the objects polymorphically.

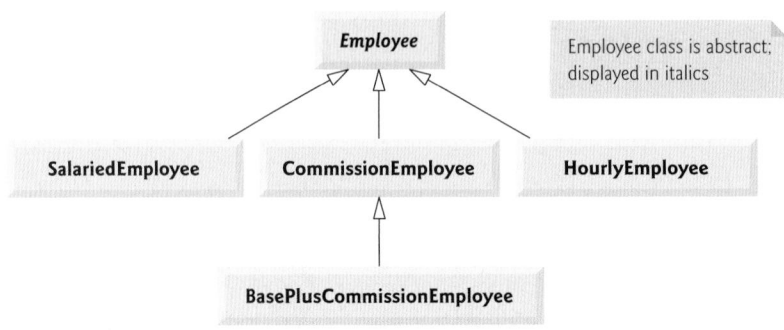

Fig. 13.11 | `Employee` hierarchy UML class diagram.

13.6.1 Creating Abstract Base Class `Employee`

Class `Employee` (Figs. 13.13–13.14, discussed in further detail shortly) provides functions `earnings` and `print`, in addition to various *get* and *set* functions that manipulate Employee's data members. An `earnings` function certainly applies generically to all employees, but each earnings calculation depends on the employee's class. So we declare `earnings` as pure `virtual` in base class `Employee` because a default implementation does not make sense for that function—there is not enough information to determine what amount `earnings` should return. Each derived class overrides `earnings` with an appropriate implementation. To calculate an employee's earnings, the program assigns the address of an employee's object to a base class `Employee` pointer, then invokes the `earnings` function on that object. We maintain a `vector` of `Employee` pointers, each of which points to an `Employee` object (of course, there cannot be `Employee` objects, because `Employee` is an abstract class—because of inheritance, however, all objects of all derived classes of `Employee` may nevertheless be thought of as `Employee` objects). The program iterates through the `vector` and calls function `earnings` for each `Employee` object. C++ processes these function calls polymorphically. Including `earnings` as a pure `virtual` function in `Employee` forces every direct derived class of `Employee` that wishes to be a concrete class to override `earnings`. This enables the designer of the class hierarchy to demand that each derived class provide an appropriate pay calculation, if indeed that derived class is to be concrete.

Function `print` in class `Employee` displays the first name, last name and social security number of the employee. As we will see, each derived class of `Employee` overrides function `print` to output the employee's type (e.g., `"salaried employee:"`) followed by the rest of the employee's information.

The diagram in Fig. 13.12 shows each of the five classes in the hierarchy down the left side and functions `earnings` and `print` across the top. For each class, the diagram shows the desired results of each function. Note that class `Employee` specifies "= 0" for function `earnings` to indicate that this is a pure `virtual` function. Each derived class overrides this function to provide an appropriate implementation. We do not list base class `Employee`'s *get* and *set* functions because they are not overridden in any of the derived classes—each of these functions is inherited and used "as is" by each of the derived classes.

Let us consider class `Employee`'s header file (Fig. 13.13). The `public` member functions include a constructor that takes the first name, last name and social security number as arguments (line 12); *set* functions that set the first name, last name and social security number (lines 14, 17 and 20, respectively); *get* functions that return the first name, last name and social security number (lines 15, 18 and 21, respectively); pure `virtual` function `earnings` (line 24) and `virtual` function `print` (line 25).

Recall that we declared `earnings` as a pure `virtual` function because we first must know the specific `Employee` type to determine the appropriate `earnings` calculations. Declaring this function as pure `virtual` indicates that each concrete derived class *must* provide an appropriate `earnings` implementation and that a program can use base-class `Employee` pointers to invoke function `earnings` polymorphically for any type of `Employee`.

Figure 13.14 contains the member-function implementations for class `Employee`. No implementation is provided for `virtual` function `earnings`. Note that the `Employee` constructor (lines 10–15) does not validate the social security number. Normally, such validation should be provided. An exercise in Chapter 12 asks you to validate a social security number to ensure that it is in the form `###-##-####`, where each # represents a digit.

	earnings	print
Employee	= 0	*firstName lastName* social security number: *SSN*
Salaried-Employee	weeklySalary	salaried employee: *firstName lastName* social security number: *SSN* weekly salary: *weeklysalary*

Hourly-Employee	*If hours <= 40*
	    wage * hours
	If hours > 40
	    (40 * wage) +
	    ((hours - 40)
	    * wage * 1.5)
		hourly employee: *firstName lastName*
		social security number: *SSN*
		hourly wage: *wage*; hours worked: *hours*

Commission-Employee	commissionRate * grossSales	commission employee: *firstName lastName* social security number: *SSN* gross sales: *grossSales*; commission rate: *commissionRate*
BasePlus-Commission-Employee	baseSalary + (commissionRate * grossSales)	base salaried commission employee: *firstName lastName* social security number: *SSN* gross sales: *grossSales*; commission rate: *commissionRate*; base salary: *baseSalary*

Fig. 13.12 | Polymorphic interface for the `Employee` hierarchy classes.

```
1   // Fig. 13.13: Employee.h
2   // Employee abstract base class.
3   #ifndef EMPLOYEE_H
4   #define EMPLOYEE_H
5
6   #include <string> // C++ standard string class
7   using std::string;
8
9   class Employee
10  {
11  public:
12     Employee( const string &, const string &, const string & );
13
14     void setFirstName( const string & ); // set first name
15     string getFirstName() const; // return first name
16
17     void setLastName( const string & ); // set last name
18     string getLastName() const; // return last name
19
```

Fig. 13.13 | Employee class header file. (Part 1 of 2.)

```
20       void setSocialSecurityNumber( const string & ); // set SSN
21       string getSocialSecurityNumber() const; // return SSN
22
23       // pure virtual function makes Employee abstract base class
24       virtual double earnings() const = 0; // pure virtual
25       virtual void print() const; // virtual
26    private:
27       string firstName;
28       string lastName;
29       string socialSecurityNumber;
30    }; // end class Employee
31
32    #endif // EMPLOYEE_H
```

Fig. 13.13 │ Employee class header file. (Part 2 of 2.)

```
1    // Fig. 13.14: Employee.cpp
2    // Abstract-base-class Employee member-function definitions.
3    // Note: No definitions are given for pure virtual functions.
4    #include <iostream>
5    using std::cout;
6
7    #include "Employee.h" // Employee class definition
8
9    // constructor
10   Employee::Employee( const string &first, const string &last,
11      const string &ssn )
12      : firstName( first ), lastName( last ), socialSecurityNumber( ssn )
13   {
14      // empty body
15   } // end Employee constructor
16
17   // set first name
18   void Employee::setFirstName( const string &first )
19   {
20      firstName = first;
21   } // end function setFirstName
22
23   // return first name
24   string Employee::getFirstName() const
25   {
26      return firstName;
27   } // end function getFirstName
28
29   // set last name
30   void Employee::setLastName( const string &last )
31   {
32      lastName = last;
33   } // end function setLastName
34
```

Fig. 13.14 │ Employee class implementation file. (Part 1 of 2.)

```
35    // return last name
36    string Employee::getLastName() const
37    {
38       return lastName;
39    } // end function getLastName
40
41    // set social security number
42    void Employee::setSocialSecurityNumber( const string &ssn )
43    {
44       socialSecurityNumber = ssn; // should validate
45    } // end function setSocialSecurityNumber
46
47    // return social security number
48    string Employee::getSocialSecurityNumber() const
49    {
50       return socialSecurityNumber;
51    } // end function getSocialSecurityNumber
52
53    // print Employee's information (virtual, but not pure virtual)
54    void Employee::print() const
55    {
56       cout << getFirstName() << ' ' << getLastName()
57          << "\nsocial security number: " << getSocialSecurityNumber();
58    } // end function print
```

Fig. 13.14 | `Employee` class implementation file. (Part 2 of 2.)

Note that `virtual` function `print` (Fig. 13.14, lines 54–58) provides an implementation that will be overridden in each of the derived classes. Each of these functions will, however, use the abstract class's version of `print` to print information common to all classes in the `Employee` hierarchy.

13.6.2 Creating Concrete Derived Class `SalariedEmployee`

Class `SalariedEmployee` (Figs. 13.15–13.16) derives from class `Employee` (line 8 of Fig. 13.15). The `public` member functions include a constructor that takes a first name, a last name, a social security number and a weekly salary as arguments (lines 11–12); a *set* function to assign a new nonnegative value to data member `weeklySalary` (lines 14); a *get* function to return `weeklySalary`'s value (line 15); a `virtual` function `earnings` that calculates a `SalariedEmployee`'s earnings (line 18) and a `virtual` function `print` that outputs the employee's type, namely, `"salaried employee: "` followed by employee-specific information produced by base class `Employee`'s `print` function and `SalariedEmployee`'s `getWeeklySalary` function (line 19).

Figure 13.16 contains the member-function implementations for `SalariedEmployee`. The class's constructor passes the first name, last name and social security number to the `Employee` constructor (line 11) to initialize the `private` data members that are inherited from the base class, but not accessible in the derived class. Function `earnings` (line 30–33) overrides pure `virtual` function `earnings` in `Employee` to provide a concrete implementation that returns the `SalariedEmployee`'s weekly salary. If we do not implement `earnings`, class `SalariedEmployee` would be an abstract class, and any attempt to instantiate an object of the class would result in a compilation error (and, of course, we

```
1   // Fig. 13.15: SalariedEmployee.h
2   // SalariedEmployee class derived from Employee.
3   #ifndef SALARIED_H
4   #define SALARIED_H
5
6   #include "Employee.h" // Employee class definition
7
8   class SalariedEmployee : public Employee
9   {
10  public:
11     SalariedEmployee( const string &, const string &,
12        const string &, double = 0.0 );
13
14     void setWeeklySalary( double ); // set weekly salary
15     double getWeeklySalary() const; // return weekly salary
16
17     // keyword virtual signals intent to override
18     virtual double earnings() const; // calculate earnings
19     virtual void print() const; // print SalariedEmployee object
20  private:
21     double weeklySalary; // salary per week
22  }; // end class SalariedEmployee
23
24  #endif // SALARIED_H
```

Fig. 13.15 | SalariedEmployee class header file.

```
1   // Fig. 13.16: SalariedEmployee.cpp
2   // SalariedEmployee class member-function definitions.
3   #include <iostream>
4   using std::cout;
5
6   #include "SalariedEmployee.h" // SalariedEmployee class definition
7
8   // constructor
9   SalariedEmployee::SalariedEmployee( const string &first,
10     const string &last, const string &ssn, double salary )
11     : Employee( first, last, ssn )
12  {
13     setWeeklySalary( salary );
14  } // end SalariedEmployee constructor
15
16  // set salary
17  void SalariedEmployee::setWeeklySalary( double salary )
18  {
19     weeklySalary = ( salary < 0.0 ) ? 0.0 : salary;
20  } // end function setWeeklySalary
21
22  // return salary
23  double SalariedEmployee::getWeeklySalary() const
24  {
```

Fig. 13.16 | SalariedEmployee class implementation file. (Part 1 of 2.)

```
25        return weeklySalary;
26    } // end function getWeeklySalary
27
28    // calculate earnings;
29    // override pure virtual function earnings in Employee
30    double SalariedEmployee::earnings() const
31    {
32        return getWeeklySalary();
33    } // end function earnings
34
35    // print SalariedEmployee's information
36    void SalariedEmployee::print() const
37    {
38        cout << "salaried employee: ";
39        Employee::print(); // reuse abstract base-class print function
40        cout << "\nweekly salary: " << getWeeklySalary();
41    } // end function print
```

Fig. 13.16 | SalariedEmployee class implementation file. (Part 2 of 2.)

want SalariedEmployee here to be a concrete class). Note that in class SalariedEmployee's header file, we declared member functions earnings and print as virtual (lines 18–19 of Fig. 13.15)—actually, placing the virtual keyword before these member functions is redundant. We defined them as virtual in base class Employee, so they remain virtual functions throughout the class hierarchy. Recall from Good Programming Practice 13.1 that explicitly declaring such functions virtual at every level of the hierarchy can promote program clarity.

Function print of class SalariedEmployee (lines 36–41 of Fig. 13.16) overrides Employee function print. If class SalariedEmployee did not override print, SalariedEmployee would inherit the Employee version of print. In that case, SalariedEmployee's print function would simply return the employee's full name and social security number, which does not adequately represent a SalariedEmployee. To print a SalariedEmployee's complete information, the derived class's print function outputs "salaried employee: " followed by the base-class Employee-specific information (i.e., first name, last name and social security number) printed by invoking the base class's print using the scope resolution operator (line 39)—this is a nice example of code reuse. The output produced by SalariedEmployee's print function contains the employee's weekly salary obtained by invoking the class's getWeeklySalary function.

13.6.3 Creating Concrete Derived Class HourlyEmployee

Class HourlyEmployee (Figs. 13.17–13.18) also derives from class Employee (line 8 of Fig. 13.17). The public member functions include a constructor (lines 11–12) that takes as arguments a first name, a last name, a social security number, an hourly wage and the number of hours worked; *set* functions that assign new values to data members wage and hours, respectively (lines 14 and 17); *get* functions to return the values of wage and hours, respectively (lines 15 and 18); a virtual function earnings that calculates an HourlyEmployee's earnings (line 21) and a virtual function print that outputs the employee's type, namely, "hourly employee: " and employee-specific information (line 22).

```
 1   // Fig. 13.17: HourlyEmployee.h
 2   // HourlyEmployee class definition.
 3   #ifndef HOURLY_H
 4   #define HOURLY_H
 5
 6   #include "Employee.h" // Employee class definition
 7
 8   class HourlyEmployee : public Employee
 9   {
10   public:
11      HourlyEmployee( const string &, const string &,
12         const string &, double = 0.0, double = 0.0 );
13
14      void setWage( double ); // set hourly wage
15      double getWage() const; // return hourly wage
16
17      void setHours( double ); // set hours worked
18      double getHours() const; // return hours worked
19
20      // keyword virtual signals intent to override
21      virtual double earnings() const; // calculate earnings
22      virtual void print() const; // print HourlyEmployee object
23   private:
24      double wage; // wage per hour
25      double hours; // hours worked for week
26   }; // end class HourlyEmployee
27
28   #endif // HOURLY_H
```

Fig. 13.17 | HourlyEmployee class header file.

```
 1   // Fig. 13.18: HourlyEmployee.cpp
 2   // HourlyEmployee class member-function definitions.
 3   #include <iostream>
 4   using std::cout;
 5
 6   #include "HourlyEmployee.h" // HourlyEmployee class definition
 7
 8   // constructor
 9   HourlyEmployee::HourlyEmployee( const string &first, const string &last,
10      const string &ssn, double hourlyWage, double hoursWorked )
11      : Employee( first, last, ssn )
12   {
13      setWage( hourlyWage ); // validate hourly wage
14      setHours( hoursWorked ); // validate hours worked
15   } // end HourlyEmployee constructor
16
17   // set wage
18   void HourlyEmployee::setWage( double hourlyWage )
19   {
20      wage = ( hourlyWage < 0.0 ? 0.0 : hourlyWage );
21   } // end function setWage
```

Fig. 13.18 | HourlyEmployee class implementation file. (Part 1 of 2.)

```
22
23   // return wage
24   double HourlyEmployee::getWage() const
25   {
26      return wage;
27   } // end function getWage
28
29   // set hours worked
30   void HourlyEmployee::setHours( double hoursWorked )
31   {
32      hours = ( ( ( hoursWorked >= 0.0 ) && ( hoursWorked <= 168.0 ) ) ?
33         hoursWorked : 0.0 );
34   } // end function setHours
35
36   // return hours worked
37   double HourlyEmployee::getHours() const
38   {
39      return hours;
40   } // end function getHours
41
42   // calculate earnings;
43   // override pure virtual function earnings in Employee
44   double HourlyEmployee::earnings() const
45   {
46      if ( getHours() <= 40 ) // no overtime
47         return getWage() * getHours();
48      else
49         return 40 * getWage() + ( ( getHours() - 40 ) * getWage() * 1.5 );
50   } // end function earnings
51
52   // print HourlyEmployee's information
53   void HourlyEmployee::print() const
54   {
55      cout << "hourly employee: ";
56      Employee::print(); // code reuse
57      cout << "\nhourly wage: " << getWage() <<
58         "; hours worked: " << getHours();
59   } // end function print
```

Fig. 13.18 | HourlyEmployee class implementation file. (Part 2 of 2.)

Figure 13.18 contains the member-function implementations for class HourlyEmployee. Lines 18–21 and 30–34 define *set* functions that assign new values to data members wage and hours, respectively. Function setWage (lines 18–21) ensures that wage is nonnegative, and function setHours (lines 30–34) ensures that data member hours is between 0 and 168 (the total number of hours in a week). Class HourlyEmployee's *get* functions are implemented in lines 24–27 and 37–40. We do not declare these functions virtual, so classes derived from class HourlyEmployee cannot override them (although derived classes certainly can redefine them). Note that the HourlyEmployee constructor, like the SalariedEmployee constructor, passes the first name, last name and social security number to the base class Employee constructor (line 11) to initialize the inherited private data members declared in the base class. In addition, HourlyEmployee's print function calls base-class function `print` (line 56) to output the `Employee`-specific information (i.e., first name, last name and social security number)—this is another nice example of code reuse.

13.6.4 Creating Concrete Derived Class CommissionEmployee

Class `CommissionEmployee` (Figs. 13.19–13.20) derives from class `Employee` (line 8 of Fig. 13.19). The member-function implementations (Fig. 13.20) include a constructor (lines 9–15) that takes a first name, a last name, a social security number, a sales amount and a commission rate; *set* functions (lines 18–21 and 30–33) to assign new values to data members `commissionRate` and `grossSales`, respectively; *get* functions (lines 24–27 and 36–39) that retrieve the values of these data members; function `earnings` (lines 43–46) to calculate a `CommissionEmployee`'s earnings; and function `print` (lines 49–55), which outputs the employee's type, namely, `"commission employee: "` and employee-specific information. The `CommissionEmployee`'s constructor also passes the first name, last name and social security number to the `Employee` constructor (line 11) to initialize `Employee`'s pri-

```
1   // Fig. 13.19: CommissionEmployee.h
2   // CommissionEmployee class derived from Employee.
3   #ifndef COMMISSION_H
4   #define COMMISSION_H
5
6   #include "Employee.h" // Employee class definition
7
8   class CommissionEmployee : public Employee
9   {
10  public:
11     CommissionEmployee( const string &, const string &,
12        const string &, double = 0.0, double = 0.0 );
13
14     void setCommissionRate( double ); // set commission rate
15     double getCommissionRate() const; // return commission rate
16
17     void setGrossSales( double ); // set gross sales amount
18     double getGrossSales() const; // return gross sales amount
19
20     // keyword virtual signals intent to override
21     virtual double earnings() const; // calculate earnings
22     virtual void print() const; // print CommissionEmployee object
23  private:
24     double grossSales; // gross weekly sales
25     double commissionRate; // commission percentage
26  }; // end class CommissionEmployee
27
28  #endif // COMMISSION_H
```

Fig. 13.19 | `CommissionEmployee` class header file.

```
1   // Fig. 13.20: CommissionEmployee.cpp
2   // CommissionEmployee class member-function definitions.
3   #include <iostream>
```

Fig. 13.20 | `CommissionEmployee` class implementation file. (Part 1 of 2.)

```cpp
 4   using std::cout;
 5
 6   #include "CommissionEmployee.h" // CommissionEmployee class definition
 7
 8   // constructor
 9   CommissionEmployee::CommissionEmployee( const string &first,
10      const string &last, const string &ssn, double sales, double rate )
11      : Employee( first, last, ssn )
12   {
13      setGrossSales( sales );
14      setCommissionRate( rate );
15   } // end CommissionEmployee constructor
16
17   // set commission rate
18   void CommissionEmployee::setCommissionRate( double rate )
19   {
20      commissionRate = ( ( rate > 0.0 && rate < 1.0 ) ? rate : 0.0 );
21   } // end function setCommissionRate
22
23   // return commission rate
24   double CommissionEmployee::getCommissionRate() const
25   {
26      return commissionRate;
27   } // end function getCommissionRate
28
29   // set gross sales amount
30   void CommissionEmployee::setGrossSales( double sales )
31   {
32      grossSales = ( ( sales < 0.0 ) ? 0.0 : sales );
33   } // end function setGrossSales
34
35   // return gross sales amount
36   double CommissionEmployee::getGrossSales() const
37   {
38      return grossSales;
39   } // end function getGrossSales
40
41   // calculate earnings;
42   // override pure virtual function earnings in Employee
43   double CommissionEmployee::earnings() const
44   {
45      return getCommissionRate() * getGrossSales();
46   } // end function earnings
47
48   // print CommissionEmployee's information
49   void CommissionEmployee::print() const
50   {
51      cout << "commission employee: ";
52      Employee::print(); // code reuse
53      cout << "\ngross sales: " << getGrossSales()
54         << "; commission rate: " << getCommissionRate();
55   } // end function print
```

Fig. 13.20 | CommissionEmployee class implementation file. (Part 2 of 2.)

vate data members. Function print calls base-class function print (line 52) to display the Employee-specific information (i.e., first name, last name and social security number).

13.6.5 Creating Indirect Concrete Derived Class BasePlusCommissionEmployee

Class BasePlusCommissionEmployee (Figs. 13.21–13.22) directly inherits from class CommissionEmployee (line 8 of Fig. 13.21) and therefore is an indirect derived class of class Employee. Class BasePlusCommissionEmployee's member-function implementations include a constructor (lines 10–16 of Fig. 13.22) that takes as arguments a first name, a last name, a social security number, a sales amount, a commission rate and a base salary. It then passes the first name, last name, social security number, sales amount and commission rate to the CommissionEmployee constructor (line 13) to initialize the inherited members. Base-PlusCommissionEmployee also contains a *set* function (lines 19–22) to assign a new value to data member baseSalary and a *get* function (lines 25–28) to return baseSalary's value. Function earnings (lines 32–35) calculates a BasePlusCommissionEmployee's earnings. Note that line 34 in function earnings calls base-class CommissionEmployee's earnings function to calculate the commission-based portion of the employee's earnings. This is a nice example of code reuse. BasePlusCommissionEmployee's print function (lines 38–43) outputs "base-salaried", followed by the output of base-class CommissionEmployee's print function (another example of code reuse), then the base salary. The resulting output begins with "base-salaried commission employee: " followed by the rest of the Base-

```
1   // Fig. 13.21: BasePlusCommissionEmployee.h
2   // BasePlusCommissionEmployee class derived from Employee.
3   #ifndef BASEPLUS_H
4   #define BASEPLUS_H
5
6   #include "CommissionEmployee.h" // CommissionEmployee class definition
7
8   class BasePlusCommissionEmployee : public CommissionEmployee
9   {
10  public:
11     BasePlusCommissionEmployee( const string &, const string &,
12        const string &, double = 0.0, double = 0.0, double = 0.0 );
13
14     void setBaseSalary( double ); // set base salary
15     double getBaseSalary() const; // return base salary
16
17     // keyword virtual signals intent to override
18     virtual double earnings() const; // calculate earnings
19     virtual void print() const; // print BasePlusCommissionEmployee object
20  private:
21     double baseSalary; // base salary per week
22  }; // end class BasePlusCommissionEmployee
23
24  #endif // BASEPLUS_H
```

Fig. 13.21 | BasePlusCommissionEmployee class header file.

```
1    // Fig. 13.22: BasePlusCommissionEmployee.cpp
2    // BasePlusCommissionEmployee member-function definitions.
3    #include <iostream>
4    using std::cout;
5
6    // BasePlusCommissionEmployee class definition
7    #include "BasePlusCommissionEmployee.h"
8
9    // constructor
10   BasePlusCommissionEmployee::BasePlusCommissionEmployee(
11      const string &first, const string &last, const string &ssn,
12      double sales, double rate, double salary )
13      : CommissionEmployee( first, last, ssn, sales, rate )
14   {
15      setBaseSalary( salary ); // validate and store base salary
16   } // end BasePlusCommissionEmployee constructor
17
18   // set base salary
19   void BasePlusCommissionEmployee::setBaseSalary( double salary )
20   {
21      baseSalary = ( ( salary < 0.0 ) ? 0.0 : salary );
22   } // end function setBaseSalary
23
24   // return base salary
25   double BasePlusCommissionEmployee::getBaseSalary() const
26   {
27      return baseSalary;
28   } // end function getBaseSalary
29
30   // calculate earnings;
31   // override pure virtual function earnings in Employee
32   double BasePlusCommissionEmployee::earnings() const
33   {
34      return getBaseSalary() + CommissionEmployee::earnings();
35   } // end function earnings
36
37   // print BasePlusCommissionEmployee's information
38   void BasePlusCommissionEmployee::print() const
39   {
40      cout << "base-salaried ";
41      CommissionEmployee::print(); // code reuse
42      cout << "; base salary: " << getBaseSalary();
43   } // end function print
```

Fig. 13.22 | BasePlusCommissionEmployee class implementation file.

PlusCommissionEmployee's information. Recall that CommissionEmployee's print displays the employee's first name, last name and social security number by invoking the print function of its base class (i.e., Employee)—yet another example of code reuse. Note that BasePlusCommissionEmployee's print initiates a chain of functions calls that spans all three levels of the Employee hierarchy.

13.6.6 Demonstrating Polymorphic Processing

To test our `Employee` hierarchy, the program in Fig. 13.23 creates an object of each of the four concrete classes `SalariedEmployee`, `HourlyEmployee`, `CommissionEmployee` and `BasePlusCommissionEmployee`. The program manipulates these objects, first with static binding, then polymorphically, using a `vector` of `Employee` pointers. Lines 31–38 create objects of each of the four concrete `Employee` derived classes. Lines 43–51 output each Employee's information and earnings. Each member-function invocation in lines 43–51 is

```
 1   // Fig. 13.23: fig13_23.cpp
 2   // Processing Employee derived-class objects individually
 3   // and polymorphically using dynamic binding.
 4   #include <iostream>
 5   using std::cout;
 6   using std::endl;
 7   using std::fixed;
 8
 9   #include <iomanip>
10   using std::setprecision;
11
12   #include <vector>
13   using std::vector;
14
15   // include definitions of classes in Employee hierarchy
16   #include "Employee.h"
17   #include "SalariedEmployee.h"
18   #include "HourlyEmployee.h"
19   #include "CommissionEmployee.h"
20   #include "BasePlusCommissionEmployee.h"
21
22   void virtualViaPointer( const Employee * const ); // prototype
23   void virtualViaReference( const Employee & ); // prototype
24
25   int main()
26   {
27      // set floating-point output formatting
28      cout << fixed << setprecision( 2 );
29
30      // create derived-class objects
31      SalariedEmployee salariedEmployee(
32         "John", "Smith", "111-11-1111", 800 );
33      HourlyEmployee hourlyEmployee(
34         "Karen", "Price", "222-22-2222", 16.75, 40 );
35      CommissionEmployee commissionEmployee(
36         "Sue", "Jones", "333-33-3333", 10000, .06 );
37      BasePlusCommissionEmployee basePlusCommissionEmployee(
38         "Bob", "Lewis", "444-44-4444", 5000, .04, 300 );
39
40      cout << "Employees processed individually using static binding:\n\n";
41
42      // output each Employee's information and earnings using static binding
43      salariedEmployee.print();
```

Fig. 13.23 | `Employee` class hierarchy driver program. (Part 1 of 4.)

```
44      cout << "\nearned $" << salariedEmployee.earnings() << "\n\n";
45      hourlyEmployee.print();
46      cout << "\nearned $" << hourlyEmployee.earnings() << "\n\n";
47      commissionEmployee.print();
48      cout << "\nearned $" << commissionEmployee.earnings() << "\n\n";
49      basePlusCommissionEmployee.print();
50      cout << "\nearned $" << basePlusCommissionEmployee.earnings()
51          << "\n\n";
52
53      // create vector of four base-class pointers
54      vector < Employee * > employees( 4 );
55
56      // initialize vector with Employees
57      employees[ 0 ] = &salariedEmployee;
58      employees[ 1 ] = &hourlyEmployee;
59      employees[ 2 ] = &commissionEmployee;
60      employees[ 3 ] = &basePlusCommissionEmployee;
61
62      cout << "Employees processed polymorphically via dynamic binding:\n\n";
63
64      // call virtualViaPointer to print each Employee's information
65      // and earnings using dynamic binding
66      cout << "Virtual function calls made off base-class pointers:\n\n";
67
68      for ( size_t i = 0; i < employees.size(); i++ )
69          virtualViaPointer( employees[ i ] );
70
71      // call virtualViaReference to print each Employee's information
72      // and earnings using dynamic binding
73      cout << "Virtual function calls made off base-class references:\n\n";
74
75      for ( size_t i = 0; i < employees.size(); i++ )
76          virtualViaReference( *employees[ i ] ); // note dereferencing
77
78      return 0;
79  } // end main
80
81  // call Employee virtual functions print and earnings off a
82  // base-class pointer using dynamic binding
83  void virtualViaPointer( const Employee * const baseClassPtr )
84  {
85      baseClassPtr->print();
86      cout << "\nearned $" << baseClassPtr->earnings() << "\n\n";
87  } // end function virtualViaPointer
88
89  // call Employee virtual functions print and earnings off a
90  // base-class reference using dynamic binding
91  void virtualViaReference( const Employee &baseClassRef )
92  {
93      baseClassRef.print();                                           '
94      cout << "\nearned $" << baseClassRef.earnings() << "\n\n";
95  } // end function virtualViaReference
```

Fig. 13.23 | Employee class hierarchy driver program. (Part 2 of 4.)

```
Employees processed individually using static binding:

salaried employee: John Smith
social security number: 111-11-1111
weekly salary: 800.00
earned $800.00

hourly employee: Karen Price
social security number: 222-22-2222
hourly wage: 16.75; hours worked: 40.00
earned $670.00

commission employee: Sue Jones
social security number: 333-33-3333
gross sales: 10000.00; commission rate: 0.06
earned $600.00

base-salaried commission employee: Bob Lewis
social security number: 444-44-4444
gross sales: 5000.00; commission rate: 0.04; base salary: 300.00
earned $500.00

Employees processed polymorphically using dynamic binding:

Virtual function calls made off base-class pointers:

salaried employee: John Smith
social security number: 111-11-1111
weekly salary: 800.00
earned $800.00

hourly employee: Karen Price
social security number: 222-22-2222
hourly wage: 16.75; hours worked: 40.00
earned $670.00

commission employee: Sue Jones
social security number: 333-33-3333
gross sales: 10000.00; commission rate: 0.06
earned $600.00

base-salaried commission employee: Bob Lewis
social security number: 444-44-4444
gross sales: 5000.00; commission rate: 0.04; base salary: 300.00
earned $500.00

Virtual function calls made off base-class references:

salaried employee: John Smith
social security number: 111-11-1111
weekly salary: 800.00
earned $800.00

hourly employee: Karen Price
social security number: 222-22-2222
hourly wage: 16.75; hours worked: 40.00
earned $670.00
```

(continued at top of next page...)

Fig. 13.23 | Employee class hierarchy driver program. (Part 3 of 4.)

(...continued from bottom of previous page)

```
commission employee: Sue Jones
social security number: 333-33-3333
gross sales: 10000.00; commission rate: 0.06
earned $600.00

base-salaried commission employee: Bob Lewis
social security number: 444-44-4444
gross sales: 5000.00; commission rate: 0.04; base salary: 300.00
earned $500.00
```

Fig. 13.23 | Employee class hierarchy driver program. (Part 4 of 4.)

an example of static binding—at compile time, because we are using name handles (not pointers or references that could be set at execution time), the compiler can identify each object's type to determine which print and earnings functions are called.

Line 54 allocates vector employees, which contains four Employee pointers. Line 57 aims employees[0] at object salariedEmployee. Line 58 aims employees[1] at object hourlyEmployee. Line 59 aims employees[2] at object commissionEmployee. Line 60 aims employee[3] at object basePlusCommissionEmployee. The compiler allows these assignments, because a SalariedEmployee *is an* Employee, an HourlyEmployee *is an* Employee, a CommissionEmployee *is an* Employee and a BasePlusCommissionEmployee *is an* Employee. Therefore, we can assign the addresses of SalariedEmployee, HourlyEmployee, CommissionEmployee and BasePlusCommissionEmployee objects to base-class Employee pointers (even though Employee is an abstract class).

The for statement at lines 68–69 traverses vector employees and invokes function virtualViaPointer (lines 83–87) for each element in employees. Function virtualViaPointer receives in parameter baseClassPtr (of type const Employee * const) the address stored in an employees element. Each call to virtualViaPointer uses baseClassPtr to invoke virtual functions print (line 85) and earnings (line 86). Note that function virtualViaPointer does not contain any SalariedEmployee, HourlyEmployee, CommissionEmployee or BasePlusCommissionEmployee type information. The function knows only about base-class type Employee. Therefore, at compile time, the compiler cannot know which concrete class's functions to call through baseClassPtr. Yet at execution time, each virtual-function invocation calls the function on the object to which baseClassPtr points at that time. The output illustrates that the appropriate functions for each class are indeed invoked and that each object's proper information is displayed. For instance, the weekly salary is displayed for the SalariedEmployee, and the gross sales are displayed for the CommissionEmployee and BasePlusCommissionEmployee. Also note that obtaining the earnings of each Employee polymorphically in line 86 produces the same results as obtaining these employees' earnings via static binding in lines 44, 46, 48 and 50. All virtual function calls to print and earnings are resolved at runtime with dynamic binding.

Finally, another for statement (lines 75–76) traverses employees and invokes function virtualViaReference (lines 91–95) for each element in the vector. Function virtualViaReference receives in its parameter baseClassRef (of type const Employee &) a reference formed by dereferencing the pointer stored in each employees element (line 76). Each call to virtualViaReference invokes virtual functions print (line 93) and earnings (line 94) via reference baseClassRef to demonstrate that polymorphic processing occurs with base-class references as well. Each `virtual`-function invocation calls the function on the object to which `baseClassRef` refers at runtime. This is another example of dynamic binding. The output produced using base-class references is identical to the output produced using base-class pointers.

13.7 (Optional) Polymorphism, Virtual Functions and Dynamic Binding "Under the Hood"

C++ makes polymorphism easy to program. It is certainly possible to program for polymorphism in non-object-oriented languages such as C, but doing so requires complex and potentially dangerous pointer manipulations. This section discusses how C++ can implement polymorphism, `virtual` functions and dynamic binding internally. This will give you a solid understanding of how these capabilities really work. More importantly, it will help you appreciate the overhead of polymorphism—in terms of additional memory consumption and processor time. This will help you determine when to use polymorphism and when to avoid it. As you will see in Chapter 22, Standard Template Library (STL), the STL components were implemented without polymorphism and `virtual` functions—this was done to avoid the associated execution-time overhead and achieve optimal performance to meet the unique requirements of the STL.

First, we will explain the data structures that the C++ compiler builds at compile time to support polymorphism at execution time. You will see that polymorphism is accomplished through three levels of pointers (i.e., "triple indirection"). Then we will show how an executing program uses these data structures to execute `virtual` functions and achieve the dynamic binding associated with polymorphism. Note that our discussion explains one possible implementation; this is not a language requirement.

When C++ compiles a class that has one or more `virtual` functions, it builds a virtual function table (*vtable*) for that class. An executing program uses the *vtable* to select the proper function implementation each time a `virtual` function of that class is called. The leftmost column of Fig. 13.24 illustrates the *vtables* for classes `Employee`, `SalariedEmployee`, `HourlyEmployee`, `CommissionEmployee` and `BasePlusCommissionEmployee`.

In the *vtable* for class `Employee`, the first function pointer is set to 0 (i.e., the null pointer). This is done because function `earnings` is a pure `virtual` function and therefore lacks an implementation. The second function pointer points to function `print`, which displays the employee's full name and social security number. [*Note:* We have abbreviated the output of each `print` function in this figure to conserve space.] Any class that has one or more null pointers in its *vtable* is an abstract class. Classes without any null *vtable* pointers (such as `SalariedEmployee`, `HourlyEmployee`, `CommissionEmployee` and `BasePlusCommissionEmployee`) are concrete classes.

Class `SalariedEmployee` overrides function `earnings` to return the employee's weekly salary, so the function pointer points to the `earnings` function of class `SalariedEmployee`. `SalariedEmployee` also overrides `print`, so the corresponding function pointer points to the `SalariedEmployee` member function that prints "salaried employee: " followed by the employee's name, social security number and weekly salary.

The `earnings` function pointer in the *vtable* for class `HourlyEmployee` points to `HourlyEmployee`'s `earnings` function that returns the employee's wage multiplied by the number of hours worked. Note that to conserve space, we have omitted the fact that hourly employees receive time-and-a-half pay for overtime hours worked. The `print` func-

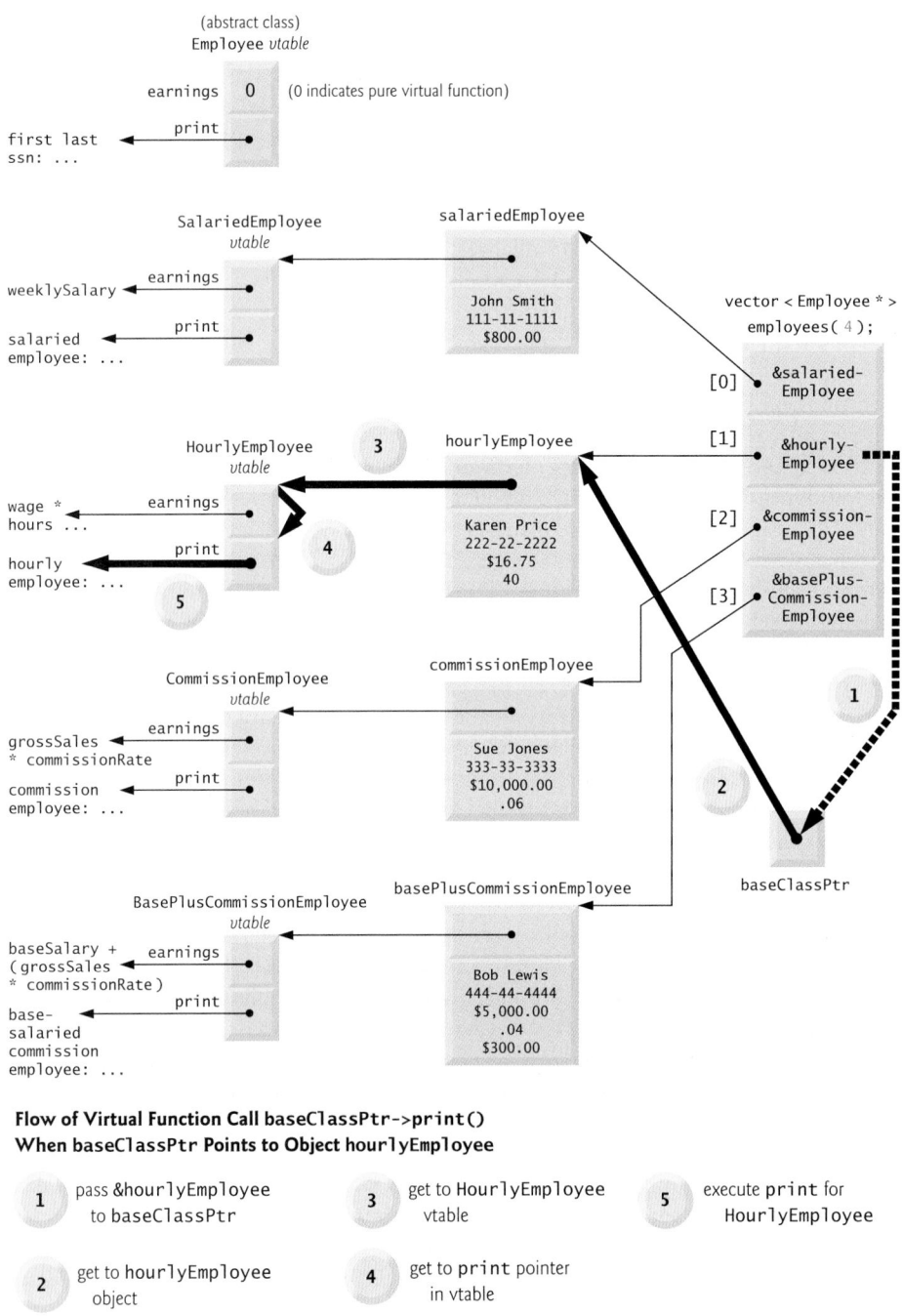

Flow of Virtual Function Call baseClassPtr->print()
When baseClassPtr Points to Object hourlyEmployee

1. pass &hourlyEmployee to baseClassPtr

2. get to hourlyEmployee object

3. get to HourlyEmployee vtable

4. get to print pointer in vtable

5. execute print for HourlyEmployee

Fig. 13.24 | How virtual function calls work.

tion pointer points to the HourlyEmployee version of the function, which prints "hourly employee: ", the employee's name, social security number, hourly wage and hours worked. Both functions override the functions in class Employee.

The earnings function pointer in the *vtable* for class CommissionEmployee points to CommissionEmployee's earnings function that returns the employee's gross sales multiplied by commission rate. The print function pointer points to the CommissionEmployee version of the function, which prints the employee's type, name, social security number, commission rate and gross sales. As in class HourlyEmployee, both functions override the functions in class Employee.

The earnings function pointer in the *vtable* for class BasePlusCommissionEmployee points to BasePlusCommissionEmployee's earnings function that returns the employee's base salary plus gross sales multiplied by commission rate. The print function pointer points to the BasePlusCommissionEmployee version of the function, which prints the employee's base salary plus the type, name, social security number, commission rate and gross sales. Both functions override the functions in class CommissionEmployee.

Notice that in our Employee case study, each concrete class provides its own implementation for virtual functions earnings and print. You have already learned that each class which inherits directly from abstract base class Employee must implement earnings in order to be a concrete class, because earnings is a pure virtual function. These classes do not need to implement function print, however, to be considered concrete—print is not a pure virtual function and derived classes can inherit class Employee's implementation of print. Furthermore, class BasePlusCommissionEmployee does not have to implement either function print or earnings—both function implementations can be inherited from class CommissionEmployee. If a class in our hierarchy were to inherit function implementations in this manner, the *vtable* pointers for these functions would simply point to the function implementation that was being inherited. For example, if BasePlus-CommissionEmployee did not override earnings, the earnings function pointer in the *vtable* for class BasePlusCommissionEmployee would point to the same earnings function as the *vtable* for class CommissionEmployee points to.

Polymorphism is accomplished through an elegant data structure involving three levels of pointers. We have discussed one level—the function pointers in the *vtable*. These point to the actual functions that execute when a virtual function is invoked.

Now we consider the second level of pointers. Whenever an object of a class with one or more virtual functions is instantiated, the compiler attaches to the object a pointer to the *vtable* for that class. This pointer is normally at the front of the object, but it is not required to be implemented that way. In Fig. 13.24, these pointers are associated with the objects created in Fig. 13.23 (one object for each of the types SalariedEmployee, Hour-lyEmployee, CommissionEmployee and BasePlusCommissionEmployee). Notice that the diagram displays each of the object's data member values. For example, the salariedEm-ployee object contains a pointer to the SalariedEmployee *vtable*; the object also contains the values John Smith, 111-11-1111 and $800.00.

The third level of pointers simply contains the handles to the objects that receive the virtual function calls. The handles in this level may also be references. Note that Fig. 13.24 depicts the vector employees that contains Employee pointers.

Now let us see how a typical virtual function call executes. Consider the call baseClassPtr->print() in function virtualViaPointer (line 85 of Fig. 13.23). Assume that baseClassPtr contains employees[1] (i.e., the address of object hourlyEmployee in employees). When the compiler compiles this statement, it determines that the call is indeed being made via a base-class pointer and that print is a virtual function.

The compiler determines that print is the *second* entry in each of the *vtables*. To locate this entry, the compiler notes that it will need to skip the first entry. Thus, the compiler compiles an offset or displacement of four bytes (four bytes for each pointer on today's popular 32-bit machines, and only one pointer needs to be skipped) into the table of machine-language object-code pointers to find the code that will execute the virtual function call.

The compiler generates code that performs the following operations [*Note:* The numbers in the list correspond to the circled numbers in Fig. 13.24]:

1. Select the ith entry of employees (in this case, the address of object hourlyEmployee), and pass it as an argument to function virtualViaPointer. This sets parameter baseClassPtr to point to hourlyEmployee.

2. Dereference that pointer to get to the hourlyEmployee object—which, as you recall, begins with a pointer to the HourlyEmployee *vtable*.

3. Dereference hourlyEmployee's *vtable* pointer to get to the HourlyEmployee *vtable*.

4. Skip the offset of four bytes to select the print function pointer.

5. Dereference the print function pointer to form the "name" of the actual function to execute, and use the function call operator () to execute the appropriate print function, which in this case prints the employee's type, name, social security number, hourly wage and hours worked.

The data structures of Fig. 13.24 may appear to be complex, but this complexity is managed by the compiler and hidden from you, making polymorphic programming straightforward. The pointer dereferencing operations and memory accesses that occur on every virtual function call require some additional execution time. The *vtables* and the *vtable* pointers added to the objects require some additional memory. You now have enough information to determine whether virtual functions are appropriate for your programs.

 Performance Tip 13.1

Polymorphism, as typically implemented with virtual functions and dynamic binding in C++, is efficient. Programmers may use these capabilities with nominal impact on performance.

 Performance Tip 13.2

Virtual functions and dynamic binding enable polymorphic programming as an alternative to switch logic programming. Optimizing compilers normally generate polymorphic code that runs as efficiently as hand-coded switch-based logic. The overhead of polymorphism is acceptable for most applications. But in some situations—real-time applications with stringent performance requirements, for example—the overhead of polymorphism may be too high.

 **Software Engineering Observation 13.11**

Dynamic binding enables independent software vendors (ISVs) to distribute software without revealing proprietary secrets. Software distributions can consist of only header files and object files—no source code needs to be revealed. Software developers can then use inheritance to derive new classes from those provided by the ISVs. Other software that worked with the classes the ISVs provided will still work with the derived classes and will use the overridden virtual functions provided in these classes (via dynamic binding).

13.8 Case Study: Payroll System Using Polymorphism and Run-Time Type Information with Downcasting, dynamic_cast, typeid and type_info

Recall from the problem statement at the beginning of Section 13.6 that, for the current pay period, our fictitious company has decided to reward BasePlusCommissionEmployees by adding 10 percent to their base salaries. When processing Employee objects polymorphically in Section 13.6.6, we did not need to worry about the "specifics." Now, however, to adjust the base salaries of BasePlusCommissionEmployees, we have to determine the specific type of each Employee object at execution time, then act appropriately. This section demonstrates the powerful capabilities of run-time type information (RTTI) and dynamic casting, which enable a program to determine the type of an object at execution time and act on that object accordingly.

Some compilers, such as Microsoft Visual C++ .NET, require that RTTI be enabled before it can be used in a program. Consult your compiler's documentation to determine whether your compiler has similar requirements. To enable RTTI in Visual C++ .NET, select the **Project** menu and then select the properties option for the current project. In the **Property Pages** dialog box that appears, select **Configuration Properties > C/C++ > Language**. Then choose **Yes (/GR)** from the combo box next to **Enable Run-Time Type Info**. Finally, click **OK** to save the settings.

The program in Fig. 13.25 uses the Employee hierarchy developed in Section 13.6 and increases by 10 percent the base salary of each BasePlusCommissionEmployee. Line 31

```
1   // Fig. 13.25: fig13_25.cpp
2   // Demonstrating downcasting and run-time type information.
3   // NOTE: For this example to run in Visual C++ .NET,
4   // you need to enable RTTI (Run-Time Type Info) for the project.
5   #include <iostream>
6   using std::cout;
7   using std::endl;
8   using std::fixed;
9
10  #include <iomanip>
11  using std::setprecision;
12
13  #include <vector>
14  using std::vector;
15
16  #include <typeinfo>
17
18  // include definitions of classes in Employee hierarchy
19  #include "Employee.h"
20  #include "SalariedEmployee.h"
21  #include "HourlyEmployee.h"
22  #include "CommissionEmployee.h"
23  #include "BasePlusCommissionEmployee.h"
24
25  int main()
26  {
```

Fig. 13.25 | Demonstrating downcasting and run-time type information. (Part 1 of 3.)

```
27      // set floating-point output formatting
28      cout << fixed << setprecision( 2 );
29
30      // create vector of four base-class pointers
31      vector < Employee * > employees( 4 );
32
33      // initialize vector with various kinds of Employees
34      employees[ 0 ] = new SalariedEmployee(
35         "John", "Smith", "111-11-1111", 800 );
36      employees[ 1 ] = new HourlyEmployee(
37         "Karen", "Price", "222-22-2222", 16.75, 40 );
38      employees[ 2 ] = new CommissionEmployee(
39         "Sue", "Jones", "333-33-3333", 10000, .06 );
40      employees[ 3 ] = new BasePlusCommissionEmployee(
41         "Bob", "Lewis", "444-44-4444", 5000, .04, 300 );
42
43      // polymorphically process each element in vector employees
44      for ( size_t i = 0; i < employees.size(); i++ )
45      {
46         employees[ i ]->print(); // output employee information
47         cout << endl;
48
49         // downcast pointer
50         BasePlusCommissionEmployee *derivedPtr =
51            dynamic_cast < BasePlusCommissionEmployee * >
52               ( employees[ i ] );
53
54         // determine whether element points to base-salaried
55         // commission employee
56         if ( derivedPtr != 0 ) // 0 if not a BasePlusCommissionEmployee
57         {
58            double oldBaseSalary = derivedPtr->getBaseSalary();
59            cout << "old base salary: $" << oldBaseSalary << endl;
60            derivedPtr->setBaseSalary( 1.10 * oldBaseSalary );
61            cout << "new base salary with 10% increase is: $"
62               << derivedPtr->getBaseSalary() << endl;
63         } // end if
64
65         cout << "earned $" << employees[ i ]->earnings() << "\n\n";
66      } // end for
67
68      // release objects pointed to by vector's elements
69      for ( size_t j = 0; j < employees.size(); j++ )
70      {
71         // output class name
72         cout << "deleting object of "
73            << typeid( *employees[ j ] ).name() << endl;
74
75         delete employees[ j ];
76      } // end for
77
78      return 0;
79   } // end main
```

Fig. 13.25 | Demonstrating downcasting and run-time type information. (Part 2 of 3.)

```
salaried employee: John Smith
social security number: 111-11-1111
weekly salary: 800.00
earned $800.00

hourly employee: Karen Price
social security number: 222-22-2222
hourly wage: 16.75; hours worked: 40.00
earned $670.00

commission employee: Sue Jones
social security number: 333-33-3333
gross sales: 10000.00; commission rate: 0.06
earned $600.00

base-salaried commission employee: Bob Lewis
social security number: 444-44-4444
gross sales: 5000.00; commission rate: 0.04; base salary: 300.00
old base salary: $300.00
new base salary with 10% increase is: $330.00
earned $530.00

deleting object of class SalariedEmployee
deleting object of class HourlyEmployee
deleting object of class CommissionEmployee
deleting object of class BasePlusCommissionEmployee
```

Fig. 13.25 | Demonstrating downcasting and run-time type information. (Part 3 of 3.)

declares four-element vector employees that stores pointers to Employee objects. Lines 34–41 populate the vector with the addresses of dynamically allocated objects of classes SalariedEmployee (Figs. 13.15–13.16), HourlyEmployee (Figs. 13.17–13.18), CommissionEmployee (Figs. 13.19–13.20) and BasePlusCommissionEmployee (Figs. 13.21–13.22).

The for statement at lines 44–66 iterates through the employees vector and displays each Employee's information by invoking member function print (line 46). Recall that because print is declared virtual in base class Employee, the system invokes the appropriate derived-class object's print function.

In this example, as we encounter BasePlusCommissionEmployee objects, we wish to increase their base salary by 10 percent. Since we process the employees generically (i.e., polymorphically), we cannot (with the techniques we've learned) be certain as to which type of Employee is being manipulated at any given time. This creates a problem, because BasePlusCommissionEmployee employees must be identified when we encounter them so they can receive the 10 percent salary increase. To accomplish this, we use operator **dynamic_cast** (line 51) to determine whether the type of each object is BasePlusCommissionEmployee. This is the downcast operation we referred to in Section 13.3.3. Lines 50–52 dynamically downcast employees[i] from type Employee * to type BasePlusCommissionEmployee *. If the vector element points to an object that *is a* BasePlusCommissionEmployee object, then that object's address is assigned to commissionPtr; otherwise, 0 is assigned to derived-class pointer derivedPtr.

If the value returned by the dynamic_cast operator in lines 50–52 is not 0, the object is the correct type and the if statement (lines 56–63) performs the special processing required for the `BasePlusCommissionEmployee` object. Lines 58, 60 and 62 invoke `Base-PlusCommissionEmployee` functions `getBaseSalary` and `setBaseSalary` to retrieve and update the employee's salary.

Line 65 invokes member function `earnings` on the object to which `employees[ i ]` points. Recall that `earnings` is declared `virtual` in the base class, so the program invokes the derived-class object's `earnings` function—another example of dynamic binding.

The `for` loop at lines 69–76 displays each employee's object type and uses the `delete` operator to deallocate the dynamic memory to which each `vector` element points. Operator `typeid` (line 73) returns a reference to an object of class `type_info` that contains the information about the type of its operand, including the name of that type. When invoked, `type_info` member function `name` (line 73) returns a pointer-based string that contains the type name (e.g., `"class BasePlusCommissionEmployee"`) of the argument passed to `typeid`. [*Note:* The exact contents of the string returned by `type_info` member function `name` may vary by compiler.] To use `typeid`, the program must include header file `<typeinfo>` (line 16).

Note that we avoid several compilation errors in this example by downcasting an `Employee` pointer to a `BasePlusCommissionEmployee` pointer (lines 50–52). If we remove the `dynamic_cast` from line 51 and attempt to assign the current `Employee` pointer directly to `BasePlusCommissionEmployee` pointer `commissionPtr`, we will receive a compilation error. C++ does not allow a program to assign a base-class pointer to a derived-class pointer because the *is-a* relationship does not apply—a `CommissionEmployee` is *not* a `BasePlusCommissionEmployee`. The *is-a* relationship applies only between the derived class and its base classes, not vice versa.

Similarly, if lines 58, 60 and 62 used the current base-class pointer from `employees`, rather than derived-class pointer `commissionPtr`, to invoke derived-class-only functions `getBaseSalary` and `setBaseSalary`, we would receive a compilation error at each of these lines. As you learned in Section 13.3.3, attempting to invoke derived-class-only functions through a base-class pointer is not allowed. Although lines 58, 60 and 62 execute only if `commissionPtr` is not 0 (i.e., if the cast can be performed), we cannot attempt to invoke derived class `BasePlusCommissionEmployee` functions `getBaseSalary` and `setBas-eSalary` on the base class `Employee` pointer. Recall that, using a base class `Employee` pointer, we can invoke only functions found in base class `Employee`—earnings, print and `Employee`'s *get* and *set* functions.

13.9 Virtual Destructors

A problem can occur when using polymorphism to process dynamically allocated objects of a class hierarchy. So far you have seen nonvirtual destructors—destructors that are not declared with keyword `virtual`. If a derived-class object with a nonvirtual destructor is destroyed explicitly by applying the `delete` operator to a base-class pointer to the object, the C++ standard specifies that the behavior is undefined.

The simple solution to this problem is to create a virtual destructor (i.e., a destructor that is declared with keyword `virtual`) in the base class. This makes all derived-class destructors `virtual` *even though they do not have the same name as the base-class destructor.* Now, if an object in the hierarchy is destroyed explicitly by applying the `delete` operator to a base-class pointer, the destructor for the appropriate class is called based on the object to which the base-class pointer points. Remember, when a derived-class object is destroyed, the base-class part of the derived-class object is also destroyed, so it is important for the destructors of both the derived class and base class to execute. The base-class destructor automatically executes after the derived-class destructor.

Good Programming Practice 13.2

If a class has virtual functions, provide a virtual destructor, even if one is not required for the class. Classes derived from this class may contain destructors that must be called properly.

Common Programming Error 13.5

Constructors cannot be virtual. Declaring a constructor virtual is a compilation error.

13.10 (Optional) Software Engineering Case Study: Incorporating Inheritance into the ATM System

We now revisit our ATM system design to see how it might benefit from inheritance. To apply inheritance, we first look for commonality among classes in the system. We create an inheritance hierarchy to model similar (yet not identical) classes in a more efficient and elegant manner that enables us to process objects of these classes polymorphically. We then modify our class diagram to incorporate the new inheritance relationships. Finally, we demonstrate how our updated design is translated into C++ header files.

In Section 3.11, we encountered the problem of representing a financial transaction in the system. Rather than create one class to represent all transaction types, we decided to create three individual transaction classes—`BalanceInquiry`, `Withdrawal` and `Deposit`— to represent the transactions that the ATM system can perform. Figure 13.26 shows the attributes and operations of these classes. Note that they have one attribute (`account-Number`) and one operation (`execute`) in common. Each class requires attribute `account-Number` to specify the account to which the transaction applies. Each class contains operation `execute`, which the ATM invokes to perform the transaction. Clearly, `Balance-Inquiry`, `Withdrawal` and `Deposit` represent *types of* transactions. Figure 13.26 reveals commonality among the transaction classes, so using inheritance to factor out the common features seems appropriate for designing these classes. We place the common functionality in base class `Transaction` and derive classes `BalanceInquiry`, `Withdrawal` and `Deposit` from `Transaction` (Fig. 13.27).

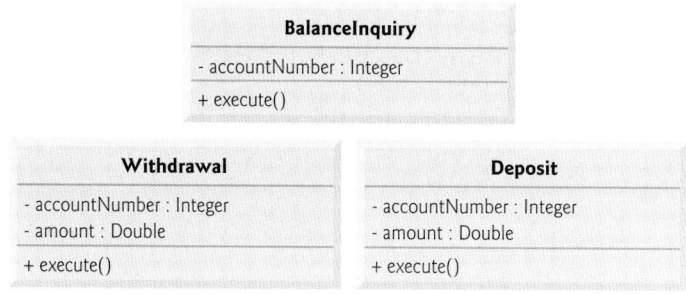

Fig. 13.26 | Attributes and operations of classes `BalanceInquiry`, `Withdrawal` and `Deposit`.

The UML specifies a relationship called a generalization to model inheritance. Figure 13.27 is the class diagram that models the inheritance relationship between base class Transaction and its three derived classes. The arrows with triangular hollow arrowheads indicate that classes BalanceInquiry, Withdrawal and Deposit are derived from class Transaction. Class Transaction is said to be a generalization of its derived classes. The derived classes are said to be specializations of class Transaction.

Classes BalanceInquiry, Withdrawal and Deposit share integer attribute account-Number, so we factor out this common attribute and place it in base class Transaction. We no longer list accountNumber in the second compartment of each derived class, because the three derived classes inherit this attribute from Transaction. Recall, however, that derived classes cannot access private attributes of a base class. We therefore include public member function getAccountNumber in class Transaction. Each derived class inherits this member function, enabling the derived class to access its accountNumber as needed to execute a transaction.

According to Fig. 13.26, classes BalanceInquiry, Withdrawal and Deposit also share operation execute, so base class Transaction should contain public member function execute. However, it does not make sense to implement execute in class Transaction, because the functionality that this member function provides depends on the specific type of the actual transaction. We therefore declare member function execute as a pure virtual function in base class Transaction. This makes Transaction an abstract class and forces any class derived from Transaction that must be a concrete class (i.e., BalanceInquiry, Withdrawal and Deposit) to implement pure virtual member function execute to make the derived class concrete. The UML requires that we place abstract class names (and pure virtual functions—abstract operations in the UML) in italics, so Transaction and its member function execute appear in italics in Fig. 13.27. Note that operation execute is not italicized in derived classes BalanceInquiry, Withdrawal and Deposit. Each derived class overrides base class Transaction's execute member function with an appropriate implementation. Note that Fig. 13.27 includes operation execute in the third compartment of classes BalanceInquiry, Withdrawal and Deposit, because each class has a different concrete implementation of the overridden member function.

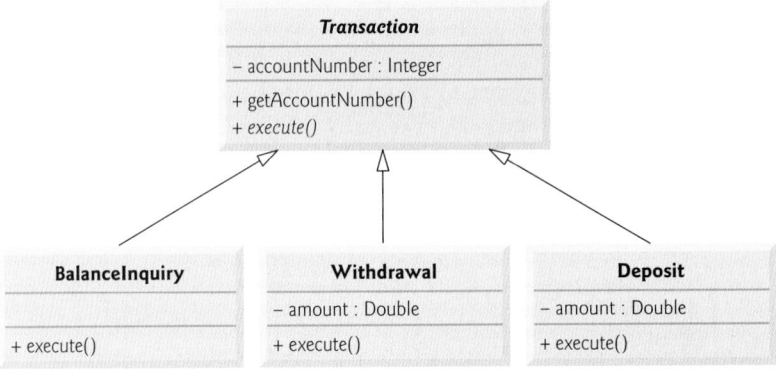

Fig. 13.27 | Class diagram modeling generalization relationship between base class Transaction and derived classes BalanceInquiry, Withdrawal and Deposit.

As you learned in this chapter, a derived class can inherit interface or implementation from a base class. Compared to a hierarchy designed for implementation inheritance, one designed for interface inheritance tends to have its functionality lower in the hierarchy—a base class signifies one or more functions that should be defined by each class in the hierarchy, but the individual derived classes provide their own implementations of the function(s). The inheritance hierarchy designed for the ATM system takes advantage of this type of inheritance, which provides the ATM with an elegant way to execute all transactions "in the general." Each class derived from Transaction inherits some implementation details (e.g., data member accountNumber), but the primary benefit of incorporating inheritance into our system is that the derived classes share a common interface (e.g., pure virtual member function execute). The ATM can aim a Transaction pointer at any transaction, and when the ATM invokes execute through this pointer, the version of execute appropriate to that transaction (i.e., implemented in that derived class's .cpp file) runs automatically. For example, suppose a user chooses to perform a balance inquiry. The ATM aims a Transaction pointer at a new object of class BalanceInquiry, which the C++ compiler allows because a BalanceInquiry *is a* Transaction. When the ATM uses this pointer to invoke execute, BalanceInquiry's version of execute is called.

This polymorphic approach also makes the system easily extensible. Should we wish to create a new transaction type (e.g., funds transfer or bill payment), we would just create an additional Transaction derived class that overrides the execute member function with a version appropriate for the new transaction type. We would need to make only minimal changes to the system code to allow users to choose the new transaction type from the main menu and for the ATM to instantiate and execute objects of the new derived class. The ATM could execute transactions of the new type using the current code, because it executes all transactions identically.

As you learned earlier in the chapter, an abstract class like Transaction is one for which the programmer never intends to instantiate objects. An abstract class simply declares common attributes and behaviors for its derived classes in an inheritance hierarchy. Class Transaction defines the concept of what it means to be a transaction that has an account number and executes. You may wonder why we bother to include pure virtual member function execute in class Transaction if execute lacks a concrete implementation. Conceptually, we include this member function because it is the defining behavior of all transactions—executing. Technically, we must include member function execute in base class Transaction so that the ATM (or any other class) can polymorphically invoke each derived class's overridden version of this function through a Transaction pointer or reference.

Derived classes BalanceInquiry, Withdrawal and Deposit inherit attribute accountNumber from base class Transaction, but classes Withdrawal and Deposit contain the additional attribute amount that distinguishes them from class BalanceInquiry. Classes Withdrawal and Deposit require this additional attribute to store the amount of money that the user wishes to withdraw or deposit. Class BalanceInquiry has no need for such an attribute and requires only an account number to execute. Even though two of the three Transaction derived classes share this attribute, we do not place it in base class Transaction—we place only features common to *all* the derived classes in the base class, so derived classes do not inherit unnecessary attributes (and operations).

Figure 13.28 presents an updated class diagram of our model that incorporates inheritance and introduces class Transaction. We model an association between class ATM and class

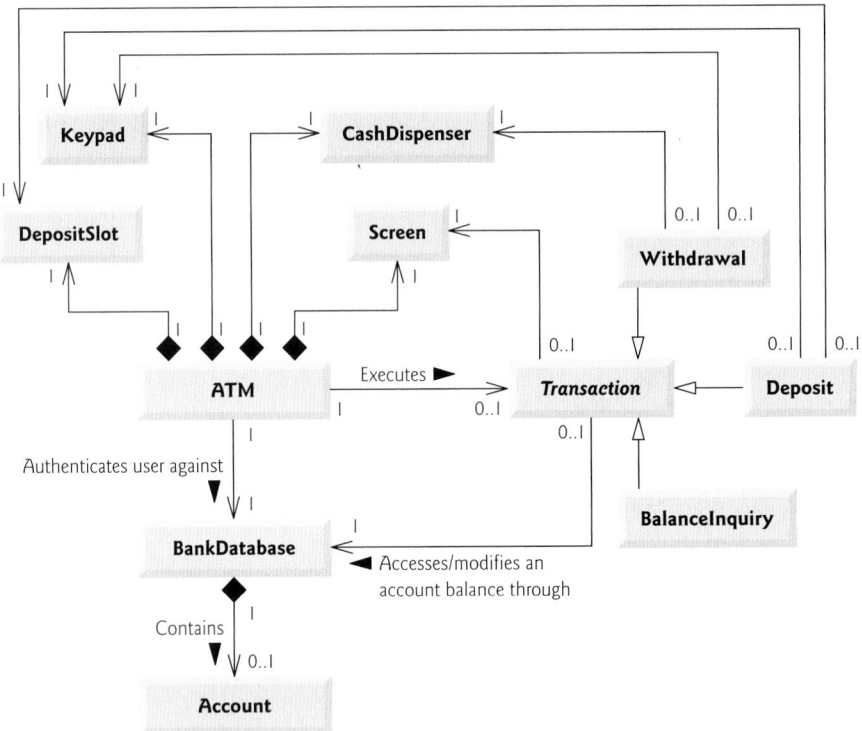

Fig. 13.28 | Class diagram of the ATM system (incorporating inheritance). Note that abstract class name `Transaction` appears in italics.

`Transaction` to show that the ATM, at any given moment, either is executing a transaction or is not (i.e., zero or one objects of type `Transaction` exist in the system at a time). Because a `Withdrawal` is a type of `Transaction`, we no longer draw an association line directly between class ATM and class `Withdrawal`—derived class `Withdrawal` inherits base class `Transaction`'s association with class ATM. Derived classes `BalanceInquiry` and `Deposit` also inherit this association, which replaces the previously omitted associations between classes `BalanceInquiry` and `Deposit` and class ATM. Note again the use of triangular hollow arrowheads to indicate the specializations of class `Transaction`, as indicated in Fig. 13.27.

We also add an association between class `Transaction` and the `BankDatabase` (Fig. 13.28). All `Transaction`s require a reference to the `BankDatabase` so they can access and modify account information. Each `Transaction` derived class inherits this reference, so we no longer model the association between class `Withdrawal` and the `BankDatabase`. Note that the association between class `Transaction` and the `BankDatabase` replaces the previously omitted associations between classes `BalanceInquiry` and `Deposit` and the `BankDatabase`.

We include an association between class `Transaction` and the `Screen` because all `Transaction`s display output to the user via the `Screen`. Each derived class inherits this association. Therefore, we no longer include the association previously modeled between `Withdrawal` and the `Screen`. Class `Withdrawal` still participates in associations with the `CashDispenser` and the `Keypad`, however—these associations apply to derived class `With-`

drawal but not to derived classes `BalanceInquiry` and `Deposit`, so we do not move these associations to base class `Transaction`.

Our class diagram incorporating inheritance (Fig. 13.28) also models `Deposit` and `BalanceInquiry`. We show associations between `Deposit` and both the `DepositSlot` and the `Keypad`. Note that class `BalanceInquiry` takes part in no associations other than those inherited from class `Transaction`—a `BalanceInquiry` interacts only with the `BankDatabase` and the `Screen`.

The class diagram of Fig. 9.20 showed attributes and operations with visibility markers. Now we present a modified class diagram in Fig. 13.29 that includes abstract base class `Transaction`. This abbreviated diagram does not show inheritance relationships (these appear in Fig. 13.28), but instead shows the attributes and operations after we have employed inheritance in our system. Note that abstract class name `Transaction` and abstract operation name `execute` in class `Transaction` appear in italics. To save space, as

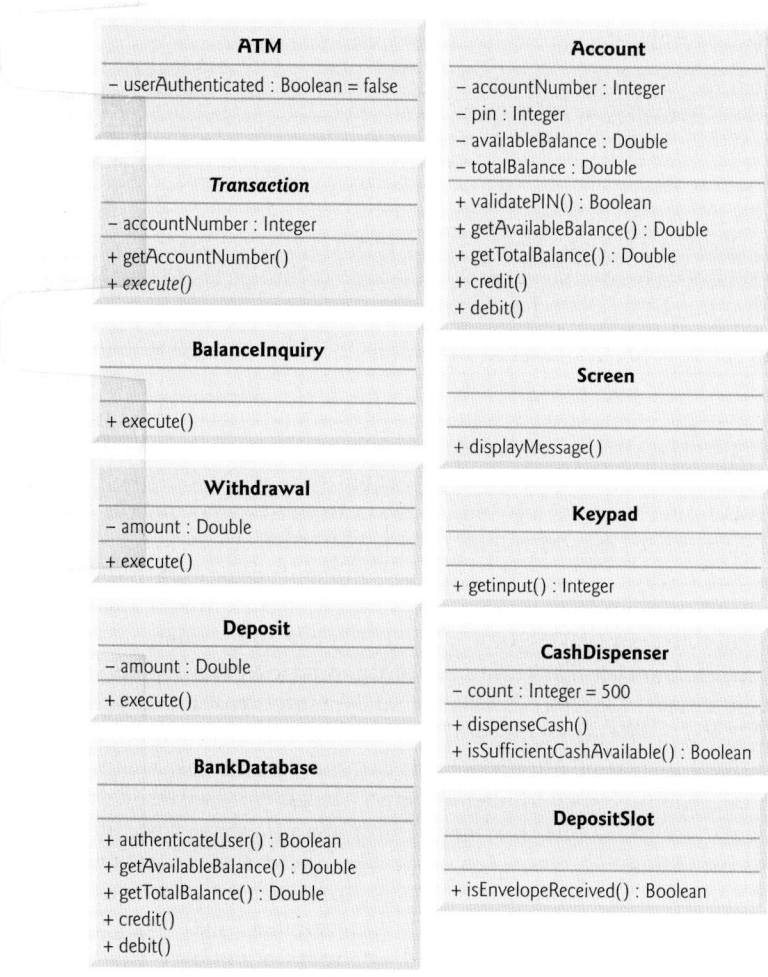

Fig. 13.29 | Class diagram after incorporating inheritance into the system.

we did in Fig. 4.24, we do not include those attributes shown by associations in Fig. 13.28—we do, however, include them in the C++ implementation in Appendix G. We also omit all operation parameters, as we did in Fig. 9.20—incorporating inheritance does not affect the parameters already modeled in Figs. 6.22–6.25.

Software Engineering Observation 13.12

A complete class diagram shows all the associations among classes and all the attributes and operations for each class. When the number of class attributes, operations and associations is substantial (as in Fig. 13.28 and Fig. 13.29), a good practice that promotes readability is to divide this information between two class diagrams—one focusing on associations and the other on attributes and operations. However, when examining classes modeled in this fashion, it is crucial to consider both class diagrams to get a complete view of the classes. For example, one must refer to Fig. 13.28 to observe the inheritance relationship between Transaction and its derived classes that is omitted from Fig. 13.29.

Implementing the ATM System Design Incorporating Inheritance

In Section 9.12, we began implementing the ATM system design in C++ code. We now modify our implementation to incorporate inheritance, using class Withdrawal as an example.

1. If a class A is a generalization of class B, then class B is derived from (and is a specialization of) class A. For example, abstract base class Transaction is a generalization of class Withdrawal. Thus, class Withdrawal is derived from (and is a specialization of) class Transaction. Figure 13.30 contains a portion of class Withdrawal's header file, in which the class definition indicates the inheritance relationship between Withdrawal and Transaction (line 9).

2. If class A is an abstract class and class B is derived from class A, then class B must implement the pure virtual functions of class A if class B is to be a concrete class. For example, class Transaction contains pure virtual function execute, so class Withdrawal must implement this member function if we want to instantiate a Withdrawal object. Figure 13.31 contains the C++ header file for class Withdrawal from Fig. 13.28 and Fig. 13.29. Class Withdrawal inherits data member accountNumber from base class Transaction, so Withdrawal does not declare this data member. Class Withdrawal also inherits references to the Screen and the BankDatabase from its base class Transaction, so we do not include these references in our code. Figure 13.29 specifies attribute amount and operation execute for class Withdrawal. Line 19 of Fig. 13.31 declares a data member for attribute amount. Line 16 contains the function prototype for operation execute. Recall that, to be a concrete class, derived class Withdrawal must provide a concrete implementation of the pure virtual function execute in base class Transaction. The prototype in line 16 signals your intent to override the base class pure virtual function. You must provide this prototype if you will provide an implementation in the .cpp file. We present this implementation in Appendix G. The keypad and cashDispenser references (lines 20–21) are data members derived from Withdrawal's associations in Fig. 13.28. In the implementation of this class in Appendix G, a constructor initializes these references to actual objects. Once again, to be able to compile the declarations of the references in lines 20–21, we include the forward declarations in lines 8–9.

```
 1    // Fig. 13.30: Withdrawal.h
 2    // Definition of class Withdrawal that represents a withdrawal transaction
 3    #ifndef WITHDRAWAL_H
 4    #define WITHDRAWAL_H
 5
 6    #include "Transaction.h" // Transaction class definition
 7
 8    // class Withdrawal derives from base class Transaction
 9    class Withdrawal : public Transaction
10    {
11    }; // end class Withdrawal
12
13    #endif // WITHDRAWAL_H
```

Fig. 13.30 | Withdrawal class definition that derives from Transaction.

```
 1    // Fig. 13.31: Withdrawal.h
 2    // Definition of class Withdrawal that represents a withdrawal transaction
 3    #ifndef WITHDRAWAL_H
 4    #define WITHDRAWAL_H
 5
 6    #include "Transaction.h" // Transaction class definition
 7
 8    class Keypad; // forward declaration of class Keypad
 9    class CashDispenser; // forward declaration of class CashDispenser
10
11    // class Withdrawal derives from base class Transaction
12    class Withdrawal : public Transaction
13    {
14    public:
15       // member function overriding execute in base class Transaction
16       virtual void execute(); // perform the transaction
17    private:
18       // attributes
19       double amount; // amount to withdraw
20       Keypad &keypad; // reference to ATM's keypad
21       CashDispenser &cashDispenser; // reference to ATM's cash dispenser
22    }; // end class Withdrawal
23
24    #endif // WITHDRAWAL_H
```

Fig. 13.31 | Withdrawal class header file based on Fig. 13.28 and Fig. 13.29.

ATM Case Study Wrap-Up

This concludes our object-oriented design of the ATM system. A complete C++ implementation of the ATM system in 877 lines of code appears in Appendix G. This working implementation uses key programming notions, including classes, objects, encapsulation, visibility, composition, inheritance and polymorphism. The code is abundantly commented and conforms to the coding practices you've learned. Mastering this code is a wonderful capstone experience for you after studying Chapters 1–13.

Software Engineering Case Study Self-Review Exercises

13.1 The UML uses an arrow with a _____ to indicate a generalization relationship.
a) solid filled arrowhead
b) triangular hollow arrowhead
c) diamond-shaped hollow arrowhead
d) stick arrowhead

13.2 State whether the following statement is *true* or *false*, and if *false*, explain why: The UML requires that we underline abstract class names and operation names.

13.3 Write a C++ header file to begin implementing the design for class Transaction specified in Fig. 13.28 and Fig. 13.29. Be sure to include private references based on class Transaction's associations. Also be sure to include public *get* functions for any of the private data members that the derived classes must access to perform their tasks.

Answers to Software Engineering Case Study Self-Review Exercises

13.1 b.

13.2 False. The UML requires that we italicize abstract class names and operation names.

13.3 The design for class Transaction yields the header file in Fig. 13.32. In the implementation in Appendix G, a constructor initializes private reference attributes screen and bankDatabase to actual objects, and member functions getScreen and getBankDatabase access these attributes. These member functions allow classes derived from Transaction to access the ATM's screen and interact with the bank's database.

```cpp
// Fig. 13.32: Transaction.h
// Transaction abstract base class definition.
#ifndef TRANSACTION_H
#define TRANSACTION_H

class Screen; // forward declaration of class Screen
class BankDatabase; // forward declaration of class BankDatabase

class Transaction
{
public:
   int getAccountNumber(); // return account number
   Screen &getScreen(); // return reference to screen
   BankDatabase &getBankDatabase(); // return reference to bank database

   // pure virtual function to perform the transaction
   virtual void execute() = 0; // overridden in derived classes
private:
   int accountNumber; // indicates account involved
   Screen &screen; // reference to the screen of the ATM
   BankDatabase &bankDatabase; // reference to the account info database
}; // end class Transaction

#endif // TRANSACTION_H
```

Fig. 13.32 | Transaction class header file based on Fig. 13.28 and Fig. 13.29.

Summary

- With `virtual` functions and polymorphism, it becomes possible to design and implement systems that are more easily extensible. Programs can be written to process objects of types that may not exist when the program is under development.

- Polymorphic programming with `virtual` functions can eliminate the need for `switch` logic. The programmer can use the `virtual` function mechanism to perform the equivalent logic automatically, thus avoiding the kinds of errors typically associated with `switch` logic.

- Derived classes can provide their own implementations of a base-class `virtual` function if necessary, but if they do not, the base class's implementation is used.

- If a `virtual` function is called by referencing a specific object by name and using the dot member-selection operator, the reference is resolved at compile time (this is called static binding); the `virtual` function that is called is the one defined for the class of that particular object.

- In many situations it is useful to define abstract classes for which the programmer never intends to create objects. Because these are used only as base classes, we refer to them as abstract base classes. No objects of an abstract class may be instantiated.

- Classes from which objects can be instantiated are called concrete classes.

- A class is made abstract by declaring one or more of its `virtual` functions to be pure. A pure `virtual` function is one with a pure specifier (= 0) in its declaration.

- If a class is derived from a class with a pure `virtual` function and that derived class does not supply a definition for that pure `virtual` function, then that `virtual` function remains pure in the derived class. Consequently, the derived class is also an abstract class.

- C++ enables polymorphism—the ability for objects of different classes related by inheritance to respond differently to the same member-function call.

- Polymorphism is implemented via `virtual` functions and dynamic binding.

- When a request is made through a base-class pointer or reference to use a `virtual` function, C++ chooses the correct overridden function in the appropriate derived class associated with the object.

- Through the use of `virtual` functions and polymorphism, a member-function call can cause different actions, depending on the type of the object receiving the call.

- Although we cannot instantiate objects of abstract base classes, we can declare pointers and references to objects of abstract base classes. Such pointers and references can be used to enable polymorphic manipulations of derived-class objects instantiated from concrete derived classes.

- Dynamic binding requires that at runtime, the call to a virtual member function be routed to the `virtual` function version appropriate for the class. A virtual function table called the *vtable* is implemented as an array containing function pointers. Each class with `virtual` functions has a *vtable*. For each `virtual` function in the class, the *vtable* has an entry containing a function pointer to the version of the `virtual` function to use for an object of that class. The `virtual` function to use for a particular class could be the function defined in that class, or it could be a function inherited either directly or indirectly from a base class higher in the hierarchy.

- When a base class provides a `virtual` member function, derived classes can override the `virtual` function, but they do not have to override it. Thus, a derived class can use a base class's version of a `virtual` function.

- Each object of a class with `virtual` functions contains a pointer to the *vtable* for that class. When a function call is made from a base-class pointer to a derived-class object, the appropriate function pointer in the *vtable* is obtained and dereferenced to complete the call at execution time. This *vtable* lookup and pointer dereferencing require nominal runtime overhead.

- Any class that has one or more 0 pointers in its *vtable* is an abstract class. Classes without any 0 *vtable* pointers are concrete classes.

- New kinds of classes are regularly added to systems. New classes are accommodated by dynamic binding (also called late binding). The type of an object need not be known at compile time for a virtual-function call to be compiled. At runtime, the appropriate member function will be called for the object to which the pointer points.

- Operator dynamic_cast checks the type of the object to which the pointer points, then determines whether this type has an *is-a* relationship with the type to which the pointer is being converted. If there is an *is-a* relationship, dynamic_cast returns the object's address. If not, dynamic_cast returns 0.

- Operator typeid returns a reference to an object of class type_info that contains information about the type of its operand, including the name of the type. To use typeid, the program must include header file <typeinfo>.

- When invoked, type_info member function name returns a pointer-based string that contains the name of the type that the type_info object represents.

- Operators dynamic_cast and typeid are part of C++'s run-time type information (RTTI) feature, which allows a program to determine an object's type at runtime.

- Declare the base-class destructor virtual if the class contains virtual functions. This makes all derived-class destructors virtual, even though they do not have the same name as the base-class destructor. If an object in the hierarchy is destroyed explicitly by applying the delete operator to a base-class pointer to a derived-class object, the destructor for the appropriate class is called. After a derived-class destructor runs, the destructors for all of that class's base classes run all the way up the hierarchy—the root class's destructor runs last.

Terminology

abstract base class
abstract class
base-class pointer to a base-class object
base-class pointer to a derived-class object
concrete class
dangerous pointer manipulation
derived-class pointer to a base-class object
derived-class pointer to a derived-class object
displacement
downcasting
dynamic binding
dynamic casting
dynamic_cast
dynamically determine function to execute
flow of control of a virtual function call
implementation inheritance
interface inheritance
iterator class
late binding
name function of class type_info
nonvirtual destructor
object's *vtable* pointer

offset into a *vtable*
override a function
polymorphic programming
polymorphism
polymorphism as an alternative to switch logic
programming in the general
programming in the specific
pure specifier
pure virtual function
RTTI (run-time type information)
static binding
switch logic
type_info class
typeid operator
<typeinfo> header file
virtual destructor
virtual function
virtual function table (*vtable*)
virtual keyword
vtable
vtable pointer

Self-Review Exercises

13.1   Fill in the blanks in each of the following statements:
- a) Treating a base-class object as a(n) _____ can cause errors.
- b) Polymorphism helps eliminate _____ logic.
- c) If a class contains at least one pure virtual function, it is a(n) _____ class.
- d) Classes from which objects can be instantiated are called _____ classes.
- e) Operator _____ can be used to downcast base-class pointers safely.
- f) Operator typeid returns a reference to a(n) _____ object.
- g) _____ involves using a base-class pointer or reference to invoke virtual functions on base-class and derived-class objects.
- h) Overridable functions are declared using keyword _____.
- i) Casting a base-class pointer to a derived-class pointer is called _____.

13.2   State whether each of the following is *true* or *false*. If *false*, explain why.
- a) All virtual functions in an abstract base class must be declared as pure virtual functions.
- b) Referring to a derived-class object with a base-class handle is dangerous.
- c) A class is made abstract by declaring that class virtual.
- d) If a base class declares a pure virtual function, a derived class must implement that function to become a concrete class.
- e) Polymorphic programming can eliminate the need for switch logic.

Answers to Self-Review Exercises

13.1   a) derived-class object. b) switch. c) abstract. d) concrete. e) dynamic_cast. f) type_info. g) Polymorphism. h) virtual. i) downcasting.

13.2   a) False. An abstract base class can include virtual functions with implementations. b) False. Referring to a base-class object with a derived-class handle is dangerous. c) False. Classes are never declared virtual. Rather, a class is made abstract by including at least one pure virtual function in the class. d) True. e) True.

Exercises

13.3   How is it that polymorphism enables you to program "in the general" rather than "in the specific"? Discuss the key advantages of programming "in the general."

13.4   Discuss the problems of programming with switch logic. Explain why polymorphism can be an effective alternative to using switch logic.

13.5   Distinguish between inheriting interface and inheriting implementation. How do inheritance hierarchies designed for inheriting interface differ from those designed for inheriting implementation?

13.6   What are virtual functions? Describe a circumstance in which virtual functions would be appropriate.

13.7   Distinguish between static binding and dynamic binding. Explain the use of virtual functions and the *vtable* in dynamic binding.

13.8   Distinguish between virtual functions and pure virtual functions.

13.9   Suggest one or more levels of abstract base classes for the Shape hierarchy discussed in this chapter and shown in Fig. 12.3. (The first level is Shape, and the second level consists of the classes TwoDimensionalShape and ThreeDimensionalShape.)

13.10   How does polymorphism promote extensibility?

13.11 You have been asked to develop a flight simulator that will have elaborate graphical outputs. Explain why polymorphic programming would be especially effective for a problem of this nature.

13.12 *(Payroll System Modification)* Modify the payroll system of Figs. 13.13–13.23 to include private data member birthDate in class Employee. Use class Date from Figs. 11.12–11.13 to represent an employee's birthday. Assume that payroll is processed once per month. Create a vector of Employee references to store the various employee objects. In a loop, calculate the payroll for each Employee (polymorphically), and add a $100.00 bonus to the person's payroll amount if the current month is the month in which the Employee's birthday occurs.

13.13 *(Shape Hierarchy)* Implement the Shape hierarchy designed in Exercise 12.7 (which is based on the hierarchy in Fig. 12.3). Each TwoDimensionalShape should contain function getArea to calculate the area of the two-dimensional shape. Each ThreeDimensionalShape should have member functions getArea and getVolume to calculate the surface area and volume of the three-dimensional shape, respectively. Create a program that uses a vector of Shape pointers to objects of each concrete class in the hierarchy. The program should print the object to which each vector element points. Also, in the loop that processes all the shapes in the vector, determine whether each shape is a TwoDimensionalShape or a ThreeDimensionalShape. If a shape is a TwoDimensionalShape, display its area. If a shape is a ThreeDimensionalShape, display its area and volume.

13.14 *(Polymorphic Screen Manager Using Shape Hierarchy)* Develop a basic graphics package. Use the Shape hierarchy implemented in Exercise 13.13. Limit yourself to two-dimensional shapes such as squares, rectangles, triangles and circles. Interact with the user. Let the user specify the position, size, shape and fill characters to be used in drawing each shape. The user can specify more than one of the same shape. As you create each shape, place a Shape * pointer to each new Shape object into an array. Each Shape class should now have its own draw member function. Write a polymorphic screen manager that walks through the array, sending draw messages to each object in the array to form a screen image. Redraw the screen image each time the user specifies an additional shape.

13.15 *(Package Inheritance Hierarchy)* Use the Package inheritance hierarchy created in Exercise 12.9 to create a program that displays the address information and calculates the shipping costs for several Packages. The program should contain a vector of Package pointers to objects of classes TwoDayPackage and OvernightPackage. Loop through the vector to process the Packages polymorphically. For each Package, invoke *get* functions to obtain the address information of the sender and the recipient, then print the two addresses as they would appear on mailing labels. Also, call each Package's calculateCost member function and print the result. Keep track of the total shipping cost for all Packages in the vector, and display this total when the loop terminates.

13.16 *(Polymorphic Banking Program Using Account Hierarchy)* Develop a polymorphic banking program using the Account hierarchy created in Exercise 12.10. Create a vector of Account pointers to SavingsAccount and CheckingAccount objects. For each Account in the vector, allow the user to specify an amount of money to withdraw from the Account using member function debit and an amount of money to deposit into the Account using member function credit. As you process each Account, determine its type. If an Account is a SavingsAccount, calculate the amount of interest owed to the Account using member function calculateInterest, then add the interest to the account balance using member function credit. After processing an Account, print the updated account balance obtained by invoking base class member function getBalance.

14

Templates

*Behind that outside pattern
the dim shapes get clearer
every day.
It is always the same shape,
only very numerous.*
—Charlotte Perkins Gilman

*Every man of genius sees the
world at a different angle
from his fellows.*
—Havelock Ellis

*…our special individuality,
as distinguished from our
generic humanity.*
—Oliver Wendell Holmes, Sr

OBJECTIVES

In this chapter you will learn:

■ To use function templates to conveniently create a group of related (overloaded) functions.

■ To distinguish between function templates and function-template specializations.

■ To use class templates to create a group of related types.

■ To distinguish between class templates and class-template specializations.

■ To overload function templates.

■ To understand the relationships among templates, friends, inheritance and static members.

14.1 Introduction

In this chapter, we discuss one of C++'s more powerful software reuse features, namely templates. Function templates and class templates enable programmers to specify, with a single code segment, an entire range of related (overloaded) functions—called function-template specializations—or an entire range of related classes—called class-template specializations. This technique is called generic programming.

We might write a single function template for an array-sort function, then have C++ generate separate function-template specializations that will sort int arrays, float arrays, string arrays and so on. We introduced function templates in Chapter 6. We present an additional discussion and example in this chapter.

We might write a single class template for a stack class, then have C++ generate separate class-template specializations, such as a stack-of-int class, a stack-of-float class, a stack-of-string class and so on.

Note the distinction between templates and template specializations: Function templates and class templates are like stencils out of which we trace shapes; function-template specializations and class-template specializations are like the separate tracings that all have the same shape, but could, for example, be drawn in different colors.

In this chapter, we present a function template and a class template. We also consider the relationships between templates and other C++ features, such as overloading, inheritance, friends and static members. The design and details of the template mechanisms discussed here are based on the work of Bjarne Stroustrup as presented in his paper, *Parameterized Types for C++*, and as published in the *Proceedings of the USENIX C++ Conference* held in Denver, Colorado, in October 1988.

This chapter is only an introduction to templates. Chapter 22, Standard Template Library (STL), presents an in-depth treatment of the template container classes, iterators and algorithms of the STL. Chapter 22 contains dozens of live-code template-based examples illustrating more sophisticated template-programming techniques than those used here.

Software Engineering Observation 14.1

Most C++ compilers require the complete definition of a template to appear in the client source-code file that uses the template. For this reason and for reusability, templates are often defined in header files, which are then #included into the appropriate client source-code files. For class templates, this means that the member functions are also defined in the header file.

14.2 **Function Templates**

Overloaded functions normally perform *similar* or *identical* operations on different types of data. If the operations are *identical* for each type, they can be expressed more compactly and conveniently using function templates. Initially, the programmer writes a single function-template definition. Based on the argument types provided explicitly or inferred from calls to this function, the compiler generates separate object-code functions (i.e., function-template specializations) to handle each function call appropriately. In C, this task can be performed using macros created with the preprocessor directive #define (see Appendix F, Preprocessor). However, macros can have serious side effects and do not enable the compiler to perform type checking. Function templates provide a compact solution, like macros, but enable full type checking.

Error-Prevention Tip 14.1

Function templates, like macros, enable software reuse. Unlike macros, function templates help eliminate many types of errors through the scrutiny of full C++ type checking.

All function-template definitions begin with keyword `template` followed by a list of template parameters to the function template enclosed in angle brackets (< and >); each template parameter that represents a type must be preceded by either of the interchangeable keywords `class` or `typename`, as in

```
template< typename T >
```

or

```
template< class ElementType >
```

or

```
template< typename BorderType, typename FillType >
```

The type template parameters of a function-template definition are used to specify the types of the arguments to the function, to specify the return type of the function and to declare variables within the function. The function definition follows and appears like any other function definition. Note that keywords `typename` and `class` used to specify function-template parameters actually mean "any built-in type or user-defined type."

Common Programming Error 14.1

Not placing keyword `class` or keyword `typename` before each type template parameter of a function template is a syntax error.

Example: Function Template `printArray`

Let us examine function template `printArray` in Fig. 14.1, lines 8–15. Function template `printArray` declares (line 8) a single template parameter T (T can be any valid identifier) for the type of the array to be printed by function `printArray`; T is referred to as a type template parameter, or type parameter. You will see nontype template parameters in Section 14.5.

When the compiler detects a `printArray` function invocation in the client program (e.g., lines 30, 35 and 40), the compiler uses its overload resolution capabilities to find a definition of function `printArray` that best matches the function call. In this case, the only printArray function with the appropriate number of parameters is the printArray function template (lines 8–15). Consider the function call at line 30. The compiler compares the type of printArray's first argument (int * at line 30) to the printArray function template's first parameter (const T * at line 9) and deduces that replacing the type parameter T with int would make the argument match the parameter. Then, the compiler substitutes int for T throughout the template definition and compiles a printArray specialization that can display an array of int values. In Fig. 14.1, the compiler creates three printArray specializations—one that expects an int array, one that expects a double array and one that expects a char array. For example, the function-template specialization for type int is

```
void printArray( const int *array, int count )
{
   for ( int i = 0; i < count; i++ )
      cout << array[ i ] << " ";

   cout << endl;
} // end function printArray
```

The name of a template parameter can be declared only once in the template parameter list of a template header but can be used repeatedly in the function's header and body. Template parameter names among function templates need not be unique.

```
1   // Fig. 14.1: fig14_01.cpp
2   // Using template functions.
3   #include <iostream>
4   using std::cout;
5   using std::endl;
6
7   // function template printArray definition
8   template< typename T >
9   void printArray( const T *array, int count )
10  {
11     for ( int i = 0; i < count; i++ )
12        cout << array[ i ] << " ";
13
14     cout << endl;
15  } // end function template printArray
16
17  int main()
18  {
19     const int ACOUNT = 5; // size of array a
20     const int BCOUNT = 7; // size of array b
21     const int CCOUNT = 6; // size of array c
22
23     int a[ ACOUNT ] = { 1, 2, 3, 4, 5 };
24     double b[ BCOUNT ] = { 1.1, 2.2, 3.3, 4.4, 5.5, 6.6, 7.7 };
25     char c[ CCOUNT ] = "HELLO"; // 6th position for null
26
27     cout << "Array a contains:" << endl;
28
```

Fig. 14.1 | Function-template specializations of function template printArray. (Part 1 of 2.)

```
29        // call integer function-template specialization
30        printArray( a, ACOUNT );
31
32        cout << "Array b contains:" << endl;
33
34        // call double function-template specialization
35        printArray( b, BCOUNT );
36
37        cout << "Array c contains:" << endl;
38
39        // call character function-template specialization
40        printArray( c, CCOUNT );
41        return 0;
42   } // end main
```

```
Array a contains:
1 2 3 4 5
Array b contains:
1.1 2.2 3.3 4.4 5.5 6.6 7.7
Array c contains:
H E L L O
```

Fig. 14.1 | Function-template specializations of function template `printArray`. (Part 2 of 2.)

Figure 14.1 demonstrates function template `printArray` (lines 8–15). The program begins by declaring five-element `int` array a, seven-element `double` array b and six-element `char` array c (lines 23–25, respectively). Then, the program outputs each array by calling `printArray`—once with a first argument a of type `int *` (line 30), once with a first argument b of type `double *` (line 35) and once with a first argument c of type `char *` (line 40). The call in line 30, for example, causes the compiler to infer that `T` is `int` and to instantiate a `printArray` function-template specialization, for which type parameter `T` is `int`. The call in line 35 causes the compiler to infer that `T` is `double` and to instantiate a second `printArray` function-template specialization, for which type parameter `T` is `double`. The call in line 40 causes the compiler to infer that `T` is `char` and to instantiate a third `printArray` function-template specialization, for which type parameter `T` is `char`. It is important to note that if `T` (line 8) represents a user-defined type (which it does not in Fig. 14.1), there must be an overloaded stream insertion operator for that type; otherwise, the first stream insertion operator in line 12 will not compile.

Common Programming Error 14.2

If a template is invoked with a user-defined type, and if that template uses functions or operators (e.g., ==, +, <=) with objects of that class type, then those functions and operators must be overloaded for the user-defined type. Forgetting to overload such operators causes compilation errors.

In this example, the template mechanism saves the programmer from having to write three separate overloaded functions with prototypes

```
void printArray( const int *, int );
void printArray( const double *, int );
void printArray( const char *, int );
```

that all use the same code, except for type `T` (as used in line 9).

Performance Tip 14.1

Although templates offer software-reusability benefits, remember that multiple function-template specializations and class-template specializations are instantiated in a program (at compile time), despite the fact that the template is written only once. These copies can consume considerable memory. This is not normally an issue, though, because the code generated by the template is the same size as the code the programmer would have written to produce the separate overloaded functions.

14.3 Overloading Function Templates

Function templates and overloading are intimately related. The function-template specializations generated from a function template all have the same name, so the compiler uses overloading resolution to invoke the proper function.

A function template may be overloaded in several ways. We can provide other function templates that specify the same function name but different function parameters. For example, function template `printArray` of Fig. 14.1 could be overloaded with another `printArray` function template with additional parameters `lowSubscript` and `highSubscript` to specify the portion of the array to output (see Exercise 14.4).

A function template also can be overloaded by providing nontemplate functions with the same function name but different function arguments. For example, function template `printArray` of Fig. 14.1 could be overloaded with a nontemplate version that specifically prints an array of character strings in neat, tabular format (see Exercise 14.5).

The compiler performs a matching process to determine what function to call when a function is invoked. First, the compiler finds all function templates that match the function named in the function call and creates specializations based on the arguments in the function call. Then, the compiler finds all the ordinary functions that match the function named in the function call. If one of the ordinary functions or function-template specializations is the best match for the function call, that ordinary function or specialization is used. If an ordinary function and a specialization are equally good matches for the function call, then the ordinary function is used. Otherwise, if there are multiple matches for the function call, the compiler considers the call to be ambiguous and the compiler generates an error message.

Common Programming Error 14.3

If no matching function definition can be found for a particular function call, or if there are multiple matches, the compiler generates an error.

14.4 Class Templates

It is possible to understand the concept of a "stack" (a data structure into which we insert items at the top and retrieve those items in last-in, first-out order) independent of the type of the items being placed in the stack. However, to instantiate a stack, a data type must be specified. This creates a wonderful opportunity for software reusability. We need the means for describing the notion of a stack generically and instantiating classes that are type-specific versions of this generic stack class. C++ provides this capability through class templates.

Software Engineering Observation 14.2

Class templates encourage software reusability by enabling type-specific versions of generic classes to be instantiated.

Class templates are called parameterized types, because they require one or more type parameters to specify how to customize a "generic class" template to form a class-template specialization.

The programmer who wishes to produce a variety of class-template specializations writes only one class-template definition. Each time an additional class-template specialization is needed, the programmer uses a concise, simple notation, and the compiler writes the source code for the specialization the programmer requires. One Stack class template, for example, could thus become the basis for creating many Stack classes (such as "Stack of double," "Stack of int," "Stack of char," "Stack of Employee," etc.) used in a program.

Creating Class Template *Stack< T >*

Note the Stack class-template definition in Fig. 14.2. It looks like a conventional class definition, except that it is preceded by the header (line 6)

```
template< typename T >
```

to specify a class-template definition with type parameter T which acts as a placeholder for the type of the Stack class to be created. The programmer need not specifically use identifier T—any valid identifier can be used. The type of element to be stored on this Stack is mentioned generically as T throughout the Stack class header and member-function definitions. In a moment, we show how T becomes associated with a specific type, such as double or int. Due to the way this class template is designed, there are two constraints for nonfundamental data types used with this Stack—they must have a default constructor (for use in line 44 to create the array that stores the stack elements), and they must support the assignment operator (lines 55 and 69).

The member-function definitions of a class template are function templates. The member-function definitions that appear outside the class template definition each begin with the header

```
template< typename T >
```

(lines 40, 51 and 65). Thus, each definition resembles a conventional function definition, except that the Stack element type always is listed generically as type parameter T. The binary scope resolution operator is used with the class-template name Stack< T > (lines 41, 52 and 66) to tie each member-function definition to the class template's scope. In this case, the generic class name is Stack< T >. When doubleStack is instantiated as type Stack< double >, the Stack constructor function-template specialization uses new to create an array of elements of type double to represent the stack (line 44). The statement

```
stackPtr = new T[ size ];
```

in the Stack class-template definition is generated by the compiler in the class-template specialization Stack< double > as

```
stackPtr = new double[ size ];
```

```
 1  // Fig. 14.2: Stack.h
 2  // Stack class template.
 3  #ifndef STACK_H
 4  #define STACK_H
 5
 6  template< typename T >
 7  class Stack
 8  {
 9  public:
10     Stack( int = 10 ); // default constructor (Stack size 10)
11
12     // destructor
13     ~Stack()
14     {
15        delete [] stackPtr; // deallocate internal space for Stack
16     } // end ~Stack destructor
17
18     bool push( const T& ); // push an element onto the Stack
19     bool pop( T& ); // pop an element off the Stack
20
21     // determine whether Stack is empty
22     bool isEmpty() const
23     {
24        return top == -1;
25     } // end function isEmpty
26
27     // determine whether Stack is full
28     bool isFull() const
29     {
30        return top == size - 1;
31     } // end function isFull
32
33  private:
34     int size; // # of elements in the Stack
35     int top; // location of the top element (-1 means empty)
36     T *stackPtr; // pointer to internal representation of the Stack
37  }; // end class template Stack
38
39  // constructor template
40  template< typename T >
41  Stack< T >::Stack( int s )
42     : size( s > 0 ? s : 10 ), // validate size
43       top( -1 ), // Stack initially empty
44       stackPtr( new T[ size ] ) // allocate memory for elements
45  {
46     // empty body
47  } // end Stack constructor template
48
49  // push element onto Stack;
50  // if successful, return true; otherwise, return false
51  template< typename T >
52  bool Stack< T >::push( const T &pushValue )
53  {
```

Fig. 14.2 | Class template Stack. (Part 1 of 2.)

```
54       if ( !isFull() )
55       {
56          stackPtr[ ++top ] = pushValue; // place item on Stack
57          return true; // push successful
58       } // end if
59
60       return false; // push unsuccessful
61    } // end function template push
62
63    // pop element off Stack;
64    // if successful, return true; otherwise, return false
65    template< typename T >
66    bool Stack< T >::pop( T &popValue )
67    {
68       if ( !isEmpty() )
69       {
70          popValue = stackPtr[ top-- ]; // remove item from Stack
71          return true; // pop successful
72       } // end if
73
74       return false; // pop unsuccessful
75    } // end function template pop
76
77    #endif
```

Fig. 14.2 | Class template Stack. (Part 2 of 2.)

Creating a Driver to Test Class Template **Stack< T >**

Now, let us consider the driver (Fig. 14.3) that exercises the Stack class template. The driver begins by instantiating object doubleStack of size 5 (line 11). This object is declared to be of class Stack< double > (pronounced "Stack of double"). The compiler associates type double with type parameter T in the class template to produce the source code for a Stack class of type double. Although templates offer software-reusability benefits, remember that multiple class-template specializations are instantiated in a program (at compile time), even though the template is written only once.

Lines 17–21 invoke push to place the double values 1.1, 2.2, 3.3, 4.4 and 5.5 onto doubleStack. The while loop terminates when the driver attempts to push a sixth value onto doubleStack (which is full, because it holds a maximum of five elements). Note that function push returns false when it is unable to push a value onto the stack.[1]

Lines 27–28 invoke pop in a while loop to remove the five values from the stack (note, in Fig. 14.3, that the values do pop off in last-in, first-out order). When the driver attempts to pop a sixth value, the doubleStack is empty, so the pop loop terminates.

---

1. Class Stack (Fig. 14.2) provides the function isFull, which the programmer can use to determine whether the stack is full before attempting a push operation. This would avoid the potential error of pushing onto a full stack. In Chapter 16, Exception Handling, if the operation cannot be completed, function push would "throw an exception." The programmer can write code to "catch" that exception, then decide how to handle it appropriately for the application. The same technique can be used with function pop when an attempt is made to pop an element from an empty stack.

```
 1   // Fig. 14.3: fig14_03.cpp
 2   // Stack class template test program.
 3   #include <iostream>
 4   using std::cout;
 5   using std::endl;
 6
 7   #include "Stack.h" // Stack class template definition
 8
 9   int main()
10   {
11      Stack< double > doubleStack( 5 ); // size 5
12      double doubleValue = 1.1;
13
14      cout << "Pushing elements onto doubleStack\n";
15
16      // push 5 doubles onto doubleStack
17      while ( doubleStack.push( doubleValue ) )
18      {
19         cout << doubleValue << ' ';
20         doubleValue += 1.1;
21      } // end while
22
23      cout << "\nStack is full. Cannot push " << doubleValue
24         << "\n\nPopping elements from doubleStack\n";
25
26      // pop elements from doubleStack
27      while ( doubleStack.pop( doubleValue ) )
28         cout << doubleValue << ' ';
29
30      cout << "\nStack is empty. Cannot pop\n";
31
32      Stack< int > intStack; // default size 10
33      int intValue = 1;
34      cout << "\nPushing elements onto intStack\n";
35
36      // push 10 integers onto intStack
37      while ( intStack.push( intValue ) )
38      {
39         cout << intValue << ' ';
40         intValue++;
41      } // end while
42
43      cout << "\nStack is full. Cannot push " << intValue
44         << "\n\nPopping elements from intStack\n";
45
46      // pop elements from intStack
47      while ( intStack.pop( intValue ) )
48         cout << intValue << ' ';
49
50      cout << "\nStack is empty. Cannot pop" << endl;
51      return 0;
52   } // end main
```

Fig. 14.3 | Class template Stack test program. (Part 1 of 2.)

```
Pushing elements onto doubleStack
1.1 2.2 3.3 4.4 5.5
Stack is full. Cannot push 6.6

Popping elements from doubleStack
5.5 4.4 3.3 2.2 1.1
Stack is empty. Cannot pop

Pushing elements onto intStack
1 2 3 4 5 6 7 8 9 10
Stack is full. Cannot push 11

Popping elements from intStack
10 9 8 7 6 5 4 3 2 1
Stack is empty. Cannot pop
```

Fig. 14.3 | Class template Stack test program. (Part 2 of 2.)

Line 32 instantiates integer stack intStack with the declaration

```
Stack< int > intStack;
```

(pronounced "intStack is a Stack of int"). Because no size is specified, the size defaults to 10 as specified in the default constructor (Fig. 14.2, line 10). Lines 37–41 loop and invoke push to place values onto intStack until it is full, then lines 47–48 loop and invoke pop to remove values from intStack until it is empty. Once again, notice in the output that the values pop off in last-in, first-out order.

*Creating Function Templates to Test Class Template **Stack< T >***
Notice that the code in function main of Fig. 14.3 is almost identical for both the double-Stack manipulations in lines 11–30 and the intStack manipulations in lines 32–50. This presents another opportunity to use a function template. Figure 14.4 defines function template testStack (lines 14–38) to perform the same tasks as main in Fig. 14.3—push a series of values onto a Stack< T > and pop the values off a Stack< T >. Function template testStack uses template parameter T (specified at line 14) to represent the data type stored in the Stack< T >. The function template takes four arguments (lines 16–19)—a reference

```
 1   // Fig. 14.4: fig14_04.cpp
 2   // Stack class template test program. Function main uses a
 3   // function template to manipulate objects of type Stack< T >.
 4   #include <iostream>
 5   using std::cout;
 6   using std::endl;
 7
 8   #include <string>
 9   using std::string;
10
11   #include "Stack.h" // Stack class template definition
12
```

Fig. 14.4 | Passing a Stack template object to a function template. (Part 1 of 2.)

```
13   // function template to manipulate Stack< T >
14   template< typename T >
15   void testStack(
16      Stack< T > &theStack, // reference to Stack< T >
17      T value, // initial value to push
18      T increment, // increment for subsequent values
19      const string stackName ) // name of the Stack< T > object
20   {
21      cout << "\nPushing elements onto " << stackName << '\n';
22
23      // push element onto Stack
24      while ( theStack.push( value ) )
25      {
26         cout << value << ' ';
27         value += increment;
28      } // end while
29
30      cout << "\nStack is full. Cannot push " << value
31         << "\n\nPopping elements from " << stackName << '\n';
32
33      // pop elements from Stack
34      while ( theStack.pop( value ) )
35         cout << value << ' ';
36
37      cout << "\nStack is empty. Cannot pop" << endl;
38   } // end function template testStack
39
40   int main()
41   {
42      Stack< double > doubleStack( 5 ); // size 5
43      Stack< int > intStack; // default size 10
44
45      testStack( doubleStack, 1.1, 1.1, "doubleStack" );
46      testStack( intStack, 1, 1, "intStack" );
47
48      return 0;
49   } // end main
```

```
Pushing elements onto doubleStack
1.1 2.2 3.3 4.4 5.5
Stack is full. Cannot push 6.6

Popping elements from doubleStack
5.5 4.4 3.3 2.2 1.1
Stack is empty. Cannot pop

Pushing elements onto intStack
1 2 3 4 5 6 7 8 9 10
Stack is full. Cannot push 11

Popping elements from intStack
10 9 8 7 6 5 4 3 2 1
Stack is empty. Cannot pop
```

Fig. 14.4 | Passing a Stack template object to a function template. (Part 2 of 2.)

to an object of type Stack< T >, a value of type T that will be the first value pushed onto the Stack< T >, a value of type T used to increment the values pushed onto the Stack< T > and a string that represents the name of the Stack< T > object for output purposes. Function main (lines 40–49) instantiates an object of type Stack< double > called doubleStack (line 42) and an object of type Stack< int > called intStack (line 43) and uses these objects in lines 45 and 46. The testStack function calls each result in a testStack function-template specialization. The compiler infers the type of T for testStack from the type used to instantiate the function's first argument (i.e., the type used to instantiate double-Stack or intStack). The output of Fig. 14.4 precisely matches the output of Fig. 14.3.

14.5 Nontype Parameters and Default Types for Class Templates

Class template Stack of Section 14.4 used only a type parameter in the template header (line 6). It is also possible to use nontype template parameters or nontype parameters, which can have default arguments and are treated as consts. For example, the template header could be modified to take an int elements parameter as follows:

```
template< typename T, int elements > // nontype parameter elements
```

Then, a declaration such as

```
Stack< double, 100 > mostRecentSalesFigures;
```

could be used to instantiate (at compile time) a 100-element Stack class-template specialization of double values named mostRecentSalesFigures; this class-template specialization would be of type Stack< double, 100 >. The class header then might contain a private data member with an array declaration such as

```
T stackHolder[ elements ]; // array to hold Stack contents
```

In addition, a type parameter can specify a default type. For example,

```
template< typename T = string > // defaults to type string
```

might specify that a Stack contains string objects by default. Then, a declaration such as

```
Stack<> jobDescriptions;
```

could be used to instantiate a Stack class-template specialization of strings named job-Descriptions; this class-template specialization would be of type Stack< string >. Default type parameters must be the rightmost (trailing) parameters in a template's type-parameter list. When one is instantiating a class with two or more default types, if an omitted type is not the rightmost type parameter in the type-parameter list, then all type parameters to the right of that type also must be omitted.

> **Performance Tip 14.2**
>
> *When appropriate, specify the size of a container class (such as an array class or a stack class) at compile time (possibly through a nontype template parameter). This eliminates the execution-time overhead of using new to create the space dynamically.*

Software Engineering Observation 14.3

Specifying the size of a container at compile time avoids the potentially fatal execution-time error if new is unable to obtain the needed memory.

In the exercises, you will be asked to use a nontype parameter to create a template for our class Array developed in Chapter 11. This template will enable Array objects to be instantiated with a specified number of elements of a specified type at compile time, rather than creating space for the Array objects at execution time.

In some cases, it may not be possible to use a particular type with a class template. For example, the Stack template of Fig. 14.2 requires that user-defined types that will be stored in a Stack must provide a default constructor and an assignment operator. If a particular user-defined type will not work with our Stack template or requires customized processing, you can define an explicit specialization of the class template for a particular type. Let's assume we want to create an explicit specialization Stack for Employee objects. To do this, form a new class with the name Stack< Employee > as follows:

```
template<>
class Stack< Employee >
{
    // body of class definition
};
```

Note that the Stack< Employee > explicit specialization is a complete replacement for the Stack class template that is specific to type Employee—it does not use anything from the original class template and can even have different members.

14.6 Notes on Templates and Inheritance

Templates and inheritance relate in several ways:

- A class template can be derived from a class-template specialization.
- A class template can be derived from a nontemplate class.
- A class-template specialization can be derived from a class-template specialization.
- A nontemplate class can be derived from a class-template specialization.

14.7 Notes on Templates and Friends

We have seen that functions and entire classes can be declared as friends of nontemplate classes. With class templates, friendship can be established between a class template and a global function, a member function of another class (possibly a class-template specialization), or even an entire class (possibly a class-template specialization).

Throughout this section, we assume that we have defined a class template for a class named X with a single type parameter T, as in:

```
template< typename T > class X
```

Under this assumption, it is possible to make a function f1 a friend of every class-template specialization instantiated from the class template for class X. To do so, use a friendship declaration of the form

```
friend void f1();
```

For example, function f1 is a friend of X< double >, X< string > and X< Employee >, etc.

It is also possible to make a function f2 a friend of only a class-template specialization with the same type argument. To do so, use a friendship declaration of the form

```
friend void f2( X< T > & );
```

For example, if T is a float, function f2(X< float > &) is a friend of class-template specialization X< float > but not a friend of class-template specification X< string >.

You can declare that a member function of another class is a friend of any class-template specialization generated from the class template. To do so, the friend declaration must qualify the name of the other class's member function using the class name and the binary scope resolution operator, as in:

```
friend void A::f3();
```

The declaration makes member function f3 of class A a friend of every class-template specialization instantiated from the preceding class template. For example, function f3 of class A is a friend of X< double >, X< string > and X< Employee >, etc.

As with a global function, another class's member function can be a friend of only a class-template specialization with the same type argument. A friendship declaration of the form

```
friend void C< T >::f4( X< T > & );
```

for a particular type T such as float makes member function

```
C< float >::f4( X< float > & )
```

a friend function of *only* class-template specialization X< float >.

In some cases, it is desirable to make an entire class's set of member functions friends of a class template. In this case, a friend declaration of the form

```
friend class Y;
```

makes every member function of class Y a friend of every class-template specialization produced from the class template X.

Finally, it is possible to make all member functions of one class-template specialization friends of another class-template specialization with the same type argument. For example, a friend declaration of the form:

```
friend class Z< T >;
```

indicates that when a class-template specialization is instantiated with a particular type for T (such as float), all members of class Z< float > become friends of class-template specialization X< float >. We use this particular relationship in several examples of Chapter 21, Data Structures.

14.8 Notes on Templates and static Members

What about static data members? Recall that, with a nontemplate class, one copy of each static data member is shared among all objects of the class, and the static data member must be initialized at file scope.

Each class-template specialization instantiated from a class template has its own copy of each `static` data member of the class template; all objects of that specialization share that one `static` data member. In addition, as with `static` data members of nontemplate classes, `static` data members of class-template specializations must be defined and, if necessary, initialized at file scope. Each class-template specialization gets its own copy of the class template's `static` member functions.

Summary

- Templates enable us to specify a range of related (overloaded) functions—called function-template specializations—or a range of related classes—called class-template specializations.

- To use function-template specializations, the programmer writes a single function-template definition. Based on the argument types provided in calls to this function, C++ generates separate specializations to handle each type of call appropriately. These are compiled along with the rest of a program's source code.

- All function-template definitions begin with the keyword `template` followed by template parameters to the function template enclosed in angle brackets (< and >); each template parameter that represents a type must be preceded by keyword `class` or `typename`. Keywords `typename` and `class` used to specify function-template parameters mean "any built-in type or user-defined type."

- Template-definition template parameters are used to specify the kinds of arguments to the function, the return type of the function and to declare variables in the function.

- The name of a template parameter can be declared only once in the type-parameter list of a template header. Formal type-parameter names among function templates need not be unique.

- A function template may be overloaded in several ways. We can provide other function templates that specify the same function name but different function parameters. A function template can also be overloaded by providing other nontemplate functions with the same function name, but different function parameters.

- Class templates provide the means for describing a class generically and for instantiating classes that are type-specific versions of this generic class.

- Class templates are called parameterized types; they require type parameters to specify how to customize a generic class template to form a specific class-template specialization.

- The programmer who wishes to use class-template specializations writes one class template. When the programmer needs a new type-specific class, the programmer uses a concise notation, and the compiler writes the source code for the class-template specialization.

- A class-template definition looks like a conventional class definition, except that it is preceded by `template< typename T >` (or `template< class T >`) to indicate this is a class-template definition with type parameter `T` which acts as a placeholder for the type of the class to create. The type `T` is mentioned throughout the class header and member-function definitions as a generic type name.

- Member-function definitions outside a class template each begin with `template< typename T >` (or `template< class T >`). Then, each function definition resembles a conventional function definition, except that the generic data in the class always is listed generically as type parameter `T`. The binary scope-resolution operator is used with the class-template name to tie each member function definition to the class template's scope.

- It is possible to use nontype parameters in the header of a class or function template.

- An explicit specialization of a class template can be provided to override a class template for a specific type.
- A class template can be derived from a class-template specialization. A class template can be derived from a nontemplate class. A class-template specialization can be derived from a class-template specialization. A nontemplate class can be derived from a class-template specialization.
- Functions and entire classes can be declared as friends of nontemplate classes. With class templates, the obvious kinds of friendship arrangements can be declared. Friendship can be established between a class template and a global function, a member function of another class (possibly a class-template specialization) or even an entire class (possibly a class-template specialization).
- Each class-template specialization instantiated from a class template has its own copy of each `static` data member of the class template; all objects of that specialization share that `static` data member. And as with `static` data members of nontemplate classes, `static` data members of class-template specializations must be defined and, if necessary, initialized at file scope.
- Each class-template specialization gets a copy of the class template's `static` member functions.

Terminology

angle brackets (< and >)
class template
class-template definition
class-template specialization
explicit specialization
`friend` of a template
function template
function-template definition
function-template specialization
generic programming
keyword `class` in a template type parameter
keyword `template`
keyword `typename`
macro
member function of a class-template
    specialization
nontype parameter

nontype template parameter
overloading a function template
parameterized type
class-template specialization
`static` data member of a class template
`static` data member of a class-template
    specialization
`static` member function of a class template
`static` member function of a class-template
    specialization
template parameter
`template< class T >`
`template< typename T >`
`typename`
type parameter
type template parameter

Self-Review Exercises

14.1 State which of the following statements are *true* and which are *false*. If a statement is *false*, explain why.

    a) The template parameters of a function-template definition are used to specify the types of the arguments to the function, to specify the return type of the function and to declare variables within the function.

    b) Keywords `typename` and `class` as used with a template type parameter specifically mean "any user-defined class type."

    c) A function template can be overloaded by another function template with the same function name.

    d) Template parameter names among template definitions must be unique.

    e) Each member-function definition outside a class template must begin with a template header.

    f) A `friend` function of a class template must be a function-template specialization.

g) If several class-template specializations are generated from a single class template with a single `static` data member, each of the class-template specializations shares a single copy of the class template's `static` data member.

14.2 Fill in the blanks in each of the following:
a) Templates enable us to specify, with a single code segment, an entire range of related functions called _____, or an entire range of related classes called _____.
b) All function-template definitions begin with the keyword _____, followed by a list of template parameters to the function template enclosed in _____.
c) The related functions generated from a function template all have the same name, so the compiler uses _____ resolution to invoke the proper function.
d) Class templates also are called _____ types.
e) The _____ operator is used with a class-template name to tie each member-function definition to the class template's scope.
f) As with `static` data members of nontemplate classes, `static` data members of class-template specializations must also be defined and, if necessary, initialized at _____ scope.

Answers to Self-Review Exercises

14.1 a) True. b) False. Keywords `typename` and `class` in this context also allow for a type parameter of a built-in type. c) True. d) False. Template parameter names among function templates need not be unique. e) True. f) False. It could be a nontemplate function. g) False. Each class-template specialization will have its own copy of the `static` data member.

14.2 a) function-template specializations, class-template specializations. b) `template`, angle brackets (< and >). c) overloading. d) parameterized. e) binary scope resolution. f) file.

Exercises

14.3 Write a function template `selectionSort` based on the sort program of Fig. 8.15. Write a driver program that inputs, sorts and outputs an `int` array and a `float` array.

14.4 Overload function template `printArray` of Fig. 14.1 so that it takes two additional integer arguments, namely `int lowSubscript` and `int highSubscript`. A call to this function will print only the designated portion of the array. Validate `lowSubscript` and `highSubscript`; if either is out of range or if `highSubscript` is less than or equal to `lowSubscript`, the overloaded `printArray` function should return 0; otherwise, `printArray` should return the number of elements printed. Then modify `main` to exercise both versions of `printArray` on arrays a, b and c (lines 23–25 of Fig. 14.1). Be sure to test all capabilities of both versions of `printArray`.

14.5 Overload function template `printArray` of Fig. 14.1 with a nontemplate version that specifically prints an array of character strings in neat, tabular, column format.

14.6 Write a simple function template for predicate function `isEqualTo` that compares its two arguments of the same type with the equality operator (`==`) and returns `true` if they are equal and `false` if they are not equal. Use this function template in a program that calls `isEqualTo` only with a variety of built-in types. Now write a separate version of the program that calls `isEqualTo` with a user-defined class type, but does not overload the equality operator. What happens when you attempt to run this program? Now overload the equality operator (with the operator function) `operator==`. Now what happens when you attempt to run this program?

14.7 Use an `int` template nontype parameter `numberOfElements` and a type parameter `element-Type` to help create a template for the `Array` class (Figs. 11.6–11.7) we developed in Chapter 11. This template will enable `Array` objects to be instantiated with a specified number of elements of a specified element type at compile time.

14.8 Write a program with class template `Array`. The template can instantiate an `Array` of any element type. Override the template with a specific definition for an `Array` of `float` elements (`class Array< float >`). The driver should demonstrate the instantiation of an `Array` of `int` through the template and should show that an attempt to instantiate an `Array` of `float` uses the definition provided in `class Array< float >`.

14.9 Distinguish between the terms "function template" and "function-template specialization."

14.10 Which is more like a stencil—a class template or a class-template specialization? Explain your answer.

14.11 What is the relationship between function templates and overloading?

14.12 Why might you choose to use a function template instead of a macro?

14.13 What performance problem can result from using function templates and class templates?

14.14 The compiler performs a matching process to determine which function-template specialization to call when a function is invoked. Under what circumstances does an attempt to make a match result in a compile error?

14.15 Why is it appropriate to refer to a class template as a parameterized type?

14.16 Explain why a C++ program would use the statement

```
Array< Employee > workerList( 100 );
```

14.17 Review your answer to Exercise 14.16. Why might a C++ program use the statement

```
Array< Employee > workerList;
```

14.18 Explain the use of the following notation in a C++ program:

```
template< typename T > Array< T >::Array( int s )
```

14.19 Why might you use a nontype parameter with a class template for a container such as an array or stack?

14.20 Describe how to provide an explicit specialization of a class template.

14.21 Describe the relationship between class templates and inheritance.

14.22 Suppose that a class template has the header

```
template< typename T > class Ct1
```

Describe the friendship relationships established by placing each of the following `friend` declarations inside this class template. Identifiers beginning with "f" are functions, identifiers beginning with "C" are classes, identifiers beginning with "Ct" are class templates and T is a template type parameter (i.e., T can represent any fundamental or class type).

a) `friend void f1();`
b) `friend void f2( Ct1< T > & );`
c) `friend void C2::f3();`
d) `friend void Ct3< T >::f4( Ct1< T > & );`
e) `friend class C4;`
f) `friend class Ct5< T >;`

14.23 Suppose that class template `Employee` has a `static` data member count. Suppose that three class-template specializations are instantiated from the class template. How many copies of the `static` data member will exist? How will the use of each be constrained (if at all)?

Stream Input/Output

OBJECTIVES

In this chapter you will learn:

- To use C++ object-oriented stream input/output.
- To format input and output.
- The stream-I/O class hierarchy.
- To use stream manipulators.
- To control justification and padding.
- To determine the success or failure of input/output operations.
- To tie output streams to input streams.

15.1 Introduction

The C++ standard libraries provide an extensive set of input/output capabilities. This chapter discusses a range of capabilities sufficient for performing most common I/O operations and overviews the remaining capabilities. We discussed some of these features earlier in the text; now we provide a more complete treatment. Many of the I/O features that we will discuss are object oriented. This style of I/O makes use of other C++ features, such as references, function overloading and operator overloading.

C++ uses type-safe I/O. Each I/O operation is executed in a manner sensitive to the data type. If an I/O member function has been defined to handle a particular data type, then that member function is called to handle that data type. If there is no match between the type of the actual data and a function for handling that data type, the compiler generates an error. Thus, improper data cannot "sneak" through the system (as can occur in C, allowing for some subtle and bizarre errors).

Users can specify how to perform I/O for objects of user-defined types by overloading the stream insertion operator (<<) and the stream extraction operator (>>). This extensibility is one of C++'s most valuable features.

Software Engineering Observation 15.1

Use the C++-style I/O exclusively in C++ programs, even though C-style I/O is available to C++ programmers.

Error-Prevention Tip 15.1

C++ I/O is type safe.

Software Engineering Observation 15.2

C++ enables a common treatment of I/O for predefined types and user-defined types. This commonality facilitates software development and reuse.

15.2 Streams

C++ I/O occurs in streams, which are sequences of bytes. In input operations, the bytes flow from a device (e.g., a keyboard, a disk drive, a network connection) to main memory. In output operations, bytes flow from main memory to a device (e.g., a display screen, a printer, a disk drive, a network connection, etc.).

An application associates meaning with bytes. The bytes could represent characters, raw data, graphics images, digital speech, digital video or any other information an application may require.

The system I/O mechanisms should transfer bytes from devices to memory (and vice versa) consistently and reliably. Such transfers often involve some mechanical motion, such as the rotation of a disk or a tape, or the typing of keystrokes at a keyboard. The time these transfers take is typically much greater than the time the processor requires to manipulate data internally. Thus, I/O operations require careful planning and tuning to ensure optimal performance.

C++ provides both "low-level" and "high-level" I/O capabilities. Low-level I/O capabilities (i.e., unformatted I/O) specify that some number of bytes should be transferred device-to-memory or memory-to-device. In such transfers, the individual byte is the item of interest. Such low-level capabilities provide high-speed, high-volume transfers but are not particularly convenient for programmers.

Programmers generally prefer a higher-level view of I/O (i.e., formatted I/O), in which bytes are grouped into meaningful units, such as integers, floating-point numbers, characters, strings and user-defined types. These type-oriented capabilities are satisfactory for most I/O other than high-volume file processing.

Performance Tip 15.1

Use unformatted I/O for the best performance in high-volume file processing.

Portability Tip 15.1

Using unformatted I/O can lead to portability problems, because unformatted data is not portable across all platforms.

15.2.1 Classic Streams vs. Standard Streams

In the past, the C++ classic stream libraries enabled input and output of chars. Because a char occupies one byte, it can represent only a limited set of characters (such as those in the ASCII character set). However, many languages use alphabets that contain more characters than a single-byte char can represent. The ASCII character set does not provide these characters; the Unicode character set does. Unicode is an extensive international character set that represents the majority of the world's commercially viable languages, mathematical symbols and much more. For more information on Unicode, visit www.unicode.org.

C++ includes the standard stream libraries, which enable developers to build systems capable of performing I/O operations with Unicode characters. For this purpose, C++ includes an additional character type called wchar_t, which can store Unicode characters. The C++ standard also redesigned the classic C++ stream classes, which processed only chars, as class templates with separate specializations for processing characters of types char and wchar_t, respectively. We use the char type of class templates with separate specializations throughout this book.

15.2.2 `iostream` Library Header Files

The C++ iostream library provides hundreds of I/O capabilities. Several header files contain portions of the library interface.

Most C++ programs include the <iostream> header file, which declares basic services required for all stream-I/O operations. The <iostream> header file defines the cin, cout, cerr and clog objects, which correspond to the standard input stream, the standard output stream, the unbuffered standard error stream and the buffered standard error stream, respectively. (cerr and clog are discussed in Section 15.2.3.) Both unformatted- and formatted-I/O services are provided.

The <iomanip> header declares services useful for performing formatted I/O with so-called parameterized stream manipulators, such as setw and setprecision.

The <fstream> header declares services for user-controlled file processing. We use this header in the file-processing programs of Chapter 17.

C++ implementations generally contain other I/O-related libraries that provide system-specific capabilities, such as the controlling of special-purpose devices for audio and video I/O.

15.2.3 Stream Input/Output Classes and Objects

The iostream library provides many templates for handling common I/O operations. For example, class template basic_istream supports stream-input operations, class template basic_ostream supports stream-output operations, and class template basic_iostream supports both stream-input and stream-output operations. Each template has a predefined template specialization that enables char I/O. In addition, the iostream library provides a set of typedefs that provide aliases for these template specializations. The **typedef** specifier declares synonyms (aliases) for previously defined data types. Programmers sometimes use typedef to create shorter or more readable type names. For example, the statement

```
typedef Card *CardPtr;
```

defines an additional type name, CardPtr, as a synonym for type Card *. Note that creating a name using typedef does not create a data type; typedef creates only a type name that may be used in the program. The typedef istream represents a specialization of basic_istream that enables char input. Similarly, the typedef ostream represents a specialization of basic_ostream that enables char output. Also, the typedef iostream represents a specialization of basic_iostream that enables both char input and output. We use these typedefs throughout this chapter.

Stream-I/O Template Hierarchy and Operator Overloading

Templates basic_istream and basic_ostream both derive through single inheritance from base template basic_ios.[1] Template basic_iostream derives through multiple inheritance[2] from templates basic_istream and basic_ostream. The UML class diagram of Fig. 15.1 summarizes these inheritance relationships.

Operator overloading provides a convenient notation for performing input/output. The left-shift operator (<<) is overloaded to designate stream output and is referred to as the stream insertion operator. The right-shift operator (>>) is overloaded to designate stream input and is referred to as the stream extraction operator. These operators are used with the standard stream objects cin, cout, cerr and clog and, commonly, with user-defined stream objects.

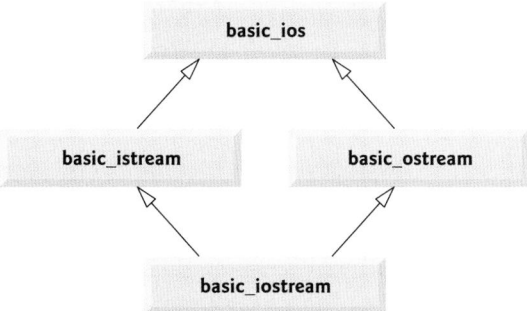

Fig. 15.1 | Stream-I/O template hierarchy portion.

---

1. Technically, templates do not inherit from other templates. However, in this chapter, we discuss templates only in the context of the template specializations that enable char I/O. These specializations are classes and thus can inherit from each other.
2. Multiple inheritance is discussed in Chapter 23, Other Topics.

Standard Stream Objects `cin`, `cout`, `cerr` *and* `clog`

The predefined object `cin` is an `istream` instance and is said to be "connected to" (or attached to) the standard input device, which usually is the keyboard. The stream extraction operator (`>>`) as used in the following statement causes a value for integer variable `grade` (assuming that `grade` has been declared as an `int` variable) to be input from `cin` to memory:

```
cin >> grade; // data "flows" in the direction of the arrows
```

Note that the compiler determines the data type of `grade` and selects the appropriate overloaded stream extraction operator. Assuming that `grade` has been declared properly, the stream extraction operator does not require additional type information (as is the case, for example, in C-style I/O). The `>>` operator is overloaded to input data items of built-in types, strings and pointer values.

The predefined object `cout` is an `ostream` instance and is said to be "connected to" the standard output device, which usually is the display screen. The stream insertion operator (`<<`), as used in the following statement, causes the value of variable `grade` to be output from memory to the standard output device:

```
cout << grade; // data "flows" in the direction of the arrows
```

Note that the compiler also determines the data type of `grade` (assuming `grade` has been declared properly) and selects the appropriate stream insertion operator, so the stream insertion operator does not require additional type information. The `<<` operator is overloaded to output data items of built-in types, strings and pointer values.

The predefined object `cerr` is an `ostream` instance and is said to be "connected to" the standard error device. Outputs to object `cerr` are unbuffered, implying that each stream insertion to `cerr` causes its output to appear immediately—this is appropriate for notifying a user promptly about errors.

The predefined object `clog` is an instance of the `ostream` class and is said to be "connected to" the standard error device. Outputs to `clog` are buffered. This means that each insertion to `clog` could cause its output to be held in a buffer until the buffer is filled or until the buffer is flushed. Buffering is an I/O performance-enhancement technique discussed in operating-systems courses.

File-Processing Templates

C++ file processing uses class templates `basic_ifstream` (for file input), `basic_ofstream` (for file output) and `basic_fstream` (for file input and output). Each class template has a predefined template specialization that enables char I/O. C++ provides a set of `typedef`s that provide aliases for these template specializations. For example, the `typedef` `ifstream` represents a specialization of `basic_ifstream` that enables char input from a file. Similarly, `typedef` `ofstream` represents a specialization of `basic_ofstream` that enables char output to a file. Also, `typedef` `fstream` represents a specialization of `basic_fstream` that enables char input from, and output to, a file. Template `basic_ifstream` inherits from `basic_istream`, `basic_ofstream` inherits from `basic_ostream` and `basic_fstream` inherits from `basic_iostream`. The UML class diagram of Fig. 15.2 summarizes the various inheritance relationships of the I/O-related classes. The full stream-I/O class hierarchy provides most of the capabilities that programmers need. Consult the class-library reference for your C++ system for additional file-processing information.

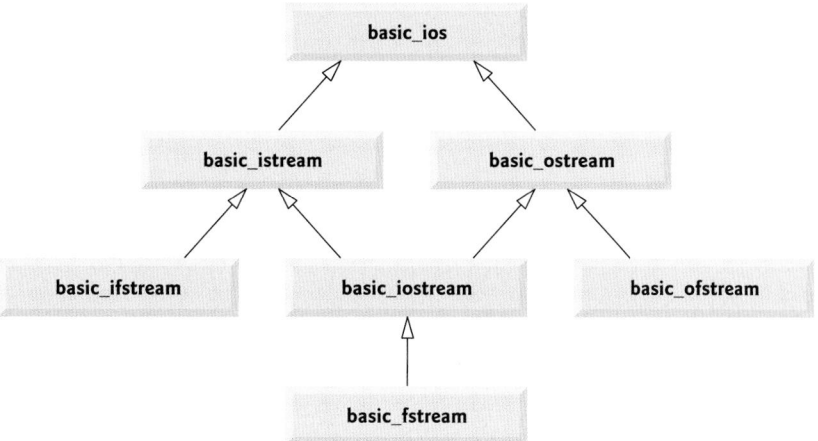

Fig. 15.2 | Stream-I/O template hierarchy portion showing the main file-processing templates.

15.3 Stream Output

Formatted and unformatted output capabilities are provided by ostream. Capabilities for output include output of standard data types with the stream insertion operator (<<); output of characters via the put member function; unformatted output via the write member function (Section 15.5); output of integers in decimal, octal and hexadecimal formats (Section 15.6.1); output of floating-point values with various precision (Section 15.6.2), with forced decimal points (Section 15.7.1), in scientific notation and in fixed notation (Section 15.7.5); output of data justified in fields of designated widths (Section 15.7.2); output of data in fields padded with specified characters (Section 15.7.3); and output of uppercase letters in scientific notation and hexadecimal notation (Section 15.7.6).

15.3.1 Output of char * Variables

C++ determines data types automatically, an improvement over C. Unfortunately, this feature sometimes "gets in the way." For example, suppose we want to print the value of a char * to a character string (i.e., the memory address of the first character of that string). However, the << operator has been overloaded to print data of type char * as a null-terminated string. The solution is to cast the char * to a void * (in fact, this should be done to any pointer variable the programmer wishes to output as an address). Figure 15.3 demonstrates printing a char * variable in both string and address formats. Note that the address prints as a hexadecimal (base-16) number. [*Note:* The reader who wants to learn more about hexadecimal numbers should read Appendix D, Number Systems.] We say more about controlling the bases of numbers in Section 15.6.1, Section 15.7.4, Section 15.7.5 and Section 15.7.7. [*Note:* The memory address shown in the output of the program in Fig. 15.3 may differ among compilers.]

15.3.2 Character Output using Member Function put

We can use the put member function to output characters. For example, the statement

```
cout.put( 'A' );
```

```
 1   // Fig. 15.3: Fig15_03.cpp
 2   // Printing the address stored in a char * variable.
 3   #include <iostream>
 4   using std::cout;
 5   using std::endl;
 6
 7   int main()
 8   {
 9      char *word = "again";
10
11      // display value of char *, then display value of char *
12      // static_cast to void *
13      cout << "Value of word is: " << word << endl
14         << "Value of static_cast< void * >( word ) is: "
15         << static_cast< void * >( word ) << endl;
16      return 0;
17   } // end main
```

```
Value of word is: again
Value of static_cast< void * >( word ) is: 00428300
```

Fig. 15.3 | Printing the address stored in a `char *` variable.

displays a single character A. Calls to put may be cascaded, as in the statement

        cout.put('A').put('\n');

which outputs the letter A followed by a newline character. As with <<, the preceding statement executes in this manner, because the dot operator (.) evaluates from left to right, and
the put member function returns a reference to the ostream object (cout) that received
the put call. The put function also may be called with a numeric expression that represents
an ASCII value, as in the following statement

        cout.put(65);

which also outputs A.

15.4 Stream Input

Now let us consider stream input. Formatted and unformatted input capabilities are provided by istream. The stream extraction operator (i.e., the overloaded >> operator) normally skips white-space characters (such as blanks, tabs and newlines) in the input stream;
later we will see how to change this behavior. After each input, the stream extraction operator returns a reference to the stream object that received the extraction message (e.g., cin
in the expression cin >> grade). If that reference is used as a condition (e.g., in a while
statement's loop-continuation condition), the stream's overloaded void * cast operator
function is implicitly invoked to convert the reference into a non-null pointer value or the
null pointer based on the success or failure of the last input operation. A non-null pointer
converts to the bool value true to indicate success and the null pointer converts to the bool
value false to indicate failure. When an attempt is made to read past the end of a stream,
the stream's overloaded void * cast operator returns the null pointer to indicate end-of-file.

Each stream object contains a set of state bits used to control the state of the stream (i.e., formatting, setting error states, etc.). These bits are used by the stream's overloaded void * cast operator to determine whether to return a non-null pointer or the null pointer. Stream extraction causes the stream's `failbit` to be set if data of the wrong type is input and causes the stream's `badbit` to be set if the operation fails. Section 15.7 and Section 15.8 discuss stream state bits in detail, then show how to test these bits after an I/O operation.

15.4.1 get and getline Member Functions

The `get` member function with no arguments inputs one character from the designated stream (including white-space characters and other non-graphic characters, such as the key sequence that represents end-of-file) and returns it as the value of the function call. This version of get returns EOF when end-of-file is encountered on the stream.

Using Member Functions *eof*, *get* and *put*

Figure 15.4 demonstrates the use of member functions eof and get on input stream cin and member function put on output stream cout. The program first prints the value of cin.eof()—i.e., false (0 on the output)—to show that end-of-file has not occurred on cin. The user enters a line of text and presses *Enter* followed by end-of-file (*<ctrl>-z* on Microsoft Windows systems, *<ctrl>-d* on UNIX and Macintosh systems). Line 17 reads each character, which line 18 outputs to cout using member function put. When end-of-file is encountered, the while statement ends, and line 22 displays the value of cin.eof(), which is now true (1 on the output), to show that end-of-file has been set on cin. Note that this program uses the version of istream member function get that takes no argu-

```cpp
 1   // Fig. 15.4: Fig15_04.cpp
 2   // Using member functions get, put and eof.
 3   #include <iostream>
 4   using std::cin;
 5   using std::cout;
 6   using std::endl;
 7
 8   int main()
 9   {
10      int character; // use int, because char cannot represent EOF
11
12      // prompt user to enter line of text
13      cout << "Before input, cin.eof() is " << cin.eof() << endl
14         << "Enter a sentence followed by end-of-file:" << endl;
15
16      // use get to read each character; use put to display it
17      while ( ( character = cin.get() ) != EOF )
18         cout.put( character );
19
20      // display end-of-file character
21      cout << "\nEOF in this system is: " << character << endl;
22      cout << "After input of EOF, cin.eof() is " << cin.eof() << endl;
23      return 0;
24   } // end main
```

Fig. 15.4 | get, put and eof member functions. (Part 1 of 2.)

```
Before input, cin.eof() is 0
Enter a sentence followed by end-of-file:
Testing the get and put member functions
Testing the get and put member functions
^Z

EOF in this system is: -1
After input of EOF, cin.eof() is 1
```

Fig. 15.4 | get, put and eof member functions. (Part 2 of 2.)

ments and returns the character being input (line 17). Function eof returns true only after the program attempts to read past the last character in the stream.

The get member function with a character-reference argument inputs the next character from the input stream (even if this is a white-space character) and stores it in the character argument. This version of get returns a reference to the istream object for which the get member function is being invoked.

A third version of get takes three arguments—a character array, a size limit and a delimiter (with default value '\n'). This version reads characters from the input stream. It either reads one fewer than the specified maximum number of characters and terminates or terminates as soon as the delimiter is read. A null character is inserted to terminate the input string in the character array used as a buffer by the program. The delimiter is not placed in the character array but does remain in the input stream (the delimiter will be the next character read). Thus, the result of a second consecutive get is an empty line, unless the delimiter character is removed from the input stream (possibly with cin.ignore()).

Comparing cin and cin.get

Figure 15.5 compares input using stream extraction with cin (which reads characters until a white-space character is encountered) and input using cin.get. Note that the call to cin.get (line 24) does not specify a delimiter, so the default '\n' character is used.

```
 1   // Fig. 15.5: Fig15_05.cpp
 2   // Contrasting input of a string via cin and cin.get.
 3   #include <iostream>
 4   using std::cin;
 5   using std::cout;
 6   using std::endl;
 7
 8   int main()
 9   {
10      // create two char arrays, each with 80 elements
11      const int SIZE = 80;
12      char buffer1[ SIZE ];
13      char buffer2[ SIZE ];
14
```

Fig. 15.5 | Input of a string using cin with stream extraction contrasted with input using cin.get. (Part 1 of 2.)

```
15        // use cin to input characters into buffer1
16        cout << "Enter a sentence:" << endl;
17        cin >> buffer1;
18
19        // display buffer1 contents
20        cout << "\nThe string read with cin was:" << endl
21           << buffer1 << endl << endl;
22
23        // use cin.get to input characters into buffer2
24        cin.get( buffer2, SIZE );
25
26        // display buffer2 contents
27        cout << "The string read with cin.get was:" << endl
28           << buffer2 << endl;
29        return 0;
30  } // end main
```

```
Enter a sentence:
Contrasting string input with cin and cin.get

The string read with cin was:
Contrasting

The string read with cin.get was:
 string input with cin and cin.get
```

Fig. 15.5 | Input of a string using `cin` with stream extraction contrasted with input using `cin.get`. (Part 2 of 2.)

Using Member Function *getline*

Member function `getline` operates similarly to the third version of the get member function and inserts a null character after the line in the character array. The `getline` function removes the delimiter from the stream (i.e., reads the character and discards it), but does not store it in the character array. The program of Fig. 15.6 demonstrates the use of the `getline` member function to input a line of text (line 15).

```
1   // Fig. 15.6: Fig15_06.cpp
2   // Inputting characters using cin member function getline.
3   #include <iostream>
4   using std::cin;
5   using std::cout;
6   using std::endl;
7
8   int main()
9   {
10     const int SIZE = 80;
11     char buffer[ SIZE ]; // create array of 80 characters
12
```

Fig. 15.6 | Inputting character data with `cin` member function `getline`. (Part 1 of 2.)

```
13      // input characters in buffer via cin function getline
14      cout << "Enter a sentence:" << endl;
15      cin.getline( buffer, SIZE );
16
17      // display buffer contents
18      cout << "\nThe sentence entered is:" << endl << buffer << endl;
19      return 0;
20   } // end main
```

```
Enter a sentence:
Using the getline member function

The sentence entered is:
Using the getline member function
```

Fig. 15.6 | Inputting character data with `cin` member function `getline`. (Part 2 of 2.)

15.4.2 `istream` Member Functions `peek`, `putback` and `ignore`

The `ignore` member function of `istream` either reads and discards a designated number of characters (the default is one character) or terminates upon encountering a designated delimiter (the default delimiter is `EOF`, which causes `ignore` to skip to the end of the file when reading from a file).

The `putback` member function places the previous character obtained by a `get` from an input stream back into that stream. This function is useful for applications that scan an input stream looking for a field beginning with a specific character. When that character is input, the application returns the character to the stream, so the character can be included in the input data.

The `peek` member function returns the next character from an input stream but does not remove the character from the stream.

15.4.3 Type-Safe I/O

C++ offers type-safe I/O. The << and >> operators are overloaded to accept data items of specific types. If unexpected data is processed, various error bits are set, which the user may test to determine whether an I/O operation succeeded or failed. If operator << has not been overloaded for a user-defined type and you attempt to input into or output the contents of an object of that user-defined type, the compiler reports an error. This enables the program to "stay in control." We discuss these error states in Section 15.8.

15.5 Unformatted I/O using `read`, `write` and `gcount`

Unformatted input/output is performed using the `read` and `write` member functions of `istream` and `ostream`, respectively. Member function `read` inputs some number of bytes to a character array in memory; member function `write` outputs bytes from a character array. These bytes are not formatted in any way. They are input or output as raw bytes. For example, the call

```
char buffer[] = "HAPPY BIRTHDAY";
cout.write( buffer, 10 );
```

outputs the first 10 bytes of buffer (including null characters, if any, that would cause output with cout and << to terminate). The call

```
cout.write( "ABCDEFGHIJKLMNOPQRSTUVWXYZ", 10 );
```

displays the first 10 characters of the alphabet.

The read member function inputs a designated number of characters into a character array. If fewer than the designated number of characters are read, failbit is set. Section 15.8 shows how to determine whether failbit has been set. Member function gcount reports the number of characters read by the last input operation.

Figure 15.7 demonstrates istream member functions read and gcount and ostream member function write. The program inputs 20 characters (from a longer input sequence) into character array buffer with read (line 15), determines the number of characters input with gcount (line 19) and outputs the characters in buffer with write (line 19).

15.6 Introduction to Stream Manipulators

C++ provides various stream manipulators that perform formatting tasks. The stream manipulators provide capabilities such as setting field widths, setting precision, setting and unsetting format state, setting the fill character in fields, flushing streams, inserting a newline into the output stream (and flushing the stream), inserting a null character into the

```
 1   // Fig. 15.7: Fig15_07.cpp
 2   // Unformatted I/O using read, gcount and write.
 3   #include <iostream>
 4   using std::cin;
 5   using std::cout;
 6   using std::endl;
 7
 8   int main()
 9   {
10      const int SIZE = 80;
11      char buffer[ SIZE ]; // create array of 80 characters
12
13      // use function read to input characters into buffer
14      cout << "Enter a sentence:" << endl;
15      cin.read( buffer, 20 );
16
17      // use functions write and gcount to display buffer characters
18      cout << endl << "The sentence entered was:" << endl;
19      cout.write( buffer, cin.gcount() );
20      cout << endl;
21      return 0;
22   } // end main
```

```
Enter a sentence:
Using the read, write, and gcount member functions
The sentence entered was:
Using the read, writ
```

Fig. 15.7 | Unformatted I/O using the read, gcount and write member functions.

output stream and skipping white space in the input stream. These features are described in the following sections.

15.6.1 Integral Stream Base: dec, oct, hex and setbase

Integers are interpreted normally as decimal (base-10) values. To change the base in which integers are interpreted on a stream, insert the hex manipulator to set the base to hexadecimal (base 16) or insert the oct manipulator to set the base to octal (base 8). Insert the dec manipulator to reset the stream base to decimal.

The base of a stream also may be changed by the setbase stream manipulator, which takes one integer argument of 10, 8, or 16 to set the base to decimal, octal or hexadecimal, respectively. Because setbase takes an argument, it is called a parameterized stream manipulator. Using setbase (or any other parameterized manipulator) requires the inclusion of the <iomanip> header file. The stream base value remains the same until changed explicitly; setbase settings are "sticky." Figure 15.8 demonstrates stream manipulators hex, oct, dec and setbase.

```
1   // Fig. 15.8: Fig15_08.cpp
2   // Using stream manipulators hex, oct, dec and setbase.
3   #include <iostream>
4   using std::cin;
5   using std::cout;
6   using std::dec;
7   using std::endl;
8   using std::hex;
9   using std::oct;
10
11  #include <iomanip>
12  using std::setbase;
13
14  int main()
15  {
16     int number;
17
18     cout << "Enter a decimal number: ";
19     cin >> number; // input number
20
21     // use hex stream manipulator to show hexadecimal number
22     cout << number << " in hexadecimal is: " << hex
23        << number << endl;
24
25     // use oct stream manipulator to show octal number
26     cout << dec << number << " in octal is: "
27        << oct << number << endl;
28
29     // use setbase stream manipulator to show decimal number
30     cout << setbase( 10 ) << number << " in decimal is: "
31        << number << endl;
32     return 0;
33  } // end main
```

Fig. 15.8 | Stream manipulators hex, oct, dec and setbase. (Part 1 of 2.)

```
Enter a decimal number: 20
20 in hexadecimal is: 14
20 in octal is: 24
20 in decimal is: 20
```

Fig. 15.8 | Stream manipulators `hex`, `oct`, `dec` and `setbase`. (Part 2 of 2.)

15.6.2 Floating-Point Precision (precision, setprecision)

We can control the precision of floating-point numbers (i.e., the number of digits to the right of the decimal point) by using either the `setprecision` stream manipulator or the `precision` member function of `ios_base`. A call to either of these sets the precision for all subsequent output operations until the next precision-setting call. A call to member function `precision` with no argument returns the current precision setting (this is what you need to use so that you can restore the original precision eventually after a "sticky" setting is no longer needed). The program of Fig. 15.9 uses both member function `precision` (line 28) and the `setprecision` manipulator (line 37) to print a table that shows the square root of 2, with precision varying from 0–9.

```
1   // Fig. 15.9: Fig15_09.cpp
2   // Controlling precision of floating-point values.
3   #include <iostream>
4   using std::cout;
5   using std::endl;
6   using std::fixed;
7
8   #include <iomanip>
9   using std::setprecision;
10
11  #include <cmath>
12  using std::sqrt; // sqrt prototype
13
14  int main()
15  {
16     double root2 = sqrt( 2.0 ); // calculate square root of 2
17     int places; // precision, vary from 0-9
18
19     cout << "Square root of 2 with precisions 0-9." << endl
20        << "Precision set by ios_base member function "
21        << "precision:" << endl;
22
23     cout << fixed; // use fixed-point notation
24
25     // display square root using ios_base function precision
26     for ( places = 0; places <= 9; places++ )
27     {
28        cout.precision( places );
29        cout << root2 << endl;
30     } // end for
31
```

Fig. 15.9 | Precision of floating-point values. (Part 1 of 2.)

```
32        cout << "\nPrecision set by stream manipulator "
33           << "setprecision:" << endl;
34
35        // set precision for each digit, then display square root
36        for ( places = 0; places <= 9; places++ )
37           cout << setprecision( places ) << root2 << endl;
38
39        return 0;
40    } // end main
```

```
Square root of 2 with precisions 0-9.
Precision set by ios_base member function precision:
1
1.4
1.41
1.414
1.4142
1.41421
1.414214
1.4142136
1.41421356
1.414213562

Precision set by stream manipulator setprecision:
1
1.4
1.41
1.414
1.4142
1.41421
1.414214
1.4142136
1.41421356
1.414213562
```

Fig. 15.9 | Precision of floating-point values. (Part 2 of 2.)

15.6.3 Field Width (width, setw)

The width member function (of base class ios_base) sets the field width (i.e., the number of character positions in which a value should be output or the maximum number of characters that should be input) and returns the previous width. If values output are narrower than the field width, fill characters are inserted as padding. A value wider than the designated width will not be truncated—the full number will be printed. The width function with no argument returns the current setting.

Common Programming Error 15.1

The width setting applies only for the next insertion or extraction (i.e., the width setting is not "sticky"); afterward, the width is set implicitly to 0 (i.e., input and output will be performed with default settings). Assuming that the width setting applies to all subsequent outputs is a logic error.

Common Programming Error 15.2

When a field is not sufficiently wide to handle outputs, the outputs print as wide as necessary, which can yield confusing outputs.

Figure 15.10 demonstrates the use of the width member function on both input and output. Note that, on input into a char array, a maximum of one fewer characters than the width will be read, because provision is made for the null character to be placed in the input string. Remember that stream extraction terminates when nonleading white space is encountered. The setw stream manipulator also may be used to set the field width.

```cpp
// Fig. 15.10: Fig15_10.cpp
// Demonstrating member function width.
#include <iostream>
using std::cin;
using std::cout;
using std::endl;

int main()
{
   int widthValue = 4;
   char sentence[ 10 ];

   cout << "Enter a sentence:" << endl;
   cin.width( 5 ); // input only 5 characters from sentence

   // set field width, then display characters based on that width
   while ( cin >> sentence )
   {
      cout.width( widthValue++ );
      cout << sentence << endl;
      cin.width( 5 ); // input 5 more characters from sentence
   } // end while

   return 0;
} // end main
```

```
Enter a sentence:
This is a test of the width member function
This
   is
    a
  test
    of
   the
   widt
       h
     memb
       er
     func
      tion
```

Fig. 15.10 | width member function of class ios_base.

[*Note:* When prompted for input in Fig. 15.10, the user should enter a line of text and press *Enter* followed by end-of-file (*<ctrl>-z* on Microsoft Windows systems, *<ctrl>-d* on UNIX and Macintosh systems).]

15.6.4 User-Defined Output Stream Manipulators

Programmers can create their own stream manipulators.[3] Figure 15.11 shows the creation and use of new nonparameterized stream manipulators bell (lines 10–13), carriageReturn (lines 16–19), tab (lines 22–25) and endLine (lines 29–32). For output stream manipulators, the return type and parameter must be of type ostream &. When line 37 inserts the endLine manipulator in the output stream, function endLine is called and line 31 outputs the escape sequence \n and the flush manipulator to the standard output stream cout. Similarly, when lines 37–46 insert the manipulators tab, bell and carriageReturn

```
1   // Fig. 15.11: Fig15_11.cpp
2   // Creating and testing user-defined, nonparameterized
3   // stream manipulators.
4   #include <iostream>
5   using std::cout;
6   using std::flush;
7   using std::ostream;
8
9   // bell manipulator (using escape sequence \a)
10  ostream& bell( ostream& output )
11  {
12     return output << '\a'; // issue system beep
13  } // end bell manipulator
14
15  // carriageReturn manipulator (using escape sequence \r)
16  ostream& carriageReturn( ostream& output )
17  {
18     return output << '\r'; // issue carriage return
19  } // end carriageReturn manipulator
20
21  // tab manipulator (using escape sequence \t)
22  ostream& tab( ostream& output )
23  {
24     return output << '\t'; // issue tab
25  } // end tab manipulator
26
27  // endLine manipulator (using escape sequence \n and member
28  // function flush)
29  ostream& endLine( ostream& output )
30  {
31     return output << '\n' << flush; // issue endl-like end of line
32  } // end endLine manipulator
33
```

Fig. 15.11 | User-defined, nonparameterized stream manipulators. (Part 1 of 2.)

---

3. Programmers also may create their own parameterized stream manipulators—consult your C++ compiler's documentation for instructions on how to do this.

```
34   int main()
35   {
36      // use tab and endLine manipulators
37      cout << "Testing the tab manipulator:" << endLine
38         << 'a' << tab << 'b' << tab << 'c' << endLine;
39
40      cout << "Testing the carriageReturn and bell manipulators:"
41         << endLine << "..........";
42
43      cout << bell; // use bell manipulator
44
45      // use carriageReturn and endLine manipulators
46      cout << carriageReturn << "-----" << endLine;
47      return 0;
48   } // end main
```

```
Testing the tab manipulator:
a       b       c
Testing the carriageReturn and bell manipulators:
-----.....
```

Fig. 15.11 | User-defined, nonparameterized stream manipulators. (Part 2 of 2.)

in the output stream, their corresponding functions—tab (line 22), bell (line 10) and carriageReturn (line 16) are called, which in turn output various escape sequences.

15.7 Stream Format States and Stream Manipulators

Various stream manipulators can be used to specify the kinds of formatting to be performed during stream-I/O operations. Stream manipulators control the output's format settings. Figure 15.12 lists each stream manipulator that controls a given stream's format state. All these manipulators belong to class ios_base. We show examples of most of these stream manipulators in the next several sections.

Stream Manipulator	Description
skipws	Skip white-space characters on an input stream. This setting is reset with stream manipulator noskipws.
left	Left justify output in a field. Padding characters appear to the right if necessary.
right	Right justify output in a field. Padding characters appear to the left if necessary.
internal	Indicate that a number's sign should be left justified in a field and a number's magnitude should be right justified in that same field (i.e., padding characters appear between the sign and the number).
dec	Specify that integers should be treated as decimal (base 10) values.

Fig. 15.12 | Format state stream manipulators from <iostream>. (Part 1 of 2.)

Stream Manipulator	Description
oct	Specify that integers should be treated as octal (base 8) values.
hex	Specify that integers should be treated as hexadecimal (base 16) values.
showbase	Specify that the base of a number is to be output ahead of the number (a leading 0 for octals; a leading 0x or 0X for hexadecimals). This setting is reset with stream manipulator noshowbase.
showpoint	Specify that floating-point numbers should be output with a decimal point. This is used normally with fixed to guarantee a certain number of digits to the right of the decimal point, even if they are zeros. This setting is reset with stream manipulator noshowpoint.
uppercase	Specify that uppercase letters (i.e., X and A through F) should be used in a hexadecimal integer and that uppercase E should be used when representing a floating-point value in scientific notation. This setting is reset with stream manipulator nouppercase.
showpos	Specify that positive numbers should be preceded by a plus sign (+). This setting is reset with stream manipulator noshowpos.
scientific	Specify output of a floating-point value in scientific notation.
fixed	Specify output of a floating-point value in fixed-point notation with a specific number of digits to the right of the decimal point.

Fig. 15.12 | Format state stream manipulators from <iostream>. (Part 2 of 2.)

15.7.1 Trailing Zeros and Decimal Points (showpoint)

Stream manipulator showpoint forces a floating-point number to be output with its decimal point and trailing zeros. For example, the floating-point value 79.0 prints as 79 without using showpoint and prints as 79.000000 (or as many trailing zeros as are specified by the current precision) using showpoint. To reset the showpoint setting, output the stream manipulator noshowpoint. The program in Fig. 15.13 shows how to use stream manipulator showpoint to control the printing of trailing zeros and decimal points for floating-point values. Recall that the default precision of a floating-point number is 6. When neither the fixed nor the scientific stream manipulator is used, the precision represents the number of significant digits to display (i.e., the total number of digits to display), not the number of digits to display after decimal point.

```
1   // Fig. 15.13: Fig15_13.cpp
2   // Using showpoint to control the printing of
3   // trailing zeros and decimal points for doubles.
4   #include <iostream>
5   using std::cout;
6   using std::endl;
7   using std::showpoint;
```

Fig. 15.13 | Controlling the printing of trailing zeros and decimal points in floating-point values. (Part 1 of 2.)

```
8
9    int main()
10   {
11      // display double values with default stream format
12      cout << "Before using showpoint" << endl
13         << "9.9900 prints as: " << 9.9900 << endl
14         << "9.9000 prints as: " << 9.9000 << endl
15         << "9.0000 prints as: " << 9.0000 << endl << endl;
16
17      // display double value after showpoint
18      cout << showpoint
19         << "After using showpoint" << endl
20         << "9.9900 prints as: " << 9.9900 << endl
21         << "9.9000 prints as: " << 9.9000 << endl
22         << "9.0000 prints as: " << 9.0000 << endl;
23      return 0;
24   } // end main
```

```
Before using showpoint
9.9900 prints as: 9.99
9.9000 prints as: 9.9
9.0000 prints as: 9

After using showpoint
9.9900 prints as: 9.99000
9.9000 prints as: 9.90000
9.0000 prints as: 9.00000
```

Fig. 15.13 | Controlling the printing of trailing zeros and decimal points in floating-point values. (Part 2 of 2.)

15.7.2 Justification (`left`, `right` and `internal`)

Stream manipulators `left` and `right` enable fields to be left justified with padding characters to the right or right justified with padding characters to the left, respectively. The padding character is specified by the `fill` member function or the `setfill` parameterized stream manipulator (which we discuss in Section 15.7.3). Figure 15.14 uses the `setw`, `left` and `right` manipulators to left justify and right justify integer data in a field.

```
1    // Fig. 15.14: Fig15_14.cpp
2    // Demonstrating left justification and right justification.
3    #include <iostream>
4    using std::cout;
5    using std::endl;
6    using std::left;
7    using std::right;
8
9    #include <iomanip>
10   using std::setw;
```

Fig. 15.14 | Left justification and right justification with stream manipulators `left` and `right`. (Part 1 of 2.)

```
11
12   int main()
13   {
14      int x = 12345;
15
16      // display x right justified (default)
17      cout << "Default is right justified:" << endl
18         << setw( 10 ) << x;
19
20      // use left manipulator to display x left justified
21      cout << "\n\nUse std::left to left justify x:\n"
22         << left << setw( 10 ) << x;
23
24      // use right manipulator to display x right justified
25      cout << "\n\nUse std::right to right justify x:\n"
26         << right << setw( 10 ) << x << endl;
27      return 0;
28   } // end main
```

```
Default is right justified:
     12345

Use std::left to left justify x:
12345

Use std::right to right justify x:
     12345
```

Fig. 15.14 | Left justification and right justification with stream manipulators `left` and `right`. (Part 2 of 2.)

Stream manipulator `internal` indicates that a number's sign (or base when using stream manipulator `showbase`) should be left justified within a field, that the number's magnitude should be right justified and that intervening spaces should be padded with the fill character. Figure 15.15 shows the `internal` stream manipulator specifying internal spacing (line 15). Note that `showpos` forces the plus sign to print (line 15). To reset the showpos setting, output the stream manipulator `noshowpos`.

```
1    // Fig. 15.15: Fig15_15.cpp
2    // Printing an integer with internal spacing and plus sign.
3    #include <iostream>
4    using std::cout;
5    using std::endl;
6    using std::internal;
7    using std::showpos;
8
9    #include <iomanip>
10   using std::setw;
11
```

Fig. 15.15 | Printing an integer with internal spacing and plus sign. (Part 1 of 2.)

```
12   int main()
13   {
14      // display value with internal spacing and plus sign
15      cout << internal << showpos << setw( 10 ) << 123 << endl;
16      return 0;
17   } // end main
```

```
+         123
```

Fig. 15.15 | Printing an integer with internal spacing and plus sign. (Part 2 of 2.)

15.7.3 Padding (`fill`, `setfill`)

The `fill` member function specifies the fill character to be used with justified fields; if no value is specified, spaces are used for padding. The `fill` function returns the prior padding character. The `setfill` manipulator also sets the padding character. Figure 15.16 demonstrates using member function `fill` (line 40) and stream manipulator `setfill` (lines 44 and 47) to set the fill character.

```
1    // Fig. 15.16: Fig15_16.cpp
2    // Using member function fill and stream manipulator setfill to change
3    // the padding character for fields larger than the printed value.
4    #include <iostream>
5    using std::cout;
6    using std::dec;
7    using std::endl;
8    using std::hex;
9    using std::internal;
10   using std::left;
11   using std::right;
12   using std::showbase;
13
14   #include <iomanip>
15   using std::setfill;
16   using std::setw;
17
18   int main()
19   {
20      int x = 10000;
21
22      // display x
23      cout << x << " printed as int right and left justified\n"
24         << "and as hex with internal justification.\n"
25         << "Using the default pad character (space):" << endl;
26
27      // display x with base
28      cout << showbase << setw( 10 ) << x << endl;
29
```

Fig. 15.16 | Using member function `fill` and stream manipulator `setfill` to change the padding character for fields larger than the values being printed. (Part 1 of 2.)

```
30      // display x with left justification
31      cout << left << setw( 10 ) << x << endl;
32
33      // display x as hex with internal justification
34      cout << internal << setw( 10 ) << hex << x << endl << endl;
35
36      cout << "Using various padding characters:" << endl;
37
38      // display x using padded characters (right justification)
39      cout << right;
40      cout.fill( '*' );
41      cout << setw( 10 ) << dec << x << endl;
42
43      // display x using padded characters (left justification)
44      cout << left << setw( 10 ) << setfill( '%' ) << x << endl;
45
46      // display x using padded characters (internal justification)
47      cout << internal << setw( 10 ) << setfill( '^' ) << hex
48         << x << endl;
49      return 0;
50   } // end main
```

```
10000 printed as int right and left justified
and as hex with internal justification.
Using the default pad character (space):
     10000
10000
0x    2710

Using various padding characters:
*****10000
10000%%%%%
0x^^^^2710
```

Fig. 15.16 | Using member function `fill` and stream manipulator `setfill` to change the padding character for fields larger than the values being printed. (Part 2 of 2.)

15.7.4 Integral Stream Base (dec, oct, hex, showbase)

C++ provides stream manipulators `dec`, `hex` and `oct` to specify that integers are to be displayed as decimal, hexadecimal and octal values, respectively. Stream insertions default to decimal if none of these manipulators is used. With stream extraction, integers prefixed with 0 (zero) are treated as octal values, integers prefixed with 0x or 0X are treated as hexadecimal values, and all other integers are treated as decimal values. Once a particular base is specified for a stream, all integers on that stream are processed using that base until a different base is specified or until the program terminates.

Stream manipulator `showbase` forces the base of an integral value to be output. Decimal numbers are output by default, octal numbers are output with a leading 0, and hexadecimal numbers are output with either a leading 0x or a leading 0X (as we discuss in Section 15.7.6, stream manipulator `uppercase` determines which option is chosen). Figure 15.17 demonstrates the use of stream manipulator `showbase` to force an integer to

```
1   // Fig. 15.17: Fig15_17.cpp
2   // Using stream manipulator showbase.
3   #include <iostream>
4   using std::cout;
5   using std::endl;
6   using std::hex;
7   using std::oct;
8   using std::showbase;
9
10  int main()
11  {
12     int x = 100;
13
14     // use showbase to show number base
15     cout << "Printing integers preceded by their base:" << endl
16        << showbase;
17
18     cout << x << endl; // print decimal value
19     cout << oct << x << endl; // print octal value
20     cout << hex << x << endl; // print hexadecimal value
21     return 0;
22  } // end main
```

```
Printing integers preceded by their base:
100
0144
0x64
```

Fig. 15.17 | Stream manipulator showbase.

print in decimal, octal and hexadecimal formats. To reset the showbase setting, output the stream manipulator noshowbase.

15.7.5 Floating-Point Numbers; Scientific and Fixed Notation (scientific, fixed)

Stream manipulators scientific and fixed control the output format of floating-point numbers. Stream manipulator scientific forces the output of a floating-point number to display in scientific format. Stream manipulator fixed forces a floating-point number to display a specific number of digits (as specified by member function precision or stream manipulator setprecision) to the right of the decimal point. Without using another manipulator, the floating-point-number value determines the output format.

Figure 15.18 demonstrates displaying floating-point numbers in fixed and scientific formats using stream manipulators scientific (line 21) and fixed (line 25). The exponent format in scientific notation might differ across different compilers.

15.7.6 Uppercase/Lowercase Control (uppercase)

Stream manipulator uppercase outputs an uppercase X or E with hexadecimal-integer values or with scientific-notation floating-point values, respectively (Fig. 15.19). Using stream manipulator uppercase also causes all letters in a hexadecimal value to be upper-

```
1   // Fig. 15.18: Fig15_18.cpp
2   // Displaying floating-point values in system default,
3   // scientific and fixed formats.
4   #include <iostream>
5   using std::cout;
6   using std::endl;
7   using std::fixed;
8   using std::scientific;
9
10  int main()
11  {
12     double x = 0.001234567;
13     double y = 1.946e9;
14
15     // display x and y in default format
16     cout << "Displayed in default format:" << endl
17        << x << '\t' << y << endl;
18
19     // display x and y in scientific format
20     cout << "\nDisplayed in scientific format:" << endl
21        << scientific << x << '\t' << y << endl;
22
23     // display x and y in fixed format
24     cout << "\nDisplayed in fixed format:" << endl
25        << fixed << x << '\t' << y << endl;
26     return 0;
27  } // end main
```

```
Displayed in default format:
0.00123457      1.946e+009

Displayed in scientific format:
1.234567e-003    1.946000e+009

Displayed in fixed format:
0.001235         1946000000.000000
```

Fig. 15.18 | Floating-point values displayed in default, scientific and fixed formats.

case. By default, the letters for hexadecimal values and the exponents in scientific-notation floating-point values appear in lowercase. To reset the uppercase setting, output the stream-manipulator nouppercase.

```
1   // Fig. 15.19: Fig15_19.cpp
2   // Stream manipulator uppercase.
3   #include <iostream>
4   using std::cout;
5   using std::endl;
6   using std::hex;
7   using std::showbase;
8   using std::uppercase;
```

Fig. 15.19 | Stream manipulator uppercase. (Part 1 of 2.)

```
9
10   int main()
11   {
12      cout << "Printing uppercase letters in scientific" << endl
13         << "notation exponents and hexadecimal values:" << endl;
14
15      // use std:uppercase to display uppercase letters; use std::hex and
16      // std::showbase to display hexadecimal value and its base
17      cout << uppercase << 4.345e10 << endl
18         << hex << showbase << 123456789 << endl;
19      return 0;
20   } // end main
```

```
Printing uppercase letters in scientific
notation exponents and hexadecimal values:
4.345E+010
0X75BCD15
```

Fig. 15.19 | Stream manipulator `uppercase`. (Part 2 of 2.)

15.7.7 Specifying Boolean Format (boolalpha)

C++ provides data type `bool`, whose values may be `false` or `true`, as a preferred alternative to the old style of using 0 to indicate `false` and nonzero to indicate `true`. A `bool` variable outputs as 0 or 1 by default. However, we can use stream manipulator `boolalpha` to set the output stream to display `bool` values as the strings `"true"` and `"false"`. Use stream manipulator **nobooalpha** to set the output stream to display `bool` values as integers (i.e., the default setting). The program of Fig. 15.20 demonstrates these stream manipulators. Line 14 displays the `bool` value, which line 11 sets to `true`, as an integer. Line 18 uses manipulator `boolalpha` to display the `bool` value as a string. Lines 21–22 then change the `bool`'s value and use manipulator `nobooalpha`, so line 25 can display the `bool` value as an integer. Line 29 uses manipulator `boolalpha` to display the `bool` value as a string. Both `boolalpha` and `nobooalpha` are "sticky" settings.

 Good Programming Practice 15.1

Displaying `bool` values as `true` or `false`, rather than nonzero or 0, respectively, makes program outputs clearer.

```
1    // Fig. 15.20: Fig15_20.cpp
2    // Demonstrating stream manipulators boolalpha and nobooalpha.
3    #include <iostream>
4    using std::boolalpha;
5    using std::cout;
6    using std::endl;
7    using std::nobooalpha;
8
9    int main()
10   {
11      bool booleanValue = true;
```

Fig. 15.20 | Stream manipulators `boolalpha` and `nobooalpha`. (Part 1 of 2.)

```
12
13      // display default true booleanValue
14      cout << "booleanValue is " << booleanValue << endl;
15
16      // display booleanValue after using boolalpha
17      cout << "booleanValue (after using boolalpha) is "
18         << boolalpha << booleanValue << endl << endl;
19
20      cout << "switch booleanValue and use noboolalpha" << endl;
21      booleanValue = false; // change booleanValue
22      cout << noboolalpha << endl; // use noboolalpha
23
24      // display default false booleanValue after using noboolalpha
25      cout << "booleanValue is " << booleanValue << endl;
26
27      // display booleanValue after using boolalpha again
28      cout << "booleanValue (after using boolalpha) is "
29         << boolalpha << booleanValue << endl;
30      return 0;
31   } // end main
```

```
booleanValue is 1
booleanValue (after using boolalpha) is true

switch booleanValue and use noboolalpha

booleanValue is 0
booleanValue (after using boolalpha) is false
```

Fig. 15.20 | Stream manipulators `boolalpha` and `noboolalpha`. (Part 2 of 2.)

15.7.8 Setting and Resetting the Format State via Member Function `flags`

Throughout Section 15.7, we have been using stream manipulators to change output format characteristics. We now discuss how to return an output stream's format to its default state after having applied several manipulations. Member function `flags` without an argument returns the current format settings as a `fmtflags` data type (of class `ios_base`), which represents the format state. Member function `flags` with a `fmtflags` argument sets the format state as specified by the argument and returns the prior state settings. The initial settings of the value that `flags` returns might differ across several systems. The program of Fig. 15.21 uses member function `flags` to save the stream's original format state (line 22), then restore the original format settings (line 30).

```
1    // Fig. 15.21: Fig15_21.cpp
2    // Demonstrating the flags member function.
3    #include <iostream>
4    using std::cout;
5    using std::endl;
6    using std::ios_base;
```

Fig. 15.21 | `flags` member function. (Part 1 of 2.)

```
 7   using std::oct;
 8   using std::scientific;
 9   using std::showbase;
10
11   int main()
12   {
13      int integerValue = 1000;
14      double doubleValue = 0.0947628;
15
16      // display flags value, int and double values (original format)
17      cout << "The value of the flags variable is: " << cout.flags()
18         << "\nPrint int and double in original format:\n"
19         << integerValue << '\t' << doubleValue << endl << endl;
20
21      // use cout flags function to save original format
22      ios_base::fmtflags originalFormat = cout.flags();
23      cout << showbase << oct << scientific; // change format
24
25      // display flags value, int and double values (new format)
26      cout << "The value of the flags variable is: " << cout.flags()
27         << "\nPrint int and double in a new format:\n"
28         << integerValue << '\t' << doubleValue << endl << endl;
29
30      cout.flags( originalFormat ); // restore format
31
32      // display flags value, int and double values (original format)
33      cout << "The restored value of the flags variable is: "
34         << cout.flags()
35         << "\nPrint values in original format again:\n"
36         << integerValue << '\t' << doubleValue << endl;
37      return 0;
38   } // end main
```

```
The value of the flags variable is: 513
Print int and double in original format:
1000    0.0947628

The value of the flags variable is: 012011
Print int and double in a new format:
01750   9.476280e-002

The restored value of the flags variable is: 513
Print values in original format again:
1000    0.0947628
```

Fig. 15.21 | `flags` member function. (Part 2 of 2.)

15.8 Stream Error States

The state of a stream may be tested through bits in class ios_base. In a moment, we show how to test these bits, in the example of Fig. 15.22.

The **eofbit** is set for an input stream after end-of-file is encountered. A program can use member function eof to determine whether end-of-file has been encountered on a stream after an attempt to extract data beyond the end of the stream. The call

```
cin.eof()
```

returns true if end-of-file has been encountered on cin and false otherwise.

The failbit is set for a stream when a format error occurs on the stream, such as when the program is inputting integers and a nondigit character is encountered in the input stream. When such an error occurs, the characters are not lost. The **fail** member function reports whether a stream operation has failed; usually, recovering from such errors is possible.

The badbit is set for a stream when an error occurs that results in the loss of data. The **bad** member function reports whether a stream operation failed. Generally, such serious failures are nonrecoverable.

```
 1   // Fig. 15.22: Fig15_22.cpp
 2   // Testing error states.
 3   #include <iostream>
 4   using std::cin;
 5   using std::cout;
 6   using std::endl;
 7
 8   int main()
 9   {
10      int integerValue;
11
12      // display results of cin functions
13      cout << "Before a bad input operation:"
14         << "\ncin.rdstate(): " << cin.rdstate()
15         << "\n    cin.eof(): " << cin.eof()
16         << "\n   cin.fail(): " << cin.fail()
17         << "\n    cin.bad(): " << cin.bad()
18         << "\n   cin.good(): " << cin.good()
19         << "\n\nExpects an integer, but enter a character: ";
20
21      cin >> integerValue; // enter character value
22      cout << endl;
23
24      // display results of cin functions after bad input
25      cout << "After a bad input operation:"
26         << "\ncin.rdstate(): " << cin.rdstate()
27         << "\n    cin.eof(): " << cin.eof()
28         << "\n   cin.fail(): " << cin.fail()
29         << "\n    cin.bad(): " << cin.bad()
30         << "\n   cin.good(): " << cin.good() << endl << endl;
31
32      cin.clear(); // clear stream
33
34      // display results of cin functions after clearing cin
35      cout << "After cin.clear()" << "\ncin.fail(): " << cin.fail()
36         << "\ncin.good(): " << cin.good() << endl;
37      return 0;
38   } // end main
```

Fig. 15.22 | Testing error states. (Part 1 of 2.)

```
Before a bad input operation:
cin.rdstate(): 0
    cin.eof(): 0
   cin.fail(): 0
    cin.bad(): 0
   cin.good(): 1

Expects an integer, but enter a character: A

After a bad input operation:
cin.rdstate(): 2
    cin.eof(): 0
   cin.fail(): 1
    cin.bad(): 0
   cin.good(): 0

After cin.clear()
cin.fail(): 0
cin.good(): 1
```

Fig. 15.22 | Testing error states. (Part 2 of 2.)

The goodbit is set for a stream if none of the bits eofbit, failbit or badbit is set for the stream.

The good member function returns true if the bad, fail and eof functions would all return false. I/O operations should be performed only on "good" streams.

The rdstate member function returns the error state of the stream. A call to cout.rdstate, for example, would return the state of the stream, which then could be tested by a switch statement that examines eofbit, badbit, failbit and goodbit. The preferred means of testing the state of a stream is to use member functions eof, bad, fail and good—using these functions does not require the programmer to be familiar with particular status bits.

The clear member function is used to restore a stream's state to "good," so that I/O may proceed on that stream. The default argument for clear is goodbit, so the statement

        cin.clear();

clears cin and sets goodbit for the stream. The statement

        cin.clear(ios::failbit)

sets the failbit. The programmer might want to do this when performing input on cin with a user-defined type and encountering a problem. The name clear might seem inappropriate in this context, but it is correct.

The program of Fig. 15.22 demonstrates member functions rdstate, eof, fail, bad, good and clear. [*Note:* The actual values output may differ across different compilers.]

The operator! member function of basic_ios returns true if the badbit is set, the failbit is set or both are set. The operator void * member function returns false (0) if the badbit is set, the failbit is set or both are set. These functions are useful in file processing when a true/false condition is being tested under the control of a selection statement or repetition statement.

15.9 Tying an Output Stream to an Input Stream

Interactive applications generally involve an istream for input and an ostream for output. When a prompting message appears on the screen, the user responds by entering the appropriate data. Obviously, the prompt needs to appear before the input operation proceeds. With output buffering, outputs appear only when the buffer fills, when outputs are flushed explicitly by the program or automatically at the end of the program. C++ provides member function tie to synchronize (i.e., "tie together") the operation of an istream and an ostream to ensure that outputs appear before their subsequent inputs. The call

```
cin.tie( &cout );
```

ties cout (an ostream) to cin (an istream). Actually, this particular call is redundant, because C++ performs this operation automatically to create a user's standard input/output environment. However, the user would tie other istream/ostream pairs explicitly. To untie an input stream, inputStream, from an output stream, use the call

```
inputStream.tie( 0 );
```

Summary

- I/O operations are performed in a manner sensitive to the type of the data.
- C++ I/O occurs in streams. A stream is a sequence of bytes.
- I/O mechanisms of the system move bytes from devices to memory and vice versa efficiently and reliably.
- C++ provides "low-level" and "high-level" I/O capabilities. Low-level I/O-capabilities specify that some number of bytes should be transferred device-to-memory or memory-to-device. High-level I/O is performed with bytes grouped into such meaningful units as integers, floats, characters, strings and user-defined types.
- C++ provides both unformatted-I/O and formatted-I/O operations. Unformatted-I/O transfers are fast, but process raw data that is difficult for people to use. Formatted I/O processes data in meaningful units, but requires extra processing time that can degrade the performance of high-volume data transfers.
- The <iostream> header file declares all stream-I/O operations.
- Header <iomanip> declares the parameterized stream manipulators.
- The <fstream> header declares file-processing operations.
- The basic_istream template supports stream-input operations.
- The basic_ostream template supports stream-output operations.
- The basic_iostream template supports both stream-input and stream-output operations.
- The basic_istream template and the basic_ostream template are each derived through single inheritance from the basic_ios template.
- The basic_iostream template is derived through multiple inheritance from both the basic_istream template and the basic_ostream template.
- The left-shift operator (<<) is overloaded to designate stream output and is referred to as the stream insertion operator.
- The right-shift operator (>>) is overloaded to designate stream input and is referred to as the stream extraction operator.

- The `istream` object `cin` is tied to the standard input device, normally the keyboard.
- The `ostream` object `cout` is tied to the standard output device, normally the screen.
- The `ostream` object `cerr` is tied to the standard error device. Outputs to `cerr` are unbuffered; each insertion to `cerr` appears immediately.
- The C++ compiler determines data types automatically for input and output.
- Addresses are displayed in hexadecimal format by default.
- To print the address in a pointer variable, cast the pointer to `void *`.
- Member function `put` outputs one character. Calls to `put` may be cascaded.
- Stream input is performed with the stream extraction operator `>>`. This operator automatically skips white-space characters in the input stream.
- The `>>` operator returns `false` after end-of-file is encountered on a stream.
- Stream extraction causes `failbit` to be set for improper input and `badbit` to be set if the operation fails.
- A series of values can be input using the stream extraction operation in a `while` loop header. The extraction returns 0 when end-of-file is encountered.
- The `get` member function with no arguments inputs one character and returns the character; `EOF` is returned if end-of-file is encountered on the stream.
- Member function `get` with a character-reference argument inputs the next character from the input stream and stores it in the character argument. This version of `get` returns a reference to the istream object for which the get member function is being invoked.
- Member function `get` with three arguments—a character array, a size limit and a delimiter (with default value newline)—reads characters from the input stream up to a maximum of limit – 1 characters and terminates, or terminates when the delimiter is read. The input string is terminated with a null character. The delimiter is not placed in the character array but remains in the input stream.
- The `getline` member function operates like the three-argument `get` member function. The `getline` function removes the delimiter from the input stream but does not store it in the string.
- Member function `ignore` skips the specified number of characters (the default is 1) in the input stream; it terminates if the specified delimiter is encountered (the default delimiter is `EOF`).
- The `putback` member function places the previous character obtained by a `get` on a stream back onto that stream.
- The `peek` member function returns the next character from an input stream but does not extract (remove) the character from the stream.
- C++ offers type-safe I/O. If unexpected data is processed by the `<<` and `>>` operators, various error bits are set, which the user may test to determine whether an I/O operation succeeded or failed. If operator `<<` has not been overloaded for a user-defined type, a compiler error is reported.
- Unformatted I/O is performed with member functions `read` and `write`. These input or output some number of bytes to or from memory, beginning at a designated memory address. They are input or output as raw bytes with no formatting.
- The `gcount` member function returns the number of characters input by the previous `read` operation on that stream.
- Member function `read` inputs a specified number of characters into a character array. `failbit` is set if fewer than the specified number of characters are read.
- To change the base in which integers output, use the manipulator `hex` to set the base to hexadecimal (base 16) or `oct` to set the base to octal (base 8). Use manipulator `dec` to reset the base to decimal. The base remains the same until changed explicitly.

- The parameterized stream manipulator setbase also sets the base for integer output. setbase takes one integer argument of 10, 8 or 16 to set the base.

- Floating-point precision can be controlled using either the setprecision stream manipulator or the precision member function. Both set the precision for all subsequent output operations until the next precision-setting call. The precision member function with no argument returns the current precision value.

- Parameterized manipulators require the inclusion of the <iomanip> header file.

- Member function width sets the field width and returns the previous width. Values narrower than the field are padded with fill characters. The field-width setting applies only for the next insertion or extraction; the field width is set to 0 implicitly (subsequent values will be output as large as necessary). Values wider than a field are printed in their entirety. Function width with no argument returns the current width setting. Manipulator setw also sets the width.

- For input, the setw stream manipulator establishes a maximum string size; if a larger string is entered, the larger line is broken into pieces no larger than the designated size.

- Programmers may create their own stream manipulators.

- Stream manipulator showpoint forces a floating-point number to be output with a decimal point and with the number of significant digits specified by the precision.

- Stream manipulators left and right cause fields to be left justified with padding characters to the right or right justified with padding characters to the left.

- Stream manipulator internal indicates that a number's sign (or base when using stream manipulator showbase) should be left justified within a field, its magnitude should be right justified and intervening spaces should be padded with the fill character.

- Member function fill specifies the fill character to be used with stream manipulators left, right and internal (space is the default); the prior padding character is returned. Stream manipulator setfill also sets the fill character.

- Stream manipulators oct, hex and dec specify that integers are to be treated as octal, hexadecimal or decimal values, respectively. Integer output defaults to decimal if none of these bits is set; stream extractions process the data in the form the data is supplied.

- Stream manipulator showbase forces the base of an integral value to be output.

- Stream manipulator scientific is used to output a floating-point number in scientific format. Stream manipulator fixed is used to output a floating-point number with the precision specified by the precision member function.

- Stream manipulator uppercase forces an uppercase X or E to be output with hexadecimal integers or with scientific-notation floating-point values, respectively. When set, uppercase causes all letters in a hexadecimal value to be uppercase.

- Member function flags with no argument returns the long value of the current format state settings. Function flags with a long argument sets the format state specified by the argument.

- The state of a stream may be tested through bits in class ios_base.

- The eofbit is set for an input stream after end-of-file is encountered during an input operation. The eof member function reports whether the eofbit has been set.

- The failbit is set for a stream when a format error occurs on the stream. The fail member function reports whether a stream operation has failed; it is normally possible to recover from such errors.

- The badbit is set for a stream when an error occurs that results in data loss. The bad member function reports whether such a stream operation failed. Such serious failures are normally non-recoverable.

- The good member function returns true if the bad, fail and eof functions would all return false. I/O operations should be performed only on "good" streams.
- The rdstate member function returns the error state of the stream.
- Member function clear restores a stream's state to "good," so that I/O may proceed on that stream.
- C++ provides the tie member function to synchronize istream and ostream operations to ensure that outputs appear before subsequent inputs.

Terminology

bad member function of basic_ios
badbit
basic_fstream class template
basic_ifstream class template
basic_ios class template
basic_iostream class template
basic_istream class template
basic_ofstream class template
basic_ostream class template
boolalpha stream manipulator
clear member function of basic_ios
dec stream manipulator
default fill character (space)
default precision
end-of-file
eof member function of basic_ios
eofbit
fail member function of basic_ios
failbit
field width
fill character
fill member function of basic_ios
fixed stream manipulator
flags member function of ios_base
fmtflags
format states
formatted I/O
fstream
gcount member function of basic_istream
get member function of basic_istream
getline member function of basic_istream
good member function of basic_ios
hex stream manipulator
ifstream
ignore member function of basic_istream
in-memory formatting
internal stream manipulator
<iomanip> header file
ios_base class
iostream

istream
leading 0 (octal)
leading 0x or 0X (hexadecimal)
left stream manipulator
noboolalpha stream manipulator
noshowbase stream manipulator
noshowpoint stream manipulator
noshowpos stream manipulator
noskipws stream manipulator
nouppercase stream manipulator
oct stream manipulator
ofstream
operator void* member function of basic_ios
operator! member function of basic_ios
ostream
output buffering
padding
parameterized stream manipulator
peek member function of basic_istream
precision member function of ios_base
predefined streams
put member function of basic_ostream
putback member function of basic_istream
rdstate member function of basic_ios
read member function of basic_istream
right stream manipulator
scientific stream manipulator
setbase stream manipulator
setfill stream manipulator
setprecision stream manipulator
setw stream manipulator
showbase stream manipulator
showpoint stream manipulator
showpos stream manipulator
skipws stream manipulator
stream input
stream manipulator
stream output
stream extraction operator (>>)
stream insertion operator (<<)

tie member function of `basic_ios`
`typedef`
type-safe I/O
unbuffered output

unformatted I/O
uppercase stream manipulator
`width` stream manipulator
`write` member function of `basic_ostream`

Self-Review Exercises

15.1 Answer each of the following:
  a) Input/output in C++ occurs as _____ of bytes.
  b) The stream manipulators that format justification are _____, _____ and _____.
  c) Member function _____ can be used to set and reset format state.
  d) Most C++ programs that do I/O should include the _____ header file that contains the declarations required for all stream-I/O operations.
  e) When using parameterized manipulators, the header file _____ must be included.
  f) Header file _____ contains the declarations required for user-controlled file processing.
  g) The `ostream` member function _____ is used to perform unformatted output.
  h) Input operations are supported by class _____.
  i) Outputs to the standard error stream are directed to either the _____ or the _____ stream object.
  j) Output operations are supported by class _____.
  k) The symbol for the stream insertion operator is _____.
  l) The four objects that correspond to the standard devices on the system include _____, _____, _____ and _____.
  m) The symbol for the stream extraction operator is _____.
  n) The stream manipulators _____, _____ and _____ specify that integers should be displayed in octal, hexadecimal and decimal formats, respectively.
  o) When used, the _____ stream manipulator causes positive numbers to display with a plus sign.

15.2 State whether the following are *true* or *false*. If the answer is *false*, explain why.
  a) The stream member function `flags` with a `long` argument sets the `flags` state variable to its argument and returns its previous value.
  b) The stream insertion operator `<<` and the stream-extraction operator `>>` are overloaded to handle all standard data types—including strings and memory addresses (stream-insertion only)—and all user-defined data types.
  c) The stream member function `flags` with no arguments resets the stream's format state.
  d) The stream extraction operator `>>` can be overloaded with an operator function that takes an `istream` reference and a reference to a user-defined type as arguments and returns an `istream` reference.
  e) The stream insertion operator `<<` can be overloaded with an operator function that takes an `istream` reference and a reference to a user-defined type as arguments and returns an `istream` reference.
  f) Input with the stream extraction operator `>>` always skips leading white-space characters in the input stream, by default.
  g) The stream member function `rdstate` returns the current state of the stream.
  h) The `cout` stream normally is connected to the display screen.
  i) The stream member function `good` returns `true` if the `bad`, `fail` and `eof` member functions all return `false`.
  j) The `cin` stream normally is connected to the display screen.

k) If a nonrecoverable error occurs during a stream operation, the bad member function will return true.

l) Output to cerr is unbuffered and output to clog is buffered.

m) Stream manipulator showpoint forces floating-point values to print with the default six digits of precision unless the precision value has been changed, in which case floating-point values print with the specified precision.

n) The ostream member function put outputs the specified number of characters.

o) The stream manipulators dec, oct and hex affect only the next integer output operation.

p) By default, memory addresses are displayed as long integers.

15.3   For each of the following, write a single statement that performs the indicated task.

a) Output the string "Enter your name: ".

b) Use a stream manipulator that causes the exponent in scientific notation and the letters in hexadecimal values to print in capital letters.

c) Output the address of the variable myString of type char *.

d) Use a stream manipulator to ensure floating-point values print in scientific notation.

e) Output the address in variable integerPtr of type int *.

f) Use a stream manipulator such that, when integer values are output, the integer base for octal and hexadecimal values is displayed.

g) Output the value pointed to by floatPtr of type float *.

h) Use a stream member function to set the fill character to '*' for printing in field widths larger than the values being output. Write a separate statement to do this with a stream manipulator.

i) Output the characters 'O' and 'K' in one statement with ostream function put.

j) Get the value of the next character in the input stream without extracting it from the stream.

k) Input a single character into variable charValue of type char, using the istream member function get in two different ways.

l) Input and discard the next six characters in the input stream.

m) Use istream member function read to input 50 characters into char array line.

n) Read 10 characters into character array name. Stop reading characters if the '.' delimiter is encountered. Do not remove the delimiter from the input stream. Write another statement that performs this task and removes the delimiter from the input.

o) Use the istream member function gcount to determine the number of characters input into character array line by the last call to istream member function read, and output that number of characters, using ostream member function write.

p) Output the following values: 124, 18.376, 'Z', 1000000 and "String".

q) Print the current precision setting, using a member function of object cout.

r) Input an integer value into int variable months and a floating-point value into float variable percentageRate.

s) Print 1.92, 1.925 and 1.9258 separated by tabs and with 3 digits of precision, using a manipulator.

t) Print integer 100 in octal, hexadecimal and decimal, using stream manipulators.

u) Print integer 100 in decimal, octal and hexadecimal, using a stream manipulator to change the base.

v) Print 1234 right justified in a 10-digit field.

w) Read characters into character array line until the character 'z' is encountered, up to a limit of 20 characters (including a terminating null character). Do not extract the delimiter character from the stream.

x) Use integer variables x and y to specify the field width and precision used to display the double value 87.4573, and display the value.

15.4 Identify the error in each of the following statements and explain how to correct it.

a) `cout << "Value of x <= y is: " << x <= y;`

b) The following statement should print the integer value of `'c'`.

`cout << 'c';`

c) `cout << ""A string in quotes"";`

15.5 For each of the following, show the output.

a) `cout << "12345" << endl;`

`cout.width( 5 );`

`cout.fill( '*' );`

`cout << 123 << endl << 123;`

b) `cout << setw( 10 ) << setfill( '$' ) << 10000;`

c) `cout << setw( 8 ) << setprecision( 3 ) << 1024.987654;`

d) `cout << showbase << oct << 99 << endl << hex << 99;`

e) `cout << 100000 << endl << showpos << 100000;`

f) `cout << setw( 10 ) << setprecision( 2 ) << scientific << 444.93738;`

Answers to Self-Review Exercises

15.1 a) streams. b) `left`, `right` and `internal`. c) flags. d) `<iostream>`. e) `<iomanip>`. f) `<fstream>`. g) `write`. h) istream. i) `cerr` or `clog`. j) ostream. k) `<<`. l) cin, cout, cerr and clog. m) `>>`. n) oct, hex and dec. o) showpos.

15.2 a) False. The stream member function `flags` with a `fmtflags` argument sets the `flags` state variable to its argument and returns the prior state settings. b) False. The stream insertion and stream extraction operators are not overloaded for all user-defined types. The programmer of a class must specifically provide the overloaded operator functions to overload the stream operators for use with each user-defined type. c) False. The stream member function `flags` with no arguments returns the current format settings as a `fmtflags` data type, which represents the format state. d) True. e) False. To overload the stream insertion operator `<<`, the overloaded operator function must take an `ostream` reference and a reference to a user-defined type as arguments and return an `ostream` reference. f) True. g) True. h) True. i) True. j) False. The `cin` stream is connected to the standard input of the computer, which normally is the keyboard. k) True. l) True. m) True. n) False. The `ostream` member function `put` outputs its single-character argument. o) False. The stream manipulators `dec`, `oct` and `hex` set the output format state for integers to the specified base until the base is changed again or the program terminates. p) False. Memory addresses are displayed in hexadecimal format by default. To display addresses as `long` integers, the address must be cast to a `long` value.

15.3 a) `cout << "Enter your name: ";`

b) `cout << uppercase;`

c) `cout << static_cast< void * >( myString );`

d) `cout << scientific;`

e) `cout << integerPtr;`

f) `cout << showbase;`

g) `cout << *floatPtr;`

h) `cout.fill( '*' );`

`cout << setfill( '*' );`

i) `cout.put( 'O' ).put( 'K' );`

j) `cin.peek();`

k) `charValue = cin.get();`

`cin.get( charValue );`

l) `cin.ignore( 6 );`

m) `cin.read( line, 50 );`

n) `cin.get( name, 10, '.' );`
   `cin.getline( name, 10, '.' );`
o) `cout.write( line, cin.gcount() );`
p) `cout << 124 << ' ' << 18.376 << ' ' << "Z " << 1000000 << " String";`
q) `cout << cout.precision();`
r) `cin >> months >> percentageRate;`
s) `cout << setprecision( 3 ) << 1.92 << '\t' << 1.925 << '\t' << 1.9258;`
t) `cout << oct << 100 << '\t' << hex << 100 << '\t' << dec << 100;`
u) `cout << 100 << '\t' << setbase( 8 ) << 100 << '\t' << setbase( 16 ) << 100;`
v) `cout << setw( 10 ) << 1234;`
w) `cin.get( line, 20, 'z' );`
x) `cout << setw( x ) << setprecision( y ) << 87.4573;`

15.4 a) Error: The precedence of the << operator is higher than that of <=, which causes the statement to be evaluated improperly and also causes a compiler error.
Correction: To correct the statement, place parentheses around the expression x <= y. This problem will occur with any expression that uses operators of lower precedence than the << operator if the expression is not placed in parentheses.

b) Error: In C++, characters are not treated as small integers, as they are in C.
Correction: To print the numerical value for a character in the computer's character set, the character must be cast to an integer value, as in the following:
   `cout << static_cast< int >( 'c' );`

c) Error: Quote characters cannot be printed in a string unless an escape sequence is used.
Correction: Print the string in one of the following ways:
   `cout << '"' << "A string in quotes" << '"';`
   `cout << "\"A string in quotes\"";`

15.5 a) 12345
   **123
   123
b) $$$$$10000
c) 1024.988
d) 0143
   0x63
e) 100000
   +100000
f)   4.45e+002

Exercises

15.6 Write a statement for each of the following:
   a) Print integer 40000 left justified in a 15-digit field.
   b) Read a string into character array variable `state`.
   c) Print 200 with and without a sign.
   d) Print the decimal value 100 in hexadecimal form preceded by 0x.
   e) Read characters into array `charArray` until the character `'p'` is encountered, up to a limit of 10 characters (including the terminating null character). Extract the delimiter from the input stream, and discard it.
   f) Print 1.234 in a 9-digit field with preceding zeros.
   g) Read a string of the form "characters" from the standard input. Store the string in character array `charArray`. Eliminate the quotation marks from the input stream. Read a maximum of 50 characters (including the terminating null character).

15.7   Write a program to test the inputting of integer values in decimal, octal and hexadecimal formats. Output each integer read by the program in all three formats. Test the program with the following input data: 10, 010, 0x10.

15.8   Write a program that prints pointer values, using casts to all the integer data types. Which ones print strange values? Which ones cause errors?

15.9   Write a program to test the results of printing the integer value 12345 and the floating-point value 1.2345 in various-sized fields. What happens when the values are printed in fields containing fewer digits than the values?

15.10   Write a program that prints the value 100.453627 rounded to the nearest digit, tenth, hundredth, thousandth and ten-thousandth.

15.11   Write a program that inputs a string from the keyboard and determines the length of the string. Print the string in a length that is twice the field width.

15.12   Write a program that converts integer Fahrenheit temperatures from 0 to 212 degrees to floating-point Celsius temperatures with 3 digits of precision. Use the formula

```
celsius = 5.0 / 9.0 * ( fahrenheit - 32 );
```

to perform the calculation. The output should be printed in two right justified columns and the Celsius temperatures should be preceded by a sign for both positive and negative values.

15.13   In some programming languages, strings are entered surrounded by either single or double quotation marks. Write a program that reads the three strings suzy, "suzy" and 'suzy'. Are the single and double quotes ignored or read as part of the string?

15.14   In Fig. 11.5, the stream extraction and stream insertion operators were overloaded for input and output of objects of the PhoneNumber class. Rewrite the stream extraction operator to perform the following error checking on input. The operator>> function will need to be reimplemented.

   a) Input the entire phone number into an array. Test that the proper number of characters has been entered. There should be a total of 14 characters read for a phone number of the form (800) 555-1212. Use ios_base-member-function clear to set failbit for improper input.

   b) The area code and exchange do not begin with 0 or 1. Test the first digit of the area-code and exchange portions of the phone number to be sure that neither begins with 0 or 1. Use ios_base-member-function clear to set failbit for improper input.

   c) The middle digit of an area code used to be limited to 0 or 1 (although this has changed recently). Test the middle digit for a value of 0 or 1. Use the ios_base-member-function clear to set failbit for improper input. If none of the above operations results in failbit being set for improper input, copy the three parts of the telephone number into the areaCode, exchange and line members of the PhoneNumber object. In the main program, if failbit has been set on the input, have the program print an error message and end, rather than print the phone number.

15.15   Write a program that accomplishes each of the following:

   a) Create a user-defined class Point that contains the private integer data members xCoordinate and yCoordinate and declares stream insertion and stream extraction overloaded operator functions as friends of the class.

   b) Define the stream insertion and stream extraction operator functions. The stream extraction operator function should determine whether the data entered is valid, and, if not, it should set the failbit to indicate improper input. The stream insertion operator should not be able to display the point after an input error occurred.

   c) Write a main function that tests input and output of user-defined class Point, using the overloaded stream extraction and stream insertion operators.

15.16 Write a program that accomplishes each of the following:

a) Create a user-defined class `Complex` that contains the private integer data members `real` and `imaginary` and declares stream insertion and stream extraction overloaded operator functions as `friends` of the class.

b) Define the stream insertion and stream extraction operator functions. The stream extraction operator function should determine whether the data entered is valid, and, if not, it should set `failbit` to indicate improper input. The input should be of the form

```
3 + 8i
```

c) The values can be negative or positive, and it is possible that one of the two values is not provided. If a value is not provided, the appropriate data member should be set to 0. The stream-insertion operator should not be able to display the point if an input error occurred. For negative imaginary values, a minus sign should be printed rather than a plus sign.

d) Write a `main` function that tests input and output of user-defined class `Complex`, using the overloaded stream extraction and stream insertion operators.

15.17 Write a program that uses a `for` statement to print a table of ASCII values for the characters in the ASCII character set from 33 to 126. The program should print the decimal value, octal value, hexadecimal value and character value for each character. Use the stream manipulators `dec`, `oct` and `hex` to print the integer values.

15.18 Write a program to show that the `getline` and three-argument `get` `istream` member functions both end the input string with a string-terminating null character. Also, show that `get` leaves the delimiter character on the input stream, whereas `getline` extracts the delimiter character and discards it. What happens to the unread characters in the stream?

16

Exception Handling

OBJECTIVES

In this chapter you will learn:

- What exceptions are and when to use them.

- To use **try**, **catch** and **throw** to detect, handle and indicate exceptions, respectively.

- To process uncaught and unexpected exceptions.

- To declare new exception classes.

- How stack unwinding enables exceptions not caught in one scope to be caught in another scope.

- To handle **new** failures.

- To use **auto_ptr** to prevent memory leaks.

- To understand the standard exception hierarchy.

I never forget a face, but in your case I'll make an exception.
—Groucho Marx

It is common sense to take a method and try it. If it fails, admit it frankly and try another. But above all, try something.
—Franklin Delano Roosevelt

O! throw away the worser part of it, And live the purer with the other half.
—William Shakespeare

If they're running and they don't look where they're going I have to come out from somewhere and catch them.
—Jerome David Salinger

O infinite virtue! com'st thou smiling from the world's great snare uncaught?
—William Shakespeare

16.1 **Introduction**

In this chapter, we introduce exception handling. An exception is an indication of a problem that occurs during a program's execution. The name "exception" implies that the problem occurs infrequently—if the "rule" is that a statement normally executes correctly, then the "exception to the rule" is that a problem occurs. Exception handling enables programmers to create applications that can resolve (or handle) exceptions. In many cases, handling an exception allows a program to continue executing as if no problem had been encountered. A more severe problem could prevent a program from continuing normal execution, instead requiring the program to notify the user of the problem before terminating in a controlled manner. The features presented in this chapter enable programmers to write robust and fault-tolerant programs that are able to deal with problems that may arise and continue executing or terminate gracefully. The style and details of C++ exception handling are based in part on the work of Andrew Koenig and Bjarne Stroustrup, as presented in their paper, "Exception Handling for C++ (revised)."[1]

Error-Prevention Tip 16.1

Exception handling helps improve a program's fault tolerance.

Software Engineering Observation 16.1

Exception handling provides a standard mechanism for processing errors. This is especially important when working on a project with a large team of programmers.

---

1. Koenig, A., and B. Stroustrup, "Exception Handling for C++ (revised)," *Proceedings of the Usenix C++ Conference*, pp. 149–176, San Francisco, April 1990.

The chapter begins with an overview of exception-handling concepts, then demonstrates basic exception-handling techniques. We show these techniques via an example that demonstrates handling an exception that occurs when a function attempts to divide by zero. We then discuss additional exception-handling issues, such as how to handle exceptions that occur in a constructor or destructor and how to handle exceptions that occur if operator new fails to allocate memory for an object. We conclude the chapter by introducing several classes that the C++ Standard Library provides for handling exceptions.

16.2 Exception-Handling Overview

Program logic frequently tests conditions that determine how program execution proceeds. Consider the following pseudocode:

> *Perform a task*
>
> *If the preceding task did not execute correctly*
> *   Perform error processing*
>
> *Perform next task*
>
> *If the preceding task did not execute correctly*
> *   Perform error processing*
>
> *. . .*

In this pseudocode, we begin by performing a task. We then test whether that task executed correctly. If not, we perform error processing. Otherwise, we continue with the next task. Although this form of error handling works, intermixing program logic with error-handling logic can make the program difficult to read, modify, maintain and debug—especially in large applications.

> **Performance Tip 16.1**
>
> *If the potential problems occur infrequently, intermixing program logic and error-handling logic can degrade a program's performance, because the program must (potentially frequently) perform tests to determine whether the task executed correctly and the next task can be performed.*

Exception handling enables the programmer to remove error-handling code from the "main line" of the program's execution, which improves program clarity and enhances modifiability. Programmers can decide to handle any exceptions they choose—all exceptions, all exceptions of a certain type or all exceptions of a group of related types (e.g., exception types that belong to an inheritance hierarchy). Such flexibility reduces the likelihood that errors will be overlooked and thereby makes a program more robust.

With programming languages that do not support exception handling, programmers often delay writing error-processing code or sometimes forget to include it. This results in less robust software products. C++ enables the programmer to deal with exception handling easily from the inception of a project.

16.3 Example: Handling an Attempt to Divide by Zero

Let us consider a simple example of exception handling (Figs. 16.1–16.2). The purpose of this example is to prevent a common arithmetic problem—division by zero. In C++, division by zero using integer arithmetic typically causes a program to terminate prematurely. In floating-point arithmetic, division by zero is allowed—it results in positive or negative infinity, which is displayed as INF or -INF.

In this example, we define a function named quotient that receives two integers input by the user and divides its first int parameter by its second int parameter. Before performing the division, the function casts the first int parameter's value to type double. Then, the second int parameter's value is promoted to type double for the calculation. So function quotient actually performs the division using two double values and returns a double result.

Although division by zero is allowed in floating-point arithmetic, for the purpose of this example, we treat any attempt to divide by zero as an error. Thus, function quotient tests its second parameter to ensure that it is not zero before allowing the division to proceed. If the second parameter is zero, the function uses an exception to indicate to the caller that a problem occurred. The caller (main in this example) can then process this exception and allow the user to type two new values before calling function quotient again. In this way, the program can continue to execute even after an improper value is entered, thus making the program more robust.

The example consists of two files—DivideByZeroException.h (Fig. 16.1) defines an exception class that represents the type of the problem that might occur in the example, and fig16_02.cpp (Fig. 16.2) defines the quotient function and the main function that calls it. Function main contains the code that demonstrates exception handling.

Defining an Exception Class to Represent the Type of Problem That Might Occur

Figure 16.1 defines class DivideByZeroException as a derived class of Standard Library class **runtime_error** (defined in header file **<stdexcept>**). Class runtime_error—a derived class of Standard Library class **exception** (defined in header file **<exception>**)—is the C++ standard base class for representing runtime errors. Class exception is the standard C++ base class for all exceptions. (Section 16.13 discusses class exception and its derived classes in detail.) A typical exception class that derives from the runtime_error class defines only a constructor (e.g., lines 12–13) that passes an error-message string to the base-class runtime_error constructor. Every exception class that derives directly or indirectly

```
 1   // Fig. 16.1: DivideByZeroException.h
 2   // Class DivideByZeroException definition.
 3   #include <stdexcept> // stdexcept header file contains runtime_error
 4   using std::runtime_error; // standard C++ library class runtime_error
 5
 6   // DivideByZeroException objects should be thrown by functions
 7   // upon detecting division-by-zero exceptions
 8   class DivideByZeroException : public runtime_error
 9   {
10   public:
11      // constructor specifies default error message
12      DivideByZeroException::DivideByZeroException()
13         : runtime_error( "attempted to divide by zero" ) {}
14   }; // end class DivideByZeroException
```

Fig. 16.1 | Class DivideByZeroException definition.

```
1   // Fig. 16.2: Fig16_02.cpp
2   // A simple exception-handling example that checks for
3   // divide-by-zero exceptions.
4   #include <iostream>
5   using std::cin;
6   using std::cout;
7   using std::endl;
8
9   #include "DivideByZeroException.h" // DivideByZeroException class
10
11  // perform division and throw DivideByZeroException object if
12  // divide-by-zero exception occurs
13  double quotient( int numerator, int denominator )
14  {
15     // throw DivideByZeroException if trying to divide by zero
16     if ( denominator == 0 )
17        throw DivideByZeroException(); // terminate function
18
19     // return division result
20     return static_cast< double >( numerator ) / denominator;
21  } // end function quotient
22
23  int main()
24  {
25     int number1; // user-specified numerator
26     int number2; // user-specified denominator
27     double result; // result of division
28
29     cout << "Enter two integers (end-of-file to end): ";
30
31     // enable user to enter two integers to divide
32     while ( cin >> number1 >> number2 )
33     {
34        // try block contains code that might throw exception
35        // and code that should not execute if an exception occurs
36        try
37        {
38           result = quotient( number1, number2 );
39           cout << "The quotient is: " << result << endl;
40        } // end try
41
42        // exception handler handles a divide-by-zero exception
43        catch ( DivideByZeroException &divideByZeroException )
44        {
45           cout << "Exception occurred: "
46              << divideByZeroException.what() << endl;
47        } // end catch
48
49        cout << "\nEnter two integers (end-of-file to end): ";
50     } // end while
51
```

Fig. 16.2 | Exception-handling example that throws exceptions on attempts to divide by zero. (Part 1 of 2.)

```
52        cout << endl;
53        return 0; // terminate normally
54    } // end main
```

```
Enter two integers (end-of-file to end): 100 7
The quotient is: 14.2857

Enter two integers (end-of-file to end): 100 0
Exception occurred: attempted to divide by zero

Enter two integers (end-of-file to end): ^Z
```

Fig. 16.2 | Exception-handling example that throws exceptions on attempts to divide by zero. (Part 2 of 2.)

from exception contains the virtual function what, which returns an exception object's error message. Note that you are not required to derive a custom exception class, such as DivideByZeroException, from the standard exception classes provided by C++. However, doing so allows programmers to use the virtual function what to obtain an appropriate error message. We use an object of this DivideByZeroException class in Fig. 16.2 to indicate when an attempt is made to divide by zero.

Demonstrating Exception Handling
The program in Fig. 16.2 uses exception handling to wrap code that might throw a "divide-by-zero" exception and to handle that exception, should one occur. The application enables the user to enter two integers, which are passed as arguments to function quotient (lines 13–21). This function divides the first number (numerator) by the second number (denominator). Assuming that the user does not specify 0 as the denominator for the division, function quotient returns the division result. However, if the user inputs a 0 value as the denominator, function quotient throws an exception. In the sample output, the first two lines show a successful calculation, and the next two lines show a failed calculation due to an attempt to divide by zero. When the exception occurs, the program informs the user of the mistake and prompts the user to input two new integers. After we discuss the code, we will consider the user inputs and flow of program control that yield these outputs.

Enclosing Code in a try Block
The program begins by prompting the user to enter two integers. The integers are input in the condition of the while loop (line 32). After the user inputs values that represent the numerator and denominator, program control proceeds into the loop's body (lines 33–50). Line 38 passes these values to function quotient (lines 13–21), which either divides the integers and returns a result, or throws an exception (i.e., indicates that an error occurred) on an attempt to divide by zero. Exception handling is geared to situations in which the function that detects an error is unable to handle it.

   C++ provides try blocks to enable exception handling. A try block consists of keyword try followed by braces ({}) that define a block of code in which exceptions might occur. The try block encloses statements that might cause exceptions and statements that should be skipped if an exception occurs.

Note that a try block (lines 36–40) encloses the invocation of function `quotient` and the statement that displays the division result. In this example, because the invocation to function `quotient` (line 38) can throw an exception, we enclose this function invocation in a try block. Enclosing the output statement (line 39) in the try block ensures that the output will occur only if function `quotient` returns a result.

Software Engineering Observation 16.2

Exceptions may surface through explicitly mentioned code in a try block, through calls to other functions and through deeply nested function calls initiated by code in a try block.

Defining a *catch* Handler to Process a *DivideByZeroException*

Exceptions are processed by catch handlers (also called exception handlers), which catch and handle exceptions. At least one catch handler (lines 43–47) must immediately follow each try block. Each catch handler begins with the keyword catch and specifies in parentheses an exception parameter that represents the type of exception the catch handler can process (`DivideByZeroException` in this case). When an exception occurs in a try block, the catch handler that executes is the one whose type matches the type of the exception that occurred (i.e., the type in the catch block matches the thrown exception type exactly or is a base class of it). If an exception parameter includes an optional parameter name, the catch handler can use that parameter name to interact with a caught exception object in the body of the catch handler, which is delimited by braces ({ and }). A catch handler typically reports the error to the user, logs it to a file, terminates the program gracefully or tries an alternate strategy to accomplish the failed task. In this example, the catch handler simply reports that the user attempted to divide by zero. Then the program prompts the user to enter two new integer values.

Common Programming Error 16.1

It is a syntax error to place code between a try block and its corresponding catch handlers.

Common Programming Error 16.2

Each catch handler can have only a single parameter—specifying a comma-separated list of exception parameters is a syntax error.

Common Programming Error 16.3

It is a logic error to catch the same type in two different catch handlers following a single try block.

Termination Model of Exception Handling

If an exception occurs as the result of a statement in a try block, the try block expires (i.e., terminates immediately). Next, the program searches for the first catch handler that can process the type of exception that occurred. The program locates the matching catch by comparing the thrown exception's type to each catch's exception-parameter type until the program finds a match. A match occurs if the types are identical or if the thrown exception's type is a derived class of the exception-parameter type. When a match occurs, the code contained within the matching catch handler executes. When a catch handler finishes processing by reaching its closing right brace (}), the exception is considered handled and the local variables defined within the catch handler (including the catch parameter) go out of scope. Program control does not return to the point at which the exception occurred (known as the throw point), because the try block has expired. Rather, control resumes with the first statement (line 49) after the last catch handler following the try block. This is known as the termination model of exception handling. [*Note:* Some languages use the resumption model of exception handling, in which, after an exception is handled, control resumes just after the throw point.] As with any other block of code, when a try block terminates, local variables defined in the block go out of scope.

Common Programming Error 16.4

Logic errors can occur if you assume that after an exception is handled, control will return to the first statement after the throw point.

Error-Prevention Tip 16.2

With exception handling, a program can continue executing (rather than terminating) after dealing with a problem. This helps ensure the kind of robust applications that contribute to what is called mission-critical computing or business-critical computing.

If the try block completes its execution successfully (i.e., no exceptions occur in the try block), then the program ignores the catch handlers and program control continues with the first statement after the last catch following that try block. If no exceptions occur in a try block, the program ignores the catch handler(s) for that block.

If an exception that occurs in a try block has no matching catch handler, or if an exception occurs in a statement that is not in a try block, the function that contains the statement terminates immediately, and the program attempts to locate an enclosing try block in the calling function. This process is called stack unwinding and is discussed in Section 16.8.

Flow of Program Control When the User Enters a Nonzero Denominator
Consider the flow of control when the user inputs the numerator 100 and the denominator 7 (i.e., the first two lines of output in Fig. 16.2). In line 16, function quotient determines that the denominator does not equal zero, so line 20 performs the division and returns the result (14.2857) to line 38 as a double (the static_cast< double > in line 20 ensures the proper return value type). Program control then continues sequentially from line 38, so line 39 displays the division result and line 40 is the end of the try block. Because the try block completed successfully and did not throw an exception, the program does not execute the statements contained in the catch handler (lines 43–47), and control continues to line 49 (the first line of code after the catch handler), which prompts the user to enter two more integers.

Flow of Program Control When the User Enters a Denominator of Zero
Now let us consider a more interesting case in which the user inputs the numerator 100 and the denominator 0 (i.e., the third and fourth lines of output in Fig. 16.2). In line 16, quotient determines that the denominator equals zero, which indicates an attempt to di-

vide by zero. Line 17 throws an exception, which we represent as an object of class DivideByZeroException (Fig. 16.1).

Note that, to throw an exception, line 17 uses keyword `throw` followed by an operand that represents the type of exception to throw. Normally, a `throw` statement specifies one operand. (In Section 16.5, we discuss how to use a `throw` statement that specifies no operands.) The operand of a `throw` can be of any type. If the operand is an object, we call it an *exception object*—in this example, the exception object is an object of type DivideByZeroException. However, a `throw` operand also can assume other values, such as the value of an expression (e.g., `throw x > 5`) or the value of an `int` (e.g., `throw 5`). The examples in this chapter focus exclusively on throwing exception objects.

Common Programming Error 16.5

Use caution when `throwing` the result of a conditional expression (`?:`), because promotion rules could cause the value to be of a type different from the one expected. For example, when throwing an `int` or a `double` from the same conditional expression, the conditional expression converts the `int` to a `double`. However, the `catch` handler always catches the result as a `double`, rather than catching the result as a `double` when a `double` is thrown, and catching the result as an `int` when an `int` is thrown.

As part of throwing an exception, the `throw` operand is created and used to initialize the parameter in the `catch` handler, which we discuss momentarily. In this example, the `throw` statement in line 17 creates an object of class DivideByZeroException. When line 17 throws the exception, function `quotient` exits immediately. Therefore, line 17 throws the exception before function `quotient` can perform the division in line 20. This is a central characteristic of exception handling: A function should throw an exception *before* the error has an opportunity to occur.

Because we decided to enclose the invocation of function `quotient` (line 38) in a `try` block, program control enters the `catch` handler (lines 43–47) that immediately follows the `try` block. This `catch` handler serves as the exception handler for the divide-by-zero exception. In general, when an exception is thrown within a `try` block, the exception is caught by a `catch` handler that specifies the type matching the thrown exception. In this program, the `catch` handler specifies that it catches DivideByZeroException objects— this type matches the object type thrown in function `quotient`. Actually, the `catch` handler catches a reference to the DivideByZeroException object created by function `quotient`'s `throw` statement (line 17).

Performance Tip 16.2

Catching an exception object by reference eliminates the overhead of copying the object that represents the thrown exception.

Good Programming Practice 16.1

Associating each type of runtime error with an appropriately named exception object improves program clarity.

The `catch` handler's body (lines 45–46) prints the associated error message returned by calling function `what` of base-class `runtime_error`. This function returns the string that the DivideByZeroException constructor (lines 12–13 in Fig. 16.1) passed to the `runtime_error` base-class constructor.

16.4 **When to Use Exception Handling**

Exception handling is designed to process synchronous errors, which occur when a statement executes. Common examples of these errors are out-of-range array subscripts, arithmetic overflow (i.e., a value outside the representable range of values), division by zero, invalid function parameters and unsuccessful memory allocation (due to lack of memory). Exception handling is not designed to process errors associated with asynchronous events (e.g., disk I/O completions, network message arrivals, mouse clicks and keystrokes), which occur in parallel with, and independent of, the program's flow of control.

Software Engineering Observation 16.3

Incorporate your exception-handling strategy into your system from the design process's inception. Including effective exception handling after a system has been implemented can be difficult.

Software Engineering Observation 16.4

Exception handling provides a single, uniform technique for processing problems. This helps programmers working on large projects understand each other's error-processing code.

Software Engineering Observation 16.5

Avoid using exception handling as an alternate form of flow of control. These "additional" exceptions can "get in the way" of genuine error-type exceptions.

Software Engineering Observation 16.6

Exception handling simplifies combining software components and enables them to work together effectively by enabling predefined components to communicate problems to application-specific components, which can then process the problems in an application-specific manner.

The exception-handling mechanism also is useful for processing problems that occur when a program interacts with software elements, such as member functions, constructors, destructors and classes. Rather than handling problems internally, such software elements often use exceptions to notify programs when problems occur. This enables programmers to implement customized error handling for each application.

Performance Tip 16.3

When no exceptions occur, exception-handling code incurs little or no performance penalties. Thus, programs that implement exception handling operate more efficiently than do programs that intermix error-handling code with program logic.

Software Engineering Observation 16.7

Functions with common error conditions should return 0 or NULL (or other appropriate values) rather than throw exceptions. A program calling such a function can check the return value to determine success or failure of the function call.

Complex applications normally consist of predefined software components and application-specific components that use the predefined components. When a predefined component encounters a problem, that component needs a mechanism to communicate the problem to the application-specific component—the predefined component cannot know in advance how each application processes a problem that occurs.

16.5 **Rethrowing an Exception**

It is possible that an exception handler, upon receiving an exception, might decide either that it cannot process that exception or that it can process the exception only partially. In such cases, the exception handler can defer the exception handling (or perhaps a portion of it) to another exception handler. In either case, the handler achieves this by rethrowing the exception via the statement

```
throw;
```

Regardless of whether a handler can process (even partially) an exception, the handler can rethrow the exception for further processing outside the handler. The next enclosing try block detects the rethrown exception, which a catch handler listed after that enclosing try block attempts to handle.

Common Programming Error 16.6

Executing an empty throw statement that is situated outside a catch handler causes a call to function terminate, which abandons exception processing and terminates the program immediately.

The program of Fig. 16.3 demonstrates rethrowing an exception. In main's try block (lines 32–37), line 35 calls function throwException (lines 11–27). The throwException

```
 1   // Fig. 16.3: Fig16_03.cpp
 2   // Demonstrating exception rethrowing.
 3   #include <iostream>
 4   using std::cout;
 5   using std::endl;
 6
 7   #include <exception>
 8   using std::exception;
 9
10   // throw, catch and rethrow exception
11   void throwException()
12   {
13      // throw exception and catch it immediately
14      try
15      {
16         cout << " Function throwException throws an exception\n";
17         throw exception(); // generate exception
18      } // end try
19      catch ( exception & ) // handle exception
20      {
21         cout << " Exception handled in function throwException"
22            << "\n Function throwException rethrows exception";
23         throw; // rethrow exception for further processing
24      } // end catch
25
26      cout << "This also should not print\n";
27   } // end function throwException
28
```

Fig. 16.3 | Rethrowing an exception. (Part 1 of 2.)

```
29   int main()
30   {
31      // throw exception
32      try
33      {
34         cout << "\nmain invokes function throwException\n";
35         throwException();
36         cout << "This should not print\n";
37      } // end try
38      catch ( exception & ) // handle exception
39      {
40         cout << "\n\nException handled in main\n";
41      } // end catch
42
43      cout << "Program control continues after catch in main\n";
44      return 0;
45   } // end main
```

```
main invokes function throwException
  Function throwException throws an exception
  Exception handled in function throwException
  Function throwException rethrows exception

Exception handled in main
Program control continues after catch in main
```

Fig. 16.3 | Rethrowing an exception. (Part 2 of 2.)

function also contains a try block (lines 14–18), from which the throw statement at line 17 throws an instance of standard-library-class exception. Function throwException's catch handler (lines 19–24) catches this exception, prints an error message (lines 21–22) and rethrows the exception (line 23). This terminates function throwException and returns control to line 35 in the try...catch block in main. The try block terminates (so line 36 does not execute), and the catch handler in main (lines 38–41) catches this exception and prints an error message (line 40). [*Note:* Since we do not use the exception parameters in the catch handlers of this example, we omit the exception parameter names and specify only the type of exception to catch (lines 19 and 38).]

16.6 Exception Specifications

An optional exception specification (also called a throw list) enumerates a list of exceptions that a function can throw. For example, consider the function declaration

```
int someFunction( double value )
   throw ( ExceptionA, ExceptionB, ExceptionC )
{
   // function body
}
```

In this definition, the exception specification, which begins with keyword throw immediately following the closing parenthesis of the function's parameter list, indicates that function someFunction can throw exceptions of types ExceptionA, ExceptionB and ExceptionC. A function can throw only exceptions of the types indicated by the specification or exceptions of any type derived from these types. If the function throws an exception that does not belong to a specified type, function unexpected is called, which normally terminates the program.

A function that does not provide an exception specification can throw any exception. Placing throw()—an empty exception specification—after a function's parameter list states that the function does not throw exceptions. If the function attempts to throw an exception, function unexpected is invoked. Section 16.7 shows how function unexpected can be customized by calling function set_unexpected.

Common Programming Error 16.7

Throwing an exception that has not been declared in a function's exception specification causes a call to function unexpected.

Error-Prevention Tip 16.3

The compiler will not generate a compilation error if a function contains a throw expression for an exception not listed in the function's exception specification. An error occurs only when that function attempts to throw that exception at execution time. To avoid surprises at execution time, carefully check your code to ensure that functions do not throw exceptions not listed in their exception specifications.

16.7 Processing Unexpected Exceptions

Function unexpected calls the function registered with function set_unexpected (defined in header file <exception>). If no function has been registered in this manner, function terminate is called by default. Cases in which function terminate is called include:

1. the exception mechanism cannot find a matching catch for a thrown exception

2. a destructor attempts to throw an exception during stack unwinding

3. an attempt is made to rethrow an exception when there is no exception currently being handled

4. a call to function unexpected defaults to calling function terminate

(Section 15.5.1 of the C++ Standard Document discusses several additional cases.) Function set_terminate can specify the function to invoke when terminate is called. Otherwise, terminate calls abort, which terminates the program without calling the destructors of any remaining objects of automatic or static storage class. This could lead to resource leaks when a program terminates prematurely.

Function set_terminate and function set_unexpected each return a pointer to the last function called by terminate and unexpected, respectively (0, the first time each is called). This enables the programmer to save the function pointer so it can be restored later. Functions set_terminate and set_unexpected take as arguments pointers to functions with void return types and no arguments.

If the last action of a programmer-defined termination function is not to exit a program, function abort will be called to end program execution after the other statements of the programmer-defined termination function are executed.

16.8 **Stack Unwinding**

When an exception is thrown but not caught in a particular scope, the function call stack is unwound, and an attempt is made to catch the exception in the next outer try...catch block. Unwinding the function call stack means that the function in which the exception was not caught terminates, all local variables in that function are destroyed and control returns to the statement that originally invoked that function. If a try block encloses that statement, an attempt is made to catch the exception. If a try block does not enclose that statement, stack unwinding occurs again. If no catch handler ever catches this exception, function terminate is called to terminate the program. The program of Fig. 16.4 demonstrates stack unwinding.

In main, the try block (lines 37–41) calls function1 (lines 27–31). Next, function1 calls function2 (lines 20–24), which in turn calls function3 (lines 11–17). Line 16 of function3 throws a runtime_error object. However, because no try block encloses the throw statement in line 16, stack unwinding occurs—function3 terminates at line 16, then returns control to the statement in function2 that invoked function3 (i.e., line 23). Because no try block encloses line 23, stack unwinding occurs again—function2 termi-

```cpp
1   // Fig. 16.4: Fig16_04.cpp
2   // Demonstrating stack unwinding.
3   #include <iostream>
4   using std::cout;
5   using std::endl;
6
7   #include <stdexcept>
8   using std::runtime_error;
9
10  // function3 throws run-time error
11  void function3() throw ( runtime_error )
12  {
13     cout << "In function 3" << endl;
14
15     // no try block, stack unwinding occur, return control to function2
16     throw runtime_error( "runtime_error in function3" );
17  } // end function3
18
19  // function2 invokes function3
20  void function2() throw ( runtime_error )
21  {
22     cout << "function3 is called inside function2" << endl;
23     function3(); // stack unwinding occur, return control to function1
24  } // end function2
25
26  // function1 invokes function2
27  void function1() throw ( runtime_error )
28  {
29     cout << "function2 is called inside function1" << endl;
30     function2(); // stack unwinding occur, return control to main
31  } // end function1
32
```

Fig. 16.4 | Stack unwinding. (Part 1 of 2.)

```
33  // demonstrate stack unwinding
34  int main()
35  {
36     // invoke function1
37     try
38     {
39        cout << "function1 is called inside main" << endl;
40        function1(); // call function1 which throws runtime_error
41     } // end try
42     catch ( runtime_error &error ) // handle run-time error
43     {
44        cout << "Exception occurred: " << error.what() << endl;
45        cout << "Exception handled in main" << endl;
46     } // end catch
47
48     return 0;
49  } // end main
```

```
function1 is called inside main
function2 is called inside function1
function3 is called inside function2
In function 3
Exception occurred: runtime_error in function3
Exception handled in main
```

Fig. 16.4 | Stack unwinding. (Part 2 of 2.)

nates at line 23 and returns control to the statement in function1 that invoked function2 (i.e., line 30). Because no try block encloses line 30, stack unwinding occurs one more time—function1 terminates at line 30 and returns control to the statement in main that invoked function1 (i.e., line 40). The try block of lines 37–41 encloses this statement, so the first matching catch handler located after this try block (line 42–46) catches and processes the exception. Line 44 uses function what to display the exception message. Recall that function what is a virtual function of class exception that can be overridden by a derived class to return an appropriate error message.

16.9 Constructors, Destructors and Exception Handling

First, let us discuss an issue that we have mentioned but not yet resolved satisfactorily: What happens when an error is detected in a constructor? For example, how should an object's constructor respond when new fails because it was unable to allocate required memory for storing that object's internal representation? Because the constructor cannot return a value to indicate an error, we must choose an alternative means of indicating that the object has not been constructed properly. One scheme is to return the improperly constructed object and hope that anyone using it would make appropriate tests to determine that it is in an inconsistent state. Another scheme is to set some variable outside the constructor. Perhaps the best alternative is to require the constructor to throw an exception that contains the error information, thus offering an opportunity for the program to handle the failure.

Exceptions thrown by a constructor cause destructors to be called for any objects built as part of the object being constructed before the exception is thrown. Destructors are called for every automatic object constructed in a try block before an exception is thrown. Stack unwinding is guaranteed to have been completed at the point that an exception handler begins executing. If a destructor invoked as a result of stack unwinding throws an exception, terminate is called.

If an object has member objects, and if an exception is thrown before the outer object is fully constructed, then destructors will be executed for the member objects that have been constructed prior to the occurrence of the exception. If an array of objects has been partially constructed when an exception occurs, only the destructors for the constructed objects in the array will be called.

An exception could preclude the operation of code that would normally release a resource, thus causing a resource leak. One technique to resolve this problem is to initialize a local object to acquire the resource. When an exception occurs, the destructor for that object will be invoked and can free the resource.

Error-Prevention Tip 16.4

When an exception is thrown from the constructor for an object that is created in a new expression, the dynamically allocated memory for that object is released.

16.10 Exceptions and Inheritance

Various exception classes can be derived from a common base class, as we discussed in Section 16.3, when we created class DivideByZeroException as a derived class of class exception. If a catch handler catches a pointer or reference to an exception object of a base-class type, it also can catch a pointer or reference to all objects of classes publicly derived from that base class—this allows for polymorphic processing of related errors.

Error-Prevention Tip 16.5

Using inheritance with exceptions enables an exception handler to catch related errors with concise notation. One approach is to catch each type of pointer or reference to a derived-class exception object individually, but a more concise approach is to catch pointers or references to base-class exception objects instead. Also, catching pointers or references to derived-class exception objects individually is error prone, especially if the programmer forgets to test explicitly for one or more of the derived-class pointer or reference types.

16.11 Processing new Failures

The C++ standard specifies that, when operator new fails, it throws a bad_alloc exception (defined in header file <new>). However, some compilers are not compliant with the C++ standard and therefore use the version of new that returns 0 on failure. For example, the Microsoft Visual Studio .NET throws a bad_alloc exception when new fails, while the Microsoft Visual C++ 6.0 returns 0 on new failure.

Compilers vary in their support for new-failure handling. Many older C++ compilers return 0 by default when new fails. Some compilers support new throwing an exception if header file <new> (or <new.h>) is included. Other compilers throw bad_alloc by default, regardless of whether header file <new> is included. Consult the compiler documentation to determine the compiler's support for new-failure handling.

In this section, we present three examples of new failing. The first example returns 0 when new fails. The second example uses the version of new that throws a bad_alloc exception when new fails. The third example uses function **set_new_handler** to handle new failures. [*Note:* The examples in Figs. 16.5–16.7 allocate large amounts of dynamic memory, which could cause your computer to become sluggish.]

new *Returning 0 on Failure*
Figure 16.5 demonstrates new returning 0 on failure to allocate the requested amount of memory. The for statement at lines 13–24 should loop 50 times and, on each pass, allocate an array of 50,000,000 double values (i.e., 400,000,000 bytes, because a double is normally 8 bytes). The if statement at line 17 tests the result of each new operation to determine whether new allocated the memory successfully. If new fails and returns 0, line 19 prints an error message, and the loop terminates. [*Note:* We used Microsoft Visual C++ 6.0 to run this example, because Microsoft Visual Studio .NET throws a bad_alloc exception on new failure instead of returning 0.]

```cpp
1   // Fig. 16.5: Fig16_05.cpp
2   // Demonstrating pre-standard new returning 0 when memory
3   // is not allocated.
4   #include <iostream>
5   using std::cerr;
6   using std::cout;
7
8   int main()
9   {
10     double *ptr[ 50 ];
11
12     // allocate memory for ptr
13     for ( int i = 0; i < 50; i++ )
14     {
15       ptr[ i ] = new double[ 50000000 ];
16
17       if ( ptr[ i ] == 0 ) // did new fail to allocate memory
18       {
19         cerr << "Memory allocation failed for ptr[ " << i << " ]\n";
20         break;
21       } // end if
22       else // successful memory allocation
23         cout << "Allocated 50000000 doubles in ptr[ " << i << " ]\n";
24     } // end for
25
26     return 0;
27   } // end main
```

```
Allocated 50000000 doubles in ptr[ 0 ]
Allocated 50000000 doubles in ptr[ 1 ]
Allocated 50000000 doubles in ptr[ 2 ]
Memory allocation failed for ptr[ 3 ]
```

Fig. 16.5 | new returning 0 on failure.

The output shows that the program performed only three iterations before new failed, and the loop terminated. Your output might differ based on the physical memory, disk space available for virtual memory on your system and the compiler you are using.

new *Throwing* bad_alloc *on Failure*

Figure 16.6 demonstrates new throwing bad_alloc on failure to allocate the requested memory. The for statement (lines 20–24) inside the try block should loop 50 times and, on each pass, allocate an array of 50,000,000 double values. If new fails and throws a bad_alloc exception, the loop terminates, and the program continues at line 28, where

```cpp
1   // Fig. 16.6: Fig16_06.cpp
2   // Demonstrating standard new throwing bad_alloc when memory
3   // cannot be allocated.
4   #include <iostream>
5   using std::cerr;
6   using std::cout;
7   using std::endl;
8
9   #include <new> // standard operator new
10  using std::bad_alloc;
11
12  int main()
13  {
14     double *ptr[ 50 ];
15
16     // allocate memory for ptr
17     try
18     {
19        // allocate memory for ptr[ i ]; new throws bad_alloc on failure
20        for ( int i = 0; i < 50; i++ )
21        {
22           ptr[ i ] = new double[ 50000000 ]; // may throw exception
23           cout << "Allocated 50000000 doubles in ptr[ " << i << " ]\n";
24        } // end for
25     } // end try
26
27     // handle bad_alloc exception
28     catch ( bad_alloc &memoryAllocationException )
29     {
30        cerr << "Exception occurred: "
31           << memoryAllocationException.what() << endl;
32     } // end catch
33
34     return 0;
35  } // end main
```

```
Allocated 50000000 doubles in ptr[ 0 ]
Allocated 50000000 doubles in ptr[ 1 ]
Allocated 50000000 doubles in ptr[ 2 ]
Exception occurred: bad allocation
```

Fig. 16.6 | new throwing bad_alloc on failure.

the catch handler catches and processes the exception. Lines 30–31 print the message "Exception occurred:" followed by the message returned from the base-class-exception version of function what (i.e., an implementation-defined exception-specific message, such as "Allocation Failure" in Microsoft Visual Studio .NET 2003). The output shows that the program performed only three iterations of the loop before new failed and threw the bad_alloc exception. Your output might differ based on the physical memory, disk space available for virtual memory on your system and the compiler you are using.

The C++ standard specifies that standard-compliant compilers can continue to use a version of new that returns 0 upon failure. For this purpose, header file <new> defines object nothrow (of type nothrow_t), which is used as follows:

```
double *ptr = new( nothrow ) double[ 50000000 ];
```

The preceding statement uses the version of new that does not throw bad_alloc exceptions (i.e., nothrow) to allocate an array of 50,000,000 doubles.

Software Engineering Observation 16.8

To make programs more robust, use the version of new *that throws* bad_alloc *exceptions on failure.*

Handling new Failures Using Function set_new_handler

An additional feature for handling new failures is function set_new_handler (prototyped in standard header file <new>). This function takes as its argument a pointer to a function that takes no arguments and returns void. This pointer points to the function that will be called if new fails. This provides the programmer with a uniform approach to handling all new failures, regardless of where a failure occurs in the program. Once set_new_handler registers a new handler in the program, operator new does not throw bad_alloc on failure; rather, it defers the error handling to the new-handler function.

If new allocates memory successfully, it returns a pointer to that memory. If new fails to allocate memory and set_new_handler did not register a new-handler function, new throws a bad_alloc exception. If new fails to allocate memory and a new-handler function has been registered, the new-handler function is called. The C++ standard specifies that the new-handler function should perform one of the following tasks:

1. Make more memory available by deleting other dynamically allocated memory (or telling the user to close other applications) and return to operator new to attempt to allocate memory again.

2. Throw an exception of type bad_alloc.

3. Call function abort or exit (both found in header file <cstdlib>) to terminate the program.

Figure 16.7 demonstrates set_new_handler. Function customNewHandler (lines 14–18) prints an error message (line 16), then terminates the program via a call to abort (line 17). The output shows that the program performed only three iterations of the loop before new failed and invoked function customNewHandler. Your output might differ based on the physical memory, disk space available for virtual memory on your system and the compiler you use to compile the program.

```
1   // Fig. 16.7: Fig16_07.cpp
2   // Demonstrating set_new_handler.
3   #include <iostream>
4   using std::cerr;
5   using std::cout;
6
7   #include <new> // standard operator new and set_new_handler
8   using std::set_new_handler;
9
10  #include <cstdlib> // abort function prototype
11  using std::abort;
12
13  // handle memory allocation failure
14  void customNewHandler()
15  {
16     cerr << "customNewHandler was called";
17     abort();
18  } // end function customNewHandler
19
20  // using set_new_handler to handle failed memory allocation
21  int main()
22  {
23     double *ptr[ 50 ];
24
25     // specify that customNewHandler should be called on
26     // memory allocation failure
27     set_new_handler( customNewHandler );
28
29     // allocate memory for ptr[ i ]; customNewHandler will be
30     // called on failed memory allocation
31     for ( int i = 0; i < 50; i++ )
32     {
33        ptr[ i ] = new double[ 50000000 ]; // may throw exception
34        cout << "Allocated 50000000 doubles in ptr[ " << i << " ]\n";
35     } // end for
36
37     return 0;
38  } // end main
```

```
Allocated 50000000 doubles in ptr[ 0 ]
Allocated 50000000 doubles in ptr[ 1 ]
Allocated 50000000 doubles in ptr[ 2 ]
customNewHandler was called
```

Fig. 16.7 | `set_new_handler` specifying the function to call when new fails.

16.12 Class `auto_ptr` and Dynamic Memory Allocation

A common programming practice is to allocate dynamic memory, assign the address of that memory to a pointer, use the pointer to manipulate the memory and deallocate the memory with `delete` when the memory is no longer needed. If an exception occurs after successful memory allocation but before the `delete` statement executes, a memory leak could occur. The C++ standard provides class template `auto_ptr` in header file `<memory>` to deal with this situation.

An object of class `auto_ptr` maintains a pointer to dynamically allocated memory. When an `auto_ptr` object destructor is called (for example, when an `auto_ptr` object goes out of scope), it performs a `delete` operation on its pointer data member. Class template `auto_ptr` provides overloaded operators `*` and `->` so that an `auto_ptr` object can be used just as a regular pointer variable is. Figure 16.10 demonstrates an `auto_ptr` object that points to a dynamically allocated object of class `Integer` (Figs. 16.8–16.9).

Line 18 of Fig. 16.10 creates `auto_ptr` object `ptrToInteger` and initializes it with a pointer to a dynamically allocated `Integer` object that contains the value 7. Line 21 uses the `auto_ptr` overloaded `->` operator to invoke function `setInteger` on the `Integer` object pointed to by `ptrToInteger`. Line 24 uses the `auto_ptr` overloaded `*` operator to dereference `ptrToInteger`, then uses the dot (`.`) operator to invoke function `getInteger` on the `Integer` object pointed to by `ptrToInteger`. Like a regular pointer, an `auto_ptr`'s `->` and `*` overloaded operators can be used to access the object to which the `auto_ptr` points.

Because `ptrToInteger` is a local automatic variable in `main`, `ptrToInteger` is destroyed when `main` terminates. The `auto_ptr` destructor forces a `delete` of the `Integer` object pointed to by `ptrToInteger`, which in turn calls the `Integer` class destructor. The memory that `Integer` occupies is released, regardless of how control leaves the block (e.g., by a `return` statement or by an exception). Most importantly, using this technique can prevent memory leaks. For example, suppose a function returns a pointer aimed at some object. Unfortunately, the function caller that receives this pointer might not `delete` the object, thus resulting in a memory leak. However, if the function returns an `auto_ptr` to the object, the object will be deleted automatically when the `auto_ptr` object's destructor gets called.

```
1   // Fig. 16.8: Integer.h
2   // Integer class definition.
3
4   class Integer
5   {
6   public:
7      Integer( int i = 0 ); // Integer default constructor
8      ~Integer(); // Integer destructor
9      void setInteger( int i ); // functions to set Integer
10     int getInteger() const; // function to return Integer
11  private:
12     int value;
13  }; // end class Integer
```

Fig. 16.8 | Class `Integer` definition.

```
1   // Fig. 16.9: Integer.cpp
2   // Integer member function definition.
3   #include <iostream>
4   using std::cout;
5   using std::endl;
```

Fig. 16.9 | Member function definition of class `Integer`. (Part 1 of 2.)

```
 6
 7   #include "Integer.h"
 8
 9   // Integer default constructor
10   Integer::Integer( int i )
11      : value( i )
12   {
13      cout << "Constructor for Integer " << value << endl;
14   } // end Integer constructor
15
16   // Integer destructor
17   Integer::~Integer()
18   {
19      cout << "Destructor for Integer " << value << endl;
20   } // end Integer destructor
21
22   // set Integer value
23   void Integer::setInteger( int i )
24   {
25      value = i;
26   } // end function setInteger
27
28   // return Integer value
29   int Integer::getInteger() const
30   {
31      return value;
32   } // end function getInteger
```

Fig. 16.9 | Member function definition of class `Integer`. (Part 2 of 2.)

```
 1   // Fig. 16.10: Fig16_10.cpp
 2   // Demonstrating auto_ptr.
 3   #include <iostream>
 4   using std::cout;
 5   using std::endl;
 6
 7   #include <memory>
 8   using std::auto_ptr; // auto_ptr class definition
 9
10   #include "Integer.h"
11
12   // use auto_ptr to manipulate Integer object
13   int main()
14   {
15      cout << "Creating an auto_ptr object that points to an Integer\n";
16
17      // "aim" auto_ptr at Integer object
18      auto_ptr< Integer > ptrToInteger( new Integer( 7 ) );
19
20      cout << "\nUsing the auto_ptr to manipulate the Integer\n";
21      ptrToInteger->setInteger( 99 ); // use auto_ptr to set Integer value
```

Fig. 16.10 | `auto_ptr` object manages dynamically allocated memory. (Part I of 2.)

```
22
23      // use auto_ptr to get Integer value
24      cout << "Integer after setInteger: " << ( *ptrToInteger ).getInteger()
25      return 0;
26   } // end main
```

```
Creating an auto_ptr object that points to an Integer
Constructor for Integer 7

Using the auto_ptr to manipulate the Integer
Integer after setInteger: 99

Terminating program
Destructor for Integer 99
```

Fig. 16.10 | auto_ptr object manages dynamically allocated memory. (Part 2 of 2.)

An `auto_ptr` can pass ownership of the dynamic memory it manages via its overloaded assignment operator or copy constructor. The last `auto_ptr` object that maintains the pointer to the dynamic memory will delete the memory. This makes `auto_ptr` an ideal mechanism for returning dynamically allocated memory to client code. When the `auto_ptr` goes out of scope in the client code, the `auto_ptr`'s destructor deletes the dynamic memory.

Software Engineering Observation 16.9

An auto_ptr has restrictions on certain operations. For example, an auto_ptr cannot point to an array or a standard-container class.

16.13 Standard Library Exception Hierarchy

Experience has shown that exceptions fall nicely into a number of categories. The C++ Standard Library includes a hierarchy of exception classes (Fig. 16.11). As we first discussed in Section 16.3, this hierarchy is headed by base-class `exception` (defined in header file `<exception>`), which contains `virtual` function `what`, which derived classes can override to issue appropriate error messages.

Immediate derived classes of base-class `exception` include `runtime_error` and `logic_error` (both defined in header `<stdexcept>`), each of which has several derived classes. Also derived from `exception` are the exceptions thrown by C++ operators—for example, `bad_alloc` is thrown by `new` (Section 16.11), `bad_cast` is thrown by `dynamic_cast` (Chapter 13) and `bad_typeid` is thrown by `typeid` (Chapter 13). Including `bad_exception` in the `throw` list of a function means that, if an unexpected exception occurs, function `unexpected` can throw `bad_exception` rather than terminating the program's execution (by default) or calling another function specified by `set_unexpected`.

Common Programming Error 16.8

Placing a catch handler that catches a base-class object before a catch that catches an object of a class derived from that base class is a logic error. The base-class catch catches all objects of classes derived from that base class, so the derived-class catch will never execute.

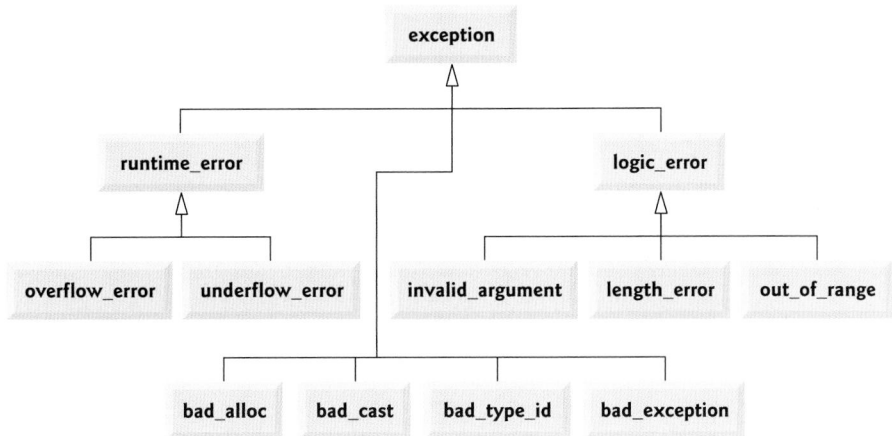

Fig. 16.11 | Standard Library exception classes.

Class `logic_error` is the base class of several standard exception classes that indicate errors in program logic. For example, class `invalid_argument` indicates that an invalid argument was passed to a function. (Proper coding can, of course, prevent invalid arguments from reaching a function.) Class `length_error` indicates that a length larger than the maximum size allowed for the object being manipulated was used for that object. Class `out_of_range` indicates that a value, such as a subscript into an array, exceeded its allowed range of values.

Class `runtime_error`, which we used briefly in Section 16.8, is the base class of several other standard exception classes that indicate execution-time errors. For example, class `overflow_error` describes an arithmetic overflow error (i.e., the result of an arithmetic operation is larger than the largest number that can be stored in the computer) and class `underflow_error` describes an arithmetic underflow error (i.e., the result of an arithmetic operation is smaller than the smallest number that can be stored in the computer).

Common Programming Error 16.9

Programmer-defined exception classes need not be derived from class `exception`. Thus, writing `catch( exception anyException )` is not guaranteed to `catch` all exceptions a program could encounter.

Error-Prevention Tip 16.6

To `catch` all exceptions potentially thrown in a `try` block, use `catch(...)`. One weakness with catching exceptions in this way is that the type of the caught exception is unknown at compile time. Another weakness is that, without a named parameter, there is no way to refer to the exception object inside the exception handler.

Software Engineering Observation 16.10

The standard `exception` hierarchy is a good starting point for creating exceptions. Programmers can build programs that can `throw` standard exceptions, `throw` exceptions derived from the standard exceptions or `throw` their own exceptions not derived from the standard exceptions.

> **Software Engineering Observation 16.11**
>
> *Use catch(...) when recovery does not depend on the exception type (e.g., releasing common resources). The exception can be rethrown to alert more specific enclosing catch handlers.*

16.14 Other Error-Handling Techniques

We have discussed several ways to deal with exceptional situations prior to this chapter. The following summarizes these and other error-handling techniques:

- Ignore the exception. If an exception occurs, the program might fail as a result of the uncaught exception. This is devastating for commercial software products or for special-purpose software designed for mission-critical situations, but, for software developed for your own purposes, ignoring many kinds of errors is common.

> **Common Programming Error 16.10**
>
> *Aborting a program component due to an uncaught exception could leave a resource—such as a file stream or an I/O device—in a state in which other programs are unable to acquire the resource. This is known as a "resource leak."*

- Abort the program. This, of course, prevents a program from running to completion and producing incorrect results. For many types of errors, this is appropriate, especially for nonfatal errors that enable a program to run to completion (potentially misleading the programmer to think that the program functioned correctly). This strategy is inappropriate for mission-critical applications. Resource issues also are important here. If a program obtains a resource, the program should release that resource before program termination.

- Set error indicators. The problem with this approach is that programs might not check these error indicators at all points at which the errors could be troublesome.

- Test for the error condition, issue an error message and call exit (in <cstdlib>) to pass an appropriate error code to the program's environment.

- Use functions setjump and longjump. These <csetjmp> library functions enable the programmer to specify an immediate jump from a deeply nested function call to an error handler. Without using setjump or longjump, a program must execute several returns to exit the deeply nested function calls. Functions setjump and longjump are dangerous, because they unwind the stack without calling destructors for automatic objects. This can lead to serious problems.

- Certain specific kinds of errors have dedicated capabilities for handling them. For example, when operator new fails to allocate memory, it can cause a new_handler function to execute to handle the error. This function can be customized by supplying a function name as the argument to set_new_handler, as we discuss in Section 16.11.

Summary

- An exception is an indication of a problem that occurs during a program's execution.
- Exception handling enables programmers to create programs that can resolve problems that occur at execution time—often allowing programs to continue executing as if no problems had been encountered. More severe problems may require a program to notify the user of the problem before terminating in a controlled manner.

- Exception handling enables the programmer to remove error-handling code from the "main line" of the program's execution, which improves program clarity and enhances modifiability.
- C++ uses the termination model of exception handling.
- A try block consists of keyword try followed by braces ({}) that define a block of code in which exceptions might occur. The try block encloses statements that might cause exceptions and statements that should not execute if exceptions occur.
- At least one catch handler must immediately follow a try block. Each catch handler specifies an exception parameter that represents the type of exception the catch handler can process.
- If an exception parameter includes an optional parameter name, the catch handler can use that parameter name to interact with a caught exception object.
- The point in the program at which an exception occurs is called the throw point.
- If an exception occurs in a try block, the try block expires and program control transfers to the first catch in which the exception parameter's type matches that of the thrown exception.
- When a try block terminates, local variables defined in the block go out of scope.
- When a try block terminates due to an exception, the program searches for the first catch handler that can process the type of exception that occurred. The program locates the matching catch by comparing the thrown exception's type to each catch's exception-parameter type until the program finds a match. A match occurs if the types are identical or if the thrown exception's type is a derived class of the exception-parameter type. When a match occurs, the code contained within the matching catch handler executes.
- When a catch handler finishes processing, the catch parameter and local variables defined within the catch handler go out of scope. Any remaining catch handlers that correspond to the try block are ignored, and execution resumes at the first line of code after the try…catch sequence.
- If no exceptions occur in a try block, the program ignores the catch handler(s) for that block. Program execution resumes with the next statement after the try…catch sequence.
- If an exception that occurs in a try block has no matching catch handler, or if an exception occurs in a statement that is not in a try block, the function that contains the statement terminates immediately, and the program attempts to locate an enclosing try block in the calling function. This process is called stack unwinding.
- Exception handling is for synchronous errors, which occur when a statement executes.
- Exception handling is not designed to process errors associated with asynchronous events, which occur in parallel with, and independent of, the program's flow of control.
- To throw an exception, use keyword throw followed by an operand that represents the type of exception to throw. Normally, a throw statement specifies one operand.
- The operand of a throw can be of any type.
- The exception handler can defer the exception handling (or perhaps a portion of it) to another exception handler. In either case, the handler achieves this by rethrowing the exception.
- Common examples of exceptions are out-of-range array subscripts, arithmetic overflow, division by zero, invalid function parameters and unsuccessful memory allocations.
- Class exception is the standard C++ base class for exceptions. Class exception provides virtual function what that returns an appropriate error message and can be overridden in derived classes.
- An optional exception specification enumerates a list of exceptions that a function can throw. A function can throw only exceptions of the types indicated by the exception specification or exceptions of any type derived from these types. If the function throws an exception that does not belong to a specified type, function unexpected is called and the program normally terminates.

- A function with no exception specification can throw any exception. The empty exception specification throw() indicates that a function does not throw exceptions. If a function with an empty exception specification attempts to throw an exception, function unexpected is invoked.

- Function unexpected calls the function registered with function set_unexpected. If no function has been registered in this manner, function terminate is called by default.

- Function set_terminate can specify the function to invoke when terminate is called. Otherwise, terminate calls abort, which terminates the program without calling the destructors of objects that are declared static and auto.

- Functions set_terminate and set_unexpected each return a pointer to the last function called by terminate and unexpected, respectively (0, the first time each is called). This enables the programmer to save the function pointer so it can be restored later.

- Functions set_terminate and set_unexpected take as arguments pointers to functions with void return types and no arguments.

- If a programmer-defined termination function does not exit a program, function abort will be called after the programmer-defined termination function completes execution.

- Unwinding the function call stack means that the function in which the exception was not caught terminates, all local variables in that function are destroyed and control returns to the statement that originally invoked that function.

- Class runtime_error (defined in header <stdexcept>) is the C++ standard base class for representing runtime errors.

- Exceptions thrown by a constructor cause destructors to be called for any objects built as part of the object being constructed before the exception is thrown.

- Destructors are called for every automatic object constructed in a try block before an exception is thrown.

- Stack unwinding completes before an exception handler begins executing.

- If a destructor invoked as a result of stack unwinding throws an exception, terminate is called.

- If an object has member objects, and if an exception is thrown before the outer object is fully constructed, then destructors will be executed for the member objects that have been constructed before the exception occurs.

- If an array of objects has been partially constructed when an exception occurs, only the destructors for the constructed array element objects will be called.

- When an exception is thrown from the constructor for an object that is created in a new expression, the dynamically allocated memory for that object is released.

- If a catch handler catches a pointer or reference to an exception object of a base-class type, it also can catch a pointer or reference to all objects of classes derived publicly from that base class—this allows for polymorphic processing of related errors.

- The C++ standard document specifies that, when operator new fails, it throws a bad_alloc exception (defined in header file <new>).

- Function set_new_handler takes as its argument a pointer to a function that takes no arguments and returns void. This pointer points to the function that will be called if new fails.

- Once set_new_handler registers a new handler in the program, operator new does not throw bad_alloc on failure; rather, it defers the error handling to the new-handler function.

- If new allocates memory successfully, it returns a pointer to that memory.

- If an exception occurs after successful memory allocation but before the `delete` statement executes, a memory leak could occur.
- The C++ Standard Library provides class template `auto_ptr` to deal with memory leaks.
- An object of class `auto_ptr` maintains a pointer to dynamically allocated memory. An `auto_ptr` object's destructor performs a `delete` operation on the `auto_ptr`'s pointer data member.
- Class template `auto_ptr` provides overloaded operators `*` and `->` so that an `auto_ptr` object can be used just as a regular pointer variable is. An `auto_ptr` also transfers ownership of the dynamic memory it manages via its copy constructor and overloaded assignment operator.
- The C++ Standard Library includes a hierarchy of exception classes. This hierarchy is headed by base-class `exception`.
- Immediate derived classes of base class `exception` include `runtime_error` and `logic_error` (both defined in header `<stdexcept>`), each of which has several derived classes.
- Several operators throw standard exceptions—operator `new` throws `bad_alloc`, operator `dynamic_cast` throws `bad_cast` and operator `typeid` throws `bad_typeid`.
- Including `bad_exception` in the throw list of a function means that, if an unexpected exception occurs, function `unexpected` can throw `bad_exception` rather than terminating the program's execution or calling another function specified by `set_unexpected`.

Terminology

abort function	new failure handler
arithmetic overflow error	`nothrow` object
arithmetic underflow error	`out_of_range` exception
asynchronous event	`overflow_error` exception
`auto_ptr` class template	resumption model of exception handling
`bad_alloc` exception	rethrow an exception
`bad_cast` exception	robust application
`bad_exception` exception	`runtime_error` exception
`bad_typeid` exception	`set_new_handler` function
`catch(...)`	`set_terminate` function
catch all exceptions	`set_unexpected` function
catch an exception	stack unwinding
catch handler	`<stdexcept>` header file
catch keyword	synchronous errors
empty exception specification	`terminate` function
exception	termination model of exception handling
exception class	throw an exception
exception handler	throw an unexpected exception
exception handling	throw keyword
`<exception>` header file	throw list
exception object	throw without arguments
exception parameter	throw point
exception specification	try block
fault-tolerant programs	try keyword
handle an exception	`underflow_error` exception
`invalid_argument` exception	`unexpected` function
`length_error` exception	`what` virtual function of class exception
`logic_error` exception	
`<memory>` header file	

Self-Review Exercises

16.1 List five common examples of exceptions.

16.2 Give several reasons why exception-handling techniques should not be used for conventional program control.

16.3 Why are exceptions appropriate for dealing with errors produced by library functions?

16.4 What is a "resource leak"?

16.5 If no exceptions are thrown in a try block, where does control proceed to after the try block completes execution?

16.6 What happens if an exception is thrown outside a try block?

16.7 Give a key advantage and a key disadvantage of using catch(...).

16.8 What happens if no catch handler matches the type of a thrown object?

16.9 What happens if several handlers match the type of the thrown object?

16.10 Why would a programmer specify a base-class type as the type of a catch handler, then throw objects of derived-class types?

16.11 Suppose a catch handler with a precise match to an exception object type is available. Under what circumstances might a different handler be executed for exception objects of that type?

16.12 Must throwing an exception cause program termination?

16.13 What happens when a catch handler throws an exception?

16.14 What does the statement throw; do?

16.15 How does the programmer restrict the exception types that a function can throw?

16.16 What happens if a function throws an exception of a type not allowed by the exception specification for the function?

16.17 What happens to the automatic objects that have been constructed in a try block when that block throws an exception?

Answers to Self-Review Exercises

16.1 Insufficient memory to satisfy a new request, array subscript out of bounds, arithmetic overflow, division by zero, invalid function parameters.

16.2 (a) Exception handling is designed to handle infrequently occurring situations that often result in program termination, so compiler writers are not required to implement exception handling to perform optimally. (b) Flow of control with conventional control structures generally is clearer and more efficient than with exceptions. (c) Problems can occur because the stack is unwound when an exception occurs and resources allocated prior to the exception might not be freed. (d) The "additional" exceptions make it more difficult for the programmer to handle the larger number of exception cases.

16.3 It is unlikely that a library function will perform error processing that will meet the unique needs of all users.

16.4 A program that terminates abruptly could leave a resource in a state in which other programs would not be able to acquire the resource, or the program itself might not be able to reacquire a "leaked" resource.

16.5 The exception handlers (in the catch handlers) for that try block are skipped, and the program resumes execution after the last catch handler.

16.6   An exception thrown outside a try block causes a call to terminate.

16.7   The form catch(...) catches any type of exception thrown in a try block. An advantage is that all possible exceptions will be caught. A disadvantage is that the catch has no parameter, so it cannot reference information in the thrown object and cannot know the cause of the exception.

16.8   This causes the search for a match to continue in the next enclosing try block if there is one. As this process continues, it might eventually be determined that there is no handler in the program that matches the type of the thrown object; in this case, terminate is called, which by default calls abort. An alternative terminate function can be provided as an argument to set_terminate.

16.9   The first matching exception handler after the try block is executed.

16.10   This is a nice way to catch related types of exceptions.

16.11   A base-class handler would catch objects of all derived-class types.

16.12   No, but it does terminate the block in which the exception is thrown.

16.13   The exception will be processed by a catch handler (if one exists) associated with the try block (if one exists) enclosing the catch handler that caused the exception.

16.14   It rethrows the exception if it appears in a catch handler; otherwise, function unexpected is called.

16.15   Provide an exception specification listing the exception types that the function can throw.

16.16   Function unexpected is called.

16.17   The try block expires, causing destructors to be called for each of these objects.

Exercises

16.18   List various exceptional conditions that have occurred throughout this text. List as many additional exceptional conditions as you can. For each of these exceptions, describe briefly how a program typically would handle the exception, using the exception-handling techniques discussed in this chapter. Some typical exceptions are division by zero, arithmetic overflow, array subscript out of bounds, exhaustion of the free store, etc.

16.19   Under what circumstances would the programmer not provide a parameter name when defining the type of the object that will be caught by a handler?

16.20   A program contains the statement

```
throw;
```

Where would you normally expect to find such a statement? What if that statement appeared in a different part of the program?

16.21   Compare and contrast exception handling with the various other error-processing schemes discussed in the text.

16.22   Why should exceptions not be used as an alternate form of program control?

16.23   Describe a technique for handling related exceptions.

16.24   Until this chapter, we have found that dealing with errors detected by constructors can be awkward. Exception handling gives us a better means of handling such errors. Consider a constructor for a String class. The constructor uses new to obtain space from the free store. Suppose new fails.

Show how you would deal with this without exception handling. Discuss the key issues. Show how you would deal with such memory exhaustion with exception handling. Explain why the exception-handling approach is superior.

16.25 Suppose a program throws an exception and the appropriate exception handler begins executing. Now suppose that the exception handler itself throws the same exception. Does this create infinite recursion? Write a program to check your observation.

16.26 Use inheritance to create various derived classes of runtime_error. Then show that a catch handler specifying the base class can catch derived-class exceptions.

16.27 Write a conditional expression that returns either a double or an int. Provide an int catch handler and a double catch handler. Show that only the double catch handler executes, regardless of whether the int or the double is returned.

16.28 Write a program that generates and handles a memory-exhaustion exception. Your program should loop on a request to create dynamic memory through operator new.

16.29 Write a program illustrating that all destructors for objects constructed in a block are called before an exception is thrown from that block.

16.30 Write a program illustrating that member object destructors are called for only those member objects that were constructed before an exception occurred.

16.31 Write a program that demonstrates several exception types being caught with the catch(...) exception handler.

16.32 Write a program illustrating that the order of exception handlers is important. The first matching handler is the one that executes. Attempt to compile and run your program two different ways to show that two different handlers execute with two different effects.

16.33 Write a program that shows a constructor passing information about constructor failure to an exception handler after a try block.

16.34 Write a program that illustrates rethrowing an exception.

16.35 Write a program that illustrates that a function with its own try block does not have to catch every possible error generated within the try. Some exceptions can slip through to, and be handled in, outer scopes.

16.36 Write a program that throws an exception from a deeply nested function and still has the catch handler following the try block enclosing the call chain catch the exception.

17

File Processing

I read part of it all the way through.
—Samuel Goldwyn

I can only assume that a "Do Not File" document is filed in a "Do Not File" file.
—Senator Frank Church
Senate Intelligence
Subcommittee Hearing, 1975

A great memory does not make a philosopher, any more than a dictionary can be called grammar.
—John Henry, Cardinal Newman

OBJECTIVES

In this chapter you will learn:

- To create, read, write and update files.
- Sequential file processing.
- Random-access file processing.
- To use high-performance unformatted I/O operations.
- The differences between formatted-data and raw-data file processing.
- To build a transaction-processing program using random-access file processing.

17.1 Introduction

Storage of data in variables and arrays is temporary. Files are used for data persistence—permanent retention of large amounts of data. Computers store files on secondary storage devices, such as magnetic disks, optical disks and tapes. In this chapter, we explain how to build C++ programs that create, update and process data files. We consider both sequential files and random-access files. We compare formatted-data file processing and raw-data file processing. We examine techniques for input of data from, and output of data to, string streams rather than files in Chapter 18.

17.2 The Data Hierarchy

Ultimately, all data items that digital computers process are reduced to combinations of zeros and ones. This occurs because it is simple and economical to build electronic devices that can assume two stable states—one state represents 0 and the other represents 1. It is remarkable that the impressive functions performed by computers involve only the most fundamental manipulations of 0s and 1s.

The smallest data item that computers support is called a bit (short for "binary digit"—a digit that can assume one of two values). Each data item, or bit, can assume either the value 0 or the value 1. Computer circuitry performs various simple bit manipulations, such as examining the value of a bit, setting the value of a bit and reversing a bit (from 1 to 0 or from 0 to 1).

Programming with data in the low-level form of bits is cumbersome. It is preferable to program with data in forms such as decimal digits (i.e., 0, 1, 2, 3, 4, 5, 6, 7, 8 and 9), letters (i.e., A through Z and a through z) and special symbols (i.e., $, @, %, &, *, (,), -, +, ", :, ?, / and many others). Digits, letters and special symbols are referred to as characters. The set of all characters used to write programs and represent data items on a particular computer is called that computer's character set. Because computers can process only 1s and 0s, every character in a computer's character set is represented as a pattern of 1s and 0s. Bytes are composed of eight bits. Programmers create programs and data items with characters; computers manipulate and process these characters as patterns of bits. For example, C++ provides data type char. Each char occupies one byte of memory. C++ also provides data type wchar_t, which can occupy more than one byte (to support larger character sets, such as the Unicode® character set). For more information on Unicode®, visit www.unicode.org.

Just as characters are composed of bits, fields are composed of characters. A field is a group of characters that conveys some meaning. For example, a field consisting of uppercase and lowercase letters can represent a person's name.

Data items processed by computers form a data hierarchy (Fig. 17.1), in which data items become larger and more complex in structure as we progress from bits, to characters, to fields and to larger data aggregates.

Typically, a record (which can be represented as a class in C++) is composed of several fields (called data members in C++). In a payroll system, for example, a record for a particular employee might include the following fields:

1. Employee identification number

2. Name

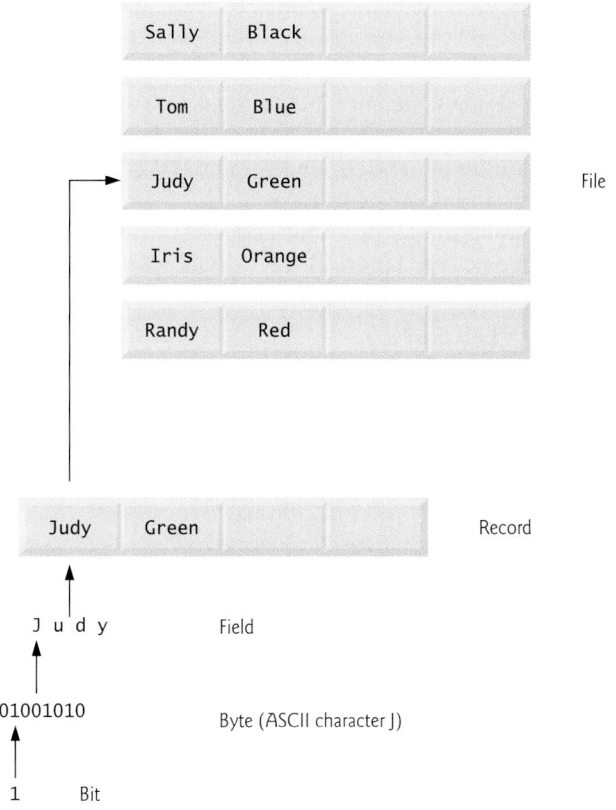

Fig. 17.1 | Data hierarchy.

3. Address

4. Hourly pay rate

5. Number of exemptions claimed

6. Year-to-date earnings

7. Amount of taxes withheld

Thus, a record is a group of related fields. In the preceding example, each field is associated with the same employee. A file is a group of related records.[1] A company's payroll file normally contains one record for each employee. Thus, a payroll file for a small company might contain only 22 records, whereas one for a large company might contain 100,000 records. It is not unusual for a company to have many files, some containing millions, billions, or even trillions of characters of information.

To facilitate the retrieval of specific records from a file, at least one field in each record is chosen as a record key. A record key identifies a record as belonging to a particular person or entity and distinguishes that record from all others. In the payroll record described previously, the employee identification number normally would be chosen as the record key.

There are many ways of organizing records in a file. A common type of organization is called a sequential file, in which records typically are stored in order by a record-key field. In a payroll file, records usually are placed in order by employee identification number. The first employee record in the file contains the lowest employee identification number, and subsequent records contain increasingly higher ones.

Most businesses use many different files to store data. For example, a company might have payroll files, accounts-receivable files (listing money due from clients), accounts-payable files (listing money due to suppliers), inventory files (listing facts about all the items handled by the business) and many other types of files. A group of related files often are stored in a database. A collection of programs designed to create and manage databases is called a database management system (DBMS).

17.3 Files and Streams

C++ views each file as a sequence of bytes (Fig. 17.2). Each file ends either with an end-of-file marker or at a specific byte number recorded in a system-maintained, administrative data structure. When a file is *opened*, an object is created, and a stream is associated with the object. In Chapter 15, we saw that objects cin, cout, cerr and clog are created when

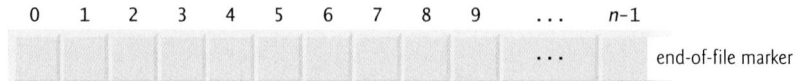

Fig. 17.2 | C++'s view of a file of *n* bytes.

---

1. Generally, a file can contain arbitrary data in arbitrary formats. In some operating systems, a file is viewed as nothing more than a collection of bytes. In such an operating system, any organization of the bytes in a file (such as organizing the data into records) is a view created by the application programmer.

<iostream> is included. The streams associated with these objects provide communication channels between a program and a particular file or device. For example, the cin object (standard input stream object) enables a program to input data from the keyboard or from other devices, the cout object (standard output stream object) enables a program to output data to the screen or other devices, and the cerr and clog objects (standard error stream objects) enable a program to output error messages to the screen or other devices.

   To perform file processing in C++, header files <iostream> and <fstream> must be included. Header <fstream> includes the definitions for the stream class templates basic_ifstream (for file input), basic_ofstream (for file output) and basic_fstream (for file input and output). Each class template has a predefined template specialization that enables char I/O. In addition, the fstream library provides a set of typedefs that provide aliases for these template specializations. For example, the typedef ifstream represents a specialization of basic_ifstream that enables char input from a file. Similarly, typedef ofstream represents a specialization of basic_ofstream that enables char output to files. Also, typedef fstream represents a specialization of basic_fstream that enables char input from, and output to, files.

   Files are opened by creating objects of these stream template specializations. These templates "derive" from class templates basic_istream, basic_ostream and basic_iostream, respectively. Thus, all member functions, operators and manipulators that belong to these templates (which we described in Chapter 15) also can be applied to file streams. Figure 17.3 summarizes the inheritance relationships of the I/O classes that we have discussed to this point.

17.4 Creating a Sequential File

C++ imposes no structure on a file. Thus, a concept like that of a "record" does not exist in a C++ file. Therefore, the programmer must structure files to meet the application's requirements. In the following example, we see how the programmer can impose a simple record structure on a file.

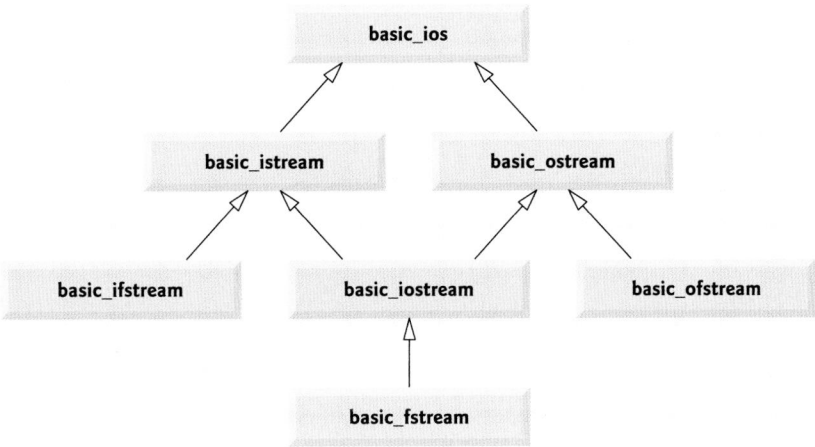

Fig. 17.3 | Portion of stream I/O template hierarchy.

Figure 17.4 creates a sequential file that might be used in an accounts-receivable system to help manage the money owed by a company's credit clients. For each client, the program obtains the client's account number, name and balance (i.e., the amount the client owes the company for goods and services received in the past). The data obtained for each client constitutes a record for that client. The account number serves as the record key in this application; that is, the program creates and maintains the file in account number order. This program assumes the user enters the records in account number order. In a comprehensive

```cpp
 1   // Fig. 17.4: Fig17_04.cpp
 2   // Create a sequential file.
 3   #include <iostream>
 4   using std::cerr;
 5   using std::cin;
 6   using std::cout;
 7   using std::endl;
 8   using std::ios;
 9
10   #include <fstream> // file stream
11   using std::ofstream; // output file stream
12
13   #include <cstdlib>
14   using std::exit; // exit function prototype
15
16   int main()
17   {
18      // ofstream constructor opens file
19      ofstream outClientFile( "clients.dat", ios::out );
20
21      // exit program if unable to create file
22      if ( !outClientFile ) // overloaded ! operator
23      {
24         cerr << "File could not be opened" << endl;
25         exit( 1 );
26      } // end if
27
28      cout << "Enter the account, name, and balance." << endl
29         << "Enter end-of-file to end input.\n? ";
30
31      int account;
32      char name[ 30 ];
33      double balance;
34
35      // read account, name and balance from cin, then place in file
36      while ( cin >> account >> name >> balance )
37      {
38         outClientFile << account << ' ' << name << ' ' << balance << endl;
39         cout << "? ";
40      } // end while
41
42      return 0; // ofstream destructor closes file
43   } // end main
```

Fig. 17.4 | Creating a sequential file. (Part 1 of 2.)

```
Enter the account, name, and balance.
Enter end-of-file to end input.
? 100 Jones 24.98
? 200 Doe 345.67
? 300 White 0.00
? 400 Stone -42.16
? 500 Rich 224.62
? ^Z
```

Fig. 17.4 | Creating a sequential file. (Part 2 of 2.)

accounts receivable system, a sorting capability would be provided for the user to enter records in any order—the records then would be sorted and written to the file.

Let us examine this program. As stated previously, files are opened by creating ifstream, ofstream or fstream objects. In Fig. 17.4, the file is to be opened for output, so an ofstream object is created. Two arguments are passed to the object's constructor—the filename and the file-open mode (line 19). For an ofstream object, the file-open mode can be either ios::out to output data to a file or ios::app to append data to the end of a file (without modifying any data already in the file). Existing files opened with mode ios::out are truncated—all data in the file is discarded. If the specified file does not yet exist, then ofstream creates the file, using that filename.

Line 19 creates an ofstream object named outClientFile associated with the file clients.dat that is opened for output. The arguments "clients.dat" and ios::out are passed to the ofstream constructor, which opens the file. This establishes a "line of communication" with the file. By default, ofstream objects are opened for output, so line 19 could have executed the statement

```
ofstream outClientFile( "clients.dat" );
```

to open clients.dat for output. Figure 17.5 lists the file-open modes.

Common Programming Error 17.1

Use caution when opening an existing file for output (ios::out), especially when you want to preserve the file's contents, which will be discarded without warning.

Mode	Description
ios::app	Append all output to the end of the file.
ios::ate	Open a file for output and move to the end of the file (normally used to append data to a file). Data can be written anywhere in the file.
ios::in	Open a file for input.
ios::out	Open a file for output.
ios::trunc	Discard the file's contents if they exist (this also is the default action for ios::out).
ios::binary	Open a file for binary (i.e., nontext) input or output.

Fig. 17.5 | File open modes.

An ofstream object can be created without opening a specific file—a file can be attached to the object later. For example, the statement

```
ofstream outClientFile;
```

creates an ofstream object named outClientFile. The ofstream member function open opens a file and attaches it to an existing ofstream object as follows:

```
outClientFile.open( "clients.dat", ios::out );
```

 Common Programming Error 17.2

Not opening a file before attempting to reference it in a program will result in an error.

After creating an ofstream object and attempting to open it, the program tests whether the open operation was successful. The if statement at lines 22–26 uses the overloaded ios operator member function operator! to determine whether the open operation succeeded. The condition returns a true value if either the failbit or the badbit is set for the stream on the open operation. Some possible errors are attempting to open a nonexistent file for reading, attempting to open a file for reading or writing without permission and opening a file for writing when no disk space is available.

If the condition indicates an unsuccessful attempt to open the file, line 24 outputs the error message "File could not be opened," and line 25 invokes function exit to terminate the program. The argument to exit is returned to the environment from which the program was invoked. Argument 0 indicates that the program terminated normally; any other value indicates that the program terminated due to an error. The calling environment (most likely the operating system) uses the value returned by exit to respond appropriately to the error.

Another overloaded ios operator member function—operator void *—converts the stream to a pointer, so it can be tested as 0 (i.e., the null pointer) or nonzero (i.e., any other pointer value). When a pointer value is used as a condition, C++ converts a null pointer to the bool value false and converts a non-null pointer to the bool value true. If the failbit or badbit (see Chapter 15) has been set for the stream, 0 (false) is returned. The condition in the while statement of lines 36–40 invokes the operator void * member function on cin implicitly. The condition remains true as long as neither the failbit nor the badbit has been set for cin. Entering the end-of-file indicator sets the failbit for cin. The operator void * function can be used to test an input object for end-of-file instead of calling the eof member function explicitly on the input object.

If line 19 opened the file successfully, the program begins processing data. Lines 28–29 prompt the user to enter either the various fields for each record or the end-of-file indicator when data entry is complete. Figure 17.6 lists the keyboard combinations for entering end-of-file for various computer systems.

Line 36 extracts each set of data and determines whether end-of-file has been entered. When end-of-file is encountered or bad data is entered, operator void * returns the null pointer (which converts to the bool value false) and the while statement terminates. The user enters end-of-file to inform the program to process no additional data. The end-of-file indicator is set when the user enters the end-of-file key combination. The while statement loops until the end-of-file indicator is set.

Computer system	Keyboard combination
UNIX/Linux/Mac OS X	*<ctrl-d>* (on a line by itself)
Microsoft Windows	*<ctrl-z>* (sometimes followed by pressing *Enter*)
VAX (VMS)	*<ctrl-z>*

Fig. 17.6 | End-of-file key combinations for various popular computer systems.

Line 38 writes a set of data to the file `clients.dat`, using the stream insertion operator `<<` and the `outClientFile` object associated with the file at the beginning of the program. The data may be retrieved by a program designed to read the file (see Section 17.5). Note that, because the file created in Fig. 17.4 is simply a text file, it can be viewed by any text editor.

Once the user enters the end-of-file indicator, `main` terminates. This invokes the `out-ClientFile` object's destructor function implicitly, which closes the `clients.dat` file. The programmer also can close the `ofstream` object explicitly, using member function `close` in the statement

```
outClientFile.close();
```

Performance Tip 17.1

Closing files explicitly when the program no longer needs to reference them can reduce resource usage (especially if the program continues execution after closing the files).

In the sample execution for the program of Fig. 17.4, the user enters information for five accounts, then signals that data entry is complete by entering end-of-file (^Z is displayed for Microsoft Windows). This dialog window does not show how the data records appear in the file. To verify that the program created the file successfully, the next section shows how to create a program that reads this file and prints its contents.

17.5 Reading Data from a Sequential File

Files store data so it may be retrieved for processing when needed. The previous section demonstrated how to create a file for sequential access. In this section, we discuss how to read data sequentially from a file.

Figure 17.7 reads records from the `clients.dat` file that we created using the program of Fig. 17.4 and displays the contents of these records. Creating an `ifstream` object opens a file for input. The `ifstream` constructor can receive the filename and the file open mode as arguments. Line 31 creates an `ifstream` object called `inClientFile` and associates it with the `clients.dat` file. The arguments in parentheses are passed to the `ifstream` constructor function, which opens the file and establishes a "line of communication" with the file.

Good Programming Practice 17.1

Open a file for input only (using `ios::in`) if the file's contents should not be modified. This prevents unintentional modification of the file's contents and is an example of the principle of least privilege.

```cpp
1   // Fig. 17.7: Fig17_07.cpp
2   // Reading and printing a sequential file.
3   #include <iostream>
4   using std::cerr;
5   using std::cout;
6   using std::endl;
7   using std::fixed;
8   using std::ios;
9   using std::left;
10  using std::right;
11  using std::showpoint;
12
13  #include <fstream> // file stream
14  using std::ifstream; // input file stream
15
16  #include <iomanip>
17  using std::setw;
18  using std::setprecision;
19
20  #include <string>
21  using std::string;
22
23  #include <cstdlib>
24  using std::exit; // exit function prototype
25
26  void outputLine( int, const string, double ); // prototype
27
28  int main()
29  {
30     // ifstream constructor opens the file
31     ifstream inClientFile( "clients.dat", ios::in );
32
33     // exit program if ifstream could not open file
34     if ( !inClientFile )
35     {
36        cerr << "File could not be opened" << endl;
37        exit( 1 );
38     } // end if
39
40     int account;
41     char name[ 30 ];
42     double balance;
43
44     cout << left << setw( 10 ) << "Account" << setw( 13 )
45        << "Name" << "Balance" << endl << fixed << showpoint;
46
47     // display each record in file
48     while ( inClientFile >> account >> name >> balance )
49        outputLine( account, name, balance );
50
51     return 0; // ifstream destructor closes the file
52  } // end main
53
```

Fig. 17.7 | Reading and printing a sequential file. (Part 1 of 2.)

```
54   // display single record from file
55   void outputLine( int account, const string name, double balance )
56   {
57      cout << left << setw( 10 ) << account << setw( 13 ) << name
58         << setw( 7 ) << setprecision( 2 ) << right << balance << endl;
59   } // end function outputLine
```

```
Account   Name          Balance
100       Jones           24.98
200       Doe            345.67
300       White            0.00
400       Stone          -42.16
500       Rich           224.62
```

Fig. 17.7 | Reading and printing a sequential file. (Part 2 of 2.)

Objects of class ifstream are opened for input by default. We could have used the statement

```
ifstream inClientFile( "clients.dat" );
```

to open clients.dat for input. Just as with an ofstream object, an ifstream object can be created without opening a specific file, because a file can be attached to it later.

The program uses the condition !inClientFile to determine whether the file was opened successfully before attempting to retrieve data from the file. Line 48 reads a set of data (i.e., a record) from the file. After the preceding line is executed the first time, account has the value 100, name has the value "Jones" and balance has the value 24.98. Each time line 48 executes, it reads another record from the file into the variables account, name and balance. Line 49 displays the records, using function outputLine (lines 55–59), which uses parameterized stream manipulators to format the data for display. When the end of file has been reached, the implicit call to operator void * in the while condition returns the null pointer (which converts to the bool value false), the ifstream destructor function closes the file and the program terminates.

To retrieve data sequentially from a file, programs normally start reading from the beginning of the file and read all the data consecutively until the desired data is found. It might be necessary to process the file sequentially several times (from the beginning of the file) during the execution of a program. Both istream and ostream provide member functions for repositioning the **file-position pointer** (the byte number of the next byte in the file to be read or written). These member functions are **seekg** ("seek get") for istream and **seekp** ("seek put") for ostream. Each istream object has a "get pointer," which indicates the byte number in the file from which the next input is to occur, and each ostream object has a "put pointer," which indicates the byte number in the file at which the next output should be placed. The statement

```
inClientFile.seekg( 0 );
```

repositions the file-position pointer to the beginning of the file (location 0) attached to in-ClientFile. The argument to seekg normally is a long integer. A second argument can be specified to indicate the **seek direction**. The seek direction can be **ios::beg** (the default) for positioning relative to the beginning of a stream, **ios::cur** for positioning relative to the current position in a stream or `ios::end` for positioning relative to the end of a stream. The file-position pointer is an integer value that specifies the location in the file as a number of bytes from the file's starting location (this is also referred to as the offset from the beginning of the file). Some examples of positioning the "get" file-position pointer are

```
// position to the nth byte of fileObject (assumes ios::beg)
fileObject.seekg( n );

// position n bytes forward in fileObject
fileObject.seekg( n, ios::cur );

// position n bytes back from end of fileObject
fileObject.seekg( n, ios::end );

// position at end of fileObject
fileObject.seekg( 0, ios::end );
```

The same operations can be performed using `ostream` member function `seekp`. Member functions `tellg` and `tellp` are provided to return the current locations of the "get" and "put" pointers, respectively. The following statement assigns the "get" file-position pointer value to variable `location` of type `long`:

```
location = fileObject.tellg();
```

Figure 17.8 enables a credit manager to display the account information for those customers with zero balances (i.e., customers who do not owe the company any money), credit (negative) balances (i.e., customers to whom the company owes money), and debit (positive) balances (i.e., customers who owe the company money for goods and services received in the past). The program displays a menu and allows the credit manager to enter one of three options to obtain credit information. Option 1 produces a list of accounts with zero balances. Option 2 produces a list of accounts with credit balances. Option 3 produces a list of accounts with debit balances. Option 4 terminates program execution. Entering an invalid option displays the prompt to enter another choice.

```
1   // Fig. 17.8: Fig17_08.cpp
2   // Credit inquiry program.
3   #include <iostream>
4   using std::cerr;
5   using std::cin;
6   using std::cout;
7   using std::endl;
8   using std::fixed;
9   using std::ios;
10  using std::left;
11  using std::right;
12  using std::showpoint;
13
14  #include <fstream>
15  using std::ifstream;
16
```

Fig. 17.8 | Credit inquiry program. (Part 1 of 4.)

```
17   #include <iomanip>
18   using std::setw;
19   using std::setprecision;
20
21   #include <string>
22   using std::string;
23
24   #include <cstdlib>
25   using std::exit; // exit function prototype
26
27   enum RequestType { ZERO_BALANCE = 1, CREDIT_BALANCE, DEBIT_BALANCE, END };
28   int getRequest();
29   bool shouldDisplay( int, double );
30   void outputLine( int, const string, double );
31
32   int main()
33   {
34      // ifstream constructor opens the file
35      ifstream inClientFile( "clients.dat", ios::in );
36
37      // exit program if ifstream could not open file
38      if ( !inClientFile )
39      {
40         cerr << "File could not be opened" << endl;
41         exit( 1 );
42      } // end if
43
44      int request;
45      int account;
46      char name[ 30 ];
47      double balance;
48
49      // get user's request (e.g., zero, credit or debit balance)
50      request = getRequest();
51
52      // process user's request
53      while ( request != END )
54      {
55         switch ( request )
56         {
57            case ZERO_BALANCE:
58               cout << "\nAccounts with zero balances:\n";
59               break;
60            case CREDIT_BALANCE:
61               cout << "\nAccounts with credit balances:\n";
62               break;
63            case DEBIT_BALANCE:
64               cout << "\nAccounts with debit balances:\n";
65               break;
66         } // end switch
67
68         // read account, name and balance from file
69         inClientFile >> account >> name >> balance;
```

Fig. 17.8 | Credit inquiry program. (Part 2 of 4.)

```
70
71          // display file contents (until eof)
72          while ( !inClientFile.eof() )
73          {
74             // display record
75             if ( shouldDisplay( request, balance ) )
76                outputLine( account, name, balance );
77
78             // read account, name and balance from file
79             inClientFile >> account >> name >> balance;
80          } // end inner while
81
82          inClientFile.clear(); // reset eof for next input
83          inClientFile.seekg( 0 ); // reposition to beginning of file
84          request = getRequest(); // get additional request from user
85       } // end outer while
86
87       cout << "End of run." << endl;
88       return 0; // ifstream destructor closes the file
89    } // end main
90
91    // obtain request from user
92    int getRequest()
93    {
94       int request; // request from user
95
96       // display request options
97       cout << "\nEnter request" << endl
98          << " 1 - List accounts with zero balances" << endl
99          << " 2 - List accounts with credit balances" << endl
100         << " 3 - List accounts with debit balances" << endl
101         << " 4 - End of run" << fixed << showpoint;
102
103      do // input user request
104      {
105         cout << "\n? ";
106         cin >> request;
107      } while ( request < ZERO_BALANCE && request > END );
108
109      return request;
110   } // end function getRequest
111
112   // determine whether to display given record
113   bool shouldDisplay( int type, double balance )
114   {
115      // determine whether to display zero balances
116      if ( type == ZERO_BALANCE && balance == 0 )
117         return true;
118
119      // determine whether to display credit balances
120      if ( type == CREDIT_BALANCE && balance < 0 )
121         return true;
122
```

Fig. 17.8 | Credit inquiry program. (Part 3 of 4.)

```
123     // determine whether to display debit balances
124     if ( type == DEBIT_BALANCE && balance > 0 )
125        return true;
126
127     return false;
128  } // end function shouldDisplay
129
130  // display single record from file
131  void outputLine( int account, const string name, double balance )
132  {
133     cout << left << setw( 10 ) << account << setw( 13 ) << name
134        << setw( 7 ) << setprecision( 2 ) << right << balance << endl;
135  } // end function outputLine
```

```
Enter request
 1 - List accounts with zero balances
 2 - List accounts with credit balances
 3 - List accounts with debit balances
 4 - End of run
? 1

Accounts with zero balances:
300        White              0.00

Enter request
 1 - List accounts with zero balances
 2 - List accounts with credit balances
 3 - List accounts with debit balances
 4 - End of run
? 2

Accounts with credit balances:
400        Stone            -42.16

Enter request
 1 - List accounts with zero balances
 2 - List accounts with credit balances
 3 - List accounts with debit balances
 4 - End of run
? 3

Accounts with debit balances:
100        Jones             24.98
200        Doe              345.67
500        Rich             224.62

Enter request
 1 - List accounts with zero balances
 2 - List accounts with credit balances
 3 - List accounts with debit balances
 4 - End of run
? 4
End of run.
```

Fig. 17.8 | Credit inquiry program. (Part 4 of 4.)

17.6 Updating Sequential Files

Data that is formatted and written to a sequential file as shown in Section 17.4 cannot be modified without the risk of destroying other data in the file. For example, if the name "White" needs to be changed to "Worthington," the old name cannot be overwritten without corrupting the file. The record for White was written to the file as

        300 White 0.00

If this record were rewritten beginning at the same location in the file using the longer name, the record would be

        300 Worthington 0.00

The new record contains six more characters than the original record. Therefore, the characters beyond the second "o" in "Worthington" would overwrite the beginning of the next sequential record in the file. The problem is that, in the formatted input/output model using the stream insertion operator << and the stream extraction operator >>, fields—and hence records—can vary in size. For example, values 7, 14, –117, 2074, and 27383 are all ints, which store the same number of "raw data" bytes internally (typically four bytes on today's popular 32-bit machines). However, these integers become different-sized fields when output as formatted text (character sequences). Therefore, the formatted input/output model usually is not used to update records in place.

Such updating can be done awkwardly. For example, to make the preceding name change, the records before 300 White 0.00 in a sequential file could be copied to a new file, the updated record then would be written to the new file, and the records after 300 White 0.00 would be copied to the new file. This requires processing every record in the file to update one record. If many records are being updated in one pass of the file, though, this technique can be acceptable.

17.7 Random-Access Files

So far, we have seen how to create sequential files and search them to locate information. Sequential files are inappropriate for instant-access applications, in which a particular record must be located immediately. Common instant-access applications are airline reservation systems, banking systems, point-of-sale systems, automated teller machines and other kinds of transaction-processing systems that require rapid access to specific data. A bank might have hundreds of thousands (or even millions) of other customers, yet, when a customer uses an automated teller machine, the program checks that customer's account in a few seconds or less for sufficient funds. This kind of instant access is made possible with random-access files. Individual records of a random-access file can be accessed directly (and quickly) without having to search other records.

As we have said, C++ does not impose structure on a file. So the application that wants to use random-access files must create them. A variety of techniques can be used. Perhaps the easiest method is to require that all records in a file be of the same fixed length. Using same-size, fixed-length records makes it easy for a program to calculate (as a function of the record size and the record key) the exact location of any record relative to the beginning of the file. We soon will see how this facilitates immediate access to specific records, even in large files.

Figure 17.9 illustrates C++'s view of a random-access file composed of fixed-length records (each record, in this case, is 100 bytes long). A random-access file is like a railroad train with many same-size cars—some empty and some with contents.

Data can be inserted into a random-access file without destroying other data in the file. Data stored previously also can be updated or deleted without rewriting the entire file. In the following sections, we explain how to create a random-access file, enter data into the file, read the data both sequentially and randomly, update the data and delete data that is no longer needed.

17.8 Creating a Random-Access File

The `ostream` member function `write` outputs a fixed number of bytes, beginning at a specific location in memory, to the specified stream. When the stream is associated with a file, function `write` writes the data at the location in the file specified by the "put" file-position pointer. The `istream` member function `read` inputs a fixed number of bytes from the specified stream to an area in memory beginning at a specified address. If the stream is associated with a file, function `read` inputs bytes at the location in the file specified by the "get" file-position pointer.

Writing Bytes with `ostream` Member Function `write`
When writing an integer `number` to a file, instead of using the statement

```
outFile << number;
```

which for a four-byte integer could print as few digits as one or as many as 11 (10 digits plus a sign, each requiring a single byte of storage), we can use the statement

```
outFile.write( reinterpret_cast< const char * >( &number ),
   sizeof( number ) );
```

which always writes the binary version of the integer's four bytes (on a machine with four-byte integers). Function `write` treats its first argument as a group of bytes by viewing the object in memory as a `const char *`, which is a pointer to a byte (remember that a `char` is one byte). Starting from that location, function `write` outputs the number of bytes specified by its second argument—an integer of type `size_t`. As we will see, `istream` function `read` can subsequently be used to read the four bytes back into integer variable `number`.

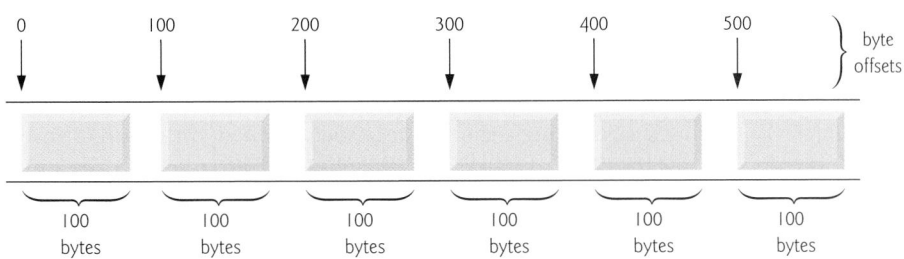

Fig. 17.9 | C++ view of a random-access file.

Converting Between Pointer Types with the `reinterpret_cast` *Operator*

Unfortunately, most pointers that we pass to function `write` as the first argument are not of type const char *. To output objects of other types, we must convert the pointers to those objects to type const char *; otherwise, the compiler will not compile calls to function `write`. C++ provides the `reinterpret_cast` operator for cases like this in which a pointer of one type must be cast to an unrelated pointer type. You can also use this cast operator to convert between pointer and integer types, and vice versa. Without a `reinterpret_cast`, the `write` statement that outputs the integer `number` will not compile because the compiler does not allow a pointer of type int * (the type returned by the expression `&number`) to be passed to a function that expects an argument of type const char *—as far as the compiler is concerned, these types are incompatible.

A `reinterpret_cast` is performed at compile time and does not change the value of the object to which its operand points. Instead, it requests that the compiler reinterpret the operand as the target type (specified in the angle brackets following the keyword `reinterpret_cast`). In Fig. 17.12, we use `reinterpret_cast` to convert a `ClientData` pointer to a const char *, which reinterprets a `ClientData` object as bytes to be output to a file. Random-access file-processing programs rarely write a single field to a file. Normally, they write one object of a class at a time, as we show in the following examples.

Error-Prevention Tip 17.1

It is easy to use reinterpret_cast *to perform dangerous manipulations that could lead to serious execution-time errors.*

Portability Tip 17.1

Using reinterpret_cast *is compiler-dependent and can cause programs to behave differently on different platforms. The* reinterpret_cast *operator should not be used unless absolute necessary.*

Portability Tip 17.2

A program that reads unformatted data (written by write*) must be compiled and executed on a system compatible with the program that wrote the data, because different systems may represent internal data differently.*

Credit Processing Program

Consider the following problem statement:

> *Create a credit-processing program capable of storing at most 100 fixed-length records for a company that can have up to 100 customers. Each record should consist of an account number that acts as the record key, a last name, a first name and a balance. The program should be able to update an account, insert a new account, delete an account and insert all the account records into a formatted text file for printing.*

The next several sections introduce the techniques for creating this credit-processing program. Figure 17.12 illustrates opening a random-access file, defining the record format using an object of class `ClientData` (Figs. 17.10–17.11) and writing data to the disk in binary format. This program initializes all 100 records of the file `credit.dat` with empty objects, using function `write`. Each empty object contains 0 for the account number, the null string (represented by empty quotation marks) for the last and first name and 0.0 for the balance. Each record is initialized with the amount of empty space in which the account data will be stored.

```
 1   // Fig. 17.10: ClientData.h
 2   // Class ClientData definition used in Fig. 17.12-Fig. 17.15.
 3   #ifndef CLIENTDATA_H
 4   #define CLIENTDATA_H
 5
 6   #include <string>
 7   using std::string;
 8
 9   class ClientData
10   {
11   public:
12      // default ClientData constructor
13      ClientData( int = 0, string = "", string = "", double = 0.0 );
14
15      // accessor functions for accountNumber
16      void setAccountNumber( int );
17      int getAccountNumber() const;
18
19      // accessor functions for lastName
20      void setLastName( string );
21      string getLastName() const;
22
23      // accessor functions for firstName
24      void setFirstName( string );
25      string getFirstName() const;
26
27      // accessor functions for balance
28      void setBalance( double );
29      double getBalance() const;
30   private:
31      int accountNumber;
32      char lastName[ 15 ];
33      char firstName[ 10 ];
34      double balance;
35   }; // end class ClientData
36
37   #endif
```

Fig. 17.10 | ClientData class header file.

Objects of class string do not have uniform size because they use dynamically allocated memory to accommodate strings of various lengths. This program must maintain fixed-length records, so class ClientData stores the client's first and last name in fixed-length char arrays. Member functions setLastName (Fig. 17.11, lines 37–45) and setFirstName (Fig. 17.11, lines 54–62) each copy the characters of a string object into the corresponding char array. Consider function setLastName. Line 40 initializes the const char * lastNam-eValue with the result of a call to string member function data, which returns an array containing the characters of the string. [*Note:* This array is not guaranteed to be null terminated.] Line 41 invokes string member function size to get the length of lastName-String. Line 42 ensures that length is fewer than 15 characters, then line 43 copies length characters from lastNameValue into the char array lastName. Member function set-FirstName performs the same steps for the first name.

```cpp
1   // Fig. 17.11: ClientData.cpp
2   // Class ClientData stores customer's credit information.
3   #include <string>
4   using std::string;
5
6   #include "ClientData.h"
7
8   // default ClientData constructor
9   ClientData::ClientData( int accountNumberValue,
10     string lastNameValue, string firstNameValue, double balanceValue )
11  {
12     setAccountNumber( accountNumberValue );
13     setLastName( lastNameValue );
14     setFirstName( firstNameValue );
15     setBalance( balanceValue );
16  } // end ClientData constructor
17
18  // get account-number value
19  int ClientData::getAccountNumber() const
20  {
21     return accountNumber;
22  } // end function getAccountNumber
23
24  // set account-number value
25  void ClientData::setAccountNumber( int accountNumberValue )
26  {
27     accountNumber = accountNumberValue; // should validate
28  } // end function setAccountNumber
29
30  // get last-name value
31  string ClientData::getLastName() const
32  {
33     return lastName;
34  } // end function getLastName
35
36  // set last-name value
37  void ClientData::setLastName( string lastNameString )
38  {
39     // copy at most 15 characters from string to lastName
40     const char *lastNameValue = lastNameString.data();
41     int length = lastNameString.size();
42     length = ( length < 15 ? length : 14 );
43     strncpy( lastName, lastNameValue, length );
44     lastName[ length ] = '\0'; // append null character to lastName
45  } // end function setLastName
46
47  // get first-name value
48  string ClientData::getFirstName() const
49  {
50     return firstName;
51  } // end function getFirstName
52
```

Fig. 17.11 | ClientData class represents a customer's credit information. (Part 1 of 2.)

```
53   // set first-name value
54   void ClientData::setFirstName( string firstNameString )
55   {
56      // copy at most 10 characters from string to firstName
57      const char *firstNameValue = firstNameString.data();
58      int length = firstNameString.size();
59      length = ( length < 10 ? length : 9 );
60      strncpy( firstName, firstNameValue, length );
61      firstName[ length ] = '\0'; // append null character to firstName
62   } // end function setFirstName
63
64   // get balance value
65   double ClientData::getBalance() const
66   {
67      return balance;
68   } // end function getBalance
69
70   // set balance value
71   void ClientData::setBalance( double balanceValue )
72   {
73      balance = balanceValue;
74   } // end function setBalance
```

Fig. 17.11 | `ClientData` class represents a customer's credit information. (Part 2 of 2.)

In Fig. 17.12, line 18 creates an `ofstream` object for the file `credit.dat`. The second argument to the constructor—`ios::binary`—indicates that we are opening the file for output in binary mode, which is required if we are to write fixed-length records. Lines 31–32 cause the `blankClient` to be written to the `credit.dat` file associated with `ofstream` object `outCredit`. Remember that operator `sizeof` returns the size in bytes of the object contained in parentheses (see Chapter 8). The first argument to function `write` on line 31 must be of type `const char *`. However, the data type of `&blankClient` is `ClientData *`. To convert `&blankClient` to `const char *`, line 31 uses the cast operator `reinterpret_cast`, so the call to `write` compiles without issuing a compilation error.

```
1    // Fig. 17.12: Fig17_12.cpp
2    // Creating a randomly accessed file.
3    #include <iostream>
4    using std::cerr;
5    using std::endl;
6    using std::ios;
7
8    #include <fstream>
9    using std::ofstream;
10
11   #include <cstdlib>
12   using std::exit; // exit function prototype
13
14   #include "ClientData.h" // ClientData class definition
15
```

Fig. 17.12 | Creating a random-access file with 100 blank records sequentially. (Part 1 of 2.)

```
16   int main()
17   {
18      ofstream outCredit( "credit.dat", ios::binary );
19
20      // exit program if ofstream could not open file
21      if ( !outCredit )
22      {
23         cerr << "File could not be opened." << endl;
24         exit( 1 );
25      } // end if
26
27      ClientData blankClient; // constructor zeros out each data member
28
29      // output 100 blank records to file
30      for ( int i = 0; i < 100; i++ )
31         outCredit.write( reinterpret_cast< const char * >( &blankClient ),
32            sizeof( ClientData ) );
33
34      return 0;
35   } // end main
```

Fig. 17.12 | Creating a random-access file with 100 blank records sequentially. (Part 2 of 2.)

17.9 Writing Data Randomly to a Random-Access File

Figure 17.13 writes data to the file credit.dat and uses the combination of fstream functions seekp and write to store data at exact locations in the file. Function seekp sets the "put" file-position pointer to a specific position in the file, then write outputs the data. Note that line 19 includes the header file ClientData.h defined in Fig. 17.10, so the program can use ClientData objects.

```
1    // Fig. 17.13: Fig17_13.cpp
2    // Writing to a random-access file.
3    #include <iostream>
4    using std::cerr;
5    using std::cin;
6    using std::cout;
7    using std::endl;
8    using std::ios;
9
10   #include <iomanip>
11   using std::setw;
12
13   #include <fstream>
14   using std::fstream;
15
16   #include <cstdlib>
17   using std::exit; // exit function prototype
18
19   #include "ClientData.h" // ClientData class definition
20
```

Fig. 17.13 | Writing to a random-access file. (Part 1 of 3.)

```
21   int main()
22   {
23      int accountNumber;
24      char lastName[ 15 ];
25      char firstName[ 10 ];
26      double balance;
27
28      fstream outCredit( "credit.dat", ios::in | ios::out | ios::binary );
29
30      // exit program if fstream cannot open file
31      if ( !outCredit )
32      {
33         cerr << "File could not be opened." << endl;
34         exit( 1 );
35      } // end if
36
37      cout << "Enter account number (1 to 100, 0 to end input)\n? ";
38
39      // require user to specify account number
40      ClientData client;
41      cin >> accountNumber;
42
43      // user enters information, which is copied into file
44      while ( accountNumber > 0 && accountNumber <= 100 )
45      {
46         // user enters last name, first name and balance
47         cout << "Enter lastname, firstname, balance\n? ";
48         cin >> setw( 15 ) >> lastName;
49         cin >> setw( 10 ) >> firstName;
50         cin >> balance;
51
52         // set record accountNumber, lastName, firstName and balance values
53         client.setAccountNumber( accountNumber );
54         client.setLastName( lastName );
55         client.setFirstName( firstName );
56         client.setBalance( balance );
57
58         // seek position in file of user-specified record
59         outCredit.seekp( ( client.getAccountNumber() - 1 ) *
60            sizeof( ClientData ) );
61
62         // write user-specified information in file
63         outCredit.write( reinterpret_cast< const char * >( &client ),
64            sizeof( ClientData ) );
65
66         // enable user to enter another account
67         cout << "Enter account number\n? ";
68         cin >> accountNumber;
69      } // end while
70
71      return 0;
72   } // end main
```

Fig. 17.13 | Writing to a random-access file. (Part 2 of 3.)

```
Enter account number (1 to 100, 0 to end input)
? 37
Enter lastname, firstname, balance
? Barker Doug 0.00
Enter account number
? 29
Enter lastname, firstname, balance
? Brown Nancy -24.54
Enter account number
? 96
Enter lastname, firstname, balance
? Stone Sam 34.98
Enter account number
? 88
Enter lastname, firstname, balance
? Smith Dave 258.34
Enter account number
? 33
Enter lastname, firstname, balance
? Dunn Stacey 314.33
Enter account number
? 0
```

Fig. 17.13 | Writing to a random-access file. (Part 3 of 3.)

Lines 59–60 position the "put" file-position pointer for object outCredit to the byte location calculated by

$$(client.getAccountNumber() - 1) * sizeof(ClientData)$$

Because the account number is between 1 and 100, 1 is subtracted from the account number when calculating the byte location of the record. Thus, for record 1, the file-position pointer is set to byte 0 of the file. Note that line 28 uses the fstream object outCredit to open the existing credit.dat file. The file is opened for input and output in binary mode by combining the file-open modes ios::in, ios::out and ios::binary. Multiple file-open modes are combined by separating each open mode from the next with the bitwise inclusive OR operator (|). Opening the existing credit.dat file in this manner ensures that this program can manipulate the records written to the file by the program of Fig. 17.12, rather than creating the file from scratch.

17.10 Reading from a Random-Access File Sequentially

In the previous sections, we created a random-access file and wrote data to that file. In this section, we develop a program that reads the file sequentially and prints only those records that contain data. These programs produce an additional benefit. See if you can determine what it is; we will reveal it at the end of this section.

The istream function read inputs a specified number of bytes from the current position in the specified stream into an object. For example, lines 57–58 from Fig. 17.14 read the number of bytes specified by sizeof(ClientData) from the file associated with ifstream object inCredit and store the data in the client record. Note that function read requires a first argument of type char *. Since &client is of type ClientData *,

&client must be cast to char * using the cast operator reinterpret_cast. Note that line 24 includes the header file clientData.h defined in Fig. 17.10, so the program can use ClientData objects.

Figure 17.14 reads every record in the credit.dat file sequentially, checks each record to determine whether it contains data, and displays formatted outputs for records containing data. The condition in line 50 uses the ios member function eof to determine when the end of file is reached and causes execution of the while statement to terminate. Also, if an error occurs when reading from the file, the loop terminates, because inCredit evaluates to false. The data input from the file is output by function outputLine (lines 65–72), which takes two arguments—an ostream object and a clientData structure to be output. The ostream parameter type is interesting, because any ostream object (such as cout) or any object of a derived class of ostream (such as an object of type ofstream) can

```
1   // Fig. 17.14: Fig17_14.cpp
2   // Reading a random access file sequentially.
3   #include <iostream>
4   using std::cerr;
5   using std::cout;
6   using std::endl;
7   using std::fixed;
8   using std::ios;
9   using std::left;
10  using std::right;
11  using std::showpoint;
12
13  #include <iomanip>
14  using std::setprecision;
15  using std::setw;
16
17  #include <fstream>
18  using std::ifstream;
19  using std::ostream;
20
21  #include <cstdlib>
22  using std::exit; // exit function prototype
23
24  #include "ClientData.h" // ClientData class definition
25
26  void outputLine( ostream&, const ClientData & ); // prototype
27
28  int main()
29  {
30     ifstream inCredit( "credit.dat", ios::in );
31
32     // exit program if ifstream cannot open file
33     if ( !inCredit )
34     {
35        cerr << "File could not be opened." << endl;
36        exit( 1 );
37     } // end if
```

Fig. 17.14 | Reading a random-access file sequentially. (Part 1 of 2.)

```
38
39       cout << left << setw( 10 ) << "Account" << setw( 16 )
40          << "Last Name" << setw( 11 ) << "First Name" << left
41          << setw( 10 ) << right << "Balance" << endl;
42
43       ClientData client; // create record
44
45       // read first record from file
46       inCredit.read( reinterpret_cast< char * >( &client ),
47          sizeof( ClientData ) );
48
49       // read all records from file
50       while ( inCredit && !inCredit.eof() )
51       {
52          // display record
53          if ( client.getAccountNumber() != 0 )
54             outputLine( cout, client );
55
56          // read next from file
57          inCredit.read( reinterpret_cast< char * >( &client ),
58             sizeof( ClientData ) );
59       } // end while
60
61       return 0;
62    } // end main
63
64    // display single record
65    void outputLine( ostream &output, const ClientData &record )
66    {
67       output << left << setw( 10 ) << record.getAccountNumber()
68          << setw( 16 ) << record.getLastName()
69          << setw( 11 ) << record.getFirstName()
70          << setw( 10 ) << setprecision( 2 ) << right << fixed
71          << showpoint << record.getBalance() << endl;
72    } // end function outputLine
```

Account	Last Name	First Name	Balance
29	Brown	Nancy	-24.54
33	Dunn	Stacey	314.33
37	Barker	Doug	0.00
88	Smith	Dave	258.34
96	Stone	Sam	34.98

Fig. 17.14 | Reading a random-access file sequentially. (Part 2 of 2.)

be supplied as the argument. This means that the same function can be used, for example, to perform output to the standard-output stream and to a file stream without writing separate functions.

What about that additional benefit we promised? If you examine the output window, you will notice that the records are listed in sorted order (by account number). This is a consequence of how we stored these records in the file, using direct-access techniques. Compared to the insertion sort we used in Chapter 7, sorting using direct-access techniques is relatively fast. The speed is achieved by making the file large enough to hold every possible record that might be created. This, of course, means that the file could be occupied sparsely most of the time, resulting in a waste of storage. This is another example of the space-time trade-off: By using large amounts of space, we are able to develop a much faster sorting algorithm. Fortunately, the continuous reduction in price of storage units has made this less of an issue.

17.11 Case Study: A Transaction-Processing Program

We now present a substantial transaction-processing program (Fig. 17.15) using a random-access file to achieve "instant" access processing. The program maintains a bank's account information. The program updates existing accounts, adds new accounts, deletes accounts and stores a formatted listing of all current accounts in a text file. We assume that the program of Fig. 17.12 has been executed to create the file credit.dat and that the program of Fig. 17.13 has been executed to insert the initial data.

```
1   // Fig. 17.15: Fig17_15.cpp
2   // This program reads a random access file sequentially, updates
3   // data previously written to the file, creates data to be placed
4   // in the file, and deletes data previously in the file.
5   #include <iostream>
6   using std::cerr;
7   using std::cin;
8   using std::cout;
9   using std::endl;
10  using std::fixed;
11  using std::ios;
12  using std::left;
13  using std::right;
14  using std::showpoint;
15
16  #include <fstream>
17  using std::ofstream;
18  using std::ostream;
19  using std::fstream;
20
21  #include <iomanip>
22  using std::setw;
23  using std::setprecision;
24
25  #include <cstdlib>
26  using std::exit; // exit function prototype
27
28  #include "ClientData.h" // ClientData class definition
29
30  int enterChoice();
31  void createTextFile( fstream& );
32  void updateRecord( fstream& );
33  void newRecord( fstream& );
34  void deleteRecord( fstream& );
```

Fig. 17.15 | Bank account program. (Part 1 of 6.)

```
35    void outputLine( ostream&, const ClientData & );
36    int getAccount( const char * const );
37
38    enum Choices { PRINT = 1, UPDATE, NEW, DELETE, END };
39
40    int main()
41    {
42       // open file for reading and writing
43       fstream inOutCredit( "credit.dat", ios::in | ios::out );
44
45       // exit program if fstream cannot open file
46       if ( !inOutCredit )
47       {
48          cerr << "File could not be opened." << endl;
49          exit ( 1 );
50       } // end if
51
52       int choice; // store user choice
53
54       // enable user to specify action
55       while ( ( choice = enterChoice() ) != END )
56       {
57          switch ( choice )
58          {
59             case PRINT: // create text file from record file
60                createTextFile( inOutCredit );
61                break;
62             case UPDATE: // update record
63                updateRecord( inOutCredit );
64                break;
65             case NEW: // create record
66                newRecord( inOutCredit );
67                break;
68             case DELETE: // delete existing record
69                deleteRecord( inOutCredit );
70                break;
71             default: // display error if user does not select valid choice
72                cerr << "Incorrect choice" << endl;
73                break;
74          } // end switch
75
76          inOutCredit.clear(); // reset end-of-file indicator
77       } // end while
78
79       return 0;
80    } // end main
81
82    // enable user to input menu choice
83    int enterChoice()
84    {
85       // display available options
86       cout << "\nEnter your choice" << endl
87            << "1 - store a formatted text file of accounts" << endl
```

Fig. 17.15 | Bank account program. (Part 2 of 6.)

```
88          << "   called \"print.txt\" for printing" << endl
89          << "2 - update an account" << endl
90          << "3 - add a new account" << endl
91          << "4 - delete an account" << endl
92          << "5 - end program\n? ";
93
94      int menuChoice;
95      cin >> menuChoice; // input menu selection from user
96      return menuChoice;
97   } // end function enterChoice
98
99   // create formatted text file for printing
100  void createTextFile( fstream &readFromFile )
101  {
102      // create text file
103      ofstream outPrintFile( "print.txt", ios::out );
104
105      // exit program if ofstream cannot create file
106      if ( !outPrintFile )
107      {
108         cerr << "File could not be created." << endl;
109         exit( 1 );
110      } // end if
111
112      outPrintFile << left << setw( 10 ) << "Account" << setw( 16 )
113         << "Last Name" << setw( 11 ) << "First Name" << right
114         << setw( 10 ) << "Balance" << endl;
115
116      // set file-position pointer to beginning of readFromFile
117      readFromFile.seekg( 0 );
118
119      // read first record from record file
120      ClientData client;
121      readFromFile.read( reinterpret_cast< char * >( &client ),
122         sizeof( ClientData ) );
123
124      // copy all records from record file into text file
125      while ( !readFromFile.eof() )
126      {
127         // write single record to text file
128         if ( client.getAccountNumber() != 0 ) // skip empty records
129            outputLine( outPrintFile, client );
130
131         // read next record from record file
132         readFromFile.read( reinterpret_cast< char * >( &client ),
133            sizeof( ClientData ) );
134      } // end while
135  } // end function createTextFile
136
137  // update balance in record
138  void updateRecord( fstream &updateFile )
139  {
```

Fig. 17.15 | Bank account program. (Part 3 of 6.)

```
140     // obtain number of account to update
141     int accountNumber = getAccount( "Enter account to update" );
142
143     // move file-position pointer to correct record in file
144     updateFile.seekg( ( accountNumber - 1 ) * sizeof( ClientData ) );
145
146     // read first record from file
147     ClientData client;
148     updateFile.read( reinterpret_cast< char * >( &client ),
149         sizeof( ClientData ) );
150
151     // update record
152     if ( client.getAccountNumber() != 0 )
153     {
154         outputLine( cout, client ); // display the record
155
156         // request user to specify transaction
157         cout << "\nEnter charge (+) or payment (-): ";
158         double transaction; // charge or payment
159         cin >> transaction;
160
161         // update record balance
162         double oldBalance = client.getBalance();
163         client.setBalance( oldBalance + transaction );
164         outputLine( cout, client ); // display the record
165
166         // move file-position pointer to correct record in file
167         updateFile.seekp( ( accountNumber - 1 ) * sizeof( ClientData ) );
168
169         // write updated record over old record in file
170         updateFile.write( reinterpret_cast< const char * >( &client ),
171             sizeof( ClientData ) );
172     } // end if
173     else // display error if account does not exist
174         cerr << "Account #" << accountNumber
175             << " has no information." << endl;
176 } // end function updateRecord
177
178 // create and insert record
179 void newRecord( fstream &insertInFile )
180 {
181     // obtain number of account to create
182     int accountNumber = getAccount( "Enter new account number" );
183
184     // move file-position pointer to correct record in file
185     insertInFile.seekg( ( accountNumber - 1 ) * sizeof( ClientData ) );
186
187     // read record from file
188     ClientData client;
189     insertInFile.read( reinterpret_cast< char * >( &client ),
190         sizeof( ClientData ) );
191
```

Fig. 17.15 | Bank account program. (Part 4 of 6.)

```
192     // create record, if record does not previously exist
193     if ( client.getAccountNumber() == 0 )
194     {
195        char lastName[ 15 ];
196        char firstName[ 10 ];
197        double balance;
198
199        // user enters last name, first name and balance
200        cout << "Enter lastname, firstname, balance\n? ";
201        cin >> setw( 15 ) >> lastName;
202        cin >> setw( 10 ) >> firstName;
203        cin >> balance;
204
205        // use values to populate account values
206        client.setLastName( lastName );
207        client.setFirstName( firstName );
208        client.setBalance( balance );
209        client.setAccountNumber( accountNumber );
210
211        // move file-position pointer to correct record in file
212        insertInFile.seekp( ( accountNumber - 1 ) * sizeof( ClientData ) );
213
214        // insert record in file
215        insertInFile.write( reinterpret_cast< const char * >( &client ),
216           sizeof( ClientData ) );
217     } // end if
218     else // display error if account already exists
219        cerr << "Account #" << accountNumber
220           << " already contains information." << endl;
221  } // end function newRecord
222
223  // delete an existing record
224  void deleteRecord( fstream &deleteFromFile )
225  {
226     // obtain number of account to delete
227     int accountNumber = getAccount( "Enter account to delete" );
228
229     // move file-position pointer to correct record in file
230     deleteFromFile.seekg( ( accountNumber - 1 ) * sizeof( ClientData ) );
231
232     // read record from file
233     ClientData client;
234     deleteFromFile.read( reinterpret_cast< char * >( &client ),
235        sizeof( ClientData ) );
236
237     // delete record, if record exists in file
238     if ( client.getAccountNumber() != 0 )
239     {
240        ClientData blankClient; // create blank record
241
242        // move file-position pointer to correct record in file
243        deleteFromFile.seekp( ( accountNumber - 1 ) *
244           sizeof( ClientData ) );
```

Fig. 17.15 | Bank account program. (Part 5 of 6.)

```
245
246        // replace existing record with blank record
247        deleteFromFile.write(
248           reinterpret_cast< const char * >( &blankClient ),
249           sizeof( ClientData ) );
250
251        cout << "Account #" << accountNumber << " deleted.\n";
252     } // end if
253     else // display error if record does not exist
254        cerr << "Account #" << accountNumber << " is empty.\n";
255  } // end deleteRecord
256
257  // display single record
258  void outputLine( ostream &output, const ClientData &record )
259  {
260     output << left << setw( 10 ) << record.getAccountNumber()
261        << setw( 16 ) << record.getLastName()
262        << setw( 11 ) << record.getFirstName()
263        << setw( 10 ) << setprecision( 2 ) << right << fixed
264        << showpoint << record.getBalance() << endl;
265  } // end function outputLine
266
267  // obtain account-number value from user
268  int getAccount( const char * const prompt )
269  {
270     int accountNumber;
271
272     // obtain account-number value
273     do
274     {
275        cout << prompt << " (1 - 100): ";
276        cin >> accountNumber;
277     } while ( accountNumber < 1 || accountNumber > 100 );
278
279     return accountNumber;
280  } // end function getAccount
```

Fig. 17.15 | Bank account program. (Part 6 of 6.)

The program has five options (option 5 is for terminating the program). Option 1 calls function createTextFile to store a formatted list of all the account information in a text file called print.txt that may be printed. Function createTextFile (lines 100–135) takes an fstream object as an argument to be used to input data from the credit.dat file. Function createTextFile invokes istream member function read (lines 132–133) and uses the sequential-file-access techniques of Fig. 17.14 to input data from credit.dat. Function outputLine, discussed in Section 17.10, is used to output the data to file print.txt. Note that createTextFile uses istream member function seekg (line 117) to ensure that the file-position pointer is at the beginning of the file. After choosing Option 1, the print.txt file contains

```
Account    Last Name      First Name      Balance
29         Brown          Nancy           -24.54
33         Dunn           Stacey          314.33
37         Barker         Doug              0.00
88         Smith          Dave            258.34
96         Stone          Sam              34.98
```

Option 2 calls updateRecord (lines 138–176) to update an account. This function updates only an existing record, so the function first determines whether the specified record is empty. Lines 148–149 read data into object client, using istream member function read. Then line 152 compares the value returned by getAccountNumber of the client structure to zero to determine whether the record contains information. If this value is zero, lines 174–175 print an error message indicating that the record is empty. If the record contains information, line 154 displays the record, using function outputLine, line 159 inputs the transaction amount and lines 162–171 calculate the new balance and rewrite the record to the file. A typical output for Option 2 is

```
Enter account to update (1 - 100): 37
37         Barker         Doug              0.00

Enter charge (+) or payment (-): +87.99
37         Barker         Doug             87.99
```

Option 3 calls function newRecord (lines 179–221) to add a new account to the file. If the user enters an account number for an existing account, newRecord displays an error message indicating that the account exists (lines 219–220). This function adds a new account in the same manner as the program of Fig. 17.12. A typical output for Option 3 is

```
Enter new account number (1 - 100): 22
Enter lastname, firstname, balance
? Johnston Sarah 247.45
```

Option 4 calls function deleteRecord (lines 224–255) to delete a record from the file. Line 227 prompts the user to enter the account number. Only an existing record may be deleted, so, if the specified account is empty, line 254 displays an error message. If the account exists, lines 247–249 reinitialize that account by copying an empty record (blankClient) to the file. Line 251 displays a message to inform the user that the record has been deleted. A typical output for Option 4 is

```
Enter account to delete (1 - 100): 29
Account #29 deleted.
```

Note that line 43 opens the credit.dat file by creating an fstream object for both reading and writing, using modes ios::in and ios::out "or-ed" together.

17.12 Input/Output of Objects

This chapter and Chapter 15 introduced C++'s object-oriented style of input/output. However, our examples concentrated on I/O of traditional data types rather than objects of user-defined types. In Chapter 11, we showed how to input and output objects using operator overloading. We accomplished object input by overloading the stream extraction operator >> for the appropriate `istream`. We accomplished object output by overloading the stream insertion operator << for the appropriate `ostream`. In both cases, only an object's data members were input or output, and, in each case, they were in a format meaningful only for objects of that particular abstract data type. An object's member functions are not input and output with the object's data; rather, one copy of the class's member functions remains available internally and is shared by all objects of the class.

When object data members are output to a disk file, we lose the object's type information. We store only data bytes, not type information, on the disk. If the program that reads this data knows the object type to which the data corresponds, the program will read the data into objects of that type.

An interesting problem occurs when we store objects of different types in the same file. How can we distinguish them (or their collections of data members) as we read them into a program? The problem is that objects typically do not have type fields (we studied this issue carefully in Chapter 13).

One approach would be to have each overloaded output operator output a type code preceding each collection of data members that represents one object. Then object input would always begin by reading the type-code field and using a `switch` statement to invoke the proper overloaded function. Although this solution lacks the elegance of polymorphic programming, it provides a workable mechanism for retaining objects in files and retrieving them as needed.

Summary

- Files are used for data persistence—permanent retention of large amounts of data.
- The smallest data item that computers support is called a bit (short for "binary digit"—a digit that can assume one of two values, 0 or 1).
- Digits, letters and special symbols are referred to as characters.
- The set of all characters used to write programs and represent data items on a particular computer is called that computer's character set.
- Bytes are composed of eight bits.
- Just as characters are composed of bits, fields are composed of characters. A field is a group of characters that conveys some meaning.
- Typically, a record (i.e., a class in C++) is composed of several fields (i.e., data members in C++).
- At least one field in a record is chosen as a record key to identify a record as belonging to a particular person or entity that is distinct from all other records in the file.
- In a sequential file, records typically are stored in order by a record-key field.
- A group of related files often are stored in a database.
- A collection of programs designed to create and manage databases is called a database management system (DBMS).

- C++ views each file as a sequential stream of bytes.
- Each file ends either with an end-of-file marker or at a specific byte number recorded in a system-maintained, administrative data structure.
- Header `<fstream>` includes the definitions for the stream class templates `basic_ifstream` (for file input), `basic_ofstream` (for file output) and `basic_fstream` (for file input and output).
- For an `ofstream` object, the file-open mode can be either `ios::out` to output data to a file or `ios::app` to append data to the end of a file (without modifying any data already in the file).
- The file-open mode `ios::ate` opens a file for output and moves to the end of the file. This is normally used to append data to a file, but data can be written anywhere in the file.
- Existing files opened with mode `ios::out` are truncated (i.e., all data in the file is discarded).
- By default, `ofstream` objects are opened for output.
- The `ofstream` member function `open` opens a file and attaches it to an existing `ofstream` object.
- An overloaded `ios` operator member function—`operator void*`—converts the stream to a pointer, so it can be tested as 0 (i.e., the null pointer) or nonzero (i.e., any other pointer value).
- You can use the `ofstream` member function `close` to close the `ofstream` object explicitly.
- Both `istream` and `ostream` provide member functions for repositioning the file-position pointer (the byte number of the next byte in the file to be read or written). These member functions are `seekg` ("seek get") for `istream` and `seekp` ("seek put") for `ostream`.
- The seek direction can be `ios::beg` (the default) for positioning relative to the beginning of a stream, `ios::cur` for positioning relative to the current position in a stream or `ios::end` for positioning relative to the end of a stream.
- Member functions `tellg` and `tellp` are provided to return the current locations of the "get" and "put" pointers, respectively.
- Individual records of a random-access file can be accessed directly (and quickly) without the need to search other records.
- The `ostream` member function `write` outputs a fixed number of bytes, beginning at a specific location in memory, to the specified stream. When the stream is associated with a file, function `write` writes the data at the location in the file specified by the "put" file-position pointer.
- The `istream` member function `read` inputs a fixed number of bytes from the specified stream to an area in memory beginning at a specified address. If the stream is associated with a file, function `read` inputs bytes at the location in the file specified by the "get" file-position pointer.
- `string` member function `data` converts a string to a non-null-terminated C-style character array.

Terminology

binary digit
bit
byte
character field
character set
`cin` (standard input)
`clog` (standard error buffered)
`close` member function of `ofstream`
database
database management system (DBMS)
`data` function of `string`
data hierarchy

data persistence
decimal digit
end-of-file
field
file
file name
file-position pointer
`fstream`
`<fstream>` header file
instant-access application
`ios::app` file open mode
`ios::ate` file open mode

ios::beg seek starting point
ios::binary file open mode
ios::cur seek direction
ios::end seek direction
ios::in file open mode
ios::out file open mode
ios::trunc file open mode
offset from the beginning of a file
open a file
open member function of ofstream
random-access file
record

record key
secondary storage device
seek direction
seekg istream member function
seekp ostream member function
sequential file
size function of string
special symbol
tellg istream member function
tellp ostream member function
transaction-processing system
truncate an existing file

Self-Review Exercises

17.1 Fill in the blanks in each of the following:
  a) Ultimately, all data items processed by a computer are reduced to combinations of _____ and _____.
  b) The smallest data item a computer can process is called a _____.
  c) A(n) _____ is a group of related records.
  d) Digits, letters and special symbols are referred to as _____.
  e) A group of related files is called a(n) _____.
  f) Member function _____ of the file streams fstream, ifstream and ofstream closes a file.
  g) The istream member function _____ reads a character from the specified stream.
  h) Member function _____ of the file streams fstream, ifstream and ofstream opens a file.
  i) The istream member function _____ is normally used when reading data from a file in random-access applications.
  j) Member functions _____ and _____ of istream and ostream, set the file-position pointer to a specific location in an input or output stream, respectively.

17.2 State which of the following are *true* and which are *false*. If *false*, explain why.
  a) Member function read cannot be used to read data from the input object cin.
  b) The programmer must create the cin, cout, cerr and clog objects explicitly.
  c) A program must call function close explicitly to close a file associated with an ifstream, ofstream or fstream object.
  d) If the file-position pointer points to a location in a sequential file other than the beginning of the file, the file must be closed and reopened to read from the beginning of the file.
  e) The ostream member function write can write to standard-output stream cout.
  f) Data in sequential files always is updated without overwriting nearby data.
  g) Searching all records in a random-access file to find a specific record is unnecessary.
  h) Records in random-access files must be of uniform length.
  i) Member functions seekp and seekg must seek relative to the beginning of a file.

17.3 Assume that each of the following statements applies to the same program.
  a) Write a statement that opens file oldmast.dat for input; use an ifstream object called inOldMaster.
  b) Write a statement that opens file trans.dat for input; use an ifstream object called inTransaction.

c) Write a statement that opens file `newmast.dat` for output (and creation); use `ofstream` object `outNewMaster`.

d) Write a statement that reads a record from the file `oldmast.dat`. The record consists of integer `accountNumber`, string `name` and floating-point `currentBalance`; use `ifstream` object `inOldMaster`.

e) Write a statement that reads a record from the file `trans.dat`. The record consists of integer `accountNum` and floating-point `dollarAmount`; use `ifstream` object `inTransaction`.

f) Write a statement that writes a record to the file `newmast.dat`. The record consists of integer `accountNum`, string `name`, and floating-point `currentBalance`; use `ofstream` object `outNewMaster`.

17.4 Find the error(s) and show how to correct it (them) in each of the following.

a) File `payables.dat` referred to by `ofstream` object `outPayable` has not been opened.

```
outPayable << account << company << amount << endl;
```

b) The following statement should read a record from the file `payables.dat`. The `ifstream` object `inPayable` refers to this file, and `istream` object `inReceivable` refers to the file `receivables.dat`.

```
inReceivable >> account >> company >> amount;
```

c) The file `tools.dat` should be opened to add data to the file without discarding the current data.

```
ofstream outTools( "tools.dat", ios::out );
```

Answers to Self-Review Exercises

17.1 a) 1s, 0s. b) bit. c) file. d) characters. e) database. f) `close`. g) `get`. h) `open`. i) `read`. j) `seekg`, `seekp`.

17.2 a) False. Function `read` can read from any input stream object derived from `istream`.

b) False. These four streams are created automatically for the programmer. The `<iostream>` header must be included in a file to use them. This header includes declarations for each stream object.

c) False. The files will be closed when destructors for `ifstream`, `ofstream` or `fstream` objects execute when the stream objects go out of scope or before program execution terminates, but it is a good programming practice to close all files explicitly with `close` once they are no longer needed.

d) False. Member function `seekp` or `seekg` can be used to reposition the put or get file-position pointer to the beginning of the file.

e) True.

f) False. In most cases, sequential file records are not of uniform length. Therefore, it is possible that updating a record will cause other data to be overwritten.

g) True.

h) False. Records in a random-access file normally are of uniform length.

i) False. It is possible to seek from the beginning of the file, from the end of the file and from the current position in the file.

17.3 a) `ifstream inOldMaster( "oldmast.dat", ios::in );`

b) `ifstream inTransaction( "trans.dat", ios::in );`

c) `ofstream outNewMaster( "newmast.dat", ios::out );`

d) `inOldMaster >> accountNumber >> name >> currentBalance;`

e) `inTransaction >> accountNum >> dollarAmount;`

f) `outNewMaster << accountNum << name << currentBalance;`

17.4 a) Error: The file `payables.dat` has not been opened before the attempt is made to output data to the stream.
Correction: Use ostream function `open` to open `payables.dat` for output.
b) Error: The incorrect `istream` object is being used to read a record from the file named `payables.dat`.
Correction: Use `istream` object `inPayable` to refer to `payables.dat`.
c) Error: The file's contents are discarded because the file is opened for output (`ios::out`).
Correction: To add data to the file, open the file either for updating (`ios::ate`) or for appending (`ios::app`).

Exercises

17.5 Fill in the blanks in each of the following:
a) Computers store large amounts of data on secondary storage devices as _____.
b) A(n) _____ is composed of several fields.
c) To facilitate the retrieval of specific records from a file, one field in each record is chosen as a _____.
d) The vast majority of information stored in computer systems is stored in _____ files.
e) A group of related characters that conveys meaning is called a(n) _____.
f) The standard stream objects declared by header `<iostream>` are _____, _____, _____ and _____.
g) ostream member function _____ outputs a character to the specified stream.
h) ostream member function _____ is generally used to write data to a randomly accessed file.
i) istream member function _____ repositions the file-position pointer in a file.

17.6 State which of the following are *true* and which are *false*. If *false*, explain why.
a) The impressive functions performed by computers essentially involve the manipulation of zeros and ones.
b) People prefer to manipulate bits instead of characters and fields because bits are more compact.
c) People specify programs and data items as characters; computers then manipulate and process these characters as groups of zeros and ones.
d) A person's 5-digit zip code is an example of a numeric field.
e) A person's street address is generally considered to be an alphabetic field in computer applications.
f) Data items represented in computers form a data hierarchy in which data items become larger and more complex as we progress from fields to characters to bits, etc.
g) A record key identifies a record as belonging to a particular field.
h) Most organizations store all information in a single file to facilitate computer processing.
i) When a program creates a file, the file is automatically retained by the computer for future reference; i.e., files are said to be persistent.

17.7 Exercise 17.3 asked the reader to write a series of single statements. Actually, these statements form the core of an important type of file-processing program, namely, a file-matching program. In commercial data processing, it is common to have several files in each application system. In an accounts-receivable system, for example, there is generally a master file containing detailed information about each customer, such as the customer's name, address, telephone number, outstanding balance, credit limit, discount terms, contract arrangements and, possibly, a condensed history of recent purchases and cash payments.

As transactions occur (e.g., sales are made and cash payments arrive), they are entered into a file. At the end of each business period (a month for some companies, a week for others and a day in some cases), the file of transactions (called `trans.dat` in Exercise 17.3) is applied to the master file (called `oldmast.dat` in Exercise 17.3), thus updating each account's record of purchases and payments. During an updating run, the master file is rewritten as a new file (`newmast.dat`), which is then used at the end of the next business period to begin the updating process again.

File-matching programs must deal with certain problems that do not exist in single-file programs. For example, a match does not always occur. A customer on the master file might not have made any purchases or cash payments in the current business period, and therefore no record for this customer will appear on the transaction file. Similarly, a customer who did make some purchases or cash payments may have just moved to this community, and the company may not have had a chance to create a master record for this customer.

Use the statements from Exercise 17.3 as a basis for writing a complete file-matching accounts-receivable program. Use the account number on each file as the record key for matching purposes. Assume that each file is a sequential file with records stored in increasing order by account number.

When a match occurs (i.e., records with the same account number appear on both the master and transaction files), add the dollar amount on the transaction file to the current balance on the master file, and write the `newmast.dat` record. (Assume purchases are indicated by positive amounts on the transaction file and payments are indicated by negative amounts.) When there is a master record for a particular account but no corresponding transaction record, merely write the master record to `newmast.dat`. When there is a transaction record but no corresponding master record, print the error message `"Unmatched transaction record for account number ..."` (fill in the account number from the transaction record).

17.8　　After writing the program of Exercise 17.7, write a simple program to create some test data for checking out the program. Use the following sample account data:

Master file Account number	Name	Balance
100	Alan Jones	348.17
300	Mary Smith	27.19
500	Sam Sharp	0.00
700	Suzy Green	−14.22

Transaction file Account number	Transaction amount
100	27.14
300	62.11
400	100.56
900	82.17

17.9 Run the program of Exercise 17.7, using the files of test data created in Exercise 17.8. Print the new master file. Check that the accounts have been updated correctly.

17.10 It is possible (actually common) to have several transaction records with the same record key. This occurs because a particular customer might make several purchases and cash payments during a business period. Rewrite your accounts-receivable file-matching program of Exercise 17.7 to provide for the possibility of handling several transaction records with the same record key. Modify the test data of Exercise 17.8 to include the following additional transaction records:

Account number	Dollar amount
300	83.89
700	80.78
700	1.53

17.11 Write a series of statements that accomplish each of the following. Assume that we have defined class `Person` that contains `private` data members

```
char lastName[ 15 ];
char firstName[ 15 ];
char age[ 4 ];
```

and `public` member functions

```
// accessor functions for lastName
void setLastName( string );
string getLastName() const;

// accessor functions for firstName
void setFirstName( string );
string getFirstName() const;

// accessor functions for age
void setAge( string );
string getAge() const;
```

Also assume that any random-access files have been opened properly.
a) Initialize the file nameage.dat with 100 records that store values lastName = "unassigned", firstName = "" and age = "0".
b) Input 10 last names, first names and ages, and write them to the file.
c) Update a record that already contains information. If the record does not contain information, inform the user "No info".
d) Delete a record that contains information by reinitializing that particular record.

17.12 You are the owner of a hardware store and need to keep an inventory that can tell you what different tools you have, how many of each you have on hand and the cost of each one. Write a program that initializes the random-access file hardware.dat to 100 empty records, lets you input the data concerning each tool, enables you to list all your tools, lets you delete a record for a tool that you no longer have and lets you update *any* information in the file. The tool identification number should be the record number. Use the following information to start your file:

Record #	Tool name	Quantity	Cost
3	Electric sander	7	57.98
17	Hammer	76	11.99
24	Jig saw	21	11.00
39	Lawn mower	3	79.50
56	Power saw	18	99.99
68	Screwdriver	106	6.99
77	Sledge hammer	11	21.50
83	Wrench	34	7.50

17.13 (*Telephone Number Word Generator*) Standard telephone keypads contain the digits 0 through 9. The numbers 2 through 9 each have three letters associated with them, as is indicated by the following table:

Digit	Letter
2	A B C
3	D E F
4	G H I
5	J K L
6	M N O
7	P R S
8	T U V
9	W X Y

Many people find it difficult to memorize phone numbers, so they use the correspondence between digits and letters to develop seven-letter words that correspond to their phone numbers. For example, a person whose telephone number is 686-2377 might use the correspondence indicated in the above table to develop the seven-letter word "NUMBERS."

Businesses frequently attempt to get telephone numbers that are easy for their clients to remember. If a business can advertise a simple word for its customers to dial, then no doubt the business will receive a few more calls.

Each seven-letter word corresponds to exactly one seven-digit telephone number. The restaurant wishing to increase its take-home business could surely do so with the number 825-3688 (i.e., "TAKEOUT").

Each seven-digit phone number corresponds to many separate seven-letter words. Unfortunately, most of these represent unrecognizable juxtapositions of letters. It is possible, however, that the owner of a barber shop would be pleased to know that the shop's telephone number, 424-7288, corresponds to "HAIRCUT." The owner of a liquor store would, no doubt, be delighted to find that the store's telephone number, 233-7226, corresponds to "BEERCAN." A veterinarian with the phone number 738-2273 would be pleased to know that the number corresponds to the letters "PETCARE."

Write a C++ program that, given a seven-digit number, writes to a file every possible seven-letter word corresponding to that number. There are 2187 (3 to the seventh power) such words. Avoid phone numbers with the digits 0 and 1.

17.14 Write a program that uses the `sizeof` operator to determine the sizes in bytes of the various data types on your computer system. Write the results to the file `datasize.dat`, so that you may print the results later. The results should be displayed in two-column format with the type name in the left column and the size of the type in right column, as in:

```
char                 1
unsigned char        1
short int            2
unsigned short int   2
int                  4
unsigned int         4
long int             4
unsigned long int    4
float                4
double               8
long double         10
```

[*Note:* The sizes of the built-in data types on your computer might differ from those listed above.]

Class **string** and String Stream Processing

OBJECTIVES

In this chapter you will learn:

- To use class **string** from the C++ Standard Library to treat **string**s as full-fledged objects.

- To assign, concatenate, compare, search and swap **string**s.

- To determine **string** characteristics.

- To find, replace and insert characters in a **string**.

- To convert **string**s to C-style strings and vice versa.

- To use **string** iterators.

- To perform input from and output to **string**s in memory.

18.1   Introduction

The C++ class template `basic_string` provides typical string-manipulation operations such as copying, searching, etc. The template definition and all support facilities are defined in namespace `std`; these include the `typedef` statement

```
typedef basic_string< char > string;
```

that creates the alias type `string` for `basic_string< char >`. A `typedef` also is provided for the `wchar_t` type. Type `wchar_t`[1] stores characters (e.g., two-byte characters, four-byte characters, etc.) for supporting other character sets. We use `string` exclusively throughout this chapter. To use `strings`, include header file `<string>`.

A `string` object can be initialized with a constructor argument such as

```
string text( "Hello" ); // creates string from const char *
```

which creates a `string` containing the characters in `"Hello"`, or with two constructor arguments as in

```
string name( 8, 'x' ); // string of 8 'x' characters
```

which creates a `string` containing eight `'x'` characters. Class `string` also provides a default constructor (which creates an empty string) and a copy constructor. An empty `string` is a `string` that does not contain any characters.

A `string` also can be initialized via the alternate construction syntax in the definition of a `string` as in

```
string month = "March"; // same as: string month( "March" );
```

---

1. Type `wchar_t` commonly is used to represent Unicode®, which does have 16-bit characters, but the size of `wchar_t` is not fixed by the standard. The Unicode Standard outlines a specification to produce consistent encoding of the world's characters and symbols. To learn more about the Unicode Standard, visit `www.unicode.org`.

Remember that operator = in the preceding declaration is not an assignment; rather it is an implicit call to the `string` class constructor, which does the conversion.

Note that class `string` provides no conversions from `int` or `char` to `string` in a `string` definition. For example, the definitions

```
string error1 = 'c';
string error2( 'u' );
string error3 = 22;
string error4( 8 );
```

result in syntax errors. Note that assigning a single character to a `string` object is permitted in an assignment statement as in

```
string1 = 'n';
```

Common Programming Error 18.1

Attempting to convert an `int` or `char` to a `string` via an initialization in a declaration or via a constructor argument is a compilation error.

Unlike C-style `char *` strings, `strings` are not necessarily null terminated. [*Note:* The C++ standard document provides only a description of the interface for class `string`— implementation is platform dependent.] The length of a `string` can be retrieved with member function `length` and with member function `size`. The subscript operator, `[]`, can be used with `strings` to access and modify individual characters. Like C-style strings, `strings` have a first subscript of 0 and a last subscript of `length() - 1`.

Most `string` member functions take as arguments a starting subscript location and the number of characters on which to operate.

The stream extraction operator (>>) is overloaded to support `strings`. The statement

```
string stringObject;
cin >> stringObject;
```

reads a `string` from the standard input device. Input is delimited by white-space characters. When a delimiter is encountered, the input operation is terminated. Function `getline` also is overloaded for `strings`. The statement

```
string string1;
getline( cin, string1 );
```

reads a `string` from the keyboard into `string1`. Input is delimited by a newline (`'\n'`), so `getLine` can read a line of text into a `string` object.

18.2 `string` Assignment and Concatenation

Figure 18.1 demonstrates `string` assignment and concatenation. Line 7 includes header `<string>` for class `string`. The `strings` `string1`, `string2` and `string3` are created in lines 12–14. Line 16 assigns the value of `string1` to `string2`. After the assignment takes place, `string2` is a copy of `string1`. Line 17 uses member function `assign` to copy `string1` into `string3`. A separate copy is made (i.e., `string1` and `string3` are independent objects). Class `string` also provides an overloaded version of member function `assign` that copies a specified number of characters, as in

```
targetString.assign( sourceString, start, numberOfCharacters );
```

where sourceString is the `string` to be copied, `start` is the starting subscript and numberOfCharacters is the number of characters to copy.

Line 22 uses the subscript operator to assign `'r'` to string3[2] (forming `"car"`) and to assign `'r'` to string2[0] (forming `"rat"`). The `strings` are then output.

```
1   // Fig. 18.1: Fig18_01.cpp
2   // Demonstrating string assignment and concatenation.
3   #include <iostream>
4   using std::cout;
5   using std::endl;
6
7   #include <string>
8   using std::string;
9
10  int main()
11  {
12     string string1( "cat" );
13     string string2;
14     string string3;
15
16     string2 = string1; // assign string1 to string2
17     string3.assign( string1 ); // assign string1 to string3
18     cout << "string1: " << string1 << "\nstring2: " << string2
19        << "\nstring3: " << string3 << "\n\n";
20
21     // modify string2 and string3
22     string2[ 0 ] = string3[ 2 ] = 'r';
23
24     cout << "After modification of string2 and string3:\n" << "string1: "
25        << string1 << "\nstring2: " << string2 << "\nstring3: ";
26
27     // demonstrating member function at
28     for ( int i = 0; i < string3.length(); i++ )
29        cout << string3.at( i );
30
31     // declare string4 and string5
32     string string4( string1 + "apult" ); // concatenation
33     string string5;
34
35     // overloaded +=
36     string3 += "pet"; // create "carpet"
37     string1.append( "acomb" ); // create "catacomb"
38
39     // append subscript locations 4 through end of string1 to
40     // create string "comb" (string5 was initially empty)
41     string5.append( string1, 4, string1.length() - 4 );
42
43     cout << "\n\nAfter concatenation:\nstring1: " << string1
44        << "\nstring2: " << string2 << "\nstring3: " << string3
45        << "\nstring4: " << string4 << "\nstring5: " << string5 << endl;
46     return 0;
47  } // end main
```

Fig. 18.1 | Demonstrating `string` assignment and concatenation. (Part 1 of 2.)

```
string1: cat
string2: cat
string3: cat

After modification of string2 and string3:
string1: cat
string2: rat
string3: car

After concatenation:
string1: catacomb
string2: rat
string3: carpet
string4: catapult
string5: comb
```

Fig. 18.1 | Demonstrating `string` assignment and concatenation. (Part 2 of 2.)

Lines 28–29 output the contents of `string3` one character at a time using member function **at**. Member function at provides checked access (or range checking); i.e., going past the end of the `string` throws an `out_of_range` exception. (See Chapter 16 for a detailed discussion of exception handling.) Note that the subscript operator, [], does not provide checked access. This is consistent with its use on arrays.

Common Programming Error 18.2

Accessing a `string` subscript outside the bounds of the `string` using function at is a logic error that causes an `out_of_range` exception.

Common Programming Error 18.3

Accessing an element beyond the size of the `string` using the subscript operator is an unreported logic error.

String `string4` is declared (line 32) and initialized to the result of concatenating `string1` and `"apult"` using the overloaded addition operator, +, which for class `string` denotes concatenation. Line 36 uses the addition assignment operator, +=, to concatenate `string3` and `"pet"`. Line 37 uses member function **append** to concatenate `string1` and `"acomb"`.

Line 41 appends the string `"comb"` to empty `string` `string5`. This member function is passed the `string` (`string1`) to retrieve characters from, the starting subscript in the `string` (4) and the number of characters to append (the value returned by `string1.length() - 4`).

18.3 Comparing strings

Class `string` provides member functions for comparing `strings`. Figure 18.2 demonstrates class `string`'s comparison capabilities.

The program declares four `strings` with lines 12–15 and outputs each `string` (lines 17–18). The condition in line 21 tests `string1` against `string4` for equality using the overloaded equality operator. If the condition is `true`, `"string1 == string4"` is output. If the condition is `false`, the condition in line 25 is tested. All the `string` class overloaded operator functions demonstrated here as well as those not demonstrated here (`!=`, `<`, `>=` and `<=`) return `bool` values.

```cpp
1   // Fig. 18.2: Fig18_02.cpp
2   // Demonstrating string comparison capabilities.
3   #include <iostream>
4   using std::cout;
5   using std::endl;
6
7   #include <string>
8   using std::string;
9
10  int main()
11  {
12     string string1( "Testing the comparison functions." );
13     string string2( "Hello" );
14     string string3( "stinger" );
15     string string4( string2 );
16
17     cout << "string1: " << string1 << "\nstring2: " << string2
18        << "\nstring3: " << string3 << "\nstring4: " << string4 << "\n\n";
19
20     // comparing string1 and string4
21     if ( string1 == string4 )
22        cout << "string1 == string4\n";
23     else // string1 != string4
24     {
25        if ( string1 > string4 )
26           cout << "string1 > string4\n";
27        else // string1 < string4
28           cout << "string1 < string4\n";
29     } // end else
30
31     // comparing string1 and string2
32     int result = string1.compare( string2 );
33
34     if ( result == 0 )
35        cout << "string1.compare( string2 ) == 0\n";
36     else // result != 0
37     {
38        if ( result > 0 )
39           cout << "string1.compare( string2 ) > 0\n";
40        else // result < 0
41           cout << "string1.compare( string2 ) < 0\n";
42     } // end else
43
44     // comparing string1 (elements 2-5) and string3 (elements 0-5)
45     result = string1.compare( 2, 5, string3, 0, 5 );
46
47     if ( result == 0 )
48        cout << "string1.compare( 2, 5, string3, 0, 5 ) == 0\n";
49     else // result != 0
50     {
```

Fig. 18.2 | Comparing `strings`. (Part I of 2.)

```
51        if ( result > 0 )
52            cout << "string1.compare( 2, 5, string3, 0, 5 ) > 0\n";
53        else // result < 0
54            cout << "string1.compare( 2, 5, string3, 0, 5 ) < 0\n";
55    } // end else
56
57    // comparing string2 and string4
58    result = string4.compare( 0, string2.length(), string2 );
59
60    if ( result == 0 )
61        cout << "string4.compare( 0, string2.length(), "
62            << "string2 ) == 0" << endl;
63    else // result != 0
64    {
65        if ( result > 0 )
66            cout << "string4.compare( 0, string2.length(), "
67                << "string2 ) > 0" << endl;
68        else // result < 0
69            cout << "string4.compare( 0, string2.length(), "
70                << "string2 ) < 0" << endl;
71    } // end else
72
73    // comparing string2 and string4
74    result = string2.compare( 0, 3, string4 );
75
76    if ( result == 0 )
77        cout << "string2.compare( 0, 3, string4 ) == 0" << endl;
78    else // result != 0
79    {
80        if ( result > 0 )
81            cout << "string2.compare( 0, 3, string4 ) > 0" << endl;
82        else // result < 0
83            cout << "string2.compare( 0, 3, string4 ) < 0" << endl;
84    } // end else
85
86    return 0;
87 } // end main
```

```
string1: Testing the comparison functions.
string2: Hello
string3: stinger
string4: Hello

string1 > string4
string1.compare( string2 ) > 0
string1.compare( 2, 5, string3, 0, 5 ) == 0
string4.compare( 0, string2.length(), string2 ) == 0
string2.compare( 0, 3, string4 ) < 0
```

Fig. 18.2 | Comparing strings. (Part 2 of 2.)

Line 32 uses string member function compare to compare string1 to string2. Variable result is assigned 0 if the strings are equivalent, a positive number if string1 is lexicographically greater than string2 or a negative number if string1 is lexicographically less than `string2`. Because a `string` starting with `'T'` is considered lexicographically greater than a string starting with `'H'`, `result` is assigned a value greater than 0, as confirmed by the output. A lexicon is a dictionary. When we say that a string is lexicographically less than another, we mean that the first string is alphabetically less than the second. The computer uses the same criterion as you would use in alphabetizing a list of names.

Line 45 uses an overloaded version of member function `compare` to compare portions of `string1` and `string3`. The first two arguments (2 and 5) specify the starting subscript and length of the portion of `string1` ("sting") to compare with `string3`. The third argument is the comparison `string`. The last two arguments (0 and 5) are the starting subscript and length of the portion of the comparison `string` being compared (also "sting"). The value assigned to `result` is 0 for equality, a positive number if `string1` is lexicographically greater than `string3` or a negative number if `string1` is lexicographically less than `string3`. Because the two pieces of `string`s being compared here are identical, `result` is assigned 0.

Line 58 uses another overloaded version of function `compare` to compare `string4` and `string2`. The first two arguments are the same—the starting subscript and length. The last argument is the comparison `string`. The value returned is also the same—0 for equality, a positive number if `string4` is lexicographically greater than `string2` or a negative number if `string4` is lexicographically less than `string2`. Because the two pieces of `string`s being compared here are identical, `result` is assigned 0.

Line 74 calls member function `compare` to compare the first 3 characters in `string2` to `string4`. Because "Hel" is less than "Hello", a value less than zero is returned.

18.4 Substrings

Class `string` provides member function `substr` for retrieving a substring from a `string`. The result is a new `string` object that is copied from the source `string`. Figure 18.3 demonstrates `substr`.

```cpp
1   // Fig. 18.3: Fig18_03.cpp
2   // Demonstrating string member function substr.
3   #include <iostream>
4   using std::cout;
5   using std::endl;
6
7   #include <string>
8   using std::string;
9
10  int main()
11  {
12     string string1( "The airplane landed on time." );
13
14     // retrieve substring "plane" which
15     // begins at subscript 7 and consists of 5 elements
16     cout << string1.substr( 7, 5 ) << endl;
17     return 0;
18  } // end main
```

Fig. 18.3 | Demonstrating `string` member function `substr`. (Part 1 of 2.)

plane

Fig. 18.3 | Demonstrating `string` member function `substr`. (Part 2 of 2.)

The program declares and initializes a `string` on line 12. Line 16 uses member function `substr` to retrieve a substring from `string1`. The first argument specifies the beginning subscript of the desired substring; the second argument specifies the substring's length.

18.5 Swapping strings

Class `string` provides member function `swap` for swapping `strings`. Figure 18.4 swaps two `strings`.

Lines 12–13 declare and initialize `strings` `first` and `second`. Each `string` is then output. Line 18 uses `string` member function `swap` to swap the values of `first` and `second`. The two `strings` are printed again to confirm that they were indeed swapped. The `string` member function `swap` is useful for implementing programs that sort strings.

```
1   // Fig. 18.4: Fig18_04.cpp
2   // Using the swap function to swap two strings.
3   #include <iostream>
4   using std::cout;
5   using std::endl;
6
7   #include <string>
8   using std::string;
9
10  int main()
11  {
12     string first( "one" );
13     string second( "two" );
14
15     // output strings
16     cout << "Before swap:\n first: " << first << "\nsecond: " << second;
17
18     first.swap( second ); // swap strings
19
20     cout << "\n\nAfter swap:\n first: " << first
21        << "\nsecond: " << second << endl;
22     return 0;
23  } // end main
```

```
Before swap:
 first: one
second: two

After swap:
 first: two
second: one
```

Fig. 18.4 | Using function `swap` to swap two `strings`.

18.6 string Characteristics

Class string provides member functions for gathering information about a string's size, length, capacity, maximum length and other characteristics. A string's size or length is the number of characters currently stored in the string. A string's capacity is the number of characters that can be stored in the string without allocating more memory. The capacity of a string must be at least equal to the current size of the string, though it can be greater. The exact capacity of a string depends on the implementation. The maximum size is the largest possible size a string can have. If this value is exceeded, a length_error exception is thrown. Figure 18.5 demonstrates string class member functions for determining various characteristics of strings.

```cpp
1   // Fig. 18.5: Fig18_05.cpp
2   // Demonstrating member functions related to size and capacity.
3   #include <iostream>
4   using std::cout;
5   using std::endl;
6   using std::cin;
7   using std::boolalpha;
8
9   #include <string>
10  using std::string;
11
12  void printStatistics( const string & );
13
14  int main()
15  {
16     string string1;
17
18     cout << "Statistics before input:\n" << boolalpha;
19     printStatistics( string1 );
20
21     // read in only "tomato" from "tomato soup"
22     cout << "\n\nEnter a string: ";
23     cin >> string1; // delimited by whitespace
24     cout << "The string entered was: " << string1;
25
26     cout << "\nStatistics after input:\n";
27     printStatistics( string1 );
28
29     // read in "soup"
30     cin >> string1; // delimited by whitespace
31     cout << "\n\nThe remaining string is: " << string1 << endl;
32     printStatistics( string1 );
33
34     // append 46 characters to string1
35     string1 += "1234567890abcdefghijklmnopqrstuvwxyz1234567890";
36     cout << "\n\nstring1 is now: " << string1 << endl;
37     printStatistics( string1 );
38
```

Fig. 18.5 | Printing string characteristics. (Part 1 of 2.)

```
39        // add 10 elements to string1
40        string1.resize( string1.length() + 10 );
41        cout << "\n\nStats after resizing by (length + 10):\n";
42        printStatistics( string1 );
43
44        cout << endl;
45        return 0;
46    } // end main
47
48    // display string statistics
49    void printStatistics( const string &stringRef )
50    {
51        cout << "capacity: " << stringRef.capacity() << "\nmax size: "
52            << stringRef.max_size() << "\nsize: " << stringRef.size()
53            << "\nlength: " << stringRef.length()
54            << "\nempty: " << stringRef.empty();
55    } // end printStatistics
```

```
Statistics before input:
capacity: 0
max size: 4294967293
size: 0
length: 0
empty: true

Enter a string: tomato soup
The string entered was: tomato
Statistics after input:
capacity: 15
max size: 4294967293
size: 6
length: 6
empty: false

The remaining string is: soup
capacity: 15
max size: 4294967293
size: 4
length: 4
empty: false

string1 is now: soup1234567890abcdefghijklmnopqrstuvwxyz1234567890
capacity: 63
max size: 4294967293
size: 50
length: 50
empty: false

Stats after resizing by (length + 10):
capacity: 63
max size: 4294967293
size: 60
length: 60
empty: false
```

Fig. 18.5 | Printing string characteristics. (Part 2 of 2.)

The program declares empty `string` `string1` (line 16) and passes it to function `printStatistics` (line 19). Function `printStatistics` (lines 49–55) takes a reference to a `const` `string` as an argument and outputs the capacity (using member function `capacity`), maximum size (using member function `max_size`), size (using member function `size`), length (using member function `length`) and whether the `string` is empty (using member function `empty`). The initial call to `printStatistics` indicates that the initial values for the capacity, size and length of `string1` are 0.

The size and length of 0 indicate that there are no characters stored in `string`. Because the initial capacity is 0, when characters are placed in `string1`, memory is allocated to accommodate the new characters. Recall that the size and length are always identical. In this implementation, the maximum size is 4294967293. Object `string1` is an empty `string`, so function `empty` returns `true`.

Line 23 reads a string from the command line. In this example, `"tomato soup"` is input. Because a space character is a delimiter, only `"tomato"` is stored in `string1`; however, `"soup"` remains in the input buffer. Line 27 calls function `printStatistics` to output statistics for `string1`. Notice in the output that the length is 6 and that the capacity is 15.

Performance Tip 18.1

To minimize the number of times memory is allocated and deallocated, some `string` class implementations provide a default capacity above and beyond the length of the `string`.

Line 30 reads `"soup"` from the input buffer and stores it in `string1`, thereby replacing `"tomato"`. Line 32 passes `string1` to `printStatistics`.

Line 35 uses the overloaded += operator to concatenate a 46-character-long string to `string1`. Line 37 passes `string1` to `printStatistics`. Notice that the capacity has increased to 63 elements and the length is now 50.

Line 40 uses member function `resize` to increase the length of `string1` by 10 characters. The additional elements are set to null characters. Notice that in the output the capacity has not changed and the length is now 60.

18.7 Finding Strings and Characters in a `string`

Class `string` provides `const` member functions for finding substrings and characters in a `string`. Figure 18.6 demonstrates the find functions.

```
1   // Fig. 18.6: Fig18_06.cpp
2   // Demonstrating the string find member functions.
3   #include <iostream>
4   using std::cout;
5   using std::endl;
6
7   #include <string>
8   using std::string;
9
10  int main()
11  {
12     string string1( "noon is 12 pm; midnight is not." );
13     int location;
```

Fig. 18.6 │ Demonstrating the `string` `find` functions. (Part 1 of 2.)

```
14
15      // find "is" at location 5 and 25
16      cout << "Original string:\n" << string1
17         << "\n\n(find) \"is\" was found at: " << string1.find( "is" )
18         << "\n(rfind) \"is\" was found at: " << string1.rfind( "is" );
19
20      // find 'o' at location 1
21      location = string1.find_first_of( "misop" );
22      cout << "\n\n(find_first_of) found '" << string1[ location ]
23         << "' from the group \"misop\" at: " << location;
24
25      // find 'o' at location 29
26      location = string1.find_last_of( "misop" );
27      cout << "\n\n(find_last_of) found '" << string1[ location ]
28         << "' from the group \"misop\" at: " << location;
29
30      // find '1' at location 8
31      location = string1.find_first_not_of( "noi spm" );
32      cout << "\n\n(find_first_not_of) '" << string1[ location ]
33         << "' is not contained in \"noi spm\" and was found at:"
34         << location;
35
36      // find '.' at location 12
37      location = string1.find_first_not_of( "12noi spm" );
38      cout << "\n\n(find_first_not_of) '" << string1[ location ]
39         << "' is not contained in \"12noi spm\" and was "
40         << "found at:" << location << endl;
41
42      // search for characters not in string1
43      location = string1.find_first_not_of(
44         "noon is 12 pm; midnight is not." );
45      cout << "\nfind_first_not_of(\"noon is 12 pm; midnight is not.\")"
46         << " returned: " << location << endl;
47      return 0;
48   } // end main
```

```
Original string:
noon is 12 pm; midnight is not.

(find) "is" was found at: 5
(rfind) "is" was found at: 25

(find_first_of) found 'o' from the group "misop" at: 1

(find_last_of) found 'o' from the group "misop" at: 29

(find_first_not_of) '1' is not contained in "noi spm" and was found at:8

(find_first_not_of) '.' is not contained in "12noi spm" and was found at:12

find_first_not_of("noon is 12 pm; midnight is not.") returned: -1
```

Fig. 18.6 | Demonstrating the `string` `find` functions. (Part 2 of 2.)

String `string1` is declared and initialized in line 12. Line 17 attempts to find `"is"` in `string1` using function `find`. If `"is"` is found, the subscript of the starting location of that string is returned. If the `string` is not found, the value `string::npos` (a `public static` constant defined in class `string`) is returned. This value is returned by the `string` find-related functions to indicate that a substring or character was not found in the `string`.

Line 18 uses member function `rfind` to search `string1` backward (i.e., right-to-left). If `"is"` is found, the subscript location is returned. If the string is not found, `string::npos` is returned. [*Note:* The rest of the find functions presented in this section return the same type unless otherwise noted.]

Line 21 uses member function `find_first_of` to locate the first occurrence in `string1` of any character in `"misop"`. The searching is done from the beginning of `string1`. The character `'o'` is found in element 1.

Line 26 uses member function `find_last_of` to find the last occurrence in `string1` of any character in `"misop"`. The searching is done from the end of `string1`. The character `'o'` is found in element 29.

Line 31 uses member function `find_first_not_of` to find the first character in `string1` not contained in `"noi spm"`. The character `'1'` is found in element 8. Searching is done from the beginning of `string1`.

Line 37 uses member function `find_first_not_of` to find the first character not contained in `"12noi spm"`. The character `'.'` is found in element 12. Searching is done from the end of `string1`.

Lines 43–44 use member function `find_first_not_of` to find the first character not contained in `"noon is 12 pm; midnight is not."`. In this case, the `string` being searched contains every character specified in the string argument. Because a character was not found, `string::npos` (which has the value –1 in this case) is returned.

18.8 Replacing Characters in a `string`

Figure 18.7 demonstrates `string` member functions for replacing and erasing characters. Lines 13–17 declare and initialize `string` `string1`. Line 23 uses `string` member function `erase` to erase everything from (and including) the character in position 62 to the end of `string1`. [*Note*: Each newline character occupies one element in the `string`.]

Lines 29–36 use `find` to locate each occurrence of the space character. Each space is then replaced with a period by a call to `string` member function `replace`. Function `replace` takes three arguments: the subscript of the character in the `string` at which replacement should begin, the number of characters to replace and the replacement string. Member function `find` returns `string::npos` when the search character is not found. In line 35, 1 is added to `position` to continue searching at the location of the next character.

Lines 40–48 use function `find` to find every period and another overloaded function `replace` to replace every period and its following character with two semicolons. The arguments passed to this version of `replace` are the subscript of the element where the replace operation begins, the number of characters to replace, a replacement character string from which a substring is selected to use as replacement characters, the element in the character string where the replacement substring begins and the number of characters in the replacement character string to use.

```cpp
// Fig. 18.7: Fig18_07.cpp
// Demonstrating string member functions erase and replace.
#include <iostream>
using std::cout;
using std::endl;

#include <string>
using std::string;

int main()
{
   // compiler concatenates all parts into one string
   string string1( "The values in any left subtree"
      "\nare less than the value in the"
      "\nparent node and the values in"
      "\nany right subtree are greater"
      "\nthan the value in the parent node" );

   cout << "Original string:\n" << string1 << endl << endl;

   // remove all characters from (and including) location 62
   // through the end of string1
   string1.erase( 62 );

   // output new string
   cout << "Original string after erase:\n" << string1
      << "\n\nAfter first replacement:\n";

   int position = string1.find( " " ); // find first space

   // replace all spaces with period
   while ( position != string::npos )
   {
      string1.replace( position, 1, "." );
      position = string1.find( " ", position + 1 );
   } // end while

   cout << string1 << "\n\nAfter second replacement:\n";

   position = string1.find( "." ); // find first period

   // replace all periods with two semicolons
   // NOTE: this will overwrite characters
   while ( position != string::npos )
   {
      string1.replace( position, 2, "xxxxx;;yyy", 5, 2 );
      position = string1.find( ".", position + 1 );
   } // end while

   cout << string1 << endl;
   return 0;
} // end main
```

Fig. 18.7 | Demonstrating functions `erase` and `replace`. (Part I of 2.)

```
Original string:
The values in any left subtree
are less than the value in the
parent node and the values in
any right subtree are greater
than the value in the parent node

Original string after erase:
The values in any left subtree
are less than the value in the


After first replacement:
The.values.in.any.left.subtree
are.less.than.the.value.in.the


After second replacement:
The;;alues;;n;;ny;;eft;;ubtree
are;;ess;;han;;he;;alue;;n;;he
```

Fig. 18.7 | Demonstrating functions `erase` and `replace`. (Part 2 of 2.)

18.9 Inserting Characters into a `string`

Class `string` provides member functions for inserting characters into a `string`. Figure 18.8 demonstrates the `string` `insert` capabilities.

The program declares, initializes and then outputs strings `string1`, `string2`, `string3` and `string4`. Line 22 uses `string` member function **insert** to insert `string2`'s content before element 10 of `string1`.

Line 25 uses `insert` to insert `string4` before `string3`'s element 3. The last two arguments specify the starting and last element of `string4` that should be inserted. Using `string::npos` causes the entire `string` to be inserted.

```
 1    // Fig. 18.8: Fig18_08.cpp
 2    // Demonstrating class string insert member functions.
 3    #include <iostream>
 4    using std::cout;
 5    using std::endl;
 6
 7    #include <string>
 8    using std::string;
 9
10    int main()
11    {
12       string string1( "beginning end" );
13       string string2( "middle " );
14       string string3( "12345678" );
15       string string4( "xx" );
16
```

Fig. 18.8 | Demonstrating the `string` `insert` member functions. (Part 1 of 2.)

```
17      cout << "Initial strings:\nstring1: " << string1
18          << "\nstring2: " << string2 << "\nstring3: " << string3
19          << "\nstring4: " << string4 << "\n\n";
20
21      // insert "middle" at location 10 in string1
22      string1.insert( 10, string2 );
23
24      // insert "xx" at location 3 in string3
25      string3.insert( 3, string4, 0, string::npos );
26
27      cout << "Strings after insert:\nstring1: " << string1
28          << "\nstring2: " << string2 << "\nstring3: " << string3
29          << "\nstring4: " << string4 << endl;
30      return 0;
31  } // end main
```

```
Initial strings:
string1: beginning end
string2: middle
string3: 12345678
string4: xx

Strings after insert:
string1: beginning middle end
string2: middle
string3: 123xx45678
string4: xx
```

Fig. 18.8 | Demonstrating the `string insert` member functions. (Part 2 of 2.)

18.10 Conversion to C-Style Pointer-Based `char` `*` Strings

Class `string` provides member functions for converting `string` class objects to C-style pointer-based strings. As mentioned earlier, unlike pointer-based strings, `strings` are not necessarily null terminated. These conversion functions are useful when a given function takes a pointer-based string as an argument. Figure 18.9 demonstrates conversion of `strings` to pointer-based strings.

The program declares a `string`, an `int` and two `char` pointers (lines 12–15). The `string string1` is initialized to `"STRINGS"`, `ptr1` is initialized to `0` and `length` is initialized to the length of `string1`. Memory of sufficient size to hold a pointer-based string equivalent of `string string1` is allocated dynamically and attached to `char` pointer `ptr2`.

Line 18 uses `string` member function **copy** to copy object `string1` into the `char` array pointed to by `ptr2`. Line 19 manually places a terminating null character in the array pointed to by `ptr2`.

Line 23 uses function `c_str` to copy object `string1` and automatically add a terminating null character. This function returns a `const char *` which is output by the stream insertion operator.

Line 29 assigns the `const char *` `ptr1` a pointer returned by class `string` member function **data**. This member function returns a non-null-terminated C-style character array. Note that we do not modify `string string1` in this example. If `string1` were to

```
1   // Fig. 18.9: Fig18_09.cpp
2   // Converting to C-style strings.
3   #include <iostream>
4   using std::cout;
5   using std::endl;
6
7   #include <string>
8   using std::string;
9
10  int main()
11  {
12     string string1( "STRINGS" ); // string constructor with char* arg
13     const char *ptr1 = 0; // initialize *ptr1
14     int length = string1.length();
15     char *ptr2 = new char[ length + 1 ]; // including null
16
17     // copy characters from string1 into allocated memory
18     string1.copy( ptr2, length, 0 ); // copy string1 to ptr2 char*
19     ptr2[ length ] = '\0'; // add null terminator
20
21     cout << "string string1 is " << string1
22        << "\nstring1 converted to a C-Style string is "
23        << string1.c_str()   << "\nptr1 is ";
24
25     // Assign to pointer ptr1 the const char * returned by
26     // function data(). NOTE: this is a potentially dangerous
27     // assignment. If string1 is modified, pointer ptr1 can
28     // become invalid.
29     ptr1 = string1.data();
30
31     // output each character using pointer
32     for ( int i = 0; i < length; i++ )
33        cout << *( ptr1 + i ); // use pointer arithmetic
34
35     cout << "\nptr2 is " << ptr2 << endl;
36     delete [] ptr2; // reclaim dynamically allocated memory
37     return 0;
38  } // end main
```

```
string string1 is STRINGS
string1 converted to a C-Style string is STRINGS
ptr1 is STRINGS
ptr2 is STRINGS
```

Fig. 18.9 | Converting `string`s to C-style strings and character arrays.

be modified (e.g., the `string`'s dynamic memory changes its address due to a member function call such as `string1.insert( 0, "abcd" );`), `ptr1` could become invalid—which could lead to unpredictable results.

Lines 32–33 use pointer arithmetic to output the character array pointed to by `ptr1`. In lines 35–36, the C-style string pointed to by `ptr2` is output and the memory allocated for `ptr2` is `delete`d to avoid a memory leak.

Common Programming Error 18.4

Not terminating the character array returned by data *with a null character can lead to execution-time errors.*

Good Programming Practice 18.1

Whenever possible, use the more robust string *class objects rather than C-style pointer-based strings.*

18.11 Iterators

Class `string` provides iterators for forward and backward traversal of `string`s. Iterators provide access to individual characters with syntax that is similar to pointer operations. Iterators are not range checked. Note that in this section we provide "mechanical examples" to demonstrate the use of iterators. We discuss more robust uses of iterators in Chapter 22. Figure 18.10 demonstrates iterators.

```cpp
1   // Fig. 18.10: Fig18_10.cpp
2   // Using an iterator to output a string.
3   #include <iostream>
4   using std::cout;
5   using std::endl;
6
7   #include <string>
8   using std::string;
9
10  int main()
11  {
12     string string1( "Testing iterators" );
13     string::const_iterator iterator1 = string1.begin();
14
15     cout << "string1 = " << string1
16        << "\n(Using iterator iterator1) string1 is: ";
17
18     // iterate through string
19     while ( iterator1 != string1.end() )
20     {
21        cout << *iterator1; // dereference iterator to get char
22        iterator1++; // advance iterator to next char
23     } // end while
24
25     cout << endl;
26     return 0;
27  } // end main
```

```
string1 = Testing iterators
(Using iterator iterator1) string1 is: Testing iterators
```

Fig. 18.10 | Using an iterator to output a `string`.

Lines 12–13 declare `string string1` and `string::const_iterator iterator1`. A `const_iterator` is an iterator that cannot modify the `string`—in this case the `string`—through which it is iterating. Iterator `iterator1` is initialized to the beginning of `string1` with the `string` class member function `begin`. Two versions of `begin` exist—one that returns an `iterator` for iterating through a non-`const` `string` and a `const` version that returns a `const_iterator` for iterating through a `const` `string`. Line 15 outputs `string1`.

Lines 19–23 use iterator `iterator1` to "walk through" `string1`. Class `string` member function `end` returns an `iterator` (or a `const_iterator`) for the position past the last element of `string1`. Each element is printed by dereferencing the iterator much as you would dereference a pointer, and the iterator is advanced one position using operator `++`.

Class `string` provides member functions `rend` and `rbegin` for accessing individual `string` characters in reverse from the end of a `string` toward the beginning. Member functions `rend` and `rbegin` can return `reverse_iterators` and `const_reverse_iterators` (based on whether the `string` is non-const or const). In the exercises, we ask the reader to write a program that demonstrates these capabilities. We will use iterators and reverse iterators more in Chapter 22.

Error-Prevention Tip 18.1

Use `string` member function `at` (rather than iterators) when you want the benefit of range checking.

Good Programming Practice 18.2

When the operations involving the iterator should not modify the data being processed, use a `const_iterator`. This is another example of employing the principle of least privilege.

18.12 String Stream Processing

In addition to standard stream I/O and file stream I/O, C++ stream I/O includes capabilities for inputting from, and outputting to, `strings` in memory. These capabilities often are referred to as in-memory I/O or string stream processing.

Input from a `string` is supported by class `istringstream`. Output to a `string` is supported by class `ostringstream`. The class names `istringstream` and `ostringstream` are actually aliases defined by the `typedef`s

```
typedef basic_istringstream< char > istringstream;
typedef basic_ostringstream< char > ostringstream;
```

Class templates `basic_istringstream` and `basic_ostringstream` provide the same functionality as classes `istream` and `ostream` plus other member functions specific to in-memory formatting. Programs that use in-memory formatting must include the `<sstream>` and `<iostream>` header files.

One application of these techniques is data validation. A program can read an entire line at a time from the input stream into a `string`. Next, a validation routine can scrutinize the contents of the `string` and correct (or repair) the data, if necessary. Then the program can proceed to input from the `string`, knowing that the input data is in the proper format.

Outputting to a `string` is a nice way to take advantage of the powerful output formatting capabilities of C++ streams. Data can be prepared in a `string` to mimic the edited screen format. That `string` could be written to a disk file to preserve the screen image.

An ostringstream object uses a string object to store the output data. The str member function of class ostringstream returns a copy of that string.

Figure 18.11 demonstrates an ostringstream object. The program creates ostringstream object outputString (line 15) and uses the stream insertion operator to output a series of strings and numerical values to the object.

Lines 27–28 output string string1, string string2, string string3, double double1, string string4, int integer, string string5 and the address of int integer—all to outputString in memory. Line 31 uses the stream insertion operator and the call outputString.str() to display a copy of the string created in lines 27–28. Line 34 demonstrates that more data can be appended to the string in memory by simply issuing another stream insertion operation to outputString. Lines 35–36 display string outputString after appending additional characters.

```cpp
1   // Fig. 18.11: Fig18_11.cpp
2   // Using a dynamically allocated ostringstream object.
3   #include <iostream>
4   using std::cout;
5   using std::endl;
6
7   #include <string>
8   using std::string;
9
10  #include <sstream> // header file for string stream processing
11  using std::ostringstream; // stream insertion operators
12
13  int main()
14  {
15     ostringstream outputString; // create ostringstream instance
16
17     string string1( "Output of several data types " );
18     string string2( "to an ostringstream object:" );
19     string string3( "\n        double: " );
20     string string4( "\n           int: " );
21     string string5( "\naddress of int: " );
22
23     double double1 = 123.4567;
24     int integer = 22;
25
26     // output strings, double and int to ostringstream outputString
27     outputString << string1 << string2 << string3 << double1
28        << string4 << integer << string5 << &integer;
29
30     // call str to obtain string contents of the ostringstream
31     cout << "outputString contains:\n" << outputString.str();
32
33     // add additional characters and call str to output string
34     outputString << "\nmore characters added";
35     cout << "\n\nafter additional stream insertions,\n"
36        << "outputString contains:\n" << outputString.str() << endl;
37     return 0;
38  } // end main
```

Fig. 18.11 | Using a dynamically allocated ostringstream object. (Part 1 of 2.)

```
outputString contains:
Output of several data types to an ostringstream object:
        double: 123.457
           int: 22
address of int: 0012F540

after additional stream insertions,
outputString contains:
Output of several data types to an ostringstream object:
        double: 123.457
           int: 22
address of int: 0012F540
more characters added
```

Fig. 18.11 | Using a dynamically allocated `ostringstream` object. (Part 2 of 2.)

An `istringstream` object inputs data from a `string` in memory to program variables. Data is stored in an `istringstream` object as characters. Input from the `istringstream` object works identically to input from any file. The end of the `string` is interpreted by the `istringstream` object as end-of-file.

Figure 18.12 demonstrates input from an `istringstream` object. Lines 15–16 create `string input` containing the data and `istringstream` object `inputString` constructed to contain the data in `string input`. The `string input` contains the data

```
Input test 123 4.7 A
```

```
1   // Fig. 18.12: Fig18_12.cpp
2   // Demonstrating input from an istringstream object.
3   #include <iostream>
4   using std::cout;
5   using std::endl;
6
7   #include <string>
8   using std::string;
9
10  #include <sstream>
11  using std::istringstream;
12
13  int main()
14  {
15      string input( "Input test 123 4.7 A" );
16      istringstream inputString( input );
17      string string1;
18      string string2;
19      int integer;
20      double double1;
21      char character;
```

Fig. 18.12 | Demonstrating input from an `istringstream` object. (Part 1 of 2.)

```
22
23      inputString >> string1 >> string2 >> integer >> double1 >> character;
24
25      cout << "The following items were extracted\n"
26         << "from the istringstream object:" << "\nstring: " << string1
27         << "\nstring: " << string2 << "\n   int: " << integer
28         << "\ndouble: " << double1 << "\n  char: " << character;
29
30      // attempt to read from empty stream
31      long value;
32      inputString >> value;
33
34      // test stream results
35      if ( inputString.good() )
36         cout << "\n\nlong value is: " << value << endl;
37      else
38         cout << "\n\ninputString is empty" << endl;
39
40      return 0;
41   } // end main
```

```
The following items were extracted
from the istringstream object:
string: Input
string: test
   int: 123
double: 4.7
  char: A

inputString is empty
```

Fig. 18.12 | Demonstrating input from an `istringstream` object. (Part 2 of 2.)

which, when read as input to the program, consist of two strings ("Input" and "test"), an int (123), a double (4.7) and a char ('A'). These characters are extracted to variables `string1`, `string2`, `integer`, `double1` and `character` in line 23.

The data is then output in lines 25–28. The program attempts to read from input-String again in line 32. The `if` condition in line 35 uses function good (Section 15.8) to test if any data remains. Because no data remains, the function returns `false` and the `else` part of the `if...else` statement is executed.

Summary

- C++ class template `basic_string` provides typical string-manipulation operations such as copying, searching, etc.
- The `typedef` statement

      typedef basic_string< char > string;

  creates the alias type `string` for `basic_string< char >`. A typedef also is provided for the wchar_t type. Type wchar_t normally stores two-byte (16-bit) characters for supporting other character sets. The size of wchar_t is not fixed by the standard.

- To use strings, include C++ Standard Library header file `<string>`.
- Class `string` provides no constructors that convert from `int` or `char` to `string`.
- Assigning a single character to a `string` object is permitted in an assignment statement.
- `string`s are not necessarily null terminated.
- Most `string` member functions take as arguments a starting subscript location and the number of characters on which to operate.
- Class `string` provides overloaded `operator=` and member function `assign` for `string` assignments.
- The subscript operator, `[]`, provides read/write access to any element of a `string`.
- `string` member function `at` provides checked access—going past either end of the `string` throws an `out_of_range` exception. The subscript operator, `[]`, does not provide checked access.
- Class `string` provides the overloaded `+` and `+=` operators and member function `append` to perform `string` concatenation.
- Class `string` provides overloaded `==`, `!=`, `<`, `>`, `<=` and `>=` operators for `string` comparisons.
- `string` member function `compare` compares two `string`s (or substrings) and returns `0` if the `string`s are equal, a positive number if the first `string` is lexicographically greater than the second or a negative number if the first string is lexicographically less than the second.
- `string` member function `substr` retrieves a substring from a `string`.
- `string` member function `swap` swaps the contents of two `string`s.
- `string` member functions `size` and `length` return the size or length of a `string` (i.e., the number of characters currently stored in the `string`).
- `string` member function `capacity` returns the total number of characters that can be stored in the `string` without increasing the amount of memory allocated to the `string`.
- `string` member function `max_size` returns the maximum size a `string` can have.
- `string` member function `resize` changes the length of a `string`.
- Class `string` find functions `find`, `rfind`, `find_first_of`, `find_last_of` and `find_first_not_of` locate substrings or characters in a `string`.
- `string` member function `erase` deletes elements of a `string`.
- `string` member function `replace` replaces characters in a `string`.
- `string` member function `insert` inserts characters in a `string`.
- `string` member function `c_str` returns a `const char *` pointing to a null-terminated C-style character string that contains all the characters in a `string`.
- `string` member function `data` returns a `const char *` pointing to a non-null-terminated C-style character array that contains all the characters in a `string`.
- Class `string` provides member functions `end` and `begin` to iterate through individual elements.
- Class `string` provides member functions `rend` and `rbegin` for accessing individual `string` characters in reverse from the end of a `string` toward the beginning.
- Input from a `string` is supported by type `istringstream`. Output to a `string` is supported by type `ostringstream`.
- `ostringstream` member function `str` returns a `string` copy of a `string`.

Terminology

append member function of class string
assign member function of class string
at member function of class string
basic_string class template
begin member function of class string
c_str member function of class string
capacity of a string
capacity member function of class string
checked access
compare member function of class string
const_iterator
const_reverse_iterator
copy member function of class string
data member function of class string
empty string
end member function of class string
erase member function of class string
find member function of class string
find_first_not_of member function of
    class string
find_first_of member function of class
    string
find_last_of member function of class string
getline member function of class string
in-memory I/O

insert member function of class string
istringstream class
iterator
length member function of class string
length of a string
lexicographical comparison
max_size member function of class string
maximum size of a string
ostringstream class
range checking
rbegin member function of class string
rend member function of class string
replace member function of class string
resize member function of class string
reverse_iterator
rfind member function of class string
size member function of class string
<sstream> header file
str member function of class ostringstream
string::npos constant
string stream processing
substr member function of class string
swap member function of class string
wchar_t type

Self-Review Exercises

18.1   Fill in the blanks in each of the following:
    a)   Header _____ must be included for class string.
    b)   Class string belongs to the _____ namespace.
    c)   Function _____ deletes characters from a string.
    d)   Function _____ finds the first occurrence of any character from a string.

18.2   State which of the following statements are *true* and which are *false*. If a statement is *false*, explain why.
    a)   Concatenation of string objects can be performed with the addition assignment operator, +=.
    b)   Characters within a string begin at index 0.
    c)   The assignment operator, =, copies a string.
    d)   A C-style string is a string object.

18.3   Find the error(s) in each of the following, and explain how to correct it (them):
    a)
```
string string1( 28 ); // construct string1
string string2( 'z' ); // construct string2
```
    b)
```
// assume std namespace is known
const char *ptr = name.data(); // name is "joe bob"
ptr[ 3 ] = '-';
cout << ptr << endl;
```

Answers to Self-Review Exercises

18.1 a) <string>. b) std. c) erase. d) find_first_of.

18.2 a) True.
   b) True.
   c) True.
   d) False. A string is an object that provides many different services. A C-style string does not provide any services. C-style strings are null terminated; strings are not necessarily null terminated. C-style strings are pointers and strings are not.

18.3 a) Constructors for class string do not exist for integer and character arguments. Other valid constructors should be used—converting the arguments to strings if need be.
   b) Function data does not add a null terminator. Also, the code attempts to modify a const char. Replace all of the lines with the code:

```
cout << name.substr( 0, 3 ) + "-" + name.substr( 4 ) << endl;
```

Exercises

18.4 Fill in the blanks in each of the following:
   a) Class string member functions _____ and _____ convert strings to C-style strings.
   b) Class string member function _____ is used for assignment.
   c) _____ is the return type of function rbegin.
   d) Class string member function _____ is used to retrieve a substring.

18.5 State which of the following statements are *true* and which are *false*. If a statement is *false*, explain why.
   a) strings are always null terminated.
   b) Class string member function max_size returns the maximum size for a string.
   c) Class string member function at can throw an out_of_range exception.
   d) Class string member function begin returns an iterator.

18.6 Find any errors in the following and explain how to correct them:
   a) std::cout << s.data() << std::endl; // s is "hello"
   b) erase(s.rfind("x"), 1); // s is "xenon"
   c) string& foo()
      {
          string s("Hello");
          ...   // other statements
          return;
      } // end function foo

18.7 (*Simple Encryption*) Some information on the Internet may be encrypted with a simple algorithm known as "rot13," which rotates each character by 13 positions in the alphabet. Thus, 'a' corresponds to 'n', and 'x' corresponds to 'k'. rot13 is an example of symmetric key encryption. With symmetric key encryption, both the encrypter and decrypter use the same key.
   a) Write a program that encrypts a message using rot13.
   b) Write a program that decrypts the scrambled message using 13 as the key.
   c) After writing the programs of part (a) and part (b), briefly answer the following question: If you did not know the key for part (b), how difficult do you think it would be to break the code? What if you had access to substantial computing power (e.g., supercomputers)? In Exercise 18.26 we ask you to write a program to accomplish this.

18.8 Write a program using iterators that demonstrates the use of functions rbegin and rend.

18.9   Write a program that reads in several `strings` and prints only those ending in "r" or "ay". Only lowercase letters should be considered.

18.10   Write a program that demonstrates passing a `string` both by reference and by value.

18.11   Write a program that separately inputs a first name and a last name and concatenates the two into a new `string`.

18.12   Write a program that plays the game of Hangman. The program should pick a word (which is either coded directly into the program or read from a text file) and display the following:

```
Guess the word:    XXXXX
```

Each X represents a letter. The user tries to guess the letters in the word. The appropriate response yes or no should be displayed after each guess. After each incorrect guess, display the diagram with another body part filled. After seven incorrect guesses, the user should be hanged. The display should look as follows:

```
      0
     /|\
      |
     / \
```

After each guess, display all user guesses. If the user guesses the word correctly, the program should display

```
Congratulations!!! You guessed my word. Play again? yes/no
```

18.13   Write a program that inputs a `string` and prints the `string` backward. Convert all uppercase characters to lowercase and all lowercase characters to uppercase.

18.14   Write a program that uses the comparison capabilities introduced in this chapter to alphabetize a series of animal names. Only uppercase letters should be used for the comparisons.

18.15   Write a program that creates a cryptogram out of a `string`. A cryptogram is a message or word in which each letter is replaced with another letter. For example the `string`

```
The bird was named squawk
```

might be scrambled to form

```
cin vrjs otz ethns zxqtop
```

Note that spaces are not scrambled. In this particular case, `'T'` was replaced with `'x'`, each `'a'` was replaced with `'h'`, etc. Uppercase letters become lowercase letters in the cryptogram. Use techniques similar to those in Exercise 18.7.

18.16   Modify Exercise 18.15 to allow the user to solve the cryptogram. The user should input two characters at a time: The first character specifies a letter in the cryptogram, and the second letter specifies the replacement letter. If the replacement letter is correct, replace the letter in the cryptogram with the replacement letter in uppercase.

18.17   Write a program that inputs a sentence and counts the number of palindromes in it. A palindrome is a word that reads the same backward and forward. For example, "tree" is not a palindrome, but "noon" is.

18.18   Write a program that counts the total number of vowels in a sentence. Output the frequency of each vowel.

18.19   Write a program that inserts the characters "******" in the exact middle of a `string`.

18.20 Write a program that erases the sequences "by" and "BY" from a `string`.

18.21 Write a program that inputs a line of text, replaces all punctuation marks with spaces and uses the C-string library function `strtok` to tokenize the `string` into individual words.

18.22 Write a program that inputs a line of text and prints the text backwards. Use iterators in your solution.

18.23 Write a recursive version of Exercise 18.22.

18.24 Write a program that demonstrates the use of the `erase` functions that take `iterator` arguments.

18.25 Write a program that generates the following from the `string` "abcdefghijklmnopqrstu-vwxyz{":

```
            a
           bcb
          cdedc
         defgfed
        efghihgfe
       fghijkjihgf
      ghijklmlkjihg
     hijklmnonmlkjih
    ijklmnopqponmlkji
   jklmnopqrsrqponmlkj
  klmnopqrstutsrqponmlk
 lmnopqrstuvwvutsrqponml
mnopqrstuvwxyxwvutsrqponm
nopqrstuvwxyz{zyxwvutsrqpon
```

18.26 In Exercise 18.7, we asked you to write a simple encryption algorithm. Write a program that will attempt to decrypt a "rot13" message using simple frequency substitution. (Assume that you do not know the key.) The most frequent letters in the encrypted phrase should be replaced with the most commonly used English letters (a, e, i, o, u, s, t, r, etc.). Write the possibilities to a file. What made the code breaking easy? How can the encryption mechanism be improved?

18.27 Write a version of the selection sort routine (Fig. 8.28) that sorts `strings`. Use function swap in your solution.

18.28 Modify class `Employee` in Figs. 13.6–13.7 by adding a `private` utility function called `isValidSocialSecurityNumber`. This member function should validate the format of a social security number (e.g., ###-##-####, where # is a digit). If the format is valid, return `true`; otherwise return `false`.

Featuring
Early Classes
& Objects
with the
UML™ 2

Web Programming

OBJECTIVES

In this chapter you will learn:

- The Common Gateway Interface (CGI) protocol.
- The Hypertext Transfer Protocol (HTTP) and HTTP headers.
- Web server's functionality.
- The Apache HTTP Server.
- To request documents from a Web server.
- To implement CGI scripts.
- To send input to CGI scripts using XHTML forms.

19.1 Introduction

With the advent of the World Wide Web, the Internet gained tremendous popularity. This greatly increased the volume of requests users made for information from Web sites. It became evident that the degree of interactivity between the user and the Web site would be crucial. The power of the Web resides not only in serving content to users, but also in responding to user requests and generating Web content dynamically.

In this chapter, we discuss specialized software—called a Web server—that responds to client (e.g., Web browser) requests by providing resources (e.g., XHTML[1] documents) for display on clients. For example, when a user enters a Uniform Resource Locator (URL) address, such as www.deitel.com, into a Web browser, the user is requesting a specific document from a Web server. The Web server maps the URL to a file on the server (or to a file on the server's network) and returns the requested document to the client. During this interaction, the Web server and the client communicate through the Hypertext Transfer Protocol (HTTP), a platform-independent protocol for transferring requests and files that answer those requests over the Internet (i.e., between Web servers and Web browsers).

Our Web server discussion introduces the Apache HTTP Server. For illustration purposes, we use Microsoft's Internet Explorer Web browser to request documents and, later,

---

1. The Extensible HyperText Markup Language (XHTML) has replaced the HyperText Markup Language (HTML) as the primary way of describing Web content. Readers not familiar with XHTML should read Appendix J, Introduction to XHTML, before reading this chapter.

to display content returned from "CGI scripts." We discuss the Apache HTTP Server and CGI scripts in Section 19.5 and Section 19.7, respectively.

19.2 HTTP Request Types

HTTP defines several request types (also known as request methods), each of which specifies how a client sends a request to a server. The two most common are get and post. These request types retrieve and send client form data from and to a Web server. A form is an XHTML element that may contain text fields, radio buttons, check boxes and other graphical user interface components that allow users to enter and submit data into a Web page. Forms can also contain hidden fields, which are not exposed as GUI components. Hidden fields are used to pass additional data not specified by the user to the form handler on the Web server. You will see examples of hidden fields later in the chapter.

A get request gets (or retrieves) information from a server. Such requests often retrieve an HTML document or an image. A post request posts (or sends) data to a server, such as authentication information or data from a form that gathers user input. Usually, post requests are used to post a message to a news group or a discussion forum, pass user input to a data-handling process and store or update the data on a server. A get request sends form data as part of the URL (e.g., www.searchsomething.com/search?query=*userquery*). In this fictitious request, the information following the ? (query=*userquery*) indicates user-specified input. For example, if the user performs a search on "Massachusetts," the last part of the URL would be ?query=Massachusetts. A get request limits the query string (e.g., query=Massachusetts) to a predefined number of characters that varies from server to server. If the query string exceeds this limit, a post request must be used.

Software Engineering Observation 19.1

The data sent in a post request is not part of the URL and cannot be seen by users. Forms that contain many fields often are submitted to Web servers via post requests. Sensitive form fields, such as passwords, should be sent using this request type.

Figure 19.1 lists request types other than get and post. These methods are not frequently used.

Request type	Description
delete	Such a request is normally used to delete a file from a server. This may not be available on some servers because of its inherent security risks (e.g., the client could delete a file that is critical to the execution of the server or an application).
head	Such a request is normally used when the client wants only the response's headers, such as its content type and content length.
options	Such a request returns information to the client indicating the HTTP options supported by the server, such as the HTTP version (1.0 or 1.1) and the request methods the server supports.

Fig. 19.1 | HTTP's other request types. (Part 1 of 2.)

Request type	Description
put	Such a request is normally used to store a file on the server. This may not be available on some servers because of its inherent security risks (e.g., the client could place an executable application on the server, which, if executed, could damage the server—perhaps by deleting critical files or occupying resources).
trace	Such a request is normally used for debugging. The implementation of this method automatically returns an XHTML document to the client containing the request header information (data sent by the browser as part of the request).

Fig. 19.1 | HTTP's other request types. (Part 2 of 2.)

An HTTP request often sends data to a server-side form handler—a program that resides on the Web server and is created by a server-side programmer to handle client requests. For example, when a user participates in a Web-based survey, the Web server receives the information specified in the form as part of the request, and the form handler processes the survey. We demonstrate how to create server-side form handlers throughout the examples in this chapter.

Browsers often cache (i.e., save on a local disk) Web pages for quick reloading, to reduce the amount of data that the browser needs to download over the Internet. Web browsers often cache the server's responses to get requests. A static Web page, such as a course syllabus, is cached in the event that the user requests the same resource again. However, browsers typically do not cache the responses to post requests, because subsequent post requests might not contain the same information. For example, in an online survey, many users could visit the same Web page and respond to a question. The page could also display the survey results. Each new response changes the overall results of the survey, so any requests to view the survey results should be sent using the post method. Similarly, the post method should be used to request a Web page containing discussion forum posts, as these posts may change frequently. Otherwise, the browser may cache the results after the user's first visit and display these same results for each subsequent visit.

19.3 Multitier Architecture

A Web server is part of a multitier application, sometimes referred to as an *n*-tier application. Multitier applications divide functionality into separate tiers (i.e., logical groupings of functionality). Tiers can be located on the same computer or on separate computers. Figure 19.2 presents the basic structure of a three-tier application.

The bottom tier (also called the information tier or the data tier) maintains data for the application. This tier typically stores data in a relational database management system (RDBMS). For example, a retail store might have a database of product information, such as descriptions, prices and quantities of items in stock. The same database also might contain customer information, such as user names for logging into the online store, billing addresses and credit card numbers.

The middle tier (also called the business logic tier) implements business logic to control interactions between application clients and application data. It acts as an interme-

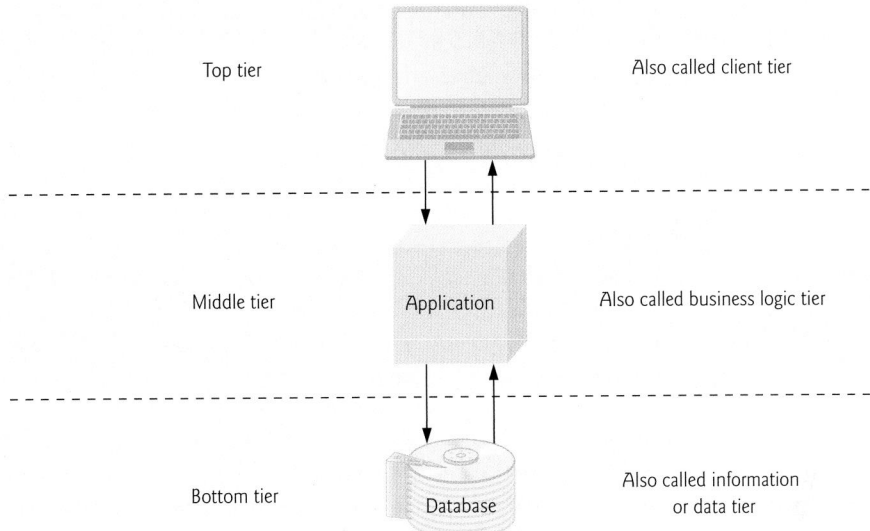

Top tier — Also called client tier

Middle tier — Application — Also called business logic tier

Bottom tier — Database — Also called information or data tier

Fig. 19.2 | Three-tier application model.

diary between data in the information tier and the application clients. The middle-tier business logic receives client requests from the top tier (e.g., a request to view a product catalog), retrieves and processes data from the information tier, and sends the result back to the client.

Business logic in the middle tier enforces business rules and ensures that data is reliable before updating the database or sending data to a user. Business rules dictate how clients can and cannot access application data and how applications process data. For example, a business rule can specify how to convert numeric grades to letter grades.

The top tier (also called the client tier) is the application's user interface. Users interact directly with the application through the user interface. The client tier interacts with the middle tier to make requests and to retrieve data from the information tier. The client tier then displays to the user the data retrieved from the middle tier.

19.4 Accessing Web Servers

To request documents from Web servers, users must know the URLs at which those documents reside. Users can request documents from local Web servers (i.e., ones residing on users' machines) or remote Web servers (i.e., ones residing on machines across a network).

To understand how a Web browser is able to locate documents on a Web server, it is helpful for you to know the following terms:

1. Host: A host is a computer that stores and maintains resources, such as Web pages, databases and multimedia files.

2. Domain: A domain represents a group of hosts on the Internet. Each domain has a domain name, also known as a Web address, which uniquely identifies the location of a business or organization on the Internet.

3. Fully qualified domain name: A fully qualified domain name (FQDN), also known as the machine name, contains a host (for example, www for World Wide Web) and a domain name, including a top-level domain (TLD). The top-level domain is the last and most significant component of a fully qualified domain name.

Local Web servers can be accessed in two ways: through the machine name, or through `localhost`—a host name that references the local machine. We use `localhost` in this book for demonstration purposes. To determine the machine name in Windows 98, right click **Network Neighborhood**, and select **Properties** from the context menu to display the **Network** dialog. In the **Network** dialog, click the **Identification** tab. The computer name displays in the **Computer name:** field. Click **Cancel** to close the **Network** dialog. In Windows 2000, right click **My Network Places** and select **Properties** from the context menu to display the **Network and Dialup Connections** explorer. In the explorer, click **Network Identification**. The **Full computer name:** field in the **System Properties** window displays the computer name. In Windows XP, select **Start > Control Panel**, which displays the **Control Panel** window. Double click **System** in the **Control Panel** window, which opens the **System Properties** window. Select the **Computer Name** tab in the **System Properties** window; the **Full computer name:** field displays the computer name.

To request documents from the Web server, users must know the fully qualified domain names (machine names) on which the Web server software resides. For example, to access the documents from Deitel's Web server, you must know the FQDN www.deitel.com. The FQDN www.deitel.com indicates that the host is www and the top-level domain is com. In a FQDN, the TLD often describes the type of organization that owns the domain. For example, usually the com TLD refers to a commercial business, the org TLD to a nonprofit organization and the edu TLD to an educational institution. In addition, each country has its own TLD, such as cn for China, et for Ethiopia, om for Oman and us for the United States.

Each FQDN corresponds to a numeric address called an IP (Internet Protocol) address, which is much like a street address. Just as people use street addresses to locate houses or businesses in a city, computers use IP addresses to locate other computers on the Internet. Each internet host computer has a unique IP address. Each address comprises four sets of numbers separated by periods, such as 63.110.43.82. A Domain Name System (DNS) server is a computer that maintains a database of FQDNs and their corresponding IP addresses. The process of translating FQDNs to IP addresses is called a DNS lookup. For example, to access the Deitel Web site, type the FQDN www.deitel.com into a Web browser. The DNS lookup translates www.deitel.com into the IP address of the Deitel Web server (63.110.43.82). The IP address of `localhost` is always 127.0.0.1. This address, also known as the loopback address, can be used to test Web applications on your local computer.

19.5 Apache HTTP Server

The Apache HTTP server, maintained by the Apache Software Foundation, is currently the most popular Web server because of its stability, cost, efficiency and portability. It is an open-source software (i.e., its source code is freely available) that runs on UNIX, Linux and Windows platforms.

To download the Apache HTTP server, visit `httpd.apache.org`.[2] For instructions on installing Apache, visit `www.deitel.com` or `httpd.apache.org`. If the Apache HTTP server is installed as a service, then it is already running after installation. Otherwise, start the server by selecting the **Start** menu, then **All Programs > Apache HTTP Server 2.0.52 > Control Apache Server > Start**. To stop the Apache HTTP server, select **Start > All Programs > Apache HTTP Server 2.0.52 > Control Apache Server > Stop**. For Linux users, we put instructions on how to start/stop the Apache HTTP server and run the examples at our Web site, `www.deitel.com`.

19.6 Requesting XHTML Documents

This section shows how to request an XHTML document from the Apache HTTP server. In the Apache HTTP server directory structure, XHTML documents must be saved in the `htdocs` directory. On Windows platforms, the `htdocs` directory resides in `C:\Program Files\Apache Group\Apache2`. On Linux platforms, the `htdocs` directory resides in the `/usr/local/httpd` directory.[3] Copy the `test.html` document from the Chapter 19 examples directory on the book's CD-ROM into the `htdocs` directory. To request the document, launch a Web browser, such as Internet Explorer or Netscape, and enter the URL in the **Address** field (i.e., `http://localhost/test.html`). Figure 19.3 shows the result of requesting `test.html`. [*Note:* In Apache, the root directory of the Web server refers to the default directory, `htdocs`, so we do not enter the directory name before the file name (i.e., `test.html`) in the **Address** field.]

19.7 Introduction to CGI

The Common Gateway Interface (CGI) is a standard protocol for enabling applications (commonly called CGI programs or CGI scripts) to interact with Web servers and (indirectly) with clients (e.g., Web browsers). CGI is often used to generate dynamic Web content using client input, databases and other information services. A Web page is dynamic if its content is generated programmatically when the page is requested, unlike static Web content, which is not generated programmatically when the page is requested (i.e., the page already exists before the request is made). For example, we can use a static Web page

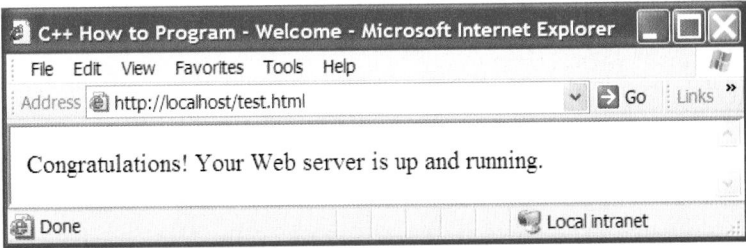

Fig. 19.3 | Requesting `test.html` from Apache.

---

2. In this chapter, we use version 2.0.52.
3. Linux users may already have Apache installed by default. The `htdocs` directory may be found in a number of places, depending on the Linux distribution.

to ask a user to input a ZIP code, then redirect the user to a CGI script that generates a dynamic Web page customized for people in that geographical area. In this chapter, we introduce the basics of CGI and use C++ to write our first CGI scripts.

The Common Gateway Interface is "common" in the sense that it is not specific to any particular operating system (such as Linux or Windows) or to any one programming language. CGI was designed to be used with virtually any programming language, such as C, C++, Perl, Python or Visual Basic.

CGI was developed in 1993 by NCSA (National Center for Supercomputing Applications—www.ncsa.uiuc.edu) for use with its popular HTTPd Web server. Unlike Web protocols and languages that have formal specifications, the initial concise description of CGI written by NCSA proved simple enough that CGI was adopted as an unofficial standard worldwide. CGI support was incorporated quickly into other Web servers, including Apache.

19.8 Simple HTTP Transactions

Before exploring how CGI operates, it is necessary to have a basic understanding of networking and how the World Wide Web works. In this section, we examine the inner workings of the Hypertext Transfer Protocol (HTTP) and discuss what goes on behind the scenes when a browser makes a request and then displays the response. HTTP describes a set of methods and headers that allows clients and servers to interact and exchange information in a uniform and predictable way.

A Web page in its simplest form is an XHTML document, which is a plain text file that contains markings (markup or elements) that describe the structure of the data the document contains. For example, the XHTML

```
<title>My Web Page</title>
```

indicates to the browser that the text between the `<title>` start tag and the `</title>` end tag is the title of the Web page. XHTML documents also can contain hypertext information (usually called hyperlinks), which are links to other Web pages or to other locations on the same page. When a user activates a hyperlink (usually by clicking it with the mouse), the Web browser "follows" the hyperlink by loading the new Web page (or a different part of the same Web page) from the Web server that contains the Web page.

Each XHTML file available for viewing over the Web has a URL associated with it. A URL contains the protocol of the resource (such as `http`), the machine name or IP address for the resource and the name (including the path) of the resource. For example, in the URL

```
http://www.deitel.com/books/downloads.html
```

the protocol is `http`, the machine name is `www.deitel.com`. The name of the resource being requested, `/books/downloads.html` (an XHTML document), is the remainder of the URL. This portion of the URL specifies both the name of the resource (`downloads.html`) and its path (`/books`), which helps the Web server processing the request to determine where the resource is located on the Web server. Note that an XHTML document ends with the `.html` file extension. The path could represent an actual directory in the Web server's file system. However, for security reasons, the path often refers to a virtual directory—an alias or fake name for a physical directory on disk. In this case, the server translates the path into a real location on the server (or even on another computer), thus hiding the true location of the resource. In fact, it is even possible that the resource is created dynamically and does not reside anywhere on the server's computer. As we will see, URLs also can be used to specify the user's input to a program on the server.

Now we consider how a browser, when given a URL, performs a simple HTTP transaction to retrieve and display a Web page. Figure 19.4 illustrates the transaction in detail. The transaction is performed between a Web browser and a Web server.

In Step 1 of Fig. 19.4, the browser sends an HTTP request to the server. The request (in its simplest form) looks like the following:

```
GET /books/downloads.html HTTP/1.1
Host: www.deitel.com
```

The word GET, an HTTP method, indicates that the client sends a get request and wishes to retrieve a resource. The remainder of the request provides the name and path of the resource

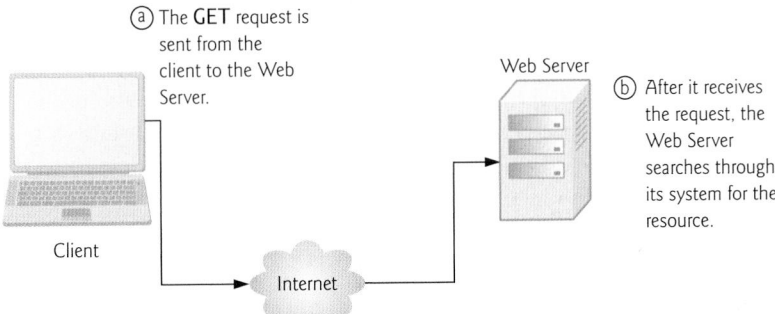

Fig. 19.4 | Client interacting with server and Web server. Step 1: The get request, GET /books/downloads.html HTTP/1.1. (Part 1 of 2.)

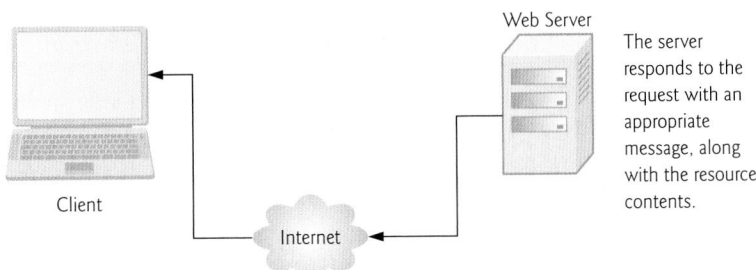

Fig. 19.4 | Client interacting with server and Web server. Step 2: The HTTP response, HTTP/1.1 200 OK. (Part 2 of 2.)

(/books/downloads.html) and the protocol's name and version number (HTTP/1.1). After the Web server receives the request, it searches through the system for the resource.

Any server that understands HTTP (version 1.1) will be able to translate this request and respond appropriately. Step 2 of Fig. 19.4 shows the results of a successful request. The server first sends a response indicating the HTTP version, followed by a numeric code and a phrase describing the status of the transaction. For example,

```
HTTP/1.1 200 OK
```

indicates success;

```
HTTP/1.1 404 Not found
```

informs the client that the requested resource was not found on the server in the specified location.

The server then sends one or more HTTP headers, which provide information about the data being sent to the client. In this case, the server is sending an XHTML document, so the HTTP header reads

```
Content-Type: text/html
```

The information in the `Content-Type` header identifies the MIME (Multipurpose Internet Mail Extensions) type of the content. Each document from the server has a MIME type by which the browser determines how to process the data it receives. For example, the MIME type `text/plain` indicates that the data contains text that should be displayed without attempting to interpret any of the content as XHTML markup. Similarly, the MIME type `image/gif` indicates that the content is a GIF image. When this MIME type is received by the browser, it attempts to display the data as an image.

The headers are followed by a blank line, which indicates to the client that the server has finished sending HTTP headers. The server then sends the contents of the requested document (e.g., `downloads.html`). The connection is terminated when the transfer of the resource is complete (in this case, when the end of the document `downloads.html` is reached). The client-side browser interprets the XHTML it receives and renders (or displays) the results.

19.9 Simple CGI Scripts

As long as an XHTML file on the server remains unchanged, its associated URL will display the same content in clients' browsers each time the file is accessed. To change the content of the XHTML file (e.g., to include new links or the latest company news), someone must alter the file manually on the server, probably with a text editor or Web-page-design software.

This need for manual change is a problem for Web page authors who want to create interesting and dynamic Web pages. To have a person continually alter a Web page is tedious. For example, if you want your Web page always to display the current date or weather conditions, the page will require continuous updating.

First CGI Script

Figure 19.5 shows our first CGI script. Note that the program consists mainly of cout statements (lines 16–29). Until now, the output of cout always has been displayed on the screen. However, technically speaking, the default target for cout is standard output. When a C++ program is executed as a CGI script, the standard output is redirected by the Web server to the client Web browser. To execute the program as a CGI script, we placed the compiled C++ executable file in the Web server's cgi-bin directory. For the purpose of this chapter, we have changed the executable file extension from .exe to .cgi.[4] Assuming that the Web server is on your local computer, you can execute the script by typing

    http://localhost/cgi-bin/localtime.cgi

in your browser's **Address** or **Location** field. If you are requesting this script from a remote Web server, you will need to replace localhost with the server's machine name or IP address.

```cpp
// Fig. 19.5: localtime.cpp
// Displays the current date and time in a Web browser.
#include <iostream>
using std::cout;

#include <ctime> // definitions of time_t, time, localtime and asctime
using std::time_t;
using std::time;
using std::localtime;
using std::asctime;

int main()
{
   time_t currentTime; // variable for storing time

   cout << "Content-Type: text/html\n\n"; // output HTTP header

   // output XML declaration and DOCTYPE
   cout << "<?xml version = \"1.0\"?>"
      << "<!DOCTYPE html PUBLIC \"-//W3C//DTD XHTML 1.1//EN\" "
      << "\"http://www.w3.org/TR/xhtml11/DTD/xhtml11.dtd\">";

   time( &currentTime ); // store time in currentTime

   // output html element and some of its contents
   cout << "<html xmlns = \"http://www.w3.org/1999/xhtml\">"
      << "<head><title>Current date and time</title></head>"
      << "<body><p>" << asctime( localtime( &currentTime ) )
      << "</p></body></html>";
   return 0;
} // end main
```

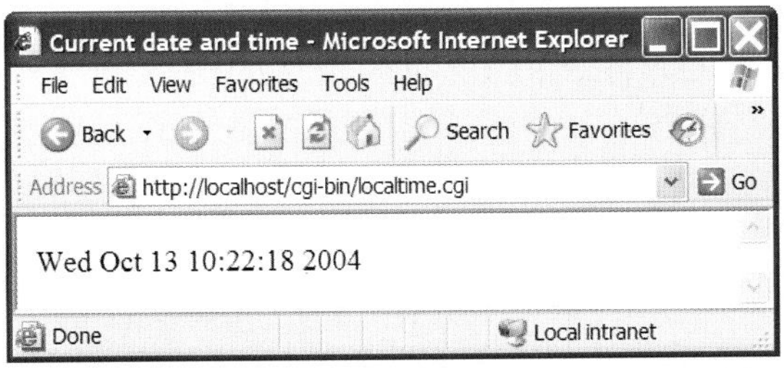

Fig. 19.5 | First CGI script.

---

4. On a server running Microsoft Windows, the executable may be run directly in .exe form.

The notion of standard output is similar to that of standard input, which we have seen associated with `cin`. Just as standard input refers to the standard source of input into a program (normally, the keyboard), standard output refers to the standard destination of output from a program (normally, the screen). It is possible to redirect (or *pipe*) standard output to another destination. Thus, in our CGI script, when we output an HTTP header (line 16) or XHTML elements (lines 19–21 and 26–29), the output is sent to the Web server, as opposed to the screen. The server sends that output to the client over HTTP, which interprets the headers and elements as if they were part of a normal server response to an XHTML document request.

It is fairly straightforward to write a C++ program that outputs the current time and date (to the monitor of the local computer). In fact, this requires only a few lines of code (lines 14, 23 and 28). Line 14 declares `currentTime` as a variable of type `time_t`. Function `time` (line 23) gets the current time, which is represented as the number of seconds elapsed since midnight January 1, 1970, and stores the retrieved value to the location specified by the parameter (in this case, `currentTime`). C++ library function `localtime` (line 28), when passed a `time_t` variable (e.g., `currentTime`), returns a pointer to an object containing the "broken-down" local time (i.e., days, hours, etc. are placed in individual member variables). Function `asctime` (line 28), which takes a pointer to an object containing "broken-down" time, returns a string such as

```
Wed Oct 31 13:10:37 2004
```

What if we wish to send the current time to a client's browser window for display (rather than outputting it to the screen)? CGI makes this possible by redirecting the output of a program to the Web server itself, which then sends the output to a client's browser.

How Web Server Redirects the Output

Figure 19.6 illustrates this process in more detail. In Step 1, the client requests the resource named `localtime.cgi` from the server, just as it requested `downloads.html` in the previous example (Fig. 19.4). If the server was not configured to handle CGI scripts, it might just return the contents of the C++ executable file to the client, as if it were any other document. However, based on the Web server configuration, the server executes `localtime.cgi` (implemented using C++) and sends the CGI script's output to the Web browser.

A properly configured Web server, however, will recognize that different types of resources should be handled differently. For example, when the resource is a CGI script, the script must be executed by the server before it is sent. A CGI script is designated in one of two ways: either it has a special filename extension (such as `.cgi` or `.exe`) or it is located in a specific directory (often `cgi-bin`). In addition, the server administrator must give permission explicitly for remote clients to be able to access and execute CGI scripts.[5]

In Step 2 of Fig. 19.6, the server recognizes that the resource is a CGI script and executes the script. In Step 3, the output produced by the script's three `cout` statements (lines 16, 19–21 and 26–29 of Fig. 19.5) is sent to the standard output and is returned to the Web server. Finally, in Step 4, the Web server adds a message to the output that indicates the status of the HTTP transaction (such as `HTTP/1.1 200 OK`, for success) and sends the entire output from the CGI program to the client.

---

5. If you are using the Apache HTTP Server and would like more information on configuration, consult the Apache home page at `httpd.apache.org/docs-2.0/`.

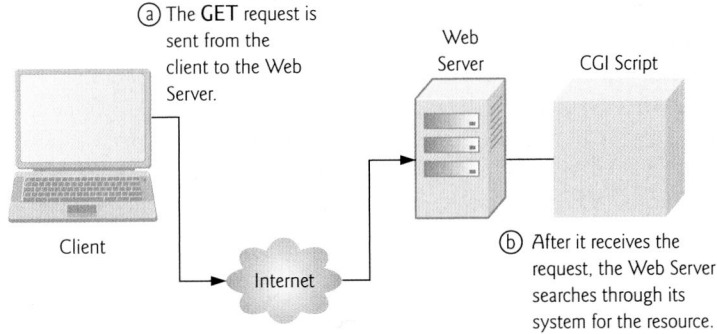

Fig. 19.6 | Step 1: The `get` request, `GET /cgi-bin/localtime.cgi HTTP/1.1`. (Part 1 of 4.)

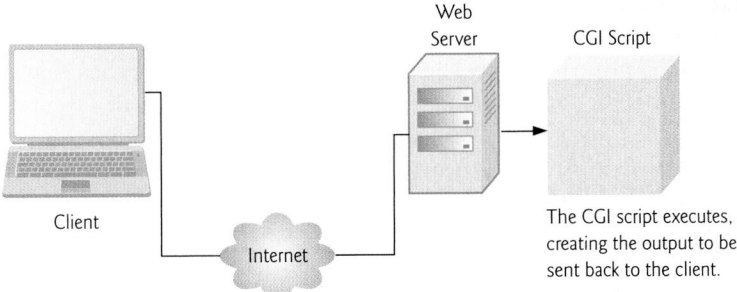

Fig. 19.6 | Step 2: The Web server starts the CGI script. (Part 2 of 4.)

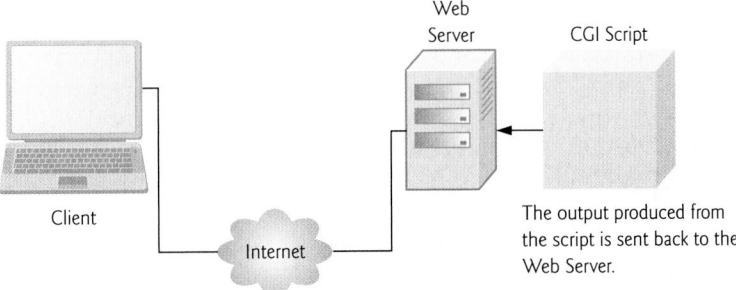

Fig. 19.6 | Step 3: The script output is sent to the Web server. (Part 3 of 4.)

The client-side browser then processes the XHTML document and displays the results. It is important to note that the browser is unaware of what has transpired on the server. In other words, as far as the browser is concerned, it requests a resource like any

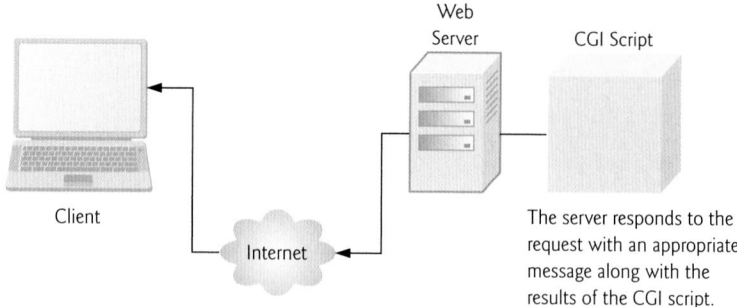

Fig. 19.6 | Step 4: The HTTP response, HTTP/1.1 200 OK. (Part 4 of 4.)

other and receives a response like any other. The browser receives and interprets the script's output just as if it were a simple, static XHTML document.

In fact, you can view the content that the browser receives by executing local-time.cgi from the command line, as we normally would execute any of the programs from the previous chapters. [*Note:* The filename extension must be changed to .exe prior to executing it from the command line on a system running Windows.] Figure 19.7 shows the output. For the purpose of this chapter, we formatted the output for human readability. Notice that, with the CGI script, we must output the Content-Type header, whereas, for an XHTML document, the Web server would include the header.

The CGI script prints the Content-Type header, a blank line and the data (XHTML, plain text, etc.) to standard output. When the CGI script is executed on the Web server, the Web server retrieves the script's output, inserts the HTTP response to the beginning and delivers the content to the client. Later we will see other content types that may be used in this manner, as well as other headers that may be used in addition to Content-Type.

 Common Programming Error 19.1

Forgetting to place a blank line after a header is a syntax error.

```
Content-Type: text/html

<?xml version = "1.0"?>
<!DOCTYPE html PUBLIC "-//W3C//DTD XHTML 1.1//EN"
   "http://www.w3.org/TR/xhtml11/DTD/xhtml11.dtd">

<html xmlns = "http://www.w3.org/1999/xhtml">
   <head>
      <title>Current date and time</title>
   </head>

   <body>
      <p>Wed Oct 13 10:22:18 2004</p>
   </body>
</html>
```

Fig. 19.7 | Output of localtime.cgi when executed from the command line.

Displaying Environment Variables
The program of Fig. 19.8 outputs the environment variables that the Apache HTTP Server sets for CGI scripts. These variables contain information about the client and server environment, such as the type of Web browser being used and the location of a document on the server. Lines 14–23 initialize an array of `string` objects with the names of the CGI environment variables. [*Note:* Environment variables are server-specific. Servers other than Apache HTTP Server may not provide all of these environment variables.] Line 37 begins the XHTML table in which the data will be displayed.

```cpp
1   // Fig. 19.8: environment.cpp
2   // Program to display CGI environment variables.
3   #include <iostream>
4   using std::cout;
5
6   #include <string>
7   using std::string;
8
9   #include <cstdlib>
10  using std::getenv;
11
12  int main()
13  {
14     string environmentVariables[ 24 ] = {
15        "COMSPEC", "DOCUMENT_ROOT", "GATEWAY_INTERFACE",
16        "HTTP_ACCEPT", "HTTP_ACCEPT_ENCODING",
17        "HTTP_ACCEPT_LANGUAGE", "HTTP_CONNECTION",
18        "HTTP_HOST", "HTTP_USER_AGENT", "PATH",
19        "QUERY_STRING", "REMOTE_ADDR", "REMOTE_PORT",
20        "REQUEST_METHOD", "REQUEST_URI", "SCRIPT_FILENAME",
21        "SCRIPT_NAME", "SERVER_ADDR", "SERVER_ADMIN",
22        "SERVER_NAME","SERVER_PORT","SERVER_PROTOCOL",
23        "SERVER_SIGNATURE","SERVER_SOFTWARE" };
24
25     cout << "Content-Type: text/html\n\n"; // output HTTP header
26
27     // output XML declaration and DOCTYPE
28     cout << "<?xml version = \"1.0\"?>"
29        << "<!DOCTYPE html PUBLIC \"-//W3C//DTD XHTML 1.1//EN\" "
30        << "\"http://www.w3.org/TR/xhtml11/DTD/xhtml11.dtd\">";
31
32     // output html element and some of its contents
33     cout << "<html xmlns = \"http://www.w3.org/1999/xhtml\">"
34        << "<head><title>Environment Variables</title></head><body>";
35
36     // begin outputting table
37     cout << "<table border = \"0\" cellspacing = \"2\">";
38
39     // iterate through environment variables
40     for ( int i = 0; i < 24; i++ )
41     {
```

Fig. 19.8 | Retrieving environment variables via function `getenv`. (Part 1 of 3.)

```
42          cout << "<tr><td>" << environmentVariables[ i ] << "</td><td>";
43
44          // attempt to retrieve value of current environment variable
45          char *value = getenv( environmentVariables[ i ].c_str() );
46
47          if ( value != 0 ) // environment variable exists
48             cout << value;
49          else
50             cout << "Environment variable does not exist.";
51
52          cout << "</td></tr>";
53       } // end for
54
55       cout << "</table></body></html>";
56       return 0;
57    } // end main
```

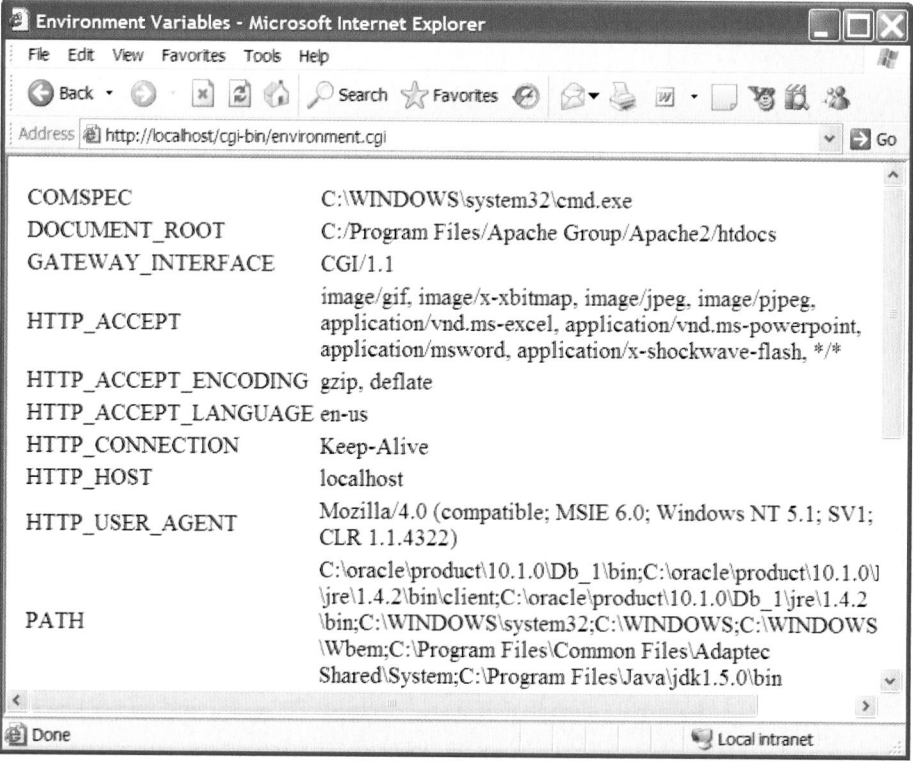

Fig. 19.8 | Retrieving environment variables via function `getenv`. (Part 2 of 3.)

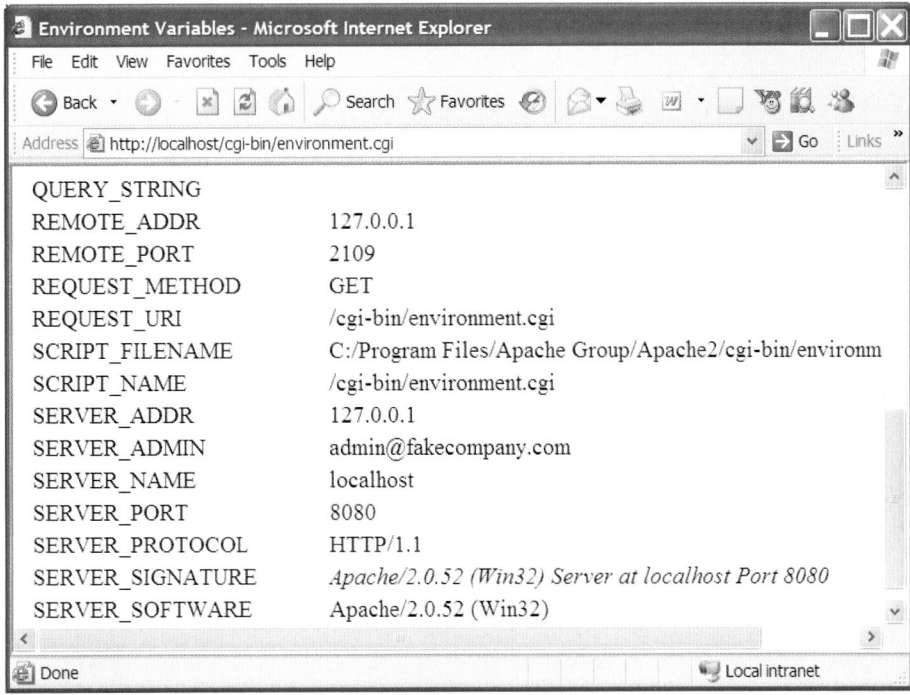

Fig. 19.8 | Retrieving environment variables via function `getenv`. (Part 3 of 3.)

Lines 42–52 output each row of the table. Let us examine each of these lines closely. Line 42 outputs an XHTML `<tr>` (table row) start tag, which indicates the beginning of a new table row. Line 52 outputs a corresponding `</tr>` end tag, which indicates the end of the row. Each row of the table contains two table cells—the name of an environment variable and the data associated with that variable (if the variable exists). The `<td>` start tag (line 42) begins a new table cell. The `for` loop (lines 40–53) iterates through each of the 24 `string` objects. Each environment variable's name is output in the left table cell (line 42). Line 45 attempts to retrieve the value associated with the environment variable by calling function `getenv` of `<cstdlib>` and passing it the string value returned from the function call `environmentVariables[ i ].c_str()`. Function `c_str` returns a C-style `char *` string containing the contents of the `environmentVariables[ i ]` string. Function `getenv` returns a `char *` string containing the value of a specified environment variable or a null pointer if the environment variable does not exist.

Lines 47–50 output the contents of the right table cell. If the current environment variable exists (i.e., `getenv` did not return a null pointer), line 48 outputs the `value` returned by function `getenv`. If the environment variable does not exist on the server executing the script, line 50 outputs an appropriate message. The sample execution shown in Fig. 19.8 was produced by running this example on Apache HTTP Server, so the output contains data associated with each of the environment variables. The results on other servers may vary. For example, if you were to run this example on Microsoft Internet Information Services (IIS), several of the table cells in the right column would display the message "Environment variable does not exist."

19.10 Sending Input to a CGI Script

Though preset environment variables provide much information, we would like to be able to supply any type of data to our CGI scripts, such as a user's name or a search-engine query. The environment variable QUERY_STRING provides a mechanism to do just that. The QUERY_STRING variable contains information that is appended to a URL in a get request. For example, the URL

www.*somesite*.com/cgi-bin/script.cgi?state=California

causes the Web browser to request a CGI script (cgi-bin/script.cgi) with query string (state=California) from www.*somesite*.com. The Web server stores the query string following the ? in the QUERY_STRING environment variable. The query string provides parameters that customize the request for a particular client. Note that the question mark (?) is not part of the resource requested, nor is it part of the query string. It serves as a delimiter (or separator) between the two.

Figure 19.9 shows a simple example of a CGI script that reads data passed through the QUERY_STRING. The data in the query string can be formatted in a variety of ways. The CGI script reading the query string must know how to interpret the formatted data. In the example in Fig. 19.9, the query string contains a series of name-value pairs delimited by ampersands (&), as in name=Jill&age=22.

In line 16 of Figure 19.9, we pass "QUERY_STRING" to function getenv, which returns the query string or a null pointer if the server has not set a QUERY_STRING environment variable. [*Note:* The Apache HTTP Server sets QUERY_STRING even if a request does not contain a query string—in this case, the variable contains an empty string. However, some servers, such as Microsoft's IIS, set this variable only if a query string actually exists.] If the QUERY_STRING environment variable exists (i.e., getenv does not return a null pointer), line 17 invokes getenv again, this time assigning the returned query string to string variable query. After outputting a header, some XHTML start tags and the title (lines 19–29), we test if query contains data (line 32). If not, we output a message instructing the user to add a query string to the URL. We also provide a link to a URL that includes a sample query string. Query string data may be specified as part of a hyperlink in a Web page when encoded in this manner. The contents of the query string are output by line 36.

This example simply demonstrated how to access data passed to a CGI script in the query string. Later chapter examples show how to break a query string into useful pieces of information that can be manipulated using separate variables.

19.11 Using XHTML Forms to Send Input

Having a client enter input directly into a URL is not a user-friendly approach. Fortunately, XHTML provides the ability to include forms on Web pages that provide a more intuitive way for users to input information to be sent to a CGI script.

XHTML *form Element*

The `form element` encloses an XHTML form. The `form` element generally takes two attributes. The first is `action`, which specifies the server resource to execute when the user submits the form. For our purposes, the `action` usually will be a CGI script that processes the form's data. The second attribute used in the `form` element is `method`, which identifies the type of HTTP request (i.e., `get` or `post`) to use when the browser submits the form to the Web server. In this section, we show examples using both `get` and `post` requests to illustrate them in detail.

An XHTML form may contain any number of elements. Figure 19.10 gives a brief description of several form elements.

```cpp
1   // Fig. 19.9: querystring.cpp
2   // Demonstrating QUERY_STRING.
3   #include <iostream>
4   using std::cout;
5
6   #include <string>
7   using std::string;
8
9   #include <cstdlib>
10  using::getenv;
11
12  int main()
13  {
14     string query = "";
15
16     if ( getenv( "QUERY_STRING" ) ) // QUERY_STRING variable exists
17        query = getenv( "QUERY_STRING" ); // retrieve QUERY_STRING value
18
19     cout << "Content-Type: text/html\n\n"; // output HTTP header
20
21     // output XML declaration and DOCTYPE
22     cout << "<?xml version = \"1.0\"?>"
23        << "<!DOCTYPE html PUBLIC \"-//W3C//DTD XHTML 1.1//EN\" "
24        << "\"http://www.w3.org/TR/xhtml11/DTD/xhtml11.dtd\">";
25
26     // output html element and some of its contents
27     cout << "<html xmlns = \"http://www.w3.org/1999/xhtml\">"
28        << "<head><title>Name/Value Pairs</title></head><body>";
29     cout << "<h2>Name/Value Pairs</h2>";
30
31     // if query contained no data
32     if ( query == "" )
33        cout << "Please add some name-value pairs to the URL above.<br/> Or"
34           << " try <a href=\"querystring.cgi?name=Joe&age=29\">this</a>.";
35     else // user entered query string
36        cout << "<p>The query string is: " << query << "</p>";
37
38     cout << "</body></html>";
39     return 0;
40  } // end main
```

Fig. 19.9 | Reading input from `QUERY_STRING`. (Part 1 of 2.)

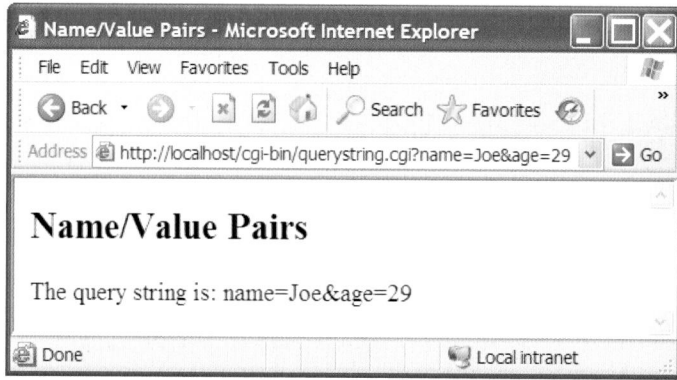

Fig. 19.9 | Reading input from QUERY_STRING. (Part 2 of 2.)

Element name	type attribute value (for input elements)	Description
input	text	Provides a single-line text field for text input.
	password	Like text, but each character typed by the user appears as an asterisk (*).
	checkbox	Displays a checkbox that can be checked (true) or unchecked (false).
	radio	Radio buttons are like checkboxes, except that only one radio button in a group of radio buttons can be selected at a time.
	button	A push button.
	submit	A push button that submits form data according to the form's action.
	image	The same as submit, but displays an image rather than a push button.
	reset	A push button that resets form fields to their default values.
	file	Displays a text field and button that allow the user to specify a file to upload to a Web server. When clicked, the button opens a file dialog that allows the user to select a file.
	hidden	Hidden form data that can be used by the form handler on the server. These inputs are not visible to the user.
select		Drop-down menu or selection box. This element is used with the option element to specify a series of selectable items.
textarea		This is a multiline text field in which text can be input or displayed.

Fig. 19.10 | XHTML form elements.

Using *get* Request

Figure 19.11 demonstrates a basic XHTML form using the HTTP get method. The form is output in lines 34–36 with the form element. Notice that attribute method has the value "get" and attribute action has the value "getquery.cgi" (i.e., the script actually calls itself to handle the form data, once it is submitted).

The form contains two input fields. The first (line 35) is a single-line text field (type = "text") named word. The second (line 36) displays a button, labeled **Submit Word** (value = "Submit Word"), to submit the form data.

The first time the script is executed, there should be no value in QUERY_STRING (unless the user has appended the query string to the URL). [*Note:* Recall that on some servers

```
 1   // Fig. 19.11: getquery.cpp
 2   // Demonstrates GET method with XHTML form.
 3   #include <iostream>
 4   using std::cout;
 5
 6   #include <string>
 7   using std::string;
 8
 9   #include <cstdlib>
10   using std::getenv;
11
12   int main()
13   {
14      string nameString = "";
15      string wordString = "";
16      string query = "";
17
18      if ( getenv( "QUERY_STRING" ) ) // QUERY_STRING variable exists
19         query = getenv( "QUERY_STRING" ); // retrieve QUERY_STRING value
20
21      cout << "Content-Type: text/html\n\n"; // output HTTP header
22
23      // output XML declaration and DOCTYPE
24      cout << "<?xml version = \"1.0\"?>"
25         << "<!DOCTYPE html PUBLIC \"-//W3C//DTD XHTML 1.1//EN\" "
26         << "\"http://www.w3.org/TR/xhtml11/DTD/xhtml11.dtd\">";
27
28      // output html element and some of its contents
29      cout << "<html xmlns = \"http://www.w3.org/1999/xhtml\">"
30         << "<head><title>Using GET with Forms</title></head><body>";
31
32      // output xhtml form
33      cout << "<p>Enter one of your favorite words here:</p>"
34         << "<form method = \"get\" action = \"getquery.cgi\">"
35         << "<input type = \"text\" name = \"word\"/>"
36         << "<input type = \"submit\" value = \"Submit Word\"/></form>";
37
38      if ( query == "" ) // query is empty
39         cout << "<p>Please enter a word.</p>";
40      else // user entered query string
41      {
42         int wordLocation = query.find_first_of( "word=" ) + 5;
43         wordString = query.substr( wordLocation );
44
45         if ( wordString == "" ) // no word was entered
46            cout << "<p>Please enter a word.</p>";
47         else // word was entered
48            cout << "<p>Your word is: " << wordString << "</p>";
49      } // end else
50
51      cout << "</body></html>";
52      return 0;
53   } // end main
```

Fig. 19.11 | Using get method with an XHTML form. (Part 1 of 3.)

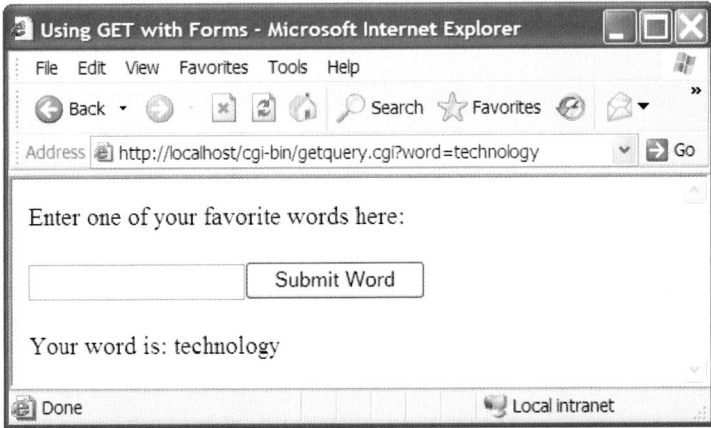

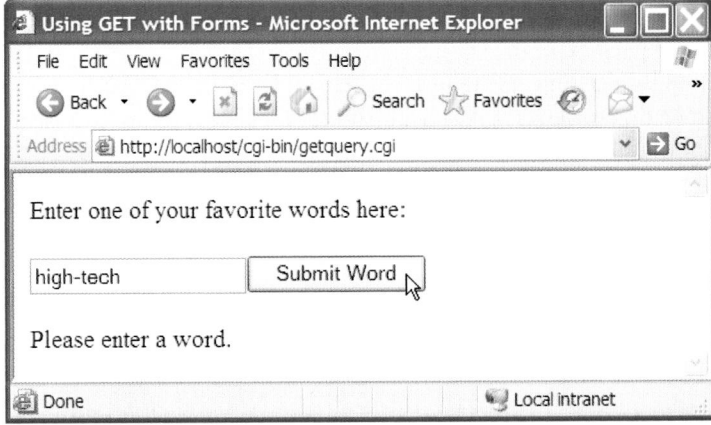

Fig. 19.11 | Using **get** method with an XHTML form. (Part 2 of 3.)

Fig. 19.11 | Using `get` method with an XHTML form. (Part 3 of 3.)

QUERY_STRING may not even exist when the query string is empty.] Once the user enters a word into the word text field and clicks **Submit Word**, the script is requested again. This time, the name of the input field (word) and the value entered by the user are placed in the QUERY_STRING environment variable. That is, if the user enters the word "technology" and clicks **Submit Word**, QUERY_STRING is assigned the value word=technology. Note that the query string is also appended to the URL in the browser's **Address** field with a question mark (?) in front of it.

During the second execution of the script, the query string is decoded. Lines 42 uses string method find_first_of to search query for the first occurrence of word=, which returns an integer value corresponding to the location in the string where the first match was found. Line 42 then adds 5 to the value returned by find_first_of to set wordLocation equal to the position in the string containing the first character of the user's favorite word. Function substr (line 43) returns the remainder of the string starting at wordLocation. Line 43 then assigns this string to wordString. Line 45 determines whether the user entered a word. If so, line 48 outputs the word entered by the user.

Using *post* Request

The two preceding examples used `get` to pass data to the CGI scripts through an environment variable (i.e., QUERY_STRING). Web browsers typically interact with Web servers by submitting forms using HTTP post. CGI programs read the contents of post requests using standard input. For comparison purposes, let us now reimplement the application of Fig. 19.11, using the post method (as in Fig. 19.12). Notice that the code in the two figures is virtually identical. The XHTML form (lines 43–45) indicates that we are now using the post method to submit the form data.

```
1   // Fig. 19.12: post.cpp
2   // Demonstrates POST method with XHTML form.
3   #include <iostream>
4   using std::cout;
5   using std::cin;
6
7   #include <string>
8   using std::string;
9
10  #include <cstdlib>
11  using std::getenv;
12  using std::atoi;
13
14  int main()
15  {
16     char postString[ 1024 ] = ""; // variable to hold POST data
17     string dataString = "";
18     string nameString = "";
19     string wordString = "";
20     int contentLength = 0;
21
22     // content was submitted
23     if ( getenv( "CONTENT_LENGTH" ) )
24     {
25        contentLength = atoi( getenv( "CONTENT_LENGTH" ) );
26        cin.read( postString, contentLength );
27        dataString = postString;
28     } // end if
29
30     cout << "Content-Type: text/html\n\n"; // output header
31
32     // output XML declaration and DOCTYPE
33     cout << "<?xml version = \"1.0\"?>"
34        << "<!DOCTYPE html PUBLIC \"-//W3C//DTD XHTML 1.1//EN\" "
35        << "\"http://www.w3.org/TR/xhtml11/DTD/xhtml11.dtd\">";
36
37     // output XHTML element and some of its contents
38     cout << "<html xmlns = \"http://www.w3.org/1999/xhtml\">"
39        << "<head><title>Using POST with Forms</title></head><body>";
40
41     // output XHTML form
42     cout << "<p>Enter one of your favorite words here:</p>"
43        << "<form method = \"post\" action = \"post.cgi\">"
44        << "<input type = \"text\" name = \"word\" />"
45        << "<input type = \"submit\" value = \"Submit Word\" /></form>";
46
47     // data was sent using POST
48     if ( contentLength > 0 )
49     {
50        int nameLocation = dataString.find_first_of( "word=" ) + 5;
51        int endLocation = dataString.find_first_of( "&" ) - 1;
52
```

Fig. 19.12 | Using post method with an XHTML form. (Part 1 of 3.)

```
53          // retrieve entered word
54          wordString = dataString.substr(
55             nameLocation, endLocation - nameLocation );
56
57          if ( wordString == "" ) // no data was entered in text field
58             cout << "<p>Please enter a word.</p>";
59          else // output word
60             cout << "<p>Your word is: " << wordString << "</p>";
61       } // end if
62       else // no data was sent
63          cout << "<p>Please enter a word.</p>";
64
65       cout << "</body></html>";
66       return 0;
67    } // end main
```

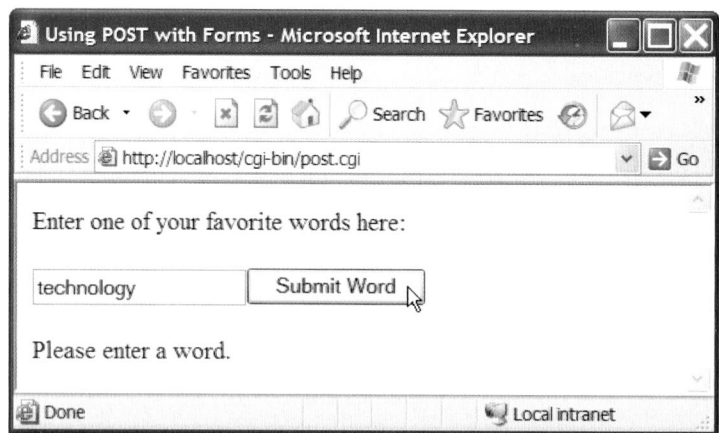

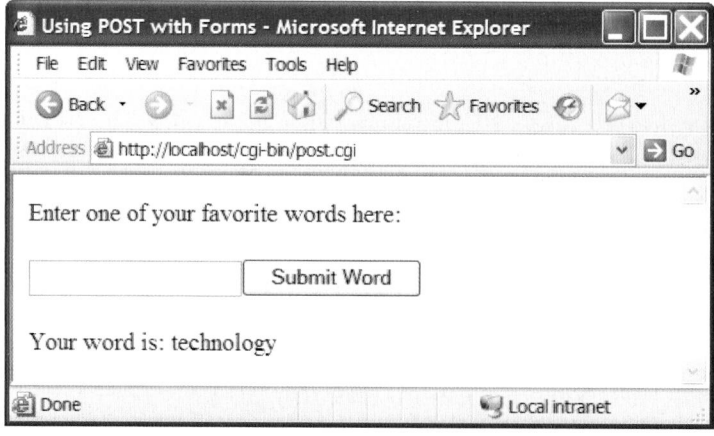

Fig. 19.12 | Using **post** method with an XHTML form. (Part 2 of 3.)

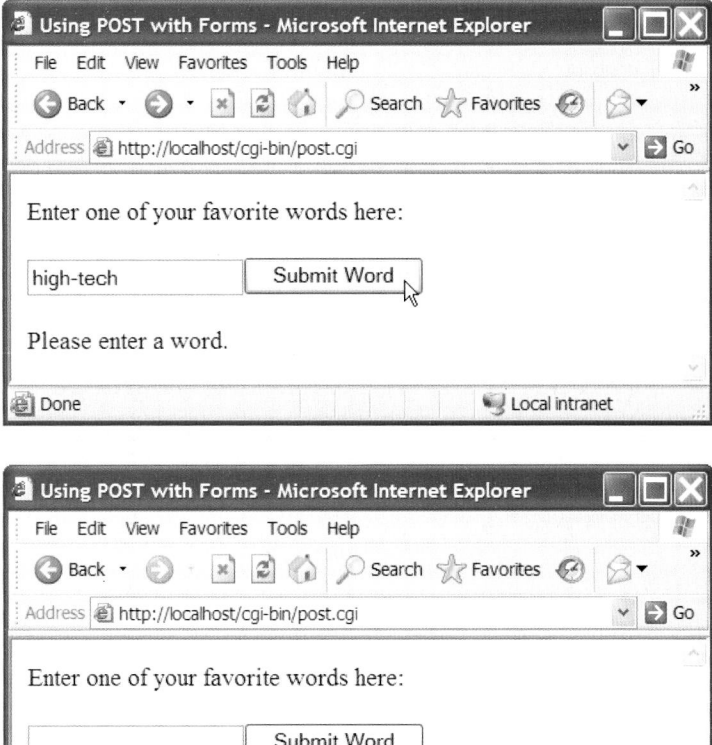

Fig. 19.12 | Using post method with an XHTML form. (Part 3 of 3.)

The Web server sends post data to a CGI script via standard input. The data is encoded (i.e., formatted) just as in QUERY_STRING (that is, with name-value pairs connected by equals signs and ampersands), but the QUERY_STRING environment variable is not set. Instead, the post method sets the environment variable CONTENT_LENGTH, to indicate the number of characters of data that were sent in a post request.

The CGI script uses the value of the CONTENT_LENGTH environment variable to process the correct amount of data. Line 23 determines whether CONTENT_LENGTH contains a value. If so, line 25 reads in the value and converts it to an integer by calling <cstdlib> function atoi. Line 26 calls function cin.read to read characters from standard input and stores the characters in array postString. Line 27 converts postString's data to a string by assigning it to dataString.

In earlier chapters, we read data from standard input using an expression such as

```
cin >> data;
```

The same approach might work in our CGI script as a replacement for the `cin.read` statement. Recall that `cin` reads data from standard input up to and including the first newline character, space or tab, whichever comes first. The CGI specification (freely available at `cgi-spec.golux.com/cgi-120-00a.html`) does not require a newline to be appended after the last name-value pair. Although some browsers append a newline or `EOF`, they are not required to do so. If `cin` is used with a browser that sends only the name-value pairs (as per the CGI specification), `cin` must wait for a newline that will never arrive. In this case, the server eventually "times out" and the CGI script terminates. Therefore, `cin.read` is preferred over `cin`, because the programmer can specify exactly how much data to read.

The CGI scripts in this section, while useful for explaining how `get` and `post` operate, do not include many of the features described in the CGI specification. For example, if we enter the words `didn't translate` into the text field and click the `submit` button, the script informs us that our word is `didn%27t+translate`.

What has happened here? Web browsers "URL encode" the XHTML form data they send. This means that spaces are replaced with plus signs, and other symbols (e.g., apostrophes) are translated into their ASCII value in hexadecimal format and preceded with a percent sign. URL encoding is necessary because URLs cannot contain certain characters, such as spaces and apostrophes.

19.12 Other Headers

A CGI script can supply other HTTP headers in addition to `Content-Type`. In most cases, the server passes these extra headers to the client without executing them. For example, the following `Refresh` header redirects the client to a new location after a specified amount of time:

```
Refresh: "5; URL = http://www.deitel.com/newpage.html"
```

Five seconds after the Web browser receives this header, the browser requests the resource at the specified URL. Alternatively, the `Refresh` header can omit the URL, in which case it will refresh the current page after the given time has expired.

The CGI specification indicates that certain types of headers output by a CGI script are to be handled by the server, rather than be passed directly to the client. The first of these is the `Location` header. Like `Refresh`, `Location` redirects the client to a new location:

```
Location: http://www.deitel.com/newpage.html
```

If used with a relative (or virtual) URL (i.e., `Location: /newpage.html`), the `Location` header indicates to the server that the redirection is to be performed on the server side without sending the `Location` header back to the client. In this case, it appears to the user as if the document rendered in the Web browser was the resource the user requested, when in fact the document rendered is the resource specified in the `Location` header.

The CGI specification also includes a `Status` header, which instructs the server to output a specified status header line (such as `HTTP/1.1 200 OK`). Normally, the server will send the appropriate status line to the client (adding, for example, the `200 OK` status line in most cases). However, CGI allows programmers to change the response status. For example, sending a

```
Status: 204 No Response
```

header indicates that, although the request was successful, the client should not display a new page in the browser window. This header might be useful if you want to allow users to submit forms without relocating to a new page.

We have now covered the fundamentals of the CGI specification. To review, CGI allows scripts to interact with servers in three basic ways:

1. through the output of headers and content to the server via standard output

2. by the server's setting of environment variables (including the URL-encoded QUERY_STRING) whose values are available within the script (via getenv)

3. through POSTed, URL-encoded data that the server sends to the script's standard input.

19.13 Case Study: An Interactive Web Page

Figures 19.13–19.14 show the implementation of a simple interactive portal for the fictitious Bug2Bug Travel Web site. The example queries the client for a name and password, then displays information about weekly travel specials based on the data entered. For simplicity, the example does not encrypt the data sent to the server. Ideally, sensitive data like a password should be encrypted. Encryption is beyond the scope of this book.

Figure 19.13 displays the opening page. It is a static XHTML document containing a form that POSTs data to the portal.cgi CGI script (line 16). The form contains one field to collect the user's name (line 18) and one to collect the user's password (line 19). [*Note:* Not like the CGI scripts, which are placed in the cgi-bin directory of the Web server, this XHTML document was placed in the htdocs directory of the Web server.]

```
 1   <?xml version = "1.0"?>
 2   <!DOCTYPE html PUBLIC "-//W3C//DTD XHTML 1.1//EN"
 3      "http://www.w3.org/TR/xhtml11/DTD/xhtml11.dtd">
 4
 5   <!-- Fig. 19.13: travel.html    -->
 6   <!-- Bug2Bug Travel Homepage    -->
 7
 8   <html xmlns = "http://www.w3.org/1999/xhtml">
 9      <head>
10         <title>Bug2Bug Travel</title>
11      </head>
12
13      <body>
14         <h1>Welcome to Bug2Bug Travel</h1>
15
16         <form method = "post" action = "/cgi-bin/portal.cgi">
17            <p>Please enter your name and password:</p>
18            <input type = "text" name = "namebox" />
19            <input type = "password" name = "passwordbox" />
20            <p>password is not encrypted</p>
21            <input type = "submit" name = "button" />
22         </form>
23      </body>
24   </html>
```

Fig. 19.13 | Interactive portal to create a password-protected Web page. (Part 1 of 2.)

Fig. 19.13 | Interactive portal to create a password-protected Web page. (Part 2 of 2.)

Figure 19.14 contains the CGI script. First, let us examine how the user's name and password are retrieved from standard input and stored in `strings`. The `string` library `find` function searches `dataString` (line 30) for an occurrence of `namebox=`. Function `find` returns a location in the string where `namebox=` was found. To retrieve the value associated with `namebox=`—the value entered by the user—we move the position in the string forward 8 characters. The program now contains an integer "pointing" to the starting location. Recall that a query string contains name-value pairs separated by equals signs and ampersands. To find the ending location for the data we wish to retrieve, we search for the `&` character (line 31). The length of the entered word is determined by the calculation `endNamelocation - namelocation`. We use a similar approach to determine the start and end locations of the password (lines 32–33). Lines 36–38 assign the form-field values to variables `nameString` and `passwordString`. We use `nameString` in line 52 to output a personalized greeting to the user. The current weekly specials are displayed in lines 53–56.

```
1   // Fig. 19.14: portal.cpp
2   // Handles entry to Bug2Bug Travel.
3   #include <iostream>
4   using std::cout;
5   using std::cin;
6
7   #include <string>
8   using std::string;
9
10  #include <cstdlib>
11  using std::getenv;
12  using std::atoi;
13
```

Fig. 19.14 | Interactive portal handler. (Part 1 of 3.)

```
14   int main()
15   {
16      char postString[ 1024 ] = "";
17      string dataString = "";
18      string nameString = "";
19      string passwordString = "";
20      int contentLength = 0;
21
22      // data was posted
23      if ( getenv( "CONTENT_LENGTH" ) )
24         contentLength = atoi( getenv( "CONTENT_LENGTH" ) );
25
26      cin.read( postString, contentLength );
27      dataString = postString;
28
29      // search string for input data
30      int namelocation = dataString.find( "namebox=" ) + 8;
31      int endNamelocation = dataString.find( "&" );
32      int password = dataString.find( "passwordbox=" ) + 12;
33      int endPassword = dataString.find( "&button" );
34
35      // get values for name and password
36      nameString = dataString.substr(
37         namelocation, endNamelocation - namelocation );
38      passwordString = dataString.substr( password, endPassword - password );
39
40      cout << "Content-Type: text/html\n\n"; // output HTTP header
41
42      // output XML declaration and DOCTYPE
43      cout << "<?xml version = \"1.0\"?>"
44         << "<!DOCTYPE html PUBLIC \"-//W3C//DTD XHTML 1.1//EN\" "
45         << "\"http://www.w3.org/TR/xhtml11/DTD/xhtml11.dtd\">";
46
47      // output html element and some of its contents
48      cout << "<html xmlns = \"http://www.w3.org/1999/xhtml\">"
49         << "<head><title>Bug2Bug Travel</title></head><body>";
50
51      // output specials
52      cout << "<h1>Welcome " << nameString << "!</h1>"
53         << "<p>Here are our weekly specials:</p>"
54         << "<ul><li>Boston to Taiwan ($875)</li>"
55         << "<li>San Diego to Hong Kong ($750)</li>"
56         << "<li>Chicago to Mexico City ($568)</li></ul>";
57
58      if ( passwordString == "coast2coast" ) // password is correct
59         cout << "<hr /><p>Current member special: "
60            << "Seattle to Tokyo ($400)</p>";
61      else // password was incorrect
62         cout << "<p>Sorry. You have entered an incorrect password</p>";
63
64      cout << "</body></html>";
65      return 0;
66   } // end main
```

Fig. 19.14 | Interactive portal handler. (Part 2 of 3.)

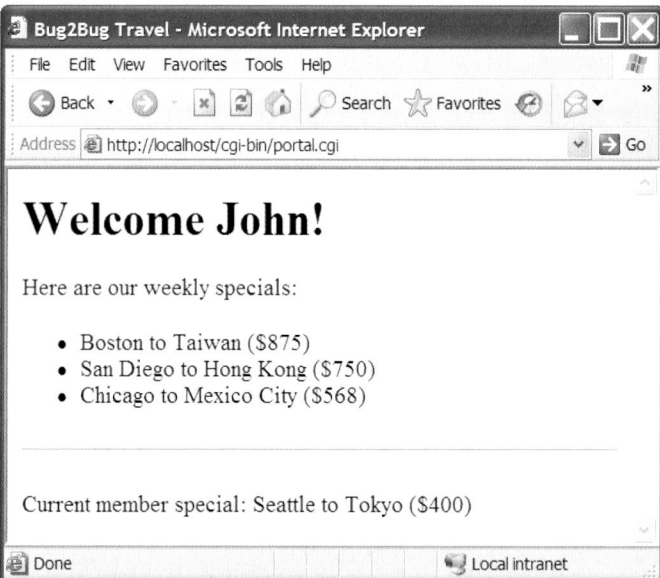

Fig. 19.14 | Interactive portal handler. (Part 3 of 3.)

If the member password is correct, lines 59–60 output additional specials. If the password is incorrect, the client is informed that the password was invalid and no additional specials are displayed.

Note that we use a static Web page and a separate CGI script here. We could have incorporated the opening XHTML form and the processing of the data into a single CGI script, as we did in previous examples in this chapter. We ask the reader to do this in Exercise 19.8.

Performance Tip 19.1

It is always much more efficient for the server to provide static content rather than execute a CGI script, because it takes time for the server to load the script from hard disk into memory and execute the script (whereas an XHTML file needs to be sent only to the client). It is a good practice to use a mix of static XHTML (for content that generally remains unchanged) and CGI scripting (for dynamic content). This practice allows the Web server to respond to clients more efficiently than if only CGI scripting were used.

19.14 Cookies

In the preceding two sections, we discussed two ways in which information may be passed between programs (or executions of the same program) through a browser. This section concentrates on storing state information on the client computer with cookies. Cookies are essentially small text files that a Web server sends to your browser, which then saves the cookies on your computer. Many Web sites use cookies to track users' progress through their site (as in a shopping-cart application) or to help customize the site for an individual user.

Cookies cannot break into your computer, nor can they erase your hard drive. However, they can be used to identify users and keep track of how often users visit a site or what users buy at a site. For this reason, cookies are considered to be a security and privacy concern. Popular Web browsers provide support for cookies. These browsers also allow users who are concerned about their privacy and security to disable this support. Most major Web sites use cookies. As a programmer, you should be aware of the possibility that cookies might be disabled by your clients. Figures 19.15–19.17 use cookies to store and manipulate information about a user.

```
 1   <?xml version = "1.0"?>
 2   <!DOCTYPE html PUBLIC "-//W3C//DTD XHTML 1.1//EN"
 3      "http://www.w3.org/TR/xhtml11/DTD/xhtml11.dtd">
 4
 5   <!-- Fig. 19.15: cookieform.html -->
 6   <!-- Cookie Demonstration          -->
 7
 8   <html xmlns = "http://www.w3.org/1999/xhtml">
 9      <head>
10         <title>Writing a cookie to the client computer</title>
11      </head>
12
13      <body>
14         <h1>Click Submit to save your cookie data.</h1>
15
16         <form method = "post" action = "/cgi-bin/writecookie.cgi">
17            <p>Name:<br />
18               <input type = "text" name = "name" />
19            </p>
20            <p>Age:<br />
21               <input type = "text" name = "age" />
22            </p>
23            <p>Favorite Color:<br />
```

Fig. 19.15 | XHTML document containing a form to **post** data to the server (Part 1 of 2.)

```
24                 <input type = "text" name = "color" />
25             </p>
26             <p>
27                 <input type = "submit" name = "button" value = "Submit" />
28             </p>
29         </form>
30     </body>
31 </html>
```

Fig. 19.15 | XHTML document containing a form to post data to the server (Part 2 of 2.)

```
 1  // Fig. 19.16: writecookie.cpp
 2  // Program to write a cookie to a client's machine.
 3  #include <iostream>
 4  using std::cin;
 5  using std::cout;
 6
 7  #include <string>
 8  using std::string;
 9
10  #include <cstdlib>
11  using std::getenv;
12  using std::atoi;
13
```

Fig. 19.16 | Writing a cookie. (Part 1 of 3.)

```
14   int main()
15   {
16      char query[ 1024 ] = "";
17      string dataString = "";
18      string nameString = "";
19      string ageString = "";
20      string colorString = "";
21      int contentLength = 0;
22
23      // expiration date of cookie
24      string expires = "Friday, 14-MAY-10 16:00:00 GMT";
25
26      // data was entered
27      if ( getenv( "CONTENT_LENGTH" ) )
28      {
29         contentLength = atoi( getenv( "CONTENT_LENGTH" ) );
30         cin.read( query, contentLength ); // read data from standard input
31         dataString = query;
32
33         // search string for data and store locations
34         int nameLocation = dataString.find( "name=" ) + 5;
35         int endName = dataString.find( "&" );
36         int ageLocation = dataString.find( "age=" ) + 4;
37         int endAge = dataString.find( "&color" );
38         int colorLocation = dataString.find( "color=" ) + 6;
39         int endColor = dataString.find( "&button" );
40
41         // get value for user's name
42         nameString = dataString.substr(
43            nameLocation, endName - nameLocation );
44
45         if ( ageLocation > 0 ) // get value for user's age
46            ageString = dataString.substr(
47               ageLocation, endAge - ageLocation );
48
49         if ( colorLocation > 0 ) // get value for user's favorite color
50            colorString = dataString.substr(
51               colorLocation, endColor - colorLocation );
52
53         // set cookie
54         cout << "Set-Cookie: Name=" << nameString << "age:"
55            << ageString << "color:" << colorString
56            << "; expires=" << expires << "; path=\n";
57      } // end if
58
59      cout << "Content-Type: text/html\n\n"; // output HTTP header
60
61      // output XML declaration and DOCTYPE
62      cout << "<?xml version = \"1.0\"?>"
63         << "<!DOCTYPE html PUBLIC \"-//W3C//DTD XHTML 1.1//EN\" "
64         << "\"http://www.w3.org/TR/xhtml11/DTD/xhtml11.dtd\">";
65
```

Fig. 19.16 | Writing a cookie. (Part 2 of 3.)

```
66      // output html element and some of its contents
67      cout << "<html xmlns = \"http://www.w3.org/1999/xhtml\">"
68          << "<head><title>Cookie Saved</title></head><body>";
69
70      // output user's information
71      cout << "<p>A cookie has been set with the following"
72          << " data:</p><p>Name: " << nameString  << "<br/></p>"
73          << "<p>Age: " << ageString << "<br/></p>"
74          << "<p>Color: " << colorString << "<br/></p>"
75          << "<p>Click <a href=\"/cgi-bin/readcookie.cgi\">"
76          << "here</a> to read saved cookie data.</p></body></html>";
77      return 0;
78   } // end main
```

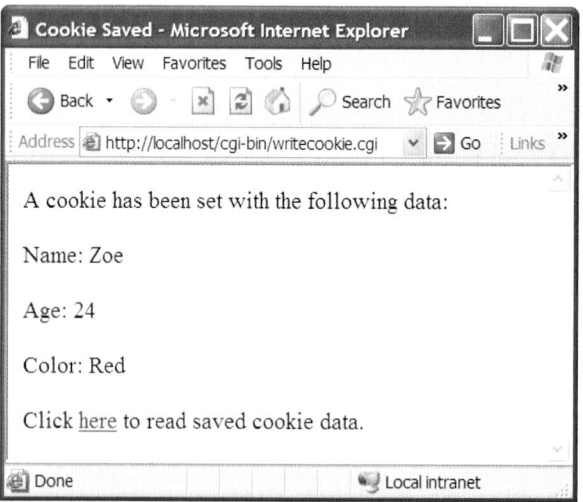

Fig. 19.16 | Writing a cookie. (Part 3 of 3.)

Figure 19.15 is an XHTML page that contains a form in which values are to be input. The form posts its information to writecookie.cgi (Fig. 19.16). This CGI script retrieves the data contained in the CONTENT_LENGTH environment variable. Line 24 of Fig. 19.16 declares and initializes string expires to store the expiration date of the cookie, which determines how long the cookie resides on the client's machine. This value can be a string, like the one in this example, or it can be a relative value. For instance, "+30d" sets the cookie to expire after 30 days. For the purposes of this chapter the expiration date is deliberately set to expire in the year 2010 to ensure that the program will run properly well into the future. You may set the expiration date of this example to any future date as needed. The browser deletes cookies when they expire.

After obtaining the data from the form, the program creates a cookie (lines 54–56). In this example, we create a cookie that stores a line of text containing the name-value pairs of the posted data, delimited by a colon character (:). The line must be output before the header is written to the client. The line of text begins with the Set-Cookie: header, indicating that the browser should store the incoming data in a cookie. We set three attributes for the cookie: a name-value pair containing the data to be stored, a name-value pair containing the expiration date and a name-value pair containing the URL of the server domain (e.g., www.deitel.com) for which the cookie is valid. For this example, path is not set to any value, making the cookie readable from any server in the domain of the server that originally wrote the cookie. Note that these name-value pairs are separated by semicolons (;). We use only colon characters within our cookie data so as not to conflict with the format of the Set-Cookie: header. When we enter the same data as displayed in Fig. 19.15, lines 54–56 store the data "Name=Zoeage:24color:Red" to the cookie. Lines 59–76 send a Web page indicating that the cookie has been written to the client.

Portability Tip 19.1

*Web browsers store the cookie information in a vendor-specific manner. For example, Microsoft's Internet Explorer stores cookies as text files in the **Temporary Internet Files** directory on the client's machine. Netscape stores its cookies in a single file named* cookies.txt.

Figure 19.17 reads the cookie written in Fig. 19.16 and displays the stored information. When a client sends a request to a server, the client Web browser locates any cookies previously written by that server. These cookies are sent by the browser back to the server as part of the request. On the server, the environment variable HTTP_COOKIE stores the client's cookies. Line 20 calls function getenv with the HTTP_COOKIE environment variable as the parameter and stores the returned value in dataString. The name-value pairs are decoded and stored in strings (lines 23–34) according to the encoding scheme used in Fig. 19.16. Lines 36–55 output the contents of the cookie as a Web page.

```cpp
1   // Fig. 19.17: readcookie.cpp
2   // Program to read cookie data.
3   #include <iostream>
4   using std::cin;
5   using std::cout;
6
7   #include <string>
8   using std::string;
9
10  #include <cstdlib>
11  using std::getenv;
12
13  int main()
14  {
15     string dataString = "";
16     string nameString = "";
17     string ageString = "";
18     string colorString = "";
19
20     dataString = getenv( "HTTP_COOKIE" ); // get cookie data
21
22     // search through cookie data string
23     int nameLocation = dataString.find( "Name=" ) + 5;
24     int endName = dataString.find( "age:" );
25     int ageLocation = dataString.find( "age:" ) + 4;
26     int endAge = dataString.find( "color:" );
27     int colorLocation = dataString.find( "color:" ) + 6;
```

Fig. 19.17 | Program to read cookies sent from the client's computer. (Part 1 of 2.)

```
28
29     // store cookie data in strings
30     nameString = dataString.substr(
31        nameLocation, endName - nameLocation );
32     ageString = dataString.substr(
33        ageLocation, endAge - ageLocation );
34     colorString = dataString.substr( colorLocation );
35
36     cout << "Content-Type: text/html\n\n"; // output HTTP header
37
38     // output XML declaration and DOCTYPE
39     cout << "<?xml version = \"1.0\"?>"
40        << "<!DOCTYPE html PUBLIC \"-//W3C//DTD XHTML 1.1//EN\" "
41        << "\"http://www.w3.org/TR/xhtml11/DTD/xhtml11.dtd\">";
42
43     // output html element and some of its contents
44     cout << "<html xmlns = \"http://www.w3.org/1999/xhtml\">"
45        << "<head><title>Read Cookies</title></head><body>";
46
47     if ( dataString != "" ) // data was found
48        cout << "<h3>The following data is saved in a cookie on"
49           << " your computer</h3><p>Name: " << nameString << "<br/></p>"
50           << "<p>Age: " << ageString << "<br/></p>"
51           << "<p>Color: " << colorString << "<br/></p>";
52     else // no data was found
53        cout << "<p>No cookie data.</p>";
54
55     cout << "</body></html>";
56     return 0;
57  } // end main
```

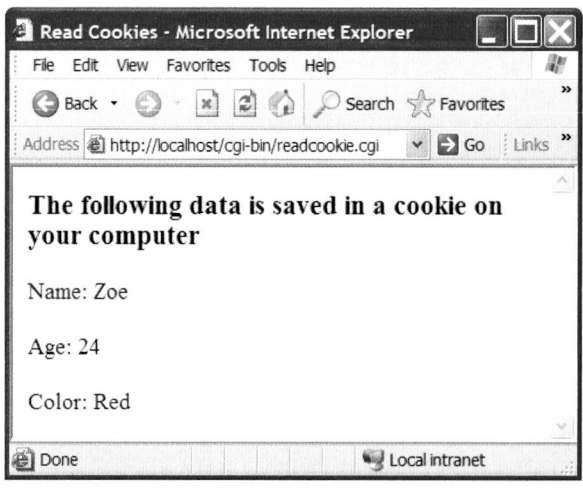

Fig. 19.17 | Program to read cookies sent from the client's computer. (Part 2 of 2.)

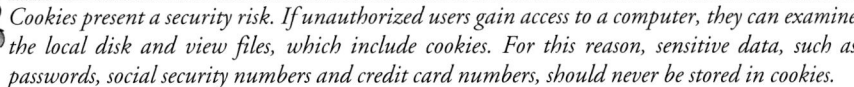

Software Engineering Observation 19.2

Cookies present a security risk. If unauthorized users gain access to a computer, they can examine the local disk and view files, which include cookies. For this reason, sensitive data, such as passwords, social security numbers and credit card numbers, should never be stored in cookies.

19.15 Server-Side Files

In the preceding section, we demonstrated how to maintain state information about a user via cookies. The other mechanism by which to do so is to create server-side files (i.e., files that are located on the server or on the server's network). This is a slightly more secure method by which to maintain vital information. In this mechanism, only someone with access and permission to change files on the server can alter files. Figures 19.18–19.19 ask users for contact information, then store it on the server. Figure 19.20 shows the file that is created by the script.

The XHTML document in Fig. 19.18 posts the form data to the CGI script in Fig. 19.19. In the CGI script, lines 45–92 decode the parameters that were sent by the client. Line 105 creates an instance of the output file stream (outFile) that opens a file for appending. If the file clients.txt does not exist, it is created. Lines 114–116 output the personal information to the file. (See Fig. 19.20 for the contents of the file.) The remainder of the program outputs an XHTML document that summarizes the user's information.

```
1   <?xml version = "1.0"?>
2   <!DOCTYPE html PUBLIC "-//W3C//DTD XHTML 1.1//EN"
3      "http://www.w3.org/TR/xhtml11/DTD/xhtml11.dtd">
4
5   <!-- Fig. 19.18: savefile.html         -->
6   <!-- Form to input client information  -->
7
8   <html xmlns = "http://www.w3.org/1999/xhtml">
9      <head>
10        <title>Please enter your contact information</title>
11     </head>
12
13     <body>
14        <p>Please enter your information in the form below.</p>
15        <p>Note: You must fill in all fields.</p>
16        <form method = "post" action = "/cgi-bin/savefile.cgi">
17           <p>
18              First Name:
19              <input type = "text" name = "firstname" size = "10" />
20              Last Name:
21              <input type = "text" name = "lastname" size = "15" />
22           </p>
23           <p>
24              Address:
25              <input type = "text" name = "address" size = "25" /><br />
26              Town: <input type = "text" name = "town" size = "10" />
27              State: <input type = "text" name = "state" size = "2" /><br/>
```

Fig. 19.18 | XHTML document to read user's contact information. (Part 1 of 2.)

```
28                  Zip Code: <input type = "text" name = "zipcode" size = "5" />
29                  Country: <input type = "text" name = "country" size = "10" />
30            </p>
31            <p>
32                  E-mail Address: <input type = "text" name = "email" />
33            </p>
34                  <input type = "submit" value = "Enter" />
35                  <input type = "reset" value = "Clear" />
36          </form>
37       </body>
38    </html>
```

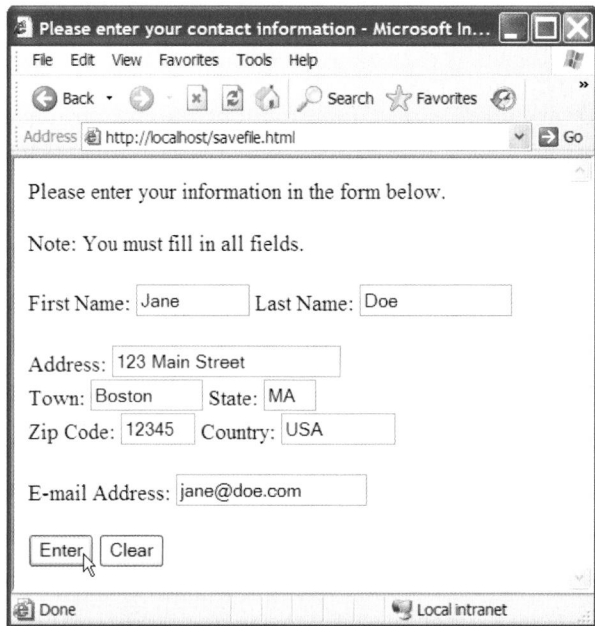

Fig. 19.18 | XHTML document to read user's contact information. (Part 2 of 2.)

```
1    // Fig. 19.19: savefile.cpp
2    // Program to enter user's contact information into a
3    // server-side file.
4    #include <iostream>
5    using std::cerr;
6    using std::cin;
7    using std::cout;
8    using std::ios;
9
10   #include <fstream>
11   using std::ofstream;
```

Fig. 19.19 | Creating a server-side file to store user data. (Part 1 of 4.)

```
12
13   #include <string>
14   using std::string;
15
16   #include <cstdlib>
17   using std::getenv;
18   using std::atoi;
19   using std::exit;
20
21   int main()
22   {
23      char postString[ 1024 ] = "";
24      int contentLength = 0;
25
26      // variables to store user data
27      string dataString = "";
28      string firstname = "";
29      string lastname = "";
30      string address = "";
31      string town = "";
32      string state = "";
33      string zipcode = "";
34      string country = "";
35      string email = "";
36
37      // data was posted
38      if ( getenv( "CONTENT_LENGTH" ) )
39         contentLength = atoi( getenv( "CONTENT_LENGTH" ) );
40
41      cin.read( postString, contentLength );
42      dataString = postString;
43
44      // search for first '+' character
45      string::size_type charLocation = dataString.find( "+" );
46
47      // search for next '+' character
48      while ( charLocation < string::npos ) )
49      {
50         dataString.replace( charLocation, 1, " " );
51         charLocation = dataString.find( "+", charLocation + 1 );
52      } // end while
53
54      // find location of firstname
55      int firstStart = dataString.find( "firstname=" ) + 10;
56      int endFirst = dataString.find( "&lastname" );
57      firstname = dataString.substr( firstStart, endFirst - firstStart );
58
59      // find location of lastname
60      int lastStart = dataString.find( "lastname=" ) + 9;
61      int endLast = dataString.find( "&address" );
62      lastname = dataString.substr( lastStart, endLast - lastStart );
63
```

Fig. 19.19 | Creating a server-side file to store user data. (Part 2 of 4.)

```
64     // find location of address
65     int addressStart = dataString.find( "address=" ) + 8;
66     int endAddress = dataString.find( "&town" );
67     address = dataString.substr( addressStart, endAddress - addressStart );
68
69     // find location of town
70     int townStart = dataString.find( "town=" ) + 5;
71     int endTown = dataString.find( "&state" );
72     town = dataString.substr( townStart, endTown - townStart );
73
74     // find location of state
75     int stateStart = dataString.find( "state=" ) + 6;
76     int endState = dataString.find( "&zipcode" );
77     state = dataString.substr( stateStart, endState - stateStart );
78
79     // find location of zip code
80     int zipStart = dataString.find( "zipcode=" ) + 8;
81     int endZip = dataString.find( "&country" );
82     zipcode = dataString.substr( zipStart, endZip - zipStart );
83
84     // find location of country
85     int countryStart = dataString.find( "country=" ) + 8;
86     int endCountry = dataString.find( "&email" );
87     country = dataString.substr( countryStart, endCountry - countryStart );
88
89     // find location of e-mail address
90     int emailStart = dataString.find( "email=" ) + 6;
91     int endEmail = dataString.find( "&submit" );
92     email = dataString.substr( emailStart, endEmail - emailStart );
93
94     cout << "Content-Type: text/html\n\n"; // output header
95
96     // output XML declaration and DOCTYPE
97     cout << "<?xml version = \"1.0\"?>"
98          << "<!DOCTYPE html PUBLIC \"-//W3C//DTD XHTML 1.1//EN\" "
99          << "\"http://www.w3.org/TR/xhtml11/DTD/xhtml11.dtd\">";
100
101    // output html element and some of its contents
102    cout << "<html xmlns = \"http://www.w3.org/1999/xhtml\">"
103         << "<head><title>Contact Information entered</title></head><body>";
104
105    ofstream outFile( "clients.txt", ios::app ); // output to file
106
107    if ( !outFile ) // file was not opened properly
108    {
109       cerr << "Error: could not open contact file.";
110       exit( 1 );
111    } // end if
112
113    // append data to clients.txt file
114    outFile << firstname << " " << lastname << "\n" << address << "\n"
115         << town << " " << state << " " << country << " " << zipcode
116         << "\n" << email << "\n\n";
```

Fig. 19.19 | Creating a server-side file to store user data. (Part 3 of 4.)

```
117
118      // output data to user
119      cout << "<table><tbody><tr><td>First Name:</td><td>" << firstname
120         << "</td></tr><tr><td>Last Name:</td><td>" << lastname
121         << "</td></tr><tr><td>Address:</td><td>" << address
122         << "</td></tr><tr><td>Town:</td><td>" << town
123         << "</td></tr><tr><td>State:</td><td>" << state
124         << "</td></tr><tr><td>Zip Code:</td><td>" << zipcode
125         << "</td></tr><tr><td>Country:</td><td>" << country
126         << "</td></tr><tr><td>Email:</td><td>" << email
127         << "</td></tr></tbody></table></body>\n</html>\n";
128      return 0;
129   } // end main
```

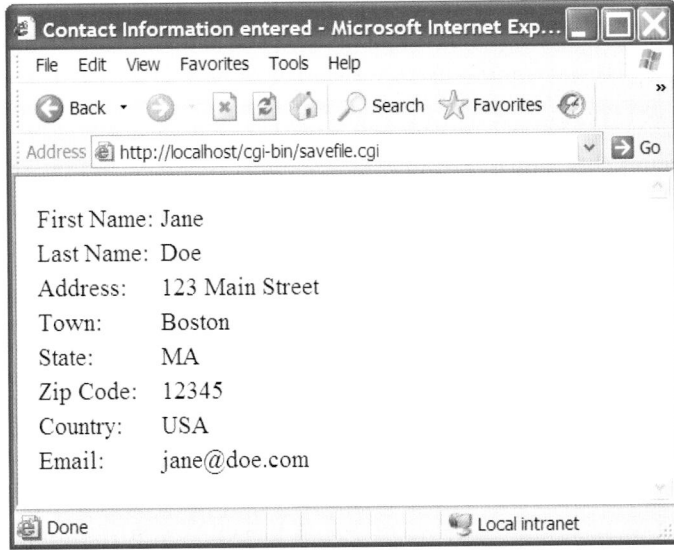

Fig. 19.19 | Creating a server-side file to store user data. (Part 4 of 4.)

```
Jane Doe
123 Main Street
Boston MA USA 12345
jane@doe.com
```

Fig. 19.20 | Contents of `clients.txt` data file.

There are a few important points to make about this program. First, we do not perform any validation on the data before writing it to disk. Normally, the script would check for bad data, incomplete data, etc. Second, our file is located in the `cgi-bin` directory, which is publicly accessible. Someone who knew the filename would find it relatively easy to access someone else's contact information.

This script is not robust enough for deployment on the Internet, but it does provide an example of the use of server-side files to store information. Once the files are stored on the server, users cannot change them unless they are allowed to do so by the server administrator. Thus, storing these files on the server is safer than storing user data in cookies. [*Note:* Many systems store user information in password-protected databases for higher levels of security.]

Note that, in this example, we show how to write data to a server-side file. In the next section we show how to retrieve data from a server-side file, using the techniques used for reading from a file in Chapter 17, File Processing.

19.16 Case Study: Shopping Cart

Many businesses' Web sites contain shopping-cart applications, which allow customers to buy items conveniently on the Web. The sites record what the consumer wants to purchase and provide an easy, intuitive way to shop online. They do so by using an electronic shopping cart, just as people would use physical shopping carts in retail stores. As users add items to their shopping carts, the sites update the carts' contents. When users "check out," they pay for the items in their shopping carts. To see a real-world electronic shopping cart, we suggest going to the online bookstore Amazon.com (www.amazon.com).

The shopping cart implemented in this section (Figs. 19.21–19.24) allows users to purchase books from a fictitious bookstore that sells four books (see Fig. 19.23). This example uses four scripts, two server-side files and cookies.

Figure 19.21 shows the first of these scripts—the login page. This script is the most complex of all the scripts in this section. The first `if` condition (line 37) determines

```
1   // Fig. 19.21: login.cpp
2   // Program to output an XHTML form, verify the
3   // username and password entered, and add members.
4   #include <iostream>
5   using std::cerr;
6   using std::cin;
7   using std::cout;
8   using std::ios;
9
10  #include <fstream>
11  using std::fstream;
12
13  #include <string>
14  using std::string;
15
16  #include <cstdlib>
17  using std::getenv;
18  using std::atoi;
19  using std::exit;
20
21  void header();
22  void writeCookie();
23
24  int main()
25  {
```

Fig. 19.21 | Program that outputs a login page. (Part 1 of 6.)

```
26      char query[ 1024 ] = "";
27      string dataString = "";
28
29      // strings to store username and password
30      string userName = "";
31      string passWord = "";
32
33      int contentLength = 0;
34      bool newMember = false;
35
36      // data was posted
37      if ( getenv( "CONTENT_LENGTH" ) )
38      {
39         // retrieve query string
40         contentLength = atoi( getenv( "CONTENT_LENGTH" ) );
41         cin.read( query, contentLength );
42         dataString = query;
43
44         // find username location
45         int userLocation = dataString.find( "user=" ) + 5;
46         int endUser = dataString.find( "&" );
47
48         // find password location
49         int passwordLocation = dataString.find( "password=" ) + 9;
50         int endPassword = dataString.find( "&new" );
51
52         if ( endPassword > 0 ) // new membership requested
53         {
54            newMember = true;
55            passWord = dataString.substr(
56               passwordLocation, endPassword - passwordLocation );
57         } // end if
58         else // existing member
59            passWord = dataString.substr( passwordLocation );
60
61         userName = dataString.substr(
62            userLocation, endUser - userLocation );
63      } // end if
64
65      // no data was retrieved
66      if ( dataString == "" )
67      {
68         header();
69         cout << "<p>Please login.</p>";
70
71         // output login form
72         cout << "<form method = \"post\" action = \"/cgi-bin/login.cgi\">"
73            << "<p>User Name: <input type = \"text\" name = \"user\"/><br/>"
74            << "Password: <input type = \"password\" name = \"password\"/>"
75            << "<br/>New? <input type = \"checkbox\" name = \"new\""
76            << " value = \"1\"/></p>"
77            << "<input type = \"submit\" value = \"login\"/></form>";
78      } // end if
```

Fig. 19.21 | Program that outputs a login page. (Part 2 of 6.)

```
79    else // process entered data
80    {
81       string fileUsername = "";
82       string filePassword = "";
83       bool userFound = false;
84
85       // open user data file for reading and writing
86       fstream userData( "userdata.txt", ios::in | ios::out);
87
88       if ( !userData ) // could not open file
89       {
90          cerr << "Could not open database.";
91          exit( 1 );
92       } // end if
93
94       // add new member
95       if ( newMember )
96       {
97          // read username and password from file
98          while ( !userFound && userData >> fileUsername >> filePassword )
99          {
100            if ( userName == fileUsername ) // name is already taken
101               userFound = true;
102         } // end while
103
104         if ( userFound ) // user name is taken
105         {
106            header();
107            cout << "<p>This name has already been taken.</p>"
108               << "<a href=\"/cgi-bin/login.cgi\">Try Again</a>";
109         } // end if
110         else // process data
111         {
112            writeCookie(); // write cookie
113            header();
114
115            // write user data to file
116            userData.clear(); // clear eof, allow write at end of file
117            userData << "\n" << userName << "\n" << passWord;
118
119            cout << "<p>Your information has been processed."
120               << "<a href=\"/cgi-bin/shop.cgi\">Start Shopping</a></p>";
121         } // end else
122      } // end if
123      else // search for password if entered
124      {
125         bool authenticated = false;
126
127         // read in user data
128         while ( !userFound && userData >> fileUsername >> filePassword )
129         {
```

Fig. 19.21 | Program that outputs a login page. (Part 3 of 6.)

```
130                  // username was found
131                  if ( userName == fileUsername )
132                  {
133                     userFound = true;
134
135                     // determine whether password is correct
136                     // and assign bool result to authenticated
137                     authenticated = ( passWord == filePassword );
138                  } // end if
139               } // end while
140
141               // user is authenticated
142               if ( authenticated )
143               {
144                  writeCookie();
145                  header();
146
147                  cout << "<p>Thank you for returning, " << userName << "!</p>"
148                     << "<a href=\"/cgi-bin/shop.cgi\">Start Shopping</a>";
149               } // end if
150               else // user not authenticated
151               {
152                  header();
153
154                  if ( userFound ) // password is incorrect
155                     cout << "<p>You have entered an incorrect password. "
156                        << "Please try again.</p>"
157                        << "<a href=\"/cgi-bin/login.cgi\">Back to login</a>";
158                  else // user is not registered
159                     cout << "<p>You are not a registered user.</p>"
160                        << "<a href=\"/cgi-bin/login.cgi\">Register</a>";
161               } // end else
162            } // end else
163         } // end else
164
165      cout << "</body>\n</html>\n";
166      return 0;
167   } // end main
168
169   // function to output header
170   void header()
171   {
172      cout << "Content-Type: text/html\n\n"; // output header
173
174      // output XML declaration and DOCTYPE
175      cout << "<?xml version = \"1.0\"?>"
176         << "<!DOCTYPE html PUBLIC \"-//W3C//DTD XHTML 1.1//EN\" "
177         << "\"http://www.w3.org/TR/xhtml11/DTD/xhtml11.dtd\">";
178
179      // output html element and some of its contents
180      cout << "<html xmlns = \"http://www.w3.org/1999/xhtml\">"
181         << "<head><title>Login Page</title></head><body>";
182   } // end function header
```

Fig. 19.21 | Program that outputs a login page. (Part 4 of 6.)

```
183
184   // function to write cookie data
185   void writeCookie()
186   {
187      string expires = "Friday, 14-MAY-10 16:00:00 GMT";
188      cout << "Set-Cookie: CART=; expires=" << expires << "; path=\n";
189   } // end function writeCookie
```

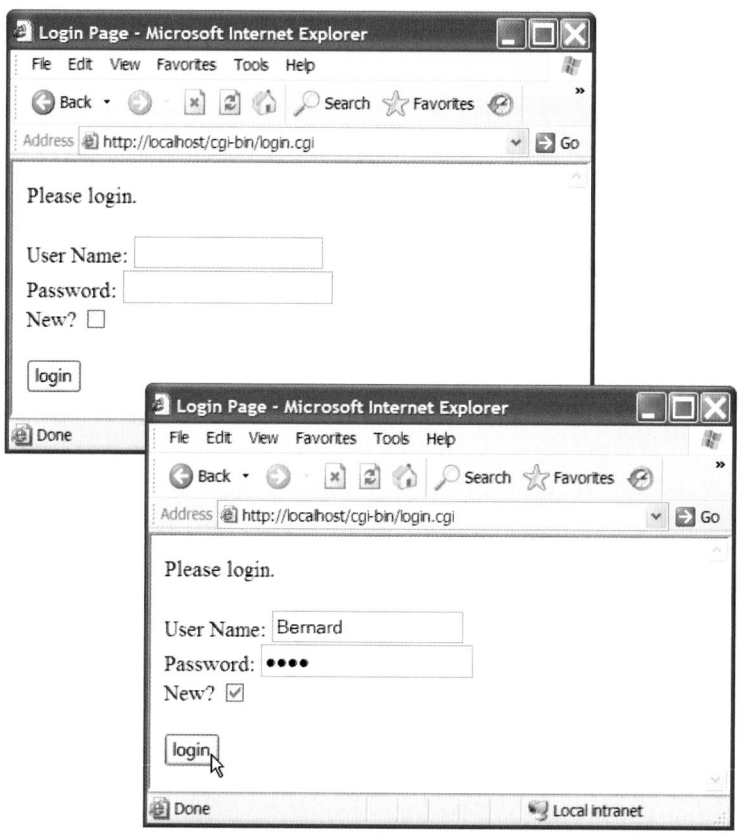

Fig. 19.21 | Program that outputs a login page. (Part 5 of 6.)

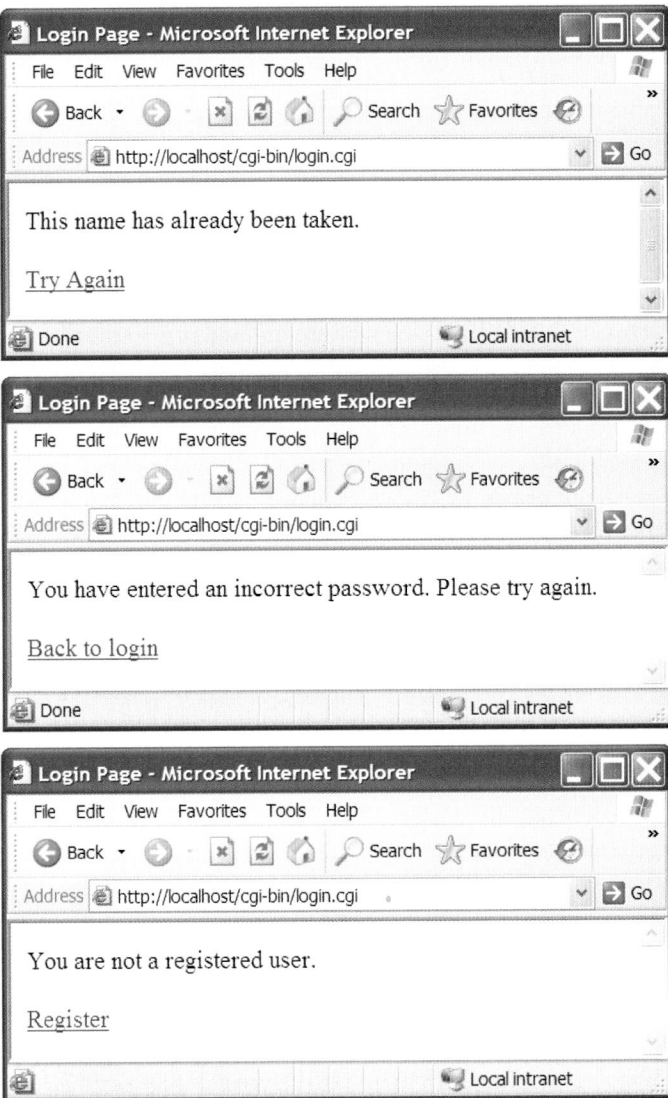

Fig. 19.21 | Program that outputs a login page. (Part 6 of 6.)

whether data was posted to the program. The second `if` condition (line 66) determines whether `dataString` remains empty (i.e., there was no submitted data to decode or the decoding did not complete successfully). The first time we run this program, the first condition fails and the second condition succeeds, so lines 72–77 output an XHTML form to the user, as shown in the first screen capture of Fig. 19.21. When the user fills out the form and clicks the **login** button, `login.cgi` is requested again—the request contains posted data this time, so the condition in line 37 evaluates to `true` and the condition in line 66 evaluates to `false`.

If the user submitted data, program control continues into the `else` block that begins in line 79, where the script processes the data. Line 86 opens `userdata.txt`—the file that contains all usernames and passwords for existing members. If the user checked the **New** checkbox on the Web page to create a new membership, the condition in line 95 evaluates to `true`, and the script attempts to record the user's information in the `userdata.txt` file on the server. Lines 98–102 read through this file, comparing each username with the name entered. If the username already appears in the file, the loop in lines 98–102 terminates before reaching the end of the file, and lines 107–108 output an appropriate message to the user, and a hyperlink back to the form is provided. If the username entered does not already exist in `userdata.txt`, line 117 adds the new user information to the file in the format

```
Bernard
blue
```

Each username and password is separated by a newline character. Lines 119–120 provide a hyperlink to the script of Fig. 19.22, which allows users to purchase items.

The last possible scenario for this script is for returning users (lines 123–162). This portion of the program executes when the user enters a name and password but does not select the **New** checkbox (i.e., the `else` of line 123 is evaluated). In this case, we assume that the user already has a username and password in `userdata.txt`. Lines 128–139 read through `userdata.txt` in an attempt to locate the username entered. If the username is found (line 131), we determine whether the password entered matches the password stored in the file (line 137). If so, `bool` variable `authenticated` is set to `true`. Otherwise, `authenticated` remains `false`. If the user has been authenticated (line 142), line 144 calls function `write-Cookie` to initialize a cookie named CART (line 188), which is used by other scripts to store data indicating which books the user has added to the shopping cart. Note that this cookie replaces any existing cookie of the same name, causing data from prior sessions to be deleted. After creating the cookie, the script outputs a message welcoming the user back to the Web site and providing a link to `shop.cgi`, where the user can purchase books (lines 147–148).

If the user was not authenticated, the program determines why (lines 154–160). If the user was found but not authenticated, a message is output indicating that the password is invalid (line 155–157). A hyperlink is provided to the login page (`<a href="/cgi-bin/login.cgi">`), where the user can attempt to login again. If neither the username nor the password was found, an unregistered user has attempted to login. Lines 159–160 output a message indicating that the user does not have the proper authorization to access the page and providing a link that allows the user to attempt another login.

Figure 19.22 uses the values in `catalog.txt` (Fig. 19.25) to output in an XHTML table the items that the user can purchase (lines 45–82). The last column for each row includes a button for adding the item to the shopping cart. Lines 63–65 output the different values for each book, and lines 71–76 output a form containing the `submit` button for adding each book to the shopping cart. Hidden form fields are specified for each book and its associated information. Note that the resulting XHTML document sent to the client contains several forms, one for each book. However, the user can submit only one form at a time. The name-value pairs of the hidden fields within the submitted form are posted to the `viewcart.cgi` script.

```cpp
1    // Fig. 19.22: shop.cpp
2    // Program to display available books.
3    #include <iostream>
4    using std::cerr;
5    using std::cout;
6    using std::ios;
7
8    #include <fstream>
9    using std::ifstream;
10
11   #include <string>
12   using std::string;
13
14   #include <cstdlib>
15   using std::exit;
16
17   void header();
18
19   int main()
20   {
21      // variables to store product information
22      char book[ 50 ] = "";
23      char year[ 50 ] = "";
24      char isbn[ 50 ] = "";
25      char price[ 50 ] = "";
26
27      string bookString = "";
28      string yearString = "";
29      string isbnString = "";
30      string priceString = "";
31
32      ifstream userData( "catalog.txt", ios::in ); // open file for input
33
34      // file could not be opened
35      if ( !userData )
36      {
37         cerr << "Could not open database.";
38         exit( 1 );
39      } // end if
40
41      header(); // output header
42
43      // output available books
44      cout << "<center><br/>Books available for sale<br/><br/>"
45         << "<table border = \"1\" cellpadding = \"7\" >";
46
47      // file is open
48      while ( userData )
49      {
50         // retrieve data from file
51         userData.getline( book, 50 );
52         bookString = book;
```

Fig. 19.22 | CGI script that allows users to buy a book. (Part 1 of 3.)

```
53
54        userData.getline( year, 50 );
55        yearString = year;
56
57        userData.getline( isbn, 50 );
58        isbnString = isbn;
59
60        userData.getline( price, 50 );
61        priceString = price;
62
63        cout << "<tr><td>" << bookString << "</td><td>" << yearString
64           << "</td><td>" << isbnString << "</td><td>" << priceString
65           << "</td>";
66
67        // file is still open after reads
68        if ( userData )
69        {
70           // output form with buy button
71           cout << "<td><form method=\"post\" "
72              << "action=\"/cgi-bin/viewcart.cgi\">"
73              << "<input type=\"hidden\" name=\"add\" value=\"true\"/>"
74              << "<input type=\"hidden\" name=\"isbn\" value=\""
75              << isbnString << "\"/>" << "<input type=\"submit\" "
76              << "value=\"Add to Cart\"/>\n</form></td>\n";
77        } // end if
78
79        cout << "</tr>\n";
80     } // end while
81
82     cout << "</table></center><br/>"
83        << "<a href=\"/cgi-bin/checkout.cgi\">Check Out</a>"
84        << "</body></html>";
85     return 0;
86  } // end main
87
88  // function to output header information
89  void header()
90  {
91     cout << "Content-Type: text/html\n\n"; // output header
92
93     // output XML declaration and DOCTYPE
94     cout << "<?xml version = \"1.0\"?>"
95        << "<!DOCTYPE html PUBLIC \"-//W3C//DTD XHTML 1.1//EN\" "
96        << "\"http://www.w3.org/TR/xhtml11/DTD/xhtml11.dtd\">";
97
98     // output html element and some of its contents
99     cout << "<html xmlns = \"http://www.w3.org/1999/xhtml\">"
100       << "<head><title>Shop Page</title></head><body>";
101 } // end function header
```

Fig. 19.22 | CGI script that allows users to buy a book. (Part 2 of 3.)

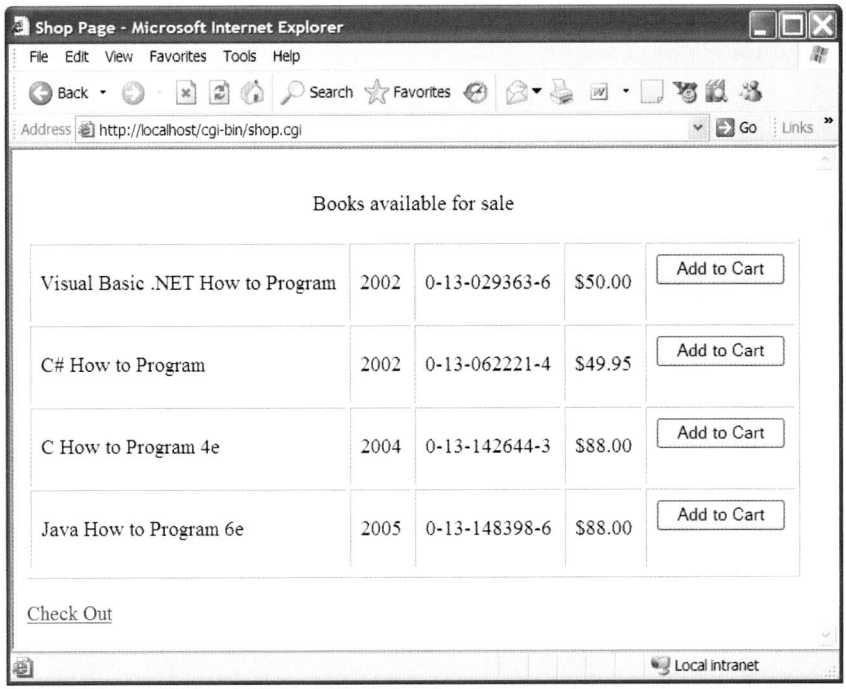

Fig. 19.22 | CGI script that allows users to buy a book. (Part 3 of 3.)

When a user purchases a book, the `viewcart.cgi` script is requested, and the ISBN for the book to be purchased is sent to the script via a hidden form field. Figure 19.23 begins by reading the value of the cookie stored on the user's system (line 35). Any existing cookie data is stored in `string cookieString` (line 36). The entered ISBN number from the form of Fig. 19.22 is stored in `string isbnEntered` (line 52). The script then determines whether the cart already contains data (line 61). If not, the `cookieString` is given the value of the entered ISBN number (line 62). If the cookie already contains data, the entered ISBN is appended to the existing cookie data (line 64). The new book is stored in the `CART` cookie in lines 67–68. Line 84 outputs the cart's contents in a table by calling function `displayShoppingCart`.

Function `displayShoppingCart` displays the items in the shopping cart in a table. Line 109 opens the server-side file `catalog.txt`. If the file opens successfully, lines 122–155 get each book's information (including its title, copyright, ISBN and price) from the file. Lines 125–138 store these pieces of data in `string` objects. Lines 140–148 count how many times the current ISBN appears in the cookie (i.e., in the shopping cart). If the current book appears in the user's cart, lines 151–154 display a table row containing the book's title, copyright, ISBN and price, as well as the number of copies of the book the user has chosen to purchase.

```
1   // Fig. 19.23: viewcart.cpp
2   // Program to view books in the shopping cart.
3   #include <iostream>
4   using std::cerr;
5   using std::cin;
6   using std::cout;
7   using std::ios;
8
9   #include <fstream>
10  using std::ifstream;
11
12  #include <string>
13  using std::string;
14
15  #include <cstdlib>
16  using std::getenv;
17  using std::atoi;
18  using std::exit;
19
20  void displayShoppingCart( const string & );
21
22  int main()
23  {
24     char query[ 1024 ] = ""; // variable to store query string
25     string cartData; // variable to hold contents of cart
26
27     string dataString = "";
28     string cookieString = "";
29     string isbnEntered = "";
30     int contentLength = 0;
31
32     // retrieve cookie data
33     if ( getenv( "HTTP_COOKIE" ) )
34     {
35        cartData = getenv( "HTTP_COOKIE" );
36        cookieString = cartData;
37     } // end if
38
39     // data was entered
40     if ( getenv( "CONTENT_LENGTH" ) )
41     {
42        contentLength = atoi( getenv( "CONTENT_LENGTH" ) );
43        cin.read( query, contentLength );
44        dataString = query;
45
46        // find location of isbn value
47        int addLocation = dataString.find( "add=" ) + 4;
48        int endAdd = dataString.find( "&isbn" );
49        int isbnLocation = dataString.find( "isbn=" ) + 5;
50
51        // retrieve isbn number to add to cart
52        isbnEntered = dataString.substr( isbnLocation );
53
```

Fig. 19.23 | CGI script that allows users to view their carts' contents. (Part 1 of 4.)

```cpp
54          // write cookie
55          string expires = "Friday, 14-MAY-10 16:00:00 GMT";
56          int cartLocation = cookieString.find( "CART=" ) + 5;
57
58          if ( cartLocation > 4 ) // cookie exists
59             cookieString = cookieString.substr( cartLocation );
60
61          if ( cookieString == "" ) // no cookie data exists
62             cookieString = isbnEntered;
63          else // cookie data exists
64             cookieString += "," + isbnEntered;
65
66          // set cookie
67          cout << "Set-Cookie: CART=" << cookieString << "; expires="
68             << expires << "; path=\n";
69       } // end if
70
71       cout << "Content-Type: text/html\n\n"; // output HTTP header
72
73       // output XML declaration and DOCTYPE
74       cout << "<?xml version = \"1.0\"?>"
75          << "<!DOCTYPE html PUBLIC \"-//W3C//DTD XHTML 1.1//EN\" "
76          << "\"http://www.w3.org/TR/xhtml11/DTD/xhtml11.dtd\">";
77
78       // output html element and some of its contents
79       cout << "<html xmlns = \"http://www.w3.org/1999/xhtml\">"
80          << "<head><title>Shopping Cart</title></head>"
81          << "<body><center><p>Here is your current order:</p>";
82
83       if ( cookieString != "" ) // cookie data exists
84          displayShoppingCart( cookieString );
85       else
86          cout << "The shopping cart is empty.";
87
88       // output links back to book list and to check out
89       cout << "</center><br/>";
90       cout << "<a href=\"/cgi-bin/shop.cgi\">Back to book list</a><br/>";
91       cout << "<a href=\"/cgi-bin/checkout.cgi\">Check Out</a>";
92       cout << "</body></html>\n";
93       return 0;
94    } // end main
95
96    // function to display items in shopping cart
97    void displayShoppingCart( const string &cookieRef )
98    {
99       char book[ 50 ] = "";
100      char year[ 50 ] = "";
101      char isbn[ 50 ] = "";
102      char price[ 50 ] = "";
103
104      string bookString = "";
105      string yearString = "";
106      string isbnString = "";
```

Fig. 19.23 | CGI script that allows users to view their carts' contents. (Part 2 of 4.)

```
107      string priceString = "";
108
109      ifstream userData( "catalog.txt", ios::in ); // open file for input
110
111      if ( !userData ) // file could not be opened
112      {
113         cerr << "Could not open database.";
114         exit( 1 );
115      } // end if
116
117      cout << "<table border = 1 cellpadding = 7 >";
118      cout << "<tr><td>Title</td><td>Copyright</td><td>ISBN</td>"
119         << "<td>Price</td><td>Count</td></tr>";
120
121      // file is open
122      while ( !userData.eof() )
123      {
124         // retrieve book information
125         userData.getline( book, 50 );
126         bookString = book;
127
128         // retrieve year information
129         userData.getline( year, 50 );
130         yearString = year;
131
132         // retrieve isbn number
133         userData.getline( isbn, 50 );
134         isbnString = isbn;
135
136         // retrieve price
137         userData.getline( price, 50 );
138         priceString = price;
139
140         int match = cookieRef.find( isbnString, 0 );
141         int count = 0;
142
143         // match has been made
144         while ( match >= 0 && isbnString != "" )
145         {
146            count++;
147            match = cookieRef.find( isbnString, match + 13 );
148         } // end while
149
150         // output table row with book information
151         if ( count != 0 )
152            cout << "<tr><td>" << bookString << "</td><td>" << yearString
153               << "</td><td>" << isbnString << "</td><td>" << priceString
154               << "</td><td>" << count << "</td></tr>";
155      } // end while
156
157      cout << "</table>"; // end table
158  } // end function displayShoppingCart
```

Fig. 19.23 | CGI script that allows users to view their carts' contents. (Part 3 of 4.)

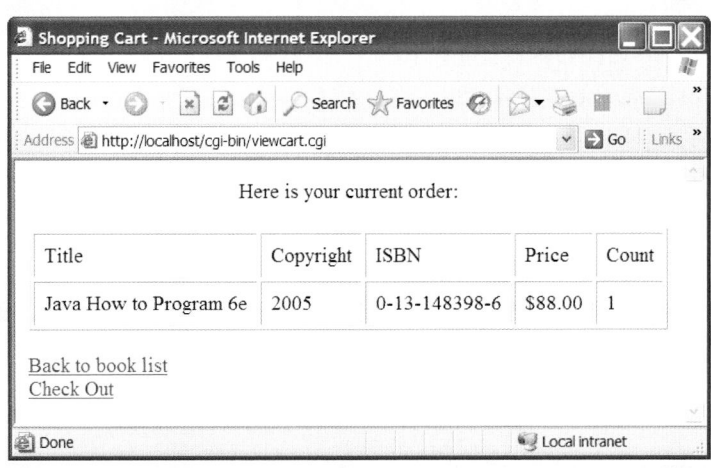

Fig. 19.23 | CGI script that allows users to view their carts' contents. (Part 4 of 4.)

Figure 19.24 is the page that is displayed when the user chooses to check out (i.e., purchase the books in the shopping cart). This script outputs a message to the user and calls `writeCookie` (line 13), which effectively erases the current information in the shopping cart.

Figure 19.25 shows the contents of the `catalog.txt` file. This file must reside in the same directory as the CGI scripts for this shopping-cart application to work correctly.

```
1  // Fig. 19.24: checkout.cpp
2  // Program to log out of the system.
3  #include <iostream>
4  using std::cout;
5
6  #include <string>
7  using std::string;
8
9  void writeCookie();
10
11  int main()
12  {
13     writeCookie(); // write the cookie
14     cout << "Content-Type: text/html\n\n"; // output header
15
16     // output XML declaration and DOCTYPE
17     cout << "<?xml version = \"1.0\"?>"
18        << "<!DOCTYPE html PUBLIC \"-//W3C//DTD XHTML 1.1//EN\" "
19        << "\"http://www.w3.org/TR/xhtml11/DTD/xhtml11.dtd\">";
20
```

Fig. 19.24 | Check out program. (Part 1 of 2.)

```
21      // output html element and its contents
22      cout << "<html xmlns = \"http://www.w3.org/1999/xhtml\">"
23          << "<head><title>Checked Out</title></head><body><center>"
24          << "<p>You have checked out<br />"
25          << "You will be billed accordingly<br />To login again, "
26          << "<a href=\"/cgi-bin/login.cgi\">click here</a>"
27          << "</center></body></html>\n";
28      return 0;
29  } // end main
30
31  // function to write cookie
32  void writeCookie()
33  {
34      // string containing expiration date
35      string expires = "Friday, 14-MAY-10 16:00:00 GMT";
36
37      // set cookie
38      cout << "Set-Cookie: CART=; expires=" << expires << "; path=\n";
39  } // end writeCookie
```

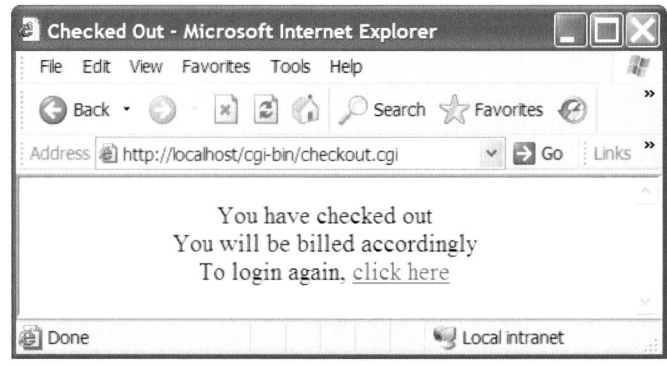

Fig. 19.24 | Check out program. (Part 2 of 2.)

```
Visual Basic .NET How to Program
2002
0-13-029363-6
$50.00
C# How to Program
2002
0-13-062221-4
$49.95
C How to Program 4e
2004
0-13-142644-3
$88.00
Java How to Program 6e
2005
0-13-148398-6
$88.00
```

Fig. 19.25 | Contents of `catalog.txt`.

19.17 Internet and Web Resources

Apache

`httpd.apache.org`
This is the product home page for the Apache HTTP server. Users may download Apache from this site.

`www.apacheweek.com`
This online magazine contains articles about Apache jobs, product reviews and other information concerning Apache software.

`linuxtoday.com/stories/18780.html`
This site contains an article about the Apache HTTP server and the platforms that support it. It also contains links to other Apache articles.

CGI

`www.gnu.org/software/cgicc/cgicc.html`
This site contains a free open-source CGI library for creating CGI scripts in C++.

`www.hotscripts.com`
This site contains a rich collection of scripts for performing image manipulation, server administration, networking, etc. using CGI.

`www.jmarshall.com/easy/cgi`
This page contains a brief explanation of CGI for those with programming experience.

`www.w3.org/CGI`
This World Wide Web Consortium page discusses CGI security issues.

`www.w3.org/Protocols`
This World Wide Web Consortium site contains information on the HTTP specification and links to news, mailing lists and published articles.

Summary

- A Web server responds to client (e.g., Web browser) requests by providing resources (e.g., XHTML documents).

- Hypertext Transfer Protocol (HTTP) is a platform-independent protocol for transferring requests and files over the Internet (i.e., between Web servers and Web browsers).

- HTTP defines several request types (also known as request methods), each of which specifies how a client sends a requests to a server.

- The two most common HTTP request types are `get` and `post`. These request types retrieve and send client form data from and to a Web server.

- A `form` is an XHTML element that may contain text fields, radio buttons, check boxes and other graphical user interface components that allow users to enter and submit data into a Web page.

- A `get` request gets (or retrieves) information from a server. Such requests often retrieve an HTML document or an image.

- A `post` request posts (or sends) data to a server, such as authentication information or data from a form that gathers user input.

- Usually, `post` requests are used to post a message to a news group or a discussion forum, pass user input to a data-handling process and store or update the data on a server.

- An HTTP request often sends data to a server-side form handler—a program that resides on the Web server and is created by a server-side programmer to handle client requests.

- Browsers often cache (i.e., save on a local disk) Web pages for quick reloading, to reduce the amount of data that the browser needs to download over the Internet.
- A Web server is part of a multitier application, sometimes referred to as an *n*-tier application.
- Multitier applications divide functionality into separate tiers (i.e., logical groupings of functionality). Tiers can be located on the same computer or on separate computers.
- The information tier (also called the data tier or the bottom tier) maintains data for the application. The information tier typically stores data in a relational database management system (RDBMS).
- The middle tier (also called the business logic tier) implements business logic to control interactions between application clients and application data.
- Business logic in the middle tier enforces business rules and ensures that data is reliable before updating the database or presenting data to a user.
- The client tier, or top tier, is the application's user interface.
- Users can request documents from local Web servers (i.e., ones residing on users' machines) or remote Web servers (i.e., ones residing on machines across a network).
- Local Web servers can be accessed in two ways: through the machine name, or through `local-host`—a host name that references the local machine.
- A host is a computer that stores and maintains resources, such as Web pages, databases and multimedia files.
- A domain represents a group of hosts on the Internet.
- Each domain has a domain name, also known as a Web address, which uniquely identifies the location of a business or organization on the Internet.
- A fully qualified domain name (FQDN), also known as the machine name, contains a host (for example, www for World Wide Web) and a domain name, including a top-level domain (TLD).
- The top-level domain is the last and most significant component of a fully qualified domain name.
- Each FQDN corresponds to a numeric address called an IP (Internet Protocol) address, which is much like the street address of a house.
- A Domain Name System (DNS) server is a computer that maintains a database of FQDNs and their corresponding IP addresses. The process of translating FQDNs to IP addresses is called a DNS lookup.
- In the Apache HTTP server directory structure, XHTML documents must be saved in the `htdocs` directory.
- The Common Gateway Interface (CGI) is a standard protocol for enabling applications (commonly called CGI programs or CGI scripts) to interact with Web servers and (indirectly) with clients (e.g., Web browsers).
- CGI is often used to generate dynamic Web content using client input, databases and other information services.
- A Web page is dynamic if its content is generated programmatically when the page is requested, unlike static Web content, which is not generated programmatically when the page is requested (i.e., the page already exists before the request is made).
- HTTP describes a set of methods and headers that allows clients and servers to interact and exchange information in a uniform and predictable way.
- An XHTML document is a plain text file that contains markings (markup or elements) that describe the structure of the data the document contains.

- XHTML documents also can contain hypertext information (usually called hyperlinks), which are links to other Web pages or to other locations on the same page.
- A URL contains the protocol of the resource (such as `http`), the machine name or IP address for the resource and the name (including the path) of the resource.
- The HTTP `get` method indicates the client wishes to retrieve a resource.
- The information in the `Content-Type` header identifies the MIME (Multipurpose Internet Mail Extensions) type of the content.
- Each type of data sent from the server has a MIME type by which the browser determines how to process the data it receives.
- It is possible to redirect (or pipe) standard output to another destination.
- Function `time` gets the current time, which is represented as the number of seconds elapsed since midnight January 1, 1970, and stores the retrieved value to the location specified by the parameter.
- C++ library function `localtime`, when passed a `time_t` variable, returns a pointer to an object containing the "broken-down" local time (i.e., days, hours, etc. are placed in individual object members).
- Function `asctime`, which takes a pointer to an object containing "broken-down" time, returns a string such as `Wed Oct 31 13:10:37 2004`.
- Environment variables contain information about the client and server environment, such as the type of Web browser being used and the location of the document on the server.
- The value associated with an environment variable can be obtained by calling function `getenv` of `<cstdlib>` and passing it the name of the environment variable.
- The `QUERY_STRING` environment variable contains information that is appended to a URL in a `get` request.
- The `form` element encloses an XHTML form and generally takes two attributes. The first is `action`, which specifies the server resource to execute when the user submits the form. The second is `method`, which identifies the type of HTTP request (i.e., `get` or `post`) to use when the browser submits the form to the Web server.
- The `post` method sets the environment variable `CONTENT_LENGTH`, to indicate the number of characters of data that were sent in a `post` request.
- Function `atoi` of `<cstdlib>` can be used to convert the value contained in `CONTENT_LENGTH` to an integer.
- The `Refresh` header redirects the client to a new location after a specified amount of time.
- The `Location` header redirects the client to a new location.
- The `Status` header instructs the server to output a specified status header line (such as `HTTP/1.1 200 OK`).
- Cookies are essentially small text files that a Web server sends to your browser, which then saves them on your computer. Cookies are sent by the browser back to the server with each subsequent request to the same path until the cookies expire or are deleted.
- The `Set-Cookie:` header indicates that the browser should store the incoming data in a cookie.
- The environment variable `HTTP_COOKIE` stores the client's cookies.
- State information can be maintained using cookies or by creating server-side files (i.e., files that are located on the server or on the server's network).
- Only someone with access and permission to change files on the server can do so.

Terminology

action attribute of form element
Apache HTTP Server
asctime function
bottom tier
business logic
business logic tier
business rule
cache
CGI (Common Gateway Interface)
CGI program
CGI script
client tier
CONTENT_LENGTH environment variable
Content-Type header
cookie
data tier
DNS lookup
domain
domain name
domain name system (DNS) server
dynamic vs. static Web content
dynamic Web content
element
end tag
environment variable
Extensible HyperText Markup Language
    (XHTML)
form XHTML element (<form>...</form>)
fully qualified domain name (FQDN)
GET HTTP method
get HTTP request type
getenv function of <cstdlib>
host
htdocs directory
HTTP_COOKIE environment variable
HTTP header
HTTPd Web server
hyperlink
hypertext
Hypertext Transfer Protocol (HTTP)

information tier
Internet Protocol (IP) address
local Web server
localhost
localtime function
Location header
loopback address
markup
method attribute of form element
middle tier
Multipurpose Internet Mail Extension (MIME)
multitier application
n-tier application
open source software
pipe
post HTTP request type
query string
QUERY_STRING environment variable
Refresh header
relational database management system
    (RDBMS)
remote Web server
request method
server-side file
server-side form handler
Set-Cookie: HTTP header
start tag
static Web content
Status header
tier
time function
time_t
title XHTML element (<title>...</title>)
top-level domain (TLD)
top tier
Universal Resource Locator (URL)
virtual directory
Web address
Web server

Self-Review Exercises

19.1   Fill in the blanks in each of the following statements:
   a)   The two most common HTTP request types are _____ and _____.
   b)   Browsers often _____ Web pages for quick reloading.
   c)   In a three-tier application, a Web server is typically part of the _____ tier.

d) In the URL `http://www.deitel.com/books/downloads.html`, `www.deitel.com` is the _____ of the server, where a client can find the desired resource.

e) A(n) _____ document is a text file containing markings that describe to a Web browser how to display and format the information in the document.

f) The environment variable _____ provides a mechanism for supplying data to CGI scripts.

g) A common way of reading input from the user is to implement the XHTML _____ element.

19.2 State whether each of the following is *true* or *false*. If *false*, explain why.

a) Web servers and clients communicate with each other through the platform-independent HTTP.

b) Web servers often cache Web pages for reloading.

c) The information tier implements business logic to control the type of information that is presented to a particular client.

d) A dynamic Web page is a Web page that is not created programmatically.

e) We put data into a query string using a format that consists of a series of name-value pairs joined with exclamation points (!).

f) Using a CGI script is more efficient than using an XHTML document.

g) The `post` method of submitting form data is preferable to `get` when sending personal information to the Web server.

Answers to Self-Review Exercises

19.1 a) `get` and `post`. b) cache. c) middle. d) machine name. e) XHTML. f) `QUERY_STRING`. g) `form`.

19.2 a) True. b) True. c) False. The middle tier implements business logic to control interactions between application clients and application data. d) False. A dynamic Web page is a Web page that *is* created programmatically. e) False. The pairs are joined with an ampersand (&). f) False. XHTML documents are more efficient than CGI scripts, because they do not need to be executed on the server side before they are output to the client. g) True.

Exercises

19.3 Define the following terms:
a) HTTP.
b) Multitier application.
c) Request method.

19.4 Explain the difference between the `get` request type and the `post` request type. When is it ideal to use the `post` request type?

19.5 Write a CGI script that prints the squares of the integers from 1 to 10 on separate lines.

19.6 Write a CGI script that receives as input three numbers from the client and displays a statement indicating whether the three numbers could represent an equilateral triangle (all three sides are the same length), an isosceles triangle (two sides are the same length) or a right triangle (the square of one side is equal to the sum of the squares of the other two sides).

19.7 Write a soothsayer script that allows the user to submit a question. When the question is submitted, the script should choose a random response from a list of answers (such as "It could be", "Probably not", "Definitely", "Not looking too good" and "Yes") and display the answer to the client.

19.8 Modify the program of Figs. 19.13–19.14 to incorporate the opening XHTML form and the processing of the data into a single CGI script (i.e., combine the XHTML of Fig. 19.13 into the CGI script of Fig. 19.14). When the CGI script is requested initially, the form should be displayed. When the form is submitted, the CGI script should display the result.

19.9 Modify the viewcart.cgi script (Fig. 19.23) to enable users to remove some items from the shopping cart.

Searching and Sorting

OBJECTIVES

In this chapter you will learn:

■ To search for a given value in a vector using binary search.

■ To sort a vector using the recursive merge sort algorithm.

■ To determine the efficiency of searching and sorting algorithms.

20.1 Introduction

Searching data involves determining whether a value (referred to as the search key) is present in the data and, if so, finding the value's location. Two popular search algorithms are the simple linear search (introduced in Section 7.7) and the faster but more complex binary search, which is introduced in this chapter.

Sorting places data in order, typically ascending or descending, based on one or more sort keys. A list of names could be sorted alphabetically, bank accounts could be sorted by account number, employee payroll records could be sorted by social security number, and so on. Previously, you learned about insertion sort (Section 7.8) and selection sort (Section 8.6). This chapter introduces the more efficient, but more complex merge sort. Figure 20.1 summarizes the searching and sorting algorithms discussed in the examples and exercises of this book. This chapter also introduces Big O notation, which is used to estimate the worst-case runtime for an algorithm—that is, how hard an algorithm may have to work to solve a problem.

20.2 Searching Algorithms

Looking up a phone number, accessing a Web site and checking the definition of a word in a dictionary all involve searching large amounts of data. Searching algorithms all accomplish the same goal—finding an element that matches a given search key, if such an element does, in fact, exist. There are, however, a number of things that differentiate search algorithms from one another. The major difference is the amount of effort they require to complete the search. One way to describe this effort is with Big O notation. For searching and sorting algorithms, this is particularly dependent on the number of data elements.

In Chapter 7, we discussed the linear search algorithm, which is a simple and easy-to-implement searching algorithm. We will now discuss the efficiency of the linear search algorithm as measured by Big O notation. Then, we will introduce a searching algorithm that is relatively efficient but more complex and difficult to implement.

20.2.1 Efficiency of Linear Search

Suppose an algorithm simply tests whether the first element of a vector is equal to the second element of the vector. If the vector has 10 elements, this algorithm requires one comparison. If the vector has 1000 elements, the algorithm still requires one comparison. In fact, the algorithm is completely independent of the number of elements in the vector.

Chapter	Algorithm	Location
Searching Algorithms		
7	Linear search	Section 7.7
20	Binary search	Section 20.2.2
	Recursive linear search	Exercise 20.8
	Recursive binary search	Exercise 20.9
21	Binary tree search	Section 21.7
	Linear search of a linked list	Exercise 21.21
23	`binary_search` standard library function	Section 22.5.6
Sorting Algorithms		
7	Insertion sort	Section 7.8
8	Selection sort	Section 8.6
20	Recursive merge sort	Section 20.3.3
	Bubble sort	Exercises 20.5 and 20.6
	Bucket sort	Exercise 20.7
	Recursive quicksort	Exercise 20.10
21	Binary tree sort	Section 21.7
23	`sort` standard library function	Section 22.5.6
	Heap sort	Section 22.5.12

Fig. 20.1 | Searching and sorting algorithms in this text.

This algorithm is said to have a constant runtime, which is represented in Big O notation as $O(1)$. An algorithm that is $O(1)$ does not necessarily require only one comparison. $O(1)$ just means that the number of comparisons is *constant*—it does not grow as the size of the vector increases. An algorithm that tests whether the first element of a vector is equal to any of the next three elements will always require three comparisons, but in Big O notation it is considered $O(1)$. $O(1)$ is often pronounced "on the order of 1" or more simply "order 1."

An algorithm that tests whether the first element of a vector is equal to *any* of the other elements of the vector requires at most $n - 1$ comparisons, where n is the number of elements in the vector. If the vector has 10 elements, this algorithm requires up to nine comparisons. If the vector has 1000 elements, this algorithm requires up to 999 comparisons. As n grows larger, the n part of the expression "dominates," and subtracting one becomes inconsequential. Big O is designed to highlight these dominant terms and ignore terms that become unimportant as n grows. For this reason, an algorithm that requires a total of $n - 1$ comparisons (such as the one we described in this paragraph) is said to be $O(n)$. An $O(n)$ algorithm is referred to as having a linear runtime. $O(n)$ is often pronounced "on the order of n" or more simply "order n."

Now suppose you have an algorithm that tests whether *any* element of a vector is duplicated elsewhere in the vector. The first element must be compared with every other element in the vector. The second element must be compared with every other element except the first (it was already compared to the first). The third element must be compared with every other element except the first two. In the end, this algorithm will end up making $(n - 1) +$ $(n - 2) + \ldots + 2 + 1$ or $n^2/2 - n/2$ comparisons. As n increases, the n^2 term dominates and the n term becomes inconsequential. Again, Big O notation highlights the n^2 term, leaving $n^2/2$. As we will soon see, however, constant factors are omitted in Big O notation.

Big O is concerned with how an algorithm's runtime grows in relation to the number of items processed. Suppose an algorithm requires n^2 comparisons. With four elements, the algorithm will require 16 comparisons; with eight elements, 64 comparisons. With this algorithm, doubling the number of elements quadruples the number of comparisons. Consider a similar algorithm requiring $n^2/2$ comparisons. With four elements, the algorithm will require eight comparisons; with eight elements, 32 comparisons. Again, doubling the number of elements quadruples the number of comparisons. Both of these algorithms grow as the square of n, so Big O ignores the constant, and both algorithms are considered to be $O(n^2)$, which is referred to as quadratic runtime and pronounced "on the order of n-squared" or more simply "order n-squared."

When n is small, $O(n^2)$ algorithms (running on today's billion-operation-per-second personal computers) will not noticeably affect performance. But as n grows, you will start to notice the performance degradation. An $O(n^2)$ algorithm running on a million-element vector would require a trillion "operations" (where each could actually require several machine instructions to execute). This could require a few hours to execute. A billion-element vector would require a quintillion operations, a number so large that the algorithm could take decades! $O(n^2)$ algorithms are easy to write, as you have seen in previous chapters. In this chapter, you will see algorithms with more favorable Big O measures. These efficient algorithms often take a bit more cleverness and effort to create, but their superior performance can be well worth the extra effort, especially as n gets large and as algorithms are compounded into larger programs.

The linear search algorithm runs in $O(n)$ time. The worst case in this algorithm is that every element must be checked to determine whether the search key exists in the vector. If the size of the vector is doubled, the number of comparisons that the algorithm must perform is also doubled. Note that linear search can provide outstanding performance if the element matching the search key happens to be at or near the front of the vector. But we seek algorithms that perform well, on average, across all searches, including those where the element matching the search key is near the end of the vector.

Linear search is the easiest search algorithm to implement, but it can be slow compared to other search algorithms. If a program needs to perform many searches on large vectors, it may be better to implement a different, more efficient algorithm, such as the binary search which we present in the next section.

 **Performance Tip 20.1**

Sometimes the simplest algorithms perform poorly. Their virtue is that they are easy to program, test and debug. Sometimes more complex algorithms are required to realize maximum performance.

20.2.2 Binary Search

The binary search algorithm is more efficient than the linear search algorithm, but it requires that the vector first be sorted. This is only worthwhile when the vector, once sorted, will be searched a great many times—or when the searching application has stringent performance requirements. The first iteration of this algorithm tests the middle element in the vector. If this matches the search key, the algorithm ends. Assuming the vector is sorted in ascending order, then if the search key is less than the middle element, the search key cannot match any element in the second half of the vector and the algorithm continues with only the first half of the vector (i.e., the first element up to, but not including, the middle element). If the search key is greater than the middle element, the search key cannot match any element in the first half of the vector and the algorithm continues with only the second half of the vector (i.e., the element after the middle element through the last element). Each iteration tests the middle value of the remaining portion of the vector. If the element does not match the search key, the algorithm eliminates half of the remaining elements. The algorithm ends either by finding an element that matches the search key or by reducing the subvector to zero size.

As an example, consider the sorted 15-element vector

2   3   5   10   27   30   34   51   56   65   77   81   82   93   99

and a search key of 65. A program implementing the binary search algorithm would first check whether 51 is the search key (because 51 is the middle element of the vector). The search key (65) is larger than 51, so 51 is discarded along with the first half of the vector (all elements smaller than 51.) Next, the algorithm checks whether 81 (the middle element of the remainder of the vector) matches the search key. The search key (65) is smaller than 81, so 81 is discarded along with the elements larger than 81. After just two tests, the algorithm has narrowed the number of elements to check to three (56, 65 and 77). The algorithm then checks 65 (which indeed matches the search key), and returns the index (9) of the vector element containing 65. In this case, the algorithm required just three comparisons to determine whether an element of the vector matched the search key. Using a linear search algorithm would have required 10 comparisons. [*Note:* In this example, we have chosen to use a vector with 15 elements, so that there will always be an obvious middle element in the vector. With an even number of elements, the middle of the vector lies between two elements. We implement the algorithm to choose the larger of those two elements.]

Figures 20.2–20.3 define class `BinarySearch` and its member functions respectively. Class `BinarySearch` is similar to `LinearSearch` (Section 7.7)—it has a constructor, a search function (`binarySearch`), a `displayElements` function, two `private` data members and a `private` utility function (`displaySubElements`). Lines 18–28 of Fig. 20.3 define the constructor. After initializing the vector with random `int`s from 10–99 (lines 24–25), line 27 calls the Standard Library function `sort` on the vector `data`. Function *sort* takes two *random-access iterators* and sorts the elements in vector `data` in ascending order. A random-access iterator is an iterator that allows access to any data item in the vector at any time. In this case, we use `data.begin()` and `data.end()` to encompass the entire vector. Recall that the binary search algorithm will work only on a sorted vector.

Lines 31–61 define function `binarySearch`. The search key is passed into parameter `searchElement` (line 31). Lines 33–35 calculate the `low` end index, `high` end index and `middle` index of the portion of the vector that the program is currently searching. At the beginning of the function, the `low` end is 0, the `high` end is the size of the vector minus 1 and the `middle` is the average of these two values. Line 36 initializes the `location` of the found element to -1—the value that will be returned if the search key is not found. Lines 38–58 loop until `low` is greater than `high` (this occurs when the element is not found) or

```
 1   // Fig 20.2: BinarySearch.h
 2   // Class that contains a vector of random integers and a function
 3   // that uses binary search to find an integer.
 4   #include <vector>
 5   using std::vector;
 6
 7   class BinarySearch
 8   {
 9   public:
10      BinarySearch( int ); // constructor initializes vector
11      int binarySearch( int ) const; // perform a binary search on vector
12      void displayElements() const; // display vector elements
13   private:
14      int size; // vector size
15      vector< int > data; // vector of ints
16      void displaySubElements( int, int ) const; // display range of values
17   }; // end class BinarySearch
```

Fig. 20.2 | BinarySearch class definition.

```
 1   // Fig 20.3: BinarySearch.cpp
 2   // BinarySearch class member-function definition.
 3   #include <iostream>
 4   using std::cout;
 5   using std::endl;
 6
 7   #include <cstdlib> // prototypes for functions srand and rand
 8   using std::rand;
 9   using std::srand;
10
11   #include <ctime> // prototype for function time
12   using std::time;
13
14   #include <algorithm> // prototype for sort function
15   #include "BinarySearch.h" // class BinarySearch definition
16
17   // constructor initializes vector with random ints and sorts the vector
18   BinarySearch::BinarySearch( int vectorSize )
19   {
20      size = ( vectorSize > 0 ? vectorSize : 10 ); // validate vectorSize
21      srand( time( 0 ) ); // seed using current time
22
23      // fill vector with random ints in range 10-99
24      for ( int i = 0; i < size; i++ )
25         data.push_back( 10 + rand() % 90 ); // 10-99
26
27      std::sort( data.begin(), data.end() ); // sort the data
28   } // end BinarySearch constructor
29
30   // perform a binary search on the data
31   int BinarySearch::binarySearch( int searchElement ) const
32   {
```

Fig. 20.3 | BinarySearch class member-function definition. (Part 1 of 2.)

```
33      int low = 0; // low end of the search area
34      int high = size - 1; // high end of the search area
35      int middle = ( low + high + 1 ) / 2; // middle element
36      int location = -1; // return value; -1 if not found
37
38      do // loop to search for element
39      {
40         // print remaining elements of vector to be searched
41         displaySubElements( low, high );
42
43         // output spaces for alignment
44         for ( int i = 0; i < middle; i++ )
45            cout << "   ";
46
47         cout << " * " << endl; // indicate current middle
48
49         // if the element is found at the middle
50         if ( searchElement == data[ middle ] )
51            location = middle; // location is the current middle
52         else if ( searchElement < data[ middle ] ) // middle is too high
53            high = middle - 1; // eliminate the higher half
54         else // middle element is too low
55            low = middle + 1; // eliminate the lower half
56
57         middle = ( low + high + 1 ) / 2; // recalculate the middle
58      } while ( ( low <= high ) && ( location == -1 ) );
59
60      return location; // return location of search key
61   } // end function binarySearch
62
63   // display values in vector
64   void BinarySearch::displayElements() const
65   {
66      displaySubElements( 0, size - 1 );
67   } // end function displayElements
68
69   // display certain values in vector
70   void BinarySearch::displaySubElements( int low, int high ) const
71   {
72      for ( int i = 0; i < low; i++ ) // output spaces for alignment
73         cout << "   ";
74
75      for ( int i = low; i <= high; i++ ) // output elements left in vector
76         cout << data[ i ] << " ";
77
78      cout << endl;
79   } // end function displaySubElements
```

Fig. 20.3 | BinarySearch class member-function definition. (Part 2 of 2.)

location does not equal -1 (indicating that the search key was found). Line 50 tests whether the value in the middle element is equal to searchElement. If this is true, line 51 assigns middle to location. Then the loop terminates and location is returned to the caller. Each iteration of the loop tests a single value (line 50) and eliminates half of the remaining values in the vector (line 53 or 55).

Lines 25–41 of Fig. 20.4 loop until the user enters the value -1. For each other number the user enters, the program performs a binary search on the data to determine whether it matches an element in the vector. The first line of output from this program is the vector of ints, in increasing order. When the user instructs the program to search for 38, the program first tests the middle element, which is 67 (as indicated by *). The search key is less than 67, so the program eliminates the second half of the vector and tests the middle element from the first half of the vector. The search key equals 38, so the program returns the index 3.

Efficiency of Binary Search

In the worst-case scenario, searching a sorted vector of 1023 elements will take only 10 comparisons when using a binary search. Repeatedly dividing 1023 by 2 (because, after each comparison, we are able to eliminate half of the vector) and rounding down (because we also remove the middle element) yields the values 511, 255, 127, 63, 31, 15, 7, 3, 1 and 0. The number 1023 ($2^{10} - 1$) is divided by 2 only 10 times to get the value 0, which indicates that there are no more elements to test. Dividing by 2 is equivalent to one comparison in the binary search algorithm. Thus, a vector of 1,048,575 ($2^{20} - 1$) elements takes a maximum of 20 comparisons to find the key, and a vector of over one billion elements takes a maximum of 30 comparisons to find the key. This is a tremendous improvement in performance over the linear search. For a one-billion-element vector, this is a difference between an average of 500 million comparisons for the linear search and a maximum of only 30 comparisons for the binary search! The maximum number of comparisons needed for the binary search of any sorted vector is the exponent of the first power of 2 greater than the number of elements in the vector, which is represented as $\log_2 n$. All logarithms grow at roughly the same rate, so in Big O notation the base can be omitted. This results in a Big O of $O(\log n)$ for a binary search, which is also known as logarithmic runtime and pronounced "on the order of log *n*" or more simply "order log *n*."

20.3 Sorting Algorithms

Sorting data (i.e., placing the data into some particular order, such as ascending or descending) is one of the most important computing applications. A bank sorts all checks by account number so that it can prepare individual bank statements at the end of each month. Telephone companies sort their lists of accounts by last name and, further, by first name to make it easy to find phone numbers. Virtually every organization must sort some data, and often, massive amounts of it. Sorting data is an intriguing, computer-intensive problem that has attracted intense research efforts.

An important point to understand about sorting is that the end result—the sorted vector—will be the same no matter which algorithm you use to sort the vector. The choice of algorithm affects only the runtime and memory use of the program. In previous chapters, we have introduced the selection sort and insertion sort—simple algorithms to implement, but inefficient. The next section examines the efficiency of these two algorithms using Big O notation. The last algorithm—merge sort, which we introduce in this chapter—is much faster but is harder to implement.

```cpp
 1   // Fig 20.4: Fig20_04.cpp
 2   // BinarySearch test program.
 3   #include <iostream>
 4   using std::cin;
 5   using std::cout;
 6   using std::endl;
 7
 8   #include "BinarySearch.h" // class BinarySearch definition
 9
10   int main()
11   {
12      int searchInt; // search key
13      int position; // location of search key in vector
14
15      // create vector and output it
16      BinarySearch searchVector ( 15 );
17      searchVector.displayElements();
18
19      // get input from user
20      cout << "\nPlease enter an integer value (-1 to quit): ";
21      cin >> searchInt; // read an int from user
22      cout << endl;
23
24      // repeatedly input an integer; -1 terminates the program
25      while ( searchInt != -1 )
26      {
27         // use binary search to try to find integer
28         position = searchVector.binarySearch( searchInt );
29
30         // return value of -1 indicates integer was not found
31         if ( position == -1 )
32            cout << "The integer " << searchInt << " was not found.\n";
33         else
34            cout << "The integer " << searchInt
35               << " was found in position " << position << ".\n";
36
37         // get input from user
38         cout << "\n\nPlease enter an integer value (-1 to quit): ";
39         cin >> searchInt; // read an int from user
40         cout << endl;
41      } // end while
42
43      return 0;
44   } // end main
```

```
26 31 33 38 47 49 49 67 73 74 82 89 90 91 95

Please enter an integer value (-1 to quit): 38

26 31 33 38 47 49 49 67 73 74 82 89 90 91 95
                  *
26 31 33 38 47 49 49
         *                          (Continued at top of next page…)
```

Fig. 20.4 | BinarySearch test program. (Part 1 of 2.)

(...Continued from previous page)

```
26 31 33 38 47 49 49 67 73 74 82 89 90 91 95

Please enter an integer value (-1 to quit): 38

26 31 33 38 47 49 49 67 73 74 82 89 90 91 95
            *
26 31 33 38 47 49 49
         *
The integer 38 was found in position 3.


Please enter an integer value (-1 to quit): 91

26 31 33 38 47 49 49 67 73 74 82 89 90 91 95
            *
                     73 74 82 89 90 91 95
                              *
                              90 91 95
                                 *
The integer 91 was found in position 13.


Please enter an integer value (-1 to quit): 25

26 31 33 38 47 49 49 67 73 74 82 89 90 91 95
            *
26 31 33 38 47 49 49
         *
26 31 33
      *
26
 *
The integer 25 was not found.


Please enter an integer value (-1 to quit): -1
```

Fig. 20.4 | BinarySearch test program. (Part 2 of 2.)

20.3.1 Efficiency of Selection Sort

Selection sort is an easy-to-implement, but inefficient, sorting algorithm. The first iteration of the algorithm selects the smallest element in the vector and swaps it with the first element. The second iteration selects the second-smallest element (which is the smallest element of the remaining elements) and swaps it with the second element. The algorithm continues until the last iteration selects the second-largest element and swaps it with the second-to-last element, leaving the largest element in the last index. After the ith iteration, the smallest i elements of the vector will be sorted into increasing order in the first i elements of the vector.

The selection sort algorithm iterates $n - 1$ times, each time swapping the smallest remaining element into its sorted position. Locating the smallest remaining element requires $n - 1$ comparisons during the first iteration, $n - 2$ during the second iteration, then $n - 3$, ... , 3, 2, 1. This results in a total of $n(n - 1) / 2$ or $(n^2 - n)/2$ comparisons. In Big O notation, smaller terms drop out and constants are ignored, leaving a final Big O of $O(n^2)$.

20.3.2 Efficiency of Insertion Sort

Insertion sort is another simple, but inefficient, sorting algorithm. The first iteration of this algorithm takes the second element in the vector and, if it is less than the first element, swaps it with the first element. The second iteration looks at the third element and inserts it into the correct position with respect to the first two elements, so all three elements are in order. At the ith iteration of this algorithm, the first i elements in the original vector will be sorted.

Insertion sort iterates $n - 1$ times, inserting an element into the appropriate position in the elements sorted so far. For each iteration, determining where to insert the element can require comparing the element to each of the preceding elements in the vector. In the worst case, this will require $n - 1$ comparisons. Each individual repetition statement runs in $O(n)$ time. For determining Big O notation, nested statements mean that you must multiply the number of comparisons. For each iteration of an outer loop, there will be a certain number of iterations of the inner loop. In this algorithm, for each $O(n)$ iteration of the outer loop, there will be $O(n)$ iterations of the inner loop, resulting in a Big O of $O(n * n)$ or $O(n^2)$.

20.3.3 Merge Sort (A Recursive Implementation)

Merge sort is an efficient sorting algorithm, but is conceptually more complex than selection sort and insertion sort. The merge sort algorithm sorts a vector by splitting it into two equal-sized subvectors, sorting each subvector and then merging them into one larger vector. With an odd number of elements, the algorithm creates the two subvectors such that one has one more element than the other.

The implementation of merge sort in this example is recursive. The base case is a vector with one element. A one-element vector is, of course, sorted, so merge sort immediately returns when it is called with a one-element vector. The recursion step splits a vector of two or more elements into two equal-sized subvectors, recursively sorts each subvector, then merges them into one larger, sorted vector. [Again, if there is an odd number of elements, one subvector is one element larger than the other.]

Suppose the algorithm has already merged smaller vectors to create sorted vectors A:

    4   10   34   56   77

and B:

    5   30   51   52   93

Merge sort combines these two vectors into one larger, sorted vector. The smallest element in A is 4 (located in the zeroth index of A). The smallest element in B is 5 (located in the zeroth index of B). In order to determine the smallest element in the larger vector, the algorithm compares 4 and 5. The value from A is smaller, so 4 becomes the first element in the merged vector. The algorithm continues by comparing 10 (the second element in A) to 5 (the first element in B). The value from B is smaller, so 5 becomes the second element in the larger vector. The algorithm continues by comparing 10 to 30, with 10 becoming the third element in the vector, and so on.

Figure 20.5 defines class `MergeSort` and lines 31–34 of Fig. 20.6 define the `sort` function. Line 33 calls function `sortSubVector` with 0 and `size - 1` as the arguments. The arguments correspond to the beginning and ending indices of the vector to be sorted, causing `sortSubVector` to operate on the entire vector. Function `sortSubVector` is

```
 1   // Fig 20.5: MergeSort.h
 2   // Class that creates a vector filled with random integers.
 3   // Provides a function to sort the vector with merge sort.
 4   #include <vector>
 5   using std::vector;
 6
 7   // MergeSort class definition
 8   class MergeSort
 9   {
10   public:
11      MergeSort( int ); // constructor initializes vector
12      void sort(); // sort vector using merge sort
13      void displayElements() const; // display vector elements
14   private:
15      int size; // vector size
16      vector< int > data; // vector of ints
17      void sortSubVector( int, int ); // sort subvector
18      void merge( int, int, int, int ); // merge two sorted vectors
19      void displaySubVector( int, int ) const; // display subvector
20   }; // end class SelectionSort
```

Fig. 20.5 | MergeSort class definition.

```
 1   // Fig 20.6: MergeSort.cpp
 2   // Class MergeSort member-function definition.
 3   #include <iostream>
 4   using std::cout;
 5   using std::endl;
 6
 7   #include <vector>
 8   using std::vector;
 9
10   #include <cstdlib> // prototypes for functions srand and rand
11   using std::rand;
12   using std::srand;
13
14   #include <ctime> // prototype for function time
15   using std::time;
16
17   #include "MergeSort.h" // class MergeSort definition
18
19   // constructor fill vector with random integers
20   MergeSort::MergeSort( int vectorSize )
21   {
22      size = ( vectorSize > 0 ? vectorSize : 10 ); // validate vectorSize
23      srand( time( 0 ) ); // seed random number generator using current time
24
25      // fill vector with random ints in range 10-99
26      for ( int i = 0; i < size; i++ )
27         data.push_back( 10 + rand() % 90 );
28   } // end MergeSort constructor
```

Fig. 20.6 | MergeSort class member-function definition. (Part 1 of 3.)

```cpp
29
30   // split vector, sort subvectors and merge subvectors into sorted vector
31   void MergeSort::sort()
32   {
33      sortSubVector( 0, size - 1 ); // recursively sort entire vector
34   } // end function sort
35
36   // recursive function to sort subvectors
37   void MergeSort::sortSubVector( int low, int high )
38   {
39      // test base case; size of vector equals 1
40      if ( ( high - low ) >= 1 ) // if not base case
41      {
42         int middle1 = ( low + high ) / 2; // calculate middle of vector
43         int middle2 = middle1 + 1; // calculate next element over
44
45         // output split step
46         cout << "split:   ";
47         displaySubVector( low, high );
48         cout << endl << "         ";
49         displaySubVector( low, middle1 );
50         cout << endl << "              ";
51         displaySubVector( middle2, high );
52         cout << endl << endl;
53
54         // split vector in half; sort each half (recursive calls)
55         sortSubVector( low, middle1 ); // first half of vector
56         sortSubVector( middle2, high ); // second half of vector
57
58         // merge two sorted vectors after split calls return
59         merge( low, middle1, middle2, high );
60      } // end if
61   } // end function sortSubVector
62
63   // merge two sorted subvectors into one sorted subvector
64   void MergeSort::merge( int left, int middle1, int middle2, int right )
65   {
66      int leftIndex = left; // index into left subvector
67      int rightIndex = middle2; // index into right subvector
68      int combinedIndex = left; // index into temporary working vector
69      vector< int > combined( size ); // working vector
70
71      // output two subvectors before merging
72      cout << "merge:   ";
73      displaySubVector( left, middle1 );
74      cout << endl << "         ";
75      displaySubVector( middle2, right );
76      cout << endl;
77
78      // merge vectors until reaching end of either
79      while ( leftIndex <= middle1 && rightIndex <= right )
80      {
```

Fig. 20.6 | `MergeSort` class member-function definition. (Part 2 of 3.)

```
81          // place smaller of two current elements into result
82          // and move to next space in vector
83          if ( data[ leftIndex ] <= data[ rightIndex ] )
84             combined[ combinedIndex++ ] = data[ leftIndex++ ];
85          else
86             combined[ combinedIndex++ ] = data[ rightIndex++ ];
87       } // end while
88
89       if ( leftIndex == middle2 ) // if at end of left vector
90       {
91          while ( rightIndex <= right ) // copy in rest of right vector
92             combined[ combinedIndex++ ] = data[ rightIndex++ ];
93       } // end if
94       else // at end of right vector
95       {
96          while ( leftIndex <= middle1 ) // copy in rest of left vector
97             combined[ combinedIndex++ ] = data[ leftIndex++ ];
98       } // end else
99
100      // copy values back into original vector
101      for ( int i = left; i <= right; i++ )
102         data[ i ] = combined[ i ];
103
104      // output merged vector
105      cout << "            ";
106      displaySubVector( left, right );
107      cout << endl << endl;
108   } // end function merge
109
110   // display elements in vector
111   void MergeSort::displayElements() const
112   {
113      displaySubVector( 0, size - 1 );
114   } // end function displayElements
115
116   // display certain values in vector
117   void MergeSort::displaySubVector( int low, int high ) const
118   {
119      // output spaces for alignment
120      for ( int i = 0; i < low; i++ )
121         cout << "   ";
122
123      // output elements left in vector
124      for ( int i = low; i <= high; i++ )
125         cout << " " << data[ i ];
126   } // end function displaySubVector
```

Fig. 20.6 | `MergeSort` class member-function definition. (Part 3 of 3.)

defined in lines 37–61. Line 40 tests the base case. If the size of the vector is 1, the vector is already sorted, so the function simply returns immediately. If the size of the vector is greater than 1, the function splits the vector in two, recursively calls function sortSub-Vector to sort the two subvectors, then merges them. Line 55 recursively calls function sortSubVector on the first half of the vector, and line 56 recursively calls function sort-

SubVector on the second half of the vector. When these two function calls return, each half of the vector has been sorted. Line 59 calls function merge (lines 64–108) on the two halves of the vector to combine the two sorted vectors into one larger sorted vector.

Lines 79–87 in function merge loop until the program reaches the end of either subvector. Line 83 tests which element at the beginning of the vectors is smaller. If the element in the left vector is smaller, line 84 places it in position in the combined vector. If the element in the right vector is smaller, line 86 places it in position in the combined vector. When the while loop has completed (line 87), one entire subvector is placed in the combined vector, but the other subvector still contains data. Line 89 tests whether the left vector has reached the end. If so, lines 91–92 fill the combined vector with the elements of the right vector. If the left vector has not reached the end, then the right vector must have reached the end, and lines 96–97 fill the combined vector with the elements of the left vector. Finally, lines 101–102 copy the combined vector into the original vector. Figure 20.7 creates and uses a MergeSort object. The output from this program displays the splits and merges performed by merge sort, showing the progress of the sort at each step of the algorithm.

Efficiency of Merge Sort
Merge sort is a far more efficient algorithm than either insertion sort or selection sort (although that may be difficult to believe when looking at the rather busy Fig. 20.7). Consider the first (nonrecursive) call to function sortSubVector. This results in two recursive calls to function sortSubVector with subvectors each approximately half the size of the original vector, and a single call to function merge. This call to function merge requires, at worst,

```
1   // Fig 20.7: Fig20_07.cpp
2   // MergeSort test program.
3   #include <iostream>
4   using std::cout;
5   using std::endl;
6
7   #include "MergeSort.h" // class MergeSort definition
8
9   int main()
10  {
11     // create object to perform merge sort
12     MergeSort sortVector( 10 );
13
14     cout << "Unsorted vector:" << endl;
15     sortVector.displayElements(); // print unsorted vector
16     cout << endl << endl;
17
18     sortVector.sort(); // sort vector
19
20     cout << "Sorted vector:" << endl;
21     sortVector.displayElements(); // print sorted vector
22     cout << endl;
23     return 0;
24  } // end main
```

Fig. 20.7 | MergeSort test program. (Part 1 of 3.)

```
Unsorted vector:
 30 47 22 67 79 18 60 78 26 54

split:     30 47 22 67 79 18 60 78 26 54
           30 47 22 67 79
                         18 60 78 26 54

split:     30 47 22 67 79
           30 47 22
                   67 79

split:     30 47 22
           30 47
                 22

split:     30 47
           30
              47

merge:     30
              47
           30 47

merge:     30 47
                 22
           22 30 47

split:                 67 79
                       67
                          79

merge:                 67
                          79
                       67 79

merge:     22 30 47
                       67 79
           22 30 47 67 79

split:                     18 60 78 26 54
                           18 60 78
                                    26 54

split:                     18 60 78
                           18 60
                                 78

split:                     18 60
                           18
                              60

merge:                     18
                              60
                           18 60
```

(Continued at top of next page…)

Fig. 20.7 | MergeSort test program. (Part 2 of 3.)

(...Continued from bottom of previous page)

```
merge:                      18 60
                                 78
                            18 60 78

split:                            26 54
                                  26
                                     54

merge:                            26
                                     54
                                  26 54

merge:                      18 60 78
                                     26 54
                            18 26 54 60 78

merge:      22 30 47 67 79
                            18 26 54 60 78
             18 22 26 30 47 54 60 67 78 79

Sorted vector:
  18 22 26 30 47 54 60 67 78 79
```

Fig. 20.7 | MergeSort test program. (Part 3 of 3.)

$n - 1$ comparisons to fill the original vector, which is *O(n)*. (Recall that each element in the vector is chosen by comparing one element from each of the subvectors.) The two calls to function sortSubVector result in four more recursive calls to function sortSubVector, each with a subvector approximately one quarter the size of the original vector, along with two calls to function merge. These two calls to function merge each require, at worst, $n/2 - 1$ comparisons, for a total number of comparisons of *O(n)*. This process continues, each call to sortSubVector generating two additional calls to sortSubVector and a call to merge, until the algorithm has split the vector into one-element subvectors. At each level, *O(n)* comparisons are required to merge the subvectors. Each level splits the size of the vectors in half, so doubling the size of the vector requires one more level. Quadrupling the size of the vector requires two more levels. This pattern is logarithmic and results in $\log_2 n$ levels. This results in a total efficiency of *O(n log n)*. Figure 20.8 summarizes many of the searching and sorting algorithms covered in this book and lists the Big O for each of them. Figure 20.9 lists the Big O values we have covered in this chapter along with a number of values for *n* to highlight the differences in the growth rates.

Algorithm	Location	Big O
Searching Algorithms		
Linear search	Section 7.7	*O(n)*
Binary search	Section 20.2.2	*O(log n)*

Fig. 20.8 | Searching and sorting algorithms with Big O values. (Part 1 of 2.)

Algorithm	Location	Big O
Recursive linear search	Exercise 20.8	$O(n)$
Recursive binary search	Exercise 20.9	$O(\log n)$
Sorting Algorithms		
Insertion sort	Section 7.8	$O(n^2)$
Selection sort	Section 8.6	$O(n^2)$
Merge sort	Section 20.3.3	$O(n \log n)$
Bubble sort	Exercises 16.3 and 16.4	$O(n^2)$
Quick sort	Exercise 20.10	Worst case: $O(n^2)$ Average case: $O(n \log n)$

Fig. 20.8 | Searching and sorting algorithms with Big O values. (Part 2 of 2.)

n	Approximate decimal value	$O(\log n)$	$O(n)$	$O(n \log n)$	$O(n^2)$
2^{10}	1000	10	2^{10}	$10 \cdot 2^{10}$	2^{20}
2^{20}	1,000,000	20	2^{20}	$20 \cdot 2^{20}$	2^{40}
2^{30}	1,000,000,000	30	2^{30}	$30 \cdot 2^{30}$	2^{60}

Fig. 20.9 | Approximate number of comparisons for common Big O notations.

Summary

- Searching data involves determining whether a search key is present in the data and, if so, finding its location.
- Sorting involves arranging data into order.
- The linear search algorithm searches each element in the vector sequentially until it finds the correct element. If the element is not in the vector, the algorithm tests each element in the vector, and when the end of the vector is reached, informs the user that the element is not present. If the element is in the vector, linear search tests each element until it finds the correct one.
- A major difference among searching algorithms is the amount of effort they require in order to return a result.
- One way to describe the efficiency of an algorithm is with Big O notation (*O*), which indicates how hard an algorithm may have to work to solve a problem.
- For searching and sorting algorithms, Big O describes how the amount of effort of a particular algorithm varies depending on how many elements are in the data.
- An algorithm that is $O(1)$ is said to have a constant runtime. This does not mean that the algorithm requires only one comparison. It just means that the number of comparisons does not grow as the size of the vector increases.
- An $O(n)$ algorithm is referred to as having a linear runtime.

- Big O is designed to highlight dominant factors and ignore terms that become unimportant with high values of n.
- Big O notation is concerned with the growth rate of algorithm runtimes, so constants are ignored.
- The linear search algorithm runs in $O(n)$ time.
- The worst case in linear search is that every element must be checked to determine whether the search element exists. This occurs if the search key is the last element in the vector or is not present.
- The binary search algorithm is more efficient than the linear search algorithm, but it requires that the vector first be sorted. This is only worthwhile when the vector, once sorted, will be searched a great many times—or when the searching application has stringent performance requirements.
- The first iteration of binary search tests the middle element in the vector. If this is the search key, the algorithm returns its location. If the search key is less than the middle element, binary search continues with the first half of the vector. If the search key is greater than the middle element, binary search continues with the second half of the vector. Each iteration of binary search tests the middle value of the remaining vector and, if the element is not found, eliminates half of the remaining elements.
- Binary search is more efficient than linear search because, with each comparison it eliminates from consideration half of the elements in the vector.
- Binary search runs in $O(\log n)$ time because each step removes half of the remaining elements from consideration.
- If the size of the vector is doubled, binary search requires only one extra comparison to complete successfully.
- Selection sort is a simple, but inefficient, sorting algorithm.
- The first iteration of selection sort selects the smallest element in the vector and swaps it with the first element. The second iteration of selection sort selects the second-smallest element (which is the smallest remaining element) and swaps it with the second element. Selection sort continues until the last iteration selects the second-largest element and swaps it with the second-to-last index, leaving the largest element in the last index. At the ith iteration of selection sort, the smallest i elements of the whole vector are sorted into the first i indices.
- The selection sort algorithm runs in $O(n^2)$ time.
- The first iteration of insertion sort takes the second element in the vector and, if it is less than the first element, swaps it with the first element. The second iteration of insertion sort looks at the third element and inserts it in the correct position with respect to the first two elements. After the ith iteration of insertion sort, the first i elements in the original vector are sorted. Only $n - 1$ iterations are required.
- The insertion sort algorithm runs in $O(n^2)$ time.
- Merge sort is a sorting algorithm that is faster, but more complex to implement, than selection sort and insertion sort.
- The merge sort algorithm sorts a vector by splitting the vector into two equal-sized subvectors, sorting each subvector and merging the subvectors into one larger vector.
- Merge sort's base case is a vector with one element. A one-element vector is already sorted, so merge sort immediately returns when it is called with a one-element vector. The merge part of merge sort takes two sorted vectors (these could be one-element vectors) and combines them into one larger sorted vector.
- Merge sort performs the merge by looking at the first element in each vector, which is also the smallest element in the vector. Merge sort takes the smallest of these and places it in the first element of the larger, sorted vector. If there are still elements in the subvector, merge sort looks at

the second element in that subvector (which is now the smallest element remaining) and compares it to the first element in the other subvector. Merge sort continues this process until the larger vector is filled.

- In the worst case, the first call to merge sort has to make $O(n)$ comparisons to fill the n slots in the final vector.

- The merging portion of the merge sort algorithm is performed on two subvectors, each of approximately size $n/2$. Creating each of these subvectors requires $n/2 - 1$ comparisons for each subvector, or $O(n)$ comparisons total. This pattern continues, as each level works on twice as many vectors, but each is half the size of the previous vector.

- Similar to binary search, this halving results in log n levels, each level requiring $O(n)$ comparisons, for a total efficiency of $O(n \log n)$.

Terminology

Big O notation	order log n
binary search	order n
constant runtime	order n-squared
linear runtime	quadratic runtime
logarithmic runtime	random-access iterator
merge sort	search key
merge two vectors	searching data
$O(1)$	sort key
$O(\log n)$	sort Standard Library function
$O(n \log n)$	sorting data
$O(n)$	split the vector in merge sort
$O(n^2)$	worst-case runtime for an algorithm
order 1	

Self-Review Exercises

20.1 Fill in the blanks in each of the following statements:
   a) A selection sort application would take approximately _____ times as long to run on a 128-element vector as on a 32-element vector.
   b) The efficiency of merge sort is _____.

20.2 What key aspect of both the binary search and the merge sort accounts for the logarithmic portion of their respective Big Os?

20.3 In what sense is the insertion sort superior to the merge sort? In what sense is the merge sort superior to the insertion sort?

20.4 In the text, we say that after the merge sort splits the vector into two subvectors, it then sorts these two subvectors and merges them. Why might someone be puzzled by our statement that "it then sorts these two subvectors"?

Answers to Self-Review Exercises

20.1 a) 16, because an $O(n^2)$ algorithm takes 16 times as long to sort four times as much information. b) $O(n \log n)$.

20.2   Both of these algorithms incorporate "halving"—somehow reducing something by half. The binary search eliminates from consideration one-half of the vector after each comparison. The merge sort splits the vector in half each time it is called.

20.3   The insertion sort is easier to understand and to implement than the merge sort. The merge sort is far more efficient ($O(n \log n)$) than the insertion sort ($O(n^2)$).

20.4   In a sense, it does not really sort these two subvectors. It simply keeps splitting the original vector in half until it provides a one-element subvector, which is, of course, sorted. It then builds up the original two subvectors by merging these one-element vectors to form larger subvectors, which are then merged, and so on.

Exercises

[*Note:* Most of the exercises shown here are duplicates of exercises from Chapters 7–8. We include the exercises again here as a convenience for readers studying searching and sorting in this chapter.]

20.5   (*Bubble Sort*) Implement bubble sort—another simple yet inefficient sorting technique. It is called bubble sort or sinking sort because smaller values gradually "bubble" their way to the top of the vector (i.e., toward the first element) like air bubbles rising in water, while the larger values sink to the bottom (end) of the vector. The technique uses nested loops to make several passes through the vector. Each pass compares successive pairs of elements. If a pair is in increasing order (or the values are equal), the bubble sort leaves the values as they are. If a pair is in decreasing order, the bubble sort swaps their values in the vector.

The first pass compares the first two elements of the vector and swaps them if necessary. It then compares the second and third elements in the vector. The end of this pass compares the last two elements in the vector and swaps them if necessary. After one pass, the largest element will be in the last index. After two passes, the largest two elements will be in the last two indices. Explain why bubble sort is an $O(n^2)$ algorithm.

20.6   (*Enhanced Bubble Sort*) Make the following simple modifications to improve the performance of the bubble sort you developed in Exercise 20.5:

    a) After the first pass, the largest number is guaranteed to be in the highest-numbered element of the vector; after the second pass, the two highest numbers are "in place"; and so on. Instead of making nine comparisons (for a 10-element vector) on every pass, modify the bubble sort to make only the eight necessary comparisons on the second pass, seven on the third pass, and so on.

    b) The data in the vector may already be in the proper order or near-proper order, so why make nine passes (of a 10-element vector) if fewer will suffice? Modify the sort to check at the end of each pass whether any swaps have been made. If none have been made, the data must already be in the proper order, so the program should terminate. If swaps have been made, at least one more pass is needed.

20.7   (*Bucket Sort*) A bucket sort begins with a one-dimensional vector of positive integers to be sorted and a two-dimensional vector of integers with rows indexed from 0 to 9 and columns indexed from 0 to $n - 1$, where n is the number of values to be sorted. Each row of the two-dimensional vector is referred to as a *bucket*. Write a class named `BucketSort` containing a function called `sort` that operates as follows:

    a) Place each value of the one-dimensional vector into a row of the bucket vector, based on the value's "ones" (rightmost) digit. For example, 97 is placed in row 7, 3 is placed in row 3 and 100 is placed in row 0. This procedure is called a *distribution pass*.

b) Loop through the bucket vector row by row, and copy the values back to the original vector. This procedure is called a *gathering pass*. The new order of the preceding values in the one-dimensional vector is 100, 3 and 97.

c) Repeat this process for each subsequent digit position (tens, hundreds, thousands, etc.).

On the second (tens digit) pass, 100 is placed in row 0, 3 is placed in row 0 (because 3 has no tens digit) and 97 is placed in row 9. After the gathering pass, the order of the values in the one-dimensional vector is 100, 3 and 97. On the third (hundreds digit) pass, 100 is placed in row 1, 3 is placed in row 0 and 97 is placed in row 0 (after the 3). After this last gathering pass, the original vector is in sorted order.

Note that the two-dimensional vector of buckets is 10 times the length of the integer vector being sorted. This sorting technique provides better performance than a bubble sort, but requires much more memory—the bubble sort requires space for only one additional element of data. This comparison is an example of the space–time trade-off: The bucket sort uses more memory than the bubble sort, but performs better. This version of the bucket sort requires copying all the data back to the original vector on each pass. Another possibility is to create a second two-dimensional bucket vector and repeatedly swap the data between the two bucket vectors.

20.8 (*Recursive Linear Search*) Modify Exercise 7.33 to use recursive function `recursiveLinearSearch` to perform a linear search of the vector. The function should receive the search key and starting index as arguments. If the search key is found, return its index in the vector; otherwise, return –1. Each call to the recursive function should check one index in the vector.

20.9 (*Recursive Binary Search*) Modify Fig. 20.3 to use recursive function `recursiveBinarySearch` to perform a binary search of the vector. The function should receive the search key, starting index and ending index as arguments. If the search key is found, return its index in the vector. If the search key is not found, return –1.

20.10 (*Quicksort*) The recursive sorting technique called quicksort uses the following basic algorithm for a one-dimensional vector of values:

a) *Partitioning Step*: Take the first element of the unsorted vector and determine its final location in the sorted vector (i.e., all values to the left of the element in the vector are less than the element, and all values to the right of the element in the vector are greater than the element—we show how to do this below). We now have one element in its proper location and two unsorted subvectors.

b) *Recursion Step*: Perform *Step 1* on each unsorted subvector. Each time *Step 1* is performed on a subvector, another element is placed in its final location of the sorted vector, and two unsorted subvectors are created. When a subvector consists of one element, that element is in its final location (because a one-element vector is already sorted).

The basic algorithm seems simple enough, but how do we determine the final position of the first element of each subvector? As an example, consider the following set of values (the element in bold is the partitioning element—it will be placed in its final location in the sorted vector):

37 2 6 4 89 8 10 12 68 45

Starting from the rightmost element of the vector, compare each element with **37** until an element less than **37** is found; then swap **37** and that element. The first element less than **37** is 12, so **37** and 12 are swapped. The new vector is

12 2 6 4 89 8 10 **37** 68 45

Element 12 is in italics to indicate that it was just swapped with **37**.

Starting from the left of the vector, but beginning with the element after 12, compare each element with 37 until an element greater than 37 is found—then swap 37 and that element. The first element greater than 37 is 89, so 37 and 89 are swapped. The new vector is

12 2 6 4 37 8 10 *89* 68 45

Starting from the right, but beginning with the element before 89, compare each element with 37 until an element less than 37 is found—then swap 37 and that element. The first element less than 37 is 10, so 37 and 10 are swapped. The new vector is

12 2 6 4 *10* 8 37 89 68 45

Starting from the left, but beginning with the element after 10, compare each element with 37 until an element greater than 37 is found—then swap 37 and that element. There are no more elements greater than 37, so when we compare 37 with itself, we know that 37 has been placed in its final location of the sorted vector. Every value to the left of 37 is smaller than it, and every value to the right of 37 is larger than it.

Once the partition has been applied on the previous vector, there are two unsorted subvectors. The subvector with values less than 37 contains 12, 2, 6, 4, 10 and 8. The subvector with values greater than 37 contains 89, 68 and 45. The sort continues recursively, with both subvectors being partitioned in the same manner as the original vector.

Based on the preceding discussion, write recursive function `quickSortHelper` to sort a one-dimensional integer vector. The function should receive as arguments a starting index and an ending index on the original vector being sorted.

21

Data Structures

OBJECTIVES

In this chapter you will learn:

- To form linked data structures using pointers, self-referential classes and recursion.

- To create and manipulate dynamic data structures such as linked lists, queues, stacks and binary trees.

- To use binary search trees for high-speed searching and sorting.

- To understand various important applications of linked data structures.

- To understand how to create reusable data structures with class templates, inheritance and composition.

Much that I bound,
I could not free;
Much that I freed
returned to me.
—Lee Wilson Dodd

'Will you walk a little
faster?' said a whiting
to a snail,
'There's a porpoise close
behind us, and he's
treading on my tail.'
—Lewis Carroll

There is always room
at the top.
—Daniel Webster

Push on — keep moving.
—Thomas Morton

I'll turn over a new leaf.
—Miguel de Cervantes

21.1 Introduction

We have studied fixed-size data structures such as one-dimensional arrays, two-dimensional arrays and structs. This chapter introduces dynamic data structures that grow and shrink during execution. Linked lists are collections of data items "lined up in a row"—insertions and removals are made anywhere in a linked list. Stacks are important in compilers and operating systems: Insertions and removals are made only at one end of a stack—its top. Queues represent waiting lines; insertions are made at the back (also referred to as the tail) of a queue and removals are made from the front (also referred to as the head) of a queue. Binary trees facilitate high-speed searching and sorting of data, efficient elimination of duplicate data items, representation of file system directories and compilation of expressions into machine language. These data structures have many other interesting applications.

We discuss several popular and important data structures and implement programs that create and manipulate them. We use classes, class templates, inheritance and composition to create and package these data structures for reusability and maintainability.

Studying this chapter is solid preparation for Chapter 22, Standard Template Library (STL). The STL is a major portion of the C++ Standard Library. The STL provides containers, iterators for traversing those containers and algorithms for processing the elements of those containers. You will see that the STL has taken each of the data structures we discuss in this chapter and packaged them into templatized classes. The STL code is carefully written to be portable, efficient and extensible. Once you understand the principles and construction of data structures as presented in this chapter, you will be able to make the best use of the prepackaged data structures, iterators and algorithms in the STL, a world-class set of reusable components.

The chapter examples are practical programs that you will be able to use in more advanced courses and in industry applications. The programs employ extensive pointer manipulation. The exercises include a rich collection of useful applications.

We encourage you to attempt the major project described in the special section Building Your Own Compiler. You have been using a C++ compiler to translate your programs to machine language so that you could execute these programs on your computer. In this project, you will actually build your own compiler. It will read a file of statements written in a simple, yet powerful, high-level language similar to early versions of the popular language BASIC. Your compiler will translate these statements into a file of Simpletron Machine Language (SML) instructions—SML is the language you learned in the Chapter 8 special section, Building Your Own Computer. Your Simpletron Simulator program will then execute the SML program produced by your compiler! Implementing this project using an object-oriented approach will give you a wonderful opportunity to exercise most of what you have learned in this book. The special section carefully walks you through the specifications of the high-level language and describes the algorithms you will need to convert each type of high-level language statement into machine-language instructions. If you enjoy being challenged, you might attempt the many enhancements to both the compiler and the Simpletron Simulator suggested in this chapter's exercises.

21.2 Self-Referential Classes

A self-referential class contains a pointer member that points to a class object of the same class type. For example, the definition

```
class Node
{
public:
    Node( int ); // constructor
    void setData( int ); // set data member
    int getData() const; // get data member
    void setNextPtr( Node * ); // set pointer to next Node
    Node *getNextPtr() const; // get pointer to next Node
private:
    int data; // data stored in this Node
    Node *nextPtr; // pointer to another object of same type
}; // end class Node
```

defines a type, Node. Type Node has two private data members—integer member data and pointer member nextPtr. Member nextPtr points to an object of type Node—another object of the same type as the one being declared here, hence the term "self-referential class." Member nextPtr is referred to as a link—i.e., nextPtr can "tie" an object of type Node to another object of the same type. Type Node also has five member functions—a constructor that receives an integer to initialize member data, a setData function to set the value of member data, a getData function to return the value of member data, a setNextPtr function to set the value of member nextPtr and a getNextPtr function to return the value of member nextPtr.

Self-referential class objects can be linked together to form useful data structures such as lists, queues, stacks and trees. Figure 21.1 illustrates two self-referential class objects linked together to form a list. Note that a slash—representing a null (0) pointer—is placed in the link member of the second self-referential class object to indicate that the link does not point to another object. The slash is only for illustration purposes; it does not correspond to the backslash character in C++. A null pointer normally indicates the end of a data structure just as the null character ('\0') indicates the end of a string.

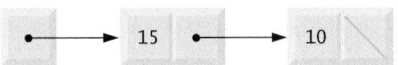

Fig. 21.1 | Two self-referential class objects linked together.

> ### Common Programming Error 21.1
>
> *Not setting the link in the last node of a linked data structure to null (0) is a (possibly fatal) logic error.*

21.3 Dynamic Memory Allocation and Data Structures

Creating and maintaining dynamic data structures requires dynamic memory allocation, which enables a program to obtain more memory at execution time to hold new nodes. When that memory is no longer needed by the program, the memory can be released so that it can be reused to allocate other objects in the future. The limit for dynamic memory allocation can be as large as the amount of available physical memory in the computer or the amount of available virtual memory in a virtual memory system. Often, the limits are much smaller, because available memory must be shared among many programs.

The new operator takes as an argument the type of the object being dynamically allocated and returns a pointer to an object of that type. For example, the statement

```
Node *newPtr = new Node( 10 ); // create Node with data 10
```

allocates sizeof(Node) bytes, runs the Node constructor and assigns the address of the new Node object to newPtr. If no memory is available, new throws a bad_alloc exception. The value 10 is passed to the Node constructor which initializes the Node's data member to 10.

The delete operator runs the Node destructor and deallocates memory allocated with new—the memory is returned to the system so that the memory can be reallocated in the future. To free memory dynamically allocated by the preceding new, use the statement

```
delete newPtr;
```

Note that newPtr itself is not deleted; rather the space newPtr points to is deleted. If pointer newPtr has the null pointer value 0, the preceding statement has no effect. It is not an error to delete a null pointer.

The following sections discuss lists, stacks, queues and trees. The data structures presented in this chapter are created and maintained with dynamic memory allocation, self-referential classes, class templates and function templates.

21.4 Linked Lists

A linked list is a linear collection of self-referential class objects, called nodes, connected by pointer links—hence, the term "linked" list. A linked list is accessed via a pointer to the first node of the list. Each subsequent node is accessed via the link-pointer member stored in the previous node. By convention, the link pointer in the last node of a list is set to null (0) to mark the end of the list. Data is stored in a linked list dynamically—each node is created as necessary. A node can contain data of any type, including objects of other classes. If nodes contain base-class pointers to base-class and derived-class objects related by inheritance, we can have a linked list of such nodes and use virtual function calls to process these objects polymorphically. Stacks and queues are also linear data structures and, as we will see, can be viewed as constrained versions of linked lists. Trees are nonlinear data structures.

Lists of data can be stored in arrays, but linked lists provide several advantages. A linked list is appropriate when the number of data elements to be represented at one time is unpredictable. Linked lists are dynamic, so the length of a list can increase or decrease as necessary. The size of a "conventional" C++ array, however, cannot be altered, because the array size is fixed at compile time. "Conventional" arrays can become full. Linked lists become full only when the system has insufficient memory to satisfy dynamic storage allocation requests.

Performance Tip 21.1

An array can be declared to contain more elements than the number of items expected, but this can waste memory. Linked lists can provide better memory utilization in these situations. Linked lists allow the program to adapt at runtime. Note that class template vector *(introduced in Section 7.11) implements a dynamically resizable array-based data structure.*

Linked lists can be maintained in sorted order by inserting each new element at the proper point in the list. Existing list elements do not need to be moved.

Performance Tip 21.2

Insertion and deletion in a sorted array can be time consuming—all the elements following the inserted or deleted element must be shifted appropriately. A linked list allows efficient insertion operations anywhere in the list.

Performance Tip 21.3

The elements of an array are stored contiguously in memory. This allows immediate access to any array element, because the address of any element can be calculated directly based on its position relative to the beginning of the array. Linked lists do not afford such immediate "direct access" to their elements. So accessing individual elements in a linked list can be considerably more expensive than accessing individual elements in an array. The selection of a data structure is typically based on the performance of specific operations used by a program and the order in which the data items are maintained in the data structure. For example, it is typically more efficient to insert an item in a sorted linked list than a sorted array.

Linked list nodes are normally not stored contiguously in memory. Logically, however, the nodes of a linked list appear to be contiguous. Figure 21.2 illustrates a linked list with several nodes.

Performance Tip 21.4

Using dynamic memory allocation (instead of fixed-size arrays) for data structures that grow and shrink at execution time can save memory. Keep in mind, however, that pointers occupy space and that dynamic memory allocation incurs the overhead of function calls.

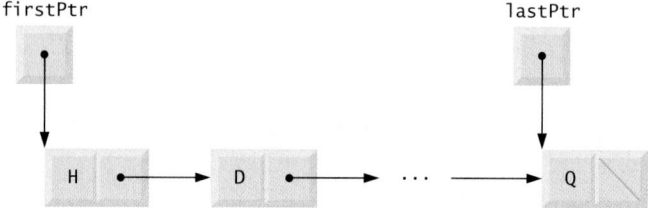

Fig. 21.2 | A graphical representation of a list.

Linked List Implementation

The program of Figs. 21.3–21.5 uses a List class template (see Chapter 14 for information on class templates) to manipulate a list of integer values and a list of floating-point values. The driver program (Fig. 21.5) provides five options: 1) Insert a value at the beginning of the list, 2) insert a value at the end of the list, 3) delete a value from the beginning of the list, 4) delete a value from the end of the list and 5) end the list processing. A detailed discussion of the program follows. Exercise 21.20 asks you to implement a recursive function that prints a linked list backward, and Exercise 21.21 asks you to implement a recursive function that searches a linked list for a particular data item.

The program uses class templates ListNode (Fig. 21.3) and List (Fig. 21.4). Encapsulated in each List object is a linked list of ListNode objects. Class template ListNode (Fig. 21.3) contains private members data and nextPtr (lines 19–20), a constructor to initialize these members and function getData to return the data in a node. Member data stores a value of type NODETYPE, the type parameter passed to the class template. Member nextPtr stores a pointer to the next ListNode object in the linked list. Note that line 13 of the ListNode class template definition declares class List< NODETYPE > as a friend. This makes all member functions of a given specialization of class template List friends of the corresponding specialization of class template ListNode, so they can access the private members of ListNode objects of that type. Because the ListNode template parameter

```
 1   // Fig. 21.3: Listnode.h
 2   // Template ListNode class definition.
 3   #ifndef LISTNODE_H
 4   #define LISTNODE_H
 5
 6   // forward declaration of class List required to announce that class
 7   // List exists so it can be used in the friend declaration at line 13
 8   template< typename NODETYPE > class List;
 9
10   template< typename NODETYPE>
11   class ListNode
12   {
13      friend class List< NODETYPE >; // make List a friend
14
15   public:
16      ListNode( const NODETYPE & ); // constructor
17      NODETYPE getData() const; // return data in node
18   private:
19      NODETYPE data; // data
20      ListNode< NODETYPE > *nextPtr; // next node in list
21   }; // end class ListNode
22
23   // constructor
24   template< typename NODETYPE>
25   ListNode< NODETYPE >::ListNode( const NODETYPE &info )
26      : data( info ), nextPtr( 0 )
27   {
28      // empty body
29   } // end ListNode constructor
```

Fig. 21.3 | ListNode class-template definition. (Part 1 of 2.)

```
30
31   // return copy of data in node
32   template< typename NODETYPE >
33   NODETYPE ListNode< NODETYPE >::getData() const
34   {
35      return data;
36   } // end function getData
37
38   #endif
```

Fig. 21.3 | ListNode class-template definition. (Part 2 of 2.)

```
1    // Fig. 21.4: List.h
2    // Template List class definition.
3    #ifndef LIST_H
4    #define LIST_H
5
6    #include <iostream>
7    using std::cout;
8
9    #include "listnode.h" // ListNode class definition
10
11   template< typename NODETYPE >
12   class List
13   {
14   public:
15      List(); // constructor
16      ~List(); // destructor
17      void insertAtFront( const NODETYPE & );
18      void insertAtBack( const NODETYPE & );
19      bool removeFromFront( NODETYPE & );
20      bool removeFromBack( NODETYPE & );
21      bool isEmpty() const;
22      void print() const;
23   private:
24      ListNode< NODETYPE > *firstPtr; // pointer to first node
25      ListNode< NODETYPE > *lastPtr; // pointer to last node
26
27      // utility function to allocate new node
28      ListNode< NODETYPE > *getNewNode( const NODETYPE & );
29   }; // end class List
30
31   // default constructor
32   template< typename NODETYPE >
33   List< NODETYPE >::List()
34      : firstPtr( 0 ), lastPtr( 0 )
35   {
36      // empty body
37   } // end List constructor
38
```

Fig. 21.4 | List class-template definition. (Part 1 of 4.)

```
39   // destructor
40   template< typename NODETYPE >
41   List< NODETYPE >::~List()
42   {
43      if ( !isEmpty() ) // List is not empty
44      {
45         cout << "Destroying nodes ...\n";
46
47         ListNode< NODETYPE > *currentPtr = firstPtr;
48         ListNode< NODETYPE > *tempPtr;
49
50         while ( currentPtr != 0 ) // delete remaining nodes
51         {
52            tempPtr = currentPtr;
53            cout << tempPtr->data << '\n';
54            currentPtr = currentPtr->nextPtr;
55            delete tempPtr;
56         } // end while
57      } // end if
58
59      cout << "All nodes destroyed\n\n";
60   } // end List destructor
61
62   // insert node at front of list
63   template< typename NODETYPE >
64   void List< NODETYPE >::insertAtFront( const NODETYPE &value )
65   {
66      ListNode< NODETYPE > *newPtr = getNewNode( value ); // new node
67
68      if ( isEmpty() ) // List is empty
69         firstPtr = lastPtr = newPtr; // new list has only one node
70      else // List is not empty
71      {
72         newPtr->nextPtr = firstPtr; // point new node to previous 1st node
73         firstPtr = newPtr; // aim firstPtr at new node
74      } // end else
75   } // end function insertAtFront
76
77   // insert node at back of list
78   template< typename NODETYPE >
79   void List< NODETYPE >::insertAtBack( const NODETYPE &value )
80   {
81      ListNode< NODETYPE > *newPtr = getNewNode( value ); // new node
82
83      if ( isEmpty() ) // List is empty
84         firstPtr = lastPtr = newPtr; // new list has only one node
85      else // List is not empty
86      {
87         lastPtr->nextPtr = newPtr; // update previous last node
88         lastPtr = newPtr; // new last node
89      } // end else
90   } // end function insertAtBack
91
```

Fig. 21.4 | List class-template definition. (Part 2 of 4.)

```
92   // delete node from front of list
93   template< typename NODETYPE >
94   bool List< NODETYPE >::removeFromFront( NODETYPE &value )
95   {
96      if ( isEmpty() ) // List is empty
97         return false; // delete unsuccessful
98      else
99      {
100         ListNode< NODETYPE > *tempPtr = firstPtr; // hold tempPtr to delete
101
102         if ( firstPtr == lastPtr )
103            firstPtr = lastPtr = 0; // no nodes remain after removal
104         else
105            firstPtr = firstPtr->nextPtr; // point to previous 2nd node
106
107         value = tempPtr->data; // return data being removed
108         delete tempPtr; // reclaim previous front node
109         return true; // delete successful
110      } // end else
111   } // end function removeFromFront
112
113   // delete node from back of list
114   template< typename NODETYPE >
115   bool List< NODETYPE >::removeFromBack( NODETYPE &value )
116   {
117      if ( isEmpty() ) // List is empty
118         return false; // delete unsuccessful
119      else
120      {
121         ListNode< NODETYPE > *tempPtr = lastPtr; // hold tempPtr to delete
122
123         if ( firstPtr == lastPtr ) // List has one element
124            firstPtr = lastPtr = 0; // no nodes remain after removal
125         else
126         {
127            ListNode< NODETYPE > *currentPtr = firstPtr;
128
129            // locate second-to-last element
130            while ( currentPtr->nextPtr != lastPtr )
131               currentPtr = currentPtr->nextPtr; // move to next node
132
133            lastPtr = currentPtr; // remove last node
134            currentPtr->nextPtr = 0; // this is now the last node
135         } // end else
136
137         value = tempPtr->data; // return value from old last node
138         delete tempPtr; // reclaim former last node
139         return true; // delete successful
140      } // end else
141   } // end function removeFromBack
142
```

Fig. 21.4 | List class-template definition. (Part 3 of 4.)

```
143    // is List empty?
144    template< typename NODETYPE >
145    bool List< NODETYPE >::isEmpty() const
146    {
147       return firstPtr == 0;
148    } // end function isEmpty
149
150    // return pointer to newly allocated node
151    template< typename NODETYPE >
152    ListNode< NODETYPE > *List< NODETYPE >::getNewNode(
153       const NODETYPE &value )
154    {
155       return new ListNode< NODETYPE >( value );
156    } // end function getNewNode
157
158    // display contents of List
159    template< typename NODETYPE >
160    void List< NODETYPE >::print() const
161    {
162       if ( isEmpty() ) // List is empty
163       {
164          cout << "The list is empty\n\n";
165          return;
166       } // end if
167
168       ListNode< NODETYPE > *currentPtr = firstPtr;
169
170       cout << "The list is: ";
171
172       while ( currentPtr != 0 ) // get element data
173       {
174          cout << currentPtr->data << ' ';
175          currentPtr = currentPtr->nextPtr;
176       } // end while
177
178       cout << "\n\n";
179    } // end function print
180
181    #endif
```

Fig. 21.4 | List class-template definition. (Part 4 of 4.)

```
1    // Fig. 21.5: Fig21_05.cpp
2    // List class test program.
3    #include <iostream>
4    using std::cin;
5    using std::cout;
6    using std::endl;
7
```

Fig. 21.5 | Manipulating a linked list. (Part 1 of 4.)

```
 8   #include <string>
 9   using std::string;
10
11   #include "List.h" // List class definition
12
13   // function to test a List
14   template< typename T >
15   void testList( List< T > &listObject, const string &typeName )
16   {
17      cout << "Testing a List of " << typeName << " values\n";
18      instructions(); // display instructions
19
20      int choice; // store user choice
21      T value; // store input value
22
23      do // perform user-selected actions
24      {
25         cout << "? ";
26         cin >> choice;
27
28         switch ( choice )
29         {
30            case 1: // insert at beginning
31               cout << "Enter " << typeName << ": ";
32               cin >> value;
33               listObject.insertAtFront( value );
34               listObject.print();
35               break;
36            case 2: // insert at end
37               cout << "Enter " << typeName << ": ";
38               cin >> value;
39               listObject.insertAtBack( value );
40               listObject.print();
41               break;
42            case 3: // remove from beginning
43               if ( listObject.removeFromFront( value ) )
44                  cout << value << " removed from list\n";
45
46               listObject.print();
47               break;
48            case 4: // remove from end
49               if ( listObject.removeFromBack( value ) )
50                  cout << value << " removed from list\n";
51
52               listObject.print();
53               break;
54         } // end switch
55      } while ( choice != 5 ); // end do...while
56
57      cout << "End list test\n\n";
58   } // end function testList
59
```

Fig. 21.5 | Manipulating a linked list. (Part 2 of 4.)

```
60   // display program instructions to user
61   void instructions()
62   {
63      cout << "Enter one of the following:\n"
64         << "  1 to insert at beginning of list\n"
65         << "  2 to insert at end of list\n"
66         << "  3 to delete from beginning of list\n"
67         << "  4 to delete from end of list\n"
68         << "  5 to end list processing\n";
69   } // end function instructions
70
71   int main()
72   {
73      // test List of int values
74      List< int > integerList;
75      testList( integerList, "integer" );
76
77      // test List of double values
78      List< double > doubleList;
79      testList( doubleList, "double" );
80      return 0;
81   } // end main
```

```
Testing a List of integer values
Enter one of the following:
  1 to insert at beginning of list
  2 to insert at end of list
  3 to delete from beginning of list
  4 to delete from end of list
  5 to end list processing
? 1
Enter integer: 1
The list is: 1

? 1
Enter integer: 2
The list is: 2 1

? 2
Enter integer: 3
The list is: 2 1 3

? 2
Enter integer: 4
The list is: 2 1 3 4

? 3
2 removed from list
The list is: 1 3 4

? 3
1 removed from list
The list is: 3 4
```
(continued at top of next page...)

Fig. 21.5 | Manipulating a linked list. (Part 3 of 4.)

(...continued from previous page)

```
? 4
4 removed from list
The list is: 3

? 4
3 removed from list
The list is empty

? 5
End list test

Testing a List of double values
Enter one of the following:
   1 to insert at beginning of list
   2 to insert at end of list
   3 to delete from beginning of list
   4 to delete from end of list
   5 to end list processing
? 1
Enter double: 1.1
The list is: 1.1

? 1
Enter double: 2.2
The list is: 2.2 1.1

? 2
Enter double: 3.3
The list is: 2.2 1.1 3.3

? 2
Enter double: 4.4
The list is: 2.2 1.1 3.3 4.4

? 3
2.2 removed from list
The list is: 1.1 3.3 4.4

? 3
1.1 removed from list
The list is: 3.3 4.4

? 4
4.4 removed from list
The list is: 3.3

? 4
3.3 removed from list
The list is empty

? 5
End list test

All nodes destroyed

All nodes destroyed
```

Fig. 21.5 | Manipulating a linked list. (Part 4 of 4.)

NODETYPE is used as the template argument for List in the friend declaration, ListNodes specialized with a particular type can be processed only by a List specialized with the same type (e.g., a List of int values manages ListNode objects that store int values).

Lines 24–25 of the List class template (Fig. 21.4) declare private data members firstPtr (a pointer to the first ListNode in a List) and lastPtr (a pointer to the last ListNode in a List). The default constructor (lines 32–37) initializes both pointers to 0 (null). The destructor (lines 40–60) ensures that all ListNode objects in a List object are destroyed when that List object is destroyed. The primary List functions are insertAt-Front (lines 63–75), insertAtBack (lines 78–90), removeFromFront (lines 93–111) and removeFromBack (lines 114–141).

Function isEmpty (lines 144–148) is called a predicate function—it does not alter the List; rather, it determines whether the List is empty (i.e., the pointer to the first node of the List is null). If the List is empty, true is returned; otherwise, false is returned. Function print (lines 159–179) displays the List's contents. Utility function getNewNode (lines 151–156) returns a dynamically allocated ListNode object. This function is called from functions insertAtFront and insertAtBack.

Error-Prevention Tip 21.1

Assign null (0) to the link member of a new node. Pointers should be initialized before they are used.

The driver program (Fig. 21.5) uses function template testList to enable the user to manipulate objects of class List. Lines 74 and 78 create List objects for types int and double, respectively. Lines 75 and 79 invoke the testList function template with these List objects.

Member Function *insertAtFront*

Over the next several pages, we discuss each of the member functions of class List in detail. Function insertAtFront (Fig. 21.4, lines 63–75) places a new node at the front of the list. The function consists of several steps:

1. Call function getNewNode (line 66), passing it value, which is a constant reference to the node value to be inserted.

2. Function getNewNode (lines 151–156) uses operator new to create a new list node and return a pointer to this newly allocated node, which is assigned to newPtr in insertAtFront (line 66).

3. If the list is empty (line 68), then both firstPtr and lastPtr are set to newPtr (line 69).

4. If the list is not empty (line 70), then the node pointed to by newPtr is threaded into the list by copying firstPtr to newPtr->nextPtr (line 72), so that the new node points to what used to be the first node of the list, and copying newPtr to firstPtr (line 73), so that firstPtr now points to the new first node of the list.

Figure 21.6 illustrates function insertAtFront. Part (a) of the figure shows the list and the new node before the insertAtFront operation. The dashed arrows in part (b) illustrate *Step 4* of the insertAtFront operation that enables the node containing 12 to become the new list front.

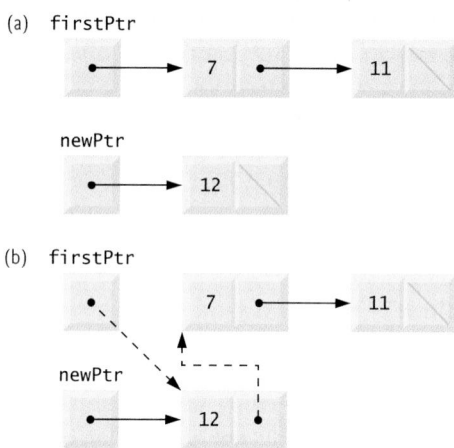

Fig. 21.6 | Operation insertAtFront represented graphically.

Member Function *insertAtBack*

Function insertAtBack (Fig. 21.4, lines 78–90) places a new node at the back of the list. The function consists of several steps:

1. Call function getNewNode (line 81), passing it value, which is a constant reference to the node value to be inserted.

2. Function getNewNode (lines 151–156) uses operator new to create a new list node and return a pointer to this newly allocated node, which is assigned to newPtr in insertAtBack (line 81).

3. If the list is empty (line 83), then both firstPtr and lastPtr are set to newPtr (line 84).

4. If the list is not empty (line 85), then the node pointed to by newPtr is threaded into the list by copying newPtr into lastPtr->nextPtr (line 87), so that the new node is pointed to by what used to be the last node of the list, and copying newPtr to lastPtr (line 88), so that lastPtr now points to the new last node of the list.

Figure 21.7 illustrates an insertAtBack operation. Part (a) of the figure shows the list and the new node before the operation. The dashed arrows in part (b) illustrate *Step 4* of function insertAtBack that enables a new node to be added to the end of a list that is not empty.

Member Function *removeFromFront*

Function removeFromFront (Fig. 21.4, lines 93–111) removes the front node of the list and copies the node value to the reference parameter. The function returns false if an attempt is made to remove a node from an empty list (lines 96–97) and returns true if the removal is successful. The function consists of several steps:

1. Assign tempPtr the address to which firstPtr points (line 100). Eventually, tempPtr will be used to delete the node being removed.

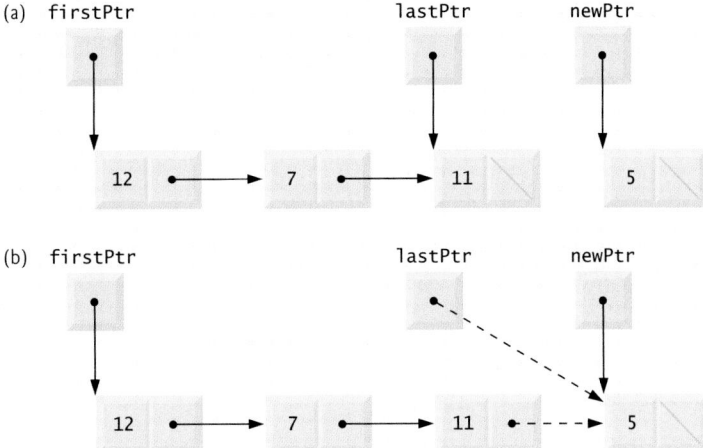

Fig. 21.7 | Operation `insertAtBack` represented graphically.

2. If `firstPtr` is equal to `lastPtr` (line 102), i.e., if the list has only one element prior to the removal attempt, then set `firstPtr` and `lastPtr` to zero (line 103) to dethread that node from the list (leaving the list empty).

3. If the list has more than one node prior to removal, then leave `lastPtr` as is and set `firstPtr` to `firstPtr->nextPtr` (line 105); i.e., modify `firstPtr` to point to what was the second node prior to removal (and is now the new first node).

4. After all these pointer manipulations are complete, copy to reference parameter `value` the `data` member of the node being removed (line 107).

5. Now `delete` the node pointed to by `tempPtr` (line 108).

6. Return `true`, indicating successful removal (line 109).

Figure 21.8 illustrates function `removeFromFront`. Part (a) illustrates the list before the removal operation. Part (b) shows the actual pointer manipulations for removing the front node from a nonempty list.

Member Function *removeFromBack*

Function `removeFromBack` (Fig. 21.4, lines 114–141) removes the back node of the list and copies the node value to the reference parameter. The function returns `false` if an attempt is made to remove a node from an empty list (lines 117–118) and returns `true` if the removal is successful. The function consists of several steps:

1. Assign to `tempPtr` the address to which `lastPtr` points (line 121). Eventually, `tempPtr` will be used to delete the node being removed.

2. If `firstPtr` is equal to `lastPtr` (line 123), i.e., if the list has only one element prior to the removal attempt, then set `firstPtr` and `lastPtr` to zero (line 124) to dethread that node from the list (leaving the list empty).

3. If the list has more than one node prior to removal, then assign `currentPtr` the address to which `firstPtr` points (line 127) to prepare to "walk the list."

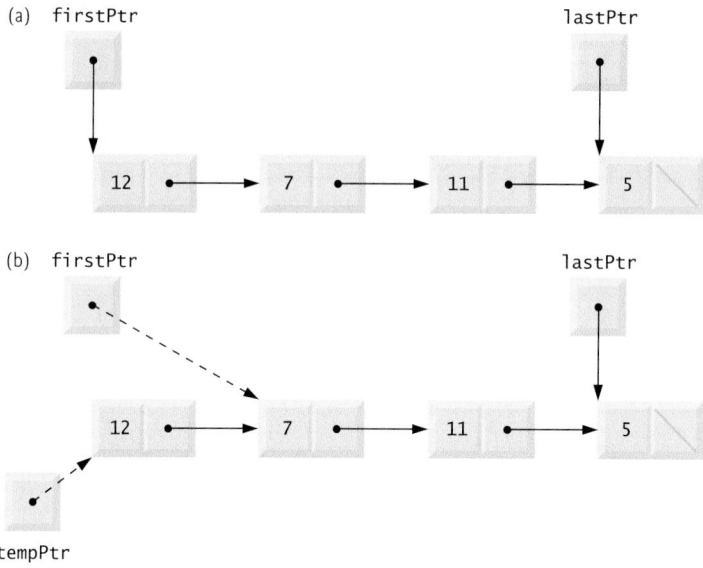

Fig. 21.8 | Operation removeFromFront represented graphically.

4. Now "walk the list" with currentPtr until it points to the node before the last node. This node will become the last node after the remove operation completes. This is done with a while loop (lines 130–131) that keeps replacing currentPtr by currentPtr->nextPtr, while currentPtr->nextPtr is not lastPtr.

5. Assign lastPtr to the address to which currentPtr points (line 133) to dethread the back node from the list.

6. Set currentPtr->nextPtr to zero (line 134) in the new last node of the list.

7. After all the pointer manipulations are complete, copy to reference parameter value the data member of the node being removed (line 137).

8. Now delete the node pointed to by tempPtr (line 138).

9. Return true (line 139), indicating successful removal.

Figure 21.9 illustrates removeFromBack. Part (a) of the figure illustrates the list before the removal operation. Part (b) of the figure shows the actual pointer manipulations.

Member Function print

Function print (lines 159–179) first determines whether the list is empty (line 162). If so, it prints "The list is empty" and returns (lines 164–165). Otherwise, it iterates through the list and outputs the value in each node. The function initializes currentPtr as a copy of firstPtr (line 168), then prints the string "The list is: " (line 170). While currentPtr is not null (line 172), currentPtr->data is printed (line 174) and current-Ptr is assigned the value of currentPtr->nextPtr (line 175). Note that if the link in the last node of the list is not null, the printing algorithm will erroneously print past the end

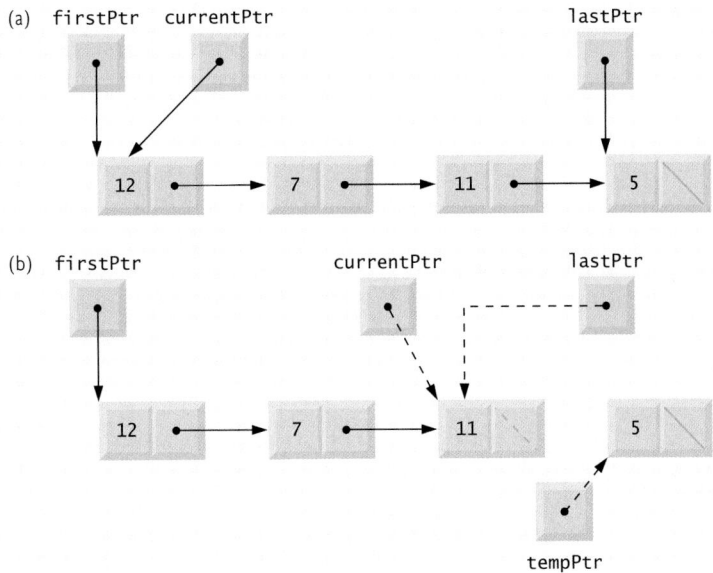

Fig. 21.9 | Operation `removeFromBack` represented graphically.

of the list. The printing algorithm is identical for linked lists, stacks and queues (because we base each of these data structures on the same linked list infrastructure).

Linear and Circular Singly Linked and Doubly Linked Lists

The kind of linked list we have been discussing is a singly linked list—the list begins with a pointer to the first node, and each node contains a pointer to the next node "in sequence." This list terminates with a node whose pointer member has the value 0. A singly linked list may be traversed in only one direction.

A circular, singly linked list (Fig. 21.10) begins with a pointer to the first node, and each node contains a pointer to the next node. The "last node" does not contain a 0 pointer; rather, the pointer in the last node points back to the first node, thus closing the "circle."

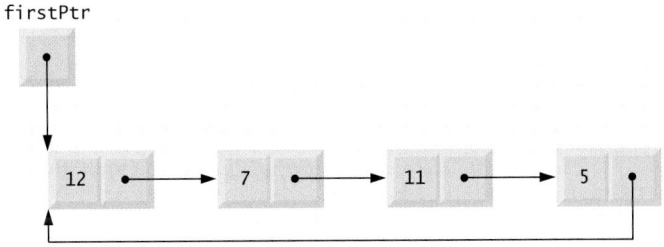

Fig. 21.10 | Circular, singly linked list.

A doubly linked list (Fig. 21.11) allows traversals both forward and backward. Such a list is often implemented with two "start pointers"—one that points to the first element of the list to allow front-to-back traversal of the list and one that points to the last element to allow back-to-front traversal. Each node has both a forward pointer to the next node in the list in the forward direction and a backward pointer to the next node in the list in the backward direction. If your list contains an alphabetized telephone directory, for example, a search for someone whose name begins with a letter near the front of the alphabet might begin from the front of the list. Searching for someone whose name begins with a letter near the end of the alphabet might begin from the back of the list.

In a circular, doubly linked list (Fig. 21.12), the forward pointer of the last node points to the first node, and the backward pointer of the first node points to the last node, thus closing the "circle."

21.5 Stacks

In Chapter 14, Templates, we explained the notion of a stack class template with an underlying array implementation. In this section, we use an underlying pointer-based linked-list implementation. We also discuss stacks in Chapter 22, Standard Template Library (STL).

A stack data structure allows nodes to be added to the stack and removed from the stack only at the top. For this reason, a stack is referred to as a last-in, first-out (LIFO) data structure. One way to implement a stack is as a constrained version of a linked list. In such an implementation, the link member in the last node of the stack is set to null (zero) to indicate the bottom of the stack.

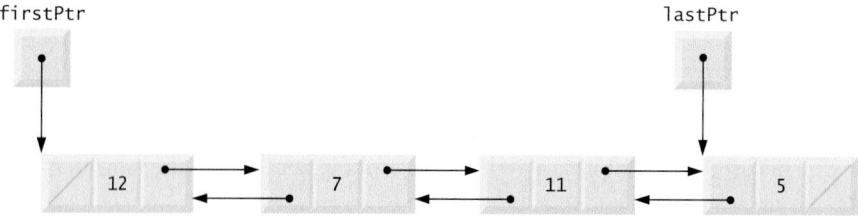

Fig. 21.11 | Doubly linked list.

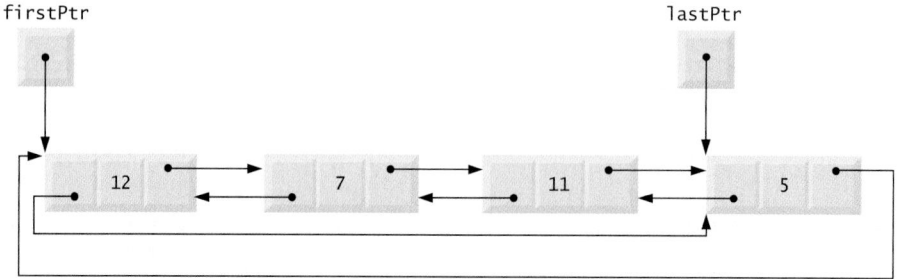

Fig. 21.12 | Circular, doubly linked list.

The primary member functions used to manipulate a stack are push and pop. Function push inserts a new node at the top of the stack. Function pop removes a node from the top of the stack, stores the popped value in a reference variable that is passed to the calling function and returns true if the pop operation was successful (false otherwise).

Stacks have many interesting applications. For example, when a function call is made, the called function must know how to return to its caller, so the return address is pushed onto a stack. If a series of function calls occurs, the successive return values are pushed onto the stack in last-in, first-out order, so that each function can return to its caller. Stacks support recursive function calls in the same manner as conventional nonrecursive calls. Section 6.11 discusses the function call stack in detail.

Stacks provide the memory for, and store the values of, automatic variables on each invocation of a function. When the function returns to its caller or throws an exception, the destructor (if any) for each local object is called, the space for that function's automatic variables is popped off the stack and those variables are no longer known to the program.

Stacks are used by compilers in the process of evaluating expressions and generating machine-language code. The exercises explore several applications of stacks, including using them to develop your own complete working compiler.

We will take advantage of the close relationship between lists and stacks to implement a stack class primarily by reusing a list class. First, we implement the stack class through private inheritance of the list class. Then we implement an identically performing stack class through composition by including a list object as a private member of a stack class. Of course, all of the data structures in this chapter, including these two stack classes, are implemented as templates to encourage further reusability.

The program of Figs. 21.13–21.14 creates a Stack class template (Fig. 21.13) primarily through private inheritance (line 9) of the List class template of Fig. 21.4. We want the Stack to have member functions push (lines 13–16), pop (lines 19–22), isStackEmpty (lines 25–28) and printStack (lines 31–34). Note that these are essentially the insertAtFront, removeFromFront, isEmpty and print functions of the List class template. Of course, the List class template contains other member functions (i.e., insertAtBack and

```
 1   // Fig. 21.13: Stack.h
 2   // Template Stack class definition derived from class List.
 3   #ifndef STACK_H
 4   #define STACK_H
 5
 6   #include "List.h" // List class definition
 7
 8   template< typename STACKTYPE >
 9   class Stack : private List< STACKTYPE >
10   {
11   public:
12      // push calls the List function insertAtFront
13      void push( const STACKTYPE &data )
14      {
15         insertAtFront( data );
16      } // end function push
17
```

Fig. 21.13 | Stack class-template definition. (Part 1 of 2.)

```
18        // pop calls the List function removeFromFront
19        bool pop( STACKTYPE &data )
20        {
21            return removeFromFront( data );
22        } // end function pop
23
24        // isStackEmpty calls the List function isEmpty
25        bool isStackEmpty() const
26        {
27            return isEmpty();
28        } // end function isStackEmpty
29
30        // printStack calls the List function print
31        void printStack() const
32        {
33            print();
34        } // end function print
35    }; // end class Stack
36
37    #endif
```

Fig. 21.13 | Stack class-template definition. (Part 2 of 2.)

removeFromBack) that we would not want to make accessible through the public interface to the Stack class. So when we indicate that the Stack class template is to inherit from the List class template, we specify private inheritance. This makes all the List class template's member functions private in the Stack class template. When we implement the Stack's member functions, we then have each of these call the appropriate member function of the List class—push calls insertAtFront (line 15), pop calls removeFromFront (line 21), isStackEmpty calls isEmpty (line 27) and printStack calls print (line 33)—this is referred to as delegation.

The stack class template is used in main (Fig. 21.14) to instantiate integer stack intStack of type Stack< int > (line 11). Integers 0 through 2 are pushed onto intStack (lines 16–20), then popped off intStack (lines 25–30). The program uses the Stack class template to create doubleStack of type Stack< double > (line 32). Values 1.1, 2.2 and 3.3 are pushed onto doubleStack (lines 38–43), then popped off doubleStack (lines 48–53).

```
1    // Fig. 21.14: Fig21_14.cpp
2    // Template Stack class test program.
3    #include <iostream>
4    using std::cout;
5    using std::endl;
6
7    #include "Stack.h" // Stack class definition
8
9    int main()
10   {
11       Stack< int > intStack; // create Stack of ints
12
```

Fig. 21.14 | A simple stack program. (Part 1 of 3.)

```
13        cout << "processing an integer Stack" << endl;
14
15        // push integers onto intStack
16        for ( int i = 0; i < 3; i++ )
17        {
18           intStack.push( i );
19           intStack.printStack();
20        } // end for
21
22        int popInteger; // store int popped from stack
23
24        // pop integers from intStack
25        while ( !intStack.isStackEmpty() )
26        {
27           intStack.pop( popInteger );
28           cout << popInteger << " popped from stack" << endl;
29           intStack.printStack();
30        } // end while
31
32        Stack< double > doubleStack; // create Stack of doubles
33        double value = 1.1;
34
35        cout << "processing a double Stack" << endl;
36
37        // push floating-point values onto doubleStack
38        for ( int j = 0; j < 3; j++ )
39        {
40           doubleStack.push( value );
41           doubleStack.printStack();
42           value += 1.1;
43        } // end for
44
45        double popDouble; // store double popped from stack
46
47        // pop floating-point values from doubleStack
48        while ( !doubleStack.isStackEmpty() )
49        {
50           doubleStack.pop( popDouble );
51           cout << popDouble << " popped from stack" << endl;
52           doubleStack.printStack();
53        } // end while
54
55        return 0;
56     } // end main
```

```
processing an integer Stack
The list is: 0

The list is: 1 0

The list is: 2 1 0
```
(continued at top of next page...)

Fig. 21.14 | A simple stack program. (Part 2 of 3.)

(...continued from previous page)

```
2 popped from stack
The list is: 1 0

1 popped from stack
The list is: 0

0 popped from stack
The list is empty

processing a double Stack
The list is: 1.1

The list is: 2.2 1.1

The list is: 3.3 2.2 1.1

3.3 popped from stack
The list is: 2.2 1.1

2.2 popped from stack
The list is: 1.1

1.1 popped from stack
The list is empty

All nodes destroyed

All nodes destroyed
```

Fig. 21.14 | A simple stack program. (Part 3 of 3.)

Another way to implement a Stack class template is by reusing the List class template through composition. Figure 21.15 is a new implementation of the Stack class template that contains a List< STACKTYPE > object called stackList (line 38). This version of the Stack class template uses class List from Fig. 21.4. To test this class, use the driver program in Fig. 21.14, but include the new header file—Stackcomposition.h in line 6 of that file. The output of the program is identical for both versions of class Stack.

```
1   // Fig. 21.15: Stackcomposition.h
2   // Template Stack class definition with composed List object.
3   #ifndef STACKCOMPOSITION_H
4   #define STACKCOMPOSITION_H
5
6   #include "List.h" // List class definition
7
8   template< typename STACKTYPE >
9   class Stack
10  {
11  public:
12     // no constructor; List constructor does initialization
```

Fig. 21.15 | Stack class template with a composed List object. (Part 1 of 2.)

```
13
14      // push calls stackList object's insertAtFront member function
15      void push( const STACKTYPE &data )
16      {
17         stackList.insertAtFront( data );
18      } // end function push
19
20      // pop calls stackList object's removeFromFront member function
21      bool pop( STACKTYPE &data )
22      {
23         return stackList.removeFromFront( data );
24      } // end function pop
25
26      // isStackEmpty calls stackList object's isEmpty member function
27      bool isStackEmpty() const
28      {
29         return stackList.isEmpty();
30      } // end function isStackEmpty
31
32      // printStack calls stackList object's print member function
33      void printStack() const
34      {
35         stackList.print();
36      } // end function printStack
37   private:
38      List< STACKTYPE > stackList; // composed List object
39   }; // end class Stack
40
41   #endif
```

Fig. 21.15 | Stack class template with a composed List object. (Part 2 of 2.)

21.6 Queues

A queue is similar to a supermarket checkout line—the first person in line is serviced first, and other customers enter the line at the end and wait to be serviced. Queue nodes are removed only from the head of the queue and are inserted only at the tail of the queue. For this reason, a queue is referred to as a first-in, first-out (FIFO) data structure. The insert and remove operations are known as enqueue and dequeue.

Queues have many applications in computer systems. Computers that have a single processor can service only one user at a time. Entries for the other users are placed in a queue. Each entry gradually advances to the front of the queue as users receive service. The entry at the front of the queue is the next to receive service.

Queues are also used to support print spooling. For example, a single printer might be shared by all users of a network. Many users can send print jobs to the printer, even when the printer is already busy. These print jobs are placed in a queue until the printer becomes available. A program called a spooler managers the queue to ensure that, as each print job completes, the next print job is sent to the printer.

Information packets also wait in queues in computer networks. Each time a packet arrives at a network node, it must be routed to the next node on the network along the path to the packet's final destination. The routing node routes one packet at a time, so additional packets are enqueued until the router can route them.

A file server in a computer network handles file access requests from many clients throughout the network. Servers have a limited capacity to service requests from clients. When that capacity is exceeded, client requests wait in queues.

The program of Figs. 21.16–21.17 creates a Queue class template (Fig. 21.16) through private inheritance (line 9) of the List class template of Fig. 21.4. We want the Queue to have member functions enqueue (lines 13–16), dequeue (lines 19–22), isQueueEmpty (lines 25–28) and printQueue (lines 31–34). Note that these are essentially the insertAtBack, removeFromFront, isEmpty and print functions of the List class template. Of course, the List class template contains other member functions (i.e., insertAtFront and removeFromBack) that we would not want to make accessible through the public interface

```cpp
1   // Fig. 21.16: Queue.h
2   // Template Queue class definition derived from class List.
3   #ifndef QUEUE_H
4   #define QUEUE_H
5
6   #include "List.h" // List class definition
7
8   template< typename QUEUETYPE >
9   class Queue : private List< QUEUETYPE >
10  {
11  public:
12     // enqueue calls List member function insertAtBack
13     void enqueue( const QUEUETYPE &data )
14     {
15        insertAtBack( data );
16     } // end function enqueue
17
18     // dequeue calls List member function removeFromFront
19     bool dequeue( QUEUETYPE &data )
20     {
21        return removeFromFront( data );
22     } // end function dequeue
23
24     // isQueueEmpty calls List member function isEmpty
25     bool isQueueEmpty() const
26     {
27        return isEmpty();
28     } // end function isQueueEmpty
29
30     // printQueue calls List member function print
31     void printQueue() const
32     {
33        print();
34     } // end function printQueue
35  }; // end class Queue
36
37  #endif
```

Fig. 21.16 | Queue class-template definition.

to the Queue class. So when we indicate that the Queue class template is to inherit the List class template, we specify private inheritance. This makes all the List class template's member functions private in the Queue class template. When we implement the Queue's member functions, we have each of these call the appropriate member function of the list class—enqueue calls insertAtBack (line 15), dequeue calls removeFromFront (line 21), isQueueEmpty calls isEmpty (line 27) and printQueue calls print (line 33). Again, this is called delegation.

Figure 21.17 uses the Queue class template to instantiate integer queue intQueue of type Queue< int > (line 11). Integers 0 through 2 are enqueued to intQueue (lines 16–20), then dequeued from intQueue in first-in, first-out order (lines 25–30). Next, the program instantiates queue doubleQueue of type Queue< double > (line 32). Values 1.1, 2.2 and 3.3 are enqueued to doubleQueue (lines 38–43), then dequeued from doubleQueue in first-in, first-out order (lines 48–53).

```cpp
1   // Fig. 21.17: Fig21_17.cpp
2   // Template Queue class test program.
3   #include <iostream>
4   using std::cout;
5   using std::endl;
6
7   #include "Queue.h" // Queue class definition
8
9   int main()
10  {
11     Queue< int > intQueue; // create Queue of integers
12
13     cout << "processing an integer Queue" << endl;
14
15     // enqueue integers onto intQueue
16     for ( int i = 0; i < 3; i++ )
17     {
18        intQueue.enqueue( i );
19        intQueue.printQueue();
20     } // end for
21
22     int dequeueInteger; // store dequeued integer
23
24     // dequeue integers from intQueue
25     while ( !intQueue.isQueueEmpty() )
26     {
27        intQueue.dequeue( dequeueInteger );
28        cout << dequeueInteger << " dequeued" << endl;
29        intQueue.printQueue();
30     } // end while
31
32     Queue< double > doubleQueue; // create Queue of doubles
33     double value = 1.1;
34
35     cout << "processing a double Queue" << endl;
36
```

Fig. 21.17 | Queue-processing program. (Part 1 of 2.)

```
37      // enqueue floating-point values onto doubleQueue
38      for ( int j = 0; j < 3; j++ )
39      {
40         doubleQueue.enqueue( value );
41         doubleQueue.printQueue();
42         value += 1.1;
43      } // end for
44
45      double dequeueDouble; // store dequeued double
46
47      // dequeue floating-point values from doubleQueue
48      while ( !doubleQueue.isQueueEmpty() )
49      {
50         doubleQueue.dequeue( dequeueDouble );
51         cout << dequeueDouble << " dequeued" << endl;
52         doubleQueue.printQueue();
53      } // end while
54
55      return 0;
56  } // end main
```

```
processing an integer Queue
The list is: 0

The list is: 0 1

The list is: 0 1 2

0 dequeued
The list is: 1 2

1 dequeued
The list is: 2

2 dequeued
The list is empty

processing a double Queue
The list is: 1.1

The list is: 1.1 2.2

The list is: 1.1 2.2 3.3

1.1 dequeued
The list is: 2.2 3.3

2.2 dequeued
The list is: 3.3

3.3 dequeued
The list is empty

All nodes destroyed

All nodes destroyed
```

Fig. 21.17 | Queue-processing program. (Part 2 of 2.)

21.7 Trees

Linked lists, stacks and queues are linear data structures. A tree is a nonlinear, two-dimensional data structure. Tree nodes contain two or more links. This section discusses binary trees (Fig. 21.18)—trees whose nodes all contain two links (none, one or both of which may be null).

Basic Terminology

For the purposes of this discussion, refer to nodes A, B, C and D in Fig. 21.18. The root node (node B) is the first node in a tree. Each link in the root node refers to a child (nodes A and D). The left child (node A) is the root node of the left subtree (which contains only node A), and the right child (node D) is the root node of the right subtree (which contains nodes D and C). The children of a single node are called siblings (e.g., nodes A and D are siblings). A node with no children is called a leaf node (e.g., nodes A and C are leaf nodes). Computer scientists normally draw trees from the root node down—exactly the opposite of how trees grow in nature.

Binary Search Trees

This section discusses a special binary tree called a binary search tree. A binary search tree (with no duplicate node values) has the characteristic that the values in any left subtree are less than the value in its parent node, and the values in any right subtree are greater than the value in its parent node. Figure 21.19 illustrates a binary search tree with 9 values. Note that the shape of the binary search tree that corresponds to a set of data can vary, depending on the order in which the values are inserted into the tree.

Implementing the Binary Search Tree Program

The program of Figs. 21.20–21.22 creates a binary search tree and traverses it (i.e., walks through all its nodes) three ways—using recursive inorder, preorder and postorder traversals. We explain these traversal algorithms shortly.

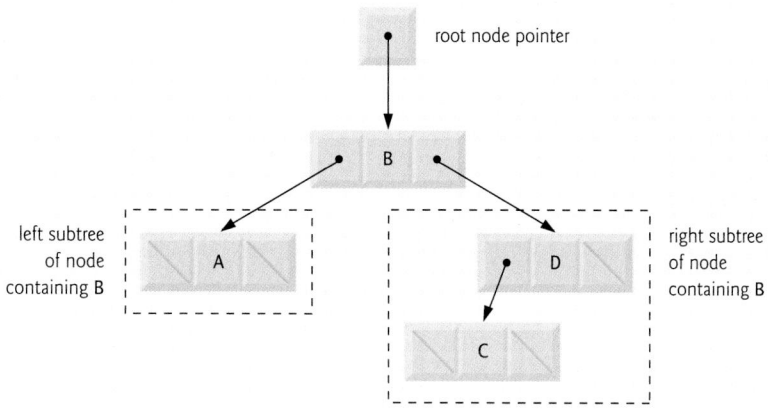

Fig. 21.18 | A graphical representation of a binary tree.

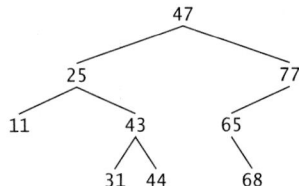

Fig. 21.19 | A binary search tree.

We begin our discussion with the driver program (Fig. 21.22), then continue with the implementations of classes TreeNode (Fig. 21.20) and Tree (Fig. 21.21). Function main (Fig. 21.22) begins by instantiating integer tree intTree of type Tree< int > (line 15). The program prompts for 10 integers, each of which is inserted in the binary tree by calling insertNode (line 24). The program then performs preorder, inorder and postorder traversals (these are explained shortly) of intTree (lines 28, 31 and 34, respectively). The program then instantiates floating-point tree doubleTree of type Tree< double > (line 36). The program prompts for 10 double values, each of which is inserted in the binary tree by calling insertNode (line 46). The program then performs preorder, inorder and postorder traversals of doubleTree (lines 50, 53 and 56, respectively).

```
1   // Fig. 21.20: Treenode.h
2   // Template TreeNode class definition.
3   #ifndef TREENODE_H
4   #define TREENODE_H
5
6   // forward declaration of class Tree
7   template< typename NODETYPE > class Tree;
8
9   // TreeNode class-template definition
10  template< typename NODETYPE >
11  class TreeNode
12  {
13     friend class Tree< NODETYPE >;
14  public:
15     // constructor
16     TreeNode( const NODETYPE &d )
17        : leftPtr( 0 ), // pointer to left subtree
18          data( d ), // tree node data
19          rightPtr( 0 ) // pointer to right substree
20     {
21        // empty body
22     } // end TreeNode constructor
23
24     // return copy of node's data
25     NODETYPE getData() const
26     {
27        return data;
28     } // end getData function
```

Fig. 21.20 | TreeNode class-template definition. (Part 1 of 2.)

```
29    private:
30       TreeNode< NODETYPE > *leftPtr; // pointer to left subtree
31       NODETYPE data;
32       TreeNode< NODETYPE > *rightPtr; // pointer to right subtree
33    }; // end class TreeNode
34
35    #endif
```

Fig. 21.20 | TreeNode class-template definition. (Part 2 of 2.)

```
1     // Fig. 21.21: Tree.h
2     // Template Tree class definition.
3     #ifndef TREE_H
4     #define TREE_H
5
6     #include <iostream>
7     using std::cout;
8     using std::endl;
9
10    #include "Treenode.h"
11
12    // Tree class-template definition
13    template< typename NODETYPE > class Tree
14    {
15    public:
16       Tree(); // constructor
17       void insertNode( const NODETYPE & );
18       void preOrderTraversal() const;
19       void inOrderTraversal() const;
20       void postOrderTraversal() const;
21    private:
22       TreeNode< NODETYPE > *rootPtr;
23
24       // utility functions
25       void insertNodeHelper( TreeNode< NODETYPE > **, const NODETYPE & );
26       void preOrderHelper( TreeNode< NODETYPE > * ) const;
27       void inOrderHelper( TreeNode< NODETYPE > * ) const;
28       void postOrderHelper( TreeNode< NODETYPE > * ) const;
29    }; // end class Tree
30
31    // constructor
32    template< typename NODETYPE >
33    Tree< NODETYPE >::Tree()
34    {
35       rootPtr = 0; // indicate tree is initially empty
36    } // end Tree constructor
37
38    // insert node in Tree
39    template< typename NODETYPE >
40    void Tree< NODETYPE >::insertNode( const NODETYPE &value )
41    {
```

Fig. 21.21 | Tree class-template definition. (Part 1 of 3.)

```
42        insertNodeHelper( &rootPtr, value );
43    } // end function insertNode
44
45    // utility function called by insertNode; receives a pointer
46    // to a pointer so that the function can modify pointer's value
47    template< typename NODETYPE >
48    void Tree< NODETYPE >::insertNodeHelper(
49       TreeNode< NODETYPE > **ptr, const NODETYPE &value )
50    {
51       // subtree is empty; create new TreeNode containing value
52       if ( *ptr == 0 )
53          *ptr = new TreeNode< NODETYPE >( value );
54       else // subtree is not empty
55       {
56          // data to insert is less than data in current node
57          if ( value < ( *ptr )->data )
58             insertNodeHelper( &( ( *ptr )->leftPtr ), value );
59          else
60          {
61             // data to insert is greater than data in current node
62             if ( value > ( *ptr )->data )
63                insertNodeHelper( &( ( *ptr )->rightPtr ), value );
64             else // duplicate data value ignored
65                cout << value << " dup" << endl;
66          } // end else
67       } // end else
68    } // end function insertNodeHelper
69
70    // begin preorder traversal of Tree
71    template< typename NODETYPE >
72    void Tree< NODETYPE >::preOrderTraversal() const
73    {
74       preOrderHelper( rootPtr );
75    } // end function preOrderTraversal
76
77    // utility function to perform preorder traversal of Tree
78    template< typename NODETYPE >
79    void Tree< NODETYPE >::preOrderHelper( TreeNode< NODETYPE > *ptr ) const
80    {
81       if ( ptr != 0 )
82       {
83          cout << ptr->data << ' '; // process node
84          preOrderHelper( ptr->leftPtr ); // traverse left subtree
85          preOrderHelper( ptr->rightPtr ); // traverse right subtree
86       } // end if
87    } // end function preOrderHelper
88
89    // begin inorder traversal of Tree
90    template< typename NODETYPE >
91    void Tree< NODETYPE >::inOrderTraversal() const
92    {
93       inOrderHelper( rootPtr );
94    } // end function inOrderTraversal
```

Fig. 21.21 | Tree class-template definition. (Part 2 of 3.)

```
 95
 96   // utility function to perform inorder traversal of Tree
 97   template< typename NODETYPE >
 98   void Tree< NODETYPE >::inOrderHelper( TreeNode< NODETYPE > *ptr ) const
 99   {
100      if ( ptr != 0 )
101      {
102         inOrderHelper( ptr->leftPtr ); // traverse left subtree
103         cout << ptr->data << ' '; // process node
104         inOrderHelper( ptr->rightPtr ); // traverse right subtree
105      } // end if
106   } // end function inOrderHelper
107
108   // begin postorder traversal of Tree
109   template< typename NODETYPE >
110   void Tree< NODETYPE >::postOrderTraversal() const
111   {
112      postOrderHelper( rootPtr );
113   } // end function postOrderTraversal
114
115   // utility function to perform postorder traversal of Tree
116   template< typename NODETYPE >
117   void Tree< NODETYPE >::postOrderHelper(
118      TreeNode< NODETYPE > *ptr ) const
119   {
120      if ( ptr != 0 )
121      {
122         postOrderHelper( ptr->leftPtr ); // traverse left subtree
123         postOrderHelper( ptr->rightPtr ); // traverse right subtree
124         cout << ptr->data << ' '; // process node
125      } // end if
126   } // end function postOrderHelper
127
128   #endif
```

Fig. 21.21 | Tree class-template definition. (Part 3 of 3.)

Now we discuss the class-template definitions. We begin with the TreeNode class template (Fig. 21.20) definition that declares Tree< NODETYPE > as its friend (line 13). This makes all member functions of a given specialization of class template Tree (Fig. 21.21) friends of the corresponding specialization of class template TreeNode, so they can access the private members of TreeNode objects of that type. Because the TreeNode template parameter NODETYPE is used as the template argument for Tree in the friend declaration, TreeNodes specialized with a particular type can be processed only by a Tree specialized with the same type (e.g., a Tree of int values manages TreeNode objects that store int values).

Lines 30–32 declare a TreeNode's private data—the node's data value, and pointers leftPtr (to the node's left subtree) and rightPtr (to the node's right subtree). The constructor (lines 16–22) sets data to the value supplied as a constructor argument and sets pointers leftPtr and rightPtr to zero (thus initializing this node to be a leaf node). Member function getData (lines 25–28) returns the data value.

```
1    // Fig. 21.22: Fig21_22.cpp
2    // Tree class test program.
3    #include <iostream>
4    using std::cout;
5    using std::cin;
6    using std::fixed;
7
8    #include <iomanip>
9    using std::setprecision;
10
11   #include "Tree.h" // Tree class definition
12
13   int main()
14   {
15      Tree< int > intTree; // create Tree of int values
16      int intValue;
17
18      cout << "Enter 10 integer values:\n";
19
20      // insert 10 integers to intTree
21      for ( int i = 0; i < 10; i++ )
22      {
23         cin >> intValue;
24         intTree.insertNode( intValue );
25      } // end for
26
27      cout << "\nPreorder traversal\n";
28      intTree.preOrderTraversal();
29
30      cout << "\nInorder traversal\n";
31      intTree.inOrderTraversal();
32
33      cout << "\nPostorder traversal\n";
34      intTree.postOrderTraversal();
35
36      Tree< double > doubleTree; // create Tree of double values
37      double doubleValue;
38
39      cout << fixed << setprecision( 1 )
40         << "\n\n\nEnter 10 double values:\n";
41
42      // insert 10 doubles to doubleTree
43      for ( int j = 0; j < 10; j++ )
44      {
45         cin >> doubleValue;
46         doubleTree.insertNode( doubleValue );
47      } // end for
48
49      cout << "\nPreorder traversal\n";
50      doubleTree.preOrderTraversal();
51
52      cout << "\nInorder traversal\n";
53      doubleTree.inOrderTraversal();
```

Fig. 21.22 | Creating and traversing a binary tree. (Part 1 of 2.)

```
54
55        cout << "\nPostorder traversal\n";
56        doubleTree.postOrderTraversal();
57
58        cout << endl;
59        return 0;
60   } // end main
```

```
Enter 10 integer values:
50 25 75 12 33 67 88 6 13 68

Preorder traversal
50 25 12 6 13 33 75 67 68 88
Inorder traversal
6 12 13 25 33 50 67 68 75 88
Postorder traversal
6 13 12 33 25 68 67 88 75 50

Enter 10 double values:
39.2 16.5 82.7 3.3 65.2 90.8 1.1 4.4 89.5 92.5

Preorder traversal
39.2 16.5 3.3 1.1 4.4 82.7 65.2 90.8 89.5 92.5
Inorder traversal
1.1 3.3 4.4 16.5 39.2 65.2 82.7 89.5 90.8 92.5
Postorder traversal
1.1 4.4 3.3 16.5 65.2 89.5 92.5 90.8 82.7 39.2
```

Fig. 21.22 | Creating and traversing a binary tree. (Part 2 of 2.)

The Tree class template (Fig. 21.21) has as private data rootPtr (line 22), a pointer to the root node of the tree. Lines 17–20 of the class template declare the public member functions insertNode (that inserts a new node in the tree) and preOrderTraversal, inOrderTraversal and postOrderTraversal, each of which walks the tree in the designated manner. Each of these member functions calls its own separate recursive utility function to perform the appropriate operations on the internal representation of the tree, so the program is not required to access the underlying private data to perform these functions. Remember that the recursion requires us to pass in a pointer that represents the next subtree to process. The Tree constructor initializes rootPtr to zero to indicate that the tree is initially empty.

The Tree class's utility function insertNodeHelper (lines 47–68) is called by insert-Node (lines 39–43) to recursively insert a node into the tree. *A node can only be inserted as a leaf node in a binary search tree.* If the tree is empty, a new TreeNode is created, initialized and inserted in the tree (lines 53–54).

If the tree is not empty, the program compares the value to be inserted with the data value in the root node. If the insert value is smaller (line 57), the program recursively calls insertNodeHelper (line 58) to insert the value in the left subtree. If the insert value is larger (line 62), the program recursively calls insertNodeHelper (line 64) to insert the value in the right subtree. If the value to be inserted is identical to the data value in the root node, the program prints the message " dup" (line 65) and returns without inserting the duplicate value into the tree. Note that insertNode passes the address of rootPtr to insertNode-

Helper (line 42) so it can modify the value stored in rootPtr (i.e., the address of the root node). To receive a pointer to rootPtr (which is also a pointer), insertNodeHelper's first argument is declared as a pointer to a pointer to a TreeNode.

Each of the member functions inOrderTraversal (lines 90–94), preOrderTraversal (lines 71–75) and postOrderTraversal (lines 109–113) traverses the tree and prints the node values. For the purpose of the following discussion, we use the binary search tree in Fig. 21.23.

Inorder Traversal Algorithm

Function inOrderTraversal invokes utility function inOrderHelper to perform the inorder traversal of the binary tree. The steps for an inorder traversal are:

1. Traverse the left subtree with an inorder traversal. (This is performed by the call to inOrderHelper at line 102.)

2. Process the value in the node—i.e., print the node value (line 103).

3. Traverse the right subtree with an inorder traversal. (This is performed by the call to inOrderHelper at line 104.)

The value in a node is not processed until the values in its left subtree are processed, because each call to inOrderHelper immediately calls inOrderHelper again with the pointer to the left subtree. The inorder traversal of the tree in Fig. 21.23 is

     6 13 17 27 33 42 48

Note that the inorder traversal of a binary search tree prints the node values in ascending order. The process of creating a binary search tree actually sorts the data—thus, this process is called the binary tree sort.

Preorder Traversal Algorithm

Function preOrderTraversal invokes utility function preOrderHelper to perform the preorder traversal of the binary tree. The steps for an preorder traversal are:

1. Process the value in the node (line 83).

2. Traverse the left subtree with a preorder traversal. (This is performed by the call to preOrderHelper at line 84.)

3. Traverse the right subtree with a preorder traversal. (This is performed by the call to preOrderHelper at line 85.)

The value in each node is processed as the node is visited. After the value in a given node is processed, the values in the left subtree are processed. Then the values in the right subtree are processed. The preorder traversal of the tree in Fig. 21.23 is

     27 13 6 17 42 33 48

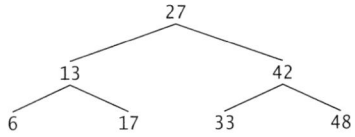

Fig. 21.23 | A binary search tree.

Postorder Traversal Algorithm

Function `postOrderTraversal` invokes utility function `postOrderHelper` to perform the postorder traversal of the binary tree. The steps for an postorder traversal are:

1. Traverse the left subtree with a postorder traversal. (This is performed by the call to `postOrderHelper` at line 122.)

2. Traverse the right subtree with a postorder traversal. (This is performed by the call to `postOrderHelper` at line 123.)

3. Process the value in the node (line 124).

The value in each node is not printed until the values of its children are printed. The `postOrderTraversal` of the tree in Fig. 21.23 is

```
6  17  13  33  48  42  27
```

Duplicate Elimination

The binary search tree facilitates duplicate elimination. As the tree is being created, an attempt to insert a duplicate value will be recognized, because a duplicate will follow the same "go left" or "go right" decisions on each comparison as the original value did when it was inserted in the tree. Thus, the duplicate will eventually be compared with a node containing the same value. The duplicate value may be discarded at this point.

Searching a binary tree for a value that matches a key value is also fast. If the tree is balanced, then each branch contains about half the number of nodes in the tree. Each comparison of a node to the search key eliminates half the nodes. This is called an $O(\log n)$ algorithm (Big O notation is discussed in Chapter 20). So a binary search tree with n elements would require a maximum of $\log_2 n$ comparisons either to find a match or to determine that no match exists. This means, for example, that when searching a (balanced) 1000-element binary search tree, no more than 10 comparisons need to be made, because $2^{10} > 1000$. When searching a (balanced) 1,000,000-element binary search tree, no more than 20 comparisons need to be made, because $2^{20} > 1,000,000$.

Overview of the Binary Tree Exercises

In the exercises, algorithms are presented for several other binary tree operations such as deleting an item from a binary tree, printing a binary tree in a two-dimensional tree format and performing a level-order traversal of a binary tree. The level-order traversal of a binary tree visits the nodes of the tree row by row, starting at the root node level. On each level of the tree, the nodes are visited from left to right. Other binary tree exercises include allowing a binary search tree to contain duplicate values, inserting string values in a binary tree and determining how many levels are contained in a binary tree.

Summary

- Dynamic data structures grow and shrink during execution.
- Linked lists are collections of data items "lined up in a row"—insertions and removals are made anywhere in a linked list.
- Stacks are important in compilers and operating systems: Insertions and removals are made only at one end of a stack—its top.

- Queues represent waiting lines; insertions are made at the back (also referred to as the tail) of a queue and removals are made from the front (also referred to as the head).
- Binary trees facilitate high-speed searching and sorting of data, efficient elimination of duplicate data items, representation of file system directories and compilation of expressions into machine language.
- A self-referential class contains a pointer member that points to a class object of the same class type.
- Self-referential class objects can be linked together to form useful data structures such as lists, queues, stacks and trees.
- The limit for dynamic memory allocation can be as large as the amount of available physical memory in the computer or the amount of available virtual memory in a virtual memory system.
- A linked list is a linear collection of self-referential class objects, called nodes, connected by pointer links—hence, the term "linked" list.
- A linked list is accessed via a pointer to the first node of the list. Each subsequent node is accessed via the link-pointer member stored in the previous node.
- Linked lists, stacks and queues are linear data structures. Trees are nonlinear data structures.
- A linked list is appropriate when the number of data elements to be represented at one time is unpredictable.
- Linked lists are dynamic, so the length of a list can increase or decrease as necessary.
- A singly linked list begins with a pointer to the first node, and each node contains a pointer to the next node "in sequence."
- A circular, singly linked list begins with a pointer to the first node, and each node contains a pointer to the next node. The "last node" does not contain a null pointer; rather, the pointer in the last node points back to the first node, thus closing the "circle."
- A doubly linked list allows traversals both forward and backward.
- A doubly linked list is often implemented with two "start pointers"—one that points to the first element of the list to allow front-to-back traversal of the list and one that points to the last element to allow back-to-front traversal. Each node has both a forward pointer to the next node in the list in the forward direction and a backward pointer to the next node in the backward direction.
- In a circular, doubly linked list, the forward pointer of the last node points to the first node, and the backward pointer of the first node points to the last node, thus closing the "circle."
- A stack data structure allows nodes to be added to the stack and removed from the stack only at the top.
- A stack is referred to as a last-in, first-out (LIFO) data structure.
- The primary member functions used to manipulate a stack are push and pop. Function push inserts a new node at the top of the stack. Function pop removes a node from the top of the stack.
- A queue is similar to a supermarket checkout line—the first person in line is serviced first, and other customers enter the line at the end and wait to be serviced.
- Queue nodes are removed only from the head of the queue and are inserted only at the tail of the queue.
- A queue is referred to as a first-in, first-out (FIFO) data structure. The insert and remove operations are known as enqueue and dequeue.
- Binary trees are trees whose nodes all contain two links (none, one or both of which may be null).
- The root node is the first node in a tree.

- Each link in the root node refers to a child. The left child is the root node of the left subtree, and the right child is the root node of the right subtree.
- The children of a single node are called siblings. A node with no children is called a leaf node.
- A binary search tree (with no duplicate node values) has the characteristic that the values in any left subtree are less than the value in its parent node, and the values in any right subtree are greater than the value in its parent node.
- A node can only be inserted as a leaf node in a binary search tree.
- An inorder traversal of a binary tree traverses the left subtree inorder, processes the value in the root node and then traverses the right subtree inorder. The value in a node is not processed until the values in its left subtree are processed.
- A preorder traversal processes the value in the root node, traverses the left subtree preorder, then traverses the right subtree preorder. The value in each node is processed as the node is encountered.
- A postorder traversal traverses the left subtree postorder, traverses the right subtree postorder, then processes the value in the root node. The value in each node is not processed until the values in both its subtrees are processed.
- The binary search tree facilitates duplicate elimination. As the tree is being created, an attempt to insert a duplicate value will be recognized and the duplicate value may be discarded.
- The level-order traversal of a binary tree visits the nodes of the tree row by row, starting at the root node level. On each level of the tree, the nodes are visited from left to right.

Terminology

binary search tree
binary tree
binary tree sort
child node
circular, doubly linked list
circular, singly linked list
data structure
delegation
dequeue
doubly linked list
duplicate elimination
dynamic data structures
enqueue
first-in, first-out (FIFO)
head of a queue
inorder traversal of a binary tree
inserting a node
last-in, first-out (LIFO)
leaf node
left child
left subtree
level-order traversal
linear data structure
link

linked list
node
nonlinear data structure
parent node
pointer link
pop
postorder traversal of a binary tree
preorder traversal of a binary tree
print spooling
push
queue
right child
right subtree
root node
self-referential structure
siblings
singly linked list
spooler
stack
tail of a queue
top of a stack

Self-Review Exercises

21.1   Fill in the blanks in each of the following:
   a) A self-_____ class is used to form dynamic data structures that can grow and shrink at execution time
   b) The _____ operator is used to dynamically allocate memory and construct an object; this operator returns a pointer to the object.
   c) A(n) _____ is a constrained version of a linked list in which nodes can be inserted and deleted only from the start of the list and node values are returned in last-in, first-out order.
   d) A function that does not alter a linked list, but looks at the list to determine whether it is empty, is an example of a(n) _____ function.
   e) A queue is referred to as a(n) _____ data structure, because the first nodes inserted are the first nodes removed.
   f) The pointer to the next node in a linked list is referred to as a(n) _____.
   g) The _____ operator is used to destroy an object and release dynamically allocated memory.
   h) A(n) _____ is a constrained version of a linked list in which nodes can be inserted only at the end of the list and deleted only from the start of the list.
   i) A(n) _____ is a nonlinear, two-dimensional data structure that contains nodes with two or more links.
   j) A stack is referred to as a(n) _____ data structure, because the last node inserted is the first node removed.
   k) The nodes of a(n) _____ tree contain two link members.
   l) The first node of a tree is the _____ node.
   m) Each link in a tree node points to a(n) _____ or _____ of that node.
   n) A tree node that has no children is called a(n) _____ node.
   o) The four traversal algorithms we mentioned in the text for binary search trees are _____, _____, _____ and _____.

21.2   What are the differences between a linked list and a stack?

21.3   What are the differences between a stack and a queue?

21.4   Perhaps a more appropriate title for this chapter would have been "Reusable Data Structures." Comment on how each of the following entities or concepts contributes to the reusability of data structures:
   a) classes
   b) class templates
   c) inheritance
   d) `private` inheritance
   e) composition

21.5   Manually provide the inorder, preorder and postorder traversals of the binary search tree of Fig. 21.24.

Answers to Self-Review Exercises

21.1   a) referential. b) `new`. c) stack. d) predicate. e) first-in, first-out (FIFO). f) link. g) `delete`. h) queue. i) tree. j) last-in, first-out (LIFO). k) binary. l) root. m) child or subtree. n) leaf. o) inorder, preorder, postorder and level order.

21.2   It is possible to insert a node anywhere in a linked list and remove a node from anywhere in a linked list. Nodes in a stack may only be inserted at the top of the stack and removed from the top of a stack.

21.3   A queue data structure allows nodes to be removed only from the head of the queue and inserted only at the tail of the queue. A queue is referred to as a first-in, first-out (FIFO) data structure. A stack data structure allows nodes to be added to the stack and removed from the stack only at the top. A stack is referred to as a last-in, first-out (LIFO) data structure.

21.4   a) Classes allow us to instantiate as many data structure objects of a certain type (i.e., class) as we wish.

b) Class templates enable us to instantiate related classes, each based on different type parameters—we can then generate as many objects of each template class as we like.

c) Inheritance enables us to reuse code from a base class in a derived class, so that the derived-class data structure is also a base-class data structure (with `public` inheritance, that is).

d) Private inheritance enables us to reuse portions of the code from a base class to form a derived-class data structure; because the inheritance is `private`, all `public` base-class member functions become `private` in the derived class. This enables us to prevent clients of the derived-class data structure from accessing base-class member functions that do not apply to the derived class.

e) Composition enables us to reuse code by making a class object data structure a member of a composed class; if we make the class object a `private` member of the composed class, then the class object's `public` member functions are not available through the composed object's interface.

21.5   The inorder traversal is

    11 18 19 28 32 40 44 49 69 71 72 83 92 97 99

The preorder traversal is

    49 28 18 11 19 40 32 44 83 71 69 72 97 92 99

The postorder traversal is

    11 19 18 32 44 40 28 69 72 71 92 99 97 83 49

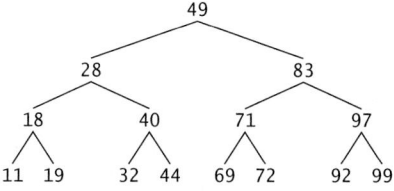

Fig. 21.24 | A 15-node binary search tree.

Exercises

21.6   Write a program that concatenates two linked list objects of characters. The program should include function `concatenate`, which takes references to both list objects as arguments and concatenates the second list to the first list.

21.7 Write a program that merges two ordered list objects of integers into a single ordered list object of integers. Function merge should receive references to each of the list objects to be merged and reference to a list object into which the merged elements will be placed.

21.8 Write a program that inserts 25 random integers from 0 to 100 in order in a linked list object. The program should calculate the sum of the elements and the floating-point average of the elements.

21.9 Write a program that creates a linked list object of 10 characters and creates a second list object containing a copy of the first list, but in reverse order.

21.10 Write a program that inputs a line of text and uses a stack object to print the line reversed.

21.11 Write a program that uses a stack object to determine if a string is a palindrome (i.e., the string is spelled identically backward and forward). The program should ignore spaces and punctuation.

21.12 Stacks are used by compilers to help in the process of evaluating expressions and generating machine language code. In this and the next exercise, we investigate how compilers evaluate arithmetic expressions consisting only of constants, operators and parentheses.

Humans generally write expressions like 3 + 4 and 7 / 9 in which the operator (+ or / here) is written between its operands—this is called *infix notation*. Computers "prefer" *postfix notation* in which the operator is written to the right of its two operands. The preceding infix expressions would appear in postfix notation as 3 4 + and 7 9 /, respectively.

To evaluate a complex infix expression, a compiler would first convert the expression to postfix notation and evaluate the postfix version of the expression. Each of these algorithms requires only a single left-to-right pass of the expression. Each algorithm uses a stack object in support of its operation, and in each algorithm the stack is used for a different purpose.

In this exercise, you will write a C++ version of the infix-to-postfix conversion algorithm. In the next exercise, you will write a C++ version of the postfix expression evaluation algorithm. Later in the chapter, you will discover that code you write in this exercise can help you implement a complete working compiler.

Write a program that converts an ordinary infix arithmetic expression (assume a valid expression is entered) with single-digit integers such as

```
(6 + 2) * 5 - 8 / 4
```

to a postfix expression. The postfix version of the preceding infix expression is

```
6 2 + 5 * 8 4 / -
```

The program should read the expression into character array infix and use modified versions of the stack functions implemented in this chapter to help create the postfix expression in character array postfix. The algorithm for creating a postfix expression is as follows:
1) Push a left parenthesis '(' onto the stack.
2) Append a right parenthesis ')' to the end of infix.
3) While the stack is not empty, read infix from left to right and do the following:
> If the current character in infix is a digit, copy it to the next element of postfix.
> If the current character in infix is a left parenthesis, push it onto the stack.
> If the current character in infix is an operator,
>> Pop operators (if there are any) at the top of the stack while they have equal or higher precedence than the current operator, and insert the popped operators in postfix.

Push the current character in infix onto the stack.

If the current character in infix is a right parenthesis

Pop operators from the top of the stack and insert them in postfix until a left parenthesis is at the top of the stack.

Pop (and discard) the left parenthesis from the stack.

The following arithmetic operations are allowed in an expression:

+   addition
-   subtraction
*   multiplication
/   division
^   exponentiation
%   modulus

[*Note:* We assume left to right associativity for all operators for the purpose of this exercise.] The stack should be maintained with stack nodes, each containing a data member and a pointer to the next stack node.

Some of the functional capabilities you may want to provide are:

a) function convertToPostfix that converts the infix expression to postfix notation
b) function isOperator that determines whether c is an operator
c) function precedence that determines whether the precedence of operator1 is less than, equal to or greater than the precedence of operator2 (the function returns −1, 0 and 1, respectively)
d) function push that pushes a value onto the stack
e) function pop that pops a value off the stack
f) function stackTop that returns the top value of the stack without popping the stack
g) function isEmpty that determines if the stack is empty
h) function printStack that prints the stack

21.13 Write a program that evaluates a postfix expression (assume it is valid) such as

6 2 + 5 * 8 4 / -

The program should read a postfix expression consisting of digits and operators into a character array. Using modified versions of the stack functions implemented earlier in this chapter, the program should scan the expression and evaluate it. The algorithm is as follows:

1) Append the null character ('\0') to the end of the postfix expression. When the null character is encountered, no further processing is necessary.
2) While '\0' has not been encountered, read the expression from left to right.

If the current character is a digit,

Push its integer value onto the stack (the integer value of a digit character is its value in the computer's character set minus the value of '0' in the computer's character set).

Otherwise, if the current character is an *operator*,

Pop the two top elements of the stack into variables x and y.

Calculate y *operator* x.

Push the result of the calculation onto the stack.

3) When the null character is encountered in the expression, pop the top value of the stack. This is the result of the postfix expression.

[*Note*: In *Step 2* above, if the operator is '/', the top of the stack is 2 and the next element in the stack is 8, then pop 2 into x, pop 8 into y, evaluate 8 / 2 and push the result, 4, back onto the stack. This note also applies to operator '-'.] The arithmetic operations allowed in an expression are

+   addition
-   subtraction

      *   multiplication
      /   division
      ^   exponentiation
      %   modulus

[*Note:* We assume left to right associativity for all operators for the purpose of this exercise.] The stack should be maintained with stack nodes that contain an `int` data member and a pointer to the next stack node. You may want to provide the following functional capabilities:

  a) function `evaluatePostfixExpression` that evaluates the postfix expression
  b) function `calculate` that evaluates the expression op1 operator op2
  c) function `push` that pushes a value onto the stack
  d) function `pop` that pops a value off the stack
  e) function `isEmpty` that determines if the stack is empty
  f) function `printStack` that prints the stack

21.14 Modify the postfix evaluator program of Exercise 21.13 so that it can process integer operands larger than 9.

21.15 *(Supermarket Simulation)* Write a program that simulates a checkout line at a supermarket. The line is a queue object. Customers (i.e., customer objects) arrive in random integer intervals of 1–4 minutes. Also, each customer is served in random integer intervals of 1–4 minutes. Obviously, the rates need to be balanced. If the average arrival rate is larger than the average service rate, the queue will grow infinitely. Even with "balanced" rates, randomness can still cause long lines. Run the supermarket simulation for a 12-hour day (720 minutes) using the following algorithm:

  1) Choose a random integer between 1 and 4 to determine the minute at which the first customer arrives.
  2) At the first customer's arrival time:
    Determine customer's service time (random integer from 1 to 4);
    Begin servicing the customer;
    Schedule arrival time of next customer (random integer 1 to 4 added to the current time).
  3) For each minute of the day:
    If the next customer arrives,
      Say so,
      Enqueue the customer;
      Schedule the arrival time of the next customer;
    If service was completed for the last customer;
      Say so
      Dequeue next customer to be serviced
      Determine customer's service completion time
        (random integer from 1 to 4 added to the current time).

Now run your simulation for 720 minutes, and answer each of the following:

  a) What is the maximum number of customers in the queue at any time?
  b) What is the longest wait any one customer experiences?
  c) What happens if the arrival interval is changed from 1–4 minutes to 1–3 minutes?

21.16 Modify the program of Figs. 21.20–21.22 to allow the binary tree object to contain duplicates.

21.17 Write a program based on Figs. 21.20–21.22 that inputs a line of text, tokenizes the sentence into separate words (you may want to use the `strtok` library function), inserts the words in a binary search tree and prints the inorder, preorder and postorder traversals of the tree. Use an OOP approach.

21.18 In this chapter, we saw that duplicate elimination is straightforward when creating a binary search tree. Describe how you would perform duplicate elimination using only a one-dimensional array. Compare the performance of array-based duplicate elimination with the performance of binary-search-tree-based duplicate elimination.

21.19 Write a function depth that receives a binary tree and determines how many levels it has.

21.20 (*Recursively Print a List Backward*) Write a member function printListBackward that recursively outputs the items in a linked list object in reverse order. Write a test program that creates a sorted list of integers and prints the list in reverse order.

21.21 (*Recursively Search a List*) Write a member function searchList that recursively searches a linked list object for a specified value. The function should return a pointer to the value if it is found; otherwise, null should be returned. Use your function in a test program that creates a list of integers. The program should prompt the user for a value to locate in the list.

21.22 (*Binary Tree Delete*) In this exercise, we discuss deleting items from binary search trees. The deletion algorithm is not as straightforward as the insertion algorithm. There are three cases that are encountered when deleting an item—the item is contained in a leaf node (i.e., it has no children), the item is contained in a node that has one child or the item is contained in a node that has two children.

If the item to be deleted is contained in a leaf node, the node is deleted and the pointer in the parent node is set to null.

If the item to be deleted is contained in a node with one child, the pointer in the parent node is set to point to the child node and the node containing the data item is deleted. This causes the child node to take the place of the deleted node in the tree.

The last case is the most difficult. When a node with two children is deleted, another node in the tree must take its place. However, the pointer in the parent node cannot be assigned to point to one of the children of the node to be deleted. In most cases, the resulting binary search tree would not adhere to the following characteristic of binary search trees (with no duplicate values): *The values in any left subtree are less than the value in the parent node, and the values in any right subtree are greater than the value in the parent node.*

Which node is used as a *replacement node* to maintain this characteristic? Either the node containing the largest value in the tree less than the value in the node being deleted, or the node containing the smallest value in the tree greater than the value in the node being deleted. Let us consider the node with the smaller value. In a binary search tree, the largest value less than a parent's value is located in the left subtree of the parent node and is guaranteed to be contained in the rightmost node of the subtree. This node is located by walking down the left subtree to the right until the pointer to the right child of the current node is null. We are now pointing to the replacement node, which is either a leaf node or a node with one child to its left. If the replacement node is a leaf node, the steps to perform the deletion are as follows:

1) Store the pointer to the node to be deleted in a temporary pointer variable (this pointer is used to delete the dynamically allocated memory).
2) Set the pointer in the parent of the node being deleted to point to the replacement node.
3) Set the pointer in the parent of the replacement node to null.
4) Set the pointer to the right subtree in the replacement node to point to the right subtree of the node to be deleted.
5) Delete the node to which the temporary pointer variable points.

The deletion steps for a replacement node with a left child are similar to those for a replacement node with no children, but the algorithm also must move the child into the replacement node's position in the tree. If the replacement node is a node with a left child, the steps to perform the deletion are as follows:

1) Store the pointer to the node to be deleted in a temporary pointer variable.
2) Set the pointer in the parent of the node being deleted to point to the replacement node.
3) Set the pointer in the parent of the replacement node to point to the left child of the replacement node.
4) Set the pointer to the right subtree in the replacement node to point to the right subtree of the node to be deleted.
5) Delete the node to which the temporary pointer variable points.

Write member function `deleteNode`, which takes as its arguments a pointer to the root node of the tree object and the value to be deleted. The function should locate in the tree the node containing the value to be deleted and use the algorithms discussed here to delete the node. The function should print a message that indicates whether the value is deleted. Modify the program of Figs. 21.20–21.22 to use this function. After deleting an item, call the `inOrder`, `preOrder` and `postOrder` traversal functions to confirm that the delete operation was performed correctly.

21.23 (*Binary Tree Search*) Write member function `binaryTreeSearch`, which attempts to locate a specified value in a binary search tree object. The function should take as arguments a pointer to the root node of the binary tree and a search key to be located. If the node containing the search key is found, the function should return a pointer to that node; otherwise, the function should return a null pointer.

21.24 (*Level-Order Binary Tree Traversal*) The program of Figs. 21.20–21.22 illustrated three recursive methods of traversing a binary tree—inorder, preorder and postorder traversals. This exercise presents the *level-order traversal* of a binary tree, in which the node values are printed level by level, starting at the root node level. The nodes on each level are printed from left to right. The level-order traversal is not a recursive algorithm. It uses a queue object to control the output of the nodes. The algorithm is as follows:

1) Insert the root node in the queue
2) While there are nodes left in the queue,
      Get the next node in the queue
      Print the node's value
      If the pointer to the left child of the node is not null
          Insert the left child node in the queue
      If the pointer to the right child of the node is not null
          Insert the right child node in the queue.

Write member function `levelOrder` to perform a level-order traversal of a binary tree object. Modify the program of Figs. 21.20–21.22 to use this function. [*Note:* You will also need to modify and incorporate the queue-processing functions of Fig. 21.16 in this program.]

21.25 (*Printing Trees*) Write a recursive member function `outputTree` to display a binary tree object on the screen. The function should output the tree row by row, with the top of the tree at the left of the screen and the bottom of the tree toward the right of the screen. Each row is output vertically. For example, the binary tree illustrated in Fig. 21.24 is output as follows:

Note that the rightmost leaf node appears at the top of the output in the rightmost column and the root node appears at the left of the output. Each column of output starts five spaces to the right of the previous column. Function `outputTree` should receive an argument `totalSpaces` representing the number of spaces preceding the value to be output (this variable should start at zero, so the root node is output at the left of the screen). The function uses a modified inorder traversal to output the tree—it starts at the rightmost node in the tree and works back to the left. The algorithm is as follows:

> While the pointer to the current node is not null
>> Recursively call `outputTree` with the right subtree of the current node and
>>> `totalSpaces + 5`
>> Use a for structure to count from 1 to `totalSpaces` and output spaces
>> Output the value in the current node
>> Set the pointer to the current node to point to the left subtree of the current node
>> Increment `totalSpaces` by 5.

Special Section: Building Your Own Compiler

In Exercise 8.18 and Exercise 8.19, we introduced Simpletron Machine Language (SML) and you implemented a Simpletron computer simulator to execute programs written in SML. In this section, we build a compiler that converts programs written in a high-level programming language to SML. This section "ties" together the entire programming process. You will write programs in this new high-level language, compile these programs on the compiler you build and run them on the simulator you built in Exercise 8.19. You should make every effort to implement your compiler in an object-oriented manner.

21.26 (*The Simple Language*) Before we begin building the compiler, we discuss a simple, yet powerful, high-level language similar to early versions of the popular language BASIC. We call the language *Simple*. Every Simple *statement* consists of a *line number* and a Simple *instruction*. Line numbers must appear in ascending order. Each instruction begins with one of the following Simple *commands*: `rem`, `input`, `let`, `print`, `goto`, `if...goto` and `end` (see Fig. 21.25). All commands except `end` can be used repeatedly. Simple evaluates only integer expressions using the +, -, * and / operators. These operators have the same precedence as in C++. Parentheses can be used to change the order of evaluation of an expression.

Our Simple compiler recognizes only lowercase letters. All characters in a Simple file should be lowercase (uppercase letters result in a syntax error unless they appear in a `rem` statement, in which case they are ignored). A *variable name* is a single letter. Simple does not allow descriptive

Command	Example statement	Description
rem	50 rem this is a remark	Text following rem is for documentation purposes and is ignored by the compiler.
input	30 input x	Display a question mark to prompt the user to enter an integer. Read that integer from the keyboard, and store the integer in x.
let	80 let u = 4 * (j - 56)	Assign u the value of 4 * (j - 56). Note that an arbitrarily complex expression can appear to the right of the equals sign.
print	10 print w	Display the value of w.
goto	70 goto 45	Transfer program control to line 45.
if...goto	35 if i == z goto 80	Compare i and z for equality and transfer control to line 80 if the condition is true; otherwise, continue execution with the next statement.
end	99 end	Terminate program execution.

Fig. 21.25 | Simple commands.

variable names, so variables should be explained in remarks to indicate their use in a program. Simple uses only integer variables. Simple does not have variable declarations—merely mentioning a variable name in a program causes the variable to be declared and initialized to zero automatically. The syntax of Simple does not allow string manipulation (reading a string, writing a string, comparing strings, etc.). If a string is encountered in a Simple program (after a command other than rem), the compiler generates a syntax error. The first version of our compiler will assume that Simple programs are entered correctly. Exercise 21.29 asks the student to modify the compiler to perform syntax error checking.

Simple uses the conditional if...goto statement and the unconditional goto statement to alter the flow of control during program execution. If the condition in the if...goto statement is true, control is transferred to a specific line of the program. The following relational and equality operators are valid in an if...goto statement: <, >, <=, >=, == and !=. The precedence of these operators is the same as in C++.

Let us now consider several programs that demonstrate Simple's features. The first program (Fig. 21.26) reads two integers from the keyboard, stores the values in variables a and b and computes and prints their sum (stored in variable c).

The program of Fig. 21.27 determines and prints the larger of two integers. The integers are input from the keyboard and stored in s and t. The if...goto statement tests the condition s >= t. If the condition is true, control is transferred to line 90 and s is output; otherwise, t is output and control is transferred to the end statement in line 99, where the program terminates.

Simple does not provide a repetition statement (such as C++'s for, while or do...while). However, Simple can simulate each of C++'s repetition statements using the if...goto and goto statements. Figure 21.28 uses a sentinel-controlled loop to calculate the squares of several integers. Each integer is input from the keyboard and stored in variable j. If the value entered is the sentinel value -9999, control is transferred to line 99, where the program terminates. Otherwise, k is assigned the square of j, k is output to the screen and control is passed to line 20, where the next integer is input.

Using the sample programs of Fig. 21.26, Fig. 21.27 and Fig. 21.28 as your guide, write a Simple program to accomplish each of the following:

a) Input three integers, determine their average and print the result.

b) Use a sentinel-controlled loop to input 10 integers and compute and print their sum.

c) Use a counter-controlled loop to input seven integers, some positive and some negative, and compute and print their average.

d) Input a series of integers and determine and print the largest. The first integer input indicates how many numbers should be processed.

e) Input 10 integers and print the smallest.

f) Calculate and print the sum of the even integers from 2 to 30.

g) Calculate and print the product of the odd integers from 1 to 9.

```
  1    10 rem    determine and print the sum of two integers
  2    15 rem
  3    20 rem    input the two integers
  4    30 input a
  5    40 input b
  6    45 rem
  7    50 rem    add integers and store result in c
  8    60 let c = a + b
  9    65 rem
 10    70 rem    print the result
 11    80 print c
 12    90 rem    terminate program execution
 13    99 end
```

Fig. 21.26 | Simple program that determines the sum of two integers.

```
  1    10 rem    determine the larger of two integers
  2    20 input s
  3    30 input t
  4    32 rem
  5    35 rem    test if s >= t
  6    40 if s >= t goto 90
  7    45 rem
  8    50 rem    t is greater than s, so print t
  9    60 print t
 10    70 goto 99
 11    75 rem
 12    80 rem    s is greater than or equal to t, so print s
 13    90 print s
 14    99 end
```

Fig. 21.27 | Simple program that finds the larger of two integers.

```
  1    10 rem    calculate the squares of several integers
  2    20 input j
  3    23 rem
  4    25 rem    test for sentinel value
  5    30 if j == -9999 goto 99
```

Fig. 21.28 | Calculate the squares of several integers. (Part 1 of 2.)

```
6    33 rem
7    35 rem    calculate square of j and assign result to k
8    40 let k = j * j
9    50 print k
10   53 rem
11   55 rem    loop to get next j
12   60 goto 20
13   99 end
```

Fig. 21.28 | Calculate the squares of several integers. (Part 2 of 2.)

21.27 (*Building a Compiler; Prerequisite: Complete Exercises 8.18, 8.19, 21.12, 21.13 and 21.26*) Now that the Simple language has been presented (Exercise 21.26), we discuss how to build a Simple compiler. First, we consider the process by which a Simple program is converted to SML and executed by the Simpletron simulator (see Fig. 21.29). A file containing a Simple program is read by the compiler and converted to SML code. The SML code is output to a file on disk, in which SML instructions appear one per line. The SML file is then loaded into the Simpletron simulator, and the results are sent to a file on disk and to the screen. Note that the Simpletron program developed in Exercise 8.19 took its input from the keyboard. It must be modified to read from a file so it can run the programs produced by our compiler.

The Simple compiler performs two *passes* of the Simple program to convert it to SML. The first pass constructs a *symbol table* (object) in which every *line number* (object), *variable name* (object) and *constant* (object) of the Simple program is stored with its type and corresponding location in the final SML code (the symbol table is discussed in detail below). The first pass also produces the corresponding SML instruction object(s) for each of the Simple statements (object, etc.). As we will see, if the Simple program contains statements that transfer control to a line later in the program, the first pass results in an SML program containing some "unfinished" instructions. The second pass of the compiler locates and completes the unfinished instructions, and outputs the SML program to a file.

First Pass

The compiler begins by reading one statement of the Simple program into memory. The line must be separated into its individual *tokens* (i.e., "pieces" of a statement) for processing and compilation (standard library function strtok can be used to facilitate this task). Recall that every statement begins with a line number followed by a command. As the compiler breaks a statement into tokens, if the token is a line number, a variable or a constant, it is placed in the symbol table. A line number is placed in the symbol table only if it is the first token in a statement. The symbolTable object is an array of tableEntry objects representing each symbol in the program. There is no restriction on the number of symbols that can appear in the program. Therefore, the symbolTable

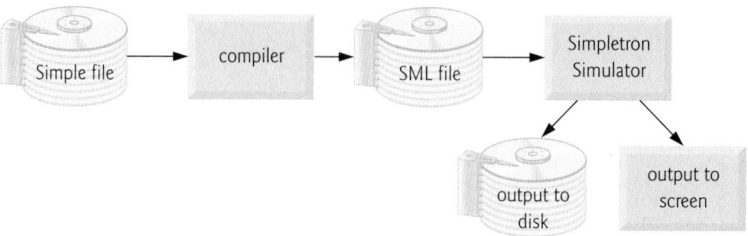

Fig. 21.29 | Writing, compiling and executing a Simple language program.

for a particular program could be large. Make the symbolTable a 100-element array for now. You can increase or decrease its size once the program is working.

Each tableEntry object contains three members. Member symbol is an integer containing the ASCII representation of a variable (remember that variable names are single characters), a line number or a constant. Member type is one of the following characters indicating the symbol's type: 'C' for constant, 'L' for line number and 'V' for variable. Member location contains the Simpletron memory location (00 to 99) to which the symbol refers. Simpletron memory is an array of 100 integers in which SML instructions and data are stored. For a line number, the location is the element in the Simpletron memory array at which the SML instructions for the Simple statement begin. For a variable or constant, the location is the element in the Simpletron memory array in which the variable or constant is stored. Variables and constants are allocated from the end of Simpletron's memory backward. The first variable or constant is stored in location at 99, the next in location at 98, etc.

The symbol table plays an integral part in converting Simple programs to SML. We learned in Chapter 8 that an SML instruction is a four-digit integer composed of two parts—the *operation code* and the *operand*. The operation code is determined by commands in Simple. For example, the simple command input corresponds to SML operation code 10 (read), and the Simple command print corresponds to SML operation code 11 (write). The operand is a memory location containing the data on which the operation code performs its task (e.g., operation code 10 reads a value from the keyboard and stores it in the memory location specified by the operand). The compiler searches symbolTable to determine the Simpletron memory location for each symbol so the corresponding location can be used to complete the SML instructions.

The compilation of each Simple statement is based on its command. For example, after the line number in a rem statement is inserted in the symbol table, the remainder of the statement is ignored by the compiler because a remark is for documentation purposes only. The input, print, goto and end statements correspond to the SML *read*, *write*, *branch* (to a specific location) and *halt* instructions. Statements containing these Simple commands are converted directly to SML (note that a goto statement may contain an unresolved reference if the specified line number refers to a statement further into the Simple program file; this is sometimes called a forward reference).

When a goto statement is compiled with an unresolved reference, the SML instruction must be *flagged* to indicate that the second pass of the compiler must complete the instruction. The flags are stored in 100-element array flags of type int in which each element is initialized to -1. If the memory location to which a line number in the Simple program refers is not yet known (i.e., it is not in the symbol table), the line number is stored in array flags in the element with the same subscript as the incomplete instruction. The operand of the incomplete instruction is set to 00 temporarily. For example, an unconditional branch instruction (making a forward reference) is left as +4000 until the second pass of the compiler. The second pass of the compiler is described shortly.

Compilation of if...goto and let statements is more complicated than for other statements— they are the only statements that produce more than one SML instruction. For an if...goto, the compiler produces code to test the condition and to branch to another line if necessary. The result of the branch could be an unresolved reference. Each of the relational and equality operators can be simulated using SML's *branch zero* or *branch negative* instructions (or a combination of both).

For a let statement, the compiler produces code to evaluate an arbitrarily complex arithmetic expression consisting of integer variables and/or constants. Expressions should separate each operand and operator with spaces. Exercise 21.12 and Exercise 21.13 presented the infix-to-postfix conversion algorithm and the postfix evaluation algorithm used by compilers to evaluate expressions. Before proceeding with your compiler, you should complete each of these exercises. When a compiler encounters an expression, it converts the expression from infix notation to postfix notation and then evaluates the postfix expression.

How is it that the compiler produces the machine language to evaluate an expression containing variables? The postfix evaluation algorithm contains a "hook" where the compiler can generate SML instructions rather than actually evaluating the expression. To enable this "hook" in the compiler, the postfix evaluation algorithm must be modified to search the symbol table for each symbol it encounters (and possibly insert it), determine the symbol's corresponding memory location and *push the memory location onto the stack (instead of the symbol)*. When an operator is encountered in the postfix expression, the two memory locations at the top of the stack are popped and machine language for effecting the operation is produced, using the memory locations as operands. The result of each subexpression is stored in a temporary location in memory and pushed back onto the stack so that the evaluation of the postfix expression can continue. When postfix evaluation is complete, the memory location containing the result is the only location left on the stack. This is popped, and SML instructions are generated to assign the result to the variable at the left of the `let` statement.

Second Pass

The second pass of the compiler performs two tasks: Resolve any unresolved references, and output the SML code to a file. Resolution of references occurs as follows:

- a) Search the `flags` array for an unresolved reference (i.e., an element with a value other than -1).
- b) Locate the object in array `symbolTable`, containing the symbol stored in the `flags` array (be sure that the type of the symbol is `'L'` for line number).
- c) Insert the memory location from member `location` into the instruction with the unresolved reference (remember that an instruction containing an unresolved reference has operand 00).
- d) Repeat *Steps 1, 2* and *3* until the end of the `flags` array is reached.

After the resolution process is complete, the entire array containing the SML code is output to a disk file with one SML instruction per line. This file can be read by the Simpletron for execution (after the simulator is modified to read its input from a file). Compiling your first Simple program into an SML file and then executing that file should give you a real sense of personal accomplishment.

A Complete Example

The following example illustrates a complete conversion of a Simple program to SML as it will be performed by the Simple compiler. Consider a Simple program that inputs an integer and sums the values from 1 to that integer. The program and the SML instructions produced by the first pass of the Simple compiler are illustrated in Fig. 21.30. The symbol table constructed by the first pass is shown in Fig. 21.31.

Simple program	SML location & instruction	Description
`5 rem sum 1 to x`	*none*	rem ignored
`10 input x`	00 +1099	read x into location 99
`15 rem check y == x`	*none*	rem ignored
`20 if y == x goto 60`	01 +2098	load y (98) into accumulator
	02 +3199	sub x (99) from accumulator
	03 +4200	branch zero to unresolved location
`25 rem    increment y`	*none*	rem ignored

Fig. 21.30 | SML instructions produced after the compiler's first pass. (Part 1 of 2.)

Simple program	SML location & instruction		Description
30 let y = y + 1	04	+2098	load y into accumulator
	05	+3097	add 1 (97) to accumulator
	06	+2196	store in temporary location 96
	07	+2096	load from temporary location 96
	08	+2198	store accumulator in y
35 rem add y to total		*none*	rem ignored
40 let t = t + y	09	+2095	load t (95) into accumulator
	10	+3098	add y to accumulator
	11	+2194	store in temporary location 94
	12	+2094	load from temporary location 94
	13	+2195	store accumulator in t
45 rem loop y		*none*	rem ignored
50 goto 20	14	+4001	branch to location 01
55 rem output result		*none*	rem ignored
60 print t	15	+1195	output t to screen
99 end	16	+4300	terminate execution

Fig. 21.30 | SML instructions produced after the compiler's first pass. (Part 2 of 2.)

Symbol	Type	Location
5	L	00
10	L	00
'x'	V	99
15	L	01
20	L	01
'y'	V	98
25	L	04
30	L	04
1	C	97
35	L	09
40	L	09
't'	V	95
45	L	14
50	L	14
55	L	15
60	L	15
99	L	16

Fig. 21.31 | Symbol table for program of Fig. 21.30.

Most Simple statements convert directly to single SML instructions. The exceptions in this program are remarks, the if...goto statement in line 20 and the let statements. Remarks do not translate into machine language. However, the line number for a remark is placed in the symbol table in case the line number is referenced in a goto statement or an if...goto statement. Line 20 of the program specifies that if the condition y == x is true, program control is transferred to line 60. Because line 60 appears later in the program, the first pass of the compiler has not as yet placed 60 in the symbol table (statement line numbers are placed in the symbol table only when they appear as the first token in a statement). Therefore, it is not possible at this time to determine the operand of the SML *branch zero* instruction at location 03 in the array of SML instructions. The compiler places 60 in location 03 of the flags array to indicate that the second pass completes this instruction.

We must keep track of the next instruction location in the SML array, because there is not a one-to-one correspondence between Simple statements and SML instructions. For example, the if...goto statement of line 20 compiles into three SML instructions. Each time an instruction is produced, we must increment the *instruction counter* to the next location in the SML array. Note that the size of Simpletron's memory could present a problem for Simple programs with many statements, variables and constants. It is conceivable that the compiler will run out of memory. To test for this case, your program should contain a *data counter* to keep track of the location at which the next variable or constant will be stored in the SML array. If the value of the instruction counter is larger than the value of the data counter, the SML array is full. In this case, the compilation process should terminate and the compiler should print an error message indicating that it ran out of memory during compilation. This serves to emphasize that, although the programmer is freed from the burdens of managing memory by the compiler, the compiler itself must carefully determine the placement of instructions and data in memory, and must check for such errors as memory being exhausted during the compilation process.

A Step-by-Step View of the Compilation Process

Let us now walk through the compilation process for the Simple program in Fig. 21.30. The compiler reads the first line of the program

```
5 rem sum 1 to x
```

into memory. The first token in the statement (the line number) is determined using strtok (see Chapter 8 and Chapter 21 for a discussion of C++'s C-style string-manipulation functions). The token returned by strtok is converted to an integer using atoi, so the symbol 5 can be located in the symbol table. If the symbol is not found, it is inserted in the symbol table. Since we are at the beginning of the program and this is the first line, no symbols are in the table yet. So 5 is inserted into the symbol table as type L (line number) and assigned the first location in SML array (00). Although this line is a remark, a space in the symbol table is still allocated for the line number (in case it is referenced by a goto or an if...goto). No SML instruction is generated for a rem statement, so the instruction counter is not incremented.

The statement

```
10 input x
```

is tokenized next. The line number 10 is placed in the symbol table as type L and assigned the first location in the SML array (00, because a remark began the program so the instruction counter is currently 00). The command input indicates that the next token is a variable (only a variable can appear in an input statement). Because input corresponds directly to an SML operation code, the compiler has to determine the location of x in the SML array. Symbol x is not found in the symbol table, so it is inserted into the symbol table as the ASCII representation of x, given type V, and assigned location 99 in the SML array (data storage begins at 99 and is allocated backward). SML code can now be generated for this statement. Operation code 10 (the SML read operation code) is multiplied by 100, and the location of x (as determined in the symbol table) is added to complete the instruction. The instruction is then stored in the SML array at location 00. The instruction counter is incremented by 1, because a single SML instruction was produced.

The statement

```
15 rem    check y == x
```

is tokenized next. The symbol table is searched for line number 15 (which is not found). The line number is inserted as type L and assigned the next location in the array, 01 (remember that rem statements do not produce code, so the instruction counter is not incremented).

The statement

```
20 if y == x goto 60
```

is tokenized next. Line number 20 is inserted in the symbol table and given type L with the next location in the SML array 01. The command if indicates that a condition is to be evaluated. The variable y is not found in the symbol table, so it is inserted and given the type V and the SML location 98. Next, SML instructions are generated to evaluate the condition. Since there is no direct equivalent in SML for the if...goto, it must be simulated by performing a calculation using x and y and branching based on the result. If y is equal to x, the result of subtracting x from y is zero, so the *branch zero* instruction can be used with the result of the calculation to simulate the if...goto statement. The first step requires that y be loaded (from SML location 98) into the accumulator. This produces the instruction 01 +2098. Next, x is subtracted from the accumulator. This produces the instruction 02 +3199. The value in the accumulator may be zero, positive or negative. Since the operator is ==, we want to *branch zero*. First, the symbol table is searched for the branch location (60 in this case), which is not found. So 60 is placed in the flags array at location 03, and the instruction 03 +4200 is generated (we cannot add the branch location, because we have not assigned a location to line 60 in the SML array yet). The instruction counter is incremented to 04.

The compiler proceeds to the statement

```
25 rem    increment y
```

The line number 25 is inserted in the symbol table as type L and assigned SML location 04. The instruction counter is not incremented.

When the statement

```
30 let y = y + 1
```

is tokenized, the line number 30 is inserted in the symbol table as type L and assigned SML location 04. Command let indicates that the line is an assignment statement. First, all the symbols on the line are inserted in the symbol table (if they are not already there). The integer 1 is added to the symbol table as type C and assigned SML location 97. Next, the right side of the assignment is converted from infix to postfix notation. Then the postfix expression (y 1 +) is evaluated. Symbol y is located in the symbol table, and its corresponding memory location is pushed onto the stack. Symbol 1 is also located in the symbol table, and its corresponding memory location is pushed onto the stack. When the operator + is encountered, the postfix evaluator pops the stack into the right operand of the operator, pops the stack again into the left operand of the operator and produces the SML instructions

```
04 +2098   (load y)
05 +3097   (add 1)
```

The result of the expression is stored in a temporary location in memory (96) with instruction

```
06 +2196    (store temporary)
```

and the temporary location is pushed on the stack. Now that the expression has been evaluated, the result must be stored in y (i.e., the variable on the left side of =). So the temporary location is loaded into the accumulator, and the accumulator is stored in y with the instructions

```
07 +2096    (load temporary)
08 +2198    (store y)
```

The reader will immediately notice that SML instructions appear to be redundant. We will discuss this issue shortly.

When the statement

```
35 rem    add y to total
```

is tokenized, line number 35 is inserted in the symbol table as type L and assigned location 09.

The statement

```
40 let t = t + y
```

is similar to line 30. The variable t is inserted in the symbol table as type V and assigned SML location 95. The instructions follow the same logic and format as line 30, and the instructions 09 +2095, 10 +3098, 11 +2194, 12 +2094 and 13 +2195 are generated. Note that the result of t + y is assigned to temporary location 94 before being assigned to t (95). Once again, the reader will note that the instructions in memory locations 11 and 12 appear to be redundant. Again, we will discuss this shortly.

The statement

```
45 rem    loop y
```

is a remark, so line 45 is added to the symbol table as type L and assigned SML location 14.

The statement

```
50 goto 20
```

transfers control to line 20. Line number 50 is inserted in the symbol table as type L and assigned SML location 14. The equivalent of goto in SML is the *unconditional branch* (40) instruction that transfers control to a specific SML location. The compiler searches the symbol table for line 20 and finds that it corresponds to SML location 01. The operation code (40) is multiplied by 100, and location 01 is added to it to produce the instruction 14 +4001.

The statement

```
55 rem    output result
```

is a remark, so line 55 is inserted in the symbol table as type L and assigned SML location 15.

The statement

```
60 print t
```

is an output statement. Line number 60 is inserted in the symbol table as type L and assigned SML location 15. The equivalent of print in SML is operation code 11 (*write*). The location of t is determined from the symbol table and added to the result of the operation code multiplied by 100.

The statement

```
99 end
```

is the final line of the program. Line number 99 is stored in the symbol table as type L and assigned SML location 16. The end command produces the SML instruction +4300 (43 is *halt* in SML), which is written as the final instruction in the SML memory array.

This completes the first pass of the compiler. We now consider the second pass. The flags array is searched for values other than -1. Location 03 contains 60, so the compiler knows that instruction 03 is incomplete. The compiler completes the instruction by searching the symbol table for 60, determining its location and adding the location to the incomplete instruction. In this case, the search determines that line 60 corresponds to SML location 15, so the completed instruction 03 +4215 is produced, replacing 03 +4200. The Simple program has now been compiled successfully.

To build the compiler, you will have to perform each of the following tasks:

a) Modify the Simpletron simulator program you wrote in Exercise 8.19 to take its input from a file specified by the user (see Chapter 17). The simulator should output its results to a disk file in the same format as the screen output. Convert the simulator to be an object-oriented program. In particular, make each part of the hardware an object. Arrange the instruction types into a class hierarchy using inheritance. Then execute the program polymorphically by telling each instruction to execute itself with an exe-cuteInstruction message.

b) Modify the infix-to-postfix conversion algorithm of Exercise 21.12 to process multi-digit integer operands and single-letter variable name operands. [*Hint:* C++ Standard Library function strtok can be used to locate each constant and variable in an expression, and constants can be converted from strings to integers using standard library function atoi (<csdtlib>).] [*Note:* The data representation of the postfix expression must be altered to support variable names and integer constants.]

c) Modify the postfix evaluation algorithm to process multidigit integer operands and variable name operands. Also, the algorithm should now implement the "hook" discussed previously so that SML instructions are produced rather than directly evaluating the expression. [*Hint:* Standard library function strtok can be used to locate each constant and variable in an expression, and constants can be converted from strings to integers using standard library function atoi.] [*Note:* The data representation of the postfix expression must be altered to support variable names and integer constants.]

d) Build the compiler. Incorporate parts (b) and (c) for evaluating expressions in let statements. Your program should contain a function that performs the first pass of the compiler and a function that performs the second pass of the compiler. Both functions can call other functions to accomplish their tasks. Make your compiler as object oriented as possible.

21.28   (*Optimizing the Simple Compiler*) When a program is compiled and converted into SML, a set of instructions is generated. Certain combinations of instructions often repeat themselves, usually in triplets called *productions*. A production normally consists of three instructions such as *load*, *add* and *store*. For example, Fig. 21.32 illustrates five of the SML instructions that were produced in the compilation of the program in Fig. 21.30. The first three instructions are the production that adds 1 to y. Note that instructions 06 and 07 store the accumulator value in temporary location 96 and load the value back into the accumulator so instruction 08 can store the value in location 98. Often a production is followed by a load instruction for the same location that was just stored. This code can be *optimized* by eliminating the store instruction and the subsequent load instruction that operate on the same memory location, thus enabling the Simpletron to execute the program faster. Figure 21.33 illustrates the optimized SML for the program of Fig. 21.30. Note that there are four fewer instructions in the optimized code—a memory-space savings of 25 percent.

Modify the compiler to provide an option for optimizing the Simpletron Machine Language code it produces. Manually compare the nonoptimized code with the optimized code, and calculate the percentage reduction.

1	04	+2098	*(load)*
2	05	+3097	*(add)*
3	06	+2196	*(store)*
4	07	+2096	*(load)*
5	08	+2198	*(store)*

Fig. 21.32 | Nonoptimized code from the program of Fig. 21.30.

Simple program	SML location & instruction		Description
5 rem sum 1 to x	*none*		rem ignored
10 input x	00	+1099	read x into location 99
15 rem check y == x	*none*		rem ignored
20 if y == x goto 60	01	+2098	load y (98) into accumulator
	02	+3199	sub x (99) from accumulator
	03	+4211	branch to location 11 if zero
25 rem increment y	*none*		rem ignored
30 let y = y + 1	04	+2098	load y into accumulator
	05	+3097	add 1 (97) to accumulator
	06	+2198	store accumulator in y (98)
35 rem add y to total	*none*		rem ignored
40 let t = t + y	07	+2096	load t from location (96)
	08	+3098	add y (98) accumulator
	09	+2196	store accumulator in t (96)
45 rem loop y	*none*		rem ignored
50 goto 20	10	+4001	branch to location 01
55 rem output result	*none*		rem ignored
60 print t	11	+1196	output t (96) to screen
99 end	12	+4300	terminate execution

Fig. 21.33 | Optimized code for the program of Fig. 21.30.

21.29 (*Modifications to the Simple Compiler*) Perform the following modifications to the Simple compiler. Some of these modifications may also require modifications to the Simpletron Simulator program written in Exercise 8.19.

    a) Allow the modulus operator (%) to be used in let statements. Simpletron Machine Language must be modified to include a modulus instruction.

    b) Allow exponentiation in a let statement using ^ as the exponentiation operator. Simpletron Machine Language must be modified to include an exponentiation instruction.

    c) Allow the compiler to recognize uppercase and lowercase letters in Simple statements (e.g., 'A' is equivalent to 'a'). No modifications to the Simulator are required.

    d) Allow input statements to read values for multiple variables such as input x, y. No modifications to the Simpletron Simulator are required.

e) Allow the compiler to output multiple values in a single `print` statement such as `print a, b, c`. No modifications to the Simpletron Simulator are required.

f) Add syntax-checking capabilities to the compiler so error messages are output when syntax errors are encountered in a Simple program. No modifications to the Simpletron Simulator are required.

g) Allow arrays of integers. No modifications to the Simpletron Simulator are required.

h) Allow subroutines specified by the Simple commands `gosub` and `return`. Command `gosub` passes program control to a subroutine, and command `return` passes control back to the statement after the `gosub`. This is similar to a function call in C++. The same subroutine can be called from many `gosub` commands distributed throughout a program. No modifications to the Simpletron Simulator are required.

i) Allow repetition statements of the form

```
for x = 2 to 10 step 2
    Simple statements
next
```

This `for` statement loops from 2 to 10 with an increment of 2. The `next` line marks the end of the body of the `for`. No modifications to the Simpletron Simulator are required.

j) Allow repetition statements of the form

```
for x = 2 to 10
    Simple statements
next
```

This `for` statement loops from 2 to 10 with a default increment of 1. No modifications to the Simpletron Simulator are required.

k) Allow the compiler to process string input and output. This requires the Simpletron Simulator to be modified to process and store string values. [*Hint:* Each Simpletron word can be divided into two groups, each holding a two-digit integer. Each two-digit integer represents the ASCII decimal equivalent of a character. Add a machine-language instruction that will print a string beginning at a certain Simpletron memory location. The first half of the word at that location is a count of the number of characters in the string (i.e., the length of the string). Each succeeding half word contains one ASCII character expressed as two decimal digits. The machine-language instruction checks the length and prints the string by translating each two-digit number into its equivalent character.]

l) Allow the compiler to process floating-point values in addition to integers. The Simpletron Simulator must also be modified to process floating-point values.

21.30 (*A Simple Interpreter*) An interpreter is a program that reads a high-level language program statement, determines the operation to be performed by the statement and executes the operation immediately. The high-level language program is not converted into machine language first. Interpreters execute slowly because each statement encountered in the program must first be deciphered. If statements are contained in a loop, the statements are deciphered each time they are encountered in the loop. Early versions of the BASIC programming language were implemented as interpreters.

Write an interpreter for the Simple language discussed in Exercise 21.26. The program should use the infix-to-postfix converter developed in Exercise 21.12 and the postfix evaluator developed in Exercise 21.13 to evaluate expressions in a `let` statement. The same restrictions placed on the Simple language in Exercise 21.26 should be adhered to in this program. Test the interpreter with the Simple programs written in Exercise 21.26. Compare the results of running these programs in the interpreter with the results of compiling the Simple programs and running them in the Simpletron Simulator built in Exercise 8.19.

21.31 *(Insert/Delete Anywhere in a Linked List)* Our linked list class template allowed insertions and deletions at only the front and the back of the linked list. These capabilities were convenient for us when we used `private` inheritance and composition to produce a stack class template and a queue class template with a minimal amount of code by reusing the list class template. Actually, linked lists are more general than those we provided. Modify the linked list class template we developed in this chapter to handle insertions and deletions anywhere in the list.

21.32 *(List and Queues without Tail Pointers)* Our implementation of a linked list (Figs. 21.3–21.5) used both a `firstPtr` and a `lastPtr`. The `lastPtr` was useful for the `insertAtBack` and `removeFromBack` member functions of the `List` class. The `insertAtBack` function corresponds to the `enqueue` member function of the `Queue` class. Rewrite the `List` class so that it does not use a `lastPtr`. Thus, any operations on the tail of a list must begin searching the list from the front. Does this affect our implementation of the `Queue` class (Fig. 21.16)?

21.33 Use the composition version of the stack program (Fig. 21.15) to form a complete working stack program. Modify this program to `inline` the member functions. Compare the two approaches. Summarize the advantages and disadvantages of inlining member functions.

21.34 *(Performance of Binary Tree Sorting and Searching)* One problem with the binary tree sort is that the order in which the data is inserted affects the shape of the tree—for the same collection of data, different orderings can yield binary trees of dramatically different shapes. The performance of the binary tree sorting and searching algorithms is sensitive to the shape of the binary tree. What shape would a binary tree have if its data was inserted in increasing order? in decreasing order? What shape should the tree have to achieve maximal searching performance?

21.35 *(Indexed Lists)* As presented in the text, linked lists must be searched sequentially. For large lists, this can result in poor performance. A common technique for improving list searching performance is to create and maintain an index to the list. An index is a set of pointers to various key places in the list. For example, an application that searches a large list of names could improve performance by creating an index with 26 entries—one for each letter of the alphabet. A search operation for a last name beginning with 'Y' would first search the index to determine where the 'Y' entries begin and "jump into" the list at that point and search linearly until the desired name is found. This would be much faster than searching the linked list from the beginning. Use the `List` class of Figs. 21.3–21.5 as the basis of an `IndexedList` class. Write a program that demonstrates the operation of indexed lists. Be sure to include member functions `insertInIndexedList`, `searchIndexedList` and `deleteFromIndexedList`.

Standard Template Library (STL)

The shapes a bright container can contain!

—Theodore Roethke

Journey over all the universe in a map.

—Miguel de Cervantes

O! thou hast damnable iteration, and art indeed able to corrupt a saint.

—William Shakespeare

That great dust heap called "history."

—Augustine Birrell

The historian is a prophet in reverse.

—Friedrich von Schlegel

Attempt the end, and never stand to doubt; Nothing's so hard but search will find it out.

—Robert Herrick

OBJECTIVES

In this chapter you will learn:

- To be able to use the template STL containers, container adapters and "near containers."

- To be able to program with the dozens of STL algorithms.

- To understand how algorithms use iterators to access the elements of STL containers.

- To become familiar with the STL resources available on the Internet and the World Wide Web.

22.1 Introduction to the Standard Template Library (STL)

We have repeatedly emphasized the importance of software reuse. Recognizing that many data structures and algorithms commonly are used by C++ programmers, the C++ standard committee added the Standard Template Library (STL) to the C++ Standard Library. The STL defines powerful, template-based, reusable components that implement many common data structures, and algorithms used to process those data structures. The STL offers proof of concept for generic programming with templates—introduced in Chapter 14, Templates, and demonstrated in detail in Chapter 21, Data Structures. [*Note:* In industry, the features presented in this chapter are commonly referred to as the Standard Template Library or STL. However, these terms are not used in the C++ standard document, because these features are simply considered to be part of the C++ Standard Library.]

The STL was developed by Alexander Stepanov and Meng Lee at Hewlett-Packard and is based on their research in the field of generic programming, with significant contributions from David Musser. As you will see, the STL was conceived and designed for performance and flexibility.

This chapter introduces the STL and discusses its three key components—containers (popular templatized data structures), iterators and algorithms. The STL containers are data structures capable of storing objects of any data type. We will see that there are three container categories—first-class containers, adapters and near containers.

Performance Tip 22.1

For any particular application, several different STL containers might be appropriate. Select the most appropriate container that achieves the best performance (i.e., balance of speed and size) for that application. Efficiency was a crucial consideration in STL's design.

Performance Tip 22.2

Standard Library capabilities are implemented to operate efficiently across many applications. For some applications with unique performance requirements, it might be necessary to write your own customized implementations.

Each STL container has associated member functions. A subset of these member functions is defined in all STL containers. We illustrate most of this common functionality in our examples of STL containers `vector` (a dynamically resizable array which we introduced in Chapter 7, Arrays and Vectors), `list` (a linked list) and `deque` (a double-ended queue, pronounced "deck"). We introduce container-specific functionality in examples for each of the other STL containers.

STL iterators, which have properties similar to those of pointers, are used by programs to manipulate the STL-container elements. In fact, standard arrays can be manipulated as STL containers, using standard pointers as iterators. We will see that manipulating containers with iterators is convenient and provides tremendous expressive power when combined with STL algorithms—in some cases, reducing many lines of code to a single statement. There are five categories of iterators, each of which we discuss in Section 22.1.2 and use throughout this chapter.

STL algorithms are functions that perform such common data manipulations as searching, sorting and comparing elements (or entire containers). Approximately 70 algorithms are implemented in the STL. Most of them use iterators to access container elements. Each algorithm has minimum requirements for the types of iterators that can be used with it. We will see that each first-class container supports specific iterator types, some more powerful than others. A container's supported iterator type determines whether the container can be used with a specific algorithm. Iterators encapsulate the mechanism used to access container elements. This encapsulation enables many of the STL algorithms to be applied to several containers without regard for the underlying container implementation. As long as a container's iterators support the minimum requirements of the algorithm, then the algorithm can process that container's elements. This also enables programmers to create new algorithms that can process the elements of multiple container types.

Software Engineering Observation 22.1

The STL approach allows general programs to be written so that the code does not depend on the underlying container. Such a programming style is called generic programming.

In Chapter 21, we studied data structures. We built linked lists, queues, stacks and trees. We carefully wove link objects together with pointers. Pointer-based code is complex, and the slightest omission or oversight can lead to serious memory-access violations and memory-leak errors with no compiler complaints. Implementing additional data structures, such as `deques`, priority queues, sets and maps, requires substantial extra work. In addition, if many programmers on a large project implement similar containers and algorithms for different tasks, the code becomes difficult to modify, maintain and debug. An advantage of the STL is that programmers can reuse the STL containers, iterators and algorithms to implement common data representations and manipulations. This reuse can save substantial development time, money and effort.

Software Engineering Observation 22.2

Avoid reinventing the wheel; program with the reusable components of the C++ Standard Library. STL includes many of the most popular data structures as containers and provides various popular algorithms to process data in these containers.

Error-Prevention Tip 22.1

When programming pointer-based data structures and algorithms, we must do our own debugging and testing to be sure our data structures, classes and algorithms function properly. It is easy to make errors when manipulating pointers at this low level. Memory leaks and memory-access violations are common in such custom code. For most programmers, and for most of the applications they will need to write, the prepackaged, templatized containers of the STL are sufficient. Using the STL helps programmers reduce testing and debugging time. One caution is that, for large projects, template compile time can be significant.

This chapter introduces the STL. It is by no means complete or comprehensive. However, it is a friendly, accessible chapter that should convince you of the value of the STL in software reuse and encourage further study.

22.1.1 Introduction to Containers

The STL container types are shown in Fig. 22.1. The containers are divided into three major categories—sequence containers, associative containers and container adapters.

Standard Library container class	Description
Sequence containers	
vector	rapid insertions and deletions at back direct access to any element
deque	rapid insertions and deletions at front or back direct access to any element
list	doubly linked list, rapid insertion and deletion anywhere
Associative containers	
set	rapid lookup, no duplicates allowed
multiset	rapid lookup, duplicates allowed
map	one-to-one mapping, no duplicates allowed, rapid key-based lookup
multimap	one-to-many mapping, duplicates allowed, rapid key-based lookup
Container adapters	
stack	last-in, first-out (LIFO)
queue	first-in, first-out (FIFO)
priority_queue	highest-priority element is always the first element out

Fig. 22.1 | Standard Library container classes.

STL Containers Overview

The sequence containers (also referred to as sequential containers) represent linear data structures, such as vectors and linked lists. Associative containers are nonlinear containers that typically can locate elements stored in the containers quickly. Such containers can store sets of values or key/value pairs. The sequence containers and associative containers are collectively referred to as the first-class containers. As we saw in Chapter 21, stacks and queues actually are constrained versions of sequential containers. For this reason, STL implements stacks and queues as container adapters that enable a program to view a sequential container in a constrained manner. There are four other container types that are considered "near-containers"—C-like pointer-based arrays (discussed in Chapter 7), strings (discussed in Chapter 18), bitsets for maintaining sets of flag values and valarrays for performing high-speed mathematical vector operations (this last class is optimized for computation performance and is not as flexible as the first-class containers). These four types are considered "near containers" because they exhibit capabilities similar to those of the first-class containers, but do not support all the first-class-container capabilities.

STL Container Common Functions

All STL containers provide similar functionality. Many generic operations, such as member function size, apply to all containers, and other operations apply to subsets of similar containers. This encourages extensibility of the STL with new classes. Figure 22.2 describes the functions common to all Standard Library containers. [*Note:* Overloaded operators operator<, operator<=, operator>, operator>=, operator== and operator!= are not provided for priority_queues.]

Common member functions for all STL containers	Description
default constructor	A constructor to provide a default initialization of the container. Normally, each container has several constructors that provide different initialization methods for the container.
copy constructor	A constructor that initializes the container to be a copy of an existing container of the same type.
destructor	Destructor function for cleanup after a container is no longer needed.
empty	Returns `true` if there are no elements in the container; otherwise, returns `false`.
size	Returns the number of elements currently in the container.
operator=	Assigns one container to another.
operator<	Returns `true` if the first container is less than the second container; otherwise, returns `false`.
operator<=	Returns `true` if the first container is less than or equal to the second container; otherwise, returns `false`.
operator>	Returns `true` if the first container is greater than the second container; otherwise, returns `false`.
operator>=	Returns `true` if the first container is greater than or equal to the second container; otherwise, returns `false`.
operator==	Returns `true` if the first container is equal to the second container; otherwise, returns `false`.
operator!=	Returns `true` if the first container is not equal to the second container; otherwise, returns `false`.
swap	Swaps the elements of two containers.
Functions found only in first-class containers	
max_size	Returns the maximum number of elements for a container.
begin	The two versions of this function return either an `iterator` or a `const_iterator` that refers to the first element of the container.
end	The two versions of this function return either an `iterator` or a `const_iterator` that refers to the next position after the end of the container.
rbegin	The two versions of this function return either a `reverse_iterator` or a `const_reverse_iterator` that refers to the last element of the container.
rend	The two versions of this function return either a `reverse_iterator` or a `const_reverse_iterator` that refers to the next position after the last element of the reversed container.
erase	Erases one or more elements from the container.
clear	Erases all elements from the container.

Fig. 22.2 | STL container common functions.

STL Container Header Files

The header files for each of the Standard Library containers are shown in Fig. 22.3. The contents of these header files are all in `namespace std`.[1]

First-Class Container Common **typedefs**

Figure 22.4 shows the common `typedefs` (to create synonyms or aliases for lengthy type names) found in first-class containers. These `typedefs` are used in generic declarations of variables, parameters to functions and return values from functions. For example, `value_type` in each container is always a `typedef` that represents the type of value stored in the container.

Standard Library container header files	
`<vector>`	
`<list>`	
`<deque>`	
`<queue>`	Contains both `queue` and `priority_queue`.
`<stack>`	
`<map>`	Contains both `map` and `multimap`.
`<set>`	Contains both `set` and `multiset`.
`<bitset>`	

Fig. 22.3 | Standard Library container header files.

typedef	Description
`value_type`	The type of element stored in the container.
`reference`	A reference to the type of element stored in the container.
`const_reference`	A constant reference to the type of element stored in the container. Such a reference can be used only for *reading* elements in the container and for performing `const` operations.
`pointer`	A pointer to the type of element stored in the container.
`iterator`	An iterator that points to the type of element stored in the container.
`const_iterator`	A constant iterator that points to the type of element stored in the container and can be used only to *read* elements.

Fig. 22.4 | `typedef`s found in first-class containers. (Part 1 of 2.)

---

1. Some older C++ compilers do not support the new-style header files. Many of these compilers provide their own versions of the header-file names. See your compiler documentation for more information on the STL support your compiler provides.

typedef	Description
reverse_iterator	A reverse iterator that points to the type of element stored in the container. This type of iterator is for iterating through a container in reverse.
const_reverse_iterator	A constant reverse iterator that points to the type of element stored in the container and can be used only to *read* elements. This type of iterator is for iterating through a container in reverse.
difference_type	The type of the result of subtracting two iterators that refer to the same container (operator – is not defined for iterators of lists and associative containers).
size_type	The type used to count items in a container and index through a sequence container (cannot index through a list).

Fig. 22.4 | typedefs found in first-class containers. (Part 2 of 2.)

Performance Tip 22.3

STL generally avoids inheritance and virtual functions in favor of using generic programming with templates to achieve better execution-time performance.

Portability Tip 22.1

Programming with STL will enhance the portability of your code.

When preparing to use an STL container, it is important to ensure that the type of element being stored in the container supports a minimum set of functionality. When an element is inserted into a container, a copy of that element is made. For this reason, the element type should provide its own copy constructor and assignment operator. [*Note:* This is required only if default memberwise copy and default memberwise assignment do not perform proper copy and assignment operations for the element type.] Also, the associative containers and many algorithms require elements to be compared. For this reason, the element type should provide an equality operator (==) and a less-than operator (<).

Software Engineering Observation 22.3

The STL containers technically do not require their elements to be comparable with the equality and less-than operators unless a program uses a container member function that must compare the container elements (e.g., the sort function in class list). Unfortunately, some prestandard C++ compilers are not capable of ignoring parts of a template that are not used in a particular program. On compilers with this problem, you may not be able to use the STL containers with objects of classes that do not define overloaded less-than and equality operators.

22.1.2 Introduction to Iterators

Iterators have many features in common with pointers and are used to point to the elements of first-class containers (and for a few other purposes, as we will see). Iterators hold state information sensitive to the particular containers on which they operate; thus, iterators are implemented appropriately for each type of container. Certain iterator operations are uniform across containers. For example, the dereferencing operator (*) dereferences an iterator so that you can use the element to which it points. The ++ operation on an iterator moves it to the next element of the container (much as incrementing a pointer into an array aims the pointer at the next element of the array).

STL first-class containers provide member functions begin and end. Function begin returns an iterator pointing to the first element of the container. Function end returns an iterator pointing to the first element past the end of the container (an element that doesn't exist). If iterator i points to a particular element, then ++i points to the "next" element and *i refers to the element pointed to by i. The iterator resulting from end can be used only in an equality or inequality comparison to determine whether the "moving iterator" (i in this case) has reached the end of the container.

We use an object of type iterator to refer to a container element that can be modified. We use an object of type const_iterator to refer to a container element that cannot be modified.

Using istream_iterator *for Input and Using* ostream_iterator *for Output*

We use iterators with sequences (also called ranges). These sequences can be in containers, or they can be input sequences or output sequences. The program of Fig. 22.5 demonstrates input from the standard input (a sequence of data for input into a program), using an istream_iterator, and output to the standard output (a sequence of data for output from a program), using an ostream_iterator. The program inputs two integers from the user at the keyboard and displays the sum of the integers.[2]

Line 15 creates an istream_iterator that is capable of extracting (inputting) int values in a type-safe manner from the standard input object cin. Line 17 dereferences iterator inputInt to read the first integer from cin and assigns that integer to number1. Note that the dereferencing operator * applied to inputInt gets the value from the stream associated with inputInt; this is similar to dereferencing a pointer. Line 18 positions iterator inputInt to the next value in the input stream. Line 19 inputs the next integer from inputInt and assigns it to number2.

Line 22 creates an ostream_iterator that is capable of inserting (outputting) int values in the standard output object cout. Line 25 outputs an integer to cout by assigning to *outputInt the sum of number1 and number2. Notice the use of the dereferencing operator * to use *outputInt as an *lvalue* in the assignment statement. If you want to output another value using outputInt, the iterator must be incremented with ++ (both the prefix and postfix increment can be used, but the prefix form should be preferred for performance reasons.).

Error-Prevention Tip 22.2

*The * (dereferencing) operator of any const iterator returns a const reference to the container element, disallowing the use of non-const member functions.*

---

2. The examples in this chapter precede each use of an STL function and each definition of an STL container object with the "std::" prefix rather than placing the using declarations or directives at the beginning of the program, as was shown in most prior examples. Differences in compilers and the complex code generated when using STL make it difficult to construct a proper set of using declarations or directives that enable the programs to compile without errors. To allow these programs to compile on the widest variety of platforms, we chose the "std::" prefix approach.

```cpp
 1   // Fig. 22.5: Fig22_05.cpp
 2   // Demonstrating input and output with iterators.
 3   #include <iostream>
 4   using std::cout;
 5   using std::cin;
 6   using std::endl;
 7
 8   #include <iterator> // ostream_iterator and istream_iterator
 9
10   int main()
11   {
12      cout << "Enter two integers: ";
13
14      // create istream_iterator for reading int values from cin
15      std::istream_iterator< int > inputInt( cin );
16
17      int number1 = *inputInt; // read int from standard input
18      ++inputInt; // move iterator to next input value
19      int number2 = *inputInt; // read int from standard input
20
21      // create ostream_iterator for writing int values to cout
22      std::ostream_iterator< int > outputInt( cout );
23
24      cout << "The sum is: ";
25      *outputInt = number1 + number2; // output result to cout
26      cout << endl;
27      return 0;
28   } // end main
```

```
Enter two integers: 12 25
The sum is: 37
```

Fig. 22.5 | Input and output stream iterators.

 Common Programming Error 22.1

Attempting to dereference an iterator positioned outside its container is a runtime logic error. In particular, the iterator returned by end cannot be dereferenced or incremented.

 Common Programming Error 22.2

Attempting to create a non-const iterator for a const container results in a compilation error.

Iterator Categories and Iterator Category Hierarchy

Figure 22.6 shows the categories of iterators used by the STL. Each category provides a specific set of functionality. Figure 22.7 illustrates the hierarchy of iterator categories. As you follow the hierarchy from top to bottom, each iterator category supports all the functionality of the categories above it in the figure. Thus the "weakest" iterator types are at the top and the most powerful one is at the bottom. Note that this is not an inheritance hierarchy.

The iterator category that each container supports determines whether that container can be used with specific algorithms in the STL. Containers that support random-access iterators can be used with all algorithms in the STL. As we will see, pointers into arrays

Category	Description
input	Used to read an element from a container. An input iterator can move only in the forward direction (i.e., from the beginning of the container to the end) one element at a time. Input iterators support only one-pass algorithms—the same input iterator cannot be used to pass through a sequence twice.
output	Used to write an element to a container. An output iterator can move only in the forward direction one element at a time. Output iterators support only one-pass algorithms—the same output iterator cannot be used to pass through a sequence twice.
forward	Combines the capabilities of input and output iterators and retains their position in the container (as state information).
bidirectional	Combines the capabilities of a forward iterator with the ability to move in the backward direction (i.e., from the end of the container toward the beginning). Bidirectional iterators support multipass algorithms.
random access	Combines the capabilities of a bidirectional iterator with the ability to directly access any element of the container, i.e., to jump forward or backward by an arbitrary number of elements.

Fig. 22.6 | Iterator categories.

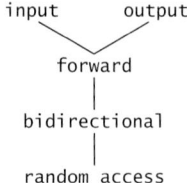

Fig. 22.7 | Iterator category hierarchy.

can be used in place of iterators in most STL algorithms, including those that require random-access iterators. Figure 22.8 shows the iterator category of each of the STL containers. Note that only vectors, deques, lists, sets, multisets, maps and multimaps (i.e., the first-class containers) are traversable with iterators.

Software Engineering Observation 22.4

Using the "weakest iterator" that yields acceptable performance helps produce maximally reusable components. For example, if an algorithm requires only forward iterators, it can be used with any container that supports forward iterators, bidirectional iterators or random-access iterators. However, an algorithm that requires random-access iterators can be used only with containers that have random-access iterators.

Predefined Iterator **typedefs**

Figure 22.9 shows the predefined iterator typedefs that are found in the class definitions of the STL containers. Not every typedef is defined for every container. We use const

Container	Type of iterator supported
Sequence containers (first class)	
vector	random access
deque	random access
list	bidirectional
Associative containers (first class)	
set	bidirectional
multiset	bidirectional
map	bidirectional
multimap	bidirectional
Container adapters	
stack	no iterators supported
queue	no iterators supported
priority_queue	no iterators supported

Fig. 22.8 | Iterator types supported by each Standard Library container.

Predefined typedefs for iterator types	Direction of ++	Capability
iterator	forward	read/write
const_iterator	forward	read
reverse_iterator	backward	read/write
const_reverse_iterator	backward	read

Fig. 22.9 | Iterator typedefs.

versions of the iterators for traversing read-only containers. We use reverse iterators to traverse containers in the reverse direction.

Error-Prevention Tip 22.3

Operations performed on a const_iterator return const references to prevent modification to elements of the container being manipulated. Using const_iterators in preference to iterators where appropriate is another example of the principle of least privilege.

Iterator Operations
Figure 22.10 shows some operations that can be performed on each iterator type. Note that the operations for each iterator type include all operations preceding that type in the figure. Note also that, for input iterators and output iterators, it is not possible to save the iterator and then use the saved value later.

Iterator operation	Description
All iterators	
++p	Preincrement an iterator.
p++	Postincrement an iterator.
Input iterators	
*p	Dereference an iterator.
p = p1	Assign one iterator to another.
p == p1	Compare iterators for equality.
p != p1	Compare iterators for inequality.
Output iterators	
*p	Dereference an iterator.
p = p1	Assign one iterator to another.
Forward iterators	Forward iterators provide all the functionality of both input iterators and output iterators.
Bidirectional iterators	
--p	Predecrement an iterator.
p--	Postdecrement an iterator.
Random-access iterators	
p += i	Increment the iterator p by i positions.
p -= i	Decrement the iterator p by i positions.
p + i	Expression value is an iterator positioned at p incremented by i positions.
p - i	Expression value is an iterator positioned at p decremented by i positions.
p[i]	Return a reference to the element offset from p by i positions
p < p1	Return true if iterator p is less than iterator p1 (i.e., iterator p is before iterator p1 in the container); otherwise, return false.
p <= p1	Return true if iterator p is less than or equal to iterator p1 (i.e., iterator p is before iterator p1 or at the same location as iterator p1 in the container); otherwise, return false.
p > p1	Return true if iterator p is greater than iterator p1 (i.e., iterator p is after iterator p1 in the container); otherwise, return false.
p >= p1	Return true if iterator p is greater than or equal to iterator p1 (i.e., iterator p is after iterator p1 or at the same location as iterator p1 in the container); otherwise, return false.

Fig. 22.10 | Iterator operations for each type of iterator.

22.1.3 Introduction to Algorithms

The STL provides algorithms that can be used generically across a variety of containers. STL provides many algorithms you will use frequently to manipulate containers. Inserting, deleting, searching, sorting and others are appropriate for some or all of the STL containers.

The STL includes approximately 70 standard algorithms. We provide live-code examples of most of these and summarize the others in tables. The algorithms operate on container elements only indirectly through iterators. Many algorithms operate on sequences of elements defined by pairs of iterators—a first iterator pointing to the first element of the sequence and a second iterator pointing to one element past the last element of the sequence. Also, it is possible to create your own new algorithms that operate in a similar fashion so they can be used with the STL containers and iterators.

Algorithms often return iterators that indicate the results of the algorithms. Algorithm find, for example, locates an element and returns an iterator to that element. If the element is not found, find returns the "one past the end" iterator that was passed in to define the end of the range to be searched, which can be tested to determine whether an element was not found. The find algorithm can be used with any first-class STL container. STL algorithms create yet another opportunity for reuse—using the rich collection of popular algorithms can save programmers much time and effort.

If an algorithm uses less powerful iterators, the algorithm can also be used with containers that support more powerful iterators. Some algorithms demand powerful iterators; e.g., sort demands random-access iterators.

Software Engineering Observation 22.5

The STL is implemented concisely. Until now, class designers would have associated the algorithms with the containers by making the algorithms member functions of the containers. The STL takes a different approach. The algorithms are separated from the containers and operate on elements of the containers only indirectly through iterators. This separation makes it easier to write generic algorithms applicable to many container classes.

Software Engineering Observation 22.6

The STL is extensible. It is straightforward to add new algorithms and to do so without changes to STL containers.

Software Engineering Observation 22.7

STL algorithms can operate on STL containers and on pointer-based, C-like arrays.

Portability Tip 22.2

Because STL algorithms process containers only indirectly through iterators, one algorithm can often be used with many different containers.

Figure 22.11 shows many of the mutating-sequence algorithms—i.e., the algorithms that result in modifications of the containers to which the algorithms are applied.

Mutating-sequence algorithms		
copy	remove	reverse_copy
copy_backward	remove_copy	rotate
fill	remove_copy_if	rotate_copy

Fig. 22.11 | Mutating-sequence algorithms. (Part 1 of 2.)

Mutating-sequence algorithms		
fill_n	remove_if	stable_partition
generate	replace	swap
generate_n	replace_copy	swap_ranges
iter_swap	replace_copy_if	transform
partition	replace_if	unique
random_shuffle	reverse	unique_copy

Fig. 22.11 | Mutating-sequence algorithms. (Part 2 of 2.)

Figure 22.12 shows many of the nonmodifying sequence algorithms—i.e., the algorithms that do not result in modifications of the containers to which they are applied. Figure 22.13 shows the numerical algorithms of the header file `<numeric>`.

22.2 Sequence Containers

The C++ Standard Template Library provides three sequence containers—vector, list and deque. Class template vector and class template deque both are based on arrays. Class template list implements a linked-list data structure similar to our List class presented in Chapter 21, but more robust.

One of the most popular containers in the STL is vector. Recall that we introduced class template vector in Chapter 7 as a more robust type of array. A vector changes size dynamically. Unlike C and C++ "raw" arrays (see Chapter 7), vectors can be assigned to one another. This is not possible with pointer-based, C-like arrays, because those array names are constant pointers and cannot be the targets of assignments. Just as with C arrays, vector subscripting does not perform automatic range checking, but class template vector does provide this capability via member function at (also discussed in Chapter 7).

Nonmodifying sequence algorithms		
adjacent_find	find	find_if
count	find_each	mismatch
count_if	find_end	search
equal	find_first_of	search_n

Fig. 22.12 | Nonmutating sequence algorithms.

Numerical algorithms from header file `<numeric>`	
accumulate	partial_sum
inner_product	adjacent_difference

Fig. 22.13 | Numerical algorithms from header file `<numeric>`.

Performance Tip 22.4

Insertion at the back of a vector *is efficient. The* vector *simply grows, if necessary, to accommodate the new item. It is expensive to insert (or delete) an element in the middle of a* vector— *the entire portion of the* vector *after the insertion (or deletion) point must be moved, because* vector *elements occupy contiguous cells in memory just as C or C++ "raw" arrays do.*

Figure 22.2 presented the operations common to all the STL containers. Beyond these operations, each container typically provides a variety of other capabilities. Many of these capabilities are common to several containers, but they are not always equally efficient for each container. The programmer must choose the container most appropriate for the application.

Performance Tip 22.5

Applications that require frequent insertions and deletions at both ends of a container normally use a deque *rather than a* vector. *Although we can insert and delete elements at the front and back of both a* vector *and a* deque, *class* deque *is more efficient than* vector *for doing insertions and deletions at the front.*

Performance Tip 22.6

Applications with frequent insertions and deletions in the middle and/or at the extremes of a container normally use a list, *due to its efficient implementation of insertion and deletion anywhere in the data structure.*

In addition to the common operations described in Fig. 22.2, the sequence containers have several other common operations—front to return a reference to the first element in the container, back to return a reference to the last element in the container, push_back to insert a new element at the end of the container and pop_back to remove the last element of the container.

22.2.1 vector Sequence Container

Class template vector provides a data structure with contiguous memory locations. This enables efficient, direct access to any element of a vector via the subscript operator [], exactly as with a C or C++ "raw" array. Class template vector is most commonly used when the data in the container must be sorted and easily accessible via a subscript. When a vector's memory is exhausted, the vector allocates a larger contiguous area of memory, copies the original elements into the new memory and deallocates the old memory.

Performance Tip 22.7

Choose the vector *container for the best random-access performance.*

Performance Tip 22.8

Objects of class template vector *provide rapid indexed access with the overloaded subscript operator* [] *because they are stored in contiguous memory like a C or C++ raw array.*

Performance Tip 22.9

It is faster to insert many elements at once than one at a time.

An important part of every container is the type of iterator it supports. This determines which algorithms can be applied to the container. A vector supports random-access iterators—i.e., all iterator operations shown in Fig. 22.10 can be applied to a vector iterator. All STL algorithms can operate on a vector. The iterators for a vector are normally implemented as pointers to elements of the vector. Each STL algorithm that takes iterator arguments requires those iterators to provide a minimum level of functionality. If an algorithm requires a forward iterator, for example, that algorithm can operate on any container that provides forward iterators, bidirectional iterators or random-access iterators. As long as the container supports the algorithm's minimum iterator functionality, the algorithm can operate on the container.

Using Vector and Iterators

Figure 22.14 illustrates several functions of the vector class template. Many of these functions are available in every first-class container. You must include header file <vector> to use class template vector.

```cpp
 1  // Fig. 22.14: Fig22_14.cpp
 2  // Demonstrating Standard Library vector class template.
 3  #include <iostream>
 4  using std::cout;
 5  using std::endl;
 6
 7  #include <vector> // vector class-template definition
 8  using std::vector;
 9
10  // prototype for function template printVector
11  template < typename T > void printVector( const vector< T > &integers2 );
12
13  int main()
14  {
15     const int SIZE = 6; // define array size
16     int array[ SIZE ] = { 1, 2, 3, 4, 5, 6 }; // initialize array
17     vector< int > integers; // create vector of ints
18
19     cout << "The initial size of integers is: " << integers.size()
20        << "\nThe initial capacity of integers is: " << integers.capacity();
21
22     // function push_back is in every sequence collection
23     integers.push_back( 2 );
24     integers.push_back( 3 );
25     integers.push_back( 4 );
26
27     cout << "\nThe size of integers is: " << integers.size()
28        << "\nThe capacity of integers is: " << integers.capacity();
29     cout << "\n\nOutput array using pointer notation: ";
30
31     // display array using pointer notation
32     for ( int *ptr = array; ptr != array + SIZE; ptr++ )
33        cout << *ptr << ' ';
34
```

Fig. 22.14 | Standard Library vector class template. (Part 1 of 2.)

```
35      cout << "\nOutput vector using iterator notation: ";
36      printVector( integers );
37      cout << "\nReversed contents of vector integers: ";
38
39      // two const reverse iterators
40      vector< int >::const_reverse_iterator reverseIterator;
41      vector< int >::const_reverse_iterator tempIterator = integers.rend();
42
43      // display vector in reverse order using reverse_iterator
44      for ( reverseIterator = integers.rbegin();
45          reverseIterator!= tempIterator; ++reverseIterator )
46          cout << *reverseIterator << ' ';
47
48      cout << endl;
49      return 0;
50  } // end main
51
52  // function template for outputting vector elements
53  template < typename T > void printVector( const vector< T > &integers2 )
54  {
55      typename vector< T >::const_iterator constIterator; // const_iterator
56
57      // display vector elements using const_iterator
58      for ( constIterator = integers2.begin();
59          constIterator != integers2.end(); ++constIterator )
60          cout << *constIterator << ' ';
61  } // end function printVector
```

```
The initial size of integers is: 0
The initial capacity of integers is: 0
The size of integers is: 3
The capacity of integers is: 4

Output array using pointer notation: 1 2 3 4 5 6
Output vector using iterator notation: 2 3 4
Reversed contents of vector integers: 4 3 2
```

Fig. 22.14 | Standard Library vector class template. (Part 2 of 2.)

Line 17 defines an instance called integers of class template vector that stores int values. When this object is instantiated, an empty vector is created with size 0 (i.e., the number of elements stored in the vector) and capacity 0 (i.e., the number of elements that can be stored without allocating more memory to the vector).

Lines 19 and 20 demonstrate the size and capacity functions; each initially returns 0 for vector v in this example. Function size—available in every container—returns the number of elements currently stored in the container. Function **capacity** returns the number of elements that can be stored in the vector before the vector needs to dynamically resize itself to accommodate more elements.

Lines 23–25 use function **push_back**—available in all sequence containers—to add an element to the end of the vector. If an element is added to a full vector, the vector increases its size—some STL implementations have the vector double its capacity.

Performance Tip 22.10

It can be wasteful to double a vector's *size when more space is needed. For example, a full* vector *of 1,000,000 elements resizes to accommodate 2,000,000 elements when a new element is added. This leaves 999,999 unused elements. Programmers can use* resize *to control space usage better.*

Lines 27 and 28 use size and capacity to illustrate the new size and capacity of the vector after the three push_back operations. Function size returns 3—the number of elements added to the vector. Function capacity returns 4, indicating that we can add one more element before the vector needs to add more memory. When we added the first element, the vector allocated space for one element, and the size became 1 to indicate that the vector contained only one element. When we added the second element, the capacity doubled to 2 and the size became 2 as well. When we added the third element, the capacity doubled again to 4. So we can actually add another element before the vector needs to allocation more space. When the vector eventually fills its allocated capacity and the program attempts to add one more element to the vector, the vector will double its capacity to 8 elements.

The manner in which a vector grows to accommodate more elements—a time consuming operation—is not specified by the C++ Standard Document. C++ library implementors use various clever schemes to minimize the overhead of resizing a vector. Hence, the output of this program may vary, depending on the version of vector that comes with your compiler. Some library implementors allocate a large initial capacity. If a vector stores a small number of elements, such capacity may be a waste of space. However, it can greatly improve performance if a program adds many elements to a vector and does not have to reallocate memory to accommodate those elements. This is a classic space-time trade-off. Library implementors must balance the amount of memory used against the amount of time required to perform various vector operations.

Lines 32–33 demonstrate how to output the contents of an array using pointers and pointer arithmetic. Line 36 calls function printVector (defined at lines 53–61) to output the contents of a vector using iterators. Function template printVector receives a const reference to a vector (integers2) as its argument. Line 55 defines a const_iterator called constIterator that iterates through the vector and outputs its contents. Notice that the declaration in line 55 is prefixed with the keyword typename. Because printVector is a function template and vector< T > will be specialized differently for each function-template specialization, the compiler cannot tell at compile time whether or not vector< T >::const_iterator is a type. In particular specialization, const_iterator could be a static variable. The compiler needs this information to compile the program correctly. Therefore, you must tell the compiler that a qualified name, whether the qualifier is a dependent type, is expected to be a type in every specialization.

A const_iterator enables the program to read the elements of the vector, but does not allow the program to modify the elements. The for statement at lines 58–60 initializes constIterator using vector member function begin, which returns a const_iterator to the first element in the vector—there is another version of begin that returns an iterator that can be used for non-const containers. Note that a const_iterator is returned because the identifier integers2 was declared const in the parameter list of function printVector. The loop continues as long as constIterator has not reached the end of the vector. This is determined by comparing constIterator to the result of integers2.end(), which returns an iterator indicating the location past the last element of the vector. If constIterator is equal to this value, the end of the vector has been reached. Functions begin and end are available for all first-class containers. The body of the loop dereferences iterator constIterator to get the value in the current element of the vector. Remember that the iterator acts like a pointer to the element and that operator * is overloaded to return a reference to the element. The expression ++constIterator (line 59) positions the iterator to the next element of the vector.

Performance Tip 22.11

Use prefix increment when applied to STL iterators because the prefix increment operator does not return a value that must be stored in a temporary object.

Error-Prevention Tip 22.4

Only random-access iterators support <. It is better to use != and end to test for the end of a container.

Line 40 declares a const_reverse_iterator that can be used to iterate through a vector backward. Line 41 declares a const_reverse_iterator variable tempIterator and initializes it to the iterator returned by function **rend** (i.e., the iterator for the ending point when iterating through the container in reverse). All first-class containers support this type of iterator. Lines 44–46 use a for statement similar to that in function printVector to iterate through the vector. In this loop, function **rbegin** (i.e., the iterator for the starting point when iterating through the container in reverse) and tempIterator delineate the range of elements to output. As with functions begin and end, rbegin and rend can return a const_reverse_iterator or a reverse_iterator, based on whether or not the container is constant.

Performance Tip 22.12

For performance reasons, capture the loop ending value before the loop and compare against that, rather than having a (potentially expensive) function call for each iteration.

Vector Element-Manipulation Functions

Figure 22.15 illustrates functions that enable retrieval and manipulation of the elements of a vector. Line 17 uses an overloaded vector constructor that takes two iterators as arguments to initialize integers. Remember that pointers into an array can be used as iterators. Line 17 initializes integers with the contents of array from location array up to—but not including—location array + SIZE.

```
1   // Fig. 22.15: Fig22_15.cpp
2   // Testing Standard Library vector class template
3   // element-manipulation functions.
4   #include <iostream>
5   using std::cout;
6   using std::endl;
```

Fig. 22.15 | vector class template element-manipulation functions. (Part 1 of 3.)

```
7
8   #include <vector> // vector class-template definition
9   #include <algorithm> // copy algorithm
10  #include <iterator> // ostream_iterator iterator
11  #include <stdexcept> // out_of_range exception
12
13  int main()
14  {
15     const int SIZE = 6;
16     int array[ SIZE ] = { 1, 2, 3, 4, 5, 6 };
17     std::vector< int > integers( array, array + SIZE );
18     std::ostream_iterator< int > output( cout, " " );
19
20     cout << "Vector integers contains: ";
21     std::copy( integers.begin(), integers.end(), output );
22
23     cout << "\nFirst element of integers: " << integers.front()
24        << "\nLast element of integers: " << integers.back();
25
26     integers[ 0 ] = 7; // set first element to 7
27     integers.at( 2 ) = 10; // set element at position 2 to 10
28
29     // insert 22 as 2nd element
30     integers.insert( integers.begin() + 1, 22 );
31
32     cout << "\n\nContents of vector integers after changes: ";
33     std::copy( integers.begin(), integers.end(), output );
34
35     // access out-of-range element
36     try
37     {
38        integers.at( 100 ) = 777;
39     } // end try
40     catch ( std::out_of_range outOfRange ) // out_of_range exception
41     {
42        cout << "\n\nException: " << outOfRange.what();
43     } // end catch
44
45     // erase first element
46     integers.erase( integers.begin() );
47     cout << "\n\nVector integers after erasing first element: ";
48     std::copy( integers.begin(), integers.end(), output );
49
50     // erase remaining elements
51     integers.erase( integers.begin(), integers.end() );
52     cout << "\nAfter erasing all elements, vector integers "
53        << ( integers.empty() ? "is" : "is not" ) << " empty";
54
55     // insert elements from array
56     integers.insert( integers.begin(), array, array + SIZE );
57     cout << "\n\nContents of vector integers before clear: ";
58     std::copy( integers.begin(), integers.end(), output );
59
```

Fig. 22.15 | vector class template element-manipulation functions. (Part 2 of 3.)

```
60      // empty integers; clear calls erase to empty a collection
61      integers.clear();
62      cout << "\nAfter clear, vector integers "
63         << ( integers.empty() ? "is" : "is not" ) << " empty" << endl;
64      return 0;
65   } // end main
```

```
Vector integers contains: 1 2 3 4 5 6
First element of integers: 1
Last element of integers: 6

Contents of vector integers after changes: 7 22 2 10 4 5 6

Exception: invalid vector<T> subscript

Vector integers after erasing first element: 22 2 10 4 5 6
After erasing all elements, vector integers is empty

Contents of vector integers before clear: 1 2 3 4 5 6
After clear, vector integers is empty
```

Fig. 22.15 │ vector class template element-manipulation functions. (Part 3 of 3.)

Line 18 defines an ostream_iterator called output that can be used to output integers separated by single spaces via cout. An ostream_iterator< int > is a type-safe output mechanism that outputs only values of type int or a compatible type. The first argument to the constructor specifies the output stream, and the second argument is a string specifying the separator for the values output—in this case, the string contains a space character. We use the ostream_iterator (defined in header <iterator>) to output the contents of the vector in this example.

Line 21 uses algorithm copy from the Standard Library to output the entire contents of vector integers to the standard output. Algorithm copy copies each element in the container starting with the location specified by the iterator in its first argument and continuing up to—but not including—the location specified by the iterator in its second argument. The first and second arguments must satisfy input iterator requirements—they must be iterators through which values can be read from a container. Also, applying ++ to the first iterator must eventually cause it to reach the second iterator argument in the container. The elements are copied to the location specified by the output iterator (i.e., an iterator through which a value can be stored or output) specified as the last argument. In this case, the output iterator is an ostream_iterator (output) that is attached to cout, so the elements are copied to the standard output. To use the algorithms of the Standard Library, you must include the header file <algorithm>.

Lines 23–24 use functions front and back (available for all sequence containers) to determine the first and last element of the vector, respectively. Notice the difference between functions front and begin. Function front returns a reference to the first element in the vector, while function begin returns a random access iterator pointing to the first element in the vector. Also notice the difference between functions back and end. Function back returns a reference to the last element in the vector, while function end returns a random access iterator pointing to the end of the vector (the location after the last element).

Common Programming Error 22.3

The vector *must not be empty; otherwise, results of the* front *and* back *functions are undefined.*

Lines 26–27 illustrate two ways to subscript through a vector (which also can be used with the deque containers). Line 26 uses the subscript operator that is overloaded to return either a reference to the value at the specified location or a constant reference to that value, depending on whether the container is constant. Function at (line 27) performs the same operation, but with bounds checking. Function at first checks the value supplied as an argument and determines whether it is in the bounds of the vector. If not, function at throws an out_of_bounds exception defined in header <stdexcept> (as demonstrated in lines 36–43). Figure 22.16 shows some of the STL exception types. (The Standard Library exception types are discussed in Chapter 16, Exception Handling.)

Line 30 uses one of the three overloaded insert functions provided by each sequence container. Line 30 inserts the value 22 before the element at the location specified by the iterator in the first argument. In this example, the iterator is pointing to the second element of the vector, so 22 is inserted as the second element and the original second element becomes the third element of the vector. Other versions of insert allow inserting multiple copies of the same value starting at a particular position in the container, or inserting a range of values from another container (or array), starting at a particular position in the original container.

Lines 46 and 51 use the two erase functions that are available in all first-class containers. Line 46 indicates that the element at the location specified by the iterator argument should be removed from the container (in this example, the element at the beginning of the vector). Line 51 specifies that all elements in the range starting with the location of the first argument up to—but not including—the location of the second argument should be erased from the container. In this example, all the elements are erased from the vector. Line 53 uses function empty (available for all containers and adapters) to confirm that the vector is empty.

Common Programming Error 22.4

Erasing an element that contains a pointer to a dynamically allocated object does not delete *that object; this can lead to a memory leak.*

Line 56 demonstrates the version of function insert that uses the second and third arguments to specify the starting location and ending location in a sequence of values (pos-

STL exception types	Description
out_of_range	Indicates when subscript is out of range—e.g., when an invalid subscript is specified to vector member function at.
invalid_argument	Indicates an invalid argument was passed to a function.
length_error	Indicates an attempt to create too long a container, string, etc.
bad_alloc	Indicates that an attempt to allocate memory with s (or with an allocator) failed because not enough memory was available.

Fig. 22.16 | Some STL exception types.

sibly from another container; in this case, from array of integers array) that should be inserted into the vector. Remember that the ending location specifies the position in the sequence after the last element to be inserted; copying is performed up to—but not including—this location.

Finally, line 61 uses function clear (found in all first-class containers) to empty the vector. This function calls the version of erase used in line 51 to empty the vector.

[*Note:* Other functions that are common to all containers and common to all sequence containers have not yet been covered. We will cover most of these in the next few sections. We will also cover many functions that are specific to each container.]

22.2.2 list Sequence Container

The list sequence container provides an efficient implementation for insertion and deletion operations at any location in the container. If most of the insertions and deletions occur at the ends of the container, the deque data structure (Section 22.2.3) provides a more efficient implementation. Class template list is implemented as a doubly linked list—every node in the list contains a pointer to the previous node in the list and to the next node in the list. This enables class template list to support bidirectional iterators that allow the container to be traversed both forward and backward. Any algorithm that requires input, output, forward or bidirectional iterators can operate on a list. Many of the list member functions manipulate the elements of the container as an ordered set of elements.

In addition to the member functions of all STL containers in Fig. 22.2 and the common member functions of all sequence containers discussed in Section 22.2, class template list provides nine other member functions—splice, push_front, pop_front, remove, remove_if, unique, merge, reverse and sort. Several of these member functions are list-optimized implementations of STL algorithms presented in Section 22.5. Figure 22.17 demonstrates several features of class list. Remember that many of the functions presented in Figs. 22.14–22.15 can be used with class list. Header file <list> must be included to use class list.

```
1   // Fig. 22.17: Fig22_17.cpp
2   // Standard library list class template test program.
3   #include <iostream>
4   using std::cout;
5   using std::endl;
6
7   #include <list> // list class-template definition
8   #include <algorithm> // copy algorithm
9   #include <iterator> // ostream_iterator
10
11  // prototype for function template printList
12  template < typename T > void printList( const std::list< T > &listRef );
13
14  int main()
15  {
16     const int SIZE = 4;
17     int array[ SIZE ] = { 2, 6, 4, 8 };
18     std::list< int > values; // create list of ints
```

Fig. 22.17 | Standard Library list class template. (Part 1 of 3.)

```
19          std::list< int > otherValues; // create list of ints
20
21          // insert items in values
22          values.push_front( 1 );
23          values.push_front( 2 );
24          values.push_back( 4 );
25          values.push_back( 3 );
26
27          cout << "values contains: ";
28          printList( values );
29
30          values.sort(); // sort values
31          cout << "\nvalues after sorting contains: ";
32          printList( values );
33
34          // insert elements of array into otherValues
35          otherValues.insert( otherValues.begin(), array, array + SIZE );
36          cout << "\nAfter insert, otherValues contains: ";
37          printList( otherValues );
38
39          // remove otherValues elements and insert at end of values
40          values.splice( values.end(), otherValues );
41          cout << "\nAfter splice, values contains: ";
42          printList( values );
43
44          values.sort(); // sort values
45          cout << "\nAfter sort, values contains: ";
46          printList( values );
47
48          // insert elements of array into otherValues
49          otherValues.insert( otherValues.begin(), array, array + SIZE );
50          otherValues.sort();
51          cout << "\nAfter insert, otherValues contains: ";
52          printList( otherValues );
53
54          // remove otherValues elements and insert into values in sorted order
55          values.merge( otherValues );
56          cout << "\nAfter merge:\n   values contains: ";
57          printList( values );
58          cout << "\n   otherValues contains: ";
59          printList( otherValues );
60
61          values.pop_front(); // remove element from front
62          values.pop_back(); // remove element from back
63          cout << "\nAfter pop_front and pop_back:\n   values contains: "
64          printList( values );
65
66          values.unique(); // remove duplicate elements
67          cout << "\nAfter unique, values contains: ";
68          printList( values );
69
70          // swap elements of values and otherValues
71          values.swap( otherValues );
```

Fig. 22.17 | Standard Library `list` class template. (Part 2 of 3.)

```
72       cout << "\nAfter swap:\n   values contains: ";
73       printList( values );
74       cout << "\n   otherValues contains: ";
75       printList( otherValues );
76
77       // replace contents of values with elements of otherValues
78       values.assign( otherValues.begin(), otherValues.end() );
79       cout << "\nAfter assign, values contains: ";
80       printList( values );
81
82       // remove otherValues elements and insert into values in sorted order
83       values.merge( otherValues );
84       cout << "\nAfter merge, values contains: ";
85       printList( values );
86
87       values.remove( 4 ); // remove all 4s
88       cout << "\nAfter remove( 4 ), values contains: ";
89       printList( values );
90       cout << endl;
91       return 0;
92    } // end main
93
94    // printList function template definition; uses
95    // ostream_iterator and copy algorithm to output list elements
96    template < typename T > void printList( const std::list< T > &listRef )
97    {
98       if ( listRef.empty() ) // list is empty
99          cout << "List is empty";
100      else
101      {
102         std::ostream_iterator< T > output( cout, " " );
103         std::copy( listRef.begin(), listRef.end(), output );
104      } // end else
105   } // end function printList
```

```
values contains: 2 1 4 3
values after sorting contains: 1 2 3 4
After insert, otherValues contains: 2 6 4 8
After splice, values contains: 1 2 3 4 2 6 4 8
After sort, values contains: 1 2 2 3 4 4 6 8
After insert, otherValues contains: 2 4 6 8
After merge:
   values contains: 1 2 2 2 3 4 4 4 6 6 8 8
   otherValues contains: List is empty
After pop_front and pop_back:
   values contains: 2 2 2 3 4 4 4 6 6 8
After unique, values contains: 2 3 4 6 8
After swap:
   values contains: List is empty
   otherValues contains: 2 3 4 6 8
After assign, values contains: 2 3 4 6 8
After merge, values contains: 2 2 3 3 4 4 6 6 8 8
After remove( 4 ), values contains: 2 2 3 3 6 6 8 8
```

Fig. 22.17 | Standard Library `list` class template. (Part 3 of 3.)

Lines 18–19 instantiate two `list` objects capable of storing integers. Lines 22–23 use function `push_front` to insert integers at the beginning of `values`. Function push_front is specific to classes `list` and `deque` (not to `vector`). Lines 24–25 use function push_back to insert integers at the end of `values`. Remember that function push_back is common to all sequence containers.

Line 30 uses `list` member function `sort` to arrange the elements in the `list` in ascending order. [*Note:* This is different from the `sort` in the STL algorithms.] A second version of function `sort` that allows the programmer to supply a binary predicate function that takes two arguments (values in the list), performs a comparison and returns a `bool` value indicating the result. This function determines the order in which the elements of the `list` are sorted. This version could be particularly useful for a `list` that stores pointers rather than values. [*Note:* We demonstrate a unary predicate function in Fig. 22.28. A unary predicate function takes a single argument, performs a comparison using that argument and returns a `bool` value indicating the result.]

Line 40 uses `list` function `splice` to remove the elements in `otherValues` and insert them into `values` before the iterator position specified as the first argument. There are two other versions of this function. Function `splice` with three arguments allows one element to be removed from the container specified as the second argument from the location specified by the iterator in the third argument. Function `splice` with four arguments uses the last two arguments to specify a range of locations that should be removed from the container in the second argument and placed at the location specified in the first argument.

After inserting more elements in `otherValues` and sorting both `values` and `other-Values`, line 55 uses `list` member function `merge` to remove all elements of `otherValues` and insert them in sorted order into `values`. Both `list`s must be sorted in the same order before this operation is performed. A second version of `merge` enables the programmer to supply a predicate function that takes two arguments (values in the list) and returns a `bool` value. The predicate function specifies the sorting order used by `merge`.

Line 61 uses `list` function `pop_front` to remove the first element in the `list`. Line 62 uses function `pop_back` (available for all sequence containers) to remove the last element in the `list`.

Line 66 uses `list` function `unique` to remove duplicate elements in the `list`. The `list` should be in sorted order (so that all duplicates are side by side) before this operation is performed, to guarantee that all duplicates are eliminated. A second version of `unique` enables the programmer to supply a predicate function that takes two arguments (values in the list) and returns a `bool` value specifying whether two elements are equal.

Line 71 uses function `swap` (available to all containers) to exchange the contents of `values` with the contents of `otherValues`.

Line 78 uses `list` function `assign` to replace the contents of `values` with the contents of `otherValues` in the range specified by the two iterator arguments. A second version of `assign` replaces the original contents with copies of the value specified in the second argument. The first argument of the function specifies the number of copies. Line 87 uses `list` function `remove` to delete all copies of the value 4 from the `list`.

22.2.3 deque Sequence Container

Class `deque` provides many of the benefits of a `vector` and a `list` in one container. The term `deque` is short for "double-ended queue." Class `deque` is implemented to provide efficient indexed access (using subscripting) for reading and modifying its elements, much like a vector. Class deque is also implemented for efficient insertion and deletion operations at its front and back, much like a list (although a list is also capable of efficient insertions and deletions in the middle of the list). Class deque provides support for random-access iterators, so deques can be used with all STL algorithms. One of the most common uses of a deque is to maintain a first-in, first-out queue of elements. In fact, a deque is the default underlying implementation for the queue adaptor (Section 22.4.2).

Additional storage for a deque can be allocated at either end of the deque in blocks of memory that are typically maintained as an array of pointers to those blocks.[3] Due to the noncontiguous memory layout of a deque, a deque iterator must be more intelligent than the pointers that are used to iterate through vectors or pointer-based arrays.

Performance Tip 22.13

In general, deque has slightly higher overhead than vector.

Performance Tip 22.14

Insertions and deletions in the middle of a deque are optimized to minimize the number of elements copied, so it is more efficient than a vector but less efficient than a list for this kind of modification.

Class deque provides the same basic operations as class vector, but adds member functions push_front and pop_front to allow insertion and deletion at the beginning of the deque, respectively.

Figure 22.18 demonstrates features of class deque. Remember that many of the functions presented in Fig. 22.14, Fig. 22.15 and Fig. 22.17 also can be used with class deque. Header file <deque> must be included to use class deque.

Line 13 instantiates a deque that can store double values. Lines 17–19 use functions push_front and push_back to insert elements at the beginning and end of the deque. Remember that push_back is available for all sequence containers, but push_front is available only for class list and class deque.

```
1   // Fig. 22.18: Fig22_18.cpp
2   // Standard Library class deque test program.
3   #include <iostream>
4   using std::cout;
5   using std::endl;
6
7   #include <deque> // deque class-template definition
8   #include <algorithm> // copy algorithm
9   #include <iterator> // ostream_iterator
10
11  int main()
12  {
13     std::deque< double > values; // create deque of doubles
```

Fig. 22.18 | Standard Library deque class template. (Part 1 of 2.)

---

3.   This is an implementation-specific detail, not a requirement of the C++ standard.

```
14    std::ostream_iterator< double > output( cout, " " );
15
16    // insert elements in values
17    values.push_front( 2.2 );
18    values.push_front( 3.5 );
19    values.push_back( 1.1 );
20
21    cout << "values contains: ";
22
23    // use subscript operator to obtain elements of values
24    for ( unsigned int i = 0; i < values.size(); i++ )
25       cout << values[ i ] << ' ';
26
27    values.pop_front(); // remove first element
28    cout << "\nAfter pop_front, values contains: ";
29    std::copy( values.begin(), values.end(), output );
30
31    // use subscript operator to modify element at location 1
32    values[ 1 ] = 5.4;
33    cout << "\nAfter values[ 1 ] = 5.4, values contains: ";
34    std::copy( values.begin(), values.end(), output );
35    cout << endl;
36    return 0;
37 } // end main
```

```
values contains: 3.5 2.2 1.1
After pop_front, values contains: 2.2 1.1
After values[ 1 ] = 5.4, values contains: 2.2 5.4
```

Fig. 22.18 | Standard Library deque class template. (Part 2 of 2.)

The for statement at lines 24–25 uses the subscript operator to retrieve the value in each element of the deque for output. Note that the condition uses function size to ensure that we do not attempt to access an element outside the bounds of the deque.

Line 27 uses function pop_front to demonstrate removing the first element of the deque. Remember that pop_front is available only for class list and class deque (not for class vector).

Line 32 uses the subscript operator to create an *lvalue*. This enables values to be assigned directly to any element of the deque.

22.3 Associative Containers

The STL's associative containers provide direct access to store and retrieve elements via keys (often called search keys). The four associative containers are multiset, set, multimap and map. Each associative container maintains its keys in sorted order. Iterating through an associative container traverses it in the sort order for that container. Classes multiset and set provide operations for manipulating sets of values where the values are the keys—there is not a separate value associated with each key. The primary difference between a multiset and a set is that a multiset allows duplicate keys and a set does not. Classes multimap and map provide operations for manipulating values associated with keys (these values are sometimes referred to as mapped values). The primary difference between a `multimap` and a `map` is that a `multimap` allows duplicate keys with associated values to be stored and a `map` allows only unique keys with associated values. In addition to the common member functions of all containers presented in Fig. 22.2, all associative containers also support several other member functions, including `find`, `lower_bound`, `upper_bound` and `count`. Examples of each of the associative containers and the common associative container member functions are presented in the next several subsections.

22.3.1 `multiset` Associative Container

The `multiset` associative container provides fast storage and retrieval of keys and allows duplicate keys. The ordering of the elements is determined by a comparator function object. For example, in an integer `multiset`, elements can be sorted in ascending order by ordering the keys with comparator function object `less< int >`. We discuss function objects in detail in Section 22.7. The data type of the keys in all associative containers must support comparison properly based on the comparator function object specified—keys sorted with `less< T >` must support comparison with `operator<`. If the keys used in the associative containers are of user-defined data types, those types must supply the appropriate comparison operators. A `multiset` supports bidirectional iterators (but not random-access iterators).

Figure 22.19 demonstrates the `multiset` associative container for a `multiset` of integers sorted in ascending order. Header file `<set>` must be included to use class `multiset`. Containers `multiset` and `set` provide the same member functions.

Line 10 uses a `typedef` to create a new type name (alias) for a `multiset` of integers ordered in ascending order, using the function object `less< int >`. Ascending order is the default for a `multiset`, so `std::less< int >` can be omitted in line 10. This new type (`Ims`) is then used to instantiate an integer `multiset` object, `intMultiset` (line 19).

 Good Programming Practice 22.1

Use typedefs to make code with long type names (such as multisets) easier to read.

The output statement at line 22 uses function `count` (available to all associative containers) to count the number of occurrences of the value 15 currently in the `multiset`.

```
1   // Fig. 22.19: Fig22_19.cpp
2   // Testing Standard Library class multiset
3   #include <iostream>
4   using std::cout;
5   using std::endl;
6
7   #include <set> // multiset class-template definition
8
9   // define short name for multiset type used in this program
10  typedef std::multiset< int, std::less< int > > Ims;
11
12  #include <algorithm> // copy algorithm
13  #include <iterator> // ostream_iterator
14
```

Fig. 22.19 | Standard Library `multiset` class template. (Part 1 of 3.)

```cpp
15   int main()
16   {
17      const int SIZE = 10;
18      int a[ SIZE ] = { 7, 22, 9, 1, 18, 30, 100, 22, 85, 13 };
19      Ims intMultiset; // Ims is typedef for "integer multiset"
20      std::ostream_iterator< int > output( cout, " " );
21
22      cout << "There are currently " << intMultiset.count( 15 )
23         << " values of 15 in the multiset\n";
24
25      intMultiset.insert( 15 ); // insert 15 in intMultiset
26      intMultiset.insert( 15 ); // insert 15 in intMultiset
27      cout << "After inserts, there are " << intMultiset.count( 15 )
28         << " values of 15 in the multiset\n\n";
29
30      // iterator that cannot be used to change element values
31      Ims::const_iterator result;
32
33      // find 15 in intMultiset; find returns iterator
34      result = intMultiset.find( 15 );
35
36      if ( result != intMultiset.end() ) // if iterator not at end
37         cout << "Found value 15\n"; // found search value 15
38
39      // find 20 in intMultiset; find returns iterator
40      result = intMultiset.find( 20 );
41
42      if ( result == intMultiset.end() ) // will be true hence
43         cout << "Did not find value 20\n"; // did not find 20
44
45      // insert elements of array a into intMultiset
46      intMultiset.insert( a, a + SIZE );
47      cout << "\nAfter insert, intMultiset contains:\n";
48      std::copy( intMultiset.begin(), intMultiset.end(), output );
49
50      // determine lower and upper bound of 22 in intMultiset
51      cout << "\n\nLower bound of 22: "
52         << *( intMultiset.lower_bound( 22 ) );
53      cout << "\nUpper bound of 22: " << *( intMultiset.upper_bound( 22 ) );
54
55      // p represents pair of const_iterators
56      std::pair< Ims::const_iterator, Ims::const_iterator > p;
57
58      // use equal_range to determine lower and upper bound
59      // of 22 in intMultiset
60      p = intMultiset.equal_range( 22 );
61
62      cout << "\n\nequal_range of 22:" << "\n   Lower bound: "
63         << *( p.first ) << "\n   Upper bound: " << *( p.second );
64      cout << endl;
65      return 0;
66   } // end main
```

Fig. 22.19 | Standard Library `multiset` class template. (Part 2 of 3.)

```
There are currently 0 values of 15 in the multiset
After inserts, there are 2 values of 15 in the multiset

Found value 15
Did not find value 20

After insert, intMultiset contains:
1 7 9 13 15 15 18 22 22 30 85 100

Lower bound of 22: 22
Upper bound of 22: 30

equal_range of 22:
   Lower bound: 22
   Upper bound: 30
```

Fig. 22.19 | Standard Library `multiset` class template. (Part 3 of 3.)

Lines 25–26 use one of the three versions of function `insert` to add the value 15 to the `multiset` twice. A second version of `insert` takes an iterator and a value as arguments and begins the search for the insertion point from the iterator position specified. A third version of `insert` takes two iterators as arguments that specify a range of values to add to the `multiset` from another container.

Line 34 uses function `find` (available to all associative containers) to locate the value 15 in the `multiset`. Function `find` returns an `iterator` or a `const_iterator` pointing to the earliest location at which the value is found. If the value is not found, `find` returns an `iterator` or a `const_iterator` equal to the value returned by a call to `end`. Line 41 demonstrates this case.

Line 46 uses function `insert` to insert the elements of array a into the `multiset`. At line 48, the `copy` algorithm copies the elements of the `multiset` to the standard output. Note that the elements are displayed in ascending order.

Lines 52 and 53 use functions `lower_bound` and `upper_bound` (available in all associative containers) to locate the earliest occurrence of the value 22 in the `multiset` and the element *after* the last occurrence of the value 22 in the `multiset`. Both functions return `iterators` or `const_iterators` pointing to the appropriate location or the iterator returned by `end` if the value is not in the `multiset`.

Line 56 instantiates an instance of class `pair` called p. Objects of class `pair` are used to associate pairs of values. In this example, the contents of a `pair` are two `const_iterators` for our integer-based `multiset`. The purpose of p is to store the return value of `multiset` function `equal_range` that returns a `pair` containing the results of both a `lower_bound` and an `upper_bound` operation. Type `pair` contains two `public` data members called `first` and `second`.

Line 60 uses function `equal_range` to determine the `lower_bound` and `upper_bound` of 22 in the `multiset`. Line 63 uses `p.first` and `p.second`, respectively, to access the `lower_bound` and `upper_bound`. We dereferenced the iterators to output the values at the locations returned from `equal_range`.

22.3.2 set Associative Container

The set associative container is used for fast storage and retrieval of unique keys. The implementation of a set is identical to that of a multiset, except that a set must have unique keys. Therefore, if an attempt is made to insert a duplicate key into a set, the duplicate is ignored; because this is the intended mathematical behavior of a set, we do not identify it as a common programming error. A set supports bidirectional iterators (but not random-access iterators). Figure 22.20 demonstrates a set of doubles. Header file <set> must be included to use class set.

```cpp
1   // Fig. 22.20: Fig22_20.cpp
2   // Standard Library class set test program.
3   #include <iostream>
4   using std::cout;
5   using std::endl;
6
7   #include <set>
8
9   // define short name for set type used in this program
10  typedef std::set< double, std::less< double > > DoubleSet;
11
12  #include <algorithm>
13  #include <iterator> // ostream_iterator
14
15  int main()
16  {
17     const int SIZE = 5;
18     double a[ SIZE ] = { 2.1, 4.2, 9.5, 2.1, 3.7 };
19     DoubleSet doubleSet( a, a + SIZE );
20     std::ostream_iterator< double > output( cout, " " );
21
22     cout << "doubleSet contains: ";
23     std::copy( doubleSet.begin(), doubleSet.end(), output );
24
25     // p represents pair containing const_iterator and bool
26     std::pair< DoubleSet::const_iterator, bool > p;
27
28     // insert 13.8 in doubleSet; insert returns pair in which
29     // p.first represents location of 13.8 in doubleSet and
30     // p.second represents whether 13.8 was inserted
31     p = doubleSet.insert( 13.8 ); // value not in set
32     cout << "\n\n" << *( p.first )
33        << ( p.second ? " was" : " was not" ) << " inserted";
34     cout << "\ndoubleSet contains: ";
35     std::copy( doubleSet.begin(), doubleSet.end(), output );
36
37     // insert 9.5 in doubleSet
38     p = doubleSet.insert( 9.5 ); // value already in set
39     cout << "\n\n" << *( p.first )
40        << ( p.second ? " was" : " was not" ) << " inserted";
41     cout << "\ndoubleSet contains: ";
42     std::copy( doubleSet.begin(), doubleSet.end(), output );
```

Fig. 22.20 | Standard Library set class template. (Part 1 of 2.)

```
43      cout << endl;
44      return 0;
45  } // end main
```

```
doubleSet contains: 2.1 3.7 4.2 9.5

13.8 was inserted
doubleSet contains: 2.1 3.7 4.2 9.5 13.8

9.5 was not inserted
doubleSet contains: 2.1 3.7 4.2 9.5 13.8
```

Fig. 22.20 | Standard Library set class template. (Part 2 of 2.)

Line 10 uses typedef to create a new type name (DoubleSet) for a set of double values ordered in ascending order, using the function object less< double >.

Line 19 uses the new type DoubleSet to instantiate object doubleSet. The constructor call takes the elements in array a between a and a + SIZE (i.e., the entire array) and inserts them into the set. Line 23 uses algorithm copy to output the contents of the set. Notice that the value 2.1—which appeared twice in array a—appears only once in doubleSet. This is because container set does not allow duplicates.

Line 26 defines a pair consisting of a const_iterator for a DoubleSet and a bool value. This object stores the result of a call to set function insert.

Line 31 uses function insert to place the value 13.8 in the set. The returned pair, p, contains an iterator p.first pointing to the value 13.8 in the set and a bool value that is true if the value was inserted and false if the value was not inserted (because it was already in the set). In this case, 13.8 was not in the set, so it was inserted. Line 38 attempts to insert 9.5, which is already in the set. The output of lines 39–40 shows that 9.5 was not inserted.

22.3.3 multimap Associative Container

The multimap associative container is used for fast storage and retrieval of keys and associated values (often called key/value pairs). Many of the functions used with multisets and sets are also used with multimaps and maps. The elements of multimaps and maps are pairs of keys and values instead of individual values. When inserting into a multimap or map, a pair object that contains the key and the value is used. The ordering of the keys is determined by a comparator function object. For example, in a multimap that uses integers as the key type, keys can be sorted in ascending order by ordering them with comparator function object less< int >. Duplicate keys are allowed in a multimap, so multiple values can be associated with a single key. This is often called a one-to-many relationship. For example, in a credit-card transaction-processing system, one credit-card account can have many associated transactions; in a university, one student can take many courses, and one professor can teach many students; in the military, one rank (like "private") has many people. A multimap supports bidirectional iterators, but not random-access iterators. Figure 22.21 demonstrates the multimap associative container. Header file <map> must be included to use class multimap.

Performance Tip 22.15

A multimap is implemented to efficiently locate all values paired with a given key.

Line 10 uses typedef to define alias Mmid for a multimap type in which the key type is int, the type of a key's associated value is double and the elements are ordered in ascending order. Line 14 uses the new type to instantiate a multimap called pairs. Line 16 uses function count to determine the number of key/value pairs with a key of 15.

```cpp
1   // Fig. 22.21: Fig22_21.cpp
2   // Standard Library class multimap test program.
3   #include <iostream>
4   using std::cout;
5   using std::endl;
6
7   #include <map> // map class-template definition
8
9   // define short name for multimap type used in this program
10  typedef std::multimap< int, double, std::less< int > > Mmid;
11
12  int main()
13  {
14     Mmid pairs; // declare the multimap pairs
15
16     cout << "There are currently " << pairs.count( 15 )
17        << " pairs with key 15 in the multimap\n";
18
19     // insert two value_type objects in pairs
20     pairs.insert( Mmid::value_type( 15, 2.7 ) );
21     pairs.insert( Mmid::value_type( 15, 99.3 ) );
22
23     cout << "After inserts, there are " << pairs.count( 15 )
24        << " pairs with key 15\n\n";
25
26     // insert five value_type objects in pairs
27     pairs.insert( Mmid::value_type( 30, 111.11 ) );
28     pairs.insert( Mmid::value_type( 10, 22.22 ) );
29     pairs.insert( Mmid::value_type( 25, 33.333 ) );
30     pairs.insert( Mmid::value_type( 20, 9.345 ) );
31     pairs.insert( Mmid::value_type( 5, 77.54 ) );
32
33     cout << "Multimap pairs contains:\nKey\tValue\n";
34
35     // use const_iterator to walk through elements of pairs
36     for ( Mmid::const_iterator iter = pairs.begin();
37        iter != pairs.end(); ++iter )
38        cout << iter->first << '\t' << iter->second << '\n';
39
40     cout << endl;
41     return 0;
42  } // end main
```

Fig. 22.21 | Standard Library multimap class template. (Part 1 of 2.)

```
There are currently 0 pairs with key 15 in the multimap
After inserts, there are 2 pairs with key 15

Multimap pairs contains:
Key     Value
5       77.54
10      22.22
15      2.7
15      99.3
20      9.345
25      33.333
30      111.11
```

Fig. 22.21 | Standard Library `multimap` class template. (Part 2 of 2.)

Line 20 uses function `insert` to add a new key/value pair to the `multimap`. The expression `Mmid::value_type( 15, 2.7 )` creates a `pair` object in which `first` is the key (15) of type `int` and `second` is the value (2.7) of type `double`. The type `Mmid::value_type` is defined as part of the `typedef` for the `multimap`. Line 21 inserts another `pair` object with the key 15 and the value 99.3. Then lines 23–24 output the number of pairs with key 15.

Lines 27–31 insert five additional `pairs` into the `multimap`. The `for` statement at lines 36–38 outputs the contents of the `multimap`, including both keys and values. Line 38 uses the `const_iterator` called `iter` to access the members of the `pair` in each element of the `multimap`. Notice in the output that the keys appear in ascending order.

22.3.4 map Associative Container

The map associative container is used for fast storage and retrieval of unique keys and associated values. Duplicate keys are not allowed in a map, so only a single value can be associated with each key. This is called a one-to-one mapping. For example, a company that uses unique employee numbers, such as 100, 200 and 300, might have a map that associates employee numbers with their telephone extensions—4321, 4115 and 5217, respectively. With a map you specify the key and get back the associated data quickly. A map is commonly called an associative array. Providing the key in a map's subscript operator `[]` locates the value associated with that key in the map. Insertions and deletions can be made anywhere in a map.

Figure 22.22 demonstrates the map associative container and uses the same features as Fig. 22.21 to demonstrate the subscript operator. Header file `<map>` must be included to

```
1   // Fig. 22.22: Fig22_22.cpp
2   // Standard Library class map test program.
3   #include <iostream>
4   using std::cout;
5   using std::endl;
6
7   #include <map> // map class-template definition
8
9   // define short name for map type used in this program
10  typedef std::map< int, double, std::less< int > > Mid;
11
```

Fig. 22.22 | Standard Library map class template. (Part 1 of 2.)

```
12   int main()
13   {
14      Mid pairs;
15
16      // insert eight value_type objects in pairs
17      pairs.insert( Mid::value_type( 15, 2.7 ) );
18      pairs.insert( Mid::value_type( 30, 111.11 ) );
19      pairs.insert( Mid::value_type( 5, 1010.1 ) );
20      pairs.insert( Mid::value_type( 10, 22.22 ) );
21      pairs.insert( Mid::value_type( 25, 33.333 ) );
22      pairs.insert( Mid::value_type( 5, 77.54 ) ); // dup ignored
23      pairs.insert( Mid::value_type( 20, 9.345 ) );
24      pairs.insert( Mid::value_type( 15, 99.3 ) ); // dup ignored
25
26      cout << "pairs contains:\nKey\tValue\n";
27
28      // use const_iterator to walk through elements of pairs
29      for ( Mid::const_iterator iter = pairs.begin();
30         iter != pairs.end(); ++iter )
31         cout << iter->first << '\t' << iter->second << '\n';
32
33      pairs[ 25 ] = 9999.99; // use subscripting to change value for key 25
34      pairs[ 40 ] = 8765.43; // use subscripting to insert value for key 40
35
36      cout << "\nAfter subscript operations, pairs contains:\nKey\tValue\n";
37
38      // use const_iterator to walk through elements of pairs
39      for ( Mid::const_iterator iter2 = pairs.begin();
40         iter2 != pairs.end(); ++iter2 )
41         cout << iter2->first << '\t' << iter2->second << '\n';
42
43      cout << endl;
44      return 0;
45   } // end main
```

```
pairs contains:
Key     Value
5       1010.1
10      22.22
15      2.7
20      9.345
25      33.333
30      111.11

After subscript operations, pairs contains:
Key     Value
5       1010.1
10      22.22
15      2.7
20      9.345
25      9999.99
30      111.11
40      8765.43
```

Fig. 22.22 | Standard Library map class template. (Part 2 of 2.)

use class map. Lines 33 and 34 use the subscript operator of class map. When the subscript is a key that is already in the map (line 33), the operator returns a reference to the associated value. When the subscript is a key that is not in the map (line 34), the operator inserts the key in the map and returns a reference that can be used to associate a value with that key. Line 33 replaces the value for the key 25 (previously 33.333 as specified in line 21) with a new value, 9999.99. Line 34 inserts a new key/value pair in the map (called creating an association).

22.4 Container Adapters

The STL provides three container adapters—stack, queue and priority_queue. Adapters are not first-class containers, because they do not provide the actual data-structure implementation in which elements can be stored and because adapters do not support iterators. The benefit of an adapter class is that the programmer can choose an appropriate underlying data structure. All three adapter classes provide member functions push and pop that properly insert an element into each adapter data structure and properly remove an element from each adapter data structure. The next several subsections provide examples of the adapter classes.

22.4.1 stack Adapter

Class stack enables insertions into and deletions from the underlying data structure at one end (commonly referred to as a last-in, first-out data structure). A stack can be implemented with any of the sequence containers: vector, list and deque. This example creates three integer stacks, using each of the sequence containers of the Standard Library as the underlying data structure to represent the stack. By default, a stack is implemented with a deque. The stack operations are push to insert an element at the top of the stack (implemented by calling function push_back of the underlying container), pop to remove the top element of the stack (implemented by calling function pop_back of the underlying container), top to get a reference to the top element of the stack (implemented by calling function back of the underlying container), empty to determine whether the stack is empty (implemented by calling function empty of the underlying container) and size to get the number of elements in the stack (implemented by calling function size of the underlying container).

Performance Tip 22.16

Each of the common operations of a stack is implemented as an inline function that calls the appropriate function of the underlying container. This avoids the overhead of a second function call.

Performance Tip 22.17

For the best performance, use class deque or vector as the underlying container for a stack.

Figure 22.23 demonstrates the stack adapter class. Header file <stack> must be included to use class stack.

Lines 20, 23 and 26 instantiate three integer stacks. Line 20 specifies a stack of integers that uses the default deque container as its underlying data structure. Line 23 specifies a stack of integers that uses a vector of integers as its underlying data structure. Line 26 specifies a stack of integers that uses a list of integers as its underlying data structure.

Function pushElements (lines 49–56) pushes the elements onto each stack. Line 53 uses function push (available in each adapter class) to place an integer on top of the stack. Line 54 uses stack function top to retrieve the top element of the stack for output. Function top does not remove the top element.

Function popElements (lines 59–66) pops the elements off each stack. Line 63 uses stack function top to retrieve the top element of the stack for output. Line 64 uses function pop (available in each adapter class) to remove the top element of the stack. Function pop does not return a value.

```cpp
1   // Fig. 22.23: Fig22_23.cpp
2   // Standard Library adapter stack test program.
3   #include <iostream>
4   using std::cout;
5   using std::endl;
6
7   #include <stack> // stack adapter definition
8   #include <vector> // vector class-template definition
9   #include <list> // list class-template definition
10
11  // pushElements function-template prototype
12  template< typename T > void pushElements( T &stackRef );
13
14  // popElements function-template prototype
15  template< typename T > void popElements( T &stackRef );
16
17  int main()
18  {
19     // stack with default underlying deque
20     std::stack< int > intDequeStack;
21
22     // stack with underlying vector
23     std::stack< int, std::vector< int > > intVectorStack;
24
25     // stack with underlying list
26     std::stack< int, std::list< int > > intListStack;
27
28     // push the values 0-9 onto each stack
29     cout << "Pushing onto intDequeStack: ";
30     pushElements( intDequeStack );
31     cout << "\nPushing onto intVectorStack: ";
32     pushElements( intVectorStack );
33     cout << "\nPushing onto intListStack: ";
34     pushElements( intListStack );
35     cout << endl << endl;
36
37     // display and remove elements from each stack
38     cout << "Popping from intDequeStack: ";
39     popElements( intDequeStack );
```

Fig. 22.23 | Standard Library stack adapter class. (Part 1 of 2.)

```
40      cout << "\nPopping from intVectorStack: ";
41      popElements( intVectorStack );
42      cout << "\nPopping from intListStack: ";
43      popElements( intListStack );
44      cout << endl;
45      return 0;
46   } // end main
47
48   // push elements onto stack object to which stackRef refers
49   template< typename T > void pushElements( T &stackRef )
50   {
51      for ( int i = 0; i < 10; i++ )
52      {
53         stackRef.push( i ); // push element onto stack
54         cout << stackRef.top() << ' '; // view (and display ) top element
55      } // end for
56   } // end function pushElements
57
58   // pop elements from stack object to which stackRef refers
59   template< typename T > void popElements( T &stackRef )
60   {
61      while ( !stackRef.empty() )
62      {
63         cout << stackRef.top() << ' '; // view (and display) top element
64         stackRef.pop(); // remove top element
65      } // end while
66   } // end function popElements
```

```
Pushing onto intDequeStack: 0 1 2 3 4 5 6 7 8 9
Pushing onto intVectorStack: 0 1 2 3 4 5 6 7 8 9
Pushing onto intListStack: 0 1 2 3 4 5 6 7 8 9

Popping from intDequeStack: 9 8 7 6 5 4 3 2 1 0
Popping from intVectorStack: 9 8 7 6 5 4 3 2 1 0
Popping from intListStack: 9 8 7 6 5 4 3 2 1 0
```

Fig. 22.23 | Standard Library stack adapter class. (Part 2 of 2.)

22.4.2 queue Adapter

Class queue enables insertions at the back of the underlying data structure and deletions from the front (commonly referred to as a first-in, first-out data structure). A queue can be implemented with STL data structure list or deque. By default, a queue is implemented with a deque. The common queue operations are push to insert an element at the back of the queue (implemented by calling function push_back of the underlying container), pop to remove the element at the front of the queue (implemented by calling function pop_front of the underlying container), front to get a reference to the first element in the queue (implemented by calling function front of the underlying container), back to get a reference to the last element in the queue (implemented by calling function back of the underlying container), empty to determine whether the queue is empty (implemented by calling function empty of the underlying container) and size to get the number of elements in the queue (implemented by calling function size of the underlying container).

Performance Tip 22.18

Each of the common operations of a queue is implemented as an inline function that calls the appropriate function of the underlying container. This avoids the overhead of a second function call.

Performance Tip 22.19

For the best performance, use class deque or list as the underlying container for a queue.

Figure 22.24 demonstrates the queue adapter class. Header file `<queue>` must be included to use a queue.

Line 11 instantiates a queue that stores double values. Lines 14–16 use function push to add elements to the queue. The while statement at lines 21–25 uses function empty (available in all containers) to determine whether the queue is empty (line 21). While there are more elements in the queue, line 23 uses queue function front to read (but not remove) the first element in the queue for output. Line 24 removes the first element in the queue with function pop (available in all adapter classes).

```cpp
1   // Fig. 22.24: Fig22_24.cpp
2   // Standard Library adapter queue test program.
3   #include <iostream>
4   using std::cout;
5   using std::endl;
6
7   #include <queue> // queue adapter definition
8
9   int main()
10  {
11     std::queue< double > values; // queue with doubles
12
13     // push elements onto queue values
14     values.push( 3.2 );
15     values.push( 9.8 );
16     values.push( 5.4 );
17
18     cout << "Popping from values: ";
19
20     // pop elements from queue
21     while ( !values.empty() )
22     {
23        cout << values.front() << ' '; // view front element
24        values.pop(); // remove element
25     } // end while
26
27     cout << endl;
28     return 0;
29  } // end main
```

```
Popping from values: 3.2 9.8 5.4
```

Fig. 22.24 | Standard Library queue adapter class templates.

22.4.3 priority_queue Adapter

Class `priority_queue` provides functionality that enables insertions in sorted order into the underlying data structure and deletions from the front of the underlying data structure. A priority_queue can be implemented with STL sequence containers vector or deque. By default, a priority_queue is implemented with a vector as the underlying container. When elements are added to a priority_queue, they are inserted in priority order, such that the highest-priority element (i.e., the largest value) will be the first element removed from the priority_queue. This is usually accomplished via a sorting technique called heapsort that always maintains the largest value (i.e., highest-priority element) at the front of the data structure—such a data structure is called a heap. The comparison of elements is performed with comparator function object less< T > by default, but the programmer can supply a different comparator.

The common priority_queue operations are **push** to insert an element at the appropriate location based on priority order of the priority_queue (implemented by calling function push_back of the underlying container, then reordering the elements using heapsort), **pop** to remove the highest-priority element of the priority_queue (implemented by calling function pop_back of the underlying container after removing the top element of the heap), **top** to get a reference to the top element of the priority_queue (implemented by calling function front of the underlying container), **empty** to determine whether the priority_queue is empty (implemented by calling function empty of the underlying container) and **size** to get the number of elements in the priority_queue (implemented by calling function size of the underlying container).

Performance Tip 22.20

Each of the common operations of a priority_queue is implemented as an inline function that calls the appropriate function of the underlying container. This avoids the overhead of a second function call.

Performance Tip 22.21

For the best performance, use class vector or deque as the underlying container for a priority_queue.

Figure 22.25 demonstrates the priority_queue adapter class. Header file **<queue>** must be included to use class priority_queue.

```
1   // Fig. 22.25: Fig22_25.cpp
2   // Standard Library adapter priority_queue test program.
3   #include <iostream>
4   using std::cout;
5   using std::endl;
6
7   #include <queue> // priority_queue adapter definition
8
9   int main()
10  {
11      std::priority_queue< double > priorities; // create priority_queue
12
```

Fig. 22.25 | Standard Library priority_queue adapter class. (Part 1 of 2.)

```
13      // push elements onto priorities
14      priorities.push( 3.2 );
15      priorities.push( 9.8 );
16      priorities.push( 5.4 );
17
18      cout << "Popping from priorities: ";
19
20      // pop element from priority_queue
21      while ( !priorities.empty() )
22      {
23         cout << priorities.top() << ' '; // view top element
24         priorities.pop(); // remove top element
25      } // end while
26
27      cout << endl;
28      return 0;
29   } // end main
```

```
Popping from priorities: 9.8 5.4 3.2
```

Fig. 22.25 | Standard Library `priority_queue` adapter class. (Part 2 of 2.)

Line 11 instantiates a `priority_queue` that stores `double` values and uses a `vector` as the underlying data structure. Lines 14–16 use function `push` to add elements to the `priority_queue`. The `while` statement at lines 21–25 uses function `empty` (available in all containers) to determine whether the `priority_queue` is empty (line 21). While there are more elements, line 23 uses `priority_queue` function `top` to retrieve the highest-priority element in the `priority_queue` for output. Line 24 removes the highest-priority element in the `priority_queue` with function `pop` (available in all adapter classes).

22.5 **Algorithms**

Until the STL, class libraries of containers and algorithms were essentially incompatible among vendors. Early container libraries generally used inheritance and polymorphism, with the associated overhead of `virtual` function calls. Early libraries built the algorithms into the container classes as class behaviors. The STL separates the algorithms from the containers. This makes it much easier to add new algorithms. With the STL, the elements of containers are accessed through iterators. The next several subsections demonstrate many of the STL algorithms.

Performance Tip 22.22

The STL is implemented for efficiency. It avoids the overhead of `virtual` function calls.

Software Engineering Observation 22.8

STL algorithms do not depend on the implementation details of the containers on which they operate. As long as the container's (or array's) iterators satisfy the requirements of the algorithm, STL algorithms can work on C-style, pointer-based arrays, on STL containers and on user-defined data structures.

Software Engineering Observation 22.9

Algorithms can be added easily to the STL without modifying the container classes.

22.5.1 `fill`, `fill_n`, `generate` and `generate_n`

Figure 22.26 demonstrates algorithms `fill`, `fill_n`, `generate` and `generate_n`. Functions `fill` and `fill_n` set every element in a range of container elements to a specific value. Functions **generate** and **generate_n** use a generator function to create values for every element

```
 1   // Fig. 22.26: Fig22_26.cpp
 2   // Standard Library algorithms fill, fill_n, generate and generate_n.
 3   #include <iostream>
 4   using std::cout;
 5   using std::endl;
 6
 7   #include <algorithm> // algorithm definitions
 8   #include <vector> // vector class-template definition
 9   #include <iterator> // ostream_iterator
10
11   char nextLetter(); // prototype of generator function
12
13   int main()
14   {
15      std::vector< char > chars( 10 );
16      std::ostream_iterator< char > output( cout, " " );
17      std::fill( chars.begin(), chars.end(), '5' ); // fill chars with 5s
18
19      cout << "Vector chars after filling with 5s:\n";
20      std::copy( chars.begin(), chars.end(), output );
21
22      // fill first five elements of chars with As
23      std::fill_n( chars.begin(), 5, 'A' );
24
25      cout << "\n\nVector chars after filling five elements with As:\n";
26      std::copy( chars.begin(), chars.end(), output );
27
28      // generate values for all elements of chars with nextLetter
29      std::generate( chars.begin(), chars.end(), nextLetter );
30
31      cout << "\n\nVector chars after generating letters A-J:\n";
32      std::copy( chars.begin(), chars.end(), output );
33
34      // generate values for first five elements of chars with nextLetter
35      std::generate_n( chars.begin(), 5, nextLetter );
36
37      cout << "\n\nVector chars after generating K-O for the"
38         << " first five elements:\n";
39      std::copy( chars.begin(), chars.end(), output );
40      cout << endl;
41      return 0;
42   } // end main
```

Fig. 22.26 | Algorithms `fill`, `fill_n`, `generate` and `generate_n`. (Part 1 of 2.)

```
43
44   // generator function returns next letter (starts with A)
45   char nextLetter()
46   {
47      static char letter = 'A';
48      return letter++;
49   } // end function nextLetter
```

```
Vector chars after filling with 5s:
5 5 5 5 5 5 5 5 5 5

Vector chars after filling five elements with As:
A A A A A 5 5 5 5 5

Vector chars after generating letters A-J:
A B C D E F G H I J

Vector chars after generating K-O for the first five elements:
K L M N O F G H I J
```

Fig. 22.26 | Algorithms `fill`, `fill_n`, `generate` and `generate_n`. (Part 2 of 2.)

in a range of container elements. The generator function takes no arguments and returns a value that can be placed in an element of the container.

Line 15 defines a 10-element `vector` that stores `char` values. Line 17 uses function `fill` to place the character `'5'` in every element of `vector chars` from `chars.begin()` up to, but not including, `chars.end()`. Note that the iterators supplied as the first and second argument must be at least forward iterators (i.e., they can be used for both input from a container and output to a container in the forward direction).

Line 23 uses function `fill_n` to place the character `'A'` in the first five elements of `vector chars`. The iterator supplied as the first argument must be at least an output iterator (i.e., it can be used for output to a container in the forward direction). The second argument specifies the number of elements to fill. The third argument specifies the value to place in each element.

Line 29 uses function `generate` to place the result of a call to generator function `nextLetter` in every element of `vector chars` from `chars.begin()` up to, but not including, `chars.end()`. The iterators supplied as the first and second arguments must be at least forward iterators. Function `nextLetter` (defined at lines 45–49) begins with the character `'A'` maintained in a `static` local variable. The statement at line 48 postincrements the value of `letter` and returns the old value of `letter` each time `nextLetter` is called.

Line 35 uses function `generate_n` to place the result of a call to generator function `nextLetter` in five elements of `vector chars`, starting from `chars.begin()`. The iterator supplied as the first argument must be at least an output iterator.

22.5.2 equal, `mismatch` and `lexicographical_compare`

Figure 22.27 demonstrates comparing sequences of values for equality using algorithms `equal`, `mismatch` and `lexicographical_compare`.

Line 29 uses function **equal** to compare two sequences of values for equality. Each sequence need not necessarily contain the same number of elements—equal returns `false`

```cpp
 1   // Fig. 22.27: Fig22_27.cpp
 2   // Standard Library functions equal, mismatch and lexicographical_compare.
 3   #include <iostream>
 4   using std::cout;
 5   using std::endl;
 6
 7   #include <algorithm> // algorithm definitions
 8   #include <vector> // vector class-template definition
 9   #include <iterator> // ostream_iterator
10
11   int main()
12   {
13      const int SIZE = 10;
14      int a1[ SIZE ] = { 1, 2, 3, 4, 5, 6, 7, 8, 9, 10 };
15      int a2[ SIZE ] = { 1, 2, 3, 4, 1000, 6, 7, 8, 9, 10 };
16      std::vector< int > v1( a1, a1 + SIZE ); // copy of a1
17      std::vector< int > v2( a1, a1 + SIZE ); // copy of a1
18      std::vector< int > v3( a2, a2 + SIZE ); // copy of a2
19      std::ostream_iterator< int > output( cout, " " );
20
21      cout << "Vector v1 contains: ";
22      std::copy( v1.begin(), v1.end(), output );
23      cout << "\nVector v2 contains: ";
24      std::copy( v2.begin(), v2.end(), output );
25      cout << "\nVector v3 contains: ";
26      std::copy( v3.begin(), v3.end(), output );
27
28      // compare vectors v1 and v2 for equality
29      bool result = std::equal( v1.begin(), v1.end(), v2.begin() );
30      cout << "\n\nVector v1 " << ( result ? "is" : "is not" )
31         << " equal to vector v2.\n";
32
33      // compare vectors v1 and v3 for equality
34      result = std::equal( v1.begin(), v1.end(), v3.begin() );
35      cout << "Vector v1 " << ( result ? "is" : "is not" )
36         << " equal to vector v3.\n";
37
38      // location represents pair of vector iterators
39      std::pair< std::vector< int >::iterator,
40         std::vector< int >::iterator > location;
41
42      // check for mismatch between v1 and v3
43      location = std::mismatch( v1.begin(), v1.end(), v3.begin() );
44      cout << "\nThere is a mismatch between v1 and v3 at location "
45         << ( location.first - v1.begin() ) << "\nwhere v1 contains "
46         << *location.first << " and v3 contains " << *location.second
47         << "\n\n";
48
49      char c1[ SIZE ] = "HELLO";
50      char c2[ SIZE ] = "BYE BYE";
51
52      // perform lexicographical comparison of c1 and c2
53      result = std::lexicographical_compare( c1, c1 + SIZE, c2, c2 + SIZE );
```

Fig. 22.27 | Algorithms `equal`, `mismatch` and `lexicographical_compare`. (Part 1 of 2.)

```
54        cout << c1 << ( result ? " is less than " :
55           " is greater than or equal to " )  << c2 << endl;
56        return 0;
57     } // end main
```

```
Vector v1 contains: 1 2 3 4 5 6 7 8 9 10
Vector v2 contains: 1 2 3 4 5 6 7 8 9 10
Vector v3 contains: 1 2 3 4 1000 6 7 8 9 10

Vector v1 is equal to vector v2.
Vector v1 is not equal to vector v3.

There is a mismatch between v1 and v3 at location 4
where v1 contains 5 and v3 contains 1000

HELLO is greater than or equal to BYE BYE
```

Fig. 22.27 | Algorithms equal, mismatch and lexicographical_compare. (Part 2 of 2.)

if the sequences are not of the same length. The == operator (whether built-in or over-loaded) performs the comparison of the elements. In this example, the elements in vector v1 from v1.begin() up to, but not including, v1.end() are compared to the elements in vector v2 starting from v2.begin(). In this example, v1 and v2 are equal. The three iterator arguments must be at least input iterators (i.e., they can be used for input from a sequence in the forward direction). Line 34 uses function equal to compare vectors v1 and v3, which are not equal.

There is another version of function equal that takes a binary predicate function as a fourth parameter. The binary predicate function receives the two elements being compared and returns a bool value indicating whether the elements are equal. This can be useful in sequences that store objects or pointers to values rather than actual values, because you can define one or more comparisons. For example, you can compare Employee objects for age, social security number, or location rather than comparing entire objects. You can compare what pointers refer to rather than comparing the pointer values (i.e., the addresses stored in the pointers).

Lines 39–43 begin by instantiating a pair of iterators called location for a vector of integers. This object stores the result of the call to mismatch (line 43). Function mismatch compares two sequences of values and returns a pair of iterators indicating the location in each sequence of the mismatched elements. If all the elements match, the two iterators in the pair are equal to the last iterator for each sequence. The three iterator arguments must be at least input iterators. Line 45 determines the actual location of the mismatch in the vectors with the expression location.first - v1.begin(). The result of this calculation is the number of elements between the iterators (this is analogous to pointer arithmetic, which we studied in Chapter 8). This corresponds to the element number in this example, because the comparison is performed from the beginning of each vector. As with function equal, there is another version of function mismatch that takes a binary predicate function as a fourth parameter.

Line 53 uses function lexicographical_compare to compare the contents of two character arrays. This function's four iterator arguments must be at least input iterators. As you know, pointers into arrays are random-access iterators. The first two iterator arguments specify the range of locations in the first sequence. The last two specify the range of locations in the second sequence. While iterating through the sequences, the lexicographical_compare checks if the element in the first sequence is less than the corresponding element in the second sequence. If so, the function returns true. If the element in the first sequence is greater than or equal to the element in the second sequence, the function returns false. This function can be used to arrange sequences lexicographically. Typically, such sequences contain strings.

22.5.3 remove, remove_if, remove_copy and remove_copy_if

Figure 22.28 demonstrates removing values from a sequence with algorithms remove, remove_if, remove_copy and remove_copy_if.

Line 26 uses function remove to eliminate all elements with the value 10 in the range from v.begin() up to, but not including, v.end() from v. The first two iterator arguments must be forward iterators so that the algorithm can modify the elements in the sequence. This function does not modify the number of elements in the vector or destroy the eliminated elements, but it does move all elements that are not eliminated toward the beginning of the vector. The function returns an iterator positioned after the last vector element that was not deleted. Elements from the iterator position to the end of the vector have undefined values (in this example, each "undefined" position has value 0).

Line 36 uses function remove_copy to copy all elements that do not have the value 10 in the range from v2.begin() up to, but not including, v2.end() from v2. The elements are placed in c, starting at position c.begin(). The iterators supplied as the first two arguments must be input iterators. The iterator supplied as the third argument must be an output iterator so that the element being copied can be inserted into the copy location. This function returns an iterator positioned after the last element copied into vector c. Note, in line 31, the use of the vector constructor that receives the number of elements in the vector and the initial values of those elements.

```cpp
1   // Fig. 22.28: Fig22_28.cpp
2   // Standard Library functions remove, remove_if,
3   // remove_copy and remove_copy_if.
4   #include <iostream>
5   using std::cout;
6   using std::endl;
7
8   #include <algorithm> // algorithm definitions
9   #include <vector> // vector class-template definition
10  #include <iterator> // ostream_iterator
11
12  bool greater9( int ); // prototype
13
14  int main()
15  {
16     const int SIZE = 10;
17     int a[ SIZE ] = { 10, 2, 10, 4, 16, 6, 14, 8, 12, 10 };
18     std::ostream_iterator< int > output( cout, " " );
```

Fig. 22.28 | Algorithms remove, remove_if, remove_copy and remove_copy_if. (Part 1 of 3.)

```
19    std::vector< int > v( a, a + SIZE ); // copy of a
20    std::vector< int >::iterator newLastElement;
21
22    cout << "Vector v before removing all 10s:\n   ";
23    std::copy( v.begin(), v.end(), output );
24
25    // remove all 10s from v
26    newLastElement = std::remove( v.begin(), v.end(), 10 );
27    cout << "\nVector v after removing all 10s:\n   ";
28    std::copy( v.begin(), newLastElement, output );
29
30    std::vector< int > v2( a, a + SIZE ); // copy of a
31    std::vector< int > c( SIZE, 0 ); // instantiate vector c
32    cout << "\n\nVector v2 before removing all 10s and copying:\n   ";
33    std::copy( v2.begin(), v2.end(), output );
34
35    // copy from v2 to c, removing 10s in the process
36    std::remove_copy( v2.begin(), v2.end(), c.begin(), 10 );
37    cout << "\nVector c after removing all 10s from v2:\n   ";
38    std::copy( c.begin(), c.end(), output );
39
40    std::vector< int > v3( a, a + SIZE ); // copy of a
41    cout << "\n\nVector v3 before removing all elements"
42       << "\ngreater than 9:\n   ";
43    std::copy( v3.begin(), v3.end(), output );
44
45    // remove elements greater than 9 from v3
46    newLastElement = std::remove_if( v3.begin(), v3.end(), greater9 );
47    cout << "\nVector v3 after removing all elements"
48       << "\ngreater than 9:\n   ";
49    std::copy( v3.begin(), newLastElement, output );
50
51    std::vector< int > v4( a, a + SIZE ); // copy of a
52    std::vector< int > c2( SIZE, 0 ); // instantiate vector c2
53    cout << "\n\nVector v4 before removing all elements"
54       << "\ngreater than 9 and copying:\n   ";
55    std::copy( v4.begin(), v4.end(), output );
56
57    // copy elements from v4 to c2, removing elements greater
58    // than 9 in the process
59    std::remove_copy_if( v4.begin(), v4.end(), c2.begin(), greater9 );
60    cout << "\nVector c2 after removing all elements"
61       << "\ngreater than 9 from v4:\n   ";
62    std::copy( c2.begin(), c2.end(), output );
63    cout << endl;
64    return 0;
65 } // end main
66
67 // determine whether argument is greater than 9
68 bool greater9( int x )
69 {
70    return x > 9;
71 } // end function greater9
```

Fig. 22.28 | Algorithms remove, remove_if, remove_copy and remove_copy_if. (Part 2 of 3.)

```
Vector v before removing all 10s:
   10 2 10 4 16 6 14 8 12 10
Vector v after removing all 10s:
   2 4 16 6 14 8 12

Vector v2 before removing all 10s and copying:
   10 2 10 4 16 6 14 8 12 10
Vector c after removing all 10s from v2:
   2 4 16 6 14 8 12 0 0 0

Vector v3 before removing all elements
greater than 9:
   10 2 10 4 16 6 14 8 12 10
Vector v3 after removing all elements
greater than 9:
   2 4 6 8

Vector v4 before removing all elements
greater than 9 and copying:
   10 2 10 4 16 6 14 8 12 10
Vector c2 after removing all elements
greater than 9 from v4:
   2 4 6 8 0 0 0 0 0 0
```

Fig. 22.28 | Algorithms remove, remove_if, remove_copy and remove_copy_if. (Part 3 of 3.)

Line 46 uses function `remove_if` to delete all those elements in the range from `v3.begin()` up to, but not including, `v3.end()` from v3 for which our user-defined unary predicate function greater9 returns true. Function greater9 (defined at lines 68–71) returns true if the value passed to it is greater than 9; otherwise, it returns false. The iterators supplied as the first two arguments must be forward iterators so that the algorithm can modify the elements in the sequence. This function does not modify the number of elements in the vector, but it does move to the beginning of the vector all elements that are not eliminated. This function returns an iterator positioned after the last element in the vector that was not deleted. All elements from the iterator position to the end of the vector have undefined values.

Line 59 uses function `remove_copy_if` to copy all those elements in the range from `v4.begin()` up to, but not including, `v4.end()` from v4 for which the unary predicate function greater9 returns true. The elements are placed in c2, starting at position `c2.begin()`. The iterators supplied as the first two arguments must be input iterators. The iterator supplied as the third argument must be an output iterator so that the element being copied can be inserted into the copy location. This function returns an iterator positioned after the last element copied into c2.

22.5.4 replace, replace_if, replace_copy and replace_copy_if

Figure 22.29 demonstrates replacing values from a sequence using algorithms replace, replace_if, replace_copy and replace_copy_if.

Line 25 uses function `replace` to replace all elements with the value 10 in the range from `v1.begin()` up to, but not including, `v1.end()` in v1 with the new value 100. The iterators supplied as the first two arguments must be forward iterators so that the algorithm can modify the elements in the sequence.

```cpp
 1   // Fig. 22.29: Fig22_29.cpp
 2   // Standard Library functions replace, replace_if,
 3   // replace_copy and replace_copy_if.
 4   #include <iostream>
 5   using std::cout;
 6   using std::endl;
 7
 8   #include <algorithm>
 9   #include <vector>
10   #include <iterator> // ostream_iterator
11
12   bool greater9( int ); // predicate function prototype
13
14   int main()
15   {
16      const int SIZE = 10;
17      int a[ SIZE ] = { 10, 2, 10, 4, 16, 6, 14, 8, 12, 10 };
18      std::ostream_iterator< int > output( cout, " " );
19
20      std::vector< int > v1( a, a + SIZE ); // copy of a
21      cout << "Vector v1 before replacing all 10s:\n   ";
22      std::copy( v1.begin(), v1.end(), output );
23
24      // replace all 10s in v1 with 100
25      std::replace( v1.begin(), v1.end(), 10, 100 );
26      cout << "\nVector v1 after replacing 10s with 100s:\n   ";
27      std::copy( v1.begin(), v1.end(), output );
28
29      std::vector< int > v2( a, a + SIZE ); // copy of a
30      std::vector< int > c1( SIZE ); // instantiate vector c1
31      cout << "\n\nVector v2 before replacing all 10s and copying:\n   ";
32      std::copy( v2.begin(), v2.end(), output );
33
34      // copy from v2 to c1, replacing 10s with 100s
35      std::replace_copy( v2.begin(), v2.end(), c1.begin(), 10, 100 );
36      cout << "\nVector c1 after replacing all 10s in v2:\n   ";
37      std::copy( c1.begin(), c1.end(), output );
38
39      std::vector< int > v3( a, a + SIZE ); // copy of a
40      cout << "\n\nVector v3 before replacing values greater than 9:\n   ";
41      std::copy( v3.begin(), v3.end(), output );
42
43      // replace values greater than 9 in v3 with 100
44      std::replace_if( v3.begin(), v3.end(), greater9, 100 );
45      cout << "\nVector v3 after replacing all values greater"
46         << "\nthan 9 with 100s:\n   ";
47      std::copy( v3.begin(), v3.end(), output );
48
49      std::vector< int > v4( a, a + SIZE ); // copy of a
50      std::vector< int > c2( SIZE ); // instantiate vector c2
```

Fig. 22.29 | Algorithms `replace`, `replace_if`, `replace_copy` and `replace_copy_if`. (Part 1 of 2.)

```
51        cout << "\n\nVector v4 before replacing all values greater "
52           << "than 9 and copying:\n   ";
53        std::copy( v4.begin(), v4.end(), output );
54
55        // copy v4 to c2, replacing elements greater than 9 with 100
56        std::replace_copy_if(
57           v4.begin(), v4.end(), c2.begin(), greater9, 100 );
58        cout << "\nVector c2 after replacing all values greater "
59           << "than 9 in v4:\n   ";
60        std::copy( c2.begin(), c2.end(), output );
61        cout << endl;
62        return 0;
63     } // end main
64
65     // determine whether argument is greater than 9
66     bool greater9( int x )
67     {
68        return x > 9;
69     } // end function greater9
```

```
Vector v1 before replacing all 10s:
   10 2 10 4 16 6 14 8 12 10
Vector v1 after replacing 10s with 100s:
   100 2 100 4 16 6 14 8 12 100

Vector v2 before replacing all 10s and copying:
   10 2 10 4 16 6 14 8 12 10
Vector c1 after replacing all 10s in v2:
   100 2 100 4 16 6 14 8 12 100

Vector v3 before replacing values greater than 9:
   10 2 10 4 16 6 14 8 12 10
Vector v3 after replacing all values greater
than 9 with 100s:
   100 2 100 4 100 6 100 8 100 100

Vector v4 before replacing all values greater than 9 and copying:
   10 2 10 4 16 6 14 8 12 10
Vector c2 after replacing all values greater than 9 in v4:
   100 2 100 4 100 6 100 8 100 100
```

Fig. 22.29 | Algorithms replace, replace_if, replace_copy and replace_copy_if. (Part 2 of 2.)

Line 35 uses function replace_copy to copy all elements in the range from v2.begin() up to, but not including, v2.end() from v2, replacing all elements with the value 10 with the new value 100. The elements are copied into c1, starting at position c1.begin(). The iterators supplied as the first two arguments must be input iterators. The iterator supplied as the third argument must be an output iterator so that the element being copied can be inserted into the copy location. This function returns an iterator positioned after the last element copied into c1.

Line 44 uses function replace_if to replace all those elements in the range from v3.begin() up to, but not including, v3.end() in v3 for which the unary predicate function greater9 returns true. Function greater9 (defined at lines 66–69) returns true if the value passed to it is greater than 9; otherwise, it returns false. The value 100 replaces each value greater than 9. The iterators supplied as the first two arguments must be forward iterators so that the algorithm can modify the elements in the sequence.

Lines 56–57 use function replace_copy_if to copy all elements in the range from v4.begin() up to, but not including, v4.end() from v4. Elements for which the unary predicate function greater9 returns true are replaced with the value 100. The elements are placed in c2, starting at position c2.begin(). The iterators supplied as the first two arguments must be input iterators. The iterator supplied as the third argument must be an output iterator so that the element being copied can be inserted into the copy location. This function returns an iterator positioned after the last element copied into c2.

22.5.5 Mathematical Algorithms

Figure 22.30 demonstrates several common mathematical algorithms from the STL, including random_shuffle, count, count_if, min_element, max_element, accumulate, for_each and transform.

```cpp
1   // Fig. 22.30: Fig22_30.cpp
2   // Mathematical algorithms of the Standard Library.
3   #include <iostream>
4   using std::cout;
5   using std::endl;
6
7   #include <algorithm> // algorithm definitions
8   #include <numeric> // accumulate is defined here
9   #include <vector>
10  #include <iterator>
11
12  bool greater9( int ); // predicate function prototype
13  void outputSquare( int ); // output square of a value
14  int calculateCube( int ); // calculate cube of a value
15
16  int main()
17  {
18     const int SIZE = 10;
19     int a1[ SIZE ] = { 1, 2, 3, 4, 5, 6, 7, 8, 9, 10 };
20     std::vector< int > v( a1, a1 + SIZE ); // copy of a1
21     std::ostream_iterator< int > output( cout, " " );
22
23     cout << "Vector v before random_shuffle: ";
24     std::copy( v.begin(), v.end(), output );
25
26     std::random_shuffle( v.begin(), v.end() ); // shuffle elements of v
27     cout << "\nVector v after random_shuffle: ";
28     std::copy( v.begin(), v.end(), output );
29
30     int a2[ SIZE ] = { 100, 2, 8, 1, 50, 3, 8, 8, 9, 10 };
31     std::vector< int > v2( a2, a2 + SIZE ); // copy of a2
32     cout << "\n\nVector v2 contains: ";
33     std::copy( v2.begin(), v2.end(), output );
```

Fig. 22.30 | Mathematical algorithms of the Standard Library. (Part 1 of 3.)

```
34
35      // count number of elements in v2 with value 8
36      int result = std::count( v2.begin(), v2.end(), 8 );
37      cout << "\nNumber of elements matching 8: " << result;
38
39      // count number of elements in v2 that are greater than 9
40      result = std::count_if( v2.begin(), v2.end(), greater9 );
41      cout << "\nNumber of elements greater than 9: " << result;
42
43      // locate minimum element in v2
44      cout << "\n\nMinimum element in Vector v2 is: "
45         << *( std::min_element( v2.begin(), v2.end() ) );
46
47      // locate maximum element in v2
48      cout << "\nMaximum element in Vector v2 is: "
49         << *( std::max_element( v2.begin(), v2.end() ) );
50
51      // calculate sum of elements in v
52      cout << "\n\nThe total of the elements in Vector v is: "
53         << std::accumulate( v.begin(), v.end(), 0 );
54
55      // output square of every element in v
56      cout << "\n\nThe square of every integer in Vector v is:\n";
57      std::for_each( v.begin(), v.end(), outputSquare );
58
59      std::vector< int > cubes( SIZE ); // instantiate vector cubes
60
61      // calculate cube of each element in v; place results in cubes
62      std::transform( v.begin(), v.end(), cubes.begin(), calculateCube );
63      cout << "\n\nThe cube of every integer in Vector v is:\n";
64      std::copy( cubes.begin(), cubes.end(), output );
65      cout << endl;
66      return 0;
67   } // end main
68
69   // determine whether argument is greater than 9
70   bool greater9( int value )
71   {
72      return value > 9;
73   } // end function greater9
74
75   // output square of argument
76   void outputSquare( int value )
77   {
78      cout << value * value << ' ';
79   } // end function outputSquare
80
81   // return cube of argument
82   int calculateCube( int value )
83   {
84      return value * value * value;
85   } // end function calculateCube
```

Fig. 22.30 | Mathematical algorithms of the Standard Library. (Part 2 of 3.)

```
Vector v before random_shuffle: 1 2 3 4 5 6 7 8 9 10
Vector v after random_shuffle: 5 4 1 3 7 8 9 10 6 2

Vector v2 contains: 100 2 8 1 50 3 8 8 9 10
Number of elements matching 8: 3
Number of elements greater than 9: 3

Minimum element in Vector v2 is: 1
Maximum element in Vector v2 is: 100

The total of the elements in Vector v is: 55

The square of every integer in Vector v is:
25 16 1 9 49 64 81 100 36 4

The cube of every integer in Vector v is:
125 64 1 27 343 512 729 1000 216 8
```

Fig. 22.30 | Mathematical algorithms of the Standard Library. (Part 3 of 3.)

Line 26 uses function `random_shuffle` to reorder randomly the elements in the range from `v.begin()` up to, but not including, `v.end()` in v. This function takes two random-access iterator arguments.

Line 36 uses function `count` to count the elements with the value 8 in the range from `v2.begin()` up to, but not including, `v2.end()` in v2. This function requires its two iterator arguments to be at least input iterators.

Line 40 uses function `count_if` to count those elements in the range from `v2.begin()` up to, but not including, `v2.end()` in v2 for which the predicate function `greater9` returns true. Function `count_if` requires its two iterator arguments to be at least input iterators.

Line 45 uses function `min_element` to locate the smallest element in the range from `v2.begin()` up to, but not including, `v2.end()` in v2. The function returns a forward iterator located at the smallest element or, if the range is empty, returns `v2.end()`. The function requires its two iterator arguments to be at least input iterators. A second version of this function takes as its third argument a binary function that compares the elements in the sequence. The binary function takes two arguments and returns a `bool` value.

Good Programming Practice 22.2

It is a good practice to check that the range specified in a call to min_element is not empty and that the return value is not the "past the end" iterator.

Line 49 uses function `max_element` to locate the largest element in the range from `v2.begin()` up to, but not including, `v2.end()` in v2. The function returns an input iterator located at the largest element. The function requires its two iterator arguments to be at least input iterators. A second version of this function takes as its third argument a binary predicate function that compares the elements in the sequence. The binary function takes two arguments and returns a `bool` value.

Line 53 uses function `accumulate` (the template of which is in header file `<numeric>`) to sum the values in the range from `v.begin()` up to, but not including, `v.end()` in v. The function's two iterator arguments must be at least input iterators and its third argument represents the initial value of the total. A second version of this function takes as its fourth argument a general function that determines how elements are accumulated. The general function must take two arguments and return a result. The first argument to this function is the current value of the accumulation. The second argument is the value of the current element in the sequence being accumulated.

Line 57 uses function `for_each` to apply a general function to every element in the range from v.begin() up to, but not including, v.end() in v. The general function should take the current element as an argument and should not modify that element. Function `for_each` requires its two iterator arguments to be at least input iterators.

Line 62 uses function `transform` to apply a general function to every element in the range from v.begin() up to, but not including, v.end() in v. The general function (the fourth argument) should take the current element as an argument, should not modify the element and should return the transformed value. Function `transform` requires its first two iterator arguments to be at least input iterators and its third argument to be at least an output iterator. The third argument specifies where the transformed values should be placed. Note that the third argument can equal the first. Another version of `transform` accepts five arguments—the first two arguments are input iterators that specify a range of elements from one source container, the third argument is an input iterator that specifies the first element in another source container, the fourth argument is an output iterator that specifies where the transformed values should be placed and the last argument is a general function that takes two arguments. This version of `transform` takes one element from each of the two input sources and applies the general function to that pair of elements, then places the transformed value at the location specified by the fourth argument.

22.5.6 Basic Searching and Sorting Algorithms

Figure 22.31 demonstrates some basic searching and sorting capabilities of the Standard Library, including `find`, `find_if`, `sort` and `binary_search`.

```cpp
1   // Fig. 22.31: Fig22_31.cpp
2   // Standard Library search and sort algorithms.
3   #include <iostream>
4   using std::cout;
5   using std::endl;
6
7   #include <algorithm> // algorithm definitions
8   #include <vector> // vector class-template definition
9   #include <iterator>
10
11  bool greater10( int value ); // predicate function prototype
12
13  int main()
14  {
15     const int SIZE = 10;
16     int a[ SIZE ] = { 10, 2, 17, 5, 16, 8, 13, 11, 20, 7 };
17     std::vector< int > v( a, a + SIZE ); // copy of a
18     std::ostream_iterator< int > output( cout, " " );
19
20     cout << "Vector v contains: ";
21     std::copy( v.begin(), v.end(), output ); // display output vector
22
```

Fig. 22.31 | Basic searching and sorting algorithms of the Standard Library. (Part 1 of 3.)

```
23      // locate first occurrence of 16 in v
24      std::vector< int >::iterator location;
25      location = std::find( v.begin(), v.end(), 16 );
26
27      if ( location != v.end() ) // found 16
28         cout << "\n\nFound 16 at location " << ( location - v.begin() );
29      else // 16 not found
30         cout << "\n\n16 not found";
31
32      // locate first occurrence of 100 in v
33      location = std::find( v.begin(), v.end(), 100 );
34
35      if ( location != v.end() ) // found 100
36         cout << "\nFound 100 at location " << ( location - v.begin() );
37      else // 100 not found
38         cout << "\n100 not found";
39
40      // locate first occurrence of value greater than 10 in v
41      location = std::find_if( v.begin(), v.end(), greater10 );
42
43      if ( location != v.end() ) // found value greater than 10
44         cout << "\n\nThe first value greater than 10 is " << *location
45            << "\nfound at location " << ( location - v.begin() );
46      else // value greater than 10 not found
47         cout << "\n\nNo values greater than 10 were found";
48
49      // sort elements of v
50      std::sort( v.begin(), v.end() );
51      cout << "\n\nVector v after sort: ";
52      std::copy( v.begin(), v.end(), output );
53
54      // use binary_search to locate 13 in v
55      if ( std::binary_search( v.begin(), v.end(), 13 ) )
56         cout << "\n\n13 was found in v";
57      else
58         cout << "\n\n13 was not found in v";
59
60      // use binary_search to locate 100 in v
61      if ( std::binary_search( v.begin(), v.end(), 100 ) )
62         cout << "\n100 was found in v";
63      else
64         cout << "\n100 was not found in v";
65
66      cout << endl;
67      return 0;
68   } // end main
69
70   // determine whether argument is greater than 10
71   bool greater10( int value )
72   {
73      return value > 10;
74   } // end function greater10
```

Fig. 22.31 | Basic searching and sorting algorithms of the Standard Library. (Part 2 of 3.)

```
Vector v contains: 10 2 17 5 16 8 13 11 20 7

Found 16 at location 4
100 not found

The first value greater than 10 is 17
found at location 2

Vector v after sort: 2 5 7 8 10 11 13 16 17 20

13 was found in v
100 was not found in v
```

Fig. 22.31 | Basic searching and sorting algorithms of the Standard Library. (Part 3 of 3.)

Line 25 uses function `find` to locate the value 16 in the range from `v.begin()` up to, but not including, `v.end()` in `v`. The function requires its two iterator arguments to be at least input iterators and returns an input iterator that either is positioned at the first element containing the value or indicates the end of the sequence (as is the case in line 33).

Line 41 uses function `find_if` to locate the first value in the range from `v.begin()` up to, but not including, `v.end()` in `v` for which the unary predicate function `greater10` returns `true`. Function `greater10` (defined at lines 71–74) takes an integer and returns a `bool` value indicating whether the integer argument is greater than 10. Function `find_if` requires its two iterator arguments to be at least input iterators. The function returns an input iterator that either is positioned at the first element containing a value for which the predicate function returns `true` or indicates the end of the sequence.

Line 50 uses function `sort` to arrange the elements in the range from `v.begin()` up to, but not including, `v.end()` in `v` in ascending order. The function requires its two iterator arguments to be random-access iterators. A second version of this function takes a third argument that is a binary predicate function taking two arguments that are values in the sequence and returning a `bool` indicating the sorting order—if the return value is `true`, the two elements being compared are in sorted order.

Common Programming Error 22.5

Attempting to sort *a container by using an iterator other than a random-access iterator is a compilation error. Function* sort *requires a random-access iterator.*

Line 55 uses function `binary_search` to determine whether the value 13 is in the range from `v.begin()` up to, but not including, `v.end()` in `v`. The sequence of values must be sorted in ascending order first. Function `binary_search` requires its two iterator arguments to be at least forward iterators. The function returns a `bool` indicating whether the value was found in the sequence. Line 61 demonstrates a call to function `binary_search` in which the value is not found. A second version of this function takes a fourth argument that is a binary predicate function taking two arguments that are values in the sequence and returning a `bool`. The predicate function returns `true` if the two elements being compared are in sorted order.

22.5.7 swap, iter_swap and swap_ranges

Figure 22.32 demonstrates algorithms `swap`, `iter_swap` and `swap_ranges` for swapping elements. Line 20 uses function `swap` to exchange two values. In this example, the first and second elements of array a are exchanged. The function takes as arguments references to the two values being exchanged.

```
1   // Fig. 22.32: Fig22_32.cpp
2   // Standard Library algorithms iter_swap, swap and swap_ranges.
3   #include <iostream>
4   using std::cout;
5   using std::endl;
6
7   #include <algorithm> // algorithm definitions
8   #include <iterator>
9
10  int main()
11  {
12     const int SIZE = 10;
13     int a[ SIZE ] = { 1, 2, 3, 4, 5, 6, 7, 8, 9, 10 };
14     std::ostream_iterator< int > output( cout, " " );
15
16     cout << "Array a contains:\n    ";
17     std::copy( a, a + SIZE, output ); // display array a
18
19     // swap elements at locations 0 and 1 of array a
20     std::swap( a[ 0 ], a[ 1 ] );
21
22     cout << "\nArray a after swapping a[0] and a[1] using swap:\n    ";
23     std::copy( a, a + SIZE, output ); // display array a
24
25     // use iterators to swap elements at locations 0 and 1 of array a
26     std::iter_swap( &a[ 0 ], &a[ 1 ] ); // swap with iterators
27     cout << "\nArray a after swapping a[0] and a[1] using iter_swap:\n    ";
28     std::copy( a, a + SIZE, output );
29
30     // swap elements in first five elements of array a with
31     // elements in last five elements of array a
32     std::swap_ranges( a, a + 5, a + 5 );
33
34     cout << "\nArray a after swapping the first five elements\n"
35        << "with the last five elements:\n    ";
36     std::copy( a, a + SIZE, output );
37     cout << endl;
38     return 0;
39  } // end main
```

```
Array a contains:
   1 2 3 4 5 6 7 8 9 10
Array a after swapping a[0] and a[1] using swap:
   2 1 3 4 5 6 7 8 9 10
Array a after swapping a[0] and a[1] using iter_swap:
   1 2 3 4 5 6 7 8 9 10
Array a after swapping the first five elements
with the last five elements:
   6 7 8 9 10 1 2 3 4 5
```

Fig. 22.32 | Demonstrating swap, iter_swap and swap_ranges.

Line 26 uses function `iter_swap` to exchange the two elements. The function takes two forward iterator arguments (in this case, pointers to elements of an array) and exchanges the values in the elements to which the iterators refer.

Line 32 uses function `swap_ranges` to exchange the elements in the range from a up to, but not including, a + 5 with the elements beginning at position a + 5. The function requires three forward iterator arguments. The first two arguments specify the range of elements in the first sequence that will be exchanged with the elements in the second sequence starting from the iterator in the third argument. In this example, the two sequences of values are in the same array, but the sequences can be from different arrays or containers.

22.5.8 copy_backward, merge, unique and reverse

Figure 22.33 demonstrates STL algorithms copy_backward, merge, unique and reverse. Line 28 uses function `copy_backward` to copy elements in the range from v1.begin() up to, but not including, v1.end() in v1, placing the elements in results by starting from the element before results.end() and working toward the beginning of the vector. The function returns an iterator positioned at the last element copied into the results (i.e., the beginning of results, because of the backward copy). The elements are placed in results in the same order as v1. This function requires three bidirectional iterator arguments (iterators that can be incremented and decremented to iterate forward and backward through a sequence, respectively). The main difference between copy and copy_backward is that the iterator returned from copy is positioned *after* the last element copied and the iterator returned from copy_backward is positioned *at* the last element copied (which is really the first element in the sequence). Also, copy requires two input iterators and an output iterator as argument.

```cpp
1   // Fig. 22.33: Fig22_33.cpp
2   // Standard Library functions copy_backward, merge, unique and reverse.
3   #include <iostream>
4   using std::cout;
5   using std::endl;
6
7   #include <algorithm> // algorithm definitions
8   #include <vector> // vector class-template definition
9   #include <iterator> // ostream_iterator
10
11  int main()
12  {
13     const int SIZE = 5;
14     int a1[ SIZE ] = { 1, 3, 5, 7, 9 };
15     int a2[ SIZE ] = { 2, 4, 5, 7, 9 };
16     std::vector< int > v1( a1, a1 + SIZE ); // copy of a1
17     std::vector< int > v2( a2, a2 + SIZE ); // copy of a2
18     std::ostream_iterator< int > output( cout, " " );
19
20     cout << "Vector v1 contains: ";
21     std::copy( v1.begin(), v1.end(), output ); // display vector output
22     cout << "\nVector v2 contains: ";
23     std::copy( v2.begin(), v2.end(), output ); // display vector output
```

Fig. 22.33 | Demonstrating copy_backward, merge, unique and reverse. (Part 1 of 2.)

```
24
25        std::vector< int > results( v1.size() );
26
27        // place elements of v1 into results in reverse order
28        std::copy_backward( v1.begin(), v1.end(), results.end() );
29        cout << "\n\nAfter copy_backward, results contains: ";
30        std::copy( results.begin(), results.end(), output );
31
32        std::vector< int > results2( v1.size() + v2.size() );
33
34        // merge elements of v1 and v2 into results2 in sorted order
35        std::merge( v1.begin(), v1.end(), v2.begin(), v2.end(),
36           results2.begin() );
37
38        cout << "\n\nAfter merge of v1 and v2 results2 contains:\n";
39        std::copy( results2.begin(), results2.end(), output );
40
41        // eliminate duplicate values from results2
42        std::vector< int >::iterator endLocation;
43        endLocation = std::unique( results2.begin(), results2.end() );
44
45        cout << "\n\nAfter unique results2 contains:\n";
46        std::copy( results2.begin(), endLocation, output );
47
48        cout << "\n\nVector v1 after reverse: ";
49        std::reverse( v1.begin(), v1.end() ); // reverse elements of v1
50        std::copy( v1.begin(), v1.end(), output );
51        cout << endl;
52        return 0;
53    } // end main
```

```
Vector v1 contains: 1 3 5 7 9
Vector v2 contains: 2 4 5 7 9

After copy_backward, results contains: 1 3 5 7 9

After merge of v1 and v2 results2 contains:
1 2 3 4 5 5 7 7 9 9

After unique results2 contains:
1 2 3 4 5 7 9

Vector v1 after reverse: 9 7 5 3 1
```

Fig. 22.33 | Demonstrating `copy_backward`, `merge`, `unique` and `reverse`. (Part 2 of 2.)

Lines 35–36 use function `merge` to combine two sorted ascending sequences of values into a third sorted ascending sequence. The function requires five iterator arguments. The first four must be at least input iterators and the last must be at least an output iterator. The first two arguments specify the range of elements in the first sorted sequence (`v1`), the second two arguments specify the range of elements in the second sorted sequence (`v2`) and the last argument specifies the starting location in the third sequence (`results2`) where the elements will be merged. A second version of this function takes as its sixth argument a binary predicate function that specifies the sorting order.

Note that line 32 creates vector `results2` with the number of elements `v1.size()` + `v2.size()`. Using the `merge` function as shown here requires that the sequence where the results are stored be at least the size of the two sequences being merged. If you do not want to allocate the number of elements for the resulting sequence before the `merge` operation, you can use the following statements:

```
std::vector< int > results2();
std::merge ( v1.begin(), v1.end(), v2.begin(), v2.end(),
   std::back_inserter( results2 ) );
```

The argument `std::back_inserter( results2 )` uses function template `back_inserter` (header file `<iterator>`) for the container `results2`. A `back_inserter` calls the container's default `push_back` function to insert an element at the end of the container. More importantly, if an element is inserted into a container that has no more space available, the container grows in size. Thus, the number of elements in the container does not have to be known in advance. There are two other inserters—`front_inserter` (to insert an element at the beginning of a container specified as its argument) and `inserter` (to insert an element before the iterator supplied as its second argument in the container supplied as its first argument).

Line 43 uses function `unique` on the sorted sequence of elements in the range from `results2.begin()` up to, but not including, `results2.end()` in `results2`. After this function is applied to a sorted sequence with duplicate values, only a single copy of each value remains in the sequence. The function takes two arguments that must be at least forward iterators. The function returns an iterator positioned after the last element in the sequence of unique values. The values of all elements in the container after the last unique value are undefined. A second version of this function takes as a third argument a binary predicate function specifying how to compare two elements for equality.

Line 49 uses function `reverse` to reverse all the elements in the range from `v1.begin()` up to, but not including, `v1.end()` in `v1`. The function takes two arguments that must be at least bidirectional iterators.

22.5.9 inplace_merge, unique_copy and reverse_copy

Figure 22.34 demonstrates STL algorithms `inplace_merge`, `unique_copy` and `reverse_copy`. Line 24 uses function `inplace_merge` to merge two sorted sequences of elements in the same container. In this example, the elements from `v1.begin()` up to, but not including, `v1.begin()` + 5 are merged with the elements from `v1.begin()` + 5 up to, but not including, `v1.end()`. This function requires its three iterator arguments to be at least bidirectional iterators. A second version of this function takes as a fourth argument a binary predicate function for comparing elements in the two sequences.

```
1   // Fig. 22.34: Fig22_34.cpp
2   // Standard Library algorithms inplace_merge,
3   // reverse_copy and unique_copy.
4   #include <iostream>
5   using std::cout;
6   using std::endl;
```

Fig. 22.34 | Demonstrating `inplace_merge`, `unique_copy` and `reverse_copy`. (Part 1 of 2.)

```
7
8    #include <algorithm> // algorithm definitions
9    #include <vector> // vector class-template definition
10   #include <iterator> // back_inserter definition
11
12   int main()
13   {
14      const int SIZE = 10;
15      int a1[ SIZE ] = { 1, 3, 5, 7, 9, 1, 3, 5, 7, 9 };
16      std::vector< int > v1( a1, a1 + SIZE ); // copy of a
17      std::ostream_iterator< int > output( cout, " " );
18
19      cout << "Vector v1 contains: ";
20      std::copy( v1.begin(), v1.end(), output );
21
22      // merge first half of v1 with second half of v1 such that
23      // v1 contains sorted set of elements after merge
24      std::inplace_merge( v1.begin(), v1.begin() + 5, v1.end() );
25
26      cout << "\nAfter inplace_merge, v1 contains: ";
27      std::copy( v1.begin(), v1.end(), output );
28
29      std::vector< int > results1;
30
31      // copy only unique elements of v1 into results1
32      std::unique_copy(
33         v1.begin(), v1.end(), std::back_inserter( results1 ) );
34      cout << "\nAfter unique_copy results1 contains: ";
35      std::copy( results1.begin(), results1.end(), output );
36
37      std::vector< int > results2;
38
39      // copy elements of v1 into results2 in reverse order
40      std::reverse_copy(
41         v1.begin(), v1.end(), std::back_inserter( results2 ) );
42      cout << "\nAfter reverse_copy, results2 contains: ";
43      std::copy( results2.begin(), results2.end(), output );
44      cout << endl;
45      return 0;
46   } // end main
```

```
Vector v1 contains: 1 3 5 7 9 1 3 5 7 9
After inplace_merge, v1 contains: 1 1 3 3 5 5 7 7 9 9
After unique_copy results1 contains: 1 3 5 7 9
After reverse_copy, results2 contains: 9 9 7 7 5 5 3 3 1 1
```

Fig. 22.34 | Demonstrating inplace_merge, unique_copy and reverse_copy. (Part 2 of 2.)

Lines 32–33 use function **unique_copy** to make a copy of all the unique elements in the sorted sequence of values from v1.begin() up to, but not including, v1.end(). The copied elements are placed into vector results1. The first two arguments must be at least input iterators and the last must be at least an output iterator. In this example, we did not preallocate enough elements in results1 to store all the elements copied from v1. Instead, we use function back_inserter (defined in header file <iterator>) to add elements to the end of v1. The back_inserter uses class vector's capability to insert elements at the end of the vector. Because the back_inserter inserts an element rather than replacing an existing element's value, the vector is able to grow to accommodate additional elements. A second version of the unique_copy function takes as a fourth argument a binary predicate function for comparing elements for equality.

Lines 40–41 use function reverse_copy to make a reversed copy of the elements in the range from v1.begin() up to, but not including, v1.end(). The copied elements are inserted into results2 using a back_inserter object to ensure that the vector can grow to accommodate the appropriate number of elements copied. Function reverse_copy requires its first two iterator arguments to be at least bidirectional iterators and its third to be at least an output iterator.

22.5.10 Set Operations

Figure 22.35 demonstrates Standard Library functions includes, set_difference, set_intersection, set_symmetric_difference and set_union for manipulating sets of sorted values. To demonstrate that Standard Library functions can be applied to arrays and containers, this example uses only arrays (remember, a pointer into an array is a random-access iterator).

Lines 27 and 33 call function includes in the conditions of if statements. Function includes compares two sets of sorted values to determine whether every element of the second set is in the first set. If so, includes returns true; otherwise, it returns false. The first two iterator arguments must be at least input iterators and must describe the first set of values. In line 27, the first set consists of the elements from a1 up to, but not including, a1 + SIZE1. The last two iterator arguments must be at least input iterators and must describe the second set of values. In this example, the second set consists of the elements from a2 up to, but not including, a2 + SIZE2. A second version of function includes takes a fifth argument that is a binary predicate function for comparing elements for equality.

```
1   // Fig. 22.35: Fig22_35.cpp
2   // Standard Library algorithms includes, set_difference,
3   // set_intersection, set_symmetric_difference and set_union.
4   #include <iostream>
5   using std::cout;
6   using std::endl;
7
8   #include <algorithm> // algorithm definitions
9   #include <iterator> // ostream_iterator
10
11  int main()
12  {
13     const int SIZE1 = 10, SIZE2 = 5, SIZE3 = 20;
14     int a1[ SIZE1 ] = { 1, 2, 3, 4, 5, 6, 7, 8, 9, 10 };
15     int a2[ SIZE2 ] = { 4, 5, 6, 7, 8 };
16     int a3[ SIZE2 ] = { 4, 5, 6, 11, 15 };
17     std::ostream_iterator< int > output( cout, " " );
18
```

Fig. 22.35 | set operations of the Standard Library. (Part 1 of 3.)

```
19        cout << "a1 contains: ";
20        std::copy( a1, a1 + SIZE1, output ); // display array a1
21        cout << "\na2 contains: ";
22        std::copy( a2, a2 + SIZE2, output ); // display array a2
23        cout << "\na3 contains: ";
24        std::copy( a3, a3 + SIZE2, output ); // display array a3
25
26        // determine whether set a2 is completely contained in a1
27        if ( std::includes( a1, a1 + SIZE1, a2, a2 + SIZE2 ) )
28           cout << "\n\na1 includes a2";
29        else
30           cout << "\n\na1 does not include a2";
31
32        // determine whether set a3 is completely contained in a1
33        if ( std::includes( a1, a1 + SIZE1, a3, a3 + SIZE2 ) )
34           cout << "\na1 includes a3";
35        else
36           cout << "\na1 does not include a3";
37
38        int difference[ SIZE1 ];
39
40        // determine elements of a1 not in a2
41        int *ptr = std::set_difference( a1, a1 + SIZE1,
42           a2, a2 + SIZE2, difference );
43        cout << "\n\nset_difference of a1 and a2 is: ";
44        std::copy( difference, ptr, output );
45
46        int intersection[ SIZE1 ];
47
48        // determine elements in both a1 and a2
49        ptr = std::set_intersection( a1, a1 + SIZE1,
50           a2, a2 + SIZE2, intersection );
51        cout << "\n\nset_intersection of a1 and a2 is: ";
52        std::copy( intersection, ptr, output );
53
54        int symmetric_difference[ SIZE1 + SIZE2 ];
55
56        // determine elements of a1 that are not in a2 and
57        // elements of a2 that are not in a1
58        ptr = std::set_symmetric_difference( a1, a1 + SIZE1,
59           a3, a3 + SIZE2, symmetric_difference );
60        cout << "\n\nset_symmetric_difference of a1 and a3 is: ";
61        std::copy( symmetric_difference, ptr, output );
62
63        int unionSet[ SIZE3 ];
64
65        // determine elements that are in either or both sets
66        ptr = std::set_union( a1, a1 + SIZE1, a3, a3 + SIZE2, unionSet );
67        cout << "\n\nset_union of a1 and a3 is: ";
68        std::copy( unionSet, ptr, output );
69        cout << endl;
70        return 0;
71  } // end main
```

Fig. 22.35 | set operations of the Standard Library. (Part 2 of 3.)

```
a1 contains: 1 2 3 4 5 6 7 8 9 10
a2 contains: 4 5 6 7 8
a3 contains: 4 5 6 11 15

a1 includes a2
a1 does not include a3

set_difference of a1 and a2 is: 1 2 3 9 10

set_intersection of a1 and a2 is: 4 5 6 7 8

set_symmetric_difference of a1 and a3 is: 1 2 3 7 8 9 10 11 15

set_union of a1 and a3 is: 1 2 3 4 5 6 7 8 9 10 11 15
```

Fig. 22.35 | set operations of the Standard Library. (Part 3 of 3.)

Lines 41–42 use function `set_difference` to find the elements from the first set of sorted values that are not in the second set of sorted values (both sets of values must be in ascending order). The elements that are different are copied into the fifth argument (in this case, the array `difference`). The first two iterator arguments must be at least input iterators for the first set of values. The next two iterator arguments must be at least input iterators for the second set of values. The fifth argument must be at least an output iterator indicating where to store a copy of the values that are different. The function returns an output iterator positioned immediately after the last value copied into the set to which the fifth argument points. A second version of function `set_difference` takes a sixth argument that is a binary predicate function indicating the order in which the elements were originally sorted. The two sequences must be sorted using the same comparison function.

Lines 49–50 use function `set_intersection` to determine the elements from the first set of sorted values that are in the second set of sorted values (both sets of values must be in ascending order). The elements common to both sets are copied into the fifth argument (in this case, array `intersection`). The first two iterator arguments must be at least input iterators for the first set of values. The next two iterator arguments must be at least input iterators for the second set of values. The fifth argument must be at least an output iterator indicating where to store a copy of the values that are the same. The function returns an output iterator positioned immediately after the last value copied into the set to which the fifth argument points. A second version of function `set_intersection` takes a sixth argument that is a binary predicate function indicating the order in which the elements were originally sorted. The two sequences must be sorted using the same comparison function.

Lines 58–59 use function `set_symmetric_difference` to determine the elements in the first set that are not in the second set and the elements in the second set that are not in the first set (both sets must be in ascending order). The elements that are different are copied from both sets into the fifth argument (the array `symmetric_difference`). The first two iterator arguments must be at least input iterators for the first set of values. The next two iterator arguments must be at least input iterators for the second set of values. The fifth argument must be at least an output iterator indicating where to store a copy of the values that are different. The function returns an output iterator positioned immediately after the last value copied into the set to which the fifth argument points. A second version of function `set_symmetric_difference` takes a sixth argument that is a binary predicate function indicating the order in which the elements were originally sorted. The two sequences must be sorted using the same comparison function.

Line 66 uses function `set_union` to create a set of all the elements that are in either or both of the two sorted sets (both sets of values must be in ascending order). The elements are copied from both sets into the fifth argument (in this case the array `unionSet`). Elements that appear in both sets are only copied from the first set. The first two iterator arguments must be at least input iterators for the first set of values. The next two iterator arguments must be at least input iterators for the second set of values. The fifth argument must be at least an output iterator indicating where to store the copied elements. The function returns an output iterator positioned immediately after the last value copied into the set to which the fifth argument points. A second version of function `set_union` takes a sixth argument that is a binary predicate function indicating the order in which the elements were originally sorted. The two sequences must be sorted using the same comparison function.

22.5.11 `lower_bound`, `upper_bound` and `equal_range`

Figure 22.36 demonstrates Standard Library functions `lower_bound`, `upper_bound` and `equal_range`. Line 24 uses function `lower_bound` to find the first location in a sorted sequence of values at which the third argument could be inserted in the sequence such that the sequence would still be sorted in ascending order. The first two iterator arguments must be at least forward iterators. The third argument is the value for which to determine the lower bound. The function returns a forward iterator pointing to the position at which the insert can occur. A second version of function `lower_bound` takes as a fourth argument a binary predicate function indicating the order in which the elements were originally sorted.

Line 30 uses function `upper_bound` to find the last location in a sorted sequence of values at which the third argument could be inserted in the sequence such that the sequence would still be sorted in ascending order. The first two iterator arguments must be at least forward iterators. The third argument is the value for which to determine the upper bound. The function returns a forward iterator pointing to the position at which the insert can occur. A second version of function `upper_bound` takes as a fourth argument a binary predicate function indicating the order in which the elements were originally sorted.

```
1   // Fig. 22.36: Fig22_36.cpp
2   // Standard Library functions lower_bound, upper_bound and
3   // equal_range for a sorted sequence of values.
4   #include <iostream>
5   using std::cout;
6   using std::endl;
7
8   #include <algorithm> // algorithm definitions
9   #include <vector> // vector class-template definition
10  #include <iterator> // ostream_iterator
11
12  int main()
13  {
14     const int SIZE = 10;
15     int a1[ SIZE ] = { 2, 2, 4, 4, 4, 6, 6, 6, 6, 8 };
```

Fig. 22.36 | Algorithms `lower_bound`, `upper_bound` and `equal_range`. (Part 1 of 3.)

```
16        std::vector< int > v( a1, a1 + SIZE ); // copy of a1
17        std::ostream_iterator< int > output( cout, " " );
18
19        cout << "Vector v contains:\n";
20        std::copy( v.begin(), v.end(), output );
21
22        // determine lower-bound insertion point for 6 in v
23        std::vector< int >::iterator lower;
24        lower = std::lower_bound( v.begin(), v.end(), 6 );
25        cout << "\n\nLower bound of 6 is element "
26           << ( lower - v.begin() ) << " of vector v";
27
28        // determine upper-bound insertion point for 6 in v
29        std::vector< int >::iterator upper;
30        upper = std::upper_bound( v.begin(), v.end(), 6 );
31        cout << "\nUpper bound of 6 is element "
32           << ( upper - v.begin() ) << " of vector v";
33
34        // use equal_range to determine both the lower- and
35        // upper-bound insertion points for 6
36        std::pair< std::vector< int >::iterator,
37                   std::vector< int >::iterator > eq;
38        eq = std::equal_range( v.begin(), v.end(), 6 );
39        cout << "\nUsing equal_range:\n   Lower bound of 6 is element "
40           << ( eq.first - v.begin() ) << " of vector v";
41        cout << "\n   Upper bound of 6 is element "
42           << ( eq.second - v.begin() ) << " of vector v";
43        cout << "\n\nUse lower_bound to locate the first point\n"
44           << "at which 5 can be inserted in order";
45
46        // determine lower-bound insertion point for 5 in v
47        lower = std::lower_bound( v.begin(), v.end(), 5 );
48        cout << "\n   Lower bound of 5 is element "
49           << ( lower - v.begin() ) << " of vector v";
50        cout << "\n\nUse upper_bound to locate the last point\n"
51           << "at which 7 can be inserted in order";
52
53        // determine upper-bound insertion point for 7 in v
54        upper = std::upper_bound( v.begin(), v.end(), 7 );
55        cout << "\n   Upper bound of 7 is element "
56           << ( upper - v.begin() ) << " of vector v";
57        cout << "\n\nUse equal_range to locate the first and\n"
58           << "last point at which 5 can be inserted in order";
59
60        // use equal_range to determine both the lower- and
61        // upper-bound insertion points for 5
62        eq = std::equal_range( v.begin(), v.end(), 5 );
63        cout << "\n   Lower bound of 5 is element "
64           << ( eq.first - v.begin() ) << " of vector v";
65        cout << "\n   Upper bound of 5 is element "
66           << ( eq.second - v.begin() ) << " of vector v" << endl;
67        return 0;
68     } // end main
```

Fig. 22.36 | Algorithms `lower_bound`, `upper_bound` and `equal_range`. (Part 2 of 3.)

```
Vector v contains:
2 2 4 4 4 6 6 6 6 8

Lower bound of 6 is element 5 of vector v
Upper bound of 6 is element 9 of vector v
Using equal_range:
   Lower bound of 6 is element 5 of vector v
   Upper bound of 6 is element 9 of vector v

Use lower_bound to locate the first point
at which 5 can be inserted in order
   Lower bound of 5 is element 5 of vector v

Use upper_bound to locate the last point
at which 7 can be inserted in order
   Upper bound of 7 is element 9 of vector v

Use equal_range to locate the first and
last point at which 5 can be inserted in order
   Lower bound of 5 is element 5 of vector v
   Upper bound of 5 is element 5 of vector v
```

Fig. 22.36 | Algorithms lower_bound, upper_bound and equal_range. (Part 3 of 3.)

Line 38 uses function **equal_range** to return a pair of forward iterators containing the combined results of performing both a lower_bound and an upper_bound operation. The first two iterator arguments must be at least forward iterators. The third argument is the value for which to locate the equal range. The function returns a pair of forward iterators for the lower bound (eq.first) and upper bound (eq.second), respectively.

Functions lower_bound, upper_bound and equal_range are often used to locate insertion points in sorted sequences. Line 47 uses lower_bound to locate the first point at which 5 can be inserted in order in v. Line 54 uses upper_bound to locate the last point at which 7 can be inserted in order in v. Line 62 uses equal_range to locate the first and last points at which 5 can be inserted in order in v.

22.5.12 Heapsort

Figure 22.37 demonstrates the Standard Library functions for performing the heapsort sorting algorithm. Heapsort is a sorting algorithm in which an array of elements is arranged into a special binary tree called a heap. The key features of a heap are that the largest element is always at the top of the heap and the values of the children of any node in the binary tree are always less than or equal to that node's value. A heap arranged in this manner is often called a maxheap. Heapsort is discussed in detail in computer science courses called "Data Structures" and "Algorithms."

```
1   // Fig. 22.37: Fig22_37.cpp
2   // Standard Library algorithms push_heap, pop_heap,
3   // make_heap and sort_heap.
4   #include <iostream>
5   using std::cout;
6   using std::endl;
```

Fig. 22.37 | Using Standard Library functions to perform a heapsort. (Part 1 of 3.)

```cpp
7
8   #include <algorithm>
9   #include <vector>
10  #include <iterator>
11
12  int main()
13  {
14     const int SIZE = 10;
15     int a[ SIZE ] = { 3, 100, 52, 77, 22, 31, 1, 98, 13, 40 };
16     std::vector< int > v( a, a + SIZE ); // copy of a
17     std::vector< int > v2;
18     std::ostream_iterator< int > output( cout, " " );
19
20     cout << "Vector v before make_heap:\n";
21     std::copy( v.begin(), v.end(), output );
22
23     std::make_heap( v.begin(), v.end() ); // create heap from vector v
24     cout << "\nVector v after make_heap:\n";
25     std::copy( v.begin(), v.end(), output );
26
27     std::sort_heap( v.begin(), v.end() ); // sort elements with sort_heap
28     cout << "\nVector v after sort_heap:\n";
29     std::copy( v.begin(), v.end(), output );
30
31     // perform the heapsort with push_heap and pop_heap
32     cout << "\n\nArray a contains: ";
33     std::copy( a, a + SIZE, output ); // display array a
34     cout << endl;
35
36     // place elements of array a into v2 and
37     // maintain elements of v2 in heap
38     for ( int i = 0; i < SIZE; i++ )
39     {
40        v2.push_back( a[ i ] );
41        std::push_heap( v2.begin(), v2.end() );
42        cout << "\nv2 after push_heap(a[" << i << "]): ";
43        std::copy( v2.begin(), v2.end(), output );
44     } // end for
45
46     cout << endl;
47
48     // remove elements from heap in sorted order
49     for ( unsigned int j = 0; j < v2.size(); j++ )
50     {
51        cout << "\nv2 after " << v2[ 0 ] << " popped from heap\n";
52        std::pop_heap( v2.begin(), v2.end() - j );
53        std::copy( v2.begin(), v2.end(), output );
54     } // end for
55
56     cout << endl;
57     return 0;
58  } // end main
```

Fig. 22.37 | Using Standard Library functions to perform a heapsort. (Part 2 of 3.)

```
Vector v before make_heap:
3 100 52 77 22 31 1 98 13 40
Vector v after make_heap:
100 98 52 77 40 31 1 3 13 22
Vector v after sort_heap:
1 3 13 22 31 40 52 77 98 100

Array a contains: 3 100 52 77 22 31 1 98 13 40

v2 after push_heap(a[0]): 3
v2 after push_heap(a[1]): 100 3
v2 after push_heap(a[2]): 100 3 52
v2 after push_heap(a[3]): 100 77 52 3
v2 after push_heap(a[4]): 100 77 52 3 22
v2 after push_heap(a[5]): 100 77 52 3 22 31
v2 after push_heap(a[6]): 100 77 52 3 22 31 1
v2 after push_heap(a[7]): 100 98 52 77 22 31 1 3
v2 after push_heap(a[8]): 100 98 52 77 22 31 1 3 13
v2 after push_heap(a[9]): 100 98 52 77 40 31 1 3 13 22

v2 after 100 popped from heap
98 77 52 22 40 31 1 3 13 100
v2 after 98 popped from heap
77 40 52 22 13 31 1 3 98 100
v2 after 77 popped from heap
52 40 31 22 13 3 1 77 98 100
v2 after 52 popped from heap
40 22 31 1 13 3 52 77 98 100
v2 after 40 popped from heap
31 22 3 1 13 40 52 77 98 100
v2 after 31 popped from heap
22 13 3 1 31 40 52 77 98 100
v2 after 22 popped from heap
13 1 3 22 31 40 52 77 98 100
v2 after 13 popped from heap
3 1 13 22 31 40 52 77 98 100
v2 after 3 popped from heap
1 3 13 22 31 40 52 77 98 100
v2 after 1 popped from heap
1 3 13 22 31 40 52 77 98 100
```

Fig. 22.37 | Using Standard Library functions to perform a heapsort. (Part 3 of 3.)

Line 23 uses function `make_heap` to take a sequence of values in the range from `v.begin()` up to, but not including, `v.end()` and create a heap that can be used to produce a sorted sequence. The two iterator arguments must be random-access iterators, so this function will work only with arrays, `vectors` and `deques`. A second version of this function takes as a third argument a binary predicate function for comparing values.

Line 27 uses function `sort_heap` to sort a sequence of values in the range from `v.begin()` up to, but not including, `v.end()` that are already arranged in a heap. The two iterator arguments must be random-access iterators. A second version of this function takes as a third argument a binary predicate function for comparing values.

Line 41 uses function `push_heap` to add a new value into a heap. We take one element of array `a` at a time, append that element to the end of vector `v2` and perform the push_heap operation. If the appended element is the only element in the vector, the vector is already a heap. Otherwise, function push_heap rearranges the elements of the vector into a heap. Each time push_heap is called, it assumes that the last element currently in the vector (i.e., the one that is appended before the push_heap function call) is the element being added to the heap and that all other elements in the vector are already arranged as a heap. The two iterator arguments to push_heap must be random-access iterators. A second version of this function takes as a third argument a binary predicate function for comparing values.

Line 52 uses **pop_heap** to remove the top heap element. This function assumes that the elements in the range specified by its two random-access iterator arguments are already a heap. Repeatedly removing the top heap element results in a sorted sequence of values. Function pop_heap swaps the first heap element (v2.begin(), in this example) with the last heap element (the element before v2.end() - i, in this example), then ensures that the elements up to, but not including, the last element still form a heap. Notice in the output that, after the pop_heap operations, the vector is sorted in ascending order. A second version of this function takes as a third argument a binary predicate function for comparing values.

22.5.13 min and max

Algorithms min and max determine the minimum of two elements and the maximum of two elements, respectively. Figure 22.38 demonstrates min and max for int and char values.

22.5.14 STL Algorithms Not Covered in This Chapter

Figure 22.39 summarizes the STL algorithms that are not covered in this chapter.

```
1   // Fig. 22.38: Fig22_38.cpp
2   // Standard Library algorithms min and max.
3   #include <iostream>
4   using std::cout;
5   using std::endl;
6
7   #include <algorithm>
8
9   int main()
10  {
11     cout << "The minimum of 12 and 7 is: " << std::min( 12, 7 );
12     cout << "\nThe maximum of 12 and 7 is: " << std::max( 12, 7 );
13     cout << "\nThe minimum of 'G' and 'Z' is: " << std::min( 'G', 'Z' );
14     cout << "\nThe maximum of 'G' and 'Z' is: " << std::max( 'G', 'Z' );
15     cout << endl;
16     return 0;
17  } // end main
```

```
The minimum of 12 and 7 is: 7
The maximum of 12 and 7 is: 12
The minimum of 'G' and 'Z' is: G
The maximum of 'G' and 'Z' is: Z
```

Fig. 22.38 | Algorithms min and max.

Algorithm	Description
inner_product	Calculate the sum of the products of two sequences by taking corresponding elements in each sequence, multiplying those elements and adding the result to a total.
adjacent_difference	Beginning with the second element in a sequence, calculate the difference (using operator –) between the current and previous elements, and store the result. The first two input iterator arguments indicate the range of elements in the container and the third indicates where the results should be stored. A second version of this algorithm takes as a fourth argument a binary function to perform a calculation between the current element and the previous element.
partial_sum	Calculate a running total (using operator +) of the values in a sequence. The first two input iterator arguments indicate the range of elements in the container and the third indicates where the results should be stored. A second version of this algorithm takes as a fourth argument a binary function that performs a calculation between the current value in the sequence and the running total.
nth_element	Use three random-access iterators to partition a range of elements. The first and last arguments represent the range of elements. The second argument is the partitioning element's location. After this algorithm executes, all elements before the partitioning element are less than that element and all elements after the partitioning element are greater than or equal to that element. A second version of this algorithm takes as a fourth argument a binary comparison function.
partition	This algorithm is similar to nth_element, but it requires less powerful bidirectional iterators, making it more flexible than nth_element. Algorithm partition requires two bidirectional iterators indicating the range of elements to partition. The third element is a unary predicate function that helps partition the elements so that all elements in the sequence for which the predicate is true are to the left (toward the beginning of the sequence) of all elements for which the predicate is false. A bidirectional iterator is returned indicating the first element in the sequence for which the predicate returns false.
stable_partition	This algorithm is similar to partition except that elements for which the predicate function returns true are maintained in their original order and elements for which the predicate function returns false are maintained in their original order.
next_permutation	Next lexicographical permutation of a sequence.
prev_permutation	Previous lexicographical permutation of a sequence.
rotate	Use three forward iterator arguments to rotate the sequence indicated by the first and last argument by the number of positions indicated by subtracting the first argument from the second argument. For example, the sequence 1, 2, 3, 4, 5 rotated by two positions would be 4, 5, 1, 2, 3.

Fig. 22.39 | Algorithms not covered in this chapter. (Part 1 of 2.)

Algorithm	Description
`rotate_copy`	This algorithm is identical to `rotate` except that the results are stored in a separate sequence indicated by the fourth argument—an output iterator. The two sequences must have the same number of elements.
`adjacent_find`	This algorithm returns an input iterator indicating the first of two identical adjacent elements in a sequence. If there are no identical adjacent elements, the iterator is positioned at the end of the sequence.
`search`	This algorithm searches for a subsequence of elements within a sequence of elements and, if such a subsequence is found, returns a forward iterator that indicates the first element of that subsequence. If there are no matches, the iterator is positioned at the end of the sequence to be searched.
`search_n`	This algorithm searches a sequence of elements looking for a subsequence in which the values of a specified number of elements have a particular value and, if such a subsequence is found, returns a forward iterator that indicates the first element of that subsequence. If there are no matches, the iterator is positioned at the end of the sequence to be searched.
`partial_sort`	Use three random-access iterators to sort part of a sequence. The first and last arguments indicate the sequence of elements. The second argument indicates the ending location for the sorted part of the sequence. By default, elements are ordered using operator < (a binary predicate function can also be supplied). The elements from the second argument iterator to the end of the sequence are in an undefined order.
`partial_sort_copy`	Use two input iterators and two random-access iterators to sort part of the sequence indicated by the two input iterator arguments. The results are stored in the sequence indicated by the two random-access iterator arguments. By default, elements are ordered using operator < (a binary predicate function can also be supplied). The number of elements sorted is the smaller of the number of elements in the result and the number of elements in the original sequence.
`stable_sort`	The algorithm is similar to `sort` except that all equal elements are maintained in their original order.

Fig. 22.39 | Algorithms not covered in this chapter. (Part 2 of 2.)

22.6 Class `bitset`

Class `bitset` makes it easy to create and manipulate bit sets, which are useful for representing a set of bit flags. `bitset`s are fixed in size at compile time. The declaration

```
bitset< size > b;
```

creates bitset b, in which every bit is initially 0. The statement

        b.set(bitNumber);

sets bit bitNumber of bitset b "on." The expression b.set() sets all bits in b "on."
The statement

        b.reset(bitNumber);

sets bit bitNumber of bitset b "off." The expression b.reset() sets all bits in b "off." The
statement

        b.flip(bitNumber);

"flips" bit bitNumber of bitset b (e.g., if the bit is on, flip sets it off). The expression
b.flip() flips all bits in b. The statement

        b[bitNumber];

returns a reference to the bit bitNumber of bitset b. Similarly,

        b.at(bitNumber);

performs range checking on bitNumber first. Then, if bitNumber is in range, at returns a
reference to the bit. Otherwise, at throws an out_of_range exception. The statement

        b.test(bitNumber);

performs range checking on bitNumber first. Then, if bitNumber is in range, test returns
true if the bit is on, false if the bit is off. Otherwise, test throws an out_of_range exception. The expression

        b.size()

returns the number of bits in bitset b. The expression

        b.count()

returns the number of bits that are set in bitset b. The expression

        b.any()

returns true if any bit is set in bitset b. The expression

        b.none()

returns true if none of the bits is set in bitset b. The expressions

        b == b1
        b != b1

compare the two bitsets for equality and inequality, respectively.
    Each of the bitwise assignment operators &=, |= and ^= can be used to combine bit-
sets. For example,

        b &= b1;

performs a bit-by-bit logical AND between bitsets b and b1. The result is stored in b.
Bitwise logical OR and bitwise logical XOR are performed by

```
b |= b1;
b ^= b2;
```

The expression

```
b >>= n;
```

shifts the bits in bitset b right by n positions. The expression

```
b <<= n;
```

shifts the bits in bitset b left by n positions. The expressions

```
b.to_string()
b.to_ulong()
```

convert bitset b to a string and an unsigned long, respectively.

Sieve of Eratosthenes with bitset

Figure 22.40 revisits the Sieve of Eratosthenes for finding prime numbers that we discussed in Exercise 7.29. A bitset is used instead of an array to implement the algorithm. The program displays all the prime numbers from 2 to 1023, then allows the user to enter a number to determine whether that number is prime.

Line 20 creates a bitset of size bits (size is 1024 in this example). By default, all the bits in the bitset are set "off." Line 21 calls function flip to set all bits "on." Numbers 0 and 1 are not prime numbers, so lines 22–23 call function reset to set bits 0 and 1 "off." Lines 29–36 determine all the prime numbers from 2 to 1023. The integer finalBit (line 26) is used to determine when the algorithm is complete. The basic algorithm is that a number is prime if it has no divisors other than 1 and itself. Starting with the number 2, we can eliminate all multiples of that number. The number 2 is divisible only by 1 and itself, so it is prime. Therefore, we can eliminate 4, 6, 8 and so on. The number 3 is divisible only by 1 and itself. Therefore, we can eliminate all multiples of 3 (keep in mind that all even numbers have already been eliminated).

```
1   // Fig. 22.40: Fig22_40.cpp
2   // Using a bitset to demonstrate the Sieve of Eratosthenes.
3   #include <iostream>
4   using std::cin;
5   using std::cout;
6   using std::endl;
7
8   #include <iomanip>
9   using std::setw;
10
11  #include <cmath>
12  using std::sqrt; // sqrt prototype
13
14  #include <bitset> // bitset class definition
15
16  int main()
17  {
18     const int SIZE = 1024;
```

Fig. 22.40 | Class bitset and the Sieve of Eratosthenes. (Part 1 of 3.)

```
19        int value;
20        std::bitset< SIZE > sieve; // create bitset of 1024 bits
21        sieve.flip(); // flip all bits in bitset sieve
22        sieve.reset( 0 ); // reset first bit (number 0)
23        sieve.reset( 1 ); // reset second bit (number 1)
24
25        // perform Sieve of Eratosthenes
26        int finalBit = sqrt( static_cast< double > ( sieve.size() ) ) + 1;
27
28        // determine all prime numbers from 2 to 1024
29        for ( int i = 2; i < finalBit; i++ )
30        {
31           if ( sieve.test( i ) ) // bit i is on
32           {
33              for ( int j = 2 * i; j < SIZE; j += i )
34                 sieve.reset( j ); // set bit j off
35           } // end if
36        } // end for
37
38        cout << "The prime numbers in the range 2 to 1023 are:\n";
39
40        // display prime numbers in range 2-1023
41        for ( int k = 2, counter = 1; k < SIZE; k++ )
42        {
43           if ( sieve.test( k ) ) // bit k is on
44           {
45              cout << setw( 5 ) << k;
46
47              if ( counter++ % 12 == 0 ) // counter is a multiple of 12
48                 cout << '\n';
49           } // end if
50        } // end for
51
52        cout << endl;
53
54        // get value from user to determine whether value is prime
55        cout << "\nEnter a value from 2 to 1023 (-1 to end): ";
56        cin >> value;
57
58        // determine whether user input is prime
59        while ( value != -1 )
60        {
61           if ( sieve[ value ] ) // prime number
62              cout << value << " is a prime number\n";
63           else // not a prime number
64              cout << value << " is not a prime number\n";
65
66           cout << "\nEnter a value from 2 to 1023 (-1 to end): ";
67           cin >> value;
68        } // end while
69
70        return 0;
71     } // end main
```

Fig. 22.40 | Class bitset and the Sieve of Eratosthenes. (Part 2 of 3.)

```
The prime numbers in the range 2 to 1023 are:
    2    3    5    7   11   13   17   19   23   29   31   37
   41   43   47   53   59   61   67   71   73   79   83   89
   97  101  103  107  109  113  127  131  137  139  149  151
  157  163  167  173  179  181  191  193  197  199  211  223
  227  229  233  239  241  251  257  263  269  271  277  281
  283  293  307  311  313  317  331  337  347  349  353  359
  367  373  379  383  389  397  401  409  419  421  431  433
  439  443  449  457  461  463  467  479  487  491  499  503
  509  521  523  541  547  557  563  569  571  577  587  593
  599  601  607  613  617  619  631  641  643  647  653  659
  661  673  677  683  691  701  709  719  727  733  739  743
  751  757  761  769  773  787  797  809  811  821  823  827
  829  839  853  857  859  863  877  881  883  887  907  911
  919  929  937  941  947  953  967  971  977  983  991  997
 1009 1013 1019 1021

Enter a value from 2 to 1023 (-1 to end): 389
389 is a prime number

Enter a value from 2 to 1023 (-1 to end): 88
88 is not a prime number

Enter a value from 2 to 1023 (-1 to end): -1
```

Fig. 22.40 | Class `bitset` and the Sieve of Eratosthenes. (Part 3 of 3.)

22.7 Function Objects

Many STL algorithms allow you to pass a function pointer into the algorithm to help the algorithm perform its task. For example, the `binary_search` algorithm that we discussed in Section 22.5.6 is overloaded with a version that requires as its fourth parameter a pointer to a function that takes two arguments and returns a `bool` value. The `binary_search` algorithm uses this function to compare the search key to an element in the collection. The function returns `true` if the search key and element being compared are equal; otherwise, the function returns `false`. This enables `binary_search` to search a collection of elements for which the element type does not provide an overloaded equality `==` operator.

STL's designers made the algorithms more flexible by allowing any algorithm that can receive a function pointer to receive an object of a class that overloads the parentheses operator with a function named `operator()`, provided that the overloaded operator meets the requirements of the algorithm—in the case of `binary_search`, it must receive two arguments and return a `bool`. An object of such a class is known as a *function object* and can be used syntactically and semantically like a function or function pointer—the overloaded parentheses operator is invoked by using a function object's name followed by parentheses containing the arguments to the function.

Function objects provide several advantages over function pointers. Since function objects are commonly implemented as class templates that are included into each source code file that uses them, the compiler can inline an overloaded `operator()` to improve performance. Also, since they are objects of classes, function objects can have data members that `operator()` can use to perform its task.

Predefined Function Objects of the Standard Template Library

Many predefined function objects can be found in the header <functional>. Figure 22.41 lists several of the STL function objects, which are all implemented as class templates. We used the function object less< T > in the set, multiset and priority_queue examples, to specify the sorting order for elements in a container.

Using the STL **Accumulate** *Algorithm*

Figure 22.42 demonstrates the accumulate numeric algorithm (discussed in Fig. 22.30) to calculate the sum of the squares of the elements in a vector. The fourth argument to accumulate is a binary function object (that is, a function object for which operator() takes two arguments) or a function pointer to a binary function (that is, a function that takes two arguments). Function accumulate is demonstrated twice—once with a function pointer and once with a function object.

STL function objects	Type	STL function objects	Type
divides< T >	arithmetic	logical_or< T >	logical
equal_to< T >	relational	minus< T >	arithmetic
greater< T >	relational	modulus< T >	arithmetic
greater_equal< T >	relational	negate< T >	arithmetic
less< T >	relational	not_equal_to< T >	relational
less_equal< T >	relational	plus< T >	arithmetic
logical_and< T >	logical	multiplies< T >	arithmetic
logical_not< T >	logical		

Fig. 22.41 | Function objects in the Standard Library.

```cpp
1   // Fig. 22.42: Fig22_42.cpp
2   // Demonstrating function objects.
3   #include <iostream>
4   using std::cout;
5   using std::endl;
6
7   #include <vector> // vector class-template definition
8   #include <algorithm> // copy algorithm
9   #include <numeric> // accumulate algorithm
10  #include <functional> // binary_function definition
11  #include <iterator> // ostream_iterator
12
13  // binary function adds square of its second argument and the
14  // running total in its first argument, then returns the sum
15  int sumSquares( int total, int value )
16  {
17     return total + value * value;
18  } // end function sumSquares
```

Fig. 22.42 | Binary function object. (Part 1 of 2.)

```
19
20   // binary function class template defines overloaded operator()
21   // that adds the square of its second argument and running
22   // total in its first argument, then returns sum
23   template< typename T >
24   class SumSquaresClass : public std::binary_function< T, T, T >
25   {
26   public:
27      // add square of value to total and return result
28      T operator()( const T &total, const T &value )
29      {
30         return total + value * value;
31      } // end function operator()
32   }; // end class SumSquaresClass
33
34   int main()
35   {
36      const int SIZE = 10;
37      int array[ SIZE ] = { 1, 2, 3, 4, 5, 6, 7, 8, 9, 10 };
38      std::vector< int > integers( array, array + SIZE ); // copy of array
39      std::ostream_iterator< int > output( cout, " " );
40      int result;
41
42      cout << "vector integers contains:\n";
43      std::copy( integers.begin(), integers.end(), output );
44
45      // calculate sum of squares of elements of vector integers
46      // using binary function sumSquares
47      result = std::accumulate( integers.begin(), integers.end(),
48         0, sumSquares );
49
50      cout << "\n\nSum of squares of elements in integers using "
51         << "binary\nfunction sumSquares: " << result;
52
53      // calculate sum of squares of elements of vector integers
54      // using binary function object
55      result = std::accumulate( integers.begin(), integers.end(),
56         0, SumSquaresClass< int >() );
57
58      cout << "\n\nSum of squares of elements in integers using "
59         << "binary\nfunction object of type "
60         << "SumSquaresClass< int >: " << result << endl;
61      return 0;
62   } // end main
```

```
vector integers contains:
1 2 3 4 5 6 7 8 9 10

Sum of squares of elements in integers using binary
function sumSquares: 385

Sum of squares of elements in integers using binary
function object of type SumSquaresClass< int >: 385
```

Fig. 22.42 | Binary function object. (Part 2 of 2.)

Lines 15–18 define a function sumSquares that squares its second argument value, adds that square and its first argument total and returns the sum. Function accumulate will pass each of the elements of the sequence over which it iterates as the second argument to sumSquares in the example. On the first call to sumSquares, the first argument will be the initial value of the total (which is supplied as the third argument to accumulate; 0 in this program). All subsequent calls to sumSquares receive as the first argument the running sum returned by the previous call to sumSquares. When accumulate completes, it returns the sum of the squares of all the elements in the sequence.

Lines 23–32 define a class SumSquaresClass that inherits from the class template binary_function (in header file <functional>)—an empty base class for creating function objects in which operator receives two parameters and returns a value. Class binary_function accepts three type parameters that represent the types of the first argument, second argument and return value of operator, respectively. In this example, the type of these parameters is T (line 24). On the first call to the function object, the first argument will be the initial value of the total (which is supplied as the third argument to accumulate: 0 in this program) and the second argument will be the first element in vector integers. All subsequent calls to operator receive as the first argument the result returned by the previous call to the function object, and the second argument will be the next element in the vector. When accumulate completes, it returns the sum of the squares of all the elements in the vector.

Lines 47–48 call function accumulate with a pointer to function sumSquares as its last argument.

The statement at lines 55–56 calls function accumulate with an object of class SumSquaresClass as the last argument. The expression SumSquaresClass< int >() creates an instance of class SumSquaresClass (a function object) that is passed to accumulate, which sends the object the message (invokes the function) operator. The statement could be written as two separate statements, as follows:

```
SumSquaresClass< int > sumSquaresObject;
result = std::accumulate( integers.begin(), integers.end(),
    0, sumSquaresObject );
```

The first line defines an object of class SumSquaresClass. That object is then passed to function accumulate.

22.8 STL Internet and Web Resources

The following is a collection of Internet and World Wide Web STL resources. These sites include tutorials, references, FAQs, articles, books, interviews and software.

Tutorials

www.cs.brown.edu/people/jak/programming/stl-tutorial/tutorial.html
This STL tutorial is organized by examples, philosophy, components and extending the STL. You will find code examples using the STL components, useful explanations and helpful diagrams.

www.yrl.co.uk/phil/stl/stl.htmlx
This STL tutorial provides information on function templates, class templates, the STL components, containers, iterators, adaptors and function objects.

`www.xraylith.wisc.edu/~khan/software/stl/os_examples/examples.html`
This site is helpful for people just learning about the STL. You will find an introduction to the STL and ObjectSpace STL Tool Kit examples.

References
`www.sgi.com/tech/stl`
The Silicon Graphics Standard Template Library Programmer's Guide is a useful resource for STL information. You can download the STL from this site and find the latest information, design documentation and links to other STL resources.

`www.cppreference.com/cpp_stl.html`
This site lists the constructors, operators and functions supported by each STL container.

Articles, Books and Interviews
`www.byte.com/art/9510/sec12/art3.htm`
The *Byte Magazine* site has a copy of an article on the STL written by Alexander Stepanov. Stepanov, one of the creators of the Standard Template Library, provides information on the use of the STL in generic programming.

`www.sgi.com/tech/stl/drdobbs-interview.html`
A Dr. Dobb's journal interview with Alexander Stepanov.

ANSI/ISO C++ Standard
`www.ansi.org`
You can purchase a copy of the C++ standard document from this site.

Software
`www.cs.rpi.edu/~musser/stl-book`
The RPI STL site includes information on how STL differs from other C++ libraries and on how to compile programs that use STL. The site lists the STL files and provides example programs that use STL, STL Container Classes and STL Iterator Categories. It also provides an STL-compatible compiler list, FTP sites for STL source code and related materials.

`msdn.microsoft.com/visualc`
This is the Microsoft Visual C++ home page. Here you can find the latest Visual C++ news, updates, technical resources, samples and downloads.

`www.borland.com/cbuilder`
This is the Borland C++Builder home page. Here you can find a variety of C++ resources, including several C++ newsgroups, information on the latest product enhancements, FAQs and many other resources for programmers using C++Builder.

Summary

- The Standard Template Library defines powerful, template-based, reusable components that implement many common data structures, and algorithms used to process those data structures.
- The STL has three key components—containers, iterators and algorithms.
- The STL containers are data structures capable of storing objects of any data type. There are three container categories—first-class containers, adapters and near containers.
- STL algorithms are functions that perform such common data manipulations as searching, sorting and comparing elements or entire containers.
- The containers are divided into three major categories—sequence containers, associative containers and container adapters.

- The sequence containers represent linear data structures, such as vectors and linked lists.

- Associative containers are nonlinear containers that quickly locate elements stored in them, such as sets of values or key/value pairs.

- Sequence containers and associative containers are collectively referred to as first-class containers.

- First-class container function begin returns an iterator pointing to the first element of a container. Function end returns an iterator pointing to the first element past the end of the container (an element that doesn't exist and is typically used in a loop to indicate when to terminate processing of the container's elements).

- An istream_iterator is capable of extracting values in a type-safe manner from an input stream. An ostream_iterator is capable of inserting values in an output stream.

- Input and output iterators can move only in the forward direction (i.e., from the beginning of the container to the end) one element at a time.

- A forward iterator combines the capabilities of input and output iterators.

- A bidirectional iterator has the capabilities of a forward iterator and the ability to move in the backward direction (i.e., from the end of the container toward the beginning).

- A random-access iterator has the capabilities of a bidirectional iterator and the ability to directly access any element of the container.

- Containers that support random-access iterators, such as vector, can be used with all algorithms in the STL.

- The STL provides three sequence containers—vector, list and deque. Class template vector and class template deque both are based on arrays. Class template list implements a linked-list data structure.

- Function capacity returns the number of elements that can be stored in a vector before the vector dynamically resizes itself to accommodate more elements.

- Sequence container function push_back adds an element to the end of a container.

- To use the algorithms of the STL, you must include the header file <algorithm>.

- Algorithm copy copies each element in a container starting with the location specified by the iterator in its first argument and up to—but not including—the location specified by the iterator in its second argument.

- Function front returns a reference to the first element in a sequence container. Function begin returns an iterator pointing to the beginning of a sequence container.

- Function back returns a reference to the last element in a sequence container. Function end returns an iterator pointing to the element one past the end of a sequence container.

- Sequence container function insert inserts value(s) before the element at a specific location.

- Function erase (available in all first-class containers) removes specific element(s) from the container.

- Function empty (available in all containers and adapters) returns true if the container is empty.

- Function clear (available in all first-class containers) empties the container.

- The list sequence container provides an efficient implementation for insertion and deletion operations at any location in the container. Header file <list> must be included to use class template list.

- The list member function push_front inserts values at the beginning of a list.

- The list member function sort arranges the elements in the list in ascending order.

- The list member function splice removes elements in one list and inserts them into another list at a specific position.

- The list member function unique removes duplicate elements in a list.
- The list member function assign replaces the contents of one list with the contents of another.
- The list member function remove deletes all copies of a specified value from a list.
- Class template deque provides the same operations as vector, but adds member functions push_front and pop_front to allow insertion and deletion at the beginning of a deque, respectively. Header file <deque> must be included to use class template deque.
- The STL's associative containers provide direct access to store and retrieve elements via keys.
- The four associative containers are multiset, set, multimap and map.
- Class templates multiset and set provide operations for manipulating sets of values where the values are the keys—there is not a separate value associated with each key. Header file <set> must be included to use class templates set and multiset.
- The primary difference between a multiset and a set is that a multiset allows duplicate keys and a set does not.
- Class templates multimap and map provide operations for manipulating values associated with keys.
- The primary difference between a multimap and a map is that a multimap allows duplicate keys with associated values to be stored and a map allows only unique keys with associated values.
- Function count (available to all associative containers) counts the number of occurrences of the specified value currently in a container.
- Function find (available to all associative containers) locates a specified value in a container.
- Functions lower_bound and upper_bound (available in all associative containers) locate the earliest occurrence of the specified value in a container and the element after the last occurrence of the specified value in a container, respectively.
- Function equal_range (available in all associative containers) returns a pair containing the results of both a lower_bound and an upper_bound operation.
- The multimap associative container is used for fast storage and retrieval of keys and associated values (often called key/value pairs).
- Duplicate keys are allowed in a multimap, so multiple values can be associated with a single key. This is called a one-to-many relationship.
- Header file <map> must be included to use class templates map and multimap.
- Duplicate keys are not allowed in a map, so only a single value can be associated with each key. This is called a one-to-one mapping.
- A map is commonly called an associative array.
- The STL provides three container adapters—stack, queue and priority_queue.
- Adapters are not first-class containers, because they do not provide the actual data structure implementation in which elements can be stored and they do not support iterators.
- All three adapter class templates provide member functions push and pop that properly insert an element into and remove an element from each adapter data structure, respectively.
- Class template stack enables insertions into and deletions from the underlying data structure at one end (commonly referred to as a last-in, first-out data structure). Header file <stack> must be included to use class template stack.
- The stack member function top returns a reference to the top element of the stack (implemented by calling function back of the underlying container).
- The stack member function empty determines whether the stack is empty (implemented by calling function empty of the underlying container).

- The `stack` member function `size` returns get the number of elements in the `stack` (implemented by calling function `size` of the underlying container).
- Class template `queue` enables insertions at the back of the underlying data structure and deletions from the front of the underlying data structure (commonly referred to as a first-in, first-out data structure). Header file `<queue>` must be included to use a `queue` or a `priority_queue`.
- The `queue` member function `front` returns a reference to the first element in the `queue` (implemented by calling function `front` of the underlying container).
- The `queue` member function `back` returns a reference to the last element in the `queue` (implemented by calling function `back` of the underlying container).
- The `queue` member function `empty` determines whether the `queue` is empty (implemented by calling function `empty` of the underlying container).
- The `queue` member function `size` returns get the number of elements in the `queue` (implemented by calling function `size` of the underlying container).
- Class template `priority_queue` provides functionality that enables insertions in sorted order into the underlying data structure and deletions from the front of the underlying data structure.
- The common `priority_queue` operations are push, pop, top, empty and `size`.
- Algorithms `fill` and `fill_n` set every element in a range of container elements to a specific value.
- Algorithms `generate` and `generate_n` use a generator function to create values for every element in a range of container elements.
- Algorithm `equal` compares two sequences of values for equality.
- Algorithm `mismatch` compares two sequences of values and returns a pair of iterators indicating the location in each sequence of the mismatched elements.
- Algorithm `lexicographical_compare` compares the contents of two character arrays.
- Algorithm `remove` eliminates all elements with a specific value in a certain range.
- Algorithm `remove_copy` copies all elements that do not have a specific value in a certain range.
- Algorithm `remove_if` deletes all elements that satisfy the `if` condition in a certain range.
- Algorithm `remove_copy_if` copies all elements that satisfy the `if` condition in a certain range.
- Algorithm `replace` replaces all elements with a specific value in certain range.
- Algorithm `replace_copy` copies all elements with a specific value in a certain range.
- Algorithm `replace_if` replaces all elements that satisfy the `if` condition in a certain range.
- Algorithm `replace_copy_if` copies all elements that satisfy the `if` condition in a certain range.
- Algorithm `random_shuffle` reorders randomly the elements in a certain range.
- Algorithm `count` counts the elements with a specific value in a certain range.
- Algorithm `count_if` counts the elements that satisfy the `if` condition in a certain range.
- Algorithm `min_element` locates the smallest element in a certain range.
- Algorithm `max_element` locates the largest element in a certain range.
- Algorithm `accumulate` sums the values in a certain range.
- Algorithm `for_each` applies a general function to every element in a certain range.
- Algorithm `transform` applies a general function to every element in a certain range and replaces each element with the result of the function.
- Algorithm `find` locates a specific value in a certain range.
- Algorithm `find_if` locates the first value in a certain range that satisfies the `if` condition.

- Algorithm `sort` arranges the elements in a certain range in ascending order or an order specified by a predicate.
- Algorithm `binary_search` determines whether a specific value is in a certain range.
- Algorithm `swap` exchanges two values.
- Algorithm `iter_swap` exchanges the two elements.
- Algorithm `swap_ranges` exchanges the elements in a certain range.
- Algorithm `copy_backward` copies elements in a certain range and places the elements in results backward.
- Algorithm `merge` combines two sorted ascending sequences of values into a third sorted ascending sequence.
- Algorithm `unique` removes duplicated elements in a sorted sequence of elements in a certain range.
- Algorithm `reverse` reverses all the elements in a certain range.
- Algorithm `inplace_merge` merges two sorted sequences of elements in the same container.
- Algorithm `unique_copy` makes a copy of all the unique elements in the sorted sequence of values in a certain range.
- Algorithm `reverse_copy` makes a reversed copy of the elements in a certain range.
- The set function `includes` compares two sets of sorted values to determine whether every element of the second set is in the first set.
- The set function `set_difference` finds the elements from the first set of sorted values that are not in the second set of sorted values (both sets of values must be in ascending order).
- The set function `set_intersection` determines the elements from the first set of sorted values that are in the second set of sorted values (both sets of values must be in ascending order).
- The set function `set_symmetric_difference` determines the elements in the first set that are not in the second set and the elements in the second set that are not in the first set (both sets of values must be in ascending order).
- The set function `set_union` creates a set of all the elements that are in either or both of the two sorted sets (both sets of values must be in ascending order).
- Algorithm `lower_bound` finds the first location in a sorted sequence of values at which the third argument could be inserted in the sequence such that the sequence would still be sorted in ascending order.
- Algorithm `upper_bound` finds the last location in a sorted sequence of values at which the third argument could be inserted in the sequence such that the sequence would still be sorted in ascending order.
- Algorithm `make_heap` takes a sequence of values in a certain range and creates a heap that can be used to produce a sorted sequence.
- Algorithm `sort_heap` sorts a sequence of values in a certain range that are already arranged in a heap.
- Algorithm `pop_heap` removes the top heap element.
- Algorithms `min` and `max` determine the minimum of two elements and the maximum of two elements, respectively.
- Class template `bitset` makes it easy to create and manipulate bit sets, which are useful for representing a set of bit flags.
- A function object is an instance of a class that overloads `operator()`.
- STL provides many predefined function objects, which can be found in header `<functional>`.

- Binary function objects are function objects that take two arguments and return a value. Class template `binary_function` is an empty base class for creating binary function objects.

Terminology

accumulate algorithm

adapter

algorithm

`<algorithm>` header file

assign member function of `list`

associative array

associative container

back member function of sequence containers

back_inserter function template

begin member function of first-class containers

bidirectional iterator

binary function

binary function object

binary_function class template

binary_search algorithm

capacity member function of vector

comparator function object

const_iterator

const_reverse_iterator

container

container adapter

copy_backward algorithm

count algorithm

count_if algorithm

`<deque>` header file

deque sequence container

empty member function of containers

end member function of containers

equal algorithm

equal_range algorithm

equal_range function of associative container

erase member function of containers

fill algorithm

fill_n algorithm

find algorithm

find function of associative container

find_if algorithm

first data member of pair

first-class container

flip function of bitset

for_each algorithm

forward iterator

front_inserter function template

front member function of sequence container

function object

`<functional>` header file

generate algorithm

generate_n algorithm

heap

heapsort sorting algorithm

includes algorithm

inplace_merge algorithm

input iterator

input sequence

insert member function of containers

inserter function template

istream_iterator

iterator

iter_swap algorithm

key/value pair

less< int >

lexicographical_compare algorithm

`<list>` header file

list sequence container

lower_bound algorithm

lower_bound function of associative container

make_heap algorithm

`<map>` header file

map associative container

max algorithm

max_element algorithm

merge algorithm

min algorithm

min_element algorithm

mismatch algorithm

multimap associative container

multiset associative container

mutating-sequence algorithm

near container

`<numeric>` header file

one-to-one mapping

ostream_iterator

output iterator

output sequence

pop_back function

pop_front function

pop_heap algorithm

pop member function of container adapters

priority_queue adapter class template

push_heap algorithm

push member function of container adapters

queue adapter class template
<queue> header file
random-access iterator
random_shuffle algorithm
range
rbegin member function of vector
remove algorithm
remove member function of list
remove_copy algorithm
remove_copy_if algorithm
remove_if algorithm
rend member function of containers
replace algorithm
replace_copy algorithm
replace_copy_if algorithm
replace_if algorithm
reset function of bitset
reverse algorithm
reverse_copy algorithm
reverse_iterator
search key
second data member of pair
sequence

sequence container
set associative container
set_difference algorithm
<set> header file
set_intersection algorithm
set_symmetric_difference algorithm
set_union algorithm
size member function of containers
sort algorithm
sort_heap algorithm
sort member function of list
splice member function of list
stack adapter class template
<stack> header file
Standard Template Library (STL)
swap algorithm
swap member function of list
swap_range algorithm
top member function of container adapters
unique algorithm
unique_copy algorithm
unique member function of list
upper_bound algorithm

Self-Review Exercises

State whether the following are *true* or *false* or fill in the blanks. If the answer is *false*, explain why,.

22.1 (T/F) The STL makes abundant use of inheritance and virtual functions.

22.2 The two types of STL containers are sequence containers and _____ containers.

22.3 The five main iterator types are _____, _____, _____, _____ and _____.

22.4 (T/F) An iterator acts like a pointer to an element.

22.5 (T/F) STL algorithms can operate on C-like pointer-based arrays.

22.6 (T/F) STL algorithms are encapsulated as member functions within each container class.

22.7 (T/F) The remove algorithm does not decrease the size of the vector from which elements are being removed.

22.8 The three STL container adapters are _____, _____ and _____.

22.9 (T/F) Container member function end yields the position of the last element of the container.

22.10 STL algorithms operate on container elements indirectly, using _____.

22.11 The sort algorithm requires a _____ iterator.

Answers to Self-Review Exercises

22.1 False. These were avoided for performance reasons.

22.2 Associative.

22.3   Input, output, forward, bidirectional, random access.

22.4   False. It is actually vice versa.

22.5   True.

22.6   False. STL algorithms are not member functions. They operate indirectly on containers, through iterators.

22.7   True.

22.8   `stack`, `queue`, `priority_queue`.

22.9   False. It actually yields the position just after the end of the container.

22.10   Iterators.

22.11   Random-access.

Exercises

22.12   Write a function template `palindrome` that takes a `vector` parameter and returns `true` or `false` according to whether the `vector` does or does not read the same forward as backward (e.g., a vector containing 1, 2, 3, 2, 1 is a palindrome, but a `vector` containing 1, 2, 3, 4 is not).

22.13   Modify Fig. 22.40, the Sieve of Eratosthenes, so that, if the number the user inputs into the program is not prime, the program displays the prime factors of the number. Remember that a prime number's factors are only 1 and the prime number itself. Every nonprime number has a unique prime factorization. For example, the factors of 54 are 2, 3, 3 and 3. When these values are multiplied together, the result is 54. For the number 54, the prime factors output should be 2 and 3.

22.14   Modify Exercise 22.13 so that, if the number the user inputs into the program is not prime, the program displays the prime factors of the number and the number of times each prime factor appears in the unique prime factorization. For example, the output for the number 54 should be

```
The unique prime factorization of 54 is: 2 * 3 * 3 * 3
```

Recommended Reading

Ammeraal, L. *STL for C++ Programmers*. New York: John Wiley, 1997.

Austern, M. H. *Generic Programming and the STL: Using and Extending the C++ Standard Template Library*. Reading, MA: Addison-Wesley, 1998

Glass, G., and B. Schuchert. *The STL <Primer>*. Upper Saddle River, NJ: Prentice Hall PTR, 1995.

Henricson, M., and E. Nyquist. *Industrial Strength C++: Rules and Recommendations*. Upper Saddle River, NJ: Prentice Hall, 1997.

Josuttis, N. *The C++ Standard Library: A Tutorial and Handbook*. Reading, MA: Addison-Wesley, 1999.

Koenig, A., and B. Moo. *Ruminations on C++*. Reading, MA: Addison-Wesley, 1997.

Meyers, S. *Effective STL: 50 Specific Ways to Improve Your Use of the Standard Template Library*. Reading, MA: Addison-Wesley, 2001.

Musser, D. R., and A. Saini. *STL Tutorial and Reference Guide: C++ Programming with the Standard Template Library*. Reading, MA: Addison-Wesley, 1996.

Musser, D. R., and A. A. Stepanov. "Algorithm-Oriented Generic Libraries," *Software Practice and Experience,* Vol. 24, No. 7, July 1994.

Nelson, M. *C++ Programmer's Guide to the Standard Template Library.* Foster City, CA: Programmer's Press, 1995.

Pohl, I. *C++ Distilled: A Concise ANSI/ISO Reference and Style Guide.* Reading, MA: Addison-Wesley, 1997.

Pohl, I. *Object-Oriented Programming Using C++, Second Edition.* Reading, MA: Addison-Wesley, 1997.

Robson, R. *Using the STL: The C++ Standard Template Library.* New York: Springer Verlag, 2000.

Schildt, H. *STL Programming from the Ground Up,* New York: Osborne McGraw-Hill, 1999.

Stepanov, A., and M. Lee. "The Standard Template Library," *Internet Distribution* 31 October 1995 <www.cs.rpi.edu/~musser/doc.ps>.

Stroustrup, B. "Making a `vector` Fit for a Standard," *The C++ Report,* October 1994.

Stroustrup, B. *The Design and Evolution of C++.* Reading, MA: Addison-Wesley, 1994.

Stroustrup, B. *The C++ Programming Language, Third Edition.* Reading, MA: Addison-Wesley, 1997.

Vilot, M. J. "An Introduction to the Standard Template Library," *The C++ Report,* Vol. 6, No. 8, October 1994.

Other Topics

OBJECTIVES

In this chapter you will learn:

- To use **const_cast** to temporarily treat a **const** object as a non-**const** object.
- To use **namespace**s.
- To use operator keywords.
- To use **mutable** members in **const** objects.
- To use class-member pointer operators `.*` and `->*`.
- To use multiple inheritance.
- The role of **virtual** base classes in multiple inheritance.

23.1 Introduction

We now consider several advanced C++ features. First, you will learn about the `const_cast` operator, which allows programmers to add or remove the `const` qualification of a variable. Next, we discuss `namespace`s, which can be used to ensure that every identifier in a program has a unique name and can help resolve naming conflicts caused by using libraries that have the same variable, function or class names. We then present several operator keywords that are useful for programmers who have keyboards that do not support certain characters used in operator symbols, such as !, &, ^, ~ and |. We continue our discussion with the `mutable` storage-class specifier, which enables a programmer to indicate that a data member should always be modifiable, even when it appears in an object that is currently being treated as a `const` object by the program. Next we introduce two special operators that we can use with pointers to class members to access a data member or member function without knowing its name in advance. Finally, we introduce multiple inheritance, which enables a derived class to inherit the members of several base classes. As part of this introduction, we discuss potential problems with multiple inheritance and how `virtual` inheritance can be used to solve those problems.

23.2 `const_cast` Operator

C++ provides the `const_cast` operator for casting away `const` or `volatile` qualification. A program declares a variable with the `volatile` qualifier when that program expects the variable to be modified by hardware or other programs not known to the compiler. Declaring a variable `volatile` indicates that the compiler should not optimize the use of that variable because doing so could affect the ability of those other programs to access and modify the `volatile` variable.

In general, it is dangerous to use the `const_cast` operator, because it allows a program to modify a variable that was declared `const`, and thus was not supposed to be modifiable. There are cases in which it is desirable, or even necessary, to cast away const-ness. For example, older C and C++ libraries might provide functions with non-const parameters and that do not modify their parameters. If you wish to pass `const` data to such a function, you would need to cast away the data's const-ness; otherwise, the compiler would report error messages.

Similarly, you could pass non-`const` data to a function that treats the data as if it were constant, then returns that data as a constant. In such cases, you might need to cast away the const-ness of the returned data, as we demonstrate in Fig. 23.1.

In this program, function `maximum` (lines 11–14) receives two C-style strings as `const char *` parameters and returns a `const char *` that points to the larger of the two strings. Function `main` declares the two C-style strings as non-`const char` arrays (lines 18–19); thus, these arrays are modifiable. In `main`, we wish to output the larger of the two C-style strings, then modify that C-style string by converting it to uppercase letters.

Function `maximum`'s two parameters are of type `const char *`, so the function's return type also must be declared as `const char *`. If the return type is specified as only `char *`, the compiler issues an error message indicating that the value being returned cannot be converted from `const char *` to `char *`—a dangerous conversion, because it attempts to treat data that the function believes to be `const` as if it were is non-`const` data.

```
1   // Fig. 23.1: fig23_01.cpp
2   // Demonstrating const_cast.
3   #include <iostream>
4   using std::cout;
5   using std::endl;
6
7   #include <cstring> // contains prototypes for functions strcmp and strlen
8   #include <cctype> // contains prototype for function toupper
9
10  // returns the larger of two C-style strings
11  const char *maximum( const char *first, const char *second )
12  {
13     return ( strcmp( first, second ) >= 0 ? first : second );
14  } // end function maximum
15
16  int main()
17  {
18     char s1[] = "hello"; // modifiable array of characters
19     char s2[] = "goodbye"; // modifiable array of characters
20
21     // const_cast required to allow the const char * returned by maximum
22     // to be assigned to the char * variable maxPtr
23     char *maxPtr = const_cast< char * >( maximum( s1, s2 ) );
24
25     cout << "The larger string is: " << maxPtr << endl;
26
27     for ( size_t i = 0; i < strlen( maxPtr ); i++ )
28        maxPtr[ i ] = toupper( maxPtr[ i ] );
29
30     cout << "The larger string capitalized is: " << maxPtr << endl;
31     return 0;
32  } // end main
```

```
The larger string is: hello
The larger string capitalized is: HELLO
```

Fig. 23.1 | Demonstrating operator `const_cast`.

Even though function `maximum` believes the data to be constant, we know that the original arrays in `main` do not contain constant data. Therefore, `main` should be able to modify the contents of those arrays as necessary. Since we know these arrays are modifiable, we use `const_cast` (line 23) to cast away the `const`-ness of the pointer returned by `maximum`, so we can then modify the data in the array representing the larger of the two C-style strings. We can then use the pointer as the name of a character array in the `for` statement (lines 27–28) to convert the contents of the larger string to uppercase letters. Without the `const_cast` in line 23, this program will not compile, because you are not allowed to assign a pointer of type `const char *` to a pointer of type `char *`.

Error-Prevention Tip 23.1

In general, a `const_cast` should be used only when it is known in advance that the original data is not constant. Otherwise, unexpected results may occur.

23.3 namespaces

A program includes many identifiers defined in different scopes. Sometimes a variable of one scope will "overlap" (i.e., collide) with a variable of the same name in a different scope, possibly creating a naming conflict. Such overlapping can occur at many levels. Identifier overlapping occurs frequently in third-party libraries that happen to use the same names for global identifiers (such as functions). This can cause compiler errors.

Good Programming Practice 23.1

Avoid identifiers that begin with the underscore character, which can lead to linker errors. Many code libraries use names that begin with underscores.

The C++ standard attempts to solve this problem with namespaces. Each `namespace` defines a scope in which identifiers and variables are placed. To use a namespace member, either the member's name must be qualified with the `namespace` name and the binary scope resolution operator (`::`), as in

    MyNameSpace`::`*member*

or a `using` declaration or `using` directive must appear before the name is used in the program. Typically, such `using` statements are placed at the beginning of the file in which members of the `namespace` are used. For example, placing the following `using` directive at the beginning of a source-code file

    `using namespace` *MyNameSpace*`;`

specifies that members of `namespace` *MyNameSpace* can be used in the file without preceding each member with *MyNameSpace* and the scope resolution operator (`::`).

A `using` declaration (e.g., `using std::cout;`) brings one name into the scope where the declaration appears. A `using` directive (e.g., `using namespace std;`) brings all the names from the specified namespace into the scope where the directive appears.

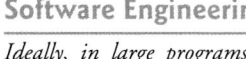

Software Engineering Observation 23.1

Ideally, in large programs, every entity should be declared in a class, function, block or namespace. This helps clarify every entity's role.

Error-Prevention Tip 23.2

Precede a member with its namespace *name and the scope resolution operator (::) if the possibility exists of a naming conflict.*

Not all namespaces are guaranteed to be unique. Two third-party vendors might inadvertently use the same identifiers for their namespace names. Figure 23.2 demonstrates the use of namespaces.

```cpp
 1   // Fig. 23.2: fig23_02.cpp
 2   // Demonstrating namespaces.
 3   #include <iostream>
 4   using namespace std; // use std namespace
 5
 6   int integer1 = 98; // global variable
 7
 8   // create namespace Example
 9   namespace Example
10   {
11      // declare two constants and one variable
12      const double PI = 3.14159;
13      const double E = 2.71828;
14      int integer1 = 8;
15
16      void printValues(); // prototype
17
18      // nested namespace
19      namespace Inner
20      {
21         // define enumeration
22         enum Years { FISCAL1 = 1990, FISCAL2, FISCAL3 };
23      } // end Inner namespace
24   } // end Example namespace
25
26   // create unnamed namespace
27   namespace
28   {
29      double doubleInUnnamed = 88.22; // declare variable
30   } // end unnamed namespace
31
32   int main()
33   {
34      // output value doubleInUnnamed of unnamed namespace
35      cout << "doubleInUnnamed = " << doubleInUnnamed;
36
37      // output global variable
38      cout << "\n(global) integer1 = " << integer1;
39
40      // output values of Example namespace
41      cout << "\nPI = " << Example::PI << "\nE = " << Example::E
42         << "\ninteger1 = " << Example::integer1 << "\nFISCAL3 = "
43         << Example::Inner::FISCAL3 << endl;
44
```

Fig. 23.2 | Demonstrating the use of namespaces. (Part 1 of 2.)

```
45       Example::printValues(); // invoke printValues function
46       return 0;
47    } // end main
48
49    // display variable and constant values
50    void Example::printValues()
51    {
52       cout << "\nIn printValues:\ninteger1 = " << integer1 << "\nPI = "
53          << PI << "\nE = " << E << "\ndoubleInUnnamed = "
54          << doubleInUnnamed << "\n(global) integer1 = " << ::integer1
55          << "\nFISCAL3 = " << Inner::FISCAL3 << endl;
56    } // end printValues
```

```
doubleInUnnamed = 88.22
(global) integer1 = 98
PI = 3.14159
E = 2.71828
integer1 = 8
FISCAL3 = 1992

In printValues:
integer1 = 8
PI = 3.14159
E = 2.71828
doubleInUnnamed = 88.22
(global) integer1 = 98
FISCAL3 = 1992
```

Fig. 23.2 | Demonstrating the use of namespaces. (Part 2 of 2.)

Using the *std* Namespace

Line 4 informs the compiler that namespace std is being used. The contents of header file <iostream> are all defined as part of namespace std. [*Note:* Most C++ programmers consider it poor practice to write a using directive such as line 4 because the entire contents of the namespace are included, thus increasing the likelihood of a naming conflict.]

The using namespace directive specifies that the members of a namespace will be used frequently throughout a program. This allows the programmer to access all the members of the namespace and to write more concise statements such as

```
cout << "double1 = " << double1;
```

rather than

```
std::cout << "double1 = " << double1;
```

Without line 4, either every cout and endl in Fig. 23.2 would have to be qualified with std::, or individual using declarations must be included for cout and endl as in:

```
using std::cout;
using std::endl;
```

The using namespace directive can be used for predefined namespaces (e.g., std) or programmer-defined namespaces.

Defining Namespaces

Lines 9–24 use the keyword `namespace` to define namespace `Example`. The body of a namespace is delimited by braces ({}). Namespace `Example`'s members consist of two constants (`PI` and `E` at lines 12–13), an `int` (`integer1` at line 14), a function (`printValues` at line 16) and a nested namespace (`Inner` at lines 19–23). Notice that member `integer1` has the same name as global variable `integer1` (line 6). Variables that have the same name must have different scopes—otherwise compilation errors occur. A namespace can contain constants, data, classes, nested namespaces, functions, etc. Definitions of namespaces must occupy the global scope or be nested within other namespaces.

Lines 27–30 create an unnamed namespace containing the member `doubleInUnnamed`. The unnamed namespace has an implicit `using` directive, so its members appear to occupy the global namespace, are accessible directly and do not have to be qualified with a namespace name. Global variables are also part of the global namespace and are accessible in all scopes following the declaration in the file.

Software Engineering Observation 23.2

Each separate compilation unit has its own unique unnamed namespace; i.e., the unnamed namespace replaces the `static` linkage specifier.

Accessing Namespace Members with Qualified Names

Line 35 outputs the value of variable `doubleInUnnamed`, which is directly accessible as part of the unnamed namespace. Line 38 outputs the value of global variable `integer1`. For both of these variables, the compiler first attempts to locate a local declaration of the variables in `main`. Since there are no local declarations, the compiler assumes those variables are in the global namespace.

Lines 41–43 output the values of `PI`, `E`, `integer1` and `FISCAL3` from namespace `Example`. Notice that each must be qualified with `Example::` because the program does not provide any `using` directive or declarations indicating that it will use members of namespace `Example`. In addition, member `integer1` must be qualified, because a global variable has the same name. Otherwise, the global variable's value is output. Notice that `FISCAL3` is a member of nested namespace `Inner`, so it must be qualified with `Example::Inner::`.

Function `printValues` (defined at lines 50–56) is a member of `Example`, so it can access other members of the `Example` namespace directly without using a namespace qualifier. The output statement in lines 52–55 outputs `integer1`, `PI`, `E`, `doubleInUnnamed`, global variable `integer1` and `FISCAL3`. Notice that `PI` and `E` are not qualified with `Example`. Variable `doubleInUnnamed` is still accessible, because it is in the unnamed namespace and the variable name does not conflict with any other members of namespace `Example`. The global version of `integer1` must be qualified with the unary scope resolution operator (`::`), because its name conflicts with a member of namespace `Example`. Also, `FISCAL3` must be qualified with `Inner::`. When accessing members of a nested namespace, the members must be qualified with the namespace name (unless the member is being used inside the nested namespace).

Common Programming Error 23.1

Placing `main` in a namespace is a compilation error.

Aliases for Namespace Names

Namespaces can be aliased. For example the statement

```
namespace CPPHTP5E = CPlusPlusHowToProgram5E;
```

creates the alias CPPHTP5E for CPlusPlusHowToProgram5E.

23.4 Operator Keywords

The C++ standard provides operator keywords (Fig. 23.3) that can be used in place of several C++ operators. Operator keywords are useful for programmers who have keyboards that do not support certain characters such as !, &, ^, ~, |, etc.

Figure 23.4 demonstrates the operator keywords. This program was compiled with Microsoft Visual C++ .NET, which requires the header file <iso646.h> (line 8) to use the operator keywords. In GNU C++, line 8 should be removed and the program should be compiled as follows:

```
g++ -foperator-names Fig23_04.cpp -o Fig23_04
```

The compiler option -foperator-names indicates that the compiler should enable use of the operator keywords in Fig. 23.3. Other compilers may not require you to include a header file or to use a compiler option to enable support for these keywords. For example, the Borland C++ 5.6.4 compiler implicitly permits these keywords.

Operator	Operator keyword	Description
Logical operator keywords		
&&	and	logical AND
||	or	logical OR
!	not	logical NOT
Inequality operator keyword		
!=	not_eq	inequality
Bitwise operator keywords		
&	bitand	bitwise AND
|	bitor	bitwise inclusive OR
^	xor	bitwise exclusive OR
~	compl	bitwise complement
Bitwise assignment operator keywords		
&=	and_eq	bitwise AND assignment
|=	or_eq	bitwise inclusive OR assignment
^=	xor_eq	bitwise exclusive OR assignment

Fig. 23.3 | Operator keyword alternatives to operator symbols.

```cpp
1   // Fig. 23.4: fig23_04.cpp
2   // Demonstrating operator keywords.
3   #include <iostream>
4   using std::boolalpha;
5   using std::cout;
6   using std::endl;
7
8   #include <iso646.h> // enables operator keywords in Microsoft Visual C++
9
10  int main()
11  {
12     bool a = true;
13     bool b = false;
14     int c = 2;
15     int d = 3;
16
17     // sticky setting that causes bool values to display as true or false
18     cout << boolalpha;
19
20     cout << "a = " << a << "; b = " << b
21        << "; c = " << c << "; d = " << d;
22
23     cout << "\n\nLogical operator keywords:";
24     cout << "\n   a and a: " << ( a and a );
25     cout << "\n   a and b: " << ( a and b );
26     cout << "\n    a or a: " << ( a or a );
27     cout << "\n    a or b: " << ( a or b );
28     cout << "\n     not a: " << ( not a );
29     cout << "\n     not b: " << ( not b );
30     cout << "\na not_eq b: " << ( a not_eq b );
31
32     cout << "\n\nBitwise operator keywords:";
33     cout << "\nc bitand d: " << ( c bitand d );
34     cout << "\nc bit_or d: " << ( c bitor d );
35     cout << "\n   c xor d: " << ( c xor d );
36     cout << "\n   compl c: " << ( compl c );
37     cout << "\nc and_eq d: " << ( c and_eq d );
38     cout << "\n c or_eq d: " << ( c or_eq d );
39     cout << "\nc xor_eq d: " << ( c xor_eq d ) << endl;
40     return 0;
41  } // end main
```

```
a = true; b = false; c = 2; d = 3

Logical operator keywords:
   a and a: true
   a and b: false
    a or a: true
    a or b: true
     not a: false
     not b: true
a not_eq b: true
```
(continued at top of next page...)

Fig. 23.4 | Demonstrating the operator keywords. (Part 1 of 2.)

(...continued from bottom of previous page)

```
Bitwise operator keywords:
c bitand d: 2
c bit_or d: 3
    c xor d: 1
    compl c: -3
c and_eq d: 2
 c or_eq d: 3
c xor_eq d: 0
```

Fig. 23.4 | Demonstrating the operator keywords. (Part 2 of 2.)

The program declares and initializes two `bool` variables and two integer variables (lines 12–15). Logical operations (lines 24–30) are performed with `bool` variables a and b using the various logical operator keywords. Bitwise operations (lines 33–39) are performed with the `int` variables c and d using the various bitwise operator keywords. The result of each operation is output.

23.5 `mutable` Class Members

In Section 23.2, we introduced the `const_cast` operator, which allowed us to remove the "const-ness" of a type. A `const_cast` operation can also be applied to a data member of a `const` object from the body of a `const` member function of that object's class. This enables the `const` member function to modify the data member, even though the object is considered to be `const` in the body of that function. Such an operation might be performed when most of an object's data members should be considered `const`, but a particular data member still needs to be modified.

As an example, consider a linked list that maintains its contents in sorted order. Searching through the linked list does not require modifications to the data of the linked list, so the search function could be a `const` member function of the linked-list class. However, it is conceivable that a linked-list object, in an effort to make future searches more efficient, might keep track of the location of the last successful match. If the next search operation attempts to locate an item that appears later in the list, the search could begin from the location of the last successful match, rather than from the beginning of the list. To do this, the `const` member function that performs the search must be able to modify the data member that keeps track of the last successful search.

If a data member such as the one described above should always be modifiable, C++ provides the storage-class specifier `mutable` as an alternative to `const_cast`. A `mutable` data member is always modifiable, even in a `const` member function or `const` object. This reduces the need to cast away "const-ness."

Portability Tip 23.1

The effect of attempting to modify an object that was defined as constant, regardless of whether that modification was made possible by a `const_cast` or C-style cast, varies among compilers.

Both `mutable` and `const_cast` allow a data member to be modified; they are used in different contexts. For a `const` object with no `mutable` data members, operator `const_cast` must be used every time a member is to be modified. This greatly reduces the chance of a member being accidentally modified because the member is not permanently modifiable. Operations involving const_cast are typically hidden in a member function's implementation. The user of a class might not be aware that a member is being modified.

Software Engineering Observation 23.3

mutable members are useful in classes that have "secret" implementation details that do not contribute to the logical value of an object.

Mechanical Demonstration of a **mutable** *Data Member*

Figure 23.5 demonstrates using a mutable member. The program defines class Test-Mutable (lines 8–22), which contains a constructor, function getValue and a private data member value that is declared mutable. Lines 16–19 define function getValue as a const member function that returns a copy of value. Notice that the function increments mutable data member value in the return statement. Normally, a const member function cannot modify data members unless the object on which the function operates—i.e., the one to which this points—is cast (using const_cast) to a non-const type. Because value is mutable, this const function is able to modify the data.

```cpp
 1   // Fig. 23.5: fig23_05.cpp
 2   // Demonstrating storage-class specifier mutable.
 3   #include <iostream>
 4   using std::cout;
 5   using std::endl;
 6
 7   // class TestMutable definition
 8   class TestMutable
 9   {
10   public:
11      TestMutable( int v = 0 )
12      {
13         value = v;
14      } // end TestMutable constructor
15
16      int getValue() const
17      {
18         return value++; // increments value
19      } // end function getValue
20   private:
21      mutable int value; // mutable member
22   }; // end class TestMutable
23
24   int main()
25   {
26      const TestMutable test( 99 );
27
28      cout << "Initial value: " << test.getValue();
29      cout << "\nModified value: " << test.getValue() << endl;
30      return 0;
31   } // end main
```

Fig. 23.5 | Demonstrating a mutable data member. (Part 1 of 2.)

```
Initial value: 99
Modified value: 100
```

Fig. 23.5 | Demonstrating a `mutable` data member. (Part 2 of 2.)

Line 26 declares `const TestMutable` object `test` and initializes it to 99. Line 28 calls the `const` member function `getValue`, which adds one to `value` and returns its previous contents. Notice that the compiler allows the call to member function `getValue` on the object `test` because it is a `const` object and `getValue` is a `const` member function. However, `getValue` modifies variable `value`. Thus, when line 29 invokes `getValue` again, the new `value` (100) is output to prove that the `mutable` data member was indeed modified.

23.6 Pointers to Class Members (.* and ->*)

C++ provides the `.*` and `->*` operators for accessing class members via pointers. This is a rarely used capability that is used primarily by advanced C++ programmers. We provide only a mechanical example of using pointers to class members here. Figure 23.6 demonstrates the pointer-to-class-member operators.

```cpp
1  // Fig. 23.6: fig23_06.cpp
2  // Demonstrating operators .* and ->*.
3  #include <iostream>
4  using std::cout;
5  using std::endl;
6
7  // class Test definition
8  class Test
9  {
10 public:
11    void test()
12    {
13       cout << "In test function\n";
14    } // end function test
15
16    int value; // public data member
17 }; // end class Test
18
19 void arrowStar( Test * ); // prototype
20 void dotStar( Test * ); // prototype
21
22 int main()
23 {
24    Test test;
25    test.value = 8; // assign value 8
26    arrowStar( &test ); // pass address to arrowStar
27    dotStar( &test ); // pass address to dotStar
28    return 0;
29 } // end main
30
```

Fig. 23.6 | Demonstrating the .* and ->* operators. (Part 1 of 2.)

```
31    // access member function of Test object using ->*
32    void arrowStar( Test *testPtr )
33    {
34       void ( Test::*memPtr )() = &Test::test; // declare function pointer
35       ( testPtr->*memPtr )(); // invoke function indirectly
36    } // end arrowStar
37
38    // access members of Test object data member using .*
39    void dotStar( Test *testPtr2 )
40    {
41       int Test::*vPtr = &Test::value; // declare pointer
42       cout << ( *testPtr2 ).*vPtr << endl; // access value
43    } // end dotStar
```

```
In test function
8
```

Fig. 23.6 | Demonstrating the . * and ->* operators. (Part 2 of 2.)

The program declares class Test (lines 8–17), which provides public member function test and public data member value. Lines 19–20 provide prototypes for the functions arrowStar (defined at lines 32–36) and dotStar (defined at lines 39–43), which demonstrate the ->* and . * operators, respectively. Lines 24 creates object test, and line 25 assigns 8 to its data member value. Lines 26–27 call functions arrowStar and dotStar with the address of the object test.

Line 34 in function arrowStar declares and initializes variable memPtr as a pointer to a member function. In this declaration, Test::* indicates that the variable memPtr is a pointer to a member of class Test. To declare a pointer to a function, enclose the pointer name preceded by * in parentheses, as in (Test::*memPtr). A pointer to a function must specify, as part of its type, both the return type of the function it points to and the parameter list of that function. The return type of the function appears to the left of the left parenthesis and the parameter list appears in a separate set of parentheses to the right of the pointer declaration. In this case, the function has a void return type and no parameters. The pointer memPtr is initialized with the address of class Test's member function named test. Note that the header of the function must match the function pointer's declaration—i.e., function test must have a void return type and no parameters. Notice that the right side of the assignment uses the address operator (&) to get the address of the member function test. Also, notice that neither the left side nor the right side of the assignment in line 34 refers to a specific object of class Test. Only the class name is used with the binary scope resolution operator (::). Line 35 invokes the member function stored in memPtr (i.e., test), using the ->* operator. Because memPtr is a pointer to a member of a class, the ->* operator must be used rather than the -> operator to invoke the function.

Line 41 declares and initializes vPtr as a pointer to an int data member of class Test. The right side of the assignment specifies the address of the data member value. Line 42 dereferences the pointer testPtr2, then uses the . * operator to access the member to which vPtr points. Note that the client code can create pointers to class members for only those class members that are accessible to the client code. In this example, both member function test and data member value are publicly accessible.

Common Programming Error 23.2

Declaring a member-function pointer without enclosing the pointer name in parentheses is a syntax error.

Common Programming Error 23.3

Declaring a member-function pointer without preceding the pointer name with a class name followed by the scope resolution operator (::) is a syntax error.

Common Programming Error 23.4

Attempting to use the -> or * operator with a pointer to a class member generates syntax errors.

23.7 Multiple Inheritance

In Chapters 9 and 10, we discussed single inheritance, in which each class is derived from exactly one base class. In C++, a class may be derived from more than one base class—a technique known as multiple inheritance in which a derived class inherits the members of two or more base classes. This powerful capability encourages interesting forms of software reuse but can cause a variety of ambiguity problems. Multiple inheritance is a difficult concept that should be used only by experienced programmers. In fact, some of the problems associated with multiple inheritance are so subtle that newer programming languages, such as Java and C#, do not enable a class to derive from more than one base class.

Good Programming Practice 23.2

Multiple inheritance is a powerful capability when used properly. Multiple inheritance should be used when an "is a" relationship exists between a new type and two or more existing types (i.e., type A "is a" type B and type A "is a" type C).

Software Engineering Observation 23.4

Multiple inheritance can introduce complexity into a system. Great care is required in the design of a system to use multiple inheritance properly; it should not be used when single inheritance and/or composition will do the job.

A common problem with multiple inheritance is that each of the base classes might contain data members or member functions that have the same name. This can lead to ambiguity problems when you attempt to compile. Consider the multiple-inheritance example (Fig. 23.7, Fig. 23.8, Fig. 23.9, Fig. 23.10, Fig. 23.11). Class Base1 (Fig. 23.7) contains one protected int data member—value (line 20), a constructor (lines 10–13) that sets value and public member function getData (lines 15–18) that returns value.

```
1   // Fig. 23.7: Base1.h
2   // Definition of class Base1
3   #ifndef BASE1_H
4   #define BASE1_H
5
```

Fig. 23.7 | Demonstrating multiple inheritance—Base1.h. (Part 1 of 2.)

```
6   // class Base1 definition
7   class Base1
8   {
9   public:
10     Base1( int parameterValue )
11     {
12        value = parameterValue;
13     } // end Base1 constructor
14
15     int getData() const
16     {
17        return value;
18     } // end function getData
19  protected: // accessible to derived classes
20     int value; // inherited by derived class
21  }; // end class Base1
22
23  #endif // BASE1_H
```

Fig. 23.7 | Demonstrating multiple inheritance—Base1.h. (Part 2 of 2.)

Class Base2 (Fig. 23.8) is similar to class Base1, except that its protected data is a char named letter (line 20). Like class Base1, Base2 has a public member function get-Data, but this function returns the value of char data member letter.

Class Derived (Figs. 23.9–23.10) inherits from both class Base1 and class Base2 through multiple inheritance. Class Derived has a private data member of type double

```
1   // Fig. 23.8: Base2.h
2   // Definition of class Base2
3   #ifndef BASE2_H
4   #define BASE2_H
5
6   // class Base2 definition
7   class Base2
8   {
9   public:
10     Base2( char characterData )
11     {
12        letter = characterData;
13     } // end Base2 constructor
14
15     char getData() const
16     {
17        return letter;
18     } // end function getData
19  protected: // accessible to derived classes
20     char letter; // inherited by derived class
21  }; // end class Base2
22
23  #endif // BASE2_H
```

Fig. 23.8 | Demonstrating multiple inheritance—Base2.h.

named `real` (line 21), a constructor to initialize all the data of class `Derived` and a `public` member function `getReal` that returns the value of `double` variable `real`.

Notice how straightforward it is to indicate multiple inheritance by following the colon (`:`) after `class Derived` with a comma-separated list of base classes (line 14). In Fig. 23.10, notice that constructor `Derived` explicitly calls base-class constructors for each of its base classes—`Base1` and `Base2`—using the member-initializer syntax (line 9). The base-class constructors are called in the order that the inheritance is specified, not in the order in which their constructors are mentioned; also, if the base-class constructors are not explicitly called in the member-initializer list, their default constructors will be called implicitly.

The overloaded stream insertion operator (Fig. 23.10, lines 18–23) uses its second parameter—a reference to a `Derived` object—to display a `Derived` object's data. This operator function is a `friend` of `Derived`, so `operator<<` can directly access all of class `Derived`'s protected and private members, including the `protected` data member `value` (inherited from class `Base1`), `protected` data member `letter` (inherited from class `Base2`) and `private` data member `real` (declared in class `Derived`).

Now let us examine the `main` function (Fig. 23.11) that tests the classes in Figs. 23.7–23.10. Line 13 creates `Base1` object `base1` and initializes it to the `int` value 10, then creates the pointer `base1Ptr` and initializes it to the null pointer (i.e., 0). Line 14 creates `Base2` object `base2` and initializes it to the `char` value `'Z'`, then creates the pointer `base2Ptr` and initializes it to the null pointer. Line 15 creates `Derived` object `derived` and initializes it to contain the `int` value 7, the `char` value `'A'` and the `double` value 3.5.

```
1   // Fig. 23.9: Derived.h
2   // Definition of class Derived which inherits
3   // multiple base classes (Base1 and Base2).
4   #ifndef DERIVED_H
5   #define DERIVED_H
6
7   #include <iostream>
8   using std::ostream;
9
10  #include "Base1.h"
11  #include "Base2.h"
12
13  // class Derived definition
14  class Derived : public Base1, public Base2
15  {
16     friend ostream &operator<<( ostream &, const Derived & );
17  public:
18     Derived( int, char, double );
19     double getReal() const;
20  private:
21     double real; // derived class's private data
22  }; // end class Derived
23
24  #endif // DERIVED_H
```

Fig. 23.9 | Demonstrating multiple inheritance—`Derived.h`.

```
1   // Fig. 23.10: Derived.cpp
2   // Member function definitions for class Derived
3   #include "Derived.h"
4
5   // constructor for Derived calls constructors for
6   // class Base1 and class Base2.
7   // use member initializers to call base-class constructors
8   Derived::Derived( int integer, char character, double double1 )
9      : Base1( integer ), Base2( character ), real( double1 ) { }
10
11  // return real
12  double Derived::getReal() const
13  {
14     return real;
15  } // end function getReal
16
17  // display all data members of Derived
18  ostream &operator<<( ostream &output, const Derived &derived )
19  {
20     output << "   Integer: " << derived.value << "\n  Character: "
21        << derived.letter << "\nReal number: " << derived.real;
22     return output; // enables cascaded calls
23  } // end operator<<
```

Fig. 23.10 | Demonstrating multiple inheritance—Derived.cpp.

```
1   // Fig. 23.11: fig23_11.cpp
2   // Driver for multiple inheritance example.
3   #include <iostream>
4   using std::cout;
5   using std::endl;
6
7   #include "Base1.h"
8   #include "Base2.h"
9   #include "Derived.h"
10
11  int main()
12  {
13     Base1 base1( 10 ), *base1Ptr = 0; // create Base1 object
14     Base2 base2( 'Z' ), *base2Ptr = 0; // create Base2 object
15     Derived derived( 7, 'A', 3.5 ); // create Derived object
16
17     // print data members of base-class objects
18     cout << "Object base1 contains integer " << base1.getData()
19        << "\nObject base2 contains character " << base2.getData()
20        << "\nObject derived contains:\n" << derived << "\n\n";
21
22     // print data members of derived-class object
23     // scope resolution operator resolves getData ambiguity
24     cout << "Data members of Derived can be accessed individually:"
25        << "\n   Integer: " << derived.Base1::getData()
```

Fig. 23.11 | Demonstrating multiple inheritance. (Part 1 of 2.)

```
26              << "\n  Character: " << derived.Base2::getData()
27              << "\nReal number: " << derived.getReal() << "\n\n";
28      cout << "Derived can be treated as an object of either base class:\n";
29
30      // treat Derived as a Base1 object
31      base1Ptr = &derived;
32      cout << "base1Ptr->getData() yields " << base1Ptr->getData() << '\n';
33
34      // treat Derived as a Base2 object
35      base2Ptr = &derived;
36      cout << "base2Ptr->getData() yields " << base2Ptr->getData() << endl;
37      return 0;
38   } // end main
```

```
Object base1 contains integer 10
Object base2 contains character Z
Object derived contains:
    Integer: 7
  Character: A
Real number: 3.5

Data members of Derived can be accessed individually:
    Integer: 7
  Character: A
Real number: 3.5

Derived can be treated as an object of either base class:
base1Ptr->getData() yields 7
base2Ptr->getData() yields A
```

Fig. 23.11 | Demonstrating multiple inheritance. (Part 2 of 2.)

Lines 18–20 display each object's data values. For objects base1 and base2, we invoke each object's getData member function. Even though there are two getData functions in this example, the calls are not ambiguous. In line 18, the compiler knows that base1 is an object of class Base1, so class Base1's version of getData is called. In line 19, the compiler knows that base2 is an object of class Base2, so class Base2's version of getData is called. Line 20 displays the contents of object derived using the overloaded stream insertion operator.

Resolving Ambiguity Issues That Arise When a Derived Class Inherits Member Functions of the Same Name from Multiple Base Classes

Lines 24–27 output the contents of object derived again by using the *get* member functions of class Derived. However, there is an ambiguity problem, because this object contains two getData functions, one inherited from class Base1 and one inherited from class Base2. This problem is easy to solve by using the binary scope resolution operator. The expression derived.Base1::getData() gets the value of the variable inherited from class Base1 (i.e., the int variable named value) and derived.Base2::getData() gets the value of the variable inherited from class Base2 (i.e., the char variable named letter). The double value in real is printed without ambiguity with the call derived.getReal()—there are no other member functions with that name in the hierarchy.

Demonstrating the Is-A Relationships in Multiple Inheritance
The *is-a* relationships of single inheritance also apply in multiple-inheritance relationships. To demonstrate this, line 31 assigns the address of object derived to the Base1 pointer base1Ptr. This is allowed because an object of class Derived *is an* object of class Base1. Line 32 invokes Base1 member function getData via base1Ptr to obtain the value of only the Base1 part of the object derived. Line 35 assigns the address of object derived to the Base2 pointer base2Ptr. This is allowed because an object of class Derived *is an* object of class Base2. Line 36 invokes Base2 member function getData via base2Ptr to obtain the value of only the Base2 part of the object derived.

23.8 Multiple Inheritance and virtual Base Classes

In Section 23.7, we discussed multiple inheritance, the process by which one class inherits from two or more classes. Multiple inheritance is used, for example, in the C++ standard library to form class basic_iostream (Fig. 23.12).

Class basic_ios is the base class for both basic_istream and basic_ostream, each of which is formed with single inheritance. Class basic_iostream inherits from both basic_istream and basic_ostream. This enables objects of class basic_iostream to provide the functionality of both basic_istreams and basic_ostreams. In multiple-inheritance hierarchies, the situation described in Fig. 23.12 is referred to as diamond inheritance.

Because classes basic_istream and basic_ostream each inherit from basic_ios, a potential problem exists for basic_iostream. Class basic_iostream could contain two copies of the members of class basic_ios—one inherited via class basic_istream and one inherited via class basic_ostream). Such a situation would be ambiguous and would result in a compilation error, because the compiler would not know which version of the members from class basic_ios to use. Of course, basic_iostream does not really suffer from the problem we mentioned. In this section, you will see how using virtual base classes solves the problem of inheriting duplicate copies of an indirect base class.

Compilation Errors Produced When Ambiguity Arises in Diamond Inheritance
Figure 23.13 demonstrates the ambiguity that can occur in diamond inheritance. The program defines class Base (lines 9–13), which contains pure virtual function print (line 12). Classes DerivedOne (lines 16–24) and DerivedTwo (lines 27–35) each publicly inherit from class Base and override the print function. Class DerivedOne and class DerivedTwo each contain what the C++ standard refers to as a base-class subobject—i.e., the members of class Base in this example.

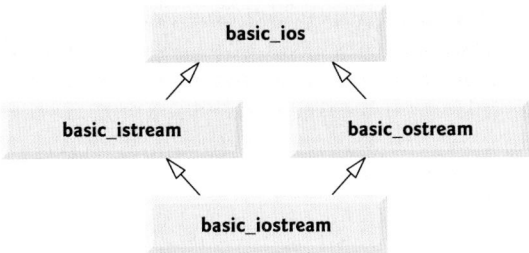

Fig. 23.12 | Multiple inheritance to form class basic_iostream.

```
1    // Fig. 23.13: fig23_13.cpp
2    // Attempting to polymorphically call a function that is
3    // multiply inherited from two base classes.
4    #include <iostream>
5    using std::cout;
6    using std::endl;
7
8    // class Base definition
9    class Base
10   {
11   public:
12      virtual void print() const = 0; // pure virtual
13   }; // end class Base
14
15   // class DerivedOne definition
16   class DerivedOne : public Base
17   {
18   public:
19      // override print function
20      void print() const
21      {
22         cout << "DerivedOne\n";
23      } // end function print
24   }; // end class DerivedOne
25
26   // class DerivedTwo definition
27   class DerivedTwo : public Base
28   {
29   public:
30      // override print function
31      void print() const
32      {
33         cout << "DerivedTwo\n";
34      } // end function print
35   }; // end class DerivedTwo
36
37   // class Multiple definition
38   class Multiple : public DerivedOne, public DerivedTwo
39   {
40   public:
41      // qualify which version of function print
42      void print() const
43      {
44         DerivedTwo::print();
45      } // end function print
46   }; // end class Multiple
47
48   int main()
49   {
50      Multiple both; // instantiate Multiple object
51      DerivedOne one; // instantiate DerivedOne object
52      DerivedTwo two; // instantiate DerivedTwo object
53      Base *array[ 3 ]; // create array of base-class pointers
```

Fig. 23.13 | Attempting to call a multiply inherited function polymorphically. (Part 1 of 2.)

```
54
55       array[ 0 ] = &both; // ERROR--ambiguous
56       array[ 1 ] = &one;
57       array[ 2 ] = &two;
58
59       // polymorphically invoke print
60       for ( int i = 0; i < 3; i++ )
61          array[ i ] -> print();
62
63       return 0;
64    } // end main
```

```
C:\Projects\cpphtp5\examples\ch23\Fig23_20\Fig23_20.cpp(55): error C2594:
'=' : ambiguous conversions from 'Multiple *' to 'Base *'
```

Fig. 23.13 | Attempting to call a multiply inherited function polymorphically. (Part 2 of 2.)

Class Multiple (lines 38–46) inherits from both classes DerivedOne and DerivedTwo. In class Multiple, function print is overridden to call DerivedTwo's print (line 44). Notice that we must qualify the print call with the class name DerivedTwo to specify which version of print to call.

Function main (lines 48–64) declares objects of classes Multiple (line 50), DerivedOne (line 51) and DerivedTwo (line 52). Line 53 declares an array of Base * pointers. Each array element is initialized with the address of an object (lines 55–57). An error occurs when the address of both—an object of class Multiple—is assigned to array[0]. The object both actually contains two subobjects of type Base, so the compiler does not know which subobject the pointer array[0] should point to, and it generates a compilation error indicating an ambiguous conversion.

Eliminating Duplicate Subobjects with virtual Base-Class Inheritance

The problem of duplicate subobjects is resolved with virtual inheritance. When a base class is inherited as virtual, only one subobject will appear in the derived class—a process called virtual base-class inheritance. Figure 23.14 revises the program of Fig. 23.13 to use a virtual base class.

```
1    // Fig. 23.14: fig23_14.cpp
2    // Using virtual base classes.
3    #include <iostream>
4    using std::cout;
5    using std::endl;
6
7    // class Base definition
8    class Base
9    {
10   public:
11      virtual void print() const = 0; // pure virtual
12   }; // end class Base
```

Fig. 23.14 | Using virtual base classes. (Part 1 of 3.)

```
13
14   // class DerivedOne definition
15   class DerivedOne : virtual public Base
16   {
17   public:
18      // override print function
19      void print() const
20      {
21         cout << "DerivedOne\n";
22      } // end function print
23   }; // end DerivedOne class
24
25   // class DerivedTwo definition
26   class DerivedTwo : virtual public Base
27   {
28   public:
29      // override print function
30      void print() const
31      {
32         cout << "DerivedTwo\n";
33      } // end function print
34   }; // end DerivedTwo class
35
36   // class Multiple definition
37   class Multiple : public DerivedOne, public DerivedTwo
38   {
39   public:
40      // qualify which version of function print
41      void print() const
42      {
43         DerivedTwo::print();
44      } // end function print
45   }; // end Multiple class
46
47   int main()
48   {
49      Multiple both; // instantiate Multiple object
50      DerivedOne one; // instantiate DerivedOne object
51      DerivedTwo two; // instantiate DerivedTwo object
52
53      // declare array of base-class pointers and initialize
54      // each element to a derived-class type
55      Base *array[ 3 ];
56      array[ 0 ] = &both;
57      array[ 1 ] = &one;
58      array[ 2 ] = &two;
59
60      // polymorphically invoke function print
61      for ( int i = 0; i < 3; i++ )
62         array[ i ]->print();
63
64      return 0;
65   } // end main
```

Fig. 23.14 | Using virtual base classes. (Part 2 of 3.)

```
DerivedTwo
DerivedOne
DerivedTwo
```

Fig. 23.14 | Using `virtual` base classes. (Part 3 of 3.)

The key change in the program is that classes `DerivedOne` (line 15) and `DerivedTwo` (line 26) each inherit from class `Base` by specifying `virtual public Base`. Since both of these classes inherit from `Base`, they each contain a `Base` subobject. The benefit of `virtual` inheritance is not clear until class `Multiple` inherits from both `DerivedOne` and `DerivedTwo` (line 37). Since each of the base classes used `virtual` inheritance to inherit class `Base`'s members, the compiler ensures that only one subobject of type `Base` is inherited into class `Multiple`. This eliminates the ambiguity error generated by the compiler in Fig. 23.13. The compiler now allows the implicit conversion of the derived-class pointer (`&both`) to the base-class pointer `array[ 0 ]` at line 56 in `main`. The `for` statement at lines 61–62 polymorphically calls `print` for each object.

Constructors in Multiple-Inheritance Hierarchies with `virtual` Base Classes

Implementing hierarchies with `virtual` base classes is simpler if default constructors are used for the base classes. The examples in Figs. 23.13 and 23.14 use compiler-generated default constructors. If a `virtual` base class provides a constructor that requires arguments, the implementation of the derived classes becomes more complicated, because the most derived class must explicitly invoke the virtual base class's constructor to initialize the members inherited from the `virtual` base class.

 Software Engineering Observation 23.5

Providing a default constructor for `virtual` *base classes simplifies hierarchy design.*

Additional Information on Multiple Inheritance

Multiple inheritance is a complex topic typically covered in more advanced C++ texts. The following URLs provide additional information about multiple inheritance.

`cplus.about.com/library/weekly/aa121302a.htm`
A tutorial on multiple inheritance with a detailed example.

`cpptips.hyperformix.com/MultipleInher.html`
Provides technical tips that explain several issues regarding multiple inheritance.

`www.parashift.com/c++-faq-lite/multiple-inheritance.html`
Part of the *C++ FAQ Lite*. Provides a detailed technical explanation of multiple inheritance and virtual inheritance.

23.9 Closing Remarks

We sincerely hope you have enjoyed learning C++ and object-oriented programming with *C++ How to Program, 5/e*. We would greatly appreciate your comments, criticisms, corrections and suggestions for improving the text. Please address all correspondence to our e-mail address:

deitel@deitel.com

Good luck!

Summary

- C++ provides the const_cast operator for casting away const or volatile qualification.

- A program declares a variable with the volatile qualifier when that program expects the variable to be modified by other programs. Declaring a variable volatile indicates that the compiler should not optimize the use of that variable because doing so could affect the ability of those other programs to access and modify the volatile variable.

- In general, it is dangerous to use the const_cast operator, because it allows a program to modify a variable that was declared const, and thus was not supposed to be modifiable.

- There are cases in which it is desirable, or even necessary, to cast away const-ness. For example, older C and C++ libraries might provide functions with non-const parameters and that do not modify their parameters. If you wish to pass const data to such a function, you would need to cast away the data's const-ness; otherwise, the compiler would report error messages.

- If you pass non-const data to a function that treats the data as if it were constant, then returns that data as a constant, you might need to cast away the const-ness of the returned data to access and modify that data.

- A program includes many identifiers defined in different scopes. Sometimes a variable of one scope will "overlap" with a variable of the same name in a different scope, possibly creating a naming conflict. The C++ standard attempts to solve this problem with namespaces.

- Each namespace defines a scope in which identifiers are placed. To use a namespace member, either the member's name must be qualified with the namespace name and the binary scope resolution operator (::) or a using directive or declaration must appear before the name is used in the program.

- Typically, using statements are placed at the beginning of the file in which members of the namespace are used.

- Not all namespaces are guaranteed to be unique. Two third-party vendors might inadvertently use the same identifiers for their namespace names.

- A using namespace directive specifies that the members of a namespace will be used frequently throughout a program. This allows the programmer to access all the members of the namespace.

- A using namespace directive can be used for predefined namespaces (e.g., std) or programmer-defined namespaces.

- A namespace can contain constants, data, classes, nested namespaces, functions, etc. Definitions of namespaces must occupy the global scope or be nested within other namespaces.

- An unnamed namespace has an implicit using directive, so its members appear to occupy the global namespace, are accessible directly and do not have to be qualified with a namespace name. Global variables are also part of the global namespace.

- When accessing members of a nested namespace, the members must be qualified with the namespace name (unless the member is being used inside the nested namespace).

- Namespaces can be aliased.

- The C++ standard provides operator keywords that can be used in place of several C++ operators. Operator keywords are useful for programmers who have keyboards that do not support certain characters such as !, &, ^, ~, |, etc.

- If a data member should always be modifiable, C++ provides the storage-class specifier mutable as an alternative to const_cast. A mutable data member is always modifiable, even in a const member function or const object. This reduces the need to cast away "const-ness."

- Both mutable and const_cast allow a data member to be modified; they are used in different contexts. For a const object with no mutable data members, operator const_cast must be used every time a member is to be modified. This greatly reduces the chance of a member being accidentally modified because the member is not permanently modifiable.

- Operations involving const_cast are typically hidden in a member function's implementation. The user of a class might not be aware that a member is being modified.

- C++ provides the .* and ->* operators for accessing class members via pointers. This is rarely used capability that is used primarily by advanced C++ programmers.

- Declaring a pointer to a function requires that you enclose the pointer name preceded by an * in parentheses. A pointer to a function must specify, as part of its type, both the return type of the function it points to and the parameter list of that function.

- In C++, a class may be derived from more than one base class—a technique known as multiple inheritance, in which a derived class inherits the members of two or more base classes.

- A common problem with multiple inheritance is that each of the base classes might contain data members or member functions that have the same name. This can lead to ambiguity problems when you attempt to compile.

- The *is-a* relationships of single inheritance also apply in multiple-inheritance relationships.

- Multiple inheritance is used, for example, in the C++ Standard Library to form class basic_iostream. Class basic_ios is the base class for both basic_istream and basic_ostream, each of which is formed with single inheritance. Class basic_iostream inherits from both basic_istream and basic_ostream. This enables objects of class basic_iostream to provide the functionality of both basic_istreams and basic_ostreams. In multiple-inheritance hierarchies, the situation described here is referred to as diamond inheritance.

- Because classes basic_istream and basic_ostream each inherit from basic_ios, a potential problem exists for basic_iostream. If not implemented correctly, class basic_iostream could contain two copies of the members of class basic_ios—one inherited via class basic_istream and one inherited via class basic_ostream). Such a situation would be ambiguous and would result in a compilation error, because the compiler would not know which version of the members from class basic_ios to use.

- The ambiguity in diamond inheritance occurs when a derived-class object inherits two or more base-class subobjects. The problem of duplicate subobjects is resolved with virtual inheritance. When a base class is inherited as virtual, only one subobject will appear in the derived class—a process called virtual base-class inheritance.

- Implementing hierarchies with virtual base classes is simpler if default constructors are used for the base classes. If a virtual base class provides a constructor that requires arguments, the implementation of the derived classes becomes more complicated, because the most derived class must explicitly invoke the virtual base class's constructor to initialize the members inherited from the virtual base class.

Terminology

.* operator
->* operator
and operator keyword
and_eq operator keyword
base-class subobject
bitand operator keyword
bitor operator keyword
bitwise assignment operator keywords
bitwise operator keywords
cast away const-ness
comma-separated list of base classes
compl operator keyword
const_cast operator
diamond inheritance
global namespace

inequality operator keywords
logical operator keywords
most derived class
multiple inheritance
mutable data member
namespace
namespace alias
namespace keyword
naming conflict
nested namespace
not operator keyword
not_eq operator keyword
operator keyword
or operator keyword
or_eq operator keyword

pointer-to-member operators
unnamed namespace
`using` declaration
`using namespace` declaration
`virtual` base class

`virtual` inheritance
`volatile` qualifier
`xor` operator keyword
`xor_eq` operator keyword

Self-Review Exercises

23.1 Fill in the blanks for each of the following:
a) The _____ operator qualifies a member with its namespace.
b) The _____ operator allows an object's "const-ness" to be cast away.
c) Because an unnamed namespace has an implicit `using` directive, its members appear to occupy the _____, are accessible directly and do not have to be qualified with a `namespace` name.
d) Operator _____ is the operator keyword for inequality.
e) A class may be derived from more than one base class; such derivation is called _____.
f) When a base class is inherited as _____, only one subobject of the base class will appear in the derived class.

23.2 State which of the following are *true* and which are *false*. If a statement is *false*, explain why.
a) When passing a non-const argument to a const function, the `const_cast` operator should be used to cast away the "const-ness" of the function.
b) namespaces are guaranteed to be unique.
c) Like class bodies, namespace bodies also end in semicolons.
d) namespaces cannot have namespaces as members.
e) A `mutable` data member cannot be modified in a const member function.

Answers to Self-Review Exercises

23.1 a) binary scope resolution (`::`). b) `const_cast`. c) global `namespace`. d) `not_eq`. e) multiple inheritance. f) `virtual`.

23.2 a) False. It is legal to pass a non-const argument to a const function. However, when passing a const reference or pointer to a non-const function, the `const_cast` operator should be used to cast away the "const-ness" of the reference or pointer
b) False. Programmers might inadvertently choose the namespace already in use.
c) False. namespace bodies do not end in semicolons.
d) False. namespaces can be nested.
e) False. A `mutable` data member is always modifiable, even in a const member function.

Exercises

23.3 Fill in the blanks for each of the following:
a) Keyword _____ specifies that a namespace or namespace member is being used.
b) Operator _____ is the operator keyword for logical OR.
c) Storage specifier _____ allows a member of a const object to be modified.
d) The _____ qualifier specifies that an object can be modified by other programs.
e) Precede a member with its _____ name and the scope resolution operator _____ if the possibility exists of a scoping conflict.
f) The body of a namespace is delimited by _____.
g) For a const object with no _____ data members, operator _____ must be used every time a member is to be modified.

23.4 Write a namespace, Currency, that defines constant members ONE, TWO, FIVE, TEN, TWENTY, FIFTY and HUNDRED. Write two short programs that use Currency. One program should make all constants available and the other should make only FIVE available.

23.5 Given the `namespaces` in Fig. 23.15, determine whether each statement is *true* or *false*. Explain any *false* answers.

```
 1   namespace CountryInformation
 2   {
 3      using namespace std;
 4      enum Countries { POLAND, SWITZERLAND, GERMANY,
 5                       AUSTRIA, CZECH_REPUBLIC };
 6      int kilometers;
 7      string string1;
 8
 9      namespace RegionalInformation
10      {
11         short getPopulation(); // assume definition exists
12         MapData map; // assume definition exists
13      } // end RegionalInformation
14   } // end CountryInformation
15
16   namespace Data
17   {
18      using namespace CountryInformation::RegionalInformation;
19      void *function( void *, int );
20   } // end Data
```

Fig. 23.15 | `namespaces` for Exercise 23.5.

a) Variable `kilometers` is visible within `namespace Data`.
b) Object `string1` is visible within `namespace Data`.
c) Constant `POLAND` is not visible within `namespace Data`.
d) Constant `GERMANY` is visible within `namespace Data`.
e) Function `function` is visible to `namespace Data`.
f) Namespace `Data` is visible to `namespace CountryInformation`.
g) Object `map` is visible to `namespace CountryInformation`.
h) Object `string1` is visible within `namespace RegionalInformation`.

23.6 Compare and contrast `mutable` and `const_cast`. Give at least one example of when one might be preferred over the other. [*Note:* This exercise does not require any code to be written.]

23.7 Write a program that uses `const_cast` to modify a `const` variable. [*Hint:* Use a pointer in your solution to point to the `const` identifier.]

23.8 What problem do `virtual` base classes solve?

23.9 Write a program that uses `virtual` base classes. The class at the top of the hierarchy should provide a constructor that takes at least one argument (i.e., do not provide a default constructor). What challenges does this present for the inheritance hierarchy?

23.10 Find the error(s) in each of the following. When possible, explain how to correct each error.
a)
```
namespace Name {
    int x;
    int y;
    mutable int z;
};
```
b) `int integer = const_cast< int >( double );`
c) `namespace PCM( 111, "hello" );   // construct namespace`

Operator Precedence and Associativity Chart

A.1 Operator Precedence

Operators are shown in decreasing order of precedence from top to bottom (Fig. A.1).

Operator	Type	Associativity
::	binary scope resolution	left to right
::	unary scope resolution	
()	parentheses	left to right
[]	array subscript	
.	member selection via object	
->	member selection via pointer	
++	unary postfix increment	
--	unary postfix decrement	
typeid	runtime type information	
dynamic_cast < *type* >	runtime type-checked cast	
static_cast< *type* >	compile-time type-checked cast	
reinterpret_cast< *type* >	cast for nonstandard conversions	
const_cast< *type* >	cast away const-ness	

Fig. A.1 | Operator precedence and associativity chart. (Part 1 of 3.)

Operator	Type	Associativity
++	unary prefix increment	right to left
--	unary prefix decrement	
+	unary plus	
-	unary minus	
!	unary logical negation	
~	unary bitwise complement	
sizeof	determine size in bytes	
&	address	
*	dereference	
new	dynamic memory allocation	
new[]	dynamic array allocation	
delete	dynamic memory deallocation	
delete[]	dynamic array deallocation	
(*type*)	C-style unary cast	right to left
.*	pointer to member via object	left to right
->*	pointer to member via pointer	
*	multiplication	left to right
/	division	
%	modulus	
+	addition	left to right
-	subtraction	
<<	bitwise left shift	left to right
>>	bitwise right shift	
<	relational less than	left to right
<=	relational less than or equal to	
>	relational greater than	
>=	relational greater than or equal to	
==	relational is equal to	left to right
!=	relational is not equal to	
&	bitwise AND	left to right
^	bitwise exclusive OR	left to right
|	bitwise inclusive OR	left to right
&&	logical AND	left to right
||	logical OR	left to right
?:	ternary conditional	right to left

Fig. A.1 | Operator precedence and associativity chart. (Part 2 of 3.)

Operator	Type	Associativity
=	assignment	right to left
+=	addition assignment	
-=	subtraction assignment	
*=	multiplication assignment	
/=	division assignment	
%=	modulus assignment	
&=	bitwise AND assignment	
^=	bitwise exclusive OR assignment	
|=	bitwise inclusive OR assignment	
<<=	bitwise left-shift assignment	
>>=	bitwise right-shift assignment	
,	comma	left to right

Fig. A.1 | Operator precedence and associativity chart. (Part 3 of 3.)

B

ASCII Character Set

ASCII character set

	0	1	2	3	4	5	6	7	8	9
0	nul	soh	stx	etx	eot	enq	ack	bel	bs	ht
1	lf	vt	ff	cr	so	si	dle	dc1	dc2	dc3
2	dc4	nak	syn	etb	can	em	sub	esc	fs	gs
3	rs	us	sp	!	"	#	$	%	&	'
4	(	)	*	+	,	-	.	/	0	1
5	2	3	4	5	6	7	8	9	:	;
6	<	=	>	?	@	A	B	C	D	E
7	F	G	H	I	J	K	L	M	N	O
8	P	Q	R	S	T	U	V	W	X	Y
9	Z	[	\	]	^	_	`	a	b	c
10	d	e	f	g	h	i	j	k	l	m
11	n	o	p	q	r	s	t	u	v	w
12	x	y	z	{	|	}	~	del		

Fig. B.1 | ASCII character set.

The digits at the left of the table are the left digits of the decimal equivalent (0–127) of the character code, and the digits at the top of the table are the right digits of the character code. For example, the character code for "F" is 70, and the character code for "&" is 38.

C

Fundamental Types

Figure C.1 lists C++'s fundamental types. The C++ Standard Document does not provide the exact number of bytes required to store variables of these types in memory. However, the C++ Standard Document does indicate how the memory requirements for fundamental types relate to one another. By order of increasing memory requirements, the signed integer types are `signed char`, `short int`, `int` and `long int`. This means that a `short int` must provide at least as much storage as a `signed char`; an `int` must provide at least as much storage as a `short int`; and a `long int` must provide at least as much storage as an `int`. Each signed integer type has a corresponding unsigned integer type that has the same memory requirements. Unsigned types cannot represent negative values, but can represent twice as many positive values than their associated signed types. By order of increasing

Integral Types	Floating-Point Types
bool	float
char	double
signed char	long double
unsigned char	
short int	
unsigned short int	
int	
unsigned int	
long int	
unsigned long int	
wchar_t	

Fig. C.1 | C++ fundamental types.

memory requirements, the floating-point types are float, double and long double. Like integer types, a double must provide at least as much storage as a float and a long double must provide at least as much storage as a double.

The exact sizes and ranges of values for the fundamental types are implementation dependent. The header files <climits> (for the integral types) and <cfloat> (for the floating-point types) specify the ranges of values supported on your system.

The range of values a type supports depends on the number of bytes that are used to represent that type. For example, consider a system with 4 byte (32 bits) ints. For the signed int type, the nonnegative values are in the range 0 to 2,147,483,647 ($2^{31} - 1$). The negative values are in the range –1 to –2,147,483,648 (-2^{31}). This is a total of 2^{32} possible values. An unsigned int on the same system would use the same number of bits to represent data, but would not represent any negative values. This results in values in the range 0 to 4,294,967,295 ($2^{32} - 1$). On the same system, a short int could not use more than 32 bits to represent its data and a long int must use at least 32 bits.

C++ provides the data type bool for variables that can hold only the values true and false.

D

Number Systems

OBJECTIVES

In this appendix you will learn:

- To understand basic number systems concepts, such as base, positional value and symbol value.

- To understand how to work with numbers represented in the binary, octal and hexadecimal number systems.

- To abbreviate binary numbers as octal numbers or hexadecimal numbers.

- To convert octal numbers and hexadecimal numbers to binary numbers.

- To convert back and forth between decimal numbers and their binary, octal and hexadecimal equivalents.

- To understand binary arithmetic and how negative binary numbers are represented using two's complement notation.

D.1 Introduction

In this appendix, we introduce the key number systems that C++ programmers use, especially when they are working on software projects that require close interaction with machine-level hardware. Projects like this include operating systems, computer networking software, compilers, database systems and applications requiring high performance.

When we write an integer such as 227 or –63 in a C++ program, the number is assumed to be in the decimal (base 10) number system. The digits in the decimal number system are 0, 1, 2, 3, 4, 5, 6, 7, 8 and 9. The lowest digit is 0 and the highest is 9—one less than the base of 10. Internally, computers use the binary (base 2) number system. The binary number system has only two digits, namely 0 and 1. Its lowest digit is 0 and its highest is 1—one less than the base of 2.

As we will see, binary numbers tend to be much longer than their decimal equivalents. Programmers who work in assembly languages, and in high-level languages like C++ that enable them to reach down to the machine level, find it cumbersome to work with binary numbers. So two other number systems—the octal number system (base 8) and the hexadecimal number system (base 16)—are popular primarily because they make it convenient to abbreviate binary numbers.

In the octal number system, the digits range from 0 to 7. Because both the binary and the octal number systems have fewer digits than the decimal number system, their digits are the same as the corresponding digits in decimal.

The hexadecimal number system poses a problem because it requires 16 digits—a lowest digit of 0 and a highest digit with a value equivalent to decimal 15 (one less than the base of 16). By convention, we use the letters A through F to represent the hexadecimal digits corresponding to decimal values 10 through 15. Thus in hexadecimal we can have numbers like 876 consisting solely of decimal-like digits, numbers like 8A55F consisting of digits and letters and numbers like FFE consisting solely of letters. Occasionally, a hexadecimal number spells a common word such as FACE or FEED—this can appear strange to programmers accustomed to working with numbers. The digits of the binary, octal, decimal and hexadecimal number systems are summarized in Fig. D.1–Fig. D.2.

Each of these number systems uses positional notation—each position in which a digit is written has a different positional value. For example, in the decimal number 937 (the 9, the 3 and the 7 are referred to as symbol values), we say that the 7 is written in the ones position, the 3 is written in the tens position and the 9 is written in the hundreds position. Note that each of these positions is a power of the base (base 10) and that these powers begin at 0 and increase by 1 as we move left in the number (Fig. D.3).

Binary digit	Octal digit	Decimal digit	Hexadecimal digit
0	0	0	0
1	1	1	1
	2	2	2
	3	3	3
	4	4	4
	5	5	5
	6	6	6
	7	7	7
		8	8
		9	9
			A (decimal value of 10)
			B (decimal value of 11)
			C (decimal value of 12)
			D (decimal value of 13)
			E (decimal value of 14)
			F (decimal value of 15)

Fig. D.1 | Digits of the binary, octal, decimal and hexadecimal number systems.

Attribute	Binary	Octal	Decimal	Hexadecimal
Base	2	8	10	16
Lowest digit	0	0	0	0
Highest digit	1	7	9	F

Fig. D.2 | Comparing the binary, octal, decimal and hexadecimal number systems.

Positional values in the decimal number system			
Decimal digit	9	3	7
Position name	Hundreds	Tens	Ones
Positional value	100	10	1
Positional value as a power of the base (10)	10^2	10^1	10^0

Fig. D.3 | Positional values in the decimal number system.

For longer decimal numbers, the next positions to the left would be the thousands position (10 to the 3rd power), the ten-thousands position (10 to the 4th power), the hundred-thousands position (10 to the 5th power), the millions position (10 to the 6th power), the ten-millions position (10 to the 7th power) and so on.

In the binary number 101, the rightmost 1 is written in the ones position, the 0 is written in the twos position and the leftmost 1 is written in the fours position. Note that each position is a power of the base (base 2) and that these powers begin at 0 and increase by 1 as we move left in the number (Fig. D.4). So, $101 = 2^2 + 2^0 = 4 + 1 = 5$.

For longer binary numbers, the next positions to the left would be the eights position (2 to the 3rd power), the sixteens position (2 to the 4th power), the thirty-twos position (2 to the 5th power), the sixty-fours position (2 to the 6th power) and so on.

In the octal number 425, we say that the 5 is written in the ones position, the 2 is written in the eights position and the 4 is written in the sixty-fours position. Note that each of these positions is a power of the base (base 8) and that these powers begin at 0 and increase by 1 as we move left in the number (Fig. D.5).

For longer octal numbers, the next positions to the left would be the five-hundred-and-twelves position (8 to the 3rd power), the four-thousand-and-ninety-sixes position (8 to the 4th power), the thirty-two-thousand-seven-hundred-and-sixty-eights position (8 to the 5th power) and so on.

In the hexadecimal number 3DA, we say that the A is written in the ones position, the D is written in the sixteens position and the 3 is written in the two-hundred-and-fifty-sixes position. Note that each of these positions is a power of the base (base 16) and that these powers begin at 0 and increase by 1 as we move left in the number (Fig. D.6).

For longer hexadecimal numbers, the next positions to the left would be the four-thousand-and-ninety-sixes position (16 to the 3rd power), the sixty-five-thousand-five-hundred-and-thirty-sixes position (16 to the 4th power) and so on.

Positional values in the binary number system			
Binary digit	1	0	1
Position name	Fours	Twos	Ones
Positional value	4	2	1
Positional value as a power of the base (2)	2^2	2^1	2^0

Fig. D.4 | Positional values in the binary number system.

Positional values in the octal number system			
Decimal digit	4	2	5
Position name	Sixty-fours	Eights	Ones
Positional value	64	8	1
Positional value as a power of the base (8)	8^2	8^1	8^0

Fig. D.5 | Positional values in the octal number system.

Positional values in the hexadecimal number system			
Decimal digit	3	D	A
Position name	Two-hundred-and-fifty-sixes	Sixteens	Ones
Positional value	256	16	1
Positional value as a power of the base (16)	16^2	16^1	16^0

Fig. D.6 | Positional values in the hexadecimal number system.

D.2 Abbreviating Binary Numbers as Octal and Hexadecimal Numbers

The main use for octal and hexadecimal numbers in computing is for abbreviating lengthy binary representations. Figure D.7 highlights the fact that lengthy binary numbers can be expressed concisely in number systems with higher bases than the binary number system.

A particularly important relationship that both the octal number system and the hexadecimal number system have to the binary system is that the bases of octal and hexadecimal (8 and 16 respectively) are powers of the base of the binary number system (base 2).

Decimal number	Binary representation	Octal representation	Hexadecimal representation
0	0	0	0
1	1	1	1
2	10	2	2
3	11	3	3
4	100	4	4
5	101	5	5
6	110	6	6
7	111	7	7
8	1000	10	8
9	1001	11	9
10	1010	12	A
11	1011	13	B
12	1100	14	C
13	1101	15	D
14	1110	16	E
15	1111	17	F
16	10000	20	10

Fig. D.7 | Decimal, binary, octal and hexadecimal equivalents.

Consider the following 12-digit binary number and its octal and hexadecimal equivalents. See if you can determine how this relationship makes it convenient to abbreviate binary numbers in octal or hexadecimal. The answer follows the numbers.

Binary number	Octal equivalent	Hexadecimal equivalent
100011010001	4321	8D1

To see how the binary number converts easily to octal, simply break the 12-digit binary number into groups of three consecutive bits each, starting from the right, and write those groups over the corresponding digits of the octal number as follows:

100	011	010	001
4	3	2	1

Note that the octal digit you have written under each group of thee bits corresponds precisely to the octal equivalent of that 3-digit binary number, as shown in Fig. D.7.

The same kind of relationship can be observed in converting from binary to hexadecimal. Break the 12-digit binary number into groups of four consecutive bits each, starting from the right, and write those groups over the corresponding digits of the hexadecimal number as follows:

1000	1101	0001
8	D	1

Notice that the hexadecimal digit you wrote under each group of four bits corresponds precisely to the hexadecimal equivalent of that 4-digit binary number as shown in Fig. D.7.

D.3 Converting Octal and Hexadecimal Numbers to Binary Numbers

In the previous section, we saw how to convert binary numbers to their octal and hexadecimal equivalents by forming groups of binary digits and simply rewriting them as their equivalent octal digit values or hexadecimal digit values. This process may be used in reverse to produce the binary equivalent of a given octal or hexadecimal number.

For example, the octal number 653 is converted to binary simply by writing the 6 as its 3-digit binary equivalent 110, the 5 as its 3-digit binary equivalent 101 and the 3 as its 3-digit binary equivalent 011 to form the 9-digit binary number 110101011.

The hexadecimal number FAD5 is converted to binary simply by writing the F as its 4-digit binary equivalent 1111, the A as its 4-digit binary equivalent 1010, the D as its 4-digit binary equivalent 1101 and the 5 as its 4-digit binary equivalent 0101 to form the 16-digit 1111101011010101.

D.4 Converting from Binary, Octal or Hexadecimal to Decimal

We are accustomed to working in decimal, and therefore it is often convenient to convert a binary, octal, or hexadecimal number to decimal to get a sense of what the number is "really" worth. Our diagrams in Section D.1 express the positional values in decimal. To convert a number to decimal from another base, multiply the decimal equivalent of each digit by its positional value and sum these products. For example, the binary number 110101 is converted to decimal 53 as shown in Fig. D.8.

To convert octal 7614 to decimal 3980, we use the same technique, this time using appropriate octal positional values, as shown in Fig. D.9.

To convert hexadecimal AD3B to decimal 44347, we use the same technique, this time using appropriate hexadecimal positional values, as shown in Fig. D.10.

D.5 Converting from Decimal to Binary, Octal or Hexadecimal

The conversions in Section D.4 follow naturally from the positional notation conventions. Converting from decimal to binary, octal, or hexadecimal also follows these conventions.

Suppose we wish to convert decimal 57 to binary. We begin by writing the positional values of the columns right to left until we reach a column whose positional value is greater than the decimal number. We do not need that column, so we discard it. Thus, we first write:

Positional values: 64   32   16   8   4   2   1

Then we discard the column with positional value 64, leaving:

Positional values: 32   16   8   4   2   1

Converting a binary number to decimal					
Positional values:	32	16	8	4	2	1
Symbol values:	1	1	0	1	0	1
Products:	1*32=32	1*16=16	0*8=0	1*4=4	0*2=0	1*1=1
Sum:	= 32 + 16 + 0 + 4 + 0s + 1 = 53					

Fig. D.8 | Converting a binary number to decimal.

Converting an octal number to decimal			
Positional values:	512	64	8	1
Symbol values:	7	6	1	4
Products	7*512=3584	6*64=384	1*8=8	4*1=4
Sum:	= 3584 + 384 + 8 + 4 = 3980			

Fig. D.9 | Converting an octal number to decimal.

Converting a hexadecimal number to decimal			
Positional values:	4096	256	16	1
Symbol values:	A	D	3	B
Products	A*4096=40960	D*256=3328	3*16=48	B*1=11
Sum:	= 40960 + 3328 + 48 + 11 = 44347			

Fig. D.10 | Converting a hexadecimal number to decimal.

Next we work from the leftmost column to the right. We divide 32 into 57 and observe that there is one 32 in 57 with a remainder of 25, so we write 1 in the 32 column. We divide 16 into 25 and observe that there is one 16 in 25 with a remainder of 9 and write 1 in the 16 column. We divide 8 into 9 and observe that there is one 8 in 9 with a remainder of 1. The next two columns each produce quotients of 0 when their positional values are divided into 1, so we write 0s in the 4 and 2 columns. Finally, 1 into 1 is 1, so we write 1 in the 1 column. This yields:

```
Positional values: 32   16      8      4      2      1
Symbol values:      1    1       1      0      0      1
```

and thus decimal 57 is equivalent to binary 111001.

To convert decimal 103 to octal, we begin by writing the positional values of the columns until we reach a column whose positional value is greater than the decimal number. We do not need that column, so we discard it. Thus, we first write:

```
Positional values:      512          64       8       1
```

Then we discard the column with positional value 512, yielding:

```
Positional values:                   64       8       1
```

Next we work from the leftmost column to the right. We divide 64 into 103 and observe that there is one 64 in 103 with a remainder of 39, so we write 1 in the 64 column. We divide 8 into 39 and observe that there are four 8s in 39 with a remainder of 7 and write 4 in the 8 column. Finally, we divide 1 into 7 and observe that there are seven 1s in 7 with no remainder, so we write 7 in the 1 column. This yields:

```
Positional values: 64      8      1
Symbol values:      1       4      7
```

and thus decimal 103 is equivalent to octal 147.

To convert decimal 375 to hexadecimal, we begin by writing the positional values of the columns until we reach a column whose positional value is greater than the decimal number. We do not need that column, so we discard it. Thus, we first write:

```
Positional values: 4096    256      16       1
```

Then we discard the column with positional value 4096, yielding:

```
Positional values:         256      16       1
```

Next we work from the leftmost column to the right. We divide 256 into 375 and observe that there is one 256 in 375 with a remainder of 119, so we write 1 in the 256 column. We divide 16 into 119 and observe that there are seven 16s in 119 with a remainder of 7 and write 7 in the 16 column. Finally, we divide 1 into 7 and observe that there are seven 1s in 7 with no remainder, so we write 7 in the 1 column. This yields:

```
Positional values: 256     16      1
Symbol values:      1       7       7
```

and thus decimal 375 is equivalent to hexadecimal 177.

D.6 Negative Binary Numbers: Two's Complement Notation

The discussion so far in this appendix has focused on positive numbers. In this section, we explain how computers represent negative numbers using *two's complement notation*. First we explain how the two's complement of a binary number is formed, then we show why it represents the negative value of the given binary number.

Consider a machine with 32-bit integers. Suppose

```
int value = 13;
```

The 32-bit representation of `value` is

```
00000000 00000000 00000000 00001101
```

To form the negative of `value` we first form its *one's complement* by applying C++'s bitwise complement operator (~):

```
onesComplementOfValue = ~value;
```

Internally, `~value` is now `value` with each of its bits reversed—ones become zeros and zeros become ones, as follows:

```
value:
00000000 00000000 00000000 00001101
```

```
~value  (i.e., value's ones complement):
11111111 11111111 11111111 11110010
```

To form the two's complement of `value`, we simply add 1 to `value`'s one's complement. Thus

```
Two's complement of value:
11111111 11111111 11111111 11110011
```

Now if this is in fact equal to –13, we should be able to add it to binary 13 and obtain a result of 0. Let us try this:

```
  00000000 00000000 00000000 00001101
 +11111111 11111111 11111111 11110011
 -----------------------------------
  00000000 00000000 00000000 00000000
```

The carry bit coming out of the leftmost column is discarded and we indeed get 0 as a result. If we add the one's complement of a number to the number, the result will be all 1s. The key to getting a result of all zeros is that the twos complement is one more than the one's complement. The addition of 1 causes each column to add to 0 with a carry of 1. The carry keeps moving leftward until it is discarded from the leftmost bit, and thus the resulting number is all zeros.

Computers actually perform a subtraction, such as

```
x = a - value;
```

by adding the two's complement of `value` to `a`, as follows:

```
x = a + (~value + 1);
```

Suppose a is 27 and value is 13 as before. If the two's complement of value is actually the negative of value, then adding the two's complement of value to a should produce the result 14. Let us try this:

```
a (i.e., 27)        00000000 00000000 00000000 00011011
+(~value + 1)      +11111111 11111111 11111111 11110011
                   ------------------------------------
                    00000000 00000000 00000000 00001110
```

which is indeed equal to 14.

Summary

- An integer such as 19 or 227 or −63 in a C++ program is assumed to be in the decimal (base 10) number system. The digits in the decimal number system are 0, 1, 2, 3, 4, 5, 6, 7, 8 and 9. The lowest digit is 0 and the highest is 9—one less than the base of 10.

- Internally, computers use the binary (base 2) number system. The binary number system has only two digits, namely 0 and 1. Its lowest digit is 0 and its highest is 1—one less than the base of 2.

- The octal number system (base 8) and the hexadecimal number system (base 16) are popular primarily because they make it convenient to abbreviate binary numbers.

- The digits of the octal number system range from 0 to 7.

- The hexadecimal number system poses a problem because it requires 16 digits—a lowest digit of 0 and a highest digit with a value equivalent to decimal 15 (one less than the base of 16). By convention, we use the letters A through F to represent the hexadecimal digits corresponding to decimal values 10 through 15.

- Each number system uses positional notation—each position in which a digit is written has a different positional value.

- A particularly important relationship of both the octal and the hexadecimal number systems to the binary system is that their bases (8 and 16 respectively) are powers of the base of the binary number system (base 2).

- To convert an octal to a binary number, replace each octal digit with its three-digit binary equivalent.

- To convert a hexadecimal to a binary number, simply replace each hexadecimal digit with its four-digit binary equivalent.

- Because we are accustomed to working in decimal, it is convenient to convert a binary, octal or hexadecimal number to decimal to get a sense of the number's "real" worth.

- To convert a number to decimal from another base, multiply the decimal equivalent of each digit by its positional value and sum the products.

- Computers represent negative numbers using two's complement notation.

- To form the negative of a value in binary, first form its one's complement by applying C++'s bitwise complement operator (~). This reverses the bits of the value. To form the two's complement of a value, simply add one to the value's one's complement.

Terminology

base	base 16 number system
base 2 number system	binary number system
base 8 number system	bitwise complement operator (~)
base 10 number system	conversions

decimal number system
digit
hexadecimal number system
negative value
octal number system

one's complement notation
positional notation
positional value
symbol value
two's complement notation

Self-Review Exercises

D.1 The bases of the decimal, binary, octal and hexadecimal number systems are _____, _____, _____ and _____ respectively.

D.2 In general, the decimal, octal and hexadecimal representations of a given binary number contain (more/fewer) digits than the binary number contains.

D.3 (*True/False*) A popular reason for using the decimal number system is that it forms a convenient notation for abbreviating binary numbers simply by substituting one decimal digit per group of four binary bits.

D.4 The (octal / hexadecimal / decimal) representation of a large binary value is the most concise (of the given alternatives).

D.5 (*True/False*) The highest digit in any base is one more than the base.

D.6 (*True/False*) The lowest digit in any base is one less than the base.

D.7 The positional value of the rightmost digit of any number in either binary, octal, decimal or hexadecimal is always _____.

D.8 The positional value of the digit to the left of the rightmost digit of any number in binary, octal, decimal or hexadecimal is always equal to _____.

D.9 Fill in the missing values in this chart of positional values for the rightmost four positions in each of the indicated number systems:

decimal	1000	100	10	1
hexadecimal	. . .	256	. . .	. . .
binary	. . .	. . .	. . .	. . .
octal	512	. . .	8	. . .

D.10 Convert binary 110101011000 to octal and to hexadecimal.

D.11 Convert hexadecimal FACE to binary.

D.12 Convert octal 7316 to binary.

D.13 Convert hexadecimal 4FEC to octal. [*Hint:* First convert 4FEC to binary, then convert that binary number to octal.]

D.14 Convert binary 1101110 to decimal.

D.15 Convert octal 317 to decimal.

D.16 Convert hexadecimal EFD4 to decimal.

D.17 Convert decimal 177 to binary, to octal and to hexadecimal.

D.18 Show the binary representation of decimal 417. Then show the one's complement of 417 and the two's complement of 417.

D.19 What is the result when a number and its two's complement are added to each other?

Answers to Self-Review Exercises

D.1   10, 2, 8, 16.

D.2   Fewer.

D.3   False. Hexadecimal does this.

D.4   Hexadecimal.

D.5   False. The highest digit in any base is one less than the base.

D.6   False. The lowest digit in any base is zero.

D.7   1 (the base raised to the zero power).

D.8   The base of the number system.

D.9   Fill in the missing values in this chart of positional values for the rightmost four positions in each of the indicated number systems:

decimal	1000	100	10	1
hexadecimal	4096	256	16	1
binary	8	4	2	1
octal	512	64	8	1

D.10   Octal 6530; Hexadecimal D58.

D.11   Binary 1111 1010 1100 1110.

D.12   Binary 111 011 001 110.

D.13   Binary 0 100 111 111 101 100; Octal 47754.

D.14   Decimal 2+4+8+32+64=110.

D.15   Decimal 7+1*8+3*64=7+8+192=207.

D.16   Decimal 4+13*16+15*256+14*4096=61396.

D.17   Decimal 177
to binary:

```
256 128 64 32 16 8 4 2 1
128 64 32 16 8 4 2 1
(1*128)+(0*64)+(1*32)+(1*16)+(0*8)+(0*4)+(0*2)+(1*1)
10110001
```

to octal:

```
512 64 8 1
64 8 1
(2*64)+(6*8)+(1*1)
261
```

to hexadecimal:

```
256 16 1
16 1
(11*16)+(1*1)
(B*16)+(1*1)
B1
```

D.18   Binary:

```
512 256 128 64 32 16 8 4 2 1
256 128 64 32 16 8 4 2 1
(1*256)+(1*128)+(0*64)+(1*32)+(0*16)+(0*8)+(0*4)+(0*2)+(1*1)
110100001
```

One's complement: 001011110
Two's complement: 001011111
Check: Original binary number + its two's complement

```
110100001
001011111
---------
000000000
```

D.19   Zero.

Exercises

D.20   Some people argue that many of our calculations would be easier in the base 12 number system because 12 is divisible by so many more numbers than 10 (for base 10). What is the lowest digit in base 12? What would be the highest symbol for the digit in base 12? What are the positional values of the rightmost four positions of any number in the base 12 number system?

D.21   Complete the following chart of positional values for the rightmost four positions in each of the indicated number systems:

	1000	100	10	1
decimal				
base 6	. . .	. . .	6	. . .
base 13	. . .	169	. . .	. . .
base 3	27	. . .	. . .	. . .

D.22   Convert binary 100101111010 to octal and to hexadecimal.

D.23   Convert hexadecimal 3A7D to binary.

D.24   Convert hexadecimal 765F to octal. [*Hint:* First convert 765F to binary, then convert that binary number to octal.]

D.25   Convert binary 1011110 to decimal.

D.26   Convert octal 426 to decimal.

D.27   Convert hexadecimal FFFF to decimal.

D.28   Convert decimal 299 to binary, to octal and to hexadecimal.

D.29   Show the binary representation of decimal 779. Then show the one's complement of 779 and the two's complement of 779.

D.30   Show the two's complement of integer value −1 on a machine with 32-bit integers.

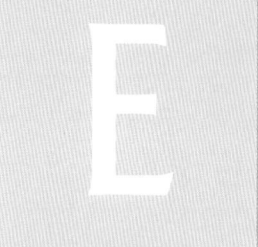

C Legacy Code Topics

E

We'll use a signal I have tried and found far-reaching and easy to yell. Waa-hoo!
—Zane Grey

It is quite a three-pipe problem.
—Sir Arthur Conan Doyle

But yet an union in partition.
—William Shakespeare

OBJECTIVES

In this chapter you will learn:

- To redirect keyboard input to come from a file and redirect screen output to a file.

- To write functions that use variable-length argument lists.

- To process command-line arguments.

- To process unexpected events within a program.

- To allocate memory dynamically for arrays, using C-style dynamic memory allocation.

- To resize memory dynamically allocated, using C-style dynamic memory allocation.

E.1 Introduction

This chapter presents several topics not ordinarily covered in introductory courses. Many of the capabilities discussed here are specific to particular operating systems, especially UNIX/LINUX/Mac OS X and/or Windows. Much of the material is for the benefit of C++ programmers who will need to work with older C legacy code.

E.2 Redirecting Input/Output on UNIX/LINUX/ Mac OS X and Windows Systems

Normally, the input to a program is from the keyboard (standard input), and the output from a program is displayed on the screen (standard output). On most computer systems—UNIX, LINUX, Mac OS X and Windows systems in particular—it is possible to redirect inputs to come from a file, and redirect outputs to be placed in a file. Both forms of redirection can be accomplished without using the file-processing capabilities of the standard library.

There are several ways to redirect input and output from the UNIX command line. Consider the executable file `sum` that inputs integers one at a time, keeps a running total of the values until the end-of-file indicator is set, then prints the result. Normally the user inputs integers from the keyboard and enters the end-of-file key combination to indicate that no further values will be input. With input redirection, the input can be stored in a file. For example, if the data are stored in file `input`, the command line

```
$ sum < input
```

causes program `sum` to be executed; the redirect input symbol (<) indicates that the data in file `input` (instead of the keyboard) is to be used as input by the program. Redirecting input in a Windows **Command Prompt** is performed identically.

Note that $ represents the UNIX command-line prompt. (UNIX prompts vary from system to system and between shells on a single system.) Redirection is an operating-system function, not another C++ feature.

The second method of redirecting input is piping. A pipe (|) causes the output of one program to be redirected as the input to another program. Suppose program random outputs a series of random integers; the output of random can be "piped" directly to program sum using the UNIX command line

```
$ random | sum
```

This causes the sum of the integers produced by random to be calculated. Piping can be performed in UNIX, LINUX, Mac OS X and Windows.

Program output can be redirected to a file by using the redirect output symbol (>). (The same symbol is used for UNIX, LINUX, Mac OS X and Windows.) For example, to redirect the output of program random to a new file called out, use

```
$ random > out
```

Finally, program output can be appended to the end of an existing file by using the append output symbol (>>). (The same symbol is used for UNIX, LINUX, Mac OS X and Windows.) For example, to append the output from program random to file out created in the preceding command line, use the command line

```
$ random >> out
```

E.3 Variable-Length Argument Lists[1]

It is possible to create functions that receive an unspecified number of arguments. An ellipsis (. . .) in a function's prototype indicates that the function receives a variable number of arguments of any type. Note that the ellipsis must always be placed at the end of the parameter list, and there must be at least one argument before the ellipsis. The macros and definitions of the variable arguments header <cstdarg> (Fig. E.1) provide the capabilities necessary to build functions with variable-length argument lists.

Figure E.2 demonstrates function average that receives a variable number of arguments. The first argument of average is always the number of values to be averaged, and the remainder of the arguments must all be of type double.

Function average uses all the definitions and macros of header <cstdarg>. Object list, of type va_list, is used by macros va_start, va_arg and va_end to process the variable-length argument list of function average. The function invokes va_start to initialize object list for use in va_arg and va_end. The macro receives two arguments—object list and the identifier of the rightmost argument in the argument list before the ellipsis—count in this case (va_start uses count here to determine where the variable-length argument list begins).

Next, function average repeatedly adds the arguments in the variable-length argument list to the total. The value to be added to total is retrieved from the argument list by invoking macro va_arg. Macro va_arg receives two arguments—object list and the type of the value expected in the argument list (double in this case)—and returns the value

---

1.   In C++, programmers use function overloading to accomplish much of what C programmers accomplish with variable-length argument lists.

Identifier	Description
va_list	A type suitable for holding information needed by macros va_start, va_arg and va_end. To access the arguments in a variable-length argument list, an object of type va_list must be declared.
va_start	A macro that is invoked before the arguments of a variable-length argument list can be accessed. The macro initializes the object declared with va_list for use by the va_arg and va_end macros.
va_arg	A macro that expands to an expression of the value and type of the next argument in the variable-length argument list. Each invocation of **va_arg** modifies the object declared with va_list so that the object points to the next argument in the list.
va_end	A macro that performs termination housekeeping in a function whose variable-length argument list was referred to by the va_start macro.

Fig. E.1 | The type and the macros defined in header `<cstdarg>`.

```
1   // Fig. E.2: figE_02.cpp
2   // Using variable-length argument lists.
3   #include <iostream>
4   using std::cout;
5   using std::endl;
6   using std::ios;
7
8   #include <iomanip>
9   using std::setw;
10  using std::setprecision;
11  using std::setiosflags;
12  using std::fixed;
13
14  #include <cstdarg>
15  using std::va_list;
16
17  double average( int, ... );
18
19  int main()
20  {
21     double double1 = 37.5;
22     double double2 = 22.5;
23     double double3 = 1.7;
24     double double4 = 10.2;
25
26     cout << fixed << setprecision( 1 ) << "double1 = "
27        << double1 << "\ndouble2 = " << double2 << "\ndouble3 = "
28        << double3 << "\ndouble4 = " << double4 << endl
```

Fig. E.2 | Using variable-length argument lists. (Part 1 of 2.)

```
29              << setprecision( 3 )
30              << "\nThe average of double1 and double2 is "
31              << average( 2, double1, double2 )
32              << "\nThe average of double1, double2, and double3 is "
33              << average( 3, double1, double2, double3 )
34              << "\nThe average of double1, double2, double3"
35              << " and double4 is "
36              << average( 4, double1, double2, double3, double4 )
37              << endl;
38       return 0;
39    }  // end main
40
41    // calculate average
42    double average( int count, ... )
43    {
44       double total = 0;
45       va_list list;   // for storing information needed by va_start
46
47       va_start( list, count );
48
49       // process variable-length argument list
50       for ( int i = 1; i <= count; i++ )
51          total += va_arg( list, double );
52
53       va_end( list ); // end the va_start
54       return total / count;
55    }  // end function average
```

```
double1 = 37.5
double2 = 22.5
double3 = 1.7
double4 = 10.2

The average of double1 and double2 is 30.000
The average of double1, double2, and double3 is 20.567
The average of double1, double2, double3 and double4 is 17.975
```

Fig. E.2 | Using variable-length argument lists. (Part 2 of 2.)

of the argument. Function average invokes macro va_end with object list as an argument before returning. Finally, the average is calculated and returned to main. Note that we used only double arguments for the variable-length portion of the argument list.

Variable-length argument lists promote variables of type float to type double. These argument lists also promote integral variables that are smaller than int to type int (variables of type int, unsigned, long and unsigned long are left alone).

Software Engineering Observation E.1

Variable-length argument lists can be used only with fundamental type arguments and with arguments of C-style struct types that do not contain C++ specific features such as virtual functions, constructors, destructors, references, const data members and virtual base classes.

> **Common Programming Error E.1**
>
> *Placing an ellipsis in the middle of a function parameter list is a syntax error. An ellipsis may be placed only at the end of the parameter list.*

E.4 Using Command-Line Arguments

On many systems—Windows, UNIX, LINUX and Mac OS X in particular—it is possible to pass arguments to main from a command line by including parameters int **argc** and char *__argv__[] in the parameter list of main. Parameter argc receives the number of command-line arguments. Parameter argv is an array of char *'s pointing to strings in which the actual command-line arguments are stored. Common uses of command-line arguments include printing the arguments, passing options to a program and passing filenames to a program.

Figure E.3 copies a file into another file one character at a time. The executable file for the program is called copyFile (i.e., the executable name for the file). A typical command line for the copyFile program on a UNIX system is

```
$ copyFile input output
```

This command line indicates that file input is to be copied to file output. When the program executes, if argc is not 3 (copyFile counts as one of the arguments), the program

```cpp
1   // Fig. E.3: figE_03.cpp
2   // Using command-line arguments
3   #include <iostream>
4   using std::cout;
5   using std::endl;
6   using std::ios;
7
8   #include <fstream>
9   using std::ifstream;
10  using std::ofstream;
11
12  int main( int argc, char *argv[] )1
13  {
14     // check number of command-line arguments
15     if ( argc != 3 )
16        cout << "Usage: copyFile infile_name outfile_name" << endl;
17     else
18     {
19        ifstream inFile( argv[ 1 ], ios::in );
20
21        // input file could not be opened
22        if ( !inFile )
23        {
24           cout << argv[ 1 ] << " could not be opened" << endl;
25           return -1;
26        } // end if
27
```

Fig. E.3 | Using command-line arguments. (Part 1 of 2.)

```
28          ofstream outFile( argv[ 2 ], ios::out );
29
30          // output file could not be opened
31          if ( !outFile )
32          {
33             cout << argv[ 2 ] << " could not be opened" << endl;
34             inFile.close();
35             return -2;
36          } // end if
37
38          char c = inFile.get(); // read first character
39
40          while ( inFile )
41          {
42             outFile.put( c );    // output character
43             c = inFile.get();    // read next character
44          } // end while
45       } // end else
46
47       return 0;
48    } // end main
```

Fig. E.3 | Using command-line arguments. (Part 2 of 2.)

prints an error message (line 16). Otherwise, array `argv` contains the strings `"copyFile"`, `"input"` and `"output"`. The second and third arguments on the command line are used as file names by the program. The files are opened by creating `ifstream` object `inFile` and `ofstream` object `outFile` (lines 19 and 28). If both files are opened successfully, characters are read from file `input` with member function `get` and written to file `output` with member function `put` until the end-of-file indicator for file `input` is set (lines 40–44). Then the program terminates. The result is an exact copy of file `input`. Note that not all computer systems support command-line arguments as easily as UNIX, LINUX, Mac OS X and Windows. Some VMS and older Macintosh systems, for example, require special settings for processing command-line arguments. See the manuals for your system for more information on command-line arguments.

E.5 Notes on Compiling Multiple-Source-File Programs

As stated earlier in the text, it is normal to build programs that consist of multiple source files (see Chapter 9, Classes: A Deeper Look, Part 1). There are several considerations when creating programs in multiple files. For example, the definition of a function must be entirely contained in one file—it cannot span two or more files.

In Chapter 6, we introduced the concepts of storage class and scope. We learned that variables declared outside any function definition are of storage class `static` by default and are referred to as global variables. Global variables are accessible to any function defined in the same file after the variable is declared. Global variables also are accessible to functions in other files; however, the global variables must be declared in each file in which they are used. For example, if we define global integer variable `flag` in one file, and refer to it in a second file, the second file must contain the declaration

```
extern int flag;
```

prior to the variable's use in that file. In the preceding declaration, the storage class-specifier `extern` indicates to the compiler that variable `flag` is defined either later in the same file or in a different file. The compiler informs the linker that unresolved references to variable `flag` appear in the file. (The compiler does not know where `flag` is defined, so it lets the linker attempt to find `flag`.) If the linker cannot locate a definition of `flag`, a linker error is reported. If a proper global definition is located, the linker resolves the references by indicating where `flag` is located.

Performance Tip E.1

Global variables increase performance because they can be accessed directly by any function— the overhead of passing data to functions is eliminated.

Software Engineering Observation E.2

Global variables should be avoided unless application performance is critical or the variable represents a shared global resource such as `cin`, because they violate the principle of least privilege, and they make software difficult to maintain.

Just as `extern` declarations can be used to declare global variables to other program files, function prototypes can be used to declare functions in other program files. (The `extern` specifier is not required in a function prototype.) This is accomplished by including the function prototype in each file in which the function is invoked, then compiling each source file and linking the resulting object code files together. Function prototypes indicate to the compiler that the specified function is defined either later in the same file or in a different file. The compiler does not attempt to resolve references to such a function—that task is left to the linker. If the linker cannot locate a function definition, an error is generated.

As an example of using function prototypes to extend the scope of a function, consider any program containing the preprocessor directive `#include <cstring>`. This directive includes in a file the function prototypes for functions such as `strcmp` and `strcat`. Other functions in the file can use `strcmp` and `strcat` to accomplish their tasks. The `strcmp` and `strcat` functions are defined for us separately. We do not need to know where they are defined. We are simply reusing the code in our programs. The linker resolves our references to these functions. This process enables us to use the functions in the standard library.

Software Engineering Observation E.3

Creating programs in multiple source files facilitates software reusability and good software engineering. Functions may be common to many applications. In such instances, those functions should be stored in their own source files, and each source file should have a corresponding header file containing function prototypes. This enables programmers of different applications to reuse the same code by including the proper header file and compiling their application with the corresponding source file.

Portability Tip E.1

Some systems do not support global variable names or function names of more than six characters. This should be considered when writing programs that will be ported to multiple platforms.

It is possible to restrict the scope of a global variable or function to the file in which it is defined. The storage-class specifier `static`, when applied to a file scope variable or a function, prevents it from being used by any function that is not defined in the same file. This is referred to as internal linkage. Global variables (except those that are `const`) and functions that are not preceded by `static` in their definitions have external linkage—they can be accessed in other files if those files contain proper declarations and/or function prototypes.

The global variable declaration

```
static double pi = 3.14159;
```

creates variable `pi` of type `double`, initializes it to `3.14159` and indicates that `pi` is known only to functions in the file in which it is defined.

The `static` specifier is commonly used with utility functions that are called only by functions in a particular file. If a function is not required outside a particular file, the principle of least privilege should be enforced by using `static`. If a function is defined before it is used in a file, `static` should be applied to the function definition. Otherwise, `static` should be applied to the function prototype.

When building large programs from multiple source files, compiling the program becomes tedious if making small changes to one file means that the entire program must be recompiled. Many systems provide special utilities that recompile only source files dependant on the modified program file. On UNIX systems, the utility is called `make`. Utility `make` reads a file called `Makefile` that contains instructions for compiling and linking the program. Systems such as Borland C++ and Microsoft Visual C++ for PCs provide `make` utilities and "projects." For more information on `make` utilities, see the manual for your particular system.

E.6 Program Termination with `exit` and `atexit`

The general utilities library (`<cstdlib>`) provides methods of terminating program execution other than a conventional return from function `main`. Function `exit` forces a program to terminate as if it executed normally. The function often is used to terminate a program when an error is detected in the input or if a file to be processed by the program cannot be opened.

Function `atexit` registers a function in the program to be called when the program terminates by reaching the end of `main` or when `exit` is invoked. Function `atexit` takes a pointer to a function (i.e., the function name) as an argument. Functions called at program termination cannot have arguments and cannot return a value.

Function `exit` takes one argument. The argument is normally the symbolic constant `EXIT_SUCCESS` or `EXIT_FAILURE`. If `exit` is called with `EXIT_SUCCESS`, the implementation-defined value for successful termination is returned to the calling environment. If `exit` is called with `EXIT_FAILURE`, the implementation-defined value for unsuccessful termination is returned. When function `exit` is invoked, any functions previously registered with `atexit` are invoked in the reverse order of their registration, all streams associated with the program are flushed and closed, and control returns to the host environment. Figure E.4 tests functions `exit` and `atexit`. The program prompts the user to determine whether the program should be terminated with `exit` or by reaching the end of `main`. Note that function `print` is executed at program termination in each case.

```
1   // Fig. E.4: figE_04.cpp
2   // Using the exit and atexit functions
3   #include <iostream>
4   using std::cout;
5   using std::endl;
6   using std::cin;
7
8   #include <cstdlib>
9   using std::atexit;
10  using std::exit;
11
12  void print();
13
14  int main()
15  {
16     atexit( print ); // register function print
17
18     cout << "Enter 1 to terminate program with function exit"
19        << "\nEnter 2 to terminate program normally\n";
20
21     int answer;
22     cin >> answer;
23
24     // exit if answer is 1
25     if ( answer == 1 )
26     {
27        cout << "\nTerminating program with function exit\n";
28        exit( EXIT_SUCCESS );
29     }  // end if
30
31     cout << "\nTerminating program by reaching the end of main"
32        << endl;
33
34     return 0;
35  }  // end main
36
37  // display message before termination
38  void print()
39  {
40     cout << "Executing function print at program termination\n"
41        << "Program terminated" << endl;
42  }  // end function print
```

```
Enter 1 to terminate program with function exit
Enter 2 to terminate program normally
2

Terminating program by reaching the end of main
Executing function print at program termination
Program terminated
```

Fig. E.4 | Using functions exit and atexit. (Part 1 of 2.)

```
Enter 1 to terminate program with function exit
Enter 2 to terminate program normally
1

Terminating program with function exit
Executing function print at program termination
Program terminated
```

Fig. E.4 | Using functions exit and atexit. (Part 2 of 2.)

E.7 The volatile Type Qualifier

The volatile type qualifier is applied to a definition of a variable that may be altered from outside the program (i.e., the variable is not completely under the control of the program). Thus, the compiler cannot perform optimizations (such as speeding program execution or reducing memory consumption, for example) that depend on "knowing that a variable's behavior is influenced only by program activities the compiler can observe."

E.8 Suffixes for Integer and Floating-Point Constants

C++ provides integer and floating-point suffixes for specifying the types of integer and floating-point constants. The integer suffixes are: u or U for an unsigned integer, l or L for a long integer, and ul or UL for an unsigned long integer. The following constants are of type unsigned, long and unsigned long, respectively:

```
174u
8358L
28373ul
```

If an integer constant is not suffixed, its type is int; if the constant cannot be stored in an int, it is stored in a long.

The floating-point suffixes are f or F for a float and l or L for a long double. The following constants are of type long double and float, respectively:

```
3.14159L
1.28f
```

A floating-point constant that is not suffixed is of type double. A constant with an improper suffix results in either a compiler warning or an error.

E.9 Signal Handling

An unexpected event, or signal, can terminate a program prematurely. Some unexpected events include interrupts (pressing *Ctrl+C* on a UNIX, LINUX, Mac OS X or Windows system), illegal instructions, segmentation violations, termination orders from the operating system and floating-point exceptions (division by zero or multiplying large floating-point values). The signal-handling library provides function signal to trap unexpected events. Function signal receives two arguments—an integer signal number and a pointer to the signal-handling function. Signals can be generated by function raise, which takes an integer signal number as an argument. Figure E.5 summarizes the standard signals defined in header file `<csignal>`. The next example demonstrates functions `signal` and `raise`.

Figure E.6 traps an interactive signal (`SIGINT`) with function `signal`. The program calls `signal` with `SIGINT` and a pointer to function `signalHandler`. (Remember that the name of a function is a pointer to the function.) Now, when a signal of type `SIGINT` occurs, function `signalHandler` is called, a message is printed and the user is given the option to continue normal execution of the program. If the user wishes to continue execution, the signal handler is reinitialized by calling `signal` again (some systems require the signal handler to be reinitialized), and control returns to the point in the program at which the signal was detected. In this program, function `raise` is used to simulate an interactive signal. A random number between 1 and 50 is chosen. If the number is 25, then `raise` is called to generate the signal. Normally, interactive signals are initiated outside the program. For example, pressing *Ctrl+C* during program execution on a UNIX, LINUX, Mac OS X or Windows system generates an interactive signal that terminates program execution. Signal handling can be used to trap the interactive signal and prevent the program from terminating.

Signal	Explanation
SIGABRT	Abnormal termination of the program (such as a call to abort).
SIGFPE	An erroneous arithmetic operation, such as a divide by zero or an operation resulting in overflow.
SIGILL	Detection of an illegal instruction.
SIGINT	Receipt of an interactive attention signal.
SIGSEGV	An invalid access to storage.
SIGTERM	A termination request sent to the program.

Fig. E.5 | Signals defined in header `<csignal>`.

```
1   // Fig. E.6: figE_06.cpp
2   // Using signal handling
3   #include <iostream>
4   using std::cout;
5   using std::cin;
6   using std::endl;
7
8   #include <iomanip>
9   using std::setw;
10
11  #include <csignal>
12  using std::raise;
13  using std::signal;
14
```

Fig. E.6 | Using signal handling. (Part 1 of 3.)

```
15   #include <cstdlib>
16   using std::exit;
17   using std::rand;
18   using std::srand;
19
20   #include <ctime>
21   using std::time;
22
23   void signalHandler( int );
24
25   int main()
26   {
27      signal( SIGINT, signalHandler );
28      srand( time( 0 ) );
29
30      // create and output random numbers
31      for ( int i = 1; i <= 100; i++ )
32      {
33         int x = 1 + rand() % 50;
34
35         if ( x == 25 )
36            raise( SIGINT ); // raise SIGINT when x is 25
37
38         cout << setw( 4 ) << i;
39
40         if ( i % 10 == 0 )
41            cout << endl; // output endl when i is a multiple of 10
42      } // end for
43
44      return 0;
45   } // end main
46
47   // handles signal
48   void signalHandler( int signalValue )
49   {
50      cout << "\nInterrupt signal (" << signalValue
51           << ") received.\n"
52           << "Do you wish to continue (1 = yes or 2 = no)? ";
53
54      int response;
55
56      cin >> response;
57
58      // check for invalid responses
59      while ( response != 1 && response != 2 )
60      {
61         cout << "(1 = yes or 2 = no)? ";
62         cin >> response;
63      } // end while
64
65      // determine if it is time to exit
66      if ( response != 1 )
67         exit( EXIT_SUCCESS );
```

Fig. E.6 | Using signal handling. (Part 2 of 3.)

```
68
69      // call signal and pass it SIGINT and address of signalHandler
70      signal( SIGINT, signalHandler );
71   } // end function signalHandler
```

```
   1   2   3   4   5   6   7   8   9  10
  11  12  13  14  15  16  17  18  19  20
  21  22  23  24  25  26  27  28  29  30
  31  32  33  34  35  36  37  38  39  40
  41  42  43  44  45  46  47  48  49  50
  51  52  53  54  55  56  57  58  59  60
  61  62  63  64  65  66  67  68  69  70
  71  72  73  74  75  76  77  78  79  80
  81  82  83  84  85  86  87  88  89  90
  91  92  93  94  95  96  97  98  99
Interrupt signal (2) received.
Do you wish to continue (1 = yes or 2 = no)? 1
  100
```

```
   1   2   3   4
Interrupt signal (2) received.
Do you wish to continue (1 = yes or 2 = no)? 2
```

Fig. E.6 | Using signal handling. (Part 3 of 3.)

E.10 Dynamic Memory Allocation with calloc and realloc

In Chapter 10, we discussed C++-style dynamic memory allocation with new and delete. C++ programmers should use new and delete, rather than C's functions malloc and free (header <cstdlib>). However, most C++ programmers will find themselves reading a great deal of C legacy code, and therefore we include this additional discussion on C-style dynamic memory allocation.

The general utilities library (<cstdlib>) provides two other functions for dynamic memory allocation—calloc and realloc. These functions can be used to create and modify dynamic arrays. As shown in Chapter 8, Pointers and Pointer-Based Strings, a pointer to an array can be subscripted like an array. Thus, a pointer to a contiguous portion of memory created by calloc can be manipulated as an array. Function calloc dynamically allocates memory for an array and initializes the memory to zeroes. The prototype for calloc is

```
void *calloc( size_t nmemb, size_t size );
```

It receives two arguments—the number of elements (nmemb) and the size of each element (size)—and initializes the elements of the array to zero. The function returns a pointer to the allocated memory or a null pointer (0) if the memory is not allocated.

Function realloc changes the size of an object allocated by a previous call to malloc, calloc or realloc. The original object's contents are not modified, provided that the memory allocated is larger than the amount allocated previously. Otherwise, the contents are unchanged up to the size of the new object. The prototype for realloc is

```
        void *realloc( void *ptr, size_t size );
```

Function realloc takes two arguments—a pointer to the original object (ptr) and the new size of the object (size). If ptr is 0, realloc works identically to malloc. If size is 0 and ptr is not 0, the memory for the object is freed. Otherwise, if ptr is not 0 and size is greater than zero, realloc tries to allocate a new block of memory. If the new space cannot be allocated, the object pointed to by ptr is unchanged. Function realloc returns either a pointer to the reallocated memory or a null pointer.

Common Programming Error E.2

Using the delete operator on a pointer resulting from malloc, calloc and realloc. Using realloc or free on a pointer resulting from the new operator.

E.11 **The Unconditional Branch: goto**

Throughout the text we have stressed the importance of using structured programming techniques to build reliable software that is easy to debug, maintain and modify. In some cases, performance is more important than strict adherence to structured-programming techniques. In these cases, some unstructured programming techniques may be used. For example, we can use break to terminate execution of a repetition structure before the loop-continuation condition becomes false. This saves unnecessary repetitions of the loop if the task is completed before loop termination.

Another instance of unstructured programming is the **goto** statement—an unconditional branch. The result of the goto statement is a change in the flow of control of the program to the first statement after the label specified in the goto statement. A label is an identifier followed by a colon. A label must appear in the same function as the goto statement that refers to it. Figure E.7 uses goto statements to loop 10 times and print the counter value each time. After initializing count to 1, the program tests count to determine whether it is greater than 10. (The label start is skipped, because labels do not per-

```
 1   // Fig. E.7: figE_07.cpp
 2   // Using goto.
 3   #include <iostream>
 4   using std::cout;
 5   using std::endl;
 6
 7   #include <iomanip>
 8   using std::left;
 9   using std::setw;
10
11   int main()
12   {
13      int count = 1;
14
15      start: // label
16         // goto end when count exceeds 10
17         if ( count > 10 )
18            goto end;
```

Fig. E.7 | Using goto. (Part 1 of 2.)

```
19
20          cout << setw( 2 ) << left << count;
21          ++count;
22
23          // goto start on line 17
24          goto start;
25
26     end: // label
27          cout << endl;
28
29     return 0;
30  }  // end main
```

```
1  2  3  4  5  6  7  8  9  10
```

Fig. E.7 | Using goto. (Part 2 of 2.)

form any action.) If so, control is transferred from the goto to the first statement after the label end. Otherwise, count is printed and incremented, and control is transferred from the goto to the first statement after the label start.

In Chapters 4–5, we stated that only three control structures are required to write any program—sequence, selection and repetition. When the rules of structured programming are followed, it is possible to create deeply nested control structures from which it is difficult to escape efficiently. Some programmers use goto statements in such situations as a quick exit from a deeply nested structure. This eliminates the need to test multiple conditions to escape from a control structure.

Performance Tip E.2

The goto statement can be used to exit deeply nested control structures efficiently but can make code more difficult to read and maintain.

Error-Prevention Tip E.1

The goto statement should be used only in performance-oriented applications. The goto statement is unstructured and can lead to programs that are more difficult to debug, maintain and modify.

E.12 Unions

A union (defined with keyword union) is a region of memory that, over time, can contain objects of a variety of types. However, at any moment, a union can contain a maximum of one object, because the members of a union share the same storage space. It is the programmer's responsibility to ensure that the data in a union is referenced with a member name of the proper data type.

Common Programming Error E.3

The result of referencing a union member other than the last one stored is undefined. It treats the stored data as a different type.

Portability Tip E.2

If data are stored in a union as one type and referenced as another type, the results are implementation dependent.

At different times during a program's execution, some objects might not be relevant, while one other object is—so a union shares the space instead of wasting storage on objects that are not being used. The number of bytes used to store a union will be at least enough to hold the largest member.

Performance Tip E.3

Using unions conserves storage.

Portability Tip E.3

The amount of storage required to store a union is implementation dependent.

A union is declared in the same format as a struct or a class. For example,

```
union Number
{
    int x;
    double y;
};
```

indicates that Number is a union type with members int x and double y. The union definition must precede all functions in which it will be used.

Software Engineering Observation E.4

Like a struct or a class declaration, a union declaration simply creates a new type. Placing a union or struct declaration outside any function does not create a global variable.

The only valid built-in operations that can be performed on a union are assigning a union to another union of the same type, taking the address (&) of a union and accessing union members using the structure member operator (.) and the structure pointer operator (->). unions cannot be compared.

Common Programming Error E.4

Comparing unions is a compilation error, because the compiler does not know which member of each is active and hence which member of one to compare to which member of the other.

A union is similar to a class in that it can have a constructor to initialize any of its members. A union that has no constructor can be initialized with another union of the same type, with an expression of the type of the first member of the union or with an initializer (enclosed in braces) of the type of the first member of the union. unions can have other member functions, such as destructors, but a union's member functions cannot be declared virtual. The members of a union are public by default.

Common Programming Error E.5

Initializing a union in a declaration with a value or an expression whose type is different from the type of the union's first member is a compilation error.

A union cannot be used as a base class in inheritance (i.e., classes cannot be derived from unions). unions can have objects as members only if these objects do not have a constructor, a destructor or an overloaded assignment operator. None of a union's data members can be declared static.

Figure E.8 uses the variable value of type union Number to display the value stored in the union as both an int and a double. The program output is implementation dependent. The program output shows that the internal representation of a double value can be quite different from the representation of an int.

An anonymous union is a union without a type name that does not attempt to define objects or pointers before its terminating semicolon. Such a union does not create a type but does create an unnamed object. An anonymous union's members may be accessed directly in the scope in which the anonymous union is declared just as are any other local variables—there is no need to use the dot (.) or arrow (->) operators.

```cpp
1   // Fig. E.8: figE_08.cpp
2   // An example of a union.
3   #include <iostream>
4   using std::cout;
5   using std::endl;
6
7   // define union Number
8   union Number
9   {
10     int integer1;
11     double double1;
12  };  // end union Number
13
14  int main()
15  {
16     Number value; // union variable
17
18     value.integer1 = 100; // assign 100 to member integer1
19
20     cout << "Put a value in the integer member\n"
21          << "and print both members.\nint:    "
22          << value.integer1 << "\ndouble: " << value.double1
23          << endl;
24
25     value.double1 = 100.0;  // assign 100.0 to member double1
26
27     cout << "Put a value in the floating member\n"
28          << "and print both members.\nint:    "
29          << value.integer1 << "\ndouble: " << value.double1
30          << endl;
31
32     return 0;
33  } // end main
```

Fig. E.8 | Printing the value of a union in both member data types. (Part 1 of 2.)

```
Put a value in the integer member
and print both members.
int:   100
double: -9.25596e+061
Put a value in the floating member
and print both members.
int:   0
double: 100
```

Fig. E.8 | Printing the value of a union in both member data types. (Part 2 of 2.)

Anonymous unions have some restrictions. Anonymous unions can contain only data members. All members of an anonymous union must be public. And an anonymous union declared globally (i.e., at file scope) must be explicitly declared static. Figure E.9 illustrates the use of an anonymous union.

E.13 Linkage Specifications

It is possible from a C++ program to call functions written and compiled with a C compiler. As stated in Section 6.17, C++ specially encodes function names for type-safe linkage. C, however, does not encode its function names. Thus, a function compiled in C will not be recognized when an attempt is made to link C code with C++ code, because the C++ code expects a specially encoded function name. C++ enables the programmer to provide linkage specifications to inform the compiler that a function was compiled on a C compiler and to prevent the name of the function from being encoded by the C++ compiler. Linkage specifications are useful when large libraries of specialized functions have been developed, and the user either does not have access to the source code for recompilation into C++ or does not have time to convert the library functions from C to C++.

```
 1   // Fig. E.9: figE_09.cpp
 2   // Using an anonymous union.
 3   #include <iostream>
 4   using std::cout;
 5   using std::endl;
 6
 7   int main()
 8   {
 9      // declare an anonymous union
10      // members integer1, double1 and charPtr share the same space
11      union
12      {
13         int integer1;
14         double double1;
15         char *charPtr;
16      };  // end anonymous union
17
```

Fig. E.9 | Using an anonymous union. (Part 1 of 2.)

```
18      // declare local variables
19      int integer2 = 1;
20      double double2 = 3.3;
21      char *char2Ptr = "Anonymous";
22
23      // assign value to each union member
24      // successively and print each
25      cout << integer2 << ' ';
26      integer1 = 2;
27      cout << integer1 << endl;
28
29      cout << double2 << ' ';
30      double1 = 4.4;
31      cout << double1 << endl;
32
33      cout << char2Ptr << ' ';
34      charPtr = "union";
35      cout << charPtr << endl;
36
37      return 0;
38   }  // end main
```

```
1 2
3.3 4.4
Anonymous union
```

Fig. E.9 | Using an anonymous union. (Part 2 of 2.)

To inform the compiler that one or several functions have been compiled in C, write the function prototypes as follows:

```
extern "C" function prototype    // single function

extern "C"    // multiple functions
{
    function prototypes
}
```

These declarations inform the compiler that the specified functions are not compiled in C++, so name encoding should not be performed on the functions listed in the linkage specification. These functions can then be linked properly with the program. C++ environments normally include the standard C libraries and do not require the programmer to use linkage specifications for those functions.

Summary

- On many systems—UNIX, LINUX, Mac OS X or Windows systems in particular—it is possible to redirect input to a program and output from a program. Input is redirected from the UNIX, LINUX, Mac OS X or Windows command lines using the redirect input symbol (<) or a pipe (|). Output is redirected from the UNIX, LINUX, Mac OS X or Windows command lines using the redirect output symbol (>) or the append output symbol (>>). The redirect output symbol simply stores the program output in a file, and the append output symbol appends the output to the end of a file.

- The macros and definitions of the variable arguments header <cstdarg> provide the capabilities necessary to build functions with variable-length argument lists.

- An ellipsis (…) in a function prototype indicates that the function receives a variable number of arguments.

- Type va_list is suitable for holding information needed by macros va_start, va_arg and va_end. To access the arguments in a variable-length argument list, an object of type va_list must be declared.

- Macro va_start is invoked before the arguments of a variable-length argument list can be accessed. The macro initializes the object declared with va_list for use by macros va_arg and va_end.

- Macro va_arg expands to an expression of the value and type of the next argument in the variable-length argument list. Each invocation of va_arg modifies the va_list object so that the object points to the next argument in the list.

- Macro va_end facilitates a normal return from a function whose variable argument list was referred to by the va_start macro.

- On many systems—UNIX, LINUX, Mac OS X and Windows in particular—it is possible to pass command-line arguments to main by including in main's parameter list the parameters int argc and char *argv[]. Parameter argc is the number of command-line arguments. Parameter argv is an array of char *'s containing the command-line arguments.

- The definition of a function must be entirely contained in one file—it cannot span two or more files.

- Global variables must be declared in each file in which they are used.

- Function prototypes can be used to declare functions in other program files. (The extern specifier is not required in a function prototype.) This is accomplished by including the function prototype in each file in which the function is invoked, then compiling the files together.

- The storage-class specifier static, when applied to a file scope variable or a function, prevents it from being used by any function that is not defined in the same file. This is referred to as internal linkage. Global variables and functions that are not preceded by static in their definitions have external linkage—they can be accessed in other files if those files contain proper declarations and/or function prototypes.

- The static specifier is commonly used with utility functions that are called only by functions in a particular file. If a function is not required outside a particular file, the principle of least privilege should be enforced by using static.

- When building large programs from multiple source files, compiling the program becomes tedious if making small changes to one file means that the entire program must be recompiled. Many systems provide special utilities that recompile only the modified program file. On UNIX systems, the utility is called make. Utility make reads a file called Makefile that contains instructions for compiling and linking the program.

- Function exit forces a program to terminate as if it had executed normally.

- Function atexit registers a function in a program to be called upon normal termination of the program—i.e., either when the program terminates by reaching the end of main, or when exit is invoked.

- Function atexit takes a pointer to a function (e.g., a function name) as an argument. Functions called at program termination cannot have arguments and cannot return a value.

- Function exit takes one argument—normally the symbolic constant EXIT_SUCCESS or the symbolic constant EXIT_FAILURE. If exit is called with EXIT_SUCCESS, the implementation-defined value for successful termination is returned to the calling environment. If exit is called with EXIT_FAILURE, the implementation-defined value for unsuccessful termination is returned.

- When function exit is invoked, any functions registered with atexit are invoked in the reverse order of their registration, all streams associated with the program are flushed and closed and control returns to the host environment.

- The volatile qualifier is used to prevent optimizations of a variable, because it can be modified from outside the program's scope.

- C++ provides integer and floating-point suffixes for specifying the types of integer and floating-point constants. The integer suffixes are u or U for an unsigned integer, l or L for a long integer and ul or UL for an unsigned long integer. If an integer constant is not suffixed, its type is determined by the first type capable of storing a value of that size (first int, then long int). The floating-point suffixes are f or F for a float and l or L for a long double. A floating-point constant that is not suffixed is of type double.

- The signal-handling library provides the capability to register a function to trap unexpected events with function signal. Function signal receives two arguments—an integer signal number and a pointer to the signal-handling function.

- Signals can also be generated with function raise and an integer argument.

- The general-utilities library (cstdlib) provides functions calloc and realloc for dynamic memory allocation. These functions can be used to create dynamic arrays.

- Function calloc receives two arguments—the number of elements (nmemb) and the size of each element (size)—and initializes the elements of the array to zero. The function returns a pointer to the allocated memory or if the memory is not allocated, the function returns a null pointer.

- Function realloc changes the size of an object allocated by a previous call to malloc, calloc or realloc. The original object's contents are not modified, provided that the amount of memory allocated is larger than the amount allocated previously.

- Function realloc takes two arguments—a pointer to the original object (ptr) and the new size of the object (size). If ptr is null, realloc works identically to malloc. If size is 0 and the pointer received is not null, the memory for the object is freed. Otherwise, if ptr is not null and size is greater than zero, realloc tries to allocate a new block of memory for the object. If the new space cannot be allocated, the object pointed to by ptr is unchanged. Function realloc returns either a pointer to the reallocated memory or a null pointer.

- The result of the goto statement is a change in the program's flow of control. Program execution continues at the first statement after the label in the goto statement.

- A label is an identifier followed by a colon. A label must appear in the same function as the goto statement that refers to it.

- A union is a data type whose members share the same storage space. The members can be almost any type. The storage reserved for a union is large enough to store its largest member. In most cases, unions contain two or more data types. Only one member, and thus one data type, can be referenced at a time.

- A union is declared in the same format as a structure.

- A union can be initialized only with a value of the type of its first member or another object of the same union type.

- C++ enables the programmer to provide linkage specifications to inform the compiler that a function was compiled on a C compiler and to prevent the name of the function from being encoded by the C++ compiler.

- To inform the compiler that one or several functions have been compiled in C, write the function prototypes as follows:

```
extern "C" function prototype   // single function
```

```
extern "C"   // multiple functions
{
    function prototypes
}
```

These declarations inform the compiler that the specified functions are not compiled in C++, so name encoding should not be performed on the functions listed in the linkage specification. These functions can then be linked properly with the program.

- C++ environments normally include the standard C libraries and do not require the programmer to use linkage specifications for those functions.

Terminology

append output symbol >>	`long integer suffix (1 or L)`
`argv`	`make`
`atexit`	`Makefile`
`calloc`	`malloc`
command-line arguments	`pipe |`
`const`	`piping`
`<csignal>`	`raise`
`<cstdarg>`	`realloc`
dynamic arrays	redirect input symbol <
event	redirect output symbol >
`exit`	segmentation violation
`EXIT_FAILURE`	`signal`
`EXIT_SUCCESS`	signal-handling library
`extern "C"`	static storage-class specifier
extern storage-class specifier	`trap`
external linkage	`union`
`float suffix (f or F)`	`unsigned integer suffix (u or U)`
floating-point exception	`unsigned long integer suffix (ul or UL)`
`free`	`va_arg`
goto statement	`va_end`
I/O redirection	`va_list`
illegal instruction	`va_start`
internal linkage	variable-length argument list
interrupt	`volatile`
`long double suffix (1 or L)`	

Self-Review Exercises

E.1 Fill in the blanks in each of the following:

a) Symbol _____ redirects input data from the keyboard to come from a file.

b) The _____ symbol is used to redirect the screen output to be placed in a file.

c) The _____ symbol is used to append the output of a program to the end of a file.

d) A(n) _____ is used to direct the output of a program as the input of another program.

e) A(n) _____ in the parameter list of a function indicates that the function can receive a variable number of arguments.

f) Macro _____ must be invoked before the arguments in a variable-length argument list can be accessed.

g) Macro _____ is used to access the individual arguments of a variable-length argument list.

h) Macro _____ performs termination housekeeping in a function whose variable argument list was referred to by macro va_start.

i) Argument _____ of main receives the number of arguments in a command line.

j) Argument _____ of main stores command-line arguments as character strings.

k) The UNIX utility _____ reads a file called _____ that contains instructions for compiling and linking a program consisting of multiple source files. The utility recompiles a file only if the file (or a header it uses) has been modified since it was last compiled.

l) Function _____ forces a program to terminate execution.

m) Function _____ registers a function to be called upon normal termination of the program.

n) An integer or floating-point _____ can be appended to an integer or floating-point constant to specify the exact type of the constant.

o) Function _____ can be used to register a function to trap unexpected events.

p) Function _____ generates a signal from within a program.

q) Function _____ dynamically allocates memory for an array and initializes the elements to zero.

r) Function _____ changes the size of a block of dynamically allocated memory.

s) A(n) _____ is an entity containing a collection of variables that occupy the same memory, but at different times.

t) The _____ keyword is used to introduce a union definition.

Answers to Self-Review Exercises

E.1 a) redirect input (<). b) redirect output (>). c) append output (>>). d) pipe (|). e) ellipsis (...). f) va_start. g) va_arg. h) va_end. i) argc. j) argv. k) make, Makefile. l) exit. m) atexit. n) suffix. o) signal. p) raise. q) calloc. r) realloc. s) union. t) union.

Exercises

E.2 Write a program that calculates the product of a series of integers that are passed to function product using a variable-length argument list. Test your function with several calls, each with a different number of arguments.

E.3 Write a program that prints the command-line arguments of the program.

E.4 Write a program that sorts an integer array into ascending order or descending order. The program should use command-line arguments to pass either argument -a for ascending order or -d for descending order. [*Note*: This is the standard format for passing options to a program in UNIX.]

E.5 Read the manuals for your system to determine what signals are supported by the signal-handling library (<csignal>). Write a program with signal handlers for the signals SIGABRT and SIG-INT. The program should test the trapping of these signals by calling function abort to generate a signal of type SIGABRT and by pressing *Ctrl+C* to generate a signal of type SIGINT.

E.6 Write a program that dynamically allocates an array of integers using a function from <cstdlib>, not the new operator. The size of the array should be input from the keyboard. The elements of the array should be assigned values input from the keyboard. Print the values of the array. Next, reallocate the memory for the array to half of the current number of elements. Print the values remaining in the array to confirm that they match the first half of the values in the original array.

E.7 Write a program that takes two file names as command-line arguments, reads the characters from the first file one at a time and writes the characters in reverse order to the second file.

E.8   Write a program that uses goto statements to simulate a nested looping structure that prints a square of asterisks as shown in Fig. E.10. The program should use only the following three output statements:

```
cout << '*';
cout << ' ';
cout << endl;
```

E.9   Provide the definition for union Data containing char charcter1, short short1, long long1, float float1 and double double1.

E.10   Create union Integer with members char charcter1, short short1, int integer1 and long long1. Write a program that inputs values of type char, short, int and long and stores the values in union variables of type union Integer. Each union variable should be printed as a char, a short, an int and a long. Do the values always print correctly?

E.11   Create union FloatingPoint with members float float1, double double1 and long double longDouble. Write a program that inputs values of type float, double and long double and stores the values in union variables of type union FloatingPoint. Each union variable should be printed as a float, a double and a long double. Do the values always print correctly?

E.12   Given the union

```
union A
{
   double y;
   char *zPtr;
};
```

which of the following are correct statements for initializing the union?

a) A p = b;   // b is of type A
b) A q = x;   // x is a double
c) A r = 3.14159;
d) A s = { 79.63 };
e) A t = { "Hi There!" };
f) A u = { 3.14159, "Pi" };
g) A v = { y = −7.843, zPtr = &x };

```
*****
*   *
*   *
*   *
*****
```

Fig. E.10 | Example for Exercise E.8.

F

Preprocessor

OBJECTIVES

In this chapter you will learn:

- To use #include for developing large programs.
- To use #define to create macros and macros with arguments.
- To understand conditional compilation.
- To display error messages during conditional compilation.
- To use assertions to test if the values of expressions are correct.

Hold thou the good; define it well.
—Alfred, Lord Tennyson

I have found you an argument;
but I am not obliged to find
you an understanding.
—Samuel Johnson

A good symbol is the best
argument, and is a missionary
to persuade thousands.
—Ralph Waldo Emerson

Conditions are
fundamentally sound.
—Herbert Hoover [December
1929]

The partisan, when he is
engaged in a dispute, cares
nothing about the rights of
the question, but is anxious
only to convince his hearers
of his own assertions.
—Plato

F.1 Introduction

This chapter introduces the preprocessor. Preprocessing occurs before a program is compiled. Some possible actions are inclusion of other files in the file being compiled, definition of symbolic constants and macros, conditional compilation of program code and conditional execution of preprocessor directives. All preprocessor directives begin with #, and only white-space characters may appear before a preprocessor directive on a line. Preprocessor directives are not C++ statements, so they do not end in a semicolon (;). Preprocessor directives are processed fully before compilation begins.

Common Programming Error F.1

Placing a semicolon at the end of a preprocessor directive can lead to a variety of errors, depending on the type of preprocessor directive.

Software Engineering Observation F.1

Many preprocessor features (especially macros) are more appropriate for C programmers than for C++ programmers. C++ programmers should familiarize themselves with the preprocessor, because they might need to work with C legacy code.

F.2 The #include Preprocessor Directive

The #include preprocessor directive has been used throughout this text. The #include directive causes a copy of a specified file to be included in place of the directive. The two forms of the #include directive are

```
#include <filename>
#include "filename"
```

The difference between these is the location the preprocessor searches for the file to be included. If the file name is enclosed in angle brackets (< and >)—used for standard library header files—the preprocessor searches for the specified file in an implementation-dependent manner, normally through predesignated directories. If the file name is enclosed in quotes, the preprocessor searches first in the same directory as the file being compiled, then in the same implementation-dependent manner as for a file name enclosed in angle brackets. This method is normally used to include programmer-defined header files.

The `#include` directive is used to include standard header files such as `<iostream>` and `<iomanip>`. The `#include` directive is also used with programs consisting of several source files that are to be compiled together. A header file containing declarations and definitions common to the separate program files is often created and included in the file. Examples of such declarations and definitions are classes, structures, unions, enumerations and function prototypes, constants and stream objects (e.g., `cin`).

F.3 The `#define` Preprocessor Directive: Symbolic Constants

The `#define` preprocessor directive creates symbolic constants—constants represented as symbols—and macros—operations defined as symbols. The `#define` preprocessor directive format is

> `#define` *identifier replacement-text*

When this line appears in a file, all subsequent occurrences (except those inside a string) of *identifier* in that file will be replaced by *replacement-text* before the program is compiled. For example,

> `#define PI 3.14159`

replaces all subsequent occurrences of the symbolic constant `PI` with the numeric constant `3.14159`. Symbolic constants enable the programmer to create a name for a constant and use the name throughout the program. Later, if the constant needs to be modified throughout the program, it can be modified once in the `#define` preprocessor directive—and when the program is recompiled, all occurrences of the constant in the program will be modified. [*Note:* Everything to the right of the symbolic constant name replaces the symbolic constant. For example, `#define PI = 3.14159` causes the preprocessor to replace every occurrence of `PI` with `= 3.14159`. Such replacement is the cause of many subtle logic and syntax errors.] Redefining a symbolic constant with a new value without first undefining it is also an error. Note that `const` variables in C++ are preferred over symbolic constants. Constant variables have a specific data type and are visible by name to a debugger. Once a symbolic constant is replaced with its replacement text, only the replacement text is visible to a debugger. A disadvantage of `const` variables is that they might require a memory location of their data type size—symbolic constants do not require any additional memory.

Common Programming Error F.2

Using symbolic constants in a file other than the file in which the symbolic constants are defined is a compilation error (unless they are #included from a header file).

Good Programming Practice F.1

Using meaningful names for symbolic constants helps make programs more self-documenting.

F.4 The #define Preprocessor Directive: Macros

[*Note:* This section is included for the benefit of C++ programmers who will need to work with C legacy code. In C++, macros can often be replaced by templates and inline functions.] A macro is an operation defined in a #define preprocessor directive. As with symbolic constants, the macro-identifier is replaced with the replacement-text before the program is compiled. Macros may be defined with or without arguments. A macro without arguments is processed like a symbolic constant. In a macro with arguments, the arguments are substituted in the replacement-text, then the macro is expanded—i.e., the replacement text replaces the macro-identifier and argument list in the program. [*Note:* There is no data type checking for macro arguments. A macro is used simply for text substitution.]

Consider the following macro definition with one argument for the area of a circle:

```
#define CIRCLE_AREA( x ) ( PI * ( x ) * ( x ) )
```

Wherever CIRCLE_AREA(y) appears in the file, the value of y is substituted for x in the replacement text, the symbolic constant PI is replaced by its value (defined previously) and the macro is expanded in the program. For example, the statement

```
area = CIRCLE_AREA( 4 );
```

is expanded to

```
area = ( 3.14159 * ( 4 ) * ( 4 ) );
```

Because the expression consists only of constants, at compile time the value of the expression can be evaluated, and the result is assigned to area at runtime. The parentheses around each x in the replacement text and around the entire expression force the proper order of evaluation when the macro argument is an expression. For example, the statement

```
area = CIRCLE_AREA( c + 2 );
```

is expanded to

```
area = ( 3.14159 * ( c + 2 ) * ( c + 2 ) );
```

which evaluates correctly, because the parentheses force the proper order of evaluation. If the parentheses are omitted, the macro expansion is

```
area = 3.14159 * c + 2 * c + 2;
```

which evaluates incorrectly as

```
area = ( 3.14159 * c ) + ( 2 * c ) + 2;
```

because of the rules of operator precedence.

 Common Programming Error F.3

Forgetting to enclose macro arguments in parentheses in the replacement text is an error.

Macro CIRCLE_AREA could be defined as a function. Function circleArea, as in

```
double circleArea( double x ) { return 3.14159 * x * x; }
```

performs the same calculation as CIRCLE_AREA, but the overhead of a function call is associated with function circleArea. The advantages of CIRCLE_AREA are that macros insert code directly in the program—avoiding function overhead—and the program remains readable because CIRCLE_AREA is defined separately and named meaningfully. A disadvantage is that its argument is evaluated twice. Also, every time a macro appears in a program, the macro is expanded. If the macro is large, this produces an increase in program size. Thus, there is a trade-off between execution speed and program size (if disk space is low). Note that inline functions (see Chapter 3) are preferred to obtain the performance of macros and the software engineering benefits of functions.

Performance Tip F.1

Macros can sometimes be used to replace a function call with inline code prior to execution time. This eliminates the overhead of a function call. Inline functions are preferable to macros because they offer the type-checking services of functions.

The following is a macro definition with two arguments for the area of a rectangle:

```
#define RECTANGLE_AREA( x, y ) ( ( x ) * ( y ) )
```

Wherever RECTANGLE_AREA(a, b) appears in the program, the values of a and b are substituted in the macro replacement text, and the macro is expanded in place of the macro name. For example, the statement

```
rectArea = RECTANGLE_AREA( a + 4, b + 7 );
```

is expanded to

```
rectArea = ( ( a + 4 ) * ( b + 7 ) );
```

The value of the expression is evaluated and assigned to variable rectArea.

The replacement text for a macro or symbolic constant is normally any text on the line after the identifier in the #define directive. If the replacement text for a macro or symbolic constant is longer than the remainder of the line, a backslash (\) must be placed at the end of each line of the macro (except the last line), indicating that the replacement text continues on the next line.

Symbolic constants and macros can be discarded using the #undef preprocessor directive. Directive #undef "undefines" a symbolic constant or macro name. The scope of a symbolic constant or macro is from its definition until it is either undefined with #undef or the end of the file is reached. Once undefined, a name can be redefined with #define.

Note that expressions with side effects (e.g., variable values are modified) should not be passed to a macro, because macro arguments may be evaluated more than once.

Common Programming Error F.4

Macros often end up replacing a name that wasn't intended to be a use of the macro but just happened to be spelled the same. This can lead to exceptionally mysterious compilation and syntax errors.

F.5 Conditional Compilation

Conditional compilation enables the programmer to control the execution of preprocessor directives and the compilation of program code. Each of the conditional preprocessor directives evaluates a constant integer expression that will determine whether the code will be compiled. Cast expressions, `sizeof` expressions and enumeration constants cannot be evaluated in preprocessor directives because these are all determined by the compiler and preprocessing happens before compilation.

The conditional preprocessor construct is much like the `if` selection structure. Consider the following preprocessor code:

```
#ifndef NULL
    #define NULL 0
#endif
```

These directives determine if the symbolic constant `NULL` is already defined. The expression `#ifndef NULL` includes the code up to `#endif` if `NULL` is not defined, and skips the code if `NULL` is defined. Every `#if` construct ends with `#endif`. Directives `#ifdef` and `#ifndef` are shorthand for `#if defined( `*name*` )` and `#if !defined( `*name*` )`. A multiple-part conditional preprocessor construct may be tested using the `#elif` (the equivalent of `else if` in an `if` structure) and the `#else` (the equivalent of `else` in an `if` structure) directives.

During program development, programmers often find it helpful to "comment out" large portions of code to prevent it from being compiled. If the code contains C-style comments, `/*` and `*/` cannot be used to accomplish this task, because the first `*/` encountered would terminate the comment. Instead, the programmer can use the following preprocessor construct:

```
#if 0
    code prevented from compiling
#endif
```

To enable the code to be compiled, simply replace the value 0 in the preceding construct with the value 1.

Conditional compilation is commonly used as a debugging aid. Output statements are often used to print variable values and to confirm the flow of control. These output statements can be enclosed in conditional preprocessor directives so that the statements are compiled only until the debugging process is completed. For example,

```
#ifdef DEBUG
    cerr << "Variable x = " << x << endl;
#endif
```

causes the `cerr` statement to be compiled in the program if the symbolic constant `DEBUG` has been defined before directive `#ifdef DEBUG`. This symbolic constant is normally set by a command-line compiler or by settings in the IDE (e.g., Visual Studio .NET) and not by an explicit `#define` definition. When debugging is completed, the `#define` directive is removed from the source file, and the output statements inserted for debugging purposes are ignored during compilation. In larger programs, it might be desirable to define several different symbolic constants that control the conditional compilation in separate sections of the source file.

Common Programming Error F.5

Inserting conditionally compiled output statements for debugging purposes in locations where C++ currently expects a single statement can lead to syntax errors and logic errors. In this case, the conditionally compiled statement should be enclosed in a compound statement. Thus, when the program is compiled with debugging statements, the flow of control of the program is not altered.

F.6   The #error and #pragma Preprocessor Directives

The #error directive

```
#error tokens
```

prints an implementation-dependent message including the *tokens* specified in the directive. The tokens are sequences of characters separated by spaces. For example,

```
#error 1 - Out of range error
```

contains six tokens. In one popular C++ compiler, for example, when a #error directive is processed, the tokens in the directive are displayed as an error message, preprocessing stops and the program does not compile.

The #pragma directive

```
#pragma tokens
```

causes an implementation-defined action. A pragma not recognized by the implementation is ignored. A particular C++ compiler, for example, might recognize pragmas that enable the programmer to take advantage of that compiler's specific capabilities. For more information on #error and #pragma, see the documentation for your C++ implementation.

F.7   The # and ## Operators

The # and ## preprocessor operators are available in C++ and ANSI/ISO C. The # operator causes a replacement-text token to be converted to a string surrounded by quotes. Consider the following macro definition:

```
#define HELLO( x ) cout << "Hello, " #x << endl;
```

When HELLO(John) appears in a program file, it is expanded to

```
cout << "Hello, " "John" << endl;
```

The string "John" replaces #x in the replacement text. Strings separated by white space are concatenated during preprocessing, so the above statement is equivalent to

```
cout << "Hello, John" << endl;
```

Note that the # operator must be used in a macro with arguments, because the operand of # refers to an argument of the macro.

The ## operator concatenates two tokens. Consider the following macro definition:

```
#define TOKENCONCAT( x, y )  x ## y
```

When TOKENCONCAT appears in the program, its arguments are concatenated and used to replace the macro. For example, TOKENCONCAT(O, K) is replaced by OK in the program. The ## operator must have two operands.

F.8 Predefined Symbolic Constants

There are six predefined symbolic constants (Fig. F.1). The identifiers for each of these begin and (and, except for __cplusplus, end) with *two* underscores. These identifiers and the defined preprocessor operator (Section F.5) cannot be used in #define or #undef directives.

F.9 Assertions

The assert macro—defined in the <cassert> header file—tests the value of an expression. If the value of the expression is 0 (false), then assert prints an error message and calls function abort (of the general utilities library—<cstdlib>) to terminate program execution. This is a useful debugging tool for testing whether a variable has a correct value. For example, suppose variable x should never be larger than 10 in a program. An assertion may be used to test the value of x and print an error message if the value of x is incorrect. The statement would be

```
assert( x <= 10 );
```

If x is greater than 10 when the preceding statement is encountered in a program, an error message containing the line number and file name is printed, and the program terminates. The programmer may then concentrate on this area of the code to find the error. If the symbolic constant NDEBUG is defined, subsequent assertions will be ignored. Thus, when assertions are no longer needed (i.e., when debugging is complete), we insert the line

```
#define NDEBUG
```

Symbolic constant	Description
__LINE__	The line number of the current source code line (an integer constant).
__FILE__	The presumed name of the source file (a string).
__DATE__	The date the source file is compiled (a string of the form "Mmm dd yyyy" such as "Aug 19 2002").
__STDC__	Indicates whether the program conforms to the ANSI/ISO C standard. Contains value 1 if there is full conformance and is undefined otherwise.
__TIME__	The time the source file is compiled (a string literal of the form "hh:mm:ss").
__cplusplus	Contains the value 199711L (the date the ISO C++ standard was approved) if the file is being compiled by a C++ compiler, undefined otherwise. Allows a file to be set up to be compiled as either C or C++.

Fig. F.1 | The predefined symbolic constants.

in the program file rather than deleting each assertion manually. As with the DEBUG symbolic constant, NDEBUG is often set by compiler command-line options or through a setting in the IDE.

Most C++ compilers now include exception handling. C++ programmers prefer using exceptions rather than assertions. But assertions are still valuable for C++ programmers who work with C legacy code.

Summary

- All preprocessor directives begin with # and are processed before the program is compiled.
- Only white-space characters may appear before a preprocessor directive on a line.
- The `#include` directive includes a copy of the specified file. If the file name is enclosed in quotes, the preprocessor begins searching in the same directory as the file being compiled for the file to be included. If the file name is enclosed in angle brackets (< and >), the search is performed in an implementation-defined manner.
- The `#define` preprocessor directive is used to create symbolic constants and macros.
- A symbolic constant is a name for a constant.
- A macro is an operation defined in a `#define` preprocessor directive. Macros may be defined with or without arguments.
- The replacement text for a macro or symbolic constant is any text remaining on the line after the identifier (and, if any, the macro argument list) in the `#define` directive. If the replacement text for a macro or symbolic constant is too long to fit on one line, a backslash (\) is placed at the end of the line, indicating that the replacement text continues on the next line.
- Symbolic constants and macros can be discarded using the `#undef` preprocessor directive. Directive `#undef` "undefines" the symbolic constant or macro name.
- The scope of a symbolic constant or macro is from its definition until it is either undefined with `#undef` or the end of the file is reached.
- Conditional compilation enables the programmer to control the execution of preprocessor directives and the compilation of program code.
- The conditional preprocessor directives evaluate constant integer expressions. Cast expressions, `sizeof` expressions and enumeration constants cannot be evaluated in preprocessor directives.
- Every `#if` construct ends with `#endif`.
- Directives `#ifdef` and `#ifndef` are provided as shorthand for `#if defined(`name`)` and `#if !defined(`name`)`.
- A multiple-part conditional preprocessor construct is tested with directives `#elif` and `#else`.
- The `#error` directive prints an implementation-dependent message that includes the tokens specified in the directive and terminates preprocessing and compiling.
- The `#pragma` directive causes an implementation-defined action. If the pragma is not recognized by the implementation, the pragma is ignored.
- The # operator causes the following replacement text token to be converted to a string surrounded by quotes. The # operator must be used in a macro with arguments, because the operand of # must be an argument of the macro.
- The ## operator concatenates two tokens. The ## operator must have two operands.

- There are six predefined symbolic constants. Constant `__LINE__` is the line number of the current source code line (an integer). Constant `__FILE__` is the presumed name of the file (a string). Constant `__DATE__` is the date the source file is compiled (a string). Constant `__TIME__` is the time the source file is compiled (a string). Note that each of the predefined symbolic constants begins (and, with the exception of `__cplusplus`, ends) with two underscores.

- The `assert` macro—defined in the `<cassert>` header file—tests the value of an expression. If the value of the expression is 0 (false), then `assert` prints an error message and calls function `abort` to terminate program execution.

Terminology

\ (backslash) continuation character	`__FILE__`
abort	header file
argument	`#if`
assert	`#ifdef`
`<cassert>`	`#ifndef`
concatenation preprocessor operator `##`	`#include "filename"`
conditional compilation	`#include <filename>`
conditional execution of preprocessor	`__LINE__`
convert-to-string preprocessor directive	macro
`__cplusplus`	macro with arguments
`<cstdio>`	operator `#`
`<cstdlib>`	`#pragma`
`__DATE__`	predefined symbolic constants
debugger	preprocessing directive
`#define`	preprocessor
directives	replacement text
`#elif`	scope of a symbolic constant or macro
`#else`	standard library header files
`#endif`	symbolic constant
`#error`	`__TIME__`
expand a macro	`#undef`

Self-Review Exercises

F.1 Fill in the blanks in each of the following:

a) Every preprocessor directive must begin with _____.

b) The conditional compilation construct may be extended to test for multiple cases by using the _____ and the _____ directives.

c) The _____ directive creates macros and symbolic constants.

d) Only _____ characters may appear before a preprocessor directive on a line.

e) The _____ directive discards symbolic constant and macro names.

f) The _____ and _____ directives are provided as shorthand notation for `#if defined(`*name*`)` and `#if !defined(`*name*`)`.

g) _____ enables the programmer to control the execution of preprocessor directives and the compilation of program code.

h) The _____ macro prints a message and terminates program execution if the value of the expression the macro evaluates is 0.

i) The _____ directive inserts a file in another file.

j) The _____ operator concatenates its two arguments.

k) The _____ operator converts its operand to a string.

l) The character _____ indicates that the replacement text for a symbolic constant or macro continues on the next line.

F.2 Write a program to print the values of the predefined symbolic constants __LINE__, __FILE__, __DATE__ and __TIME__ listed in Fig. F.1.

F.3 Write a preprocessor directive to accomplish each of the following:

a) Define symbolic constant YES to have the value 1.

b) Define symbolic constant NO to have the value 0.

c) Include the header file common.h. The header is found in the same directory as the file being compiled.

d) If symbolic constant TRUE is defined, undefine it, and redefine it as 1. Do not use #ifdef.

e) If symbolic constant TRUE is defined, undefine it, and redefine it as 1. Use the #ifdef preprocessor directive.

f) If symbolic constant ACTIVE is not equal to 0, define symbolic constant INACTIVE as 0. Otherwise, define INACTIVE as 1.

g) Define macro CUBE_VOLUME that computes the volume of a cube (takes one argument).

Answers to Self-Review Exercises

F.1 a) #. b) #elif, #else. c) #define. d) white space. e) #undef. f) #ifdef, #ifndef. g) Conditional compilation. h) assert. i) #include. j) ##. k) #. l) \.

F.2 (See below.)

```
 1   // exF_02.cpp
 2   // Self-Review Exercise F.2 solution.
 3   #include <iostream>
 4
 5   using std::cout;
 6   using std::endl;
 7
 8   int main()
 9   {
10      cout << "__LINE__ = " << __LINE__ << endl
11           << "__FILE__ = " << __FILE__ << endl
12           << "__DATE__ = " << __DATE__ << endl
13           << "__TIME__ = " << __TIME__ << endl
14           << "__cplusplus = " << __cplusplus << endl;
15
16      return 0;
17
18   } // end main
```

```
__LINE__ = 9
__FILE__ = c:\cpp4e\ch19\ex19_02.CPP
__DATE__ = Jul 17 2002
__TIME__ = 09:55:58
__cplusplus = 199711L
```

   a) `#define YES 1`
   b) `#define NO 0`
   c) `#include "common.h"`
   d) `#if defined(TRUE)`
         `#undef TRUE`
         `#define TRUE 1`
     `#endif`
   e) `#ifdef TRUE`
         `#undef TRUE`
         `#define TRUE 1`
     `#endif`
   f) `#if ACTIVE`
         `#define INACTIVE 0`
     `#else`
         `#define INACTIVE 1`
     `#endif`
   g) `#define CUBE_VOLUME( x )  ( ( x ) * ( x ) * ( x ) )`

Exercises

F.4   Write a program that defines a macro with one argument to compute the volume of a sphere. The program should compute the volume for spheres of radii from 1 to 10 and print the results in tabular format. The formula for the volume of a sphere is

$$(4.0 / 3) * \pi * r^3$$

where π is 3.14159.

F.5   Write a program that produces the following output:

```
The sum of x and y is 13
```

The program should define macro SUM with two arguments, x and y, and use SUM to produce the output.

F.6   Write a program that uses macro MINIMUM2 to determine the smaller of two numeric values. Input the values from the keyboard.

F.7   Write a program that uses macro MINIMUM3 to determine the smallest of three numeric values. Macro MINIMUM3 should use macro MINIMUM2 defined in Exercise F.6 to determine the smallest number. Input the values from the keyboard.

F.8 Write a program that uses macro PRINT to print a string value.

F.9 Write a program that uses macro PRINTARRAY to print an array of integers. The macro should receive the array and the number of elements in the array as arguments.

F.10 Write a program that uses macro SUMARRAY to sum the values in a numeric array. The macro should receive the array and the number of elements in the array as arguments.

F.11 Rewrite the solutions to Exercise F.4 to Exercise F.10 as inline functions.

F.12 For each of the following macros, identify the possible problems (if any) when the preprocessor expands the macros:

a) `#define SQR( x ) x * x`
b) `#define SQR( x ) ( x * x )`
c) `#define SQR( x ) ( x ) * ( x )`
d) `#define SQR( x ) ( ( x ) * ( x ) )`

ATM Case Study Code

G.1 ATM Case Study Implementation

This appendix contains the complete working implementation of the ATM system that we designed in the "Software Engineering Case Study" sections found at the ends of Chapters 1–7, 9 and 13 . The implementation comprises 877 lines of C++ code. We consider the classes in the order in which we identified them in Section 3.11:

- ATM
- Screen
- Keypad
- CashDispenser
- DepositSlot
- Account
- BankDatabase
- Transaction
- BalanceInquiry
- Withdrawal
- Deposit

We apply the guidelines discussed in Section 9.12 and Section 13.10 to code these classes based on how we modeled them in the UML class diagrams of Fig. 13.28 and Fig. 13.29. To develop the definitions of classes' member functions, we refer to the activity diagrams presented in Section 5.11 and the communication and sequence diagrams presented in Section 7.12. Note that our ATM design does not specify all the program logic and may not specify all the attributes and operations required to complete the ATM implementation. This is a normal part of the object-oriented design process. As we implement the system, we complete the program logic and add attributes and behaviors as necessary to construct the ATM system specified by the requirements document in Section 2.8.

We conclude the discussion by presenting a C++ program (`ATMCaseStudy.cpp`) that starts the ATM and puts the other classes in the system in use. Recall that we are developing a first version of the ATM system that runs on a personal computer and uses the computer's keyboard and monitor to approximate the ATM's keypad and screen. We also only simulate the actions of the ATM's cash dispenser and deposit slot. We attempt to implement the system, however, so that real hardware versions of these devices could be integrated without significant changes in the code.

G.2 Class ATM

Class `ATM` (Figs. G.1–G.2) represents the ATM as a whole. Figure G.1 contains the `ATM` class definition, enclosed in `#ifndef`, `#define` and `#endif` preprocessor directives to ensure that this definition only gets included once in a program. We discuss lines 6–11 shortly.

```
1   // ATM.h
2   // ATM class definition. Represents an automated teller machine.
3   #ifndef ATM_H
4   #define ATM_H
5
6   #include "Screen.h" // Screen class definition
7   #include "Keypad.h" // Keypad class definition
8   #include "CashDispenser.h" // CashDispenser class definition
9   #include "DepositSlot.h" // DepositSlot class definition
10  #include "BankDatabase.h" // BankDatabase class definition
11  class Transaction; // forward declaration of class Transaction
12
13  class ATM
14  {
15  public:
16     ATM(); // constructor initializes data members
17     void run(); // start the ATM
18  private:
19     bool userAuthenticated; // whether user is authenticated
20     int currentAccountNumber; // current user's account number
21     Screen screen; // ATM's screen
22     Keypad keypad; // ATM's keypad
23     CashDispenser cashDispenser; // ATM's cash dispenser
24     DepositSlot depositSlot; // ATM's deposit slot
25     BankDatabase bankDatabase; // account information database
26
27     // private utility functions
28     void authenticateUser(); // attempts to authenticate user
29     void performTransactions(); // performs transactions
30     int displayMainMenu() const; // displays main menu
31
32     // return object of specified Transaction derived class
33     Transaction *createTransaction( int );
34  }; // end class ATM
35
36  #endif // ATM_H
```

Fig. G.1 | Definition of class ATM, which represents the ATM.

Lines 16–17 contain the function prototypes for the class's public member functions. The class diagram of Fig. 13.29 does not list any operations for class ATM, but we now declare a public member function run (line 17) in class ATM that allows an external client of the class (i.e., ATMCaseStudy.cpp) to tell the ATM to run. We also include a function prototype for a default constructor (line 16), which we discuss shortly.

Lines 19–25 of Fig. G.1 implement the class's attributes as private data members. We determine all but one of these attributes from the UML class diagrams of Fig. 13.28 and Fig. 13.29. Note that we implement the UML Boolean attribute userAuthenticated in Fig. 13.29 as a bool data member in C++ (line 19). Line 20 declares a data member not found in our UML design—an int data member currentAccountNumber that keeps track of the account number of the current authenticated user. We will soon see how the class uses this data member.

Lines 21–24 create objects to represent the parts of the ATM. Recall from the class diagram of Fig. 13.28 that class ATM has composition relationships with classes Screen, Keypad, CashDispenser and DepositSlot, so class ATM is responsible for their creation. Line 25 creates a BankDatabase, with which the ATM interacts to access and manipulate bank account information. [*Note:* If this were a real ATM system, the ATM class would receive a reference to an existing database object created by the bank. However, in this implementation we are only simulating the bank's database, so class ATM creates the BankDatabase object with which it interacts.] Note that lines 6–10 #include the class definitions of Screen, Keypad, CashDispenser, DepositSlot and BankDatabase so that the ATM can store objects of these classes.

Lines 28–30 and 33 contain function prototypes for private utility functions that the class uses to perform its tasks. We will see how these functions serve the class shortly. Note that member function createTransaction (line 33) returns a Transaction pointer. To include the class name Transaction in this file, we must at least include a forward declaration of class Transaction (line 11). Recall that a forward declaration tells the compiler that a class exists, but that the class is defined elsewhere. A forward declaration is sufficient here, as we are using Transaction only as a return type—if we were creating an actual Transaction object, we would need to #include the full Transaction header file.

ATM Class Member-Function Definitions

Figure G.2 contains the member-function definitions for class ATM. Lines 3–7 #include the header files required by the implementation file ATM.cpp. Note that including the ATM header file allows the compiler to ensure that the class's member functions are defined correctly. This also allows the member functions to use the class's data members.

Line 10 declares an enum named MenuOption that contains constants corresponding to the four options in the ATM's main menu (i.e., balance inquiry, withdrawal, deposit and

```
1   // ATM.cpp
2   // Member-function definitions for class ATM.
3   #include "ATM.h" // ATM class definition
4   #include "Transaction.h" // Transaction class definition
5   #include "BalanceInquiry.h" // BalanceInquiry class definition
6   #include "Withdrawal.h" // Withdrawal class definition
7   #include "Deposit.h" // Deposit class definition
```

Fig. G.2 | ATM class member-function definitions. (Part 1 of 4.)

```
8
9     // enumeration constants represent main menu options
10    enum MenuOption { BALANCE_INQUIRY = 1, WITHDRAWAL, DEPOSIT, EXIT };
11
12    // ATM default constructor initializes data members
13    ATM::ATM()
14       : userAuthenticated ( false ), // user is not authenticated to start
15         currentAccountNumber( 0 ) // no current account number to start
16    {
17       // empty body
18    } // end ATM default constructor
19
20    // start ATM
21    void ATM::run()
22    {
23       // welcome and authenticate user; perform transactions
24       while ( true )
25       {
26          // loop while user is not yet authenticated
27          while ( !userAuthenticated )
28          {
29             screen.displayMessageLine( "\nWelcome!" );
30             authenticateUser(); // authenticate user
31          } // end while
32
33          performTransactions(); // user is now authenticated
34          userAuthenticated = false; // reset before next ATM session
35          currentAccountNumber = 0; // reset before next ATM session
36          screen.displayMessageLine( "\nThank you! Goodbye!" );
37       } // end while
38    } // end function run
39
40    // attempt to authenticate user against database
41    void ATM::authenticateUser()
42    {
43       screen.displayMessage( "\nPlease enter your account number: " );
44       int accountNumber = keypad.getInput(); // input account number
45       screen.displayMessage( "\nEnter your PIN: " ); // prompt for PIN
46       int pin = keypad.getInput(); // input PIN
47
48       // set userAuthenticated to bool value returned by database
49       userAuthenticated =
50          bankDatabase.authenticateUser( accountNumber, pin );
51
52       // check whether authentication succeeded
53       if ( userAuthenticated )
54       {
55          currentAccountNumber = accountNumber; // save user's account #
56       } // end if
57       else
58          screen.displayMessageLine(
59             "Invalid account number or PIN. Please try again." );
60    } // end function authenticateUser
```

Fig. G.2 | ATM class member-function definitions. (Part 2 of 4.)

```
61
62   // display the main menu and perform transactions
63   void ATM::performTransactions()
64   {
65      // local pointer to store transaction currently being processed
66      Transaction *currentTransactionPtr;
67
68      bool userExited = false; // user has not chosen to exit
69
70      // loop while user has not chosen option to exit system
71      while ( !userExited )
72      {
73         // show main menu and get user selection
74         int mainMenuSelection = displayMainMenu();
75
76         // decide how to proceed based on user's menu selection
77         switch ( mainMenuSelection )
78         {
79            // user chose to perform one of three transaction types
80            case BALANCE_INQUIRY:
81            case WITHDRAWAL:
82            case DEPOSIT:
83               // initialize as new object of chosen type
84               currentTransactionPtr =
85                  createTransaction( mainMenuSelection );
86
87               currentTransactionPtr->execute(); // execute transaction
88
89               // free the space for the dynamically allocated Transaction
90               delete currentTransactionPtr;
91
92               break;
93            case EXIT: // user chose to terminate session
94               screen.displayMessageLine( "\nExiting the system..." );
95               userExited = true; // this ATM session should end
96               break;
97            default: // user did not enter an integer from 1-4
98               screen.displayMessageLine(
99                  "\nYou did not enter a valid selection. Try again." );
100               break;
101         } // end switch
102      } // end while
103   } // end function performTransactions
104
105   // display the main menu and return an input selection
106   int ATM::displayMainMenu() const
107   {
108      screen.displayMessageLine( "\nMain menu:" );
109      screen.displayMessageLine( "1 - View my balance" );
110      screen.displayMessageLine( "2 - Withdraw cash" );
111      screen.displayMessageLine( "3 - Deposit funds" );
112      screen.displayMessageLine( "4 - Exit\n" );
```

Fig. G.2 | ATM class member-function definitions. (Part 3 of 4.)

```
113        screen.displayMessage( "Enter a choice: " );
114        return keypad.getInput(); // return user's selection
115   } // end function displayMainMenu
116
117   // return object of specified Transaction derived class
118   Transaction *ATM::createTransaction( int type )
119   {
120        Transaction *tempPtr; // temporary Transaction pointer
121
122        // determine which type of Transaction to create
123        switch ( type )
124        {
125           case BALANCE_INQUIRY: // create new BalanceInquiry transaction
126              tempPtr = new BalanceInquiry(
127                 currentAccountNumber, screen, bankDatabase );
128              break;
129           case WITHDRAWAL: // create new Withdrawal transaction
130              tempPtr = new Withdrawal( currentAccountNumber, screen,
131                 bankDatabase, keypad, cashDispenser );
132              break;
133           case DEPOSIT: // create new Deposit transaction
134              tempPtr = new Deposit( currentAccountNumber, screen,
135                 bankDatabase, keypad, depositSlot );
136              break;
137        } // end switch
138
139        return tempPtr; // return the newly created object
140   } // end function createTransaction
```

Fig. G.2 | ATM class member-function definitions. (Part 4 of 4.)

exit). Note that setting BALANCE_INQUIRY to 1 causes the subsequent enumeration constants to be assigned the values 2, 3 and 4, as enumeration constant values increment by 1.

Lines 13–18 define class ATM's constructor, which initializes the class's data members. When an ATM object is first created, no user is authenticated, so line 14 uses a member initializer to set userAuthenticated to false. Likewise, line 15 initializes currentAccountNumber to 0 because there is no current user yet.

ATM member function run (lines 21–38) uses an infinite loop (lines 24–37) to repeatedly welcome a user, attempt to authenticate the user and, if authentication succeeds, allow the user to perform transactions. After an authenticated user performs the desired transactions and chooses to exit, the ATM resets itself, displays a goodbye message to the user and restarts the process. We use an infinite loop here to simulate the fact that an ATM appears to run continuously until the bank turns it off (an action beyond the user's control). An ATM user has the option to exit the system, but does not have the ability to turn off the ATM completely.

Inside member function run's infinite loop, lines 27–31 cause the ATM to repeatedly welcome and attempt to authenticate the user as long as the user has not been authenticated (i.e., !userAuthenticated is true). Line 29 invokes member function displayMessageLine of the ATM's screen to display a welcome message. Like Screen member function displayMessage designed in the case study, member function displayMessageLine (declared in line 13 of Fig. G.3 and defined in lines 20–23 of Fig. G.4) displays a message to the user, but this member function also outputs a newline after displaying the message. We have added this member function during implementation to give class Screen's clients more control over the placement of displayed messages. Line 30 of Fig. G.2 invokes class ATM's private utility function authenticateUser (lines 41–60) to attempt to authenticate the user.

We refer to the requirements document to determine the steps necessary to authenticate the user before allowing transactions to occur. Line 43 of member function authenticateUser invokes member function displayMessage of the ATM's screen to prompt the user to enter an account number. Line 44 invokes member function getInput of the ATM's keypad to obtain the user's input, then stores the integer value entered by the user in a local variable accountNumber. Member function authenticateUser next prompts the user to enter a PIN (line 45), and stores the PIN input by the user in a local variable pin (line 46). Next, lines 49–50 attempt to authenticate the user by passing the accountNumber and pin entered by the user to the bankDatabase's authenticateUser member function. Class ATM sets its userAuthenticated data member to the bool value returned by this function—userAuthenticated becomes true if authentication succeeds (i.e., accountNumber and pin match those of an existing Account in bankDatabase) and remains false otherwise. If userAuthenticated is true, line 55 saves the account number entered by the user (i.e., accountNumber) in the ATM data member currentAccountNumber. The other member functions of class ATM use this variable whenever an ATM session requires access to the user's account number. If userAuthenticated is false, lines 58–59 use the screen's displayMessageLine member function to indicate that an invalid account number and/or PIN was entered and the user must try again. Note that we set currentAccountNumber only after authenticating the user's account number and the associated PIN—if the database could not authenticate the user, currentAccountNumber remains 0.

After member function run attempts to authenticate the user (line 30), if userAuthenticated is still false, the while loop in lines 27–31 executes again. If userAuthenticated is now true, the loop terminates and control continues with line 33, which calls class ATM's utility function performTransactions.

Member function performTransactions (lines 63–103) carries out an ATM session for an authenticated user. Line 66 declares a local Transaction pointer, which we aim at a BalanceInquiry, Withdrawal or Deposit object representing the ATM transaction currently being processed. Note that we use a Transaction pointer here to allow us to take advantage of polymorphism. Also note that we use the role name included in the class diagram of Fig. 3.20—currentTransaction—in naming this pointer. As per our pointer-naming convention, we append "Ptr" to the role name to form the variable name currentTransactionPtr. Line 68 declares another local variable—a bool called userExited that keeps track of whether the user has chosen to exit. This variable controls a while loop (lines 71–102) that allows the user to execute an unlimited number of transactions before choosing to exit. Within this loop, line 74 displays the main menu and obtains the user's menu selection by calling an ATM utility function displayMainMenu (defined in lines 106–115). This member function displays the main menu by invoking member functions of the ATM's screen and returns a menu selection obtained from the user through the ATM's keypad. Note that this member function is const because it does not modify the contents of the object. Line 74 stores the user's selection returned by displayMainMenu in local variable mainMenuSelection.

After obtaining a main menu selection, member function `performTransactions` uses a `switch` statement (lines 77–101) to respond to the selection appropriately. If `main-MenuSelection` is equal to any of the three enumeration constants representing transaction types (i.e., if the user chose to perform a transaction), lines 84–85 call utility function `createTransaction` (defined in lines 118–140) to return a pointer to a newly instantiated object of the type that corresponds to the selected transaction. Pointer `currentTransactionPtr` is assigned the pointer returned by `createTransaction`. Line 87 then uses `currentTransactionPtr` to invoke the new object's execute member function to execute the transaction. We will discuss `Transaction` member function execute and the three `Transaction` derived classes shortly. Finally, when the `Transaction` derived class object is no longer needed, line 90 releases the memory dynamically allocated for it.

Note that we aim the `Transaction` pointer `currentTransactionPtr` at an object of one of the three `Transaction` derived classes so that we can execute transactions polymorphically. For example, if the user chooses to perform a balance inquiry, `mainMenuSelection` equals `BALANCE_INQUIRY`, leading `createTransaction` to return a pointer to a `BalanceInquiry` object. Thus, `currentTransactionPtr` points to a `BalanceInquiry`, and invoking `currentTransactionPtr->execute()` results in `BalanceInquiry`'s version of execute being called.

Member function `createTransaction` (lines 118–140) uses a `switch` statement (lines 123–137) to instantiate a new `Transaction` derived class object of the type indicated by the parameter type. Recall that member function `performTransactions` passes `mainMenuSelection` to this member function only when `mainMenuSelection` contains a value corresponding to one of the three transaction types. Therefore type equals either `BALANCE_INQUIRY`, `WITHDRAWAL` or `DEPOSIT`. Each `case` in the `switch` statement aims the temporary pointer `tempPtr` at a newly created object of the appropriate `Transaction` derived class. Note that each constructor has a unique parameter list, based on the specific data required to initialize the derived class object. A `BalanceInquiry` requires only the account number of the current user and references to the ATM's `screen` and the `bankDatabase`. In addition to these parameters, a `Withdrawal` requires references to the ATM's `keypad` and `cashDispenser`, and a `Deposit` requires references to the ATM's `keypad` and `depositSlot`. Note that, as you will soon see, the `BalanceInquiry`, `Withdrawal` and `Deposit` constructors each specify reference parameters to receive the objects representing the required parts of the ATM. Thus, when member function `createTransaction` passes objects in the ATM (e.g., `screen` and `keypad`) to the initializer for each newly created `Transaction` derived class object, the new object actually receives *references* to the ATM's composite objects. We discuss the transaction classes in more detail in Section G.9–Section G.12.

After executing a transaction (line 87 in `performTransactions`), `userExited` remains `false` and the `while` loop in lines 71–102 repeats, returning the user to the main menu. However, if a user does not perform a transaction and instead selects the main menu option to exit, line 95 sets `userExited` to `true`, causing the condition of the `while` loop (`!userExited`) to become `false`. This `while` is the final statement of member function `performTransactions`, so control returns to the calling function run. If the user enters an invalid main menu selection (i.e., not an integer from 1–4), lines 98–99 display an appropriate error message, `userExited` remains `false` and the user returns to the main menu to try again.

When `performTransactions` returns control to member function run, the user has chosen to exit the system, so lines 34–35 reset the ATM's data members `userAuthenticated` and `currentAccountNumber` to prepare for the next ATM user. Line 36 displays a goodbye message before the ATM starts over and welcomes the next user.

G.3 Class Screen

Class Screen (Figs. G.3–G.4) represents the screen of the ATM and encapsulates all aspects of displaying output to the user. Class Screen approximates a real ATM's screen with a computer monitor and outputs text messages using cout and the stream insertion operator (<<). In this case study, we designed class Screen to have one operation—displayMessage. For greater flexibility in displaying messages to the Screen, we now declare three Screen member functions—displayMessage, displayMessageLine and displayDollarAmount. The prototypes for these member functions appear in lines 12–14 of Fig. G.3.

Screen Class Member-Function Definitions
Figure G.4 contains the member-function definitions for class Screen. Line 11 #includes the Screen class definition. Member function displayMessage (lines 14–17) takes a string as an argument and prints it to the console using cout and the stream insertion operator (<<). The cursor stays on the same line, making this member function appropriate for displaying prompts to the user. Member function displayMessageLine (lines 20–23) also prints a string, but outputs a newline to move the cursor to the next line. Finally, member function displayDollarAmount (lines 26–29) outputs a properly formatted dollar amount (e.g., $123.45). Line 28 uses stream manipulators fixed and setprecision to output a value formatted with two decimal places. See Chapter 15, Stream Input/Output, for more information about formatting output.

```
1   // Screen.h
2   // Screen class definition. Represents the screen of the ATM.
3   #ifndef SCREEN_H
4   #define SCREEN_H
5
6   #include <string>
7   using std::string;
8
9   class Screen
10  {
11  public:
12     void displayMessage( string ) const; // output a message
13     void displayMessageLine( string ) const; // output message with newline
14     void displayDollarAmount( double ) const; // output a dollar amount
15  }; // end class Screen
16
17  #endif // SCREEN_H
```

Fig. G.3 | Screen class definition.

```
1   // Screen.cpp
2   // Member-function definitions for class Screen.
3   #include <iostream>
4   using std::cout;
5   using std::endl;
6   using std::fixed;
7
```

Fig. G.4 | Screen class member-function definitions. (Part I of 2.)

```
8   #include <iomanip>
9   using std::setprecision;
10
11  #include "Screen.h" // Screen class definition
12
13  // output a message without a newline
14  void Screen::displayMessage( string message ) const
15  {
16     cout << message;
17  } // end function displayMessage
18
19  // output a message with a newline
20  void Screen::displayMessageLine( string message ) const
21  {
22     cout << message << endl;
23  } // end function displayMessageLine
24
25  // output a dollar amount
26  void Screen::displayDollarAmount( double amount ) const
27  {
28     cout << fixed << setprecision( 2 ) << "$" << amount;
29  } // end function displayDollarAmount
```

Fig. G.4 | Screen class member-function definitions. (Part 2 of 2.)

G.4 Class Keypad

Class Keypad (Figs. G.5–G.6) represents the keypad of the ATM and is responsible for receiving all user input. Recall that we are simulating this hardware, so we use the computer's keyboard to approximate the keypad. A computer keyboard contains many keys not found on the ATM's keypad. However, we assume that the user presses only the keys on the computer keyboard that also appear on the keypad—the keys numbered 0–9 and the *Enter* key. Line 9 of Fig. G.5 contains the function prototype for class Keypad's one member function getInput. This member function is declared const because it does not change the object.

```
1   // Keypad.h
2   // Keypad class definition. Represents the keypad of the ATM.
3   #ifndef KEYPAD_H
4   #define KEYPAD_H
5
6   class Keypad
7   {
8   public:
9      int getInput() const; // return an integer value entered by user
10  }; // end class Keypad
11
12  #endif // KEYPAD_H
```

Fig. G.5 | Keypad class definition.

Keypad Class Member-Function Definition

In the Keypad implementation file (Fig. G.6), member function getInput (defined in lines 9–14) uses the standard input stream cin and the stream extraction operator (>>) to obtain input from the user. Line 11 declares a local variable to store the user's input. Line 12 reads input into local variable input, then line 13 returns this value. Recall that getInput obtains all the input used by the ATM. Keypad's getInput member function simply returns the integer input by the user. If a client of class Keypad requires input that satisfies some particular criteria (i.e., a number corresponding to a valid menu option), the client must perform the appropriate error checking. [*Note:* Using the standard input stream cin and the stream extraction operator (>>) allows noninteger input to be read from the user. Because the real ATM's keypad permits only integer input, however, we assume that the user enters an integer and do not attempt to fix problems caused by noninteger input.]

G.5 Class `CashDispenser`

Class CashDispenser (Figs. G.7–G.8) represents the cash dispenser of the ATM. The class definition (Fig. G.7) contains the function prototype for a default constructor (line 9). Class CashDispenser declares two additional public member functions—dispenseCash (line 12) and isSufficientCashAvailable (line 15). The class trusts that a client (i.e., Withdrawal) calls dispenseCash only after establishing that sufficient cash is available by calling isSufficientCashAvailable. Thus, dispenseCash simply simulates dispensing the requested amount without checking whether sufficient cash is available. Line 17 declares private constant INITIAL_COUNT, which indicates the initial count of bills in the cash dispenser when the ATM starts (i.e., 500). Line 18 implements attribute count (modeled in Fig. 13.29), which keeps track of the number of bills remaining in the CashDispenser at any time.

CashDispenser Class Member-Function Definitions

Figure G.8 contains the definitions of class CashDispenser's member functions. The constructor (lines 6–9) sets count to the initial count (i.e., 500). Member function dispenseCash (lines 13–17) simulates cash dispensing. If our system were hooked up to a real

```cpp
1   // Keypad.cpp
2   // Member-function definition for class Keypad (the ATM's keypad).
3   #include <iostream>
4   using std::cin;
5
6   #include "Keypad.h" // Keypad class definition
7
8   // return an integer value entered by user
9   int Keypad::getInput() const
10  {
11     int input; // variable to store the input
12     cin >> input; // we assume that user enters an integer
13     return input; // return the value entered by user
14  } // end function getInput
```

Fig. G.6 | Keypad class member-function definition.

```
1   // CashDispenser.h
2   // CashDispenser class definition. Represents the ATM's cash dispenser.
3   #ifndef CASH_DISPENSER_H
4   #define CASH_DISPENSER_H
5
6   class CashDispenser
7   {
8   public:
9      CashDispenser(); // constructor initializes bill count to 500
10
11     // simulates dispensing of specified amount of cash
12     void dispenseCash( int );
13
14     // indicates whether cash dispenser can dispense desired amount
15     bool isSufficientCashAvailable( int ) const;
16  private:
17     const static int INITIAL_COUNT = 500;
18     int count; // number of $20 bills remaining
19  }; // end class CashDispenser
20
21  #endif // CASH_DISPENSER_H
```

Fig. G.7 | CashDispenser class definition.

```
1   // CashDispenser.cpp
2   // Member-function definitions for class CashDispenser.
3   #include "CashDispenser.h" // CashDispenser class definition
4
5   // CashDispenser default constructor initializes count to default
6   CashDispenser::CashDispenser()
7   {
8      count = INITIAL_COUNT; // set count attribute to default
9   } // end CashDispenser default constructor
10
11  // simulates dispensing of specified amount of cash; assumes enough cash
12  // is available (previous call to isSufficientCashAvailable returned true)
13  void CashDispenser::dispenseCash( int amount )
14  {
15     int billsRequired = amount / 20; // number of $20 bills required
16     count -= billsRequired; // update the count of bills
17  } // end function dispenseCash
18
19  // indicates whether cash dispenser can dispense desired amount
20  bool CashDispenser::isSufficientCashAvailable( int amount ) const
21  {
22     int billsRequired = amount / 20; // number of $20 bills required
23
24     if ( count >= billsRequired )
25        return true; // enough bills are available
26     else
27        return false; // not enough bills are available
28  } // end function isSufficientCashAvailable
```

Fig. G.8 | CashDispenser class member-function definitions.

hardware cash dispenser, this member function would interact with the hardware device to physically dispense cash. Our simulated version of the member function simply decreases the count of bills remaining by the number required to dispense the specified amount (line 16). Note that line 15 calculates the number of $20 bills required to dispense the specified amount. The ATM allows the user to choose only withdrawal amounts that are multiples of $20, so we divide amount by 20 to obtain the number of billsRequired. Also note that it is the responsibility of the client of the class (i.e., Withdrawal) to inform the user that cash has been dispensed—CashDispenser cannot interact directly with Screen.

Member function isSufficientCashAvailable (lines 20–28) has a parameter amount that specifies the amount of cash in question. Lines 24–27 return true if the Cash-Dispenser's count is greater than or equal to billsRequired (i.e., enough bills are available) and false otherwise (i.e., not enough bills). For example, if a user wishes to withdraw $80 (i.e., billsRequired is 4), but only three bills remain (i.e., count is 3), the member function returns false.

G.6 Class DepositSlot

Class DepositSlot (Figs. G.9–G.10) represents the deposit slot of the ATM. Like the version of class CashDispenser presented here, this version of class DepositSlot merely simulates the functionality of a real hardware deposit slot. DepositSlot has no data members and only one member function—isEnvelopeReceived (declared in line 9 of Fig. G.9 and defined in lines 7–10 of Fig. G.10)—that indicates whether a deposit envelope was received.

```
1   // DepositSlot.h
2   // DepositSlot class definition. Represents the ATM's deposit slot.
3   #ifndef DEPOSIT_SLOT_H
4   #define DEPOSIT_SLOT_H
5
6   class DepositSlot
7   {
8   public:
9      bool isEnvelopeReceived() const; // tells whether envelope was received
10  }; // end class DepositSlot
11
12  #endif // DEPOSIT_SLOT_H
```

Fig. G.9 | DepositSlot class definition.

```
1   // DepositSlot.cpp
2   // Member-function definition for class DepositSlot.
3   #include "DepositSlot.h" // DepositSlot class definiton
4
5   // indicates whether envelope was received (always returns true,
6   // because this is only a software simulation of a real deposit slot)
7   bool DepositSlot::isEnvelopeReceived() const
8   {
9      return true; // deposit envelope was received
10  } // end function isEnvelopeReceived
```

Fig. G.10 | DepositSlot class member-function definition.

Recall from the requirements document that the ATM allows the user up to two minutes to insert an envelope. The current version of member function isEnvelopeReceived simply returns true immediately (line 9 of Fig. G.10), because this is only a software simulation, and we assume that the user has inserted an envelope within the required time frame. If an actual hardware deposit slot were connected to our system, member function isEnvelopeReceived might be implemented to wait for a maximum of two minutes to receive a signal from the hardware deposit slot indicating that the user has indeed inserted a deposit envelope. If isEnvelopeReceived were to receive such a signal within two minutes, the member function would return true. If two minutes elapsed and the member function still had not received a signal, then the member function would return false.

G.7 Class Account

Class Account (Figs. G.11–G.12) represents a bank account. Lines 9–15 in the class definition (Fig. G.11) contain function prototypes for the class's constructor and six member functions, which we discuss shortly. Each Account has four attributes (modeled in Fig. 13.29)—accountNumber, pin, availableBalance and totalBalance. Lines 17–20 implement these attributes as private data members. Data member availableBalance represents the amount of funds available for withdrawal. Data member totalBalance represents the amount of funds available, plus the amount of deposited funds still pending confirmation or clearance.

Account Class Member-Function Definitions

Figure G.12 presents the definitions of class Account's member functions. The class's constructor (lines 6–14) takes an account number, the PIN established for the account, the

```
1   // Account.h
2   // Account class definition. Represents a bank account.
3   #ifndef ACCOUNT_H
4   #define ACCOUNT_H
5
6   class Account
7   {
8   public:
9      Account( int, int, double, double ); // constructor sets attributes
10     bool validatePIN( int ) const; // is user-specified PIN correct?
11     double getAvailableBalance() const; // returns available balance
12     double getTotalBalance() const; // returns total balance
13     void credit( double ); // adds an amount to the Account balance
14     void debit( double ); // subtracts an amount from the Account balance
15     int getAccountNumber() const; // returns account number
16  private:
17     int accountNumber; // account number
18     int pin; // PIN for authentication
19     double availableBalance; // funds available for withdrawal
20     double totalBalance; // funds available + funds waiting to clear
21  }; // end class Account
22
23  #endif // ACCOUNT_H
```

Fig. G.11 | Account class definition.

initial available balance and the initial total balance as arguments. Lines 8–11 assign these values to the class's data members using member initializers.

Member function validatePIN (lines 17–23) determines whether a user-specified PIN (i.e., parameter userPIN) matches the PIN associated with the account (i.e., data member pin). Recall that we modeled this member function's parameter userPIN in the UML class diagram of Fig. 6.37. If the two PINs match, the member function returns true (line 20); otherwise, it returns false (line 22).

Member functions getAvailableBalance (lines 26–29) and getTotalBalance (lines 32–35) are *get* functions that return the values of double data members availableBalance and totalBalance, respectively.

```cpp
1   // Account.cpp
2   // Member-function definitions for class Account.
3   #include "Account.h" // Account class definition
4
5   // Account constructor initializes attributes
6   Account::Account( int theAccountNumber, int thePIN,
7      double theAvailableBalance, double theTotalBalance )
8      : accountNumber( theAccountNumber ),
9        pin( thePIN ),
10       availableBalance( theAvailableBalance ),
11       totalBalance( theTotalBalance )
12  {
13     // empty body
14  } // end Account constructor
15
16  // determines whether a user-specified PIN matches PIN in Account
17  bool Account::validatePIN( int userPIN ) const
18  {
19     if ( userPIN == pin )
20        return true;
21     else
22        return false;
23  } // end function validatePIN
24
25  // returns available balance
26  double Account::getAvailableBalance() const
27  {
28     return availableBalance;
29  } // end function getAvailableBalance
30
31  // returns the total balance
32  double Account::getTotalBalance() const
33  {
34     return totalBalance;
35  } // end function getTotalBalance
36
37  // credits an amount to the account
38  void Account::credit( double amount )
39  {
40     totalBalance += amount; // add to total balance
41  } // end function credit
```

Fig. G.12 | Account class member-function definitions. (Part 1 of 2.)

```
42
43    // debits an amount from the account
44    void Account::debit( double amount )
45    {
46       availableBalance -= amount; // subtract from available balance
47       totalBalance -= amount; // subtract from total balance
48    } // end function debit
49
50    // returns account number
51    int Account::getAccountNumber() const
52    {
53       return accountNumber;
54    } // end function getAccountNumber
```

Fig. G.12 | Account class member-function definitions. (Part 2 of 2.)

Member function credit (lines 38–41) adds an amount of money (i.e., parameter amount) to an Account as part of a deposit transaction. Note that this member function adds the amount only to data member totalBalance (line 40). The money credited to an account during a deposit does not become available immediately, so we modify only the total balance. We assume that the bank updates the available balance appropriately at a later time. Our implementation of class Account includes only member functions required for carrying out ATM transactions. Therefore, we omit the member functions that some other bank system would invoke to add to data member availableBalance (to confirm a deposit) or subtract from data member totalBalance (to reject a deposit).

Member function debit (lines 44–48) subtracts an amount of money (i.e., parameter amount) from an Account as part of a withdrawal transaction. This member function subtracts the amount from both data member availableBalance (line 46) and data member totalBalance (line 47), because a withdrawal affects both measures of an account balance.

Member function getAccountNumber (lines 51–54) provides access to an Account's accountNumber. We include this member function in our implementation so that a client of the class (i.e., BankDatabase) can identify a particular Account. For example, BankDatabase contains many Account objects, and it can invoke this member function on each of its Account objects to locate the one with a specific account number.

G.8 Class BankDatabase

Class BankDatabase (Figs. G.13–G.14) models the bank's database with which the ATM interacts to access and modify a user's account information. The class definition (Fig. G.13) declares function prototypes for the class's constructor and several member functions. We discuss these momentarily. The class definition also declares the BankDatabase's data members. We determine one data member for class BankDatabase based on its composition relationship with class Account. Recall from Fig. 13.28 that a BankDatabase is composed of zero or more objects of class Account. Line 24 of Fig. G.13 implements data member accounts—a vector of Account objects—to implement this composition relationship. Lines 6–7 allow us to use vector in this file. Line 27 contains the function prototype for a private utility function getAccount that allows the member functions of the class to obtain a pointer to a specific Account in the accounts vector.

```
1   // BankDatabase.h
2   // BankDatabase class definition. Represents the bank's database.
3   #ifndef BANK_DATABASE_H
4   #define BANK_DATABASE_H
5
6   #include <vector> // class uses vector to store Account objects
7   using std::vector;
8
9   #include "Account.h" // Account class definition
10
11  class BankDatabase
12  {
13  public:
14     BankDatabase(); // constructor initializes accounts
15
16     // determine whether account number and PIN match those of an Account
17     bool authenticateUser( int, int ); // returns true if Account authentic
18
19     double getAvailableBalance( int ); // get an available balance
20     double getTotalBalance( int ); // get an Account's total balance
21     void credit( int, double ); // add amount to Account balance
22     void debit( int, double ); // subtract amount from Account balance
23  private:
24     vector< Account > accounts; // vector of the bank's Accounts
25
26     // private utility function
27     Account * getAccount( int ); // get pointer to Account object
28  }; // end class BankDatabase
29
30  #endif // BANK_DATABASE_H
```

Fig. G.13 | BankDatabase class definition.

BankDatabase *Class Member-Function Definitions*

Figure G.14 contains the member-function definitions for class BankDatabase. We implement the class with a default constructor (lines 6–15) that adds Account objects to data member accounts. For the sake of testing the system, we create two new Account objects with test data (lines 9–10), then add them to the end of the vector (lines 13–14). Note

```
1   // BankDatabase.cpp
2   // Member-function definitions for class BankDatabase.
3   #include "BankDatabase.h" // BankDatabase class definition
4
5   // BankDatabase default constructor initializes accounts
6   BankDatabase::BankDatabase()
7   {
8      // create two Account objects for testing
9      Account account1( 12345, 54321, 1000.0, 1200.0 );
10     Account account2( 98765, 56789, 200.0, 200.0 );
11
```

Fig. G.14 | BankDatabase class member-function definitions. (Part 1 of 3.)

```
12     // add the Account objects to the vector accounts
13     accounts.push_back( account1 ); // add account1 to end of vector
14     accounts.push_back( account2 ); // add account2 to end of vector
15  } // end BankDatabase default constructor
16
17  // retrieve Account object containing specified account number
18  Account * BankDatabase::getAccount( int accountNumber )
19  {
20     // loop through accounts searching for matching account number
21     for ( size_t i = 0; i < accounts.size(); i++ )
22     {
23        // return current account if match found
24        if ( accounts[ i ].getAccountNumber() == accountNumber )
25           return &accounts[ i ];
26     } // end for
27
28     return NULL; // if no matching account was found, return NULL
29  } // end function getAccount
30
31  // determine whether user-specified account number and PIN match
32  // those of an account in the database
33  bool BankDatabase::authenticateUser( int userAccountNumber,
34     int userPIN )
35  {
36     // attempt to retrieve the account with the account number
37     Account * const userAccountPtr = getAccount( userAccountNumber );
38
39     // if account exists, return result of Account function validatePIN
40     if ( userAccountPtr != NULL )
41        return userAccountPtr->validatePIN( userPIN );
42     else
43        return false; // account number not found, so return false
44  } // end function authenticateUser
45
46  // return available balance of Account with specified account number
47  double BankDatabase::getAvailableBalance( int userAccountNumber )
48  {
49     Account * const userAccountPtr = getAccount( userAccountNumber );
50     return userAccountPtr->getAvailableBalance();
51  } // end function getAvailableBalance
52
53  // return total balance of Account with specified account number
54  double BankDatabase::getTotalBalance( int userAccountNumber )
55  {
56     Account * const userAccountPtr = getAccount( userAccountNumber );
57     return userAccountPtr->getTotalBalance();
58  } // end function getTotalBalance
59
60  // credit an amount to Account with specified account number
61  void BankDatabase::credit( int userAccountNumber, double amount )
62  {
```

Fig. G.14 | BankDatabase class member-function definitions. (Part 2 of 3.)

```
63        Account * const userAccountPtr = getAccount( userAccountNumber );
64        userAccountPtr->credit( amount );
65    } // end function credit
66
67    // debit an amount from of Account with specified account number
68    void BankDatabase::debit( int userAccountNumber, double amount )
69    {
70        Account * const userAccountPtr = getAccount( userAccountNumber );
71        userAccountPtr->debit( amount );
72    } // end function debit
```

Fig. G.14 | BankDatabase class member-function definitions. (Part 3 of 3.)

that the Account constructor has four parameters—the account number, the PIN assigned to the account, the initial available balance and the initial total balance.

Recall that class BankDatabase serves as an intermediary between class ATM and the actual Account objects that contain users' account information. Thus, the member functions of class BankDatabase do nothing more than invoke the corresponding member functions of the Account object belonging to the current ATM user.

We include private utility function getAccount (lines 18–29) to allow the Bank-Database to obtain a pointer to a particular Account within vector accounts. To locate the user's Account, the BankDatabase compares the value returned by member function getAccountNumber for each element of accounts to a specified account number until it finds a match. Lines 21–26 traverse the accounts vector. If the account number of the current Account (i.e., accounts[i]) equals the value of parameter accountNumber, the member function immediately returns the address of the current Account (i.e., a pointer to the current Account). If no account has the given account number, then line 28 returns NULL. Note that this member function must return a pointer, as opposed to a reference, because there is the possibility that the return value could be NULL—a reference cannot be NULL, but a pointer can.

Note that vector function size (invoked in the loop-continuation condition in line 21) returns the number of elements in a vector as a value of type size_t (which is usually unsigned int). As a result, we declare the control variable i to be of type size_t, too. On some compilers, declaring i as an int would cause the compiler to issue a warning message, because the loop-continuation condition would compare a signed value (i.e., an int) and an unsigned value (i.e., a value of type size_t).

Member function authenticateUser (lines 33–44) proves or disproves the identity of an ATM user. This member function takes a user-specified account number and user-specified PIN as arguments and indicates whether they match the account number and PIN of an Account in the database. Line 37 calls utility function getAccount, which returns either a pointer to an Account with userAccountNumber as its account number or NULL to indicate that userAccountNumber is invalid. We declare userAccountPtr to be a const pointer because, once the member function aims this pointer at the user's Account, the pointer should not change. If getAccount returns a pointer to an Account object, line 41 returns the bool value returned by that object's validatePIN member function. Note that Bank-Database's authenticateUser member function does not perform the PIN comparison itself—rather, it forwards userPIN to the Account object's validatePIN member function to do so. The value returned by Account member function validatePIN indicates whether the user-specified PIN matches the PIN of the user's Account, so member function authenticateUser simply returns this value to the client of the class (i.e., ATM).

BankDatabase trusts the ATM to invoke member function authenticateUser and receive a return value of true before allowing the user to perform transactions. BankDatabase also trusts that each Transaction object created by the ATM contains the valid account number of the current authenticated user and that this is the account number passed to the remaining BankDatabase member functions as argument userAccountNumber. Member functions getAvailableBalance (lines 47–51), getTotalBalance (lines 54–58), credit (lines 61–65) and debit (lines 68–72) therefore simply retrieve a pointer to the user's Account object with utility function getAccount, then use this pointer to invoke the appropriate Account member function on the user's Account object. We know that the calls to getAccount within these member functions will never return NULL, because userAccountNumber must refer to an existing Account. Note that getAvailableBalance and getTotalBalance return the values returned by the corresponding Account member functions. Also note that credit and debit simply redirect parameter amount to the Account member functions they invoke.

G.9 Class Transaction

Class Transaction (Figs. G.15–G.16) is an abstract base class that represents the notion of an ATM transaction. It contains the common features of derived classes BalanceInquiry, Withdrawal and Deposit. Figure G.15 expands upon the Transaction header file first developed in Section 13.10. Lines 13, 17–19 and 22 contain function prototypes for the class's constructor and four member functions, which we discuss shortly. Line 15 defines a virtual destructor with an empty body—this makes all derived-class destructors virtual (even those defined implicitly by the compiler) and ensures that dynamically allocated derived-class objects get destroyed properly when they are deleted via a base-class pointer. Lines 24–26 declare the class's private data members. Recall from the class diagram of Fig. 13.29 that class Transaction contains an attribute accountNumber (implemented in line 24) that indicates the account involved in the Transaction. We derive data members screen (line 25) and bankDatabase (line 26) from class Transaction's associations modeled in Fig. 13.28—all transactions require access to the ATM's screen and the bank's database, so we include references to a Screen and a BankDatabase as data members of class Transaction. As you will soon see, Transaction's constructor initializes these references. Note that the forward declarations in lines 6–7 signify that the header file contains references to objects of classes Screen and BankDatabase, but that the definitions of these classes lie outside the header file.

```
1   // Transaction.h
2   // Transaction abstract base class definition.
3   #ifndef TRANSACTION_H
4   #define TRANSACTION_H
5
6   class Screen; // forward declaration of class Screen
7   class BankDatabase; // forward declaration of class BankDatabase
8
```

Fig. G.15 | Transaction class definition. (Part 1 of 2.)

```
9   class Transaction
10  {
11  public:
12     // constructor initializes common features of all Transactions
13     Transaction( int, Screen &, BankDatabase & );
14
15     virtual ~Transaction() { } // virtual destructor with empty body
16
17     int getAccountNumber() const; // return account number
18     Screen &getScreen() const; // return reference to screen
19     BankDatabase &getBankDatabase() const; // return reference to database
20
21     // pure virtual function to perform the transaction
22     virtual void execute() = 0; // overridden in derived classes
23  private:
24     int accountNumber; // indicates account involved
25     Screen &screen; // reference to the screen of the ATM
26     BankDatabase &bankDatabase; // reference to the account info database
27  }; // end class Transaction
28
29  #endif // TRANSACTION_H
```

Fig. G.15 | Transaction class definition. (Part 2 of 2.)

```
1   // Transaction.cpp
2   // Member-function definitions for class Transaction.
3   #include "Transaction.h" // Transaction class definition
4   #include "Screen.h" // Screen class definition
5   #include "BankDatabase.h" // BankDatabase class definition
6
7   // constructor initializes common features of all Transactions
8   Transaction::Transaction( int userAccountNumber, Screen &atmScreen,
9      BankDatabase &atmBankDatabase )
10     : accountNumber( userAccountNumber ),
11       screen( atmScreen ),
12       bankDatabase( atmBankDatabase )
13  {
14     // empty body
15  } // end Transaction constructor
16
17  // return account number
18  int Transaction::getAccountNumber() const
19  {
20     return accountNumber;
21  } // end function getAccountNumber
22
23  // return reference to screen
24  Screen &Transaction::getScreen() const
25  {
26     return screen;
27  } // end function getScreen
28
```

Fig. G.16 | Transaction class member-function definitions. (Part 1 of 2.)

```
29   // return reference to bank database
30   BankDatabase &Transaction::getBankDatabase() const
31   {
32      return bankDatabase;
33   } // end function getBankDatabase
```

Fig. G.16 | Transaction class member-function definitions. (Part 2 of 2.)

Class Transaction has a constructor (declared in line 13 of Fig. G.15 and defined in lines 8–15 of Fig. G.16) that takes the current user's account number and references to the ATM's screen and the bank's database as arguments. Because Transaction is an abstract class, this constructor will never be called directly to instantiate Transaction objects. Instead, the constructors of the Transaction derived classes will use base-class initializer syntax to invoke this constructor.

Class Transaction has three public *get* functions—getAccountNumber (declared in line 17 of Fig. G.15 and defined in lines 18–21 of Fig. G.16), getScreen (declared in line 18 of Fig. G.15 and defined in lines 24–27 of Fig. G.16) and getBankDatabase (declared in line 19 of Fig. G.15 and defined in lines 30–33 of Fig. G.16). Transaction derived classes inherit these member functions from Transaction and use them to gain access to class Transaction's private data members.

Class Transaction also declares a pure virtual function execute (line 22 of Fig. G.15). It does not make sense to provide an implementation for this member function, because a generic transaction cannot be executed. Thus, we declare this member function to be a pure virtual function and force each Transaction derived class to provide its own concrete implementation that executes that particular type of transaction.

G.10 Class BalanceInquiry

Class BalanceInquiry (Figs. G.17–G.18) derives from abstract base class Transaction and represents a balance-inquiry ATM transaction. BalanceInquiry does not have any data members of its own, but it inherits Transaction data members accountNumber, screen and bankDatabase, which are accessible through Transaction's public *get* functions. Note that line 6 #includes the definition of base class Transaction. The Balance-Inquiry constructor (declared in line 11 of Fig. G.17 and defined in lines 8–13 of Fig. G.18) takes arguments corresponding to the Transaction data members and simply forwards them to Transaction's constructor, using base-class initializer syntax (line 10 of Fig. G.18). Line 12 of Fig. G.17 contains the function prototype for member function execute, which is required to indicate the intention to override the base class's pure virtual function of the same name.

Class BalanceInquiry overrides Transaction's pure virtual function execute to provide a concrete implementation (lines 16–37 of Fig. G.18) that performs the steps involved in a balance inquiry. Lines 19–20 get references to the bank database and the ATM's screen by invoking member functions inherited from base class Transaction. Lines 23–24 retrieve the available balance of the account involved by invoking member function getAvailableBalance of bankDatabase. Note that line 24 uses inherited member function getAccountNumber to get the account number of the current user, which it then passes to getAvailableBalance. Lines 27–28 retrieve the total balance of

```
 1   // BalanceInquiry.h
 2   // BalanceInquiry class definition. Represents a balance inquiry.
 3   #ifndef BALANCE_INQUIRY_H
 4   #define BALANCE_INQUIRY_H
 5
 6   #include "Transaction.h" // Transaction class definition
 7
 8   class BalanceInquiry : public Transaction
 9   {
10   public:
11      BalanceInquiry( int, Screen &, BankDatabase & ); // constructor
12      virtual void execute(); // perform the transaction
13   }; // end class BalanceInquiry
14
15   #endif // BALANCE_INQUIRY_H
```

Fig. G.17 | BalanceInquiry class definition.

```
 1   // BalanceInquiry.cpp
 2   // Member-function definitions for class BalanceInquiry.
 3   #include "BalanceInquiry.h" // BalanceInquiry class definition
 4   #include "Screen.h" // Screen class definition
 5   #include "BankDatabase.h" // BankDatabase class definition
 6
 7   // BalanceInquiry constructor initializes base-class data members
 8   BalanceInquiry:: BalanceInquiry( int userAccountNumber, Screen &atmScreen,
 9      BankDatabase &atmBankDatabase )
10      : Transaction( userAccountNumber, atmScreen, atmBankDatabase )
11   {
12      // empty body
13   } // end BalanceInquiry constructor
14
15   // performs transaction; overrides Transaction's pure virtual function
16   void BalanceInquiry::execute()
17   {
18      // get references to bank database and screen
19      BankDatabase &bankDatabase = getBankDatabase();
20      Screen &screen = getScreen();
21
22      // get the available balance for the current user's Account
23      double availableBalance =
24         bankDatabase.getAvailableBalance( getAccountNumber() );
25
26      // get the total balance for the current user's Account
27      double totalBalance =
28         bankDatabase.getTotalBalance( getAccountNumber() );
29
```

Fig. G.18 | BalanceInquiry class member-function definitions. (Part 1 of 2.)

```
30        // display the balance information on the screen
31        screen.displayMessageLine( "\nBalance Information:" );
32        screen.displayMessage( " - Available balance: " );
33        screen.displayDollarAmount( availableBalance );
34        screen.displayMessage( "\n - Total balance:      " );
35        screen.displayDollarAmount( totalBalance );
36        screen.displayMessageLine( "" );
37    } // end function execute
```

Fig. G.18 | `BalanceInquiry` class member-function definitions. (Part 2 of 2.)

the current user's account. Lines 31–36 display the balance information on the ATM's screen. Recall that `displayDollarAmount` takes a `double` argument and outputs it to the screen formatted as a dollar amount. For example, if a user's `availableBalance` is 700.5, line 33 outputs $700.50. Note that line 36 inserts a blank line of output to separate the balance information from subsequent output (i.e., the main menu repeated by class `ATM` after executing the `BalanceInquiry`).

G.11 Class Withdrawal

Class `Withdrawal` (Figs. G.19–G.20) derives from `Transaction` and represents a withdrawal ATM transaction. Figure G.19 expands upon the header file for this class developed in Fig. 13.31. Class `Withdrawal` has a constructor and one member function `execute`, which we discuss shortly. Recall from the class diagram of Fig. 13.29 that class `Withdrawal` has one attribute, `amount`, which line 16 implements as an `int` data member. Figure 13.28 models

```
1   // Withdrawal.h
2   // Withdrawal class definition. Represents a withdrawal transaction.
3   #ifndef WITHDRAWAL_H
4   #define WITHDRAWAL_H
5
6   #include "Transaction.h" // Transaction class definition
7   class Keypad; // forward declaration of class Keypad
8   class CashDispenser; // forward declaration of class CashDispenser
9
10  class Withdrawal : public Transaction
11  {
12  public:
13     Withdrawal( int, Screen &, BankDatabase &, Keypad &, CashDispenser & );
14     virtual void execute(); // perform the transaction
15  private:
16     int amount; // amount to withdraw
17     Keypad &keypad; // reference to ATM's keypad
18     CashDispenser &cashDispenser; // reference to ATM's cash dispenser
19     int displayMenuOfAmounts() const; // display the withdrawal menu
20  }; // end class Withdrawal
21
22  #endif // WITHDRAWAL_H
```

Fig. G.19 | `Withdrawal` class definition.

```cpp
 1   // Withdrawal.cpp
 2   // Member-function definitions for class Withdrawal.
 3   #include "Withdrawal.h" // Withdrawal class definition
 4   #include "Screen.h" // Screen class definition
 5   #include "BankDatabase.h" // BankDatabase class definition
 6   #include "Keypad.h" // Keypad class definition
 7   #include "CashDispenser.h" // CashDispenser class definition
 8
 9   // global constant that corresponds to menu option to cancel
10   const static int CANCELED = 6;
11
12   // Withdrawal constructor initialize class's data members
13   Withdrawal::Withdrawal( int userAccountNumber, Screen &atmScreen,
14      BankDatabase &atmBankDatabase, Keypad &atmKeypad,
15      CashDispenser &atmCashDispenser )
16      : Transaction( userAccountNumber, atmScreen, atmBankDatabase ),
17        keypad( atmKeypad ), cashDispenser( atmCashDispenser )
18   {
19      // empty body
20   } // end Withdrawal constructor
21
22   // perform transaction; overrides Transaction's pure virtual function
23   void Withdrawal::execute()
24   {
25      bool cashDispensed = false; // cash was not dispensed yet
26      bool transactionCanceled = false; // transaction was not canceled yet
27
28      // get references to bank database and screen
29      BankDatabase &bankDatabase = getBankDatabase();
30      Screen &screen = getScreen();
31
32      // loop until cash is dispensed or the user cancels
33      do
34      {
35         // obtain the chosen withdrawal amount from the user
36         int selection = displayMenuOfAmounts();
37
38         // check whether user chose a withdrawal amount or canceled
39         if ( selection != CANCELED )
40         {
41            amount = selection; // set amount to the selected dollar amount
42
43            // get available balance of account involved
44            double availableBalance =
45               bankDatabase.getAvailableBalance( getAccountNumber() );
46
47            // check whether the user has enough money in the account
48            if ( amount <= availableBalance )
49            {
50               // check whether the cash dispenser has enough money
51               if ( cashDispenser.isSufficientCashAvailable( amount ) )
52               {
```

Fig. G.20 | Withdrawal class member-function definitions. (Part 1 of 3.)

```
53                          // update the account involved to reflect withdrawal
54                          bankDatabase.debit( getAccountNumber(), amount );
55
56                          cashDispenser.dispenseCash( amount ); // dispense cash
57                          cashDispensed = true; // cash was dispensed
58
59                          // instruct user to take cash
60                          screen.displayMessageLine(
61                             "\nPlease take your cash from the cash dispenser." );
62                      } // end if
63                      else // cash dispenser does not have enough cash
64                          screen.displayMessageLine(
65                             "\nInsufficient cash available in the ATM."
66                             "\n\nPlease choose a smaller amount." );
67                  } // end if
68                  else // not enough money available in user's account
69                  {
70                      screen.displayMessageLine(
71                         "\nInsufficient funds in your account."
72                         "\n\nPlease choose a smaller amount." );
73                  } // end else
74              } // end if
75              else // user chose cancel menu option
76              {
77                  screen.displayMessageLine( "\nCanceling transaction..." );
78                  transactionCanceled = true; // user canceled the transaction
79              } // end else
80          } while ( !cashDispensed && !transactionCanceled ); // end do...while
81      } // end function execute
82
83      // display a menu of withdrawal amounts and the option to cancel;
84      // return the chosen amount or 0 if the user chooses to cancel
85      int Withdrawal::displayMenuOfAmounts() const
86      {
87          int userChoice = 0; // local variable to store return value
88
89          Screen &screen = getScreen(); // get screen reference
90
91          // array of amounts to correspond to menu numbers
92          int amounts[] = { 0, 20, 40, 60, 100, 200 };
93
94          // loop while no valid choice has been made
95          while ( userChoice == 0 )
96          {
97              // display the menu
98              screen.displayMessageLine( "\nWithdrawal options:" );
99              screen.displayMessageLine( "1 - $20" );
100             screen.displayMessageLine( "2 - $40" );
101             screen.displayMessageLine( "3 - $60" );
102             screen.displayMessageLine( "4 - $100" );
103             screen.displayMessageLine( "5 - $200" );
104             screen.displayMessageLine( "6 - Cancel transaction" );
105             screen.displayMessage( "\nChoose a withdrawal option (1-6): " );
```

Fig. G.20 | Withdrawal class member-function definitions. (Part 2 of 3.)

```
106
107        int input = keypad.getInput(); // get user input through keypad
108
109        // determine how to proceed based on the input value
110        switch ( input )
111        {
112           case 1: // if the user chose a withdrawal amount
113           case 2: // (i.e., chose option 1, 2, 3, 4 or 5), return the
114           case 3: // corresponding amount from amounts array
115           case 4:
116           case 5:
117              userChoice = amounts[ input ]; // save user's choice
118              break;
119           case CANCELED: // the user chose to cancel
120              userChoice = CANCELED; // save user's choice
121              break;
122           default: // the user did not enter a value from 1-6
123              screen.displayMessageLine(
124                 "\nIvalid selection. Try again." );
125        } // end switch
126     } // end while
127
128     return userChoice; // return withdrawal amount or CANCELED
129  } // end function displayMenuOfAmounts
```

Fig. G.20 | Withdrawal class member-function definitions. (Part 3 of 3.)

associations between class Withdrawal and classes Keypad and CashDispenser, for which lines 17–18 implement references keypad and cashDispenser, respectively. Line 19 is the function prototype of a private utility function that we soon discuss.

Withdrawal *Class Member-Function Definitions*
Figure G.20 contains the member-function definitions for class Withdrawal. Line 3 #includes the class's definition, and lines 4–7 #include the definitions of the other classes used in Withdrawal's member functions. Line 11 declares a global constant corresponding to the cancel option on the withdrawal menu. We will soon discuss how the class uses this constant.

Class Withdrawal's constructor (defined in lines 13–20 of Fig. G.20) has five parameters. It uses a base-class initializer in line 16 to pass parameters userAccountNumber, atmScreen and atmBankDatabase to base class Transaction's constructor to set the data members that Withdrawal inherits from Transaction. The constructor also takes references atmKeypad and atmCashDispenser as parameters and assigns them to reference data members keypad and cashDispenser using member initializers (line 17).

Class Withdrawal overrides Transaction's pure virtual function execute with a concrete implementation (lines 23–81) that performs the steps involved in a withdrawal. Line 25 declares and initializes a local bool variable cashDispensed. This variable indicates whether cash has been dispensed (i.e., whether the transaction has completed successfully) and is initially false. Line 26 declares and initializes to false a bool variable transactionCanceled that indicates whether the transaction has been canceled by the user. Lines 29–30 get references to the bank database and the ATM's screen by invoking member functions inherited from base class Transaction.

Lines 33–80 contain a do…while statement that executes its body until cash is dispensed (i.e., until cashDispensed becomes true) or until the user chooses to cancel (i.e., until transactionCanceled becomes true). We use this loop to continuously return the user to the start of the transaction if an error occurs (i.e., the requested withdrawal amount is greater than the user's available balance or greater than the amount of cash in the cash dispenser). Line 36 displays a menu of withdrawal amounts and obtains a user selection by calling private utility function displayMenuOfAmounts (defined in lines 85–129). This member function displays the menu of amounts and returns either an int withdrawal amount or the int constant CANCELED to indicate that the user has chosen to cancel the transaction.

Member function displayMenuOfAmounts (lines 85–129) first declares local variable userChoice (initially 0) to store the value that the member function will return (line 87). Line 89 gets a reference to the screen by calling member function getScreen inherited from base class Transaction. Line 92 declares an integer array of withdrawal amounts that correspond to the amounts displayed in the withdrawal menu. We ignore the first element in the array (index 0) because the menu has no option 0. The while statement at lines 95–126 repeats until userChoice takes on a value other than 0. We will see shortly that this occurs when the user makes a valid selection from the menu. Lines 98–105 display the withdrawal menu on the screen and prompt the user to enter a choice. Line 107 obtains integer input through the keypad. The switch statement at lines 110–125 determines how to proceed based on the user's input. If the user selects a number between 1 and 5, line 117 sets userChoice to the value of the element in amounts at index input. For example, if the user enters 3 to withdraw $60, line 117 sets userChoice to the value of amounts[3] (i.e., 60). Line 118 terminates the switch. Variable userChoice no longer equals 0, so the while at lines 95–126 terminates and line 128 returns userChoice. If the user selects the cancel menu option, lines 120–121 execute, setting userChoice to CANCELED and causing the member function to return this value. If the user does not enter a valid menu selection, lines 123–124 display an error message and the user is returned to the withdrawal menu.

The if statement at line 39 in member function execute determines whether the user has selected a withdrawal amount or chosen to cancel. If the user cancels, lines 77–78 execute to display an appropriate message to the user and set transactionCanceled to true. This causes the loop-continuation test in line 80 to fail and control to return to the calling member function (i.e., ATM member function performTransactions). If the user has chosen a withdrawal amount, line 41 assigns local variable selection to data member amount. Lines 44–45 retrieve the available balance of the current user's Account and store it in a local double variable availableBalance. Next, the if statement at line 48 determines whether the selected amount is less than or equal to the user's available balance. If it is not, lines 70–72 display an appropriate error message. Control then continues to the end of the do…while, and the loop repeats because both cashDispensed and transactionCanceled are still false. If the user's balance is high enough, the if statement at line 51 determines whether the cash dispenser has enough money to satisfy the withdrawal request by invoking the cashDispenser's isSufficientCashAvailable member function. If this member function returns false, lines 64–66 display an appropriate error message and the do…while repeats. If sufficient cash is available, then the requirements for the withdrawal are satisfied, and line 54 debits amount from the user's account in the database. Lines 56–57 then instruct the cash dispenser to dispense the cash to the user and set cashDispensed to true. Finally, lines 60–61 display a message to the user that cash has been dispensed. Because cashDispensed is now true, control continues after the do...while. No additional statements appear below the loop, so the member function returns control to class ATM.

Notice that, in the function calls in lines 64–66 and lines 70–72, we divide the argument to Screen member function displayMessageLine into two string literals, each placed on a separate line in the program. We do so because each argument is too long to fit on a single line. C++ concatenates (i.e., combines) string literals adjacent to each other, even if they are on separate lines. For example, if you write "Happy " "Birthday" in a program, C++ will view these two adjacent string literals as the single string literal "Happy Birthday". As a result, when lines 64–66 execute, displayMessageLine receives a single string as a parameter, even though the argument in the function call appears as two string literals.

G.12 Class Deposit

Class Deposit (Figs. G.21–G.22) derives from Transaction and represents a deposit ATM transaction. Figure G.21 contains the Deposit class definition. Like derived classes BalanceInquiry and Withdrawal, Deposit declares a constructor (line 13) and member function execute (line 14)—we discuss these momentarily. Recall from the class diagram of Fig. 13.29 that class Deposit has one attribute amount, which line 16 implements as an int data member. Lines 17–18 create reference data members keypad and depositSlot that implement the associations between class Deposit and classes Keypad and DepositSlot modeled in Fig. 13.28. Line 19 contains the function prototype for a private utility function promptForDepositAmount that we will discuss shortly.

```cpp
1   // Deposit.h
2   // Deposit class definition. Represents a deposit transaction.
3   #ifndef DEPOSIT_H
4   #define DEPOSIT_H
5
6   #include "Transaction.h" // Transaction class definition
7   class Keypad; // forward declaration of class Keypad
8   class DepositSlot; // forward declaration of class DepositSlot
9
10  class Deposit : public Transaction
11  {
12  public:
13     Deposit( int, Screen &, BankDatabase &, Keypad &, DepositSlot & );
14     virtual void execute(); // perform the transaction
15  private:
16     double amount; // amount to deposit
17     Keypad &keypad; // reference to ATM's keypad
18     DepositSlot &depositSlot; // reference to ATM's deposit slot
19     double promptForDepositAmount() const; // get deposit amount from user
20  }; // end class Deposit
21
22  #endif // DEPOSIT_H
```

Fig. G.21 | Deposit class definition.

***Deposit* Class Member-Function Definitions**
Figure G.22 presents the implementation file for class Deposit. Line 3 #includes the De-posit class definition, and lines 4–7 #include the class definitions of the other classes used in Deposit's member functions. Line 9 declares a constant CANCELED that corresponds to the value a user enters to cancel a deposit. We will soon discuss how the class uses this constant.

Like class Withdrawal, class Deposit contains a constructor (lines 12–19) that passes three parameters to base class Transaction's constructor using a base-class initializer (line 15). The constructor also has parameters atmKeypad and atmDepositSlot, which it assigns to its corresponding data members (line 16).

Member function execute (lines 22–62) overrides pure virtual function execute in base class Transaction with a concrete implementation that performs the steps required in a deposit transaction. Lines 24–25 get references to the database and the screen. Line 27 prompts the user to enter a deposit amount by invoking private utility function

```
1   // Deposit.cpp
2   // Member-function definitions for class Deposit.
3   #include "Deposit.h" // Deposit class definition
4   #include "Screen.h" // Screen class definition
5   #include "BankDatabase.h" // BankDatabase class definition
6   #include "Keypad.h" // Keypad class definition
7   #include "DepositSlot.h" // DepositSlot class definition
8
9   const static int CANCELED = 0; // constant representing cancel option
10
11  // Deposit constructor initializes class's data members
12  Deposit::Deposit( int userAccountNumber, Screen &atmScreen,
13     BankDatabase &atmBankDatabase, Keypad &atmKeypad,
14     DepositSlot &atmDepositSlot )
15     : Transaction( userAccountNumber, atmScreen, atmBankDatabase ),
16       keypad( atmKeypad ), depositSlot( atmDepositSlot )
17  {
18     // empty body
19  } // end Deposit constructor
20
21  // performs transaction; overrides Transaction's pure virtual function
22  void Deposit::execute()
23  {
24     BankDatabase &bankDatabase = getBankDatabase(); // get reference
25     Screen &screen = getScreen(); // get reference
26
27     amount = promptForDepositAmount(); // get deposit amount from user
28
29     // check whether user entered a deposit amount or canceled
30     if ( amount != CANCELED )
31     {
32        // request deposit envelope containing specified amount
33        screen.displayMessage(
34           "\nPlease insert a deposit envelope containing " );
35        screen.displayDollarAmount( amount );
36        screen.displayMessageLine( " in the deposit slot." );
```

Fig. G.22 | Deposit class member-function definitions. (Part 1 of 2.)

```
37
38          // receive deposit envelope
39          bool envelopeReceived = depositSlot.isEnvelopeReceived();
40
41          // check whether deposit envelope was received
42          if ( envelopeReceived )
43          {
44              screen.displayMessageLine( "\nYour envelope has been received."
45                  "\nNOTE: The money just will not be available until we"
46                  "\nverify the amount of any enclosed cash, and any enclosed "
47                  "checks clear." );
48
49              // credit account to reflect the deposit
50              bankDatabase.credit( getAccountNumber(), amount );
51          } // end if
52          else // deposit envelope not received
53          {
54              screen.displayMessageLine( "\nYou did not insert an "
55                  "envelope, so the ATM has canceled your transaction." );
56          } // end else
57      } // end if
58      else // user canceled instead of entering amount
59      {
60          screen.displayMessageLine( "\nCanceling transaction..." );
61      } // end else
62  } // end function execute
63
64  // prompt user to enter a deposit amount in cents
65  double Deposit::promptForDepositAmount() const
66  {
67      Screen &screen = getScreen(); // get reference to screen
68
69      // display the prompt and receive input
70      screen.displayMessage( "\nPlease enter a deposit amount in "
71          "CENTS (or 0 to cancel): " );
72      int input = keypad.getInput(); // receive input of deposit amount
73
74      // check whether the user canceled or entered a valid amount
75      if ( input == CANCELED )
76          return CANCELED;
77      else
78      {
79          return static_cast< double >( input ) / 100; // return dollar amount
80      } // end else
81  } // end function promptForDepositAmount
```

Fig. G.22 | Deposit class member-function definitions. (Part 2 of 2.)

promptForDepositAmount (defined in lines 65–81) and sets data member amount to the value returned. Member function promptForDepositAmount asks the user to enter a deposit amount as an integer number of cents (because the ATM's keypad does not contain a decimal point; this is consistent with many real ATMs) and returns the double value representing the dollar amount to be deposited.

Line 67 in member function `promptForDepositAmount` gets a reference to the ATM's screen. Lines 70–71 display a message on the screen asking the user to input a deposit amount as a number of cents or "0" to cancel the transaction. Line 72 receives the user's input from the keypad. The `if` statement at lines 75–80 determines whether the user has entered a real deposit amount or chosen to cancel. If the user chooses to cancel, line 76 returns the constant `CANCELED`. Otherwise, line 79 returns the deposit amount after converting from the number of cents to a dollar amount by casting `input` to a `double`, then dividing by 100. For example, if the user enters 125 as the number of cents, line 79 returns 125.0 divided by 100, or 1.25—125 cents is $1.25.

The `if` statement at lines 30–61 in member function `execute` determines whether the user has chosen to cancel the transaction instead of entering a deposit amount. If the user cancels, line 60 displays an appropriate message, and the member function returns. If the user enters a deposit amount, lines 33–36 instruct the user to insert a deposit envelope with the correct amount. Recall that `Screen` member function `displayDollarAmount` outputs a `double` formatted as a dollar amount.

Line 39 sets a local `bool` variable to the value returned by `depositSlot`'s `isEnvelopeReceived` member function, indicating whether a deposit envelope has been received. Recall that we coded member function `isEnvelopeReceived` (lines 7–10 of Fig. G.10) to always return `true`, because we are simulating the functionality of the deposit slot and assume that the user always inserts an envelope. However, we code member function `execute` of class `Deposit` to test for the possibility that the user does not insert an envelope—good software engineering demands that programs account for all possible return values. Thus, class `Deposit` is prepared for future versions of `isEnvelopeReceived` that could return `false`. Lines 44–50 execute if the deposit slot receives an envelope. Lines 44–47 display an appropriate message to the user. Line 50 then credits the deposit amount to the user's account in the database. Lines 54–55 will execute if the deposit slot does not receive a deposit envelope. In this case, we display a message to the user stating that the ATM has canceled the transaction. The member function then returns without modifying the user's account.

G.13 Test Program ATMCaseStudy.cpp

`ATMCaseStudy.cpp` (Fig. G.23) is a simple C++ program that allows us to start, or "turn on," the ATM and test the implementation of our ATM system model. The program's `main` function (lines 6–11) does nothing more than instantiate a new `ATM` object named `atm` (line 8) and invoke its `run` member function (line 9) to start the ATM.

```
 1   // ATMCaseStudy.cpp
 2   // Driver program for the ATM case study.
 3   #include "ATM.h" // ATM class definition
 4
 5   // main function creates and runs the ATM
 6   int main()
 7   {
 8      ATM atm; // create an ATM object
 9      atm.run(); // tell the ATM to start
10      return 0;
11   } // end main
```

Fig. G.23 | `ATMCaseStudy.cpp` starts the ATM system.

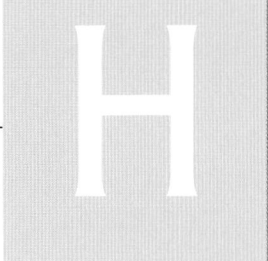

UML 2: Additional Diagram Types

H.1 Introduction

If you read the optional Software Engineering Case Study sections in Chapters 2–7, 9 and 13, you should now have a comfortable grasp of the UML diagram types that we use to model our ATM system. The case study is intended for use in first- or second-semester courses, so we limit our discussion to a concise subset of the UML. The UML 2 provides a total of 13 diagram types. The end of Section 2.8 summarizes the six diagram types that we use in the case study. This appendix lists and briefly defines the seven remaining diagram types.

H.2 Additional Diagram Types

The following are the seven diagram types that we have chosen not to use in our Software Engineering Case Study.

- Object diagrams model a "snapshot" of the system by modeling a system's objects and their relationships at a specific point in time. Each object represents an instance of a class from a class diagram, and several objects may be created from one class. For our ATM system, an object diagram could show several distinct Account objects side by side, illustrating that they are all part of the bank's account database.

- Component diagrams model the artifacts and components—resources (which include source files)—that make up the system.

- Deployment diagrams model the rsystem's runtime requirements (such as the computer or computers on which the system will reside), memory requirements, or other devices the system requires during execution.

- Package diagrams model the hierarchical structure of packages (which are groups of classes) in the system at compile time and the relationships that exist between the packages.

- Composite structure diagrams model the internal structure of a complex object at runtime. New in UML 2, they allow system designers to hierarchically decompose a complex object into smaller parts. Composite structure diagrams are beyond the scope of our case study. They are more appropriate for larger industrial applications, which exhibit complex groupings of objects at execution time.

- Interaction overview diagrams, new in UML 2, provide a summary of control flow in the system by combining elements of several types of behavioral diagrams (e.g., activity diagrams, sequence diagrams).

- Timing diagrams, also new in UML 2, model the timing constraints imposed on stage changes and interactions between objects in a system.

To learn more about these diagrams and advanced UML topics, please visit www.uml.org and the Web resources listed at the ends of Section 1.17 and Section 2.8.

C++ Internet and Web Resources

This appendix contains a list of C++ resources that are available on the Internet and the World Wide Web. These resources include FAQs (Frequently Asked Questions), tutorials, links to the ANSI/ISO C++ standard, information about popular C++ compilers and access to free compilers, demos, books, tutorials, software tools, articles, interviews, conferences, journals and magazines, online courses, newsgroups and career resources. For additional information about the American National Standards Institute (ANSI) and its activities related to C++, visit www.ansi.org.

I.I Resources

www.cplusplus.com
This site contains information about the history and development of C++ as well as tutorials, documentation, reference material, source code and forums.

www.possibility.com/Cpp/CppCodingStandard.html
The *C++ Coding Standard* site examines the C++ standard and the standardizing process. The site includes such topics as standards enforcement, formatting, portability and documentation and offers links to additional C++ Web resources.

http://www.research.att.com/~bs/bs_faq2.html
The C++ Style and Technique FAQ by Bjarne Stroustrup, the creator of the language, provides answers to common questions about C++.

help-site.com/cpp.html
Help-site.com provides links to C++ resources on the Web, including tutorials and a C++ FAQ.

www.glenmccl.com/tutor.htm
This reference site discusses topics such as object-oriented design and writing robust code. The site provides introductions to C++ language topics, including keyword `static`, data type `bool`, namespaces, the Standard Template Library and memory allocation.

www.programmersheaven.com/zone3

This site provides links to articles, tutorials, development tools, an extensive collection of free C++ libraries and source code.

www.hal9k.com/cug

The *C/C++ Users Group (CUG)* site contains C++ resources, journals, shareware and freeware.

www.devx.com

DevX is a comprehensive resource for programmers that provides the latest news, tools and techniques for various programming languages. The *C++ Zone* offers tips, discussion forums, technical help and online newsletters.

www.cprogramming.com

This site contains interactive tutorials, quizzes, articles, journals, compiler downloads, book recommendations and free source code.

www.acm.org/crossroads/xrds3-2/ovp32.html

The Association for Computing Machinery's (ACM) site offers a comprehensive listing of C++ resources, including recommended texts, journals and magazines, published standards, newsletters, FAQs and newsgroups.

www.comeaucomputing.com/resources

Comeau Computing's site links to technical discussions, FAQs (including one devoted to templates), user groups, newsgroups and an online C++ compiler.

www.exciton.cs.rice.edu/CppResources

The site provides a document that summarizes the technical aspects of C++. The site also discusses the differences between Java and C++.

www.accu.informika.ru/resources/public/terse/cpp.htm

The Association of C & C++ Users (ACCU) site contains links to C++ tutorials, articles, developer information, discussions and book reviews.

www.cuj.com

The *C/C++ User's Journal* is an online magazine that contains articles, tutorials and downloads. The site features news about C++, forums and links to information about development tools.

directory.google.com/Top/Computers/Programming/Languages/C++/Resources/Directories

Google's C++ resources directory ranks the most useful C++ sites.

www.compinfo-center.com/c++.htm

This site provides links to C++ FAQs, newsgroups and magazines.

www.apl.jhu.edu/~paulmac/c++-references.html

This site contains book reviews and recommendations for introductory, intermediate and advanced C++ programmers and links to online C++ resources, including books, magazines and tutorials.

www.cmcrossroads.com/bradapp/links/cplusplus-links.html

This site divides links into categories, including Resources and Directories, Projects and Working Groups, Libraries, Training, Tutorials, Publications and Coding Conventions.

www.codeproject.com

Articles, code snippets, user discussions, books and news about C++, C# and .NET programming are available at this site.

www.austinlinks.com/CPlusPlus

Quadralay Corporation's site links to numerous C++ resources, including Visual C++/MFC Libraries, C++ programming information, C++ career resources and a list of tutorials and other online tools for learning C++.

www.csci.csusb.edu/dick/c++std

Links to the ANSI/ISO C++ Standard and the `comp.std.c++` Usenet group are available at this site.

`www.research.att.com/~bs/homepage.html`

This is the home page for Bjarne Stroustrup, designer of the C++ programming language. This site provides a list of C++ resources, FAQs and other useful C++ information.

I.2 Tutorials

`www.cprogramming.com/tutorial.html`

This site offers a step-by-step tutorial, with sample code, that covers file I/O, recursion, binary trees, template classes and more.

`www.programmersheaven.com/zone3/cat34`

Free tutorials that are appropriate for many skill levels are available at this site.

`www.programmershelp.co.uk/c%2B%2Btutorials.php`

This site contains free online courses and a comprehensive list of C++ tutorials. This site also provides FAQs, downloads and other resources.

`www.codeproject.com/script/articles/beginners.asp`

This site lists tutorials and articles available for C++ beginners.

`www.eng.hawaii.edu/Tutor/Make`

This site provides a tutorial that describes how to create makefiles.

`www.cpp-home.com`

Free tutorials, discussions, chat rooms, articles, compilers, forums and online quizzes related to C++ are available at this site. The C++ tutorials cover such topics as ActiveX/COM, MFC and graphics.

`www.codebeach.com`

Code Beach contains source code, tutorials, books and links to major programming languages, including C++, Java, ASP, Visual Basic, XML, Python, Perl and C#.

`www.kegel.com/academy/tutorials.html`

This site provides links to tutorials on C, C++ and assembly languages.

I.3 FAQs

`www.faqs.org/faqs/by-newsgroup/comp/comp.lang.c++.html`

This site consists of links to FAQs and tutorials gathered from the `Comp.Lang.C++` newsgroup.

`www.eskimo.com/~scs/C-faq/top.html`

This C FAQ list contains topics such as pointers, memory allocation and strings.

`www.technion.ac.il/technion/tcc/usg/Ref/C_Programming.html`

This site contains C/C++ programming references, including FAQs and tutorials.

`www.faqs.org/faqs/by-newsgroup/comp/comp.compilers.html`

This site contains a list of FAQs generated in the `comp.compilers` newsgroup.

I.4 Visual C++

`msdn.microsoft.com/visualc`

Microsoft's Visual C++ page provides information about the latest release of Visual C++ .NET.

`www.freeprogrammingresources.com/visualcpp.html`

This site contains free programming resources for Visual C++ programmers, including tutorials and sample programming applications.

`www.mvps.org/vcfaq`

The *Most Valuable Professional (MVP)* site contains a Visual C++ FAQ.

`www.onesmartclick.com/programming/visual-cpp.html`

This site contains Visual C++ tutorials, online books, tips, tricks, FAQs and debugging.

I.5 Newsgroups

`ai.kaist.ac.kr/~ymkim/Program/c++.html`
This site offers tutorials, libraries, popular compilers, FAQs and newsgroups, including `comp.lang.c++`.

`www.coding-zone.co.uk/cpp/cnewsgroups.shtml`
This site includes links to several C++ newsgroups including `comp.lang.c`, `comp.lang.c++` and `comp.lang.c++.moderated`, to name a few.

I.6 Compilers and Development Tools

`msdn.microsoft.com/visualc`
The *Microsoft Visual C++* site provides product information, overviews, supplemental materials and ordering information for the Visual C++ compiler.

`lab.msdn.microsoft.com/express/visualc/`
You can download the Microsoft Visual C++ Express Beta for free from this Web site.

`msdn.microsoft.com/visualc/vctoolkit2003/`
Visit this site to download the Visual C++ Toolkit 2003

`www.borland.com/bcppbuilder`
This is a link to the *Borland C++ Builder 6*. A free command-line version is available for download.

`www.thefreecountry.com/developercity/ccompilers.shtml`
This site lists free C and C++ compilers for a variety of operating systems.

`www.faqs.org/faqs/by-newsgroup/comp/comp.compilers.html`
This site lists FAQs generated within the `comp.compilers` newsgroup.

`www.compilers.net/Dir/Free/Compilers/CCpp.htm`
Compilers.net is designed to help users locate compilers.

`developer.intel.com/software/products/compilers/cwin/index.htm`
The *Intel® C++ Compiler 8.1 for Windows* is available at this site.

`www.intel.com/software/products/compilers/clin/index.htm`
The *Intel® C++ Compiler 8.1 for Linux* is available at this site.

`www.symbian.com/developer/development/cppdev.html`
Symbian provides a C++ Developer's Pack and links to various resources, including code and development tools for C++ programmers (particularly those working with the Symbian operating system).

`www.gnu.org/software/gcc/gcc.html`
The *GNU Compiler Collection (GCC)* site includes links to download GNU compilers for C++, C, Objective C and other languages.

`www.bloodshed.net/devcpp.html`
Bloodshed Dev-C++ is a free integrated development environment for C++.

Third Party Vendors That Provide Libraries for Precise Financial Calculations

`www.roguewave.com/products/sourcepro/analysis/`
RogueWave Software's SourcePro Analysis libraries include classes for precise monetary calculations, data analysis and essential mathematical algorithms.

`www.boic.com/numorder.htm`
Base One International Corporation's Bas/1 Number class implements highly precise mathematical calculations.

I.7 Standard Template Library

Tutorials

`www.cs.brown.edu/people/jak/programming/stl-tutorial/tutorial.html`
This STL tutorial is organized by examples, philosophy, components and extending STL. You will find code examples using the STL components, useful explanations and helpful diagrams.

`www.xraylith.wisc.edu/~khan/software/stl/os_examples/examples.html`
This site is helpful for people just learning about the STL. You will find an introduction to the STL and ObjectSpace STL Tool Kit examples.

`cplus.about.com/od/stltutorial/l/blstl.htm`
This tutorial discusses all of the features of the STL.

`www.yolinux.com/TUTORIALS/LinuxTutorialC++STL.html`
This Linux-focused site includes an STL tutorial and examples.

`www.cs.rpi.edu/~musser/stl-book`
The RPI STL site includes information on how STL differs from other C++ libraries and on how to compile programs that use STL. A list of STL include files, example programs that use STL, STL Container Classes, and STL Iterator Categories are available. The site also provides an STL-compatible compiler list, FTP sites for STL source code and related materials.

References

`www.sgi.com/tech/stl`
The Silicon Graphics Standard Template Library Programmer's Guide is a useful resource for STL information. You can download STL source code from this site, and find the latest information, design documentation and links to other STL resources.

`www.byte.com/art/9510/sec12/art3.htm`
The *Byte Magazine* site has a copy of an article written by one of the creators of the Standard Template Library, Alexander Stepanov, that provides information on the use of the STL in generic programming.

ANSI/ISO C++ Standard

`www.ansi.org`
You can purchase a copy of the C++ Standard from this site.

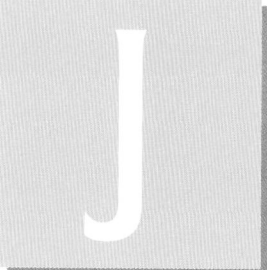

Introduction to XHTML

OBJECTIVES

In this appendix you will learn:

- To understand important components of XHTML documents.
- To use XHTML to create World Wide Web pages.
- To add images to Web pages.
- To understand how to create and use hyperlinks to navigate Web pages.
- To mark up lists of information.
- To create forms.

J.1 Introduction

In this appendix, we introduce XHTML[1]—the Extensible HyperText Markup Language for creating Web content. Unlike procedural programming languages such as C, Fortran, Cobol and Visual Basic, XHTML is a markup language that specifies the format of text that is displayed in a Web browser, such as Microsoft's Internet Explorer or Netscape's Communicator.

One key issue when using XHTML is the separation of the presentation of a document (i.e., the document's appearance when rendered by a browser) from the structure of the document's information. Throughout this appendix, we will discuss this issue in depth.

In this appendix, we build several complete Web pages featuring text, hyperlinks, images, horizontal rules and line breaks. We also discuss more substantial XHTML features, including presentation of information in tables and incorporating forms for collecting information from a Web-page visitor. By the end of this appendix, you will be familiar with the most commonly used XHTML features and will be able to create more complex Web documents. In this appendix, we do not present any C++ programming.

J.2 Editing XHTML

In this appendix, we write XHTML in its source-code form. We create XHTML documents by typing them in with a text editor (e.g., Notepad, Wordpad, vi or emacs), saving the documents with either an .html or .htm file-name extension.

---

1. XHTML has replaced the HyperText Markup Language (HTML) as the primary means of describing Web content. XHTML provides more robust, richer and more extensible features than HTML. For more on XHTML/HTML, visit www.w3.org/markup.

Good Programming Practice J.1

Assign documents file names that describe their functionality. This practice can help you identify documents faster. It also helps people who want to link to a page, by giving them an easy-to-remember name. For example, if you are writing an XHTML document that contains product information, you might want to call it products.html.

Machines running specialized software called a Web server store XHTML documents. Clients (e.g., Web browsers) request specific resources, such as XHTML documents, from the Web server. For example, typing www.deitel.com/books/downloads.htm into a Web browser's address field requests downloads.htm from the Web server running at www.deitel.com. This document is located in a directory named books.

J.3 First XHTML Example

In this appendix, we present XHTML markup and provide screen captures that show how Internet Explorer renders (i.e., displays) the XHTML. Every XHTML document we show has line numbers for the reader's convenience. These line numbers are not part of the XHTML documents.

Our first example (Fig. J.1) is an XHTML document named main.html that displays the message Welcome to XHTML! in the browser. The key line in the program is line 14, which tells the browser to display Welcome to XHTML! Now let us consider each line of the program.

```
1   <?xml version = "1.0"?>
2   <!DOCTYPE html PUBLIC "-//W3C//DTD XHTML 1.1//EN"
3     "http://www.w3.org/TR/xhtml11/DTD/xhtml11.dtd">
4
5   <!-- Fig. J.1: main.html -->
6   <!-- Our first Web page. -->
7
8   <html xmlns = "http://www.w3.org/1999/xhtml">
9      <head>
10        <title>Our first Web page</title>
11     </head>
12
13     <body>
14        <p>Welcome to XHTML!</p>
15     </body>
16  </html>
```

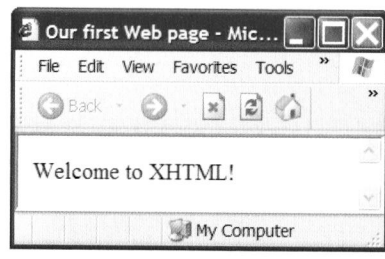

Fig. J.1 | First XHTML example.

Lines 1–3 are required in XHTML documents to conform with proper XHTML syntax. Lines 5–6 are XHTML comments. XHTML document creators insert comments to improve markup readability and to describe the content of a document. Comments also help other people read and understand an XHTML document's markup and content. Comments do not cause the browser to perform any action when the user loads the XHTML document into the Web browser to view the document. XHTML comments always start with `<!--` and end with `-->`. Each of our XHTML examples includes comments that specify the figure number and file name and provide a brief description of the example's purpose. Subsequent examples include comments in the markup, especially to highlight new features.

Good Programming Practice J.2

Place comments throughout your markup. Comments help other programmers understand the markup, assist in debugging and list useful information that you do not want the browser to render. Comments also help you understand your own markup when you revisit a document for modifications or updates in the future.

XHTML markup contains text that represents the content of a document and elements that specify a document's structure. Some important elements of an XHTML document include the `html` element, the `head` element and the `body` element. The `html` element encloses the head section (represented by the `head` element) and the body section (represented by the `body` element). The head section contains information about the XHTML document, such as the title of the document. The head section also can contain special document-formatting instructions called style sheets and client-side programs called scripts for creating dynamic Web pages. The body section contains the page's content that the browser displays when the user visits the Web page.

XHTML documents delimit an element with start and end tags. A start tag consists of the element name in angle brackets (e.g., `<html>`). An end tag consists of the element name preceded by a / in angle brackets (e.g., `</html>`). In this example, lines 8 and 16 define the start and end of the `html` element. Note that the end tag in line 16 has the same name as the start tag, but is preceded by a / inside the angle brackets. Many start tags define attributes that provide additional information about an element. Browsers can use this additional information to determine how to process the element. Each attribute has a name and a value, separated by an equal sign (=). Line 8 specifies a required attribute (`xmlns`) and value (`http://www.w3.org/1999/xhtml`) for the `html` element in an XHTML document.

Common Programming Error J.1

Not enclosing attribute values in either single or double quotes is a syntax error.

Common Programming Error J.2

Using uppercase letters in an XHTML element or attribute name is a syntax error.

An XHTML document divides the `html` element into two sections—head and body. Lines 9–11 define the Web page's head section with a `head` element. Line 10 specifies a `title` element. This is called a nested element, because it is enclosed in the `head` element's start and end tags. The head element also is a nested element, because it is enclosed in the html element's start and end tags. The `title` element describes the Web page. Titles usually appear in the title bar at the top of the browser window and also as the text identifying a page when users add the page to their list of **Favorites** or **Bookmarks,** which enable users to return to their favorite sites. Search engines (i.e., sites that allow users to search the Web) also use the `title` for cataloging purposes.

Good Programming Practice J.3

Indenting nested elements emphasizes a document's structure and promotes readability.

Common Programming Error J.3

XHTML does not permit tags to overlap—a nested element's end tag must appear in the document before the enclosing element's end tag. For example, the nested XHTML tags <head><title>hello</head></title> cause a syntax error, because the enclosing head element's ending </head> tag appears before the nested title element's ending </title> tag.

Good Programming Practice J.4

Use a consistent `title` naming convention for all pages on a site. For example, if a site is named "Bailey's Web Site," then the `title` of the main page might be "Bailey's Web Site—Links." This practice can help users better understand the Web site's structure.

Line 13 opens the document's body element. The body section of an XHTML document specifies the document's content, which may include text and tags.

Some tags, such as the paragraph tags (`<p>` and `</p>`) in line 14, mark up text for display in a browser. All text placed between the `<p>` and `</p>` tags form one paragraph. When the browser renders a paragraph, a blank line usually precedes and follows paragraph text.

This document ends with two closing tags (lines 15–16). These tags close the body and html elements, respectively. The ending `</html>` tag in an XHTML document informs the browser that the XHTML markup is complete.

To view this example in Internet Explorer, perform the following steps:

1. Copy the Appendix J examples onto your machine (these examples are available on the CD-ROM that accompanies this book).

2. Launch Internet Explorer, and select **Open...** from the **File** Menu. This displays the **Open** dialog.

3. Click the **Open** dialog's **Browse...** button to display the **Microsoft Internet Explorer** file dialog.

4. Navigate to the directory containing the Appendix J examples, and select the file `main.html`; then click **Open**.

5. Click **OK** to have Internet Explorer (or any other browser) render the document. Other examples are opened in a similar manner.

At this point, your browser window should appear similar to the sample screen capture shown in Fig. J.1.

J.4 Headers

Some text in an XHTML document might be more important than other text. For example, the text in this section is considered more important than a footnote. XHTML provides six headers, called header elements, for specifying the relative importance of information. Figure J.2 demonstrates these elements (h1 through h6).

```
1   <?xml version = "1.0"?>
2   <!DOCTYPE html PUBLIC "-//W3C//DTD XHTML 1.1//EN"
3      "http://www.w3.org/TR/xhtml11/DTD/xhtml11.dtd">
4
5   <!-- Fig. J.2: header.html -->
6   <!-- XHTML headers.          -->
7
8   <html xmlns = "http://www.w3.org/1999/xhtml">
9      <head>
10         <title>XHTML headers</title>
11      </head>
12
13      <body>
14
15         <h1>Level 1 Header</h1>
16         <h2>Level 2 header</h2>
17         <h3>Level 3 header</h3>
18         <h4>Level 4 header</h4>
19         <h5>Level 5 header</h5>
20         <h6>Level 6 header</h6>
21
22      </body>
23   </html>
```

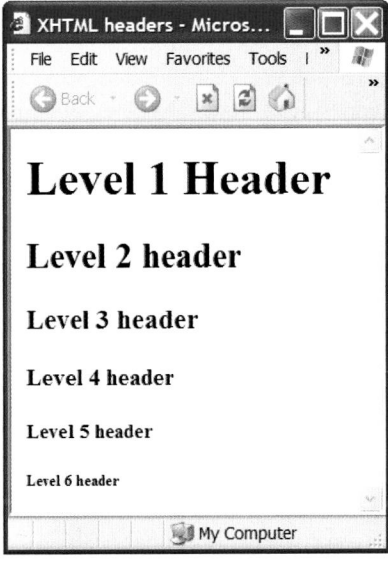

Fig. J.2 | Header elements h1 through h6.

Header element h1 (line 15) is considered the most significant header and is rendered in a larger font than the other five headers (lines 16–20). Each successive header element (i.e., h2, h3, etc.) is rendered in a smaller font.

Portability Tip J.1

The text size used to display each header element can vary significantly between browsers.

Look-and-Feel Observation J.1

Placing a header at the top of every XHTML page helps viewers understand the purpose of each page.

Look-and-Feel Observation J.2

Use larger headers to emphasize more important sections of a Web page.

J.5 Linking

One of the most important XHTML features is the hyperlink, which references (or links to) other resources, such as XHTML documents and images. In XHTML, both text and images can act as hyperlinks. Web browsers typically underline text hyperlinks and color their text blue by default, so that users can distinguish hyperlinks from plain text. In Fig. J.3, we create text hyperlinks to four different Web sites. Line 17 introduces the <strong> tag. Browsers typically display text marked up with <strong> in a bold font.

Links are created using the a (anchor) element. Line 21 defines a hyperlink that links the text Deitel to the URL assigned to attribute href, which specifies the location of a linked resource, such as a Web page, a file or an e-mail address. This particular anchor element links to a Web page located at http://www.deitel.com. When a URL does not indicate a specific document on the Web site, the Web server returns a default Web page. This page often is called index.html; however, most Web servers can be configured to use any file as the default Web page for the site. (Open http://www.deitel.com in one browser window and http://www.deitel.com/index.html in a second browser window to con-

```
 1   <?xml version = "1.0"?>
 2   <!DOCTYPE html PUBLIC "-//W3C//DTD XHTML 1.1//EN"
 3      "http://www.w3.org/TR/xhtml11/DTD/xhtml11.dtd">
 4
 5   <!-- Fig. J.3: links.html         -->
 6   <!-- Introduction to hyperlinks. -->
 7
 8   <html xmlns = "http://www.w3.org/1999/xhtml">
 9      <head>
10         <title>Introduction to hyperlinks</title>
11      </head>
12
13      <body>
14
15         <h1>Here are my favorite sites</h1>
```

Fig. J.3 | Linking to other Web pages. (Part 1 of 2.)

```
16
17        <p><strong>Click a name to go to that page.</strong></p>
18
19        <!-- create four text hyperlinks -->
20        <p>
21            <a href = "http://www.deitel.com">Deitel</a>
22        </p>
23
24        <p>
25            <a href = "http://www.prenhall.com">Prentice Hall</a>
26        </p>
27
28        <p>
29            <a href = "http://www.yahoo.com">Yahoo!</a>
30        </p>
31
32        <p>
33            <a href = "http://www.usatoday.com">USA Today</a>
34        </p>
35
36    </body>
37  </html>
```

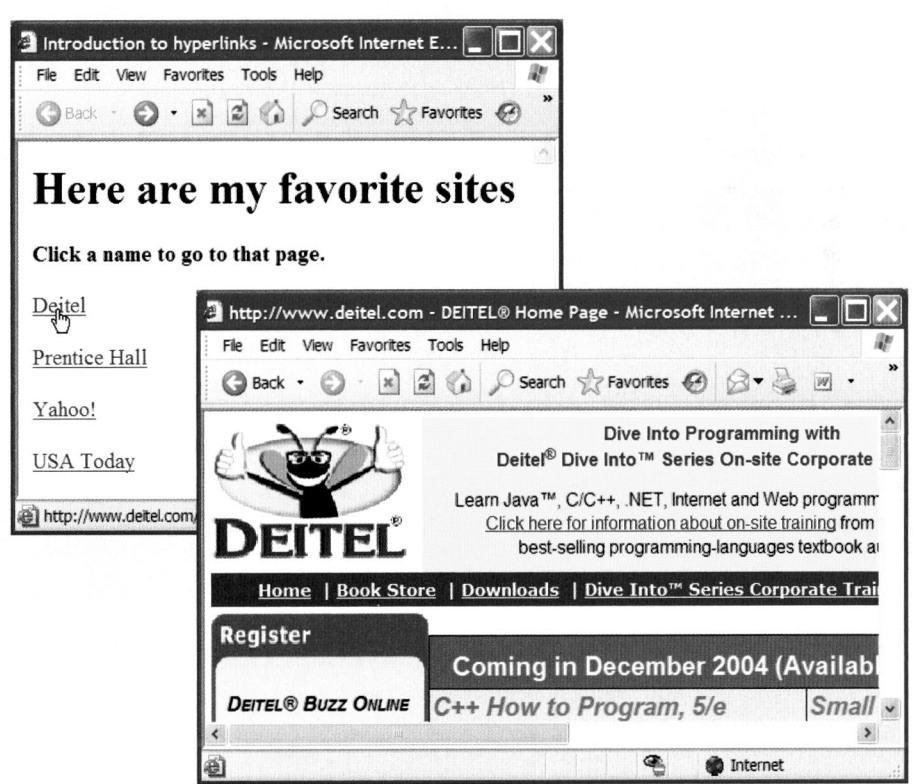

Fig. J.3 | Linking to other Web pages. (Part 2 of 2.)

firm that they are identical.) If the Web server cannot locate a requested document, the server returns an error indication to the Web browser, and the browser displays an error message to the user.

Anchors can link to e-mail addresses through a `mailto:` URL. When someone clicks this type of anchored link, most browsers launch the default e-mail program (e.g., Outlook Express) to enable the user to write an e-mail message to the linked address. Figure J.4 demonstrates this type of anchor.

Lines 17–19 contain an e-mail link. The form of an e-mail anchor is `<a href = "mailto:`*emailaddress*`">...</a>`. In this case, we link to the e-mail address `deitel@deitel.com`.

J.6 Images

The examples discussed so far demonstrated how to mark up documents that contain only text. However, most Web pages contain both text and images. In fact, images are an equal and essential part of Web-page design. The two most popular image formats used by Web developers are Graphics Interchange Format (GIF) and Joint Photographic Experts Group (JPEG) images. Users can create images, using specialized pieces of software, such as Adobe® PhotoShop Elements and Jasc® Paint Shop Pro (`www.jasc.com`). Images may also be acquired from various Web sites, such as `gallery.yahoo.com`. Figure J.5 demonstrates how to incorporate images into Web pages.

Good Programming Practice J.5

Always include the width and the height of an image inside the `<img>` tag. When the browser loads the XHTML file, it will know immediately from these attributes how much screen space to provide for the image and will lay out the page properly, even before it downloads the image.

```
 1   <?xml version = "1.0"?>
 2   <!DOCTYPE html PUBLIC "-//W3C//DTD XHTML 1.1//EN"
 3       "http://www.w3.org/TR/xhtml11/DTD/xhtml11.dtd">
 4
 5   <!-- Fig. J.4: contact.html    -->
 6   <!-- Adding email hyperlinks. -->
 7
 8   <html xmlns = "http://www.w3.org/1999/xhtml">
 9      <head>
10         <title>Adding e-mail hyperlinks</title>
11      </head>
12
13      <body>
14
15         <p>My email address is
16            <a href = "mailto:deitel@deitel.com">
17               deitel@deitel.com
18            </a>
19            . Click the address and your browser will
20            open an e-mail message and address it to me.
21         </p>
22      </body>
23   </html>
```

Fig. J.4 | Linking to an e-mail address. (Part 1 of 2.)

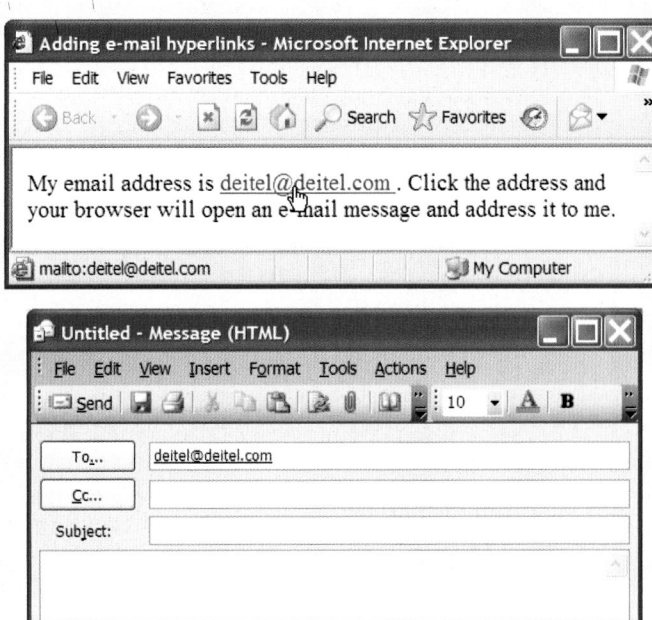

Fig. J.4 | Linking to an e-mail address. (Part 2 of 2.)

> **Performance Tip J.1**
>
> *Including the* width *and* height *attributes in an* <img> *tag will help the browser load and render pages faster.*

```
 1   <?xml version = "1.0"?>
 2   <!DOCTYPE html PUBLIC "-//W3C//DTD XHTML 1.1//EN"
 3      "http://www.w3.org/TR/xhtml11/DTD/xhtml11.dtd">
 4
 5   <!-- Fig. J.5: picture.html    -->
 6   <!-- Adding images with XHTML. -->
 7
 8   <html xmlns = "http://www.w3.org/1999/xhtml">
 9      <head>
10         <title>Adding images in XHTML</title>
11      </head>
12
13      <body>
14
15         <p>
16            <img src = "cool8se.jpg" height = "238" width = "181"
17               alt = "An imaginary landscape." />
18
19            <img src = "fish.jpg" height = "238" width = "181"
20               alt = "A picture of a fish swimming." />
21         </p>
```

Fig. J.5 | Placing images in XHTML files. (Part 1 of 2.)

```
22
23      </body>
24   </html>
```

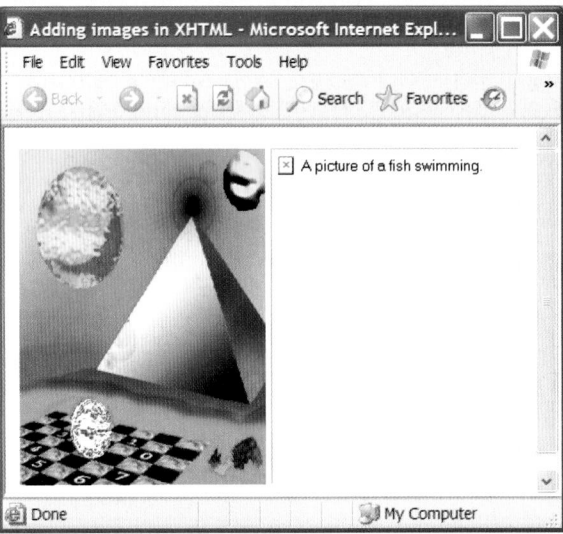

Fig. J.5 | Placing images in XHTML files. (Part 2 of 2.)

 Common Programming Error J.4

Entering new dimensions for an image that change its inherent width-to-height ratio might distort the appearance of the image. For example, if your image is 200 pixels wide and 100 pixels high, you should ensure that any new dimensions have a 2:1 width-to-height ratio.

Lines 16–17 use an img element to insert an image in the document. The image file's location is specified with the img element's src attribute. In this case, the image is located in the same directory as this XHTML document, so only the image's file name is required. Optional attributes width and height specify the image's width and height, respectively. The document author can scale an image by increasing or decreasing the values of the image width and height attributes. If these attributes are omitted, the browser uses the image's actual width and height. Images are measured in pixels ("picture elements"), which represent dots of color on the screen. The image in Fig. J.5 is 181 pixels wide and 238 pixels high.

Every img element in an XHTML document has an alt attribute. If a browser cannot render an image, the browser displays the alt attribute's value. A browser might not be able to render an image for several reasons. It might not support images—as is the case with a text-based browser (i.e., a browser that can display only text)—or the client may have disabled image viewing to reduce download time. Figure J.5 shows Internet Explorer rendering the alt attribute's value when a document references a nonexistent image file (fish.jpg).

The alt attribute is important for creating accessible Web pages for users with disabilities, especially those with vision impairments and text-based browsers. Specialized software called a speech synthesizer often is used by people with disabilities. Such software applications "speak" the alt attribute's value so that the user knows what the browser is displaying.

Some XHTML elements (called empty elements) contain only attributes and do not mark up text (i.e., text is not placed between the start and end tags). Empty elements (e.g., img) must be terminated, either by using the forward slash character (/) inside the closing right angle bracket (>) of the start tag or by explicitly including the end tag. When using the forward slash character, we add a space before the forward slash to improve readability (as shown at the ends of lines 17 and 20). Rather than using the forward slash character, lines 19–20 could be written with a closing </img> tag as follows:

```
<img src = "cool8se.jpg" height = "238" width = "181"
   alt = "An imaginary landscape."></img>
```

By using images as hyperlinks, Web developers can create graphical Web pages that link to other resources. In Fig. J.6, we create six different image hyperlinks.

Lines 16–19 create an image hyperlink by nesting an img element within an anchor (a) element. The value of the img element's src attribute value specifies that this image (links.jpg) resides in a directory named buttons. The buttons directory and the XHTML document are in the same directory. Images from other Web documents also can be referenced (after obtaining permission from the document's owner) by setting the src attribute to the name and location of the image.

```
 1   <?xml version = "1.0"?>
 2   <!DOCTYPE html PUBLIC "-//W3C//DTD XHTML 1.1//EN"
 3      "http://www.w3.org/TR/xhtml11/DTD/xhtml11.dtd">
 4
 5   <!-- Fig. J.6: nav.html           -->
 6   <!-- Using images as link anchors. -->
 7
 8   <html xmlns = "http://www.w3.org/1999/xhtml">
 9      <head>
10         <title>Using images as link anchors</title>
11      </head>
12
13      <body>
14
15         <p>
16            <a href = "links.html">
17               <img src = "buttons/links.jpg" width = "65"
18                  height = "50" alt = "Links Page" />
19            </a><br />
20
21            <a href = "list.html">
22               <img src = "buttons/list.jpg" width = "65"
23                  height = "50" alt = "List Example Page" />
24            </a><br />
25
26            <a href = "contact.html">
27               <img src = "buttons/contact.jpg" width = "65"
28                  height = "50" alt = "Contact Page" />
29            </a><br />
30
```

Fig. J.6 | Using images as link anchors. (Part 1 of 2.)

```
31          <a href = "header.html">
32              <img src = "buttons/header.jpg" width = "65"
33                  height = "50" alt = "Header Page" />
34          </a><br />
35
36          <a href = "table.html">
37              <img src = "buttons/table.jpg" width = "65"
38                  height = "50" alt = "Table Page" />
39          </a><br />
40
41          <a href = "form.html">
42              <img src = "buttons/form.jpg" width = "65"
43                  height = "50" alt = "Feedback Form" />
44          </a><br />
45      </p>
46
47    </body>
48  </html>
```

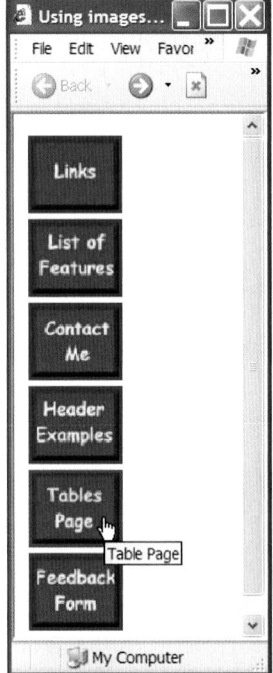

Fig. J.6 | Using images as link anchors. (Part 2 of 2.)

In line 19, we introduce the br element, which most browsers render as a line break. Any markup or text following a br element is rendered on the next line. Like the img element, br is an example of an empty element terminated with a forward slash. We add a space before the forward slash to enhance readability.

J.7 Special Characters and More Line Breaks

When marking up text, certain characters or symbols (e.g., <) might be difficult to embed directly into an XHTML document. Some keyboards do not provide these symbols, or the presence of these symbols could cause syntax errors. For example, the markup

```
<p>if x < 10 then increment x by 1</p>
```

results in a syntax error, because it uses the less-than character (<), which is reserved for start tags and end tags such as <p> and </p>. XHTML provides special characters or entity references (in the form &*code*;) for representing these characters. We could correct the previous line by writing

```
<p>if x &lt; 10 then increment x by 1</p>
```

which uses the special character < for the less-than symbol.

Figure J.7 demonstrates how to use special characters in an XHTML document. For a list of special characters, see Appendix K. Lines 26–27 contain other special characters, which are expressed either as word abbreviations (e.g., &amp for ampersand and &copy for copyright) or as hexadecimal values (e.g., & is the hexadecimal representation of &). Hexadecimal numbers are base-16 numbers—digits in a hexadecimal number have values from 0 to 15 (a total of 16 different values). The letters A–F represent the hexadecimal digits corresponding to decimal values 10–15. Thus, in hexadecimal notation, we can have numbers like 876 consisting solely of decimal-like digits, numbers like DA19F consisting of digits and letters, and numbers like DCB consisting solely of letters. We discuss hexadecimal numbers in detail in Appendix D.

In lines 33–35, we introduce three new elements. Most browsers render the del element as strike-through text. With this format, users can easily indicate document revisions. To superscript text (i.e., raise text on a line with a decreased font size) or subscript text (i.e., lower text on a line with a decreased font size), use the sup and sub elements, respectively. We also use special characters < for a less-than sign and ¼ for the fraction 1/4 (line 37).

```
 1   <?xml version = "1.0"?>
 2   <!DOCTYPE html PUBLIC "-//W3C//DTD XHTML 1.1//EN"
 3      "http://www.w3.org/TR/xhtml11/DTD/xhtml11.dtd">
 4
 5   <!-- Fig. J.7: contact2.html      -->
 6   <!-- Inserting special characters. -->
 7
 8   <html xmlns = "http://www.w3.org/1999/xhtml">
 9      <head>
10         <title>Inserting special characters</title>
11      </head>
12
13      <body>
14
```

Fig. J.7 | Inserting special characters into XHTML. (Part 1 of 2.)

```
15       <!-- special characters are    -->
16       <!-- entered using form &code; -->
17       <p>
18          Click
19          <a href = "mailto:deitel@deitel.com">here
20          </a> to open an e-mail message addressed to
21          deitel@deitel.com.
22       </p>
23
24       <hr /> <!-- inserts a horizontal rule -->
25
26       <p>All information on this site is <strong>&copy;</strong>
27          Deitel <strong>&amp;</strong> Associates, Inc. 2005.</p>
28
29       <!-- to strike through text use <del> tags    -->
30       <!-- to subscript text use <sub> tags         -->
31       <!-- to superscript text use <sup> tags       -->
32       <!-- these tags are nested inside other tags -->
33       <p><del>You may download 3.14 x 10<sup>2</sup>
34          characters worth of information from this site.</del>
35          Only <sub>one</sub> download per hour is permitted.</p>
36
37       <p>Note: <strong>&lt; &frac14;</strong> of the information
38          presented here is updated daily.</p>
39
40    </body>
41 </html>
```

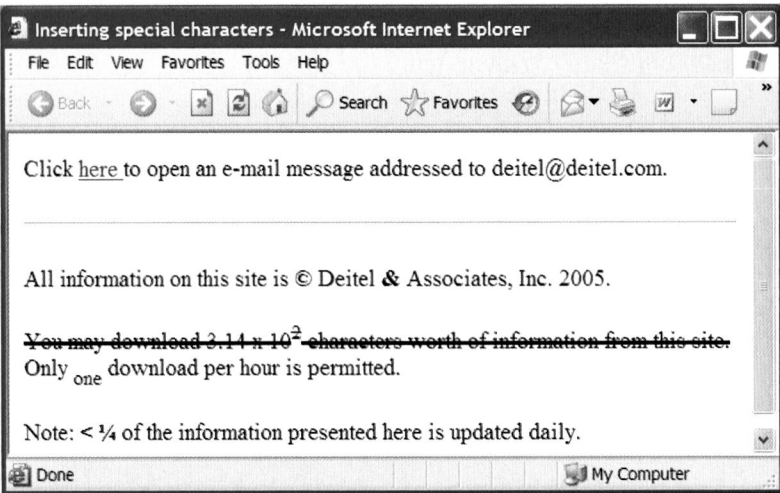

Fig. J.7 | Inserting special characters into XHTML. (Part 2 of 2.)

In addition to special characters, this document introduces a horizontal rule, indicated by the `<hr />` tag in line 24. Most browsers render a horizontal rule as a horizontal line. The `<hr />` tag also inserts a line break above and below the horizontal line.

J.8 Unordered Lists

Up to this point, we have presented basic XHTML elements and attributes for linking to resources, creating headers, using special characters and incorporating images. In this section, we discuss how to organize information on a Web page using lists. Later in the appendix, we introduce another feature for organizing information, called a table. Figure J.8 displays text in an unordered list (i.e., a list that does not order its items by letter or number). The unordered list element ul creates a list in which each item begins with a bullet (called a disc).

Each entry in an unordered list (element ul in line 20) is an li (list item) element (lines 23, 25, 27 and 29). Most Web browsers render these elements with a line break and a bullet symbol indented from the beginning of the new line.

J.9 Nested and Ordered Lists

Lists may be nested to represent hierarchical relationships, as in an outline format. Figure J.9 demonstrates nested lists and ordered lists (i.e., list that order items by letter or number).

```
 1  <?xml version = "1.0"?>
 2  <!DOCTYPE html PUBLIC "-//W3C//DTD XHTML 1.1//EN"
 3     "http://www.w3.org/TR/xhtml11/DTD/xhtml11.dtd">
 4
 5  <!-- Fig. J.8: links2.html              -->
 6  <!-- Unordered list containing hyperlinks. -->
 7
 8  <html xmlns = "http://www.w3.org/1999/xhtml">
 9     <head>
10        <title>Unordered list containing hyperlinks</title>
11     </head>
12
13     <body>
14
15        <h1>Here are my favorite sites</h1>
16
17        <p><strong>Click on a name to go to that page.</strong></p>
18
19        <!-- create an unordered list -->
20        <ul>
21
22           <!-- add four list items -->
23           <li><a href = "http://www.deitel.com">Deitel</a></li>
24
25           <li><a href = "http://www.w3.org">W3C</a></li>
26
27           <li><a href = "http://www.yahoo.com">Yahoo!</a></li>
28
29           <li><a href = "http://www.cnn.com">CNN</a></li>
30
31        </ul>
32
33     </body>
34  </html>
```

Fig. J.8 | Unordered lists in XHTML. (Part 1 of 2.)

The first ordered list begins in line 33. Attribute **type** specifies the sequence type (i.e., the set of numbers or letters used in the ordered list). In this case, setting **type** to **"I"** specifies upper-case roman numerals. Line 47 begins the second ordered list and sets attribute **type** to **"a"**, specifying lowercase letters for the list items. The last ordered list (lines 71–75) does not use attribute **type**. By default, the list's items are enumerated from one to three.

A Web browser indents each nested list to indicate a hierarchal relationship. By default, the items in the outermost unordered list (line 18) are preceded by discs. List items nested inside the unordered list of line 18 are preceded by circles. Although not demonstrated in this example, subsequent nested list items are preceded by squares. Unordered list items can be explicitly set to discs, circles or squares by setting the **ul** element's **type** attribute to **"disc"**, **"circle"** or **"square"**, respectively.

J.10 Basic XHTML Tables

This section presents the XHTML table—a frequently used feature that organizes data into rows and columns. Our first example (Fig. J.10) uses a table with six rows and two columns to display price information for fruit.

```
1   <?xml version = "1.0"?>
2   <!DOCTYPE html PUBLIC "-//W3C//DTD XHTML 1.1//EN"
3      "http://www.w3.org/TR/xhtml11/DTD/xhtml11.dtd">
4
5   <!-- Fig. J.9: list.html                    -->
6   <!-- Advanced Lists: nested and ordered. -->
7
8   <html xmlns = "http://www.w3.org/1999/xhtml">
9      <head>
10        <title>Advanced lists</title>
11     </head>
12
```

Fig. J.9 | Nested and ordered lists in XHTML. (Part 1 of 3.)

```
13      <body>
14
15         <h1>The Best Features of the Internet</h1>
16
17         <!-- create an unordered list -->
18         <ul>
19            <li>You can meet new people from countries around
20               the world.</li>
21
22            <li>
23               You have access to new media as it becomes public:
24
25               <!-- start nested list, use modified bullets -->
26               <!-- list ends with closing </ul> tag          -->
27               <ul>
28                  <li>New games</li>
29                  <li>
30                     New applications
31
32                     <!-- ordered nested list -->
33                     <ol type = "I">
34                        <li>For business</li>
35                        <li>For pleasure</li>
36                     </ol>
37
38                  </li>
39
40                  <li>Around the clock news</li>
41                  <li>Search engines</li>
42                  <li>Shopping</li>
43                  <li>
44                     Programming
45
46                     <!-- another nested ordered list -->
47                     <ol type = "a">
48                        <li>XML</li>
49                        <li>Java</li>
50                        <li>XHTML</li>
51                        <li>Scripts</li>
52                        <li>New languages</li>
53                     </ol>
54
55                  </li>
56
57               </ul> <!-- ends nested list started in line 27 -->
58
59            </li>
60
61            <li>Links</li>
62            <li>Keeping in touch with old friends</li>
63            <li>It is the technology of the future!</li>
64
65         </ul>    <!-- ends unordered list started in line 18 -->
```

Fig. J.9 | Nested and ordered lists in XHTML. (Part 2 of 3.)

```
66
67          <h1>My 3 Favorite <em>CEOs</em></h1>
68
69          <!-- ol elements without type attribute have -->
70          <!-- numeric sequence type (i.e., 1, 2, ...) -->
71          <ol>
72              <li>Lawrence J. Ellison</li>
73              <li>Steve Jobs</li>
74              <li>Michael Dell</li>
75          </ol>
76
77      </body>
78  </html>
```

Fig. J.9 | Nested and ordered lists in XHTML. (Part 3 of 3.)

Tables are defined with the `table` element. Lines 16–18 specify the start tag for a table element that has several attributes. The `border` attribute specifies the table's border width in pixels. To create a table without a border, set `border` to "0". This example assigns attribute `width` "40%", to set the table's width to 40 percent of the browser's width. A developer can also set attribute `width` to a specified number of pixels.

As its name implies, attribute **summary** (line 17) describes the table's contents. Speech devices use this attribute to make the table more accessible to users with visual impairments. The **caption** element (line 22) describes the table's content and helps text-based browsers interpret the table data. Text inside the <caption> tag is rendered above the table by most browsers. Attribute **summary** and element **caption** are two of many XHTML features that make Web pages more accessible to users with disabilities.

```
1   <?xml version = "1.0"?>
2   <!DOCTYPE html PUBLIC "-//W3C//DTD XHTML 1.1//EN"
3      "http://www.w3.org/TR/xhtml11/DTD/xhtml11.dtd">
4
5   <!-- Fig. J.10: table1.html  -->
6   <!-- Creating a basic table. -->
7
8   <html xmlns = "http://www.w3.org/1999/xhtml">
9      <head>
10        <title>Creating a basic table</title>
11     </head>
12
13     <body>
14
15        <!-- the <table> tag begins table -->
16        <table border = "1" width = "40%"
17           summary = "This table provides information about
18              the price of fruit">
19
20           <!-- <caption> tag summarizes table's   -->
21           <!-- contents to help visually impaired -->
22           <caption><strong>Price of Fruit</strong></caption>
23
24           <!-- <thead> is first section of table -->
25           <!-- it formats table header area      -->
26           <thead>
27              <tr> <!-- <tr> inserts one table row -->
28                 <th>Fruit</th> <!-- insert heading cell -->
29                 <th>Price</th>
30              </tr>
31           </thead>
32
33           <!-- all table content is enclosed within <tbody> -->
34           <tbody>
35              <tr>
36                 <td>Apple</td> <!-- insert data cell -->
37                 <td>$0.25</td>
38              </tr>
39
40              <tr>
41                 <td>Orange</td>
42                 <td>$0.50</td>
43              </tr>
44
```

Fig. J.10 | XHTML table. (Part 1 of 2.)

```
45              <tr>
46                  <td>Banana</td>
47                  <td>$1.00</td>
48              </tr>
49
50              <tr>
51                  <td>Pineapple</td>
52                  <td>$2.00</td>
53              </tr>
54          </tbody>
55
56          <!-- <tfoot> is last section of table -->
57          <!-- it formats table footer          -->
58          <tfoot>
59              <tr>
60                  <th>Total</th>
61                  <th>$3.75</th>
62              </tr>
63          </tfoot>
64
65      </table>
66
67    </body>
68 </html>
```

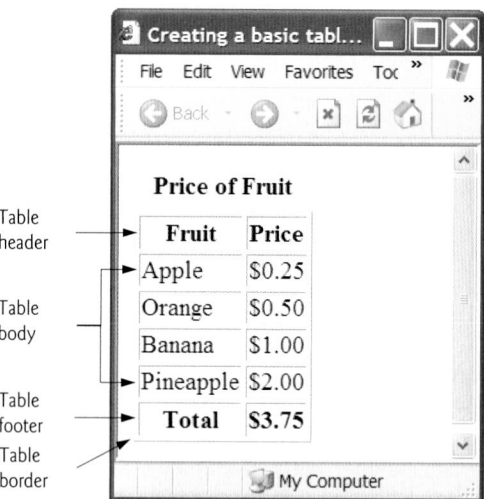

Fig. J.10 | XHTML table. (Part 2 of 2.)

 Error-Prevention Tip J.1

Try resizing the browser window to see how the width of the window affects the width of the table.

A table has three distinct sections—head, body and foot. The head section (or header cell) is defined with a **thead** element (lines 26–31), which contains header information, such as column names. Each **tr** element (lines 27–30) defines an individual table row.

The columns in the head section are defined with th elements. Most browsers center text formatted by th (table header column) elements and display it in bold. Table header elements are nested inside table row elements.

The body section, or table body, contains the table's primary data. The table body (lines 34–54) is defined in a tbody element. Data cells contain individual pieces of data and are defined with td (table data) elements.

The foot section (lines 58–63) is defined with a tfoot (table foot) element and represents a footer. Text commonly placed in the footer includes calculation results and footnotes. Like other sections, the foot section can contain table rows and each row can contain columns.

J.11   Intermediate XHTML Tables and Formatting

In the previous section, we explored the structure of a basic table. In Fig. J.11, we enhance our discussion of tables by introducing elements and attributes that allow the document author to build more complex tables.

Common Programming Error J.5

When using colspan and rowspan to adjust the size of table data cells, keep in mind that the modified cells will occupy more than one column or row; other rows or columns of the table must compensate for the extra rows or columns spanned by individual cells. If you do not, the formatting of your table will be distorted, and you could inadvertently create more columns and rows than you originally intended.

The table begins at line 17. Element colgroup (lines 22–27) groups and formats columns. The col element (line 26) specifies two attributes in this example. The align attribute determines the alignment of text in the column. The span attribute determines how many columns the col element formats. In this case, we set align's value to "right" and span's value to "1" to right-align text in the first column (the column containing the picture of the camel in the sample screen capture).

```
 1    <?xml version = "1.0"?>
 2    <!DOCTYPE html PUBLIC "-//W3C//DTD XHTML 1.1//EN"
 3        "http://www.w3.org/TR/xhtml11/DTD/xhtml11.dtd">
 4
 5    <!-- Fig. J.11: table2.html      -->
 6    <!-- Intermediate table design. -->
 7
 8    <html xmlns = "http://www.w3.org/1999/xhtml">
 9       <head>
10          <title>Intermediate table design</title>
11       </head>
12
13       <body>
14
15          <h1>Table Example Page</h1>
16
17          <table border = "1">
18             <caption>Here is a more complex sample table.</caption>
```

Fig. J.11 | Complex XHTML table. (Part 1 of 3.)

```
19
20              <!-- <colgroup> and <col> tags are -->
21              <!-- used to format entire columns -->
22              <colgroup>
23
24                 <!-- span attribute determines how  -->
25                 <!-- many columns <col> tag affects -->
26                 <col align = "right" span = "1" />
27              </colgroup>
28
29              <thead>
30
31                 <!-- rowspans and colspans merge specified    -->
32                 <!-- number of cells vertically or horizontally   -->
33                 <tr>
34
35                    <!-- merge two rows -->
36                    <th rowspan = "2">
37                       <img src = "camel.gif" width = "205"
38                          height = "167" alt = "Picture of a camel" />
39                    </th>
40
41                    <!-- merge four columns -->
42                    <th colspan = "4" valign = "top">
43                       <h1>Camelid comparison</h1><br />
44                       <p>Approximate as of 9/2002</p>
45                    </th>
46                 </tr>
47
48                 <tr valign = "bottom">
49                    <th># of Humps</th>
50                    <th>Indigenous region</th>
51                    <th>Spits?</th>
52                    <th>Produces Wool?</th>
53                 </tr>
54
55              </thead>
56
57              <tbody>
58
59                 <tr>
60                    <th>Camels (bactrian)</th>
61                    <td>2</td>
62                    <td>Africa/Asia</td>
63                    <td rowspan = "2">Llama</td>
64                    <td rowspan = "2">Llama</td>
65                 </tr>
66
67                 <tr>
68                    <th>Llamas</th>
69                    <td>1</td>
70                    <td>Andes Mountains</td>
71                 </tr>
```

Fig. J.11 | Complex XHTML table. (Part 2 of 3.)

```
72
73              </tbody>
74
75          </table>
76
77      </body>
78  </html>
```

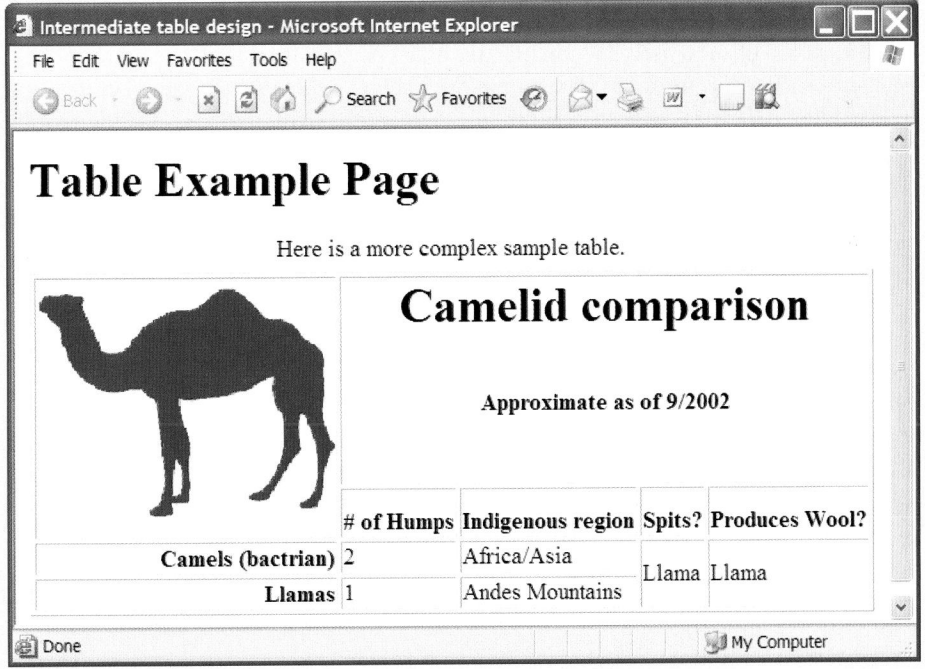

Table cells are sized to fit the data they contain. Document authors can create larger data cells by using attributes rowspan and colspan. The values assigned to these attributes specify the number of rows or columns occupied by a cell. The th element at lines 36–39 uses the attribute rowspan = "2" to allow the cell containing the picture of the camel to use two vertically adjacent cells (thus the cell *spans* two rows). The th element at lines 42–45 uses the attribute colspan = "4" to widen the header cell (containing Camelid comparison and Approximate as of 9/2002) to span four cells.

Line 42 introduces attribute valign, which aligns data vertically and may be assigned one of four values—"top" aligns data with the top of the cell, "middle" vertically centers data (the default for all data and header cells), "bottom" aligns data with the bottom of the cell and "baseline" ignores the fonts used for the row data and sets the bottom of all text in the row on a common baseline (i.e., the horizontal line to which each character in a word is aligned).

J.12 Basic XHTML Forms

When browsing Web sites, users often need to provide information such as e-mail addresses, search keywords and zip codes. XHTML provides a mechanism, called a **form**, for collecting such user information.

Data that users enter on a Web page normally is sent to a Web server that provides access to a site's resources (e.g., XHTML documents or images). These resources are located either on the same machine as the Web server or on a machine that the Web server can access through the network. When a browser requests a Web page or file that is located on a server, the server processes the request and returns the requested resource. A request contains the name and path of the desired resource and the method of communication (called a **protocol**). XHTML documents use the Hypertext Transfer Protocol (HTTP).

Figure J.12 sends the form data to the Web server, which passes the form data to a CGI (Common Gateway Interface) script (i.e., a program) written in C++, C, Perl or some other language. The script processes the data received from the Web server and typically returns information to the Web server. The Web server then sends the information in the form of an XHTML document to the Web browser. [*Note*: This example demonstrates client-side functionality. If the form is submitted (by clicking **Submit Your Entries**), an error occurs.]

```
1   <?xml version = "1.0"?>
2   <!DOCTYPE html PUBLIC "-//W3C//DTD XHTML 1.1//EN"
3      "http://www.w3.org/TR/xhtml11/DTD/xhtml11.dtd">
4
5   <!-- Fig. J.12: form.html   -->
6   <!-- Form design example 1. -->
7
8   <html xmlns = "http://www.w3.org/1999/xhtml">
9      <head>
10        <title>Form design example 1</title>
11     </head>
12
13     <body>
14
15        <h1>Feedback Form</h1>
16
17        <p>Please fill out this form to help
18           us improve our site.</p>
19
20        <!-- <form> tag begins form, gives -->
21        <!-- method of sending information -->
22        <!-- and location of form scripts  -->
23        <form method = "post" action = "/cgi-bin/formmail">
24
25           <p>
26
27              <!-- hidden inputs contain non-visual -->
28              <!-- information                       -->
29              <input type = "hidden" name = "recipient"
30                 value = "deitel@deitel.com" />
```

Fig. J.12 | Simple form with hidden fields and a text box. (Part 1 of 2.)

```
31
32              <input type = "hidden" name = "subject"
33                 value = "Feedback Form" />
34
35              <input type = "hidden" name = "redirect"
36                 value = "main.html" />
37          </p>
38
39          <!-- <input type = "text"> inserts text box -->
40          <p>
41            <label>Name:
42                <input name = "name" type = "text" size = "25"
43                   maxlength = "30" />
44            </label>
45          </p>
46
47          <p>
48
49              <!-- input types "submit" and "reset" -->
50              <!-- insert buttons for submitting    -->
51              <!-- and clearing form's contents      -->
52              <input type = "submit" value =
53                 "Submit Your Entries" />
54
55              <input type = "reset" value =
56                 "Clear Your Entries" />
57          </p>
58
59       </form>
60
61    </body>
62 </html>
```

Fig. J.12 | Simple form with hidden fields and a text box. (Part 2 of 2.)

Forms can contain visual and non-visual components. Visual components include clickable buttons and other graphical user interface components with which users interact. Non-visual components, called hidden inputs, store any data that the document author specifies, such as e-mail addresses and XHTML document file names that act as links. The form begins at line 23 with the form element. Attribute method specifies how the form's data is sent to the Web server.

Using method = "post" appends form data to the browser request, which contains the protocol (i.e., HTTP) and the requested resource's URL. Scripts located on the Web server's computer (or on a computer accessible through the network) can access the form data sent as part of the request. For example, a script may take the form information and update an electronic mailing list. The other possible value, method = "get", appends the form data directly to the end of the URL. For example, the URL /cgi-bin/formmail might have the form information name = bob appended to it.

The action attribute in the <form> tag specifies the URL of a script on the Web server; in this case, it specifies a script that e-mails form data to an address. Most Internet Service Providers (ISPs) have a script like this on their site; ask the Web-site system administrator how to set up an XHTML document to use the script correctly.

Lines 29–36 define three input elements that specify data to provide to the script that processes the form (also called the form handler). These three input elements have type attribute "hidden", which allows the document author to send form data that is not entered by a user to a script.

The three hidden inputs are an e-mail address to which the data will be sent, the e-mail's subject line and a URL where the browser will be redirected after submitting the form. Two other input attributes are name, which identifies the input element, and value, which provides the value that will be sent (or posted) to the Web server.

Good Programming Practice J.6

Place hidden input elements at the beginning of a form, immediately after the opening <form> tag. This placement allows document authors to locate hidden input elements quickly.

We introduce another type of input in lines 38–39. The "text" input inserts a text box into the form. Users can type data in text boxes. The label element (lines 37–40) provides users with information about the input element's purpose.

Common Programming Error J.6

Forgetting to include a label element for each form element is a design error. Without these labels, users cannot determine the purpose of individual form elements.

The input element's size attribute specifies the number of characters visible in the text box. Optional attribute maxlength limits the number of characters input into the text box. In this case, the user is not permitted to type more than 30 characters into the text box.

There are two types of input elements in lines 52–56. The "submit" input element is a button. When the user presses a "submit" button, the browser sends the data in the form to the Web server for processing. The value attribute sets the text displayed on the button (the default value is **Submit**). The "reset" input element allows a user to reset all form elements to their default values. The value attribute of the "reset" input element sets the text displayed on the button (the default value is **Reset**).

J.13 More Complex XHTML Forms

In the previous section, we introduced basic forms. In this section, we introduce elements and attributes for creating more complex forms. Figure J.13 contains a form that solicits user feedback about a Web site.

The `textarea` element (lines 42–44) inserts a multiline text box, called a `textarea`, into the form. The number of rows is specified with the **rows attribute** and the number of columns (i.e., characters) is specified with the **cols attribute**. In this example, the tex-tarea is four rows high and 36 characters wide. To display default text in the text area, place the text between the `<textarea>` and `</textarea>` tags. Default text can be specified in other `input` types, such as textboxes, by using the `value` attribute.

The `"password"` input in lines 52–53 inserts a password box with the specified `size`. A password box allows users to enter sensitive information, such as credit card numbers and passwords, by "masking" the information input with asterisks. The actual value input is sent to the Web server, not the asterisks that mask the input.

Lines 60–78 introduce the checkbox form element. Checkboxes enable users to select from a set of options. When a user selects a checkbox, a check mark appears in the check box. Otherwise, the checkbox remains empty. Each `"checkbox"` input creates a new checkbox. Checkboxes can be used individually or in groups. Checkboxes that belong to a group are assigned the same `name` (in this case, `"thingsliked"`).

We continue our discussion of forms by presenting a third example that introduces several more form elements from which users can make selections (Fig. J.14). In this example, we introduce two new `input` types. The first type is the radio button (lines 90–113), specified with type `"radio"`. Radio buttons are similar to checkboxes, except that only one radio button in a group of radio buttons may be selected at any time. All radio buttons in a group have the same `name` attribute; they are distinguished by their different `value` attributes. The attribute–value pair checked = `"checked"` (line 92) indicates which radio button, if any, is selected initially. The `checked` attribute also applies to checkboxes.

```
1   <?xml version = "1.0"?>
2   <!DOCTYPE html PUBLIC "-//W3C//DTD XHTML 1.1//EN"
3      "http://www.w3.org/TR/xhtml11/DTD/xhtml11.dtd">
4
5   <!-- Fig. J.13: form2.html  -->
6   <!-- Form design example 2. -->
7
8   <html xmlns = "http://www.w3.org/1999/xhtml">
9      <head>
10        <title>Form design example 2</title>
11     </head>
12
13     <body>
14
15        <h1>Feedback Form</h1>
16
17        <p>Please fill out this form to help
18           us improve our site.</p>
19
```

Fig. J.13 | Form with textareas, password boxes and checkboxes. (Part 1 of 3.)

```
20          <form method = "post" action = "/cgi-bin/formmail">
21
22             <p>
23                 <input type = "hidden" name = "recipient"
24                    value = "deitel@deitel.com" />
25
26                 <input type = "hidden" name = "subject"
27                    value = "Feedback Form" />
28
29                 <input type = "hidden" name = "redirect"
30                    value = "main.html" />
31             </p>
32
33             <p>
34                 <label>Name:
35                    <input name = "name" type = "text" size = "25" />
36                 </label>
37             </p>
38
39             <!-- <textarea> creates multiline textbox -->
40             <p>
41                 <label>Comments:<br />
42                    <textarea name = "comments" rows = "4"
43                       cols = "36">Enter your comments here.
44                    </textarea>
45                 </label></p>
46
47             <!-- <input type = "password"> inserts -->
48             <!-- textbox whose display is masked   -->
49             <!-- with asterisk characters          -->
50             <p>
51                 <label>E-mail Address:
52                    <input name = "email" type = "password"
53                       size = "25" />
54                 </label>
55             </p>
56
57             <p>
58                 <strong>Things you liked:</strong><br />
59
60                 <label>Site design
61                 <input name = "thingsliked" type = "checkbox"
62                    value = "Design" /></label>
63
64                 <label>Links
65                 <input name = "thingsliked" type = "checkbox"
66                    value = "Links" /></label>
67
68                 <label>Ease of use
69                 <input name = "thingsliked" type = "checkbox"
70                    value = "Ease" /></label>
71
```

Fig. J.13 | Form with textareas, password boxes and checkboxes. (Part 2 of 3.)

```
72                <label>Images
73                <input name = "thingsliked" type = "checkbox"
74                   value = "Images" /></label>
75
76                <label>Source code
77                <input name = "thingsliked" type = "checkbox"
78                   value = "Code" /></label>
79           </p>
80
81           <p>
82              <input type = "submit" value =
83                 "Submit Your Entries" />
84
85              <input type = "reset" value =
86                 "Clear Your Entries" />
87           </p>
88
89        </form>
90
91     </body>
92  </html>
```

Feedback Form

Please fill out this form to help us improve our site.

Name: [   ]

Comments:
Enter your comments here.

E-mail Address: [   ]

Things you liked:
Site design ☐ Links ☐ Ease of use ☐ Images ☐
Source code ☐

[Submit Your Entries]
[Clear Your Entries]

Feedback Form

Please fill out this form to help us improve our site.

Name: joe bob

Comments:
Your site is great! I would like
to see more XHTML Web resources.

E-mail Address: ●●●●●●●●●●●●

Things you liked:
Site design ☐ Links ☐ Ease of use ☐ Images ☐
Source code ☑

[Submit Your Entries]
[Clear Your Entries]

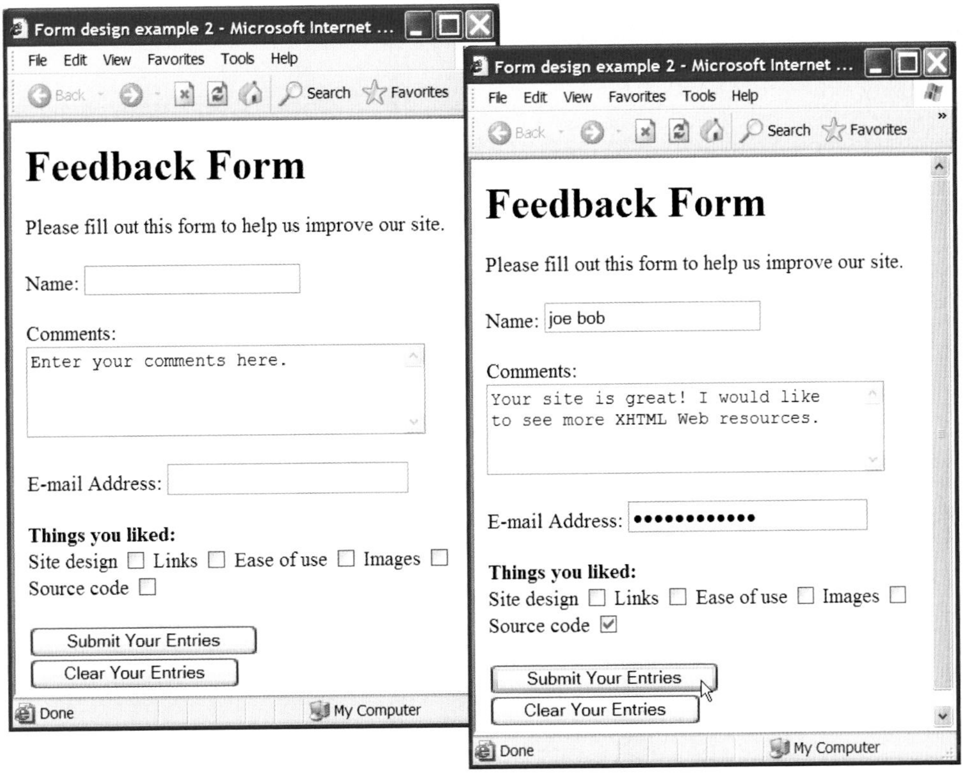

Fig. J.13 | Form with textareas, password boxes and checkboxes. (Part 3 of 3.)

Common Programming Error J.7

When your form has several checkboxes with the same name, you must make sure that they have dif-ferent values, or the scripts running on the Web server will not be able to distinguish between them.

Common Programming Error J.8

When using a group of radio buttons in a form, forgetting to set the name attributes to the same name is a logic error that lets the user select all of the radio buttons at the same time.

The select element (lines 123–136) provides a drop-down list from which the user can select an item. The name attribute identifies the drop-down list. The option element (lines 124–135) adds items to the drop-down list. The option element's selected attribute specifies which item initially is displayed as the selected item in the select element.

```
1    <?xml version = "1.0"?>
2    <!DOCTYPE html PUBLIC "-//W3C//DTD XHTML 1.1//EN"
3       "http://www.w3.org/TR/xhtml11/DTD/xhtml11.dtd">
4
5    <!-- Fig. J.14: form3.html   -->
6    <!-- Form design example 3. -->
7
8    <html xmlns = "http://www.w3.org/1999/xhtml">
9       <head>
10         <title>Form design example 3</title>
11      </head>
12
13      <body>
14
15         <h1>Feedback Form</h1>
16
17         <p>Please fill out this form to help
18            us improve our site.</p>
19
20         <form method = "post" action = "/cgi-bin/formmail">
21
22            <p>
23               <input type = "hidden" name = "recipient"
24                  value = "deitel@deitel.com" />
25
26               <input type = "hidden" name = "subject"
27                  value = "Feedback Form" />
28
29               <input type = "hidden" name = "redirect"
30                  value = "main.html" />
31            </p>
32
33            <p>
34               <label>Name:
35                  <input name = "name" type = "text" size = "25" />
36               </label>
37            </p>
38
```

Fig. J.14 | Form including radio buttons and drop-down lists. (Part 1 of 4.)

```
39          <p>
40             <label>Comments:<br />
41                <textarea name = "comments" rows = "4"
42                   cols = "36"></textarea>
43             </label>
44          </p>
45
46          <p>
47             <label>E-mail Address:
48                <input name = "email" type = "password"
49                   size = "25" />
50             </label>
51          </p>
52
53          <p>
54             <strong>Things you liked:</strong><br />
55
56             <label>Site design
57                <input name = "thingsliked" type = "checkbox"
58                   value = "Design" />
59             </label>
60
61             <label>Links
62                <input name = "thingsliked" type = "checkbox"
63                   value = "Links" />
64             </label>
65
66             <label>Ease of use
67                <input name = "thingsliked" type = "checkbox"
68                   value = "Ease" />
69             </label>
70
71             <label>Images
72                <input name = "thingsliked" type = "checkbox"
73                   value = "Images" />
74             </label>
75
76             <label>Source code
77                <input name = "thingsliked" type = "checkbox"
78                   value = "Code" />
79             </label>
80
81          </p>
82
83          <!-- <input type = "radio" /> creates one radio    -->
84          <!-- button. The difference between radio buttons -->
85          <!-- and checkboxes is that only one radio button -->
86          <!-- in a group can be selected.                  -->
87          <p>
88             <strong>How did you get to our site?:</strong><br />
89
```

Fig. J.14 | Form including radio buttons and drop-down lists. (Part 2 of 4.)

```
 90              <label>Search engine
 91                 <input name = "howtosite" type = "radio"
 92                    value = "search engine" checked = "checked" />
 93              </label>
 94
 95              <label>Links from another site
 96                 <input name = "howtosite" type = "radio"
 97                    value = "link" />
 98              </label>
 99
100              <label>Deitel.com Web site
101                 <input name = "howtosite" type = "radio"
102                    value = "deitel.com" />
103              </label>
104
105              <label>Reference in a book
106                 <input name = "howtosite" type = "radio"
107                    value = "book" />
108              </label>
109
110              <label>Other
111                 <input name = "howtosite" type = "radio"
112                    value = "other" />
113              </label>
114
115         </p>
116
117         <p>
118            <label>Rate our site:
119
120               <!-- <select> tag presents a drop-down -->
121               <!-- list with choices indicated by    -->
122               <!-- <option> tags                      -->
123               <select name = "rating">
124                  <option selected = "selected">Amazing</option>
125                  <option>10</option>
126                  <option>9</option>
127                  <option>8</option>
128                  <option>7</option>
129                  <option>6</option>
130                  <option>5</option>
131                  <option>4</option>
132                  <option>3</option>
133                  <option>2</option>
134                  <option>1</option>
135                  <option>Awful</option>
136               </select>
137
138            </label>
139         </p>
140
```

Fig. J.14 | Form including radio buttons and drop-down lists. (Part 3 of 4.)

```
141            <p>
142               <input type = "submit" value =
143                  "Submit Your Entries" />
144
145               <input type = "reset" value = "Clear Your Entries" />
146            </p>
147
148         </form>
149
150      </body>
151   </html>
```

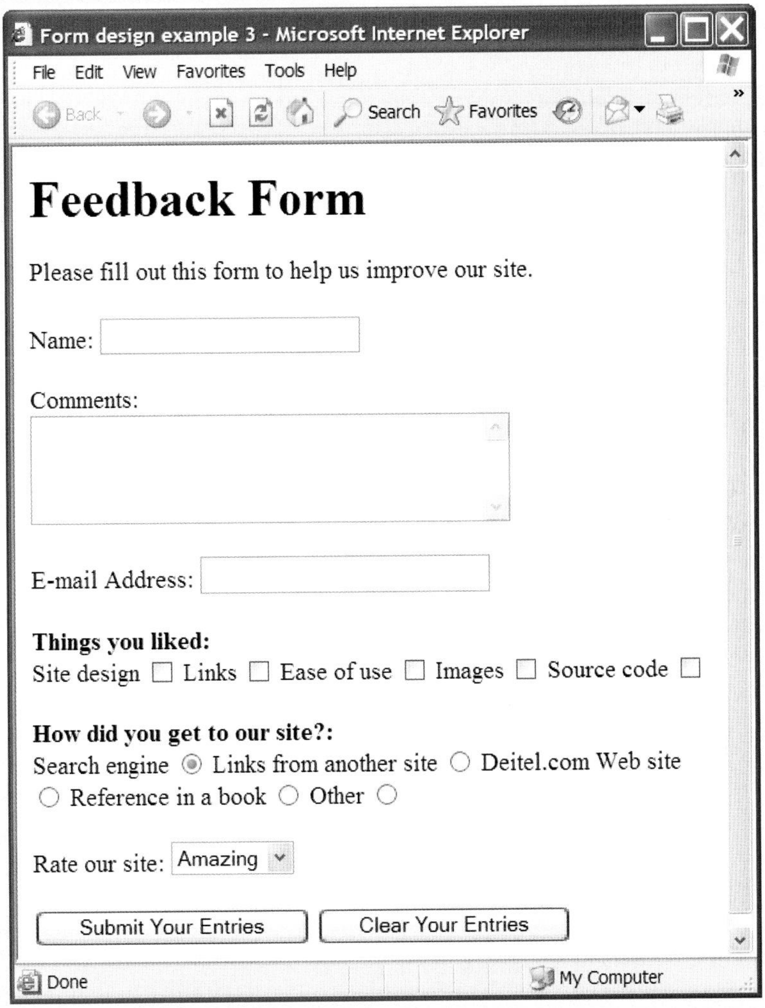

Fig. J.14 | Form including radio buttons and drop-down lists. (Part 4 of 4.)

J.14 Internet and World Wide Web Resources

www.w3.org/TR/xhtml11

The *XHTML 1.1 Recommendation* contains general information, information on compatibility issues, document type definition information, definitions, terminology and much more relating to XHTML.

www.xhtml.org

XHTML.org provides XHTML development news and links to other XHTML resources, which include books and articles.

www.w3schools.com/xhtml/default.asp

The *XHTML School* provides XHTML quizzes and references. This page also contains links to X–HTML syntax, validation and document type definitions.

hotwired.lycos.com/webmonkey/00/50/index2a.html

This site provides an article about XHTML. Key sections of the article overview XHTML and discuss tags, attributes and anchors.

wdvl.com/Authoring/Languages/XML/XHTML

The Web Developers' Virtual Library provides an introduction to XHTML. This site also contains articles, examples and links to other technologies.

Summary

- XHTML (Extensible Hypertext Markup Language) is a markup language for creating Web pages.

- A key issue when using XHTML is the separation of the presentation of a document (i.e., the document's appearance when rendered by a browser) from the structure of the information in the document.

- In XHTML, text is marked up with elements, delimited by tags that are names contained in pairs of angle brackets. Some elements may contain additional markup called attributes, which provide additional information about the element.

- A machine that runs specialized piece of software called a Web server stores XHTML documents.

- XHTML documents that are syntactically correct are guaranteed to render properly. XHTML documents that contain syntax errors might not display properly.

- Every XHTML document contains a start `<html>` tag and an end `</html>` tag.

- Comments in XHTML always begin with `<!--` and end with `-->`. The browser ignores all text inside a comment.

- Every XHTML document contains a `head` element, which generally contains information, such as a title, and a `body` element, which contains the page content. Information in the `head` element generally is not rendered in the display window but could be made available to the user through other means.

- The `title` element names a Web page. The title usually appears in the colored bar (called the title bar) at the top of the browser window and also appears as the text identifying a page when users add your page to their list of **Favorites** or **Bookmarks**.

- The body of an XHTML document is the area in which the document's content is placed. The content may include text and tags.

- All text placed between the `<p>` and `</p>` tags form one paragraph.

- XHTML provides six headers (`h1` through `h6`) for specifying the relative importance of information. Header element `h1` is considered the most significant header and is rendered in a larger font than the other five headers. Each successive header element (i.e., `h2`, `h3`, etc.) is rendered in a smaller font.

- Web browsers typically underline text hyperlinks and color them blue by default.

- The `<strong>` tag usually causes a browser to render text in a bold font.

- Users can insert links with the a (anchor) element. The most important attribute for the a element is `href`, which specifies the resource (e.g., page, file, e-mail address) being linked.

- Anchors can link to an e-mail address using a `mailto:` URL. When someone clicks this type of anchored link, most browsers launch the default e-mail program (e.g., Outlook Express) to initiate e-mail messages to the linked addresses.

- The `img` element's `src` attribute specifies an image's location. Optional attributes `width` and `height` specify the image width and height, respectively. Images are measured in pixels ("picture elements"), which represent dots of color on the screen.

- The `alt` attribute makes Web pages more accessible to users with disabilities, especially those with vision impairments.

- Some XHTML elements are empty elements, contain only attributes and do not mark up text. Empty elements (e.g., img) must be terminated, either by using the forward slash character (/) or by explicitly writing an end tag.

- The `br` element causes most browsers to render a line break. Any markup or text following a br element is rendered on the next line.

- XHTML provides special characters or entity references (in the form &*code*;) for representing characters that cannot be marked up.

- Most browsers render a horizontal rule, indicated by the `<hr />` tag, as a horizontal line. The hr element also inserts a line break above and below the horizontal line.

- The unordered list element `ul` creates a list in which each item in the list begins with a bullet symbol (called a disc). Each entry in an unordered list is an `li` (list item) element. Most Web browsers render these elements with a line break and a bullet symbol at the beginning of the line.

- Lists may be nested to represent hierarchical data relationships.

- Attribute `type` specifies the sequence type (i.e., the set of numbers or letters used in the ordered list).

- XHTML tables mark up tabular data and are one of the most frequently used features in XHTML.

- The `table` element defines an XHTML table. Attribute `border` specifies the table's border width, in pixels. Tables without borders set this attribute to `"0"`.

- Element `summary` summarizes the table's contents and is used by speech devices to make the table more accessible to users with visual impairments.

- Element `caption` describe's the table's content. The text inside the `<caption>` tag is rendered above the table in most browsers.

- A table can be split into three distinct sections: head (`thead`), body (`tbody`) and foot (`tfoot`). The head section contains information such as table titles and column headers. The table body contains the primary table data. The table foot contains information such as footnotes.

- Element `tr`, or table row, defines individual table rows. Element `th` defines a header cell. Text in th elements usually is centered and displayed in bold by most browsers. This element can be present in any section of the table.

- Data within a row are defined with `td`, or table data, elements.

- Element `colgroup` groups and formats columns. Each `col` element can format any number of columns (specified with the `span` attribute).

- The document author has the ability to merge data cells with the `rowspan` and `colspan` attributes. The values assigned to these attributes specify the number of rows or columns occupied by the cell. These attributes can be placed inside any data-cell tag.

- XHTML provides forms for collecting information from users. Forms contain visual components, such as buttons that users click. Forms may also contain non-visual components, called hidden inputs, which are used to store any data, such as e-mail addresses and XHTML document file names used for linking.

- A form begins with the form element. Attribute method specifies how the form's data is sent to the Web server.

- The "text" input inserts a text box into the form. Text boxes allow the user to input data.

- The input element's size attribute specifies the number of characters visible in the input element. Optional attribute maxlength limits the number of characters input into a text box.

- The "submit" input submits the data entered in the form to the Web server for processing. Most Web browsers create a button that submits the form data when clicked. The "reset" input allows a user to reset all form elements to their default values.

- The textarea element inserts a multiline text box, called a text area, into a form. The number of rows in the text area is specified with the rows attribute and the number of columns (i.e., characters) is specified with the cols attribute.

- The "password" input inserts a password box into a form. A password box allows users to enter sensitive information, such as credit-card numbers and passwords, by "masking" the information input with another character. Asterisks are the masking character used for password boxes. The actual value input is sent to the Web server, not the asterisks that mask the input.

- The checkbox input allows the user to make a selection. When the checkbox is selected, a check mark appears in the checkbox. Otherwise, the checkbox is empty. Checkboxes can be used individually and in groups. Checkboxes that are part of the same group have the same name.

- A radio button is similar in function and use to a checkbox, except that only one radio button in a group can be selected at any time. All radio buttons in a group have the same name attribute value and have different attribute values.

- The select input provides a drop-down list of items. The name attribute identifies the drop-down list. The option element adds items to the drop-down list. The selected attribute, like the checked attribute for radio buttons and checkboxes, specifies which list item is displayed initially.

Terminology

<!--...--> (XHTML comment)
a element (<a>...</a>)
action attribute
alt attribute
& (& special character)
anchor
angle brackets (< >)
attribute
body element
border attribute
br (line break) element
browser request
<caption> tag
checkbox
checked attribute
col element
colgroup element

cols attribute
colspan attribute
comments in XHTML
© (© special character)
disc
element
e-mail anchor
empty tag
form
form element
head element
header
header cell)
header elements (h1 through h6)
height attribute
hexadecimal code
hidden input element

<hr /> tag (horizontal rule)
href attribute
.htm (XHTML file-name extension)
.html (XHTML file-name extension)
<html> tag
hyperlink
image hyperlink
img element
input element
level of nesting
<li> (list item) tag
linked document
mailto: URL
markup language
maxlength attribute
method attribute
name attribute
nested list
nested tag
ol (ordered list) element
p (paragraph) element
password box
"radio" (attribute value)
rows attribute (textarea)
rowspan attribute (tr)
selected attribute
size attribute (input
special character
src attribute (img)
type attribute
<strong> tag

sub element
subscript
superscript
syntax
table element
tag
tbody element
td element
text editor
textarea
textarea element
tfoot (table foot) element
<thead>...</thead>
title element
tr (table row) element
unordered-list element (ul)
valign attribute (th)
value attribute
Web page
Web server
width attribute
World Wide Web (WWW)
XHTML (Extensible Hypertext Markup Language)
XHTML comment
XHTML form
XHTML markup
XHTML tag
XML declaration
xmlns attribute

XHTML Special Characters

The table of Fig. K.1 shows many commonly used XHTML special characters—called *character entity references* by the World Wide Web Consortium. For a complete list of character entity references, see the site

www.w3.org/TR/REC-html40/sgml/entities.html

Character	XHTML encoding	Character	XHTML encoding
non-breaking space		ê	&#234;
§	&#167;	ì	&#236;
©	&#169;	í	&#237;
®	&#174;	î	&#238;
π	&#188;	ñ	&#241;
∫	&#189;	ò	&#242;
Ω	&#190;	ó	&#243;
à	&#224;	ô	&#244;
á	&#225;	õ	&#245;
â	&#226;	÷	&#247;
ā	&#227;	ù	&#249;
å	&#229;	ú	&#250;
ç	&#231;	û	&#251;
è	&#232;	•	&#8226;
é	&#233;	™	&#8482;

Fig. K.1 | XHTML special characters.

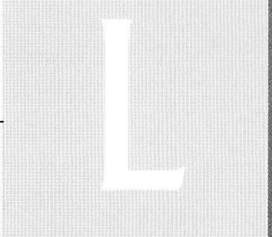

Using the
Visual Studio
.NET Debugger

OBJECTIVES

In this appendix you will learn:

- To set breakpoints to debug programs.
- To run a program through the debugger.
- To set, disable and remove a breakpoint.
- To use the **Continue** command to continue execution.
- To use the **Locals** window to view and modify the values of variables.
- To use the **Watch** window to evaluate expressions.
- To use the **Step Into**, **Step Out** and **Step Over** commands to control execution.
- To use the **Autos** window to view variables that are used in the surrounding statements.

L.1 Introduction

In Chapter 2, you learned that there are two types of errors—compilation errors and logic errors—and you learned how to eliminate compilation errors from your code. Logic errors (also called bugs) do not prevent a program from compiling successfully, but do cause the program to produce erroneous results when it runs. Most C++ compiler vendors provide software called a debugger, which allows you to monitor the execution of your programs to locate and remove logic errors. The debugger will be one of your most important program development tools. This appendix demonstrates key features of the Visual Studio .NET debugger. Chapter M discusses the features and capabilities of the GNU C++ debugger. We provide several free *Dive Into™ Series* publications to help students and instructors familiarize themselves with the debuggers provided with various other development tools. These publications are available on the CD that accompanies the text and can be downloaded from `www.deitel.com/books/downloads`.

L.2 Breakpoints and the Continue Command

We begin our study of the debugger by investigating breakpoints, which are markers that can be set at any executable line of code. When program execution reaches a breakpoint, execution pauses, allowing you to examine the values of variables to help determine whether logic errors exist. For example, you can examine the value of a variable that stores the result of a calculation to determine whether the calculation was performed correctly. Note that attempting to set a breakpoint at a line of code that is not executable (such as a comment) will actually set the breakpoint at the next executable line of code in that function.

To illustrate the features of the debugger, we use the program listed in Fig. L.3, which creates and manipulates an object of class `Account` (Figs. L.1–L.2). Execution begins in `main` (lines 12–30 of Fig. L.3). Line 14 creates an `Account` object with an initial balance of $50.00. `Account`'s constructor (lines 10–22 of Fig. L.2) accepts one argument, which specifies the `Account`'s initial `balance`. Line 17 of Fig. L.3 outputs the initial account balance using `Account` member function `getBalance`. Line 19 declares a local variable `withdrawalAmount`, which stores a withdrawal amount read from the user. Line 21 prompts the user for the withdrawal amount, and line 22 inputs the amount into `withdrawalAmount`. Line 25 subtracts the withdrawal from the `Account`'s `balance` using its `debit` member function. Finally, line 28 displays the new `balance`.

```
 1   // Fig. L.1: Account.h
 2   // Definition of Account class.
 3
 4   class Account
 5   {
 6   public:
 7      Account( int ); // constructor initializes balance
 8      void credit( int ); // add an amount to the account balance
 9      void debit( int ); // subtract an amount from the account balance
10      int getBalance(); // return the account balance
11   private:
12      int balance; // data member that stores the balance
13   }; // end class Account
```

Fig. L.1 | Header file for the Account class.

```
 1   // Fig. L.2: Account.cpp
 2   // Member-function definitions for class Account.
 3   #include <iostream>
 4   using std::cout;
 5   using std::endl;
 6
 7   #include "Account.h" // include definition of class Account
 8
 9   // Account constructor initializes data member balance
10   Account::Account( int initialBalance )
11   {
12      balance = 0; // assume that the balance begins at 0
13
14      // if initialBalance is greater than 0, set this value as the
15      // balance of the Account; otherwise, balance remains 0
16      if ( initialBalance > 0 )
17         balance = initialBalance;
18
19      // if initialBalance is negative, print error message
20      if ( initialBalance < 0 )
21         cout << "Error: Initial balance cannot be negative.\n" << endl;
22   } // end Account constructor
23
24   // credit (add) an amount to the account balance
25   void Account::credit( int amount )
26   {
27      balance = balance + amount; // add amount to balance
28   } // end function credit
29
30   // debit (subtract) an amount from the account balance
31   void Account::debit( int amount )
32   {
33      if ( amount <= balance ) // debit amount does not exceed balance
34         balance = balance - amount;
35
```

Fig. L.2 | Definition for the Account class. (Part 1 of 2.)

```
36        else // debit amount exceeds balance
37            cout << "Debit amount exceeded account balance.\n" << endl;
38    } // end function debit
39
40    // return the account balance
41    int Account::getBalance()
42    {
43        return balance; // gives the value of balance to the calling function
44    } // end function getBalance
```

Fig. L.2 | Definition for the Account class. (Part 2 of 2.)

```
 1    // Fig. L.3: figL_03.cpp
 2    // Create and manipulate Account objects.
 3    #include <iostream>
 4    using std::cin;
 5    using std::cout;
 6    using std::endl;
 7
 8    // include definition of class Account from Account.h
 9    #include "Account.h"
10
11    // function main begins program execution
12    int main()
13    {
14        Account account1( 50 ); // create Account object
15
16        // display initial balance of each object
17        cout << "account1 balance: $" << account1.getBalance() << endl;
18
19        int withdrawalAmount; // stores withdrawal amount read from user
20
21        cout << "\nEnter withdrawal amount for account1: "; // prompt
22        cin >> withdrawalAmount; // obtain user input
23        cout << "\nattempting to subtract " << withdrawalAmount
24            << " from account1 balance\n\n";
25        account1.debit( withdrawalAmount ); // try to subtract from account1
26
27        // display balances
28        cout << "account1 balance: $" << account1.getBalance() << endl;
29        return 0; // indicate successful termination
30    } // end main
```

Fig. L.3 | Test class for debugging.

In the following steps, you will use breakpoints and various debugger commands to examine the value of the variable withdrawalAmount declared in Fig. L.3.

1. *Enabling the debugger.* The debugger is enabled by default. If it is not enabled, you have to change the settings of the *Solution Configurations* combo box (Fig. L.4) in the toolbar. To do this, click the combo box's down arrow to access the *Solution Configurations* combo box, then select **Debug**. The toolbar will display **Debug** in the *Solution Configurations* combo box.

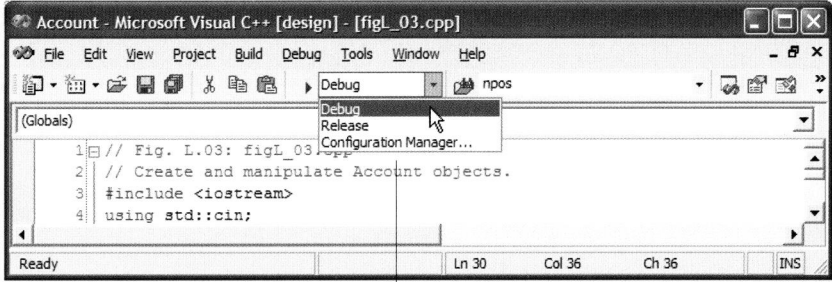

Solution Configurations combo box

Fig. L.4 | Enabling the debugger.

2. ***Inserting breakpoints in Visual Studio .NET.*** To insert a breakpoint in Visual Studio .NET, click inside the margin indicator bar (the gray margin at the left of the code window in Fig. L.5) next to the line of code at which you wish to break or right click that line of code and select **Insert Breakpoint**. You can set as many breakpoints as necessary. Set breakpoints at lines 21 and 25 of your code. A solid maroon circle appears in the margin indicator bar where you clicked, indicating that a breakpoint has been set (Fig. L.5). When the program runs, the debugger suspends execution at any line that contains a breakpoint. The program is said to be in break mode when the debugger pauses the program's execution. Breakpoints can be set before running a program, in break mode and while a program is running.

3. ***Beginning the debugging process.*** After setting breakpoints in the code editor, select **Build > Build Solution** to compile the program, then select **Debug > Start** to begin the debugging process. During debugging of a C++ program, a **Command Prompt** window appears (Fig. L.6), allowing program interaction (input and output). The program pauses when execution reaches the breakpoint at line 21. At this point, the title bar of the IDE will display **[break]** (Fig. L.7), indicating that the IDE is in break mode.

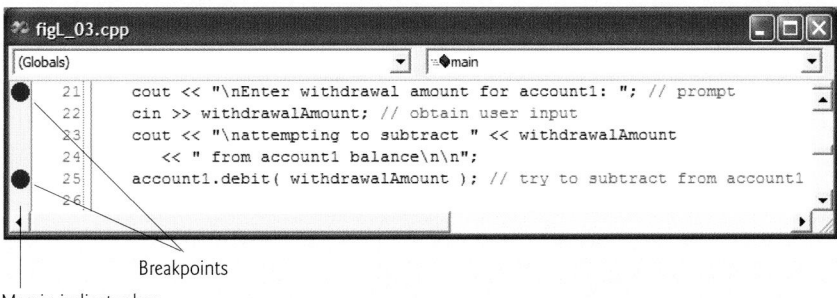

Breakpoints

Margin indicator bar

Fig. L.5 | Setting two breakpoints.

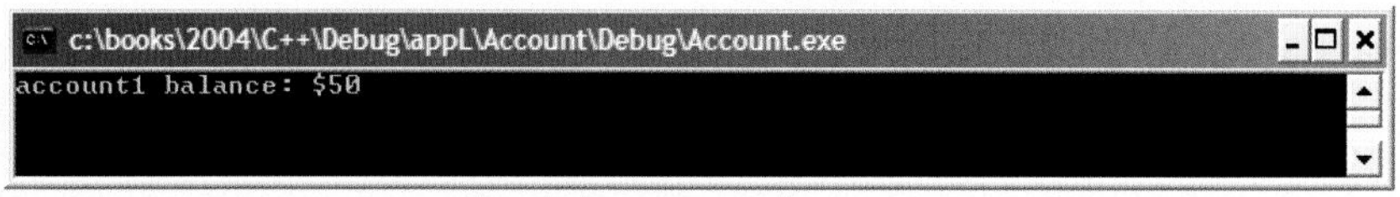

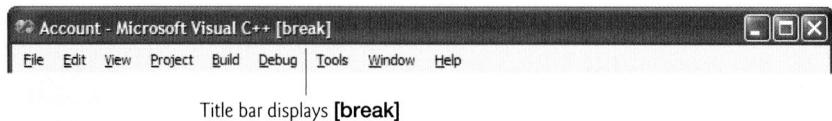

Fig. L.6 | **Inventory** program running.

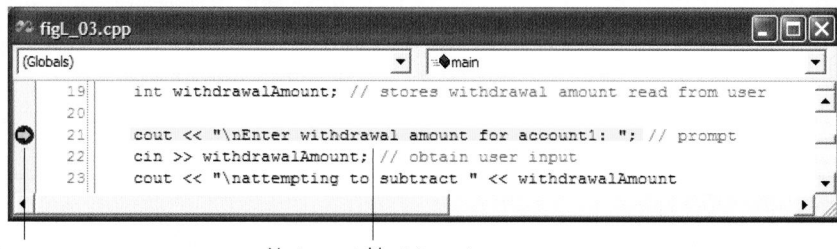

Title bar displays **[break]**

Fig. L.7 | Title bar of the IDE displaying **[break]**.

4. *Examining program execution.* Program execution suspends at the first break-point (line 21), and the IDE becomes the active window (Fig. L.8). The yellow arrow to the left of line 21 indicates that this line contains the next statement to execute. [*Note:* We have added the yellow highlighting to these images. Your code will not contain this highlighting.]

5. *Using the **Continue** command to resume execution.* To resume execution, select **Debug > Continue**. The Continue command will execute any statements between the next executable statement and the next breakpoint or the end of main, which-ever comes first. The program continues executing and pauses for input at line 22. Input 13 as the withdrawal amount. The program executes until it stops at the next breakpoint, line 25. Notice that when you place your mouse pointer over the variable name withdrawalAmount, the value that the variable stores is dis-played in a *Quick Info* box (Fig. L.9). In a sense, you are peeking inside the com-puter at the value of one of your variables. As you'll see, this can help you spot logic errors in your programs.

6. *Setting a breakpoint at the **return** statement.* Set a breakpoint at line 29 in the source code by clicking in the margin indicator bar to the left of line 29 (Fig. L.9). This will prevent the program from closing immediately after display-ing its result. When there are no more breakpoints at which to suspend execution, the program will execute to completion and the **Command Prompt** window will close. If you do not set this breakpoint, you will not be able to view the program's output before the console window closes.

Fig. L.8 | Program execution suspended at the first breakpoint.

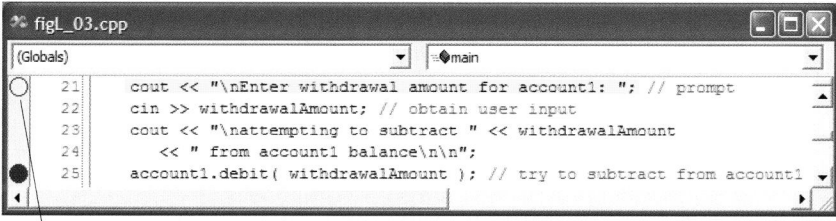

```
% figL_03.cpp
(Globals)                              ▼  ◆main                            ▼
     25    account1.debit( withdrawalAmount ); // try to subtract from account1
     26
     27    // display balances
     28    cout << "account1 balance: $" << account1.getBalance() << endl;
●    29    return 0; // indicate successful termination
```

Fig. L.9 | Setting a breakpoint at line 29.

7. *Continuing program execution.* Use the **Debug > Continue** command to execute line 25. The program displays the result of its calculation (Fig. L.10).

8. *Disabling a breakpoint.* To disable a breakpoint, right click a line of code on which a breakpoint has been set (or the breakpoint itself) and select **Disable Breakpoint**. The disabled breakpoint is indicated by a hollow maroon circle (Fig. L.11). Disabling rather than removing a breakpoint allows you to re-enable the breakpoint (by clicking inside the hollow circle) in a program. This also can be done by right clicking the line marked by the hollow maroon circle (or the maroon circle itself) and selecting **Enable Breakpoint**.

9. *Removing a breakpoint.* To remove a breakpoint that you no longer need, right click a line of code on which a breakpoint has been set and select **Remove Breakpoint**. You also can remove a breakpoint by clicking the maroon circle in the margin indicator bar.

10. *Finishing program execution.* Select **Debug > Continue** to execute the program to completion.

```
c:\books\2004\C++\Debug\appL\Account\Debug\Account.exe
account1 balance: $50
Enter withdrawal amount for account1: 13
attempting to subtract 13 from account1 balance
account1 balance: $37
```

Fig. L.10 | Program output.

```
% figL_03.cpp
(Globals)                              ▼  ◆main                            ▼
○    21    cout << "\nEnter withdrawal amount for account1: "; // prompt
     22    cin >> withdrawalAmount; // obtain user input
     23    cout << "\nattempting to subtract " << withdrawalAmount
     24       << " from account1 balance\n\n";
●    25    account1.debit( withdrawalAmount ); // try to subtract from account1
```

Disabled breakpoint

Fig. L.11 | Disabled breakpoint.

In this section, you learned how to enable the debugger and set breakpoints so that you can examine the results of code while a program is running. You also learned how to continue execution after a program suspends execution at a breakpoint and how to disable and remove breakpoints.

L.3 The Locals and Watch Windows

In the preceding section, you learned that the *Quick Info* feature allows you to examine the value of a variable. In this section, you will learn how to use the Locals window to assign new values to variables while your program is running. You will also use the Watch window to examine the value of more complex expressions.

1. *Inserting breakpoints.* Set a breakpoint at line 25 in the source code by clicking in the margin indicator bar to the left of line 25 (Fig. L.12). Set another breakpoint at line 28 of the code by clicking in the margin indicator bar to the left of line 28.

2. *Starting debugging.* Select **Debug > Start**. Type 13 at the **Enter withdrawal amount for account1:** prompt (Fig. L.13) and press *Enter* so that your program reads the value you just entered. The program executes until the breakpoint at line 25.

3. *Suspending program execution.* When the program reaches line 25, Visual C++ .NET suspends program execution and switches the program into break mode (Fig. L.14). At this point, the statement in line 22 (Fig. L.3) has input the withdrawalAmount that you entered (13), the statement in lines 23–24 has output that the program will attempt to withdraw money and the statement in line 25 is the next statement that will be executed.

4. *Examining data.* Once the program has entered break mode, you can explore the values of your local variables using the debugger's **Locals** window. To view the **Locals** window, select **Debug > Windows > Locals**. The values for account1 and withdrawalAmount (13) are displayed (Fig. L.15).

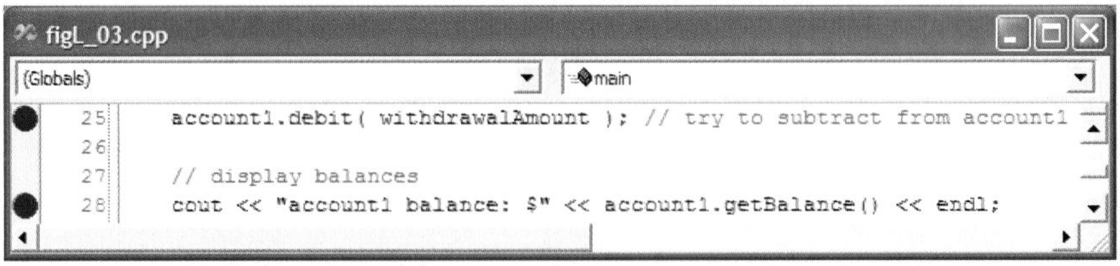

Fig. L.12 | Setting breakpoints at lines 25 and 28.

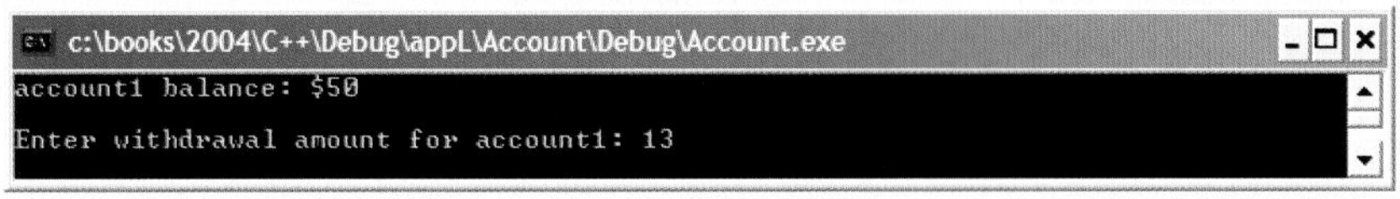

Fig. L.13 | Entering withdrawal amount before breakpoint is reached.

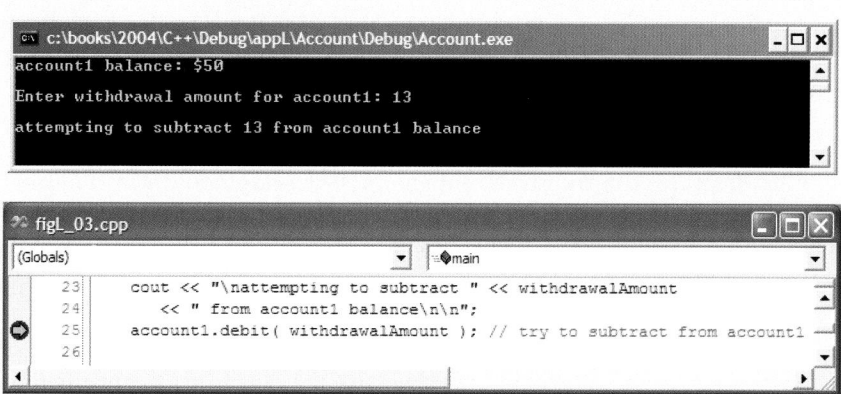

Fig. L.14 | Program execution suspended when debugger reaches the breakpoint at line 25.

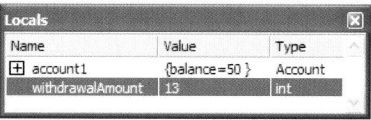

Fig. L.15 | Examining variable `withdrawalAmount`.

5. *Evaluating arithmetic and boolean expressions.* Visual Studio .NET allows you to evaluate arithmetic and boolean expressions using the **Watch** window. There are four different **Watch** windows, but we will be using only the first window. Select **Debug > Windows > Watch > Watch 1**. In the first row of the **Name** column (which should be blank initially), type `(withdrawalAmount + 3) * 5`, then press *Enter*. Notice that the **Watch** window can evaluate arithmetic expressions. In this case, it displays the value 80 (Fig. L.16). In the next row of the **Name** column in the **Watch** window, type `withdrawalAmount == 3`, then press *Enter*. This expression determines whether the value contained in `withdrawalAmount` is 3. Expressions containing the `==` symbol are treated as boolean expressions. The value returned is `false` (Fig. L.16), because `withdrawalAmount` does not currently contain the value 3.

Evaluating an
arithmetic expression
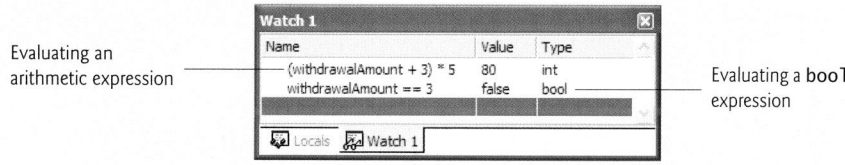
Evaluating a `bool`
expression

Fig. L.16 | Examining the values of expressions.

6. *Resuming execution.* Select **Debug > Continue** to resume execution. Line 25 executes, debiting the account with the withdrawal amount, and the program is once again suspended at line 28. Select **Debug > Windows > Locals**. The updated account1 value is now displayed in red to indicate that it has been modified since the last breakpoint (Fig. L.17). The value in withdrawalAmount is not in red because it has not been updated since the last breakpoint. Click the plus box to the left of account1 in the **Name** column of the **Locals** window. This allows you to view each of account1's data member values individually.

7. *Modifying values.* Based on the value input by the user (13), the account balance output by the program should be $37. However, you can use the debugger to change the values of variables in the middle of the program's execution. This can be valuable for experimenting with different values and for locating logic errors in programs. You can use the **Locals** window to change the value of a variable. In the **Locals** window, click the **Value** field in the balance row to select the value 37. Type 33, then press *Enter*. The debugger changes the value of balance and displays its new value in red (Fig. L.18).

8. *Setting a breakpoint at the **return** statement.* Set a breakpoint at line 29 in the source code by clicking in the margin indicator bar to the left of line 29 (Fig. L.19). This will prevent the program from closing immediately after displaying its result. If you do not set this breakpoint, you will not be able to view the program's output before the console window closes.

9. *Viewing the program result.* Select **Debug > Continue** to continue program execution. Function main executes until the return statement on line 29 and displays the result. Notice that the result is $33 (Fig. L.20). This shows that the previous step changed the value of balance from the calculated value (37) to 33.

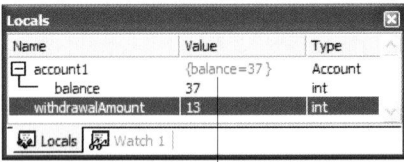

Value of the account1 variable displayed in red

Fig. L.17 | Displaying the value of local variables.

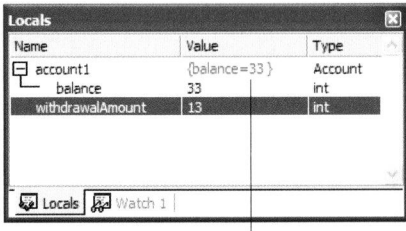

Value modified in the debugger

Fig. L.18 | Modifying the value of a variable.

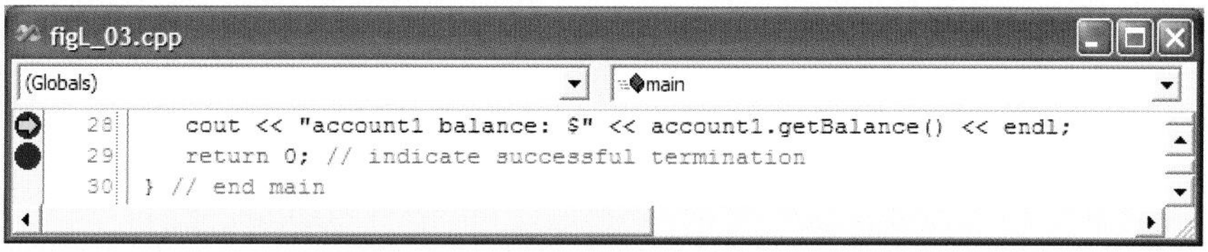

Fig. L.19 | Setting a breakpoint at line 29.

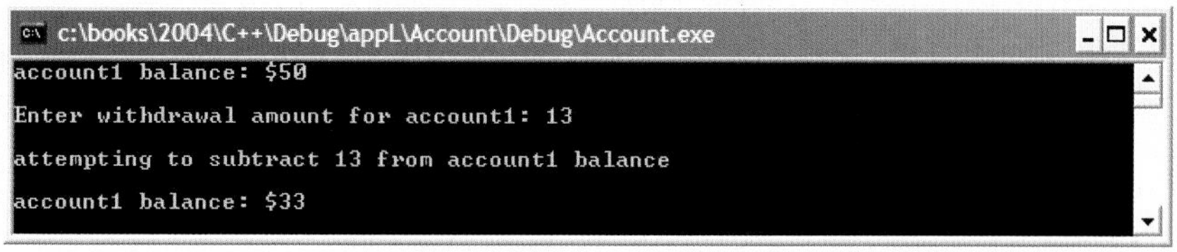

Fig. L.20 | Output displayed after modifying the `account1` variable.

10. *Stopping the debugging session.* Select **Debug > Stop Debugging**. This will close the **Command Prompt** window. Remove all remaining breakpoints.

In this section, you learned how to use the debugger's **Watch** and **Locals** windows to evaluate arithmetic and boolean expressions. You also learned how to modify the value of a variable during your program's execution.

L.4 Controlling Execution Using the Step Into, Step Over, Step Out and Continue Commands

Sometimes you will need to execute a program line by line to find and fix logic errors. Walking through a portion of your program this way can help you verify that a function's code executes correctly. In this section, you will learn how to use the debugger for this task. The commands you learn in this section allow you to execute a function line by line, execute all the statements of a function at once or execute only the remaining statements of a function (if you have already executed some statements within the function).

1. *Setting a breakpoint.* Set a breakpoint at line 25 by clicking in the margin indicator bar (Fig. L.21).

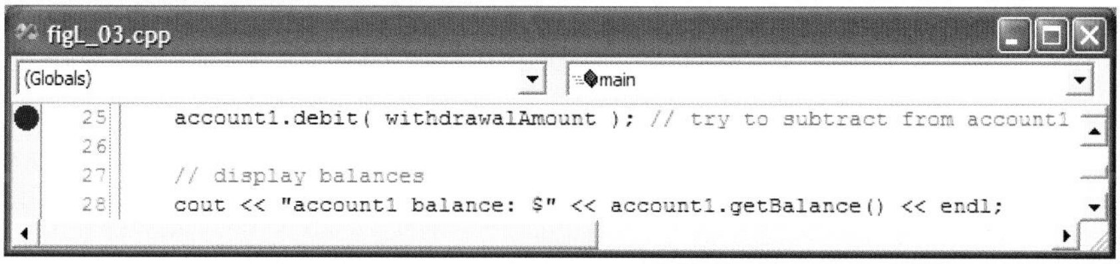

Fig. L.21 | Setting a breakpoint in the program

2. *Starting the debugger.* Select **Debug > Start**. Enter the value 13 at the **Enter withdrawal amount for account1:** prompt. Execution will halt when the program reaches the breakpoint at line 25.

3. *Using the **Step Into** command.* The **Step Into command** executes the next statement in the program (the yellow highlighted line of Fig. L.24) and immediately halts. If the statement to be executed as a result of the **Step Into** command is a function call, control is transferred to the called function. The **Step Into** command allows you to enter a function and confirm its execution by individually executing each statement inside the function. Select **Debug > Step Into** to enter the debit function (Fig. L.22). If the debugger is not at line 33, select **Debug > Step Into** again to reach that line.

4. *Using the **Step Over** command.* Select **Debug > Step Over** to execute the current statement (line 33 in Fig. L.22) and transfer control to line 34 (Fig. L.23). The **Step Over command** behaves like the **Step Into** command when the next statement to execute does not contain a function call. You will see how the **Step Over** command differs from the **Step Into** command in *Step 10*.

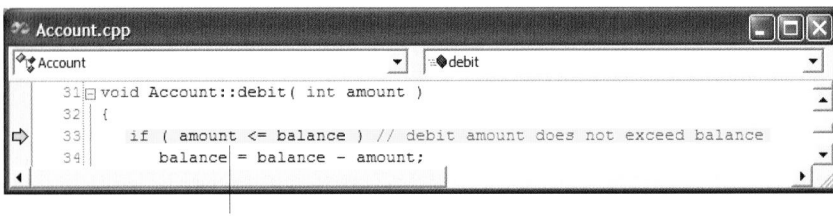

Next statement to execute

Fig. L.22 | Stepping into the debit function.

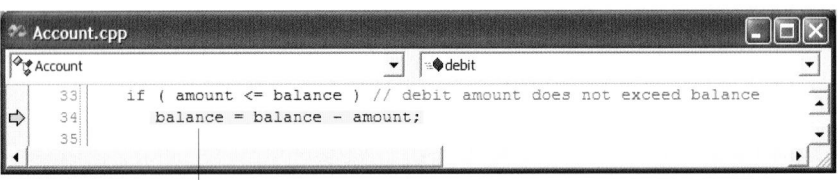

Control is transferred to the next statement

Fig. L.23 | Stepping over a statement in the debit function.

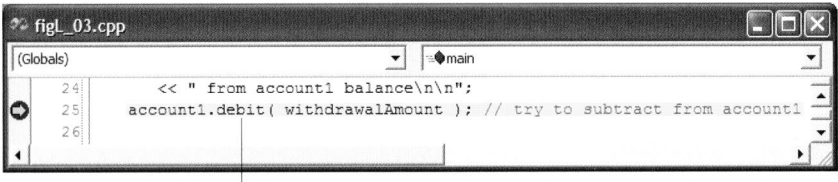

Next statement to execute is a function call

Fig. L.24 | Using the **Step Into** command to execute a statement.

5. *Using the Step Out command.* Select **Debug > Step Out** to execute the remaining statements in the function and return control to the next executable statement (line 28 in Fig. L.3), which contains the function call. Often, in lengthy functions, you will want to look at a few key lines of code, then continue debugging the caller's code. The Step Out command is useful for such situations, where you do not want to continue stepping through the entire function line by line.

6. *Setting a breakpoint.* Set a breakpoint (Fig. L.25) at the return statement of main at line 29 of Fig. L.3. You will make use of this breakpoint in the next step.

7. *Using the Continue command.* Select **Debug > Continue** to exectue until the next breakpoint is reached at line 29. This feature saves time when you do not want to step line by line through many lines of code to reach the next breakpoint.

8. *Stopping the debugger.* Select **Debug > Stop Debugging** to end the debugging session. This will close the **Command Prompt** window.

9. *Starting the debugger.* Before we can demonstrate the next debugger feature, you must start the debugger again. Start it, as you did in *Step 2*, and enter as input the same value (13). The debugger pauses execution at line 25.

10. *Using the Step Over command.* Select **Debug > Step Over** (Fig. L.26) Recall that this command behaves like the **Step Into** command when the next statement to execute does not contain a function call. If the next statement to execute contains a function call, the called function executes in its entirety (without pausing execution at any statement inside the function), and the yellow arrow advances to the next executable line (after the function call) in the current function. In this case, the debugger executes line 25, located in main (Fig. L.3). Line 25 calls the debit function. The debugger then pauses execution at line 28, the next executable line in the current function, main.

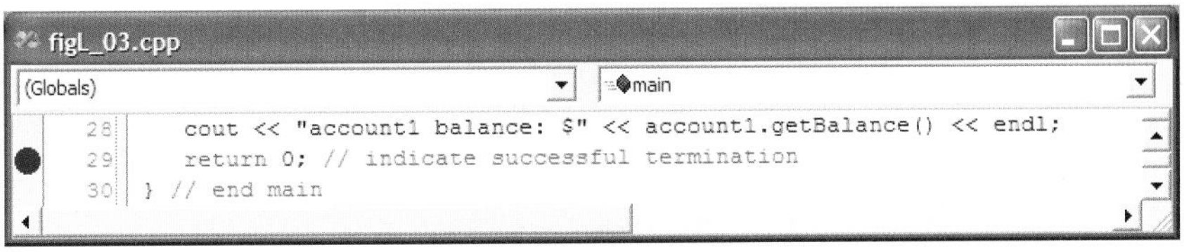

Fig. L.25 | Setting a second breakpoint in the program.

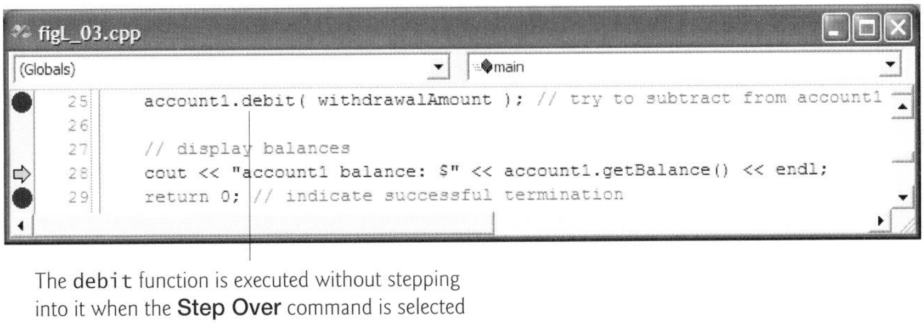

The debit function is executed without stepping into it when the **Step Over** command is selected

Fig. L.26 | Using the debugger's **Step Over** command.

11. *Stopping the debugger.* Select **Debug > Stop Debugging**. This will close the **Command Prompt** window. Remove all remaining breakpoints.

In this section, you learned how to use the debugger's **Step Into** command to debug functions called during your program's execution. You saw how the **Step Over** command can be used to step over a function call. You used the **Step Out** command to continue execution until the end of the current function. You also learned that the **Continue** command continues execution until another breakpoint is found or the program exits.

L.5 The Autos Window

In this section, we present the Autos window, which displays the variables used in the previous statement executed and the next command to execute. The **Autos** window allows you to focus on variables that were just used, and those that will be used and modified in the next statement.

1. *Setting breakpoints.* Set breakpoints at lines 14 and 22 by clicking in the margin indicator bar (Fig. L.27).

2. *Using the* **Autos** *window.* Start the debugger by selecting **Debug > Start**. When execution halts at the breakpoint at line 14, open the **Autos** window (Fig. L.28) by selecting **Debug > Windows > Autos**. The **Autos** window allows you to view the contents of the variables used in the last statement that was executed. This allows you to verify that the previous statement executed correctly. The **Autos** window also lists the values in the next statement to be executed. Notice that the **Autos** window lists the account1 variable, its value and its type. Viewing the values stored in an object lets you verify that your program is manipulating these variables correctly. Notice that account1 contains a large negative value. This value, which may be different each time the program executes, is account1's uninitialized value. This unpredictable (and often undesirable) value demonstrates why it is important to initialize all C++ variables before use.

3. *Using the* **Step Over** *command.* Select **Debug > Step Over** to execute line 14. The **Autos** window (Fig. L.29) updates the value of account1 after it is initialized. The value of account1 is displayed in red to indicate that it changed.

4. *Continuing execution.* Select **Debug > Continue**. Program execution will stop at the second breakpoint, set at line 22. The **Autos** window (Fig. L.30) displays uninitialized local variable withdrawalAmount, which has a large negative value.

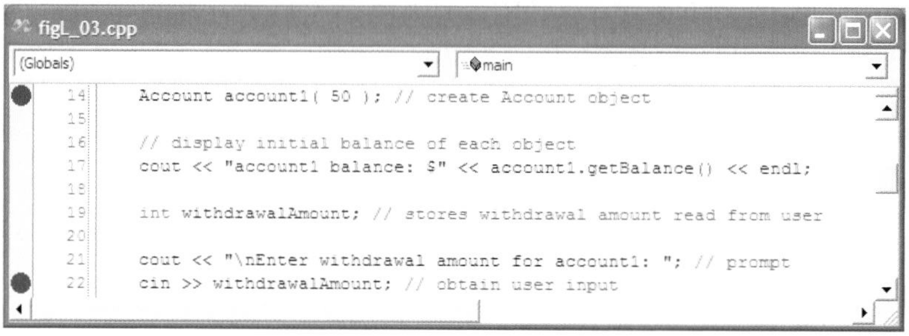

Fig. L.27 | Setting breakpoints in the program.

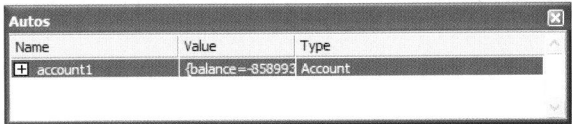

Fig. L.28 | **Autos** window displaying the state of `account1` object.

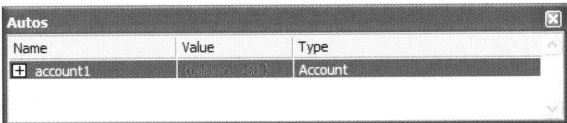

Fig. L.29 | **Autos** window displaying the state of `account1` object after initialization.

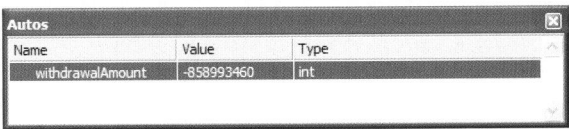

Fig. L.30 | **Autos** window displaying local variable `withdrawalAmount`.

5. *Entering data.* Select **Debug > Step Over** to execute line 22. At the program's input prompt, enter a value for the withdrawal amount. The **Autos** window (Fig. L.29) will update the value of local variable `withdrawalAmount` with the value you entered. [*Note:* The first line of the **Autos** window contains the `istream` object (`cin`) you used to input data.]

6. *Stopping the debugger.* Select **Debug > Stop Debugging** to end the debugging session. Remove all remaining breakpoints.

In this section, you learned about the **Autos** window, which allows you to view the variables used in the most recent command.

Summary

- Most C++ compiler vendors provide software called a debugger, which allows you to monitor the execution of your programs to locate and remove logic errors.

- Breakpoints are markers that can be set at any executable line of code. When program execution reaches a breakpoint, execution pauses.

- The debugger is enabled by default. If it is not enabled, you have to change the settings of the *Solution Configurations* combo box.

- To insert a breakpoint, either click inside the margin indicator bar next to the line of code or right click that line of code and select **Insert Breakpoint**. A solid maroon circle appears where you clicked, indicating that a breakpoint has been set.

- When the program runs, it suspends execution at any line that contains a breakpoint. It is then said to be in break mode, and the title bar of the IDE will display **[break]**.

- A yellow arrow indicates that this line contains the next statement to execute.

- When you place your mouse pointer over a variable name, the value that the variable stores is displayed in a *Quick Info* box.

- To disable a breakpoint, right click a line of code on which a breakpoint has been set and select **Disable Breakpoint**. The disabled breakpoint is indicated by a hollow maroon circle.

- To remove a breakpoint that you no longer need, right click a line of code on which a breakpoint has been set and select **Remove Breakpoint**. You also can remove a breakpoint by clicking the maroon circle in the margin indicator bar.

- Once the program has entered break mode, you can explore the values of your variables using the debugger's **Locals** window. To view the **Locals** window, select **Debug > Windows > Locals**.

- You can evaluate arithmetic and boolean expressions using one of the **Watch** windows. The first **Watch** window is displayed by selecting **Debug > Windows > Watch > Watch 1**.

- Updated variables are displayed in red to indicate that they have been modified since the last breakpoint.

- Clicking the plus box next to an object in the **Name** column of the **Locals** window allows you to view each of object's data member values individually.

- You can click the **Value** field of a variable to change its value in the **Locals** window.

- The **Step Into** command executes the next statement (the yellow highlighted line) in the program. If the next statement is to execute a function call and you select **Step Into**, control is transferred to the called function.

- The **Step Over** command behaves like the **Step Into** command when the next statement to execute does not contain a function call. If the next statement to execute contains a function call, the called function executes in its entirety, and the yellow arrow advances to the next executable line in the current function.

- Select **Debug > Step Out** to execute the remaining statements in the function and return control to the function call.

- The **Continue** command will execute any statements between the next executable statement and the next breakpoint or the end of `main`, whichever comes first.

- The **Autos** window allows you to view the contents of the variables used in the last statement that was executed. The **Autos** window also lists the values in the next statement to be executed.

Terminology

Autos window	margin indicator bar
break mode	*Quick Info* box
breakpoint	*Solution Configurations* combo box
bug	**Step Into** command
Continue command	**Step Out** command
debugger	**Step Over** command
disabling a breakpoint	**Watch** window
Locals window	yellow arrow in break mode

Self-Review Exercises

L.1   Fill in the blanks in each of the following statements:

  a) When the debugger suspends program execution at a breakpoint, the program is said to be in _____ mode.

b) The _____ feature in Visual Studio .NET allows you to "peek into the computer" and look at the value of a variable.

c) You can examine the value of an expression by using the debugger's _____ window.

d) The _____ command behaves like the **Step Into** command when the next statement to execute does not contain a function call.

L.2   State whether each of the following is *true* or *false*. If *false*, explain why.

a) When program execution suspends at a breakpoint, the next statement to be executed is the statement after the breakpoint.

b) When a variable's value is changed, it becomes yellow in the **Autos** and **Locals** windows.

c) During debugging, the **Step Out** command executes the remaining statements in the current function and returns program control to the place where the function was called.

Answers to Self-Review Exercises

L.1   a) break. b) *Quick Info* box. c) **Watch**. d) **Step Over**.

L.2   a) False. When program execution suspends at a breakpoint, the next statement to be executed is the statement at the breakpoint. b) False. A variable turns red when its value is changed. c) True.

Using the GNU C++ Debugger

OBJECTIVES

In this appendix you will learn:

- To use the **run** command to run a program in the debugger.
- To use the **break** command to set a breakpoint.
- To use the **continue** command to continue execution.
- To use the **print** command to evaluate expressions.
- To use the **set** command to change variable values during program execution.
- To use the **step**, **finish** and **next** commands to control execution.
- To use the **watch** command to see how a data member is modified during program execution.
- To use the **delete** command to remove a breakpoint or a watchpoint.

M.1 Introduction

In Chapter 2, you learned that there are two types of errors—compilation errors and logic errors—and you learned how to eliminate compilation errors from your code. Logic errors do not prevent a program from compiling successfully, but they do cause the program to produce erroneous results when it runs. GNU includes software called a debugger that allows you to monitor the execution of your programs so you can locate and remove logic errors.

The debugger will be one of your most important program development tools. Many IDEs provide their own debuggers similar to the one included in GNU or provide a graphical user interface to GNU's debugger. This appendix demonstrates key features of GNU's debugger. Appendix L discusses the features and capabilities of the Visual Studio .NET debugger. We provide several free *Dive Into™ Series* publications to help students and instructors familiarize themselves with the debuggers provided with various development tools. These publications are available on the CD that accompanies the text and can be downloaded from `www.deitel.com/books/downloads`.

M.2 Breakpoints and the `run`, `stop`, `continue` and `print` Commands

We begin our study of the debugger by investigating breakpoints, which are markers that can be set at any executable line of code. When program execution reaches a breakpoint, execution pauses, allowing you to examine the values of variables to help determine whether logic errors exist. For example, you can examine the value of a variable that stores the result of a calculation to determine whether the calculation was performed correctly. Note that attempting to set a breakpoint at a line of code that is not executable (such as a comment) will actually set the breakpoint at the next executable line of code in that function.

To illustrate the features of the debugger, we use the program listed in Fig. M.3, which creates and manipulates an object of class `Account` (Figs. M.1–M.2). Execution begins in `main` (lines 12–30 of Fig. M.3). Line 14 creates an `Account` object with an initial balance of $50.00. `Account`'s constructor (lines 10–22 of Fig. M.2) accepts one argument, which specifies the `Account`'s initial `balance`. Line 17 of Fig. M.3 outputs the initial account balance using `Account` member function `getBalance`. Line 19 declares a local variable `withdrawalAmount` which stores a withdrawal amount read from the user. Line 21 prompts the user for the withdrawal amount; line 22 inputs the amount into `withdrawalAmount`. Line 25 subtracts the withdrawal from the `Account`'s `balance` using its `debit` member function. Finally, line 28 displays the new `balance`.

```
1   // Fig. M.1: Account.h
2   // Definition of Account class.
3
4   class Account
5   {
6   public:
7      Account( int ); // constructor initializes balance
8      void credit( int ); // add an amount to the account balance
9      void debit( int ); // subtract an amount from the account balance
10     int getBalance(); // return the account balance
11  private:
12     int balance; // data member that stores the balance
13  }; // end class Account
```

Fig. M.1 | Header file for the Account class.

```
1   // Fig. M.2: Account.cpp
2   // Member-function definitions for class Account.
3   #include <iostream>
4   using std::cout;
5   using std::endl;
6
7   #include "Account.h" // include definition of class Account
8
9   // Account constructor initializes data member balance
10  Account::Account( int initialBalance )
11  {
12     balance = 0; // assume that the balance begins at 0
13
14     // if initialBalance is greater than 0, set this value as the
15     // balance of the Account; otherwise, balance remains 0
16     if ( initialBalance > 0 )
17        balance = initialBalance;
18
19     // if initialBalance is negative, print error message
20     if ( initialBalance < 0 )
21        cout << "Error: Initial balance cannot be negative.\n" << endl;
22  } // end Account constructor
23
24  // credit (add) an amount to the account balance
25  void Account::credit( int amount )
26  {
27     balance = balance + amount; // add amount to balance
28  } // end function credit
29
30  // debit (subtract) an amount from the account balance
31  void Account::debit( int amount )
32  {
33     if ( amount <= balance ) // debit amount does not exceed balance
34        balance = balance - amount;
35
```

Fig. M.2 | Definition for the Account class. (Part 1 of 2.)

```
36        else // debit amount exceeds balance
37            cout << "Debit amount exceeded account balance.\n" << endl;
38    } // end function debit
39
40    // return the account balance
41    int Account::getBalance()
42    {
43        return balance; // gives the value of balance to the calling function
44    } // end function getBalance
```

Fig. M.2 | Definition for the Account class. (Part 2 of 2.)

```
1     // Fig. M.3: figM_03.cpp
2     // Create and manipulate Account objects.
3     #include <iostream>
4     using std::cin;
5     using std::cout;
6     using std::endl;
7
8     // include definition of class Account from Account.h
9     #include "Account.h"
10
11    // function main begins program execution
12    int main()
13    {
14        Account account1( 50 ); // create Account object
15
16        // display initial balance of each object
17        cout << "account1 balance: $" << account1.getBalance() << endl;
18
19        int withdrawalAmount; // stores withdrawal amount read from user
20
21        cout << "\nEnter withdrawal amount for account1: "; // prompt
22        cin >> withdrawalAmount; // obtain user input
23        cout << "\nattempting to subtract " << withdrawalAmount
24            << " from account1 balance\n\n";
25        account1.debit( withdrawalAmount ); // try to subtract from account1
26
27        // display balances
28        cout << "account1 balance: $" << account1.getBalance() << endl;
29        return 0; // indicate successful termination
30    } // end main
```

Fig. M.3 | Test class for debugging.

In the following steps, you will use breakpoints and various debugger commands to examine the value of the variable `withdrawalAmount` declared in line 19 of Fig. M.3.

1. *Compiling the program for debugging.* The GNU debugger works only with executable files that were compiled with the `-g` compiler option, which generates information that is used by the debugger to help you debug your programs. Compile the program with the -g command-line option by typing g++ -g -o figM_03 figM_03.cpp Account.cpp.

2. *Starting the debugger.* Type `gdb` `figM_03` (Fig. M.4). This command will start the GNU debugger and display the (gdb) prompt at which you can enter commands.

3. *Running a program in the debugger.* Run the program through the debugger by typing `run` (Fig. M.5). If you do not set any breakpoints before running your program in the debugger, the program will run to completion.

4. *Inserting breakpoints using the GNU debugger.* You set a breakpoint at a specific line of code in your program. The line numbers used in these steps are from the source code in Fig. M.3. Set a breakpoint at line 17 in the source code by typing `break 17`. The `break command` inserts a breakpoint at the line number specified after the command. You can set as many breakpoints as necessary. Each breakpoint is identified in terms of the order in which it was created. The first breakpoint created is known as `Breakpoint 1`. Set another breakpoint at line 25 by typing `break 25` (Fig. M.6). When the program runs, it suspends execution at any line that contains a breakpoint and the program is said to be in break mode. Breakpoints can be set even after the debugging process has begun. [*Note:* If you do not have a numbered listing for your code, you can use the `list` command to output your code with line numbers. For more information about the `list` command type `help` `list` from the gdb prompt.]

```
~/Debug$ gdb figM_03
GNU gdb 6.1-debian
Copyright 2004 Free Software Foundation, Inc.
GDB is free software, covered by the GNU General Public License, and you are
welcome to change it and/or distribute copies of it under certain conditions.
Type "show copying" to see the conditions.
There is absolutely no warranty for GDB.  Type "show warranty" for details.
This GDB was configured as "i386-linux"...Using host libthread_db library "/
lib/libthread_db.so.1".

(gdb)
```

Fig. M.4 | Starting the debugger to run the program.

```
(gdb) run
Starting program: /home/student/Debug/figM_03
account1 balance: $50

Enter withdrawal amount for account1: 13

attempting to subtract 13 from account1 balance

account1 balance: $37

Program exited normally.
(gdb)
```

Fig. M.5 | Running the program with no breakpoints set.

```
(gdb) break 17
Breakpoint 1 at 0x80487d8: file figM_03.cpp, line 17.
(gdb) break 25
Breakpoint 2 at 0x8048871: file figM_03.cpp, line 25.
(gdb)
```

Fig. M.6 | Setting two breakpoints in the program.

5. ***Running the program and beginning the debugging process.*** Type run to execute your program and begin the debugging process (Fig. M.7). The program pauses when execution reaches the breakpoint at line 17. At this point, the debugger notifies you that a breakpoint has been reached and displays the source code at that line (17). That line of code contains the next statement that will execute.

6. ***Using the `continue` command to resume execution.*** Type continue. The continue command causes the program to continue running until the next breakpoint is reached (line 25). Enter 13 at the prompt. The debugger notifies you when execution reaches the second breakpoint (Fig. M.8). Note that figM_03's normal output appears between messages from the debugger.

```
(gdb) run
Starting program: /home/student/Debug/figM_03

Breakpoint 1, main () at figM_03.cpp:17
17          cout << "account1 balance: $" << account1.getBalance() << endl;
(gdb)
```

Fig. M.7 | Running the program until it reaches the first breakpoint.

```
(gdb) continue
Continuing.
account1 balance: $50

Enter withdrawal amount for account1: 13

attempting to subtract 13 from account1 balance


Breakpoint 2, main () at figM_03.cpp:25
25          account1.debit( withdrawalAmount ); // try to subtract from
account1
(gdb)
```

Fig. M.8 | Continuing execution until the second breakpoint is reached.

7. *Examining a variable's value.* Type print withdrawalAmount to display the current value stored in the withdrawalAmount variable (Fig. M.9). The print command allows you to peek inside the computer at the value of one of your variables. This command will help you find and eliminate logic errors in your code. Note that the value displayed is 13—the value read in and assigned to withdrawalAmount in line 22 of Fig. M.3. Use the print command to output the contents of the account1 object. When an object is output through the debugger with the print command, the object is output with braces surrounding the object's data members. In this case, there is a single data member—balance—which has a value of 50.

8. *Using convenience variables.* When the print command is used, the result is stored in a convenience variable such as $1. Convenience variables, which are temporary variables, named using a dollar sign followed by an integer, are created by the debugger as you print values during your debugging session. A convenience variable can be used in the debugging process to perform arithmetic and evaluate boolean expressions. Type print $1. The debugger displays the value of $1 (Fig. M.10), which contains the value of withdrawalAmount. Note that printing the value of $1 creates a new convenience variable—$3.

9. *Continuing program execution.* Type continue to continue the program's execution. The debugger encounters no additional breakpoints, so it continues executing and eventually terminates (Fig. M.11).

```
(gdb) print withdrawalAmount
$1 = 13
(gdb) print account1
$2 = {balance = 50}
(gdb)
```

Fig. M.9 | Printing the values of variables.

```
(gdb) print $1
$3 = 13
(gdb)
```

Fig. M.10 | Printing a convenience variable.

```
(gdb) continue
Continuing.
account1 balance: $37

Program exited normally.
(gdb)
```

Fig. M.11 | Finishing execution of the program.

10. ***Removing a breakpoint.*** You can display a list of all of the breakpoints in the program by typing `info break`. To remove a breakpoint, type `delete`, followed by a space and the number of the breakpoint to remove. Remove the first breakpoint by typing `delete 1`. Remove the second breakpoint as well. Now type `info break` to list the remaining breakpoints in the program. The debugger should indicate that no breakpoints are set (Fig. M.12).

11. ***Executing the program without breakpoints.*** Type `run` to execute the program. Enter the value 13 at the prompt. Because you successfully removed the two breakpoints, the program's output is displayed without the debugger entering break mode (Fig. M.13).

12. ***Using the `quit` command.*** Use the `quit` command to end the debugging session (Fig. M.14). This command causes the debugger to terminate.

```
(gdb) info break
Num Type           Disp Enb Address    What
1   breakpoint     keep y   0x080487d8 in main at figM_03.cpp:17
        breakpoint already hit 1 time
2   breakpoint     keep y   0x08048871 in main at figM_03.cpp:25
        breakpoint already hit 1 time
(gdb) delete 1
(gdb) delete 2
(gdb) info break
No breakpoints or watchpoints.
(gdb)
```

Fig. M.12 | Viewing and removing breakpoints.

```
(gdb) run
Starting program: /home/student/Debug/figM_03
account1 balance: $50

Enter withdrawal amount for account1: 13

attempting to subtract 13 from account1 balance

account1 balance: $37

Program exited normally.
(gdb)
```

Fig. M.13 | Program executing with no breakpoints set.

```
(gdb) quit
~/Debug$
```

Fig. M.14 | Exiting the debugger using the `quit` command.

In this section, you learned how to enable the debugger using the `gdb` command and run a program with the `run` command. You saw how to set a breakpoint at a particular line number in the `main` function. The `break` command can also be used to set a breakpoint at a line number in another file or at a particular function. Typing `break`, then the filename, a colon and the line number will set a breakpoint at a line in another file. Typing `break`, then a function name will cause the debugger to enter the break mode whenever that function is called.

Also in this section, you saw how the `help list` command will provide more information on the `list` command. If you have any questions about the debugger or any of his commands, type `help` or `help` followed by the command name for more information.

Finally, you learned to examine variables with the `print` command and remove breakpoints with the `delete` command. You learned how to use the `continue` command to continue execution after a breakpoint is reached and the `quit` command to end the debugger.

M.3 The print and set Commands

In the preceding section, you learned how to use the debugger's `print` command to examine the value of a variable during program execution. In this section, you will learn how to use the `print` command to examine the value of more complex expressions. You will also learn the **set command**, which allows the programmer to assign new values to variables. We assume you are working in the directory containing this appendix's examples and have compiled for debugging with the `-g` compiler option.

1. *Starting debugging.* Type `gdb figM_03` to start the GNU debugger.

2. *Inserting a breakpoint.* Set a breakpoint at line 25 in the source code by typing `break 25` (Fig. M.15).

3. *Running the program and reaching a breakpoint.* Type `run` to begin the debugging process (Fig. M.16). This will cause `main` to execute until the breakpoint at line 25 is reached. This suspends program execution and switches the program into break mode. The statement in line 25 is the next statement that will execute.

4. *Evaluating arithmetic and boolean expressions.* Recall from Section M.2 that once the program has entered break mode, you can explore the values of the program's variables using the debugger's `print` command. You can also use the `print` command to evaluate arithmetic and boolean expressions. Type `print withdrawalAmount - 2`. Note that the `print` command returns the value 11 (Fig. M.17). However, this command does not actually change the value of `withdrawalAmount`. Type `print withdrawalAmount == 11`. Expressions containing the `==` symbol are treated as boolean expressions. The value returned is `false` (Fig. M.17) because `withdrawalAmount` does not currently contain the value 11—`withdrawalAmount` is still 13.

```
(gdb) break 25
Breakpoint 1 at 0x8048871: file figM_03.cpp, line 25.
(gdb)
```

Fig. M.15 | Setting a breakpoint in the program.

```
(gdb) run
Starting program: /home/student/Debug/figM_03
account1 balance: $50

Enter withdrawal amount for account1: 13

attempting to subtract 13 from account1 balance


Breakpoint 1, main () at figM_03.cpp:25
25          account1.debit( withdrawalAmount ); // try to subtract from
account1
(gdb)
```

Fig. M.16 | Running the program until the breakpoint at line 25 is reached.

```
(gdb) print withdrawalAmount - 2
$1 = 11
(gdb) print withdrawalAmount == 11
$2 = false
(gdb)
```

Fig. M.17 | Printing expressions with the debugger.

5. *Modifying values.* The debugger allows you to change the values of variables during the program's execution. This can be valuable for experimenting with different values and for locating logic errors in programs. You can use the debugger's set command to change the value of a variable. Type set withdrawalAmount = 42. The debugger changes the value of withdrawalAmount. Type print withdrawalAmount to display its new value (Fig. M.18).

6. *Viewing the program result.* Type continue to continue program execution. Line 25 of Fig. M.3 executes, passing withdrawalAmount to Account member function debit. Function main then displays the new balance. Note that the result is $8 (Fig. M.19). This shows that the preceding step changed the value of withdrawalAmount from its initial value (13) to 42.

7. *Using the quit command.* Use the quit command to end the debugging session (Fig. M.20). This command causes the debugger to terminate.

In this section, you learned how to use the debugger's print command to evaluate arithmetic and boolean expressions. You also learned how to use the set command to modify the value of a variable during your program's execution.

```
(gdb) set withdrawalAmount = 42
(gdb) print withdrawalAmount
$3 = 42
(gdb)
```

Fig. M.18 | Setting the value of a variable while in break mode.

```
(gdb) continue
Continuing.
account1 balance: $8

Program exited normally.
(gdb)
```

Fig. M.19 | Using a modified variable in the execution of a program.

```
(gdb) quit
~/Debug$
```

Fig. M.20 | Exiting the debugger using the quit command.

M.4 Controlling Execution Using the step, finish and next Commands

Sometimes you will need to execute a program line by line to find and fix errors. Walking through a portion of your program this way can help you verify that a function's code executes correctly. In this section, you will learn how to use the debugger for this task. The commands you learn here allow you to execute a function line by line, execute all the statements of a function at once or execute only the remaining statements of a function (if you have already executed some statements within the function). Once again, we assume you are working in the directory containing this appendix's examples and have compiled for debugging with the -g compiler option.

1. *Starting the debugger.* Start the debugger by typing gdb figM_03.

2. *Setting a breakpoint.* Type break 25 to set a breakpoint at line 25.

3. *Running the program.* Run the program by typing run. After the program displays its two output messages, the debugger indicates that the breakpoint has been reached and displays the code at line 25. The debugger and program then pause and wait for the next command to be entered.

4. *Using the step command.* The step command executes the next statement in the program. If the next statement to execute is a function call, control transfers to the called function. The step command enables you to enter a function and study the individual statements of that function. For instance, you can use the print and set commands to view and modify the variables within the function. Type step to enter the debit member function of class Account (Fig. M.2). The debugger indicates that the step has been completed and displays the next executable statement (Fig. M.21)—in this case, line 33 of class Account (Fig. M.2).

5. *Using the finish command.* After you have stepped into the debit member function, type finish. This command executes the remaining statements in the function and returns control to the place where the function was called. The finish command executes the remaining statements in member function debit, then pauses at line 28 in main (Fig. M.22). In lengthy functions, you may want to look at a few key lines of code, then continue debugging the caller's code. The finish

```
(gdb) step
Account::debit (this=0xbffffd70, amount=13) at Account.cpp:33
33          if ( amount <= balance ) // debit amount does not exceed balance
(gdb)
```

Fig. M.21 | Using the step command to enter a function.

```
(gdb) finish
Run till exit from #0  Account::debit (this=0xbffffd70, amount=13)
    at Account.cpp:33
main () at figM_03.cpp:28
28          cout << "account1 balance: $" << account1.getBalance() << endl;
(gdb)
```

Fig. M.22 | Using the finish command to complete execution of a function and return to the calling function.

command is useful for situations in which you do not want to continue stepping through the entire function line by line.

6. *Using the **continue** command to continue execution.* Enter the continue command to continue execution. No additional breakpoints are reached, so the program terminates.

7. *Running the program again.* Breakpoints persist until the end of the debugging session in which they are set—even after execution of the program, all breakpoints are maintained. The breakpoint you set in *Step 2* will be there in the next execution of the program. Type run to run the program. As in *Step 3*, the program runs until the breakpoint at line 25 is reached, then the debugger pauses and waits for the next command (Fig. M.23).

8. *Using the **next** command.* Type next. This command behaves like the step command, except when the next statement to execute contains a function call. In that case, the called function executes in its entirety and the program advances to the next executable line after the function call (Fig. M.24). In *Step 4*, the step com-

```
(gdb) run
Starting program: /home/student/Debug/figM_03
account1 balance: $50

Enter withdrawal amount for account1: 13

attempting to subtract 13 from account1 balance

Breakpoint 1, main () at figM_03.cpp:25
25          account1.debit( withdrawalAmount ); // try to subtract from
account1
(gdb)
```

Fig. M.23 | Restarting the program.

```
(gdb) next
28          cout << "account1 balance: $" << account1.getBalance() << endl;
(gdb)
```

Fig. M.24 | Using the `next` command to execute a function in its entirety.

mand enters the called function. In this example, the `next` command causes `Ac-count` member function `debit` to execute, then the debugger pauses at line 28.

9. *Using the **quit** command.* Use the `quit` command to end the debugging session (Fig. M.25). While the program is running, this command causes the program to immediately terminate rather than execute the remaining statements in `main`.

In this section, you learned how to use the debugger's `step` and `finish` commands to debug functions called during your program's execution. You saw how the `next` command can be used to step over a function call. You also learned that the `quit` command ends a debugging session.

M.5 The watch Command

In this section, we present the watch command, which tells the debugger to watch a data member. When that data member is about to change, the debugger will notify you. In this section, you will learn how to use the `watch` command to see how the `Account` object's data member `balance` is modified during the execution of the program.

1. *Starting the debugger.* Start the debugger by typing `gdb figM_03`.

2. *Running the program.* Type `break 14` to set a breakpoint at line 14. Run the program with the command `run`. The debugger and program will pause at the breakpoint at line 14 (Fig. M.26).

3. *Watching a class's data member.* Set a watch on `account1`'s `balance` data member by typing `watch account1.balance` (Fig. M.27). This watch is labeled as `watch-point 2` because watchpoints are labeled with the same numbers as breakpoints. You can set a watch on any variable or data member of an object currently in scope during execution of the debugger. Whenever the value of a watched variable changes, the debugger enters break mode and notifies you that the value has changed.

4. *Continuing the program.* Step into the `Account` constructor with the command `step`. The debugger will display line 12 of Fig. M.2, which is the first line in the constructor. Use the `step` command again to execute this line of code. The debugger will now notify you that data member `balance`'s value will change (Fig. M.28). When the program begins, an instance of `Account` is created. When the constructor for this object runs, data member `balance` is first assigned the value 0. The debugger notifies you that the value of `balance` has been changed.

```
(gdb) quit
The program is running.  Exit anyway? (y or n) y
~/Debug$
```

Fig. M.25 | Exiting the debugger using the `quit` command.

```
(gdb) run
Starting program: /home/student/Debug/figM_03

Breakpoint 1, main () at figM_03.cpp:14
14          Account account1( 50 ); // create Account object
(gdb)
```

Fig. M.26 | Running the program until the first breakpoint.

```
(gdb) watch account1.balance
Hardware watchpoint 2: account1.balance
(gdb)
```

Fig. M.27 | Setting a watchpoint on a data member.

```
(gdb) step
Account (this=0xbffffd70, initialBalance=50) at Account.cpp:12
12          balance = 0; // assume that the balance begins at 0
(gdb) step
Hardware watchpoint 2: account1.balance

Old value = 1073833120
New value = 0
Account (this=0xbffffd70, initialBalance=50) at Account.cpp:16
16          if ( initialBalance > 0 )
(gdb)
```

Fig. M.28 | Stepping into the constructor.

5. *Finishing the constructor.* Type step to execute line 16, then type step again to execute line 17. The debugger will notify you that data member balance's value has changed from 0 to 50 (Fig. M.29).

6. *Withdrawing money from the account.* Type continue to continue execution and enter a withdrawal value at the prompt. The program executes normally. Line 25 of Fig. M.3 calls Account member function debit to reduce the Account

```
(gdb) step
17              balance = initialBalance;
(gdb) step
Hardware watchpoint 2: account1.balance

Old value = 0
New value = 50
Account (this=0xbffffd70, initialBalance=50) at Account.cpp:20
20          if ( initialBalance < 0 )
(gdb)
```

Fig. M.29 | Reaching a watchpoint notification.

object's balance by a specified amount. Line 34 of Fig. M.2 inside function debit changes the value of balance. The debugger notifies you of this change and enters break mode (Fig. M.30).

7. *Continuing execution.* Type continue—the program will finish executing function main because the program does not attempt any additional changes to balance. The debugger removes the watch on account1's balance data member because the variable goes out of scope when function main ends. Removing the watchpoint causes the debugger to enter break mode. Type continue again to finish execution of the program (Fig. M.31).

8. *Restarting the debugger and resetting the watch on the variable.* Type run to restart the debugger. Once again, set a watch on account1 data member balance by typing watch account1.balance. This watchpoint is labeled as watchpoint 3. Type continue to continue execution (Fig. M.32).

```
(gdb) continue
Continuing.
account1 balance: $50

Enter withdrawal amount for account1: 13

attempting to subtract 13 from account1 balance

Hardware watchpoint 2: account1.balance

Old value = 50
New value = 37
0x08048a01 in Account::debit (this=0xbffffd70, amount=13) at Account.cpp:34
34              balance = balance - amount;
(gdb)
```

Fig. M.30 | Entering break mode when a variable is changed.

```
(gdb) continue
Continuing.
end of function
account1 balance: $37

Watchpoint 2 deleted because the program has left the block in
which its expression is valid.
0x4012fa65 in exit () from /lib/libc.so.6
(gdb) continue
Continuing.

Program exited normally.
(gdb)
```

Fig. M.31 | Continuing to the end of the program.

```
(gdb) run
Starting program: /home/student/Debug/figM_03

Breakpoint 1, main () at figM_03.cpp:14
14          Account account1( 50 ); // create Account object
(gdb) watch account1.balance
Hardware watchpoint 3: account1.balance
(gdb) continue
Continuing.
Hardware watchpoint 3: account1.balance

Old value = 1073833120
New value = 0
Account (this=0xbffffd70, initialBalance=50) at Account.cpp:16
16          if ( initialBalance > 0 )
(gdb)
```

Fig. M.32 | Resetting the watch on a data member.

9. ***Removing the watch on the data member.*** Suppose you want to watch a data member for only part of a program's execution. You can remove the debugger's watch on variable balance by typing delete 3 (Fig. M.33). Type continue—the program will finish executing without reentering break mode.

In this section, you learned how to use the watch command to enable the debugger to notify you of changes to the value of a data member throughout the life of a program. You also learned how to use the delete command to remove a watch on a data member before the end of the program.

```
(gdb) delete 3
(gdb) continue
Continuing.
account1 balance: $50

Enter withdrawal amount for account1: 13

attempting to subtract 13 from account1 balance

end of function
account1 balance: $37

Program exited normally.
(gdb)
```

Fig. M.33 | Removing a watch.

Summary

- GNU includes software called a debugger, which allows you to monitor the execution of your programs to locate and remove logic errors.

- The GNU debugger works only with executable files that were compiled with the -g compiler option, which generates information that is used by the debugger to help you debug your programs.

- The gdb command will start the GNU debugger and enable you to use its features. The run command will run a program through the debugger.

- Breakpoints are markers that can be set at any executable line of code. When program execution reaches a breakpoint, execution pauses.

- The break command inserts a breakpoint at the line number specified after the command.

- When the program runs, it suspends execution at any line that contains a breakpoint and is said to be in break mode.

- The continue command causes the program to continue running until the next breakpoint is reached.

- The print command allows you to peek inside the computer at the value of one of your variables.

- When the print command is used, the result is stored in a convenience variable such as $1. Convenience variables are temporary variables that can be used in the debugging process to perform arithmetic and evaluate boolean expressions.

- You can display a list of all of the breakpoints in the program by typing info break.

- To remove a breakpoint, type delete, followed by a space and the number of the breakpoint to remove.

- Use the quit command to end the debugging session.

- The set command allows the programmer to assign new values to variables.

- The step command executes the next statement in the program. If the next statement to execute is a function call, control transfers to the called function. The step command enables you to enter a function and study the individual statements of that function.

- The finish command executes the remaining statements in the function and returns control to the place where the function was called.

- The next command behaves like the step command, except when the next statement to execute contains a function call. In that case, the called function executes in its entirety and the program advances to the next executable line after the function call.

- The watch command sets a watch on any variable or data member of an object currently in scope during execution of the debugger. Whenever the value of a watched variable changes, the debugger enters break mode and notifies you that the value has changed.

Terminology

break command	info break command
break mode	next command
breakpoint	print command
continue command	quit command
debugger	run command
delete command	set command
finish command	step command
-g compiler option	watch command
gdb command	

Self-Review Exercises

M.1   Fill in the blanks in each of the following statements:
a) A breakpoint cannot be set at a(n) _____ .
b) You can examine the value of an expression by using the debugger's _____ command.
c) You can modify the value of a variable by using the debugger's _____ command.
d) During debugging, the _____ command executes the remaining statements in the current function and returns program control to the place where the function was called.
e) The debugger's _____ command behaves like the step command when the next statement to execute does not contain a function call.
f) The watch debugger command allows you to view all changes to a(n) _____ .

M.2   State whether each of the following is *true* or *false*. If *false*, explain why.
a) When program execution suspends at a breakpoint, the next statement to be executed is the statement after the breakpoint.
b) Watches can be removed using the debugger's remove command.
c) The -g compiler option must be used when compiling programs for debugging.

Answers to Self-Review Exercises

M.1   a) non-executable line. b) print. c) set. d) finish. e) next. f) data member.

M.2   a) False. When program execution suspends at a breakpoint, the next statement to be executed is the statement at the breakpoint. b) False. Watches can be removed using the debugger's delete command. c) True.

Bibliography

Alhir, S. *UML in a Nutshell.* Cambridge, MA: O'Reilly & Associates, Inc., 1998.

Allison, C. "Text Processing I." *The C Users Journal* Vol. 10, No. 10, October 1992, 23–28.

Allison, C. "Text Processing II." *The C Users Journal* Vol. 10, No. 12, December 1992, 73–77.

Allison, C. "Code Capsules: A C++ Date Class, Part I," *The C Users Journal* Vol. 11, No. 2, February 1993, 123–131.

Allison, C. "Conversions and Casts." *The C/C++ Users Journal* Vol. 12, No. 9, September 1994, 67–85.

Almarode, J. "Object Security." *Smalltalk Report* Vol. 5, No. 3 November/December 1995, 15–17.

American National Standard, Programming Language C++. (ANSI Document ISO/IEC 14882), New York, NY: American National Standards Institute, 1998.

Anderson, A. E. and W. J. Heinze. *C++ Programming and Fundamental Concepts.* Englewood Cliffs, NJ: Prentice Hall, 1992.

Baker, L. *C Mathematical Function Handbook.* New York, NY: McGraw Hill, 1992.

Bar-David, T. *Object-Oriented Design for C++.* Englewood Cliffs, NJ: Prentice Hall, 1993.

Beck, K. "Birds, Bees, and Browsers–Obvious Sources of Objects." *The Smalltalk Report* Vol. 3, No. 8, June 1994,13.

Becker, P. "Shrinking the Big Switch Statement." *Windows Tech Journal* Vol. 2, No. 5, May 1993, 26–33.

Becker, P. "Conversion Confusion." *C++ Report* October 1993, 26–28.

Berard, E. V. *Essays on Object-Oriented Software Engineering: Volume I.* Englewood Cliffs, NJ: Prentice Hall, 1993.

Binder, R. V. "State-Based Testing." *Object Magazine* Vol. 5, No. 4, August 1995, 75–78.

Binder, R. V. "State-Based Testing: Sneak Paths and Conditional Transitions." *Object Magazine* Vol. 5, No. 6, October 1995, 87–89.

Blum, A. *Neural Networks in C++: An Object-Oriented Framework for Building Connectionist Systems.* New York, NY: John Wiley & Sons, 1992.

Booch, G. *Object Solutions: Managing the Object-Oriented Project.* Reading, MA: Addison-Wesley, 1996.

Booch, G. *Object-Oriented Analysis and Design with Applications, Third Edition.* Reading: MA: Addison-Wesley, 2005.

Booch, G., J. Rumbaugh, and I. Jacobson. *The Unified Modeling Language User Guide.* Reading, MA: Addison-Wesley, 1999.

Cargill, T. *C++ Programming Style.* Reading, MA: Addison-Wesley, 1993.

Carroll, M. D. and M. A. Ellis. *Designing and Coding Reusable C++*. Reading, MA: Addison-Wesley, 1995.

Coplien, J. O. and D. C. Schmidt. *Pattern Languages of Program Design*. Reading, MA: Addison-Wesley, 1995.

Deitel, H. M, P. J. Deitel and D. R. Choffnes. *Operating Systems, Third Edition*. Upper Saddle River, NJ: Prentice Hall, 2004.

Deitel, H. M and P. J. Deitel. *Java How to Program, Sixth Edition*. Upper Saddle River, NJ: Prentice Hall, 2005.

Deitel, H. M. and P. J. Deitel. *C How to Program, Fourth Edition*. Upper Saddle River, NJ: Prentice Hall, 2004.

Duncan, R. "Inside C++: Friend and Virtual Functions, and Multiple Inheritance." *PC Magazine* 15 October 1991, 417–420.

Ellis, M. A. and B. Stroustrup. *The Annotated C++ Reference Manual*. Reading, MA: Addison-Wesley, 1990.

Embley, D. W., B. D. Kurtz and S. N. Woodfield. *Object-Oriented Systems Analysis: A Model-Driven Approach*. Englewood Cliffs, NJ: Yourdon Press, 1992.

Entsminger, G. and B. Eckel. *The Tao of Objects: A Beginner's Guide to Object-Oriented Programming*. New York, NY: Wiley Publishing, 1990.

Firesmith, D.G. and B. Henderson-Sellers. "Clarifying Specialized Forms of Association in UML and OML." *Journal of Object-Oriented Programming* May 1998: 47–50.

Flamig, B. *Practical Data Structures in C++*. New York, NY: John Wiley & Sons, 1993.

Fowler, M. *UML Distilled: A Brief Guide to the Standard Object Modeling Language, Third Edition*. Reading, MA: Addison-Wesley, 2004.

Gehani, N. and W. D. Roome. *The Concurrent C Programming Language*. Summit, NJ: Silicon Press, 1989.

Giancola, A. and L. Baker. "Bit Arrays with C++." *The C Users Journal* Vol. 10, No. 7, July 1992, 21–26.

Glass, G. and B. Schuchert. *The STL <Primer>*. Upper Saddle River, NJ: Prentice Hall PTR, 1995.

Gooch, T. "Obscure C++." *Inside Microsoft Visual C++* Vol. 6, No. 11, November 1995, 13–15.

Hansen, T. L. *The C++ Answer Book*. Reading, MA: Addison-Wesley, 1990.

Henricson, M. and E. Nyquist. *Industrial Strength C++: Rules and Recommendations*. Upper Saddle River, NJ: Prentice Hall, 1997.

International Standard: Programming Languages—C++. ISO/IEC 14882:1998. New York, NY: American National Standards Institute, 1998.

Jacobson, I. "Is Object Technology Software's Industrial Platform?" *IEEE Software Magazine* Vol. 10, No. 1, January 1993, 24–30.

Jaeschke, R. *Portability and the C Language*. Indianapolis, IN: Sams Publishing, 1989.

Johnson, L.J. "Model Behavior." *Enterprise Development* May 2000: 20–28.

Josuttis, N. *The C++ Standard Library: A Tutorial and Reference*. Boston, MA: Addison-Wesley, 1999.

Knight, A. "Encapsulation and Information Hiding." *The Smalltalk Report* Vol. 1, No. 8 June 1992, 19–20.

Koenig, A. "What is C++ Anyway?" *Journal of Object-Oriented Programming* April/May 1991, 48–52.

Koenig, A. "Implicit Base Class Conversions." *The C++ Report* Vol. 6, No. 5, June 1994, 18–19.

Koenig, A. and B. Stroustrup. "Exception Handling for C++ (Revised)," *Proceedings of the USENIX C++ Conference,* San Francisco, CA, April 1990.

Koenig, A. and B. Moo. *Ruminations on C++: A Decade of Programming Insight and Experience.* Reading, MA: Addison-Wesley, 1997.

Kruse, R. L. and A. J. Ryba. *Data Structures and Program Design in C++.* Upper Saddle River, NJ: Prentice Hall, 1999.

Langer, A. and K. Kreft. *Standard C++ IOStreams and Locales: Advanced Programmer's Guide and Reference.* Reading, MA: Addison-Wesley, 2000.

Lejter, M., S. Meyers and S. P. Reiss. "Support for Maintaining Object-Oriented Programs," *IEEE Transactions on Software Engineering* Vol. 18, No. 12, December 1992, 1045–1052.

Lippman, S. B. and J. Lajoie. *C++ Primer, Third Edition,* Reading, MA: Addison-Wesley, 1998.

Lorenz, M. *Object-Oriented Software Development: A Practical Guide.* Englewood Cliffs, NJ: Prentice Hall, 1993.

Lorenz, M. "A Brief Look at Inheritance Metrics." *The Smalltalk Report* Vol. 3, No. 8 June 1994, 1, 4–5.

Martin, J. *Principles of Object-Oriented Analysis and Design.* Englewood Cliffs, NJ: Prentice Hall, 1993.

Martin, R. C. *Designing Object-Oriented C++ Applications Using the Booch Method.* Englewood Cliffs, NJ: Prentice Hall, 1995.

Matsche, J. J. "Object-Oriented Programming in Standard C." *Object Magazine* Vol. 2, No. 5, January/February 1993, 71–74.

McCabe, T. J. and A. H. Watson. "Combining Comprehension and Testing in Object-Oriented Development." *Object Magazine* Vol. 4, No. 1, March/April 1994, 63–66.

McLaughlin, M. and A. Moore. "Real-Time Extensions to the UML." *Dr. Dobb's Journal* December 1998: 82–93.

Melewski, D. "UML Gains Ground." *Application Development Trends* October 1998: 34–44.

Melewski, D. "UML: Ready for Prime Time?" *Application Development Trends* November 1997: 30–44.

Melewski, D. "Wherefore and What Now, UML?" *Application Development Trends* December 1999: 61–68.

Meyer, B. *Object-Oriented Software Construction, Second Edition.* Englewood Cliffs, NJ: Prentice Hall, 1997.

Meyer, B. *Eiffel: The Language.* Englewood Cliffs, NJ: Prentice Hall, 1992.

Meyer, B. and D. Mandrioli. *Advances in Object-Oriented Software Engineering.* Englewood Cliffs, NJ: Prentice Hall, 1992.

Meyers, S. "Mastering User-Defined Conversion Functions." *The C/C++ Users Journal* Vol. 13, No. 8, August 1995, 57–63.

Meyers, S. *More Effective C++: 35 New Ways to Improve Your Programs and Designs.* Reading, MA: Addison-Wesley, 1996.

Meyers, S. *Effective C++: 50 Specific Ways to Improve Your Programs and Designs, Second Edition.* Reading, MA: Addison-Wesley, 1998.

Meyers, S. *Effective STL: 50 Specific Ways to Improve Your Use of the Standard Template Library.* Reading, MA: Addison-Wesley, 2001.

Muller, P. *Instant UML.* Birmingham, UK: Wrox Press Ltd, 1997.

Murray, R. *C++ Strategies and Tactics.* Reading, MA: Addison-Wesley, 1993.

Musser, D. R. and A. A. Stepanov. "Algorithm-Oriented Generic Libraries." *Software Practice and Experience* Vol. 24, No. 7, July 1994.

Musser, D. R., G. J. Derge and A. Saini. *STL Tutorial and Reference Guide: C++ Programming with the Standard Template Library, Second Edition.* Reading, MA: Addison-Wesley, 2001.

Nerson, J. M. "Applying Object-Oriented Analysis and Design." *Communications of the ACM,* Vol. 35, No. 9, September 1992, 63–74.

Nierstrasz, O., S. Gibbs and D. Tsichritzis. "Component-Oriented Software Development." *Communications of the ACM* Vol. 35, No. 9, September 1992, 160–165.

Perry, P. "UML Steps to the Plate." *Application Development Trends* May 1999: 33–36.

Pinson, L. J. and R. S. Wiener. *Applications of Object-Oriented Programming.* Reading, MA: Addison-Wesley, 1990.

Pittman, M. "Lessons Learned in Managing Object-Oriented Development." *IEEE Software Magazine* Vol. 10, No. 1, January 1993, 43–53.

Plauger, P. J. *The Standard C Library.* Englewood Cliffs, NJ: Prentice Hall, 1992.

Plauger, D. "Making C++ Safe for Threads." *The C Users Journal* Vol. 11, No. 2, February 1993, 58–62.

Pohl, I. *C++ Distilled: A Concise ANSI/ISO Reference and Style Guide.* Reading, MA: Addison-Wesley, 1997.

Press, W. H., S. A. Teukolsky, W. T. Vetterling and B. P. Flannery. *Numerical Recipes in C: The Art of Scientific Computing.* Cambridge, MA: Cambridge University Press, 1992.

Prieto-Diaz, R. "Status Report: Software Reusability." *IEEE Software* Vol. 10, No. 3, May 1993, 61–66.

Prince, T. "Tuning Up Math Functions." *The C Users Journal* Vol. 10, No. 12, December 1992.

Prosise, J. "Wake Up and Smell the MFC: Using the Visual C++ Classes and Applications Framework." *Microsoft Systems Journal* Vol. 10, No. 6, June 1995, 17–34.

Rabinowitz, H. and C. Schaap. *Portable C.* Englewood Cliffs, NJ: Prentice Hall, 1990.

Reed, D. R. "Moving from C to C++." *Object Magazine* Vol. 1, No. 3, September/October 1991, 46–60.

Ritchie, D. M. "The UNIX System: The Evolution of the UNIX Time-Sharing System." *AT&T Bell Laboratories Technical Journal* Vol. 63, No. 8, Part 2, October 1984, 1577–1593.

Ritchie, D. M., S. C. Johnson, M. E. Lesk and B. W. Kernighan. "UNIX Time-Sharing System: The C Programming Language." *The Bell System Technical Journal* Vol. 57, No. 6, Part 2, July/August 1978, 1991–2019.

Rosler, L. "The UNIX System: The Evolution of C—Past and Future." *AT&T Laboratories Technical Journal* Vol. 63, No. 8, Part 2, October 1984, 1685–1699.

Robson, R. *Using the STL: The C++ Standard Template Library.* New York, NY: Springer Verlag, 2000.

Rubin, K. S. and A. Goldberg. "Object Behavior Analysis." *Communications of the ACM* Vol. 35, No. 9, September 1992, 48–62.

Rumbaugh, J., M. Blaha, W. Premerlani, F. Eddy and W. Lorensen. *Object-Oriented Modeling and Design.* Englewood Cliffs, NJ: Prentice Hall, 1991.

Rumbaugh, J., Jacobson, I. and G. Booch. *The Unified Modeling Language Reference Manual, Second Edition.* Reading, MA: Addison-Wesley, 2005.

Saks, D. "Inheritance." *The C Users Journal* May 1993, 81–89.

Schildt, H. *STL Programming from the Ground Up.* Berkeley, CA: Osborne McGraw-Hill, 1999.

Schlaer, S. and S. J. Mellor. *Object Lifecycles: Modeling the World in States.* Englewood Cliffs, NJ: Prentice Hall, 1992.

Sedgwick, R. *Bundle of Algorithms in C++, Parts 1–5: Fundamentals, Data Structures, Sorting, Searching, and Graph Algorithms (Third Edition).* Reading, MA: Addison-Wesley, 2002.

Sessions, R. *Class Construction in C and C++: Object-Oriented Programming.* Englewood Cliffs, NJ: Prentice Hall, 1992.

Skelly, C. "Pointer Power in C and C++." *The C Users Journal* Vol. 11, No. 2, February 1993, 93–98.

Snyder, A. "The Essence of Objects: Concepts and Terms." *IEEE Software Magazine* Vol. 10, No. 1, January 1993, 31–42.

Stepanov, A. and M. Lee. "The Standard Template Library." 31 October 1995 <www.cs.rpi.edu/~musser/doc.ps>.

Stroustrup, B. "The UNIX System: Data Abstraction in C." *AT&T Bell Laboratories Technical Journal* Vol. 63, No. 8, Part 2, October 1984, 1701–1732.

Stroustrup, B. "What is Object-Oriented Programming?" *IEEE Software* Vol. 5, No. 3, May 1988, 10–20.

Stroustrup, B. "Parameterized Types for C++." *Proceedings of the USENIX C++ Conference* Denver, CO, October 1988.

Stroustrup, B. "Why Consider Language Extensions?: Maintaining a Delicate Balance." *The C++ Report* September 1993, 44–51.

Stroustrup, B. "Making a vector Fit for a Standard." *The C++ Report* October 1994.

Stroustrup, B. *The Design and Evolution of C++.* Reading, MA: Addison-Wesley, 1994.

Stroustrup, B. *The C++ Programming Language, Special Third Edition.* Reading, MA: Addison-Wesley, 2000.

Taligent's Guide to Designing Programs: Well-Mannered Object-Oriented Design in C++. Reading, MA: Addison-Wesley, 1994.

Taylor, D. *Object-Oriented Information Systems: Planning and Implementation.* New York, NY: John Wiley & Sons, 1992.

Tondo, C. L. and S. E. Gimpel. *The C Answer Book.* Englewood Cliffs, NJ: Prentice Hall, 1989.

Urlocker, Z. "Polymorphism Unbounded." *Windows Tech Journal* Vol. 1, No. 1, January 1992, 11–16.

Van Camp, K. E. "Dynamic Inheritance Using Filter Classes." *The C/C++ Users Journal* Vol. 13, No. 6, June 1995, 69–78.

Vilot, M. J. "An Introduction to the Standard Template Library." *The C++ Report* Vol. 6, No. 8, October 1994.

Voss, G. *Object-Oriented Programming: An Introduction.* Berkeley, CA: Osborne McGraw-Hill, 1991.

Voss, G. "Objects and Messages." *Windows Tech Journal* February 1993, 15–16.

Wang, B. L. and J. Wang. "Is a Deep Class Hierarchy Considered Harmful?" *Object Magazine* Vol. 4, No. 7, November/December 1994, 35–36.

Weisfeld, M. "An Alternative to Large Switch Statements." *The C Users Journal* Vol. 12, No. 4, April 1994, 67–76.

Weiskamp, K. and B. Flamig. *The Complete C++ Primer, Second Edition.* Orlando, FL: Academic Press, 1993.

Wiebel, M. and S. Halladay. "Using OOP Techniques Instead of *switch* in C++." *The C Users Journal* Vol. 10, No. 10, October 1993, 105–112.

Wilde, N. and R. Huitt. "Maintenance Support for Object-Oriented Programs." *IEEE Transactions on Software Engineering* Vol. 18, No. 12, December 1992, 1038–1044.

Wilde, N., P. Matthews and R. Huitt. "Maintaining Object-Oriented Software." *IEEE Software Magazine* Vol. 10, No. 1, January 1993, 75–80.

Wilson, G. V. and P. Lu. *Parallel Programming Using C++.* Cambridge, MA: MIT Press, 1996.

Wilt, N. "Templates in C++." *The C Users Journal* May 1993, 33–51.

Wirfs-Brock, R., B. Wilkerson and L. Wiener. *Designing Object-Oriented Software.* Englewood Cliffs, NJ: Prentice Hall PTR, 1990.

Wyatt, B. B., K. Kavi and S. Hufnagel. "Parallelism in Object-Oriented Languages: A Survey." *IEEE Software* Vol. 9, No. 7, November 1992, 56–66.

Yamazaki, S., K. Kajihara, M. Ito and R. Yasuhara. "Object-Oriented Design of Telecommunication Software." *IEEE Software Magazine* Vol. 10, No. 1, January 1993, 81–87.

Index

X

Y

Z

End User License Agreements

Prentice Hall License Agreement and Limited Warranty

READ THE FOLLOWING TERMS AND CONDITIONS CAREFULLY BEFORE OPENING THIS SOFTWARE PACKAGE. THIS LEGAL DOCUMENT IS AN AGREEMENT BETWEEN YOU AND PRENTICE-HALL, INC. (THE "COMPANY"). BY OPENING THIS SEALED SOFT-WARE PACKAGE, YOU ARE AGREEING TO BE BOUND BY THESE TERMS AND CONDI-TIONS. IF YOU DO NOT AGREE WITH THESE TERMS AND CONDITIONS, DO NOT OPEN THE SOFTWARE PACKAGE. PROMPTLY RETURN THE UNOPENED SOFTWARE PACKAGE AND ALL ACCOMPANYING ITEMS TO THE PLACE YOU OBTAINED THEM FOR A FULL REFUND OF ANY SUMS YOU HAVE PAID.

1.GRANT OF LICENSE: In consideration of your purchase of this book, and your agreement to abide by the terms and conditions of this Agreement, the Company grants to you a nonexclusive right to use and display the copy of the enclosed software program (hereinafter the "SOFTWARE") on a single computer (i.e., with a single CPU) at a single location so long as you comply with the terms of this Agree-ment. The Company reserves all rights not expressly granted to you under this Agreement.

2.OWNERSHIP OF SOFTWARE: You own only the magnetic or physical media (the enclosed media) on which the SOFTWARE is recorded or fixed, but the Company and the software developers retain all the rights, title, and ownership to the SOFTWARE recorded on the original media copy(ies) and all subsequent copies of the SOFTWARE, regardless of the form or media on which the original or other copies may exist. This license is not a sale of the original SOFTWARE or any copy to you.

3.COPY RESTRICTIONS: This SOFTWARE and the accompanying printed materials and user manual (the "Documentation") are the subject of copyright. The individual programs on the media are copyrighted by the authors of each program. Some of the programs on the media include separate licensing agreements. If you intend to use one of these programs, you must read and follow its accompa-nying license agreement. You may not copy the Documentation or the SOFTWARE, except that you may make a single copy of the SOFTWARE for backup or archival purposes only. You may be held legally responsible for any copying or copyright infringement which is caused or encouraged by your failure to abide by the terms of this restriction.

4.USE RESTRICTIONS: You may not network the SOFTWARE or otherwise use it on more than one computer or computer terminal at the same time. You may physically transfer the SOFTWARE from one computer to another provided that the SOFTWARE is used on only one computer at a time. You may not distribute copies of the SOFTWARE or Documentation to others. You may not reverse engi-neer, disassemble, decompile, modify, adapt, translate, or create derivative works based on the SOFT-WARE or the Documentation without the prior written consent of the Company.

5. TRANSFER RESTRICTIONS: The enclosed SOFTWARE is licensed only to you and may not be transferred to any one else without the prior written consent of the Company. Any unauthorized transfer of the SOFTWARE shall result in the immediate termination of this Agreement.

6. TERMINATION: This license is effective until terminated. This license will terminate automat-ically without notice from the Company and become null and void if you fail to comply with any provi-sions or limitations of this license. Upon termination, you shall destroy the Documentation and all copies of the SOFTWARE. All provisions of this Agreement as to warranties, limitation of liability, remedies or damages, and our ownership rights shall survive termination.

7. MISCELLANEOUS: This Agreement shall be construed in accordance with the laws of the United States of America and the State of New York and shall benefit the Company, its affiliates, and assignees.

8.LIMITED WARRANTY AND DISCLAIMER OF WARRANTY: The Company warrants that the SOFTWARE, when properly used in accordance with the Documentation, will operate in substantial conformity with the description of the SOFTWARE set forth in the Documentation. The Company does not warrant that the SOFTWARE will meet your requirements or that the operation of the SOFTWARE will be uninterrupted or error-free. The Company warrants that the media on which the SOFTWARE is delivered shall be free from defects in materials and workmanship under normal use for a period of thirty

(30) days from the date of your purchase. Your only remedy and the Company's only obligation under these limited warranties is, at the Company's option, return of the warranted item for a refund of any amounts paid by you or replacement of the item. Any replacement of SOFTWARE or media under the warranties shall not extend the original warranty period. The limited warranty set forth above shall not apply to any SOFTWARE which the Company determines in good faith has been subject to misuse, neglect, improper installation, repair, alteration, or damage by you. EXCEPT FOR THE EXPRESSED WARRANTIES SET FORTH ABOVE, THE COMPANY DISCLAIMS ALL WARRANTIES, EXPRESS OR IMPLIED, INCLUDING WITHOUT LIMITATION, THE IMPLIED WARRANTIES OF MERCHANTABILITY AND FITNESS FOR A PARTICULAR PURPOSE. EXCEPT FOR THE EXPRESS WARRANTY SET FORTH ABOVE, THE COMPANY DOES NOT WARRANT, GUARANTEE, OR MAKE ANY REPRESENTATION REGARDING THE USE OR THE RESULTS OF THE USE OF THE SOFTWARE IN TERMS OF ITS CORRECTNESS, ACCURACY, RELIABILITY, CURRENTNESS, OR OTHERWISE.

IN NO EVENT, SHALL THE COMPANY OR ITS EMPLOYEES, AGENTS, SUPPLIERS, OR CONTRACTORS BE LIABLE FOR ANY INCIDENTAL, INDIRECT, SPECIAL, OR CONSEQUENTIAL DAMAGES ARISING OUT OF OR IN CONNECTION WITH THE LICENSE GRANTED UNDER THIS AGREEMENT, OR FOR LOSS OF USE, LOSS OF DATA, LOSS OF INCOME OR PROFIT, OR OTHER LOSSES, SUSTAINED AS A RESULT OF INJURY TO ANY PERSON, OR LOSS OF OR DAMAGE TO PROPERTY, OR CLAIMS OF THIRD PARTIES, EVEN IF THE COMPANY OR AN AUTHORIZED REPRESENTATIVE OF THE COMPANY HAS BEEN ADVISED OF THE POSSIBILITY OF SUCH DAMAGES. IN NO EVENT SHALL LIABILITY OF THE COMPANY FOR DAMAGES WITH RESPECT TO THE SOFTWARE EXCEED THE AMOUNTS ACTUALLY PAID BY YOU, IF ANY, FOR THE SOFTWARE.

SOME JURISDICTIONS DO NOT ALLOW THE LIMITATION OF IMPLIED WARRANTIES OR LIABILITY FOR INCIDENTAL, INDIRECT, SPECIAL, OR CONSEQUENTIAL DAMAGES, SO THE ABOVE LIMITATIONS MAY NOT ALWAYS APPLY. THE WARRANTIES IN THIS AGREEMENT GIVE YOU SPECIFIC LEGAL RIGHTS AND YOU MAY ALSO HAVE OTHER RIGHTS WHICH VARY IN ACCORDANCE WITH LOCAL LAW.

ACKNOWLEDGMENT
YOU ACKNOWLEDGE THAT YOU HAVE READ THIS AGREEMENT, UNDERSTAND IT, AND AGREE TO BE BOUND BY ITS TERMS AND CONDITIONS. YOU ALSO AGREE THAT THIS AGREEMENT IS THE COMPLETE AND EXCLUSIVE STATEMENT OF THE AGREEMENT BETWEEN YOU AND THE COMPANY AND SUPERSEDES ALL PROPOSALS OR PRIOR AGREEMENTS, ORAL, OR WRITTEN, AND ANY OTHER COMMUNICATIONS BETWEEN YOU AND THE COMPANY OR ANY REPRESENTATIVE OF THE COMPANY RELATING TO THE SUBJECT MATTER OF THIS AGREEMENT.

Should you have any questions concerning this Agreement or if you wish to contact the Company for any reason, please contact in writing at the address below.

Robin Short
Prentice Hall PTR
One Lake Street
Upper Saddle River, New Jersey 07458

The DEITEL® Suite of Products...

HOW TO PROGRAM BOOKS

C++ How to Program Fifth Edition

BOOK / CD-ROM

©2005, 1500 pp., paper
(0-13-185757-6)

The complete authoritative DEITEL® LIVE-CODE introduction to programming with C++! The Fifth Edition takes a new easy-to-follow, carefully developed early classes and early objects approach to programming in C++. The text includes comprehensive coverage of the fundamentals of object-oriented programming in C++. It includes a a new optional automated teller machine (ATM) case study that teaches the fundamentals of software engineering and object-oriented design with the UML 2.0 in Chapters 1-7, 9 and 13. Additional integrated case studies appear throughout the text, including the **Time** class (Chapter 9), the **Employee** class (Chapters 12 and 13) and the **GradeBook** class (Chapters 3-7). The book also includes a new interior design including updated colors, new fonts, new design elements and more.

Small C++ How to Program Fifth Edition

BOOK / CD-ROM

©2005, 900 pp., paper
(0-13-185758-4)

Based on chapters 1-13 (except the optional OOD/UML case study) and appendices of *C++ How to Program, Fifth Edition*, *Small C++* features a new early classes and early objects approach and comprehensive coverage of the fundamentals of object-oriented programming in C++. Key topics include applications, variables, memory concepts, data types, control statements, functions, arrays, pointers and strings, inheritance and polymorphism.

📖 Coming in Spring 2005 for both *C++ How to Program, 5/e* and *Small C++ How to Program, 5/e:* FREE C++ Web-based *Cyber Classroom* with the purchase of a new textbook. The *Cyber Classroom* includes a complete e-book, audio walkthroughs of the code examples, a FREE Lab Manual and selected student solutions. See pages 7–8 of this advertorial for more information.

Java™ How to Program Sixth Edition

BOOK / CD-ROM

©2005, 1500 pp., paper
(0-13-148398-6)

The complete authoritative DEITEL® LIVE-CODE introduction to programming with the new Java™ 2 Platform Standard Edition 5.0! New early classes and early objects approach. *Java How to Program, Sixth Edition* is up-to-date with J2SE™ 5.0 and includes comprehensive coverage of the fundamentals of object-oriented programming in Java; a new interior design including new colors, new fonts, new design elements and more; and a new optional automated teller machine (ATM) case study that teaches the fundamentals of software engineering and object oriented design with the UML 2.0 in Chapters 1-8 and 10. Additional integrated case studies appear throughout the text, including GUI and graphics (Chapters 3-12), the **Time** class (Chapter 8), the **Employee** class (Chapters 9 and 10) and the **Grade-Book Employee** (Chapters 3-8). New J2SE 5.0 topics covered included input/output, enhanced **for** loop, autoboxing, generics, new collections APIs and more.

Small Java™ How to Program, Sixth Edition

BOOK / CD-ROM

©2005, 700 pp., paper
(0-13-148660-8)

Based on chapters 1-10 of *Java™ How to Program, Sixth Edition*, *Small Java* is up-to-date with J2SE™ 5.0, features a new early classes and early objects approach and comprehensive coverage of the fundamentals of object-oriented programming in Java. Key topics include applications, variables, data types, control statements, methods, arrays, object-based programming, inheritance and polymorphism.

📖 Coming in Spring 2005 for both *Java How to Program, 6/e* and *Small Java How to Program, 6/e:* Free Java Web-based *Cyber Classroom* with the purchase of a new textbook. The *Cyber Classroom* includes a complete e-book, audio walkthroughs of the code examples, a FREE Lab Manual and selected student solutions. See pages 7–8 of this advertorial for more information.

C How to Program
Fourth Edition

BOOK / CD-ROM

©2004, 1255 pp., paper
(0-13-142644-3)

C How to Program, Fourth Edition—the world's best-selling C text—is designed for introductory through intermediate courses as well as programming languages survey courses. This comprehensive text is aimed at readers with little or no programming experience through intermediate audiences. Highly practical in approach, it introduces fundamental notions of structured programming and software engineering and gets up to speed quickly.

📖 **A Student Solutions Manual is also available is for use with this text. Use ISBN 0-13-145245-2 to order.**

Getting Started with Microsoft® Visual C++™ 6 with an Introduction to MFC

BOOK / CD-ROM

©2000, 163 pp., paper
(0-13-016147-0)

Visual C++ .NET® How To Program

BOOK / CD-ROM

©2004, 1400 pp., paper
(0-13-437377-4)

Written by the authors of the world's best-selling introductory/intermediate C and C++ textbooks, this comprehensive book thoroughly examines Visual C++® .NET. Visual C++® .NET How to Program begins with a strong foundation in the introductory and intermediate programming principles students will need in industry, including fundamental topics such as arrays, functions and control statements. Readers learn the concepts of object-oriented programming. The text then explores such essential topics as networking, databases, XML and multimedia. Graphical user interfaces are also extensively covered, giving students the tools to build compelling and fully interactive programs using the "drag-and-drop" techniques provided by Visual Studio .NET 2003.

Advanced Java™ 2 Platform How to Program

BOOK / CD-ROM

©2002, 1811 pp., paper
(0-13-089560-1)

Expanding on the world's best-selling Java textbook—Java™ How to Program—Advanced Java™ 2 Platform How To Program presents advanced Java topics for developing sophisticated, user-friendly GUIs; significant, scalable enterprise applications; wireless applications and distributed systems. Primarily based on Java 2 Enterprise Edition (J2EE), this textbook integrates technologies such as XML, JavaBeans, security, JDBC™, JavaServer Pages (JSP™), servlets, Remote Method Invocation (RMI), Enterprise JavaBeans™ (EJB), design patterns, Swing, J2ME™, Java 2D and 3D, XML, design patterns, CORBA, Jini™, JavaSpaces™, Jiro™, Java Management Extensions (JMX) and Peer-to-Peer networking with an introduction to JXTA.

C# How to Program

BOOK / CD-ROM

©2002, 1568 pp., paper
(0-13-062221-4)

C# How to Program provides a comprehensive introduction to Microsoft's C# object-oriented language. C# enables students to create powerful Web applications and components—ranging from XML-based Web services on Microsoft's .NET platform to middle-tier business objects and system-level applications. C# How to Program begins with a strong foundation in the introductory- and intermediate-programming principles students will need in industry. It then explores such essential topics as object-oriented programming and exception handling. Graphical user interfaces are extensively covered, giving readers the tools to build compelling and fully interactive programs. Internet technologies such as XML, ADO .NET and Web services are covered as well as topics including regular expressions, multithreading, networking, databases, files and data structures.

Visual Basic® .NET How to Program
Second Edition

BOOK / CD-ROM

©2002, 1400 pp., paper
(0-13-029363-6)

Learn Visual Basic .NET programming from the ground up! This book provides a comprehensive introduction to Visual Basic .NET—featuring extensive updates and increased functionality. *Visual Basic .NET How to Program, Second Edition* covers introductory programming techniques as well as more advanced topics, featuring enhanced treatment of developing Web-based applications. Other topics discussed include XML and wireless applications, databases, SQL and ADO .NET, Web forms, Web services and ASP .NET.

Internet & World Wide Web How to Program
Third Edition

BOOK / CD-ROM

©2004, 1250 pp., paper
(0-13-145091-3)

This book introduces students with little or no programming experience to the exciting world of Web-based applications. This text provides in-depth coverage of introductory programming principles, various markup languages (XHTML, Dynamic HTML and XML), several scripting languages (JavaScript, JScript .NET, ColdFusion, Flash ActionScript, Perl, PHP, VBScript and Python), Web servers (IIS and Apache) and relational databases (MySQL)—all the skills and tools needed to create dynamic Web-based applications. The text contains a comprehensive introduction to ASP .NET and the Microsoft .NET Framework. A case study illustrating how to build an online message board using ASP .NET and XML is also included. New in this edition are chapters on Macromedia ColdFusion, Macromedia Dreamweaver and a much enhanced treatment of Flash, including a case study on building a video game in Flash. After mastering the material in this book, students will be well prepared to build real-world, industrial-strength, Web-based applications.

Wireless Internet & Mobile Business How to Program

©2002, 1292 pp., paper
(0-13-062226-5)

This book offers a thorough treatment of both the management and technical aspects of this growing area, including coverage of current practices and future trends. The first half explores the business issues surrounding wireless technology and mobile business. The book then turns to programming for the wireless Internet, exploring topics such as WAP (including 2.0), WML, WMLScript, XML, XHTML™, wireless Java programming (J2ME™) and more. Other topics covered include career resources, wireless marketing, accessibility, Palm™, PocketPC, Windows CE, i-mode, Bluetooth, MIDP, MIDlets, ASP, Microsoft .NET Mobile Framework, BREW™, multimedia, Flash™ and VBScript.

Python How to Program

BOOK / CD-ROM

©2002, 1376 pp., paper
(0-13-092361-3)

This exciting textbook provides a comprehensive introduction to Python—a powerful object-oriented programming language with clear syntax and the ability to bring together various technologies quickly and easily. This book covers introductory-programming techniques and more advanced topics such as graphical user interfaces, databases, wireless Internet programming, networking, security, process management, multithreading, XHTML, CSS, PSP and multimedia. Readers will learn principles that are applicable to both systems development and Web programming.

e-Business & e-Commerce for Managers

©2001, 794 pp., cloth
(0-13-032364-0)

This comprehensive overview of building and managing e-businesses explores topics such as the decision to bring a business online, choosing a business model, accepting payments, marketing strategies and security, as well as many other important issues (such as career resources). The book features Web resources and online demonstrations that supplement the text and direct readers to additional materials. The book also includes an appendix that develops a complete Web-based shopping-cart application using HTML, JavaScript, VBScript, Active Server Pages, ADO, SQL, HTTP, XML and XSL. Plus, company-specific sections provide "real-world" examples of the concepts presented in the book.

XML How to Program

BOOK / CD-ROM

©2001, 934 pp., paper (0-13-028417-3)

This book is a comprehensive guide to programming in XML. It teaches how to use XML to create customized tags and includes chapters that address markup languages for science and technology, multimedia, commerce and many other fields. Concise introductions to Java, JavaServer Pages, VBScript, Active Server Pages and Perl/CGI provide readers with the essentials of these programming languages and server-side development technologies to enable them to work effectively with XML. The book also covers topics such as XSL, DOM™, SAX, a real-world e-commerce case study and a complete chapter on Web accessibility that addresses Voice XML. Other topics covered include XHTML, CSS, DTD, schema, parsers, XPath, XLink, namespaces, XBase, XInclude, XPointer, XSLT, XSL Formatting Objects, JavaServer Pages, XForms, topic maps, X3D, MathML, OpenMath, CML, BML, CDF, RDF, SVG, Cocoon, WML, XBRL and BizTalk™ and SOAP™ Web resources.

Perl How to Program

BOOK / CD-ROM

©2001, 1057 pp., paper (0-13-028418-1)

This comprehensive guide to Perl programming emphasizes the use of the Common Gateway Interface (CGI) with Perl to create powerful, dynamic multi-tier Web-based client/server applications. The book begins with a clear and careful introduction to programming concepts at a level suitable for beginners, and proceeds through advanced topics such as references and complex data structures. Key Perl topics such as regular expressions and string manipulation are covered in detail. The authors address important and topical issues such as object-oriented programming, the Perl database interface (DBI), graphics and security. Also included is a treatment of XML, a bonus chapter introducing the Python programming language, supplemental material on career resources and a complete chapter on Web accessibility.

e-Business & e-Commerce How to Program

BOOK / CD-ROM

©2001, 1254 pp., paper (0-13-028419-X)

This book explores programming technologies for developing Web-based e-business and e-commerce solutions, and covers e-business and e-commerce models and business issues. Readers learn a full range of options, from "build-your-own" to turnkey solutions. The book examines scores of the top e-businesses (examples include Amazon, eBay, Priceline, Travelocity, etc.), explaining the technical details of building successful e-business and e-commerce sites and their underlying business premises. Learn how to implement the dominant e-commerce models—shopping carts, auctions, name-your-own-price, comparison shopping and bots/intelligent agents—by using markup languages (HTML, Dynamic HTML and XML), scripting languages (JavaScript, VBScript and Perl), server-side technologies (Active Server Pages and Perl/CGI) and database (SQL and ADO), security and online payment technologies.

Visual Basic® 6 How to Program

BOOK / CD-ROM

©1999, 1015 pp., paper (0-13-456955-5)

ORDER INFORMATION

For ordering information,
visit us on the Web at www.prenhall.com.

INTERNATIONAL ORDERING INFORMATION

CANADA:
Pearson Education Canada
26 Prince Andrew Place
PO Box 580
Don Mills, Ontario M3C 2T8 Canada
Tel.: 416-925-2249; Fax: 416-925-0068
e-mail: phcinfo.pubcanada@pearsoned.com

EUROPE, MIDDLE EAST, AND AFRICA:
Pearson Education
Edinburgh Gate
Harlow, Essex CM20 2JE UK
Tel: 01279 623928; Fax: 01279 414130
e-mail: enq.orders@pearsoned-ema.com

BENELUX REGION:
Pearson Education
Concertgebouwplein 25
1071 LM Amsterdam
The Netherlands
Tel: 31 20 5755 800; Fax: 31 20 664 5334
e-mail: amsterdam@pearsoned-ema.com

ASIA:
Pearson Education Asia Pte. Ltd.
23/25 First Lok Yang Road
Jurong, 629733 Singapore
Tel: 65 476 4688; Fax: 65 378 0370

JAPAN:
Pearson Education Japan
Ogikubo TM Bldg. 6F. 5-26-13 Ogikubo
Suginami-ku, Tokyo 167-0051 Japan
Tel: 81 3 3365 9001; Fax: 81 3 3365 9009

INDIA:
Pearson Education
Indian Branch
482 FIE, Patparganj
Delhi – 110092 India
Tel: 91 11 2059850 & 2059851
Fax: 91 11 2059852

AUSTRALIA:
Pearson Education Australia
Unit 4, Level 2, 14 Aquatic Drive
Frenchs Forest, NSW 2086, Australia
Tel: 61 2 9454 2200; Fax: 61 2 9453 0089
e-mail: marketing@pearsoned.com.au

NEW ZEALAND/FIJI:
Pearson Education
46 Hillside Road
Auckland 10, New Zealand
Tel: 649 444 4968; Fax: 649 444 4957
E-mail: sales@pearsoned.co.nz

SOUTH AFRICA:
Maskew Miller Longman
Central Park   Block H
16th Street   Midrand   1685
South Africa
Tel: 27 21 686 6356; Fax: 27 21 686 4590

LATIN AMERICA:
Pearson Education Latin America
Attn: Tina Sheldon
1 Lake Street
Upper Saddle River, NJ 07458

The SIMPLY SERIES!

The Deitels' *Simply Series* takes an engaging new approach to teaching programming languages from the ground up. The pedagogy of this series combines the DEITEL® signature *LIVE-CODE Approach* with an *APPLICATION-DRIVEN Tutorial Approach* to teach programming with outstanding pedagogical features that help students learn. We have merged the notion of a lab manual with that of a conventional textbook, creating a book in which readers build and execute complete applications from start to finish, while learning the fundamental concepts of programming!

Simply C++
An APPLICATION-DRIVEN Tutorial Approach

©2005, 800 pp., paper (0-13-142660-5)

Simply C++ An APPLICATION-DRIVEN Tutorial Approach guides readers through building real-world applications that incorporate C++ programming fundamentals. Learn methods, functions, data types, control statements, procedures, arrays, object-oriented programming, strings and characters, pointers, references, templates, operator overloading and more in this comprehensive introduction to C++.

Simply Java™ Programming
An APPLICATION-DRIVEN Tutorial Approach

©2004, 950 pp., paper (0-13-142648-6)

Simply Java™ Programming An APPLICATION-DRIVEN Tutorial Approach guides readers through building real-world applications that incorporate Java programming fundamentals. Learn GUI design, components, methods, event-handling, types, control statements, arrays, object-oriented programming, exception-handling, strings and characters, sequential files and more in this comprehensive introduction to Java. We also include higher-end topics such as database programming, multimedia, graphics and Web applications development.

Simply C#
An APPLICATION-DRIVEN Tutorial Approach

©2004, 850 pp., paper (0-13-142641-9)

Simply C# An APPLICATION-DRIVEN Tutorial Approach guides readers through building real-world applications that incorporate C# programming fundamentals. Learn GUI design, controls, methods, functions, data types, control statements, procedures, arrays, object-oriented programming, strings and characters, sequential files and more in this comprehensive introduction to C#. We also include higher-end topics such as database programming, multimedia and graphics and Web applications development.

Simply Visual Basic® .NET
An APPLICATION-DRIVEN Tutorial Approach

Visual Studio .NET 2002 Version: *©2003, 830 pp., paper (0-13-140553-5)*

Visual Studio .NET 2003 Version: *©2004, 960 pp., paper (0-13-142640-0)*

Simply Visual Basic® .NET An APPLICATION-DRIVEN Tutorial Approach guides readers through building real-world applications that incorporate Visual Basic .NET programming fundamentals. Learn GUI design, controls, methods, functions, data types, control statements, procedures, arrays, object-oriented programming, strings and characters, sequential files and more in this comprehensive introduction to Visual Basic .NET. We also include higher-end topics such as database programming, multimedia and graphics and Web applications development. If you're using Visual Studio® .NET 2002, choose *Simply Visual Basic .NET*; or, if you're using Visual Studio .NET 2003, you can use *Simply Visual Basic .NET 2003*, which includes updated screen captures and line numbers consistent with Visual Studio .NET 2003.

MULTIMEDIA CYBER CLASSROOMS

Premium content available FREE with *Java™* and *Small Java™ How to Program*, Sixth Edition and *C++* and *Small C++ How to Program*, Fifth Edition!

Java and *Small Java How to Program, 6/e* and *C++* and *Small C++ How to Program, 5/e* will soon be available with a **FREE** Web-based *Multimedia Cyber Classroom* for students who purchase new copies of these books! The *Cyber Classroom* is an interactive, multimedia, tutorial version of DEITEL textbooks. *Cyber Classrooms* are a great value, giving students additional hands-on experience and study aids.

COMING SOON for Java and Small Java How to Program, 6/e and C++ and Small C++ How to Program, 5/e (with purchase of book)

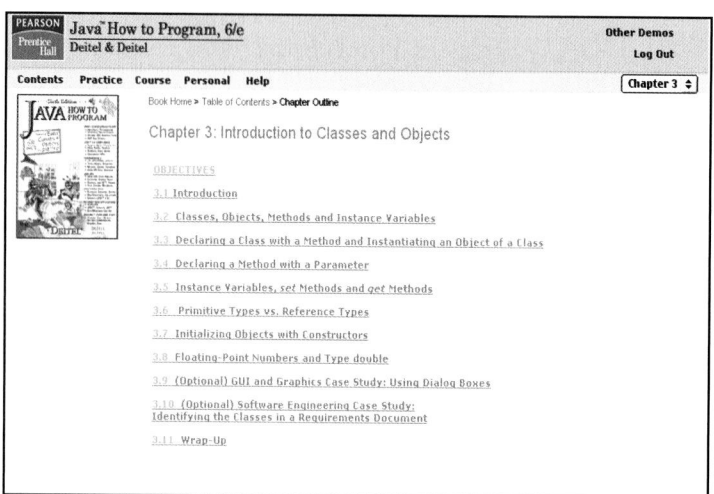

DEITEL® Multimedia Cyber Classrooms *feature the complete text of their corresponding* How to Program *titles.*

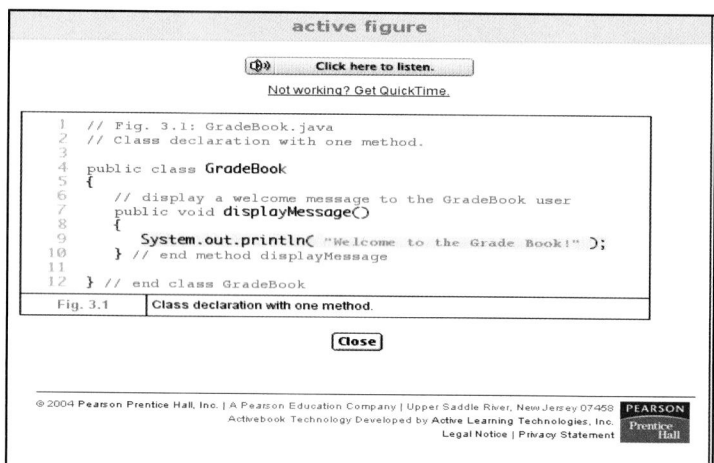

Unique audio "walkthroughs" of code examples reinforce key concepts.

MULTIMEDIA CYBER CLASSROOMS

Deitel® *Multimedia Cyber Classrooms* **include:**

- The full text, illustrations and program listings of its corresponding *How to Program* book.

- Hours of detailed, expert audio descriptions of hundreds of lines of code that help to reinforce important concepts.

- An abundance of self-assessment material, including practice exams, hundreds of programming exercises and self-review questions and answers.

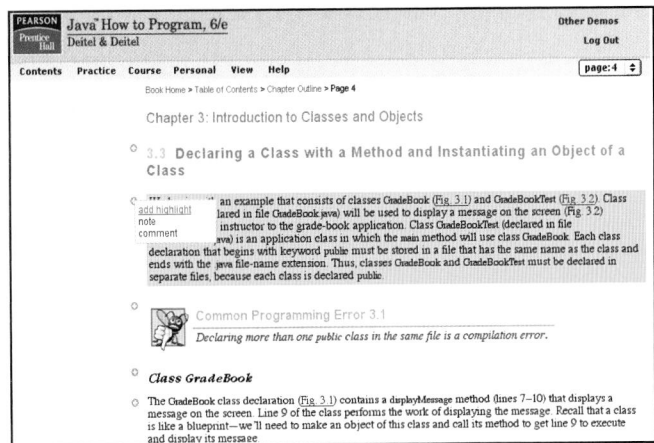

Deitel® Multimedia Cyber Classrooms *offer a host of interactive features, such as highlighting of key sections of the text...*

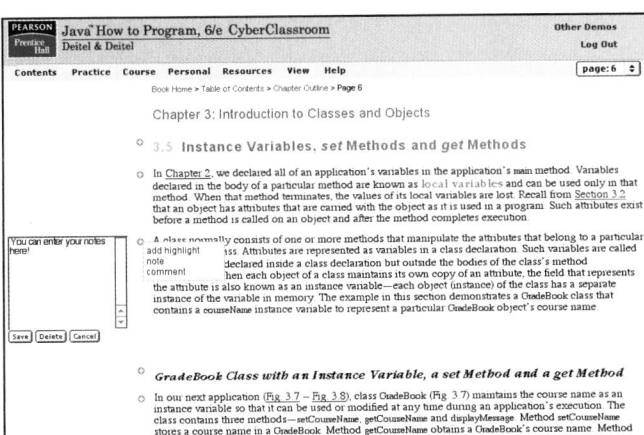

...and the ability to write notes in the margin of a given page for future reference.

- Intuitive browser-based interface designed to be easy and accessible.

- A Lab Manual featuring lab exercises as well as pre- and post-lab activities.

- Student Solutions to approximately one-half of the exercises in the textbook.

Students receive access to a protected Web site via access code cards packaged, for FREE, automatically with these new textbooks. (Simply tear the strip on the inside of the *Cyber Classroom* package to reveal access code.)

To redeem your access code or for more information, please visit:
www·prenhall·com/deitel/ cyberclassroom

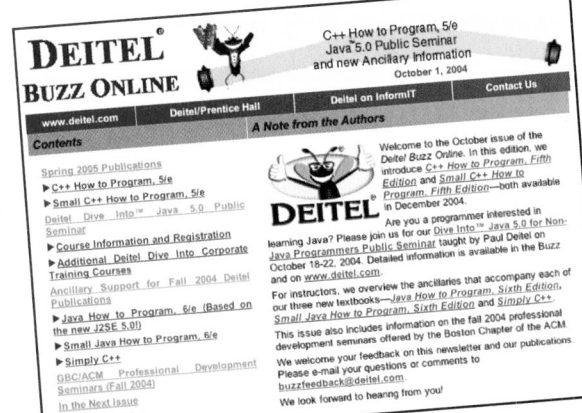
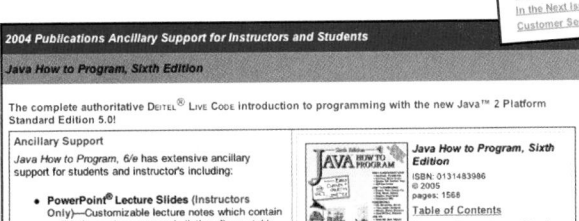

License Agreement and Limited Warranty

The software is distributed on an "AS IS" basis, without warranty. Neither the authors, the software developers, nor Prentice Hall make any representation, or warranty, either express or implied, with respect to the software programs, their quality, accuracy, or fitness for a specific purpose. Therefore, neither the authors, the software developers, nor Prentice Hall shall have any liability to you or any other person or entity with respect to any liability, loss, or damage caused or alleged to have been caused directly or indirectly by the programs contained on the media. This includes, but is not limited to, interruption of service, loss of data, loss of classroom time, loss of consulting or anticipatory profits, or consequential damages from the use of these programs. If the media itself is defective, you may return it for a replacement. Use of this software is subject to the Binary Code License terms and conditions at the back of this book. Read the licenses carefully. By opening this package, you are agreeing to be bound by the terms and conditions of these licenses. If you do not agree, do not open the package.

Please refer to end-user license agreements on the CD-ROM for further details.

Using the CD-ROM

The interface to the contents of this CD is designed to start automatically through the **AUTORUN.EXE** file. If a startup screen does not pop up automatically when you insert the CD into your computer, double click on the welcome.htm file to launch the Student CD or refer to the file **readme.txt** on the CD.

Contents of the CD-ROM

- Software downloads: links to free C++ compilers and development tools
- Examples
- Web Resources

Software and Hardware System Requirements

- 450 MHz (minimum) Pentium II or faster processor
- Microsoft® Windows® Server 2003, XP Professional, XP Home Edition, XP Media Center Edition, XP Tablet PC Edition, 2000 Professional (SP3 or later required for installation), 2000 Server (SP3 or later required for installation), or
- One of the following Linux distributions: Fedora Core 3 (Formally Red Hat Linux), Mandrakelinux 10.1 Official, Red Hat 9.0, SUSE LINUX Professional 9.2, or Turbolinux 10 Desktop
- Other than the minimum amount of RAM required by the items listed above, there are no additional RAM requirements for this CD-ROM.
- CD-ROM drive
- Internet connection
- C++ environment
- Web browser, Adobe® Acrobat® Reader® and a Zip decompression utility

Cassell's

English-Dutch
Dutch-English
Dictionary
Engels-Nederlands
Nederlands-Engels
Woordenboek

Completely revised by
J.A. JOCKIN-la BASTIDE
G. van KOOTEN

MACMILLAN PUBLISHING COMPANY
New York

CONTENTS

WENKEN VOOR HET GEBRUIK VAN DEEL II:
NEDERLANDS-ENGELS

Net als in deel I is ook hier de inrichting van de tekst gewijzigd: er is gebroken met de oude traditie van ieder trefwoord voluit op een nieuwe regel. De afleidingen en samenstellingen worden in de nieuwgevormde, samengestelde artikelen in afgekorte vorm weergegeven. In het samengestelde artikel *deinen* staat *–ning* voor *deining* en in het artikel *dempen* staat *–er* voor *demper*. In deze gevallen geeft een half kastlijntje (–) dàt gedeelte van het opvolgende trefwoord aan, dat met het voorafgaande trefwoord – vóór de eerste gemeenschappelijke klinker of medeklinker, van achteren gerekend – gelijk is.

In het samengestelde artikel *deur* staat *–bel* voor *deurbel*, *–klink* voor *deurklink* enz.

In sommige grotere samengestelde artikelen is het eerste trefwoord niet het hoofdwoord van de daarna volgende afgekorte afleidingen of samenstellingen. Men dient binnen een samengesteld artikel te zien naar het eerste, niet afgekorte trefwoord dat aan één of meerdere afgekorte voorafgaat: dat is het hoofdwoord waarop die afkorting(en) aansluiten. De lezer die een bepaald woord opzoekt komt automatisch van het voluit geschreven trefwoord binnen een samengesteld artikel bij het daarna volgende, afgekorte trefwoord dat hij zoekt terecht. In het artikel *dromen* bijvoorbeeld ziet men als eerste trefwoord *dromen* voluit, gevolgd door *dromenland* en *dromer* voluit en *dromerig* in de afgekorte vorm *–ig*. Het is in dit geval duidelijk dat de grondvorm van het afgekorte *dromerig, dromer* is.

De soms optredende complicatie van een verbindings-n of -s in samenstellingen, wordt in het gevolgde systeem als volgt aangegeven: in het samengestelde artikel *dokter*, vindt u na het tweede trefwoord *dokteren* (N.B. werkwoorden worden niet afgekort in samengestelde artikelen, tenzij er een reeks werkwoorden op elkaar volgen die een prefix gemeen hebben, zie bijvoorbeeld *doormaken*), het trefwoord *doktersassistente* voluit, gevolgd door de afgekorte vormen *–rekening* en *–visite*. De verbindings-s in doktersassistente treedt ook op in *doktersrekening* en *doktersvisite*. Opvolgende trefwoorden waarbij dat niet het geval is worden niet afgekort, maar voluit na elkaar gegeven, zie het samengestelde artikel *besseboom*.

Naast de hierboven geschetste vernieuwing van de redactie van samengestelde artikelen, zijn nog andere vernieuwingen geïntroduceerd, waarbij in het bijzonder gelet is op de bruikbaarheid van het woordenboek voor niet-nederlandstaligen. Wij menen hiermee te zijn tegemoetgekomen aan de in augustus 1973, tijdens het Vijfde Colloquium Neerlandicum te Noordwijkerhout, aangenomen resolutie, waarbij het bestuur van de Internationale Vereniging voor Nederlandistiek verzocht werd er bij de uitgevers van woordenboeken op aan te dringen te letten op de bruikbaarheid van hun uitgaven voor niet-nederlandstaligen. Bij de Nederlandse trefwoorden zijn bij deze bewerking toegevoegd: aanwijzingen voor de uitspraak, wanneer die niet met de bekend veronderstelde regels voor de uitspraak van het Nederlands in overeenstemming is[1], de klemtoon, het woordgeslacht, de vorm van het meervoud van het zelfstandig naamwoord en de vervoeging van de werkwoorden, plus de aanduiding of deze in de voltooide tijd met *hebben* of met *zijn* worden vervoegd. Bij sterke werkwoorden, waarbij in de verleden en/of voltooide tijd klinkerwisseling optreedt, zijn die 'afwijkende' vormen – op dezelfde wijze als dat met de Engelse onregelmatige werkwoorden in deel I gebeurt – op hun alfabetische plaats in het alfabet nog eens afzonderlijk vermeld, voor wat de verleden tijd betreft zowel in de vorm van het enkel- als van het meervoud.

Achterin het boek is een naar volledigheid strevende lijst van de sterke en onregelmatige werkwoorden van het Nederlands opgenomen. Bij de spelling van de trefwoorden is de voorkeurspelling gevolgd.

[1] Voor de uitspraak van woorden met een c geldt de regel: vóór medeklinker en a, o, u klinkt de c als een k, in de overige gevallen als een s. Afwijkingen van deze regel zijn afzonderlijk aangegeven.

LIJST VAN TEKENS

~	herhalingsteken	🕮	historische term
*	sterk of onregelmatig werkwoord,	➢	school en academie
	zie de lijst achterin	⌀	wapenkunde
&	en; enzovoorts	⚔	militaire term; wapens
+	attributief	⚓	marine, scheepvaart
±	ongeveer hetzelfde als	✈	vliegwezen
‖	etymologisch niet verwant	🚗	automobilisme; wegverkeer
●	verbindingen	⚡	elektriciteit
◍	eufemistisch	✝	telegrafie
☉	dichterlijk en hogere stijl	☎	telefonie
✎	verouderd	✉	post
<	versterkend	$	handelsterm
>	geringschattend	ⓡ	handelsmerk [1]
↓	zie beneden	⚕	geneeskunde
2	na een woord: eigenlijk en figuurlijk	⚖	rechtskundige term
°	na een woord: in velerlei betekenis	×	wiskunde
🐾	dierkunde	⚒	techniek
🐦	vogelkunde	△	bouwkunde
🐟	viskunde	♪	muziek
🦋	insektenkunde	⚬⚬	biljart
🌱	plantkunde	◇	kaartspel
★	sterrenkunde		

[1] Het ontbreken van het teken ⓡ bij enig woord in dit woordenboek heeft niet de betekenis dat dit woord geen merk in de zin van de Nederlandse of enige andere merkenwet zou zijn.

LIJST VAN AFKORTINGEN

aj	bijvoeglijk naamwoord	P	plat, triviaal
ad	bijwoord	*phot*	fotografie
alg.	algemeen	*pl*	meervoud
Am	vooral in Amerika	*pol*	politiek
anat	anatomie	*pr*	protestants
Austr	vooral in Australië	*pref*	voorvoegsel
B	Bijbels	*prep*	voorzetsel
biol	biologie	*pron*	voornaamwoord
Br	vooral in Groot-Brittannië	*ps*	psychologie
cj	voegwoord	R	radio
dial	dialect	*rel*	godsdienst
eig	eigenlijk	*rk*	rooms-katholiek
F	gemeenzaam	RT	radio en televisie
fig	figuurlijk	S	slang
filos	filosofie	*sb*	zelfstandig naamwoord
fon	fonetiek	sbd.	somebody
Fr	Frans	sbd.'s	somebody's
geol	geologie	*Sc*	Schots
gew.	gewoonlijk	*sp*	sport
gram	grammatica	*spec*	in het bijzonder
h.	in de voltooide tijd	*sth.*	something
	vervoegd met *hebben*	T	televisie
id.	idem	*theat*	toneel
iem.	iemand	*typ*	typografie
iems.	iemands	*v*	vrouwelijk
ij	tussenwerpsel	v.	van; voor
Ir	Iers	V.D.	voltooid deelwoord
is	in de voltooide tijd	verk. v.	verkorting van
	vervoegd met *zijn*	*va*	absoluut gebruikt werkwoord
J	schertsend	*vi*	onovergankelijk werkwoord
Lat	Latijn	*vr*	wederkerend werkwoord
m	mannelijk	*vt*	overgankelijk werkwoord
math	wiskunde	V.T.	onvoltooid verleden tijd
mv	meervoud	*ZA*	Zuid-Afrikaans
o	onzijdig		

PHONETIC SYMBOLS

DUTCH VOWELS

Several Dutch vowel sounds have no equivalent in English. As close an approximation as possible is given below. It should be borne in mind that all Dutch vowels are much shorter than the corresponding English vowels.

Sign	Dutch word	Equivalent in English and other languages	Description
ɑ	b*a*d	shorter than b*a*th	
a	b*a*den, h*aa*st	f*a*st, f*a*ther	
ɛ	b*e*d	f*a*t	
e	f*ee*st, l*e*zen	f*a*ce	
ɪ	p*i*t	p*i*t	
i	r*ie*t	fr*ee*	
ò	b*o*t	between f*u*ll and p*o*t	
ɔ	p*o*t	p*o*t	
o	b*oo*t, l*o*pen	d*a*te	
u	h*oe*d	f*oo*t	
ü	p*u*t	unstressed vowel in *a*go	
y	min*uu*t, *u*ren	Fr. min*u*te	
ø	r*eu*s	Fr. p*eu*	
ɛ:	cr*è*me	*ai*r	
ɔ:	contr*o*le	dr*a*w	in foreign words only
œ:	fr*eu*le	p*ea*rl	
ə	gav*e*	unstressed vowel in *a*go	
ã	h*a*ngar	Fr. d*a*ns	
ĩ	enf*in*	Fr. enf*in*	nasalized vowels,
õ	pensi*on*	Fr. t*on*	in foreign words only
œ̃	Verd*un*	Fr. Verd*un*	

ɑ, ɛ, ɪ, ò, ɔ, ü, short vowels
a., e., o., u., y., ø., half long vowels
a:, e:, o:, u:, y:, ø:, ɛ:, ɔ:, œ:, long vowels

DUTCH DIPHTHONGS

ai	*ai*	l*i*ne	
ɛi	*ij*s, rei*s*	*eye*	[ɛ + i]
ɔu	k*ou*d, mia*uw*	l*ou*d	[ɔ (top) + u]
a:i	dr*aai*	a (f*a*st) + i (fr*ee*)	
e:u	*eeuw*	e (f*a*ce) + u (f*oo*t)	
i:u	n*ieuw*	i (fr*ee*) + u (f*oo*t)	
o:i	n*ooi*t	o (d*a*te) + i (fr*ee*)	
œy	h*ui*s	œ (p*ea*rl) + ə (*a*go)	
u:i	r*oei*t	u (f*oo*t) + i (fr*ee*)	
y:u	d*uw*	y (Fr. min*u*te) + u (f*oo*t)	

DUTCH CONSONANTS

All Dutch consonants are pronounced as in English with the exception of those indicated below.

Sign	Dutch word	Equivalent in English and other languages	Description
c	ka*tj*e	cu*t y*our	
g	za*g*en	Scotch lo*ch*, but weaker	
j	*j*ong	*y*es	
ŋ	la*ng*	lo*ng*	
ɲ	fra*nj*e	pan*nier*	
ʃ	s*j*aal, ka*stj*e	*sh*awl	
ʒ	stella*ge*	leis*u*re	
v	*v*ater	like a soft *v*	pronounced by pressing the lower lip against the edge of the upper teeth, like Engl. v, but it is a stop without friction
x	dee*g*	Scotch lo*ch*	

STRESS

In words of two or more syllables the stress is indicated by ' preceding the syllable: ['ja͵gə(n)], [jɑs'mɛin].

II

NEDERLANDS-ENGELS

A

a [a.] (a's) *v* a; *wie ~ zegt, moet ook b zeggen* in for a penny, in for a pound; *van ~ tot z* [read a book] from A to Z, from beginning to end, from cover to cover

a = *are*

à [a.] at [four guilders, 6 per cent(.)]; *tien ~ vijftien* from ten to fifteen; *vijf ~ zes* some five or six; *over 4 ~ 5 weken* in 4 or 5 weeks

A° = *anno*

'Aagje (-s) *o nieuwsgierig ~* Paul Pry; Nos(e)y Parker

aai (-en) *m* caress, chuck (under the chin); **'aaien** (aaide, h. geaaid) *vt* stroke, caress, chuck (under the chin)

aak (aken) *m & v* ⚓ barge; **–schipper** (-s) *m* bargemaster

aal (alen) *m* 🐟 eel; *hij is zo glad als een ~* he is as slippery as an eel

'aalbes (-sen) *v* ⚘ (black, red, white) currant; **–sestruik** (-en) *m* currant bush

'aalmoes (-moezen) *v* alms, charity; *(om) een ~ vragen* ask for charity, ask for (an) alms

aalmoeze'nier (-s) *m* 1 [prison &] chaplain; 2 ⚔ (army) chaplain, **F** padre; 3 ✎ almoner

'aalscholver (-s) *m* 🦆 cormorant

'aaltje (-s) *o* eelworm

'aambeeld (-en) *o* anvil°, *anat* ook: incus; *steeds op hetzelfde ~ hameren (slaan)* always harp on one (the same) string

'aambeien *mv* h(a)emorrhoids, piles

aam'borstig asthmatic, wheezy; **–heid** *v* asthma, shortness of breath, wheeziness

aan I *prep* on, upon, at; *~ haar bed* at (by) her bedside; *~ boord* on board; *~ de deur* at the door; *~ de muur* on the wall; *vier ~ vier* four by four; *rijk ~ mineralen* rich in minerals; *er is iets stuk ~ de motor* there is something wrong with the engine; *zij is ~ het koken* she is cooking; *~ wie heb je dat gegeven?* to whom did you give it?; *het is ~ u* 1 (it is) your turn; it is for you [to play]; 2 it is up to you, it is your duty [to...]; **II** *ad* (v . k l e d i n g) *hij heeft zijn jas ~* he has his coat on; (v . v u u r , l i c h t &) *het licht is ~* the light is on; (v . b o o t , t r e i n &) *de boot is nog niet ~* the steamer is not in yet; (v . d e u r , r a a m &) *de deur staat ~* the door is ajar; (v . b i j e e n k o m s t e n) *de school is al ~*

school has begun; (v . b e w i n d) *dit kabinet blijft niet lang ~* this government will not remain in office for long; (v . l i e f d e , v r i e n d s c h a p) *het is erg ~ tussen hen* they are very fond of each other, they are as thick as thieves; (in c o m b i n a t i e m e t er) *er is niets van ~* there is not a word of truth in it; *er is niets ~* 1 it is easy; 2 it is very dull; *er is niet veel ~* it is very dull

'aanaarden¹ *vt* earth (up), hill (up)

'aanbakken (bakte 'aan, is 'aangebakken) *vi* stick to the pan [of food]

'aanbeeld = *aambeeld*

'aanbelanden (belandde 'aan, is 'aanbeland) *vi ergens ~* end up somewhere; **–belangen** *wat mij aanbelangt* as far as I am concerned; **–bellen¹** *vi* ring (the bell), give a ring; **–benen** (beende 'aan, h. 'aangebeend) *vi* **F** step out, mend one's pace

'aanbesteden¹ *vt* invite tenders for, put out to tender; **–ding** (-en) *v* tender; *bij openbare (onderhandse) ~* by public (private) tender

'aanbetalen¹ *vt* make a down payment, deposit; **–ling** (-en) *v* initial deposit, down payment, (first) instalment

'aanbevelen¹ I *vt* recommend, commend; *wij houden ons aanbevolen voor...* we solicit the favour of... [your orders]; **II** *vr zich ~* recommend oneself; **aanbevelens'waard(ig)** recommendable; **'aanbeveling** (-en) *v* recommendation; ook = *aanbevelingsbrief, aanbevelingslijst*; *kennis van Frans strekt tot ~* knowledge of French (will be) an advantage; *het verdient ~* it is to be recommended, it is advisable; *op ~ van...* on the recommendation of...; **'aanbevelingsbrief** (-brieven) *m* letter of recommendation (introduction); **–lijst** (-en) *v* nomination

aan'biddelijk adorable; **aan'bidden¹** (aan'bad, h. aan'beden en bad 'aan, h. 'aangebeden) *vt* adore², worship; **–er** (-s) *m* adorer; **aan'bidding** *v* adoration, worship

'aanbieden¹ I *vt* offer [congratulations, a gift, services &], tender [money, services, one's resignation]; present [a bill]; present [sbd.] with [a bouquet]; hand in [a telegram]; **II** *vr zich ~* 1 (p e r s o n e n) offer (oneself), volunteer; 2 (g e l e g e n h e i d) offer (itself), present

---

¹ V.T. en V.D. van dit werkwoord volgens het model: **'aan**aarden, V.T. aardde **'aan**, V.D. **'aan**geaard. Zie voor de vormen onder het grondwoord, in dit voorbeeld: *aarden*. Bij sterke en onregelmatige werkwoorden wordt u verwezen naar de lijst achterin.

itself; **–ding** (-en) *v* offer, tender; (v.
g e s c h e n k, w i s s e l) presentation;
(r e c l a m e ~) bargain, special offer; *in de ~*
on offer
'aanbijten[1] *vi* bite[2], take the bait[2], rise to the
bait[2]; **–binden**[1] *vt* tie (on), fasten; zie ook:
aangebonden; **–blaffen**[1] *vt* bark at, bay at;
–blazen[1] *vt* blow[2]; fan[2] [the fire, discord];
rouse, stir up [passions]; *fon* aspirate; **–blijven**[1]
vi continue (remain) in office; stay on
'aanblik *m* sight, look, view, aspect; *bij de eerste*
~ at first sight (glance)
'aanbod (aanbiedingen) *o* offer; *een ~ doen* make
an offer
'aanboren[1] *vt* 1 bore, sink [a well]; 2 strike
[oil &]; 3 broach [a cask]; 4 *fig* tap [other
sources]
'aanbouw *m* 1 (aanbouwsels) annex(e); 2
building [of ships]; 3 cultivation [of land]; 4
growing [of potatoes]; *in ~* under (in course
of) construction; **'aanbouwen**[1] *vt* 1 add [by
building]; 2 build [ships &]; 3 cultivate [the
land]; 4 grow [potatoes]; **'aanbouwsel** (-s) =
aanbouw 1
'aanbranden (brandde 'aan, is 'aangebrand) *vi*
burn, be burnt; *dat ruikt 'aan* (*smaakt*) *aangebrand* it
has a burnt smell (taste); *hij is gauw aangebrand*
[*fig*] he is very touchy; **–breken**[1] **I** *vt* break
into [one's provisions, one's capital], cut into
[a loaf], broach [a cask], open [a bottle]; **II** *vi* 1
(v. d a g) break, dawn; 2 (v. n a c h t) fall; 3
(v. o g e n b l i k, t i j d) come; **III** *o bij het ~
van de dag* at daybreak, at dawn; *bij het ~ van de
nacht* at nightfall
'aanbreng *m* ⚙ (marriage) portion; dowry;
'aanbrengen[1] *vt* 1 *eig* bring, carry; 2
(p l a a t s e n) place, put up [ornaments], fix
(up) [a thermometer], fit [a telephone in a
room, to the wall]; 3 (m a k e n) make [a
passage in a wall], let [a door into a wall];
introduce [a change]; 4 (g e v e n) yield [a
profit]; bring [luck]; bring in [capital]; 5
(a a n g e v e n) denounce [sbd. to the police],
inform on [one's own family]; 6 (w e r v e n)
introduce [new members]; bring in, recruit
[subscribers]; **'aanbrengpremie** (-s) *v* reward
'aandacht *v* attention; *iets onder iems. ~ brengen*
bring sth. to sbd.'s notice; *geen ~ schenken aan*
pay no attention to...; *overdreven ~ aan iem.*
schenken make a fuss of (over) sbd.; *de ~ trekken*
attract (catch) attention; *de ~ vestigen op* call
(draw) attention to..., highlight...; *zijn ~*

vestigen op... turn one's attention to...;
aan'dachtig attentive; **'aandachtsstreep**
(-strepen) *v* dash
'aandeel (-delen) *o* share, portion, part; ~ *aan*
toonder share to bearer, bearer share; ~ *op naam*
registered share; *gewoon, preferent* ~ ordinary,
preference share; *voorlopig* ~ scrip (certificate);
~ *hebben in* have a share in, have part in; zie
ook: *deel*; **–bewijs** (-wijzen) *o* share certificate;
–houder (-s) *m* shareholder; **'aandelen-
kapitaal** (-talen) *o* share capital, capital stock;
–pakket (-ten) *o* block of shares
'aandenken *o* memory, remembrance;
(v o o r w e r p) memento, keepsake
'aandienen[1] *vt* announce; *zich laten* ~ send in
(up) one's name (one's card); **–dikken** (dikte
'aan, h. 'aangedikt) *vt* thicken [a line]; heighten
[an effect, a story]; blow up [a story]
'aandoen[1] *vt* 1 put on [clothes]; 2 (v e r o o r-
z a k e n) cause [trouble], give [pain], bring
[shame, disgrace]; 3 (a a n p a k k e n) affect [the
mind &]; move [the heart &]; 4 (b i n n e n-
l o p e n) call at [a port, a station &]; *zijn longen*
zijn aangedaan his lungs are affected; *dat kun je*
hem niet ~ you cannot do that to him; *het doet*
(*ons*) *vreemd aan* it strikes us as odd; *aangenaam*
~ please [the eye]; *onaangenaam* ~ offend [the
ear &]; *aangedaan* ook: moved, touched,
affected; zie ook: *proces* &; **'aandoening** (-en)
v emotion [in his voice]; affection [of the
throat]; *een lichte ~ van koorts* ook: a touch of
fever; **aan'doenlijk I** *aj* 1 (v. v e r h a a l,
t o n e e l) moving, touching, pathetic; 2 (v.
g e m o e d) sensitive, impressionable; **II** *ad*
movingly, touchingly, pathetically; **–heid** *v* 1
(v. v e r h a a l) pathos; 2 (v. g e m o e d)
sensitiveness
'aandraaien[1] *vt* 1 turn on, turn, fasten, tighten
[the screw[2]]; 2 switch on [the light]; **–dragen**[1]
vt bring, carry; *komen ~ met* furnish [proof]
'aandrang *m* 1 (a a n d r i f t) impulse, urge; 2 ('t
a a n d r i n g e n) pressure; urgency; insistence;
3 (v. b l o e d) congestion, rush (to the head); 4
(t o e l o o p) crush; *met* ~ urgently, earnestly;
op ~ *van* at the instance of; *uit eigen* ~ of one's
own accord
'aandrift (-en) *v* impulse; instinct
'aandrijfas (-sen) *v* drive shaft, driving axle;
'aandrijven[1] **I** *vt* drive on, prompt, press,
press on, urge on; ✕ drive [a machine, nails];
II *vi* be washed ashore; **–ving** (-en) *v* ✕ drive;
met elektrische ~ ✕ electrically driven

---

[1] V.T. en V.D. van dit werkwoord volgens het model: **'aan**aarden, V.T. aardde **'aan**, V.D. **'aan**geaard. Zie voor de
vormen onder het grondwoord, in dit voorbeeld: *aarden*. Bij sterke en onregelmatige werkwoorden wordt u
verwezen naar de lijst achterin.

'aandringen¹ **I** *vi* press; insist (*op* on); *op iets* ~ press the matter, pursue one's point; **II** *o* insistence; *op* ~ *van* at the instance of; **–drukken**¹ *vt* press (firmly)

'aanduiden¹ *vt* 1 (w i j z e n) indicate, point out, show; 2 (a a n g e v e n) denote, designate, describe; 3 (b e t e k e n e n) mean, signify, mark; *nader* ~ specify; *terloops* ~ hint at; **–ding** (-en) *v* 1 indication, intimation; (t e r l o o p s) hint; 2 designation

'aandurven¹ *vt* dare; venture; *iem.* ~ dare to fight sbd., stand up to sbd.; (*iets*) *niet* ~ shrink from, be afraid to, not feel up to, stop short of; **–duwen**¹ *vt* push (firmly)

aan'een together; *dagen* ~ for days together, at a stretch; *zes uren* ~ for six hours on end; **–binden**² *vt* bind (tie) together; **–gesloten** united; serried [ranks]; **–hangen**² *vi* hang together; *het hangt als droog zand aaneen* it sticks together like grains of sand; *het hangt van leugens aaneen* it is a tissue of lies; **–hechten**² *vt* join, fasten, connect together; **–ketenen**² *vt* chain (link) together; **–kleven**² *vi* stick together; **–klinken**² *vt* rivet together; **–knopen**² *vt* tie together; **–koppelen**² *vt* couple together, couple² [railway-carriages, dogs, two people]; **–lassen**² *vt* join together; **–lijmen**² *vt* glue together; **–naaien**² *vt* sew together; **–plakken**² **I** *vt* stick together; **II** *vt* glue (paste) together; **–rijgen**² *vt* string [beads]; tack together [garments]; **–schakelen**² *vt* link together, link up; **–schakelend** *gram* copulative; **–schakeling** (-en) *v* concatenation, series, sequence; **–schrijven**² *vt* write in one; **–sluiten**² **I** *vi* fit; **II** *vr zich* ~ close the ranks; join hands, unite; zie ook: *aaneengesloten*; **–smeden**² *vt* weld together; **–vlechten**² *vt* braid together; twist (twine) together; **–voegen**² *vt* put together, join

'aanfluiting (-en) *v* mockery [of a trial]; **B** byword; *tot een* ~ *maken* make into a farce

'aanfokken¹ *vt* = *fokken*

'aangaan¹ **I** *vi* 1 (v u u r &) light, catch, strike, take fire, burn; (l i c h t) come on, go up; (v o o r s t e l l i n g &) begin; 2 (t e k e e r g a a n) take on, carry on; *dat gaat niet aan* that won't do; *bij iem.* ~ call at sbd.'s house, call on sbd.; ~ *o p* ... go up to..., make for...; **II** *vt* 1 enter into [a marriage, treaty &], contract [a marriage], conclude [a treaty], negotiate [a loan], lay [a wager &]; 2 concern, regard; *dat*

gaat u niet(s) aan ook: that's none of your business, no business (no concern) of yours; *wat dat aangaat...* as regards (respects) this, as to that; as for that; for that matter; *wat mij aangaat* so far as I am concerned, for my part, I for one, as for me; *wat gaat mij dat aan?* what's that to me?; *allen die het aangaat* all concerned; **aan'gaande** concerning, as regards..., as to...

'aangapen¹ *vt* gape at

aange'bedene (-n) *zijn* ~ his adored (one), **F** his dream-boat

'aangebonden *kort* ~ short-tempered; **–geboren** innate [ideas]; inborn [talent]; inbred [courtesy]; congenital [defect]; hereditary [disease]; native [charm]; **–gebrand** zie *aanbranden*; **–gedaan** zie *aandoen*; **–gegoten** *het zit als* ~ it fits like a glove; **–gehuwd** = *aangetrouwd*; **–gelegd** *humoristisch* ~ of a humorous turn; *religieus* ~ religiously minded

'aangelegen adjacent, adjoining, contiguous

aange'legenheid (-heden) *v* matter, concern, affair, business

'aangenaam **I** *aj* agreeable, pleasant; pleasing; gratifying; comfortable; ~ (*kennis te maken*)! pleased to meet you!; how do you do?; *het is mij* ~ *te horen* I am pleased to hear; **II** *sb het aangename van...* the amenities of... [such a life]; *het aangename met het nuttige verenigen* combine business with pleasure

'aangenomen adoptive [child]; assumed [name]; ~ *werk* job-work; zie ook: *aannemen*; **–geschoten** 1 (v o g e l) winged, wounded; 2 (d r o n k e n) **F** tipsy; zie ook: *aanschieten*; **–geschreven** zie *aanschrijven*; **–gesloten** ~ *bij* affiliated [to a party]; on [the telephone]; **–gestoken** worm-eaten [apples]; unsound [fruit]; carious [teeth]; broached [casks]; **–getekend** ✍ registered; ~ *verzenden* ✍ send by registered post; **–getrouwd** related by marriage; ~*e tante* aunt by marriage

'aangeven¹ **I** *vt* 1 (a a n r e i k e n) give, hand, reach, pass [the salt]; 2 (a a n w ij z e n) indicate [the direction]; mark [sth. on a map]; 3 (o p g e v e n) state [particulars]; notify [a disease]; give notice of [a birth]; 4 (v. b a g a g e) register; 5 (a a n d e d o u a n e) enter, declare; 6 🏛 denounce, report [sbd. to the police]; *hebt u niets aan te geven?* anything to declare?; zie ook: *maat, pas, toon &*; **II** *vr zichzelf* ~ *bij de politie* give oneself up to the police; **–er** (-s) *m* 1 🏛 denunciator, informer; 2 **$**

1,2 V.T. en V.D. volgens de modellen: 1 'aanaarden, V.T. aardde 'aan, V.D. 'aangeaard; 2 aan'eenhechten; V.T. hechtte aan'een, V.D. aan'eengehecht. Zie voor de vormen onder de grondwoorden, in deze voorbeelden: *aarden* en *hechten*. Bij sterke en onregelmatige werkwoorden wordt u verwezen naar de lijst achterin.

declarant; 3 *theat* stooge

'**aangewezen** zie *aanwijzen*

'**aangezicht** (-en) *o* = *gezicht*; *van* ~ *tot* ~ face to face; –**spijn** (-en) *v* face-ache, ✶ tic douloureux

aange'**zien**, '**aangezien** seeing that, since, as

'**aangifte** (-n) *v* notification [of birth &]; declaration [of goods, of one's income]; ⚓ information; ~ *doen van* give notice of [a birth]; declare, enter [goods]; report [a theft]; –**biljet** (-ten) *o* form of return, tax form

'**aangorden**[1] **I** *vt* gird on [a sword]; **II** *vr zich* ~ gird oneself [for the fray]

aan'**grenzend** adjacent, adjoining, neighbouring

'**aangrijnzen**[1] *vt* grin at [sbd.]; *de honger grijnst hen aan* hunger stares them in the face

'**aangrijpen**[1] *vt* 1 *eig* seize, take (seize, catch) hold of; 2 *fig* take, seize [the opportunity], seize upon [a pretext]; attack [the enemy]; tell upon [sbd.'s health]; *aangegrepen door...* seized with [fear]; deeply moved by [the sight]; **aan'grijpend** 1 (o n t r o e r e n d) touching, moving, pathetic; 2 (h u i v e r i n g w e k k e n d) thrilling; '**aangrijpingspunt** (-en) *o* point of application

'**aangroei** *m* growth, increase; '**aangroeien**[1] *vi* grow, augment, increase; (v . s c h i p) get fouled; '**aangroeisel** (-s) *o* (o p s c h e e p s - r o m p) marine fouling

'**aanhaken**[1] *vt* hook on, hitch on [to]

'**aanhalen**[1] *vt* 1 (a a n t r e k k e n) tighten [a knot]; 2 (c i t e r e n) quote, cite [an author, his words, an instance]; instance [cases]; 3 (b i j d e l i n g) bring down [a figure]; 4 (l i e f - k o z e n) fondle, caress; *je weet niet wat je aanhaalt* you don't know what you are letting yourself in for; **aan'halig** affectionate, caressing, cuddlesome, cuddly; '**aanhaling** (-en) *v* quotation, citation; –**stekens** *mv* inverted commas, quotation marks, **F** quotes; *tussen* ~ *plaatsen* put (place) in inverted commas (quotation marks)

'**aanhang** *m* supporters, following, party, followers, adherents, disciples; '**aanhangen**[1] *vt* adhere to [a party]; –**er** (-s) *m* follower, supporter, partisan, adherent; **aan'hangig** pending; ~ *maken* 1 ⚓ lay, put, bring [a matter] before a court; 2 bring in [a bill]; 3 take up [the matter with the government]; '**aanhangmotor** (-s, -motoren) *m* 1 ⚓ outboard motor; 2 (v . f i e t s) cycle motor; '**aanhangsel** (-s) *o* appendix [to a book]; rider

[of a document], codicil [of a will]; '**aanhangwagen** (-s) *m* trailer; **aan'hankelijk** affectionate, attached; –**heid** *v* attachment

'**aanhechten**[1] *vt* affix, attach

'**aanhef** *m* beginning [of a letter]; opening words [of a speech]; '**aanheffen**[1] *vt* intone [a psalm], strike up [a song], raise [a shout], set up [a cry]

'**aanhikken**[1] *vi* ~ *tegen iets* have difficulty in doing sth.; –**hitsen** (hitste 'aan, h. 'aangehitst) = *ophitsen*; –**horen**[1] *vt* listen to; *het is hem aan te horen* you can tell by his accent (voice); *het is niet om aan te horen* you couldn't bear to hear it, I can't stand it; *ten* ~ *van* in the hearing of; –**houden**[1] **I** *vt* 1 (n i e t a f b r e k e n) hold, sustain [a note]; 2 (n i e t l a t e n d o o r - g a a n) stop [a man in the street &]; hold up [a ship]; apprehend, arrest [a thief]; seize, detain [goods]; 3 (b e h o u d e n) keep on [servants &]; 4 (b l i j v e n d o o r g a a n m e t) keep up [a correspondence &]; 5 (n i e t u i t d o v e n) keep... burning; 6 (n i e t b e - h a n d e l e n) hold over [an article, the matter till the next meeting]; **II** *vi* 1 (v o o r t d u r e n) hold, last [of the weather], continue; 2 (v o l - h o u d e n) hold on[2]; *fig* persevere, persist, *ook*: pursue one's point; 3 (a a n e e n h e r b e r g &) stop; ~ *op* ⚓ make for [the coast], head for [home], keep to [the right]; **aan'houdend** continual, continuous, incessant, persistent; '**aanhouder** (-s) *m* persevering person, sticker; *de* ~ *wint* it's dogged does it; '**aanhouding** (-en) *v* 1 detainment, seizure [of goods, of a ship]; 2 arrest, apprehension [of a thief], detention [of a suspect]; –**sbevel** (-bevelen) *o* ⚓ warrant

'**aanjagen**[1] zie: *schrik, vrees*; –**er** (-s) *m* ✗ supercharger, booster

'**aankaarten**[1] *vt* bring up [matters]

'**aankap** *m* 1 felling [of trees]; 2 timber reserve, lumber exploitation

'**aankijken**[1] *vt* look at; *het* ~ *niet waard* not worth looking at; *iem. niet* ~ look away from sbd.; *de zaak nog eens* ~ wait and see; *iem. op iets* ~ blame sbd. for sth.; *met schele ogen* ~ view with jealous eyes

'**aanklacht** (-en) *v* accusation, charge, indictment; *een* ~ *indienen tegen* lodge a complaint against, bring a charge against; '**aanklagen**[1] *vt* accuse; ~ *wegens* accuse of, charge with, indict for; –**er** (-s) *m* 1 (i n 't a l g .) accuser; 2 ⚓ plaintiff; *openbaar* ~ public prosecutor

'**aanklampen**[1] (klampte 'aan, h. 'aangeklampt)

---

[1] V.T. en V.D. van dit werkwoord volgens het model: 'aan*aarden*, V.T. aard*de* 'aan, V.D. 'aan*geaard*. Zie voor de vormen onder het grondwoord, in dit voorbeeld: *aarden*. Bij sterke en onregelmatige werkwoorden wordt u verwezen naar de lijst achterin.

vt 1 ⚓ board [a vessel]; 2 *fig* accost, buttonhole [sbd.]

'**aankleden**[1] **I** *vt* dress [a child &]; get up [a play]; **II** *vr zich* ~ dress (oneself); **–ding** *v* dressing; get-up [of a play]

'**aankloppen**[1] *vi* knock (rap) at the door; *bij iem.* ~ *om geld (hulp)* apply (appeal) to sbd. for money (help)

'**aanknopen**[1] **I** *vt* tie on to; *een gesprek* ~ *met* enter into conversation with; *onderhandelingen* ~ enter into negotiations, open negotiations; *weer* ~ renew, resume; **II** *vi* ~ *bij* go on [from what was said before]; **–pingspunt** (-en) *o* point of contact; ~ *voor een gesprek* starting point for a conversation

'**aankoeken** (koekte 'aan, is 'aangekoekt) *vi* cake, incrust, encrust; stick [to the pan]

'**aankomeling** (-en) *m* beginner, novice; ☞ freshman; new-comer; '**aankomen**[1] **I** *vi* 1 *eig* come [of persons], arrive, come in [of a train &]; 2 (v. slag) go home; 3 (v. twist &) begin, start; 4 (t o e n e m e n i n g e w i c h t &) gain [8 oz. a week]; put on weight; *je moet eens* ~ just come round, drop in; *je moet er niet* ~ you must not touch it (them), (you should) leave it alone; *te laat* ~ be overdue; arrive (be) late; *ik zie* ~, *dat...* I foresee...; *ik heb 't wel zien* ~ I've seen it coming; *hij zal je zien* ~ he'll see you further (first); ● ~ *b ij iem.* call at sbd.'s house, call on sbd.; ~ *i n Londen* arrive in London; ~ *m e t een voorstel* come out with, put forward a proposal; *daarmee kan je bij hem niet* ~ 1 it will hardly do for you to propose that to him; 2 that will be no good with him; *daarmee hoef je bij mij niet aan te komen* none of that for me; don't tell me!; ~ *o p de plaats* arrive at (on) the spot; *op iem.* ~ come up to a person; *het komt hier op geld aan* it is money that matters; *het komt op nauwkeurigheid aan* accuracy is the great thing; *op de kosten komt het niet aan* the cost will be no consideration; *het komt er niet op aan* it doesn't matter; *het zal er maar op* ~ *om...* the great thing will be to...; *nu zal het erop* ~ now for it!; *als het erop aankomt* when it comes to the trial; *als het erop aankomt om te betalen...* when it comes to paying...; *het laten* ~ *op een ander* leave things to another; *het er maar op laten* ~ let things drift, trust to luck, leave it to chance; *het laten* ~ *op het laatste ogenblik* put it off to the last minute; ~ *t e g e n de muur* strike (against) the wall; **II** *o er is geen* ~ *aan* it is (they are) not to be had; **–d** *een* ~ *bediende, kantoorbediende* a junior man, clerk; *een* ~ *onderwijzer* 1

(n o g o p g e l e i d w o r d e n d) a future teacher; 2 (p a s b e g i n n e n d) a young teacher; '**aankomst** *v* arrival; *bij (mijn)* ~ on (my) arrival

'**aankondigen** (kondigde 'aan, h. 'aangekondigd) *vt* 1 (i n 't a l g.) announce; (b ij wijze van reclame) advertise; (per a a n p l a k b i l j e t) bill [a play &]; (o f f i-c i e e l) notify; 2 (v o o r s p e l l e n) herald; forebode, portend; foreshadow [a major crisis, grave developments]; 3 (b e s p r e k e n) notice, review [a book]; **–ging** (-en) *v* 1 announcement; (o f f i c i e e l) notification; notice; 2 (a d v e r t e n t i e r e c l a m e) advertisement; 3 (b e s p r e k i n g) (press) notice, review [of a book]; *tot nadere* ~ until further notice

'**aankoop** (-kopen) *m* purchase, acquisition; **–som** (-men) *v* (purchase) price; '**aankopen**[1] *vt* purchase, buy, acquire

'**aankrijgen**[1] *vt* get on [one's boots &]; get into [one's clothes]; (v. w a r e n) get in stock

'**aankruisen**[1] *vt* check (tick) off; mark with a cross, put a cross against

'**aankunnen**[1] **I** *vt* be a match for [sbd.]; be equal to [a task]; be able to cope with [the demands]; *hij kan heel wat aan* 1 he can cope with a lot of work; 2 he can manage heaps of food, a lot of drink, no end of money; **II** *vi kan men op iem aan?* can one rely upon him?

'**aankweken**[1] *vt eig* grow, cultivate[2]; *fig* foster [feelings of...]

'**aanlachen**[1] = *toelachen*

'**aanlanden**[1] *vi* land; zie ook: *belanden*

aan'**landig** onshore [breeze]

'**aanleg** *m* 1 laying out, lay-out [of avenues, roads &]; construction [of a railway]; laying [of a cable]; installation [of electric plant]; 2 (n a t u u r l ij k t a l e n t) (natural) disposition, aptitude, talent, turn [for music &]; 3 (v a t b a a r h e i d) predisposition, tendency [to consumption]; 4 (g e n e i g d h e i d) disposition [to jealousy]; 5 ⚖ instance; 6 (p l a n t-s o e n) (pleasure) grounds; ~ *hebben voor* have a turn for [music &]; have a tendency, a predisposition to [consumption]; '**aanleggen**[1] **I** *vt* 1 apply [a dressing, a standard]; place [a clinical thermometer]; 2 (t o t s t a n d b r e n g e n) lay out [a garden], construct [a railway, a road], build [a bridge], dig [a canal], install, put in [electric light]; lay on [gas, light, water]; lay [a fire]; make [a collection, a list]; 3 ⚔ level [one's rifle] (at *op*); *het* ~ manage; *het (de zaak)*

---

[1] V.T. en V.D. van dit werkwoord volgens het model: '**aan**aarden, V.T. aardde '**aan**, V.D. '**aan**geaard. Zie voor de vormen onder het grondwoord, in dit voorbeeld: *aarden*. Bij sterke en onregelmatige werkwoorden wordt u verwezen naar de lijst achterin.

handig ~ manage things (the matter) cleverly; *het verkeerd* ~ set about it the wrong way; *het zó* ~ *dat...* manage to, contrive to...; *het zuinig* ~ be economical; *het* ~ *met een meisje* carry on (take up) with a girl; *hij legt het er op aan om straf te krijgen* he is bent upon getting punished; **II** *vi* 1 (s t i l h o u'd e n) stop [at an inn]; 2 (m i k k e n) aim, take aim; *leg aan!* ⚔ present!; ~ *o p* aim at, take aim at; zie ook: *aangelegd*; **–er** (-s) *m* 1 originator [of a quarrel], instigator [of a revolt], author [of a plot]; 2 constructor, builder [of roads, canals &]; **'aanleghaven** (-s) *v* port of call; **–plaats** (-en) *v*, **–steiger** (-s) *m* landing-stage, pier

'**aanleiding** (-en) *v* occasion, inducement, motive; ~ *geven tot* give rise to, lead to, give cause for, occasion; *b i j de geringste* ~ on the slightest provocation; *n a a r* ~ *van* in pursuance of [our note]; with reference to, referring to [your letter]; having seen [your advertisement...]; in consequence of, on account of [his behaviour]; in connection with [your inquiry]; *z o n d e r de minste* ~ without any reason

'**aanlengen**[1] *vt* dilute, weaken; **–leren**[1] *vt* learn [a trade &]; acquire [a habit]; **–leunen**[1] *vi* ~ *tegen* lean against; *zich iets laten* ~ take sth. as one's due; *zich iets niet laten* ~ not put up with sth., not swallow sth., not take sth. lying down

'**aanliggend, aan'liggend** adjacent, adjoining
'**aanlijmen**[1] *vt* glue on; **–lijnen** (lijnde 'aan, h. 'aangelijnd) *vt* leash [a dog]; *fig = aankaarten*

aan'**lokkelijk** alluring, enticing, tempting, attractive; **–heid** (-heden) *v* alluringness &; charm, attraction; '**aanlokken**[1] *vt* allure, entice, tempt; (a a n t r e k k e n) attract, draw [customers]

'**aanloop** *m* run; *fig* preamble; *een* ~ *nemen* take a run; *veel* ~ *hebben* be called on by many people; *sprong met (zonder)* ~ running (standing) jump; **–haven** (-s) *v* port of call; **–kosten** *mv* initial cost(s), start-up cost(s); **–stadium** (-ia) *o* initial stage; '**aanlopen** *vi* 1 (e e n s a a n - k o m e n) call round, drop in [somewhere]; 2 (d u r e n) last; *hij liep blauw (rood, paars) aan* he got purple in the face; ~ *b i j iem.* call on sbd., drop in upon sbd.; ~ *o p* walk towards; ~ *t e g e n* run up against [a wall]; run into [sbd.]; *er (toevallig) tegen* ~ *fig* chance upon [sth.]

'**aanmaak** *m* manufacture, making; **–hout** *o* kindling; *aanmaakhoutjes* kindlings; **–kosten** *mv* cost of manufacture, manufacturing cost(s); = *aanloopkosten*; '**aanmaken**[1] *vt* 1 manufacture,

make; 2 light [a fire]; 3 dress [salad]; 4 mix [colours]

'**aanmanen**[1] *vt* exhort [to a course, to make haste], call upon [him to do his duty]; dun [for payment]; **–ning** (-en) *v* warning, exhortation; dun [for payment]

'**aanmatigen** *zich* ~ (matigde zich 'aan, h. zich 'aangematigd) arrogate to oneself; assume; presume [to advise sbd., to express an opinion]; **aan'matigend** arrogant, presumptuous, overbearing, overweening, assuming, high-handed, assertive, assumptive, pretentious; '**aanmatiging** (-en) *v* arrogance, presumption, overbearingness, assumingness, high-handedness, pretence

'**aanmelden**[1] **I** *vt* announce; **II** *vr zich* ~ announce oneself; apply [for a place]; zie verder: *zich aangeven*; **–ding** (-en) *v* 1 (b e r i c h t) announcement, notice; 2 (v o o r b e t r e k k i n g) application; 3 (v o o r w e d s t r i j d &) entry

'**aanmengen**[1] *vt* mix

aan'**merkelijk** considerable; '**aanmerken**[1] *vt* (b e s c h o u w e n, r e k e n e n) consider; *ik heb er niets (veel, weinig) op aan te merken* I have no (great, little) fault to find with it; **–king** (-en) *v* 1 (o p m e r k z a a m h e i d) consideration; 2 (o n a a n g e n a m e o p m e r k i n g) remark, observation; 3 (a f k e u r i n g) ⮐ bad mark; ~ *maken op* find fault with, criticize, pick holes in; *geen* ~ *te maken hebben* have no fault to find (with it); *in* ~ *komen* be considered [for an appointment]; be eligible [for a pension]; qualify [for a job]; *niet in* ~ *komen* be left out of account (consideration), deserve (receive) no consideration; *hij komt niet in* ~ *voor die betrekking* his application is not considered; *in* ~ *nemen* take into consideration, consider (that...), take into account, make allowance for; *zijn leeftijd in* ~ *genomen...* considering (in view of) his age; *alles in* ~ *genomen...* all things considered

'**aanmeten**[1] *vt* take one's measure for; *zich een jas laten* ~ have one's measure taken for a coat; *een aangemeten jas* a made-to-measure coat

aan'**minnig** charming, sweet

'**aanmoedigen** (moedigde 'aan, h. 'aangemoedigd) *vt* encourage; '**aanmoediging** (-en) *v* encouragement; **–spremie** (-s) *v* incentive bonus

'**aanmonsteren I** (monsterde 'aan, h. 'aangemonsterd) *vt* engage; **II** (monsterde 'aan, is 'aangemonsterd) *vi* sign on [in a ship]

---

[1] V.T. en V.D. van dit werkwoord volgens het model: '**aan**aarden, V.T. aardde '**aan**, V.D. '**aan**geaard. Zie voor de vormen onder het grondwoord, in dit voorbeeld: *aarden*. Bij sterke en onregelmatige werkwoorden wordt u verwezen naar de lijst achterin.

'**aanmunten**¹ *vt* coin, mint, monetize
aan'nemelijk acceptable [present &]; plausible [excuse]; '**aannemeling(e)** (-en) *m* (& *v*) 1 *pr* candidate for confirmation; confirmee; 2 *rk* first communicant; '**aannemen**¹ *vt* 1 take, accept, receive [it]; take in [the milk]; take delivery of [the goods]; 2 (o p n e m e n a l s l i d) admit [(ás) a member], confirm [a baptized person], receive [into the Church]; 3 (n i e t w e i g e r e n) accept [an offer &]; 4 (n i e t v e r·w e r p e n) adopt, carry [a motion], pass [a bill]; 5 (a l s w a a r) admit; 6 (o n d e r s t e l l e n) suppose; 7 (i n d i e n s t n e m e n) take on, engage; 8 (z i c h g e v e n) adopt, take on, assume [an air]; 9 (k l e u r, v o r m) take on; 10 (v . w e r k) take in [sewing]; contract for [a work]; ~! waiter!; *aangenomen!* agreed!; *aangenomen dat...* assuming that..., supposing it to be...; zie ook: *aange-nomen*; ~ *om te...* undertake to...; *als regel* ~ *om...* make it a rule to...; *tot kind* ~ adopt as a child; *boodschappen* ~ take messages; *een godsdienst* ~ embrace a religion; *de telefoon* ~ answer the telephone; zie ook: *gewoonte* & *rouw*; *goed van* ~ teachable [of a child &]; '**aannemer** (-s) *m* contractor; building contractor, (master) builder; –**sfirma** ('s) *v* firm of (building) contractors; '**aanneming** (-en) *v* 1 accept-ance, adoption, admission; 2 confirmation [in the Protestant Church]; '**aannemingssom** (-men) *v* sum (price) contracted for
'**aanpak** *m de* ~ *van dit probleem* the approach to this problem; '**aanpakken**¹ **I** *vt* 1 *eig* seize, take (lay) hold of; tackle [a problem]; deal with [a situation]; 2 (v . d e g e z o n d h e i d) tell upon [sbd.]; *hoe wil je dat* ~? how are you going to set about it, tackle it?; *het goed (verkeerd)* ~ go to work the right (wrong) way; *iem. flink* ~ take a firm line with sbd.; *iem. ruw (zacht)* ~ handle sbd. roughly (gently); *het verkeerd* ~ go the wrong way to work; *iem. verkeerd* ~ rub sbd. the wrong way; *dat pakt je nogal aan* it rather tells on you, takes it out of you; **II** *vi* **F** wire in, wire away; *je moet (flink)* ~ put your back into [the job]; '**aanpakkertje** (-s) *o* holder
'**aanpalend** adjacent, adjoining, neighbouring
'**aanpappen** (papte 'aan, h. 'aangepapt) *vi met iem.* ~ **F** strike up an acquaintance with sbd., pick up (chum up) with sbd.
'**aanpassen**¹ **I** *vt* try on [clothes]; ~ *aan* adapt to [the needs of...], adjust to [modern condi-tions]; **II** *vr zich* ~ *aan* adapt oneself to, adjust oneself to [circumstances, conditions]; '**aanpassing** (-en) *v* adaptation, adjustment; –**svermogen** *o* adaptability
'**aanplakbiljet** (-ten) *o* placard, poster, bill; –**bord** (-en) *o* bill-board, notice-board; '**aanplakken**¹ *vt* placard, post (up); paste (up); *verboden aan te plakken* stick no bills; –**er** (-s) *m* bill-sticker; '**aanplakzuil** (-en) *v* adver-tising pillar
'**aanplant** *m* 1 (h e t p l a n t e n) planting; 2 (p l a n t a g e) plantation; '**aanplanten**¹ *vt* plant; –**ting** (-en) = *aanplant*
'**aanporren**¹ *vt* rouse, shake up, spur on; –**poten¹ I** *vt* (a a n p l a n t e n) plant; **II** *vi* **F** (a a n s t a p p e n) step out; *fig* work hard; –**praten**¹ *vt iem. iets* ~ talk sbd. into sth.; –**prijzen**¹ *vt* recommend, commend highly, sound the praises of, preach up
'**aanraden**¹ **I** *vt* advise; recommend; suggest; **II** *o op* ~ *van* on (at) the advice of, on (at) the suggestion of
'**aanraken**¹ *vt* touch; '**aanraking** (-en) *v* touch, contact; *in* ~ *brengen met* bring into contact with; *in* ~ *komen met* come into touch (contact) with; *met de politie in* ~ *komen* get into trouble with the police; –**spunt** (-en) *o* point of contact
'**aanranden** (randde 'aan, h. 'aangerand) *vt* assail, assault [🕮 a woman criminally]; –**er** (-s) *m* assailant, assaulter; '**aanranding** (-en) *v* assault
'**aanrecht** (-en) *o* & *m* dresser
'**aanreiken**¹ *vt* reach, hand, pass
'**aanrekenen**¹ **I** *vt iem. iets* ~ blame sbd. for sth., hold sth. against sbd.; **II** *vr zich iets als een eer* ~ 1 take credit to oneself for...; 2 consider it an honour; zie ook: *verdienste*
'**aanrichten**¹ *vt* 1 do [harm]; work [mischief]; cause, bring about [damage]; commit [ravages]; 2 give [a dinner-party]
'**aanrijden**¹ **I** *vt iem.* ~ run into sbd.; collide with [another car]; *hij werd aangereden* he was knocked down [by a motor-car]; –**ding** (-en) *v* collision, crash, smash
'**aanroepen**¹ *vt* invoke [God's name]; call, hail [sbd., a cab, a ship]; call upon [sbd. for help]; ⚓ challenge [sbd.]; –**ping** (-en) *v* invocation; ⚓ challenge
'**aanroeren**¹ *vt fig* touch upon [a subject]; zie ook: *snaar*; –**rommelen**¹ *vi* mess, fiddle, tinker about ; –**rukken**¹ *vi* advance, march on; ~ *op* march (move) upon; *laten* ~ order [wine &]; ⚓ move up [reinforcements]

---

¹ V.T. en V.D. van dit werkwoord volgens het model: '**aan**aarden, V.T. aardde '**aan**, V.D. '**aan**geaard. Zie voor de vormen onder het grondwoord, in dit voorbeeld: *aarden*. Bij sterke en onregelmatige werkwoorden wordt u verwezen naar de lijst achterin.

'**aanschaf** (-fingen) *m* acquisition, purchase; '**aanschaffen** (schafte 'aan, h. 'aangeschaft) **I** *vt* procure, buy, get; **II** *vr zich* ~ procure, buy, get

'**aanscherpen**[1] *vt* sharpen[2]; '**aanschieten**[1] *vt* 1 (v o g e l) wing, wound; 2 (k l e r e n &) slip on [one's coat]; *vleugelen* ~ take wing; *iem.* ~ accost sbd.; zie ook: *aangeschoten*

'**aanschijn** *o* 1 (s c h ij n) appearance; 2 (g e - l a a t) face, countenance; zie ook: *zweet*

'**aanschikken**[1] *vi* draw up to the table, sit down to table; –**schoppen**[1] *vi* ~ *tegen* [*eig*] kick against; *fig* go on about, storm at [sacred cows]

aan'**schouwelijk** clear, graphic; ~ *onderwijs* object teaching, object lessons; ~ *maken* illustrate; **aan'schouwen** (aanschouwde, h. aanschouwd) *vt* behold; see; *ten* ~ *van* in the sight of, in the presence of

'**aanschrijven**[1] *vt* notify; summon; instruct; *goed (slecht) aangeschreven staan* be in good (bad, ill) repute, enjoy a good (bad) reputation; *ik sta goed (slecht) bij hem aangeschreven* I am in his good (bad) books; –**ving** (-en) *v* notification, summons; instruction(s)

'**aanschroeven**[1] *vt* 1 (s c h r o e v e n a a n) screw on; 2 (v a s t e r s c h r o e v e n) screw home; –**schuiven**[1] **I** *vt* push on, shove on; **II** *vi* = *aanschikken*

'**aanslaan**[1] **I** *vt* 1 (v a s t s l a a n) put up [a notice]; 2 (v a s t e r i n s l a a n) drive home; 3 ♪ strike [a note], touch [a string]; 4 (s c h a t t e n) estimate, rate; 5 (i n d e b e l a s t i n g) assess; *een artikel* ~ (m e t k a s - r e g i s t e r) ring up an item; *een huis* ~ put up a house for sale; *te hoog* ~ 1 (s c h a t t e n) overestimate; 2 (i n d e b e l a s t i n g) assess too high; *te laag* ~ 1 (s c h a t t e n) underestimate; 2 (i n d e b e l a s t i n g) assess too low; *voor 300 gulden (in de belasting)* ~ assess in (at) 300 guilders; **II** *vi* 1 ⚓ salute; 2 (b l a f f e n) bark, give tongue; 3 ✕ (v . m o t o r) start; 4 (d o o r a a n s l a g o p r u i t &) dim, get blurred; fur [of a boiler]; 5 *fig* (i n d r u k m a k e n) catch on; 6 (v . w o r t e l s) strike [root], root; *fig* take; ~ *tegen* strike, beat (dash, flap &) against; '**aanslag** (-slagen) *m* 1 ('t a a n s l a a n) striking; ♪ (v . p i a n i s t) touch; 2 (o p r u i t) moisture; (in k e t e l) scale, fur; 3 (i n b e l a s t i n g) assessment; 4 attempt [on sbd.'s life], [bomb] outrage; *met het geweer in de* ~ with one's rifle at the ready; *in de* ~ *brengen* cock [a rifle &]; –**biljet** (-ten) *o* notice of assessment

'**aanslibben** (slibde 'aan, is 'aangeslibd) *vi* form a deposit, silt up; –**bing** *v* accretion; alluvium, silt

'**aanslingeren**[1] *vt* crank [the motor]

'**aansluiten**[1] **I** *vt* 1 connect; link up; 2 ☎ link up with the telephone system; **II** *vi* & *va* join [of two roads]; connect, correspond [of two trains]; ~*!* close up!; ~ *op* be linked up with; connect with [the 6.30 train]; **III** *vr zich* ~ unite, join hands; *zich* ~ *b ij* 1 join [sbd., a party]; join in [a strike]; rally to [the Western bloc]; 2 become affiliated to (with) [a society]; 3 hold with [a speaker]; *verkeerd aangesloten* ☎ wrong number; *aangesloten bij* affiliated to [a party]; on [the telephone]; –**ting** (-en) *v* 1 joining; junction; 2 connection [on the telephone]; communication; 3 connection, correspondence [of trains]; ~ *hebben* connect (with *op*), correspond [of trains]; *de* ~ *missen* miss the connection; ~ *zoeken bij...* try to join..., seek contact with...; *in* ~ *op ons schrijven van...* referring to our letter of...

'**aansmeren**[1] *vt* smear, daub [a wall]; *iem. iets* ~ palm sth. off on sbd.; –**snellen**[1] *vi* run up, hurry on; ~ *o p* make a run for; –**snijden**[1] *vt* cut into [a loaf]; *een onderwerp* ~ broach (bring up) a subject; –**spannen**[1] **I** *vt* put to [horses]; *een proces* ~ take (institute) legal proceedings; **II** *va* put the horses to; –**spoelen**[1] **I** *vt* wash ashore [jetsam &]; **II** *vi* be washed ashore, be washed up

'**aansporen** (spoorde 'aan, h. 'aangespoord) *vt* spur (on) [a horse]; incite, urge, urge on [a person]; –**ring** (-en) *v* incitement; stimulus; impetus; *op* ~ *van* at the instance of

'**aanspraak** (-spraken) *v* claim; title; ~ *hebben* have people to talk to [you]; ~ *hebben op* have a claim to, be entitled to; ~ *maken op* lay claim to; **aan'sprakelijk** answerable, responsible, liable; ~ *stellen voor* hold responsible for; *zich* ~ *stellen voor* accept responsibility for; –**heid** (-heden) *v* responsibility, liability

aan'**spreekbaar** approachable, get-at-able, communicative; '**aanspreekvorm** (-en) *m* (form of) address; '**aanspreken**[1] **I** *vt* speak to, address [sbd.], accost [in the street]; *de fles (geducht)* ~ have a good go at the bottle; *zijn kapitaal* ~ break into one's capital; ● *iem.* ~ *m e t „Sir"* address sbd. as "Sir"; *iem.* ~ *o m schadevergoeding* claim damages from sbd., ⚖ sue sbd. for damages; *iem.* ~ *o v e r...* talk to sbd. about...; **II** *vi deze schilderijen spreken mij aan, spreken (mij) weinig aan* these paintings appeal

---

[1] V.T. en V.D. van dit werkwoord volgens het model: '**aan**aarden, V.T. aardde '**aan**, V.D. '**aan**geaard. Zie voor de vormen onder het grondwoord, in dit voorbeeld: *aarden*. Bij sterke en onregelmatige werkwoorden wordt u verwezen naar de lijst achterin.

to me, have little appeal (for me); **–er** (-s) *m* undertaker's man

'aanstaan[1] *vi* please ‖ (v. d e u r) be ajar ‖ (v. r a d i o) be on; *het zal hem niet* ~ he will not be pleased with it, he will not like (fancy) it;

'aanstaande, aan'staande I *aj* next, (forth)coming; ~ *Kerstmis* next Christmas; ~ *moeders* expectant mothers; ~ *onderwijzers* prospective teachers; *zijn* ~ *schoonmoeder* his prospective mother-in-law, his mother-in-law to-be; ~ *week* next week; **II** (-n) *m-v zijn* ~, *haar* ~ his fiancée, her fiancé, his future wife, her future husband

'aanstalten *mv* ~ *maken om* make ready to, prepare to; *geen* ~ *maken om* show no sign of [...ing]

'aanstampen[1] *vt* ram (down, in); tamp; **–stappen**[1] *vi* mend one's pace, step out; *op iem.* ~ step up to sbd.; **–staren**[1] *vt* stare at, gaze at, gape at

aan'stekelijk infectious[2], contagious[2], catching[2]; **'aansteken**[1] **I** *vt* 1 light [a lamp &]; kindle [a fire]; set fire to [a house]; 2 broach, tap [a cask]; 3 infect [with a disease]; **II** *vi* & *va* be infectious, be catching; zie ook: *aangestoken*; **–er** (-s) *m* lighter

'aanstellen[1] **I** *vt* appoint; ~ *tot* appoint (as), appoint to be [commander &]; **II** *vr zich* ~ pose, attitudinize; (t e k e e r g a a n) carry on; *zich dwaas* (*mal*) ~ make a fool of oneself, play the fool; **–er** (-s) *m* poseur; **aan'stellerig** affected; **aanstelle'rij** (-en) *v* affectation, attitudinizing, posing, pose; **'aanstelling** (-en) *v* appointment [to office]

'aansterken[1] *vi* get (grow) stronger, recuperate, convalesce

'aanstevenen (stevende 'aan, is 'aangestevend) *vi komen* ~ come sailing along; ~ *op* make for, head for, bear down upon

'aanstichten[1] *vt* instigate [some mischief]; hatch [a plot]; **–er** (-s) *m* instigator; **'aanstichting** (-en) *v op* ~ *van* at the instigation of

'aanstippen[1] *vt* 1 tick (check) off [items &]; 2 touch [a sore spot]; 3 touch (lightly) on [a subject]

'aanstoken[1] *vt* stir up, incite, instigate; **–er** (-s) *m* instigator, firebrand

'aanstonds, aan'stonds presently, directly, forthwith

'aanstoot *m* offence, scandal; ~ *geven* give offence, create a scandal; scandalize people; ~ *nemen aan* take offence at, take exception to, resent; **–gevend, aan'stotelijk** offensive,

scandalous, objectionable, shocking;

'aanstoten[1] **I** *vt* 1 (i e m .) nudge, jog; 2 (t o o s t e n) clink [glasses]; **II** *vi* ~ *tegen* bump up against, strike against; **–strepen**[1] *vt* mark [a passage in a book]; tick (check) off [items]; **–strijken**[1] *vt* 1 brush (over) [with paint], paint [with iodine]; 2 plaster [a wall]; 3 strike, light [a match]; **–sturen**[1] *vi* ~ *op* make for, head for[2] [the harbour &]; *fig* lead up to [sth.]; aim at

'aantal (-len) *o* number; *in* ~ *overtreffen* outnumber

'aantasten[1] *vt* 1 (g e z o n d h e i d, m e t a a l &) affect; 2 trench on [sbd.'s capital]; 3 injure [sbd.'s honour]; *in de wortel* ~ strike at the roots of

'aantekenboekje (-s) *o* notebook; **'aantekenen**[1] **I** *vt* 1 note (down), write down; mark; record; 2 🖋 register [a letter]; zie ook: 2 *appel* & *protest;* **II** *va* have their names entered at the registry office; *aangetekend verzenden* send by registered post; **–ning** (-en) *v* 1 note; annotation; entry [in a diary]; [good (bad)] mark; 2 🖋 registration; ~*en maken* take (make) notes

'aantellen[1] *va* add up [nicely]

'aantijgen (teeg 'aan, h. 'aangetegen en tijgde 'aan, h. 'aangetijgd) *vt* impute [a fault & to]; **–ging** (-en) *v* imputation

'aantikken[1] **I** *va* tap (at the door &), knock [before entering]; **II** *vi* (b i j z w e m w e d - s t r i j d) finish; (v. b e d r a g e n) add up [nicely]

'aantocht *m in* ~ *zijn* be approaching [of a thunderstorm &]; be in the offing, be on the way; ✕ be advancing, be marching on

'aantonen[1] *vt* show, demonstrate, prove; point out; zie ook: *bewijzen;* **aan'toonbaar** demonstrable

'aantrappen[1] *vt* (v. b r o m f i e t s &) start; **–treden**[1] **I** *vi* fall in, fall into line; line up, form up; **–treffen**[1] *vt* meet (with), find; come across, come upon

aan'trekkelijk attractive, likeable, inviting; **–heid** (-heden) *v* attractiveness, attraction, charm; **'aantrekken**[1] **I** *vt* 1 attract[2], draw; raise [capital &]; 2 (v a s t e r t r e k k e n) draw tighter, tighten; 3 put on [a coat, one's boots]; *zich aangetrokken voelen tot* feel attracted to(wards), feel drawn to(wards); **II** *vi* **$** (v. p r i j z e n) harden, stiffen, firm up; **III** *vr zich iets* (*erg*) ~ take sth. (heavily) to heart; *zich iems. lot* ~ interest oneself in sbd.'s behalf; *hij zal er zich niets* (*geen lor, geen zier*) *van* ~ he won't care

---

[1] V.T. en V.D. van dit werkwoord volgens het model: 'aan**aarden**, V.T. aardde 'aan, V.D. 'aangeaard. Zie voor de vormen onder het grondwoord, in dit voorbeeld: *aarden*. Bij sterke en onregelmatige werkwoorden wordt u verwezen naar de lijst achterin.

a bit (a straw); **'aantrekking** *v* attraction;
–skracht *v* pull, (power of) attraction[2]; weight
aan'vaardbaar acceptable (*voor* to);
 aan'vaarden (aanvaardde, h. aanvaard) *vt*
accept [an offer, an invitation, the conse-
quences], assume [a responsibility, the government, command]; take possession of [an
inheritance &], take up [one's appointment];
enter upon, begin [one's duties]; set out on
[one's journey]; *dadelijk (leeg) te* ~ with vacant
possession, with immediate possession; *wanneer
is het (huis) te* ~? when can I have possession?;
–ding (-en) *v* acceptance; taking possession
[of a house]; accession [to the throne]; entering
[upon one's duties]; *bij de* ~ *van mijn ambt* on
my entrance into office

'aanval (-len) *m* 1 ✠ attack°, assault, onset,
charge; 2 attack, fit [of fever &]; zie ook:
beroerte; **'aanvallen[1]** *vt* attack, assail, assault;
fall upon, set upon, lash out at [an enemy];
tackle [the player who has the ball]; charge
[with the bayonet]; **II** *vi & va* attack;
(t o e t a s t e n) fall to; ~ *op* fall upon, attack;
–d I *aj* offensive; aggressive; ~ *verbond* offensive alliance; **II** *ad* ~ *optreden* act on the offensive; **'aanvaller** (-s) *m* attacker, assailant,
aggressor

aan'vallig sweet, charming; tender [age];
–heid (-heden) *v* sweetness, charm

'aanvalsoorlog (-logen) *m* war of aggression

'aanvang *m* beginning, start, commencement;
een ~ *nemen* commence, begin; *bij de* ~ at the
beginning; zie verder: *begin*; **'aanvangen I**
(ving 'aan, is 'aangevangen) *vi* begin, start,
commence; **II** (ving 'aan, h. 'aangevangen) *vt*
do; *wat zullen wij ermee* ~? what to do with it?;
zie verder *beginnen*; **'aanvangssalaris** (-sen) *o*
commencing salary; **–snelheid** (-heden) *v*
initial velocity; **aan'vankelijk I** *aj* initial; **II**
ad in the beginning, at first, at the outset

'aanvaring (-en) *v* collision; *in* ~ *komen met*
collide with, run into, fall foul of

'aanvatten[1] *vt* catch (take, seize, lay) hold of;
iets (goed, verkeerd) ~ zie *aanpakken*; **'aanvat-
tertje** (-s) *o* holder

aan'vechtbaar questionable, debatable;
 'aanvechten[1] *vt* 1 ⊙ tempt; 2 (b e t w i s t e n)
challenge, question; **–ting** (-en) *v* temptation
'aanvegen[1] *vt* sweep [the floor]; *de vloer met iem.*
~ **F** wipe the floor with sbd., knock (hit) sbd.
for six

'aanverwant allied, related

'aanvliegen[1] I *vt iem.* ~ fly at sbd.; **II** *vi komen*
~ come flying along; (v. v l i e g t u i g)
approach; ~ *op* fly at; **'aanvliegroute** [-ru.tə]
(-s en -n) *v* approach route (path)

'aanvlijen[1] *zich* ~ *tegen* nestle against (up to)

'aanvoegen[1] *vt* add, join; ~*de wijs* subjunctive
(mood)

'aanvoelen[1] I *vt* feel; appreciate [the difficulty
&]; *zij voelen elkaar goed aan* they are well
attuned to each other; **II** *vi zacht* ~ feel soft, be
soft to the touch (to the feel); **'aanvoelings-
vermogen** *o* intuitive power; *ps* empathy;
understanding

'aanvoer (-en) *m* supply, arrival(s); **–der** (-s) *m*
1 commander, leader; *sp* captain; 2 (v.
k o m p l o t) ringleader; **'aanvoeren[1]** *vt* 1
(a a n b r e n g e n) supply; bring, convey [to]; 2
(a a n h a l e n) allege, put forward, advance
[arguments], adduce [a proof], produce
[reasons]; raise [objections to], cite [a saying, a
case]; 3 (l e i d e n) command; lead; **–ring** *v*
leadership, command; *onder* ~ *van X* under the
command of X; **'aanvoerweg** (-wegen) *m*
approach (access) road

'aanvraag (-vragen) *v* demand, inquiry [for
goods]; (v e r z o e k) request; *op* ~ [send] on
application; [tickets to be shown] on demand;
op ~ *van* at the request of; **–formulier** (-en) *o*
form of application, application form;
 'aanvragen[1] *vt* apply for, ask for; **–er** (-s) *m*
applicant

'aanvreten[1] *vt* erode; (v. m e t a l e n) corrode

'aanvullen[1] *vt* fill up [a gap]; replenish [one's
stock]; amplify [a statement]; complete [a
number], supplement [a sum]; supply [a
deficiency]; *elkander* ~ be complementary (to
one another); **–d** supplementary, complementary; **'aanvulling** (-en) *v* replenishment,
replacement [of stock]; amplification [of a
statement]; completion [of a number]; supplement, new supply; **–stroepen** *mv* ✠ reserves

'aanvuren[1] *vt* fire, stimulate, inspire; (s p o r t)
cheer; **–ring** (-en) *v* stimulation, incitement

'aanwaaien[1] *vi hij is hier komen* ~ *uit Amerika*
he has come over from America; *kennis zal
niemand* ~ there is no royal road to learning

'aanwakkeren I (wakkerde 'aan, h. 'aangewakkerd) *vt* 1 (o n g u n s t i g) stir up, fan; 2
(g u n s t i g) stimulate; **II** (wakkerde 'aan, is
'aangewakkerd) *vi* freshen [of the wind];
increase

'aanwas (-sen) *m* 1 growth, increase; 2 (v.

---

[1] V.T. en V.D. van dit werkwoord volgens het model: **'aan**aarden, V.T. aardde **'aan**, V.D. **'aan**geaard. Zie voor de
vormen onder het grondwoord, in dit voorbeeld: *aarden*. Bij sterke en onregelmatige werkwoorden wordt u
verwezen naar de lijst achterin.

g r o n d) accretion; **'aanwassen**[1] *vi* grow, increase

'aanwenden[1] *vt* use, employ, apply, bring to bear; *geld ten eigen bate* ~ convert money to one's own use; *pogingen* ~ make attempts; **–ding** *v* use, employment, application

'aanwennen[1] *vt* *zich een gewoonte (iets)* ~ make it a habit, get (fall) into the habit of...;

'aanwensel (-s) *o* (ugly) habit, trick

'aanwerven[1] *vt* enlist, recruit [soldiers]

aan'wezig 1 present; 2 (b e s t a a n d) extant; *de* ~*e voorraad* the stock on hand, the available stock; *de* ~*en* those present; **–heid** *v* 1 presence; 2 existence

aan'wijsbaar apparent; **'aanwijsstok** (-ken) *m* pointer; **'aanwijzen**[1] *vt* 1 show, point out, indicate [it]; mark [80˚]; register [10 miles an hour]; 2 (t o e w ij z e n) assign; 3 (v o o r b e p a a l d d o e l) designate; *zij zijn op zich zelf aangewezen* they are thrown on their own resources; they are entirely dependent upon themselves, *hij is de aangewezen man* he is the one to do it; *het aangewezen middel* the obvious thing; *de aangewezen weg* the proper way [to do it]; **'aanwijzend, aan'wijzend** demonstrative [pronoun]; **'aanwijzing** (-en) *v* 1 indication; 2 assignment, allocation; 3 direction [for use]; instruction, hint; 4 (i n z v o o r d e p o l i t i e) clue (to *omtrent*)

'aanwinnen[1] *vt* reclaim [land]; **'aanwinst** (-en) *vt* 1 (w i n s t) gain; 2 (b o e k e n &) acquisition, accession; 3 *fig* asset

'aanwippen[1] *vi* F drop in (on sbd.), pop in

'aanwrijven[1] *vt* *iem. iets* ~ impute sth. to sbd.

'aanzeggen[1] *vt* announce, notify, give notice of; **–ging** (-en) *v* announcement, notification, notice

'aanzet (-ten) *m* start; ♪ embouchure; **–riem** (-en) *m* (razor-)strop; **–sel** (-s) *o* crust; **–stuk** (-ken) *o* extension (piece); **'aanzetten** I *vt* 1 put... (on to); 2 fit on [a piece]; sew (on) [a button]; put ajar [the door]; turn on, tighten [a screw]; put on [the brake]; whet [a knife], set, strop [a razor]; 3 start [an engine]; put on, turn on, switch on [the radio]; urge on [a horse, a pupil]; incite [to revolt]; put [sbd.] up [to sth.]; II *vi* 1 (v. s p ij z e n) stick to the pan (to the bottom); 2 (v. k e t e l) fur; *komen* ~ come along; *komen* ~ *met* 1 *eig* come and bring; 2 *fig* come out with [a guess], bring forward [a proposal]

'aanzien[1] I *vt* look at; *wij zullen het nog wat* ~

we'll wait and see; we'll take no steps for the present; *men kan het hem* ~ he looks it; *het niet kunnen* ~ be unable to bear the look of it; be unable to stand it; *ik zie er u niet minder o m aan* I don't respect you the less for it; *iem. o p iets* ~ suspect sbd. of sth.; *iem. (iets)* ~ v o o r... take sbd. (sth.) for...; *(ten onrechte)* ~ *voor* mistake for; *waar zie je mij voor aan?* what (whom) do you take me for?; *ik zie ze er wel voor aan* I wouldn't put it past them; *zich goed (mooi) laten* ~ look promising, promise well; *het laat zich* ~ *dat...* there is every appearance that...; *naar het zich laat* ~, *zullen wij slecht weer krijgen* to judge from appearances, we are going to have bad weather; zie ook: *nek*; **II** *o* 1 look, aspect; 2 (a c h t i n g) consideration; regard, prestige, esteem; *zich het* ~ *geven van* assume an air of; *dat geeft de zaak een ander* ~ that puts another complexion on the matter; ● *(zeer) i n* ~ *zijn* be held in (great) respect, in (high) esteem; *t e n* ~ *van* with respect to, with regard to; *te dien* ~ as for that; *een man v a n* ~ a man of note (distinction); *iem. van* ~ *kennen* know sbd. by sight; *z o n d e r* ~ *des persoons* without respect of persons; **aan'zienlijk I** *aj* 1 (g r o o t) considerable [sums], substantial [loss]; 2 (v o o r - n a a m) distinguished [people], notable, ...of note, of good (high) standing; **II** *ad* < considerably [better &]

'aanzijn *o* existence; *het* ~ *geven* give life (to); *in het* ~ *roepen* call into being (existence)

'aanzitten[1] *vi* sit at table, sit down; *de aanzittenden, de aangezetenen* the guests

'aanzoek (-en) *o* 1 request, application; 2 offer (of marriage), proposal; *een* ~ *doen* propose to [a girl]; **'aanzoeken**[1] *vt* apply to [a person for...]; request

'aanzuiveren[1] *vt* pay, clear off [a debt], settle [an account]; make good [a deficit]

'aanzwellen[1] *vi* swell [into a roar]

'aanzwengelen (zwengelde 'aan, h. aangezwengeld) *vt* crank up [the motor]

aap (apen) *m* monkey²; (z o n d e r s t a a r t) ape; *een* ~ *van een jongen* a (little) rascal; *in de* ~ *gelogeerd zijn* F be in a fix; be up a tree; *daar komt de* ~ *uit de mouw* there we have it; *zich een* ~ *lachen* split one's sides with laughter; *iem. voor* ~ *zetten* make a laughing-stock of sbd.; ~*-wat-heb-je-mooie-jongen spelen* butter up; **–achtig** apish, ape-like, monkey-like; **–je** (-s) *o* 1 *eig* little monkey; 2 (r ij t u i g) cab; **–mens** (-en) *m* ape man

---

[1] V.T. en V.D. van dit werkwoord volgens het model: **'aan**aarden, V.T. aardde **'aan**, V.D. **'aan**geaard. Zie voor de vormen onder het grondwoord, in dit voorbeeld: *aarden*. Bij sterke en onregelmatige werkwoorden wordt u verwezen naar de lijst achterin.

aar (aren) *v* ear [of corn] ‖ (b l o e d v a t) vein
aard *m* 1 (g e s t e l d h e i d) nature, character, disposition; 2 (s o o r t) kind, sort; *het ligt niet in zijn ~* it is not in his nature, it is not in him; *u i t de ~ der zaak* in (by, from) the nature of the case (of things); *v a n allerlei ~* of all kinds, of every description; *de omstandigheden zijn van die ~, dat...* the circumstances are such that ...; *niets van die ~* nothing of the kind; *studeren (werken, zingen) dat het een ~ heeft* with a will, with a vengeance; zie ook *aardje*

'**aardappel** (-s en -en) *m* potato; –**meel** *o* potato flour; –**moeheid** *v* potato blight (disease, rot); –**puree** *v* mashed potatoes; –**ziekte** *v* potato blight (disease, rot)

'**aardas** *v* axis of the earth, earth's axis; –**bei** (-en) *v* strawberry; –**beving** (-en) *v* earthquake; –**bodem** *m* earth; –**bol** (-len) *m* (terrestrial) globe; '**aarde** *v* 1 earth; 2 soil; (t e e l ~) mould; 3 ⚡ earth connection; *(niet) i n goede ~ vallen* be (badly) well received [of a proposal &]; *b o v e n ~ staan* await burial; *t e r ~ bestellen* inter, commit to earth; *zich ter ~ werpen* prostrate oneself; '**aardedonker I** *aj* pitch-dark; **II** *o* pitch-darkness; **1** '**aarden** *aj* earthen; ~ *kruik* stone jar; ~ *pijp* clay pipe; **2** '**aarden** (aardde, h. geaard) *vi* thrive, do well [of a plant]; ~ *naar* take after; *ik kon er niet ~* I did not feel at home there; zie ook: *geaard*; **3** '**aarden** (aardde, h. geaard) *vt* ⚡ earth, ground; zie ook: *geaard*; '**aardewerk** *o* earthenware, crockery, pottery

'**aardgas** *o* natural gas; –**bel** (-len) *v* natural gas reserve (field, deposit, pocket); –**leiding** (-en) *v* gas pipeline (feeder)

'**aardgeest** (-en) *m* gnome; –**gordel** (-s) *m* zone
'**aardig I** *aj* 1 (l i e f, b e v a l l i g) pretty, nice; dainty; sweet; 2 (e e n a a n g e n a m e i n d r u k m a k e n d) nice, pleasant; 3 (h e u s) nice, kind; 4 (g r a p p i g) witty, smart; 5 (t a m e l i j k g r o o t) fair; *een ~ sommetje* a pretty penny, a tidy sum of money; *dat vindt hij wel* ~ he rather fancies it; *zich ~ voordoen* have a way with one; **II** *ad* 1 nicely, prettily, pleasantly; 2 < pretty [cold &]; –**heid** (-heden) *v er is geen ~ aan* there is not much fun to be got out of it; *de ~ is er af* the gilt is off; ~ *in iets hebben* take pleasure in sth.; ~ *in iets krijgen* take a fancy to sth.; *uit ~, voor de ~* for fun, for the fun of the thing; –**heidje** (-s) *o* little present
'**aardje** *o hij heeft een ~ naar zijn vaartje* he is a chip of the old block

'**aardkluit** (-en) *m & v* clod (lump) of earth; –**korst** *v* crust of the earth, earth's crust; –**kunde** *v* geology; –**laag** (-lagen) *v* layer (of earth); –**leiding** (-en) *v* ⚡ earth connection, earth wire, ground wire; –**magnetisme** *o*

terrestrial magnetism; –**mannetje** (-s) *o* gnome, goblin, brownie; –**noot** (-noten) *v* ground-nut; –**olie** *v* petroleum
'**aardrijkskunde** *v* geography; **aardrijks'kundig I** *aj* geographical [knowledge, Society &], geographic; **II** *ad* geographically; –**e** (-n) *m* geographer
aards earthly[2] [paradise], terrestrial; worldly
'**aardsatelliet** (-en) *m* earth satellite; –**schok** (-ken) *m* earthquake shock; –**schors** *v* = *aardkorst*; –**slak** (-ken) *v* slug; –**straal** (-stralen) *m & v* earth ray, dowsing ray; –**verschuiving** (-en) *v* landslip, landslide; –**worm** (-en) *m* earthworm
aars (aarzen) *m* anus; –**vin** (-nen) *v* anal fin
aartsbedrieger (-s) *m* arrant cheat; –**bisdom** (-men) *o* archbishopric; –**bisschop** (-pen) *m* archbishop; **aartsbis'schoppelijk** archiepiscopal; '**aartsdom** as stupid as an ass; –**engel** (-en) *m* archangel; –**hertog** (-togen) *m* archduke; –**hertogdom** (-men) *o* archduchy; **aartsher'togelijk** archducal; '**aartshertogin** (-nen) *v* archduchess; –**leugenaar** (-s) *m* arrant liar, arch-liar; –**lui** extremely lazy; –**luiaard** (-s) *m* inveterate idler; –**vader** (-s en -en) *m* patriarch; **aarts'vaderlijk** patriarchal; '**aartsvijand** (-en) *m* arch-enemy
'**aarzelen** (aarzelde, h. geaarzeld) *vi* hesitate, waver; *zonder ~* without hesitation, unhesitatingly; –**ling** (-en) *v* hesitation, wavering
1 aas *o* 1 bait[2]; 2 (d o o d d i e r) carrion; **2 aas** (azen) *m & o* ◇ ace; –**eter** (-s) *m* scavenger; –**gier** (-en) *m* vulture; –**je** (-s) *o een ~ wind* a breath of wind; –**vlieg** (-en) *v* bluebottle; meat-fly
A.B.(N.) = *Algemeen Beschaafd Nederlands* standard Dutch (cf. the King's English)
abat'toir [a.bɑ'twa:r] (-s) *o* abattoir, slaughterhouse
ab'c [a.be.'se.] ('s) *o* ABC[2], alphabet; **ab'c-boek** (-en) *o* primer, spelling book
ab'ces [ɑp'ses] (-sen) *o* abscess
abdi'catie [-(t)si.] (-s) *v* abdication; **abdi'ceren** (abdiceerde, h. geabdiceerd) *vi* abdicate, renounce, give up [the throne]
ab'dij (-en) *v* abbey; **ab'dis** (-sen) *v* abbess
a'beel (abelen) *m* abele
aber'ratie [a.bɛ'ra.(t)si.] *v* aberration
Abes'sijn (-en) *m* Abyssinian; –**s** Abyssinian; **Abes'sinië** *o* Abyssinia
'**ablatief** (-tieven) *m* ablative
abnor'maal abnormal; **abnormali'teit** (-en) *v* abnormality, abnormity
abomi'nabel horrible, abominable, execrable
abon'nee (-s) *m* 1 subscriber; 2 (o p t r e i n &) season-ticket holder; –**nummer** (-s) *o* subscriber's number; **abonne'ment** (-en) *o*

subscription [to...]; season-ticket;
abonne′mentskaart (-en) *v* season-ticket;
–prijs (-prijzen) *m*, **–tarief** (-rieven) *o*
subscription rate, rate of subscription;
abon′neren (abonneerde, h. geabonneerd) *vr*
zich ~ *op* subscribe to [a newspaper]; *ik ben op*
de Times geabonneerd I take in the Times
abor′teren (aborteerde, h. geaborteerd) *vt*
abort; **abor′tief** abortive, unsuccessful;
a′bortus (-sen) *m* abortion
à bout por′tant [a.bu.pɔr′tɑ̃] point-blank
′Abraham, ′Abram [′a.bra.hɑm, ′a.brɑm] *m*
Abraham; ~ *gezien hebben* be 50 years or over;
zie ook: *weten*
a′bri (′s) *m* (bus) shelter
abri′koos (-kozen) *v* apricot
ab′rupt abrupt, sudden
ab′sent 1 (a f w e z i g) absent; 2 (v e r -
s t r o o i d) absent-minded, abstracted;
absente′isme *o* absenteeism; **ab′sentie**
[-(t)si.] (-s) *v* 1 absence; non-attendance; 2
absence (of mind), absent-mindedness; **–lijst**
(-en) *v* attendance register
ab′sint *o* & *m* absinth(e)
abso′lutie [-(t)si.] *v* absolution; *de* ~ *geven rk*
absolve
absolu′tisme *o* absolutism; **–ist** (-en) *m*
absolutist; **–istisch** absolutist
abso′luut I *aj* absolute; ~ *gehoor* absolute pitch;
II *ad* absolutely, decidedly; ~ *niet* not at all, by
no means, not by any means; ~ *niets* absolutely
nothing
absor′beren (absorbeerde, h. geabsorbeerd) *vt*
absorb[2]; **ab′sorptie** [-′sɔrpsi.] *v* absorption
ab′soute [ɑp′su.tə] *v rk* absolution; *de* ~
verrichten pronounce (give) the absolution
ab′stract abstract [art]; **–ie** [-′strɑksi.] (-s) *v*
abstraction; **abstra′heren** (abstraheerde, h.
geabstraheerd) *vt* abstract
ab′surd absurd, preposterous; **absurdi′teit**
(-en) *v* absurdity, preposterousness
abt (-en) *m* abbot
a′buis (abuizen) *o* mistake, error; ~ *hebben (zijn)*
be mistaken; *per* ~ by (in) mistake, erroneously, mistakenly; **abu′sief, abu′sievelijk**
wrongly, by mistake
a′cacia [a.′ka.si.a.] (′s) *m* acacia
aca′demicus (-ci) *m* university graduate,
academic; **aca′demie** (-s en -iën) *v* academy,
university, college; *pedagogische* ~ (teachers′)
training college; **aca′demisch** academic
[year, title, question]; ~ *gevormd* college-taught,
with a university training; ~*e graad* university
degree; ~ *ziekenhuis* teaching hospital
accele′ratie [ɑkse.lə′ra.(t)si.] *v* acceleration
ac′cent [ɑk′sɛnt] (-en) *o* accent°; stress[2]; *fig*
emphasis [*mv* emphases]; **accentu′eren**

(accentueerde, h. geaccentueerd) *vt* accent;
stress[2]; *fig* emphasize, accentuate
ac′cept [ɑk′sɛpt] (-en) *o* $ 1 acceptance [of a
bill]; 2 (p r o m e s s e) promissory note;
accep′tabel acceptable; **–ant** (-en) *m* $
acceptor; **accep′teren** (accepteerde, h. geac-
cepteerd) *vt* accept; *niet* ~ refuse (acceptance
of); $ dishonour [a bill]
ac′ces [ɑk′sɛs] (-sen) *o* access, entrance
acces′soires [ɑksɛ′swa.rəs] *mv* accessories
ac′cijns [ɑk′sɛins] (-cijnzen) *m* excise(-duty)
accla′matie [ɑkla.′ma.(t)si.] *v* acclamation; *bij*
~ *aannemen* carry by acclamation
acclimati′satie [ɑkli.ma.ti.′za.(t)si.] *v* acclimati-
zation; **acclimati′seren** [s = z] **I** (acclimatiseerde, h. geacclimatiseerd) *vt* acclimatize; **II**
(acclimatiseerde, is geacclimatiseerd) *vi*
become acclimatized
acco′lade [ɑko.′la.də] (-s) *v* 1 accolade [at
bestowal of knighthood]; 2 (~t e k e n) brace;
♪ accolade
accommo′datie [ɑkɔmo.′da.(t)si.] (-s) *v* accommodation; **–vermogen** *o* faculty of accommodation
accompagne′ment [ɑkɔ̀mpaɲə′mɛnt] *o*
accompaniment; **accompa′gneren** (accom-
pagneerde, h. geaccompagneerd) *vt* accompany
accorde′on [cc = k] (-s) *o* & *m* accordion;
accordeo′nist (-en) *m* accordionist
accor′deren [cc = k] (accordeerde, h. geaccor-
deerd) *vi* 1 agree; come to terms; 2 $
compound with one′s creditors; 3 get on [well]
ac′countant [ɑ′kɑuntɔnt] (-s) *m* (chartered)
acountant, auditor; **ac′countantsdienst** (-en)
m audit(ing) service, accounts service;
–rapport (-en) *o* audit(ing) report
accredi′teren [cc = k] (accrediteerde, h. geac-
crediteerd) *vt* accredit [to, at a court];
accredi′tief (-tieven) *o* letter of credit
′accu [′ɑky.] (′s) = *accumulator*; **accumu′latie**
[-(t)si.] (-s) *v* accumulation; **–tor** (-s en - ′toren)
m accumulator, (storage) battery; *de* ~ *is leeg*
the battery is burnt out; **accumu′leren**
(accumuleerde, h. geaccumuleerd) *vt* accumulate, store
accu′raat [ɑky.-] accurate, exact, precise;
accura′tesse *v* accuracy, exactitude, precision
′accusatief [′ɑky.za.ti.f] (-tieven) *m* accusative
ace′taat [c = s] (-taten) *o* acetate
ace′ton [c = s] *o* & *m* acetone
acety′leen [a.seti.′le.n] *o* acetylene
ach ah!, alas!; ~ *en wee roepen* lament
a′chilleshiel (-en) *m* Achilles′ heel[2]; **–pees**
(-pezen) *v* Achilles tendon
1 acht eight
2 acht *v* attention, heed, care; ~ *slaan op* pay

attention to; *geef...~!* ⚓ attention!, 'shun!; *in ~ nemen* be observant of, observe [the rules, the law]; *zich in ~ nemen* 1 be on one's guard; 2 take care of one's health (of oneself); *neem u in ~ nemen voor...* mind what you do!; *zich in ~ nemen voor...* beware of..., be on one's guard against...

'**achtbaan** (-banen) *v* big dipper, switchback [at a fair]

'**achteloos** careless, negligent; **achte'loosheid** *v* carelessness, negligence; '**achten** (achtte, h. geacht) **I** *vt* 1 esteem, respect; 2 (d e n k e n, v i n d e n) deem, think, consider, judge; 3 (l e t t e n o p) pay attention to; *het beneden zich ~ om...* think it beneath one to...; *ik acht het niet raadzaam* I don't think it advisable; **II** *vr zich gelukkig ~* deem (think) oneself fortunate; *ik acht mij niet verantwoord dit te zeggen* I do not feel justified in saying this; zie ook: *geacht*; **achtens'waardig** respectable

'**achter I** *prep* behind, after, at the back of; *ik ben er ~* 1 (n u w e e t i k h e t) I've found it out; 2 (n u k e n i k h e t) I've got into it; I've got the knack of it; *~ iem. staan fig* support, stand by sbd.; **II** *ad hij is ~* 1 he is in the backroom; 2 *fig* he is behindhand (in his studies, with his lessons); he is in arrear(s) [with his payments]; *mijn horloge is ~* my watch is slow; *er ~ komen* discover, detect, find out; *er toevallig ~ komen* stumble upon; *~ raken* drop (fall) behind; get behind [with one's work]; ● *t e n ~* in arrear(s) [with his payments]; behindhand [in his studies, with his lessons]; behind [with his work]; *ten ~ bij zijn tijd* behind the times; *v a n ~* [attack] from behind; [low] at the back; [viewed] from the back; *van ~ inrijden op* run into the back of, crash into the rear of [another train]; *van ~ naar voren* [spell a word] backwards; **achter'aan** behind, in the rear, at the back; *2de klas ~* 2nd class in rear of train; '**achteraandrijving** *v* rear-wheel drive; **achter'aankomen** (kwam achter'aan, is achter'aangekomen) *vi* come last, lag behind, bring up the rear; '**achteraanzicht** (-en) *o* back (rear) view; **achter'af** in the rear; [live] out of the way; *~ bekeken...* 1 looking back, retrospectively, in retrospect; 2 after all [he is not a bad fellow]; *zich ~ houden* keep aloof; **achter'afbuurt** (-en) *v = achterbuurt;* '**achteras** (-sen) *v* rear (hind, back) axle

achter'baks I *aj* underhand, backdoor; **II** *ad* underhand, behind one's back; *iets ~ houden* keep sth. back

'**achterbalkon** (-s) *o* rear platform [of a tram-car]; **-ban** *m fig* rank and file; **-band** (-en) *m* back tyre; **-bank** (-en) *v* back seat, rear seat

'**achterblijven[1]** *vi 1 eig* stay behind, remain behind; 2 (b ij s t e r f g e v a l) be left (behind); 3 (b ij w e d s t r ij d e n &) fall (drop, lag) behind, be outdistanced; ⚓ be backward; *~ bij* fall (come) short of; *achtergebleven gebieden* backward countries, underdeveloped countries; **-er** (-s) *m* straggler, laggard

'**achterbout** (-en) *m* hind quarter; **-buurt** (-en) *v* back street, slum; **-deel** (-delen) *o* back part, hind part; **-dek** (-ken) *o* poop, after-deck; **-deur** (-en) *v* backdoor; **~tje** (s p a a r d u i t j e) nest-egg

'**achterdocht** *v* suspicion; *~ hebben (koesteren)* have suspicions, be suspicious; *~ krijgen* become suspicious; *~ opwekken* arouse suspicion; **achter'dochtig** suspicious

achter'een in succession, consecutively; at a stretch; *viermaal ~* four times running; *vier uur ~* four hours at a stretch (on end); *maanden ~* for months at a time, for months together; **achtereen'volgend** successive, consecutive; **achtereen'volgens** successively, in succession, in turn, consecutively

'**achtereind(e)** (-(e)n) *o* hind part, back part

achterel'kaar one after the other; *~ lopen* walk in single (Indian) file; *~ door* continuously, without interruption; zie ook *achtereen*

'**achteren** *naar ~* backward(s); *naar ~ gaan* **F** go to the bathroom, spend a penny; *van ~* from behind; zie verder: *achter* **II**

'**achtergebleven** zie *achterblijven*

'**achtergevel** (-s) *m* back-front; **-grond** (-en) *m* background[2]; *op de ~ blijven* keep (remain) in the background; *op de ~ raken* fall (recede) into the background; **-grondmuziek** *v* background music, muzak

achter'halen (achterhaalde, h. achterhaald) *vt* 1 (v. m i s d a d i g e r &) arrest; 2 (v. v o o r-w e r p e n) recover; 3 (v. f o u t e n, g e g e-v e n s) trace, detect; *achterhaald* out of date

'**achterhand** (-en) *v* 1 (h a n d w o r t e l) carpus; 2 (v. p a a r d) hind quarters

achter'heen *achter iem. (iets) heen zitten* keep after sbd. (sth.)

'**achterhoede** (-n en -s) *v* rear(guard); *sp* defence; *de ~ vormen* bring up the rear; **-gevecht** (-en) *v* rearguard action; **-speler** (-s) *m = achterspeler*

'**achterhoofd** (-en) *o* back of the head, occiput; *gedachten in zijn ~* thoughts at the back of his

---

[1] V.T. en V.D. volgens het model: '**achter**stellen, V.T. stelde '**achter**, V.D. '**achter**gesteld. Zie voor de vormen onder het grondwoord, in dit voorbeeld: *stellen*. Bij sterke en onregelmatige werkwoorden wordt u verwezen naar de lijst achterin.

mind; *hij is niet op zijn ~ gevallen* there are no flies on him

'**achterhouden**[1] *vt* keep back, hold back, withhold

'**achterhuis** (-huizen) *o* 1 (a c h t e r s t e g e-d e e l t e) back part of the house; 2 (g e b o u w) back premises

achter'**in** at the back [of the book, of the garden &], [sit] in the back [of a car, of a lorry], [climb, peer] into the back [of the car]

'**Achter-'Indië** *o* Further India, Indochina

'**achterkamer** (-s) *v* backroom; –**kant** (-en) *m* back; reverse (side); –**klap** *m* backbiting, scandal, slander(ing); –**kleinkind** (-eren) *o* greatgrandchild; –**lader** (-s) *m* breech-loader; –**land** (-en) *o* hinterland

achter'**lastig** ⚓ stern-heavy

'**achterlaten**[1] *vt* leave [sth. somewhere, with sbd.]; leave behind [after one's departure or death]; –**ting** *v met* ~ *van* leaving behind

'**achterlicht** (-en) *o* rear-light, tail-light, rear-lamp

'**achterliggen**[1] ~ *op, bij* lag behind [sbd.]

'**achterlijf** (-lijven) *o* abdomen [of insects]

'**achterlijk** 1 retarded, backward [= mentally deficient]; 2 behind the times; –**heid** *v* backwardness

'**achterlopen**[1] *vi* (v. u u r w e r k) be slow; *fig* lag behind, not keep up with the times

achter'**na** after; behind; ~ *gaan* follow, pursue; ~ *lopen, zitten* run after; ~ *zetten* chase, pursue

'**achternaam** (-namen) *m* surname, family name

'**achterneef** (-neven) *m* grand-nephew; second cousin; –**nicht** (-en) *v* grand-niece; second cousin

achter'**om** the back way about; behind; back; ~ *lopen* go round (at the back); ~ *zien* &, zie *omzien* &

achter'**op** behind, at the back; on the back [of an envelope]; ~ *raken* fall behind; get behind with one's work (studies); be in arrear(s) [with one's payments]; –**komen** (kwam achter'op, is achter'opgekomen) *vt* overtake [sbd.], catch [sbd.] up, come up with

achter'**over** backward, on one's back; –**drukken**[2] F pinch, pilfer; –**leunen**[2] *vi* lean back; –**vallen**[2] *vi* fall backwards

'**achterpand** (-en) *o* back; –**plaats** (-en) *v* back-yard; –**plecht** (-en) *v* poop; –**poot** (-poten) *m* hind leg; –**ruit** (-en) *v* rear window;

–**schip** (-schepen) *o* stern; *op het* ~ abaft; –**speler** (-s) *m* back

'**achterstaan**[1] *vi* ~ *bij* be inferior to; *bij niemand* ~ ook: be second to none

achter'**stallig** outstanding; overdue; ~*e huur* back rent; ~*e rente* interest arrears; ~ *zijn* be in arrear(s) with one's payments; be behind with the rent

'**achterstand** *m* arrears; ~ *inlopen* (*inhalen*) make up arrears

'**achterste I** *aj* hindmost, hind; **II** *sb* (-n) *o* 1 back part; 2 (z i t v l a k) bottom, backside, buttocks

'**achterstellen**[1] *vt* subordinate (to); discriminate (against); slight [sbd.]; ~ *bij* neglect for; –**ling** *v* neglect, slighting; *met* ~ *van* to the neglect of

'**achtersteven** (-s) *m* stern

achterste'**voren** back to front

'**achtertuin** (-en) *m* back-garden

achter'**uit I** *ad* backward(s), back; ⚓ aft; [full speed] astern; ~ *daar!* stand back!; **II** *v* 🔄 reverse; –**boeren** (boerde achter'uit, h. en is achter'uitgeboerd) *vi* go downhill; –**gaan**[3] *vi* go (walk) back(wards); *fig* go back [of civilization], decline [in vitality, prosperity], go down in the world; retrograde [in morals], fall off [in quality]; fall [of barometer]; *hard* ~ ook: sink fast

1 '**achteruitgang** (-en) *m* rear-exit

2 achter'**uitgang** *m* going down, decline

achter'**uitkijkspiegel** (-s) *m* (driving) mirror; –**krabbelen**[3] *vi* back out of sth.; –**rijden**[3] **I** *vi* 1 ride (sit) with one's back to the engine (to the driver); 2 back, reverse [of motor-car]; **II** *vt* back, reverse [a motor-car]; –**zetten**[3] *vt* 1 put (set) back [a watch]; 2 (f i n a n c i e e l &) throw back; 3 (v. g e z o n d h e i d) put back; 4 (v e r o n g e l i j k e n) slight

'**achtervoegen**[1] *vt* affix, add; '**achtervoegsel** (-s) *o* suffix

achter'**volgen** (achtervolgde, h. achtervolgd) *vt* run after[2], pursue, dog; persecute; achter'**volging** (-en) *v* pursuit; persecution; –**swedstrijd** (-en) *m* pursuit race

'**achterwaarts I** *aj* backward, retrograde; **II** *ad* backward(s), back

achter'**wege** ~ *blijven* fail to appear; ~ *laten* omit, drop

'**achterwerk** (-en) *o* = *achterste* **II** 2

'**achterwiel** (-en) *o* back (hind, rear) wheel; –**aandrijving** *v* rear-wheel drive

[1,2,3] V.T. en V.D. volgens de modellen: 1 '**achter**stellen, V.T. stelde '**achter**, V.D. '**achter**gesteld; 2 achter'**over**drukken, V.T. drukte achter'**over**, V.D. achter'**over**gedrukt; 3 achter'**uit**krabbelen, V.T. krabbelde achter'**uit**, V.D. achter'**uit**gekrabbeld. Zie voor de vormen onder de grondwoorden, in deze voorbeelden: *stellen, drukken* en *krabbelen*. Bij sterke en onregelmatige werkwoorden wordt u verwezen naar de lijst achterin.

'**achterzak** (-ken) *m* hip-pocket; **–zij(de)** (-den) *v* back; reverse (side)

'**achthoek** (-en) *m* octagon; **–ig, acht'hoekig** octagonal

'**achting** *v* esteem, regard, respect; *de* ~ *genieten van...* be held in esteem by...; ~ *hebben voor* hold in esteem; *in iems.* ~ *dalen (stijgen)* fall (rise) in sbd.'s esteem

'**achtjarig** 1 of eight years, eight-year-old; 2 octennial (= lasting eight years); '**achtste** eighth (part); '**achttal** (-len) *o* (number of) eight; '**achttien** eighteen; **–de** eighteenth (part); **acht'urendag** (-dagen) *m* eight-hour(s) day; '**achtvlak** (-ken) *o* octahedron; **–kig** octahedral; '**achtvoudig** eightfold, octuple

acquisi'teur [ɑkʋi.zi.'tø:r] (-s) *m* canvasser

acro'baat (-baten) *m* acrobat; **acroba'tiek** *v* acrobatics; **acro'batisch** acrobatic; **~e toeren** acrobatic feats

acro'niem (-en) *o* acronym

'**acte** ~ *de présence* [ɑktǝdǝpre'zãs] *geven* put in an appearance, show one's face; zie ook *akte*

ac'teren (acteerde, h. geacteerd) *vi & vt* act; **ac'teur** (-s) *m* actor, player

'**actie** ['ɑksi.] (-s) *v* 1 ⚖ action°; lawsuit; 2 agitation, campaign [in favour of]; drive [to raise funds &]; 3 ⚖ action; *een* ~ *instellen tegen* ⚖ bring an action against; *in* ~ *komen* 1 ⚖ go into action; 2 *fig* act, take action; ~ *voeren (voor)* agitate (for); *in* ~ *zijn* run; **ac'tief I** *aj* 1 active, energetic; 2 ⚖ with the colours; *actieve handelsbalans* $ favourable trade balance; **II** *ad* actively, energetically; **III** (-tiva) *o* ~ *en passief* $ assets and liabilities; '**actiegroep** ['ɑksi.-] (-en) *v* action group, action committee; **–radius** *m* radius (range) of action, flying range; '**activa** *mv* $ assets; ~ *en passiva* assets and liabilities; **acti'veren** (activeerde, h. geactiveerd) *vt* activate; **acti'vist** (-en) *m* activist; **activi'teit** (-en) *v* activity

ac'trice (-s) *v* actress

actuali'teit (-en) *v* topicality [of a theme]; actuality; *een* ~ a topic of the day; **–enprogramma** ('s) *o* news-reel

actu'aris (-sen) *m* actuary

actu'eel of present interest; topical [event, question, subject]; timely [article in the papers]

acupunc'tuur (-turen) *v* acupuncture

a'cuut acute

ad $ at [3%]

A.D. = *anno Domini*

'**adamsappel** (-s) *m* Adam's apple; **–kostuum** *o in* ~ in a state of nature

adap'tatie [- 'ta.(t)si.] (-s) *v* adaptation; **adap'teren** (adapteerde, h. geadapteerd) adapt

'**adder** (-s) *v* viper, adder; *een* ~ *aan zijn borst koesteren* nourish (cherish) a viper in one's

bosom; *er schuilt een* ~*tje onder het gras* there is a snag somewhere, there is a nigger in the woodpile

'**adel** *m* nobility; *van* ~ *zijn* be of noble birth, belong to the nobility

'**adelaar** (-s en -laren) *m* eagle; **–sblik** (-ken) *m met* ~ eagle-eyed

'**adelboek** (-en) *o* peerage; **–borst** (-en) *m* naval cadet, midshipman, **F** middy; **–brief** (-brieven) *m* patent of nobility; **–dom** *m* nobility; '**adelen** (adelde, h. geadeld) *vt* ennoble[2], raise to the peerage; '**adellijk** 1 noble; 2 high [of game], gamy; '**adelstand** *m* nobility, nobiliary rank; *in (tot) de* ~ *verheffen* ennoble, raise to the peerage

'**adem** *m* breath; *de* ~ *inhouden* hold one's breath; ~ *scheppen* take breath; *de laatste* ~ *uitblazen* breathe one's last; *b u i t e n* ~ out of breath, breathless; *buiten* ~ *raken* get out of breath; *i n één* ~ in (one and) the same breath; *n a a r* ~ *snakken* gasp; *o p* ~ *komen* recover one's breath; *op* ~ *laten komen* breathe; *v a n lange* ~ 1 long-winded [speaker, tale]; 2 [a work] requiring time and labour; **–benemend, adembe'nemend** breath-taking; '**ademen** (ademde, h. geademd) *vt & vi* breathe; *piepend* ~ wheeze; '**ademhalen** (haalde 'adem, h. 'ademgehaald) *vi* draw breath, breathe; *ruimer* ~ breathe more freely, breathe again; '**ademhaling** (-en) *v* respiration, breathing; *kunstmatige* ~ artificial respiration; '**ademhalingsoefening** (-en) *v* respiratory exercise, breathing exercise; **–organen** *mv* respiratory organs; '**ademloos** breathless[2]; **–nood** *m* dyspn(o)ea; **–pauze** (-s) *v* breathing space, breather; **–proef** (-proeven) *v* breath test; **–tocht** *m* breath

adeno'ïde vege'taties [... ve.gǝ'ta.(t)si.s] *mv* adenoids

a'dept (-en) *m* follower

ade'quaat [a.de.'kʋa.t] adequate

'**ader** (-s en -en) *v* 1 (i n h e t l i c h a a m o f h o u t) vein; 2 (v. e r t s &) vein, lode, seam; '**aderen** (aderde, h. geaderd) *vt* vein, grain; '**aderlaten** (liet 'ader, h. 'adergelaten) *vt* bleed[2]; **–ting** (-en) *v* blood-letting; bleeding[2]; '**aderlijk** venous; '**aderontsteking** (-en) *v* phlebitis; **–verkalking** *v* arteriosclerosis

ad 'fundum bottoms up!

ad'hesie [ɑt'he.zi.] *v* adhesion; *zijn* ~ *betuigen* give one's adhesion [to a plan]

ad 'interim ad interim

'**adjectief** (-tieven) *o* adjective

adju'dant (-en) *m* ⚔ adjutant; aide-de-camp, A.D.C. [to a general]

ad'junct (-en) *m* assistant

administra'teur (-s en -en) *m* 1 (i n 't a l g .)

administrator; manager; 2 ⚓ purser; 3 (v.
p l a n t a g e) estate manager; 4 (b.o e k -
h o u d e r) book-keeper, accountant;
admini'stratie [-'stra.(t)si.] (-s) *v* administration, management; **administra'tief** administrative; **admini'stratiekosten** [-'stra.(t)si.-]
mv administrative expenses; **admini'streren**
(administreerde, h. geadministreerd) *vt* administer, manage
admi'raal (-s en -ralen) *m* ⚓ admiral; ook =
admiraalvlinder; **–schap** *o* ⚓ admiralship;
admi'raalsschip (-schepen) *o* ⚓ flagship;
admi'raalvlinder (-s) *m* red admiral; **admi-
rali'teit** (-en) *v* admiralty
adoles'cent [adolɛ'sɪnt] (-en) *m* adolescent; **–ie**
[-(t)si.] *v* adolescence
adop'tant (-en) *m* adopter; **adop'teren** (adop-
teerde, h. geadopteerd) *vt* adopt; **a'doptie**
[a.'dɔpsi.] *v* adoption
ado'ratie [-(t)si.] (-s) *v* adoration; **ado'reren**
(adoreerde, h. geadoreerd) worship, adore,
venerate
ad 'rem to the point
a'dres (-sen) *o* 1 (o p b r i e f) address, direction; 2 (m e m o r i e) memorial, petition; *een ~
richten tot* address a petition to; *dan ben je aan het
verkeerde ~* you have come to the wrong shop;
per ~ care of, c/o; **–boek** (-en) *o* directory;
–kaart (-en) *v* (v o o r p o s t p a k k e t)
dispatch note; **–plaatje** (-s) *o* address stencil;
adres'sant (-en) *m* petitioner, applicant;
adres'seermachine [-ma.ʃi.nə] (-s) *v* addressing machine, addressograph; **adres'seren**
(adresseerde, h. geadresseerd) *vt* direct, address
[a letter]; **a'dresstrook** (-stroken) *v* label,
wrapper; **–wijziging** (-en) *v* change of address
Adri'atische 'Zee *v de ~* the Adriatic
adspi'rant = *aspirant*
ad'structie [-'strüksi.] *v ter ~ van* in elucidation
(explanation) of, in support of
ad'vent *m* Advent
adver'teerder (-s) *m* advertiser; **adver'tentie**
[-'tɛnsi.] (-s) *v* advertisement, **F** ad; *kleine ~s*
classified advertisements; **–blad** (-bladen) *o*
advertiser; **–bureau** [-by.ro.] (-s) *o* advertising
agency; **–kosten** *mv* advertising charges;
–pagina ('s) *v* advertisement page; **adver'teren** (adverteerde, h. geadverteerd) *vt*
& *va* advertise
ad'vies (-viezen) *o* 1 advice; 2 recommendation
[of a commission]; *op ~ van* at (by, on) the
advice of; *commissie van ~* advisory committee;
het verstrekken van ~ (a l s b e r o e p) consul-

tancy; **–bureau** [-by.ro.] (-s) *o* consultancy
firm; **–commissie** (-s) *v* advisory committee;
–orgaan (-ganen) *o*, **–raad** (-raden) *m* consultative body, consultative council; **–prijs**
(-prijzen) *m* recommended price; **advi'seren**
[s = z] (adviseerde, h. geadviseerd) *vt* 1 advice;
2 recommend [of a jury &]; **–d** advisory,
consultative; **advi'seur** [s = z] (-s) *m* adviser,
consultant; *wiskundig ~* actuary
advo'caat (-caten) *m* 1 ⚖ barrister(-at-law),
counsel; ± soliçitor, lawyer; *Sc* advocate; 2
(d r a n k) advocaat; *als ~ toegelaten worden* be
admitted to the bar; *~ van kwade zaken* shyster,
pettifogger; **advo'caat-gene'raal** (advocaten-
generaal) *m* Solicitor-General; **advo'caten-
streken** *mv*, **advocate'rij** *v* pettifoggery;
advoca'tuur *v de ~* the bar, the legal
profession
aërody'namica [a.e.ro.di.-] *v* aerodynamics;
aëro'sol [a.e.r.o.-] (-s en -solen) *o* aerosol
af off; down; *~ en aan lopen* come and go; go to
and fro; *~ en toe* off and on, every now and
then, now and again, once in a while, occasionally; *A ~* exit Λ; *allen ~* exeunt all; *het
(engagement) is ~* the engagement is off; *het
(werk) is ~* the work is finished; *hij is ~* he is
out [at a game]; *hij is minister ~* he is out (of
office); *~!* 1 down! [to a dog]; 2 *sp* [are you
ready?] go!; *hoeden ~!* hats off!; *links ~* to the
left; *goed (slecht) ~ zijn* be well (badly) off; *alle
prijzen ~ fabriek* $ all prices ex works (mill);
● *bij zwart ~* off black; *op de minuut* & *~ to*
the minute &; *v a n... ~* from [a child, his
childhood, that day &], from [two shillings]
upwards; from [this day] onwards; *nu ben je van
die... ~* now you are rid of that (those)...; *ze
zijn van elkaar ~* they have separated; *je bent nog
niet van hem ~!* you have not done with him
yet; you haven't heard (seen) the last of him
yet
afa'sie [s = z] *v* 𝕋 aphasia
'afbakenen (bakende 'af, h. 'afgebakend) *vt* 1
(w e g &) trace (out), mark out; 2 ⚓ (v a a r-
w a t e r) beacon; *duidelijk afgebakend* ook:
clearly defined
'afbeelden (beeldde 'af, h. 'afgebeeld) *vt*
represent, portray, picture, paint, depict;
–ding (-en) *v* picture, portrait, representation,
portraiture
'afbekken (bekte 'af, h. 'afgebekt) *vt* snap at,
snap sbd.'s head off; **–bellen¹** *vt* & *va* (a f b e -
s t e l l e n) countermand (put off) by telephone;
(g e s p r e k b e ë i n d i g e n) put down the

---

¹ V.T. en V.D. van dit werkwoord volgens het model: **'afbellen**, V.T. belde **'af**, V.D. **'afgebeld**. Zie voor de
vormen onder het grondwoord, in dit voorbeeld: *bellen*. Bij sterke en onregelmatige werkwoorden wordt u verwezen
naar de lijst achterin.

receiver, ring off

'afbestellen (bestelde 'af, h. 'afbesteld) *vt* countermand, cancel [the order]; **–ling** (-en) *v* cancellation

'afbetalen[1] (-en) *vt* pay off, pay (up); pay [£ 5] on account; **'afbetaling** (-en) *v* (full) payment; ~ *in termijnen* payment by instalments; £ 5 *op* ~ £ 5 on account; *op* ~ *kopen* buy on the instalment plan (system), on the hire-purchase system, F on the never-never; **–stermijn** (-en) *m* repayment [of a mortgage &], instalment

'afbetten *vt* bathe [a wound]; **–beulen** (beulde 'af, h. 'afgebeuld) **I** *vt* overdrive, fag out [sbd.], override [a horse]; **II** *vr zich* ~ work oneself to the bone, work oneself to death; **–bidden**[1] *vt* 1 (t r a c h t e n a f t e w e n d e n) avert; 2 (b i d d e n o m) pray for, invoke; **–bijten**[1] *vt* bite off [a bit]; clip [one's words]; zie ook: *bijten, afgebeten, spits;* **–bikken**[1] *vt* chip (off); **–binden**[1] **I** *vt* 1 untie [one's skates]; 2 ligature [a vein], tie (up) [an artery]; **II** *va* untie one's skates; **–bladderen**[1] *vi* peel off, scale off; **–blaffen** [1] *iem.* ~ storm at sbd.; **–blazen**[1] *vt* blow off, let off[2] [steam]; **–blijven**[1] *vi* ~ *van iem.* keep one's hands off sbd.; ~ *van iets* let (leave) sth. alone; ~*!* hands off!; **–boeken**[1] *vt* \$ 1 (a f s c h r i j v e n) write off; 2 (o v e r-b o e k e n) transfer [from one account to another]; 3 (a f s l u i t e n) close [an account]; **–boenen**[1] *vt* (d r o o g) rub; (n a t) scrub; **–borstelen**[1] **I** *vt* brush off [the dust]; brush [clothes, shoes, a person]; **II** *vr zich* ~ brush oneself up; **–bouwen**[1] *vt* finish [a building construction]; (v e r m i n d e r e n) reduce, cut (run) down [numbers of staff]

'afbraak *v* 1 demolition; 2 old materials [of a house]; rubbish; 3 § breakdown; *voor* ~ *verkopen* sell for its materials; **–prijzen** *mv* rock-bottom (distress) prices; **–produkt** (-en) *o* breakdown product

'afbranden I (brandde 'af, h. 'afgebrand) *vt* burn off [the paint]; burn down [a house]; **II** (brandde 'af, is 'afgebrand) *vi* be burnt down

af'breekbaar biodegradable, biodestructible;

'afbreken[1] **I** *vt* 1 break (off) [a flower from its stalk]; demolish, pull down [a house], break down [a bridge; chemically]; take down [a booth, a scaffolding]; 2 break off [a sentence, engagement &], divide [a word], interrupt [one's narrative]; cut short [one's holidays]; 3 cut [a connection]; 4 sever [friendship, relations]; 5 *fig* demolish, cry down, pull to pieces [an author &], write down [a book, play &]; **II**

vi 1 break (off) [of a thread]; 2 stop [in the middle of a sentence]; **III** *va* destroy, disparage; *hij is altijd aan het* ~ he is always crying (running) down people; **IV** *o* rupture, severance [of diplomatic relations]; zie ook *afgebroken;* **–d** destructive [criticism]; **'afbreking** (-en) *v* breaking off, rupture; interruption; demolition; **–steken** (-s) *o* break

'afbrengen[1] *vt* (v l o t m a k e n) $ get off; *het er goed* ~ get through very well, do well; *het er levend* ~ get off (escape) with one's life; *het er slecht* ~ come off badly, do badly; *hij was er niet van af te brengen* he could not be dissuaded from it, we could not talk (reason) him out of it; *iem. van de goede (rechte) weg* ~ lead sbd. away from the right course, lead sbd. astray

'afbreuk *v* ~ *doen aan* be detrimental to, detract from [his reputation]; *de vijand* ~ *doen* do harm to the enemy

'afbrokkelen (brokkelde 'af, is 'afgebrokkeld) *vi* crumble (off, away); **–buigen**[1] *vi* turn off; (v. w e g) branch off; **–checken**[1] [-tʃkə(n)] *vt* check against [a list]; tick off

'afdak (-daken) *o* penthouse, shed

'afdalen[1] *vi* descend, come (go) down; ~ *in bijzonderheden* go (enter) into detail(s); ~ *tot* condescend to [inferiors]; descend to [the level of, doing something]; **–d** descending; **'afdaling** (-en) *v* 1 descent; 2 *sp* downhill [in skiing]

'afdammen (damde 'af, h. 'afgedamd) *vt* dam up; **–ming** (-en) *v* damming up; dam

'afdanken[1] *vt* disband [troops]; dismiss [an army, a servant &]; pay off [the ship's crew]; superannuate [an official]; discard [a lover, clothes]; part with [a motorcar]; scrap [ships]; **'afdankertje** (-s) *o* cast-off; **'afdanking** *v* disbanding [of troops]; dismissal [of a servant &]

'afdeinzen (deinsde 'af, is 'afgedeinsd) *vi* withdraw, retreat; **–dekken**[1] *vt* 1 (t o e-d e k k e n) cover; 2 cope [a wall]

'afdeling (-en) *v* 1 (h e t a f d e l e n) division; classification; 2 (o n d e r d e e l) division, section, branch [of a party &]; 3 ✗ detachment [of soldiers], body [of horse], [landing] party; 4 (c o m p a r t i m e n t) compartment; 5 (v a n b e s t u u r, w i n k e l &) department; ward [in a hospital]; [parliamentary] ± committee; **'afdelingschef** [-ʃtʃf] (-s) *m* head of a department, floorwalker [in shop]; **–hoofd** (-en) *o* divisional head

'afdingen I *vi* bargain, chaffer; beat down the

[1] V.T. en V.D. van dit werkwoord volgens het model: 'af**bellen**, V.T. belde 'af, V.D. 'af**gebeld**. Zie voor de vormen onder het grondwoord, in dit voorbeeld: *bellen*. Bij sterke en onregelmatige werkwoorden wordt u verwezen naar de lijst achterin.

price; **II** *vt* beat down; *ik wil niets ~ op zijn verdiensten* I have no wish to detract from his merits; *daar is niets op af te dingen* there is nothing to be said against it, it is unobjectionable

'**afdoen**[1] *vt* 1 (k l e d i n g s t u k k e n &) take off; 2 (a f v e g e n) clean, wipe, dust; 3 (a f-m a k e n) finish, dispatch, expedite [a business]; 4 (u i t m a k e n) settle [a question]; 5 (v e r h a n d e l e n) $ sell; 6 (a f b e t a l e n) pay off, settle [a debt]; *hij heeft afgedaan* he has had his day; *hij heeft b ij mij afgedaan* I have done with him, I am through with him; *dat doet er niets aan t o e of af* 1 it doesn't alter the fact; 2 that's neither here nor there; *iets v a n de prijs ~, er iets ~* knock off something, take something off; *dit doet niets af van de waarde* this does not detract from the value; **–d, af'doend** *dat is ~(e)* that settles the question; *een ~ argument (bewijs)* a conclusive argument (proof); *~e maatregelen* efficacious (effectual, effective) measures; '**afdoening** (-en) *v* 1 disposal, dispatch [of the business on hand]; 2 settlement [of business]; payment [of a debt]; 3 $ sale

'**afdraaien**[1] *vt* 1 turn off [a tap, the gas]; 2 (e r ~) twist off; 3 (r a m m e l e n d o p z e g g e n) reel off, rattle off [one's lines]; 4 grind out [on a barrel-organ]; 5 run off [a stencil on a duplicating machine]; 6 show [a film]; 7 play [a gramophone record]

'**afdracht** *v* remittance [of money]; '**afdragen**[1] *vt* 1 carry down [the stairs &]; 2 wear out [clothes]; 3 remit, hand over [money]

'**afdraven**[1] *vt een paard ~* trot out a horse; **–dreggen**[1] *vt* drag; **–drijven**[1] **I** *vi* 1 float (drift) down [the river]; 2 (v. s c h i p) drift (off), make leeway; 3 (o n w e e r &) blow over; *met de stroom ~* be borne down the stream; *fig* go with the stream; **II** *vt* produce an abortion; **–drogen**[1] *vt* dry, wipe (off); (a f r a n s e l e n) beat, thrash

'**afdronk** *m* after-taste [of wine]

'**afdroogdoek** (-en) *m* tea-towel

'**afdruipen**[1] *vi* 1 (v l o e i s t o f f e n) trickle (drip) down, drain; 2 (w e g s l u i p e n) slink away, slink off [with one's tail between one's legs]; '**afdruiprek** (-ken) *o* drainer, draining board

'**afdruk** (-ken) *m* 1 (i n d r u k) imprint, print; 2 (v. b o e k o f g r a v u r e) impression; copy; 3 (v. f o t o) print; '**afdrukken**[1] *vt* 1 print (off) [a book]; 2 impress [on wax]; 3 *sp* clock [8

minutes 7.10 seconds in a race]

'**afduwen**[1] **I** *vt* push off; **II** *va* push off, shove off

'**afdwalen** (dwaalde 'af, is 'afgedwaald) *vi* 1 *eig* stray off, stray from the company; 2 *fig* stray (wander) from one's subject, depart from the question; (o p v e r k e e r d e w e g e n) go astray; **–ling** (-en) *v* 1 straying, wandering from the point; digression; 2 (f o u t) aberration

'**afdwingen**[1] *vt* compel, command [admiration, respect]; extort [a concession from]

'**afeten**[1] **I** *vt* eat off; **II** *vi* finish one's dinner &

af'faire [ɑ'fɛːrə] (-s) *v* 1 (z a a k) affair, business; 2 $ business; (t r a n s a c t i e) transaction

af'fect (-en) *o ps* affect

affec'tatie [-'ta.(t)si.] (-s) *v* affectation

af'fectie [-ksi.] (-s) *v* affection

af'fiche [ɑ'fi.ʃə] (-s) *o & v* poster, placard; playbill [of a theatre]; **affi'cheren** (afficheerde, h. geafficheerd) *vt* post up, placard; *fig* show off, parade

affili'atie [-(t)si.] *v* affiliation

affini'teit (-en) *v* affinity

af'fix (-en) *o* affix

'**affluiten**[1] *vi* whistle for a foul

af'freus horrid, horrible

af'front (-en) *o* affront; **affron'teren** (affronteerde, h. geaffronteerd) *vt* affront

af'fuit (-en) *v(m) & o* ⚔ (gun-)carriage; [fixed] mounting

'**afgaan**[1] **I** *vi* 1 (a f v a r e n) start, sail; 2 (v. v u u r w a p e n e n) go off; 3 (v. g e t ij) recede, ebb; *er ~* come off [of paint]; 4 (d e f a e-c e r e n) excrete; 5 (i n d e o g e n v a n a n d e r e n) fail dismally; *het gaat hem glad (handig, gemakkelijk) af* it comes very easy to him; *dat gaat hem goed af* it [his new dignity &] sits well on him; ● *b ij de rij ~* take them in their order; *~ o p iem.* 1 walk up to sbd., make for sbd. [the enemy]; 2 *fig* rely on sbd.; *~ op praatjes* trust (go by) what people say; *recht op zijn doel ~* go straight to the point; *~ v a n* leave [school, sbd.]; *daar gaat niets van af* there is no denying it; **II** *vt* go (walk) down [the stairs, a hill &]; **–gang** (-en) *m* failure, flop

'**afgebeten** clipped [speech]; **–gebroken** broken off, broken, interrupted; **–gedaan** zie *afdoen*; **–geladen** *de treinen waren ~ (vol)* the trains were packed, crowded [with passengers]

'**afgelasten**[1] *vt* countermand, cancel [a dinner, a football match], call off [a strike]

'**afgeleefd** decrepit, worn with age; **–gelegen**

---

[1] V.T. en V.D. van dit werkwoord volgens het model: 'af'bellen, V.T. belde 'af, V.D. 'afgebeld. Zie voor de vormen onder het grondwoord, in dit voorbeeld: *bellen*. Bij sterke en onregelmatige werkwoorden wordt u verwezen naar de lijst achterin.

distant, remote, outlying, out-of-the-way, sequestered; **–geleid** derived; ~ *woord* derivative; zie ook: *afleiden*; **–gelopen** past [year]; *nu is het* ~*!* stop it!; **–gemat** tired out, worn out, exhausted; **–gemeten** measured[2], formal, stiff; *op* ~ *toon* [speak] in measured tones, stiffly; **–gepast** adjusted; ready-made [curtains &]; ~ *geld* the exact sum (money); *met* ~ *geld betalen!* no change given!, (i n b u s, t r a m) exact fare!; **–gepeigerd** ready to drop, more dead than alive; exhausted, fagged out; **–gerond** rounded (off); *een* ~ *geheel* a self-contained unit; *een* ~*e som* a round sum; **–gescheiden** separate; *een* ~ *dominee* a dissenting minister; ~ *van* apart from; **–gesloofd** fagged (out), worn out; **–gesloten** closed &; ~ *rijweg!* no thoroughfare!; **–gestampt** ~ *vol* packed; **–gestompt** dull, impassive; **–gestorven I** *aj* deceased, dead; **II** *sb de* ~*e* the deceased, the defunct; *de* ~*en* the deceased, the dead; **–getobd** haggard [look]; careworn [with care], exhausted [with suffering]; **–getrapt** ~*e schoenen* boots down at heel; *met* ~*e schoenen aan* down at heel; **–getrokken** pale, white

'afgevaardigde (-n) *m* deputy, delegate, representative; *het Huis van Afgevaardigden* the House of Representatives [in Australia, U.S.A. &]

'afgeven¹ I *vt* 1 deliver up [what is not one's own]; hand [a parcel], hand in (over); leave [a card] on [sbd.], leave [a letter] with [sbd.]; issue [a declaration, a passport]; 2 (v a n z i c h g e v e n) give off, give out [heat &], emit [a smell &]; *een boodschap* ~ deliver a message; *een wissel* ~ *op...* draw (a bill) on...; **II** *vr zich* ~ *met een meisje* take up with a girl; *zich* ~ *met iets* meddle with sth.; *geef u daar niet mee af, met hem niet af* have nothing to do with it, with him; **III** *vi* come off [of paint]; stain [of material]; ~ *op iem. (iets)* cry (run) down sbd. (sth.)

'afgezaagd *fig* trite, stale, hackneyed, hardworked, worn-out

'afgezant (-en) *m* ambassador; envoy; messenger; (g e h e i m) emissary

'afgezien ~ *van* apart from

'afgezonderd secluded, retired, sequestered; ~ *van* separate from; ~ *wonen* live in an out-of-the-way place

Af'ghaan(s) [af'ga.n(s)] Afghan; **Af'ghanistan** *o* Afghanistan

'afgieten¹ *vt* 1 (v. k o o k s e l) pour off, strain off; 2 (v. g i p s b e e l d e n) cast; **'afgietsel** (-s) *o* (plaster) cast

'afgifte *v* delivery; *bij* ~ on delivery

'afglijden¹ *vi* slide down (off), slip down (off); stall; *fig* slide, drift [into chaos &]

'afgod (-goden) *m* idol[2], false god; **afgode'rij** (-en) *v* idolatry, idol worship; **af'godisch** idolatrous; ~ *liefhebben (vereren)* idolize; **'afgodsbeeld** (-en) *o* idol

'afgooien¹ *vt* throw down (off)

'afgraven *vt* dig off; level; **–ving** (-en) *v* quarry

'afgrazen¹ *vt* graze, browse

'afgrendelen¹ *vt* seal off [an area]

af'grijs(e)lijk horrible, horrid, ghastly; **'afgrijzen** *o* horror; *een* ~ *hebben van* abhor

'afgrond (-en) *m* abyss[2], gulf[2], precipice[2]

'afgunst *v* envy, jealousy; **af'gunstig** envious (of), jealous (of)

'afhaken¹ *vt* unhook; uncouple [a railway carriage]; **–hakken¹** *vt* cut off, chop off, lop off; **–halen¹** *vt* 1 (n a a r b e n e d e n) fetch down; 2 (o p h a l e n) collect [parcels]; 3 (p e r s o n e n) call for [a man at his house]; meet (at the station); take up [in one's car]; 4 (v. d i e r e n) zie *afstropen* 1; *de bedden* ~ strip the beds; *bonen* ~ string beans; *laten* ~ send for; *wordt afgehaald* to be left till called for; *niet afgehaalde bagage* left luggage; **–handelen¹** *vt* settle, conclude, dispatch

af'handig *iem. iets* ~ *maken* trick sbd. out of sth.

'afhangen¹ *vi* hang down; depend[2]; ~ *van* depend (up)on, be dependent on; *dat zal er van* ~ that depends; **–d** hanging, drooping

af'hankelijk dependent (on *van*); **–heid** *v* dependence (on *van*)

'afhechten¹ *vt* (b r e i w e r k) cast off; (n a a i w e r k) fasten off; **–hellen¹** *vi* slope down; **–helpen¹** *vt* 1 help off, help down [from a horse &]; 2 rid [sbd. of his money]; **–houden¹ I** *vt* 1 keep [one's eyes] off, keep... from [evil courses &]; 2 deduct, stop [so much from sbd.'s pay]; *van zich* ~ keep [one's enemies] at bay (at a distance); **II** *vi* bear off; *van land* ~ stand from the shore; *links (rechts)* ~ turn to the left (right); zie ook *boot*; **–jakkeren¹** *vt* override [a horse], overdrive, jade [one's servants], wear out [with work]; **–kalven** (kalfde 'af, is 'afgekalfd) *vi* cave in; **–kammen¹** *vt* cut up, run down, pull to pieces [a book]; **–kanten¹** *vt* cant, bevel, square; (b r e i w e r k) cast off; **–kapen¹** *vt* filch (pilfer) from

'afkappen¹ *vt* cut off, chop off, lop off; **–pingsteken** (-s) *o* apostrophe

'afkeer *m* aversion, dislike; *een* ~ *inboezemen*

¹ V.T. en V.D. van dit werkwoord volgens het model: 'af**bellen**, V.T. belde 'af, V.D. 'af**gebeld**. Zie voor de vormen onder het grondwoord, in dit voorbeeld: *bellen*. Bij sterke en onregelmatige werkwoorden wordt u verwezen naar de lijst achterin.

inspire an aversion; *een ~ hebben van* have a dislike of (to), feel (have) an aversion to (for, from); dislike; be allergic to; *een ~ krijgen van* take a dislike to, take an aversion to; **'afkeren**[1] **I** *vt* turn away [one's eyes]; avert [a blow]; **II** *vr zich ~* turn away; **af'kerig** averse; *~ van* averse from (to); *iem. ~ maken van* make sbd. take an aversion to; *~ worden van* take an aversion (a dislike) to; **–heid** *v* aversion **'afketsen**[1] **I** *vi* glance off, ricochet; *fig* fall through; **II** *vt* reject [an offer], defeat [a motion] **'afkeuren**[1] *vt* 1 (z e d e l i j k) condemn, disapprove (of); rebuke; 2 (n i e t a a n n e m e n) reject [a man] as unfit; 3 (b u i t e n d i e n s t s t e l l e n) condemn [a house as unfit to live in], scrap [ships &]; declare [meat] unfit for use; *hij is afgekeurd* he was rejected (not passed) by the doctor; **–d I** *aj* disapproving, [look] of disapproval; **II** *ad* disapprovingly; **afkeurens'waard(ig)** condemnable, objectionable, censurable, blameworthy; **'afkeuring** (-en) *v* 1 disapprobation, disapproval, condemnation, censure; 2 ✕ rejection [by the Army doctor]; 3 ✍ bad mark **'afkicken** [-kɪkə(n)] (kickte 'af, is 'afgekickt) *vi* S kick it, kick the habit; **–kijken**[1] **I** *vt iets van iem. ~* 1 learn sth. from sbd. by watching him; 2 ✍ copy, **F** crib sth. from sbd.; *de straat ~* look down the street; **II** *va* ✍ copy, **F** crib; **–klaren**[1] *vt* (v l o e i s t o f) clarify, clear; **–klauteren**[1], **–klimmen**[1] *vt* clamber (climb) down; **–klemmen**[1] *vt* clamp; ✕ strangulate; ✕ disconnect; **–kloppen**[1] **I** *vt* (k l e r e n &) flick [the dust] off; **II** *va* (u i t b i j g e l o o f) touch wood; **–kluiven**[1] *vt* gnaw off, pick [a bone]; **–knabbelen**[1] *vt* nibble off, nibble at; **–knagen**[1] *vt* gnaw off; **–knappen**[1] *vi* 1 *eig* snap (off); 2 *fig* have a breakdown; **–knijpen**[1] *vt* pinch (nip) off; **–knippen**[1] *vt* clip (off), cut (off); snip (off) [a piece]; **–knotten**[1] *vt* 1 truncate [a cone]; 2 top [a tree] **'afkoelen**[1] **I** *vt* cool (down)[2]; **II** *vi* 1 cool (down)[2]; 2 (v a n h e t w e e r) grow cooler; **'afkoeling** (-en) *v* 1 cooling (down)[2]; 2 fall in temperature; **–speriode** (-s en -n) *v* cooling-off period **'afkoken** (kookte 'af, h. en is 'afgekookt) *vt* boil **'afkomen**[1] *vi* 1 (e r a f k o m e n) come down; get off (his horse &); 2 (k l a a r k o-m e n) get finished; 3 (o f f i c i e e l b e k e n d-w o r d e n) be published; 4 (m e t g e l d) **F** cough up; *er goed (goedkoop of genadig,*

slecht) ~· get off well (cheaply, badly); *er ~ m e t een boete* get off (be let off) with a fine; *er met ere ~* come out of it with honour; *er met de schrik ~* get off with a fright; *~ o p* make for; *ik zag hem op mij ~* I saw him coming towards me, coming up to me; *~ v a n* be derived from [Latin &]; *ik kon niet van hem ~* I could not get rid of him; *ik kon niet van mijn waren ~* I was left with my goods; **II** *vt* come down [the stairs &]; **'afkomst** *v* descent, extraction, origin, birth; **af'komstig** *~ uit (van)* coming from; a native of [Dublin]; *hij is uit A. ~* he hails from Λ.; *~ van* coming from [my father], emanating from [his pen]; *dat is van hem ~* that proceeds from him; that comes from his pen **'afkondigen** (kondigde 'af, h. 'afgekondigd) *vt* proclaim, promulgate [a decree], publish [the banns], declare, call [a strike]; **–ging** (-en) *v* proclamation, publication **'afkooksel** (-s) *o* decoction **'afkoop** (-kopen) *m* buying off, redemption, ransom; **–som** (-men) *v* ransom, redemption money; **'afkopen**[1] *vt* 1 buy (purchase) from; 2 (l o s k o p e n) buy off [a strike], ransom, redeem **'afkoppelen**[1] *vt* uncouple [railway carriages]; ✕ disconnect, throw out of gear **'afkorten**[1] *vt* shorten, abbreviate; **–ting** (-en) *v* abbreviation; *...is een ~ van... ...is* short for... **'afkrabben**[1] *vt* scrape (scratch) off, scrape; **–kraken**[1] *vt* slash, **F** slate, do down [a book]; **–krijgen**[1] *vt* 1 (k l a a r k r i j g e n) get finished; 2 (a f n e m e n) take (down) [from the cupboard &]; *ik kon hem niet van zijn plaats (stoel) ~* I could not get him away from where he stood, from his chair; *ik kon er geen cent ~* I could not get off one cent; *ik kon er de vlek niet ~* I could not get the stain out; **–kunnen**[1] **I** *vi* (a f g e m a a k t k u n n e n w o r d e n) get finished; *meer dan hij afkan* more than he can manage, more than he can handle (cope with); *je zult er niet meer ~* you won't be able to back out of it, they won't let you off; *het zal er niet ~* I'm sure we (they) can't afford it; *hij kan niet van huis af* he can't leave home; *hij kon niet van die man af* he couldn't get rid of that fellow; **II** *vt het alleen niet ~* 1 be unable to manage the thing (things) alone; 2 be unable to cope with so much work alone; *het wel ~* be able to manage, to cope; **–kussen**[1] *vt* kiss away [tears]; *laten wij het maar ~* let us kiss and be friends **'aflaat** (-laten) *m rk* indulgence; *volle ~* plenary indulgence

'afladen[1] *vt* unload, discharge; zie ook *afgeladen*

af'landig off-shore [breeze]

'aflaten[1] **I** *vt* let down; **II** *vi* (o p h o u d e n) cease, desist (from), leave off ...ing

'afleggen[1] *vt* 1 lay down [a burden, arms &], take (put) off [one's cloak &]; 2 (v o o r g o e d w e g l e g g e n) lay aside[2] [one's arrogance, mourning &]; 3 (l ij k) lay out [a corpse]; 4 (d o e n) make [a declaration, a statement &]; 5 cover [a distance, so many miles]; 6 (v. p l a n t) layer; *het* ~ have (get) the worst of it, be worsted, go to the wall; fail [of a student]; (s t e r v e n) die; *het* ~ *tegen* be unable to hold one's own against, be no match for; zie ook: *bezoek, eed* &; **–er** (-s) *m* 1 layer-out [of a corpse]; 2 ⚶ layer; 3 cast-off coat, trousers &

'afleiden[1] *vt* 1 (n a a r b e n e d e n) lead down; 2 (i n a n d e r e r i c h t i n g) divert [the course of a river, sbd.'s attention]; distract, take off [one's mind, students from their studies]; 3 (t r e k k e n u i t) derive [words from Latin &]; 4 (b e s l u i t e n) deduce, infer, conclude [from sbd.'s words &]; *hij is gauw afgeleid* he is easily distracted; **'afleiding** (-en) *v* 1 diversion [of water &]; derivation [of words]; distraction, diversion [of the mind, ook: = amusement]; 2 *gram* derivative; **'afleidingsmanoeuvre, –maneuver** [-ma.nœ.vɔr] (-s) *v* & *o* diversion; *fig* red herring, smoke-screen

'afleren[1] *vt* 1 (i e t s) unlearn [the habit, the practice of]; 2 (i e m. i e t s) break sbd. of a habit; *ik heb het lachen afgeleerd* 1 I have broken myself of the habit of laughing; 2 I have unlearned the practice of laughing; *ik zal het je* ~ *om*... I'll teach you to...

'afleveren[1] *vt* deliver; **–ring** (-en) *v* 1 delivery [of goods]; 2 number, part, instalment [of a publication]; *in ~en laten verschijnen* serialize

'aflezen[1] *vt* read (out); read [ook: the thermometer]; **–likken**[1] *vt* lick [it] off; lick [one's fingers]; **–loeren**[1] *vt alles* ~ spy out everything

'afloop (-lopen) *m* 1 (v. g e b e u r t e n i s) end, termination; 2 (u i t s l a g) issue, result; 3 (v. t e r m ij n) expiration; *ongeluk met dodelijke* ~ fatal accident; *na* ~ *van het examen* when the examination is (was) over, after the examination; *na* ~ *van deze termijn* on expiry of this term; **'aflopen**[1] **I** *vi* 1 (n a a r b e n e d e n) run down; 2 (a f h e l l e n) slope; 3 (t e n e i n d e l o p e n) run out, expire [of a contract]; 4 (e i n d i g e n) turn out [badly &]; end; 5 (v.

u u r w e r k) run down; go off [of alarm]; 6 (v. k a a r s) run, gutter; 7 ⚓ (v. s c h e p e n) leave the ways, be launched; *het zal gauw met hem* ~ all will soon be over with him; *het zal niet goed met je* ~ you will come to grief; *hoe zal het* ~? what will be the end of it?; *op iem.* ~ go (run) up to sbd.; *laten* ~ launch [a vessel]; pay out [a cable]; let [the alarm] run down; terminate [a contract]; **II** *vt* 1 (n a a r b e n e d e n) run (walk, go) down [a hill &]; 2 (s t u k l o p e n) wear [one's shoes &] out (by walking), wear down [one's heels]; 3 (d o o r l o p e n) beat, scour [the woods]; *fig* finish [a course]; pass through [a school]; 4 (p l u n d e r e n) plunder [a vessel]; *alle huizen* ~ run from house to house; *de stad* ~ go through (search) the whole town; zie ook *afgelopen*; *zich de benen* ~ walk off one's legs; **–d** sloping; outgoing [tide]

af'losbaar redeemable, repayable; **'aflossen**[1] *vt* 1 (i e m.) ⚶ relieve [the guard]; take sbd.'s place; 2 (a f b e t a l e n) pay off [a debt], redeem [a bond, a mortgage]; *elkaar* ~ take turns; **–sing** (-en) *v* 1 (v. w a c h t &) relief; 2 (a f b e t a l i n g) instalment; (v. l e n i n g &) redemption

'afluisterapparaat (-raten) *o* detectophone, **S** bug; **'afluisteren**[1] *vt* overhear, eavesdrop; listen in to (bug, tap) [telephone conversations]

'afmaaien[1] *vt* mow, cut, reap [corn]; **–maken**[1] **I** *vt* finish [a letter], complete [a building]; 2 (b e ë i n d i g e n, u i t m a k e n) settle [the matter]; 3 (d o d e n) kill, dispatch [a victim]; 4 agree (up)on [a price]; *het* ~ *met zijn meisje* break off the engagement) off; **II** *vr zich van iets* (*met een grapje*) ~ pass off the matter with a joke; *zich met een paar woorden van een kwestie* ~ dismiss a question with a few words

'afmarche [-marʃ] = *afmars*; **'afmarcheren**[1] *vi* march off; **'afmars** *m* & *v* marching off, march

'afmatten (matte 'af, h. 'afgemat) *vt* fatigue, wear out, tire out; **af'mattend** fatiguing, tiring, trying

'afmelden[1] *zich* ~ check out; **–meren**[1] *vi* moor [a ship]

'afmeten[1] *vt* measure (off); *anderen naar zichzelf* ~ judge others by oneself; zie ook *afgemeten*; **–ting** (-en) *v* measurement; dimension

'afmijnen[1] *vt* bid at a public auction

'afmonsteren I (monsterde 'af, h. 'afgemonsterd) *vt* pay off, discharge [the crew]; **II** (monsterde 'af, is 'afgemonsterd) *vi* be paid off;

---

[1] V.T. en V.D. van dit werkwoord volgens het model: **'af**bellen, V.T. belde **'af**, V.D. **'af**gebeld. Zie voor de vormen onder het grondwoord, in dit voorbeeld: *bellen*. Bij sterke en onregelmatige werkwoorden wordt u verwezen naar de lijst achterin.

–ring (-en) *v* paying off, discharge
'afname *v* bij ~ van *100 stuks* when taking a hundred; zie *afneming;* **af'neembaar** detachable, removable; (v. b e h a n g &) washable; **'afnemen**[1] **I** *vt* 1 take (away) [a book, his rights & from a man, a child from school]; take off [a bandage], take down [a picture &]; 2 (a f z e t t e n) take off [one's hat to sbd.]; 3 (s c h o o n v e g e n) clean [the windows &]; 4 (k o p e n) $ buy; *de kaarten* ~ cut; zie ook: *biecht, eed* &; **II** *vi* decrease, decline [of forces]; diminish [of stocks]; abate [of a storm]; wane [of the moon & *fig*]; draw in [of the days]; **III** *va* 1 cut [at cards]; 2 clear away, remove the cloth [after dinner]; **–er** (-s) *m* client, buyer, purchaser; **'afneming** *v* 1 decrease, diminution, abatement [of a storm], wane[2]; 2 deposition [from the Cross]
'afnokken *vi* (nokte 'af, is 'afgenokt) knock off
afo'risme (-n) *o* aphorism
'afpakken[1] *vt* snatch (away) [sth. from sbd.]; **–palen**[1] *vt* 1 fence off, enclose; 2 stake out; **–passen**[1] *vt* pace [a field &]; *geld* ~ give the exact sum (money); zie ook: *afgepast;* **–peigeren** (peigerde 'af, h. afgepeigerd) **I** *vt = afbeulen;* **II** *vr zich* ~ wear oneself out; zie ook *afgepeigerd;* **'afpellen**[1] *vt* peel, pare off; **–perken** (perkte 'af, h. afgeperkt) *vt* 1 (a f b a k e n e n) peg out, delimit; 2 (i n p e r k e n) fence in
'afpersen[1] *vt* extort [money & from]; blackmail; force, draw [tears & from]; wring, wrest [a promise from]; **–er** (-s) *m* blackmailer, extortioner; **'afpersing** *v* extortion, exaction; blackmail
'afpijnigen[1] *vt* rack [one's brains]; **–pikken**[1] *vt* peck off; *iem. iets* ~ [*fig*] **F** pinch sth. from sbd.; **–pingelen**[1] **I** *vi* haggle, chaffer; **II** *vt* beat down
'afplatten (platte 'af, h. 'afgeplat) *vt* flatten; **–ting** *v* flattening
'afplukken[1] *vt* pluck (off), pick; **–poeieren** (poeierde 'af, h. 'afgepoeierd) *vt iem.* ~ send sbd. about his business; rebuff sbd., put sbd. off; **–prijzen** (prijsde 'af, h. 'afgeprijsd) *vt* mark down; **–raden**[1] *vt iem....* ~ advise sbd. against..., dissuade sbd. from...; **–raffelen** (raffelde 'af, h. 'afgeraffeld) = *afroffelen;* **–raken**[1] *vi* be broken off [of an engagement]; ~ *van* 1 (w e g k o m e n) get away from; get off, get clear of [a dangerous spot &]; 2 (k w ij t r a k e n) get rid of [sbd., wares]; *van de drank* ~ drop the drink habit; *van elkaar* ~ get

separated; drift apart[2]; *van zijn onderwerp* ~ wander from one's subject; *van de weg* ~ lose one's way, lose oneself, go astray; **–rammelen**[1] *vt* 1 rattle off, reel off [one's lines]; 2 = *afranselen;* **–ranselen**[1] *vt* thrash, beat (up), flog, whack
'afrasteren (rasterde 'af, h. 'afgerasterd) *vt* rail off (in), fence off (in); **–ring** (-en) *v* railing, fence
'afratelen[1] *vt* reel off [one's lesson], rattle off; **–reageren**[1] *vt* work off [one's bad temper]; *ps* abreast; **–reizen**[1] **I** *vi* depart, set out (on one's journey), leave (for *naar*); **II** *vt* travel all over [Europe &]; tour [the country]
'afrekenen[1] **I** *vt* (a f t e l l e n) take off, deduct; **II** *vi* settle, square up; *ik heb met hem afgerekend* we have settled accounts[2]; I have squared accounts with him; I have settled with him; **–ning** (-en) *v* settlement; statement (of account), account
'afremmen[1] **I** *vt* slow down[2]; *fig* put a brake on [spending]; **II** *va* slow down[2]; *fig* put on the brake(s); **–richten**[1] *vt* train [for a match &]; coach [for an examination]; break [a horse]; **–rijden**[1] **I** *vi* ride (drive) off, ride (drive) away; *sp* start; **II** *vt* 1 (n a a r b e n e d e n r ij d e n) ride (drive) down [a hill]; 2 (o e f e n e n) exercise [a horse]; 3 (a f j a k k e r e n) override [one's horses]; *beide benen werden hem afgereden* both his legs were cut off [by a train]
'Afrika *o* Africa; **Afri'kaan** (-kanen) *m* African; **Afri'kaander** (-s) *m = Afrikaner;* **Afri'kaans** African; **afri'kaantje** (-s) *o* African marigold; **Afri'kaner** (-s) *m ZA* Afrikaner
'afristen[1] *vt* strip (off), string
'afrit (-ten) *m* 1 start [on horseback]; 2 slope [of a hill]; exit [of motorway]
'Afro-Azi'atisch Afro-Asian, Afro-Asiatic
'afroeien[1] **I** *vi* row off (away); **II** *vt* 1 row down [the river]; 2 *sp* coach [the crew]
'afroep *m levering op* ~ delivery at buyer's request; **'afroepen**[1] *vt* call [the hours, a blessing upon]; call over [the names]
'afroffelen[1] *vt* bungle, scamp [one's work]; **–rollen**[1] *vt* unroll, unreel; **–romen**[1] *vt* cream, skim [milk]; **–ronden**[1] *vt* round, round off; zie ook *afgerond*
'afrossen (roste 'af, h. 'afgerost) *vt* thrash, beat (up), whack; **–sing** (-en) *v* thrashing, beating (up), whacking
'afruimen[1] **I** *vt* clear [the table]; **II** *va* clear away; **–rukken**[1] *vt* tear away (off, down); snatch (away), pluck off

---

[1] V.T. en V.D. van dit werkwoord volgens het model: **'afbellen**, V.T. belde **'af**, V.D. **'afgebeld**. Zie voor de vormen onder het grondwoord, in dit voorbeeld: *bellen*. Bij sterke en onregelmatige werkwoorden wordt u verwezen naar de lijst achterin.

'**afschaafsel** (-s) *o* shavings
'**afschaduwen**[1] *vt* adumbrate, shadow forth;
 –wing (-en) *v* adumbration, shadow
'**afschaffen** (schafte 'af, h. 'afgeschaft) *vt* 1 (v.
 w e t &) abolish; 2 (v. m i s b r u i k) do away
 with; 3 (v. d e h a n d d o e n) part with, give
 up [one's car]; **–fing** *v* abolition [of a law, of
 slavery]; giving up [of one's car &]
'**afschampen**[1] *vi* glance off
'**afscheid** *o* parting, leave, leave-taking, farewell, adieu(s); ~ *nemen* take (one's) leave, say
 goodbye; ~ *nemen van* take leave of, say
 goodbye to, bid farewell to; '**afscheiden**[1] I *vt*
 1 separate; sever; mark off &; zie *scheiden*; 2
 (u i t s c h e i d e n) secrete; **II** *vr zich* ~ 1 (v.
 p e r s o n e n) separate, secede; break away [of
 colonies &]; 2 (v. s t o f f e n) be secreted; zie
 ook *afgescheiden*; **–ding** (-en) *v* 1 (v. l o k a l i -
 t e i t) separation; partition; 2 (v. v o c h t)
 secretion; 3 (v. p a r tij) secession, separation;
 breakaway; '**afscheidsgroet** (-en) *m* farewell,
 valediction; **–receptie** [-sεπsι.] (-s) *v* farewell
 reception; **–rede** (-s) *v* valedictory address
'**afschenken**[1] *vt* pour off, decant; **–schepen**
 (scheepte 'af, h. 'afgescheept) *vt* 1 ⚓ ship
 [goods]; 2 *fig* send [sbd.] about his business;
 put [sbd.] off; **–scheppen**[1] *vt* skim [milk];
 skim off [the cream, the fat]; **–scheren**[1] *vt* 1
 shave (off) [the beard]; 2 shear (off) [wool];
 –schermen (schermde 'af, h. 'afgeschermd) *vt*
 screen; **–scheuren**[1] I *vt* tear off; tear down [a
 poster]; **II** *vr zich* ~ *van* tear oneself away from,
 break away from; **–schieten**[1] I *vt* 1 (v u u r -
 w a p e n) discharge, fire (off), let off; (p i j l)
 shoot, let fly; 2 (w e g s c h i e t e n) shoot off;
 (r a k e t) launch; 3 (a f d e l e n) partition off [a
 room]; (m e t g o r d ij n) curtain off; (m e t
 p l a n k e n) board off; **II** *vi* ~ *op iem.* rush at
 sbd.; ~ *van* slip (off) from; **–schilderen**[1] *vt*
 paint, depict, portray; **–schilferen**[1] *vi* & *vt*
 scale, peel (flake) off; **–schminken**[1] [-ʃmi.ŋ
 kə(n)] *zich* ~ take off one's make-up (one's
 grease paint); **–schoppen**[1] *vt* & *vi* = *aftrappen*
'**afschraapsel** (-s) *o* scrapings; '**afschrabben**[1],
 –schrapen[1], **–schrappen**[1] *vt* scrape (off) [a
 carrot]; zie ook: *schrappen*; **–schrapsel** (-s) *o*
 scrapings
'**afschrift** (-en) *o* copy; *gewaarmerkt* ~ certified
 copy; exemplification; *een* ~ *maken van* make
 (take) a copy of; '**afschrijven** I *vt* 1 finish
 [what one is writing]; 2 copy [from original or
 another's work]; 3 write off [so much for
 depreciation, as lost]; *iem.* ~ 1 put sbd. off,

write a message of excuse; 2 declare the deal
off; **II** *vi X en Y hebben afgeschreven* 1 X and Y
have copied; 2 X and Y have written to
excuse themselves; **III** *vr zich laten* ~ have
one's name taken off the books [of a club &];
remove one's name from the list [of sub-
scribers]; **–ving** (-en) *v* copying; $ writing off;
~ *voor waardevermindering* $ depreciation
'**afschrik** *m* horror; *een* ~ *hebben van* hold in
abhorrence, abhor; *tot* ~ as a deterrent;
'**afschrikken**[1] *vt* deter [from going &];
discourage; scare [wild animals]; *hij laat zich
niet gauw* ~ he is not easily daunted; *hij liet zich
niet* ~ *door...* he was not to be deterred by...;
'**afschrikkend, afschrik'wekkend** deterrent
[effect]; forbidding [appearance]; *een* ~ *middel*
(*voorbeeld*) a deterrent
'**afschudden**[1] *vt* shake off; **–schuimen**[1] *vt* 1
skim [metals]; 2 scour [the seas]; **–schuinen**[1]
vt bevel, chamfer, flue, splay; **–schuiven**[1] I *vt*
push off, move away [a chair from...]; push
back [a bolt]; *de schuld van zich* ~ shift (shove)
the blame on another man's shoulders; **II** *vi* 1
slide (slip) down; 2 (b e t a l e n) **S** shell out;
–schutten[1] *vt* partition (off), screen (off)
'**afschuw** *m* abhorrence, horror; *een* ~ *hebben van*
hold in abhorrence, abhor; **af'schuwelijk**
horrible, horrid, lurid, abominable, execrable;
afschuw'wekkend revolting, repulsive
'**afslaan**[1] I *vt* 1 *eig* knock (beat, strike) off; 2
beat off [the enemy], repulse [an attack]; 3 (d e
b a j o n e t) unfix; 4 (d e t h e r m o m e t e r)
beat down; 5 (d e p r ij s) reduce [the price],
knock down [a penny]; 6 (w e i g e r e n) refuse
[a request], decline [an invitation], reject [an
offer]; *dat kan ik niet* ~, dat *sla ik niet af* I won't
(can't) say no to that; I can't (won't) refuse it;
hij slaat niets af dan vliegen nothing comes amiss
to him; **II** *vi* 1 (a f b u i g e n) turn off [to the
right]; 2 (v. p r ij z e n) go down; 3 (v.
m o t o r) cut out; *links, rechts* ~ (i n h e t
v e r k e e r) turn left, right; *van een ladder* ~
dash down from a ladder; (*flink*) *van zich* ~ hit
out
'**afslachten**[1] *vt* kill off, slaughter, massacre
'**afslag** (-slagen) *m* 1 abatement, reduction [of
prices]; 2 (sale by) Dutch auction; 3 (v.
a u t o w e g) exit; *bij* ~ *veilen* (*verkopen*) sell by
Dutch auction; '**afslager** (-s) *m* auctioneer
'**afslanken** (slankte 'af, is 'afgeslankt) *vi* & *vt*
slim; **–slijten**[1] *vt* & *vi* wear down; wear off
(out)[2]; **–sloven**[1] *zich* ~ drudge, slave, toil and
moil; zie ook *afgesloofd*

---

[1] V.T. en V.D. van dit werkwoord volgens het model: 'afbellen, V.T. belde 'af, V.D. 'afgebeld. Zie voor de
vormen onder het grondwoord, in dit voorbeeld: *bellen*. Bij sterke en onregelmatige werkwoorden wordt u verwezen
naar de lijst achterin.

'afsluitdijk (-en) *m* dam; 'afsluiten¹ I *vt* 1 lock [a door]; 2 (d o o r s l u i t e n v e r s p e r r e n) lock up [a garden &]; block, close [a road]; 3 (i n s l u i t e n) fence off [a garden]; 4 (v. t o e v o e r) turn off [the gas], cut off [the steam, the supply]; 5 (o p m a k e n) $ balance [the books], close [an account]; 6 (t o t s t a n d b r e n g e n) conclude [a bargain, a contract]; effect [an insurance]; 7 (b e ë i n- d i g e n) close [a period]; II *vi* lock up; III *vr* *zich* ~ seclude oneself from the world (from society); zie ook: *afgesloten*; **–ting** (-en) *v* 1 (i n 't a l g.) closing; 2 (v. c o n t r a c t) conclusion; 3 (a f s l u i t m i d d e l) barrier, partition, enclosure; 'afsluitkraan (-kranen) *v* stopcock 'afsmeken¹ *vt* implore, invoke (on *over*); **–snauwen¹** *vt* snarl at, snap at, snub; *hij werd afgesnauwd* ook: he had his head snapped off; **–snijden¹** *vt* cut (off) [ook: gas &]; zie ook: 1 *pas*; **–snoepen¹** *vt iem. iets* ~ steal a march on sbd.; **–snoeren¹** *vt* 𝔗 tie up, strangulate; **–soppen¹** *vt* wash [tiles &]; **–spannen¹** *vt* 1 unyoke [oxen]; unharness [a horse]; 2 (a f m e t e n m e t h a n d) span; **–spelen¹** I *vt* (d o e n s l i j t e n) wear out; (m e t b a n d- r e c o r d e r) play back; II *vr het drama dat zich daar heeft afgespeeld* the drama that was enacted there; *de gebeurtenissen spelen zich af in Londen* the events take place in London; *de handeling speelt zich af in Frankrijk* the scene is laid in France 'afspiegelen¹ I *vt* reflect, mirror; II *vr zich* ~ be reflected, be mirrored [in a lake &]; **–ling** (-en) *v* reflection 'afsplijten¹ *vt* & *vi* split off; **–splitsen¹** I *vt* split off; II *vr zich* ~ split off; (p o l i t i e k) secede; **–spoelen¹** *vt* wash, rinse; wash away; **–sponsen¹**, **–sponzen¹** *vt* sponge (down, over) 'afspraak (-spraken) *v* agreement; appointment [to meet], engagement; arrangement; *een* ~ *maken om...* make an arrangement to...; *agree upon ...ing; zich houden aan de* ~ stand by the agreement, stick to one's word; *t e g e n d e* ~ contrary to (our) agreement; *v o l g e n s* ~ according to (our) agreement, as agreed; [meet] by appointment; **–je** (-s) *o* 𝔉 date; *een* ~ *maken* date [a girl]; make a date [with sbd.]; 'afspreken¹ *vt* agree upon, arrange; *het was afgesproken voor de gelegenheid* it was preconcerted, got up (for the occasion); *de afgesproken plaats* the place agreed upon; *het was een afgesproken zaak* it was an arranged thing, a concerted piece of acting, a put-up job; *afge-*

sproken! done!, that's a bargain! 'afspringen¹ *vi* 1 (n a a r b e n e d e n) leap down, jump off; 2 (l o s g a a n) come off, fly off; 3 (o n d e r h a n d e l i n g e n) break down; 4 (k o o p) come to nothing; ~ *op* 1 spring at [sbd.]; 2 = *afstuiten*; **–staan¹** I *vt* cede [territory], yield [possession, one's place]; resign [office, a right &]; surrender [a privilege]; give up, hand over [property &]; II *vi* ~ *van* stand away (back) from; *zijn oren staan af* his ears stick (stand) out 'afstammeling (-en) *m* descendant; *~en* progeniture; ~ *in de rechte lijn* lineal descendant; ~ *in de zijlinie* collateral descendant; 'afstammen¹ *vi* ~ *van* be descended [in the (fe)male line] from, spring from, come of [a noble stock], be derived from [Latin &]; 'afstamming *v* descent [of man], [of Indian] extraction, ancestry; derivation [of words]; **–sleer** *v* descent theory 'afstand (-en) *m* 1 distance²; 2 (v. t r o o n) abdication; 3 (v. r e c h t) relinquishment; 4 (v. e i g e n d o m o f r e c h t) cession, surrender, renunciation; ~ *doen van* renounce, give up, waive [a claim, a right]; abdicate [a power, the throne]; cede [a property, right]; forgo [an advantage]; part with [property]; ~ *nemen* ⚔ take distance; ● *o p e e n* ~ at a (some) distance; *hij is erg op een* ~ he is very stand-offish; *op een* ~ *blijven* = *zich op een* ~ *houden*; *op een* ~ *houden* keep at a distance, keep [sbd.] at arm's length; *zich op een* ~ *houden* keep at a distance; *fig* keep one's distance, keep aloof; *v a n* ~ *tot* ~ at regular distances, at intervals; **af'standelijk** detached; 'afstandsbediening *v* remote control; **–marche** (-marʃ] = *afstandsmars*; **–mars** (-en) *m* & *v* ⚔ route-march; **–meter** (-s) *m* ⚔ range-finder; **–rit** (-ten) *m* long-distance ride (run) 'afstapje (-s) *o denk om het* ~ mind the step; 'afstappen¹ I *vi* step down; get off [one's bike], alight [from one's horse], dismount; ~ *b ij een vriend* put up with a friend; ~ *i n een hotel* put up at a hotel; ~ *o p iem.* step up to sbd.; ~ *v a n het onderwerp* change (drop) the subject; II *vt* pace [the room]; walk [a horse] 'afsteken¹ I *vt* 1 (m e t b e i t e l) bevel; (m e t s p a) cut; 2 (d o e n o n t b r a n d e n) let off [fireworks]; 3 (k o r t e r e w e g n e m e n) take a short cut; *een bezoek* ~ pay a visit; *een speech* ~ make a speech; II *vi* 1 ⚓ push off [from the shore]; 2 contrast [with its surroundings]; *gunstig* ~ *bij* contrast favourably with; ~

---

¹ V.T. en V.D. van dit werkwoord volgens het model: 'afbellen, V.T. belde 'af, V.D. 'afgebeld. Zie voor de vormen onder het grondwoord, in dit voorbeeld: *bellen*. Bij sterke en onregelmatige werkwoorden wordt u verwezen naar de lijst achterin.

tegen stand out against, be outlined against
'afstel *o* zie *uitstel*; 'afstellen[1] *vt* ✗ adjust;
'afstelling *v* ✗ adjustment

'afstemmen[1] *vt* 1 reject [a motion]; 2 *R* tune
(in), syntonize [a wireless set]; ~ *op* 1 *R* tune
(in) to [a station]; 2 *fig* tune to; attune to
[modern life &]

'afstempelen[1] *vt* (v. r e k e n i n g e n &)
stamp; 'afstempeling *v* stamping [of shares
&]

'afsterven[1] *vi* die; zie ook *afgestorven*; 'afste-
venen (stevende 'af, is 'afgestevend) *vi* ~ *op*
make for, bear down upon; 'afstijgen[1] I *vi* get
off [one's horse], dismount [from horseback];
II *vt* go down [a hill &]; 'afstoffen[1] *vt* dust;
'afstompen I (stompte 'af, h. 'afgestompt) *vt*
blunt[2]; *fig* dull; II (stompte 'af, is afgestompt)
vi become dull[2]; zie ook *afgestompt*

af'stotelijk = *afstotend*; 'afstoten[1] I *vt* 1 *eig* push
down (off), knock off (down), thrust down; 2
(i e m.) repel; 3 (b i j t r a n s p l a n t a t i e) ✗
reject; 4 (z i c h o n t d o e n v a n) dispose of
[shares &]; discharge [personnel]; II *va* repel,
be repellent; 'afstotend, af'stotend repelling,
repellent, repulsive; 'afstoting (-en) *v* 1
repulsion; 2 ✗ rejection [of the transplant]; 3 $
disposal [of share &]; discharge [of personnel]

'afstraffen[1] *vt* punish; chastise, correct; *fig*
trounce, **F** give a dressing-down; 'afstraffing
(-en) *v* punishment; correction; *fig* trouncing,
F dressing-down

'afstralen[1] *vt* & *vi* radiate [heat, joy &]; 'afstra-
ling (-en) *v* radiation; reflection

'afstrijken[1] *vt* strike [a match, bushel]; *een
afgestreken theelepel* a level teaspoonful;
–stropen[1] *vt* 1 *eig* strip (off) [the skin, a
covering]; skin [an eel]; flay [a fox]; strip [a
hare]; 2 *fig* ravage, harry [the country];
–studeren[1] *vi* finish one's studies; –stuiten[1]
vi rebound; ~ *op* 1 *eig* glance off [the cuirass],
rebound from [a wall]; 2 *fig* be frustrated by,
be foiled by [one's tenacity]; –stuiven[1] *vi* 1
(v. z a k e n) fly off; 2 (v. p e r s o n e n) rush
(tear) down [the stairs &]; ~ *op* make a rush
for, rush at

'aftakdoos (-dozen) *v* ✗ branch box
'aftakelen I (takelde 'af, h. 'afgetakeld) *vt*
unrig, dismantle [a ship]; II (takelde 'af, is
'afgetakeld) *vi hij is aan het* ~ he is on the
decline; *zij is aan het* ~ she is going off; *hij ziet
er erg afgetakeld uit* he looks rather decrepit (a
wreck); –ling *v* ⚓ unrigging &; *fig* decay
'aftakken (takte 'af, is 'afgetakt) *vt* branch, (✗

ook) tap; 'aftakking (-en) *v* 1 (d e t a k)
branch, (✗ ook) tap; 2 (h e t a f t a k k e n)
branching, (✗ ook) tapping

af'tands long in the tooth[2]; *fig* past one's prime
'aftapkraan (-kranen) *v* drain-cock; 'aftappen[1]
vt draw (off); tap [a tree, telegraph or telephone wires, calls &], drain [a pond]; bottle
[beer &]

'aftasten[1] *vt* scan [*T* a picture; an air space with
a radar beam]; feel, grope [an object];
(p e i l e n) put out feelers; 'aftekenen[1] I *vt* 1
(n a t e k e n e n) draw, delineate; 2 (m e t
t e k e n s a a n g e v e-n) mark off; 3 (v o o r
g e z i e n) sign; II *vr zich* ~ *tegen* stand out
against, be outlined against

'aftellen[1] I *vt* 1 (t e l l e n) count (off, out); 2
(b i j s p e l e n) count out; 3 (b i j l a n -
c e r i n g) count down; 4 (a f t r e k k e n)
deduct; II *o het* ~ *voor de lancering* the count-
down; 'aftelrijmpje (-s) *o* counting-out
rhyme

'aftobben[1] *zich* ~ weary oneself out, worry
oneself; zie ook *afgetobd*

'aftocht *m* retreat[2]; *de* ~ *blazen* [*fig*] beat a
retreat

'aftrap (-pen) *m sp* kick-off; *de* ~ *doen* kick off;
'aftrappen[1] I *vt* kick down (off); *hem van de
kamer* ~ kick him out of the room; II *vi* (b i j
v o e t b a l) kick off; *van zich* ~ kick out; zie
ook *afgetrapt*

'aftreden[1] I *vi* 1 *eig* step down; go off [the
stage]; 2 (v. m i n i s t e r s &) resign (office),
retire (from office); II *o zijn* ~ his resignation,
his retirement; 'aftredend retiring, outgoing

'aftrek *m* 1 deduction; 2 $ (v e r k o o p) sale,
demand; *goede* ~ *vinden* meet with a large sale,
find a ready market, sell well; *ze vinden weinig* ~
there is little demand for them; *na (onder)* ~
van... after deducting [expenses]; less [10 %];
vóór ~ *van belasting* before-tax [*aj*]; af'trekbaar
deductible; 'aftrekken[1] I *vt* 1 (n e e r t r e k -
k e n) draw off (down), pull (tear) off; 2 (v.
g e l d) deduct; 3 (v. g e t a l) subtract; 4 (v.
v u u r w a p e n) fire (off) [a gun]; 5
(k r u i d e n &) extract; ~ *van* 1 draw... from,
pull away... from; 2 × subtract, take [5] from
[10]; *zijn (de) handen van iem.* ~ wash one's
hands of sbd.; II *vi* 1 × subtract; 2 (w e g -
g a a n) withdraw, march off, ⚔ retreat; 3 (v.
o n w e e r) blow over; 4 (a f s c h i e t e n) pull
the trigger; *de* ~*de wacht* ⚔ the old guard; zie
ook *afgetrokken*; –er (-s) *m* × subtrahend;
'aftrekking (-en) *v* deduction; × subtraction;

---

[1] V.T. en V.D. van dit werkwoord volgens het model: 'afbellen, V.T. belde 'af, V.D. 'afgebeld. Zie voor de
vormen onder het grondwoord, in dit voorbeeld: *bellen*. Bij sterke en onregelmatige werkwoorden wordt u verwezen
naar de lijst achterin.

'**aftrekpost** (-en) *m* deductible item [from taxable income]; **–sel** (-s) *o* infusion, extract; **–som** (-men) *v* × subtraction sum; **–tal** (-len) *o* × minuend

'**aftroeven** (troefde 'af, h. 'afgetroefd) *vt* 1 ◊ trump; 2 *fig* put [sbd.] in his place; **–troggelen** (troggelde 'af, h. 'afgetroggeld) *vt* wheedle (coax) out of, trick [sbd.] out of; '**aftuigen**[1] *vt* 1 unharness [a horse]; 2 ⚓ unrig [a ship]; 3 *fig* thrash, beat (up); **–turven** (turfde 'af, h. 'afgeturfd) *vt* score, notch, tick off

'**afvaardigen** (vaardigde 'af, h. 'afgevaardigd) *vt* delegate, depute; return [members of Parliament]; **–ging** (-en) *v* delegation, deputation

'**afvaart** (-en) *v* sailing, departure

1 '**afval** *m* (a f v a l l i g h e i d v. g e l o o f) apostasy; (i n d e p o l i t i e k) defection

2 '**afval** (-len) *o* & *m* (h e t a f g e v a l l e n e i n 't a l g.) waste (matter), refuse (matter), rubbish; (b ij h e t s l a c h t e n) offal, garbage; (b ij h e t b e w e r k e n) clippings, cuttings, parings; (v. e t e n) leavings; (a f g e w a a i d e v r u c h t e n) windfall; '**afvallen**[1] *vi* 1 (n a a r b e n e d e n) fall (off), tumble down; 2 (v e r v a l l e n) fall away, lose flesh, lose [six pounds] (in weight); 3 (v a n g e l o o f) apostatize; 4 (v. z ij n p a r t ij) desert [one's party, one's friends &]; secede [from...]; 5 (b ij s p e l e n) drop out [of the race]; *er zal voor hem wel wat ~* he is sure to have his pickings out of it; *iem. ~* fall away from sbd.; let sbd. down; **af'vallig** apostate; unfaithful; *~ worden* backslide; zie ook *afvallen* 3, 4; **–e** (-n) *m-v* (v. g e l o o f) apostate; (v. p a r t ij) renegade, deserter; **–heid** *v* (v. g e l o o f) apostasy; (v. p a r t ij) desertion, defection; '**afvalprodukt** (-en) *o* waste product; **–stoffen** *mv* [chemical, radioactive] waste, waste materials; **–verwerking** *v* waste disposal; **–water** *o* effluent [of factory into stream]; **–wedstrijd** (-en) *m* *sp* (eliminating) heat

'**afvaren**[1] **I** *vi* sail, depart, start, leave; **II** *vt* go down [the river]; **–vegen**[1] *vt* wipe (off); *haar handen ~ aan een schort* wipe her hands on an apron; **–vinken** (vinkte 'af, h. afgevinkt) *vt* tick off [items on a list]; **–vissen**[1] *vt* fish (out), whip [a stream], draw [a pond]; **–vlakken**[1] *vt* make flat, flatten

'**afvloeien**[1] *vi* flow down, flow off; *fig* be discharged gradually; '**afvloeiing** (-en) *v* flowing down, flowing off; *fig* gradual discharge; **–sregeling** (-en) *v* personnel reduction agreement

'**afvoer** *m* 1 carrying off, discharge [of a liquid]; 2 conveyance, transport, removal [of goods]; 3 = *afvoerbuis*; **–buis** (-buizen) *v* outlet-pipe, waste-pipe, drain-pipe; '**afvoeren**[1] *vt* 1 (a f l e i d e n) carry off [water]; 2 (v e r v o e r e n) convey, transport, remove; 3 (a f s c h r ij v e n) remove [sbd.'s name from the list], strike off [the list]; '**afvoerkanaal** (-nalen) *o* drainage canal; outlet

'**afvragen**[1] **I** *vt* ask (for), demand; **II** *vr zich ~* ask oneself; *zij vroegen zich af...* they wondered...; **–vuren**[1] *vt* fire off, fire, discharge

'**afwachten**[1] **I** *vt* wait (stay) for, await; abide [the consequences]; wait [one's turn]; bide [one's time]; *dat moeten we nog ~, dat dient men af te wachten* that remains to be seen; **II** *vi* wait (and see); *een ~de houding aannemen* assume an attitude of expectation; follow a wait-and-see policy; **–ting** *v* expectation; *in ~ van de dingen die komen zouden* in (eager) expectation of what was to come; *in ~ van een regeling* pending a settlement; *in ~ uwer berichten* awaiting your news

'**afwas** *m* washing-up; **–automaat** [-o.t o.-, -ɔuto.-] (-maten) *m* (automatic) dishwasher; **af'wasbaar** washable; '**afwasbak** (-ken) washing-up bowl; **–kwast** (-en) *m* dish-mop; **–machine** [-ma.ʃi.nə] (-s) *v* = *afwasautomaat*; **–middel** (-en) *o* detergent; '**afwassen**[1] **I** *vt* wash, wash off; (d e v a a t) wash up; **II** *va* wash up; '**afwaswater** *o* dish-water

'**afwateren**[1] *vt* & *vi* drain; **–ring** (-en) *v* drainage; drain

'**afweer** *m* defence; **–geschut** *o* anti-aircraft artillery; **–houding** *v* defensive attitude; **–kanon** (-nen) *o* anti-aircraft gun; **–mechanisme** (-n) *o* defense mechanism; **–reactie** [-ksi.] (-s) *v* defensive reaction; **–stof** (-fen) *v* anti-body; **–vuur** *o* defensive fire

'**afwegen**[1] *vt* weigh; weigh out [sugar]; *tegen elkaar ~* balance, compare the pro's and cons; **–weken**[1] **I** *vt* remove by soaking; **II** *vi* come off; **–wenden**[1] **I** *vt* turn away [one's eyes]; divert [the attention]; avert [a danger]; ward off, parry [a blow], stave off [a calamity, ruin]; **II** *vr zich ~* turn away; **–wennen**[1] *vt* *iem. iets ~* break sbd. of the habit of ...ing; *zich iets ~* get out of a (bad) habit, break oneself of a habit; **–wentelen**[1] *vt* roll off (down); *de schuld op iem. anders ~* shift the blame on to another; **–weren**[1] *vt* keep off; avert [danger]; ward off, parry [a blow]; counter [an attack]

'**afwerken**[1] *vt* finish, finish off, give the finish-

---

[1] V.T. en V.D. van dit werkwoord volgens het model: 'af**bellen**, V.T. belde 'af, V.D. 'af**gebeld**. Zie voor de vormen onder het grondwoord, in dit voorbeeld: *bellen*. Bij sterke en onregelmatige werkwoorden wordt u verwezen naar de lijst achterin.

ing touch(es) to; get (work) through [the programme]; (v. n a a d) overcast; zie ook: *afbeulen*; **–king** *v* finishing (off); finish
'**afwerpen**[1] *vt* cast off, throw off, shake off, fling off; throw down; hurl down; cast, shed [the horns, the skin]; ≠ drop [bombs, arms], parachute [a man, troops]; *fig* yield [profit, results]; zie ook: *masker*; **–weten**[1] *vi het laten* ~ cry off; *ergens van* ~ 1 know sth. about; 2 know a thing or two about
af'wezig 1 absent [from school &]; away [from home], not at home; 2 *fig* absent-minded; *de afwezige(n)* the absentee(s); **–heid** *v* 1 absence; non-attendance; 2 *fig* absent-mindedness; *bij* ~ *van* in the absence of
'**afwijken**[1] *vi* 1 (v. n a a l d) deviate; 2 (v. l ij n) diverge; 3 (v. w e g) deflect [to the west]; 4 *fig* deviate [from a course, rule, a predecessor, the truth &]; wander [from the right path]; depart [from custom, a method, truth]; differ [from sample]; vary; **–d, af'wijkend** deviating[2], divergent[2]; different [readings]; dissentient [views]; at variance [with the truth]; aberrant [forms]; *ps* deviant [social behaviour]; '**afwijking** (-en) *v* deviation, deflection; divergence [from a course, line &]; departure [from a rule, a habit]; variation, difference [in a text]; (g e e s t e l ij k) aberrance, aberration; (l i c h a m e l ij k) abnormity, anomaly; *in* ~ *van* contrary to [this rule]
'**afwijzen**[1] *vt* refuse admittance to, turn away [intending visitors]; turn down [proposal, offer]; reject [a candidate, a lover, an offer]; refuse [a request]; decline [an invitation]; deny [a charge]; dismiss [a claim]; *afgewezen worden* fail [in an examination]; **af'wijzend** *er werd* ~ *beschikt op zijn verzoek* his request met with a refusal; ~ *staan tegenover* be averse to, from; '**afwijzing** (-en) *v* refusal, denial [of a request]; rejection [of a candidate, of an offer]
'**afwikkelen**[1] *vt* unroll, unwind, wind off [a rope &]; *fig* wind up [a business], settle [affairs]; fulfil [a contract]; **–ling** (-en) *v* unrolling, unwinding; *fig* winding up [of a business]; settlement [of affairs]; fulfilment [of a contract]
'**afwimpelen** (wimpelde 'af, h. 'afgewimpeld) *vt* brush aside [a proposal], wave aside [compliments]; **–winden**[1] *vt* wind off, unwind, unreel
'**afwisselen I** *vi* 1 (e l k a a r) alternate; 2 (v e r s c h i l l e n) vary; **II** *vt* 1 (i e m.) relieve [sbd.], take turns with [sbd.]; 2 (i e t s)

alternate, interchange; vary; *elkaar* ~ 1 (p e r - s o n e n) relieve one another, take turns; 2 (z a k e n) succeed each other, alternate; ...*afgewisseld door...* relieved by[2]...; **af'wisselend I** *aj* 1 (o n g e l ij k) various; 2 (v o l a f w i s s e - l i n g) varied, variegated; 3 (w i s s e l e n d) alternate; *met* ~ *geluk* with varying success; **II** *ad* alternately, by turns, in turn; '**afwisseling** (-en) *v* 1 (v e r a n d e r i n g) change, variation; 2 (v e r s c h e i d e n h e i d) variety; 3 (o p e e n v o l g i n g) alternation [of day and night], succession [of the seasons]; *t e r* ~, *v o o r de* ~ for a change, by way of a change
'**afwissen**[1] *vt* wipe (off); **–wrijven**[1] *vt* rub (off)
'**afzadelen**[1] *vt* unsaddle; **–zagen**[1] *vt* saw off; zie ook: *afgezaagd*
'**afzakken**[1] **I** *vi* (v. k l e r e n) come (slip) down; 2 (v. b u i) blow (pass) over; 3 (v. p e r s o n e n) withdraw, drop away; **II** *vt de rivier* ~ sail (float) down the stream; '**afzak- kertje** (-s) *o* **F** one for the road
'**afzeggen**[1] *vt* countermand; *het* (*laten*) ~ send an excuse; *iem.* ~ put sbd. off
'**afzenden**[1] *vt* send (off), dispatch, forward, ship; **–er** (-s) *m* sender, shipper; ~ *X* from X; '**afzending** *v* 1 sending; 2 **$** dispatch, forwarding; shipment
1 '**afzet** *m* **$** sale; ~ *vinden* zie *aftrek*
2 '**afzet** *m sp* (b ij s p r o n g) take-off
'**afzetgebied** (-en) *o* outlet, market; '**afzetten[1]
I** *vt* 1 (a f n e m e n) take off [one's hat]; take [from the fire]; 2 (u i t v e r v o e r m i d d e l) put (set) down [sbd. at the post office &], drop [a passenger]; 3 (d o e n b e z i n k e n) deposit [mud]; 4 (v. l e d e m a t e n) cut off, amputate; 5 (a f s t o t e n) push off [a boat]; 6 (a f p a l e n) peg out, stake out [an area]; 7 (a f s l u i t e n) block, close [a road]; (i n d e l e n g t e) line [with soldiers]; (m e t t o u w e n) rope off; 8 (o m h e i n e n) fence in; 9 (o m b o o r d e n) set off [with pearls &], trim [a dress with...]; 10 (o n t s l a a n) depose [a king], dismiss [a functionary], deprive [a clergyman]; 11 (v e r k o p e n) sell; 12 (s t o p z e t t e n) ✘ shut off, switch off, turn off [the wireless]; stop [the alarm]; 13 (t e v e e l l a t e n b e t a l e n) fleece [one's customers]; *iem.* ~ *voor vijf gulden* swindle (cheat, do) sbd. out of five guilders; *ik kon het niet van mij* ~ I couldn't put away the thought from me, dismiss the idea, put it out of my head; *een stoel van de muur* ~ move away a chair from the wall; **II** *vi* ⚓ push off; **III** *vr zich* ~ *sp* take off [for a jump]; *zich* ~ *tegen* [*fig*]

---

[1] V.T. en V.D. van dit werkwoord volgens het model: '**afbellen**, V.T. belde '**af**, V.D. '**afgebeld**. Zie voor de vormen onder het grondwoord, in dit voorbeeld: *bellen*. Bij sterke en onregelmatige werkwoorden wordt u verwezen naar de lijst achterin.

dissociate oneself from; **–er** (-s) *m* swindler, extortioner; **afzette'rij** (-en) *v* swindling, swindle; **'afzetting** (-en) *v* 1 dismissal [of a functionary], deprivation [of a clergyman], deposition [of a king]; 2 ⚔ amputation; 3 (b e z i n k i n g) deposition; (b e z i n k s e l) deposit; (v . i j s , r i j p) formation; 4 (a f - s l u i t i n g) [police] cordon; **–gesteente** (-n en -s) *o* sedimentary rocks

af'zichtelijk hideous

'afzien[1] **I** *vt* look down [the road]; *heel wat moeten* ~ have to go through quite a lot; **II** *vi* ~ *van* 1 (a f k i j k e n) copy from [one's neighbour]; 2 (o p g e v e n) relinquish, renounce, waive [a claim, a right &]; forgo, give up [an advantage, a right]; abandon, give up [the journey, the attempt]; *er van* ~ cry off [from a bargain]; zie ook: *afgezien*; **af'zienbaar** *in* (*binnen*) *afzienbare tijd* in the near future, in (within) the foreseeable future, within a measurable time

af'zijdig *zich* ~ *houden* hold (keep, stand) aloof

'afzoeken[1] *vt* search, ransack [a room]; beat [the woods], scour [the country]; *de stad* ~ hunt through the town; **–zoenen**[1] *vt* = *afkussen*

'afzonderen (zonderde 'af, h. 'afgezonderd) **I** *vt* separate (from *van*); prescind (from *van*); set apart; put aside [money]; isolate [patients], segregate [the sexes]; **II** *vr zich* ~ seclude oneself [from society], retire [from the world]; zie ook *afgezonderd*; **–ring** (-en) *v* separation; isolation, retirement, seclusion [from the world]; privacy; *in* ~ in seclusion; **af'zonderlijk I** *aj* separate, private, special; *elk deel* ~ each separate volume; *~e gevallen* individual cases; **II** *ad* separately; individually; [dine] apart

'afzuigen[1] *vt* suck (up), draw off [by suction]; **'afzuiginstallatie** [-(t)si.] (-s) *v* suction apparatus; **–kap** (-pen) *v* hood [over the kitchen range]

'afzwaaien[1] *vi* ✕ be released, demob; **–zwakken** (zwakte 'af, h. ' afgezwakt) *vt* tone down[2]; **–zwemmen**[1] *vi* 1 swim off; 2 (v o o r d i p l o m a) pass the final swimming test; **II** *vt* swim down [the river]; swim [a distance]

1 'afzweren (zwoer 'af. h. 'afgezworen) *vt* swear off [drink, a habit &]; abjure [a heresy, cause]; forswear [sbd.'s company]; renounce [the world]; **2 'afzweren** (zwoor 'af en zweerde 'af, is 'afgezworen) *vi* ulcerate away;

'afzwering (-en) *v* abjuration; renunciation

a'gaat (agaten) *m* & *o* agate; **a'gaten** *aj* agate

a'genda ('s) *v* 1 agenda, order-paper; 2 (pocket) diary

'agens (a'gentia) *o* agent

a'gent (-en) *m* 1 agent; representative; 2 ~ (*van politie*) policeman, constable, officer; **–schap** (-pen) *o* agency; (v . b a n k) branch (office); **agen'tuur** (-turen) *v* agency

a'geren (ageerde, h. geageerd) *vi* ~ *voor* (*tegen*) agitate for (against) [capital punishment &]

agglome'raat (-raten) *o* agglomerate; **agglome'ratie** [-(t)si.] (-s) *v* agglomeration; *stedelijke* ~ conurbation

aggra'veren (aggraveerde, h. geaggraveerd) *vt* aggravate, exaggerate [symptoms]

aggre'gaat (-gaten) *o* 1 aggregate; 2 ✕ unit; **aggre'gatietoestand** [-'ga.(t)si.-] (-en) *m* state of matter (of aggregation)

'agio *o* premium

agi'tatie [-'ta.(t)si.] *v* agitation, flutter, excitement; **agi'tator** (-s en -'toren) *m* agitator; **agi'teren** (agiteerde, h. geagiteerd) *vt* agitate; flutter, fluster, flurry

a'gnosticus (-ci) *m* agnostic

a'gogisch agogic

a'grariër (-s) *m* farmer; **a'grarisch** *~e hervorming* land reform; *~e produkten* agricultural products, farm products

a'gressie (-s) *v* aggression; ~ *plegen* (*jegens*) aggress (on); **agres'sief** aggressive; **agressivi'teit** *v* aggressiveness; **a'gressor** (-s) *m* aggressor

ah!, aha! aha!

a'horn (-en) *m*, **a'hornboom** (-bomen) *m* maple (tree)

a.h.w. = *als het ware* as it were

a.i. = *ad interim*

air [ɛːr] *o* air; look, appearance; *een* ~ *aannemen, zich ~s geven* give oneself airs

a'jakkes!, a'jasses! *ij* bah!, faugh!

a'jour [a.'ʒuːr] open-work

a'juin (-en) *m* onion

ake'lei (-en) *v* columbine

'akelig I *aj* dreary, dismal, nasty; *ik ben er nog* ~ *van* I still feel quite upset; *ik word er* ~ *van* it makes me (feel) sick; *wat* ~ *goedje!* what vile (nasty) stuff!; *dat* ~*e mens* that hateful woman; *die* ~*e vent* **F** that rotten chap (fellow); *die* ~*e wind* that wretched wind; **II** *ad* < ~ *geleerd* & awfully learned &

'Aken *o* Aix-la-Chapelle, Aachen

akke'fietje (-s) *o* (bad) job, affair; ook: trifle

---

[1] V.T. en V.D. van dit werkwoord volgens het model: **'afbellen**, V.T. belde **'af**, V.D. **'afgebeld**. Zie voor de vormen onder het grondwoord, in dit voorbeeld: *bellen*. Bij sterke en onregelmatige werkwoorden wordt u verwezen naar de lijst achterin.

'akker (-s) *m* field; **–bouw** *m* agriculture, farming, tillage [of the land]; **–winde** *v* bindweed

akke'vietje = *akkefietje*

ak'koord (-en) **I** *o* 1 agreement, arrangement, settlement; 2 $ composition [with one's creditors]; 3 ♪ chord; *een ~ aangaan (sluiten, treffen)* come to an agreement; *het op een ~je gooien* compromise; come to terms (with); **II** *aj* correct; *~ bevinden* find correct; *~ gaan met* agree to [a resolution]; agree with [the last speaker]; *~! agreed!*

akoe'stiek *v* acoustics; a'koestisch acoustic(al)

ako'lei = *akelei*

ako'niet (-en) *v* 🜍 aconite; *o* (v e r g i f) aconite

'akte (-n en -s) *v* document; [legal] instrument; deed [of sale &]; diploma, certificate; *rk* act [of faith, hope, and charity, of contrition]; act [of a play]; *~ van beschuldiging* indictment; *~ van oprichting* memorandum of association; *~ van overdracht (verkoop, vennootschap &)* deed of conveyance (sale, partnership &); *~ van overlijden* death certificate; *~ nemen van* take note of; *~ opmaken van* make a record of;
'aktentas (-sen) *v* brief case, portfolio

1 al, 'alle I *aj* all; every; *alle dagen &*, every day *&*; *alle drie* all three (of them); *er is alle reden om...* there is every reason to...; *al het mogelijke* all that is possible; zie ook: *mogelijk* **II**; *al het vee* all the cattle; *wij (gij, zij) allen* we (you, they) all, all of us (you, them); *gekleed en al* dressed as he was; *met schil en al* skin and all; *al met al* all in all; **II** *sb het al* the universe; *zij is zijn al* she is his all (in all); zie ook: *met*

2 al *ad* already, yet; *dat is ~ even moeilijk* quite as difficult; *het wordt ~ groter* it is growing larger and larger; *~ lang* long before this, for a long time past; *~ maar* all the while, continually; *~ (wel) zes maanden geleden* as long as six months ago; *dat is ~ zeer ongelukkig* very unfortunate indeed; *~ de volgende dag* the very next day; *~ in de 16e eeuw* as early as, as (so) far back as the 16th century; *hoe ver ben je ~?* how far have you got yet?; *zijn ze ~ getrouwd?* are they married yet?; *nu (toen) ~* even now (then); *~ zingende* singing (all the while), as he sang; *~ te zwaar* too heavy; *het is maar ~ te waar* it's only too true; *niet ~ te best* none too good, rather bad(ly); *niet ~ te wijd* not too wide; *u kunt het ~ of niet geloven* whether you believe it or not; *ik twijfelde of hij mij ~ dan niet gehoord had* I was in doubt whether he had heard me or not

3 al *cj* though, although, even if, even though; *~ is hij nog zo rijk* however rich he may be

a'larm *o* 1 alarm; 2 commotion, uproar; *~ blazen* sound the (an) alarm; *~ maken (slaan)* give (raise) the alarm; *loos ~ maken* make a false alarm; **alar'meren** (alarmeerde, h. gealarmeerd) *vt* give the alarm [to the soldiers], alarm [the population]; **–d** alarming; a'larminstallatie [-(t)si.] (-s) *v* alarm (device); **–klok** (-ken) *v* alarm-bell; **–pistool** (-pistolen) *o* blank (cartridge) pistol; **–signaal** [-si‚ɲa.l] (-nalen) *o* alarm(-signal); **–toestand** *m* ⚔ alert

Alba'nees Albanian; Al'banië *o* Albania

al'bast (-en) *o* alabaster; **–en** *aj* alabaster

'albatros (-sen) *m* albatross

'albe (-n) *v* alb

'albino ('s) *m* albino

'album (-s) *o* album

alche'mie, alchi'mie *v* alchemy; alche'mist, alchi'mist (-en) *m* alchemist

'alcohol (-holen) *m* alcohol; **–gehalte** *o* alcoholic content; **–houdend** alcoholic; alco'holica *mv* alcoholic drinks; alco'holisch alcoholic; alcoho'lisme *o* alcoholism; **–ist** (-en) *m* alcoholic; 'alcoholvrij non-alcoholic

al'daar there, at that place

alde'hyde [y = i.] (-n en -s) *o* aldehyde

al'door all the time

al'dus thus, in this way

al'eer before; *voor en ~* before

alexan'drijn (-en) *m* alexandrine

'alfa ('s) *v* alpha

'alfabet (-bɛt] (-ten) *o* alphabet; alfa'betisch **I** *aj* alphabetical; **II** *ad* alphabetically, in alphabetical order; alfabeti'seren [s = z] (alfabetiseerde, h. gealfabetiseerd) *vt* arrange alphabetically (in alphabetical order)

'alfavakken *mv* humanities, arts

'alge (-n) *v* alga [*mv* algae]

'algebra *v* algebra; alge'braïsch algebraic

al'geheel complete, entire, total, whole; zie ook: *geheel*

'algemeen, alge'meen **I** *aj* 1 (a l l e n o f a l l e s o m v a t t e n d) universal [history, suffrage &], general [rule]; 2 (o v e r a l v e r s p r e i d) general, common; 3 (o p e n-b a a r) general, public; 4 (o n b e p a a l d) general, vague; *dat is hans erg ~* that is very common now; *met algemene stemmen* unanimously; **II** *ad* generally, universally; *~ in gebruik* ook: in general (common) use; **III** *o in het ~* in general, on the whole; *o v e r het ~* generally speaking, on the whole; **–heid** (-heden) *v* universality, generality; *vage algemeenheden* commonplaces, platitudes; *in algemeenheden spreken* speak in vague terms

Al'gerië, Alge'rije *o* Algeria; Alge'rijn(s) (-en) *m* (*aj*) Algerian

al'hier here, at this place

alhoe'wel (al)though

'alias *ad* alias, otherwise (called)

'alibi ('s) *o* alibi

'alikruik (-en) *v* periwinkle, winkle
alimen'tatie [-(t)si.] *v* alimony
a'linea ('s) *v* paragraph
al'kali (-iën) *o* alkali; **al'kalisch** alkaline
al'koof (-koven) *v* alcove, recess [in a wall]
'allebei, alle'bei both (of them)
alle'daags 1 *eig* daily [wear], everyday [clothes], quotidian [fever]; 2 *fig* common, commonplace [topic], ordinary, plain [face], stale, trivial, trite [saying]; **–heid** (-heden) *v* triteness, triviality
al'lee (-leeën) *v* avenue
al'leen I *aj* 1 alone; single-handed; by oneself; 2 [feel] lonely; *de gedachte ~ is...* the mere (bare) thought; **II** *ad* only, merely; *ik dacht ~ maar dat...* I only thought...; *niet ~..., maar ook...* not only..., but also...; **–handel** *m* monopoly; **–heerschappij** *v* absolute monarchy (power, rule), autocracy; **–heerser** (-s) *m* absolute monarch, autocrat; **–spraak** (-spraken) *v* monologue, soliloquy; **–staand** single, isolated [case], detached [house]; **–staande** (-n) *m-v* single, unattached man or woman; **–verkoop** *m* sole sale, sole agency; **–vertegenwoordiger** (-s) *m* sole agent
'allegaar, alle'gaar = *allemaal*; **alle'gaartje** (-s) *o* hotchpotch, medly
allego'rie (-ieën) *v* allegory; **alle'gorisch** allegoric
'allemaal, alle'maal all, one and all
alle'machtig I *ij* (*wel*) ~! well, I never!; by Jove!; **II** *ad* < awfully
'alleman everybody; zie ook: *Jan*; **'allemansgeheim** (-en) *o* open secret; **–vriend** (-en) *m hij is een ~* he is friends with everybody
'allen all (of them); zie 1 *al*
al'lengs, 'allengs by degrees, gradually
aller'aardigst most charming; **–'armst** very poorest; **–be'lachelijkst** most ridiculous; **'allerbest, aller'best I** *aj* very best, best of all; ~*e vriend* dear(est) friend; *het ~e* the very best thing you can do (buy, get &); **II** *ad* best (of all); zie ook: *best*; **aller'christelijkst** [ch = k] most Christian; **–'eerst I** *aj* very first; **II** *ad* first of all; **'allerergst, aller'ergst** very worst, worst of all
aller'geen (-genen) *o* allergen
allerge'ringst least (smallest) possible; *niet het ~e* not the least little bit
aller'gie (-ieën) *v* allergy; **al'lergisch** allergic (to *voor*); **allergo'loog** (-logen) *m* allergist
'allerhande of all sorts, all sorts (kinds) of
Aller'heiligen *m* All Saints' Day
aller'heiligst most holy; *het Allerheiligste* 1 the Holy of Holies, Tabernacle; 2 *rk* the Eucharist; **–'hoogst** very highest; supreme; **–'laatst, 'allerlaatst I** *aj* very last; **II** *ad* last of all
'allerlei, aller'lei I *aj* of all sorts, all sorts

(kinds) of; miscellaneous; **II** *o* 1 all sorts of things; 2 (i n d e k r a n t) miscellaneous
'allerliefst, aller'liefst I *aj* 1 loved, very dearest; 2 (a a r d i g) charming, sweet; **II** *ad* most charmingly, sweetly; *het ~ hoor ik Wagner* best of all I like to hear W.; **'allermeest, aller'meest** most, most of all; *op zijn ~* at the very most; **aller'minst, 'allerminst I** *aj* (very) least, least possible; **II** *ad* least of all; zie ook: *minst*; **'allernaast, aller'naast** very nearest; very next; **'allernieuwst, aller'nieuwst** very newest (latest); **'allernodigst, aller'nodigst** most necessary; *het ~e* 1 what is most needed; 2 the common (least dispensable) necessaries; **'alleruiterst, aller'uiterst** (very) utmost; **aller'wegen** everywhere
Aller'zielen *m* All Souls' Day
'alles all, everything; ~ *en nog wat* the whole bag of tricks; ~ *of niets* all or nothing; *niets van dat* ~ nothing of the sort; ~ *op zijn tijd* there's a time for everything; *dat is ook niet* ~ it is anything but pleasant, it is no joke; *geld is niet* ~ money is not everything; ~ *te zamen genomen* on the whole, taking it all in all; ● *boven* ~ above all; ~ *o p* ~ *zetten* go all out; *v a n* ~ all sorts of things; *van* ~ *en nog wat* this that and the other, one thing and another; *v o o r* ~ above all; *veiligheid voor ~!* safety first!; **'allesbehalve, allesbe'halve** anything but, not at all, far from; **'allesbe'heersend** predominating [idea &], of paramount importance; **'allesetend** omnivorous; **'alleszins** in every respect, in every way, in all respects; highly, very, wholly
alli'age [g = 3] (-s) *v* & *o* alloy
alli'antie [-(t)si.] (-s) *v* alliance
al'licht, 'allicht (w e l l i c h t) probably, perhaps; ~, *zeg!* of course!, obviously!; *je kunt het ~ proberen* no harm in trying
alli'gator (-s) *m* alligator
allit(t)e'ratie [-(t)si.] (-s) *v* alliteration; **allit(t)e'reren** (allit(t)ereerde, h. geallit(t)ereerd) *vi* alliterate; ~*d* alliterative [verse]
al'longe [a'lõзə] (-s) *v* $ allonge, rider
al'lure (-s) *v* ~*s* airs; *van* (*grote*) ~ in the grand manner
al'lusie [s = z] (-s) *v* allusion; **allu'sief** allusive
alluvi'aal alluvial; **al'luvium** *o* alluvium, alluvion
'almacht *v* omnipotence; **al'machtig** almighty, omnipotent, all-powerful; *de Almachtige* the Almighty, the Omnipotent
'almanak (-ken) *m* almanac
'alom everywhere; **alomtegen'woordig** omnipresent, ubiquitous

'alom'vattend all-embracing
'aloud ancient, antique
'alpaca *o* 1 (w e e f s e l) alpaca; 2 (l e g e r i n g) German silver
'Alpen *mv de* ~ the Alps; **alpen-** Alpine [club, flora, hut, pass, peak, rose &]; 'alpenweide (-n) *v* alpine pasture, alp; **al'pine** Alpine [race]; **alpi'nisme** *o* mountaineering; **–ist** (-en) *m* mountaineer, (mountain) climber, Alpinist
al'pino (-s) *m,* **al'pinomuts** (-en) *v* beret
al'ras (very) soon
al'ruin (-en) *v* mandrake, mandragora
als 1 (g e l ij k) like [a father &]; 2 (z o a l s : b ij o p s o m m i n g) (such) as [ducks, drakes &]; 3 (q u a) as [a father]; as [president]; by way of [a toothpick]; 4 (a l s o f) as if [he wanted to say...]; 5 (w a n n e e r) when, whenever; 6 (i n d i e n) if; 7 (v a a k n a c o m p a r a t i e f) than; *rijk ~ hij is, kan hij dat betalen* being rich; *rijk ~ hij is, zal hij dat niet kunnen betalen* however rich he may be; ~ *het ware* as it were
als'dan then
alsje'blieft = *alstublieft*
als'mede and also, as well as, and... as well, together with; **als'nog** yet, still; **als'of** as if, as though; *doen* ~ pretend, make believe, play-act; **als'ook** in addition, too, along with; zie ook *alsmede*
alstu'blieft 1 (o v e r r e i k e n d) here is... [the key &], here you are; 2 (v e r z o e k e n d) (if you) please; 3 (t o e s t e m m e n d) yes, please; thank you
alt (-en) *v* alto; (m a n n e l ij k e) ook: counter-tenor; (v r o u w e l ij k e) ook: contralto
'altaar (-taren) *o* altar; **–stuk** (-ken) *o* altar piece
'altblokfluit (-en) *v* alto recorder, tenor recorder
alterna'tief (-tieven) *o* & *aj* alternative
alter'neren (alterneerde, h. gealterneerd) *vi* alternate
al'thans at least, at any rate, anyway
'altijd, al'tijd always, ever; ~ *door* all the time; ~ *en eeuwig* for ever (and ever); ~ *nog* always; *nog* ~ still; *nog* ~ *niet* not ...yet; ~ *weer* always, time and again; *voor* ~ for ever; **–durend** everlasting; **–groen** evergreen; ~ *gewas* evergreen
'altoos, al'toos = *altijd*
altru'ïsme *o* altruism; **–'ïst** (-en) *m* altruist; **–'ïstisch** *aj* (& *ad*) altruistic(ally)
'altsleutel (-s) *m* alto clef; **–stem** (-men) *v* contralto (voice); **–viool** (-violen) *v* viola, tenor violin
a'luin (-en) *m* alum; **–aarde** *v* alumina, alum earth

alu'minium *o Am* aluminum, *Br* aluminium; **–folie** *o* tinfoil
al'vast *zo, dat is* ~ *gebeurd* well, that's that; *dat is* ~ *verkeerd* that's wrong to begin with
al'vleesklier (-en) *v* pancreas
al'vorens before, previous to
al'waar where; wherever
al'weer again, once again
al'wetend all-knowing, omniscient
'alzijdig = *veelzijdig*
'alzo, al'zo thus, in this manner, so
amalga'matie [-(t)si.] *v* amalgamation; **amalga'meren** (amalgameerde, h. geamalgameerd) *vt* amalgamate
a'mandel (-en en -s) *v* 1 🌰 almond; 2 (k l i e r) tonsil; **–ontsteking** (-en) *v* tonsilitis; **–pers** *o,* **–spijs** *v* almond paste; **–vormig** almond-shaped
amanu'ensis (-ensissen en -enses) *m* assistant [in physics and chemistry]
ama'teur (-s) *m* amateur; **amateu'risme** *o* amateurism; **–istisch** amateurish, small-time
ama'zone [-'zo:nə] (-s) *v* 1 horsewoman; 2 (k o s t u u m) riding habit
'ambacht (-en) *o* trade, (handi)craft; *op een* ~ *doen bij* apprentice [sbd.] to; *timmerman van zijn* ~ a carpenter by trade; *twaalf ~en en dertien ongelukken* [he is] a Jack-of-all-trades and master of none; **'ambachtsman** (-lieden en -lui) *m* artisan; **–onderwijs** *o* technical instruction
ambas'sade (-s) *v* embassy; **ambassa'deur** (-s) *m* ambassador
'amber *m* amber
ambi'ëren (ambieerde, h. geambieerd) *vt* aspire after (to); **am'bitie** [-(t)si.] (-s) *v* 1 zeal; 2 ambition; **ambiti'eus** [-(t)si.'øs] 1 zealous, full of zeal; 2 ambitious
ambiva'lent ambivalent; **–ie** [-(t)si.] *v* ambivalence
ambro'zijn *o* ambrosia
ambt [amt] (-en) *o* 1 office, place, post, function; 2 (k e r k e l ij k) ministry; **'ambtelijk** official; **'ambteloos** out of office; ~ *burger* private citizen; **'ambtenaar** (-s en -naren) *m* official [in the Government service], civil servant, officer, [public] functionary; clerk; ~ *van de burgerlijke stand* registrar; **'ambtena-renapparaat** *o* civil service; **ambtena'rij** *v* officialdom, officialism, bureaucracy, **F** red tape, bumbledom; **'ambtgenoot** (-noten) *m* colleague; **'ambtsaanvaarding** *v* entrance into office; **–eed** (-eden) *m* oath of office; **–geheim** (-en) *o* 1 official secret [of a minister &]; 2 professional secret [of a doctor]; *het* ~ 1 official secrecy; 2 professional secrecy; **–gewaad** (-waden) *o* robes of office; **–halve,**

ambts'halve officially; **'ambtsketen** (-s) *v* chain of office; **–misdrijf** (-drijven) *o*, **–overtreding** (-en) *v* misfeasance, abuse of power; **–periode** (-s en -n) *v*, **–termijn** (-en) *m* term of office; **–woning** (-en) *v* official residence

ambu'lance [- 'lãs(ə)] (-s en -n) *v* ambulance; field hospital

a'mechtig breathless, out of breath

'amen (*o*) amen

amende'ment (-en) *o* amendment (to *op*); **amen'deren** (amendeerde, h. geamendeerd) *vt* amend

A'merika *o* America; **Ameri'kaan(s)** American

ame'thist (-en) *m* & *o* amethyst

ameuble'ment (-en) *o* suite (set) of furniture

amfeta'mine *v* amphetamine

amfi'bie (-bieën) *m* amphibian; **–vaartuig** (-en) *o* amphibian; **–voertuig** (-en) *o* amphibious vehicle; **am'fibisch** amphibious [animal; ✕ operation]

amfithe'ater (-s) *o* amphitheatre; **–sgewijs** in tiers

ami'caal I *aj* friendly; **II** *ad* in a friendly way; **a'mice** [a'mi.sə] (dear) friend

am'monia *m* ammonia; **ammoni'ak** *m* ammonia

ammu'nitie [-(t)si.] *v* (am)munition

amne'sie [ɑmne.'zi.] *v* amnesia

amnes'tie (-ieën) *v* amnesty; (*algemene*) ~ general pardon; ~ *verlenen* (*aan*) amnesty

a'moebe [a.'mø.bə] (-n) *v* amoeba [*mv* amoebae]

'amok *o* amuck; ~ *maken* run amuck

amo'reel non-moral

a'morf amorphous

amorti'satiefonds [- 'za.(t)si.-] (-en) *o*, **–kas** (-sen) *v* sinking fund; **amorti'seren** (amortiseerde, h. geamortiseerd) *vt* amortize, redeem

amou'reus [ou = u.] amorous [disposition, looks, words]; amatory [interests, successes]

amo'veren (amoveerde, h. geamoveerd) *vt* pull down [houses]

'ampel ample

'amper hardly, scarcely; barely [thirty]

am'père (-s) *m* ampere; **–meter** (-s) *m* ammeter

ampli'tude (-s en -n) *v* amplitude

am'pul (-len) *v* 1 ampulla [*mv* ampullae]; 2 (v o o r i n j e c t i e s t o f) ampoule; 3 *rk* cruet

ampu'tatie [- 'ta.(t)si.] (-s) *v* amputation; **ampu'teren** (amputeerde, h. geamputeerd) *vt* amputate

amu'let (-ten) *v* amulet, talisman, charm

amu'sant [s = z] amusing; **amuse'ment** [s = z] (-en) *o* amusement, entertainment, pastime; **amuse'mentsbedrijf** *o* entertainment industry; **–film** (-s) *m* entertainment film; **amu'seren** [s = z] (amuseerde, h. geamu-

seerd) **I** *vt* amuse; **II** *vr zich* ~ enjoy (amuse) oneself; *amuseer je!* I hope you will enjoy yourself!, have a good time!

a'naal anal

anachro'nisme (-n) *o* anachronism; **–istisch** anachronistic

anako'loet *v* anacoluthon, anacoluthia

anakro- = *anachro-*

analfa'beet (-beten) *m* illiterate; **analfabe'tisme** *o* illiteracy

ana'list (-en) *m* analyst, analytical chemist

analo'gie (-ieën) *v* analogy; *naar* ~ *van* on the analogy of, by analogy with; **ana'loog** analogous (to *aan*); *analoge rekenmachine* analogue computer

ana'lyse [- 'li.zə] (-n en -s) *v* analysis [*mv* analyses]; **analy'seren** [-li.'ze.rə(n)] (analyseerde, h. geanalyseerd) *vt* analyse; **ana'lyticus** [- 'li.ti.küs] (-ci) *m* (psycho)analyst; **ana'lytisch** [y = i.] **I** *aj* analytical [geometry &], analytic; **II** *ad* analytically

anam'nese [s = z] *v* 🗲 anamnesis

ana'nas (-sen) *m* & *v* pine-apple

anar'chie *v* anarchy; **anar'chisme** *o* anarchism; **–ist** (-en) *m* anarchist; **–istisch** 1 anarchist [theories &]; 2 (o r d e l o o s) anarchic(al)

anato'mie *v* anatomy; **ana'tomisch** anatomical; **ana'toom** (-tomen) *m* anatomist

anciënni'teit [ɑnsi.ɛni.'tɛit] *v* seniority; *naar* ~ by seniority

'ander I *aj* other [= different, second]; *een* ~*e dag* another day, some other day; *om de* ~*e dag* every other day; *een* ~*e keer* some other time; ~*e kleren aantrekken* change one's clothes; *hij was een* ~ *mens* he was a changed man; *de* ~*e week* next week; *met* ~*e woorden* in other words; **II** *pron een* ~ another (man); ~*en* others, other people; *de een n a de* ~ one after the other; *o m de* ~ by turns, in turn; zie ook: *om*; *o n d e r* ~*e* among other things; *het ene verlies o p het* ~*e* loss upon loss; **–daags** ~*e koorts* tertian fever; **–deels** on the other hand; **–half, ander'half** one and a half; ~ *maal zo lang* one and a half times the length of..., half as long again; ~ *uur* an hour and a half; *anderhalve man (en een paardekop)* a handful of people; **'andermaal** (once) again, once more, a second time; **–mans** another man's, other people's

'anders I *aj* other [than he is], different [from us]; **II** *pron iemand* ~ somebody (any one) else, another (person), other people; *iets (niets)* ~ something (nothing) else; *als u niets* ~ *te doen hebt* if you are not otherwise engaged; *wat (wie)* ~*?* what (who) else?; *dat is wat* ~ that's another affair (matter); *ik heb wel wat* ~ *te doen* I've

other things to do, I've other fish to fry; **III** *ad* 1 otherwise, differently; 2 at other times; 3 in other respects; ~ *niet?* nothing else?, is that all?; *net als* ~ just as usual; *het is niet* ~ it cannot be helped; *het kan niet* ~ 1 it cannot be done in any other way; 2 there's no help for it; *ik kan niet* ~ I can do no other, I have no choice; *ik kan niet* ~ *dan erkennen dat...* I cannot but recognize that..., I can't help recognizing that...; *hoe vlug hij* ~ *is, dit...* quick(-witted) as he is at other times (as a rule), this...;
anders'denkend 1 of another opinion; 2 (i n g o d s d i e n s t) dissenting; ~*en* 1 such as think (believe) otherwise; 2 dissentients; **–ge'zind** otherwise-minded, dissenting; **–'om,** **'andersom** the other way round; *het is precies* ~ it is quite the reverse; **'anderszins** otherwise; **'anderzijds** on the other hand
'Andes *de* ~ the Andes
an'dijvie *v* endive
anek'dote *v* (-s en -n) anecdote, **F** yarn; **anek'dotisch** anecdotal
ane'mie [ɑne.-] *v* an(a)emia; **a'nemisch** an(a)emic
ane'moon (-monen) *v* anemone
anesthe'sie [anɛste.'zi.] *v* anaesthesia; **anesthe'sist** [-'zɪst] (-en) *m* anaesthetist
'angel (-s) *m* 1 sting [of a wasp]; 2 (fish)hook
'Angelen *mv* Angles
Angel'saks (-en) *m* Anglo-Saxon; **Angel'saksisch** *aj* & *o* Anglo-Saxon
'angelus *o* angelus
an'gina [ɑŋ'ɡi.na.] *v* 🍐 angina, quinsy; ~ *pectoris* ['pɪkto:rɪs] angina pectoris
angli'caan(s) [ɑŋɡli.-] Anglican
An'glist [ɑŋ'ɡlɪst] (-en) *m* Anglicist
anglo'fiel [ɑŋɡlo.-] (-en) *m* Anglophile
An'gola [ɑŋ'ɡo.la.] *o* Angola; **Ango'lees I** *aj* Angolan; **II** *o* Angolese; **III** (-lezen) *m* Angolese
an'gorakat [ɑŋ'ɡo:-] (-ten) *v* Angora cat
angst (-en) *m* 1 fear, terror; 2 (s t e r k e r) [mental] anguish, agony; 3 *ps* anxiety [complex, neurosis]; *uit* ~ *voor...* for fear of; *radeloze* ~ **F** blue funk; *duizend* ~*en uitstaan* be in mortal fear; **angstaan'jagend** terrifying, fearsome; **'angstgevoel** (-ens) *o* feeling of anxiety; **'angstig** afraid [a l l é é n p r e d i k a-t i e f !]; fearful; anxious [moment]; **'angst-kreet** (-kreten) *m* cry of distress; **–toestand** (-en) *m* anxiety state; **angst'vallig** scrupulous; **–'wekkend** alarming; **'angstzweet** *o* cold perspiration, cold sweat
a'nijs *m* anise; **–zaad** *o* aniseed
ani'line *v* aniline
ani'meermeisje (-s) *o* nightclub hostess; **ani'meren** (animeerde, h. geanimeerd) *vt* encourage, stimulate; *een geanimeerd gesprek* an

animated (a lively) discussion; **'animo** *m* & *o* gusto, zest, spirit; *er was weinig* ~ *voor het plan* the plan was not too well received
animosi'teit [s = z] *v* animosity
anje'lier (-en), **'anjer** (-s) *v* [red, white] carnation, pink
'anker (-s) *o* 1 ⚓ anchor[2]; 2 (a a n m u u r) brace, cramp-iron; 3 (v . m a g n e e t) armature; 4 (m a a t) anker; *het* ~ *laten vallen* ⚓ drop anchor; *het* ~ *lichten* ⚓ weigh anchor; *het* ~ *werpen* ⚓ cast anchor; *v o o r* ~ *liggen* ⚓ be (lie, ride) at anchor; **–boei** (-en) *v* anchor-buoy; **'ankeren** (ankerde, h. geankerd) *vi* ⚓ anchor, cast (drop) anchor; **'ankergrond** (-en) *m* anchoring ground, anchorage; **–plaats** (-en) *v* moorage, mooring, anchorage; **–touw** (-en) *o* cable
'anklet [a = ɛ] (-s) *m* short [men's] sock, anklet
an'nalen *mv* annals
an'nex *huis met* ~*e brouwerij* house with brewery joined on to it
anne'xatie [-(t)si.] (-s) *v* annexation; **anne'xeren** (annexeerde, h. geannexeerd) *vt* annex
'anno in the year; ~ *Domini* in the year of our Lord
an'nonce [ɑ'nõsə] (-s) *v* advertisement, **F** ad; **annon'ceren** (annonceerde, h. geannonceerd) *vt* announce
anno'teren (annoteerde, h. geannoteerd) *vt* annotate
annuï'teit (-en) *v* annuity
annu'leren (annuleerde, h. geannuleerd) *vt* cancel, annul; **–ring** *v* cancellation, annulment
a'node (-n en -s) *v* anode
ano'niem anonymous; **anonimi'teit** *v* anonymity; **a'nonymus** [y = i.] (-mi) *m* anonymous writer
anor'ganisch inorganic [chemistry]
'ansichtkaart [s = z] (-en) *v* picture postcard
an'sjovis (-sen) *m* anchovy
antago'nisme *o* antagonism
antece'dent (-en) *o* 1 (l o g i s c h & *gram*) antecedent; 2 (a n d e r g e v a l) precedent; *zijn* ~*en* his antecedents, his record
anteda'teren (antedateerde, h. geantedateerd) *vt* antedate
an'tenne (-n en -s) *v RT* aerial, antenna
antibi'oticum (-ca) *o* antibiotic
anticham'breren [ch = ʃ] (antichambreerde, h. geantichambreerd) *vi* be kept waiting; cool one's heels
antici'patie [-'pa.(t)si.] *v* anticipation; **antici'peren** (anticipeerde, h. geanticipeerd) *vt* anticipate
anticon'ceptie [-'sɛpsi.] *v* contraception; **anticonceptio'neel** contraceptive; ~ *middel*

contraceptive
antida′teren (antidateerde, h. geantidateerd) =
antedateren
an′tiek I *aj* antique, old [furniture]; ancient,
old-fashioned; **II** *o* (v o o r w e r p e n) antiques;
III *mv* (k u n s t e n a a r s) *de* ~*en* the classics;
–zaak (-zaken) *v* antique shop
anti′geen (-genen) *o* antigen
antikleri′kaal anticlerical
anti′krist (-en) *m* Antichrist
An′tillen *de* ~ the Antilles; *de Grote (Kleine)* ~
the Greater (Lesser) Antilles; **Antilli′aan(s)**
(-ianen) *m* (& *aj*) Antillian
anti′lope (-n) *v* antelope
antima′kassar (-s) *m* antimacassar
Antio′chië *o* Antioch
antipa′pisme *o* anticlericalism; hatred of
Roman-Catholicism
′antipassaat *m* anti-trade (wind)
antipa′thie (-ieën) *v* antipathy, dislike;
antipa′thiek antipathetic, unlikeable
anti′pode (-n) *m* antipode
anti′quaar [-′kʋaːr] (-quaren) *m* 1 antique
dealer; 2 second-hand bookseller, antiquarian
bookseller; **anti′quair** [-′kɛːr] (-s) *m* antique
dealer; **antiquari′aat** [-kʋa:-] (-riaten) *o* 1
(h e t v a k) antiquarian bookselling; 2 (d e
w i n k e l) second-hand bookshop, antiquarian
bookshop; **anti′quarisch** [-′kʋa:-] second-
hand, antiquarian; **antiqui′teiten** [-kʋi.-] *mv*
antiques
antise′miet (-en) *m* anti-Semite;
antise′mitisch anti-Semitic; **antisemi′tisme**
o anti-Semitism
anti′septisch antiseptic
anti′slip non-skid [tyre]
′antistof (-fen) *v* antibody
anti′tankgeschut [-′tɪŋk] *o* anti-tank gun
anti′these [s = z] (-n en -s) *v* antithesis [*mv*
antitheses]
anti′vries *o*, **anti′vriesmiddel** (-en) *o* anti-
freeze
antra′ciet *m* & *o* anthracite
antropolo′gie *v* anthropology; **antropo′lo-
gisch** anthropologic
′Antwerpen *o* Antwerp
′antwoord (-en) *o* 1 (o p e e n b r i e f,
v r a a g &) answer, reply; (o p e e n a n t-
w o o r d) rejoinder; *gevat* ~ repartee, ready
answer; *i n* ~ *op* in reply (answer) to; **–apparaat** (-raten) *o* answer-phone machine;
–coupon [ou = u.] (-s) *m* reply coupon;
′antwoorden (antwoordde, h. geantwoord) **I**
vt answer, reply; rejoin, retort; **II** *va* & *vi*
answer, reply; (b r u t a a l) talk back; ~ *op*
reply to, answer [a letter]; **′antwoordkaart**
(-en) *v* business reply card

′anus *m* anus, vent
A° = *anno*
a′orta (′s) *v* aorta
AO′W [a.o.′ʋe.] *v* = *Algemene Ouderdomswet*; **F**
old-age pension; **AO′W′er** (-s) *m* old-age
pensioner
a′pache [a.′pɑxə] (-n) *m* Apache; apache [street
robber]
a′part apart; separate; *een* ~ *ras* a race apart; ~
berekenen charge extra for; zie verder: *afzonderlijk*; **–heid** *v* ZA apartheid: (race, racial)
segregation; **–je** (-s) *o* private talk
apa′thie *v* apathy; **a′pathisch** apathetic
′apegapen *op* ~ *liggen* be at one's last gasp;
–kool *v* **F** gammon, bosh; **–kop** (-pen) *m*
monkey; **–liefde** *v* blind love, foolish fondness; **–nootje** (-s) *o* peanut
Apen′nijnen *mv* Apennines; **Apen′nijns**
Apennine [peninsula]
′apepak (-ken) *o* **F** gala uniform
aperi′tief [-pe.-] (-tieven) *o* & *m* apéritif
a′pert obvious, evident
ape′zat **F** dead-drunk; **′apezuur** *o* *zich het* ~
schrikken be frightened out of one's wits; **a′pin**
(-nen) *v* she-monkey, she-ape [tailless]
a′plomb [a.′plõ] *o* aplomb, self-possession,
coolness, assurance
apoca′lyptisch [y = ı] apocalyptic
apo′crief apocryphal; *de* ~*e boeken* the
Apocrypha
apo′dictisch apodictic
apolo′gie (-ieën) *v* apology°
a′postel (-en en -s) *m* apostle; **–schap,
aposto′laat** *o* apostolate, apostleship;
apos′tolisch apostolic
apo′strof (-fen en -s) *v* apostrophe
apo′theek (-theken) *v* pharmacy, chemist's
(shop), dispensary; **apo′theker** (-s) *m* pharma-
cist, (pharmaceutical, dispensing) chemist
apothe′ose [s = z] (-n) *v* apotheosis
appa′raat (-raten) *o* apparatus, zie ook: *toestel*;
fig [government, production &] machinery,
machine; *huishoudelijke apparaten* domestic
(electrical) appliances; **appara′tuur** *v* equipment
apparte′ment (-en) *o* apartment
1 ′appel (-en en -s) *m* apple (ook = pupil of the
eye); *door de zure* ~ *heen bijten* make the best of
a bad job; *voor een* ~ *en een ei* **F** for a (mere)
song; *de* ~ *valt niet ver van de boom* it runs in the
blood; like father, like son
2 ap′pel (-s) *o* 1 ⚖ appeal; 2 ✕ roll-call; parade;
~ *aantekenen* give notice of appeal, lodge an
appeal; ~ *houden* call the roll, take the roll-call;
ze goed onder ~ *hebben* have them well in hand
′appelbeignet [-bɛɲe.] (-s) *m* apple fritter; **–bol**
(-len) *m* apple dumpling; **–boom** (-bomen) *m*

apple tree; **–flap** (-flappen) *v* apple turnover;
–flauwte (-n en -s) *v een* ~ *krijgen* pretend to
faint
appel′lant (-en) *m* appellant; **appel′leren**
(apelleerde, h. geapelleerd) *vi* ﬆ appeal, lodge
an appeal; ~ *aan* appeal to [reason, the senti-
ments]
′appelmoes *o* & *v* apple-sauce; **–sap** *o* apple
juice; **–schimmel** (-s) *m* dapple-grey (horse);
–taart (-en) *v* apple-tart; **–tje** (-s) *o* (small)
apple; *een* ~ *met iem. te schillen hebben* have a
bone to pick with sbd.; have a rod in pickle for
sbd.; have an account to settle with sbd.; *een* ~
voor de dorst a nest-egg; *een* ~ *voor de dorst
bewaren* provide against a rainy day; **–wangen**
mv rosy cheeks; **–wijn** *m* cider
appe′tijtelijk appetizing; *er* ~ *uitzien* look
attractive
applaudis′seren [-di.-] (applaudisseerde, h.
geapplaudisseerd) *vi* applaud, clap, cheer;
ap′plaus *o* applause
appor′teren (apporteerde, h. geapporteerd) *vi*
fetch and carry, retrieve
appreci′atie [aprɛ.si.′a.(t)si.] (-s) *v* appreciation;
appreci′ëren (apprecieerde, h. geapprecieerd)
vt appreciate, value
ap′pret [a′prɛt] *o* starch; **appre′teren** (appre-
teerde, h. geappreteerd) *vt* finish
approvian′deren (approviandeerde, h. geap-
proviandeerd) *vt* provision [a garrison &]
a′pril *m* April; *eerste* ~ first of April; *één* ~ All
Fools' Day; *één* ~ *!* April Fool!
apro′pos [a.pro.′po:] **I** *ad* apropos, to the point;
II *ij* by the way, by the bye; talking of...; **III** *o*
& *m om op ons* ~ *terug te komen...* to return to
our subject; *hij laat zich niet van zijn* ~ *brengen* he
is not to be put out
aqua′duct (-en) *o* aqueduct
′aqualong (-en) *v* aqualung
aqua′rijn (-en) *m* & *o* aquamarine
aqua′rel (-len) *v* aquarelle, water-colour
a′quarium (-s en -ria) *o* aquarium
ar (-ren) *v* sleigh, sledge
ara′besk (-en) *vi* arabesque
A′rabië *o* Arabia; **Ara′bier** (-en) *m* Arab [man
& horse]; **A′rabisch I** *aj* Arabian [Desert, Sea
&], Arab [horse, country, state, League]; (v .
t a a l & g e t a l l e n) Arabic; **II** *o* Arabic
à raison van [a.rɛ′zɔ:-] *at* [15 p.]
a′rak *m* arrack, rack
′arbeid *m* labour, work°; *zware* ~ toil; *aan de* ~
gaan set to work; *aan de* ~ *zijn* be at work; ~
adelt there is nobility in labour;
′arbeid(s)besparend labour-saving;
′arbeiden (arbeidde, h. gearbeid) *vi* labour,
work; **′arbeider** (-s) *m* worker, working man,
labourer, hand, operative, workman; **′arbei-**

dersbeweging (-en) *v* labour movement;
–klasse (-n) *v* working class(es); **–wijk** (-en) *v*
workmen's quarter; **–′zelfbestuur** *o* autoges-
tion
′arbeidsbemiddeling *v* (*bureau, dienst voor*) ~ =
arbeidsbureau; **–beurs** (-beurzen) *v* = *arbeidsbureau*; **–bureau** [-by.ro.] (-s) *o* labour exchange,
employment exchange; **–contractant** (-en) *m*
(i n o v e r h e i d s d i e n s t) public servant
appointed on agreement; **–geschil** (-len) *o*
labour dispute; **–inspectie** [-spɛksi.] (-s) *v*
trade (industrial) supervision; factory inspection; **–intensief** [-zi.f] requiring much labour;
bedrijven die ~ *zijn* industries that are heavy
users of labour; **–kracht** (-en) *v* = *werkkracht*;
–leer *v* ergonomics; **–loon, arbeids′loon**
(-lonen) *o* wages; **–markt** *v* labour market;
arbeidsonge′schikt unfit for work, disabled;
′arbeidsovereenkomst (-en) *v* labour
contract, labour agreement; *collectieve* ~ collective agreement; *het onderhandelen over een collectieve* ~ collective bargaining; **–plaats** (-en) *v*
job; **–prestatie** [-(t)si.] (-s) (labour) efficiency,
output, productivity; **–reserve** [-zɛrvə] *v*
labour reserve; **–terrein** *o* field (sphere) of
activity, domain; **–therapeut** [-te.ra.pœyt]
(-en) *m* occupational therapist; **–therapie** *v*
occupational therapy; **–tijd** (-en) *m* working
hours; **–tijdverkorting** *v* shortening (reduction) of working hours; reduced hours;
–verdeling (-en) *v* division of labour;
–vermogen *o* working power, energy; ~ *van
beweging* kinetic (actual) energy; ~ *van plaats*
potential energy; **–voorwaarden** *mv* [favour-
able] terms of employment; [healthy] working
conditions; **–vrede** *m* & *v* labour peace;
ar′beidzaam industrious
ar′biter (-s) *m* arbiter, arbitrator; *sp* umpire;
arbi′trage [g = ʒ] *v* arbitration
ar′cadisch Arcadian
ar′ceren (arceerde, h. gearceerd) *vt* hatch, shade
ar′chaïsch archaic; **archa′isme** (-n) *o* archaism
archeolo′gie *v* archaeology; **archeo′logisch**
archaeological; **archeo′loog** (-logen) *m*
archaeologist
ar′chief (-chieven) *o* 1 archives, records; 2
record office; 3 $ files
′archipel [′arɡi.-,′arʃi.pɛl] (-s) *m* archipelago
archi′tect [arɡi.-, arʃi.-] (-en) *m* architect;
architec′tonisch architectonic, architectural;
architec′tuur *v* architecture
archi′traaf (-traven) *v* architrave
archi′varis (-sen) *m* archivist, keeper of the
records
Ar′dennen *de* ~ the Ardennes
ar′duin *o* freestone, ashlar
′are (-n) *v* are [= 100 sq. m.]

'areligi'eus ['a.re.li.gi'øs] areligious, religionless

a'rena ('s) *v* arena; bullring [for bullfights], ring [of circus]

'arend (-en) *m* eagle; 'arendsblik (-ken) *m met* ~ eagle-eyed; −jong (-en) *o* eaglet; −nest (-en) *o* eagle's nest, aerie; −neus (-neuzen) *m* aquiline nose

'argeloos 1 guileless, inoffensive; 2 unsuspecting; arge'loosheid *v* 1 guilelessness, inoffensiveness; 2 confidence

Argen'tijn(s) (-en) *m* (&*aj*) Argentine; Argen'tinië *o* the Argentine, Argentina

'arglist *v* craft(iness), cunning, guile; arg'listig crafty, cunning, guileful

argu'ment (-en) *o* argument, plea; argumen'tatie [-(t)si.] (-s) *v* argumentation; argumen'teren (argumenteerde, h. geargumenteerd) *vi* argue

'argusogen *mv met* ~ argus-eyed

'argwaan *m* suspicion, mistrust; ~ *hebben* entertain (have) suspicions, misdoubt; ~ *krijgen* become suspicious, **F** smell a rat; arg'wanend suspicious

'aria ('s) *v* air, aria

'Ariër (-s) *m* Aryan; 'Arisch Aryan

aristo'craat (-craten) *m* aristocrat; aristocra'tie [-'(t)si.] (-ieën) *v* aristocracy; aristo'cratisch aristocratic

Aris'toteles *m* Aristotle

ark (-en) *v* ark; *de ~e Noachs* Noah's ark; ~ *des Verbonds* Ark of the Covenant

1 arm (-en) *m* arm [of a man, the sea, a balance &]; branch [of a river]; bracket [of a lamp]; *de* ~ *der wet* the limb of the law; *haar de* ~ *bieden* give (offer) her one's arm; *met een meisje a a n de* ~ with a girl on his arm; ~ *i n* ~ arm in arm; *iem. in de* ~ *nemen* consult sbd.; *zich in de* ~*en werpen van* throw oneself into the arms of; *m e t open* ~*en ontvangen* receive with open arms; *met de* ~*en over elkaar* with folded arms

2 arm *aj* poor², indigent, needy; *ook*: penniless; *zo* ~ *als Job (als de mieren, als de straat, als een kerkrat)* as poor as Job (as a church mouse); *een* ~*e* a poor man, a pauper; *de* ~*en* the poor; *de* ~*en van geest* the poor in spirit; ~ *aan* poor in [minerals]

arma'tuur (-turen) *v* armature

'armband (-en) *m* bracelet; −horloge [-lo.ʒə] (-s) *o* wrist-watch

'armelijk poor, shabby; 'armenhuis (-huizen) = *armhuis*; −zorg *v* ⬜ poor-relief; arme'tierig poor, wretched

arme'zondaarsbankje (-s) *o* penitent form; −gezicht *o een* ~ *zetten* put on a hangdog look

'armhuis (-huizen) *o* ⬜ almshouse, workhouse; arm'lastig ~ *worden* ⬜ come upon the parish (the rates)

'armleuning (-en) *v* arm, arm-rest

'armoe(de) *v* 1 poverty; *het is daar* ~ *troef* they are in dire want; *t o t* ~ *geraken (vervallen)* be reduced to poverty; *u i t* ~ from poverty; *tot* ~ *brengen* reduce to poverty; *tot* ~ *vervallen* be reduced to poverty; ar'moedig poor, needy, poverty-stricken, shabby; −heid *v* poverty; penury, poorness; 'armoedje *o mijn* ~ what little I have, my few sticks of furniture; 'armoedzaaier (-s) *m* poor devil

'armsgat (-gaten) *o* arm-hole; 'armslag *m* elbow-room²; 'armslengte (-n) *v op* ~ at arm's length; 'armstoel (-en) *m* arm-chair

arm'tierig = *armetierig*

'armvol (-len) *m* armful

arm'zalig pitiful, miserable; paltry, beggarly

a'roma ('s) *o* aroma, flavour; aro'maten *mv* flavourings; aro'matisch aromatic

'aronskelk (-en) *m* arum

a'room (aromen) *o* = *aroma*

arrange'ment [ɑrãʒə'mɛnt] (-en) *o* ♪ arrangement, orchestration; arran'geren [g = ʒ] (arrangeerde, h. gearrangeerd) *vt* arrange²; get up

'arreslede (-n) *v*, 'arreslee (-sleeën) *v* sleigh, sledge

ar'rest (-en) *o* 1 (v a s t h o u d i n g) custody, arrest; 2 (b e s l a g n a m e) seizure; 3 (b e s l u i t) decision, judgement; *in* ~ under arrest; *in* ~ *nemen* = *arresteren* 1; *in* ~ *stellen* place under arrest; arres'tant (-en) *m* arrested person, prisoner; arres'tantenkamer (-s) *v*, −lokaal (-kalen) *o* detention room; arres'tatie [-(t)si.] (-s) *v* arrest, apprehension; −bevel (-velen) *o* ⚖ warrant of arrest; arres'teren (arresteerde, h. gearresteerd) *vt* 1 arrest, take into custody, apprehend [an offender]; 2 confirm [the minutes]

arri'veren (arriveerde, is gearriveerd) *vi* arrive

arro'gant arrogant, presumptuous, uppish; arro'gantie [-(t)si.] *v* arrogance, presumption

arrondisse'ment [-di.-] (-en) *o* district; −srechtbank (-en) *v* county court

arse'naal (-nalen) *o* arsenal; armoury

ar'senicum *o*, arse'niek *o* arsenic

ar'tesisch [-zi.s] ~*e put* artesian well

articu'latie [-(t)si.] (-s) *v* articulation; articu'leren (articuleerde, h. gearticuleerd) *vt* articulate

ar'tiest (-en) *m* artist; (i n c i r c u s e. d.) artiste, performer

ar'tikel (-en en -s) *o* 1 (i n 't a l g.) article; (w e t e n s c h a p p e l ij k) *ook*: paper; 2 (a f-d e l i n g) section, clause [of a law]; 3 (i n w o o r d e n b o e k) entry; 4 $ article, commodity; (b e p a a l d s o o r t) line; ~*en* $ *ook*: goods, [own brand] items [at a supermarket];

ar'tikelsgewijs, –gewijze by clause
artille'rie [ɑrtılə'ri. of -ti.jə-] (-ieën) *v* artillery, ordnance; *rijdende* ~ horse artillery; **artille'rist** (-en) *m* artilleryman, gunner
'Artis *v* the Amsterdam Zoo
arti'sjok (-ken) *v* artichoke
artistici'teit *v* artistry; **artis'tiek** artistic; **artis'tiekerig F** arty
arts (-en) *m* physician, general practioner; **–enbezoeker** (-s) *m* pharmaceutical representative, salesman; **artse'nij** (-en) *v* medicine, physic; **–bereidkunde** *v* pharmaceutics, pharmacy
a.s. = *aanstaande* **I**
1 as (-sen) *v* 1 axle, axle-tree [of a carriage]; 2 axis [of the earth & *fig, mv* axes]; 3 𝕏 shaft; arbor; spindle; *vervoer per* ~ road transport
2 as *v* ash [= powdery residue, also of a cigar], ashes [ook = remains of human body]; [hot] embers; cinders; ~ *is verbrande turf* if ifs and ans were pots and pans; *in de* ~ *leggen* lay in ashes, reduce to ashes; *uit zijn* ~ *verrijzen* rise from its ashes; zie ook: *rusten*; **–bak** (-ken) *m* 1 ash-tray; 2 (v u i l n i s b a k) ash-bin; **–belt** (-en) *m* & *v* ash-pit, refuse dump
as'best *o* asbestos
'asblond ash-blond(e)
as'ceet [ɑ'se.t, ɑs'ke.t] (-ceten) *m* ascetic; **as'cese** [ɑ'se.zə, ɑs'ke.zə] *v* asceticism; **as'cetisch** [ɑ'se.ti.s, ɑs'ke.ti.s] ascetic
ascor'binezuur [ɑskɔr-] *o* ascorbic acid
'asem *m* **F** *geen* ~ *geven* keep silent, keep mum, not breathe a word
a'septisch aseptic
'asfalt (-en) *o* asphalt, bitumen; **asfal'teren** (asfalteerde, h. geasfalteerd) *vt* asphalt; **'asfaltpapier** *o* bituminized (asphalt) paper; **–weg** (-wegen) *m* asphalt (bituminous) road
'asgrauw ashen(-grey), ashy
a'siel [s = z] (-en) *o* asylum; home; shelter; *politiek* ~ political asylum; **a'sielrecht** *o* right of asylum
asje'blief(t) [ɑʃə'bli.f(t)] 1 (e n o f!) I should think so!, you bet!; (n e e m a a r!) well now!, my word!; 2 = *alstublieft*
asjeme'nou! *ij* **F** good heavens!
'asmogendheden *mv* ☖ Axis powers
asoci'aal [-si.'a.l] antisocial, unsocial
as'pect (-en) *o* aspect
as'perge [g = ʒ] (-s) *v* asparagus
aspi'rant (-en) *m* applicant; candidate
aspi'ratie [-(t)si.] (-s) *v* aspiration, ambition
Ⓦ aspi'rine (-s) *v* aspirin
assem'blage [ɑsɑm'bla.ʒə] *v* (car) assembly; **–bedrijf** (-drijven) *o* (car) assembly plant
assem'blee [ɑsɑm-] (-s) *v* assembly [of UNO]
assem'bleren [ɑsɑm-] (assembleerde, h. geassembleerd) *vt* assemble [cars]

'Assepoester, 'assepoes(ter) *v* Cinderella²
assimi'latie [-(t)si.] (-s) *v* assimilation; **assimi'leren** (assimileerde, h. geassimileerd) *vt* assimilate
assi'stent (-en) *m* assistant; **–e** (-n) *v* assistant, lady help; **–ie** [-(t)si.] *v* assistance, help; **assi'steren** (assisteerde, h. geassisteerd) *vt* & *va* assist
associ'atie [-(t)si.] (-s) *v* association°; $ partnership; **associ'é** (-s) *m* $ partner; **associ'ëren** (associeerde, h. geassocieerd) *zich* ~ $ enter into partnership (with *met*)
assorti'ment (-en) *o* assortment
assura'deur (-en en -s) *m* insurer; ⚓ underwriter; **assu'rantie** [-(t)si.] (-iën en -s) *v* 1 [fire, accident] insurance; 2 [life] assurance; **–bezorger** (-s) *m* insurance agent; **–premie** (-s) *v* (insurance) premium; **assu'reren** (assureerde, h. geassureerd) *vt* 1 insure, effect an insurance [against fire]; 2 assure [one's life]
As'syrië [y = i.] *o* Assyria; **–r** (-s) *m* Assyrian; **As'syrisch** *aj* & *o* Assyrian
'aster (-s) *v* aster
'astma *o* asthma; **–lijder** (-s) *m* asthmatic (patient); **ast'matisch** asthmatic
astrolo'gie *v* astrology; **astro'logisch** astrological; **astro'loog** (-logen) *m* astrologer
astro'naut (-en) *m* astronaut
astrono'mie *v* astronomy; **astro'nomisch** astronomical [figures], astronomic; **astro'noom** (-nomen) *m* astronomer
'asvaalt (-en) *v* = *asbelt*
'aswenteling (-en) *v* rotation
As'woensdag *m* Ash Wednesday
asym'metrisch [y = i.] asymmetric(al), dissymmetric
at (aten) V.T. v. *eten*
ata'visme (-n) *o* atavism, throw-back; **–istisch** atavistic
atelier [ɑtəl'je.] (-s) *o* 1 studio; atelier [of an artist]; 2 workshop, work-room [of an artisan]
'aten V.T. meerv. v. *eten*
'aterling (-en) *m* disgusting fellow
A'theens Athenian
athe'isme *o* atheism; **–ïst** (-en) *m* atheist; **–'ïstisch** atheistic
A'thene *o* Athens; **A'thener** (-s) *m* Athenian
athe'neum [a.tə'ne.üm] (-s en -nea) *o* ⚐ ± secondary modern school
At'lantische Oce'aan *m* Atlantic (Ocean)
'atlas (-sen) *m* atlas
at'leet (-leten) *m* athlete; **atle'tiek I** *v* athletics; **at'letisch** athletic
atmos'feer (-feren) *v* atmosphere; **atmos'ferisch** atmospheric; ~*e storing* static
a'tol (-len) *o* atoll

a'tomisch atomic
ato'naal atonal
a'toom (atomen) *o* atom; **a'toom-** atomic,
nuclear; **a'toombom** (-men) *v* atom bomb,
atomic bomb; **–centrale** (-s) *v* atomic power-
station; **–energie** [-*gi.* of -ʒi.] *v* atomic energy;
–gewicht (-en) *o* atomic weight; **–kern** (-en)
v atomic nucleus [*mv* nuclei]; **–kop** (-pen) *m*
atomic war-head; **–proef** (-proeven) *v* atomic
(nuclear) test; **–splitsing** *v* fission; **–tijdperk** *o*
atomic age; **–wapen** (-s) *o* nuclear weapon
atro'fie *v* atrophy; **atrofi'ëren** (atrofieerde, *vt*
h., *vi* is geatrofieerd) *vi* & *vt* atrophy
atta'ché [ch = ʃ] (-s) *m* attaché
atten'deren (attendeerde, h. geattendeerd) *vt* ~
op draw attention to; **at'tent** 1 (o p l e t t e n d)
attentive; 2 (v o l a t t e n t i e s) considerate (to
voor), thoughtful (of, for *voor*); *iem.* ~ *maken op*
draw sbd.'s attention to; **–ie** [-(t)si.] (-s) *v* 1
attention; 2 consideration, thoughtfulness
at'test (-en) *o* certificate; (g e t u i g s c h r i f t)
testimonial; **attes'tatie** [-(t)si.] (-s) *v* attesta-
tion; testimonial, certificate
at'tractie [ɑ'trɑksi.] (-s) *v* attraction; **attrac'tief**
attractive; **attractivi'teit** *v* attractiveness
attri'buut (-buten) *o* attribute
au! [ɔu] ouch!, ow!
a.u.b. = *alstublieft*
au'bade [au = o.] (-s) *v* aubade
audi'ëntie [o.-, ɔudi.'ɪn(t)si.] (-s) *v* audience; ~
aanvragen bij ask (request) an audience of; ~
verlenen grant an audience; *op* ~ *gaan bij de*
minister have an audience of the minister
'audio-visu'eel [s = z] audio-visual
audi'teren [au = ɔu en o.] (auditeerde, h.
geauditeerd) *vi* audition; **au'ditie**
[ɔu'di.(t)si., o.-] (-s) *v* audition
audi'torium [au = ɔu en o.] (-s en -ria) *o* 1
auditory [= part of building & assembly of
listeners]; 2 audience [= assembly of listeners]
'Augiasstal *de* ~ *reinigen* clean the Augean
stables
au'gurk (-en) *v* gherkin
augus'tijn (-en) *m* Augustinian, Austin friar;
(t y p o g r a f i e) cicero
au'gustus *m* August
'aula ('s) *v* auditorium
au 'pair [o.'pɪːr] au pair
aure'ool [au = ɔu en o.] (-reolen) *v* aureole,
halo
aus'piciën *mv onder de* ~ *van* under the auspices
of, sponsored by; under the aegis of
Aus'tralië *o* Australia; **Aus'traliër** (-s) *m*
Australian; **Aus'tralisch** Australian
'autaar ['ɔuta:r] = *altaar*
autar'kie *v* autarky, self-sufficiency;
au'tarkisch autarkic(al), selfsufficient

au'teur [au = o. en ɔu] (-s) *m* author; **–srecht** *o*
copyright
authentici'teit [au = ɔu en o.] *v* authenticity;
authen'tiek authentic
au'tisme *o ps* autism; **–istisch** autistic
'auto [au = ɔu en o.] ('s) *m* car, motor-car;
–band (-en) *m* (automobile, motor) tyre;
–bezitter (-s) *m* car owner
autobiogra'fie (-ieën) *v* autobiography;
autobio'grafisch autobiographical
'autobus [au = o. en ɔu] (-sen) *m* & *v* motor-
bus, coach
'autocoureur ['o.to.-, 'ɔuto.ku:rør] (-s) *m* =
coureur 1
auto'craat (-craten) *m* autocrat; **autocra'tie**
[-'(t)si.] (-ieën) *v* autocracy; **auto'cratisch**
autocratic
autodi'dact (-en) *m* autodidact, self-taught man
auto'geen autogenous [welding]
auto'gram (-men) *o* autograph
'autokerkhof [au = o. en ɔu] (-hoven) *o* car
dump
auto'maat [au = ɔu en o.] (-maten) automatic
machine, [cigarette, stamp, ticket &] machine,
penny-in-the-slot machine, slot-machine,
vending machine; **automa'tiek** (-en) *v*
automat; **auto'matisch** automatic, self-acting;
~*e handeling* automatism; **automati'seren**
[s = z] (automatiseerde, h. geautomatiseerd) *vt*
automate, computerize; **–ring** *v* automation,
computerization; **automa'tisme** (-n) *o* automatism
automo'biel [au = o. en ɔu] (-en) *m* motor-car,
Am automobile; **automobi'lisme** *o* motoring;
–ist (-en) *m* motorist
'automonteur [au = ɔu en o.] (-s) *m* motor
mechanic
autono'mie [au = ɔu en o.] *v* autonomy;
auto'noom autonomous, autonomic
'autonummer [au = o. en ɔu] (-s) *o* registration number, car number; **–park** (-en) *o* 1
(t e r r e i n) car park; 2 (d e a u t o's) fleet of
(motor-)cars; **–pech** *m* car breakdown; **–ped**
(-s) *m* scooter; **–radio** ('s) *m* car radio; **–rijden**
I (reed 'auto, h. 'autogereden) *vi* drive [a car],
motor; II *o* motoring; **–rijder** (-s) *m* motorist;
–rijschool (-scholen) *v* driving-school, school
of motoring
autori'seren [s = z] (autoriseerde, h. geautori-
seerd) *vt* authorize
autori'tair [ɔu-, o.to.ri.'tɪːr] authoritative [air,
manner, tones], officious; (i n z. ± n i e t-
d e m o c r a t i s c h) authoritarian [regime,
State]; **autori'teit** (-en) *v* authority°
'autoslaaptrein [au = o. en ɔu] (-en) *m* car
sleeper train; **–snelweg** (-wegen) *m Br*
motorway, *Am* super highway, turnpike;

–tentoonstelling (-en) *v* motor show; **–verhuur** *m* car hire; ~ *zonder chauffeur* self-drive (car hire); **–verkeer** *o* motor traffic; **–weg** (-wegen) *m* motorway, motor road; **–wrak** (-ken) *o* car wreck

a'val *o* guarantee [of a bill]; *voor* ~ *tekenen* guarantee

a'vances [a.'vãsǝs] *mv* advances, approaches, overtures

avant-'garde [a.vã'gɑrdǝ] **I** *v* avant-garde; **II** *aj* avant-garde; **avant-gar'distisch** avant-garde

'avegaar (-s) *m* auger

'averechts I *aj* purl [stitch]; *fig* wrong [way, ideas &]; preposterous [means]; **II** *ad* wrongly, the wrong way (round); ~ *breien* purl

ave'rij *v* damage; ~ *grosse* general average; ~ *particulier* particular average; ~ *krijgen* 1 suffer damage; 2 break down

a'versie [s = z] *v* aversion

'avond (-en) *m* evening, night; *de* ~ *te voren* the evening (night) before; *de* ~ *vóór de slag* the eve of the battle; *des* ~*s,* *'s* ~*s* 1 (t ij d) in the evening, at night; 2 (g e w o o n t e) of an evening; *b ij* ~ in the evening, at night; *t e g e n de* ~ towards evening; *het wordt* ~ night is falling; **–blad** (-bladen) *o* evening paper; **–cursus** [-züs] (-sen) *m* evening-classes; **–eten** *o* supper; **–gebed** (-beden) *o* night prayers; **–japon** (-nen) *m* evening gown (frock); **–je**

(-s) *o* evening (party); *een gezellig* ~ a social evening; *een* ~ *uit* a night out; **–kleding** *v* evening dress; **–klok** *v* curfew; *de* ~ *instellen* impose a curfew; **–land** *o* Occident; **–maal** *o* supper, evening-meal; *het Avondmaal* the Lord's Supper, Holy Communion; *het Laatste Avondmaal* the Last Supper; **–rood** *o* afterglow, red evening-sky; **–schemering** *v* evening twilight; **–school** (-scholen) *v* night-school, evening school, evening classes; **–ster** *v* evening star; **–stond** (-en) *m* evening (hour); **–voorstelling** (-en) *v* evening performance

avon'turen (-tuurde, h. ge-tuurd) *vt* risk, venture; **avontu'rier** (-s) *m* adventurer; **avon'tuur** (-turen) *o* adventure; **–lijk I** *aj* adventurous [life]; risky [plan &]; *een* ~ *leven* ook: a life of adventures; **II** *ad* adventurously

à 'vue [a.'vy.] at sight

axi'oma ('s) *o* axiom

a'zalea ('s) *v* azalea

'azen (aasde, h. geaasd) *vi* ~ *op* [*fig*] covet

Azi'aat (-iaten) *m* Asian, Asiatic; **Azi'atisch** Asian, Asiatic; **'Azië** *o* Asia

a'zijn (-en) *m* vinegar; **–zuur** *o* acetic acid

'azimut *o* azimuth

A'zoren *mv de* ~ the Azores

a'zuren *aj* azure, sky-blue; **a'zuur** *o* azure, sky blue

B

b [be.] ('s) *v* b

ba [bɑ] *ij* bah!, pooh!, pshaw!, pah!; zie ook *boe*

'baadje (-s) *o* (sailor's) jacket; *iem. op zijn ~ geven* **F** dust (trim) sbd.'s jacket

baai (-en) 1 *v* (i n h a m) bay ‖ 2 *m & o* (s t o f) baize ‖ 3 *m* (t a b a k) cross-cut Maryland; **–en** *aj* baize

'baaierd *m* chaos, welter

baak (baken) *v* = *baken*

baal (balen) *v* 1 (g e p e r s t) bale [of cotton &]; (g e s t o r t) bag [of rice &]; 2 ten reams [of paper]; *(de) balen (tabak) van iets hebben* = *balen*

'Baäl *m* Baal

baan (banen) *v* 1 path, way, road; 2 (r e n - b a a n) (race-)course, (running) track; 3 (l o o p b a a n) orbit [of planet, (earth) satellite]; trajectory [of projectile]; 4 (t e n n i s~) court; 5 (v. s p o o r w e g) track; 6 (v. a u t o w e g, *sp* v. z w e m b a s s i n &) lane; 7 (i j s~) (skating) rink; 8 (g l ij~) slide; 9 (k e g e l~) alley; 10 (s t r o o k) breadth, width [of cloth &]; 11 (v. v l a g) stripe; 12 = *baantje*; *zich ~ breken* make (push, force) one's way; *fig* ook: gain ground; *ruim ~ maken* clear the way; ● *in een ~ brengen* put into orbit, orbit [an artificial satellite]; *in een ~ draaien* orbit; *in een ~ (om de aarde) komen* come into orbit; *vlucht in een ~* orbital flight; *het gesprek in andere banen leiden* turn the conversation into other channels; *op de lange ~ schuiven* put off (indefinitely), shelve, postpone; *dat is nu van de ~* that question has been shelved, that's off now;
–brekend pioneer [work], epoch-making [discovery]; **–breker** (-s) *m* pioneer, pathfinder; **–schuiver** (-s) *m* fender, track-clearer; **'baantje** (-s) *o* 1 slide [on snow]; 2 job; billet, berth; *een gemakkelijk (lui) ~* **F** a soft job; **'baantjesjager** (-s) *m* place-hunter; **'baanvak** (-ken) *o* section [of a railroad line]; **–veger** (-s) *m* sweeper; **–wachter** (-s) *m* signalman

baar (baren) **I** *v* 1 (g o l f) wave, billow ‖ 2 (l ij k ~) bier; 3 (d r a a g~) litter, stretcher ‖ 4 (s t a a f) bar, ingot ‖ 5 (z a n d b a n k) bar; **II** als *aj ~ geld* ready money

baard (-en) *m* beard [of man, animals, grasses &]; barb, wattle [of a fish]; feather [of a quill]; whiskers [of a cat]; whalebone, baleen [of a whale]; bit [of a key]; *een ~ van een week* a week's growth of beard; *hij heeft de ~ in de keel* his voice is breaking; *iets in zijn ~ brommen* mutter something in one's beard; *zijn ~ laten staan* grow a beard; *om 's keizers ~ spelen* play

for love; zie ook: 2 *mop*; **–aap** (-apen) **F** *m* beaver; **–eloos** beardless; **–ig** bearded

'baarlijk *de ~e duivel* the devil himself; *~e nonsens* utter (rank) nonsense, gibberish

'baarmoeder (-s) *v* womb, uterus

baars (baarzen) *m* perch, bass

baas (bazen) *m* **I** master; foreman [in a factory]; **F** boss; 2 (a l s a a n s p r e k i n g) **P** governor, mister; *de ~* **F** the old man [at the office &]; *is de ~* **F** is your man [= husband] in?; *een leuke ~* 1 **F** a funny chap; 2 **F** a jolly buffer; *het is een ~ hoor!* **F** what a whopper!; *hij is de ~ (van het spul)* **F** he runs the show; *hij is een ~* he is a dab (at *in*); *zijn vrouw is de ~* the wife wears the breeches; *de ~ blijven* remain top dog; *de ~ spelen* lord it (over), overbear; *om de inflatie de ~ te worden* to get inflation under control; *de socialisten zijn de ~ (geworden)* the socialists are in control, have gained control; *zij werden ons de ~* they got the better of us; *hij is mij de ~* he beats me [in...]; *he is one too many for me*, he has the whip hand of me; *er is altijd ~ boven ~* a man always finds his master; *zijn eigen ~ zijn* be one's own master

baat (baten) *v* **I** (v o o r d e e l) profit, benefit; 2 (g e n e z i n g) relief; *te ~ nemen* avail oneself of, take [the opportunity]; use, employ [means]; *~ vinden bij* be benefited by, derive benefit from; *zonder ~* without avail; zie ook: *bate* & 2 *baten*; **–zucht** *v* selfishness, self-interest; **baat'zuchtig** selfish, self-interested

'babbel (-s) *m* 1 (p e r s o o n) chatterbox; 2 (b a b b e l t j e) chat; **–aar** (-s) *m* 1 tattler; chatterbox, gossip; telltale; 2 (s n o e p) bull's-eye; **–achtig** talkative; **'babbelen** (babbelde, h. gebabbeld) *vi* 1 chatter, babble, prattle, tittle, chit-chat; 2 talk (in class); 3 tittle-tattle, gossip; **'babbeltje** (-s) *o* chat; **'babbelziek** talkative; **–zucht** *v* talkativeness

'Babel *o* Babel

'baby ('s) ['be.bi.] *m* baby; **–box** (-en) *m* playpen

'Babylon [y = i] *o* Babylon; **Baby'loniër** (-s) *m* Babylonian; **Baby'lonisch** Babylonian [captivity, exile]; *een ~e spraakverwarring* a perfect Babel

'babysit(ter) ['be.bi.-] (-s) *m-v* baby-sitter; **'babysitten** *vi* baby-sit; **'babyuitzet** (-ten) *m & o* baby linen, layette

baccalaure'aat *o* baccalaureate, bachelor's degree

baccha'naal [bɑgɑ.-] (-nalen) *o* bacchanal

ba'cil (-len) *m* bacillus [*mv* bacilli]; **–lendrager**

(-s) *m* (germ-)carrier

back [bɪk] (-s) *m sp* back

'bacon ['be.kən] *o* & *m* bacon

bac'terie (-iën) *v* bacterium [*mv* bacteria]; **bacteri'eel** bacterial; **bacteriolo'gie** *v* bacteriology; **bacterio'logisch** bacteriological; **bacterio'loog** (-logen) *m* bacteriologist

1 bad (baden) *o* bath [= vessel, or room for bathing in]; *een ∼ geven* bath [the baby]; *een ∼ nemen* have (take) a bath [in the bathroom]; have (take) a bathe [in the sea, river]

2 bad (baden) V.T. v. *bidden*

'badcel (-len) *v* shower cabinet; **1 baden** (baadde, h. gebaad) **I** *vi* bathe²; *in bloed ∼* bathe in blood; **II** *vt* bath [a child]; **III** *vr zich ∼* bathe [= take a bath or bathe]; *(zich) in tranen ∼* be bathed in tears; *(zich) in weelde ∼* be rolling in luxury

2 'baden V.T. meerv. v. *bidden*

3 'baden meerv. v. 1 *bad*

'badgast (-en) *m* visitor [at a watering place; at a seaside resort]; **–handdoek** (-en) *m* bath towel; **–hokje** (-s) *o* bathing box; **–huis** (-huizen) *o*, **–inrichting** (-en) *v* (public) baths; **–jas** (-sen) *m* & *v* bathing wrap; **–kamer** (-s) *v* bathroom; **–kuip** (-en) *v* bath, bath-tub; **–mantel** (-s) *m* bathing wrap; **–meester** (-s) *m* bath(s) superintendent; **–muts** (-en) *v* bathing cap; **–pak** (-ken) *o* bathing suit; **–plaats** (-en) *v* (n i e t a a n z e e) spa, watering place; (a a n z e e) seaside resort; **–schuim** *o* foam bath, bath foam, bubble bath; **–seizoen** (-en) *o* bathing season; **–spons** (-en en -sponzen) *v* bath sponge; **–stof** *v* towelling, terry (cloth); **–water** *o* bath-water; *het kind met het ∼ wegwerpen* throw out the baby with the bath-water; **–zeep** *v* bath soap; **–zout** (-en) *o* bath salts

ba'gage [-'ga.ʒə] *v* luggage; ook: (🚢 en vooral *Am*) baggage; **–bureau** [-by.ro.] (-s) *o* luggage office; **–depot** [-de.po.] (-s) *o* & *m* cloak-room; **–drager** (-s) *m* (luggage) carrier; **–net** (-ten) *o* (luggage) rack; **–reçu** [-rəsy.] ('s) *o* luggage ticket; **–ruimte** *v* 🚢 boot; **–wagen** (-s) *m* luggage van

baga'tel (-len) *v* & *o* trifle, bagatelle, fillip; **bagatelli'seren** [s = z] (bagatelliseerde, h. gebagatelliseerd) *vt* make light of [a matter]; minimize [the gravity of ..., its importance], play down

'bagger *v* mud, slush; **'baggeren** (baggerde, h. gebaggerd) **I** *vt* dredge; **II** *vi door de modder ∼* wade through the mud; **'baggerlaarzen** *mv* waders; **–machine** [-ma.ʃi.nə] (-s) *v* dredging machine, dredger; **–molen** (-s) *m* dredger; **–schuit** (-en) *v* dredge, mud-barge

bah! [bɑ] bah!, pooh!, pshaw!, pah!

'Bahrein *o* Bahrain

'baileybrug ['be.li.-] (-gen) *v* Bailey bridge

'baisse ['bɛ.sə] *v* fall; *à la ∼ speculeren* speculate for a fall, sell short, bear; **baissi'er** [bɛ.si.'e.] (-s) *m* bear

'bajes *v in de ∼* **S** in quod, in the nick, in jug; **–klant** (-en) *m* jail bird

bajo'net (-ten) *v* bayonet; *met gevelde ∼* with fixed bayonets; **–sluiting** (-en) *v* bayonet catch (joint)

bak (-ken) *m* 1 trough [for animal food, mortar &]; cistern, tank [for water]; bin [for dust]; bucket [of a dredging-machine]; basket [for bread]; tray [in a trunk]; body [of a carriage]; 2 = **F** 2 *mop*

'bakbeest (-en) *o* colossus

'bakblik (-ken) *o* baking tin

'bakboord *o* port; *aan ∼* port-side, to port; *iem. van ∼ naar stuurboord zenden* send sbd. from pillar to post

'baken (-s) *o* beacon; *als ∼ dienen* beacon; *de ∼s verzetten* change one's policy, change one's tack; *de ∼s zijn verzet* times have changed; **–licht** (-en) *o* beacon light

'baker (-s) *v* monthly nurse, (dry-)nurse; **'bakeren** (bakerde, h. gebakerd) **I** *vt* swaddle; **II** *vr zich ∼* bask [in the sun]; **III** *vi uit ∼ gaan* go out nursing; zie ook: *gebakerd*; **'bakerkind** (-eren) *o* infant in arms; **–mat** (-ten) *v* cradle² [of freedom]; **–praat** *m* old wives' tales, gossip; **–rijmpje** (-s) *v* nursery rhyme; **–speld** (-en) *v* large safety-pin; **–sprookje** (-s) *o* nursery tale, old wives' tale

'bakfiets (-en) *m* & *v* carrier tricycle, carrier cycle

'bakje (-s) *o* **F** cup [of coffee]

'bakkebaard (-en) *m* (side-)whisker(s)

bakke'leien (bakkeleide, h. gebakkeleid) *vi* tussle, be at loggerheads

'bakken* **I** *vt* (i n o v e n) bake; (i n p a n) fry; *iem. een poets ∼* play sbd. a trick; **II** *va* 1 make bread; 2 🖐 fail [in an examination], **S** plough; *laten ∼* **S** pluck [sbd.], plough [sbd.]; **III** *vi* bake [bread]; *aan de pan ∼* stick to the pan; **'bakker** (-s) *m* baker; **bakke'rij** (-en) *v* bakery, bakehouse; baker's shop; **'bakkersknecht** (-s en -en) *m* baker's man; **–tor** (-ren) *v* cockroach; **–winkel** (-s) *m* baker's shop

'bakkes (-en) *o* **P** mug, **F** phiz; *hou je ∼ !* **F** shut up!

'bakoven (-s) *m* (baking) oven; **–pan** (-nen) *v* frying-pan; **–plaat** (-platen) *v* baking sheet; **–poeder** *o* & *m* baking powder; **–sel** (-s) *o* batch, baking; **–steen** (-stenen) *o* & *m* brick; *drijven (zinken) als een ∼* float (sink) like a stone; *zakken als een ∼* fail ignominiously [in one's exam]; **–stenen** *aj* brick; **–vis** (-sen) *v* teen-ager (girl)

'bakzeil ~ *halen* ⚓ back the sails; *fig* back down, climb down

1 bal (-len) *m* ball [also of the foot]; bowl [solid, of wood]; (t e e l ~) testicle; *de* ~ *misslaan* miss the ball; *fig* be beside (wide of) the mark; *de* ~ *aan het rollen brengen* set the ball rolling; *er geen* ~ *van weten* **S** not know the first thing about it; *geen* ~ *geven om* **S** not care a rap (damn, fig)

2 bal (-s) *o* ball; ~ *masqué* masked ball

balan'ceren (balanceerde, h. gebalanceerd) *vt & vi* balance, poise; **ba'lans** (-en) *v* 1 (w e e g s c h a a l) balance, (pair of) scales; 2 ✗ beam; 3 $ balance-sheet; *de* ~ *opmaken* 1 $ draw up the balance-sheet; 2 *fig* strike a balance; **–opruiming** (-en) *v* clearance sale

'balboekje (-s) *o* (ball) programme, (dance) card

bal'dadig wanton; **–heid** (-heden) *v* wantonness; *hij deed het uit louter* ~ he did it out of pure mischief

balda'kijn (-s en -en) *o & m* canopy, baldachin

'balderen (balderde, h. gebalderd) *vi* court, display, call

Bale'arisch *de* ~*e Eilanden* the Balearic Islands

ba'lein (-en) 1 *o* (v. w a l v i s) whalebone, baleen; 2 *v* (v. k o r s e t) busk; *de* ~*en* ook: the steels [of a corset], the ribs [of an umbrella]

'balen (baalde, h. gebaald) *vi* ~ *van iets* **F** be fed up with sth., be sick of sth., pall with sth.

balg (-en) *m* bellows [of a camera]

'balie (-s) *v* 1 bar; 2 (v. k a n t o o r) counter; 3 (v. b r u g) railing, parapet; *tot de* ~ *toegelaten worden* be called to the bar; **–kluiver** (-s) *m* loafer

'baljapon (-nen) *m* ball dress

'baljuw (-s) *m* bailiff; **–schap** (-pen) *o* bailiwick

balk (-en) *m* beam; ♩ staff, stave; ∅ bar; *dat mag wel aan de* ~ it is to be marked with a white stone; *het over de* ~ *gooien* play ducks and drakes with one's money; *het niet over de* ~ *gooien* be rather close-fisted

'Balkan *m de* ~ the Balkans; *het* ~*schiereiland* the Balkan peninsula; *de* ~*staten* the Balkan States

'balken (balkte, h. gebalkt) *vi* bray; *fig* bawl

bal'kon (-s) *o* 1 (a a n h u i s) balcony; 2 (v. t r a m) platform; 3 (i n s c h o u w b u r g) balcony, dress circle

bal'lade (-s en -n) *v* 1 ballad; 2 [mediaeval French] ballade

'ballast *m* ballast

'ballen (balde, h. gebald) **I** *vi* 1 ball [= grow into a lump]; 2 play at ball; **II** *vt* ball; *de vuist* ~ clench, double one's fist; **'ballenjongen** (-s) *m* ball boy

balle'rina ('s) *v* ballerina; **bal'let** *o* ballet; **–danser** (-s) *m* ballet dancer; **–danseres** (-sen) *v* ballet dancer, ballet girl

'balletje (-s) *o* small ball; *een* ~ *over iets opgooien* **F** fly a kite, throw out a feeler

bal'letmeester (-s) *m* ballet master; **–school** (-scholen) *v* ballet school

'balling (-en) *m* exile; **–schap** *v* exile, banishment

ballis'tiek *v* ballistics; **bal'listisch** ballistic

bal'lon (-s en -nen) *m* 1 (l u c h t b a l) balloon; 2 (v. l a m p) globe; **–band** (-en) *m* balloon tire; **–vaarder** (-s) *m* balloonist; **–vaart** (-en) *v* balloon flight

ballo'tage [-'ta.ʒə] (-s) *v* ballot(ing), voting by ballot; **ballo'teren** (balloteerde, h. geballoteerd) *vt* ballot, vote by ballot

ba'lorig petulant, cross; *er* ~ *van worden* get out of all patience with it; **–heid** *v* petulance

'balpen (-nen) *m* ballpoint, ball-point pen

balsa'mine (-n) *v* = *balsemien*

'balsem (-s) *m* balm²; balsam; **'balsemen** (balsemde, h. gebalsemd) *vt* embalm²

balse'mien (-en) *v* balsam

'balspel (-spelen) *o* ball game

bal'sturig obstinate, refractory, intractable, stubborn

'Baltisch Baltic; *de* ~*e Zee* the Baltic

balu'strade (-s en -n) *v* balustrade [of a terrace &]; banisters [of a staircase]

'balzaal (-zalen) *v* ball-room

'balzak (-ken) *m* scrotum

'bamboe *o & m, aj* bamboo

ban (-nen) *m* excommunication; *in de* ~ *doen* (k e r k e l ij k) excommunicate; *fig* put (place) under a ban, proscribe, ostracize; *in de* ~ *van haar schoonheid* under the spell of her beauty

ba'naal banal, trite, commonplace

ba'naan (-nanen) *v* banana

banali'teit (-en) *v* banality, platitude

ba'naneschil (-len) *v* banana skin (peel)

'banbliksem (-s) *m* anathema, excommunication

1 band *o* (s t o f n a a m) tape; ribbon

2 band (-en) *m* 1 tie [for fastening], tape [used in dressmaking and for parcels, documents, sound recording]; fillet, braid [for the hair]; string [of an apron, bonnet &]; 2 (d r a a g- b a n d) sling [for injured arm &]; (b r e u k- b a n d) truss; 3 (o m a r m, h o e d &)-band; 4 (o m t e v e r b i n d e n) bandage; 5 (v. t o n) hoop; (v. a u t o, f i e t s) tyre; 7 ♂ cushion; 8 (i n d e a n a t o m i e) ligament; 9 (v. b o e k) binding; cover; (l o s) case; [ring, spring] binder; 10 (b o e k d e e l) volume; 11 R [frequency, wave] band; 12 *fig* tie [of blood, friendship], bond [of love, captivity &], link [with the people, with home]; [political] affiliation; *lopende* ~ ✗ conveyor (belt); assembly line; *aan de lopende* ~

[murders, novels &] one after another; *iem.*
a a n ~en leggen put a restraint on sbd.; *aan de ~
liggen* be tied up; *u i t de ~ springen* kick over the
traces

3 band [bɪnt] (-s) *m ♪* band

'**bandelichter** (-s) *m* tyre lever

bande'lier (-s en -en) *m* shoulder-belt, bandoleer

'**bandeloos** lawless, licentious, riotous

'**bandenspanning** *v* tyre pressure

'**bandepech** *m* puncture, tyre trouble

bande'rol (-rollen) *v* band [for cigar]; **ban-
derol'leren** (banderolleerde, h. gebande-
rolleerd) *vt* band [cigars]

ban'diet (-en) *m* bandit, ruffian, brigand

'**bandijzer** *o* bale tie, metal strapping

bandi'tisme *o* banditry

'**bandjir** (-s) *m Ind* spate

'**bandopname** (-n en -s) *v* tape recording;
–opnemer (-s), **–recorder** [-rikɔrdər] (-s) *m*
tape recorder

'**banen** (baande, h. gebaand) *vt een weg ~* clear
(break) a way; *nieuwe wegen ~* break new
ground; *de weg ~ voor* pave the way for; *zich een
weg ~ door* make (force, push) one's way
through; *zich al strijdend een weg ~* fight one's
way; zie ook: *gebaand*

bang I *aj* afraid [a l l é é n p r e d i k a t i e f];
fearful; (s c h u c h t e r) timorous, timid;
(o n g e r u s t) anxious; *~ voor* 1 afraid of
[death, tigers &], in fear of [a person]; 2 afraid
for, fearing for [one's life]; *daar ben ik niet ~
voor* I'm not afraid of that; *~ maken* frighten,
make afraid, scare; *~ zijn* be afraid; *~ zijn om...*
be afraid to..., fear to...; *~ zijn dat* be afraid
that, fear that; *wees maar niet ~!* ook: no fear!;
zie ook: *dood*; *zo ~ als een wezel* as timid as a
hare; **II** *ad* fearfully &; **–erd** (-s) *m*, **–erik**
(-riken) *m* coward, **S** funk

'**Bangla'desh** *o* Bangladesh

bangmake'rij *v* intimidation

ba'nier (-en) *v* banner, standard

'**banjir** = *bandjir*

'**banjo** ('s) *m* banjo

bank (-en) *v* 1 (z i t ~) bench, [garden] seat; 2
(v . b a n k s t e l) settee; 3 (s c h o o l ~) desk;
4 (k e r k b a n k) pew; 5 (m i s t-, z a n d-
b a n k &) bank; 6 **$** bank; *~ van lening* pawn-
shop; *de ~ houden* keep (hold) the bank; *door de
~ (genomen)* on the average; **–bediende** (-n en
-s) *m-v* bank clerk (official); **–biljet** (-ten) *o*
bank-note; **–breuk** (-en) *v* bankruptcy; *bedrieg-
lijke ~* fraudulent bankruptcy; **–directeur**
(-en) *m* bank manager; **–disconto** ('s) *o* bank
rate, bank discount

ban'ket (-ten) *o* 1 (g a s t m a a l) banquet [=
dinner with speeches &]; 2 (g e b a k) (fancy)

cakes, pastry; (m e t a m a n d e l p e r s)
almound pastry; **–bakker** (-s) *m* confectioner;
banketbakke'rij (-en) *v* confectioner's
(shop); **banket'teren** (banketteerde, h. geban-
ketteerd) *vi* banquet, feast

'**bankgeheim** *o* banking secrecy; **–houder** (-s)
m 1 *sp* banker; 2 (v . p a n d h u i s) pawnbroker; **ban'kier** (-s) *m* banker; **–shuis**
(-huizen) *o* banking house; '**bankinstelling**
(-en) *v* banking house; '**bankje** (-s) *o* 1 small
bench, stool; 2 banknote; '**bankkluis**
(-kluizen) *v* bank vault, strongroom; **–krediet**
(-en) *o* bank credit (loan); **–loper** (-s) *m* bank
messenger; **–overval** (-len) *m* bank raid;
–papier *o* paper currency, bank-notes; **–rekening** (-en) *v* bank(ing) account

bank'roet (-en) *o* bankruptcy, failure; *~ gaan*
become a bankrupt, go bankrupt; *frauduleus ~*
fraudulent bankruptcy; **bankroe'tier** (-s) *m*
bankrupt

'**banksaldo** ('s en -di) *o* balance [with a bank];
–schroef (-schroeven) *v* vice; **–stel** (-len) *o*
lounge suite, three-piece suite; **–werker** (-s) *m*
fitter, bench hand; **II** *ad* < awfully, very
–wezen *o* banking

'**banneling** (-en) *m* exile; '**bannen*** *vt* 1 (v e r-
b a n n e n) banish[2], exile; 2 (u i t d r i j v e n)
exorcise [evil spirits]

'**bantamgewicht** *o* bantam weight

'**banvloek** (-en) *m* anathema, ban

bap'tist (-en) *m* baptist

1 bar (-s) *m &* *v* bar

2 bar I *aj* barren [tract of land]; inclement
[weather]; biting [cold]; rough [manner]; *het is
~* it's a bit thick; **II** *ad* < awfully, very

ba'rak (-ken) *v ※* hut; *~ken* ook: ※ barracks

bar'baar (barbaren) *m* barbarian; **bar'baars**
barbarous, barbaric, barbarian; **–heid** (-heden)
v barbarousness, barbarity; **barba'rij** *v* barbarism; **barba'risme** (-n) *o* barbarism

bar'beel (-belen) *m* barbel

bar'bier (-s) *m* barber

barbitu'raat (-raten) *o* barbiturate

bard (-en) *m* bard

'**baren** (baarde, h. gebaard) *vt* give birth to,
bring forth, bear [into the world]; *opzien ~*
create a stir; *zorg ~* cause anxiety, give trouble;
de tijd baart rozen time and straw make medlars
ripe; zie ook *oefening*; '**barensnood** *m in ~* in
labour, in travail; **–weeën** *mv* throes, pains of
childbirth, birth pains, labour pains

ba'ret (-ten) *v* [student's, magistrate's] cap;
[soldier's, woman's] beret

Bar'goens *o* (thieves') flash; *fig* jargon, gibberish, lingo, **F** double Dutch

'**baring** (-en) *v* delivery; child-birth, parturition

'**bariton** (-s) *m* baritone

bark (-en) *v ⚓* bark, barque

bar′kas (-sen) *v* launch, longboat

′barkeeper [′ba.rki.pɔr] (-s) *m* bar keeper;
　–kruk (-ken) *v* bar stool

barm′hartig merciful, charitable; **–heid**
　(-heden) *v* mercy, mercifulness, charity; *uit ~*
　out of charity

′barnsteen *o* & *m* amber; **′barnstenen** *aj*
　amber

ba′rok *aj*, *v* baroque

′barometer (-s) *m* barometer; **–stand** (-en) *m*
　height of the barometer, barometer reading;
　baro′metrisch barometric(al)

ba′ron (-nen) *m* baron; **baro′nes(se)** (-nessen)
　v baroness; **baro′nie** (-ieën) *v* barony

′barrevoets barefoot

barri′cade (-n en -s) *v* barricade; *een ~ opwer-*
pen raise (put up) a barricade; **barrica-**
′deren (barricadeerde, h. gebarricadeerd) *vt*
　barricade

barri′ère (-s) *v* barrier

bars stern, hard-featured [look]; grim [aspect];
　harsh, gruff, rough [voice]

barst (-en) *m* & *v* crack, burst, flaw; *geen ~* **F** zie
zier; **′barsten*** *vi* burst*, crack [of glass &],
　split [of wood]; chap [of the skin]; *barst!* hell!;
een ~de hoofdpijn a splitting headache; *(tot) ~s*
(toe) vol crammed

Bartholo′meusnacht [-′me.üs-] *m* Massacre of
　St. Bartholomew

′Bartje(n)s *volgens ~* according to Cocker

bas (-sen) 1 *v* (i n s t r u m e n t) double-bass,
　contrabass; 2 *m* (z a n g e r) bass

ba′salt [s = z] *o* basalt, whimstone

bas′cule (-s) *v* weighing machine

′base [s = z] (-n) *v* base

ba′seren [s = z] (baseerde, h. gebaseerd) **I** *vt ~*
op base, found, ground on; **II** *vr zich ~ op* take
　one's stand on, base one's case on

′bases meerv. v. *basis*

ba′silicum [s = z] *o* basil

basi′liek [s = z] (-en) *v* basilica

′basis [-zəs] (-ses en -sissen) *v* (g r o n d s l a g) ba-
　sis; (w i s k u n d e, ⚔) base; (l e g e r k a m p) base,
　station; *de ~ leggen voor* lay the foundation of;
op ~ van on the basis of, on the principle that

′basisch [-zi.s] basic

′basisindustrie [-zəs-] (-ieën) *v* basic industry;
　–loon (-lonen) *o* basic wage; **–onderwijs** *o*
　elementary education

Bask (-en) *m* Basque; **–isch I** *aj* Basque; **II** *o*
　Basque

bas′kuul (-kules) *v* = *bascule*

bas-reliëf [bɑrəl′jɛf] (-s) *o* bas-relief, low relief

′bassen (baste, h. gebast) *vi* bay, bark

bas′sin [bɑ′sɛ̃] (-s) *o* 1 ⚓ basin; reservoir; 2
　(z w e m ~) pool

bas′sist (-en) *m* bass (singer); (b a s s p e l e r)
　bass player; **′bassleutel** (-s) *m* bass clef,
　F-clef; **–stem** (-men) *v* bass (voice)

bast (-en) *m* 1 bark, rind [of a tree]; bast [=
　inner bark]; 2 pod, husk, shell [of pulse]; **F** *in*
z'n blote ~ in his birthday suit

′basta *ij (daarmee) ~!* and there's an end of it!,
　so there!, enough!

′bastaard (-en en -s) *m* (& *aj*) 1 bastard; 2 ⚬ &
　⚬ mongrel; 3 ⚬ hybrid; *tot ~ maken* bastard-
　ize; **bastaar′dij** *v* bastardy; **′bastaardnachte-**
gaal (-galen) *m* hedge-sparrow; **–ras** (-sen) *o*
　mongrel breed; **–suiker** *m* = *basterdsuiker*;
　–vloek (-en) *m* mild oath; **–woord** *o* loan-
　word; **′basterd(-)** = *bastaard*(-); **′basterd-**
suiker *m* caster (castor) sugar

basti′on (-s) *o* bastion

′basviool (-violen) *v* bass-viol, violoncello

Ba′taaf(s) Batavian

batal′jon (-s) *o* battalion

′bate *ten ~ van* for the benefit of, in behalf of, in
　aid of; 1 **′baten** *mv* profits; *de ~ en lasten* the
　assets and liabilities; 2 **′baten** (baatte, h.
　gebaat) *vt* avail; *niet(s) ~* be of no use, of no
　avail; *wat baat het?* what's the use (the good)?;
daar ben je niet mee gebaat that will not benefit
　you, that will not serve your interests; *gebaat*
worden door... profit by; **′batig** *~ saldo* credit
　balance, surplus

′batikken (batikte, h. gebatikt) *vt* & *vi* batik

ba′tist *o* batiste, lawn, cambric; **–en** *aj* batiste,
　lawn, cambric

batte′rij (-en) *v* ⚔ & ⚡ battery

bau′xiet *o* bauxite

bavi′aan (-ianen) *m* baboon

ba′za(a)r (-s) *m* 1 (o o s t e r s e　m a r k t-
　p l a a t s) bazaar; 2 (w a r e n h u i s) stores; 3
　(v o o r　l i e f d a d i g　d o e l) bazaar, fancy
　fair, jumble-sale

′Bazel *o* Basel, Basle

′bazelen (bazelde, h. gebazeld) *vi* twaddle,
　drivel

′bazig masterful, bossy; **ba′zin** (-nen) *v*
　mistress

ba′zooka [-′zu:-] (′s) *m* bazooka

ba′zuin (-en) *v* ♪ trombone; **B** trumpet

B.B = *Bescherming Bevolking* Civil Defense

b.b.h.h. = *bezigheden buitenshuis hebbende* away all
　day [in advertisements]

be′ademen[1] *vt* ⚕ apply artificial respiration

---

[1] V.T. en V.D. van dit werkwoord volgens het model: be′ademen, V.T. be′ademde, V.D. be′ademd (ge- valt dus
weg in het V.D.). Zie voor de vormen onder het grondwoord, in dit voorbeeld: *ademen*. Bij sterke en onregelmatige
werkwoorden wordt u verwezen naar de lijst achterin.

[to]; breathe upon [a window-pane]

be'ambte (-n) *m* functionary, official, employee

be'amen (beaamde, h. beaamd) *vt* say yes to, assent to

be'angstigen (beangstigde, h. beangstigd) *vt* alarm

be'antwoorden[1] *vt* & *vi* answer, reply to [a letter, speaker]; return [love &]; acknowledge [greetings]; *aan de beschrijving* ~ answer (to) the description; *aan het doel* ~ answer (serve, fulfil) the purpose; *aan de verwachtingen* ~ come up to expectations; **–ding** *v* answering, replying; *ter* ~ *van* in answer (reply) to

be'bakenen (bebakende, h. bebakend) *vt* beacon; **–ning** (-en) *v* 1 (d e h a n d e l i n g) beaconing; 2 (d e b a k e n s) beacons

be'bloed blood-stained, covered with blood

be'boeten[1] *vt* fine, mulct, amerce

be'bossen (beboste, h. bebost) *vt* afforest; **–sing** *v* afforestation

be'bouwbaar arable, tillable, cultivable; **be'bouwd** 1 built on [plot]; ~*e kom* built-up area; 2 cultivated [land], under cultivation; ~ *met graan* under corn; **be'bouwen**[1] *vt* 1 build upon [a building plot]; develop [a housing estate]; 2 cultivate, till [the soil, the ground]; **–wing** (-en) *v* 1 building upon [a plot]; development [of the City of London]; 2 cultivation [of the ground], tillage [of the soil]

be'broeden[1] *vt* brood, sit (on eggs); *bebroed* hard-set [egg]

be'cijferen[1] *vt* calculate, figure out

beconcur'reren[1] *vt* compete with

bed (-den) *o* bed[2]; ook: bedside; *het* ~ *houden* stay in bed; *i n (zijn)* ~ in bed; *in* ~ *leggen, naar* ~ *brengen* put to bed; *naar* ~ *gaan* go to bed, **S** hit the hay (the sack); *met iem. naar* ~ *gaan* sleep with sbd; *aan zijn* ~ at his bedside; *o p zijn* ~ on (in) his bed; *t e* ~ in bed; *te* ~ *liggen met reumatiek* be laid up (be down) with rheuma-

be'daagd elderly, aged   [tism

be'daard calm, composed, quiet; zie ook *bedaren;* **–heid** *v* calmness, composure, quietness

be'dacht ~ *zijn op* think of, be mindful (thoughtful) of; *niet* ~ *op* not prepared for; **be'dachtzaam** 1 (o v e r l e g g e n d) thoughtful; 2 (o m z i c h t i g) cautious; **–heid** *v* 1 thoughtfulness; 2 cautiousness

be'dankbrief (-brieven) *m* 1 acknowledgement, (letter of) thanks; 2 refusal; **be'danken**[1] **I** *vt* (d a n k b e t u i g e n) thank; **II** *vi* & *va* 1 (z ij n d a n k u i t s p r e k e n) return (render)

thanks; 2 (n i e t a a n n e m e n) decline [the honour &]; 3 (a f t r e d e n) resign; 4 (v o o r tijdschrift, lidmaatschap) withdraw one's subscription, withdraw one's name [from the society]; *wel bedankt!* thank you very much!; ~ *voor een betrekking* 1 decline the offer of a post (place); 2 send in one's papers, resign; ~ *voor een uitnodiging* decline an invitation; **be'dankje** (-s) *o* 1 acknowledgement, (letter of) thanks; 2 refusal; *ik heb er niet eens een* ~ *voor gehad* I've not even got a "thank you" for it

be'daren I (bedaarde, is bedaard) *vi* calm down, quiet down, compose oneself; abate, subside [of a storm, tumult &]; **II** (bedaarde, h. bedaard) *vt* calm, soothe, quiet; appease, still; assuage, allay [pain]; *tot* ~ *brengen = vt*; *tot* ~ *komen = vi*; zie ook *bedaard*

'bedbank (-en) *v* bed-settee

'beddegoed *o* bedding, bed-clothes; **–laken** (-s) *o* sheet; **'beddenwinkel** (-s) *m* bedroom furniture shop; **'beddepan** (-nen) *v* warming pan; **–sprei** (-s) *v* bedspread, counterpane, coverlet; **–tijk** (-en) 1 *o* (s t o f) ticking; 2 *m* (v o o r w e r p) (bed)tick

'bedding (-en) *v* 1 bed, watercourse [of a river]; 2 layer, stratum [*mv* strata] [of matter]; 3 ⚔ platform [of a gun], rest

'bede (-n) *v* 1 (g e b e d) prayer; 2 (s m e e k-b e d e) supplication, appeal, entreaty

be'deesd timid, bashful, shy; **–heid** *v* timidity, bashfulness, shyness

'bedehuis (-huizen) *o* house (place) of worship

be'dekken[1] *vt* cover, cover up; **–king** (-en) *v* cover; **be'dekt** covered [with straw &]; veiled [hint]; *op* ~*e wijze* covertly; **–bloeiend** ~*e plant* cryptogam; **bedekt'zadig** angiospermous

'bedelaar (-s) *m* beggar; **–ster** (-s) *v,* **bedela'res** (-sen) *v* beggar-woman; **bedela'rij** *v* begging; **'bedelarmband** (-en) *m* charm bracelet; **–brief** (-brieven) *m* begging letter; **1 'bedelen** (bedelde, h. gebedeld) **I** *vi* beg; beg (ask) alms, beg charity; *er om* ~ beg for it; **II** *vt* beg

2 be'delen (bedeelde, h. bedeeld) *vt* endow; *bedeeld met* endowed with, blessed with; **–ling** (-en) *v* 1 distribution (of alms); 2 *fig* order, dispensation; *in de* ~ *zijn, van de* ~ *krijgen* 🕮 be on the parish; *in deze* ~, *onder de tegenwoordige* ~ in this dispensation, under the present dispensation

'bedelmonnik (-niken) *m* mendicant friar; **–nap** (-pen) *m* begging bowl; **–orde** (-n en -s) *v* mendicant order; **–staf** *m* *tot de* ~ *brengen*

---

[1] V.T. en V.D. van dit werkwoord volgens het model: **be'**ademen, V.T. **be'**ademde, V.D. **be'**ademd (**ge-** valt dus weg in het V.D.). Zie voor de vormen onder het grondwoord, in dit voorbeeld: *ademen*. Bij sterke en onregelmatige werkwoorden wordt u verwezen naar de lijst achterin.

reduce to beggary; **–tje** (-s) *o* charm [for a bracelet]
be'delven[1] *vt* bury; *bedolven onder [fig]* snowed under with
'bedelvolk *o* beggarly people, beggars; **–zak** (-ken) *m* (beggar's) wallet
be'denkelijk I *aj* critical, risky [of operations &]; serious, grave [of cases &]; doubtful [of looks &]; questionable [assertion]; *dat ziet er ~ uit* things look serious; *een ~ gezicht zetten* put on a serious (doubtful) face; *een ~e overeenkomst vertonen met...* look suspiciously like...; **II** *ad* alarmingly [thin &]; suspiciously [alike];
be'denken[1] **I** *vt* 1 (n i e t v e r g e t e n) remember, bear in mind [that...]; 2 (o v e r- w e g e n) consider, take into consideration, reflect [that]; 3 (u i t d e n k e n) think of, bethink oneself of, devise; invent, contrive, hit upon; 4 (e e n f o o i & g e v e n) remember [the waiter]; *als men bedenkt dat...* considering that...; *een vriend in zijn testament ~* put a friend in one's will; **II** *vr zich ~* think better of it, change one's mind; *zich wel ~ alvorens te...* think twice before ...ing; *zonder (zich te) ~* without thinking, without hesitation; *zie ook bedacht*; **–king** (-en) *v* objection; *geen ~ hebben tegen* have no objection to...; **be'denktijd** *m* time to consider
be'derf *o* corruption [of what is good, of language &]; decay [of a tooth &]; depravation [of morals]; [moral] taint; *aan ~ onderhevig* perishable; *tot ~ overgaan* go bad; **–elijk** perishable [goods]; **–'werend** antiseptic;
be'derven* **I** *vt* spoil [a piece of work, a child &]; taint, vitiate [the air]; disorder [the stomach]; corrupt [the language &]; deprave [the morals]; ruin [sbd.'s prospects &]; mar [the effect]; **II** *vi* go bad; *zie ook: bedorven*
'bedevaart (-en) *v* pilgrimage; **–ganger** (-s) *m* pilgrim; **–plaats** (-en) *v* place of pilgrimage
'bedgenoot (-noten) *m* bedfellow
be'diende (-n en -s) *m* 1 (man-)servant, man; 2 waiter, attendant [at hotel or restaurant]; 3 employee [of a firm]; 4 clerk [in an office]; 5 assistant [in a shop]; **be'dienen**[1] **I** *vt* 1 serve, attend to [customers]; 2 wait upon [people at table &]; 3 ⚔ serve [the guns]; 4 ✗ work [a pump], operate [an engine], control [from a distance, electronically]; *een stervende ~ rk* administer the last sacraments to a dying man; **II** *vr zich ~* help oneself [to some meat &]; 1 help oneself [to some meat &]; 2 avail oneself of [an opportunity]; use; **III** *vi & va* 1 wait (at

table); 2 serve (in the shop); **be'diening** *v* 1 (i n h o t e l &) attendance, service; waiting (at table); ⚔ serving, service [of the guns]; 3 ✗ working [of a pump], operation [of a machine], [remote] control; *rk* administration of the last sacraments; **–sgeld** *o* [15%] service charge; house charge
be'dierf (bedierven) V.T. v. *bederven*
be'dijken (bedijkte, h. bedijkt) *vt* dam up, dam in, embank; **–king** (-en) *v* embankment; dikes
be'dilal [-'dɪl-] (-len) *m* fault-finder, caviller, carper; **be'dillen** (bedilde, h. bedild) *vt* censure, carp at; **be'dillerig, be'dilziek** censorious; **–zucht** *v* censoriousness
be'ding (-en) *o* condition, proviso, stipulation; *onder één ~* on one condition; **be'dingen**[1] *vt* stipulate (that), bargain for [a price], obtain [better terms]; *dat was er niet bij bedongen* that was not included in the bargain
bediscussi'ëren[1] *vt* discuss
be'disselen (bedisselde, h. bedisseld) *vt fig* arrange [matters], manage
'bedjasje (-s) *o* bed-jacket; **bed'legerig** bedridden, laid up, confined to one's bed
bedoe'ïen [be.du.'i.n] (-en) *m* Bedouin [*mv* Bedouin]
be'doeld *(de) ~e...* the... in question; **be'doelen**[1] *vt* 1 (z i c h t e n d o e l s t e l- l e n) intend; (e e n b e d o e l i n g h e b b e n) mean; 3 (w i l l e n z e g g e n) mean (to say); *het was goed bedoeld* it was meant for the best, I (he) meant it kindly; *hij bedoelt het goed met je* he means well by you; *een goed bedoelde raad* a well-intentioned piece of advice; *ik heb er geen kwaad mee bedoeld!* it was meant for the best, no offence was meant!; *ik begrijp wat je bedoelt* I see your point; *wat bedoelt u daarmee?* what do you mean by it?; **–ling** (-en) *v* 1 (v o o r n e m e n) intention, design, purpose, aim, 🔒 intent; 2 (b e t e k e n i s) meaning, purport; *het ligt niet i n onze ~ om...* we have no intention to...; *m e t de beste ~* with the best intentions; *met een bepaalde ~* purposively; *z o n d e r bepaalde ~* unintentionally; *zonder kwade ~* no offence being meant; no harm being meant
be'doen[1] **F** *zich ~* wet one's pants, wet oneself
be'dompt close, stuffy, frowsty; **–heid** *v* closeness, stuffiness
be'dorven V.D. v. *bederven*; *~ kind* spoiled child; *~ lucht* foul air; *~ maag* disordered stomach; *~ vis (vlees)* tainted fish (meat); *~ zeden* depraved morals
be'dotten (bedotte, h. bedot) *vt* take in, cheat,

bilk; **–er** (-s) *m* cheat; **bedotte'rij** *v* take-in, trickery, monkey business

be'drading (-en) *v* ✺ wiring

be'drag (-dragen) *o* amount of; **be'dragen**[1] *vt* amount to the amount of; *ten ~e van* to the amount of; **be'dragen**[1] *vt* amount to

be'dreigen[1] *vt* threaten, menace; **–ging** (-en) *v* threat, menace

be'dremmeld confused, perplexed; **–heid** *v* confusion, perplexity

be'dreven skilful, skilled, experienced, practised, expert; ~ *in* (well) versed in; **–heid** *v* skill, skilfulness, expertness; *zijn ~ in* his proficiency in

be'driegen* **I** *vt* 1 deceive, cheat, take in, impose upon; 2 (o n t r o u w z ij n) be unfaithful to [one's husband, one's wife]; *bedrogen echtgenoot* cuckold; *hij heeft ons voor een grote som bedrogen* he has cheated us out of a large amount; *hij kwam bedrogen uit* his hopes were deceived, he was disappointed; **II** *vr als ik mij niet bedrieg* if I am not mistaken; **III** *va* cheat [at cards &]; **–er** (-s) *m* deceiver, impostor, cheat, fraud; *de ~ bedrogen* the biter bit; **bedriege'rij** (-en) *v* deceit, deception, imposture, fraud; **be'drieglijk** deceitful [acting]; fraudulent [practices]; deceptive, fallacious, delusive [arguments &]; **–heid** *v* deceitfulness, fraudulence; deceptiveness, delusiveness, fallacy

be'drijf (-drijven) *o* 1 (h a n d e l i n g) action, deed; 2 (b e r o e p) business, trade; 3 (v. t o-n e e l s t u k) act [of a play]; 4 (e x p l o i t a t i e) working; 5 (n ij v e r h e i d) industry; 6 (d i e n s t) [gas, railway &] service; 7 (o n d e r-n e m i n g) business, concern, undertaking, [chemical] works; *b u i t e n ~* (standing) idle; *buiten ~ stellen* close down; *i n ~* in (full) operation; *in ~ stellen* put into operation; *o n d e r de bedrijven door* in the meantime, meanwhile

be'drijfsauto [-o.to., -ɔuto.] ('s) *m* commercial vehicle; **be'drijfseconomie** *v* business economics; **–geneeskunde** *v* industrial medicine; **–installatie** [-(t)si.] (-s) *v* working plant; **–kapitaal** (-talen) *o* working capital; **–klaar** in working order; **–kosten** *mv* working expenses; *vaste ~* overhead charges; **–kunde** *v* business administration; **–leider** (-s) *m* works manager; **–leiding** *v* (industrial) management; **–leven** *o* trade and industry; **–resultaat** [-zül-] (-taten) *o* operating results; **–sluiting** (-en) *v* close down; **–tak** (-ken) *m* industrial branch

be'drijven[1] *vt* commit, perpetrate; zie ook

bedreven; **–d** *gram* active; **be'drijvig** active, busy, bustling; **–heid** *v* activity, stir

'bedrinken[1] *zich ~* get drunk, **F** get tight, fuddle oneself

be'droefd sad, sorrowful, grieved; **–heid** *v* sadness, sorrow, grief; **be'droeven** (bedroefde, h. bedroefd) **I** *vt* give (cause) pain (to), afflict, grieve, distress; *het bedroeft mij dat...* I am grieved (distressed) to learn (see) that...; **II** *vr zich ~ (over)* grieve, be grieved (at it, to see &); **–d I** *aj* sad, pitiable, deplorable; **II** *ad ~ weinig* precious little (few)

be'drog *o* deceit, deception, imposture, fraud; [optical] illusion; ~ *plegen* cheat [at play &]; **be'drogen** V.T. meerv. en V.D. v *bedriegen*; **be'droog (bedrogen)** V.T. v. *bedriegen*

be'druipen[1] *vt* baste [meat]; *zich kunnen ~* pay one's way, be selfsupporting

be'drukken[1] *vt* print (over); **be'drukt** 1 *eig* printed [cotton &]; 2 *fig* depressed, dejected; **–heid** *v* depression, dejection

'bedsprei (-en) *v = beddesprei*; **–stede** (-n) *v*, **–stee** (-steeën) *v* cupboard-bed; **'bedtafeltje** (-s) *o* bedside table; **–tijd** *m* bedtime

be'ducht ~ *voor* apprehensive of [danger], apprehensive for [his life, safety]

be'duiden[1] *vt* 1 (a a n d u i d e n, b e t e k e n e n) mean, signify; 2 (d u i d e l ij k m a k e n) make clear [something to...], indicate; *het heeft niets te ~* it does not matter; it is of no importance; **–d** considerable

be'duimelen (beduimelde, h. beduimeld) *vt* thumb; *beduimeld* well-thumbed [book]

be'duusd dazed, **F** flabbergasted, taken aback

be'duvelen (beduvelde, h. beduveld) *vt* fool, hoodwink, double-cross, finagle

be'dwang *o* restraint, control; *goed in ~ hebben* have well in hand; *in ~ houden* hold (keep) in check, keep under control; *zich in ~ houden* control oneself

'bedwateren I *vi* wet one's bed; **II** *o* bedwetting; ✺ enuresis

be'dwelmen (bedwelmde, h. bedwelmd) *vt* stun, stupefy, drug; intoxicate; **–d** stunning [beauty]; stupefying; intoxicating [liquor]; ~ *middel* ook: narcotic, drug; **be'dwelming** (-en) *v* stupefaction, stupor

be'dwingen[1] **I** *vt* restrain, subdue, control, check, curb; *een oproer ~* repress (put down, quell) a rebellion; *zijn toorn ~* contain one's anger; *zijn tranen ~* keep back one's tears; **II** *vr zich ~* contain oneself, restrain oneself

be'ëdigd 1 (v. p e r s o n e n) sworn (in); 2 (v.

[1] V.T. en V.D. van dit werkwoord volgens het model: **be'**ademen, V.T. **be'**ademde, V.D. **be'**ademd (**ge-** valt dus weg in het V.D.). Zie voor de vormen onder het grondwoord, in dit voorbeeld: *ademen*. Bij sterke en onregelmatige werkwoorden wordt u verwezen naar de lijst achterin.

v e r k l a r i n g) sworn, on oath; ~*e verklaring* affidavit; ~ *makelaar* sworn broker; **be'ëdigen** (beëdigde, h. beëdigd) *vt* 1 (i e m.) swear in [a functionary]; administer the oath to [the witnesses]; 2 (i e t s) swear to, confirm on oath; **–ging** (-en) *v* 1 swearing in [of a functionary]; 2 administration of the oath [to witnesses]; 3 confirmation on oath

be'ëindigen[1] *vt* bring to an end, finish, conclude; terminate [a contract]; **–ging** *v* conclusion; termination [of a contract]

beek (beken) *v* brook, rill, rivulet; **–je** (-s) *o* brooklet, rill, runnel

beeld (-en) *o* 1 (s p i e g e l b e e l d) image, reflection; 2 (a f b e e l d i n g) image, picture, portrait; 3 (s t a n d b e e l d) statue; 4 (z i n n e-b e e l d) image, symbol; 5 (r e d e f i g u u r) figure (of speech), metaphor; 6 (s c h o o n-h e i d) beauty, **F** beaut; *zich een ~ vormen van* form a notion of, visualize, image to oneself, realize; *in ~ brengen = afbeelden; n a a r Gods ~ (en gelijkenis) geschapen* created after (in) the image of God; **–band** (-en) *m* video-tape; **–buis** (-buizen) *v T* cathode tube; *op de ~* **F** on the small screen, on the box; **'beeldenaar** (-s) *m* effigy, head [of a coin]; **'beeldend** expressive; pictorial; ~*e kunsten* plastic arts; **'beeldendienst** *m* image-worship; **–storm** *m* iconoclasm; **–stormer** (-s) *m* iconoclast

'beeldhouwen (beeldhouwde, h. gebeeld-houwd) *vt* sculpture; **–er** (-s) *m* sculptor; **'beeldhouwkunst** *v* sculpture; **–werk** (-en) *o* sculpture

'beeldig charming, lovely, sweet; **'beeldje** (-s) *o* image, figurine, statuette; **'beeldmerk** (-en) *o* ideograph, ideogram; **–rijk** full of images, vivid [style]; **–roman** (-s) *m* = *beeldverhaal*; **–scherm** (-en) *o* screen; **–schoon** divinely beautiful; **–snijder** (-s) *m* (wood-)carver; **–spraak** *v* figurative language; metaphor, imagery; **–stormer** (-s) *m* = *beeldenstormer*; **–verhaal** (-halen) *o* comic strip; **'beeltenis** (-sen) *v* image, portrait, likeness

beemd (-en) *m* meadow, field, pasture, ⊙ lea

been *o* 1 (benen) leg; 2 (beenderen) (d e e l v. g e r a a m t e) bone; 3 (s t o f n a a m) bone; *benen maken, de benen nemen* take to one's heels; *het ~ stijf houden* stand firm, dig one's toes in, dig in one's heels; *er geen ~ in zien om...* make no bones about ...ing, make nothing of ...ing; ● *m e t één ~ in het graf staan* have one foot in the grave; *met het verkeerde ~ uit bed stappen* get out of bed on the wrong side; *o p de ~ blijven* keep (on) one's feet; *op de ~ brengen* levy, raise [an army]; *iem. op de ~ helpen* set (put) sbd. on his legs; *op de ~ houden* keep going; *zich op de ~ houden = op de been blijven*; *op één ~ kan men niet lopen* two make a pair; *op zijn laatste benen lopen* be on one's last legs; *op eigen benen staan* stand on one's own feet (legs); *op de ~ zijn* 1 *eig* be on one's feet; 2 (o p z ij n) ook: be stirring; 3 (r o n d l o p e n) be about, be on the move; 4 (n a z i e k t e) be on one's legs, be up and about again; *vlug (wel) t e r ~ zijn* be a good walker; *het zijn sterke benen die de weelde kunnen dragen* set a beggar on horseback and he'll ride to the devil; **–beschermer** (-s) *m* leg-guard, pad; **–breuk** (-en) *v* fracture of a bone; fracture of the leg

'beendergestel *o* skeleton; osseous system; **–meel** *o* bone-dust

'beeneter (-s) *m* caries, necrosis; **–houwer** (-s) *m* = *slager*; **–kap** (-pen) *v* legging, gaiter; **–merg** *o* bone marrow; **–tje** (-s) *o* (small) bone; ~ *over rijden* do the outside edge; *iem. een* ~ *lichten (zetten)* trip sbd. up; *zijn beste* ~ *voor-zetten* put one's best foot foremost; **–vlies** (-vliezen) *o* periosteum; **–windsel** (-s) *o* puttee

beer (beren) *m* 1 bear ‖ 2 (m a n n e t j e s-v a r k e n) boar ‖ 3 (s c h o o r) buttress; 4 (w a t e r k e r i n g) dam ‖ 5 (m e s t) night-soil; *de Grote Beer* the Great Bear, Ursa Major; *de Kleine Beer* the Little Bear, Ursa Minor; *de huid van de ~ verkopen voor men hem geschoten heeft* count one's chickens before they are hatched; zie ook: *ongelikt*; **–put** (-ten) *m* cesspool, cesspit

be'ërven[1] *vt* inherit

beest (-en) *o* (zelden *v*) 1 animal; 2 beast², brute² [ook = lower animal]; 3 ⚓ fluke, fluky shot; *een ~ van een kerel* a brute (of a man); *de ~ spelen (uithangen)* raise hell (the devil, Cain); **–achtig I** *aj* beastly, bestial, brutal, brutish; **II** *ad* in a beastly way, bestially &; < beastly [drunk, dull, wet]; **'beestenboel** *m een* ~ a beastly mess; **–spel** (-len) *o* menagerie; **–voe(de)r** *o* fodder; **–wagen** (-s) *m* cattle-truck; **–weer** *o* beastly weather; **'beestig I** *aj* beastly; **II** *ad* < beastly

1 beet (beten) *m* 1 (h a n d e l i n g) bite; 2 (h a p j e) bit, morsel, mouthful; *hij heeft* ~ he has a bite (got a rise)

2 beet (beten) V.T. v *bijten*

3 beet (beten) *v* = *biet*

'beethebben[2] *vt iem.* ~ have got hold of sbd.; zie ook: 1 *beet* & *beetnemen*

[1,2] V.T. en V.D. van dit werkwoord volgens het model: 1 **be'**ademen, V.T. **be'**ademde, V.D. **be'**ademd (**ge-** valt dus weg in het V.D.); 2 **'beet**pakken, V.T. pakte **'beet**, V.D. **'beet**gepakt. Zie voor de vormen onder het grond-woord, in deze voorbeelden: *ademen* en *pakken*. Bij sterke en onregelmatige werkwoorden wordt u verwezen naar de lijst achterin.

'**beetje** (-s) *o* (little) bit, little; *het ~ geld dat ik heb* 1 the little money I have; 2 what money I have; *lekkere ~s* titbits, dainties; *alle ~s helpen* every little helps; *bij ~s* bit by bit, little by little

'**beetkrijgen**[2] *vt* catch; zie ook *beetpakken*; **–nemen**[2] *vt* 1 (v o o r d e g e k h o u d e n) pull sbd.'s leg; 2 (b e d o t t e n) take [sbd.] in; *je hebt je laten ~* **F** you've been had (**S** sold); **–pakken**[2] *vt* seize, take (get) hold of, grip, grasp

'**beetwortel** (-en en -s) *m* beet(root); '**beetwortelsuiker** *m* beet(root) sugar

'**beevaart** (-en) *v* = *bedevaart*

bef (-fen) *v* bands

be'faamd noted, famous, renowned; **–heid** *v* fame, renown

be'gaafd gifted, talented; **–heid** (-heden) *v* gifts, talents

1 **be'gaan** (beging, h. begaan) **I** *vt* 1 (l o p e n o v e r) walk (upon); tread; 2 (b e d r ij v e n) commit [an error], make [a mistake], perpetrate [a crime]; **II** *va laat hem maar ~!* leave him alone!; leave it to him; **2 be'gaan** *aj* trodden [path], beaten [track]; *~ zijn met* feel sorry for, pity; *de begane grond* the (solid) ground; the ground level; the ground floor; **–baar** passable, practicable [pass, road]

be'geerlijk desirable; **be'geerte** (-n) *v* desire; (s e k s u e e l) lust

bege'leiden (begeleidde, h. begeleid) *vt* accompany [a lady]; attend [a royal personage &]; ♪ accompany, play the accompaniment; (⚓) escort, ⚓ convoy; *~d schrijven* covering letter; *~de omstandigheden* attendant (concomitant) circumstances; **–er** (-s) *m* 1 companion; 2 ♪ accompanist; **bege'leiding** (-en) *v* accompaniment; *met ~ van...* ♪ to the accompaniment of...

bege'nadigen (begenadigde, h. begenadigd) *vt* 1 pardon, reprieve; 2 bless [with]; *een begenadigd kunstenaar* an inspired artist; **–ging** (-en) *v* pardon, reprieve

be'geren (begeerde, h. begeerd) *vt* desire, wish, want, covet; **begerens'waard(ig)** desirable; **be'gerig** desirous, covetous, eager, (g u l z i g) edacious, (i n h a l i g) greedy; *~ naar* avid of, eager for, greedy of; *~ om te...* desirous to..., eager to...; *~e blikken werpen op* cast covetous eyes on; **–heid** *v* covetousness, eagerness, greediness, avidity

be'geven[1] **I** *vt zijn benen begaven hem* his legs gave way; *zijn krachten ~ hem* his strength begins to fail him; *zijn moed begaf hem* his heart

sank; **II** *va de ketting kan het ~* the chain may give; **III** *vr ik zou mij daar niet in ~* I should not venture on that sort of thing; *zich ~ in gevaar* expose oneself to danger; *zich ~ naar* go to, repair to, set out (start) [for home]; zie ook *rust, weg* &

be'gieten[1] *vt* water

be'giftigen (begiftigde, h. begiftigd) *vt* endow [an institution]; *iem. ~ met...* endow sbd. with..., confer... on sbd.

be'gijn (-en) *v,* **be'gijntje** (-s) *o* Beguine

be'gin *o* beginning, commencement, outset, opening, start, inception; *een ~ van brand* an outbreak of fire; *het ~ van het einde* the beginning of the end; *alle ~ is moeilijk* all beginnings are difficult; *een goed ~ is het halve werk* well begun is half done; *een verkeerd ~* a bad (false) start; *een ~ maken* make a beginning (a start); *een ~ maken met* begin, start [work &]; ● *bij het ~ beginnen* begin at the beginning; *i n het ~* at (in) the beginning [of the year]; at first [all went well]; *al in het ~* at the (very) outset; from the outset [we could not hit it off]; *(in het) ~ (van) januari* at the beginning of January, early in January; *v a n het ~ af aan* from the first, from the beginning; *van het ~ tot het einde* from beginning to end, from start to finish, throughout; **–fase** (-s en -n) *v* initial phase; **–letter** (-s) *v* initial; **–neling** (-en) *m* beginner, tyro, novice; **be'ginnen** * **I** *vt* begin, commence, start; *een school ~* open a school; *met Frans ~* take up French; *wat moet ik ~?* what to do?; *wat ben ik begonnen!* what have I let myself in for!; *~ te drinken* 1 (f e i t) begin to drink, begin drinking; 2 (a l s g e w o o n t e) take to drinking (drink); **II** *vi* begin; set in [of winter]; come on [rain, illness, night]; start; *begin maar!* go ahead!; *zij zijn begonnen!* they started it!; *om te ~ ...* to begin with..., to start with..., for a start...; ● *a a n iets ~* begin (up)on sth., begin sth.; *daar begin ik niet aan* I don't go in for that sort of thing; *m e t iets ~* begin with sth.; *~ met te zeggen dat...* begin by saying that...; *er is niets met hem te ~* he is quite unmanageable; *er is niets mee te ~* 1 it won't do, it's hopeless; 2 I can make nothing of it; *o m te ~...* to begin with..., to start with...; *men moet iets hebben om te ~* to start upon; *~ (te praten) o v e r* begin (start) on, broach [a subject, politics]; *v a n voren af aan ~* begin [it] over again; start afresh [in business]; *~ v o o r zich zelf* set up (start) for oneself; **–er** (-s) *m* beginner, tyro, novice; **be'ginpunt** (-en) *o*

[1,2] V.T. en V.D. van dit werkwoord volgens het model: 1 **be'ademen**, V.T. **be'**ademde, V.D. **be'**ademd (**ge-** valt dus weg in het V.D.); 2 '**beetpakken**, V.T. pakte '**beet**, V.D. '**beet**gepakt. Zie voor de vormen onder het grondwoord, in deze voorbee!lden: *ademen* en *pakken*. Bij sterke en onregelmatige werkwoorden wordt u verwezen naar de lijst achterin.

starting point; **–salaris** (-sen) *o* commencing salary

be'ginsel (-en en -s) *o* principle; *de (eerste)* ~*en* the elements, the rudiments; the ABC [of science]; *i n* ~ in principle; *u i t* ~ on principle; **–loos** without principle(s); > unprincipled; **–vast** firm in one's principle(s); **–verklaring** (-en) *v* platform [of a party], statement (declaration) of policy

be'ginselheid (-heden) *v* initial velocity; **–stadium** (-s en -dia) *o* initial stage

be'gluren[1] *vt* spy upon; peep at; ogle [a girl]

be'gon (begonnen) V.T. v. *beginnen*

be'gonia ('s) *v* begonia

be'gonnen V.T. meerv. en V.D. v. *beginnen*

bé'goochelen[1] *vt* bewitch; delude; **–ling** (-en) *v* spell; delusion

be'graafplaats (-en) *v* burial-ground, cemetery, churchyard, graveyard; **be'grafenis** (-sen) *v* funeral, burial, interment; **–gezicht** (-en) *o* funereal expression; **–kosten** *mv* funeral expenses; **–ondernemer** (-s) *m* undertaker, mortician; **–onderneming** (-en) *v* undertaker's business; **–plechtigheid** (-heden) *v* funeral ceremony; (k e r k e l ij k) burial-service; **–stoet** (-en) *m* funeral procession; **be'graven**[1] **I** *vt* bury, ⊙ inter

be'grensd limited; **be'grenzen**[1] *vt* bound; (b e p e r k e n) limit; **–zing** (-en) *v* limitation

be'grijpelijk understandable, comprehensible, intelligible; **begrijpelijker'wijs, –'wijze** understandably, for obvious reasons; **be'grijpelijkheid** *v* comprehensibility, intelligibility; **be'grijpen**[1] *vt* understand, comprehend, conceive, grasp; *verkeerd* ~ misunderstand; *alles inbegrepen* all included, inclusive (of everything); *het niet op iem. begrepen hebben* have no friendly feelings towards sbd.; *dat kun je* ~! **F** not likely!

be'grinden (begrindde, h. begrind), **be'grinten** (begrintte, h. begrint) *vt* gravel

be'grip (-pen) *o* 1 (i d e e) idea, notion, conception; 2 (b e v a t t i n g) understanding, comprehension, apprehension; *kort* ~ summary, epitome; *traag van* ~ slow in the uptake; *zich een* ~ *van iets vormen (maken)* form an idea (a notion) of sth.; *dat gaat mijn* ~ *te boven* it passes my understanding, it is beyond my comprehension, it is beyond me; ~ *hebben voor* appreciate [other people's problems], sympathize with [your difficulties], be understanding of [their point of view]; *volgens mijn* ~*pen* according to my notions of...; **–sverwarring** (-en) *v*

confusion of ideas

be'groeid overgrown, grown over (with), covered (with); **be'groeiing** (-en) *v* vegetation

be'groeten[1] *vt* salute, greet; *gaan* ~ (go and) pay one's respects to...; **–ting** (-en) *v* salutation, greeting

be'groten (begrootte, h. begroot) *vt* estimate (at *op*); **be'groting** (-en) *v* estimate; *de* ~ the budget, the [Army, Navy, Air] estimates; **be'grotingspost** (-en) *m* item on a budget; **–tekort** (-en) *o* budgetary deficit

be'gunstigde (-n) *m-v* beneficiary; **be'gunstigen** (begunstigde, h. begunstigd) *vt* 1 favour; 2 (z e d e l ij k s t e u n e n) countenance; **–er** (-s) *m* patron; **be'gunstiging** (-en) *v* favour; patronage, preferential treatment; (a l s s t e l s e l) favouritism; *onder* ~ *van...* favoured by..., under favour of [(the) night]

be'ha [be.'ha.] ('s) *m* bra

be'haaglijk pleasant, comfortable; **F** snug; **–ziek** coquettish; **–zucht** *v* coquetry

be'haard hairy, hirsute

be'hagen I (behaagde, h. behaagd) *vt* please; **II** *o* pleasure; ~ *scheppen in* find pleasure in, take delight (pleasure) in

be'halen[1] *vt* obtain, gain, win; *daar is geen eer aan te* ~ zie 2 *eer* (*inleggen met iets*); zie ook *overwinning, prijs, winst*

be'halve 1 (u i t g e z o n d e r d) except, but, save, apart from; 2 (m e t i n b e g r i p v a n) besides, in addition to

be'handelen[1] *vt* 1 (i e m.) treat [well, ill]; deal [cruelly &] with (by); (r u w) knock about; handle [kindly, roughly]; attend [medically]; 2 (i e t s) handle, manipulate [an instrument]; treat [a sprained ankle]; treat of [a subject]; deal with [a case, a matter, a question]; 🜊 hear [civil cases], try [criminal cases]; **–ling** (-en) *v* treatment [of a man, a patient]; [medical] attendance; handling [of an instrument]; discussion [of a bill]; 🜊 hearing [of a civil case], trial [of a criminal case]; *de zaak is i n* ~ the matter is being dealt with, under discussion; *wanneer zal de zaak in* ~ *komen?* when will the matter come up for discussion (be dealt with)?; *hij is o n d e r* ~ he is under medical treatment; **be'handelkamer** (-s) *v* consulting room

be'hang *o* = *behangsel*; **be'hangen**[1] *vt* hang [with festoons]; paper [a room]; **–er** (-s) *m* paper-hanger; (b e h a n g e r e n s t o f-f e e r d e r) upholsterer; **be'hangsel** (-s) *o*, **–papier** (-en) *o* (wall)paper, paper-hangings

---

[1] V.T. en V.D. van dit werkwoord volgens het model: **be'**ademen, V.T. **be'**ademde, V.D. **be'**ademd (**ge-** valt dus weg in het V.D.). Zie voor de vormen onder het grondwoord, in dit voorbeeld: *ademen.* Bij sterke en onregelmatige werkwoorden wordt u verwezen naar de lijst achterin.

be'hartigen (behartigde, h. behartigd) *vt* look after, attend to; (b e v o r d e r e n) promote, further; –ging *v* promotion, care

be'heer *o* management, control, direction, administration; *i n eigen* ~ under direct management; *o n d e r zijn* ~ 1 under his management &; 2 during his administration; –der (-s) *m* manager, director, administrator; ~ *van een failliete boedel* trustee

be'heersen[1] **I** *vt* command, master [one's passions], control [oneself], dominate [a man, the surrounding country], rule, govern, sway [a people &]; be master of [a language, of the situation]; **II** *vr zich* ~ control oneself; –sing (-en) *v* command [of a language], control, dominion, sway, rule; be'heerst 1 (k a l m) self-possessed, composed; restrained; 2 (g e - m a t i g d) controlled

be'heksen[1] *vt* bewitch

be'helpen[1] *zich* ~ make shift, make do, manage to get on

be'helzen (behelsde, h. behelsd) *vt* contain; ~*de dat...* to the effect that...

be'hendig dext(e)rous, deft, adroit; –heid (-heden) *v* dexterity, deftness, skill, adroitness

be'hept ~ *met* afflicted with, troubled with, affected with

be'heren (beheerde, h. beheerd) *vt* manage, control [affairs], superintend; administer [an estate], conduct [a business]; ~*d vennoot* managing (acting) partner

be'hoeden[1] *vt* protect, guard, preserve (from *voor*)

be'hoedzaam prudent, cautious, wary; –heid *v* prudence, caution, cautiousness, wariness

be'hoefte (-n) *v* want, need [of money, for quiet]; ~ *hebben aan* stand in need of, be in want of, want; *zijn* ~ *doen* relieve oneself (nature), do one's needs; zie ook: *voorzien*; –tig needy, indigent, destitute; *in* ~*e omstandigheden* in penury

be'hoeve *ten* ~ *van* for the benefit of, in behalf of, in aid of; be'hoeven[1] *vt* want, need, require; *men behoeft niet te ...om* there is no need to ..., it is not necessary to ...; *er behoeft niet gezegd te worden, dat...* there is no occasion (for me) to say that...

be'hoorlijk **I** *aj* proper, fit(ting); decent [coat, salary &]; siz(e)able [piece, cupboard]; ~*e kennis van...* fair knowledge of...; **II** *ad* properly, decently; < pretty [cold]; **be'horen I** (behoorde, h. behoord) *vi* 1 (t o e b e h o r e n) belong to; 2 (b e t a m e n) be fit (proper); *je*

behoort (behoorde) *te gehoorzamen* you should (ought to) obey; ~ *b ij* go with; *bij elkaar* ~ belong together; ~ *t o t de besten* be among the best; **II** *sb* ~ *naar* ~ as it should be, duly, properly, fittingly. Zie ook: *toebehoren*

be'houd *o* preservation [of one's health]; conservation [of energy]; salvation [of the soul &]; *met* ~ *van zijn salaris* on full pay, [holidays] with pay; **1** be'houden[1] *vt* keep, retain, preserve; **2** be'houden *aj* safe, safe and sound; be'houdend conservative [party]; be'houdens except for, but for; barring [mistakes &]; ~ *nadere goedkeuring van...* subject to the approval of...; ~ *onvoorziene omstandigheden* if no unforeseen circumstances arise; ~ *zijn recht om...* without prejudice to his right to...; be'houdzucht *v* conservatism

be'huild tear-stained [eyes], blubbered [face]

be'huisd *klein* ~ *zijn* be confined (cramped) for room, live at close quarters; *ruim* ~ *zijn* have plenty of room; be'huizing (-en) *v* 1 housing; 2 house, dwelling

be'hulp *o met* ~ *van* with the help (assistance) of [friends], with the aid of (crutches); –zaam helpful, obliging, ready to help; *iem.* ~ *zijn* (*bij*)... help, assist sbd. (in)...; *iem. de behulpzame hand bieden* hold out a helping hand to sbd., lend sbd. a helping hand

be'huwd [brother &] in-law

'beiaard ['bɛia:rt] (-s en -en) *m* chimes, carillon; beiaar'dier (-s) *m* carillon player

'beide both; *m e t ons* (*z'n*) ~*n* we two, the two of us; *met ons* ~*n kunnen wij dat wel* between us; *een van* ~(*n*) one of the two, either; *geen van* ~(*n*) neither; *alle* ~ both of them; *wij, gij* ~*n* both of us, both of you; *ons* ~*r vriend* our mutual friend; *in* ~ *gevallen* in either case

'beiden (beidde, h. gebeid) *vt* abide, wait for

'beiderlei of both sorts; *o p* ~ *wijs* both ways, either way; *v a n* ~ *kunne* of both sexes, of either sex; 'beiderzijds on both sides

'Beier (-en) *m* Bavarian

'beieren (beierde, h. gebeierd) *vi* (& *vt*) chime, ring (the bells)

'Beieren *o* Bavaria; 'Beiers Bavarian

'beige ['bɛːʒə] *aj* & *o* beige

beig'net [bɛ'ɲe.] (-s) *m* fritter

be'ijveren[1] *zich* ~ *om...* do one's utmost to..., lay oneself out to...

be'ijzeld icy [roads]

be'invloeden (beïnvloedde, h. beïnvloed) *vt* influence, affect

'beitel (-s) *m* chisel; 'beitelen (beitelde, h.

---

[1] V.T. en V.D. van dit werkwoord volgens het model: be'ademen, V.T. be'ademde, V.D. be'ademd (ge- valt dus weg in het V.D.). Zie voor de vormen onder het grondwoord, in dit voorbeeld: *ademen*. Bij sterke en onregelmatige werkwoorden wordt u verwezen naar de lijst achterin.

gebeiteld) *vt* chisel [a block of marble]

beits (-en) *m* & *o* mordant, stain; **'beitsen** (beitste, h. gebeitst) *vt* stain

be'jaard aged; **be'jaarden** *mv* the aged, old people; **–tehuis** (-huizen) *o* old people's home; **–zorg** *v* care for the aged

be'jammeren¹ *vt* deplore, bewail, lament

be'jegenen (bejegende, h. bejegend) *vt* use [ill &], treat [politely &]; **–ning** (-en) *v* treatment

be'jubelen¹ *vt* cheer, acclaim, extol

bek (-ken) *m* mouth [of a horse &, also ✂]; beak, bill [of a bird]; snout [of fish &]; jaws [of a vice]; bit [of pincers]; *hou je ~!* shut up!; *een grote ~ hebben* be rude, be impudent; zie ook: *mond*

be'kaaid *er ~ afkomen* come off badly, fare badly

'bekaf knocked up, done up, dog-tired

be'kakt haughty, supercilious

be'kapping (-en) *v* roofing

be'keerde (-n) *m* = *bekeerling*; **be'keerling** (-en) *m* convert, proselyte

be'kend 1 known; 2 (w e l b e k e n d) well-known, noted, famous [author &], > notorious [criminal]; familiar [face, ground]; *~ (zijn) in Amsterdam* (be) acquainted or known in A.; *~ met* acquainted with, familiar with; *~ maken* announce, make known, publish; *als ~ aannemen (veronderstellen)* take for granted; *iem. met iets ~ maken* acquaint sbd. with sth.; *~ worden* 1 (v. p e r s o n e n &) become known; 2 (v. g e h e i m) become known, get about (abroad); *met iem. ~ raken* get acquainted with sbd.; *~ zijn* be known; *het is ~* is a well-known fact; *~ zijn om* be known for; *het is algemeen ~* it is a matter of common knowledge; *er zijn gevallen ~ van...* there are cases on record of...; *~ zijn (staan) als...* be known as...; *~ staan als de bonte hond* have a bad reputation; *ik ben hier (goed) ~* I know the place (well), I know these parts; *ik ben hier niet ~* I am a stranger (to the place); *voor zover mij ~* as far as I know, for all I know; to (the best of) my knowledge; **–e** (-n) *m-v* acquaintance; **–heid** *v* acquaintance, conversance, familiarity [with French, a fact &]; *~ geven aan* make public; *grote ~ genieten* be widely known; **–making** (-en) *v* announcement, notice [in the papers]; publication [of a report]; [official] proclamation

be'kennen¹ I *vt* confess, own, admit [one's guilt]; **B** know [a woman]; *er was geen huis te ~* there was no sign of a house, there was not a

house to be seen; *de moord ~* ✂ confess to the murder; *kleur ~* follow suit [at cards]; II *va* ✂ plead guilty; **be'kentenis** (-sen) *v* confession, admission, avowal; *een volledige ~ afleggen* make a full confession; make a clean breast [of...]

'beker (-s) *m* cup, chalice, goblet, beaker, bowl; mug [of cocoa]; (v. d o b b e l s t e n e n) dice-box

be'keren¹ I *vt* convert²; reclaim [a sinner]; ook: proselytize; II *vr zich ~* (t o t a n d e r e g o d s d i e n s t) be converted, become a convert; (v. z o n d a a r) reform, repent; **–ring** (-en) *v* 1 (t o t a n d e r g e l o o f) conversion; 2 (v. z o n d a a r) reclamation

'bekerwedstrijd (-en) *m* cup match, cup tie

be'keuren¹ *vt* *iem. ~* take sbd.'s name; **–ring** (-en) *v* ticket

be'kijk *o veel ~s hebben* attract a great deal of notice; **be'kijken**¹ *vt* look at, view; *de zaak van alle kanten ~* turn the matter over in one's mind; *zo heb ik het nog niet bekeken* I have not thought of it that way

be'kisting (-en) *v* (v. b e t o n) shuttering, formwork

'bekken (-s) *o* 1 (s c h o t e l) bowl, basin; 2 (i n h e t l i c h a a m) pelvis; 3 ♪ cymbal; 4 (v. r i v i e r) (catchment) basin; **bekke'nist** (-en) *m*, **'bekkenslager** (-s) *m* ♪ cymbalist

'bekketrekken *vi* clown

be'klaagde (-n) *m-v* (the) accused; **–nbankje** (-s) *o* dock

be'kladden¹ *vt* bespatter, blot; *fig* asperse, smear, slander [a person]

be'klag *o* complaint; *zijn ~ doen over... bij* complain of... to...; *zijn ~ indienen (bij)* lodge a complaint (with); **be'klagen** I *vt* (i e t s) lament, deplore; (i e m.) pity, commiserate; II *vr zich ~* complain; *zich ~ over... bij...* complain of... to...; **beklagens'waard(ig)** (much) to be pitied, pitiable, lamentable

be'klant *goed ~e winkel* well-patronized shop

be'kleden¹ *vt* 1 (b e d e k k e n) clothe, cover, upholster [chairs], drape, dress [a figure]; coat, line [with tinfoil], face [with layer of other material]; metal, sheathe [a ship's sides]; ✂ lag [a boiler with a strip of wood]; 2 *fig* (i n n e m e n) hold, fill [a place], occupy [a post]; *~ met* endow with, (in)vest with [power]; **–ding** (-en) *v* clothing, covering &, upholstery [of chairs]

be'klemd (b e n a u w d) oppressed; *~e breuk* ⚕ strangulated hernia; **–heid** *v* oppression; **be'klemmen**¹ *vt* oppress; **–ming** (-en) *v* 1

---

¹ V.T. en V.D. van dit werkwoord volgens het model: **be'**ademen, V.T. **be'**ademde, V.D. **be'**ademd (**ge-** valt dus weg in het V.D.). Zie voor de vormen onder het grondwoord, in dit voorbeeld: *ademen*. Bij sterke en onregelmatige werkwoorden wordt u verwezen naar de lijst achterin.

oppression; 2 (v. b r e u k) ⚓ strangulation; 3 (o p d e b o r s t) constriction

be'klemtonen (beklemtoonde, h. beklemtoond) *vt* stress², *fig* emphasize

be'klijven (beklijfde, h. en is beklijfd) *vi* remain, stick

be'klimmen¹ *vt* climb [a tree, a mountain], mount [a throne]; ascend [a mountain, the throne]; scale [a wall]; **–ming** (-en) *v* climbing, mounting, ascent

be'klinken¹ *vt fig* settle [an affair]; clinch [the deal, a question]; *de zaak was spoedig beklonken* the matter was soon settled

be'kloppen¹ *vt* 1 tap; 2 ⚓ percuss, sound

be'knellen¹ *vt* pinch; *bekneld raken* get jammed, get wedged

be'knibbelen¹ *vt* pinch [sbd. for food], skimp, stint [sbd. in money, praise &]

be'knopt concise, brief, succinct; **–heid** *v* conciseness, briefness, brevity, succinctness

be'knorren¹ *vt* chide, scold

be'knotten¹ *vt* curtail

be'kocht *ik voelde mij* ~ I felt taken in; *hij is er aan* ~ he has paid too dear for it; *u bent er niet aan* ~ you have got your money's worth; zie ook: *bekopen*

be'koelen¹ *vi* (& *vt*) cool (down)²

be'kogelen (bekogelde, h. bekogeld) *vt* pelt [with eggs &]; [*fig*] *iem. met vragen* ~ fire questions at sbd.

be'kokstoven (bekokstoofde, h. bekokstoofd) *vt = bekonkelen*

be'komen I (bekwam, h. bekomen) *vt* 1 (k r ij g e n) get, receive, obtain; 2 (v. s p ij - z e n) agree with, suit; *dat zal je slecht* ~ you will be sorry for it; II (bekwam, is bekomen) *vi* recover [from the shock]

be'kommerd concerned, anxious; be'kommeren (bekommerde, h. bekommerd) *zich* ~ *om* (*over*) care about, trouble about, be anxious about; *zonder zich te* ~ *om* heedless of, regardless of; be'kommernis (-sen) *v* anxiety, solicitude, trouble, care

be'komst *zijn* ~ *hebben van* F be fed up with

be'konkelen¹ *vt* plot, hatch, scheme

be'koorlijk charming, enchanting; **–heid** (-heden) *v* charm, enchantment

be'kopen¹ *vt hij moest het met de dood* ~ he had to pay for it with his life; zie ook: *bekocht*

be'koren (bekoorde, h. bekoord) *vt* charm, enchant, fascinate; *rk* tempt; *dat kan mij niet* ~ that does not appeal to me; **–ring** (-en) *v* charm, enchantment, fascination; *rk* tempta-

tion; *onder de* ~ *komen van* fall under the spell of

be'korten¹ *vt* shorten [a distance]; abridge [a book]; cut short [a speech]; **–ting** (-en) *v* shortening, abridgement

be'kostigen (bekostigde, h. bekostigd) *vt* defray (bear) the cost of, pay the expenses of; *dat kan ik niet* ~ I cannot afford it

be'krachtigen (bekrachtigde, h. bekrachtigd) *vt* confirm [a statement]; ratify [a treaty]; sanction [a custom, a law]; **–ging** (-en) *v* confirmation; ratification; sanction; [royal] assent

be'krassen¹ *vt* scratch (all) over

be'kreunen¹ *zich* ~ = *zich bekommeren*

be'krimpen¹ *zich* ~ cut down [on food]

bekriti'seren [s = z] (bekritiseerde, h. bekritiseerd) *vt* criticize, censure

be'krompen 1 (p e r s o n e ņ, g e e s t) narrow-minded, narrow; 2 (b e g i n s e l e n) hidebound; 3 confined [space]; 4 slender [means], straitened [circumstances]; **–heid** *v* narrow-mindedness

be'kronen¹ *vt* 1 crown; 2 award a (the) prize to; zie ook: *bekroond*; **–ning** (-en) *v* 1 crowning; 2 award, prize; be'kroond prize (winning) [ox, poem, essay, fellowship]

be'kruipen¹ *vt de lust bekroop hem om...* a desire to... came over him

'bekvechten *vi* wrangle, squabble

be'kwaam capable, able, clever; fit; **–heid** (-heden) *v* capability, ability, capacity, aptitude; skill, proficiency; *zijn bekwaamheden* his capacities (faculties, abilities, accomplishments); be'kwamen (bekwaamde, h. bekwaamd) *vr zich* ~ fit oneself, qualify [for a post]; read [for an examination]

be'kwijlen *vi* beslaver, beslobber

bel (-len) *v* 1 (v. m e t a a l) bell; 2 (l u c h t - b l a a s j e) bubble; zie ook: *kat*

be'labberd = *beroerd*

be'lachelijk I *aj* ridiculous, ludicrous, laughable; ~ *maken* ridicule; *zich* ~ *maken* make oneself ridiculous, make a fool of oneself; II *ad* ridiculously

be'laden¹ *vt* load, lade, burden²

be'lagen (belaagde, h. belaagd) *vt* threaten, beset; **–er** (-s) *m* enemy, attacker

be'landen¹ *vi* land; *waar is mijn pen beland?* what has become of my pen?; *doen* ~ land

be'lang (-en) *o* 1 (v o o r d e e l) interest; 2 (b e l a n g r ij k h e i d) importance; ~ *hebben bij* have an interest in, be interested in; *er* ~ *bij hebben om...* find it one's interest to...; ~ *stellen in* take an interest in, be interested in, interest

<hr>

¹ V.T. en V.D. van dit werkwoord volgens het model: be'ademen, V.T. be'ademde, V.D. be'ademd (**ge-** valt dus weg in het V.D.). Zie voor de vormen onder het grondwoord, in dit voorbeeld: *ademen*. Bij sterke en onregelmatige werkwoorden wordt u verwezen naar de lijst achterin.

oneself in; ~ *gaan stellen in* become interested in; • *ik doe het in uw* ~ I do it in your interest; *het is in ons aller* ~ it is to the interest of all of us; *het is v a n* ~ it is important, it is of importance; *van groot* ~ of consequence; *van geen* ~ of no importance; *van het hoogste* ~ of the first (of vital) importance; *van weinig* ~ of little consequence (moment); **–eloos** disinterested; be**'langenconflict** (-en) *o* clash of interests; **–gemeenschap** (-pen) *v* community of interests; **–groep** (-en) *v* pressure group; **–groepering** (-en) *v* combine; syndicate; **–sfeer** (-sferen) *v* sphere of interests; belang**'hebbende** (-n) *m-v* party concerned, party interested; be**'langrijk I** *aj* important, of importance; considerable [amount &]; marked [difference]; *een* ~ *man* a man of weight, a notability; **II** *ad* < considerably [better &]; **–heid** *v* importance; belang**'stellend I** *aj* interested; **II** *ad* with interest; **–en** *mv* those interested; be**'langstelling** *v* interest (in *voor*); *bewijzen (blijken) van* ~ marks of sympathy; *iems.* ~ *wekken voor* interest sbd. in; *met* ~ with interest; belang**'wekkend** interesting
be**'last** ~ *en beladen* heavy-laden, heavily loaded; *een erfelijk* ~*e* a victim of heredity; **–baar** dutiable [at the custom-house], taxable [income, capital, profits], assessable, rat(e)able [property]; be**'lasten** (belastte, h. belast) **I** *vt* 1 (l a s t o p l e g g e n) burden; 2 ✗ load; 3 (b e l a s t i n g o p l e g g e n) tax [subjects], rate [city people]; impose a tax on [liquors]; 4 $ burst [with a sum]; *iem. met* ~ charge sbd. with sth.; *belast zijn met (de zorg voor)* be in charge of; *erfelijk belast zijn* have a hereditary taint; **II** *vr zich* ~ *met* undertake, take upon oneself, charge oneself with; **–d** incriminating [evidence]
be**'lasteren**[1] *vt* calumniate, slander, malign, defame; **–ring** (-en) *v* calumniation, defamation
be**'lasting** (-en) *v* 1 (h e t b e l a s t e n) burdening &; taxation [of subjects]; 2 ✗ weight, load [on arch &]; 3 (r ij k s ~) tax(es); duty [on petrol]; (p l a a t s e l ij k) rates; 4 (d e d i e n s t, d e f i s c u s) inland revenue; ~ *op openbare vermakelijkheden* (public) entertainment tax, amusement tax; ~ *over de toegevoegde waarde* zie *B.T.W.*; ~ *heffen van* levy a tax (taxes) on; *in de* ~ *vallen* be liable to taxation; **–aangifte** (-n) *v* (tax) return; **–aanslag** (-slagen) *m* assessment; **–aftrek** *m* tax deduction; **–ambtenaar** (-s en -naren) *m* tax official, revenue official;

–betaler (-s) *m* taxpayer, ratepayer; **–biljet** (-ten) *o* notice of assessment; **–consulent** [-zy.lɪnt] (-en) *m* tax consultant; **–druk** *m* tax burden; **–faciliteit** (-en) *v* tax relief (concession); **–inspecteur** (-s) *m* assessor; **–jaar** (-jaren) *o* fiscal year; **–kantoor** (-toren) *o* tax-collector's office; **–ontduiking** *v* tax-evasion, tax-dodging; belasting**'plichtig** *aj* taxable, ratable; **~en** taxpayers, ratepayers; be**'lastingschuld** (-en) *v* tax(es) due; belasting**'schuldig** = *belastingplichtig;* be**'lastingstelsel** (-s) *o* system of taxation, tax system, fiscal system; **–verlaging** (-en) *v* tax abatement (relief, reduction); **–vrij** tax-free, duty-free
be**'lazeren** (belazerde, h. belazerd) *vt* **P** cheat, swindle, defraud; *ben je belazerd?* are you mad?
'bel**boei** (-en) *v* bell-buoy
be**'ledigen** (beledigde, h. beledigd) *vt* insult, affront, offend, hurt [one's feelings], (g r o f) outrage; **–d** offensive, insulting, opprobrious; ~ *worden* **F** become (get) personal; be**'lediging** (-en) *v* (v. i e m.) insult, affront; (v. g e v o e l e n s) offence, outrage
be**'leefd I** *aj* polite, civil, courteous; **II** *ad* politely &; *wij verzoeken u* ~ we kindly request you; ~ *maar dringend* gently but firmly; be**'leefdheid** (-heden) *v* politeness, civility, courteousness, courtesy; *de burgerlijke* ~ common politeness; *beleefdheden* civilities; compliments; *dat laat ik aan uw* ~ *over* I leave it to your discretion; **–sbezoek** (-en) *o* courtesy visit; beleefdheids**'halve** out of politeness, out of courtesy; be**'leefdheidsvorm** (-en) *m* form of etiquette; (a a n s p r e e k v o r m) form of address
be**'leenbaar** pawnable; **–brief** (-brieven) *m* pawn ticket
be**'leg** *o* ✗ siege; *het* ~ *slaan voor* lay siege to; zie ook: *opbreken, staat* &
be**'legen** matured [cigars, wine &]; ripe [cheese], stale [bread]
be**'legeraar** (-s) *m* besieger; be**'legeren**[1] *vt* besiege; **–ring** (-en) *v* siege
be**'leggen**[1] *vt* 1 cover, overlay [with a coating of...]; 2 invest [money]; 3 (b ij e e n r o e p e n) convene, call [a meeting]; 4 (o p t o u w z e t t e n) arrange [a meeting]; **–er** (-s) *m* $ investor; be**'legging** (-en) *v* $ investment; **–sfondsen** *mv* investment stock
be**'legsel** (-s) *o* trimming [of a gown]; be**'legstuk** (-ken) *o* lining piece
be**'leid** *o* 1 prudence, discretion, generalship; 2

---

[1] V.T. en V.D. van dit werkwoord volgens het model: be**'ademen**, V.T. be**'ademde**, V.D. be**'ademd** (ge- valt dus weg in het V.D.). Zie voor de vormen onder het grondwoord, in dit voorbeeld: *ademen*. Bij sterke en onregelmatige werkwoorden wordt u verwezen naar de lijst achterin.

[foreign] policy; *met ~ te werk gaan* proceed tactfully

be'lemmeren (belemmerde, h. belemmerd) *vt* hamper, hinder, impede, obstruct, stand in the way of; *in de groei belemmerd* stunted in growth; **–ring** (-en) *v* hindrance, impediment, obstruction, handicap, obstacle

be'lendend adjacent, adjoining, neighbouring

be'lenen[1] *vt* pawn; borrow money on [securities]; **–ning** (-en) *v* pawning; loan against security

be'lerend lecturing, didactic

be'let *o ~!* don't come in!, occupied!; *~ geven* not be at home [to visitors]; *~ hebben* be engaged; *hij heeft ~* he cannot receive you; *~ krijgen* be denied; *~ laten vragen* send to inquire if Mr and Mrs So-and-So are at home

'bel-etage ['bɪle.ta.ʒə] (-s) *v* ground floor

be'letsel (-s en -en) *o* hindrance, obstacle, impediment; **be'letten** (belette, h. belet) *vt* 1 (i e t s) prevent; 2 (m e t i n f i n i t i e f) hinder (prevent) from, preclude from

be'leven[1] *vt* 1 live to see; 2 go through [many adventures, three editions]; *zijn 80ste verjaardag nog ~* live to be eighty; **be'levenis** (-sen) *v* experience

be'lezen *aj* well-read; **–heid** *v* (range of) reading; *zijn grote ~* his extensive (wide) reading

'belfort (-s) *o* bell tower, belfry

Belg (-en) *m* Belgian; **'België** *o* Belgium; **'Belgisch** Belgian

'Belgrado *o* Belgrade

'belhamel (-s) *m* bell-wether; (d e u g n i e t) rascal

be'lichamen (belichaamde, h. belichaamd) *vt* embody; **–ming** (-en) *v* embodiment

be'lichten[1] *vt* 1 illuminate, throw (a) light on; 2 light [a picture]; 3 expose [in photography]; **be'lichting** (-en) *v* 1 illumination, light; 2 lighting [of a picture]; 3 exposure [in photography]; **–smeter** (-s) *m* exposure meter

be'lieven I (beliefde, h. beliefd) *vt* please; *wat belieft u?* (b ij u i t e r s t a n) (I beg your) pardon?; **II** *o naar ~* at pleasure, at will; [add sugar] to taste

be'lijden[1] *vt* 1 confess [one's guilt]; 2 profess [a religion]; **be'lijdenis** (-sen) *v* 1 confession [of faith]; 2 (g o d s d i e n s t) profession, creed, denomination; 3 (a a n n e m i n g t o t l i d m a a t) confirmation; *zijn ~ doen* be confirmed; **be'lijder** (-s) *m* 1 adherent [of a faith], professor [of a religion]; 2 confessor [in

spite of persecution and torture]; *Eduard de Belijder* ⌾ Edward the Confessor

'belknop (-pen) *m* bell-button, bell-push

bella'donna *v* belladonna

'bellen (belde, h. gebeld) *vi & vt* ring [the bell]; *er wordt gebeld* there is a ring (at the bell, at the door); *ik zal je ~* I'll give you a ring

bellet'trie *v* belles-lettres

be'loeren[1] *vt* watch, spy upon, peep at

be'lofte (-n) *v* promise; (p l e c h t i g) pledge, undertaking; ⚖ affirmation; *zijn ~ breken* break one's promise; *zijn ~ houden* keep one's promise; *~ maakt schuld* promise is debt

be'loken *~ Pasen* Low Sunday

be'lommerd shady

be'lonen[1] *vt* reward; recompense, remunerate; **–ning** (-en) *v* reward; recompense, remuneration; *ter ~ van* as a reward for, in reward of, in return for; *een ~ uitloven* offer a reward

be'loop *o alles op zijn ~ laten* let things take their course, let things drift; **be'lopen**[1] *vi* amount to [of a sum]

be'loven[1] *vt* promise; (p l e c h t i g) vow; *fig* bid fair [to be a success]; *de oogst belooft veel* the crops are very promising, promise well; *het belooft mooi weer te worden* there is every promise of fine weather; *dat belooft wat!* that looks promising!

'belroos *v* ✚ erysipelas

belt (-en) *m & v = asbelt*

be'luisteren[1] *vt* overhear [a conversation]; catch [a change of tone]; listen in to [a broadcast]; ✚ auscultate

be'lust *~ zijn op* be eager for, be keen on

be'machtigen[1] *vt* secure, seize, take possession of, possess oneself of

be'mannen (bemande, h. bemand) *vt* man [a ship]; *bemand* manned [spacecraft, space flight]; **–ning** (-en) *v* crew

be'mantelen (bemantelde, h. bemanteld) *vt* cloak[2], *fig* veil, palliate; gloze over, gloss over

be'merken[1] *vt* perceive, notice, find

be'mesten[1] *vt* manure, dress; (d o o r b e -. v l o e i i n g) warp; (m e t k u n s t m e s t) fertilize; **–ting** (-en) *v* manuring, dressing; (m e t k u n s t m e s t) fertilization

be'middelaar (-s) *m* mediator, go-between

be'middeld in easy circumstances, well-to-do

be'middelen (bemiddelde, h. bemiddeld) *vt* mediate [a peace]; *~d optreden* act as a mediator, mediate; **be'middeling** (-en) *v* mediation; *door ~ van* through the agency (intermediary, medium) of...; **–spoging** (-en) *v*

---

mediatory effort

be'mind (be)loved; *zich ~ maken* make oneself loved [by...], popular [with...], endear oneself [to...]; **–e** (-n) *m-v* loved one, (well-)beloved, lover, sweetheart, betrothed; **be'minnelijk** 1 (p a s s i e f) lovable; 2 (a c t i e f) amiable; **be'minnen**[1] *vt* be fond of, love, cherish

be'modderd muddy, mud-stained

be'moederen[1] *vt* mother

be'moedigen (bemoedigde, h. bemoedigd) *vt* encourage, cheer up; **–ging** (-en) *v* encouragement

be'moeial [bə'mu.jɑl] (-len) *m* busybody, meddler; **be'moeien** (bemoeide, h. bemoeid) *zich ~ met* meddle with, interfere with [what's not one's business]; *zich met zijn eigen zaken ~* mind one's own business; *hij bemoeit zich niet met anderen* he keeps himself to himself; *niet mee ~!* let well alone!; *je moet je niet zo met alles ~* you mustn't always be meddling; **be'moeienis** (-sen), **be'moeiing** (-en) *v ik heb er geen ~ mee* I have nothing to do with it; *door zijn ~* through his efforts

be'moeilijken (bemoeilijkte, h. bemoeilijkt) *vt* hamper, hinder, thwart

be'moeiziek meddlesome; **–zucht** *v* meddlesomeness

be'monsteren[1] *vt* sample; *bemonsterde offerte* sampled offer, offer with sample(s)

be'morsen[1] *vt* soil, dirty, bedabble

be'most mossy, moss-grown

ben (-nen) *v* basket, hamper

be'nadelen [-de.-] (benadeelde, h. benadeeld) *vt* hurt, harm, injure, prejudice; **–ling** (-en) *v* injury; ⚕ lesion

be'naderen (benaderde, h. benaderd) *vt* 1 (n a b ij k o m e n) approximate; 2 (s c h a t t e n) estimate; 3 (i e m a n d, e e n v r a a g s t u k) approach; *moeilijk te ~* unapproachable; **–ring** (-en) *v* (v. g e t a l l e n &) approximation; *de ~ van een probleem* the approach to a problem; *bij ~* approximately

be'nadrukken (benadrukte, h. benadrukt) *vt* stress, emphasize, underline

be'naming (-en) *v* name, appellation; *verkeerde ~* misnomer

be'nard critical; *in ~e omstandigheden* in straitened circumstances, in distress; *in deze ~e tijden* in these hard (trying) times

be'nauwd 1 (v e r t r e k) close, stuffy; (w e e r) stifling, sultry; oppressive; 2 tight in the chest, oppressed; 3 (b a n g) fearful, timid, timorous; anxious [hours]; 4 (n a u w) tight; *het is hier erg*

~ 1 it is very close here; 2 we are rather cramped for room; *hij kreeg het ~* 1 he was hard pressed; 2 he became afraid; *wees maar niet ~!* no fear!, don't be afraid!; **–heid** (-heden) *v* 1 closeness; 2 tightness of the chest; 3 anxiety, fear; **be'nauwen** (benauwde, h. benauwd) *vt* oppress; **–d** oppressive; **be'nauwing** (-en) *v* oppression

'bende (-n en -s) *v* band [of rebels], troop [of children]; gang [of ruffians]; pack [of beggars]; *de hele ~* the whole lot; *een hele ~* a lot of [mistakes]; *wat een ~!* 1 (v. p e r s o n e n) what a (disorderly) crew!; 2 (v. t o e s t a n d) what a mess!; **–hoofd** (-en) *o*, **–leider** *m* (-s) gang leader

be'neden I *prep* below, beneath, under; *dat is ~ mijn waardigheid* that is beneath me; *hij staat ~ mij* he is under me, my inferior; *inkomens ~ £ 200* incomes under £ 200; *over ~... blijven* fall greatly short of...; *~ verwachting* not up to (below) expectations; **II** *ad* 1 downstairs, down; 2 below (ook = at the foot of the page); *wij wonen ~* we live on the ground-floor; *~ (aan de bladzijde)* at the foot (bottom) of the page, below; *n a a r ~* downstairs; downward(s), down; [jump] on to the ground; *5de regel v a n ~* from bottom; **–buur** (-buren) *m* neighbour on the lower storey, ground-floor neighbour; **–eind(e)** (-(e)n) *o* lower end, bottom; **–hoek** (-en) *m* bottom corner; *~ links (rechts)* bottom left-hand (right-hand) corner; **–huis** (-huizen) *o* ground floor; **–loop** (-lopen) *m* lower course [of a river]; **–stad** *v* lower town; **–ste** lowest, lowermost, undermost, bottom; **–verdieping** (-en) *v* ground floor; **Be'nedenwindse 'Eilanden** *mv* Leeward Islands

benedic'tijn [be.nə-] (-en) *m* Benedictine (monk)

bene'fietvoorstelling [be.nə-] (-en) *v* benefit performance, benefit night

be'nemen[1] *vt* take away [one's breath]; *het uitzicht ~* obstruct the view; *de moed ~* dishearten; *iem. de lust ~ om...* spoil sbd.'s pleasure in...

1 'benen *aj* bone

2 'benen (beende, h. gebeend) *vi* walk (quickly)

'benenwagen *m met de ~ gaan* ride Shanks's(s) mare

be'nepen petty; small-minded; pinched [face]; *met een ~ hart* with a faint heart; *met een ~ stemmetje* in a timid voice; **–heid** *v* small-mindedness, pettiness, pinchedness

---

[1] V.T. en V.D. van dit werkwoord volgens het model: **be'**ademen, V.T. **be'**ademde, V.D. **be'**ademd (**ge-** valt dus weg in het V.D.). Zie voor de vormen onder het grondwoord, in dit voorbeeld: *ademen.* Bij sterke en onregelmatige werkwoorden wordt u verwezen naar de lijst achterin.

be′neveld 1 foggy, misty, hazy; dim [of sight, intelligence]; 2 (h a l f d r o n k e n) muzzy, fuddled; **be′nevelen** (benevelde, h. beneveld) *vt* 1 befog, cloud, dim; 2 (d o o r d e d r a n k) bemuse, fuddle

be′nevens (together) with, besides, in addition to

′bengel (-s) *m* 1 clapper [of a bell]; 2 bell; 3 naughty boy, **F** pickle

′bengelen (bengelde, h. gebengeld) *vi* dangle, swing [on the gallows]

be′nieuwd ~ *zijn* be curious to know; *zeer* ~ *zijn* be anxious to know; zie ook: *benieuwen;* **be′nieuwen** (benieuwde, h. benieuwd) *vt het zal mij* ~ *of hij komt* I wonder if he is going to turn up

′benig bony

be′nijdbaar enviable; **be′nijden** (benijdde, h. benijd) *vt* envy, be envious of; **benijdens-′waard(ig)** enviable

Be′nin *o* Benin

be′nodigd required, necessary, wanted; **–heden** *mv* needs, necessaries, requisites, materials

be′noembaar eligible; **be′noemd** ~ *getal* concrete number; **be′noemen**[1] *vt* appoint, nominate; *hem* ~ *tot...* appoint him (to be)...; **–ming** (-en) *v* appointment, nomination; *zijn* ~ *tot...* his appointment to be (a)..., as (a)...

be′noorden (to the) north of

′bent *v* set, clique, party; **–genoot** (-noten) *m* partisan, fellow

be′nul *o* notion; *ik heb er geen flauw* ~ *van* I have not the foggiest (slightest) idea

be′nutten (benutte, h. benut) *vt* utilize, make use of, avail oneself of

B. en W. = *Burgemeester en Wethouders,* zie *burgemeester*

ben′zeen *o* benzene

ben′zine *v* 1 petrol; *Am* gasoline; 2 benzine [for cleaning clothes &]; **–blik** (-ken) *o* petrol can; **–bom** (-men) *v* petrol bomb, Molotov cocktail; **–meter** (-s) *m* petrol gauge; **–motor** (-s en -toren) *m* petrol engine; **–pomp** (-en) *v* petrol pump; **–station** [-sta.(t)ʃɔn] (-s) *o* filling station; **–tank** [-tɛŋk] (-s) *m* fuel tank

be′oefenaar (-s en -naren) *m* practitioner [of pugilism &]; student [of English]; cultivator [of the art of painting]; **be′oefenen**[1] *vt* study [a science, an art], cultivate [an art]; practise, follow [a profession]; practise [virtue]; **–ning** *v* study [of a science, an art], practice, cultivation [of an art]

be′ogen (beoogde, h. beoogd) *vt* have in view, aim at, intend; *het had niet de beoogde uitwerking* it did not work

be′oordelen[1] *vt* judge of [sth.], judge [sbd.]; review, criticize [a book, play &]; *hem ~ naar...* judge him by...; **be′oordeling** (-en) *v* 1 judg(e)ment; 2 (v. b o e k &) criticism, review; (v. s c h o o l w e r k) marking; *dit is ter* ~ *van...* this is at the discretion of...; **–sfout** (-en) *v* misjudgement, miscalculation

be′oorlogen (beoorloogde, h. beoorloogd) *vt* wage (make) war on (against)

be′oosten (to the) east of, eastward of

be′paalbaar determinable, definable; **be′paald I** *aj* fixed [hour, price]; 2 (d u i d e l ij k o m-l ij n d) definite [object], positive [answer], distinct [inclination]; 3 (v a s t s t a a n d) stated [hours for...], appointed [times for...]; 4 *gram* definite [article]; *in* ~*e gevallen* in certain (particular, specific) cases; *het bij de wet* ~*e* the provisions enacted (laid down) by law; *niets* ~*s* nothing definite; **II** *ad* positively, quite, decidedly [fine, impossible &]; *u moet* ~ *gaan* you should go by all means; *u moet* ~ *gaan* you should make a point of going; *hij moet daar* ~ *iets mee op het oog hebben* I am sure he must have a definite object in view; *als je nu* ~ *gaan wilt, dan...* if you are determined on going, then...; *hij is nu niet* ~ *slim* he is not exactly clever; **–elijk** particularly, specifically; **–heid** *v* definiteness, positiveness

be′pakken[1] *vt* pack; **–king** (-en) *v* ✗ pack; *met volle* ~ in full marching kit

be′palen (bepaalde, h. bepaald) **I** *vt* 1 fix [a time, price], appoint [an hour for...], stipulate [a condition]; 2 (b ij b e s l u i t) provide, lay down, decree, enact; 3 (d o o r o n d e r z o e k) ascertain, determine [the weight &]; 4 (o m-s c h r ij v e n) define [an idea]; 5 (u i t m a k e n) decide, determine [the success]; *nader te* ~ to be fixed, to be determined later on; **II** *vr zich* ~ *t o t* restrict oneself to, confine oneself to; **–d** defining, determining; ~ *lidwoord* definite article; **be′paling** (-en) *v* 1 (v. u u r &) fixing; 2 (v. b e g r i p) definition; 3 (i n c o n t r a c t) stipulation, condition, clause; 4 (i n w e t &) provision, regulation; 5 (d o o r o n d e r z o e k) determination; 6 *gram* adjunct

be′pantseren[1] *vt* armour; *bepantserd* ook: armour-plated

be′peinzen[1] *vt* meditate (on), muse (up)on

be′perken (beperkte, h. beperkt) **I** *vt* limit, restrict, confine; cut down, curtail [expenses,

---

[1] V.T. en V.D. van dit werkwoord volgens het model: **be′**ademen, V.T. **be′**ademde, V.D. **be′**ademd (**ge-** valt dus weg in het V.D.). Zie voor de vormen onder het grondwoord, in dit voorbeeld: *ademen.* Bij sterke en onregelmatige werkwoorden wordt u verwezen naar de lijst achterin.

output], reduce [the service]; modify, qualify [the sense of a word]; *de brand* ~ localize the fire; **II** *vr zich* ~ *tot* limit (restrict) oneself to; **–d** restrictive [clause &]; **be'perking** (-en) *v* limitation, restriction, restraint; reduction; [credit, economic] squeeze; **be'perkt** limited [area, means, franchise, sense], confined [space], restricted [application]; *~e aansprake-lijkheid* limited liability; ~ *tot* limited to, restricted to; **–heid** (-heden) *v* limitedness, limitation

be'plakken[1] *vt* paste (over)

be'planten[1] *vt* plant; **–ting** (-en) *v* planting; plantation

be'pleisteren[1] *vt* plaster (over); **–ring** (-en) *v* plastering

be'pleiten[1] *vt* plead, advocate

be'poederen, be'poeieren[1] *vt* powder

be'poten[1] *vt* plant, set [with]

be'praten[1] *vt* 1 (i e t s) talk about, discuss; 2 (i e m.) talk... round, persuade; *iem.* ~ *om...* talk sbd. into ...ing; *zich laten* ~ allow oneself to be persuaded, to be talked into ...ing

be'proefd well-tried [system], approved [methods]; efficacious [remedy]; tried [friend]; *zwaar* ~ bereaved [family]; sorely tried [people]; **be'proeven**[1] *vt* 1 (p r o b e r e n) try, attempt, endeavour [it]; 2 (o p d e p r o e f s t e l l e n) try, test; visit [with affliction]; **–ving** (-en) *v* trial, ordeal, affliction

be'raad *o* deliberation, consideration; *iets in* ~ *houden* think it over, consider it; *in* ~ *nemen* consider; *na rijp* ~ after mature deliberation, on careful consideration; **be'raadslagen** (beraadslaagde, h. beraadslaagd) *vi* deliberate; ~ *m e t* consult with; ~ *o v e r* deliberate upon; **–ging** (-en) *v* deliberation, consultation; **1 be'raden** *aj* 1 well-advised; deliberate; 2 (v a s t b e s l o t e n) resolute; **2 be'raden**[1] *zich* ~ think [sth.] over

be'ramen (beraamde, h. beraamd) *vt* 1 (b e - d e n k e n) devise [a plan]; plan [a journey &]; plot [his death]; 2 (s c h a t t e n) estimate [at fifty pounds]; **–ming** (-en) *v* (r a m i n g) estimate

'berberis (-sen) *v* 🌿 barberry

'berde zie *brengen*

be'rechten (berechtte, h. berecht) *vt* ⚖ try [a criminal]; adjudicate [a civil case]; **–ting** (-en) *v* ⚖ trial [of a criminal]; adjudication [of a civil case]

be'redderen[1] *vt* arrange, put in order

be'reden mounted [police]

berede'neren[1] *vt* reason about (upon), discuss, argue

be'reid ready, prepared, willing; *zich* ~ *verklaren* express one's willingness; **be'reiden** (bereidde, h. bereid) *vt* 1 prepare [the meals]; 2 dress [leather]; 3 give [a cordial welcome, a surprise]; **be'reidheid** *v* readiness, willing-ness; **be'reiding** (-en) *v* preparation [of a meal]; **bereid'vaardig, bereid'willig** ready, willing, obliging

be'reik *o* reach[2], range[2]; *b i n n e n ieders* ~ within the reach of all[2]; [price] within the means of all; *b u i t e n mijn* ~ beyond (out of) my reach[2]; **–baar** attainable, within (easy) reach, on (at) call; **be'reiken**[1] *vt* reach[2], attain[2]; *fig* achieve; *we* ~ *er niets mee* it does not get us anywhere, it gets us nowhere

be'reisd (widely-)travelled; **be'reizen**[1] *vt* travel over; visit

be'rekend ~ *o p* calculated (meant) for; ~ *v o o r zijn taak* equal to (up to) his task; **be'rekenen**[1] *vt* 1 (u i t r e k e n e n) calculate, compute [the number]; 2 (a a n r e k e n e n) charge [five pounds]; *teveel* ~ overcharge; **–d** scheming, craftily [person]; **be'rekening** (-en) *v* calculation, computation

'berekuil (-en) *m* bear-pit; **–muts** (-en) *v* bearskin (cap)

berg (-en) *m* mountain[2], mount; (i n e i g e n -n a m e n) Mount [Everest]; *gouden ~en beloven* promise mountains of gold; *over* ~ *en dal* up hill and down dale; *de haren rijzen mij te ~e* it makes my hair stand on end; *de* ~ *heeft een muis gebaard* the mountain has brought forth a mouse; **–achtig** mountainous, hilly; **berg'af** downhill; **berg'afwaarts** downhill, down the slope; **'bergbeklimmer** (-s) *m* mountain climber, mountaineer; **–bewoner** (-s) *m* mountaineer

'bergen* I *vt* 1 (l e g g e n) put; 2 (o p s l a a n) store; 3 (b e v a t t e n) hold, contain; 4 (s t r a n d g o e d e r e n) salve; 5 (e e n l ij k, r u i m t e c a p s u l e) recover; **II** *vr zich* ~ get out of the way; *berg je!* hide yourself!; get away!; save yourself!; *niet weten zich te* ~ *van schaamte* not to know where to hide

'bergengte (-n en -s) *v* defile

'berger (-s) *m* salvor

'berghelling (-en) *v* mountain slope

'berghok (-ken) *o* shed

'berghut (-ten) *v* climbers' hut, mountain hut, Alpine hut

'berging *v* 1 (v. s t r a n d g o e d e r e n) sal-

---

[1] V.T. en V.D. van dit werkwoord volgens het model: **be'**ademen, V.T. **be'**ademde, V.D. **be'**ademd (**ge-** valt dus weg in het V.D.). Zie voor de vormen onder het grondwoord, in dit voorbeeld: *ademen*. Bij sterke en onregelmatige werkwoorden wordt u verwezen naar de lijst achterin.

vage; 2 (v. r u i m t e c a p s u l e) recovery;
'**bergingsmaatschappij** (-en) *v* salvage
company; **–vaartuig** (-en) *o* salvage vessel,
salvor

'**bergkam** (-men) *m* mountain ridge; **–keten**
(-s) *v* chain (range) of mountains, mountain
range, mountain chain, rand; **–kloof** (-kloven)
v cleft, gorge, chasm, ravine, gully; **–kristal**
(-len) *o* rock-crystal; **–land** (-en) *o* mountainous country

'**bergloon** (-lonen) *o* ⚓ salvage (money)

berg'op uphill; '**bergpad** (-paden) *o* mountain
path; **–pas** (-sen) *m* mountain pass; **–plaats**
(-en) *v* depository; shed

'**Bergrede** *v* Sermon on the Mount; '**bergrug**
(-gen) *m* mountain ridge

'**bergruimte** (-s en -n) *v* storage room, *Br*
box-room

'**bergschoen** (-en) *m* mountaineering boot;
–sport *v* mountaineering; **–storting** (-en) *v*
landslide, landslip; **–top** (-pen) *m* mountain
top; mountain peak, pinnacle; **–wand** (-en) *m*
mountain side, mountain slope

be'richt (-en) *o* 1 (n i e u w s) news, tidings; 2
(k e n n i s g e v i n g) message, notice, advice;
communication; report; 3 (i n k r a n t) paragraph; **~ van ontvangst** acknowledgement (of
receipt); **~ krijgen** receive (get) news, hear
[from sbd.]; **~ sturen** (*zenden*) send word

be'richten (berichtte, h. bericht) *vt* let [us]
know, send word [whether...], inform [of your
arrival], report; zie ook: *ontvangst*

be'ridderen (beridderde, h. beridderd) =
beredderen

be'rijdbaar passable, practicable [of roads];
be'rijden[1] *vt* ride over, drive over [a road];
ride [a horse, a bicycle]

be'rijmen[1] *vt* rhyme, versify, put into verse;
–ming (-en) *v* rhyming, rhymed version

be'rijpt frosted, hoar

be'rin [be:-] (-nen) *v* she-bear

be'rispen (berispte, h. berispt) *vt* blame,
reprove, rebuke, reprehend, reprimand,
censure, admonish, rate; **–ping** (-en) *v*
reproof, rebuke, reprimand

berk (-en), '**berkeboom** (-bomen) *m* birch,
birch tree; '**berkehout** *o* birch-wood;
'**berken** *aj* birchen

Ber'lijn *o* Berlin, **–er** (-s) *m* Berliner; **–s** Berlin;
~ blauw Prussian blue

berm (-en) *m* (grass) verge [of a road], [hard,
soft] shoulder; (v e r h o o g d) bank; **–lamp**
(-en) *v* spotlight

Bern *o* Berne; '**Berner** Bernese [Oberland];
Berne [Convention]

be'roemd famous, renowned, illustrious,
celebrated; **~ maken F** put on the map; **–heid**
(-heden) *v* fame, renown; **een ~** a celebrity;
be'roemen[1] **zich ~** boast, brag; **zich ~ op**
boast of, pride oneself on, glory in

be'roep (-en) *o* 1 (v a k) profession, trade,
business, calling, occupation; 2 ⚖ appeal; 3
(p r e d i k a n t) call; **~ aantekenen** lodge an
appeal; **een ~ doen op** appeal to [sbd. for sth.];
call on [sbd.'s help]; *i n (hoger)* **~ gaan** appeal to
a higher court, appeal against a decision; **zijn
~ maken v a n** professionalize; *...van ~* ...by
profession, by trade, professional...; *Anna N.
z o n d e r ~* ...(of) no occupation; **be'roepen**[1]
I *vt* call [a clergyman]; **II** *vr zich ~ op* refer to
[your evidence], plead [ignorance], invoke
[article 34]; **be'roepengids** (-en) *m*, **–lijst**
(-en) *v* yellow pages; **be'roeps(-)** vaak:
professional; **be'roepsgeheim** (-en) *o* professional secret; *het ~* professional secrecy [in
journalism &]; **beroeps'halve** by virtue of
one's profession, professionally; **be'roeps-
keuze** *v* choice of a profession (of a career);
voorlichting bij ~ vocational guidance; **–leger**
(-s) *o* regular army; **–misdadiger** (-s) *m*
professional criminal; **–officier** (-en) *m*
regular officer; **–speler** (-s) *m* professional
(player); **–sport** *v* professionalism; **–ziekte** (-n
en -s) *v* occupational (industrial) disease

be'roerd I *aj* unpleasant, miserable, wretched,
F rotten; **II** *ad <* wretchedly [bad &];

be'roeren[1] *vt eig* touch lightly; *fig* stir, disturb,
perturb; **–ring** (-en) *v* commotion, disturbance, turmoil; perturbation; *in ~ brengen = fig
beroeren;* **be'roerling** (-en) *m* rotter; **be'roerte**
(-n en -s) *v* stroke (of apoplexy), (apoplectic)
fit, seizure; *een (aanval van) ~ krijgen, door een ~
getroffen worden* have an apoplectic fit (a stroke)

be'roet sooty

be'rokkenen (berokkende, h. berokkend) *vt*
cause [sorrow], give [pain]; *leed ~* bring misery
upon; *schade ~* do damage to

be'rooid penniless, down and out

be'rouw *o* repentance, contrition, compunction, remorse; **~ hebben over** (*van*) repent
(of), regret, feel sorry for; **be'rouwen**
(berouwde, h. berouwd) *vt* 1 (p e r s o o n l i j k)
repent (of), regret; 2 (o n p e r s o o n l i j k) *het
zal u ~* you will repent it; 3 (a l s d r e i g e-
m e n t) you shall repent (rue) it, you will be
sorry for it; *die dag zal u ~* you will rue the

---

[1] V.T. en V.D. van dit werkwoord volgens het model: **be'**ademen, V.T. **be'**ademde, V.D. **be'**ademd (**ge-** valt dus
weg in het V.D.). Zie voor de vormen onder het grondwoord, in dit voorbeeld: *ademen.* Bij sterke en onregelmatige
werkwoorden wordt u verwezen naar de lijst achterin.

day; **be'rouwvol** repentant, contrite, penitent; ~ *zondaar* prodigal

be'roven[1] *vt* rob [a traveller]; *iem. van iets* ~ rob, deprive sbd. of sth.; *zich van het leven* ~ take one's own life; **–ving** (-en) *v* robbery

'berrie (-s) *v* (hand-)barrow; stretcher [for the wounded]

'berst = *barst*; **'bersten*** = *barsten*

be'rucht notorious; disreputable, ...of ill repute [of persons, places &]; ~ *om* (*wegens*) notorious for; **–heid** *v* notoriety, notoriousness, disreputableness

berusten[1] *vi* ~ *b ij* rest with, be in the keeping of, be deposited with [of a document &]; be lodged in [of power], be vested in [of a right]; ~ *i n iets* acquiesce in sth., resign oneself to sth.; ~ *o p* be based (founded) on, rest on [solid grounds], be due to [a misunderstanding]; **–d** resigned; **be'rusting** *v* resignation, acquiescence, submission; *de stukken zijn onder zijn* ~ the documents rest with him, are in his hands, are in his custody

1 bes *v* ♪ B flat

2 bes (-sen) *v* 🐝 berry [of coffee &]; **~sen** [black, red, white] currants

3 bes (-sen) *v* old woman, gammer

be'schaafd *aj* 1 (n i e t b a r b a a r s) civilized [nations]; 2 (u i t e r l ij k) well-bred [people], polished, refined [manners, society], polite [society]; 3 (g e e s t e l ij k) cultivated, educated, cultured; **–heid** *v* refinement, good breeding

be'schaamd I *aj* ashamed, shamefaced, abashed; (s c h u c h t e r) bashful; ~ *maken* make [sbd.] feel ashamed; ~ *staan* be ashamed; ~ *doen staan* make [sbd.] feel ashamed, put to shame; *wij werden in onze verwachtingen (niet)* ~ our hopes (expectations) were (not) falsified; ~ *zijn over* be ashamed of; **II** *ad* shamefacedly; (s c h u c h t e r) bashfully

be'schadigen (beschadigde, h. beschadigd) *vt* damage; **–ging** (-en) *v* damage

be'schaduwen[1] *vt* shade, overshadow

be'schamen[1] *vt* 1 put to shame, confound [sbd.]; 2 falsify [sbd.'s expectations]; betray [our trust]; **–d** humiliating

be'schaven[1] *vt fig* refine, polish, civilize; **–ving** (-en) *v* civilization; culture, refinement

be'scheid (-en) *o* answer; *de (officiële)* ~*en* the (official) papers, documents

be'scheiden modest; unpretending, unassuming, unobtrusive; **–heid** *v* modesty

be'schenken[1] *vt* ~ *met* present with, bestow,

confer [a title, a favour &] on, endow with [a privilege]

be'schermeling(e) (-(e)n) *m* (-*v*) protégé(e);

be'schermen (beschermde, h. beschermd) *vt* protect, screen, shelter; *beschermd t e g e n de wind* sheltered (screened) from the wind; ~ *v o o r* protect from (against); **–d** 1 protecting [hand &]; protective [duties]; protectionist [system]; 2 patronizing [tone]; **be'schermengel** (-en) *m* guardian angel; **be'schermer** (-s) *m* protector; ook: = *beschermheer*; **be'schermheer** (-heren) *m* patron; **–schap** (-pen) *o* patronage; **be'schermheilige** (-n) *m* (-*v*) patron(ess), patron saint; **be'scherming** (-en) *v* 1 (b e s c h u t t i n g) protection; 2 (b e - g u n s t i g i n g) patronage; *Bescherming Bevolking* ± Civil Defence; *i n* ~ *nemen tegen* shield from; *o n d e r* ~ *van* under cover of [the night]

be'scheuren[1] *zich* ~ **P** split one's sides, laugh fit to burst

be'schieten[1] *vt* 1 ⚔ fire at (upon), (i n z. m e t g r a n a t e n) shell; 2 (b e k l e d e n) board, wainscot [a wall]; **–ting** (-en) *v* firing, (i n z. m e t g r a n a t e n) shelling

be'schijnen[1] *vt* shine upon; light up

be'schikbaar available, at sbd.'s disposal; *niet* ~ unavailable; **be'schikken**[1] *vi gunstig* (*ongunstig*) ~ *o p* grant (refuse) [a request]; ~ *o v e r* have the disposal of, have at one's disposal; dispose of [one's time]; command [a majority, 50 seats in the Lower House]; *u kunt over mij* ~ I am at your disposal; zie ook *wikken*; **–king** (-en) *v* 1 disposal; 2 [ministerial] decree; *de* ~ *hebben over...* have the disposal of..., have at one's disposal; *b ij* ~ *van de president* by order of the president; *het staat t e uwer* ~ it is at your disposal; *ter* ~ *stellen van* place (put) at the disposal of; *ter* ~ *zijn* be available

be'schilderen[1] *vt* paint, paint over; *beschilderde ramen* stained-glass windows

be'schimmeld mouldy; **be'schimmelen**[1] *vi* go (grow) mouldy

be'schimpen[1] *vt* taunt, jeer (at)

be'schoeien (beschoeide, h. beschoeid) *vt* campshed; **be'schoeiing** (-en) *v* campshot, campshedding, campsheeting

be'schonken drunk, intoxicated, tipsy

be'schoren *het was mij* ~ it fell to my lot

be'schot (-ten) *o* 1 (b e k l e e d s e l) wainscoting; 2 (a f s c h e i d i n g) partition

be'schouwelijk contemplative;

   be'schouwen[1] *vt* look at, view, contemplate;

---

[1] V.T. en V.D. van dit werkwoord volgens het model: **be'**ademen, V.T. **be'**ademde, V.D. **be'**ademd (**ge-** valt dus weg in het V.D.). Zie voor de vormen onder het grondwoord, in dit voorbeeld: *ademen*. Bij sterke en onregelmatige werkwoorden wordt u verwezen naar de lijst achterin.

consider, regard, envisage; ~ *als* consider [it one's duty], regard as [confidential], look upon as [a crime], hold (to be) [responsible], take [sbd. to be crazy, the news as true]; (*alles*) *wel beschouwd* after all, all things considered; *op zichzelf beschouwd* in itself; *oppervlakkig beschouwd* on the face of it; **–d** contemplative, speculative; **be'schouwer** (-s) *m* spectator, contemplator; **–wing** (-en) *v* 1 (a l s h a n d e l i n g) contemplation; 2 (b e s p i e g e l i n g) speculation, contemplation; 3 (b e o o r d e l i n g, b e s p r e k i n g) consideration; 4 (d e n k - w ij z e) view; *bij nadere* ~ on closer examination; *b u i t e n* ~ *laten* leave out of consideration, leave out of account (out of the question), not take into consideration, ignore, prescind from

be'schrijven¹ *vt* 1 (s c h r ij v e n o p) write upon; 2 describe, draw [a circle &]; 3 (s c h i l d e r e n) describe [a voyage &]; 4 (s c h r i f t e l ij k b ij e e n r o e p e n) convoke [a meeting]; **–d** descriptive [style, geometry]; **be'schrijving** (-en) *v* description; **–sbrief** (-brieven) *m* convocation, notice of a meeting

be'schroomd I *aj* timid, timorous, diffident, shy; **II** *ad* timidly

be'schuit (-en) *v* rusk

be'schuldigde (-n) *m-v de* ~ the accused; **be'schuldigen** (beschuldigde, h. beschuldigd) *vt* incriminate [sbd.]; accuse [other people], impeach [sbd. of treason, heresy &]; indict [sbd. for riot, as a rioter]; ~ *van* accuse of [a fault, theft], charge with [carelessness, complicity], tax with [ingratitude], impeach of [high crime], indict for [riot]; **–d** accusatory; **be'schuldiging** (-en) *v* accusation, charge, indictment, impeachment; *een* ~ *inbrengen tegen iem.* bring a charge against sbd.; *een* ~ *richten tot* level charges at; *onder* ~ *van* on a charge of

be'schutten (beschutte, h. beschut) *vt* shelter², screen², protect²; ~ *voor (tegen)* shelter from [heat, danger &], protect from (against) [danger, injury]; **–ting** (-en) *v* shelter, protection; ~ *geven (verlenen)* give shelter [from heat, danger &]; ~ *zoeken* take shelter [in a cave, under a tree, with friends; from the rain, dangers &]

be'sef *o* 1 sense, notion; 2 realization [of the situation]; *geen flauw* ~ *hebben van* not have the faintest notion of; *tot het* ~ *komen van* realize; **be'seffen** (besefte, h. beseft) *vt* realize, be aware; *wij* ~ *heel goed dat* we fully appreciate that

'besje (-s) *o* old woman, gammer; **–shuis** (-huizen) *o* old women's almshouse

be'slaan¹ I *vt* 1 ✗ (...s l a a n o m), hoop [a cask]; (...s l a a n o p) stud [a door with nails], mount [a pistol with silver]; shoe [a horse]; 2 (k l o p p e n d r o e r e n) beat up [the batter]; 3 take up [much room], occupy [much space], contain [300 pages], fill [the whole space]; **II** *vi* & *va* become steamy, get dim [of panes]; get covered over [with moisture]; **be'slag** (-slagen) *o* 1 ✗ (a l s v e r s i e r i n g) mounting; (a a n d e u r) ironwork, studs, (iron, brass) fittings; (a a n h e i p a a l) binding; (a a n t o n) hoops, bands; (a a n s t o k) tip, ferrule; (v. p a a r d) (horse)shoes; 2 (v. deeg) batter; (v o o r b r o u w s e l) mash; 3 (o p t o n g) fur; 4 ♟ attachment; seizure; ♃ embargo; *de zaak heeft haar* ~ the matter is settled; ~ *leggen op* levy a distress upon [sbd.'s goods], seize; ♃ put (lay) an embargo on; ~ *leggen op iemand(s tijd)* 1 (v. p e r s o n e n) trespass on sbd.'s time; 2 (v. z a k e n) engross sbd., take up all his time; *in* ~ *nemen* seize [goods smuggled]; *fig* take up [much time, much room]; engross [sbd.'s attention];

be'slagen 1 shod [of a horse]; 2 steamy, steamed [windows], dimmed with moisture [of glass]; furred, coated [tongue]; zie ook: *beslaan* & *ijs*; **be'slaglegging** (-en) *v* = *beslag* 4

be'slapen¹ *vt dit bed is al* ~ this bed has been slept in; *zich ergens op* ~ sleep on (over) it, take counsel of one's pillow

be'slechten¹ *vt* settle, compose [a quarrel]; zie ook *pleit*

be'slissen (besliste, h. beslist) **I** *vt* decide; (s c h e i d s r e c h t e r l ij k) arbitrate (upon), rule; ~ *ten gunste van* decide for (in favour of); ~ *ten nadele van* decide against; **II** *va* decide; **–d** decisive [battle], final [match, trial], conclusive [proof], determinant [factor]; critical [moment]; casting [vote]; **be'slissing** (-en) *v* decision; ♟ ruling; *een* ~ *nemen* make a decision, come to a decision; **–swedstrijd** (-en) *m* final; play-off; decider

be'slist decided, resolute, firm, peremptory; **–heid** *v* decision, resolution, firmness; peremptoriness

be'slommering (-en) *v* care, worry

be'sloten resolved, determined; *ik ben* ~ I am resolved, I have made up my mind; *vast* ~ of set purpose; ~ *naamloze vennootschap* ± limited liability company; ~ *jacht* private shooting; ~ *vergadering* private meeting

¹ V.T. en V.D. van dit werkwoord volgens het model: **be'ademen**, V.T. **be'ademde**, V.D. **be'ademd** (**ge-** valt dus weg in het V.D.). Zie voor de vormen onder het grondwoord, in dit voorbeeld: *ademen*. Bij sterke en onregelmatige werkwoorden wordt u verwezen naar de lijst achterin.

be'sluipen[1] *vt* 1 (o p j a c h t) stalk [deer]; 2 *fig* steal upon [sbd.]

be'sluit (-en) *o* 1 (b i j z i c h z e l f) resolve; resolution, determination; decision; 2 (v . v e r g a d e r i n g &) resolution [of a meeting]; decree [set forth by authority]; 3 (g e v o l g - t r e k k i n g) conclusion; 4 (e i n d e) conclusion, close; *Koninklijk B~* Order in Council; *een ~ nemen* 1 (i n v e r g a d e r i n g) pass (adopt) a resolution; 2 (v . p e r s o o n) take a decision, make up one's mind; *een kloek ~ nemen* form a bold resolution; *tot ~* in conclusion, to conclude; *tot een ~ komen* come to a conclusion (resolution); *hij kan nooit tot een ~ komen* he cannot make up his mind; **be'sluiteloos** undecided, irresolute; **besluite'loosheid** *v* irresolution, indecision, infirmity of purpose; **be'sluiten**[1] **I** *vt* 1 (e i n d i g e n) end, conclude [a speech]; 2 (g e v o l g t r e k k i n g m a k e n) conclude, infer (from *uit*); 3 (e e n b e s l u i t n e m e n) decide, resolve, determine [to do, on doing]; *ergens toe ~* make up one's mind; *dat heeft me doen ~ te gaan* that has decided me to go; **II** *vi ~ met het volkslied* wind up with the national anthem; **III** *va* decide; *hij kan maar tot niets ~* he cannot decide on anything; zie ook: *besloten;* **besluit'vaardig** resolute; **be'sluit-vorming** *v* decision-making

be'smeren[1] *vt* besmear, smear, daub; spread [with butter], (m e t b o t e r) butter [bread]

be'smet contaminated, infected; polluted [water]; (b i j w e r k s t a k i n g) tainted [goods]; **–telijk** contagious[2], infectious[2], catching[2]; **be'smetten** (besmette, h. besmet) *vt* contaminate [by contact & morally], infect [the body & the mind]; pollute[2] [water], taint[2] [meat]; **be'smetting** (-en) *v* contagion, contamination, infection, pollution, taint; **–shaard** (-en) *m* source of infection

be'smeuren (besmeurde, h. besmeurd) *vt* besmear, besmirch[2], soil[2], stain[2]

be'snaren (besnaarde, h. besnaard) *vt* string

be'sneeuwd covered with snow, snow-covered, snowy

be'snijden[1] *vt* 1 cut, carve [wood]; 2 (r i t u e e l & ✝) circumcise; **be'snijdenis** (-sen) *v* circumcision

be'snoeien[1] *vt fig* cut down; retrench, curtail [expenses &]; **be'snoeiing** (-en) *v fig* retrenchment, curtailment; **~en** cutbacks

be'snuffelen[1] *vt* smell at, sniff at

be'spannen[1] *vt ♪* string [a violin]; *met paarden ~* horse-drawn; *met vier paarden ~ wagen* coach

and four, four-in-hand

be'sparen[1] *vt dat leed werd haar bespaard* she was spared that grief; *zich (de moeite) ~* save (spare) oneself [the trouble, the effort]; **–ring** (-en) *v* saving; economy; *ter ~ van kosten* to save expenses

be'spatten[1] *vt* splash, (be)spatter

be'spelen[1] *vt* play on [an instrument, a billiards table &], play [an instrument], touch [the lyre]; play in [a theatre]

be'speuren[1] *vt* perceive, descry

be'spieden[1] *vt* spy upon, watch

be'spiegelend contemplative [life]; speculative [philosophy]; **be'spiegeling** (-en) *v* speculation, contemplation; *~en houden over* speculate on

be'spijkeren[1] *vt* stud [a door &] with nails; *met planken ~* nail planks on to

be'spikkelen[1] *vt* speckle

bespio'neren[1] *vt* spy upon

be'spoedigen (bespoedigde, h. bespoedigd) *vt* accelerate [a motion], hasten, speed up [a work], expedite [a process]

be'spottelijk I *aj* ridiculous, ludicrous; *~ ma-\ken* ridicule, deride, hold up to ridicule; *zich ~ aanstellen* make a fool of oneself, lay oneself open to ridicule; **II** *ad* ridiculously; **be'spotten**[1] *vt* mock, deride, ridicule, quip; **–ting** (-en) *v* mockery, derision, ridicule

be'spreekbureau [-by.ro.] (-s) *o* booking-office; (i n t h e a t e r) box-office; **be'spreken**[1] *vt* 1 talk about, talk [it] over, discuss; 2 (b e o o r d e l e n) review [a book &]; 3 (v o o r u i t n e m e n) book [a berth, a place], secure, engage, reserve [seats], bespeak [a book at the library]; **–king** (-en) *v* 1 discussion [of some subject], talk, conference; 2 review [of a book]; 3 booking [of seats]

be'sprenkelen[1] *vt* sprinkle

be'springen[1] *vt* leap (spring, pounce) upon

be'sproeien[1] *vt* water [plants]; irrigate [land]

be'spuiten[1] *vt* squirt [water] upon; spray [an insecticide] on

'besseboom (-bomen) *m* currant bush; **'bessengelei** [-ʒəlɛi] (-en) *m* & *v* currant jelly; **–jenever** *m* black-currant gin; **'bessesap** (-pen) *o* & *m* currant juice; **–struik** (-en) *m* currant bush

best I *aj* 1 (r e l a t i e f) best; 2 (a b s o l u u t) very good; *mij ~!* all right!, I have no objection; *hij is niet al te ~* he is none too well; *~e aardappelen* prime potatoes; *~e jongen* (my) dear boy; **II** *ad* best; very well; *ik zou ~ met hem*

---

[1] V.T. en V.D. van dit werkwoord volgens het model: **be'**ademen, V.T. **be'**ademde, V.D. **be'**ademd (**ge-** valt dus weg in het V.D.). Zie voor de vormen onder het grondwoord, in dit voorbeeld: *ademen.* Bij sterke en onregelmatige werkwoorden wordt u verwezen naar de lijst achterin.

willen ruilen I wouldn't mind swapping with him; *het is* ∼ *mogelijk* it is quite possible; *hij schrijft het* ∼ he writes best; **III** *sb* best; *dat kan de* ∼*e gebeuren* that may happen to the best of us; ..., *dan ben je een* ∼*e!* there is a good boy (a dear); *het* ∼*e zal zijn...* the best thing (plan) will be...; *het* ∼*e ermee!* all the best, good luck (to you)!; *het* ∼*e met je verkoudheid* I hope your cold will soon be better; *zijn* ∼ *doen* do one's best; *zijn uiterste* ∼ *doen* do one's utmost, exert oneself to the utmost; *beter zijn* ∼ *doen* try harder; *er het* ∼*e van hopen* hope for the best; *er het* ∼ *van maken* make the best of it; *iem. het* ∼*e wensen* wish sbd. all the best; ● *op zijn* ∼ [Shakespeare] at his best; [fifty] at the utmost, at most, at best; *Juffrouw X zal iets* t e n ∼*e geven* Miss X is going to oblige the company; *alles zal ten* ∼*e keren* everything will turn out for the best

be'staan[1] I *vi* be, exist; subsist [= continue to exist]; *hoe bestaat 't?* how is it possible?; ● ∼ *i n* consist in; ∼*u i t* consist of, be composed of; ∼ *v a n* live on (upon); *iem. van na(bij)* ∼ be near sbd. in blood; ∼ *v o o r* live for; *hij heeft het* ∼ *om...* he had the nerve to...; **II** *o* 1 (h e t z ij n) being, existence; 2 (o n d e r h o u d) subsistence; *een aangenaam* ∼ a pleasant life; *een behoorlijk* ∼ a decent living; *de strijd om het* ∼ the struggle for life; *hij heeft een goed* ∼ he has a fair competency; *het vijftigjarig* ∼ *herdenken van* commemorate the fiftieth anniversary of; –**baar** possible; **be'staand** existing, in existence; **be'staansminimum** (-nima) *o* subsistence minimum; –**voorwaarden** *mv* living conditions

1 be'stand *aj* ∼ *zijn tegen* be able to resist, be proof against; ∼ *tegen het weer* weather-proof
2 be'stand (-en) *o* truce

be'standdeel (-delen) *o* element, component, (constituent) part, ingredient

be'standslijn (-en) *v* armistice (cease-fire) line

be'steden (besteedde, h. besteed) *vt* spend, pay [a certain sum]; *geld (tijd)* ∼ *aan* spend money (time) on; *het is aan hem besteed* he can appreciate that; *het is aan hem niet besteed* it [the joke, advice &] is wasted (lost) on him; *goed (nuttig)* ∼ make (a) good use of; *slecht* ∼ make a bad use of; **be'steding** (-en) *v* expenditure, spending; –**beperking** *v* austerity, economic squeeze

be'stek (-ken) *o* 1 (b ij a a n n e m i n g) △ specification(s); 2 ⚓ (g e g i s t ∼) (dead) reckoning; 3 (e e t g e r e i v o o r é é n

p e r s o o n) fork, knife and spoon; cover; *het* ∼ *opmaken* ⚓ determine (reckon) the ship's position; *b i n n e n het* ∼ *van dit werk* within the scope of this work; *veel i n een klein* ∼ much in a small compass; *in kort* ∼ in brief, in a nutshell

beste'kamer (-s) *v* convenience, w.c., privy

be'stel *o* [new, old, present] order (of things), set-up, [totalitarian &] regime, [financial, army &] system, scheme; *het (heersende)* ∼ the Establishment

be'stelauto [-o.to., -ɔuto.] ('s) *m* delivery van; –**biljet** (-ten) *o,* –**bon** (-nen en -s) *m* order-form; –**dienst** (-en) *m* parcels delivery (service)

be'stelen[1] *vt* rob

be'stelkaart (-en) *v* order-form; **be'stellen**[1] *vt* 1 (b e z o r g e n) deliver [letters &]; 2 (o m t e b e z o r g e n) order [goods from]; 3 (o n t - b i e d e n) send for [sbd.]; *bij wie bestelt u uw boeken?* from whom do you order your books?; –**er** (-s) *m* 1 ⚓ postman; 2 parcels delivery man; 3 (k r u i e r) porter; **be'stelling** (-en) *v* 1 ⚓ delivery; 2 $ order; ∼*en aannemen (doen, uitvoeren)* receive (place, fill) orders; ∼*en doen bij* place orders with; *op zijn i n* ∼ they are on order; *o p (volgens)* ∼ (made) to order; **be'stelloon** (-lonen) *o* porterage; –**wagen** (-s) *m* delivery van

'bestemaatjes *ze zijn* ∼ they are very thick together; *met iedereen* ∼ *zijn* be hail-fellow-well-met with everybody

be'stemmen[1] *vt* destine, intend, mark out; ∼ *v o o r* destine for [some service]; appropriate, set apart, allocate [a sum] for...; appoint, fix [a day] for...; *dat was voor u bestemd* that was intended (meant) for you; **be'stemming** (-en) *v* 1 (place of) destination, 2 [a man's] lot, destiny; *met* ∼ ⚓ bound for [Marseille]; –**splan** (-nen) *o* development plan

be'stempelen[1] *vt* stamp; ∼ *met de naam van...* designate as..., style..., describe as..., label as...

be'stendig I *aj* continual, constant, lasting; steady; ∼ *weer* settled weather, set fair; **II** *ad* continually, constantly; **be'stendigen** (bestendigde, h. bestendigd) *vt* continue, confirm [in office]; perpetuate [indefinitely]; –**ging** *v* continuance; perpetuation

be'sterven[1] *hij zal het nog* ∼ it wil be the death of him; *zij bestierf het bijna van schrik (van het lachen)* she nearly jumped out of her skin (nearly died with laughing); *het woord bestierf op zijn lippen* the word died on his lips; *vlees laten*

---

[1] V.T. en V.D. van dit werkwoord volgens het model: **be'**ademen, V.T. **be'**ademde, V.D. **be'**ademd (**ge-** valt dus weg in het V.D.). Zie voor de vormen van het grondwoord, in dit voorbeeld: *ademen.* Bij sterke en onregelmatige werkwoorden wordt u verwezen naar de lijst achterin.

~ hang meat; zie ook: *bestorven*
be'stier *o*, be'stiering (-en) *v* guidance
be'stijgen (besteeg, h. bestegen) *vt* ascend, climb [a mountain]; mount [the throne, a horse]; **–ging** (-en) *v* ascent, climbing, mounting
be'stikken¹ *vt* stitch, embroider
be'stoken¹ *vt* batter, shell [a fortress]; harass [the enemy], press hard; ~ **met vragen** ply (assail) with questions
be'stormen¹ *vt* storm, assault [a fortress], assail, bombard [people with questions]; besiege [with requests]; *de bank werd bestormd* there was a run (rush) on the bank; **–er** (-s) *m* stormer, assaulter; be'storming (-en) *v* storming, assault; rush [of a fortress, on a bank]
be'storven *dat ligt hem in de mond* ~ it is constantly on his lips
be'stoven 1 dusty; 2 🐝 pollinated
be'straffen¹ *vt* punish; (b e r i s p e n) reproach, rebuke, reprimand; ~*d* reproachful, reproving [look]; **–fing** (-en) *v* punishment
be'stralen¹ *vt* shine upon, irradiate; ☀ ray; **–ling** (-en) *v* irradiation; ☀ radiation; *Röntgen~* radiotherapy
be'straten (bestraatte, h. bestraat) *vt* pave; **–ting** (-en) *v* (d e h a n d e l i n g; d e s t e n e n) paving; (d e s t e n e n) pavement
be'strijden¹ *vt* 1 (i e m.) fight (against), combat, contend with; 2 (i e t s) fight (against), combat [abuses, prejudice]; control [insects, diseases]; dispute, contest [a point], oppose [a proposal]; defray [the expenses], meet [the costs]; **–er** (-s) *m* fighter, adversary, opponent; be'strijding *v* fight [against cancer]; control [of insects, of diseases]; fighting; *ter ~ der kosten* to meet the costs, for the defrayment of expenses; **–smiddel** (-en) *o* pesticide
be'strijken¹ *vt* 1 spread (over) [with mortar &]; 2 🔫 cover, command, sweep; ~ **met** coat (spread) with; *een groot terrein* ~ cover a wide field
be'strooien¹ *vt* strew, sprinkle
bestu'deren¹ *vt* study, read up [a subject]; *bestudeerd* affected [attitude]; **–ring** *v* study
be'stuiven¹ *vt* 1 cover with dust; 2 🐝 pollinate; 3 dust [crops with insecticide]; **–ving** (-en) *v* 🐝 pollination
be'sturen¹ *vt* govern, rule [a country]; manage [affairs]; conduct [a business], run [a house]; 🔧 steer [a ship]; drive [a car]; ✈ fly [an aeroplane]; *draadloos bestuurd* wireless-controlled, radio-controlled; **–ring** (-en) *v* 🔧 steering &;

dubbele ~ ◄ ◄ dual control; *linkse (rechtse)* ~ ◄ left-hand (right-hand) drive; be'stuur (-sturen) *o* 1 government, rule; administration [of a country]; 2 (l e i d i n g) administration, management, direction, control [of an undertaking]; 3 (l i c h a a m) board, governing body, committee, executive [of a party]; *het plaatselijk* ~ 1 (c o n c r e e t) the local authorities; 2 (a b s t r a c t) local government; be'stuurbaar dirigible [balloon]; manageable; **–heid** *v* ⚓ steerage; be'stuurder (-s en -en) *m* 1 governor, director, administrator; 2 🔫 driver; 3 ✈ pilot; be'stuurlijk administrative; be'stuursambtenaar (-s en -naren) *m* government official, civil servant; **–functie** [-fünksi.] (-s) *v* executive function; **–lid** (-leden) *o* member of the board &, zie *bestuur* 3; **–tafel** (-s) *v* board table, committee table; **–vergadering** (-en) *v* committee meeting, meeting of the board, board meeting
'bestwil *om uw* ~ for your good; *een leugentje om* ~ a white lie
'bèta ('s) *v* beta
be'taalbaar payable; ~ *stellen* make payable, domicile; be'taald paid (for); *het iem.* ~ *zetten* pay sbd. out, take it out of sbd.; *met* ~ *antwoord* reply paid [telegram]; ~ *voetbal* professional football; be'taaldag (-dagen) *m* 1 day of payment; 2 pay-day; **–kantoor** (-toren) *o*, **–kas** (-sen) *v* pay-office; **–meester** (-s) *m* paymaster; **–middel** (-en) *o wettig* ~ legal tender, legal currency; **–pas** (-sen) *m* bank card; **–staat** (-staten) *m* pay-sheet; be'talen (betaalde, h. betaald) **I** *vt* pay [one's debts, the servants &], pay for [the drinks, flowers &]; *zij kunnen het (best)* ~ they can afford it; *wie zal dat* ~*?* who is to pay?; *zich goed laten* ~ charge heavily; ~ *met* pay with [ingratitude &]; pay in [gold]; *het is met geen geld te* ~ money cannot buy it; **II** *va* pay, settle; *dat betaalt goed* it pays (you well); ~*e slecht* 1 they are not punctual in paying; 2 they underpay their workmen (employees &); be'taling (-en) *v* payment; *tegen* ~ *van...* on payment of; *ter* ~ *van* in payment of; be'talingsbalans (-en) *v* balance of payments; **–condities** [-(t)si.s] *mv* terms of payment; **–termijn** (-en) *m* 1 term (of payment, for the payment of...); 2 instalment; **–voorwaarden** *mv* terms of (payment); *op gemakkelijke* ~ on easy terms
be'tamelijk decent, becoming, proper, befitting; be'tamen (betaamde, h. betaamd) *vi* become, beseem; behove; *het betaamt u niet...*

---

¹ V.T. en V.D. van dit werkwoord volgens het model: be'ademen, V.T. be'ademde, V.D. be'ademd (**ge-** valt dus weg in het V.D.). Zie voor de vormen onder het grondwoord, in dit voorbeeld: *ademen*. Bij sterke en onregelmatige werkwoorden wordt u verwezen naar de lijst achterin.

ook: it is not for you to...
be'tasten[1] *vt* handle, feel, 𝕋 palpate
'bètastralen *mv* beta rays; 'bètatron (-s) *o*
betatron; 'bètawetenschappen *mv* (natural)
sciences
be'tegelen (betegelde, h. betegeld) *vt* tile
be'tekenen[1] *vt* 1 (w i l l e n z e g g e n) mean,
signify; 2 (v o o r s p e l l e n) signify, portend,
spell; 3 𝕥𝕥 serve [a notice, writ] upon [sbd.]; *het
heeft niet veel te ~* 1 it does not amount to
much; 2 it is nothing much; *het heeft niets te ~* it
does not matter; it is of no importance; *wat
heeft dat te ~?* what does it all mean?, what's all
this?; **-ning** (-en) *v* 𝕥𝕥 (legal) notice, service
(of writ); be'tekenis (-sen) *v* 1 meaning,
sense, signification; acceptation [= aangenomen betekenis]; pregnancy [= volle bete-
kenis]; 2 (b e l a n g) significance, importance,
consequence; *het is van ~* it is significant; it is
important; *van enige ~* of some significance
(consequence); *het is van geen ~* it is of no
importance (consequence), it does not signify;
mannen van ~ men of note; *een schrijver van ~* a
distinguished writer; **-leer** *v* semantics,
semasiology; **-verandering** (-en) *v* change
of meaning, semantic change
'beten V.T. meerv. v. *bijten*
be'tengelen (betengelde, h. betengeld) *vt* lath
'beter I *aj* better [weather &]; better (i.e.
improved), well (i.e. recovered) [of a patient];
hij is ~ 1 he is better, a better man [than his
brother]; 2 he is better (= improved) [of a
patient]; 3 he is well again, he is (has) recovered [of a patient]; *het ~ hebben* be better off; *het
kan nog ~* you (he, they) can do better yet; *zij
hopen het ~ te krijgen* they hope to better themselves; *de volgende keer ~* better luck next time;
~ maken set right, put right, cure [some defect
&]; set up, bring round [a patient]; *dat maakt
de zaak niet ~* that does not improve (help)
matters; *~ weten* know better than that; *de
zaken gaan ~* business is looking up; *ik ben er
niets ~ van geworden* I did not get anything out
of it, I have gained nothing of it; *~ worden* I
become (get) better, mend, improve [of the
outlook &]; 2 be getting well (better) [after
illness]; **II** *ad* better; *des te ~!* so much the
better!; *hij deed ~ te zwijgen* he had better be
silent; **III** *sb als u niets ~s te doen hebt* if you are
not better engaged
1 be'teren[1] *vt* tar
2 'beteren (beterde, h. en is gebeterd) **I** *vi*
become (get) better, mend, improve, recover

[in health]; *aan de ~de hand zijn* be getting
better, be doing well, be on the mend; **II** *vr
zich (zijn leven) ~* mend one's ways; 'beter-
schap *v* improvement [in health], recovery; *~!*
I hope you will soon be well again!; *~ beloven*
promise to behave better (in future).
be'teugelen (beteugelde, h. beteugeld) *vt*
bridle, curb, check, keep in check, restrain
be'teuterd confused, perplexed, puzzled; *~
kijken* be taken aback
be'tichten (betichtte, h. beticht) *vt iem. ~ van*
accuse sbd. of, charge sbd. with, tax sbd. with
be'timmeren[1] *vt* line with wood; **-ring** (-en) *v*
woodwork [of a room]
be'titelen (betitelde, h. betiteld) *vt* title, entitle,
style; **-ling** (-en) *v* style, title
be'togen (betoogde, h. betoogd) **I** *vt* argue; **II**
vi make a [public] demonstration, demonstrate;
-er (-s) *m* demonstrator; be'toging (-en) *v*
[public] demonstration
be'ton *o* concrete; *gewapend ~* reinforced
concrete, ferro-concrete
be'tonen[1] **I** *vt* show [courage, favour, kind-
ness], manifest [one's joy]; **II** *vr zich ~* show
oneself [grateful], prove oneself [equal to]
be'tonijzer *o* reinforcement (reinforcing) steel;
-molen (-s) *m* concrete mixer
1 be'tonnen (betonde, h. betond) *vt* buoy
2 be'tonnen *aj* concrete
be'tonning (-en) *v* 1 (d e h a n d e l i n g)
buoying; 2 (d e t o n n e n) buoys
be'tonwerker (-s) *m* concrete worker,
concreter
be'toog (-togen) *o* argument(s); *dat behoeft geen ~*
it is obvious; **-kracht** *v* argumentative power;
-trant *m* argumentation
be'toon *o* demonstration, show, manifestation
be'toveren[1] *vt* bewitch[2], enchant[2], cast a spell
on[2], *fig* fascinate, charm; **-d** bewitching,
enchanting, fascinating, charming
'betovergrootmoeder (-s) *v* great-great-grand-
mother; **-vader** (-s) *m* great-great-grandfather
be'tovering (-en) *v* enchantment, bewitchment,
spell, fascination, glamour
be'traand tearful, wet with tears
be'trachten[1] *vt de deugd ~* practise virtue; *zijn
plicht ~* do one's duty
be'trappen[1] *vt* catch, detect; *iem. op diefstal ~*
catch sbd. (in the act of) stealing; *iem. op een fout
~* catch sbd. out (tripping); *op heter daad ~* take
in the (very) act, catch sbd. red-handed; *iem. op
een leugen ~* catch sbd. in a lie
be'treden[1] *vt* tread (upon), set foot upon (in);

---

[1] V.T. en V.D. van dit werkwoord volgens het model: **be'**ademen, V.T. **be'**ademde, V.D. **be'**ademd (**ge-** valt dus
weg in het V.D.). Zie voor de vormen onder het grondwoord, in dit voorbeeld: *ademen*. Bij sterke en onregelmatige
werkwoorden wordt u verwezen naar de lijst achterin.

enter [a building, a room &]; *de kansel ~* mount the pulpit

be'treffen[1] *vt* concern, regard, touch, affect, pertain; *waar het zijn eer betreft* where his honour is concerned; *voor zover het... betreft* so far as... is (are) concerned; *wat* [*uitgaan* &] *betreft* in the way of [entertainment &]; *wat mij betreft* as for me, as to me, I for one, personally, I; *wat dat betreft* as to that; **–de** concerning, regarding, with respect (regard) to, relative to

be'trekkelijk *aj* relative [pronoun &]; comparative [poverty &]; *alles is ~* all things go by comparison; **–heid** *v* relativity; **be'trekken**[1] **I** *vt* 1 (t r e k k e n i n) move into [a house]; 2 (l a t e n k o m e n) get, order [goods from X &]; *iem. in iets ~* involve (implicate) sbd. in an affair, mix sbd. up in it; bring sbd. into the discussion &; draw sbd. into a conflict; **II** *vi* become overcast [of the sky], cloud over[2] [of the sky, sbd.'s face]; zie ook: *betrokken;* **be'trekking** (-en) *v* 1 (v e r h o u d i n g) relation; relationship [of master and servant, with God]; 2 (b a a n) post, position, place, job, situation [as servant], [official] appointment; *diplomatieke ~en* diplomatic relations; *dat heeft daar geen ~ op* that does not relate to it, has no reference to it; that does not bear upon it; *het vraagteken heeft ~ op...* the question mark refers to...; ● *in ~* in employment; *in ~ staan met* have relations with; *in goede ~ staan met* be on good terms with; *met ~ tot* with regard (respect) to, in (with) reference to; *zonder ~* out of employment, unemployed

be'treuren[1] *vt* regret, deplore, lament, bewail, mourn for [a lost person], mourn [the loss of...]; zie ook *mensenleven;* **betreurens-** **'waard(ig)** regrettable, deplorable, lamentable

be'trokken 1 cloudy, overcast [sky]; 2 clouded, gloomy [face]; *de ~ autoriteiten* the proper authorities; *bij (in) iets ~ zijn* be concerned in (with), be a party to, be mixed up with (in); be involved in [a bankruptcy]; *financieel ~ zijn bij* have a financial interest in; *de daarbij ~ en* the persons concerned (involved); **–heid** *v* involvement

be'trouwbaar reliable, trustworthy; **–heid** *v* reliability, reliableness, trustworthiness

'betten (bette, h. gebet) *vt* bathe, dab

be'tuigen (betuigde, h. betuigd) *vt* express [sympathy, one's regret &]; protest [one's innocence]; profess [friendship]; tender [thanks]; **–ging** (-en) *v* expression [of one's feelings]; protestation [of one's innocence]; profession [of friendship]

be'tuttelen (betuttelde, h. betutteld) *vt* chide, lecture, upbraid

'betweter ['bɛt-] (-s) *m* wiseacre, pedant; **F** back-seat driver; **betwete'rij** (-en) *v* pedantry

be'twijfelen[1] *vt* doubt, question

be'twistbaar disputable, contestable [statements &], debatable [grounds], questionable [accuracy]; **be'twisten**[1] *vt* 1 (i e t s) dispute [a fact, every inch of ground], contest [a point], challenge [a statement]; 2 (i e m . i e t s) dispute [a point] with; deny; *zij betwistten ons de overwinning* they disputed the victory with us

beu *~ (van)* tired (sick) of

beug (-en) *v* long line [for fishing]

'beugel (-s) *m* guard [of a sword]; (trigger) guard [of a rifle]; ✕ shackle [of a padlock], ring, strap, brace; ⚓ gimbals [of a compass]; clasp [of lady's bag; on a bottle]; ※ (contact) bow [of an electric tramway]; braces [for straitening teeth]; (leg) iron; zie ook: *stijgbeugel; dat kan niet d o o r de ~* 1 (k a n e r n i e t m e e d o o r) that cannot pass muster; 2 (i s o n g e o o r l o o f d) this cannot be allowed; **–sluiting** (-en) *v* clasp

'beugvisserij *v* long-line fishing

1 beuk (-en) *m* & *v* △ (h o o f d ~) nave; (z ij ~) aisle

2 beuk (-en) *m,* **'beukeboom** (-bomen) *m* 🌱 beech, beech tree; **'beukehout** *o* beech-wood, beech; **1 'beuken** *aj* beech(en)

2 'beuken (beukte, h. gebeukt) *vt* beat, batter, pummel, pommel; pound [with one's fists]; *de golven ~ het strand* the waves lash the shore (the beach); *er op los ~* pound away [at sbd.]

'beukenbos (-sen) *o* beech-wood; **'beukenoot** (-noten) *v* beech-nut

'beukhamer (-s) *m* maul, mallet

beul (-en) *m* 1 hangman, executioner; 2 *fig* brute, bully, torturer; **'beulsknecht** (-s en -en) *m* hangman's assistant; **–werk** *o fig* drudgery, toil, grind

'beunhaas (-hazen) *m* interloper, dabbler; **'beunhazen** (beunhaasde, h. gebeunhaasd) *vi* dabble (in); **beunhaze'rij** (-en) *v* dabbling

'beuren (beurde, h. gebeurd) *vt* 1 lift (up) [a load]; 2 receive [money]

1 beurs *aj* overripe, bruised [fruit]

2 beurs (beurzen) *v* 1 (v o o r g e l d) purse; 2 $ (g e b o u w) exchange; Bourse [on the Continent]; 3 (s t u d i e b e u r s) scholarship,

---

[1] V.T. en V.D. van dit werkwoord volgens het model: **be'ademen,** V.T. **be'**ademde, V.D. **be'**ademd (**ge-** valt dus weg in het V.D.). Zie voor de vormen onder het grondwoord, in dit voorbeeld: *ademen.* Bij sterke en onregelmatige werkwoorden wordt u verwezen naar de lijst achterin.

bursary; grant; *i n zijn* ~ *tasten* loosen one's purse strings; *elkaar met gesloten beurzen betalen* settle on mutual terms; *n a a r de* ~ *gaan* go to 'Change; *o p de* ~, *t e r beurze* on 'Change; *hij studeert v a n een* ~ he holds a scholarship; **–berichten** *mv* quotations, stock-list; **–gebouw** (-en) *o* exchange building; **–notering** (-en) *v* stock-exchange quotation; **–overzicht** (-en) *o* exchange report; **–polis** (-sen) *v* exchange policy; **–student** (-en) *m* scholar, exhibitioner; **–tijd** (-en) *m* 'Change hours; **–waarde** *v* market value; **~n** stocks and shares **beurt** (-en) *v* turn; *een kamer een* ~ *geven* do (turn out) a room; *een* ~ *krijgen* get one's turn; *een goede* ~ *maken* make a good impression, score; *a a n de* ~ *komen* come in for one's turn; *wie is aan de* ~*?* whose turn is it; next please!; *o m de* ~, *om* ~*en* by turns, in turn; ~ *om* ~ turn (and turn) about, by turns; *ieder o p zijn* ~ everyone in his turn; *t e* ~ *vallen* fall to the share of, fall to; *v ó ó r zijn* ~ out of his turn; **–dienst** (-en) *m*, **–vaart** (-en) *v* regular (barge) service; **–elings** by turns, turn (and turn) about, in turn, alternately; **–zang** (-en) *m* alternate singing; antiphon(y) **'beuzelachtig** trifling, trivial, futile; **beuzela'rij** (-en) *v* trifle; **'beuzelen** (beuzelde, h. gebeuzeld) *vi* dawdle, trifle; **–ling** (-en) *v* trifle; **'beuzelpraat** *m* nonsense, twaddle **be'vaarbaar** navigable; **–heid** *v* navigableness, navigability **be'vaderen** (bevaderde, h. bevaderd) *vt* patronize, paternalize **be'val (bevalen)** V.T. v. **bevelen** **be'vallen¹ I** (beviel, is bevallen) *vt* please; *het zal u wel* ~ I am sure you will be pleased with it, you will like it; *hoe is 't u* ~*?* how did you like it?; *dat (zaakje) bevalt mij niet* I don't like it; **II** (beviel, is bevallen) *vi* be confined (be delivered) [of a child]; *zij moet* ~ she is going to have a baby; *zij is* ~ *van een zoon* she gave birth to a son; *aan het* ~ *zijn* be in labour **be'vallig** graceful; **–heid** (-heden) *v* grace, gracefulness **be'valling** (-en) *v* confinement, delivery; *pijnloze* ~ painless childbirth **be'vangen¹ I** *vt* seize; *de koude beving hem* the cold seized him; *door slaap* ~ overcome with (by) sleep; *door vrees* ~ seized with fear; **II** *aj* timid, bashful **1 be'varen¹** *vt* navigate, sail [the seas]; **2 be'varen** *aj* ~ *matroos* able (experienced) sailor

be'vattelijk I *aj* 1 (v l u g) intelligent, teachable; 2 (v e r s t a a n b a a r) intelligible; **II** *ad* intelligibly; **be'vatten¹** *vt* 1 (i n h o u d e n) contain, comprise; 2 (b e g r ij p e n) comprehend, grasp; **be'vatting** *v* comprehension, (mental) grasp; **–svermogen** *o* comprehension, (mental) grasp **be'vechten¹** *vt* fight (against), combat; *de zege* ~ gain the victory, carry the day **be'veiligen** (beveiligde, h. beveiligd) *vt* secure, protect, safeguard; *beveiligd tegen (voor)* secure from (against) [attack], sheltered from [rain &]; **–ging** (-en) *v* protection, safeguarding, shelter **be'vel** (-velen) *o* order, command, injunction [= authoritative order]; ~ *tot aanhouding* warrant (of arrest); ~ *tot huiszoeking* search-warrant; ~ *geven om...* give orders to...; order [sbd.] to...; *het* ~ *overnemen* take over command; *het* ~ *voeren over* be in command (control) of, command; ● *o n d e r iems.* ~*en staan* be under command; *o p* ~ 1 [cry, laugh] to order; 2 (o p h o o g b e v e l) by order; *op* ~ *van* at (by) the command of, by order of; **be'velen*** *vt* order, command, charge; commend [one's spirit into the hands of the Lord]; ~*de toon* commanding tone; **be'velhebber** (-s) *m* commander; **–schrift** (-en) *o* warrant; **–voerder** (-s) *m* commander; **–voerend** commanding, in command **'beven** (beefde, h. gebeefd) *vi* tremble [with anger or fear]; shake [with fear or cold]; quiver, waver [of the voice]; shiver [with cold]; shudder [with horror]; ~ *als een riet* tremble like an aspen leaf **'bever** 1 (-s) *m* ⚥ beaver; 2 *o* (s t o f) beaver **'beverig** trembling, shaky **be'vestigen¹** *vt* fix, fasten, attach [a thing to another]; *fig* 1 affirm [a declaration]; 2 confirm [a report]; corroborate, bear out [an opinion, a statement]; 3 consolidate [power]; 4 confirm [new members of a Church]; 5 induct [a new clergyman]; 6 uphold [a judge's decision]; **–d I** *aj* affirmative; **II** *ad* affirmatively, [answer] in the affirmative; **be'vestiging** (-en) *v* 1 fastening; 2 (b e k r a c h t i g i n g) affirmation; 3 (v a n b e r i c h t) confirmation; 4 (v a n m a c h t, p o s i t i e) consolidation; 5 (v a n l i d m a t e n) confirmation; 6 (v a n p r e d i-k a n t) induction **be'vind** *naar* ~ (*van zaken*) according to the circumstances; **be'vinden¹ I** *vt* find [sbd. guilty, correct]; **II** *vr zich* ~ (e r g e n s) be (found) [of things], be [of persons]; *zich ergens*

---

¹ V.T. en V.D. van dit werkwoord volgens het model: **be'**ademen, V.T. **be'**ademde, V.D. **be'**ademd (**ge-** valt dus weg in het V.D.). Zie voor de vormen onder het grondwoord, in dit voorbeeld: *ademen*. Bij sterke en onregelmatige werkwoorden wordt u verwezen naar de lijst achterin.

~, *zich in gevaar* ~ find oneself [somewhere]; be [in danger]; **–ding** (-en) *v* finding [of a committee]; ~*en uitwisselen* compare notes

'**beving** (-en) *v* trembling, shivering, dither

be'**vitten**[1] *vt* cavil at, carp at, criticize

be'**vlekken**[1] *vt* stain, spot, soil, defile, pollute

be'**vliegen**[1] *vt* ✈ fly [a route]

be'**vlieging** (-en) *v* caprice, whim; *een* ~ *van edelmoedigheid* a fit of generosity

be'**vloeien**[1] *vt* irrigate; be'**vloeiing** (-en) *v* irrigation

be'**vochtigen** (bevochtigde, h. bevochtigd) *vt* moisten, wet; **–er** (-s) *m* damper; be'**vochtiging** (-en) *v* moistening, wetting

be'**voegd** competent, [fully] qualified; authorized, entitled; *de* ~*e instanties* the appropriate authorities; ~ *om...* qualified to...; having power to...; *van* ~*e zijde* from an authoritative source, [hear] on good authority; **–heid** (-heden) *v* competence, competency; power [of the government, local officials &]; qualification; *...met de* ~ *om...* qualified to [teach that language]; with power to [dismiss him]

be'**voelen**[1] *vt* feel, finger, handle

be'**volen** V.D. v. *bevelen*

be'**volken** (bevolkte, h. bevolkt) *vt* people, populate; be'**volking** (-en) *v* population; be'**volkingsaanwas** *m* increase in population; **–cijfer** (-s) *o* population figure, population returns; **–dichtheid** *v* density of population, population density; **–explosie** [-ɪksplo.zi.] (-s) *v* explosion of population, population explosion; **–groei** *m = bevolkings-aanwas*; **–groep** (-en) *v* 1 section of the population; 2 [Jewish, Muslim] community; **–overschot** *o* surplus population; **–register** (-s) *o* register (of population), registry; **–statistiek** (-en) *v* statistics of population, population statistics; be'**volkt** populated

be'**voogding** *v* paternalism

be'**voordelen** (bevoordeelde, h. bevoordeeld) *vt* favour

bevoor'**oordeeld** prejudiced, prepossessed, bias(s)ed

be'**voorraden** (bevoorraadde, h. bevoorraad) *vt* supply, provision; **–ding** (-en) *v* supply, provisioning

be'**voorrechten** (bevoorrechtte, h. bevoorrecht) *vt* privilege, favour; **–ting** (-en) *v* 1 (i n 't a l g.) favouring; 2 (a l s s t e l s e l) favouritism

be'**vorderen**[1] *vt* further [a cause &]; advance;

promote [plans, sbd. to a higher office]; prefer [sbd. to an office]; aid [digestion]; benefit [health]; remove [a pupil]; ~ *tot kapitein* promote (to the rank of) captain; **–ring** (-en) *v* advancement, promotion [of plans, persons]; preferment [to an office]; furtherance [of a cause]; ☞ remove; be'**vorderlijk** ~ *voor* conducive to, beneficial to, instrumental to

be'**vrachten** (bevrachtte, h. bevracht) *vt* freight, charter [ships]; load

be'**vragen**[1] *te* ~ *bij...* (for particulars) apply to..., information to be had at ...'s, inquire at...'s; *hier te* ~ inquire within

be'**vredigen** (bevredigde, h. bevredigd) *vt* satisfy [appetite or want], gratify [a desire], appease [hunger]; *het bevredigt (je) niet* it does not give satisfaction; **–d** satisfactory, satisfying; be'**vrediging** (-en) *v* satisfaction, gratification, appeasement

be'**vreemden** (bevreemdde, h. bevreemd) *vt het bevreemdt mij, dat hij het niet deed* I wonder (am suprised to find) he...; *het bevreemdde mij* I wondered (was surprised) at it; **–ding** *v* surprise

be'**vreesd** afraid; ~ *voor* 1 apprehensive of [the consequences, danger]; 2 apprehensive for [a person or his safety]

be'**vriend** friendly [nations]; ~ *met* on friendly terms with, a friend of; ~ *worden met* become friends (friendly) with

be'**vriezen* I** *vi* 1 freeze (over, up), congeal; 2 freeze to death; *ik bevries* I am freezing; *je bevriest hier* one freezes to death here; *laten* ~ freeze [meat &]; **II** *vt* freeze; **–zing** *v* freezing (over, up), congelation

be'**vrijd** free, at liberty, liberated [from tyranny]; be'**vrijden** (bevrijdde, h. bevrijd) *vt* free, set free, set at liberty, deliver, liberate, rescue [from danger]; release [from confinement], emancipate [from a yoke]; **–er** (-s) *m* deliverer, liberator, rescuer; be'**vrijding** (-en) *v* deliverance, liberation, rescue, release, emancipation; be'**vrijdingsfront** (-en) *o* liberation front; **–leger** (-s) *o* liberation army; **–oorlog** (-logen) *m* war of liberation

be'**vroeden** (bevroedde, h. bevroed) *vt* 1 suspect, surmise; 2 realize, apprehend

be'**vroor (bevroren)** V.T. v. *bevriezen*

be'**vroos (bevrozen)** V.T. v. *bevriezen*

be'**vroren** V.T. meerv. en V.D. v. *bevriezen*; frozen [meat; credits]; frost-bitten [buds, toes]; frosted [window-panes]

be'**vrozen** V.T. meerv. en V.D. van *bevriezen*

---

[1] V.T. en V.D. van dit werkwoord volgens het model: be'**ademen**, V.T. be'**ademde**, V.D. be'**ademd** (**ge-** valt dus weg in het V.D.). Zie voor de vormen onder het grondwoord, in dit voorbeeld: *ademen*. Bij sterke en onregelmatige werkwoorden wordt u verwezen naar de lijst achterin.

be'vruchten (bevruchtte, h. bevrucht) *vt* impregnate; ⚥ fertilize; **–ting** (-en) *v* impregnation; ⚥ fertilization

be'vuilen (bevuilde, h. bevuild) *vt* dirty, soil, foul, defile, pollute; *zich* ~ soil one's pants

be'waarder (-s) *m* keeper, guardian; (v . w o n i n g) care-taker; **be'waarengel** (-en) *m* guardian angel; **–geving** *v* deposit

be'waarheid ~ *worden* come true

be'waarloon *o* storage; **–nemer** (-s) *m* depositary; **–plaats** (-en) *v* depository, [furniture] repository, storehouse; [bicycle] shelter; **–school** (-scholen) *v* infant school, kindergarten

be'waasd steamed up [window]

be'waken[1] *vt* (keep) watch over, guard; *laten* ~ set a watch over; **–er** (-s) *m* keeper, watch; (i n m u s e u m) custodian; (v . a u t o) [car] attendant; **be'waking** *v* guard, watch(ing), custody; *onder* ~ under guard; *onder* ~ *van* in the charge of

be'wandelen[1] *vt* walk, tread (upon); *de veilige weg* ~ keep on the safe side

be'wapenen[1] *vt* arm; **be'wapening** *v* armament; **be'wapeningsindustrie** (-ieën) *v* arms industry; **–wedloop** *m* arms race

be'waren (bewaarde, h. bewaard) *vt* keep [a thing, a secret, one's balance]; preserve [fruit, meat &]; maintain, keep up [one's dignity]; ~ *voor* preserve (defend, save) from, guard from (against); zie ook: *God, hemel*; **–ring** *v* keeping, preservation, custody; *in* ~ *geven* deposit [luggage, money &]; *het hem in* ~ *geven* entrust him with the care of it; *in* ~ *hebben* have in one's keeping, hold in trust; *iem. in verzekerde* ~ *nemen* take sbd. into custody

be'wasemen[1] *vt* steam, dim (cloud) with moisture

be'weegbaar movable; **–grond** (-en) *m* motive, ground; **be'weeglijk** 1 movable; mobile [features]; 2 lively [children]; **–heid** *v* 1 movableness; mobility; 2 liveliness; **be'weegreden** (-en) *v* motive, ground; **be'wegen**[1] **I** *vi* move; stir; **II** *vt* 1 move; stir; 2 (o n t r o e r e n) move, stir, affect; 3 (o v e r h a l e n) move, induce [sbd. to do it]; **III** *vr zich* ~ move, stir, budge; *zich in de hoogste kringen* ~ move in the best society (circles); *hij weet zich niet te* ~ he doesn't know how to behave, he has no manners; **be'weging** (-en) *v* 1 (h e t b e w e g e n v . i e t s) motion, **F** move; movement, stir(ring); 2 (h e t b e w e g e n m e t i e t s) motion [of the arms], movement

[of the lever]; 3 (d r u k t e) commotion, agitation, stir, bustle; 4 (l i c h a a m s b e w e g i n g) exercise; (*veel*) ~ *maken* create a commotion; make a stir; ~ *nemen* take exercise; ● *i n* ~ *brengen* set (put) in motion, set going, ⚒ start; *fig* stir [people]; *in* ~ *houden* keep going; *in* ~ *komen* begin to move, start; *in* ~ *krijgen* set (get) going; *in* ~ *zijn* 1 be moving, be in motion, be on the move [of sbd.]; 2 be in commotion [of a town &]; *u i t eigen* ~ of one's own accord; **be'wegingloos** motionless; **be'wegingsleer** *v* kinetics, mechanics, dynamics; **–oorlog** (-logen) *m* mobile (open) warfare; **–vrijheid** *v* 1 freedom of movement; 2 ⚔ 24 hours' leave

be'wegwijzeren (bewegwijzerde, h. bewegwijzerd) *vt* signpost

be'weiden[1] *vt* pasture, graze

be'wenen[1] *vt* weep for, weep, deplore, lament, bewail, mourn, mourn for

be'weren (beweerde, h. beweerd) *vt* 1 assert, contend, maintain, claim; 2 (w a t o n b e - w e z e n is) allege; 3 (m e e s t a l t e n o n r e c h t e) pretend; *hij heeft niet veel te* ~ he has not much to say for himself; *naar men beweert* by all accounts; **–ing** (-en) *v* 1 assertion, contention; 2 (o n b e w e z e n) allegation

be'werkelijk laborious, requiring or involving much labour, toilsome; **be'werken**[1] *vt* 1 work, dress, fashion, shape [one's material], till [the ground]; work up [materials]; 2 (o m w e r k e n) adapt [a novel for the stage]; (t o t s t a n d b r e n g e n) effect, bring about; 4 (i e m.) influence [sbd.]; > tamper with, prime [the witnesses]; *met vuisten* ~ pummel [sbd.]; *6de druk bewerkt door...* edited (revised) by...; ~ *tot* work up into; **–er** (-s) *m* cause [of sbd.'s death], worker [of mischief]; compiler [of a book], adapter [of a novel], editor [of the revised edition]; **be'werking** (-en) *v* 1 (h e t b e w e r k e n) working [of material], tillage [of the ground]; × operation [in mathematics], adaptation, dramatization [of a play]; version [of a film]; 2 (w i j z e v a n b e w e r k e n) workmanship [of a box &]; *in* ~ in preparation

be'werkstelligen (bewerkstelligde, h. bewerkstelligd) *vt* bring about, effect

be'westen (to the) west of

be'wieroken (bewierookte, h. bewierookt) *vt iem.* ~ shower praise on sbd.; extol sbd.

be'wijs (-wijzen) *o* 1 proof, evidence, demonstration; 2 (b e w i j s g r o n d) argument; 3 (b e w i j s s t u k) voucher; [doctor's, medical &]

---

[1] V.T. en V.D. van dit werkwoord volgens het model: **be'ademen**, V.T. **be'ademde**, V.D. **be'ademd** (**ge-** valt dus weg in het V.D.). Zie voor de vormen onder het grondwoord, in dit voorbeeld: *ademen*. Bij sterke en onregelmatige werkwoorden wordt u verwezen naar de lijst achterin.

certificate; 4 (b l i j k) mark; *indirect* ~ ⚖ circumstantial evidence; ~ *van goed gedrag* certificate of good character (conduct); ~ *van herkomst* (*oorsprong*) certificate of origin; ~ *van lidmaatschap* certificate of membership; ~ *van ontvangst* receipt; *ten bewijze waarvan* in support (proof) of which; **-baar** provable, demonstrable; **-exemplaar** [-ɛksəm-] (-plaren) *o* (v. b o e k) free copy, voucher copy; (v. k r a n t) reference copy; **-grond** (-en) *m* argument; **-je** *o* (-s) small trace (of), suspicion of; **-kracht** *v* evidential force, conclusiveness, conclusive force, cogency [of an argument]; **-last** *m* burden (onus) of proof; **-materiaal** *o* evidence; **-plaats** (-en) *v* quotation in support, reference; **-stuk** (-ken) *o* evidence; ⚖ exhibit; title-deed [as evidence of a right]; **-voering** (-en) *v* argumentation; **be'wijzen**[1] *vt* 1 (a a n t o n e n) prove, demonstrate [a proposition], establish [the truth of...], make out, make good [a claim, one's point]; 2 (b e t o n e n) show [favour], confer [a favour] upon, render [a service, the last funeral honours]; zie ook *dienst*, 2 *eer*, *gunst* &

be'willigen (bewilligde, h. bewilligd) *vi* ~ *in* grant, consent to

be'wind *o* administration, government, rule; *het* ~ *voeren* hold the reins of government; *het* ~ *voeren over* rule (over); *aan het* ~ *komen* accede to the throne [of a king], come into power [of a minister]; *aan het* ~ *zijn* be in power; **be'windsman** (-lieden) *m* minister, member of the government; **be'windvoerder** (-s) *m* ⚖ receiver; trustee

be'wogen *fig* 1 moved, affected; 2 feeling [language]; ~ *debat* heated debate; ~ *tijden* stirring times

be'wolken (bewolkte, h. en is bewolkt) *vi* cloud over (up), become overcast; **-king** (-en) *v* cloud(s); **be'wolkt** clouded, cloudy, overcast

be'wonderaar (-s) *m*, **-ster** (-s) *v* admirer, fan; **be'wonderen** (bewonderde, h. bewonderd) *vt* admire; **bewonderens'waard(ig)** admirable; **be'wondering** *v* admiration

be'wonen[1] *vt* inhabit, occupy, live in, dwell in, reside in [a place]; **-er** (-s) *m* inhabitant [of a country], tenant, inmate, occupant, occupier [of a room, a house]; resident [and not a visitor]; **be'woning** *v* occupation [of a house], (in)habitation; **be'woonbaar** (in)habitable

be'woording(en) *v* (*mv*) wording; *in algemene* ~*en* in general terms; *in krachtige* ~*en gesteld* strongly worded

be'wust 1 conscious; 2 (b e d o e l d) in question; *ik was het mij niet* ~ I did not realize it, I was unaware of it; *hij was het zich ten volle* ~ he was fully aware of it; *zij werd het zich* ~ she became conscious of it; *hij was zich van geen kwaad* ~ he was not conscious of having done anything wrong; ~ *of onbewust* wittingly or unwittingly; *heb je de* ~*e persoon gezien?* have you seen the person in question?; **be'wusteloos** unconscious; ~ *slaan* beat insensible, knock senseless; **-heid, bewuste'loosheid** *v* unconsciousness, senselessness, insensibility; **be'wustheid** *v* consciousness; **be'wustwording** *v* awaking; **be'wustzijn** *o* consciousness, (full) knowledge; *het* ~ *verliezen* lose consciousness; *b ij zijn volle* ~ fully conscious; *b u i t e n* ~ unconscious; *weer t o t* ~ *komen* recover (regain) consciousness; **be'wustzijnsverruimend** psychedelic, consciousness-expanding, mind-expanding, **S** mind-blowing

be'zaaien[1] *vt* sow, seed; ~ *met* sow (seed) with[2]; *fig* strew with

be'zaan (-zanen) *v* ⚓ miz(z)en; **-smast** (-en) *m* miz(z)enmast

be'zadigd sedate, staid, dispassionate [views]

be'zegelen[1] *vt* seal[2] [sbd.'s fate]

be'zeilen[1] *vt* sail [the seas]; *er is geen land met hem te* ~ he is quite unmanageable

'bezem (-s) *m* broom; (v. t w i j g e n) besom; *nieuwe* ~*s vegen schoon* new brooms sweep clean; **-steel** (-stelen) *m* broomstick

be'zeren (bezeerde, h. bezeerd) **I** *vt* hurt, injure; **II** *vr zich* ~ hurt oneself

be'zet 1 taken [of a seat]; 2 (b e z i g) engaged, occupied, busy; 3 ⚔ occupied [of a town]; 4 (m e t j u w e l e n) set [with rubies]; *alles* ~*!* full up!; *is deze plaats* ~*?* is this seat taken?; *ik ben zó* ~ *dat...* I am so busy that...; *al mijn uren zijn* ~ all my hours are taken up; *de rollen waren goed* ~ the cast was an excellent one; *de zaal was goed* ~ there was a large audience

be'zeten *aj* possessed; *als* ~*(en)* like mad; ~ *van* obsessed by; **-e** (-n) *m-v* one possessed; **-heid** *v* mania

be'zetten[1] *vt* occupy [a town]; take [seats]; fill [a post]; cast [a piece, play]; ~ *met* set with [diamonds]. Zie ook: *bezet*; **be'zetting** (-en) *v* 1 (h e t b e z e t t e n) occupation; 2 (v. t o n e e l s t u k) cast; 3 (v. o r k e s t) strength; **-sleger** *o* army of occupation; **be'zettoon** (-tonen) *m* engaged signal

be'zichtigen (bezichtigde, h. bezichtigd) *vt* have a look at, view, inspect; *te* ~ on view;

[1] V.T. en V.D. van dit werkwoord volgens het model: **be'**ademen, V.T. **be'**ademde, V.D. **be'**ademd (**ge-** valt dus weg in het V.D.). Zie voor de vormen onder het grondwoord, in dit voorbeeld: *ademen*. Bij sterke en onregelmatige werkwoorden wordt u verwezen naar de lijst achterin.

–ging (-en) *v* view(ing), inspection

be′zield animated, inspired; **be′zielen** (bezielde, h. bezield) *vt* animate, inspire; *wat bezielt je toch?* **F** what has come over you?; **–d** inspiring [influence, leadership]; **be′zieling** *v* animation, inspiration

be′zien[1] *vt* look at, view; *het staat te ~* it remains to be seen; **beziens′waardig** worth seeing; **–heid** (-heden) *v* curiosity; *de beziens-waardigheden* the sights [of a town], the places of interest

′bezig busy, at work, occupied, engaged; *is hij weer ~?* is he at it again?; *a a n iets ~ zijn* have sth. in hand, be at work (engaged) on sth.; *hij is er druk aan ~* he is hard at work upon it, hard at it; *~ zijn m e t...* be busy ...ing, be busy at (on), be working on

′bezigen (bezigde, h. gebezigd) *vt* use, employ

′bezigheid (-heden) *v* occupation, employment; *bezigheden* pursuits; *huishoudelijke bezigheden* household duties (chores); **′bezighouden** (hield bezig, h. bezigehouden) *vt iem. ~* keep sbd. busy; *het gezelschap (aangenaam) ~* entertain the company; *de kinderen nuttig ~* keep the children usefully occupied; *deze gedachte houdt mij voortdurend bezig* this thought haunts me; *zich met iets ~* occupy (busy) oneself with sth.

be′zijden *het is ~ de waarheid* it is beside the truth

be′zingen[1] *vt* sing (of), chant

be′zinken[1] *vi* settle (down); *fig* sink [in the mind]; **be′zinking** (-en) *v* sedimentation; **be′zinkingssnelheid** (-heden) *v* sedimentation rate; **be′zinksel** (-s) *o* sediment, deposit, lees, dregs, residue

be′zinnen[1] **I** *va* reflect; *bezint eer gij begint* look before you leap; **II** *vr zich ~* think, reflect, change one's mind; *zich lang ~* think long; **–ning** *v* conciousness; *zijn ~ verliezen* lose one's senses; *weer tot ~ komen* come to one's senses again; *iem. tot ~ brengen* bring sbd. to his senses

be′zit *o* possession; (e i g e n d o m) property; (t. o. s c h u l d e n) assets; *fig* asset; $ holdings [of securities, sterling &]; *in het ~ zijn van* be in possession of, be possessed by; *wij zijn in het ~ van uw brief* we have your letter; *in het volle ~ van zijn geestesvermogens* in full possession of his mental faculties; **–neming** *v* occupancy, occupation; **be′zittelijk** possessive [pronoun]; **be′zitten**[1] *vt* possess, own, have; $ hold [securities]; *zijn ziel in lijdzaamheid ~* possess one's soul in patience; *de ~de klassen*

the propertied classes; **–er** (-s) *m* possessor, owner, proprietor; $ holder [of securities]; **be′zitting** (-en) *v* possession; property; *zijn persoonlijke ~en* his personal effects

be′zocht (much) frequented [place]; *druk ~* ook: numerously attended [meeting]; *goed ~* well-attended; *door spoken ~* haunted

be′zoedelen (bezoedelde, h. bezoedeld) *vt* soil, sully, contaminate, stain, pollute, defile, blemish, besmirch; **–ling** (-en) *v* contamination, stain, pollution, defilement, blemish

be′zoek (-en) *o* 1 (v i s i t e) visit, call; [cinema-, museum-, theatre- &] going; 2 (m e n s e n) visitor(s), guests, company; 3 (a a n w e z i g z i j n) attendance; *een ~ afleggen* (*brengen*) make a call, pay a visit; *een ~ beantwoorden* return a call; *er is ~, we hebben ~* we have visitors; *wij ontvangen vandaag geen ~* we are not at home to anybody to-day; *ik was daar op ~* I was on a visit there; **–dag** (-dagen) *m* visitors' (visiting) day [at a hospital &]; **be′zoeken**[1] *vt* visit [a person, place, museum &]; go (come) to see, call on, see [a friend, a man], call at [a house, the Jansens'], attend [church, school, a lecture &]; frequent [the theatres]; **–er** (-s) *m* visitor, caller, guest; frequenter [of a theatre], [theatre-&] goer; **be′zoeking** (-en) *v* visitation, affliction, trial; **be′zoekuur** (-uren) *o* visiting hour

be′zoldigen (bezoldigde, h. bezoldigd) *vt* pay, salary; **–ging** (-en) *v* pay, salary

be′zondigen[1] *zich ~ aan* indulge in [alcohol]

be′zonken *fig* well-considered, mature [judgement]

be′zonnen level-headed, sober-minded, staid, sedate

be′zopen (d r o n k e n) sozzled, dead drunk; (d w a a s) fatuous, crazy, idiotic

be′zorgd anxious, solicitous; *~ voor* anxious (uneasy, concerned) about, solicitous about (for); *zich ~ maken* worry (about *over*); **–heid** (-heden) *v* anxiety, uneasiness, solicitude, concern, apprehension; worry

be′zorgen[1] *vt* 1 (b r e n g e n) deliver [goods, letters &]; 2 (v e r s c h a f f e n) procure, get, find [sth. for sbd.]; gain, win [him many friends], earn [him a certain reputation]; 3 give, cause [trouble &]; *we kunnen het u laten ~* you can have it delivered at your house; **–er** (-s) *m* delivery-man; bearer [of a letter]; [milk &] roundsman; **be′zorging** (-en) *v* delivery [of letters, parcels &]

be′zuiden (to the) south of

be′zuinigen (bezuinigde, h. bezuinigd) *vi*

---

[1] V.T. en V.D. van dat werkwoord volgens het model: **be′**ademen, V.T. **be′**ademde, V.D. **be′**ademd (**ge-** valt dus weg in het V.D.). Zie voor de vormen onder het grondwoord, in dit voorbeeld: *ademen*. Bij sterke en onregelmatige werkwoorden wordt u verwezen naar de lijst achterin.

economize, retrench, reduce one's expenses, cut down expenses, reduce expenditure; ~ *op* economize on; **be′zuiniging** (-en) *v* economy, retrenchment, cut [in wages]; **be′zuinigingsmaatregel** (-en en -s) *m* measure of economy, economy measure

be′zuipen[1] *vr zich* ~ fuddle oneself, booze

be′zuren (bezuurde, h. bezuurd) *vt iets moeten* ~ suffer (pay dearly, smart) for sth.

be′zwaar (-zwaren) *o* 1 difficulty, objection; scruple [= concientious objection]; 2 (n a - d e e l) drawback; *dat is geen* ~ that's no problem; *heeft u er* ~ *tegen...* do you mind...; *bezwaren maken* 1 raise objections, object (to *tegen*); 2 make difficulties, have scruples about doing

be′zwaard burdened[2]; *fig* oppressed; heavy-laden; *voelt u zich* ~? is there anything weighing on your mind?, have you any grievance?; *zich* ~ *voelen* have scruples; *met* ~ *gemoed* with a heavy heart; ~ *met een hypotheek* encumbered (with a mortgage), mortgaged

be′zwaarlijk I *aj* difficult, hard; **II** *ad* with difficulty; **be′zwaarschrift** (-en) *o* petition; (t e g e n b e l a s t i n g) appeal

be′zwadderen (bezwadderde, h. bezwadderd) *vt fig* besmirch

be′zwangerd *met geuren* ~ laden (heavy) with odours

be′zwaren (bezwaarde, h. bezwaard) *vt* burden[2], load[2], weight [with a load]; oppress, weigh (lie) heavy upon [the stomach, the mind]. Zie ook: *bezwaard*; **–d** burdensome [tax], onerous [terms], aggravating [circumstances], damaging [facts], incriminating [evidence]

be′zweek (bezweken) V.T. v. *bezwijken*

be′zweet perspiring, in a sweat

be′zweken V.T. meerv. en V.D. v. *bezwijken*

be′zweren[1] *vt* 1 (m e t e e d) swear (to), make oath [that...]; 2 (b a n n e n) exorcise, cónjure, lay [ghosts, a storm]; charm [snakes]; avert, ward off [a danger]; 3 (s m e k e n) conjúre, adjure [sbd. not to...]; **be′zwering** (-en) *v* 1 swearing; 2 exorcism; 3 conjuration, adjuration; **–sformulier** (-en) *o* incantation, charm, spell

be′zwijken[*] *vi* succumb [to wounds, to a disease], yield [to temptation], give way, break down, collapse [also of things]

be′zwijmen (bezwijmde, is bezwijmd) *vi* faint (away), swoon; **–ming** (-en) *v* fainting fit, faint, swoon

b.g.g. = *bij geen gehoor* if there is no answer

b.h. = *bustehouder*

bi′aisband [bi.′e.-] *o* bias binding

bibbe′ratie [- ′ra.(t)si.] *v* the shivers; **′bibberen** (bibberde, h. gebibberd) *vi* shiver [with cold], tremble [with fear]; **′bibberig** shaky, tremulous

′bibliobus (-sen) *m* & *v* mobile library; **biblio′fiel I** (-en) *m* bibliophile, philobiblist; **II** *aj* bibliophilic, philobiblic; **biblio′graaf** (-grafen) *m* bibliographer; **bibliogra′fie** (-ieën) *v* bibliography; **biblio′grafisch** bibliographical; **bibliothe′caris** (-sen) *m* librarian; **biblio′theek** (-theken) *v* library

bibs *mv* **F** buttocks, bottom

′biceps (-en) *m* biceps

′bidbankje (-s) *o* praying desk; **–dag** (-dagen) *m* day of prayer; **′bidden* I** *vi* 1 pray [to God], say one's prayers; (v ó ó r h e t e t e n) ask a blessing; 3 (n a h e t e t e n) say grace; ~ *om* pray for; ~ *en smeken* beg and pray (implore); **II** *vt* pray [to God]; beg, entreat, implore [sbd. to...]; *niet zo vlug, wat ik u* ~ *mag* pray not so fast; **′bidprentje** (-s) *o* 1 mortuary card; 2 devotional picture; **–stoel** (-en) *m* prie-dieu (chair); **–stond** (-en) *m* prayer meeting; intercession service [for peace]

biecht (-en) *v* confession; *de* ~ *afnemen rk* confess [a penitent]; *fig* question [sbd.] closely; ~ *horen* hear confession; *te* ~ *gaan* go to confession; **–eling(e)** (-en) *m* (*v*) confessant; **′biechten** (biechtte, h. gebiecht) *vt* & *vi* confess; *gaan* ~ go to confession; **′biechtgeheim** (-en) *o* secret of the confessional; **–stoel** (-en) *m* confessional (box); **–vader** (-s) *m* confessor

′bieden* I *vt* 1 (a a n b i e d e n) offer, present; 2 (o p v e r k o p i n g , ◊) bid; *vijf gulden* ~ *op* offer 5 guilders for; **II** *va* bid, make bids; ~ *op* make a bid for; *meer* ~ *dan een ander* outbid sbd.; **–er** (-s) *m* bidder

′biefstuk (-ken) *m* rumpsteak

biels *mv* sleepers [under the rails]

bier *o* beer, ale; **–blikje** (-s) *o* beer-can; **–brouwer** (-s) *m* (beer-)brewer; **bierbrouwe′rij** (-en) *v* brewery; **′bierbuik** (-en) *m* pot-belly; **–fles** (-sen) *v* beer-bottle; **–glas** (-glazen) *o* beer-glass; **–huis** (-huizen) *o* beerhouse, ale-house; **–kaai** *v het is vechten tegen de* ~ it is lost labour; **–pomp** (-en) *v* beer-engine; **–ton** (-nen) *v*, **–vat** (-vaten) *o* beer-cask, beer-barrel; **–viltje** (-s) *o* beer-mat

1 bies (biezen) *v zijn biezen pakken* clear out

---

[1] V.T. en V.D. van di̱t werkwoord volgens het model: **be′ademen**, V.T. **be′ademde**, V.D. **be′ademd** (**ge**- valt dus weg in het V.D.). Zie voor de vormen onder het grondwoord, in dit voorbeeld: *ademen*. Bij sterke en onregelmatige werkwoorden wordt u verwezen naar de lijst achterin.

2 bies (biezen) *v* 1 border; 2 piping [on trousers &]; **–band** (-en) *o* & *m* seam binding

'bieslook *o* chive

biest *v* beestings

biet (-en) *v* beet; **–suiker** *m* beet sugar

'biezen *aj* rush, rush-bottomed [chair]

big (-gen) *v* young pig, piglet, pigling

biga'mie *v* bigamy; *in ~ levend* bigamous

'biggelen ('biggelde, h. gebiggeld) *vi* trickle; *tranen ~ langs haar wangen* tears trickle down her cheeks

'biggen (bigde, h. gebigd) *vi* farrow, cast [pigs]; **'biggetje** (-s) *o* piggy

bi'got bigot(ed)

1 bij (-en) *v* bee

2 bij I *prep* by, with, near, about &; *~ zijn aankomst* on (at) his arrival; *~ de artillerie (marine)* in the artillery (navy); *~ avond* in the evening; *~ de Batavieren* with the Batavians; *~ brand* in case of fire; *zijn broer was ~ hem* his brother was with him; *~ zijn dood* at his death; *~ het dozijn* by the dozen; *~ een glas bier* over a glass of beer; *~ honderden* by (in) hundreds; [they came] in their hundreds; *dat is ~ Europa (~ Fichte) reeds vermeld* already mentioned under Europe (in Fichte); *~ al zijn geleerdheid...* with all his learning; *~ het lezen* when reading; *~ goed weer* if it is fine; *ik heb het niet ~ mij* I've not got it with me; *er werd geen geld ~ hem gevonden* 1 no money was found (up)on him; 2 no money was found in his house; *~ zijn leven* during his life; *hij is (iets) ~ het spoor* he is (something) on (in) the railway; *er stond een streepje ~ zijn naam* against his name; *~ ons* 1 with us; 2 in this country; *~ het vallen van de avond* at nightfall; *~ het venster* near (by) the window; *het is ~ vijven* going on for five; *~ de zestig* close upon sixty; *~ Waterloo* near Waterloo; *de slag ~ Waterloo* the battle of Waterloo; *~ deze woorden* at these words; **II** *ad hij is goed ~* he has (all) his wits about him, **F** he is all there; *ik ben niet ~* I've got behind; *ik ben nog niet ~* I am still behind; *het boek is ~* is up to date; *de boeken zijn ~* $ are posted up; *hij is er ~* he is present; *hij is er niet ~* he is not attending to what I say (to his work &); *je bent er ~ ~!* you are in for it!; *zonder mij was je er ~ geweest* but for me you would have been done for; **–baantje** (-s) *o* side-line; **–bedoeling** (-en) *v* hidden motive, by-end; **–behorend** accessory; *met ~(e)...* with... to match

'bijbel (-s) *m* bible; **–plaats** (-en) *v* scriptural passage; **'bijbels** *aj* biblical, of the bible, scriptural; *~e geschiedenis* sacred history; **'bijbeltaal** *v* biblical language; **–tekst** (-en) *m* Scripture text; **–vast** well-read in Scripture; **–verklaring** (-en) *v* exegesis; **–vertaling** (-en) *v* translation of the bible; *de Engelse ~* the English version of the Bible; (v a n 1 6 6 1) the Authorized Version; (v a n 1 8 8 4) the Revised Version

'bijbenen¹ keep pace (step) with [sbd.], keep up with (abreast with) [sth.]; be able to follow [what is said]

'bijbetalen¹ *vt* pay in addition, pay extra; **–ling** (-en) *v* additional (extra) payment

'bijbetekenis (-sen) *v* additional meaning, connotation

'bijblad (-bladen) *o* supplement [to a newspaper]

'bijblijven¹ *vi* 1 (m e t l o p e n) keep pace; (m e t z ij n t ij d) keep up to date; 2 (i n h e t g e h e u g e n) remain, stick in one's memory; *ik kan niet ~* I can't keep up (with you); *het is mij altijd bijgebleven* it has remained with me all along

'bijbrengen¹ *vt* 1 (i e t s) bring forward [evidence], produce [proofs]; 2 (i e m .) bring round, bring to, restore to consciousness; 3 (i e m . i e t s) impart [knowledge] to, instil [it] into sbd.'s mind, teach [a pupil French]

bijde'hand smart, quick-witted, bright, spry; **–je** (-s) *o het (hij) is een ~* he is a smart little fellow; *zij is een ~* **F** she is all there, there are no flies on her; **'bijdehands** *~ paard* near (left) horse

'bijdraaien¹ *vi* ⚓ heave to, bring to; *fig* come round

'bijdrage (-n) *v* contribution ° ; *een ~ leveren tot* make a contribution to(wards); **'bijdragen¹** *vt* contribute [money to a fund &]; *zijn deel (het zijne) ~ ook:* play one's part; *zie ook steentje*

bij'een together; **–behoren** (hoorde bij'een, h. bij'eenbehoord) *vi* belong together; **–brengen²** *vt* bring together [people]; collect [money], raise [funds]; **–drijven²** *vt* drive together, round up; **–houden²** *vt* keep together; **–komen²** *vi* 1 (v. p e r s o n e n) meet, assemble, get together; 2 (v. k l e u - r e n) go together, match; **–komst** (-en) *v* meeting, gathering, assembly; **–roepen²** *vt* call together, call, convene, convoke, summon; **–schrapen²** *vt* scrape together, scratch up [a living &]; **–zoeken²** *vt* get together, gather, find

---

¹,² V.T. en V.D. van dit werkwoord volgens het model: 1 **'bij**draaien, V.T. draaide **'bij**, V.D. **'bij**gedraaid; 2 **bij'een**schrapen, V.T. schraapte **bij'een**, V.D. bij'eengeschraapt. Zie voor de vormen onder het grondwoord, in deze voorbeelden: *draaien* en *schrapen*. Bij sterke en onregelmatige werkwoorden wordt u verwezen naar de lijst achterin.

'**bijenhouder** (-s) *m* bee-keeper, bee-master, apiarist; **–koningin** (-nen) *v* queen-bee; **–korf** (-korven) *m* beehive; **–stal** (-len) *m* apiary; **–teelt** *v* apiculture; **–volk** (-en) *o* hive, swarm (of bees); **–was** *m* & *o* beeswax; **–zwerm** (-en) *m* swarm of bees

'**bijfiguur** (-guren) *v* secondary figure [in drawing]; minor character [in novel &]; **–film** (-s) *m* supporting film

'**bijgaand** enclosed, annexed; ~ *schrijven* the accompanying letter

'**bijgebouw** (-en) *o* outbuilding, outhouse, annex(e); **–gedachte** (-n) *v* 1 by-thought; 2 ulterior motive

'**bijgeloof** *o* superstition; **bijge'lovig** superstitious; **–heid** (-heden) *v* superstitiousness

'**bijgeluid** (-en) *o* accompanying noise, background noise; **–genaamd** nicknamed, surnamed; **–gerecht** (-en) *o* side-dish

bijge'val by any chance, perhaps; *als je* ~... if you happen (chance) to...; **bijge'volg** in consequence, consequently

'**bijhouden**[1] *vt* (iem., iets) keep up with, keep pace with [sbd., sth.]; (zijn glas &) hold out [one's glass]; $ (de boeken) 1 keep up to date [the books]; 2 keep [the books]; (zijn talen &) keep up [one's French, German]; *er is geen* ~ *aan* it is impossible to cope with (keep up with)

'**bijkans, bij'kans** almost, nearly

'**bijkantoor** (-toren) *o* 1 branch office; 2 ☏ sub-office; **–keuken** (-s) *v* scullery

'**bijknippen**[1] *vt* trim

'**bijkok** (-s) *m* under-cook

'**bijkomen**[1] *vi* 1 (na flauwte) come to oneself again, come round; 2 (na ziekte) gain [in weight; four pounds &], put on weight; zie ook *komen*; **–d** ~*e (on)kosten* additional (extra) costs, extras; ~*e omstandigheden* attendant circumstances; **bij'komstig** of minor importance; **–heid** (-heden) *v* thing of minor importance

bijl (-en) *v* axe, hatchet; *voor de* ~ *gaan* F be for it, get it

'**bijladen**[1] *vt* fill up; ⚡ recharge

'**bijlage** (-n) *v* appendix, enclosure, addendum

'**bijlbundel** (-s) *m* ⚏ fasces (*mv*)

'**bijleggen**[1] *vt* 1 (leggen bij) add [to]; 2 (uitmaken) make up, accommodate, arrange, compose, settle [differences]; *het weer* ~ make it up again; *ik moet er nog (geld)* ~ I lose on it, I'm a loser by it

'**bijles** (-sen) *v* extra lesson, coaching

'**bijlichten**[1] *vt iem.* ~ give sbd. a light

'**bijltje** (-s) *o* little axe; *het* ~ *er bij neerleggen* leave off, give up, chuck; *ik heb (hij heeft) al lang met dat* ~ *gehakt* I am (he is) an old hand at it, he is an old stager; **–sdag** *m* day of reckoning

'**bijmaan** (-manen) *v* mock-moon, moon dog

'**bijna** almost, nearly, next to, all but; ~ *niet* hardly, scarcely; ~ *niets (niemand, nooit)* hardly anything (anybody, ever)

'**bijnaam** (-namen) *m* 1 (tweede naam) surname; 2 (scheldnaam) nickname, byname, sobriquet; **–nier** (-en) *v* adrenal gland

bijoute'rieën [bi.ʒu.tə-] *mv* jewellery; **bijoute'riekistje** (-s) *o* jewel-case

'**bijpassen**[1] *vt* pay in addition, pay extra; **–d** ...to match, ...to go with it (them)

'**bijprodukt** (-en) *o* by-product; spin-off; **–rijder** (-s) *m* driver's mate; **–rivier** (-en) *v* tributary (stream), affluent; **–rol** (-len) *v* secondary part, minor rôle

'**bijschaven**[1] *vt fig* polish, smooth

'**bijschilderen**[1] *vt* 1 paint in [figures &]; 2 touch up, work up [here and there]

'**bijschrift** (-en) *o* inscription, legend, motto; marginal note; postscript; letterpress [to an illustration]; '**bijschrijven**[1] *vt* write up [the books]; *er wat* ~ add something [in writing]; **–ving** (-en) *v* $ credit statement

'**bijschuiven** I *vt* draw (pull) up [one's chair to the table]; II *vi* close up

'**bijslaap** *m* cohabitation; **–slag** *m* extra allowance; zie ook: *toeslag* 1; **–smaak** (-smaken) *m* taste, flavour, tang²; *fig* tinge

'**bijspringen**[1] *vt iem.* ~ stand by sbd.; help sbd. out

'**bijstaan**[1] *vt* assist, help, aid, succour; '**bijstand** *m* assistance, help, aid, succour; ~ *verlenen* lend assistance

'**bijstellen**[1] *vt* (re)adjust; **–ling** (-en) *v gram* apposition

'**bijster** I *aj het spoor* ~ *zijn* 1 *eig* be thrown off the scent; 2 *fig* have lost one's way; be at sea, be at fault; II *ad* < *hij is niet* ~ *knap* he is not particularly clever; *het is* ~ *koud* it is extremely cold

'**bijstorten**[1] *vt* make an additional payment of...

'**bijsturen**[1] *vi* correct [the course]

bijt (-en) *v* hole (made in the ice)

'**bijtanken**[1] *vi* refuel

'**bijtellen**[1] *vt* count in

'**bijten*** I *vt* bite²; II *vi* bite²; *hij wou er niet in* ~ he did not bite; *in het stof (zand)* ~ 1 bite the dust; 2 (ruiter) be thrown, be unhorsed; *o p*

<hr>

[1] V.T. en V.D. van dit werkwoord volgens het model: '**bij**draaien, V.T. draaide '**bij**, V.D. '**bij**gedraaid. Zie voor de vormen onder het grondwoord, in dit voorbeeld: *draaien*. Bij sterke en onregelmatige werkwoorden wordt u verwezen naar de lijst achterin.

zijn nagels ~ bite one's nails; *v a n zich af* ~ show fight, not take it lying down; **–d** biting, caustic, corrosive; nipping [cold]; *fig* biting, caustic, cutting, mordant, pungent, poignant; ~*e spot* sarcasm

bij′tijds in (good) time

′bijtmiddel (-en) *o* mordant, caustic, corrosive

′bijtrekken[1] **I** *vt* draw, pull [a chair &] near(er); join, add [an adjacent plot] on to [one's own garden &]; **II** *vi het zal wel* ~ it is sure to tone down [to the colour of the surrounding part]; *hij zal wel* ~ he'll come round in the end

′bijtring (-en) *m* teething ring

bijv. = *bijvoorbeeld*

′bijvak (-ken) *o* subsidiary subject

′bijval *m* approval, approbation, applause; *stormachtige* ~ (*in*)*oogsten* be received with a storm of applause; ~ *vinden* meet with approval [proposal]; catch on [plays]; **′bijvallen**[1] *vt iem.* ~ concur in (fall in with) sbd.'s opinions (ideas &), agree with sbd.; **′bijvalsbetuiging(en)** *v* (*mv*) applause; shouts of applause, cheers

′bijvegen[1] *vt* sweep up

′bijverdienen[1] earn sth. extra; **′bijverdienste** (-n) *v* extra earnings

′bijvoeding *v* extra feeding

′bijvoegen[1] *v* add, join, subjoin, annex; **–ging** (-en) *v* addition; *onder* ~ *van...* adding..., enclosing...; **bij′voeglijk I** *aj* adjectival; ~ *naamwoord* adjective; **II** *ad* adjectively; **′bijvoegsel** (-s) *o* 1 addition; 2 supplement, appendix

bij′voorbeeld for instance, for example, say [three]

′bijvullen[1] *vt* replenish, fill up

′bijwagen (-s) *m* trailer [of a tram-car]; **–weg** (-wegen) *m* by-road, by-path

′bijwerken[1] *vt* 1 (*i e t s*) touch up [a picture], bring up to date [a book]; $ post up [the books]; make up [arrears]; 2 (*e e n l e e r l i n g*) coach; *bijgewerkt tot 1977* brought up to 1977; **–king** (-en) *v* ⚕ side-effect [of a drug]

′bijwijzen[1] *vi* follow with one's finger

′bijwonen[1] *vt* be present at [some function], attend [divine service, a lecture, mass], witness [a scene]

′bijwoord (-en) *o gram* adverb; **bij′woordelijk** adverbial

′bijzaak (-zaken) *v* matter of secondary (minor) importance, accessory matter; side-issue, side-show; *geld is* ~ money is no object [with him]

′bijzettafeltje (-s) *o* occasional table;

′bijzetten[1] *vt* 1 place or put near (to, by); 2 (*b e g r a v e n*) inter; 3 ⚓ set [a sail]; *kracht* ~ *aan* emphasize, add (lend) force to, press [a demand]; zie ook *luister, zeil*, **–ting** (-en) *v* interment

bij′ziend near-sighted, myopic; **–heid** *v* near-sightedness, myopia

′bijzijn *o* presence; *in het* ~ *van* in the presence of

′bijzin (-nen) *m gram* (subordinate) clause

′bijzit (-ten) *v* concubine; **′bijzitter** (-s) *m* 1 ⚖ second examiner; 2 ⚖ assessor

′bijzon (-nen) *v* mock-sun, sun-dog

bij′zonder [bi.-] **I** *aj* particular, special; peculiar, strange; *in het* ~ in particular, especially; **II** *ad* < particularly, exceptionally, uncommonly, specially [active]; **–heid** (-heden) *v* particularity; particular, detail; peculiarity

bi′kini ('s) *m* bikini

′bikkel (-s) *m* knucklebone; **′bikkelen** (bikkelde, h. gebikkeld) *vi* play at knucklebones; **′bikkel′hard** hard as stone, stony

′bikken (bikte, h. gebikt) *vt* chip [a stone]; scale [a boiler] ‖ (*e t e n*) eat

bil (-len) *v* buttock; rump [of oxen]; *voor de* ~*len geven* spank

bilate′raal bilateral

bil′jart (-en) *o* 1 (*h e t s p e l*) billiards; 2 (*d e t a f e l*) billiard(s) table; ~ *spelen* play (at) billiards; *een partij* ~ a game of billiards; **–bal** (-len) *m* billiard-ball; **bil′jarten** (biljartte, h. gebiljart) *vi* play (at) billiards; **bil′jartkeu** (-en en -s) *v* billiard ceu; **–laken** (-s) *o* billiard-cloth; **–spel** (-spelen) *o* (game of) billiards; **–zaal** (-zalen) *v* billiard(s) room

bil′jet (-ten) *o* 1 (*k a a r t*) ticket; 2 (*b a n k*~) (bank-)note; 3 (*a a n p l a k*~) poster; 4 (*s t r o o i*~) handbill

bil′joen (-en) *o* billion [= million millions]; *Am* trillion

′billijk fair, just, reasonable; $ moderate [prices]; *het is niet meer dan* ~ it is only fair; **′billijken** (billijkte, h. gebillijkt) *vt* approve of; **billijker′wijs, –′wijze** in fairness, in justice; **′billijkheid** *v* fairness, justice; reasonableness [of demands]

′bimbam ding-dong

bimetal′lisme *o* bimetallism

′binden* I *vt* bind˚ [a book, sheaves, a prisoner, tie [a knot, sbd.'s hands]; tie up [a parcel]; thicken [soup, gravy]; make [brooms]; *iem. iets op het hart* ~ enjoin sth. on sbd.; ~ *aan* tie to [a post &]; *de kinderen* ~ *mij aan huis* I am

---

[1] V.T. en V.D. van dit werkwoord volgens het model: **′bij**draaien, V.T. draaide **′bij**, V.D. **′bij**gedraaid. Zie voor de vormen onder het grondwoord, in dit voorbeeld: *draaien*. Bij sterke en onregelmatige werkwoorden wordt u verwezen naar de lijst achterin.

tied down to my home by the children; **II** *vr*
zich ~ bind oneself, commit oneself; **–d**
binding [on both parties]; **'bindgaren** (-s) *o*
string; **'binding** (-en) *v* tie, bond; (v. s k i)
ski-binding; **'bindmiddel** *o* binder, cement²;
fig link; **–vlies** (-vliezen) *o* conjunctiva;
–weefsel (-s) *o* connective tissue

bink (-en) **S** *m* chap

'binnen I *prep* within; ~ *enige dagen* in a few
days; ~ *veertien dagen* within a fortnight; **II** *ad*
~*!* come in!; *wie is er* ~*?* who is inside
(within)?; *hij is* ~ he is indoors; *fig* he is a
made man; ● *n a a r* ~ *gaan* go (walk) in; *naar*
~ *gekeerd* [with the hairy side] in; [with his
toes] turned in; *naar* ~ *zenden* send in; *iem. t e* ~
schieten come to sbd.; *het wilde me niet te* ~
schieten I could not remember it (think of it), I
could not hit upon it; *v a n* ~ 1 (on the) inside;
[it looks fine] whithin; 2 [it came] from within;
van ~ *en van buiten* inside and out; **–baan**
(-banen) *v* inside track; **–bad** (-baden) *o* indoor
swimming-pool; **–bal** (-len) *m* [football]
bladder; **–band** (-en) *m* (inner) tube

'binnenblijven[1] *vi* remain (keep) indoors, stay
in

'binnenbocht (-en) *v* inside(-bend); **–brand**
(-en) *m* indoor fire

'binnenbrengen[1] *vt* bring in, take in; ⚓ bring
[a ship] into port

'binnendeur (-en) *v* inner door; **–dijks,**
binnen'dijks (lying) on the inside of a dike,
on the landside of the dike

binnen'door ~ *gaan* 1 take a short cut; 2 go
through the house

'binnendringen[1] **I** *vt* penetrate, invade; *een huis*
~ penetrate into a house; **II** *vi* force one's way
into a (the) house

'binnendruppelen[1] *vi fig* trickle in

'binnengaan[1] *vi* & *vt* enter

binnen'gaats ⚓ in the roads

'binnenhalen[1] *vt* gather in; zie ook: *inhalen*

'binnenhaven (-s) *v* 1 inner harbour; 2 inland
port; **–hoek** (-en) *m* interior angle; **–hof**
(-hoven) *o* inner court

'binnenhouden[1] *vt* 1 keep [sbd.] in; 2 retain
[food on one's stomach]

'binnenhuisarchitect [-ɑrgi.-, -ɑrʃi.tɛkt] (-en)
m interior decorator; **–architectuur** *v* interior
decoration

'binnenhuisje (-s) *o* interior

binnen'in on the inner side, inside, within

'binnenkant (-en) *m* inside

'binnenkomen[1] *vi* 1 (p e r s o n e n, t r e i n,

g e l d &) come in; get in(to a room), enter; 2
⚓ come into port; *laat haar* ~ show (ask) her
in; **–komst** (-en) *v* entrance, entry, coming in

binnen'kort before long, shortly

'binnenkrijgen[1] *vt* get down [food]; get in
[outstanding debts]; *water* ~ (v . s c h i p) make
water

'binnenland (-en) *o* interior; *in binnen- en*
buitenland at home and abroad; **–s** inland
[letter, navigation], home [market, news];
home-made [products], interior, domestic,
intestine [quarrels], internal [policy]; ~ *bestuur*
▭ civil service; *ambtenaar bij het* ~ *bestuur* ▭
civil servant; ~*e zaken* home affairs; zie ook:
ministerie &

'binnenlaten[1] *vt* let in, show in; admit

'binnenleiden[1] *vt* usher in

'binnenloodsen[1] *vt* pilot [a ship] into port

'binnenlopen[1] **I** *vi* 1 run in; 2 ⚓ put into port;
even ~ drop in før a minute; **II** *vt* 1 run into [a
house]; 2 ⚓ put into [port]

'binnenmeer (-meren) *o* inland lake; **–meid**
(-en) *v*, **–meisje** (-s) *o* parlourmaid; **–muur**
(-muren) *m* inner wall; **–pad** (-paden) *o*
by-path; **–pagina** ('s) *v* inside page; **–plaats**
(-en) *v* inner court, inner yard, courtyard [of a
prison]

'binnenpraten[1] *vt* (v . v l i e g t u i g) talk down

'binnenpret *v* secret amusement

'binnenrijden[1] *vi* ride, drive in(to a place)

'binnenroepen[1] *vt* call in

'binnenrukken[1] *vi* march in(to the town &)

'binnenscheepvaart *v* inland navigation;
–schipper (-s) *m* bargeman, bargemaster

binnens'huis indoors, within doors; **–'kamers**
in one's room; *fig* in private, privately

'binnensluipen[1] *vi* steal into [a house]

'binnensmokkelen[1] *vt* smuggle (in)

binnens'monds under one's breath; ~ *spreken*
speak indistinctly, mumble

'binnenspeler (-s) *m sp* inside right (or left)
forward; **–stad** (-steden) *v* inner part of a
town

'binnenstappen[1] *vi* step in(to the room)

'binnenste I *aj* inmost; **II** *o* inside; *in zijn* ~ in
his heart of hearts, deep down;
binnenste'buiten inside out

'binnenstormen[1] *vi* rush in(to a house)

'binnenstromen[1] *vi* stream (flow, pour) in;
stream (flock, flow, pour) into the country &

'binnenstuiven[1] *vi = binnenstormen*

'binnentarief (-rieven) *o* $ internal tariff

'binnentreden[1] *vi* enter [the room]

---

[1] V.T. en V.D. van dit werkwoord volgens het model: **'binnen**halen, V.T. haalde **'binnen**, V.D. **'binnen**gehaald.
Zie voor de vormen onder het grondwoord, in dit voorbeeld: *halen*. Bij sterke en onregelmatige werkwoorden wordt
u verwezen naar de lijst achterin.

'binnentrekken[1] *vi* = *binnenrukken*
'binnenvaart *v* inland navigation
'binnenvallen[1] *vi* 1 ⚓ put into port; 2 invade [a country]; 3 drop in [on a friend]
'binnenvetter (-s) *m fig* secret hoarder;
  –waarts I *aj* inward; **II** *ad* inward(s);
  –wateren *mv* inland waterways; **–weg** (-wegen) *m* 1 by-road, by-path; (k o r t e r) short cut; 2 (v. h. v e r k e e r) secondary road; **–werk** *o* 1 inside work; 2 works [of a watch]; 3 interior [of a piano]; 4 filler [for cigars]; **–werks** *~e maat* inside diameter
'binnenwippen[1] drop in, **F** blow in [upon sbd.]
'binnenzak (-ken) *m* inside pocket; **–zee** (-zeeën) *v* inland sea; **–zij(de)** (-den) *v* inside, inner side; **–zool** (-zolen) *v* insole
bi'nomium *o* binomial; *het ~ van Newton* the binomial theorem
bint (-en) *o* tie-beam, joist
bioche'mie *v* biochemistry
bio'graaf (-grafen) *m* biographer; **biogra'fie** (-ieën) *v* biography; **bio'grafisch** biographical
biolo'geren (biologeerde, h. gebiologeerd) *vt* mesmerize; **biolo'gie** *v* biology, natural history; **bio'logisch** biological; **bio'loog** (-logen) *m* biologist
bio'scoop (-scopen) *m* cinema, picture-theatre; *naar de ~ gaan* go to the pictures; **–bezoeker** (-s) *m* filmgoer; *in 1977 bedroeg het aantal ~s...* ook: in 1977 cinema attendances numbered...; **–voorstelling** (-en) *v* picture show, cinema show
bio'sfeer *v* biosphere
bio'toop (-topen) *v* biotope
bips F *mv* bottom, buttocks, behind
'Birma *o* Burma; **Bir'maan(s)** Burmese [*mv* Burmese]
1 bis [bi.s] *ad* encore
2 bis [bi.s] *v* ♪ B sharp
'bisambont ['bi.zɑm-] *o* musquash, musk-rat; **–rat** (-ten) *v* musk-rat, musquash
bis'cuit [bɪs'kʋi.] (-s) *o* & *m* biscuit
'bisdom (-men) *o* diocese; bishopric
biseksu'eel bisexual
Bis'kaje *Golf van ~* Gulf of Biscay
'bismut *o* bismuth
'bisschop (-pen) *m* bishop (ook = mulled wine); **bis'schoppelijk** episcopal;
  'bisschopsmijter (-s) *m* mitre; **–staf** (-staven) *m* crosier
bissec'trice [bi.sɛk-] (-n) *v* bisector, bisecting line
bis'seren [bi.-] (bisseerde, h. gebisseerd) **I** *vt*

encore; **II** *va* demand an encore
'bit (-ten) *o* bit
bits snappish, snappy, acrimonious, tart; sharp
'bitter I *aj* bitter[2] [drink, disappointment, tone &]; *een glaasje ~* a (glass of) gin and bitters; **–heid** (-heden) *v* bitterness[2], *fig* acerbity, acrimony; **–koekje** (-s) *o* macaroon; **–zout** *o* magnesium sulphate, Epsom salt(s)
bi'tumen *o* bitumen
'bivak (-ken) *o* bivouac; *ergens z'n ~ opslaan* [*fig*] stay temporarily; **bivak'keren** (bivakkeerde, h. gebivakkeerd) bivouac
bi'zar I *aj* bizarre, grotesque, odd; **II** *ad* in a bizarre way, grotesquely
'bizon (-s) *m* bison, buffalo
'blaadje (-s) *o* 1 leaflet [= young leaf & part of compound leaf]; 2 sheet [of paper]; > (news) paper, **F** rag; 3 tray [of wood or metal]; *bij iem. in een goed* (*slecht*) *~ staan* be in sbd.'s good (bad) books
blaag (blagen) *m-v* naughty boy or girl, brat
blaam *v* 1 blame, censure; 2 blemish; *hem treft geen ~* no blame attaches to him; *een ~ werpen op* put (cast) a slur on; *zich van alle ~ zuiveren* exculpate oneself; zie ook *vrees*
blaar (blaren) *v* 1 (z w e l l i n g) blister; 2 (b l e s) blaze, white spot
blaas (blazen) *v* 1 (in l i c h a a m) bladder; 2 (in v l o e i s t o f) bubble
'blaasbalg (-en) *m* bellows; *een ~* a pair of bellows; **–instrument** (-en) *o* wind instrument
'blaasje (-s) *o* 1 vesicle, bleb; 2 bubble, bladder
'blaaskaak (-kaken) *v* gas-bag, braggart; **blaaskake'rij** (-en) *v* gassing, swagger, braggadocio
'blaaskapel (-len) *v* brass band
'blaasontsteking (-en) *v* cystitis
'blaasorkest (-en) *o* wind-band; **–pijp** (-en) *v* blow-pipe; *~je* breathalyzer
'blaassteen (-stenen) *m* 🪨 calculus; **–worm** (-en) *m* bladder-worm
blad *o* 1 (bladen, bla(de)ren) leaf [of a tree, of a book]; 2 (bladen) sheet [of paper, metal], blade [of an oar, of a saw & 🪓], top [of a table]; 3 (bladen) tray [for glasses]; *geen ~ voor de mond nemen* not mince one's words, not mince matters; *van het ~ spelen* play at sight; **–aarde** *v* leaf-mould; **–deeg** = *bladerdeeg*

'bladder (-s) *v* (*m*) blister [in paint]; 'bladderen (bladderde, h. gebladderd) *vi* blister
'bladen meerv. v. *blad*
'bladerdeeg *o* puff-paste
1 'bladeren (bladerde, h. gebladerd) *vi* ~ *in*
turn over the leaves [of a book], leaf (through)
[a book]; 2 'bladeren meerv. v. *blad* 1
'bladgoud *o* gold-leaf; **–groen** *o* leaf-green,
chlorophyll; **–groente** (-n en -s) *v* greens,
leafy vegetable; **–knop** (-pen) *m* leaf-bud;
–koper *o* sheet-copper, leaf-brass; **–luis**
(-luizen) *v* plant-louse, green fly, aphid, aphis
[*mv* aphides]; **–spiegel** (-s) *m* type area; **–steel**
(-stelen) *m* leaf-stalk; **–stil** *het was* ~ there was
a dead calm, not a leaf stirred; **–tin** *o* tinfoil;
–vormig leaf-like, leaf-shaped; **–vulling** (-en)
v fill-up, stop-gap; **–wijzer** (-s) *m* book-
mark(er); **–zij(de)** (-den) *v* page
'blaffen (blafte, h. geblaft) *vi* bark[2] (at *tegen*);
–er (-s) *m* barker[2]
'blaken (blaakte, h. geblaakt) *vi* ~ *van gezondheid*
be in rude health, glow with health; ~ *van
vaderlandsliefde* burn with patriotism; **–d**
burning, ardent; (z o n) blazing, scorching; *in*
~*e welstand* in the pink of health
'blaker (-s) *m* flat candlestick
'blakeren (blakerde, h. geblakerd) *vt* burn,
scorch
bla'mage [- 'ma.ʒə] (-s) *v* disgrace (to *voor*);
bla'meren (blameerde, h. geblameerd) **I** *vt*
iem. ~ bring shame upon sbd.; **II** *vr zich* ~
disgrace oneself
'blanco blank; ~ *stemmen* abstain (from voting);
tien ~ *stemmen* ten abstentions; ~ *volmacht* blank
power of attorney
blank **I** *aj* white, fair [skin]; naked [sword]; ~
schuren scour bright; *de weiden staan* ~ the
meadows are flooded; **II** *o* (d o m i n o s p e l)
blank; 'blanke (-n) *m-v* white man (woman);
de ~*n* the whites
blan'ketsel (-s) *o* paint; face powder
'blaren meerv. v. *blad* 1
bla'sé [bla.'ze.] blasé: cloyed with pleasure
blasfe'meren (blasfemeerde, h. geblasfemeerd)
vi blaspheme; blasfe'mie *v* blasphemy
'blaten (blaatte, h. geblaat) *vi* bleat
'blauw **I** *aj* blue; ~*e druif* black grape; *een* ~*e
maandag* a very short time; *de zaak* ~ ~ *laten* let
the matter rest; *iemand een* ~ *oog slaan* give sbd.
a black eye; *een* ~*e plek* a bruise; ~*e zone*
restricted parking zone; **II** *o* blue; **–achtig**
bluish
'Blauwbaard, 'blauwbaard *m* Bluebeard;
'blauwbekken (blauwbekte, h. geblauwbekt)
staan ~ stand in the cold; 'blauwdruk (-ken)
m blueprint; blauwe'regen (-s) *m* 🌿 wistaria;
'blauwkous (-en) *v* bluestocking; **–sel** (-s) *o*

powder-blue; *door het* ~ *halen* blue; **–tje** (-s) *o*
een ~ *lopen* **F** get the mitten, be jilted [by a
girl]; **–zuur** *o* Prussic acid
'blazen* **I** *vi* blow˚; (v . k a t) spit; ~ *op* blow
[the flute, a whistle]; sound, wind [the horn];
sound [the trumpet]; **II** *vt* blow [one's tea, the
flute, glass &], blow, play [an instrument]. Zie
ook: *aftocht, alarm* &; 1 'blazer (-s) *m*
(p e r s o o n) blower; *de* ~*s* 🎵 the wind
2 'blazer ['ble.zər] (-s) *m* (j a s j e) blazer
bla'zoen (-en) *o* blazon, coat of arms
bleef (bleven) V.T. v. *blijven*
1 bleek *aj* pale, pallid, wan; ~ *van toorn* pale
with anger
2 bleek *v* bleach-field
3 bleek (bleken) V.T. v. *blijken*
'bleekgezicht (-en) *o* pale-face; **–heid** *v*
paleness, pallor; **–jes** palish; **–middel** (-en) *o*
bleaching agent; **–neus** (-neuzen) *m* tallow-
face; **–neusje** (-s) *o* delicate child, sickly-
looking child; **–poeder** *o* & *m* bleaching-
powder; **–veld** (-en) *o* bleach-field; **–water** *o*
bleach(ing liquor); **–zucht** *v* chlorosis, green
sickness; bleek'zuchtig chlorotic
blei (-en) *v* 🐟 white bream
1 'bleken (bleekte, h. gebleekt) *vt* & *vi* bleach
2 'bleken V.T. meerv. v. *blijken*
'blèren ['blɛː rə(n)] (blèrde, h. geblèrd) *vi* bawl,
howl
bles (-sen) 1 *v* blaze; 2 *m* horse with a blaze
bles'seren (blesseerde, h. geblesseerd) *vt* injure,
wound, hurt; bles'sure (-n) *v*, bles'suur
(-suren) *v* injury, wound, hurt
bleu timid, shy, bashful
bleven V.T. meerv. v. *blijven*
bliek (-en) *m* 🐟 = *blei* & *sprot*
blies (bliezen) V.T. v. *blazen*
'blieven (bliefde, h. gebliefd) = *believen*
'blij(de) glad, joyful, joyous, cheerful, pleased;
hij is er ~ *mee* he is delighted (happy) with it; *ik
ben er* ~ *om* (*over*) I am glad of it; *iem.* ~ *maken*
please sbd., make sbd. happy; *zich* ~ *maken met
een dode mus* have found a mare's nest; 'blijd-
schap *v* gladness, joy, mirth; *met* ~ *geven wij
kennis van...* we are happy to announce...;
'blijheid *v* gladness, joyfulness, joy

blijk (-en) *o* token, mark, proof, sign; ~ *geven
van* give evidence (proof) of, show; **–baar**
apparent, evident, obvious; 'blijken* *vi* be
evident, appear, be obvious; *het blijkt nu* it is
evident now; *uit alles blijkt dat...* everything
goes to show that...; *hij bleek de maker te zijn* he
turned out (proved) to be the maker; *het is
nodig gebleken te...* it has been found necessary
to...; *het zal wel* ~ *uit de stukken* it will appear
(be apparent, be evident) from the documents;
het moet nog ~ it remains to be seen; it is to be

proved; *doen ~ van* give proof of; *niet de minste aandoening laten ~* not betray (show) the least emotion; *je moet er niets van laten ~* you must not appear to know anything about it; *–s* as appears from, from

blij′moedig joyful, cheerful, jovial, merry, gay, glad

′blijspel (-spelen) *o* comedy; **–dichter** (-s) *m* writer of comedies

′blijven* *vi* 1 remain [for weeks in Paris], stay [here!]; 2 (i n e e n t o e s t a n d) remain [faithful, fine, our friend]; go [unnoticed, unpunished]; 3 (o v e r b l ij v e n) remain, be left [of former glory]; 4 (d o o d b l ij v e n) die, be killed, perish; 5 (d o o r g a a n m e t) continue to..., keep ...ing; *waar blijft hij toch?* where can he be?; *waar is het (hij) gebleven?* what has become of it (him)?; *waar zijn we gebleven?* where did we leave off (stop)?; *waar was ik gebleven?* where had I got to?; *waar blijft het eten toch?* where *is* dinner?; *waar blijft de tijd!* how time flies!; *hij blijft lang, hoor!* 1 how long he is staying!; 2 he is a long time (in) coming (back); *blijf je het hele concert?* are you going to sit out the whole concert?; *goed ~* keep [of food]; *~ eten* stay to dinner; *~ leven* live (on); zie ook: *hangen* &; ● *hij blijft b ij ons* he is going to stay with us; *alles blijft bij het oude* everything remains as it was; *maar daar bleef het niet bij* but that was not all; *ik blijf bij wat ik gezegd heb* I stick to what I have said; *hij blijft er bij, dat...* he persists in saying that...; *het blijft er dus bij dat...* so it is settled that...; *daarbij bleef het* there the matter rested, that was that; *dat blijft o n d e r ons* this is strictly between ourselves; *blijf v a n mij (ervan) af!* hands off!; *daarmee moet je mij van het lijf ~!* none of that for me!; **–d** lasting [peace, evidence]; enduring, abiding [value]; permanent [abode, wave]; **′blijvertje** (-s) *o dat is geen ~* that child will never grow old; **S** it's a goner

1 blik (-ken) *m* glance, look; *zijn brede ~* his broad view; *zijn heldere ~* 1 his bright look; 2 his keen insight; *een ~ slaan (werpen) op* cast a glance at; *begerige ~ken werpen (laten vallen) op* cast covetous eyes on; ● *b ij de eerste ~* at the first glance; *i n één ~* at a glance; *m e t één ~ overzien* take it in at a (single) glance

2 blik (-ken) *o* 1 (m e t a a l) tin, tin plate, white iron; 2 (v o o r w e r p) dustpan; tin [of meat], can [of peaches &]; *kreeft in ~* tinned (canned) lobster; *stoffer en ~* brush and dustpan; **–groenten** *mv* tinned (canned) vegetables; **–je** (-s) *o* tin [of meat], can; **1 ′blikken** *aj* tin

2 ′blikken (blikte, h. geblikt) *vt* look, glance; *zonder ~ of blozen* without turning a hair

′blikkeren (blikkerde, h. geblikkerd) *vi* glitter, flash

′blikkerig tinny, brassy

′blikopener (-s) *m* tin-opener, can opener; **–schade** *v* bodywork damage

′bliksem (-s) *m* lightning; *arme ~* poor devil; *wat ~!* **F** what the hell!; *als de ~* (as) quick as lightning, like blazes; *naar de ~ gaan* go to the dogs, go to pot; *loop naar de ~!* go to blazes!; **–actie** [-ɑksi.] (-s) *v* lightning action; **–afleider** (-s) *m* lightning conductor[2]; **–bezoek** (-en) *o* flying visit; **′bliksemen** (bliksemde, h. gebliksemd) *vi* lighten; (v . d e o g e n &) flash; *het bliksemt* it lightens, there is a flash of lightning; zie ook: *donderen;* **′bliksemflits** (-en) *m* flash (streak) of lightning; **′bliksems I** *aj die ~e kerel* that confounded fellow; **II** *ad* < deucedly; **III** *ij* the deuce!; **′bliksemschicht** (-en) *m* thunderbolt, flash of lightning; **–snel** quick as lightning, with lightning speed; lightning [victory &]; **F** like winking; **–straal** (-stralen) *m* & *v* flash of lightning; *als een ~ uit heldere hemel* like a bolt from the blue

′blikslager (-s) *m* tin-smith

′blikvanger (-s) *m* eye-catcher

1 blind (-en) *o* shutter

2 blind *aj* blind[2]; *~ als een mol* as blind as a bat; *~e deur* blind (dead) door; *~e gehoorzaamheid* blind obedience; *~ geloof (vertrouwen)* implicit faith; *~e kaart* skeleton map, blank map; *~e klip* sunken rock; *~e muur* blank (dead) wall; *~e passagier* stowaway; *~e steeg* blind alley; *~ toeval* mere chance; *~e vlek* blind spot; *~ a a n één oog* blind of (in) one eye; *~ v o o r het feit dat...* blind to the fact that...; zie ook: *blinde;* **–doek** (-en) *m* bandage; **′blinddoeken** (blinddoekte, h. geblinddoekt) *vt* blindfold; **′blinddruk** (-ken) *m* blind-blocking, blind-tooling, blind-stamping; **′blinde** (-n) *m-v* 1 blind man, blind woman; *de ~n* the blind; 2 ◊ dummy; *de ~* at random; blindly; *met de ~ spelen* ◊ play dummy

blinde′darm (-en) *m* 1 caecum; 2 (= w o r m-v o r m i g a a n h a n g s e l) vermiform appendix; **–ontsteking** (-er) *v* 1 appendicitis; 2 (v a n h e t c a e c u m) typhlitis

′blindelings blindfold; blindly; *~ gehoorzamen* obey implicitly; **–gehoorzamen** obey implicitly; *~ spelen* play at blindman's buff; **′blindenge′leidehond** (-en) *m* guide dog; **′blindeninstituut** (-tuten) *o* institution for the blind, home for the blind; **′blinden-schrift** *o* Bráille

blin′deren (blindeerde, h. geblindeerd) *vt* blind; *geblindeerde auto's* ⚔ armoured cars

′blindganger (-en) *m* ⚔ dud; **′blindge′boren** blind-born, born blind; **′blindheid** *v* blindness; *met ~ geslagen* struck blind[2]; *fig* blinded;

'**blindtypen** [y = i.] (typte 'blind, h. 'blindge-typt) *vi* touch type; '**blindvliegen** (vloog 'blind, h. 'blindgevlogen) **I** *vi* fly blind; **II** *o* blind flying

'**blinken*** *vi* shine, gleam; *het is niet alles goud wat er blinkt* all that glitters is not gold

blo bashful, timid; *better ~ Jan dan do Jan* discretion is the better part of valour

bloc *en ~* [à'blɔk] in the lump; in a body; *en ~ weigeren* refuse in mass

'**blocnote** [-no.t] (-s) *m* (scribbling-)block, (writing-)pad

'**blode** = *blo*

1 bloed *o* blood; *blauw ~* blue blood; *kwaad ~ zetten* stir strong feelings, stir up bad blood; *nieuw ~ (in een vereniging &)* fresh blood; *het zit i n het ~* it runs in the blood; *het ~ kruipt waar het niet gaan kan* blood is thicker than water; **–aandrang** *m* congestion, rush of blood (to the head); **–arm** anaemic; **–armoede** *v* anaemia; **–baan** (-banen) *v* blood-stream; **–bad** (-baden) *o* blood-bath, carnage, massacre, (wholesale) slaughter; *een ~ aanrichten onder…* make a slaughter of…, massacre…; **–bank** (-en) *v* blood bank; **–bezinking** (-en) *v* sedimentation rate; '**bloeddoor'lopen** bloodshot; '**bloeddorst** *m* thirst for blood, bloodthirstiness; '**bloeddorstig** bloodthirsty; '**bloeddruk** *m* [high, low] blood pressure; **–eigen** very own; **–eloos** bloodless; '**bloeden** (bloedde, h. gebloed) *vi* bleed[2]; *u i t zijn neus ~* bleed at (from) the nose; *hij zal er v o o r moeten ~* they will make him bleed for it; *t o t ~s toe* till the blood came; '**bloeder** (-s) *m* bleeder; **–ig** bloody; **–ziekte** *v* haemophilia; '**bloedgeld** *o* blood-money, price of blood; **–getuige** (-n) *m-v* martyr; **–gever** (-s) *m* blood donor; **–groep** (-en) *v* blood group; **–heet** sizzling hot; **–hond** (-en) *m* bloodhound; **–ig** bloody, sanguinary; **–ing** (-en) *v* bleeding, h(a)emorrhage; **–je** (-s) *o ~s van kinderen* poor little mites; **–koraal** (-ralen) *o & v* red coral; **–lichaampje** (-s) *o* blood corpuscle; **–neus** (-neuzen) *m* bleeding nose; *hem een ~ slaan* make his nose bleed; **–onderzoek** (-en) *o* blood test; **–plas** (-sen) *m* pool of blood; **–plasma** *o* (blood) plasma; **–proef** (-proeven) *v* blood test; **–prop** (-pen) *v* blood clot, thrombus; **–rood** blood-red, scarlet; **–schande** *v* incest; **bloed'schendig**, **–'schennig** incestuous; '**bloedsomloop** *m* circulation of the blood, blood circulation; '**bloedspuwing** (-en) *v* spitting of blood; **–stelpend** styptic; **~ middel** styptic; **–suiker** *m* blood sugar; **–transfusie** [-fy.zi.] (-s) *v* blood transfusion; **–uitstorting** (-en) *v* extravasation of blood, effusion of blood, haematoma; **–vat**

(-vaten) *o* blood-vessel; **–vergieten** *o* bloodshed; **–vergiftiging** (-en) *v* blood-poisoning, sepsis; **–verlies** *o* loss of blood; **–verwant(e)** (-en) *m (v)* (blood-)relation, relative, kinsman, kinswoman; *naaste ~* near relative; **–verwantschap** (-pen) *v* blood-relationship, consanguinity; **–vlek** (-ken) *v* bloodstain; **–worst** (-en) *v* black pudding, blood sausage; **–wraak** *v* vendetta; **–ziekte** (-n en -s) *v* blood disease; **–zuiger** (-s) *m* leech, blood-sucker[2]; **–zuiverend** blood-cleansing

bloei *m* flowering; bloom[2], flower[2], *fig* prosperity; *in ~ staan* be in blossom; *in de ~ der jaren* in the prime of life; *in volle ~* in full blossom, in (full) bloom; '**bloeien** (bloeide, h. gebloeid) *vi* bloom, blossom, flower; *fig* flourish, prosper, thrive; **–d** *aj* blossoming, [early-, late-]flowering; *fig* flourishing, prosperous, thriving; '**bloeimaand** *v* May; **–tijd** (-en) *m* flowering time, florescence; *fig* flourishing period; **–wijze** (-n) *v* ☙ inflorescence

bloem (-en) *v* 1 *eig & fig* flower; 2 (v . m e e l) flour; **–bak** (-ken) *m* flower-box; **–bed** (-den) *o* flower-bed; **–blad** (-bladen) *o* petal; **–bol** (-len) *m* (flower) bulb; '**bloembollenteelt** *v* bulb growing; **–veld** (-en) *o* bulb field

'**bloemencorso** ('s) *m & o* floral procession, flower pageant, flower parade; **–handelaar** (-s en -laren) *m* florist; '**bloemenschikken** *o* flower-arranging; **–stalletje** (-s) *o* flower-stall; **–teelt** *v* floriculture; **–vaas** (-vazen) *v* (flower) vase; **–winkel** (-s) *m* flower shop, florist's shop

'**bloemetje** (-s) *o* little flower, floweret; *de ~s buiten zetten* go on the spree, be on a spree, **F** paint the town red, make whoopee; '**bloemig** floury, mealy [potatoes]; **bloe'mist** (-en) *m* florist, floriculturist; **bloemiste'rij** (-en) *v* 1 floriculture; 2 florist's (garden, business, shop)

'**bloemkelk** (-en) *m* ☙ calyx; **–knop** (-pen) *m* flower-bud; **–kool** (-kolen) *v* cauliflower; **–kooloor** (-oren) *o* cauliflower ear; **–krans** (-en) *m* garland, wreath (chaplet) of flowers; **–kroon** (-kronen) *v* corolla; **–lezing** (-en) *v* anthology; **–perk** (-en) *o* flower-bed; **–pje** (-s) *o* 1 little flower, floweret; 2 (v. b l o e i w i j z e) floret; **–pot** (-ten) *m* flowerpot; **–rijk** flowery[2]; *fig* florid; **–scherm** (-en) *o* ☙ umbel; **–schikken** *o* flower-arranging; **–steel** (-stelen), **–stengel** (-s) *m* flowerstalk; **–stuk** (-ken) *o* 1 (v. b l o e m i s t) bouquet; 2 (s c h i l d e r ij) flower-piece

bloes (bloezes, bloezen) *v* blouse, shirt

'**bloesem** (-s) *m* blossom, bloom, flower; '**bloesemen** (bloesemde, h. gebloesemd) *vi* blossom, bloom, flower

blok (-ken) *o* 1 block [of anything, also for chopping or hammering on], log [of wood]; billet [of firewood], chump [= short thick lump of wood], clog [to leg]; brick [= building block]; pig [of lead]; 2 bloc [of parties, of nations]; *het* ~ ⏍ the stocks; *een* ~ *aan het been hebben* be clogged; *dat is een* ~ *aan zijn been* it is a drag on him; *iem. voor het* ~ *zetten* leave sbd. no choice, give sbd. Hobson's choice; **–boek** (-en) *o* block book; **–druk** (-ken) *m* block printing; **–fluit** (-en) *v* recorder; **–hoofd** (-en) *o* (air-raid) warden; **–huis** (-huizen) *o* 1 blockhouse, loghouse; 2 (v. s p o o r w e g) signalbox; **–hut** (-ten) *v* (*m*) log-cabin

blok'kade (-s) *v* blockade; *de* ~ *doorbreken* run the blockade

'blokken (blokte, h. geblokt) *vi* ~ (*op*) plod (at), **F** swot (at), mug (at), grind (at)

'blokkendoos (-dozen) *v* box of bricks

blok'keren (blokkeerde, h. geblokkeerd) *vt* blockade [a port]; block [a road &; $ an account], freeze [an account]; **–ring** (-en) *v* blockade [of a port]; blocking [of a road &; $ of an account]; freezing [of an account]

'blokletter (-s) *v* block capital, block letter; **–schrift** *o* block capitals, print; **–stelsel** (-s) *o* block system; **–vorming** *v* forming of blocks

blom (-men) *v* flower; [*fig*] *een jonge* ~ a young (and pretty) girl

blond blond, fair, light; **blon'deren** (blondeerde, h. geblondeerd) dye blond, bleach; **blon'dine** (-s) *v* blonde, fair-haired girl

blonk (blonken) V.T. v. *blinken*

'bloodaard (-s) *m* coward

bloot I *aj* 1 naked, bare; 2 (a l l e e n m a a r) bald, mere; *de blote feiten* the bald facts; *een* ~ *toeval* a mere accident; *met het blote oog* with the naked eye; *onder de blote hemel* in the open; *...op het blote lijf dragen* wear... next (next to) the skin; **II** *ad* barely, merely; **–geven**[1] *zich* ~ show one's hand, lay oneself open[2]; *fig* commit oneself; *zich niet* ~ be non-committal; **–leggen**[1] *vt* lay bare[2], reveal [plans], expose [secrets]; *fig* state, uncover; **–liggen**[1] *vi* lie bare, lie open; **'blootshoofds, bloots'hoofds** bareheaded; **'blootstaan**[1] *vi* ~ *aan* be exposed to; **–stellen**[1] **I** *vt* expose; **II** *vr zich* ~ *aan* expose oneself to [the weather]; lay oneself open to [criticism]

'blootsvoets, bloots'voets barefoot

blos *m* 1 blush [of embarrassment], flush [of excitement]; 2 bloom [of health]

'blouse ['blu.zə] (-s) *v* blouse°, shirt

'blozen (bloosde, h. gebloosd) *vi* blush, flush, colour; *doen* ~ cause [sbd.] to blush, make [sbd.] blush; ~ *om* (*over*) blush at [sth.]; **–d** 1 blushing; 2 ruddy, rosy

'blubber *m* mud, slush

bluf *m* brag(ging), boast(ing), **F** swank; **'bluffen** (blufte, h. gebluft) *vi* brag, boast, **F** swank; ~ *op* boast of; **bluffe'rij** (-en) *v* bragging, boasting, braggadocio

'blunder (-s) *m* blunder, howler; **'blunderen** (blunderde, h. geblunderd) *vi* blunder

'blusapparaat (-raten) *o* fire-extinguisher; **–middel** (-en) *o* fire-extinguisher; **'blussen** (bluste, h. geblust) *vt* 1 extinguish, put out; 2 slack, slake [lime]

blut *aj* 1 hard up, **F** broke; 2 (n a s p e l) **F** cleaned out; *iem.* ~ *maken* **F** clean sbd. out

bluts (-en) *v* (d e u k) dent; **'blutsen** (blutste, h. geblutst) *vt* (d e u k e n) dent

blz. = *bladzijde*

'boa ['bo.a.] ('s) *m* boa [snake & fur necklet]

'bobbel (-s) *m* 1 bubble; 2 (g e z w e l) lump; **'bobbelen** (bobbelde, h. gebobbeld) *vi* bubble; **–lig** lumpy

'bobslee (-sleeën en -sleden) *v* bob-sled, bobsleigh

'bochel (-s) *m* 1 hump, hunch; 2 (p e r s o o n) humpback, hunchback; zie ook: *lachen*

1 bocht *o* & *m* trash, rubbish; (v. d r a n k) rot-gut

2 bocht (-en) *v* bend, turn(ing), winding [of a road, river &]; trend [of the coast]; flexion, curve [in a line]; bight [in a rope]; coil [of a cable]; bight [of the sea]; bay; *voor iem. in de* ~ *springen* take sbd.'s part; *zich in* ~*en wringen* tie oneself in knots; **–ig** winding, tortuous, sinuous

'bockbier *o* bock(-beer)

bod *o* 1 $ offer; 2 (o p v e r k o p i n g) bid; *een hoger* ~ *doen dan* outbid [sbd.]; *aan* ~ *komen* get a chance; *een* ~ *doen* make a bid; *een* ~ *doen op* make a bid for[2]

'bode (-n en -s) *m* 1 messenger[2]; 2 (v r a c h t - r i j d e r) carrier; 3 (v. g e m e e n t e &) beadle; 4 ⚖ usher

bo'dega ('s) *m* bodega

'bodem (-s) *m* 1 bottom [of a cask, the sea]; 2 [English] ground, soil, territory; 3 ⚓ bottom, ship, vessel; *de* ~ *inslaan* stave in [a cask]; *fig* shatter [plans, hopes]; dash [expectations]; *op de* ~ *van de zee* at the bottom of the sea; *vaste* ~ *onder de voeten hebben* be on firm ground; *op*

---

[1] V.T. en V.D. van dit werkwoord volgens het model: **'bloot**stellen, V.T. stelde **'bloot**, V.D. **'bloot**gesteld. Zie voor de vormen onder het grondwoord, in dit voorbeeld: *stellen*. Bij sterke en onregelmatige werkwoorden wordt u verwezen naar de lijst achterin.

vreemde ~ on foreign soil; *tot de* ~ *leegdrinken* drain to the dregs; **–gesteldheid** *v* nature of the soil, soil conditions; **–kunde** *v* soil science, pedology; **–loos** bottomless; *'t is een bodemloze put* it's like pouring money down a drain; **–onderzoek** *o* soil research; **–prijs** (-prijzen) *m* minimum price; **–schatten** *mv* mineral resources

'**boden** V.T. meerv. v. *bieden*

boe bo(o)!; ~ *roepen* boo, hoot; *geen* ~ *of ba zeggen* not open one's lips; *zij durft geen* ~ *of ba te zeggen* she cannot say boo to a goose

'**Boeddha,** '**boeddha** ('s) *m* Buddha; '**Boeddhabeeld** (-en) *o* Buddha; **boed'dhisme** *o* Buddhism; **–ist** (-en) *m* Buddhist; **–istisch** Buddhist [monk &], Buddhistic

'**boedel** (-s) *m* (personal) estate, property, goods and chattels, movables; *de* ~ *aanvaarden* take possession of the estate; *de* ~ *beschrijven* make (draw up) an inventory; **–afstand** *m* cession; **–beschrijving** (-en) *v* inventory; **–scheiding** (-en) *v* division of an estate, division of property

boef (boeven) *m* 1 knave, rogue, villain; (v. k i n d) rascal; 2 ✠ criminal, **F** crook; (t u c h t h u i s b o e f) convict, jail-bird; **–je** (-s) *o* gutter-snipe, street arab

boeg (-en) *m* ⚓ bow(s); *het o v e r een andere* ~ *wenden (gooien)* ⚓ change one's tack[2], try another tack[2]; *v o o r de* ~ *hebben* have to deal with [much work]; *wat wij nog voor de* ~ *hebben* what lies ahead of us, what is ahead; **–beeld** (-en) *o* figurehead

boeg'seren (boegseerde, h. geboegseerd) *vt* tow [a boat]

'**boegspriet** (-en) *m* 1 ⚓ bowsprit; **–lopen** *o sp* walking the greasy pole

1 boei (-en) *v* (a a n v o e t e n) shackle, fetter; (a a n h a n d e n) handcuff; *in ~en* in irons, in chains; *iem. de ~en aandoen* handcuff sbd.; *iem. in de ~en sluiten* put sbd. in irons

2 boei (-en) *v* ⚓ buoy; *met een kop als een* ~ as red as a beetroot

'**boeien** (boeide, h. geboeid) *vt* put in irons; handcuff; *fig* captivate, enthral(l), fascinate, grip [the audience], arrest [the attention, the eye]; **–d** captivating, enthralling, fascinating, arresting, absorbing; '**boeienkoning** (-en) *m* escapologist

'**boeier** (-s) *m* ⚓ small yacht

boek (-en) *o* 1 book; 2 quire [of paper]; *dat is voor mij een gesloten* ~ that is a sealed book to me; *te* ~ *staan als…* be reputed (as)…, be reputed to be…, pass for…; *te* ~ *stellen* set down, record

boeka'nier (-s) *m* buccaneer

'**Boekarest** *o* Bucharest

'**boekband** (-en) *m* binding; '**boekbespreking** (-en) *v* (book) review, criticism; **–binden** *o* bookbinding, bookbinder's trade; **–binder** (-s) *m* bookbinder; **boekbinde'rij** (-en) *v* 1 bookbinding; 2 bookbinder's shop, bookbinding establishment, bookbindery; '**boekdeel** (-delen) *o* volume; *dat spreekt boekdelen* that speaks volumes; **–druk** *m* typographic printing; **–drukken** *o* (book) printing; **–drukker** (-s) *m* (book) printer; **boekdrukke'rij** (-en) *v* printing office; '**boekdrukkunst** *v* (art of) printing, typography; '**boekebon** (-nen) *m* book token; **–legger** (-s) *m* book-mark(er); '**boeken** (boekte, h. geboekt) *vt* book [an order]; enter (in the books); *fig* record, register; *succes* ~ score a success; *een post* ~ make an entry; *in iems. credit (debet)* ~ place [a sum] to sbd.'s credit (debit); *op nieuwe rekening* ~ carry to new account; '**boekenclub** (-s) *v* book club; **–geleerdheid** *v* book-learning; **–kast** (-en) *v* bookcase; **–lijst** (-en) *v* list of books; **–molen** (-s) *m* revolving book-stand; **–plank** (-en) *v* book-shelf; **–rek** (-ken) *o* book-rack; **–stalletje** (-s) *o* (second-hand) bookstall; **–steun** (-en) *m* book-end; **–taal** *v* bookish language; **–tas** (-sen) *v* satchel; **–wijsheid** *v* book-learning; **–worm, –wurm** (-en) *m* bookworm; **boeke'rij** (-en) *v* library

boe'ket (-ten) *o & m* 1 [bu.'kɛt] bouquet, nosegay; 2 [bu.'kɛ] bouquet, aroma, flavour [of wine]

'**boekhandel** (-s) *m* 1 bookselling, book trade; 2 bookseller's shop, bookshop; **–aar** (-s en -laren) *m* bookseller

'**boekhouden I** (hield '**boek**, h. '**boekgehouden**) *vi* $ keep books (accounts); **II** *o* bookkeeping; *dubbel (enkel)* ~ book-keeping by double entry (by single entry); **–er** (-s) *m* book-keeper; '**boekhouding** (-en) *v* book-keeping; (a f d e l i n g) accounts (accounting) department; '**boekhoudmachine** [-ma.ʃi.nə] (-s) *v* book-keeping machine

'**boeking** (-en) *v* entry; '**boekjaar** (-jaren) *o* financial (fiscal) year; '**boekje** (-s) *o* small book, booklet; *ik zal een* ~ *over (van) u opendoen* I'll let people know what (the) sort of man you are; *b u i t e n zijn* ~ *gaan* go beyond one's powers; exceed one's orders; *bij iem. i n (g)een goed* ~ *staan* be in sbd.'s good (bad) books; *v o l g e n s het* ~ by the book

'**boekomslag** (-slagen) *m* dust jacket; '**boekstaven** (boekstaafde, h. geboekstaafd) *vt* set down, record, chronicle; '**boekverkoper** (-s) *m* bookseller; **–verkoping** (-en) *v* book auction; **–waarde** *v* book value

'**boekweit** *v* buckwheat

'**boekwerk** (-en) *o* book, work, volume;

–winkel (-s) *m* bookshop, bookstore
boel *m* een ~ (quite) a lot, lots [of sth.]; *een* ~ *geld* a lot (lots) of money; *de hele* ~ the whole lot; the whole thing; **F** the whole show; *een (hele)* ~ *beter (meer)* **F** a jolly sight better (more); *een hele* ~ *mensen* an awful lot of people; *het was een dooie (saaie)* ~ it was a dull affair; *een mooie* ~*!* a pretty kettle of fish, **F** a nice go (mess); *het is een vuile* ~ it is a mess; *de* ~ *erbij neergooien* **F** chuck it
'boeldag (-dagen) *m* auction
'boeltje (-s) *o zijn* ~ **F** his traps; *zijn* ~ *pakken* pack up one's traps
'boeman (-nen) *m* bogey(-man), bugaboo
'boemel *aan de* ~ on the spree; **–aar** (-s) *m* reveller, rake, run-about, fly-by-night;
'boemelen (boemelde, h. geboemeld) *vi* 1 **F** knock about; 2 go the pace, be on the spree; **'boemeltrein** (-en) *m* slow train
'boemerang (-s) *m* boomerang
'boender (-s) *m* scrubbing-brush, scrubber;
'boenen (boende, h. geboend) *vt* scrub; rub; polish; **'boenwas** *m & o* beeswax
boer (-en) *m* 1 farmer; (k e u t e r ~) peasant; (b u i t e n m a n) countryman; 2 ◊ knave, jack; 3 *fig* boor, yokel; 4 (o p r i s p i n g) belch, **F** burp; *een* ~ *laten* belch, **F** burp; *de* ~ *opgaan* go round the country hawking; **boerde'rij** (-en) *v* farm; farm-house
'boeren (boerde, h. geboerd) *vi* 1 farm, be a farmer; 2 (o p r i s p e n) belch, **F** burp; *hij heeft goed geboerd* he has managed his affairs well
boeren'arbeider (-s) *m* farmhand; **'boeren-bedrijf** *o* farming; **–bedrog** *o* humbug, monkey business, take-in; **boeren'bont** *o* (s t o f) gingham; **–'bruiloft** (-en) *v* country wedding; **–'dans** (-en) *m* country dance; **boeren'hoeve** (-n) *v*, **boeren'hofste(d)e** (-steden, -steeën) *v* farmstead, farm, homestead; **–'jongen** (-s) *m* country lad; ~*s* (d r a n k) brandy and raisins **–'kinkel** (-s) *m* yokel, country lout; **–'knecht** (-en en -s) *m* farm-hand; **–'kool** (-kolen) *v* ⚘ kale, kail; **–'lummel** (-s) *m* clodhopper, bumpkin, lout; **–'meisje** (-s) *o* country girl, country lass; ~*s* (d r a n k) brandy and apricots; **'Boerenoorlog** *m* Boer War; **'boerenoorlog** (-logen) *m* peasants' war; **boeren'pummel** *m* bumpkin; **–'slimheid** *v* cunning, craftiness; **–'stand** (-en) *m* peasantry; **–'vrouw** (-en) *v* country-woman; **–'wagen** (-s) *m* farm(er's) cart; **–'zoon** (-s en -zonen) *m* farmer's son; **–'zwaluw** (-en) *v* barnswallow; **boe'rin** (-nen) *v* 1 countrywoman; 2 farmer's wife; **boers** rustic, boorish
Boe'roendi *o* Burundi
boert (-en) *v* bantering, jest, joke; **–ig** jocular

Boe'tan *o* Bhutan
'boete (-n en -s) *v* 1 (b o e t e d o e n i n g) penance; 2 (g e l d b o e t e) penalty, fine; ~ *betalen* pay a fine; ~ *doen* do penance; *50 £* ~ *krijgen* be fined *£ 50;* ~ *opleggen* impose a fine; *op* ~ *van* under (on) penalty of; **–doening** (-en) *v* penance, penitential exercise; **–kleed** (-kleederen) *o* penitential robe (garment), hair-shirt; *het* ~ *aanhebben* stand in a white sheet; **–ling(e)** (-en) *m(-v)* penitent; **'boeten** (boette, h. geboet) **I** *vt* (h e r s t e l l e n) mend [nets, sth.]; atone [an offence], expiate [sin]; *iets* ~ *met zijn leven* pay for sth. with one's life; **II** *vi* ~ *voor* expiate, atone for [an offence]; *hij zal ervoor* ~ he shall pay (suffer) for it
boe'tiek (-s) *v = boutique*
'boetpredikatie [-(t)si.] (-s en -iën) *v* penitential homily; **–psalm** (-en) *m* penitential psalm
boet'seerklei *v* modelling clay; **boet'seren** (boetseerde, h. geboetseerd) *vt* model
boet'vaardig contrite, penitent, repentant; **–heid** *v* contriteness, contrition, penitence, repentance; *het sacrament van* ~ *rk* the sacrament of penance
'boevenstreek (-streken) *m & v* villainy, roguish (knavish) trick, piece of knavery; **–taal** *v* flash (language), thieves' slang (cant); **–tronie** (-s) *v* hangdog face; **–wagen** (-s) *m* police van, **F** black Maria, *Am* patrol wagon
'boezel(aar) (-s) *m* apron
'boezem (-s) *m* 1 bosom, breast; 2 auricle [of the heart]; 3 bay [of the sea]; 4 reservoir [of a polder]; *de hand in eigen* ~ *steken* search one's own heart; **–vriend** (-en) *m*, **'boezem-vriendin** (-nen) *v* bosom friend
boeze'roen (-s en -en) *m & o* (workman's) blouse
bof *m* 1 ⚕ (z w e l l i n g) mumps; 2 (g e l u k) stroke of luck, **F** fluke; **'boffen** (bofte, h. geboft) *vi* be lucky, be in luck; *daar bof je bij!* lucky for you!; **–er** (-s) *m* **F** lucky dog
'bogaard (-en) *m = boomgaard*
1 'bogen (boogde, h. geboogd) *vi* ~ *op* glory in, boast
2 'bogen V.T. meerv. v. *buigen*
Bo'heems Bohemian; **Bo'hemen** *o* Bohemia
bohe'mien [bo.he.'miẽ] (-s) *m* Bohemian
'boiler (-s) *m* (hot-water) heater
bok (-ken) *m* 1 ⚕ (he-)goat; (v. r e e &) buck; 2 (v o o r g y m n a s t i e k) vaulting buck; 3 (v. r i j t u i g) box; 4 ⚓ rest; 5 (s c h r a a g) [sawyer's] jack; 6 (h i j s t o e s t e l) derrick; 7 (f o u t) blunder, **F** bloomer, howler; *een* ~ *schieten* [*fig*] make a blunder; *als een* ~ *op de haverkist* as keen as mustard
bo'kaal (-kalen) *m* goblet, beaker, cup
'bokken (bokte, h. gebokt) *vi* 1 (v. p a a r d)

buck, buckjump; 2 *fig* be sulky

'**bokkepoot** (-poten) *m* = *bokspoot*; **–pruik** (-en) *v* de ~ op hebben be in a (black) temper; **–sprong** (-en) *m* caper, capriole; ~*en maken* [cut capers

'**bokkig** surly, churlish

'**bokking** (-en) *m* 1 (v e r s) bloater; 2 (g e r o o k t) red herring

'**boksbal** (-len) *m sp* punch(ing)-ball; **–beugel** (-s) *m* knuckle-duster; '**boksen** (bokste, h. gebokst) *vi* box; '**bokser** (-s) *m* 1 boxer, prize-fighter; 2 🐕 boxer; '**bokshandschoen** (-en) *m* & *v* boxing glove; **–kampioen** (-en) *m* boxing champion

'**bokspoot** (-poten) *m* goat's paw; *met bokspoten* goat-footed

'**bokspringen** *o* vaulting; zie ook: *haasje-over*; **bok-sta'vast** *o* high cockalorum

'**bokswedstrijd** (-en) *m* boxing match, prizefight

'**boktor** (-ren) *v* capricorn beetle

1 bol *aj* convex [glasses]; bulging [sails]; chubby [cheeks]; ~ *staan* belly, bulge

2 bol (-len) *m* ball, sphere; globe [of a lamp]; bulb [of a plant & thermometer]; crown [of a hat]; *zijn* ~ **F** his pate; *een knappe* ~ a clever fellow, **F** a dab (at *in*)

'**boldriehoek** (-en) *m* spherical triangle; **–smeting** *v* spherical trigonometry

bo'leet (-leten) *m* boletus

'**bolgewas** (-sen) *o* 🌱 bulbous plant

'**bolhoed** (-en) *m* bowler (hat)

Bolivi'aan(s) (-ianen) *m* (*aj*) Bolivian; **Bo'livië** *o* Bolivia

bolle'boos (-bozen) *m* **F** dab [at something]; *hij is een ~ in het zwemmen* he is a first-rate (crack) swimmer

'**bollen** (bolde, h. gebold) *vi* puff up, swell (fill) out

'**bollenkweker** (-s) *m* bulb-grower; **–teelt** *v* bulb-growing; **–veld** (-en) *o* bulb-field

'**bolletje** (-s) *o* globule

'**bolrond** convex; spherical

bolsje'wiek (-en) *m* bolshevik, bolshevist; **bolsje'wisme** *o* bolshevism; **–istisch** bolshevik, bolshevist

'**bolster** (-s) *m* 🌱 shell, husk, hull; *ruwe ~ blanke pit* rough diamond

'**bolus** (-sen) *m* 1 bole [clay]; 2 🐍 bolus [large pill]; 3 (g e b a k) treacle cake

'**bolvorm** (-en) *m* spherical shape; **–ig, bol'vormig** spherical, globular, bulb-shaped, bulbous

'**bolwerk** (-en) *o* rampart, bastion; *fig* bulwark, stronghold [of liberty &]

'**bolwerken** (bolwerkte, h. gebolwerkt) *vt het ~* manage, bring it off

bom (-men) *v* bomb; *zure ~* pickled gherkin; *de* ~ *is gebarsten* the fat is in the fire, the storm has broken; *hij heeft een ~ duiten* he has lots of money; **–aanslag** (-slagen) *m* bomb outrage; **–alarm** *o* bomb alarm; **bombarde'ment** (-en) *o* bombardment°; (m e t g r a n a t e n) shelling; **bombar'deren** (bombardeerde, h. gebombardeerd) *vt* bombard° [also in nuclear physics]; (i n z. ✈) bomb; (i n z. m e t g r a n a t e n) shell; *met vragen ~* bombard [sbd.] with questions; *iem. ~ tot...* **F** make sbd. a... on the spur of the moment, pitchfork sbd. into...

bom'barie *v* fuss, tumult; *~ maken over iets* make a fuss about sth.

'**bombast** *m* bombast, fustian; **bom'bastisch** bombastic, fustian

'**bombrief** (-brieven) *m* bomb letter, letter bomb

'**bomen** (boomde, h. geboomd) **I** *vt* punt, pole [a boat]; **II** *vi* (p r a t e n) yarn, spin a yarn

'**bomgat** (-gaten) *o* bung-hole

'**bomijs** *o* cat-ice

'**bominslag** (-slagen) *m* bomb hit; **–krater** (-s) *m* bomb crater; **–melding** (-en) *v* bomb alert

'**bommen** (bomde, h. gebomd) *vi* boom; *'t kan mij niet ~* **F** I don't care a rap, (a) fat lot I care!

'**bommenlast** (-en) *m* bomb load; **–luik** (-en) *o* bomb(-bay) door; **–tapijt** (-en) *o* bomb carpet; **–werper** (-s) *m* bomber

'**bomscherf** (-scherven) *v* fragment of a bomb, splinter of a bomb; **–vrij** bomb-proof, shellproof

bon (-nen) *m* ticket (o o k b e k e u r i n g), check; voucher [for the payment of money]; coupon [of an agency, for meat &]; [book, gift] token; *o p de* ~ [sell food &] on the ration; *iem. op de* ~ *zetten* (b e k e u r e n) take sbd.'s name

bona 'fide in good faith

'**bonboekje** (-s) *o* coupon-book; (v. d i s t r i b u t i e) ration-book

bon'bon (-s) *m* bonbon, sweet, [chocolate, peppermint] cream, [liqueur] chocolate; *een doos ~s* ook: a box of chocolates; **bonbon'nière** [-'jɛrə] (-s) *v* bonbon dish, bonbonnière

1 bond (-en) *m* alliance, association, union, league, confederacy, confederation

2 bond (bonden) V.T. v. *binden*

'**bondgenoot** (-noten) *m* ally, confederate; **–schap** (-pen) *v* alliance, confederacy; **bondgenoot'schappelijk** allied

'**bondig** succinct, concise

'**bondsdag** (-dagen) *m* federal diet; **–kanselier** (-s) *m* federal chancellor; '**Bondsrepubliek** *v de ~ Duitsland* the Federal Republic of Germany; '**bondsstaat** (-staten) *m* federal state

'**bonekruid** *o* 🌱 savory; '**bonensoep** (-en) *v* bean-soup; '**bonestaak** (-staken) *m* bean-stalk,

beanpole²
'**bongerd** (-s) *m* orchard
bonho'mie [bɔnɔ'mi.] *v* geniality, bonhomie
'**bonis** *hij is een man in* ~ he is well off
'**bonje** *v* **F** row, ructions
'**bonjour** [bõ'ʒu:r] 1 (b i j k o m e n o f
o n t m o e t e n) good morning, good day; 2
(b i j w e g g a a n) good-bye!; **bon'jouren**
(bonjourde, h. gebonjourd) *vt iem. er uit* ~
bundle sbd. off, out of the room &
bonk (-en) *m* lump; chunk; *hij is één* ~ *zenuwen*
he is a bundle of nerves; *een* ~ *van een kerel* a
hulking lump of a fellow
'**bonken** (bonkte, h. gebonkt) *vi* ~ *op* thump
[(on) the door]
'**bonkig** bony, chunky
bonne'fooi *op de* ~ on spec, hit or miss
1 bons (bonzen) *m* thump, bump, thud; ~ *!*
bang!; *de* ~ *geven* **F** give the sack (boot, mitten,
push), jilt; *de* ~ *krijgen* **F** get the sack (the boot,
the push)
2 bons (bonzen) *m* [trades-union, party] boss
1 bont *aj* particoloured [dresses]; motley
[assembly, crowd]; manycoloured, varicoloured, varied, variegated [flowers]; spotted
[cows]; piebald, pied [horses]; gay [colours];
colourful² [life, scene]; > gaudy [dress]; ~
hemd coloured shirt; ~ *schort* print apron; ~*e
was* coloured washing; *in* ~*e rij* 1 in motley
rows; 2 the gentlemen paired off with the
ladies; *het te* ~ *maken* go too far; ~ *en blauw
slaan* beat black and blue; zie ook *bekend*
2 bont *o* fur; **–en** *aj* fur, furry, furred; **–jas**
(-sen) *m* & *v* fur coat; **–je** (-s) *o* fur collar;
–mantel (-s) *m* fur coat; **–muts** (-en) *v* fur
cap; **–werk** *o* furriery; **–werker** (-s) *m* furrier
'**bonus** (-sen) *m* bonus; **–aandeel** (-delen) *o*
bonus share
bon-vi'vant [bõvi.'vã] (-s) *m* man about town
'**bonze** (-n) *m* 1 bonze [= Buddhist priest]; 2 *fig*
[trades-union, party] boss
'**bonzen** (bonsde, h. gebonsd) *vi* throb, thump
[of the heart]; *o p de deur* ~ bang at the door,
batter the door; *t e g e n iem. (aan)* ~ bump (up)
against sbd.
bood (**boden**) V.T. v. *bieden*
'**boodschap** (-pen) *v* 1 message; errand; 2
(e e n i n k o o p) purchase; *de blijde* ~ the
Gospel; *een blijde* ~ good news; *grote (kleine)* ~
F number two (one); *een* ~ *achterlaten (bij)* leave
word (with); *de* ~ *brengen dat...* bring word
that...; ~*pen doen* 1 be shopping [for oneself]; 2
run errands [for others]; *een* ~ *laten doen* send
on an errand; *stuur hem maar even een* ~ just
send him word; '**boodschappen** (bood-
schapte, h. geboodschapt) *vt* bring word,
announce; **–jongen** (-s) *m* errand-boy; *ik ben je*

~ *niet!* you cannot order me around!; **–mand**
(-en) *v* shopping basket; **–net** (-ten) *o* string
bag; **–tas** (-sen) *v* shopping bag; '**bood-
schapper** (-s) *m* messenger
1 boog (bogen) *m* 1 [archer's] bow; 2 (v. g e -
w e l f) arch; 3 (v. c i r k e l) arc; 4 (b o c h t)
curve; 5 *♩* tie; *de* ~ *kan niet altijd gespannen zijn*
the bow cannot always be stretched (strung);
zie ook: *pijl*
2 boog (**bogen**) V.T. v. *buigen*
'**boogbrug** (-gen) *v* arch(ed) bridge; **–gewelf**
(-welven) *o* arched vault; **–lamp** (-en) *v*
[electric] arc-lamp; **–passer** (-s) *m* wing
divider; **–raam** (-ramen) *o* arched window;
–schieten *o* archery; **–schutter** (-s) *m* archer,
bowman; **★** *de B*~ the Archer, Sagittarius;
–venster (-s) *o* arched window; **–vormig**
arched
boom (bomen) *m* 1 🌿 tree; 2 ⚒ beam [of a
plough, in a loom]; 3 ⚓ punting pole; boom
[for stretching the sail]; 4 (t e r a f s l u i t i n g)
bar [of a door]; barrier; 5 (v. w a g e n) shaft;
pole; *een* ~ *van een kerel, een kerel als een* ~ a
strapping fellow; *een* ~ *opzetten* have a chat, **F**
spin a yarn; *hoge bomen vangen veel wind* high
(huge) winds blow on high hills; *door de bomen
het bos niet zien* not see the wood for the trees;
–bast (-en) bark, rind; **–gaard** (-en) *m*
orchard; **–grens** *v* tree line, timber line;
–kikvors (-en) *m* tree-frog; **–klever** (-s) *m*
nuthatch; **–kruiper** (-s) *m* (tree-)creeper;
–kweker (-s) *m* nursery-man; **boom-
kwekerij** (-en) *v* 1 (a l s h a n d e l i n g)
cultivation of trees; 2 (k w e e k p l a a t s)
nursery; '**boommarter** (-s) *m* pine marten;
–pieper (-s) *m* tree-pipit; **–schors** (-en) *v*
(tree-)bark; **–stam** (-men) *m* (tree-)trunk,
stem, bole; **–stomp** (-en) *m*, **–stronk** (-en) *m*
tree-stump; **–tak** (-ken) *m* (tree-)branch,
bough; **–zaag** (-zagen) *v* pit-saw
boon (bonen) *v* bean; *blauwe* ~ **F** bullet; *bruine
bonen* kidney beans; *tuinbonen* broad beans; *witte
bonen* white beans; *ik ben een* ~ *als het niet waar is*
I'm blest (I'm a Dutchman) if it's not true; *in de
bonen zijn* be at sea; **–kruid** *o* = *bonekruid*;
–soep (-en) *v* = *bonensoep*; **–staak** (-staken) *m*
= *bonestaak*; **–tje** (-s) *o* bean; *heilig* ~ (little)
saint; ~ *komt om zijn loontje* his chickens have
come home to roost; *zijn eigen* ~*s doppen*
manage one's own affairs
boor (boren) *v* 1 brace and bit, gimlet, drill,
borer; 2 taster [for cheese &]; *appel*~ corer
boord (-en) 1 *m* (r a n d) border [of a carpet &],
edge [of a forest], brim [of a cup], bank [of a
river]; 2 *o* & *m* (k r a a g) collar; 3 *o* & *m* ⚓
board; *dubbele* ~ double collar; *omgeslagen* ~
turndown collar; *staande* ~ stand-up collar;

• *a a n ~ van het schip* on board the ship; *aan ~ brengen* put on board; *aan ~ gaan* go on board; *te Genua aan ~ gaan* take ship, embark at Genoa; *aan ~ hebben* have on board, carry [wireless]; *aan ~ nemen* take on board; *een man o v e r ~!* man overboard!; *over ~ gooien (werpen)* throw overboard[2], jettison[2]; fling [principles] to the winds; *over ~ slaan* be swept overboard; *v a n ~ gaan* go ashore, disembark; **–band** *o* binding, edging; **'boordeknoopje** (-s) *o* collar stud; **'boorden** (boordde, h. geboord) *vt* border, edge, hem; **'boordevol** filled to the brim, brimful; **'boordje** (-s) *o* = *boord* 2; **'boordlicht** (-en) *o* sidelight; **–lint** *o* tape; **–radio** ('s) *m* ship's radio; **–schutter** (-s) *m* (*air-*)gunner; **'boordsel** (-s) *o* edging, border

boordwerktuig'kundige (-n) *m* ✈ flight engineer

'booreiland (-en) *o* drilling platform, drilling rig; **–gat** (-gaten) *o* bore-hole; **–ijzer** (-s) *o* bit; **–kop** (-pen) *m* drill head; **–machine** [-ma.-ʃi.nə] (-s) *v* drilling machine, boring machine; **–put** (-ten) *m* drilling hole; **–tje** (-s) *o* gimlet; **–toren** (-s) *m* (drilling) derrick

'boorwater *o* boric lotion; **–zalf** *v* boric ointment; **–zuur** *o* bor(ac)ic acid

boos 1 (k w a a d) angry, cross, annoyed; 2 (k w a a d a a r d i g) malign, malicious [influence]; 3 (s l e c h t) bad [wheather, dream], evil [spirits, tongues]; *het boze oog* the evil eye; *zo ~ als wat* as cross as two sticks; *~ worden, zich ~ maken* become angry, lose one's temper (with *op*); *~ zijn o m (over)* be angry at; *~ zijn o p* be angry (cross) with; **boos'aardig** [s = z] malicious, malign; **–heid** *v* malice; **'boosdoener** (-s) *m* malefactor, evildoer, culprit; **–heid** (-heden) *v* 1 anger; 2 wickedness; **–wicht** (-en) *m* wretch, villain

boot (boten) *m &* *v* boat, steamer, vessel; *toen was de ~ aan* then the fat was in the fire; *de ~ afhouden [fig]* play for time; *de ~ missen* miss the bus; *laat je niet in de ~ nemen* don't let yourself be fooled; *uit de ~ vallen [fig]* opt out; **–reis** (-reizen) *v* boat-journey, boat-trip; **'bootshaak** (-haken) *m* boat-hook; **–lengte** (-n en -s) *v* boat's length; **–man** (-lieden) *m* boat-swain; **'boottocht** (-en) *m* boat-excursion, boat-trip; **–trein** (-en) *m* boat-train; **–werker** (-s) *m* docker, dock worker

bord (-en) *o* 1 plate; (d i e p) soup-plate, (p l a t) dinner-plate, (h o u t e n) trencher; 2 (s c h o o l b o r d) blackboard; (a a n p l a k ~, d a m ~ &) board; (i n z. v o o r h e t v e r k e e r & u i t h a n g ~) sign

bordeaux(wijn) [bɔr'do.-] *m* (r o d e) claret; Bordeaux (wine)

bor'deel (-delen) *o* brothel, bawdy (disorderly) house, house of ill fame

'bordenrek (-ken) *o* plate-rack; **–wasser** (-s) *m* dishwasher; **–wisser** (-s) *m* (s c h o o l) eraser

borde'rel [-'rɛl] (-len) *o* list, docket

bor'des (-sen) *o* (flight of) steps

'bordje (-s) *o* 1 (small) plate; 2 (notice-)board, sign; *de ~s zijn verhangen* the tables are turned

'bordpapier *o* cardboard, pasteboard

bor'duren (borduurde, h. geborduurd) *vi & vt* embroider[2]; **bor'duurgaas** (-gazen) *o* canvas; **–garen** (-s) *o* embroidery thread; **–naald** (-en) *o* embroidery needle; **–raam** (-ramen) *o* embroidery frame; **–sel** (-s) *o*, **–werk** (-en) *o* embroidery; **–wol** *v* crewel

'boren (boorde, h. geboord) *vt* bore, drill, pierce [a hole &], sink [a well]; *in de grond ~* ⚓ sink [a ship]; *fig* ruin [sbd.], torpedo [a plan]

1 borg (-en) *m* 1 (p e r s o o n) surety, guarantee, guarantor; 2 (z a a k) security, guaranty; 3 ⚖ bail; *~ staan voor, zich ~ stellen voor* stand surety (⚖ go bail) for [a friend]; answer for, warrant, guarantee [the fulfilment of...]; give security

2 borg (**borgen**) V.T. v. *bergen*

1 'borgen (borgde, h. geborgd) *vi* give credit

2 'borgen V.T. meerv. v. *bergen*

'borgtocht (-en) *m* security, surety; ⚖ bail; *onder ~ vrijlaten* ⚖ release on bail

'boring (-en) *v* boring; (v. c i l i n d e r) bore; *~en* ook: drilling operations

'borrel (-s) *m* dram, nip, peg; **S** snorter, snifter; **'borrelen** (borrelde, h. geborreld) *vi* 1 (b e l-l e n m a k e n) bubble, burble; 2 (b o r r e l s d r i n k e n) have drinks; **'borrelpraat** *m* trifling club chat, tattle; **–uur** (-uren) *o* cocktail hour

1 borst (-en) *v* 1 [right, left] breast, [broad] chest, ⊙ bosom; 2 breast, front [of a dress, a coat, a shirt]; *een hoge ~ (op)zetten* throw out one's chest, give oneself airs; *a a n de ~* breastfeed [baby]; *het o p de ~ hebben* be chesty; *het stuit mij t e g e n de ~* it goes against the grain with me; *u i t volle ~* at the top of one's voice, lustily

2 borst (-en) *m* lad; *brave ~* good fellow; *een jonge ~* stripling; *een stevige ~* a strapping lad

3 borst (**borsten**) V.T. v. *bersten*

'borstaandoening (-en) *v* chest affection; **–beeld** (-en) *o* 1 bust; 2 effigy; **–been** (-deren) *o* breast-bone, sternum

'borstel (-s) *m* 1 (v o o r k l e r e n &) brush; 2 (s t ij v e h a r e n) bristle; **'borstelen** (borstelde, h. geborsteld) *vt* brush; **'borstelig** bristly, bristling

'borsten V.T. meerv. v. *bersten*

'borstharnas (-sen) *o* breast-plate, cuirass; **–holte** (-n) *v* cavity of the chest; **–kanker** *m*

breast cancer; **–kas** (-sen) *v* chest, thorax;
–kruis (-en) *o* pectoral cross; **–kwaal**
(-kwalen) *v* chest complaint, chest trouble;
–middel (-en) *o* pectoral (medicine); **–plaat**
(-platen) *v* 1 ⚓ breast-plate, cuirass; 2
(s u i k e r g o e d) fudge; **–riem** (-en) *m* breast-
strap; **–rok** (-ken) *m* (under)vest; **–slag**
(-slagen) *m* breast-stroke; **–spier** (-en) *v*
pectoral muscle; **–stuk** (-ken) *o* 1 (v .
g e s l a c h t b e e s t) breast, brisket; 2 (v.
h a r n a s) breast-plate, corslet; 3 (v . i n s e k t)
thorax, corslet; **–vin** (-nen) *v* pectoral fin;
–vlies (-vliezen) *o* pleura; **–vliesontsteking**
(-en) *v* pleurisy; **–voeding** *v* breast feeding;
mother's milk; *het kind krijgt ~* the child is
breast-fed; **–wering** (-en) parapet°; ⚓ ook:
breastwork; **–wijdte** (-n en -s) *v* chest measurement; **–zak** (-ken) *m* breast-pocket

1 bos (-sen) *m* bunch [of radishes, daffodils,
keys], bottle [of hay], bundle [of grass, straw,
papers &], truss [of straw]; tuft, shock [of hair]

2 bos (-sen) *o* wood; (u i t g e s t r e k t) forest;
iem. het ~ insturen F lead sbd. up the garden
(path); **–achtig** woody, woodlike, bosky;
–beheer *o* forest administration; **–bes** (-sen) *v*
bilberry, whortleberry; **–bouw** *m* forestry;
–bouwkunde *v* sylviculture, forestry; **–brand**
(-en) *m* forest-fire; **–duif** (-duiven) *v* wood-
pigeon, ring-dove; **–god** (-goden) *m* sylvan
deity, faun; **–grond** (-en) *m* woodland;
1 'bosje (-s) *o* grove, thicket, shrubbery

2 'bosje (-s) *o* = 1 *bos*

'Bosjesman (-nen) *m* Bushman

'boskabouter (-s) *m* wood goblin; **–kat** (-ten) *v*
wild cat; **–neger** (-s) *m* Bush Negro, maroon;
–nimf (-en) *v* wood-nymph; **–rand** (-en) *m*
edge of the wood(s); **–rijk** woody, wooded;
bos'schage [-'ɣa.ʒə] (-s) *o* grove, spinney;
'bosuil (-en) *m* tawny owl; **–viooltje** (-s) *o*
wood-violet; **–wachter** (-s) *m* forester;
boswachte'rij (-en) *v* forestry; **'bosweg**
(-wegen) *m* forest road

1 bot *eig* blunt [of a knife]; *fig* dull, obtuse,
stupid [fellow]; blunt [answer], flat [refusal]

2 bot *~ vangen* draw a blank

3 bot (-ten) 1 *m* 🐟 flounder ‖ 2 *v* 🌿 bud

4 bot (-ten) *o* bone

bo'tanicus (-ci) *m* botanist; **bota'nie** *v* botany;
bo'tanisch botanical; **botani'seertrommel**
[s = z] (-s) *v* botanical collecting box;
botani'seren [s = z] (botaniseerde, h. gebota-
niseerd) *vi* botanize

'botenhuis (-huizen) *o* boat-house;
–verhuurder (-s) *m* boatman

'boter (-s) *v* 1 butter; 2 ⓜ margarine, **F** marge;
het is ~ aan de galg gesmeerd it's to no purpose; *~
bij de vis* cash down; *met zijn neus in de ~ vallen*

come at the right moment; **–bloem** (-en) *v* 🌼
buttercup; **–briefje** (-s) *o* **F** (marriage) lines;
'boteren (boterde, h. geboterd) *vt* butter
[bread]; *het botert niet tussen ons* we don't hit it
off together; **'boterfabriek** (-en) *v* creamery,
butter factory; **'boterham** (-men) *m* & *v* (slice
of, some) bread and butter; *dubbele ~*
sandwich; *een goede ~ verdienen* make a decent
living; **–(me)papier** *o* greaseproof paper,
sandwich paper; **–trommeltje** (-s) *o* sandwich
box; **'boterletter** (-s) *v* almond-paste letter;
–pot (-ten) *m* butter pot, butter crock; ⟍
–vlootje (-s) *o* butter-dish

'botheid *v* bluntness[2], dulness[2], obtuseness[2]

'botje (-s) *o* – *bij ~ leggen* pool money, club
together

'botsautootje [-.o.to.-, -ɔuto.-] (-s) *o* dodgem
car, dodgem; **'botsen** (botste, h. en is gebotst)
vi – *tegen* 1 (v . v o e r t u i g e n) collide with,
crash into; 2 (a n d e r s) bump against, strike
against, dash against; **–sing** (-en) *v* collision[2],
[air, road, train] crash; *fig* clash; *in ~ komen met*
collide with[2]; *fig* clash with

Bot'swana *o* Botswana

'bottelen (bottelde, h. gebotteld) *vt* bottle

'botten (botte, is gebot) *vi* bud

'botter (-s) *m* fishing boat

'botterik (-riken) *m* blockhead

'botvieren (vierde 'bot, h. 'botgevierd) *vt* zijn
hartstochten (lusten) ~ give rein to one's passions

'botweg bluntly; *~ weigeren* refuse point-blank
(flatly)

boud bold

bou'deren [bu.-] (boudeerde, h. geboudeerd) *vi*
sulk

bou'doir [bu.'dwa:r] (-s) *o* boudoir

'boudweg boldly

bouf'fante [bu.-] (-s) *v* comforter, (woollen)
muffler

bou'gie [bu.'ʒi.] (-s) *v* ✕spark(ing) plug;
–sleutel (-s) *m* sparking-plug spanner

bouillon [bu.l'jòn] *m* broth, beef tea, clear
soup; stock [from stews, used for soups];
–blokje (-s) *o* beef cube

boule'vard [bu.lə'va:r] *m* boulevard; **–blad**
(-bladen) *o* tabloid; **–pers** *v* yellow press,
gutter press

bour'gogne(wijn) [bu:r'ɡòɲə-] *m* burgundy

Bour'gondië [bu:r-] *o* Burgundy; **–r** (-s) *m*
Burgundian; **Bour'gondisch** Burgundian

bout (-en) *m* 1 ✕ bolt; [wooden] pin; 2 (i n
s t r i j k i j z e r) heater; (s t r i j k i j z e r) iron ‖ 3
(v . d i e r) leg, quarter, drumstick [of fowls]

bou'tade [bu.-] (-s) *v* witticism, sally

bou'tique [bu.'ti.k] (-s) *v* boutique

bouw *m* 1 building, construction, erection [of
houses]; 2 structure [of a crystal &], frame [of

the body], build [of the body, a violin &]; 3 (v. l a n d) cultivation, culture; 4 = *bouwbedrijf*; *krachtig van* ~ of powerful build; **–bedrijf** (-drijven) *o* building trade, construction industry; **–beleid** *o* building policy; **–doos** (-dozen) *v* box of bricks; **'bouwen** (bouwde, h. gebouwd) **I** *vt* 1 build [a house], construct [a factory, an aircraft]; throw [a party]; **II** *vi* build; *op iem. (iets)* ~ rely on sbd. (on sth.); **–er** (-s) *m* builder; constructor; **'bouwfonds** (-en) *o* building society; **–grond** (-en) *m* building ground, building site, building plot; **–keet** (-keten) *v* building shed; **–kunde** *v* structural (building) engineering; **bouw'kundig** structural (civil) [engineer]; architectural [journal]; **–e** (-n) *m* structural (construction) engineer; **'bouwkunst** *v* architecture; **–land** *o* arable land, farmland; **–materialen** *mv* building materials; **–meester** (-s) *m* architect, builder; **–pakket** (-ten) *o* building set, construction set; **–plaat** (-platen) *v* cut out; **–plan** (-nen) *o* building scheme, plan; **–politie** [-po.li.(t)si.] *v* building inspectors; **–put** (-ten) *m* excavation, excavated building-site; **–rijp** ready for building; **–sel** (-s) *o* structure; **–steen** (-stenen) *m* building stone; *bouwstenen* materials [for an essay &]; **–stijl** (-en) *m* architecture, style (of building); **–stoffen** *mv* materials; **–stop** (-pen) *m* building freeze; **–terrein** (-en) *o* building-site, building-plot; **–trant** *m* style of building; **–vak** (-ken) *o* building trade; **–vakarbeider** (-s) *m*, **–vakker** (-s) *m* building(-trade) worker, builder; **–val** (-len) *m* ruin, ruins; **bouw'vallig** going to ruin, tumbledown, dilapidated, ramshackle, crazy; **'bouwverbod** (-boden) *o* building ban; **–vergunning** (-en) *v* building permit (licence); **–werk** (-en) *o* building

'boven I *prep* above [par, criticism, one's station &]; [fly, hover] over; over, upwards of [fifty &]; beyond [one's means]; ~ *de deur stond...* over the door; ~ *het lawaai (uit)* above the tumult (noise); *het gaat (stijgt)* ~ *het menselijke uit* it transcends the human; *hij is* ~ *de veertig* he is over forty; **II** *ad* above (in one's room, in this book); upstairs; *hij is* ~ he is upstairs; *deze kant* ~ this side up; *als* ~ as above; ● *n a a r* ~ up; *naar* ~ *brengen* take up [luggage]; bring up [a miner from the pit]; *naar* ~ *gaan* go upstairs; *naar* ~ *kijken* look up(wards); *t e* ~ *gaan* be above [one's strength]; surpass [everything], exceed [the amount]; zie ook: *begrip* &; *te* ~ *komen* overcome, surmount [difficulties]; *wij zijn het nu te* ~ we have got over it now; *v a n* ~ 1 from upstairs; 2 from above, from on high [comes all blessing]; *zoveelste regel van* ~ from the top; *spits van* ~ pointed at the top; *van*

~ *naar beneden* from the top downward; *van* ~ *tot beneden* from top to bottom; **boven'aan** at the upper end, at the top; ~ *op de lijst staan* be at the top (at the head) of the list, head the list; **'bovenaards, boven'aards** superterrestrial, supernatural [phenomena]; heavenly [music]; **boven'af van** ~ from above, from the top, from the surface; **'bovenal, boven'al** above all (things), especially; **'bovenarm** (-en) *m* upper arm; **bovenbe'doeld** above (-mentioned); **'bovenbeen** (-benen) *o* upper (part of the) leg, thigh; **–blad** (-bladen) *o* table-top; **–bouw** *m* superstructure; **–buur** (-buren) *m* upstairs neighbour; **–dek** (-ken) *o* ⚓ upper deck; **boven'dien** besides, moreover; **'bovendorpel** (-s) *m*, **–drempel** (-s) *m* lintel; **'bovendrijven** (dreef 'boven, h. 'bovengedreven) *vi* float on the surface; *fig* prevail [of an opinion]; **'boveneind(e)** (-en) *o* upper end, top, head [of the table]; **–gedeelte** (-n en -s) *o* upper part; **–gemeld**, **bovenge'meld, 'bovengenoemd**, **bovenge'noemd** above(-mentioned); **'bovengronds** above-ground, elevated [railway]; ⚡ overhead [wires]; surface [miner]; **–hand** *v de* ~ *krijgen* get (take) the upper hand; **–hoek** (-en) *m* top corner; ~ *links (rechts)* top left-hand (right-hand) corner; **–huis** (-huizen) *o* 1 upper part of a house; 2 upstairs flat; **boven'in** at the top; **'bovenkaak** (-kaken) *v* upper jaw; **–kamer** (-s) *v* upper room, upstairs room; *het scheelt hem in zijn* ~ **F** he is a little wrong in the upper storey, he has a tile loose; **–kant** (-en) *m* top, upper side; **'bovenkomen** (kwam 'boven, is 'bovengekomen) *vi* rise to the surface, come to the surface, come to the top [of the water]; come up(stairs); *laat hem* ~ show him up(stairs); **'bovenlaag** (-lagen) *v* upper (top) layer; **–landen** *mv* uplands; **–last** (-en) *m* ⚓ deck-load, deck-cargo; **–le(d)er** *o* upper leather, uppers; **–leiding** (-en) *v* ⚡ overhead wires; **–licht** (-en) *o* skylight, transom-window; **–lijf** (-lijven) *o* upper part of the body; **–lip** (-lippen) *v* upper lip; **–loop** (-lopen) *m* upper course [of a river]; **–mate**, **boven'mate, boven'matig** extremely, exceedingly; **boven'menselijk** superhuman; **–na'tuurlijk** supernatural; **boven'op** on (the) top, on top of [the others &]; *er (weer)* ~ *brengen (helpen)* 1 pull, bring [a patient] round (through), get [a patient] on his legs again; 2 put [a business man] on his feet again; *er weer* ~ *komen* pull through, pull round; *er* ~ *zijn* be a made man; **–'over** along the top; **'bovenschip** (-schepen) *o* ⚓ upperworks; **–staand** *aj* above(-mentioned); *het* ~*e* the above; **–stad**

(-steden) *v* upper town; **'bovenste I** *aj* uppermost, upper, topmost, top; *een ~ beste* **F** a trump, a clipper; **II** *sb het ~* the upper part, the top; **'bovenstuk** (-ken) *o* upper part, top; **–toon** (-tonen) *m* overtone; *de ~ voeren* (pre)dominate; **boven'uit** (*men hoorde zijn stem*) *er ~* above (the noise, the tumult &); **'bovenverdieping** (-en) *v* upper storey, upper floor, top floor; **'bovenvermeld, bovenver'meld** above(-mentioned), aforementioned; **'bovenwijdte** *v* bust size; **'Bovenwindse 'Eilanden** *mv* Windward Islands; **'bovenzij(de)** (-zijden) *v = bovenkant*; **boven'zinnelijk** transcendental, supersensual

bowl [bo.l] (-s) *m* 1 (k o m) bowl; 2 (d r a n k) (claret &) cup

'bowlen ['bo.lə(n)] (bowlde, h. gebowld) *vi* bowl

box (-en) *m* 1 (in s t a l) box; 2 (in g a r a g e) lock-up; 3 (v. k i n d e r e n) playpen; 4 📬 (post-office) box

'boycot ['bɔikɔt] (-ten) *m* boycott; **'boycotten** (boycotte, h. geboycot) *vt* boycott

'boze *m de B~* the Evil One; *het is uit den ~* it is wrong

'braadkip (-pen) *v,* **'braadkuiken** (-s) *o* broiler hen, broiler; **–oven** (-s) *m* roaster; **–pan** (-nen) *v* 1 (m e t s t e e l, k o e k e p a n) frying pan; 2 (m e t d e k s e l, v u u r v a s t e t a f e l p a n) casserole; **–sle(d)e** (-sleeën, -sleden) *v* baking dish, roasting pan; **–spit** (-speten) *o* spit, broach; **–vet** (-ten) *o* 1 dripping; 2 frying-fat; **–worst** (-en) *v* roast sausage

braaf ± good, honest, > worthy [people]; honest and respectable [servant-girls]; *~!* good (old) dog!; **–heid** *v* honesty

1 braak *aj* fallow; *~ liggen* lie fallow[2]

2 braak (braken) *v* 1 breaking [into a house], burglary; 2 brake [for hemp]

'braakbal (-len) *m* pellet; **–middel** (-en) *o* emetic; **–sel** *o* vomit

braam (bramen) *v* 1 ✗ wire-edge, burr [of a knife] ‖ 2 (b r a a m b e s) blackberry; **–struik** (-en) *m* blackberry bush, bramble

'brabbelen (brabbelde, h. gebrabbeld) *vt & vi* jabber; **'brabbeltaal** *v* jabber, gibberish

brace'let [brasə'lɪt] (-ten) *m* bracelet, bangle

bracht (brachten) V.T. v. *brengen*

'braden* I *vt* roast [on a spit], fry [in a pan], grill, broil [on a fire, on a gridiron], bake [in an oven]; **II** *vi* roast &; zie ook: *gebraden*

'Brahma ['bra.ma.] *m* Brahma; **brah'maan** (-manen) *m* Brahman, Brahmin

'braille(schrift) ['brɑjə-] *o* braille

1 brak *aj* brackish, saltish, briny

2 brak (-ken) *m* 🐕 beagle

3 brak (**braken**) V.T. v. *breken*

1 'braken (braakte, h. gebraakt) **I** *vt* break [hemp] ‖ vomit[2] [blood, smoke &]; belch forth [flames, smoke &]; **II** *vi* vomit

2 'braken V.T. meerv. v. *breken*

'brallen (bralde, h. gebrald) *vi* brag

bram (-men) *m* topgallant sail; **–steng** (-en) *v* topgallant mast

bran'card [brɑŋ'ka:r] (-s) *m* stretcher

'branche ['brɑ̃ʃə] (-s) *v* 1 line [of business], trade; 2 (f i l i a a l) branch

brand (-en) *m* 1 *eig* fire, conflagration; 2 (b r a n d s t o f) fuel, firing; 3 (i n h e t l i c h a a m) heat; 4 (u i t s l a g) eruption; 5 (i n h e t k o r e n) smut, blight; *~!* fire! *er is ~* there is a fire; *~ stichten* raise a fire; *i n ~ raken* catch (take) fire; ignite; *in ~ staan* be on fire, be burning; *in ~ steken* set on fire, set fire to; ignite; *iem. u i t de ~ helpen* **F** help sbd. out of a scrape; **–alarm** *o* fire-alarm, firecall; **–assurantie** [-(t)si.] (-s) *v* fire insurance; **–baar** combustible, (in)flammable; **–blaar** (-blaren) *v* blister from a burn; **–blusapparaat** (-raten) *o* fire-extinguisher; **–bom** (-men) *v* incendiary bomb, incendiary, fire bomb; **–brief** (-brieven) *m fig* pressing letter; **–deur** (-en) *v* emergency door

brande'bourg [-'bu:r] (-s) *m* frog

'brandemmer (-s) *m* fire-bucket; **'branden** (brandde, h. gebrand) **I** *vi* burn, be on fire; *het brandt hem o p de tong* (*om het te zeggen*) he is burning to tell the secret; *~ v a n liefde* burn with love; *~ van verlangen* (*om*)... be burning (dying) to...; **II** *vt* burn [wood, lime, charcoal]; brand [cattle]; roast [coffee]; scald [with hot liquid]; distil [spirits]; cauterize [a wound]; stain [glass]; zie ook: *gebrand*; **–d I** *aj* burning [fire &]; lighted [candle, cigar]; ardent [love]; **II** *ad ~ heet* burning (scalding) hot; **brander** (-s) *m* 1 burner [of a lamp, of a gascooker &]; 2 distiller [of spirits]; 3 fire-ship; **–ig** *ik heb een ~ gevoel in mijn ogen* my eyes burn (smart); *een ~e lucht* (*smaak*) a burnt smell (taste)

'brandewijn (-en) *m* brandy

'brandgang (-en) *m* fire lane; **–gevaar** *o* danger from fire; fire-risk; **–glas** (-glazen) *o* burning glass; **–haard** (-en) *m* seat (source) of a fire; **–hout** *o* firewood; **–ijzer** (-s) *o* 1 (v o o r w o n d) cauterizing iron; 2 (v o o r m e r k) branding iron

'branding (-en) *v* breakers, surf

'brandkast (-en) *v* safe, strong-box; **–kastkraker** (-s) *m* safe buster (cracker); **–klok** (-ken) *v* fire-bell; **–kraan** (-kranen) *v* fire-plug; **–ladder** (-s) *v* fire-ladder, fire-escape; **–lucht** *v* smell of fire, burnt smell; **–meester** (-s) *m* chief fireman; **–melder** (-s) *m* fire-alarm; **–merk** (-en) *o* brand, stigma; **'brandmerken**

(brandmerkt, h. gebrandmerkt) *vt* brand², *fig* stigmatize; '**brandmuur** (-muren) *m* fireproof wall; **–offer** (-s) *o* holocaust, burnt offering; **–plek** (-ken) *v* burn; **–polis** (-sen) *v* fire-policy; **–punt** (-en) *o* focus [*mv* foci] [of a lens]; *fig* focus [of interest]; centre [of civilization]; *in één* ~ *verenigen* (*brengen*) focus; **–puntsafstand** (-en) *m* focal distance; **–schade** *v* damage (caused) by fire, fire-loss; '**brandschatten** (brandschatte, h. gebrandschat) *vt* lay under contribution; **–ting** (-en) *v* contribution; '**brandschel** (-len) *v* fire-alarm; **–scherm** (-en) *o* safety curtain, fire-curtain; '**brandschilderen** (brandschilderde, h. gebrandschilderd) *vt* 1 (v. g l a s &) stain; 2 (e m a i l-l e r e n) enamel; *gebrandschilderd raam* stained-glass window; '**brandschoon** scrupulously clean; **F** spic-and-span; **–slang** (-en) *v* fire-hose, hose pipe; **–spiritus** *m* methylated spirit; **–spuit** (-en) *v* fire-engine; *drijvende* ~ fire-float; **–spuitgast** (-en) *m* fireman; **–stapel** (-s) *m* (funeral) pile; *o p de* ~ at the stake; *t o t de* ~ *veroordelen* condemn to the stake; **–stichter** (-s) *m* incendiary, arsonist, fire raiser; **–stichting** (-en) *v* arson, incendiarism, fire-raising; **–stof** (-fen) *v* fuel, firing; **–strook** (-stroken) *v* fire-break; **–trap** (-pen) *m* fire-escape; **–verf** *v* enamel; **–verzekering** (-en) *v* fire insurance; **–vrij** fire-proof; **–wacht** (-en) *v* fire-watcher, fire-warden

'**brandweer** (-weren) *v* fire-brigade; fire department; **–auto** [-o.to., -ɔuto.] ('s) *m* fire-engine; **–kazerne** (-s) *v* (fire-)brigade premises; fire-station; **–man** (-nen en -lieden) *m* fireman

'**brandwond** (-en) *v* burn [from fire]; scald [from hot liquids]; *derdegraads* ~*en* third-degree burns; **–zalf** (-zalven) *v* anti-burn ointment

'**branie** (-s) *m* 1 (d u r f) daring, pluck; (o p s c h e p p e r ij) swagger, **F** swank; 2 (d u r f a l) dare-devil; (o p s c h e p p e r) swell; *de* ~ *uithangen* do the grand (the swell); **–achtig** swaggering

bras (-sen) *m* ⚓ brace

'**brasem** (-s) *m* bream

'**braspartij** (-en) *v* orgy, revel; '**brassen** (braste, h. gebrast) **I** *vi* feast, revel ‖ **II** *v* ⚓ brace; **–er** (-s) *m* feaster, reveller; **brasse'rij** (-en) *v* feasting, revel, orgy

bra'vo *ij* bravo! [to actor &], good!, well done!; hear, hear! [to orator]

bra'voure [-'vu:r] *v* (d a p p e r h e i d) bravado; (m u z i k a l e v a a r d i g h e i d) bravura

Brazili'aan(s) Brazilian; Bra'zilië *o* Brasil

breed I *aj* broad [chest, smile, street], wide [street, river, brim &]; *lang en* ~ (*in den brede*)

uiteenzetten set forth at large, at length; **II** *ad het niet* ~ *hebben* be in straitened circumstances, not be well off; *wie het* ~ *heeft, laat het* ~ *hangen* they that have plenty of butter can lay it on thick; *iets* ~ *zien* take a wide view; zie ook: *opgeven, uitmeten* &; **–gerand** broad-brimmed; **–geschouderd** broad-shouldered; **–heid** *v* breadth², width²; breed'**sprakig** verbose, diffuse, lengthy, long-winded, prolix; **–heid** *v* verbosity, prolixity, diffuseness

'**breedte** (-n en -s) *v* breadth, width [of a piece of cloth]; [geographical] latitude; *in de* ~ in breadth; breadthwise, breadthways, broadwise; **–cirkel** (-s) *m* parallel of latitude; **–graad** (-graden) *m* degree of latitude

breed'**voerig I** *aj* ample [discussion]; circumstantial [account]; **II** *ad* amply, at length, in detail; **–heid** *v* ampleness

'**breekbaar** breakable, fragile, brittle; (v. s t r a l e n) refrangible; **–heid** *v* fragility, brittleness; '**breekijzer** (-s) *o* crowbar, crow, jemmy; **–punt** (-en) *o* breaking point

'**breeuwen** (breeuwde, h. gebreeuwd) *vt* caulk

'**breidel** (-s) *m* bridle²; '**breidelen** (breidelde, h. gebreideld) *vt* bridle, check, curb; '**breidelloos** unbridled

'**breien** (breide, h. gebreid) *vi* & *vt* knit [stockings]; '**breikatoen** *o* & *m* knitting cotton; **–kous** (-en) *v* knitting, stocking; **–machine** [-ma.ʃi.nə] (-s) *v* knitting machine

brein *o* brain, intellect, mind; *fig* (c o m p l o t) mastermind; *elektronisch* ~ electronic brain

'**breinaald** (-en) *v* knitting needle; **–patroon** (-tronen) *o* knitting pattern; **–pen** (-nen) *v* knitting needle; **–ster** (-s) *v* knitter; *de beste* ~ *laat wel eens een steek vallen* it is a good horse that never stumbles; **–werk** (-en) *o* knitting; **–wol** *v* knitting wool

'**brekebeen** (-benen) *m-v* duffer, bungler; '**breken*** **I** *vi* break, be broken; ~ *d o o r* break through [the enemy, the clouds]; *m e t iem.* ~ break with sbd.; *met een gewoonte* ~ 1 break oneself of a habit; 2 break through a practice; *u i t de gevangenis* ~ break out of prison; **II** *vt* break [a glass, one's fall, the law, the record, resistance, a vow &], smash [a jug], fracture [a bone]; refract [the light]; zie ook: *hals* &; **–er** (-s) *m* breaker; '**breking** (-en) *v* breaking; refraction [of light]; **–shoek** (-en) *m* angle of refraction

brem *m* ⚘ broom

'**bremzout** salt as brine

'**brengen*** *vt* 1 carry [in vehicle, ship, hand], convey [goods &]; put [one's handkerchief to one's nose]; see [sbd. home]; 2 (n a a r d e s p r e k e r) bring; 3 (v a n d e s p r e k e r a f) take; *het ver* ~ go far [in the world]; make one's way; *wat brengt u hier?* what brings you here? *wat brengt hem ertoe te...* what makes him [say that...]; *dit brengt ons niets verder* this gets us nowhere; ● *iem. a a n het twijfelen ~* make sbd. doubt; *n a a r voren ~* put forward, mention; *iem. o p iets ~* get sbd. on the subject, lead sbd. up to it; *iem. op een idee ~* suggest an idea to sbd.; *het gesprek ~ op* lead the conversation to the subject of; *het getal ~ op* raise the number to; *t e berde ~* put forward, mention; *het zich te binnen ~* call it to mind, recall it; *iem. er t o e ~ te...* bring (persuade, get) sbd. to...; *hij was er niet toe te ~* he couldn't be made to do it; *het t o t generaal ~* rise to be a general; *het tot niets ~* come to nothing; *tot wanhoop ~* drive to despair; zie ook: *aanraking, bed* &; **–er** (-s) *m* bearer; *~ dezes* bearer

bres (-sen) *v* breach; *een ~ schieten in...* make a breach in...²; *i n de ~ springen voor* stand in the breach for; *o p de ~ staan [voor iem.]* stand in the breach

Bre'tagne [brə'tɑɲə] *o* Brittany

bre'tels *mv* braces, suspenders

Bre'ton (-s) *m* Breton; **–s** *aj* & *o* Breton

breuk (-en) *v* burst, crack [in glass &]; break [with a tradition]; rupture, split [between friends]; fracture [of a leg, an arm], rupture [of a blood-vessel], hernia [of the intestines]; fraction [in arithmetics]; $ breakage; *gewone ~* vulgar fraction; *onechte ~* improper fraction; *repeterende ~* repeater, repeating fraction; *gemengd repeterende ~* mixed repeater; *zuiver repeterende ~* pure repeater; *samengestelde ~* complex fraction; *tiendelige ~* decimal fraction; **–band** (-en) *m* truss; **–lijn** (-en) *v* line of fissure, rift; **–vlak** (-ken) *o* (i n a a r d l a a g) fault(-plane); (i n g e s t e e n t e) fracture

bre'vet (-ten) *o* patent, brevet, certificate

bre'vier (-en) *o rk* breviary; *zijn ~ bidden (lezen)* recite one's breviary; **bre'vieren** (brevierde, h. gebrevierd) *vi rk* recite one's breviary

bridge [brɪdʒ] *o* bridge; **'bridgen** (bridgede, h. gebridged) *vi* play bridge

brief (brieven) *m* letter, epistle; *een ~ op poten* **F** a snorter; *per ~* by letter; **–geheim** *o* privacy (secrecy) of correspondence; **–hoofd** (-en) *o* letter-head; **–je** (-s) *o* note; *dat geef ik u op een ~* you may take it from me; **–kaart** (-en) *v* postcard; *dubbele ~* letter-card; *~ met betaald antwoord* reply-postcard; **–opener** (-s) *m* paper-knife; **–ord(e)ner** (-s) *m* (letter) file; **–papier** *o* writing-paper, note-paper; **–port(o)** (-porti, porto's) *o* & *m* letter postage; **–stijl** (-en) *m* epistolary style; **–telegram** (-men) *o* letter telegram; **–vorm** *m* epistolary form; **–weger** (-s) *m = brieveweger*; **–wisseling** (-en) *v* correspondence; *~ houden* carry on (keep up)

a correspondence

bries *v* breeze; **'briesen** (brieste, ħ. gebriest) *vi* snort [of horses], roar [of lions]; *fig* foam [with rage]; seeth [with anger]

'brievehoofd (-en) *o = briefhoofd;* **'brieven- bakje** (-s) *o* letter tray: in-tray, out-tray; **–besteller** (-s) *m* postman; **–boek** (-en) *o* 1 letter-book; 2 model letter-writer; **–bus** (-sen) *v* letter-box [of a house, at a post office], pillar-box [in the street], post-box; **–post** *v* mail, post; **'brieveweger** (-s) *m* letter-balance

bri'gade (-s en -n) *v* ᕽᕽ brigade; *vliegende ~* flying squad; **–commandant** (-en) *m* ᕽᕽ brigadier; **briga'dier** (-s) *m* police sergeant

brij (-en) *m* 1 (v o e d s e l) porridge, mush; 2 (v. s n e e u w, m o d d e r) slush; (v. p a p i e r &) pulp

brik (-ken) *v* 1 brig [ship] ‖ 2 break [carriage]

bri'ket (-ten) *v* briquette

bril (-len) *m* 1 (pair of) spectacles; (t e r b e s c h e r m i n g t e g e n s t o f, s c h e r p l i c h t &) goggles; 2 seat [of a water-closet]; *blauwe (groene, zwarte) ~* dark glasses, smoked glasses; *alles door een rooskleurige ~ bekijken* look at (view) things through rose-coloured spectacles

bril'jant I *aj* brilliant; **II** (-en) *m* brilliant

brillan'tine [brɪljɑn-, bri.jɑn-] *v* brilliantine

'brilledoos (-dozen) *v*, **'brillehuisje** (-s) *o*, **'brillekoker** (-s) *m* spectacle-case; **'brillen** (brilde, h. gebrild) *vi* wear spectacles; **'bril- montuur** (-turen) *o* spectacle-frame; **–slang** (-en) *v* cobra

brink (-en) *m* village green

bri'santbom [s = z] (-men) *v* highly explosive bomb

Brit (-ten) *m* Briton, > Britisher; *de ~ten* (i n 't a l g., g e z a m e n l ij k) the British

brits (-en) *v* wooden couch; plank-bed

Brits British; **Brit'tanje, Brit'tannië** *o* Britain

'broche ['brɔʃə] (-s) *v* brooch

bro'cheren [brɔ'ʃeːrə(n)] (brocheerde, h. gebrocheerd) *vt* stitch, sew [a book]; **bro'chure** [brɔ'ʃyːrə] (-s) *v* pamphlet, brochure

'broddelaar (-s) *m* bungler, botcher; **'brod- delen** (broddelde, h. gebroddeld) *vi* bungle, botch; **'broddelwerk** (-en) *o* bungling, bungle, botch

'brodeloos breadless; *iem. ~ maken* throw sbd. out of employment

'broed *o* brood, hatch; fry [of fish]; **–ei** (-eren) *o* brood egg; **'broeden** (broedde, h. gebroed) *vi* brood, sit (on eggs); *op iets zitten ~* brood over, hatch [a plot]

'broeder (-s en -en) *m* 1 brother; 2 (g e e s t e- l ij k e) brother, friar; 3 (z i e k e n ~) male

nurse; *de zwakke ~s* the weaker brethren;
–dienst *m* brotherly service; *vrijstelling wegens ~*
exemption owing to one's brother's (military)
service; **–liefde** *v* fraternal (brotherly) love;
–lijk brotherly, fraternal; **–moord** (-en) *m*
fratricide; **–moordenaar** (-s) *m* fratricide;
–schap (-pen) 1 *o* & *v* (e i g e n s c h a p)
fraternity, brotherhood; 2 *v* (v e r e n i g i n g)
rk brotherhood, confraternity, sodality; *~*
sluiten met fraternize with; **–volk** (-en en -eren)
o sister nation

'**broedhen** (-nen) *v* brood-hen; **–machine**
[-ma.ʃi.nə] (-s) *v* incubator; **–plaats** (-en) *v*
breeding place; '**broeds** wanting to brood,
broody; '**broedsel** (-s) *o = broed*

'**broeibak** (-ken) *m* hotbed; '**broeien** (broeide,
h. gebroeid) *vi* (v. d. l u c h t) be sultry; (v.
h o o i) heat, get heated, get hot; *daar (er) broeit
iets* there is some mischief brewing; *dat heeft al
lang gebroeid* that has been smouldering for ever
so long; *er broeit een onweer* a storm is gathering;
'**broeierig** stifling, sweltering; '**broeikas**
(-sen) *v* hothouse, forcing-house; **–nest** (-en) *o*
hotbed²

broek (-en) *v* (pair of) trousers; *Am* pants; **F**
breeches; *korte ~* breeches, knickerbockers;
shorts; *de vrouw heeft de ~ aan* the wife wears
the breeches; *iem. a c h t e r d e ~ zitten* keep sbd.
up to scratch; *v o o r d e ~ geven* spank [a child];
voor de ~ krijgen be spanked; **–eman** (-nen) *m*
tiny tot, little mite, toddler; **–je** (-s) *o* shorts;
zo'n jong ~ a whipper-snapper (of a young
fellow); **–pak** (-ken) *o* trouser suit; **–rok** (-ken)
m culottes, divided skirt; '**broeksband** (-en) *v*
waist-band; **–pijp** (-en) *v* trouser-leg, trouser;
'**broekzak** (-ken) *m* trouser(s) pocket

broer (-s) *m = broeder*; **–tje** (-s) *o* little brother;
baby brother; *ik heb er een ~ aan dood* I hate
(detest) it; *het is ~ en zusje* it is six of one and
half a dozen of the other

broes (broezen) *v* rose [of shower-bath, water-
ing-can]

brok (-ken) *m* & *v* & *o* piece, bit, morsel, lump,
fragment; *hij voelde een ~ in de keel* he felt a
lump in his throat; *~ken maken [fig]* blunder

bro'kaat *o* brocade

'**brokje** (-s) *o* bit, morsel; *een lekker ~* a titbit;
'**brokkelen** (brokkelde, h. gebrokkeld) *vt* & *vi*
crumble; '**brokkelig** crumbly, friable, brittle;
'**brokken** (brokte, h. gebrokt) *vt* break [bread];
zie ook: *melk*; '**brokstuk** (-ken) *o* fragment,
piece, scrap

'**brombeer** (-beren) *m* grumbler

'**bromfiets** (-en) *m* & *v* moped, motorized
bicycle, auto-cycle; **–er** (-s) *m* moped rider,
mopedalist

'**brommen** (bromde, h. gebromd) *vi* 1 (v.

i n s e k t e n) drone, hum, buzz; 2 (v. p e r-
s o n e n) growl, grumble; 3 (i n g e v a n-
g e n i s) do time, do [a month]; 4 (o p
b r o m f i e t s) ride on a moped; '**brommer**
(-s) *m = brombeer, bromfiets, bromvlieg*; **–ig**
grumpy, grumbling; '**brompot** (-ten) *m =
brombeer*; **–tol** (-len) *m* humming-top; **–vlieg**
(-en) *v* bluebottle, flesh-fly

bron (-nen) *v* source², spring², well², fountain-
head, fountain², ☉ fount; *fig* origin; *~ van
bestaan* means of living; *~ van inkomsten* source
of income (of revenue); *uit goede ~ iets vernemen*
have sth. from a reliable source, on good
authority; **–bemaling** *v* de-watering, drainage

'**bronchiën** ['brɔŋɡi.ən] bronchi, *enkelvoud:*
bronchea; **bron'chitis** *v* bronchitis

'**bronnenstudie** (-s) *v* study of literary or
historical sources

brons *o* bronze; **–kleurig** bronze-coloured

bronst *v* (v. m a n n e t j e s d i e r) rut; (v.
v r o u w t j e s d i e r) heat; **–ig** (v. m a n n e-
t j e s d i e r) ruttish, (v. v r o u w t j e s d i e r) in
heat

'**bronstijd** *m* bronze age

'**bronsttijd** *m* rutting season

'**bronwater** (-en) *o* 1 spring water; 2 mineral
water

'**bronzen I** (bronsde, h. gebronsd) *vt* bronze; **II**
aj bronze

brood (broden) *o* bread; *een ~* a loaf [of bread];
ons dagelijks ~ our daily bread; *wiens ~ men eet,
diens woord men spreekt* ± it is bad policy to
quarrel with one's bread and butter; *zijn ~
hebben* earn one's bread; *goed zijn ~ hebben* be
well off; *iem. het ~ uit de mond stoten* take the
bread out of sbd.'s mouth; *zijn ~ verdienen* earn
one's bread; *geen droog ~ verdienen* not earn a
penny; *ergens geen ~ in zien* not think sth. will
pay bread; *iemand a a n een stuk ~ helpen* put
sbd. in the way to earn a living; *hij doet het o m
den brode* he does it for a living; *iem. iets o p zijn
~ geven* cast (fling, throw) sth. in sbd.'s teeth;
broodbakke'rij *v* 1 (b e d r i j f) bread-baking,
baker's trade; 2 (-en) (g e b o u w) bakehouse,
bakery; **–bezorger** (-s) *m* baker's delivery-
man; **–boom** (-bomen) *m* bread-fruit tree;
–deeg *o* dough (for bread); **brood'dronken**
wanton; '**broodfabriek** (-en) *v* bread-factory,
bakery; **–heer** (-heren) *m* employer; **–je** (-s) *o*
roll; *zoete ~s bakken* eat humble pie; **–korst**
(-en) *v* bread-crust; **–kruimel** (-s) *m* (bread)
crumb; **–mager** as lean as a rake; **–mand**
(-en) *v* bread-basket; **–mes** (-sen) *o* bread-
knife; **–nijd** *m* professional jealousy; **–nodig**
highly necessary, much-needed; **–plank** (-en)
v bread-board; **–rooster** (-s) *m* & *o* toaster;
–schrijver (-s) *m* hack (writer); **–trommel**

(-s) *v* bread-tin; **–vrucht** (-en) *v* bread-fruit; **–winner** (-s) *m* bread-winner; **–winning** (-en) *v* (means of) living, livelihood; **–zak** (-ken) *m* 1 bread-bag; 2 ✗ haversack

broom *o* 1 (e l e m e n t) bromine; 2 (g e n e e s-m i d d e l) potassium bromide; **broom′kali** *m* potassium bromide; **′broomzuur** *o* bromic acid

broos *aj* frail, brittle, fragile

bros crisp, brittle

brosse [brɔs] *Fr haar en* ~ crew cut

brouil′leren [bru.(l)′je: rə(n)] (brouilleerde, h. gebrouilleerd) *vt* set at variance; zie ook: *gebrouilleerd*

′brouwen* I *vt* brew; *fig* brew, concoct, plot [evil, mischief] ‖ **II** *vi* speak with a burr; **–er** (-s) *m* brewer; **brouwe′rij** (-en) *v* brewery; zie ook: *leven* **II** 3; **′brouwerspaard** (-en) *o* dray-horse

′brouwsel (-s) *o* brew, concoction[2]

brug (-gen) *v* 1 bridge; 2 (o e f e n t o e s t e l) parallel bars; *over de* ~ *komen* pay up, cough up; *flink over de* ~ *komen* **F** come down handsomely; **–balans** (-en) *v* weighing-machine; **–dek** (-en) *o* roadway [of a bridge]

′Brugge *o* Bruges

′bruggegeld (-en) *o* (bridge-)toll; **–hoofd** (-en) *o* 1 abutment; 2 ✗ bridgehead; **–wachter** (-s) *m = brugwachter;* **′brugleuning** (-en) *v* railing; (v. s t e e n) parapet

′Brugman *praten kunnen als* ~ **F** have the gift of the gab

′brugpijler (-s) *m* pier, pillar; **–wachter** (-s) *m* bridge-man

brui *m ik geef er de* ~ *van* **F** I chuck the thing (the whole show)

bruid (-en) *v* bride; **–egom** (-s) *m* bridegroom; **′bruidsbed** (-bedden) *o* bridal bed, nuptial couch; **–boeket** (-ten) *o* & *m* wedding-bouquet; **–dagen** *mv* bridal days; **–japon** (-nen) *m* wedding-dress, bridal gown; **–jonker** (-s) *m* 1 bridesman, groomsman, best man; 2 bride's page; **–meisje** (-s) *o* bridesmaid; **–nacht** (-en) *m* wedding night; **–paar** (-paren) *o* bride and bridegroom; newly-married couple; **–schat** (-ten) *m* dowry, dower, dot; **–sluier** (-s) *m* wedding-veil; **–stoet** (-en) *m* wedding-procession; **–suikers** *mv* sugar(ed) almonds; **–taart** (-en) *v* wedding cake; **–tooi** *m* bridal attire, bride's dress and jewellery; **′bruigom** (-s) *m = bruidegom*

′bruikbaar serviceable, useful, fit for use; workable [definition, scheme]; **–heid** *v* serviceableness, usefulness, utility; **′bruikleen** *o* & *m* (free) loan; *in* ~ *afstaan* lend

′bruiloft (-en) *v* wedding [ook: golden, silver &], wedding-party, ⊙ nuptials; ~ *houden*

celebrate one's wedding; have (attend) a wedding-party; **′bruiloftsdag** (-dagen) *m* wedding-day; **–feest** (-en) *o* wedding-party; **–gast** (-en) *m* wedding-guest; **–maal** (-malen) *o* wedding-banquet; **–taart** (-en) *v* wedding-cake

bruin I *aj* brown; tanned [by the sun]; (v. p a a r d) bay; ~*e beuk* copper beech; ~*e suiker* brown sugar; ~ *worden* (v a n h u i d d o o r z o n o f k u n s t m a t i g) get a tan, tan; **II** *o* brown; zie ook: *bruintje;* **–achtig** brownish; **′bruinen** (bruinde, *vt* h., *vi* is gebruind) *vt* & *vi* brown; (v a n h u i d d o o r z o n o f k u n s t m a t i g) tan; **brui′neren** (bruineerde, h. gebruineerd) *vt* burnish; **′bruinharig** brown-haired; **–kool** (-kolen) *v* brown coal, lignite; **–ogig** brown-eyed; **–tje** (-s) *o* 1 bay horse; 2 Bruin [the bear]; *dat kan* ~ *niet trekken* I cannot afford it; **–vis** (-sen) *m* porpoise

′bruisen (bruiste, h. gebruist) *vi* effervesce, fizz [of drinks]; seethe, roar [of the sea]; *fig* bubble [with energy]; **′bruispoeder** (-s) *o* & *m* effervescent powder

′brulaap (-apen) *m* howling-monkey; **–boei** (-en) *v* whistling-buoy; **′brullen** (brulde, h. gebruld) *vi* roar

bru′nette (-n en -s) *v* brunette

′Brunswijk *o* Brunswick

′Brussel *o* Brussels; **–s** Brussels; ~*e kant* Brussels lace; ~ *lof* chicory

bru′taal I *aj* 1 (z i c h a a n n i e t s s t o r e n d) bold, cool; 2 (a l t e v r ij m o e d i g) forward, pert, saucy, brash, **F** cheeky; impudent, impertinent; *zo* ~ *als de beul* as bold as brass; ~ *zijn tegen iem.* cheek (sauce) sbd., give sbd. lip; *een* ~ *mens heeft de halve wereld* fortune favours the bold; **II** *ad* coolly &; *het* ~ *volhouden* brazen it out; **–tje** (-s) *o* impertinent girl, **F** hussy; **–weg** coolly; **brutali′seren** [s = z] *vt iem.* ~ give sbd. lip, cheek (sauce) sbd.; **brutali′teit** (-en) *v* forwardness &; impudence, impertinence, effrontery; *hij had de* ~ *om...* **F** he had the cheek to...

′bruto gross [income, national product, weight &]

bruusk brusque, abrupt, blunt, off-hand

bruut I *aj* brutal, brutish; ~ *geweld* brute force; **II** (bruten) *m* brute; **–heid** (-heden) *v* brutality, brutishness

B.S. = *Burgerlijke stand*

B.T.W. [be.te.′ve.] *v = belasting over de toegevoegde waarde* value-added tax, VAT

bubs *de hele* ~ the whole caboodle, all the lot

budget [′büdʒɪt, büd′ʒɪt] (-s en -ten) *o* budget; **budget′tair** [büdʒɛ′tɪ: r] budgetary; **budget′teren** (budgetteerde, h. gebudgetteerd) **I** *vi* budget; **II** *vt* budget for; **–ring** *v* budgeting

'**buffel** (-s) *m* 🐃 buffalo; '**buffelen** (buffelde, h. gebuffeld) *vi* gobble, gorge oneself

'**buffer** (-s) *m* buffer; **–staat** (-staten) *m* bufferstate; **–voorraad** (-raden) *m* buffer stock; **–zone** (-n en -s) *v* buffer zone

buf'fet [by'fɛt] (-ten) *o* 1 (m e u b e l) sideboard, buffet; 2 (t a p k a s t i n s t a t i o n &) refreshment bar, buffet; *koud* ~ buffet dinner (luncheon); **–bediende** (-n) *m* barman; **–juffrouw** (-en) *v* barmaid

'**bugel** (-s) *m* bugle

bui (-en) *v* 1 shower [of rain, hail or arrows, stones &], squall [of wind, with rain or snow]; 2 (g r i l) freak, whim; 3 fit [of humour, of coughing]; *b ij* ~*en* by fits and starts; *i n een goede* ~ *zijn* be in a good humour; *in een boze* (*kwade*) ~ *zijn* be in a (bad) temper, be out of humour; *in een royale* ~ *zijn* be in a generous mood

'**buidel** (-s) *m* bag, pouch [ook = purse], sac; **–dier** (-en) *o* marsupial (animal); **–rat** (-ten) *v* opossum

'**buigbaar** pliable, flexible, pliant; '**buigen* I** *vi* bend, bow; curve; *hij boog en vertrok* he made his bow; ~ *als een knipmes* make a deep bow; ~ *of barsten* bend or break; ~ *voor* bow to[2]; bow before [sbd.]; **II** *vt* bend [a branch, the knee, sbd.'s will], bow [the head, the back, sbd.'s will]; **III** *vr zich* ~ bend (down), bow (down), stoop [of persons]; curve [of a line]; deflect, make a bend, trend [of a path &]; *zich* ~ *over* [*fig*] examine, look into [the problem]; '**buiging** (-en) *v* bow [of head or body]; curts(e)y [of a lady]; declension [of a word]; deflection [of a beam]; **–suitgang** (-en) *m* (in)flexional ending; '**buigspier** (-en) *v* flexor; **–tang** (-en) *v* pliers; '**buigzaam** flexible, supple[2], pliant[2]; **–heid** *v* flexibility, suppleness[2], pliancy[2]

'**buiig** ['bœyɔx] showery, gusty, squally

buik (-en) *m* belly [of man, animals & things], abdomen, > paunch; ● stomach, **F** tummy; *ik heb er mijn* ~ *vol van* **F** I am fed up with it; *zijn* ~ *vol eten* eat one's fill; *zijn* ~ *vasthouden van het lachen* hold one's sides with laughter; *twee handen op één* ~ hand in glove; **–band** (-en) *m* abdominal belt; **–dans** (-en) *m* belly dance; **–holte** (-n en -s) *v* abdominal cavity; **–ig** (big-)bellied, bulging; **–je** (-s) *o* tummy; (d i k) potbelly, paunch; **J** corporation; **–kramp** (-en) *v* gripes; **F** collywobbles; **–landing** (-en) *v* belly landing; **–loop** *m* diarrhoea; **–pijn** (-en) *v* stomach ache, **F** tummy ache; **–riem** (-en) *m* girth, belly-band; *de* ~ *aanhalen* tighten the belt[2]; '**buikspreken I** (sprak '**buik**, h. '**buik**gesproken) *vi* ventriloquize; **II** *o* ventriloquy,

ventriloquism; '**buikspreker** (-s) *m* ventriloquist; **–tyfus** [-ti.füs] *m* enteric (fever), typhoid; **–vin** (-nen) *v* 🐟 ventral fin; '**buikvlies** (-vliezen) *o* peritoneum; **–ontsteking** (-en) *v* peritonitis; '**buikziek** (v. p e e r) sleepy

buil (-en) *v* swelling; lump, bump, bruise; *daar kun je je geen* ~ *aan vallen* it won't ruin (kill) you '**builen** (builde, h. gebuild) *vt* bolt

'**builenpest** *v* bubonic plague

'**builtje** (-s) *o* sachet, [tea-]bag

1 buis (buizen) *o* (k l e d i n g s t u k) jacket

2 buis (buizen) *v* tube [ook 📺], pipe, conduit, duct; *de* ~ *T* **F** the box, the little screen; **–leiding** (-en) *v* conduit, duct, pipe, tube, pipeline(s); **–post** *v* pneumatic dispatch; **–verlichting** (-en) *v* tube (fluorescent) lighting; **–vormig** tubular

'**buiswater** *o* spray, bow wave

buit *m* booty, spoils, prize, plunder, loot; *met de* ~ *gaan strijken* carry off the prize (the swag)

'**buitelaar** (-s en -laren) *m* tumbler; '**buitelen** (buitelde, h. en is gebuiteld) *vi* tumble; **–ling** (-en) *v* tumble

'**buiten I** *prep* outside [the town], out of [the room, breath &], without [doors], beyond [one's reach, all question]; *hij kon niet* ~ *haar* he could not do without her; ~ *iets blijven, zich er* ~ *houden* keep out of sth.; (*niet*) ~ *iets kunnen* (not) be able to do without sth.; *iem. er* ~ *laten* leave sbd. out of sth.; *ergens* ~ *staan* be (entirely) out of; ~ (*en behalve*) *zijn salaris* besides (over and above) his salary; ~ *mij was er niemand* there was no one except me, but me; *dat is* ~ *mij om gegaan* I have nothing to do with it; *het werd* ~ *mij om gedaan* it was done without my knowledge, behind my back; *hij was* ~ *zichzelf* he was beside himself; **II** *ad* outside, out, outdoors, out of doors, without; *hij is* ~ 1 he is outside; 2 he is in the country; *hij woont* ~ he lives in the country; ● *n a a r* ~ *!* (go) outside!; *naar* ~ *gaan* 1 go outside, leave the house; 2 go into the country; *naar* ~ *opengaan* open outwards; *zijn voeten naar* ~ *zetten* turn out one's toes; *t e* ~ *gaan* exceed; *zich te* ~ *gaan aan* indulge too freely in, partake too freely of; *v a n* ~ [come, as seen] from without; [open] from the outside; *een meisje van* ~ a girl from the country, a country-girl; *van* ~ *gesloten* locked on the outside; *van* ~ *kennen* know by heart; *van* ~ *leren* learn by heart; *van* ~ *en van binnen* outside and in; **III** (-s) *o* country house, country seat; zie *grens*; **–aards** extraterrestrial; **–baan** (-banen) *v sp* outside track; **–bad** (-baden) *o* open-air swimming-pool, lido; **–band** (-en) *m* (outer) cover; **–beentje** (-s) *o* 1 illegitimate child; 2 *fig* **F** crank, maverick;

buiten'boordmotor (-s en -toren) *m* outboard motor; **'buitendeur** (-en) *v* 1 outer door; 2 street-door; **buiten'dien** moreover, besides; **'buitendienst** (-en) *m* field (outside) service; **–dijks, buiten'dijks** on the outside of the dike; **buiten'echtelijk** (r e l a t i e) extra-marital; (k i n d) illegitimate, born out of wedlock; **~ kind F** side-blow, by-blow, side-slip; **buiten'gaats** outside; offshore, in the offing; **'buitengemeen, buitenge'meen I** *aj* extraordinary, uncommon, exceptional; **II** *ad* < extraordinarily, uncommonly, exceptionally; **buitenge'rechtelijk** extrajudicial, out of court, private [settlement]; **'buitengewoon, buitenge'woon I** *aj* extraordinary; **~ gezant** envoy extraordinary; **~ hoogleraar** extraordinary professor; *buitengewone uitgaven* extras; *niets ~s* nothing out of the common; zie ook: *buitengemeen;* **II** *ad* < extraordinarily, uncommonly; **'buitenhaven** (-s) *v* outer harbour; **–hoek** (-en) *m* 1 exterior angle [of a △]; 2 outer corner [of the eye]; **–hof** (-hoven) *o* outer court, fore-court; **–huis** (-huizen) *o* country house, cottage

buite'nissig out-of-the-way, eccentric; **–heid** (-heden) *v* oddity, eccentricity

'buitenkansje (-s) *o* (stroke of) good luck, godsend, windfall; **–kant** (-en) *m* outside, exterior; **buiten'kerkelijk** irreligious, non-church; **'buitenland** *o* foreign country (countries); *i n h e t ~* abroad, in foreign parts; *n a a r het ~* abroad; *u i t h e t ~* from abroad; **–lander** (-s) *m* foreigner; **–lands** foreign [affairs &]; exotic [fruit]; *een ~e reis* a trip abroad; *van ~ fabrikaat* of foreign make, foreign-made; **–leven** *o* country-life; **–lucht** *v* 1 open air; 2 country air; **–lui** *mv* country people; *burgers en ~* town folk and country folk; **–man** (-lieden, -lui) *m* countryman; **buiten'mate** = *bovenmate;* **'buitenmens** (-en) *m-v* countryman; **buitenmo'del** ✠ non-regulation; **'buitenmuur** (-muren) *m* outer wall; **buiten'om** [go] round the house &; **'buitenopname** (-n en -s) *v* exterior (shot); **–plaats** (-en) *v* country seat; **–post** (-en) *m* 1 ✠ outpost; 2 out-station; **buitens'huis** out of doors, outdoors; *~ eten* eat (dine) out; **–'lands** abroad, in foreign parts; **'buitensluiten** (sloot 'buiten, h. 'buitengesloten) *vt* exclude, shut out; **–ting** *v* exclusion; **buiten'spel** *sp* offside; **'buitenspeler** (-s) *m* left (right) wing; **–spiegel** (-s) *m* 🚗 driving mirror; **buiten'sporig I** *aj* extravagant, excessive, exorbitant [price]; **II** *ad* extravagantly, excessively, to excess; **–heid** (-heden) *v* extravagance, excessiveness, exorbitance; **'buitenstaander** (-s) *m* outsider; **'buitenste** outmost, outer(most), exterior;

'buitentarief (-rieven) *o* $ external tariff; **–verblijf** (-blijven) *o* country house, country seat; **–waarts I** *aj* outward; **II** *ad* outward(s); **–wacht** (-en) *v* outpost; *ik heb het van de ~* 1 heard it from an outsider; **–weg** (-wegen) *m* country-road, rural road; **–wereld** *v* outer (outside, external) world; **–werk** (-en) *o* 1 ✠ outwork; 2 outdoor-work; **–wijk** (-en) *v* suburb; *de ~en* ook: the outskirts; **–zak** (-ken) *m* outside pocket, outer pocket; **–zij(de)** (-den) *v* outside exterior

'buitmaken (maakte 'buit, h. 'buitgemaakt) *vt* seize, take, capture

'buizenpost *v* = *buispost*

'buizerd (-s) *m* buzzard

'bukken (bukte, h. gebukt) **I** *vt* bend [the head]; **II** *vi* stoop; duck [to avoid a blow]; *gebukt gaand o n d e r...* bending under, bowed (weighed) down by; *~ v o o r* bow to (before), submit to; **III** *vr* zich *~* stoop; duck

buks (-en) *v* ✠ rifle

1 bul (-len) *m* (s t i e r) bull

2 bul 1 (papal) bull; 2 ✍ diploma

'bulderbast (-en) *m* blusterer; **'bulderen** (bulderde, h. gebulderd) *vi* boom [of cannon &], bluster, roar [of wind, sea, persons], bellow [of persons]; *~ tegen* bellow at; *~d gelach* uproarious laughter

'buldog (-gen) *m* bulldog

Bul'gaar (-garen) *m*, **Bulgaars** *aj* & *o* Bulgarian; **Bulga'rije** Bulgaria

bulk *m* ⚓ bulk; **–artikelen** *mv* bulk goods

'bulken (bulkte, h. gebulkt) *vi* low, bellow, bawl, roar; *~ van het geld* roll in money

'bulldozer ['bu.l-] (-s) *m* bulldozer

'bullebak (-ken) *m* bully, browbeater, bugbear, ogre; **–bijter** (-s) *m* bulldog; *fig* bully

'bullen *mv* **F** things

'bullepees (-pezen) *v* (*m*) policeman's rod

bulle'tin [by.lə'tɛ̃] (-s) *o* bulletin, newsletter

bult (-en) *m* 1 hunch [of a man], hump [of man or camel]; 2 boss, lump [= swelling]; **–ig** 1 hunchbacked, humpbacked; 2 lumpy [old mattress]

'bumper (-s) *m* bumper; *~ aan ~* bumper to bumper

bun (-nen) *v* creel

'bundel (-s) *m* bundle [of clothes, rods &], sheaf [of arrows, papers]; beam [of light]; *een ~ gedichten* a volume of verse; **'bundelen** (bundelde, h. gebundeld) *vt* gather, bring together, collect; tie up together

'bunder (-s) *o* hectare

'bungalow ['büŋga.lo.] (-s) *m* bungalow

'bungelen (bungelde, h. gebungeld) *vi* dangle

'bunker (-s) *m* 1 bunker; 2 ✠ casemate, (k l e i n) [concrete] blockhouse, pill-box,

[German] bunker; (t e g e n l u c h t a a n v a l)
air-raid shelter; **'bunkeren** (bunkerde, h.
gebunkerd) *vi* bunker, coal
'bunzing (-s en -en) *m* polecat, fitchew
burcht (-en) *m* & *v* castle, stronghold², citadel²;
–heer (-heren) *m* ⌂ castellan; **–vrouw(e)**
(-en) *v* ⌂ chatelaine
bu'reau [by.'ro.] (-s) *o* 1 (m e u b e l) desk,
writingtable; 2 (l o k a a l) bureau [*mv* bureaux],
office; [police] station; 3 (b e d r ij f) [travel,
publicity, private detective] agency; **–chef**
[-ʃɛf] (-s) *m* head-clerk
bureau'craat [by.ro.-] (-craten) *m* bureaucrat;
bureaucra'tie [-'(t)si.] *v* bureaucracy, **F** red
tape; **bureau'cratisch** bureaucratic
bu'reaukosten [by.'ro.-] *mv* office expenses;
–lamp (-en) *v* desk lamp; **bu'reau-mi'nistre**
[-mi.'ni.strə] (bureaux-ministres) *o* pedestal
writing-table; **bu'reauredacteur** (-s en -en) *m*
desk-editor; **–stoel** (-en) *m* desk chair; **–werk**
o office work, clerical work
bu'reel (-relen) *o* office, bureau
'burengerucht *o* disturbance; ~ *maken* cause a
nuisance by noise
burg (-en) *m* & *v* = *burcht*
burge'meester (-s) *m* 1 burgomaster [on the
Continent]; 2 mayor [in England]; ~ *en wethouders* the burgomaster [in England: the mayor]
and aldermen; **–sbuik** (-en) *m* **J** corporation
'burger (-s) *m* 1 citizen; commoner [not a
nobleman]; **J** & ✒ (n i e t i n E n g.) burgher;
2 civilian [non-military man]; *in* ~ in plain
clothes, **F** in civvies; ⚔ in mufti; *agent in* ~
plainclothes (police)man; *een brave* ~ *worden*
settle down; *dat geeft de* ~ *moed* that is encour-
aging; **–bevolking** (-en) *v* civil(ian) population; **–deugd** (-en) *v* civic virtue; **burge'rij**
(-en) *v* 1 (a l s s t a n d) commonalty, com-
moners, middle classes; *de kleine* ~ the lower
classes; 2 (d e i n g e z e t e n e n) citizens,
citizenry [of Amsterdam &]; **'burgerkleding**
v plain (civilian) clothes; *in* ~ zie *burger*; **–kost**
m plain fare; **–lijk** 1 civil [engineering, law,
rights &]; civic [functions], civilian [life]; 2 (v i
d e b u r g e r s t a n d) middle-class; 3 (n i e t
f ij n o f v o o r n a a m) middle-class, bourgeois, plain, homely; zie ook: *ambtenaar, stand,
beleefdheid*; **–luchtvaart** *v* civil aviation; **–man**,
burger'man (-lieden en -lui) *m* middle-class
man, bourgeois; **'burgeroorlog** (-logen) *m*
civil war; **–pakje** (-s) *o* ⚔ **S** civvies; **–plicht**
(-en) *m* & *v* civic duty; **–recht** (-en) *o* civil
right, citizenship, freedom of a city; *dat woord
heeft* ~ *verkregen* the word has been adopted
into the language; *zijn* ~ *verliezen* forfeit one's
civil rights; **'burgerschap** *o* citizenship;
'burgerschapskunde *v* civics; **–rechten** *mv*

civic rights; **'burgerstand** (-en) *m* middle
classes; **burger'vader** (-en en -s) *m* 1 father of
the city, burgomaster; 2 mayor [in England];
'burgerwacht (-en) *v* citizen guard, civic
guard, home guard; **–zin** *m* civic spirit, civic
sense
'burggraaf (-graven) *m* (t i t e l) ⚑ ʼscount;
–gravin (-nen) *v* viscountess
bur'lesk burlesque, farcical; **–e** ( ) *v*
burlesque, farce
bur'saal (-salen) *m* scholar, exhibitioner
1 bus (-sen) *v* 1 (v o o r g r o e n t e n &) tin,
can; 2 (v o o r g e l d, b r i e v e n) (money-)
box, (letter-)box; poor-box [in a church],
collecting-box; 3 ✕ bush, box; 4 (f o n d s)
club; *in de* ~ *blazen* dip deep in one's purse;
dat klopt (sluit) als een ~ it is perfectly logical;
u i t de ~ *komen* result; *een brief o p de* ~ *doen* post
a letter
2 bus (-sen) *m* & *v* (a u t o b u s) bus; (v o o r
l a n g e a f s t a n d e n) coach; **–chauffeur**
[-ʃo.fø:r] (-s) *m* bus driver; **–conducteur** (-s)
m ticket-collector, **F** jumper; **–dienst** (-en) *m*
bus service; **–halte** (-n en -s) *v* bus stop
'buskruit *o* gunpowder; *hij heeft het* ~ *niet
uitgevonden* he will never set the Thames on
fire; *opvliegen als* ~ flare up at the least thing
'buslichting (-en) *v* collection
'buslijn (-en) *v* bus line, bus service; **–station**
[-sta.(t)ʃɔn] (-s) *o* bus station
'buste ['by.stə] (-n en -s) *v* bust, (v. v r o u w
v a a k:) bosom; **–houder** (-s) *m* brassière, bra
bu'taan *o* butane; Calor gas
'butagas *o* compressed
butane, Calor gas
'butler (-s) *m* butler
buts (-en) *v* dent
buur (buren) *m* neighbour; **–kind** (-eren) *o*
neighbour's child; **–land** (-en) *o* neigh-
bour(ing) country; **–man** (-lieden) *m* neighbour; **–meisje** (-s) *o* girl next door; **–praatje**
(-s) *o* neighbourly talk, gossip; **–schap** (-pen)
1 *o* neighbourhood; 2 *v = buurtschap*
buurt (-en) *v* neighbourhood, vicinity; (w ij k)
quarter; *het is in de* ~ it is quite near; *een winkelier in de* ~ a neighbouring shopkeeper; *hier in
de* ~ hereabout(s); near here; (ver) *u i t de* ~ far
off, a long way off; *dat woont u i t de* ~ don't go near
him; **'buurten** (buurtte, h. gebuurt) *vi* pay a
visit to a neighbour; **'buurhuis** (-huizen) *o*
community centre; **–schap** (-pen) *v* hamlet;
–spoor (-sporen) *o* local railway; **–verkeer** *o*
local service
'buurvrouw (-en) *v* neighbour, neighbour's wife
b.v. = *bij voorbeeld* zie *voorbeeld*
B.W. = *burgerlijk wetboek* zie *wetboek*
By'zantium *o* Byzantium; **Byzan'tijn(s)** (-en)
m (*aj*) Byzantine

C

c [se.] ('s) *v* c
ca = *centiare*
ca. ['sɪrka.] = *circa*
caba'ret [kaba'rɛ(t)] (-s) *o* cabaret; **cabare'tier** [kabarɛ'tje.] (-s) *m* cabaret performer
ca'bine (-s) *v* 1 cabin; 2 (v. v r a c h t a u t o) cab; 3 (v. b i o s c o o p) projection room
cabrio'let (-ten) *m* (r ij t u i g) cabriolet; ⇔ convertible
ca'cao [ka'kɔu] *m* cocoa; **–boon** (-bonen) *v* cocoa-bean; **–boter** *v* cocoa-butter; **–poeder** *o* & *m* cocoa-powder
ca'chet [ka.'ʃɛ(t)] (-ten) *o* 1 seal, signet; 2 (e i g e n a a r d i g e s t e m p e l) cachet, stamp [of distinction]; *een zeker ~ hebben* bear a distinctive stamp
ca'chot [ka'ʃɔt] (-ten) *o* lock-up, **S** clink; ⚔ cells
'cactus (-sen) *m* cactus [*mv* cacti]
ca'dans (-en) *v* cadence
ca'deau [ka'do.] (-s) *o* present; *iem. iets ~ geven* give sbd. sth. as a present, make sbd. a present of sth.; *ik zou het niet ~ willen hebben* I would not have it as a gift; *dat kun je van mij ~ krijgen!* you can have (keep) it!; **–bon** (-nen) *m* gift token
ca'dens (-en) *v* ♪ cadenza
ca'det (-s en -ten) *m* cadet; **–tenschool** (-scholen) *v* military school, cadet college
ca'fé (-s) *o* café, coffee-house; (m e t v e r g u n n i n g) ± public house, **F** pub; **ca'fé-chan'tant** [-ʃã'tã] (café-chantants) *o* cabaret; **ca'féhouder** (-s) *m* café proprietor; (m e t v e r g u n n i n g) ± public-house keeper, publican
cafe'ïne [kafe.'i.nə] *v* caffeine; **–vrij** caffeine-free, decaffeinated
ca'fé-restau'rant [ka'fe.rɪsto.'rã] (café-restaurants) *o* café-restaurant; **cafe'taria** [kafə-] ('s) *v* cafetaria
ca'hier [ka'je.] (-s) *o* exercise-book
caissière [kɛ.s'jɛ:rə] (-s) *v* cashier
cais'son [kɛ'sõ] (-s) *m* caisson
cake [ke.k] (-s) *m* cake
cal = *calorie*
'calcium *o* calcium
calcu'latie [-(t)si.] (-s) *v* calculation, estimation; (v. b o u w w e r k) costing; **calcu'lator** (-s) *m* calculator, computing clerk; **calcu'leren** (calculeerde, h. gecalculeerd) calculate, estimate, compute; (v. b o u w w e r k) cost
ca'lèche [ka'lɛʃ] (-s) *v* calash

caleido'scoop (-scopen) *m* kaleidoscope; **–'scopisch** kaleidoscopic
Cali'fornië *o* California; **–r** (-s) *m*, **Cali'fornisch** Californian
calo'rie (-ieën) *v* calorie; **calori'meter** (-s) *m* calorimeter; **ca'lorisch** caloric
cal'queerlinnen [qu = k] *o* tracing-cloth; **–papier** (-en) *o* transfer paper, tracing-paper; **cal'queren** (calqueerde, h. gecalqueerd) *vt* trace, calk
Cal'varieberg *m* (Mount) Calvary
Cal'vijn *m* Calvin; **calvi'nisme** *o* Calvinism; **–ist** (-en) *m* Calvinist; **–istisch** Calvinistic
ca'mee (-meeën) *v* cameo
ca'melia ('s) *v* camellia
'camera ('s) *v* camera; *~ obscura* [-ɔp'sky:ra.] camera obscura; **–man** (-nen) *m* cameraman; **–wagen** (-s) *m* dolly
camou'flage [kamu.'fla.ʒə] *v* camouflage; **camou'fleren** (camoufleerde, h. gecamoufleerd) *vt* camouflage
cam'pagne [-'paɲə] (-s) *v* ⚔ campaign[2]; season [of opera]; working season [of a sugar factory]; *fig* ook: [export] drive
'camping ['kɛmpɪŋ] (-s) *m* camping site, caravan park
'campus (-sen) *m* campus
'Canada *o* Canada; **Cana'dees** *m* (-dezen) & *aj* Canadian
ca'naille [ka'na(l)jə] (-s) *o* 1 (g e s p u i s) rabble, mob, riff-raff; 2 (m a n) scamp; 3 (v r o u w) vixen
cana'pé (-s) *m* 1 sofa, settee; *Am* davenport; 2 (h a p j e) canapé
ca'nard [ka'na:r] *m* canard, newspaper hoax
Ca'narische 'Eilanden *mv* Canaries
canne'leren (cannelleerde, h. gecannelleerd) *vt* channel, flute
'canon (-s) *m* canon°; (l i e d) catch; **cano'niek** canonical; *~ recht* canon law; **canoni'satie** [-'za.(t)si.] (-s) *v* canonization; **canoni'seren** [s = z] (canoniseerde, h. gecanoniseerd) *vt* canonize
can'tate (-n en -s) *v* cantata
cantha'rel (-len) *m* chanterelle
ca'nule (-s) *v* can(n)ula
'canvas *o* canvas
C.A.O. [se.a.'o.] *v* = *collectieve arbeidsovereenkomst*; zie *arbeidsovereenkomst*
ca'outchouc [ka'u.tʃu.k] *o* & *m* caoutchouc, india-rubber
capaci'teit (-en) *v* capacity; ability

cape [ke.p] (-s) *v* (k o rt) cape; (l a n g) cloak
capil'lair [-'lɛːr] capillary; **capillari'teit** *v* capillarity
capiton'neren (capitonneerde, h. gecapitonneerd) *vt* pad
Capi'tool *o* Capitol
capitu'latie [-(t)si.] (-s) *v* capitulation, surrender (to *voor*); **capitu'leren** (capituleerde, h. gecapituleerd) *vt* capitulate, surrender (to *voor*)
caprici'eus [kɑprisi.'øːs] capricious
capri'ool (-olen) *v* caper; *zijn (haar) capriolen* ook: his (her) antics; *capriolen maken* cut capers
cap'sule (-s) *v* capsule, cachet; (v. f l e s) lead cap
'captie ['kɑpsi.] (-s) *v* ~s *maken* 1 raise captious objections; 2 recalcitrate
capu'chon [kɑpy.'ʃòn] (-s) *m* hood
Cara'ïbisch *het* ~ *gebied* the Caribbean
caram'bole [kɑrɑm'bo.l] (-s) *m* cannon; **carambo'leren** (caramboleerde, h. gecaramboleerd) *vi* ♋ cannon [against, with]
'caravan ['kɛrɑvɑn] (-s) *m* caravan
car'bid [-'bi.t] *o* carbide
car'bol *o* & *m* carbolic acid; **–zeep** (-zepen) *v* carbolic soap; **–zuur** *o* = *carbol*
carboni'seren [s = z] (carboniseerde, h. gecarboniseerd) *vt* carbonize
car'bonpapier *o* carbon paper
carbura'teur (-s) *m*, **carbu'rator** (-s en - 'toren) *m* carburettor
car'danas (-sen) *v* propellor shaft; **car'dankoppeling** (-en) *v* universal joint
cardio'graaf (-grafen) *m* cardiograph; **cardio'gram** (-men) *o* cardiogram; **cardiolo'gie** *v* cardiology; **cardio'loog** (-logen) *m* cardiologist
carga'door (-s) *m* ship-broker; **'cargalijst** (-en) *v* manifest; **'cargo** ('s) *m* cargo
'cariës ['kaːri.ɛs] *v* caries
caril'lon [kɑri.l'ʃòn] (-s) *o* & *m* carillon, chimes
carita'tief = *charitatief*
'carnaval (-s) *o* carnival
car'ré (-s) *o* & *m* square
carri'ère [kɑri.'rɛ] (-s) *v* career; ~ *maken* make a career for oneself; **–jager** (-s) *m* careerist
carrosse'rie (-ieën) *v* coach-work, body
carrou'sel [ou = u.] (-s) *m* & *o* merry-go-round
carte [kɑrt] *à la* ~ *eten* dine à la carte; ~ *blanche* carte blanche; *iem.* ~ *blanche geven* give sbd. a free hand
'carter (-s) *o* crank-case
cartogra'fie *v* cartography
carto'theek (-theken) *v* filing cabinet, card-index cabinet, card index
cas'cade [kɑs'ka.də] (-n en -s) *v* cascade
'casco ['kɑsko.] ('s) *o* body, hull [of ship]

ca'sino [s = z] ('s) *o* casino
cas'satie [-(t)si.] *v* cassation, appeal; ~ *aantekenen* give notice of appeal; **cas'seren** (casseerde, h. gecasseerd) *vt* 1 reverse, quash [a judgment in appeal]; 2 ⚔ cashier [an officer]
cas'sette (-n en -s) *v* 1 money-box; 2 casket [for jewels &]; 3 canteen [of cutlery]; 4 box [for books]; 5 writing-desk; 6 cassette [for cassette recorder and player]
casta'gnetten [kɑstɑ'ɲɛtə(n)] *mv* castanets
Castili'aan (-anen) *m* Castilian; **–s** Castilian; **Cas'tilië** *o* Castile
'castorolie *v* castor oil
cas'traat (-traten) *m* castrato; **cas'treren** (castreerde, h. gecastreerd) *vt* castrate, geld, emasculate
'casu [s = z] *in* ~ in (this) case
casu 'quo [ka.zy. 'kʋo.] or, as the case may be
catalogi'seren [s = z] (catalogiseerde, h. gecatalogiseerd) *vt* catalogue; **ca'talogus** (-gi en -gussen) *m* catalogue; **–prijs** (-prijzen) *m* list price
cata'ract (-en) *v* cataract
ca'tarre [ka'tɑr] (-s) *v* catarrh
catastro'faal catastrophic, disastrous; **cata'strofe** (-n en -s) *v* catastrophe, disaster
cate'cheet [kɑtə'xe.t] (-cheten) *m* catechist; **cate'chetisch** catechetic; **catechi'sant** [s = z] (-en) *m* catechumen; **catechi'satie** [-'za.(t)si.] (-s) *v* confirmation class(es); **cate'chismus** (-sen) *m* catechism
categori'aal grouped (classified) according to category; **catego'rie** (-ieën) *v* category; **cate'gorisch** categorical
ca'theter (-s) *m* catheter
cau'saal [s = z] *v* causal; **causali'teit** *v* causality; **'causatief** causative
cause'rie [ko.zə'ri.] (-ieën) *v* causerie, talk; *een* ~ *houden* give a talk; **cau'seur** [ko.'zøː r] (-s) *m* conversationalist
'cautie ['kɔutsi.] (-s) *v* = *borgtocht*
caval'cade (-s en -n) *v* cavalcade
cavale'rie *v* cavalry, horse; **cavale'rist** (-en) *m* cavalryman, trooper
cava'lier [kɑvɑ'lje.] (-s) *m* cavalier
'cavia ('s) *v* guinea-pig
ca'yennepeper [ka.'jɛ.nəpe.pər] *m* Cayenne pepper
'cedel *v* & *o* (-s) = *ceel*
'ceder (-s) *m* cedar; ~ *van de Libanon* cedar of Lebanon
ce'deren (cedeerde, h. gecedeerd) *vt* ⚖ assign; **'cederhouten** *aj* cedar
ce'dille [se.'di.jə] (-s) *v* cedilla
ceel (celen) *v* & *o* 1 list; 2 $ (dock) warrant
cein'tuur [ei = ɛ] (-s en -turen) *v* belt, sash

cel (-len) *v* cell; **F** ook = *celstraf* & *cello*; **–deling** *v* cell division

cele'brant [se.lə-] (-en) *m* celebrant; **cele'breren** (celebreerde, h. gecelebreerd) *vt* & *vi* celebrate

celi'baat *o* celibacy; **celiba'tair** [-'tɛːr] *m* (-s) *m* celibate, (old) bachelor

'celkern (-en) *v* nucleus

cel'list (-en) *m* violoncellist, cellist; **'cello** ['sɛlo., 'tʃɛlo.] ('s) *m* cello

cello'faan *o* cellophane

cellu'lair [-'lɛːr] ~*e opsluiting* solitary confinement

cellu'loid [-'lɔit] *o* celluloid

cellu'lose [-'lo.zə] *v* cellulose

'Celsius *m* Celsius; *20°* ~ 20 degrees centigrade

'celstraf *v* solitary confinement; **–vormig** cellular; **–weefsel** *o* cellular tissue

ce'ment *o* & *m* cement; **–en** *aj* cement; **cemen'teren** (cementeerde, h. gecementeerd) *vt* cement

'censor [s = z] (-s en -soren) *m* censor, licenser [of plays]; **censu'reren** [s = z] (censureerde, h. gecensureerd) *vt* censor [letters]

'census [-züs] *m* census

cen'suur [s = z] *v* censorship; *onder* ~ *staan* be censored; *onder* ~ *stellen* censor

cent (-en) *m* cent [$^1/_{100}$ of a guilder]; ~*en* **F** money; ~*en hebben* have plenty of money; *ik heb geen* ~ I haven't a penny; *het is geen* ~ *waard* it is not worth a red cent; *het kan me geen* ~ *schelen* I don't care a cent; *tot de laatste* ~ to the last farthing; zie ook *duit*

cen'taur [sɛn'tɔur] (-en) *m* centaur

'centenaar (-s) *m* hundredweight; quintal

'center (-s) *m sp* centre

'centerboor (-boren) *v* centrebit

'centeren (centerde, h. gecenterd) *vi* & *vt sp* centre

'centiare (-n en -s) *v* centiare, square metre; **–gram** (-men) *o* centigramme; **–liter** (-s) *m* centilitre; **–meter** (-s) *m* 1 centimetre [$^1/_{100}$ part of a metre]; 2 (m e e t l i n t) tape-measure

cen'traal central; centric(al); *met centrale verwarming* centrally heated; ~ *staan bij* be central to [their idea, programme], be at the centre of [their strategy]; *deze kwestie staat* ~ *bij het conflict* ook: the conflict centres on this issue; **–station** (-s) *o* central station; **cen'trale** (-s) *v* 1 ☿ generating station, power-station; 2 ☎ exchange; 3 $ bureau, agency; **centrali'satie** [-'za.(t)si.] *v* centralization; **centrali'seren** [s = z] (centraliseerde, h. gecentraliseerd) *vt* centralize

cen'treren (centreerde, h. gecentreerd) *vt* centre

centrifu'gaal centrifugal; **centri'fuge** [g = ʒ] (-s) *v* 1 centrifugal machine; 2 (v. w a s - a u t o m a a t) spin-drier; **centrifu'geren** (centrifugeerde, h. gecentrifugeerd) *vt* (v. d. w a s) spin

centripe'taal centripetal

'centrum (-s en -tra) *o* centre

cera'miek [se.-, ke.-] *v* ceramics; **ce'ramisch** ceramic

cere'braal cerebral²

cere'monie (-s en -iën) *v* ceremony; **cere-moni'eel I** *aj* ceremonial; **II** *het* ~ the ceremonial; **cere'moniemeester** (-s) *m* Master of (the) Ceremonies; **ceremoni'eus** ceremonious

ce'rise [sə'ri.zə] cerise, cherry-red

certifi'caat (-caten) *o* certificate; ~ *van aandeel* share certificate; ~ *van oorsprong* certificate of origin

cerve'laatworst (-en) *v* saveloy

'cessie (-s) *v* cession; **cessio'naris** (-sen) *m* cessionary, assign(ee)

ce'suur [se.'zy:r] (-suren) *v* caesura

cf = [*Lat*] *confer* vergelijk

cg = *centigram*

cha'grijn [ʃa-] *o* chagrin, vexation; **cha'grijnig** chagrined, peevish, fretful

cham'breren [ch = ʃ] (chambreerde, h. gechambreerd) *vt* (v . w ij n) bring to room temperature

cham'pagne [ʃam'paɲə] (-s) *m* champagne, **F** fizz, **S** bubbly

champi'gnon [ʃampi.'ɲɔ̀n] (-s) *m* [edible] mushroom

chan'geant [ʃã'ʒã.] ~ *zijde* shot silk

chan'tage [ʃan'ta.ʒə] *v* blackmail; ~ *plegen jegens* blackmail [sbd.]; **chan'teren** (chanteerde, h. gechanteerd) *vt* blackmail; **chan'teur** (-s) *m* 1 ♪ singer, vocalist; 2 (a f p e r s e r) blackmailer

'chaos ['xa.ɔs] *m* chaos; *orde scheppen in de* ~ bring (make) order out of chaos, reduce chaos to order; **cha'otisch** chaotic

chape'ron [ʃapə'rõ] (-s) *m*, **chaperonne** (-s) *v* chaperon; **chaperon'neren** (chaperonneerde, h. gechaperonneerd) *vt* chaperon

cha'piter [ʃa-] (-s) *o* chapter; *nu wij toch a a n dat* ~ *bezig zijn* as (now) we are upon the subject; *om o p ons* ~ *terug te komen* to return to our subject; *dat is een heel ander* ~ (but) that is quite something else

'charge ['ʃarʒə] (-s) *v* charge; *getuige à* ~ ⚖ witness for the prosecution; **char'geren** (chargeerde, h. gechargeerd) *vi* 1 ⚔ charge; 2 *fig* exaggerate, overact, overdraw

cha'risma [xa.-] ('s) *o* charisma, charism; **charis'matisch** charismatic

'charitas ['xa:-] *v* charity; **charita'tief** charitable 'charlatan ['ʃɑr-] (-s) *m* charlatan, quack, mountebank

char'mant [ʃɑr-] charming; 'charme (-s) *m* charm; char'meren (charmeerde, h. gecharmeerd) *vt* charm; zie ook: *gecharmeerd*

char'taal [xɑr-] ~ *geld* notes and coin

'charter ['(t)ʃɑrtər] (-s) *o* charter; 'charteren (charterde, h. gecharterd) *vt* charter; 'chartervliegtuig (-en) *o* charter plane; –vlucht (-en) *v* charter flight

chas'seur [ʃɑ'sø:r] (-s) *m* page(-boy), **F** buttons, *Am* bell-hop

chas'sis [ʃɑ'si.] *o* 1 chassis [of a motor-car &]; 2 plate-holder [for a camera]

chauf'feren [ʃo.-] (chauffeerde, h. gechauffeerd) *vi* drive [a car]; chauf'feur (-s) *m* (i n d i e n s t b ij i e m.) chauffeur; (b e s t u u r d e r) driver; zie ook: *autoverhuur*

chauvi'nisme [ʃo.-] *o* chauvinism; –ist (-en) *m* chauvinist; –istisch chauvinistic

'checken [tʃɪ-] (checkte, h. gecheckt) *vt* check, examine

chef [ʃɛf] (-s) *m* chief, head; (v. a f d e l i n g) office-manager; (p a t r o o n) employer; (d i r e c t e u r) manager; **F** boss; ~ *de bureau* head-clerk; ~ *de cuisine*, ~*-kok* chef;~*-d'oeuvre* masterpiece; ~ *van het protocol* head of protocol; ~*-staf* ⚔ Chief of Staff

chemi'caliën [ch = x] *mv* chemicals; 'chemicus (-ci) *m* 1 chemist; 2 analytical chemist; che'mie *v* chemistry; 'chemisch chemical; ~ *reinigen* dry-clean; *het* ~ *reinigen* dry-cleaning; ~*e wasserij* dry-cleaning works

cheque [ʃɛk] (-s) *m* cheque; –boek (-en) *o* cheque-book

'chertepartij ['ʃɛrtə-] (-en) *v* $ charter-party

cheru'bijn [xe:-] (-en) *m* cherub

che'vron [ʃɔ-] (-s) *m* chevron, stripe

chic [ʃi.k] **I** *aj* smart, stylish, fashionable [hotel]; **II** *ad* smartly &; **III** *m* smartness &; *de* ~ the smart set; *kale* ~ shabby-genteel people

chi'cane [ʃi.-] (-s) *v* chicane(ry); chica'neren (chicaneerde, h. gechicaneerd) *vi* chicane, quibble; chica'neur (-s) *m* quibbler; chica'neus captious

'Chili *o* Chile

'chimpansee [ch = ʃ] (-s) *m* chimpanzee

'China [ch = ʃ] *o* China; Chi'nees **I** *aj* Chinese, China; **II** *o het* ~ Chinese; **III** (-nezen) *m* Chinese; *de Chinezen* the Chinese; zie ook: *raar*; Chi'nezenbuurt (-en) *v*, Chi'nezenwijk (-en) *v* Chinese quarter, [New York's &] Chinatown

chique [ʃi.k] = *chic* **I** & **II**

chi'rurg [ch = ʃ] (-en) *m* surgeon; chirur'gie [ʃi.rür'ʒi.] *v* surgery; chi'rurgisch surgical

'chloor [ch = x] *m* & *o* chlorine; chlo'reren

(chloreerde, h. gechloreerd) *vt* chlorinate

chloro'form [ch = x] *m* chloroform

chloro'fyl [xlo.ro.'fi.l] *o* chlorophyll

choco'la(-) [ʃo.ko.'la] = *chocolade(-);* choco'laatje (-s) *o* chocolate, **F** choc; choco'lade *m* chocolate; –bonbon (-s) *m* chocolate cream; –reep (-repen) *m* bar of chocolate

'cholera [ch = x] *v* (malignant) cholera

cho'lericus [ch = x] (-ci) *m* choleric (irascible) person; cho'lerisch choleric

choleste'rol [xo.lɪs-] *m* cholesterol

cho'queren [ʃɔ'ke:rə(n)] (choqueerde, h. gechoqueerd) *vt* shock

choreo'graaf [ch = x] (-grafen) *m* choreographer; choreogra'fie (-ieën) *v* choreography

'christelijk [ch = k of x] Christian; 'christen (-en) *m* Christian; –dom *o* Christianity; –heid *v* Christendom; chris'tin (-nen) *v* Christian, Christian lady (woman); 'Christus *m* Christ; *in 200 na* ~ in 200 A.D.; *in 200 voor* ~ in 200 B.C.

chro'matisch [ch = x] chromatic

chromo'soom [xro.mo.'zo.m] (-somen) *o* chromosome

'chronisch [ch = x] chronic

chronolo'gie [ch = x] (-ieën) *v* chronology; chrono'logisch chronological

'chronometer ['xro.no.me.tər] (-s) *m* chronometer

'chroom [ch = x] *o* chromium; –geel *o* chrome yellow; –le(d)er *o* chrome leather; –staal *o* chrome steel

chry'sant [kri.- of xri.'zɑnt] (-en) *v* ꕔ chrysanthemum

c.i. = *civiel-ingenieur*

ci'borie (-s en -iën) *v rk* ciborium

cicho'rei [si.xo.'rɑi] (-en) *m* & *v* chicory

'cider *m* cider

Cie. = *compagnie*

'cijfer (-s) *o* 1 figure; 2 cipher [in cryptography]; 3 ⟿ mark; *Arabische (Romeinse)* ~*s* Arabic (Roman) numerals; 'cijferen (cijferde, h. gecijferd) *vi* cipher; 'cijferkunst *v* arithmetic; –lijst (-en) *v* ⟿ marks list; –schrift (-en) *o* 1 numerical notation; 2 cipher, code; *in* ~ in cipher; –telegram (-men) *o* code message

cijns (cijnzen) *m* tribute, tribute-money

ciko'rei (-en) *m* & *v* = *cichorei*

ci'linder (-s) *m* cylinder; –bureau [-by.ro.] (-s) *o* roll-top desk; –inhoud *m* cubic capacity; –kop (-pen) *m* cylinder head; –vormig, ci'lindrisch cylindrical

cim'baal (-balen) *v* ♪ cymbal; cimba'list (-en) *m* ♪ cymbalist

'cineac, cine'ac (-s) *m* newsreel theatre;

cine'ast (-en) *m* film maker; 'cinema ('s) *m* cinema, picture-theatre; cinema'scope [-'sko.p] *in* ~ wide-screen

ci'pier (-s) *m* warder, jailer, gaoler, turnkey

ci'pres (-sen) *m* cypress

'circa ['sɪrka.] about, some [5 millions], circa

cir'cuit [sɪr'kvi.(t)] (-s) *o* circuit; *gesloten tv-*~ closed-circuit television

circu'laire [-'lɪːrə] (-s) *v* circular letter, circular

circu'latie [-'la.(t)si.] *v* circulation; *in* ~ *brengen* put into circulation; –bank (-en) *v* bank of issue; –stoornis (-sen) *v* circulatory disorder; –systeem [y = i.] (-stemen) *o* circulatory system; circu'leren (circuleerde, h. gecirculeerd) *vi* circulate; *laten* ~ circulate, send round [lists &]

circum'flex (-en) *m* & *o* circumflex (accent)

'circus (-sen) *o* & *m* circus; –artiest (-en) *m* circus performer; –directeur (-en) *m* circus master; –tent (-en) *v* circus tent

'cirkel (-s) *m* circle; –boog (-bogen) *m* arc of a circle; 'cirkelen (cirkelde, h. gecirkeld) *vi* circle; ~ *om de aarde* circle the earth; 'cirkelgang (-en) *m* circular course; *fig* circle; –omtrek (-ken) *m* circumference of a circle; –redenering (-en) *v* circular reasoning; –vormig circular; –zaag (-zagen) *v* ✗ circular saw

'cirruswolk (-en) *v* cirr(h)us (cloud)

cis [si.s] (-sen) *v* ♪ C sharp

cise'leren [s = z] (ciseleerde, h. geciseleerd) *vt* chase

ci'taat (-taten) *o* quotation

cita'del (-len en -s) *v* citadel

'citer (-s) *v* zither

ci'teren (citeerde, h. geciteerd) *vt* quote [a saying]; cite [book, author]; ⚡ cite, summon

ci'troen (-en) *m* & *v* lemon; –geel *aj* lemon-coloured; –limonade *v* lemonade; –pers (-en) *v* lemon-squeezer; –sap *o* lemon juice; –schijfje (-s) *o* slice of lemon; –schil (-len) *v* lemon peel; –vlinder (-s) *m* brimstone butterfly; –zuur *o* citric acid

'citrus (-sen) *m* citrus; –vrucht (-en) *v* citrus fruit

ci'viel 1 (b u r g e r l ij k) civil; 2 (b i l l ij k) moderate, reasonable [prices]; ci'vielinge'nieur [-Inʒe.-, -Inʒəni.'øː r] (-s) *m* civil engineer; civili'satie [-za.(t)si.] (-s) *v* civilization; civili'seren [s = z] (civiliseerde, h. geciviliseerd) *vt* civilize

clandes'tien [-dɛs-] clandestine, secret, illicit, illegal; *een* ~*e zender* R a pirate transmitter

classi'cisme *o* classicism;'classicus (-ci) *m* classicist

classifi'catie [-'ka.(t)si.] (-s) *v* classification; classifi'ceren (classificeerde, h. geclassifi-

ceerd) *vt* classify, class

claus (clausen, clauzen) *v* cue

claustrofo'bie *v* claustrophobia

clau'sule [s = z] (-s) *v* clause, proviso

claxon (-s) *m* horn, hooter; claxon'neren (claxonneerde, h. geclaxonneerd) *vi* sound the (one's) horn, honk, hoot

'clearinginstituut ['kli:rɪŋ-] (-tuten) *o* clearing institute

cle'matis [kle.-] (-sen) *v* clematis

cle'ment [kle.-] lenient, clement; cle'mentie [-(t)si.] *v* clemency, leniency

'clerus *m* clergy

cli'ché [kli.'ʃe.] (-s) *o* 1 plate [of type], block [of illustration]; 2 [photo] negative; 3 *fig* cliché, worn-out phrase, ready-made answer; cli'cheren (clicheerde, h. geclicheerd) *vt* stereotype

cli'ënt (-en) *m* 1 client [⚖ of a patrician &, ⚖ of a lawyer]; 2 $ customer [of a shop]; cliën'teel *v*, clien'tèle [kli.ɑ̃'tɛː lə] *v* clientele, customers, clients

cligno'teur [kli.ɲo.'tøː r] (-s) *m* 🚗 winker, trafficator, flashing signal (indicator)

'climax *m* climax

clo'set [s = z] (-s) *o* water-closet, F loo; –bak (-ken) *m* lavatory basin, lavatory pan; –borstel (-s) *m* lavatory brush; –papier *o* toilet-paper; –pot (-ten) *m* lavatory bowl

close-up [klo.'zũp] (-s) *m* close-up

clou [klu.] *m* feature, chief attraction

clown [klɔun] (-s) *m* clown, funny-man; –achtig, 'clownerig, clow'nesk clownish

club (-s) *v* club; –fauteuil [-fo.tœyj] (-s) *m* club (arm-)chair

cm = *centimeter*

Co. = *compagnon*

coa'litie [-(t)si.] (-s) *v* coalition

'coassistent (-en) *m* medical student who walks the hospital

'cobra ('s) *v* 🐍 cobra

coca'ïne *v* cocaine

'cockpit (-s) *m* cockpit

'cocktail ['kɔkte.l] (-s) *m* cocktail; –jurk (-en) *v* cocktail dress; –partij (-en) *v* cocktail party

co'con (-s) *m* cocoon

'code (-s) *m* code; co'deren (codeerde, h. gecodeerd) *vt* code; 'codetelegram (-men) *o* code message; –woord (-en) *o* code word

'codex (codices) *m* codex [*mv* codices]

codi'cil (-len) *o* codicil

codifi'catie [-'ka.(t)si.] (-s) *v* codification; codifi'ceren (codificeerde, h. gecodificeerd) *vt* codify

coëdu'catie [-'ka.(t)si.] *v* coeducation

coëffi'cient [ko.ɛfi.'sjɛnt] (-en) *m* coefficient

coëxi'stentie [-(t)si.] *v* coexistence;

coëxi'steren (coëxisteerde, h. gecoëxisteerd) *vi* coexist

co'gnac [kò'ɲɑk] *m* cognac, brandy

cognosse'ment [kònɔsə-] (-en) *o* = *connossement*

co'hesie [s = z] *v* cohesion

co'hort(e) (-en) *v* cohort

coif'feren [kʋɑ'fe:rə(n)] (coiffeerde, h. gecoiffeerd) *vt* dress (do) the hair; **coif'feur** (-s) *m* hairdresser; **coif'fure** (-s) *v* coiffure, hair-style, hairdo

coïnci'dentie [-(t)si.] (-s) *v* coincidence

coï'teren (coïteerde, h. gecoïteerd) *vi* cohabit, copulate; **'coïtus** *m* coition

cokes [ko.ks] *v* coke

col (-s) *m* 1 (b e r g p a s) col; 2 (k r a a g v. t r u i) polo-neck

col'bert [kɔl'bɛːr] *o* & *m* 1 (j a s j e) jacket; 2 (k o s t u u m) lounge-suit; **–kostuum** (-s) *o* lounge-suit

collabora'teur (-s) *m* collaborator; **collabo'ratie** [-'ra.(t)si.] *v* collaboration; **collabo'reren** (collaboreerde, h. gecollaboreerd) *vi* collaborate

col'lage [g = ʒ] (-s) *v* collage [a picture]

col'laps *m* collapse

collate'raal collateral

col'latie [-(t)si.] (-s) *v* collation; **collatio'neren** [-(t)si.o-] (collationeerde, h. gecollationeerd) *vt* collate, check

collec'tant (-en) *m* collector; **col'lecte** (-s en -n) *v* collection; *een ~ houden* make a collection; **–bus** (-sen) *v* collecting-box; **collec'teren** (collecteerde, h. gecollecteerd) **I** *vt* collect; **II** *va* make a collection; **col'lecteschaal** (-schalen) *v* collection-plate

col'lectie [kɔ'lɛksi.] (-s) *v* collection

collec'tief collective

col'lega ('s) *m* colleague

col'lege [g = ʒ] (-s) *o* 1 college [of cardinals &]; board [of guardians]; 2 ☞ lecture; *~ geven* ☞ give a course of lectures, lecture (on *over*); *~ lopen* (*volgen*) attend the lectures; **–gelden** *mv* lecture fees; **–zaal** (-zalen) *v* lecture-room, lecture-hall

collegi'aal [kɔle.gi.'a.l] (in a) brotherly (spirit)

'colli ('s) *o* package, bale, bag, barrel &

col'lier [kɔl'je.] (-s) *m* necklace

'collo ('s) *o* = *colli*

colon'nade (-s) *v* colonnade, portico

co'lonne (-s) *v* column; *auto-~* motorcade; *vijfde ~* fifth column; *lid van de vijfde ~* fifth columnist

colo'radokever (-s) *m* Colorado beetle

colpor'tage [g = ʒ] *v* colportage; **colpor'teren** (colporteerde, h. gecolporteerd) *vt* hawk, peddle [wares]; *fig* retail, spread [a report]; **colpor'teur** (-s) *m* 1 $ canvasser; 2 hawker [of

religious books &]

'coltrui (-en) *v* polo-neck sweater, roll-neck sweater

colum'barium (-s en -ria) *o* columbarium

Co'lumbia *o* Colombia

'coma ('s) *o* coma; **coma'teus** comatose

combat'tant (-en) *m* combatant

'combi ('s) *m* estate car, shooting-brake

combi'natie [-(t)si.] (-s) *v* combination; $ combine; **–vermogen** *o* power of combining

com'bine [kòm'bi.nə, -'bain] (-s) *v* combine; **combi'neren** (combineerde, h. gecombineerd) *vt* combine

'combo ('s) *m* combo [small jazz band]

comes'tibles [ko.mɛs'ti.bləs] *mv* comestibles, provisions; table delicacies

com'fort [kõ'fɔ:r, kòm'fɔ:r] *o* (conveniences conducive to) personal comfort; **comfor'tabel** [kòmfɔr'ta.bəl] **I** *aj* (v a n h u i z e n) commodious, supplied with all conveniences, with every comfort, comfortable; **II** *ad* conveniently, comfortably

comi'té [kòmi.'te.] (-s) *o* committee

comman'dant (-en) *m* ⚓ commandant, commander, officer in command; ⚓ captain; **comman'deren** (commandeerde, h. gecommandeerd) **I** *vt* order, command, be in command of; *hij commandeert iedereen maar* he orders people about; *zij laten zich niet ~* they will not be ordered about; **II** *vi* & *va* 1 command; *in* command; 2 order people about; **comman'deur** (-s) *m* commander [of an order of knighthood]

commandi'tair [-'tɛːr] *~ vennoot* sleeping (silent, dormant) partner; *~e vennootschap* limited partnership

com'mando ('s) 1 *o* (word of) command; 2 *m* (s p e c i a l e m i l i t a i r e g r o e p) commando; 3 *m* (l i d d a a r v a n) commando; zie verder: *bevel*; **–brug** (-gen) *v* ⚓ (navigating) bridge; **–post** (-en) *m* command post; **–toren** (-s) *m* conning-tower

comme il 'faut [kɔmi.l'fo.] correct, good form

commen'saal (-s en -salen) *m* boarder, lodger; ⚞ commensal

commen'taar (-taren) *m* & *o* commentary; comment; *~ overbodig* comment is needless; *~ leveren op* make comment on, comment (up)on; *zich van ~ onthouden* give no comment; **commentari'ëren** (commentarieerde, h. gecommentarieerd) *vt* comment upon; **commen'tator** (-s en -'toren) *m* commentator

com'mercie *v* commerce, business; *de ~* the business world; **commerci'eel** commercial

com'mies (-miezen) *m* 1 (departmental) clerk; 2 (v. d o u a n e) custom-house officer

commissari'aat (-riaten) *o* 1 commissionership; 2 police-station; **commis'saris** (-sen) *m* 1 commissioner; 2 (v. m a a t s c h a p p ij) supervisory director; 3 (v. o r d e) steward; 3 (v. p o l i t i e) superintendent of police, chief constable; *Hoge C~* High Commissioner; *~ der Koningin* provincial governor

com'missie (-s) *v* 1 committee, board; 2 $ commission; *~ van onderzoek* fact-finding commission; *~ van toezicht* board of visitors [of a school], visiting committee; *in ~* $ [sell] on commission; [send] on consignment; **–handel** *m* commission business; **–loon** *o* $ commission; **commissio'nair** [-'nɛːr] (-s) *m* 1 $ commission-agent; 2 commissionaire, porter; *~ in effecten* $ stockbroker; **commissori'aal** *iets ~ maken* refer sth. to a committee

commit'tent (-en) *m* principal

com'mode (-s) *v* chest of drawers

communau'tair [-no.'tɛːr] regarding the E.E.C., the Common Market

com'mune (-s) *v* commune

communi'cant (-en) *m rk* communicant

communi'catie [-'ka.(t)si.] (-s) *v* communication; **–middel** (-en) *o* means of communication; **–satelliet** (-en) *m* communication satellite; **–stoornis** (-sen) *v* failure of communication, breakdown in communications [between... and...]; **communi'ceren** (communiceerde, h. gecommuniceerd) *vi* 1 communicate; 2 *rk = te communie gaan*

com'munie (-s en -iën) *v* communion; *zijn ~ doen rk* receive Holy Communion for the first time; *de ~ ontvangen rk* take Holy Communion; *te ~ gaan rk* go to Communion; **–bank** (-en) *v* communion rail(s)

communi'qué [qu = k] (-s) *o* communiqué

commu'nisme *o* communism; **–ist** (-en) *m* communist; **–istisch** communist [party, Manifesto], communistic [system]

com'pact compact, dense

compa'gnie [gn = ɲ] (-s en -ieën) *v ⚓ & $* company; **–schap** (-pen) *v* $ partnership; **compa'gnon** [gn = ɲ] (-s) *m* $ partner

compa'rant (-en) *m* ⚖ appearer, party (to a suit); **compa'reren** (compareerde, h. en is gecompareerd) *vi* appear (in court); **compa'ritie** [-'ri.(t)si.] (-s en -iën) *v* appearance

comparti'ment (-en) *o* compartment

com'pendium (-s en -ia) *o* compendium

compen'satie [-pɛn'za.(t)si.] (-s) *v* compensation; **compen'seren** [s = z] (compenseerde, h. gecompenseerd) *vt* compensate, counterbalance, make up for

compe'tent competent; **compe'tentie** [-'tɛn(t)si.] (-s) *v* competence; *het behoort niet tot mijn ~* it is out of my domain

compe'titie [-'ti.(t)si.] (-s) *v* 1 competition; 2 *sp* league

compi'latie [-(t)si.] (-s) *v* compilation; **compi'lator** (-s en -'toren) *m* compiler; **compi'leren** (compileerde, h. gecompileerd) *vt & vi* compile

com'pleet complete

comple'ment (-en) *o* complement; **complemen'tair** [-'tɛːr] complementary

com'plet [kɔm'plɛ] (-s) *m & o* ensemble

comple'teren [kòmple.-] (completeerde, h. gecompleteerd) *vt* complete

com'plex (-en) *aj & o* complex; **complexi'teit** *v* complexity

compli'catie [-(t)si.] (-s) *v* complication; **compli'ceren** (compliceerde, h. gecompliceerd) *vt* complicate; zie ook: *gecompliceerd*

compli'ment (-en) *o* compliment; *de ~en aan allemaal* best remembrances (love) to all; *de ~en aan Mevrouw* kind regards to Mrs...; *~ van mij, de ~en van mij en zeg dat...* give him (them) my compliments and say that...; *zonder ~* without (standing upon) ceremony; *zonder veel (verdere) ~en* [dismiss him] without more ado, off-hand; *zijn ~ afsteken (bij de dames)* pay one's respects to the ladies; *geen ~en afwachten van iem.* stand no nonsense from sbd.; *de ~en doen (maken)* give (make, pay, send) one's compliments; *veel ~en hebben* be very exacting; put on airs; *iem. een (zijn) ~ maken over iets* compliment sbd. (up)on sth.; *hij houdt van ~en maken* he is given to paying compliments; **complimen'teren** (complimenteerde, h. gecomplimenteerd) *vt iem. ~* compliment sbd. [on, upon sth.]; **complimen'teus** complimentary; **compli'mentje** (-s) *o* compliment; *~s maken* turn compliments

compo'nent (-en) *m* component

compo'neren (componeerde, h. gecomponeerd) *vt & vi* compose; **compo'nist** (-en) *m* composer; **compo'sitie** [-'zi.(t)si.] (-s) *v* composition

com'post *o & m* compost

com'pote [kòm'pɔ(ː)t] (-s) *m & v* compote, stewed fruit

com'pressor (-s en -'soren) *m* ⚒ compressor

compri'meren (comprimeerde, h. gecomprimeerd) *vt* compress, condense

compro'mis [-'mɪs, -'mi.] (-sen) *o* compromise; *een ~ sluiten* compromise; *een ~voorstel* a compromise proposal

compromit'teren (compromitteerde, h. gecompromitteerd) **I** *vt* compromise; **II** *vr zich ~* compromise oneself, commit oneself

comptabili'teit *v* 1 accountability; 2 accountancy; audit-office

com'puter [-'pju.-] (-s) *m* computer; **compu-**

teri'seren [s = z] (computeriseerde, h. gecomputeriseerd) *vt* computerize; **–ring** *v* computerization

con'caaf concave

concen'tratie [-(t)si.] (-s) *v* concentration; **–kamp** (-en) *o* concentration camp; **–vermogen** *o* power(s) of concentration; **concen'treren** (concentreerde, h. geconcentreerd) **I** *vt* concentrate [troops, power, attention &, in chemistry], focus [one's attention &]; **II** *vr zich* ~ concentrate

con'centrisch concentric

con'cept (-en) *o* (rough) draft

con'ceptie [- 'stpsi.] (-s) *v* conception

con'cept-reglement [-re.-] (-en) *o* draft regulations

con'cern [kòn'sɔ.(r)n] (-s) *o* concern

con'cert (-en) *o* 1 concert; 2 recital [by one performer]; 3 concerto [for solo instrument]; **concer'teren** (concerteerde, h. geconcerteerd) *vi* give a concert; **con'certmeester** (-s) *m* leader; **–stuk** (-ken) *o* concert piece; **–vleugel** (-s) *m* concert grand; **–zaal** (-zalen) *v* concert hall; **–zanger** (-s) *m*, **–zangeres** (-sen) *v* concert singer

con'cessie (-s) *v* concession; ~ *aanvragen* apply for a concession; ~*s doen* make concessions; ~ *verlenen* grant a concession; **–houder** (-s) *m*, **concessio'naris** (-sen) *m* concessionaire

conciërge [kòn'sjɛrʒə] (-s) *m* door-keeper, hall-porter, care-taker [of flats &]

con'cilie (-s en -iën) *o* council [of prelates]

concipi'ëren (concipieerde, h. geconcipieerd) *vt* draft [a plan]

con'claaf (-claven) *o*, **conclave** (-n) *o* conclave

conclu'deren (concludeerde, h. geconcludeerd) *vt* conclude (from *uit*); **con'clusie** [s = z] *v* conclusion

concor'daat (-daten) *o* concordat

concor'dantie [-(t)si.] (-s en -iën) *v* (Bible) concordance

con'cours [- 'ku:r(s)] (-en) *o* & *m* competition; ~ *hippique* [-ku:ri'pi.k] horse show

con'creet concrete; **concreti'seren** [s = z] (concretiseerde, h. geconcretiseerd) **I** *vt* shape [one's attitude, a plan]; **II** *vr zich* ~ take shape, materialize

concubi'naat *o* concubinage; **concu'bine** (-s) *v* concubine, mistress

concur'rent [-ky.'rɛnt] (-en) **I** *aj* ordinary [creditor]; **II** *m* competitor, rival; **concur'rentie** [-(t)si.] *v* competition, rivalry; **–beding** *o* competition clause; **concur'reren** (concurreerde, h. geconcurreerd) *vi* compete [with...]; **–d** competitive [price]; rival [firms]

conden'satie [- 'za.(t)si.] *v* condensation; **conden'sator** (-s en - 'toren) *m* condenser;

conden'seren (condenseerde, *vt* h., *vi* is gecondenseerd) condense; *gecondenseerde melk* evaporated milk; **con'densstreep** (-strepen) *v* ✈ contrail, vapour trail

con'ditie [-(t)si.] (-s en -iën) *v* (v o o r-w a a r d e) condition; *onze* ~*s zijn...* our terms are...; *in goede* ~ [kept] in good repair [of a house &]; in good form [of a person]; in good condition [of a horse &]; **–training** [-tre.-] *v* fitness training

conditio'neren (conditioneerde, h. geconditioneerd) *vt* 1 condition; 2 stipulate

condolé'ance [- 'ɑsə] (-s) *v* condolence, sympathy; **–bezoek** (-en) *o* call of condolence; **–brief** (-brieven) *m* letter of condolence, letter of sympathy; **condole'antie** [-(t)si.] (-s) *v* condolence, sympathy; **condo'leren** (condoleerde, h. gecondoleerd) *vt* condole, express one's sympathy; *iem.* ~ condole with sbd. [on a loss], sympathize with sbd. [in his loss]; *ik condoleer u van harte* accept my heartfelt sympathy

con'doom (-domen) *o* condom, sheath, **F** French letter

'condor (-s) *m* condor

conduc'teur (-s) *m* 1 (v. t r e i n) guard; 2 (v. b u s, t r a m) conductor, ticket-collector; **conduc'trice** (-s) *v* conductress, **F** clippie

con'duitelijst [- 'dʌi.-] (-en) *v*, **–staat** (-staten) *m* ✠ confidential report

con'fectie [- 'fɛksi.] *v* ready-made clothing, ready-made clothes, **F** off the peg (clothes), reach-me-downs; **–pak** (-ken) *o* ready-made suit

confede'ratie [-fe.də'ra.(t)si.] (-s) *v* confederation, confederacy

conferen'cier [kònfe.rã'sje.] (-s) *m* (v. c a b a-r e t) compere

confe'rentie [-fə'rɛn(t)si.] (-s) *v* conference, discussion, **F** palaver; **–tafel** (-s) *v* conference table; **–tolk** (-en) *m* conference interpreter; **–zaal** (-zalen) *v* conference room; **confe'reren** (confereerde, h. geconfereerd) *vi* confer (consult) together, hold a conference; ~ *over* confer upon

con'fessie (-s) *v* confession; **confessio'neel** denominational [teaching &]

con'fetti *m* confetti

confi'dentie [-(t)si.] (-s) *v* confidence; **confidenti'eel** confidential

confis'catie [-(t)si.] (-s) *v* confiscation, seizure; **confis'queren** [qu = k] (confisqueerde, h. geconfisqueerd) *vt* confiscate, seize

confi'turen *mv* preserves, jam

con'flict (-en) *o* conflict; *in* ~ *komen met...* come into conflict with, conflict (clash) with; **–situatie** [-(t)si.] (-s) *v* situation of conflict,

conflict situation

con'form in conformity with; **confor'meren** (conformeerde, h. geconformeerd) *vr zich ~* conform oneself; **confor'misme** *o* conformity; **-ist** (-en) *m* conformist; **-istisch** conformist

con'frater (-s) *m* colleague, confrère

confron'tatie [-(t)si.] (-s) *v* confrontation; **confron'teren** (confronteerde, h. geconfronteerd) *vt* confront [with...]; *geconfronteerd met de werkelijkheid* faced with reality

con'fuus confused, abashed, ashamed

con'gé [kõ'ʒe.] *o* & *m* dismissal; *iem. zijn ~ geven* F give sbd. the sack, dismiss sbd; *hij kreeg zijn ~* F he got the sack, he was dismissed

con'gestie [kɔŋ'gɛsti.](-s) *v* congestion[2] [ℑ, of traffic &]

conglome'raat [kɔŋglo.-] (-raten) *o* conglomerate

congre'gatie [-gre.'ga.(t)si.] (-s) *v* congregation; *rk* ook: sodality [for the laity]

con'gres [-'grɛs] (-sen) *o* congress; **-lid** (-leden) *o* member of a (the) congress; (v. h. Am. C o n g r e s) Member of Congress, Congressman; **congres'seren** (congresseerde, h. gecongresseerd) *vi* meet, hold a meeting, sit (in congress); **con'grestolk** (-en) *m* congress interpreter

congru'ent congruent; **-ie** [-(t)si.] (-s) *v* congruence

coni'feer (-feren) *m* ℀ conifer

con'junctie [-'jüŋksi.] (-s) *v* conjunction; **'conjunctief** (-tieven) *m* subjunctive; **conjunc'tuur** (-turen) *v* conjuncture; $ economic (trade, business) conditions; state of the market, state of trade (and industry); (p e r i o d e) trade cycle, business cycle

con'nectie [kɔ'nɛksi.] (-s) *v* connection; *~s hebben* have influence [with the minister]

connosse'ment (-en) *o* bill of lading, B/L

'correctdor (-s en -toren) *m* ⬡ second master, vice-principal

consa'creren (consacreerde, h. geconsacreerd) *vt rk* consecrate

consciënti'eus [-ʃɪnsi.'ø.s] conscientious

con'scriptie [-'skrɪpsi.] *v* conscription

conse'cratie [-se.'kra.(t)si.] (-s) *v rk* consecration; **conse'creren** (consecreerde, h. geconsecreerd) *vt rk* consecrate

conse'quent [-sə'kvɛnt] (logically) consistent; **conse'quentie** [-(t)si.] (-s) *v* 1 (logical) consistency; 2 (g e v o l g) consequence

conserva'tief I *aj* conservative; II (-tieven) *m* conservative; **conserva'tisme** *o* conservatism

conser'vator (-s en -'toren) *m* custodian, curator [of a museum]

conserva'torium (-s en -ria) *o* school of music,

conservatoire, conservatory

con'serven *mv* preserves; **-fabriek** (-en) *v* preserving factory, canning factory, cannery; **-industrie** (-ieën) *v* preserving industry, canning industry; **conser'veren** (conserveerde, h. geconserveerd) *vt* preserve, keep

conside'ratie [-(t)si.] (-s) *v* consideration

consig'natie [-si.'ɲa.(t)si.] (-s) *v* consignment; *in ~ zenden* send on consignment, consign

con'signe [-'si.ɲə] (-s) *o* 1 orders, instructions; 2 password

consig'neren [-si.'ɲe:-] (consigneerde, h. geconsigneerd) *vt* 1 $ consign [goods]; 2 ⚔ confine [troops] to barracks

consi'storie (-s) *o* consistory; **-kamer** (-s) *v* vestry

con'sole [-'sɔ:lə] (-s) *v* 1 △ console; 2 console table

consoli'datie [-(t)si.] *v* consolidation; **consoli'deren** (consolideerde, h. geconsolideerd) *vt* consolidate

'consonant (-en) *v* consonant

con'sorten *mv* associates; *X en ~ X and his company*, F *X and his likes*

con'sortium [-tsi.üm] (-s) *o* $ consortium, syndicate, ring

con'stant constant; **-e** (-n) *v* constant

consta'teren (constateerde, h. geconstateerd) *vt* state; ascertain, establish [a fact]; ℑ diagnose; *er werd geconstateerd dat...* ook: it was found that...; **-ring** (-en) *v* statement; *tot de ~ komen dat* find that, observe that

constel'latie [-(t)si.] (-s) *v* (s t e r r e n b e e l d) constellation; (s i t u a t i e) situation, F line-up

conster'natie [-(t)si.] (-s) *v* consternation, dismay

consti'patie [-(t)si.] *v* constipation

constitu'eren (constitueerde, h. geconstitueerd) I *vt* constitute; II *vr zich tot... ~* constitute themselves into...; **consti'tutie** [-(t)si.] (-s) *v* constitution; **constitutio'neel** constitutional

construc'teur (-s) *m* designer; **con'structie** [-'strüksi.] (-s) *v* construction; **construc'tief** constructive; **constru'eren** (construeerde, h. geconstrueerd) *vt* construct

'consul (-s) *m* consul; **consu'laat** (-laten) *o* consulate; **~-gene'raal** (consulaten-generaal) *o* consulate general; **consu'lair** [-'lɛ:r] consular

consu'lent (-en) *m* 1 adviser; 2 advisory expert

'consul-gene'raal (consuls-generaal) *m* consul general

con'sult (-en) *o* consultation; **consul'tatie** [-(t)si.] (-s) *v* consultation; **-bureau** [-by.ro.] (-s) *o* health centre, (infant) welfare centre; **consul'teren** (consulteerde, h. geconsulteerd) *vt* consult [a doctor]; *~d geneesheer* consulting

physician
consu'ment [s = z] (-en) *m* consumer;
–enbond (-en) *m* consumers' association,
consumers' union; **consu'meren** (consu-
meerde, h. geconsumeerd) *vt* consume;
con'sumptie [-'züm(p)si.] (-s) *v* 1 consumption; 2 food and drinks; **–goederen** *mv*
consumer goods; **–maatschappij** *v* consumer
society
con'tact (-en) *o* contact, touch; ~ *hebben met* be
in contact with, be in touch with; ~ *maken*
(*nemen, opnemen*) *met* make contact with, contact
[sbd.]; ~*en leggen* make contacts; **–doos**
(-dozen) *v* (wall) socket, plug-box; **–draad**
(-draden) *m* contact wire; **–lens** (-lenzen) *v*
contact lens; **–man** (-nen en -lieden) contact
(man); **–sleuteltje** (-s) *o* ignition key
con'tainer [-'te.nər] (-s) *m* (freight) container
contami'natie [-(t)si.] (-s) *v* contamination,
blend
con'tant I *aj* cash; *à* ~ for cash; ~*e betaling* cash
payment; **II** *ad* ~ *betalen* pay cash; **III** *mv* ~*en*
ready money, (hard) cash
contempla'tief contemplative, meditative
contempo'rain [-tāpo'ri.] contemporary
con'tent content(ed), happy
conti'nent (-en) *o* continent; **continen'taal**
continental
contin'gent [-tɪŋ'gɛnt] (-en) *o* ✂ contingent²; $
quota²; **contingen'teren** (contingenteerde, h.
gecontingenteerd) *vt* establish quotas for
[imports], quota, limit by quotas; **–ring** *v* quota
system, quota restriction, quota
conti'nu continuous; **–bedrijf** (-drijven) *o*
continuous industry; **continu'eren** (conti-
nueerde, h. gecontinueerd) *vt* & *vi* continue;
continuï'teit *v* continuity;
con'tour [-'tu:r] (-en) *m* contour, outline
'contra contra, versus, against
'contrabande *v* contraband (goods)
'contrabas (-sen) *v* double-bass
con'tract (-en) *o* contract; **contrac'tant** (-en)
m contracting party; **con'tractbreuk** (-en)
v breach of contract; **contrac'teren** (con-
tracteerde, h. gecontracteerd) *vi* & *vt* contract
(for)
con'tractie [-'traksi.] (-s) *v* contraction
contractu'eel I *aj* contractual; **II** *ad* by contract
'contradans (-en) *m* contra dance, contredance
contra'dictie [-'dɪksi.] (-s) *v* contradiction
'contrafagot (-ten) *m* ♪ double-bassoon
'contragewicht (-en) *o* counterpoise, counter-
weight
'contra-indicatie [-(t)si.] (-s) *v* counter indication
'contramerk (-en) *o* 1 pass-out check (ticket); 2
countermark

'contramine *v in de* ~ *zijn* $ speculate for a fall;
hij is altijd in de ~ he is always in the humour
of opposition
'contrapunt (-en) *o* counterpoint
'contrarevolutie [-re.vo.ly.(t)si.] (-s) *v* counter-
revolution
contrari'ëren (contrarieerde, h. gecontrarieerd)
vt act (go) contrary to the wishes of, thwart the
plans of
contrasig'neren [-si.'ɲe: rə(n)] (contrasig-
neerde, h. gecontrasigneerd) *vt* countersign
'contraspionage [g = ʒ] *v* counter-espionage
con'trast (-en) *o* contrast; **constras'teren**
(contrasteerde, h. gecontrasteerd) *vi* contrast
contre'coeur [kõtrə'kœ: r] *à* ~ half heartedly
con'treien *mv* regions; *in deze* ~ in these parts
contribu'ant (-en) *m* subscribing member;
contribu'eren (contribueerde, h. gecontri-
bueerd) *vt* & *vi* contribute; **contri'butie**
[-(t)si.] (-s) *v* subscription
con'trole [-'trɔ: lə] (-s) *v* check(ing), supervision, control; ~ *uitoefenen op de...* check the...;
–kamer (-s) *v* control room; **–post** (-en) *m*
checkpoint; **contro'leren** [-tro.-] (contro-
leerde, h. gecontroleerd) *vt* check, examine,
verify, control; test; supervise; **contro'leur**
(-s) *m* 1 (i n 't a l g.) controller; 2 (a a n
s c h o u w b u r g &) ticket inspector
contro'verse (-n en -s) *v* controversy; **contro-
versi'eel** controversial
conveni'ëren (convenieerde, h. geconvenieerd)
vi suit; *het convenieert mij niet* I cannot afford it;
als het u convenieert if it suits your convenience
con'ventie [-(t)si.] (-s) *v* convention;
conventio'neel conventional, orthodox
conver'geren (convergeerde, h. geconver-
geerd) *vi* converge
conver'satie [-'za.(t)si.] (-s) *v* conversation; *hij
heeft geen* ~ 1 he has no conversational powers;
2 he has no friends; *zij hebben veel* ~ they see
much company; **–les** (-sen) *v* conversation
lesson; **conver'seren** [s = z] (converseerde, h.
geconverseerd) *vi* converse
con'versie [s = z] *v* conversion; **conver'teerbaar** convertible; **conver'teren** (conver-
teerde, h. geconverteerd) *vt* convert [into...];
convertibili'teit *v* convertibility
con'vex convex
convo'catie [-'ka.(t)si.] (-s) *v* 1 convocation; 2
notice (of a meeting); **convo'ceren**
[-'se: rə(n)] (convoceerde, h. geconvoceerd)
vt convene, convoke
coöpe'ratie [ko.o.pə'ra.(t)si.] (-s) *v* 1 co-operation; 2 co-operative stores; **coöpera'tief**
co-operative
coöp'tatie [ko.ɔp'ta.(t)si.] (-s) *v* co-optation
coördi'naten [ko.ɔr-] *mv* co-ordinates;

coördi'natie [-(t)si.] (-s) *v* co-ordination; coördi'neren (coördineerde, h. gecoördineerd) *vt* co-ordinate

copi'eus **I** *aj* plentiful [dinner]; **II** *ad* ~ *dineren* partake of a plentiful dinner

'coproductie [-düksi.] (-s) *v* co-production

copu'leren (copuleerde, h. gecopuleerd) *vi* copulate

Co'rinthe *o* Corinth; Co'rinthiër (-s) *m* Corinthian; Co'rinthisch Corinthian

'corner (-s) *m sp* & $ corner

coro'nair [-'nɛːr] coronary [thrombosis &]

corpo'ratie [-(t)si.] (-s) *v* corporate body, corporation; corpora'tief corporative

corps [kɔːr, kɔrps] (corpora) *o* corps, body; zie ook: *studentencorps*; *het* ~ *diplomatique* the Diplomatic Corps, the Diplomatic Body; *het* ~ *leraren* the teaching staff; *en* ~ in a body

corpu'lent corpulent, stout; –ie [-(t)si.] *v* corpulence, stoutness

corpuscu'lair [-lɛ.r] corpuscular

cor'rect correct; –heid *v* correctness; cor'rectie [-'rɛksi.] (-s) *v* correction; –teken (-s) *o* correction mark; cor'rector (-s en -'toren) *m* (proof-)reader, corrector

correspon'dent (-en) *m* correspondent; [foreign] correspondence clerk; correspon'dentie [-(t)si.] (-s) *v* correspondence; correspon'deren (correspondeerde, h. gecorrespondeerd) *vi* correspond

corri'dor [-'dɔːr] (-s) *m* corridor

corri'geren [g = g en ʒ] (corrigeerde, h. gecorrigeerd) *vt* & *vi* correct[2]; mark [papers], read [proofs]

cor'rosie [s = z] *v* corrosion

corrum'peren (corrumpeerde, h. gecorrumpeerd) *vt* & *vi* corrupt; cor'rupt corrupt; –ie [-'rüpsi.] (-s) *v* corruption

cor'sage [-'sa.ʒə] (-s) *v* & *o* corsage

corse'let (-s en -ten) *o* corslet

'corso ('s) *m* & *o* parade, procession

cor'vee (-s) *v* 1 ⚔ fatigue duty; fatigue party; 2 *het is een* ~ it's quite a job; ~ *hebben* do the chores

cory'fee [ko:ri.-] (-feeën) *m* & *v* coryphaeus; coryphee

cos. = *cosinus*; 'cosinus *m* cosine

cos'metica *mv* cosmetics

'Costa 'Rica *o* Costa Rica

'cotangens *v* cotangent

cote'rie (-s en -ieën) *v* coterie, clique, (exclusive) set

cou'chette [ku.'ʃɛtə] (-s) *v* berth

cou'lant [ou = u.] $ accommodating

cou'lisse [ku.'lɪsə, ku.'li.sə] (-n en -s) *v* sidescene, wing; *achter de* ~*n* behind the scenes, in the wings; als *aj* back-stage [influence]

cou'loir [ku.'lwaːr] (-s) *m* lobby [of Lower House]

coup [ku.] (-s) *m* coup, stroke, move

coupe [ku.p] (-s) *v* 1 cut [of dress]; 2 cup [as a drink]

cou'pé [ku.'pe.] (-s) *m* 1 (v . t r e i n) compartment; 2 (r ij t u i g) coupé, brougham

'coupenaad ['ku.p-] (-naden) *m* dart

cou'peren [ou = u.] (coupeerde, h. gecoupeerd) **I** *vt* cut [the cards]; make cuts [in a play]; forestall [disagreeable consequences]; dock [a tail], crop [ears]; *een gecoupeerde staart* a bobtail; **II** *va* cut [the cards]

cou'peur (-s) *m*, cou'peuse [s = z] (-s) *v* cutter

cou'plet [ou = u.] (-ten) *o* stanza; (t w e e - r e g e l i g) couplet

cou'pon [ou = u.] (-s) *m* 1 $ coupon; remnant [of dress-material], cutting; –blad (-bladen) *o* coupon-sheet; –boekje (-s) *o* book of coupons, book of tickets

cou'pure [ou = u.] (-s) *v* cut; *in* ~*s van* £ *5* en £ *10* in denominations of £ 5 and £ 10

1 cou'rant [ou = u.] **I** *aj* current, marketable; **II** *o Nederlands* ~ Dutch currency

2 cou'rant [ou = u.] (-en) *v* = *krant*

cour'bette [ku:r'bɛt] (↖s) *v* curvet

cou'reur [ou = u.] (-s) *m* 1 (m e t a u t o) racing driver, racing motorist; 2 (m e t m o t o r) racing motor-cyclist; 3 (m e t f i e t s) racing cyclist, racer

cour'tage [ku.r'ta.ʒə] (-s) *v* brokerage

courti'sane [ku.rti.'za.nə] (-s) *v* courtesan

cou'vert [ku.'vɛːr] (-s) *o* 1 cover [of letter & plate, napkin, knife and fork]; 2 envelope; *onder* ~ under cover

cou'veuse [ku.'vø.zə] (-s) *v* incubator; –kind (-eren) *o* premature baby

'coveren ['küvərə(n)] (coverde, h. gecoverd) *vt* retread [a tyre]

'cowboy ['kɔubɔi] (-s) *m* cowboy; –film (-s) *m* cowboy film, western; –pak (-ken) *o* cowboy suit

c.q. = *casu quo*

cra'paud [krɑ'po.] (-s) *m* easy-chair

craque'lé [krɑkə'le.] *o* crackling; craque'leren (craqueleerde, h. gecraqueleerd) *vt* craze

'crawl(slag) ['krɔ:l-] (-slagen) *m* crawl(-stroke)

cre'atie [kre.'a.(t)si.] (-s) *v* creation; crea'tief creative, originative; creativi'teit *v* creativeness; crea'tuur (-turen) *o* creature

crèche [krɛ:ʃ] (-s) *v* crèche, day-nursery

'crediet *o* credit; credi'teren (crediteerde, h. gecrediteerd) *vt iem.* ~ *voor* place [a sum] to sbd.'s credit, credit sbd. with; credi'teur (-s en -en) *m* creditor; 'creditnota ('s) *v* credit note; –zijde (-n) *v* credit side, creditor side

'credo ('s) *o* credo [during Mass]; [Apostles',

political] creed
cre′ëren (creëerde, h. gecreëerd) *vt* create [a part &]
cre′matie [-(t)si.] (-s) *v* cremation; **crema′torium** (-s en -ria) *o* crematorium, crematory
crème [krɛːm] **I** (-s) *v* cream; **II** *aj* cream (-coloured)
cre′meren [kre.-] (cremeerde, h. gecremeerd) *vt* cremate
cre′ool (-olen) *m*, **creoolse** (-n) *v* Creole
creo′soot [kre.o.′zo.t] *m* & *o* creosote
crêpe [krɛːp] *m* crêpe [ook = crêpe rubber]
′crêpepapier [krɛːp-] (-en) *o* crêpe paper
cre′peren (crepeerde, is gecrepeerd) *vi* die [of animals]
cric (-s) *m* (car, lifting) jack
′cricket [′krɪkət] *o* cricket
criminali′teit *v* 1 (h e t   m i s d a d i g e) criminality; 2 (d e   m i s d a a d   c o l l e c t i e f) crime; *het toenemen van de* ~ the increase in crime; zie ook: *jeugdcriminaliteit*; **crimi′neel** criminal; (*de*) *criminele jeugd* delinquent youth; **criminolo′gie** *v* criminology; **crimino′loog** (-logen) *m* criminologist
crino′line (-s) *v* crinoline, hoop petticoat, hoop
′crisis [′kri.zɪs] (-sen en crises) *v* crisis* [*mv* crises], critical stage, turning-point; (i n z. e c o n o m i s c h) depression, slump; (n o o d-t o e s t a n d   v.   d.   l a n d b o u w &) emergency; *tot een* ~ *komen* come to a crisis (a head); **–maatregel** (-en) *m* emergency measure; **–tijd** (-en) *m* time of crisis; *de* ~ the depression
cri′terium (-ria) *o* criterion [*mv* criteria], test
criti′caster (-s) *m* criticaster; **′criticus** (-ci) *m* critic
cro′quant [qu = k] crisp
1 cro′quet [kro.′kɛt] (-ten) *v* (v o e d s e l) croquette
2 ′croquet [′krɔkət] *o* *sp* croquet
cru [kry.] crude, blunt
cruci′fix (-en) *o* crucifix
cruise [kru:z] (-s) *m* cruise
crypt(e) [y = ɪ] (-en) *v* crypt
c.s. = *cum suis*
′Cuba *o* Cuba; **Cu′baan** (-banen) *m* Cuban; **–s** Cuban
culi′nair [-′nɛːr] culinary
culmi′natie [-(t)si.] (-s) *v* culmination; **–punt** (-en) *o* culminating point[2]; **culmi′neren** (culmineerde, h. geculmineerd) *vi* culminate[2]
culti′veren (cultiveerde, h. gecultiveerd) *vt* cultivate
cul′ture (-s) *v* (v e r b o u w   v.   g e w a s s e n   i n   h e t   g r o o t) plantation
cultu′reel cultural

′cultus (culten) *m* cult[2]
cul′tuur (-turen) *v* 1 (b e s c h a v i n g) culture; 2 (t e e l t) culture, cultivation; 3 culture [= set of bacteria]; **–filosoof** (-sofen) *m* social philosopher; **–geschiedenis** *v* social history; **–historicus** (-ci) *m* social historian; **–his′torisch** socio-historical; **–volk** (-en en -eren) *o* civilized nation
cum ′suis [küm′sy.ɪs] and others
cumu′latie [-(t)si.] (-s) *v* accumulation; **cumula′tief** cumulative
′cumuluswolk (-en) *v* cumulus (cloud)
cup (-s) *m* 1 *sp* cup; 2 (v. b e h a) cup
′Cupido, ′cupido (′s) *m* Cupid
cura′tele *v* guardianship; *onder* ~ *staan* be in ward, be under guardianship; *onder* ~ *stellen* put in ward, deprive of the management of one's affairs; **cu′rator** (-s en - ′toren) *m* 1 guardian; curator, keeper [of a museum &]; 2 governor [of a school]; 3 ⚖ trustee, official receiver [in bankruptcy]; **cura′torium** (-ria) *o* board of governors [of a school]
1 ′curie *v* *rk* [Roman] curia
2 cu′rie *v* (v. r a d i o a c t i e v e   s t r a l i n g) curie
curi′eus curious, odd, queer; **curiosi′teit** [s = z] (-en) *v* curiosity
cur′sief (-sieven) **I** *o* italic type, italics; **II** *aj* in italics, italicized; **III** *ad* in italics; **–je** (-s) *o* (regular) column [in newspaper]; **–letters** *mv* italics
cur′sist [-′zɪst] (-en) *m* student of a course (of lectures)
cursi′veren (cursiveerde, h. gecursiveerd) *vt* italicize, print in italics; *wij* ~ the italics are ours, our italics
′cursus [-züs, -zəs] (-sen) *m* course, curriculum; [evening] classes
′curve (-n) *v* curve
′custos (custodes) *m* 1 keeper, custodian; 2 catchword
c.v. = *commanditaire vennootschap*; *centrale verwarming*
cyaan′kali [y = i.] *m* cyanide, prussic acid
cyber′netica [si.bɪr′ne.ti.ka.] cybernetics; **cyber′netisch** cybernetic
cy′claam [y = i.] (-clamen) *v* cyclamen
Cy′claden [y = i.] *de* ~ the Cyclades
′cyclisch [y = i.] cyclic(al)
cyclo′naal [y = i.] cyclonic(al); **cy′cloon** (-clonen) *m* cyclone
cy′cloop [y = i.] (-clopen) *m* cyclops
cyclo′style [si.klo.′sti.l] (-s) *m* cyclostyle; **cyclosty′leren** (cyclostyleerde, h. gecyclostyleerd) *vt* cyclostyle
cyclo′tron [y = i.] (-s) *o* cyclotron
′cyclus [y = i.] (-sen en cycli) *m* cycle

'**cynicus** [y = i.] (-ci) *m* cynic; '**cynisch**
cynical; **cy'nisme** *o* cynicism
'**cypers** [si.pərs] ~*e kat* Cyprian cat
Cypri'oot [y = i.] (-oten) *m* Cypriot, Cyprian;

'**Cyprisch** Cyprian, Cypriot; '**Cyprus** *o*
Cyprus
'**cyste** ['ki.stə] (-n) *v* cyst
cytolo'gie [y = i.] *v* cytology

D

d [de.] ('s) *v* d

daad (daden) *v* deed, act, action, feat, achievement; *man van de* ~ man of action; *de ~ bij het woord voegen* suit the action to the word; zie ook: *betrappen* & *raad;* **daad'werkelijk** 1 (w e r k e l ij k, m e t t e r d a a d) actual; 2 (k r a c h t i g) active [support &]

daags I *aj* daily; *mijn ~e jas* my everyday (weekday) coat; **II** *ad* by day; *des anderen* ~, ~ *daarna* the next day; ~ *te voren* the day before, the previous day; *driemaal* ~ three times a day

'daalder (-s) *m* [coin symbol] Dutch coin; *f* 1,50-worth

daar I *ad* there; **II** *cj* as (i n v ó ó r z i n), because (i n n a z i n); **daaraan'volgend** following, next; **daar'achter** behind it (that), at the back of that; **–be'neden** 1 under it; 2 down there; *...van 21 jaar en* ~ *...*and under; **'daarbij, daar'bij** 1 near it; 2 over and above this, besides, moreover, in addition, at that; *50 gedood,* ~ *3 officieren* including (among them, among whom) three officers; *zij hebben* ~ *het leven verloren* they have lost their lives in it; **daar'binnen** within, in there; **–'boven** 1 up there, above; 2 over it; *50%en iets* ~ and something over; *sommen van £ 500 en* ~ and upwards; *God* ~ God above, God on high; **–'buiten** outside; zie verder: *buiten;* **'daardoor, daar'door** 1 (p l a a t s e l ij k) through it; 2 (o o r z a k e l ij k) by that, by doing so, by these means; **daaren'boven** moreover, besides; **–'tegen** on the other hand, on the contrary; *hij is..., zijn broer* ~ *is zeer...* ook: whereas his brother is very...; **'daargelaten** leaving aside; *dat* ~ apart from that; *nog* ~ *dat...* let alone (not to mention) that; **daar'ginder, daar'ginds** over there; out there [in Africa &]; **'daarheen, daar'heen** there, thither; **'daarin** in there; in it (this, that); **daar'langs** along that road (path, line &); **'daarlaten** (liet 'daar, h. 'daargelaten) *vt* *dat wil ik nog* ~ this I'll leave out of consideration. Zie ook: *daargelaten;* **'daarme(d)e, daar'me(d)e** with that; **'daarna, daar'na** after that; in the second place; **'daarnaar** by that, accordingly; **'daarnaast, daar'naast** beside it, at (by) the side of it; next to it; **daar'net** just now; **'daarom, daar'om** therefore, for that reason; ~ *ga ik er niet heen* ook: that's why I am not going; **daarom'heen** around (it); about it; **'daaromstreeks** thereabouts; **'daaromtrent, daarom'trent I** *prep* about that, concerning

that; **II** *ad* thereabouts; **'daaronder, daar'onder** 1 under it (that); underneath, 2 among them; **'daarop** 1 on it, on that; 2 there-upon, upon (after) this; **daarop'volgend** following, next; **'daarover, daar'over** 1 over it (that), across it; 2 about (concerning) that, on that subject; **'daartegen, daar'tegen** against that; **daartegen'over** opposite; ~ *staat dat...* but then..., on the other hand..., however...; **'daartoe, daar'toe** for it, for that purpose, to that end; **'daartussen, daar'tussen** between (them), among them; *en niets* ~ and nothing in between; **'daaruit, daar'uit** out (of it), from that (this), thence; **'daarvan, daar'van** 1 of that; 2 from that; **'daarvandaan, daarvan'daan** away from there, thence; (r e d e n) that's why, therefore; 1 **'daarvoor, daar'voor** for that; for it; for that purpose; ~ *komt hij* that is what he has come for; 2 **daar'voor** before (that); before it (them)

daas dazed; foolish [plans]

1 **dacht** (dachten) V.T. v. *denken*

2 **dacht** *mij* ~ V.T. van *dunken*

dactylosco'pie [y = i.] *v* finger-print identification; **dactylo'scopisch** finger-print [examination &]

'dactylus [y = i.] (-tyli en -tylen) *m* dactyl

'dadel (-s) *v* date; **–boom** (-bomen) *m* date tree

'dadelijk I *aj* immediate, direct; **II** *ad* immediately, at once, right away, directly, instantly; *zo* ~ presently

'dadelpalm (-en) *m* date-palm

'dader (-s) *m* author, doer, wrong-doer, culprit

'dading (-en) *v* [symbol] settlement, arrangement

dag (dagen) *m* day; ~*!* zie *goedendag;* ~ *en nacht* night and day, day and night, round the clock; *de (ge)hele* ~ all day (long); *de jongste* ~ the Day of Judgment; *de oude* ~ old age; *de* ~ *daarna* the following day; *de* ~ *tevoren* the day before, the previous day; *de* ~ *des Heren* the Lord's Day [= Sunday]; *de* ~ *van morgen* to-morrow; *dezer* ~*en* the other day, lately; ook = *één dezer* ~*en* one of these days, some day soon; *betere* ~*en gekend hebben* have seen better days; *het wordt* ~ day is breaking; *het is kort* ~ time is short; *het is morgen vroeg* ~ we have to get up early to-morrow; ● ~ *a a n* ~ day by day, day after day; *het aan de* ~ *brengen* bring it to light; *aan de* ~ *komen* come to light; *aan de* ~ *leggen* display, manifest, show; *bij* ~ by day; *bij de* ~ *leven* live by the day; (i n) *de laatste* ~*en* during the last few days, lately, of late; *in vroeger* ~*en* in former days, formerly; ~ *in* ~ *uit* day in day out; *later o p de* ~ later in the day(-time); *op de* ~ *(af)* to the (very) day; *midden op de* ~ 1 in the middle of the day; 2 in broad daylight; *op een (goeie)* ~, *op zekere* ~ one (fine) day; *op zijn oude* ~ in his old age; *t e n ~e van...* in the days of...; *heden ten ~e* nowadays; *t o t op deze* ~ to this (very) day; *v a n ~ tot* ~ from day to day, day by day; *... van de* ~ current [affairs, politics]; *v o o r ~ en dauw* at dawn, before daybreak; *iets voor de ~ halen* produce sth., take it out, bring it out; *voor de ~ komen* appear, show oneself, turn up [of persons]; become apparent, show [of things]; *voor de ~ ermee!* out with it!; *hij kwam er niet mee voor de* ~ he didn't produce it [the promised thing], he didn't come out with it [his guess], he didn't put it [the idea] forward

'**dagblad** (-bladen) *o* (daily) newspaper, daily paper, newspaper; –**correspondent** (-en) *m* newspaper correspondent; –**pers** *v* daily press

'**dagblind** day-blind; –**boek** (-en) *o* 1 diary; 2 $ day-book; –**boot** (-boten) *m* & *v* day-boat, day-steamer; –**bouw** *m* open-cast mining, surface mining; –**dief** (-dieven) *m* idler; –**dienst** (-en) *m* 1 day-service; 2 day-duty; '**dagdieven** (dagdiefde, h. gedagdiefd) *vi* idle; **dagdieve'rij** (-en) *v* idling; '**dagdromen** *o* day-dreaming

dagelijks I *aj* daily, everyday [clothes, life], ★ diurnal; *het ~ bestuur* 1 (v. g e m e e n t e) ± the mayor and aldermen; 2 (v. v e r e n i-g i n g) the executive (committee); **II** *ad* every day, daily; **1** '**dagen** (daagde, h. gedaagd) **I** *vi* dawn; **II** *vt* summon, summons; **2** '**dagen** meerv. v. *dag*; '**dagenlang I** *aj* lasting for days; **II** *ad* for days on end; **dag-en-'nachtevening** *v* equinox; '**dageraad** *m* daybreak, dawn²; '**daggeld** (-en) *o* $ call-money; day's wage(s), daily wage(s); –**gelder** (-s) *m* day-labourer; –**geldlening** (-en) *v* $ day-to-day loan, call loan; –**hit** (-ten) *v* day-girl; –**indeling** (-en) *v* = *dagverdeling*; –**je** (-s) *o* day; *het er een ~ van nemen* make a day of it; –**jesmensen** *mv* day trippers, cheap trippers; –**kaart** (-en) *v* day-ticket; –**koers** (-en) *m* day's rate of exchange, current rate of exchange; –**licht** *o* daylight; *dat kan het ~ niet verdragen* that cannot bear the light of day; *iem. in een kwaad ~ stellen* get sbd. in wrong [with sbd. else]; *bij ~* by daylight; –**loner** (-s) *m* day-labourer; –**loon** (-lonen) *o* day's wage(s), daily wage(s); –**marche** [-marʃ] (-en) *m* & *v*. –**mars** (-en) *m* & *v* day's march; –**meisje** (-s) *o* day-girl, daily help, daily; –**orde** *v* order of the day; –**order** (-s) *v* & *o* ✗ order of the day; –**pauwoog** (-ogen) *m* peacock butterfly; –**ploeg** (-en) *v* day-shift; –**reis** (reizen) *v* day's journey;

–**retour** [ou = u.] (-s) *o* day-return ticket; –**school** (-scholen) *v* day-school; –**schotel** (-s) *m* & *v* special dish for the day; –**taak** (-taken) *v* day's work; '**dagtekenen** (dagtekende, h. gedagtekend) *vi* & *vt* date; –**ning** (-en) *v* date; '**dagtochtje** (-s) *o* day trip

'**dagvaarden** (dagvaardde, h. gedagvaard) *vt* cite, summon, summons, subpoena; –**ding** (-en) *v* summons, subpoena, writ

'**dagverdeling** (-en) *v* division of the day; time-table, schedule; –**vlinder** (-s) *m* (diurnal) butterfly; –**werk** *o* daily work; *als..., dan had ik wel* ~ there would never be an end of it

'**dahlia** ['da.li.a] ('s) *v* dahlia

'**dak** (daken) *o* roof; *een ~ boven zijn hoofd hebben* have a roof over one's head; *o n d e r ~ brengen* give [sbd.] shelter; *onder één ~ wonen met* live under the same roof with; *ik kon nergens onder* ~ *komen* nobody could take me in, could put me up; *onder ~ zijn* be under cover [of a person]; *fig* be provided for; *iem. o p zijn ~ komen [fig]* take sbd. to task; *dat krijg ik op mijn* ~ they'll lay it at my door, they'll blame it on me; *iem. iets op zijn ~ schuiven (sturen)* shove the blame (sth.) on sbd., saddle sbd. with sth.; *o v e r de ~en klauteren* scramble over the roof-tops; *v a n de ~en prediken* proclaim from the house-tops; *het gaat van een leien ~je* it goes smoothly (swimmingly), the thing goes on wheels (without a hitch); –**balk** (-en) *m* roof-beam; –**bedekking** (-en) *v* roofing; roofing material; –**dekker** (-s) *m* = *dekker*; –**goot** (-goten) *v* gutter; –**kamertje** (-s) *o* attic, garret; –**kapel** (-len) *v* dormer-window; –**licht** (-en) *o* sky-light; –**loos** homeless, roofless; –**loze** (-n) *m-v* waif; *de ~n* ook: the homeless; –**pan** (-nen) *v* (roofing) tile; –**pijp** (-en) *v* gutter-pipe; –**rand** (-en) *m* (o n d e r-s t e) eaves; –**riet** *o* thatch; –**ruiter** (-s) *m* 1 ridge-piece, ridge-board; 2 (t o r e n t j e) ridge turret; –**spaan** (-spanen) *v* shingle; –**spar** (-ren) *m* rafter; –**stoel** (-en) *m* truss; –**tuin** (-en) *m* roof garden; –**venster** (-s) *o* dormer-window, garret-window; –**vorst** (-en) *v* ridge [of a (the) roof]; –**werk** *o* roofing

dal (dalen) *o* valley, ⊙ vale; dale; dell, dingle

'**dalen** (daalde, is gedaald) *vi* descend, land [of an airplane]; sink, drop [of the voice], go down [of the sun, of prices &], fall [of prices, the barometer]; *de stem laten ~* drop (lower) one's voice; –**ling** (-en) *v* descent, fall, drop, decline

1 dam (-men) *m* dam, dike, causeway, barrage [to hold back water], weir [across a river]; *een* ~ *opwerpen tegen* cast (throw) up a dam against; dam up², stem² [the progress of evil]

2 dam (-men) *v* king [at draughts]; ~ *halen*

crown a man, go to king; ~ *spelen* play at
draughts

da'mast (-en) *o*, da'masten *aj* damask

'dambord (-en) *o* draught-board

'dame (-s) *v* 1 lady; 2 partner [at dance &];
'damesachtig ladylike; –blad (-bladen) *o*
women's magazine; –fiets (-en) *m* & *v* ladies'
bicycle; –kapper (-s) *m* ladies' hairdresser;
–kleding *v* ladies' wear; –kleermaker (-s) *m*
ladies' tailor; –mantel (-s) *m* lady's coat;
–mode *v de* ~ ladies' fashion; ~*s* ladies' wear;
–tasje (-s) *o* lady's bag, vanity bag; –verband
o sanitary towel, sanitary napkin; –zadel (-s) *o*
& *m* side-saddle [for horse]; lady's saddle [for
bicycle]

'damhert (-en) *o* fallow-deer

'dammen (damde, h. gedamd) *vi* play at
draughts; –er (-s) *m* draught-player

damp (-en) *m* vapour, steam, smoke, fume;
'dampen (dampte, h. gedampt) *vi* steam [of
soup &], smoke; (*zitten*) ~ sit and smoke, blow
clouds; 'dampig 1 vaporous, vapoury, hazy; 2
(k o r t a d e m i g) broken-winded; 'damp-
kring (-en) *m* atmosphere

'damschijf (-schijven) *v* (draughts)man; –spel
(-len) *o* 1 draughts, game at (of) draughts; 2
draught-board and men

dan I *ad* then; *zeg het,* ~ *ben je een beste vent* tell it,
there's (that's) a good boy; *ik had* ~ *toch maar
gelijk* so I was right after all; *ga* ~ *toch* do go; *en
ik* ~? and what about me?; *wat is er* ~? now,
what's the matter?; *wat zeur je* ~? why all the
fuss?; *als je wilt,* ~ *kun je gaan* you can go, if
you want to; *maar hij heeft* ~ *ook...* after all he
has...; *nu eens hier,* ~ *weer daar* now here, now
there; II *cj* than; *groter* ~ bigger than; *hij is te
oud,* ~ *dat wij...* he is too old for us to...; *of hij
komt,* ~ *of hij gaat* whether he comes or
whether he goes

'dancing ['da.nsɪŋ] (-s) *m* dance-hall

'dandy ['dɛndi.] ('s) *m* dandy, coxcomb

'danig I *aj* < very great; *ik heb een* ~*e honger* I
feel awfully hungry; II *ad* very, very much,
greatly [disappointed], vigorously [defending
themselves], badly, severely [hurt], sadly
[disappointed], sorely [mistaken, afflicted]

dank *m* thanks; *geen* ~! don't mention it!; *zijn
hartelijke* ~ *betuigen* express one's heartfelt
thanks; *ik heb er geen* ~ *van gehad* much thanks I
have got for it!; ~ *weten* thank; ~ *zij zijn hulp*
thanks to his help; *Gode zij* ~ thank God; *in* ~
gratefully [accepted]; [received] with thanks; *in*
~ *terug* returned with thanks; zie ook *stank*;
'dankbaar thankful, grateful; –heid *v* thankfulness, gratitude; 'dankbetuiging (-en) *v*
expression of thanks, letter of thanks, vote of
thanks; *onder* ~ with thanks; –dag (-dagen) *m*

thanksgiving day; 'danken (dankte, h.
gedankt) I *vt* thank; *te* ~ *hebben* owe, be
indebted for [to sbd.]; *hij heeft het zichzelf te* ~ he
has himself to thank for it; *dank u* 1 (b ij
w e i g e r i n g) no, thank you; 2 (b ij a a n n e-
m i n g) thank you; *dank u zeer* thank you very
much, thanks awfully; *niet te* ~! don't mention
it!; II *vi* 1 give thanks; 2 say grace [after
meals]; *daar dank ik voor* thank you very much;
ik zou je ~! not likely!; thank you for nothing!;
'dankfeest (-en) *o* 1 thanksgiving feast; 2
harvest festival; –gebed (-beden) *o* 1 (prayer
of) thanksgiving; 2 grace [before and after
meals]; –lied (-eren) *o* song of thanksgiving;
–offer (-s) *o* thank-offering; 'dankzeggen (zei
of zegde 'dank, h. 'dankgezegd) *vi* give thanks,
render (return) thanks, thank [sbd.]; –zegging
(-en) *v* thanksgiving

dans (-en) *m* dance; *de* ~ *ontspringen* have a
narrow escape; –club (-s) *v* dancing-club;
'dansen (danste, h. gedanst) *vi* dance°; *hij
danst naar haar pijpen* he dances to her piping
(to her tune); –er (-s) *m*, danse'res (-sen) *v*
dancer; partner [at a dance]; dan'seuse
[-'sø.zə] (-s) *v* dancer, ballet-dancer; 'dansfi-
guur (-guren) *v* & *o* dance figure; –je (-s) *o*
dance, F hop; *een* ~ *maken* have a dance, S
shake a leg; –kunst *v* (art of) dancing; –leraar
(-s en -raren) *m* dancing master; –les (-sen) *v*
dancing-lesson; (a l g e m e e n) dancing
classes; –muziek *v* dance music; –orkest
(-en) *o* dance band, dance-orchestra; –partij
(-en) *v* dancing-party, dance, F hop; –pas
(-sen) *m* dancing-step, step; –school
(-scholen) *v* dancing-school; –vloer *m* dance
floor; –wijsje (-s) *o* dance tune; –zaal (-zalen)
v ball-room, dancing-room, dance-hall

'dapper I *aj* brave, valiant, gallant, valorous;
een ~ *ventje* a plucky little fellow; II *ad* bravely
&; ~ *meedoen* join heartily in the game; *er* ~ *op
los zingen* sing (away) lustily; *zich* ~ *houden*
behave gallantly, bear oneself bravely, F keep
one's pecker up; –heid *v* bravery, valour,
gallantry, prowess

dar (-ren) *m* drone

Darda'nellen *mv de* ~ the Dardanelles

darm (-en) *m* intestine, gut; ~*en* ook: bowels;
dikke (dunne) ~ large (small) intestine; *nuchtere*
~ jejunum; *twaalfvingerige* ~ duodenum;
–kanaal (-nalen) *o* intestinal tube; –ontsteking (-en) *v* enteritis

'dartel frisky, frolicsome, playful, skittish,
sportive; wanton; 'dartelen (dartelde, h.
gedarteld) *vi* frisk, frolic, gambol; dally;
'dartelheid *v* friskiness, playfulness; wantonness

darwi'nisme *o* Darwinism; –ist (-en) *m*,

darwi'nistisch *aj* Darwinian, Darwinist

1 das (-sen) *m* ᴥ badger

2 das (-sen) *v* 1 (neck-)tie; 2 (inz. = sjaal) scarf, (dik, voor warmte) = *bouffante*; 3 ᴥ cravat; *iem. de ~ omdoen* be sbd.'s undoing, **F** do for sbd.

'dashond (-en) *m* ᴥ badger-dog

'dasspeld (-en) *v* tie-pin, scarf-pin

dat I *aanw. vnw.* that; *~ alles* all that; *~ moest je doen* that's what you ought to do; *~ zijn mijn vrienden* those are my friends; *het is je ~!* **F** that's the stuff!; *het is nog niet je ~* not quite what it ought to be; *hij heeft niet ~* not even that much; *wat zijn ~?* what are those?; *wie zijn ~?* who are they?; *~ zijn...* those are..., they are...; *ben jij ~?* is that you?; *wat zou ~?* what of it?; *wat moet ~?* what's all that?; *en ~ is ~* so much for that; *~ is het nu juist* that's just it; *hoe weet je ~?* how do you know?; **II** *betr. vnw.* that, which; *de dag ~ hij kwam* the day he came; **III** *cj* (that); *en regenen ~ het deed!* how it rained!

'data *mv* (gegevens) data; **–bank** (-en) *v* data bank

da'teren (dateerde, *vt* h., *vi* is gedateerd) *vt* (& *vi*) date (from *uit*)

'datgene that; *~ wat* that which

'datief (-tieven) *m* dative

'dato dated...; *twee maanden na ~* two months after date; **'datum** (data) *m* date

dauw *m* dew; **–droppel** (-s) *m*, **–druppel** (-s) *m* dew-drop; **'dauwen** (dauwde, h. gedauwd) *vi* dew; *het dauwt* the dew is falling; *het begint te ~* it is beginning to dew; **'dauwworm** *m* 🜊 ringworm

d.a.v. = *daaraanvolgend*

'daveren (daverde, h. gedaverd) *vi* thunder, resound; shake; *de zaal daverde van de toejuichingen* the house rang with cheers; *een ~d succes* a roaring succes

'davidster (-ren) *v* Star of David

'davit (-s) *m* davit

'dazen (daasde, h. gedaasd) *vi* **F** waffle, talk rot, talk through one's hat

d.d. = *de dato*

de [də] the

'dealer ['di.lər] (-s) *m* dealer

de'bâcle [de.'ba.kəl] *v* & *o* debacle; collapse; **F** flop

deballo'teren [de.-] (deballoteerde, h. gedeballoteerd) *vt* blackball

de'bat [de.-] (-ten) *o* debate, discussion; **de'bater** [di.'be:tər] (-s) *m* debater; **debat'teren** [de.-] (debatteerde, h. gedebatteerd) *vi* debate, discuss; *~ over* debate (on), discuss

'debet ['de.bɪt] **I** *o* debit; **II** *aj u bent mij nog ~* you still owe me something; *ook hij is er ~ aan*

he, too, is guilty of it; **–post** (-en) *m* debit item; **–zijde** (-n) *v* debit side, Debtor side

de'biel [de.-] **I** *aj* mentally deficient (defective); **II** *m-v* mental deficient (defective)

de'biet [də-] *o* sale; *een groot ~ hebben* meet with (find, command) a ready sale, sell well

debili'teit [de.-] *v* mental deficiency

debi'teren [de.-] (debiteerde, h. gedebiteerd) *vt* \$ debit [sbd. with an amount]; dish up [arguments, lies]; *een aardigheid ~* crack a joke

debi'teur [de.-] (-s en -en) *m* debtor

deblok'keren [de.-] (deblokkeerde, h. gedeblokkeerd) *vt* \$ unblock, unfreeze; **–ring** (-en) *v* \$ unblocking, unfreezing

debra'yeren [de.bra.'je:.rə(n)] (debrayeerde, h. gedebrayeerd) *vi* declutch

debu'tant [de.-] (-en) *m*, **debu'tante** (-n en -s) *v* débutant(e); **debu'teren** (debuteerde, h. gedebuteerd) *vi* make one's début; **de'buut** [də- en de.-] (-buten) *o* début, first appearance [of an actor &]

de'caan [de.-] (-canen) *m* dean

de'cade [de.-] (-s en -n) decade

deca'dent [de.-] decadent; **–ie** [-(t)si.] *v* decadence

'decagram (-men) *o* decagramme; **–liter** (-s) *m* decalitre; **–meter** (-s) *m* decametre

deca'naat [de.-] (-naten) *o* deanship, deanery

decan'teren [de.-] (decanteerde, h. gedecanteerd) *vt* decant

de'cember [de.-] *m* December

de'cennium [de.-] (-niën en -nia) *o* decennium, decade

de'cent [de.-] decent, seemly

decentrali'satie [de.sɪntra.li.'za.(t)si.] (-s) *v* decentralization, devolution; **decentrali'seren** [s = z] (decentraliseerde, h. gedecentraliseerd) *vt* decentralize

de'ceptie [de.'sɪpsi.] (-s) *v* disappointment

de'charge [de.'ʃarʒə] *v* discharge; *~ verlenen* give a discharge; *getuige à décharge* 🜊 witness for the defence; **dechar'geren** (dechargeerde, h. gedechargeerd) *vt* give [sbd.] a release, give formal approval of the actions of [sbd.]

'decibel ['de.si.bɪl] (-s) *m* decibel

deci'deren [de.-] (decideerde, h. gedecideerd) *vt* & *vi* decide; zie ook: *gedecideerd*

'decigram (-men) *o* decigramme; **–liter** (-s) *m* decilitre

deci'maal I *aj* decimal; **II** (-malen) *v* decimal place; *tot in 5 decimalen* to 5 decimal places; **–teken** (-s) *o* decimal point

deci'meren (decimeerde, h. gedecimeerd) *vt* decimate

'decimeter (-s) *m* decimetre

decla'matie [de.kla.'ma.(t)si.] (-s) *v* declamation, recitation; **decla'mator** (-s en -'toren) *m* elocutionist, reciter; **decla'meren** (decla-meerde, h. gedeclameerd) *vt* & *vi* declaim, recite

decla'ratie [de.kla.'ra.(t)si.] (-s) *v* declaration [of Paris, at a custom-house], entry [at a custom-house], voucher [for money]; expense account; **decla'reren** (declareerde, h. gedeclareerd) *vt* charge [expences]; declare [dutiable goods]

decli'natie [de.kli.'na.(t)si.] (-s) *v* declination [of star, compass]; *gram* declension

deco'deren [de.-] (decodeerde, h. gedecodeerd) *vt* decode

decolle'té [de.-] (-s) *o* low neckline

de'cor [de.'kɔ:r] (-s) *o* scenery, scenes, [film] set; **decora'teur** (-s) *m* 1 (painter and) decorator, ornamental painter; 2 scene-painter; **deco'ratie** [-(t)si.] (-s) *v* decoration [ook = order of knighthood, cross, star]; ornament; *de ~s* the scenery, the scenes; **decora'tief** decorative, ornamental; **deco'reren** (decoreerde, h. gedecoreerd) *vt* 1 decorate, ornament [a wall]; 2 decorate [a general &]; **de'cor-ontwerper** (-s) *m* scene (scenic, set) designer, stage decorator

de'corum [de.'kɔ:rüm] *o* decorum; *het ~* ook: the proprieties, the decencies; *het ~ bewaren* keep up appearances

de'creet [də-] (-creten) *o* decree; **decre'teren** [de.kre.-] (decreteerde, h. gedecreteerd) *vt* decree, ordain

de'dain [de.'dἳ.] *o* contempt, hauteur, disdain

de 'dato [de.] dated...

'deden V.T. meerv. v. *doen*

dedu'ceren [de.-] (deduceerde, h. gededuceerd) *vt* deduce; infer; **de'ductie** [de.'düksi.] (-s) *v* deduction; **deduc'tief** deductive

deed (deden) V.T. v. *doen*

deeg *o* dough, (v. gebak) paste; **–achtig** doughy; **–roller** (-s) *m* rolling-pin

1 deel (delen) *o* 1 part, portion, share; 2 (boek ~) volume; 3 (deel van symfonie) movement; *ik heb er geen ~ aan* I am no party to it; *ik heb er geen ~ in* I have no share in it; *zijn ~ krijgen* come into one's own; come in for one's share [of vicissitudes &]; *~ uitmaken van...* form part of...; be a member of...; ● *in allen dele* in every respect; *in genen dele* not at all, by no means; *iem. ten ~ vallen* fall to sbd.'s lot (share); *ten dele* partly; *voor een ~* partly; *voor een goed ~ = goeddeels; voor een groot ~ = grotendeels; voor het grootste ~* zie *gedeelte*

2 deel (delen) *v* 1 (plank) deal, board [under 2 in. thick]; 2 (dorsvloer) treshing-floor

deel'achtig *iem. iets ~ maken* impart sth. to sbd.; *iets ~ worden* obtain, participate in [the grace of God]; **'deelbaar** divisible [number], partible; **–heid** *v* divisibility; **'deelgenoot** (-noten) *m* 1

sharer [of my happiness], partner; 2 $ partner; *iem. ~ maken van een geheim* disclose (confide) a secret to sbd.; **–schap** (-pen) *o* partnership; **'deelge'rechtigd** entitled to a share; **'deel-hebber** (-s) *m* 1 participant, participator; 2 $ partner, copartner, joint proprietor

'deelname *v = deelneming* 2; **'deelnemen** (nam 'deel, h. 'deelgenomen) *vi ~ aan* participate in, take part in, join in [the conversation &], assist at [a dinner]; *~ in* participate in, share in, share [sbd.'s feelings]; **–er** (-s) *m* 1 participant, participator, partner; 2 competitor, entrant, contestant [in a match &], entry [for a race, contest]; **'deelneming** *v* 1 sympathy, compassion, commiseration, concern, pity; 2 participation (in *aan*); entry [for sporting event &]; *iem. zijn ~ betuigen = condoleren*

'deelpachter (-s) *m* sharecropper

deels ~..., **~...** partly..., partly...; *~ door..., ~ door...* what with... and...

'deelsom (-men) *v* division sum; **–staat** (-staten) *m* federal state; **–tal** (-len) *o* dividend; **–teken** (-s) *o gram* diaeresis; × division sign (mark); **'deeltje** (-s) *v* particle; **–sversneller** (-s) *m* cyclotron; **'deelwoord** (-en) *o* participle; *tegenwoordig (verleden, voltooid) ~* present (past) participle

'deemoed *m* humility, meekness; **dee'moedig** humble, meek; apologetic; **dee'moedigen** (deemoedigde, h. gedeemoedigd) **I** *vt* humble, mortify [a person]; **II** *vr zich ~* humble oneself; **dee'moedigheid** *v* humility, humbleness

Deen (Denen) *m* Dane; **–s I** *aj* Danish; **II** *o het ~* Danish; **III** *v een ~e* a Danish woman

'deerlijk I *aj* sad, grievous, piteous, pitiful, miserable; **II** *ad* grievously, piteously &; *~ gewond* badly wounded; *zich ~ vergissen* be greatly (sorely) mistaken

'deern(e) (-s en -(e)n) *v* girl, lass, wench; > hussy

'deernis *v* pity, commiseration, compassion; *~ hebben met* take (have) pity on, pity; **deernis'waard(ig)** pitiable; **–'wekkend** pitiful

de 'facto [de.] de facto

defai'tisme [de.fἐ.-] *o* defeatism; **–ist** (-en) *m*, **–istisch** *aj* defeatist

de'fect [də-] **I** (-en) *o* defect, deficiency; [engine] trouble; **II** *aj* defective, faulty, [machinery] out of order; *er is iets ~* there is something wrong [with the engine]; *~ raken* get out of order, break down, go wrong

de'fensie [de.-] *v* defence; **defen'sief I** *aj* defensive; **II** *ad* defensively; *~ optreden* act on the defensive; **III** *o* defensive; *in het ~* on the defensive

'deficit ['de.fi. (t)si.t] (-s) *o* deficit, deficiency, shortfall

defi'lé [de.-] (-s) *o* 1 (b e r g p a s) defile; 2 (v o o r b ij m a r c h e r e n) march past; *een ~ afnemen* take the salute; **defi'leren** (defileerde, h. gedefileerd) *vi* defile; ~ (*voor*) march past

defini'ëren [de.-] (definieerde, h. gedefinieerd) *vt* define; **defi'nitie** [de.fi.'ni.(t)si.] (-s) *v* definition

defini'tief [de.-] **I** *aj* definitive; final [agreement, decision], definite [answer, reductions]; permanent [appointment]; **II** *ad* definitively; finally; [coming, say] definitely; ~ *benoemd worden* be permanently appointed

de'flatie [de.'fla.(t)si.] *v* $ deflation; **deflatio'nistisch, defla'toir** [-'tʋa:r en -'to.r] deflationary

'deftig I *aj* grave [mien], dignified, stately [bearing], portly [gentlemen], distinguished [air], fashionable [quarters]; (o v e r d r e v e n ~) genteel [woman]; *zogenaamd* ~ la-di-da; **II** *ad* gravely &; ~ *doen* assume a solemn and pompous air; **–heid** *v* gravity, stateliness, portliness; (o v e r d r e v e n) genteelness

'degelijk I *aj* substantial [food]; solid [grounds &]; thorough [work &]; sterling [fellow, qualities]; sound [education, knowledge]; **II** *ad* thoroughly; *ik heb het wel ~ gezien* I did see it; *het is wel ~ waar* it is really true; **–heid** *v* solidity, thoroughness, sterling qualities, soundness

'degen (-s) *m* sword; *de ~s kruisen* cross swords

de'gene [də-] (-n) he, she; *~n die* those (they) who

degene'ratie [de.ɡənə'ra.(t)si.] (-s) *v* degeneracy, degeneration; **degene'reren** (degenereerde, is gedegenereerd) *vi* degenerate; zie ook: *gedegenereerd*

'degenslikker (-s) *m* sword-swallower; **–stoot** (-stoten) *m* sword thrust

degra'datie [de.ɡra.'da.(t)si.] (-s) *v* degradation, demotion; ⚓ reduction to the ranks; ⚓ disrating; *sp* relegation; **degra'deren** (degradeerde, h. gedegradeerd) *vt* 1 degrade, demote; reduce to a lower rank; 2 ⚓ reduce to the ranks; ⚓ disrate; *sp* relegate

'deinen (deinde, h. gedeind) *vi* heave, roll; **–ning** (-en) *v* swell; *fig* excitement, commotion

'deinzen (deinsde, is gedeinsd) *vi* recoil

dejeu'ner [de.ʒœ.'ne.] (-s) *o* 1 breakfast; 2 (t w e e d e o n t b ij t) lunch(eon); **dejeu'neren** (dejeuneerde, h. gedejeuneerd) *vi* 1 breakfast, have breakfast; 2 lunch, have lunch

dek (-ken) *o* 1 cover, covering; 2 bed-clothes; 3 horse-cloth; 4 ⚓ deck; *aan* ~ ⚓ on deck; **–balk** (-en) *m* deck beam; **–bed** (-den) *o* quilt, eider-down, duvet; **–blad** (-bladen) *o* (v a n

s i g a a r) wrapper

1 'deken (-en en -s) *m* dean

2 'deken (-s) *v* blanket; *onder de ~s kruipen* **F** turn in

'dekhengst (-en) *m* stud-horse, stallion, sire; **'dekken** (dekte, h. gedekt) **I** *vt* cover [one's head, one's bishop, expenses, a debt, a horse, the retreat &]; (m e t p a n n e n) tile, (m e t l e i) slate, (m e t r i e t) thatch; screen, shield [a functionary]; (b e v r u c h t e n) serve; *sp* mark [an opponent]; *gedekt zijn* 1 be secured against loss; 2 be covered [of functionaries, soldiers &]; *zich gedekt houden* lie low; *houd u gedekt!* 1 be covered; 2 *fig* be careful!; **II** *vr zich* ~ 1 cover oneself [put on one's hat]; 2 shield oneself, screen oneself [behind others]; 3 $ secure oneself against loss(es); **III** *va* lay the cloth, set the table; ~ *voor 20 personen* lay (covers) for twenty; **'dekker** (-s) *m* (p a n n e n ~) tiler, (l e i ~) slater, (r i e t ~) thatcher; **'dekking** (-en) *v* cover; ⚓ cover; *fig* cloak, shield, guard; ~ *zoeken* ⚓ seek (take) cover (from *voor*); **'dekkleed** (-kleden) *o* cover

'deklaag (-lagen) *v* top (surface) layer, protective cover

'deklading (-en) *v* = *deklast*; **–last** (-en) *m* deck-cargo, deck-load

'dekmantel (-s) *m* cloak[2], *fig* veil; cover; *onder de ~ van...* under the cloack (cover) of...

dekoloni'satie [de.ko.lo.ni.'za.(t)si.] (-s) *v* decolonization

'dekpassagier [-ʒi:r] (-s) *m* deck-passenger

'dekriet *o* thatch; **–schaal** (-schalen) *v* vegetable dish; **–schild** (-en) *o* wing-sheath, wing-case; **–schuit** (-en) *v* covered barge

'deksel (-s) *o* cover; lid; *te ~!, wat ~!* **F** the deuce!, the devil!

'deksels = *drommels*

'deksteen (-stenen) *m* slab [of a stone]; capstone; copingstone, coping [of a wall]

'dekstoel (-en) *m* deck-chair

'dekstro *o* thatch; **–veren** *mv* ❧ coverts; **–verf** (-verven) *v* body-colour; **–zeil** (-en) *o* tarpaulin

del (-len) *v* hollow, dip; ‖ (s l o r d i g e v r o u w) **P** slut, slattern

dele'gatie [de.lə'ɡa.(t)si.] (-s) *v* delegation; **dele'geren** (delegeerde, h. gedelegeerd) *vt* delegate

'delen (deelde, h. gedeeld) **I** *vt* divide [a sum of money &], share [sbd.'s feelings]; split [the difference]; **II** *vi* divide; ~ *i n* participate in, share in, share [sbd.'s feelings]; ~ *in iems. droefheid* sympathize with sbd.; ~ *m e t* share with; *samen* ~ go halves, go fifty-fifty; **'deler** (-s) *m* 1 (p e r s o o n) divider; 2 (g e t a l) divisor; (*grootste*) *gemene* ~ (highest) common factor 'delfstof (-fen) *v* mineral; 'delfstoffenkunde *v* = *delfstofkunde*; –rijk *o* mineral kingdom; 'delfstofkunde *v* mineralogy

delfts *o* (a a r d e w e r k) delftware, dęlf(t)

'delgen (delgde, h. gedelgd) *vt* pay off, amortize, discharge, redeem [a loan], extinguish [a debt]; –ging *v* extinction [of a debt], redemption [of a loan], amortization, payment

delibe'ratie [de.li.bɔ'ra.(t)si.] (-s) *v* deliberation; delibe'reren (delibereerde, h. gedelibereerd) *vi* deliberate

deli'caat [de.-] I *aj* delicate°, ticklish; II *ad* delicately, tactfully; delica'tesse (-n) *v* 1 delicacy°; 2 dainty (bit); ~*n* table delicacies, delicatessen; ~*nwinkel* delicatessen

de'lict [de.-] (-en) *o* offence

'deling (-en) *v* 1 partition [of real property]; 2 × division

delin'quent [de.lɪŋ'kvɛnt] I (-en) *m* delinquent, offender; II *aj* delinquent

de'lirium [de.-] *o* delirium, delirium tremens; ~ *hebben* F see snakes, have the horrors

'delta ('s) *v* delta

'delven* *vi* & *vt* dig; –er (-s) *m* digger

demago'gie [de.-] *v* demagogy; dema'gogisch demagogic; dema'goog (-gogen) *m* demagogue

demar'catie [de.mar'ka.(t)si.] (-s) *v* demarcation; –lijn (-en) *v* line of demarcation, demarcation line, dividing line

de'marche [de.'marʃə] (-s) *v* demarche, diplomatic step

de'ment [de.-] dement, demented

1 demen'teren [de.-] (dementeerde, is gedementeerd) *vi* (k i n d s w o r d e n) grow senile, become dement(ed)

2 demen'teren [de.-] (dementeerde, h. gedementeerd) *vt* (o n t k e n n e n) deny [a fact], disavow, disclaim

demen'ti [de.mã'ti.] ('s) *o* denial, disclaimer; *een* ~ *geven* give the lie

de'mi [dɔ-] ('s) *m* = *demi-saison*; de'mi-fi'nale (-s) *v sp* semi-final; de'mi-sai'son [-sɛ'zõ] (-s) *m* spring overcoat; summer overcoat; autumn overcoat

demissionair [de.mɪsjo.'nɛ.r] ~ *zijn* be under resignation; ~ *kabinet* outgoing cabinet

demobili'satie [de.mo.bi.li.'za.(t)si.] (-s) *v* demobilization; demobili'seren [s = z] (demobiliseerde, h. gedemobiliseerd) *vt* demobilize

demo'craat [de.-] (-en) *m* democrat; democra'tie [- '(t)si.] (-ieën) *v* democracy; ~ demo'cratisch democratic; democrati'seren [s = z] (democratiseerde, h. gedemocratiseerd) *vt* democratize; –ring *v* democratization

'demon (de'monen) *m* demon; de'monisch demoniac(al)

demon'strant [de.-] (-en) *m* demonstrator; demonstra'teur (-s) *m* demonstrator [of an article, for a company]; demon'stratie [-(t)si.] (-s) *v* demonstration; display [by aircraft]; demonstra'tief demonstrative, ostentatious [behaviour &]; demon'streren (demonstreerde, h. gedemonstreerd) *vt* & *vi* demonstrate

demon'teren [de.-] (demonteerde, h. gedemonteerd) *vt* dismount [a gun]; ✕ dismantle [machines, mines]

demorali'satie [de.mo.ra.li.'za.(t)si.] *v* demoralization; demorali'seren [s = z] (demoraliseerde, h. gedemoraliseerd) *vt* demoralize

'dempen (dempte, h. gedempt) *vt* fill up (in) [a canal &]; quench, smother [fire]; quell, crush, stamp out [a revolt]; damp [a furnace]; muffle, deaden [the sound]; subdue [light]; *met gedempte stem* in a hushed (muffled) voice; –er (-s) *m* 1 ✕ damper; 2 ♪ mute; 'demping (-en) *v* filling up; quenching &

den (-nen) *m* fir, fir tree; *grove* ~ pine; –appel (-s) *m* = *denneappel*

denatu'reren [de.-] (denatureerde, h. gedenatureerd) *vt* denature; *gedenatureerd alcohol* methylated spirit

'denderen (denderde, h. gedenderd) *vi* rumble; –d *aj* & *ad* F smashing

'Denemarken *o* Denmark

deni'grerend [de.-] derogatory

'denim *o* denim

'denkbaar imaginable, conceivable, thinkable; 'denkbeeld (-en) *o* idea, notion; (m e n i n g) view; denk'beeldig imaginary; 'denkelijk I *aj* probable, likely; II *ad* probably; *hij zal* ~ *niet komen* he is not likely to come; 'denken* I *vi* & *vt* think; *...denk ik* ...I think, I suppose; *...zou ik* ~ I should think; *ik denk het wel, ik denk van wel* I think so, I should imagine so; *ik denk het niet, ik denk van niet* I think not, I don't suppose so; *wat denk je wel?* 1 what are you thinking of?; 2 who do you think you are?; *kun je net* ~ *!* what an idea!, not likely!; *dat kun je* ~ *!* F *dat had je gedacht!* fancy me doing that!, F catch me!, not I!; *ik denk er heen te gaan* I think of going (there); *ik denk er het mijne van* I know what to think of it; *het laat zich* ~ it may be imagined; ● ~ *a a n iets* think of sth.; *daar is geen* ~ *aan* it is out of the question, F forget it; *ik moet er niet aan* ~ I cannot bear to think of it, it does not bear thinking; *denk eraan dat...* mind you..., be sure to..., remember to...; *denk eens aan!* imagine, just think of it, fancy that!; *ik denk er niet aan!* I'll do nothing of the kind!, absolutely not!, I would not dream of it!; *ik* denk er niet aan om... I have no idea of ...ing, I do not intend to...; *ik dacht er niet aan dat...* I didn't realize that...; *nu ik eraan denk* now I come to think of it; *doen ~ aan* make [sbd.] think of; remind [them] of [his brother &]; *...dacht ik b ij mijzelf* I thought to myself; *zonder er b ij te ~* without thinking, thoughtlessly; *o m iets ~* think of (remember) sth.; *denk er om!* mind!; *o v e r iets ~* think about (of) sth.; *ik denk er niet over* I wouldn't even dream of it; *hoe denk je erover?* how about it?; *ik zal er eens over ~* I'll see about it; *ik denk er nu anders over* I now feel differently, I take a different view now; *daar kun je verschillend over ~* that is a matter of opinion; **II** *o het ~* [Marxist, modern] thought; [creative, critical, crude, historical] thinking; **–er** (-s) *m* thinker; **'denkfout** (-en) *v* error of thought; **–patroon** (-tronen) *o* pattern of thinking; **–proces** (-sen) *o* thinking process, thought process; **–vermogen** (-s) *o* faculty of thinking, thinking faculty; intellectual power; **–werk** *o* brain-work, **F** cerebration; **–wijs, –wijze** (-wijzen) *v* way of thinking, way(s) of thought, habit of thought

'denneappel (-s) *m* fir-cone; **–boom** (-bomen) *m* fir-tree; **–hout** *o* fir-wood; **'dennen** *aj* fir; **'dennenaald** (-en) *v* fir-needle; **'dennenbos** (-sen) *o* fir-wood

de'odorans, deodo'rant [de.-] (-tia, -s) *o* deodorant

Dep. = *departement*; **departe'ment** [de.-] (-en) *o* department, government office; *~ van Binnenlandse Zaken* Home Office; *~ van Buitenlandse Zaken* Foreign Office; *~ van Marine* Navy Office; *~ van Oorlog* War Office

depen'dance [de.pã'dãsə] (-s) *v* annex(e) [to a hotel]

deplo'rabel [de.-] pitiable

depo'neren [de.-] (deponeerde, h. gedeponeerd) *vt* put down [sth.]; deposit [a sum of money], lodge [a document with sbd.]; zie ook: *gedeponeerd*

depor'tatie [de.pɔr'ta.(t)si.] (-s) *v* deportation, transportation; **depor'teren** (deporteerde, h. gedeporteerd) *vt* deport, transport

de'posito [de.'po.zi.to.] ('s) *o* deposit; *in ~ on* deposit; **–bank** (-en) *v* deposit bank

de'pot [de.'po.] (-s) *o* & *m* **1** ☒ depot; **2** $ depot; **–houder** (-s) *m* $ (sole) agent

'deppen (depte, h. gedept) *vt* dab

depreci'atie [de.pre.si.'a.(t)si.] *v* depreciation

de'pressie [de.-] (-s) *v* depression; **depres'sief** depressive; **depri'meren** [de.-] (deprimeerde, h. gedeprimeerd) *vt* depress, dispirit

Dept. = *departement*

depu'tatie [de.py.'ta.(t)si.] (-s) *v* deputation

derail'leren [de.rɑ'je:rə(n)] (derailleerde, is

gederailleerd) *vi* go (run) off the metals

deran'geren [de.rã'ʒe:rə(n)] (derangeerde, h. gederangeerd) **I** *vt* inconvenience; **II** *vr zich ~* put oneself out, trouble

'derde I *aj* third; *~ man* 1 third person; 2 third player; *~ wereld* Third World; *ten ~* thirdly; **II** (-n) *sb* 1 third (part); 2 third person, third party; 3 third player; *aansprakelijkheid jegens ~n* third-party risks

derde'machtsvergelijking (-en) *v* cubic equation; **–wortel** (-s) *m* cube root

'derdedaags quartan [fever]; **'derderangs** third-rate

'deren (deerde, h. gedeerd) *vt* harm, hurt; *wat deert het ons?* what do we care?; *het deerde hem niet, dat...* it was nothing to him that...

'dergelijk such, suchlike, like, similar; *en ~e* and the like; *iets ~s* something like it; some such thing, [say] something to that effect (in that strain)

der'halve therefore, consequently, so

deri'vaat [de:-] (-vaten) *o* derivate, derivative

'dermate in such a manner, to such a degree

'derrie *v* muck

'dertien thirteen; **–de** thirteenth (part); **'dertig** thirty; **–jarig** of thirty years; *de D~e oorlog* the Thirty Years' War; **–ste** thirtieth (part)

'derven (derfde, h. gederfd) *vt* be (go) without, be deprived of, forgo [wages]; **–ving** *v* privation, want, loss

'derwaarts thither, that way

1 des of the, of it, of that; *~ avonds* zie *avond*; *~ te beter* all the better, so much the better; *hoe meer..., ~ te meer...* the more..., the more...

2 des *v* ♪ d flat

desalniette'min [dɛs-] nevertheless, for all that

desavou'eren [de.za.vu.'e:rə(n)] (desavoueerde, h. gedesavoueerd) *vt* repudiate, disavow

'desbetreffend pertinent (relating, relative) to the matter in question

'desem (-s) *m* leaven; **'desemen** (desemde, h. gedesemd) *vt* leaven

deser'teren [de.zɪr-] (deserteerde, is gedeserteerd) *vi* desert; **deser'teur** (-s) *m* deserter; **de'sertie** [-(t)si.] (-s) *v* desertion

desge'lijks likewise, also, as well; **–ge'wenst** if so wished, if desired

'desillusie ['dɛ.zi.ly.zi.] (-s) *v* disillusionment, disenchantment; **desillusio'neren** (desillusioneerde, h. gedesillusioneerd) *vt* disillusion, disenchant

desinfec'teermiddel (-en) *o* disinfectant; **desinfec'teren** (desinfecteerde, h. gedesinfecteerd) *vt* disinfect; **desin'fectie** [-'fɛksi.] *v* disinfection; **–middel** (-en) *o* disinfectant

desinte'gratie [-(t)si.] *v* disintegration; **desinte'greren** (desintegreerde, is gedes-

integreerd) *vi* disintegrate
des'kundig *aj* expert; **~e**, *m-v* expert; **–heid**
expert knowledge, expertise
desniettegen'staande, desniette'min for all
that, nevertheless
des'noods, 'desnoods if need be, **F** at a pinch
deso'laat [de.zo.-] disconsolate, ruined
deson'danks [dɪs-] nevertheless, for all that
desorgani'satie [-'za.(t)si.] *v* disorganization;
desorgani'seren [s = z] (desorganiseerde, h.
gedesorganiseerd) *vt* disorganize
des'poot (-poten) *m* despot; **des'potisch**
despotic; **despo'tisme** *o* despotism
des'sert [dɛ'sɛr(t)] (-en) *o* dessert; *bij het* **~** at
dessert; **–lepel** (-s) *m* dessert-spoon
des'sin [dɛ'sɪ̃] (-s) *o* design, pattern
des'sous [dɛ'su.] *mv* ladies underwear; *fig*
background [of an affair]
'destijds at the (that) time
de'structie [dɛ'strüksi.] *v* destruction;
destruc'tief destructive
desver'langd if desired; **'deswege** for that
reason, on that account
detache'ment [de.taʃə-] (-en) *o* detachment,
draft, party; **deta'cheren** (detacheerde, h.
gedetacheerd) *vt* detach, detail, draft (off)
de'tail [de.'tɑi] (-s) *o* detail; *en* **~** **$** (by) retail; *in*
~s in detail; *in* **~s** *treden* enter (go) into
detail(s); **–foto** ('s) *v* close-up; **–handel** *m* 1
retail trade; 2 retail business, shopkeeping;
–kwestie (-s) *v* matter of detail; **detail'leren**
(detailleerde, h. gedetailleerd) *vt* detail, particu-
larize, specify; zie ook: *gedetailleerd*; **de'taillist**
(-en) *m* retailer, retail dealer; **de'tailprijs**
(-prijzen) *m* retail price; **–verkoop** (-kopen) *m*
retail sale
detec'tive [de.tɪk-] (-s) *m* detective; *particulier* **~**
private detective, private eye; **–roman** (-s) *m*
detective novel; **~s** ook: detective fiction;
–verhaal (-halen) *o* detective story, **F**
whodunit
determi'neren [de.tɪr-] (determineerde, h.
gedetermineerd) *vt* determine;
determi'nisme *o* determinism
deti'neren [de.-] (detineerde, h. gedetineerd) *vt*
detain
deto'neren [de.-] (detoneerde, h. gedetoneerd)
vi 1 be out of tune; *fig* be out of keeping; 2
detonate
deugd (-en) *v* virtue [ook = quality]; (good)
quality; *lieve* **~**! good gracious!; **'deugdelijk I**
aj sound, valid; **II** *ad* duly; **–heid** *v* soundness,
validity; **'deugdzaam** virtuous [women];
–heid *v* virtuousness; virtue
'deugen (deugde, h. gedeugd) *vi* be good, be
fit; *niet* **~** be good for nothing, be no good,
not be worth one's salt; *dit deugt niet* it is not

any good, this won't do; *je werk deugt niet* your
work is bad; *a l s onderwijzer deugt hij niet* as a
teacher he is inefficient; *hij deugt niet v o o r
onderwijzer* he will never make a good teacher,
he will never do for a teacher; **'deugniet** (-en)
m good-for-nothing, ne'er-do-well, rogue,
rascal
deuk (-en) *v* dent, dint, **F** dinge; **'deuken**
(deukte, h. gedeukt) *vt* dent, indent; **'deuk-
hoed** (-en) *m* soft felt hat, trilby (hat)
deun (-en) tune, song, singsong, chant; **–tje**
(-s) *o* air, tune
deur (-en) *v* door; *dat doet de* **~** *dicht* **F** that puts
the lid on it, that settles it; *bij iem. de* **~** *platlopen*
be either coming or going; *ik ga (kom) de* **~** *niet
uit* I never go out; *iem. de* **~** *uitzetten* turn sbd.
out; *iem. de* **~** *wijzen* show sbd. the door; *een
open* **~** *intrappen* force an open door; ● *a a n de*
~ at the door; *b ij de* **~** near (at) the door;
b u i t e n de **~** out of doors; *i n de* **~** in his door,
in the doorway; *m e t gesloten* **~en** behind closed
doors; 🕮 in camera; *met open* **~en** with open
doors; 🕮 in open court; *met de* **~** *in huis vallen*
go straight to the point; *het gevaar staat v o o r de*
~ the danger is imminent; *de winter staat voor de*
~ winter is at hand; *voor een gesloten* **~** *staan* find
the door locked; **–bel** (-len) *v* door-bell;
–klink (-en) *v* door-latch; **–klopper** (-s) *m*
door-knocker; **–knop** (-pen) *m* door-handle,
door-knob; **–kozijn** (-en) *o* door-frame; **–lijst**
(-en) *v* door-frame; **–mat** (-ten) *v* door-mat;
–opening (-en) *v* doorway; **–post** (-en) *m*
door-post, door-jamb; **–slot** (-sloten) *o* door-
lock; **–stijl** (-en) *m* = *deurpost*
'deurwaarder (-s) *m* process-server; usher;.
'deurwaardersexploot (-ploten) *o* writ (of
execution)
deux-'pièces [dø.'pjɛ.s] *v* two-piece
devalu'atie [de.va.ly.'a.(t)si.] (-s) *v* devaluation;
devalu'eren (devalueerde, h. gedevalueerd) *vt*
devaluate, devalue
devi'atie [de.vi.'a.(t)si.] (-s) *v* deviation
de'vies [də-] (-viezen) *o* device, motto; *deviezen*
$ (foreign) exchange, (v a l u t a) (foreign)
currency
de'voot [de.-] devout, pious; **de'votie** [-(t)si.]
(-s) *v* devotion, piety
☉ **de'welke** [də-] who, which, that
'deze this, these; **~** *en gene* this one and the
other; **~** *of gene* somebody or other; this or that
man; zie ook: *gene*; *de 10de* **~** *r* the 10th inst.;
schrijver **~s** the present writer; *b ij* **~n** herewith,
hereby; *i n* **~n** in this matter; *n a (voor)* **~n** after
(before) this (date); *t e n* **~** in this respect
de'zelfde [də-] the same; *precies* **~** the very
same
'dezerzijds on this side, on our part

de'zulken [də-] such
dhr. = *de heer*
d.i. = *dat is* that is, i.e.
'dia ('s) *m* slide, transparency
dia'betes [-'be.təs] *m* diabetes; **dia'beticus** (-ci) *m* diabetic
dia'bolisch diabolic(al)
dia'bolo ('s) *m* diabolo
diaco'nes (-sen) *v* 1 deaconess; 2 sicknurse; **–senhuis** (-huizen) *o* 1 home for deaconesses; 2 nursing-home
dia'deem (-demen) *m* & *o* diadem
dia'fragma ('s) *o* diaphragm
dia'gnose [s = z] (-n en -s) *v* diagnosis [*mv* diagnoses]; *de ~ stellen* diagnose the case; **diagnosti'seren** [s = z] (diagnostiseerde, h. gediagnostiseerd) diagnose
diago'naal I *aj* diagonal; **II** (-nalen) *v* diagonal (line)
dia'gram (-men) *o* diagram
di'aken (-en en -s) *m* deacon
dia'lect (-en) *o* dialect; **dia'lecticus** (-ci) *m* dialectician; **dialec'tiek** *v* dialectic(s); **dia'lectisch** 1 dialectal [word]; 2 dialectical [philosophy, materialism]
dia'loog (-logen) *m* dialogue
dia'mant (-en) *m* & *o* diamond; *geslepen ~* cut diamond; *ongeslepen ~* rough diamond; **diaman'tair** [-'tɛːr] (-s) *m* jeweller; **dia'manten** *aj* diamond; **dia'mantslijper** (-s) *m* diamond-polisher, diamond-cutter; **diamantslijpe'rij** (-en) *v* diamond-polishing factory; **dia'mantwerker** (-s) *m* diamond-worker
'diameter (-s) *m* diameter
diame'traal diametrical
diaposi'tief [s = z] (-tieven) *o* slide, transparency; **'diaprojector** (-s) *m* slide projector; **–raampje** (-s) *o* slide frame
diar'ree *v* diarrhoea
'diaschuif (-schuiven) *v* slide carrier; **dia'scoop** (-scopen) *m* slide projector; **'diaviewer** [-vju.ər] *m* slide viewer
dicht I *aj* 1 closed [doors, car]; 2 dense [clouds, fog, forests &], close [texture], thick [fog, woods], tight [ships]; clogged [nose]; *de deur was ~* the door was closed (shut); *hij is zo ~ als een pot* he is very close; **II** *ad* closely [interwoven]; densely [populated]
'dichtader *v* poetic vein
'dichtbevolkt, dichtbe'volkt densely populated; **dicht'bij** close by, hard by, near; *van ~* at close quarters; **'dichtbinden**[1] *vt* tie up

'dichtbundel (-s) *m* volume of verse
'dichtdoen[1] *vt* shut, close; **–draaien**[1] *vt* turn off [a tap]
1 'dichten (dichtte, h. gedicht) *vt* & *vi* make verses; write poetry
2 'dichten (dichtte, h. gedicht) *vt* stop (up), close [a dyke]
'dichter (-s) *m* poet; **dichte'res** (-sen) *v* poetess; **'dichterlijk** poetic(al)
'dichtgaan[1] *vi* 1 (v. d e u r &) shut, close; 2 (v. w o n d e) heal over (up), close; **–gooien**[1] *vt* slam [a door]; fill up [a ditch], fill in [a well]; **–groeien**[1] *vi* (w o n d) heal; (b o s s c h a g e) close; (v e r s t o p p e n) clog up; **–heid** *v* density; **–houden**[1] *vt* keep closed (shut); hold [one's nose], stop [one's ears]; **–knijpen**[1] *vt* clench, clasp [hands]; shut tightly [eyes]; *half ~* screw up [eyes]; **–knippen**[1] *vt* snap shut, close with a snap; **–knopen**[1] *vt* button up
'dichtkunst *v* (art of) poetry, poetic art; **–maat** (-maten) *v* metre; *in ~* in verse
'dichtmaken[1] *vt* close, stop [a hole]; shut [one's book], do up [her dress]; **–metselen**[1] *vt* brick up, wall up, mure up; **–naaien**[1] *vt* sew up; **–plakken**[1] *vt* seal (up)
'dichtregel (-s en -en) *m* verse
'dichtschroeien[1] *vt* sear; cauterize [a wound]; **–schroeven**[1] *vt* screw down (up); **–schuiven**[1] *vt* shut; **–slaan**[1] **I** *vt* slam, bang [a door]; **II** *vi* slam [a door]; **–slibben**[1] *vi* silt up; **–smijten**[1] *vt* slam shut; **–spelden**[1] *vt* pin up; **–spijkeren**[1] *vt* nail up; board up [a window]; **–stoppen**[1] *vt* stop, plug; **–trekken**[1] *vt* pull [the door] to, draw [the curtains]; **–vallen**[1] *vi* (d e u r) click shut; (o g e n) close
'dichtvorm (-en) *m* poetic form; *in ~* in verse
'dichtvouwen[1] *vt* fold up; **–vriezen**[1] *vi* freeze over (up)
'dichtwerk (-en) *o* poetical work, poem
dic'taat (-taten) *o* 1 dictation; 2 (h e t g e d i c-t e e r d e) notes; **–cahier** [-ka.je.] (-s) *o* (lecture) notebook; **dicta'foon** (-s) *m* dictaphone
dic'tator (-s) *m* dictator; **dictatori'aal** dictatorial; **dicta'tuur** (-turen) *v* dictatorship
dic'tee (-s) *o*; **dic'teerapparaat** (-raten) *o*, **–machine** [-ma.ʃi.nə] (-s) *v* dictating machine; **–snelheid** *v* dictation speed; **dic'teren** (dicteerde, h. gedicteerd) *vt* & *vi* dictate
'dictie ['dɪksi.] *v* diction, utterance
dictio'naire [dɪkʃo.'nɛː.rə] (-s) *v* dictionary
di'dacticus (-ci) *m* didactician; **didac'tiek** *v* didactics; **di'dactisch** didactic

---

[1] V.T. en V.D. van dit werkwoord volgens het model: **'dicht**draaien, V.T. draaide **'dicht**, V.D. **'dicht**gedraaid. Zie voor de vormen onder het grondwoord, in dit voorbeeld: *draaien*. Bij sterke en onregelmatige werkwoorden wordt u verwezen naar de lijst achterin.

die I *aanw. vnw.* that, those; ~ *met de groene jas* the one in the green coat, he of the green coat; *Meneer ~ en ~* (Mr) So-and-so; *in ~ en ~ plaats* in such and such a place; ~ *is goed, zeg!* I like that!; **II** *betr. vnw.* which, who, that

di'eet (diëten) *o* diet, regimen; ~ *houden, op ~ leven* be on a diet, diet (oneself); *hem op* (*streng*) ~ *stellen* put him on a diet, diet him

1 dief (dieven) *m* (s c h e u t) bud, shoot

2 dief (dieven) *m* thief; *houd*(*t*) *de ~!* stop thief!; *het is ~ en diefjesmaat* the one is as great a thief as the other; *wie eens steelt is altijd een ~* once a thief, always a thief; *met dieven moet men dieven vangen* set a thief to catch a thief; *als een ~ in de nacht* as (like) a thief in the night; **–achtig** thievish; **–stal** (-len) *m* theft, robbery, ⚖ larceny

'diegene [-ge.-] he, she; ~*n die* those who

'dienaangaande with respect to that, on that score, as to that

'dienaar (-s en -naren) *m* servant; *uw dienstwillige ~ H.* Yours faithfully H.; **diena'res(se)** (-sen) *v* servant

'dienblad (-bladen) *o* (dinner, tea) tray; **–couvert** [-ku.vɛr] (-s) *o* server

'diender (-s) *m* policeman, constable; *dooie ~* **F** stick

'dienen (diende, h. gediend) **I** *vt* serve [the Lord, two masters &]; *dat kan u niet ~* that won't serve your purpose; *waarmee kan ik u ~?* 1 (b ij d i e n s t a a n b i e d i n g) what can I do for you?; 2 (i n w i n k e l) can I help you?; *om u te ~* 1 at your service; 2 right you are!; **II** *vi* & *va* serve [in the army, navy], be in service [of girls &]; *aan tafel ~* wait at table; *gaan ~* go (out) to service; *het dient te gebeuren* it ought to (must) be done; *deze dient om u aan te kondigen, dat...* the present is to let you know that...; • ~ *a l s verontschuldiging* serve as an excuse; ~ *b ij de artillerie* serve in the artillery; ~ *bij rijke mensen* serve with rich people; *nergens t o e ~* serve no purpose, be no good; *waartoe zou het ~?* what's the good?; *waartoe dient dit knopje?* what is the use of this switch?; ~ *t o t bewijs* serve as a proof; *tot niets ~ = nergens toe ~*; *laat u dit tot een waarschuwing ~* let this be a warning to you; *iem. v a n advies ~* advise sbd.; *iem. van antwoord ~* 1 answer sbd.; 2 (i r o n.) serve sbd. out; *van zo iets ben ik niet gediend* none of that for me

'dienluik (-en) *o* service hatch

dienovereen'komstig accordingly

dienst (-en) *m* service; *commissie van goede ~en* good offices commission (committee); *iem. een ~ bewijzen* do (render) sbd. a service, do sbd. a good office; *goede ~en bewijzen* do good service; *u hebt mij een slechte ~ bewezen* you have done me

an ill service (a disservice, a bad turn); ~ *doen* perform the duties of one's office; be on duty [of police &]; *die jas kan nog ~ doen* that coat may be useful yet; ~ *doen als...* serve as, serve for, do duty as...; *de ~ doen* officiate [of a clergyman]; ~ *hebben* 1 be on duty; 2 be in attendance [at court]; *geen ~ hebben* 1 be off duty [of a soldier, of a doctor &]; 2 be out of employment [of servants]; ~ *nemen* ✗ enlist; *de ~ opzeggen* give warning, give a (month's) notice; *de ~ uitmaken* [*fig*] run the show; *de ~ weigeren* refuse to act [of a thing]; refuse to obey [of persons]; *een ~ zoeken* look out for a place; *de ene ~ is de andere waard* one good turn deserves another; ● *b u i t e n ~* 1 (v. p e r-s o o n) off duty; retired [colonel &]; 2 (v. s c h i p &) taken out of the service; 3 (a l s o p s c h r i f t v. s p o o r w e g r ij t u i g &) not to be used!; *buiten ~ stellen* lay up, scrap [a ship &]; *i n ~ gaan* go into service; ✗ enter the service; *in ~ hebben* employ [600 men and women]; *in ~ komen* enter upon one's duties, take up office; ✗ enter the service [the army]; *in ~ nemen* take [sbd.] into one's service (employ), engage [a servant &]; *in ~ stellen* put [a steamer] on the service; *in ~ stellen van* place [television] at the service of [propaganda]; *in ~ treden = in ~ komen*; *in ~ zijn* 1 be in service, be serving; 2 be on duty; 3 ✗ be in the army; *in mijn ~* in my employ; *n a de ~* after (divine) service; *o n d e r ~ gaan* ✗ enlist; *onder ~ zijn* ✗ be in the army; *t e n ~ e van* for the use of...; *t o t de* (*heilige*) ~ *toegelaten* admitted to holy orders; *tot uw ~!* [na: thank you] not at all, don't mention it!; *het is tot uw ~* it is at your service, at your disposal; *het zal u v a n ~ zijn* it will be of use to you; it will render you good service; *waarmee kan ik u van ~ zijn?* zie *dienen*; *z o n d e r ~* out of employment; **–auto** [-ɔuto, -o.to.] ('s) *m* official car; **'dienstbaar** liable to service, subservient, menial; (*een volk*) ~ *maken* subjugate; ~ *maken aan* make subservient to; **–heid** *v* servitude, subservience; **'dienstbetoon** *o* service(s) rendered; **–betrekking** (-en) *v* service; **–bode** (-n en -s) *v* (domestic) servant, maid-servant; **–boek** (-en) *o* service book [of the Church]; **–brief** (-brieven) *m* (official) missive; **–doend** 1 in waiting [at court]; 2 ✗ on duty; 3 (w a a r n e m e n d) acting; ~*e beambte* official in charge; **–er** (-s) *v* waitress; **–ig** serviceable, useful; ~ *voor* conducive to, beneficial to; **–ijver** *m* (professional) zeal; **–jaar** (-jaren) *o* 1 financial year, fiscal year; 2 year of service, in: *dienstjaren* years of service, years in office; **–kleding** *v* uniform; **–klopper** (-s) *m* martinet; **–knecht** (-en) *m* servant, man-servant; ⊙ **–maagd** (-en) *v*

servant, handmaid; **–meid** (-en) *v* (maid-)
servant; **–meisje** (-s) *o* servant-girl; **–order**
(-s) *v* service order; **–personeel** *o* servants;
–plicht *m* & *v* compulsory (military) service;
algemene ~ general conscription;
dienst′plichtig liable to (military) service; ~*e*
m conscript; **′dienstregeling** (-en) *v* time-
table, ⚓ (& *Am*) schedule; **–reis** (-reizen) *v*
official journey, (duty) tour; **–tijd** (-en) *m* 1
(v. iedere dag) working-hours, hours of
attendance; 2 (v. iems. loopbaan) term
of office; 3 ⚓ period of service;
dienst′vaardig obliging; **–heid** *v* obligingness; **′dienstverband** *o* engagement; **–verle-
nend** [-le.-] ~*e bedrijven* service industries;
–vertrek (-ken) *o* office; **–weigeraar** (-s) *m*
(met gewetensbezwaren) ⚓ conscien-
tious objector; **–weigeren** (weigerde ′dienst,
h. ′dienstgeweigerd) *vi* object to military
service; refuse to serve in the army; refuse to
enter the service; **–weigering** *v* refusal to
obey orders; **dienst′willig** obliging; *uw* ~*e* zie
dienaar; **′dienstwoning** (-en) *v* official residence; **–zaak** (-zaken) *v*, **–zaken** *mv* official
business
′dientafeltje (-s) *o* dinner-wagon, dumb-waiter
dientenge′volge [-tɪn-] in consequence, hence,
as a result
′dienwagen (-s) *m* trolley, dinner-wagon
1 diep 1 *aj* deep [water, bow, mourning,
colour, sleep, sigh &], profound [interest,
secret, bow]; *in* ~*e gedachten* deep in thought;
II *ad* deeply, profoundly; ~ *gevallen* fallen low;
~ *in de dertig* well on in the thirties; ~ *in de
nacht* far into the night, very late in the night;
~ *in de schulden* deep in debt; **III** als *o* in: *in het
~ste van zijn hart in the depths of his heart, in
his heart of hearts
2 diep (-en) *o* deep; canal; channel of a
harbour; *het grondeloze* ~ ☉ the unfathomed
deep
′diepbedroefd deeply afflicted; **–denkend**
deep-thinking; **–druk** *m* rotogravure; **–gaand**
searching [inquiry]; profound [difference]; ⚓
with a deep draught; **–gang** *m* ⚓ draught; *fig*
depth; *een* ~ *hebben van 10 voet* draw 10 feet of
water; **–liggend** sunken, deep-set [eyes];
–lood (-loden) *o* sounding-lead, deep-sea lead;
–ploeg (-en) *m* trench-plough
′diepte (-n en -s) *v* deep [= the sea]; depth[2]; *fig*
deepness, profoundness; *naar de* ~ *gaan* go to
the bottom; **–bom** (-men) *v* depth-charge;
–meter (-s) *m* depth-gauge; **–psychologie** [y
= i.] *v* depth psychology; **–punt** (-en) *o* lowest
point; the depth(s); ... *heeft het* ~ *bereikt* ... is at
its lowest ebb
′diepvries *m* deep-freeze [vegetables &]; **–kast**

(-en) *v*, **–kist** (-en) *v* deep-freeze, freezer; **–vak**
(-ken) *o* deep-freeze chamber (compartment)
diep′zeeonderzoek (-en) *o* deep-sea research
diep′zinnig deep, profound, abstruse; **–heid**
(-heden) *v* depth, profoundness, profundity,
abstruseness
dier (-en) *o* animal, beast
′dierbaar dear, beloved, dearly beloved; *dierbare
herinneringen* cherished memories; *mijn* ~*ste wens*
my dearest wish
′dierenarts *m* veterinary surgeon, **F** vet; **–asiel**
[s = z] (-en) *o* animal home; **–bescherming** *v*
protection of animals; *de* ~ the Society for the
Prevention of Cruelty to Animals; **–beul** (-en)
m tormentor of animals; **–dag** *m* (world)
animal day; **–fabel** (-s) *v* beast fable, animal
fable; **–handel** *m* 1 (alg.) animal trade; 2 (-s)
pet shop; **–handelaar** (-s en -laren) *m* naturalist; **–park** (-en) *o* zoological garden(s), zoo;
–psychology [y = i.] animal psychology,
zoopsychology; **–riem** *m* ★ zodiac; **–rijk** *o*
animal kingdom; **–temmer** (-s) *m* tamer (of
wild beasts); **–tuin** (-en) *m* zoological
garden(s), **F** zoo; **–vriend** (-en) *m* animal
lover; **–wereld** *v* animal world, fauna;
′dierevel (-len) *o* hide; **′diergaarde** (-n en -s)
v zoological garden(s), zoo; **–geneeskunde** *v*
veterinary medicine; **–kunde** *v* zoology;
dier′kundig zoological; **–e** (-n) *m* zoologist;
′dierlijk animal [fat, food, magnetism &],
bestial [instincts], brutal, brutish [lusts]; **–heid**
v animality; bestiality, brutality; **′diersoort**
(-en) *v* species of animals
1 dies *aj* therefore, consequently; *en wat* ~ *meer
zij* and so on, and so forth
2 ′dies [′di.ɪs] *m* ⚓ ± Founders' Day, [Oxford
University] Commemoration
′dieselmotor [s = z] (-s en -toren) *m* Diesel
engine; **–olie** *v* Diesel oil
dië′tist (-en) *m* dietician
diets *iem. iets* ~ *maken* make one believe sth.
Diets *o* (mediaeval) Dutch
die′vegge (-n) *v* (female) thief; **′dieven** (diefde,
h. gediefd) *vt* steal, pilfer, thieve; **′dieven-
bende** (-n en -s) *v* gang of thieves; **–hol**
(-holen) *o* thieves' den; **–lantaarn, –lantaren**
(-s) *v* dark lantern, bull's-eye; **–taal** *v* = *boeven-
taal*; **–wagen** (-s) *m* = *boevenwagen*; **dieve′rij**
(-en) *v* theft, robbery, thieving
differenti′aal [t = (t)s] (-ialen) *v* × differential;
–rekening *v* × differential calculus; **diffe-
renti′eel** [t = (t)s] **I** *aj differentiële rechten* differential duties; **II** (-iëlen) *v* ⚒ differential;
differenti′ëren (differentieerde, h. gedifferen-
tieerd) *vt* differentiate
dif′fusie [s = z] *v* diffusion; **dif′fuus** diffuse
difte′rie, difte′ritis *v* diphtheria

dif'tong (-en) *v* diphthong; **difton'gering** [-tɔŋ'ge:-] (-en) *v* diphthongization
di'gestie *v* digestion
'diggel (-en) *m* potsherd; *aan ~en vallen* F fall to smithereens
digi'taal digital
digni'taris (-sen) *m* dignitary
dij (-en) *v* thigh; **–been** (-deren) *o* thigh-bone, femur
dijk (-en) *m* dike, bank, dam; *aan de ~ zetten* get rid of [a functionary]; **–bestuur** (-sturen) *o* board of inspection of dikes; **–breuk** (-en) *v* bursting of a dike; **–graaf** (-graven) *m* dike-reeve; **–schouw** *m* inspection of a dike (of dikes); **–werker** (-s) *m* dike-maker, diker
dijn zie *mijn*
'dijspier (-en) *v* thigh muscle
dik I *aj* thick´, big, bulky, burly, stout; *~ en vet* plump; *Karel de Dikke* Charles the Fat; *de ~ke dame* the fat lady; *een ~ke honderd gulden* a hundred guilders odd; *~ke melk* curdled milk; *een ~ uur* a good hour; *~ke vrienden* great (close, fast, firm) friends; *ze zijn ~ke vrienden* F they are very thick (together); *een ~ke wang* a swollen cheek; *~ke wangen* plump cheeks; *~ doen* swagger, boast; *maak je niet ~* don't get excited, **S** keep your hair on; *~ worden* grow fat, put on flesh, fill out; **II** *ad* thickly; *het er ~ opleggen* F lay it on thick, pile it on; *de... ligt er ~ op* the... is quite obvious; *er ~ in zitten* have plenty of money; **III** *o* thick (part); grounds [of coffee]; *door ~ en dun met iem. meegaan* go through thick and thin with sbd.; **–buik** (-en) *m* F fatty; **dik'buikig** big-bellied, corpulent; **'dikdoener** (-s) *m* braggart, windbag; **–ig** swaggering, ostentatious, braggart; **'dikheid** *v* thickness, corpulency, bigness; **dik'huidig** *aj* thick-skinned²; *~e dieren, ~en* thickskinned quadrupeds, pachyderms; **'dikkerd** (-s) *m = dikzak*; **–je** (-s) *o* F roly-poly; **'dikkop** (-pen) *m* 1 thickhead; 2 🐸 tadpole; **'dikte** (-n en -s) *v* thickness, bigness &; **⚡** swelling
'dikwijls often, frequently
'dikzak (-ken) *m* big fellow, F fatty
di'lemma ('s) *o* dilemma; *iem. voor een ~ stellen* place sbd. on the horns of a dilemma
dilet'tant(e) (-en) *m* (-*v*) dilettante [*mv* dilettanti], amateur; **dilet'tanterig** amateurish; **dilettan'tisme** *o* dilettantism, amateurishness
dili'gence [di.li.'ʒãsǝ] (-s) *v* stage-coach, coach
'dille *v* 🌿 dill
diluvi'aal diluvial; **di'luvium** *o* diluvium
di'mensie [s = z] (-s) *v* dimension
'dimlicht (-en) *o met ~(en) rijden* drive on dipped headlights; **'dimmen** (dimde, h. gedimd) *vt & vi* dip [the headlights]
di'ner [di.'ne.] (-s) *o* dinner, dinner party;

di'neren (dineerde, h. gedineerd) *vi* dine
ding (-en) *o* thing; *een aardig ~* a bright young thing [of a girl]; *het is een heel ~* it is not an easy thing; *alle goede ~en in drieën* third time is lucky
'dingen* *vi* chaffer, bargain, haggle; *~ naar* compete for, try to obtain [a post &]
'dinges *mijnheer* ~ Mr So-and-so; **'dingsigheidje** (-s) *o* gadget, dinkey
'dinsdag (-dagen) *m* Tuesday; **–s I** *aj* Tuesday; **II** *ad* on Tuesdays
dio'cees (-cesen) *o* diocese; **dioce'saan** [s = z] (-sanen) *aj & m* diocesan; **dio'cese** (-n) *v = diocees*
diop'trie (-ieën) *v* dioptre, diopter
di'ploma ('s) *o* certificate, diploma
diplo'maat (-maten) *m* diplomat, diplomatist; **diplo'matenkoffertje** (-s) *o* attaché-case, dispatch case; **diploma'tie** [-'(t)si.] *v* diplomacy; **diploma'tiek I** *aj* diplomatic; *langs ~e weg* through diplomatic channels; **II** *v* diplomatics; **diplo'matisch** diplomatic
diplo'meren (diplomeerde, h. gediplomeerd) *vt* certificate; *gediplomeerd verpleegster* ook: qualified (trained) nurse
di'rect I *aj* direct; straight; **II** *ad* directly, promptly, at once, straightaway
direc'teur (-en en -s) *m* director, managing director [of a company]; manager [of a theatre]; governor [of a prison]; superintendent [of a hospital]; 📮 postmaster; principal, headmaster [of a school]; ♪ (musical) conductor, choirmaster; **–generaal** (-directeurs-generaal en directeuren-generaal) *m* director-general [of the B.B.C.]; *~ der Posterijen* 📮 Postmaster General
di'rectheid *v* directness
di'rectie [-'rɪksi.] (-s) *v* board; management; **direc'tief** (-tieven) *o* directive; **di'rectiekeet** [-'rɪksi.-] (-keten) *v* building shed
direc'toire [di.rɪk'tʋa:r] (-s) *m* knickers, panties
directo'raat (-raten) *o* directorate; **direc'trice** (-s) *v* directress; manageress [of a hotel], (lady-)principal, headmistress [of a school]; superintendent, matron [of a hospital]
diri'geerstok (-ken) *m* baton; **diri'gent** (-en) *m* (musical) conductor [of an orchestra], (v a n k o o r) choirmaster; **diri'geren** (dirigeerde, h. gedirigeerd) *vt* direct [troops]; ♪ conduct [an orchestra]; **diri'gisme** *o* dirigism(e)
1 dis [di.s] (-sen) *v* ♪ D sharp
2 dis ☉ **dis** [dɪs] (-sen) *m* table, board
dis'agio *o* discount
dis'cipel [dɪ'si.pǝl] (-en en -s) *m* disciple [of Christ, of any leader of thought &]; pupil [of a school]
discipli'nair [-'nɛ:r] disciplinary; **disci'pline** (-s) *v* discipline; *ijzeren ~* tight rein;

discipli'neren (disciplineerde, h. gedisciplineerd) *vt* discipline

'discobar (-s) *m* & *v* record shop

discon'teren (disconteerde, h. gedisconteerd) *vt* discount; dis'conto ('s) *o* (rate of) discount, (bank) rate

disco'theek (-theken) *v* 1 record library; 2 (a m u s e m e n t s g e l e g e n h e i d) discotheque

dis'creet modest [behaviour]; considerate [handling of the business]; discreet [person]

discre'pantie [-kre.'pan(t)si.] (-s) discrepancy, difference

dis'cretie [-(t)si.] *v* 1 modesty; considerateness; 2 (g e h e i m h o u d i n g) secrecy; 3 (g o e d - v i n d e n) discretion

discrimi'natie [-(t)si.] (-s) *v* discrimination; discrimi'neren (discrimineerde, h. gediscrimineerd) *vt* discriminate against

'discus (-sen) *m* discus, disc, disk

dis'cussie (-s) *v* discussion, debate, argument; *in* ∼ *brengen, ter* ∼ *stellen* bring up for discussion, bring (call) in(to) question, challenge; **-leider** (-s) *m* (panel) chairman; discussi'ëren (discussieerde, h. gediscussieerd) *vi* = *discuteren*; dis'cussiestuk (-ken) *o* working paper

'discusvormig discoid; **-werpen** *o* throwing the discus; **-werper** (-s) *m* discus thrower

discu'tabel arguable, debatable; discu'teren (discuteerde, h. gediscuteerd) *vi* discuss, argue; *m e t i e m.* ∼ argue with sbd.; *o v e r i e t s* ∼ discuss, talk over, ventilate a subject

'disgenoot (-noten) *m* neighbour at table, fellow-guest; *de disgenoten* the guests

'disharmonie *v* disharmony, discord

'diskrediet *o* discredit; *in* ∼ *brengen* bring into discredit, bring (throw) discredit on, discredit

diskwalifi'catie [-(t)si.] (-s) *v* disqualification; diskwalifi'ceren (diskwalificeerde, h. gediskwalificeerd) *vt* disqualify

dis'pache [-pa.ʃ] (-s) *v* average adjustment; dispa'cheur (-s) *m* average adjuster

dispen'satie [-'za.(t)si.] (-s) *v* dispensation (*from* van); dispen'seren [s = z] (dispenseerde, h. gedispenseerd) *vt* dispense (*from* van)

dispo'neren (disponeerde, h. gedisponeerd) *vi* ∼ *o p* $ value on; ∼ *o v e r* dispose of; zie ook: *gedisponeerd*; dispo'nibel available, at one's disposal; dispo'sitie [-'zi.(t)si.] (-s) *v* disposition, disposal

dispu'teren (disputeerde, h. gedisputeerd) *vi* dispute, argue; dis'puut (-puten) *o* dispute, disputation, argument; (c l u b) debating club

'dissel (-s) *m* 1 pole [of a carriage] ‖ 2 [carpenter's] adze; **-boom** (-bomen) *m* pole

dis'senter (-s) *m pol* dissident; dissenter

disser'tatie [-(t)si.] (-s) *v* dissertation; ∾ thesis [*mv* theses] [for a degree]

dissi'dent (-en) *m* dissident; (c o m m u n i s - t i s c h) deviationist

disso'nant (-en) *m* ♪ discord; *dat was de enige* ∼ that was the only discordant note

dis'tantie [-(t)si.] (-s) *v* distance; *fig* reserve; ∼ *bewaren* keep (stand, hold) aloof from; distanti'ëren [-(t)si.'e:rǝ(n)] (distantieerde, h. gedistantieerd) *zich* ∼ *van* ⚔ detach oneself from [the enemy]; *fig* move away from, dissociate oneself from [those views &]

'distel (-s en -en) *m* & *v* thistle; **-vink** (-en) *m* & *v* goldfinch

distil'laat (-laten) *o* distillate; distilla'teur (-s) *m* distiller; distil'latie [-(t)si.] *v* distillation; distilleerde'rij (-en) *v* distillery; distil'leer-ketel (-s) *m* still; **-kolf** (-kolven) *v* receiver of a still; **-toestel** (-len) *o* still; distil'leren (distilleerde, h. gedistilleerd) *vt* distil

dis'tinctie [-'tɪnksi.] (-s) *v* refinement, elegance, distinction; distinc'tief (-tieven) *o* (distinctive) badge

distribu'eren (distribueerde, h. gedistribueerd) *vt* distribute; (i n t i j d e n v a n o o r l o g o f s c h a a r s t e) ration; distri'butie [-(t)si.] (-s) *v* distribution; (i n t i j d e n v a n o o r l o g o f s c h a a r s t e) rationing

dis'trict (-en) *o* district

dit this; ∼ *alles* all this; ∼ *zijn mijn kleren* these are my clothes; 'ditje (-s) *o* ∼*s en datjes* 1 customary banalities; 2 trifles, knick-knacks; *wij praatten over* ∼*s en datjes* we were talking about (of) this and that, about one thing and another; 'ditmaal this time, for this once

'dito ditto, do

'diva ('s) *v* diva, prima donna

'divan (-s) *m* couch, divan; **-bed** (-den) *o* bed-settee, sofa bed

diver'geren (divergeerh. en is gedivergeerd) *vi* diverge

di'vers various; ∼*en* sundries, miscellaneous (articles, items, news &)

divi'dend (-en) *o* dividend; **-belasting** *v* dividend (coupon) tax; **-bewijs** (-wijzen) *o* dividend coupon

di'visie [s = z] (-s en -iën) *v* division°

dm = *decimeter*

d.m.v. = *door middel van*

do *v* ♪ do

'dobbelbeker (-s) *m* dice cup, shaker, dicebox; 'dobbelen (dobbelde, h. gedobbeld) *vi* dice, play dice, gamble; 'dobbelspel (-spelen) *o* dice-playing, game at dice; **-steen** (-stenen) *m* die [*mv* dice]; cube [of bread &]

'dobber (-s) *m* float [of a fishing-line]; *een harde* ∼ *hebben om...* be hard put to it to [do sth.];

'**dobberen** (dobberde, h. gedobberd) *vi* bob (up and down), float; *fig* fluctuate [between hope and fear]

do'**cent** (-en) *m* teacher; **–enkamer** (-s) *v* common room, staff room; do'**ceren** (doceerde, h. gedoceerd) *vi* & *vt* teach

doch but

docht *mij* V.T. v. *dunken*

'**dochter** (-s) *v* daughter; **–maatschappij** (-en) *v* subsidiary company

do'**ciel** docile, submissive

'**doctor** (-s en -'toren) *m* doctor; docto'**raal** (-ralen) *o* final examination for a degree; docto'**raat** (-raten) *o* doctorate, doctor's degree; docto'**randus** (-di en -dussen) *m* candidate for the doctorate (for a doctor's degree); docto'**reren** (doctoreerde, is gedoctoreerd) *vi* graduate, take one's degree; '**doctorsbul** (-len) *v* doctor's diploma

doctri'**nair** [-'nɛːr] doctrinaire

docu'**ment** (-en) *o* document; documen'**tair** [-'tɛːr] documentary; **–e** (-s) *v* documentary (film), actuality film; documen'**tatie** [-(t)si.] *v* documentation; docu'**mentenkoffertje** (-s) *o* dispatch-box (-case); documen'**teren** (documenteerde, h. gedocumenteerd) *vt* document; zie ook: *gedocumenteerd*

'**doddig** sweet, adorable; *Am* cute

'**dode** (-n) *m-v* dead man, dead woman; *de ~* ook: the deceased; *de ~n* the dead; *een ~* a dead man (body); *één ~* one dead, one killed; *het aantal ~n* the number of lives lost [in an accident], the casualties; '**dodelijk I** *aj* mortal [blow], fatal [wounds]; deadly [hatred]; lethal [weapons]; **II** *ad* mortally, fatally [wounded]; deadly [dull]; '**dodemansknop** (-pen) *m* dead-man's handle (pedal); '**doden** (doodde, h. gedood) *vt* kill², slay, put (do) to death; *fig* mortify [the flesh]; *de tijd ~* kill time; '**dodenakker** (-s) *m* God's acre, cemetery; **–cel** [-stl] (-len) *v* condemned cell, deathcell; **–cultus** *m* cult of the dead; **–dans** (-en) *m* death-dance, Dance of Death [by Dürer]; **–masker** (-s) *o* ·death-mask; **–mis** (-sen) *v* requiem mass; **–rijk** *o* realm of the dead; **–wacht** (-en) *v* lyke-wake

'**doedelen** (doedelde, h. gedoedeld) *vi* 1 ♩ play the bagpipe; 2 tootle; '**doedelzak** (-ken) *m* bagpipe, (bag)pipes

doe-het-'**zelf** do-it-yourself [kit &]; doe-het-'**zelver** (-s) *m* do-it-yourselfer, hobbyist

1 doek (-en) *m* 1 cloth; 2 (o m s l a g d o e k) shawl; *hij had zijn arm in een ~* he wore his arm in a sling; *u i t de ~en doen* disclose

2 doek (-en) 1 *o* & *m* cloth [of woven stuff]; ⚓ sail; 2 *o* canvas [of a painter]; curtain [of theatre]; screen [of cinema]; **–je** (-s) *o* 1 (piece of) cloth, rag; 2 fichu; *~ voor het bloeden* pallia-

tive; *er geen ~s om winden* not mince matters; **–speld** (-en) *v* brooch

doel (-en) *o* target˚, mark; *sp* goal; *fig* mark, aim, goal, purpose, object; design; (v . r e i s) destination); *een goed ~* a good (worthy) cause (intention; *het ~ heiligt de middelen* the end justifies the means; *recht op zijn ~ afgaan* go (come) straight to the point; *zijn ~ bereiken* gain (attain, secure, achieve) one's object (one's end); *zijn ~ missen* miss one's aim; *een ~ nastreven* pursue an object (end); *zijn ~ treffen* hit the mark; *het ~ voorbijstreven* overshoot the mark, defeat its own object; ● *m e t het ~ om...* for the purpose of ...ing, with a view to...; with intent to... [steal]; *t e n ~ hebben* be intended to... [ensure his safety &]; *zich ten ~ stellen* make it one's object to...; *v o o r een goed ~* for a good intention; *dat was genoeg voor mijn ~* that was enough for my purpose; **doelbe'wust** purposeful, purposive; '**doeleinde** (-n) *o* end, purpose; '**doelen** (doelde, h. gedoeld) *vi ~ op* aim at, allude to; *dat doelt op mij* it is aimed at me; '**doelgemiddelde** (-n en -s) *o* goal average; **–groep** (-en) *v* target group; **–lijn** (-en) *v* goal line; '**doelloos** aimless, meaningless; **–heid** *v* aimlessness; '**doelman** (-nen) *m = doelverdediger*; **doel'matig** appropriate (to the purpose), suitable, efficient; **–heid** *v* suitability, efficiency; '**doelpaal** (-palen) *m sp* goal post; **–punt** (-en) *o sp* goal; *een ~ maken* score (a goal); **–schop** (-pen) *m* goal-kick; **–stelling** (-en) *v* aim; **–trap** (-pen) *m* goal-kick; **doel'treffend** efficient, effective, to the purpose; '**doelverdediger** (-s) *m* goal-keeper; **–wit** *o* target˚, mark; *fig* mark, aim, goal, purpose, object

doem *m* curse; '**doemen** (doemde, h. gedoemd) *vt* condemn, foredoom; *tot mislukking gedoemd* doomed to failure

doen* I *vt* 1 (i n h e t a l g.) do, work [harm, a service &]; 2 (v ó ó r i n f i n i t i e f) make [sbd. go, people laugh]; 3 (s t e k e n , w e g-b e r g e n) put [it in one's pocket &]; 4 (o p k n a p p e n) do [one's hair, a room]; 5 (o p b r e n g e n , k o s t e n) be worth, be, fetch [2 guilders a pound]; 6 (m a k e n) make [a journey], take [a walk &]; 7 (u i t s p r e k e n) make [a promise, vow], take [an oath]; 8 (t e r h e r h a l i n g v a n h e t w e r k w.) do [of onvertaald: he will cheat you, as he has (done) me; will you get it or shall I?]; zie ook: *afbreuk, dienst, groet, keuze &; het ~ (v . m a c h i n e)* work, go; *die vaas doet het* produces its effect; *dat doet het hem* that's what does it; it works; *geld doet het hem* it's money makes the mare to go; *het doet er niet(s) toe* it does not matter; that is neither here nor there, no matter; *hij kan het* (*goed*) ~ he can (well) afford it; he is comfortably off; *hij kan het er mee* ~ he can take his change out of that; *hij doet het om het geld* he does it for the money; *hij doet het er om* he does it on purpose; *het is hem er om te* ~ *aan te tonen, dat...* he is concerned to show that...; *het is hem alleen om het geld te* ~ it is only money that he is after; *daarom is het niet te* ~ that is not the point; *is het je daarom te* ~? is that what you are after?; *het zijne* ~ play one's part; *iets* ~ do something; *als je hem iets durft te* ~ if you dare hurt (touch) him; *als ik er iets aan kan* ~ if I can do anything about it; *ik zal zien of ik er iets aan kan* ~ I'll see about it; *ik kan er niets aan* ~ 1 I can do nothing about it (in the matter), 2 I cannot help it; *er is niets aan te* ~ it cannot be helped, there is no help for it; *je moet hem niets* ~, *hoor!* mind you don't hurt (touch) him; *zij hebben veel te* ~ 1 they have a lot of work to do; 2 they do a roaring business; *wat doet het buiten?* what is the weather doing?; *wat doet het er toe?* what does it matter?; *wat doet dat huis?* what's the rent of the house?; *wat doet hij?* what's his business (trade, profession)?; *wij hebben wel wat beters te* ~ we have better things to do; *ik heb het weer gedaan* I'm always blamed; **II** *vi* do; *wat is hier te* ~? what is doing here?, what's up?, what is going on here?; ~ *alsof...* pretend to, make as if, make believe to; *je doet maar!* (do) as you please, please yourself; *je moet maar* ~ *alsof je thuis was* make yourself at home!; *hij doet maar zo* he is only pretending (shamming); *daaraan heeft hij verkeerd* (*wijs*) *gedaan* he has done wrong (wisely) to...; *onverschillig* ~ feign indifference; *vreemd* ~ act (behave) strangely; *doe wel en zie niet om* do well and shame the devil; *doe zoals ik* do as I do; ● *zij* ~ *niet aan postzegels verzamelen* they don't go in for collecting stamps; *zij doet niet meer aan...* she has given up...; *ik kan daar niet aan* ~ I can't occupy myself with that; *zij* ~ *in wijnen* they deal in wines; *daar kun je jaren m e e* ~ that will last you for years; *hij had gedaan m e t eten* (*schrijven*) he had finished (done) dinner (writing &); *wij hadden met hem te* ~ we pitied him, we were (we felt) sorry for him; *pas op, als je met hem te* ~ *hebt* when dealing with him; *...je zult met mij te* ~ *krijgen* you shall have to do with me; *als je... dan krijg je met mij te* ~ ...we shall get into a row; *met een gulden kun je niet veel* ~ a guilder does not go far; *hoe lang doe je o v e r dat werk?* how long does it take you?; *daar is heel wat over te* ~ *geweest* there has been a lot of talk about it, it has made a great stir. Zie ook: *doende* & *gedaan;* **III** *o* doing(s); *hij weet ons* ~ *en laten* he knows all our doings; *er is geen* ~ *aan* it

cannot be done; ● *i n betere* ~ in better circumstances, better situated, better off; *in goede(n)* ~ *zijn* be well-to-do, well off, in easy circumstances; *hij is niet in zijn gewone* ~ he is not his usual self; *upset; u i t zijn gewone* ~ off (out of) one's beat; upset; *niets v a n* ~ *hebben met* have nothing to do with; *dat is al heel aardig v o o r zijn* ~ for him; **–de** doing; ~ *zijn met* ...be busy ...ing; *al* ~ *leert men* practice makes perfect; **'doeniet** (-en) *m* do-nothing, idler; **'doenlijk** practicable, feasible

does (doezen) *m* poodle [cable, feasible

'doetje (-s) *o* **F** silly, softy

'doezelen (doezelde, h. gedoezeld) *vi* doze, be drowsy; **'doezelig** dozy, drowsy

dof dull [of colour, light, sound, mind &]; dim [light]; lacklustre [eyes], lustreless [pearls]; dead [gold]

'doffer (-s) *m* cock-pigeon

'dofheid *v* dullness, dimness, lack of lustre

doft (-en) *v* thwart, (rower's) bench

dog (-gen) *m* mastiff, bulldog

'dogma ('s en -ta) *o* dogma; **dog'maticus** (-ci) *m* dogmatist; **dogma'tiek** *v* dogmatics; **dog'matisch** dogmatic

dok (-ken) *o* ⚓ dock; *drijvend* ~ floating dock

'doken V.T. meerv. v. *duiken*

'dokgeld (-en) *o* dockage; **~en** dock-dues

'dokken (dokte, h. gedokt) **I** *vt* dock, put into dock; **II** *vi* dock, go into dock; (b e t a l e n) **F** fork out, cough up

dok'saal (-salen) *o* = *oksaal*

'dokter (-s en dok'toren) *m* doctor, physician; *hij is onder ~s handen* he is under medical treatment; **'dokteren** (dokterde, h. gedokterd *vi* 1 (v. d o k t e r) practise; 2 (v. p a t i ë n t) be under the doctor; ~ *aan* tinker at; **'dokters-assistente** (-n) *v* receptionist; **–rekening** *v* doctor's bill; **–visite** [-zi.tə] (-s) *v* doctor's visit

'dokwerker (-s) *m* dock labourer, docker

1 dol I *aj* mad; frantic, wild; *is het niet* ~? isn't it ridiculous?; *een ~le hond* a mad dog; *~le pret* hilarious fun; *~le schroef* screw that won't bite, stripped screw; *hij is* ~ *met haar* he is wild (crazy) about her; *hij is* ~ *op erwtensoep* he is very fond of pea-soup; *iem.* ~ *maken* drive sbd. mad (wild); ~ *worden* run mad; *het is om* ~ *te worden* it is enough to drive you mad, it is maddening; **II** *ad* madly; *~veel van iets houden* be mad about it; *hij is* ~ *verliefd* he is madly in love (with her), he is mad on her; **III** *o door het ~le heen zijn* be mad (frantic) with joy, be wild

2 dol (-len) *m* ⚓ thole, row lock

'dolblij mad with joy, overjoyed

'dolboord (-en) *o* gunwale

'doldriest reckless; **dol'driftig** furious

'dolen (doolde, h. gedoold) *vi* 1 wander (about),

roam, rove, ramble; 2 err [be mistaken]
dolf (**dolven**) V.T. v. *delven*
dol'fijn (-en) *m* 🐟 dolphin
'dolgelukkig deliriously happy
'dol'graag ~ ! with the greatest pleasure!, ever
so much!; *ik zou het ~ willen* I'd love to
'dolheid (-heden) *v* wildness, madness, frenzy
'dolik *v* cockle, corn-cockle, darnel
dolk (-en) *m* dagger, poniard, stiletto, dirk;
–mes (-sen) *o* bowie-knife; **–steek** (-steken)
m, **–stoot** (-stoten) *m* stab (with a dagger),
stab² [in the back]
'dollar (-s) *m* dollar
dolle'kervel *m* hemlock
'dolleman (-nen) *m* madman, madcap; **–swerk**
o het is ~ it is sheer madness, a mad thing to
do; **'dollen** (dolde, h. gedold) *vi* lark
'dolmen (-s) *m* dolmen
dolo'miet *o* dolomite
'dolven V.T. meerv. v. *delven*
dol'zinnig mad, frantic; **–heid** (-heden) *v*
madness, frenzy
1 dom I *aj* stupid, dull; *een ~me streek* a stupid
(silly, foolish) thing; *hij is zo ~ nog niet* (*als hij er
uitziet*) he is not such a fool as he looks; *hij
houdt zich van de(n) ~me* he pretends ignorance,
plays possum; *het geluk is met de ~men* fortune
favours fools; **II** *ad* stupidly
2 dom (domkerken) *m* cathedral (church)
3 dom *m* (t i t e l) dom
domani'aal domanial
do'mein (-en) *o* domain², crown land,
demesne; *publiek ~* public property
'domheer (-heren) *m* canon, prebendary
'domheid (-heden) *v* stupidity, dullness;
domheden ook: stupid (silly, foolish) things
domi'cilie (-s en -iën) *o* domicile; *~ kiezen*
choose one's domicile; **domicili'ëren** (domi-
cilieerde, h. gedomicilieerd) *vt* domicile
domi'nant (-en) *v* ♪ dominant
'dominee (-s) *m* clergyman; minister [esp. in
Nonconformist & Presbyterian Churches];
vicar, rector [in Church of England]; >
parson; [Lutheran] pastor; *~ W. Brown* the
Reverend W. Brown; *~ Niemöller* Pastor
Niemöller
domi'neren (domineerde, h. gedomineerd) **I** *vt*
dominate (over), lord it over, command; **II** *vi*
(pre)-dominate ‖ play (at) dominoes; **–d**
dominating, possessive
domini'caan (-canen) *m* Dominican
Domini'caanse Repu'bliek *v de ~* the
Dominican Republic, Santo Domingo
dominica'nes (-sen) *v* Dominican nun
'domino ('s) 1 *m* domino; 2 *sp* dominoes;
'dominoën (dominode, h. gedominood) *vi*
play (a game of) dominoes; **'dominospel**

(-len) *o* 1 (game of) dominoes; 2 set of dominoes; **–steen** (-stenen) *m* domino
'domkapittel (-s) *o* (dean and) chapter; **–kerk**
(-en) *v* cathedral (church)
'domkop (-pen) *m* blockhead, dunce, duffer,
dolt, numskull, dullard, nitwit; **'domme-
kracht** (-en) *v* ✗ jack
'dommel *m in de ~ zijn* be in a doze;
'dommelen (dommelde, h. gedommeld) *vi*
doze, drowse; **'dommelig** dozy, drowsy
'dommerik (-riken) *m*, **'domoor** (-oren) *m* =
domkop
'dompelaar (-s) *m* 1 🐦 diver; 2 ✗ plunger; 3
☿ immersion heater; **'dompelen** (dompelde,
h. gedompeld) **I** *vt* plunge², dip, duck,
immerse; **II** *vr zich ~ in* plunge into ♪
'domper (-s) *m* extinguisher; *een ~ zetten op*
dampen, cast a damp over, pour (throw) cold
water on
'dompig close, stuffy
'domproost (-en) *m* dean
domp'teur (-s) *m* (animal) trainer, (animal)
tamer
'domtoren (-s) *m* cathedral tower
'domweg 1 stupidly, without thinking; 2
(e e n v o u d i g w e g) just, simply
dona'teur (-s) *m* donor; **do'natie** [-(t)si.] (-s) *v*
donation, gift
'Donau *m* Danube
'donder (-s) *m* thunder²; *arme ~* poor devil; *het
kan me geen ~ schelen* I don't care a damn; *daar
kun je ~ op zeggen* you bet, you can bet your life
on it; *iem. op zijn ~ geven* give sbd. a proper
dressing down; *als door de ~ getroffen* thunderstruck; **–bui** (-en) *v* thunderstorm; **–bus** (-sen)
v 🔫 blunderbuss
'donderdag (-dagen) *m* Thursday; **–s I** *aj*
Thursday; **II** *ad* on Thursdays
'donderen (donderde, h. gedonderd) *vi*
thunder² [against abuses, in one's ears], fulmi-
nate²; *hij keek of hij het in Keulen hoorde ~* he
stared like a stuck pig; (v a l l e n) **P** pitch,
tumble (down the stairs); **–d** thundering²,
thunderous²; **'dondergod** *m* thunder-god,
thunderer; **'donderjagen** (donderjaagde, h.
gedonderjaagd) *vi* raise hell; **'donders F I** *aj*
devilish, confounded; **II** *ad* < deucedly; *~ blij*
(*groot*) thundering glad (great); **III** *ij* the deuce!;
'donderslag (-slagen) *m* thunderclap, peal of
thunder; *een ~ uit heldere hemel* a bolt from the
blue; **–steen** (-stenen) *m* **F** little rascal;
–straal (-stralen) *m* & *v* streak of lightning;
(s c h e l d w o o r d) **F** rogue, rascal, scoundrel;
–wolk (-en) *v* thundercloud
dong (**dongen**) V.T. v. *dingen*
don'jon [dõ'ʒõ] (-s) *m* dungeon, keep
Don Juan [dõʒy.'ã, dòngu.'ɑn] *m* Don Juan²,

lady-killer

'**donker I** *aj* dark², obscure, gloomy, sombre, dusky, dim, ☉ darksome, darkling; *het ziet er ~ voor hem uit* things look pretty black (gloomy) for him; **II** *ad* darkly; *hij keek ~* he looked gloomy; *hij ziet alles ~ in* he takes a gloomy view of things; **III** *o het ~* the dark; *bij ~* at dark; *in het ~* in the dark²; *in het ~ tasten* 1 grope (walk) in darkness; 2 be in the dark [about the future &]; *na ~* after dark; *vóór ~* before dark; –**blauw** dark-blue, deep-blue; –**bruin** dark-brown, deepbrown; –**geel** deep-yellow; –**heid** *v* darkness, obscurity; –**rood** dark-red, deep-red; –**te** *v* darkness, obscurity

'**donor** (-s) *m* donor

dons *o* down, fluff; zie ook: *poederdons*; –**achtig** downy, fluffy; '**donzen** *aj* down; zie ook: *donzig*; –**zig** downy, fluffy

dood *aj* dead [also of capital, weight &]; *zo ~ als een pier* as dead as a door-nail; *de dode hand* mortmain; *een dode stad* a dead-alive town; *ze lieten hem voor ~ liggen* they left him for dead; *zich ~ drinken* drink oneself to death; *zich ~ houden* sham dead; *zich ~ lachen* die (with, of) laughing, laugh one's head off, laugh oneself helpless; *ik lach me ~!* **F** it's too killing; zie ook: *kniezen* &; *iem. ~ verklaren* send sbd. to Coventry; **II** *m & v* death; *~ en verderf* death and destruction; *het is de ~ in de pot* it is a dead-alive business; *er uitziend als de ~ van Ieperen* ghastly white, wretchedly thin; *de een zijn ~ is de ander zijn brood* one man's meat is another man's poison; *duizend doden sterven* die a thousand deaths; *een natuurlijke ~ sterven* die a natural death; *de ~ vinden* meet one's death; *de ~ in de golven vinden* find a watery grave; *hij is er (zo bang) als de ~ voor* he is mortally afraid of it, he is scared stiff (of it); *de ~ nabij* at death's door; ● *hij heeft het gehaald bij de ~ af* he has been at death's door; *n a de ~* after death; *o m de (dooie) ~ niet!* not for anything!, not on your life!; *by no means, not at all* [stupid &]; *dat zou ik om de ~ niet willen* not for the life of me; *hij is t e n dode opgeschreven* he is doomed (to death); *t e r ~ brengen* put to death; *t o t in de ~ getrouw* faithful unto death; *u i t de ~ opstaan* rise from the dead; –'**af** dead-beat, knocked up; –'**arm** very poor, as poor as Job, as poor as a church mouse; –**be'daard** quite calm, as cool as a cucumber; –**bidder** (-s) *m* undertaker's man; –**bijten**¹ *vt* bite to death; –**blijven** *vi ter*

plaatse ~ die on the spot; –**bloeden** (bloedde 'dood, is 'doodgebloed) *vi* bleed to death; *fig* fizzle out, die down; –**doener** (-s) *m* **F** clincher; –**drukken**¹ *vt* press (squeeze) to death; –**een'voudig I** *aj* very easy, as easy as lying, quite simple; **II** *ad* simply; –'**eerlijk** honest to the core; –'**eng** creepy, eerie; –'**ernstig** serious; –**gaan**¹ *vi* die; –**geboren** still-born²; *fig* foredoomed to failure; *het boek was een ~ kindje* the book fell still-born from the press; –**ge'makkelijk** quite easy; –**gemoede'reerd** cooly, calmly; –**gewoon I** *aj* quite common; ordinary, common or garden; **II** *ad* simply; –**goed** extremely kind-hearted, kind to a fault; –**gooien**¹ *vt* kill by throwing stones at...; *iem. ~ met geleerde woorden* knock sbd. down (bombard) with learned words; –**graver** (-s) *m* 1 grave-digger; 2 ❀ sexton-beetle; –**hongeren** (hongerde 'dood, *vi* is, *vt* h. 'doodgehongerd) starve to death; –**jammer** a great pity; –**kalm** = *doodbedaard*; –**kist** (-en) *v* coffin; –**lachen**¹ *vr zich ~* nearly die laughing, split one's sides with laugher; *ik lach me dood!* that's a scream!, that's absolutely killing!; *'t is om je dood te lachen* it's too funny for words; –'**leuk** quite coolly, as cool as a cucumber; –**lopen**¹ **I** *vi* have a dead end [of a street]; *~de straat* cul-de-sac, blind alley; *~de weg* (o p s c h r i f t) no through road; **II** *vr zich ~* tire oneself out with walking; –'**mak** meek as a lamb; –**maken**¹ *vt* kill, do to death; –'**makkelijk** = *doodgemakkelijk*; –**martelen**¹ *vt* torture to death; –'**moe(de)** dead-tired, dead-beat, tired to death; –'**nuchter** quite sober; zie ook: *doodleuk*; –**onge'lukkig** utterly miserable; –**on'schuldig** as innocent as a lamb; –'**op** = *doodaf*; –**praten**¹ *vt* talk out [a bill]

doods deathly, deathlike [silence], dead, dead-alive [town]; '**doodsakte** (-n en -s) *v* death certificate; –**angst** (-en) *m* 1 (d o d e l ij k e a n g s t) mortal fear; 2 (a n g s t d e s d o o d s) death agony; –'**bang** mortally afraid [of...], dead scared [of...], scared stiff; –**bed** (-den) *o* death-bed; –**beenderen** *mv* (dead man's) bones; –**be'nauwd** = *doodsbang*; –**bericht** (-en) *o* 1 announcement of sbd.'s death; 2 obituary (notice); –**bleek** deathly pale, as white as a sheet; '**doodschamen**¹ *vr zich ~* die for shame; –**schieten**¹ *vt* shoot (dead); –**schoppen**¹ *vt* kick to death; '**doodsgevaar** (-varen) *o* peril of death, danger of life, deadly

---

¹ V.T. en V.D. van dit werkwoord volgens het model: '**dood**drukken, V.T. drukte '**dood**, V.D. '**dood**gedrukt. Zie voor de vormen onder het grondwoord, in dit voorbeeld: *drukken*. Bij sterke en onregelmatige werkwoorden wordt u verwezen naar de lijst achterin.

danger; **–hemd** (-en) *o* shroud, winding-sheet;
–hoofd (-en) *o* death's-head, skull; **–kist** (-en)
= *doodkist*; **–kleed** (-kleden) *o* 1 (l i j k w a d e)
shroud, winding-sheet; 2 (d o o d k i s t k l e e d)
pall; **–kleur** *v* livid colour; **–klok** (-ken) *v*
death-bell, passing-bell, knell; **–kop** (-pen) *m*
F = *doodshoofd*

'doodslaan[1] *vt* kill, slay, [a man], beat to death;
fig silence [sbd. in a discussion]; **–slag**
(-slagen) *m* homicide, manslaughter; **–smak**
(-ken) *m* deadly crash (fall)

'doodsnood *m* (death) agony; **–oorzaak**
(-zaken) *v* cause of death; **–schrik** *m* mortal
fright; *iem. een ~ op het lijf jagen* frighten sbd.
out of his wits; **–snik** *m* last gasp; **–strijd**
(-en) *m* death-struggle, agony; **–stuip** (-en) *v*
spasm of death

'doodsteek (-steken) *m* death-blow[2], finishing
stroke[2]; **–steken**[1] *vt* stab (to death); **–stil**
stock-still; still as death, deathly silent; [listen]
dead silent; *hij stond ~* he stood as still as a
statue; **–straf** (-fen) *v* capital punishment,
death penalty

'doodsuur (-uren) *o* hour of death, dying (last,
mortal) hour; **–verachting** *v* contempt for
death; **–vijand** (-en) *m* mortal enemy; **–zweet**
o death-sweat, sweat of death

'dood'tij *o* slack water; neap(-tide); **'dood-
trappen**[1] *vt* kick to death; **–vallen**[1] *vi* fall
(drop) dead; *ik mag ~ als...* strike me dead if...;
–ver'legen very bashful, very timid;
–verven[1] *vt met een betrekking gedoodverfd worden*
be popularly designated for a place (post); *hij
werd ermee gedoodverfd* it was attributed to him, it
was laid at his door; **–vonnis** (-sen) *o*
sentence of death, death-sentence; *het ~
uitspreken over* pass sentence of death on;
–vriezen[1] *vi* freeze (be frozen) to death;
–werken[1] *zich ~* work oneself to death; *iem.
zich laten ~* slave sbd. to death; **–ziek** mortally
ill; **–zonde** (-n) *v rk* mortal sin; **–zwijgen**[1] *vt*
not talk about, hush up; ignore

doof deaf; *zo ~ als een kwartel* as deaf as a post;
oostindisch ~ zijn sham deafness; ● *~ a a n één
oor* deaf on (in) one ear; *aan dat oor was hij ~* he
was deaf on that side; *~ v o o r* deaf to; *~ blijven
voor...* turn a deaf ear to...; **–achtig** somewhat
deaf; **–heid** *v* deafness; **–pot** (-ten) *m* extinguisher; *in de ~ stoppen* hush up (cover up) [the
matter], draw a curtain

'doofstom, doof'stom deaf and dumb;
doof'stomheid *v* deaf-muteness;
doof'stomme (-n) *m-v* deaf-mute;

doof'stommeninstituut (-tuten) *o* institution
for the deaf and dumb

dooi *m* thaw; **'dooien** (dooide, h. gedooid) *vi*
thaw; *het dooit* it is thawning; *het begint te ~* the
thaw is setting in

'dooier (-s) *m* yolk

'dooiwe(d)er *o* thaw

dook (doken) V.T. v. *duiken*

'doolhof (-hoven) *m* labyrinth, maze; **–weg**
(-wegen) *m* wrong way; *op ~en geraken* go
astray

doop *m* baptism, christening; *de ~ ontvangen* be
baptized, be christened; *ten ~ houden* hold
(present) at the font; **–akte** (-n en -s) *v* certificate of baptism; **–bekken** (-s) *o* (baptismal)
font; **–boek** (-en) *o* register of baptisms; **–ceel**
(-celen) *v* & *o* certificate of baptism; *iems. ~
lichten* lay bare sbd.'s past; **–feest** (-en) *o*
christening feast; **–formulier** (-en) *o* service
for baptism; **–gelofte** (-n) *v* baptismal vow(s);
–getuige (-n) *m-v* sponsor; **–hek** (-ken) *o*
baptistery screen; **–jurk** (-en) *v* christening
robe; **–kapel** (-len) *v* baptistery; **–kind** (-eren)
o godchild; **–kleed** (-kleden) *o* christening
robe; chrisom; **–leerling** (-en) *m* catechumen;
–maal (-malen) *o* christening feast; **–moeder**
(-s) *v* godmother; **–naam** (-namen) *m* Christian name; **–plechtigheid** (-heden) *v* christening ceremony, (v. s c h i p &) naming
ceremony; **–register** (-s) *o* register of
baptisms; **–sel** (-s) *o* baptism; **doopsge'zinde**
(-n) *m-v* Mennonite; **'doopvader** (-s) *m*
godfather; **–vont** (-en) *v* (baptismal) font;
–water *o* baptismal water

door I *prep* through; by; due to, on account of
[the rain, his illness &]; *het ene jaar ~ het andere*
one year with another; *~ alle eeuwen* through all
ages; *~ heel Europa* throughout Europe, all
over Europe; *~ mij geschreven* written by me; *ik
rende ~ de gang* I ran along the corridor; *ik liep
~ de kamer* I walked across the room; *~ de stad*
through the town; *~ de week* during the week,
on week-days; **II** *ad* through; *ik ben het boek ~* I
have got through the book; *de dag (het jaar) ~*
throughout the day (the year); *al maar ~* all the
time, on and on; *iems. hele leven ~* all through a
man's life, all his life; *ze zijn er ~* they have got
through; *de verloving is er ~* the engagement has
come off; *~ en ~ eerlijk* thoroughly (completely) honest; *iets ~ en ~ kennen* know a thing
thoroughly (through and through); *~ en ~
koud* chilled to the marrow, the bones; *~ en ~
nat* wet through, wet to the skin

door'bakken well-baked [bread]; *niet* ~ slack-baked

'doorberekenen (berekende 'door, h. 'doorberekend) *vt* pass on [the higher prices to the consumer]; *de verhoging* ~ *in de prijzen* pass the increase on in higher prices; **–betalen**[1] *vt* continue to pay wages [during temporary absence &]; **–bijten**[1] *vt* bite through; **–bladeren**[1] *vt* turn over the leaves of [a book], leaf, riffle, browse (through) [a book]; **–blazen**[1] *vt* blow through; **door'boren** (doorboorde, h. doorboord) *vt* 1 (m e t i e t s p u n t i g s) pierce, perforate; 2 (m e t e e n w a p e n) transfix [with a lance], run through [with a sword], stab [with a dagger]; impale [with a spear]; 3 (m e t k o g e l s) riddle [with bullets]; 4 (m e t z ij n b l i k k e n) transfix [him]; ~ *de blik* piercing look; **'doorbraak** (-braken) *v* bursting [of a dike]; breach [in a dike]; ⚓, *fig* break-through; **–braden**[1] *vt* roast well (thoroughly); *goed door'braden* well-done [steak]; **–branden**[1] **I** *vi* 1 (b l ij v e n b r a n d e n) burn on, burn away; 2 burn through; *de lamp is doorgebrand* ☼ the bulb has burnt out; *de zekering is doorgebrand* ☼ the fuse has blown; **II** *vt* burn through

1 'doorbreken[1] **I** *vt* break [a piece of bread &]; break through [the enemy]; run [a blockade]; **II** *vi* & *va* burst [of a dike, an abscess], break through [of the sun]; cut [of teeth through gums]; **2 door'breken** (doorbrak, h. doorbroken) *vt* break through

'doorbrengen[1] *vt* pass [one's days], spend [days, money]; run through [a fortune]; **–buigen**[1] *vi* bend, give way, sag

door'dacht well-considered, well thought-out

door'dat because, on account of; ~ *hij niet...* by (his) not having...

1 'doordenken[1] *vt* consider fully, think out, reflect; **2 door'denken** (doordacht, h. doordacht) **I** *vt* think out [a thought]; **II** *vi* think things out

door-de-'weeks weekday [clothes, morning, name &]; *een* ~ *e dag* a weekday; **'doordouwer** (-s) *m* persevering person, pusher; **'doordraaien**[1] *vi* continue turning; **–draven**[1] *vi* trot on; *fig* rattle on

door'drenkt drenched (with), permeated (with)

'doordrijven[1] *vt* force through [measures]; *zijn wil (zin)* ~ carry one's point, have one's own way; **–er** (-s) *m* self-willed whole-hogger; **doordrijve'rij** (-en) *v* obstinate assertion of one's will

door'dringbaar penetrable [by shot &]; pervious, permeable [to a fluid]; **1 'doordringen**[1] *vi* penetrate [into sth.]; *het dringt niet tot hem door* he doesn't realize it, he doesn't take it in, it doesn't register with him; **2 door'dringen** (doordrong, h. doordrongen) *vt* pierce, penetrate, pervade; zie ook: *doordrongen*; **door'dringend** penetrating [odour], piercing [cold, wind, looks, cry], searching [cold, look], strident [sound], permeating [light]; **–heid** *v* piercingness; searchingness; (power of) penetration; **door'drongen** ~ *van* penetrated by [a sense of...]; impressed with [the truth]; imbued with [his own importance]

'doordrukken[1] **I** *vi* 1 press through; 2 continue pressing; 3 go on printing; **II** *vt* push through

door'een pell-mell, in confusion; ~ *genomen* on an average; **–gooien**[2] *vt* jumble together, make hay of [papers &]; **–halen**[2] *vt* = *dooreengooien* & *dooreenhaspelen*; **–haspelen**[2] *vt* mix up, muddle up; **–lopen**[2] *vi* 1 flow together; 2 run together; intermingle; **–schudden**[2] *vt* shake up; *je wordt dooreengeschud in de trein* one is jolted; **–strengelen**[2] *vt* intertwine; **–weven**[2] *vt* interweave

'doorgaan[1] **I** *vi* 1 (v e r d e r g a a n) go (walk) on; 2 (v o o r t g a n g h e b b e n) come off, take place; 3 (d o o r b r e k e n) break [of an abscess]; 4 (b l ij v e n g e l d e n) hold (good); 5 (g o e d g e k e u r d w o r d e n) go through, pass [of a bill], be carried [of a motion]; *ga (nu) door!* go on!; *de koop gaat niet door* the deal is off; *er van* ~ zie *ervandoor*; ● ~ *m e t* go on with [his studies]; go on, continue, keep [doing something]; *o p (o v e r) iets* ~ pursue the subject; ~ *v o o r* be considered, be thought (to be), pass for; *zij wilden hem laten* ~ *voor de prins* they wanted to pass him off as the prince; **II** *vt* go through [the street, accounts], pass through [the doorway]; **'doorgaand** ~*e reizigers* through passengers; ~*e trein* through (non-stop) train; ~ *verkeer* through traffic; **'doorgaans** generally, usually, normally, commonly, as a rule; **'doorgang** (-en) *m* passage, way, thoroughfare; *geen* ~ no thoroughfare; *...zal geen* ~ *hebben* ...will not take place; **'doorgangshuis** (-huizen) *o* temporary stay institution; **–kamp** (-en) *o* transit camp

'doorgeefkast (-en) *v* two-way cupboard; **–luik** (-en) *o* service hatch

'doorgelegen ~ *plek* bedsore; **–gestoken**

[1,2] V.T. en V.D. van dat werkwoord volgens het model: 1 'doorbladeren, V.T. bladerde 'door, V.D. 'doorgebladerd; 2 door'eengooien, V.T. gooide door'een, V.D. door'eengegooid. Zie voor de vormen onder de grondwoorden, in deze voorbeelden *bladeren* en *gooien*. Bij sterke en onregelmatige werkwoorden wordt u verwezen naar de lijst achterin.

pierced; zie ook: *kaart*; **–geven**[1] *vt* pass, pass [it] on, hand down, hand on; **–gewinterd** seasoned [soldier &], hard-core [politician]

door'gloeien (doorgloeide, h. doorgloeid) *vt* inflame, fire

'doorgraven[1] *vt* dig through, cut (through); **–ving** (-en) *v* digging (through); cutting [of the Isthmus of Suez]

door'groefd rugged [face]

door'gronden (doorgrondde, h. doorgrond) *vt* fathom [a mystery], get to the bottom of [sth.], see into [the future], see through [sbd.]

'doorhakken[1] *vt* cut (through), cleave

'doorhalen[1] *vt* 1 (d o o r t r e k k e n) pull through [a cord]; 2 (d o o r s t r e p e n) strike (cross) out [a word]; 3 (o v e r d e h e k e l h a l e n) haul over the coals [sbd.]; slash, cut up, slate [a book, an author]; *hij zal het er wel ~ zie halen;* **–ling** (-en) *v* erasure, cancellation

'doorhebben[1] *vt* see through [a person, it], get wise [to sth.], realize [it]; *iets ~* (b e g r ij p e n) comprehend, **S** tape; (e r a c h t e r k o m e n) **S** rumble sth.

door'heen through; *ik ging er ~* I went through [the ice]; *zich ergens ~ slaan* labour through

'doorhelpen[1] *vt* help (*fig* see) through; **–hollen**[1] **I** *vi* hurry on; **II** *vt* hurry through [the country], gallop through [a book];

door'huiveren (doorhuiverde, h. doorhuiverd) *vt* thrill

'doorjagen[1] *vt er ~* run through [a fortune &]; *een wetsvoorstel er ~* rush a bill through

'doorkijk (-en) *m* vista; **–bloes** (-bloezes, -bloezen) *v* see-through blouse; **'doorkijken**[1] *vt* look over, look (go) through [a list], glance through [the newspapers]

door'klieven (doorkliefde, h. doorkliefd) *vt* cleave; **'doorknagen**[1] *vt* gnaw through

door'kneed *~ in* versed in, well-read in [history], steeped in [the philosophy of...], seasoned in [a science]

'doorknippen[1] *vt* cut (through)

'doorknoopjurk (-en) *v* button-through gown

'doorkomen[1] **I** *vt* pass, get through[2]; tide through [difficulties]; **II** *vi* get through[2], come through[2]; *er was geen ~ aan* you couldn't get through [the crowd]; *hij zal er wel ~* he is sure to pass [his exam]; *zijn tandjes zullen gauw ~* it will soon cut its teeth; *de zon zal gauw ~* the sun will soon break through; **–krijgen**[1] *vt* get through; *iem. (iets) ~* see through sbd. (sth.);

door'kruisen (doorkruiste, h. doorkruist) *vt* cross [the mind], traverse [the streets]; inter-

sect [the country, of railways], scour [the seas, a forest]; *fig* thwart [sbd.'s plans]

'doorlaat (-laten) *m* culvert; **–post** (-en) *m* checkpoint; **'doorlaten**[1] *vt* let [sbd., sth.] through, pass [a candidate], transmit [the light]

'doorlekken[1] *vt* leak through; **door'leven** (doorleefde, h. doorleefd) *vt* go (pass) through [moments of..., dangers &]

'doorlezen I *vt* read through, go through, peruse; **II** *vi* read on, go on reading; **–zing** *v* reading, perusal

'doorlichten[1] *vt* ※ X-ray; **–ting** (-en) *v* ※ X-ray examination

'doorliggen[1] *vi* get bedsores, become bedsore

'doorloop (-lopen) *m* passage; 1 **'doorlopen I** *vi* go (walk, run) on; keep going (walking, running); (v. k l e u r e n) run; *~ (mensen)!* pass along!, move on!; *loop door!* **F** get along (with you)!; *loop wat door!* hurry up a bit!; **II** *vt* 1 go (walk, run) through [a wood]; 2 go through [a piece of music, accounts]; run over [the contents]; 3 wear out [one's shoes] by walking; *doorgelopen voeten* sore feet; **2 door'lopen** (doorliep, h. doorlopen) *vt* walk through; pass through [a school]; 1 **'doorlopend**, *aj* continuous, non-stop [performance]; **2 door'lopend** *ad* continuously; *~ genummerd* consecutively numbered

door'luchtig illustrious; (most) serene; **–heid** (-heden) *v* illustriousness; *Zijne Doorluchtigheid* His Serene Highness

'doormaken[1] *vt* go (pass) through [a crisis &]; **–marcheren**[1] [ch = ʃ] **I** *vi* march on; **II** *vt* march through; **–meten**[1] *vt* ※ test [electrical apparatus, flex &]

door'midden in half, [break] in two; [tear it] across

'doorn (-en en -s) *m* 1 thorn, prickle, spine; 2 tang [of a knife]; *dat is hem een ~ in het oog* it is an eyesore to him, a thorn in his side; *een ~ in het vlees* a thorn in the flesh; **–achtig** thorny, spinous; **–appel** (-s) *m* thorn-apple

door'nat wet through, wet to the skin, soaked, drenched

'doornemen[1] *vt* go through, go over [a paper, book &]

'doŏrnenkroon (-kronen) *v* crown of thorns; **'doornhaag** (-hagen) *v* thorn-hedge, hawthorn hedge; **'doornig** thorny[2]; **'Doorn-roosje** *v & o* the Sleeping Beauty; **'doorn-struik** (-en) *m* thorn-bush

'doornummeren[1] *vt* number consecutively

door'ploegen (doorploegde, h. doorploegd) *vt*

---

[1] V.T. en V.D. van dit werkwoord volgens het model: **'doorbladeren.** V.T. bladerde **'door,** V.D. **'door**gebladerd. Zie voor de vormen onder het grondwoord, in dit voorbeeld: *bladeren.* Bij sterke en onregelmatige werkwoorden wordt u verwezen naar de lijst achterin.

plough [the sea]; **'doorpraten**[1] **I** *vi* go on talking, talk on; **II** *vt* talk [it] out;
door'priemen (doorpriemde, h. doorpriemd) *vt* pierce; **'doorprikken**[1] *vt* prick, pierce
door'regen *aj* streaked, streaky [bacon]
'doorreis *v* passage (journey) through; *op mijn ~ door A.* on my way through A.; **1** **'doorreizen**[1] *vi* go on; **2** **door'reizen** (doorreisde, h. doorreisd) *vt* travel through
'doorrennen[1] **I** *vi* race along; **II** *vt* race through[2] [the fields, a curriculum]
'doorrijden[1] **I** *vi* ride (drive) on; *wat ~* ride (drive) faster; **II** *vt* ride (drive) through [the country]; **'doorrijhoogte** *v* headroom
'doorrit (-ten) *m* passage
'doorroeren[1] *vt* stir; **–roesten**[1] *vt* corrode, rust; **–rollen**[1] **I** *vi* continue rolling; *er ~* **F** escape (pass) by the skin of one's teeth, scrape through; **II** *vt* roll through
'doorschemeren[1] *vi* shine (show) through; *laten ~* hint, give to understand; **–scheuren**[1] *vt* rend, tear (up)
1 **'doorschieten**[1] **I** *vi* continue to shoot (fire); **II** *vt* shoot through; **2** **door'schieten** (doorschoot, h. doorschoten) *vt* 1 riddle [with shot]; 2 interleave [a book]
'doorschijnen[1] *vi* shine (show) through; **door'schijnend** translucent, diaphanous
'doorschrappen[1] *vt* cross (strike) out, cancel; **–schudden**[1] *vt* shake thoroughly; shake (up) [a mixture][2]; shuffle [the cards]; **–seinen**[1] *vt* 🎵 transmit [a message]; **–sijpelen**[1] *vi* ooze through, percolate
'doorslaan[1] *vi* 1 *eig* go on beating; 2 (v. balans) dip; 3 (v. machine) race; 4 ⚡ (v. zekering) blow (out); 5 *fig* run on [in talking]; 6 **S** (v. medeplichtige) squeal, blow the gaff; 7 (v. vochtige muur) sweat; *de balans doen ~* turn the scale[2]; **II** *vt* sever [sth.] with a blow; ✗ punch [a metal plate]; ⚡ blow [a fuse]; zie ook: *doorschrappen*; **III** *vr zich er ~* zie *slaan*; **–d ~** *bewijs* conclusive proof
'doorslag (-slagen) *m* 1 (d r e v e l) punch; 2 (k o p i e) carbon copy, **F** flimsy; 3 turn of the scale; *dat gaf de ~* that's what turned the scale (what settled the matter), that did it; **door-slag'gevend** decisive [importance, proof, factor], deciding [factor, voice]; **'doorslagpa-pier** *o* copy(ing) paper
'doorslapen[1] *vi* sleep on, sleep without a break; **–slepen**[1] *vt* drag (pull) through[2]; **–slijten**[1] *vt* & *vi* wear through; **–slikken**[1] *vt* swallow

(down); **–smelten**[1] **I** *vi* ⚡ blow (out); **II** *vt* ⚡ blow [a fuse]; **–smeren**[1] *vt* 🔧 grease
'doorsne(d)e (-sneden) *v* [longitudinal, transverse] section; profile; diameter; *in ~* (g e m i d d e l d) on an (the) average; **'doorsneeprijs** (-prijzen) *m* $ average price; **1** **'doorsnijden**[1] *vt* cut (through); **2** **door'snijden** (doorsneed, h. doorsneden) *vt* cut, traverse, intersect, cross; *elkaar ~* intersect
door'snuffelen (doorsnuffelde, h. doorsnuffeld) *vt* ransack, rummage (in); **–'spekken** (doorspekte, h. doorspekt) *vt* lard[2], *fig* interlard; **'doorspelen**[1] **I** *vi* play on; **II** *vt* ♪ play over; **–spoelen**[1] *vt* rinse (through) [stockings &]; flush [a drain]; *fig* wash down [one's food]; **–spreken**[1] **I** *vi* speak on, go on speaking; **II** *vt* discuss; **door'staan** (doorstond, h. doorstaan) *vt* stand [the wear and tear, the test]; sustain [a siege, hardships, a comparison]; go through [many trials], endure [pain]; weather [the storm]; **'doorstappen**[1] *vi* mend one's pace
'doorsteek (-steken) *m* (k o r t e r e w e g) short cut; **1** **'doorsteken**[1] 1 *vt* pierce [the dikes], prick [a bubble]; 2 *vi* (k o r t e r e w e g n e m e n) take a short cut; zie ook: *kaart*; **2** **door'steken** (doorstak, h. doorstoken) *vt* run through, stab, pierce
'doorstoten[1] **I** *vt* thrust (push) through; **II** *vi* ∞ play a follow; **–strepen**[1] *vt = doorschrappen*
door'stromen (doorstroomde, h. doorstroomd) *vt* stream (flow, run) through; **–ming** *v* flow[2], circulation[2]
'doorstuderen[1] *vi* continue one's studies; **–sturen**[1] *vt = doorzenden*
'doortasten[1] *vi* push on, go ahead, take strong action; **door'tastend I** *aj* energetic; *een ~ man* a man of action; **II** *ad* energetically
door'timmerd solidly built
door'tintelen (doortintelde, h. doortinteld) *vt* thrill
'doortocht (-en) *m* passage, march through; *zich een ~ banen* force one's way through
'doortrappen[1] *vi* pedal on; **door'trapt** sly, cunning, tricky; **–heid** *v* wiliness, cunning
1 **'doortrekken**[1] *vt* 1 pull through [a thread in sewing]; 2 (s t u k m a k e n) pull asunder [a string]; 3 go through, march through [the country, the streets]; 4 continue [a line], extend [a railway]; *de W.C. ~* flush the toilet, pull the plug; **2** **door'trekken** (doortrok, h. doortrokken) *vt* permeate, pervade, imbue, soak; zie ook: *doortrokken*; **door'trokken** permeated [with a smell], imbued [with a

doctrine], steeped [in prejudice], soaked [in, with]

'doorvaart (-en) *v* passage; **–hoogte** (-n en -s) *v* headway, headroom; **'doorvaren I** (voer 'door, is 'doorgevaren) *vi* sail on; pass [under a bridge]; **II** (door'voer, h. door'varen) *vt* pass through

'doorverbinden[1] *vt* 🕾 put [me] through (to *met*); **'doorverkopen**[1] *vt* resell; **door'vlechten** (doorvlocht, h. doorvlochten) *vt* interweave, intertwine, interlace; **'doorvliegen**[1] **I** *vt* fly through [the country]; run over [the contents]; gallop through [a curriculum]; **II** *vi* ✈ fly on [to Paris]

door'voed well-fed

'doorvoer (-en) *m* transit; **'doorvoeren**[1] *vt* 1 $ convey [goods] in transit; 2 carry through, follow out [a principle]; **'doorvoerhandel** *m* transit trade; **–rechten** *mv* $ transit duties

door'vorsen (doorvorste, h. doorvorst) *vt* fathom, get to the bottom (of sth.)

door'waadbaar fordable; **door'waden** (doorwaadde, h. doorwaad) *vt* wade through, ford [a river]

door'waken (doorwaakte, h. doorwaakt) *vt* watch through [the night]; *doorwaakte nachten* wakeful nights

door'weekt soaked, sodden, soggy; **door'weken** (doorweekte, h. doorweekt) *vt* soak, steep

1 'doorwerken I *vi* work on, keep working; **II** *vt* work through; **2 door'werken** (doorwerkte, h. doorwerkt) *vt* work [with gold]; *een doorwerkte studie* an elaborate study

door'weven (doorweefde, h. doorweven) *vt* interweave [with...]; **–'worstelen** (doorworstelde, h. doorworsteld) *vt* struggle (toil, plough, wade) through [a book]

door'wrocht elaborate

'doorzagen[1] **I** *vt* saw through; *iem.* ~ 1 pester sbd. with questions; 2 **F** bore sbd. stiff; **II** *vi* saw on; **–zakken**[1] *vi* sag; (b r a s s e n) go on a spree; *doorgezakte voet* fallen arch; **–zenden**[1] *vt* send on [sth.]; forward [letters]; transmit [a memorial to the proper authority]

'doorzetten[1] **I** *vt* carry (see) ...through, see [a thing] out, go on with [it]; **II** *va* persevere, carry on, **F** stick it; **–er** (-s) *m* go-getter; **'doorzettingsvermogen** *o* perseverance

door'zeven (doorzeefde, h. doorzeefd) *vt* riddle [with bullets]

'doorzicht *o* penetration, discernment, insight; **door'zichtig** transparent; **–heid** *v* transpar-

ency; **1 door'zien** (doorzag, h. doorzien) *vt* see through [a man &]; **2 'doorzien**[1] *vt* = *doorkijken*

'doorzijpelen[1] *vi* = *doorsijpelen*; **door'zoeken** (doorzocht, h. doorzocht) *vt* search, go through [a man's pockets], ransack [a house], rummage [a desk]

doos (dozen) *v* box, case; *in de* ~ **S** in quod; *uit de oude* ~ antiquated; **–vrucht** (-en) *v* capsular fruit, capsule

dop (-pen) *m* 1 shell [of an egg, a nut], husk [of some seeds], pod [of peas], cup [of an acorn]; 2 top, cap [of a fountain-pen]; cover [of a tobacco-pipe]; button [of a foil]; *hoge* ~ top-hat; *een advocaat i n de* ~ a budding lawyer; *hij is pas u i t de* ~ just out of the shell; *goed uit zijn ~pen kijken* have all one's eyes about one; *kijk uit je ~pen* look where you're going

'dopeling (-en) *m* child (person) to be baptized; **'dopen** (doopte, h. gedoopt) *vt* 1 baptize, christen [a child, a church bell, a ship] name [a ship]; 2 dip; sop [bread in tea]; *hij werd Jan gedoopt* he was christened John; **–er** (-s) *m* baptizer; *Johannes de Doper* John the Baptist

'doperwt ['dɔpɛrt] (-en) *v* green pea; **–hei(de)** *v* heath, bell-heather; **–hoed** (-en) *m* **F** billycock; **'doppen** (dopte, h. gedopt) **I** *vt* shell [eggs, peas]; husk [corn]; **II** *vi* ~ *voor* cap [= take off one's hat to sbd.]; **'dopper** (-s) *m* = *doperwt*; **'dopsleutel** (-s) *m* socket wrench, box wrench

dor barren, arid, dry

'doren (-s) = *doorn*

'dorheid *v* barrenness, aridity, dryness

'Dorisch Dorian, (i n z . △) Doric

dorp (-en) *o* village

'dorpel (-s) *m* threshold

'dorpeling (-en) *m* villager; **dorps** countrified, rustic; **–bewoner** (-s) *m* villager; **–dominee** (-s) *m* country vicar; **–gek** (-ken) *m* village idiot; **–herberg** (-en) *v* country inn, village inn; **–kerk** (-en) *v* village church; **–meisje** (-s) *o* country lass, country girl; **–pastoor** (-s) *m* village priest; **–pastorie** (-ieën) *v* country rectory; **–plein** *o* village square; **–school** (-scholen) *v* village school

'dorren (dorde, is gedord) *vi* wither, fade

'dorsen (dorste, h. gedorst) *vt & vi* thresh; **'dorsmachine** [-ma.ʃi.nə] (-s) *v* threshing machine

1 dorst *m* thirst[2]; *de* ~ *naar roem* the thirst for glory; ~ *hebben* (*krijgen*) be (get) thirsty

2 dorst (dorsten) V.T. v. *durven*

---

[1] V.T. en V.D. van dit werkwoord volgens het model: **'door**bladeren. V.T. bladerde **'door**, V.D. **'door**gebladerd. Zie voor de vormen onder het grondwoord, in dit voorbeeld: *bladeren*. Bij sterke en onregelmatige werkwoorden wordt u verwezen naar de lijst achterin.

1 'dorsten (dorstte, h. gedorst) *vi* be thirsty; *fig* thirst (for, after)

2 'dorsten V.T. meerv. v. *durven*

'dorstig thirsty; **–heid** *v* thirstiness, thirst; **dorst'lessend** refreshing, thirst-quenching; **–ver'wekkend** producing thirst

'dorsvlegel (-s) *m* flail; **–vloer** (-en) *m* threshing-floor

dos *m* attire, raiment, dress

do'seren [s = z] (doseerde, h. gedoseerd) *vt* dose; **–ring** (-en) *v* dosage; **'dosis** [-zɪs] (doses) *v* dose, quantity; *te grote* ~ overdose; *te kleine* ~ underdose

'dossen (doste, h. gedost) *zich* ~ smarten oneself up

dossier [dɔsi.'e.] (-s) *o* dossier, file

dot (-ten) *m* & *v* knot [of hair, worsted &], tuft [of grass]; *een* ~ *van een kind* (*hoedje*) a duck of a child (of a hat); *wat een* ~! what a dear!

'dotterbloem (-en) *v* marsh marigold

douairi'ère [duɑr'jɛ: rə] (-s) *v* dowager

dou'ane [du.'a.nə] (-n) *v* customs house, custom-house; *de* ~ ook: the Customs; **–beambte** (-n) *m* customs officer, custom-house officer; **–formaliteiten** *mv* customs formalities; **–kantoor** (-toren) *o* customs house, custom-house; **–loods** (-en) *v* customs shed; **–onderzoek** *o* customs examination; **–post** (-en) *m* customs station; **–rechten** *mv* customs (duties); **–tarief** (-rieven) *o* customs tariff; **dou'ane-unie** (-s) *v* customs union; **dou'aneverklaring** (-en) *v* customs declaration; **doua'nier** [du.a.n'je.] (-s) *m* = *douanebeambte*

dou'blé [ou = u.] *o* gold-(silver-)plated work

dou'bleren [ou = u.] (doubleerde, h. gedoubleerd) **I** *vt* 1 double [a part, a rôle]; 2 ↝ repeat [a class]; **II** *vi* ◊ double; **dou'blet** (-s) *o* 1 double [of stamps; ◊]; 2 doublet [of words]; **dou'blure** (-s) *v* understudy [of an actor]

dou'ceurtje [ou = u.] (-s) *o* tip, gratuity

'douche [du.ʃ(ə)] (-s) *v* shower(-bath); *een koude* ~ [*fig*] a cold shower; **–cel** (-len) *v* shower cabinet; **'douchen** (douchte, h. gedoucht) *vi* take a shower, shower

'douw(en) ['dɔu(ə(n))] **F** = *duw(en)*

'dove (-n) *m-v* deaf man, deaf woman &; **'doveman** *m* deaf man; *dat is niet aan* ~*s oren gezegd* that did not fall on deaf ears

'doven (doofde, h. gedoofd) *vt* 1 extinguish, put out; 2 *vi* die down²

dove'netel (-s) *v* ⚘ dead-nettle

'dovig somewhat deaf

do'zijn (-en) *o* dozen; *per* ~ [sell them] by the dozen; [pack them] in dozens; *drie* (*vier* &) ~ three (four &) dozen; *een paar* ~ some dozens

Dr. = *doctor*

dra = *weldra*

1 draad (draden) *m* thread [of cotton, screw & *fig*]; fibre, filament [of plant or root]; wire [of metal]; filament [of electric bulb]; string [of French beans]; grain [of wood]; *een* ~ *in een naald steken* thread a needle; *de* (*rode*) ~ *die er doorheen loopt* the (leading) thread running through it; *de draden in handen hebben* hold the clue, have got hold of the threads [of the mystery]; *de* ~ *kwijt zijn* have lost the thread (of one's argument &); *geen droge* ~ *aan het lijf hebben* not have a dry thread (stitch) on one; *de* ~ *weer opvatten* take up the thread of (one's narrative); *alle dagen een draadje, is een hemdsmouw in het jaar* many a little makes a mickle; ● *aan een zijden* ~(*je*) *hangen* hang by a thread; (*kralen*) *aan een* ~ *rijgen* thread beads; *met* (*op*) *de* ~ with the grain; *tegen de* ~ against the grain²; *versleten tot op de* ~ threadbare; *voor de* ~ *komen* speak up; **2 draad** *o* & *m* (*stofnaam*) thread [of cotton]; wire [of metal]; **–glas** *o* wire(d) glass; **–harig** wire-haired [terrier]; **–loos** wireless; **–nagel** (-s) *m* wire-nail; **–omroep** *m* wire broadcasting; **–schaar** (-scharen) *v* wire-cutter; **–tang** (-en) *v* pliers, nippers; **–trekker** (-s) *m* wire-drawer; **–vormig** thread-like; **–werk** (-en) *o* 1 filigree; 2 wire-work

1 'draagbaar *aj* bearable; portable [loads]; wearable [clothes]

2 'draagbaar (-baren) *v* litter, stretcher

'draagbalk (-en) *m* beam, girder; **–band** (-en) *m* strap; sling [for arm]; **–golf** (-golven) *v* ⚡ carrier wave; **–koets** (-en) *v* palanquin; **–kracht** *v* ability to bear [something, also financial loads]; capacity to pay; carrying-capacity [of a ship]; range [of guns, of the voice]; **draag'krachtig** well-to-do, prosperous; **'draaglijk I** *aj* 1 tolerable [= endurable & fairly good], bearable; 2 passable, rather decent, middling; **II** *ad* tolerably; **–loon** *o* porterage; **–raket** (-ten) *v* carrier rocket, booster rocket; **–riem** (-en) *m* strap; **–stoel** (-en) *m* ⚏ sedan (chair); **–tas** (-sen) *v* carrier bag; **–vermogen** *o* = *draagkracht*; **–vlak** (-ken) *o* ✈ plane, bearing surface; aerofoil (*Am* airfoil); **–vleugelboot** (-boten) *m* & *v* hydrofoil; **–wijdte** *v* 1 ✕ range; 2 *fig* bearing, full significance [of one's words]

draai (-en) *m* turn; twist [of a rope], turning, winding [of the road]; ~ (*om de oren*) box on the ear; *hij gaf er een* ~ *aan* he gave it a twist; *zijn* ~ *hebben* be as pleased as Punch (about it); *hij nam zijn* ~ *te kort* he took too short a bend; **–baar** revolving; **–bank** (-en) *v* lathe; **–boek** (-en) *o* shooting script, screenplay, continuity; **–brug** (-gen) *v* swing-bridge; **–cirkel** (-s) *m*

turning circle; **–deur** (-en) *v* revolving door;
'draaien (draaide, h. gedraaid) **I** *vi* 1 *eig* turn
[in all directions], spin [quickly round], whirl
[rapidly round and round in orbit or curve],
twist [spirally], gyrate [in circle or spiral],
revolve, rotate [on axis], shift, veer [from one
position to another, round to the East &]; 2 *fig*
shuffle, prevaricate, tergiversate; *zitten te ~*
wriggle [on a chair]; *het (alles) draait mij, mijn
hoofd draait* my head swims; *in deze bioscoop
draait de film* this cinema is showing the film;
de fabriek draait (volop, op volle toeren) the factory
is working (to capacity), is running (at full
capacity), is in full swing; *blijven ~* [*fig*] keep
going; *alles draait om dat feit* everything turns
(hinges, pivots) on that fact; *om de zaak heen ~*
beat about the bush; **II** *vt* turn [the spit, a
wheel, ivory &]; roll [a cigarette, pills]; wind
[round one's finger]; zie ook: *orgel* &; *een film ~*
1 (v e r t o n e n) show a film; 2 (o p n e m e n)
shoot a film; *een nummer ~* ☏ dial; (*grammofoon)platen ~* play records; *hij weet alles zo te ~
dat...* he gives things a twist so that...; **III** *vr
zich ~* turn [to the right, left]; **–d** turning &;
rota(to)ry [motion]; **'draaier** (-s) *m* 1 [wood,
ivory] turner; 2 *fig* shuffler, prevaricator; 3
(h a l s w e r v e l) axis; **–ig** giddy, dizzy;
'draaihek (-ken) *o* turnstile; **'draaiing** (-en) *v*
turn(ing); rotation; **'draaikolk** (-en) *m* & *v*
whirlpool, eddy, vortex²; **–kraan** (-kranen) *v*
rotary (swing, slewing) crane; **–licht** (-en) *o*
revolving-light; **–molen** (-s) *m* roundabout,
merry-go-round, whirligig; **–orgel** (-s) *o*
barrel-organ; **–punt** (-en) *o* turning-point;
centre of rotation, fulcrum; **–schijf** (-schijven)
v 1 turn-table [of a railway; of a gramophone];
2 ☏ dial; 3 (potter's) wheel; **–spit** (-ten) *o* spit;
–stoel (-en) *m* revolving chair; **–stroom** *m* ⚡
rotary current, three-phase current; (i n
s a m e n s t.) three-phase [motor &]; **–tafel** (-s)
v turn-table [of record player]; **–tol** (-len) *m*
spinning-top; *fig* weathercock; **–toneel**
(-nelen) *o* revolving stage

draak (draken) *m* 1 🐉 dragon²; 2 (t o n e e l -
s t u k) melodrama; *de ~ steken met* poke fun at
[sbd.], make fun of [the regulations]

drab *v* & *o* dregs, lees; sediment; **–big** turbid,
dreggy

dracht (-en) *v* 1 (l a s t) charge, load; 2 (z w a n -
g e r s c h a p) gestation, pregnancy; 3
(k l e d e r d r a c h t) dress, costume, garb; 4
(e t t e r) matter; 5 (d r a a g w ij d t e) range

'drachtig pregnant; with young, in pup

'drad(er)ig thready, stringy; ropy [of liquids]

1 draf *m* trot; *i n volle ~* at full trot; *o p een ~* at a
trot

2 draf *m* (v e e v o e d e r) draff, hog-wash

dra'gee [g = ʒ] (-s) *v* dragée

'dragen* **I** *vt* bear [a load, arms, a name, the
cost, interest &], wear [a beard, clothes,
spectacles, diamonds, a look of... &], carry
[sth., arms, a watch, interest, one's head high];
support [the roof, a character, part]; **II** *vi* & *va*
1 bear [of the ice, a tree]; 2 discharge [of a
wound]; 3 ✗ carry [of fire-arms]; *~de vrucht-
bomen* fruit-trees in (full) bearing; **–er** (-s) *m*
bearer², carrier, porter; wearer [of contact
lenses]

'dragon *m* tarragon

dra'gonder (-s) *m* dragoon; *een ~ (van een wijf)* a
virago

drai'neerbuis [drɛ-] (-buizen) *v* drain(age)
pipe; **drai'neren** (draineerde, h. gedraineerd)
vt drain; **–ring** (-en) *v* drainage, draining

'drakerig melodramatic

'dralen (draalde, h. gedraald) *vi* linger, tarry;
dawdle; *zonder ~* without (further) delay

'drama (*'s*) *o* drama; **drama'tiek** *v* drama;
dra'matisch dramatic; **dramati'seren** [s = z]
(dramatiseerde, h. gedramatiseerd) *vt* drama-
tize, emotionalize; **–ring** (-en) *v* dramatization;
drama'turg (-en) *m* dramatist, dramaturge;
script reader; **dramatur'gie** *v* dramaturgy

drang *m* pressure, urgency, impulse, urge [of
impulse, instinct], drive [= strong impulse];
onder de ~ der omstandigheden under (the) pressure of circumstances

'dranghek (-ken) *o* crush-barrier

drank (-en) *m* 1 drink, beverage; 2 ℞ medicine,
mixture, draught, [love, magic] potion; *sterke
~* strong drink, spirits, liquor; *aan de ~ zijn* be
given to drink, be addicted to liquor; *zie ook
raken;* **–bestrijder** (-s) *m* teetotaller; **–bestrijding** *v* temperance movement; **–misbruik** *o*
excessive drinking; **–orgel** (-s) *o* **J** sponge,
soaker, tippler; **–smokkel** *m* bootlegging;
–smokkelaar (-s) *m* bootlegger, **S** moon-
shiner; **–verbod** (-boden) *o* prohibition;
–verkoop (-kopen) *m* sale of intoxicants;
–verkoper (-s) *m* liquor-seller; **–winkel** (-s) *m*
gin-shop, liquor-shop; **–zucht** *v* dipsomania;
drank'zuchtige (-n) *m-v* dipsomaniac

dra'peren (drapeerde, h. gedrapeerd) *vt* drape;
drape'rie (-ieën) *v* drapery

'drasland (-en) *o* marshland, swamp; **'drassig**
marshy, swampy, soggy; **–heid** *v* marshiness

'drastisch drastic

'draven (draafde, h. gedraafd) *vi* trot; **–er** (-s) *m*
trotter; **drave'rij** (-en) *v* trotting-match

1 dreef (dreven) *v* 1 alley, lane; 2 field, region;
iem. op ~ helpen help sbd. on; *op ~ komen* get
into one's swing, get into one's stride; *op ~
zijn* be in the vein; be in splendid form

2 dreef (**dreven**) V.T. v. *drijven*

dreg (-gen) *v* drag, grapnel; **–anker** (-s) *o* grapnel; **'dregge** (-n) *v = dreg;* **'deggen** (dregde, h. gedregd) *vi* drag (for *naar*)

'dreigbrief (-brieven) *m* threatening letter; **dreige'ment** (-en) *o* threat, menace; **'dreigen** (dreigde, h. gedreigd) *vi* & *vt* threaten, menace; *hij dreigde in het water te vallen* he was in danger of falling into the water; *het dreigt te regenen* it looks like rain; *er dreigt een onweer* a storm is threatening (brewing), it looks like thunder; *er dreigt oorlog* it threatens war; *er dreigt een staking* a strike is threatened; *er ~ moeilijkheden* there's trouble brewing; **–d I** *aj* threatening, menacing [looks, dangers &]; imminent, impending [perils]; lowering [clouds]; ugly [situation]; *de ~e hongersnood* (*staking* &) the threatened famine (strike &); **II** *ad* threateningly, menacingly; **'dreiging** (-en) *v* threat, menace

'dreinen (dreinde, h. gedreind) *vi* whine, whimper, pule

drek *m* dirt, muck; (u i t w e r p s e l e n) dung, excrement, droppings

'drempel (-s) *m* threshold; **–waarde** *v* threshold (liminal) value

'drenkeling (-en) *m* 1 drowned person; 2 drowning person

'drenken (drenkte, h. gedrenkt) *vt* water [cattle, horses &]; drench [the earth]; *~ in* steep (soak) in

'drentelen (drentelde, h. en is gedrenteld) *vi* saunter

'drenzen (drensde, h. gedrensd) *vi = dreinen;* **'drenzerig** whining, fretful, crabbed, cross

dres'seren (dresseerde, h. gedresseerd) *vt* break (in) [horses], train [dogs], break in [schoolboys]; *gedresseerde olifanten* performing elephants; **dres'seur** (-s) *m* trainer; (v. p a a r d) horse-breaker

dres'soir [-'swa:r] (-s) *o* & *m* sideboard

dres'suur *v* breaking in² [of horses, schoolboys], *sp* dressage [of a horse for show jumping &], training [of animals]

'dreumes (-mesen) *m* mite, toddler

dreun (-en) *m* 1 (v. g e l u i d) drone, rumble, roar(ing), boom; 2 (b i j o p z e g g e n) singsong, chant; 3 (o p s t o p p e r) **F** biff, pound, sock; *op een ~* in monotone; **'dreunen** (dreunde, h. gedreund) *vi* drone, rumble, roar, boom; (*doen*) *~* shake [the house]

'drevel (-s) *m* drift, punch; **'drevelen** (drevelde, h. gedreveld) *vt* drift, punch

'dreven V.T. meerv. v *drijven*

'dribbelaar (-s) *m* toddler; **'dribbelen** (dribbelde, h. en is gedribbeld) *vi* 1 toddle; trip; 2 *sp* dribble; **'dribbelpasjes** *mv* tripping steps

drie three; *wij ~ën* the three of us; *het is bij ~ën* it's going on for three; it's almost three

o'clock; *in ~ën delen* divide in three; zie ook: *ding* &; **–daags** three days'...; **–delig** tripartite; three-piece [suit]; **–dik** threefold, treble, three-ply; **driedimensio'naal** threedimensional; **'driedraads** three-ply; **–'dubbel** treble, triple, threefold; **Drie'ëenheid** *v* (Holy) Trinity; **drie'ënig** triune; **'drieërlei** of three sorts; **drie'fasen, –'fasig** [s = z] ⚡ three-phase [current]

'driehoek (-en) *m* triangle; (t e k e n g e r e e d-s c h a p) set square; **–ig** triangular, three-cornered; **'driehoeksmeting** (-en) *v* trigonometry; (v. t e r r e i n) triangulation; **–ruil** *m* triangular (ex)change [of houses &]; **–verhouding** (-en) *v* triangular relationship; three-cornered love affair

'driehoofdig three-headed [monster], triceps [muscle]; **–jaarlijks** triennial; **–jarig** of three years, three-year-old; **–kant(ig)** three-cornered; **–klank** (-en) *m* ♪ triad

'driekleur (-en) *v* tricolour; **drie'kleurendruk** (-ken) *m* three-colour printing; **'driekleurig** three-coloured

Drie'koningen *m* Twelfthnight, Epiphany

'driekwart three-quarter(s); **–smaat** (-maten) *v* ♪ three-four time

drie'ledig threefold; **'drielettergrepig** trisyllabic; *~ woord* trisyllable; **'drieling** (-en) *m* triplets; **–luik** (-en) *o* triptych; **–maal** three times, thrice; **–maandelijks** quarterly; *~e betaling* quarterage; *een ~ tijdschrift* a quarterly

'drieman (-nen) *m* triumvir; **–schap** (-pen) *o* triumvirate

'driemaster (-s) *m* three-master; **driemo'torig** three-engined; **'driepoot** (-poten) *m* tripod; **–regelig** of three lines, threeline...; *~ vers* triplet; **–span** (-nen) *o* team of three horses (oxen); **–sprong** (-en) *m* three-forked road

driest audacious, bold

'driestemmig, drie'stemmig for three voices, three-part

'driestheid (-heden) *v* audacity, boldness

'drietal (-len) *o* (number of) three, trio; **drie'talig** trilingual; **'drietallig** ternary

'drietand (-en) *m* trident; **–ig** three-pronged [fork]

'drietrapsraket (-ten) *o* & *v* three-stage rocket; **–versnellingsnaaf** (-naven) *v* threespeed hub

'drievoet (-en) *m* tripod, trivet; **–ig** three-footed, three-legged

'drievoud (-en) *o* treble; *in ~* in triplicate; **–ig** triple, threefold; **Drie'vuldigheid** *v* (Holy) Trinity

'driewerf three times, thrice; **–wieler** (-s) *m* tricycle; **–zijdig** three-sided, trilateral

drift (-en) *v* 1 drove [of oxen], flock [of sheep]; 2 ⚓ drift [of a ship]; 3 (w o e d e, h a r t st o c h t) passion; 4 *ps* impulse, urge; *in* ~ in a fit of passion; *in* ~ *geraken* lose one's temper; *o p* ~ ⚓ adrift; **–bui** (-en) *v* fit of temper; **driftig I** *aj* 1 (o p v l i e g e n d) passionate, quick-tempered, fiery, hasty; (w o e d e n d) angry; 2 ⚓ adrift; ~ *worden, zich* ~ *maken* fly into a passion, lose one's temper; **II** *ad* passionately; angrily; **–heid** *v* passionateness, quick temper, hastiness of temper; **'driftkop** (-pen) *m* hothead, spitfire, tartar; **–leven** *o* instinctive life

'drijfanker (-s) *o* drift-anchor; **–as** (-sen) *v* driving shaft; **–beitel** (-s) *m* chasing-chisel; **–hamer** (-s) *m* chasing-hammer; **–hout** *o* driftwood; **–ijs** *o* drift-ice, floating ice; **–jacht** (-en) *v* drive, battue; **–kracht** *v* 1 ✗ motive power; 2 *fig* driving force, moving power; *voornaamste* ~ prime mover; **–'nat** soaking wet, sopping wet; **–riem** (-en) *m* driving-belt; **–stang** (-en) *v* connecting-rod; **–veer** (-veren) *v* moving spring[2]; *fig* mainspring, incentive, motive; *wat was zijn* ~ *tot die daad?* by what motive was he actuated?; **–werk** (-en) *o* 1 chased work, chasing; 2 ✗ driving-gear; **–wiel** (-en) *o* driving-wheel; **–zand** *o* quicksand(s); **'drijven* I** *vi* 1 float [on or in liquid], swim [on the surface]; 2 (m e e g e v o e r d w o r d e n) drift; 3 (n a t z ij n) be soaking wet; **II** *vt* 1 drive[2], propel[2], impel[2], *fig* actuate, prompt [to an action]; 2 chase [gold, silver]; *een zaak* ~ run a business; *het te ver* ~ carry it [economy, the thing] too far; *iem. in het nauw* ~ press sbd. hard; *het t o t het uiterste* ~ push things to the last extremity (to an extreme); *iem. tot het uiterste* ~ drive sbd. to extremities; **III** *va* be fanatically zealous [in some cause]; *door afgunst gedreven* prompted by jealousy; *door stoom gedreven* driven by steam; **–er** (-s) *m* 1 beater [of game]; driver, drover [of cattle]; 2 chaser [in metal]; 3 *fig* zealot, fanatic; 4 ✗ & ⚓ float; **drijve'rij** (-en) *v* fanaticism, zealotry, bigotry

1 dril (-len) *m* (b o o r) drill
2 dril *v* (v l e e s n a t) jelly
3 dril *o* (w e e f s e l) drill
'drilboor (-boren) *v* drill
'drillen (drilde, h. gedrild) *vt* 1 ✗ drill; 2 drill [soldiers &]; ⚲ cram [pupils for an examination]; **'drilschool** (-scholen) *v* cramming-school
'dringen* I *vi* push, crowd, throng; *de tijd dringt* time presses; ~ *d o o r* pierce, penetrate; force (push) one's way through [the crowd]; ~ *i n = binnendringen; naar voren* ~ force one's way (through); **II** *vt* push, crowd; press [against sth.]; *wanneer het hart* (*u*) *tot spreken dringt* when your heart urges (prompts) you to speak; *ze*

drongen hem de straat op they hustled him out into the street; **–d** urgent, pressing
'drinkbaar drinkable; **'drinkbak** (-ken) *m* drinking-trough, watering-trough; **–bakje** (-s) *o* (bird's) trough; **–beker** (-s) *m* cup, goblet; **'drinkebroer** (-s) *m* toper, tippler, wine-bibber; **'drinken* I** *vt* drink [water &]; have, take [a glass of wine with sbd]; **II** *vi* drink; *o p iems. gezondheid* ~ drink (to) sbd.'s health; *veel* (*zwaar*) ~ drink deep; **III** *va* drink; **IV** *o* drinking [is bad]; beverage, drink(s); **–er** (-s) *m* (great) drinker, toper, tippler; **'drinkgelag** (-lagen) *o* drinking-bout, carousal; **–geld** (-en) *o* 1 ✗ drink-money; 2 gratuity, tip; **–glas** (-glazen) *o* drinking-glass, tumbler; **–lied** (-eren) *o* drinking-song; **–plaats** (-en) *v* watering-place; **–water** *o* drinking-water; **–watervoorziening** *v* water-supply

droef sad, afflicted; **–enis** *v* grief, sorrow, affliction; **droef'geestig** melancholy, gloomy, wistful; **–heid** *v* melancholy, gloominess; **'droefheid** *v* sadness, affliction, sorrow
droeg (droegen) V.T. v. *dragen*
droes *m* 1 (g o e d a a r d i g e) strangles; 2 (k w a d e) glanders
'droesem (-s) *m* dregs, lees; **–ig** dreggy, turbid
'droevig sad [man]; pitiful, sorry [sight]; mournful, rueful [countenance]
'drogbeeld (-en) *o* illusion, phantom
'droge *o* *op het* ~ on dry land; *zie ook vis* &; **'drogen** (droogde, h. gedroogd) **I** *vt* dry; wipe; **II** *vi* dry; **droge'naaldets** (-en) *v* dry point
dro'gist (-en) *m* chemist, druggist; **drogiste'rij** (-en) *v* chemist's (shop), druggist's (shop)
'drogreden (-en) *v* fallacy
drol (-len) **P** *m* turd
drom (-men) *m* crowd, throng
drome'daris [drɔmə-] (-sen) *m* dromedary
'dromen (droomde, h. gedroomd) *vi* & *vt* dream?; **'dromenland** *o* dreamland, never-never land; **'dromer** *m* dreamer; **–ig** dreamy; **drome'rij** (-en) *v* day-dreaming, reverie
'drommel (-s) *m* deuce, devil; *arme* ~ poor devil; *wat* ~ *!* what the deuce; *om de* ~ *niet!* not on your life!; *hij is om de* ~ *niet dom* he is by no means stupid; **–s I** *aj* devilish, deuced, confounded; **II** *ad* < devilish; ~ *goed weten* know jolly well; **III** *ij* the deuce!, what the dickens (devil)!, confound it!
'drommen (dromde, h. en is gedromd) *vi* throng, crowd [around sbd., to the city]
drong (drongen) V.T. v. *dringen*
1 dronk (-en) *m* draught, drink [of water &]; *een* ~ *instellen* propose a toast; **2 dronk (dronken)** V.T. v *drinken*; **'dronkaard** (-s) *m*,

'**dronkelap** (-pen) *m* drunkard, **F** soak, sponge; '**dronkemanspraat** *m* drunken twaddle; **1** '**dronken** [p r e d i k a t i e f] drunk, tight; [a t t r i b u t i e f] drunken, tipsy, cock-eyed; **2** '**dronken** V.T. meerv. v. *drinken*; '**dronkenschap** (-pen) *v* drunkenness, inebriety

droog I *aj* dry² [bread, cough, humour &], arid² [ground, subject &]; parched [lips]; *fig* dry-as-dust; *het zal wel ~ blijven* the fine (dry) weather will continue; *geen ~ brood verdienen* not earn enough for one's bread and cheese; *hij is nog niet ~ achter de oren* he is only just out of the shell; *het droge* zie *droge*; **II** *ad* drily², dryly²; **–bloeier** (-s) *m* ⚘ meadow saffron; **–bloemen** *mv* everlastings, everlasting flowers; **–doek** (-en) *m* tea-towel; **–dok** (-ken) *o* dry-dock, graving-dock; **–heid** *v* dryness, aridity; **–je** *o op een ~ zitten* have nothing to drink; **–jes** (= *droogweg;* **–kap** (-pen) *v* electric hair-dryer; **–koken** (kookte 'droog, is 'drooggekookt) *vi* & *vt* boil dry; **–komiek I** (-en) *m* man of dry humour; **II** *aj* full of quiet fun (dry humour); **III** *ad* with dry humour, drily, dryly; **–leggen**¹ *vt* 1 drain [a marsh]; reclaim [a lake]; 2 *fig* make [a country] dry; **–legging** (-en) *v* draining; reclaiming [of a lake]; *fig* making dry [of a country]; prohibition [of alcohol]; **–lijn** (-en) *v* clothes-line; **–lopen**¹ *vi* run dry; **–machine** [-ma.ʃi.nə] (-s) *v* drying-machine; **–maken**¹ *vt* dry [what is wet]; zie ook: *droogleggen*; **droogmake'rij** (-en) *v* 1 reclaimed land; 2 reclamation of land; '**droogmaking** (-en) *v* = *drooglegging;* **–malen**¹ *vt* = *droogleggen* 1; **–oven** (-s) *m* (drying-)kiln; **–rek** (-ken) *o* drying-rack; clothes-horse; **–stempel** (-s) *o* die stamp; **–stoppel** (-s) *m* dry old stick, dry-as-dust; **–te** (-n) *v* 1 dryness, drought; 2 shoal, sand-bank; **–trommel** (-s) *v* tumble drier; **–vallen**¹ *vi* fall dry; **–weg** drily, dryly, with dry humour; **–zolder** (-s) *m* drying-loft

droom (dromen) *m* dream; *dromen zijn bedrog* dreams are deceptive; *uit de ~ helpen* undeceive; **–beeld** (-en) *o* vision; **–boek** (-en) *o* dream-book; **–gezicht** (-en) *o* vision; **–uitlegger** (-s) *m* interpreter of dreams; **–wereld** *v* dream world

droop (**dropen**) V.T. v *druipen*

1 drop (-pen) *m* 1 drop; 2 drip(ping) [of water from the roof]

2 drop [drɔp] *v* & *o* liquorice, licorice

'**dropen** V.T. meerv. v. *druipen*

'**droppel-** & = *druppel-* &

'**dropwater** *o* licorice-water

'**drossen** (droste, is gedrost) *vi* run away

drs. = *doctorandus*

'**druggebruik** [drüggə-] *o* use of drugs, drug-taking; **–gebruiker** (-s) *m* drug user, drug-taker; **–handel** *m* drug traffic, drug trafficking, **S** drug pushing; **–handelaar** (-s en -laren) *m* drug trafficker, **S** drug pusher; **drugs** *mv* [hard, soft] drugs; *~ gebruiken* be on drugs

dru'ïde (-n) *m* druid

druif (druiven) *v* grape; *de druiven zijn zuur* the grapes are sour; **–luis** (-luizen) *v* vine-pest, phylloxera

'**druilen** (druilde, h. gedruild) *vi* mope, pout; '**druilerig** moping [person]; drizzling [weather]; '**druiloor** (-oren) *m-v* mope, moper

'**druipen*** *vi* drip; *~ van het bloed* drip with blood; '**druiper** (-s) *m* ⚤ gonorrhoea, **S** clap; '**druipnat** dripping (wet); **–neus** (-neuzen) *m* 1 running nose; 2 sniveller; **–steen** (-stenen) *m* stalactite [hanging from roof of cave], stalagmite [rising from floor]

'**druiveblad** (-bladen en -bladeren) *o* vine-leaf; '**druivenkas** (-sen) *v* vinery; **–kwekerij** (-en) *v* 1 grape culture; 2 grapery; **–oogst** (-en) *m* grape-harvest, vintage; **–pers** (-en) *v* wine-press; **–plukker** (-s) *m* grape gatherer, vintager; **–tros** (-sen) *m* bunch (cluster) of grapes; '**druivepit** (-ten) *v* grape-stone; **–sap** *o* grape juice; **–suiker** *m* grape-sugar, glucose, dextrose

1 druk I *aj* 1 (v. p l a a t s e n) busy [street], crowded [meeting], bustling [town], lively [place]; 2 (v. p e r s o n e n) busy, bustling, fussy; lively, noisy [children]; 3 (v. v e r - s i e r i n g) loud [patterns]; *een ~ gebruik maken van...* make a frequent use of...; *een ~ gesprek* a lively conversation; *een ~ke handel* a brisk trade; *de ~ke uren* the busy hours, the rush hours; *~ verkeer* heavy traffic [on the road]; *een ~ke zaak* a well-patronized business; *het is mij hier te ~* things are too lively for me here; *het ~ hebben* be (very) busy; *het ontzettend ~ hebben* be rushed; *zij hadden het ~ over hem* he was made the general theme of their conversation; *ze hebben het niet ~ in die winkel* there is not much doing in that shop; *zich ~ maken* get excited; worry, bother, fuss (about *om, over*); *hij maakt het zich niet ~* he takes things easy; **II** *ad* busily; *~ bezochte vergadering* well-attended meeting; *~ bezochte winkel* well-patronized shop; zie ook: *bezig, stemmen* **III**

---

¹ V.T. en V.D. van dit werkwoord volgens het model: '**droog**maken, V.T. maakte '**droog**, V.D. '**droog**gemaakt. Zie voor de vormen onder het grondwoord, in dit voorbeeld: *maken*. Bij sterke en onregelmatige werkwoorden wordt u verwezen naar de lijst achterin.

2 druk (-ken) *m* 1 pressure[2] [of the hand, of the atmosphere &, also = oppression]; squeeze [of the hand]; *fig* burden [of taxation]; 2 print(ing), [small] print, type; [5th] impression, edition; ~ *uitoefenen op* bring pressure to bear upon [sbd.]; *in* ~ *verschijnen* appear in print

'**drukcabine** (-s) *v* pressurized cabin

'**drukfout** (-en) *v* misprint, printer's error, typographical error

'**drukinkt** *m* printer's (printing) ink; '**drukken** (drukte, h. gedrukt) **I** *vt* 1 press[2]; squeeze, *fig* weigh (heavy) upon, oppress [sbd.], depress [prices, the market]; 2 print [books, calico &]; *iem. a a n zijn borst (het hart)* ~ press sbd. to one's breast (heart); *iem. i n zijn armen* ~ clasp sbd. in one's arms; *de hoed diep in de ogen* ~ pull one's hat over one's eyes; *iem. iets o p het hart* ~ impress (enjoin) sth. upon sbd.; **II** *vi* press; pinch [of shoes]; *zich* ~ **F** flunk; ~ *op* press (on); *fig* weigh (heavy) upon; *op de knop* ~ press the button; zie ook: *gedrukt*; **-d** burdensome [load], heavy [air]; oppressive [load, heat], close, stifling [atmosphere], sultry [weather], crushing; '**drukker** (-s) *m* printer; **drukke'rij** (-en) *v* printing-office, printing-works; '**drukknoopje** (-s) *o* press-button, press-stud; '**drukknop** (-pen) *m* push-button; **-kosten** *mv* cost of printing; **-kunst** *v* (art of) printing, typography; **-letter** (-s) *v* 1 type; 2 (t e g e n o v e r s c h r i j f l e t t e r) print letter; **-meter** (-s) *m* pressure-gauge; **-pan** (-nen) *v* pressure-cooker; **-pers** (-en) *v* printing-press, press; **-proef** (-proeven) *v* proof [for correction]; *vuile* ~ galley-proof, galley-sheet

'**drukte** *v* stir, (hustle and) bustle; [seasonal] pressure; fuss; *kouwe* ~ **F** swank, la-di-da *veel* ~ *over iets maken* make a noise (a great fuss) about sth.; **-maker** (-s) *m* **F** fuss-pot; zie ook: *opschepper*

'**druktoets** (-en) *m* push key, push button; **-verband** (-en) *o* pressure bandage (dressing); **-werk** (-en) *o* printed matter; *een* ~ 🏷 a printed paper; *als* ~ *verzenden* send as printed matter

drum (-s) *m* ♪ drum; '**drummen** (drumde, h. gedrumd) *vi* ♪ drum; **-er** (-s) *m* ♪ drummer; '**drumstel** (-len) *o* drums, set of drums

drup (-pen) *m* = 1 *drop*; '**druppel** (-s) *m* drop (of water); globule, bead; *het is een* ~ *op een gloeiende plaat* it's a drop in the ocean; '**druppelen** (druppelde, h. en is gedruppeld) *vi* drop; *het druppelt* drops of rain are falling; *het water druppelt van het dak* the water is dripping (trickling) from the roof; '**druppelsgewijs, -gewijze** by drops

Ds. ~ *W. Brown* the Reverend W. Brown, the Rev. W. Brown

D-trein (-en) *m* corridor train

dua'lisme *o* dualism; **-istisch** dualistic

'**dubbel I** *aj* double; twofold; dual; ~*e bodem* false bottom; *de* ~*e hoeveelheid* double the quantity; ~*e naam* double-barrelled name, hyphenated name; *zijn* ~*e natuur* his dual nature; ~*e punt* zie 3 *punt*; ~*e schroef* twinscrew; **II** *ad* doubly; ~ *en dwars verdiend* more than deserved; ~ *zo groot* (*lang* & *als*) twice the size (length &) (of); ~ *zien* see double; **III** (-en) *m een* ~*e* a duplicate [of a stamp], a double [at dominoes]; **-dekker** (-s) *m* biplane, doubledecker; **dubbel'focusbril** (-len) *m* bifocal glasses, bifocals; '**dubbelganger** (-s) *m* double; **dubbel'hartig** double-faced, doublehearted; **-heid** *v* double-dealing, duplicity; **dubbel'koolzure 'soda** *m* & *v* bicarbonate of soda; '**dubbelloops** double-barrelled; **-parkeren** (parkeerde 'dubbel, h. 'dubbelgeparkeerd) *vi* & *vt* double-park; **-punt** (-en) *v* & *o* colon; **-rol** (-len) *v een* ~ *spelen* double (as); **-spel** (-spelen) *o sp* double [at tennis]; *dames-*(*heren-*)~ ladies' (men's) doubles; *gemengd* ~ mixed doubles; **-spion** (-nen) *m* double agent; **-spoor** (-sporen) *o* double track; **-stek(k)er** (-s) *m* multiple plug; **-tje** (-s) *o* "dubbeltje", ten cent piece; *het is een* ~ *op zijn kant* it will be touch and go; *een* ~ *tweemaal omkeren* look twice at one's money; **-vouwen** (vouwde 'dubbel, h. 'dubbelgevouwen) *vt* fold in two; double up [with laughter]; **-zien** (zag 'dubbel, h. 'dubbelgezien) *vi* see double, suffer from diplopia; **dubbel'zinnig** ambiguous, equivocal; **-heid** (-heden) *v* ambiguity, double entendre

'**dubben** (dubde, h. gedubd) *vi* be in two minds; waver

dubi'eus dubious, doubtful; *dubieuze vordering* $ doubtful (bad) debt

'**dubio** *hij stond in* ~ he was in two minds

'**duchten** (duchtte, h. geducht) *vt* fear, dread, apprehend; '**duchtig I** *aj* fearful, strong; **II** *ad* < fearfully, terribly

du'el [dy.'tl] (-s en -len) *o* duel, single combat; **duel'leren** (duelleerde, h. geduelleerd) *vt* fight a duel, duel

du'et [dy'ct] (-ten) *o* ♪ duet

duf stuffy; fusty; *fig* fusty, musty

'**duffel I** *o* duffel, duffle, pilot cloth; **II** (-s) *m* duffel coat

'**dufheid** *v* fustiness, stuffiness; *fig* fustiness, mustiness

'**duidelijk** clear, plain, distinct, obvious, self-evident, explicit; marked [improvement, influence, preference]; **-heid** *v* clearness, plainness &; **duidelijkheids'halve** for the sake of clearness

'**duiden** (duidde, h. geduid) **I** *vi ~ op iets* point to sth.; **II** *vt* interpret; *ten kwade ~* take amiss (in bad part); **–ding** (-en) *v* interpretation
duif (duiven) *v* 🐦 pigeon, dove²; *de gebraden duiven vliegen een mens niet in de mond* don't think the plums will drop into your mouth while you sit still; zie ook *havik*, *schieten* **I**; **–je** (-s) *o* (small) pigeon; *mijn ~!* my dove!
duig (-en) *v* stave; *in ~en vallen* drop to pieces; *fig* fall through, miscarry [of plans &]; *in ~en doen vallen* stave in; *fig* cause to fall through, make [plans] miscarry
duik (-en) *m* dive; **–bommenwerper** (-s) *m* dive-bomber; **–boot** (-boten) *m & v* submarine, [German] U-boat; **–bril** (-len) *m sp* diving goggles; **–elaar** (-s) *m* (p o p p e t j e) tumbler; '**duikelen** (duikelde, h. en is geduikeld) *vi* 1 tumble, fall head over heels; 2 *fig* fall flat; **–ling** (-en) *v* 1 (i n d e l u c h t) somersault; 2 (v a l) tumble; *een ~ maken = duikelen*; '**duiken*** *vi* dive, plunge, dip; *i n elkaar gedoken* huddled (up), hunched (up), crouched (down); *in zijn stoel gedoken* ensconced in his chair; *o n d e r de tafel ~* duck under the table; '**duiker** (-s) *m* 1 diver (ook 🐦); 2 🔧 culvert; **–helm** (-en) *m* diving-helmet; **–klok** (-ken) *v* diving-bell; **–pak** (-ken) *o* diving-dress, diving-suit; **–toestel** (-len) *o* diving-apparatus;'**duikmasker** (-s) *o sp* face mask; **–sport** *v* skin-diving; **–vlucht** (-en) *v* dive
duim (-en) *m* 1 thumb [of the hand]; 2 inch = $2^1/_2$ cm; 3 🔧 hook [also of a door]; *ik heb hem onder de ~* he is under my thumb; **–afdruk** (-ken) *m* thumb-print; **–breed** *o geen ~* not an inch; '**duimeling** (-en) *m* thumb-stall; **–lot** (-ten) *m* 1 thumb-stall; 2 thumb; '**duimen** (duimde, h. geduimd) *vi ik zal voor je ~* ± I'll keep my fingers crossed; **–dik** *het ligt er ~ bovenop* (it is) as plain as pike staff; **–draaien** (draaide 'duimen, h. 'duimengedraaid) *vi* twiddle (twirl) one's thumbs²; '**duimpje** (-s) *o* thumb; *iets op zijn ~ kennen* have a thing at one's finger-ends; '**duimschroef** (-schroeven) *v* thumbscrew; *(iem.) de duimschroeven aanzetten* put on the thumbscrews; *fig* put on the screw; **–stok** (-ken) *m* (folding) rule
duin (-en) *v & o* dune
'**Duinkerken** *o* Dunkirk
'**duinpan** (-nen) *v* dip (hollow) in the dunes; **–roos** (-rozen) *v* Scotch rose; **–zand** *o* sand (of the dunes)
'**duister I** *aj* dark², obscure², dim²; gloomy²; *fig* mysterious; **II** *o het ~* the dark; *iem. in het ~ laten* keep (leave) sbd. in the dark; *in het ~ tasten* be (grope) in the dark; zie ook: *donker*; **–heid** (-heden) *v* darkness², obscurity; **–ling** (-en) *m* obscurant(ist); **–nis** (-sen) *v* darkness,

dark, obscurity
duit (-en) *m & v* 🔟 doit; *een aardige (flinke) ~* a pretty penny; *hij heeft geen (rooie) ~* he has not a penny to bless himself with, he hasn't a bean; *een hele (een slordige) ~ kosten* cost a pretty penny; *ook een ~ in het zakje doen* contribute one's mite; put in a word; *~en hebben* **F** have plenty of money; *op de ~en zijn* be close-fisted; zie ook: *cent*, '**duitendief** (-dieven) *m* money-grubber
Duits I *aj* German; 🔟 Teutonic [Order of Knights]; **II** *sb het ~* German; *een ~e* a German woman; **–er** (-s) *m* German; **–land** *o* Germany
'**duiveëi** (-eren) *o* pigeon's egg.
'**duivel** (-en en -s) *m* devil², demon, fiend; *een arme ~* a poor devil; *de ~ en zijn moer* the devil and his dam; *wat ~ is dat nou?* what the deuce have we here?; *de ~ hale me, als...* (the) deuce take me, if...; *het is of de ~ er mee speelt* the devil is in it; *loop naar de ~!* **F** go to hell!; *iem. naar de ~ wensen* wish sbd. at the devil; *de ~ in hebben* have one's monkey up; *als je van de ~ spreekt, trap je op zijn staart* talk of the devil and he is sure to appear; **–achtig** devilish, fiendish, diabolic(al); **–banner** (-s) *m*, **–bezweerder** (-s) *m* exorcist; **–banning** *v*, **–bezwering** *v* exorcism; **duive'lin** (-nen) *v* she-devil; '**duivels I** *aj* devilish, diabolic(al), fiendish; (w o e d e n d) furious; *[iem.] ~ maken* infuriate; *het is om ~ te worden* it would vex a saint; *het is een ~e kerel* he is a devil of a fellow; *die ~e kerel* that confounded fellow; *het is een ~ werk* it is a devilish business, the devil and all of a job; **II** *ad* diabolically; < devilish, deuced(ly); **III** *ij* the deuce, the devil!; '**duivelsdrek** *m* asafoetida; **–kind** (-eren) *o* imp, child of Satan; **–kunstenaar** (-s) *m* magician, sorcerer; **duivelskunstena'rij** (-en) *v* devilish arts, magic; '**duivels'toejager** (-s) *m* **F** factotum, handyman; '**duivelswerk** (-en) *o* devilish work; '**duiveltje** (-s) *o* (little) devil, imp; *een ~ in een doosje* a Jack-in-the-box
'**duivenhok** (-ken) *o*, '**duivenkot** (-ten) *o* pigeon-house, dovecot; **–melker** (-s) *m* pigeon-fancier; **–slag** (-slagen) *o* pigeon-loft; **–til** (-len) *v* pigion-house, dovecot, columbarium
'**duizelen** (duizelde, h. geduizeld) *vi* grow dizzy (giddy); *ik duizel* I feel dizzy (giddy); *het (hoofd) duizelt mij* my head swims (whirls), my brain reels; '**duizelig** dizzy, giddy, vertiginous; **–heid** *v* dizziness, giddiness [of persons], swimming of the head; '**duizeling** (-en) *v* vertigo, fit of giddiness, swimming of the head; *een ~ overviel hem* he was seized (taken) with giddiness; **duizeling'wekkend** dizzy, giddy, vertiginous

'**duizend** (-en) a (one) thousand; *iem. uit ~en* one in a thousand; **–blad** *o* milfoil, yarrow; **duizend-en-'één-nacht** *m* the Arabian Nights' (Entertainments), a Thousand and One Nights; '**duizendjarig** of a thousand years, millennial; *het ~ rijk* the millennium; **–kunstenaar** (-s) *m* magician, sorcerer; **–poot** (-poten) *m* centipede, millipede; **–schoon** (-schonen) *v* ⚘ sweet william; **–ste** thousandth (part); **–stemmig** many-voiced, myriad-voiced; **–tal** (-len) *o* a thousand; **–voud** *o* multiple of a thousand; **–voudig** a thousand-fold

du'**kaat** (-katen) *m* ducat

duk'**dalf** (-dalven) *m* ⚓ dolphin

'**dulden** (duldde, h. geduld) *vt* bear, suffer, endure [pain]; stand, tolerate [practices, actions]; *het (Jan) niet ~* not tolerate it (John); *zij ~ hem daar, hij wordt geduld, méér niet* he is there on sufferance

dun I *aj* thin[2], slender [waists]; small [ale], washy [beer], clear [soup], rare [air]; *het is ~ 1* it is a poor performance, poor stuff; 2 it is mean; **II** *ad* thinly [spread, inhabited]; **–doek** *o* bunting, flag; **–drukpapier** *o* thin paper, India paper; **–heid** *v* thinness[2]; rareness [of the air]

dunk *m* opinion; *een grote (hoge) ~ hebben van* have a high opinion of, think much (highly) of; *geen hoge ~ hebben van* have but a poor opinion of, think poorly of; have no opinion of, think little (nothing) of; '**dunken*** *vi* think; *mij dunkt* I think, it seems to me; *mij dacht (docht)* I thought; *wat dunkt u?* what you think?

'**dunnen I** (dunde, h. gedund) *vt* thin (out); *gedunde gelederen* depleted ranks; **II** (dunde, is gedund) *vi* thin; '**dunnetjes I** *ad* thinly; zie ook: *overdoen*; **II** *aj het is ~* zie *dun*; '**dunsel** *o* thinnings

'**duo** ('s) 1 *o* (t w e e t a l) pair, (i n c a b a r e t, r e v u e &) duo; ♪ duet ‖ 2 *m* (v . m o t o r-f i e t s) pillion; *~ rijden* ride pillon; **–passagier** [g = ʒ] (-s) *m* pillion-rider; **–zitting** (-en) *v* pillion

'**dupe** (-s) *m-v* dupe, victim; *ik ben er de ~ van* I am to suffer for it; du'**peren** (dupeerde, h. gedupeerd) *vt* fail, disappoint, trick

dupli'**caat** (-caten) *o* duplicate; **dupli'cator** (-s) *m* duplicator

du'**pliek** (-en) *v* rejoinder

'**duplo** *in ~* in duplicate; *in ~ opmaken* draw up in duplicate, duplicate

'**duren** (duurde, h. geduurd) *vt* last, endure; *het duurde uren voor hij...* it was hours before...; *dit kan wel eindeloos ~* this can go on (continue) for ever; *duurt het lang?* will it take (be) long?); *wat*

duurt het lang voor jij komt what a time you are!; *het duurde lang eer hij kwam* he was (pretty) long in coming; *het zal lang ~ eer...* it will be long before...; *het duurt mij te lang* it is too long for me; *zo lang als het duurde* while (as long as) it lasted

durf *m* daring, **F** pluck; **–al** (-len) *m* dare-devil; '**durven*** *vt* dare; *dat zou ik niet ~ beweren* I should not venture (be bold enough) to say such a thing, I am not prepared to say that; zie ook: *gedurfd*

dus I *ad* thus, in that way; **II** *cj* consequently, so, therefore; *we zien ~, dat...* ook: we see, then, that...; **–danig I** *aj* such; **II** *ad* 1 in such a way (manner), so; 2 to such an extent, so much; **–ver(re)** *tot ~* so far, hitherto, up to the present, up to this time, up to now

dut (-ten) *m* doze, snooze, nap; **–je** (-s) *o* = *dut*; *een ~ doen* take a nap; '**dutten** (dutte, h. gedut) *vi* doze, snooze, take a nap, have forty winks; *zitten ~* doze

1 **duur** *m* duration; continuance; length [of service, of a visit]; life [of an electric bulb]; *o p den ~* in the long run, in the end; *van korte ~* of short duration; short-lived; *van lange ~* of long standing; of long duration; long-lived; *het was niet van lange ~* it did not last long

2 **duur I** *aj* dear, expensive, costly; *hoe ~ is dat?* how much is it?, what is the price?; *een dure eed zweren* swear a solemn oath; *het is mijn dure plicht* it is my bounden duty; **II** *ad* dear(ly); *het zal u ~ te staan komen* you shall pay dearly for this; *~ verkopen* $ sell dear; *fig* sell [one's life] dearly; '**duurbaar** = *dierbaar*

'**duurkoop** dear; zie ook *goedkoop*; '**duurte** *v* dearness, expensiveness; **–toeslag** (-slagen) *m* cost-of-living allowance

'**duurzaam** durable, lasting [peace]; hard-wearing, that wears well [stuff]; *duurzame gebruiksgoederen* consumer durables; **–heid** *v* durability, durableness

'**duvels'toejager** (-s) *m* factotum, handy-man

duw (-en) *m* push, thrust, shove; '**duwen** (duwde, h. geduwd) *vt* & *vi* push, thrust, shove; '**duwschroef** (-schroeven) *v* ⚙ pusher screw; **–tje** (-s) *o* nudge, shove, prod; *iem. een ~ geven* ook: nudge sbd.

D.V. = *deo volente* God willing

dw. = *dienstwillige*

'**dwaalbegrip** (-pen) *o* false notion, fallacy; **–geest** (-en) *m* wandering (erring) spirit; **–leer** (-leren) *v* false doctrine, heresy; **–licht** (-en) *o* will-o'-the-wisp; **–spoor** (-sporen) *o* wrong track; *iem. op een ~ brengen* lead sbd. astray; *op een ~ geraken* go astray; **–ster** (-ren) *v* planet; **–weg** (-wegen) *m* wrong way, zie verder: *dwaalspoor*

dwaas I *aj* foolish, silly; ~ *genoeg heb ik*... I was fool enough to...; zie ook: *aanstellen*; **II** *ad* foolishly, in a silly way; **III** (dwazen) *m* fool; **–heid** (-heden) *v* folly, foolishness

'dwalen (dwaalde, h. gedwaald) *vi* 1 roam, wander; 2 (e e n v e r k e e r d i n z i c h t h e b b e n) err; ~ *is menselijk* to err is human; **–ling** (-en) *v* error

dwang *m* compulsion, constraint, coercion; **–arbeid** *m* hard (compulsory) labour; ⚖ penal servitude; **–arbeider** (-s) *m* convict; **–bevel** (-velen) *o* ⚖ warrant, writ; distress warrant [for non-payment of rates]; **–buis** (-buizen) *o* strait-jacket; **–gedachte** (-n) *v* obsession; **–handeling** (-en) *v* compulsive (obsessional) act; **–maatregel** (-en) *m* coercive measure; **dwang'matig** compulsive; **'dwangmiddel** (-en) *o* 1 means of coercion; 2 forcible means; **–positie** [-zi.(t)si.] (-s) *v* 1 ◊ squeeze; 2 *fig* embarrassing situation, plight; *iem. in een ~ brengen* force (tie) sbd.'s hands; **–som** (-men) *v* penal sum; **–voorstelling** (-en) *v* obsession, fixed idea

'dwarrelen (dwarrelde, h. en is gedwarreld) *vi* whirl; **–ling** (-en) *v* whirl(ing); **'dwarrelwind** (-en) *m* whirlwind

dwars 1 transverse, (in samenst.) cross...; 2 *fig* (t e g e n d e d r a a d i n) cross-grained, wrong-headed, contrary; ~ *door*... *heen*, ~ *over* (right) across the...; ~ *oversteken* cross [the street]; *iem. de voet ~ zetten, iem. ~ zitten* cross (thwart) sbd., **F** put sbd.'s nose out of joint; *dat zit hem ~ (in de maag)* that sticks in his gizzard, that annoys him; **–balk** (-en) *m* cross-beam; **–beuk** (-en) *m* transept; **–bomen** (dwarsboomde, h. gedwarsboomd) *vt* cross, thwart; **–dal** (-dalen) *o* transverse valley; **–door-sne(d)e** (-sneden) *v* cross-section; slice; **–drijven** (dwarsdrijfde, h. gedwarsdrijfd) *vi* take the opposite course (or view); **–drijver** (-s) *m* cross-grained (perverse) fellow; **dwarsdrijve'rij** (-en) *v* contrariness, perverseness; **'dwarsfluit** (-en) *v* German flute; **–gang** (-en) *m* transverse passage; **–heid** *v* = *dwarsdrijverij*; **–hout** (-en) *o* cross-beam; **–kijker** (-s) *m* spy,

snooper; **–laesie** [-le.zi.] transverse lesion; **–lat** (-ten) *v* 1 cross-lath; 2 *sp* cross-bar; **–ligger** (-s) *m* sleeper [under the rails]; *fig* **F** anti; **–lijn** (-en) = *dwarsstreep*; **'dwars-'scheeps** abeam; **'dwarsschip** (-schepen) *o* transept [of a church]; **–sne(d)e** (-sneden) *v* cross-section; **–straat** (-straten) *v* cross-street; **–streep** (-strepen) *v* cross-line, transverse line; **–weg** (-wegen) *m* cross-road

'dwaselijk foolishly

'dweepachtig *aj* 1 fanatical [in religious matters]; 2 gushing [in sentimental matters]; **–ziek** 1 fanatical; 2 gushingly enthusiastic; **–zucht** *v* fanaticism

dweil (-en) *m* floor-cloth, mop, swab; (s l o n s) slut; **'dweilen** (dweilde, h. gedweild) *vt* mop (up), swab, wash [floors]

'dwepen (dweepte, h. gedweept) *vi* be fanatical; ~ *met* be enthusiastic about [poetry], be dotingly fond of, **F** enthuse over [music], gush about [professor X], be a devotee of [Wagner], rave about [a girl]; **–d** zie *dweepachtig*; **'dweper** (-s) *m* 1 fanatic; 2 **F** enthusing zealot, devotee, enthusiast; **–ig** fanatic, bigoted; **dwepe'rij** (-en) *v* 1 fanaticism; 2 gushing enthusiasm

dwerg (-en) *m* dwarf, pygmy; **–achtig** dwarfish, dwarf, pygmean; **–poedel** (-s) *m* toy poodle; **–volk** (-en) *o* pygmean race

'dwingeland (-en) *m* tyrant; **dwingelan'dij** *v* tyranny; **'dwingen* I** *vt* compel, force, constrain, coerce; *hij laat zich niet* ~ he doesn't suffer himself to be forced; *dat laat zich niet* ~ you can't force it; **II** *vi* be tyrannically insistent [of a child]; *om iets* ~ be insistent on getting sth.; *dat kind kan zo* ~ always wants to have its own way; **–d** coercive [measures]; compelling [reasons]; **'dwingerig** tyrannic, insistent; **dwong** (dwongen) V.T. v. *dwingen*

d.w.z. = *dat wil zeggen* that is (to say), namely

dy'namica [y = i.] *v* dynamics; **dyna'miek** *v* dynamics

dyna'miet [y = i.] *o* dynamite

dy'namisch [y = i.] dynamic; **dy'namo** ('s) *m* dynamo

dynas'tie [y = i.] (-ieën) *v* dynasty; **–k** dynastic

dysente'rie [y = i.] *v* dysentery

E

e [e.] ('s) *v* e

e.a. = *en andere(n)* and others, and other things

eau de co'logne [o.dɔko.'lɔɲə] *v* eau de Cologne

eb, 'ebbe *v* ebb, ebb-tide; **~ en vloed** ebb-tide and flood-tide, ebb and flow

'ebbehout *o* ebony; **–en** *aj* ebony

'ebben (ebde, h. geëbd) *vi* ebb, flow back; *de zee ebt* the tide ebbs, is ebbing, is going out

ebo'niet *o* ebonite, vulcanite

e'chec [e.'ʃɛk] (-s) *o* check, rebuff, repulse, failure; **~ lijden** 1 (v. p e r s o o n) meet with a rebuff; 2 (v. r e g e r i n g &) be defeated; 3 (v. o n d e r n e m i n g) fail

eche'lon [e.ʃɔ'lɔ̀n] (-s) *m* ✕ echelon

'echo ['ɛxo.] ('s) *m* echo; **'echoën** (echode, h. geëchood) *vi* & *vt* (re-)echo; **'echolood** *o* echo sounder; **–peiling** (-en) *v* echo sounding; **–put** (-ten) *m* echoing well

1 echt I *aj* authentic [letters], real [roses &], genuine [butter &], legitimate [children]; true(-born) [Briton]; out-and-out [boys]; **F** regular [blackguards]; *dat is nou ~ eens een man* he is a real man; **II** *ad* < really; *hij was ~ kwaad* he was downright angry; *het is ~ waar* it is really true

2 echt *m* marriage, matrimony, wedlock; *in de ~ treden, zich in de ~ begeven* marry; zie ook: *verbinden, verenigen*; **'echtbreekster** (-s) *v* adulteress; **–breken** *vi* commit adultery; **–breker** (-s) *m* adulterer; **–breuk** *v* adultery; **'echtelieden** *mv* married people; *de ~* the married couple; **–lijk** conjugal [rights]; matrimonial [happiness]; married [state]; marital [bliss]; **'echten** (echtte, h. geëcht) *vt* legitimate [a child]

'echter however, nevertheless; **F** though

'echtgenoot (-noten) *m* husband, spouse; *echtgenoten* zie ook *gehuwden*; **–genote** (-n) *v* wife, spouse, lady

'echtheid *v* authenticity [of a picture], genuineness

'echting *v* legitimation; **'echtpaar** (-paren) *o* (married) couple; **–scheiding** (-en) *v* divorce; **–verbintenis** (-sen) *v*, **–vereniging** (-en) *v* marriage

ecla'tant signal, striking [case &]; brilliant, sensational [success]

ec'lecticus [ɛk'lɛk-] (-ci) *m* eclectic; **ec'lectisch** eclectic

e'clips (-en) *v* eclipse; **eclip'seren** (eclipseerde, h. en is geëclipseerd) **I** *vt* eclipse; **II** *vi fig* abscond

ecolo'gie *v* ecology; **eco'logisch** ecological; **eco'loog** (-logen) *m* ecologist

econome'trie *v* econometrics

econo'mie (-ieën) *v* 1 economy; 2 (w e t e n - s c h a p) economics; *geleide* ~ planned economy; **eco'nomisch** 1 economic; 2 (z u i n i g) economical; **economi'seren** [s = z] (economiseerde, h. geëconomiseerd) *vi* economize; **eco'noom** (-nomen) *m* economist

e'cru ecru

'Ecuador *m* Ecuador

ec'zeem [ɛk'se.m] (-zemen) *o* eczema

e.d. = *en dergelijke* zie *dergelijk*

e'dammer (-s) *m* Edam (cheese)

'edel I *aj* 1 noble[2] [birth, blood, features, thoughts &]; 2 precious [metals, stones]; 3 vital [parts, organs]; *de ~en* the nobility; 🕮 the nobles; **II** *ad* nobly; **edel'achtbaar** honourable, worshipful; *Edelachtbare* Your Honour; Your Worship; **'edelgas** (-sen) *o* rare gas; **–gesteente** (-n en -s) *o* precious stone, gem; **–heid** *v* nobleness, nobility; *Hare (Zijne) Edelheid* Her (His) Grace; **–hert** (-en) *o* red deer; **–knaap** (-knapen) *m* page; **edel'man** (-lieden) *m* nobleman, noble; **edel'moedig** generous, noble(-minded); **–heid** *v* generosity, noblemindedness; **'edelsmid** (-smeden) *m* gold and silver smith; **–steen** (-stenen) *m* = *edelgesteente*; **–vrouw** (-en) *v* noblewoman

e'dict (-en) *o* edict [of Nantes &], decree

e'ditie [-(t)si.] (-s) *v* edition, issue

e'doch but, however, yet, still

educa'tief educational

eed (eden) *m* oath; *de ~ afnemen* administer the oath to, swear in [a functionary]; *een ~ doen (afleggen)* take (swear) an oath; *een ~ doen om...* swear [never] to...; *daarop heeft hij een ~ gedaan* 1 he has sworn it; 2 he has affirmed it on his oath; *onder ede* [declared] on oath; *hij staat onder ede* he is under oath; **–aflegging** (-en) *v* taking an (the) oath; **–afneming** (-en) *v* swearing in; **–breuk** (-en) *v* violation of one's oath, perjury; **'eedsaflegging** (-en) *v* = *eedaflegging*

E.E.G. *v* = *Europese Economische Gemeenschap* European Economic Community, E.E.C.

'eega ('s en eegaas), **'eegade** (-n) *m-v* spouse

'eekhoorn, 'eekhoren (-s) *m* squirrel

eelt *o* callus, callosity; **'eeltachtig** callous, horny [hands]; **–heid** *v* callosity; **'eeltig** callous, horny [hands]; **'eeltknobbel** (-s) *m* callosity

1 een [ən] a, an; ~ *vijftig* some fifty
2 een [e.n] **I** *telw.* one; *het was* ~ *en al modder* all mud, mud all over; ~ *en al oor* all ears; ~ *en ander* the things mentioned; *het* ~ *en ander* a few things, a thing or two, one thing and another; *de ene na de andere...* one... after another; *de (het)* ~ *of andere* one or other, some; *het* ~ *of ander* 1 *aj* some; 2 *sb* something or other; *de* ~ *of andere dag* some day; *het* ~ *of het ander* either... or..., one or the other; *noch het* ~ *noch het ander* neither one thing nor the other; *in* ~ *of andere vorm* in one shape or another; *die ene dag* 1 (only) that one day; 2 that day of all others; ~*-twee-drie* **F** in two shakes; *o p* ~ *na* all except one; the last but one; *ze zijn v a n* ~ *grootte (leeftijd)* they are of a size (of an age); ~ *v o o r* ~ one by one, one at a time; **II** *v* one; *drie enen* three ones; **–akter** (-s) *m* act play; **–armig** one-armed; **–cellig** unicellular; ~*e diertjes* protozoa
eend (-en) *v* 1 duck; 2 *fig* goose, ass
'eendaags lasting one day, one-day; **'eendagsvlieg** (-en) *v* ephemeron, mayfly
'eendeëi (-eren) *o* duck's egg; **–jacht** (-en) *v* duck-shooting
'eendekker (-s) *m* monoplane
'eendekroos *o* duckweed
'eendelig one-piece [swim-suit]
'eendemossel (-s) *v* barnacle
'eendenkooi (-en) *v* decoy
'eender I *aj* equal; the same; *het is my* ~ it is all the same (all one) to me; **II** *ad* equally; ~ *gekleed* dressed alike
'eendracht *v* concord, union, unity, harmony; ~ *maakt macht* union is strength; **een'drachtig I** *aj* united [efforts], harmonious, concerted [views]; **II** *ad* unitedly, as one man, [act] in unity, in concert, [work together] harmoniously
'eendvogel (-s) *m* duck; **'eeneiïg** (v. t w e e l i n g e n) identical; uniovular, monozygotic
eenge'zinswoning (-en) *v* one-family-house
'eenheid (-heden) *v* 1 (a l s m a a t) unit; 2 (a l s e i g e n s c h a p) oneness, uniformity [of purpose]; 3 (a l s d e u g d) unity; *de drie eenheden* the three (dramatic) unities; **'eenheidsprijs** (-prijzen) *m* unit price; **–staat** (-staten) *m* unitary state
'eenhoevig ungulate; **–hoofdig** monarchial; *een* ~*e regering* a monarchy; **–hoorn, –horen** (-s) *m* unicorn; **–huizig** ♀ monoecious; **–jarig** 1 of one year, one-year-old [child]; 2 ♀ annual; 3 ♙ yearling
een'kennig shy, timid; **–heid** *v* shyness, timidity
'eenlettergrepig monosyllabic, of one syllable; ~ *woord* monosyllable; **'eenling** (-en) *m*

individual; **'eenmaal** 1 once; 2 one day; ~, *andermaal, derdemaal!* going, going, gone!; ~ *is geenmaal* once is no custom; zie ook: 1 *zo* **I;** **'eenmaking** *v* unification, integration [of Europe]; **'eenmansgat** (-gaten) *o* fox-hole; **–zaak** (-zaken) *v* one-man business; **'eenmotorig** single-engined
'eenogig one-eyed; **–oog** (-ogen) *m-v* one-eyed person; *in het land der blinden is* ~ *koning* in the kingdom of blind men the one-eyed is king
een'parig I *aj* 1 unanimous [in opinion]; 2 uniform [velocity]; **II** *ad* 1 unanimously, with one accord; 2 uniformly [accelerated]; **–heid** *v* 1 unanimity; 2 uniformity
'eenpersoons for one person, one-man [show &]; single [room, bed]; twin [bed, of a pair]; single-seater [car, aeroplane]; **een'richtingsverkeer** *o* oneway traffic; *straat voor* ~ one-way-street
eens 1 once, one day (evening); (i n s p r o o k j e s) once upon a time [there was...]; 2 (i n d e t o e k o m s t) one day [you will...]; 3 just [go, fetch, tell me &]; ~ *voor al* once for all; *de* ~ *beroemde schoonheid* the once famous beauty; *hij bedankte niet* ~ he did not so much as (not even) thank us; ~ *zoveel* as much (many) again; *het* ~ *worden* come to an agreement [about the price &]; *wij zijn het* ~ *(met elkaar)* we are at one, we agree; *die twee zijn het* ~ there is an understanding between them; they are hand in glove; *ik ben het met mijzelf niet* ~ I am in two minds about it; *wij zijn het er over* ~ *dat...* we are of one mind as to..., we are agreed that...; *daar zijn we het niet over* ~ we don't see eye to eye on that point; *daarover zijn allen het* ~ there is only one opinion about that; *zij waren het onderling niet* ~ they were divided against themselves
'eensdeels ~...*anderdeels...* partly... partly...; for one thing... for another...; **eensge'zind I** *aj* unanimous, of one mind, at one, in harmony; **II** *ad* unanimously, [act] in harmony, in concert; **–heid** *v* unanimousness, unanimity, union, harmony; **'eensklaps** all at once, suddenly, all of a sudden
een'slachtig monosexual, unisexual; **eens'luidend** of the same tenor; ~ *afschrift* a true copy; ~*e verklaringen* identical statements
een'stemmig, 'eenstemmig I *aj* ♩ for one voice; *fig* unanimous; ~*e liederen* unison songs; **II** *ad* with one voice, unanimously; **–heid** *v* unanimity, harmony
'eenterm (-en) *m* × monomial; **'eentje** *o* one; *je bent me er* ~ **F** you are a one; *er* ~ *pakken* **F** have one; *in (op) mijn* ~ by myself
een'tonig I *aj* monotonous[song]; *fig* humdrum, dull [life &]; **II** *ad* monotonously;

–heid *v* monotony; *fig* sameness

een-twee-'drie at once, immediately

een'vormig uniform; **–heid** *v* uniformity

'eenvoud *m* simplicity, plainness, homeliness; *in alle* ~ without ceremony, in all simplicity; **een'voudig I** *aj* simple [sentence, dress, style, people], plain [food, words]; homely [fare, entertainment &]; **II** *ad* simply; *ik vind het* ~ *schande* I think it a downright shame; *ga* ~ *en zeg niets* (just) go and say nothing; **–heid** *v* simplicity; *in zijn* ~ in his simplicity; **eenvoudigheids'halve** for the sake of simplicity; **een'voudigweg** simply

'een(zaad)lobbig unilobed

'eenzaam I *aj* solitary, lonely, lone(some); desolate, retired; *het is hier zo* ~ 1 it is (one is, one feels) so lonely here; 2 the place is so lonely; *een eenzame* a solitary; **II** *ad* solitarily; ~ *leven* lead a solitary (secluded) life, live in solitude; **–heid** *v* solitariness, loneliness, solitude; retirement; *in de* ~ in solitude

een'zelvig I *aj* solitary, keeping oneself to oneself, self-contained; **II** *ad* ~ *leven* lead a solitary (secluded) life; **–heid** *v* solitariness

'eenzijdig, een'zijdig *aj* one-sided [views]; partial [judgements]; unilateral [disarmament]; **–heid** *v* one-sidedness, partiality

1 eer *ad* & *cj* before, sooner; rather; ~ *dat* before; *hoe* ~ *hoe liever* the sooner the better; ~ *te veel dan te weinig* rather too much than too little

2 eer *v* honour; credit; *de* ~ *aandoen om...* do [me] the honour to...; *op een manier die hun weinig* ~ *aandeed* (very) little to their honour (credit); *een schotel* ~ *aandoen* do justice to a dish; ~ *bewijzen* do (render) honour to; *iem. de laatste* ~ *bewijzen* render the last honours to sbd.; *ik heb de* ~ *u te berichten...* I have the honour to inform you...; *ik heb de* ~ *te zijn* I am; *je hebt er alle* ~ *van* you have all credit of it, you have done a fine job; *de* ~ *aan zich houden* save one's honour, put a good face on the matter; ~ *inleggen met iets* gain credit by sth.; *dat kwam zijn* ~ *te na* that he felt as a disparagement to his honour; *er een* ~ *in stellen te...* make it a point of honour to..., be proud to...; *ere wie ere toekomt* honour to whom (where) honour is due; *ere zij God!* glory to God!; ● *dat bent u a a n uw* ~ *verplicht* you are in honour bound to...; *i n (alle)* ~ *en deugd* in honour and decency; *in ere houden* honour; *iems. aandenken in ere houden* hold sbd.'s memory in esteem; *m e t e r e* with honour, with credit, honourably, creditably; *met militaire* ~ *begraven* bury with military honours; *t e zijner ere* in (to) his honour; *t e r ere van de dag* in honour of the day; *ter ere Gods* for the glory of God; *acceptatie ter ere* acceptance for honour; *t o t zijn* ~ *zij het*

gezegd to his credit be it said; *zich iets tot een* ~ *rekenen* consider sth. an honour; take credit (to oneself) for ...ing; *het zal u tot* ~ *strekken* it will be a credit to you, do you credit, reflect honour on you; **'eerbaar** virtuous, modest; *eerbare bedoelingen* honorable intentions; **–heid** *v* virtue, modesty; **'eerbetoon** *o*, **–bewijs** (-en) *v*, **–betuiging** (-en) *v*, **–bewijs** (-wijzen) *o* (mark of) honour, homage; **–bied** *m* respect, reverence; **eer'biedig** respectful, deferential, reverent; **eer'biedigen** (eerbiedigde, h. geëerbiedigd) *vt* respect; **eer'biedigheid** *v* respect, deference, devotion; **eer'biediging** *v* respect; **eerbied'waardig** respectable, venerable; (d o o r o u d e r d o m) **–'wekkend** imposing

'eerdaags one of these days, in a few days

'eerder = 1 *eer*; *nooit* ~ never before

'eergevoel *o* sense of honour

'eergisteren, eer'gisteren the day before yesterday; **eergister(en)'nacht** the night before last

'eerherstel *o* rehabilitation

'eerlang, eer'lang before long, shortly

'eerlijk I *aj* honest [people], fair [fight, play, dealings], honourable [burial, intentions]; ~*! F* honour bright!; ~ *duurt het langst* honesty is the best policy; ~ *is* ~ fair is fair; **II** *ad* honestly, fair(ly); ~ *delen!* divide fairly!; ~ *gezegd...* to be honest, honestly [I don't trust him]; ~ *spelen* play fair; ~ *zijn brood verdienen* make an honest living; ~ *of oneerlijk* by fair means or foul; ~ *waar* it is the honest truth; **–heid** *v* honesty, probity, fairness; **eerlijkheids'halve** in fairness

'eerloos infamous; **–heid** *v* infamy; **eers'halve** for honour's sake

eerst I *aj* first [aid, principles, hours, class &]; early [times]; prime [minister]; premier [position]; first-rate [singers &]; leading [shops]; initial [difficulties, expenses]; chief [clerk]; *de* ~*e de beste man* the (very) first man you meet, the next man you see, anybody, any man; *hij is niet de* ~*e de beste* he is not everybody; *bij de* ~*e de beste gelegenheid* at the first opportunity; *in de* ~*e zes maanden niet* not for six months yet; *de* ~*e steen* the foundation-stone; *de* ~*en van de stad* the upper ten of the town; *hij is de* ~*e van zijn klas* he is at the top of his class; *het* ~*e dat ik hoor* the first thing I hear; *de* ~*e...*, *de laatste...* the former..., the latter...; ● *i n het* ~ at first; *t e n* ~*e* first, in the first place, to begin with; ook: firstly; *ten* ~*e...*, *ten tweede...* ook: for one thing..., for another...; *v o o r het* ~ for the first time; **II** *ad* first; ook: at first; *beter dan* ~ better than before (than he used to); ~ *was hij zenuwachtig* 1 at first [when beginning his speech] he was nervous; 2 [long ago] he used to be nervous; *als ik maar ~ eens weg ben, dan...* when once away, I...; *~ gisteren is hij gekomen* he came only yesterday; *~ gisteren heb ik hem gezien* not before (not until) yesterday; *~ in de laatste tijd* but (only) recently; *~ morgen* not before tomorrow; *~ nu (nu ~)* only now [do I see it]; *doe dat het ~* do it first thing; *hij kwam het ~* he was the first to come, he was first; *wie het ~ komt, het ~ maalt* first come first served; **–aanwezend** senior; **–daags** in a few days, one of these days; **eerste'dagenvelop(pe)** [-āvələp] (-pen) *v* first-day cover; **–'jaarsstudent** (-en) *m* first-year student; **–'klas(se) I** *v* first-class [in a train]; **II** *aj* first-class [hotel]; **'eersteling** (-en) *m* first-born [child]; firstling [of cattle]; *fig* first-fruits; *het is een ~* it is a "first" book (picture &); **eerste'rangs** first-rate, first-class; **–'steenlegging** (-en) *v* laying of the foundation-stone; **eerstge'boorte** *v* primogeniture; **–recht** *o* birthright; **eerstge'borene** (-n) *m-v* first-born; **'eerstgenoemde** (-n) *(de)* the first-mentioned, the former; **eerst'komend, eerst'volgend** next, following

'eertijds formerly, in former times

'eervergeten devoid of all honour, lost to all sense of honour, infamous; **–vol** honourable [discharge]; creditable; **eer'waard** *aj* reverend; *uw ~e* Your Reverence; **–ig** venerable; **'eerzaam** respectable; **–zucht** *v* ambition; **eer'zuchtig** ambitious; *~ zijn* aim high

'eetbaar fit to eat, eatable, edible [bird's nest, fungus, snail], esculent; **–heid** *v* eatableness, edibility; **'eetgelegenheid** (-heden) *v* eating-place, restaurant; **–gerei** *o* dinner-things; **–hoek** (-en) *m* dinette; dining recess; **–huis** (-huizen) *o* eating-house; **–kamer** (-s) *v* dining-room; **–keteltje** (-s) *o* ⚔ mess-tin; **–keuken** (-s) *v* dining-kitchen; **–lepel** (-s) *m* table-spoon; **–lust** *m* appetite; *dat heeft mij ~ gegeven* it has given me an appetite; **–servies** (-viezen) *o* dinner-set, dinner-service; **–stokje** (-s) *o* chopstick; **–tafel** (-s) *v* dining-table; **–waren** *mv* eatables, victuals; **–zaal** (-zalen) *v* dining-room

eeuw (-en) *v* century, age; *de gouden ~* the golden age; *de twintigste ~* the twentieth century; *de ~ van Koningin Elizabeth* the age of Queen Elizabeth; *in geen ~* not for ages; **'eeuwenlang** age-long [tyranny &]; **–oud** centuries old [trees], age-old [errors]; **'eeuwfeest** (-en) *o* centenary; **'eeuwig** *aj* eternal, everlasting, perpetual; *ten ~en dage, voor ~* for ever; **II** *ad* for ever; < eternally; *het is ~ jammer* it is a thousand pities; **'eeuwigdurend, eeuwig'durend** = *eeuwig*; **'eeuwigheid**

(-heden) *v* eternity; *ik heb een ~ gewacht* I have been waiting for ages; *nooit in der ~* never; *ik heb je in geen ~ gezien* I have not seen you for ages; *tot in ~* to all eternity; *van ~ tot amen* for ever and ever; **'eeuwwisseling** (-en) *v* turn of the century; *bij de ~* at the turn of the century **efe'meer** [e.efe.-] ephemeral

ef'fect (-en) *o* 1 effect; 2 ♑ side; *nuttig ~* ✗ efficiency; *een bal ~ geven* ♑ put side on a ball; *~ hebben* take effect; *dat zal ~ maken* that will produce quite an effect; *~ sorteren* have the desired effect; zie ook: *effecten*; **–bejag** *o* straining after effect, claptrap

ef'fecten *mv* stocks (and shares), securities; **–beurs** (-beurzen) *v* stock exchange; **–handel** *m* stock-jobbing; **–handelaar** (-s) *m* stock-jobber; **–makelaar** (-s) *m* stock-broker; **–markt** (-en) *v* stockmarket

effec'tief effective, real; *in effectieve dienst* on active service; **effectu'eren** (effectueerde, h. geëffectueerd) *vt* carry out, execute

'effen smooth, even, level [ground]; plain [colour, material]; unruffled [countenance]; settled [account]; **'effenen** (effende, h. geëffend) *vt* smooth (down, over, out), level, make even; *fig* smooth [the way for sbd.]; zie ook: *vereffenen*; **'effenheid** *v* smoothness, evenness; **'effening** *v* levelling, smoothing

efficiënt [ifi.si.'tnt] 1 (v. z a k e n) efficacious [cure, method]; 2 (v. p e r s o n e n) efficient **eg** (-gen) *v* harrow, drag

e'gaal uniform, unicoloured, plain [in colour]; smooth, even [grand]; *het is mij ~* it is all the same to me

egali'satie [-'za.(t)si.] (-s) *v* levelling, equalization; **egali'seren** [s = z] (egaliseerde, h. geëgaliseerd) *vt* level, make even [ground]; equalize

e'gards [e.'ga.rs] *mv* consideration(s), regard(s), attention; *iem. met (zonder) veel ~ behandelen* treat sbd. with (little) ceremony

E'geïsche 'Zee *v* Aegean Sea

'egel (-s) *m* hedgehog

egelan'tier (-s en -en) *m* eglantine, sweet briar **'egelstelling** (-en) *v* ⚔ all-round defense position

'egge (-n) = *eg*; **'eggen** (egde, h. geëgd) *vt* & *vi* harrow, drag

ego'centrisch self-centred, self-absorbed, egocentric; **ego'ïsme** *o* egoism; **–'ïst** (-en) *m* egoist; **–'ïstisch** selfish, egoistic

E'gypte [y = i] *o* Egypt; **–naar** (-s en -naren) *m* Egyptian; **E'gyptisch** Egyptian; *~e duisternis* Egyptian darkness

E.H.B.O. [e.ha.be.'o.] = *Eerste Hulp bij Ongelukken* first-aid (association); *~-afdeling* emergency ward; *~-post* first-aid station

1 ei (-eren) *o* egg; *gebakken* ~ fried egg; *zacht (hard) gekookt* ~ soft-(hard-)boiled egg; *het* ~ *van Columbus* the egg of Columbus; *het* ~ *wil wijzer zijn dan de hen!* teach your grandmother to suck eggs!; *een half* ~ *is beter dan een lege dop* half a loaf is better than no bread; *zij kozen eieren voor hun geld* they came down a peg or two; *dat is het hele* ~*eren eten* that's all there is to it

2 ei! *ij* ah!, indeed!

e.i. = *elektrotechnisch ingenieur*; zie *elektrotechnisch*

'eicel (-len) *v* egg, ovum

'eiderdons *o* eider-down; **–eend** (-en) *v*, **–gans** (-ganzen) *v* eider (-duck)

'eierdooier (-s) *m* yolk (of egg), egg-yolk; **–dop** (-pen) *m* egg-shell; **–dopje** (-s) *o* egg-cup; **–klopper** (-s) *m* egg-whisk, egg-beater; **–koek** (-en) *m* egg-cake; **–kolen** *mv* egg coal, ovoids; **–leggend** egg-laying, oviparous; **–lepeltje** (-s) *o* egg-spoon; **–rekje** (-s) *o* egg-rack; **–saus** (-en) *v* egg-sauce; **–schaal** (-schalen) *v* egg-shell; **–stok** (-ken) *m* ovary; **–warmer** (-s) *m* egg cosy; **'eigeel** (-gelen) *o* yellow, (egg-)yolk

'eigen 1 (i n i e m s. b e z i t) own, of one's own, private, separate; 2 (a a n g e b o r e n) proper to [mankind], peculiar to [that class]; 3 (k e n m e r k e n d) characteristic, peculiar; 4 (i n t i e m) friendly, familiar, intimate; 5 (z e l f d e) the (very) same, [his] very...; ~ *broeder van...* own brother to...; *hij heeft een* ~ *huis* he has a house of his own; *in zijn* ~ *huis* in his own house; *zijn vrouws* ~ *naam* his wife's maiden name; *met de hem* ~ *beleefdheid* with his characteristic courtesy; *ik ben hier al* ~ I am quite at home here; *hij was zeer* ~ *met ons* he was on terms of great intimacy with us; *zich* ~ *maken* make oneself familiar with, master [a technique], acquire [all the knowledge needed]

'eigenaar (-s en -naren) *m* owner, proprietor; *van* ~ *verwisselen* change hands

eigen'aardig 1 (m e r k w a a r d i g) curious; 2 (b i j z o n d e r) peculiar; **–heid** (-heden) *v* peculiarity

eigena'res (-sen) *v* owner, proprietress

'eigenbaat *v* self-interest, self-seeking; **–belang** *o* self-interest, personal interest

'eigendom (-men) 1 *o* (b e z i t t i n g) property; 2 *m* (r e c h t) ownership [of the means of production]; *bewijs van* ~ title(-deed); *in* ~ *hebben* be in possession of, own; **'eigendomsbewijs** (-wijzen) *o* title deed; **–overdracht** *v* transfer of property; **–recht** *o* 1 ownership; 2 proprietary right(s) [of an estate]; 3 copyright [of a publisher]

'eigendunk *m* self-conceit; **eigen'erfde** (-n) *m* = *eigengeërfde*; **'eigengebakken** home-made;

–geërfde [-gəɛrf-] (-n) *m* freeholder; **–gemaakt** home-made; **eigenge'rechtig** self-righteous; **–ge'reid** opinionated, self-willed, stubborn; **–'handig** [done] with one's own hands; [written] in one's own hand; [to be delivered] "by hand"; ~ *geschreven brieven aan...* apply in own handwriting to...; ~ *geschreven stuk* autograph; **'eigenliefde** *v* self-love, love of self

'eigenlijk I *aj* proper, properly so called; actual, real, true; zie ook: *zin*; **II** *ad* properly speaking; really, actually; *wat betekent dit* ~? just what does this mean?; *wat is hij nu* ~? what is he exactly?; *wat wil je nu* ~? what in point of fact do you want?; *wie is die vent* ~? who is this fellow, anyway?; ~ *niet* exactly; *kunnen we dat* ~ *wel tolereren?* can we really tolerate this?

eigen'machtig I *aj* arbitrary, high-handed; **II** *ad* arbitrarily, high-handedly; **–heid** *v* arbitrariness, highhandedness

'eigennaam (-namen) *m* proper noun, proper name; **–richting** *v* taking the law into one's own hands; **–schap** (-pen) *v* property [of bodies]; 2 quality [of persons], attribute [of God]; **–tijds** contemporary; **–waan** *m* conceitedness, presumption; **–waarde** *v* gevoel van ~ feeling of one's own worth, self-esteem; **eigen'wijs** pigheaded, opinionated; ~ *zijn* always think one knows better; **–'zinnig** self-willed, wayward, wilful

eik (-en) *m* oak; **'eikeboom** (-bomen) *m* oak-tree; **eike'hakhout** *o* oak coppice; **'eikehout** *o* oak, oak-wood; **–en** *aj* oak, oaken

'eikel (-s) *m* acorn; (v. d. p e n i s) glans

'eikeloof *o* oak-leaves; **'eiken** *aj* oak, oaken; **–bos** (-sen) *o* oak-wood; **'eikeschors** *v* oak-bark; (g e m a l e n) tan

'eiland (-en) *o* island, isle; *het* ~ *Wight* the Isle of Wight; **–bewoner** (-s) *m* islander; **'eilandengroep** (-en) *v* group of islands, archipelago

'eileider (-s) *m* oviduct

eind (-en) *o* 1 end² [ook = death]; [happy] ending; close, termination, conclusion; (u i t e i n d e) end, extremity; 2 (s t u k) piece [of wood]; bit [of string]; length [of sausage]; zie ook: *eindje*; 3 in: ~ (*weegs*) part of the way; *het is een heel* ~ it is a good distance (off), a long way (off); *maar een klein* ~ only a short distance; *het* ~ *van het liedje is...* the upshot is..., the end is...; *zijn* ~ *voelen naderen* feel one's end drawing near; ● *aan het andere* ~ *van de wereld* at the back of beyond; *er komt geen* ~ *aan* there is no end to it; *komt er dan geen* ~ *aan?* shall we never see (hear) the last of it?; *er moet een* ~ *aan komen* it must stop; *hij kwam treurig aan zijn* ~ he came to a sad end; *aan alles komt een* ~ all things must have an end; *een ~ maken aan iets* put an end (a stop) to sth., make an end of sth.; *aan het kortste (langste) ~ trekken* come off worst (best), get the worst (best) of it, have the worst (better) end of the staff; *wij zijn nog niet aan het ~* the end is not yet; *het b i j het rechte ~ hebben* be right, be correct; *het bij het verkeerde ~ aanpakken* begin at the wrong end; *het bij het verkeerde ~ hebben* be mistaken, have got hold of the wrong end of the stick, be wrong; *i n (o p) het ~* at last, eventually; *een ~ in de 40* well past forty, well over forty years of age; *een ~ over zessen* well over six [o'clock]; *het loopt o p een ~* things are coming to an end (drawing to a close); *het loopt op zijn ~ met hem* his end is drawing near; *t e dien ~e* to that end, with that end in view, for that purpose; *t e g e n het ~* towards the end (close); *t e n ~e...* in order to...; *ten ~e brengen* bring to an end (conclusion); *ten ~e lopen* come to an end, draw to an end (to a close), expire [of a contract]; *ten ~e raad zijn* be at one's wits' (wit's) end; *t o t het ~ (toe)* till the end; *tot een goed ~e brengen* bring the matter to a favourable ending, bring [things] to a happy conclusion; *v a n alle ~en van de wereld* from all parts of the world; *ze stelen, daar is het ~ van weg* there is no end to it; *jokken dat hij kan, daar is het ~ van weg!* he is no end of a liar; *z o n d e r ~* without end, endless(ly); *het ~ zal de last dragen* the end will bear the consequences; *~ goed al goed* all's well that ends well; **–bedrag** (-dragen) *o* total, sum total; **–beslissing** (-en) *v*, **–besluit** (-en) *o* final decision; **–bestemming** (-en) *v* final destination, ultimate destination; **–cijfer** (-s) *o* 1 final figure; 2 ▥ final mark; 3 (t o t a a l) grand total; **–diploma** ('s) *o* (school) leaving certificate, (v. m i d d e l b a r e s c h o o l) *Br* ± General Certificate of Education, G.C.E.; **–doel** (-en) *o* final purpose, final goal, ultimate object; **'einde** (-n) *o = eind*; **'eindelijk** finally, at last, ultimately, in the end, at length; **'eindeloos I** *aj* endless, infinite, interminable; **II** *ad* infinitely, without end; *~ lang* [talking, waiting] interminably; **–heid** (-heden) *v* endlessness, infinity

'einder (-s) *m* horizon

'eindexamen (-s) *o* final examination, (school) leaving examination; **–fase** [s = z] (-n en -s) *v* final stage

'eindig finite; **'eindigen I** (eindigde, is geëindigd) *vi* end, finish, terminate, conclude; *~ i n* end in; *~ m e t te geloven dat...* end in believing that...; *~ met te zeggen* end with (by) saying that...; *~ o p een k* end in a k; **II** (eindigde, h. geëindigd) *vt* end, finish, conclude, terminate

'eindje (-s) *o* end, bit, piece; (a f s t a n d) *een*

klein ~ a short distance, a short way; *een ~ verder* a little (way) further; *een ~ sigaar* a cigar-end, a cigar-stub; *ga je een ~ mee?* will you accompany me (are you coming) part of the way? *de ~s aan elkaar knopen* make (both) ends meet; **'eindklassement** *o* final classification; **–letter** (-s) *v* final letter; **–overwinning** *v* final victory; **–paal** (-palen) *m sp* winning-post; **–produkt** (-en) *o* finished product, end-product; **–punt** (-en) *o* terminal point, end; [bus, tramway, railway] terminus; **–resultaat** (-taten) *o* (end, final) result, upshot; **–rijm** (-en) *o* final rhyme; **–spel** (-spelen) *o* end game [at chess]; **–sprint** (-en en s) *m*, **–spurt** *m sp* finishing spurt; **–stand** (-en) *m* final score; **–station** [-sta.(t)ʃon] (-s) *o* terminal station, terminus; **–streep** *v* finish(ing) line, finish; **–strijd** *m sp* finals; final fight; final struggle, final contest; **–uitslag** *m* (end, final) result; **–wedstrijd** (-en) *m* final match, final

'eirond egg-shaped, egg-like, oval

eis (-en) *m* demand, requirement; claim; petition [for a divorce]; *de gestelde ~en* the requirements; *~ tot schadevergoeding* claim for damages; *de ~en voor het toelatingsexamen* the requirements of the entrance examination; *iems. ~ afwijzen* ⚖ find against sbd.; *een ~ instellen* ⚖ institute proceedings; *een ~ inwilligen* meet a claim; *hogere ~en stellen* make higher demands (on *aan*); *hem de ~ toewijzen* ⚖ give judgement in his favour; *aan de gestelde ~en voldoen* come up to (meet) the requirements; *naar de ~ as* required, properly; **'eisen** (eiste, h. geëist) *vt* demand, require, claim; **'eiser** (-s) *m*, **eise'res** (-sen) *v* 1 claimant; 2 ⚖ plaintiff

'eivol crammed, chock-full; **–vormig** = *eirond*

'eiwit (-ten) *o* white of egg, glair, albumen; protein; **–houdend** albuminous; **–stof** (-fen) *v* albumen; protein

e.k. = *eerstkomend*

'ekster (-s) *v* magpie; **–oog** (-ogen) *o* corn [on toe]

ekwi'page [g = ʒ] (-s) *v = equipage*

ekwiva'lent = *equivalent*

el (-len) *v* yard [English]; ell [Dutch]

e'lan [e.'lã] *o* élan, dash, impetuousness

'eland (-en) *m* elk

elastici'teit *v* elasticity, springiness; **elas'tiek** (-en) *o* elastic; **–en** *aj* elastic; **–je** (-s) *o* (piece of) elastic; (r i n g v o r m i g) rubber ring; (b r e e d) rubber band; **e'lastisch** elastic, springy

'elders elsewhere; *naar ~ (vertrekken)* (move) somewhere else; *overal ~* everywhere (anywhere) else

eldo'rado ('s) *o* El Dorado

electo'raat (-raten) *o* electorate

ele'gant elegant, stylish; **–ie** [-(t)si.] *v* elegance
ele'gie [e.le.'ɡi] (-ieën) *v* elegy; **e'legisch**
elegiac

e'lektra *o* F electricity; electric appliancies;
elektri'cien [-'ʃi.] (-s) *m* electrician; **elek-
trici'teit** *v* electricity; **–svoorziening** (-en) *v*
electricity supply; **elektrifi'catie** [-(t)si.] *v*
electrification; **elektrifi'ceren** (elektrificeerde,
h. geëlektrificeerd) *vt* electrify; **e'lektrisch**
electric; **elektri'seren** [s = z] (elektriseerde, h.
geëlektriseerd) *vt* electrify; **elektro-
cardio'gram** (-men) *o* electrocardiogram;
elek'trode (-n en -s) *v* electrode; **elektro'lyse**
[-li.zə] *v* electrolysis; **e'lektromagneet**
(-neten) *m* electromagnet; **elektromag'netisch** electro-magnetic; **e'lektromonteur** (-s)
m electrician; **–motor** (-s en -toren) *m* electric
motor, electromotor; **e'lektron** (-'tronen) *o*
electron; **elek'tronenbuis** (-buizen) *v* valve;
–microscoop (-scopen) *m* electron microscope; **elek'tronica** *v* electronics;
elek'tronisch electronic; **elektro'scoop**
(-scopen) *m* electroscope; **elektro'technicus**
(-ci) *m* electrical engineer; **e'lektrotechniek** *v*
electrical engineering; **elektro'technisch**
electrical; **~ ingenieur** electrical engineer
ele'ment (-en) *o* 1 element[2]; 2 ⚥ cell; *in zijn ~
zijn* be in one's element; **elemen'tair** [-'tɛːr]
elementary

1 **elf** (elven) *v* (n a t u u r g e e s t) elf
2 **elf** eleven; **'elfde** eleventh (part);
elfen'dertigst *op zijn ~* at a snail's pace;
'elftal (-len) *o* (number of) eleven; *sp* eleven,
team, side; **elf'uurtje** (-s) *o* elevenses
elimi'natie [-(t)si.] (-s) *v* elimination;
elimi'neren (elimineerde, h. geëlimineerd) *vt*
eliminate
eli'tair [-'tɛːr] elite(-conscious); **e'lite** *v* élite,
pick, flower (of society)
e'lixer, e'lixir [e.'liksər] (-s) *o* elixir
elk every; each; any
el'kaar, el'kander each other, one another; ●
a c h t e r ~ 1 one after the other, in succession;
2 at a stretch; *uren achter ~* for hours
(together), for hours on end; *achter ~ lopen* file,
walk in single (Indian) file; *b ij ~ is het [200
gld.]* together; *bij ~ pakken (rapen &)* gather up;
d o o r ~ gebruiken use indifferently; *door ~
gebruikt kunnende worden* be interchangeable;
door ~ raken get (become) mixed up; *door ~
roeren* mix; *door ~ (genomen)* on an (the) average,
by (in) the lot; *door ~ liggen* lie in a heap, mixed
up, pell-mell; *i n ~ vallen (storten)* collapse, fall
to pieces; *in ~ zakken* collapse, sag; *in ~ zetten*
put together; ✕ assemble; *goed in ~ zitten* be
well-made, well-planned, well-organized, well
set-up; *m e t ~ together*; *n a ~* the one after

the other; after each other; *n a a s t ~* side by
side; [four, five, six] abreast; *o n d e r ~* zie *onder*
I; *o p ~* one on top of the other; *met de benen
o v e r ~* (with) legs crossed; *u i t ~ houden* tell
apart; *uit ~ vallen* fall to pieces; zie ook *uiteen*;
v a n ~ gaan separate; *fig* drift apart; *v o o r ~
willen ze het niet weten* they (are)..., but they
won't let it appear; *'t is voor ~* it's settled; *het
voor ~ krijgen* manage (it)
'elkeen every man, everyone, everybody
'elleboog (-bogen) *m* elbow; *het (ze) achter de ~
(ellebogen) hebben* be a slyboots; *de ellebogen vrij
hebben* have elbow-room; *zijn ellebogen steken
erdoor* he is out at elbows
el'lende *v* misery, miseries, wretchedness;
–ling (-en) *m* wretch, miscreant; **el'lendig**
miserable, wretched [feeling, weather]; *zich ~
voelen* feel low, feel miserable
'ellenlang many yards long; *fig* longdrawn;
'ellepijp (-en) *v* ulna
el'lips (-en) *v* ellipsis [of word]; ellipse [oval];
el'liptisch elliptic(al)
1 **els** (elzen) *v* [shoemaker's] awl, bradawl
2 **els** (elzen) *m* ✤ alder
El Salva'dor *o* (El) Salvador
'Elzas *m de ~* Alsace; **~-'Lotharingen** *o*
Alsace-Lorraine
'elzeboom (-bomen) *m* alder-tree; **–hout** *o*
alder-wood; **–katje** (-s) *o* alder-catkin; 'elzen
aj alder
e'mail [e.'ma.j] *o* enamel; **email'leren** (email-
leerde, h. geëmailleerd) *vt* enamel; **email'leur**
(-s) *m* enameller
emanci'patie [-(t)si.] (-s) *v* emancipation;
emanci'peren (emancipeerde, h. geëmanci-
peerd) *vt* emancipate
embal'lage [ɑmbɑ'la.ʒə] *v* packing;
embal'leren (emballeerde, h. geëmballeerd) *vt*
pack (up); **embal'leur** (-s) *m* packer
em'bargo *o* embargo; *onder ~ leggen* lay an
embargo on, embargo; **em'bleem** (-blemen) *o*
emblem; **embo'lie** *v* embolism
'embryo ('s) *o* embryo; **embryo'naal**
embryonic
emeri'taat *o* superannuation [of professors and
clergymen]; *met ~ gaan* retire; **e'meritus**
emeritus, retired
emfy'seem [-fi.'ze.m] *o* emphysema
'emier (-s) *m* emir, ameer
emi'grant (-en) *m* emigrant; **emi'gratie** [-(t)si.]
(-s) *v* emigration; **emi'greren** (emigreerde, is
geëmigreerd) *vi* emigrate
emi'nent eminent; **–ie** [-(t)si.] (-s) *v* eminence
e'missie (-s) *v* issue [of shares]
'emmer (-s) *m* pail, bucket; 'emmeren
(emmerde, h. geëmmerd) *vi* F whine, bore,
bother

emolu'menten *mv* emoluments, perquisites, fringe benefits

e'motie [-(t)si.] (-s) *v* emotion; **emotionali'teit** *v* emotionality; **emotio'neel** emotional, affective

empa'thie *v* empathy

em'pirisch empiric(al)

emplace'ment [ăm-] (-en) *o* emplacement [of gun]; railway-yard

em'plooi [ăm-, ŭm-] *o* 1 employ, employment; 2 part, rôle

emplo'yé [ămplʋa'je.] (-s) *m* employee

emul'geren (emulgeerde, h. geëmulgeerd) *vt* emulsify; **e'mulsie** (-s) *v* emulsion

en and; *èn...*, *èn...* both... and...; ... ~ *zo* and such, and the like, and all that

en bloc [ă'blɔk] en bloc; lock, stock and barrel; [tender their resignation] in a body; [reject proposals] in their entirety

enca'dreren [ăka.-] (encadreerde, h. geëncadreerd) *vt* 1 frame; 2 ✗ officer [a battalion]; enroll [recruits]

encanail'leren [ăka.na'je: rə(n)] (encanailleerde, h. geëncanailleerd) *vr zich ~* keep low company, cheapen oneself

en'clave [ă-, ŭn-] (-s) *v* enclave

en corps [ă'kɔːr] in a body

ency'cliek [ăsi-, ŭnsi.-] (-en) *v* encyclical (letter)

encyclope'die [ă-, ŭnsi.klo.pe.'di.] (-ieën) *v* encyclop(a)edia; **encyclo'pedisch** encyclop(a)edic

end (-en) = *eind*

'endeldarm (-en) *m* rectum

endo'crien endocrine [gland]; **endocrino'loog** (-logen) *m* endocrinologist

endo'geen endogenous, endogenetic

endos'sant [ă-, ŭn-] (-en) *m* endorser; **endosse'ment** (-en) *o* endorsement; **endos'seren** (endosseerde, h. geëndosseerd) *vt* endorse

'enenmale *ten ~* entirely, wholly, utterly, totally, completely, absolutely

ener'gie [e.n.ŭr'ʒi.] (-ieën) *v* 1 energy; 2 power [from coal, water]; **–bron** (-nen) *v* source of power, power source; **ener'giek** energetic; **ener'gievoorziening** (-en) *v* power supply

'enerlei of the same kind; zie ook: *eender*

ener'veren (enerveerde, h. geënerveerd) *vt* agitate, fluster; enervate

'enerzijds on the one side

en'face en'face full face [portrait]

en'fin [ă'fɛ̃] in short...; ~ *!* well, ...; *maar ~* anyhow, anyway, but there,...

eng 1 (n a u w) narrow [passage, street &]; tight, [coat &]; 2 (a k e l i g) creepy, eerie, weird, uncanny

engage'ment [ăga.ʒǝ-] *o* 1 engagement [ook: betrothal]; 2 *fig* [political] commitment;

enga'geren (engageerde, h. geëngageerd) **I** *vt* engage; **II** *vr zich ~* become engaged (to *met*); zie ook: *geëngageerd*

'engel (-en) *m* angel[2]; *mijn reddende ~* my saviour; **–achtig** angelic; **–achtigheid** *v* angelic nature

'Engeland *o* (a a r d r ij k s k.) England; (s t a a t k. t h a n s m e e s t a l) Britain; ☉ Albion

'engelbewaarder (-s) *m* guardian angel; **'engelenbak** (-ken) *m* gallery; **–geduld** *o* angelic patience; **–haar** *o* angel hair [for Christmas tree]; **–koor** (-koren) *o* angelic choir, angel choir; **–schaar** (-scharen) *v* host of angels; **–zang** *m* hymn of angels

'Engels I *aj* English [language, girl]; (s t a a t k. t h a n s m e e s t a l) British [army, navy, consul]; (i n s a m e n s t.) Anglo[-Dutch trade]; *de ~e Kerk* the Anglican Church; the Church of England; *~e pleister* court-plaster; *~e sleutel* ✗ monkey-wrench; *~e ziekte* rachitis, rickets; *lijdend aan ~e ziekte* rickety; *~ zout* Epsom salt(s); **II** *o het ~* English; **III** *v een ~e* an Englishwoman; *zij is een ~e* ook: she is English; **IV** *mv de ~en* the English, the British; **–gezind** Anglophile; **–man** (Engelsen) *m* Englishman, Briton; **–talig** English-speaking [countries, South Africans], English-language [churches, press]

'engeltje (-s) *o* (little) angel, cherub

'engerd (-s) *m* horrible fellow, **F** creep

'engerling (-en) *m* grub of the cockchafer

eng'hartig narrow-minded; **'engheid** *v* narrowness, tightness

en 'gros [ă'gro.] $ wholesale

'engte (-n en -s) *v* 1 strait[2]; defile, narrow passage; 2 ('t e n g zij n) narrowness

'enig I *aj* sole [heir], single [instance], only [child], unique [specimen]; *een ~e vent* a smashing fellow; *dat (vaasje) is ~ !* that is something unique; *dat (die) is ~* that's a good one, that is capital!; *het was ~ !* it was marvellous, delightful!; *het is ~ in zijn soort* it is (of its kind) unique; *de ~e...* ook: the one and only...; *de ~e die...* the one man who..., the only one to...; *het ~e dat hij zei* the only thing he said; **II** *pron* some, any; *~en hunner* some of them; **III** *ad ~ en alleen omdat...* uniquely because...; **'enigerlei** any, of some sort; **'eniger'mate** in a measure, in some degree

'eniggeboren only-begotten; **'enigszins** somewhat, a little, slightly, rather; *als u ook maar ~ moe bent* if you are tired at all; *indien ~ mogelijk* if at all possible; *zo gauw ik maar ~ kan* as soon as I possibly can; *alle ~ belangrijke* mensen all people of any importance

1 'enkel (-s) *m* ankle; *tot aan de* ~*s* up to the ankles, ankle-deep

2 'enkel I *aj* single; ~*e reis* single (journey); *geen* ~*e kans* not a single chance; *een* ~*e keer* once in a while, occasionally; *een* ~*e vergissing* an occasional mistake; *een* ~ *woord* just a word, a word or two; ~*e boeken* (*uren* &) a few books (hours &); zie ook: *keer* &; **II** *ad* only, merely; **'enkeling** (-en) *m* individual; **'enkelspel** (-spelen) *o sp* single [at tennis]; *dames-* (*heren-*)~ ladies' (men's) singles; **–spoor** (-sporen) *o* single track

'enkelvoud (-en) *o* singular (number); **enkel'voudig** 1 singular [number]; 2 simple [tenses]

e'norm enormous, huge, immense, tremendous; **enormi'teit** (-en) *v* enormity; ~*en verkondigen* make shocking remarks, say the most awful things

en pas'sant [āpɑ'sā] by the way, in passing

en pro'fil [āpro.'fi.l] in profile

en'quête [ā'k t.tə] (-s) *v* inquiry, investigation

ensce'neren [ās̄-] (ensceneerde, h. geënsceneerd) *vt* stage; **ensce'nering** (-en) *v* (a b s t r a c t) staging²; (c o n c r e e t) setting

en'semble [ā'sāblə] (-s) *o* ensemble, [theatrical] company

ent (-en) *v* graft

enta'meren [ā-] (entameerde, h. geëntameerd) *vt* enter upon, broach [a subject]; start on, begin, address oneself to [a task]

'enten (entte, h. geënt) *vt* 1 graft [upon]; 2 = *inenten*

'enteren (enterde, h. geënterd) *vt* board; **'enterhaak** (-haken) *m* grappling-iron

enthousi'asme [ātu.zi.'asmə] *o* enthusiasm, warmth; **enthousi'ast I** (-en) *m* enthusiast; **II** *aj* enthusiastic

'enting *v* grafting; **'entmes** (-sen) *o* grafting knife

entou'rage [ātu'ra.ʒə] (-s) *v* entourage, surroundings, environment; (g e v o l g) attendants, retinue

entr'acte [ā'traktə] (-s en -n) *v* entr'acte, interval, interlude

entre-'deux [ātrə'dø] *o* & *m* [lace] insertion

en'tree [ā'tre.] (-s) *v* 1 (t o e l a t i n g) entrance, admittance, admission; 2 (b i n n e n t r e d e n) entrance, [ceremonial] entry; 3 (p l a a t s) entrance, (entrance-)hall; 4 (t o e l a t i n g s-p r i j s) entrance-fee [of a club], admission [of a theatre], *sp* gate-money [received at football match]; 5 (s c h o t e l) entrée; ~ *betalen* pay for admission; *zijn* ~ *maken* enter first; *fig* make one's bow; *tegen* ~ at a charge; *vrij* ~ admission free; **–biljet** (-ten) *o* (admission) ticket; **–geld** (-en)

o door-money, admission; (a l s l i d) admission fee

entre'pot [ātrə'po.] (-s) *o* bonded warehouse; *in* ~ *opslaan* bond [goods]

entre'sol [ātrə'sɔl] (-s) *m* mezzanine (floor)

entstof (-fen) *v* vaccine, serum

enve'lop(pe) [āvə'lɔp] (-pen) *v* envelope

enz., enzo'voort(s), 'enzovoort(s) etc., and so on

en'zym [y = i.] (-en) *o* enzyme

'eolusharp (-en) *v* Aeolian harp

epau'let [e.po.'lɪt] (-ten) *v* 1 ✠ epaulet(te); 2 shoulderknot

epi'centrum (-tra en -trums) *o* epicentre

epicu'rist (-en) *m* epicure, epicurean; **–isch** epicurean

epide'mie (-ieën) *v* epidemic; **epi'demisch** epidemic(al)

e'piek *v* epic poetry

epi'goon (-gonen) *m* epigone

epi'gram (-men) *o* epigram

epilep'sie *v* epilepsy; **epi'lepticus** (-ci) *m* epileptic

epi'leren (epileerde, h. geëpileerd) *vt* depilate

epi'loog (-logen) *m* epilogue

'episch epic

episco'paal *aj* episcopal, *de episcopalen* the episcopalians; **episco'paat** *o* episcopacy

epi'sode [s = z] (-n en -s) *v* episode; *korte* ~ incident

e'pistel (-s) *o* & *m* epistle

e'pos (epen en epossen) *o* epic, epic poem, epopee; (p r i m i t i e f, n i e t o p s c h r i f t) epos

e'quator [e.'kʋa.-] *m* equator; **equatori'aal** equatorial; *E~ Guinee* Equatorial Guinea

equi'page [e.k.(ʋ)i.'pa.ʒə] (-s) *v* 1 ⚓ crew; 2 carriage

e'quipe [e.'ki.p] (-s) *v sp* team, side

equipe'ment [e.ki.-] (-en) *o* ✠ equipment

equiva'lent [e.kʋi.-] (-en) *o* equivalent

er there; ~ *zijn* ~ *die nooit...* there are people who never...; *hoeveel heb je* ~ how many have you (got)?; *ik heb* ~ *nog twee* I have (still) two left; *ik ken* ~ *zo* I know some like that; *wat is* ~? what's the matter?; what is it?; *is* ~ *iets?* what's wrong?, is anything the matter?; *ik ben* ~ *nog niet gewoon* I have not been there yet; *we zijn* ~ here we are; ~ *komt niemand* nobody comes; ~ *gebeurt nooit iets* nothing ever happens; zie ook: *worden* &

'era ['e:ra.] ('s) *v* era

er'barmelijk pitiful, pitiable, miserable, wretched, lamentable; **er'barmen** (erbarmde, h. erbarmd) *vr zich* ~ *over* have pity (mercy) on; **–ming** *v* pity, compassion

'ere *v* = 2 *eer*; **'ereambt** (-en) *o*, **–baantje** (-s) *o* honorary post (office); **–blijk** (-en) *o* mark of respect, tribute; **–boog** (-bogen) *m* triumphal arch; **'ereburger** (-s) *m* freeman; **–schap** *o* freedom [of a city]; **'erecode** (-s) *m* code of honour

e'rectie [-ksi.] (-s) *v* erection

'eredienst (-en) *m* (public) worship; **–diploma** ('s) *o* award of honour; **–divisie** [s = z] (-s) *sp* first division [in league football]; **–doctoraat** (-raten) *o* honorary degree, honorary doctorate; **–kroon** (-kronen) *v* crown of honour; **–kruis** (-en) *o* cross of merit; **–lid** (-leden) *o* honorary member; **–medaille** [-mɑdɑ(l)jə] (-s) *v* medal of honour; **–metaal** *o* medal of honour

ere'miet (-en) *m* = *heremiet*

'eren (eerde, h. geëerd) *vt* honour, revere

'erepalm (-en) *m* palm of honour; **–plaats** (-en) *v* place of honour; **–poort** (-en) *v* triumphal arch; **–prijs** (-prijzen) *m* prize ‖ ⚘ speedwell, veronica; **–ronde** (-n en -s) *v sp* lap of honour; **–schuld** (-en) *v* debt of honour²; **–teken** (-en en -s) *o* mark (badge) of honour; **–titel** (-s) *m* title of honour, honorary title; **–voorzitter** (-s) m honorary president; **–voorzitterschap** (-pen) *o* honorary presidency; **–wacht** (-en) *v* guard of honour; **–woord** (-en) *o* 1 word of honour; 2 ⚔ parole; *op mijn* ~ upon my word; *op zijn* ~ *vrijlaten* ⚔ liberate on parole

erf (erven) *o* grounds; premises; (o o s t e r s) compound; (v. b o e r d e r ij) (farm)yard

'erfdeel (-delen) *o* portion, heritage; *vaderlijke* ~ patrimony; **–dochter** (-s) *v* heiress; **'erfelijk** hereditary; 𝔶 congenital; **–heid** *v* heredity; **–heidsleer** *v* genetics; **'erfenis** (-sen) *v* inheritance, heritage, legacy [of the past, of the war]; **'erfgenaam** (-namen) *m* heir; **–gename** (-n) *v* heiress; **–gerechtigd** heritable; **–goed** (-eren) *o* inheritance, estate; *vaderlijk* ~ patrimony; **–laatster** (-s) *v* testatrix; **–land** (-en) *o* patrimonial land; **–later** (-s) *m* testator; **–lating** (-en) *v* bequest; legacy; **–opvolging** (-en) *v* succession; **–pacht** (-en) *v* 1 (d e v e r b i n t e n i s) hereditary tenure, long lease; 2 (h e t g e l d) groundrent; *in* ~ on long lease; **–pachter** (-s) *m* long-lease tenant; **–prins** (-en) *m* hereditary prince; **–recht** *o* 1 law of inheritance (succession); 2 right of inheritance (succession); **–schuld** (-en) *v* debt(s) payable by the heirs; **–stuk** (-ken) *o* heirloom; **–vijand** (-en) *m* sworn (traditional, hereditary) enemy; **–zonde** *v* original sin

erg I *aj* bad, ill, evil; *het is* ~ it is (very) bad; *de zieke is* ~ *vandaag* he is (very) bad to-day; II *ad* badly; < badly, very, very much, sorely [needed], severely [felt]; *ik heb het* ~ *nodig*

I want it very badly; *vind je het* ~ ...*?* do you mind ...*?*; zie ook: *erger* & *ergst*; **III** *o voor ik er* ~ *in had* before I was aware of it, before I knew where I was; *hij had er geen* ~ *in* he was not aware of any harm (of it); *hij deed het zonder* ~ quite unintentionally

'ergens somewhere; *zo* ~ if anywhere; ~ *vind ik* **F** I think somehow; ~ *herinnert het aan* ... it is somehow reminiscent of...

'erger worse; *al* ~ worse and worse; ~ *worden* grow worse; *om* ~ *te voorkomen* to prevent worse following

'ergeren (ergerde, h. geërgerd) **I** *vt* 1 annoy, irritate, **F** peeve; 2 scandalize; **B** offend; *het ergert mij* it annoys (vexes) me; *anderen* ~ make a nuisance of oneself; **II** *vr zich* ~ take offence [at sth.], be indignant [with sbd.]; **'ergerlijk** 1 annoying, irritating, provoking, irksome, vexatious, aggravating; 2 offensive, shocking, scandalous; **'ergernis** (-sen) *v* 1 annoyance, nuisance, irritation, aggravation, vexation; (s t e r k e r) anger; 2 umbrage, offence, scandal; *tot mijn grote* ~ to my great annoyance

'ergo ergo, therefore, consequently

ergst worst; *op het* ~*e voorbereid* prepared for the worst; *op zijn* ~ at (the) worst, at its worst; zie ook: *geval*

'erica ('s) *v* ⚘ heath

er'kennen (erkende, h. erkend) *vt* acknowledge [to be...], recognize [a government]; admit, own, confess, avow; *een erkende handelaar* a recognized dealer; *een erkende instelling* ook: an approved institution; **–ning** (-en) *v* acknowledg(e)ment, recognition [of a government]; admission [of a fact]

er'kentelijk thankful, grateful; **–heid** *v* thankfulness, gratitude

er'kentenis *v* = *erkenning* & *erkentelijkheid*

'erker (-s) *m* 1 (v i e r k a n t) bay-window; 2 (r o n d) bow-window; 3 (a a n b o v e n v e r-d i e p i n g) oriel window

ermi'tage [g = ʒ] (-s) *v* = *hermitage*

ernst *m* earnestness, earnest, seriousness, gravity [of the situation]; *is het u* ~*?* are you serious*?*; *het wordt nu* ~ things are getting serious now; *in* ~ in earnest, earnestly, seriously; *in alle (volle)* ~ in good (full, sober) earnest; *u moet het niet in* ~ *opvatten* don't take it seriously; **'ernstig I** *aj* earnest [wish, word]; serious [look, matter, rival, wound &], grave [concern, fault, symptom]; serious-minded [persons]; pensive [look]; solemn [child, look]; **II** *ad* earnestly &; badly [wounded]

ero'deren (erodeerde, h. geërodeerd) *vt* erode

ero'geen erogenous, ero(to)genic

er'op on it (them &); ~ *of eronder* sink or swim, kill or cure

e'rosie *v* erosion
ero'tiek *v* eroti(ci)sm; e'rotisch erotic
er'rata *mv* errata
erts (-en) *o* ore; **–ader** (-s en -en) *v* mineral
vein, lode; **–boot** (-boten) *m* & *v* ore carrier
eru'diet erudite; eru'ditie [-(t)si.] *v* erudition
e'ruptie [-'rüpsi.] (-s) *v* eruption
ervan'door ~ *gaan* bolt, take to one's heels, run
away [also of a couple of lovers]; *de paarden*
gingen ~ the horses bolted, ran away; *ik ga* ~
I'm off; *ik moet* ~ I must be off
1 er'varen* *vt* 1 (o n d e r v i n d e n) experience;
2 (g e w a a r w o r d e n) perceive; 3 (v e r -
n e m e n) learn
2 er'varen *aj* experienced, expert, skilled,
practised [in...]; **–heid** *v* experience, skill;
er'varing (-en) *v* experience; *uit eigen* ~ from
one's own experience
'erve (-n) *v* = *erf*
1 'erven *mv* heirs; *de* ~ X X heirs
2 'erven (erfde, h. geërfd) I *vt* inherit; II *va*
come into money
er'voer (ervoeren) V.T. v. *ervaren*
erwt [ɛrt] (-en) *v* pea; 'erwtensoep *v* (thick)
pea-soup
1 es (-sen) *v* ♪ E flat
2 es (-sen) *m* ♣ ash, ash-tree
esca'latie [-(t)si.] *v* escalation; esca'leren
(escaleerde, *vi* is, *vt* h. geëscaleerd) *vi* & *vt*
escalate
esca'pade (-s) *v* escapade, adventurous prank
eschatolo'gie *v* eschatology
es'corte (-s) *o* escort; escor'teren (escorteerde,
h. geëscorteerd) *vt* escort
escu'laap (-lapen) *m fig* Aesculapius
'esdoorn, **–doren** (-s) *m* maple (tree)
es'kader (-s) *o* ⚓ squadron; eska'dron (-s) *o* ⚔
squadron
'Eskimo ('s) *m* Eskimo
eso'terisch [s = z] esoteric
esp (-en) *m* aspen
espagno'let [ɪspaɲo.'lɛt] (-ten) *v* = *spanjolet*
'espeblad (-bladen, -bladeren) *o* aspen leaf;
–boom (-bomen) *m* aspen; 'espen *aj* aspen
espla'nade (-n) *v* esplanade
'essehout *o* ash-wood; **–en** *aj* ashen; 'essen *aj*
ash
es'sence [ɪ'sãsə] (-s en -n) *v* essence
es'sentie [-(t)si.] *v de* ~ the substance, the
inbeing; essenti'eel I *aj* essential; II *o het*
essentiële what is essential; the quintessence, gist
[of the matter]
esta'fette (-n en -s) 1 *m* courier; 2 *v* (w e d -
s t r ij d) relay; **–loop** (-lopen) *m sp* relay race
'ester (-s) *m* ester
es'theet (-theten) *m* aesthete; es'thetica *v*
aesthetics; es'thetisch aesthetic

'Estland *o* Esthonia
etablisse'ment [e.ta.bli.-] (-en) *o* establishment
e'tage [e.'ta.ʒə] (-s) *v* floor, stor(e)y
eta'gère [e.ta.'ʒɛːrə] (-s) *v* whatnot, bracket
e'tagewoning [e.'ta.ʒə-] (-en) *v* flat
eta'lage [e.ta.'la.ʒə] (-s) 1 (h e t r a a m, d e
r u i m t e) shop-window, show-window; 2
(h e t u i t g e s t a l d e) display; ~*s kijken*
window-shop; **–materiaal** (-ialen) *o* display
material(s); **–pop** (-pen) *v* (window) dummy;
eta'leren (etaleerde, h. geëtaleerd) I *vt* display;
II *va* do the window-dressing; III *o* window-
dressing; eta'leur (-s) *m* window-dresser
e'tappe *v* (-n en -s) 1 halting-place; 2 stage [in
route]; 3 ⚔ supply-depot; *iem. t e (n)*
~ *vragen* invite sbd. to dinner; *hij is bij ons ten*
~ he is dining with us; *v o o r het* ~ before dinner;
z o n d e r ~ *naar bed gaan* go to bed without
supper; 'etenstijd (-en) *m* dinner-time,
meal-time; **–uur** (-uren) *o* dinner-hour;
'etentje (-s) *o* dinner, small dinner party;
'eter (-s) *m* eater
eter'niet *o* asbestos cement
'etgras, **–groen** *o* after-grass, aftermath
'ether ['e.tər] (-s) *m* 1 ether; 2 R air; *door (in, uit)*
de ~ over (on, off) the air; e'therisch ethereal
'ethica, e'thiek, 'ethika *v* ethics
Ethi'opië *o* Ethiopia; Ethi'opiër (-s) *m*,
Ethi'opisch *aj* Ethiopian
'ethisch ethical
eti'ket (-ten) *b* label; etiket'teren (etiketteerde,
h. geëtiketteerd) *vt* label
etiolo'gie *v* (a)etiology
eti'quette [e.ti.'kɛtə] *v* etiquette
'etmaal (-malen) *o* (space of) 24 hours
'etnisch I *aj* ethnic(al); II *ad* ethnically;
etno'graaf (-grafen) *m* ethnographer;
etnogra'fie *v* ethnography; etno'grafisch
ethnographic(ally); etnolo'gie *v* ethnology;
etno'logisch ethnological(ly); etno'loog
(-logen) *m* ethnologist
ets (-en) *v* etching; 'etsen (etste, h. geëtst) *vt* &
vi etch; 'etser (-s) *m* etcher; 'etskunst *v* (art

of) etching; **–naald** (-en) *v* etching-needle
'**ettelijke** a number of, some, several
'**etter** *m* matter, pus, purulent discharge;
–achtig purulent; '**etteren** (etterde, h. geët-
terd) *vi* fester, suppurate, ulcerate, run; '**etter-
gezwel** (-len) *o* abscess, gathering; '**etterig**
purulent; '**ettering** (-en) *v* suppuration
e'**tude** (-s) *v* ♪ study
e'**tui** [e.'tɥi.] (-s) *o* case, etui, etwee
etymolo'**gie** [y = i.] (-ieën) *v* etymology;
ety**mo'logisch** etymological; etymo'**loog**
(-logen) *m* etymologist
eucharis'**tie** [œy-] *v* rk Eucharist; **–viering**
(-en) *v* celebration of the Eucharist;
eucha'**ristisch** rk Eucharistic
eufe'**misme** [œy-] (-n) *o* euphemism; **–istisch**
euphemistic
eufo'**nie** [œy-] *v* euphony; eu'**fonisch**
euphonic
eufo'**rie** [œy-] *v* euphoria; eu'**forisch** euphoric
'**eunuch** ['œy-] (-en) *m* eunuch
'**Euromarkt** *v* Common Market; Eu'**ropa** *o*
Europe; Euro**pe'aan** (-eanen) *m*, Euro'**pees**
aj European
Eu'**stachius** [ø:- of œy-] *buis van* ~ Eustachian
tube
euthana'**sie** [œyta.na'zi.] *v* euthanasia; mercy
killing
'**euvel I** *ad* ~ *duiden* (*opnemen*) take amiss, take in
bad part; *duid het mij niet* ~ don't take it ill of
me; **II** *aj* ~*e moed* insolence; **III** (-en) *o* evil,
fault; **–daad** (-daden) *v* evil deed, crime
e.v. = *en volgende* f.f., and following
'**Eva** *v* Eve
E.V.A. = *Europese Vrijhandelsassociatie* European
Free-Trade Association, E.F.T.A.
evacu'**atie** [e.va.ky.'a.(t)si.] (-s) *v* evacuation;
evacu'**é(e)** (-s) *m* (-*v*) evacuee; evacu'**eren**
(evacueerde, h. geëvacueerd) *vt* 1 evacuate [a
place]; 2 invalid home, send home [wounded
soldiers]
evalu'**atie** [-(t)si.] (-s) *v* evaluation; evalu'**eren**
(evalueerde, h. geëvalueerd) *vt* evaluate
evan'**gelie** (-iën en -s) *o* gospel; *het* ~ *van
Johannes* the Gospel according to St. John; *het is
nog geen* ~ *wat hij zegt* it is not gospel truth what
he says; **–woord** (-en) *o* gospel; evangeli-
'**satie** [-'za.(t)si.] *v* evangelization, mission
work; evan'**gelisch** evangelic(ally); evan-
geli'**seren** [s = z] (evangeliseerde, h. geëvan-
geliseerd) *vt* evangelize; evange'**list** (-en) *m*
evangelist
'**even I** *aj* even [numbers, numbered]; ~ *of
oneven* odd or even; *het is mij om het* ~ it is all
the same (all one) to me; *om het* ~ *wie* no
matter who; **II** *ad* 1 (g e l ij k) equally; 2
(e v e n t j e s) just; ~... *als*... as... as...; *overal* ~

breed of uniform breadth; *een* ~ *groot aantal* an
equal number; *zij zijn* ~ *groot* 1 they are equally
tall; 2 they are of a size; *haal eens* ~... just go
and fetch me...; *wacht* ~ wait a minute (bit); ~
aangaan bij iem. put in at sbd.
'**evenaar** (-s) *m* 1 equator; 2 index, tongue [of a
balance]
'**evenals** (just) as, (just) like
eve'**naren** (evenaarde, h. geëvenaard) *vt* equal,
match, be a match for, come up to
'**evenbeeld** (-en) *o* image, picture
even'**eens** also, likewise, as well
evene'**ment** (-en) *o* event
'**evengoed** 1 as well; 2 all the same
'**evenknie** (-knieën) *v* equal; **–mens** (-en) *m*
fellow-man
even'**min**, even'**min** no more; ~ *te vertrouwen
als*... no more to be trusted than...; *en zijn broer*
~ nor his brother either
even'**naaste** (-n) *m* fellowman
even'**nachtslijn** *v* equator
even'**redig** *aj* proportional [numbers, represen-
tation]; *omgekeerd* ~ *met* inversely proportional
to; *recht* ~ *met* directly proportional to; **–heid**
(-heden) *v* proportion
'**eventjes** just, only just, (just) a minute
eventuali'**teit** (-en) *v* contingency; possibility;
eventu'**eel I** *aj* contingent [expenses];
possible [defeat]; potential [buyer]; *eventuele
mogelijkheid* off chance; *eventuele onkosten worden
vergoed* any expenses will be made good; *de
eventuele schade wordt vergoed* the damage, if any,
will be made good; **II** *ad* this being the case;
mocht hij ~ *weigeren*... in the event of his refu-
sing...
'**even'veel** as much, as many
even'**wel** nevertheless, however
'**evenwicht** *o* equilibrium, balance, (equi)poise;
het ~ *bewaren* keep one's balance; *het* ~ *herstellen*
redress (restore) the balance; *het* ~ *verliezen* lose
one's balance; *het* ~ *verstoren* upset the balance;
in ~ in equilibrium, evenly balanced; *in* ~
brengen bring into equilibrium, equilibrate,
balance; *in* ~ *houden* keep in equilibrium,
balance; *uit* ~ *zijn* off-balance; even'**wichtig**
1 well-balanced[2]; 2 *fig* level-headed; '**even-
wichtsbalk** (-en) *m* *sp* balance beam; **–leer** *v*
statics; **–orgaan** (-ganen) *o* organ of equilibrium; **–stoornis** (-sen) *v* disequilibrium
even'**wijdig** parallel; ~*e lijn* parallel (line);
–heid *v* parallelism
'**evenzeer**, even'**zeer** as much
even'**zo** likewise; ~ *groot als*... (just) as large
as...; *zijn broer* ~ his brother as well, his
brother too
'**everzwijn** (-en) *o* 🐗 wild boar
evi'**dent** evident, plain, clear

evolu'eren (evolueerde, h. en is geëvolueerd) *vi* evolve; evo'lutie [-(t)si.] (-s) *v* evolution; evo'lutieleer *v* theory of evolution

ex ex, late, past, sometime [president &]

ex'act exact [sciences]; precise

ex'amen (-s en -mina) *o* examination **F** exam; ~ *afleggen* undergo an examination; ~ *afnemen* examine; *ik ga* ~ *doen* I am going in for an examination; *ik moet* ~ *doen* I must go up for (my) examination, take my examination, sit for an examination; *voor zijn* ~ *slagen* pass (one's examination); **–commissie** (-s) *v* examining board, examination board; **–geld** (-en) *o* examination fee; **–opgaaf** (-gaven) *v*, **–opgave** (-n) *v* examination paper; **–vak** (-ken) *o* examination subject; **–vrees** *v* examination fright; **exami'nandus** (-di) *m* examinee; **exami'nator** (-s en -'toren) *m* examiner; **exami'neren** (examineerde, h. geëxamineerd) *vt* & *vi* examine (on *in*)

excel'lent excellent; **–ie** [-(t)si.] (-s) *v* excellency; *Ja, Excellentie* Yes, Your Excellency

excentri'citeit (-en) *v* eccentricity, oddity; **excen'triek** 1 *aj* eccentric(al); 2 (-en) *o* ✗ eccentric [gear]; **excen'triekeling** (-en) *m* eccentric, **F** freak; **ex'centrisch** eccentric

ex'ceptie [-'sɛpsi.] (-s) *v* exception; 🏛 demurrer, bar; **exceptio'neel** exceptional, unusual

excer'peren (excerpeerde, h. geëxcerpeerd) *vt* make an abstract of; **ex'cerpt** (-en) *o* abstract

ex'ces (-sen) *o* excess

exclu'sief [s = z] 1 exclusive; 2 (n i e t i n-b e g r e p e n) exclusive of..., excluding..., ...not included, ...extra; **exclusivi'teit** *v* exclusiveness, exclusivity

excommuni'catie [-(t)si.] (-s) *v* excommunication; **excommuni'ceren** (excommuniceerde, h. geëxcommuniceerd) *vt* excommunicate

ex'cretie [-(t)si.] (-s) *v* excretion

ex'cursie [s = z] (-s) *v* excursion

excu'seren [s = z] (excuseerde, h. geëxcuseerd) **I** *vt* excuse; **II** *vr zich* ~ 1 excuse oneself; 2 send an excuse; **ex'cuus** (-cuses) *o* excuse, apology; *hij maakte zijn* ~ he apologized; *ik vraag u* ~ I beg your pardon

exe'crabel execrable, abominable, detestable

execu'tant (-en) *m* executant, performer; **execu'teren** (executeerde, h. geëxecuteerd) *vt iem.* ~ 1 (t e r e c h t s t e l l e n) execute sbd.; 2 🏛 sell sbd.'s goods under execution; **execu'teur** (-s en -en) *m* executor; **execu'teur-testamen'tair** [-'tɛ:r] (execu-teurs-testamentair) *m* executor; **exe'cutie** [-(t)si.] (-s) *v* execution°; *bij* ~ *laten verkopen* 🏛 sell under execution; **–peleton** (-s) *o* ✗ firing-party, firing-squad; **execu'tieve** *v* executive (authority); **executori'aal** *executoriale verkoop* distress sale, compulsory sale; **execu'trice** (-s) *v* executrix

exe'geet (-geten) *m* exegete; **exe'gese** [s = z] (-n) *v* exegesis

exem'plaar (-plaren) *o* specimen; copy [of a book &]

excer'ceren (exerceerde, h. geëxerceerd) *vi* & *vt* drill; *aan het* ~ at drill; **exer'citie** [-(t)si.] (-s en -iën) *v* drill; **–terrein** (-en) *o* ✗ parade (-ground)

exhibitio'nisme [-(t)si.-] *o* exhibitionism; **–istisch** exhibitionist

existentia'lisme [-(t)si.-] *o* existentialism; **–ist** *m* existentialist; **–istisch** existentialist; **exis'tentie** *v* existence; **existenti'eel** existential; **exis'teren** (existeerde, h. geëxisteerd) *vi* exist

ex-'libris (-libris en -librissen) *o* ex-libris [ook *mv*], bookplate

exoga'mie *v* exogamy

exo'geen exogenous

exorbi'tant exorbitant, excessive

ex'otisch exotic

ex'pansie [s = z] *v* expansion; **expan'sief** expansive; **ex'pansiepolitiek** *v* policy of expansion; **–vat** (-vaten) *o* expansion tank

expedi'ëren (expedieerde, h. geëxpedieerd) *vt* forward, send, dispatch, ship [goods]; **expedi'teur** (-s en -en) *m* forwarding-agent, shipping-agent; **expe'ditie** [-(t)si.] (-s) *v* 1 ✗ expedition; 2 $ forwarding, dispatch, shipping [of goods]; **–kosten** *mv* forwarding charges

experi'ment (-en) *o* experiment; **experi-rimen'teel** experimental; **experimen'teren** (experimenteerde, h. geëxperimenteerd) *vi* experiment

ex'pert [ɛks'pɛːr] (-s) *m* expert; (s c h a t t e r) appraiser; surveyor [of Lloyd's &]; **exper'tise** [s = z] (-s en -n) 1 appraisement, survey; 2 certificate of survey

explici'teren (expliciteerde, h. geëxpliciteerd) *vt* state explicitly

explo'deren (explodeerde, is geëxplodeerd) *vi* explode

exploi'tant [-plva-] (-en) *m* owner [of a mine &], operator [of air service]; **exploi'tatie** [-(t)si.] (-s) *v* exploitation², working, operation [of air service]; *in* ~ in working order; **–kosten** *mv* working-expenses, operating costs; **exploi'teren** (exploiteerde, h. geëxploi-teerd) *vt* exploit², work [a mine], run [hotel], operate [air service]; *fig* ook: trade on [sbd.'s credulity]

ex'ploot (-ploten) *o* writ; *iem. een* ~ *betekenen* serve a writ upon sbd.

ex'plosie [s = z] (-s) *v* explosion; explo'sief explosive; ex'plosiemotor (-toren) *m* internal combustion engine

expo'nent (-en) *m* exponent², index

'export *m* $ export(ation), exports; expor'teren (exporteerde, h. geëxporteerd) *vt* export; expor'teur (-s) *m* $ exporter; 'exporthandel *m* export trade

expo'sant [s = z] (-en) *m* exhibitor; expo'seren (exposeerde, h. geëxposeerd) *vt* exhibit, show; expo'sitie [-'zi.(t)si.] (-s) *v* 1 (k u n s t) exhibition, show; 2 (a n d e r s) exposition° [ook ♪, *rk*]

ex'pres I *aj* ~*se bestelling* ⌕ express delivery; II *ad* [do] on purpose, deliberately; III *m* = *exprestrein*; –goed (-eren) *o* parcels; *als* ~ by passenger train; ex'presse (-n) *v* ⌕ express-delivery letter

ex'pressie (-s) *v* expression; expres'sief expressive; expressio'nisme *o* expressionism; expressio'nist (-en) *m* expressionist; –isch expressionist [painter, painting], expressionistic

ex'prestrein (-en) *m* express (train)

ex'quis [ɪks'ki.s] exquisite

ex'tase [s = z] *v* ecstasy, rapture; *in* ~ enraptured; *in* ~ *geraken* go into ecstasies [over sth.]; *in* ~ *zijn* be in an ecstasy; ex'tatisch ecstatic

ex'tenso [s = z] *in* ~ at great length

ex'tern I *aj* non-resident [master]; ~*e leerlingen* day-pupils, day-scholars; II *mv de* ~*en* the day-pupils, day-boys

'extra extra, special, additional; 'extraatje (-s) *o* extra

ex'tract (-en) *o* extract; extra'heren (extraheerde, h. geëxtraheerd) *vt* extract

ex'traneus [-ne.üs] (-neï) *m* extramural student

extrapo'latie [-(t)si.] (-s) *v* extrapolation; extrapo'leren (extrapoleerde, h. geëxtrapoleerd) *vt* extrapolate

'extraterritori'aal exterritorial, extraterritorial

extra'vert (-en) *m, aj* extrovert

ex'treem extreme; extre'mist (-en) *m* extremist; extre'mistisch extremist

extremi'teit (-en) *v* extremity

'ezel (-s) *m* 1 ⌕ ass², donkey; 2 easel [of a painter]; *een* ~ *stoot zich geen tweemaal aan dezelfde steen* once bitten twice shy, the burnt child dreads the fire; 'ezelachtig asinine², *fig* stupid; –heid (-heden) *v* (asinine) stupidity; eze'lin (-nen) *v* she-ass, jenny-ass; –nemelk *v* ass's milk; 'ezelsbrug (-gen) *v*, 'ezelsbruggetje (-s) *o* aid (in study &); –kop (-pen) *m* 1 ass's head; 2 *fig* dunce, ass; –oor (-oren) *o* 1 ass's ear; 2 dog-ear [of a book]; –veulen (-s) *o* 1 ass's foal; 2 *fig* dunce, ass; 'ezel(s)wagen (-s) *m* donkey-cart

F

f [ɛf] ('s) *v* f;-**f.** = *florijn, gulden*
fa [fa.] *v* ♪ fa, f
fa. = *firma*
faam *v* fame; reputation [as a scholar]
'fabel (-en en -s) *v* fable²; *fig* myth; **–achtig**
 fabulous; **–leer** *v* mythology; **–tje** (-s) *o* fabri-
 cation, fiction
fabri'cage [g = ʒ] *v*, **fabri'catie** [-(t)si.] *v*
 manufacture; **fabri'ceren** (fabriceerde, h.
 gefabriceerd) *vt* manufacture; *fig* fabricate [lies
 &]
fa'briek (-en) *v* factory; works, mill; plant;
 fa'brieken (fabriekte, h. gefabriekt) *vt* make;
 fa'brieksarbeider (-s) *m* (factory-)hand,
 factory-worker, mill-hand; **–gebouw** (-en) *o*
 factory-building; **–geheim** (-en) *o* trade
 secret; **–meisje** (-s) *o* factory girl; **–merk**
 (-en) *o* trade mark; **–prijs** (-prijzen) *m* manufacturer's price; **–schip** (-schepen) *o* ♨ factory
 (ship); **–stad** (-steden) *v* manufacturing town;
 –terrein (-en) *o* factory site; **–werk** *o*
 machine-made article(s)
fabri'kaat (-katen) *o* make; *auto van Frans* ~
 French-made car; **fabri'kant** (-en) *m* 1 manufacturer; 2 factory-owner, mill-owner;
 fabri'keren (fabrikeerde, h. gefabrikeerd) *vt* =
 fabriceren
fabu'leren (fabuleerde, h. gefabuleerd) *vt*
 invent, fabricate, lie
fabu'leus fabulous
fa'çade (-s en -n) *v* facade, front
face-à-'main [fa.sa.'mɛ̃] (-s) *m* lorgnette
fa'cet (-ten) *o* facet; aspect
'facie (-s) *o* & *v* face, F phiz, S mug
facili'teit (-ten) *v* facility
fac'simile [fɑk'si.mi.le.] ('s) *o* facsimile, auto-
 type
'factie ['fɑksi.] (-s en -iën) *v* faction
fac'toor (-toren) *m* factor, agent
'factor (-'toren) *m* factor²
facto'rij (-en) *v* factory, trading-post
fac'totum (-s) *o* factotum
factu'reren (factureerde, h. gefactureerd) *vt*
 invoice; **factu'rist** (-en) *m* $ invoice clerk;
 fac'tuur (-turen) *v* $ invoice; **–prijs** (-prijzen)
 m $ invoice price
faculta'tief optional [subjects]
facul'teit (-en) *v* faculty; *de medische* ~ the
 faculty of medicine
fae'caliën [fe.-] *mv* faeces; **'faeces** ['fe.tsəs] *mv*
 faeces
fa'got (-ten) *m* bassoon; **fagot'tist** (-en) *m*

bassoonist
faïence [fa.'jã:sə] (-s) *v* faience
fail'leren [fɑ(l)'je:rə(n)] (failleerde, is gefail-
 leerd) *vi* fail, become a bankrupt; be adjudged
 (adjudicated) bankrupt; **fail'liet** [fɑ'ji.t] **I** *o*
 1 failure, bankruptcy; 2 (-en) *m* bankrupt; **II** *aj*
 ~*e boedel*, ~*e massa* bankrupt's estate; ~ *gaan*
 fail, become (go) bankrupt; **F** smash; **S** bust
 up; ~ *verklaren* adjudge (adjudicate) bankrupt;
 –verklaring (-en) *v* adjudication order;
 faillisse'ment (-en) *o* failure, bankruptcy;
 (*zijn*) ~ *aanvragen* file one's petition (in bankruptcy); *in staat van* ~ (*verkerend*) in bankruptcy; **faillisse'mentsaanvraag** (-vragen) *v*,
 –aanvrage (-n) *v* petition (in bankruptcy);
 –wet (-ten) *v* Bankruptcy act
'fait accom'pli ['fɛtakòm'pli] (faits accomplis)
 m fait accompli
'faki(e)r (-s) *m* fakir
'fakkel (-s) *v* torch; ⚶ flare; **–drager** (-s) *m*
 torch-bearer; **–loop** (-lopen) *m* torch race;
 –(op)tocht (-en) *m* torch-light procession
falderalde'riere folderol
'falen (faalde, is gefaald) *vi* fail, miss, make a
 mistake, err
'falie (-s) *v* F *iem. op zijn* ~ *geven* dust sbd.'s
 jacket
falie'kant wrong; ~ *uitkomen* go wrong; ~
 verkeerd completely (all) wrong
'fallus (-sen) *m* phallus
fal'saris (-sen) *m* falsifier, forger
fal'set (-ten) *m* & *o* falsetto; **–stem** (-men) *v*
 head voice
fa'meus **I** *aj* famous; *het is* ~*!* it is enormous!; **II**
 ad [enjoy oneself] splendidly, gloriously
famili'aar familiar, informal; *al te* ~ too free
 (and easy); ~ *met iem. zijn* be on familiar terms
 with sbd.; **familiari'teit** (-en) *v* familiarity;
 zich ~*en veroorloven jegens* take liberties with sbd.
fa'milie (-s) *v* family, relations, relatives; *de*
 Koninklijke ~ the royal family; *de* ~ *X* the X
 family; *zijn* ~ his relations, his people; *ik ben* ~
 van hem I am related to him; *van goede* ~ of a
 good family, well-connected; ~ *en kennissen*
 relatives and friends; **–aangelegenheden** *mv*
 family affairs (business); **–band** (-en) *m* family
 tie; **–berichten** *mv* births, marriages and
 deaths [column]; **–drama** ('s) *o* domestic
 drama; **–feest** (-en) *o* family celebration; **–graf**
 (-graven) *o* family vault; **–kring** (-en) *m* family
 circle, domestic circle; **–kwaal** (-kwalen) *v*
 family complaint; **–leven** *o* family life; **–lid**

(-leden) *o* member of the family, relation, relative; *familieleden* **F** folks; **–naam** (-namen) *m* 1 surname; 2 family name; **–pension** [-pāsi.òn] (-s) *o* private boarding-house, private hotel; **–raad** (-raden) *m* family council; **–stuk** (-ken) *o* family piece, heirloom; **–trek** (-ken) *m* family trait; **–trots** *m* family pride; **–twist** (-en) *m* family quarrel; **–wapen** (-s) *o* ⊘ family arms; **–ziek** clannish

fan [fɪn] (-s) *m* fan

fa'naticus (-ci) *m* fanatic; **fana'tiek** fanatical; **–eling** (-en) *m* fanatic; **fana'tisme** *o* fanaticism

'fanclub [fɪn-] (-s) *v* fan club

fan'fare (-n en -s) *v* ♩ 1 fanfare, flourish; 2 (k o r p s) brass band; **–korps** (-en) *o* brass band

fanta'seren [s = z] (fantaseerde, h. gefantaseerd) **I** *vt* 1 invent [things]; 2 ♩ improvise; **II** *vi* 1 indulge in fancies, imagine things; 2 ♩ improvise; **fanta'sie** [s = z] (-ieën) *v* phantasy, fancy, [rich] imagination; **–stof** (-fen) *v* dress-material in fancy shades; **fan'tast** (-en) *m* fantast, phantast; **–isch** fantastic°; fanciful [project; writer]; visionary; **~** (*goed, mooi*) < **F** marvellous, wonderful; terrific

'farao ('s) *m* Pharaoh

'farce (-n en -s) *v* 1 farce, mockery ‖ 2 stuffing [in cookery]; **far'ceren** (farceerde, h. gefarceerd) *vt* stuff

fari'zeeër (-s) *m* pharisee, hypocrite; **fari'zees, fari'zeïsch** pharisaic

farma'ceut [- 'sœyt] (-en) *m* (pharmaceutical) chemist; **–isch** pharmaceutical; **farma'cie** *v* pharmacy

'Faröer ['fa: røɔr] *nw* Faeroes, Faroe Islands

fasci'neren [fɑsi.-] (fascineerde, h. gefascineerd) *vt* fascinate; **~d** [*fig*] magnetic, intriguing

fas'cisme [fɑ's(j)ɪsmə] *o* fascism; **–ist** (-en) *m*, **fas'cistisch** *aj* fascist

'fase [s = z] (-s en -n) *v* phase; stage; period; vgl. *stadium*; **fa'seren** [s = z] (faseerde, h. gefaseerd) *vt* phase; stagger [holidays]

fat (-ten) *m* dandy, fop, **F** swell

fa'taal fatal; **fata'lisme** *o* fatalism; **fata'list** (-en) *m* fatalist; **–isch** fatalistic

'fata mor'gana ('s) *v* fata morgana, mirage

fat'soen (-en) *o* 1 (v o r m) fashion, form, shape, make, cut; 2 (d e c o r u m) decorum, (good) manners; 3 (n a a m) respectability; *zijn ~ houden* behave (decently); *zijn ~ ophouden* keep up appearances; ● *met* (*goed*) *~* decently; *erg op zijn ~ zijn* be a great stickler for the proprieties; *u'i t zijn ~ zijn* be out of shape; *v o o r zijn ~* for the sake of decency, to keep up appearances; **fatsoe'neren** (fatsoeneerde, h.

gefatsoeneerd) *vt* fashion, shape, model;

fat'soenlijk I *aj* 1 (n e t) respectable [people]; reputable [neighbourhood]; decent [behaviour, clothes, fellow]; 2 (w o u l d - b e a a n z i e n - l i j k) genteel; *~e armen* deserving poor; *~e armoede* gilded poverty, shabby gentility; **II** *ad* respectably; decently; **–heid** *v* 1 respectability; decency; 2 gentility; **fat'soenshalve** for decency's sake; **–rakker** (-s) *m* stickler for proprieties; bigot

'fatterig foppish, dandified; **–heid** *v* foppishness, dandyism

faun (-en) *m* faun

'fauna *v* fauna

faus'set [fo.'sɪt] = *falset*

fau'teuil [fo.'tœyj] (-s) *m* 1 arm-chair, easy chair; 2 fauteuil, stall [in theatre]

favo'riet I *aj* favourite; **II** (-en) *m* favourite; *hij is ~* he is the favourite

fa'zant (-en) *m* pheasant; **fa'zantehaan** (-hanen) *m* cock-pheasant; **–hen** (-nen) *v* hen-pheasant; **–jacht** (-en) *v* pheasant shooting; **fa'zantenpark** *o* pheasant preserve

febru'ari *m* February

fede'raal federal; **federa'list** (-en) *m* federalist; **fede'ratie** [-(t)si.] (-s) *v* federation; **federa'tief** federative

fee (feeën) *v* fairy; **'feeënland** *o* fairyland; **feeë'rie** (-ieën) *v* fairy play; **feeë'riek** fairylike

feeks (-en) *v* vixen, termagant, shrew, virago

feest (-en) *o* feast, festival, festivity, fête; (f e e s t j e, f u i f) party; *een waar ~* a treat; **–avond** (-en) *m* festive evening, festive night; **–commissie** (-s) *v* entertainment committee; **–dag** (-dagen) *m* 1 feast-day, festive day, festal day, high day; [national, public] holiday; 2 [church] holy-day; *op zon- en feestdagen* on Sundays and holidays; **–dis** (-sen) *m* festive board; **–dronk** (-en) *m* toast; **–drukte** *v* festive excitement (commotion, turmoil, bustle); **'feestelijk** festive, festal; *dank je ~* no, thank you; I'll thank you!, nothing doing!; **–heid** (-heden) *v* festivity; merry-making, rejoicings; *met grote ~* amid much festivity; **'feesten** (feestte, h. gefeest) *vi* feast, make merry, celebrate; **'feestgewaad** (-waden) *o* festive attire, festal dress; **–je** (-s) *o* party; **–maal** (-malen) *o*, **–maaltijd** (-en) *m* banquet; **–neus** (-neuzen) *m* false nose; **–programma** ('s) *o* program of (the) festivities; **–rede** (-s) *v* speech of the day; **–redenaar** (-s) *m* speaker of the day; **–stemming** *v* festive mood; **–terrein** (-en) *o* festive grounds; **–verlichting** *v* illumination; **–vieren** (vierde 'feest, h. 'feestgevierd) *vi* feast, make merry, celebrate; **–viering** (-en) *v* feasting, celebration of a (the) feast, feast, festival; **'feestvreugde** *v* festive joy, festive mirth

feil (-en) *v* fault, error, mistake; **'feilbaar** fallible, liable to error; **–heid** *v* fallibility; **'feilen** (feilde, h. gefeild) *vi* err, make a mistake; **'feilloos** faultless, indefectable

feit (-en) *o* fact; *in* ~*e* = *feitelijk* **II**; **–elijk I** *aj* actual, real; ~*e gegevens* factual data; **II** *ad* in point of fact, in fact [you are right]; virtually [the same case]; **'feitenkennis** *v* factual knowledge; **–materiaal** *o* body of facts, factual material, factual evidence

fel fierce [heat &]; *zij zijn er* ~ *op* they are very keen on it; **–gekleurd** gaudy; **–heid** *v* fierceness

felici'tatie [-(t)si.] (-s) *v* congratulation; **–brief** (-brieven) *m* letter of congratulation; **felici'teren** (feliciteerde, h. gefeliciteerd) **I** *vt* congratulate (on *met*); **II** *va* offer one's congratulations

'femelaar (-s) *m*, **–ster** (-s) *v* canter, canting hypocrite, sniveller; **'femelen** (femelde, h. gefemeld) *vi* cant, snivel

femi'nisme *o* feminism; **–ist(e)** (-en) *m*(*v*) feminist

'feniks (-en) *m* phoenix

fe'nol (-nolen) *o* phenol

feno'meen (-menen) *o* phenomenon [*mv* phenomena]; **fenome'naal** phenomenal, exceptional

feo'daal Ⓤ feudal

ferm 1 (f l i n k , d e g e l i j k) fine [boy]; smart [blow]; 2 (v. k a r a k t e r) energetic; spirited

fer'ment (-en) *o* ferment; **fermen'tatie** [-(t)si.] *v* fermentation; **fermen'teren** (fermenteerde, h. gefermenteerd) *vi* ferment

fer'vent fervent, passionate

fes'tijn (-en) *o* feast, banquet

'festival (-s) *o* (musical) festival

festivi'teit (-en) *v* festivity

fes'toen (-en) *o* & *m* 1 (g u i r l a n d e) festoon [of flowers &]; 2 = *feston*

fes'ton (-s) *o* & *m* (g e b o r d u u r d e r a n d) scallop; **feston'neren** (festonneerde, h. gefestonneerd) *vt* scallop [handkerchiefs &]; buttonhole [lace]

fê'teren (fêteerde, h. gefêteerd) *vt* fête, lionize, make much of

fetisj ['fe.ti.ʃ] (-en) *m* fetish

feu'daal [fø'da.l] = *feodaal*

feuille'ton [fœyjə'tɔn] (-s) *o* 1 (v e r v o l g - v e r h a a l) serial (story); 2 (a n d e r s) feuilleton

fi'asco ('s) *o* fiasco; **F** wash-out, flop; *een* ~ *worden* (zijn) be a failure, fall flat

'fiat I *o* fiat; **II** *ij* done!; that's a bargain; **fiat'teren** (fiatteerde, h. gefiatteerd) *vt* 1 give

on's fiat to; authorize, **F** o.k.; 2 pass for press

'fiber *o* & *m* fibre

fi'brine *v* fibrin

'fiche ['fi.ʃə] (-s) *o* & *v* 1 (p e n n i n g) counter, fish, marker; 2 (v. k a a r t s y s t e e m) index card, filing card; **fi'cheren** (ficheerde, h. geficheerd) *vt* card-index

'fictie [fiksi.] (-s) *v* fiction; **fic'tief** fictitious [names], fictive [characters, persons], imaginary [profits]

fi'deel jolly, jovial

fiduci'air [fi.dy.si.'ɛ: r] fiduciary

fi'ducie *v* confidence, trust; *niet veel* ~ *hebben in* not have much faith in

'Fidji ['fi.ʒi.] *de* ~-*eilanden* the Fiji islands

'fiedel (-s) *m* **F** fiddle; **'fiedelen** (fiedelde, h. gefiedeld) *vi* & *vt* **F** fiddle

fielt (-en) *m* rogue, rascal, scoundrel; **–achtig** rascally, scoundrelly; **–enstreek** (-streken) *m* & *v* knavish trick, piece of knavery; **–erig** = *fieltachtig*

fier proud; **–heid** *v* pride

fiets (-en) *m* & *v* bicycle, cycle, **F** bike; **–band** (-en) *m* (cycle-)tyre; **–bel** (-len) *v* bicycle-bell, cycle-bell; **–benodigdheden** *mv* cycle accessories; **'fietsen** (fietste, h. en is gefietst) *vi* cycle, **F** bike; *wat gaan* ~ **F** go for a spin; **'fietsenhok** (-ken) *o* bicycle shed; **–rek** (-ken) *o* bicycle stand; **–stalling** (-en) *v* (bi)cycle store; **'fietser** (-s) *m* cyclist; **'fietshok** (-ken) *o* = *fietsenhok*; **–ketting** (-en) *m* & *v* bicycle chain; **–lamp** (-en) *v*, **–lantaarn**, **–lantaren** (-s) *v* cycle-lamp; **–pad** (-paden) *o* cycling-track, cycle-track; *Am* bikeway; **–pomp** (-en) *v* inflator, cycle-pump; **–rek** (-ken) *o* = *fietsenrek*; **–tas** (-sen) *v* cycle-bag; **–tocht** (-en) *m* cycling-tour, **F** spin

figu'rant (-en) *m* super, walking gentleman; **–e** (-n) *v* super, walking lady

figura'tief figurative; **figu'reren** (figureerde, h. gefigureerd) *vi* figure; (t o n e e l) walk on; **fi'guur** (-guren) *v* & *o* figure [of the body, decorative, geometrical, emblematical, historical, in dancing, in grammar, of speech]; [illustrative] diagram; character [in drama, in history]; *een droevig* (*goed*) ~ *maken* (*slaan*) cut (make) a poor (good) figure; *zijn* ~ *redden* save one's face; **–lijk** figurative; **–naad** (-naden) *v* dart; **–zaag** (-zagen) *v* fret-saw; **fi'guurzagen I** *vi* do fretwork; **II** *o* fretwork

fijn I *aj* 1 (s c h e r p) fine [point, tooth, ear, gold, distinctions], fine-tooth(ed) [comb]; 2 (v. k w a l i t e i t) choice [food, wines]; exquisite [taste]; 3 (v. o n d e r s c h e i d i n g) nice [difference], delicate [ear for music], subtle [distinction], shrewd [remarks]; 4 (o r t h o - d o x) precise, godly; 5 (v o o r n a a m , c h i c) smart [people], **F** swell [neighbourhood, clothes]; (*dat is*) ~! good!, **F** capital!, famous!, (it's) great! **S** ripping!; *een ~e vent* **F** a man and a brother; **II** *o het ~e van de zaak* the ins and outs of the matter; **III** *ad* finely; *het is ~ koud* 1 the cold is biting; 2 it is nice and cold; **–besnaard** finely strung, delicate, refined; **–gebouwd** of delicate build; **'fijngevoelig** delicate, sensitive; **–heid** (-heden) *v* delicacy, sensitiveness; **'fijnhakken**[1] *vt* cut (chop) small, mince; **–heid** (-heden) *v* fineness, choiceness, delicacy, nicety [of taste], subtlety; **–knijpen**[1] *vt* squeeze; **–korrelig** fine-grained; **–maken**[1] *vt* pulverize, crush; **–malen**[1] *vt* grind (down); **–proever** (-s) *m* gastronomer; *fig* connoisseur; **–stampen**[1] *vt* crush, bray, pound, pulverize; **–tjes** smartly, cleverly, [guess] shrewdly, [remark] slyly; zie ook: *fijn* **III**; **–wrijven**[1] *vt* rub (grind) down, bray, pulverize

fijt (-en) *v* & *o* whitlow

fik (-ken) *m* (h o n d) dog(gie), bow-wow; || (b r a n d) blaze, fire; *in de ~ staan* (*steken*) be (set) ablaze

'fikken *mv* **F** paws; *blijf er af met je ~!* paws off!

'fiks I *aj* good, sound; *een ~e klap* a smart (hard) blow; **II** *ad* well, soundly, thoroughly

filan'troop (-tropen) *m* philanthropist; **filantro'pie** *v* philanthropy; **filan'tropisch** philanthropic

filate'lie *v* philately; **filate'list** (-en) *m* philatelist; **–isch** philatelic

fil d'é'cosse [fi.lde.'kɔs] *o* lisle thread; *kousen van ~* lisle stockings

'file (-s) *v* row, file, line, queue

fi'leren (fileerde, h. gefileerd) *vt* fillet [fish]; **fi'let** [-'le.] (-s) *m* & *o* fillet [of fish &], undercut [of beef]

'filevorming (-en) *v* traffic congestion

filhar'monisch philharmonic

fili'aal (-ialen) *o* branch establishment, branch office, branch; (v. g r o o t w i n k e l b e d r ij f) chain store; **–bedrijf** (-drijven) *o* chain store

film (-s) *m* film°; *aan de ~ zijn, voor de ~ spelen* act for the films; *naar de ~ gaan* go to the pictures (**F** the flicks); **–acteur** (-s) *m* film actor; **'filmen** (filmde, h. gefilmd) *vt* film; **'filmindustrie** *v* film industry; **'filmisch** cinematic; **'filmjournaal** [-ʒu: r-] (-s) *o* newsreel; **–keuring** *v* 1 film censorship; 2 (d e c o m m i s s i e) board of film censors, viewing board; **–kunst** *v* film art; **–operateur** (-s) *m* 1 (d i e o p n e e m t) cameraman; 2 (d i e

v e r t o o n t) projectionist; **filmo'theek** (-theken) *v* film library; **'filmscenario** [-se.-] ('s) *o* film script, screenplay; **–ster** [-stɛr] (-ren) *v* film star, screen star; **–sterretje** (-s) *o* film starlet; **–studio** ('s) *m* film studio; **–toestel** (-len) *o* cine-camera; **–verhuur** *m* distribution; **–verhuurder** (-s) *m* distributor

filolo'gie *v* philology; **filo'logisch** philological; **filo'loog** (-logen) *m* philologist

filoso'feren (filosofeerde, h. gefilosofeerd) *vi* philosophize; **filoso'fie** (-ieën) *v* philosophy; **filo'sofisch** philosophical; **filo'soof** (-sofen) *m* philosopher

'filter (-s) *m* & *o* filter, percolator; **'filteren** (filterde, h. gefilterd) *vi* & *vt* filter; (v. k o f f i e) percolate; **'filtersigaret** (-ten) *v* filter-tip cigarette; **fil'traat** (-traten) *o* filtrate; **fil'treerpapier** (-en) *o* filter(ing)-paper; **fil'treren** (filtreerde, h. gefiltreerd) *vt* filter, filtrate; (v. k o f f i e) percolate

'Fin (-nen) *m* Finn

fi'naal I *aj* final; complete, total; *finale uitverkoop* wind-up sale; **II** *ad* quite [impossible]

fi'nale (-s) *v* 1 finale; 2 *sp* final; *halve ~* semi-final; **fina'list** (-en) *m* finalist

financi'eel financial; **fi'nanciën** *mv* 1 finances; 2 (f i n a n c i e w e z e n) finance; **finan'cier** (-s) *m* financier; **finan'cieren** (financierde, h. gefinancierd) *vt* finance; **–ring** *v* financing; necessary funds, capital

fi'neer *o* veneer; **fi'neren** (fineerde, h. gefineerd) *vt* 1 refine [gold]; 2 veneer [wood]

fi'nesse (-s) *v* finesse, nicety; *de ~s (van een zaak)* ook: the ins and outs

fin'geren [fɪŋ'ge:rə(n)] (fingeerde, h. gefingeerd) *vt* feign, simulate; zie ook: *gefingeerd*

'finish ['fɪnɪʃ] *m sp* finish; **'finishen** (finishte, h. gefinisht) *vi sp* finish

'Finland *o* Finland; **'Fins** Finnish

fi'ool (fiolen) *v* phial; *de fiolen des toorns* the vials of wrath

'firma ('s) *v* 1 style [of a firm]; 2 firm, house (of business)

firma'ment *o* firmament, sky

'firmanaam (-namen) *m* firm, style; **fir'mant** (-en) *m* partner

fis [fi.s] (-sen) *v* ♪ **F** sharp

fis'caal fiscal

'fiscus *m* treasury, exchequer, Inland Revenue

'fistel (-s) *v* fistula

fit fit; *~ blijven* keep fit

'fitis (-sen) *m* willow-warbler

'fitter (-s) *m* (gas-)fitter

---

[1] V.T. en V.D. van dit werkwoord volgens het model: **'fijn**maken, V.T. maakte **'fijn**, V.D. **'fijn**gemaakt. Zie voor de vormen onder het grondwoord, in dit voorbeeld: *maken*. Bij sterke en onregelmatige werkwoorden wordt u verwezen naar de lijst achterin.

'**fitting** (-s en -en) *m* fitting; lampholder, socket
fix'atie [-(t)si.] (-s) *v* fixation; **fixa'tief** (-tieven) *o* 1 fixative; 2 (v o o r h e t h a a r) fixature; **fi'xeerbad** (-baden) *o* fixing-bath; **–middel** (-en) *o* fixer; **fi'xeren** (fixeerde, h. gefixeerd) *vt* 1 fix, fixate; 2 fix [a person with one's eyes], stare at [her]
fjord (-en) *m* fiord, fjord
fl. = *florijn, gulden*
fla'con (-s) *m* 1 flask; 2 scent-bottle
'**fladderen** (fladderde, h. en is gefladderd) *vi* flit [of bats &]; flitter, flutter, hover [from flower to flower]
flageo'let [flaʒo.'lɛt] (-ten) *m* ♩ flageolet
fla'grant glaring [error, injustice &]
flair [flɛːr] *m* & *o* flair
'**flakkeren** (flakkerde, h. geflakkerd) *vi* flicker, waver
flam'bard [flɑmˈbaːr] (-s) *m* slouch hat, wide-awake
flam'bouw (-en) *v* torch
fla'mingo [fla.'mɪŋo.] ('s) *m* flamingo
fla'nel(len) *o* (& *aj*) flannel; **fla'nelletje** (-s) *o* flannel vest; **fla'nelsteek** (-steken) *m* herring-bone stitch
fla'neren (flaneerde, h. geflaneerd) *vi* stroll, lounge, saunter, laze about; **fla'neur** (-s) *m* lounger, saunterer, idler
flank (-en) *v* flank, side; *i n de* ~ *vallen* take in flank; *rechts (links) u i t de* ~*!* by the right (the left); **–aanval** (-len) *m* flank attack[2]; **flank'eren** (flankeerde, h. geflankeerd) *vt* flank[2]
'**flansen** (flanste, h. geflanst) *vt in elkaar* ~ knock together, rip up, whip up [a meal]
flap (-pen) **I** *m* slap, box [on the ear]; **II** *ij* flop!; **–drol** (-len) **F** *m* milksop, craven; **–hoed** (-en) *m* = *flambard*; **–oren** *met* ~ flap-eared; '**flappen** (flapte, h. geflapt) *vi* flap; ook = *uit-flappen*; '**flaptekst** (-en) *m* blurb; **flap'uit** (-en) *m* blab(ber)
'**flarden** *mv* rags, tatters; *aan* ~ [be] in tatters, in rags, [tear] to rags
flat [flɛt] (-s) *m* flat; *Am* apartment; zie ook: *flatgebouw*
'**flater** (-s) *m* blunder, **F** howler
'**flatgebouw** ['flɛt-] (-en) *o* block of flats, *Am* apartment building
flat'teren (flatteerde, h. geflatteerd) *vt* flatter; *de balans* ~ cook (salt) the balance-sheet; *het flatteert u niet* it [the photo] doesn't flatter you; *een geflatteerd portret* a flattering portrait; **flat'teus** flattering, becoming
flauw I *aj* 1 faint [resistance, notions, light, of heart, with hunger]; 2 insipid [food, remarks], mild [jokes], vapid [conversation]; 3 dim, pale [outline]; 4 $ flat [of the market]; 5 poor-

spirited [fellows]; *hij heeft er geen* ~ *begrip van* he has not got the faintest notion of it; zie ook *idee*; *ik had er een* ~ *vermoeden van* I had an inkling of it; *dat is* ~ *van je* (how) silly!; **II** *ad* faintly, dimly; **flauwe'kul** *m* rubbish, fiddle-sticks, stuff and nonsense, all my eyes (and Betty Martin); **P** bull shit; '**flauwerd** (-s) *m*, '**flauwerik** (-riken) *m* 1 (k i n d e r a c h t i g) silly; 2 (b a n g) **S** funk; **flauw'hartig** faint-hearted; **–heid** *v* faint-heartedness; '**flauw-heid** (-heden) *v* faintness, insipidity; '**flauwig-heid** (-heden) *v*, **flauwi'teit** (-en) *v* silly thing, silly joke; '**flauwte** (-n en -s) *v* swoon, fainting fit, faint; '**flauwtjes** faintly; '**flauwvallen** (viel 'flauw, is 'flauwgevallen) *vi* go off in a swoon, have a fainting fit, swoon, faint
'**fleemkous** (-en) *v*, '**fleemster** (-s) *v* coaxer
fleer (fleren) *m* box on the ear
'**flegma** *o* phlegm, stolidity; **flegma'tiek** phlegmatic(al), stolid
'**flemen** (fleemde, h. gefleemd) *vi* coax; **–er** (-s) *m* coaxer
flens (flenzen) *m* ✗ flange
'**flensje** (-s) *o* thin pancake
fles (-sen) *v* bottle; *Leidse* ~ Leyden jar; *op de* ~ *gaan* **S** go to pot, go bust; *(veel) van de* ~ *houden* be fond of the bottle; '**flesopener** (-s) *m* bottle opener; '**flessebier** *o* bottled beer; **–gas** *o* bottled gas; **–hals** (-halzen) *m* bottle-neck; **–kind** (-eren) *o* bottle-baby, bottle-fed child; **–melk** *v* milk in bottles, bottled milk; **flessen** (fleste, h. geflest) *vt* swindle, cheat, **F** diddle; '**flessenrek** (-ken) *o* bottle-rack; **–trekker** (-s) *m* swindler; **flessentrekke'rij** (-en) *v* swindle, swindling
flets pale, faded, washy; **–heid** *v* paleness, fadedness, washiness
fleur *m* & *v* bloom, flower, prime; '**fleurig** blooming; *fig* bright, gay; **–heid** *v* bloom; *fig* brightness, gaiety
flex'ibel flexible[2]; **flexibili'teit** *v* flexibility[2]
'**flikflooien** (flikflooide, h. geflikflooid) *vt* & *vi* cajole, wheedle, fawn on [sbd.]; **–er** (-s) *m* fawner, cajoler, wheedler
'**flikje** (-s) *o* chocolate drop
'**flikken** (flikte, h. geflikt) *vt* patch, cobble [shoes]; **P** manage, do; *het 'm* ~ manage to do sth., bring sth. about; *iem. iets* ~ play sbd. a trick, do sth. to sbd.
'**flikker** (-s) *m* **P** 1 (z i e r) *het kan me geen* ~ *schelen* I don't care a damn; *hij weet er geen* ~ *van* he knows nothing about it, he hasn't got a clue; 2 (l i c h a a m) *iem. op zijn* ~ *slaan* give sbd. a hiding; *[fig] iem. op zijn* ~ *geven* give sbd. a drubbing; 3 > male homosexual
'**flikkeren** (flikkerde, h. geflikkerd) *vi* flicker, glitter, twinkle; **P** = *smijten*; **–ring** (-en) *v*

flicker(ing), glittering, twinkling; **'flikkerlicht** (-en) *o* flash-light

flink I *aj* 1 (v. z a k e n) good [walk, telling-off, number, size &], considerable [sum], substantial [progress]; goodly [size, volumes], sizable [desk, table], generous [piece], thorough [overhaul], sound [drubbing], smart [rap, pace &]; 2 (v. p e r s o n e n) fine [boy, lass, woman]; sturdy, stout, lusty, robust, strapping, stalwart, hardy [fellows], notable [housekeeper]; *hij is niet ~* 1 he is not strong; 2 he is not energetic enough; *hij is nog ~* he is still going strong; *wees nou een ~e jongen!* be a brave chap now!; **II** *ad* soundly, vigorously, thoroughly; *iem. ~ aframmelen* give sbd. a good (sound) drubbing; *~ eten* eat heartily (well); *hij kan ~ lopen* he is a good walker; *~ optreden* deal firmly (with), take a firm line; *het regent ~* it is raining hard; *zij zongen er ~ op los* they sang lustily; *ik heb hem ~ de waarheid gezegd* I have given him a piece of my mind, I have taken him up roundly; **–gebouwd** strongly built, well set-up; **–heid** *v* thoroughness; spirit; **–weg** without mincing matters

'flinter (-s) *m* flake; thin slice; paring, shaving; strip

'flippen (flipte, is geflipt) *vi* **S** have a bad trip

flirt [flœ:rt] (-en) 1 *m-v* (p e r s o o n) flirt; 2 *m* (h a n d e l i n g) flirtation; **'flirten** (flirtte, h. geflirt) *vi* flirt

flits (-en) *m* flash; **'flitsen** (flitste, h. geflitst) *vi* flash; **'flitslamp** (-en) *v* flash lamp, (k l e i n) flash bulb; **–licht** *o* flash-light

'flitspuit (-en) *v* spray

'flodder (-s) *v losse ~s* blank cartridges; **'flodderbroek** (-en) *v* floppy trousers; **'flodderen** (flodderde, h. geflodderd) *vi* 1 flounder (splash) through the dirt; 2 hang loosely, flop; 3 work in a careless (sluttish) way; **–rig** floppy; baggy; slipshod; **'flodderkous** (-en) *v* frump

floep *ij* pop!; (i n w a t e r) flop!

floers (-en) *o* (black) crape; *fig* veil

'flonkeren (flonkerde, h. geflonkerd) *vi* sparkle, twinkle; **–ring** (-en) *v* sparkling, twinkling

floot (floten) V.T.v. *fluiten*

flop *m* **F** flop, fiasco

'flora *v* flora

flo'reren (floreerde, h. gefloreerd) *vi* flourish, prosper, thrive

flo'ret (-retten) *v* & *o* (d e g e n) foil

floris'sant [-ri.-] flourishing, prospering, thriving

'floten V.T. meerv. v. *fluiten*

flot'tielje (-s) *v* flotilla

fluctu'atie [-(t)si.] *v* fluctuation; **fluctu'eren** (fluctueerde, h. gefluctueerd) *vi* fluctuate

'fluïdum *o* 1 (g a s, v l o e i s t o f) fluid; 2 (s p i - r i t i s t i s c h) aura

fluim (-en) *v* phlegm, **S** gob; *een ~ van een vent* a squirt

'fluistercampagne [-pɑɲə] (-s) *v* whispering campaign; **'fluisteren** (fluisterde, h. gefluisterd) *vt* & *vi* whisper; *het iem. in het oor ~* whisper it in his ear; *er wordt gefluisterd dat...* it is whispered that...; **–d** whisperingly, in a whisper; **'fluistergewelf** (-welven) *o* whispering gallery; **'fluistering** (-en) *v* whispering, whisper

fluit (-en) *v* flute; *op de ~ spelen* play (on) the flute; **–concert** (-en) *o* concert for flute; **F** *een ~ geven* (u i t j o u w e n) boo, hiss; **'fluiten* I** *vi* whistle [on one's fingers, of a bullet, the wind &]; ♪ play (on) the flute; warble, sing [of birds]; hiss [in theatre]; *je kan er naar ~* you may whistle for it; **II** *vt* whistle [a tune]; **'fluitenkruid** *o* cow parsley; **flui'tist** (-en) *m* ♪ flute-player, flautist, flutist; **'fluitje** (-s) *o* whistle; **'fluitketel** (-s) *m* whistling kettle; **–register** (-s) *o* ♪ flute-stop; **–spel** *o* flute-playing; **–speler** (-s) *m* flute-player, flautist, flutist

fluks quickly

'fluor *o* fluorine

fluores'centie [fly.o.rɛ'sɪn(t)si.] (-s) *v* fluorescence; **–lamp** (-en) *v* fluorescent lamp; **fluores'cerend** fluorescent

fluo'ride (-n) *o* fluoride; **fluori'deren** (fluorideerde, h. gefluorideerd) *vt* fluoridate; **–ring** *v* fluoridation

flu'weel (-welen) *o* velvet; *op ~ zitten* [*fig*] be on velvet; **–achtig** velvety, velvet-like; **flu'welen** *aj* velvet; *met ~ handschoenen* [handle sbd.] with kid gloves; **flu'welig** velvety, velvet-like

flux de 'bouche [fly.də'bu.ʃ] *o* flow of words, gift of the gab

'fnuiken (fnuikte, h. gefnuikt) *vt* destroy, break, clip (the wings of)²; **–d** pernicious

fo'bie (-ieën) *v* phobia

foe'draal (-dralen) *o* case, sheath, cover

foef (foeven) *v*, **'foefje** (-s) *o* trick, **F** dodge

'foei! fie!, for shame!, phooey!

'foelie (-s) *v* 1 mace [of nutmeg]; 2 (tin-)foil [of a looking-glass]

foe'rage [g = ʒ] *v* forage; **foera'geren** (foerageerde, h. gefoerageerd) *vi* forage

foe'rier (-s) *m* quartermaster-sergeant

'foeteren (foeterde, h. gefoeterd) *vi* storm and swear; grumble (at *over, tegen*)

'foetsie *ij* gone, **S** napoo

'foetus [oe = ø:] (-sen) *m* foetus, fetus

föhn [føn] *m* foehn, föhn

fok (-ken) *v* 1 ⚓ foresail; 2 **F** specs: spectacles

'fokhengst (-en) *m* breeding stallion, sire, stud-horse

'fokkemast (-en) *m* foremast

'fokken (fokte, h. gefokt) *vt* breed, rear [cattle]; **-er** (-s) *m* (cattle-)breeder, stock-breeder; **fokke'rij** (-en) *v* 1 (cattle-)breeding, stock-breeding; 2 (stock-)farm; **'fokvee** *o* breeding-cattle

'folder (-s) *m* folder

foli'ant (-en) *m* folio (volume)

'folie *v* foil

'folio ('s) *o* folio

folk'lore *v* folklore

'folteraar (-s) *m* torturer, tormentor; **'folteren** (folterde, h. gefolterd) *vt* put to the rack[2]; *fig* torture, torment; **-ring** (-en) *v* torture, torment; **'folterkamer** (-s) *v* torture chamber

fond [fõ] *o* & *m* background; *fig* bottom; *au* [o.] ~ actually, fundamentally [he is right]

fonda'ment (-en) *o* 1 foundation(s); 2 **F** anus

fon'dant (-s) *m* fondant

fonde'ment (-en) *o* = *fondament*

fonds (-en) *o* 1 $ fund, stock; 2 club; 3 (publisher's) list; *zijn ~en zijn gerezen* his shares have risen; **-dokter** (-s) *m* panel doctor; **-enmarkt** (-en) *v* stockmarket; **-patiënt** [-pa.si.ɛnt] (-en) *m* panel patient; **-praktijk** (-en) *v* panel practice

fo'neem (-nemen) *o* phoneme; **fone'tiek** *v* phonetics; **fo'netisch** phonetic(al)

'fonkelen (fonkelde, h. gefonkeld) *vi* sparkle, scintillate; **-ling** (-en) *v* sparkling, scintillation; **'fonkelnieuw** brand-new

fono'graaf (-grafen) *m* phonograph

fonta'nel (-len) *v* fontanel

fon'tein (-en) *v* fountain[2]; **-tje** (-s) *o* (wall) wash-basin

fooi (-en) *v* tip, gratuity; *fig* pittance; *hem een* (*pond*) ~ *geven* tip him (a pound); **'fooienpot** (-ten) *m* tronc; **-stelsel** *o* tipping system

'foppen (fopte, h. gefopt) *vt* fool, cheat, gull, hoax, S cod; **foppe'rij** (-en) *v* hoax, trickery; **'fopspeen** (-spenen) *v* (baby's) comforter, dummy

for'ceren (forceerde, h. geforceerd) *vt* force [sbd., one's voice, a door, locks, defences]

fo'rel (-len) *v* trout

fo'rens (-en en -renzen) *m* non-resident; ± suburban, commuter; **fo'rensenplaats** (-en) *v* dormitory suburb; **-trein** (-en) *m* suburban train, *Am* commuter train

fo'rensisch ~*e geneeskunde* forensic medicine

fo'renzen (forensde, h. geforensd) **I** *vi* commute; **II** = *mv* v. *forens*

'forma *v* pro ~ for form's sake

for'maat (-maten) *o* format, size[2]; *...van (groot)* ~ [individuals] of large calibre, of great stature,

[problems] of great magnitude, major [figures, problems]; *een denker van Europees* ~ a thinker of European stature

formali'seren [s = z] (formaliseerde, h. geformaliseerd) *vt* formalize; **-ring** (-en) *v* formalization; **forma'listisch** formalist(ic); **formali'teit** (-en) *v* formality

for'matie [-(t)si.] (-s) *v* 1 formation; 2 ✠ establishment; *b o v e n de* ~ ✠ supernumerary; *i n* ~ *vliegen* ✈ fly in formation

for'meel I *aj* formal; ceremonial; **II** *ad* formally; ~ *weigeren* flatly refuse

for'meren (formeerde, h. geformeerd) *vt* form; **-ring** *v* formation

formi'dabel formidable, mighty

for'mule (-s) *v* formula [*mv* ook *formulae*];

formu'leren (formuleerde, h. geformuleerd) *vt* formulate [a wish], word [a notion]; *anders* ~ reword; **-ring** (-en) *v* formulation, wording

formu'lier (-en) *o* 1 form [to be filled up]; 2 formulary [for belief or ritual]

for'nuis (-nuizen) *o* kitchen-range, [electric, gas] cooker

fors robust [fellows], strong [voice, wind, style], vigorous [style]; heavy [defeat, loss]; zie verder *fiks*; **-gebouwd** strongly built; **-heid** *v* robustness, strength, vigour

1 fort (-en) *o* ✠ fort

2 fort [fɔːr] [Fr] *o* & *m* forte, strong point

fortifi'catie [-(t)si.] (-s en -iën) *v* fortification

for'tuin [-'tœyn] 1 *v* fortune [= chance]; 2 (-en) *o* fortune [= wealth]; ~ *maken* make one's fortune; *zijn* ~ *zoeken* seek one's fortune; **-lijk** lucky; **-tje** (-s) *o* 1 small fortune; 2 piece of good fortune, windfall; **-zoeker** (-s) *m* fortune-hunter, adventurer

'forum (-s) *o* forum[2]; (a l s g r o e p d e s k u n d i g e n) panel; (a l s d i s c u s s i e) teach-in; *voor het* ~ *der publieke opinie brengen* bring before the bar of public opinion

fos'faat (-faten) *o* phosphate

'fosfor *m* & *o* phosphorus

fosfores'centie [fɔsfo.rɛ'sɛn(t)si.] *v* phosphorescence; **fosfores'ceren** (fosforesceerde, h. gefosforesceerd) *vi* phosphoresce; **-d** phosphorescent

'fosforzuur *o* phosphoric acid

fos'siel I *aj* fossil; **II** (-en) *o* fossil; **-enkunde** *v* palaeontology

'foto ('s) *v* photograph, **F** photo; (i n k r a n t &) picture; **-album** (-s) *o* photograph album; **foto-e'lektrisch** ~*e cel* photocell, photoelectric cell; **'fotofinish** *m sp* photo-finish; **fotoge'niek** [-ʒe.'ni.k] photogenic; **foto'graaf** (-grafen) *m* photographer; **fotogra'feren** (fotografeerde, h. gefotografeerd) *vt* & *va* photograph; *zich laten* ~ have one's photo

(picture) taken; **fotogra'fie** (-ieën) *v* 1 (d e
k u n s t) photography; 2 (b e e l d)
photo(graph); **foto'grafisch** photographic;
fotogra'vure (-s) *v* photogravure; **fotoko'pie**
(-ieën) *v* photocopy; **fotokopi'eerapparaat**
(-raten) *o* photostat, copier; **fotokopi'ëren**
(fotokopieerde, h. gefotokopieerd); *vt*
photostat, photocopy; **'fotomodel** (-len) *o*
cover-girl; **–montage** [g = ʒ] (-s) *v* 1 (d e
h a n d e l i n g) photo composing; 2 (h e t
g e h e e l) composite picture; **–toestel** (-len) *o*
camera; **–wedstrijd** (-en) *m* photographic
competition
fouil'leren [fu.(l)'je: rə(n)] (fouilleerde, h.
gefouilleerd) *vt* search [a suspect], frisk; **–ring**
(-en) *v* search
four'neren [ou = u.] (fourneerde, h. gefour-
neerd) *vt* furnish
fout (-en) **I** *v* fault; mistake, error, blunder; **II** *aj*
wrong; **fou'tief** wrong; **'foutloos** faultless,
perfect, impeccable
fo'yer [fʋa'je.] (-s) *m* foyer, lobby
fraai beautiful, handsome, pretty, nice, fine; *een*
~e hand schrijven write a fair hand; *dat is ~!*
(i r o n i s c h) that is nice (of you); **–heid**
(-heden) *v* beauty, prettiness &; **'fraaiigheid**
(-heden) *v* fine thing
'fractie ['frɑksi.] (-s) *v* 1 fraction; 2 [political]
group; party; *(in) een ~ van een seconde* **F** (in) a
split second; **–voorzitter** (-s) *m* leader of a
parliamentary group; ± whip [in Britain];
fractio'neel [frɑksi.-] fractional
frac'tuur (-turen) *v* 𝔵 fracture
fra'giel [g = ʒ] fragile; **fragili'teit** *v* fragility
frag'ment (-en) *o* fragment; **fragmen'tarisch**
fragmentary, scrappy [knowledge]
frak (-ken) *m* dress-coat
fram'boos (-bozen) *v* raspberry; **fram'boze-**
struik (-en) *m* raspberry bush
'frame [fre.m] (-s) *o* frame
Fran'çaise [frɑn'sɛ: zə] (-s) *v* Frenchwoman
francis'caan (-canen) *m* Franciscan
'franco 1 ✆ post-free, post-paid, postage paid;
2 $ carriage paid; free [on board &]
franco'foon French-speaking
franc-tir'eur [frãti.'rø: r] (francs-tireurs) *m*
franc-tireur, sniper
'franje (-s) *v* fringe; *fig* frills
1 frank frank; *~ en vrij* frank and free
2 frank (-en) *m* franc
fran'keerkosten *mv* postage [of a letter],
carriage [of a parcel]; **–machine** [-ma.ʃi.nə]
(-s) *v* franking machine; **–zegel** (-s) *m* postage
stamp; **fran'keren** (frankeerde, h. gefrankeerd) *vt* ✆ prepay; (p o s t z e g e l s o p-
p l a k k e n) stamp [a letter]; *gefrankeerd* post-
paid; *gefrankeerde enveloppe* stamped envel-

ope; *onvoldoende gefrankeerd* understamped;
–ring (-en) *v* ✆ prepayment, postage; *~ bij*
abonnement ✆ paid
'Frankrijk *o* France; **'Frans I** *aj* French; **II** *o het*
~ French; *daar is geen woord ~* bij *[fig]* that is
plain English; **III** *v een ~e* a Frenchwoman; **IV**
mv de ~en the French; **–man** (Fransen) *m*
Frenchman; **Fran'soos** (-sozen) *m* **F** Frenchy;
'Franstalig French-speaking
frap'pant striking; **frap'peren** (frappeerde, h.
gefrappeerd) *vt* 1 (t r e f f e n) strike; 2 (k o u d
m a k e n) ice [drinks]
'frase [s = z] (-n en -s) *v* phrase; *holle ~n*
vapourings; **fra'seren** [s = z] (fraseerde, h.
gefraseerd) *vt* & *vi* phrase
'frater (-s) *m* (Christian) brother, friar
'fratsen *mv* caprices, whims, pranks; **–maker**
(-s) *m* buffoon
'fraude (-s) *v* fraud [on the revenue];
frau'deren (fraudeerde, h. gefraudeerd) *vi*
practise fraud(s); **fraudu'leus** fraudulent
frees (frezen) *v* 𝕏 (milling) cutter
'freesia [s = z] ('s) *v* freezia
'freesmachine [-ma.ʃi.nə] (-s) *v* milling
machine
fre'gat [frə-] (-ten) *o* frigate
fre'quent [fre.'kvʌnt] frequent; **frequen'teren**
(frequenteerde, h. gefrequenteerd) *vt* frequent;
fre'quentie [-(t)si.] (-s) *v* frequency, incidence;
–modulatie [-(t)si.] (-s) *v* frequency modulation, F.M.
'fresco ('s) *o* fresco; *al ~ schilderen* paint in
fresco, fresco
fret (-ten) 1 *o* 🐾 ferret ‖ 2 *m* 𝕏 auger
'fretten (frette, h. gefret) *vi* ferret
Freudi'aan(s) [eu = ɔi] Freudian
'freule ['frœ:lə] (-s) *v* honourable miss (lady)
'frezen (freesde, h. gefreesd) *vt* 𝕏 mill; **–er** (-s)
m 𝕏 miller
'friemelen (friemelde, h. gefriemeld) *vi* fumble
fries (friezen) 1 *v* & *o* △ frieze ‖ 2 *o* (s t o f) frieze
Fries I *aj* Frisian; **II** *o het ~* Frisian; **III** (Friezen)
m Frisian
friet (-en) *v = frites*
Frie'zin (-nen) *v* Frisian (woman)
fri'gide [g = ʒ] frigid, sexually unresponsive
frik (-ken) *m* **F** schoolmaster
frika'del (-len) *v* minced-meat ball
fris I *aj* fresh [morning, complexion, wind &],
refreshing [drinks]; cool [room]; *een ~ meisje* a
girl as fresh as a rose; *zo ~ als een hoentje* as fit
as a fiddle, as fresh as paint; *met ~se moed* with
fresh courage; **II** *ad* freshly, fresh; **–drank**
(-en) *m* soft drink
fri'seerijzer [s = z] (-s) *o*, **fri'seertang** (-en) *v*
curling-tongs; **fri'seren** (friseerde, h. gefri-
seerd) *vt* crisp, curl, frizz

'**frisheid** v freshness; coolness; **–jes** a little fresh
frites [fri:t] mv French fried potatoes, French
fries, (potato) chips; **–kraam** (-kramen) v
French-fries stand, chips stand
fri'tuurvet o deep fat; *in ~ bakken* deep-fry
frivoli'té o tatting
frivoli'teit (-en) v frivolity; **fri'vool** frivolous
'**fröbelschool** [ö = ø] (-scholen) v kindergarten
'**frommelen** (frommelde h. gefrommeld) vt
rumple, crumple
frons (-en en fronzen) v frown, wrinkle;
'**fronsen** (fronste, h. gefronst) vt *het voorhoofd
(de wenkbrauwen)* ~ frown, knit one's brows
front (-en) o front, façade; frontage [= 1 front
of a building &; 2 extent of frontal &; 3 expo-
sure]; (i n k o l e n m ij n) (coal-)face; ~ *maken
naar de straat* front (towards) the street; ~
maken tegen zijn vervolgers front one's pursuers;
● *a a n h e t ~* ✗ at the front; *m e t h e t ~ naar...*
fronting...; *v o o r h e t ~* ✗ in front of the line
(of the troops); **fron'taal** ~ *tegen elkaar botsen*
collide head-on; *frontale botsing* head-on collision; '**frontaanval** (-len) m frontal attack
frontis'pice [-'pi.s] (-s) o frontispiece
'**frontje** (-s) o front, S dick(e)y
frot'té o sponge cloth
fruit o fruit
fruiten (fruitte, h. gefruit) vt fry
'**fruitig** fruity [wine]
'**fruitmand** (-en) v fruit basket; **–schaal**
(-schalen) v fruit dish; **–winkel** (-s) m fruit
shop; fruiterer's shop
frus'tratie [-(t)si.] (-(t)si.s) v frustration; **frus'treren**
(frustreerde, h. gefrustreerd) vt frustrate
'**frutselen** (frutselde, h. gefrutseld) vi trifle,
tinker; fumble
'**fuga** ('s) v fugue
fuif (fuiven) v celebration, party, spree, F
beano; *een ~ geven* throw a party; **–nummer**
(-s) o F gay blade
fuik (-en) v trap; *in de ~ lopen* walk (fall) into the
trap
'**fuiven** (fuifde, h. gefuifd) I vi feast, celebrate,
revel, make merry; II vt feast [sbd. (with *op*)],
treat (to *op*)
fulmi'neren (fulmineerde, h. gefulmineerd) vi
fulminate, thunder; ~ *tegen* declaim (inveigh)
against
'**functie** ['füŋksi.] (-s) v function; *in ~ treden*

enter upon one's duties; *in ~ zijn* be in function; *in zijn ~ van* in his capacity of;
functio'naris [füŋksi.-] (-sen) m functionary,
office-holder, official; **functio'neel** functional; **functio'neren** (functioneerde, h.
gefunctioneerd) vi function
funda'ment (-en) o foundation(s);
fundamen'teel fundamental, basal
fun'datie [-(t)si.] (-s en -iën) v foundation;
fun'deren (fundeerde, h. gefundeerd) vt 1
found; 2 $ fund [a debt]; **–ring** (-en) v founda-
tion
fu'nest fatal, disastrous
fun'geren [füŋ'ge:rə(n)] (fungeerde, h. gefun-
geerd) vi officiate; ~ *als* act as, perform the
duties of; **–d** acting, in charge, pro tem
'**furie** (-s en -iën) v fury[2]; **furi'eus** furious
fu'rore v ~ *maken* create a furore
fu'seepen [-'ze.pɪn] (-en) v ✗ kingbolt
fuse'lier [s = z] (-s) m 1 fusilier; 2 ✚ private
(soldier)
fu'seren [s = z] (fuseerde, is gefuseerd) vt & vi
= *fusioneren*; '**fusie** [s = z] (-s) v amalgamation,
fusion, merger; *een ~ aangaan, een ~ tot stand
brengen tussen* amalgamate, fuse
fusil'leren [fy.zi.(l)'je:rə(n)] (fusilleerde, h.
gefusilleerd) vt shoot (down)
fusio'neren [s = z] (fusioneerde, h. gefusio-
neerd) vt & vi amalgamate, fuse
fust (-en) o cask, barrel; *leeg ~* empty boxes,
dummies; *wijn op ~* wine in the wood
fut m & v spirit, F spunk; *de ~ is eruit* F he has
no kick (pep, snap) left in him
futili'teit (-en) v futility
'**futloos** spiritless
futu'risme o futurism; **–ist** (-en) m,
futu'ristisch aj futurist; **futurolo'gie** v
futurology
fuut (futen) m ✍ grebe
'**fysica** ['fi.zi.ka.] v physics, natural science;
'**fysicus** (-ci) m physicist
fy'siek [fi.'zi.k] I aj physical; II (-en) o physique,
physical structure
fysiolo'gie [fi.zi.-] v physiology; **fysio'logisch**
physiological; **fysio'loog** (-logen) m physiol-
ogist
fysiothera'peut [-te:ra.'pœyt] (-en) m physio-
therapist; **–'pie** v physiotherapy
'**fysisch** ['fi.zi.s] physical

G

g [ge.] ('s) v g̊
1 gaaf (gaven) $v = $ gave
2 gaaf *aj* 1 *eig* sound, whole, entire; 2 *fig* pure, perfect, flawless [technique, work of art &]; **–heid** v 1 *eig* soundness, wholeness; 2 *fig* purity, perfectness, flawlessness
gaai (-en) *m* **☙** jay
gaal (galen) v (i n w e e f s e l) thin place
gaan* I *vi* 1 go°; 2 (v ó ó r i n f i n i t i e v e n) go and..., go to...; *ik ging hem bezoeken* I went to see him; *hij ging jagen* he went (out) shooting; ∼ *liggen* zie *liggen*; *zullen wij* ∼ *lopen?* shall we walk it?; *wij* ∼ *verhuizen* we are going to move; *hij is* ∼ *wandelen* he has gone for a walk; *ik ga, hoor!* I am off; *ik ga al* I am going; *ze zien hem liever* ∼ *dan komen* they like his room better than his company; *daar ga je!, daar gaat-ie!* here goes!; *...en hij ging* and off he went, [saying...] he left, he walked away; *hoe gaat het (met u)?* how are you?, how do you do?; *hoe gaat het met uw broer (voet* &) how is your brother (your foot &)?; *hoe gaat het met uw proces (werk)?* how is your lawsuit (your work) getting on?; *het zal hem niet beter* ∼ he will fare no better; *het gaat hem goed* he is doing well; *het ging hem niet goed* things did not go well with him; *hoe is het?, het gaat nogal* pretty middling, not too bad; *hoe is het met je...? o, het gaat (wel)* fairly well; *het stuk ging 150 keer* the play had a run of 150 nights; *dat boek zal wel (goed)* ∼ will sell well; *als alles goed gaat* if everything goes off (turns out) well; *onze handel gaat goed* our trade is going; *deze horloges* ∼ *goed* 1 these watches go well, keep good time; 2 these watches sell well; *het ga je goed!* good luck to you!; *de zee ging hoog* there was a heavy sea on; *het (dat) gaat niet* that won't do (work), it can't be done; *zijn zaken* ∼ *niet* he isn't doing well; *het zal niet* ∼! no go!, **F** nothing doing!; *het gaat slecht* things are going badly; *het ging slecht* things went off badly; *het ging hem slecht* he was doing badly; *zij gingen verder* they walked on; *ga verder!* go on!; *het ging verkeerd* things turned out badly; *zo gaat het!* that's the way of things; *zo is het gegaan* that is how it came about; *het zal wel* ∼ it will go all right; *het ga zoals het gaat* come what may; ● *er a a n* ∼ **F** buy it, be for it, *dat gaat b o v e n alles* that surpasses everything; that comes first (of all); *er gaat niets boven...* there is nothing like... [a good cigar &]; *dat gaat er bij mij niet i n* that won't go down with me; *de weg gaat l a n g s een kanaal* the road runs along a

canal; *h i e r m e e gaat het niet* this will not do; *m e t de pen gaat het nog niet* I (he &) cannot yet manage a (his) pen; *met de trein* ∼ go by train (by rail); ∼ *met* **F** walk' out with [a girl]; *n a a r de bioscoop* ∼ go to the pictures; *waar* ∼ *ze naar toe?* where are they going?; *daar gaat het (niet) o m* that is (not) the point; *daar gaat het juist om* that's just the point; *het gaat om uw toekomst* your future is at stake; *5 gaat 6 keer o p 30* 5 into 30 goes 6 times; *6 op de 5 gaat niet* 6 into 5 will not go; *o v e r Brussel* ∼ go via (by way of) Brussels; *de dokter gaat over vele patiënten* the doctor attends many patients; *het gesprek gaat over...* the conversation is about (on) [war, peace &]; *zij gaat over het geld* she has the spending; *wie gaat erover?* who is in charge?; *wij* ∼ *t o t A.* we are going as far as A.; *zij gingen tot 1000 gulden* they went as high as 1000 guilders; *u i t eten* ∼ dine out; *uit werken* ∼ go out to work; *er v a n door* ∼ zie *ervandoor*; **II** *vt* go; zie 2 *gang* &; **III** *vr zich laten* ∼ let oneself go; **IV** *o* going, walking; *het* ∼ *valt hem moeilijk* he walks with difficulty; **'gaande** going; *de* ∼ *en komende man* comers and goers; ∼ *houden* keep going; *de belangstelling* ∼ *houden* keep the interest from flagging; *het gesprek* ∼ *houden* keep up the conversation; ∼ *maken* stir, arouse, move [sbd.'s pity]; provoke [sbd.'s anger]; *wat is er* ∼? what is going on?, what is the matter?; **gaande'rij** (-en) v gallery; **'gaandeweg** gradually, by degrees, little by little; **gaans** *een uur* ∼ an hour's walk
gaap (gapen) *m* yawn; *de* ∼ the gapes
gaar 1 done [meat]; 2 *fig* clever, knowing [fellows]; *goed* ∼ well-done; *juist* ∼ done to a turn; *niet* ∼ underdone [meat]; *te* ∼ overdone; **–keuken** (-s) v eating-house
'gaarne willingly, readily, gladly; with pleasure; ∼ *doen* 1 like to...; 2 be quite willing to...; *iets* ∼ *erkennen* admit sth. frankly; zie ook: *mogen* &, *graag* **II**
gaas *o* gauze; (k i p p e ∼) wire-netting; **–achtig** gauzy
'gaatje (-s) *o* (small) hole
gabar'dine (-s) v gabardine
Ga'bon *o* Gabon
'gade (-n) 1 *m* husband, consort; 2 v wife, consort
'gadeslaan (sloeg 'gade, h. 'gadegeslagen) *vt* observe, watch
'gading v liking; *alles is van zijn* ∼ nothing comes amiss to him, all's fish that comes to his

net; *het is niet van mijn* ~ it is not what I want
gaf (gaven) V.T. v. *geven*
'**gaffel** (-s) *v* 1 pitchfork, fork; 2 ⚓ gaff;
–**vormig** forked; –**zeil** (-en) *o* ⚓ trysail
'**gage** ['ga.ʒə] (-s) *v* 1 wage(s); 2 ⚓ pay
'**gaine** ['gɪ.nə] *v* girdle
'**gajes** ['ga.jəs] **S** *o* rabble, hoi polloi
gal *v* gall, bile; *zijn* ~ *uitbraken* vent one's bile
[on sbd.]; *de* ~ *loopt hem over* his blood is up;
iems. ~ *doen overlopen* stir (up) sbd.'s bile
'**gala** *o* gala; full dress; *in* ~ in full dress, [dine]
in state; '**gala-avond** (-en) *m* gala night;
'**galadiner** [-di.ne.] (-s) *o* state dinner;
–**kleding** *v* full dress
ga'lant I *aj* gallant; II (-s en -en) *m* intended,
betrothed, fiancé
galante'rie (-ieën) *v* gallantry; ~**ën** fancy goods
galan'tine *v* galantine
'**galappel** (-s) *m* gall-nut
'**galavoorstelling** (-en) *v* gala performance
'**galblaas** (-blazen) *v* gall-bladder; –**bult** (-en) *m*
~**en** hives
ga'lei (-en) *v* ⚓ galley; –**boef** (-boeven) *m*,
–**slaaf** (-slaven) *m* galleyslave; –**straf** *v* forced
labour in the galleys
gale'rie (-s en -ieën) *v* (picture) gallery
gale'rij (-en) *v* gallery°; [Indonesian] veranda(h)
galg (-en) *v* gallows; gallows-tree; *op moord staat
de* ~ murder is a hanging matter; *tot de* ~
veroordelen sentence to death on the gallows;
voor ~ *en rad (voor de* ~) *opgroeien* be heading
straight for the gallows; '**galgebrok** (-ken) *m*
= *galgenaas*; –**humor** *m* grim humour; –**maal** *o*
last meal, parting meal; '**galgenaas** (-azen) *o*
gallows bird, rogue, ruffian; '**galgestrop**
(-pen) *m* & *v* = *galgenaas*; –**tronie** (-s) *v*
hangdog look
gal'joen (-en en -s) *o* galleon
'**gallen** (galde, h. gegald) *vt* take the gall from [a
fish]
galli'cisme (-n) *o* gallicism
'**Gallië** *o* Gaul; –**r** (-s) *m* Gaul
'**gallig** bilious²; –**heid** *v* biliousness²
'**Gallisch** Gallic
galm (-en) *m* sound, resounding, reverberation;
'**galmen** (galmde, h. gegalmd) *vi* 1 sound,
resound; 2 bawl, chant [of persons]; '**galmgat**
(-gaten) *o* belfry window, sound hole
'**galnoot** (-noten) *v* gall-nut
ga'lon (-nen en -s) *o* & *m* (gold or silver) lace,
braid, galloon, piping; **galon'neren** (galon-
neerde, h. gegalonneerd) *vt* lace, braid
ga'lop (-s) *m* 1 gallop; 2 (d a n s) galop; *korte* ~
canter; *in* ~ at a gallop; *in volle* ~ (at) full
gallop; **galop'peren** (galoppeerde, h. gega-
loppeerd) *vi* 1 gallop [of a horse]; 2 galop [of a
dancer]

'**galsteen** (-stenen) *m* gall-stone, bile-stone
galvani'satie [-za.(t)si.] *v* galvanization;
gal'vanisch galvanic; **galvani'seren** [s = z]
(galvaniseerde, h. gegalvaniseerd) *vt* galvanize;
galva'nisme *o* galvanism
'**galwesp** (-en) *v* gall-fly; –**ziekte** (-n en -s) *v*,
–**zucht** *v* bilious complaint
'**Gambia** *o* Gambia
gam'biet (-en) *o* gambit
ga'mel (-len) *v* mess-tin
'**gamma** ('s) *v* & *o* 1 ♪ gamut, scale; 2 (l e t t e r)
gamma; –**stralen** *mv* gamma rays; –**wetenschappen** *mv* ± social sciences
'**gammel** 1 (v e r v a l l e n, w r a k) ramshackle, decrepit; 2 (v e r s l e t e n, a f g e -
l e e f d) worn out; 3 (s l a p, l u s t e l o o s) **F**
seedy
1 **gang** (-en) *m* 1 [subterranean] passage [of a
house], corridor [of a house, train]; 2 alley [=
narrow street]; 3 gallery [of a mine]; **2 gang**
(-en) *m* 1 (v. p e r s o o n) gait, walk; 2 (v.
h a r d l o p e r, p a a r d) pace; 3 (v. a u t o,
t r e i n &) speed, rate; 4 (v. z a a k) progress;
5 (v. z i e k t e, g e s c h i e d e n i s) course,
march; 6 (v. m a a l t i j d) course; 7 ✗ (v.
m a c h i n e) running, working; 8 ✗ (v.
s c h r o e f) thread; 9 (i n h e t s c h e r m e n)
pass; ~ *van zaken* course of things; *de gewone
(normale)* ~ *van zaken* the usual procedure, the
usual course of things, the customary routine;
voor de goede ~ *van zaken* for a smooth running,
for the proper working; *de verdere* ~ *van zaken*
further developments; *er zit* ~ *in (de handeling)*
it is full of go; *ga uw* ~! 1 please yourself!; 2
(t o e m a a r !) go ahead !, go on!; ⚔ **S** carry
on!; *hij gaat zijn eigen* ~ he goes his own way;
laat hem zijn ~ *maar gaan* let him have his way;
alles gaat weer zijn gewone ~ things go on as
usual; ~ *maken sp* ~*en nagaan* watch
sbd., have sbd. shadowed; *ik zal u die* ~ *sparen*
I'll spare you that walk; ● *a a n d e* ~ *blijven* go
on, continue (working &); *aan de* ~ *brengen
(helpen, maken)* set going, start; *aan de* ~ *gaan*
get going, set to work; *aan de* ~ *zijn* 1 (v.
p e r s o o n) be at work; 2 (v. v o o r s t e l -
l i n g &) have started, be in progress; *wat is er
aan de* ~? what is going on?; *hij is weer aan de* ~
he is at it again; *i n volle* ~ *zijn* be in full
swing²; *o p* ~ *brengen* set going, start; *op* ~
houden keep going; *op* ~ *komen* get going; *op* ~
krijgen get going; '**gangbaar** current; ~ *zijn*
pass [of coins]; be still available [of tickets]; **$**
have a ready sale [of articles]; –**heid** *v*
currency; '**gangboord** (-en) *o* & *m* ⚓
gangway; –**loper** (-s) *m* corridor-carpet;
–**maker** (-s) *m sp* pace-maker; –**pad** (-paden)
o 1 path; 2 gangway; 3 (i n k e r k, v l i e g -

t u i g) aisle

gan'green [gɑŋ'gre.n] *o* gangrene, necrosis

'gangspil (-len) *o* capstan

'gangster ['gɛŋstər] (-s) *m* gangster

'gannef (gannefen en ganneven) *m* crook; rogue

1 gans (ganzen) *v* goose[2]; *sprookjes van Moeder de Gans* Mother Goose's tales

2 gans I *aj* whole, all; ~ *Londen* the whole of London [was burnt down]; all London [was at the races]; **II** *ad* wholly, entirely; ~ *niet* not at all

'gansje (-s) *o* gosling, little goose[2]; **'ganze-bloem** (-en) *v* ox-eye (daisy); **–lever** (-s) *v* goose-liver; **'ganzenbord** (-en) *o* game of goose; **'ganzenborden** (ganzenbordde, h. geganzenbord) *vi* play the game of goose; **'ganzenhoeder** (-s) *m* gooseherd; **–mars** (-en) *m* Indian file, single file; **–pas** (-sen) *m* goose step; **'ganzeveer** (-veren) *v* goose-quill

'gapen (gaapte, h. gegaapt) *vi* gape [in amazement, also of oysters, chasms, wounds]; yawn [from hunger, drowsiness]; *een ~de afgrond* a yawning abyss (precipice); **–er** (-s) *m* gaper; **'gaping** (-en) *v* gap, hiatus

'gappen (gapte, h. gegapt) *vt & vi* F pinch, S nab, nip

ga'rage [-ʒə] (-s) *v* garage; **–houder** (-s) *m* garage keeper, garage proprietor

garan'deren (garandeerde, h. gegarandeerd) *vt* warrant, guarantee; zie ook: *gegarandeerd*; **ga'rant** (-en) *m* guarantor; **ga'rantie** [-(t)si.] (-s) *v* guarantee, warrant, security, warranty; *onder ~ vallen* be under warranty; **–bewijs** (-wijzen) *o* warranty

gard (-en) *v* rod

'garde *v* 1 (-s) guard; ‖ 2 (-n) = *gard*; *de koninklijke ~* the Royal Guards; *de oude ~* the old guard

gar'denia ('s) *v* gardenia

garde'robe [-ɾɔːbə] (-s) *v* 1 wardrobe; 2 cloak-room [in a theatre, railway station &]; **–juffrouw** (-en) *v* cloak-room attendant

ga'reel (-relen) *o* harness, (horse-)collar; *in het ~ in harness*[2]; *in het ~ brengen* bring into line

1 'garen (-s) *o* thread, yarn; ~ *en band* haberdashery; *wollen ~* worsted; **2 'garen** *aj* thread

3 'garen = *vergaren*

garen-en-'bandwinkel (-s) *m* haberdashery

garf (garven) *v* sheaf; *in garven binden* sheave

gar'naal (-nalen) *m* shrimp; *een geheugen als een ~* a memory like a sieve; **gar'nalenvangst** (-en) *v* shrimping; **–visser** (-s) *m* shrimper

gar'neersel (-s) *o* trimming; **gar'neren** (garneerde, h. gegarneerd) *vt* trim [a dress, hat &], garnish [a dish]; **–ring** (-en) *v* trimming; garnish [of food]

garni'tuur (-turen) *o* 1 trimming [of a gown]; 2 set of jewels; 3 set of mantelpiece ornaments

garni'zoen (-en) *o* garrison; ~ *leggen in een plaats* garrison a town; *hij lag te G. in ~* he was garrisoned at G; **garni'zoenscommandant** (-en) *m* town major; **–plaats** (-en) *v* ✕ garrison town

'garstig rancid; **–heid** *v* rancidness

garve (-n) *v* = *garf*; **'garven** (garfde, h. gegarfd) *vt* sheave, sheaf

gas (-sen) *o* gas; ~ *geven* open (out) the throttle, **F** step on the gas; ~ *op de plank geven* **F** step on the juice; ~ *terugnemen* throttle down; **–aanval** (-len) *m* gas attack; **–achtig** 1 gaseous [body &]; 2 gassy [smell]; **'gasbel** (-len) *v* = *aardgasbel*; **–brander** (-s) *m* gas-burner, gas-jet; **–buis** (-buizen) *v* gas-pipe; **–fabriek** (-en) *v* gas-works; **–fitter** (-s) *m* gas-fitter; **–fornuis** (-nuizen) *o* gas-cooker (-stove); **–geiser** [-zər] (-s) *m* gas-heater; **–generator** (-s en -toren) *m* gas producer; **–haard** (-en) *m* gas-fire; **–houder** (-s) *m* gas-holder, gasometer; **–kachel** (-s) *v* gas-stove; **–kamer** (-s) *v* gas-chamber [for executing human beings]; lethal chamber [for killing animals]; **–komfoor** (-foren) *o* gas-ring; **–kraan** (-kranen) *v* gas-tap; **–lamp** (-en) *v* gas-lamp; **–lantaarn, –lantaren** (-s) *v* gas-light, gas-lamp; **–leiding** (-en) *v* 1 gas-main [in the street]; 2 gas-pipes [in the house]; **–licht** *o* gas-light; **–lucht** *v* smell of gas, gassy smell; **–masker** (-s) *o* gas-mask; **–meter** (-s) *m* gas-meter; **–motor** (-s en -toren) *m* gas-engine; **–oven** (-s) *m* 1 (i n h u i s h o u d i n g) gas stove; 2 ✕ gas furnace; **–pedaal** (-dalen) *o* & *m* accelerator (pedal); **–pit** (-ten) *v* gas-burner; (g a s a r m) gas bracket; **–rekening** (-en) *v* gas-bill; **'gassen** (gaste, h. gegast) *vt* ✕ gas; **'gasslang** (-en) *v* gas-tube; **–stel** (-len) *o* = *gasfornuis* en *gaskomfoor*

gast (-en) *m* guest; visitor; *stevige ~* robust fellow; *bij iem. te ~ zijn* be sbd.'s guest; **–arbeider** (-s) *m* foreign (immigrant, migratory) worker; **–dirigent** (-en) *m* guest conductor; **'gastenboek** (-en) *o* visitors' book; **gas'teren** (gasteerde, h. gegasteerd) *vi* be starring; **'gastheer** (-heren) *m* host; **–hoogleraar** (-s en -raren) *m* visiting professor; **–huis** (-huizen) *o* hospital; **–maal** (-malen) *o* feast, banquet

'gastrol (-len) *v* star-part

gastrono'mie *v* gastronomy; **gastro'nomisch** gastronomic; **gastro'noom** (-nomen) *m* gastronomer

'gasturbine (-s) *v* gas-turbine

'gastvoorstelling (-en) *v* starring-performance; **'gastvrij, gast'vrij** hospitable; *heel ~ zijn* keep open house; **gast′vrijheid** *v* hospitality; **′gastvrouw** (-en) *v* hostess

′gasverlichting (-en) *v* gas-lighting; **–verwarming** (-en) *v* gas heating; **–vlam** (-men) *v* gas-flame; **–vormig** gasiform, gaseous; **–vorming** (-en) *v* gasification

gat (gaten) *o* hole, opening, gap [in a wall &]; cavity (in tooth); **P** arse; *een ~ > F* a hole [of a place]; *een ~ in de dag slapen* sleep all the morning; *een ~ in de lucht springen* jump for joy; *een ~ stoppen* stop a gap; *het ene ~ met het andere stoppen* rob Peter to pay Paul; *zich een ~ in het hoofd vallen* break one's head; *ergens geen ~ in zien* not see a way out of it, not see one's way to... [do something]; ● *iets in de ~en hebben* have got wind of sth.; **F** have twigged sth.; *iem. in de ~en hebben* have found out sbd; *iem. in de ~en houden* keep one's eye on sbd.; *in de ~en krijgen* get wind of [sth]; spot [sbd.]

gauw I *aj* 1 (v. b e w e g i n g) quick, swift; 2 (v. v e r s t a n d) quick; *ik was hem te ~ af* I was too quick for him; **II** *ad* quickly, quick; soon; in a hurry; *~ wat!* be quick!, hurry up!; *ik kom ~* I'm coming soon; *dat zal hij niet zo ~ weer doen* he won't do that again in a hurry; *zo ~ hij mij zag* as soon as he saw me; **–dief** (-dieven) *m* thief, rogue; **gauwdieve′rij** (-en) *v* thieving; **′gauwigheid** *v* quickness[2], swiftness; *in de ~* 1 in a hurry; 2 in my hurry

′gave (-n) *v* gift[2]

′gaven V.T. meerv. v. *geven*

ga′zel(le) (-len) *v* gazelle

′gazen *aj* gauze

ga′zon (-s) *o* lawn, green; **–sproeier** (-s) *m* (lawn) sprinkler

ge [gə] = *gij*

ge′aard disposed; **–heid** (-heden) *v* disposition, temper, nature

geabon′neerde (-n) *m-v* = *abonnee*

geacciden′teerd [-aksi.-] uneven, hilly [ground]

geache′veerd [ch = ∫] carefully finished, completed, perfected

ge′acht respected, esteemed; *G~e heer* Dear Sir

geadres′seerde (-n) *m-v* addressee; consignee [of goods]

geaffec′teerd affected; **–heid** *v* affectedness, affectation

Gealli′eerden *mv* Allied Powers

ge′armd arm in arm

geavan′ceerd advanced, progressive

geb. = *geboren*

ge′baand beaten [road]; *~e wegen bewandelen* (*gaan*) follow the beaten track

ge′baar (-baren) *o* gesture[2], gesticulation; motion, sign; *gebaren maken* gesticulate, make gestures

ge′babbel *o* chatter, babble, prattle, tattle, chit-chat; (r o d d e l) tittle-tattle, gossip

ge′bak *o* pastry, cake(s), confectionery

ge′bakerd *heet ~* hot-headed

ge′bakje (-s) *o* pastry (ook = *~s*), tart(let)

ge′balk *o* braying, bray

ge′baren (gebaarde, h. gebaard) *vi* gesticulate; motion; **ge′barenspel** *o* 1 gesticulation, gestures; 2 pantomime, dumb-show; **–taal** *v* sign-language

ge′bazel *o* twaddle, drivel, balderdash

ge′bed (-beden) *o* prayer; *het ~ des Heren* the Lord's Prayer; *een ~ doen* say a prayer, pray

ge′bedel *o* begging

ge′beden V.D. v. *bidden*; **ge′bedenboek** (-en) *o* prayer-book; **ge′bedsgenezer** (-s) *m* faith healer; **–riem** (-en) *m* phylactery; **–molen** (-s) *m* prayer wheel

ge′beente (-n) *o* bones

ge′beft with bands

ge′beier *o* chiming, ringing

ge′bekt *goed ~ zijn* have the gift of the gab; zie ook: *vogeltje*

ge′bel *o* ringing

ge′belgd offended (at *over*); **–heid** resentment; anger

ge′bergte (-n en -s) *o* (chain of) mountains

ge′beten V.D. v. *bijten*; *~ zijn op iem.* have a grudge (spite) against sbd.

ge′beurde *het ~* what (had) happened, the happenings, the occurrence(s), the incident; **ge′beuren** (gebeurde, is gebeurd) *vi* happen, chance, occur, come about, come to pass, be; *het is me gebeurd, dat...* it has happened to me that...; *er ~ rare dingen* 1 strange things happen; 2 things come about (so) strangely; *wanneer zal net ~?* when is it to come about (come off, be)?; *dat zal me niet weer ~* that will not happen to me again; *wat er ook ~ moge* happen (come) what may; *het moet ~!* it must be done!; *het zal je ~!* fancy that happening!; *dat gebeurt niet!* you will do nothing of the kind!; *wat ermee gebeurde, is onbekend* what happened to it is unknown; *voor ik wist wat er gebeurde* before I knew where I was; **ge′beurtenis** (-sen) *v* event, occurrence; *een blijde ~* a happy event; *een toevallige ~* a contingency

ge′beuzel *o* dawdling, trifling

ge′bied (-en) *o* territory, dominion; area; [mining] district, [arctic] region; ♓ jurisdiction; *fig* domain, sphere, department, province, field, range; *o p het ~ van de kunst* in the domain (field, realm(s)) of art; *dat behoort niet t o t mijn ~* that is not within my province

ge′bieden (gebood, h. geboden) **I** *vt* command, order,bid; **II** *vi* command, order; *~ over* command; **–d** imperious; imperative [neces-

sity]; *de ~e wijs* the imperative (mood);
ge'bieder (-s) *m* ruler, master, lord
ge'biesd *oranje ~* orange-piped
ge'bint(e) (-en) *o* cross-beams
ge'bit (-ten) *o* 1 (e c h t) set of teeth, teeth; 2
(v a l s) (set of) false teeth, denture(s); 3 (v.
i j z e r) bit [of horses]
ge'blaas *o* blowing; (v. k a t) spitting
ge'blaat *o* bleating
ge'bladerte *o* foliage, leaves
ge'blaf *o* bark(ing)
ge'bleken V.D. v. *blijken*
ge'bleven V.D. v. *blijven*
ge'bloemd flowered
ge'blok *o* plodding, **F** swotting
ge'blokt chequered
ge'blonken V.D. v. *blinken*
ge'bluf *o* boast(ing), brag(ging), **F** swank
ge'bocheld [- 'bɔ̀gəlt] **I** *aj* hunchbacked, humpbacked; **II** *m-v ~e* hunchback, humpback
'**gebod** (-boden) *o* command; *de ~en* 1 the [ten]
commandments; 2 (h u w e l ij k s a f k o n d i -
g i n g) the banns
ge'boden V.D. v. *bieden* & *gebieden*; required,
necessary, called for
ge'boefte *o* riff-raff, rabble
ge'bogen V.D. v. *buigen*
ge'bonden V.D. v. *binden*; bound [books]; tied
[hands &]; latent [heat]; thick [soup, sauce]; *~
stijl* poetic style, verse; *je bent zo ~* it is such a
tie; *niet ~* uncommitted, non-aligned [nations]
ge'bons *o* thumping &, zie *bonzen*
ge'boomte (-n) *o* trees
ge'boorte (-n) *v* birth; *b ij de ~* at birth; *n a de ~*
post-natal; *een Fransman v a n ~* a Frenchman
by birth, [he is] French-born; *een Groninger van
~* a native of Groningen; *–akte* (-n en -s) *v*
birth-certificate; *–dag* (-dagen) *m* birthday;
–datum (-s en -data) *m* date of birth, birthdate; *–grond* *m* native soil; *–huis* *o* birth-
place, house where... was born; *–jaar* (-jaren)
o year of sbd.'s birth; *–land* *o* native land
(country), (o f f i c i e e l) country of birth
ge'boortenbeperking *v* birth-control; *v*
–cijfer (-s) *o* birth-rate; *–golf* (-golven) *v*
(birth) bulge; *–overschot* (-ten) *o* excess of
births; *–regeling* (-en) *v* birth control;
–register (-s) *o* register of births
ge'boorteplaats (-en) *v* birth-place, place of
(one's) birth; *–recht* *o* birthright; *–stad*
(-steden) *v* native town; *zijn ~ Londen* & his
native London &; **ge'boortig** *~ uit A.* born
in (at) A., a native of A.; **ge'boren** born; *hij is
een ~ Fransman* he is a Frenchman by birth; *hij
is een ~ Groninger* he is a native of Groningen;
Mevrouw A., ~ B. Mrs. A., née B., maiden
name B.; *~ en getogen* born and bred

ge'borgen V.D. v. *bergen*; secure; **–heid** *v*
security
gebor'neerd limited, narrow-minded, narrow
ge'borrel *o* 1 (o p b o r r e l e n) bubbling; 2
(d r i n k e n v a n b o r r e l s) tippling
ge'borsten V.D. v. *bersten*
ge'bouw (-en) *o* building, edifice², structure²,
fig fabric
Gebr. = *Gebroeders*
ge'braad *o* roast, roast meat
ge'brabbel *o* gibberish, jabber
ge'bracht V.D. v. *brengen*
ge'braden roasted [potatoes], roast [meat]
ge'bral *o* **F** brag, wind, gas
ge'brand burnt &; zie *branden*; *~ zijn op* be keen
(**F** hot) on [sth.]; be agog [to know...]
ge'bras *o* feasting, revelling
ge'breid knitted; *~e goederen* knitted goods,
knitwear
ge'brek (-breken) *o* 1 (t e k o r t) want, lack,
shortage-(of *aan*); 2 (a r m o e d e) want [=
poverty]; 3 (f o u t) defect, fault, shortcoming;
4 (l i c h a a m s~) infirmity; *~ hebben ~ ~
lijden*; *~ hebben aan* be in want of, be short of;
aan niets ~ hebben want for nothing; *~ lijden*
suffer want, be in want; *~ aan eerbied* disrespect; *~ aan organisatie* inorganization; *er is ~
aan steenkolen* there is a famine in coal; *geen
~ aan klachten* no lack (want) of complaints; •
b ij ~ aan... for want of...; in default of; *bij ~
aan iets beters* for lack of something better; *bij ~
daaraan* failing that, in the absence of such; *i n
~e blijven te...* fail to...; *in ~e blijven te betalen*
default; *u i t ~ aan* for want of; *hij heeft de ~en
zijner deugden* he has the defects of his qualities;
–kelijk infirm, crippled; **ge'brekkig I** *aj* 1
(v. p e r s o n e n) invalid [by injury], infirm
[through age]; 2 (v. z a k e n) defective
[machines], faulty [English]; **II** *ad zich ~
uitdrukken* express oneself badly (imperfectly,
poorly); murder the King's English; **–heid** *v*
defectiveness, faultiness
ge'brild spectacled
ge'broddel *o* bungling, botch
ge'broed *o* brood
ge'broeders *mv* brothers; *de ~ P.* the P. brothers, **$** P. Brothers, P. Bros
ge'broken V.D. v. *breken*; *~ getal* fractional
number, fraction; *~ rib* ☞ ook: fractured rib
ge'brom *o* buzz(ing), humming, drone; growling [of a dog, of a person]; *fig* grumbling
gebrouil'leerd [-bru.(l)'je:rt] on bad terms, not
on speaking terms
ge'bruik (-en) *o* 1 use [of cosmetics, opium &];
2 employment [of special means]; 3 consumption [of food]; 4 custom, usage, habit, practice
[followed in various countries]; *~ maken van*

use, make use of [sth.]; avail oneself of [an offer, opportunity]; *een goed ~ maken van* make good use of [sth.], put [it] to good use, turn [one's time] to good account; *veel (druk) ~ maken van* use freely, make a great use of; ● *b u i t e n ~* out of use; *i n ~ (hebben)* (have) in use; *in ~ nemen (stellen)* put into use; *n a a r aloud ~* according to time-honoured custom; *t e n ~e van* for the use of; *v o o r dagelijks ~* for everyday use, for daily wear; **–elijk** usual, customary; **ge'bruiken** (gebruikte, h. gebruikt) *vt* 1 use, make use of, employ [means]; 2 partake of, take [food, a drink, sugar, the waters]; 3 (v e r b r u i k e n) consume; *hij kan (van) alles ~* he has a use for everything; *ik kan het (hem) niet ~* I have no use for it (for him); *Gods naam ijdellijk ~* **B** take God's name in vain; *wat ~* take (have) some refreshment; *wat wilt u ~?* what will you have?, what's yours?; **–er** (-s) *m* user; **ge'bruikmaking** *v met ~ van* using, by means of; **ge'bruiksaanwijzing** (-en) *v* directions for use; **–goederen** *mv* utility goods; *(duurzame ~)* durable consumer goods; **–klaar** ready (for use); **–voorwerp** (-en) *o* article (thing) of use, useful object; *~en* utilities; **–waarde** *v* utility

ge'bruis *o* 1 effervescence; 2 seething, roaring
ge'brul *o* roaring²
ge'bulder *o* rumbling, booming &, zie *bulderen*; ook: roar
ge'bulk *o* bellowing, lowing &, zie *bulken*
gechar'meerd [ch = ʃ] *~ zijn van* be taken with
gecommit'teerde [-mi.-] (-n) *m* delegate; (b ij e x a m e n) supervisor
gecompli'ceerd complicated [affair]; complex [character, problem, situation &]; compound [fracture]; **–heid** *v* complexity
geconsig'neerde [-si.ɲe:r-] *m* $ consignee
ge'daagde (-n) *m-v* defendant
ge'daan V.D. v. *doen*; finished; *~ geven* dismiss; *~ krijgen* **F** get the sack [of servants]; *ik kan niets van hem ~ krijgen* I have no influence with him; *het (iets) ~ krijgen* bring it off; *het is niets ~* it's no good; *ik kan alles van hem ~ krijgen* he will do anything for me; *het is met hem ~* it is all over (**F** all up) with him; **F** he is done for, he is finished; zie ook: *doen, zaak*
ge'daante (-n en -s) *v* shape, form, figure; *i n de ~ van...* in the shape of...; *zich in zijn ware ~ vertonen* show oneself in one's true colours; *o n d e r beiderlei ~n* in both kinds; *v a n ~ veranderen* change one's shape; *van ~ verwisselen* 1 change one's shape; 2 ook: be subject to metamorphosis [of insects]; **–verwisseling** (-en) *v* metamorphosis
ge'daas *o* balderdash, **S** tosh
ge'dacht V.D. v. *denken*; **ge'dachte** (-n) *v*

thought, idea; reflection; notion; *~n zijn tolvrij* thought is free; *de ~ daaraan* the thought of it; *de ~ alleen al* the mere thought; *de ~ dat ik zo iets zou kunnen doen* the idea of my doing such a thing; *ik heb mijn eigen ~n daarover* I have an idea of my own about it; *zijn ~n erbij houden* keep one's mind on what one is doing; *zijn ~n er niet bij hebben* be absent-minded, be wool-gathering; *zijn ~en erover laten gaan* give one's mind to the subject; just give a thought to the matter; *waar zijn uw ~n?* what are you thinking of?; ● *b ij de ~ aan* when thinking of, at the thought of; *i n ~n* in thought, in spirit; *ik zal het in ~ houden* I'll keep it in mind (remember it); *in ~n verzonken* lost in thought; *in ~n zijn* be (deep) in thought; *o p de ~ komen* hit upon the idea; *hoe is hij op die ~ gekomen?* what can have suggested the idea to him?; *t o t andere ~n komen* change one's mind, come to think differently about the matter; *hij kwam tot betere ~n* better thoughts came to him; *dat is mij u i t de ~ gegaan* it has gone out of my mind; *dat moet je je maar uit je ~n zetten* you must put it out of your mind; *v a n ~ veranderen* change one's mind, think better of it; *van ~n wisselen* exchange views; *van ~ zijn dat* be of the opinion that; *van ~ zijn om...* think of ...ing, mean to...; *zijn ~n verzamelen* recollect one's thoughts, concentrate one's thoughts; **ge'dachteloos** thoughtless; **–heid** *v* thoughtlessness; **ge'dachtenassociatie** [-sja.(t)si.] (-s) *v* association of ideas, thought association; **–gang** (-en) *m* train (line) of thought; **ge'dachtenis** (-sen) *v* 1 (h e r i n n e r i n g) memory, remembrance; 2 (v o o r w e r p ter h e r i n n e r i n g) memento, souvenir, keepsake; *ter ~ van* in memory of; **ge'dachtenlezen** *o* thought-reading, mind-reading; **–loop** (-lopen) *m = gedachtengang*; **–overbrenging** *v* thought-transference; **–reeks** (-en) *v* train of thoughts; **–sprong** (-en) *m* mental leap (jump), mental switch; **–streep** (-strepen) *v* dash; **–vlucht** *v ps* flight of ideas; **–wereld** *v* world of thought; **–wisseling** (-en) *v* exchange of views; **ge'dachtig** mindful (of); *wees mijner ~* remember me [in your prayers]
ge'dartel *o* gambolling, frisking
gedeci'deerd [-de.si.-] firm decided, resolute
gedecolle'teerd [-de.-] décolleté(e), low-necked [dress], [woman] in a low-necked dress
ge'deelte (-n en -s) *o* part, section, piece; instalment; *bij ~n* [pay] in instalments; *v o o r een groot ~* largely; *voor het grootste ~* for the most (greater, better) part; **–lijk I** *aj* partial; *~e betaling* part-payment; **II** *ad* partly, in part
ge'degen 1 native [gold]; 2 (g r o n d i g) thorough [enquiry]; (d e g e l ij k) sound, solid

[knowledge]; (w e t e n s c h a p p e l ij k ~) scholarly [study]

gedege'neerd [-de.-] degenerate; *een* ~e a degenerate

ge'deist F *zich* ~ *houden* lie doggo

gedele'geerde [-de.-] (-n) *m* delegate

ge'demilitari'seerd [s:= z] demilitarized

ge'denkboek (-en) *o* memorial book; ~*en* annals, records; **–dag** (-dagen) *m* anniversary; **ge'denken** (gedacht, h. gedacht) *vt* remember [in one's prayers], commemorate; **ge'denk-jaar** (-jaren) *o* memorial year; **–penning** (-en) *m* commemorative medal; **–plaat** (-platen) *v* (memorial) plaque, table; **–schrift** (-en) *o* memoir; **–steen** (-stenen) *m* memorial tablet (stone); **–teken** (-s en -en) *o* monument, memorial; **gedenk'waardig** memorable; **ge'denkzuil** (-en) *v* commemorative column

gedepo'neerd [-de.-] registered [trade mark]

gedepor'teerde [-de.-] (-n) *m* deportee

gedepu'teerde [-de.-] (-n) *m* deputy, delegate

gedesoriën'teerd [-dɪs-] disoriented

gedetail'leerd [-de.tɑ'je:rt] **I** *aj* detailed; **II** *ad* in detail

gedeti'neerde [-de.-] (-n) *m* prisoner

ge'dicht (-en) *o* poem; **–enbundel** (-s) *m* volume of verse (poems)

ge'dierte (-n en -s) *o* 1 (d i e r e n) animals, beasts; 2 (o n g e d i e r t e) vermin

ge'dijen (gedijde, h. en is gedijd) *vi* thrive, prosper, flourish

ge'ding (-en) *o* 차 lawsuit, action, cause, case; *fig* controversy; *kort* ~ summary proceedings (procedure), proceedings for a rule nisi; *in het* ~ *brengen* argue, bring into discussion; *in het* ~ *komen* come into play; *in het* ~ *zijn* be at issue, be in question, be at stake

gedispo'neerd *ik ben er niet toe* ~ I am not in the mood for it

gedistin'geerd [-tɪŋ'ge:rt] distingué, distinguished; refined [taste]

ge'dobbel *o* gambling², dicing

ge'docht V.D. v. *dunken*

gedocumen'teerd well-documented [report &]; $ documentary [draft]

ge'doe *o* doings, bustle, carryings-on; F brouhaha; *het hele* ~*(tje)* the whole affair, the whole business

ge'dogen (gedoogde, h. gedoogd) *vt* suffer, permit, allow, tolerate

ge'doken V.D. v. *duiken*

ge'dolven V.D. v. *delven*

ge'donder *o* 1 *eig* thunder; 2 *fig* trouble, bother ition

ge'dongen V.D. v. *dingen*

ge'draaf *o* running, trotting (about)

ge'draai *o* turning; wriggling; *fig* shuffling

ge'draal *o* lingering, tarrying, delay

ge'drag (-dragingen) *o* [moral] conduct, behaviour, bearing; [outward] demeanour, deportment [also in chemical experiment]

1 ge'dragen (gedroeg, h. gedragen) *zich* ~ behave, conduct oneself; *zich netjes* ~ behave (oneself)

2 ge'dragen V.D. v. *dragen* en *gedragen*; lofty, exalted, elevated [tone]

ge'dragingen *mv* v. *gedrag*

ge'dragscijfer (-s) *o* ✍ conduct mark; **–lijn** *v* line of conduct, line of action, course, policy; **–patroon** (-tronen) *o* behavioural pattern, pattern of behaviour, pattern of conduct; **–regel** (-s) *m* rule of conduct; **–stoornis** (-sen) *v* behavioural disturbance; **–wetenschappen** *mv* behavioural sciences

ge'drang *o* crowd, throng, crush; *in het* ~ *komen* get in a crowd; *fig* be hard pressed; suffer, be neglected [of discipline &]

ge'drentel *o* sauntering

ge'dreun *o* droning &, zie *dreunen*

ge'dreven V.D. v. *drijven*

ge'dribbel *o* toddling; (v o e t b a l) dribbling

ge'drocht (-en) *o* monster, misgrowth; **–elijk** monstrous

ge'drongen V.D. v. *dringen*; 1 compact, terse [style]; 2 thick-set [body]; *wij voelen ons* ~ *te...* we feel prompted to...

ge'dronken V.D. v. *drinken*

ge'dropen V.D. v. *druipen*

ge'druis *o* noise, roar; hubbub

ge'drukt 1 printed [books, cottons &]; 2 depressed, dejected, in low spirits; 3 $ depressed, weak [of the market]

ge'ducht 1 *aj* formidable, redoubtable, feared; < tremendous [ook = huge]; **II** *ad* fearfully, tremendously

ge'duld *o* patience, forbearance; ~ *overwint alles* patience overcomes all things; ~ *hebben* (*oefenen*) have (exercise) patience; be patient [under trials]; *iems.* ~ *op de proef stellen* try sbd.'s patience; *wij verloren ons* ~ we lost patience; *mijn* ~ *is op, mijn* ~ *is ten einde* my patience is at an end; *met* ~ with patience, patiently; **–ig** patient; **–oefening** (-en) *v* trial of patience; **–werk** *o* work (task) requiring great patience

gedu'peerde (-n) *m-v* sufferer, victim

ge'durende *prep* during, for, ook: pending; over; ~ *twee dagen* for two days (at a stretch); ~ *de laatste vijf jaar* over the last five years; ~ *het onderzoek* pending the inquiry

ge'durfd daring

ge'durig continual, incessant

ge'duvel *o* bother, botheration, nuisance

ge'duw *o* pushing, jostling, elbowing
ge'dwarrel *o* whirling, whirl
ge'dwee meek, docile, submissive
ge'dweep *o* fanaticism; gushing enthusiasm
ge'dwing *o* insistency, insistent begging
ge'dwongen I V.D. v. *dwingen*; **II** *aj* forced [avowal, laugh, loan &]; enforced [absence, idleness]; constrained [manner]; compulsory [service]; **III** *ad* forcedly &; [laugh] in a strained manner; *hij deed het* ~ he did it under compulsion
geef *te* ~ for nothing; *het is te* ~ it is dirt-cheap; **–ster** (-s) *v* giver, donor
geel I *aj* yellow; **II** (gelen) *o* yellow; *het* ~ *van een ei* the yolk; **–achtig** yellowish; **–filter** (-s) *m* & *o* yellow filter; **–gors** (-en) *v* yellowhammer, yellowbunting; **–koper** *o* brass; **–koperen** *aj* brass; **–tje** (-s) *o* S 25-guilders note; **–zucht** *v* jaundice, ☿ icterus
geëmotio'neerd [-(t)ʃjo.-] moved, affected
geen no, none, not any, not one; ~ *van allen* none of them; ~ *ander kan dat* nobody else, no other; ~ *van beiden* neither of them; ~ *cent* not a (red) cent, not a (single) farthing; ~ *één* not a (single) one; *hij kent* ~ *Engels* he doesn't know (any) English; ~ *enkel geval* not a single case; ~ *geld meer* no money left; ~ *geld en ook* ~ *soldaten* no money nor soldiers either; *hij heet* ~ *Jan* he isn't called J.; *dat is* ~ *spelen* (*vechten* &) that is not playing the game, that is not (what you call) fighting; ~ *hunner* none (neither) of them
geëndos'seerde [gɔã-, gɔın-] (-n) *m* $ endorsee
geen'eens not even, not so much as
geënga'geerd [-ãga.'ʒe:rt] 1 engaged; 2 *fig* committed [writer]; **–heid** *v* commitment
'geenszins, geens'zins not at all, by no means
geep (gepen) *v* 🐟 garfish
'geervalk (-en) *m* & *v* gerfalcon
geest (-en) *m* 1 (tegenover lichaam) spirit¹, mind, intellect; 2 (geestigheid) wit; 3 (onlichamelijk wezen) spirit, ghost, spectre, phantom, apparition; [good, evil] genius; *de* ~ *des tijds* the spirit of the age; ~ *van wijn* spirit(s) of wine; *boze* ~*en* evil spirits; *zijn boze* ~ his evil genius; *zijn goede* ~ his good genius; *er heerste een prettige* ~ there was a pleasant atmosphere; *de Griekse* ~ the Greek genius; *een grote* ~ a great mind; *hoe groter* ~, *hoe groter beest* the greater the intellect, the worse the man; *de Heilige Geest* the Holy Ghost; *vliegende* ~ ammonia; ~ *van zout* spirits of salt; *de* ~ *geven* expire, breathe one's last, give up the ghost; *de* ~ *krijgen* be inspired, be in the mood; *er uitzien als een* ~ look like a ghost; ● *in de* ~ *wik bij u* in (the) spirit; *in die* ~ *is het boek geschreven* that is the strain in which the book is written; *in die* ~ *handelen* act

along these lines; *hij maakte nog een paar opmerkingen in deze* ~ in the same strain, to the same effect; *naar de* ~ *zowel als naar de letter* in (the) spirit as well as in (the) letter; *voor de geest brengen* (*roepen, halen*) call to mind, call up before the mind (our minds); *zich weer voor de* ~ *halen* recapture; *het staat mij nog voor de* ~ it is still present to my mind; *voor de* ~ *zweven* zie *zweven*; *de* ~ *is gewillig, maar het vlees is zwak* B the spirit is willing, but the flesh is weak; zie ook *tegenwoordigheid*; **'geestdodend, geest'dodend** dull, monotonous
'geestdrift *v* enthusiasm; *in* ~ *brengen* rouse to enthusiasm; enrapture; *in* ~ *geraken* become enthusiastic; **geest'driftig** enthusiastic(al)
geestdrijve'rij (-en) *v* fanaticism
'geestelijk I *aj* 1 (niet stoffelijk) spiritual [comfort]; 2 (van het verstand) intellectual, mental [gifts, health, hygiene]; 3 (niet werelds) sacred [songs]; religious [orders], clerical, ecclesiastical [duties]; ~*e zaken* things spiritual; **II** *ad* mentally [disturbed, handicapped]; **–e** (-n) *m* clergyman, divine; *rk* priest; ~*n en leken* clerics and laymen; **–heid** *v* clergy, ministry
'geesteloos spiritless, insipid, dull; **'geestenbezweerder** (-s) *m* exorcist; **–bezwering** (-en) *v* exorcism, **–rijk** *o*, **–wereld** *v* spirit world
'geestesgaven *mv* intellectual gifts, mental powers; **–gesteldheid** (-heden) *v* mental condition, state of mind, mentality; **–houding** (-en) *v* mental attitude, mentality; **–oog** *o* mind's eye; **–produkt** (-en) *o* brain child; **–toestand** (-en) *m* = *geestesgesteldheid*; **–stoornis** (-sen) *v* (mental) derangement; **–wetenschappen** *mv* ± humanities; **–ziek** mentally ill (sick); **–zieke** (-n) *m-v* mental patient; **–ziekte** (-n en -s) *v* mental sickness, illness (disease) of the mind
'geestig witty, smart; **–heid** (-heden) *v* wit, wittiness; *geestigheden* witty things, witticisms
'geestkracht *v* energy, strength of mind, intellectual power; **–rijk** witty; ~*e dranken* spirituous liquors, spirits; **geestver'heffend** elevating (the mind); **'geestvermogens** *mv* intellectual faculties, mental powers; **–verruimend** mind-expanding, hallucinogenic [drugs]; **–verrukking** (-en) *v* rapture, trance; **–verschijning** (-en) *v* apparition, phantom; **–vervoering** *v* exaltation, rapture; **'geestverwant I** *aj* congenial; **II** (-en) *m* congenial (kindred) spirit; [political] supporter; **–schap** (-pen) *v* congeniality of mind
geeuw (-en) *m* yawn; **'geeuwen** (geeuwde, h. gegeeuwd) *vi* yawn
geëvacu'eerde [gɔe.-] (-n) *m-v* evacuee

geëxal'teerd over-excited, exaggerated
ge'femel *o* cant(ing)
gefin'geerd [-fɪŋ'geːrt] fictitious [name], feigned; ~*e factuur* $ pro forma invoice
ge'fladder *o* fluttering, flutter, flitting
ge'fleem *o*, **ge'flikflooi** *o* coaxing, wheedling
ge'flikker *o* twinkling, twinkle, flashing, flash
ge'flirt [-'flœːrt] *o* flirting, flirtation
ge'flonker *o* sparkling, sparkle, twinkling; twinkle
ge'floten V.D. v. *fluiten*
ge'fluister *o* whisper(ing), whispers
ge'fluit *o* whistling [of a person, an engine]; warbling, singing [of birds]; hissing, catcalls [in theatre &]
gefortu'neerd rich, wealthy; *de ~en* the rich
ge'gadigde (-n) *m-v* interested party; intending purchaser; would-be contractor; applicant, candidate
ge'galm *o* 1 sound, resounding; 2 bawling; [monotonous] chant
gegaran'deerd guaranteed; (s t e l l i g) definitely, absolutely, **F** and no mistake
ge'geten V.D. v. *eten*
ge'geven **I** *aj* given; *in de ~ omstandigheden* in the circumstances, as things are; **II** (-s) *o* datum [*mv* data]; fundamental idea, subject [of a play &]
ge'giechel *o* giggling, titter(ing)
ge'gier *o* scream(ing)
ge'gil *o* screaming, yelling, screams, yells
ge'ginnegap *o* giggling, sniggering
ge'gleden V.D. v. *glijden*
ge'glommen V.D. v. *glimmen*
ge'goed well-to-do, well-off, in easy circumstances; *de meer ~en* those better off; **–heid** *v* wealth, easy circumstances
ge'golden V.D. v. *gelden*
ge'golfd 1 waved [hair]; 2 corrugated [iron]
ge'gons *o* buzz(ing), hum(ming) [of insects]; whirr(ing) [of wheels &]
ge'goochel *o* juggling[2]
ge'gooi *o* throwing
ge'goten V.D. v. *gieten*; cast [steel, iron]; [*fig*] *het zit als ~* it fits like a glove
ge'grabbel *o* grabbling, scrambling, scramble [for money &]
ge'grepen V.D. v. *grijpen*
ge'grinnik *o* snigger, chortle
ge'groefd grooved [beams]; fluted [columns]
ge'grom *o* grumbling, growling[2]
ge'grond well-grounded, well-founded, just; *dit zijn ~e redenen om dankbaar te zijn* these are strong reasons for gratitude; **–heid** *v* justice; soundness
ge'haaid sharp, knowing, wily
ge'haast hurried [work]; ~ *zijn* be in a hurry

ge'haat hated, hateful, odious
ge'had V.D. v. *hebben*
ge'hakketak *o* wrangling, bickering(s), squabble(s)
ge'hakt *o* minced meat; *bal(letje)* ~ minced-meat ball; **–bal** (-len) *m* meat-ball; **–molen** (-s) *m* mincer
ge'halte (-n en -s) *o* grade [of ore], alloy [of gold or silver], proof [of alcohol], percentage [of fat], standard[2]; *van degelijk* ~ of (sterling) quality; *van gering* ~ low-grade [ore]; *fig* of a low standard
ge'hamer *o* hammering
ge'hard 1 hardened, hardy [of body]; 2 tempered [steel]; ~ *tegen* inured to; **–heid** *v* hardiness, inurement
ge'harrewar *o* bickering(s), squabble(s)
ge'haspel *o* 1 bungling; 2 trouble; zie ook: *geharrewar*
ge'havend battered, dilapidated, damaged
ge'hecht attached; ~ *aan* attached to; **–heid** *v* attachment
ge'heel **I** *aj* whole, entire, complete; ~ *Engeland* the whole of England, all England; *gehele getallen* whole numbers; *de gehele mens* the entire man; *de gehele stad* the whole town; zie verder *heel*; **II** *ad* wholly; entirely, completely, all [alone, ears &]; ~ (*en al*) completely, quite; ~ *of gedeeltelijk* in whole or in part; **III** (gehelen) *o* whole; *een ~ uitmaken* (*vormen*) form a whole; ● *i n h e t* ~ in all...; *in het ~ niet* not at all; *in het* ~ *niets* nothing at all; *in zijn* ~ [the Church &] in its entirety; [swallow it] whole; [look on things] as a whole; *o v e r het* ~ (*genomen*) (up)on the whole; **ge'heelonthouder** (-s) *m* teetotaller, total abstainer; ~ *zijn* **F** be on the water-wagon; **–svereniging** (-en) *v* temperance society; **ge'heelonthouding** *v* total abstinence, teetotalism
ge'heim **I** *aj* secret [door, session, understanding &]; clandestine [trade]; occult [sciences]; private [ballots &]; *het moet ~ blijven* it must remain a secret, it must be kept (a) secret; *je moet het ~ houden* (*voor hen*) keep it (a) secret (from them); *wat ben je er ~ mee!* how secret(ive) (mysterious) you are about it!; *voor mij is hier niets* ~ there are no secrets from me here; **II** (-en) *o* secret, mystery; *publiek* ~ open secret; *een ~ bewaren* keep a secret; *in het* ~ in secret, secretly, in secrecy; **–enis** (-sen) *v* mystery; **–houdend** secret, secretive, close; **–houding** *v* secrecy; **–schrift** (-en) *o* cipher, cryptography; **–taal** (-talen) *v* secret language, code (language); **–zegel** (-s) *o* privy seal; **geheim'zinnig** mysterious; *hij is er erg ~ mee* he is very mysterious about it; **–heid** (-heden) *v* mysteriousness, mystery

ge'helmd helmeted
ge'hemelte (-n en -s) *o* palate
ge'hesen V.D. v. *hijsen*
ge'heugen (-s) *o* memory; *een goed* ~ a strong (retentive) memory; *een slecht* ~ poor memory; *als mijn* ~ *me niet bedriegt* if my memory serves me; *iets in het* ~ *houden* keep (bear) sth. in mind; **–verlies** *o* loss of memory, amnesia
ge'heven V.D. v. *heffen*
ge'hijg *o* panting, gasping
ge'hinnik *o* neighing, whinnying
ge'hobbel *o* jolting
ge'hoest *o* coughing
ge'hol *o* running
ge'holpen V.D. v. *helpen*
ge'hoor *o* 1 (z i n t u i g) hearing; 2 (t o e h o o r-d e r s) audience, auditory; 3 (g e l u i d) sound; *een goed* ~ a good ear for music; *geen* ~ no ear for music; *bij geen* ~ if there's no answer; ~ *geven aan de roepstem van...* give ear to the call of..., obey the call of...; ~ *geven aan een verzoek* comply with a request; ~ *krijgen* get (obtain) a hearing; *ik klopte, maar ik kreeg geen* ~ 1 I could not make myself heard; 2 ook: there was no answer; ~ *verlenen* give an audience, receive in audience; ● *ik was o n d e r zijn* ~ I sat under him (that clergyman); *o p het* ~ *spelen* ♩ play by ear; *t e n gehore brengen* ♩ play, sing; **–apparaat** (-raten) *o* hearing aid; **–beentjes** *mv* the ossicles: anvil (incus), stirrup (stapes), hammer (malleus); **–buis** (-buizen) *v* 1 acoustic duct [of the ear]; 2 ear-trumpet [for deaf people]; **–gang** (-en) *m* auditory canal; **–gestoord** hard of hearing
ge'hoornd horned, cornuted
ge'hoororganen *mv* auditory organs;
ge'hoorsafstand *m binnen* ~ within hearing, within earshot, within call; **ge'hoorzaal** (-zalen) *v* auditory, auditorium
ge'hoorzaam obedient; **–heid** *v* obedience;
ge'hoorzamen (gehoorzaamde, h. gehoor-zaamd) **I** *vt* obey; *niet* ~ refuse obedience, disobey; *hij weet zich te doen* ~ he knows how to enforce obedience; **II** *vi* obey; ⚔ obey orders; ~ *aan* obey, be obedient to; ~*d aan* in obedience to...
ge'hoorzenuw (-en) *v* auditory nerve
ge'horend = *gehoornd*
ge'horig noisy, not sound-proof
ge'hots *o* jolting
ge'houden ~ *zijn om...* be bound to...; **–heid** *v* obligation
ge'hucht (-en) *o* hamlet
ge'huichel *o* dissembling, hypocrisy; **–d** feigned, sham
ge'huil *o* howling [of dogs &], crying [of a child]

ge'huisvest lodged, housed
gehu'meurd *goed* ~ good-tempered (well-disposed); *slecht* ~ ill-tempered
ge'huppel *o* hopping, skipping
ge'huwd *aj* married; *~en* married people (persons, couples)
'geigerteller [ˈgɛigər-] (-s) *m* Geiger counter
ge'ijkt *~e termen* current (standing) expressions
geil 1 rank [of the soil]; 2 lascivious, lewd, hot [of persons]; **–heid** *v* 1 rankness; 2 lascivious-ness, lewdness
gein *m* (g r a p p i g h e i d, p l e z i e r) fun; (g r a p) joke
geïnteres'seerd interested; [watch sth.] with interest; *de ~en* the persons interested, those concerned
geïnter'neerde (-n) *m* internee; *de ~n* ook: the interned
'geintje (-s) **F** ⚓ joke, lark, prank
geïntri'geer *o* scheming, intriguing
'geiser [s = z] (-s) *m* geyser·
geit (-en) *v* 1 (s o o r t n a a m) goat; 2 (v r o u-w e l i j k d i e r) she-goat; *vooruit met de ~!* off you go!, go it!; **'geitele(d)er** *o* goatskin; **–melk** *v* goat's milk; **'geitenhoeder** (-s) *m* goatherd; **–melker** (-s) *m* 🦇 nightjar, goat-sucker; **'geitevel** (-len) *o* goatskin; **'geitje** (-s) *o* 🐑 kid
ge'jaag *o* hunting; *fig* driving, hurrying;
ge'jaagd hurried, agitated, nervous; **–heid** *v* hurry, agitation
ge'jacht *o* hurry(ing), hustling, hustle
ge'jammer *o* lamenting, lamentation(s)
ge'jank *o* yelping, whining, whine
ge'jengel *o* whining, whine
ge'jodel *o* yodelling
ge'joel *o* shouting, shouts
ge'jok *o* fibbing, story-telling
ge'jouw *o* hooting, booing
ge'jubel *o*, **ge'juich** *o* cheering, cheers, shout-ing, shouts

gek I *aj* 1 (k r a n k z i n n i g) mad, crazy, crack-brained, **F** cracked; **S** moony, loony, loopy, nuts, daffy; 2 (o n w i j s) mad, foolish [pranks], nonsensical, silly [remarks]; 3 (v r e e m d) odd, funny, queer, curious; 4 (b e s p o t t e-l i j k) funny, queer; *dat is* ~ that is funny; that is queer; *het is nog zo* ~ *niet* there's something in that; *zo iets ~s* such a funny (queer) thing; ~ *genoeg, hij...* oddly enough, he...; *te* ~ *om los te lopen* too ridiculous; *die gedachte maakt je* ~ the thought is enough to drive you mad; *je wordt er* ~ *van* it's maddening; ~ *opzien (staan kijken)* look foolish, **F** sit up [at being told that...]; ~ *worden* go (run) mad; **S** go off the hooks; ~ *worden op...* run mad after...; *dat ziet er* ~ *uit* it is awkward; *zich* ~ *zoeken* seek till one is half crazy; ● *hij is ~ m e t dat kind* he is mad about the child; *hij is ~ o p zeldzame postzegels* he is mad after (about, on) rare stamps; *~ v a n woede* mad with rage; *het ~ke (van het geval) is* the funny part of it is, the odd thing is; **II** *ad* like a madman; foolishly, oddly, funnily; **III** (-ken) *m* 1 (k r a n k z i n n i g e) madman, lunatic; 2 (d w a a s) fool; 3 (m o d e g e k) fop; 4 (s c h o o r s t e e n k a p) cowl, chimney-cap; *hij is een grote ~* he is a downright fool; *een halve ~* a half-mad fellow; *ouwe ~* old fool; *de ~ scheren (steken) met iem. = voor de gek houden; de ~ steken met iets* make sport of sth.; poke fun at sth.; *iem. voor de ~ houden* make a fool of sbd., make fun of sbd., pull sbd.'s leg; fool sbd.; josh sbd.; *voor ~ spelen* play the fool; *iem. voor ~ laten staan* make sbd. look a fool (foolish); *als een ~ staan kijken* look foolish; *ik heb als een ~ moeten vliegen (lopen)* I had to run like mad; *de ~ken krijgen de kaart* fortune favours fools; *één ~ kan meer vragen dan honderd wijzen kunnen beantwoorden* one fool can ask more than ten wise men can answer

ge'**kabbel** *o* babbling, babble [of a brook]; *het ~ der golven* the lapping of the waves

ge'**kakel** *o* cacling², cackle²

ge'**kanker** *o* **F** grousing, grumbling

ge'**kant** *~ tegen* set against, opposed to, hostile to

ge'**karteld** 1 milled [coins]; 2 ⚬ crenate(d)

ge'**kef** *o* yapping

ge'**keken** V.D. v. *kijken*

ge'**kerm** *o* groaning, groans, moans, lamentation(s)

ge'**keuvel** *o* chat, chit-chat, tattle, gossip

ge'**keven** V.D. v. *kijven*

'**gekheid** (-heden) *v* folly, foolishness, foolery, madness; *Gekheid!* Fiddlesticks!; *het is geen ~* 1 I am not joking; 2 it is no joke; *uit ~* for a joke, for fun; *alle ~ op een stokje* joking apart; *zonder ~* seriously, no kidding; *~ maken* joke; *je moet hier geen ~ uithalen!* no foolery here!; *hij verstaat geen ~* he cannot take a joke

ge'**kibbel** *o* bickering(s), squabble(s)

ge'**kietel** *o* tickling

ge'**kijf** *o* quarrelling, wrangling, dispute

ge'**kir** *o* cooing

ge'**kittel** *o* tickling, titillation

'**gekken** (gekte, h. gegekt) *vi* jest, joke

'**gekkenhuis** (-huizen) *o* madhouse; **–praat** *m* foolish talk, nonsense; **–werk** *o* (sheer) madness

ge'**klaag** *o* complaining, lamentation

ge'**klad** *o* daubing

ge'**klap** *o eig* 1 clapping [of hands]; 2 cracking [of a whip]; *fig* prattle, tattle

ge'**klapper** *o* flapping [of a sail]; chattering [of the teeth]

ge'**klapwiek** *o* flapping of wings, wing-beat

ge'**klater** *o* splash(ing)

ge'**kleed** dressed [persons, dolls]; *geklede jas* frock-coat; *dat staat (niet) ~* it is (not) dressy; *fig* **F** it is (not) the thing

ge'**klep** *o* tolling [of bells]; clatter [of pigeon's wings]; clapping [of storks]

ge'**klepper** *o* clatter(ing); zie ook: *geklep*

ge'**klets** *o* cackle, twaddle; **S** jaw, rubbish, tosh

ge'**kletter** *o* clattering &, zie *kletteren*

ge'**kleurd** coloured; *~ glas* stained glass; *~e platen* colour plates; *er ~ op staan* [*fig*] look a fool

ge'**klik** *o* tale-telling

ge'**klommen** V.D. v. *klimmen*

ge'**klonken** V.D. v. *klinken*

ge'**klop** *o* 1 knocking [at a door]; 2 throbbing [of the pulse]

ge'**klots** *o* dashing, [of the waves], splashing, sloshing

ge'**kluns** *o* **S** bungling, clumsiness

ge'**kloven** V.D. v. *kluiven* en v. *klieven*

ge'**knaag** *o* gnawing

ge'**knabbel** *o* nibbling

ge'**knars** *o* gnashing [of the teeth], grinding

ge'**knepen** V.D. v. *knijpen*

ge'**knetter** *o* crackling

ge'**kneusd** bruised

ge'**kneveld** moustached; zie ook: *knevelen*

ge'**knies** *o* fretting, moping

ge'**knipt** *~ voor* cut out for [a teacher], to the manner born for [the job]

ge'**knoei** *o* bungling &, zie *knoeien*; zie ook: *gekonkel*

ge'**knor** *o* grumbling; grunting, grunt

ge'**knutsel** *o* pottering; zie ook: *knutselwerk*

ge'**kocht** V.D. v. *kopen*

gekon'**fijt** candied

ge'**konkel** *o* intriguing, plotting, intrigues; **F** jiggery-pokery

ge'**korven** V.D. v. *kerven*

ge'**kout** *o* talk, chat(ting)

ge'**kozen** V.D. v. *kiezen*

ge'**kraai** *o* crowing²

ge'**kraak** *o* creaking; *met een luid ~* with a loud crash

ge'**krabbel** *o* 1 scratching; 2 *zijn ~* his scrawl, his scribbling

ge'**krakeel** *o* quarrelling, wrangling

ge'**kras** *o* 1 croaking [of raven], screeching [of owl]; 2 scratching [of a pen]

ge'**kregen** V.D. v. *krijgen*

ge'**kreten** V.D. v. *krijten*

ge'**kreukeld** rumpled, creased, wrinkled

ge'**kreun** *o* groaning, groans, moan(ing)

ge'**kriebel** *o* 1 tickling; 2 = *krabbelschrift*

ge'krijs *o* screeching
gekri'oel *o* swarming
ge'kroesd frizzy, crisp, fuzzy
ge'kromd curved
ge'krompen V.D. v. *krimpen*
ge'kropen V.D. v. *kruipen*
'gekscheren (gekscheerde, h. gegekscheerd) *vi* jest, joke, banter; ~ *met* poke fun at; *hij laat niet met zich* ~ he is not to be trifled with; *zonder* ~ joking apart
ge'kuch *o* coughing
ge'kuip *o* = *gekonkel*
ge'kunsteld artificial, mannered, affected, unnatural; **–heid** *v* artificiality, mannerism
ge'kwaak *o* quack-quack, quacking [of ducks]; croaking [of frogs or ravens]
ge'kwebbel *o* chattering, chatter
ge'kweel *o* warbling
ge'kweten V.D. v. *kwijten*
ge'kwezel *o* cant(ing)
ge'kwijl *o* drivelling², slobber
ge'kwispel *o* (tail-)wagging
ge'laagd stratified; **–heid** *v* stratification
ge'laarsd booted; *de Gelaarsde Kat* Puss in Boots
ge'laat (-laten) *o* countenance, face; **–kunde** *v* physiognomy; **gelaat'kundige** (-n) *m* physiognomist; **ge'laats-** facial; **ge'laats- kleur** *v* complexion; **–trek** (-ken) *m* feature; **–uitdrukking** (-en) *v* facial expression
ge'lach *o* laughter, laughing; mirth; *een homerisch* ~ Homeric laughter
ge'laden (v u u r w a p e n) charged, loaded; (a c c u) charged; *fig* (s f e e r) tense
ge'lag (-lagen) *o het* ~ *betalen* pay for the drinks; *fig* pay the piper; *het is een hard* ~ *(voor hem)* it is hard lines (on him)
ge'lagkamer (-s) *v* bar-room, tap-room
gelamen'teer *o* lamenting, lamentations
ge'lang *naar* ~ [their action was] in keeping; *naar* ~... according as... [we are rich or poor], as... [we grow older, we...]; *naar* ~ *van* in proportion to, according to; *naar* ~ *van omstan- digheden* according to the circumstances of the case; as circumstances may require
ge'lasten (gelastte, h. gelast) *vt* order, charge, instruct; **ge'lastigde** (-n) *m* proxy, delegate, deputy
ge'laten resigned; **–heid** *v* resignation
gela'tine [g = ʒ] *v* gelatine; **–achtig** gelatinous; **–pudding** (-en) *m* jelly
ge'lauwerd crowned with laurel
geld (-en) *o* money; *(afgepast)* zie *afgepast*; *gereed* ~ ready money, cash; ~ *en goed* money and property; *kinderen half* ~ children at half price; *klein* ~ change, small coin; *slecht* ~ bad (base) coin; *vals* ~ counterfeit money; *wegge- gooid* ~ money down the drain; *de nodige* ~*en*

the necessary moneys; *alles draait om het* ~ money makes the world go round; *er is geen* ~ *onder de mensen* there is no money stirring; *goed* ~ *naar kwaad* ~ *gooien* throw good money after bad, throw the helve after the hatchet; *zijn* ~ *in het water gooien (smijten)* throw away one's money, throw one's money down the drain; *het* ~ *groeit mij niet op de rug* do you think I am made of money?; ~ *hebben* have some money, have private means; ~ *hebben als water* have tons of money; *dat zal* ~ *kosten* it will cost a pretty penny; ~ *slaan* coin money; ~ *slaan uit* make money (capital) out of...; ~ *speelt geen rol* money is no object; ~ *stinkt niet* money tells no tales; ~ *stukslaan* make the money fly; *heb je al* ~ *terug?* have you got your change?; ~*en toestaan voor...* vote money towards...; ~ *verdienen als water* coin money; ~ *verkwisten* squander money; *zwemmen in het* ~ be rolling in money; ● *duizend gulden a a n* ~ in cash; *een meisje m e t* ~ a moneyed girl; *het is met geen* ~ *te betalen* it's priceless; *zijn... t e* ~*e maken* convert one's... into cash, realize; *iem.* ~ *u i t de zak kloppen* relieve sbd. of his money, take sbd.'s money off him; *v a n zijn* ~ *leven* live on one's capital (private means); *v o o r geen* ~ *van de wereld* not for the world; *voor* ~ *of goede woorden* for love or money; *een meisje z o n d e r* ~ a moneyless (dowerless) girl; *geen* ~ *geen Zwitsers* nothing for nothing; *het* ~ *moet rollen* money is round, it will roll; ~ *verzoet de arbeid* ± money makes labour(s) sweet; **–adel** *m* moneyed aristocracy; **–belegging** (-en) *v* investment; **–beurs** (-beurzen) *v* purse; **–boete** (-n) *v* (money-)fine; **–buidel** (-s) *m* money-bag; · **–dorst** *m* thirst for money; **–duivel** (-s) *m* 1 demon of money; 2 (v r e k) money-grubber; **–elijk I** *aj* monetary [matters]; pecuniary [considerations], financial [support]; money [contributions, reward]; **II** *ad* financially
'gelden* **I** *vi* 1 (k o s t e n) cost, be worth; 2 (v . k r a c h t zijn) be in force, obtain, hold (good); 3 (b e t r e k k i n g h e b b e n o p) concern, apply to, refer to; *dat geldt niet* that does not count; *dat geldt van (voor) ons allen* it holds good with regard to all of us, it is true of all of us; *het geldt mij méér dan al het andere (dan schatten)* it outweighs all the rest with me; *mijn eerste gedachte gold hem* my first thought was of him; *zulke redenen* ~ *hier niet* do not hold in this case; *zulke redenen* ~ *bij mij niet* carry no weight with me; *die wetten* ~ *hier niet* do not hold (good), cannot be applied here; ~ *als,* ~ *voor* be considered (to be); *deze regeling geldt niet voor personen die...* this scheme does not apply to persons who...; *zijn invloed doen (laten)* ~ assert one's influence, make one's influence felt; *zich*

doen ~ 1 (v . p e r s o n e n) assert oneself; 2 (v . z a k e n) assert itself, make itself felt; *dat laat ik* ~ I grant (admit) that; **II** (o n p e r - s o o n l i j k) *wie geldt het hier?* who is aimed at?; *het geldt hier te...* the great point is...; *het geldt uw leven* your life is at stake; *als het ... geldt* when it is a question of...; *wanneer het u zelf geldt* when you are concerned

'geldgebrek *o* want of money; ~ *hebben* be short of money, be hard-pressed; **–handel** *m* money-trade; **–handelaar** (-s en -laren) *m* money-broker

'geldig valid; ~ *voor de wet* valid in law; ~ *voor een maand na de dag van afgifte* valid (available) for a month after the day of issue; 'geldig- heid *v* validity; **–sduur** *m* period of validity

'geldingsdrang *m ps* need for recognition; desire to be important

'geldkist (-en) *v* strong-box; **–kistje** (-s) *o* cash-box; **–la(de)** (-laden) *v* cash-drawer, till; **–lening** (-en) *v* loan; **–magnaat** (-naten) *m* financial magnate; **–markt** (-en) *v* money- market; **–middelen** *mv* pecuniary resources, means; **F** the where withal; *zijn* ~ ook: his finances; **–nood** *m* shortage of money; *in* ~ *zijn* be short of money, be hard-pressed; **–ontwaarding** *v* inflation; **–sanering** (-en) *v* currency reform; **–schaarste** *v* scarcity of money; **–schieter** (-s) *m* money-lender; **–som** (-men) *v* sum of money; **–soort** (-en) *v* kind of money, coin; **–stuk** (-ken) *o* coin; 'geldswaarde *v* money value, value in money, monetary value; **gelds'waardige pa'pieren** *mv* securities; 'geldverspilling (-en) *v* waste of money; **–wezen** *o* finance; **–wisselaar** (-s) *m* money-changer; **–wolf** (-wolven) *m* money-grubber; **–zaak** (-zaken) *v* money affair; money matter; **–zak** (-ken) *m* money-bag²; **–zending** (-en) *v* remittance; **–zorgen** *mv* money troubles (worries); **–zucht** *v* love of money; **geld'zuchtig** covetous, money-grubbing, mercenary; 'geldzuivering (-en) *v* currency reform

1 ge'leden ago; *het is lang* ~ it is long since, long ago, a long time ago

2 ge'leden V.D. v. *lijden*

ge'lederen *mv* v. *gelid*

ge'leding (-en) *v* 1 articulation, joint [of the bones]; 2 ✕ joint; 3 indentation [of coastline]; 4 *fig* section [of the people]

ge'leed jointed, articulated

ge'leerd learned; *dat is mij te* ~ that is beyond me, beyond my comprehension; **–e** (-n) *m-v* 1 learned man, scholar; learned woman, scholar; 2 [atomic] scientist; **–heid** (-heden) *v* learning, erudition, scholarship

ge'legen V.D. v. *liggen*; 1 lying, situated; 2 convenient; *het is er zó mee* ~ that is how matters stand; *als het u* ~ *komt* if it suits your convenience, at your convenience; *net* ~ at an opportune moment, just in time; *het komt mij niet* ~ it is not convenient (to me) just now; *daar is veel aan* ~ it is of great importance, it matters a great deal; *daar is niets aan* ~ it is of no consequence; *ik laat mij veel aan hem* ~ *liggen* I interest myself in him; *te ~er tijd* zie *tijd*

ge'legenheid (-heden) *v* opportunity; occasion; *er was* ~ *om te dansen* there was a place to dance; *de ~ aangrijpen om...* seize the opportu- nity to... (for..., of ...ing); *iem. (de)* ~ *geven om...* give (afford) sbd. an opportunity to... (for ...ing), put sbd. in the way of...; ~ *geven* (v . p o o i e r) procure, pander; *de* ~ *hebben om...* have an opportunity to... (of ...ing); *(de)* ~ *krijgen* get, find, be given an opportunity (to, of, for); *wanneer hij er de* ~ *toe zag* when he saw his opportunity; *een* ~ *voorbij laten gaan* miss an opportunity; *als de* ~ *zich aanbiedt* when the opportunity offers, when occasion arises; ● *b ij* ~ 1 on occasion, occasionally [I go there]; 2 at the first opportunity [I mean to do it]; *bij een andere* ~ on some other occasion; *bij deze* ~ on this occasion; *bij de een of andere* ~ as oppor- tunity occurs; *bij de eerste* ~ at (on) the first opportunity; *bij de eerste* ~ *vertrekken* sail by first steamer, leave by the next train; *bij elke (iedere)* ~ on every occasion, on all occasions; *bij feestelijke gelegenheden* on festive occasions; *bij voorkomende* ~ when opportunity offers, when occasion arises; *bij gelegenheden ben ik in het zwart* for social events I wear black; *bij* ~ *van zijn huwelijk* on the occasion of his marriage; *iem. i n de* ~ *stellen om...* give sbd. an opportunity to...; *in de* ~ *zijn om...* be in a position to..., have opportunities to...; *o p eigen* ~ on one's own; *p e r eerste* ~ = *bij de eerste* ~; *t e r* ~ *van* on the occasion of; *de* ~ *maakt de dief* opportunity makes the thief; **ge'legenheidsdief** (-dieven) *m* sneak-thief; **–gedicht** (-en) *o* occasional verses; **–gezicht** (-en) *o* face put for the occasion; **–kleding** *v* full dress, formal dress; **–stuk** (-ken) *o* occasional piece

ge'lei [ʒəˈlɛi] (-en) *m & v* 1 (v o o r v l e e s &) jelly; 2 (v . v r u c h t e n) jelly, preserve(s); *paling in* ~ jellied eel(s); **–achtig** jelly-like

ge'leibiljet (-ten) *o* permit; **–brief** (-brieven) *m* safe-conduct

ge'leid guided; *~e economie* planned economy; ~ *projectiel* guided missile

ge'leide *o* 1 guidance, care, protection; 2 ⚓ escort; 3 ⚓ convoy; *mag ik u mijn* ~ *aanbieden?* may I offer to accompany you (to see you home)?; *onder* ~ *van* escorted by; **–hond** (-en) *m* guide-dog (for the blind)

ge'leidelijk I *aj* gradual; II *ad* gradually, by degrees, little by little; *heel* ~ inchmeal; –heid *v* gradualness
ge'leiden (geleidde, h. geleid) *vt* 1 lead, conduct, accompany [persons]; 2 conduct [electricity, heat]; –er (-s) *m* 1 guide, conductor; 2 (w a r m t e, e l e k t r.) conductor; ge'leiding (-en) *v* 1 (a b s t r a c t) leading, conducting; conduction [of electricity, heat]; 2 (c o n c r e e t) conduit, pipe, ⚡ wire; –svermogen *o* conductivity; ge'leidraad (-draden) *m* ⚡ conducting-wire
ge'leken V.D. v. *lijken* en *gelijken*
ge'letterd lettered², literary; ~*e* man of letters; *de* ~*en* ook: the literati
ge'leuter *o* drivel, twaddle, **F** rot
ge'lezen read; *het* ~*e* the things (books &) read
ge'lid (-lederen) *o* 1 joint [of, in the body]; 2 ⚔ rank, file; *de gelederen der liberalen* the ranks of the liberals; *dubbele (enkele) gelederen* ⚔ double (single) files; *de gelederen sluiten* close the ranks; *i n* ~ *opstellen* ⚔ align; *zich in* ~ *opstellen* ⚔ draw up; *in de voorste gelederen* in the front ranks; *u i t het* ~ zie *lid*; *uit het* ~ *treden* leave the ranks, ⚔ fall out
ge'liefd 1 beloved, dear; 2 = *geliefkoosd*; –e (-n) *m-v* sweetheart, beloved, [his] lady-love, inamorata; [her] lover, inamorato; *de* ~*n* the lovers; ge'liefhebber *o* amateurism, dilettantism, dabbling [in politics &]; –koosd favourite; 1 ge'lieven *mv* lovers; ge'lieven (geliefde, h. geliefd) *vt* please; *gelieve mij te zenden* please send me; *als het hem gelieft te komen* when he chooses to come
'gelig yellowish
ge'lijk I *aj* 1 (h e t z e l f d e) similar, identical [things]; [they are] alike, equal, even [quantities]; 2 (g e l i j k w a a r d i g) equivalent; 3 (e f f e n) even, level, smooth; ~ *en gelijkvormig* congruent [triangles]; *dat is mij* ~ it is all the same to me; *mijn horloge is* ~ my watch is right; *wij zijn* ~ we are even (quits); *40* ~ *!* forty all!, [bij tennis] deuce!; ~ *spel* *sp* draw; *twee en drie is* ~ *aan vijf* two and three equal (make) five; *zich* ~ *blijven* act consistently; *ze zijn* ~ *in grootte (jaren)* they are of a size, of an age; ~ *van hoogte* of the same height; zie ook: *maat, munt* &; II *ad* 1 (e v e n m a t i g) equally; 2 (e e n d e r) alike, similarly; 3 (i n g e l i j k e p o r t i e s) equally, evenly; 4 (t e g e l i j k e r t i j d) at the same time; III *cj* as, ⚓ like; IV *o* right; *iem.* ~ *geven* grant that sbd. is right, agree with sbd., back sbd. up; ~ *hebben* be right, be correct;

soms: be in the right; ~ *heb je!* quite right too!, right you are; *hij heeft groot* ~ *dat hij het niet doet* he is quite right not to do it; *hij wil altijd* ~ *hebben* he always wants to know better; ~ *krijgen* be put in the right; *iem. in het* ~ *stellen* declare that sbd. is right; decide in sbd.'s favour; *de uitkomst heeft hem in het* ~ *gesteld* has proved him right, has justified him; zie ook: *gelijke*; **gelijk'benig** isosceles [triangle]; ge'lijke (-n) *m-v* equal; *hij heeft zijns* ~ *niet* there is no one like him, he has no equal; *van 's* ~*n!* (the) same to you!; ge'lijkelijk equally; zie verder *gelijk* II; ge'lijken (geleek, h. geleken) I *vt* be like, resemble, look like; II *vi* ~ *op* be like &; zie ook: 2 *lijken*; ge'lijk- en gelijk'vormigheid *v* congruence; ge'lijkenis (-sen) *v* 1 (o v e r e e n k o m s t) likeness, resemblance [to *met*], similitude; 2 parable; gelijkge'rechtigd having equal rights, equal; –heid *v* equality; gelijkge'zind of one mind, likeminded, consentient; ge'lijkheid *v* 1 equality; 2 parity [among members of a church]; 3 similarity, likeness; 4 evenness, smoothness [of a path, road]; zie ook: *voet*; gelijk'hoekig equiangular; ge'lijklopend 1 (v. l i j n e n) parallel; 2 (v. u u r w e r k e n) keeping good time; gelijk'luidend 1 ♪ consonant; homonymous [words]; 2 of the same tenor, identical [clauses]; ~ *afschrift* true copy; –heid *v* 1 ♪ consonance; 2 conformity; ge'lijkmaken¹ I *vt* equalize [quantities]; 2 level [with], raze [to the ground]; II *vi sp* equalize; –er (-s) *m sp* equalizer; ge'lijkmaking *v* equalization; leveling; gelijk'matig equal, equable, even [temper &]; uniform [size, acceleration]; –heid *v* equability, equableness, evenness, uniformity; gelijk'moedig I *aj* of equable temperament; II *ad* with equanimity; –heid *v* equanimity; gelijk'namig of the same name; having the same denominator [of fractions]; ⚡ similar [poles]; ~ *maken* reduce to a common denominator [of fractions]; ge'lijkrichter (-s) *m* rectifier; ge'lijkschakelen¹ *vt* coordinate; *fig* synchronize; –ling *v* coordination; *fig* synchronization; gelijk'slachtig homogeneous; gelijk'soortig homogeneous, similar; –heid *v* homogeneousness, similarity; ge'lijkspelen¹ *vi sp* draw (a game); –staan¹ *vi* be equal, be on a level; ~ *met* be equal to, be equivalent to, be tantamount to, amount to [an insult &]; be on a level (on a par) with [a minister &]; –stellen¹ *vt* put on a level (on a par); –stelling (-en) *v* equalization; levelling;

---

¹ V.T. en V.D. van dit werkwoord volgens het model: ge'lijkmaken, V.T. maakte ge'lijk, V.D. ge'lijkgemaakt. Zie voor de vormen onder het grondwoord, in dit voorbeeld: *maken*. Bij sterke en onregelmatige werkwoorden wordt u verwezen naar de lijst achterin.

assimilation; **gelijk'straats** at street-level;·
ge'lijkstroom *m* direct current; **–teken** (-s) *o*
sign of equality; **gelijk'tijdig** simultaneous,
synchronous; **–heid** *v* simultaneousness,
simultaneity, synchronism; **gelijk'vloers** on
the ground floor; ~*e kruising* level crossing;
gelijk'vormig of the same form, similar;
–heid (-heden) *v* similarity; **gelijk'waardig**
equal in value, equivalent; equal [members,
partners]; **–heid** (-heden) *v* equivalence;
equality [between the sexes]; **ge'lijkzetten**[1] *vt*
de klok ~ set the clock (right); ~ *met* set by;
hun horloges met elkaar ~ synchronize their
watches; **gelijk'zijdig** equilateral [triangles]
ge'lijnd, gelini'eerd ruled
ge'lispel *o* lisping, lisp
ge'lobd lobed, lobate
ge'loei *o* lowing, bellowing; roaring, roar; wail
[of sirens]
ge'lofte (-n) *v* vow [of chastity, obedience,
poverty], promise; *de* ~ *afleggen rk* take the
vow; *een* ~ *doen* make a vow
ge'logen V.D. v. *liegen*
ge'loken V.D. v. *luiken*; *met* ~ *ogen* with eyes
closed
ge'lonk *o* ogling
ge'loof (-loven) *o* 1 (k e r k e l ij k) faith, creed,
belief [in God]; 2 (n i e t k e r k e l ij k) credit,
credence; trust; belief [in ghosts]; *de twaalf
artikelen des* ~*s* the Apostles' Creed; *het* ~ *verzet
bergen* faith will remove mountains; *een blind* ~
hebben in have an implicit faith in; ~ *hechten*
(*slaan*) *aan* give credence to, give credit to,
believe; *het verdient geen* ~ it deserves no credit;
~ *vinden* be credited; *op goed* ~ on trust;
ge'loofsartikel (-en en -s) *o* article of faith;
–belijdenis (-sen) *v* confession of faith,
profession of faith, creed; *de apostolische* ~ the
Apostles' Creed; **–brieven** *mv* 1 letters of
credence, credentials [of an ambassador]; 2
documentary proof of one's election; **–dwang**
m coercion (constraint) in religious matters,
religious constraint; **–genoot** (-noten) *m*
co-religionist; **–ijver** *m* religious zeal; **–leer** *v*
doctrine (of faith); **–overtuiging** (-en) *v*
religious conviction; **–punt** (-en) *o* doctrinal
point; **–vervolging** (-en) *v* religious persecution; **–verzaker** (-s) *m* apostate, renegade;
–verzaking *v* apostasy; **–vrijheid** *v* religious
liberty; **–waarheid** (-heden) *v* religious truth;
–zaak (-zaken) *v* matter of faith;
geloof'waardig credible [of things]; trustworthy, reliable [of persons]; **–heid** *v* credi-

bility, trustworthiness, reliability
ge'loop *o* running
ge'loven (geloofde, h. geloofd) *vi* & *vt* 1
believe; 2 (m e n e n) believe, think, be of
opinion; *het is niet te* ~! it's incredible!; *je kunt
me* ~ *of niet* believe it or not; *je kunt niet* ~ *hoe...*
you can't think (imagine) how...; *geloof dat
maar!* you can take it from me!; *dat geloof ik!* I
should think so!, I dare say; *ze* ~ *het wel* they
don't bother, they couldn't care less; *iem. op zijn
woord* ~ believe sbd. on his word, take sbd.'s
word for it; ● ~ *a a n spoken* believe in ghosts;
niet ~ *aan* disbelieve in; *hij moest eraan* ~ there
was no help for it, he had to...; *mijn jas moest er
aan* ~ my coat had to go; ~ *i n God* believe in
God; **ge'lovig** 1 believing; 2 earnest [Chris-
tian, prayer]; *de* ~*en* the faithful, the believers;
–heid *v* 1 faith; 2 earnestness
ge'lui *o* ringing, tolling, peal of bells, chime
ge'luid (-en) *o* sound, noise; **–dempend**
sound-deadening; **–demper** (-s) *m* 1 silencer
[of engine, fire-arm]; 2 ♪ mute [for violin,
trumpet], sordine [for violin]; 3 muffler [for
engine, piano]; **–dicht** soundproof; **–gevend**
sounding; **–loos** soundless; **ge'luidsband**
(-en) *m* recording tape, *Am* dictabelt;
–barrière [-bari.ːːrə] (-s) *v* sound barrier,
sonic barrier; **–bron** (-nen) *v* sound source;
–film (-s) *m* sound film, sound picture; **–golf**
(-golven) *v* sound wave; **–hinder** *m* noise
pollution; **–installatie** [-(t)si.] (-s) *v* sound
equipment; **–isolatie** [-zo.la.(t)si.] *v* sound
proofing, sound isolation; **–knal** (-len) sonic
bang, sonic boom; **–leer** *v* acoustics;
–opname (-n) *v* sound recording; **–signaal**
[-si.ɲa.l] (-nalen) *o* sound signal; **–snelheid** *v*
sonic speed, speed of sound; **–spoor** (-sporen)
o sound track; **–technicus** (-ci) *m* sound
engineer, sound mixer; **–trilling** (-en) *v* sound
vibration
ge'luier *o* idling, lazing, laziness
ge'luimd in the mood [for...], in the humour
[to...]; *goed* (*slecht*) ~ in a good (bad) temper
ge'luk *o* 1 (a l s g e v o e l) happiness, felicity [=
intense happiness], bliss; 2 (z e g e n) blessing;
3 (g u n s t i g t o e v a l) fortune, (good) luck,
chance; 4 (s u c c e s) success; *als je* ~ *hebt...*
with some luck...; *wat een* ~! what a mercy!;
stom ~ sheer luck; *dat is nu nog eens een* ~ that is
a piece of good fortune, indeed; *dat ontbrak nog
maar aan mijn* ~ [*iron*] that would be all I'd
need; *een* ~ *bij een ongeluk* a blessing in disguise;
~ *ermee!* I wish you joy of it!; *het* ~ *dient u* you

<hr>

[1] V.T. en V.D. van dit werkwoord volgens het model: **ge'lijk**maken, V.T. maakte **ge'lijk**, V.D. **ge'lijk**gemaakt. Zie
voor de vormen onder het grondwoord, in dit voorbeeld: *maken*. Bij sterke en onregelmatige werkwoorden wordt u
verwezen naar de lijst achterin.

are always in luck; *meer ~ dan wijsheid* more lucky than wise; *zijn ~ beproeven* try one's luck; *~ hebben* be fortunate, be in luck; *het ~ hebben om...* have the good fortune to...; *hij mag nog van ~ spreken* he may thank his lucky stars, he may consider himself lucky; ● *bij ~* by chance; *op goed ~ (af)* at a venture, at random, at haphazard, on the off-chance, **F** on spec; hit or miss; **–aanbrengend** bringing luck, lucky; **–je** (-s) *o* piece (stroke) of good fortune, windfall; **ge'lukken** (gelukte, is gelukt) *vi* succeed; *alles gelukt hem* he is successful in everything; *als het gelukt* if the thing succeeds; *het gelukte hem...* he succeeded in ...ing; *het gelukte hem niet...* ook: he failed to...; **ge'lukkig I** *aj* 1 (v. g e v o e l) happy; 2 (v. k a n s) lucky, fortunate; 3 ⸗goed gekozen &) felicitous; *een ~e dag* 1 a happy day; 2 a lucky day; *een ~e gedachte* a happy thought; *een ~ huwelijk* a happy marriage; *~ in het spel, ongelukkig in de liefde* lucky at play (at cards), unlucky in love; *wie is de ~e?* who is the lucky one?; **II** *ad* 1 (b e - p e r k e n d) [live] happily, 2 (z i n s b e p a - l e n d) = *gelukkigerwijs*; *~!* thank goodness!; **gelukkiger'wijs, –'wijze** fortunately, happily, luckily; **ge'luksdag** (-dagen) *m* 1 happy day; 2 lucky day; **–kind** (-eren) *o* favourite (spoiled child) of fortune, **F** lucky dog; **–nummer** (-s) *o* lucky number; **–poppetje** (-s) *o* mascot; **–ster** [-stɛr] (-ren) *v* lucky star; **–telegram** (-men) *o* greetings telegram, congratulatory telegram; **–vogel** (-s) *m* **F** lucky dog; **ge'lukwens** (-en) *m* congratulation; **ge'lukwensen** (wenste ge'luk, h. ge'lukgewenst) *vt* congratulate (on *met*); wish [a person] good luck; wish [a person] joy (of it *ermee*); **geluk'zalig** blessed, blissful; *de ~en* the blessed; **–heid** (-heden) *v* blessedness, bliss, felicity, beatitude; **ge'lukzoeker** (-s) *m* adventurer, fortune-hunter

ge'lul *o* **F** rot, rubbish, drivel, nonsense

ge'maakt 1 made; ready-made, ready-to-wear [clothes]; 2 affected, pretentious, finical [ways]; **–heid** *v* affectation, mannerism

1 ge'maal (-malen) *o* 1 (h e t m a l e n) grinding; 2 (i n p o l d e r) pumping-engine (-station)

2 ge'maal (-s en -malen) *m* (e c h t g e n o o t) consort, spouse

ge'machtigde (-n) *m* proxy, deputy; (v a n p o s t w i s s e l) endorsee

ge'mak (-ken) *o* 1 (g e m a k k e l ij k h e i d) ease, facility; 2 (r u s t i g h e i d) ease; 3 (g e r i e f) comfort, convenience; *hou je ~!* 1 don't move; 2 keep quiet!; *zijn ~ (ervan) nemen* take one's ease; ● *met ~* easily; *een huis met vele ~ken* a house with many conveniences; *op zijn*

~ at ease; niet op zijn ~ ill at ease; *hij had het op zijn ~ kunnen doen* he might have... and done it easily; *doe het op uw ~* take it easy; take your time; *op zijn ~ gesteld* easy-going; *iem. op zijn ~ stellen* put sbd. at ease; *op zijn ~ winnen* have a walk-over [of a race-horse]; *iem. op zijn ~ zetten* put sbd. at ease; *zit je daar op je ~?* **F** are you quite comfy there?; *v a n z ij n ~ houden* love one's ease, like one's comforts; *van alle moderne ~ken voorzien* fitted with all modern conveniences; *v o o r h e t ~* for convenience('s sake); **ge'makkelijk I** *aj* easy [sums, chairs &]; commodious [house]; comfortable [armchairs]; *zij hebben het niet ~* they are not having an easy time; *hij is wat ~* he likes to take his ease (to take things easy); *hij is niet ~, hoor!* **F** he is an ugly customer to deal with; he is hard to please; *het zich ~ maken* make oneself comfortable, take one's ease; take things easy; *neem een van die ~e stoelen* take one of those easy chairs; **II** *ad* [done] easily, at one's ease, with ease; conveniently [arranged], comfortably [settled]; *~ te bereiken van...* within easy reach of...; *zit je daar ~?* are you comfortable there?; *die stoel zit ~* that is an easy chair; **–heid** *v* facility, ease, easiness, commodiousness, comfortableness; **gemaks'halve** for convenience('s sake); **ge'makzucht** *v* love of ease; **gemak'zuchtig** easy-going

gema'lin (-nen) *v* consort, spouse, lady

gema'nierd well-behaved, well-mannered

gemanie'reerd mannered; **–heid** *v* mannerism

gemari'neerd marinaded [herring]

ge'martel *o* tormenting, torturing

ge'matigd moderate [claims]; measured [terms, words]; temperate [zones]; *de ~en* the moderates; **–heid** *v* 1 moderation; 2 temperateness

ge'mauw *o* mewing

'gember *m* ginger; **–bier** *o* ginger ale, ginger beer

ge'meden V.D. v. *mijden*

ge'meen I *aj* 1 (a l g e m e e n) common, public; 2 (g e m e e n s c h a p p e l ij k) common, joint; 3 (g e w o o n) common, ordinary; 4 (o r d i - n a i r) common, vulgar, low; 5 (s l e c h t i n z ij n s o o r t) bad, inferior, vile; 6 (m i n) mean, base, scurvy; 7 (z e d e n k w e t s e n d, v u i l) obscene, foul, filthy, smutty; *een gemene jaap* an ugly gash; *die gemene jongens* those mean (bad) boys; *een gemene streek* a dirty trick; *gemene taal* foul language, foul talk; *een gemene vent* a shabby fellow, a blackguard, a scamp; *de gemene zaak* the public cause, zie ook: *zaak*; *~ hebben met* have in common with; *iets ~ maken* make it common property; **II** *ad* basely, meanly &; < beastly [cold &]; **III** *o* rabble, mob

ge'meend serious

gemeen′goed *o* common property

ge′meenheid (-heden) *v* 1 meanness, baseness &; 2 mean action, shabby trick

ge′meenlijk commonly, usually

ge′meenplaats (-en) *v* commonplace [expression], platitude, ready-made answer (opinion)

ge′meenschap (-pen) *v* 1 (a a n r a k i n g) *eig* connection, communication², *fig* commerce, intercourse [also sexual]; 2 (m a a t s c h a p) fellowship, community; communion [of saints]; 3 (g e m e e n s c h a p p e l ij k h e i d) community [of interests]; *Europese G~pen* European Communities; *~ hebben met* have intercourse with [persons]; communicate with [a passage &]; *in ~ van goederen* in community of goods; **gemeen′schappelijk I** *aj* common [friend, market, room]; joint [property, interests, statement]; *voor ~e kosten (rekening)* on joint account; **II** *ad* in common, jointly; *~ optreden* act together, act in concert

ge′meenschapsgevoel *o* communal sense; **–huis** (-huizen) *o* community centre; **–zin** *m* sense of community (solidarity)

ge′meente (-n en -s) *v* 1 (b u r g e r l ij k e) municipality; 2 (k e r k e l ij k e) parish; 3 (k e r k g a n g e r s) congregation; **–ambtenaar** (-s en -naren) *m* municipal official; **–bestuur** (-sturen) *o* municipality, [the Mayor and his] corporation; **–huis** (-huizen) *o* town hall; **–lijk** municipal; **–naren** *mv* inhabitants; **–raad** (-raden) *m* town (municipal, parish) council; **–raadslid** (-leden) *o* town councillor; **–raadsverkiezing** (-en) *v* municipal election; **–reiniging** (-en) *v* municipal scavenging department; **–school** (-scholen) *v* municipal school; **–secretaris** (-sen) *m* town clerk; **–verordening** (-en) *v* by-law; **–werken** *mv* municipal works; **–wet** (-ten) *v* Municipal Corporations Act; **–woning** (-en) *v* council-house

ge′meenzaam familiar; *~ met* familiar with; **–heid** (-heden) *v* familiarity

ge′meld (above-)said, above-mentioned

′gemelijk peevish, sullen, fretful, morose

gemene′best (-en) *o* commonwealth

ge′mengd mixed [number, company, marriage]; assorted [biscuits]; miscellaneous; *~ bedrijf* mixed farming; *~e berichten, ~ nieuws* miscellaneous news; *voor ~ koor* ♩ for mixed voices

ge′menigheidje (-s) *o* (bit of) trickery, dirty trick

gemi′auw *o* mewing

ge′middeld I *aj* average, mean; **II** *ad* on an average, on the average; **–e** (-n en -s) *o* average

ge′mier *o* *wat een ~!* bother!, what a bore!, botheration!

ge′mijmer *o* reverie, musing, meditation

ge′mijterd mitred

ge′mis *o* want, lack; *een ~ vergoeden* make up for a deficiency; *het ~ aan...* the lack of...

ge′mocht V.D. v. *mogen*

ge′modder *o* messing in the mud; *fig* bungling; *wat een ~!* what a mess!

ge′moed (-eren) *o* mind, heart; *in ~e* in (all) conscience; *zijn ~ luchten* vent one's feelings, pour out one's heart; *de ~eren waren verhit* feeling was running high

ge′moedelijk kind(-hearted), good-natured, genial; heart-to-heart [talk]; *~ met iem. spreken* have a heart-to-heart talk with sbd.; **–heid** (-heden) *v* kind-heartedness, good nature

gemoede′reerd *dood~* coolly, serenely

ge′moedsaandoening (-en) *v* emotion; **–bezwaar** (-zwaren) *o* conscientious scruple; **–gesteldheid** *v* frame of mind, temper, disposition; **–leven** *o* inner life; **–rust** *v* peace of mind, tranquillity (of mind), serenity; **–stemming** (-en) *v* mood; zie ook: *gemoedsgesteldheid*; **–toestand** (-en) *m* state of mind, disposition of mind, temper

ge′moeid *...is er mee ~* ...is at stake; *...is involved; daar is veel ... mee ~* it takes a lot of...

ge′mok *o* sulking

ge′molken V.D. v. *melken*

ge′mompel *o* mumbling, muttering, murmur

ge′moogd V.D. v. *mogen*

ge′mopper *o* grumbling, **S** grousing

ge′mor *o* murmuring, grumbling

ge′morrel *o* fumbling

ge′mors *o* messing, slopping

gems (gemzen) *v* chamois

′gemsle(d)er = *gemzele(d)er*

ge′mummel *o* mumbling

ge′munt coined; *op wie heb je het ~?* who do you aim at?, who is it meant for?; *hij heeft het op haar geld ~* he is after her money; *hij heeft het altijd al op mij ~* he always picks on me

ge′murmel *o* purl(ing), gurgling, murmur(ing)

ge′mutst *goed (slecht) ~* in a good (bad) temper

′gemzele(d)er *o* chamois, shammy (leather)

gen (genen) *o* gene

ge′naakbaar accessible², approachable²; **–heid** *v* accessibility, approachableness

ge′naamd named, called

ge′nade *v* grace [of God], mercy [from our fellow-men]; 🕀 pardon; *geen ~!* ✕ no quarter!; *goeie (grote) ~!* good gracious!, bless my soul!; *Uwe Genade* Your Grace; *~ voor recht laten gelden* temper justice with mercy; *iem. ~ schenken* pardon sbd.; *(geen) ~ vinden in de ogen van...* find (no) favour in the eyes of...; ● *a a n de ~ van... overgeleverd zijn* be at the mercy of..., be left to the tender mercies of...; *d o o r Gods ~* by the grace of God; *weer in ~ aangenomen worden* be restored to grace (to favour); *o m ~ bidden (smeken)* pray (cry) for mercy; *zich o p ~ of ongenade overgeven* surrender at discretion; *van anderer ~ afhangen* be dependent upon the bounty of others; *z o n d e r ~* without mercy; **–brood** *o* bread of charity, bread of dependence; *hij eet het ~* he eats the bread of charity, he lives upon charity; **–loos** merciless, ruthless; hip and thigh; **–middel** (-en) *o* means of grace; *de ~en der Kerk* rk the sacraments; **–schot** (-schoten) *o* coup de grace, death-blow; **–slag** (-slagen) *m* finishing stroke, death-blow; **ge'nadig I** *aj* merciful, gracious; *een ~ knikje* a gracious (condescending) nod; *God zij ons ~* God have mercy upon us; *wees hem ~* be merciful to him; **II** *ad* 1 mercifully; *er ~ afkomen* get off lightly; 2 graciously, patronizingly, condescendingly

ge'naken (genaakte, is genaakt) *vt & vi* approach, draw near; *hij is niet te ~* he is inaccessible (unapproachable)

gê'nant [ʒə'nɑnt] embarrassing, awkward

ge'nas (genazen) V.T. v. *genezen*

gen'darme [ʒã'dɑrm(ə)] (-n en -s) *m* gendarme; **gendarme'rie** *v* gendarmerie

'gene that, the former; *aan ~ zijde van de rivier* beyond the river; *~ de..., deze de...* the former..., the latter...

genealo'gie [ge.ne.-] (-ieën) *v* genealogy; **genea'logisch** genealogical; **genea'loog** (-logen) *m* genealogist

ge'neesheer (-heren) *m* physician, doctor; *~-directeur* medical superintendent

ge'neeskracht *v* curative power, healing power; **genees'krachtig** curative, healing [properties]; medicinal [springs], officinal [herbs]

ge'neeskunde *v* medicine, medical science; **genees'kundig** medical; *(gemeentelijke) ~e dienst* public health department; *arts van de (gemeentelijke) ~e dienst* medical officer of health; **–e** (-n) *m = geneesheer*; **ge'neeskunst** *v* medecine, medical science

ge'neeslijk curable; **–heid** *v* curability; **ge'neesmethode** [-me.to.-] (-n en -s) *v* therapy; **–middel** (-en) *o* remedy, medicine; **–wijze** (-n) *v* curative (medical) method, method of treatment

ge'negen V.D. v. *nijgen*; inclined, disposed (to...); *iem. ~ zijn* feel favourably (friendly) disposed towards sbd.; **–heid** (-heden) *v* affection, inclination

ge'neigd *~ om te (tot)* ... inclined, disposed, apt to..., < prone to...; **–heid** (-heden) *v* inclination, disposition, aptness, proneness, propensity

ge'nepen V.D. v. *nijpen*

1 gene'raal [ge.-] *aj* general; *generale bas* thoroughbass; zie ook: *repetitie*; **2 gene'raal** (-s) *m* general; **gene'raal-ma'joor** (-s) *m* major-general; **generali'satie** [-za.(t)si.] (-s) *v* generalization, generalizing; **generali'seren** [s = z] (generaliseerde, h. gegeneraliseerd) *vi* generalize; **–ring** (-en) *v* generalization; **genera'lissimus** *m* ✕ generalissimo

gene'ratie [ge.nɔ'ra.(t)si.] (-s) *v* generation

gene'rator [ge.-] (-s en -toren) *m* generator, [gas] producer

ge'neren [ʒ ə -] (geneerde, h. gegeneerd) *vr zich ~* feel embarrassed; *geneer je maar niet!* 1 don't be shy! (there's plenty more); 2 don't stand on ceremony; *geneer u maar niet voor mij* never (don't) mind me; *zij geneerden zich het aan te nemen* they were nice about accepting it; *zij ~ zich zo iets te doen* they are ashamed (think shame) of doing a thing like that

gene'reus [ge.-] generous

ge'nerfd nervate

'generhande, 'generlei no manner of, no... whatever

generosi'teit [ge.-; s = z] *v* generosity

ge'neselijk(-) = *geneeslijk(-)*

ge'netica [ge.-] *v* genetics; **ge'neticus** (-ci) *m* geneticist; **ge'netisch** genetic(al)

Ge'nève [ʒ ə 'nɪ: və] *o* Geneva

☉ **ge'neugte** (-n) *v* pleasure, delight, delectation

ge'neurie *o* humming

ge'nezen* I *vt* cure² [a patient, malaria], heal [wounds, the sick], restore [people] to health; *iem. ~ van...* cure² sbd. of...; **II** *vi* get well again [of persons, wounds]; heal [of wounds]; recover (from *van*) [of persons]; **III** V.D. v. *genezen*; **–zing** (-en) *v* cure, recovery, healing

geni'aal [ge.-] **I** *aj* [man, stroke, work] of genius; brilliant [idea, general]; *iets ~s* a touch of genius; **II** *ad* with genius; brilliantly; **geniali'teit** *v* genius

1 ge'nie [ʒ ə 'ni.] (-ieën) *o* genius; *een ~* a man of genius

2 ge'nie [ʒ ə 'ni.] *v de ~* ✕ the Royal Engineers

ge'niep *in het ~* in secret, secretly, on the sly, stealthily; **–erig, –ig I** *aj* sneaking; **II** *ad = in het geniep*; **–igerd** (-s) *m* sneak

ge'nies *o* sneezing

ge'niesoldaat [ʒ ə -] (-daten) *m* ✕ engineer

ge'nieten* I *vt* enjoy [sbd.'s favour, poor health], savour [a wine &]; *een goede opvoeding genoten hebben* have received a good education; *een salaris ~* receive (be in receipt of) a salary; **II** *vi ~ van* enjoy [one's dinner, the performance]; **III** *va* enjoy it; **–er** (-s) *m* epicurean, sensualist; **ge'nieting** (-en) *v*

enjoyment
ge'nietroepen [ʒə-] *mv* ⚒ engineers
geni'taliën [ge.-] *mv* genitals; **F** (privy) parts
'genitief (-tieven) *m* genitive
'genius (geniën) *m* genius [*mv* genii]
geno'cide [ge.-] *v* genocide
ge'nodigde (-n) *m-v* person invited, guest
ge'noeg enough, sufficient(ly); ~ *hebben van iem.* have had enough of sbd.; ~ *hebben van alles* have enough of everything, have no lack of anything; *er schoon ~ van hebben* **F** be fed up with it; *meer dan ~* more than enough, enough and to spare; ~ *zijn* suffice, be sufficient; *zo is het* ~ ook: that will do; *vreemd ~, hij...* oddly enough, he...; *het moet u ~ zijn, dat ik...* you ought to be satisfied with the assurance that I...; *men kan niet voorzichtig ~ zijn* one cannot be too careful; **-doening** *v* satisfaction, reparation
ge'noegen (-s) *o* pleasure, delight; satisfaction; *u zult er ~ van beleven* it (he) will give you satisfaction; *dat zal hem ~ doen* he will be pleased (with it), be pleased (satisfied) to hear it; *dat doet mij ~* I am very glad to hear it; *wil je mij het ~ doen bij mij te eten?* will you do me the pleasure (the favour) of dining with me?; *zijn ~ eten* eat one's fill; *wij hebben het ~ u mede te delen* we have pleasure in informing you...; *met wie heb ik het ~ (te spreken)?* may I ask whom I have the pleasure of speaking to?; ~ *nemen met* be satisfied with, be content with, put up with; *daarmee neem ik geen ~* I won't put up with that; ~ *scheppen in, (zijn) ~ vinden in* take (a) pleasure in; ● *met* ~ with pleasure; *met alle* ~ I shall be delighted!; *was het n a a r ~?* were you satisfied with it (with them)?; *neem er van naar* ~ take as much (many) as you like; *ik kon niets naar zijn ~ doen* I couldn't possibly please (satisfy) him in anything; *als het niet naar* ~ *is* if it does not give satisfaction; *t e n ~ van...* to the satisfaction of...; *adieu, t o t ~!* good-bye!, I hope we shall meet again!; *tot mijn ~* to my satisfaction; *hij reist v o o r zijn* ~ for pleasure; **ge'noeglijk I** *aj* pleasant, agreeable, enjoyable; contented; **II** *ad* pleasantly; contentedly; **-heid** (-heden) *v* pleasantness, agreeableness; contentedness
ge'noegzaam sufficient; **-heid** *v* sufficiency
ge'noemd 1 named, called; 2 [the person] mentioned, (the) said person
ge'nomen V.D. v. *nemen*
1 ge'noot (-noten) *m* fellow, companion
2 ge'noot (genoten) V.T. v. *genieten*
ge'nootschap (-pen) *o* [learned] society
'genot (genietingen) *o* 1 joy, pleasure, delight; 2 enjoyment; 3 usufruct; ~ *verschaffen* afford pleasure; *onder het ~ van...* while enjoying...;
ge'noten V.T. meerv. en V.D. v. *genieten;*

ge'notmiddel (-en) *o* luxury; **ge'notrijk, ge'notvol** delightful
'genotype [y = i.] (-n) *o* genotype
ge'notziek pleasure-loving; **-zoeker** (-s) *m* pleasure seeker; **-zucht** *v* love of pleasure; **genot'zuchtig** pleasure-seeking
'genre ['ʒãrə] (-s) *o* genre, kind, style
Gent *o* Ghent
genti'aan [gɛn(t)si.'a.n] (-ianen) *v* gentian
1 'Genua *o* Genoa
2 'genua ('s) *v* ⚓ Genoa (jib)
genuan'ceerd differentiated [opinion]
Genu'ees (-nuezen) Genoese [*mv* Genoese]
geode'sie [ge.o.de.'zi.] *v* geodesy
ge'oefend practised, trained, expert
geo'fysica [ge.o.'fi.zi.ka.] geophysics
geo'graaf (-grafen) *m* geographer; **geogra'fie** *v* geography; **geo'grafisch** geographical
geolo'gie *v* geology; **geo'logisch** geological; **geo'loog** (-logen) *m* geologist
geome'trie *v* geometry
ge'oorloofd lawful, allowed, permitted, admissible, allowable
'geowetenschappen *mv* geo-sciences
ge'paard 1 in pairs, in couples, coupled; 2 ⚭ geminate; *dat gaat ~ met...* that is attended by..., that is coupled with...; that involves...; *en de daarmee ~ gaande...* the ... attendant upon it [old age] and its attendant... [ills]
ge'pakt ~ *en gezakt* all ready to depart
ge'pantserd armoured, armour-plated (-clad); ~*e vuist* mailed fist; ~ *tegen* proof against
geparen'teerd related (to *aan*)
ge'past fit, fitting, befitting, proper, suitable, becoming; ~ *geld* zie *afgepast*; **-heid** *v* fitness, propriety, suitability, becomingness
ge'peins *o* musing, meditation(s), pondering; *in diep ~ verzonken* absorbed in thought, in a brown study
gepensio'neerde (-n) *m-v* pensioner
ge'pepen V.D. v. *pijpen*
ge'peperd peppered, peppery; *fig* 1 highly seasoned [stories], spiced [jests]; 2 exorbitant [bills], stiff [prices]
ge'peupel *o* mob, populace, rabble; **F** ragtag (and bobtail)
ge'peuter *o* picking; fumbling
ge'pieker *o* brooding
ge'piep *o* chirping, squeaking
gepi'keerd I *aj* piqued (at *over*); *hij is* ~ he is in a fit of pique; *gauw* ~ touchy; **II** *ad* with a touch of feeling; **-heid** *v* pique
ge'pimpel *o* toping, tippling
ge'pingel *o* haggling
ge'plaag *o* teasing
ge'plas *o* splashing, splash
ge'ploeter *o* splashing; *fig* drudging

ge'plozen V.D. v. *pluizen*
ge'poch *o* boasting, brag(ging)
gepor'teerd ~ *zijn voor* favour, have a liking for
gepo'seerd [s = z] staid, steady
ge'praat *o* talk, tattle
ge'preek *o* preaching, sermonizing, lecturing
ge'prevel *o* muttering, mumbling
ge'prezen V.D. v. *prijzen*
ge'prikkeld irritated, huffish; ...*zei hij* ~ ...he said irritably; **ge'prikkeldheid** *v* irritation
gepromo'veerde (-n) *m-v* graduate
ge'pronk *o* ostentation
gepronon'ceerd pronounced[2]
geproportio'neerd [-pɔrsi.-] [well-, ill-] proportioned
ge'pruikt periwigged
ge'pruil *o* pouting, sulkiness
ge'pruts *o* pottering, tinkering
ge'pruttel *o* 1 simmering [of a kettle]; 2 grumbling [of a person]
ge'raakt hit, touched; *fig* piqued, offended; **-heid** *v* pique, irritation
ge'raamte (-n en -s) *o* skeleton [of animal or vegetable body]; carcass [of ship]; shell [of a house]; frame, framework [of anything]
ge'raas *o* noise, din, hubbub, roar
ge'raaskal *o* raving(s)
ge'radbraakt *zich* ~ *voelen* feel knocked up, feel used up (exhausted)
ge'raden *het* ~ *achten* think it advisable; *het is je* ~ you'd better (do it)
geraffi'neerd 1 refined[2] [sugar; taste]; 2 (s l u w) cunning, crafty; *een* ~*e schelm* a thorough-paced rogue
ge'raken (geraakte, is geraakt) *vi* get, come to, arrive, attain; zie ook: *raken*; *i n gesprek* ~ get into conversation; *i n iems. gunst* ~ win sbd.'s favour; *in verval* ~ fall into decay; *o n d e r dieven* ~ fall among thieves; *t e water* ~ fall into the water; *t o t zijn doel* ~ attain one's end
ge'rammel *o* clanking, rattling
ge'rand edged [lace]; rimmed [glasses]; bordered [parterres]; milled [coins]
ge'ranium (-s) *v* geranium
ge'rant [ʒe:'rã] (-s en -en) *m* manager
ge'ratel *o* rattling
gera'vot *o* romping
1 ge'recht *aj* just, condign [punishment], righteous [ire]
2 ge'recht (-en) *o* 1 ᵫ court (of justice), tribunal; 2 course; [egg &] dish; *voor het* ~ *dagen* summon; *voor het* ~ *moeten verschijnen* have to appear in court; **ge'rechtelijk I** *aj* judicial [murder, sale]; legal [adviser]; ~*e geneeskunde* forensic medicine; **II** *ad* judicially; legally; *iem.* ~ *vervolgen* proceed against sbd., bring an action against sbd.

ge'rechtigd authorized, qualified, entitled
ge'rechtigheid (-heden) *v* justice
ge'rechtsbode (-n en -s) *m* usher; **-dag** (-dagen) *m* court-day; **-dienaar** (-s en -naren) *m* = *politieagent*; **-gebouw** (-en) *o* court house; **-hof** (-hoven) *o* court (of justice); **-kosten** *mv* legal charges; costs; **-zaal** (-zalen) *v* courtroom
ge'redelijk readily
ge'reden V.D. v. *rijden*
gerede'neer *o* arguing
ge'reed 1 ready [money, to do something]; 2 finished [product]; ~ *houden* hold ready, hold in readiness; *zich* ~ *houden* hold oneself in readiness, stand by [to assist]; ~ *leggen* put in readiness, lay out; ~ *liggen* be (lie) ready; (*zich*) ~ *maken* make (get) ready, prepare; ~ *staan* be (stand) ready; ~ *zetten* put ready, set out [the tea-things], lay [dinner]; **-heid** *v* readiness; *in* ~ *brengen* put in readiness, get ready
ge'reedschap (-pen) *o* tools, instruments, implements, utensils; **ge'reedschapskist** (-en) *v* tool-box, tool-chest, kit; **-maker** (-s) *m* tool maker
gerefor'meerd Calvinist; *de* ~*en* the Calvinists
ge'regeld I *aj* regular, orderly, fixed; ~*e veldslag* pitched battle; **II** *ad* regularly; **-heid** *v* regularity
ge'regen V.D. v. *rijgen*
ge'rei *o* things [for tea &], tackle [for shaving &]; [fishing] gear
ge'reis *o* travelling
ge'rekt long-drawn(-out), long-winded, protracted; *ietwat* ~ *ook:* lengthy
ge'remd *ps* inhibited; **-heid** (-heden) *v ps* inhibition
1 'geren (geerde, h. gegeerd) **I** *vi* slant; (v. r o k) flare; **II** *vt* gore
2 ge'ren *o* running
gerenom'meerd famous, renowned
gerepatri'eerde [-re.pa.-] (-n) *m-v* repatriate
gereser'veerd [s = z] reserved[2]; **-heid** *v* reserve
ge'reten V.D. v. *rijten*
ge'reutel *o* [dying man's] death-rattle
ge'rezen V.D. v. *rijzen*
geri'ater [ge:-] (-s) *m* geriatrician; **geria'trie** *v* geriatrics; **geri'atrisch** geriatric
ge'ribd ribbed
ge'richt *o het jongste* ~ judgment day
ge'rief *o* convenience, comfort; *veel* ~ *bieden* offer many comforts; *ten gerieve van...* for the convenience of...; **ge'rief(e)lijk** commodious, convenient, comfortable
ge'rieven (geriefde, h. geriefd) *vt* accommodate, oblige [persons]
ge'rijmel *o* rhyming

ge'ring small, scanty, slight, trifling, inconsiderable; low; *van niet ~e bekwaamheid* of no mean ability; *een ~e dunk hebben van* have a poor opinion of; *een ~e kans* a slender chance, a slim chance; *met ~ succes* with scant success; **–heid** *v* smallness, scantiness; **–schatten** (schatte ge'ring, h. ge'ringgeschat) *vt* hold cheap, have a low opinion of, disparage; **–schattend** slighting; **–schatting** *v* disdain, disregard, slight

ge'rinkel *o* jingling

ge'ritsel *o* rustling, rustle

Ger'maan (-manen) *m* Teuton; **–s** Teutonic, Germanic; **Ger'manië** *o* Germany; **germa-'nisme** (-n) *o* germanism; **germa'nist** (-en) *m* Germanist

ge'rochel *o* death-rattle

ge'roddel *o* talk, gossip

ge'roep *o* calling, shouting, shouts, call

ge'roerd touched; moved [person]

ge'roezemoes *o* bustle; buzz(ing), hubbub

ge'roffel *o* roll, rub-a-dub [of a drum]

ge'roken V.D. v. *rieken* en v. *ruiken*

ge'rol *o* rolling

ge'rommel *o* rumbling [of a cart, of thunder]

ge'ronk *o* snoring [of a sleeper]; snorting [of an engine], drone [of aircraft], zie *ronken*

ge'ronnen curdled [milk], clotted [blood]

gerontolo'gie [ge:-] *v* gerontology; **geronto'loog** (-logen) *m* gerontologist

gerouti'neerd [ou = u.] (thoroughly) experienced, expert, practised

gerst *v* barley; **'gerstekorrel** (-s) *m* 1 barleycorn; 2 (g e z w e l a a n o o g l i d) sty; 3 (w e e f s e l) huckaback; **'gerstkorrel** (-s) *m* = *gerstekorrel*

ge'rucht (-en) *o* rumour, report, whisper; noise; *er loopt een ~ dat...* it is rumoured that...; *~ maken* make a noise; *het (een) ~ verspreiden (dat)...* spread a rumour, noise it abroad (that)...; ● *bij ~e* [know] by (from) hearsay; *i n een kwaad ~ staan* be in bad repute; *hij is v o o r geen klein ~(je) vervaard* he is not easily frightened; **–makend** sensational

ge'rug(ge)steund backed (up), supported (by)

ge'ruim *een ~e tijd* a long time, a considerable time

ge'ruis *o* noise [of moving thing], rustling, rustle [of a dress, leaf], murmur [of a stream], rushing [of a torrent]; **–loos** noiseless, silent

ge'ruit checked, chequered

ge'rust I *aj* quiet; easy; *u kunt er ~ op zijn dat...* you may rest assured that...; *wees daar maar ~ op* make your mind easy on that point (about that); *ik ben er niet ~ op* I feel uneasy about it, I have some misgivings; **II** *ad* [sleep] quietly; *ik durf ~ beweren, dat...* I venture to say that...; *u*

kunt er ~ heengaan without fear; *zij kunnen ~ wegblijven* they may stay away and welcome; *u kunt ~ zeggen, dat...* you may freely say (say with a clear conscience) that...; *wij kunnen dat ~ zeggen* we may safely say that; **–heid** *v* peace of mind, tranquillity; **–stellen** (stelde ge'rust, h. ge'rustgesteld) *vt* set [sbd.'s mind] at rest (at ease), reassure [sbd.]; **–stellend** reassuring; **–stelling** (-en) *v* reassurance

ge'sar *o* teasing

ge'schal *o* shouting, sound [of voices]; clang [of a horn]

ge'schapen V.D. v. *scheppen*

ge'scharrel *o* scraping &, zie *scharrelen*

ge'schater *o* burst (shout) of laughter; *hun ~* their peals of laughter

ge'scheiden separated [gardens]; divided [into parts]; divorced [women]; [living] apart

ge'schel *o* ringing

ge'scheld *o* abuse (of *op*)

ge'schenen V.D. v. *schijnen*

ge'schenk (-en) *o* present, gift; *iets ten ~e geven* make a present of sth., present (sbd.) with sth.; **–bon** (-s en -nen) *m* gift voucher, gift token; **–zending** (-en) *v* gift parcel

ge'scherm *o* fencing, zie *schermen*

gescher'mutsel *o* skirmishing

ge'scherts *o* joking, banter

ge'scheten V.D. v. *schijten*

ge'schetter *o* flourish, blare; *fig* bragging

ge'schiedboeken *mv* annals, records

ge'schieden (geschiedde, is geschied) *vi* happen, come to pass, occur, chance; befall, take place; *Uw wil geschiede* Thy will be done!

ge'schiedenis (-sen) *v* history; story; *de hele ~* the whole affair; *een mooie ~!* a pretty story!, a pretty kettle of fish!; *het is weer de oude ~* it is the old story over again; *een rare ~* a queer story; *het is een saaie (taaie) ~* it is a flat affair, a tedious business; *dat zal spoedig tot de ~ behoren* that will soon be a thing of the past; **–boek** (-en) *o* history book; **ge'schiedkunde** *v* history; **geschied'kundig** historical; **–e** (-n) *m* historian; **ge'schiedrol** (-len) *v* record, archives; **–schrijver** *mv* historical writer, historian, historiographer [= official historian]; **–schrijving** *v* writing of history, historiography

ge'schift F crack-brained, dotty

ge'schikt fit [person, to do..., to be..., for...]; able, capable, efficient [man, servant &]; suitable, suited [to or for the purpose], appropriate [to the occasion]; practical [solution]; eligible [candidate], proper [time, way]; *een ~e vent* F a decent chap; *~ zijn voor* lend oneself (itself) [to the purpose, the occasion]; make a good [teacher]; *dat is er niet ~ voor* that's no good; **–heid** *v* fitness, capability, ability; suitability

ge'schil (-len) *o* difference, dispute, quarrel; **–punt** (-en) *o* point (matter) at issue, point of difference

ge'schimp *o* scoffing, abuse

ge'schitter *o* glitter(ing)

ge'schok *o* jolting, shaking

ge'scholden V.D. v. *schelden*

ge'scholen V.D. v. *schuilen*

ge'schommel *o* swinging &, zie *schommelen*

ge'schonden V.D. v. *schenden*

ge'schonken V.D. v. *schenken*

ge'schoold trained [voices &], skilled [labourers]

ge'schop *o* kicking

ge'schoren V.D. v. *scheren*

ge'schoten V.D. v. *schieten*

ge'schoven V.D. v. *schuiven*

ge'schraap *o* 1 scraping [on the violin]; 2 throat-clearing; 3 *fig* money-grubbing

ge'schreden V.D. v. *schrijden*

ge'schreeuw *o* cry, cries, shrieks, shouts; *veel ~ en weinig wol* much ado about nothing

ge'schrei *o* weeping, crying

ge'schreven V.D. v. *schrijven*

ge'schrift (-en) *o* 1 writing; 2 document, letter, paper &; *in ~e* in writing; zie ook: *valsheid*

ge'schrijf *o* scribbling, writing

ge'schrokken V.D. v. *schrikken*

ge'schubd scaled, scaly

ge'schuifel *o* shuffling, scraping [of feet]

ge'schut *o* artillery, guns, ordnance; *grof ~* heavy artillery, heavy guns[2]; *licht ~* light artillery; *een stuk ~* a piece of ordnance; *het zware ~* the heavy guns; **–koepel** (-s) *m* (gun-)turret; **–poort** (-en) *v* porthole; **–toren** (-s) *m* (gun-)turret; **–vuur** *o* gunfire

'gesel (-en en -s) *m* scourge[2] [of war, of God], lash[2] [of satire]; **'geselen** (geselde, h. gegeseld) *vt* lash[2], scourge[2], flagellate, whip; *it* flog; **–ling** (-en) *v* lashing[2], scourging[2], flagellation, whipping; *it* flogging; **'geselkoord** (-en) *o* & *v* lash; **–paal** (-palen) *m* whipping-post; **–roede** (-n) *v* scourge[2], lash[2]; **–slag** (-slagen) *m* lash; **–straf** (-fen) *v* lashing, whipping; *it* flogging

geser'reerd terse, succinct

ge'sis *o* hissing

gesitu'eerd *beter ~* well-(better-)off; *de beter ~en* the better-off, the more substantial class; *de minder ~en* the less well-to-do

ge'sjachel [-ʃɑ-] *o*, **ge'sjacher** [-ʃɑ-] *o* bartering; traffic

ge'sjochten F done for, down and out

ge'sjouw *o* toiling

ge'slaagd successful

1 ge'slacht (-en) *o* 1 (g e n e r a t i e) generation; 2 (f a m i l i e) race, family [of men], lineage; genus [*mv* genera] [of animals, plants]; 3 (k u n n e) [male, female] sex; 4 *gram* [masculine, feminine, neuter] gender; *het andere ~* the opposite sex; *het menselijk ~* the human race, mankind; *het schone ~* the fair sex; *het sterke ~* the sterner sex; *het zwakke ~* the weaker sex

2 ge'slacht *o* killed meat, butcher's meat

ge'slachtelijk sexual

ge'slachtkunde *v* genealogy

ge'slachtloos sexless [beings]; asexual; ⚥ agamic, agamous

ge'slachtsboom (-bomen) *m* genealogical tree, pedigree

ge'slachtsdaad *v* sexual act; coitus; **–delen** *mv* genitals, private parts; **–drift** *v* sexual urge, desire, sex instinct, libido; **–gemeenschap** *v* intercourse, coition, coitus, sex, intimacy, love-making; *~ hebben met* have intercourse with, have sex with, lie with; **–kenmerken** *mv* sex characteristics; **–klier** (-en) *v* 🜨 sexual gland; ⚥ germ gland

ge'slachtsnaam (-namen) *m* family name

ge'slachtsorgaan (-ganen) *o* sexual organ

ge'slachtsregister (-s) *o* genealogical register

ge'slachtsrijp sexually mature; **–heid** *v* sexual maturity

ge'slachtswapen (-s) *o* family arms

ge'slachtsziekte (-n en -s) *v* venereal disease

ge'slagen V.D. v. *slaan*; beaten; *~ goud* beaten gold; *~ vijanden* declared enemies

ge'sleep *o* dragging

ge'slenter *o* sauntering, lounging

ge'slepen I V.D. v. *slijpen*; **II** *aj* sharp, whetted [knives]; cut [glass]; *fig* cunning, sly; **III** *ad* cunningly, slyly; **–heid** *v* cunning, slyness

ge'sleten V.D. v. *slijten*

ge'slinger *o* ⚓ roll

ge'sloken V.D. v. *sluiken*

ge'slof *o* shuffling

ge'sloof *o* drudgery

ge'slonken V.D. v. *slinken*

ge'slopen V.D. v. *sluipen*

ge'sloten V.D. v. *sluiten*; 1 shut [doors], closed [doors, books, car, circuit, economy, system; to traffic]; sealed [envelope]; (o p s l o t) locked; 2 ⚔ serried [ranks], close [formation]; 3 *fig* uncommunicative, close; *~ jachttijd* close season, fence-season; **–heid** *v* uncommunicativeness, closeness

ge'sluierd 1 veiled [lady]; 2 fogged [plate]

ge'smaal *o* reviling, scoffing, contumely

ge'smak *o* smacking [of lips]

ge'smeek *o* supplication(s), entreaty

ge'smeten V.D. v. *smijten*

ge'smoes *o* 1 whispering; 2 underhand

dealings

ge'**smolten** V.D. v. *smelten*; melted [butter], molten [lead]

ge'**smul** *o* feasting, banqueting

ge'**snap** *o* (tittle-)tattle, prattle, small talk

ge'**snater** *o* chatter(ing)

ge'**snauw** *o* snarling, snubbing

ge'**sneden** V.D. v. *snijden*; cut; sliced [bread]; gelded [tomcat]

ge'**snik** *o* sobbing, sobs

ge'**snoef** *o* boasting, boast, bragging

ge'**snor** *o* whirr(ing)

ge'**snork** *o* snoring

ge'**snoten** V.D. v. *snuiten*

ge'**snotter** *o* snivelling

ge'**snoven** V.D. v. *snuiven*

ge'**snuffel** *o* ferreting, rummaging

ge'**soes** *o* dozing

gesoig'**neerd** [-swɑ'ɲeːrt] = *verzorgd* 2

gesp (-en) *m* & *v* buckle, clasp

ge'**spannen** bent [of a bow]; taut, tight [rope]; nervous, on edge; strained² [relations], tense² [situation &]; zie ook: *verwachting* & *voet*

ge'**spartel** *o* sprawling, floundering

ge'**speel** *o* playing

ge'**speend** ~ *van* deprived of, devoid of, without

'**gespen** (gespte, h. gegespt) *vt* buckle

ge'**speten** V.D. v. *spijten*

ge'**spierd** muscular, sinewy, brawny; *fig* nervous [language]

ge'**spin** *o* 1 spinning; 2 purring [of a cat]

ge'**spleten** V.D. v. *splijten*; split, cleft; ~ *verhemelte* cleft palate

ge'**spogen** V.D. v. *spugen*

ge'**sponnen** V.D. v. *spinnen*

ge'**spoord** spurred

ge'**spot** *o* mocking, jeering, scoffing &

ge'**spoten** V.D. v. *spuiten*

ge'**sprek** (-ken) *o* conversation, talk; ☏ call; *fig* dialogue [of the Church with the State]; *in* ~ ☏ number engaged (*Am* number busy); *een* ~ *voeren* hold a conversation; ge'**spreksgroep** (-en) *v* discussion group; –**partner** (-s) *m-v* interlocutor; ge'**sproken** V.D. v. *spreken*

ge'**sprongen** V.D. v. *springen*

ge'**sproten** V.D. v. *spruiten*

ge'**spuis** *o* rabble, riff-raff, scum

ge'**staag**, ge'**stadig I** *aj* steady, continual, constant; **II** *ad* steadily, constantly; ge'**stadigheid** *v* steadiness, constancy

ge'**stalte** (-n en -s) *v* figure, shape, stature

ge'**stamel** *o* stammering

ge'**stamp** *o* 1 stamping; 2 ⚓ pitching [of a steamer]

ge'**stand** *zijn woord* ~ *doen* redeem one's promise (word, pledge), keep one's word

'**geste** ['ʒɛstə] (-n en -s) *v* gesture²

ge'**steente** (-n en -s) *o* 1 (precious) stones; 2 stone, rock; *vast* ~ solid rock

ge'**stegen** V.D. v. *stijgen*

ge'**stel** (-len) *o* system, constitution

ge'**steld** ~ *dat het zo is* supposing it to be the case; *de* ~*e machten* (*overheid*) the constituted authorities, **J** the powers that be; *het is er zó mee* ~ that's how the matter stands; ~ *zijn op* be fond of [a good dinner, a friend]; stand on [getting things well done &]; be a stickler for [ceremony]; *daar ben ik niet op* ~ I don't appreciate that, I want none of that; –**heid** *v* state, condition; nature [of the soil &]

ge'**stemd** 1 ♪ tuned; 2 *fig* disposed; *ik ben er niet toe* ~ I am not in the vein for it; *gunstig* ~ *zijn jegens* be favourably disposed towards

ge'**sternte** (-n) *o* star, constellation, stars; *onder een gelukkig* ~ *geboren* born under a lucky star

ge'**steun** *o* moaning, groaning

ge'**steven** V.D. v. *stijven*

1 ge'**sticht** (-en) *o* (i n 't a l g.) establishment, institution; (v o o r d a k l o z e n &) asylum, home

2 ge'**sticht** *aj fig* edified; *hij was er niets* ~ *over* he was not pleased at all about it

gesticu'**latie** [ɡɛsti.ky.'la.(t)si.] (-s) *v* gesticulation; gesticu'**leren** (gesticuleerde, h. gegesticuleerd) *vi* gesticulate

ge'**stoei** *o* romping

☉ ge'**stoelte** (-n en -s) *o* seat, chair

gestof'**feerd** (partly) furnished [rooms]

ge'**stoken** V.D. v. *steken*

ge'**stolen** V.D. v. *stelen*

ge'**stommel** *o* clatter(ing)

ge'**stonken** V.D. v. *stinken*

ge'**stoord** disturbed; *geestelijk* ~ mentally deranged (handicapped)

ge'**storven** V.D. v. *sterven*

ge'**stotter** *o* stuttering, stammering

ge'**stoven** V.D. v. *stuiven*

ge'**streden** V.D. v. *strijden*

ge'**streept** striped

ge'**streken** V.D. v. *strijken*

ge'**strekt** stretched; *in* ~*e draf* (at) full gallop; ~*e hoek* straight angle

ge'**streng** = 2 *streng*

gestructu'**reerd** structured

gestu'**deerd** ~ *iem.* (university) graduate

ge'**suf** *o* day-dreaming, dozing

ge'**suikerd** sugared, sugary, candied

ge'**suis** *o* = *suizing*

ge'**sukkel** *o* 1 pottering &; 2 ailing

ge'**taand** tawny, tanned

ge'**takt** branched, branchy, branching

ge'**tal** (-len) *o* number; *i n groten* ~*e* in (great) numbers; *t e n* ~*e van* to the number of..., ...in number; **–lenprijs** (-prijzen) *m* trade discount (price)

ge'talm *o* lingering, loitering, dawdling

ge'talsterkte *v* numerical strength

ge'tand 1 toothed; 2 ⚙ dentate; 3 ✕ toothed, cogged

ge'tapt 1 drawn [beer]; skimmed [milk]; 2 *fig* popular [with the boys &]

ge'teem *o* drawl(ing), whine, whining

ge'tekend drawn, signed; marked

ge'teut *o* dawdling, loitering

ge'tier *o* noise, clamour, vociferation

ge'tij (-den) *o* 1 (e b b e e n v l o e d) tide [high or low]; 2 = *getijde*; *het* ~ *keert* the tide turns; *dood* ~ neap tide; zie ook: *baken*

☉ **ge'tijde** (-n) *o* 1 (t i j d r u i m t e) season; 2 = *getij*; *de* ~*n rk* the hours; **ge'tijdenboek** (-en) *o rk* breviary

ge'tijhaven (-s) *v* tidal harbour; **–rivier** (-en) *v* tidal river; **–stroom** (-stromen) *m* tidal current; **–tafel** (-s) *v* tide-table

ge'tik *o* ticking [of a clock]; tapping [at a door]; click(ing) [of an engine &]

ge'tikt nuts, daft, weird, loopy, crack-brained

ge'timmer *o* carpentering

ge'timmerte (-n) *o* structure

ge'tingel *o* tinkling

ge'tintel *o* sparkling &, zie *tintelen*

ge'titeld titled [person]; [book &] entitled

ge'tjilp *o* chirping, twitter

ge'tob *o* 1 bother, worry; 2 toiling, drudgery

ge'toet(er) *o* tooting, hoot(ing)

ge'togen V.D. v. *tijgen*; zie ook: *geboren*

ge'tokkel *o* thrumming, twanging &, zie *tokkelen*

ge'touw (-en) *o* gear, loom; zie ook: *touw*

ge'tralied grated, latticed, barred

ge'trappel *o* stamping, trampling

ge'trapt ~*e verkiezingen* elections at two removes, indirect elections

ge'treiter *o* teasing, nagging

ge'treur *o* pining, mourning

ge'treuzel *o* dawdling, lingering

ge'trippel *o* tripping, patter, pitter-patter

getroe'bleerd (mentally) deranged, **F** a bit touched, a bit cracked

ge'troffen V.D. v. *treffen*

ge'trokken V.D. v. *trekken*

ge'trommel *o* 1 drumming, rattle of drums; 2 strumming [on a piano]

ge'troosten (getroostte, h. getroost) *zich* ~ bear patiently, put up with; *zich een grote inspanning* ~ make a great effort; *zich de moeite* ~ *om...* go (put oneself) to the trouble of ...ing; *zich veel moeite* ~ spare no pains

ge'trouw = *trouw* **I** & **II**; *zijn* ~*en* his trusty followers, his stalwarts, his henchmen

'getto ('s) *o* ghetto

ge'tuige (-n) *m* & *v* 1 ⚖ witness; 2 (b i j h u w e l i j k) best man; 3 (b i j d u e l) second; ~ *mijn armoede* witness my poverty; *schriftelijke* ~*n* written references; *ik zal u goede* ~*n geven* I'll give you a good character; *iem. tot* ~ *roepen* call (take) sbd. to witness; ~ *zijn van* be a witness of, witness; **ge'tuigen** (getuigde, h. getuigd) **I** *vt* testify to, bear witness [that...]; **II** *vi* appear as a witness, give evidence; *dat getuigt t e g e n...* that is what testifies against...; ~ *v a n* attest to..., bear witness to...; *dat getuigt van zijn...* that testifies to his..., that bears testimony to his...; ~ *v o o r* testify in favour of; *dat getuigt voor hem* that speaks in his favour; **ge'tuigenbank** (-en) *v* witness-box; **–bewijs** (-wijzen) *o* proof by witnesses, oral evidence; **–geld** (-en) *o* conduct money; **ge'tuigenis** (-sen) *o* & *v* evidence, testimony; ~ *afleggen van* bear witness to, give evidence of; ~ *dragen van* bear testimony (evidence) to; **ge'tuigenverhoor** (-horen) *o* examination (hearing) of the witnesses; **–verklaring** (-en) *v* deposition, testimony, evidence; **ge'tuigschrift** (-en) *o* certificate, testimonial; [servant's] character

ge'twist *o* quarrelling, wrangling, bickering(s)

geul (-en) *v* gully, channel, watercourse

geur (-en) *m* smell, odour, fragrance, flavour, aroma, perfume, scent; *in* ~*en en kleuren* in detail; **'geuren** (geurde, h. gegeurd) *vi* 1 smell, be fragrant, give forth scent (perfume); 2 **F** swank; ~ *met* show off [one's learning], sport, **F** flash [a gold watch]; **'geurig** sweet-smelling, odoriferous, fragrant, aromatic; **–heid** *v* perfume, smell, fragrance; **'geurmaker** (-s) *m* swagger

1 geus (geuzen) *m* ▢ Beggar: Protestant [during the revolt of the Netherlands against Spain]

2 geus (geuzen) *v* ⚓ jack

'gevaar (-varen) *o* danger, peril, risk; *er is geen* ~ *bij* there is no danger; *daar is geen* ~ *voor* no danger (no fear) of that; ~ *voor brand* danger of fire; *een* ~ *voor de vrede* a danger to peace; ~ *lopen om...* run the risk of ...ing; ● *b u i t e n* ~ out of danger [of a patient &]; *i n* ~ *brengen* endanger, imperil; (v. r e p u t a t i e) compromise, jeopardize; *in* ~ *verkeren* be in danger (peril); *o p* ~ *af van u te beledigen* at the risk of offending you; *z o n d e r* ~ without danger, without (any) risk; **ge'vaarlijk** dangerous, perilous, risky, hazardous; *het* ~*e ervan* the danger of it; ~*e zone* danger zone (area); **–heid** *v* dangerousness &

ge'vaarte (-n en -s) *o* colossus, monster, leviathan

ge'vaarvol perilous, hazardous

ge'val (-len) *o* 1 case; 2 **J** affair; *het* ~ *zijn* be the case; *een gek* ~ a queer business (situation), a strange affair; *een lastig* ~ an awkward case; *bij* ~ by any chance, possibly; *dat is met hem ook het* ~ that's the same with him, he is in the same position; ● *i n* ~ *van* in case of [need], in the event of [war]; *in negen van de tien* ~*len* in nine cases out of ten; *in elk* ~ in any case, at all events; at any rate, anyhow; *in het ergste* ~ if the worst comes to the worst; *in het gunstigste* ~ at (the) best; *in geen* ~ in no case, on no account; *in uw* ~ *zou ik...* if it were my case I should...; *v a n* ~ *tot* ~ individually; *v o o r het* ~ *dat...* in case... [you should...]; *wat wou nu het* ~ it so turned out that..., it happened that...

ge'vallen (geviel, is gevallen) *vi* happen; *zich laten* ~ put up with

ge'vangen captive; zie *geven* II; **ge'vangenbewaarder** (-s) *m* warder, jailer, turnkey; **ge'vangene** (-n) *m-v* prisoner, captive; **ge'vangenenkamp** (-en) = *gevangenkamp*; **ge'vangenhouden**[1] *vt* detain, keep in prison (in custody); **–ding** *v* detention; **ge'vangenis** (-sen) *v* 1 (g e b o u w) prison, jail, gaol; **S** nick, quod; 2 (s t r a f) imprisonment, goal; *de* ~ *ingaan* be sent to prison; **–kleren** *mv* prison clothes; **–kost** *m* prison food; **–straf** (-fen) *v* imprisonment; *tot* ~ *veroordelen* sentence to prison; **–wezen** *o* prison system; **ge'vangenkamp** (-en) *o* prison camp, prisoners' camp; **ge'vangennemen**[1] *vt* 1 ⚔ arrest, apprehend, capture; 2 ⚔ take prisoner, take captive; **–ming** (-en) *v* arrest, apprehension, capture; **ge'vangenschap** *v* (i n z. k r ij g s ~) captivity; (a l s s t r a f) imprisonment; **–wagen** (-s) *m* prison van; **F** black Maria; **ge'vangenzetten**[1] *vt* put in prison, imprison; **–ting** (-en) *v* imprisonment; **ge'vangenzitten**[1] *vi* be in prison (in jail); **ge'vankelijk** ~ *wegvoeren* 1 ⚔ take away in custody; 2 ⚔ march off under guard

ge'varendriehoek (-en) *m* red warning (advance danger) triangle; **–zone** [-zɔnə] *v* danger zone (area)

ge'vat quick-witted [debater]; witty [answer], clever, smart [retort]; **–heid** (-heden) *v* quick-wittedness, ready wit, quickness at repartee, smartness

ge'vecht (-en) *o* ⚔ fight, combat, battle, action, engagement; *de* ~*en duren nog voort* ⚔ the fighting still goes on; *buiten* ~ *stellen* ⚔ put out of action, disable; **ge'vechtsklaar** combat-ready, clear for action; **–linie** (-s) *v* line of battle

ge'vederd feathered; **ge'vederte** *o* feathers, feathering

ge'veins *o* dissembling, dissimulation; **ge'veinsd** feigned, simulated, hypocritical; **–heid** *v* dissembling, dissimulation, hypocrisy

'gevel (-s) *m* front, façade; **–breedte** (-t en -s) *v* frontage; **–dak** (-daken) *o* gabled roof; **–spits** (-en) *v*, **–top** (-pen) *m* gable; **–toerist** (-en) *m* cat burglar

'geven* I *vt* give [money, a cry]; make a present of [it], present with [a thing]; afford, yield, produce; give out [heat]; ◊ deal [the cards]; *mag ik u wat kip* ~? may I help you to some chicken?; *geef mij nog een kopje* let me have another cup; *geef mij maar Amsterdam* commend me to Amsterdam; *dat zal wel niets* ~ it will be of no avail, it will be no use (no good); *het geeft 50%* it yields 50 per cent.; *rente (interest)* ~ bear interest; *welk stuk wordt er gegeven?* what is on (to-night)?; *een toneelstuk* ~ produce (put on) a play; *ik gaf hem veertig jaar* I took him to be forty, I put him down at forty; *het geeft je wat of je al...* it is no use telling him (to tell him); *wat geeft het?* (h e l p e n) what's the use (the good)?; (h i n d e r e n) what does it matter?; (w a t z o u d a t) what of that?; *wat moet dat* ~? what will be the end of it?; zie ook: *brui, cadeau, gewonnen, les, rekenschap, vuur* &; *God geve dat het niet gebeurt* God grant that it does not happen; *gave God dat ik hem nooit gezien had!* would to God I had never seen him; ● *het roken er a a n* ~ give up smoking; *er een andere uitleg aan* ~ put a different construction (up)on it; *niets* ~ *o m* not care for; *veel* ~ *om* care much for; *weinig* ~ *om* care little for [jewels]; not mind [privations], make little of [pains]; II *vr zich* ~ *zoals men is* give oneself in one's true character; *zich gevangen* ~ give oneself up [to justice], surrender; zie ook: *gewonnen*; III *vi* & *va* 1 give; 2 ◊ deal; ~ *en nemen* give and take; *u moet* ~ ◊ it is your deal, the deal is with you; *er is verkeerd gegeven* ◊ there was a misdeal; *geef hem ervan langs!* let him have it!; *te denken* ~ give food for thought; **–er** (-s) *m* giver, donor; ◊ dealer

ge'vest (-en) *o* hilt

ge'vestigd fixed [opinion]; ~*e belangen* vested interests; *zijn* ~*e reputatie* his (old-, well-)established reputation

ge'vierd famous; zie ook: *vieren*

ge'vind 1 🐟 finned, finny; 2 🌿 pinnate

---

[1] V.T. en V.D. van dit werkwoord volgens het model: **ge'vangen**zetten, V.T. zette **ge'vangen**, V.D. **ge'vangen**-gezet. Zie voor de vormen onder het grondwoord, in dit voorbeeld: *zetten*. Bij sterke en onregelmatige werkwoorden wordt u verwezen naar de lijst achterin.

ge'vingerd fingered, ⚜ & ⚜ digitate
ge'vit *o* fault-finding, cavilling
ge'vlamd flamed [tulips]; watered [silk]
ge'vlei *o* flattering &, zie *vleien*
ge'vlekt spotted, stained; piebald [horse]
ge'vleugeld winged[2]; *~e woorden* winged
  words, well-known sayings
ge'vlij *o bij iem. in het ~ zien te komen* make up to
  sbd., try to ingratiate oneself with sbd.
ge'vlochten V.D. v. *vlechten*
ge'vloden V.D. v. *vlieden*
ge'vloek *o* cursing, swearing
ge'vlogen V.D. v. *vliegen*
ge'vloten V.D. v. *vlieten*
ge'vochten V.D. v. *vechten*
ge'voeg *o zijn ~ doen* relieve nature
ge'voeglijk decently; *wij kunnen nu ~...* we may
  as well...; **–heid** *v* decency, propriety
ge'voel (-ens) *o* 1 (a l s a a n d o e n i n g)
  feeling, sensation, sentiment, sense; feel; 2
  (a l s z i n) feeling, touch; *het ~ hebben dat...*
  have the feeling that...; *het ~ voor...* the sense
  of...; *m e t ~* with expression, with much
  feeling; *o p het ~* by the feel; [read] by touch;
  zacht op het ~ soft to the feel (touch);
ge'voelen[1] I *vt = voelen*; II (-s) *o* feeling;
  opinion; *edele ~s* noble sentiments; *n a a r mijn*
  ~ in my opinion; *wij verschillen v a n ~* we are
  of a different opinion [about this], we differ;
ge'voelig I *aj* 1 (v e e l g e v o e l h e b-
  b e n d) feeling, susceptible, impressionable,
  sensitive [people]; 2 (l i c h t g e r a a k t) touchy;
  3 (p ij n l ij k) tender [feet]; 4 (h a r d) smart
  [blow]; severe [cold &]; 5 (i n d e f o t o-
  g r a f i e) sensitive [plates]; *een ~e nederlaag* a
  heavy defeat; *~e plek* tender spot; *fig* sore
  point; *~ o p het punt van* over sensitive about
  honour; *~ v o o r* sensitive to [kindness]; *~ zijn*
  voor ook: appreciate [sbd.'s kindness]; *~ maken*
  sensitize [a plate &]. Zie ook: *snaar*; II *ad*
  feelingly; **–heid** (-heden) *v* sensitiveness;
  tenderness; *gevoeligheden kwetsen* wound (offend)
  susceptibilities; ge'voelloos unfeeling; insensible [to emotion]; numb [foot, arm]; *~ maken*
  anaesthetize; **–heid** *v* unfeelingness; insensibility; ge'voelsleven *o* emotional-life, inner life;
  –mens (-en) *m* emotional person; **–waarde** *v*
  emotional value; **–zenuw** (-en) *v* sensory
  nerve; **–zin** *m* sense of touch (feeling);
ge'voelvol feeling
ge'vogelte *o* birds, fowl(s), poultry
ge'volg (-en) *o* 1 (p e r s o n e n) followers, suite,
  train, retinue; 2 (u i t o o r z a a k) consequence, result; effect [of the wars on the
  nations]; *geen nadelige ~en ondervinden van* be
  none the worse for; *de ~en zijn voor hem* he
  must take the consequences; ● *~ geven a a n een*

opdracht carry an order into effect; *~ geven aan*
een verzoek grant a request; *~ geven aan een wens*
comply with a wish, carry out (fulfil) a wish;
m e t goed ~ with success, successfully; *t e n ~e*
hebben cause [sbd.'s death &], result in [a big
profit], bring on; *ten ~e van* in consequence of,
as a result of, owing to; *z o n d e r ~* without
success, unsuccessful(ly); **–aanduidend** *gram*
consecutive; **–lijk** consequently; **–trekking**
(-en) *v* conclusion, deduction, inference; *een ~*
maken draw a conclusion (from *uit*)
ge'volmachtigde (-n) *m* plenipotentiary [of a
  country]; proxy [in business]
ge'vonden V.D. v. *vinden*
ge'vorderd advanced, late; *op ~e leeftijd* at an
  advanced age; *op een ~ uur* at a late hour
ge'vorkt forked, furcated
ge'vraag *o* asking, inquiring, questioning; **–d**
  asked, requested, $ in request (demand)
ge'vreeën F V.D. v. *vrijen*
ge'vreesd dreaded
ge'vroren V.D. v. *vriezen*
ge'vuld well-lined [purse]; full, plump [figure]
ge'waad (-waden) *o* garment, dress, garb, attire
ge'waagd hazardous, risky; risqué [joke]; *aan*
  elkaar ~ zijn be well-matched
ge'waand supposed, pretended, feigned
gewaar'deerd valued [friends, help]
ge'waarmerkt certified, attested, authenticated
ge'waarworden (werd ge'waar, is ge'waarge-
  worden) *vt* become aware of, perceive, notice;
  find out, discover; **–ding** (-en) *v* 1 (a a n-
  d o e n i n g) sensation; 2 (v e r m o g e n)
  perception
ge'wag *~ maken van = gewagen*; ge'wagen
  (gewaagde, h. gewaagd) *vi ~ van* mention,
  make mention of
ge'wapend armed [soldiers, peace, eye]; *~ beton*
  reinforced concrete; *~ glas* wired glass;
  –erhand by force of arms
ge'wapper *o* fluttering
ge'warrel *o* whirl(ing)
ge'was (-sen) *o* 1 growth, crop(s), harvest; 2
  plant
gewat'teerd quilted, wadded [quilt]
ge'wauwel *o* twaddle, drivel, F (tommy-)rot
ge'weeklaag *o* lamentation(s)
ge'ween *o* weeping, crying
ge'weer (-weren) *o* gun, rifle, ✎ musket; *i n het*
  ~ komen 1 ⚔ turn out [of the guard]; stand to
  [of a company in the field]; 2 *fig* be up in arms
  (against *tegen*); *het ~ presenteren* present arms;
  o v e r... ~! ⚔ slope... arms!; **–fabriek** (-en) *v*
  small-arms factory; **–kogel** (-s) *m* (rifle) bullet;
  –kolf (-kolven) *v* rifle butt; **–loop** (-lopen) *m*
  (gun-)barrel; **–maker** (-s) *m* gunsmith,
  gunmaker; **–rek** (-ken) *o* arm-rack; **–riem**

(-en) *m* rifle-sling; **–schot** (-schoten) *o* gun-shot, rifleshot; **–vuur** *o* rifle-fire, musketry, fusillade

ge'weest V.D. v. *wezen* en v. *zijn*

ge'wei (-en) *o* (h o r e n s) horns, antlers [of a deer]

ge'wei(de) 1 (i n g e w a n d e n) bowels, entrails; 2 (u i t w e r p s e l e n) droppings

ge'weifel *o* hesitation, wavering

ge'weken V.D. v. *wijken*

ge'weld *o* 1 (main) force, violence; 2 noise; ~ *aandoen* do violence to[2], *fig* strain, stretch [the truth &]; *zich zelf ~ aandoen* do violence to one's nature (one's feelings); *zich ~ aandoen om (niet) te...* make an effort (not) to...; ~ *gebruiken* use force, use violence; *met ~* by (main) force, by violence; *hij wou er met alle ~ heen* he wanted to go by all means, at any cost; *hij wou met alle ~ voor ons betalen* he insisted on paying for us; *fysiek ~* [*fig*] the mailed fist; **–daad** (-daden) *v* act of violence; *tot gewelddaden overgaan* offer violence; **geweld'dadig** violent, forcible; **–heid** (-heden) *v* violence; **ge'weldenaar** (-s en -naren) *m* tyrant, oppressor; **ge'weldig I** *aj* (h e v i g) violent; (m a c h t i g) powerful, mighty, enormous, < terrible; *ze zijn ~!* **F** they are wonderful (marvellous, terrific, fabulous, super)!; **II** *ad* < dreadfully, terribly, awfully; **ge'weldloosheid** *v* non-violence; **–pleging** (-en) *v* violence

ge'welf (-welven) *o* vault, arched roof, dome, archway; **–d** vaulted, arched, domed

ge'wemel *o* swarming &, zie *wemelen*

ge'wend accustomed; ~ *aan* accustomed to, used to; ~ *zijn om...* be in the habit of ...ing; *ben je hier al ~?* do you feel at home here?; *hij is niet veel* ~ he is not used to better things; *jong ~, oud gedaan* as the twig is bent the tree is inclined

ge'wennen (gewende, *vt* h., *vi* is gewend) *vt* & *vi* = *wennen*; zie ook *gewend*; **–ning** *v* habituation, habit-formation

ge'wenst wished(-for), desired; desirable

ge'werveld vertebrate

ge'west (-en) *o* region, province; *betere ~en* better lands, the fields of heavenly bliss; **–elijk** regional, provincial; **–vorming** (-en) *v* regionalization

1 ge'weten (-s) *o* conscience; *een rekbaar, ruim ~ hebben* have an elastic conscience; *d o o r zijn ~ gekweld* conscience smitten (stricken); *het m e t zijn ~ overeenbrengen* reconcile it to one's conscience; *iets op zijn ~ hebben* have something on one's conscience; *heel wat op zijn ~ hebben* have a lot to answer for; *z o n d e r ~ = gewetenloos* **I**

2 ge'weten V.D. v. *weten* en v. *wijten*

ge'wetenloos I *aj* unscrupulous, unprincipled; **II** *ad* unscrupulously; **geweten'loosheid** *v* unscrupulousness, unprincipledness; **ge'wetensbezwaar** (-zwaren) *o* (conscientious) scruple, conscientious objection; **–bezwaarde** (-n) *m* conscientious objector, **F** conchie, conchy, C. O.; **–dwang** *m* moral constraint; **–geld** (-en) *o* conscience money; **–vraag** (-vragen) *v* question of conscience; **–vrijheid** *v* freedom of conscience; **–wroeging** (-en) *v* sting (pangs, qualms, twinges) of conscience, compunction(s); **–zaak** (-zaken) *v* matter of conscience; *van iets een ~ maken* make sth. a matter of conscience

ge'wettigd justified, legitimate

ge'weven woven, textile [fabrics]

1 ge'wezen late, former, ex-

2 ge'wezen V.D. v. *wijzen*

ge'wicht (-en) *o* weight[2], *fig* importance; *dood (eigen)* ~ dead weight; *soortelijk* ~ specific gravity; *(geen)* ~ *hechten aan* attach (no) importance to; ~ *in de schaal leggen* carry weight; *zijn ~ in de schaal werpen* throw the weight of one's (his) influence into the scale; ● *b ij het ~ verkopen* sell by weight; *een man v a n ~* a man of weight (consequence); *een zaak van groot ~* a matter of weight (moment, importance); *van het grootste ~* all-important; **–heffen** *o* weight-lifting; **–heffer** (-s) *m* (weight-)lifter;

ge'wichtig important, weighty, momentous, of weight; ~ *doen* assume consequential airs; ~ *doend* consequential, pompous, self-important; **gewichtigdoene'rij** (-en) *v* pomposity; (v . a m b t e n a r e n) bumbledom; **ge'wichtigheid** *v* importance, weightiness; **ge'wichtloosheid** *v* weightlessness; **ge'wichtseenheid** (-heden) *v* unit of weight; **–verlies** *o* loss of weight

ge'wiekst knowing, sharp, **F** deep; **–heid** *v* knowingness &

ge'wiekt winged

ge'wijd consecrated [Host], sacred [music &]

ge'wijsde (-n) *o* ⚖ final judgment; *in kracht van ~ gaan* ⚖ become final

ge'wild 1 in demand, in favour, much sought after, popular; 2 studied [= affected], would-be

ge'willig willing; **–heid** *v* willingness

ge'win *o* gain, profit; *vuil ~* filthy lucre; **–zucht** *v* = *winzucht*

ge'wis certain, sure; **–heid** *v* certainty, certitude

ge'woel *o* stir, bustle, turmoil

ge'wogen V.D. v. *wegen*

ge'wonde (-n) *m-v* wounded person; *de ~n* the wounded

ge'wonden V.D. v. *winden*

ge'wonnen V.D. v. *winnen*; *zo ~ zo geronnen*

light(ly) come, light(ly) go; *het* ~ *geven* give it up, give up the point; *zich* ~ *geven* yield the point [in an argument]; own defeat, throw up the sponge; zie ook: *spel*
ge'woon I *aj* 1 (g e w e n d) accustomed, used to; customary, usual, wonted; 2 (n i e t b u i t e n g e w o o n) common [people, cold]; ordinary [people, shares, members]; plain [people]; [professor] in ordinary; *de gewone man* the man in the street; *het is heel* ~ it is quite common, nothing out of the common; ~ *raken aan* get accustomed (used) to; ~ *zijn aan* be accustomed (used) to...; ~ *zijn om...* be in the habit of ...ing; *bij was* ~ *om...* ook: he used to...; II *ad* commonly; F simply, just; [everything is going on] as usual; *het was* ~ *verrukkelijk* F it was simply ravishing; *het is* ~ *niet waar* F it is just not true; **–heid** *v* commonness; **–lijk** usually, as a rule, normally, mostly, generally, ordinarily; *als* ~ as usual
ge'woonte (-n en -s) *v* 1 (g e b r u i k) custom, use, usage; 2 (a a n w e n s e l) habit, wont; 3 (a a n g e w e n d e h a n d e l w ij z e) practice; *zijn* ~*s* his ways; *ouder* ~ as usual, from old habit; *dat is een* ~ *van hem* that is a custom with him, a habit of his; *een* ~ *aannemen* contract a habit; *die* ~ *afleggen* get out of that habit; ● *zoals de* ~ *is, als n a a r* ~, *volgens* ~ as usual, according to custom; *t e g e n zijn* ~ contrary to his wont; *t o t een* ~ *vervallen* fall into a habit; *alleen u i t* ~ from (sheer force of) habit; ~ *is een tweede natuur* use is a second nature; **–misdadiger** (-s) *m* habitual criminal; **–recht** *o* common law
ge'woonweg F simply, just
ge'worden (geword, is geworden) come to hand; *het is mij* ~ it has come to hand; *ik zal het u doen* (*laten*) ~ I'll let you have it; *iem. laten* ~ let sbd. have his way
ge'worpen V.D. v. *werpen*
ge'worven V.D. v. *werven*
ge'woven F V.D. v. *wuiven*
ge'wreven V.D. v. *wrijven*
ge'wricht (-en) *o* joint, articulation; ge'wrichtsontsteking (-en) *v* arthritis; **–reumatiek** *v* rheumatoid arthritis
ge'wrocht (-en) *o* work, masterpiece, creation
ge'wroet *o* rooting &; *fig* insidious agitation, intrigues
ge'wroken V.D. v. *wreken*
ge'wrongen V.D. v. *wringen*; distorted
ge'wurm *o* toiling and moiling
Gez. = *Gezusters*
ge'zaag *o* sawing; *fig* scraping [on a violin]
ge'zag *o* authority; ~ *hebben over, het* ~ *voeren over* command; *op eigen* ~ on one's own authority; **–drager** (-s) *m* authority; **–hebbend** authori-

tative; **–hebber** (-s) *m* director, administrator; ge'zagscrisis [-zɪs] (-ses en -sissen) *v* crisis of authority; **–getrouw** law-abiding; ge'zagvoerder (-s) *m* ⚓ master, captain; ✈ chief pilot, captain
ge'zakt 1 (i n z a k k e n g e d a a n) bagged; 2 ⚓ F plucked; zie ook: *gepakt*
ge'zalfde (-n) *m* [the Lord's] anointed
ge'zamenlijk I *aj* joint [owners, account]; collective [interests, action]; aggregate, total [amount]; complete [works of Scott &]; II *ad* jointly, together
ge'zang (-en) *o* 1 (h e t z i n g e n) singing; warbling [of birds]; 2 (h e t t e z i n g e n of g e z o n g e n l i e d) song; 3 (k e r k g e z a n g) hymn; **–boek** (-en) *o* hymn-book
ge'zanik *o* bother, botheration
ge'zant (-en) *m* 1 minister; 2 (a m b a s s a-d e u r, a f g e z a n t) ambassador, envoy; *pauselijk* ~ (papal) nuncio; **–schap** (-pen) *o* embassy, legation
ge'zapig indolent, easy-going, languid
ge'zegd above-said, above-mentioned; **–e** (-n en -s) *o* 1 saying, expression, phrase, dictum, (o p m e r k i n g) statement; 2 *gram* predicate
ge'zegeld 1 sealed [envelope]; 2 stamped [paper]
ge'zegen V.D. v. *zijgen*
ge'zegend blessed; ~ *met...* ook: happy in the possession of...
ge'zeggen *vt zich laten* ~ listen to reason; obey
ge'zeglijk biddable, docile, amenable; **–heid** *v* docility
ge'zeken V.D. v. *zeiken*
ge'zel (-len) *m* 1 mate, companion, fellow; 2 workman, journeyman [baker &]
ge'zellig 1 (v. p e r s o o n) companionable, sociable, convivial; 2 (v. v e r t r e k &) snug, cosy; 3 (g e z e l l i g l e v e n d) social, gregarious [animals]; ~*e bijeenkomst* social meeting; *een* ~*e boel* a pleasant affair; ge'zelligheid *v* companionableness, sociability, conviviality; snugness, cosiness; *voor de* ~ for company; **–svereniging** (-en) *v* social club, students' society
gezel'lin (-nen) *v* companion, mate
ge'zelschap (-pen) *o* company°, society; *ons* (*het Koninklijk* &) ~ our (the royal &) party; *besloten* ~ private party, club; *iem.* ~ *houden* bear, keep sbd. company; ● *i n* ~ *van* in (the) company of, in company with, accompanied by; *wil jij v a n het* ~ *zijn?* will you be of the party?; *bij is zijn* ~ *waard* he is good company; ge'zelschapsbiljet (-ten) *o* party ticket; **–dame** (-s) *v* (lady-)companion; **–reis** (-reizen) *v* conducted party tour; **–spel** (-spelen) *o* round game

ge′zet 1 set [hours]; 2 corpulent, thickset, stout, stocky

ge′zeten V.D. v. *zitten*; ~ *burger* substantial citizen

ge′zetheid *v* corpulence, stoutness, stockiness

ge′zeur *o* (m o e i l ij k h e i d) bother; (g e z a n i k) drivel, twaddle

′gezicht (-en) *o* 1 (v e r m o g e n) (eye)sight; 2 (a a n g e z i c h t) face; **S** mug; 3 (u i t d r u k - k i n g) looks, countenance; 4 (h e t g e z i e n e) view, sight; 5 (v i s i o e n) vision; *~en trekken* pull (make) faces (at *tegen*); *een vrolijk* (*treurig*) *~ zetten* put on a cheerful (sad) face; ● *b ij* (*op*) *het ~ van...* at sight of; *i n het ~ van de kust* in sight of the coast; *in het ~ komen* heave in sight; *in het ~ krijgen* catch sight of, sight; *hem in het ~ uitlachen* laugh in his face; *hem in zijn ~ zeggen* tell him to his face; *o p het eerste ~* at first sight; *zo op het eerste ~ is het...* on the face of it, it is...; *iem. op zijn ~ geven* tan sbd.'s hide; *u i t het ~ verdwijnen* disappear, vanish (from sight); *uit het ~ verliezen* lose sight of; *uit het ~ zijn* be out of sight; *hem v a n ~ kennen* know him by sight; *scherp van ~* sharp-sighted; (*ergens*) *even je ~ laten zien* **F** show the flag; **ge′zichtsbedrog** *o* optical illusion; **–einder** *m* horizon; **–hoek** (-en) *m* optic (visual) angle; **–kring** (-en) *m* horizon, ken; **–orgaan** (-organen) *o* organ of sight; **–punt** (-en) *o* point of view, viewpoint; sight; **–scherpte** *v* visual acuity; **–veld** (-en) *o* field of vision; **–verlies** *o* loss of (eye) sight; *fig* loss of face; **–vermogen** *o* visual faculty, visual power; *zijn ~* his eyesight; **–zenuw** (-en) *v* optic nerve

ge′zien esteemed, respected; *hij is daar niet ~* he is not liked (not popular) there; *~...* in view of... [the danger &]; *mij niet ~!* **F** nothing doing!

ge′zin (-nen) *o* family, household; *het grote ~* the large family

ge′zind inclined, disposed; *...-minded*; *iem. goed* (*slecht*) *~ zijn* be kindly (unfriendly) disposed towards sbd.; **–heid** (-heden) *v* 1 inclination, disposition; 2 persuasion; **ge′zindte** (-n) *v* persuasion, sect

ge′zinshelpster (-s) *v* home help; **–hoofd** (-en) *o* 1 head of the family; 2 householder; **–hulp** (-en) *v* home help; **–leven** *o* family life; **–planning** [-plɛn-] *v* family planning; **–verzorgster** (-s) *v* trained mother's help; **–voogd** (-en) *m* family guardian

ge′zocht V.D. v. *zoeken*; 1 in demand, in request, sought after [articles, wares]; 2 (n i e t n a t u u r l ij k) studied, affected; 3 (v e r g e - z o c h t) far-fetched

ge′zoden V.D. v. *zieden*

ge′zoek *o* seeking, search

ge′zoem *o* buzz(ing), hum(ming)

ge′zoen *o* kissing

ge′zogen V.D. v. *zuigen*

ge′zond I *aj* healthy[2] [life, man &]; wholesome[2] [food]; sound[2] [body, mind, policy &]; *fig* sane [judgment, views]; [a l l é é n p r e d i k a t i e f] [a man] in good health; *uw ~ verstand* your common sense; *de zaak is ~* it's all right, the business is safe; *~ en wel* fit and well, safe and sound; *zo ~ als een vis* as fit as a fiddle; *~ naar ziel en lichaam* sound in body and mind; *~ van lijf en leden* sound in life and limb; *~ bidden* heal by prayer; *~ blijven* keep fit; *~ maken* restore to health, cure; *weer ~ worden* recover (one's health); **II** *ad* [live] healthily; [reason] soundly[2]; **–bidden** *o* faith-healing; **–bidder** (-s) *m* faith-healer

ge′zonden V.D. v. *zenden*

ge′zondheid *v* health; healthiness &; *fig* soundness; *~ is de grootste schat* health is better than wealth; *o p iems. ~ drinken* drink sbd.'s health; *op uw ~!* your health! *v o o r zijn ~* for health; **ge′zondheidsattest** (-en) *o* health certificate; **–commissie** (-s) *v* 1 Board of Health, Health Committee; 2 Medical Board; **–dienst** *m* public health service, health department; **–leer** *v* hygiene; **–maatregel** (-en en -s) *m* sanitary measure; **–onderzoek** (-en) *o* algemeen ~ check-up, medical (examination); **–redenen** *mv* considerations of health; *om ~* 1 for reasons of health; 2 on the ground of ill health; **–toestand** (-en) *m* (state of) health; *de ~ der ... is uitstekend* the... are in excellent health

ge′zongen V.D. v. *zingen*

ge′zonken V.D. v. *zinken*

ge′zonnen V.D. v. *zinnen*

ge′zopen V.D. v. *zuipen*

ge′zouten salt* [food]; [p r e d i k a t i e f] salted

ge′zucht *o* sighing, sighs

ge′zusters *mv* sisters; *de ~ D.* the D. sisters

ge′zwam *o* jaw, blah; **S** tosh

ge′zwegen V.D. v. *zwijgen*

ge′zwel (-len) *o* swelling, growth, tumour

ge′zwendel *o* swindling

ge′zwets *o* vapourings, wind, **F** gas

ge′zwind swift, quick; *met ~e pas* at the double

ge′zwoeg *o* drudgery, toiling

ge′zwolgen V.D. v. *zwelgen*

ge′zwollen V.D. v. *zwellen*; *fig* stilted [style, tone]; bombastic [speech], turgid [language]; **–heid** (-heden) *v* swollen state; *fig* turgidity [of style]

ge′zwommen V.D. v. *zwemmen*

ge′zworen V.D. v. *zweren*; sworn [friends, enemies]; *een ~e* a juror, a juryman; *de ~en* the jury ge′zworven V.D. v. *zwerven*

G.G. (& G.) D. = *Gemeentelijke Geneeskundige en Gezondheidsdienst* ± Municipal Public Health Department

′Ghana *o* Ghana; Gha′nees Ghanaian

gids (-en) *m* guide², (b o e k) ook: guide-book, handbook; *Gids voor Londen* Guide to London

′giechelen (giechelde, h. gegiecheld) *vi* giggle, titter

giek (-en) *m* ⚓ gig

1 gier (-en) *m* 🦅 vulture

2 gier *v* (m e s t) liquid manure

′gierbrug (-gen) *v* flying-bridge

1 ′gieren (gierde, h. gegierd) *vi* scream; (v . w i n d) howl; ~ *van het lachen* (*de pret*) scream (shriek) with laughter, delight; *het was om te* ~ F it was screamingly funny

2 ′gieren (gierde, h. gegierd) *vi* ⚓ jaw, sheer

′gierig I *aj* miserly, niggardly, stingy, avaricious, close-fisted; II *ad* stingily, avariciously; **–aard** (-s) *m* miser, niggard, skinflint; **–heid** *v* avarice, miserliness, stinginess

′gierpont (-en) *v* flying-bridge

gierst *v* millet

′giervalk (-en) *m* & *v* gyrfalcon; **–zwaluw** (-en) *v* swift

′gietbeton *o* poured concrete; **–bui** (-en) *v* downpour; ′gieten* I *vt* 1 pour [water]; 2 found [guns], cast [metals &], mould [candles &]; II *vi* (*het regent dat*) *het giet* it is pouring, it is raining cats and dogs; ′gieter (-s) *m* 1 watering-can, watering-pot; 2 founder, caster [of metals]; giete′rij (-en) *v* foundry; ′gietijzer *o* cast iron; **–staal** *o* cast steel; **–stuk** (-ken) *o* casting; **–vorm** (-en) *m* casting-mould; **–werk** (-en) *o* cast work

gif (-fen) *o* = 1 *gift*; **–beker** (-s) *m* = *giftbeker*; **–blaas** (-blazen) *v* = *giftblaas*; **–gas** (-sen) *o* = *giftgas*; **–kikker** (-s) *m* crosspatch, hothead; **–klier** (-en) *v* = *giftklier*; **–menger** (-s) *m*, **–mengster** (-s) *v* = *giftmenger, -mengster*; **–plant** (-en) *v* = *giftplant*; **–slang** (-en) *v* = *giftslang*; 1 gift (-en) *o* 1 (i n ′t a l g .) poison²; 2 (v . d i e r) venom²; 3 (v . z i e k t e) virus²

2 gift (-en) *v* (g e s c h e n k) gift, present, donation, gratuity

′giftand (-en) *m* = *gifttand*; ′giftbeker (-s) *m* poisoned cup; **–blaas** (-blazen) *v* venom bag; **–gas** (-sen) *o* poison-gas; ′giftig 1 poisonous, venomous²; *fig* virulent; 2 S waxy [= angry]; **–heid** *v* 1 poisonousness, venomousness²; *fig* virulence; 2 (b o o s h e i d) anger; ′giftklier (-en) *v* poison-gland, venom gland; **–menger** (-s) *m*, **–mengster** (-s) *v* poisoner; **–plant** (-en) *v* poisonous plant; **–slang** (-en) *v* poisonous snake; **–tand** (-en) *m* poison-fang; gif(t)vrij non-poisonous

gi′gant (-en) *m* giant; **–isch** giant, gigantic

′gigolo [′dʒi.go.-] (′s) *m* gigolo, S lounge lizard

gij you, ⊙ ye; ⊙ [a l l é é n e n k e l v .] thou; gij′lieden you, F you fellows, you people

′gijpen (gijpte, h. gegijpt) *vi* ⚓ gybe, jibe

′gijzelaar (-s) *m* 1 hostage; 2 prisoner for debt; ′gijzelen (gijzelde, h. gegijzeld) *vt* 1 seize and keep as hostage(s); 2 imprison for debt; **–ling** (-en) *v* 1 seizure and keeping as hostage(s); 2 imprisonment for debt

gil (-len) *m* yell, shriek, scream

gild (-en) *o*, ′gilde (-n) *o* & *v* ⊞ guild, corporation, craft; ′gildebroeder (-s) *m* ⊞ freeman of a guild; **–huis** (-huizen) *o* ⊞ guildhall

′gillen (gilde, h. gegild) *vi* yell, shriek, scream; *het was om te* ~ F it was a scream; **–er** (-s) *m* F scream, howler

′ginder over there, yonder

ginds I *aj* yonder, ⊙ yon; ~*e boom* the tree over there; *aan* ~*e kant* on the other side, over the way, over there; II *ad* over there

ging (gingen) V.T. v. *gaan*

′ginnegappen (ginnegapte, h. geginnegapt) *vi* giggle, snigger

gips (-en) *o* 1 (m e n g s e l) plaster (of Paris); 2 (m i n e r a a l) gypsum; *in het* ~ *liggen* lie in plaster; **–afgietsel** (-s) *o* plaster cast; **–beeld** (-en) *o* plaster image, plaster figure; 1 ′gipsen *aj* plaster; 2 ′gipsen (gipste, h. gegipst) *vt* plaster; ′gipsmodel (-len) *o* plaster cast; **–verband** (-en) *o* plaster of Paris dressing; **–vorm** (-en) *m* plaster mould

gi′raal ~ *geld* deposit money, money in account

gi′raf(fe) [ʒiː′raf(ə)] (-n en -fes) giraffe

gi′reren (gireerde, h. gegireerd) *vt* $ transfer; 📠 pay through (by) giro; ′giro *m* $ 1 clearing; 2 *de* ~(*dienst*) 📠 giro; **–bank** (-en) *v* $ clearing-bank; **–betaalkaart** (-en) *v* giro cheque; **–dienst** (-en) *m* = *giro* 2; **–kaart** (-en) *v* giro transfer card; **–nummer** (-s) *o* giro transfer account number, giro number; **–rekening** (-en) *v* $ transfer account, giro account

gis *v* guess, conjecture; *op de* ~ at random

′gispen (gispte, h. gegispt) *vt* blame, censure; **–ping** (-en) *v* blame, censure

′gissen (giste, h. gegist) I *vt* guess, conjecture, surmise; II *vi* guess; ~ *naar iets* guess at sth.; **–sing** (-en) *v* guess, conjecture; estimation; *het is maar een* ~ it is mere guesswork; *naar* ~ at a rough guess (estimate)

gist *m* yeast, barm; ′gisten (gistte, h. gegist) *vi* ferment², work; *het had al lang gegist* things had been in a ferment for a long time

′gisteren yesterday; *hij is niet van* ~ he was not born yesterday, there are no flies on him, he knows a thing or two; *de Times van* ~ yesterday's (issue of the) Times; *gister(en)avond* last night, yesterday evening; *gister(en)morgen* yesterday morning

'**gisting** (-en) *v* working, fermentation², ferment² [ook = agitation, excitement]; *in ~ verkeren* be in a ferment²

git (-ten) *o* & *v* jet

gi'taar (-taren) *v* guitar; **gita'rist** (-en) *m* guitarist

'**gitten** *aj* (made of) jet; '**gitzwart** jet-black

'**glaasje** (-s) *o* 1 (small) glass; 2 slide [of a microscope]; *hij heeft te diep in het ~ gekeken* he has had a drop too much; *een ~ nemen* have a glass

gla'cé I *aj* kid; II (-s) *o* kid (leather); III (-s) *m* (h a n d s c h o e n) kid glove; **–handschoen** (-en) *m = glacé* III

gla'ceren (glaceerde, h. geglaceerd) *vt* glaze [tiles]; ice, frost [pastry, cakes]

glad I *aj eig* slippery [roads, ground]; sleek [hair]; *eig & fig* smooth [surface, chin, skin, style, verse &]; glib [tongue]; *fig* cunning, cute, clever [fellow]; *een –de ring* a plain ring; *dat is nogal ~* **F** that goes without saying; II *ad* smooth(ly); *~ lopen* run smooth(ly); *je hebt het ~ mis* you are quite wrong; *dat zal je niet ~ zitten* you're not going to get away with that; *ik ben het ~ vergeten* I have clean forgotten it; *dat was ~ verkeerd* that was quite wrong

'**gladakker** (-s) *m* 1 ⚓ pariah dog; 2 *fig* (s c h u r k) rascal, scamp; 3 (s l i m m e r d) **F** sly dog, slyboots

'**gladgeschoren** clean-shaven; **–harig** sleek-haired, smooth-haired; **–heid** *v* smoothness², slipperiness

gladi'ator (-s en - 'toren) *m* gladiator

gladi'ool (-iolen) *v* gladiolus [*mv* gladioli]

'**gladjanus** (-sen) *m* **F** sly dog, slyboots;

'**gladmaken** (maakte 'glad, h. 'gladgemaakt) *vt* smooth, polish; **–schaaf** (-schaven) *v* ✕ smoothing-plane; **–strijken** (streek 'glad, h. 'gladgestreken) *vt* smooth (out)²; **–weg** clean [forgotten]; [refuse] flatly; **–wrijven** (wreef 'glad, h. 'gladgewreven) *vt* polish

glans (glansen en glanzen) *m* 1 shine [of boots], gloss [of hair], lustre²; *fig* gleam [in his eye]; glory, splendour, brilliancy, glamour; 2 polish; *~ verlenen aan* lend lustre to; *hij is met ~ geslaagd* he has passed with flying colours; **–loos** lustreless [stuff], lacklustre [eyes]; **–papier** *o* glazed (coated) paper; **–periode** (-n en -s) *v* heyday, golden age; **–punt** (-en) *o* acme, height, highlight; **–rijk** I *aj* splendid, glorious, radiant, brilliant; II *ad* gloriously, brilliantly; *het ~ afleggen tegen* fail signally; *de vergelijking ~ doorstaan* compare very favourably (with);

'**glanzen** (glansde, h. geglansd) I *vi* gleam, shine; II *vt* gloss [cloth]; glaze [paper]; burnish

[steel &]; polish [marble, rice]; brighten [metal]; **–d** gleaming, glossy; '**glanzig** shining, glossy, glittering

glas (glazen) *o* 1 glass; 2 chimney [of a lamp]; *zes glazen* ⚓ six bells; *het ~ heffen* raise one's glass; *zijn eigen glazen ingooien* cut (bite) off one's nose to spite one's face, stand in one's own light, quarrel with one's bread and butter; *onder ~ kweken* grow under glass; **–achtig** glass-like, glassy, vitreous; **–blazen** I (blies 'glas, h. 'glasgeblazen) *vi* blow glass; II *o* glass-blowing; **–blazer** (-s) *m* glass-blower; **glasblaze'rij** (-en) *v* glass-works; **glas'dicht** glazed; '**glasfabriek** (-en) *v* glass-works; **–fiber** [-faibər] *o* & *m* glass fibre; **–handel** (-s) *m* glass-trade; **–hard** hard as nails; *hij weigerde ~* he refused flatly (bluntly); **–helder** clear as glass; *fig* crystal-clear; **glas-in-'lood** leaded (lights); *~ ruitje* quarrel; '**glasoven** (-s) *m* glass-furnace; **–potlood** (-loden) *o* chinagraph pencil; **–ruit** (-en) *v* window-pane; **–scherf** (-scherven) *v* piece of broken glass; **–schilder** (-s) *m* stained-glass artist, glass-painter; **–schilderen** *o* glass-painting; **–slijper** (-s) *m* glass-grinder; **–snijder** (-s) *m* glass-cutter; **–verzekering** (-en) *v* plate-glass insurance; **–vezel** (-s) *v* glass fibre; **–werk** (-en) *o* 1 glass-work, (table) glass-ware, glasses, glass things; 2 glazing [windows &]; **–wol** *v* glass mineral wool; 1 '**glazen** *aj* (of) glass, glassy; *~ deur* glass door, glazed door; *een ~ oog* a glass eye; 2 '**glazen** *meerv. v. glas*; **glaze'nier** (-s) *m = glasschilder*; '**glazenkast** (-en) *v* glazed cabinet, glazed cupboard; **–maker** (-s) *m* 1 (m e n s) glazier; 2 (i n s e k t) dragon-fly; **–spuit** (-en) *v* window-cleaning syringe; **–wasser** (-s) *m* window-cleaner; **glazenwasse'rij** (-en) *v* window-cleaning company; '**glazig** glassy; waxy [potato]

gla'zuren (glazuurde, h. geglazuurd) *vt* glaze; **gla'zuur** *o* 1 glaze [of pottery]; 2 enamel [of teeth]

gleed (**gleden**) V.T. v. *glijden*

'**gletsjer** (-s) *m* glacier

gleuf (gleuven) *v* groove, slot, slit

'**glibberen** (glibberde, is geglibberd) *vi* slither, slip; **–rig** slithery, slippery

'**glijbaan** (-banen) *v* slide; **–bank** (-en) *v* sliding-seat [in a gig]; **–bekisting** (-en) *v* formwork; **–boot** (-boten) *m* & *v* hydroplane (motorboat); '**glijden*** *vi* glide [over the water &]; slide [on ice]; slip [over a patch of oil, from one's hands, off the table]; *laten ~* slide [a drawer &]; slip [a coin into sbd.'s hand]; run [one's fingers over, one's eyes along...]; *zich laten ~* slip [off one's horse]; slide [down the banisters]; *d o o r de vingers ~* slip through one's

fingers; *o v e r iets heen* ~ slide over a delicate subject; **'glijvlucht** (-en) *v* glide
'glimlach *m* smile; **'glimlachen** (glimlachte, h. geglimlacht) *vi* smile; ~ *over (tegen)* smile at
'glimmen* *vi* 1 shine; glimmer, gleam; 2 glow [under the ashes]; *haar neus glimt* her nose is shiny; **–d** shining, shiny
'glimmer (-s) *o* mica
glimp (-en) *m* glimpse; glimmer [of hope &]; *hij gaf er een ~ aan* he varnished it over; *een ~ van waarheid* some colour of truth
'glimworm (-en) *m* glow-worm, firefly
'glinsteren (glinsterde, h. geglinsterd) *vi* glitter, sparkle, shimmer, glint; **–ring** (-en) *v* glittering, sparkling, sparkle, shimmering, shimmer, glint
'glippen (glipte, is geglipt) *vi* slip; *er door* ~ slip through
glo'baal I *aj* rough; broad [picture]; **II** *ad* roughly, in the gross
'globe (-s en -n) *v* globe; **–trotter** (-s) *m* globe-trotter
gloed *m* blaze, glow; *fig* ardour, fervour, verve; *in* ~ *geraken* warm up [to one's subject]; **–nieuw** brand-new
'gloeidraad (-draden) *m* ☀ filament; **'gloeien** (gloeide, h. gegloeid) **I** *vi* 1 (v. m e t a l e n) glow, be red-hot (white-hot); 2 (v. w a n g e n &) burn; ~ *van* glow (be aglow) with, burn with, be aflame with; **II** *vt* bring to a red (white) heat; **–d I** *aj* glowing; red-hot [iron]; burning [cheeks]; *fig* ardent; *~e kolen* hot (live) coals; **II** *ad* ~ *heet* 1 burning hot, baking hot; 2 (v. m e t a l e n) red-hot; 3 (v. w a t e r) scalding hot; **'gloeihitte** *v* red (white) heat; intense heat; **–kousje** (-s) *o* gas-mantle, incandescent mantle; **–lamp** (-en) *v* glow-lamp, bulb; **–licht** *o* incandescent light
glom (glommen) V.T. v. *glimmen*
'glooien (glooide, h. geglooid) *vi* slope; **–d** sloping; **'glooiing** (-en) *v* slope, escarp
'gloren (gloorde, h. gegloord) *vi* 1 glimmer; 2 dawn; *bij het* ~ *van de dag* at dawn, at peep of day
'glorie *v* glory, lustre, splendour; **–rijk, glori'eus** [*glo:*ri'ø.s] glorious
glos'sarium (-ria) *o* glossary
glu'cose [s = z] *v* glucose
'gluipen (gluipte, h. gegluipt) *vi* sneak, skulk; **'gluiper(d)** (-s) *m* sneak, skulking fellow; **'gluiperig** sneaking
'glunder genial; **'glunderen** (glunderde, h. geglunderd) *vi* beam (with geniality)
'gluren (gluurde, h. gegluurd) *vi* peep, > leer
glyce'rine [y = i.] *v* glycerine
'gniffelen (gniffelde, h. gegniffeld) *vi* chuckle
gnoe (-s) *m* ☙ gnu, wildebeest

gnoom (gnomen) *m* gnome, goblin
'gnuiven (gnuifde, h. gegnuifd) *vi* chuckle
goal [go.l] (-s) *m* goal
gobe'lin [go.bə'lĭ] (-s) *o* & *m* gobelin, Gobelin tapestry
God *m* God; ~ *bewaar me* God forbid!, save us!; ~ *weet waar* Heaven (Goodness) knows where; *om ~'s wil* for God's sake; *zo* ~ *wil* God willing; ~ *zij gedankt* thank God; *leven als* ~ *in Frankrijk* be in clover; **god** (goden) *m* god; **god'dank** thank God!; **'goddelijk** divine [providence, beauty], heavenly; **–heid** *v* diviness, divinity; **'goddeloos I** *aj* godless, impious, ungodly, wicked, unholy; *een ~ kabaal* a dreadful (infernal) noise; **II** *ad* 1 godlessly, impiously; 2 < dreadfully;.
godde'loosheid (-heden) *v* godlessness, ungodliness, impiety, wickedness; **'godendienst** (-en) *m* idolatry; **–dom** *o* (heathen) gods; **–drank** *m* nectar; **–leer** *v* mythology; **–spijs** *v* ambrosia; **god'gans(elijk)** *de ~e dag* the whole blessed day; **'godgeklaagd** *het is* ~ it is a crying shame; **'godgeleerd** theological; **–e** (-n) *m* theologian, divine; **'godgeleerdheid** *v* theology; **'godheid** (-heden) *v* 1 divinity [of Christ], godhead; 2 deity; **go'din** (-nen) *v* goddess; **god'lof** thank God (heavens); **'godloochenaar** (-s) *m* atheist; **–ning** (-en) *v* atheism; **'Godmens** *m* God-man; **'godsakker** (-s) *m* God's acre, churchyard
'godsdienst (-en) *m* 1 religion; 2 divine worship; **gods'dienstig I** *aj* religious [people]; devotional [literature]; **II** *ad* religiously; **–heid** *v* religiousness, piety; **'godsdienstijver** *m* religious zeal; **–leraar** (-s en -raren) *m* religious teacher; **–oefening** (-en) *v* divine service; **–onderwijs** *o* religious teaching; **–onderwijzer** (-s) *m* religious teacher; **–oorlog** (-logen) *m* religious war; **–plechtigheid** (-heden) *v* religious ceremony (rite); **–twist** (-en) *m* religious dissension; **–vrijheid** *v* religious liberty, freedom of religion; **–waanzin** *m* religious mania
'godsgericht (-en) *o* 1 judgment of God; 2 = *godsoordeel*; **–geschenk** (-en) *o* gift of God; godsend; **'Godsgezant** (-en) *m* divine messenger; **'godshuis** (-huizen) *o* 1 house of God, place of worship; 2 charitable institution, almshouse; **–lamp** (-en) *v* sanctuary lamp; **–lasteraar** (-s) *m* blasphemer; **–lastering** (-en) *v* blasphemy; **gods'lasterlijk** blasphemous, profane; **gods'mogelijk** *hoe is het ~* how on earth (how the hell) is it possible; **'godsnaam** *in ~ ga weg!* for Heaven's sake go!; *ga in ~* go in the name of God; *in ~ dan maar* all right! [I'll go]; *waar heb je het in ~ over?* what it

on earth are you talking about?; **'godsonmo-gelijk** absolutely impossible; **'godsoordeel** (-delen) *o* ⊡ (trial by) ordeal; **–vrede** (-s) *m* truce of God; **–vrucht** *v* piety, devotion; **–wil** *om* ∼ for Heaven's sake; goodness gracious; **'godvergeten I** *aj* godforsaken [country, place]; graceless [rascal]; **II** *ad* < infernally, infamously; **god'vrezend** godfearing, pious; **god'vruchtig** devout, pious; **–heid** *v* devotion, piety; **god'zalig** godly

1 goed I *aj* 1 (n i e t s l e c h t) good; 2 (n i e t v e r k e e r d) right, correct; 3 (g o e d h a r t i g) kind; 4 (g e z o n d) well; *een* ∼ *eind* a goodly distance; *een* ∼ *jaar* 1 a good year [for fruit]; 2 a round (full) year; *een* ∼ *rekenaar* a clever (good) hand at figures; *een* ∼ *uur* a full (a good) hour; *hij is een* ∼*e veertiger* he is (has) turned forty; ∼ *volk* honest people; *Goede Vrijdag* Good Friday; *de Goede Week* r*k* Holy Week; ∼*!* good!; *die is* ∼*!* that's a good one!; *mij* ∼*!* all right!, I don't mind!; *net* ∼*!* serve him (you, them) right!; *nu,* ∼*!* well!; all right!; *ook* ∼*!* just as well!; *al te* ∼ *is buurmans gek* all lay goods on a willing horse; *(alles)* ∼ *en wel* that's all very well, (all) well and good [but...]; *wij zijn* ∼ *en wel aangekomen* safe and sound; *het is maar* ∼ *dat* it's a good thing that, it's as well that; *dat is maar* ∼ *ook!* and a (very) good thing (it is), too!; ∼ *zo!* well done!, good business that!; *het zou* ∼ *zijn als...* it would be a good thing if...; *hij is niet* ∼ 1 he is not well; 2 he is not in his right mind; *ben je niet* ∼*?* are you mad?; *hij was zo* ∼ *niet of hij moest...* he had to... whether he liked it or not; *wees zo* ∼ *mij te laten weten...* be so kind as to, be kind enough to...; *zou u zo* ∼ *willen zijn mij het zout aan te reiken?* ook: would you mind passing the salt?; *hij is zo* ∼ *als dood* he is as good as (all but) dead, nearly dead; *zo* ∼ *als niemand* next to nobody; *zo* ∼ *als niets* next to nothing; *het is zo* ∼ *als onmogelijk* it is well-nigh impossible; *zo* ∼ *als zeker* next to certain, all but certain, almost certain; *het weer* ∼ *maken, weer* ∼ *worden* make it up (again); *hij is* ∼ *af* zie *af*; ● *hij is* ∼ *i n talen* he is good at languages, **F** he is a whale at languages; *hij is weer* ∼ *o p haar* he is friends with her again; ∼ *v o o r...* gld. good for... guilders; *hij is* ∼ *voor zijn evenmens* kind to his fellowmen; *hij is er* ∼ *voor* he is good for it [that sum]; *hij is nergens* ∼ *voor* he is a good-for-nothing sort of fellow, he is no good; *het is ergens (nergens)* ∼ *voor* it serves some (no) purpose; *daar ben ik te* ∼ *voor* I am above that;

hij is er niet te ∼ *voor* he is not above that; *zich te* ∼ *doen* do oneself well; *zij deden zich te* ∼ *aan mijn wijn* they were having a go at my wine; *nog iets te* ∼ *hebben (van)* 1 have something in store; 2 (n o g t e v o r d e r e n) zie *tegoed*; *ik heb nog geld te* ∼ money is owing to me; *ik heb nog geld van hem te* ∼ he owes me money; *t e n* ∼*e beïnvloed* influenced for good; *verandering ten* ∼*e* change for the good (for the better); *u moet het mij ten* ∼*e houden* you must not take it ill of me; *dat zal u ten* ∼*e komen* it will benefit you; *jullie hebt* ∼ *praten* it is all very well for you to say so; zie ook: *houden, uitzien* &; *ik wens u alles* ∼*s* I wish you well; *niets dan* ∼*s* nothing but good; **II** *ad* well; ∼ *wat geld* a good deal of money; *als ik het* ∼ *heb* if I'm not mistaken; *zo* ∼ *en zo kwaad als hij kon* as best he might, somehow or other; *het is* ∼ *te zien* it is easily seen; *men kan net zo* ∼*...* one might just as well...; *hij doet (maakt) het* ∼ he is doing well; *hij kan* ∼ *leren* he is good at learning; *hij kan* ∼ *rekenen* he is good at sums; *hij kan* ∼ *schaatsen* he is a clever skater; *het smaakt* ∼ it tastes good; zie ook: *goede*

2 goed *o* 1 (h e t g o e d e) good; 2 (k l e d i n g- s t u k k e n) clothes, things; 3 (r e i s g o e d) luggage, things; 4 (g e r e i) things; 5 (k o o p- w a a r) wares, goods; 6 (b e z i t t i n g) goods, property, possession; 7 (l a n d g o e d) estate; 8 (s t o f f e n) stuff, material [for dresses]; *lijf en* ∼ life and property; *de strijd tussen* ∼ *en kwaad* the struggle between good and evil; *meer* ∼ *dan kwaad* more good than harm; *aardse* ∼*eren* worldly goods; *ik kan geen* ∼ *bij hem doen* I can do no good in his eyes; *gestolen* ∼ *gedijt niet* ill-gotten goods seldom prosper; *het hoogste* ∼ the highest good; *het kleine* ∼ the small fry; *onroerend* ∼ real property, real estate, immovables; *roerend* ∼ personal property, movables; *schoon* ∼ a change of linen; clean things; *vaste* ∼*eren* = *onroerend* ∼; *vuil* ∼ dirty linen; *mijn goeie* ∼ **F** my Sunday best; *dat zoete* ∼ that (sort of) sweet stuff

goed'aardig I *aj* 1 (v. m e n s e n) good-natured, benignant; 2 (v. z i e k t e n) benign [tumour], mild [form of measles]; **II** *ad* good-naturedly, benignantly; **–heid** *v* good nature [of a person, an animal]; benignity, mildness [of a disease]

'goedbedoeld well-meant; **–betaald** well-paid; **–bloed** (-s) *m een (Joris)* ∼ **F** a softy; **–deels** for the greater part; **–doen**[1] *vi* do good; **–dunken**[1] **I** *vi* think fit; **II** *o* approbation; *naar* ~ as you think fit, at discretion; *handel naar* ~ use your own discretion

'**goede** *o* good; *het* ~ *doen* do what is right; *te veel van het* ~ too much of a good thing

goede'middag good afternoon!; –'**morgen** good morning!; –'**nacht** good night!;

goeden'avond (b i j k o m s t) good evening!; (b i j v e r t r e k) good night!; –'**dag** (b i j k o m s t) good day!, hallo!; (b i j a f s c h e i d) good-bye!, bye-bye!; ~ *zeggen* (i n h e t v o o r b i j g a a n) say good morning, give the time of day, say hallo; (b i j v e r t r e k) say good-bye, bid farewell

'**goederen** *mv* goods; –**kantoor** (-toren) *o* goods office; –**loods** (-en) *v* goods shed; –**station** [-sta.(t)ʃɔn] (-s) *o* goods station; –**trein** (-en) *m* freight train, goods train; –**verkeer** *o* goods traffic; –**vervoer** *o* carriage of goods; –**voorraad** (-raden) *m* stock(-in-trade); –**wagen** (-s) *m* goods van [of a train], truck

goeder'hand *van* ~ from a good source

goeder'tieren merciful, clement; –**heid** *v* mercy, clemency

'**goedgebouwd** well-built

goed'geefs liberal, generous, open-handed; –**heid** *v* liberality, generosity, open-handedness

goedge'lovig credulous; –**heid** *v* credulity

'**goedgemikt** well-aimed; –**gevuld** well-lined [purse]; full [house, figure]; **goedge'zind** friendly

goed'gunstig kind; –**heid** *v* kindness

goed'hartig I *aj* good-natured, good-tempered, kind-hearted; **II** *ad* good-naturedly, kindheartedly; –**heid** (-heden) *v* good nature, kind-heartedness

'**goedheid** *v* goodness, kindness; *hemelse* ~ ! good heavens!, good gracious!; *wilt u de* ~ *hebben...* will you have the kindness to..., will you be so kind as to...; '**goedhouden** [1] zie *houden* **III**; '**goedig** good-natured; –**heid** *v* good nature; '**goedje** *o dat* ~ that (sort of) stuff

'**goedkeuren** [1] *vt* 1 approve (of) [a measure]; 2 pass [a person, play, film]; ✗ pass [him] fit (for service); –**d** approving; ~ *knikken* nod one's assent; '**goedkeuring** *v* 1 approval, approbation; assent; 2 ↩ good mark; *zijn* ~ *hechten aan* approve of; *zijn* ~ *onthouden* (*aan*) not approve (of); *o n d e r nadere* ~ *van* subject to the approval of; *t e r* ~ *voorleggen* submit for approval

goed'koop cheap[2]; low-budget; ~ *is duurkoop* cheap goods are dearest in the long run; cheap bargains are dear; –'**lachs** fond of laughter, easily amused; *zij is erg* ~ she laughs very easily; –'**leers** teachable, docile; '**goed-maken** [1] *vt* 1 (v e r b e t e r e n) put right, repair [a mistake]; 2 (a a n v u l l e n, i n h a l e n, h e r s t e l l e n) make good, make up for [a loss]; *het weer* ~ make (it) up again;

goed'moedig = *goedhartig*; '**goedpraten** [1] *vt iets* ~ gloze (varnish) sth. over, explain sth. away, gloss over, whitewash; '**goedschiks** with a good grace, willingly; ~ *of kwaadschiks* willy-nilly; **goeds'moeds** 1 with a good courage; 2 of good cheer; '**goedvinden** [1] ↑ *vt* think fit, approve of; *hij zal het wel* ~ he won't mind; **II** *o* approval; *m e t* ~ *van...* with the consent of...; *met onderling* ~ by mutual consent; *doe* (*handel*) *n a a r eigen* ~ use your own discretion; *naar eigen* ~ *handelen* act on one's own discretion; **goed'willig** willing; '**goedzak** (-ken) *m* = *goeierd*; **goege'meente** *v de* ~ the general public, the public at large; '**goeierd** (-s) *m* 1 dear (kind) soul, good fellow; 2 > simpleton, **F** juggins

'**gok** *m* gamble; *een* ~*je* **F** a flutter; –**automaat** [au = ɔu en o.] (-maten) *o* fruitmachine; '**gokken** (gokte, h. gegokt) *vi* gamble; –**er** (-s) *m* gambler; **gokke'rij** (-en) *v* gamble, gambling; '**goktent** (-en) *v* gambling house; disorderly house

gold (**golden**) V.T. v. *gelden*

1 golf [gɔlf] (**golven**) *v* 1 wave° [ook R], billow; stream [of blood]; 2 (i n h a m) bay, gulf

2 golf [gɔlf] *o sp* golf; –**baan** (-banen) *v sp* golf-course, golf-links

'**golfbeweging** (-en) *v* undulatory motion, undulation; –**breker** (-s) *m* breakwater, pier, bulwark; –**dal** (-dalen) *o* trough (of the sea); –**ijzer** *o* corrugated iron; –**karton** *o* corrugated cardboard; –**lengte** (-n en -s) *v* wave-length; –**lijn** (-en) *v* wavy (sinuous) line; –**slag** *m* dash of the waves; –**stok** (-ken) *m sp* golf-club; '**Golfstroom** *m* Gulf-Stream; '**golven** (golfde, h. gegolfd) *vt* & *vi* wave, undulate; zie ook *gegolfd*; –**d** waving, wavy [hair], undulating [countryside]; rolling [fields]; flowing [robes]; '**golving** (-en) *v* waving, undulation

gom (-men) *m* & *o* gum; *Arabische* ~ gum arabic; zie ook: *vlakgom*; –**achtig** gummy; –**bal** (-len) *m* gum, gum-drop; **gomelas'tiek** [gɔme-] *o* (india-)rubber; '**gomhars** (-en) *o* & *m* gum-resin; '**gommen** (gomde, h. gegomd)

---

[1] V.T. en V.D. van dit werkwoord volgens het model: '**goed**keuren, V.T. keurde '**goed**, V.D. '**goed**gekeurd. Zie voor.de vormen onder het grondwoord, in dit voorbeeld: *keuren*. Bij sterke en onregelmatige werkwoorden wordt u verwezen naar de lijst achterin.

vt gum

'**gondel** (-s) *v* gondola; **gonde'lier** (-s) *m* gondolier; '**gondellied** (-eren) *o* barcarol(l)e

gong (-s) *m* gong

goniome'trie *v* goniometry

gonor'rhoea [go.nɔ'rø.] *v* gonorrhea, **S** clap

'**gonzen** (gonsde, h. gegonsd) *vi* buzz, hum, drone, whirr; *het gonst van geruchten* the air buzzes with rumours

'**goochelaar** (-s) *m* juggler, conjurer, illusionist; juggler; '**goochela'rij** (-en) *v* conjuring, conjuring trick(s); juggling, jugglery; '**goochelen** (goochelde, h. gegoocheld) *vi* conjure, perform conjuring tricks; juggle²; ~ *met cijfers* juggle with figures; '**goochelkunst** (-en) *v* 1 prestidigitation; 2 = *goocheltoer*; **–toer** (-en) *m*, **–truc** [-try.k] (-s) conjuring trick

'**goochem** knowing, shrewd, **F** all there; **–erd** (-s) *m* **F** slyboots

gooi (-en) *m* cast, throw; *een ~ naar iets doen* 1 have a shot at sth., have a try at sth.; 2 make a bid for sth.; '**gooien** (gooide, h. gegooid) **I** *vt* fling, cast, throw; *d o o r elkaar ~* jumble; *iets i n het vuur ~* throw (fling, toss) sth. into the fire; *m e t de deur ~* slam the door; *iem. met iets ~* throw (pitch, shy) sth. at sbd.; *iem. met stenen ~* pelt sbd. with stones; *iets n a a r iem. ~* toss (throw) sth. to sbd.; *o p papier ~* dash off [an article &]; *het (de schuld) op iem. ~* lay the blame (for it) on sbd.; *het op iets anders ~* turn the talk to something else; zie ook: *balk* & *boeg*; **II** *va* throw; *jij moet ~* it is your turn to throw; *gooi jij ook eens* have a throw, too; **gooi-en-'smijt-film** (-s) *m* slapstick film; **–kraam** (-kramen) *v* cock-shy

goor dingy; *fig* nasty; **–heid** *v* dinginess; *fig* nastiness

1 goot (goten) *v* gutter, gully, kennel, drain; **2 goot** (goten) V.T. v. *gieten*; '**gootsteen** (-stenen) *m* (kitchen) sink; **–water** *o* gutter-water; slops

'**gordel** (-s) *m* girdle [round waist], belt² [of leather, of forts], ⊙ zone; *een stoot onder de ~ toebrengen* hit below the belt²; **–dier** (-en) *o* ﹩ armadillo; **–riem** (-en) *m* belt; **–roos** *v* ✝ shingles

'**gorden** (gordde, h. gegord) **I** *vt* gird; **II** *vr zich ten strijde ~* gird oneself (up) for the fight

gordi'aans *de ~e knoop* the Gordian knot; zie ook: *knoop*

gor'dijn (-en) *o* & *v* curtain [of window, in theatre]; (o p r o l l e n) blind; *ijzeren ~* iron curtain; **–koord** (-en) *o* & *v* curtain-cord; **–rail** [-re.l] *v*, **gor'dijnreel** (-s) *v* curtain-rail; **–ring** (-en) *m* curtain-ring; **–roe(de)** (-den) *v* curtain-rod, curtain-pole

'**gording** (-s en -en) *v* ⚓ bunt-line

'**gorgeldrank** (-en) *m* gargle; '**gorgelen** (gorgelde, h. gegorgeld) *vi* gargle

go'rilla ('s) *m* gorilla

gors (gorzen) *v* ✦ bunting

gort *m* groats, grits; (s p e c i a a l) barley; (p a p) gruel

'**gortig** *het al te ~ maken* go too far

'**gossie!, gossie'mijne F** gosh!

1 'Goten *mv* Goths

2 'goten V.T. meerv. v. *gieten*

go'tiek *v* Gothic (style), Gothicism; '**gotisch** Gothic; *~e letter* Gothic letter, black letter; '**Gotisch** *o* Gothic

goud *o* gold; *het is ~ waard* it is worth its weight in gold; *het is alles geen ~ wat er blinkt* it is not all gold that glitters; **–achtig** gold-like, golden; **–blond** golden; **–brokaat** *o* gold-brocade; **–bruin** auburn [hair]; golden brown; **–clausule** [s = z] (-s) *v* gold clause; **–dekking** (-en) *v* ＄ gold cover; **–delver** (-s) *m* gold-digger; **–dorst** *m* thirst for (of) gold, lust of gold, gold-thirst; **–draad** (-draden) *m* & *o* 1 gold-wire; 2 gold-thread; **–druk** *m* gold-printing; '**gouden** gold, golden²; ~ *bril* gold-rimmed spectacles; ~ *standaard* gold standard; **gouden'regen** (-s) *m* laburnum; '**gouderts** (-en) *o* gold-ore; **–fazant** (-en) *m* golden pheasant; **–geel** gold-coloured, golden; **–geld** *o* gold coin, gold; **–graver** (-s) *m* gold-digger; **–houdend** gold-bearing, auriferous; **–kleur** *v* gold colour; **–kleurig** golden, gold-coloured; **–klomp** (-en) *m* nugget of gold; **–koorts** *v* gold-fever; **–le(d)er** *o* gilt leather; **–le(de)ren** *aj* gilt-leather; **–merk** (-en) *o* hallmark [on gold]; **–mijn** (-en) *v* gold-mine²; **–renet** [-rɔnt] (-ten) *v* golden rennet

Gouds Gouda [cheese]

'**goudsbloem** (-en) *v* marigold; '**goudschaal** (-schalen) *v* gold-balance, gold-scales, assay-balance; *zijn woorden op een ~ wegen* weigh one's every word; **–smid** (-smeden) *m* goldsmith; **–stuk** (-ken) *o* gold coin; '**goudveld** (-en) *o* gold-field; **–vink** (-en) *m* & *v* ✦ bullfinch; **–vis** (-sen) *m* 1 ⌬ goldfish; 2 *fig* ~(*je*) rich heiress; **–viskom** (-men) *v* globe (for goldfish), goldfish bowl; **–voorraad** (-raden) *m* gold stock(s); **–werk** (-en) *o* gold-work; **–zoeker** (-s) *m* gold-seeker

gouver'nante [gu.-] (-s) *v* governess

gouverne'ment [gu.vɛrnə'mɛnt] (-en) *o* government; **gouverne'mentsambtenaar** (-s en -naren) *m* government officer (official, servant); **–dienst** (-en) *m* government service; *in ~* in the government service

gouver'neur [gu.vɔr'nø:r] (-s) *m* 1 governor; 2 (o n d e r w i j z e r) tutor; **gouver'neur-gene'raal** [-ge.-] (gouverneurs-generaal) *m* governor-general; **gouver'neurs–** gubernatorial

gouw (-en) *v* district, province

'gouwenaar (-s) *m* long clay, **F** churchwarden

'gozer (-s) *m* **S** bloke, guy, chap

graad (graden) *m* 1 degree°; 2 (r a n g) rank, grade, degree; 3 (v a n b l o e d v e r w a n t - s c h a p) remove; *14 graden vorst* 14 degrees of frost; *een ~ halen* take one's [university] degree; ● *b ij 0 graden* at zero; *i n graden verdelen* graduate; *o p 52 graden noorderbreedte en 16 graden westerlengte* in latitude 52° north and in longitude 16° west; **–boog** (-bogen) *m* protractor, graduated arc, quadrant scale; **–meter** (-s) *m* graduator; *fig* criterion, standard; **–verdeling** (-en) *v* graduation

graaf (graven) *m* 1 earl [in England]; 2 count [on the Continent]; **–lijk** = *grafelijk*

'graafmachine [-ma.ʃi.nə] (-s) *v* excavator

'graafschap (-pen) *o* 1 (g e b i e d) county, shire; 2 countship, earldom

'graafwerk (-en) *o* digging, excavation(s); **–wesp** (-en) *v* digger-wasp

graag I *aj* eager; **II** *ad* gladly, readily, willingly; with pleasure; *hij doet het ~* he likes to do it, he likes it; *ik zou niet ~* I would not care to; *wil je nog wat...? heel ~* thank you!; *~ of niet* take it or leave it!; zie ook: *gaarne;* **–te** *v* eagerness, appetite

'graaien (graaide, h. gegraaid) *vt & vi* grab; grabble

graal *m* (Holy) Grail; **–ridder** (-s) *m* Knight of the Round Table

graan (granen) *o* corn, grain; *granen* cereals; **–beurs** (-beurzen) *v* corn-exchange; **–bouw** *m* corn-growing; **–gewassen** *mv* cereals; **–handel** (-s) *m* corn-trade; **–handelaar** (-s en -laren) *m* corn-dealer, corn-merchant; **–korrel** (-s) *m* grain of corn; **–oogst** (-en) *m* grain-crop(s), cereal crop; **–pakhuis** (-huizen) *o* granary, **–schuur** (-schuren) *v* granary²; **–silo** ('s) *m* = *graanpakhuis,* **–tje** (-s) *o een ~ pikken* **F** have a quick drink; *een ~ meepikken* profit by, gain by; **–zolder** (-s) *m* corn-loft; **–zuiger** (-s) *m* grain elevator

graat (graten) *v* fish-bone, bone; *rood (niet zuiver) op de ~* 1 not fresh [of fish]; 2 *fig* unreliable; unorthodox [in politics]; 3 red [= a socialist, communist]; *fijn op de ~* orthodox; *van de ~ vallen* 1 be faint with hunger; 2 lose flesh; 3 faint

'grabbel *te ~ gooien* throw [among children] to be scrambled for; *zijn eer te ~ gooien* throw away one's honour; *zijn geld te ~ gooien [fig]* make ducks and drakes of one's money;

'grabbelen (grabbelde, h. gegrabbeld) *vi* scramble [for a thing], grabble [in...]; **'grab-**

belton (-nen) *v* bran-tub, bran-pie, lucky dip

gracht (-en) *v* 1 canal [in a town]; 2 ditch, moat [round a town]; *ik woon op een ~* I live in a canal street; **–enhuis** (-huizen) *o* [Amsterdam] canal(side) house

graci'eus [gra.si.'øs] graceful

gra'datie [-(t)si.] (-s en -iën) *v* gradation; **'gradenboog** (-bogen) *m* = *graadboog;* **gra'deren** (gradeerde, h. gegradeerd) *vt* graduate

gradu'eel [difference] of (in) degree

graf (graven) *o* grave, ☉ tomb, sepulchre; *witgepleisterde graven* **B** whited sepulchres; *het Heilige Graf* the Holy Sepulchre; *zijn eigen ~ graven* dig one's own grave; *een ~ in de golven vinden* find a watery grave; **F** go to Davy Jones's locker; ● *hij sprak a a n het ~* he spoke at the graveside; *dat zal hem i n het ~ brengen* that will bring him to his grave; *het geheim met zich meenemen in het ~* carry the secret with one to the grave; *hij zou zich in zijn ~ omkeren* he would turn in his grave; *t e n grave dalen* sink into the grave; *iem. ten grave dragen* bear sbd. to burial; *dit zal hem ten grave slepen* it will bring him (carry him off) to his grave; *t o t aan het ~* till death

'grafelijk 1 of a count, of an earl; 2 like a count, like an earl; zie *graaf*

'grafgewelf (-welven) *o* sepulchral vault; (o n d e r k e r k) crypt; **–heuvel** (-s) *m* 1 burial mound, grave-mound; 2 ▯ barrow, tumulus [*mv* tumuli]

'graficus (-ci) *m* graphic artist

gra'fiek (-en) *v* 1 (k u n s t) graphic arts, graphics; (v o o r t b r e n g s e l e n d a a r v a n) drawings; 2 (v o o r s t e l l i n g) graph, diagram

gra'fiet *o* graphite, plumbago

'grafisch graphic; *~e kunst* graphic arts, graphics; (s t a t i s t i e k) *~e voorstelling* graph, diagram

'grafkamer (-s) *v* burial chamber; **–kapel** (-len) *v* mortuary chapel; **–kelder** (-s) *m* (family) vault; **–krans** (-en) *m* (funeral) wreath; **–kuil** (-en) *m* grave; **–legging** (-en) *v* interment, sepulture; *de ~ van Christus* the Entombment of Christ; **–lucht** *v* sepulchral smell; **–monument** (-en) *o* mortuary monument

grafolo'gie *v* graphology; **grafo'loog** (-logen) *m* graphologist, handwriting expert

'grafrede (-s) *v* funeral oration; **–schennis** *v* desecration of graves (a grave); **–schrift** (-en) *o* epitaph; **–steen** (-stenen) *m* gravestone, tombstone; **–stem** (-men) *v* sepulchral voice; **–tombe** (-s en -n) *v* tomb; **–waarts** to the grave; **–zerk** (-en) *v* = *grafsteen;* **–zuil** (-en) *m*

sepulchral pillar
1 gram (-men) *o* gramme
2 gram *v zijn ~ halen* obtain satisfaction (compensation), get one's own back
gram'matica ('s) *v* grammar; **grammati'caal** grammatical'
grammo'foon (-s en -fonen) *m* gramophone, record player; **–muziek** *v* gramophone music, recorded music; **F** canned (tinned) music; **–naald** (-en) *v* gramophone needle; **–plaat** (-platen) *v* (gramophone) record, disk
'gramschap *v* anger, wrath; **gram'storig** angry, wrathful
1 gra'naat (-naten) *m* (s t e e n) garnet
2 gra'naat (-naten) *v* ✠ shell; (hand) grenade
3 gra'naat *o* (s t o f n a a m) garnet
gra'naatappel (-en en -s) *m* pomegranate
gra'naatscherf (-scherven) *v* shell splinter; **–trechter** (-s) *m* shell hole, shell crater; **–vuur** *o* shell fire
grandi'oos grandiose, grand
'grand-seig'neur ['grãsī'jø.r] (grands-seigneurs) *m* fine gentleman; **F** swell; *de ~ uithangen* do the grand, play the swell
gra'niet *o* granite; **–blok** (-ken) *o* block of granite; **gra'nieten** *aj* granite
granu'leren (granuleerde, h. gegranuleerd) *vt* granulate
grap (-pen) *v* joke, jest; **F** gag; *een dure ~* an expensive business (affair); *een mooie ~!* a nice affair!; *dat zou me een ~ zijn!* I wouldn't that be fun (some fun)?; 2 **F** that would be a nice go!; *~pen maken* joke, cut jokes; *~pen uithalen* play tricks; *je moet hier geen ~pen uithalen* you must not play off your (any) jokes here, don't come your tricks over me; *hij maakte er een ~(je) van* he laughed it off; *voor de ~* in (for) fun, by way of a joke; **'grapjas** (-sen) *m,* **'grappenmaker** (-s) *m* wag, joker; **grappenmake'rij** (-en) *v* drollery, waggery; **'grappig I** *aj* funny, amusing, droll, comic, facetious; (b i j z o n d e r) quaint; jocose, jocular; comical; *het ~ste was* the funniest part of it was, the best joke of all was; **II** *ad* funnily, drolly, comically, facetiously; jocosely, jocularly; **–heid** (-heden) *v* fun, drollery, comicality, facetiousness; jocosity, jocularity
gras (-sen) *o* grass; *Engels ~* ⚘ sea-pink, thrift; *hij laat er geen ~ over groeien* he doesn't let the grass grow under his feet; *iem. het ~ voor de voeten wegmaaien* cut the ground from under sbd.'s feet; **–achtig** grass-like, grassy; **–baan** (-banen) *v sp* 1 grass-court [for lawntennis]; 2 grass-track [for racing]; **–boter** *v* grass-butter, May-butter; **–duinen** (grasduinde, h. gegrasduind) *vi ergens in ~* browse [among books &, in a book]; **–gewas** (-sen) *o* 1 grass crop; 2

graminaceous plant; **–groen** as green as grass, grassgreen; **–halm** (-en) *m* grass-blade, blade of grass; **–je** (-s) *o* blade of grass; **–land** (-en) *o* grassland; **–linnen** *o* grass-cloth; cotton fabric; **–maaier** (-s) *m* 1 (p e r s o o n) grass-mower; 2 = *grasmaaimachine*; **–maaimachine** [-ma.ʃi.nə] (-s) *v* lawn-mower, grass-cutter; **–maand** [-ma.ʃi.nə] (-s) *v* April; **–mat** (-ten) *v* turf, sward; **–mus** (-sen) *v* 🐦 whitethroat; **–perk** (-en) *o* grass-plot, lawn; **–rol** (-len) *v,* **–roller** (-s) *m* garden-roller; **–spriet** (-en) *m* blade of grass; **–veld** (-en) *o* grass-field; lawn, grass-plot; **–vlakte** (-n en -s) *v* grassy plain, prairie; **–zode** (-n) *v* (turf) sod
'gratie ['gra.(t)si.] (-tiën) *v* 1 (g e n a d e) pardon, grace; (v. d o o d s t r a f) reprieve; 2 (b e v a l l i g h e i d) grace; *~ verlenen (aan)* pardon; *verzoek om ~* appeal for mercy; ● *bij de ~ Gods* by the grace of God; *weer i n de ~ komen* be restored to grace (in favour); *in de ~ trachten te komen bij* ingratiate oneself with; *bij iem. in de ~ zijn* be in favour with sbd., be in sbd.'s good books; *bij iem. u i t de ~ raken* lose favour with sbd., fall from grace; *bij iem. u i t de ~ zijn* be out of favour with sbd., be no longer in sbd.'s good books
gratifi'catie [-(t)si.] (-s en -tiën) *v* bonus, gratuity
'gratig bony
'gratis I *aj* gratis, free (of charge); *~ monster* $ free sample; **II** *ad* gratis, free (of charge)
gratu'it [gra.ty'vi.t] *aj* gratuitous [remark]
1 grauw (-en) *m* growl, snarl
2 grauw *o* rabble, mob
3 grauw *aj* grey; *fig* drab; **–achtig** greyish, grizzly
'grauwen (grauwde, h. gegrauwd) *vi* snarl; *~ en snauwen* growl and grumble, snap and snarl
'grauwtje (-s) *o* donkey
gra'veerder (-s) *m* engraver; **gra'veerkunst** *v* art of engraving; **–naald** (-en) *v,* **–staal** *o,* **–stift** (-en) *v* engraving-needle, burin; **–werk** (-en) *o* engraving
1 'graven* I *vt* dig [a hole, pit, well &]; ✠ burrow [a hole]; sink [a mine, a well]; **II** *vi* dig, ✠ burrow
2 'graven meerv. v. *graf* en *graaf*
's-Graven'hage *o* The Hague
'graver (-s) *m* digger
gra'veren (graveerde, h. gegraveerd) *vt & vi* engrave; **gra'veur** (-s) *m* engraver
gra'vin (-nen) *v* countess
gra'vure (-n en -s) *v* engraving, plate
'grazen (graasde, h. gegraasd) *vi* graze, pasture, feed; *iem. te ~ nemen* 1 take sbd. in; 2 get one's own back

'**grazig** grassy; **B** ~*e weiden* green pastures
1 greep (grepen) *m* 1 (h e t g r i j p e n) grip, grasp; > clutch; 2 *v* handful [of salt &]; 3 (h a n d v a t) grip [of a weapon &], clutch [of a crane], handle [of a tool &], pull [of a bell], hilt [of a sword], haft [of a dagger]; 4 (v o r k) (dung-)fork; *een gelukkige* ~ a lucky hit; *hier en daar een* ~ *doen in...* dip into the subject here and there; *een* ~ *doen naar* make a grab at; *fig* make a bid for [power]
2 greep (grepen) V.T. v. *grijpen*
Gregori'aans *aj* (& *sb*) Gregorian (chant)
grei'neren (greineerde, h. gegreineerd) *vt* granulate
'**greintje** (-s) *o* particle, atom, spark; *geen* ~ *ijdelheid* not a grain of vanity; *geen* ~ *verschil* not a bit of difference;
grena'dier (-s) *m* ✗ grenadier
grena'dine *v* grenadine
'**grendel** (-s) *m* bolt [of a door, of a rifle &], slot; '**grendelen** (grendelde, h. gegrendeld) *vt* bolt
'**grenehout** *o* deal; '**grenen** *aj* deal
grens (grenzen) *v* 1 limit, boundary; 2 (b e p e r k i n g) bound; 3 (p o l i t i e k e s c h e i l ij n) frontier, border; (n a t u u r l ij k e s c h e i l ij n) border; *alles heeft zijn grenzen* there are limits (to everything); *de grenzen te buiten gaan* go beyound all bounds, exceed all bounds; *zijn... kent geen grenzen* his... knows no bounds; ● *b i n n e n zekere grenzen* within certain limits; *binnen de grenzen blijven van...* keep within the bounds of...; *o p de* ~ *van* [*fig*] on the verge of; *o v e r de* ~ *zetten* conduct across the frontier; **–bewoner** (-s) *m* frontier inhabitant, borderer; **–gebied** (-en) *o* border (frontier) area, borderland; *fig* borderland, twilight zone; **–geschil** (-len) *o* frontier (border) dispute; **–geval** (-len) *o* borderline case; **–incident** (-en) *o* border incident; **–kantoor** (-toren) *o* frontier customhouse; **–land** (-en) *o* borderland; **–lijn** (-en) *v* border line; boundary; *pol* line of demarcation; **–nut** *o* marginal utility; **–paal** (-palen) *m* boundary post, landmark; **–rechter** (-s) *m sp* linesman; **–regeling** (-en) *v* frontier settlement; **–rivier** (-en) *v* river forming a border; **–station** [-sta.(t)ʃòn] (-s) *o* frontier station; **–steen** (-stenen) *m* boundary stone; **–verkeer** *o* frontier (border) traffic; **–vesting** (-en) *v* frontier fortress; **–waarde** (-n) *v* 1 × ultimate (limit) value; 2 $ marginal utility [of an article]; **–wacht** (-en) *v* (p o s t) frontier outpost; *m* (s o l d a a t) frontier guard;
'**grenzeloos** boundless, unlimited; '**grenzen** (grensde, h. gegrensd) *vi* ~ *aan* border on, abut on; *fig* border on (upon), verge on (upon); *dit land grenst ten noorden aan...* is bounded on the

North by...
'**grepen** V.T. meerv. v. *grijpen*
'**greppel** (-s) *v* trench, ditch, drain
'**gretig** avid [of], eager [for], greedy [of]; **–heid** *v* avidity, eagerness, greediness
'**gribus** (-sen) *m* slum; 2 hovel, **F** hole
grief (grieven) *v* grievance; (o n r e c h t) wrong; *een* ~ *hebben* have a monkey on one's back
Griek (-en) *m* Greek²; '**Griekenland** *o* Greece; '**Grieks I** *aj* 1 (e c h t G r i e k s) Greek; 2 (n a a r G r i e k s m o d e l) Grecian; **II** *o* Greek
griend (-en) *v* low willow-ground
'**grienen** (griende, h. gegriend) *vi* cry, snivel, blubber, whimper
griep *v* influenza, **F** flu; **–epidemie** (-mieën) *v* influenza epidemic
gries *o* middlings; **–meel** *o* semolina
1 griet (-en) *v* 🐟 brill
2 griet (-en) *m* 🦅 godwit
3 griet (-en) *v* (m e i s j e) **P** skirt, piece; *Am* **F** dame
'**grieve** (-n) *v* = *grief*; '**grieven** (griefde, h. gegriefd) *vt* hurt, offend; **–d** offensive, bitter
'**griezel** (-s) *m* 1 (o o r z a a k v a n a f k e e r) horror; 2 (r i l l i n g) shudder, (the) creep(s); '**griezelen** (griezelde, h. gegriezeld) *vi* shiver, shudder; ~ *bij de gedachte* shiver (shudder) at the thought; *ik griezel ervan* it makes me shudder; it gives me the creeps; '**griezelfilm** (-s) *m* horror film; '**griezelig** gruesome, creepy, weird
grif readily, promptly
'**griffel** (-s) *v* slate-pencil; **–doos** (-dozen) *v*, **–koker** (-s) *m* pencil-case
'**griffen** (grifte, h. gegrift) *vt* grave (on *in*), inscribe (on *in*)
'**griffie** (-s) *v* office of the clerk; *ter* ~ *deponeren* [*fig*] shelve [a proposal &]; **grif'fier** (-s) *m* clerk (of the court), recorder, registrar; '**griffie-recht** (-en) *o* registration fee
griff(i)'oen (-en) *m* griffin
'**grifweg** = *grif*
grijns (grijnzen) *v* smirk, grimace; **–lach** *m* sneer; **–lachen** (grijnslachte, h. gegrijnslacht) *vi* laugh sardonically, sneer; '**grijnzen** (grijnsde, h. gegrijnsd) *vi* smirk, grimace
'**grijparm** (-en) *m* ✗ grip arm, transfer arm; 🐙 tentacle; '**grijpen* I** *vt* 1 (o m v a t t e n) catch, seize, lay hold of, grasp; 2 (n a a r z i c h t o e) grasp, grab, snatch; 3 (i n z i j n k l a u w) clutch; **II** *vi i n e l k a a r* ~ ✗ gear into one another; ~ *n a a r* grab (snatch, grasp) at [it]; reach for [his revolver &]; take up [arms]; make a bid for [power]; *o m z i c h h e e n* ~ spread [of flames]; zie ook *ineengrijpen*; **III** *o je hebt ze maar v o o r het* ~ they are as plentiful as black-

berries; *ze zijn niet voor het ~* they are not found every day, they do not grow on every bush; *voor het ~ liggen* be (lie) ready to hand, be readily available; (o p l o s s i n g) be obvious; '**grijper** (-s) *m* ✗ grab; '**grijpstaart** (-en) *m* prehensile tail; **–stuiver** (-s) *m* trifle

grijs grey; grey-haired, grey-headed; *fig* hoary [antiquity]; *~ worden = grijzen*; **–aard** (-s) *m* grey-haired man, old man; **–achtig** greyish; **–heid** *v* greyness, hoariness²; '**grijzen** (grijsde, is gegrijsd) *vi* grow (become, go, turn) grey, grey; '**grijzig** greyish

gril (-len) *v* caprice, whim, freak, fancy '**grille** ['gri.jə] (-s) *v* (v. a u t o) radiator grill '**grillen** (grilde, h. gegrild), **gril'leren** [grɪl-] (grilleerde, h. gegrilleerd) *vt* grill '**grillig** capricious, whimsical, freakish, fitful, fickle, wanton; **F** crotchety; **–heid** (-heden) *v* capriciousness, caprice, whimsicality, whimsicalness, fitfulness

gri'mas (-sen) *v* grimace, wry face; *~sen maken* grimace, make wry faces, pull faces **grime** [gri.m] (-s) *v* make-up [of actors]; **gri'meren** (grimeerde, h. gegrimeerd) **I** *vt* make up; **II** *vr zich ~* make up '**grimmig** grim, truculent; **–heid** *v* grimness **grind** *o* gravel; **–weg** (-wegen) *m* gravel-road, gravelled road '**grinniken** (grinnikte, h. gegrinnikt) *vi* chuckle, chortle, snigger '**grissen** (griste, h. gegrist) *vt* grab, snatch **1 groef** (groeven) *v = groeve* **2 groef** (**groeven**) V.T. v. *graven* **groei** *m* growth; *in de ~ zijn* be growing; *op de ~ gemaakt* made with a view to growing requirements; '**groeien** (groeide, is gegroeid) *vi* grow; *iem. b o v e n (o v e r) het hoofd ~* 1 outgrow sbd.; 2 *fig* get beyond sbd.'s control; *~ i n* exult in [the misfortunes of others &]; *u i t zijn kracht (kleren) ~* outgrow one's strength (clothes); '**groeifonds** (-en) *o* growth stock; **–kracht** *v* vegetative faculty, vigour, vitality; **–proces** (-sen) *o* process of growth; '**groeisnelheid** (-heden) *v* rate of growth, growth rate; '**groeistuip** (-en) *v ~en* growing pains, infantile convulsions; *~ weer* growing weather **groen I** *aj* green², ⊙ & *fig* verdant; *het werd hem ~ en geel voor de ogen* his head began to swim; *het licht op ~ zetten voor* give the green light (the go-ahead) to [a plan &]; *een ~e hand (~e vingers) hebben* [*fig*] have a green thumb (green fingers); *~e kaart* international motor insurance card; *~e zeep* soft soap; *~e zone* green belt; **II** 1 *o* (a l s k l e u r) green; (l e v e n d) verdure, greenery; 2 (-en) *m* greenhorn; *~* freshman, fresher; **–achtig** greenish; **–gordel** (-s) *m*

green belt; **–heid** *v* greenness², verdancy; **–ig** greenish; ⊙ viridescent; **–strook** (-stroken) *v* green belt; 2 grass-strip; centre strip [of grass] '**groente** (-n en -s) *v* 1 (o n g e k o o k t) greens, vegetables, green stuff; 2 (g e k o o k t) vegetables; **–boer** (-en) *m* greengrocer; **–kweker** (-s) *m* vegetable grower, market gardener; **–kwekerij** (-en) *v* market garden; **–man** (-nen) *m* greengrocer; **–markt** (-en) *v* vegetable market; **–soep** (-en) *v* vegetable soup; **–tuin** (-en) *m* kitchen-garden, vegetable garden; **–vrouw** (-en) *v* greengrocer('s wife); **–winkel** (-s) *m* greengrocer's (shop) '**groentijd** (-en) *m ~* noviciate; **–vink** (-en) *m* & *v* greenfinch; **–voe(de)r** *o* green fodder **groep** (-en) *v* group; cluster [of stars, islands, houses], clump [of trees, plants], batch [of children, recruits], body [of men, members], band [of robbers, fugitives] **groe'page** [-pa.ʒə] *v* (o v e r zee) joint cargo; (o v e r l a n d) combined truck load **groe'peren** (groepeerde, h. gegroepeerd) **I** *vt* group; **II** *vr zich ~* group themselves; **–ring** (-en) *v* grouping '**groepje** (-s) *o* (little) group [of people], cluster, clump [of trees]; *bij ~s* in groups; '**groepsgewijs**, **–gewijze** in groups; '**groepspraktijk** (-en) *v* group practice; '**groep(s)verband** *in ~* in groups; *werken in ~* do teamwork **groet** (-en) *m* greeting, salutation, salute; *de ~en aan allemaal!* best love to all!; *de ~ thuis* remember me to the family; *hij laat de ~en doen* he begs to be remembered to you; he sends his love; *met mijn vriendelijke ~en* with kind(est) regards; '**groeten** (groette, h. gegroet) **I** *vt* greet, salute; *gegroet, hoor!* 1 good-bye!; 2 (s a r c a s-t i s c h) good afternoon!; *groet hem van mij* kindly remember me to him; **II** *va* salute, raise (take off) one's hat, touch one's cap; '**groetenis** (-sen) *v* salutation '**groeve** (-n) *v* groove, channel, flute [in a column]; furrow² [between two ridges; in the forehead]; line [in a face]; pit [for marl], quarry [for stones]; *bij de (geopende) ~* at the graveside, at the open grave **1 'groeven** (groefde, h. gegroefd) *vt* groove; zie ook *gegroefd* **2 'groeven** V.T. meerv. v. *graven* '**groezelig** dingy, grubby, dirty; **–heid** *v* dinginess, dirtiness **grof I** *aj* 1 (n i e t f i j n) coarse [bread, cloth, hair, salt, features &]; rough [work]; large-toothed [comb]; 2 (n i e t b e w e r k t) crude [oar]; 3 (n i e t g l a d) coarse [hands], rough [towels]; 4 (l a a g) deep [voice]; 5 *fig* coarse [language], rude, abusive [words, terms]; crude [style]; gross [injustice, insult, ignorance], big [lies &]; guess [estimate]; *dadelijk ~ worden* become rude (abusive) at once; **II** *ad* coarsely &; *~ liegen* lie barefacedly; *~ spelen* play high; *~ geld verdienen* make big money; *~* (*geld*) *verteren* spend money like water; **–gebouwd** large-limbed, big-boned; **–grein** *o* grogram; **–heid** (-heden) *v* coarseness &; *grofheden* ook: rude things; **–korrelig** coarse-grained; **–smid** (-smeden) *m* blacksmith

grog [grɔk] *m* grog; **–stem** (-men) *v* husky voice

grol (-len) *v* broad joke; *~len* buffoonery

grom *m* growl; **'grommen** (gromde, h. gegromd) *vi* grumble, growl (at *tegen*); **'grompot** (-ten) *m* grumbler

grond (-en) *m* 1 (a a r d e) ground, earth, soil; 2 (l a n d) land; 3 (o n d e r s t e) ground, bottom; 4 (g r o n d s l a g) ground, foundation, substratum [of truth]; 5 *fig* (r e d e n) ground, reason; *vaste ~* firm ground; *vaste ~ onder de voeten hebben* be on firm ground; *~ hebben* (*krijgen, voelen, vinden*) feel ground, touch ground; *de ~ leggen tot...* lay the foundation(s) of...; *~ verliezen* lose ground; *ik voelde geen ~* I was out of my depth; ● *a a n d e ~ raken* (*zitten*) ⚓ run (be) aground; *aan de ~ geraakt* [*fig*] **F** down and out; *b o v e n d e ~* above ground; *d o o r d e ~ zinken* sink through the ground; *iets in de ~ kennen* know sth. thoroughly; *in de ~ is hij eerlijk* he is an honest fellow at bottom; *in de ~ hebt u gelijk* fundamentally you are right; *o n d e r d e ~* under ground, underground; *o p ~ van...* on the ground of..., on the score of..., on the strength of...; *op ~ van het feit dat...* on the ground(s) that...; *op goede ~* on good grounds; *op de ~ gooien* throw down; *op de ~ vallen* fall to the ground; *t e ~e gaan* go to rack and ruin, be ruined, come to nought; *te ~e richten* bring to ruin (nought), ruin, wreck; *t e g e n de ~ gooien* throw (dash) to the ground; *u i t de ~ van zijn hart* from the bottom of his heart; *v a n alle ~ ontbloot* without any foundation; *een dichter van de koude ~* a would-be poet; *groenten van de koude ~* open-grown vegetables; *van de ~ komen* get off the ground; **–beginsel** (-en en -s) *o* fundamental (basic, root) principle; *de ~en* the elements, rudiments, fundamentals; **–begrip** (-pen) *o* fundamental (basic) idea; **–belasting** (-en) *v* land-tax; **–bestanddeel** (-delen) *o* fundamental part; **–bezit** *o* landed property; **–bezitter** (-s) *m* landed proprietor, landholder; **–boring** (-en) *v* soil drilling, soil boring; **–dienst** (-en) *m* ⚒ ground organization; **–eigenaar** (-s en -naren) *m* = *grondbezitter*; **–eigendom** (-men) *o* = *grondbezit*

'grondel (-s) *m*, **'grondeling** (-en) *m* 🐟 gudgeon

'grondeloos bottomless, unfathomable; **gronde'loosheid** *v* bottomless depth

'gronden (grondde, h. gegrond) *vt* ground [a painting]; *fig* ground, found, base [one's belief &]; zie ook *gegrond*

'grondgebied (-en) *o* territory; **–gedachte** (-n) *v* leading thought, root idea; **–gesteldheid** (-heden) *v* nature (condition) of the soil

'grondig I *aj* 1 *fig* thorough [cleaning, overhaul, knowledge], profound [study]; 2 *eig* earthy [taste]; **II** *ad* thoroughly; *iets ~ doen* ook: **F** go the whole hog; **–heid** *v* 1 *fig* thoroughness; 2 *eig* earthiness [of taste]

'grondijs *o* ground-ice, anchor-ice; **–kamer** (-s) *v* land-control board; **–kleur** (-en) *v* 1 (v e r f) ground-colour, priming; 2 (k l e u r) primary colour; **–laag** (-lagen) *v* 1 bottom layer; 2 (v e r f) priming coat; **–lasten** *mv* land-tax; **–legger** (-s) *m* founder, father, founding father; **–legging** (-en) *v* foundation; **–lijn** (-en) *v* base; **–monster** (-s) *o* soil sample; **–nevel** (-en en -s) *m* ground mist; **–oorzaak** (-zaken) *v* original (first, root) cause; **–patroon** (-tronen) *o* basic pattern; **–personeel** *o* ⌖ ground staff; **–rechten** *mv* civil rights; **–regel** (-en en -s) *m* fundamental rule, principle, maxim; **–slag** (-slagen) *m* foundation(s)²; *fig* basis; *~en* grass-roots; *ten ~ liggen aan* underlie; **–soort** (-en) *v* kind of soil; **–sop** *o* grounds, dregs; **–stelling** (-en) *v* axiom [in geometry]; principle, maxim; **–stof** (-fen) *v* raw material; element; **–strijdkrachten** *mv* ground forces; **–tal** (-len) *o* base; **–toon** (-tonen) *m* ♪ keynote²; **–trek** (-ken) *m* main feature; **–verf** (-verven) *v* ground-colour, priming; **–verven** (grondverfde, h. gegrondverfd) *vt* ground, prime; **–verzakking** (-en) *v* subsidence

1 **'grondvesten** *mv* foundations; 2 **'grond-vesten** (grondvestte, h. gegrondvest) *vt* found, lay the foundations of, ground; **–vester** (-s) *m* founder, founding father; **–vesting** (-en) *v* foundation

'grondvlak (-ken) *o* base [of cube]; **–vorm** (-en) *m* primitive form; **–waarheid** (-heden) *v* fundamental truth; *de grondwaarheden* the basic truths; **–water** *o* (under)ground water; **–werk** (-en) *o* earthwork; **–werker** (-s) *m* navvy; **–wet** (-ten) *v* fundamental law, constitution; **–wetsherziening** (-en) *v* revision of the Constitution; **grond'wettelijk, grond'wettig** constitutional; **'grondwoord** (-en) *o* primary word, primitive word-form, etymon; **–zee** (-zeeën) *v* breaker; **–zeil** (-en) *o* ground sheet

groot I *aj* 1 (o m v a n g) large, big; voluminous; (e m o t i o n e e l) great, big [trees]; 2 (u i t g e - s t r e k t) great, large, vast; 3 (v. g e s t a l t e) tall; 4 (n i e t m e e r k l e i n) grown-up; 5 (v. b e t e k e n i s) great [men, scoundrels];

great [powers, question], grand [entrance, dinner]; major [crisis, operations &]; *een grote eter* a big (great) eater; *een ~ kwartier* a good quarter of an hour; *een ~ man* a great man; *een grote man* a tall man; *de grote massa* the masses; *de grote mast* ⚓ the mainmast; *de Grote Oceaan* the Pacific (Ocean); *de grote weg* the high road, the highway, the main road; *~ wild* big game; *~ worden* grow (up), grow tall; *wat ben je ~ geworden!* how tall you have grown!; *groter groeien* grow, increase; **II** *ad* large; *~ gelijk!* quite right!; *~ leven* live in grand style; **III** *sb de groten* the great ones (of the earth); *het grote* what is great; *~ en klein* big and small; *groot (groten) en klein(en)* great and small; *in het ~* 1 in grand style, on a large scale; in a large way; 2 $ wholesale; *iets ~s* something great (grand), a great thing; zie ook *klein* **III**; **–bedrijf** *o* large-scale industry; *het ~* ook: the big industries; **–boek** (-en) *o* 1 $ ledger; 2 Great Book of the Public Debt; **–brengen** (bracht 'groot, h. 'grootgebracht) *vt* bring up, rear; **Groot-Brit'tannië** *o* Great Britain; **'grootdoen** *vi* give oneself airs, swagger; **grootdoene'rij** (-en) *v* swagger; **groot'grondbezit** *o* large ownership; **–bezitter** (-s) *m* big landowner, big landed proprietor; **'groothandel** (-s) *m* wholesale trade; **–handelaar** (-s) *m* wholesale dealer; **–handel(s)prijs** (-prijzen) *m* wholesale price; **groot'hartig** magnanimous; generous; **'grootheid** (-heden) *v* greatness, largeness, bigness, tallness; *fig* grandeur, magnitude², quantity; *~ van ziel* magnanimity; *algebraïsche grootheden* algebraic magnitudes; *een onbekende ~* an unknown quantity²; **–swaan(zin)** *m* delusion of grandeur, megalomania; *lijder aan ~* megalomaniac; **'groothertog** (-togen) *m* grand duke; **groot'hertogdom** (-men) *o* grand duchy [of Luxembourg]; **grootherto'gin** (-nen) *v* grand duchess; **'groothoekig** *~e lens* wide-angle lens; **–houden** (hield 'groot, h. 'grootgehouden) *zich ~* keep up appearances, bear it bravely, keep a stiff upper lip; **–industrie** (-ieën) *v de ~* the big industries; **–industrieel** (-iëlen) *m* captain of industry; **–je** (-s) *o* F granny; *je ~!* not a bit!; *maak dat je ~ wijs* you tell that to the marines!; **–kapitaal** *o* 1 high finance; 2 *het ~* the big capitalists; **–kruis** (-en) *o* grand cross; **–ma(ma)** ('s) *v* grandmother; **–meester** (-s) *m* Grand Master [Mason; of an order of knighthood; of chess]; **–moe(der)** (-(der)s) *v* grandmother; **groot'moedig** magnanimous, generous; **–heid** *v* magnanimity, generosity; **'grootmogol** (-s) *m* Great Mogul; **–ouders** *mv* grandparents; **–pa(pa)** ('s) *m* F grandfather, grand-dad; **groots** 1 grand, grandiose, noble,

majestic; ambitious [plans]; 2 (t r o t s) proud, haughty; **'grootscheeps, groot'scheeps I** *aj* grand; ambitious [attempt]; large-scale [programme]; **II** *ad* in grand style; on a large scale; **'grootschrift** *o* text-hand; **'grootsheid** *v* 1 grandeur, grandiosity, nobleness, majesty; 2 (t r o t s) pride, haughtiness; **'grootsig** arrogant, haughty; **'grootspraak** *v* boast(ing), brag(ging), big words; **groot'sprakig** vainglorious, boastful; **'grootspreken** *vi* boast, brag, talk big; **–spreker** (-s) *m* boaster, braggart; **groot'steeds** *~e manieren* city manners; **'grootte** (-n *en* -s) *v* bigness, largeness, greatness, size, extent; magnitude [of stars, an offer]; *in deze ~* of this size; *op (de) ware ~* full-size(d); *een... t e r ~ van ...* the size of...; *v a n dezelfde ~ zijn* be of a size; *van de eerste ~* of the first magnitude²; **'grootvader** (-s) *m* grandfather; **–vizier** (-en *en* -s) *m* grand vizier; **–vorst** (-en) *m* grand duke; **–vorstin** (-nen) *v* grand duchess; **groot'waardigheidsbekleder** (-s) *m* high dignitary; **groot'winkelbedrijf** (-drijven) *o* 1 (c o l l e c t i e f) multiple shop organization, chain; 2 (é é n w i n k e l d a a r v a n) multiple shop, chain store; **'grootzegel** (-s) *o het ~* the great seal; **groot'zegelbewaarder** (-s) *m* keeper of the great seal; *Br* Lord Privy Seal; **'grootzeil** (-en) *o* ⚓ mainsail **gros** (-sen) *o* 1 gross [= 12 dozen]; 2 gross, mass, main body; *het ~* ook: the majority; **–lijst** (-en) *v* list of candidates **'grosse** (-n) *v* engrossment, engrossed document; **gros'seren** (grosseerde, h. gegrosseerd) *vt* engross **gros'sier** (-s) *m* wholesale dealer; **grossierde'rij** (-en) *v* 1 wholesale trade; 2 wholesale business; **gros'siersprijs** (-prijzen) *m* wholesale price, trade price **grot** (-ten) *v* grotto, cave **grote** (-n) 1 *m* grown-up person, adult; *de ~n der aarde* the great ones [of the earth]; 2 *v* (g r o t e b o o d s c h a p) F number two; 3 *o wie het kleine niet eert is het ~ niet weerd* take care of the pence and the pounds will take care of themselves; **'grotelijks** greatly, in a large measure; **'grotendeels** for the greater part, for the most part; largely [depend on] **gro'tesk** grotesque; **–e** (-n) *v* grotesque **'grotonderzoek** (-en) *o* speleology **'grovelijk** grossly; coarsely **gruis** *o* 1 coal-dust; 2 grit [of stone] **gruize(le)'menten** *mv = gruize(le)menten* **grut** *o het kleine ~* the small fry **'grutten** *mv* groats, grits **'grutter** (-s) *m* grocer; **–swaren** *mv* groceries **'grutto** ('s) *m* godwit **'gruwel** (-en) *m* 1 (g e v o e l) abomination; 2

(d a a d) atrocity, horror; *...is mij een ~* I detest
(loath, abhor)..., ...is my pet aversion (abomination); **–daad** (-daden) *v* atrocity; **–ijk I** *aj*
abominable, horrible, atrocious; **II** *ad* abominably, horribly, atrociously, < awfully; *zich ~
vervelen* be bored to death; **–kamer** (-s) *v*
chamber of horrors; **–verhaal** (-halen) *o*
horror story; **'gruwen** (gruwde, h. gegruwd)
vi shudder; *~ b ij de gedachte* shudder at the
thought; *~ v a n* abhor; **'gruwzaam** horrible,
gruesome

gruze(le)'menten *mv aan ~* to shivers
gu'ano *m* guano
Guate'mala *o* Guatemala
guer'rilla ('s) *m*, **guer'rillaoorlog** [gɪ'ri.lja.-]
(-logen) *m* guer(r)illa (warfare); **–strijder** (-s)
m guer(r)illa
'guichelheil *o* (scarlet) pimpernel
guillo'tine [gi.(l)jo.'ti.nə] (-s) *v* guillotine
Gui'nee-Bissau *o* Guinea-Bissau; **Gui'nees**
[gi.- of gu.vi.-] Guinean; *~ biggetje* guinea-pig
guir'lande [gi: r-] (-s) *v* garland, festoon,
wreath, [paper] chain
guit (-en) *m* rogue²; **'guitenstreek** (-streken) *m*
& *v* roguish trick; **'guitig** roguish, arch;
–heid (-heden) *v* roguishness, archness
gul I *aj* 1 generous, open-handed, liberal; 2
frank, open, open-hearted, genial; **II** *ad* 1
generously, liberally; 2 frankly, genially
1 'gulden *aj* golden; *de ~ middenweg* the happy
(golden) mean (medium)
2 'gulden (-s) *m* guilder
gul'hartig = *gul I* 2; **–heid** (-heden) *v* 1 generosity, open-handedness, liberality, bounty; 2
frankness, openness, open-heartedness, geniality
gulp (-en) *v* 1 gulp [of blood]; 2 (v. b r o e k)
fly; **'gulpen** (gulpte, h. gegulpt) *vi* gush, spout
'gulzig gluttonous, greedy, edacious; **–aard** (-s)
m glutton; **–heid** (-heden) *v* gluttony, greediness, greed
gum *m* & *o* = *gom*
'gummi *o* & *m* (india-)rubber; **–hak** (-ken) *v*
rubber heel; **–handschoen** (-en) *m* & *v* rubber
glove; **–stok** (-ken) *m* (rubber) truncheon;
–waren *mv* rubber articles (goods)
'gunnen (gunde, h. gegund) *vt* 1 grant; 2 not
grudge, not envy; *het is je gegund* you are
welcome to it; **–ning** (-en) *v* allotment

gunst (-en) **I** *v* favour, patronage, $ favour,
custom, goodwill; *een ~ bewijzen* do a favour,
oblige; *i n de ~ komen bij* get into favour with,
F get on the right side of; *weer bij iem. in de ~
komen* get into sbd.'s good books again; *in de ~
trachten te komen bij* ingratiate oneself with; *in de
~ staan bij iem.* be in favour with sbd., be in
sbd.'s good books; *t e n ~e van...* 1 in favour
of...; 2 in behalf of...; *u i t de ~ geraken* fall out
of favour (with *bij*); *uit de ~ zijn* be in disfavour; **II** *ij* goodness gracious!; **–bejag** *o*
favour-hunting; **–betoon** *o* marks of favour;
–bewijs (-wijzen) *o* mark of favour, favour;
–eling(e) (-en) *m(-v)* favourite
'gunstig I *aj* favourable, propitious, auspicious;
het geluk was ons ~ fortune (fate) favoured us; *op
het ~ste moment* at the flood; zie ook *geval*; **II** *ad*
favourably; *~ bekend* enjoying a good reputation
gut! *ij* = *gunst* **II**
guts (-en) *v* ⚒ gouge
1 'gutsen (gutste, h. gegutst) *vt* ⚒ gouge
2 'gutsen (gutste, h. gegutst) *vi* gush, spout [of
blood]; stream, run [of sweat]
guur bleak, raw, inclement, damp and chilly;
–heid *v* bleakness, inclemency, intemperance
[of climate]
Guy'aan [gi.'a.n] (-anen) *m* Guyanese [*mv*
Guyanese]; **–s** Guyanese; **Guy'ana** *o* Guyana
'gymbroek ['gɪm-] (-en) *v* **F** gym slip
gymnasi'aal [gɪmna.zi.'a.l] *aj* grammar-
school...; **gymnasi'ast** (-en) *m* pupil of a
grammarschool; **gym'nasium** (-s en -ia) *o*
grammar school
gym'nast (-en) *m* gymnast; **gymnas'tiek** *v*
gymnastics, physical training, P.T.; *ritmische ~*
callisthenics; **–leraar** (-s en -raren) *m* physical
training master, P.T. master; **–les** (-sen) *v*
gymnastic lesson; **–lokaal** (-kalen) *o* gymnasium; **–schoen** (-en) *m* gymnasium shoe, **F**
gym shoe; **–uitvoering** (-en) *v* gymnastic
display; **–vereniging** (-en) *v* gymnastic club;
–werktuigen *mv* gymnastic apparatus; **–zaal**
(-zalen) *v* gymnasium; **gym'nastisch**
gymnastic
'gympjes *mv*, **'gymschoenen** *mv* plimsolls
gynaecolo'gie [gi.ne.-] *v* gynaecology;
gynaeco'loog (-logen) *m* gynaecologist

H

h [ha.] ('s) *v* h
H. = *heilige*
ha! *ij* ha!, oh!, ah!; ~ *die Jan* hullo John!
Haag, Den ~ The Hague
haag (hagen) *v* hedge, hedgerow; lane [of people, of soldiers]; **–appel** (-en en -s) *m* haw, hawthorn berry; **–beuk** (-en) *m* hornbeam; **–doorn, –doren** (-s) *m* = *hagedoorn*
Haags (of The) Hague
haai (-en) *m* 🐟 shark; *fig* vulture, kite; *n a a r de* ~*en gaan* ⚓ go to Davy Jones's locker; *hij is v o o r de* ~*en* he is going to the dogs
'**haai(e)baai** (-en) *v* shrew, virago, scold
haak (haken) *m* 1 hook; 2 cradle [of desk telephone]; 3 picklock [for opening locks &]; 4 (w i n k e l~) ✗ square; 5 (k l e e r h a n g e r) peg; *haken en ogen* hooks and eyes; *fig* difficulties, squabbles, bickerings; *a a n de* ~ *slaan* hook²; *schoon aan de* ~ dressed (net) weight; *(niet) i n de* ~ (not) right; *de hoorn weer o p de* ~ *leggen* 📞 put down the receiver, ring off, hang up; *de hoorn v a n de* ~ *nemen* 📞 lift the receiver
'**haakbus** (-sen) *v* (h)arquebus
'**haakgaren** (-s) *o* crochet cotton
'**haakje** *o* (i n d e d r u k k e rij) bracket, parenthesis: ( ); *tussen (twee)* ~*s* between brackets; *fig* in parentheses; *tussen twee* ~*s, heb je ook...?* by the way, have you...?
'**haaknaald** (-en) *v,* **–pen** (-nen) *v* crochet-hook
haaks square; *niet* ~ out of square; '**haakvormig** hook-shaped, hooked
'**haakwerk** (-en) *o* crochet-work, crocheting
haal (halen) *m* stroke [in writing]; *aan de* ~ *gaan* take to one's heels, run away
'**haalbaar** practicable, realizable, feasible
haam (hamen) *o* collar [of a horse]
haan (hanen) *m* cock; *daar zal geen* ~ *naar kraaien* nobody will be the wiser; *zijn* ~ *kraait daar koning* he is (the) cock of the walk, he has it all his own way; *de rode* ~ *laten kraaien* set the house & ablaze; *de* ~ *overhalen* cock a gun; *de gebraden* ~ *uithangen* do the grand; **–tje** (-s) *o* young cock, cockerel; *hij is een* ~ he is a young hotspur; *hij is* ~ *de voorste* he is (the) cock of the walk
1 haar 1 *bez. vnmw.* her; their; 2 *pers. vnmw.* (3de nmv.) (to) her; (to) them; (4de nmv.) her; them; *het is van* ~ it is hers
2 haar (haren) *o* hair [of the head &]; *hij is geen* ~ *beter* he is not a bit (whit) better; *geen* ~ *op mijn hoofd dat er aan denkt* I don't even dream of doing such a thing; ~ *op de tanden hebben* be a

tough customer, have a sharp tongue; *het scheelde maar een* ~*, geen* ~ it was a near thing, it was touch and go; *iem. geen* ~ *krenken* not touch (harm) a hair of sbd.'s head; *ergens grijze haren van krijgen* worry about sth., lose sleep over sth.; *zijn haren rezen hem ten berge* his hair stood on end; *[het scheelde] geen* ~ very nearly, by an inch; *het scheelde maar een* ~ it was a near miss; *zijn wilde haren verliezen* sow one's wild oats; *elkaar i n het* ~ *vliegen* go for one another, come to blows; *elkaar altijd in het* ~ *zitten* quarrel constantly, always be at loggerheads; *iets m e t de haren erbij slepen* drag it in; *dat is er met de haren bijgesleept* that's far-fetched; *o p een* ~ *na* by (to) a hair, by a hair's breadth; *alles op haren en snaren zetten* leave no stone unturned; *t e g e n het* ~ *instrijken* stroke against the hair, rub [sbd.] the wrong way; zie ook *hand, huid, vos;* **–band** (-en) *m* hair ribbon, fillet, head-band; **–borstel** (-s) *m* hairbrush; **–bos** (-sen) *m* 1 tuft of hair; 2 (h a a r d o s) shock of hair; **–breed** *o* hair's-breadth, hairbreadth; **–buisje** (-s) *o* capillary vessel (tube)
haard (-en) *m* 1 hearth, fireside, fireplace; 2 stove; 3 *fig* focus [*mv* foci], seat [of the fire], centre [of infection, resistance]; *eigen* ~ *is goud waard* there is no place like home, home is home be it (n)ever so homely; *aan de huiselijke* ~, *bij de* ~ by (at) the fireside; **–ijzer** (-s) *o* 1 fender [to keep coals from rolling into room]; 2 firedog [for supporting burning wood]; **–kleedje** (-s) *o* hearth-rug
'**haardos** *m* (head of) hair
'**haardplaat** (-platen) *v* hearth-plate
'**haardracht** (-en) *v* coiffure, hairdo; **–droger** (-s) *m* hair drier
'**haardscherm** (-en) *o* fire-screen, fender; **–stede** (-n) *v* hearth, fireside; **–stel** (-len) *o* (set of) fire-irons; **–vuur** *o* fire on the hearth
'**haarfijn I** *aj* 1 as fine as a hair; 2 *fig* minute [account], subtle [distinction]; **II** *ad* minutely, [tell] in detail; **–groei** *m* hair growth, growth of the hair; **–groeimiddel** (-en) *o* hair-grower, hair-restorer, pilatory; **–kam** (-men) *m* hair-comb
'**haarkloven** (haarkloofde, h. gehaarkloofd) *vi* split hairs; **–klover** (-s) *m* hair-splitter, casuist; **haarklove'rij** (-en) *v* hair-splitting
'**haarknippen** *o* hair-cutting; **–lak** *m* hair spray
'**Haarlemmer** Haarlem; ~ *olie* Dutch drops
'**haarlijntje** (-s) *o* fine line, hairline; **–lint** (-en) *o* hair-ribbon; **–lok** (-ken) *v* lock of hair; **–loos**

hairless, without hair; **–netje** (-s) *o* hairnet;
–pijn *v* **F** a head, a hang-over; **–scherp** very
clear; **–speld** (-en) *v* hairpin, hair-slide,
bobby-pin; **–speldbocht** (-en) *v* hairpin bend;
–stukje (-s) *o* hairpiece, toupee; **–uitval** *m*
loss of hair; ♀ alopecia; **–vat** (-vaten) *o* capillary vessel; **–verf** (-verven) *v* hair-dye;
–versteviger (-s) *m* setting lotion; **–vlecht**
(-en) *v* [woman's] plait, braid; [girl's] pigtail
[hanging from the back]; **–wassing** (-en) *v*
shampoo; **–water** (-s) *o* hair-wash (lotion);
–worm (-en) *m* trichina; **–wortel** (-s) *m* root
of a hair; **–zakje** (-s) *o* hair follicle

haas (hazen) *m* 1 🐇 hare; 2 (s t u k v l e e s)
fillet, tenderloin, undercut [of beef]; **haasje-**
'over *o* leap-frog

1 haast *v* haste, speed, hurry [= undue haste]; *er
is ~ bij* it is urgent; *er is geen ~ bij* there is no
hurry; *~ hebben* be in a hurry; *~ maken* make
haste, be quick; *in ~* in a hurry; *waarom zo'n ~?*
what's the hurry?

2 haast *ad* 1 = *bijna*; 2 *kom je ~?* are you
coming soon (yet)?

'haasten (haastte, h. gehaast) **I** *vt* hurry; **II** *vr
zich ~* hasten, make haste; *haast je langzaam!*
make haste slowly!; *haast je (wat)!* hurry up!;
haast je rep je… in a hurry; zie ook *haast-je-rep-je,
gehaast*; **'haastig I** *aj* hasty, hurried; *~e spoed is
zelden goed* more haste, less speed; **II** *ad* hastily,
in haste, in a hurry, hurriedly; **haast-je-'rep-**
je post-haste, *Am* **S** lickety-split; **'haastklus**
(-sen) *m* hurry-up job; **'haastwerk** (-en) *o* rush
job, rush order

haat *m* hatred (of *tegen*), ⊙ hate; **haat'dragend**
resentful, rancorous; **–heid** *v* resentfulness,
rancour

'habbekrats *m voor een ~* for a mere song
(trifle)

ha'bijt (-en) *o* habit

habitu'é (-s) *m* regular customer (visitor),
patron

'habitus *m* habit

ha'chee [ha'ʃe.] (-s) *m* & *o* hash [of warmed-up
meat]

'hachelen (hachelde, h. gehacheld) *je kunt me de
bout ~* **F** go climb a tree

'hachelijk precarious, critical, dangerous,
perilous

'hachje (-s) *o bang voor zijn ~* anxious to save
one's skin; *zijn ~ er bij inschieten* not be able to
save one's skin

had (hadden) V.T. v. *hebben*

haf (-fen) *o* lagoon

haft (-en) *o* mayfly, ephemeron

hage'dis (-sen) *v* lizard

'hagedoorn, –doren (-s) *m* hawthorn

'hagel (-s) *m* 1 hail; 2 (o m t e s c h i e t e n)

(small) shot; **–bui** (-en) *v* shower of hail,
hailstorm; *een ~ van stenen* a shower of stones;
'hagelen (hagelde, h. gehageld) *vi* hail; *het
hagelde kogels* volleys of shot pattered down;
'hagelkorrel (-s) *m* 1 hailstone; 2 grain of
shot; **–schade** *v* damage (caused) by hail;
–slag *m* 1 hailstorm; 2 damage (caused) by
hail; 3 (o p b r o o d) ± hundreds and thousands; **–steen** (-stenen) *m* hailstone; **–wit**
white as snow

'hageprediker (-s) *m* 🕮 hedge-priest; **–preek**
(-preken) *v* 🕮 hedge-sermon

Ha'ïti *o* Haiti

1 hak (-ken) *v* 1 (g e r e e d s c h a p) hoe,
mattock, pickaxe; 2 heel; *schoenen met hoge (lage,
platte) ~ken* high-heeled (low-heeled, flat-
heeled) shoes; *met de ~ken over de sloot* [escape]
by the skin of one's teeth, only just [managed
to…]; *op de ~ nemen* make fun of

2 hak (-ken) *m* cut [of wood]; *iem. een ~ zetten*
play sbd. a nasty trick; *van de ~ op de tak
springen* jump (skip) from one subject to
another, ramble

'hakbijl (-en) *v* 1 hatchet; 2 (v. s l a g e r)
chopper, cleaver; **–bord** (-en) *o* chopping-
board

'haken (haakte, h. gehaakt) **I** *vt* 1 hook, hitch
[to…, on to…]; 2 (h a n d w e r k e n) crochet; **II**
va 1 hook, hitch; 2 (h a n d w e r k e n) do
crochetwork; *in een struik blijven ~* be caught in
a bush; **III** *vi ~ naar* hanker after, long for,
yearn for (after)

'hakenkruis (-en en -kruizen) *o* swastika

'hakhout *o* copse, coppice

'hakkebord (-en) *o* dulcimer

'hakkelen (hakkelde, h. gehakkeld) *vi* stammer,
stutter

'hakken (hakte, h. gehakt) *vt* & *vi* cut, chop,
hack, hew, hash, mince [to pieces]; *op iem. zitten
~* peck, nag at sbd.; *waar gehakt wordt vallen
spaanders* ± you can't make an omelette
without breaking eggs; zie ook: *inhakken, pan*
&

'hakketakken (hakketakte, h. gehakketakt),
hakke'teren (hakketeerde, h. gehakketeerd) *vi*
bicker, squabble, wrangle

'hakmes (-sen) *o* chopping-knife, cleaver; **–sel,**
(-s), **–stro** *o* chopped straw, chaff; **–vrucht**
(-en) *v* root crop

hal (-len) *v* hall; (covered) market

'halen (haalde, h. gehaald) **I** *vt* 1 fetch; get; draw,
pull; get; run [the comb through one's hair,
one's pen through the name]; *laten ~* send for;
een akte ~ obtain (secure) a certificate (a
diploma); *hij zal de dag niet meer ~* he won't last
out the night; *een dokter ~* go for (call in) a
doctor; *er bij ~* drag in [sbd.'s name]; *hij zal het*

wel (erdoor) ~ he's sure to pull through; *de dokter kan hem niet erdoor* ~ the doctor can't pull him through; *het wetsvoorstel erdoor* ~ carry the bill; *hij haalde het nog net* he just made it; *de post* ~ 1 fetch the mail; 2 be in time for the post; *het zal nog geen 10 stuivers* ~ it will not even fetch 10 pence; *de honderd* ~ live to be a hundred; *de trein* ~ catch the train; *iem. van de trein* ~ meet sbd. at the station; *daar is niets te* ~ nothing to be got there; *worden jullie (straks) gehaald?* is anybody coming for you?; *een huis tegen de grond* ~ pull down a house; *zijn beurs uit de zak* ~ pull out one's purse; *dat haalt niets uit* that's no good; *waar haalt hij het vandaan?* where does he get it?; zie ook: *hals* &; **II** *va* 1 ⚓ pull; 2 draw (raise) the curtain; 3 (k i n k h o e s t) whoop; *dat haalt niet bij...* **F** that is not a patch (up)on..., that cannot touch...

half I *aj* half; *halve cirkel* semicircle; ~ *één* half past twelve; ~ *Engeland* half (one half of) England; ~ *geld* half the money, half price; *een halve gulden* (w a a r d e) half a guilder; *een* ~ *jaar* half a year, six months; ~ *maart* mid-March; *tot* ~ *maart* until the middle of March; *een halve toon* ♪ a semitone; *een* ~ *uur* half an hour; *de halve wereld* half the world; zie ook: *verstaander* &; *het slaat* ~ the half-hour is striking; **II** *o* half; *twee en een* ~ two and a half; *twee halven* two halves; *ten halve iets doen* do a thing by halves; *ten halve omkeren* turn when halfway; *beter ten halve gekeerd dan ten hele gedwaald* he who stops halfway is only half in error; **III** *ad* half; ~ *te geef* half for nothing; *dat is mij maar* ~ *naar de zin* not altogether to my liking; *iets maar* ~ *verstaan* understand only half of it; *hij is niet* ~ *zo...* not half so...; **–aap** (-apen) *m* half-ape; **half'bakken, half'gebak-** *²* half-baked; **'halfbloed I** *aj* half-bred; **II** (-en en -s) *m-v* half-breed, half-caste, half-blood; **–broe(de)r** (-s) *m* half-brother; **–dek** *o* quarter-deck; **–donker** *o* semi-darkness; **half'dood** half-dead; **'half-edelsteen** (-stenen) *m* semi-precious stone; **1 'half-en-half** *ad* ~ *beloven* half promise; *ik denk er* ~ *over om...* I have half a mind to...; **2 half-en-'half** *o* & *m* = *half-om-half*; **'halffa-brikaat** (-katen) *o* semi-manufactured article; **'halfgaar, half'gaar** 1 half-done, half-baked; 2 *fig* half-baked, **F** dotty; **'halfgeleider** (-s) *m* semi-conductor; **–god** (-goden) *m* demigod; **–heid** *v* half-heartedness, irresolution; **'half-jaarlijks, half'jaarlijks I** *aj* half-yearly; **II** *ad* every six months; **'halfje** (-s) *o* **F** 1 half a glass; 2 ~ [Dutch] half-cent; **'halfklinker** (-s) *m* semivowel; **–leer** *o* half calf; *halfleren band* half binding; **–linnen** *o* half cloth; **–luid** in an undertone, under one's breath; **'halfmaande-lijks, half'maandelijks I** *aj* fortnightly; **II** *ad*

every fortnight; **half-om-'half** *o* & *m* half-and-half; fifty-fifty; **'halfrond** (-en) *o* hemisphere; **–schaduw** (-en) *o* penumbra; **half'slachtig** amphibious; *fig* half-hearted; **'halfsleets** halfworn; **–speler** (-s) *m* half-back; **half'stok** at half-mast, half-mast high; **half'vasten** *m* mid-Lent; **–'was** *m-v* apprentice; **'halfweg, half'weg** halfway; **half'wijs** half-witted; **–'zacht** medium-boiled [egg]; *fig* half-baked, dotty; **'halfzuster** (-s) *v* half-sister; **half'zwaargewicht** (-en) *m* light-heavy-weight

halle'luja ('s) *o* hallelujah
hal'lo *ij* hullo!
halluci'natie [-(t)si.] (-s) *v* hallucination; **hallucino'geen I** (-genen) *o* hallucinogen; **II** *aj* hallucinogenic
halm (-en) *m* stalk, blade
'halo ('s) *m* halo
hals (halzen) *m* 1 neck [of body, bottle, garment &]; 2 tack [of a sail]; 3 *(onnozele)* ~ simpleton; *zijn (de)* ~ *breken* break one's neck; *dat zal hem de* ~ *breken* that will be his undoing; *iem. o m* ~ *brengen* make away with sbd.; *iem. om de* ~ *vallen* fling one's arms round sbd.'s neck, fall upon sbd.'s neck; *zich iets o p de* ~ *halen* bring sth. on oneself, incur [punishment &]; catch [a disease, a cold &]; ~ *o v e r kop* head over heels, [rush] headlong [into...], [run] helterskelter; in a hurry; **–ader** (-en en -s) *v* jugular (vein); **–band** (-en) *m* collar; **–boord** (-en) *o* & *m* neckband [of a shirt]; **–brekend** breakneck; **–doek** (-en) *m* neckerchief, scarf; **–ketting** (-en) *m* & *v* neck-chain, necklace; **–lengte** (-n en -s) *v* [win by a] neck; **–misdaad** (-daden) *v* capital crime; **–slagader** (-en en -s) *v* carotid (artery); **–snoer** (-en) *o* necklace
hals'starrig I *aj* headstrong, stubborn, obstinate; **II** *ad* stubbornly, obstinately; **–heid** *v* stubbornness, obstinacy
'halster (-s) *m* halter
'halswervel (-s) *m* cervical vertebra
halt halt; ~ *houden* make a halt, halt, make a stand, stop; ~ *laten houden* ⚔ halt [soldiers]; call a halt [on the march]; *een* ~ *toeroepen aan* [*fig*] check; ~ *!* 1 ⚔ halt!; 2 stop!; ~ *...wie daar!* ⚔ stand!, who goes there?; **'halte** (-n en -s) *v* wayside station [of railway]; stopping-place, stop [of tramway or bus]
'halter (-s) *m* dumb-bell, (l a n g) bar-bell
'halve zie *half*; **halve'maan** (-manen) *v* half-moon, crescent; **–tje** (-s) *o* crescent roll; **halvemaan'vormig** semilunar, crescent-shaped; **hal'veren** (halveerde, h. gehalveerd) *vt* halve; **'halverhoogte** halfway up; **hal'vering** (-en) *v* halving; **halver'wege** halfway

ham (-men) *v* ham

'hamel (-s) *m* wether

'hamer (-s) *m* hammer, (v a n h o u t o o k:) mallet; *o n d e r de ~ brengen* bring to the hammer; *onder de ~ komen* come under the hammer, be sold by auction; *t u s s e n ~ en aanbeeld* between the devil and the deep sea; **'hameren** (hamerde, h. gehamerd) *vi & vt* hammer; **'hamerhaai** (-en) *m* hammer-head shark; **–slag** 1 (-slagen) *m* blow (stroke) of a hammer, hammer stroke, hammer blow[2]; 2 *o* hammer-scale, scale

'hamster (-s) *v* hamster; **–aar** (-s) *m* (food-) hoarder; **'hamsteren** (hamsterde, h. gehamsterd) *vi & vt* hoard (food)

'hamvraag (-vragen) *v dat is de ~* that is the crux, the crucial question

hand (-en) *v* hand; *de ~en staan hem verkeerd* he is very unhandy; *de vlakke ~* the flat of the hand; *iem. de ~ drukken (geven, schudden)* shake hands with sbd.; *iem. de ~ op iets geven* shake hands on (over) it; *de ~ hebben in iets* have a hand in sth.; *de vrije ~ hebben* have carte blanche; *de ~ houden aan* enforce [a regulation &]; *iem. de ~ boven het hoofd houden* extend one's protection to sbd.; *de ~en ineenslaan* clasp one's hands; *fig* join hands; *de ~en ineenslaan van verbazing* throw up one's hands in wonder; *iem. de vrije ~ laten* leave (give, allow) sbd. a free hand; *de laatste ~ leggen aan het werk* put the finishing touches to the work; *de ~ leggen op* lay hands on; *de ~ lenen tot iets* lend oneself to sth., be a party to sth.; *de ~ lichten met* let oneself off lightly from the labour of ...ing, make light of...; *zijn ~ niet omdraaien voor iets* make nothing of ...ing; *~en omhoog!* hold (stick) them up!; *de ~ opheffen tegen iem.* lift (raise) one's hand against sbd.; *de ~ ophouden* 1 hold out one's hand; 2 *fig* beg; *de ~en aan het werk slaan* set to work; *de ~ aan zich zelf slaan* lay violent hands on oneself; *de ~en uit de mouwen steken* put one's shoulder to the wheel, buckle to; *geen ~ uitsteken om...* not lift (raise, stir) a finger to...; *~ vol geld* **F** heaps (lots) of money; *de ~en vol hebben* have (have got) one's hands full, have one's work cut out; *de ~ vragen van een meisje* ask her hand in marriage; *geen ~ voor ogen kunnen zien* not be able to see one's hand before one; ● *a a n de ~ van deze gegevens* on the basis of these data; *aan de ~ van voorbeelden* from examples; *~ aan ~* hand in hand; *iem. iets aan de ~ doen* procure (find, get) sth. for sbd.; suggest [a means] to sbd.; *aan de beter(end)e ~ zijn* zie *beteren*; *wat is er aan de ~?* **F** what is up?; *er is iets aan de ~* there is something going on; *er is niets aan de ~* there's nothing wrong, there's nothing doing; *aan ~en en voeten binden* bind hand and foot; *iets a c h t e r*

de ~ hebben have sth. up one's sleeve; *iets (altijd) b ij de ~ hebben* have sth. at hand, ready (to hand), handy; *al vroeg bij de ~* up early; *nog niet bij de ~ zijn* not be stirring; zie ook: *bijdehand; met de degen i n de ~* sword in hand; zie ook: *hoed; wij hebben dat niet in de ~* these things are beyond (out of) our control; *~ in ~* hand in hand; *in ~en komen (vallen) van...* fall into the hands of...; *iets in ~en krijgen* get hold of sth.; *in andere ~en overgaan* change hands; *iem. iets in ~en spelen* smuggle sth. into sbd.'s hands; *hij heeft zich iets in de ~ laten stoppen* he has been taken in; *iem. in de ~ werken* play the game (into the hands) of sbd.; *iem. in de ~ werken* promote sth.; *in ~en zijn van* be in the hands of; *m e t de ~ gemaakt* hand-made, made by hand; *met de ~en in het haar zitten* be at one's wit's (wits') end; *met de ~en in de schoot zitten* sit with folded hands; *met de ~ op het hart* in all conscience; hand on heart [they affirmed]; *met beide ~en aangrijpen* jump at [a proposal], seize [the opportunity] with both hands; *met lege ~en* empty-handed; *met de ~ over het hart strijken* strain a point; *met ~ en tand* tooth and nail; *iem. n a a r zijn ~ zetten* manage sbd. (at will); *niets o m ~en hebben* have nothing to do; *o n d e r de ~* meanwhile; *iets onder ~en hebben* have a work in hand, be at work on sth.; *iem. onder ~en nemen* take sbd. in hand, take sbd. to task; *iets onder ~en nemen* (o p k n a p p e n) take in hand, undertake; clean, overhaul; *iem. o p de ~en dragen* make much of sbd.; *het publiek op zijn ~ hebben* have the audience with one; *op iems. ~ zijn* be on sbd.'s side, side with sbd.; *op ~en zijn* be near at hand, be drawing near; *op ~en en voeten* on all fours; *~ o v e r ~* hand over hand; *~ over ~ toenemen* spread, be rampant; *een voorwerp t e r ~ nemen* take it in one's hands, take it up; *een werk ter ~ nemen* undertake, take (put) in hand; *iem. iets ter ~ stellen* hand sth. to sbd.; *u i t de eerste (tweede) ~* (at) first (second) hand; *uit de eerste ~* **F** straight from the horse's mouth; *uit de vrije ~* by hand; *uit de ~ geschilderd* painted by hand; *iets uit zijn ~en geven* trust sth. out of one's hands; *(iem.) uit de ~ lopen* get out of hand; *uit de ~ verkopen* sell by private contract; *v a n hoger ~* [a revelation] from on high; [an order] from high quarters, from the government; [hear] on high authority; *iets van de ~ doen* dispose of, part with, sell sth.; *goed van de ~ gaan* sell well; *van de ~ wijzen* refuse [a request], decline [an offer], reject [a proposal]; *van ~ tot ~* from hand to hand; *van de ~ in de tand* from hand to mouth; *uit de ~ liggen* be obvious; *het zijn twee ~en op één buik* they are hand in (and) glove; *als de éne ~ de andere wast, worden ze beide schoon* one hand washes another;

veel ~en maken licht werk many hands make light work; **–appel** (-en en -s) *m* eating apple, eater; **–arbeider** (-s) *m* manual worker; **–bagage** [-bɑɡɑ.ʒə] *v* hand-luggage; **–bal** (-len) 1 *m* (b a l) handball; 2 *o* (s p e l) handball; **–bereik** *o binnen ~* within reach; **–bibliotheek** (-theken) *v* reference library; **–boeien** *mv* handcuffs, manacles; **–boek** (-en) *o* manual, handbook, textbook; **–boog** (-bogen) *m* crossbow; **–boor** (-boren) *v* (k l e i n) gimlet, (g r o o t) auger; **–breed** *o*, **–breedte** (-n en -s) *v* hand's breadth; *geen ~ wijken* not budge an inch; **–dienst** (-en) *m zie hand-en-spandiensten*; **–doek** (-en) *m* towel; *~ op rol* roller-towel; **–doekenrek** (-ken) *o*, **–doekenrekje** (-s) *o* (l o s) towel-horse, (v a s t) towel-rail; **–druk** (-ken) *m* hand pressure; handshake; *een ~ wisselen* shake hands

1 'handel (-s) *m* 1 trade; commerce; > traffic[2]; 2 (z a a k) business; *~ en wandel* conduct, life; *~ drijven* do business, trade (with *met*); *in de ~ brengen* put on the market; *in de ~ gaan (zijn)* go into (be in) business; *niet in de ~* 1 [goods] not supplied to the trade; 2 privately printed [pamphlets]

2 'handel ['hɪndəl] (-s) *o & m* ✗ handle
'handelaar (-s en -laren) *m* merchant, dealer, trader; > [drug] trafficker; **'handelbaar** tractable, manageable, docile; **'handeldrijvend** trading; **'handelen** (handelde, h. gehandeld) *vi* 1 (d o e n) act; 2 (h a n d e l d r ij v e n) trade, deal; *~ in hout* deal (trade) in timber; *~ n a a r (een beginsel)* act on (a principle); *o p de Levant ~* trade to the Levant; *o v e r een onderwerp ~* treat of (deal with) a subject; **'handeling** (-en) *v* 1 action, act; 2 action [of a play]; *H~en der Apostelen* Acts of the Apostles; *de ~en van dit genootschap* the Proceedings (Transactions) of this Society; *Handelingen van het Engels Parlement* Hansard; **handelingsbe'kwaam** ⚖ competent, capable to contract; **'handelmaatschappij** (-en) *v* trading-company; **'handelsadresboek** (-en) *o* business directory; **–agent** (-en) *m* commercial agent; **–akkoord** (-en) *o* trade agreement; **–artikel** (-en en -s) *o* article of commerce, commodity; **–attaché** [-ʃe.] (-s) *m* commercial attaché; **–balans** (-en) *v* balance of trade, trade balance; *tekort op de ~* trade gap; **–bank** (-en) *v* merchant bank; **–belang** (-en) *o* commercial interest; **–berichten** *mv* commercial news; **–betrekkingen** *mv* commercial relations; **–brief** (-brieven) *m* business letter; **–correspondent** (-en) *m* correspondence clerk; **–correspondentie** [-d(n)tsi.] (-s) *v* commercial correspondence; **–gebruik** (-en) *o* commercial custom, business practice, trade

usage; **–geest** *m* commercial spirit; **–hogeschool** (-scholen) *v* school of economics, school of commerce; **–huis** (-huizen) *o* business house, firm; **–kennis** *v* commercial practice; **–krediet** (-en) *o* trade credit; **–maatschappij** (-en) *v = handelmaatschappij*; **–man** (-lieden en -lui) *m* business man; **–merk** (-en) *o* trade mark; **–naam** (-namen) *m* trade name; **–nederzetting** (-en) *v* trading post, trading station; **–onderneming** (-en) *v* commercial enterprise (undertaking), business concern; **–overeenkomst** (-en) *v* commercial agreement, trade agreement; **–politiek** *v* commercial policy; **–recht** *o* commercial law, law merchant; **–register** (-s) *o* commercial register; **–reiziger** (-s) *m* salesman, commercial traveller; **–rekenen** *o* commercial arithmetic; **–school** (-scholen) *v* commercial school; **–stad** (-steden) *v* commercial town; **–tarief** (-rieven) *o* commercial tariff; **–term** (-en) *m* business term; **–verdrag** (-dragen) *o* treaty of commerce, commercial treaty, trade treaty; **–verkeer** *o* trade, business dealings; (i n h e t g r o o t) commerce; **–vloot** (-vloten) *v* merchant fleet; **–vriend** (-en) *m* business friend, correspondent; **–vrijheid** *v* freedom of trade; **–waar** (-waren) *v* commercial articles (goods), merchandise; **–waarde** *v* market (commercial) value; **–weg** (-wegen) *m* trade route; **–wereld** *v* commercial world; **–wet** (-ten) *v* commercial law; **–wetboek** (-en) *o* mercantile code; **–zaak** (-zaken) *v* business concern, business; **'handelwijs**, **–wijze** (-wijzen) *v* proceeding, method, way of acting

'handenarbeid *m* 1 manual labour; 2 sloyd, manual training, handicraft; **hand- en 'spandiensten** *mv* statute-labour; *~ verlenen aan (verrichten voor) de vijand* aid and abet the enemy; **'handexemplaar** (-plaren) *o* author's copy; **–gebaar** (-baren) *o* gesture, motion of the hand; **–geklap** *o* hand-clapping, applause; **–geld** *o* earnest-money, handsel; **–gemeen I** *aj ~ worden* come to blows, engage in a hand-to-hand fight, come to handgrips; **II** *o* mêlée, hand-to-hand fight, affray; **–granaat** (-naten) *v* (hand-)grenade; **–greep** (-grepen) *m* 1 (g r e e p) grasp, grip; 2 (h a n d v a t) handle; 3 (h a n d i g h e i d) knack; 4 (t r u c) trick
'handhaven (handhaafde, h. gehandhaafd) **I** *vt* maintain, vindicate [one's rights]; **II** *vr zich ~* hold one's own, keep one's ground
'handicap ['hɪndi.kɪp] (-s) *m* handicap[2];
'handicappen (handicapte, h. gehandicapt) *vt* handicap[2]
'handig I *aj* handy, clever, skilful, adroit, deft, practical; (s l i m) slick; **II** *ad* cleverly, skilfully,

adroitly &; **–heid** (-heden) *v* handiness, skill, adroitness; **~je** trick

'**handje** (-s) *o* (little) hand; *ergens een ~ van hebben* have a little way of ...ing; *een ~ helpen* lend a (helping) hand; **–vol** *o* handful, fistful; '**handkar** (-ren) *v* barrow, hand-cart, pushcart; **–koffer** (-s) *m* (suit-)case; **–kracht** *v door ~ aangedreven* hand-operated; **–kus** (-sen) *m* kiss on the hand; **–langer** (-s) *m* helper, > accomplice; **–leiding** (-en) *v* manual, guide; **–lichting** (-en) *v* emancipation; **–omdraai** *m in een ~* in a twinkling, off-hand; **–oplegging** *v* imposition (laying on) of hands; **–opsteken** *o bij (door) ~* by (a) show of hands; **–palm** (-en) *m* palm of the hand; **–reiking** (-en) *v* a helping hand, assistance; **–rem** (-men) *v* handbrake; **–schoen** (-en) *m* & *v* glove; gauntlet [□ & also for driving, fencing &]; *de ~ opnemen* take up the gauntlet; *iem. de ~ toewerpen* throw down the gauntlet (the glove); *met de ~ trouwen* marry by proxy; **–schoenenkastje** (-s) *o*, **–schoenenvakje** (-s) ⚙ glove compartment; **–schrift** (-en) *o* 1 handwriting; 2 manuscript; **–slag** (-slagen) *m* slap (with the hand); *iets op (met, onder) ~ beloven* slap hands upon sth.; **–spaak** (-spaken) *v* handspike, capstan bar; **–spiegel** (-s) *m* hand-mirror, handglass; **–tas** (-sen) *v* handbag; **hand'tastelijk** palpable; evident, obvious [lie]; *~ worden* become aggresive; paw [a girl]; **–heden** *mv* assault and battery, blows; '**handtekenen** *o* free-hand drawing; **–ning** (-en) *v* signature; **hand'vaardigheid** *v* dexterity, manual skill; '**handvat** (-vatten) *o*, '**handvatsel** (-s) *o* handle; **–vest** (-en) *o* charter [of the United Nations]; covenant [of the League of Nations]; **–vol** *v* handful; *een ~ geld* **F** a lot of money; **–vuurwapenen** *mv* small arms; **–werk** (-en) *o* 1 trade, (handi)craft; 2 (a l s p r o d u k t) hand-made...; handiwork; *fraaie ~en* fancywork; *nuttige ~en* plain needlework; **–werken** (handwerkte, h, gehandwerkt) *vi* do needlework, do fancy-work; **–werkje** (-s) *o* (piece of) fancy-work; **–werksman** (-lieden en -lui) *m* artisan; **–wijzer** (-s) *m* signpost, finger-post; **–woordenboek** (-en) *o* concise dictionary, desk dictionary; **–wortel** (-s) *m* carpus; **–zaag** (-zagen) *v* hand-saw; **–zaam** tractable, manageable; (t̄e h a n t e r e n) handy; **–zetter** (-s) *m* (hand) compositor

'**hanebalk** (-en) *v* purlin, tie-beam; *onder de ~en* in the garret; **–gekraai** *o* cock-crow(ing); **–kam** (-men) *m* 1 cock's comb; 2 🌿 cocks; comb; 3 (z w a m) chanterelle; '**hanengevecht** (-en) *o* cock-fight(ing); '**hanepoot** (-poten) *m* (l e t t e r) pot-hook, (s l e c h t s c h r i f t) scrawl; **–veer** (-veren) *v* cock's feather

hang *m een ~ naar* a leaning (bent, tendency) to(wards); nostalgy for [the past]

han'g(a)ar [hã'ga:r] (-s) *m* hangar

'**hangbrug** (-gen) *v* suspension bridge; '**hangen*** **I** *vt* hang; *ik laat me ~ als...* I'll be hanged if...!; **II** *va* hang; *ik zou nog liever ~* I'll be hanged first; *het was tussen ~ en wurgen* it was a tight squeeze; **III** *vi* hang; *het hangt als droog zand (van leugens)* aan elkaar zie aaneenhangen; *aan iems. lippen ~* hang on sbd.'s lips; *aan een spijker ~* be hung from a nail; *aan een touw ~* hang by a rope; *hij is daar blijven ~* he has stuck there; *blijven ~ aan* be caught in [a branch &]; *hij is eraan blijven ~* he was stuck with it; *er zal weinig van blijven ~* very little of it will stick in the memory; *het hoofd laten ~* hang one's head; *de lip laten ~* hang its lip [of a child], pout; *sta daar niet te ~* don't hang about, don't stand idling (lazing) there; zie ook: *draad, klok* &; **–d** hanging; pending [question]; *~e het onderzoek* pending the inquiry; **hang-en-'sluitwerk** *o* locks and hinges; '**hanger** (-s) *m* 1 hanger; 2 ear-drop, pendant; '**hangerig** listless, languid; '**hangijzer** (-s) *o een heet ~* [*fig*] a ticklish question, a knotty question (affair); **–kast** (-en) *v* hanging wardrobe; **–klok** (-ken) *v* hanging clock; **–lamp** (-en) *v* hanging lamp; **–lip** (-pen) *v* hanging lip; **–map** (-pen) *v* suspended filing folder; **–mat** (-ten) *v* hammock; **–oor** (-oren) *o* lop-ear; **–oortafel** (-s) *v* gate-legged table; '**hangop** *m* curds; '**hangplant** (-en) *v* hanging plant; **–slot** (-sloten) *o* padlock; **–snor** (-ren) *v* drooping moustache(s); **–wangen** *mv* baggy cheeks

'**hannesen** (hanneste, h. gehannest) *vi* 1 (k l e t s e n) **F** yarn; 2 (b e u z e l e n) dawdle, potter

han'sop (-pen) *m* combination night-dress

hans'worst (-en) *m* buffoon

han'teerbaar easy to handle, manageable; **han'teren** (hanteerde, h. gehanteerd) *vt* handle [one's tools], ply [the needle], wield [a weapon, the blue pencil]

'**Hanze** *v* Hanse, Hanseatic League; **–stad** (-steden) *v* Hanseatic town

hap (-pen) *m* 1 (h e t h a p p e n) bite; 2 (m o n d v o l) bite, morsel, bit; *in één ~* at one bite, at one mouthful

'**haperen** (haperde, h. gehaperd) *vi* 1 (b i j h e t s p r e k e n) falter, stammer, waver; 2 stick; *hapert er iets aan?* anything wrong (the matter)?; *het hapert hem aan geduld* he wants patience; *zonder ~* without a hitch; **–ring** (-en) *v* 1 hitch; 2 hesitation [in repeating one's lesson]

'**hapje** (-s) *o* bit, bite, morsel; '**happen** (hapte, h. gehapt) *vi* snap; bite; *~ i n* bite; *~ n a a r* snap at; '**happig** (*niet erg*) *~ op iets zijn* (not) be

keen upon a thing, (not) be eager for it
hara′kiri *o* hara-kiri
hard I *aj* hard² [stone, winter, fight, work &]; harsh [punishment, words]; tough [policy, writers]; loud [voice]; hardboiled [eggs]; *het is* ~ *(voor een mens) als...* it is hard lines upon a man if...; **II** *ad* hard, [treat a person] hardly, harshly; [talk] loud; *...is* ~ *nodig* ...is badly needed; *het gaat* ~ *tegen* ~ it is a fight to the finish; it is pull devil, pull baker; *zo* ~ *zij konden, om het* ~*st,* as hard (loud, fast &) as they could, they... their hardest (loudest &); **−board** [′hartbɔ.rt] *o* hardboard; **−draven** (harddraafde, h. geharddraafd) *vi* run in a trotting-match; run; **−draver** (-s) *m* trotter; **harddrave′rij** (-en) *v* trotting-match; ′**harden** (hardde, h. gehard) *vt* harden², temper [steel]; *het niet kunnen* ~ **F** not be able to stick it; *het is niet te* ~ it's unbearable; zie ook: *gehard*; **hard′handig** rough, harsh; ′**hardheid** (-heden) *v* hardness, harshness; **hard′hoofdig** headstrong, obstinate; −′**horend,** −′**horig** dull (hard) of hearing; −′**leers** dull, unteachable; **hard′lijvig** constipated; **−heid** *v* constipation; ′**hardloopwedstrijd** (-en) *m* footrace; **−lopen** *o* running; **−loper** (-s) *m* runner, racer; **hard′nekkig** obstinate, stubborn [people &], persistent; rebellious [diseases]; **−heid** *v* obstinacy, stubbornness, persistency; **hard′op,** ′**hardop** [dream, read, speak, say] aloud; ′**hardrijden** *o* racing; ~ *op de schaats* speed-skating; **−rijder** (-s) *m* racer; ~ *op de schaats* speed-skater; **hardrijde′rij** (-en) *v* skating-match; ′**hardsteen** (-stenen) *o* & *m* freestone, ashlar; **−stenen** *aj* freestone, ashlar; **−stikke** = *hartstikke*; **−vallen** (viel ′hard, is ′hardgevallen) *vt iem.* ~ *over...* be hard on sbd. for...; zie ook: *vallen* **I**; **hard′vochtig** hard-hearted, callous, flinty
′**harem** (-s) *m* harem, seraglio
1 ′**haren** *aj* hair [shirt]
2 ′**haren** (haarde, h. gehaard) *vt* sharpen [a scythe]
′**harent** *te(n)* ~ at her home; ~*halve* for her sake; ~*wege* as for her; *van* ~*wege* on her behalf, in her name; *om* ~*wil(le)* for her sake; ′**harerzijds** on her part, on her behalf
′**harig** hairy
′**haring** (-en) *m* 1 🐟 herring; 2 (v. t e n t) tent-peg; *als* ~*en in een ton* packed like sardines; **−haai** (-en) *m* porbeagle; **−kaken** *o* curing of herrings; **−sla** *v* herring-salad; **−ton** (-nen) *v* herring-barrel; **−vangst** (-en) *v* 1 herring-fishing; 2 catch of herrings; **−visser** (-s) *m* herring-fisher; **haringvisse′rij** *v* herring-fishery
hark (-en) *v* 1 rake; 2 ~ *van een vent* stick; muff;

′**harken** (harkte, h. geharkt) *vt* & *vi* rake;
′**harkerig I** *aj* stiff, wooden; **II** *ad* stiffly
harle′kijn, ′**harlekijn** (-s) *m* harlequin; *fig* buffoon; **harleki′nade** (-s) *v* harlequinade
harmo′nie *v* 1 (-ieën) harmony˚; 2 (-s) = *harmonieorkest;* **−leer** *v* theory of harmony; **−orkest** (-en) *o* wood-wind and brass band; **harmoni′ëren** (harmonieerde, h. geharmonieerd) *vi* harmonize (with *met*); **harmoni′eus** = *harmonisch;* **har′monika** (′s) *v* accordion; **−deur** (-en) *v* folding door; **−trein** (-en) *m* corridor-train; **harmoni′satie** [-za.(t)si.] (-s) *v* harmonization; **harmoni′seren** [s = z] (harmoniseerde, h. geharmoniseerd) *vt* harmonize; **−ring** (-en) *v* harmonization; **har′monisch** 1 harmonious; 2 harmonic [progression &]; **har′monium** (-s) *o* harmonium
′**harnas** (sen) *o* cuirass, armour: *iem. (tegen zich) in het* ~ *jagen* put sbd.'s back up, set sbd. against oneself; *hen tegen elkaar in het* ~ *jagen* set them by the ears; *in het* ~ *sterven* die in harness
harp (-en) *v* 1 ♪ harp; 2 riddle (= sieve); 3 ⚓ shackle; **−enaar** (-s en -naren) *m* harper, harp-player
har′pij (-en) *v* harpy²
har′pist(e) (-en) *m* (*v*) (lady) harpist
har′poen (-en) *m* harpoon; **harpoe′neren** (harpoeneerde, h. geharpoeneerd) *vt* harpoon
′**harpspeler** (-s) *m* harpist
′**harrewarren** (harrewarde, h. geharreward) *vi* bicker, wrangle, squabble
hars (-en) *o* & *m* resin, rosin; **−achtig** resinous; **−houdend** resinous, resiniferous
hart (-en) *o* heart²; *het* ~ *hebben om...,* have the heart to..., have the conscience to...; *niet het* ~ *hebben om* not have the heart (courage) to, not dare to; *als je het* ~ *hebt!* if you dare!; *heb het* ~ *niet* don't you dare, don't you have the cheek; *hij draagt het* ~ *op de juiste plaats* his heart is in the right place; *het* ~ *op de tong hebben* wear one's heart upon one's sleeve; *geen* ~ *hebben voor zijn werk* not have one's heart in the work; *een goed* ~ *hebben* be kind-hearted; *het* ~ *klopte mij in de keel* my heart was in my mouth; *zijn* ~ *luchten* give vent to one's feelings, speak one's mind; *zijn* ~ *ophalen aan* eat (read &) one's fill of; *iem. een* ~ *onder de riem steken* hearten sbd.; *iem. een goed* ~ *toedragen* be well disposed toward sbd.; *het* ~ *zonk hem in de schoenen* his heart sank (into his boots); *ik hou mijn* ~ *vast* I have misgivings, I tremble, I expect (fear) the worst; *iem. aan het* ~ *drukken* clasp sbd. to one's heart (bosom), embosom sbd.; ● *dat zal hem a a n het* ~ *gaan* it will go to his heart; *hij heeft het aan zijn* ~ he has a weak heart, he has (got) heart trouble; *dat is mij na aan 't* ~ *gebakken* I

hold it dear; *dat ligt mij na aan het* ~ it is very near my heart; *i n zijn* ~ *gaf hij mij gelijk* in his heart (of hearts); *in zijn* ~ *is hij...* at heart he is...; *hij is een... in* ~ *en nieren* he is a... to the backbone; *m e t* ~ *en ziel* heart and soul; *met een bezwaard (bloedend)* ~ with a heavy (bleeding) heart; *hij is een man n a a r mijn* ~ he is a man after my own heart; *het wordt mij wee o m het* ~ I am sick at heart; *iem. iets o p het* ~ *binden (drukken)* enjoin sth. upon sbd., urge sbd. to... [do sth.]; *iets op het* ~ *hebben* have sth. on one's mind; *zeggen wat men op het* ~ *heeft* speak freely, speak one's mind; *hij kon het niet o v e r zijn* ~ *krijgen om...* he did not have the heart to...; *uw welzijn gaat mij t e r* ~*e* I have your welfare at heart, I'm very concerned about your welfare; *ter* ~*e nemen* take (sth.) to heart; *dat is mij u i t het* ~ *gegrepen (gesproken)* this is quite after my heart; *uit de grond (het diepst) van zijn* ~ from the bottom of his heart; *van zijn* ~ *geen moordkuil maken* speak freely; *van* ~*e, hoor!* congratulations!; *van ganser* ~*e* [love obd.] with all one's heart; [thank sbd.] whole-heartedly, from one's heart; *waar het* ~ *van vol is, vloeit de mond van over* out of the abundance of the heart, the mouth speaketh; **–aandoening** (-en) *v* cardiac affection; **–aanval** (-len) *m* heart attack; **–ader** (-en en -s) *v* great artery, aorta; *fig* artery; **–boezem** (-s) *m* auricle (of the heart); **–brekend** heart-breaking, heart-rending; '**hartebloed** *o* heart's blood, lifeblood; **–dief** (-dieven) *m* darling, S heart-throb; **–kreet** (-kreten) *m* heartfelt cry; **–lap** (-pen) *m* = *hartedief;* **–leed** *o* grief, heartache; '**hartelijk** hearty, cordial, warm; *de* ~*e groeten van allen* kindest love (regards) from all; **–heid** (-heden) *v* heartiness, cordiality; '**harteloos** heartless; **–lust** *m naar* ~ to one's heart's content; '**harten** (-s) *v* ◊ hearts; ~*aas* [hartən-'a.s] &, ace of hearts; '**hartewens** (-en) *m* heart's desire; '**hartgebrek** (-breken) *o* cardiac defect; **hart'grondig** whole-hearted, cordial; '**hartig** 1 salt; 2 hearty [meal]; *een* ~ *woordje met iem. spreken* have a heart-to-heart talk with sbd.; **–heid** (-heden) *v* 1 saltness; 2 heartiness; '**hartinfarct** (-en) *o* cardiac infarct, coronary thrombosis, **F** coronary; **–je** (-s) *o* (little) heart; *mijn* ~*!* dear heart!; *in het* ~ *van Rusland* in the centre of Russia; *in het* ~ *van de winter* in the dead of winter; *in het* ~ *van de zomer* in the height of summer; **–kamer** (-s) *v* ventricle (of the heart); **–klep** (-pen) *v* 1 cardiac valve; 2 ✗ suction-valve; **–klopping** (-en) *v* palpitation (of the heart), heart palpitation; **–kramp** (-en) *v* spasm of the heart, heart disease, heart trouble; **–lap** (-pen) *m* = *hartelap;* **–lijder** (-s)

m, **–patiënt** [-pa.si.ɛnt] (-en) *m* heart sufferer, cardiac patient; **hart'roerend I** *aj* pathetic, moving; **II** *ad* pathetically; '**hartsgeheim** (-en) *o* secret of the heart; '**hartslag** (-slagen) *m* heart-beat, pulsation of the heart; **–specialist** (-en) *m* cardiologist; **–spier** (-en) *v* heart muscle

'**hartstikke** ~ *dood (doof)* stone-dead (-deaf); ~ *goed* super, smashing; ~ *gek* stark (staring) mad; *verder:* < **F** awfully [bad, good, nice, rich &]

'**hartstocht** (-en) *m* passion; **harts'tochtelijk** passionate(ly)

'**hartstreek** (-streken) *v* cardiac region; '**hartsvanger** (-s) *m* cutlass, hanger; **–vriend(in)** (-(inn)en) *m* (*v*) bosom friend; '**harttoon** (-tonen) *m* heart sound; **–vergroting** (-en) *v* megalocardia, cardiac dilatation, heart enlargement; **hartver'heffend**, '**hartverheffend** uplifting, exalting; '**hartverlamming** (-en) *v* paralysis of the heart, heart failure; **hartver'overend** enchanting, ravishing; **–ver'scheurend** heart-rending; '**hartversterking** (-en) *v* cordial, pick-me-up; **–vervetting** (-en) *v* fatty degeneration of the heart; **hartver'warmend** heart-warming; '**hartvormig** heart-shaped; **–zakje** (-s) *o* pericardium; **–zeer** *o* heartache, heart-break, grief

hasj [haʃ] *m* **S** hash (= hashish); **–iesj** ['haʃi.ʃ] *m* hashish

'**haspel** (-s en -en) *m* reel; '**haspelen** (haspelde, h. gehaspeld) **I** *vt* reel, wind; **II** *vi* reel, wind; *fig* bungle, potter; *door elkaar* ~ mix up, confuse

'**hatelijk I** *aj* spiteful, invidious, hateful, odious, malicious, ill-natured; **II** *ad* spitefully; **–heid** (-heden) *v* spitefulness, invidiousness, hatefulness, spite, malice; *een* ~ a gibe; '**haten** (haatte, h. gehaat) *vt* hate; *zie ook: gehaat*

hausse [ho.s] *v* rise, (s t e r k, s n e l) boom; *à la* ~ *speculeren* buy for a rise, bull; **haussier** [ho.si.'e.] (-s) *m* bull

hau'tain [o.'tɛ̃] haughty

haute-cou'ture [o.tku'ty:r] *v* haute couture

haut-reliëf [o:rəli.'ɛf] (-s) *o* high relief

ha'vannasigaar (-garen) *v* Havana

'**have** *v* property, goods, stock; ~ *en goed* goods and chattels; *levende* ~ livestock, cattle; *tilbare* ~ movables, personal property; **–loos** shabby, ragged

'**haven** (-s) *v* harbour, port[2], (m e e s t *fig*) haven; (b a s s i n e n o m g e v i n g) docks, dock; *een* ~ *aandoen* put in at a port; **–arbeider** (-s) *m* dock labourer, docker; **–dam** (-men) *m* mole, jetty, pier

'**havenen** (havende, h. gehavend) *vt* batter, ill-treat; damage; *zie ook: gehavend* '**havengeld** (-en) *o* harbour dues, dock dues; **–hoofd** (-en) *o* jetty, pier, mole; **–kantoor** (-toren) *o* harbour office; **–kwartier** (-en) *o* dockland; **–licht** (-en) *o* harbour light; **–loods** (-en) *m* harbour pilot; **–meester** (-s) *m* harbour master; **–plaats** (-en) *v* (sea)port; **–politie** [-(t)si.] *v* harbour police; **–stad** (-steden) *v* seaport town, port town, port; **–staking** (-en) *v* dock strike; **–werken** *mv* harbour-works

'**haver** *v* oats; *iem. kennen van ~ tot gort* know sbd. thoroughly (inside out); *iets van ~ tot gort vertellen* tell sth. in great detail; **–klap** *m om de ~* at every moment, on the slightest provocation; **–meel** *o* oatmeal; **–mout** *m* 1 rolled oats; 2 (a l s p a p) (oatmeal) porridge; **–stro** *o* oat-straw; **–zak** (-ken) *m* 1 oat-bag; 2 nose-bag [of a horse]

'**havezate** (-n) *v* ± manorial estate, manorial farm

'**havik** (-viken) *m* hawk, goshawk; *~en en duiven* [*fig*] hawks and doves; '**haviksneus** (-neuzen) *m* hawk-nose, aquiline nose; *met een ~* hawk-nosed; **–ogen** *mv met ~* hawk-eyed

ha'**zardspel** [ha.'za:r-] (-spelen) *o* game of chance (of hazard)

'**hazejacht** (-en) *v* hare-hunting, hare-shooting

'**hazelaar** (-s en -laren) *m* hazel(-tree)

'**hazeleger** (-s) *o* form of a hare; **–lip** (-pen) *v* harelip

'**hazelnoot** (-noten) *v* (hazel-)nut, filbert; **–worm** (-en) *m* blind-worm, slow-worm

'**hazepad** *o het ~ kiezen* take to one's heels; **–peper** *m* jugged hare; **–slaap** *m* dog-sleep, cat-nap; **–vel** (-len) *o* hare-skin; **haze'wind** (-en) *m ♀.* greyhound

'**H-bom** (-men) *v* H-bomb

h.c. = *honoris causa*

he [he.] hey!, ha!, ah!, oh!, o!, I say!; ⚓ ahoy!

'**hebbeding** (-en) *o* knick-knack

'**hebbelijkheid** (-heden) *v* (bad) habit, trick; *hebbelijkheden* ways, idiosyncracies

'**hebben* I** *vt* have; *wij ~ nu aardrijkskunde* we are doing geography now; *ik kan je hier niet ~* I have no use for you here; *daar heb ik je!* I had you there; *daar heb je hem weer!* there he is again!; *daar heb je bijv. XYZ...* there is..., now take...; *daar heb je het nou!* there you are; *hier heb je het* here you are; *dat hebben we weer gehad* that's that; [*hij zong*] *van heb ik jou daar* lustily; *een klap van heb ik jou daar* an enormous blow; zie ook: *dorst, gelijk, nodig, spijt* &; *ik heb 't* I've got it; *het gemakkelijk ~* have an easy time of it; *het goed ~* be well off, be in easy circumstances; *het hard ~* have a hard time of it; *het koud ~* be cold; *hoe heb ik het nou?* well, I'm jiggered!; *hij weet niet hoe hij het heeft* he doesn't know

whether he is standing on his head or on his heels; *het rustig ~* be quiet; *het in de buik* (*in de ingewanden*) *~* suffer from intestine troubles; *het over iem.* (*iets*) *~* be talking about sbd. (sth.); *het tegen iem. ~* be talking to sbd.; *hij zal iets aan zijn voet ~* there will be something the matter with his foot; *je hebt er niet veel aan* it is (they are) not much use; *daar hebt u niets aan* 1 it is nothing for you; 2 it will not profit you; *zijn boeken* (*stok* &) *niet bij zich ~* not have... with one; *hij heeft wel iets van zijn vader* he looks (is) somewhat like his father; *hij heeft niets van zijn vader* he is nothing like his father; *het heeft er wel iets van* it looks like it; *hebt u er iets tegen?* have you any objection?; *hij heeft iets tegen mij* he owes me a grudge; *als ma er niets tegen heeft* if ma sees no objection, if ma doesn't mind; *ik heb niets tegen hem* I have nothing against him; *daar moet ik niets van ~* I don't hold with that, I'm not having any; *hij moest niets ~ van...* he didn't take kindly to..., he didn't hold with..., he didn't like...; he wasn't having any (of it), he said; *wat heb je toch?* what is the matter (wrong) with you?; *wat heeft hij toch?* what has come over him?; *wie moet je ~?* whom do you want?; *je moet wat ~* 1 you deserve what for; 2 there must be something the matter with you; *wat heb je eraan?* what is the use (the good) of it?; *daar heb ik niets aan* that's of no use to me; *ik weet niet wat ik aan hem heb* I cannot make him out; *wat zullen we nu ~?* what's up now?; *iets niet kunnen ~* not be able to stand (bear) sth.; *ik moet nog geld van hem ~* he is still owing me; *ik wil* (*moet*) *mijn... ~* I want my...; *ik wil het niet ~* I won't have (allow) it; **II** *va* have; *~ is ~, maar krijgen is de kunst* possession is nine points of the law; **III** *o zijn hele ~ en houden* all his belongings; '**hebberig** = *hebzuchtig*

He'breeuws *aj* & *o* Hebrew

'**hebzucht** *v* greed, covetousness, avarice; **heb'zuchtig** greedy, grasping, covetous

1 hecht (-en) *o* handle, haft; hilt; zie ook *heft*

2 hecht *aj* solid, firm, strong

'**hechtdraad** (-draden) *m* basting (tacking) thread); '**hechten** (hechtte, h. gehecht) **I** *vt* 1 (v a s t m a k e n) attach, fasten, affix; 2 (v a s t-n a a i e n) stitch up, suture [a wound]; 2 *fig* attach [importance, a meaning to...]; zie ook: *goedkeuring* &; **II** *vi* & *va ~ aan iets* believe in [a method &]; *erg ~ aan de vormen* be very particular about forms; **III** *vr zich ~ aan iem.* (*iets*) become (get) attached to sbd. (sth.); zie ook: *gehecht*

'**hechtenis** *v* custody, detention; *in ~ nemen* take into custody, arrest, apprehend; *in ~ zijn* be under arrest; *uit de ~ ontslaan* free from custody

'**hechtheid** *v* solidity, firmness, strength

'**hechting** (-en) *v* suture, stitch; '**hechtma-chine** [-ma.ʃi.nə] (-s) *v* stapling-machine, stitching-machine; –**pleister** (-s) *v* sticking-plaster, adhesive plaster; –**wortel** (-s) *m* clinging root

hec'tare (-n en -s) *v* hectare

'**hectogram** (-men) *o* hectogramme; –**liter** (-s) *m* hectolitre; –**meter** (-s) *m* hectometre

'**heden I** *ad* to-day, this day; ~ *!* dear me!; ~ *over 8 dagen* this day week; ~ *over 14 dagen* this day fortnight; ~ *ten dage* nowadays; *tot* ~ up to the present, to this day; **II** *o het* ~ the present; **heden'avond** this evening, tonight; '**heden-daags I** *aj* modern, present, present-day, contemporary; *de* ~*e dames* the ladies of to-day; **II** *ad* nowadays; **heden'middag** this after-noon; –'**morgen** this morning; –'**nacht** to-night

'**hederik** (-riken) *m* = *herik*

hedo'nisme *o* hedonism; **hedo'nist** (-en) *m* hedonist; **hedo'nistisch** hedonistic, hedonic

heeft 3e pers. enkelv. tijd v. *hebben*

heel I *aj* whole, entire; *dat is een* ~ *besluit* that is quite a decision; *de hele dag* all day, the whole day; *een* ~ *getal* a whole number; [*de klok sloeg*] *het hele uur* the hour; *hij is een hele heer* (*held &*) he is quite a gentleman (hero &); *langs die hele oever* all along the bank; *het kost hele sommen* large sums, lots of money; *een* ~ *spektakel* **F** a regular row; *een hele tijd* a good while, a long time; *hij blijft soms hele weken weg* for weeks together; *er bleef geen ruit* ~ not a window was left unbroken (remained intact); *hij liet geen stuk* ~ *van het meubilair* he smashed all the furniture; [*fig*] *hij liet geen stukje* ~ *van het betoog* he slated (slashed) the argument to shreds; **II** *ad* quite; ~ *en al* wholly, totally, entirely, altogether, quite; ~ *niet* not at all; ~ *goed* (*mooi &*) very good (fine &); ~ *iets anders* quite a different thing; ~ *in de verte* far, far away; zie ook: *geheel*

heel'al *o* universe

'**heelbaar** curable; that can be healed

'**heelhuids** with a whole skin, unscathed

'**heelkunde** *v* surgery; **heel'kundige** (-n) *m* surgeon; '**heelmeester** (-s) *m* surgeon; *zachte* ~*s maken stinkende wonden* desperate ills call for desperate remedies

'**heemkunde** *v* local history and geography; local lore; '**heemraad** (-raden) *m* 1 (p e r s o o n) dike-reeve; 2 (c o l l e g e) polder authority; –**schap** (-pen) *o* 1 (a m b t) office of a dike-reeve; 2 = *heemraad* 2

heemst *v* ⚘ marsh mallow

heen away; ~ *en terug* there and back; ~ *en weer* to and fro; ~ *en weer geloop* coming and going; ~ *en weer gepraat* cross-talk, *waar moet dit* (*boek, stoel*) ~ *?* where does this (book, chair) go?; *waar moet dat* ~ *?* 1 where are you going to?; 2 *fig* what are we coming to?; *waar ik* ~ *wilde* 1 where I wanted to go to; 2 *fig* what I was driving at; **heen- en te'rugreis** (-reizen) *v* journey there and back, ⚓ voyage out and home; **heen-en-'weer** *o krijg het* ~ *!* go climb a tree; '**heengaan¹ I** *vi* go away, leave, go; pass away [= die]; *daar gaan weken mee heen* it will take weeks (to do it), it will be weeks before...; **II** *o* departure [also of a minister &]; ☉ passing away, death; –**komen** *o een goed* ~ *zoeken* seek safety in flight; –**lopen¹** *vi* run away; *ergens over* ~ make light of it; scamp one's work &; *loop heen!* **F** get along with you!; –**reis** (-reizen) *v* outward journey, ⚓ voyage out; –**rijden¹** *vi* ride (drive) away; –**snellen¹** *vi* run away; –**stappen¹** *vi* stride off; *over iets* ~ 1 *eig* step across sth.; 2 *fig* ignore sth., not mind sth.; *hij stapte over die bezwaren heen* he brushed aside these objections; –**vlieden¹** *vi* fleet; –**weg** *m* way there; –**zetten¹** *zich* ~ *over iets* get over sth.

1 heer (heren) *m* 1 (v. s t a n d) gentleman; 2 (g e b i e d e r) lord; 3 (m e e s t e r) master; 4 (c a v a l i e r) partner; 5 ◊ king; *de Heer* the Lord; *de* ~ *S.* Mr S.; *de heren Kolff & Co.* Messrs. Kolff & Co.; *die heren* those gentlemen; *Heer der Heerscharen* Lord God of Hosts; *de* ~ *des huizes* the master of the house; ~ *en meester zijn* be master; *de grote* ~ *uithangen* zie *uithangen*; *met grote heren is het kwaad kersen eten* the weakest always goes to the wall; *zo* – *zo knecht* like master, like man; *nieuwe heren, nieuwe wetten* new lords, new laws; *niemand kan twee heren dienen* nobody can serve two masters

2 heer (heren) *o dat* ~ > *that* gent; *een raar* ~ **F** a queer chap, a rum customer

3 heer (heren) *o* (l e g e r) host; –**baan** (-banen) *v* high road; –**leger** (-s) *o* = 3 *heer*

'**heerlijk I** *aj* 1 (p r a c h t i g) glorious; splendid; lovely; 2 (v. s m a a k, g e u r &) delicious, delightful, divine; 3 (v. e. h e e r l ij k h e i d) manorial, seigniorial [rights]; **II** *ad* deliciously; gloriously; –**heid** (-heden) *v* 1 (p r a c h t) splendour, magnificence, glory, grandeur; 2 (e i g e n d o m) manor, seigniory; *al die heerlijk-heden* all those good things

heerschap'pij *v* mastery, dominion, rule, lordship, empire; *elkaar de* ~ *betwisten* contend

---

¹ V.T. en V.D. van dit werkwoord volgens het model: '**heen**snellen, V.T. snelde '**heen**, V.D. '**heen**gesneld. Zie voor de vormen onder het grondwoord, in dit voorbeeld: *snellen*. Bij sterke en onregelmatige werkwoorden wordt u verwezen naar de lijst achterin.

(struggle) for mastery; ~ *voeren* bear sway, rule, lord it

'**heerscharen** *mv* hosts; zie ook: 1 *heer*

'**heersen** (heerste, h. geheerst) *vi* 1 rule, reign; 2 (v. z i e k t e &) reign, prevail, be prevalent; ~ *over* rule (over); –d ruling, prevailing, prevalent; *de ~e godsdienst* the prevailing religion; *de ~e smaak* the reigning fashion; *de ~e ziekte* the prevalent (prevailing) disease; '**heerser** (-s) *m*, **heerse'res** (-sen) *v* ruler°; '**heerszucht** *v* ambition for power, lust of power; **heers-'zuchtig** imperious, ambitious of power, dictatorial; –**heid** *v* imperious spirit, ambition for power

'**heertje** (-s) *o* dandy, **S** nut, fop, > gent

'**heerweg** (-wegen) *m* high road

1 hees hoarse; –**heid** *v* hoarseness

2 hees (hesen) V.T. v. *hijsen*

'**heester** (-s) *m* shrub

heet I *aj* hot²; torrid [zone]; ~ *van de naald* (*van de pan*) piping hot; ~ *zijn op iets* be hot (keen) on sth.; *in het ~st van de strijd* in the thick of the fight; **II** *ad het zal er ~ toegaan* it will be hot work there; **heetge'bakerd** zie *gebakerd*; '**heethoofd** (-en) *m-v Griekse* & ~*en* hot-headed Greeks &; **heet'hoofdig** hot-headed; '**heetlopen** (liep 'heet, is 'heetgelopen) *vi* = *warmlopen*; **heet'waterkruik** (-en) *v* hot-water bottle; –**toestel** (-len) *o* (hot-water) heater

hef *v* = *heffe*

'**hefboom** (-bomen) *m* lever; –**brug** (-gen) *v* lift(ing)-bridge

'**heffe** *v* dregs; *de ~ [des volks]* the scum [of the people]

'**heffen*** *vt* raise, lift, levy [taxes on]; '**heffing** (-en) *v* levying; levy; ~ *ineens* capital levy; '**hefschroefvliegtuig** (-en) *o* helicopter

heft (-en) *o* = *hecht*; *[fig] het ~ in handen hebben* be at the helm (in command)

'**heftig** vehement, violent; –**heid** *v* vehemence, violence

'**heftruck** [-trük] (-s) *m* lift truck; –**vermogen** (-s) *o* lifting capacity, lifting power

heg (-gen) *v* hedge; zie ook: *steg*

hegemo'nie *v* hegemony

'**hegge** (-n) *v* = *heg*; –**rank** (-en) *v* (white) bryony; '**heg(ge)schaar** (-scharen) *v* hedge shears, hedge clippers

1 hei *ij* ho!, hey!, hallo!; ~ *daar!* hey there!, I say!

2 hei (-en) *v* ⚒ rammer; pile-driver

3 hei *v* = *heide*

'**heibel** *m* = *herrie*

'**heibezem** (-s) *m* heather broom

'**heiblok** (-ken) *o* ram, monkey

'**heide** *v* 1 (v e l d) heath, moor; 2 ⚘ heather;

–**achtig** heathy, heathery; –**brand** (-en) *m* heath fire; –**grond** *m* heath, moor, moorland; –**honi(n)g** *m* heather honey

'**heiden** (-en) *m* 1 heathen, pagan; (t e g e n-o v e r j o o d) gentile; 2 (z i g e u n e r) gipsy; *aan de ~en overgeleverd zijn* be delivered to the gentiles; –**dom** *o* heathenism, paganism; '**heidens** *aj* heathen, pagan; heathenish; *een ~ leven* **F** an infernal noise

'**heideontginning** (-en) *v* reclaiming of moorland; –**veld** (-en) *o* heath, moor

'**heien** (heide, h. geheid) **I** *vt* ram, drive (in) [a pile], pile [the ground]; **II** *o* piling, pile-work

'**heiig** hazy

'**heikneuter** (-s) *m* yokel, bumpkin, clodhopper

heil *o* welfare, good; (g e e s t e l ij k) salvation; ~ *u!* hail to thee!; *veel ~ en zegen!* a happy New Year!; *ergens geen ~ in zien* expect no good from, not believe in...; *zijn ~ zoeken bij* seek the support of; *zijn ~ zoeken in* resort to, seek salvation in; *zijn ~ zoeken in de vlucht* seek safety in flight

'**Heiland** *m* Saviour, Redeemer

'**heilbede** (-n) *v* prayer for the well-being

'**heilbot** (-ten) *m* halibut

'**heildronk** (-en) *m* toast, health; *een ~ instellen* propose a toast

'**heilgymnastiek** [-gim-] *v* Swedish gymnastics

'**heilig I** *aj* 1 (v. p e r s o n e n & z a k e n) holy; 2 (v. z a k e n) sacred; *de Heilige Elizabeth* St. (Saint) Elizabeth; *het is mij ~e ernst* I am in real earnest; ~ *huisje [fig]* sacred cow; *het Heilige Land* the Holy Land; *in de ~e overtuiging dat...* honestly convinced that...; *de Heilige Stad* the Holy City; *niets is hem ~* nothing is sacred to (from) him; *haar wens is mij ~* her wish is sacred with me; *hij is nog ~ bij* he is a paragon (saint) in comparison with; ~ *verklaren* canonize; *het Heilige der Heiligen²* the Holy of Holies²; **II** *ad* sacredly; ~ *verzekeren* assure solemnly; *zich ~ voornemen om...* make a firm resolution to...; –**been** (-deren) *o* sacrum; –**dom** (-men) *o* 1 (p l a a t s) sanctuary; **F** sanctum [= den]; 2 (v o o r w e r p) relic; –**e** (-n) *m-v* saint; *Heiligen der Laatste Dagen* [the Church of Jesus Christ of] Latter-day Saints; zie ook: *heilig* **I**;

'**heiligen** (heiligde, h. geheiligd) *vt* sanctify [a place, us]; hallow [God's name]; keep holy [the Sabbath &]; consecrate [the host]; *geheiligd zij Uw naam* hallowed be thy name; zie ook *doel*;

'**heiligenbeeld** (-en) *o* image of a saint, holy image; '**heiligheid** *v* holiness, sacredness, sanctity; *Zijne Heiligheid (de Paus)* His Holiness; –**schennend** sacrilegious; –**schennis** *v* sacrilege, profanation; –**verklaring** (-en) *v* canonization

'**heilloos** 1 fatal, disastrous; 2 wicked

'**Heilsleger** *o* Salvation Army; '**heilsoldaat** (-daten) *m* Salvationist; **–soldate** (-n) *v* Salvationist, **F** Sally Ann

'**heilstaat** *m* ideal state; **–wens** (-en) *m* congratulation

'**heilzaam** beneficial, salutary, wholesome; **–heid** *v* beneficial influence, salutariness, wholesomeness

'**heimachine** [-ma.ʃi.nə] (-s) *v* pile-driver, monkey engine

'**heimelijk** secret, clandestine; **–heid** (-heden) *v* secrecy

'**heimwee** *o* homesickness, nostalgia; ~ *hebben* be homesick (for *naar*)

Hein *m* Harry; *magere* ~ the old gentleman with the scythe: Death; *hij is een ijzeren* ~ he is as strong as a horse

'**heinde** ~ *en ver* far and near, far and wide

'**heining** (-en) *v* enclosure, fence

'**Heintje** *m* & *o* Harry; ~ *Pik* Old Scratch

'**heipaal** (-palen) *m* pile

heir = 3 *heer*

'**heisa** *ij* huzza!; *wat een* ~ what a lot of fuss

'**heitje** (-s) *o* = *kwartje*; ~ *karweitje* bob-a-job

'**heitoestel** (-len) *o* pile-driver, monkey-engine

hek (-ken) *o* 1 [lath, wire] fence; 2 [iron] railing(s); [metal, steel] barrier; [level crossing, entrance] gate; 3 [choir] screen; 4 *sp* hurdle; 5 ⚓ stern; *het* ~ *is van de dam* it is Liberty Hall

'**hekel** (-s) *m* hackle; *fig* dislike; *ik heb een* ~ *aan* I dislike (hate); I'm allergic to; *een* ~ *krijgen aan* take a dislike to; *over de* ~ *halen* criticize; satirize

'**hekeldicht** (-en) *o* satire; **–dichter** (-s) *m* satirist; '**hekelen** (hekelde, h. gehekeld) *vt* hackle; *fig* criticize; satirize; '**hekelschrift** (-en), **–vers** (-verzen) *o* satire, diatribe

'**hekkesluiter** (-s) *m* last comer

heks (-en) *v* witch²; *fig* vixen, hag; '**heksen** (hekste, h. gehekst) *vi* use witchcraft, practise sorcery; *ik kan niet* ~ I am no wizard; '**heksendans** (-en) *m* witches' dance; **–jacht** (-en) *v* witch-hunt(ing); **–ketel** (-s) *m* witches' cauldron; *fig* chaos; **–kring** (-en) *m* hot fairy ring; **–proces** (-sen) *o* trial for witchcraft; **–sabbat** (-ten) *m* witches' sabbath; **–toer** (-en) *m het was een* ~ it was a devil of a job; *dat is zo'n* ~ *niet* that's no magic, there's nothing to it; **–werk** *o* sorcery, witchcraft, witchery; *dat is zo'n* ~ *niet* zie *heksentoer*; **hekse'rij** (-en) *v* sorcery, witchcraft, witchery

'**hekwerk** (-en) *o* railing(s), trellis-work

1 **hel** *v* hell²

2 **hel** *aj* bright, glaring, blazing

'**hela!** *ij* hallo!

he'laas *ij* alas!; unfortunately

held (-en) *m* hero; *een* ~ *zijn in* be good at;

'**heldendaad** (-daden) *v* heroic deed, exploit; **–dicht** (-en) *o* heroic poem, epic, epopee; **–dichter** (-s) *m* epic poet; **–dood** *m* & *v* heroic death; *de* ~ *sterven* die heroically; **–moed** *m* heroism; *met* ~ heroically; **–rol** (-len) *v* heroic part, part of a hero; **–schaar** (-scharen) *v* band of heroes; **–tenor** [-tɔːno:r] (-s) *m* heroic tenor; **–zang** (-en) *m* epic song

'**helder I** *aj* 1 clear, bright, lucid; serene; 2 clean; **II** *ad* 1 clearly, brightly, lucidly; serenely; 2 cleanly; ~ *rood* bright red; **–denkend** clear-headed; **–heid** *v* 1 clearness &, clarity, lucidity; 2 cleanness; **helder'ziend** 1 clear-sighted; 2 clairvoyant; *een* ~*e* a clairvoyant; **–heid** *v* 1 clear-sightedness; 2 clairvoyance

held'haftig I *aj* heroic; **II** *ad* heroically; **–heid** (-heden) *v* heroism

hel'din (-nen) *v* heroine

'**heleboel, hele'boel** many, a lot, lots

'**helemaal, hele'maal** wholly, totally, entirely, quite, altogether; ~ *achterin* right at the back; *kom je* ~ *van A.?* have you come all the way from A.?; ~ *niet* not at all; *niet* ~ quite, not altogether; ~ *niets* nothing at all

1 '**helen** (heelde, *vi* is, *vt* h. geheeld) *vi* (& *vt*) (v. w o n d e n) heal

2 '**helen** (heelde, h. geheeld) *vt* receive [stolen goods]

'**heler** (-s) *m* receiver; *de* ~ *is net zo goed als de steler* the receiver is as bad as the thief

helft (-en) *v* half; *zijn betere* ~ his better half; *de* ~ *van 10 is 5* the half of 10 is 5; *voor de* ~ *van het geld* for half the money; *de* ~ *ervan is rot* half of it is rotten, half of them are rotten; *(ik verstond niet) de* ~ *van wat hij zei* one half (what) he said; *meer dan de* ~ more than one half (of them); *de* ~ *minder* less by half; *maar tot op de* ~ only half

'**Helgoland** *o* Heligoland

'**helhond** (-en) *m* hell-hound, Cerberus

'**helihaven** (-s) *v* heliport; **heli'kopter** (-s) *m* helicopter, **F** chopper

1 '**heling** (-en) *v* (g e n e z i n g) healing

2 '**heling** *v* receiving [of stolen goods]

'**helium** *o* helium

'**hellebaard** (-en) *v* halberd; **hellebaar'dier** (-en en -s) *m* halberdier

Hel'leen (-lenen) *m* Hellene; **–s** Hellenic

'**hellen** (helde, h. geheld) *vi* incline, slant, slope, shelve; **–d** slanting, sloping, inclined, zie ook: 1 *vlak* **III**

helle'nisme *o* Hellenism; **–ist** (-en) *m* Hellenist

'**hellepijn** (-en) *v* torture of hell; '**hellevaart** *v* descent into hell; '**helleveeg** (-vegen) *v* hell-cat, termagant, shrew

'**helling** (-en) *v* 1 incline, declivity, slope; 2 gradient [of railway]; 3 ⚓ slipway, slips; *op de*

~ ⚓ in dock; *op de* ~ *nemen* overhaul [education]; **–shoek** (-en) *m* gradient

1 helm *v* 🌾 bent-grass

2 helm (-en) *m* 1 helmet; 2 (v. d u i k e r) head-piece; 3 (v. d i s t i l l e e r k o l f) head; 4 (b i j g e b o o r t e) caul; *met de* ~ *geboren* born with a caul

'**helmdraad** (-draden) *m* 🌾 filament

'**helmstok** (-ken) *m* ⚓ tiller, helm

'**helmteken** (-s) *o* ⊘ crest

help *ij* help!; *lieve* ~ good gracious!; '**helpen* I** *vt* 1 (h u l p v e r l e n e n) help, aid, assist, succour; 2 (b a t e n) avail, be of avail, be of use; 3 (b e d i e n e n) attend to [customers]; *wordt u geholpen?* are you being attended to?; *waarmee kan ik u* ~? what can I do for you?; *zo waarlijk helpe mij God almachtig!* so help me God!; *dat zal u niets* ~ that won't be much use, will be of no avail; *wat zal het* ~? of what use will it be?, what will be the good (of it)?; *hij kan het niet* ~ it is not his fault; ● *a a n iets* ~ help to, procure, get; *kunt u me* ~ *aan* can you oblige me [with a match]?; *er is geen* ~ *aan* it can't be helped; *iem. (aan) b i j zijn sommen* ~ help sbd. to do his sums; *iem. i n zijn jas* ~ help sbd. in his coat; *iem m e t geld* ~ assist sbd. with money; *iem. u i t zijn bed* ~ help sbd. out of bed; **II** *vi* help; avail, be of avail, be of use; *help!* help!; *het helpt al* it is some good already; *alles helpt* everything is helpful; *het helpt niet* it's no good, it's no use, it is of no avail; *aspirine helpt tegen de hoofdpijn* is good for a headache; **III** *vr zich* ~ help oneself; '**helper** (-s) *m*, '**helpster** (-s) *v* helper, assistant

hels I *aj* hellish, infernal, devilish; *iem.* ~ *maken* **F** drive sbd. wild; *hij was* ~ **S** he was in a wax; *een* ~ *lawaai* a hellish noise (din); ~*e machine* infernal machine; ~*e pijn* excruciating pain, agony; ~*e steen* lunar caustic, argentic (silver) nitrate; **II** *ad* < infernally, devilish(ly)

hem *pers. voornw.* him; *het is van* ~ it is his; *hij is* ~ he is it; *dat is het* ~ that's it; *daar zit het* ~ *in* that's just it (the case)

hemd (-en) *o* shirt; chemise [of a woman]; *hij heeft geen* ~ *aan zijn lijf* he has not a shirt to his back; *iem. het* ~ *van het lijf vragen* pester sbd. with questions; *het* ~ *is nader dan de rok* charity begins at home; ● *i n zijn* ~ *staan* [*fig*] cut a sorry figure; *iem. in zijn* ~ *laten staan* make sbd. look foolish; *t o t op het* ~ *toe nat* wet to the skin; *iem. tot op het* ~ *uitkleden* strip sbd. naked; '**hemdsknoop** (-knopen) *m* shirt-button; **–mouw** (-en) *v* shirt-sleeve; *in zijn* ~*en* in his shirt-sleeves

'**hemel** (-en en -s) *m* 1 (d e r g e l u k z a l i g e n) heaven; 2 (u i t s p a n s e l) sky, firmament, heavens; 3 (d a k) canopy [of throne]; tester [of bed]; *goeie (lieve)* ~! good heavens!; *de* ~ *beware ons!* God forbid!; *de* ~ *geve dat hij...!* would to God he...!; *om 's* ~*s wil* for heaven's sake; ~ *en aarde bewegen* move heaven and earth; *de* ~ *mag weten* heaven knows, goodness knows; ● *de sterren a a n de* ~ the stars in the sky; *i n de* ~ in heaven; *in de* ~ *komen* go to heaven; *t u s s e n* ~ *en aarde* between heaven and earth, [hang] in mid-air; *als de* ~ *valt hebben we allemaal een blauwe hoed* if the sky falls we shall catch larks; zie ook: *bloot, schreien &*; **–bed** (-den) *o* four-poster; **–bestormer** (-s) *m* Titan; **–bol** (-len) *m* celestial globe; **–gewelf** *o* vault of heaven, firmament; **–hoog I** *aj* sky-high, reaching (towering) to the skies; **II** *ad* sky-high, to the skies; *iem.* ~ *verheffen* exalt (laud) sbd. to the skies; **–lichaam** (-chamen) *o* heavenly body, celestial body; **–opneming** (-en) *v* assumption [of the Virgin Mary]; **–poort** (-en) *v* gate of Heaven; **–rijk** *o* kingdom of Heaven; '**hemels I** *aj* celestial, heavenly [Father &]; *het Hemelse Rijk* the Celestial Empire [China]; **II** *ad* celestially, heavenly; divinely [beautiful &]; **–blauw** sky-blue, azure; **–breed** *een* ~ *verschil* a big difference; *er is een* ~ *verschil tussen hen* they are as wide asunder as the poles; ~ *100 km* 100 km as the crow flies; **–breedte** *v* celestial latitude; **–naam** *in 's* ~, zie *godsnaam*; '**hemelstreek** (-streken) *v* 1 climate; 2 point of the compass; 3 zone; **–tergend** crying to heaven, crying; **–tje** *ij* good heavens!; **–vaart** *v* Ascension (of J.C.); '**Hemelvaartsdag** *m* Ascension Day; '**hemelvuur** *o* 1 celestial fire; 2 lightning; **–waarts** heavenward, towards Heaven; **–water** *o* rain

hemi'sfeer (-sferen) *v* hemisphere

hemofi'lie *v* haemophilia

1 hen (-nen) *v* 🐦 hen

2 hen them; ~ *die* those who

'**hendel** (-s) *o* & *m* = 2 *handel*

'**henen** = *heen*

'**hengel** (-s) *m* 1 fishing-rod; 2 (v. m i c r o-f o o n) boom; **–aar** (-s) *m* angler; '**hengelen I** (hengelde, h. gehengeld) *vi* angle; *naar een complimentje* ~ be angling (fishing) for a compliment; **II** *o het* ~ angling; '**hengelroe(de)** (-den) *v* fishing-rod; **–snoer** (-en) *o* fishing-line; **–stok** (-ken) *m* fishing rod

'**hengsel** (-s) *o* 1 handle; 2 hinge [of a door]; **–mand** (-en) *v* hand-basket

hengst (-en) *m* stallion, stud-horse

'**hengsten** (hengstte, h. gehengst) *vi* = *blokken*

'**henna** *v* henna

'**hennep** *m* hemp; ~ *en hempen*, hemp; **–olie** *v* hempseed oil; **–zaad** (-zaden) *o* hempseed

hens *alle* ~ *aan dek* ⚓ all hands on deck

her ~ *en der* here and there, hither and thither;

van eeuwen ~ ages old; *jaren* ~ ages since
her'ademen[1] *vi* breathe again; **–ming** (-en) *v*
fig relief
heral'diek I *v* heraldry; **II** *aj* heraldic;
he'raldisch *aj* heraldic
he'raut (-en) *m* herald[2]
her'barium (-s en -ria) *o* herbarium
'herbebossen (herbeboste, h. herbebost) *vt*
reafforest; **–sing** (-en) *v* reafforestation
'herbenoemen (herbenoemde, h. herbenoemd)
vt reappoint; **–ming** (-en) *v* reappointment
'herberg (-en) *v* inn, public house, **F** pub,
tavern; **'herbergen** (herbergde, h. geher-
bergd) *vt* accommodate, lodge; **herber'gier**
(-s) *m* innkeeper, landlord, host; **her'berg-**
zaam hospitable
'herbewapenen (herbewapende, h. herbewa-
pend) (*zich*) ~ rearm; **–ning** (-en) *v* rearmament; *morele* ~ moral rearmament
her'boren born again, reborn, regenerate
'herbouw *m* rebuilding; **her'bouwen**[1]*vt*
rebuild
'herculesarbeid *m* Herculean labour
'herdenken[1] *vt* commemorate, call to remembrance; **her'denking** (-en) *v* commemoration;
ter ~ *van* in commemoration of; **–zegel** (-s) *m*
commemorative stamp
'herder (-s) *m* 1 (v. s c h a p e n) shepherd, (v.
v e e) herdsman, (m e e s t i n s a m e n s t.)
[swine-]herd; 2 (g e e s t e l ij k e) shepherd,
pastor; 3 = *herdershond; de Goede Herder* the
Good Shepherd; **herde'rin** (-nen) *v* shepherdess; **'herderlijk** pastoral; ~ *ambt* pastorate,
pastorship; ~ *schrijven* pastoral (letter);
'herdersambt (-en) *o* pastorship, pastorate;
–dicht (-en) *o* pastoral (poem); **~en** bucolics;
–fluit (-en) *v* shepherd's pipe; **–hond** (-en) *m*
shepherd's dog, sheepdog; *Duitse* ~ Alsatian;
–spel (-spelen) *o* pastoral (play); **–staf**
(-staven) *m* 1 sheep-hook, [shepherd's] crook;
2 [bishop's] crosier; **–tas** (-sen) *v* shepherd's
pouch; **–tasje** (-s) *o* 🌼 shepherd's-purse;
–uurtje (-s) *o* lovers' tryst; **–zang** (-en) *m*
pastoral (song), eclogue
'herdruk (-ken) *m* reprint, new edition; *in* ~
reprinting; **her'drukken**[1] *vt* reprint
'hereboer (-en) *m* gentleman-farmer
here'miet (-en) *m* hermit
heremijn'tijd [-mə(n)'tɛit] *ij* Good heavens!
'herendienst (-en) *m* forced labour; statute
labour; **heren'dubbelspel** (-spelen) *o* men's
doubles; **–'enkelspel** (-spelen) *o* men's
singles; **'herenhuis** (-huizen) *o* 1 manor-

house; 2 gentleman's house
her'enigen (herenigde, h. herenigd) *vt* reunite;
–ging (-en) *v* reunion; [German] reunification
'herenkleding *v* men's wear; **–leventje** *o een* ~
hebben live like a prince, be in clover; **–mode**
(-s) *v* (gentle)men's fashion; **~s** men's wear;
winkelier in **~s** (men's) outfitter, clothier
'herexamen (-s) *o* re-examination
herfst *m* autumn, *Am* fall; **–achtig** autumnal;
–aster (-s) *v* Michaelmas daisy; **–bloem** (-en)
v autumnal flower; **–dag** (-dagen) *m* autumn
day, day in autumn; **–draden** *mv* air-threads,
gossamer; **–ig** autumnal, autumn-like;
–maand (-en) *v* autumn month, September;
–tijd *m* autumn time; **–tijloos** (-lozen) *v*
meadow saffron; **–vakantie** [-(t)si.] (-s) *v*
autumn holidays
her'geven[1] *vt* 1 give again; 2 ◊ deal again
'hergroeperen[1] *vt* regroup; **–ring** *v* regrouping
her'haald repeated; **~e** *malen* repeatedly, again
and again; **–elijk** repeatedly, again and again;
her'halen I *vt* repeat, say (over) again,
reiterate; (k o r t) recapitulate; **II** *vr zich* ~
repeat oneself (itself); **her'haling** (-en) *v*
repetition; *bij* ~ again and again; repeatedly; *in*
~en *vervallen* repeat oneself; **her'halings-**
cursus [-züs] (-sen) *m* refresher course; **–oefe-**
ning (-en) *v* recapitulatory exercise; **~en** ✠
(military) training [of reservists]; **–teken** (-s) *o*
repeat
'herijken[1] *vt* regauge
'herik (-riken) *m* charlock
her'inneren (herinnerde, h. herinnerd) **I** *vt aan*
iets ~ recall sth.; *iem. aan iets* ~ remind sbd. of
sth.; **II** *vr zich* ~ remember, (re)call to mind,
recollect, recall; *voor zover ik mij herinner* to the
best of my recollection, as far as I can
remember; **her'innering** (-en) *v* 1 memory;
remembrance, recollection, reminiscence; 2
(a a n d e n k e n) souvenir, memento, keepsake;
3 (g e h e u g e n o p f r i s s i n g) reminder; *iem.*
iets in ~ *brengen* remind sbd. of sth.; *ter* ~ *aan* in
memory (remembrance) of; **her'innerings-**
medaille [-me.da(l)jə] (-s) *v* commemorative
medal; **–vermogen** *o* memory
'herkansing (-en) *v sp* supplementary heat;
(s c h o o l) re-examination
'herkauwen[1] *vt* & *vi* ruminate, chew the cud;
fig repeat (the same thing); **–d** ~ *dier* =
herkauwer; **'herkauwer** (-s) *m* 🐄 ruminant;
–wing *v* rumination
her'kenbaar recognizable, knowable (by *aan*);
her'kennen[1] *vt* recognize (by *aan*); know

---

[1] V.T. en V.D. van dit werkwoord volgens het model: **her'**ademen, V.T. **her'**ademde, V.D. **her'**ademd (**ge-** in het
V.D. valt weg). Zie voor de vormen onder het grondwoord, in dit voorbeeld: *ademen*. Bij sterke en onregelmatige
werkwoorden wordt u verwezen naar de lijst achterin.

again; *ik herkende hem aan zijn stem* ook: I knew him by his voice; **her′kenning** (-en) *v* recognition; **her′kenningsmelodie** (-ieën) *v* R signature tune; **–teken** (-en en -s) *o* mark of recognition; identification mark, ↝ marking
′herkeuren[1] *vt* examine again, re-examine; **–ring** (-en) *v* (medical) re-examination
her′kiesbaar re-eligible, eligible for re-election; *zich niet ~ stellen* not seek re-election; **her′kiezen**[1] *vt* re-elect; **–zing** (-en) *v* re-election
′herkomst (-en) *v* origin
her′krijgen[1] *vt* get back, recover, regain [one′s health, vigour]; **–ging** (-en) *v* recovery
her′leidbaar reducible; **her′leiden**[1] *vt* reduce, convert; **her′leiding** (-en) *v* reduction, conversion; **–stabel** (-len) *v* reduction table, conversion table
her′leven[1] *vi* revive, return to life, requicken, live again; *doen ~* revive, bring to life again; requicken; **–ving** *v* revival, resurgence
her′lezen[1] *vt* re-read, read (over) again; **–zing** (-en) *v* re-reading, second reading
hermafro′diet (-en) *m-v* hermaphrodite
Her′mandad *m* Hermandad; *de heilige ~* [fig] the police, the law
herme′lijn 1 (-en) *m* ⚬ ermine [white], stoat [red]; 2 *o* (b o n t) ermine; **–en** *aj* ermine
′hermesstaf (-staven) *m* caduceus
her′metisch hermetical
her′nemen[1] *vt* 1 take again [something]; ⚔ retake, recapture [a fortress], take up [the offensive] again; 2 resume, reply; **–ming** *v* retaking, recapture
′hernhutter (-s) *m* Moravian brother [*mv* Moravian brethren]
′hernia (′s) *v* 𝕋 (i n z. v. t u s s e n w e r v e l-s c h ij f) slipped disc (disk); (a n d e r s) hernia
her′nieuwen (hernieuwde, h. hernieuwd) *vt* renew; **–wing** (-en) *v* renewal, resurgence
hero′ïek heroic(al); **hero′ïne** *v* heroin; **he′roïsch** heroic(al); **hero′ïsme** *o* heroism
herontdekken (herontdekte, h. herontdekt) *vt* rediscover; **–king** (-en) *v* rediscovery
her′openen[1] *vt* re-open; **–ning** (-en) *v* re-opening
′heropvoeding *v* re-education
′heroriëntatie [-(t)si.] (-s) *v* reorientation
′heros (he′roën) *m* hero
her′overen (heroverde, h. heroverd) *vt* reconquer, recapture, retake, recover [from the enemy]; **–ring** (-en) *v* reconquest, recapture
′herrie *v* 1 noise, din, uproar, racket, hulla-

baloo; 2 F row; *~ hebben* F have a row, be at odds; *~ krijgen* F get into a row; *~ maken, ~ schoppen* F kick up a row (a shindy), S raise a stink; **–maker** (-s) *m*, **–schopper** (-s) *m* noisy fellow; rowdy
her′rijzen[1] *vi* 1 rise again; 2 rise (from the dead)
her′roepbaar revocable, repealable; **her′roepen**[1] *vt* recall, revoke, rescind [a decision]; recant [a statement], repeal, annul [a law], retract [a promise]; **–ping** (-en) *v* recall, revocation [of the Edict of Nantes], repeal, recantation, retractation, annulment
her′schapen transformed, turned [into]
′herschatten[1] *vt* revalue; **–ting** (-en) *v* revaluation
her′scheppen[1] *vt* recreate, create anew, regenerate, transform, turn (into *in*); **–ping** (-en) *v* recreation, regeneration, transformation
her′scholen[1] *vt* retrain; **′herscholing** *v* retraining
′hersenarbeid *m* brain-work; **–bloeding** (-en) *v* cerebral haemorrhage; **–cel** (-len) *v* brain cell; **–en** *mv de grote ~* the cerebrum; *de kleine ~* the cerebellum; zie *hersens*; **–gymnastiek** [-glm-] *v* mental gymnastics; (v r a a g s p e l) quiz; **–loos** brainless; **–ontsteking** (-en) *v* encephalitis; **–pan** (-nen) *v* brain-pan, cranium; **′hersens** *mv* brain [as organ], brains [as matter & intelligence]; *met een prima stel ~* with a first-rate brain; *z′n ~ afpijnigen* cudgel one′s brains; *iem. de ~ inslaan* knock sbd.′s brains out, bash sbd.′s brains in; *hoe krijgt hij het i n zijn ~?* how does he get it into his head? *dat zal hij wel u i t zijn ~ laten* he will think twice before doing it; he will not even dare to think of doing such a thing; **′hersenschim** (-men) *v* idle fancy, chimera;
hersen′schimmig chimerical; **′hersenschors** *v* brain cortex, cerebral cortex;
–schudding (-en) *v* concussion (of the brain); **–spoeling** *v* brainwashing; **–stam** *m* brain stem; **–trombose** [-bo.zə] *v* cerebral thrombosis; **–tumor** (-s en -moren) *m* tumor of the brain, brain tumor; **–verweking** (-en) *v* softening of the brain; **–vlies** (-vliezen) *o* cerebral membrane; **–vliesontsteking** *v* meningitis; **–weefsel** (-s) *o* brain tissue; **–werk** *o* brain-work; **–winding** (-en) *v* convolution of the brain; **–ziekte** (-n en -s) *v* brain disease
her′stel *o* reparation, repair [of what is broken], recovery [after illness, of business, of prices

---

[1] V.T. en V.D. van dit werkwoord volgens het model: **her**′ademen, V.T. **her**′ademde, V.D. **her**′ademd (**ge-** in het V.D. valt weg). Zie voor de vormen onder het grondwoord, in dit voorbeeld: *ademen*. Bij sterke en onregelmatige werkwoorden wordt u verwezen naar de lijst achterin.

&], restoration [of confidence, of order, of a building], re-establishment [of sbd.'s health, of the monarchy], $ rally [of shares]; redress [of grievances]; reinstatement [of an official]; **–baar** repairable, reparable, remediable, restorable, retrievable; **–betalingen** *mv* reparations; **her'stellen I** (herstelde, h. hersteld) *vt* repair, mend [shoes &], remedy [an evil]; correct [mistakes], right [a wrong], redress [grievances], set [it] right, make good [the damage, the loss &], retrieve [a loss, an error &]; restore [order, confidence], re-establish [authority]; reinstate [an official]; *in zijn eer ~* rehabilitate; *een gebruik in ere ~* revive a custom; **II** (herstelde, is hersteld) *va* recover [from an illness]; *herstel!* ✂ as you were!; **III** (herstelde, h. hersteld) *vr zich ~* recover oneself, pull oneself together; recover [from]; **–de** (-n) *m-v* convalescent; **her'steller** (-s) *m* repairer, restorer; **her'stelling** (-en) *v* repairing, repair, restoration, re-establishment, recovery; *~en doen* make repairs; **her'stellingsoord** (-en) *o* (p l a a t s , s t r e e k) health-resort; (i n r i c h t i n g) sanatorium; (t e h u i s v o o r h e r s t e l l e n d e n) convalescent home; **–teken** (-s) *o* ♪ natural (sign); **her'stel(lings)werk** *o* repairs, repair work; **her'stellingswerkplaats** (-en) *v* repair shop

'**herstemmen**[1] *vi* vote again; **–ming** (-en) *v* second ballot

'**herstructureren**[1] *vt* restructure; **–ring** (-en) *v* restructuring

hert (-en) *o* deer [*mv* deer]; (m a n n e t j e s~) stag; *vliegend ~* ✺ stag-beetle; '**hertebout** (-en) *m* haunch of venison; **–jacht** (-en) *v* stag-hunting; deer-stalking; **–le(d)er** = *hertsle(d)er*

'**hertelling** (-en) *v* recount [of votes]

'**hertenkamp** (-en) *m* deer-park; '**hertevlees** *o* venison

'**hertog** (-togen) *m* duke; **–dom** (-men) *o* duchy; **her'togelijk** ducal

'**s-Hertogen'bosch** *o* Bois-le-Duc

herto'gin (-nen) *v* duchess

'**hertrouwen**[1] *vi* remarry, marry again

1 'hertshoorn *o* & *m* (s t o f n a a m) hartshoorn

2 'hertshoorn, –horen (-s) *m* (v o o r w e r p) stag's horn; '**hertsle(d)er** *o* deerskin

hertz *m* hertz

her'vatten[1] *vt* resume, return to [work, a conversation]; **–ting** (-en) *v* resumption

'**herverdeling** (-en) *v* redistribution [of wealth]

'**herverkaveling** (-en) *v* re-allocation [of arable land]

'**herverzekeren**[1] *v* reinsure; **–ring** (-en) *v* reinsurance

her'vinden[1] *vt* find again

her'vormd *aj* reformed; *de ~en* the Protestants; **her'vormen**[1] *vt* reform; **–er** (-s) *m* reformer; **her'vorming** (-en) *v* 1 (v. d. m a a t s c h a p - p i j &) reform; 2 (v. d. k e r k) reformation; **Her'vormingsdag** *m* Reformation Day

'**herwaarderen**[1] *vt* revalue; **-ring** (-en) *v* $ revaluation

'**herwaarts** hither, this way

her'winnen[1] *vt* regain [one's footing, consciousness]; win back [money]; recover [a loss, lost ground]; retrieve [a battle]

her'zien[1] *vt* revise [a book, a treaty &]; reconsider [a policy]; review [a lawsuit]; **her'ziening** (-en) *v* revision [of a book, a treaty &]; reconsideration [of a policy]; review [of a lawsuit]

hes (-sen) *v* smock

'**hesen** V.T. meerv. v. *hijsen*

'**Hessen** *o* Hesse; **–sisch** Hessian

het [hǝt, ǝt] the, it; he, she; *3 shilling ~ pond* 3 sh. a pound; *3 shilling ~ stuk* 3 sh. each

hete'luchtverwarming (-en) *v* space-heating

1 'heten (heette, h. geheet) *vt* heat [= make hot]

2 'heten* I *vt* 1 name, call; 2 ✎ order, bid [sbd. welcome]; **II** *vi* be called, be named; *hoe heet dat?* what is it called?; *hoe heet hij?* what is his name?; *vraag hem hoe hij heet* go and ask his name; *het heet dat hij... is* it is reported (said) that he...; *zoals het heet* as the saying is; *zo waar ik... heet* as truly as my name is...; *hij heet Jan naar zijn vader* he is called John after his father

'**heterdaad** *iem. op ~ betrappen* catch sbd. in the act, catch sbd. red-handed

hetero'geen heterogeneous; **heterogeni'teit** *v* heterogeneity

heteroseksu'eel heterosexual

het'geen [hǝt-, ǝt'ge.n] that which, what; which; **–'welk** which

'**hetze** (-s) *v* agitation, (smear) campaign; (i n k r a n t) yellow-press campaign

het'zelfde the same

het'zij *cj* 1 (n e v e n s c h i k k e n d) either... or; 2 (o n d e r s c h i k k e n d) whether ... or

heug *tegen ~ en meug* reluctantly, against one's wish

'**heugen** (heugde, h. geheugd) *het heugt mij* I remember; *dat zal u ~* you won't forget that in a hurry; **–is** *v* remembrance, recollection,

---

[1] V.T. en V.D. van dit werkwoord volgens het model: her'ademen, V.T. her'ademde, V.D. her'ademd (**ge-** in het V.D. valt weg). Zie voor de vormen onder het grondwoord, in dit voorbeeld: *ademen*. Bij sterke en onregelmatige werkwoorden wordt u verwezen naar de lijst achterin.

memory; **'heuglijk** memorable; joyful, pleasant

heul *o* comfort

'heulen (heulde, h. geheuld) *vi* ~ *met* be in league with, be in collusion with

heup (-en) *v* hip; *hij heeft 't op de* ~*en* he is in one of his tempers; **–been** (-deren) *o* hip-bone; **–broek** (-en) *v* hipster trousers; **–wiegen** (heupwiegde, h. geheupwiegd) *vi* swing (sway, roll) one's hips; **–zwaai** (-en) *m* (w o r s t e - l e n) cross-buttock; (a a n   d e   r i n g e n) hip roll

⊙ **heur** = 1 *haar*

'heus I *aj* 1 courteous, kind; 2 real, live; **II** *ad* 1 (h o f f e l ij k) courteously, kindly; 2 < really; *ik heb het zelf gezien*, ~! really, truly; *Heus?* really?, have you though?; **–heid** (-heden) *v* courtesy, kindness

'heuvel (-en en -s) *m* hill; **–achtig** hilly; **–landschap** (-pen) *o* hilly landscape; **–rug** (-gen) *m* range of hills; **–tje** (-s) *o* knoll; hillock, mound; **–top** (-pen) *m* hill top

'hevel (-s) *m* siphon; **'hevelen** (hevelde, h. geheveld) *vt* siphon

'hevig I *aj* vehement, violent [storm &], severe, heavy [fighting], intense [heat, pain]; **II** *ad* vehemently; violently; < greatly, badly [bleeding &]; **–heid** *v* vehemence, violence, intensity, severity

he'xameter (-s) *m* hexameter

H.H. = *heren* gentlemen

hi'aat (-aten) *m* & *o* hiatus, gap

hief (hieven) V.T. v. *heffen*

hiel (-en) *m* heel; *iem. op de* ~*en zitten* be close upon sbd.'s heels; *nauwelijks heb ik de* ~*en gelicht, of...* no sooner have I turned my back than...; *zijn* ~*en laten zien* show a clean pair of heels; **–been** (-deren) *o* heel-bone

hield (hielden) V.T. v. *houden*

'hielenlikker (-s) *m* lickspittle, toady

hielp (hielpen) V.T. v. *helpen*

'hielstuk (-ken) *o* counter

hiep, hiep, hoe'ra! *ij* hip, hip, hurrah!

hier *ad* here; ~ *en daar* here and there; *wel* ~ *en daar!* **F** the deuce!, by Jove!; ~ *en daar over spreken* talk about this and that; ~ *te lande* in this country; ~ *ter stede* in this town; **–aan** to this; by this &; **hier'achter** 1 behind (this); 2 hereafter, hereinafter [in deeds &]

hiërar'chie [hi:rɑr'gi.] (-chieën) *v* hierarchy; **hië'rarchisch** hierarchical

hierbe'neden down here, here below; **'hierbij, hier'bij** 1 herewith, enclosed; 2 hard by; 3 hereby, herewith [I declare]; **hier'binnen** within this place or room, in here, within; **–'boven** up here, above; **–'buiten** outside (this); **'hierdoor, hier'door** 1 (o o r z a a k) by

this; 2 through here; **'hierheen, hier'heen** 1 hither, here; 2 this way; **'hierin, hier'in** in here, herein, in this; **'hierlangs** this way, past here; **–me(d)e** with this; **'hierna, hier'na** after this, hereafter; **'hiernaar** after this, from this; **hier'naast** next door; **–'namaals I** *ad* hereafter; *het leven* ~ the future life; **II** *o* hereafter, after-world; **–'nevens** enclosed, annexed

hiëro'gliefen [hi:.ro.-] *mv* = *hiëroglyfen*; **hiëro'glifisch** = *hiëroglyfisch*; **hiëro'glyfen** [-'gli.-] *mv* hieroglyphics; **hiëro'glyfisch** hieroglyphic

'hierom 1 round this; 2 for this reason; **hierom'heen** round this; **'hieromtrent** 1 about this, on this subject; 2 hereabout(s)

hier'onder 1 underneath, below; 2 at the foot [of the page]; 3 among these; **'hierop** upon this, hereupon; **–'over** 1 opposite, over the way; 2 on (about) this subject, about this; **–tegen** against this; **hiertegen'over** opposite; against this; ~ *staat dat ...* on the other hand...; **'hiertoe** to this purpose; *tot* ~ thus far, so far; **hier'tussen** between these; **'hieruit** from this, hence; **–van** of this (that), about this, hereof; **–voor** 1 for this, in exchange, in return (for this); 2 [hi.r'vo:r] before (this)

nieuw (hieuwen) V.T. v. *houwen*

hieven V.T. meerv. v. *heffen*

nij he; *is het een* ~ *of een zij?* a he or a she?

'hijgen (hijgde, h. gehijgd) *vt* pant, gasp (for breath); ~ *naar* [*fig*] pant for (after)

hijs *m* hoisting, hoist; *een hele* ~ quite a job; **–balk** (-en) *m* hoisting beam; **–blok** (-ken) *o* pulley-block; **'hijsen*** *vt* hoist [a sail, a flag &], pull up; run up [a flag]; **'hijskraan** (-kranen) *v* crane; **–toestel** (-len) *o* hoisting apparatus, hoist; **–touw** (-en) *o* hoisting rope

hik (-ken) *m* hiccup, hiccough; **'hikken** (hikte, h. gehikt) *vi* hiccup, hiccough

hilari'teit *v* hilarity

'hinde (-n) *v* hind, doe

'hinder *m* hindrance, impediment, obstacle; *ik heb er geen* ~ *van* it does not hinder me; it is no trouble to me, it is not in my way; **'hinderen** (hinderde, h. gehinderd) **I** *vt* hinder, impede, incommode, inconvenience, trouble; *het hindert mij bij mijn werk* it hinders me in my work; *dat hinderde hem* that's what annoyed him; **II** *va* hinder, be in the way; *dat hindert niet* it does not matter; **'hinderlaag** (-lagen) *v* ambush, ambuscade; *een* ~ *leggen* lay an ambush; *in* ~ *liggen* lie in ambush; *in een* ~ *lokken* ambush; *in een* ~ *vallen* be ambushed; **'hinderlijk** annoying, troublesome [persons]; inconvenient [things]; **'hindernis** (-sen) *v* hindrance, obstacle; *wedren met* ~*sen* obstacle race;

'**hinderpaal** (-palen) *m* obstacle, impediment, hindrance; *iem. hinderpalen in de weg leggen* put (throw) obstacles in sbd.'s way; *alle hinderpalen uit de weg ruimen* remove all obstacles; **–wet** *v* nuisance act

'**Hindoe** (-s) *m*, **Hindoes** *aj* Hindu, Hindoo; **hindoe'isme** *o* Hinduism

hing (hingen) V.T. v. *hangen*

'**hinkelbaan** (-banen) *v* hopscotch; '**hinkelen** (hinkelde, h. gehinkeld) *vi* hop, play at hopscotch

'**hinken** (hinkte, h. gehinkt) *vi* 1 limp, walk with a limp; F dot and carry one; 2 *sp* hop, play at hopscotch; ~ *op twee gedachten* halt between two opinions; '**hinkepoot** (-poten) *m* limper, cripple; **hink-stap-'sprong** *m* hop-step-and-jump

'**hinniken** (hinnikte, h. gehinnikt) *vi* neigh, whinny

hip with-it [girl]; trendy [clothing]; S hip [disc jockey], groovy [scene], F swinging [town]

'**hippie** (-s) *m-v* hippie (boy, girl)

'**hippisch** equestrian

hippo'droom (-dromen) *m & o* hippodrome

his'toricus (-ci) *m* historian; **his'torie** (-s en -iën) *v* history, story; zie *geschiedenis*; **–schrijver** (-s) *m* historiographer; **his'torisch I** *aj* historical [novel, materialism &], historic [building, event, monument, procession]; *het is ~!* it actually happened; **II** *ad* historically

1 hit (-ten) *m* ≈. (i n z. S h e t l a n d) pony, nag

2 hit (-ten) *v* (d i e n s t m e i s j e) F slavey; S skivvy

3 hit (-s) *m* (s u c c e s) F hit, ♪ ook: hit tune; '**hitparade** (-s) *v* hit parade

'**hitsig** hot-blooded

'**hitte** *v* heat²; **–bestendig** heat-resistant; **–golf** (-golven) *v* heat-wave

'**hittepetit** (-ten) *v* F chit

H.K.H. = *Hare Koninklijke Hoogheid*

hl = *hectoliter*

H.M. = *Hare Majesteit*

h'm [hüm] *ij* ahem!

ho! *ij* ho!; zie ook: 1 *hei*

H.O. = *hoger onderwijs*, zie *onderwijs*

'**hobbel** (-s) *m* knob; bump; '**hobbelen** (hobbelde, h. gehobbeld) *vi* 1 rock (to and fro), jolt [in a cart]; 2 ride on a rocking-horse; '**hobbelig** rugged, uneven, bumpy; '**hobbelpaard** (-en) *o* rocking-horse

'**hobbezak** (-ken) *m* (k l e d i n g s t u k) sack, sacklike dress; (p e r s o o n) jumbo

'**hobby** [y = i.] ('s) *m* hobby

ho'bo ('s) *m* oboe; **hobo' 'ïst** (-en) *m* oboist, oboe-player

'**hockey** ['hɔki.] *o* hockey

hocus-'pocus *m & o* hocus-pocus, F hanky-panky; ~ *pas!* hey presto!

hoe how; ~*! ik mijn huis verkopen* what, I sell my house!; ~ *dan ook* anyhow, anyway; ~ *zo?* how so?, what do you mean?; ~ *langer*, ~ *erger* worse and worse; ~ *meer...*, ~ *minder...* the more..., the less...; ~ *rijk hij ook zij* however rich he may be; ~ *het ook zij* however that may be; *zij weet* ~ *de mannen zijn* she knows what men are like; *ik zou gaarne weten* ~ *of wat* I should like to know where I stand; *het* ~ *en wat weet hij niet* he does not know the ins and outs of the case

hoed (-en) *m* 1' (v o o r h e e r) hat; 2 (v o o r d a m e) hat, bonnet; *hoge* ~ top-hat, topper; *de* ~ *afnemen (voor iem.)* raise (take off) one's hat (to sbd.); *daar neem ik mijn (de)* ~ *voor af* I take off my hat to that; *met de* ~ *in de hand komt men door het ganse land* cap in hand will take you through the land

'**hoedanig** how, what; **hoe'danigheid** (-heden) *v* quality; *in zijn* ~ *van...* in his capacity as..., in his capacity of...

'**hoede** *v* guard; care, protection; *o n d e r zijn* ~ *nemen* take under one's protection, take charge of; *(niet) o p zijn* ~ *zijn* be on (off) one's guard (against *voor*)

'**hoededoos** (-dozen) *v* hat-box, [lady's] bandbox; **–lint** (-en) *o* hatband

'**hoeden** (hoedde, h. gehoed) **I** *vt* guard, take care of, tend [flocks], keep, herd, watch, look after [the cattle]; **II** *vr zich* ~ *voor* beware of, guard against [mistakes]

'**hoedenmaakster** (-s) *v* milliner; **–maker** (-s) *m* hatter; **–winkel** (-s) *m* hat-shop; '**hoedepen** (-nen) *v* hat-pin; **–plank** (-en) *v* ◄ parcel shelf

'**hoeder** (-s) *m* keeper², *fig* guardian; (v . v e e) herdsman; (m e e s t i n s a m e n s t.) [swine-] herd; *mijns broeders* ~ **B** my brother's keeper

'**hoedje** (-s) *o* (little) hat; *onder één* ~ *spelen met* be in league with; *nu is hij onder een* ~ *te vangen* F he sings small now

hoef (hoeven) *m* hoof; **–blad** *o* coltsfoot; **–dier** (-en) *o* hoofed animal, ungulate; **–getrappel** *o* clatter of hoofs; **–ijzer** (-s) *o* horseshoe, shoe; **–nagel** (-s) *m* horseshoe nail; **–slag** (-slagen) *m* hoofbeat; **–smid** (-smeden) *m* farrier; **–stal** (-len) *m* frame

'**hoegenaamd, hoege'naamd** ~ *niets* absolutely nothing, nothing whatever, nothing at all

hoe'grootheid *v* quantity, size

hoek (-en) *m* 1 angle [between meeting lines or planes], corner [enclosed by meeting walls]; 2 hook, fish-hook; *dode* ~ blind angle; *iem. i n een* ~ *drijven* corner sbd.; *een jongen in de* ~ *zetten* put a boy in the cranny; *in alle* ~*en en gaten* in every nook and corner; *o m de* ~ round the corner; *ga de* ~ *om* go round the corner; *o n d e r een* ~ *van* at an angle of [40°]; *o p de* ~ at (on) the corner; *hij kan zo aardig u i t de* ~ *komen* he can come out with a joke (witty remark &) quite unexpectedly; *hij kwam flink uit de* ~ **F** he came down handsomely; zie ook: *wind*; **–huis** (-huizen) *o* corner house; **–ig** angular[2]; *fig* rugged; **–je** (-s) *o* corner, nook; *bij het* ~ *van de haard* at the fireside; *het* ~ *omgaan* **S** kick the bucket; *het* ~ *te boven zijn* have turned the corner; **–kast** (-en) *v* corner cupboard; **–man** (-nen) *m* (b e u r s) jobber; **–plaats** (-en) *v* corner-seat; **–punt** (-en) *o* angular point; **–schop** (-pen) *m sp* corner; **–steen** (-stenen) *m* corner-stone[2], quoin; **–tand** (-en) *m* canine (tooth), eye-tooth

hoen (-deren en -ders) *o* hen, fowl; **'hoender-achtig** gallinaceous; **–hof** (-hoven) *m* poultry-yard, chicken-yard; **–hok** (-ken) *o* poultry-house, henhouse; **–park** (-en) *o* poultry-farm; **'hoenders** *mv* (barn-door) fowls, poultry, chickens; **'hoenderteelt** *v* chicken breeding (farming); **'hoentje** (-s) *o* chicken, pullet

'hoepel (-s) *m* hoop [of a cask]; **'hoepelen** (hoepelde, h. gehoepeld) *vi* play with a (the) hoop, trundle a hoop; **'hoepelrok** (-ken) *m* hoop-petticoat, crinoline; **–stok** (-ken) *m* hoop-stick

hoer (-en) *v* whore, harlot, prostitute

hoe'ra! *ij* hurrah, hurray; *driemaal* ~ *voor...* three cheers for...

'hoerenkast (-en) *v* brothel, bawdy house; **hoe'reren** (hoereerde, h. gehoereerd) *vi* whore; **hoere'rij** (-en) *v* whoring; fornication; **'hoertje** (-s) *o* floosie, floozie

hoes (hoezen) *v* cover, dust sheet; (v. g r a m - m o f o o n p l a a t) sleeve; **–laken** (-s) *o* fitted sheet

hoest *m* cough; **–bui** (-en) *v* fit of coughing; **–drankje** (-s) *o* cough mixture; **'hoesten** (hoestte, h. gehoest) *vi* cough; **'hoestmiddel** (-en) *o* cough remedy; **–pastille** [-pɑsti.jə] (-s) *v* cough lozenge

'hoeve (-n) *v* farm, farmstead, homestead

'hoeveel, hoe'veel how much [money], how many [books]; **hoe'veelheid** (-heden) *v* quantity, amount; **hoe'veelste** *de* ~ *keer?* how many times (have I told you)?; *de* ~ *van de maand hebben wij?* what day of the month is it?; *de* ~ *bent u?* what is your number?

'hoeven (hoefde, h. gehoefd) = *behoeven*

'hoever(re), hoe'ver(re) *in* ~ how far

hoe'wel *cj* although, though

hoe'zee *ij* hurrah, huzza!

hoe'zeer however much

1 hof (hoven) *m* garden

2 hof (hoven) *o* court [of arbitration, cassation &]; *het* ~ *maken* pay one's court (addresses) to, make love to; *aan het* ~ at court; **–bal** (-s) *o* court ball, state ball; **–dame** (-s) *v* court lady, lady-in-waiting, (o n g e h u w d) maid of honour; **–dignitaris** (-sen) *m* court official; **–etiquette** [-e.ti.kɛtə] *v* court etiquette; **'hoffelijk** courteous; **–heid** (-heden) *v* courteousness, courtesy; **'hofhouding** (-en) *v* court, household; **'hofje** (-s) *o* 1 almshouse; 2 court; **'hofjonker** (-s) *m* page; **–kapel** (-len) *v* court chapel; 2 **♪** court band; **–kliek** (-en) *v* court clique; **–kring** (-en) *m in* ~*en* in court circles; **–leverancier** (-s) *m* purveyor to His (Her) Majesty, by appointment (to His Majesty, to Her Majesty); **–maarschalk** (-en) *m* Lord Chamberlain; knight marshall; Master of Ceremonies; **–meester** (-s) *m* ♃ steward; **hofmeeste'res** (-sen) *v* ♃ stewardess; **'hofmeier** (-s) *m* major-domo; **–nar** (-ren) *m* court jester, court fool; **–prediker** (-s) *m* court chaplain; **–ste(d)e** (-steden) *v* homestead, farmstead, farm

hoge'drukgebied (-en) *o* high(-pressure) area, high, anticyclone; **'hogelijk** = *hooglijk*; **'hogepriester** (-s) *m* high priest

'hoger higher; **–hand** *v van* ~ zie *hand*; **'Hogerhuis** *o* Upper House, House of Lords; **hoger'op** higher; ~ *willen* have higher aspirations, be ambitious; **hoge'school** (-scholen) *v* university; *a a n de* ~ in the University; *o p de* ~ at college

1 hok (-ken) *o* kennel [for dogs], sty [for pigs], pen [for sheep, poultry], [pigeon-, poultry-] house, cage [for lions], hutch [for rabbits], shed [for coals &]; [*fig*] den [= room]; **S** quod [= prison]; *het* ~ the shop [= one's school]; *een* ~ (*van een kamer*) a poky little room, **F** a hole

2 hok (-ken) *o* (v. g a r v e n, s c h o v e n) shock

'hokje (-s) *o* compartment; pigeon-hole [for papers]; cubicle [of bathing establishment &]; (v i e r k a n t v a k j e) square; (o p i n v u l - b i l j e t) box

1 'hokken (hokte, h. gehokt) *vi* come to a standstill; *er hokt iets* there's a hitch somewhere; *het gesprek hokte* the talk hung for a time

2 'hokken (hokte, h. gehokt) *vi* (i n c o n c u - b i n a a t l e v e n) **S** shack up; *bij elkaar* ~ huddle together; *zij* ~ *altijd thuis* they are stay-at-homes

'hokkerig poky, cramped

'hokvast *hij is* (*erg*) ~ he is a stay-at-home

1 hol (holen) *o* cave [under ground], cavern; hole [of an animal], den, lair [of wild beast]; *fig* den; **F** hole

2 hol *m op* ~ *raken* (*slaan*) bolt, run away; *iem. het*

hoofd op ~ *brengen* turn sbd's head; *zijn hoofd is op* ~ it has turned his head

3 hol I *aj* hollow² [stalks, cheeks, phrases, tones], empty² [vessels, phrases], cavernous [eyes], concave [lenses]; ~*le weg* sunken road; ~*le zee* rough sea; *in het* ~*le (in het* ~*st) van de nacht* at dead (in the dead) of night; **II** *ad* hollow

'**hola** hallo!; hold on!, stop!

'**holbewoner** (-s) *m* cave-dweller, troglodyte

'**holderdebolder** head over heels, helter-skelter; ~ *door elkaar* pell-mell

'**holebeer** (-beren) *m* cave-bear; '**holemens** (-en) *m* cave-man; '**holenkunde** *v* speleology; –**kunst** *v* cave-art

'**holheid** *v* hollowness², emptiness²; –**klinkend** hollow(-sounding)

'**Holland** *o* Holland; –**er** (-s) *m* Dutchman; *vliegende* ~ 1 ⚓ Flying Dutchman; 2 *sp* (boy's) racer; *de* ~*s* the Dutch; –**s I** *aj* Dutch; **II** *o het* ~ Dutch; **III** *v een* ~*e* a Dutchwoman

'**hollen** (holde, h. gehold) *vi* run; *het is altijd* ~ *of stilstaan met hem* he is always running into extremes; *een* ~*d paard* a runaway horse; '**holletje** *o* scamper; *op een* ~ at a scamper

'**hologig** hollow-eyed

holo'**grafisch** holograph(ic)

'**holrond** concave

'**holster** (-s) *m* holster

'**holte** (-n en -s) *v* hollow [of the hand, in the ground &], cavity [in a solid body], socket [of the eye, of the hip], pit [of the stomach]

hom (-men) *v* milt, soft roe

homeo'**paat** (-paten) *m* homoeopath

homeopa'**thie** *v* homoeopathy; homeo'**patisch** homoeopathic(al)

'**hommel** (-s) *v* 1 (d a r) drone; 2 bumblebee

'**hommeles** *het is* ~ *tussen hen* they are at odds, **F** there is a row

'**homo** ('s) *m* **F** queer, **S** queen, pansy, sissy; homo'**fiel** homosexual, **F** queer; homofi'**lie** *v* homosexuality

homo'**geen** homogeneous; homogeni'**teit** *v* homogeneity, homogeneousness

homolo'**gatie** [-(t)si.] (-s) *v* sanction

homo'**niem I** (-en) *o* homonym; **II** *aj* homonymous

homoseksuali'**teit** *v* homosexuality; homo-seksu'**eel** homosexual, **F** queer

homp (-en) *v* hunk, lump, chunk [of bread &]

'**hompelen** (hompelde, h. gehompeld) *vi* hobble, limp

hond (-en) *m* dog², hound²; *jonge* ~ puppy, pup; *jij stomme* ~*!* you mooncalf!; *vliegende* ~ flying-fox; *blaffende* ~*en bijten niet* his bark is worse than his bite; *men moet geen slapende* ~*en wakker maken* let sleeping dogs lie; *de* ~ *in de pot vinden*

go without one's dinner; *wie een* ~ *wil slaan, kan licht een stok vinden* it is easy to find a staff to beat a dog; *veel* ~*en zijn der hazen dood* nobody can hold out against superior numbers;

'**hondebaantje** (-s) *o* **F** rotten job; –**brood** *o* dog-biscuit; –**hok** (-ken) *o* (dog-)kennel; –**kar** (-ren) *v* cart drawn by dogs; –**ketting** (-en) *m* & *v* dog-chain; –**leven** (-s) *o* dog's life; –**mepper** (-s) *m* doghunter; '**hondenasiel** [s = z] (-en) *o* home for dogs, dogs' home; –**belasting** *v* dog-tax; –**tentoonstelling** (-en) *v* dogshow; '**hondepenning** (-en) *m* dog-licence badge; –**ras** (-sen) *o* breed of dogs

'**honderd** a (one) hundred; ~*en mensen* hundreds of people; *bij* ~*en* by the hundred; *alles is i n het* ~ everything is at sixes and sevens; *alles loopt in het* ~ everything goes awry (wrong); *de boel in het* ~ *laten lopen* make a muddle (a mess) of it; *vijf t e n* ~ five per cent.; ~ *uit praten* talk nineteen to the dozen; –**duizend** a (one) hundred thousand; ~*en* hundreds of thousands; –**jarig** *aj* a hundred years old, centenary, centennial, secular; ~ *bestaan,* ~ *gedenkfeest* centenary; *een* ~*e* a centenarian; –**ste** hundredth (part); –**tal** (-len) *o* (a, one) hundred, (a) five score; –**voud** *o* centuple; –**voudig** a hundredfold, centuple

'**honderiem** (-en) *m* dog's leash, slip; –**vlees** *o* dog's meat; –**wacht** *v* ⚓ dog-watch, middle watch; –**weer** *o* **F** beastly weather; –**ziekte** *v* distemper; –**zweep** (-zwepen) *v* dog-whip; **honds I** *aj* currish [fellow]; brutal [treatment &]; **II** *ad* brutally; '**hondsdagen** *mv* dog-days; **honds'dolheid** *v* rabies, canine madness; (b i j m e n s) hydrophobia; '**hondsdraf** *v* ground-ivy; –**haai** (-en) *m* dog-fish; –**heid** (-heden) *v* currishness; brutality; zie *honds*; –**roos** *v* dog-rose; –**ster** *v* dog-star; –**vot** (-ten) *v* & *o* rascal, scoundrel, scamp

Hon'**duras** *o* Honduras

'**honen** (hoonde, h. gehoond) *vt* jeer at, taunt, insult, fleer; –**d** scornful, jeeringly

Hon'**gaar** [hŏ'ga:r] (-garen) *m*, Hon'**gaars** *aj* & *o* Hungarian; Honga'**rije** *o* Hungary

'**honger** *m* hunger; ~ *hebben* be hungry; ~ *krijgen* get hungry; ~ *lijden* starve; *van* ~ *sterven* die of hunger; ~ *is de beste kok (saus),* ~ *maakt rauwe bonen zoet* hunger is the best sauce; –**dood** *m* & *v* death from hunger (starvation); '**hongeren** (hongerde, h. gehongerd) *vi* hunger, be hungry; '**hongerig** hungry; '**hongerkunstenaar** (-s) *m* fasting champion, professional starver; –**kuur** (-kuren) *v* hunger (fasting) cure; –**lijder** (-s) *m* starveling; –**loon** (-lonen) *o* starvation wages, pittance; '**hongersnood** (-noden) *m* famine; '**hongerstaker** (-s) *m* hunger striker; –**staking** (-en) *v*

hunger strike; *in ~ gaan* go on hunger strike
'**honi(n)g** *m* honey; *iem. ~ om de mond smeren*
butter sbd. up; **–bij** (-en) *v* honey-bee; **–dauw**
m honeydew; **–raat** (-raten) *v* honeycomb;
–zoet as sweet as honey, honey-sweet[2]; *fig*
honeyed, mellifluous [words]

honk (-en) *o* home, *sp* goal, base; *b ij ~ blijven* 1
stay near, stay at home; 2 *fig* keep to the point;
v a n ~ gaan leave home; *van ~ zijn* be absent,
be away from home; **–bal** *o* baseball; **–vast** =
hokvast

'**honnepon** (-nen) *v* & *m* sweetie
hon'neurs *mv* honours; *de ~ waarnemen* do the
honours [of the house]
hono'rair [-'rɛːr] honorary
hono'rarium (-s en -ria) *o* fee
hono'reren (honoreerde, h. gehonoreerd) *vt* 1
pay; 2 $ honour [a bill]; *niet ~* $ dishonour [a
bill]
ho'noris 'causa [-za.] honorary; *hij werd tot
doctor ~ benoemd* the honorary degree was
conferred upon him, he was given the honorary degree of doctor of laws &
hoofd (-en) *o* head°; **F** noddle; **S** loaf, knob,
nut; chief, leader; principal [of a school,
university]; heading [of a paper, an article];
headline(s) [of an article]; *~ van school* headmaster; *een ~ groter* taller by a head; *~ links
(rechts)!* ⚔ eyes... left (right)!; *zijn ~ is er mee
gemoeid* it may cost him his head; *het ~ bieden
aan* make head against, stand up to [sbd.],
brave, face [dangers &], meet [a difficulty],
cope with, deal with [this situation]; bear up
against [misfortunes]; *zich het ~ breken over* rack
one's brains over (about) sth.; *een goed ~ hebben
voor wiskunde* have a good head for mathematics; *ergens een hard ~ in hebben* have great doubts
about sth.; *het ~ vol hebben van...* have one's
head full of...; *het ~ boven water houden* keep
one's head above water; *het ~ hoog houden* carry
(hold) one's head high; *het ~ in de schoot leggen*
give in, resign; *mijn ~ loopt om* my head is in a
whirl; *het ~ opsteken* raise its head (their heads);
de ~en bij elkaar steken lay (put) their heads
together; *zijn ~ stoten [fig]* meet with a rebuff;
het ~ verliezen lose one's head; *het ~ niet verliezen*
keep one's head; *het ~ in de nek werpen* bridle
up; ● *veel a a n het ~ hebben* have lots of things
to attend to; *aan het ~ staan van* be at the head
of; be in charge of [a prison &]; *niet wel b ij het
(zijn) ~ zijn* not be in one's right mind; *wat ons
b o v e n het ~ hangt* what is hanging over our
heads; *dat is mij d o o r het ~ gegaan* it has
slipped my memory; it has completely gone
out of my head; *iets i n zijn ~ halen* get (take)
sth. into one's head; *iets in zijn ~ hebben* have
sth. in one's mind; *hoe kon hij het in zijn ~*

krijgen? how could he get it into his head?; *zich
iets in 't ~ zetten* take (get) sth. into one's head;
zich een gat in het ~ vallen zie *gat*; *m e t opgeheven
~* with head erect; *met het ~ tegen de muur lopen*
run one's head against a wall; *iem. iets n a a r het
(zijn) ~ gooien* throw sth. at sbd.'s head; *fig* fling
sth. in sbd.'s teeth; *iem. beledigingen naar het ~
slingeren* hurl insults at sbd.; *naar het ~ stijgen* go
to one's head; *z'n ~ om de deur steken* pop one's
head in; *het zal o p uw ~ neerkomen* be it on your
head(s); *iets o v e r het ~ zien* overlook sth.; *3
gulden p e r ~* 3 guilders per head; *u i t ~e van*
on account of, owing to; *uit dien ~e* on that
account, for that reason; *iets uit zijn ~ kennen*
(*leren, opzeggen*) know (learn, say) sth. by heart;
berekeningen uit het ~ maken make calculations in
one's head; *uit het ~ spelen* play from memory;
v a n het ~ tot de voeten from head to foot, from
top to toe, all over; *van het ~ tot de voeten
gewapend* armed cap-a-pie (to the teeth); *iem.
van ~ tot voeten opnemen* look sbd. up and down;
iem. v o o r het ~ stoten rebuff sbd.; *~ voor ~*
individually; *zoveel ~en, zoveel zinnen* (so) many
men, (so) many minds; **hoofd-** main, principal; chief [engineer, merit &]; '**hoofdagent**
(-en) *m* 1 $ general agent; 2 ± police sergeant;
–akte (-n en -s) *v* headmaster's certificate;
–altaar (-taren) *o* & *m rk* high altar; **–ambtenaar** (-naren en -s) *m* higher official, senior
officer; **–arbeider** (-s) *m* brain-worker;
–artikel (-en en -s) *o* leading article, leader,
editorial; **–assistent** (-en) *m* chief (senior)
assistant; **–beginsel** (-en en -s) *o* chief principle; **–bestanddeel** (-delen) *o* main constituent; **–bestuur** *o* managing committee,
executive committee, general committee; **$**
governing (central) board of directors; governing body; **–bewerking** (-en) *v* × elementary
operation; **–bewoner** (-s) *m* principal occupier; **–boekhouder** (-s) *m* head bookkeeper;
–breken(s) trouble, care, worry; **–bron**
(-nen) *v* head-spring, chief source; **–buis**
(-buizen) *v* main (tube); **–bureau** [-by.ro.] (-s)
o 1 head-office [of a company]; 2 police
headquarters (office); **–commissaris** (-sen) *m*
(chief) commissioner (of police); **–deksel** (-s)
o head-gear; **–deur** (-en) *v* main door, main
entrance; **–doek** (-en) *m* kerchief, turban [of a
native]; **–doel** *o* main object, principal aim;
–eind(e) (-en) *o* head [of a bed &]; '**hoofdelijk** per capita; **~e stemming** voting by roll-call;
zie ook: *omslag*; '**hoofdfiguur** (-guren) *v*
principal figure; **–film** (-s) *m* feature film,
main film, big film; **–gebouw** (-en) *o* main
building; **–geld** *o* capitation, poll-tax, head-
money; **–gerecht** (-en) *o* main course; **–haar**
(-haren) *o* hair of the head; **–ingang** (-en) *m*

main entrance; **–inspecteur** (-s) *m* chief inspector; **–kaas** *m* (pork) brawn; **–kantoor** (-toren) *o* head-office, head-quarters; **–kleur** (-en) *v* primary colour; **–knik** (-ken) *m* nod of the head; **–kraan** (-kranen) *v* main cock; **–kussen** (-s) *o* pillow; **–kwartier** (-en) *o* ⚔ headquarters; *het grote* ~ ⚔ general headquarters, G.H.Q.; **–leiding** (-en) *v* 1 general management; 2 (v. gas, water &) main, mains; **–letter** (-s) *v* capital (letter); **–lijn** (-en) *v* main line, trunk-line [of a railway]; *de ~en* the main features; **–man** (-nen en -lieden) *m* chief; **–moot** (-moten) *v* principal part; **–officier** (-en) *m* field-officer; **–onderwijzer** (-s) *m* head-teacher; **–persoon** (-sonen) *m* principal person, central figure; *de hoofdpersonen (van de roman)* the principal characters; **–pijn** (-en) *v* headache; ~ *hebben (krijgen)* have (get) a headache; **–postkantoor** (-toren) *o* ⚓ head post office; (i n L o n d e n) General Post Office; **–prijs** (-prijzen) *m* first prize [in a lottery]; **–punt** (-en) *o* main point; **–redacteur** (-en en -s) *m* chief editor, editor-in-chief; **–regel** (-en en -s) *m* principal rule; **–rekenen** *o* mental arithmetic; **–rol** (-len) *v* principal part (rôle), leading part; **–schakelaar** (-s) *m* main switch; **–schakeldoos** (-dozen) *v*, **–schakelkast** (-en) *v* service box; **–schotel** (-s) *m* & *v* principal dish; *fig* principal feature; **–schudden** *o* shaking (shake) of the head; **–schuldige** (-n) *m-v* chief culprit; **–slagader** *v* aorta; **–som** (-men) *v* 1 (h e t t o t a a l) sum total; 2 (h e t k a p i t a a l) principal; **–stad** (-steden) *v* capital city, capital, metropolis; (v . p r o v i n c i e , g r a a f s c h a p) chief town, county town; **hoofd'stedelijk** metropolitan; **'hoofdstel** (-len) *o* head-stall; **–steun** (-en) *m* head-rest; **–straat** (-straten) *v* principal street, main street, (main) thoroughfare; **–stuk** (-ken) *o* chapter; **–telwoord** (-en) *o* cardinal number; **–toon** (-tonen) *m* 1 main stress; 2 ♪ keynote²; **–trek** (-ken) *m* principal trait (characteristic), main feature; *in ~ken* in outline; **–vak** (-ken) *o* principal subject; **–verkeersweg** (-wegen) *m* arterial road; **–verpleegster** (-s) *v* head-nurse, sister in charge; **–weg** (-wegen) *m* main road; main route, highroad; **–wond(e)** (-en) *v* wound in the head, head wound; **–woord** (-en) *o* headword; **–wortel** (-s) *m* ⚘ main root, tap-root; **–zaak** (-zaken) *v* main point, main thing; *hoofdzaken ook:* essentials; *in* ~ in the main, on the whole, substantially; **hoofd'zakelijk** principally, chiefly, mainly; **'hoofdzetel** (-s) *m* principal seat, head-quarters; **–zin** (-nen) *m gram* principal sentence; **–zonde** (-n) *v* deadly sin; **–zuster** (-s) *v* head-nurse, sister (in charge)

hoofs courtly; **–heid** *v* courtliness

hoog I *aj* high [favour, hills, jump, opinion, temperature, words &]; tall [tree, glass], lofty [roof]; senior [officers]; *een hoge g* ♪ a top G; *hoge druk* high pressure; *onder hoge druk* at high pressure; *het hoge noorden* the extreme North; ~ *en droog* high and dry; *het is mij te* ~ that is beyond me, above my comprehension; *de sneeuw ligt* ~ the snow lies deep; ~ *staan* be high [of prices]; *hij woont twee (drie* &) ~ two stairs up; **II** *m een hoge* **F** a bigwig, **S** a big shot, a V.I.P.; ⚔ **F** a brass hat; *(hele) hogen* ⚔ **S** (top) brass; *God in den hoge* God on high; *uit den hoge* from on high; **III** *ad* [play, sing] high; highly [paid, placed]; **'hoogachten** (achtte 'hoog, h. 'hooggeacht) *vt* (hold in high) esteem, respect; ~*d* yours faithfully, yours truly; **–ting** *v* esteem, respect, regard; *met (de meeste)* ~ yours truly; **'hoogaltaar** (-taren) *o* & *m* high altar; **'hoogbedaagd, –bejaard** very old, aged, advanced in years; **–blond** sandy; **–bouw** *m* high-rise flats, high-rise (office) blocks, multi-storey building; **–conjunctuur** *v* boom; **hoog'dravend I** *aj fig* high-sounding, high-flown, highfalutin(g), grandiloquent, pompous; **II** *ad* pompously; **–heid** *v* grandiloquence, pompousness; **'hoogdruk** (-ken) *m* letter-press [printing]; **'Hoogduits** *aj* & *o* (High) German; **'hoogfrequent** [-fre.kvεnt] high-frequency; **–gaand** high; ~*e ruzie hebben* have high words; ~*e zee* heavy sea; **–geacht** (highly) esteemed; *H~e heer* Dear Sir; **–gebergte** (-n en -s) *o* high mountains; **–geboren** high-born; **–geëerd** highly honoured; **–geleerd** very learned; **–gelegen** high; **–geplaatst** highly placed, highplaced; **hooge'rechtshof** *o* Supreme Court [of the USA]; **'hooggeschat** (highly) valued; **–gespannen** high-strung, high; **–gestemd** high-pitched; **hoog'hartig** proud, haughty; *op zijn* ~*e manier* in his off-hand manner; **–heid** *v* haughtiness; **'hoogheid** (-heden) *v* highness; height; grandeur; *Zijne Koninklijke Hoogheid* His Royal Highness; **–houden** (hield 'hoog, h. 'hooggehouden) *vt* uphold, maintain; **–koor** (-koren) *o* sanctuary; **–land** (-en) *o* highland; **'Hooglanden** *mv* Highlands; **–er** (-s) *m* Highlander; **hoog'leraar** (-s en -raren) *m* (University) professor; **–schap** (-pen) *o* professorship; **'Hooglied** *o het* ~ *van Salomo* the Song of Solomon, the Song of Songs, the Canticles; **'hooglijk** highly, greatly; **–lopend** = *hooggaand*; **–mis** (-sen) high mass; **–moed** *m* pride, haughtiness; ~ *komt voor de val* pride will have a fall; **hoog'moedig** proud, haughty; **'hoogmoedswaan(zin)** *m* = *grootheidswaan(zin)*; **hoog'mogend** *aj* high and mighty;

Hunne Hoogmogenden Their High Mightinesses;
'hoognodig very (highly) necessary, urgently needed, much-needed; *het ~e* what is strictly necessary; **–oven** (-s) *m* blast-furnace; **–rood** 1 bright red; 2 flushed [face &]; **–schatten** (schatte 'hoog, h. 'hooggeschat) *vt* esteem highly; **–schatting** *v* esteem; **–seizoen** (-en) *o* high season, peak season; **–spanning** *v* high tension; **–spannings...** high-tension...; **–springen** *o sp* high jump

hoogst I *aj* highest, supreme; top [class, prices &]; *op zijn (het) ~ zijn* be at its height [of quarrel, storm &]; *op zijn (het) ~* at (the) most; *ten ~e* 1 at (the) most; 2 highly, greatly, extremely; *een boete van ten ~e* £ 5 a fine not exceeding £ 5; **II** *ad* highly, very, greatly, extremely, quite

'hoogstaand of high standing, eminent, distinguished, superior, high-minded

hoogst'aangeslagene (-n) *m-v* highest taxpayer

'hoogstand (-en) *m* handstand

hoogst'biedende (-n) *m* highest bidder

'hoogsteigen *in ~ persoon* in his own proper person; **'hoogstens** at (the) most, at the utmost, at the outside, at best; **'hoogstwaarschijnlijk I** *aj* highly probable; **II** *ad* most probably

'hoogte (-n en -s) *v eig* 1 (h e t h o o g z ij n) height [of a hill &], altitude [of the stars, above the sea-level]; 2 (v e r h e v e n h e i d) height, elevation, eminence; *fig* height; $ highness [of prices]; ♪ pitch [of the voice]; level [in social, moral & intellectual matters]; *de ~ hebben (krijgen)* be (get) tipsy; *geen ~ van iets hebben* not understand sth.; *daar kan ik geen ~ van krijgen* it is above my comprehension, it beats me; *de ~ ingaan* rise²; *fig* go up, look up [of prices]; *~ verliezen* ⬳ lose altitude; ● *i n de ~ steken* cry up [a book &]; *o p de ~ van Gibraltar* ⚓ off Gibraltar; *op dezelfde ~ als...* on a level with, on a par with; *op geringe (grote) ~* [fly] at low (high) altitude; *op de ~ blijven* stay in the picture, keep oneself posted (up); keep abreast of the times; *iem. op de ~ brengen* post sbd. (up); *iem. op de ~ houden* keep sbd. posted (informed); *iem. op de ~ stellen van* inform sbd. of; *zich op de ~ stellen van iets* acquaint oneself with sth.; *op de ~ van zijn tijd zijn* be well abreast of the times; *op de ~ van de Franse taal* familiar with the French language; *goed op de ~ van iets zijn* be well-informed, be in the picture, be well-posted on a subject; *t o t op zekere ~* to a certain extent; *iem. u i t de ~ behandelen* treat sbd. loftily, in an off-hand manner; *uit de ~ neerzien op* look down upon; *uit de ~ zijn* **F** be uppish; **–cirkel** (-s) *m = breedtecirkel*; **–lijn** (-en) *v* 1 perpendic-

ular [in a triangle]; 2 contour line [in a map]; **–meter** (-s) *m* altimeter; **–punt** (-en) *o* culminating point²; *fig* high point, peak, pinnacle, zenith; *op het ~* at the height (at the flood) [of his glory]; **–record** [-kɔːr] (-s) *o* ⬳ height (altitude) record; **–roer** (-en) *o* ⬳ elevator; **–vrees** *v* acrophobia, height fear; *~ hebben* be afraid of heights; **–zon** (-nen) *v* artificial sun(light); (a p p a r a a t) sun-lamp

'hoogtij *~ vieren* reign supreme, run riot, be rampant; **–dag** (-dagen) *m* great day [of the Christian year &], holy day [in Islam's calendar &]

'hooguit = *hoogstens*; **'hoogveen** *o* peat-moot; **–verheven** lofty, exalted, sublime; **–verraad** *o* high treason; **–vlakte** (-n en -s) *v* plateau, tableland; **–vliegend** high-flying, soaring; **–vlieger** (-s) *m* 1 ⮞ high-flying pigeon; 2 *fig* genius; **hoog'waardig** venerable, eminent; **hoog'waardigheid** *v* eminence; **–sbekleder** (-s) *m* dignitary; **hoog'water** *o* high water, high tide; **–lijn** (-en) *v* high-water mark, tidemark

hooi *o* hay; *te veel ~ op zijn vork nemen* bite off more than one can chew; have too many irons in the fire; *te ~ en te gras* by fits and starts, occasionally; **–berg** (-en) *m* haystack, hayrick; **–bouw** *m* haymaking, hay harvest; **–broei** *m* overheated hay; **'hooien** (hooide, h. gehooid) *vt* make hay; **–er** (-s) *m* haymaker; **'hooikist** (-en) *v* haybox; **–koorts** *v* hay fever; **–land** (-en) *o* hayfield; **–maand** *v* July; **–mijt** (-en) *v* haystack; **–oogst** *m* hay harvest; **–opper** (-s) *m* haycock; **–schelf** (-schelven) *v* haystack; **–schudder** (-s) *m* tedder; **–schuur** *v* haybarn; **–tijd** (-en) *m* hay(making) time, hay harvest; **–vork** (-en) *v* hayfork; **–wagen** (-s) *m* 1 hay cart; 2 ⬳ daddy-long-legs; **–zolder** (-s) *m* hayloft

hoon *m* contumely, insult, taunt, scorn; **–gelach** *o* scornful laughter

1 hoop (hopen) *m* 1 heap², pile [of things]; 2 heap, crowd, multitude [of people]; **F** lot [of trouble &]; *de grote ~* the multitude, the masses; *b ij hopen* in heaps; *geld bij hopen* **F** heaps (lots) of money; *t e ~ lopen* gather in a crowd

2 hoop *v* hope, hopes; *weinig ~ geven* hold out little hope; *~ hebben* have a hope, have hopes [of...]; *er is weinig ~ op* there is little hope of this; ● *i n de ~ dat* in the hope that, hoping that...; *o p ~ van...* hoping for...; *t u s s e n ~ en vrees* between fear and hope; **hoop'gevend** promising, hopeful; **'hoopvol** hopeful, optimistic

'hoorapparaat (-raten) *o* hearing aid, deaf-aid, ear aid; **–baar** audible; **–col'lege** [-le.ʒə] (-s) *o* lecture; **–der** (-s) *m* hearer, listener, auditor

1 hoorn (-en en -s) *m* horn [on head of cattle, deer, snail; wind-instrument of the hunter &]; ☒ bugle; ☎ (l u i s t e r~) receiver; (s p r e e k~) mouthpiece; ~ *des overvloeds* horn of plenty; **2 hoorn** *o* (s t o f n a a m) horny; **–achtig** horny; **–blazer** (-s) *m* 1 horn-blower; 2 ☒ bugler; **hoorn'dol** crazy²; **'hoorndrager** (-s) *m* horned animal; *fig* cuckold; **'hoorn** *aj* horn; **'hoorngeschal** *o* 1 sound of horns; 2 trumpet sound; **'hoornig** horny; **hoor'nist** (-en) *m* ♪ horn-player; **'hoornsignaal** [-si̯ɲa.l] (-nalen) *o* ☒ bugle call; **–vee** *o* horned cattle, horned beasts

'hoornvlies (-vliezen) *o* cornea; **–ontsteking** (-en) *v* keratitis, inflammation of the cornea; **–transplantatie** [-(t)si.] (-s) *v* corneal graft(ing)

'hoorspel (-spelen) *o* radio play; **–toestel** (-len) *o* = *hoorapparaat*

hoos (hozen) *v* violent whirlwind; *water~* water-spout; **–vat** (-vaten) *o* scoop, bailer

1 hop *v* 🐾 hop, hops

2 hop (-pen) *m* 🦚 hoopoe

3 hop! *ij* gee-up

'hopakker (-s) *m* hop-field

'hope *v* = 2 *hoop;* **'hopelijk** *ad* it is to be hoped (that...); **'hopeloos** hopeless, desperate; **'hopen** (hoopte, h. gehoopt) **I** *vt* hope (for); *het beste* ~ hope for the best; **II** *vi* hope; ~ *op* hope for

'hopje (-s) *o* coffee-flavoured sweet, *Am* coffee candy

'hopman (-s & -lieden) *m* (p a d v i n d e r ij) scoutmaster

'hoppe *v* = 1 *hop*

'hoppen (hopte, h. gehopt) *vt* hop

'hopsa! *ij* hey-day!

'hopsen (hopste, h. gehopst) *vi* jig

hor (-ren) *v* wire-blind, screen

'horde (-n en -s) *v* 1 (v l e c h t w e r k) hurdle; ‖ 2 (t r o e p) horde, troop, band; **'hordenloop** (-lopen) *m* hurdle-race, hurdles

'horecabedrijf (-drijven) *o* 1 hotel, restaurant and catering industry; 2 hotel, restaurant, or café

1 'horen (hoorde, h. gehoord) **I** *vt* 1 hear; 2 (v e r n e m e n) hear, learn; *ik heb niets meer van hem gehoord* I have not heard from him, I had no news from him; *heb je nog wat van hem gehoord?* heard [any news] about him?; *gaan ~ wat er is* go and hear what is up; *een geluid laten ~* utter (produce) a sound; *het is niet te ~* it cannot be heard; *ik heb het ~ zeggen* I have heard it said; *ik heb het van ~ zeggen* I had it from hearsay; **II** *vi* & *va* hear; *je krijgt, hoor!* do you hear!; *hoor eens, wat...?* (I) say, what...?; *hoor*

eens, dat gaat niet! look here, that won't do!; ~ *n a a r* listen to [advice]; *hij wil er niet v a n ~* he will not hear of it; *wie niet ~ wil, moet voelen* he who will not be taught must suffer; ~*de doof zijn* be like those who having ears hear not, sham deafness; **III** *o het was een leven dat ~ en zien je verging* the noise was deafening; ~ *en zien verging ons* we were bewildered

2 'horen (hoorde, h. gehoord) = *behoren* **I**; zie ook: *wat* **II**

3 'horen (-s) *m* = 1 *hoorn*

'horige (-n) *m* ▥ serf, villain

'horizon(t) (-zonnen, -zonten) *m* horizon, sky-line; *a a n (o n d e r) de ~* on (below) the horizon; **horizon'taal** horizontal; (b ij k r u i s w o o r d r a a d s e l) across

'horlepijp (-en) *v* hornpipe

hor'loge [hɔr'lo.ʒə] (-s) *o* watch; *3 uur op mijn ~* by my watch; **–bandje** (-s) *o* watch-strap; **–glas** (-glazen) *o* watch-glass; **–kast** (-en) *v* watch-case; **–ketting** (-en) *m* & *v* watch-chain; **–maker** (-s) *m* watchmaker; **–sleutel** (-s) *m* watch-key

hor'moon (-monen) *o* hormone

horo'scoop (-scopen) *m* horoscope; *iems. ~ trekken* cast sbd.'s horoscope, cast sbd.'s nativity

'horrelvoet (-en) *m* clubfoot

hors d'oeuvre [ɔr'dœ:vrə] (-s) *o* hors d'œuvres

horst (-en) *m* aerie, aery

hort (-en) *m* jerk, jolt, jog, push; *met ~en en stoten* by fits and starts; **'horten** (hortte, h. gehort) *vi* jolt, be jerky²; **–d** jerky²

hor'tensia [-'tɛnzi.a.] (-s) *v* hydrangea

'hortus (-sen) *m* botanical garden

'horzel (-s) *v* horse-fly, hornet, gad-fly

'hospes (-sen en -pites) *m* landlord; **'hospita** ('s) *v* landlady

'hospitaal (-talen) *o* hospital; **–linnen** *o* water-proof sheeting; **–schip** (-schepen) *o* hospital ship; **–soldaat** (-daten) *m* hospital orderly, aid man

hospi'tant (-en) *m* teacher-trainee; **hospi'teren** (hospiteerde, h. gehospiteerd) *vi* 🕮 attend a lesson as a visitor

'hossen (hoste, h. gehost) *vi* jig, jolt

'hostie (-s en -iën) *v* host

'hot *ij* gee-up!; ~ *en haar* right and left; ~ *en haar door elkaar* higgledy-piggledy

ho'tel (-s) *o* hotel; **–bedrijf** (-drijven) *o* hotel trade, hotel industry, hotel business

hotelde'botel **F** upset, confused, in a muddle, at sea

ho'telhouder (-s) *m* hotelier, hotel-keeper; **–rat** (-ten) *v* hotel thief; **–schakelaar** (-s) *m* two-way switch; **–school** (-scholen) *v* catering and hotel-management school

'**hotsen** (hotste, h. gehotst) *vi* jolt, bump, shake
'**Hottentot** (-ten) *m*, '**Hottentots** *aj* Hottentot
1 hou *ij* stop! ho!
2 hou ~ en trouw loyal and faithful
'**houdbaar** (v e r d e d i g b a a r) tenable; *boter die
(niet)* ~ *is* butter that will (not) keep; **–heid** *v* 1
tenability; 2 (v . e e t w a r e n) keeping qualities; '**houden*** I *vt* 1 (v a s t h o u d e n) hold; 2
(i n h o u d e n) hold, contain; 3 (e r o p
n a h o u d e n) keep [pigs, an inn, servants]; 4
(b e h o u d e n) keep [the change]; 5 (v i e r e n)
keep, observe, celebrate [a feast]; 6 (n a k o -
m e n) keep [a promise]; 7 (u i t s p r e k e n)
make, deliver [a speech &], give [an address];
hij was niet te ~ he could not be checked, he
could not be kept quiet; *houdt de dief!* stop
thief!; *5 ik houd er 3* carry three; zie ook: *bed,
kamer, steek* &; *'t met een andere vrouw* ~ carry on
with another woman; ● *wij moeten het a a n de
gang* ~ we must keep the thing going; *het aan
zich* ~ reserve it to oneself; *je moet ze b ij elkaar
~* you should keep them together; *hen er
b u i t e n* ~ keep them out of it; *ik kan u niet i n
dienst* ~ I can't continue you in my service; *in
ere* ~ zie *eer*; *een stuk (brief* &) *o n d e r zich* ~
keep it (back); *ik kan ze maar niet u i t elkaar* ~ I
can't tell them apart, I can't tell which is
which; *u moet die jongens v a n elkaar* ~ keep
these boys apart; *ik houd hem v o o r een vriend* I
consider him to be a friend; *ik hield hem voor een
Amerikaan* I (mis)took him for an American;
ik houd het voor onvermijdelijk I regard it as
inevitable; *ik houd het voor een slecht teken* I
consider it a bad sign; *ik houd het ervoor dat...* I
take it that...; *waar houdt u mij voor?* what do
you take me for?: *zich* ~ *voor* consider oneself
[a better man]; *iets voor zich* ~ keep it [the
money &] for oneself; keep it [the secret] to
oneself; *hij kan niets vóór zich* ~ he can't keep
his counsel; **II** *va* & *vi* hold; keep; *links (rechts)
~!* keep (to the) left (right)!; *het zal erom* ~ *of...*
it will be touch and go whether...; *met iets zitten
te* ~ zie *zitten*; *van iets* ~ like sth., be fond of
sth.; *veel van iem.* ~ be fond of sbd., love sbd.;
III *vr zich* ~ *alsof...* make as if..., pretend to...;
zich doof ~ pretend not to hear, sham deafness;
zich goed ~ 1 (v . p e r s o n e n) keep one's
countenance, control oneself; 2 (v . z a k e n)
keep [of apples]; wear well [of clothes]; 3 (v .
w e e r) hold; *zich goed* ~ *(voor zijn leeftijd)* carry
one's years well; *hij kon zich niet meer goed* ~ he
could not help laughing (crying); *zich goed* ~ 1
keep well!; 2 never say die!; *zich ver* ~ *van* hold
aloof from [a question &]; *zich ziek* ~ pretend
to be ill; *zich* ~ *aan* stick to [the facts &], abide
by [a decision], keep [a strict diet, a treaty &];
zich aan iems. woord ~ take sbd. at his word; *ik*

weet nu waar ik mij aan te ~ *heb* I now know
where I stand; zie ook: *been* &; **IV** *o* zie *hebben*
III; **–er** (-s) *m* holder, keeper, bearer; '**houd-
greep** (-grepen) *m*, hold; '**houding** (-en) *v* 1
bearing, carriage, posture, attitude; 2 ⚔
position of "attention"; *de* ~ *aannemen* ⚔ come
to attention; *een (gemaakte)* ~ *aannemen* strike an
attitude; *een dreigende (gereserveerde)* ~ *aannemen*
assume a threatening (guarded) attitude; *zich
een* ~ *geven* assume an air; *om zich een* ~ *te geven*
in order to save his face; *in de* ~ *staan* ⚔ stand
at attention; '**houdstermaatschappij** (-en) *v*
holding company

hout *o* wood; timber; piece of wood; *de Haarlemmer Hout* the Haarlem Wood; *alle* ~ *is geen
timmerhout* every reed will not make a pipe; *dat
snijdt geen* ~ that does not hold good, that cuts
no ice; *hij is uit hetzelfde* ~ *gesneden* he is the
same stamp; *hij is uit het goede* ~ *gesneden* he is of
the right stuff; *hij kreeg van dik* ~ *zaagt men
planken* he got a sound threshing; **–aankap**
(-pen) *m* 1 felling of trees; 2 timber reserve,
lumber exploitation; **–achtig** woody,
ligneous; **–bewerker** (-s) *m* woodworker;
–blazer (-s) *m* woodwind player; **–blok** (-ken)
o (wood) log; **–duif** (-duiven) *v* wood-pigeon;
'**houten** *aj* wooden [shoes, leg &]; ~ *klaas*
stick; '**houterig** wooden²; '**houtgravure** (-n
en -s) *v* wood engraving; **–hakker** (-s) *m*
wood-cutter; **–handel** (-s) *m* timber trade;
–handelaar (-s) *m* timber merchant; **–haven**
(-s) *v* timber port; '**houtje** (-s) *o* bit of wood;
op (zijn) eigen ~ on one's own hook, off one's
own bat; *we moesten op een* ~ *bijten* we had
nothing (little) to eat; *van 't* ~ *zijn* be a Roman
Catholic; **houtje-'touwtje-jas** (-sen) *m* duffle
coat; '**houtlijm** *m* joiner's glue; **–loods** (-en) *v*
wood-shed; **–luis** (-luizen) *v* wood-louse;
–mijt (-en) *v* 1 stack of wood; 2 (b r a n d -
s t a p e l) pile; **–molm** *m* dry rot; **–pulp** *v*
wood pulp; **–rijk** woody, well-wooded;
–schroef (-schroeven) *v* wood-screw;
–schuur (-schuren) *v* wood-shed; '**houtskool**
v charcoal; **–tekening** (-en) *v* charcoal
drawing; '**houtsne(d)e** (-sneden) *v* woodcut;
–snijder (-s) *m* 1 wood-cutter; 2 wood-carver;
–snijkunst *v* 1 wood-cutting; 2 wood-
carving; **–snijwerk** *o* wood carving; **–snip**
(-pen) *v* 🦜 woodcock; **–soort** (-en) *v* kind of
wood; **–spaander** (-s) *m* chip of wood; **–teer**
m & *o* wood tar; **–veiling** (-en) *v*, **–verkoping**
(-en) *v* timber sale; **–verbinding** (-en) *v* joint,
scarf; **–vester** (-s) *m* forester; **houtveste'rij**
(-en) *v* forestry; '**houtvezel** (-s) *v* wood-fibre;
–vlot (-ten) *o* (timber) raft; **–vlotter** (-s) *m*
raftsman; **–vrij** free from wood-pulp; **–waren**
mv wooden ware; **–werk** *o* woodwork; **–wol** *v*

wood-wool; **–worm** (-en) *m* wood-worm;
–zaagmolen (-s) *m* saw-mill; **–zager** (-s) *m*
wood-sawyer; **houtzage′rij** (-en) *v* saw-mill;
′**houtzolder** (-s) *m* wood-loft

hou′vast *o* handhold; *fig* hold; *dat geeft ons enig ~*
that's something to go by (to go on); *zijn ~*
verliezen loose one's footing

houw (-en) *m* cut, gash; **–degen** (-s) *m* 1
broadsword; 2 *fig* tough fighter, rugged old
soldier

hou′weel (-welen) *o* pickaxe, mattock

′**houwen*** *vi* hew, hack, cut, slash; zie ook:
slaan

hou′witser (-s) *m* howitzer

ho′vaardig proud, haughty; **hovaar′dij** *v*
pride, haughtiness

′**hoveling** (-en) *m* courtier

′**hoven** meerv. v. *hof*

hove′nier (-s) *m* gardener

′**hozen** (hoosde, h. gehoosd) *vi* & *vt* scoop, bail
(out), bale

H.S. = *Heilige Schrift*

hs. = *handschrift*

H.T.S = *Hogere Technische School* ± secondary
technical school

hu! *ij* 1 (v o o r u i t) gee!; 2 (s t o p) whoa!; 3 (v.
a f g r ij z e n) ugh

′**hufter** (-s) **F** *m* lout, bumpkin

′**hugenoot** (-noten) *m* Huguenot

′**huichelaar** (-s) *m*, **–ster** (-s) *v* hypocrite,
dissembler; ′**huichelachtig** hypocritical;
huichela′rij (-en) *v* hypocrisy, humbug,
dissembling, dissimulation; ′**huichelen**
(huichelde, h. gehuicheld) **I** *vt* simulate, feign,
sham; **II** *vi* dissemble, play the hypocrite

huid (-en) *v* skin [of human or animal body],
hide [raw or dressed], fell [with the hair]; *een*
dikke (*harde*) *~ hebben* be thick-skinned; *iem. de*
~ vol schelden shower abuse on sbd., slang sbd.;
men moet de ~ van de beer niet verkopen, voordat men
hem geschoten heeft sell not the skin before you
have caught the bear, don't count your chickens before they are hatched; *zijn ~ wagen* risk
one's life; ● *m e t ~ en haar verslinden* swallow
whole; *iem. o p zijn ~ geven* (*komen*) **S** tan a
person's hide; **–arts** (-en) *m* skin doctor,
dermatologist; **–enkoper** (-s) *m* fellmonger

′**huidig** present [age], modern, present-day
[difficulties, knowledge, needs]; *ten ~en dage*
nowadays; *tot op de ~e dag* to this day

′**huidje** (-s) *o* skin, film; ′**huidplooi** (-en) *v*
crease, fold (in skin); ′**huidskleur** (-en) *v*
colour of the skin; ′**huidspecialist** [-spe.si.a.-]
(-en) *m* = *huidarts*; **–transplantatie** [-(t)si.] (-s)
v skin-grafting; **–uitslag** *m* rash, eruption (of
the skin), skin eruption; **–ziekte** (-n en -s) *v*
skin disease

huif (huiven) *v* 1 (h o o f d d e k s e l) coif; 2 (v.
w a g e n) hood, awning, tilt; **–kar** (-ren) *v*
tilt-cart, hooded cart

huig (-en) *v* uvula

′**huik** (-en) *v* ◫ hooded cloak; *de ~ naar de wind*
hangen (trim to the times and) hang one's cloak
to the wind

′**huilbui** (-en) *v* fit of crying (of weeping);
′**huilebalk** (-en) *m* cry-baby, sissy; ′**huile-**
balken (huilebalkte, h. gehuilebalkt) *vi*
blubber, whine; ′**huilen** (huilde, h. gehuild) *vi*
1 (s c h r e i e n) cry, weep; 2 (v. d i e r) howl,
whine; 3 (v. w i n d) howl; *het is om* (*van*) *te ~* I
could cry!; *~ met de wolven in het bos* run with
the hare and hunt with the hounds; *het ~ stond*
hem nader dan het lachen he was on the verge of
tears; ′**huilerig** tearful

huis (huizen) *o* house, home; *het ~ des Heren* the
House of God; *het Koninklijk ~* the Royal
family; *het ~ van Oranje* the House of Orange;
men kan huizen op hem bouwen one can always
depend on him; *er is geen ~ met hem te houden*
there is no doing anything with him, he is
impossible; ● *ik kom veel bij hen a a n ~* I see a
good deal of them; *~ aan ~* [go] from door to
door; door-to-door [canvassing], house-to-
house [visiting]; (*dicht*) *b ij ~* near home;
bezigheden i n ~ activities in the home; *er is geen*
brood in ~ there is no bread in the house; *wij*
gaan n a a r ~ we are going home; *naar ~ sturen*
send home; ✄ release [troops]; dissolve
[Parliament]; *uit ~ zetten* turn out of [evict
from] the house; *t e mijnen huize* at my house;
ten huize van... at the house of...; *hij is v a n ~* he
is away from home; *hij is van goeden huize* he
comes of a good family; *van ~ gaan* leave
home; *van ~ komen* come from one's house; *nog*
verder van ~ even worse off; *van ~ tot ~* from
house to house; *van ~ uit is hij...* originally he
is a...; *van ~ en hof verdreven* driven out of
house and home; *elk ~ heeft zijn kruis* there is a
skeleton in every cupboard; **–adres** (-sen) *o*
home address; **–apotheek** (-theken) *v* (family)
medicine chest; **–arrest** *o* confinement in one's
home; *~ hebben* 1 ✄ be confined to quarters; 2
be confined to one's house; **–arts** (-en) *m*
family doctor, general practitioner, G.P.;
–baas (-bazen) *m* landlord; **huis′bakken**
home-made; *fig* prosaic, pedestrian; ′**huisbe-**
diende (-n en -s) *m-v* domestic servant; **–bel**
(-len) *v* street-door bell; **–bewaarder** (-s) *m*
care-taker; custodian; **–bezoek** (-en) *o* (v.
a r t s) home visit; (v. g e e s t e l ij k e) parochial
visit, parish visiting; *op ~ gaan* visit, go visiting; **–brand** *m* domestic fuel; **–brandolie** *v*
domestic fuel oil; **–deur** (-en) *o* street-door;
–dier (-en) *o* domestic animal; **–dokter** (-s) *m*

= *huisarts*; **–eigenaar** (-s en -naren) *m* 1 house-owner; 2 (h u i s b a a s) landlord; 'huiselijk I *aj* domestic, household; home; homelike, homy; ~*e aangelegenheden* family affairs; domestic affairs; ~*e kring* domestic circle; *het ~ leven* home life; *een ~ man* a man of domestic habits, a home-loving man; ~*e plichten* household duties; **II** *ad* in a homely manner, informally; **–heid** *v* domesticity; 'huisgenoot (-noten) *m* housemate, inmate; *de huisgenoten* the inmates, the whole family; **–gezin** (-nen) *o* family household; **–goden** *mv* household gods; **–heer** (-heren) *m* 1 landlord; 2 master of the house

'huishoudboek (-en) *o* housekeeping book; huis'houdelijk 1 economical, thrifty; 2 domestic, household; *zaken van* ~*e aard* domestic affairs; *voor* ~ *gebruik* for household purposes; ~*e artikelen* household ware; ~*e uitgaven* household expenses; ~*e vergadering* private meeting; 'huishouden I *vi* (hield 'huis, h. 'huisgehouden) keep house; *vreselijk* ~ (*onder*) make (play) havoc (with, among); **II** *o* 1 household, establishment, family; 2 housekeeping; *een* ~ *van Jan Steen* a house where everything is at sixes and sevens; *het* ~ *doen* keep house; 'huishoudgeld (-en) *o* housekeeping money; 'huishouding (-en) *v* 1 housekeeping; 2 household, family; 'huishoudkunde *v* domestic economy; **–school** (-scholen) *v* domestic science school, school of domestic economy; **–schort** (-en) *v* & *o* overall, apron dress; **–ster** (-s) *v* housekeeper; **–zeep** *v* household soap

'huishuur (-huren) *v* rent; **–industrie** *v* home industry; 'huisje (-s) *o* 1 small house, cottage; 2 (v. s l a k) shell; 3 (v. b r i l) case; 'huisjesmelker (-s) *m* rack-renter; **–slak** (-ken) *v* snail; 'huiskamer (-s) *v* sitting-room, living-room; **–kapel** (-len) *v* 1 private chapel; 2 ♪ private band; **–knecht** (-en en -s) *m* 1 man-servant, footman; 2 boots [of an hotel]; **–krekel** (-s) *m* house-cricket; 'huislijk(-) = *huiselijk*(-); 'huislook *o* houseleek; **–middel** (-en) *o* domestic remedy; **–moeder** (-s) *v* mother of a (the) family; **–mus** (-sen) *v* 1 ♂ (house-)sparrow; 2 *fig* stay-at-home; **–naaister** (-s) *v* seamstress who comes to the house; **–nummer** (-s) *o* number (of the house); **–onderwijs** *o* private tuition; **–onderwijzer** (-s) *m* private teacher, tutor; **–orde** (-n) *v* 1 rules of the house; 2 family order [of knighthood]; **–raad** *o* (household) furniture, household goods; **–schilder** (-s) *m* house-painter; **–sleutel** (-s) *m* latchkey, house-key; **–telefoon** (-s) *m* house telephone; **huis-tuin-en** 'keuken common or garden; 'huisvader (-s)

m father of a (the) family, pater familias; 'huisvesten (huisvestte, h. gehuisvest) *vt* house, lodge, take in, put up; 'huisvesting *v* lodging, accommodation, housing; ~ *verlenen* = *huisvesten*; 'huisvestingsbureau [-by.ro.] (-s) *o* housing office; 'huisvlijt *v* 1 home industry; 2 (u i t l i e f h e b b e r ij) home handicrafts; **–vredebreuk** *v* disturbance of domestic peace; **–vriend** (-en) *m* family friend; **–vrouw** (-en) *v* housewife; **–vuil** *o* household refuse; **–waarts** homeward(s); ~ *gaan* go home; **–werk** *o* 1 (v. b e d i e n d e n) housework; 2 ▭ home tasks, homework; **S** prep; **–zoeking** (-en) *v* house search; *er werd* ~ *gedaan* the house was searched; **–zwaluw** (-en) *v* (house-)martin

'huiveren (huiverde, h. gehuiverd) *vi* shiver [with cold or fear], shudder [with horror]; *ik huiverde b ij de gedachte* I shuddered to think of it; *hij huiverde er v o o r* he shrank from it; 'huiverig shivery, chilly; ~ *om zo iets te doen* shy of doing such a thing; 'huivering (-en) *v* shiver(s), shudder; *een* ~ *voer mij door de leden* a shudder went through me; *fig* hesitation, scruple; huivering'wekkend horrible, ghastly

'huizehoog I *aj* mountainous [seas]; **II** *ad* ~ *springen (van vreugde)* jump (leap) out of one's skin; ~ *uitsteken boven* rise head and shoulders above; 'huizen (huisde, h. gehuisd) *vi* house, live; 'huizenblok (-ken) *o* residential block; **–rij** (-en) *v* row of houses

'hulde *v* homage; tribute; ~ *brengen* do (pay) homage [to sbd.]; pay a tribute [to a man of merit]; **–betoon** *o* homage; **–blijk** (-en) *o* tribute, testimonial; 'huldigen (huldigde, h. gehuldigd) *vt* do (pay) homage to²; hold [an opinion], believe in [a method]; 'huldiging (-en) *v* homage; 'huldigingseed (-eden) *m* oath of allegiance

'hullen (hulde, h. gehuld) I *vt* envelop, wrap (up); *fig* shroud [in mystery]; **II** *vr zich* ~ wrap oneself (up) [in a cloak]

hulp (-en) *v* help, aid, assistance; succour, relief; *eerste* ~ *bij ongelukken* first aid; ~ *in de huishouding* lady help; ~ *en bijstand* aid and assistance; *t e* ~ *komen* come (go) to [sbd.'s] aid, come to the rescue [of the crew &]; *te* ~ *roepen* call in; *te* ~ *snellen* hasten (run) to the rescue; *z o n d e r* ~ without anyone's help (assistance), unaided, unassisted; **–actie** [-aksi.] (-s) *v* relief action, relief measures; hulpe'hoevend helpless, infirm; *hij is* ~ ook: he is an invalid; 'hulpbetoon *o* assistance; **–bisschop** (-pen) *m rk* auxiliary bishop; **–bron** (-nen) *v* resource; **–dienst** (-en) *m telefonische* ~ telephone emergency service [in Britain: (Telephone) Samari-tans]; **–eloos** helpless; **–geroep** *o* cry for help; **–kracht** (-en) *v* & *m* additional (temporary) worker; help(er), assistant; **–kreet** (-kreten) *m* cry for help; **–lijn** (-en) *v* 1 (m e e t k u n d e) auxiliary line; 2 *♩* ledger-line; **–mechanisme** (-n) *o* servo-mechanism; **–middel** (-en) *o* expedient, makeshift; *fotografische ~en* photographic aids; *zijn ~en* ook: his resources; *rijk aan ~* resourceful; **–motor** (-s en -toren) *m* auxiliary motor, auxiliary engine; *rijwiel met ~* motor-assisted bicycle, powered pedal-cycle; **–ploeg** (-en) *v* breakdown gang; **–post** (-en) *m* aid post; **–postkantoor** (-toren) *o* sub(post)office; **–prediker** (-s) *m* curate; **–stuk** (-ken) *o* ✗ accessory; (v. s t o f z u i g e r) attachment; (v. b u i z e n) fitting; **–troepen** *mv* ✕ auxiliaries, auxiliary troops, reinforcements; **hulp'vaardig** willing to help, helpful; **–heid** *v* willingness to help; **'hulpverlening** *v* assistance; relief work; **–werkwoord** (-en) *o* auxiliary (verb)

huls (hulzen) *v* 1 ⚘ pod, husk, shell; 2 ✕ (cartridge-)case; 3 (straw) case [for bottle]; 4 carton

'hulsel (-s) *o* = *omhulsel*

hulst *m* holly

1 hum *o* **F** = *humeur*

2 hum! *ij* = *h'm!*

hu'maan humane; **humani'ora** *mv* humanities; **huma'nisme** *o* humanism; **–ist** (-en) *m* humanist; **–istisch** humanistic; **humani'tair** [-'tɪːr] humanitarian; **humani'teit** *v* humaneness, humanity

'humbug *m* humbug

hu'meur (-en) *o* humour, mood, temper; *in zijn ~* in a good humour; *niet in zijn ~*, *uit zijn ~* out of humour, in a (bad) temper; **hu'meurig** moody, crabby, grumpy, subject to moods, having tempers; **–heid** (-heden) *v* moodiness

'hummel (-s) *m*, **'hummeltje** (-s) *o* (little) tot, mite

'hummen (humde, h. gehumd) *vi* hem [to call attention]; clear one's throat

'humor *m* humour; **humo'rist** (-en) *m* humorist; **–isch** comic(al), humorous

humus *m* humus, vegetable mould

Hun (-nen) *m* Hun²

hun their, them; *het ~ne, de ~nen* theirs

'hunebed (-den) *o* [the Borger] Hunebed, ± dolmen, cromlech

'hunkeren (hunkerde, h. gehunkerd) *vi* hanker; *~ naar* hanker after; *ik hunker er naar hem te zien* I am longing (anxious) to see him

'hunnent *te(n) ~* at their house; *~halve* for their sake(s); *~wege* as for them; *van ~wege* on their behalf, in their name; *om ~wil(le)* for their sake(s); **'hunnerzijds** on their part, on their

behalf

'huplakee *ij* whoops!, oops

'huppelen (huppelde, h. gehuppeld) *vi* hop, skip; **'huppen** (hupte, h. gehupt) *vi* hop, skip, jump; **hups** kind; nice; **'hupsakee** *ij* = *huplakee*

'huren (huurde, h. gehuurd) *vt* hire, rent [a house &]; hire, engage [servants]; ⚓ charter [a ship]

1 'hurken *mv* *op zijn ~* squatting; **2 'hurken** (hurkte, h. gehurkt) *vi* squat (down)

hut (-ten) *v* 1 cottage, hut, hovel, ⊙ cot; 2 ⚓ cabin [of a ship]; **–bagage** [-ga.3ə] *v* cabin-luggage

'hutje (-s) *o* *met ~ en mutje* with bag and baggage; *het hele ~mutje* the whole caboodle

'hutkoffer (-s) *m* cabin-trunk

'hutselen (hutselde, h. gehutseld) *vt* shake up, mix up

'hutspot (-ten) *m* hotchpotch², hodgepodge²; [as Dutch speciality:] mashed potatoes, carrots and onions with meat

huur (huren) *v* 1 rent, rental, hire; 2 (l o o n) wages; 3 (h u u r t ij d) lease; *in ~* on hire; *auto's te ~* cars for hire; *huis te ~* house to let; *te ~ of te koop* to be let or sold; *vrij van ~* rent-free; **–auto** [au = ɔu of o.] ('s) *m* hire(d) car; **–bescherming** *v* legal guarantee against eviction from a rented house; **'huurcontract** (-en) *o* lease; **–compensatie** [-za.(t)si.] (-s) *v* (governmental) rent subsidy; **–der** (-s) *m* hirer; (v. h u i s) tenant, lessee; **–huis** (-huizen) *o* rented house, hired house; house to let; **–kazerne** (-s) *v* tenement house, **F** warren; **–koetsier** (-s) *m* hackney-coachman, cabman; **–koop** *m* hire-purchase (system); *in ~* on the hire-purchase system; **–leger** (-s) *o* mercenary army; **–ling** (-en) *m* hireling, mercenary; **–penningen** *mv* rent; **–prijs** (-prijzen) *m* rent; **–rijtuig** (-en) *o* hackney-carriage, cab; **–tijd** (-en) *m* term of lease, lease; **–troepen** *mv* mercenary troops, mercenaries; **–verhoging** (-en) *v* rent increase; **–waarde** (-en) *v* rental (value); **–wet** *v* Rent Act

'huwbaar marriageable; nubile; **–heid** *v* marriageable age; nubility; **'huwelijk** (-en) *o* marriage, matrimony, wedlock, wedding; *een ~ aangaan (sluiten)* contract a marriage; *een goed ~ doen* marry well; *een rijk ~ doen* marry a fortune; *in het ~ treden* marry; *een meisje ten ~ vragen* ask a girl in marriage, propose to a girl; **'huwelijksaankondiging** (-en) *v* wedding announcement; **–aanzoek** (-en) *o* proposal, offer (of marriage); **–advertentie** [-tɪnsi.] (-s en -tiën) *v* matrimonial advertisement; **–afkondiging** (-en) *v* 1 public notice of (a) marriage; 2 (k e r k e l ij k) banns; **–belofte**

(-n) *v* promise of marriage; **–bootje** *o* Hymen's boat; *in het ~ stappen* embark on matrimony; **–bureau** [-by.ro.] (-s) *o* matrimonial agency, marriage bureau; **–cadeau** [-do.] (-s) *o* wedding present; **–contract** (-en) *o* marriage settlement, marriage articles; **–feest** (-en) *o* wedding, wedding-feast, wedding-party; **–geluk** *o* wedded happiness; **–gift** (-en) *v*, **–goed** (-eren) *o* marriage portion, dowry; **–inzegening** (-en) *v* marriage (wedding) ceremony; **–leven** *o* married life; **–plicht** (-en) *m* & *v* conjugal duty; **–reis** (-reizen) *v* wedding-trip, honeymoon (trip); **–trouw** *v* conjugal fidelity; **–voorwaarden** *mv* marriage contract; **'huwen** (huwde, *vt* h., *vi* is gehuwd) *vt* & *vi* marry, wed; ~ *met* marry; *gehuwd met een Duitser* married to a German

hu'zaar (-zaren) *m* ⚔ hussar; **hu'zarensla** *v* Russian salad

hya'cint [hi.a.'sɪnt] (-en) *v* ⚘ hyacinth

hy'bridisch [hi.-] hybrid

'hydra ['hi.-] ('s) *v* hydra

hy'draat [hi.-] (-draten) *o* hydrate

hy'draulica [hi.-] *v* hydraulics; **hy'draulisch** hydraulic(ally)

hydro-dynamica [y = i.] *v* hydrodynamics; **hydro-e'lektrisch** hydro-electric

hy'ena [hi.'e.na.] ('s) *v* hyena

hygi'ëne [hi.gi.'e.nə] *v* hygiene; **hygi'ënisch** hygienic(al)

'hygrometer ['hi.-] (-s) *m* hygrometer

'hymne ['hɪmnə] (-n) *v* hymn

hyper'bolisch [hi.-] hyperbolical; **hyper'bool**

(-bolen) *v* hyperbole

'hypergevoelig ['hi.-] hypersensitive; **–modern** hypermodern; **–nerveus** tense; **hyper'tensie** [hi.-] *v* hypertension; **hypertro'fie** *v* hypertrophy

hyp'nose [hɪ.p'no.zə] *v* hypnosis; **hyp'notisch** hypnotic(al); **hypnoti'seren** [s = z] (hypnotiseerde, h. gehypnotiseerd) *vt* hypnotize; **hypnoti'seur** [s = z] (-s) *m* hypnotist; **hypno'tisme** *o* hypnotism

hypo'chonder [hi.-] (-s) *m* hypochondriac; **hypochon'drie** *v* hypochondria; **hypo'chondrisch** hypochondriac(al)

hypo'criet [hi.-] (-en) *m* hypocrite; **hypocri'sie** [s = z] *v* hypocrisy; **hypo'critisch** hypocritical

hypo'fyse [hi.po'fi.zə] (-n) *v* pituitary body (gland), hypophysis

hypote'nusa [hi.po.tə'ny.za.] ('s) *v* hypotenuse

hypothe'cair [hi.po.te.'kɛːr] *~e schuld* mortgage debt; **hypo'theek** (-theken) *v* mortgage; *met een ~ bezwaard* mortgaged; **–akte** (-n en -s) *v* mortgage deed; **–bank** (-en) *v* mortgage bank; **–bewaarder** (-s) *m* registrar of mortgages; **–gever** (-s) *m* mortgagor; **–houder** (-s) *m*, **–nemer** (-s) *m* mortgagee; **–kantoor** (-toren) *o* mortgage registry; **hypothe'keren** (hypothekeerde, h. gehypothekeerd) *vt* mortgage

hypo'these [hi.po.'te.zə] (-n en -s) *v* hypothesis [*mv* hypotheses]; **hypo'thetisch** hypothetic(al)

hys'terica [his-] ('s), *v* **hys'tericus** (-ci) *m* hysteric; **hyste'rie** *v* hysteria; **hys'terisch** hysterical; *een ~e aanval krijgen* go into hysterics; **F** go off the hooks

I

i [i.] ('s) *v* i

i'a (v. e z e l) hee-haw; i'aën (iade, h. geïaad) *vi* hee-haw

ib., ibid. = *ibidem* in the same place

'ibis (-sen) *m* 🐦 ibis

i.c. = *in casu* in this case

i'co(o)n (iconen) *v* icon, ikon

id. = *idem*

ide'aal I *aj* ideal; II (idealen) *o* ideal; *een ~ van een echtgenoot* an ideal husband; ideali'seren [s = z] (idealiseerde, h. geïdealiseerd) *vt & va* idealize; idea'lisme *o* idealism; idea'list (-en) *m* idealist; –isch idealistic(al)

i'dee (ideeën) *o & v* idea, thought, notion; *precies mijn ~!* quite my opinion!; *naar mijn ~* in my view; *je hebt er geen ~ van* you have no notion of it; *een hoog ~ hebben van* have a high opinion of; *er niet het minste (flauwste) ~ van hebben* not have the least idea; *ik heb géén ~!* F search me!; *ik heb zo'n ~ dat...* I have a notion that...; *naar mijn ~* in my opinion; *op het ~ komen om...* get it into one's head to..., hit upon an idea; i'deeënbus (-sen) *v* suggestion box; idee-'fixe [-fi.ks] (-n) *o & v* fixed idea

'idem the same, ditto, do.

iden'tiek identical

identifi'catie [-(t)si.] *v* identification; identifi'ceren (identificeerde, h. geïdentificeerd) I *vt* identify; II *vr zich* – prove one's identity

identi'teit *v* identity; identi'teitsbewijs (-wijzen) *o*, –kaart (-en) *v* identity card; –plaatje (-s) *o* identity disk

ideolo'gie (-gieën) *v* ideology; ideo'logisch ideological; ideo'loog (-logen) *m* ideologue, ideologist

idio'matisch idiomatic(al); idi'oom (idiomen) *o* idiom

idi'oot I *aj* idiotic(al), foolish; II (idioten) *m* idiot, fool, nitwit; idio'tisme (-n) *o* 1 idiocy; 2 *gram* idiom

ido'laat ~ *van* infatuated with; idola'trie *v* idolatry; i'dool (idolen) *o* idol

i'dylle [i.'dɪlə] (-n en -s) *v* idyl(l); –lisch idyllic(al)

'ieder every; each; any; *een ~* everyone; anyone; ieder'een, 'iedereen everybody, everyone

'iegelijk *een ~* everybody

iel thin, scanty; ethereal

'iemand somebody, someone; anybody, anyone; a man, one; *zeker ~* "Somebody"

'iemker (-s) *m* = *imker*

iep (-en) *m*, 'iepeboom (-bomen) *m* elm,

elm-tree; 'iepen *aj* elm; iepziekte *v* (Dutch) elm disease

Ier (-en) *m* Irishman; *de ~en* the Irish; –land *o* Ireland, ⊙ Hibernia, Erin; –s I *aj* Irish; II *o het* ~ Irish; III *v een* ~e an Irishwoman

iet zie 1 *niet* II; iets I *voornw.* something, anything; *er is ~, een zeker ~ in zijn stem dat...* there is (a certain) something in his voice; *is er ~?* is anything the matter?, anything wrong?; *echt ~ voor haar!* how like her!; *er is nog ~* there is something else, there is another thing; *[die jurk] is net ~ voor jou!* the very thing for you!; II *ad* 1 (b e v e s t i g e n d) somewhat, a little; 2 (v r a g e n d & o n t k e n n e n d) any; 'ietsje *o een ~* a shade [better]; a thought [shorter]; a trifle [too short, too tough]; *met een ~...* with something of..., with a touch of...; 'ietwat = *iets en ietsje*

'iezegrim (-men en -s) *m* surly fellow, crab, grumbler; ieze'grimmig surly, crabbed

'iglo ('s) *m* igloo

i-'grec [-'grɛk] (-s) *v* [the letter] y

'ijdel 1 vain [= empty, useless & conceited]; 2 idle [hope]; –heid (-heden) *v* vanity, vainness; *~ der ijdelheden* B vanity of vanities; –tuit (-en) *v* vain person

ijk (ijken) *m* verification and stamping of weights and measures; 'ijken (ijkte, h. geijkt) *vt* gauge, verify and stamp; zie ook: *geijkt*; –er (-s) *m* gauger; inspector of weights and measures; 'ijkkantoor (-toren) *o* gauging-office; –maat (-maten) *v* standard measure; –meester (-s) *m* = *ijker*

1 ijl *v in aller ~* at the top of one's speed, with all speed, in great haste

2 ijl *aj* thin, rare; *~e lucht* rarefied air; *de ~e ruimte* (vacant) space

'ijlbode (-n en -s) *m* courier, express messenger; 'ijlen *vi* 1 (ijlde, is geijld) hasten, hurry (on); speed; 2 (ijlde, h. geijld) rave, wander, be delirious; *de patiënt ijlt* the patient is wandering in his (her) mind; 'ijlgoed (-eren) *o* express goods; *als ~* by express delivery

ijl'hoofdig 1 light-headed; delirious; 2 feather-brained, feather-headed

'ijlings hastily, in great haste, post-haste

ijs *o* ice; (o m t e e t e n) ice-cream; *het ~ breken* break the ice; *zich op glad ~ wagen* tread on dangerous ground, skate over thin ice; *(goed) beslagen t e n ~ komen* be fully prepared (for...); *niet o v e r één nacht ~ gaan* not move in

too hurried a manner, take no risks; **–afzetting** *v* icing; **–baan** (-banen) *v* skating-rink,
ice-rink; **–beer** (-beren) *m* polar bear, white
bear; **–beren** (ijsbeerde, h. geijsbeerd) *vi* walk
(pace) up and down; **–berg** (-en) *m* iceberg;
–bestrijder (-s) *m ↝* de-icer; **–bloemen** *mv*
frost flowers; **–blokje** (-s) *o* ice-cube; **–breker**
(-s) *m* ice-breaker; **–club** (-s) *v* skating-club;
'ijsco ('s) *m* ice; **–man** (-nen) *m* ice-cream
vendor; **'ijselijk** horrible, frightful, shocking,
terrible, dreadful; **'ijsfabriek** (-en) *v* ice-
factory, ice-works; **–gang** *m* breaking up and
drifting of the ice, ice drift; **–glas** *o* frosted
glass; **–heiligen** *mv* Ice Saints; **–hockey**
[-hɔki.] *o sp* ice-hockey; **–je** (-s) *o* ice, ice-
cream; **–kap** (-pen) *v* ice sheet (cap), ice
mantle; **–kast** (-en) *v* refrigerator, icebox, **F**
fridge; *in de ~ zetten (leggen, bergen)* [*fig*] keep on
ice, put in cold storage; **–kegel** (-s) *m* icicle;
–kelder (-s) *m* ice-house; **–klomp** (-en) *m*
lump of ice; **–korst** (-en) *v* crust of ice; **–koud
I** *aj* cold as ice, icy-cold², icy², frigid²; *ik werd
er ~ van* a chill came over me; **II** *ad* icily²;
frigidly²; **F** = *doodleuk*; **–kristal** (-len) *o* ice
crystal

'IJsland *o* Iceland; **'IJslander** (-s) *m* Icelander;
'IJslands I *aj* Icelandic; **~** *mos* Iceland moss
(lichen); **II** *o* Icelandic

'ijslolly [y = i.] ('s) *m* iced lollipop, ice lolly;
–machine [-ma.ʃi.nə] (-s) *v* freezing-machine;
–pegel (-s) *m* icicle; **–salon** (-s) *m* ice-cream
parlour, *Am* soda fountain; **–schol** (-len) *v*,
–schots (-en) *v* floe (flake) of ice, ice-floe;
–spoor (-sporen) *o* ice-spur, crampon; **–tijd**
(-en) *m* ice-age, glacial age; **–venter** (-s) *m*
ice-cream vendor; **–vlakte** (-n en -s) *v* ice-
plain, ice-field, sheet of ice; **–vogel** (-s) *m ↝*
kingfisher; **–vorming** (-en) *v* ice formation;
–vrij ice-free; **–wafel** (-s) *v* ice-cream wafer;
–water *o* iced water, ice-water; **–zak** (-ken) *m*
ice-bag, ice-pack; **–zee** (-zeeën) *v* polar sea,
frozen ocean; *de Noordelijke IJszee* the Arctic
(Ocean); *de Zuidelijke IJszee* the Antarctic
(Ocean)

'ijver *m* diligence, zeal, ardour; **'ijveraar** (-s en
-raren) *m*, **–ster** (-s) *v* zealot; **'ijveren** (ijverde,
h. geijverd) *vi* be zealous; **~** *t e g e n* declaim
against, preach down; **~** *v o o r*... be zealous for
(in the cause of)...; **–rig** diligent, industrious,
zealous, assiduous, fervent; *hij was ~ bezig aan
zijn werk* he was intent upon his work; **'ijver-
zucht** *v* jealousy, envy; **ijver'zuchtig** jealous,
envious

'ijzel *m* glazed frost; **'ijzelen** (ijzelde, h. geij-
zeld) *het ijzelt* there is a glazed frost

'ijzen (ijsde, h. geijsd) *vi* shudder; *ik ijsde er van*
it sent a shudder through me

'ijzer (-s) *o* iron [ook = branding-iron & flat-
iron for smoothing]; (v. s c h a a t s) runner; zie
ook: *hoefijzer, oorijzer; oud ~* scrap iron; *men
moet het ~ smeden als het heet is* strike the iron
while it is hot, make hay while the sun shines;
men kan geen ~ met handen breken you cannot
make a silk purse out of a sow's ear; **–achtig**
iron-like, irony; **–draad** (-draden) *o & m* (iron)
wire; **–en** *aj* iron²; **–erts** (-en) *o* iron ore;
–gaas *o* (g r o f) wire-netting, (f i j n) wire-
gauze; **–garen** *o* two-cord yarn, patent-strong
yarn; **ijzergiete'rij** (-en) *v* iron foundry,
ironworks; **'ijzerhandel** (-s) *m* iron trade,
ironmongery; **–handelaar** (-s en -laren) *m*
ironmonger; **–hard** as hard as iron, iron-hard;
–houdend containing iron, ferruginous
[earth, water]; **–hout** *o* ironwood; **–roest** *m &
o* rust (of iron); **ijzersmede'rij** (-en) *v* forge;
ijzersmelte'rij (-en) *v* iron-smelting works;
'ijzersterk strong as iron, iron; **–tijd** *m* iron
age; **–vijlsel** *o* iron filings; **–vreter** (-s) *m*
fire-eater, swashbuckler; **–waren** *mv*
hardware, ironmongery; **–werk** (-en) *o* ironwork; **–winkel** (-s) *m* ironmonger's shop

'ijzig icy; ook = *ijzingwekkend*; **ijzing'wekkend**
gruesome, appalling; ook = *ijselijk*

ik I *het* **~** the ego; *zijn eigen ~* his own self; *mijn
tweede ~* my other self; **–figuur** (-guren) *v & m*
first-person narrator [in a novel &]; **–vorm** *m
in de ~ geschreven* [novel] with a first-person
narrator

'Ilias *v* Iliad

ille'gaal underground, clandestine; **illegali'teit**
(-en) *v* resistance movement

illumi'natie [-(t)si.] (-s) *v* illumination;
illumi'neren (illumineerde, h. geïllumineerd)
vt illuminate

il'lusie [ɪˈly.zi.] (-s) *v* illusion; *iem. de ~ (zijn ~s)
benemen* disillusion(ize) sbd., rob sbd. of his
illusions; *zich geen ~s maken over* be under no
illusions about, have no illusions about;
illu'soir [i.ly.ˈzva:r, -ˈzo:r] illusory

il'luster illustrious

illu'stratie [-(t)si.] (-s) *v* illustration; **illu'strator**
(-s) *m* illustrator; **illu'strerem** (illustreerde, h.
geïllustreerd) *vt* illustrate

'image [ɪmɪdʒ] *v & o* image; **imagi'nair** [-ʒi.-
ˈnɛː r] imaginary

imbe'ciel [-be.ˈsi.l] (-en) *aj & m-v* imbecile;
imbecili'teit *v* imbecility

imi'tatie [-(t)si.] (-s) *v* imitation; **–le(d)er** *o*
imitation leather; **imi'teren** (imiteerde, h.
geïmiteerd) *vt* imitate

'imker [ˈɪmkər] (-s) *m* beekeeper, apiarist

immateri'eel immaterial, insubstantial

im'mens immense, huge

'immer ever; **–meer** ever, evermore

'immers I *ad ik heb het ~ gezien* I have seen it,
haven't I?; *hij is ~ thuis?* he is in, isn't he?; II *cj*
for; *men moet altijd zijn best doen ~ vlijt alleen
kan...* for it is only industry that...
immi'grant (-en) *m* immigrant; immi'gratie
[-(t)si.] (-s) *v* immigration; immi'greren
(immigreerde, is geïmmigreerd) *vi* immigrate
immorali'teit *v* immorality; immo'reel
immoral
immor'telle (-n) *v* immortelle, everlasting
immuni'satie [-'za.(t)si.] *v* immunization;
immuni'seren [s = z] (immuniseerde, h.
geïmmuniseerd) *vt* immunize, make (render)
immune; immuni'teit (-en) *v* immunity;
im'muun immune; ~ *maken* render immune
[from...], immunize [from...]
im'passe (-en en -s) *v* deadlock; *in een ~* at a
deadlock; *uit de ~ geraken* solve (break, end)
the deadlock
'imperatief, impera'tief I *aj* imperative; II *m
de ~* the imperative (mood)
imperi'aal (-ialen) *o* & *v* top [for passengers on
bus, coach]; roof rack [for luggage]
imperia'lisme *o* imperialism; imperia'list
(-en) *m* imperialist; -isch imperialist(ical);
im'perium (-s en -ria) *o* empire
imperti'nent impertinent, rude
impli'catie [-(t)si.] (-s) *v* implication;
impli'ceren (impliceerde, h. geïmpliceerd) *vt*
implicate, imply; impli'ciet implicit, implied
impondera'bilia *mv* imponderables
impo'neren (imponeerde, h. geïmponeerd) *vt*
impress (forcibly), awe; -d imposing, impressive
impopu'lair [-'lɛ:r] unpopular
'import (-en) *m* import(ation); impor'teren
(importeerde, h. geïmporteerd) *vt* import;
impor'teur (-s) *m* importer
impo'sant [s = z] imposing, impressive
impo'tent impotent; -ie [-(t)si.] *v* impotence
impre'sario [-prɛ'sa:ri.o.] ('s) *m* impresario
im'pressie (-s) *v* impression;
impressio'nisme *o* impressionism;
impressio'nist (-en) *m* impressionist; -isch
impressionist [painter, painting], impression-
istic
improduk'tief unproductive
improvi'satie [-'za.(t)si.] (-s) *v* improvisation,
impromptu; improvi'sator (-s en -'toren) *m*
improvisateur; improvi'seren (improviseerde,
h. geïmproviseerd) *vt* & *vi* improvise, extemporize, speak extempore; impro'viste
[ɛ̃pro.'vi.st(ə)] *à l'~* ex tempore; *à l'~ spreken*

extemporize
im'puls (-en) *m* impulsion, impulse; ℳ pulse;
impul'sief [s = z] impulsive, on impulse;
impulsivi'teit *v* impulsiveness
1 in *prep* in; into; at; on; ~ *de commissie zitting
hebben* be on the committee; ~ *Arnhem* at
Arnhem; ~ *Londen* in London; ~ *Parijs* at
Paris, in Paris; *twee plaatsen ~ een vliegtuig*
[reserve] two seats on a plane; *goed ~ talen*
good at languages; *doctor ~ de medicijnen, de
theologie* & doctor of medicine, of theology &;
60 minuten ~ het uur to the hour; [*er zijn er*] ~
de veertig forty odd; *hij is ~ de veertig* he is
turned forty; ~ *geen drie weken* not for three
weeks; *dat wil er bij mij niet ~* that won't go
down with me; *zij was ~ het zwart (gekleed)* she
was (dressed) in black, she wore black; ~ *zijn*
F 1 (in t r e k) be in; 2 (g o e d b ij) be with
it; 2 in... (in samenstellingen met *aj
o f ad*) very [~*droevig* & very sad(ly) &],
intensive(ly), deep(ly)
in ab'stracto in the abstract
in'achtneming *v* observance; *met ~ van* having
regard to, regard being had to
inaccu'raat inaccurate
'inademen¹ *vt* breathe (in), inhale, inspire;
-ming (-en) *v* breathing (in), inhalation,
inspiration, intake of breath
inade'quaat [-'kva.t] inadequate
inaugu'ratie [-(t)si.] (-s) *v* inauguration;
inaugu'reel inaugural [address];
inaugu'reren (inaugureerde, h. geïnaugu-
reerd) *vt* inaugurate
'inbaar collectable [bills, debts]
'inbakeren¹ I *vt* swaddle [an infant]; II *vr zich
~* muffle (wrap) oneself up
'inbedroefd very sad, deeply afflicted
'inbeelden (beeldde 'in, h. 'ingebeeld) *zich ~*
imagine, fancy; *zich heel wat ~* rather fancy
oneself; -ding (-en) *v* 1 imagination, fancy; 2
(v e r w a a n d h e i d) (self-)conceit
'inbegrepen = *met inbegrip van...*; *alles ~* all in,
everything included; *niet ~* exclusive of...;
'inbegrip *met ~ van* including, inclusive of
[charges], [charges] included
'inbeitelen¹ *vt* chisel, carve with a chisel
inbe'slagneming (-en) *v* 🏛 seizure, attachment
inbe'zitneming (-en) *v* taking possession [of];
-stelling (-en) *v* handing over; 🏛 delivery
'inbijten (beet 'in, is 'ingebeten) *vi* (v. z u u r)
bite into, corrode; -d corrosive
'inbinden¹ I *vt* bind [books]; *laten ~* have
[books] bound; II *vi fig* climb down

---

¹ V.T. en V.D. van dit werkwoord volgens het model: 'inademen, V.T. ademde 'in, V.D. 'ingeademd. Zie voor de
vormen onder het grondwoord, in dit voorbeeld: *ademen*. Bij sterke en onregelmatige werkwoorden wordt u
verwezen naar de lijst achterin.

'**inblazen**[1] *vt* blow into; *fig* prompt, suggest; *nieuw leven* ~ breathe new life into; **–zing** (-en) *v* prompting(s), instigation, suggestion
'**inblij** very glad, as pleased as Punch
'**inblikken** (blikte 'in, h. 'ingeblikt) *vt* can, tin
'**inboedel** (-s) *m* furniture, household effects
'**inboeken**[1] *vt* book, enter
'**inboeten** *vt veel aan invloed* ~ lose much in influence; *er het leven bij* ~ pay for it with one's life
'**inboezemen** (boezemde 'in, h. 'ingeboezemd) *vt* inspire with [courage], strike [terror] into
in '**bonis** well-to-do, in easy circumstances
'**inboorling** (-en) *m* native, aborigine
'**inborst** *v* character, nature, disposition
'**inbouwen**[1] *vt* build in, let into, fit
'**inbraak** (-braken) *v* house-breaking, burglary; **–vrij** burglar-proof
'**inbranden**[1] *vt* burn (in)
'**inbreken**[1] *vi* break into a house, commit burglary; *er is bij ons ingebroken* our house has been broken into; **–er** (-s) *m* burglar, housebreaker
'**inbreng** *m* capital brought in [to undertaking]; *fig* contribution; '**inbrengen**[1] *vt* bring in, gather in [the crops]; bring in [capital]; *je hebt hier niets in te brengen* you have nothing to say here; *daar kan ik niets tegen* ~ 1 I can offer no objection; 2 it leaves me without a reply
'**inbreuk** (-en) *v* infringement [of rights], infraction [of the law], encroachment [on rights]; ~ *maken op* infringe [the law, rights], encroach upon [rights]
'**inburgeren** (burgerde 'in, h. en is 'ingeburgerd) *hij is hier helemaal ingeburgerd* he has struck root here, he feels quite at home here; *die woorden hebben zich ingeburgerd* these words have found their way into the language
incar'**natie** [-(t)si.] (-s) *v* incarnation; incar'**neren** (incarneerde, h. geïncarneerd) *vt* incarnate
incas'**seerder** (-s) *m* collector; incas'**seren** (incasseerde, h. geïncasseerd) *vt* cash [a bill], collect [debts]; *fig* **F** take [a blow, a hiding]; incas'**sering** (-en) *v* cashing-collection; **–svermogen** *o* resilience
in'**casso** ('s) *o* collection [of bills, debts &]; **–bureau** [-by.ro.] (-s) *o* collection agency [of debts]; **–kosten** *mv* collecting-charges
in '**casu** [s = z] in this case
'**incest** *m* incest; **incestu'eus** incestuous
inci'**dent** (-en) *o* incident; **inciden'teel** incidental

in'**cluis** included; **inclu'sief** [s = z] inclusive of..., including...
in'**cognito** incognito, **F** incog
incom'**pleet** incomplete
in con'**creto** in the concrete
inconse'**quent** [-'kvɛnt] inconsistent; **–ie** [-(t)si.] (-s) *v* inconsistency
inconstitutio'**neel** [-(t)si.-] inconstitutional
inconveni'**ënt** (-en) *o* drawback
incou'**rant** [ou = u.] unsalable, unmarketable [articles]; unlisted [securities]
incu'**batie** [-(t)si.] *v* incubation; **–tijd** *m* incubation period, latent period
incu'**nabel** (-en) *m* early printed book, incunabulum
in'**dachtig** mindful of...; *wees mijner* ~ remember me
'**indammen** (damde 'in, h. 'ingedamd) *vt* embank, dam[2]
'**indampen**[1] *vt* evaporate, boil down
inde'**cent** indecent, shocking
'**indekken**[1] *zich* ~ *tegen* safeguard against
'**indelen**[1] *vt* 1 divide; (i n k l a s s e n) class(ify), group; (i n g r a d e n) graduate; 2 ⚥ incorporate (in, with *bij*); **–ling** (-en) *v* 1 division; classification, grouping; graduation; 2 ⚥ incorporation
'**indenken** *zich ergens* ~ try to realize it, think oneself into the spirit of...; *zich iets* ~ image sth., conceive sth.
inder'**daad** indeed, really; **–'haast** in a hurry, hurriedly; **–'tijd** at the time
'**indeuken**[1] *vt* dent, indent [a hat &]
'**index** (-en en -dices) *m* index, table of contents; *op de* ~ *plaatsen* place on the index; **–cijfer** (-s) *o* index figure
'**India** *o* India
Indi'**aan** (-ianen) *m* (Red) Indian; **–s** *aj* Indian
'**Indiaas** Indian
indi'**catie** [-(t)si.] (-s) *v* indication
'**Indië** *o* ⚏ 1 (British) India; 2 the (Dutch) Indies, the East Indies
in'**dien** if, in case
'**indienen**[1] *vt* present [the bill, a petition to...]; tender [one's resignation]; bring in, introduce [a bill, a motion]; move [an address]; lodge [a complaint]; make [a protest]; **–ning** *v* presentation [of a petition &]; introduction [of a bill in Parliament]
in'**diensttreding** *v* entrance upon one's duties; ~ *1 juli* duties (to) commence on July 1
'**Indiër** (-s) *m* Indian
indi'**gestie** *v* indigestion

[1] V.T. en V.D. van dit werkwoord volgens het model: '**inademen**, V.T. ademde '**in**, V.D. '**ingeademd**. Zie voor de vormen onder het grondwoord, in dit voorbeeld: *ademen*. Bij sterke en onregelmatige werkwoorden wordt u verwezen naar de lijst achterin.

'**indigo** *m* indigo; **–blauw** indigo-blue

'**indijken** (dijkte '**in**, h. 'ingedijkt) *vt* dike, dike (dam) in, embank; **–king** (-en) *v* diking, embankment

'**indikken** (dikte '**in**, *vt* h., *vi* is 'ingedikt) *vt* & *vi* thicken, concentrate

'**indirect** indirect, oblique

'**Indisch** Indian

indis'**creet** indiscreet; **indis'cretie** [-(t)si.] (-s) *v* indiscretion

indivi'**du** (-en en 's) *o* individual; *een verdacht ~* a shady character; **individuali'teit** *v* individuality; **individu'eel** individual

'**Indo** ('s) *m* Eurasian, half-caste

Indo-'China [-'ʃi.-] *o* Indo-China

indoctri'**natie** [-(t)si.] *v* indoctrination; **indoctri'neren** (indoctrineerde, h. geïndoctrineerd) *vt* indoctrinate

Indo-europe'aan (-eanen) *m* 1 (I n d o g e r-m a a n) Indo-European; 2 (h a l f b l o e d) Eurasian; **Indo-euro'pees** 1 (I n d o g e r m.) Indo-European; 2 (v. g e m e n g d b l o e d) Eurasian; **Indoger'maan** (-manen) *m* Indo-European; **–s** *aj* & *o* Indo-Germanic

indo'**lent** indolent; **–ie** [-(t)si.] *v* indolence

'**indommelen** (dommelde '**in**, is 'ingedommeld) *vi = indutten*

'**indompelen**[1] *vt* plunge in, dip in, immerse; **–ling** *v* immersion

Indo'nesië [s = z] *o* Indonesia; **Indo'nesiër** (-s) *m*, **Indo'nesisch** *aj* Indonesian

'**indopen**[1] *vt* dip in(to)

'**indraaien**[1] *vt* screw in; *zich ergens ~* worm oneself into a post

'**indrijven**[1] **I** *vt* drive into; **II** *vi* float into

'**indringen**[1] **I** *vt* penetrate (into), enter by force; **II** *vr zich ~* intrude, **S** horn in [on]; *zich ~ bij iem.* 1 obtrude oneself upon sbd. (upon sbd.'s company); 2 insinuate onself into sbd.'s favour; **in'dringend** *fig* profound; emphatic; '**indringer** (-s) *m* intruder; **in'dringerig** intrusive, obtrusive

'**indrinken**[1] *vt* drink (in), imbibe

'**indroevig** intensely sad, heart-breaking

'**indrogen**[1] *vi* dry up

'**indroppelen** = *indruppelen*

'**indruisen** (druiste '**in**, h. en is 'ingedruist) *vi ~ tegen* run counter to [all conventions], interfere with [one's interests], clash with [a previous statement], be at variance with [truth], be contrary to [laws, customs &]

'**indruk** (-ken) *m* impression[2]; imprint; *~ maken* make an impression; *de ~ maken van...* give an

impression of...; *onder de ~ komen* be impressed (by, with *van*); *hij was nog onder de ~* he had not got over it yet; '**indrukken**[1] *vt* push in, stave in [something]; impress, imprint [a seal &];

indruk'wekkend impressive, imposing

'**indruppelen**[1] **I** *vi* drip in; **II** *vt* drip in, instil

in '**dubio** in doubt

indu'**ceren** (induceerde, h. geïnduceerd) *vt* induce; **in'ductie** [ɪn'dʉksi.] (-s) *v* induction; **induc'tief** inductive; **in'ductieklos** (-sen) *m* & *v* induction coil; **–stroom** (-stromen) *m* induced current; **in'ductor** (-'toren) *m* inductor

industriali'**satie** [-'za.(t)si.] *v* industrialization; **industriali'seren** [s = z] (industrialiseerde, h. geïndustrialiseerd) *vt* industrialize; **–ring** *v* industrialization

indus'**trie** (-trieën) *v* industry; **–arbeider** (-s) *m* industrial worker; **–centrum** (-s en -tra) *o* industrial centre; **–diamant** (-en) *m* & *o* industrial diamond; **industri'eel I** *aj* industrial; **II** (-iëlen) *m* industrialist, manufacturer; **indus'triegebied** (-en) *o* industrial area; **–school** (-scholen) *v* technical school; **–stad** (-steden) *v* industrial town; **–terrein** (-en) *o* industrial site; industrial estate

'**indutten** (dutte '**in**, is 'ingedut) *vi* doze off, drop off, go to sleep

'**induwen**[1] *vt* push in, push into, shove in

in'**eendraaien**[2] *vt* twist together; **–frommelen**[2] *vt* crumple up; **–gedoken** zie *duiken*; **–grijpen**[2] *vi* interlock; **–krimpen**[2] *vi* writhe, shrink, cringe; **–kronkelen**[2] *zich ~* coil up, curl up; **–lopen**[2] *vi* run into each other [of colours]; communicate [of rooms]

in'**eens** all at once; *~ te betalen* payable in one sum

in'**eenschuiven**[2] *vt* telescope (into each other); **–slaan**[2] *vt* strike together; zie ook: *hand*; **–storten**[2] *vt* collapse[2]; **–storting** (-en) *v* collapse[2]; **–strengelen**[2] *vt* intertwine, interlace; **–vloeien**[2] *vi* flow together, run into each other [of colours]; **–zakken**[2] *vi* collapse

'**inenten**[1] *vt* vaccinate, inoculate; **–ting** (-en) *v* [smallpox] vaccination, [yellow fever] inoculation

in'**faam** infamous

'**infanterie, infante'rie** *v* infantry, foot; **infante'rist** (-en) *m* infantryman

infan'**tiel** infantile; **infanti'lisme** *o* infantilism

in'**farct** (-en) *o* (cardiac) infarct

infec'**teren** (infecteerde, h. geïnfecteerd) *vt* infect[2]; **in'fectie** [-'fɛksi.] (-s) *v* infection[2];

–**haard** (-en) *m* focus of infection; –**ziekte** (-n en -s) *v* infectious disease

inferi'eur *aj* inferior (= lower in rank & of poor quality); *een ~e* one of inferior rank, an inferior, a subordinate; **inferiori'teit** *v* inferiority

infil'trant (-en) *m* infiltrator; **infil'tratie** [-(t)si.] (-s) *v* infiltration; **infil'treren** (infiltreerde, *vt* h., *vi* is geïnfiltreerd) *vi* & *vt* infiltrate

'**infinitief** (-tieven) *m* infinitive

in'flatie [-(t)si.] (-s) *v* inflation; **infla'toir** [-'tʋaːr of -'toːr] inflationary

influen'ceren [-fly.ɑn-] (influenceerde, h. geïnfluenceerd) *vt* influence, affect

influ'enza *v* influenza, **F** flu

'**influisteren**[1] *vt* whisper [in sbd.'s ear], prompt, suggest; –**ring** (-en) *v* whispering, prompting, suggestion

infor'mant (-en) *m* informant; **infor'matie** [-(t)si.] (-s en -tiën) *v* 1 information; 2 inquiry; *~s geven* give information; *~s inwinnen* make inquiries; –**bureau** [-by.ro.] (-s) *o* inquiry-office, information bureau (centre); **informa'tief** informative; **infor'matiever-werking** *v* data processing; **informa'trice** (-s) *v* inquiry clerk; (t e l e f.) information operator

infor'meel informal, unofficial

infor'meren (informeerde, h. geïnformeerd) *vt* inquire [after it], make inquiry (inquiries) [about it]; *~ bij* inquire of [sbd.]

'**infrarood** infra-red

'**infrastructuur** *v* infrastructure

in'fusiediertjes [s = z] *mv* infusoria

'**ingaan**[1] **I** *vi* enter, go (walk) into; *dat artikel zal er wel ~* **F** is sure to catch (take) on; (v. v a k a n t i e, a b o n n e m e n t &) begin; (v a n k r a c h t w o r d e n) date (take effect, run) from; *(dieper) ~ o p iets* go into the subject, labour a point; *nader ~ op* go further into the matter; *op een aanbod ~* take up an offer; *op een offerte ~* entertain an offer; *op een verzoek ~* comply with (grant) a request; *er niet op ~* take no notice of it, make no comment, let it pass, ignore it; *~ t e g e n* 1 zie *indruisen*; 2 (z i c h v e r z e t t e n) oppose, counter-act, go against; **II** *vt* enter; *de eeuwigheid ~* pass into eternity; *zijn zeventigste jaar ~* enter upon one's seventieth year; *de geschiedenis ~* go down in history; *de wijde wereld ~* go out into the world

'**ingang** (-en) *m* entrance, way in, entry; *~ vinden* find acceptance, **F** go down (with the public); *met ~ van 6 sept.* (as) from Sept. 6

'**ingebeeld** 1 imaginary; 2 (v e r w a a n d)

(self-)conceited, pretentious, presumptuous; *~e zieke (ziekte)* imaginary invalid (illness)

'**ingeblikt** tinned, *Am* canned [fruit]; canned [sound]

'**ingeboren** innate, native

'**ingebouwd** built-in, fitted; installed, mounted

inge'brekestelling *v* notice of default, prompt note

'**ingehouden** subdued, restrained [force], pent-up [rage]; *met ~ adem* with bated breath

'**ingekankerd** inveterate [hatred]

'**ingelegd** 1 inlaid, tessellated, mosaic [floors, table]; 2 = *ingemaakt*

'**ingemaakt** preserved, potted [foods, vegetables], pickled [pork]

'**ingemeen** vile

'**ingenaaid** (v. b o e k) stitched, sewn; *~ etiket* sewed-in label

ingeni'eur [ɪnʒənˈjøːr, ɪnʒe.-] (-s) *m* engineer

ingenieus [-ʒe.ni.ˈøs] ingenious

'**ingenomen** taken; *~ met iets zijn* be taken with sth.; *ik ben er erg mee ~* I am highly pleased with it; *hij is zeer met zichzelf ~* he rather fancies himself; **inge'nomenheid** *v* satisfaction; *~ met zichzelf* self-complacency

ingé'nue [ɛ̃ʒe.ˈny.] (-s) *v* ingenue

'**ingeroest** *fig* inveterate, deep-rooted

'**ingeschreven** inscribed; *~ leerlingen* pupils on the books (on the rolls); *~ veelhoeken* inscribed polygons; *~e* entrant

'**ingesloten** enclosed; zie ook: *inbegrepen*

'**ingesneden** indented [coast-line]

'**ingespannen I** *aj* strenuous [work]; hard [thinking]; intent [gaze]; **II** *ad* strenuously [working]; [think] hard; intently [listening, looking at]; *goed ~ zijn* be well set-up, have all that is necessary

'**ingetogen** modest; **inge'togenheid** *v* modesty

inge'val in case

'**ingevallen** hollow [cheeks], sunken [eyes]

'**ingeven**[1] *vt* administer [medicine]; *fig* prompt, suggest [a thought, a word]; inspire with [an idea, hope &], dictate [by fear]; –**ving** (-en) *v* prompting, suggestion, inspiration; *plotselinge ~* brainwave; *als b ij ~* as if by inspiration; *n a a r de ~ van het ogenblik handelen* act on the spur of the moment

'**ingevoerd** *goed ~* well established [salesman]

inge'volge in pursuance of, pursuant to, in compliance with, in obedience to

'**ingevroren** ice-bound, frost-bound, frozen in

'**ingewand(en)** *o* (*mv*) bowels, intestines, entrails

---

[1] V.T. en V.D. van dit werkwoord volgens het model: '**in**ademen, V.T. ademde '**in**, V.D. '**in**geademd. Zie voor de vormen onder het grondwoord, in dit voorbeeld: *ademen*. Bij sterke en onregelmatige werkwoorden wordt u verwezen naar de lijst achterin.

'ingewijd initiated; *een ~e* an initiate, an insider
inge'wikkeld intricate, complicated [arrangements, machinery]; complex; sophisticated [machines]; **–heid** *v* intricacy, complexity
'ingeworteld deep-rooted, inveterate
'ingezet set-in, put-in, inserted
'ingezetene (-n) *m-v* inhabitant, resident
'ingezonden sent in; *~ mededeling* paragraph advertisement; *~ stuk* letter to the editor (to the press)
'ingieten[1] *vt* pour in, infuse
'ingooi (-en) *m sp* throw in; 'ingooien[1] *vt de ruiten ~* smash (break) the windows; zie ook: *glas*
'ingraven[1] *zich ~* ✄ dig (oneself) in; burrow [of a rabbit]
ingredi'ënt (-en) *o* ingredient
'ingreep (-grepen) *m* ✚ operation, surgery
'ingriffen[1] *vt* engrave
'ingrijpen[1] *vi* intervene; **in'grijpend** radical, far-reaching [change]
'ingroeien[1] *vi* grow in (into)
'inhaalmanœuvre [-ma.nø.vɔr] (-s) *v* passing (overtaking) manœuvre; **–strook** (-stroken) *v* overtaking lane; **–verbod** (-boden) *o* overtaking prohibition
'inhaken[1] *vi* hook in(to); link [arms]; *~op* go on from what was said before, follow up (take up) a point
'inhakken[1] **I** *vt* hew in, break open; **II** *vi op de vijand ~* pitch into the enemy; *dat zal er ~* it will run into a lot of money
inha'latie [-(t)si.] (-s) *v* inhalation; **–toestel** (-len) *o* inhaler
'inhalen[1] *vt* 1 (n a a r b i n n e n t r e k k e n) take in [sails]; haul in [a rope]; get in, gather in [crops]; inhale [smoke, air]; 2 (b i n n e n - h a l e n) receive in state [a prince &]; 3 (a c h t e r h a l e n) come up with, overtake, catch up[2]; ⚓ overhaul; 4 (b ij w e r k e n) make up for [lost time]; *de achterstand ~* make up arrears, make up leeway; *~ verboden* ⛔ no overtaking
inha'leren (inhaleerde, h. geïnhaleerd) *vt & va* inhale
in'halig greedy, grasping, covetous; **–heid** *v* greed, covetousness
'inham (-men) *m* creek, bay, bight, inlet
'inhameren[1] *vt* hammer in, hammer home
'inhebben[1] *vt* hold, contain, ⚓ carry
in'hechtenisneming (-en) *v* apprehension, arrest; *bevel tot ~* warrant
in'heems native, indigenous [population,

products], home-bred [cattle], home [produce, market], endemic [diseases]
'inheien[1] *vt* drive in [piles]
inhe'rent [-he:-] inherent; *~ zijn aan* inhere in
'inhoud (-en) *m* contents [of a book &]; tenor, purport [of a letter]; content [of a cube], capacity [of a vessel]; *korte ~* abstract, summary; *een brief van de volgende ~* ook: to the following effect; **in'houdelijk** in substance, in content(s); 'inhouden[1] **I** *vt* 1 (b e v a t t e n) contain, hold; 2 (t e g e n h o u d e n) hold in, rein in [a horse]; hold [one's breath]; check, restrain, keep back [one's anger, tears]; retain [food]; 3 (a f h o u d e n) deduct [a month's salary], stop [allowance, pocket-money]; *dit houdt niet in, dat...* this does not imply that...; *de pas ~* step short; **II** *vr zich ~* contain (restrain) oneself; zie ook *ingehouden*; **–ding** (-en) *v* retention [of food]; stoppage [of wages], deduction [of salary]; 'inhoudsmaat (-maten) *v* measure of capacity, cubic measure; **–opgaaf**, **–opgave** (-gaven) *v* table of contents, contents table, contents list
'inhouwen[1] *vt & vi = inhakken*
'inhuldigen[1] *vt* inaugurate, install; **–ging** (-en) *v* inauguration, installation
inhu'maan inhumane
'inhuren[1] *vt* hire again; *opnieuw ~* renew the lease
initi'aal [-(t)si.-] (-ialen) *v* initial
initi'atie [-(t)si.'a(t)si.] (-s) *v* initiation
initia'tief [-(t)si.a.-] (-tieven) *o* initiative; *het particulier ~* private enterprise; *geen ~ hebben* be lacking initiative; *het ~ nemen* take the initiative (the lead); *op ~ van* at (on) the initiative of; *op eigen ~ handelen* act on one's own initiative (of one's own accord)
initi'eel [-(t)si.-] initial [costs]
'injagen[1] *vt* drive in(to); *iem. de dood ~* send sbd. to his death
in'jectie [-'jɛksi.] (-s) *v* injection; **–motor** (-s en -toren) *m* (fuel) injection engine; **–naald** (-en) *v* hypodermic needle; **–spuitje** (-s) *o* hypodermic syringe
'inkankeren[1] *vi* eat into, corrode; become inveterate; zie ook: *ingekankerd*
'inkapselen (kapselde 'in, h. 'ingekapseld) *vt* encyst, encapsulate[2]
'inkeer *m* repentance; *tot ~ komen* repent
'inkepen[1] *vt* indent, notch, nick; **–ping** (-en) *v* indentation, notch, nick
'inkeren[1] *vi tot zich zelf ~* retire into oneself; search one's own heart; repent

---

[1] V.T. en V.D. van dit werkwoord volgens het model: 'inademen, V.T. ademde 'in, V.D. 'ingeademd. Zie voor de vormen onder het grondwoord, in dit voorbeeld: *ademen*. Bij sterke en onregelmatige werkwoorden wordt u verwezen naar de lijst achterin.

'**inkerven**[1] *vt* = *inkepen*
'**inkijk** *m* view, glimpse [into]; '**inkijken**[1] **I** *vi* look in [at the window]; *mag ik bij u ~?* may I look on with you?; **II** *vt* glance over [a letter], browse through (look into) [a book]
'**inklaren**[1] *vt* $ clear [goods]; **–ring** (-en) *v* $ clearance, clearing
'**inkleden**[1] *vt* 1 clothe² [ook = word]; 2 *rk* give the habit to [a postulant]
'**inklemmen**[1] *vt* jam in, wedge in
'**inklimmen**[1] *vi* climb in(to)
'**inklinken** (klonk 'in, is 'ingeklonken) *vi* set
'**inkoken** (kookte 'in, *vt* h., *vi* is 'ingekookt) *vt* & *vi* boil down
'**inkomen**[1] **I** *vi* enter, come in; *~de rechten* import duties; *daar kan ik ~* I can understand that (enter into your feelings), I can see that; *daar komt niets van in* that's out of the question altogether; **II** (-s) *o* income; **–klasse** (-n) *v* income bracket (group); '**inkomensgroep** (-en) *v* income group; **–politiek** *v* income policy
'**inkomst** (-en) *v* entry; *~en* income [of a person], earnings, gainings, profits; revenue [of a State]; *~en en uitgaven* receipts and expenditure; **–enbelasting** (-en) *v* income tax
'**inkoop** (-kopen) *m* purchase; *inkopen doen* make purchases, buy things; go (be) shopping; **–organisatie** [-za.(t)si.] (-s) *v* buying organization; **–(s)prijs** (-prijzen) *m* cost price; '**inkopen**[1] **I** *vt* 1 buy, purchase; 2 (t e r u g - k o p e n) buy in; **II** *vr zich ~* (*in een zaak*) buy oneself into a business; **–er** (-s) *m* purchaser, $ buyer [for business house]
'**inkoppen**[1] *vt* head home [a ball]
'**inkorten**[1] *vt* shorten, curtail; **–ting** (-en) *v* shortening, curtailment
'**in krijgen**[1] *vt* get in; *ik kon niets ~* I could not get down a morsel; zie ook: *water*
'**inkrimpen**[1] **I** *vi* shrink; contract; *het getal... was ingekrompen tot...* had dwindled to...; **II** *vt* (p e r s o n e e l, p r o d u k t i e &) reduce, cut back; **III** *vr zich ~* retrench (curtail) one's expenses; **–ping** (-en) *v* shrinking [of bodies]; contraction [of credit]; dwindling [of numbers]; reduction; curtailment, retrenchment
'**inkt** (-en) *m* ink; *Oostindische ~* Indian ink; '**inkten** (inktte, h. geïnkt) *vt* ink; '**inktfles** (-sen) *v* ink-bottle; **–gom** *m* & *o* ink-eraser; **–koker** (-s) *m* inkstand, ink-well; **–lap** (-pen) *m* penwiper; **–lint** (-en) *o* ink ribbon; **–pot** (-ten) *m* inkpot, ink-well; **–potlood** (-loden) *o*

copying-pencil, indelible pencil; **–stel** (-len) *o* inkstand; **–vis** (-sen) *m* ꩜. ink-fish, cuttle-fish, squid; **–vlek** (-ken) *v* blot of ink, ink-stain
'**inkuilen** (kuilde 'in, h. 'ingekuild) *vt* ensilage, ensile, clamp [potatoes]
'**inkwartieren** (kwartierde 'in, h. 'ingekwartierd) *vt* billet, quarter; **–ring** (-en) *v* billeting, quartering; *wij hebben ~* we have soldiers billeted on us
'**inlaat** (-laten) *m* inlet; **–klep** (-pen) *v* inlet valve
'**inladen**[1] *vt* 1 load [goods]; ⚓ put on board; ship [goods]; 2 ⚒ entrain [soldiers]
'**inlander** (-s) *m* native; '**inlands** home, home-grown, home-made [products], home-bred [cattle]; native, indigenous [tribes]; *een ~e* a native woman
'**inlas** (-sen) *m* insert; '**inlassen**[1] *vt* insert, intercalate; **–sing** (-en) *v* insertion, intercalation
'**inlaten**[1] **I** *vt* let in, admit; **II** *vr zich ~ met iem.* associate with sbd., have dealings with sbd.; *ik wil er mij niet mee ~* I will have nothing to do with it; *u hoeft u niet met mijn zaken in te laten* you need not concern yourself with (in) my affairs
'**inleg** *m* 1 (v. r o k) tuck; 2 (a a n g e l d) entrance money [of member]; stake(s) [wagered]; deposit [in a bank]; **–geld** (-en) *o* = *inleg* 2; '**inleggen**[1] *vt* lay in, put in [something]; inlay [wood with ivory &]; preserve [fruit &]; pickle [pork]; deposit [money at a bank]; stake [at cards &]; put on [an extra train]; take in [a dress]; zie ook: *eer*; **–er** (-s) *m* depositor; '**inlegvel** (-len) *o* inset, insert, supplementary sheet; **–werk** *o* inlaid work, marquetry, mosaic
'**inleiden**[1] *vt* introduce, usher in [a person]; open [the subject]; **–d** introductory, opening, preliminary; '**inleider** (-s) *m* speaker appointed (invited) to introduce the discussion (to open the subject), lecturer of the evening; '**inleiding** (-en) *v* introduction; introductory lecture; preamble, exordium
'**inleven**[1] *vr zich in iem. ~* put oneself in sbd.'s shoes, imagine oneself in another (someone else's) situation
'**inleveren**[1] *vt* deliver up [arms]; send in, give in, hand in [documents]; give in [their exercises]; **–ring** *v* delivery; giving in, handing in
'**inlichten** (lichtte 'in, h. 'ingelicht) *vt* inform; *~ over* (*omtrent*) give information about; '**inlichting** (-en) *v* information; *~en geven* give

---

[1] V.T. en V.D. van dit werkwoord volgens het model: '**in**ademen, V.T. ademde 'in, V.D. 'in**ge**ademd. Zie voor de vormen onder het grondwoord, in dit voorbeeld: *ademen*. Bij sterke en onregelmatige werkwoorden wordt u verwezen naar de lijst achterin.

information; ~en inwinnen gather information, make inquiries; ~en krijgen get (obtain) information; –endienst (-en) m intelligence service

'inliggend enclosed

'inlijsten¹ vt frame

'inlijven (lijfde 'in, h. 'ingelijfd) vt incorporate (in, with bij); annex (to bij); –ving (-en) v incorporation; annexation

'inloodsen¹ vt pilot in [a ship], take [a ship] into port

'inlopen¹ I vi 1 (i n g a a n) enter, walk into [a house]; turn into [a street]; drop in [(up)on sbd. bij iem.]; 2 (i n h a l e n, w i n n e n) gain (on op); hij zal er niet ~ he is not going to walk into the trap; iem. er laten ~ fool sbd., take sbd. in; hij wilde me er laten ~ he wanted to catch me; II vt de achterstand ~ 1 make up arrears; 2 sp gain on one's competitors; een motor ~ ✗ run in an engine; schoenen ~ break in shoes

'inlossen¹ vt redeem; –sing (-en) v redemption

'inluiden¹ vt ring in²; herald (usher in) [a new era]

'inluizen (luisde 'in, vi is, vt h. 'ingeluisd) I vi F erin luizen walk into a trap, get caught straight, be the dupe; II vt iem. ergens ~ double-cross sbd., betray sbd.

'inmaak m preservation; onze ~ our preserves; –fles (-sen) v preserving-bottle; –pot (-ten) m preserving-jar; 'inmaken¹ vt 1 preserve, pickle [pork]; 2 sp overwhelm [by 5 goals to 0]

'inmenging (-en) v meddling, interference, intervention

'inmetselen¹ vt wall up, immure

in 'middels in the meantime, meanwhile

'innaaien¹ vt sew, stitch [books]

'inname v taking, capture [of a town]; 'innemen¹ vt 1 (n a a r b i n n e n h a l e n) take in [chairs, cargo, sails &]; ship [the oars]; 2 (n e m e n, g e b r u i k e n) take [physic, poison]; 3 (b e s l a a n) take (up), occupy [space, place]; 4 (v e r o v e r e n) ✗ take, capture [a town]; fig captivate, charm; 5 (o p z a m e l e n) collect [tickets]; 6 (i n n a a i e n) take in [a garment]; brandstof (benzine) ~ fuel, fill up; kolen ~ bunker, coal; water ~ water; de mensen tegen zich ~ prejudice people against oneself, antagonize people; de mensen voor zich ~ prepossess people in one's favour; zie ook: ingenomen; in 'nemend taking, winning, prepossessing, engaging, attractive, endearing [ways]; ~ zijn have a way with one; –heid v charm, endearing ways; 'inneming (-en) v taking, capture [of a town]

'innen (inde, h. geïnd) vt collect [debts, bills], cash [a cheque], get in [debts]; te ~ wissel bill receivable

'innerlijk I aj inner [life], inward [conviction], internal [feelings], intrinsic [value]; II ad inwardly; internally

'innig I aj heartfelt [thanks, words], tender [love], close [co-operation, friendship], earnest, fervent; II ad [love] tenderly, dearly; closely [connected], earnestly, fervently; –heid v heartfelt affection, tenderness, earnestness, fervour

'inning v collection [of debts, bills], cashing [of a cheque]; –skosten mv collecting-charges

'inoogsten¹ vt reap²

'inpakken¹ I vt pack (up), wrap up, parcel up; zal ik het voor u ~? shall I wrap it up (do it up) for you?; II vr zich ~ wrap (oneself) up; III va pack; hij kan wel ~ F he can hop it (pack off)

'inpalmen (palmde 'in, h. 'ingepalmd) vt haul in [a rope]; fig appropriate [sth.]; iem. ~ get round sbd.

'inpassen¹ vt fit in, fit [conditions] into [the framework of a treaty]

'inpeperen¹ vt ik zal het hem ~ I'll make him pay for it, I'll take it out of him

'inperken (perkte 'in, h. 'ingeperkt) vt 1 fence in; 2 restrict

in 'petto in reserve, in store, up one's sleeve

'inpikken¹ vt F (z i c h m e e s t e r m a k e n v a n) pinch; 2 (k l a a r s p e l e n) het (iets) ~ set about it, manage it

'inplakken¹ vt paste in

'inplanten¹ vt implant², fig inculcate; –ting (-en) v implantation², fig inculcation

in 'pleno plenary [session]

'inpolderen (polderde 'in, h. 'ingepolderd) vt reclaim; –ring (-en) v reclamation

'inpompen¹ vt pump into; lessen ~ cram (lessons)

'inprenten (prentte 'in, h. 'ingeprent) vt imprint, impress, stamp, inculcate [sth.] on [sbd.]

'inproppen¹ vt cram in(to)

inquisi'teur [ɪŋkʋi.zi.'tøː r] (-s) m inquisitor; inqui'sitie [-'zi.(t)si.] v inquisition

'inregenen¹ vi rain in

'inreisvisum [-züm] (-s en -sa) o entry visa

'inrekenen¹ vt run in [a drunken man]

'inrichten¹ I vt 1 (r e g e l e n) arrange; 2 (m e u b i l e r e n) fit up, furnish; ingericht als... fitted up as a... [bedroom &]; een goed ingericht huis a well-appointed home; bent u al ingericht?

---

¹ V.T. en V.D. van dit werkwoord volgens het model: 'inademen, V.T. ademde 'in, V.D. 'ingeademd. Zie voor de vormen onder het grondwoord, in dit voorbeeld: ademen. Bij sterke en onregelmatige werkwoorden wordt u verwezen naar de lijst achterin.

are you settled in yet?; **II** *vr zich* ~ furnish one's house, set up house; **–ting** (-en) *v* 1 (r e g e l i n g) arrangement; lay-out; 2 (m e u b i l e r i n g) furnishing, fitting up; 3 (m e u b e l s) furniture; 4 (s t i c h t i n g, i n s t e l l i n g) establishment, institution; 5 ✗ apparatus, appliance, device

'inrijden[1] **I** *vt* ride (drive) into [a town]; break in [a horse]; ✗ run in [a motor-car]; **II** *vi* ~ *op* run into, crash into [another train]; *op elkaar* ~ collide

'inrit (-ten) *m* way in, entrance; *verboden* ~! no entry!

'inroepen[1] *vt* invoke, call in [sbd.'s help]

'inroesten[1] *vi* rust; zie ook: *ingeroest*

'inruil *m* (v a n g e b r u i k t v o o r n i e u w) trade-in, part-exchange; **'inruilen**[1] *vt* exchange [for...]; (v a n g e b r u i k t v o o r n i e u w) trade in [one's car]; **'inruilwaarde** *v* trade-in value

'inruimen[1] *vt plaats* ~ make room (for)

'inrukken[1] **I** *vt* ✗ march into [a town]; **II** *vi* ✗ march back to barracks; (v. b r a n d w e e r &) withdraw; *laten* ~ ✗ dismiss; *ingerukt mars!* ✗ dismiss!; *ruk in!* **S** hop it!

'inschakelen[1] **I** *vt* ✗ throw into gear; ⚡ switch on, (d o o r s t e k k e r) plug in [a radiator &]; *fig* bring in [workers], call in [a detective &], include [in the Government]; **II** *va* ⚙ let in the clutch

'inschenken[1] *vt & vi* pour (out) [tea &]; fill [a glass]

'inschepen (scheepte 'in, h. 'ingescheept) **I** *vt* embark, ship; **II** *vr zich* ~ (*naar*) embark, take ship (for); **–ping** *v* embarkation, embarking

'inscherpen[1] *vt iem. iets* ~ inculcate, impress sth. upon sbd.

'inscheuren[1] *vt & vi* tear; ⚡ *vi* rupture

'inschieten[1] *vt* dash into [a house]; *er geld bij* ~ lose money over it; *er het leven bij* ~ lose one's life in the affair; *dat moest er bij* ~ there was no time left for it

in'schikkelijk obliging, compliant, complaisant, accommodating; **–heid** *v* obligingness, complaisance, compliance; **'inschikken**[1] *vi* close up, sit or stand closer

'inschoppen[1] kick in [a door]; job sbd. [into a well-paid place]; *de wereld* ~ **F** spawn

'inschrift (-en) *o* inscription

'inschrijfgeld (-en) *o* registration fee; **'inschrijven** **I** *vt* inscribe; book, enrol(l), register [items, names &]; enter [names, students, horses]; *zich laten* ~ enrol(l) oneself,

enter one's name; **II** *vi* send in a tender; ~ *o p aandelen* apply for shares; ~ *op een lening* subscribe to a loan; *v o o r de bouw van een nieuwe school* ~ tender for a new school; **–er** (-s) *m* subscriber [to a charity, a loan &]; applicant [for shares]; tenderer; *laagste* ~ holder of the lowest tender; **'inschrijving** (-en) *v* 1 enrolment, registration [of names &]; 2 (v o o r t e n t o o n s t e l l i n g &) entry; 3 (o p l e n i n g &) subscription; 4 (o p a a n d e l e n) application; 5 (b ij a a n b e s t e d i n g) (public) tender; *de* ~ *openen* call for tenders; *bij* ~ *bij* ~ by tender; **–sbiljet** (-ten) *o* 1 tender [for a work]; 2 $ form of application

'inschuiven[1] **I** *vt* push in, shove in; **II** *vi* = *inschikken*

in'scriptie [-'skrɪpsi.] (-s) *v* inscription

in'sekt (-en) *o* insect; **in'sektenkunde** *v* entomology, insectology; **–poeder** *o & m* insect powder; **insekti'cide** (-n) *v* insecticide, pesticide

insemi'natie [-(t)si.] *v kunstmatige* ~ artificial insemination

insge'lijks likewise, in the same manner; *het beste met u! Insgelijks!* (the) same to you!

in'signe [ɪn'si.ɲə] (-s) *o* badge; *de* ~*s*, ook: the insignia (of office)

'insijpelen[1] *vi* trickle in, filter in

insinu'atie [-(t)si.] (-s) *v* insinuation, innuendo; **insinu'eren** (insinueerde, h. geïnsinueerd) *vt* insinuate

'inslaan[1] **I** *vt* 1 (s l a a n i n...) drive in [a nail, a pole]; 2 (s t u k s l a a n) beat in, dash in, smash [the windows]; 3 (o p d o e n) lay in (up) [provisions]; 4 (n e m e n) take, turn into [a road]; *een vat de bodem* ~ stave in a cask; zie ook: *bodem*; *iem. de hersens* ~ knock sbd.'s brains out; **II** *vi* 1 (v. b l i k s e m, p r o j e c t i e l) strike; 2 *fig* (i n d r u k m a k e n) go home [of a remark, speech &]; make a hit [of a play &];

'inslag (-slagen) *m* 1 woof; zie ook: *schering*; 2 ✗ (v a n p r o j e c t i e l) striking; 3 *fig* tendency, strain [of mysticism], [her strong practical] streak

'inslapen (sliep 'in, is 'ingeslapen) *vi* fall asleep; *fig* pass away

'inslikken[1] *vt* swallow

'insluimeren (sluimerde 'in, is 'ingesluimerd) *vi* fall into a slumber, doze off

'insluipen[1] *vi* steal in, sneak in; *fig* slip in, creep in; **–ping** *v* stealing in

'insluiten[1] *vt* lock in [oneself, sbd.], lock up [a thief]; enclose [a meadow, a letter]; hem in,

---

[1] V.T. en V.D. van dit werkwoord volgens het model: **'in**ademen, V.T. ademde **'in**, V.D. **'in**geademd. Zie voor de vormen onder het grondwoord, in dit voorbeeld: *ademen*. Bij sterke en onregelmatige werkwoorden wordt u verwezen naar de lijst achterin.

surround [a field &]; invest [a town]; include, involve, comprise, embrace [the costs for..., everything]; *dit sluit niet in, dat...* this does not imply that...; **–ting** (-en) *v* enclosure, investment; inclusion

'**inslurpen**[1] *vt* gulp down

'**insmeren**[1] *vt* grease, smear, oil

'**insmijten**[1] *vt* throw in, smash, break

'**insneeuwen** (sneeuwde 'in, is 'ingesneeuwd) *vi* snow in; *ingesneeuwd zijn* be snowed up, be snow-bound

'**insnijden**[1] *vt* cut into, incise; **–ding** (-en) *v* 1 incision [with a lancet]; 2 indentation [of the coast-line]

'**insnoeren**[1] *vt* constrict

'**insnuiven**[1] *vt* sniff in, inhale

insol'**vent** insolvent; **–ie** [-(t)si.] *v* insolvency

'**inspannen**[1] I *vt* put [the horses] to; *fig* exert [one's strength]; strain [every nerve]; II *vr zich* ~ exert oneself, endeavour, do one's utmost [to do sth.]; **in'spannend** strenuous [work]; '**inspanning** (-en) *v* exertion; effort; *met ~ van alle krachten* using every effort

in 'spe prospective, ...to-be

inspeci'**ënt** [-spe.si.'ɛnt] (-en) *m* stage manager

inspec'**teren** (inspecteerde, h. geïnspecteerd) *vt* inspect; **inspec'teur** (-s) *m* inspector; in'**spectie** [-'spɛksi.] (-s) *v* inspection; **–reis** (-reizen) *v* tour of inspection; **inspec'trice** (-s) *v* woman inspector, inspectress

'**inspelen**[1] I *vt* play in [an instrument]; II *vi sp* warm up; *op elkaar ingespeeld raken* get used to each other's ways

inspici'**ënt** [-spi.si.'ɛnt] (-en) *m* = *inspeciënt*

inspi'**ratie** [-(t)si.] (-s) *v* inspiration; inspi'**reren** (inspireerde, h. geïnspireerd) *vt* inspire

'**inspraak** *v* 1 dictate, dictates [of the heart]; 2 input, consultation; '**inspreken**[1] *vt moed ~* inspire with courage, hearten

'**inspringen**[1] *vi* 1 (v. h o e k) recess; 2 (v. h u i s) stand back from the street, recede; *voor hem ~* take his place; *doen ~* indent [a line]

'**inspuiten**[1] *vt* inject; **–ting** (-en) *v* injection

'**instaan**[1] *vt ~ voor de echtheid* guarantee the genuineness; *voor iem. ~* answer for sbd.; *~ voor iets* (*voor de waarheid*) vouch for sth. (for the truth)

installa'**teur** (-s) *m* [central heating] installer; ⚡ electrician; **instal'latie** [-(t)si.] (-s) *v* 1 installation [of a functionary], inauguration, enthronement [of a bishop], induction [of a clergyman]; 2 ⚒ [electric, heating] installation;

[radar, stereo] equipment; plant [in industrial process]; **–kosten** *mv* cost of installation, installation costs; **instal'leren** (installeerde, h. geïnstalleerd) *vt* 1 install, instate [an official], enthrone [a bishop], induct [a clergyman], inaugurate [a new governor]; 2 install [electric light]

'**instampen**[1] *vt* ram in; *het iem. ~* hammer (drum, pound) it into sbd.'s head

in'**standhouding** *v* maintenance, preservation, upkeep

in'**stantie** [-(t)si.] (-s) *v* 1 ⚖ instance, resort; 2 (o v e r h e i d s o r g a a n) [education, civil, military &] authority, [international &] agency; *in eerste* (*laatste*) ~ in the first instance (in the last resort)

'**instappen**[1] *vi* step in(to), get in; *de conducteur roept:* ~*!* (take your) seats, please!; *wij moesten ~* we had to get in

'**insteken**[1] *vt* put in; *een draad ~* thread a needle

'**instellen**[1] *vt* 1 adjust [instruments], focus [a microscope &]; 2 set up [a board]; institute [an inquiry, proceedings &]; establish [a passenger-service]; zie ook: *dronk* &; **–ling** (-en) *v* 1 institution; 2 *fig* & *ps* attitude

'**instemmen**[1] *vi ~ met* agree with [an opinion]; approve of [a plan]; **–ming** *v* agreement; approval [of a plan]

insti'**gatie** [-(t)si.] *v* instigation; *op ~ van* at the instigation of

in'**stinct** (-en) *o* instinct; **instinc'tief, instinct'matig** I *aj* instinctive; II *ad* instinctively, by instinct

'**instinken** (stonk in, is ingestonken) *vi* F *erin stinken* get caught, fall into a trap, be the dupe; *iem. ergens laten ~* deceive sbd., double-cross sbd., dupe sbd.

institutio'**neel** [-(t)si.o.'ne.l] institutional [investor &]; **insti'tuut** (-tuten) *o* 1 institute, institution; 2 boarding-school

'**instoppen**[1] I *vt* tuck in [a child in bed]; stuff [the shawl &] in; *er van alles ~* put in all sorts of things; *de kinderen er eerst ~* pack off the children to bed first; II *vr zich ~* tuck oneself up

'**instorten**[1] I *vi* fall (tumble) down, fall in, collapse [of a house]; relapse [of patients]; II *vt* pour into; *fig* infuse [the grace of God]; **–ting** (-en) *v* collapse[2], *fig* downfall; relapse [of patient]; infusion [of grace]

'**instromen**[1] *vt* flow in, stream in, pour in (into)

instruc'**teur** (-s) *m* instructor, ✗ drillsergeant; in'**structie** [-ksi.] (-s) *v* 1 instruction [=

---

[1] V.T. en V.D. van dit werkwoord volgens het model: '**inademen**, V.T. ademde '**in**, V.D. '**ingeademd**. Zie voor de vormen onder het grondwoord, in dit voorbeeld: *ademen*. Bij sterke en onregelmatige werkwoorden wordt u verwezen naar de lijst achterin.

teaching & direction], briefing; 2 ⚔ preliminary inquiry into the case; ~ **geven** instruct, direct [sbd.]; **instruc'tief** instructive; **instru'eren** (instrueerde, h. geïnstrueerd) *vt* 1 instruct; 2 ⚔ prepare [a case]

instru'ment (-en) *o* instrument; **instrumen'taal** instrumental; **instrumen'tarium** (-s en -taria) *o* (set of) instruments; **instrumen'tatie** [-(t)si.] (-s) *v* instrumentation; **instru'mentenbord** (-en) *o* instrument panel, dash-board; **instrumen'teren** (instrumenteerde, h. geïnstrumenteerd) *vt* instrument; **instru'mentmaker** (-s) *m* instrument-maker

'instuderen[1] *vt* practise [a sonata], study [a rôle], rehearse [a play &]; *ze zijn het stuk aan het* ~ the play is in rehearsal

'instuif (-stuiven) *m* open-house party, gettogether; informal reception; **'instuiven**[1] *vi* fly in (into), rush in (into)

'instulpen (stulpte 'in, is 'ingestulpt) *vi* (v a n d a r m) invaginate

'insturen[1] *vt* 1 steer in(to); 2 send in(to)

insubordi'natie [-(t)si.] *v* (act of) insubordination

Insu'linde *o* poetical name for the former Dutch East Indies

insu'line *v* insulin

in'sult (-en) *o* ⚕ attack, fit

in'tact intact, unimpaired

'inteelt *v* inbreeding

in'tegendeel on the contrary

in'teger upright, honest, conscientious, incorruptible

inte'graal integral; **–rekening** *v* integral calculus

inte'gratie [-(t)si.] *v* integration; **inte'greren** (integreerde, h. geïntegreerd) *vt* integrate; **inte'grerend** integral

integri'teit *v* integrity

'intekenaar (-s en -naren) *m* subscriber; **'intekenbiljet** (-ten) *o* subscription form; **'intekenen**[1] *vt* subscribe [to a work]; ~ *voor 50 gulden* subscribe 50 guilders (for); **'intekening** (-en) *v* subscription; **–slijst** = *intekenlijst*; **'intekenlijst** (-en) *v* subscription list; **–prijs** *m* subscription price

intel'lect *o* intellect; **intellectua'listisch** intellectualist; **intellectu'eel I** *aj* intellectual; **II** (-uelen) *m* intellectual

intelli'gent intelligent; **intelli'gentie** [-(t)si.] *v* intelligence; **–quotiënt** [-ko.ʃɪnt] (-en) *o* intelligence quotient, I.Q.; **–test** (-s) *m* intelli-

gence test; **intelli'gentsia** *v* intelligentsia

inten'dance [Intɛn'dɑ̃s(ə)] (-s) *v* ⚔ Army Service Corps; **inten'dant** (-en) *m* intendant; ⚔ A.S.C. officer

in'tens intense; **inten'sief** [s = z] intensive; **intensi'teit** *v* intensity; **intensi'veren** (intensiveerde, h. geïntensiveerd) *vt* intensify; **–ring** *v* intensification

in'tentie [-(t)si.] (-s) *v* intention

intercontinen'taal intercontinental

inter'dict (-en) *o* interdict

'interen I (teerde 'in, is 'ingeteerd) *vi* eat into one's capital, live on one's fat; **II** (teerde 'in, h. 'ingeteerd) *vt* *50 gulden* ~ be 50 guilders to the bad

interes'sant interesting; *het* ~*e* the interesting part of the case; *iets* ~*s* something interesting; *veel* ~*s* much of interest; **inte'resse** (-s) *v* interest; **interes'seren** (interesseerde, h. geïnteresseerd) **I** *vt* interest; *er* (*zwaar*) *bij geïnteresseerd* (closely, deeply) interested in it; **II** *vr zich* ~ *voor iem.* take an interest in sbd., interest oneself in sbd.; *zich voor iets* ~ take an interest in sth., be interested in sth.; be curious about sth.; zie ook: *geïnteresseerd*

'interest (-en) *m* interest; *m e t* ~ *terugbetalen* return with interest[2]; ~ *o p* ~ at compound interest; *op* ~ *plaatsen* put out at interest; *t e g e n* ~ at interest; **–rekening** (-en) *v* 1 $ interest-account; 2 × calculation of interest

interfe'rentie [-(t)si.] *v* interference [of vibrations, waves]; **interfe'reren** (interfereerde, h. geïnterfereerd) *vi* interfere

interi'eur [Intəri.'ør] (-s) *o* interior

inter'kerkelijk interdenominational

inter'landwedstrijd (-en) *m* international contest (match)

inter'linie (-s) *v* (interlinear) space; lead; **interlini'ëren** (interlinieerde, h. geïnterlinieerd) *vt* space lines; lead

interlo'kaal I *aj* ~ *gesprek* ☎ trunk call; **II** *ad* ☎ by trunk call

inter'mezzo [-'mɛdzo.] ('s en -mezzi) *o* intermezzo[2]

intermit'terend intermittent

in'tern 1 internal [questions, affairs, medicine &]; 2 (i n w o n e n d) resident; ~*e leerling* boarder; ~*e onderwijzer* resident teacher; ~*e patiënt* in-patient; ~ *zijn* live in; **inter'naat** (-naten) *o* ⛪ boarding-school

internatio'naal [-(t)sjo.-] international; **Internatio'nale** *v* International(e); **internationali'seren** [s = z] (internationaliseerde, h.

---

[1] V.T. en V.D. van dit werkwoord volgens het model: **'inademen**, V.T. ademde **'in**, V.D. **'ingeademd**. Zie voor de vormen onder het grondwoord, in dit voorbeeld: *ademen*. Bij sterke en onregelmatige werkwoorden wordt u verwezen naar de lijst achterin.

geïnternationaliseerd) *vt* internationalize

inter'neren (interneerde, h. geïnterneerd) *vt* intern; **inter'nering** (-en) *v* internment; **–skamp** (-en) *o* internment camp

inter'nist (-en) *m* specialist in internal medicine

inter'nuntius [-(t)si.üs] (-sen en -tiï) *m* internuncio

interpel'lant (-en) *m* interpellator, questioner; **interpel'latie** [-(t)si.] (-s) *v* interpellation, question; **interpel'leren** (interpelleerde, h. geïnterpelleerd) *vt* interpellate, ask a question

interplane'tair [-'tɛːr] interplanetary

interpo'latie [-(t)si.] (-s) *v* interpolation; **interpo'leren** (interpoleerde, h. geïnterpoleerd) *vt* interpolate

interpre'tatie [-(t)si.] (-s) *v* interpretation; **interpre'teren** (interpreteerde, h. geïnterpreteerd) *vt* interpret

inter'punctie [-ksi.] *v* punctuation

interrum'peren (interrumpeerde, h. geïnterrumpeerd) *vt* interrupt; **inter'ruptie** [-psi.] (-s) *v* interruption

interstel'lair [-'lɛːr] interstellar

'interval (-len) *o* ♩ interval

interveni'ënt (-en) *m* intervener; $ acceptor for honour; **interveni'ëren** (intervenieerde, h. geïntervenieerd) *vi* intervene; **inter'ventie** [-(t)si.] (-s) *v* intervention

inter'view [-'vju.] (-s) *o* interview; **inter'viewen** (interviewde, h. geïnterviewd) *vt* interview; **–er** (-s) *m* interviewer

interzo'naal interzonal

in'tiem I *aj* intimate; **~e** *bijzonderheden* inner details; *zij zijn zeer* **~** (*met elkaar*) they are on very intimate terms; **II** *ad* intimately

in'tijds in good time (season)

intimi'datie [-(t)si.] (-s) *v* intimidation; **intimi'deren** (intimideerde, h. geïntimideerd) *vt* intimidate, browbeat, cow

intimi'teit (-en) *v* intimacy

'intocht (-en) *m* entry; *zijn* **~** *houden* make one's entry

intole'rantie [-(t)si.] *v* intolerance

'intomen[1] *vt* curb, rein in [one's horse]; *fig* check, restrain

into'natie [-(t)si.] (-s) *v* intonation; **into'neren** (intoneerde, h. geïntoneerd) *vt* intone

intoxi'catie [-(t)si.] (-s) *v* intoxication, poisoning

intransi'tief [s = z] intransitive

'intrappen I (trapte 'in, h. 'ingetrapt) *vt* kick in (open); *een open deur* **~** force an open door; **II** *vi* (trapte 'in, is 'ingetrapt) *ergens* **~** [*fig*] fall for

a trick, walk into a trap

'intrede *v* entrance, entry; beginning [of winter]; **'intreden**[1] *vi* enter; set in [of thaw]; fall [of silence]; *zijn* ...*ste jaar* **~** enter upon one's ...th year; *de dood is onmiddellijk ingetreden* death was instantaneous; **'intree** = *intrede*; **–rede** (-s) *v* inaugural speech (address), maiden speech

'intrek *m zijn* **~** *nemen* put up at [a hotel], take up one's abode [somewhere]; **in'trekbaar** retractable; **'intrekken**[1] **I** *vt* 1 draw in, retract[2] [claws, horns &]; *fig* withdraw [a grant, a sanction, money], retire [notes, bonds]; revoke [a decree], cancel [a permission]; 2 march into [a town]; **II** *vi* move in [into a house]; zie ook: *zijn intrek nemen*; **–king** *v* withdrawal, cancellation, revocation, retractation

'intrest(-) = *interest*(-)

intri'gant(e) (-en) *m(-v)* intriguer, schemer, plotter, wire-puller; **in'trige** [-ʒə] (-s) *v* 1 intrigue; 2 plot [of a drama]; **intri'geren** (intrigeerde, h. geïntrigeerd) **I** *vi* intrigue, plot, scheme; **II** *vt dat intrigeert mij* that's what puzzles me

intrin'siek intrinsic(al)

introdu'cé (-s) *m* guest; **introdu'ceren** (introduceerde, h. geïntroduceerd) *vt* introduce; **intro'ductie** [-ksi.] (-s) *v* introduction

intro'vert (-en) *m* (& *aj*) introvert

intu'ïtie [ɪnty.'i.(t)si.] (-s) *v* intuition; **intuï'tief** intuitive

in'tussen 1 meanwhile, in the meantime; 2 (t o c h) yet

inun'datie [-(t)si.] (-s) *v* inundation; **inun'deren** (inundeerde, h. geïnundeerd) *vt* inundate

'inval (-len) *m* 1 invasion [of a country], irruption, incursion [into a place], [police] raid [on a café]; 2 fancy, sally of wit; *een dwaze* **~** a whimsy; *een gelukkige* **~** a happy thought; *een idiote* **~** a brain-storm, a crazy idea; *wonderlijke* **~** freak, whim; *het is daar de zoete* **~** they keep open house there; *ik kwam op de* **~** it occurred to me, the thought flashed upon me; *een* **~** *doen in* invade [a country]; raid [a café]

inva'lide I *aj* invalid, disabled [soldier]; **II** (-n) *m-v* invalid, disabled soldier; **inva'lidenwagentje** (-s) *o* invalid chair, invalid vehicle; **invalidi'teit** *v* disablement, disability; **invalidi'teitsrente** (-n en -s) *v* disability pension; **–uitkering** (-en) *v* disability benefit; **–wet** (-ten) *v* disability insurance act, disabled

---

[1] V.T. en V.D. van dit werkwoord volgens het model: **'in**ademen, V.T. ademde **'in**, V.D. **'in**geademd. Zie voor de vormen onder het grondwoord, in dit voorbeeld: *ademen*. Bij sterke en onregelmatige werkwoorden wordt u verwezen naar de lijst achterin.

pensions act

'**invallen**[1] *vi* 1 (v. h u i s) collapse, tumble down, fall in; 2 (v. l i c h t) fall; 3 (v. n a c h t) fall; 4 (v. v o r s t &) set in; 5 ♪ join in; 6 (b ij s p e l, i n h e t g e s p r e k) cut in; 7 (i n d i e n s t) deputize; substitute; 8 (v a n g e - d a c h t e n) come into one's head; 9 (v a n w a n g e n) fall in; *het viel mij in* it occurred to me, the thought flashed upon me; *het wou mij niet ~* I could not hit upon it, I could not remember it; *~ in een land* invade a country; *~ voor een collega* substitute for a colleague; *bij ~de duisternis* at dark; *~de lichtstralen* incident rays; **–er** (-s) *m* 1 (v e r v a n g e r) substitute, *sp* deputizer, reserve, stand-in; 2 (i n e e n l a n d) invader; '**invalshoek** (-en) *m* angle of incidence; **–weg** (-en) *m* access road, approach road

'**invaren**[1] *vi* sail in (into)

in'vasie [s = z] (-s) *v* invasion

inven'taris (-sen) *m* inventory; *de ~ opmaken* draw up an inventory, take stock; **inventari'satie** [- 'za.(t)si.] *v* stock-taking; **inventari'seren** (inventariseerde, h. geïnventariseerd) *vt* draw up an inventory of, take stock of; **inven'tarisuitverkoop** *m* stock-taking sale **inven'tief** inventive, ingenious; **inventivi'teit** *v* inventiveness

in'versie [s = z] (-s) *v* inversion

inves'teren (investeerde, h. geïnvesteerd) *vt* $ invest; **inves'tering** (-en) *v* $ investment; **–saftrek** *m* investment allowance

investi'tuur *v* investiture

'**invetten** (vette 'in, h. 'ingevet) *vt* grease, oil

invi'tatie [-(t)si.] (-s) *v* invitation; **–kaart** (-en) *v* invitation card; **in'vite** [- 'vi.t] (-s) *v* ◊ call (for trumps), lead; **invi'té** [ē-] (-s) *m* guest; **invi'teren** (inviteerde, h. geïnviteerd) *vt* invite [to dinner &]

'**invlechten**[1] *vt* plait in, intertwine; entwine; *fig* put in, insert [a few remarks]

'**invliegen**[1] **I** *vi* fly into; fly in; *er ~* [*fig*] be caught, walk into the trap; **II** *vt* ✈ test [a machine]; **–er** (-s) *m* ✈ test pilot

'**invloed** (-en) *m* influence; **F** pull; effect [of the war, of the slump], impact [of the war, of western civilization &]; *zijn ~ bij* his influence with; *zijn ~ aanwenden bij* use one's influence with; *~ hebben op* 1 have an influence upon (over), have a hold on; 2 affect [the results]; *~ uitoefenen* exercise (an) influence; *onder de ~ staan van* be influenced by; *onder de ~ zijn van* be under the influence of; *onder de ~ van sterke*

drank under the influence of drink; **–rijk** influential; '**invloedssfeer** (-sferen) *v* sphere of influence

'**invochten** (vochtte 'in, h. 'ingevocht) *vt* damp [the washing]

'**invoegen**[1] *vt* put in, insert, intercalate; *vi* (b ij a u t o r ij d e n) filter in; **–ging** (-en) *v*, '**invoegsel** (-s en -en) *o* insertion

'**invoer** (-en) *m* import; importation; (d e g o e d e r e n) imports; *de ~ verlagen en de uitvoer verhogen* reduce imports and increase exports; **–artikel** (-en) *o* article of import, importation; *~en* ook: imports; '**invoeren** *vt* 1 $ import; 2 introduce; '**invoerhandel** *m* import trade; **–haven** (-s) *v* import harbour; '**invoering** *v* introduction; '**invoerpremie** (-s) *v* bounty on importation; **–rechten** *mv* import duties; **–stop** (-s) *m* import ban, suspension of imports; **–verbod** (-verboden) *o* import prohibition, import embargo (ban); **–vergunning** (-en) *v* import licence

'**invorderen**[1] *vt* collect [money]; **–ring** (-en) *v* collection

'**invreten** (vrat 'in, is 'ingevreten) *vi* eat into, corrode; *~d* corrosive; **–ting** *v* corrosion

'**invriezen**[1] **I** *vi* be frozen in; **II** *vt* quick-freeze, deep-freeze

in'vrijheidstelling *v* liberation, release

'**invulbiljet** (-ten), **–formulier** (-en) *o* blank form; '**invullen**[1] *vt* fill up [a ballot-paper]; fill in [a cheque &]; *een formulier ~* complete a form; **–ling** (-en) *v* filling up, filling in, completion [of a form]

'**inwaarts I** *aj* inward; **II** *ad* inward(s)

'**inwachten**[1] *vt* await [a reply]; *sollicitaties worden ingewacht* applications are invited

in'wendig I *aj* inward, interior, internal [parts]; inner [man]; home [mission]; *voor ~ gebruik* to be taken interiorly (inwardly); **II** *ad* inwardly, internally; on the inside; **III** *o het ~e* the interior (part, parts)

'**inwerken**[1] **I** *vi ~ op* act (operate) upon, affect, influence; *op elkaar ~* interact; *op zich laten ~* absorb; **II** *vr zich ~* post oneself (thoroughly) up, work one's way in; read up [on a subject]; **III** *vt* break in [sbd.]; **–king** (-en) *v* action, influence

in'werkingtreding *v* coming into force

'**inwerpen**[1] *vt* throw in, smash [a window]

'**inweven**[1] *vt* weave in, interweave

'**inwijden**[1] *vt* consecrate [a church]; inaugurate [a building]; initiate [adepts]; (v o o r h e t e e r s t g e b r u i k e n) **F** break in; *iem. in het*

---

[1] V.T. en V.D. van dit werkwoord volgens het model: '**inademen**, V.T. ademde '**in**, V.D. '**ingeademd**. Zie voor de vormen onder het grondwoord, in dit voorbeeld: *ademen*. Bij sterke en onregelmatige werkwoorden wordt u verwezen naar de lijst achterin.

geheim ~ initiate sbd. in(to) the secret, let sbd.
in on the secret; **–ding** (-en) *v* consecration [of
church &]; inauguration [of a public building
&]; initiation [of adepts]

'inwikkelen[1] *vt* wrap (up)

'inwilligen (willigde 'in, h. 'ingewilligd) *vt*
grant; **–ging** (-en) *v* granting

'inwinnen[1] *vt inlichtingen* ~ (*omtrent*) gather
information, make inquiries (about), apply for
information; inquire (of *bij*); zie ook: *raad*

in'wisselbaar exchangeable [for]; convertible
[into]; **'inwisselen**[1] *vt* change, convert
[foreign currency]; collect, cash in [a cheque];
~ *voor* exchange for; **–ling** (-en) *v* changing,
(ex)change

'inwonen[1] *vi* live in, (v a n k i n d e r e n) live at
home; ~ *bij* live (lodge) with; ~*d geneesheer*
house-physician, resident physician (surgeon);
een ~*d onderwijzer* a resident master; **–er** (-s) *m*
inhabitant, resident; (h u u r d e r) lodger;
'inwoning *v* 1 lodging; 2 (d o o r w o n i n g-
t e k o r t) sharing of a house; *plaats van* ~ place
of residence; zie ook: *kost*

'inworp (-en) *m sp* throw-in

'inwortelen[1] *vi* take root, become deeply
rooted

'inwrijven[1] *vt* rub in(to), rub

inz. = *inzonderheid*

'inzaaien[1] *vt* sow

'inzage *v* inspection; ~ *nemen van* inspect,
examine [reports &]; *ter* ~ on approval [of
books &]; open to inspection [of letters]; *de
stukken liggen ter* ~ *ten kantore van...* the reports
may be seen at the office of...

in'zake in the matter of, on the subject of, re
[your letter], concerning, [crisis] over [Korea
&]

'inzakken[1] *vi* sink down, sag, collapse

'inzamelen[1] *vt* collect, gather, ⊙ garner; **–ling**
(-en) *v* collection, gathering; *een* ~ *houden* make
a collection

'inzegenen[1] *vt* bless, consecrate; **–ning** (-en) *v*
blessing, consecration

'inzeilen[1] *vi* sail into, enter [the harbour]

'inzenden[1] *vt* send in; **–er** (-s) *m* contributor,
writer [of a letter to the editor]; sender; exhibitor [for an exposition]; **'inzending** (-en) *v*
exhibit [for a show]; contribution [to a period-
ical]; entry [for a competition]; sending in

'inzepen[1] *vt* soap [before washing], lather
[before shaving]

'inzet (-ten) *m* 1 stake, stakes [in games]; 2
upset price [at auction]; 3 ♩ start; 4 *fig*

employment [of troops, workmen]; devoting
[of one's life to a cause], devotion; **–stuk**
(-ken) *o* ⚔ insert; **'inzetten**[1] **I** *vt* set in [the
sleeves of a frock]; put in [window-panes &];
insert [a piston &]; set [diamonds &]; stake
[money at cards &]; start [a house at auction
for...]; ♩ start [a hymn]; launch [an attack]; *fig*
employ [troops, workmen]; devote [one's
energies, one's life, oneself to one's country
&]; **II** *vi & va* 1 ♩ begin to play (to sing &),
strike up; 2 *sp* put down one's stake(s), stake
one's money, stake [heavily]; *de zomer zet goed in*
summer starts well; **–er** (-s) *m* first bidder

'inzicht (-en) *o* 1 (b e g r i p) insight; 2
(m e n i n g) view; 3 (b e o o r d e l i n g)
judg(e)ment, opinion; *naar mijn* ~ in my view;
naar zijn ~(*en*) *handelen* act according to one's
(own) views; **'inzien I** *vt* look into, glance
over [a newspaper, a letter], skim [a book];
see, realize [the danger, one's error]; *het ernstig
(optimistisch)* ~ take a grave (an optimistic)
view of things; **II** *o bij nader* ~ on reflection,
on second thoughts; *mijns* ~*s* in my opinion
(view), to my thinking

'inzinken[1] *vi* sink² (down); *fig* decline; **–king**
(-en) *v* sinking, decline; ⚕ (w e d e r i n s t o r-
t i n g) relapse; *ps* [mental, nervous] breakdown

'inzitten[1] *vi ik zit er erg mee in* I am in an awful
fix; *hij zit er niets mee in* he doesn't bother about
that; *hij zat er over in* he was worried about it;
er warmpjes in zitten be comfortably off; zie ook:
dik **II**; in'zittenden *mv de* ~ the occupants

'inzoet intensely sweet

in'zonderheid especially

'inzouten[1] *vt* salt

'inzuigen[1] *vt* suck in, suck up, imbibe

'inzwachtelen[1] *vt* swathe, bandage

i'on (ionen) *o* ion; i'onentheorie *v* ionic
theory; ioni'satie [-'za.(t)si.] *v* ionization;
ioni'seren (ioniseerde, h. geïoniseerd) *vt*
ionize; iono'sfeer *v* ionosphere

i.p.v. = *in plaats van* instead of

Ir. = *ingenieur*

I'raaks Iraqi

I'raans Iranian

I'rak *o* Iraq; Ira'kees (-kezen) *m* Iraqi

I'ran [i.'ran, i.'ra.n] *o* Iran; I'raniër (-s) *m*
Iranian

'iris (-sen) *v* iris

iro'nie *v* irony; i'ronisch ironical, wry

irratio'neel [-(t)si.-] irrational

irre'ëel [Ire.'e.l] unreal

irre'levant irrelevant, not to the point

---

[1] V.T. en V.D. van dit werkwoord volgens het model: **'**inademen, V.T. ademde **'**in, V.D. **'**ingeademd. Zie voor de
vormen onder het grondwoord, in dit voorbeeld: *ademen*. Bij sterke en onregelmatige werkwoorden wordt u
verwezen naar de lijst achterin.

irri'gatie [-(t)si.] (-s) v irrigation; irri'gator (-s en -'toren) m irrigator; ⚶ douche, syringe; irri'geren (irrigeerde, h. geïrrigeerd) vt & va irrigate

irri'tant irritating; fig galling; irri'tatie [-(t)si.] (-s) v irritation; irri'teren (irriteerde, h. geïrriteerd) vt irritate

is 3de pers. enkelv. tegenwoordige tijd v. zijn

'ischias v sciatica

is'lam [-'la.m] m de ~ Islam; isla'miet (-en) m Islamite; isla'mitisch Islamitic, Islamic

'isme (-n en -s) o ism

iso'baar [s = z] (-baren) m isobar

iso'latie [i.zo.'la.(t)si.] (-s) v 1 isolation; 2 ⚡ insulation; –band, –lint (-en) o insulating tape; –materiaal o insulating material, insulant; lagging; iso'lator (-s en -'toren) m

insulator; isole'ment o isolation; iso'leren (isoleerde, h. geïsoleerd) vt 1 isolate; 2 ⚡ insulate; –ring (-en) v 1 isolation; 2 ⚡ insulation

iso'therm [s = z] (-en) m isotherm

iso'toop [s = z] (-topen) m isotope

'Israël o Israel; Isra'ëli ('s) m Israeli; Israë'liet (-en) m Israelite; Isra'ëlisch Israeli; Israë'litisch Israelitish

Itali'aan (-ianen) m Italian; –s I aj Italian; II o het ~ Italian; III v een ~e an Italian woman (lady); I'talië o Italy

i.v.m. = in verband met in connection with

i'voor (ivoren) m & o ivory; I'voorkust v Ivory Coast; i'voren ivory

I'wriet o (modern) Hebrew

J

j [je.] ['s] *v* j

ja I *ad* 1 yes; 2 (v e r s t e r k e n d) indeed, ⊙ nay, ↖ yea; 3 (a a r z e l e n d) m-yes; ~, ~! yes, yes!, well, well!; *is hij uit?, ik meen (van)* ~ did he got out? I think he did; has he gone out? I think he has; ~ *zeggen* say yes [to life]; *hij zei van* ~ he said yes; *op alles* ~ *en amen zeggen* say yes and amen to everything; *met* ~ *beantwoorden* answer in the affirmative; **II** ('s) *o* yes

'jaaglijn (-en) *v* towing-line; **–pad** (-paden) *o* tow-path; **–schuit** (-en) *v* tow-boat

jaap (japen) *m* cut, gash, slash

jaar (jaren) *o* year; *het* ~ *onzes Heren* the year of our Lord, the year of grace; *de jaren dertig, veertig* & the thirties, the forties; *nog vele jaren na dezen!* many happy returns of the day!; *de jaren nog niet hebben om...* not be old enough to...; *eens of tweemaal 's* ~*s* once or twice a year; *het hele* ~ *door* all the year round, throughout the year; *de laatste jaren* of late years, in recent years; ● *i n het* ~ *nul* in the year one; *in het begin van het* ~ at the turn of the year; ~ *in* ~ *uit* year in year out; *m e t de jaren* with the years; *n a* ~ *en dag* after many years; *o m het andere* ~ every other year; ~ *o p* ~ year by year; *op jaren komen* be getting on in years; *op jaren zijn* be well on in years; *o v e r een* ~ in a year; *vandaag over een* ~ this day twelvemonth; *p e r* ~ per annum; *eens per* ~ once a year; *s i n d s* ~ *en dag* for years and years; *v a n* ~ *tot* ~ from year's end to year's end; every year; *een jongen van mijn jaren* a boy my age; **–beurs** (-beurzen) *v* industries fair, trade fair, [Leipzig &] fair; **–boek** (-en) *o* year-book, annual; **~en** annals; **–cijfers** *mv* annual returns; **–club** (-s) *v* fraternity whose members came up in the same year; **–feest** (-en) *o* annual feast, anniversary; **–gang** (-en) *m* 1 (annual) volume [of a periodical]; 2 vintage [of wine]; **–geld** (-en) *o* 1 pension; 2 annuity; **–genoot** (-noten) *m* someone of the same age as oneself; fellow-student who came up the same year as oneself; **–getij(de)** (-tijden) *o* season; **–kring** (-en) *m* 1 annual cycle [in almanac]; 2 ⚘ annual ring [of a tree]; **–lijks I** *aj* yearly, annual; **II** *ad* yearly, annually, every year; **–loon** (-lonen) *o* (annual) salary; **–markt** (-en) *v* (annual) fair; **–rekening** (-en) *v* annual account; **–salaris** *o* annual (yearly) salary; **–stukken** *mv* annual accounts; **–tal** (-len) *o* year [in chronology], date; **–telling** (-en) *v* era; **–vergadering** (-en) *v* annual meeting; **–verslag** (-verslagen) *o* annual report; **–wedde** (-n) *v* (annual) salary; **–wisseling** *v* turn of the year; *bij de* ~ at the turn of the year

ja'bot [ʒa.'bo.] (-s) *m* & *o* jabot, frill

'jabroer (-s) *m* F yes-man

1 jacht (-en) *v* hun(ting), shooting, chase; pursuit²; ~ *maken op* hunt [elephants &]; give chase to [a ship], be in pursuit of²; ~ *maken op effect* strain after effect; *op (de)* ~ *gaan* go (out) shooting (hunting); *op* ~ *naar* on the hunt for

2 jacht (-en) *o* ⚓ yacht

'jachtakte (-n en -s) *v* shooting-licence, game-licence; **–bommenwerper** (-s) *m* ⮕ fighter-bomber; **–buks** (-en) *v* hunting-rifle; **'jachten** (jachtte, h. gejacht) *vt* & *vi* hurry, hustle; **'jachtgeweer** (-weren) *o* (sporting-)gun; **–grond** (-en) *m* hunting-ground; **–haven** (-s) *v* marina; **–hond** (-en) *m* sporting-dog, hound; **–hoorn** (-s), **–horen** (-s) *m* hunting-horn; **–huis** (-huizen) *o* hunting-lodge, hunting-box; **–ig** hurried, hasty, hard-pressed; **–luipaard** (-en) *o* cheetah; **–opziener** (-s) *m* gamekeeper; **–paard** (-en) *o* hunter; **–partij** (-en) *v* 1 hunting-party, hunt; 2 shooting-party, shoot; **–recht** *o* shooting-rights; **–schotel** *m* & *v* hotpot; **–slot** (-sloten) *o* hunting lodge (seat); **–stoet** (-en) *m* hunting-party; **–terrein** (-en) *o* = jachtveld; **–tijd** (-en) *m* shooting-season; **–veld** (-en) *o* hunting-field, hunting-ground; *eeuwige* ~*en* happy hunting-grounds; *particulier* ~ preserve; **–vlieger** (-s) *m* ⮕ fighter pilot; **–vliegtuig** (-en) *o* ⮕ fighter; **–wet** (-wetten) *v* game-act

'jacketkroon ['dʒækit-] (-kronen) *v* jacket crown

jac'quet [ʒa'kɪt] (-s en -ten) *o* & *v* morning-coat, cut-away (coat)

'jaeger ['je.gər] Jaeger; ~ *ondergoed* Jaeger (woollen) underclothes

'jagen* I *vt* 1 hunt [wild animals, game]; shoot [hares, game]; chase [deer &]; 2 *fig* drive, hurry on [one's servants &]; *zich een kogel d o o r het hoofd* ~ put a bullet through one's head; *iets e r d o o r jagen* rush sth. through; *de vijanden u i t het land* ~ drive the enemy out of the country; **II** *va* & *vi* 1 hunt, shoot; 2 race, rush, tear; *de* ~*de wolken* the scudding clouds; ~ *n a a r eer* hunt after honours; ~ *o p hazen* hunt the hare; zie ook: *lijf, vlucht* &; **'jager** (-s) *m* 1 hunter, sportsman; 2 ⚔ rifleman; 3 ⮕ fighter; 4 driver of a towing-horse; *de* ~*s* ⚔ ook: the Rifles; **–meester** (-s) *m* huntsman; zie ook: *opper-*

jager(meester); '**jagerslatijn** *o* tall story (stories); **–taal** *v* sportsman's language; **–tas** (-tassen) *v* game-bag

'**jaguar** ['ja.gu.ɑr] (-s) *m* jaguar

'**jajem** ['ja.jəm] *m* S Dutch gin

1 jak (-ken) *o* jacket

2 jak (-ken) *m* ⚕ yak

'**jakhals** (-halzen) *m* ⚕ jackal

'**jakkeren** (jakkerde, h. gejakkerd) *vi* tear (along), race, drive furiously

'**jakkes!** *ij* faugh!, bah!

'**jaknikker** (-s) *m* 1 (j a b r o e r) F yes-man; 2 ✗ (p o m p) nodding donkey

jako'bijn (-en) *m*, **jako'bijns** *aj* Jacobin

'**jakobsladder** (-s) *v* Jacob's ladder; bucket chain

ja'loers jealous, envious (of *op*); *iem. ~ maken* F put sbd.'s nose out of joint; **–heid** (-heden) *v* jealousy; **jaloe'zie** [ʒa.-] (-zieën) *v* 1 (j a l o e r s h e i d) jealousy; 2 (b l i n d) Venetian blind, (sun-)blind

jam [ʒɑm] *m* & *v* jam

'**jambe** (-n) *v* iambus, iamb; '**jambisch** iambic

'**jammer** (-en) *o* & *m* misery; *het is ~* it is a pity; *het is eeuwig ~* it is a thousand pities; *ik vind het ~* (*dat*) I regret, I'm sorry; *hoe ~!, wat ~!* what a pity!, what a shame!; '**jammeren** (jammerde, h. gejammerd) *vi* lament, wail; '**jammerhout** (-en) *o* F fiddle; **–klacht** (-en) *v* lamentation; **–lijk I** *aj* miserable, pitiable, piteous, pitiful, woeful, wretched; **II** *ad* miserably, piteously, woefully, wretchedly

'**jampot** ['ʒɑmpɔt] (-ten) *m* jam-jar, jam-pot

Jan *m* John; *~ (en) alleman* all the world and his wife, Jack Everybody; *~ Compagnie* John Company; *~ Klaassen* merry-andrew, Jack Pudding; *~ Klaassen en Katrijn* Punch and Judy; *~, Piet en Klaas* Tom, Dick, and Harry; *~ Rap en zijn maat* ragtag and bobtail; *~ zonder Land* John Lackland; *~ zonder Vrees* John the Fearless; *boven ~ zijn* have got round the corner; '**janboel** *m* muddle, mess; **janboeren'fluitjes** *op z'n ~* in a slipshod way, in a happy-go-lucky way; **jan'hagel** 1 *o* rabble; 2 *m* kind of biscuit; **jan'hen** (-nen) *m = keukenpiet*

'**janken** (jankte, h. gejankt) *vi* yelp, whine, squeal

jan'klaassen *m* (g e k h e i d) tomfoolery; (d r u k t e) fuss; zie ook: *Jan*; **–spel** (-len) *o* Punch and Judy show

'**janmaat** (-s) *m* F Jack, Jack-tar; **janple'zier** (-en en -s) *m* char-à-banc, charabanc; **jan'salie** (-s) *m* stick-in-the-mud; '**Jantje** *o* F Johnnie, Jack; *de j~s* ⚓ the bluejackets; *zich met een j~-van-leiden van iets afmaken* shirk the difficulty; *een ~ Sekuur* a punctilious fellow

janu'ari *m* January

jan-van-'gent (-s) *m* gannet

Ja'pan *o* Japan; **Ja'panner** (-s) *m* Japanese, F Jap, *mv* Japanese; **Ja'pans I** *aj* Japanese; **II** *o het ~* Japanese

'**japen** (jaapte, h. gejaapt) *vt* gash, slash

ja'pon (-nen en -s) *m* dress, gown; **–stof** (-fen) *v* dress material

'**jarenlang I** *aj* of years, of many years' standing; **II** *ad* for years (together)

jar'gon (-s) *o* jargon

'**jarig I** *aj* a year old; *zij is vandaag ~* it is her birthday to-day; **II** *m-v de ~e* the person celebrating his (her) birthday

jarre'tel(le) [ʒɑrə'tɛl] (-s) *v* suspender; **–gordel** (-s) *m* suspender-belt

jas (-sen) *m* & *v* coat; (j a s j e) jacket; **–beschermer** (-s) *m* dress guard

jas'mijn (-en) *v* 1 jasmine, jessamine; 2 mock-orange

'**jaspanden** *mv* coat-tails

'**jaspis** (-sen) *m* & *o* jasper

'**jasschort** (-en) *v* & *o* overall, dust-coat

'**jassen** (jaste, h. gejast) *vt* peel [potatoes]; *piepers ~* F bash spuds

'**jasses** = *jakkes*

'**jaszak** (-ken) *m* coat-pocket

jat (-ten) *v* S *~ten* hands, paws; '**jatten** (jatte, h. gejat) *vt* S pinch, swipe

Ja'vaan (-vanen) *m* Javanese, *mv* Javanese; **–s I** *aj* Javanese; **II** *o het ~* Javanese; **III** *v een ~e* a Javanese woman

ja'wel yes; indeed

'**jawoord** *o* consent, yes; *het ~ geven* say yes

jazz [dʒɛs] *m* jazz; **–band** (-s) *m* jazzband

je 1 *pers. vnmw.* you; **II** *bez. vnmw.* your; *dat is ~ van hèt* that's absolutely it, it's the thing

jee! [je.] *ij* oh dear!

'**jegens** *prep* towards, to; [honest] with

Je'hova *m* Jehovah; *~'s getuigen* Jehovah's Witnesses

'**jekker** (-s) *m* jacket

je'lui = *jullie*

'**Jemen** *o* (the) Yemen

je'never *m* gin, Hollands, geneva; **–bes** (-sen) *v* juniper berry; **–neus** (-neuzen) *m* bottle-nose; **–stokerij** (-en) *v* gin-distillery

'**jengelen** (jengelde, h. gejengeld) *vi* whine

'**jennen** (jende, h. gejend) *vt* F needle, tease

jeremi'ade (-s en -n) *v* jeremiad; **jeremi'ëren** (jeremieerde, h. gejeremieerd) *vi* lament

jeugd *v* youth; *tweede ~* F Indian summer; **–beweging** (-en) *v* youth movement; **–criminaliteit** (-en) *v* juvenile delinquency; **–herberg** (-en) *v* youth hostel; **–vader** youth hosteller; '**jeugdig** youthful; **–heid** *v* youthfulness, youth; '**jeugdleider** (-s) *m* youth leader,

leader of a youthgroup; **–organisatie** [-(t)si.] (-s) *v* youth organization; **'jeugdportret** (-ten) *o* youth portrait; **–puistjes** *mv* acne, pimples; **–sentiment** *o* nostalgia for one's youth; **–verkeersbrigade** (-s) *v* school safety patrol [in U.S.A.], school crossing patrol [in Britain]; **–verkeersbrigadiertje** (-s) *o* patrol member; **–vriend** (-en) *m*, **–vriendin** (-nen) *v* childhood friend, old friend; **–werk** (-en) *o* (v a n k u n s t e n a a r) early work; (i n v e r e n i-g i n g s v e r b a n d) youth welfare (work); **–zonde** (-n) *v* youthful transgression (indiscretion)

'jeuig ['ʒø.əx] = *sjeuig*

jeuk *m* itching, itch, pruritus; **'jeuken** (jeukte, h. gejeukt) *vi* itch; *de handen jeuken mij (om)* I was itching (to); *mijn maag jeukt* I feel peckish; **'jeukerig** itchy, itching

jeune pre'mier [ʒœːn prə'mje:] (jeunes premiers) *m* juvenile (lead)

jezu'ïet (-en) *m* Jesuit; **–enorde** *v* order of Jesuits

'Jezus *m* Jesus; ~ *Christus* Jesus Christ

Jhr. = *jonkheer*

jicht *v* gout; **–ig** gouty; **–knobbel** (-s) *m* chalk-stone; **–lijder** (-s) *m* gouty sufferer (patient); **–pijnen** *mv* gouty pains

'Jiddisch ['jIdi.ʃ] *o* Yiddish

jij you; **'jijbak** (-ken) *m dat is een* ~ F that's stealing sbd.'s thunder; **'jijen** (jijde, h. gejijd) *vt* ~ *en jouwen* behave (speak) (over)familiarly [towards]

jioe-'jitsoe *o* jiu-jitsu

Jkvr. = *jonkvrouw* 2

jl. = *jongstleden*

'jobstijding (-en) *v* (piece of) bad news

joch, 'jochie (-s) *o* F boy, kid, sonny

jockey ['dʒɔki.] (-s) *m* jockey

'jodelen (jodelde, h. gejodeld) *vi & vt* yodel

'jodenbuurt (-en) *v* Jewish quarter, Jews' quarter; **–dom** *o* 1 (d e l e e r) Judaism; 2 (d e j o d e n) Jews, Jewry; **–vervolging** (-en) *v* persecution of the Jews, Jew-baiting

jo'dide (-n) *o* iodide

jo'din (-nen) *v* Jewess

'jodium *o* iodine; **–tinctuur** *v* tincture of iodine

jodo'form *o* iodoform

joeg (joegen) V.T. van *jagen*

Joego'slaaf (-slaven) *m* Yugoslav; **Joego'slavië** *o* Yugoslavia; **Joego'slavisch** Yugoslav

'joelen (joelde, h. gejoeld) *vi* shout

'jofel fine, splendid, capital, topping

johan'nieter (-s) *m* Knight of St. John

'jokkebrok (-ken) *m-v* fibber, story-teller; **'jokken** (jokte, h, gejokt) *vi* fib, tell fibs, tell stories; **'jokkentje** (-s) *o* fib, story, white lie;

jokker'nij (-en) *v* joke, jest

jol (-len) *v* 1 yawl, jolly-boat; 2 (k l e i n e r e) dinghy

'jolig jolly, merry; **–heid** *v* jollity; **jo'lijt** *v & o* fun, frolics

'jonassen (jonaste, h. gejonast) *vt* toss [a person] in a blanket

jong I *aj* young; ~*e kaas* new cheese; *van ~e datum* of recent date; *de ~ste berichten* the latest news; *de ~ste gebeurtenissen* recent events; *de ~ste oorlog* the late war; ~*ste vennoot* junior partner; **II** *o* young one, [wolf's, bear's &] cub; *de ~en* the young ones, the young of...; ~*en krijgen* (*werpen*) litter; **'jonge** *m* (j e n e v e r) Hollands; **jonge'dame** (-s) *v* young lady; **–'dochter** (-s) *v* 1 girl; 2 spinster; **–'heer** (-heren) *m* young gentleman; **–'juffrouw** (-en) *v* young lady; *een oude* ~ an old maid; **'jongeling** (-en) *m* young man, youth, lad; **jonge'lui** *mv* young people; **–'man** (-nen) *m* young man

1 'jongen (-s) *m* 1 boy, lad; 2 (v r i j e r) boyfriend, sweetheart; ~, ~! dear, dear!, oh dear!; *ouwe* ~! old boy!; *zware* ~ F tough (guy)

2 'jongen (jongde, h. gejongd) *vi* bring forth young (ones), litter, kitten [of cat], pup, whelp [of dog], kid [of goat], calve [of cow], foal [of mare], yean, lamb [of ewe], fawn [of deer], whelp [of lion], pig [of sow]

'jongensachtig boyish; **–gek** (-ken) *v* girl fond of boys; **–jaren** *mv* (years of) boyhood; **–kop** (-pen) *m* (k a p s e l) Eton crop; **–school** (-scholen) *v* boys' school; **–streek** (-streken) *m & v* boyish trick

'jonger I *aj* younger, junior; *twee jaar* ~ *dan hij* (*zij*) ook: two years his (her) junior; **II** *mv* de ~*en* the younger generation; *de ~en van Jezus* Jesus' disciples

'jongetje (-s) *o* little boy

jongge'borene (-n) *m-v* new-born baby; **–ge'huwden** *mv de* ~ the newly married couple, F the newly-weds; **–ge'zel** (-len) *m* bachelor, single man

jong'leren (jongleerde, h. gejongleerd) *vi* juggle; **jong'leur** (-s) *m* juggler

jong'maatje (-s) *o* 1 apprentice; 2 shipboy; **jong'mens** (jonge'lieden, jonge'lui) *o* young man

jongs *van* ~ *af* from one's childhood up; *ik ken hem van* ~ *af* I know him man and boy

jongst'leden last; *de 12de maart* ~ on March 12th last

jonk (-en) *m* ⚓ junk

'jonker (-s) *m* (young) nobleman; (country-) squire; **'jonkheer** (-heren) *m* "jonkheer"; **'jonkvrouw** (-en) *v* 1 maid; 2 (f r e u l e) honourable miss (lady); **jonk'vrouwelijk** maidenlike, maiden(ish), maidenly

1 jood (joden) *m* Jew

2 jood *o* (j o d i u m) iodine; **–'kali** *m* potassium iodide

Joods 1 Jewish [life &]; 2 Judaic [law]

jool *m* fun, frolic, jollity, jollification; ☞ [students'] rag

Joost *m* dat mag ~ weten goodness knows

Jor'daan *m* de ~ the (river) Jordan; **–s** Jordanian; **Jor'danië** *o* Jordan; **–r** (-s) *m* Jordanian

'Joris *m* George; ~ Goedbloed F softy, nincompoop

'jota ('s) *v* iota

jou you; *is het van ~?* is it yours?; *van heb ik ~ daar* immense, enormous

jour [ʒuːr] (-s) *m* at-home day, at-home; ~ houden be at home, receive

jour'naal [ʒuːrˈnaːl] (-nalen) *o* 1 journal [ook $]; 2 ⚓ logbook; 3 (f i l m) newsreel; **journali'seren** [s = z] (journaliseerde, h. gejournaliseerd) *vt* $ journalize; **journa'list** (-en) *m* journalist, newspaperman, pressman; F newshawk; **journalis'tiek I** *v* journalism; **II** *aj* journalistic

jouw your

'jouwen (jouwde, h. gejouwd) *vi* hoot, boo

jovi'aal genial; *joviale kerel* F blade; **joviali'teit** *v* geniality, bonhomie

'Jozef *m* Joseph²; *de ware ~* Mr Right

jr. = *junior*

jubelen (jubelde, h. gejubeld) *vi* jubilate, be jubilant, exult; ~ van vreugde shout for joy; **'jubelfeest** (-en) *o* jubilee; **–jaar** (-jaren) *o* jubilee year; **–kreet** (-kreten) *m* shout of joy; **–zang** (-en) *m* paean

jubi'laris (-sen) *m* person celebrating his jubilee; hero of the feast; **jubi'leren** (jubileerde, h. gejubileerd) *vi* 1 jubilate, be jubilant; 2 celebrate one's jubilee; **jubi'leum** [- ˈle.üm] (-s en -ea) *o* jubilee

'juchtle(d)er *o* Russia leather; **'juchtleren** *aj* Russia leather

'judaskus (-sen) *m* Judas kiss; **–penning** (-en) *m* honesty; **'judassen** (judaste, h. gejudast) *vt* tease, nag, badger

'judo *o* judo; **ju'doka** ('s) *m-v* judoka

juf (-fen en -s) *v* F = juffrouw; **'juffer** (-s) *v* 1 young lady, miss; 2 ⚓ pole, beam; 3 paving-beetle, rammer; **–shondje** (-s) *o* toy dog; zie ook: beven; **'juffertje** (-s) *v* missy; **~-in-'t-'groen** (juffertjes-in-'t-groen) *o* 🌿 love-in-a-mist; **'juffrouw** (-en) *v* miss, (young) lady; (a l s a a n s p r e k i n g) 1 miss; 2 madam; *de ~ the young lady*; *onze ~* (k i n d e r j u f f r o u w) our nurse; (o n d e r w ij z e r e s) our teacher; ~ van gezelschap lady-companion

'juichen (juichte, h. gejuicht) *vi* shout, jubilate;

~ over exult at (in); *de ~de menigte* the cheering crowd; **'juichkreet** (-kreten), **–toon** (-tonen) *m* shout of joy, cheer

juist I *aj* exact, correct, right, proper, precise; *het ~e midden* the happy (golden) mean; *het ~e woord* the right (proper) word; ~, *dat is het* right, exactly; *zeer ~* very well; hear! hear! [to an orator]; **II** *ad* just; exactly; correctly; *ik wou ~... I* was just going to...; *zeer ~ gezegd* that's it exactly; ~ *wat ik hebben moet* the very thing I want; ~ *daarom* for that very reason; *waarom ~ zo'n vent?* why he of all people?; *waarom ~ hier?* why here of all places?; **–heid** *v* exactness, exactitude, correctness, precision

ju'jube [ʒy.ˈʒy.bə] (-s) *m* & *v* jujube

juk (-ken) *o* yoke; beam [of balance]; *het ~ afschudden (afwerpen)* shake (throw) off the yoke; *onder het ~ brengen* bring under the yoke

'jukbeen (-deren) *o* cheek-bone

'juli *m* July

'jullie I *pers. vnmw.* you, F you fellows, you people; *is het van ~?* is it yours?; **II** *bez. vnmw.* your

jun. = *junior*

'juni *m* June

'junior (-ioren en -iores) junior; *P. ~*, ook: the younger P.

ju'pon [ʒy.ˈpòn] (-s) *m* petticoat

ju'reren [ʒy.ˈre.rə(n)] (jureerde, h. gejureerd) *va* act as a judge or umpire in a competition

ju'ridisch juridical; legal [adviser, aspect, ground]; **juris'dictie** [-ˈdɪksi.] (-s en -dictiën) *v* jurisdiction; **jurispru'dentie** [-ˈdɪn(t)si.] *v* jurisprudence; collective body of judgements given; **ju'rist** (-en) *m* 1 jurist, barrister, lawyer; 2 law-student; **juriste'rij** *v* legal quibbling

jurk (-en) *v* frock, dress, gown

'jury [ˈʒy:ri.] ('s) *v* jury; **–lid** (-leden) *o* 1 member of the jury, judge; 2 ⚖ juror, juryman, jurywoman; **–rechtspraak** *v* trial by jury

jus [ʒy.] *m* gravy; **–kom** (-men) *v* gravy-boat; **–lepel** (-s) *m* gravy-spoon

jus'titie [-ˈti.(t)si.] *v* justice; judicature; *de ~* ook: the law; the police [are after him]; **justiti'eel** judicial

Jut (-ten) *m* Jutlander, Jute; || *hoofd (kop) van ~* try-your-strength machine

'jute *v* jute; **–fabriek** (-en) *v* jute mill; **–zak** (-ken) *m* gunny bag

'jutter (-s) *m* = strandjutter

ju'weel (-welen) *o* jewel², gem²; *een ~ van bouwkunst* an architectural gem; *een ~ van een vrouw* a jewel of a woman; **ju'welen** *aj* jewelled; **ju'welenkistje** (-s) *o* jewel-box, jewel-case; **juwe'lier** (-s) *m* jeweller; **–swinkel** (-s) *m* jeweller's (shop)

K

k [ka.] ('s) *v* k

ka *v* = *kaai*

kaai (-en) *v* quay, wharf; embankment [along river]; **–geld** (-en) *o* quayage, wharfage, pierage

'kaaiman (-s en -nen) *m* cayman, caiman, alligator

'kaaimuur (-muren) *m* quay wall; **–werker** (-s) *m* wharf-labourer, wharf-porter

kaak (kaken) *v* 1 jaw, jaw-bone; 2 gill [of fish]; 3 mandible [of an insect]; *aan (op) de* ~ *stellen* (put into the) pillory, denounce, expose, show up; *met beschaamde kaken* shamefaced; **–been** (-deren) *o* jaw-bone, mandible

'kaakje (-s) *o* biscuit

'kaakslag (-slagen) *m* slap in the face

kaal *eig* 1 (m e n s) bald; 2 (v o g e l) callow, unfledged; 3 (b o o m) leafless, bare; 4 (k l e r e n) threadbare; 5 (v e l d e n, h e i) barren; 6 (m u r e n) bare, naked; *fig* shabby; *zo* ~ *als een biljartbal* as bold a a coot; *zo* ~ *als een rat* as poor as a 'church mouse; *er* ~ *afkomen* come away with a flea in one's ear, fare badly; ~ *vreten* eat bare; **–geknipt** close-cropped [heads]; **–geschoren** (close-)shaven; shorn [sheep]; **–heid** *v* baldness [of head]; bareness [of wall &]; threadbareness, shabbiness[2] [of a coat]; barrenness [of a tract of land];

kaal'hoofdig baldheaded; **–heid** *v* baldness; **☊** alopecia; **'kaalkop** (-pen) *m* baldpate, baldhead; **–slag** *m* clear-cutting, deforestation

kaam *v*, **'kaamsel** *o* mould

'kaantjes *mv* greaves, cracklings

kaap (kapen) *v* cape, headland, promontory; *de Kaap de Goede Hoop* the Cape of Good Hope; **'Kaapstad** *v* Cape Town

'kaapstander (-s) *m* capstan

'kaapvaarder (-s) *m* privateer; **–vaart** *v* privateering

kaar (karen) *v* basket

'kaard(e) (-en) *v* card; **'kaardebol** (-len) *m* teasel; **–distel** (-s) *m* & *v* teasel; **'kaarden** (kaardde, h. gekaard) *vt* card [wool]; **'kaard-wol** *v* carding wool

kaars (-en) *v* 1 [tallow, wax] candle; [wax] taper; 2 ☊ (v. p a a r d e b l o e m) blowball; *in de* ~ *vliegen* burn one's wings; **'kaarsenfabriek** (-en) *v* candle-factory; **–maker** (-s) *m* candle-maker; **'kaarsepit** (-ten) *v* candle-wick; **–snuiter** (-s) *m* (pair of) snuffers; **'kaarslicht** *o* candlelight; *bij* ~ by candlelight; **–recht** straight as an arrow; ~ *zitten* sit bolt upright;

–snuiter = *kaarsesnuiter*; **–vet** *o* tallow

kaart (-en) *v* 1 (s p e e l k a a r t, n a a m k a a r t, v o o r a a n t e k e n i n g e n &) card; 2 (z e e k a a r t) chart; 3 (l a n d k a a r t) map; 4 (t o e g a n g s k a a r t) ticket; *een doorgestoken* ~ a put-up job, a trumped-up charge; *groene* ~ green card; *goede* ~*en hebben* have a good hand; *alle* ~*en op tafel leggen (gooien)* put (throw) all one's cards on the table; *het is een (geen) haalbare* ~ it is (not) on the cards; *alle* ~*en in handen hebben* hold all the cards; *iem. de* ~ *leggen* tell sbd.'s fortunes from the cards; *de* ~ *van het land kennen* know the lie of the land; ~ *spelen* play (at) cards; *open* ~ *spelen* lay one's cards on the table; act above-board, be frank; ● *in* ~ *brengen* map [a region], chart [a coast]; *iem. in de* ~ *kijken* look at sbd.'s cards; *zich in de* ~ *laten kijken* show one's hand; *in iems.* ~ *spelen* play into sbd.'s hands, play sbd.'s game; *op* ~ *brengen* card-index [addresses &]; *alles op één* ~ *zetten* stake one's all on one (a single) throw, put all one's eggs in one basket; **–avondje** (-s) *o* card-party; **–club** (-s) *v* card(-playing) club; **'kaarten** (kaartte, h. gekaart) *vi* play (at) cards; **'kaartenbakje** (-s) *o* card-tray; **–huis** (-huizen) *o* house of cards; *als een* ~ *in elkaar vallen* come down like a house of cards; **–kamer** (-s) *v* ⚓ chart-room; **–maker** (-s) *m* cartographer, map maker; **'kaartje** (-s) *o* 1 (n a a m) card; 2 (t r e i n &) ticket; *zijn* ~ *afgeven (bij)* leave one's card (upon); *een* ~ *leggen* have a game of cards; **'kaartlegster** (-s) *v* fortune-teller (by cards); **–spel** (-spelen en -len) *o* 1 (h e t s p e l e n) card-playing, cards; 2 (e e n p a r t ij) game at (of) cards; 3 (s o o r t v a n s p e l) card game; 4 (p a k k a a r t e n) pack of cards; **–speler** (-s) *m* card-player; **–systeem** [-s i.s-] (-temen) *o* card-index (system); **–verkoop** *m* sale of tickets; ~ *van 8 tot 10* box-office open from 8 till 10

kaas (kazen) *m* cheese; *zich de* ~ *niet van het brood laten eten* stand up for oneself, fight back; *hij heeft er geen* ~ *van gegeten* he doesn't understand anything about it, he doesn't know the first thing about it; **–achtig** cheesy, cheese-like, caseous; **–bereiding** *v* cheese-making; **–boer** (-en) *m* 1 cheese-maker; 2 (v e r k o p e r) cheesemonger; **–boor** (-boren) *v* cheese-taster; **–doek** (-en) *m* cheese cloth; **–handel** *m* cheese-trade; **–handelaar** (-s en -laren) *m* cheesemonger; **–jeskruid** *o* mallow; **–kop** (-pen) *m* Belgian nickname for a Dutchman;

–koper (-s) *m* cheesemonger; **–korst** (-en) *v* cheese-rind, rind of cheese; **–made** (-n) *v* cheese-maggot; **–maker** (-s) *m* cheese-maker; **–markt** (-en) *v* cheese-market; **–mes** (-sen) *o* 1 cheese-cutter; 2 (m e s j e) cheese-knife; **–pakhuis** (-huizen) *o* cheese-warehouse; **–pers** (-en) *v* cheese-press; **–schaaf** (-schaven) *v* cheese slicer; **–stof** *v* casein; **–stolp** (-en) *v* cheese-cover; **–vorm** (-en) *m* cheese-mould; **–winkel** (-s) *m* cheese-shop

'Kaatje *v* & *v* Kitty, Kate

'kaatsbal (-len) *m* hand-ball; **'kaatsen** (kaatste, h. gekaatst) *vi* play at ball; *wie kaatst moet de bal verwachten* if you play at bowls you must look for rubbers; **'kaatsspel** *o* Dutch tennis

ka'baal *o* noise, din, hubbub, racket; **~** *maken* (*schoppen, trappen*) kick up a row

'kabbelen (kabbelde, h. gekabbeld) *vi* ripple, babble, purl, lap; **–ling** *v* rippling, babble, lapping, purl

'kabel (-s) *m* ⚓ & ⟟ cable; **–baan** (-banen) *v* cable railway, funicular railway; **–ballon** (-s) *m* captive balloon; **–bericht** (-en) *o* cable-message, cablegram, cable; **–garen** (-s) *o* rope-yarn

kabel'jauw (-en) *m* cod, cod-fish; **–vangst** *v* cod-fishing

'kabellengte (-n en -s) *v* cable's length; **–net** (-ten) *o* grid; **–schip** (-schepen) *o* cable-ship; **–spoorweg** (-wegen) *m* cable-railway; telpher line; **–telegram** (-men) *o* = *kabelbericht*; **–televisie** *v* cable television; **–touw** (-en) *o* cable

kabi'net (-ten) *o* (m e u b e l) cabinet; (k a m e r t j e) closet; (k u n s t v e r z a m e-l i n g) picture-gallery, museum, ✎ cabinet; (r e g e r i n g) cabinet, government; **–formaat** *o* cabinet-size; **kabi'netscrisis** (-sen en -crises) *v* cabinet crisis; **–formateur** (-s) *m* cabinetmaker; **–kwestie** *v* cabinet question; *de ~ stellen* ask for a vote of confidence

ka'bouter (-s) *m* elf, gnome, dwarf, brownie [also = junior girl guide]

'kachel (-s) *v* stove; *elektrisch ~tje* electric fire (heater); **–glans** *m* blacklead; **–hout** *o* kindling, fire-wood; **–pijp** (-en) *v* 1 stove-pipe; 2 **F** chimney-pot hat, stove-pipe; **–smid** (-smeden) *m* stove-maker

ka'daster (-s) *o* 1 land registry; 2 Offices of the Land registry; **kadas'traal** cadastral

ka'daver (-s) *o* (dead) body; ✝ subject

'kade (-n) *v* quay, wharf; embankment [along a river]; **–geld** (-en) *o* quayage, wharfage; **–muur** (-muren) *m* quay wall

'kader (-s) *o* ⚔ (regimental) cadre, skeleton [of a regiment]; *fig* framework; box [in newspaper &]; *b i n n e n het ~ van* whithin the framework

of [this organization]; *i n het ~ van* in connection with [the reorganization, the exhibition]; under [this agreement, a scheme]; **–cursus** [s = z] (-sen) *m* training-course for executives

ka'detje (-s) *o* French roll [of bread]

ka'duuk used up, decrepit; broken

kaf *o* chaff; *het ~ van het koren scheiden* separate chaff from wheat, sift the grain from the husk; *als ~ voor de wind* like chaff before the wind

'kaffer (-s) *m* boor, lout

kaft (-en) *m* & *v* wrapper, cover, jacket

'kaftan (-s) *m* caftan

'kaften (kaftte, h. gekaft) *vt* cover [a book]; **'kaftpapier** *o* wrapping-paper

'kaïk (-en) *m* caique

'Kaïnsteken *o* brand (mark) of Cain

'kajak (-s en -ken) *m* kayak

ka'juit (-en) *v* cabin; **ka'juitsjongen** (-s) *m* cabin-boy; **–poort** (-en) *v* porthole

kak *m* muck, mire, **P** shit, crap; (b l u f) *kale* (*kouwe*) **~** bunkum, baloney, hot air, swank, **S** eyewash

'kakebeen = *kaakbeen*

'kakelbont motley, variegated, chequered

'kakelen (kakelde, h. gekakeld) *vi* cackle[2], *fig* gabble, chatter

kake'ment (-en) *o* jaw(s)

'kaken (kaakte, h. gekaakt) *vt* cure [herrings]

'kaketoe (-s) *m* cockatoo

'kaki *o* khaki

'kakken (kakte, h. gekakt) *vi* **P** shit, crap; *iem. te ~ zetten* ridicule sbd., make a fool of sbd.

'kakkerlak (-ken) *m* cockroach, blackbeetle

kakofo'nie (-nieën) *v* cacophony

ka'lander (-s) *m* ✻ weevil; || *v* ✗ calender

kal(e)'bas (-sen) *v* calabash, gourd

ka'lender (-s) *m* calendar; **–jaar** (-jaren) *o* calendar year

kalf (kalveren) *o* 1 ⚲ calf; 2 (b o v e n-d r e m p e l) lintel; 3 *fig* calf; *een ~ van een jongen* a calf, a booby; *als het ~ verdronken is, dempt men de put* after the horse has bolted (is stolen) the stable-door is locked; *het gouden ~ aanbidden* worship the golden calf; zie ook: *mesten*

kal'faten (kalfaatte, h. gekalfaat), **kal'fateren** (kalfaterde, h. gekalfaterd) *vt* ⚓ caulk

'kalfsbiefstuk (-ken) *m* veal steak; **–borst** (-en) *v* breast of veal; **–bout** (-en) *m* joint of veal; **–gehakt** *o* minced veal; **–karbonade** (-s en -n) *v* veal cutlet; **–kop** (-pen) *m* calf's head; **–kotelet** (-ten) *v* veal cutlet; **–lapje** (-s) *o* veal steak; **–le(d)er** *o* calf, calfskin, calfleather; *in kalfsleren band* bound in calf; **–oester** (-s) *v* veal collop; **–schnitzel** [-ʃni.tzəl] (-s) *o* & *m* scallop of veal; **–vlees** *o* veal; **–zwezerik** (-en) *m* sweetbread '**kali** *m* potassium

ka'liber (-s) *o* calibre[2], bore

ka'lief (-en) *m* caliph; **kali'faat** (-faten) *o* caliphate

'**kalium** *o* potassium

kalk *m* 1 lime; 2 (g e b l u s t e) slaked lime; 3 (o n g e b l u s t e) quicklime; 4 (m e t s e l) mortar; 5 (p l e i s t e r) plaster; **–aarde** *v* calcareous earth; **–achtig** limy, calcareous; **–bak** (-ken) *m* hod; **kalkbrande'rij** (-en) *v* limekiln; '**kalkei** (-eren) *o* preserved egg; '**kalken** (kalkte, h. gekalkt) *vt* 1 lime [skins &]; roughcast, plaster [a wall]; 2 (= schrijven) write, chalk; '**kalkgroeve** (-n) *v* limestone quarry; **–houdend** calcareous, calciferous

kal'koen (-en) *m* ♂ turkey

'**kalkoven** (-s) *m* limekiln; **–put** (-ten) *m* lime pit; **–steen** *o* & *m* limestone; **–water** *o* lime water; **–zandsteen** *m* sand-lime bricks

kalm calm, quiet, composed, peaceful, untroubled; ~ (*aan*)! easy!, steady!; *blijf* ~ take it easy; *doe* (*het*) ~ *aan* go easy (on *met*), **S** cool it; ~ *en bedaard* calm and quiet, cool and collected; **kal'meren I** (kalmeerde, h. gekalmeerd) *vt* calm, soothe, appease, tranquillize; **II** (kalmeerde, is gekalmeerd) *vi* calm down, compose oneself; ~*d middel* sedative, tranquillizer, calmative

'**kalmoes** *m* sweet flag

'**kalmpjes** calmly; ~ *aan*! easy!, steady!, easy does it!; '**kalmte** *v* calm, calmness, composure; quiet, quietude, repose

ka'lotje (-s) *o* 1 (v. h e e r) skull-cap; 2 (v a n g e e s t e l ij k e) calotte

'**kalven** (kalfde, h. gekalfd) *vi* calve; '**kalverachtig** calf-like; '**kalveren** meerv. v. *kalf*; '**kalverliefde** (-s) *v* calf-love

kam (-men) *m* comb [for the hair]; crest [of a cock, helmet, hill &]; bridge [of violin]; ✕ cam, cog [of wheel]; hand [of bananas]; *over één* ~ *scheren* lump (together) with, treat all alike

ka'meel (-melen) *m* camel [also for raising ships]; **–drijver** (-s) *m* camel-driver; **–haar** *o* camel's hair

kamele'on [ka.me.le.'òn] (-s) *o* & *m* chameleon[2]; **–tisch** chameleontic; *fig* unreliable

kame'nier (-s) *v* (lady's) maid

'**kamer** (-s) *v* 1 room, chamber; 2 chamber [of a gun]; 3 ventricle [of the heart]; *donkere* ~ dark room; *de Eerste Kamer* the First Chamber; [in Britain] the Upper House; *gemeubileerde* ~*s* furnished apartments; *de Tweede Kamer* the Second Chamber; [in Britain] the Lower House; *de Kamer van Koophandel* the Chamber of Commerce; *de Kamer der Volksvertegenwoordigers* the [Belgian] Chamber of Deputies; *de* ~ *bijeenroepen* convoke the House; ~*s te huur*

hebben have apartments (rooms) to let; *zijn* ~ *houden* keep one's room; *de* ~ *ontbinden* (*openen, sluiten*) dissolve (open, prorogue) the Chamber; *hij woont op* ~*s* he lives in lodgings; *ik woon hier op* ~*s* I am in rooms here; *hij is niet op zijn* ~ he is not in his room

kame'raad (-raden) *m* comrade, mate, fellow, companion, **F** chum, pal; **–schap** *v* companionship, (good-)fellowship, comradeship; **kameraad'schappelijk I** *aj* friendly, **F** chummy; **II** *ad* in a friendly manner

'**kamerarrest** *o* confinement to one's room; ~ *hebben* **J** have to keep one's room; **–bewoner** (-s) *m*, **–bewoonster** (-s) *v* lodger; **–breed** ~ *tapijt* wall-to-wall carpeting; **–debat** (-ten) *o* Parliamentary debate; **–deur** (-en) *v* room-door; **–dienaar** (-s en -naren) *m* 1 valet, man(-servant); 2 (a a n h e t h o f) groom (of the chamber), chamberlain; **–genoot** (-noten) *m* room-mate; **–gymnastiek** [-ɣImnᴂsti.k] *v* indoor gymnastics; **–heer** (-heren) *m* chamberlain, gentleman in waiting [at court]; **–huur** *v* room-rent; **–jas** (-sen) *m* dressing-gown; **–lid** (-leden) *o* member of the Chamber, member of Parliament [in Britain]; **–meisje** (-s) *o* chambermaid; **–muziek** *v* chamber music

Kame'roen *o* Cameroon

'**kamerontbinding** (-en) *v* dissolution of the Chamber(s); **–orkest** (-en) *o* chamber orchestra; **–plant** (-en) *v* indoor plant; **–pot** (-ten) *m* chamber (pot); **–scherm** (-en) *o* draught-screen, folding-screen; **–temperatuur** *v* room temperature; **–verhuurder** (-s) *m*, **–verhuurster** (-s) *v* lodging-house keeper; **–verslag** (-slagen) *o* report of the Parliamentary debates; **–zetel** (-s) *m* seat (in Parliament)

'**kamfer** *m* camphor; **–boom** (-bomen) *m* camphor-tree; **–spiritus** *m* camphorated spirits

'**kamgaren** (-s) *o* & *aj* worsted

'**kamhagedis** (-sen) *v* iguana

'**kamig** mouldy

ka'mille *v* camomile; **–thee** *m* camomile tea

kami'zool (-zolen) *o* camisole

'**kammen** (kamde, h. gekamd) **I** *vt* comb; card [wool]; **II** *vr zich* ~ comb one's hair

1 kamp (-en) *o* ✕ camp[2]

2 kamp (-en) *m* combat, fight, struggle, contest

3 kamp *aj* ~ *geven* yield, throw up the sponge; *het bleef* ~ the race (the sports &) ended in a tie (in a draw)

kam'panje (-s) *v* ⚓ poop(-deck)

'**kampcommandant** (-en) *m* camp commandant

kam'peerauto [-ɔuto., -o.to.] ('s) *m*, **–bus** (-sen) *v* camper (van); **–centrum** (-s en -tra) *o*

= *kampeerterrein*; **–der** (-s) *m* camper; **–terrein** (-en) *o* camping ground, camping site; **–wagen** (-s) *m* caravan

kampe'ment (-en) *o* encampment, camp

'kampen (kampte, h. gekampt) *vi* fight, combat, struggle, contend, wrestle; *te ~ hebben met* have to contend with

kam'peren (kampeerde, h. gekampeerd) **I** *vt* (en)camp; **II** *vi* camp, be (lie) encamped, camp out; **III** *o* camping

kamper'foelie (-s) *v* honeysuckle; *wilde ~* woodbine

kampi'oen (-en) *m* champion°; **–schap** (-pen) *o sp* championship

'kamprechter (-s) *m* umpire; **–vechter** (-s) *m* fighter, wrestler; champion

'kampvuur (-vuren) *o* camp-fire; **–wacht** (-en) *v* camp guard

'kamrad (-raderen) *o* cog-wheel; **–vormig** comb-shaped; **–wol** *v* combing-wool

kan (-nen) *v* 1 jug, can, mug, tankard; 2 litre; *het is in ~nen en kruiken* the matter (everything) is settled, fixed (up)

ka'naal (-nalen) *o* 1 (g r a c h t) canal; 2 (v a a r g e u l, *T, fig*) channel; *het Kanaal* the Channel

'Kanaän *o* Canaan; **Kanaä'niet** (-en) *m* Canaanite

kanali'satie [-'za.(t)si.] (-s) *v* canalization; **kanali'seren** (kanaliseerde, h. gekanaliseerd) *vt* canalize

ka'narie (-s) *m* canary; **–geel** canary-yellow; **–kooi** (-en) *v* canary-bird cage; **–piet** (-en) *m* canary; **–zaad** (-zaden) *o* canary-seed

kan'deel *v* caudle

'kandelaar (-s en -laren) *m* candlestick; **kande'laber** (-s) *m* candelabra

kandi'daat (-daten) *m* candidate [for appointment or honour]; applicant [for an office]; *iem. ~ stellen* nominate sbd., put sbd. up; *zich ~ stellen* 1 become a candidate; 2 contest a seat in Parliament, stand for [Amsterdam]; *~ in de letteren* Bachelor of Arts; *~ in de rechten* Bachelor of Laws; **kandi'daatsexamen** (-s) *o* little-go; **kandi'daatstelling** *v* nomination; **kandida'tuur** (-turen) *v* candidature, candidateship, nomination

kan'dij *v* candy; **–suiker** *m* sugar-candy

ka'neel *m* & *o* cinnamon

'kangoeroe (-s) *m* kangaroo

'kanis (-sen) *m* (h o o f d) **F** nut, pate, noddle; *hou je ~* hold your trap; *iem. op z'n ~ geven* tan sbd.'s hide

'kanjer (-s) *m* a big one, **F** spanker, whopper

'kanker *m* ☞ cancer; ☞ canker; *fig* canker; **–aar** (-s) *m* **F** grouser, grumbler; **–achtig** cancerous, cancroid; **–bestrijding** *v* fight against

cancer; **'kankeren** (kankerde, h. gekankerd) *vi* 1 cancer; 2 *fig* canker; 3 **F** grouse, grumble; **'kankergezwel** (-len) *o* cancerous tumour, cancerous growth; **–lijder** (-s) *m* cancer patient; **–onderzoek** *o* cancer research; **–pit** (-ten) *m* grumbler, croaker

kanni'baal (-balen) *m* cannibal; **–s** cannibalistic; **kanniba'lisme** *v* cannibalism

'kano ('s) *m* canoe; **'kanoën** (kanode, h. gekanood) *vi* canoe

ka'non (-nen) *o* gun, cannon; **–gebulder** *o* roar (booming) of guns; **kanon'nade** (-s) *v* cannonade; **kanon'neerboot** (-boten) *m* & *v* gun-boat; **kanon'neren** (kanonneerde, h. gekanonneerd) *vt* cannonade; **ka'nonnevlees** *o* cannon-fodder; **kanon'nier** (-s) *m* gunner; **ka'nonschot** (-schoten) *o* cannon-shot; **ka'nonskogel** (-s) *m* cannon-ball; **ka'nonvuur** *o* gun-fire, cannonade

'kanosport *v* canoeing; **–vaarder** (-s) *m* canoeist

kans (-en) *v* chance, opportunity; *iem. een ~ geven* give sbd. a chance; *~ hebben om...* have a chance of...ing; *hij heeft goede ~en* he stands a good change; *weinig ~ hebben om...* stand little chance of...ing; *geen schijn van ~* not the ghost of a chance; *de ~ krijgen om...*get a chance of...ing; *de ~ lopen om...* run the risk of...ing; *~ maken* zie *~ hebben*; *een ~ missen* lose (miss) an opportunity; *de ~ schoon zien om...* see one's chance (opportunity) to...; *de ~ waarnemen* seize the opportunity; *de ~ wagen* take one's chance; *als hij ~ ziet om...* when he sees his chance to..., when he manages to...; *ik zie er geen ~ toe* I don't see my way to do it, I can't manage it; *er is alle ~ dat...* there is every chance (it is very likely) that...; *daar is geen ~ op* there is no chance of it; *de ~ keerde* the (my, his &) luck was turning; *de ~en staan gelijk* the odds are even

'kansel (-s) *m* pulpit

kansela'rij (-en) *v* chancellery; **–stijl** *m* official style, officialese; **kanse'lier** (-s en -en) *m* chancellor

'kanselredenaar (-s) *m* pulpit orator

'kansrekening *v* calculus of probabilities; **–spel** (-spelen) *o* game of chance

1 kant (-en) *m* 1 side [of a road, of a bed &]; border [of the Thames &]; edge [of the water, of a forest]; brink [of a precipice]; margin [of a printed or written page]; 2 (r i c h t i n g) side, direction; 3 aspect [of life, of the matter, of the same idea]; *dat raakt ~ noch wal* that is neither here nor there; *die ~ moet het uit met...* that way... ought to tend; *een andere ~ uitkijken* look the other way; ● *a a n d e ~ van de weg* at the side of the road, by the roadside; *aan de andere*

~ *moeten wij niet vergeten dat...* on the other hand (but then) we should not forget that...; *aan de veilige* ~ on the safe side; *dat is weer aan* ~ that job is jobbed; *de kamer aan* ~ *doen* straighten up (do) the room, put things tidy; *zijn zaken aan* ~ *doen* retire from business; *het mes snijdt aan twee* ~*en* the knife cuts both ways; *aan de* ~ *zetten* cast aside, throw over; *n a a r alle* ~*en* [look, run] in every direction; *een vaatje o p zijn* ~ *zetten* cant (tilt) a cask; *het is een dubbeltje op zijn* ~ zie *dubbeltje*; *veel o v e r zijn* ~ *laten gaan* not be so very particular (about...); *v a n alle* ~*en* on every side, from every quarter; *de zaak van alle (verschillende)* ~*en bekijken* look at the question from all sides (from different angles); *van die* ~ *bekeken...* looked at from that point...; *van vaders* ~ on the paternal (one's father's) side; *van de* ~ *van* on the part of; *van welke* ~ *komt de wind?* from which side does the wind blow?; *iem. van* ~ *helpen (maken)* put sbd. out of the way, do sbd. in; *zich van* ~ *maken* make (do) away with oneself; zie ook: 1 *zijde*

2 kant *m* (s t o f n a a m) lace

3 kant *aj* neat; ~ *en klaar* all ready; cut and dried; ready to hand

kan'teel (-telen) *m* crenel, battlement

'kanteldeur (-en) *v* up-and-over door; **'kantelen I** (kantelde, h. gekanteld) *vt* (w e n t e l e n) turn over, overturn; (o p z'n k a n t z e t t e n) cant, tilt; **II** (kantelde, is gekanteld) *vi* topple over, overturn, turn over; ⚓ capsize; *niet* ~*!* this side up

1 'kanten (kantte, h. gekant) **I** *vt* cant, square; **II** *vr zich* ~ *tegen* oppose; zie ook *gekant*

2 'kanten *aj* lace

'kantig angular

kan'tine (-s) *v* canteen; **–wagen** (-s) *m* mobile canteen

'kantje (-s) *o* page, side [of note-paper]; *het was op het* ~ *af* it was a near (close) thing, it was touch and go; *op het* ~ *af geslaagd* got trough by the skin of his teeth; *'t was op het* ~ *van onbeleefd* it was sailing near the wind

'kantklossen *o* pillow lace-making

'kantlijn (-en) *v* 1 marginal line; 2 edge [of a cube &]; *een* ~ *trekken* rule a margin

kan'ton (-s) *o* canton; **–gerecht** (-en) *o* magistrate's court; **–rechter** (-s) *m* ± justice of the peace

kan'toor (-toren) *o* office; ~ *van afzending* forwarding office; ~ *van ontvangst* delivery office; *daar ben je a a n het rechte (verkeerde)* ~ you have come to the right (wrong) shop; *o p een* ~ in an office; *t e n kantore van...* at the office of...; **–bediende** (-n en -s) *m-v* (office) clerk; **–behoeften** *mv* stationery; **–boek** (-en) *o* office book; **–boekhandel** (-s) *m* stationer's

(shop); **–boekhandelaar** (-s en -laren) *m* stationer; **–gebouw** (-en) *o* office building; **–klerk** (-en) *m* clerk [in bank, office &]; **–kruk** (-ken) *v* office stool; **–machine** [-ʃi.nə] (-s) *v* office machine; ~*s* ook: office machinery; **–meubelen** *mv* office furniture; **–personeel** *o* office staff, clerical staff, clerks; **–stoel** (-en) *m* office chair; **–tuin** (-en) *m* open-plan (landscaped) office; **–uren** *mv* office hours; **–werkzaamheden** *mv* office work

'kantrechten (kantrechtte, h. gekantrecht) *vt* square

'kanttekening (-en) *v* marginal note

'kantwerk (-en) *o* lace-work; **–ster** (-s) *v* lace-maker

ka'nunnik (-en) *m* canon

kao'lien *o* kaolin

kap (kappen) *v* 1 (h o o f d b e d e k k i n g) cap [of a cloak], hood [of a cowl]; 2 (v. v o e r-t u i g) hood; 3 (v. s c h o o r s t e e n) cowl; 4 (v. m o l e n) cap; 5 (v. l a m p) shade; 6 (v. l a a r s) top; 7 (v. h u i s) roof, roofing; 8 (v. m u u r) coping; 9 ✗ bonnet [of motor-car engine], cowl(ing) [of aircraft engine]; cap, cover

ka'pel (-len) *v* 1 chapel [house of prayer]; 2 ♪ band; 3 🦋 butterfly

kape'laan (-s) *m* chaplain, *rk* curate, assistant priest

ka'pelmeester (-s) *m* (military) bandmaster; conductor; ⚓ choirmaster [in a church or chapel]

'kapen (kaapte h. gekaapt) **I** *vi* 1 ⚓ privateer; 2 ⚓ hijack; 3 (g a p p e n) filch, pilfer; **II** *vt* 1 ⚓ capture; 2 ⚓ hijack [aircraft]; 3 (w e g-n e m e n) filch, pilfer; **'kaper** (-s) *m* 1 ⚓ privateer, raider; 2 ⚓ hijacker [of aircraft]; *er zijn* ~*s op de kust* 1 the coast is not clear; 2 there are rivals in the field; **–brief** (-brieven) *m* letter of marque (and reprisal); **–schip** (-schepen) *o* privateer, corsair; **'kaping** (-en) *v* ⚓ hijacking [of aircraft]

kapi'taal I *aj* capital [letter]; *een* ~ *huis* a fine (substantial) house; **II** (-talen) *o* capital; ~ *en interest* principal and interest; **–belegging** (-en) *v* investment (of capital); **–goederen** *mv* capital goods; **–intensief** requiring large capital assets; **kapitaal'krachtig** substantial [firm], financially strong, backed by sufficient capital; **'kapitaalmarkt** *v* capital market; **–schaarste** *v* shortage of capital; **kapi'taals-overdrachtbelasting** (-en) *v* capital transfer tax; **kapi'taalvlucht** *v* flight of capital; **–vorming** *v* capital formation; **kapitali'satie** [-'za.(t)si.] (-s) *v* capitalization; **kapitali'seren** (kapitaliseerde, h. gekapitaliseerd) *vt* capitalize; **kapita'lisme** *o* capitalism; **kapita'list** (-en) *m* capitalist; **–isch** I *aj* capitalist [country, society], capitalistic [production]; **II** *ad* capitalistically

kapi'teel (-telen) *o* capital [of a column]

kapi'tein (-s) *m* ⚓ & ⚓ captain; ⚓ master; **~-luitenant-ter-zee** commander; **~-vlieger** flight-lieutenant

Kapi'tool *o* Capitol

ka'pittel (-s) *o* chapter; **ka'pittelen** (kapittelde, h. gekapitteld) *vt iem.* ~ lecture sbd., read sbd. a lecture; **ka'pittelheer** (-heren) *m* canon; **–kerk** (-en) *v* minster

'kapje (-s) *o* 1 little cap; 2 circumflex; 3 heel (crusty end) [of a loaf]

'kaplaars (-laarzen) *v* top-boot

'kapmantel (-s) *m* dressing-jacket

'kapmes (-sen) *o* chopper, cleaver

ka'poen (-en) *m* capon

ka'pok *m* kapok

ka'pot broken, out of order, gone to pieces [of a tool &]; in holes [of a coat &]; *ik ben* ~ I am fairly knocked up; *ik ben er* ~ *van* I am dreadfully cut up by it; ~ *gaan* go to pieces; ~ *gooien* smash; ~ *maken* spoil, put out of order, break

ka'potje (-s) *o* 1 (lady's) bonnet; 2 (c o n d o o m) sheath, S French letter

'kappen (kapte, h. gekapt) **I** *vt* 1 chop [wood]; cut (down), fell [trees]; 2 dress [the hair]; **II** *vi* & *va* 1 chop &; 2 dress the hair; **III** *vr zich* ~ dress one's hair; **–er** (-s) *m* hairdresser

'kappertjes *mv* capers

'kappersbediende (-n en -s) *m-v* hairdresser's assistant; **–winkel** (-s) *m* hairdresser's (shop)

'kapseizen (kapseisde, is gekapseisd) *vi* ⚓ capsize

'kapsel (-s) *o* coiffure, hairdo, hair-style

'kapsies *mv* F ~ *maken* recalcitrate, be obstinate

kap'sones *mv* F ~ *hebben* swagger, give oneself airs

'kapspiegel (-s) *m* toilet-glass; **'kapster** (-s) *v* (lady) hairdresser

'kapstok (-ken) *m* 1 (a a n m u u r) row of pegs; 2 (i n g a n g) hat-rack, hat-stand, hall-stand, coat-rack; 3 (é é n h a a k) peg

'kaptafel (-s) *v* dressing-table

kapu'cijn (-en) *m* Capuchin

kapu'cijner (-s) *m* ⚬ marrowfat (pea)

'kapverbod *o* felling prohibition

kar (-ren) *v* cart [on 2 or 4 wheels]; **F** (f i e t s) bike

kar. = *karaat*

ka'raat (-s en -raten) *o* carat; *18-~s* 18-carat [gold]

kara'bijn (-en) *v* carbine

ka'raf (-fen) *v* 1 water-bottle; 2 decanter [for wine]

ka'rakter (-s) *o* 1 (a a r d) character; nature; 2

(l e t t e r t e k e n) character; **–eigenschappen** *mv* qualities of character; **–fout** (-en) *v* defect of character; **karakteri'seren** [s = z] (karakteriseerde, h. gekarakteriseerd) *vt* characterize; **karakteris'tiek** I *aj* characteristic; **II** *ad* characteristically; **III** (-en) *v* characterization; **ka'rakterkunde** *v* characterology, ethology; **–loos** characterless; **karakter'loosheid** *v* characterlessness, lack of character; **ka'rakterschets** (-en) *v* characterization; **–speler** (-s) *m* character actor; **–stuk** (-ken) *o* character piece; **–trek** (-ken) *m* trait of character, feature; **–vorming** *v* character-building

kara'mel (-s en -len) *v* caramel

ka'rate *o* karate

kara'vaan (-vanen) *v* caravan

kar'bies (-biezen) *v* shopping basket

karbo'nade (-s en -n) *v* chop, cutlet

kar'bonkel (-s en -en) *m* & *o* carbuncle

kar'bouw (-en) *m* (water) buffalo

kardi'naal (-nalen) **I** *m* cardinal; *tot* ~ *verheffen* raise to the purple; **II** *aj* cardinal [point, error]; **–schap** *o* cardinalship; **kardinaalshoed** (-en) *m* cardinal's hat

kare'kiet = *karkiet*

'Karel *m* Charles; ~ *de Grote* Charlemagne; ~ *de Kale* Charles the Bald; ~ *de Stoute* Charles the Bold

karia'tide (-n) *v* caryatid

'karig **I** *aj* scanty, frugal [meal], sparing [use]; *(niet)* ~ *zijn met* (not) be chary (sparing) of; **II** *ad* scantily, frugally, sparingly, with a sparing hand; **–heid** *v* scantiness, frugality, sparingness

karikaturi'seren [s = z] (karikaturiseerde, h. gekarikaturiseerd) *vt* caricature; **karika'tuur** (-turen) *v* caricature; **–tekenaar** (-s) *m* caricaturist

kar'kas (-sen) *o* & *v* carcass, carcase, skeleton

kar'kiet (-en) *m* reed-warbler

kar'mijn *o* carmine

karn (-en) *v* churn; **'karnemelk** *v* buttermilk; **'karnen** (karnde, h. gekarnd) *vt* churn; **'karnpols** (-en), **–stok** (-ken) *m* dasher; **–ton** (-nen) *v* churn

Karo'linger (-s) *m*, **Karo'lingisch** *aj* Carlovingian

ka'ros (-sen) *v* coach, state carriage   gian

Kar'paten *mv* Carpathians

'karper (-s) *m* carp

kar'pet (-ten) *o* (square of) carpet

'karren (karde, h. gekard) *vi* (f i e t s e n) pedal, (r i j d e n) drive

'karrepaard (-en) *o* cart-horse; **–spoor** (-sporen) *o* rut, cart track; **–vracht** (-en) *v* cart-load; **'karspoor** = *karrespoor*

1 kar'tel (-s) *o* cartel, syndicate, combine, **F** ring

2 'kartel (-s) *m* (k e r f) notch; **'karteldarm** (-en) *m* colon; **'kartelen** (kartelde, h. gekarteld) *vt* notch; mill [coins]; zie ook: *gekarteld*; **'kartelrand** (-en) *m* milled edge

kar'telvorming *v* formation of cartels

kar'teren (karteerde, h. gekarteerd) *vt* map; (i n z. ✈) survey; **–ring** *v* mapping; (i n z. ✈) survey(ing)

kar'ton (-s) *o* cardboard, pasteboard; *een ~* a cardboard box, a carton; **karton'nagefabriek** [-tò'na.ʒə-] (-en) *v* cardboard factory; **kar'tonnen** *aj* cardboard, pasteboard; **karton'neren** (kartonneerde, h. gekartonneerd) *vt* bind in boards [books]; *gekartonneerd* (in) boards

kar'tuizer (-s) *m* Carthusian (monk)

kar'wats (-en) *v* horsewhip, riding-whip

kar'wei (-en) *v & o* job; *op ~ gaan* go out jobbing; *op ~ zijn* be on the job; **–tje** (-s) *o* job; *(allerlei) ~s* odd jobs; *het is me een ~* it is a nice job

kar'wij *v* caraway

kas (-sen) *v* 1 (t e r i n v a t t i n g) case [of a watch], socket [of a tooth]; 2 (v o o r d r u i v e n &) hothouse, greenhouse, glasshouse; 3 $ cash; pay-office; (pay-)desk; 4 [unemployment &] fund; *kleine ~* petty cash; *'s lands ~* the exchequer, the coffers of the State; *de openbare ~* the public purse; *de ~ houden* keep the cash; *de ~ opmaken* make up the cash; ● *goed b ij ~ zijn* be in cash, be in funds, have plenty of money, be heeled; *slecht (niet) bij ~ zijn* be short of cash, be out of funds, be hard up; *geld i n ~* cash in hand; **–bloem** (-en) *v* hothouse (stove) flower; **–boek** (-en) *o* cashbook; **–druiven** *mv* hothouse grapes; **–geld** (-en) *o* till-money, cash (in hand); **–groente** (-n en -s) *v* hothouse vegetables

'kasjmier *o* cashmere

'kasmiddelen *mv* cash (in hand); **–plant** (-en) *v* hothouse plant; **~je** [*fig*] delicate person; **–register** (-s) *o* cash-register

'kassa ('s) *v* 1 cash; 2 cash-desk, (pay-)desk; check-out [of supermarket]; box-office [of cinema &]; (t e l m a c h i n e) cash-register, till; *per ~* net cash

'kassaldo ('s en -di) *o* cash balance; **'kassen** (kaste, h. gekast) *vt* set [in gold &]

kasse'rol = *kastrol*

kas'sier (-s) *m* 1 cashier, (v. b a n k ook:) teller; 2 banker; **kas'siersboekje** (-s) *o* passbook; **–kantoor** (-toren) *o* banking-office

kast (-en) *v* 1 cupboard [for crockery, provisions &]; wardrobe [for clothes]; chest [for belongings]; book-case [for books]; press [in a wall]; cabinet [for valuables]; 2 **F** diggings: room; **S** quod: prison; 3 case [of a watch &];

hem i n de ~ zetten **S** put him in quod; *iem. o p de ~ jagen* **F** rile, bait, tease sbd.

kas'tanje (-s) *v* chestnut; *wilde ~* horsechestnut; *voor iem. de ~s uit het vuur halen* pull the chestnuts out of the fire for sbd., be made a cat's-paw of; **–boom** (-bomen) *m* chestnut-tree; **–bruin** chestnut, auburn

'kaste (-n) *v* caste

kas'teel (-telen) *o* 1 castle, ⚔ citadel; 2 *sp* castle, rook [in chess]

'kastegeest *m* spirit of caste, caste-feeling

'kastekort (-en) *o* deficit, deficiency

kaste'lein (-s) *m* innkeeper, landlord, publican

'kastenmaker (-s) *m* cabinetmaker

'kastenstelsel (-s) *o* caste system

kas'tijden (kastijdde, h. gekastijd) *vt* chastise, castigate, punish; **–ding** (-en) *v* chastisement, castigation

'kastje (-s) *o* (small) cupboard; (s i e r l ij k) cabinet; (v. l e e r l i n g, v o e t b a l l e r &) locker; *van het ~ naar de muur sturen* send from pillar to post; **'kastlijn** (-en) *v* dash; **–papier** *o* shelf-paper; **–rand** (-en) *m* shelf edging

kas'trol (-len) *v* casserole

kasu'aris [-zy.-] (-sen) *m* cassowary

kat (-ten) *v* ⚥ cat², tabby; *de ~ de bel aanbinden* bell the cat; *als een ~ in een vreemd pakhuis* like a fish out of water; *een ~ in de zak kopen* buy a pig in a poke; *als een ~ om de hete brij* like a cat on hot bricks; *de ~ uit de boom kijken* see which way the cat jumps, sit on the fence; *de ~ in het donker knijpen* saint it in public and sin in secret, be a slyboots (a sneak); *als de ~ weg is, dansen de muizen* when the cat's away the mice will play; *zij leven als ~ en hond* they live like cat and dog; *~ en muis sp* cat and mouse; **–achtig** catlike, feline²

kata'falk (-en) *v* catafalque

kataly'sator [s = z] (-s en - 'toren) *m* catalyst; **kataly'seren** (kataliseerde, h. gekatalyseerd) *vt* catalyze

'katapult (-en) *m* catapult

'kater (-s) *m* 1 tom cat, tom; 2 *een ~ hebben* **F** have a head, a hang-over

ka'tern (-en) *v & o* gathering

ka'theder (-s) *m* chair

kathe'draal I *aj* cathedral; **II** (-dralen) *v* cathedral (church)

ka'thode (-n en -s) *v* cathode; **–straal** (-stralen) *m & v* cathode ray

katholi'cisme *o* (Roman) Catholicism; **katho'liek** (-en) *m & aj* (Roman) Catholic

'katje (-s) *o* 1 kitten; 2 ✿ catkin; *zij is geen ~ om zonder handschoenen aan te pakken* she can look after herself, she is a spitfire; *bij nacht zijn alle ~s grauw* in the dark all cats are grey; **'katjesspel** *o* kittenish romps

ka'toen o & m cotton; *hem van ~ geven* let oneself go, **F** put some vim into it; *hun van ~ geven* give them hell; **–achtig** cottony; **–boom** (-bomen) m cotton-tree; **–bouw** m cotton-growing; **–drukker** (-s) m calico-printer; **katoendrukke'rij** (-en) v calico-printing factory; **ka'toenen** aj cotton; *~ stoffen* cotton fabrics, cottons; **ka'toenfabriek** (-en) v cotton-mill; **–flanel** o flannelette; **–fluweel** o cotton velvet, velveteen; **–markt** (-en) v cotton market; **–plantage** [-ta.ʒə] (-s) v cotton plantation; **katoenspinne'rij** (-en) v cotton mill; **ka'toentje** (-s) o print (dress); **~s** cotton prints

ka'trol (-len) v pulley; **–blok** (-ken) o pulley-block, tackle-block; **–schijf** (-schijven) v sheave

'kattebak (-ken) m 1 cat's box; 2 dickey (-seat) [of a carriage]; **–belletje** (-s) o (hasty) scribble, scrawl; **–darm** (-en) m catgut; **–gespin** o cat's purr; *het eerste gewin is* ~ first winnings don't count; **–kop** (-pen) m fig cat; **–kwaad** o naughty (monkey) tricks, mischief; **–mepper** (-s) m cat-catcher (-snatcher); **'katten** (katte, h. gekat) vt cat; **'katterig S** chippy, **F** having a head (a hangover); **'kattestaart** (-en) m 1 ⚘ cat's tail; 2 ⚘ purple loosestrife; **–vel** (-len) o catskin; **–wasje** (-s) o a lick and a promise; **'kattig** catty, cattish; **'katuil** (-en) m barn-owl; **'katvis** (-vissen) m small fry; **–zwijm** in ~ *liggen* be in a fainting fit; *in* ~ *vallen* faint, swoon

Kau'kasiër (-s) m, **Kau'kasisch** aj Caucasian

kauw (-en) v 🐦 jackdaw, daw

'kauwen (kauwde, h. gekauwd) **I** vi chew, masticate; ~ *op* chew; **II** vt chew, masticate; **'kauwgom** m & o chewing gum; **–spier** (-en) v masticatory muscle

ka'valje (-s) o wreck

'kavel (-s) m lot, parcel; **'kavelen** (kavelde, h. gekaveld) vt lot (out), parcel out, divide into lots

kavi'aar m caviar(e)

kaze'mat (-ten) v casemate

ka'zerne (-s en -n) v barracks, ook: barrack; *in* ~s *onderbrengen* barrack; **–woning** (-en) v tenement house

ka'zuifel (-s) o chasuble

K.B. [ka.'be.] = *Koninklijk Besluit*

keef (keven) V.T. van *kijven*

keek (keken) V.T. van *kijken*

keel (kelen) v throat; *een zere* ~ a sore throat; *een* ~ *opzetten* set up a cry; *iem. de* ~ *dichtknijpen* choke (throttle, strangle) sbd.; *iem. b ij de* ~ *grijpen* seize sbd. by the throat; *angst snoerde hem de* ~ *dicht* be choked with fear; *het woord bleef mij i n de* ~ *steken* the word stuck in my throat;

iem. n a a r d e ~ *vliegen* fly at sbd.'s throat; *het hangt mij de* ~ *uit* **F** I am fed up with it; **–aandoening** (-en) v throat affection; **–amandel** (-en) v tonsil; **–gat** (-gaten) o gullet; *het kwam in het verkeerde* ~ it went down the wrong way; **–geluid** (-en) o guttural sound; **–holte** (-n en -s) v pharynx; **–klank** (-en) m guttural (sound); **keel-, neus- en 'oorarts** (-en) m otorhinolaryngologist; **'keelontsteking** (-en) v inflammation of the throat, quinsy; **–pijn** (-en) v pain in the throat; ~ *hebben* have a sore throat; **–spiegel** (-s) m laryngoscope

keep (kepen) v notch, nick, indentation

'keeper ['ki.pər] (-s) m goal-keeper

keer (keren) m 1 turn; 2 time; *de ziekte heeft een goede (gunstige)* ~ *genomen* the illness has taken a favourable turn; (*voor*) *deze* ~ this time; *twee* ~ twice; *de twee keren dat hij...* the two times that he...; *een* ~ *of drie* two or three times; *drie* ~ three times, thrice; *een enkele* ~ once in a while, occasionally; *de laatste* ~ (the) last time; *de volgende* ~ next time; *i n één* ~ at one time, at one go, [kill] at a blow, [drink] at a draught; *in (binnen) de kortste keren* in no time at all, without further delay, before you can say knife (Jack Robinson), lickety-split; *o p een* ~ one day (one evening &); ~ *op* ~ time after time; *v o o r deze ene* ~ for this once; **–dam** (-men) m barrage, weir; **–koppeling** (-en) v reverse gear; **–kring** (-en) m tropic; **–punt** (-en) o turning-point [in career], crisis; **–weer** (-weren) m blind alley; **–zij(de)** (-zijden) v reverse (side), back; fig seamy side; *de* ~ *van de medaille* [fig] the other side of the coin (the picture); *aan de* ~ on the back

'keeshond (-en) m Pomeranian (dog)

keet (keten) v shed; ~ *maken* **F** make a mess; kick up a row

'keffen (kefte, h. gekeft) vi yap[2]; **–er** (-s) m yapper[2]

keg (-gen) v wedge

'kegel (-s) m 1 cone [in geometry]; 2 skittle, ninepin [game]; 3 (ij s k e g e l) icicle; **'kegelaar** (-s) m player at skittles; **'kegelbaan** (-banen) v skittle-alley, bowling-alley; **–bal** (-len) m skittle-ball; **'kegelen** (kegelde, h. gekegeld) vi play at skittles, at ninepins; **'kegelsnede** (-n) v conic section; **–spel** o (game of) skittles, ninepins; **–vlak** (-ken) o conical surface; **–vormig** conical, cone-shaped, coniform

'kegge = *keg*

kei (-en) m 1 boulder; 2 (t e r b e s t r a t i n g) paving-stone, [round] cobble(-stone); 3 fig **F** = *bolleboos*; **–hard** stone-hard; fig adamant; *een* ~ *schot* a fierce shot; *een* ~*e vrouw* a hard-boiled woman; *de radio stond ~ aan* the radio was full on, was on at full blast

keil (-en) *m* wedge; pin, peg, cotter; **–bout** (-en) *m* cotter bolt

'**keileem** *o* loam

'**keilen** (keilde, h. gekeild) *vt* fling, pitch; *steentjes over het water ~* make ducks and drakes

'**keislag** *m* stone chippings; **–steen** (-stenen) *m* = *kei* 1 & 2

'**keizer** (-s) *m* emperor; *geef den ~, wat des ~s is* **B** render unto Caesar the things which are Caesar's; *waar niets is verliest de ~ zijn recht* the King looseth his right where nought is to be had; **keize'rin** (-nen) *v* empress; '**keizerlijk** imperial; **–rijk** (-en) *o* empire; '**keizerskroon** (-kronen) *v* imperial crown; '**keizersne(d)e** (-sneden) *v* caesarean operation (section)

'**keken** V.T. meerv. van *kijken*

'**kelder** (-s) *m* cellar; vault [of a bank]; *naar de ~ gaan* 1 ⚓ go to the bottom; 2 *fig* go to the dogs; '**kelderen I** (kelderde, h. gekelderd) *vt* lay up, cellar, store (in a cellar); **II** (kelderde, is gekelderd) *vi* slump [of shares]; '**keldergat** (-gaten) *o* air-hole, vent-hole; **–luik** (-en) *o* trap-door, cellar-flap; **–meester** (-s) *m* cellarman; (v. k l o o s t e r) cellarer; **–mot** (-ten) *v* sow-bug; **–raam** (-ramen) *o* cellar-window; **–ruimte** (-n en -s) *v* cellarage; **–trap** (-pen) *m* cellar stairs; **–verdieping** (-en) *v* basement; **–woning** (-en) *v* basement

'**kelen** (keelde, h. gekeeld) *vt* cut the throat of, kill

kelk (-en) *m* 1 cup, chalice; 2 ⚘ calyx; **–blad** (-bladen) *o* sepal; **–vormig** cup-shaped

'**kelner** (-s) *m* waiter; ⚓ steward; **kelne'rin** (-nen) *v* waitress

Kelt (-en) *m* Celt; **–isch** Celtic

'**kemelshaar** *o* camel's hair

'**kemphaan** (-hanen) *m* 1 ⚔ ruff; gamecock, fighting cock; 2 *fig* fighter, bantam

'**kenau** (-s) *v* virago, tartar, battle-axe

'**kenbaar** knowable; *~ maken* make known

'**kengetal** (-tallen) *o* = *netnummer*

Keni'aan (-ianen) *m*, **–s** *aj* Kenyan

'**kenmerk** (-en) *o* 1 distinguishing mark; 2 characteristic feature; '**kenmerken** (kenmerkte, h. gekenmerkt) **I** *vt* characterize, mark; **II** *vr zich ~ door* be characterized by; **ken'merkend** characteristic (of *voor*)

'**kennel** (-s) *m* kennel

'**kennelijk I** *aj* obvious; *in ~e staat van dronkenschap* under the influence of drink, intoxicated, drunk; **II** *ad* clearly, obviously

'**kennen** (kende, h. gekend) *vt* know, be acquainted with; *dat ~ we!* I've heard that one before!; *ken u zelven* know thyself; *geen... van... ~* not know... from...; *zijn lui ~* know ·with

whom one has to deal; *hij kent geen vrees* he knows no fear; *te ~ geven* give to understand, hint, signify, intimate, express [a wish], declare; *zich doen ~ als...* show oneself a...; *zich laten ~* show oneself in one's true colours; *laat je nou niet ~ aan een gulden* don't give yourself away (don't let yourself down) in the matter of a poor guilder; *iem. leren ~* get acquainted with sbd., come (learn) to know sbd.; *zij wilden hem niet ~* **F** they cut him; ● *ik ken hem a a n zijn gang (manieren, stem)* I know him by his gait (manners, voice); *iem. niet i n iets ~* act without sbd.'s knowledge, not consult sbd.; *ze u i t elkaar ~* know them apart; '**kenner** (-s) *m* connoisseur, (good) judge (of *van*); *een ~ van het Latijn* & a Latin & scholar; **–sblik** (-ken) *m* look of a connoisseur; *met ~* with the eye of a connoisseur

'**kennis** 1 *v* [theoretical or practical] knowledge [of a thing]; acquaintance [with persons & things]; know-how; *oppervlakkige ~* smattering; 2 (kennissen) *m-v* (p e r s o o n) acquaintance; *~ is macht* knowledge is power; *~ dragen van* have knowledge (cognizance) of; *~ geven van* announce, give notice of; *~ hebben aan iem.* be acquainted with sbd.; *(geen) ~ hebben van* have (no) knowledge of; *~ maken met iem.* make sbd.'s acquaintance; *nader ~ maken met iem.* improve sbd.'s acquaintance; *~ maken met iets* get acquainted with sth.; *~ nemen van* take cognizance (note) of, acquaint oneself with; ● *b ij ~ zijn* be conscious; *weer bij ~ komen* regain consciousness; *b u i t e n ~ zijn* be unconscious, have lost consciousness; *dat is buiten mijn ~ gebeurd* without my knowledge; *met elkaar i n ~ brengen* make acquainted with each other, introduce to each other; *iem. in ~ stellen met (van)* acquaint sbd. with, inform sbd. of; *m e t ~ van zaken* with (full) knowledge; *wij zijn o n d e r ~en* we are among acquaintances (friends) here; *iets t e r (algemene) ~ brengen* give (public) notice of sth.; *ter ~ komen van* come to the knowledge of; **–geving** (-en) *v* notice, [official] notification; *voor ~ aannemen* lay [a petition] on the table; *het zal voor ~ aangenomen worden* the Government (the Board &) do not intend (propose) to take notice of it; **–leer** *v* epistemology; **–making** (-en) *v* getting acquainted, acquaintance; *b ij de eerste (nadere) ~* on first (nearer) acquaintance; *o p onze ~!* to our better acquaintance!; *t e r ~* ⚓ on approval; **–neming** *v* (taking) cognizance, examination, inspection; '**kennissenkring** (-en) *m* (circle of) acquaintances; '**kennistheorie** *v* = *kennisleer*

'**kenschetsen** (kenschetste, h. gekenschetst) *vt* characterize

ken'taur (-en) *m* = *centaur*

'kenteken (-s en -en) *o* distinguishing mark, badge, token; (v. a u t o) registration number; **'kentekenbewijs** (-wijzen) *o* registration certificate; **'kentekenen** (kentekende, h. gekentekend) *vt* characterize; **'kentekenplaat** (-platen) *v* registration plate

'kenteren (kenterde, is gekenterd) *vi* turn; **–ring** (-en) *v* 1 turn (of the tide), turning (of the tide); 2 change [of the monsoon(s)]; *er komt een ~ in de publieke opinie* the tide of popular feeling is on the turn

'kenvermogen *o* cognition

'Kenya *o* Kenya

'keper (-s) *m* twill; *op de ~ beschouwen* examine carefully; *op de ~ beschouwd* on close inspection; after all; **'keperen** (keperde, h. gekeperd) *vt* twill

'kepie (-s) *m* kepi

kera'miek = *ceramiek*

ke'ramisch = *ceramisch*

'kerel (-s) *m* fellow, chap

1 'keren (keerde, h. gekeerd) *vt* (v e g e n) sweep, clean

2 'keren I (keerde, h. gekeerd) *vt* 1 (o m - k e r e n) turn [a coat, one's face in a certain direction &]; ◊ turn up [a card]; 2 (t e g e n - h o u d e n) stem, stop, check, arrest; *hooi ~* make (toss, ted) hay; **II** (keerde, is gekeerd) *vi* turn; *i n zichzelf ~* retire within oneself; *in zichzelf gekeerd* retiring; *beter t e n halve gekeerd, dan ten hele gedwaald* he who stops halfway is only half in error; *per ~de post* by return (of post); **III** *vr zich ~* turn; *zich t e g e n iedereen ~* turn against everybody; *zich t e n goede (kwade) ~* turn out well (badly), take a turn for the better; *zich t o t God ~* turn to God

kerf (kerven) *v* notch, nick; **–stok** (-ken) *m* tally; *hij heeft veel op zijn ~* his record is none of the best

kerk (-en) *v* [established] church; [dissenting] chapel; *de ~ in het midden laten* pursue a give-and-take policy; *hoe laat begint de ~?* at what o'clock does divine service begin?; ● *i n de ~* at (in) church; in the church; *n a ~* after church; *n a a r d e ~ gaan* 1 (o m t e b i d d e n) go to church; 2 (a l s t o e r i s t) go to the church; **–ban** *m* excommunication; **–bank** (-en) *v* pew; **–bestuur** (-sturen) *o* church government; *het ~ = kerkeraad*; **–bezoek** *o* church attendance; **–boek** (-en) *o* 1 church-book, prayerbook; 2 parish register; **–concert** (-en) *o* church concert; **–dief** (-dieven) *m* church-robber; **–dienst** (-en) *m* divine service, church service, religious service; **'kerkelijk** ecclesiastical; *een ~e begrafenis* a religious burial; *een ~ feest* a church festival; *~e goederen* church

property; *een ~ huwelijk* a church (religious) wedding; *het ~ jaar* the Christian year; *~ recht = kerkrecht*; **'kerken** (kerkte, h. gekerkt) *vi* go to church; *waar kerkt hij?* what church does he attend?

'kerker (-s) *m* dungeon, prison

'kerkeraad (-raden) *m* church council; consistory [Lutheran]

'kerkeren (kerkerde, h. gekerkerd) *vt* imprison, incarcerate

'kerkezakje (-s) *o* collection-bag; **'kerkgang** *m* going to church, church-going; **–ganger** (-s) *m* church-goer; **–gebouw** (-en) *o* church (-building); **–genootschap** (-pen) *o* denomination; **–geschiedenis** *v* ecclesiastical history, church history; **–gezang** (-en) *o* 1 (h e t z i n g e n) church-singing; 2 (l i e d) (church)hymn; **–goed** (-eren) *o* church property; **–hervormer** (-s) *m* reformer; **–hervorming** (-en) *v* reformation; **–hof** (-hoven) *o* churchyard; graveyard, cemetery; *op het ~* in the churchyard; *de dader ligt op het ~* the cat has done it; **–klok** (-ken) *v* 1 church-clock; 2 church-bell; **–koor** (-koren) *o* choir; church choir; **–latijn** *o rk* Church Latin; **–leraar** (-raren & -s) *m rk* Doctor of the Church; **–meester** (-s) *m* churchwarden; **–muziek** *v* church music; **–plein** (-en) *o* parvis, church square; **–portaal** (-portalen) *o* church-porch; **–provincie** (-s en -ciën) *v* (church) province; **–raam** (-ramen) *o* church-w.ndow; **–rat** *v zo arm als een ~* as poor as a church mouse; **–recht** *o* canon law; **–roof** *m* church-robbery; **kerks F** churchy; **'kerkstoel** (-en) *m* prie-dieu (chair); **–toren** (-s) *m* church-tower, (s p i t s e) church-steeple; **–uil** (-en) *m* barn-owl; **–vader** (-s) *m* Father (of the Church), Church Father; **–vergadering** (-en) *v* church-meeting, synod; **–vervolging** (-en) *v* persecution of the Church; **–volk** *o* church-goers; **–voogd** (-en) *m rk* prelate; *pr* church-warden; **–vorst** (-en) *m* prince of the church; **–wijding** (-en) *v* consecration of a church; **–zakje** = *kerkezakje*

'kermen (kermde, h. gekermd) *vi* moan, groan

'kermis (-sen) *v* fair; *het is niet alle dagen ~* Christmas comes but once a year; *het is ~ in de hel* it's rain and shine together; *hij kwam van een koude ~ thuis* he came away with a flea in his ear; **–bed** (-den) *o* shakedown; **–gast** (-en) *m* 1 visitor of the fair; 2 (s p u l l e b a a s) showman; **–tent** (-en) *v* booth; **–terrein** (-en) *o* fair ground; **–volk** *o* showmen; **–wagen** (-s) *m* caravan

kern (-en) *v* kernel [of a nut]; stone [of a peach], § [of atom, cell] nucleus [*mv* nuclei]; *fig* substance, heart, core, kernel, pith; *een ~ van* *waarheid* a nucleus of truth; *de ~ van de zaak* the heart (substance, core, pith, kernel) of the matter; *de harde ~ van…* the hard core of…; **–achtig** pithy, terse; **–achtigheid** *v* pithiness, terseness; **–bom** (-men) *v* nuclear bomb; **–centrale** (-s) nuclear power-station; **–deling** (-en) *v* nuclear fission; **–energie** [-e.nɛrʒi.] *v* nuclear energy, nuclear power; **–explosie** [s = z] (-s) *v* nuclear explosion; **–fusie** [s = z] (-s) *v* nuclear fusion; **–fysica** [-fi.zi.-] *v* nuclear physics; **–fysicus** (-fysici) *m* nuclear physicist; **–gedachte** (-n) *v* central idea; **–gezond** 1 (v. p e r s o n e n) in perfect good health; 2 (v a n z a k e n) thoroughly sound; **–hout** *o* heartwood, duramen; **–kop** (-pen) *m* ☒ nuclear warhead; **–lading** (-en) *v* nuclear charge; **–onderzoek** *o* nuclear research; **–probleem** *o* central problem; **–proef** (-proeven) *v* nuclear test; **–punt** (-en) *o* central (crucial) point, crux; **–reactor** (-s en -'toren) *m* nuclear reactor, atomic pile; **–splitsing** *v* nuclear fission; **–spreuk** (-en) *v* pithy saying, aphorism; **–stopverdrag** *o* test-ban treaty; **–vak** (-ken) *o* key subject; **–wapen** (-s) *o* nuclear weapon; **–wetenschap** *v* nuclear physics

kero'sine [s = z] *v* kerosene, paraffin oil

'kerrie *m* curry, curry-powder

kers (-en) *v* 1 (v r u c h t) cherry; 2 ☒ cress; *~en op brandewijn* cherry brandy; **'kersebloesem** (-s) *m* cherry blossom; **–bonbon** (-s) *m* cherry chocolate; **–boom** (-bomen) *m* cherry tree; **–boomgaard** (-en) *m* cherry orchard; **–hout** *o* cherry-wood; **'kersentijd** *m* cherry season, cherry time; **'kersepit** (-ten) *v* 1 cherry stone; 2 **F** nob: head

'kerspel (-s en -en) *o* parish

'kerstavond (-en) *m* 1 (2 4 d e c.) Christmas Eve; 2 (2 5 d e c.) Christmas evening; **–boom** (-bomen) *m* Christmas tree; **–dag** (-dagen) *m* Christmas Day; *eerste ~* Christmas Day; *tweede ~* the day after Christmas Day, Boxing Day; *in de ~en* at Christmas, during Christmas time; **'kerstenen** (kerstende, h. gekerstend) *vt* christianize; **–ning** *v* christianization

'kerstfeest (-en) *o* Christmas(-feast); **–geschenk** (-en) *o* Christmas present; **'Kerstkind(je)** *o* Christ child, infant Jesus [in the crib]; **'kerstkribbe** (-n) *v* Christmas crib; **–lied** (-eren) *o* Christmas carol; **–mannetje** (-s) *o* *het ~* Father Christmas, Santa Claus; **'Kerstmis** *m* Christmas, Xmas; **'kerstnacht** (-en) *m* Christmas night; **–roos** (-rozen) *v* Christmas rose; **–spel** (-spelen) *o* Nativity play; **–tijd** *m* Christmas time, yule (tide); **–vakantie** [-(t)si.] (-s) *v* Christmas holidays; **–versiering** (-en) *v* Christmas decoration; **–week** (-weken) *v* Christmas week; **–zang**

(-en) *m* Christmas carol

'kersvers quite new, quite fresh; *~ van school* straight (fresh) from school

'kervel *m* chervil

'kerven* *vt* carve, cut, notch, slash

'ketel (-s) *m* 1 (v o o r k e u k e n) kettle, cauldron, copper; 2 ☒ boiler; **–bikker** (-s) *m* scaler; **–dal** (-dalen) *o* basin; **–huis** (-huizen) *o* boiler-house, boiler-room; **–lapper** (-s) *m* tinker; **–maker** (-s) *m* boiler-maker; **–muziek** *v* mock serenade with kettles, pans, horns &; **–steen** *o & m* (boiler-)scale, fur; **–trom** (-men) *v* kettledrum

'keten (-s en -en) *v* chain², *fig* bond; (a a n é é n s c h a k e l i n g) concatenation; *in ~en slaan* chain; **'ketenen** (ketende, h. geketend) *vt* chain, enchain, shackle

'ketsen (ketste, is geketst) *vi* misfire [of a gun]; (b i l j a r t e n) miscue; (a f s c h a m p e n) rebound; **'ketsschot** *o* misfire

'ketter (-s) *m* heretic; *hij zuipt als een ~* he drinks like a fish; *hij vloekt als een ~* he swears like a trooper; **'ketteren** (ketterde, h. geketterd) *vi* swear, rage; **kette'rij** (-en) *v* héresy, misbelief; **'ketterjacht** (-en) *v* heresy hunt; **–jager** (-s) *m* heresy hunter; **–s** *aj* heretical; **–vervolging** (-en) *v* persecution of heretics

'ketting (-en) *m & v* 1 chain [of metal links]; 2 warp [in weaving]; **–botsing** (-en) *v* pile-up; **–breuk** (-en) *v* continued fraction; **–brief** (-brieven) *m* chain-letter; **–brug** (-gen) *v* chain-bridge; **–draad** (-draden) *m* warp; **–hond** (-en) *m* watch-dog; **–kast** (-en) *v* gear-case, chain-guard; **–reactie** [-re.ɑksi.] (-s) *v* chain reaction; **–roker** (-s) *m* chain-smoker; **–slot** (-sloten) *o* chain lock; **–steek** (-steken) *m* chain stitch; **–zaag** (-zagen) *v* chain-saw

keu (-s en -en) *v* (billiard-)cue

'keuken (-s) *v* 1 kitchen; 2 (s p i j s b e r e i-d i n g) cooking; *Franse ~* French cuisine; *koude ~* cold dishes; **–buffet** [-by.fɛt] (-ten) *o* dresser; **–fornuis** (-fornuizen) *o* kitchen-range; **–gerei** *o* kitchen-utensils, kitchenware; **–kast** (-en) *v* kitchen-cupboard; **–lift** (-en) *m* dumb waiter; **–meid** (-en) *v* cook; *tweede ~* kitchen-maid; *gillende ~ = voetzoeker*; **–meidenroman** (-s) *m* cheap sentimental novel; **–prinses** (-sen) *v* cook; **–rol** (-len) *v* kitchen roll; **–stroop** *v* molasses; **–wagen** (-s) *m* kitchen-car; **–zout** *o* kitchen-salt

'Keulen *o* Cologne; *~ en Aken zijn niet op één dag gebouwd* Rome was not built in a day; **Keuls** Cologne; *~e pot* Cologne jar, stone jar

keur (-en) *v* 1 (k e u s) choice; selection; 2 (m e r k) hallmark; 3 (v e r o r d e n i n g) by-law; *~ van spijzen* choice viands (food); zie ook: 2 *kust*; **–bende** (-n en -s) *v* picked (body of) men; **–collectie** [-kɔlɪksi.] (-s) *v* choice collection; **–der** (-s) *m = keurmeester*; **'keuren** (keurde, h. gekeurd) *vt* assay [gold, silver]; [medically] examine [recruits]; inspect [food &]; taste [wine &]; *hij keurde mij geen blik waardig* he didn't deign to look at me

'keurig I *aj* choice, nice, exquisite, trim; **II** *ad* choicely &; *het past u ~* it fits you beautifully; **–heid** *v* choiceness, nicety

'keuring (-en) *v* assay(ing) [of gold &]; (medical) examination; inspection [of food]; **'keuringsdienst** (-en) *m ~ voor waren* food inspection department; **–raad** (-raden) *m* medical board; **'keurkorps** (-en) *o* picked (body of) men; **–meester** (-s) *m* assayer [of gold &]; inspector [of food &]; judge

keurs (-en en keurzen) *o*, **–lijf** (-lijven) *o* bodice; stays; *fig* curb, trammels

'keurstempel (-s) *o*, **–teken** (-s) *o* hallmark, stamp; **–troepen** *mv* picked men; **–vorst** (-en) *m* elector; **–vorstendom** (-men) *o* electorate

keus (keuzen) *v = keuze*

'keutel (-s) *m* turd

'keutelaar (-s) *m* trifler, dawdler; **'keutelen** (keutelde, h. gekeuteld) *vi* trifle, potter

'keuterboer (-en) *m* small farmer

keuvela'rij (-en) *v* chat; **'keuvelen** (keuvelde, h. gekeuveld) *vi* chat

'keuze (-n) *v* choice, selection; *een ruime ~* a large assortment, a wide choice; *een ~ doen* make a choice; *u hebt de ~* the choice lies with you; *als mij de ~ gelaten wordt* if I am given the choice; *iem. de ~ laten tussen... en...* leave sbd. to choose between... and...; *een ~ maken* make a choice; ● *b ij ~* by selection; *n a a r ~* at choice; *een leervak naar ~* an optional subject; *een... of een..., naar ~* a(n)... or a(n)... to choice; *naar (t e r) ~ van...* at the option of...; *u i t vrije ~* from choice; **–commissie** (-s) *v* selection committee; **–vak** (-vakken) *o* optional subject

'keven V.T. meerv. van *kijven*

'kever (-s) *m* beetle

kg *= kilogram*

K.I. [ka.'i.] *= kunstmatige inseminatie*

kibbela'rij (-en) *v* bickering(s), wrangle, squabble; **'kibbelen** (kibbelde, h. gekibbeld) *vi* bicker, wrangle, squabble [about]; **'kibbelpartij** (-en) *v* squabble

'kibboets (-en en kibboetsiem) *m* kibbutz [*mv* kibbutzim]

kiek (-en) *m* snap(shot)

'kiekeboe bo-peep; *~ !* bo!; *~ spelen* play (at) bo-peep

1 'kieken (-s) *o* 🐦 chicken

2 'kieken (kiekte, h. gekiekt) *vt* snapshot, snap, take.

'kiekendief (-dieven) *m* 🐦 harrier, kite

'kiekje (-s) *o* snap, snapshot; **'kiektoestel** (-len) *o* camera

1 kiel (-en) *m* blouse, smock(-frock)

2 kiel (-en) *v* ⚓ keel; *de ~ leggen van een schip* lay down a ship

'kiele'kiele tickle-tickle!; *[fig] het was ~* it was touch-and-go

'kielen (kielde, h. gekield) *vt* ⚓ keel, careen, heave down; **'kielhalen** (kielhaalde, h. gekielhaald) *vt* 1 careen; 2 (a l s s t r a f) keelhaul; **'kielvlak** (-ken) *o* ⚓ fin; **–water** *o* ⚓ wake, dead water; **–zog** *o* ⚓ wake; *in iems. ~ varen* follow in sbd.'s wake

kiem (-en) *v* germ²; *in de ~ smoren* nip in the bud; **–blad** (-bladen) *o* cotyledon; **–cel** (-len) *v* germ-cell; **'kiemen** (kiemde, is gekiemd) *vi* germinate²; **–ming** *v* germination; **'kiemkracht** *v* germination capacity; germinative power; **–vrij** germ-free

kien I *ij* ± bingo; **II** *aj* (p i e n t e r, 'b ij') **F** cute, with it; **'kienen** (kiende, h. gekiend) *vi* play at lotto, play bingo; **'kienspel** (-len) *o* lotto, bingo

'kieperen I (kieperde, h. gekieperd) *vt* **F** chuck; **II** (kieperde, is gekieperd) *vi* tumble

kier (-en) *m* & *v* narrow opening; (r e e t) chink; *op een ~ staan (zetten)* be (set) ajar

'kierewiet F touched, crackers

1 kies (kiezen) *v* molar (tooth), tooth, grinder; **2 kies** *o* (s t o f n a a m) pyrites; **3 kies I** *aj* delicate [subject]; considerate [man]; **II** *ad* [treat a subject] with delicacy; [act] considerately

'kiescollege [-le.ʒə] (-s) *o* electoral college; **–deler** (-s) *m* quota; **–district** (-en) *o* constituency, (parliamentary) borough; ward; **–gerechtigd** qualified to vote; **–e leeftijd** voting age

'kiesheid *v* delicacy, considerateness

'kieskauwen (kieskauwde, h. gekieskauwd) *vi* peck at one's food; **–er** (-s) *m* reluctant eater; **kies'keurig** dainty, nice, (over)particular, fastidious, squeamish, choosy

'kieskring (-en) *m* electoral district; **–man** (-nen) *m* elector

'kiespijn *v* toothache

'kiesrecht *o* franchise, suffrage; *algemeen ~* universal suffrage; **–schijf** (-schijven) *v* ☎ dial; **–stelsel** (-s) *o* electoral system; **–toon** (-tonen) *m* ☎ dialling tone; **–vereniging** (-en) *v* electoral association; **–wet** (-ten) *v* electoral law, ballot act

'kietelen (kietelde, h. gekieteld) *vt* & *vi* tickle

kieuw (-en) *v* gill; **–deksel** (-s) *o* gill-cover; **–holte** (-n) *v* gill-opening; **–spleet** (-spleten) *v* gill-cleft, gill-split

'**kievi(e)t** (-en) *m* lapwing, pe(e)wit;
'**kievi(e)tsei** (-eren) *o* lapwing's egg, **F** plover's egg

1 '**kiezel** *o* (s t o f n a a m) gravel; **2** '**kiezel** (-s) *m* (s t e e n t j e) pebble; –**aarde** *v* siliceous earth, silica; –**steen** (-stenen) *m* pebble; –**weg** (-wegen) *m* gravelled road; –**zand** *o* gravel; –**zuur** *o* silicic acid

'**kiezen*** **I** *vt* choose, select; elect [as a representative]; pick [one's words]; *hij is gekozen tot lid van...* he has been elected a member of...; *kiest Jansen!* vote for J.; zie ook: *hazepad, kwaad, partij, zee* &; **II** *va* 1 choose; 2 vote; *je moet ~ of delen* you must make your choice; –**er** (-s) *m* constituent, voter, elector; '**kiezerskorps** (-en) *o* electorate; –**lijst** (-en) *v* list (register) of voters, poll; –**volk** *o* electorate

kif(t) *v* 1 (a f g u n s t) envy; *dat is de ~!* sour grapes!; 2 (r u z i e) squabble, **F** row; '**kiften** (kiftte, h. gekift) *vi* squabble, **F** row

kijf *buiten ~* beyond dispute, indisputably

kijk *m* view, outlook; *mijn ~ op het leven* my outlook on life; *zijn ~ op de zaak* his view of the case; *ik heb daar een andere ~ op* I take a different view of the thing; *hij heeft een goede ~ op die dingen* he is a good judge of such things; *er is geen ~ op* it is out of the question; *hij loopt er mee te ~* he makes a show of it; *te ~ zetten* place on view, display; *het is te ~* it is on show, on view; *tot ~!* see you (again)!, **F** so long!; –**dag** (-dagen) *m* show-day, view-day; *~ twee dagen vóór de verkoop* on view two days prior to sale; **kijk'dichtheid** *v* **T** viewing figures; '**kijken*** *vi* 1 look, have a look, (g l u r e n d) peep; 2 **T** view, watch, look in (at TV); *kijk, kijk!* 1 (b e v e l e n d) look (there)!; 2 (i r o n i s c h) ah!, indeed!; *kijk eens aan!* look here!; *laat eens ~* let me see; *wij zullen eens gaan ~* we shall go and have a look; *ga eens ~ of...* just go and see if...; *ik zal eens komen ~* I am coming round one of these days; *hij komt pas ~* he is only just out of the shell; *er komt heel wat bij ~* it is rather a bit of a job; *alles wat daarbij komt ~* all that is involved; *staan ~* stand and look; *daar sta ik van te ~* that's a surprise to me; well, I am dashed; ● *~ n a a r* 1 look at [sth.]; 2 look after [the children]; 3 watch [television, a play, the boat-race]; *laat naar je ~!* be your age!; *kijk naar je eigen!* look at home!; *~ o p* look at [his watch &]; *zij ~ op geen gulden of wat* they are not particular about a few guilders; *de... kijkt hem de ogen u i t* ...looks through his eyes; *kijk uit!* look out!, watch it!; *~ staat vrij* a cat may look at a king; –**er** (-s) *m* 1 (p e r s o o n) looker-on, spectator; **T** (tele)viewer, television viewer; 2 (k ij k g l a s) spy-glass, telescope; opera-glass; (d u b b e l e)

binoculars; (v e l d) fieldglasses; *een paar heldere ~s* a pair of bright eyes (**S** peepers); '**kijkgat** (-gaten) *o* peep-hole, spy-hole; –**geld** *o* television licence fee; –**graag** curious; –**je** (-s) *o* look, glimpse, view; *een ~ gaan nemen* go and have a look, **F** have a dekko; –**kast** (-en) *v* 1 (r a r e k i e k) raree-show, peep-show; 2 **T F** box [= television set]; –**spel** (-spelen) *o* 1 (o p k e r m i s) show at a fair, booth; 2 (s p e k - t a k e l s t u k) show-piece; 3 **T** television play

'**kijven*** *vi* quarrel, wrangle; *~ op* scold

kik *m hij gaf geen ~* he did not utter a sound; '**kikken** (kikte, h. gekikt) *vi je hoeft maar te ~* you need only say the word, you only have to say so; *je mag er niet van ~* you must not breathe a word of it to anyone

'**kikker** (-s) *m* ± frog; ± cleat; –**billetje** (-s) *o* frog's leg; –**dril** *o* = *kikkerrit*; –**land** *o* frog-land [= Holland]; –**rit** *o* frog-spawn; –**visje** (-s) *o* tadpole

'**kikvors** (-en) *m* frog; –**man** (-nen) *m* frogman

1 kil (-len) *v* channel

2 kil *aj* chilly; –**heid** *v* chilliness

'**kilo** ('s), '**kilogram** (-men) *o* kilogramme; '**kilohertz** *m* kilocycle; '**kilometer** (-s) *m* kilometre; –**teller** (-s) *m* mileage recorder; –**vreter** (-s) *m* road-hog; '**kilowatt** [-vat of -vɔt] (-s) *m* kilowatt; –**uur** (-uren) *o* kilowatt-hour

'**kilte** *v* chilliness

kim (-men) *v* 1 rim [of a cask]; 2 ± bilge; 3 horizon, sea-line; –**duiking** (-en) *v* dip (of the horizon); '**kimme** = *kim 3*

ki'mono ('s) *m* kimono

kin (-nen) *v* chin

'**kina** *m* cinchona; –**bast** *m* cinchona, Jesuits' bark; –**boom** (-bomen) *m* cinchona(-tree); –**druppels** *mv* quinine drops; –**wijn** *m* quinine wine

kind (-eren) *o* child, babe, baby, infant, **F** kid; little one; *een ~ krijgen* have a child; *een ~ verwachten* expect a child; *een ~ kan de was doen* it's very easy; *daar ben ik maar een ~ bij* I'm a mere baby to that; *geen ~ aan iem. hebben* he (she) is no trouble at all; *mijn papieren ~eren* my literary babes (infants); *hij is zo onschuldig als een pasgeboren ~* he is as innocent as the babe unborn; *ik ben geen ~ meer* I'm not a kid any longer; *ik ben er als ~ in huis* I am treated like one of the family; *hij is een ~ des doods* he is a dead man; *hij werd het ~ van de rekening* he had to pay the piper; *hij is een ~ van zijn tijd* he is the child of his age; *van ~ af aan* from a child; *het ~ bij zijn naam noemen* call a spade a spade; *~ noch kraai hebben* be alone in the world; ☉ '**kindeke(n)** (-s) *o* infant; *het ~ Jezus* the infant Jesus; '**kinderachtig** **I** *aj* childish,

babyish; **II** *ad* childishly; **'kinderafdeling**
(-en) *v* (i n w i n k e l) children's department;
(i n z i e k e n h u i s) children's ward;
–aftrek *m* (tax) relief in respect of each child;
–arbeid *m* child-labour; **–arts** (-en) *m* pediat-
rician; **–bed** (-den) *o* child's bed, cot; *in het ~
liggen* be in childbed; **–bescherming** *v* protection of children, child protection; **–beul** (-en)
m bully; **–bewaarplaats** (-en) *v* crèche, day
nursery; **–bijslag** *m* family allowance; **–boek**
(-en) *o* children's book; **–doop** *m* infant
baptism; **–geneeskunde** *v* pediatrics; **–goed**
o child's clothes, babies' clothes; **–hand** (-en) *v*
child's hand; *een ~ is gauw gevuld* small hearts
have small desires; **–hoofdje** (-s) *o* (s t r a a t-
s t e e n) cobble (stone); **–jaren** *mv* (years of)
childhood, infancy; **–juffrouw** (-en) *v* nursery-
governess, nannie, nanny; **–kaart** (-en) *v* half
ticket; **–kamer** (-s) *v* nursery; **–koor** (-koren)
o children's choir; **–kost** *m* children's food; *dat
is geen ~* that is no milk for babes; **–leed** *o*
childish grief; **–liefde** *v* 1 love of (one's)
children; 2 (v o o r d e o u d e r s) filial love;
'kinderlijk childlike, childish; filial [love];
–heid *v* naïveté; **'kinderloos** childless; **–meel**
o infants' food; **–meid** (-en) *v*, **–meisje** (-s) *o*
nursemaid, nurse-girl; **–moord** (-en) *m* child-
murder, infanticide; *de ~ te Bethlehem* the
massacre of the Innocents; **–partijtje** (-s) *o*
children's party; **–pistooltje** (-s) *o* toy pistol;
–praat *m* childish talk[2], baby talk[2]; **–psychologie** *v* child psychology; **–rechtbank** (-en) *v*
juvenile court; **–rechter** (-s) *m* juvenile court
magistrate; **–rijmpje** (-s) *o* nursery rhyme;
–roof *m* kidnapping; **–schaar** *v* swarm of
children; **–schoen** (-en) *m* child's shoe; *de ~en
ontwassen zijn* be past a child; *nog in de ~en staan
(steken)* be still in its infancy; **–speelgoed** *o*
children's toys; **–spel** (-spelen) *o* child's play[2];
childhood game, children's game; **–sprookje**
(-s) *v* nursery tale; **–stem** (-men) *v* child's
voice; *~men* children's voices; **–sterfte** *v* infant
mortality; **–stoel** (-en) *m* baby-chair, high
chair; **–taal** *v* children's talk[2]; **–tehuis**
(-huizen) *o* children's home; **–uurtje** (-s) *o*
(r a d i o) children's hour; **–verlamming** *v*
infantile paralysis, poliomyelitis, polio;
–versje (-s) *o* nursery rhyme; **–verzorging** *v*
child welfare; **–verzorgster** (-s) *v* trained
children's nurse; **–voedsel** *o* infants' food;
–vriend (-en) *m* lover of children; **–wagen**
(-s) *m* baby-carriage, perambulator, **F** pram;
–weegschaal (-schalen) *v* baby-balance;
–wereld *v* children's world; **–ziekenhuis**
(-huizen) *o* children's hospital; **–ziekte** (-n en
-s) *v* children's complaint; *~(n)* [fig] growing
pains, teething trouble; **–zitje** (-s) *v* ⬤ infant

carrier; **–zorg** *v* child welfare; **'kindje** (-s) *o*
(little) child, baby, babe; *het ~ Jezus* the infant
Jesus; **'kindlief** dear child, my child

kinds doting; *~ worden* become childish; *~ zijn*
be in one's dotage; **–been** *van ~ af* from a
child; **–deel** (-delen), **–gedeelte** (-n en -s) *o*
(child's) portion; **–heid** *v* 1 (o u d e r d o m)
second childhood, dotage; 2 (j e u g d) childhood, infancy; **–kind** (-eren) *o* grandchild; *onze
~eren* our children's children

ki'nine *v* quinine; **–pil** (-len) *v* quinine pill
kink (-en) *v* twist, kink; *er is een ~ in de kabel*
there is a hitch somewhere
'kinkel (-s) *m* lout, bumpkin
'kinketting (-en) *m &v* curb(-chain)
'kinkhoest *m* (w)hooping-cough
'kinnebak (-ken) *v* jaw-bone, mandible
ki'osk (-en) *v* kiosk
kip (-pen) *v* (l e v e n d) hen, fowl; (o p t a f e l)
chicken; (a g e n t) **F** cop, copper; *als een ~
zonder kop praten* talk through one's hat, talk
nonsense; *er is geen ~ te zien* not a soul to be
seen; *~ ik heb je!* got you!; *de ~ met de gouden
eieren slachten* kill the goose with the golden
eggs; *er als de ~pen bij zijn* be on it like a bird,
be quick to...; *met de ~pen op stok gaan* go to
bed with the birds
'kipkar (-ren) *v* tip-car(t)
'kiplekker as fit as a fiddle; **'kippeborst** (-en)
v chicken-breast; *fig* pigeon-breast; **–boutje**
(-s) *o* drumstick; **–ëi** (-eren) *o* hen's egg; **–gaas**
o wire-netting, chicken wire
'kippen (kipte, h. gekipt) *vt* tip up
kippenfokke'rij (-en) *v* 1 poultry farming; 2
poultry farm; **'kippenhok** (-hokken) *o* henhouse; **–loop** (-lopen) *m* chicken-run, fowl-
run; **kippenmeste'rij** (-en) *v* broiler house
'kipper (-s) *m* ⬤ tipper
'kippesoep *v* chicken-broth; **–tje** (-s) *o* **F** bird;
–vel *o fig* goose-flesh, goose-pimples; *ik krijg
er ~ van* it makes my flesh creep; **–voer** *o*
poultry food
'kippig short-sighted
'kipwagen (-s) *m* tip-car(t)
'kirren (kirde, h. gekird) *vi* coo
'kiskassen (kiskaste, h. gekiskast) *vi* make
ducks and drakes
kist (-en) *v* 1 case, chest, box; 2 (d o o d k i s t)
coffin; **–dam** (-men) *m* coffer-dam; **'kisten**
(kistte, h. gekist) *vt* (v. l ij k) coffin; **'kisten-
maker** (-s) *m* 1 box-maker; 2 coffin-maker;
'kistje (-s) *o* 1 box [of cigars]; 2 (s c h o e n) **F**
beetle-crusher
kit (kitten) *v &* lute [clay or cement]
kits (-en) *v* ⚓ ketch; *alles ~* **F** everything o.k.
'kittelaar (-s) *m* clitoris; **'kittelen** (kittelde, h.
gekitteld) *vt & vi* tickle, titillate; **'kittelig**

ticklish; 'kitteling (-en) v tickling, titillation;
kitte'lorig touchy
'kitten (kitte, h. gekit) vt lute
'kittig smart, spruce
'klaaggeschrei o lamentation; –lied (-eren) o
lament, lamentation; ~eren lamentations [of
Jeremiah]; –lijk plaintive, mournful; 'Klaag-
muur m de ~ the Wailing Wall [of Jerusalem];
'klaagster (-s) v 1 complainer; 2 ᵗᵗ plaintiff;
'klaagtoon (-tonen) m plaintive tone; op een ~
ook: in a querulous tone; –vrouw (-en) v
hired mourner, mute; –zang (-en) v dirge,
elegy
klaar I aj 1 (h e l d e r) clear; evident; 2
(g e r e e d) ready; (v o l t o o i d) finished; ~!
ready!; done!; ~ is Kees! that's done!, that job is
jobbed; en ~ is Kees! and there you are!; ik ben
~ met ontbijten (met eten &) I have finished (my)
breakfast, I have finished eating; klare jenever
plain (neat, raw) Hollands; dat is zo ~ als een
klontje that is as clear as daylight; II ad clearly;
~ wakker broad awake, wide awake;
klaar'blijkelijk I aj clear, evident, obvious; II
ad clearly &; ~ had hij niet... he clearly
(evidently &) had not...; 'klaarhebben¹ vt
have (got) ready; altijd een antwoord ~ be always
ready with an answer; 'klaarheid v clearness,
clarity; tot ~ brengen clear up; 'klaarkomen¹ vi
get ready, get done; (o r g a s m e) P come;
–krijgen¹ vt complete, finish, get ready;
–leggen¹ vt put in readiness, lay out
'klaarlicht op ~e dag in broad daylight
'klaarliggen¹ vi lie ready; –maken¹ I vt get
ready, prepare; een drankje ~ prepare a potion;
iem. ~ voor een examen coach sbd. for an examination; medicijn (een recept) ~ make up a prescription; II vr zich ~ get ready; –spelen¹ vt
het ~ manage (it), cope; ook: pull it off;
–staan¹ vi be ready; altijd voor iem. ~ 1 be
always ready to oblige sbd.; 2 (o m t e
g e h o o r z a m e n) be at sbd.'s beck and call;
–stomen¹ vt cram [pupils]
'klaarte v clearness, lucidity
'klaarzetten¹ vt lay [dinner &]; set out [the
tea-things]
Klaas m Nicholas; ~ Vaak the sandman; een
houten klaas a stick
kla'bak (-ken) m S cop, copper
klacht (-en) v 1 complaint; lamentation; 2 ᵗᵗ
indictment, complaint; een ~ tegen iem. indienen
lodge a complaint against sbd.; 'klachten-
boek (-en) o complaintbook
klad (-den) 1 v (v l e k) blot, stain, blotch; 2 o

(o n t w e r p) rough draught, rough copy; een
~ op iems. naam werpen put (cast) a slur upon
sbd.; de ~ erin brengen spoil the trade; iem. bij de
~den pakken catch hold of sbd.; in het ~
schrijven make a rough copy; –blok (-ken) o
scribbling-pad; –boek (-en) o $ waste-book;
jotter; 'kladden (kladde, h. geklad) vi 1 stain,
blot; 2 fig daub; 'kladje (-s) o rough draught;
rough copy; 'kladpapier (-en) o scribbling-
paper; –schilder (-s) m dauber; –schrift (-en)
o rough-copybook; –werk (-en) o 1 rough
copy; 2 daub.
'klagen (klaagde, h. geklaagd) vi complain;
lament; ~ b ij complain to; ~ o v e r complain
of; hij heeft geen ~ he has no cause for complaint; zie ook: nood, steen &; –d plaintive;
'klager (-s) m 1 complainer; 2 ᵗᵗ plaintiff
'klakhoed (-en) m crush-hat, opera-hat
'klakkeloos gratuitous
'klakken (klakte, h. geklakt) vt clack [one's
tongue]
klam clammy, damp, moist
'klamboe (-s) m mosquito-net
'klamheid v clamminess, dampness, moistness
klamp (-en) m & v clamp, cleat; 'klampen
(klampte, h. geklampt) vt clamp
klan'dizie v clientele, custom, goodwill
klank (-en) m sound, ring; zijn naam heeft een
goede ~ he enjoys a good reputation; dat zijn
maar ijdele ~en idle words; –beeld (-en) o
(radio) feature; –bodem (-s) m sound-board;
–bord (-en) o sound-board, sounding-board;
klank-en-'lichtspel (-en) o son et lumière;
'klankkast (-en) v sound box, sound body,
resonance box; –kleur (-en) v timbre; –leer v
phonetics; –loos toneless; –nabootsing (-en)
v onomatopoeia; –rijk sonorous, rich [voice];
–verandering (-en) v sound-change;
–verschuiving (-en) v 1 shifting of sound; 2
permutation of consonants; –wet (-ten) v
phonetic law
klant (-en) m customer²; client; vaste ~ regular
(customer); 'klantenkring m clientele, regular
customers; –service [-sɛ:rvɪs] m customer
service; after-sales service
klap (-pen) m slap, smack, blow, buffet;
(g e l u i d) clap; iem. een ~ geven, iem. ~pen geven
(om de oren) strike sbd. a blow, box sbd.'s ears;
iem. een ~ in het gezicht geven give sbd. a slap in
the face²; –pen krijgen have one's ears boxed,
have one's face slapped; fig be hard hit, suffer
heavy losses; geen ~ zie (geen) steek; –band
(-en) m blow-out; –bankje (-s) o tip-up seat,

---

¹ V.T. en V.D. van dit werkwoord volgens het model: 'klaarmaken, V.T. maakte 'klaar, V.D. 'klaargemaakt. Zie
voor de vormen onder het grondwoord, in dit voorbeeld: maken. Bij sterke en onregelmatige werkwoorden wordt u
verwezen naar de lijst achterin.

drop seat; **–bes** (-sen) *v* gooseberry; **–deur** (-en) *v* swing-door; **–ekster** (-s) *v* 1 ☙ grey shrike; 2 *fig* gossip; **–hek** (-ken) *o* swing-gate

'klaplopen *vi* sponge (on *bij*), cadge; **–er** (-s) *m* sponger, cadger, parasite; **klaplope'rij** *v* sponging, cadging

klap'pei (-en) *v* gossip; **klap'peien** (klappeide, h. geklappeid) *vi* gossip

'klappen (klapte, h. & is geklapt) **I** *vi* clap, smack; 2 (u i t e l k a a r ~) burst; *i n de handen* ~ clap one's hands; *in de handen* ~ *voor* zie ~ *voor*; *m e t de zweep* ~ crack one's whip; *u i t de school* ~ tell tales; ~ *v o o r* applaud [a player, a speaker &]; **II** *vt zijn hakken tegen elkaar* ~ click one's heels; **III** *o het* ~ *van de zweep kennen* know the ropes

1 'klapper (-s) *m* 1 tattler; telltale; 2 clapper [of a mill]; 3 index; 4 (v u u r w e r k) cracker

2 'klapper (-s) *m* ☙ coco-nut; **–boom** (-bomen) *m* coco-nut tree; **–dop** (-pen) *m* coco-nut shell

'klapperen (klapperde, h. geklapperd) *vi* clack, rattle; chatter [of teeth]; flap [of sails, shutters &]; **'klapperman** (-nen) = *klepperman*

'klappermelk *v* coconut milk; **–noot** (-noten) *v* coco-nut; **–olie** *v* coco-nut oil

'klappertanden (klappertandde, h. geklappertand) *vi hij klappertandt* his teeth chatter

'klappertje (-s) *o* cap [for toy pistol]

'klaproos (-rozen) *v* poppy; **'Klaproosdag** *m* Poppy Day

'klapsigaar (-garen) *m* trick cigar; **–stoel** (-en) *m* folding chair; tip-up seat; **–stuk** (-ken) *o* brisket of beef; *fig* **F** hit; **–tafel** (-s) *v* folding table, drop-leaf table, gate-legged table;

'klapwieken (klapwiekte, h. geklapwiekt) *vi* clap (flap) the wings; **'klapzoen** (-en) *m* smack

'klare (-) *m een* ~ a glass of Hollands

'klaren I (klaarde, h. geklaard) *vt* 1 clear, clarify, fine [liquids]; 2 clear [goods at the custom-house, ⚓ the anchor]; *hij zal het wel* ~ he'll manage; **II** (klaarde, is geklaard) *vi* clear; *het begint te* ~ the weather begins to clear up

klari'net (-ten) *v* clarinet, clarionet; **klarinet'tist** (-en) *m* clarinettist

kla'roen (-en) *v* clarion; **–geschal** *o* clarion call

klas (-sen) = *klasse*, **–boek** (-en) = *klasseboek*; **–genoot** (-noten) = *klassegenoot*; **–leraar** (-raren) = *klasseleraar*; **–lokaal** (-kalen) = *klasselokaal*

'klasse (-n) *v* 1 class [of animals, goods &]; 2 ☙ class, [in secondary schools] form, [in elementary schools] standard, *Am* grade; [overcrowded] class-room; *alle ~n aflopen* ☙ do all one's classes; *in de* ~ ☙ in class; **–bewust** class conscious; **–boek** (-en) *o* ☙ homework

book, class diary; **–genoot** (-genoten) *m* ☙ class mate; **–justitie** [-jüsti.(t)si.] *v* justice based on class bias; **–leraar** (-leraren) *m* ☙ form master; **–lokaal** (-kalen) *o* ☙ class-room

klasse'ment (-en) *o sp* [general] classification, classified results

'klassenhaat *m* class-hatred; **–loos** classless; **–strijd** *m* class-war, class-struggle

'klassepatiënt [-pa.ʃɪnt] (-en) *m* private patient

klas'seren (klasseerde, h. geklasseerd) *vt* classify, class; **–ring** (-en) *v* classification

klas'siek I *aj* classic [simplicity], classical [music]; **II** *ad* classically; **klas'sieken** *mv de* ~ the classics

klassi'kaal I *aj* classical, class; ~ *onderwijs* class-teaching; **II** *ad* in class

'klateren (klaterde, h. geklaterd) *vi* splash [of water]; **'klatergoud** *o* tinsel[2], Dutch gold

'klauteraar (-s) *m* clamberer, climber; **'klauteren** (klauterde, h. en is geklauterd) *vi* clamber, scramble

klauw (-en) *m & v* 1 claw [of beast, bird & > man]; talon [of bird of prey]; *fig* clutch, paw; 2 ⚓ fluke [of an anchor]; **'klauwen** (klauwde, h. geklauwd) *vt & vi* claw

'klauwhamer (-s) *m* claw-hammer

klau'wier (-s) *m* ☙ shrike

'klauwplaat (-platen) *v* ⚒ chuck

'klauwzeer *o mond-en-~* foot-and-mouth disease

klave'cimbel (-s) *m & o* harpsichord

'klaver (-s) *v* clover, trefoil, shamrock; zie ook: *klaveren*; **–blad** (-bladen en -bladeren) *o* 1 clover-leaf; 2 *fig* trio; 3 (v o o r v e r k e e r) cloverleaf; **'klaveren** *mv* ◊ clubs; *~aas* & ace & of clubs; **klaver'jassen** (klaverjaste, h. geklaverjast) *vi* ◊ play jass; **klavertje'vier** *o* = *klavervier* 2; **'klaverveld** (-en) *o* clover-field; **klaver'vier** *v* 1 ◊ four of clubs; 2 ☙ four-leaved clover; **'klaverzuring** *v* wood-sorrel

kla'vier (-en) *o* 1 keyboard; 2 piano

'kledder (-s) *m* slush, sludge; **'kledderen** (kledderde, h. gekledderd) = *kliederen*; **'kledderig** slushy, squashy

'kleden (kleedde, h. gekleed) **I** *vt* dress, clothe; *dat kleedt haar (niet) goed* it is (not) becoming; **II** *vr zich* ~ dress; zie ook: *gekleed*; **'klederdracht** (-en) *v* costume; **kle'dij** *v* clothes

'kleding *v* clothes, dress, attire; **–industrie** *v* clothing industry; **–magazijn** (-en) *o* (ready-made) clothes shop; **–stuk** (-ken) *o* article of clothing, article of dress, garment

kleed *o* (kleden) 1 garment, garb, dress; 2 carpet [on the floor]; 3 table-cover; *het geestelijk* ~ the cloth; **–geld** (-en) *o* dress-allowance, pin-money; **–hokje** (-s) *o* (dressing-)cubicle; **–je** (-s) *o* rug [on the floor]; table-centre; **–kamer** (-s) *v* dressing-room;

changing-room [for football-players &]
'**kleefband** o adhesive tape; **–middel** (-en) o
glue, adhesive; **–pleister** (-s) v = hechtpleister;
–stof (-fen) v glue; gluten
'**kleerborstel** (-s) m clothes-brush; **–hanger**
(-s) m coat-hanger; (v o o r j a p o n) dress-
hanger; **–kast** (-en) v wardrobe, clothes-press;
–maker (-s) m tailor; **–makerskrijt** o French
chalk; **–makerszit** m in ~ sitting crosslegged;
–mot (-ten) v clothes-moth; **–scheuren** mv er
zonder ~ afkomen get off with a whole skin
(without a scratch)
klef 1 (v. b r o o d) doughy; 2 (v. s n e e u w)
sticky; 3 (v. h a n d e n) clammy
klei v clay; **–aarde** v clay; **–achtig** clayey;
–duif (-duiven) v sp clay pigeon; **–grond** (-en)
m clay-soil, clay-ground; **–laag** (-lagen) v
clay-layer; **–masker** (-s) o mud pack
klein I aj little, small; petty; (v. g e s t a l t e,
a f s t a n d) short; (v a n m i n d e r b e l a n g)
minor [accident, officials, strike &]; slight
[improvement, mistake &]; een ~ beetje a tiny
bit; de ~ste bijzonderheden the minutest details;
een ~e boer a small farmer; ~e druk small print;
~e stappen short steps; ~e uitgaven petty
expenses; een ~ uur less than an hour; nearly
an hour; ~ maar dapper small but plucky; ~
maar fijn small but good; **II** sb ~ en groot zie
groot **III**; de ~e the little one, the baby; in het ~
in a small way, on a small scale; [an ocean] in
miniature; $ by retail; de wereld in het ~ the
world in a nutshell; wie het ~e niet eert, is het
grote niet weerd who will not keep a penny shall
never have many; **IV** ad small; zich ~ voelen
feel small; **Klein-'Azië** o Asia Minor; '**klein-
bedrijf** o small-scale industry; het ~ ook: the
small industries; **–beeldcamera** ('s) v miniature camera; **–beeldfilm** (-s) m miniature
film, 35-mm film; **klein'burgerlijk** fig
narrow-minded, low-brow, parochial,
suburban; '**kleindochter** (-s) v grand-
daughter; **Klein'duimpje** o Tom Thumb;
klein'duimpje (-s) o hop-o'-my-thumb;
klei'neren (kleineerde, h. gekleineerd) vt
belittle, disparage; **–ring** v belittlement,
disparagement; **klein'geestig** small-minded,
narrow-minded; '**kleingeld** o (small) change,
small coin; **kleinge'lovig** of little faith; **–heid**
v little faith; '**kleinhandel** m retail trade; **–aar**
(-s) m retail dealer, retailer; '**kleinhandels-
prijs** (-prijzen) m retail price; '**kleinigheid**
(-heden) v small thing, trifle; '**kleinkind**
(-eren) o grandchild; '**kleinkrijgen** (kreeg
'klein, h. 'kleingekregen) vt iem. ~ bring sbd.
to heel, subdue (tame) sbd., break sbd. down,
browbeat sbd.; '**kleinkunst** v cabaret; '**klein-
maken** (maakte 'klein, h. 'kleingemaakt) vt
chop small; een bankbiljet ~ break a banknote;
klein'moedig faint-hearted, timid, pusillani-
mous; '**kleinood** (-noden en -'nodiën) o
jewel², gem²; **klein'steeds** provincial, parochial; **–heid** v provinciality, parochialism;
'**kleintje** (-s) o little one, baby; op de ~s passen
[fig] take care of the pence; veel ~s maken een
grote many a little makes a mickle; voor geen ~
vervaard not easily frightened (scared);
klein'zerig squeamish about pain;
klein'zielig small-minded, petty [excuse &];
hoe ~! how shabby!; '**kleinzoon** (-zonen en -s)
m grandson
'**kleitablet** (-ten) o, **–tafel** (-s) v (clay) tablet
klem I (-men) v 1 (v a l) catch, (man)trap; 2 ⚒
bench-clamp; clip; 3 ⚕ terminal; 4 (z i e k t e)
lockjaw; 5 (n a d r u k) stress², accent,
emphasis; i n de ~ zitten zie knel **I**; m e t ~
[speak] emphatically, with great force,
urgently; met ~ van redenen with cogent
reasons; **II** aj ~ lopen, raken, zijn, zitten jam, get
jammed; ~ zetten jam; **–haak** (-haken) m clip,
holdfast; '**klemmen** (klemde, h. geklemd) **I** vt
pinch [one's finger]; clench, set [one's teeth],
tighten [one's lips], clasp [one's arms round...,
sbd. to one's breast]; **II** vi stick, jam [of a door];
–d cogent [reasons]; '**klemschroef**
(-schroeven) v clamping-screw; '**klemtoon**
(-tonen) m stress, accent, emphasis; **–teken**
(-s) o stress-mark
klep (-pen) v 1 flap [of a pocket]; 2 ⚒ leaf [of a
sight]; 3 peak [of a cap]; 4 ⚒ valve; 5 damper
[of a stove]; 6 ♪ key [of a horn]
'**klepel** (-s) m clapper, tongue
'**kleppen** (klepte, h. geklept) vi 1 clack, clap; 2
toll [of a bell]
'**klepper** (-s) m 1 watchman; 2 🐎 steed; ~s ♪
castanets
'**klepperen** (klepperde, h. geklepperd) vi clack,
clap; clatter [of a stork]
'**klepperman** (-nen) m watchman
klepto'maan (-manen) m kleptomaniac;
kleptoma'nie v kleptomania
'**kleren** mv clothes; de ~ maken de man the tailor
makes the man, fine feathers make fine birds;
het raakt mijn koude ~ niet it leaves me perfectly
cold; het gaat je niet in je koude ~ zitten it takes it
out of you; iem. in de ~ steken clothe sbd.;
–hanger (-s) = kleerhanger; **–kast** (-en) =
kleerkast
kleri'kaal aj clerical; de klerikalen the clerical-
ists; **klerika'lisme** o clericalism
klerk (-en) m clerk
1 klets v 1 (-en) smack, slap [in the face]; splash
[of water]; 2 fig **F** rubbish; ~! **S** rats!, **F** rot!
2 klets! ij slap!, flap!, smack!, bang!

'**kletsen** (kletste, h. gekletst) **I** *vi* 1 splash [against something]; 2 **F** talk rubbish (rot); talk; natter, yap, gossip; **II** *vt iets in het water* ~ dash sth. into the water; **–er** (-s) *m* = *kletskous* & *kletsmeier*; '**kletsica** *v*, '**kletskoek** *m* **F** bosh and nonsense, tommyrot, gup, piffle; **–kous** (-en) *v* chatterbox, tattler; **–meier** (-s) *m* twaddler, blabber; **–nat** soaking wet, sopping wet; **–praat** *m* = 1 *klets* 2; ~ *verkopen* **F** talk rot; ~*jes* gossiping

'**kletteren** (kletterde, h. gekletterd) *vi* clatter, pelt, patter [of hail, rain]; clash [of arms]

'**kleumen** (kleumde, h. gekleumd) *vi* feel chilled, shiver

kleur (-en) *v* 1 (i n 't a l g.) colour, hue; 2 (v. g e z i c h t) complexion; 3 ◊ suit; 4 *fig* colour; ~ *bekennen* 1 ◊ follow suit; 2 *fig* show one's colours; *een* ~ *hebben als een bellefleur* have rosy cheeks; *een* ~ *krijgen* colour, blush; m e t (*in*) *levendige* (*donkere*) ~*en afschilderen* paint in bright (dark) colours; v a n ~ *verschieten* change colour; *politici van allerlei* ~ of all colours; **–boek** (-en) *o* painting-book; **–doos** (-dozen) *v* paint-box, box of paints; **–echt** fast(-dyed), colourfast, colour-proof; '**kleuren** (kleurde, h. gekleurd) **I** *vi* colour, blush; **II** *vt* colour; (f o t o) tone; zie ook: *gekleurd*; '**kleurenblind** colour-blind; **–heid** *v* colour-blindness; '**kleurendia** ('s) *m* colour transparency, colour slide; **–druk** *m* colour-printing; *in* ~ in colour; **–film** (-s) *m* colour film, film in colour; **–foto** ('s) *v* colour photograph; **–fotografie** *v* colour photography; **–gamma** ('s) *v* & *o* colour range; **–leer** *v* chromatics; **–pracht** *v* blaze of colour(s), rich (brilliant) colouring; **–spectrum** (-s en -tra) *o* chromatic spectrum; **–spel** *o* play of colours; **–televisie** [s = z] (-s) *v* colour television; '**kleurfilter** (-s) *m* & *o* colour filter; **–fixeerbad** (-baden) *o* (tone) fixing bath; **kleurge'voelig** colour sensitive; '**kleurhoudend** fast-dyed, colour-fast; **–ig** colourful, gay; **–ing** (-en) *v* colouring, coloration; **–krijt** *o* (coloured) chalk; **–ling** (-en) *m* coloured man; **–loos** colourless[2] [cheeks &]; *fig* drab; **–menging** *v* colour-blending, (-mixture); **–potlood** (-loden) *o* coloured pencil; **–rijk** coloured, colourful; **–schakering** (-en) *v* 1 shade, hue, tinge; 2 colour gradation; **–sel** (-s) *o* colour(ing); **–stof** (-fen) *v* colouring matter, pigment; ~*fen* dye-stuffs; **–tje** (-s) *o* colour

'**kleuter** (-s) *m* little one, (tiny) tot, todler, **F** kid, kiddy; **–klas(se)** (-klassen) *v* infant class; **–leidster** (-s) *v* infant-school teacher, kindergarten teacher; **–school** (-scholen) *v* infant school, kindergarten; **–zorg** *v* infant care

'**kleven** (kleefde, h. gekleefd) *vi* stick, adhere, cling; ~ *aan* stick & to; *daar kleeft geen schande*

aan no disgrace attaches to it; *daar kleeft een smet op* it is blotted with a stain; '**kleverig** sticky, gluey, viscous; **–heid** *v* stickiness, viscosity

'**kliederen** (kliederde, h. gekliederd) *vi* dabble, make a mess

kliek (-en) *v* clique, set, coterie, junto; **–geest** *m* cliquishness

'**kliekjes** *mv* scraps, leavings, left-overs, **F** scran; **–dag** (-dagen) *m* left-over day

klier (-en) *v* 1 gland; 2 = *kliergezwel*; *een* ~ (*van een vent*) **S** a rotter, a cad; **–achtig** 1 glandular; 2 scrofulous; '**klieren** (klierde, h. geklierd) *vi* **F** pester, annoy; '**kliergezwel** (-len) *o* scrofulous tumour; **–ziekte** (-n en -s) *v* scrofulous disease, scrofula

'**klieven*** *vt* cleave; *de golven* ~ cleave (plough) the waves (the waters)

klif (-fen) *o* cliff

1 '**klikken** (klikte, h. geklikt) *vi* tell (tales); *van iem.* ~ tell upon sbd.; **2** '**klikken** (klikte, h. geklikt) *vi* click [of cameras]; *het klikte meteen tussen hen* they hit it off from the start; **–r** (-s) *m*, '**klikspaan** (-spanen) *v* telltale, **F** sneak

klim *m* climb; *een hele* ~ a bit of a climb

kli'maat (-maten) *o* climate; **–gordel** (-s) *m* climatic zone (belt); **–regeling** *v* air-conditioning; **klimati'seren** [s = z] (klimatiseerde, h. geklimatiseerd) *vt* air-condition; **klimatolo-'gie** *v* climatology

'**klimijzer** (-s) *o* crampon; '**klimmen*** *vi* climb, ascend, mount; i n *een boom* ~ climb (up) a tree; *klim maar o p de canapé* (*op mijn knie*) climb on to the sofa (on to my knee); b i j *het* ~ *der jaren* as we advance in years; **–ming** *v* climbing; '**klimop** *m* & *o* ivy; '**klimpaal** (-palen) *m* climbing-pole; **–partij** (-en) *v* climb; **–plant** (-en) *v* climbing-plant, climber; **–rek** (-ken) *o* climbing frame; wall bars, monkey bars; **–roos** (-rozen) *v* rambler; **–vogel** (-s) *m* climber

kling (-en) *v* blade [of a sword]; *over de* ~ *jagen* put to the sword

'**klingelen** (klingelde, h. geklingeld) *vi* jingle, tinkle

kli'niek (-en) *v* clinic; '**klinisch** clinical

klink (-en) *v* latch [of door]; *op de* ~ on the latch; *de deur op de* ~ *doen* latch the door; *de deur van de* ~ *doen* unlatch the door

'**klinkdicht** (-en) *o* sonnet; '**klinken* I** *vi* 1 (g e l u i d g e v e n) sound, ring; 2 (a a n s t o t e n) clink (touch) glasses; *een diner dat* (*een stem die*) *klonk als een klok* a number one dinner, a voice as clear as a bell; *bekend* (*in de oren*) ~ sound familiar; **II** *vt* ✗ rivet, clinch[2]; **–d** sounding; resounding [reply, victory]; ~*e munt* **$** hard cash; ~*e naam* a name of great reputation

'klinker (-s) *m* 1 vowel [sound or letter]; 2 △ clinker, brick; 3 ✗ riveter; **–pad** (-paden) *o* brick path; **–weg** (-wegen) *m* brick-paved road

'klinkhamer (-s) *m* riveting-hammer

'klinkklaar *dat is klinkklare onzin* it is sheer (broad, pure) nonsense

'klinknagel (-s) *m* rivet

klip (-pen) *v* rock, reef; *t e g e n de ~pen op* (*drinken, liegen*) (drink, lie) outrageously; *t u s s e n de ~pen door zeilen* steer clear of the rocks; **–geit** (-en) *v* chamois

'klipper (-s) *m* ⚓ clipper

'klipzout *o* rock-salt

klis (-sen) *v* 1 ⚘ bur(r); 2 tangle; *als een ~ aan iem. hangen* stick to sbd. like a bur(r); **–kruid, –sekruid** *o* burdock

klit (-ten) *v* = *klis*; **'klitten** (klitte, h. geklit) *vi* tangle; *aan elkaar ~* cling (hang) together

K.L.M. = *Koninklijke Luchtvaart-Maatschappij* Royal Dutch Airlines

'klodder (-s) *m* clot [of blood], blob, blotch, daub [of paint]; **'klodderaar** (-s) *m* dauber; **'klodderen** (klodderde, h. geklodderd) *vt* daub [paint]

1 kloek I *aj* brave, stout, bold; *twee ~e delen* two substantial volumes; **II** *ad* bravely, stoutly, boldly

2 kloek (-en) *v* mother hen

'kloekheid *v* bravery, courage, vigour

kloek'moedig stout-hearted, valiant, courageous; **–heid** *v* stout-heartedness, bravery, courage, valour

1 klok *ij* cluck!

2 klok (-ken) *v* 1 (u u r w e r k) clock; 2 (t o r e n b e l) bell; 3 (g l a z e n s t o l p) bell-jar, bell-glass; *hij heeft de ~ horen luiden, maar hij weet niet waar de klepel hangt* he has heard about it, but he does not know what to make of it; ● *hij hangt alles a a n de grote ~* he noises everything abroad; *m e t de ~ mee* clockwise; *hij kan o p de ~ kijken* he can tell the clock; *op de ~ af* to the minute; *t e g e n de ~ in* anti-clockwise; *een man v a n de ~* a punctual man; *het is betalen wat de ~ slaat* pay(ing) is the order of the day; **–beker** (-s) *m* bell beaker; **–gelui** *o* bell-ringing, peals, chiming; **–huis** (-huizen) *o* ⚘ core [of an apple]; **–je** (-s) *o* 1 (u u r w e r k) small clock; 2 ⚘ harebell, bluebell; *het ~ van gehoorzaamheid* time to go to bed; *zoals het ~ thuis tikt, tikt het nergens* there's no place like home; **'klokke** *~ zes* on the stroke of six, at six o'clock precisely; **'klokkeluider** (-s) *m* bell-ringer; **'klokken** (klokte, h. geklokt) *vi* cluck [of hens], gobble [of turkeys], gurgle [of a liquid]; ‖ (t ij d n o t e r e n) time; (w ij d

'klokkengieter (-s) *m* bell-founder; **klok-kengiete'rij** (-en) *v* 1 (h e t g i e t e n) bell-founding; 2 (w e r k p l a a t s) bell-foundry; **'klokkenmaker** (-s) *m* clockmaker; **–spel** (-len) *o* 1 carillon, chimes; 2 ♪ (s l a g i n-s t r u m e n t) glockenspiel; **–speler** (-s) *m* carillon player; **'klokketoren** (-s) *m* bell-tower, steeple, belfry; **–touw** (-en) *o* bell-rope

'klokrok (-ken) *m* full skirt; **–sein** (-en), **–signaal** [-sɪɲaːl] (-nalen) *o* bell-signal; **–slag** (-slagen) *m* stroke of the clock; *~ vier uur* on the stroke of four; **–slot** (-sloten) *o* time-lock; **–spijs** *v* bell-metal; **–vormig** bell-shaped

klom (klommen) V.T. van *klimmen*

klomp (-en) *m* 1 (b r o k) lump; 2 (s c h o e i s e l) clog, wooden shoe, sabot; *een ~ goud* a nugget of gold; *nou breekt mijn ~!* **F** that's the limit!, that takes the cake!, that does it!; **'klompendans** (-en) *m* (Dutch folk-)dance on wooden shoes; **–maker** (-s) *m* clogmaker; **'klompschoen** (-en) *m* clog; **–voet** (-en) *m* club-foot, talipes

klonk (klonken) V.T. van *klinken*

klont (-en) *m & v* clod [of earth]; lump [of sugar &]; **'klonter** (-s) *m* clot [of blood]; **'klonteren** (klonterde, is geklonterd) *vi* clot; **'klonterig** clotted, clotty; **–heid** *v* clottiness; **'klontje** (-s) *o* lump [of sugar]

1 kloof (kloven) *v* 1 (v a n d e a a r d e) cleft, chasm, gap; 2 (a a n d e h a n d e n) chap; 3 *fig* gap; *de ~ dempen* (*overbruggen*) *tussen hen* bridge (over) the gap (gulf) between them; *de ~ verbreden* widen the gap (gulf)

2 kloof (kloven) V.T. van *klieven* en *kluiven*

'klooster (-s) *o* 1 (in h e t a l g.) cloister; 2 monastery [for men]; 3 convent [for women]; *in het ~ gaan* go into a convent; go into a monastery; **–achtig** cloistral, conventual, monastic; **–broeder** (-s) *m* 1 conventual, friar; 2 lay brother; **–cel** (-len) *v* convent cell; monastery cell; **–gang** (-en) *m* cloister; **–gelofte** (-n) *v* monastic vow; **–kerk** (-en) *v* conventual church, monastic church; **–latijn** *o* Low Latin; **–leven** *o* monastic life, convent life; **–lijk** cloistral, conventual, monastic; **–ling** (-en) *m* monk; **–en** ook: conventuals; **–linge** (-n) *v* nun; **–moeder** (-s) *v* prioress, abbess, Mother (Lady) Superior; **–orde** (-n en -s) *v* monastic order; **–regel** (-s) *m* monastic rule; **–school** (-scholen) *v* monastic school, convent school; **–vader** (-s) *m* prior, abbot, Father Superior; **–wezen** *o* monasticism, monachism; **–zuster** (-s) *v* nun

kloot (kloten) *m* 1 globe; 2 **P** ball, testicle; **–jesvolk** *o* **F** hoi polloi; **–zak** (-ken) *m* 1 *anat* scrotum; 2 **P** duffer, clodhopper

klop (-pen) *m* knock, tap, rap; *iem.* ~ *geven* beat sbd., **F** lick sbd.; ~ *krijgen* be beaten, **F** be licked (by *van*); **–geest** (-en) *m* rapping spirit, poltergeist; **–jacht** (-en) *v* battue; round-up [by police]; **–partij** (-en) *v* scuffle, affray, set-to, **F** scrap; **'kloppen** (klopte, h. geklopt) **I** *vi* & *va* knock, rap [at a door], tap [on the shoulder], pat [on the head]; beat, throb, palpitate [of the heart]; knock [of a motor]; *er wordt geklopt* there is a knock (at the door); *binnen zonder* ~ *!* please walk in!; (*het*) *klopt* (it's) right; *de cijfers* ~ *niet* the figures do not balance; *dat klopt niet* [*met*] that does not tally (square, fit in) [with], it doesn't add up [with]; *de boel* ~*d maken* square things; **II** *vt* beat [a carpet]; beat up [eggs]; break [stones]; *iem.* ~ beat sbd., **F** lick sbd.; *geld* ~ *uit* make money out of...; *iem. iets uit de zak* ~ do sbd. out of sth.; **–er** (-s) *m* 1 (door-)knocker; 2 (carpet-) beater; 3 ⚓ sounder; **'klopping** (-en) *v* beat(ing), throb(bing), palpitation, pulsation

'kloris (-sen) *m* **F** beau

klos (-sen) *m* & *v* 1 bobbin, spool, reel; 2 ⚡ coil; *hij is de* ~ **F** he's for it, he is (always) the dupe (loser); **–kant** *m* bobbin lace

'klossen (kloste, h. en is geklost) *vi* clump

klots (-en) *m* ⚓ kiss; **'klotsen** (klotste, h. geklotst) *vi* 1 dash [of the waves], slosh; 2 ⚓ kiss

'klove (-n) = 1 *kloof*

1 'kloven (kloofde, h. gekloofd) *vt* cleave [diamonds]; chop [wood]

2 'kloven V.T. meerv. van *klieven* en *kluiven*

klucht (-en) *v* farce; **'kluchtig** comical, droll, farcical, odd; **–heid** (-heden) *v* comicalness, drollery, oddness, oddity; **'kluchtspel** (-spelen) *o* farce

kluif (kluiven) *v* bone (to pick); (a l s g e r e c h t) knuckle; *dat is een hele* ~ **F** that is a tough proposition

kluis (kluizen) *v* 1 (v. k l u i z e n a a r) hermitage; cell; 2 (v. b a n k) strong-room, vault, safe-deposit; **–gat** (-gaten) *o* ⚓ hawse-hole

'kluister (-s) *v* fetter, shackle; ~*s* shackles, trammels; **'kluisteren** (kluisterde, h. gekluisterd) *vt* fetter, shackle; *aan het bed gekluisterd* confined to one's bed, bed-ridden; *aan haar stoel gekluisterd* pinned to her chair

1 kluit (-en) *m* & *v* clod, lump; *de hele* ~ **F** the whole lot; *hij is uit de* ~*en gewassen* **F** he is a tall, spanking fellow

2 kluit (-en) *m* 🐦 avocet

'kluitje (-s) *o* (small) clod, lump; *iem. met een* ~ *in het riet sturen* put sbd. off with fair words, fob sbd. off with promises; *op een* ~ [*zitten*] in a heap, huddled

'kluiven* *vt* & *vi* pick, gnaw, nibble; *iets om aan te* ~ something to gnaw; *fig* **F** a tough proposition

'kluiver (-s) *m* ⚓ jib

'kluizenaar (-s en -naren) *m* hermit, recluse; **–sleven** *o* life of a hermit

'klungel (-s) 1 *v* (v o o r w e r p) = *lor*; 2 *m-v* (p e r s o o n) bungler, muff; **'klungelen** (klungelde, h. geklungeld) *vi* 1 (k n o e i e n) bungle (one's task), muff it; 2 (b e u z e l e n) dawdle; **'klungelig** botchy; **'klungelwerk** *o* bungling, bungle

kluns (klunzen) *m* bungler, muff; **'klunzen** (klunsde, h. geklunsd) *vi = klungelen*

'klusje (-s) *o* odd job; **–sman** (-nen) *m* odd-job man, handyman

kluts *v* *de* ~ *kwijt raken* be put out; *de* ~ *kwijt zijn* be at sea, be all abroad

'klutsen (klutste, h. geklutst) *vt* beat up [eggs]

'kluwen (-s) *o* ball [of yarn, wool, string], clew

'klysma [y = i] ('s) *o* enema, clyster

km = *kilometer*

'knaagdier (-en) *o* rodent

knaak (knaken) *v* **F** = *rijksdaalder*

knaap (knapen) *m* 1 (j o n g e n) boy, lad, youth, youngster, fellow; 2 **F** (k o k k e r d) whopper; **–je** (-s) *o* little boy; clothes hanger

'knabbelen (knabbelde, h. geknabbeld) *vt* (& *vi*) nibble (at *aan*)

'knagen (knaagde, h. geknaagd) *vi* gnaw²; ~ *aan* gnaw (at)²; **–ging** (-en) *v* gnawing; ~*en van het geweten* pangs (qualms, twinges) of conscience

knak (-ken) *m* crack, snap; *fig* blow, injury, damage; *de handel een* ~ *geven* cripple (the) trade; *zijn gezondheid heeft een* ~ *gekregen* his health has received a shock, has suffered a set-back; **'knakken** (knakte, h. en is geknakt) **I** *vi* snap [of a flower]; crack [of the finger-joints]; **II** *vt* break [a flower]; injure, impair, shake [sbd.'s health]; **'knakworst** (-en) *v* frankfurter (sausage)

knal (-len) *m* crack, bang, pop, detonation, report; **–bonbon** (-s) *m* cracker; **'knallen** (knalde, h. geknald) *vi* crack [of a rifle, a whip], bang [of a gun], pop [of corks], fulminate [of gold &], detonate [of gas]; **'knalpot** (-ten) *m* silencer

1 knap (-pen) *m* crack, snap; **2 knap I** *aj* 1 (v. u i t e r l ij k) handsome, comely, good-looking; smart; 2 (v. v e r s t a n d) clever, able, capable; *een* ~ *meisje* a pretty girl; *een* ~*pe vent* 1 a handsome fellow, a good looker; 2 a clever fellow; ~ *in het Engels* well up in English; **II** *ad* 1 cleverly, ably; 2 < pretty; ~ *donker* (*duur*) pretty dark (expensive); **–heid** *v* 1 good looks; 2 cleverness, ability, skill; **–jes** cleverly; *zij kwam* ~ *voor de dag* she was neatly dressed

'**knappen** (knapte, h. en is geknapt) **I** *vi* crack, go crack; (v. v u u r) crackle; *het touw zal* ~ the string will snap; **II** *vt* crack [a bottle]; **–d** crackling [fire]; crunchy, crisp [biscuit]
'**knapperd** (-s) *m* clever fellow, clever one
'**knapperig** crisp, crunchy, brittle
'**knapzak** (-ken) *m* knapsack, haversack
knar (-ren) *m* **F** *ouwe* ~ old fogey
'**knarpen** (knarpte, h. geknarpt) *vi* crunch
'**knarsen** (knarste, h. geknarst) *vi* creak, grate; grind [also of a door]; *met de tanden* ~ gnash one's teeth; '**knarsetanden** (knarsetandde, h. geknarsetand) *vi* gnash one's teeth
knauw (-en) *m* bite; *fig* = *knak*; '**knauwen** (knauwde, h. geknauwd) *vi* gnaw, munch
knecht (-en en -s) *m* man-servant, servant, man; '**knechten** (knechtte, h. geknecht) *vt* enslave; '**knechtschap** *o* servitude
'**kneden** (kneedde, h. gekneed) *vt* knead²; *fig* mould [sbd. like wax]; '**kneedbaar** kneadable, fictile; *fig* pliable; **–bom** (-men) *v* plastic bomb
1 kneep (knepen) *v* 1 *eig* pinch; mark of a pinch; 2 *fig* trick, **F** dodge; *daar zit 'm de* ~ that's why, there's the rub; *de knepen van het vak kennen* know the ropes (the tricks of the trade)
2 kneep (knepen) V.T. v. *knijpen*
'**knekelhuis** (-huizen) *o* charnel-house, ossuary
knel I *v in de* ~ *zitten* **F** be in a scrape, **S** be up a gum-tree; **II** *aj* ~ *raken*, ~ *zitten* jam, get jammed; '**knellen** (knelde, h. gekneld) **I** *vt* pinch, squeeze; **II** *va* & *vi* pinch; **–d** *fig* oppressive; '**knelpunt** (-en) *o* bottle-neck²
'**knepen** V.T. meerv. v. *knijpen*
'**knerpen** (knerpte, h. geknerpt) *vi* crunch
'**knersen** (knerste, h. geknerst) *vi* grind, crunch
'**knetteren** (knetterde, h. geknetterd) *vi* crackle
'**knettergek** bonkers, crackers, raving mad, barmy
kneu (-en) *v* linnet
'**kneusje** (-s) *o* misfit
'**kneuterig** snug
'**kneuzen** (kneusde, h. gekneusd) **I** *vt* bruise, contuse; **II** *vr zich* ~ get bruised; **–zing** (-en) *v* bruise, contusion
'**knevel** (-s) *m* moustache [of a man]; whiskers [of an animal]
'**knevelen** (knevelde, h. gekneveld) *vt* 1 (m e t k o o r d e n) pinion, tie; 2 *fig* extort money from [people]; gag, muzzle [the press]
'**knibbelaar** (-s) *m*, **–ster** (-s) *v* haggler; '**knibbela'rij** (-en) *v* haggling; '**knibbelen** (knibbelde, h. geknibbeld) *vi* 1 haggle; 2 *sp* play at spillikins; '**knibbelspel** (-len) *o* *sp* spillikins
knie (knieën) *v* knee; *de* ~*(ën) buigen* bend (bow) the knee(s); ● *d o o r de* ~*ën gaan* give way, go down, knuckle under (to *voor*); *iets o n d e r de* ~ *hebben* have mastered sth.; *o p de* ~*ën vallen* drop

on one's knees; *voor iem. op de* ~*ën vallen* go down on one's knees to sbd.; *een kind o v e r de* ~ *leggen* lay a child over one's knee; *t o t aan de* ~*ën* kneedeep [in the water]; **–broek** (-en) *v* knickerbockers, kneebreeches; **–buiging** (-en) *v* genuflexion; *diepe* ~ deep knee-bend [in gymnastics]; **–gewricht** (-en) *o* knee-joint; **–holte** (-n en -s) *v* hollow of the knee; **–kous** (-en) *v* knee-stocking
'**knielbank** (-en) *v* kneeling stool; '**knielen** (knielde, h. en is gekniel) *vi* kneel, go down on one's knees, bend the knee; ~ *voor* [*fig*] kneel to; *geknield* kneeling, on one's knees; '**knielkussen** (-s) *o* hassock
'**kniepees** (-pezen) *v* hamstring; **–schijf** (-schijven) *v* knee-cap, knee-pan, patella
'**kniesoor** (-soren) *m*-*v* grumbler
'**knietje** (-s) *o* *iem. een* ~ *geven* give sbd. a leg-up; '**knieval** (-len) *m* prostration; *een* ~ *doen voor* bow the knee before, go down on one's knees to
'**kniezen** (kniesde, h. gekniesd) *vi* fret, mope; *zich dood* ~ fret (mope) oneself to death; *er over* ~ fret about it; **–er** (-s) *m* = *kniesoor*; '**kniezerig**, '**kniezig** fretful, mopy
knijp (-en) *v* (k r o e g) pub; pinch; *in de* ~ *zitten* **F** be in a scrape; **–bril** (-len) *m* pince-nez; '**knijpen* I** *vt* pinch², *fig* squeeze; *hij kneep mij in mijn neus* he tweaked my nose; *hij kneep het kindje in de wang* he pinched the child's cheek; **II** *vi* & *va* pinch; *hem* ~ **F** be in a funk; **–er** (-s) *m* 1 (v o o r w e r p) clip; (v o o r d e w a s) clothes-peg, clothes-pin; 2 (p e r s o o n) niggard, skinflint; '**knijpfles** (-sen) *v* squeeze bottle; **–kat** (-ten), **–lamp** (-en), **–lantaarn** (-s), **–lantaren** (-s) *v* hand-dynamo torch; **–tang** (-en) *v* pincers, nippers
knik (-ken) *m* 1 (b u i g i n g) nod, bob; 2 (b r e u k) crack; 3 (k r o m m i n g) bend; '**knikkebenen** (knikkebeende, h. geknikkebeend) *vi* wobble; '**knikkebollen** (knikkebolde, h. geknikkebold) *vi* nod; doze; '**knikken** (knikte, h. geknikt) *vi* nod; *hij knikte van ja* he nodded assent; *hij knikte van neen* he shook his head; *zijn knieën knikten* his legs gave way, his knees shook
'**knikker** (-s) *m* marble; *kale* ~ bald pate; '**knikkeren** (knikkerde, h. geknikkerd) *vi* play at marbles; zie ook: *baan*; '**knikkerspel** (-len) *o* game of marbles
1 knip (-pen) *m* 1 (i n s n ij d i n g) cut, snip; 2 fillip [with finger and thumb]; flip, flick; *hij is geen* ~ *voor de neus waard* he is not worth a straw (his salt); **2 knip** (-pen) *v* (v o o r w e r p) catch [of a door]; snap [of a bag, of a bracelet]; trap [to catch birds]; **–beugel** (-s) *m* snap [of a purse]; **–kaart** (-en) *v* card, ticket book; **–mes**

(-sen) *o* clasp-knife, jack-knife; *buigen als een ~* bow and scrape; **–ogen** (knipoogde, h. geknipoogd) *vi* wink, blink; *~ tegen* wink at; **–oogje** (-s) *o* wink (of the eyes); *iem. een ~ geven* wink at sbd.; **–patroon** (-tronen) *o* paper pattern; **'knippen** (knipte, h. geknipt) **I** *vt* 1 cut [the hair]; cut out [a dress]; punch [tickets]; clip [tickets, coupons]; trim [one's beard]; pare [one's nails]; 2 flip, flick (off) [the ashes]; 3 **S** pinch, nab [a thief]; *zich laten ~* have one's hair cut; *je moet mijn haar kort ~* crop my hair short; *het uit de Times ~* cut it from The Times; **II** *va* cut (out); **III** *vi met de ogen ~* blink; *met de vingers ~* snap one's fingers; zie ook: *geknipt*

'knipperbol (-len) *m* flashing (Belisha) beacon; **'knipperen** (knipperde, h. geknipperd) *vi met de ogen ~* blink; **'knipperlicht** (-en) *o* flashing light, winker; **–signaal** [-slɲa.l] (-nalen) *o* intermittent signal

'knipsel (-s) *o* cutting(s), clipping(s)

'knisteren (knisterde, h. geknisterd) *vi* crackle, rustle

K.N.M.I. = *Koninklijk Nederlands Meteorologisch Instituut* Royal Dutch Meteorological Institute

'knobbel (-s) *m* bump [on the skull, swelling caused by blow]; knob [at end or surface of a thing]; knot [in animal body], knurl [= knot, knob]; ⚕ tubercle; **–ig** knotty, knobby

knock-'out [nɔk'ɔut] (-s) *aj* & *m* knock-out; *iem. ~ slaan* knock sbd. out

'knoedel (-s) *m* 1 (g e r e c h t) dumpling; 2 (k n o t) knot, bun [of hair]

knoei *m* muddle; *wij zitten in de ~* we are in a fine mess!, **S** we are in the soup!; **–boel** *m* mess; **'knoeien** (knoeide, h. geknoeid) *vi* 1 *eig* mess, make a mess; 2 *fig* bungle, blunder [over one's work]; engage in underhand dealings; *~ a a n iets* meddle (mess) with sth.; *m e t a s ~* mess ashes about; *~ met de boter* adulterate butter; **–er** (-s) *m* bungler, dabbler, botcher; swindler; intriguer; **knoeie'rij** (-en) *v eig* messing, mess; *fig* underhand dealings; intrigue(s); jobbery; **'knoeipot** (-ten) *m* messy person; **–werk** *o* bungling, bungle

knoert (-en) *m* **F** *een ~ van een... a* huge..., an enormous...; **–hard** stone-hard; *fig* tough

knoest (-en) *m* knot, gnarl; **–ig** knotty, gnarled, gnarly

knoet (-en) *m* knout

'knoflook *o* & *m* garlic

knok (-ken) = *knook*

'knokig bony

'knokkel (-s) *m* knuckle

'knokken (knokte, h. geknokt) *vi* fight, **F** scrap; **'knokpartij** (-en) *v* fight, tussle; **–ploeg** (-en) *v* strong-arm squad, gang of strong boys

knol (-len) *m* 1 ⚕ tuber [of potatoes &];

2 (k n o l r a a p) turnip; 3 jade [of a horse]; 4 turnip [= watch]; *iemand ~len voor citroenen verkopen* gull a person, take a person in; **–achtig** ⚕ tuberous; **–gewas** (-sen) *o* tuberous plant; **'knollentuin** *hij is in zijn ~* he is as pleased as Punch; **'knolraap** (-rapen) *v* Swedish turnip, swede; **–selderij** *m* turnip-rooted celery

knook (knoken) *m* & *v* bone

knoop (knopen) *m* 1 knot; 2 ⚕ node, joint; 3 button; stud [of collar &]; *de blauwe ~* the blue ribbon; *de (gordiaanse) ~ doorhakken* cut the (Gordian) knot; *een ~ leggen* tie a knot; *een ~ in zijn zakdoek leggen* make a knot in one's handkerchief; *zoveel knopen lopen* ⚓ run (make) so many knots; *een ~ losmaken* untie (undo) a knot; *daar zit 'm de ~* there's the rub; **–laars** (-laarzen) *v* button-boot; **–punt** (-en) *o* junction; **'knoopsgat** (-gaten) *o* buttonhole; **'knoopsluiting** (-en) *v* button fastening, buttoning

knop (-pen) *m* knob [of a stick, door &]; pommel [of a saddle, a sword]; button, push [of an electric bell]; switch [of electric light]; ⚕ bud

'knopehaak (-haken) *m* button-hook; **'knopen** (knoopte, h. geknoopt) *vt* 1 knot, tie, button; 2 make [nets]; *het in zijn oor ~* make a mental note of it

knor (-ren) *m* grunt; *~ren krijgen* get a scolding

'knorhaan (-hanen) *m* 🐟 gurnet, gurnard

'knorren (knorde, h. geknord) *vi* 1 grunt [of pigs]; 2 *fig* grumble, growl; 3 scold; *~ op* scold; **'knorrepot** (-ten) *m* grumbler; **'knorrig** grumbling, growling, grumpy; **–heid** *v* grumbling (growling) disposition, grumpiness

knot (-ten) *v* knot [of silk, hair], ball [of wool]

1 knots (-en) *v* club, bludgeon, *een ~ van een... a* big...

2 knots F mad, crazy; *~gek zijn* have a slate loose (a bee in one's bonnet), be as mad as a March hare

'knotsvormig club-shaped

'knotten (knotte, h. geknot) *vt* 1 pollard [a willow], head down [a tree]; 2 truncate [a cone]; 3 *fig* curtail [power]

'knotwilg (-en) *m* pollard-willow

'knudde F *het is ~* it's a flop, a wash-out

'knuffelen (knuffelde, h. geknuffeld) *vt* hug, cuddle

knuist (-en) *m* & *v* fist, paw; *blijf eraf met je ~en!* paws off!

knul (-len) *m* fellow

'knuppel (-s) *m* 1 cudgel, club, bludgeon; 2 🛩 **F** joy-stick; 3 *fig* lout; *een ~ in het hoenderhok gooien* flutter the dovecotes; **'knuppelen** (knuppelde, h. geknuppeld) *vt* cudgel knus snug, cosy; **–jes** snugly

'**knutselaar** (-s) *m* handy-man, potterer; '**knut-selen** (knutselde, h. geknutseld) *vi* do handi-craft, do small jobs; potter; *in elkaar ~* put together; '**knutselwerk** *o* amateur handicraft; pottering, trifling work

ko'**balt** *o* cobalt; **–blauw** *o* & *aj* cobalt-blue

'**kobold** (-en en -s) *m* gnome, imp, goblin

kocht (kochten) V.T. van *kopen*

'**koddebeier** (-s) *m* gamekeeper

'**koddig I** *aj* droll, odd, comical; **II** *ad* drolly

koe (koeien) *v* cow; *heilige ~* sacred cow; *oude ~ien uit de sloot halen* rake up old stories, dust off an old legend; *geen oude ~ien uit de sloot halen* let bygones be bygones; *men noemt geen ~ bont of er is een vlekje aan* there is no smoke without fire; *de ~ bij de horens vatten (pakken)* take the bull by the horns, grasp the nettle; *men kan nooit weten hoe een ~ een haas vangt* a cow may catch a hare; **–handel** *m* horse-trading, bargaining, jobbery; **–hoorn** (-s), **–horen** (-s) *m* cow's horn; '**koe(ie)huid** (-en) *v* cow's hide; '**koeiekop** (-pen) *m* cow's head; '**koeieletter** (-s) *v met ~s* in big lettering; **–oog** (-ogen) *o* cow's eye; **–staart** (-en) *m* cow's tail; **–stal** (-len) *m* cowshed, cowhouse, byre

koeio'neren (koeioneerde, h. gekoeioneerd) *vt* bully

koek (-en) *m* 1 cake; 2 gingerbread; 3 (v. vuil) cake, crust; *ze gaan als ~* they sell like hot cakes; *dat is andere ~!* that's something else!, now you're talking!; *dat is gesneden ~* that's mere child's play; *het gaat erin als ~* they lap it up; *ze zijn ~ en ei* they are hand in glove; *iets voor zoete ~ opeten* take sth. for gospel; **–bakker** (-s) = *koekenbakker*; **–deeg** cake paste; '**koekebakker** (-s) *m fig* botcher

koeke'loeren (koekeloerde, h. gekoekeloerd) *vi* peer; *zitten ~* be day-dreaming, sit and stare

'**koeken** (koekte, is gekoekt) *vi* cake; '**koekenbakker** (-s) *m* pastry-cook; **koek-en-'zopie** (-s) *o* stand, esp. on ice, selling hot milk drinks and cakes; '**koekepan** (-nen) *v* frying-pan; '**koekje** (-s) *o* (sweet) biscuit; '**koektrommel** (-s) *v* biscuit tin

'**koekoek** (-en) *m* 1 ❧ cuckoo; 2 △ skylight; *het is altijd ~ één zang met hem* he is always harping on the same string; '**koekoeksbloem** (-en) *v* ragged robin; red campion; **–klok** (-ken) *v* cuckoo clock

koel I *aj* cool[2], *fig* cold [reception]; *in ~en bloede* in cold blood, cold-bloodedly; **II** *ad* coolly; **–bak** (-ken) *m* cooler; **koel'bloedig I** *aj* cool-headed, level-headed, steady, cool; **II** *ad* coolly, steadily; **–heid** *v* cool-headedness, sang froid; '**koelcel** (-len) *v* cold storage; '**koelen I** *vt* (koelde, h. gekoeld) cool; zie ook: *woede* &;

II *vi* (koelde, is gekoeld) cool (down); '**koelheid** *v* coolness[2]; *fig* coldness; '**koelhuis** (-huizen) *o* cold store, cold-storage depot

'**koelie** (-s) *m* coolie; **–werk** *o fig* donkey work, drudgery

'**koelinrichting** (-en) *v* refrigerator, refriger-ating plant; **–kamer** (-s) *v* cold store; cooling-room; **–kast** (-en) *v* refrigerator; **–middel** (-en) *o* coolant; **–schip** (-schepen) *o* refriger-ator ship; '**koelte** *v* coolness; cool [of the evening]; '**koeltje** (-s) *o* breeze; '**koeltjes** coolly, coldly; '**koelvat** (-en) *o* cooler; **–wagen** (-s) *m* refrigerator car; **–water** *o* cooling water

'**koemelk** *v* cow's milk

koen I *aj* bold, daring, hardy; **II** *ad* boldly; **–heid** *v* boldness, daring, hardihood

'**koeoog** (-ogen) = *koeieoog*

'**koepel** (-s) *m* 1 △ dome, dome-shaped top, arch, cupola; 2 (tuinhuisje) summer-house; **–dak** (-daken) *o* dome-shaped roof, dome; **–gewelf** (-welven) *o* dome-shaped vault, dome; **–graf** (-graven) *o* beehive tomb, tholos; **–kerk** (-en) *v* dome-church; **–vormig** dome-shaped

'**koepokinenting** (-en) *v* vaccination; '**koepokken** *mv* cowpox; '**koepokstof** *v* vaccine (lymph)

'**koeren** (koerde, h. gekoerd) *vi* coo

koe'**rier** (-s) *m* courier

koers (-en) *m* 1 ⚓ course, tack; 2 $ quotation, price; rate (of exchange); 3 *fig* course, line of action; *~ zetten naar* shape one's course for, make for, steer for; *uit de ~* be off course; *uit de ~ raken* be driven off one's course; *van ~ veranderen* change course; **–bericht** (-en) *o* market report; **–daling** (-en) *v* fall in prices

'**koersen** (koerste, h. gekoerst) *vi* ⚓ = *koers zetten*

'**koerslijst** (-en) *v* list of quotations; **–notering** (-en) *v* (market) quotation; **–schommeling** (-en) *v* fluctuation in price (exchange); **–verandering** (-en) *v* change of course[2], *fig* new orientation; **–verlies** (-liezen) *o* loss on stock prices, loss on exchange parities; **–verschil** (-len) *o* difference in price; **–waarde** *v* market value; **–winst** (-en) *v* exchange profits; gains

koest quiet; *~!* down, dog!; *zich ~ houden* be (keep) mum, lie low (and say nothing)

'**koestaart** (-en) = *koeiestaart*; **–stal** (-len) = *koeiestal*

'**koesteren** (koesterde, h. gekoesterd) **I** *vt* cherish [children, plants, feelings, a design to..., &], entertain [feelings &]; harbour [thoughts]; **II** *vr zich ~* bask

koet (-en) *m* coot

koeter'waals *o* gibberish, F double Dutch

'koetje (-s) *o* (small) cow; *over ~s en kalfjes praten* talk about this and that, about one thing and another, about things in general; *gepraat over ~s en kalfjes* small-talk

koets (-en) *v* coach, carriage; **–huis** (-huizen) *o* coach-house; **koet'sier** (-s) *m* driver, coachman; **'koetswerk** (-en) *o* coachwork

'koevoet (-en) *m* crowbar

'Koeweit *o* Kuwait

'koffer (-s) *m* 1 box [for articles of value], trunk [for travelling], (k l e i n e r) (suit-)case; 2 🔊 (~r u i m t e) boot, trunk; **–grammofoon** (-s en -fonen) *m* portable grammophone; **–ruimte** (-n en -s) *v* boot, trunk; **–schrijfma-chine** [-ʃi.nə] (-s) *v* portable typewriter, portable; **–tje** (-s) *o* (suit-)case

'koffie *m* coffee; *~ drinken* 1 take (have) coffee; 2 lunch; *op de ~ komen* come over for coffee; *fig* catch it; *dat is geen zuivere ~* F there is something fishy about it, it looks suspicious; **–baal** (-balen) *v* coffee bag; **–bar** (-s) *m* & *v* coffee bar; **–bes** (-sen) *v* coffee-berry; **–boom** (-bomen) *m* coffee-tree; **–boon** (-bonen) *v* coffee-bean; **–brander** (-s) *m* coffee-roaster; **koffiebrande'rij** (-en) *v* coffee-roasting factory; **'koffiebruin** coffee-brown, coffee-coloured; **–cultuur** *v* coffee-growing; **–dik** *o* coffee-grounds; *zo helder als ~* as clear as mud; **–drinken** *o* lunch; **–extract** *o* coffee essence; **–huis** (-huizen) *o* 1 (z o n d e r v e r g u n-n i n g) coffee-house; 2 (m e t v e r g u n-n i n g) (licensed) café; **–kamer** (-s) *v* refresh-ment-room; **–kan** (-nen) *v* coffee-pot; **–kopje** (-s) *v* coffee-cup; **–melk** *v* pasteurized, thick-ened milk; **–molen** (-s) *m* coffee-mill, coffee-grinder; **–pauze** (-n en -s) *v* coffee-break; **–plantage** [-taʒə] (-s) *v* coffee-plantation; **–planter** (-s) *m* coffee-planter; **–poeder** *o* & *m* instant coffee; **–pot** (-ten) *m* coffee-pot; **–room** *m* thin (single) cream; **–servies** (-viezen) *o* coffee-service, coffee-set; **–surro-gaat** (-gaten) *o* coffee-substitute; **–tafel** (-s) *v* lunch; **–tijd** *m* coffee-break; lunch time; **–zetapparaat** (-raten) *o* coffee machine, percolater

'kogel (-s) *m* ball [of a cannon & ⚔]; bullet [for small arms]; *de ~ is door de kerk* the die is cast; *de ~ krijgen* be shot; *tot de ~ veroordelen* sentence to be shot; **–baan** (-banen) *v* trajec-tory; **–flesje** (-s) *o* globe-stoppered bottle; **–gat** (-en) *o* bullet hole; **–gewricht** (-en) *o* ball-and-socket joint; **–kussen** (-s), **–lager** (-s) *o* ⚔ ball-bearing; **–regen** *m* shower (hail) of bullets; **–rond** globular, spherical; **–slin-geren** *o sp* throwing the hammer; **–stoten** *o sp* putting the weight; **–vanger** (-s) *m* butt;

–vormig globular, spherical; **–vrij** bullet-proof, shot-proof

ko'hier (-en) *o* register

1 kok (-s) *m* cook; (d i e m a a l t i j d e n u i t z e n d t) caterer; *het zijn niet allen ~s lange messen dragen* all are not hunters that blow the horn; *veel ~s bederven de brij* too many cooks spoil the broth

2 kok (-ken) coccus

ko'karde (-s) *v* cockade

'koken (kookte, h. gekookt) **I** *vi* boil; *~ van kwaadheid* boil (seethe) with rage; **II** *va zij kan goed ~* she is an excellent cook; *wie kookt voor u?* who does your cooking?; **III** *vt* boil [water &]; cook [food]; 1 **'koker** (-s) *m* boiler

2 'koker (-s) *m* case, sheath; tube; quiver [for arrows]

'kokerjuffer (-s) *v* caddis-fly; **–vrucht** (-en) *v* ⚘ follicle

ko'ket coquettish

koket'teren (koketteerde, h. gekoketteerd) *vi* coquet(te), flirt[2]; **kokette'rie** (-rieën) *v* coquetry

'kokhalzen (kokhalsde, h. gekokhalsd) *vi* retch, keck, heave; *tegen iets ~* keck at sth.

'kokker(d) (-s) *m* bouncer, F spanker, whopper; *een ~ van een neus* F a conk

kok'kin (-nen) *v* cook

'kokmeeuw (-en) *v* black-headed gull

'kokosmat (-ten) *v* coco-nut mat; coir matting; **–melk** *v* coco-nut milk; **–noot** (-noten) *v* coco-nut; **–olie** *v* coco-nut oil; **–palm** (-en) *m* coco-nut palm (tree), coco; **–vezel** (-s) *v* coco-nut fibre; **–zeep** *v* coco-soap

'koksjongen (-s) *m* cook's boy; **–maat** (-s) *m* ⚓ cook's mate

kol (-len) 1 *v* (h e k s) witch, sorceress; 2 *m* star [of a horse]

'kolbak (-ken en -s) *m* busby

1 'kolder (-s) *m* (h a r n a s) 🛡 jerkin

2 'kolder *m* 1 (p a a r d e z i e k t e) (blind) staggers; 2 (o n z i n) (wild) nonsense; *hij heeft de ~ in de kop* the temper is on him; he is in a mad frenzy

'kolen *mv* coal, coals; *ik zat op hete ~* I was kept on thorns; *vurige ~ op iems. hoofd stapelen* **B** heap coals of fire upon sbd.'s head; **–bedding** (-en) *v* coal-seam; **–bekken** (-s) *o* coal basin; **–brander** (-s) *m* charcoal-burner; **–damp** *m* carbon monoxide; (i n m i j n e n) white damp; **–dampvergiftiging** *v* carbon-monoxide poisoning; **–drager** (-s) *m* coal-heaver; **–emmer** (-s) *m* coal-scuttle; **–gruis** *o* coal-dust; **–hok** (-ken) *o* coal-hole; (s c h u u r) coal-shed; **–kit** (-ten) *v* coal-scuttle; **–laag** (-lagen) *v* layer (bed) of coals, coal-stratum; **–mijn** (-en) *v* coal-mine, coal-pit, colliery;

–**schip** (-schepen) *o* collier; –**schop** (-pen) *v*
coal-shovel, coal-scoop; –**schuur** (-schuren) *v*
coal-shed; –**station** [-sta.(t)ʃɔn] (-s) *o* coaling
station; –**stof** *o* coal-dust; –**tremmer** (-s) *m*
coal-trimmer; –**wagen** (-s) *m* 1 coal-truck; 2
(v. l o c o m o t i e f) tender

kolf (kolven) *v* 1 butt(-end) [of a rifle]; 2
receiver [of a retort]; 3 ⚗ spike, cob [of corn];
spadix [*mv* spadices]; –**je** (-s) *o dat is een ~ naar
zijn hand* that's the very thing he wants

'kolibrie (-s) *m* humming-bird

ko'liek (-en) *o* & *v* colic

kolk (-en) *m* & *v* 1 pit, pool; abyss, gulf; eddy,
whirlpool; 2 chamber [in a canal]; **'kolken**
(kolkte, h. gekolkt) *vi* eddy, whirl, swirl

ko'lom (-men) *v* column

kolo'nel (-s) *m* colonel

koloni'aal I *aj* colonial; **II** (-nialen) *m* 🕮 colonial soldier; **kolonia'lisme** *o* colonialism; –**ist**
(-en) *m* colonialist; –**istisch** colonialist;
ko'lonie (-s en -niën) *v* colony, settlement;
koloni'satie [-'za.(t)si.] (-s) *v* colonization,
settlement; **koloni'sator** (-s en -'toren) *m*
colonizer; **koloni'seren** (koloniseerde, h.
gekoloniseerd) *vt* & *vi* colonize, settle;
kolo'nist (-en) *m* colonist, settler

kolo'riet *o* coloration, colouring

ko'los (-sen) *m* colossus, leviathan; **kolos'saal I**
aj colossal; (i r o n i s c h) huge, tremendous; **II**
ad colossally, < hugely, tremendously

kom (-men) *v* basin, bowl; (v. g e w r i c h t)
socket; *de ~ van de gemeente* the centre; *bebouwde
~* built-up area

kom'aan! come!; well!

kom'af *m* descent, origin; *van adellijke ~ of*
noble birth, highborn; *van goede ~ of* a good
(respectable) family; *van lage ~ of* low birth
(descent), low-born

kom'buis (-buizen) *v* caboose, galley, cook's
house

komedi'ant (-en) *m* comedian; *hij is een echte ~*
he is always acting a part; **ko'medie** (-s) *v* 1
comedy; 2 (g e b o u w) theatre; *het is allemaal
maar ~* it's all sham, it's mere make-believe, it
is mere acting; *~ spelen* (d o e n a l s o f) put up
an act

ko'meet (-meten) *v* comet

'komen* *vi* come; *kom, kom* come now; *och kom!*
zie *och*; *ik kom al!* (I'm) coming!; *er komt regen*
we are going to have rain; *hij zal er wel ~* he is
sure to get there (to succeed); *wij kunnen er niet
~* we cannot make (both) ends meet; *er moge
van ~ wat wil* come what may; *hoe komt het
dat...?* how comes it that..., how is it that...?;
hoe kwam ik daar? how do I get there?; *hij wist
niet hoe het gekomen was* how it had come about;
zo kom je er niet this is not the right way; *fig in*

this way you'll never make it (succeed), this
will get you nowhere; *er kwam maar geen geld* no
money was forthcoming; *wij moeten maar
afwachten wat er ~ zal* await (further) developments; *is het zo ver gekomen dat...?* has it come to
this (to such a pass) that...?; *wie eerst komt, eerst
maalt* first come, first served; *ik zal hem laten ~*
I'll send for him; *ik zal het laten ~* I'll order it;
~ te spreken over get talking about; *als ik zou ~
te vallen* if I should fall; *fig* if I should (come to)
die; *hoe kwam je het boek te verliezen?* how did
you happen to lose the book?; *kom ze halen*
come and fetch (get) them; *ik kom u vertellen
dat...* I have come to tell you that...; *u moet eens
~ kijken* come and see, come and have a look
(at things); *hij kwam naast me zitten* he sat down
by my side; *hij kwam naast mij te zitten* he
happened to have his seat next to mine; *dat zal
duur ~* it will come expensive; zie ook: 2 *duur*
II; *op hoeveel komt dat?* what does it come to?;
hoe duur komt u dat te staan? what does it cost
you?; ● *er mee a a n de deur ~* hawk from door
to door, come to the house; *hoe zal ik aan het
geld ~?* how am I to come by (get) the money?,
how am I to raise the money?; *eerlijk aan iets ~*
come by sth. honestly; *kom er niet aan!* don't
touch it!; *hoe kom je daaraan?* 1 how have you
come by it?; 2 how did you find out?; how did
you get knowledge of it?; *a c h t e r iets ~* find
sth. out; *zal je b i j me ~?* will you come to
me?; *ik kom dadelijk bij je* I'll join you directly;
wij ~ niet meer bij hen we don't visit at their
house any more; *hoe kom je erbij?* what makes
you think so?; *bij elkaar ~* come together,
meet; *de kleuren ~ niet bij elkaar* the colours
don't match; *daarbij komt dat zij...* added to this
they...; *dat moest er nog bij ~!* that would be the
last straw; *er d o o r ~* get through[2], pass
through [a town]; *ik kon niet i n mijn jas ~* I
could not get into my coat; *in de kamer ~* come
into the room, enter the room; *er een beetje in ~*
catch on, get one's hand in, **F** gather speed;
ergens in kunnen ~ understand; *hij kwam n a a r
mij toe* he came up to me; *hij komt o m iets* he
has come for something or other; *o p hoeveel
komt dat beeldje?* how much is that figure?; *het
komt op 1£ per persoon* it comes to (works out
at) £ 1.00 per head; *ik kon niet op mijn fiets, mijn
paard ~* I could not get on to my bicycle, my
horse; *ik kan er niet op ~* I cannot think of it,
remember it, recall it; zie ook: *gedachte, idee,
inval*; *ik kon er niet t o e ~* I could not bring
myself to do it; *hoe bent u daartoe gekomen?* how
did you come to do it?; *~ t o t* [middel, schouder]
come up to; *tot iem. ~* come to sbd.; *tot zichzelf
~* come to one's senses; *tot een regeling ~* come
to, arrive at, reach a settlement; *zij ~ u i t een*

dorp they are from a village; *die woorden ~ uit het Grieks* those words are derived from Greek; *ik kom er niet uit* [*fig*] I can't make it out; *kun jij eruit ~?* what do you make of it?; *dat komt v a n het vele lezen* that comes of reading so much; *van lezen (werken &) zal vandaag niets ~* there will be no reading (working &) to-day; *wat zal ervan ~?* what is it going to end in?; *als er ooit iets van komt* if it ever comes to anything; *er zal niets van ~* nothing will come of it; *daar komt niets van in* that's out of the question, **F** nothing doing; *dat komt er van* that comes of being..., that's what comes from ...ing; *waar kom jij vandaan?* 1 where do you come from?; 2 where do you hail from, where are you from?

kom'foor (-foren) *o* chafing-dish, brazier; zie ook: *gaskomfoor* en *theelichtje*

kom'fort = *comfort*

1 ko'miek I *aj* comical, funny, droll; **II** *ad* in a comical (funny) way; 2 **ko'miek** (-en) *m* (low) comedian, clown, funny-man

ko'mijn *m* cum(m)in; **-ekaas** (-kazen) *m* cum(m)in-seed cheese

'komisch *aj* comic [film, opera], comical; *het ~e is dat...* the funny part of the matter is that...

kom'kommer (-s) *v* cucumber; **-sla** *v* cucumber salad; **-tijd** *m fig* dull (dead, silly) season; *de ~* ook: the slack

'komma ('s) *v* & *o* comma; *0,5 = nul ~ vijf* decimal five; **komma'punt** (-en) *v* & *o* semicolon

'kommer *m* 1 solicitude; 2 trouble, affliction, sorrow, grief; **-lijk** needy, pitiful; **-loos** free from cares, untroubled; **-nis** (-sen) *v* solicitude, anxiety, concern; **-vol** distressful, wretched

'kommetje (-s) *o* (small) cup, mug

Ko'moren *mv de ~* The Comoro Islands

kom'pas (-sen) *o* compass; **-beugel** (-s) *m* gimbals; **-huisje** (-s) *o* binnacle; **-naald** (-en) *v* needle (of a compass); **-roos** (-rozen) *v* compass-card; **-streek** (-streken) *v* point of the compass, rhumb

'kompel (-s) *m* pitman

kom'plot (-ten) *o* plot, intrigue, conspiracy; **komplot'teren** (komplotteerde, h. gekom-plotteerd) *vi* plot, intrigue, conspire

kom'pres I *aj* solid [composition]; **II** *ad* closely [printed]; **III** (-sen) *o* compress

komst *v* coming, arrival; ☉ advent [of Christ; of the motor-car and the aeroplane]; *op ~ zijn* be coming, be drawing near, be on the way

'komvormig bowl-shaped, basin-shaped

Kon. = *Koninklijk*

kon (konden) V.T. van *kunnen*

kond *~ doen* make known

'konden V.T. meerv. van *kunnen*

kon'fijten (konfijtte, h. gekonfijt) *vt* preserve, candy

'Kongo *o* Congo; **Kongo'lees I** *aj* Congolese; **II** *m* (-lezen) Congolese; *de Kongolezen* the Congolese

'kongsi(e) (-si's en -sies) *v* 1 kongsee, (secret) society; 2 $ combine, ring, trust; 3 clique

ko'nijn (-en) *o* rabbit, **F** bunny; **ko'nijnehok** (-ken) *o* rabbit-hutch; **-hol** (-holen) *o* burrow; **-jacht** *v* rabbit-shooting; **ko'nijnenberg** (-en) *m* (rabbit-)warren; **ko'nijnevel** (-len) *o* 1 rabbit's skin, rabbit-skin; (a l s b o n t) cony

'koning (-en) *m* king°; *de ~ der dieren* the king of beasts; *hij is de ~ te rijk* he is very happy; **konin'gin** (-en) *v* queen°; **~-moeder** queen mother; **~-regentes** queen regent; **~-weduwe** queen dowager; **konin'ginnedag** (-dagen) *m* the Queen's feast [in the Netherlands]; **konin'ginnenpage** [-pa.ʒə] (-s) *m* 🦋 swallow-tailed butterfly; **'koningsarend** (-en) *m* royal eagle; **'koningschap** *o* 1 royalty, kingship [of Christ &]; 2 [absolute, constitutional] monarchy; **'koningsdochter** (-s) *v* king's daughter; **-gezind** *aj* royalist; **~e** (-en) *m-v* royalist; **koningse'zindheid** *v* royalism; **'koningshuis** (-huizen) *o* royal house; **-kind** (-eren) *o* royal child; **-kroon** (-kronen) *v* royal crown; **-tijger** (-s) *m* royal tiger; **-titel** (-s) *m* title of king, regal title; **-troon** (-tronen) *m* royal throne; **-varen** (-s) *v* osmund; **-zoon** (-s en -zonen) *m* king's son; **'koninkje** (-s) *o* petty king, kingling, kinglet; **'koninklijk I** *aj* royal, regal, kingly, kinglike; *van ~e afkomst* ook: royally descended; **II** *ad* royally, regally, in regal splendour; in a kingly way; **'koninkrijk** (-en) *o* kingdom; *het ~ Denemarken* the Kingdom of Denmark; *het ~ der hemelen* the Kingdom of Heaven

'konisch conic(al), cone-shaped

'konkelaar (-s) *m* plotter, intriguer, schemer; **konkela'rij** (-en) *v* plotting, intriguing, scheming, machination(s); **'konkelen** (konkelde, h. gekonkeld) *vi* plot, intrigue, scheme; **konkel'foezen** (konkelfoesde, h. gekonkelfoesd) *vi* plot against sbd., scheme

kon'stabel (-s) *m* ⚓ gunner

kont (-en) *v* **P** arse

konter'feiten (konterfeitte, h. gekonterfeit) *vt* portray, picture; **konter'feitsel** (-s) *o* portrait, likeness

kon'vooi (-en) *o* convoy; **konvooi'eren** [-vo.'je:rə(n)] (konvooieerde, h. gekon-vooieerd) *vt* convoy

kooi (-en) *v* 1 cage [for birds, lions &]; 2 fold, pen [for sheep]; 3 decoy [for ducks]; 4 ⚓ berth, bunk; *naar ~ gaan* **F** turn in; **-eend** (-en) *v* decoy-duck; **'kooien** (kooide, h.

gekooid) *vt* 1 cage, put into a cage; 2 fold, pen; 'kooiker (-s) *m* decoy man
kook *v a a n de* ~ *brengen* bring to the boil; *aan de* ~ *zijn* be on the boil; *v a n de* ~ *zijn* 1 be off the boil; 2 *fig* be upset; –boek (-en) *o* cook(ery) book; –cursus [-kürzəs] (-sen) *m* course of cookery, cooking classes; –fornuis (-nuizen) *o* cooking range, kitchen stove, kitchener, cooker; –hitte *v* boiling-heat; –kachel (-s) *v* cooking-stove; –kunst *v* cookery, art of cooking, culinary art; –les (-sen) *v* cookery lesson; –plaat (-platen) *v* hot-plate, cooking plate; –punt (-en) *o* boiling-point; –ster (-s) *v* cook; –toestel (-len) *o* cooker, cooking-apparatus
1 kool (kolen) *v* ⚛ cabbage; *de* ~ *en de geit sparen* temporize; *iem. een* ~ *stoven* play sbd. a trick; *het is allemaal* ~ F it's all gammon
2 kool (kolen) *v* 1 (s t e e n k o o l) coal; 2 (v. h o u t) charcoal; 3 (e l e m e n t) & ☿ carbon; zie ook: *kolen*; –borstel (-s) *m* carbon brush
kool'dioxyde [-òksi.də] *o* carbon dioxide; 'koolhydraat (-draten) *o* carbohydrate
'koolmees (-mezen) *v* great tit(mouse)
kool'monoxyde [-òksi.də] *o* carbon monoxide
'koolraap (-rapen) *v* 1 Swedish turnip, swede; 2 (b o v e n d e g r o n d) kohlrabi, turnip-cabbage; kool'rabi ('s) *v* = *koolraap* 2
'koolspits (-en) *v* carbon(-point), crayon
'koolstof *v* carbon; –houdend carbonic, carbonaceous, carboniferous; –verbinding (-en) *v* carbon compound
'koolstronk (-en) *m* stalk of cabbage
'koolteer *m* & *o* coal-tar
kool'waterstof (-fen) *v* hydrocarbon
'koolwitje (-s) *o* cabbage butterfly
'koolzaad (-zaden) *o* rapeseed
'koolzuur *o* carbonic acid, carbon dioxide; –houdend carbonated [water]
'koolzwart coal-black, carbon black
koon (konen) *v* cheek
koop (kopen) *m* purchase; bargain, buy; *een* ~ *sluiten* strike a bargain; *o p de* ~ *toe* into the bargain; *t e* ~ for sale, on sale; *te* ~ *bieden* offer (put up) for sale; *te* ~ *lopen met zijn geleerdheid* show off (air) one's learning; *met zijn gevoelens te* ~ *lopen* wear one's heart on one's sleeve; *weten wat er in de wereld te* ~ *is* know what is going on in the world; –akte (-n en -s) *v* purchase deed; –avond (-en) *m* late shopping night; –briefje (-s) *o* bought note; –contract (-en) *o* contract of sale; –handel *m* trade, commerce; –je (-s) *o* (great) bargain, (good) buy; *daaraan heb ik een* ~ 1 that's a (real) bargain, that's a good buy; *op een* ~ on the cheap; –jesjager (-s) *m* bargain-hunter; –kracht *v* purchasing power, buying power; (v. h. p u b l i e k) spending

power; koop'krachtig having great purchasing power, able to buy; 'kooplieden *mv* van *koopman*; –lust *m* inclination (desire) to buy, buying propensity; koop'lustig eager to buy, fond of buying; 'koopman (-lieden en -lui) *m* merchant; dealer; (street) hawker; 'koopmansbeurs (-beurzen) *v* (commodity) exchange; –boek (-en) *o* account book; 'koopmanschap *v* trade, business; 'koop-penningen *mv* purchase money; –prijs (-prijzen) *m* purchase price; –som (-men) *v* purchase money; –stad (-steden) *v* commercial town; –vaarder (-s) *m* = *koopvaardijschip;* koopvaar'dij *v* merchant service; –schip (-schepen) *o* merchantman; –vloot (-vloten) *v* merchant fleet, merchant navy; 'koopvrouw (-en) *v* tradeswoman; (vegetable &) woman; –waar (-waren) *v* merchandise, commodities, wares; –ziek eager to buy; –zucht *v* eagerness to buy
koor (koren) *o* 1 (z a n g e r s) choir; 2 (t e g e n-o v e r s o l o; r e i) chorus; 3 (p l a a t s) choir, chancel; *in* ~ in chorus; –bank (-en) *v* choir-stall
koord (-en) *o* & *v* cord, string, rope; *de* ~*en van de beurs in handen hebben* hold the purse-strings; *op het slappe* ~ *dansen* walk (balance) on the slack-rope; –danser (-s) *m*, –danseres (-sen) *v* rope-dancer, rope-walker; 'koorde (-n) *v* chord
'koordirigent (-en) *m* choral conductor
'koordje (-s) *o* (bit of) string
'koorgezang (-en) *o* choral song(s), choral singing; –hek (-ken) *o* choir-screen; –hemd (-en) *o* surplice; –kap (-pen) *v* cope; –knaap (-knapen) *m* chorister, choirboy
koorts (-en) *v* fever; *de gele* ~ yellow fever; *koude* ~ ague; *(de)* ~ *hebben* have (a, the) fever; *de* ~ *krijgen* be taken with the fever; –aanval (-len) *m* attack (fit) of fever; –achtig I *aj* feverish[2]; II *ad* feverishly[2]; –droom (-dromen) *m* feverish dream; *koortsdromen hebben* be delirious with fever; –gloed *m* fever-heat; –ig feverish; –lijder (-s) *m* fever patient; –middel (-en) *o* febrifuge; –thermometer (-s) *m* fever (clinical) thermometer; –verwekkend pyretogenic; –vrij free from fever; –werend pyretic
'koorzang (-en) *m* = *koorgezang*; –er (-s) *m* chorister
koos (kozen) V.T. van *kiezen*
'koosjer = *kousjer*
koot (koten) *v* 1 (v. m e n s) knuckle-bone; 2 (v. p a a r d) pastern
'kootje (-s) *o* phalanx [*mv* phalanges]
kop (-pen) *m* 1 head [of a person, a nail &], F pate, S nob; *fig* head, brains; heading, headline [of newspaper article]; 2 cup [for coffee, tea]; 3

bowl [of a pipe]; 4 ☕ cupping-glass; 5 litre; 6 crest [of a wave]; 7 ✕ war-head [of rocket, torpedo]; ~ *van jut* try-your-strength machine; *een schip met 100 ~pen* with a hundred souls (hands); *een goede ~ hebben* have a good head [for names &]; *geen ~ hebben* have no head; (*hou je*) *~ dicht!* **F** shut up!; *~ op!* **F** don't let it get you down, cheer up!; *iets de ~ indrukken* nip sth. in the bud, stamp out, quell [a rebellion]; scotch [a rumour]; *de ~ nemen sp* take the lead; *zijn ~ tonen* be obstinate; *~pen zetten* cup [a patient]; ● *a a n de ~ liggen sp* lead; *o p de ~ af* exactly [five]; *iem. op zijn ~ geven* let sbd. have it; *op zijn ~ krijgen* catch it; *al ging hij op zijn ~ staan* though he should do anything; *de wereld staat op zijn ~* the world has turned topsy-turvy; *iets op de ~ tikken* 1 pick sth. up [at a sale]; 2 **S** nab sth.; *de dingen op hun ~ zetten* stand things on their head; *iem. op z'n ~ zitten* bully sbd.; *hij laat zich niet op zijn ~ zitten* **F** he doesn't suffer himself to be sat upon; *o v e r de ~ gaan* (f a i l l i e t g a a n) **F** go bust; *over de ~ schieten, over de ~ slaan* turn over; *z o n d e r ~ of staart* without either head or tail; without beginning or end; zie ook: *hoofd*; **–bal** (-len) *m sp* header

ko'peke (-n) *m* kopeck

'kopen* I *vt* buy[2], purchase; *wat koop ik er voor?* [*fig*] what good can it do me?, what's the good of that?; **II** *va* buy; *wij ~ niet bij hen* we don't deal with them; **1 'koper** (-s) *m* buyer, purchaser

2 'koper *o* copper; *geel ~* brass; *rood ~* copper; *het ~* ♪ the brass; **–achtig** coppery; brassy; **–blazers** *mv* ♪ brass winds; **–(diep)druk** (-ken) *m* copperplate printing, photogravure; **'koperdraad** (-draden) *o &* *m* brass-wire; **1 'koperen** *aj* copper, brass; **2 'koperen** (koperde, h. gekoperd) *vt* copper; **'kopererts** (-en) *o* copper-ore; **–geld** *o* coppers, copper coin; **kopergiete'rij** (-en) *v* brass-foundry; **'kopergravure** (-s en -n) *v* copperplate; **–groen** *o* verdigris; **–houdend** containing copper, cupreous; **–kleurig** copper-coloured, brass-coloured; **–mijn** (-en) *v* copper-mine; **koperplette'rij** (-en) *v* copper-mill; **'koperslager** (-s) *m* copper-smith, brazier

'kopersmarkt *v* $ buyers' market

'koperwerk *o* brass-ware

'koperwiek (-en) *v* redwing

'kopgroep (-en) *v* leading group

ko'pie (-pieën) *v* copy [of a letter]; replica [of work of art]; *voor ~ conform* a true copy; **–boek** (-en) *o* $ letter-book; **kopi'eerapparaat** (-raten) *o* copying machine, copier; **–inkt** *m* copying-ink; **kopi'ëren** (kopieerde, h. gekopieerd) *vt* copy; engross [a deed]; **kopi'' ïst**

(-en) *m* transcriber, copyist [of documents]; copying-clerk [in an office &]

ko'pij (-en) *v* copy; *er zit ~ in* it makes good copy, there is a story in it; **–recht** (-en) *o* copyright

'kopje (-s) *o* 1 head; 2 cup; 3 *ZA* kopje [hill]; 4 headline [of an article]; *wat een lief ~!* what a sweet face!; *~ duikelen* turn over and over; *~-onder doen, ~-onder gaan* take a header, get a ducking; *iem. een ~ kleiner maken* behead sbd., **F** chop sbd.'s head off; **'kopklep** (-pen) *v* overhead valve; **–lamp** (-en) *v* headlamp; **–licht** (-en) *o* headlight; **–loper** (-s) *m ~ zijn* take (be in) the lead; **–pakking** *v* cylinder head gasket

1 'koppel (-s) *o* couple [of eggs]; brace [of partridges]; ♪ coupler [of organ]

2 'koppel (-s) *m* belt [of a sword]; leash [for dogs]

'koppelaar (-s) *m* procurer, matchmaker, pimp; **–ster** (-s) *v* matchmaker, procuress; **koppela'rij** (-en) *v* matchmaking, procuring, pimping

'koppelbaas (-bazen) *m* contractor, recruiter

'koppelen (koppelde, h. gekoppeld) *vt* couple [chains &]; dock [of spacecraft]; leash [hounds]; join [words]; (v. m e n s e n) make a match; **'koppeling** (-en) *v* coupling; (v. a u t o o o k:) clutch; (r u i m t e v a a r t) docking; **–spedaal** (-dalen) *o &* *m* clutch (acceleration) pedal

'koppelriem (-en) *m* ✕ belt

'koppelstang (-en) *v* coupling-rod; connecting-rod [of an engine]; **–teken** (-s) *o* hyphen; **–verkoop** *m* linked transaction; package deal; **–werkwoord** (-en) *o* copula; **–woord** (-en) *o* copulative

'koppen (kopte, h. gekopt) *vt* 1 (v. k o p o n t d o e n) poll, cut back, head; 2 (b i j v o e t b a l) head [the ball]

'koppensnellen *o* head-hunting; **–er** (-s) *m* head-hunter

'koppig I *aj* 1 headstrong, obstinate [people], refractory; 2 heady [of liquors]; **II** *ad* obstinately; **–heid** *v* 1 obstinacy [of people]; 2 headiness [of liquors]

'koppijn *v* **F** a head

'kopra *v* copra

'kopschuw shy; *~ maken* frighten (off); *~ worden* jib; **–spijker** (-s) *m* tack; hobnail [for boots]; **–station** [-sta.(t)ʃòn] (-s) *o* terminus [*mv* termini]; **–stoot** (-stoten) *m* header; **–stem** (-men) *v* head-voice; **–stuk** (-ken) *o* headpiece; *de ~ken van de partij* **F** the big men of the party; **–telefoon** (-s) *m* headphone(s), headset; **–zorg** (-en) *v* worry; *zich ~(en) maken* worry (about *over*)

1 ko'raal (-ralen) *o* ♪ (g e z a n g) chorale
2 ko'raal (-ralen) *o* (d e s t o f) coral; **–achtig**
coralline; **–bank** (-en) *v* coral reef; **–dier** (-en)
o coral polyp; **–eiland** (-en) *o* coral island;
–mos *o* coral moss, coralline
ko'raalmuziek *v* choral music
ko'raalrif (-fen) *o* coral reef; **–visser** (-s) *m*
coral fisher, coral diver; **ko'ralen** *aj* coral,
coralline
ko'ran [-'ra.n] *m* Koran, Alcoran
kor'daat determined, resolute, firm
kor'don (-s) *o* cordon [of police &]
Ko'rea *o* Korea; **Kore'aan** (-eanen) *m*, **–s** *aj*
Korean
'koren *o* corn, grain; *het is ~ op zijn molen* that is
just what he wants, that is grist to his mill;
–aar (-aren) *v* ear of corn; **–beurs** (-beurzen) *v*
corn-exchange; **–bloem** *v* cornflower blue;
–bloem (-en) *v* cornflower, bluebottle; **–halm**
(-en) *m* corn-stalk; **–maat** (-maten) *v* corn-
measure; zie ook: 2 *licht*; **–molen** (-s) *m*
corn-mill; **–schoof** (-schoven) *v* sheaf of corn;
–schuur (-schuren) *v* granary²; **–veld** (-en) *o*
cornfield; **–wan** (-nen) *v* winnow; **–zolder**
(-s) *m* corn-loft, granary
1 korf (korven) *m* basket, hamper; hive [for
bees]
2 korf (korven) V.T. van *kerven*
'korhaan (-hanen) *m* black-cock; **–hoen** (-ders)
o grey-hen; *korhoenders* grouse
1 kor'net (-ten) *m* ✄ cornet, ensign
2 kor'net (-ten) *v* ♪ cornet
kor'noelje (-s) *v* cornel, dogberry
kor'nuit (-en) *m* comrade, companion, mate,
fellow
korpo'raal (-s) *m* ✄ corporal
korps (-en) *o* (army) corps; zie ook: *muziekkorps,
politiekorps, studentenkorps* &; **–geest** *m* esprit de
corps
'korpus (-sen) *o* body
'korrel (-s) *m* 1 grain; 2 = *vizierkorrel; op de ~
nemen* ✄ aim at; *fig* snipe at; **'korrelen**
(korrelde, h. gekorreld) *vt* grain, granulate;
–lig granular; **–ling** *v* granulation, graining;
'korreltje (-s) *o* grain, granule; *met een ~ zout*
with a pinch of salt
kor'set (-ten) *o* corset, (l i c h t,
z o n d e r b a l e i n e n) girdle
korst (-en) *v* crust [of bread]; rind [of cheese];
scab [on a wound]; **–achtig** crusty; **–deeg** *o*
short pastry; **–ig** crusty; scurfy, scabby
[wounds]; **–mos** (-sen) *o* 🌿 lichen
kort I *aj* short, brief; *~ en bondig* short and
concise, short and to the point; clear and
succinct; *~ en dik* thick-set, squat; *~ en goed* in
a word, in short; *alles ~ en klein slaan* smash
everything to atoms; *~ en (maar) krachtig* short

and sweet; *om ~ te gaan* to be brief, to make a
long story short; *iem. ~ houden* 1 keep sbd.
short (on short allowance); 2 keep sbd. on a
tight rein; *het ~ maken* make it short; *ik zal ~
zijn* I will be brief; *~ van memorie zijn* have a
short memory; *~ van stof zijn* be brief, be
shortspoken; ● *in ~e woorden* in a few words;
n a ~er of langer tijd sooner or later; *s e d e r t ~*
lately, recently; *t e ~ doen aan iems. verdiensten*
derogate from sbd.'s merits; *iem. te ~ doen*
wrong sbd.; *ik heb hem nooit een stuiver te ~
gedaan* I never wronged him of a penny; *geld te
~ komen* be short of money; *ik kom een paar
gulden te ~* I am a few guilders short; *er niet bij
te ~ komen* profit by it, get something out of it;
te ~ schieten fall short of the mark; *te ~ schieten
in...* be lacking in..., be deficient in...; *er is 20
gulden te ~* there are twenty guilders short; **II** *o
in het ~* in brief, briefly; *tot voor ~* until
recently; **III** *ad* briefly, shortly; *~ aangebonden*
zie *aangebonden*; *~ daarna (daarop)* shortly after;
het is ~ dag time is getting short; *om ~ te gaan*
the long and the short of it [is]; *~ geleden* lately,
recently; **kort'ademig** asthmatic, short of
breath, short-winded; **–heid** *v* shortness of
breath, asthma, short-windedness; **'kort'af I** *aj*
curt; *hij was erg ~ tegen me* he was very short
with me; **II** *ad* curtly; **korte'baan** short-
distance; **korte'golfontvanger** (-s) *m* short-
wave receiver; **–zender** (-s) *m* short-wave
transmitter; **'kortelings** a short time ago, not
long ago; **'korten I** (kortte, h. gekort) *vt*
shorten (a string, the hours); clip [wings];
deduct from [wage]; beguile [the time]; **II**
(kortte, is gekort) *vi* grow shorter; *de dagen ~*
the days are shortening (drawing in); **'kort-
heid** *v* shortness, brevity, succinctness;
kortheids'halve for the sake of brevity;
[called Tom] for short; **'korthoornvee** *o*
short-horned cattle, shorthorns; **'korting** (-en)
v 1 deduction [from wages]; 2 $ discount,
rebate, allowance; *~ voor contant* $ cash
discount; **'kortlopend** short-term; **'kortom,
kort'om** in short, in a word, in fine;
'kortoren (kortoorde, h. gekortoord) *vt* crop
the ears of; **'kortparkeerder** (-s) *m* short-term
parker; **–sluiting** *v* ⚡ short-circuit, short-
circuiting; **–staart** (-en) *m* bobtail; **'kort-
staarten** (kortstaartte, h. gekortstaart) *vt* dock
(the tail of); **kort'stondig** of short duration,
short-lived; **–heid** *v* shortness, brevity;
'kortweg curtly, summarily; *~, ik wil niet* to
make a long story short, I will not;
'kortwieken (kortwiekte, h. gekortwiekt) *vt*
clip the wings of; *[fig] iem. ~* clip sbd.'s wings;
kort'zicht *o wissel op ~* $ short(-dated) bill;
kort'zichtig near-sighted, short-sighted²,

purblind; **–heid** *v* near-sightedness, short-sightedness[2]

1 'korven (korfde, h. gekorfd) *vt* put into a basket (baskets); hive [bees]

2 'korven V.T. meerv van *kerven*

kor'vet (-ten) *v* corvette

'korzelig I *aj* crabbed, crusty; **II** *ad* crabbedly; **–heid** *v* crabbedness, crustiness

kosme'tiek *v* cosmetic

'kosmisch cosmic [rays]; **kosmogra'fie** *v* cosmography; **–'naut** (-en) *m* cosmonaut; **–po'liet** (-en) *m* cosmopolite, cosmopolitan; **–po'litisch** cosmopolitan; **'kosmos** *m* cosmos

kost *m* board, food, fare, victuals; livelihood; ~ *en inwoning* board and lodging, bed and board; *degelijke* ~ substantial fare; *dat is oude* ~ that is old news; *slappe* ~ cat-lap; *volle* ~ full board; *zware* ~ heavy food; *fig* strong meat; *geen* ~ *voor kinderen* no food for children; *fig* no milk for babes; *iem. de* ~ *geven* feed sbd.; *de* ~ *verdienen* earn one's keep; ● *a a n de* ~ *komen* earn one's keep, make a living; *(een jongen) i n de* ~ *doen* put out (a boy) to board; *bij een leraar in de* ~ boarded out with a teacher; *iem. in de* ~ *nemen* take sbd. in to board; *in de* ~ *zijn bij* be boarding with; *wat doet hij v o o r de* ~? what does he do for a living?; *z o n d e r* ~ without food; zie ook: *koste* & 2 *kosten*

'kostbaar 1 expensive, costly, dear [objects of art]; 2 precious [gems]; 3 valuable [furniture, time]; 4 sumptuous [banquets]; **–heid** (-heden) *v* expensiveness; costliness; sumptuousness; *kostbaarheden* valuables

'kostbaas (-bazen) *m* landlord

'koste *ten* ~ *van zijn gezondheid* at the cost of his health; *zich ten* ~ *van iem. anders vermaken* amuse oneself at the expense of someone else; *ten* ~ *leggen aan* spend [money &] on

'kostelijk I *aj* exquisite, delicious [food]; splendid, glorious; *die is* ~! that is a good one!; **II** *ad* splendidly

'kosteloos I *aj* free, gratis; **II** *ad* free of charge, gratis; **1 'kosten** (kostte, h. gekost) *vt* cost; *wat kost het?* how much is it?, what do you charge for it?; *het kan hem zijn betrekking* ~ it is as much as his place is worth; *het zal mij twee dagen* ~ it will take me two days; *al kost het mij het leven* even if it cost my life; *het kostte vijf personen het leven* it cost the lives of five persons; *het zal u veel moeite* ~ it will give you a lot of trouble; *het koste wat het wil* cost what it may, at any cost (price); *tegen de* ~*de prijs* at cost-price; **2 'kosten** *mv* expense(s), cost, 🕈 costs [of a lawsuit]; ~ *maken* go to expense, spend money; ~ *noch moeite sparen* spare neither effort nor expense; *op eigen* ~ at his (her) own expense; *op mijn* ~ at my (own) expense; *iem.*

op (hoge) ~ *jagen* put sbd. to (great) expense; *op* ~ *van ongelijk* at the loser's risk; *uit de* ~ *komen* break even; **–berekening** (-en) *v* calculation of expense; $ cost-accounting, costing; **–besparing** (-en) *v* economy

'koster (-s) *m* sexton, verger

'kostganger (-s) *m* boarder; **–geld** (-en) *o* board; **–huis** (-huizen) *o* boarding-house

'kostje (-s) *o* F chow

'kostjuffrouw (-en) *v* landlady

'kostprijs *m* $ cost-price; prime cost

'kostschool (-scholen) *v* boarding-school; **–houder** (-s) *m* boarding-school master; **–leerling** (-en) *m* boarder

kostu'meren (kostumeerde, h. gekostumeerd) *vt* & *vr* dress up (as a...); *gekostumeerd bal* fancy(-dress) ball; **kos'tuum** (-s) *o* 1 costume [of a lady]; suit [of a man]; 2 (v o o r g e k o s- t u m e e r d b a l) fancy dress; **–naaister** (-s) *v* dressmaker; **–repetitie** [-(t)si.] (-s) *v* dress rehearsal

'kostwinner (-s) *m* bread-winner; **–svergoe- ding** *v* separation allowance; **'kostwinning** *v* livelihood

kot (-ten) *o* pen [for sheep]; kennel [for dogs]; sty [for pigs]; **S** quod [= prison]

kote'let (-ten) *v* cutlet, chop

'koter (-s) *m* F kid

'kotsen (kotste, h. gekotst) *vi* throw up, puke; **'kots'misselijk** sick to death; *ik ben er* ~ *van* I am sick and tired of it

'kotter (-s) *m* ⚓ cutter

kou *v* cold; *een* ~ *in het hoofd* a cold in the head; ~ *vatten* catch (a) cold; **koud I** *aj* cold[2]; frigid [zone]; *het* ~ *hebben* be cold; *ik werd er* ~ *van* it made my blood run cold; *het laat mij* ~ it leaves me cold; *iem.* ~ *maken* (d o d e n) F do away with sbd.; **II** *ad* coldly; **III** *cj* (n a u w e- l i j k s) hardly, scarcely; **–bloedig** cold-blooded[2]; **'koude** *v* = *kou*; **'kou(de)front** (-en) *o* cold front; **'koudegolf** (-golven) *v* cold-wave; **'koudgreep** (-grepen) *v* insulated handle; **'koudheid** *v* coldness; **'koudjes I** *aj* coldish; **II** *ad* coldly; **'koudmakend** cooling; ~ *mengsel* freezing mixture; **koud'vuur** *o* gangrene; **'koukleum** (-en) *m-v* chilly person

kous (-en) *v* stocking; zie ook: *kousje*; *daarmee is de* ~ *af* that settles the matter; *m e t de* ~ *op de kop thuiskomen* come away with a flea in one's ear; *o p zijn* ~*en* in his stockinged feet; **'kouse- band** (-en) *m* garter; **'kousenwinkel** (-s) *m* hosier's shop; **'kousevoeten** *mv op* ~ in one's stockinged feet˚; **'kousje** (-s) *o* 1 wick [of a lamp]; 2 (incandescent) mantle

'kousjer kosher[2]

kout *m* talk, chat; **'kouten** (koutte, h. gekout) *vi* talk, chat

'**kouter** (-s) *o* coulter [of a plough]
'**kouvatten** (vatte 'kou, h. 'kougevat) *vi* catch cold; '**kouwelijk** chilly, sensitive to cold
ko'**zak** (-ken) *m* Cossack
'**kozen** V.T. meerv. van *kiezen*
ko'**zijn** (-en) *o* window-frame
kraag (kragen) *m* collar [of linen, of a coat]; tippet [of fur]; (g e p l o o i d) ruff; *bij de* ~ *pakken* seize [sbd.] by the collar, collar [sbd.]; –**je** (-s) *o* collaret(te)
kraai (-en) *v* **☙** crow; *bonte* ~ hooded crow; '**kraaien** (kraaide, h. gekraaid) *vi* crow; '**kraaienest** (-en) *o* crow's nest˚; '**kraaien-mars** *m de* ~ *blazen* **F** go west, **S** kick the bucket; '**kraaiepootjes** *mv* crow's-feet
kraak (kraken) *m* crack, cracking; –**amandel** (-s en -en) *v* shell-almond; –**been** *o* gristle, cartilage; –'**helder** spotlessly clean, spick-and-span; –**stem** (-men) *v* grating voice; –'**zinde-lijk** spotlessly clean
1 kraal (kralen) *v* (b o l l e t j e) bead
2 kraal (kralen) *v* (o m s l o t e n r u i m t e) kraal
'**kraaloogjes** *mv* beady eyes
kraam (kramen) *v* booth, stall, stand; *dat komt niet in zijn* ~ *te pas* that does not suit his book (his purpose, his game)
'**kraambed** *o* childbed; *in het* ~ *liggen* be confined, lie in; –**been** (-benen) *o* white-leg, milk-leg; –**inrichting** (-en) *v* maternity home, maternity hospital; –**kliniek** (-en) *v* maternity (lying-in) hospital; –**koorts** (-en) *v* puerperal fever
'**kraampje** (-s) *o* booth [at a fair]
'**kraamverpleegster** (-s) *v* maternity nurse; –**verzorgster** (-s) *v* monthly nurse; –**vrouw** (-en) *v* mother of newly-born child
1 kraan (kranen) *v* 1 (a a n v a t &) tap, cock, *Am* faucet; 2 (o m t e h ij s e n) crane, derrick
2 kraan (kranen) *m* **F** dab; *hij is een* ~ *in...* he is a dab at...
3 kraan (kranen) *m* **☙** = *kraanvogel*
'**kraanbalk** (-en) *m* cat-head; –**drijver** (-s) *m* crane-driver; –**geld** (-en) *o* **$** cranage
'**kraanvogel** (-s) *m* **☙** crane
'**kraanwagen** (-s) *m* breakdown lorry
krab (-ben) *v* (s c h r a m) scratch
'**krab(be)** (krabben) *v* (d i e r) crab
'**krabbel** (-s) *v* scratch [with the nails]; scrawl, scribble [with a pen]; thumb-nail sketch [by an artist]; doodle [while thinking or listening]; '**krabbelen** (krabbelde, h. gekrabbeld) **I** *vi* scratch; scrawl, scribble; doodle [idly, while thinking or listening]; **II** *vt* scratch; scrawl, scribble [a few lines]; '**krabbelig** scrawled, crabbed [writing]; '**krabbelschrift** *o* crabbed writing; *zijn* ~ ook: his scrawl(s); '**krabbeltje** (-s) *o* note, scrawl, word

'**krabben** (krabde, h. gekrabd) **I** *vi* scratch [with the nails]; **II** *vt* scratch; scrape; *iem. in zijn gezicht* ~ scratch sbd.'s face; **III** *vr zich* ~ scratch (oneself); *zich achter de oren* ~ scratch one's head; –**er** (-s) *m* scratcher, scraper; '**krabijzer** (-s) *o* scraping-iron, scraper
krach (-s) *m* **$** crash
kracht (-en) *v* energy, power, strength, force, vigour; (w e r k k r a c h t) employee, worker; ~ *en stof* matter and force; *de* ~ *der gewoonte* the force of habit; *zijn* ~*en beproeven (aan...)* try one's hand (at...); ~ *bijzetten aan...* zie *bijzetten*; ~ *van wet hebben* have the force of law; *zijn* ~*en herkrijgen (herstellen)* regain one's strength; *al zijn* ~*en inspannen* exert one's utmost strength; *zijn* ~*en wijden aan* devote one's energy to; ● *i n de* ~ *van hun leven* in their prime, in the prime of life; *m e t alle* ~ with might and main; *met halve* ~ **⚓** ease her!, half speed; *met vereende* ~*en* with united efforts; *met volle* ~ ful speed [ahead!]; *(weer) o p* ~*en komen* regain strength, recuperate; *u i t* ~ *van* in (by) virtue of; *v a n* ~ in force; *van* ~ *worden* come into force; *God geeft* ~ *naar kruis* God tempers the wind to the shorn lamb; –**bron** (-nen) *v* source of power; **kracht'dadig** strong, powerful, energetic; efficacious; –**heid** *v* energy; efficacy; '**krach-teloos** 1 (v. p e r s o o n) powerless, nerveless, impotent; 2 (v. w e t &) invalid; ~ *maken* enervate [of the body]; invalidate, annul, make null and void [of laws &]; **krachte'loosheid** *v* 1 powerlessness, impotence; 2 invalidity; '**krachtens** in (by) virtue of; '**krachtig I** *aj* 1 (l i c h a a m) strong, robust; 2 (m i d d e l e n &) strong, powerful, forceful, potent; 3 (m a a t-r e g e l e n &) strong, powerful, energetic, vigorous; 4 (t a a l, s t ij l) strong, powerful, forcible; 5 (v o e d s e l) nourishing; **II** *ad* strongly, ener-getically; '**krachtinstallatie** [-(t)si.] (-s) *v* (electric) power plant; –**lijn** (-en) *v* line of force; –**meting** *v* trial of strength, **F** show-down; –**overbrenging** *v* transmission of power; –**patser** (-s) *m* muscle man, strong-arm man; '**krachtseenheid** *v* dynamic unit; –**inspanning** *v* exertion, effort; '**kracht-stroom** *m* electric power; '**krachtterm** (-en) *m* strong word (expression), expletive, swear word; ~*en* strong language; –**toer** (-en) *m* tour-de-force; –**veld** (-en) *o* field of force; –**verhouding** *v* relative (comparative) strength –**verspilling** *v* waste of energy
krak I *ij* crack; ~ *zei het ijs* crack went the ice; **II** (-ken) *m* crack
kra'keel (-kelen) *o* quarrel, wrangle; **kra'kelen** (krakeelde, h. gekrakeeld) *vi* quarrel, wrangle
'**krakeling** (-en) *m* cracknel
'**kraken** (kraakte, h. gekraakt) **I** *vi* crack [of the

ice], creak, squeak [of boots]; **II** *vt* crack [nuts, *fig* a bottle, petroleum &]; *fig* **F** slate [an author, a book, a play &]; *huizen* ~ break into and occupy empty houses, squat

krakke'mikkig ramshackle, tumble-down

'kralensnoer (-en) *o* bead necklace

kram (-men) *v* cramp(-iron), staple; clasp [of a bible]

'kramer (-s) *m* pedlar, hawker; **krame'rij** (-en) *v* small wares

'krammen (kramde, h. gekramd) *vt* cramp, clamp; **'krammetje** (-s) *o* clip

kramp (-en) *v* cramp, spasm; *hij kreeg de* ~ he was seized with cramp; **kramp'achtig** spasmodic(al), convulsive, jerky; *zich* ~ *vasthouden aan* cling desparately to; **'kramphoest** *m* spasmodic cough

'kranig I *aj* brave; *een* ~*e kerel* a smart (dashing) man; *een* ~ *soldaat* a dashing soldier; *dat is een* ~ *stukje* that is a fine feat; **II** *ad* in dashing (gallant) style; ~ *voor de dag komen* make a fine show; *zij hebben zich* ~ *gehouden* they bore themselves splendidly; **–heid** *v* dash

⊙ **krank** sick, ill; ⊙ **–e** (-n) *m-v* sick person, patient; ⊙ **–heid** (-heden) *v* illness, sickness

krank'zinnig I *aj* insane, lunatic, mad, crazy; **II** *ad* exorbitantly [expensive, high]; **–e** (-n) *m-v* lunatic, madman, mad woman, **S** nut-case; **krank'zinnigengesticht** (-en) *o* lunatic asylum; **–verpleegster** (-s) *v* mental nurse; **krank'zinnigheid** *v* insanity, lunacy, madness, craziness

krans (-en) *m* wreath, garland, crown; zie ook: *kransje*; **–je** (-s) *o* (v. p e r s o n e n) club, circle; **–slagader** (-s en -en) *v* coronary artery

krant (-en) *v* (news)paper; **'kranteartikel** (-en) *o* newspaper article; **–bericht** (-en) *o* newspaper report, (newspaper) paragraph; **–knipsel** (-s) *o* press cutting; **'krantenjongen** (-s) *m* newsboy; **–kiosk** (-en) *v* newspaper-kiosk, news-stand; **–koning** (-en) *m* press baron; **–man** (-nen) *m* newsman; **–papier** *o* newsprint, newspaper; **–taal** *v* journalese; **–verkoper** (-s) *m* newsvendor, newsman

1 krap (-pen) *v* 1 (m e e k r a p) madder; ‖ 2 clasp [of a book]

2 krap I *aj* tight, narrow, skimpy; *het geld is* ~ money is tight; **II** *ad* tightly, narrowly, skimpily; *het is* ~ *aan* it's barely enough; *zij hebben het maar* ~ they are in straitened circumstances; ~ *meten* give short measure; *de tijd te* ~ *nemen* cut the time too sharp; *wij zitten hier* ~ we are cramped for room; **–jes** = 2 *krap* **II**

1 kras I *aj* 1 (v. p e r s o o n & m a a t r e g e l) strong, vigorous; 2 (v. b e w e r i n g &) **F** stiff, steep; *dat is (wat al te)* ~ **F** that's a bit stiff

(steep, thick); *hij is nog* ~ *voor zijn leeftijd* he is still hale and hearty (still going strong); **II** *ad* strongly, vigorously; *dat is nogal* ~ *gesproken* that is strong language

2 kras (-sen) *v* scratch; **'krassen** (kraste, h. gekrast) **I** *vi* scratch; scrape [of a pen, on a violin]; screech [of owl], croak, caw [of raven]; grate [of voice], jar [of sounds, upon sbd.'s ears]; **II** *vt* scratch [a name in soft stone]

krat (-ten) *o* 1 tail-board [of a carriage &]; 2 **$** crate, packing case

'krater (-s) *m* crater; **–meer** (-meren) *o* crater-lake; **–vormig** crater-shaped, crater-like

'krauwen (krauwde, h. gekrauwd) *vt* scratch

kre'diet (-en) *o* credit; *op* ~ on credit; **–bank** (-en) *v* credit bank; **–beperking** *v* credit squeeze; **–brief** (-brieven) *m* letter of credit; **–hypotheek** [-hi.po.-] (-theken) *v* equitable mortgage; **–instelling** (-en) *v* credit establishment; **krediet'waardig** *v* solvent, creditworthy; **–heid** *v* solvency, credit-worthiness

kreeft (-en) *m* & *v* 1 (z o e t w a t e r) crayfish, crawfish; 2 (z e e) lobster; *de Kreeft* ★ Cancer; **'kreeftegang** *m hij gaat de* ~ he is going backward; **–sla** *v* lobster salad; **'kreeftskeerkring** *m* tropic of Cancer

kreeg (kregen) V.T. van *krijgen*

kreek (kreken) *v* creek, cove

1 kreet (kreten) *m* cry, scream, shriek

2 kreet (kreten) V.T. van *krijten*

'kregel(ig) I *aj* peevish; ~ *maken* irritate; **II** *ad* peevishly; **'kregeligheid** *v* peevishness

'kregen V.T. meerv. van *krijgen*

krek exactly, quite (so)

'krekel (-s) *m* (house-)cricket

kreng (-en) *o* carrion; *fig* beast [of a master &], rotter; (v r o u w) bitch; *dat* ~ *van een ding* the blooming thing; *oud* ~ old crock

'krenken (krenkte, h. gekrenkt) *vt* hurt, offend, injure; *iems. gevoelens* ~ wound sbd.'s feelings; *geen haar op uw hoofd zal gekrenkt worden* not a hair of your head shall be touched; *iems. goede naam* ~ injure sbd.'s reputation; *zijn geestvermogens zijn gekrenkt* he is of unsound mind; *op gekrenkte toon* in a hurt tone; **–d I** *aj* injurious, offensive, insulting, wounding; **II** *ad* injuriously, offensively; **'krenking** (-en) *v* injury[2], *fig* mortification

krent (-en) *v* (dried) currant; (a c h t e r s t e) behind, bum; (g i e r i g a a r d) skinflint, miser; **'krenten** (krentte, h. gekrent) *vt* thin out [grapes]; **'krentenbaard** *m* impetigo; **–brood** (-broden) *o* currant-bread; *een* ~ a currant-loaf; **–broodje** (-s) *o* currant-bun; **'krentenkakker** (-s) *m* **S** tightwad, skinflint, niggard; **'krenterig I** *aj* mean, niggardly; **II** *ad* meanly

'Kreta *o* Crete

'**kreten** V.T. meerv. van *krijten*
Kre'tenzer (-s) *m* Cretan
kreuk (-en), **–el** (-s) *v* crease; '**kreukelen**
(kreukelde, *vt* h., *vi* is gekreukeld) *vt* & *vi*
crease, rumple, crumple; '**kreukelig** creased,
crumpled; '**kreuken** (kreukte, *vt* h., *vi* is
gekreukt) = *kreukelen*; '**kreukher'stellend,**
'**kreukvrij** crease-(wrinkle-)proof, crease-
resistant, non-creasing
'**kreunen** (kreunde, h.) gekreund) *vi* moan,
groan
'**kreupel** *aj* lame; ~ *lopen* walk with a limp,
limp; *een ~e* a lame person, a cripple
'**kreupelbos** (-sen) *o* thicket, brake, underwood; **–hout** *o* underwood, undergrowth
'**kreupelrijm** (-en) *o* doggerel
'**krib(be)** (kribben) *v* 1 (v o e d e r b a k) manger,
crib; 2 (s l a a p s t e e) cot; 3 (w a t e r k e r i n g)
groyne
'**kribbebijter** (-s) *m fig* crosspatch; **–bijtster**
(-s) *v* shrew, scratch-cat
'**kribbig I** *aj* peevish, crabby, testy; **II** *ad*
peevishly, testily
'**kriebel** (-s) *m* itch(ing); *ik krijg er de ~s van* **F** it
gives me the jim-jams, it's driving me crazy;
'**kriebelen** (kriebelde, h. gekriebeld) *vt* & *vi*
tickle; zie ook: *krabbelen*; '**kriebelig** ticklish; *je
wordt er ~ van* it is irritating, it gets under your
skin; zie ook: *krabbelig*; '**kriebeling** (-en) *v*
tickling; '**kriebelschrift** *o* = *krabbelschrift*
'**kriegel** peevish
kriek (-en) *v* black cherry; zie ook: *lachen*
'**krieken** (kriekte, h. gekriekt) *vi* chirp; *bij het ~
van de dag* at day-break, at peep of day
kriel 1 *o* small potatoes (apples); small fry; 2
(-en) *m-v* pygmy, midget, small child; **–haan**
(-hanen) *m* dwarf-cock; **–hen** (-nen), **–kip**
(-pen) *v,* **–kippetje** (-s) *o* dwarf-hen
'**krieuwel** *m* = *kriebel*; '**krieuwelen** (krieu-
welde, h. gekrieuweld) *vi* & *vt* = *krioelen* &
kriebelen
⊙ **krijg** (-en) *m* war; ~ *voeren* make war, wage
war (on *tegen*)
'**krijgen*** *vt* get [sth.]; receive, obtain [books,
money &]; acquire [a reputation]; catch [a
thief, measles &]; receive [a hurt]; have [a boy,
a girl, a holiday, kittens]; have [a beard]
coming; put forth, send out [leaves]; *kan ik een
boek ~?* can I have a book?; *hoeveel krijgt u van
me?* how much do I owe you?, how much is
it?; ~ *ze elkaar?* do they get married (in the
end)?; *ik zal je ~!* I'll make you pay for it!; *ik
kan het niet dicht (open)* ~ I cannot shut it (open
it); *het koud (warm)* ~ begin to feel cold (hot);
het te horen (te zien) ~ get to hear of it, get to
see it; *ik zal trachten hem te spreken te* ~ I'll try to
see him; *het uit hem* ~ get it out of him; draw it

from him; *het zijne* ~ come by one's own; *er
genoeg van* ~ have (got) enough of it, get tired
of it; *ik kan hem er niet toe* ~ I cannot get him
to do it, make him do it; *niet meer te* ~ not to
be had any more; zie ook: *benauwd, gelijk,
kwaad, lek, ongeluk, doorkrijgen* &
'**krijger** (-s) *m* warrior; **–tje** *o* ~ *spelen* play tag;
'**krijgsartikelen** *mv* ⚔ articles of war;
–banier (-en) *v* banner of war; **–dienst** *m*
military service; **–gevangene** (-n) *m* prisoner
of war; **–gevangenschap** *v* captivity;
krijgs'haftig martial,warlike; **–heid** *v* martial
spirit, warlike appearance; '**krijgskunde** *v* art
of war; **krijgs'kundig** *aj* military; ~*e* military
expert; '**krijgslied** (-eren) *o* warlike (military)
song; **–lieden** *mv* warriors, (band of) soldiers;
–list (-en) *v* stratagem, ruse of war; **–macht**
(-en) *v* (military) forces; **–man** (-lieden) *m*
warrior, soldier; **–raad** (-raden) *m* 1 council of
war; 2 ⚖ court-martial; ~ *houden* hold a
council of war; *iem. voor een* ~ *brengen* ⚖ court-
martial sbd.; **–school** (-scholen) *v* military
school (college); *hogere* ~ staff-college; **–tocht**
(-en) *m* military expedition, campaign;
–toneel (-nelen) *o* seat (theatre) of war;
–tucht *v* military discipline; **krijgs'tuchtelijk**
disciplinary; '**krijgsvolk** *o* soldiers, soldiery,
military; **–wet** (-ten) *v* martial law; **–wetenschap** (-pen) *v* military science
krijs (-en) *m* scream, shriek, screech, cry;
'**krijsen** (krijste, h. gekrijst) *vi* & *vt* scream,
shriek, screech, cry
krijt *o* 1 chalk; 2 (o m t e k e n e n) crayon;
i n het ~ *staan (bij)* be in debt (to); *m e t dubbel* ~
schrijven charge double; **–bakje** (-s) *o* chalk-
box; **–berg** (-en) *m* chalk-hill
1 '**krijten*** **I** *vi* cry, weep; **II** *vt* cry, scream
2 '**krijten** (krijtte, h. gekrijt) *vt* ⚒ chalk [one's
cue]
'**krijtgebergte** (-n en -s) *o* chalk-hills; **–je** (-s) *o*
piece of chalk; **–rots** (-en) *v* chalk-cliff;
–streep (-strepen) *v* chalk-line; **–tekening**
(-en) *v* crayon drawing; **–wit I** *o* chalk-dust,
whiting; **II** *aj* as white as chalk (as a sheet),
chalk-white
krikke'mikkig = *krakkemikkig* [Crimean War
Krim *v de* ~ the Crimea; **–oorlog** *m de* ~ the]
krimp *v de* ~ shrinking; shrinkage; *geen* ~ *hebben* be
well-off; *geen* ~ *geven* not yield; bear up, hold
out
'**krimpen*** **I** *vi* 1 (v. s t o f) shrink; 2 ⚓ (v a n
w i n d) back; *van koude* ~ shiver with cold; ~
van de pijn writhe with pain; **II** *vt* shrink [cloth];
'**krimpvrij** unshrinkable
kring (-en) *m* circle, ring; *blauwe* ~*en onder de
ogen* dark rings under the eyes; *de hogere* ~*en* the
upper circles; *in sommige* ~*en* in some quarters

'**kringelen** (kringelde, h. gekringeld) *vi* coil, curl
'**kringetje** (-s) *o* circlet, ring; ~*s blazen* blow rings of smoke; '**kringloop** *m* circular course; (v. o u d p a p i e r) recycling; *fig* circle, cycle [of life and death]
'**krinkel** (-s) *m* crinkle; '**krinkelen** (krinkelde, h. gekrinkeld) *vi* crinkle
kri'oelen (krioelde, h. gekrioeld) *vi* swarm; ~ *van* crawl with, swarm with, bristle with
krip *o* crape
kris (-sen) *v* creese [Malay dagger]
'**kriskras** criss-cross
kris'tal (-len) *o* crystal; –**achtig** crystalline; –**helder** (as clear as) crystal, crystal-clear; **kris'tallen, kristal'lijnen** *aj* crystal(line); **kristalli'satie** [-'za.(t)si.] (-s) *v* crystallization; **kristalli'seren** [s = z] (kristalliseerde, h. gekristalliseerd) *vt, vi* & *vr* crystallize (into *tot*); **kris'talsuiker** *m* granulated sugar; –**water** *o* water of crystallization
kri'tiek I *aj* critical; *een* ~ *ogenblik* a critical (crucial) moment; *een* ~ *punt bereiken* come to a head; **II** (-en) *v* 1 criticism (of *op*); 2 critique [in art or literature], review [of books]; ~ *hebben op* be critical of [a plan &]; ~ *uitoefenen* (*op*) pass criticism (on...), criticize...; *beneden* ~ below criticism, beneath contempt; –**loos** uncritical; '**kritisch** critical; ~ *staan tegenover* be critical of [a plan &]; **kriti'seren** (kritiseerde, h. gekritiseerd) [s = z] *vt* 1 criticize, censure [= criticize unfavourably]; 2 review [books]
krocht (-en) *v* 1 (c r y p t) crypt, undercroft [under a church]; 2 (s p e l o n k) cavern
kroeg (-en) *v* public house, pub; –**baas** (-bazen), –**houder** (-s) *m* publican; –**loper** (-s) *m* pub-loafer
'**kroelen** (kroelde, h. gekroeld) *vi* pet, make love
kroep *m* croup
1 kroes (kroezen) *m* 1 cup, pot, mug, noggin [for drinking]; 2 crucible [for melting]
2 kroes *aj* frizzled, frizzy, fuzzy, woolly; –**haar** *o* frizzy hair; –**kop** (-pen) *m* curly-pate, curly-head, fuzzy head, frizzly head; '**kroezen** (kroesde, h. gekroesd) *vi* curl, friz(z), crisp; zie ook *gekroesd*
kro'ket = 1 *croquet*
kroko'dil (-len) *m* & *v* crocodile; **kroko'dillele(d)er** *o* crocodile leather; *tas van* ~ crocodile bag; –**tranen** *mv* crocodile tears
'**krokus** (-sen) *m* crocus
'**krollen** (krolde, h. gekrold) *vi* caterwaul; **krols**

(v. k a t t e n) in heat
krom crooked, curved; ~*me benen* bandy-legs, bow-legs; *een* ~*me lijn* a curved line, a curve; *een* ~*me neus* a hooked nose; *een* ~*me rug* a crooked back, a crook-back; ~ *van de reumatiek* doubled up with rheumatism; –**benig** bandy-legged, bow-legged; –**groeien**[1] *vi* become (get) bent (crooked); –**heid** *v* crookedness; –**hout** (-en) *o* ⚓ knee; –**liggen**[1] *vi* stint (pinch) oneself; –**lopen**[1] *vi* 1 (v. p e r s o o n) walk with a stoop, stoop; 2 (v. w e g &) curve; '**kromme** (-n) *v* curve; '**krommen** (kromde, *vt* h., *vi* is gekromd) *vt* & *vi* bow, bend, curve; –**ming** (-en) *v* bend, curve
kromp (krompen) V.T. van *krimpen*
'**krompasser** (-s) *m* callipers
'**krompen** V.T. meerv. van *krimpen*
'**krompraten**[1] *vi* 1 talk brokenly, murder the King's English; 2 lisp; –**staf** (-staven) *m* crossier, crook; –**trekken**[1] *vi* warp; –**zwaard** (-en) *o* 1 scimitar; 2 (k o r t) falchion
'**kronen** (kroonde, h. gekroond) *vt* crown[2]; *hem tot koning* ~ crown him king
kro'niek (-en) *v* chronicle; ~*en ook:* memorials; (i n k r a n t) [sports, theatrical] column, [financial &] news; –**schrijver** (-s) *m* chronicler; (v. e. k r a n t) reporter
'**kroning** (-en) *v* crowning, coronation; '**kroningsdag** (-dagen) *m* coronation day; –**plechtigheid** (-heden) *v* coronation ceremony
'**kronkel** (-s) *m* twist, coil; –**darm** (-en) *m* ileum; '**kronkelen** (kronkelde, h. en is gekronkeld) *vi* & *vr* wind, twist; meander [of a river]; –**lig** winding, sinuous, meandering; –**ling** (-en) *v* winding; coil; convolution; '**kronkelpad** (-paden) *o* winding path; *fig* devious (circuitous) way
kroon (kronen) *v* 1 (v. v o r s t) crown; 2 (v. 't h o o f d) crown, top; 3 (l i c h t) chandelier, lustre; 4 🌿 corolla; *de* ~ *neerleggen* abdicate, resign the crown; *iem. de* ~ *van het hoofd nemen* rob sbd. of his honour; *iem. de* ~ *opzetten* crown sbd.; *de* ~ *spannen* bear the palm; *dat spant de* ~ that caps everything; *iem. naar de* ~ *steken* vie with (rival) sbd.; *de* ~ *op het werk zetten* crown it all; –**domein** (-en) *o* demesne of the crown, crown land; –**getuige** (-n) *m-v* crown witness, King's (Queen's) evidence; –**juwelen** *mv* crown jewels; –**kolonie** (-s en -iën) *v* crown colony; –**kurk** (-en) *v* crown cork; –**lijst** (-en) *v* cornice; –**luchter** (-s) *m* chandelier; –**pretendent** (-en) *m* pretender to the throne;

---

[1] V.T. en V.D. van dit werkwoord volgens het model: '**krom**groeien, V.T. groeide '**krom**, V.D. '**krom**gegroeid. Zie voor de vormen onder het grondwoord, in dit voorbeeld: *groeien*. Bij sterke en onregelmatige werkwoorden wordt u verwezen naar de lijst achterin.

–prins (-en) *m* crown prince; **–prinses** (-sen) *v* crown princess; **–sieraden** *mv* regalia; **–tje** (-s) *o* ⊘ coronet; **–vormig** crown-shaped

kroop (kropen) V.T. van *kruipen*

kroos *o* 🌿 duckweed

kroost *o* offspring, progeny, issue

kroot (kroten) *v* 🌿 beetroot

1 krop (-pen) *m* 1 crop, gizzard, craw; 2 (a l s z i e k t e) goitre

2 krop (-pen) *m* head [of cabbage, lettuce]

'kropduif (-duiven) *v* 🐦 cropper, pouter

'kropen V.T. meerv. van *kruipen*

'kropgezwel (-len) *o* goitre

1 'kroppen (kropte, h. gekropt) *vi* head [of salad]

2 'kroppen (kropte, h. gekropt) *vt* cram [a bird]; *hij kan het niet ~* zie *verkroppen*

'kropsalade, –sla *v* head (cabbage-)lettuce

krot (-ten) *o* hovel, den; *wat een ~!* what a hole!; **–opruiming** *v* slum clearance; **–woning** (-en) *v* slum dwelling

kruid (-en) *o* 🌿 herb; *daar is geen ~ voor gewassen* there is no cure for it; **–achtig** herbaceous; **–boek** (-en) *o* herbal; **'kruiden** (kruidde, h. gekruid) *vt* season[2], spice[2]; *sterk gekruid* highly seasoned[2], spicy[2]; **'kruidenaftreksel** (-s) *o* decoction of herbs; **–azijn** *m* aromatic (herb) vinegar; **–dokter** (-s) *m* herb-doctor, quack

kruide'nier (-s) *m* grocer; **kruide'niersgeest** *m* bigotry, narrow-mindedness; **–vak** *o* grocer's trade; **–waren** *mv* groceries; **–winkel** (-s) *m* grocer's (shop), grocery shop

'kruidenthee *m* herbal tea, herb-tea; **–tuin** (-en) *m* herb garden, herbary; **–wijn** (-en) *m* spiced wine; **kruide'rijen** *mv* spices; **'kruidig** spicy; **kruidje-'roer-mij-niet** (kruidjes-) *o* 1 🌿 sensitive plant; 2 *fig* touch-me-not; **'kruidkoek** (-en) *m* spiced gingerbread; **–kunde** *v* botany; **kruid'kundige** (-n) *m* botanist, herbalist; **'kruidnagel** (-s) *m* clove

'kruien (kruide, h. gekruid) **I** *vi* 1 trundle a wheelbarrow; 2 drift [of ice]; *de rivier kruit* the river is full of drift-ice; **II** *vt* wheel [in a wheelbarrow]; **'kruier** (-s) *m* porter; **–sloon** *o* porterage

kruik (-en) *v* stone bottle, jar, pitcher; *warme ~* hot-water bottle; *de ~ gaat zo lang te water tot zij breekt* so often goes the pitcher to the well that it comes home broken at last

kruim (-en) *v* & *o* crumb [inner part of bread]; **'kruimel** (-s) *m* crumb; **'kruimeldief** (-dieven) *m* petty thief, magpie; **–diefstal** (-len) *m* petty theft, pilferage; **'kruim(el)en** (kruim(el)de, *vt* h., *vi* is gekruim(el)d) *vi* & *vt* crumble; **'kruimelig** crumbly; **'kruimig** floury, mealy [potatoes]

kruin (-en) *v* (v. b e r g, h o o f d &) crown; top

'kruipen* *vi* 1 crawl[2], creep[2]; 2 🐌 creep, trail; 3 *fig* cringe [to a person]; **–d** 1 crawling[2], creeping[2]; 2 🐌 creeping, trailing; 3 🐍 reptile, reptilian; 4 *fig* cringing; *~ dier* reptile, reptilian; **'kruiperig** cringing; **'kruippakje** (-s) *o* crawlers, jumpers

kruis (-en en kruizen) *o* 1 (i n h e t a l g.) cross, 2 (l i c h a a m s d e e l) small of the back, crotch [of man]; croup [of animals], crupper [of horse]; 3 (v. b r o e k) seat; crotch; 4 ♪ sharp; 5 ⚓ (v. a n k e r) crown; 6 *fig* cross [= trial, affliction, nuisance]; *~ of munt* heads or tails; *~en mollen* sharps and flats; *iem. het heilige ~ nageven* be glad to see the back of sbd.; *een ~ slaan* make the sign of the cross, cross oneself; **–afneming** (-en) *v* deposition from the Cross, descent from the Cross; **–beeld** (-en) *o* crucifix; **–bes** (-sen) *v* gooseberry; **–beuk** (-en) *m* transept; **kruis'bloemig I** *aj* cruciferous; **II** *mv* *–en* cruciferae; **'kruisboog** (-bogen) *m* 🏹 cross-bow; **'kruiselings** crosswise, crossways; **'kruisen** (kruiste, h. gekruist) **I** *vt* 1 cross [the arms]; 2 crucify [a criminal]; 3 cross [animals, plants]; *elkaar ~* cross, cross each other [of letters &]; *gekruist ras* crossbreed; **II** *vi* ⚓ cruise; **III** *vr zich ~* cross oneself; **'kruiser** (-s) *m* cruiser; **'kruisgang** (-en) *m* △ cloister; **–gewelf** (-welven) *o* cross vault; **–gewijs, –gewijze** crosswise, crossways; **–hout** *o* cross-beam; *aan het ~* (up)on the cross; **'kruisigen** (kruisigde, h. gekruisigd) *vt* crucify; **–ging** (-en) *v* crucifixion; **'kruising** (-en) *v* 1 cross-breeding [of animals]; 2 crossbreed; cross [between... and...]; 3 crossing [of roads]; **'kruisje** (-s) *o* (small) cross, obelisk (†); *zij heeft de drie ~s achter de rug* she is turned (of) thirty; **'kruiskerk** (-en) *v* cruciform church; **–net** (-ten) *o* square fishing-net; **–peiling** (-en) *v* cross bearing; **–punt** (-en) *o* 1 (point of) intersection; 2 crossing [of a railway &]; **–ridder** (-s) *m* knight of the Cross; **–snarig** ♪ overstrung [piano]; **–snede** (-n) *v* crucial incision; **–snelheid** *v* cruising speed; **–spin** (-nen) *v* cross-spider; **–standig** decussate(d); **–steek** (-steken) *m* cross-stitch; **–teken** (-s) *o* sign of the cross; **–tocht** (-en) *m* 1 ⚓ crusade[2]; 2 ⚓ cruise; **–vaarder** (-s) *m* ⚓ crusader; **–vaart** (-en) *v* ⚓ crusade; **–verband** (-en) *o* 1 △ cross-bond; 2 ✚ cross-bandage; **–vereniging** (-en) *v* medical welfare society; **'Kruisverheffing** *v* Exaltation of the Cross; **'kruisverhoor** (-horen) *o* cross-examination; **–vormig** cross-shaped, cruciform; **–vuur** *o* cross-fire[2]; **–weg** (-wegen) *m* 1 cross-road; 2 *rk* Way of the Cross; *de ~ bidden rk* do the Stations (of the Cross); **–woordraadsel** (-s) *o* crossword puzzle

kruit o powder, gunpowder; *hij heeft al zijn ~ verschoten* he has fired his last shot; **–damp** *m* gunpowder smoke; **–hoorn** (-s), **–horen** (-s) *m* powder-horn, powder-flask; **–kamer** (-s) *v* powder-room; **–magazijn** (-en) o powder-magazine; **–molen** (-s) *m* powder-mill; **–schip** (-schepen) o gunpowder ship; **–vat** o (-vaten) powder-keg²

'kruiwagen (-s) *m* wheelbarrow; *hij heeft goede ~s* he has powerful patrons (influence, patronage)

kruize'munt *v* ⚕ mint

1 kruk (-ken) *v* 1 crutch [for cripples]; 2 handle [of a door]; 3 ✗ crank; 4 perch [for birds]; 5 stool, tabouret

2 kruk (-ken) *m* bungler; duffer

'krukas (-sen) *v* crank-shaft

'krukken (krukte, h. gekrukt) *vi* 1 (o n h a n-d i g d o e n) bungle; 2 (z i e k z i j n) be ailing; **'krukkig** clumsy

krul (-len) *v* 1 (h a a r) curl; 2 (h o u t) shaving; 3 (b ij h e t s c h r ij v e n) flourish, scroll; *er zit geen ~ in dat haar* the hair doesn't curl; *de ~ is er uit* it is out of curl; *~len zetten* set curls; **–haar** o curly hair; **–ijzer** (-s) o curling-iron; **'krullebol** (-len), **–kop** (-pen) *m* curly-head, curly-pate; **'krullen** (krulde, h. gekruld) **I** *vi* curl; **II** *vt* curl, crisp, friz(z) [the hair]; **'krullenjongen** (-s) *m* 1 carpenter's apprentice; 2 *fig* factotum; **'krulletter** (-s) *v* flourished letter; **'krullig** curly; **'krulspeld** (-en) *v* curling pin, (hair) curler; **–tang** (-en) *v* curling-tongs

kub. = *kubiek*

ku'biek, 'kubiek cubic; *de ~e inhoud* the cubic content, cubage; **ku'biekwortel** (-s) *m* cube root

ku'bisme o cubism; **–istisch** cubist; **'kubus** (-sen) *m* cube

kuch (-en) *m* (dry) cough ‖ o & *m* (b r o o d) **S** tommy; **'kuchen** (kuchte, h. gekucht) *vi* cough

'kudde (-n en -s) *v* herd [of cattle], flock [of sheep]; (v. z i e l e n h e r d e r) flock; **–dier** (-en) o *fig* herd animal, gregarious animal; **–geest** *m fig* herd-instinct (-mentality); **–mens** (-en) *m* person who follows the crowd

'kuier *m* stroll, walk; **'kuieren** (kuierde, h. en is gekuierd) *vi* stroll, walk

kuif (kuiven) *v* tuft, crest [on a bird's head]; forelock [on a man's head]; **–eend** (-en) *v* tufted duck; **–leeuwerik** (-en) *m* tufted lark

'kuiken (-s) o chicken; **kuikenmeste'rij** (-en) *v* broiler house

kuil (-en) *m* 1 pit, hole; [potato] clamp; 2 ⚓ waist; *wie een ~ graaft voor een ander, valt er zelf in* those who lay traps for others get caught themselves; harm set, harm get; **'kuilen**

(kuilde, h. gekuild) *vt* = *inkuilen*; **'kuiltje** (-s) *v* hole; dimple [in the cheek]; *met ~s in de wangen* with dimpled cheeks; **'kuilvoe(de)r** o ensilage

kuip (-en) *v* tub, vat; zie ook: *vlees*

'kuipen (kuipte, h. gekuipt) *vi* intrigue; **–er** (-s) *m* intriguer; **kuipe'rij** (-en) *v* intrigue

'kuipstoel (-en) *m* bucket-seat

kuis chaste, pure; **'kuisen** (kuiste, h. gekuist) *vt* chasten, purify; (v. b o e k) bowdlerize, expurgate; **'kuisheid** *v* chastity, purity

kuit (-en) *v* 1 calf [of the leg]; 2 ⚕ roe, spawn [female hard roe]; **~ schieten** spawn; **–been** (-deren) o splint-bone; **'kuitenflikker** (-s) *m een ~ slaan* cut a caper

kukele'ku! cock-a-doodle-doo!

'kukelen (kukelde, is gekukeld) *vi* **F** (v a l l e n) tumble, roll

kul *m flauwe ~* nonsense, **F** rot

'kunde *v* knowledge; **'kundig** able, clever, skilful; **–heid** (-heden) *v* skill, knowledge, learning; *kundigheden* accomplishments

'kunne (-n) *v* sex

'kunnen* I *vi* & *vt* be able; *het kan (niet)* it can(not) be done; *dat kan niet* that's impossible: *hij kan tekenen* he can draw; *hij kan het gedaan hebben* he may have done it; *hij kan het niet gedaan hebben* he cannot have done it; *hij kan niet begrijpen hoe...* ook: he fails to understand how...; *hij kan het weten* he ought to know; *hoe kan ik dat weten?* how am I to know?; *zo hij niet meer kon* until he was spent; *zo kon hij uren zitten* thus he would sit for hours; ● *ik kan er niet bij* I cannot reach it; *fig* that's beyond me; *het kan er mee door* it will do, it may pass; *hij kan daar niet tegen* he can't stand it [being laughed at]; it [that food] does not agree with him; *hij kon niet meer terug [fig]* he couldn't back out; **II** *o* [technical] prowess

kunst (-en) *v* 1 art; 2 trick; *beeldende ~en* plastic arts; *de schone ~en* the fine arts; *de vrije ~en* the liberal arts; *de zwarte ~* necromancy, the black art; *geen ~en alsjeblieft!* none of your games!; *~en maken* perform feats; *je moet hier geen ~en uithalen!* none of your tricks here!; *zijn ~en vertonen* show what one can do; *hij verstaat de ~ om...* he knows how to..., he has a knack of ...ing; *dat is geen ~* that's not difficult; *dat is nu juist de ~* that's the art of it; *met ~ en vliegwerk* by hook or by crook; *volgens de regelen der ~* skilfully; **–arm** (-en) *m* artificial arm; **–bloem** (-en) *v* artificial flower; **–broeder** (-s) *m* fellow-artist; **–criticus** (-ci) *m* art critic; **–drukpapier** o art paper; **'kunstenaar** (-s) *m* artist; **–schap** o artistry; **kunstena'res** (-sen) *v* artist; **'kunstenmaker** (-s) *m* acrobat; (g o o c h e l a a r) juggler; **'kunstgebit** (-ten) o set of artificial teeth, denture, dental prothesis;

–geschiedenis (-sen) *v* history of art, art history; **–greep** (-grepen) *m* artifice, trick, knack; **–handel** *m* 1 (-s) picture-shop, print-(seller's) shop; 2 dealing in works of art, art trade; **–handelaar** (-s en -laren) *m* art dealer; **–hars** (-en) *o* & *m* synthetic resin; **–historicus** (-ci) *m* art historian, historian of art; **kunsthis'torisch** of art history, [a work] on art history, art-historical [studies]; **'kunstig** ingenious; **'kunstijsbaan** (-banen) *v* (ice) rink; **'kunstje** (-s) *o* trick, knack, F dodge; *~s met de kaart* card-tricks; *dat is een koud (klein) ~* there's nothing to it, that's simple; **'kunstkabinet** (-ten) *o* art gallery; **–kenner** (-s) *m* connoisseur; **–koper** (-s) *m* art dealer; **–kritiek** (-en) *v* art criticism; **–le(d)er** *o* artificial leather; leatherette; **–licht** *o* artificial light; **–liefhebber** (-s) *m* lover of art (of the arts), art-lover; **kunst'lievend** art-loving; **'kunstmaan** (-manen) *v* earth satellite; **kunst'matig** artificial; **'kunstmest** *m* artificial manure, fertilizer; **–meststof** (-fen) *v* (artificial) fertilizer; **–middel** (-en) *o* artificial means; **kunst'minnend** art-loving; **'kunstmoeder** (-s) *v* (b r o e d m a c h i n e) incubator; **–nier** (-en) *v* artificial kidney, kidney machine; **kunst'nijverheid** *v* industrial arts, arts and crafts; **'kunstprodukt** (-en) *o* art product, work of art; **–rijden** *o ~ op de schaats* figure-skating; **–rijder** (-s) *m* 1 (t e p a a r d) equestrian, circus-rider, performer; 2 (o p s c h a a t s e n) figure-skater; **–schaats** (-en) *v* figure skate; **–schatten** *mv* art treasures; **–schilder** (-s) *m* painter, artist; **–stof** (-fen) *v* synthetic; **–stuk** (-ken) *o* tour de force, feat, performance; **–taal** (-talen) *v* artificial language; **kunst'vaardig** skilful; **–heid** *v* skill; **'kunstveiling** (-en) *v* art auction (sale); **–verlichting** *v* artificial lighting; **–verzameling** (-en) *v* art collection; **–vezel** (-s) *v* synthetic (man-made) fibre; **–vliegen I** *vi* stunt; **II** *o* stunt-flying; **–voorwerp** (-en) *o* work of art, art object; **–vorm** (-en) *m* form of art, art form; **–waarde** *v* artistic value; **–werk** (-en) *o* work of art; (w e g- e n w a t e r b o u w) constructional work; **–zij(de)** *v* artificial silk, rayon; **kunst'zinnig** artistic; **–heid** *v* artistry

ku'ras (-sen) *o* cuirass; **kuras'sier** (-s) *m* cuirassier

'kuren (kuurde, h. gekuurd) *vi zie een kuur doen*

1 kurk *o* & *m* (s t o f n a a m) cork; **2 kurk** (-en) *v* (v o o r w e r p) cork; **–'droog** bone-dry; **–eik** (-en) *m* cork-oak; **1 'kurken** (kurkte, h. gekurkt) *vt* cork; **2 'kurken** *aj* cork; **'kurketrekker** (-s) *m* corkscrew

kus (-sen) *m* kiss; **'kushandje** (-s) *o een ~ geven* kiss one's hand to, blow a kiss to; **1 'kussen** (kuste, h. gekust) *vt* kiss

2 'kussen (-s) *o* cushion; (b e d d e k u s s e n) pillow; *op het ~ zitten* be in office; **–sloop** (-slopen) *v* & *o* pillow-case, pillow-slip

1 kust (-en) *v* coast, shore

2 kust *te ~ en te keur* in plenty, of every description

'kustbatterij (-en) *v* coastal battery, shore battery; **–bewoner** (-s) *m* inhabitant of the coast; **–gebied** (-en) *o* coast(al) region, seaboard; **–licht** (-en) *o* coast-light; **–lijn** (-en) *v* coast-line; **–plaats** (-en) *v* coastal town; **–streek** (-streken) *v* coastal region; **–strook** (-stroken) *v* coastal strip; **–vaarder** (-s) *m* coaster; **–vaart** *v* coasting trade, coastwise trade; **kustvisse'rij** *v* inshore fishery; **'kustvlakte** (-n en -s) *v* coastal plain; **–wacht** *v* coast-guard; **–wachter** (-s) *m* coast-guard(sman)

kut (-ten) *v* P cunt

kuur (kuren) *v* 1 whim, freak, caprice; 2 ℞ cure; *een ~ doen (volgen)* take a cure; take (a course of medical) treatment

K. v. K. = *Kamer van Koophandel* Chamber of Commerce

kW = *kilowatt*

kwaad I *aj* 1 (s l e c h t) bad, ill, evil; 2 (b o o s) angry; *dat is (lang) niet ~* that is not (S half) bad; *het te ~ krijgen* feel queer, be on the point of breaking down or fainting; *het te ~ krijgen met...* get into trouble with [the police &]; *iem. ~ maken* make sbd. angry, provoke sbd.; *zich ~ maken, ~ worden* become (get) angry, fly into a passion, throw a fit; *~ zijn op iem.* be angry with sbd.; *hij is de ~ste niet* he is not so bad (such a bad fellow); **II** *ad het niet ~ hebben* not be badly off; *zij ziet er niet ~ uit* she is not bad to look at; **III** (kwaden) *o* 1 (w a t s l e c h t i s) wrong, evil; 2 (n a d e e l, l e t s e l) harm, wrong, injury; *een noodzakelijk ~* a necessary evil; *~ brouwen* brew mischief; *~ doen* do wrong; *niemand zal u ~ doen* nobody will harm you; *het heeft zijn goede naam veel ~ gedaan* it has done his reputation much harm; *dat kan geen ~* there is no harm in that; *hij kan bij haar geen ~ doen* he can do no wrong in her eyes; *ergens geen ~ in zien* see no harm in it; *ten kwade beïnvloed* influenced for evil; (zie ook: *duiden*; *van ~ tot erger vervallen* go from bad to worse; *van twee kwaden moet men het minste kiezen* of two evils choose the lesser; **kwaad'aardig** 1 ill-natured, malicious [people, reports]; 2 malignant [growth, tumour], virulent [diseases]; **–heid** *v* 1 malice, ill-nature; 2 malignancy, virulence; **kwaad'denkend** suspicious, distrustful; **'kwaadheid** *v* anger; **–schiks**

unwillingly; zie ook: *goedschiks*; **'kwaad-spreken** (sprak 'kwaad, h. 'kwaadgesproken) *vi* talk scandal; ~ *van* speak ill of, slander, throw mud at; **kwaad'sprekend** slanderous, backbiting; **'kwaadspreker** (-s) *m* backbiter, slanderer, scandalmonger; **kwaadspreke'rij** (-en) *v* backbiting, slander(ing), scandal; **kwaad'willig** malevolent, ill-disposed; **–heid** *v* malevolence

kwaal (kwalen) *v* complaint, disease, evil, ill; ~*tjes* aches and pains

kwab (-ben) *v* lobe; dewlap [of cow]

kwa'draat (-draten) **I** *o* square, quadrate; *2 duim in het* ~ 2 inches square; *een ezel in het* ~ a downright ass; **II** *aj* square; **–getal** (-len) *o* square number; **kwa'drant** (-en) *o* quadrant; **kwadra'tuur** *v* quadrature; *de* ~ *van de cirkel* the squaring of the circle

kwa'jongen (-s) *m* mischievous (naughty) boy; **kwa'jongensachtig** boyish, mischievous; **–streek** (-streken) *m* & *v* monkey-trick

kwak I *ij* flop!; **II** (-ken) *m* 1 (g e l u i d) flop, thud; 2 (h o e v e e l h e i d) dab [of soap &]; 3 (k l o d d e r) blob

'kwaken (kwaakte, h. gekwaakt) *vi* quack[2]; croak [of frogs]

'kwakkelen (kwakkelde, h. gekwakkeld) *vi* be ailing; **'kwakkelwinter** (-s) *m* lingering "off-and-on" winter

'kwakken (kwakte, h. gekwakt) **I** *vt* dump, plump, flop, dash (down); *dicht* ~ slam [the door]; **II** *vi* bump

'kwakzalver (-s) *m* quack (doctor); *fig* charlatan; **kwakzalve'rij** (-en) *o* quackery; charlatanry

kwal (-len) *v* jelly-fish; *een* ~ *van een vent* **S** a rotter

kwalifi'catie [-(t)si.] (-s) *v* qualification; **kwalifi'ceren** (kwalificeerde, h. gekwalificeerd) *vt* qualify

'kwalijk I *aj* bad [joke, thing], ill [effects], evil [consequences], ugly [business]; **II** *ad* 1 ill, amiss; badly [treated]; 2 hardly, scarcely; *iets* ~ *nemen* take sth. amiss, take sth. in bad part, resent sth.; *neem me niet* ~ (I) beg (your) pardon; excuse me; sorry!; *neem het hem niet* ~ don't take it ill of him; *ik kan het hem niet* ~ *nemen* I cannot blame him; *dat zou ik u* ~ *kunnen zeggen* I could hardly tell you; ~ *riekend* evil-smelling; ~ *verborgen* ill-concealed; **kwalijke'zind** 1 evil-minded; 2 ill-disposed

kwalita'tief qualitative; **kwali'teit** (-en) *v* 1 quality, capacity; *in zijn* ~ *van...* in his capacity of...; 2 **$** quality, grade

kwam (kwamen) V.T. van *komen*

kwan'suis for the look of the thing; *hij kwam* ~ *eens kijken* for form's sake; *hij deed* ~ *of hij mij*

niet zag he pretended (feigned) not to see me

kwant (-en) *m* fellow, **F** blade

kwantita'tief quantitative; **kwanti'teit** (-en) *v* quantity

kwark *m* curds; **–taart** (-en) *v* cheesecake

kwart (-en) 1 *o* fourth (part), quarter; 2 *v* ♪ (n o o t) crotchet; (i n t e r v a l) fourth; ~ *o v e r vieren* a quarter past four; ~ *v o o r vieren* a quarter to four; **kwar'taal** (-talen) *o* quarter (of a year), three months; *per* ~ quarterly; **–staat** (-staten) *m* quarterly list; **'kwarteeuw** *v* quarter of a century, quarter-century

'kwartel (-s) *m* & *v* quail; **–koning** (-en) *m* landrail, corn-crake

kwar'tet (-ten) *o* quartet(te); **'kwartfinale** (-s) *v* quarter-final; **kwar'tier** (-en) *o* quarter (of an hour, of the moon, of a town); *geen* ~ *geven* give (grant) no quarter; **kwar'tiermaker** (-s) *m* quartermaster; **–meester** (-s) *m* ⚓ & ⚓ quartermaster; **~-generaal** ⚔ quartermaster-general; **'kwartje** (-s) *o* "kwartje", twenty-five cent piece; **–svinder** (-s) *m* **F** sharper; **'kwartnoot** (-noten) *v* ♪ crotchet; **'kwarto** ('s) *o* quarto; *in* ~ in quarto, 4to

kwarts *o* quartz

'kwartslag (-slagen) *m* quarter turn

'kwartslamp (-en) *v* quartz lamp

1 kwast *m* lemon-squash [a drink]

2 kwast (-en) *m* 1 brush [of a painter]; [dish] mop; tassel [of a curtain, cushion]; 2 knot [in wood]; 3 *fig* fop, fool, coxcomb; **–ig** knotty, gnarled

kwa'trijn (-en) *o* quatrain

'kwebbel (-s) *m-v* chatterbox; **'kwebbelen** (kwebbelde, h. gekwebbeld) *vi* chatter

'kwee (kweeën) *v*, **'kweeappel** (-s en -en) *m* quince

1 kweek (kweken) *v* 🌿 couch-grass, quitch

2 kweek (kweken) *m* culture; **–bed** (-den) *o* seed-bed

'kweekgras *o* 🌿 couch-grass, quitch

'kweekplaats (-en) *v* nursery[2]; **–reactor** (-s en -toren) *m* breeder reactor; **–school** (-scholen) *v* training-college (for teachers); *fig* nursery

'kweepeer (-peren) *v* quince

kweet (kweten) V.T. van *kwijten*

'kwekeling (-en) *m*, **–e** (-n) *v* 1 pupil; 2 ⚲ pupil-teacher; **'kweken** (kweekte, h. gekweekt) *vt* grow, cultivate[2] [plants], raise [vegetables]; *fig* foster, breed [discontent]; *gekweekte champignons* cultivated mushrooms; *gekweekte rente* accrued interest; **–er** (-s) *m* grower; nurseryman; **kweke'rij** (-en) *v* nursery

'kwekken (kwekte, h. gekwekt) *vi* 1 quack; 2 (k w e b b e l e n) yap, cackle

'kwelder (-s) *v* land on the outside of a dike

'**kwelduivel** (-s) *m* = *kweller*

'**kwelen** (kweelde, h. gekweeld) *vi* & *vt* warble, carol

'**kwelgeest** (-en) *m* teaser, **F** holy terror; '**kwellen** (kwelde, h. gekweld) **I** *vt* vex, tease, torment, plague, pester, harass; **II** *vr zich* ~ torment oneself; **–er** (-s) *m* tormentor, teaser; '**kwelling** (-en) *v* vexation (of spirit), torment, trouble

'**kwelwater** *o* seeping water

'**kwestie** (-s) *v* question, matter; *dat is een andere* ~ that's another question; *een* ~ *van smaak* a matter of taste; *een* ~ *van tijd* a matter (question) of time; *zij hebben* ~ they have a quarrel; *geen* ~ *van!* that's out of the question!; *b u i t e n de* ~ outside the question; *buiten* ~ beyond (without) question; *de zaak i n* ~ the matter in question; the point at issue; **kwesti'eus** doubtful, questionable

'**kweten** V.T. meerv. van *kwijten*

'**kwetsbaar** vulnerable; '**kwetsen** (kwetste, h. gekwetst) *vt* injure[2], wound[2], hurt[2], *fig* offend; **kwet'suur** (-suren) *v* injury, wound, hurt

'**kwetteren** (kwetterde, h. gekwetterd) *vi* 1 (v. v o g e l) twitter; 2 (v. m e n s) chatter

'**kwezel** (-s) *v* devotee, sanctimonious person; **–achtig** sanctimonious; **kwezela'rij** (-en) *v* sanctimoniousness

kWh = *kilowattuur*

'**kwibus** (-sen) *m* **F** (odd) character, (queer) fellow; *rare* ~ **F** queer bird

kwiek smart, bright, sprightly, spry

kwijl *v* & *o* slaver, slobber; '**kwijlen** (kwijlde, h. gekwijld) *vi* slaver, slobber, drivel, dribble, **S** drool

'**kwijnen** (kwijnde, h. gekwijnd) *vi* 1 languish[2], pine [of persons]; wither, droop [of flowers &]; 2 *fig* flag [of a conversation]

kwijt *ik ben het* ~ 1 I have lost it [the address &]; 2 I have got rid of it [my cold &]; 3 it has slipped my memory; *die zijn we lekker* ~ he is

(that is) a good riddance; *hij is zijn verstand* ~ he is off his head; ~ *raken (worden)* lose; get rid of

'**kwijten** *vr zich* ~ *van* acquit oneself of [an obligation, a duty, a task], discharge [a responsibility, a debt]; **–ting** (-en) *v* discharge

'**kwijtschelden** (schold '**kwijt**, h. '**kwijtge**scholden) *vt* remit [punishment, a debt, a fine &]; *iem. het bedrag* ~ let sbd. off the payment of the amount; *voor ditmaal zal ik het u* ~ I will let you off for this once; **–ding** *v* remission [of sins, debts]; (free) pardon, amnesty

1 kwik *o* mercury, quicksilver

2 kwik (-ken) *v* ~*ken en strikken* frills

'**kwikbak** (-ken) *m* mercury trough; **–baro**meter (-s) *m* mercurial barometer; **–kolom** (-men) *v* mercurial column; **–lamp** (-en) *v* mercury lamp

'**kwikstaart** (-en) *m* wagtail

'**kwikthermometer** (-s) *m* mercurial thermometer; **–vergiftiging** *v* mercurial poisoning; **–zilver** *o* mercury, quicksilver

kwinke'leren (kwinkeleerde, h. gekwinkeleerd) *vi* warble, carol

'**kwinkslag** (-slagen) *m* witticism, quip, jest, joke, bon mot

kwint (-en) *v* ♪ fifth

'**kwintessens** *v* quintessence

kwin'tet (-ten) *o* quintet(te)

kwispe'door (-s en -doren) *o* & *m* spittoon, cuspidor

'**kwispel(staart)en** (kwispelde, h. gekwispeld; kwispelstaartte, h. gekwispelstaart) *vi* wag the tail

'**kwistig** lavish, liberal; ~ *met* lavish of [money]; liberal in [bestowing titles]; **–heid** *v* lavishness, prodigality, liberality

kwi'tantie [-(t)si.] (-s) *v* receipt; **–boekje** (-s) *o* receipt book; **kwi'teren** (kwiteerde, h. gekwiteerd) *vt* receipt

L

l [ɭl] ('s) v 1
1 la ('s) v ♩ la
2 la ('s en laas) v = *lade*
'laadbak (-ken) m 🚢 body, platform; **–boom** (-bomen) m ⚓ derrick; **–kist** (-en) v (freight) container; **–klep** (-pen) v tail-board; **–ruim** (-en) o cargo-hold; **–ruimte** (-n en -s) v ⚓ cargo-capacity, tonnage; **–stok** (-ken) m ⚔ ramrod, rammer; **–vermogen** o carrying-capacity
1 laag I *aj* low²; *fig* base, mean, low-minded; *lage druk* low pressure; **II** *ad* [sing, fly] low; *fig* basely, meanly; ~ *denken van* think meanly of; ~ *houden* keep down [prices, one's weight]; ~ *neerzien op* look down upon; ~ *vallen* fall low²; *fig* sink low; zie ook: 1 *lager*
2 laag (lagen) v 1 (d i k t e) layer, stratum [*mv* strata], bed; course [of bricks]; coat [of paint]; 2 (h i n d e r l a a g) ambush, snare; *alle lagen der bevolking* all sections of the population, all walks of life; *alle lagen der samenleving* all strata of society; *de vijand de volle* ~ *geven* give the enemy a broadside; *iem. de volle* ~ *geven* let sbd. have it
laag-bij-de-'gronds trite, commonplace; ~*e opmerkingen* fatuous remarks; **'laagbouw** m △ low building; **–frequent** [-fre.kʋnt] low-frequency; **–hangend** lowering [sky]; **laag'hartig** base, vile, mean; **'laagheid** (-heden) v 1 lowness; 2 *fig* baseness, meanness; *laagheden* mean things
'laagje (-s) o thin layer
'laagland (-en) o lowland; **–spanning** v low tension; **–spannings...** low-tension...;
laagstbe'taalden *mv* the low-paid; **'laagte** (-n en -s) v lowness; *in de* ~ down below;
'laagtij o low tide; **–veen** o bog; **–vlakte** (-n en -s) v low-lying plain; **'laagvormig** stratified; **–vorming** v stratification; **laag'water** o low tide; *bij* ~ at low tide (low water); **–lijn** v low-water mark
'laai(e) *in lichte(r)* ~ in a blaze, ablaze
'laakbaar condemnable, blamable, blameworthy, censurable, reprehensible
laan (lanen) v avenue; *iem. de* ~ *uitsturen* send sbd. packing; **–tje** (-s) o alley
laars (laarzen) v boot; **'laarzeknecht** (-en en -s) m bootjack; **'laarzenmaker** (-s) m bootmaker
laat I *aj* late; *hoe* ~? what time?, at what o'clock?; *hoe* ~ *is het?* what's the time?, what time is it?, what o'clock is it?; *is 't zo* ~? so

that's the time of day!, that's your little game!; *is het weer zo* ~? are you (is he) at it again?; *hoe* ~ *heb je het?* what time do you make it?; *op de late avond* late in the evening; *de trein is een uur te* ~ the train is an hour late (overdue); **II** *ad* late; *te* ~ *komen* be late; *u komt te* ~ 1 you are late [I expected you at noon]; 2 you are too late [to be of any help]; *tot* ~ *in de nacht* to a late hour; ~ *op de dag* late in the day; *beter* ~ *dan nooit* better late than never; **–bloeiend** late-flowering
laat'dunkend self-conceited, overweening, overbearing, arrogant; **–heid** v self-conceit, arrogance
'laatje (-s) o (little) drawer; *aan het* ~ *zitten* handle the cash; *dat brengt geld in het* ~ it brings in money
'laatkomer (-s) m late comer
laatst I *aj* 1 last, final; 2 (j o n g s t) latest, (most) recent; 3 (v a n t w e e) latter [part of May]; *het* ~*e artikel* 1 the last article [in this review]; 2 the last-named article [is sold out]; *zijn* ~*e artikel* 1 his latest [most recent] article; 2 his last article [before his death]; *de* ~*e dagen* the last few days; *in de* ~*e jaren* the last (recent) years; *de* ~*e (paar) maanden* the last few months; *het* ~*e nieuws* the latest news; *de* ~*e tijd* of late, recently; *de* ~*e drie weken* these three weeks; **II** *sb de* ~*e* the last-named, the latter; *dit* ~*e* this last, the latter [is always a matter of difficulty]; *de* ~*en zullen de eersten zijn* **B** the last shall be first; ● *op het* ~ at last, finally; *op zijn* ~ at (the) latest; *ten (als)* ~*e* lastly, last; *tot het* ~ to (till) the last; *voor het* ~ for the last time; **III** *ad* lately, the other day; ~ *op een middag* the other afternoon; **'laatstelijk** lastly, finally; **'laatstgeboren** last-born; **–genoemd** *aj* last-named, latter; ~*e* the latter; **–leden** = *jongstleden*
lab (-s) o **F** lab
'labbekak (-ken) m **F** milksop, wet blanket
labber'daan m salt cod
labber'doedas (-sen) m **F** blow, crack [on the head], punch, lunge
'label ['le.bəl] (-s) m label
la'biel unstable
labo'rant (-en) m laboratory worker; **labora'torium** (-s en -ria) o laboratory; **labo'reren** (laboreerde, h. gelaboreerd) *vi* labour (under *aan*)
laby'rint [la.bi:'rɪnt] (-en) o labyrinth, maze
lach m laugh, laughter; *in een* ~ *schieten* burst out

laughing, laugh outright; **–bek** (-ken) =
lachebek; **–bui** (-en) *v* fit of laughter;
'lachebek (-ken) *m zij is een* ~ she laughs very
easily; **'lachen* I** *vi* laugh; *i n zich zelf* ~ laugh
to oneself; ~ *o m iets* laugh at (over) sth.; *ik
moet om je* ~ you make me laugh; *ik moet erom* ~
it makes me laugh; *t e g e n iem.* ~ smile at sbd.;
het is niet om te ~ it is no laughing matter; *ik
kon niet spreken van het* ~ I could hardly speak
for laughing; *hij lachte als een boer die kiespijn
heeft* he laughed on the wrong side of his
mouth; *wie het laatst lacht, lacht het best* he laughs
best who laughs last; *laat me niet* ~ *!* don't make
me laugh; **II** *vr zich een aap (bochel, bult, kriek,
ongeluk, puist, stuip, tranen, ziek)* ~ split one's
sides; **–d I** *aj* laughing, smiling; **II** *ad* laugh-
ing(ly), with a laugh; **'lacher** (-s) *m de* ~*s op
zijn hand hebben (krijgen)* have the laugh on
one's side; **–ig** giggly; **–tje** (-s) *o* joke;
'lachgas *o* nitrous oxide, laughing-gas; **–lust**
m inclination to laugh, risibility; *de* ~ *opwekken*
provoke (raise) a laugh; **–salvo** ('s) *o* gale of
laughter; **–spiegel** (-s) *m* distorting mirror;
–spier (-en) *v op de* ~*en werken* provoke (raise)
a laugh; **–stuip** (-en) *v* convulsion of laughter;
lach'wekkend ludicrous, ridiculous, laughable
laco'niek laconic(al)
la'cune (-s) *v* vacancy, void, gap
'ladder (-s) *v* ladder; **'ladderen** (ladderde, h.
geladderd) *vi* ladder, run
'lade (-n) *v* 1 drawer; till [of a shop-counter]; 2
stock [of a rifle]
'laden* I *vt* 1 (w a g e n) load; 2 (s c h i p) load;
3 (v u u r w a p e n) load, charge; 4 ⚡ charge;
de verantwoording op zich ~ undertake the
responsibility; **II** *vi & va* load, take in cargo; ~
en lossen load and discharge, discharge and load
'ladenkast (-en) *v* chest of drawers; **–lichter**
(-s) *m* till-sneak
'lader (-s) *m* loader; **'lading** (-en) *v* 1 cargo;
load [of a waggon]; 2 ⚒ & ⚡ charge; ~
innemen take in cargo, load; *het schip is in* ~ the
ship is (in) loading
'ladykiller ['le.di.kılər] (-s) *m* lady-killer
lae'deren [le.'de.rə(n)] (laedeerde, h. gelae-
deerd) *vt* injure
'laesie ['le.zi.] (-s) *v* lesion
laf I *aj* 1 (f l a u w) insipid²; 2 (l a f h a r t i g)
cowardly, **S** yellow; **II** *ad* 1 insipidly²; 2 in a
cowardly manner, faint-heartedly; **–aard** (-s)
m coward, poltroon, **F** chicken; **–bek** (-ken) *m*
coward, milksop
'lafenis (-sen) *v* refreshment, comfort, relief
laf'hartig = *laf* 2; **'lafheid** *v* 1 insipidity²; 2
cowardice
lag (lagen) V.T. van *liggen*

1 **'lager** *aj* lower, inferior; *een* ~*e ambtenaar* a
minor offical; zie ook: *onderwijs*
2 **'lager** (-s) *o* ⚙ bearing(s)
'lager(bier) *o* lager (beer)
'Lagerhuis *o* House of Commons, Lower
House
lager'wal *m* leeshore; [*fig*] *aan* ~ *raken* go
downhill, come down (in the world), go to the
dogs (to pot)
la'gune (-n en -s) *v* lagoon
lak (-ken) *o & m* 1 (v e r f) lacquer; lac
[produced by insect]; varnish [for the nails]; 2
(z e g e l~) sealing-wax; 3 (~z e g e l) seal; *daar
heb ik* ~ *aan!* **F** fat lot I care!; *ik heb* ~ *aan hem*
he can go to the devil
la'kei (-en) *m* footman, lackey, > flunkey
1 **'laken** (laakte, h. gelaakt) *vt* blame, censure
2 **'laken** *o* 1 (s t o f) cloth; 2 (-s) (v. b e d) sheet;
dan krijg je van hetzelfde ~ *een pak* you will be
served with the same sauce; *hij deelt de* ~*s uit* **F**
he runs (bosses) the show; **–fabriek** (-en) *v*
cloth manufactory; **–fabrikant** (-en) *m* clothier, cloth manufacturer; **'lakens** *aj* cloth
lakens'waardig objectionable, blameworthy
'lakken (lakte, h. gelakt) *vt* 1 seal [a letter &]; 2
lacquer, varnish, japan; **'lakle(d)er** *o* patent
leather
'lakmoes *o* litmus; **–papier** *o* litmus paper
laks lax, slack, indolent
'lakschoen (-en) *m* patent leather shoe
'laksheid *v* laxness, laxity, slackness, indolence
'lakverf (-verven) *v* glossy paint; **–vernis** (-sen)
o & m lac varnish, lacquer; **–werk** *o* 1 lacquer;
2 japanned goods, lacquered ware
1 **lam** (-meren) *o* lamb; *Lam Gods* Lamb of God
2 **lam** *aj* 1 (v e r l a m d) paralysed, paralytic; 2
(o n a a n g e n a a m) tiresome, provoking; *wat
is dat* ~*, (een* ~*me boel, geschiedenis)!* how provoking!; *wat een* ~*me vent!* what a tiresome fellow!;
~ *leggen* paralyse [an industry, trade &]; *zich* ~
schrikken be frightened (startled) to death; *de
handel* ~ *slaan* paralyse (cripple) trade; *iem.* ~
slaan beat sbd. to a jelly; *zich* ~ *voelen* feel
miserable; *een* ~*me* a paralytic
1 **'lama** ('s) *m* lama [priest]
2 **'lama** ('s) *m* ⚶ llama
lambri'zering (-en) *v* wainscot(ing), panelling;
dado
la'mel (-len) *v* lamella
lamen'teren (lamenteerde, h. gelamenteerd) *vi*
lament
'lamgelegd paralysed (d o o r s t a k i n g)
strike-bound; **'lamheid** *v* paralysis; *met* ~
geslagen paralysed
lami'neren (lamineerde, h. gelamineerd) *vi & vt*
laminate
lam'lendig miserable; **'lammeling** (-en) *m*

miserable fellow; *jij ~ !* **P** (you) cad, rotter!;
lamme'nadig 1 (f u t l o o s) weak, limp,
spineless; 2 (n i e t w e l) **F** seedy; 3 (b e -
r o e r d) wretched
1 **'lammeren** (lammerde, h. gelammerd) *vi*
lamb; **2 'lammeren** meerv. van 1 *lam*;
'lammergier (-en) *m* lammergeyer;
'lammetje (-s) *o* little lamb
la'moen (-en) *o* (pair of) shafts, thill
lamp (-en) *v* lamp; ⚡ bulb; R valve; *lelijk tegen*
de ~ lopen get into trouble, come to grief; get
caught; **'lampeglas** (-glazen) *o* lamp-chimney;
–kap (-pen) *v* lamp-shade; **–pit** (-ten) *v*
lamp-wick
lam'petkan (-nen) *v* ewer, jug; **–kom** (-men) *v*
wash-basin, wash-hand basin
lampi'on (-s) *m* Chinese lantern
'lamplicht *o* lamplight
lam'prei (-en) *v* 🐟 lamprey
'lampzwart *o* lamp-black, smokeblack
'lamsbout (-en) *m* leg of lamb; **–kotelet** (-ten)
v lamb cutlet
'lamslaan (sloeg 'lam, h. 'lamgeslagen) *vt*
paralyse, cripple [trade]; *iem. ~* beat sbd. to a
jelly
'lamstraal (-stralen) *m* **P** cad, rotter
'lamsvlees *o* lamb
lan'ceerbasis [-zis] (-bases en -sissen) *v* launching site; **–inrichting** (-en) *v* launcher; **–plat-**
form (-en en -s) *o* launching pad; **–terrein**
(-en) *o* launching site; **lan'ceren** (lanceerde, h.
gelanceerd) *vt* launch² [a missile, a torpedo, a
new enterprise]; set afloat, float [an affair, a
rumour]; start [a report]; **–ring** (-en) *v* [missile,
space] launching
lan'cet (-ten) *o* lancet; **–visje** (-s) *o* lancelet;
–vormig lanceolate
land (-en) *o* 1 (t e g e n o v e r z e e) land; 2
(s t a a t) country; nation; 3 (t e g e n o v e r
s t a d) country; 4 (a k k e r) field; 5 (l a n d -
b e z i t) estate; *~ en volk* land and people; *het*
~ van belofte **B** the promised land; *de Lage*
Landen the Low Countries; *een stukje ~* a plot,
an allotment; *het ~ hebben* 1 be annoyed; 2
have a fit of the blues; *het ~ hebben aan* hate
[sbd., sth.]; *ik heb er het ~ over* 1 I am hating
myself for it; 2 I cannot stomach it; *het ~*
krijgen become annoyed, **F** get the hump; *het ~*
krijgen aan take a dislike to, come to hate [sbd.,
sth.]; *iem. het ~ op jagen* **F** give sbd. the hump,
rile sbd.; ● *a a n ~* ashore, ook: on land; *aan ~*
gaan go ashore; *aan ~ komen* land, come
ashore; *iem. aan ~ zetten* put sbd. ashore; *de*
zomer is in het ~ summer has come in; *n a a r ~*
to the shore; *o p het ~ wonen* live in the country;
o v e r ~ by land, overland; *te ~ en te water*
[transportation] by land and sea; *onze strijd-*

krachten te ~ en te water (ter zee) our land-forces
and naval forces; *de strijdkrachten te ~, ter zee en*
in de lucht the armed forces on land, at sea and
in the air; *hier te ~e* in this country; *waar zal hij*
te ~ komen? what is to become of him?; *een*
meisje v a n het ~ a country lass; **–aanwinning**
(-en) *v* reclamation of land, (land) reclamation;
–aard *m* 1 national character; 2 nationality;
–adel *m* country nobility; **–arbeider** (-s) *m*
farm worker, agricultural labourer (worker)
'landauer (-s) *m* landau
'landbouw *m* agriculture; **–bedrijf** (-drijven) *o*
agricultural enterprise, farm; **–consulent** [s =
z] (-en) *m* consulting agriculturist; **–er** (-s) *m*
farmer, tiller, agriculturist; **–gereedschappen**
mv agricultural implements; **–krediet** (-en) *o*
agricultural credit; **–kunde** *v* agriculture,
husbandry, agronomics; **landbouw'kundig**
agricultural; **–e** (-n) *m* agriculturist; **'land-**
bouwmachine [-ma.ʃi.nə] (-s) *v* agricultural
machine; *~s* ook: farm(ing) machinery, agricultural machinery; **–onderneming** (-en) *v*
agricultural enterprise; **–onderwijs** *o* agricultural education, agricultural instruction;
–produkten *mv* agricultural produce
(products), farm products (produce); **land-**
bouw'proefstation [-sta.(t)ʃɔn] (-s) *o* agricultural experiment-station; **'landbouwschool**
(-scholen) *v* agricultural college; **–tentoon-**
stelling (-en) *v* agricultural show; **–werktuig**
(-en) *o* agricultural implement, farming implement
'landdag (-dagen) *m* diet; *de Poolse ~* the Polish
Diet; *een Poolse ~* [*fig*] a regular beargarden;
–edelman (-lieden) *m* country gentleman,
squire; **–eigenaar** (-s en -naren) *m* landowner,
landed proprietor; **'landelijk** 1 (v. h. p l a t -
t e l a n d) rustic, rural, country...; 2 (v. h.
g e h e l e l a n d) national; **–heid** *v* rusticity;
'landen I (landde, h. geland) *vt* land, disembark; **II** (landde, is geland) *vi* land;
'landengte (-n en -s) *v* isthmus; **land- en**
'volkenkunde *v* geography and ethnography;
'landenwedstrijd (-en) *m* international
contest; **land- en 'zeemacht** *v* Army and
Navy; **'landerig** blue; **–heid** *v* the blues;
lande'rijen *mv* landed estates; **'landgenoot**
(-noten) *m* (fellow-)countryman, compatriot;
–genote (-n) *v* (fellow-)countrywoman;
–goed (-eren) *o* country-seat, estate, manor;
–grens (-grenzen) *v* land-frontier; **–heer**
(-heren) *m* lord of the manor; **–hoofd** (-en) *o*
abutment; **–huis** (-huizen) *o* country-house,
villa; **land'huishoudkunde** *v* rural economy;
'landhuur (-huren) *v* land-rent
'landing (-en) *v* 1 landing [of troops &]; 2
disembarkation [from ship]; ✈ landing,

descent; (v. r u i m t e v a a r t u i g i n z e e)
splash-down; 'landingsbaan (-banen) *v*
runway; –brug (-gen) *v* 1 landing-stage; 2
gangway; –gestel (-len) *o* (under-)carriage,
landing-gear; –rechten *mv* landing rights;
–strook (-stroken) *v* «⸱» airstrip; –terrein (-en)
o landing-ground; –troepen *mv* landing-
forces; –vaartuig(en) *o* (*mv*) landing-craft
land'inwaarts inland; 'landjonker (-s) *m*
(country-)squire; –kaart (-en) *v* map;
–klimaat *o* continental climate; –leger *o*
land-forces; –leven *o* country-life; –loper (-s)
m vagabond, vagrant, tramp, lay-about;
landlope'rij *v* vagabondage, vagrancy, tramp-
ing; 'landmacht *v* land-forces; *de* ~ ook: the
Army; –man (-lieden) *m* countryman;
(l a n d b o u w e r) farmer; –meten *o*
surveying; –meter (-s) *m* surveyor; –mijn
(-en) *v* landmine
lan'douw (-en) *v* field, region
'landpaal (-palen) *m* boundary mark; –rat
(-ten) *v* = *landrot*; –rente (-n en -s) *v* land-
revenue; –rot (-ten) *v fig* landlubber; 'landschap (-pen) *o* landscape; –schilder (-s) *m*
landscape painter, landscapist; –schilderkunst *v* landscape painting; 'landscheiding
(-en) *v* boundary; –schildpad (-den) *v* land
tortoise; 'landsdienaar (-s en -naren) *m*
public servant; landsdrukke'rij (-en) *v*
government printing-office, H. M. Stationery
Office; 'landsheer (-heren) *m* sovereign lord,
monarch; –man (-lieden) *m* (fellow-)coun-
tryman; –taal (-talen) *v* vernacular (language);
'landstreek (-streken) *v* region, district,
quarter; 'landsverdediging *v* 1 defence of the
country, national defence; 2 *de* ~ the land
defences; –vrouwe (-n) *v* sovereign lady;
'landtong (-en) *v* spit of land; –verhuizer (-s)
m emigrant; –verhuizing (-en) *v* emigration;
–verraad *o* high treason; –verrader (-s) *m*
traitor to one's country; –volk *o* country-
people; –voogd (-en) *m* governor (of a
country); –waarts landward(s); *meer* ~ more
inland; –weer *v* ⚔ territorial army; –weg
(-wegen) *m* 1 (d o o r e e n l a n d)
country-road, rural road, (country-)lane; 2 (o v e r
l a n d e n n i e t o v e r z e e) overland
route; –wijn (-en) *m* simple, regional wine;
–wind (-en) *m* land-wind, land-breeze;
–winning (-en) *v* = *landaanwinning*; –zij(de) *v*
land-side
lang **I** *aj* long; (v. g e s t a l t e) tall, high; *hij is
5 voet* ~ he is five feet in height; *de tafel is 5 voet*
~ the table is five feet in length; ~ *en slank* tall
and slim; *zo* ~ *als hij was viel hij* he fell at full
length; *een* ~ *gezicht* (*zetten*) (pull) a long face;
hij is nogal ~ *van stof* he is rather long-winded;

het is zo ~ *als het breed is* it is as broad as it is
long, it is six of one and half a dozen of the
other; ~ *worden* 1 (v. p e r s o o n) grow tall; 2
(v . d a g) = *lengen*; **II** *ad* long; *ik heb het hem* ~
en breed verteld I've told him the whole thing at
great length; *hoe* ~? how long [am I to wait]?;
twee jaar ~ for two years; *zijn leven* ~ all his life;
ben je hier al ~? have you been here long?, zie
ook: 2 *al*; *ik ben er nog* ~ *niet* I still have a long
way to go; *dat is* ~ *niet slecht* not bad at all; **S**
not half bad; ~ *niet sterk genoeg* not strong
enough by a long way; ~ *niet zo oud* (*als je zegt*)
nothing like so old; *hij is al* ~ *weg* he has been
gone a long time; *wat ben je* ~ *weggebleven!* what
a time you have been!; *bij* ~ *niet zo…* not nearly
so, not by a long way so; *hoe* ~*er hoe beter* 1 the
longer the better; 2 better and better; *hoe* ~*er
hoe meer* more and more; ● *waarom heb je i n zo
~ niet geschreven?* why have you not written me
for so long?; *ik heb hem in* ~ *niet gezien* I've not
seen him for a long time; *o p zijn* ~*st* at (the)
most; *s e d e r t* ~ for a long time; lang'dradig
long-winded, prolix, prosy; –heid *v* long-
windedness, prolixity; lang'durig long [illness
&], prolonged [applause &], protracted;
[connection, quarrel &] of long standing;
–heid *v* long duration, length; lange-
'afstandsbommenwerper (-s) *m* long-range
bomber; –loper (-s) *m sp* long-distance
runner; –race [-re.s] (-s) *m sp* long-distance
race; –raket (-ten) *v* long-range rocket;
'langgerekt, langge'rekt long-drawn(-out)
[sound &]; protracted, lengthy [negotiations
&]; 'langharig, lang'harig long-haired;
'langlopend long-term; –parkeerder (-s) *m*
long-term parker; –pootmug (-gen) *v* crane-
fly, daddy-long-legs
langs **I** *prep* along [the river]; past [the house];
by [this route]; **II** *ad hij ging* ~ he went past, he
passed; *iem. er van* ~ *geven* let sbd. have it, **F**
give sbd. what for; *er van* ~ *krijgen* catch it, **F**
get what for
'langslaper (-s) *m* lie-abed; –snuitkever (-s) *m*
weevil; –speelplaat (-platen) *v* long-play(ing)
record, long player, L.P.; langs'scheeps ⚓
fore and aft; 'langstlevende, langst'levende
(-n) *m-v* longest liver, survivor
langs'zij(de) alongside
'languit (at) full length; –verwacht long-
expected; lang'werpig oblong; ~ *rond* oval;
–heid *v* oblong form
'langzaam **I** *aj* slow?, tardy, lingering; ~ *maar
zeker* slow and sure; **II** *ad* 1 slowly; 2 ⚓ easy
[ahead, astern]; ~ *werkend vergif* slow poison; ~
maar zeker slowly but surely; ~ *aan!* easy!,
steady!; ~ *aan dan breekt het lijntje niet* easy does
it; langzaam-'aan-actie [-ɑksi.] (-s) *v* go-

slow; **langzamer'hand** gradually, by degrees, little by little

lank'moedig *v* long-suffering, patient; **–heid** *v* long-suffering, patience

lans (-en) *v* lance; *met gevelde ~* lance in rest; *een ~ breken met* break a lance with; *een ~ breken voor* intercede for [sbd.]; advocate [measures &], break a lance for; **lan'sier** (-s) *m* ⚔ lancer; **'lansknecht** (-en) ⬚ lansquenet

lan'taarn (-s) *v* 1 (t o t   v e r l i c h t i n g) lantern; 2 (f i e t s &) lamp; 3 (l i c h t - k o e p e l) skylight; **–opsteker** (-s) *m* lamplighter; **–paal** (-palen) *m* lamp-post; **–plaatje** (-s) *o* lantern-slide

'lanterfanten (lanterfantte, h. gelanterfant) *vi* idle, laze (about), loaf, **S** mike; **–er** (-s) *m* idler, loafer

'Laos *o* Laos

Lap (-pen) *m* Lapp, Laplander

lap (-pen) *m* 1 piece [of woven material]; rag, tatter [of cloth, paper]; 2 (o m   t e   v e r s t e l - l e n) patch; 3 (o m   t e   w r i j v e n) cloth; 4 (o v e r g e b l e v e n   s t u k   g o e d) remnant; 5 (s t u k) patch [of arable land]; slice [of meat], steak [for frying, stewing &]; 6 (k l a p) lick, slap; box [on the ears]; 7 *sp* (b a a n r o n d e) lap; *de leren ~* the shammy (leather); *dat werkt op hem als een rode ~ op een stier* it is like a red rag to a bull; *er een ~ op zetten* put a patch upon it, patch it; *de ~pen hangen erbij* it is in rags (in tatters); *een gezicht van oude ~pen* a sour face

la'pel (-len) *m* lapel

lapi'dair [-'dɛːr] lapidary

'lapje (-s) *o* (small) patch &, zie *lap*; *~s* (v l e e s) steaks; *iem. voor het ~ houden* pull sbd.'s leg; **–skat** (-ten) *v* tortoise (shell) cat

'Lapland *o* Lapland; **–er** (-s) *m* Laplander, Lapponian, Lapp; **–s** Lappish, Lapponian

'lapmiddel (-en) *o* palliative, makeshift; **'lappen** (lapte, h. gelapt) *vt* patch, piece; mend [clothes &]; wash [windows]; *hij zal het hem wel ~* he'll do (manage) it; *wie heeft mij dat gelapt?* who has played me that trick?; *dat lap ik a a n mijn laars!* **F** fat lot I care!; *een waarschuwing aan zijn laars ~* ignore a warning; *iem. er b ij ~* **S** cop a man; *alles er d o o r ~* run through a fortune &; **'lappendeken** (-s) *v* patchwork quilt; **–mand** (-en) *v* remnant basket; *in de ~ zijn* be laid up, be on the sick-list

'lapwerk *o* patchwork[2]; *fig* tinkering

'lapzwans (-en) *m* dud

lar'deerpriem (-en) *m* larding-pin; **lar'deren** (lardeerde, h. gelardeerd) *vt* lard

larf (larven) *v* = *larve*

'larie *v* nonsense, fudge; fiddlesticks!

'lariks(boom) (lariksen, lariksbomen) *m* larch

larmoy'ant [lɑrmvɑ'jɑnt] tearful, maudlin

'larve (-n) *v* larva [*mv* larvae], (o o k:) grub [of insects]

1 las (-sen) *v* weld, joint, seam, scarf

2 las (lazen) V.T. van *lezen*

'lasapparaat (-raten) *o* welder

'laser ['le.zɔr] (-s) *m* laser

'lassen (laste, h. gelast) *vt* weld [iron]; joint [a wire]; scarf [timber]; **–er** (-s) *m* [electric] welder

'lasso ('s) *m* lasso

1 last (-en) *m* 1 (o p g e l a d e n   v r a c h t) load[2], burden[2]; 2 (z w a a r t e d r u k) load[2], burden[2], weight[2]; 3 (l a d i n g) load, ⚓ cargo; 4 (o v e r - l a s t) trouble, nuisance; 5 (b e v e l) order, command; *~en* charges, rates and taxes; *baten en ~en* assets and liabilities; *~ hebben van* be incommoded by [the neighbourhood of...]; be troubled with, suffer from [a complaint], be subject to [fits of dizziness]; *~ veroorzaken* incommode, cause (give) trouble; ● *i n ~ hebben om...* be charged to...; *o p ~ van...* by order of...; *op zware ~en zitten* be heavily encumbered; *t e n ~e van* be chargeable to; *iem. iets ten ~e leggen* charge sbd. with a thing, lay it to sbd.'s charge; *iem. t o t ~ zijn* 1 incommode sbd.; 2 be a burden on sbd.; *zich v a n een ~ kwijten* acquit oneself of a charge

2 last (-en) *o* & *m* ⚓ last [= 2 tons]

'lastbrief (-brieven) *m* mandate; **–dier** (-en) *o* beast of burden, pack-animal; **–drager** (-s) *m* porter

'laster *m* slander, calumny, defamation; **–aar** (-s en -raren) *m* slanderer, calumniator; **–campagne** [-kɑmpɑɲə] (-s) *v* campaign of calumny (of slander), **F** smear campaign; **'lasteren** (lasterde, h. gelasterd) *vt* slander, calumniate, defame; *God ~* blaspheme (God); **'lasterlijk I** *aj* 1 slanderous; defamatory, libellous; 2 blasphemous; **II** *ad* 1 slanderously; 2 blasphemously; **'lasterpraatjes** *mv* slanderous talk, scandal; **–taal** *v* slander

'lastgever (-s) *m* principal; **–geving** (-en) *v* mandate, commission; **–hebber** (-s) *m* mandatary

'lastig I *aj* 1 (m o e i l ij k   u i t   t e   v o e r e n) difficult, hard; 2 (m o e i l ij k   t e   r e g e r e n) troublesome, unruly; 3 (v e r v e l e n d) annoying; awkward; 4 (v e e l e i s e n d) exacting, hard to please; 5 (o n g e m a k k e l ij k) inconvenient; *wat zijn jullie vandaag weer ~!* what nuisances you are to-day!; *de kinderen zijn helemaal niet ~* the children give no trouble; *een ~ geval* a difficult case; *een ~e vent* a troublesome customer; *~ vallen* importune, molest [sbd.]; *het spijt mij dat ik u ~ moet vallen* I am sorry to be a nuisance, sorry to trouble you; *dat zal u niet ~ vallen* it will not be difficult for you; **II** *ad* with difficulty; *dat ʒal ~ gaan* that will hardly be possible; **'lastpak** (-ken) *o* **F** handful, nuisance; **–post** (-en) *m* 1 (v a n z a k e n) nuisance; 2 (v . p e r s o n e n) nuisance; *die ~en van jongens* ook: those troublesome boys

lat (-ten) *v* 1 lath; 2 (v . e . j a l o e z i e) slat; 3 ⚙ **F** skewer; 4 *sp* (d o e l~) cross-bar; (s p r i n g~) bar; *de lange ~ten sp* the skis; *onder de ~ staan sp* keep goal; *op de ~ kopen* **F** buy on
'latafel *v* chest of drawers   [tick
'laten* **I** *hulpww.* let; *~ we gaan!* let us go!; *laat ik u niet storen* do not let me disturb you; **II** *zelfst.ww.* 1 (l a t e n i n z e k e r e t o e s t a n d) leave [things as they are]; 2 (n a l a t e n) omit, forbear, refrain from [telling &]; leave off, give up [drinking, smoking]; 3 (t o e l a t e n) let [sbd. do sth.], allow, permit, suffer [sbd. to...]; 4 (t o e w ij z e n) let have; 5 (g e l a s t e n) make, have [sbd. do sth.]; get, cause [sbd. to...]; *~ bouwen* have... built; *wij zullen het ~ doen* we shall have (get) it done; *het laat zich niet beschrijven* it cannot be described, it defies (beggars) description; *het laat zich denken* it may be imagined; *het laat zich verklaren* it can be explained; *laat dat!* don't!; stop it!; *laat (me) los!* let (me) go!; *laat het maar hier* leave it here; *je had het maar moeten ~* you should have left it undone; *hij kan het niet ~* he cannot help it, he cannot desist from it; *als je mij maar tijd wilt ~* if only you allow me time; ● *ver a c h t e r zich ~* leave far behind, outdistance; throw into the shade; *wij zullen het hier b ij ~* we'll leave it at that; *hij zal het er niet bij ~* he is not going to let the matter rest, to lie down under it; *ik kan het u niet v o o r minder ~* I can't let you have it for less; *wij zullen dat ~ voor wat het is* we'll let it rest; *ik weet niet waar hij het (al dat eten) laat* I don't know where he puts it; *waar heb ik mijn boek gelaten?* where have I put my book?; *waar heb je het geld gelaten?* what have you been and done with the money?; zie ook: *vallen,* 1 *weten, zien* &
la'tent latent
'later *aj* later; **II** *ad* later; later on
late'raal *aj* lateral
'latertje *o dat wordt een ~* it will be late, it will be well into the small hours [before we are finished]
'latex *o* & *m* latex
'lathyrus ['la.ti: rüs] (-sen) *m* sweet pea
La'tijn *o* Latin; *aan 't eind van ʒ'n ~ zijn* be at the end of one's rope; **–s** Latin; *~- Amerika* Latin America; *~- Amerikaans* Latin-American
la'trine (-s) *v* latrine
'latwerk (-en) *o* lath-work; (v . l e i b o m e n) trellis

lau'rier (-en) *m* laurel, bay; **–blad** (-blaren en -bladeren) *o* laurel-leaf, bay-leaf; **–boom** (-bomen) *m* laurel(-tree), bay(-tree)
lauw lukewarm[2]; tepid; *fig* half-hearted
'lauwer (-en) *m* laurel, bay; *~en behalen* win (reap) laurels; *op zijn ~en rusten* rest on one's laurels; **'lauweren** (lauwerde, h. gelauwerd) *vt* crown with laurels, laurel; **'lauwerkrans** (-en) *m* wreath of laurels
'lava *v* lava
'lavabo ('s) *m* lavabo
'laveloos dead drunk, sozzled
lave'ment (-en) *o* enema, clyster
'laven (laafde, h. gelaafd) **I** *vt* refresh; **II** *vr zich ~* refresh oneself; *zich aan de bron ~* drink from that source
la'vendel *v* lavender
la'veren (laveerde, h. en is gelaveerd) *vi* ⚓ tack[2] (about), beat up against the wind; *fig* manoeuvre
'laving (-en) *v* refreshment
la'waai *o* noise, din, tumult, uproar, hubbub; *~ schoppen* roister; **–bestrijding** *v* noise abatement; **la'waai(er)ig** *aj* noisy, uproarious, loud; **la'waaimaker** (-s) *m,* **–schopper** (-s) *m* blusterer, bounder, roisterer
la'wine (-s en -n) *v* avalanche
'laxans (la'xantia) *o* aperient, laxative; **la'xeer-middel** (-en) *o = laxans;* **la'xeren** (laxeerde, h. gelaxeerd) *vi* open (relax) the bowels; **–d** (gelaxeerd) *vi* open (relax) the bowels; **–d** laxative
laza'ret (-ten) *o* lazaretto
'lazarus P ~ zijn be drunk
'lazen V.T. meerv. v. *lezen*
'lazer *o* **P** *iem. op ʒ'n ~ geven* give sbd. hell, give sbd. a hiding;
'lazeren P I (lazerde, h. gelazerd) *vt* (s m ij t e n) *iem. er uit ~* chuck (fling, hurl) sbd. out; **II** (lazerde, is gelazerd) *vi* (v a l l e n) *van de trap ~* pitch down the stairs
'leasen ['li.sə(n)] (leasde, h. geleasd) *vt* lease; **'leasing** *v* leasing
'lebberen (lebberde, h. gelebberd) *vt* lap (up)
leb, 'lebbe (lebben) *v* rennet; **'lebmaag** (-magen) *v* rennet-stomach
'lector (-'toren en -s) *m* ⇦reader; **lecto'raat** (-raten) *o* ⇦ readership
lec'tuur *v* reading; reading-matter
'ledematen *mv* limbs
1 'leden V.T. meerv. v. *lijden*
2 'leden *mv.* v. *lid*
'ledenlijst (-en) *v* list (register) of members
'ledenpop (-pen) *v* lay figure, manikin; *fig* puppet
'leder = 3 *leer;* **–en** = 2 *leren*
'ledig (ledigde, h. geledigd) = *leeg;* **'ledigen** (ledigde, h. geledigd) *vt* empty; **'lediggang** *m*

idleness; **–heid** *v* 1 (h e t l e d i g z i j n)
emptiness; 2 (l e d i g g a n g, n i e t s d o e n)
idleness; *~ is des duivels oorkussen* idleness is the
parent of vice

ledi'kant (-en) *o* bedstead

1 leed I *o* 1 (l i c h a m e l i j k) harm, injury; 2
(v. d e z i e l) affliction, grief, sorrow; *in lief*
en ~ ± for better and for worse; *het doet mij ~* I
am sorry (for it); *iem. zijn ~ klagen* pour out
one's grief to sbd.; *u zal geen ~ geschieden* you
shall suffer no harm; **II** *aj met lede ogen* with
regret

2 leed (leden) V.T. v. *lijden*

'leedvermaak *o* enjoyment of others' mishaps;
–wezen *o* regret; *m e t ~* with regret; regret-
fully; *t o t mijn ~ kan ik niet...* I regret not being
able to..., to my regret

'leefbaar liveable; **–heid** *v* liveableness; **'leef-**
klimaat *o* living climate, living conditions;
–regel (-s) *m* regimen, diet; **–ruimte** *v* living
space, lebensraum; **–tijd** (-en) *m* lifetime; age;
o p die ~ at that age; *op hoge ~* at a great age; *op*
late(re) ~ late(r) in life; *op ~ komen* be getting
on in years; *op ~ zijn* be well on in life; *een*
jongen v a n mijn ~ a boy my age; *zij zijn van*
dezelfde ~ they are of an age; **'leeftijdgenoot**
(-noten) *m* contemporary; **'leeftijdsgrens**
(-grenzen) *v* age limit; **–groep** (-en) *v* age
group; **–verschil** (-len) *o* difference of age;
'leeftocht *m* provisions, victuals; **–wijze** *v*
manner of life, style of living

leeg 1 (n i e t s i n h o u d e n d) empty[2];
vacant[2]; 2 (n i e t s d o e n d) idle; **–drinken**[1] *vt*
empty, finish [one's glass]; **–gieten**[1] *vt* empty
out; **–halen**[1] *vt* clear out; (p l u n d e r e n)
strip; **–heid** *v* emptiness; **–hoofd** (-en) *o &*
m-v empty-headed person; **–loop** *m* $ down-
time; **–lopen**[1] *vi* 1 idle (about), loaf; 2 empty,
become empty; go flat [of a balloon, a tyre];
laten ~ empty [a cask]; deflate [a balloon, a
tyre]; drain [a pond]; **–loper** (-s) *m* idler,
loafer; **–maken**[1] *vt* empty; **–pompen**[1] *vt*
pump dry; *fig* drain (dry); **–staan**[1] *vi* be empty,
stand empty, be uninhabited (unoccupied); **–te**
(-n) *v* emptiness[2], *fig* void, blank

1 leek (leken) *m* layman[2]; outsider [in art &]; *de*
leken ook: the laity

2 leek (leken) V.T. van *lijken*

leem *o &* *m* loam, clay, mud; **–achtig** loamy;
–groeve (-n) *v* loam-pit; **–grond** (-en) *m*
loamy soil; **–kuil** (-en) *m* loam-pit

'leemte (-n en -s) *v* gap, lacuna [*mv* lacunae],
hiatus, deficiency

leen (lenen) *o* ⫍ fief, feudal tenure; *in ~ hebben* 1
have it lent to one; 2 ⫍ hold in feud; *te ~ on*
loan; *mag ik dat van u te ~ hebben?* may I
borrow this (from you)?; will you favour me
with the loan of it?; *te ~ geven* lend; *te ~ vragen*
ask for the loan of; **–bank** (-en) *v* loan-office;
–dienst (-en) *m* feudal service, vassalage;
–goed (-eren) *o* feudal estate; **–heer** (-heren)
m feudal lord, liege (lord); **–man** (-nen) *m*
vassal; **–plicht** (-en) *m & v* feudal duty;
leen'plichtig liege; **'leenrecht** *o* feudal right;
leen'roerig feudal, feudatory; **'leenstelsel** *o*
⫍ feudal system; **'leentjebuur** *~ spelen*
borrow (right and left); **'leenwoord** (-en) *o*
loan-word

leep I *aj* sly, cunning, shrewd, longheaded; **II**
ad slyly, shrewdly, cunningly; **–heid** *v* slyness,
cunning

1 leer (leren) *v* (l a d d e r) ladder

2 leer (leren) *v* 1 (l e e r s t e l s e l) doctrine;
teaching [of Christ]; 2 (t h e o r i e) theory; 3
(h e t l e e r l i n g z i j n) apprenticeship; *in de*
~ doen bij bind apprentice to; *in de ~ zijn* serve
one's apprenticeship [with], be bound apprentice [to a goldsmith]

3 leer *o* (s t o f n a a m) leather; *~ om ~* tit for
tat; *van ~ trekken* draw one's sword; go at it (at
them); *van een andermans ~ is het goed riemen*
snijden it is easy to cut thongs out of another
man's leather; **–achtig** leathery

'leerboek (-en) *o* text-book; lesson-book;
–dicht (-en) *o* didactic poem; **–gang** (-en) *m*
course, course of lectures; **–geld** *o* premium;
~ betalen [fig] learn it to one's cost; **–gezag** *o rk*
teaching authority (of the Church); **leer'gierig**
eager to learn, studious; **–heid** *v* eagerness to
learn, studiousness

'leerhuid *v* true skin

'leerjaren *mv* (years of) apprenticeship;
–jongen (-s) *m* apprentice; **–kracht** (-en) *v*
teacher; **–ling** (-en) *m* 1 pupil, disciple; 2 =
leerjongen; **leerling-ver'pleegster** (-s) *v*
student nurse, probationer; **~-'vlieger** (-s) *m*
aircraft apprentice

'leerlooien *va* tan; *het ~* tanning; **–er** (-s) *m*
tanner; **leerlooie'rij** (-en) *v* tannery

'leermeester (-s) *m* teacher, master, tutor;
–meisje (-s) *o* apprentice; **–middelen** *mv*
educational appliances; **–opdracht** (-en) *v*
teaching assignment, lectureship; **–plan** (-nen)
o curriculum [*mv* curricula]; **'leerplicht** *m & v*
compulsory education; **leer'plichtig** liable to
compulsory education; **'leerschool** (-scholen)

---

[1] V.T. en V.D. van dit werkwoord volgens het model: 'leeg**halen**, V.T. haalde 'leeg, V.D. 'leeg**gehaald**. Zie voor
de vormen onder het grondwoord, in dit voorbeeld: *halen*. Bij sterke en onregelmatige werkwoorden wordt u
verwezen naar de lijst achterin.

v school; *een harde ~ doorlopen* learn the hard way, go (pass) through the mill; **leer'stellig** 1 dogmatic; 2 doctrinaire; **'leerstelling** (-en) *v* tenet, dogma; **–stoel** (-en) *m* chair [of Greek History &, in college or university]; **–stof** *v* subject-matter of tuition; **–stuk** (-ken) *o* dogma, tenet; **–tijd** *m* 1 time of learning; pupil(l)age; 2 (term of) apprenticeship

'leertje (-s) *o* ✕ (v . k r a a n) washer

'leervak (-ken) *o* subject (taught)

'leerwaren *mv* leather goods; **–werk** *o* leather-work, leather goods

'leerzaam I *aj* 1 (v . p e r s o o n) docile, teachable, studious; 2 (v . b o e k &) instructive; **II** *ad* instructively; **–heid** *v* 1 docility, teachableness [of persons]; 2 instructiveness [of books]

'leesapparaat (-raten) *o* 1 reading aid; 2. (v . c o m p u t e r) optical character reader; **–baar** legible [writing]; readable [novels]; **–beurt** (-en) *v* 1 (o p s c h o o l) turn to read; 2 (l e z i n g) lecture; **–bibliotheek** (-theken) *v* lending-library; **–blindheid** *v* word-blindness, alexia; **–boek** (-en) *o* reading-book, reader; **–bril** (-len) *m* reading-glasses; **–gezelschap** (-pen) *o*, **–kring** (-en) *m* reading-club; **–les** (-sen) *v* reading lesson; **–oefening** (-en) *v* reading exercise; **–onderwijs** *o* instruction in reading; **–portefeuille** [-pɔrtəfœyjə] (-s) *m* book and magazine portfolio [of a reading-club]; **–stof** *v* reading-matter

leest (-en) *v* 1 (v . l i c h a a m) waist; 2 (v a n s c h o e n m a k e r) last; (o m t e r e k k e n) (boot-)tree; *we zullen dat op een andere ~ moeten schoeien* we shall have to put it on a new footing; *op dezelfde ~ schoeien* cast in the same mould; *op socialistische ~ geschoeid* organized on socialist lines; *op de ~ zetten* put on the last. Zie ook: *schoenmaker*

'leestafel (-s) *v* reading-table; **–teken** (-s) *o* punctuation mark, stop; *~s aanbrengen* punctuate; **–wijzer** (-s) *m* book-mark(er); **–woede** *v* mania for reading; **–zaal** (-zalen) *v* reading room; *openbare ~* public library

leeuw (-en) *m* lion²; *de Leeuw* ★ Leo; **–achtig** leonine; **'leeuwebek** (-ken) *m* 🌿 snapdragon; **–deel** *o* lion's share; **–kuil** (-en) *m* den of lions; **–manen** *mv* lion's mane; **–moed** *m* courage of a lion; *met ~ bezield* lion-hearted [man]; **'leeuwentemmer** (-s) *m* lion-tamer

'leeuwerik (-en) *m* (sky)lark

leeu'win (-nen) *v* lioness; **'leeuwtje** (-s) *o* 1 little lion; 2 Maltese dog

'leewater *o* water on the knee, synovitis

lef *o* & *m* 1 pluck, courage; 2 swagger; *het ~ hebben iets te doen* have the guts to do sth.; *als je ~ hebt* if you dare; **–doekje** (-s) *o* breast-

pocket handkerchief; **–gozer** (-s) *m*, **–schopper** (-s) *m* braggart, swanker, toff

leg *m* egg-laying; *aan de ~* in lay

le'gaal legal

le'gaat (-gaten) 1 *o* legacy, bequest; 2 *m* (v a n p a u s) legate

legali'satie [- 'za.(t)si.] (-s) *v* legalization; **legali'seren** (legaliseerde, h. gelegaliseerd) *vt* legalize

lega'taris (-sen) *m* legatee; **lega'teren** (legateerde, h. gelegateerd) *vt* bequeath

le'gatie [-(t)si.] (-s) *v* legation

'legen (leegde, h. geleegd) = *ledigen*

legen'darisch legendary, fabled; **le'gende** (-n en -s) *v* legend; *fig* myth

'leger (-s) *o* 1 ✕ army²; ✎ & *fig* host; 2 bed; form [of a hare]; lair [of wild animals]; haunt [of a wolf]; *Leger des Heils* Salvation Army; **–aalmoezenier** (-s) *m* army chaplain, **F** padre; **–afdeling** (-en) *v* unit; **–bericht** (-en) *o* army bulletin; **–commandant** (-en) *m* commander-in-chief; 1 **'legeren** ['le.gərə(n)] (legerde, h. gelegerd) *vt, vi* & *vr* ✕ encamp [of troops]

2 **le'geren** [lə'ge:rə(n)] (legeerde, h. gelegeerd) *vt* alloy [metals]

1 **'legering** ['le.gɔrɪŋ] (-en) *v* ✕ encampment

2 **le'gering** [lə'ge:rɪŋ] (-en) *v* alloy [of metals]

'legerkamp (-en) *o* army camp; **–korps** (-en) *o* army corps; **–leiding** *v* (army) command; **–plaats** (-en) *v* camp; **–predikant** (-en) *m* army chaplain, **F** padre; **–scharen** *mv* hosts, army

☉ **'legerstede** (-n) *v* couch, bed

'legertent (-en) *v* army tent; **–trein** (-en), **–tros** (-sen) *m* baggage (of an army), train (of an army)

'leges *mv* legal charges, fee

'leggen* I *vt* 1 lay, put, place [a thing somewhere]; lay [eggs]; 2 *sp* throw [in wrestling]; **II** *va* lay [of hens]; **–er** (-s) *m* 1 (p e r s o o n) layer; 2 (r e g i s t e r) register, ledger; **'leghen** (-nen) *v* layer, laying hen

'legio numberless, innumerable, no end of [possibilities]; *die zijn ~* their name (number) is legion

legi'oen (-en) *o* legion

legi'tiem legitimate, lawful; **legiti'matie** [-(t)si.] (-s) *v* legitimation; **–bewijs** (-wijzen) *o* identity card; **legiti'meren** (legitimeerde, h. gelegitimeerd) **I** *vt* legitimate; **II** *vr zich ~* prove one's identity

'legkaart (-en) *v* jigsaw puzzle; **–penning** (-en) *m* commemorative coin (medal); **–plaat** (-platen) *v* jigsaw puzzle; **–puzzel** (-s) *m* jigsaw puzzle

legu'aan (-uanen) *m* 🦎 iguana

1 lei (-en) *v* & *o* slate; *met een schone ~ beginnen* start with a clean slate (sheet)

2 lei (**leien**) F V.T. van *leggen*

'leiband (-en) *m* leading-string(s); *aan de ~ lopen* be in leading-strings[2]

'leiboom (-bomen) *m* espalier

'leidekker (-s) *m* slater

'Leiden *o* Leyden; *toen was ~ in last* then there was the devil to pay, then we (they &) were in a fix

'leiden (leidde, h. geleid) **I** *vt* lead [a person, a party, a solitary life &]; conduct [visitors, matters, a meeting]; guide [us, the affairs of state &], direct [one's actions, a rehearsal &]; *sp* lead, be in the lead; *zich laten ~ door...* be guided by...; *b ij (aan) de hand ~* lead by the hand; *leid ons niet i n verzoeking* (*rk in bekoring*) lead us not into temptation; *die weg leidt n a a r...* that road leads (conducts) to...; *dat leidt t o t niets* that leads nowhere (to nothing); **II** *va sp* lead [by ten points &]; zie ook: *geleid*; **-d** leading [persons, principle &]; guiding [motive, ground &]; executive [capacity in business and industry]; **'leider** (-s) *m* leader [of a party, some movement &]; director [of institution &]; [spiritual] guide; [sales, works] manager; **-schap** *o* leadership; **'leiding** (-en) *v* 1 (a b s t r a c t) leadership, conduct, guidance, direction, management; *sp* lead; 2 (c o n c r e e t) conduit, pipe, ☇ wire; *~ geven aan* lead; *de ~ hebben* be in control; *sp* lead; *de ~ (op zich) nemen* take the lead; *ik vertrouw hem aan uw ~ toe* I entrust him to your guidance; *onder ~ van...* under the guidance of...; [orchestra] conducted by, [a delegation] led by, [a committee] headed by...; **-water** *o* tap water, company's water; **'leidmotief** (-tieven) *o* leitmotiv[2], leading motive[2]

'leidraad (-draden) *m* guide; guide-book

'leidsel (-s) *o* rein; **'leidsman** (-lieden) *m* leader, guide[2]; **1 'leidster** [-stɛr] (-sterren) *v fig* guiding star; ☉ lodestar; **2 'leidster** [-stɔr] (-s) *v* (g e l e i d s t e r, l e i d s v r o u w) leader; guide; conductress

1 'leien F V.T. meerv. van *leggen*

2 'leien *aj* slate; *dat gaat van een ~ dakje* it goes smoothly (on wheels, without a hitch); **'leigroef** (-groeven), **-groeve** (-n) *v* slate quarry; **-kleurig** slate-coloured; **-steen** *o* & *m* slate

lek I (-ken) *o* leak [in a vessel]; leakage, escape [of gas]; puncture [in a bicycle tire]; *een ~ krijgen* spring a leak; *een ~ stoppen* stop a leak[2]; **II** *aj* leaky; *~ke band* punctured tire, flat tyre, F a flat; *~ zijn* be leaky, leak; ⚓ make water

'lekebroeder (-s) *m* lay brother

'leken V.T. meerv. van *lijken*

'lekenapostolaat *o* apostolate of the laity, lay

apostolate; **-dom** *o* laity; **'lekespel** (-spelen) *o* ± nativity play; **-zuster** (-s) *v* lay sister

lek'kage [lɛ'ka.ʒə] (-s) *v* leakage, leak; **'lekken** (lekte, h. en is gelekt) *vi* leak, be leaky, have a leak; ‖ lick [of flames]; *een ~de* (*waterkraan*) ook: a dripping tap; *de ~de vlammen* ook: the lambent flames

'lekker I *aj* 1 (v. s m a a k) nice, delicious, good; 2 (v. r e u k) nice, sweet; 3 (v. w e e r) nice, fine; *ik vind 't niet ~* I don't like it; *ik ben weer zo ~ als kip* I am as fit as a fiddle; *ik voel me niet ~* I feel out of sorts, I am (feel) under the weather; *iem. ~ maken* 1 butter sbd. up; 2 set sbd. agog; *~, dat je nu ook eens straf hebt!* serve you right!; *~ is maar een vinger lang* what is sweet cannot last long; *geef ons wat ~s* give us something nice (to eat); *het is wat ~s!* a nice job, indeed!; **II** *ad* nicely; *heb je ~ gegeten?* 1 did you enjoy your meal?; 2 did you have a nice meal?; *ik doe het ~(tjes) niet* F catch me doing it; *dat heb je nou eens ~(tjes) mis* yah, out you are!; *het is hier ~ warm* it is nice and warm here; **-bek** (-ken) *m* gourmand, epicure, dainty feeder; **-bekje** (-s) *o* fried fillet of haddock; **lekker'nij** (-en) *v* dainty, titbit, delicacy; **'lekkers** *o* sweets, sweetmeats, goodies; **'lekkertje** (-s) *o* sweet[2]

lel (-len) *v* 1 lobe [of the ear]; 2 wattle, gill [of a cock]; 3 uvula [of the throat]; 4 F (k l a p) whack, clout; 5 = *lellebel*

'lelie (-s en ☉ -iën) *v* lily; **-blank** as white as a lily, lily-white; **lelietje-van-'dalen** (lelietjes-) *o* lily of the valley

'lelijk I *aj* ugly[2] [houses, faces, rumours &]; plain [girls]; nasty [smell &]; badly [wounded &]; *~ als de nacht* as ugly as sin; *dat is ~, ik heb mijn sleutel verloren* that's awkward; *dat staat u ~* it does not become you[2]; *dat ziet er ~ uit* things look bad (black), it's a pretty mess, that's a bad outlook; *een ~ gezicht trekken* make a wry face, scowl; *~e woorden zeggen* use bad language; **II** *ad* uglily; badly; *~ vallen* have a bad fall; **-erd** (-s) *m* ugly person; **-heid** *v* ugliness, plainness

'lellebel (-len) *v* slut, hussy

1 'lemen (leemde, h. geleemd) *vt* loam, cover (coat) with loam; **2 'lemen** *aj* loam, mud [hut]; *~ voeten* feet of clay

'lemma (-ta en 's) *o* headword [in a dictionary &]

'lemmer (-s), **'lemmet** (-en) *o* blade [of a knife]

'lende (-n en -nen) *v* loin; **'lendendoek** (-en) *m* loin-cloth; **'lendepijn** (-en) *v* lumbar pain, lumbago; **-streek** *m* small of the back; **-stuk** (-ken) *o* sirloin [of beef]; **-wervel** (-s) *m* lumbar vertebra

'lenen (leende, h. geleend) **I** *vt* (a a n

i e m a n d) lend (to), (v a n i e m a n d) borrow
(of, from); **II** *vr zich ~ tot...* lend oneself (itself)
to...; **–er** (-s) *m* (a a n i e m a n d) lender, (v a n
i e m a n d) borrower
leng (-en) *m* 🐟 ling; ‖ *o* ⚓ sling
'lengen (lengde, h. & is gelengd) *vi* become
longer, lengthen, draw out [of the days];
'lengte (-s en -n) *v* 1 length; 2 (v a n
p e r s o o n) height; 3 (a a r d r ij k s k.) longitude; *tot i n ~ van dagen* for many years to
come; *in de ~ doorzagen* lengthwise, length-
ways; *3 m in de ~* 3 metres in length; *in zijn
volle ~* (at) full length; **–as** *v* longitudinal axis;
–cirkel (-s) *m* meridian; **–dal** (-dalen) *o*
longitudinal valley; **–graad** (-graden) *m*
degree of longitude; **–maat** (-maten) *v* linear
measure
'lenig lithe, supple, pliant
'lenigen (lenigde, h. gelenigd) *vt* alleviate,
relieve, assuage
'lenigheid *v* litheness, suppleness, pliancy
'leniging *v* alleviation, relief, assuagement
'lening (-en) *v* loan; *een ~ sluiten* contract a
loan; *een ~ uitschrijven* issue a loan; *een ~
verstrekken* make a loan
1 lens (lenzen) *v* lens [of a camera &]
2 lens *aj* empty; *de pomp is ~* the pump sucks;
hij is ~ **F** he is cleaned out
'lensvormig lens-shaped, lenticular
'lente (-s) *v* spring²; **–achtig** spring-like;
–bode (-n en -s) *m* harbinger of spring; **–dag**
(-dagen) *m* day in spring, spring-day; **–lied**
(-eren) *o* vernal song, spring-song; **–maand**
(-en) *v* month of spring; March; *de lentemaanden*
the spring-months; **–tijd** *m* springtime
'lenzen (lensde, h. gelensd) *vt* empty
'lepel (-s) *m* 1 (o m t e e t e n) spoon; (o m
o p t e s c h e p p e n) ladle; 2 (v o l l e
l e p e l) spoonful; 3 ear [of a hare]
'lepelaar (-s en -laren) *m* ⚑ spoonbill
'lepelblad (-bladen) *o* bowl [of a spoon];
'lepelen (lepelde, h. gelepeld) **I** *vi* use one's
spoon; **II** *vt* spoon; ladle; **'lepelvormig**
spoon-shaped
'leperd (-s) *m* slyboots, cunning fellow
'leppen (lepte, h. gelept), **'lepperen** (lepperde,
h. gelepperd) *vi* & *vt* sip, lap, lick
'lepra *v* leprosy; **–lijder** (-s), **le'proos** (-prozen)
m leper
'leraar (-s en -raren) *m* 1 🖝 teacher; 2 (g e e s -
t e l ij k e) minister; *~ in natuur- en scheikunde*
science master; **'leraarsambt** *o* 🖝 mastership;
–kamer (-s) *v* (masters') common room, staff
room; **lera'res** (-sen) *v* (woman) teacher,
mistress; *~ in natuur- en scheikunde* science
mistress; **1 'leren** (leerde, h. geleerd) **I** *vi*
learn; **II** *vt* teach [a person]; learn [lessons &];

~ lezen learn to read; *uit 't hoofd ~* memorize;
iem. ~ lezen teach sbd. to read; *wacht, ik zal je
~!* I'll teach you!
2 'leren *aj* leather
'lering (-en) *v* 1 instruction; 2 = *catechisatie*;
ergens ~ uit trekken learn from sth.
les (-sen) *v* lesson; *~ geven* give lessons, teach; *~
hebben* be having one's lesson; *de onderwijzer heeft
~* is in class; *we hebben vandaag geen ~* no lessons
to-day; *iem. de ~ lezen* lecture sbd.; *~ nemen*
(bij)... take lessons (from)...; *onder de ~* during
lessons; **–auto** [-ɔuto.,-o.to.] ('s) *m* learner car
lesbi'enne (-s) *v*, **'lesbisch** *aj* lesbian
'lesgeld *o* lesson-money, fee, tuition;
'lesgeven (gaf 'les, h. 'lesgegeven) *vi* teach,
instruct; **'lesje** (-s) *o* lesson; *iem. een ~ geven*
teach sbd. a lesson; **'leslokaal** (-kalen) *o*
class-room; **–rooster** (-s) *m* & *o* time-table
Le'sotho *o* Lesotho
'lessen (leste, 'h. gelest) *vt* quench, slake [one's
thirst]
'lessenaar (-s) *m* desk; reading-desk, writing-
desk
lest last; *~ best* the best is at the bottom; *ten
langen ~e* at long last
'lestoestel (-len) *o* 🚗 trainer; **–uur** (-uren) *o*
lesson; *per ~ betalen* pay by the lesson; **–vliegtuig** (-en) *o* trainer; **–wagen** (-s) *m* 🚗 learner
car
le'taal lethal
lethar'gie *v* lethargy; **le'thargisch** lethargic
'Letland *o* Latvia; **–s** Latvian
'letsel (-s) *o* injury, hurt, [bodily] harm; damage;
een ~ krijgen receive an injury; *zonder ~*
unharmed
1 'letten (lette, h. gelet) *vi let wel!* mind!, mark
you!; *~ op* attend to, mind, pay attention to;
take notice of; *op de kosten zal niet gelet worden*
the cost is no consideration; *let op mijn woorden*
mark my words; *gelet op...* in view of...
2 'letten (lette, h. gelet) *vt wat let me of ik...* what
prevents me from ...ing
'letter (-s en -en) *v* letter, character, type; *met
grote ~* in big letters; *kleine ~* small letter; *met
kleine ~ (gedrukt)* in small type; *i n de ~en
studeren* study literature; *n a a r de ~* to the
letter; **–dief** (-dieven) *m* plagiarist; **letter-
dieve'rij** (-en) *v* plagiarism; *~ plegen* plagiarize; **'letteren** (letterde, h. geletterd) *vt* letter,
mark; **'lettergieter** (-s) *m* type-founder;
lettergiete'rij (-en) *v* type-foundry; **'lettergreep** (-grepen) *v* syllable; **–kast** (-en) *v*
type-case; **–knecht** (-en) *m* literalist; **letter-
knechte'rij** *v* literalism; **'letterkorps** (-en) *o*
size of type; **–kunde** *v* literature;
letter'kundig literary; **–e** (-n) *m* man of
letters, literary man, bookman; **'letterlijk I** *aj*

literal; **II** *ad* literally, to the letter; *zij werden ~ gedecimeerd* they were literally decimated; **'letterraadsel** (-s) *o* word-puzzle; **–schrift** *o* writing in characters; **–slot** (-sloten) *o* letter-lock; **–soort** (-en) *v* (kind of) type; **–specie, –spijs** *v* type-metal; **–teken** (-s) *o* character; **–type** [-ti.pǝ] (-n en -s) *o* (kind of) type; **–woord** (-en) *o* acronym; **'letterzetten** *o* type-setting; **–er** (-s) *m* compositor, type-setter; **letterzette'rij** (-en) *v* composing room; **–zifte'rij** (-en) *v* hair-splitting

leugen (-s) *v* lie, falsehood; *dat is een grote (grove) ~* that is a big lie; *al is de ~ nog zo snel, de waarheid achterhaalt haar wel* liars have short memories; **'leugenaar** (-s) *m*, **–ster** (-s) *v* liar; **'leugenachtig** lying, mendacious, untruthful, false; **–heid** *v* mendacity, falseness; **'leugen-campagne** [-kɑmpɑɲǝ] (-s) *v* lying campaign, smear lying; **–detector** (-s en -toren) *m* lie-detector; **–taal** *v* lying, lies; **–tje** (-s) *o* fib; *~ om bestwil* white lie

leuk *aj* 1 (g r a p p i g) amusing, funny [story], arch [way of telling]; 2 (a a r d i g, p r e t t i g) jolly, pleasant; 3 (o n b e w o g e n) cool, dry, sly [fellow]; *dat zal ~ zijn* that will be great fun, won't it be jolly!; *ik vind het erg ~!* (I think it) fine!; *het was erg ~!* such fun!; *hij vond het niets ~* he did not much like it; *die is ~, zeg!* that's a good one; *zo ~ als wat, zei hij...* with the coolest cheek he said; *het ~ste is dat...* the richest point about the story is that...

leuk(a)e'mie [lœy-, lø.ke.'mi.] *v* leuk(a)emia

'leukerd (-s) *m* **F** funny chap; **'leukweg** dryly

'leunen (leunde, h. geleund) *vi* lean (on *op*; against *tegen*); **'leuning** (-en) *v* 1 rail; banisters, handrail [of a staircase]; parapet [of a bridge]; 2 back [of a chair]; arm(-rest) [of a chair]; **'leunstoel** (-en) *m* arm-chair

'leuren (leurde, h. geleurd) *vi* hawk; *~ met* hawk

leus (leuzen) *v* slogan, catchword, watchword

leut *v* 1 fun; 2 **F** coffee; *voor de ~* for fun

'leuteraar (-s) *m* 1 (k l e t s e r) twaddler, driveller; 2 (t a l m e r) dawdler; **'leuteren** (leuterde, h. geleuterd) *vi* 1 (k l e t s e n) twaddle, drivel; 2 (t a l m e n) dawdle; **'leuter-praat** *m* twaddle, drivel

'leutig jolly

'leuze (-n) *v = leus*

Le'vant *m* Levant; **Levan'tijn** (-en) *m* Levantine; **–s** Levantine

'leven (leefde, h. geleefd) **I** *vi* live; *leve...!* three cheers for... [France]; hurrah for... [the holidays &]; *leve de koning!* long live the King!; *~ en laten* ~ live and let live; *wie dan leeft, die dan zorgt* sufficient unto the day is the evil thereof; *van brood alleen kan men niet ~* we cannot live by bread alone; *van gras ~* live (feed) on grass;

daar kan ik niet van ~ I cannot subsist (live) on that; *alleen v o o r... ~* live only for...; **II** (-s) *o* 1 life; 2 (h e t l e v e n d d e e l) the quick; 3 (r u m o e r) noise; *~ in de brouwerij brengen* liven things up; *er komt ~ in de brouwerij* things are beginning to move (to hum); *daar had je het lieve ~ aan de gang* then there was the devil to pay; *er zit geen ~ in* there is no life (spirit) in it; *wel, al m'n ~!* Well, I never!; *een ander (nieuw) ~ beginnen* begin a new life, turn over a new leaf; *zijn ~ beteren* mend one's ways; *in ~ blijven* keep body and soul together; *~ geven aan* give life to, put life into [a statue], zie ook: *schenken*; *zijn ~ geven voor* lay down (sacrifice) one's life for [one's country]; *geen ~ hebben* lead a wretched life; *iets nieuw ~ inblazen* put new life into sth.; *het ~ erbij inschieten, het ~ laten* lose one's life; *~ maken* make a noise; ● *bij het ~ h e v i g e m a t e* intensely, with a will; *bij zijn ~* during his life, in his lifetime, in life; *bij ~ en welzijn* if I have life; *nog i n ~ zijn* be still alive; *in ~ notaris te... in his lifetime; in her ~ blijven* remain (keep) alive, live; *in het ~ houden* keep alive; *in het ~ roepen* bring (call) into being (existence), create; *zijn ~ lang* all his life; *n a a r het ~ getekend* drawn from (the) life; *iem. naar het ~ staan* seek to kill sbd.; *o m het ~ brengen* kill, do to death; *om het ~ komen* lose one's life, perish; *een strijd o p ~ en dood* a fight to the death, a life-and-death struggle; *zijn ~ op het spel zetten* take one's life in one's hands; *weer t o t ~ brengen* resuscitate; *u i t het ~ gegrepen* taken from life; *v a n mijn ~ heb ik zoiets niet gezien* never in my life; *nooit van mijn ~!* never!; *wel heb je van je ~!* Well, I never!; not on your life!, not for the life of me!; *de kans (de schrik &) van mijn ~* the chance (the fright &) of my life; *v o o r het ~ benoemd (gekozen)* for life; *z o l a n g er ~ is, is er hoop* as long as there is life there is hope; **'levend** alive [a l l e e n p r e d i k a-t i e f !]; living; quickset [hedge]; *de ~e talen* the modern languages; *~ maken (worden)* bring (come) to life; *iem. ~ verbranden* burn sbd. alive; **–barend** viviparous; **'levendig I** *aj* lively, animated [discussion], vivid [imagination], green [memories], vivacious [person], keen [interest], $ active [market], brisk [demand]; **II** *ad* in a lively manner; *ik kan mij ~ voorstellen* I can well imagine; **–heid** *v* liveliness, vivacity; **'levenloos** lifeless, inanimate

'levensadem *m* breath of life, life-breath; **–ader** *v* life-blood artery, fountain of life; *fig* life artery, life-line; **–avond** *m* evening of life; **–beginsel** (-en en -s) *o* principle of life; **–behoeften** *mv* necessaries of life; **–behoud** *o* preservation of life; **–belang** *o* vital importance; **–beschouwing** (-en) *v* weltanschauung; **–beschrijving** (-en) *v* biography, life; **–bron** (-nen) *v* source of life, lifespring; **–dagen** *mv al zijn ~* his whole life; *wel heb ik van mijn ~!* Well, I never!, did you ever!, by Jove!; **–doel** *o* aim of life, aim in life; **–drang** *m* life-force, vital force (urge); **–duur** *m* length of life; lifetime; (t e c h n i s c h) service life; life; *vermoedelijke ~* expectation of life; **–elixer** (-s), **–elixir** (-s) *o* elixir of life; **–geesten** *mv* vital spirits; *de ~ weer opwekken bij* resuscitate; *de ~ waren geweken* life was extinct; **–genieter** (-s) *m* epicure; **–gevaar** *o* danger (peril) of life; *i n ~* in peril of one's life; *m e t ~* at the peril (risk) of one's life; **levensge'vaarlijk** dangerous to life, involving risk of life, perilous; **'levensgezel** (-len) *m*, **–gezellin** (-nen) *v* partner for life; **–groot** life-sized, life-size, as large as life; *meer dan ~* larger than life, over life-size; **–houding** (-en) *v* attitude to life; **–kracht** (-en) *v* vital power, vitality; **levens'krachtig** 1 full of life; 2 = *levensvatbaar*; **'levenskwestie** (-s) *v* vital question, question of life and death; **–lang I** *aj & ad* for life, lifelong; *tot ~e gevangenschap veroordeeld worden* be sentenced to imprisonment for life, get a life sentence; **II** *sb* (= *levenslange gevangenisstraf*) **F** lifer; **–licht** *o het ~ aanschouwen* be born, see the light; **–loop** *m* course of life, career; **–lust** *m* zest for life, love of live, animal spirits; **levens'lustig** cheerful, vivacious, sprightly, buoyant; **'levensmiddelen** *mv* provisions, victuals; foodstuffs, food(s); **–bedrijf** (-drijven) *o* grocer's shop; **'levensmoe(de)** weary of life; **–omstandigheden** *mv* circumstances in life, living conditions; **–onderhoud** *o* livelihood, sustenance; *kosten van ~* cost of living, living costs; **–opvatting** (-en) *v* philosophy of life; **–pad** (-paden) *o* path of life; **–standaard** *m* standard of life, standard of living, living standard; **–teken** (-s en -en) *o* sign of life; *~en vertonen* show life; **levens'vatbaar** viable, capable of living; **–heid** *v* viability, vitality; **'levensverzekering** (-en) *v* life-assurance, life-insurance; *een ~ sluiten* take out a life-policy, insure one's life; **–(s)maatschappij** (-en) *v* life-insurance (life-assurance) company; **'levensvoorwaarde** (-n) *v* condition of life; *fig* vital condition; **–vraag** (-vragen) *v* = *levenskwestie*; **–vreugde** *v* joy of life, delight in life; **–wandel** *m* conduct in life, life; **–weg** *m* path of life; **–werk** *o* life-work; **–wijsheid** (-heden) *v* wisdom of life; **–wijze** (-n) *v* mode of life, way of living; conduct

'leventje *o* life; *dat was me een ~!* 1 what a jolly life we had of it!; 2 (i r o n i s c h) what a life!;

'levenwekkend life-giving, vivifying

'lever (-s) *v* liver

leveran'cier (-s) *m* 1 contractor, supplier, purveyor, dealer; 2 provider, caterer; *de ~s* ook: the tradesmen; leve'rantie [-'ran(t)si.] (-s) *v* supply(ing), purveyance; **'leverbaar** 1 (a f t e l e v e r e n) deliverable, ready for delivery; 2 (t e v e r s c h a f f e n) available; *beperkt ~* in short supply; **'leveren** (leverde, h. geleverd) *vt* 1 (a f l e v e r e n) deliver; 2 (v e r s c h a f f e n) furnish, supply [goods], provide; contribute [an article to a newspaper]; *achterhoedegevechten ~* fight rearguard actions; *er zijn hevige gevechten geleverd* there was heavy fighting, heavy fighting took place; *~ aan* cater for; *(aan) iem. brandstoffen ~* supply sbd. with fuel; *het bewijs ~ dat...* prove that...; *stof ~ voor* provide matter for [discussion, a novel]; *hij heeft prachtig werk geleverd* he has done splendid work; *hij zal het hem wel ~* he is sure to manage it; *wie heeft me dat geleverd?* who has played me that trick?; **–ring** (-en) *v* 1 (a f l e v e r i n g) delivery; 2 (v e r s c h a f f i n g) supply; **'leveringscondities** [-kòndi.(t)si.s] *mv* = *leveringsvoorwaarden*; **–contract** (-en) *o* delivery contract; **–datum** (-data en -s) *m* delivery date; **–termijn** (-en) *m* time (term) of delivery; **–tijd** (-en) *m* delivery period, delivery time; **–voorwaarden** *mv* terms of delivery

'leverkleurig liver-coloured; **–pastei** (-en) *v* liver pie

'levertijd (-en) *m* = *leveringstijd*

'levertraan *m* cod-liver oil; **–worst** (-en) *v* liver sausage

le'viet (-en) *m* Levite

lexico'graaf (-grafen) *m* lexicographer; **lexicogra'fie** *v* lexicography; **lexico'grafisch** lexicographical; **'lexicon** (-s) *o* lexicon

'lezen* I *vi* read [ook = give a lecture]; **II** *vt* 1 read [books]; 2 glean, gather [ears of corn]; *het stond op zijn gezicht te ~* it was written on his face, it was depicted in his face; *het boek laat zich gemakkelijk ~* reads easily, makes easy reading; zie ook: *les, mis &*; **levens'waard(ig)** readable, worth reading; **'lezer** (-s) *m*, **leze'res** (-sen) *v* 1 reader; 2 gleaner, gatherer [of grapes &]; **'lezerskring** (-en) *m* readership; circulation; **'lezing** (-en) *v* 1 (v. b a r o m e t e r &) reading; 2 (i n t e r p r e t a t i e) version; 3 (v o o r l e z i n g) lecture; *een ~ houden* give a lecture, lecture (on *over*)

li'aan (lianen), **liane** (-n) *v* 🌿 liana, liane

liai'son [li.ε'zõ] (-s) *v* liaison

'lias (-sen) *v* file

Liba'nees I *aj* Lebanese; **II** (-nezen) *m* Lebanese; *de Libanezen* the Lebanese; **'Libanon** *m* (the) Lebanon

li′bel (-len) *v* 🦟 dragon-fly

libe′raal I *aj* liberal; **II** (-ralen) *m* liberal; **liberali′seren** [s = z] (liberaliseerde, h. geliberaliseerd) *vt* liberalize; **−ring** *v* liberalization; **libera′lisme** *o* liberalism

Li′beria *o* Liberia

liber′tijn (-en) *m* libertine; **−s** licentious; (w u l p s) lascivious

′libido *m* libido

′Libië *o* Libya;**′Libiër** (-s) *m*, **′Libisch** *aj* Libyan

li′bretto (′s en libretti) *o* libretto, book (of words)

li′centie [li.′sɛn(t)si.] (-s) *v* licence; *in ~ vervaardigd* manufactured under licence; **−houder** (-s) *m* licensee

′lichaam (-chamen) *o* body°, frame; *naar ~ en ziel* in body and mind; **′lichaamsarbeid** *m* bodily labour; **−beweging** (-en) *v* physical exercise; **−bouw** *m* build, stature; **−deel** (-delen) *o* part of the body; **−gebrek** (-breken) *o* bodily defect; **−gestel** *o* constitution; **−gewicht** *o* body weight; **−houding** (-en) *v* posture, carriage of the body; **−kracht** (-en) *v* physical strength, force; **−oefening** (-en) *v* bodily exercise; **−temperatuur** (-turen) *v* body temperature, blood-heat; **li′chamelijk I** *aj* corporal [punishment], corporeal [being]; bodily [harm &]; physical [culture, education, work]; **II** *ad* corporally, physically

1 licht I *aj* 1 (n i e t d o n k e r) light² [materials], light-coloured [dresses], bright [day]; fair [hair]; 2 (n i e t z w a a r²) light [weight, bread, work, sleep, troops, step]; slight [wound, repast, cold]; mild [beer, tobacco]; 3 (v a n z e d e n) wanton [woman]; *het wordt al ~* it is getting light; *~ in het hoofd* light-headed; **II** *ad* 1 lightly, slightly; 2 easily; zie ook: *allicht*; *~ gewond* slightly wounded; *het ~ opnemen* make light of it, take it lightly; *men vergeet ~ dat...* one is apt to forget that...; *het wordt ~ een gewoonte* it tends to become a habit; **2 licht** (-en) *o* light²; *fig* luminary; *~ en schaduw* light(s) and shade(s)²; *hij is geen ~* he is no great light (luminary); *je bent me ook een ~!* what a shining light you are!; *er gaat mij een ~ op* now I begin to see light; *er ging mij een ~ op* it dawned on me; *~ geven* give off light; *iem. het ~ in de ogen niet gunnen* grudge sbd. the light of his eyes; *wij zullen eens wat ~ maken* (m e t l u c i f e r s) we'll strike a light; (d o o r l a m p l i c h t) we'll have the lamp(s) lighted; (e l e k t r i s c h) we'll turn (switch) on the light; *het ~ opsteken* light the lamp; *fig [bij iem.] z′n ~ opsteken* make inquiries, inform oneself [about sth.]; *het ~ schuwen* shun the light; *(een helder) ~ werpen op* throw (shed)

(a bright) light upon; *zijn ~ onder de korenmaat zetten* hide one's light under a bushel; *het ~ zien* see the light; ● *a a n het ~ brengen* bring to light, reveal; *aan het ~ komen* come (be brought) to light; *een boek i n het ~ geven* publish a book; *zichzelf in het ~ staan* stand in one's own light; *iets in een gunstig (ongunstig) ~ stellen* place (put) it in a favourable (unfavourable) light; paint it in bright (dark) colours; *iets in een helder ~ stellen* throw light upon sth.; *iets in een heel ander ~ zien* see sth. in a totally different light; *t e g e n het ~ houden* hold (up) to the light; *t u s s e n ~ en donker* in the twilight; *ga u i t het ~* stand out of my (the) light; **−bak** (-ken) *m* 1 (a l s r e c l a m e) illuminated sign; 2 (v a n s t r o p e r s) light; **−baken** (-s) *o* beacon (light); **−beeld** (-en) *o* lantern view; **−blauw** light (pale) blue; **−blond** light(-blond), fair; **−boei** (-en) *v* light-buoy; **−boog** (-bogen) *m* electric arc; **−bron** (-nen) *v* source of light; **−bruin** light brown; **−bundel** (-s) *m* pencil of rays, beam of light; **−druk** (-ken) *m* phototype; **−echt** fast; **−effect** (-en) *o* effect(s) of light, light-effect(s); **′lichtekooi** (-en) *v* light-o-love, prostitute; **′lichtelijk** somewhat, a little, slightly; **1 ′lichten** (lichtte, h. gelicht) *vt* 1 (o p l i c h t e n) lift, raise; 2 ⚓ weigh [anchor]; raise [a sunken ship]; 3 📮 clear [the letter-boxes]; zie ook: *doopceel, hand, hiel, voet* &; **2 ′lichten** (lichtte, h. gelicht) *vi* 1 (l i c h t g e-v e n) give light, shine; 2 (l i c h t w o r d e n) get light, dawn; 3 (w e e r l i c h t e n) lighten; *het ~ van de zee* the phosphorescence of the sea; **−d** luminous, shining [example]; phosphorescent; **′lichter** (-s) *m* ⚓ lighter; **′lichte(r)laaie** *in ~ staan* be ablaze; **′lichtfakkel** (-s) *v* ⚐ flare; **−filter** (-s) *m* & *o* light (colour) filter; **−gas** *o* illuminating gas, coal-gas; **−geel** light yellow; **lichtge′lovig** credulous; **−heid** *v* credulousness, credulity; **lichtge′raakt** quick to take offence, touchy, huffish; **−heid** *v* touchiness; **′lichtgevend** luminous; **lichtge′voelig** light-sensitive; **′lichtgewapend** light-armed; **−gewicht** (-en) *m* light-weight²; **−grijs** light grey; **−groen** light green; **licht′hartig** light-hearted; **′lichtheid** *v* lightness; easiness; **′lichting** (-en) *v* 1 📮 collection; 2 ⚔ draft, levy; *de ~ 1955* ⚔ the 1955 class; **′lichtinstallatie** [-(t)si.] (-s) *v* (electric) light-plant; **−jaar** (-jaren) *o* light-year; **−kegel** (-s) *m* cone of light; **−kever** (-s) *m* fire-fly, glow-worm; **−kogel** (-s) *m* Very light, signal flare; **−krans** (-en) *m* 1 wreath of light, halo [round a saint's head, round sun or moon]; 2 [round the sun] corona; **−krant** (-en) *v* illuminated news trailer; **−kroon** (-kronen) *v* chandelier; **−leiding** (-en) *v* (b u i t e n) electric main, (b i n n e n) electric wire; **–mast** (-en) *m* light standard; **–matroos** (-trozen) *m* ordinary seaman; **–meter** (-s) *m* 1 photometer; 2 (v a n c a m e r a) lightmeter; **–mis** (-sen) *m* libertine, rake, debauchee; **–net** (-ten) *o* (electric) mains; **–prikkel** (-s) *m* luminous stimulus; **–punt** (-en) *o* 1 luminous point; *fig* bright spot; 2 ⚓ connection; **–reclame** (-s) *v* illuminated sign(s) (advertising); **–rood** light red, pink; **–schip** (-schepen) *o* lightship; **–schuw** shunning the light²; ~ *gespuis* shady characters; **licht′schuwheid** *v* photophobia; **′lichtsein** (-en) *o*, **–signaal** [-sı̣na.l] (-nalen) *o* light signal; **–sterkte** *v* luminosity, light intensity; *de* ~ *is*... the candle-power is...; **–straal** (-stralen) *m* & *v* ray of light, beam of light; **licht′vaardig** rash; **′lichtzijde** (-n) *v* bright side; **licht′zinnig** frivolous; **–heid** (-heden) *v* levity, frivolity

lid (leden) *o* 1 (v. l i c h a a m) limb; (v a n v e r e n i g i n g) member; (v. v i n g e r) phalanx [*mv* phalanges]; (v. w e t s a r t i k e l) paragraph; (v. v e r g e l ij k i n g) term; 2 (g e w r i c h t) joint; 3 (v. v e r w a n t s c h a p) degree, generation; 4 (d e k s e l) lid [of the eye]; 5 (p e n i s) member, penis; ~ *worden van* join [a club, a party]; become a member of; ● *een arm weer i n het* ~ *zetten* reduce an arm; *een ziekte o n d e r de leden hebben* be sickening for something; *o v e r al zijn leden beven* tremble in every limb; *t o t in het vierde* ~ to the fourth generation; *mijn arm is u i t het* ~ out (of joint), dislocated; **–cactus** (-sen) *m* crab cactus; **–maat** (-maten) *m* member; **–maatschap** *o* membership; **′lid-staat** (-staten) *m* member state; **′lidwoord** (-en) *o gram* article

lied (-eren) *o* 1 song; [church] hymn; ⊙ lay [of a minstrel]; **–boek** (-en) = *liederboek*

′lieden *mv* people, folks, men

′liederboek (-en) *o* book of songs, songbook; **′liederen** meerv. v. *lied*

′liederlijk I *aj* dissolute, debauched; < wretched, beastly; ~*e taal* coarse language; II *ad* dissolutely; < abominably, horribly; **–heid** (-heden) *v* dissoluteness, debauchery

′liedje (-s) *o* song, tune, ditty, (street-)ballad; *het is altijd hetzelfde (oude)* ~ it is always the same (old) song; *een ander* ~ *zingen* [*fig*] change one's tune; *het eind van het* ~ the end of the matter, the upshot; *het* ~ *van verlangen zingen* dawdle at bedtime for a few moments' grace [of children]; **–zanger** (-s) *m* ballad-singer

1 lief I *aj* 1 (b e m i n d) dear, beloved; 2 (b e m i n n e l ij k) amiable; 3 (a a n m i n n i g) sweet, pretty; 4 (a a r d i g v o o r a n d e r e n) nice; 5 (v r i e n d e l ij k) kind; 6 (i r o n i s c h) nice, fine; *toen had je het lieve leven gaande* then

there was the devil to pay; *maar mijn lieve mensen...* but my dear people...; *dat is erg* ~ *van hem* very kind (nice) of him; *...meer dan me* ~ *is* ...more than I care for; **II** *ad* amiably, sweetly, nicely, kindly; ~ *doen* do the amiable; *iets voor* ~ *nemen* put up with sth.; *ik wou net zo* ~... I would just as soon...; zie ook: *liefst* en *liever*;

2 lief (lieven) *o* (g e l i e f d e) love, sweetheart; *in* ~ *en leed* in weal and woe

lief′dadig I *aj* charitable; **II** *ad* charitably; **–heid** *v* charity; **lief′dadigheidsinstelling** (-en) *v* charitable institution; **–voorstelling** (-en) *v* charity performance

′liefde (-s en -n) *v* love; ⚒ (c h r i s t e l ij k e) charity; *kinderlijke* ~ filial piety; *de* ~ *voor de kunst* the love of art; ~ *tot God* love of God; *de* ~ *bedrijven* make love; *uit* ~ for (out of, from) love; *een huwelijk uit* ~ a love-match; *oude* ~ *roest niet* old love never dies; **–blijk** (-en) *o* token of love; **–dienst** (-en) *m* act of charity (of kindness); **–gave** (-n) *v* alms, charity; **–leven** *o* love-life; **–loos** loveless, uncharitable; **–rijk I** *aj* charitable; **II** *ad* charitably; **′liefdesbetuiging** (-en) *v* profession of love; **–brief** (-brieven) *m* love-letter; **–geschiedenis** (-sen) *v* 1 love-story; 2 love-affair; **′liefdesmart** (-en) *v* pangs of love; **′liefde(s)verklaring** (-en) *v* declaration (of love); **′liefdevol** full of love, loving; **–werk** (-en) *o* charitable deed, good work; **–zuster** (-s) *v* sister of charity; **liefdoene′rij** *v* demonstrative affection; **′liefelijk I** *aj* lovely, sweet; **II** *ad* in a lovely manner, sweetly; **–heid** *v* loveliness, sweetness; *liefelijkheden* (feline) amenities; **′liefhebben** (had ′lief, h. ′liefgehad) *vt* love, cherish; **–d** loving, affectionate; *uw* ~*e*... yours affectionately; **′liefhebber** (-s) *m*, **–ster** (-s) *v* 1 amateur, lover; 2 = *gegadigde*; *er zijn veel* ~*s* there is a keen demand [for it]; *er zijn geen* ~*s voor* people are not interested; *hij is een* ~ *van roken* he is fond of smoking; *hij is daar geen* ~ *van* he doesn't like it; **′liefhebberen** (liefhebberde, h. liefgehebberd) *vi* do amateur work; dabble [in politics &]; **liefhebbe′rij** (-en) *v* hobby; **′liefje** (-s) *o* sweetheart, F ducks; F dreamboat; **′liefkozen** (liefkoosde, h. geliefkoosd) *vt* caress, fondle; **–zing** (-en) *v* caress; **′liefkrijgen** (kreeg ′lief, h. ′liefgekregen) *vt* get (grow) to like, grow fond of; **′lieflijk(-)** = *liefelijk*(-); **liefst I** *aj* dearest, favourite; **II** *ad* rather; *wat heb je ′t* ~? which do you like best, which do you prefer?; ~ *die soort* preferably [that sort], ...for preference; ~ *niet* rather not; **′liefste** (-n) 1 *m* sweetheart, lover; 2 *v* sweetheart, beloved; **lief′tallig I** *aj* sweet; **II** *ad* sweetly; **–heid** (-heden) *v* sweetness

'liegen* I *vi* & *va* lie, tell lies, tell stories; *lieg er nu maar niet om* don't lie about it; *de brief liegt er niet om* the letter is very explicit; *de cijfers ~ er niet om* the figures speak for themselves; *hij liegt alsof het gedrukt is* he is a terrible liar; *als ik lieg, dan lieg ik in commissie* if it is a lie, you have the tale as cheap as I; **II** *vt dat lieg je, je liegt het* that's a lie

liep (liepen) V.T. v. *lopen*

lier (-en) *v* 1 ♪ lyre; ✗ (o r g e l t j e) hurdy-gurdy; 2 ⚓ winch; *branden als een ~* burn fiercely

li'ëren (lieerde, h. gelieerd) *vi* connect, unite, join

lies (liezen) *v* groin; **–breuk** (-en) *v* inguinal hernia; **–laars** (-laarzen) *v* thigh boot

liet (lieten) V.T. v. *laten*

lieve'heersbeestje (-s) *o* ladybird; **'lieveling** (-en) *m* darling, favourite, pet, love; **–dichter** (-s) *m* favourite poet; **lieve'moederen** *daar helpt geen ~ aan* there is no help for it; **'liever** I *aj* dearer; sweeter &; **II** *ad* rather; *ik heb dit huis ~* I like this house better, I prefer this house [to that]; *hij zou ~ sterven dan...* he would rather die than...; *ik zou er ~ niet heengaan* I had rather not go; *je moest maar ~ naar bed gaan* you'd (you had) better go to bed; *je moest daar ~ niet heengaan* you had better not go; *niets ~ verlangen (wensen, willen) dan...* want nothing better than...; *je kunt stuivers krijgen, als je dat ~ hebt* if you'd rather; *~ niet!* I'd rather not!; **'lieverd** (-s) *m* darling; **–je** (-s) *o* je bent me een *~!* you're a nice one!; **'lieverkoekjes** *mv ~ worden niet gebakken* if you don't like it you may lump it; **–lede** *van ~* gradually, by degrees, little by little; **lievevrouwe'bedstro** *o* woodruff; **'lievig** quasi-sweet

'liflafje (-s) *o* fancy dish, trifle

lift (-en) *m* lift, *Am* elevator; *een ~ geven (krijgen)* give (get) a lift; *een ~ vragen* thumb a lift; **'liften** (liftte, h. en is gelift) *v* hitch-hike; (m e t v r a c h t a u t o's) lorry-hop; **–er** (-s) *m* hitch-hiker; **'liftjongen** (-s) *m* lift-boy; **–kooi** (-en) *v* cage; **–koker** (-s) *m* lift-shaft

'liga ('s) *v* league

'ligdag (-dagen) *m* ⚓ lay-day; **–geld** (-en) *o* ⚓ 1 dock dues; 2 = *overliggeld*; **'liggen** *vi* lie [also of troops]; be situated; *de lonen ~ lager* wages are lower; *dat werk ligt me niet* the job does not suit me, it's not in my line; *altijd ~ te zeuren* always be bothering; *blijven ~* remain; *hij zal enige dagen moeten blijven ~* he will have to lie up for a couple of days; *morgen vroeg blijf ik wat (langer) ~* I'll remain in bed a little longer; *hij is gaan ~* 1 he has gone to bed; 2 he has taken to his bed; *ga daar ~* lie down there; *de wind is gaan ~* the wind has abated; *ik heb het geld ~* I

have the money ready; *iets nog hebben ~* have sth. in store (on hand); *laat dat ~!* leave it there!, leave it alone!; *hij heeft het lelijk laten ~* he has made a mess of it; ● *die stad ligt a a n een rivier* is situated on a river; *hij ligt al 8 dagen aan (met) die ziekte* he has been laid up (in bed) with it for a week; *dat ligt nog maar aan u* the issue lies with you; *als het aan mij lag* if I had any say in the matter; *aan mij zal het niet ~* it will be through no fault of mine; *waar ligt het aan, dat...?* what may be the cause (of it)?; *i n zijn bed ~* lie (be) in bed; *het huis ligt o p een heuvel* stands on a hill; *het huis ligt op het oosten* it has an eastern aspect, it faces east; *de wagen ligt vast op de weg* the car holds the road well; *hij lag t e bed* he was in bed; *~ te slapen* lie sleeping; *lie ook: bedoeling &*; **–d** lying, recumbent [position &]; turn-down [collar]; **'ligging** (-en) *v* situation, lie [of a house]; [geographical] position; (v. k i n d b i j b a r i n g) presentation; **'lighal** (-len) *v* (open-air) shelter; **–kuur** (-kuren) *v* rest-cure; **–plaats** (-en) *v* ⚓ berth, moorings; **–stoel** (-en) *m* reclining-chair, lounge-chair

li'guster (-s) *m* privet

lij *v* lee; *aan ~* alee, on the lee-side

'lijdelijk passive; **–heid** *v* passiveness, passivity; **'lijden*** I *vt* suffer, endure, bear; *dorst ~* suffer thirst; *iem. wel mogen ~* rather like sbd.; *ik mag ~ dat hij...* I wish he may...; **II** *vi* suffer; *nu kan het wel ~* we can afford it now; *~ a a n hoofdpijn* suffer from (be affected with) headaches; *erg ~ aan* ook: suffer a great deal from..., be a martyr to...; *~ o n d e r iets* suffer under sth.; *zij ~ er het meest onder* they are the greatest sufferers; *te ~ hebben van* suffer from; **III** *o* suffering(s); *het ~ van Christus* the Passion of Christ; *n a ~ komt verblijden* after rain comes sunshine; *u i t zijn ~ verlossen* put out of (his) misery; **–d** suffering; *gram* passive; *de ~e partij* the suffering party, the sufferer; *de ~e partij zijn* be the loser; *~ voorwerp* direct object; *de ~e vorm van het werkwoord* the passive voice; **'lijdensgeschiedenis** (-sen) *v* Passion [of Christ]; *het is een hele ~* it is a long tale of misery (of woe); **–kelk** *m* cup of bitterness; **–preek** (-preken) *v* Passion sermon; **–week** (-weken) *v* Holy Week; **–weg** (-wegen) *m* way of the Cross; *fig* [long] martyrdom; **'lijder** (-s) *m* sufferer, patient; **'lijdzaam** patient, meek; **–heid** *v* patience, meekness

lijf (lijven) *o* body; *het a a n den lijve ondervinden (voelen)* learn what it feels like, feel it personally; *i n levenden lijve* in the flesh; *hier is hij in levenden lijve* here he is as large as life; *niet veel o m het ~ hebben* be no great matter, amount to very little; *iem. een schrik (de koorts) o p het ~*

jagen **F** give sbd. a fright (a turn); *iem. op het ~ vallen* unexpectedly drop in on sbd.; take sbd. unawares; *iem. ergens mee op het ~ vallen* spring sth. on sbd.; *o v e r zijn hele ~ beven* tremble in every limb; *iem. t e ~ gaan* go at (for) sbd.; *iem. t e g e n het ~ lopen* run into (up against) sbd.; *zich... v a n het ~ houden* keep... at arm's length; **–arts** (-en) *m* personal physician, physician in ordinary; **–blad** (-bladen) *o* favourite paper; **–eigene** (-n) *m-v* serf, thrall; **–eigenschap** *v* bondage, serfage; **–goed** (-eren) *o* body-linen; **–je** (-s) *o* bodice, corsage; **–knecht** (-en en -s) *m* valet; **–lucht** *v* body odour; **–rente** (-n en -s) *v* (life-)annuity; **'lijfsbehoud** *o* preservation of life; **–gevaar** (-varen) *o* danger of life; **'lijfsieraad** (-raden) *o* personal ornament; **–spreuk** (-en) *v* motto, favourite maxim; **–straf** (-fen) *v* corporal punishment; **–tocht** *m* subsistence; **–wacht** (-en) *m-v* bodyguard, life-guard

lijk (-en) *o* 1 corpse, (dead) body; [anatomical] subject; 2 ♺ leech [of a sail]; **–auto** [-ɔuto., -o.to.] ('s) *m* hearse, funeral car; **–baar** (-baren) *v* bier; **–bezorger** (-s) *m* undertaker; **–bezorging** (-en) *v* disposal of the dead; **–bidder** (-s) *m* undertaker's man; **–bleek** deathly pale; **–dienst** (-en) *m* funeral service; service for (the burial of) the dead; **–drager** (-s) *m* bearer [at a funeral]; **'lijkegif(t)** *o* ptomaine

1 'lijken* *vt* dat zou mij wel ~ that's what I should like

2 'lijken* *vi* 1 be (look) like, resemble; 2 seem, appear; *het lijkt alsof...* it looks as if...; *het lijkt wel dat ze...* it would appear that they...; *hij lijkt wel gek* he must be mad; *ofschoon het heel wat leek* though it made a great show; *zij zijn niet wat zij ~ they* are not what they appear (to be); *het is niet zo gemakkelijk als het lijkt* it is not so easy as it looks; *dat lijkt maar zo* it only seems so; *het lijkt er niet naar, dat ze...* there is no appearance of their ...ing; *het lijkt naar niets, het lijkt nergens naar* it is below contempt; *zij ~ op elkaar* they look like each other, they resemble each other; *zij ~ (niet) veel op elkaar* they are (not) very like; *zij ~ op elkaar als twee druppels water* they are as like as two peas; *het begint er naar (op) te ~* that's more like it; *ik lijk wel doof vandaag* I seem (to be) deaf today; *dat portret lijkt goed (niet)* it is a good (poor) likeness

'lijkenhuisje (-s) *o* mortuary; **'lijkkist** (-en) *v* coffin; **–kleed** *o* 1 (-kleden) (o v e r d e k i s t) pall; 2 (-kle-deren) (k l e d i n g s t u k) shroud, winding-sheet; **–kleur** *v* livid (cadaverous) colour; **–kleurig** livid, cadaverous; **–koets** (-en) *v* hearse; **–opening** (-en) *v* autopsy, dissection; **–plechtigheden** *mv* funeral ceremonies, obsequies; **–rede** (-s en -nen) *v*

funeral oration (speech); **–roof** *m* body-snatching; **–schouwer** (-s) *m* coroner; **–schouwing** (-en) *v* post-mortem (examination); **–staatsie** (-s) *v*, **–stoet** (-en) *m* burial procession, funeral procession, funeral; **–verbranding** (-en) *v* cremation; **–wa(de)** (-waden) *v* shroud; **–wagen** (-s) *m* hearse, funeral car; **–zang** (-en) *m* funeral song, dirge

lijm *m* glue, gum; (h a r d w o r d e n d) cement; (v o g e l l i j m) lime; **'lijmen** (lijmde, h. gelijmd) *vt* talk sbd. over, rope sbd. in; **'lijmerig** 1 sticky, gluey; 2 *fig* drawling [voice]; ~ *spreken* speak with a drawl, drawl; **'lijmkwast** (-en) *o* glue-brush; **–pot** (-ten) *m* glue-pot

lijn (-en) *v* 1 line [also of a railway &]; 2 (k o o r d) cord, rope; leash, lead [for dog]; *de ~ trekken* **S** swing the lead; *één ~ trekken* pull together, take the same line; *de harde ~ volgen* adopt a strong policy; *a a n d e ~ blijven* (t e l e - f o o n) hold on, hold the line; *aan de ~ doen* slim; *honden aan de ~* dogs on the leash; *i n grote ~en* broadly outlined; *dat ligt niet in mijn ~* that is not in my line; *m e t ~ 3* by number 3 bus, (t r a m) by number 3 car; *o m de ~ denken* watch one's figure; *op één ~ met* on a par with; *o p één ~ staan* be on a level; *op één ~ stellen met* bring (put) on a level with; *o v e r de hele ~* all along the line; *fig* all-round, overall [situation]; *v o o r de (slanke) ~* for the figure; **–baan** (-banen) *v* rope-walk; **–boot** (-boten) *m & v* liner; **–cliché** [-kli.ʃe.] (-s) *o* line engraving; **–dienst** (-en) *m* regular service; **–draaier** (-s) *m* rope-maker; **'lijnen** (lijnde, h. gelijnd) *vt* rule; *vi* (a a n d e l i j n d o e n) slim

'lijnkoek (-en) *m* linseed cake, oilcake; **–olie** (-oliën) *v* linseed oil

'lijnrecht I *aj* straight, perpendicular, diametrical; *in ~e tegenspraak met* in flat contradiction with; **II** *ad* straightly, perpendicularly, diametrically; ~ *staan tegenover* be diametrically opposed to; **–tekenen** *o* geometrical drawing; **–tje** (-s) *o* line; *ik heb hem aan het ~* I have him in my power; *iem. aan het ~ houden* keep sbd. on a string; *met een zacht (zoet) ~* with soothing words; **–toestel** (-len) *o* air-liner; **–trekken** (trok 'lijn, h. 'lijngetrokken) *vi* malinger, shirk duty, **S** swing the lead; **–trekker** (-s) *m* shirker; **lijntrekke'rij** *v* shirking; **'lijnvliegtuig** (-en) *o* airliner; **–waad** (-waden) *o* linen; **–werker** (-s) *m* lineman

'lijnzaad *o* linseed

lijp **P** daft, weak-minded

lijs (lijzen) *m-v* dawdler, slow-coach; *een lange ~* a maypole

lijst (-en) *v* list, register; frame [of a picture]; △ cornice, moulding; *i n een ~ zetten* frame [a

picture]; *o p de* ~ *zetten* place (enter) on the list;
–aanvoerder (-s) *m* first candidate (of a party)
on the list [at elections]; **'lijsten** (lijstte, h.
gelijst) *vt* frame [a picture]; **'lijstenmaker** (-s)
m frame-maker

'lijster (-s) *v* thrush; *grote* ~ missel-thrush;
zwarte ~ = *merel*; **–bes** (-sen) *v* 1 (v r u c h t)
mountain-ash berry, rowan berry; 2 (b o o m)
mountain-ash, rowan

'lijstwerk *o* framework; △ moulding

'lijvig corpulent; voluminous, bulky, thick;
–heid *v* corpulency; voluminousness, bulki-
ness, thickness

'lijwaarts leeward

'lijzig drawling, slow; **–heid** *v* drawling,
slowness

'lijzij(de) *v* leeside

1 lik (-ken) *m* 1 lick [with the tongue]; 2 box on
the ears; ~ *o p stuk geven* give tit for tat

2 lik (-ken) *v* Ⓢ (g e v a n g e n i s) nick, quod

'likdoorn (-s), **–doren** (-s) *m* corn

li'keur (-en) *v* liqueur; **–glaasje** (-s) *o* liqueur
glass; **–tje** (-s) *o* glass of liqueur

'likkebaarden (likkebaardde, h. gelikkebaard)
vi lick (smack) one's lips (one's chops); **'likken**
(likte, h. gelikt) *vi & vt* lick; **'likmevestje** ...*van*
~ F a twopenny-halfpenny...

lil *o & m* jelly, gelatine

'lila lilac

'lillen (lilde, h. gelild) *vi* quiver, tremble

'lilliputachtig Lilliputian; **'lilliputter** (-s) *m*
Lilliputian[2]

li'miet (-en) *v* limit; (v . v e i l i n g) reserve
(price); **limi'teren** (limiteerde, h. gelimiteerd)
vt limit; (o p v e i l i n g) put a reserve price on

limo'nade (-s) *v* lemonade

limou'sine [li.mu.'zi.nə] (-s) *v* limousine

'linde (-n) *v* lime-tree, lime, linden, lindentree;
–bloesem (-s) *m* lime-tree blossom; **–boom**
(-bomen) *m* = *linde*; **–hout** *o* lime-wood;
'lindenlaan (-lanen) *v* lime-tree avenue, lime
avenue

'linea ~ *recta* straight [for]; **line'air** [li.ne.'ɛ:r]
linear

linge'rie [lɛ̃ʒə'ri.] (-s en -rieën) *v* lingerie

lini'aal (-ialen) *v & o* ruler; **'linie** (-s) *v* line; *over*
de hele ~ on all points; *over de hele* ~ *zegevieren*
carry all (everything) before one; *de* ~ *passeren*
⚓ cross the line; **lini'ëren** (linieerde, h.
gelinieerd) *vt* rule; **'linieschip** (-schepen) *o*
ship of the line; **–troepen** *mv* troops of the
line

link (s l i m) artful, F cute, sharp; (g e v a a r -
l ij k) risky, dangerous

'linker left; Ø sinister; **linker'achterpoot**
(-poten) *m* near hind-leg; **–'arm** (-en) *m* left
arm; **–'been** (-benen) *o* left leg; *met zijn* ~ *uit*

bed stappen get out of bed on the wrong side;
'linkerhand (-en) *v* left hand; *hij heeft twee* ~*en*
his fingers are all thumbs; **–kant** (-en) *m* left
side; *aan de* ~ ook: on the left-hand side; *naar*
de ~ to the left; **–vleugel** (-s) *m* left wing;
linker'voorpoot (-poten) *m* near foreleg;
'linkerzij(de) (-zijden) *v* left(-hand) side; *de*
Linkerzijde the (parliamentary) Left; **links I** *aj*
1 (t e g e n o v e r r e c h t s, ook i n d e
p o l i t i e k) left; 2 (l i n k s h a n d i g) left-handed; 3 (o n h a n d i g) *fig* gauche, awkward,
clumsy; ~ *georiënteerd* leftist; *een* ~*e regering* & a
left-wing government &; **II** *ad* 1 to (on, at) the
left; 2 *fig* in a gauche way, awkwardly, clumsily; *de...* ~ *laten liggen* leave the... on the left;
iem. ~ *laten liggen* give sbd. the cold shoulder,
ignore sbd.; *naar* ~ to the left; **'linksaf,**
links'af to the left ~ *buigen* (*slaan*) bear to the
left, turn left; **links'binnen** (-s) *m sp* inside
left; **–'buiten** (-s) *m sp* outside left; **–'handig**
left-handed; **'linksheid** *v fig* gaucherie,
awkwardness, clumsiness; **links'om** to the
left; ~... *keert!* ✄ left... turn!

'linnen *o & aj* linen; ~ (*boek*)*band* cloth binding;
in ~ (*gebonden*) (in) cloth; **–goed** *o* linen;
–juffrouw (-en) *v* linen-maid; **–kamer** (-s) *v*
linen-room; **–kast** (-en) *v* linen-cupboard

li'noleum [li.'no.leüm] *o & m* linoleum, F lino;
–druk (-ken) *m,* **–snede** (-n) *v* linocut

lint (-en) *o* ribbon; **–bebouwing** *v* ribbon
development; **'lintje** (-s) *o* ribbon; *een* ~ *krijgen*
obtain an order of knighthood; **–sregen** *m*
shower of birthday honours; **'lintworm** (-en)
m tapeworm; **–zaag** (-zagen) *v* band-saw

'linze (-n) *v* lentil

lip (-pen) *v* lip; *a a n iemands* ~*pen hangen* zie
hangen; zich o p de ~*pen bijten* bite one's lips; *het*
lag mij op de ~*pen* I had it on the tip of my
tongue; *o v e r iems.* ~*pen komen* pass sbd's. lips;
lip'bloemig labiate; ~*en* labiates; **'liplezen** *o*
lip-reading; **'lippendienst** (-en) *m* lip-service;
~ *bewijzen aan* pay lip-service to; **–stift** (-en) *v*
lipstick

Ⓦ'lipssleutel (-s) *m* Yale key; **–slot** (-sloten) *o*
Yale lock

liquida'teur [li.kʋi.da.'tø:r] (-s) *m* liquidator;
liqui'datie [li.kʋi.da.(t)si.] (-s) *v* 1 liquidation,
winding-up; 2 settlement [on Stock
Exchange]; **li'quide** [li.'ki.də] liquid;
liqui'deren [li.kʋi.'de:rə(n)] (liquideerde, h.
geliquideerd) **I** *vt* liquidate, wind up [one's
affairs]; **II** *vi* go into liquidation; **liquidi'teit**
[li.kʋi.di.'tɛit] *v* liquidity

'lire (-s) *v* lira

1 lis (-sen) *m & o* 🌿 iris, blue flag, yellow flag

2 lis (-sen) *v* = *lus*

'lisdodde (-n) *v* reed-mace

'**lispelen** (lispelde, h. gelispeld) *vi* lisp

list (-en) *v* 1 (a b s t r a c t) craft, cunning; 2 (c o n c r e e t) trick, stratagem, ruse; '**listig** sly, cunning, crafty, dodgy, wily, subtle; **–heid** (-heden) *v* slyness, cunning, subtlety

lita'nie (-ieën) *v* litany

'**liter** (-s) *m* litre

lite'rair [li.tə'rɛ.r] literary; **~-his'toricus** [-küs] (-rici) *m* literary historian, historian of literature; **~-his'torisch** of literary history, [a work] on literary history; **lite'rator** (-'toren) *m* literary man, man of letters; **litera'tuur** *v* literature°; **–geschiedenis** (-sen) *v* literary history, history of literature; **–lijst** (-en) *v* reading list; **–wetenschap** *v* study of literature

litho'graaf (-grafen) *m* lithographer; **–gra'feren** (lithografeerde, h. gelithografeerd) *vt* lithograph; **–gra'fie** (-ieën) *v* 1 (k u n s t) lithography; 2 (p l a a t) lithograph

'**Litouwen** *o* Lithuania; '**Litouwer** (-s) *m,* '**Litouws** Lithuanian

lits-ju'meaux [li.ʒy.'mo.] (-s) *o* double bed, twin beds

'**litteken** (-s) *o* scar, cicatrice

'**littera-** = *litera-*

litur'gie (-ieën) *v* liturgy; **li'turgisch** liturgical

li'vrei (-en) *v* livery

l.l. = *laatstleden*

L.O. = *lager onderwijs*

lob (-ben) *v* lobe

'**lobbes** (-en) *m goeie* **~** good-natured fellow; *een* **~** *van een hond* a big, good-natured dog

lo'catie [-(t)si.] (-s) *v* location

'**loco** $ (on) spot; **~** *Amsterdam* $ ex warehouse Amsterdam; **~** *station* $ free station

'**loco-burgemeester** (-s) *m* deputy mayor

locomo'tief (-tieven) *v* engine, locomotive

'**lodderig** drowsy

1 '**loden I** *aj* lead, leaden²; *met* **~** *schoenen* with leaden feet; **II** (loodde, h. gelood) *vt* 1 (i n l o o d v a t t e n) lead; 2 (i n d e b o u w-k u n d e) plumb; 3 ⚓ (p e i l e n) sound; **III** (loodde, h. gelood) *va* ⚓ take soundings

2 '**loden I** *m & o* (s t o f n a a m) loden; **II** *aj* loden [raincoat]

'**loeder** (-s) *o & m* **P** 1 (m a n) bastard; 2 (v r o u w) bitch

loef (loeven) *v de* **~** *afsteken* (*afwinnen*) ⚓ get to windward of; *fig* outdo sbd., steal a march on sbd.; **–waarts** to windward, aweather; **–zij(de)** *v* windward side, weather-side

'**loeien** (loeide, h. geloeid) *vi* 1 low, moo [of cows], bellow [of bulls]; 2 roar [of the wind]; 3 wail [of sirens]

loens squint-eyed; **~** *kijken* squint; '**loensen** (loenste, h. geloenst) *vi* squint

loep (-en) *v* magnifying glass, magnifier, lens; *onder de* **~** *nemen* examine

loer *v op de* **~** *liggen* lie in wait, lie on the look-out, lurk; *iem. een* **~** *draaien* play sbd. a dirty trick

'**loeren** (loerde, h. geloerd) *vi* peer, spy; **~** *op iem.* lie in wait for sbd.; *op een gelegenheid* **~** watch one's opportunity

'**loeven** (loefde, h. en is geloefd) *vi* luff; '**loever(t)** *te* **~** to windward

1 **lof** *m* praise, eulogy; *God* **~** *!* praise be to God!, thank God!; *zijn eigen* **~** *verkondigen* blow one's own trumpet; *de* **~** *verkondigen* (*zingen*) *van* sing the praises of; *b o v e n alle* **~** *verheven* beyond all praise; *zij spraken m e t veel* **~** *over hem* they were loud in praise of him

2 **lof** *o* ℔ Brussels **~** chicory

3 **lof** (loven) *o rk* benediction, evening service

'**lofdicht** (-en) *o* panegyric, laudatory poem; '**loffelijk** laudable, commendable, praiseworthy; '**loflied** (-eren) *o* hymn (song) of praise; **–psalm** (-en) *m* psalm (hymn) of praise; **–rede** (-s) *v* laudatory speech, panegyric; **–spraak** *v* praise, commendation; **–trompet** *v de* **~** *steken over* trumpet forth the praises of..., sing (sound) sbd.'s praises; **–tuiting** (-en) *v* praise, commendation; **lof'waardig** = *loffelijk*; '**lofzang** (-en) *m* 1 hymn (song) of praise, panegyric; 2 doxology

1 **log I** *aj* heavy [gait], unwieldy, cumbrous, cumbersome [mass]; **II** *ad* heavily

2 **log** (-gen) *v* ⚓ log

3 **log** *v* × *log* (= logarithm); **loga'ritme** (-n) *v* logarithm; **loga'ritmentafel** (-s) *v* table of logarithms

'**logboek** (-en) *o* logbook

'**loge** ['lɔ:ʒə] (-s) *v* 1 lodge [of freemasons]; 2 box [in a theatre]; (v. p o r t i e r) lodge; *in de* **~** in the masonic hall

lo'gé [lo.'ʒə.] (-s) *m* guest, visitor; *betalend* **~** paying guest; **lo'geerbed** [lo.'ʒe:r-] (-den) *o* spare bed; **–gast** (-en) *m* guest, visitor; **–kamer** (-s) *v* spare (bed)room, visitor's room, guest-room; **loge'ment** [lo.ʒə'mɛnt] (-en) *o* inn, hotel; **–houder** (-s) *m* innkeeper, hotel-keeper

1 '**logen** (loogde, h. geloogd) *vt* steep in lye

2 '**logen** V.T. meerv. van *liegen*

'**logenstraffen** (logenstrafte, h. gelogenstraft) *vt* give the lie to, belie [hopes, a statement]; falsify [an assumption]

lo'geren [lo.'ʒe:rə(n)] (logeerde, h. gelogeerd) **I** *vi* stay, stop; *ik logeer bij mijn oom* I am staying at my uncle's (with my uncle); *u kunt bij ons* **~** you can stay with us; *ik ben daar te* **~** I am on a visit there; *we hebben mensen te* **~** *ook:* we have visitors; *ze gaan* **~** *in de Zon* they are going to put up at the Sun hotel; **II** *vt* put [sbd.] up

'**loggen** (logde, h. gelogd) *vi* heave the log

'**logger** (-s) *m* lugger

'**logica** *v* logic

lo'**gies** [lo.'ʒi.s] *o* lodging, accommodation; ⚓ quarters; ~ *en ontbijt* bed and breakfast

'**logisch I** *aj* logical; *dat is nogal* ~ **F** of course, that goes without saying; *het ~e van het geval* the logic of the case; **II** *ad* logically

logis'**tiek I** *aj* logistic; **II** *v* logistics

logope'**die** *v* speech-training; logope'**dist** (-en) *m* speech-trainer   [tresses

lok (-ken) *v* lock, curl; strand [of hair]; ~*ken*

lo'**kaal I** *aj* local; **II** (-kalen) *o* room, hall; –**tje** (-s) *o*, –**trein** (-en) *m* local (train); *A m* shuttle train; –**vredebreuk** *v* ⚖ breach of the peace

'**lokaas** (-azen) *o* bait, allurement, decoy

lokali'**satie** [-'za.(t)si.] (-s) *v* localization; lokali'**seren** (lokaliseerde, h. gelokaliseerd) *vt* localize; lokali'**teit** (-en) *v* locality; (v e r t r e k, z a a l) room, hall

'**lokartikel** (-en) *o* loss-leader; –**duif** (-duiven) *v* ⚘ stool-pigeon; –**eend** (-en) *v* ⚘ decoy-(duck)

lo'**ket** (-ten) *o* 1 (s t a t i o n) ticket-office, booking-office, ticket-window; 2 (s c h o u w b u r g) (box-)office, (box-office) window; 3 (p o s t - k a n t o o r e.d.) counter; 4 pigeon-hole [of a cabinet]; 5 (safe-deposit) box; *aan het* ~ at the counter, [sell] over the counter; –**beambte** (-n) *m-v* booking-clerk [at railway station], counter clerk [at post office]; **loket'tist(e)** (-en en -es) *m* (*v*) = *loketbeambte*

'**lokfluitje** (-s) *o* bird-call; '**lokken** (lokte, h. gelokt) *vt* lure, allure, entice, decoy; attract, draw [customers]; '**lokmiddel** (-en) *o* enticement, bait, lure; –**roep** *m* call-note; *fig* lure; –**spijs** (-spijzen) *v* bait, lure; –**stem** (-men) *v* enticing voice, siren voice; –**vogel** (-s) *m* decoy-bird, decoy²

lol (-len) *v* fun, **F** lark(s); ~ *maken* make fun, lark; *voor de* ~ for fun, for a lark; '**lolletje** (-s) *o* lark; *het was geen* ~ it was no fun; '**lollig I** *aj* jolly, funny; *het was zo* ~! it was such fun!; *het is niks* ~ it is not a bit amusing; **II** *ad* funnily

'**lolly** ['lɔli.] ('s) *m* lollipop, lolly

'**lombok** *m* red pepper

'**lommer** *o* 1 shade; 2 foliage

'**lommerd** (-s) *m* pawnbroker's shop, pawnshop; *in de* ~ in pawn; **S** in pop, at my uncle's; *in de* ~ *zetten* take to the pawnbroker's (to uncle's); –**briefje** (-s) *o* pawn-ticket; –**houder** (-s) *m* pawnbroker

'**lommerrijk** shady, shadowy

1 lomp (-en) *v* rag, tatter

2 lomp 1 (v a n v o r m) ungainly; 2 (o n h a n - d i g) clumsy, awkward, flat-footed; 3 (g r o f)

hulking; 4 (v l e g e l a c h t i g) rude, unmannerly

'**lompenkoopman** (-lieden en -lui) *m* ragman, dealer in rags

'**lomperd** (-s) *m* boor, lout; '**lompheid** (-heden) *v* 1 ungainliness; 2 clumsiness, awkwardness; 3 rudeness

'**Londen** *o* London

'**lonen** (loonde, h. geloond) *vt* pay; *het loont de moeite (niet)* it is (not) worth while; –**d** paying, remunerative

long (-en) *v* lung; –**aandoening** (-en) *v* pulmonary affection; –**arts** (-en) *m* lung specialist; –**blaasje** (-s) *o* alveolus; –**kanker** *m* lung cancer; –**kruid** *o* lungwort; –**ontsteking** (-en) *v* pneumonia; –**slagader** (-s en -en) *v* pulmonary artery; –**tering** *v* pulmonary consumption, phthisis

lonk (-en) *m* ogle; *iem.* ~*jes toewerpen* ogle sbd.; '**lonken** (lonkte, h. gelonkt) *vi* ogle; *naar iem.* ~ make eyes at sbd.

lont (-en) *v* (slow) match, fuse; ~ *ruiken* smell a rat; *de* ~ *in het kruit steken (werpen)* put the torch to the powder-magazine; *fig* put the spark to the tinder

'**loochenen** (loochende, h. geloochend) *vt* deny; –**ning** (-en) *v* denial

lood (loden) *o* 1 lead; 2 (d i e p l o o d) soundinglead, lead; 3 (s c h i e t l o o d) plumb-line; 4 (g e w i c h t) decagramme; *het is* ~ *om oud ijzer* it is six of one and half a dozen of the other; *i n het* ~ plumb, upright; *glas in* ~, *in* ~ *gevatte ruitjes* leaded lights; *m e t* ~ *in de schoenen* with leaden feet; *u i t het* ~ out of plumb; *hij was uit het* ~ *geslagen* he was taken aback; he was thrown off his balance; –**erts** (-en) *o* lead-ore; –**gieter** (-s) *m* plumber; –**gieterswerk** *o* plumbing; –**glans** *o* lead glance; –**glit** *o* litharge; –**houdend** plumbic; –**je** (-s) *o* 1 small lump of lead; 2 (p l o m b e) lead seal; *de laatste* ~*s wegen het zwaarst* it is the last straw that breaks the camel's back; *hij moest het* ~ *leggen* he had to pay the piper; he got the worst of it; –**kleur** *v* lead colour, leaden hue; –**kleurig** lead-coloured, leaden; –**lijn** (-en) *v* 1 perpendicular (line); 2 ⚓ sounding-line; *een* ~ *oprichten (neerlaten)* erect (drop) a perpendicular; –**mijn** (-en) *v* lead-mine; –**recht** perpendicular

1 loods (-en) *v* shed; (a a n g e b o u w d) lean-to; ⚐ hangar

2 loods (-en) *m* ⚓ pilot; –**boot** (-boten) *m* & *v* pilot-boat; –**dienst** *m* pilot-service; pilotage; '**loodsen** (loodste, h. geloodst) *vt* pilot²; '**loodsgeld** (-en) *o* pilotage (dues); –**mannetje** (-s) *o* pilot-fish; –**wezen** *o* pilotage '**loodvergiftiging** *v* lead poisoning; **–wit** *o* white lead; **–zwaar** heavy as lead, leaden

loof *o* foliage, leaves; [potato] tops, (i n z. g e d r o o g d a l s s t r o) haulm; **–boom** (-bomen) *m* foliage tree; **–hout** *o* handwood; **–hut** (-ten) *v* tabernacle; **Loof'huttenfeest** *o* Feast of Tabernacles; '**loofrijk** leafy; **–werk** *o* △ leaf-work, foliage

1 loog (logen) *v* & *o* lye

2 loog (logen) V.T. v. *liegen*

'**loogbak** (-ken) *m* lye-trough; **–kuip** (-en) *v* steeper; **–water** *o* lye

'**looien** (looide, h. gelooid) *vt* tan; **–er** (-s) *m* tanner; **looie'rij** (-en) *v* 1 tannery, tan-yard; 2 tanner's trade; '**looikuip** (-en) *v* tan vat; **–stof** (-fen) *v* tannin; **–zuur** *o* tannic acid

look *o* & *m* garlic, leek

loom slow, heavy; languid; *met lome schreden* with heavy feet, with lazy (tardy) steps; **–heid** *v* slackness, dul(l)ness, slowness, heaviness, lassitude, languor

loon (lonen) *o* wages, pay; 2 reward, recompense; *met behoud van* ~ with full pay; *hij kreeg* ~ *naar werken* he got his due; *hij heeft zijn verdiende* ~ it serves him right; **–actie** [-aksi.] (-s) *v* agitation for higher wages; **–arbeid** *m* wagework; **–belasting** (-en) *v* pay-as-you-earn income-tax, P.A.Y.E.; **–beslag** *o* attachment (distraint) of wages; **–briefje** (-s) *o* pay-slip; **–derving** *v* loss of pay (wages); **–dienst** (-en) *m* wage-earning; *personen in* ~ employed persons; *werk in* ~ paid labour; *werk in* ~ *verrichten* work for wages; **–eis** (-en) *m* wage(s) demand, wage claim, pay claim; **loonen 'prijsbeleid** *o* price and income policy; '**loongeschil** (-len) *o* wage dispute; **–lijst** (-en) *v* pay-list, pay-roll, wage(s) sheet; **–pauze** (-s) *v* temporary wage freeze; **–peil** *o* wage level, level of wages; **–politiek** *v* wages policy, pay (wage) policy; **–ronde** (-n) *v* wage round; **–schaal** *v* wage scale; *glijdende* ~ sliding scale (of wages); **–slaaf** (-slaven) *m* wage-slave, drudge, hack, journeyman; **–standaard** *m* rate of wages, wage rate; **–stelsel** (-s) *o* wage(s) system; **–stop** (-s) *m* wage freeze, pay freeze; *een* ~ *afkondigen* freeze wages; '**loonsverhoging** (-en) *v* rise in wages, pay rise; **–verlaging** (-en) *v* wages reduction; '**loontrekker** (-s) *m* wage-earner; **–wet** *v* [iron] law of wages; **–zakje** (-s) *o* pay-packet, wage-packet

loop (lopen) *m* 1 (h e t l o p e n) run; 2 (g a n g v. p e r s o o n) walk, gait; 3 (v. z a k e n) course; trend, march [of events]; 4 (v a n g e w e e r) barrel; *'s werelds* ~ the way of the world; *het recht moet zijn* ~ *hebben* the law must take its course; *de vrije* ~ *laten aan...* let... take their (own) course; give free course to...; *een andere* ~ *nemen* take a different turn; ● *i n de* ~ *van de dag* in the course of to-day, during to-day; *in de* ~ *der jaren* over the years; *in de* ~ *der tijden* in the course of ages (of time); *iets in zijn* ~ *stuiten* arrest (check) ...in its (their) course; *o p de* ~ *gaan* run for it, take to one's heels, **S** cut and run; bolt [also of a horse]; *o p de* ~ *zijn* be on the run; **–baan** (-banen) *v* career; **–brug** (-gen) *v* foot bridge; gangway; **–graaf** (-graven) *v* trench; **–hek** (-ken) *o* playpen; **–je** (-s) *o* 1 run; 2 ♪ run, passage; 3 (k u n s t g r e e p) trick; *met iem. een* ~ *nemen* pull sbd.'s leg; **–jongen** (-s) *m* errand-boy, office-boy; **–kat** (-ten) *v* crab; **–kraan** (-kranen) *v* travelling crane, transporter, **F** jenny; **–neus** (-neuzen) *m* running (dripping) nose; **–pas** *m* double time; *in de* ~ at the double; **–plank** (-en) *v* ⚓ gangway, duckboard; **–rek** *o* playpen

loops in (on, at) heat

'**looptijd** (-en) *m* $ currency [of a bill]; **–vlak** (-ken) *o* tread [of a tyre]; **–vogel** (-s) *m* walker

loor *te* ~ *gaan* get lost

loos 1 (s l i m) cunning, crafty, wily; 2 (n i e t e c h t) dummy [doors &], false [bottom, alarm]

loot (loten) *v* ⚘ shoot; *fig* scion, offspring

'**lopen* I** *vi* 1 (g a a n) walk; 2 (h a r d l o p e n) run; 3 (z i c h b e w e g e n) go [of machines, clocks &], run [of rivers, wheels &]; 4 (e t t e r e n) run; 5 *fig* run [of a contract, lease &]; ~ *als een haas* (*een dief*) run like a hare (like mad); *zullen we* ~? shall we walk?; *loop heen!* **F** get along with you!; *die treinen* ~ *niet* these trains are not run; *het liep anders* things turned out differently; *mijn horloge loopt goed* my watch goes well, is a good timekeeper; *de twist liep hoog* the dispute ran high; *gaan* ~ run away [also of visitors]; *zullen we wat gaan* ~? shall we go for a walk?; *hij laat alles maar* ~ he lets things slide (drift); *we zullen hem maar laten* ~ better leave him alone; give him the go-by; *men liet het metaal in een vorm* ~ they ran the metal into a mould; *zijn vingers over de toetsen laten* ~ run one's fingers over the keys; *zij* ~ *te bedelen* they go about begging; ● *het loopt i n de duizenden* it runs into thousands; *het loopt in de papieren* zie *papier*; zie ook: *inlopen*; *het loopt n a a r twaalven* it is getting on for twelve o'clock; *hij loopt naar de vijftig* he is getting on for fifty; *de gracht loopt o m de stad* goes round the town; *o p een mijn* & ~ ⚓ strike a mine &; *[de ketting] loopt o v e r een katrol* passes over a pulley; *de weg loopt over A.* goes via A.; *die zaken* ~ *over de boekhouder* these affairs are handled by the book-keeper; *ergens tegen a a n* ~ come across sth.; **II** *vt* run; *zich moe* ~ tire oneself out with walking (with running);

III *o een uur ~* (*s*) an hour's walk; *onder het ~* while walking; *het op een ~ zetten* take to one's heels; **'lopend** running [dogs, boys, bills &]; current [year]; *~e band* assembly line, conveyor-belt; *~ commentaar* running commentary; *~e golf* travelling wave; *de zevende van de ~e maand* the seventh inst. (= instant); *~e patiënt* ambulant patient; *~e rekening* 1 current account; 2 outstanding (open) claim; *~ schrift* cursive; *zich als een ~ vuurtje verspreiden* spread like wildfire; *~e schulden* running (outstanding) debts; *de ~e zaken* current affairs, the business of the day; *rekeningen ~e over de laatste drie jaren* covering the last three years; **'loper** (-s) *m* 1 (in 't alg.) runner; 2 (k r a n t e n r o n d-b r e n g e r) newsman; 3 (v. b a n k &) messenger; 4 (s c h a a k s p e l) bishop; 5 (t a p ij t) carpet; 6 (t a f e l k l e e d j e) table-runner; 7 (s l e u t e l) master-key, pass-key, skeleton-key

lor (-ren) *o* & *v* rag; *het is een ~* **F** it is a dud; it is mere trash, rubbish; *een ~ van een roman* a rubbishy novel; *geen ~* not a bit (a straw)

lor'dose [s = z] *v* **🗲** lordosis

lorg'net [lɔr'nɛt] (-ten) *v* & *o* eye-glasses, [pince-nez

'lorre *m* Poll(y) [= parrot]

'lorrie (-s) *v* lorry, trolley, truck

'lorrig trashy, rubbishy, trumpery

'lorum F *in de ~* (v e r w a r d) confused, put out, at a loss; (d r o n k e n) tight, drunk

1 los (-sen) *m* lynx

2 los I *aj* loose² [screw, dress, money, style, reports &]; detached [sentences]; *~se aantekeningen* stray notes; *~ arbeider* casual labourer, odd hand; *~se bloemen* cut flowers; *~ kruit* powder; *~se letters* movable type(s); *~se nummers* (v. e. krant) [I have] occasional (odd) numbers, a few stray copies; single copies [not sold]; *...wordt niet ~ verkocht* ...is not sold loose; *~ werkman = ~ arbeider*; **II** *ad* loosely²; *~!* let go!; *erop ~ gaan* go at [them, him]; *erop ~ leven* go the pace; live from hand to mouth; *erop ~ slaan* hit out, pitch into [them]; **los'bandig** licentious, dissolute, profligate; **–heid** (-heden) *v* licentiousness, dissoluteness, profligacy, libertinism; **'losbarsten** *vi* break out, burst, explode; (v. b u i, s t o r m) break; **–ting** (-en) *v* outbreak, burst, explosion; **los'bladig** loose-leaf...; **'losbol** (-len) *m* loose liver, profligate, rake; **'losbranden** (brandde los, h. en is losgebrand) *vt* fire off, discharge; **–breken**¹ *vi* break loose, break away; (v a n b u i, s t o r m) break; **–draaien**¹ *vt* unscrew,

loosen [a screw]; **–gaan**¹ *vi* get loose; zie ook: 1 *los* **II**; **–geld** (-en) *o* 1 ransom; 2 **$** landing-charges; **–geraakt** undone; **–geslagen** adrift; **–gespen**¹ *vt* unbuckle; **–gooien**¹ *vt* cast off, throw off; **–haken**¹ *vt* unhook; **–hangen**¹ *vi* hang loose; **–hangend** fly-away, loose [hair]; **–jes** loosely; (v l u c h t i g) lightly; **–knopen**¹ *vt* 1 unbutton; 2 untie; **–komen**¹ *vi* 1 get loose [of a person &]; 2 *fig* come out of one's shell, open out; 3 🗲 get off the ground; **–kopen**¹ *vt* buy off, ransom, redeem; **–koppelen**¹ *vt* disconnect; **–krijgen**¹ *vt* 1 get loose; 2 *fig* extract [money, a promise from sbd.]; *geld zien los te krijgen* try to raise money; **–laten**¹ **I** *vt* let loose, let go of [my hand], release, unhand; abandon [a policy, a system]; let slip [a secret]; *hij laat niets los* he is very reticent; *de gedachte laat mij niet meer los* the thought haunts me; **II** *vi* & *va* 1 let go; 2 come off [of paint &]; *laat los!* let go!; *hij laat niet los* he holds on like grim death (like a leech); **–lating** *v* release; **los'lijvig** loose (in the bowels); **los'lippig** indiscreet; **–heid** *v* indiscretion; **'loslopen**¹ *vi* be at liberty; *~de honden* unattached dogs; *~d jongmens* unattached young man; *dat zal wel ~* it is sure to come right; **–maken**¹ **I** *vt* loosen, untie, unbind, undo [a knot]; dislodge [a stone &]; *fig* disengage [moneys]; disjoin [what was united]; **II** *vr zich ~* disengage (free) oneself; *zich ~ van...* dissociate oneself from [a company], break away from; **–plaats** (-en) *v* 🗲 discharging-berth (-place); **–prijs** (-prijzen) *m* ransom²; **–raken**¹ *vi* get loose, get undone; **–rukken**¹ *vt* = losscheuren I; **II** *vr zich ~ (van)* = losscheuren **II**

löss [lœs] *v* loess

'losscheuren¹ **I** *vt* tear loose; tear (away) from; **II** *vr zich ~ (van)* tear oneself away (from), break away (from); **–schieten**¹ *vi* slip; **'lossen** (loste, h. gelost) **I** *vt* 1 (v. g o e d e r e n) unload; 2 (v. v u u r w a p e n) discharge; fire [a shot at him]; **II** *vi* unload, break bulk; **'loslaan**¹ *vi* 🗲 break adrift; **–springen**¹ *vi* spring loose (open); **–staand** detached [house]; **–stormen**¹ *vi* ~ *op* rush upon; **–tornen**¹ *vt* unsew, rip (open); **–trekken**¹ *vt* pull loose, tear loose; **–weg** casually, off-handedly; **'loswerken**¹ **I** *vt* & *vi* work loose; **II** *vr zich ~* work loose, disengage oneself

lot *o* 1 (n o o d l o t) fate, destiny, lot; 2 (l e v e n s l o t) lot; 3 (loten) (l o t e r ij b r i e f-j e) (lottery-)ticket; *dat is een ~ uit de loterij* [*fig*] that's a stroke of luck; *iem. aan zijn ~ over-*

¹ V.T. en V.D. van dit werkwoord volgens het model: 'losdraaien, V.T. draaide 'los, V.D. 'losgedraaid. Zie voor de vormen onder het grondwoord, in dit voorbeeld: *draaien*. Bij sterke en onregelmatige werkwoorden wordt u verwezen naar de lijst achterin.

laten abandon (leave) sbd. to his fate, leave sbd. to his own devices; 'loteling (-en) *m* conscript; 'loten (lootte, h. geloot) *vi* draw lots; lote'rij (-en) *v* lottery; –briefje (-s) *o* lottery-ticket; 'lotgenoot (-noten) *m* companion in distress; –geval (-len) *o* adventure

'Lotharingen ['lo.ta:-] *o* Lorraine

'loting (-en) *v* drawing of lots

lo'tion [lo.'ʃòn] (-s) *v* lotion

'lotje *van ~ getikt* crackbrained

'lotto ('s) *m* lotto

'lotus (-sen) *m* lotus

louche [lu.ʃ] shady

'louter pure [gold], mere [politeness]; ~ *leugens* only (nothing but) lies; ~ *onzin* sheer nonsense; 'louteren (louterde, h. gelouterd) *vt* purify, refine; –ring (-en) *v* purification, refining

'louwmaand *v* January

1 'loven (loofde, h. geloofd) *vt* praise, laud, extol, glorify, sing praises of; ~ *en bieden* haggle, chaffer, bargain

2 'loven *mv.* v. 3 *lof*

'lover (-s) *o* foliage; –tje (-s) *o* spangle, sequin

loxo'droom (-dromen) *m* rhumb

lo'yaal [lʋɑ.l, lo.'ja.l] loyal; loyali'teit *v* loyalty

'lozen (loosde, h. geloosd) *vt* 1 drain, void [water]; 2 heave [a sigh]; 3 get rid of [a person]

LSD [ɛlɛs'de.] *o* LSD [a drug]

'lubben (lubde, h. gelubd) *vt* 1 (c a s t r e r e n) geld, castrate; 2 (s t r i k k e n) inveigle, wheedle [sbd. into doing sth.]

lucht (-en) *v* 1 (g a s) air; 2 (u i t s p a n s e l) sky; 3 (r e u k) smell, scent[2]; ~ *geven aan zijn gevoelens (verontwaardiging)* give vent to one's feelings, vent one's indignation; *de ~ krijgen van iets* get wind (scent) of it, scent it; ● *in de ~* in the air; *dat hangt nog in de ~* it is still (somewhat) in the air; *in de ~ vliegen* explode, be blown up; *het zit in de ~* it is in the air; *in de ~ zitten kijken* stare into the air (into vacancy); *in de open ~* in the open (air); *dat is u i t de ~ gegrepen* it is without any foundation; *uit de ~ komen vallen* drop from the skies, appear out of the blue; –aanval (-len) *m* air attack, air raid; –afweer *m* 1 = *luchtverdediging;* 2 = *luchtafweergeschut;* –afweergeschut *o* anti-aircraft artillery; –alarm *o* air-raid warning, alert; –ballon (-s) *m* balloon; –band (-en) *m* tyre, pneumatic tyre; –basis [-zis] (-sen en -bases) *v* air base; –bed (-den) *o* air-bed, air-mattress; –bel (-len) *v* (air-)bubble; –belwaterpas (-sen) *o* spirit-level; –bescherming *v* air-raid precautions, A.R.P., Civil Defence, C.D.; –bombardement (-en) *o* aerial bombardment; –brug (-gen) *v* (h o g e

v o e t b r u g) overhead bridge; 2 ⇙ air-lift; –buis (-buizen) *v* 1 air-pipe; 2 (l u c h t p ij p) trachea [*mv* tracheae]; –bus (-sen) *m* & *v* air-shuttle; –dicht I *aj* airtight; II *ad* hermetically; –doel-geschut *o* anti-aircraft artillery; –doop *m ik onderging de ~* it was my first flight; –druk *m* 1 atmospheric pressure; 2 air-pressure, blast [of an explosion]; 'luchten (luchtte, h. gelucht) *vt* air[2], ventilate[2]; *fig* vent; *zijn geleerdheid ~* air one's learning; *zijn gemoed (hart) ~* relieve one's feelings, unburden one's mind (heart); *de kamers ~* air the rooms; *ik kan hem niet ~ of zien* I hate the very sight of him

'luchter (-s) *m* 1 chandelier; 2 candlestick

'luchtfilter (-s) *m* & *o* air-filter; –foto ('s) *v* air (aerial) photograph, air (aerial) view; –gat (-gaten) *o* air hole, vent(-hole); –gekoeld air-cooled; –gesteldheid *v* 1 condition of the air; 2 climate; lucht'hartig light-hearted; 'luchthaven (-s) *v* airport; 'luchtig I *aj* 1 well-aired; 2 (d u n, l i c h t) airy[2] [costumes &]; light [bread]; II *ad* airily, lightly; –heid *v* airiness, lightness, levity; 'luchtje (-s) *o* faint air; breath of air; *er is een ~ aan* it smells; *fig* F it is a bit fishy; *een ~ scheppen* take an airing; *een ~ gaan scheppen* go out for a breath of air; 'luchtkartering *v* air (aerial) survey; –kasteel (-telen) *o* castle in the air, castle in Spain; *luchtkastelen bouwen* build castles in the air; –klep (-pen) *v* air valve; –koeling *v* air-cooling; *motor met ~* air-cooled engine; –koker (-s) *m* air shaft; –kussen (-s) *o* air-cushion; –kussenvoertuig (-en) *o* ⊛ hovercraft (ook *mv*); –kuur (-kuren) *v* open-air treatment; –laag (-lagen) *v* layer of air; –landing (-en) *v* air-borne landing; –landings... air-borne [troops &]; lucht'ledig I *aj* void of air; ~*e ruimte* vacuum; II *o* vacuum; 'luchtlijn (-en) *v* airline; –macht *v* air force; –net (-ten) *o* air network; –pijp (-en) *v* windpipe, trachea [*mv* tracheae]; –pomp (-en) *v* air-pump; –post *v* air mail; –postblad (-bladen) *o* air letter, aerogramme; –recht *o* ℔ air-mail postage; –regeling *v* air-conditioning; –reis (-reizen) *v* voyage by air, air voyage, air journey; –reiziger (-s) *m* 1 ⇙ air-traveller; 2 ⚒ = *luchtschipper;* –rooster (-s) *m* & *o* air grating; –ruim *o* 1 atmosphere; [the conquest of the] air; 2 [national, Dutch &] airspace; –schip (-schepen) *o* airship; –schipper (-s) *m* aeronaut, balloonist; –schommel (-s) *m* & *v* swing-boat; –schroef (-schroeven) *v* airscrew, propeller; –sluis (-sluizen) *v* air-lock; –spiegeling (-en) *v* mirage, fata morgana; –spoorweg (-wegen) *o* elevated (overhead) railway; –storingen *mv* atmospherics; –streek (streken) *v* climate, zone; **–strijdkrachten** *mv* air force; **–stroom** (-stromen) *m* air current; **–vaart** *v* aeronautics, aviation; **–vaartmaatschappij** (-en) *v* airline (company), aviation company; **–vaartuig(en)** *o* (*mv*) aircraft; **–verdediging** *v* air defence; **–verkeer** *o* aerial traffic, air traffic; **–verkenning** *v* air reconnaissance, aerial reconnaissance; **–verschijnsel** (-en en -s) *o* atmospheric phenomenon; **–verversing** *v* ventilation; **–vervuiling** *v* air pollution; **–vloot** (-vloten) *v* air fleet; **–vracht** *v* air freight; **lucht'waardig** airworthy;

'luchtweerstand *m* air resistance; **–weg** (-wegen) *m* 1 ⚕ air route; 2 air-passage; **~en** bronchia; **–wortel** (-s) *m* aerial root; **–zak** (-ken) *m* air-pocket; **–ziek** airsick; **–ziekte** *v* airsickness

'lucifer (-s) *m* match; **–sdoosje** (-s) *o* match-box

lucra'tief lucrative

lu'diek (in) playful (form)

'lues *v* 🜊 lues, syphilis

lu'guber lugubrious, sinister, lurid

1 lui I *aj* lazy, idle, slothful; *liever ~ dan moe zijn* be born tired; **II** *ad* lazily

2 lui *mv* people, folks

'luiaard (-s) *m* 1 lazy-bones, sluggard; 2 🦥 sloth

luid loud

'luiden (luidde, h. geluid) **I** *vi* sound; *hoe luidt de brief?* how does the letter run?; *het antwoord luidt niet gunstig* the answer is unfavourable; *zoals de uitdrukking luidt* as the phrase has it (goes); **II** *va* sound, ring, peal, chime [for a birth], toll [for a death]; **III** *vt* ring, peal, chime, toll

'luidens *prep* according to

'luidkeels at the top of one's voice; **luid'ruchtig** loud, noisy, boisterous; **'luid-spreker** (-s) *m* loud-speaker; **–installatie** *v* (-s) loud-speaker system, public-address system

'luier (-s) *v* (baby's) napkin, nappy, *Am* diaper

'luieren (luierde, h. geluierd) *vi* be idle, idle, laze

'luiermand (-en) *v* 1 baby-linen basket; 2 layette, baby linen, baby clothes

'luierstoel (-en) *m* easy chair

'luifel (-s) *v* penthouse; (glass) porch [at hotel door &], awning [over railway platform]

'luiheid *v* laziness, idleness, sloth

luik (-en) *o* 1 (a a n r a a m) shutter; 2 (i n v l o e r) trapdoor; 3 ⚓ hatch; 4 (v. s c h i l-d e r ij) panel

Luik *o* Liège

'luilak (-ken) *m* lazy-bones; **'luilakken** (luilakte, h. geluilakt) *vi* idle, laze

lui'lekkerland *o* land of Cockaigne, Billy Bunterland, land of plenty

luim (-en) *v* 1 humour, mood; 2 whim, caprice; freak; *in een goede* (*kwade*) *~ zijn* be in a good (bad) temper (humour); **–ig** capricious

'luipaard (-en) *m* leopard

luis (luizen) *v* louse [*mv* lice]

'luister *m* lustre, splendour, resplendence, pomp (and splendour); **~** *bijzetten* grace, add lustre to

'luisteraar (-s) *m* listener; **'luisterbijdrage** (-n) *v* (listener's) licence fee; **luister'dichtheid** *v* R listening figures; **'luisteren** (luisterde, h. geluisterd) *vi* 1 listen; 2 R listen (in); *wie luistert aan de wand, hoort zijn eigen schand* eavesdroppers hear no good of themselves; *naar iem. ~* listen to sbd.; *~de naar de naam Fox* answering to the name of Fox; *naar het roer ~* ⚓ answer (respond to) the helm; **luister- en 'kijkgeld** *o* radio and t.v. licence fee; **'luisterpost** (-en) *m* listening-post

'luisterrijk I *aj* splendid, magnificent, glorious; **II** *ad* splendidly, magnificently, gloriously

'luistervergunning (-en) *v* radio licence; **–vink** (-en) *m* & *v* eavesdropper; **'luistervin-ken** (luistervinkte, h. geluistervinkt) eaves-drop, play the eavesdropper

luit (-en) *v* ♪ lute

'luitenant (-s) *m* 🜨 lieutenant; **~-***ter zee 2e klasse* ⚓ sub-lieutenant; **~-gene'raal** (-s) *m* 🜨 lieutenant-general; **~-kolo'nel** (-s) *m* 🜨 lieutenant-colonel; ⚕ wing commander

'luitjes *mv* people, folks

'luitspeler (-s) *m* lute-player, lutanist

'luiwagen (-s) *m* scrubbing-brush

'luiwammes (-en) *m* = *luilak*

'luizenbaan (-banen) *v* soft job; **–kam** (-men) *m* fine-tooth comb

'lukken (lukte, is gelukt) *vi* succeed; zie *geluk-ken*; **'lukraak** at random, hit or miss

lul (-len) *m* **P** 1 penis; 2 duffer, clodhopper; **'lullen** (lulde, h. geluld) *vi* **F** gas, ramble; **'lullig F** trivial, twaddling, fiddle-faddle

lumi'neus luminous, brilliant, bright

'lummel (-s) *m* lout, lubber, galoot; **–achtig** loutish, lubberly; **'lummelen** (lummelde, h. gelummeld) *vi* laze (about); **'lummelig** = *lummelachtig*

'lunapark (-en) *o* amusement park, fun fair

lunch [lünʃ] (-en en -es) *m* lunch(eon); **'lunchen** (lunchte, h. geluncht) *vi* lunch, have lunch; **'lunchpakket** (-ten) *o* packed lunch; **–room** [-ru.m] (-s) *m* tea-room(s), tea-shop

luns (lunzen) *v* linchpin

lu'pine (-n) *v* lupin(e)

'lurken (lurkte, h. gelurkt) *vi* suck

lus (-sen) *v* 1 (in t r a m) strap; 2 (v a n

s c h o e n) tag; 3 (v . t o u w) noose; 4 (a l s
o r n a m e n t) loop

lust (-en) *m* 1 inclination, liking, mind; 2 desire,
appetite; 3 delight; 4 lust [of the flesh], concu-
piscence; 5 *ps* pleasure [and displeasure]; *een ~
voor de ogen* a feast for the eyes, a sight for sore
eyes; *~ hebben*... have a mind to..., feel inclined
to...; *ik heb er geen ~ in* I have no mind to, I
don't feel like it; *het is mijn ~ en mijn leven* that
is meat and drink to me; *ja, een mens zijn ~ is
een mens zijn leven* my mind to me a kingdom is;
zij... dat het een (lieve) ~ is with a will; **'luste-
loos I** *aj* listless, apathetic; $ dull [market]; **II**
ad listlessly, apathetically; **luste'loosheid** *v*
listlessnéss, apathy, dullness; **'lusten** (lustte, h.
gelust) *vt* like; *...gaarne ~* be a lover of...; *zij ~
dat niet* they don't like it; *hij zal ervan ~* he is
going to catch it (hot)

'luster (-s) *m* lustre

'lustgevoel (-ens) *o ps* pleasure sensation; **–hof**
(-hoven) *m* pleasure-ground; *fig* (garden of)
Eden; **–ig I** *aj* merry, cheerful; ☉ blithe,
blithesome; **II** *ad* merrily, cheerfully, ☉ blithe-
ly; < lustily; **–knaap** (-knapen) *m* Ganymede;
–moord (-en) *m* sex-murder; **–oord** (-en) *o*
delightful spot, pleasure-ground

'lustrum (-tra) *o* lustrum, lustre

luthe'raan (-ranen) *m* Lutheran; **'luthers** *aj*
Lutheran

'luttel small, little; few

'luwen (luwde, is geluwd) *vi* abate, die down
[of a storm, of wind]; calm down, quiet down
[of excitement]; cool down [of friendship];
'luwte *v* lee

'luxe ['ly.ksǝ] *m* luxury; **–artikel** (-en) *o* article
of luxury; **~en** ook: luxury goods; **–brood**
(-broden) *o* fancy bread; **~-editie** [-(t)si.] (-s) *v*
de luxe edition; **–hut** (-ten) *v* ⚓ state cabin;
–leven *o* life of luxury

'Luxemburg *o* Luxembourg; **–s** Luxembourg

luxu'eus [ly.ksy.'ø.s] luxurious, de luxe

ly'ceum [li.'se.üm] (-cea en -s) *o* 1 ▣ lyceum; 2
⚭ ± grammar school, *Am* high school

lym'fatisch [lɪm'fa.ti.s] lymphatic; **'lymf(e)** *v*
lymph; **–klier** (-en) *v* lymph gland; **–vat**
(-vaten) *o* lymphatic vessel

'lynchen [ˈlɪnʃǝ(n)] (lynchte, h. gelyncht) *vt*
lynch

lynx [lɪŋks] (-en) *m* lynx

'lyricus ['li.ri.küs] (-ci) *m* lyrist; **ly'riek** *v* 1 lyric
poetry, lyrics; 2 lyricism; **'lyrisch I** *aj* lyrical
[account, verses], lyric [poetry]; **II** *ad* lyrically

⑩ **ly'sol** [li.'zɔl] *o & m* lysol

M

m [ɛm] ('s) *v* m
m = *meter*
ma ('s) *v* mamma
maag (magen) *v* stomach; **–bloeding** (-en) *v* haemorrhage from the stomach; ✴ gastrorrhagia
maagd (-en) *v* maid(en), virgin; *de Maagd* ★ Virgo; *de Heilige Maagd* the (Holy) Virgin; *de Maagd van Orléans* the Maid of Orleans; **'maagdelijk** maidenly; virgin [forest]; **–heid** *v* maidenhood, virginity; **'maagdenpalm** (-en) *m* periwinkle; **–vlies** (-vliezen) *o* hymen
'maagkanker *m* cancer of the stomach; **–kramp** (-en) *v* stomach cramp, spasm of the stomach; **–kwaal** (-kwalen) *v* stomach complaint; **–pijn** (-en) *v* stomach ache; **–sap** (-pen) *o* gastric juice; **–streek** *v* gastric region; **–zuur** *o* gastric acid; **–zweer** (-zweren) *v* gastric ulcer, stomach ulcer
'maaidorser (-s) *m*, **maai'dorsmachine** [-ma.ʃi.nə] (-s) *v* combine, combine harvester; **'maaien** (maaide, h. gemaaid) *vt & vi* mow [grass &]; reap [grain]; cut [corn &]; **–er** (-s) *m* mower, reaper; **'maailand** (-en) *o* mowing-field; **–machine** [-ma.ʃi.nə] (-s) *v* mowing-machine; reaper, reaping-machine [for grain]; **–tijd** *m* mowing-time; **–veld** *o* 1 mowing field; 2 ground (surface) level
maak *m & v in de ~* under repair; *ik heb een jas in de ~* I am having a coat made; **–loon** (-lonen) *o* charge for making, cost of making; **–sel** (-s) *o* make; **–werk** *o* [goods, books &] made to order
1 maal (malen) *v & o* (k e e r) time; *een~* once; zie ook: *eenmaal*; *een enkele ~* once in a while; *twee~* twice; *drie~* three times; *vier~* four times; zie ook: *keer*
2 maal (malen) *o* (m a a l t ij d) meal
'maalmachine [-ma.ʃi.nə] (-s) *v* masticator, crusher, grinding (crushing) machine
'maalstroom (-stromen) *m* whirlpool, vortex²; mælstrom²
'maalteken (-s) *o* multiplication sign
'maaltijd (-en) *m* [hot] meal, (f o r m e e l) repast
maan (manen) *v* moon; *afnemende ~* waning moon; *nieuwe ~* new moon; *volle ~* full moon; *wassende ~* waxing moon; *naar de ~ gaan* [fig] **F** go to the dogs; *loop naar de ~* **F** go to the devil; *alles is naar de ~* all is gone (lost); *naar de ~ reiken* cry for the moon
maand (-en) *v* month
'maandag (-dagen) *m* Monday; *een blauwe ~ a* very short time; *~ houden* take Monday off; **–s I** *aj* Monday; **II** *ad* on Mondays; **–ziek** Mondayish
'maandblad (-bladen) *o* monthly (magazine); **'maandelijks I** *aj* monthly; **II** *ad* monthly, every month; **'maandgeld** (-en) *o* monthly pay, monthly wages, monthly allowance; **–staat** (-staten) *m* monthly returns; **–verband** (-en) *o* sanitary towel, *Am* sanitary napkin
'maanfase [s = z] (-s en -n), **–gestalte** (-n) *v* phase of the moon; **–lander** (-s) *m* = *maansloep*; **–landing** (-en) *v* landing on the moon, lunar landing; **–landschap** (-pen) *o* moonscape, lunar landscape; **–licht** *o* moonlight; **–sikkel** (-s) *v* crescent; **–sloep** (-en) *v* lunar module; **–steen** (-stenen) *m* moonstone; **'maansverduistering** (-en) *v* eclipse of the moon, lunar eclipse; **'maanvlucht** (-en) *v* flight to the moon; **–ziek** moon-struck, **B** lunatic
1 maar I *cj* but; **II** *ad* but, only; *je bent ~ eens jong* you're only young once; *pas ~ op* do be careful; *kon ik het ~!* I wish I could; **III** (maren) *o* but; *er komt een ~ bij* there is a but; *geen maren!* no buts!; **IV** *ij* but!; *~, ~, hoe heb ik het nou* dear me!; **2 maar** (maren) *v = mare*
'maarschalk (-en) *m* marshal
maart *m* March; **–s** (of) March; *de ~e buien* April showers
maas (mazen) *v* mesh [of a net]; stitch [in knitting &]; *hij kroop door de mazen* he slipped through the meshes; **Maas** *v* Meuse; **'maasbal** (-len) *m* darning-ball, darning-egg
1 maat (maten) *v* 1 (a f m e t i n g) measure, size; 2 (w a a r m e e m e n m e e t) measure; 3 ♩ time, measure; (c o n c r e e t) bar; 4 (v e r s-k u n s t) metre, measure; *maten en gewichten* weights and measures; *enkele maten rust* ♩ a few bars rest; *de ~ aangeven* ♩ mark (the) time; *~ 7 hebben* take size 7; *~ houden* 1 keep within bounds; 2 ♩ keep time; *geen ~ houden* go beyond all bounds; overdo it; *geen ~ weten te houden* not be able to restrain oneself; *iem. de ~ nemen (voor een jas)* measure sbd. (take sbd.'s measure) for a coat; *de ~ slaan* ♩ beat time; *dat maakte de ~ vol* then the cup was full; **F** that put the lid on; ● *bij de ~ verkopen* sell by measure; *in de ~* ♩ in time; *in die mate dat...* to the extent that...; *in gelijke mate* in the same measure, equally; *in hoge mate* in a large measure, highly, greatly, extremely; *in de hoogste mate* highly, exceedingly, to a degree; *in mindere*

mate to a less extent; *in meerdere of mindere mate* more or less; *in ruime mate* in a large measure, to a large extent; largely, amply; *in zekere mate* in a measure; *met mate* in moderation; *alles met mate* there is a measure in all things; *met twee maten meten* apply a double standard; *n a a r ~ (gemaakt)* (made) to measure, made to order; *naar de mate van mijn vermogens* as far as lies within my power; *o n d e r de ~ blijven* 1 *eig* be undersized [of conscripts]; 2 *fig* fall short of what is expected (required), not be up to (the) standard; *o p ~* to measure; *op de ~ van de muziek* in time to the music; *u i t de ~ ♪* out of time

2 maat (-s) *m* mate, comrade, companion, *sp* partner

'**maatafdeling** (-en) *v* bespoke department; **–beker** (-s) *m = maatglas*; **–gevend** decisive [of], a criterion [of]; **–gevoel** *o* sense of rhythm; **–glas** (-glazen) *o* measuring glass (jug)

1 '**maatje** (-s) *o* mate; *zij zijn goede ~s* they are as thick as thieves; *met iedereen goede ~s zijn* be hail-fellow-well-met with everybody

2 '**maatje** (-s) *o* **F** mammy

3 '**maatje** (-s) *o* decilitre; '**maatkleding** *v* custom-made clothes, made-to-measure clothes; '**maatregel** (-s en -en) *m* measure; *halve ~en* half measures; *~en treffen* take measures

'**maatschap** (-pen) *v* partnership; **maat'schappelijk I** *aj* social; *~ kapitaal* registered capital; *~ werk* social work, social welfare; *~ werk(st)er* social worker; **II** *ad* socially; **maatschap'pij** (-en) *v* 1 (s a m e n-l e v i n g) society; 2 (g e n o o t s c h a p) society; 3 $ company; *~ op aandelen* joint-stock company; *in de ~* in society; **–leer** *v* civics

'**maatschoenmaker** (-s) *m* bespoke shoemaker; **–slag** (-slagen) *m ♪* beat; **–staf** (-staven) *m* measuring-rod, standard²; *fig* measure; gauge, criterion; *naar deze ~* by this standard; *at this rate*; *een andere ~ aanleggen* apply another standard; **–stok** (-ken) *m* 1 rule; 2 **♪** (conductor's) baton; **–streep** (-strepen) *v* 1 **♪** bar; 2 grade mark; **–werk** *o* goods (shoes, clothes) made to measure (to order)

ma'caber [mɑ'ka.bər] macabre

maca'dam [maka.'dam] *o & m* macadam

maca'roni [mɑkɑ.'ro.ni.] *m* macaroni

machiavel'listisch [mɑki.a.vɛ'listi.s] Machia-vellian

machi'naal [ma.ʃi.'na.l] [act] mechanical, automatic(al); *~ vervaardigd* machine-made; **machi'natie** [ma.ʃi.'na.(t)si.] (-s) *v* machina-tion; **ma'chine** [ma.'ʃi.nə] (-s) *v* 1 engine, machine²; *de ~* 1 the (steam-)engine; 2 the (sewing-)machine; *~s ook:* machinery;

machine'bankwerker (-s) *m* engine fitter; **ma'chinebouw** *m* engine building; **–fabriek** (-en) *v* engineering-works; **–geweer** (-weren) *o* machine-gun; **–kamer** (-s) *v* engine-room; **–olie** *v* machine oil; **–park** *o* machinery, mechanical equipment; **machine'rie(ën)** *v* (*mv*) machinery; **ma'chineschrift** *o* typescript; **–schrijven** *o* typewriting; **–tekenaar** (-s) *m* engineering draughtsman; **machi'nist** (-en) *m* engine-driver [of a train], **F** locoman; engineer [of a ship]; 2 scene-shifter [in a theatre]; *eerste ~ ⚓* chief engineer

macht (-en) *v* power, might; ⚔ force(s); *de hemelse (helse) ~en* the heavenly (hellish) powers; *vaderlijke (ouderlijke) ~* paternal authority; *de ~ der gewoonte* the force of habit; *een ~ mensen* **F** a power of people; *geen ~ hebben over zichzelf* not be able to control oneself, not be master of oneself; ● *hij was de ~ o v e r het stuur kwijtge-raakt* ⚠ he had lost control of the car; *ik ben niet b i j ~e dit te doen* I am not able to do it; it does not lie in my power to do it; *het gaat b o v e n mijn ~*, *het staat niet i n mijn ~* it is beyond my power (control), it is not in my power; *het in zijn ~ hebben om...* have the power to... (the power of ...ing); *iem. in zijn ~ hebben* have sbd. in one's power, have a hold on sbd., have sbd. at one's mercy; *18 in de 3de ~ verheffen* raise 18 to the third power; *m e t alle ~* with all his (their) might; *u i t alle ~* all he (she, they) could, to the utmost of their power, [shout] at the top of one's voice; '**machteloos** powerless, impotent [fury]; *~ staan tegenover...* be powerless against; **machte'loosheid** *v* powerlessness, impotence; '**machthebber** (-s) *m* ruler, man in power; *de ~s ook:* those in power; '**machtig** *aj* 1 powerful, mighty; 2 (z w a a r t e v e r t e r e n) rich [food], heavy [dishes]; *iets ~ worden* get hold of sth.; *een taal ~ zijn* have mastered a language, have a language at one's command; *dat is mij te ~* that is too much for me; *het werd haar te ~* she was overcome by her emotions, she broke down; **II** *ad* powerfully; *< mightily*, **F** mighty; *hij is ~ rijk* awfully rich; '**machtigen** (machtigde, h. gemachtigd) *vt* empower, authorize; **–ging** (-en) *v* authorization; '**machtsevenwicht** *o* balance of power; **–middel** (-en) *o* means of power; **–misbruik** *o* abuse of power; **–poli-tiek** *v* power politics; **–positie** (-s) *v* position of power; **–verheffing** (-en) *v* involution; **–vertoon** *o* display of power; **–wellust** *m* lust for power

Mada'gaskar *o* Madagascar

'**made** (-n) *v* maggot, grub

made'liefje (-s) *o* daisy

ma'dera *m* Madeira

ma'donna ('s) *v* madonna
madri'ga(a)l (-galen) *o* madrigal
maf I *m* F sleep; *ik heb zo'n* ~ I am so sleepy; II *aj* 1 lazy, slow; 2 dull, tedious, stupid;
'maffen (mafte, h. gemaft) *vi* sleep, S kip; *gaan* ~ hit the hay; 'maffer (-s) *m* (s t a k i n g s - b r e k e r) blackleg, scab; 'mafkees (-kezen), –ketel (-s) S stick-in-the-mud, muff, milksop
mag tegenw. tijd enkelv. v. *mogen*
maga'zijn (-en) *o* 1 warehouse; storehouse; 2 store(s) [= shop]; 3 magazine [of rifle]; –bediende (-n en -s) *m* warehouseman; –meester (-s) *m* storekeeper
'mager lean[2] [body, frame, person, meat, years]; thin[2] [boy & programme]; gaunt [person]; meagre [fare, soil, wages]; –heid, –te *v* leanness, thinness; –tjes poorly, scantily
ma'gie *v* magic art, [black, white] magic; 'magiër (-s) *m* magician
ma'girusladder (-s) *v* extension ladder
'magisch I *aj* magic [power]; II *ad* magically
magis'traal masterly [work]; magis'traat (-traten) *m* magistrate; magistra'tuur *v* magistracy; *de* ~ ook: the robe
mag'naat (-naten) *m* magnate
mag'neet (-neten) *m* magnet; (v. m o t o r) magneto; –band (-en) *m* magnetic tape; –ijzer *o* magnetic iron; –kracht *v* magnetic force; –naald (-en) *v* magnetic needle; mag'nesia [s = z] *v* magnesia; mag'nesium *o* magnesium; mag'netisch I *aj* magnetic; II *ad* magnetically; magneti'seren [s = z] (magnetiseerde, h. gemagnetiseerd) *vt* magnetize [an object]; magneti'seur (-s) *m* magnetizer; magne'tisme *o* magnetism; magneto'foon (-s) *m* = *bandrecorder*
mag'nificat [ma'ɲi-, mɑg'ni.fi.kɑt] *o* magnificat; magni'fiek [mɑɲi.'fi.k] magnificent, splendid
mag'nolia ('s) *v* magnolia
ma'honie(hout) *o* mahogany; ma'honiehouten *aj* mahogany
mail'lot [ma.'jo.] (-s) *o* tights; (v. d a n s e r s, a c r o - b a t e n &) leotard
mainte'née [mɛ̃tə'ne.] (-s) *v* kept woman, fancy woman, mistress; mainte'neren (mainteneerde, h. gemainteneerd) *vt* keep [a mistress]
maïs [mɑis] *m* maize, Indian corn; –kolf (-kolven) *v* corncob; –meel *o* corn flour
maison'nette [mɛ:sɔ'nɛt(ə)] (-s) *v* maisonette, double flat
'maïspap ['mais-] *v* mush; –vlokken *mv* corn flakes
mai'tresse [mɛ:'trɛsə] (-s en -n) *v* mistress
ma'jesteit (-en) *v* majesty; *Zijne Majesteit* His Majesty; –schennis *v* lese-majesty; majestu'eus I *aj* majestic; II *ad* majestically

ma'jeur [j = ʒ] *v* major
ma'jolica *o* & *v* majolica
ma'joor (-s) *m* ✕ major; ✍ squadron-leader
majo'rette (-s) *v* drum majorette
mak tame, gentle, meek; *fig.* manageable
'makelaar (-s) *m* broker; ~ *in assurantiën* insurance broker; ~ *in effecten* stock-broker; ~ *in huizen* house-agent; ~ *in onroerende (vaste) goederen* (real) estate agent; makelaar'dij *v* brokerage, broking; 'makerlaarsloon (-lonen) *o*, –provisie (-s) *v* brokerage; makela'rij *v* = *makelaardij*
make'lij *v* make, workmanship
'maken (maakte, h. gemaakt) *vt* 1 make [boots &]; take [a photograph]; 2 (d o e n z i j n) make, render [happy], drive [mad]; 3 (o p w e r p e n) make, raise [objections &]; 4 (u i t m a k e n) make [a difference]; 5 (d o e n) make [a journey &], do; 6 (r e p a r e r e n) mend, repair; 7 ☞ do [sums, translations &]; 8 (v o r m e n) form [an idea of...]; 9 (i n - n e m e n) make [water]; *hij kan je ~ en breken* he can put you in his pocket, he can make matchwood of you; *maak dat je wegkomt!* be off!, get out!; *wat moet ik daarvan ~?* what am I to make (think) of it?; *dat maakt zoveel* that amounts to..., that makes...; *niemand kan mij wat ~* no one can do anything to me; *hoe maak je het?* how are you?, how do you do?; *hij maakt het goed* he is (doing) well; *het goed ~* (n a r u z i e) make up; *hij zal het niet lang meer ~* he won't last much longer, he is not long for this world; *hij maakt het er ook naar* he has (only) himself to thank for it; *dat heeft er niets mee te ~* that is (has) nothing to do with it, it is neither here nor there; *je hebt hier niets te ~* you have no business here; *ik wil er niets mee te ~ hebben* I will have nothing to do with it, I will have no hand in the matter; *ik wil niet met de vent te ~ hebben* I will have nothing to say to the fellow; I will have no dealings with that fellow; *ik wil niets meer met hem te ~ hebben* I have done with him; *dat maakt niets uit* that does not matter; *hij maakt er maar wat van* he makes a poor job of it; *ik heb hem de thema laten ~* I've made him do the exercise; *ik ga mij een jas laten ~* I'm having a coat made; *zij ~ mij aan het lachen* they make me laugh; *zich boos ~* become (get) angry; *die woorden tot de zijne ~* make those words one's own; *een zienswijze tot de zijne ~* espouse a view; –er (-s) *m* maker, author
'makheid *v* tameness, meekness, meekness
'makkelijk = *gemakkelijk*
'makker (-s) *m* mate, comrade, companion
'makkie *o* F pushover, S piece of cake
ma'kreel (-krelen) *m* mackerel
1 mal (-len) *m* model, mould, gauge; stencil

2 mal I *aj* 1 foolish; silly; 2 fond (of *met, op*); *het is een ~le geschiedenis* 1 it is a funny story; 2 that is queer, it is an awkward affair; *ben je ~?* are you mad?; *iem. voor de ~ houden* make a fool of sbd.; **II** *ad* foolishly; *doe niet zo ~* **F** don't be silly (daft); zie ook: *aanstellen*

ma'laise [ma.'lɛːzə] *v* **$** depression, slump

ma'laria *v* malaria; **–lijder** (-s) *m* malaria(l) patient; **–mug** (-gen) *v* malaria mosquito, anopheles

Ma'lawi *o* Malawi

malcon'tent I *aj* discontented; **II** *sb de ~en* the malcontents

Male'diven *de ~* the Maldive Islands, the Maldives

Ma'leier (-s) *m* Malay; **Ma'leis I** *aj* Malay; **II** *o het ~* Malay; **III** *v een ~e* a Malay woman; **Ma'leisië** [s = z] *o* Malaysia; **Ma'leisiër** (-s) *m*, **Ma'leisisch** *aj* Malaysian

1 'malen* *vt* grind [corn, coffee]; *die 't eerst komt het eerst maalt* first come first served; **2 'malen** (maalde, h. gemaald) *vi wat maal ik erom?* what do I care!, who cares?; *daar maalt hij over* that is what his mind is running on; *hij is ~de* he is mad (crazy); zie ook: *zaniken*

'malheid (-heden) *v* foolishness

mal'heur [ma'lør] (-en en -s) *o* mishap

'Mali *o* Mali

'maliënkolder (-s) *m* coat of mail, hauberk

'maling *v ~ aan iets hebben* not care (a damn &) about sth.; *iem. in de ~ nemen* make a fool of sbd.

mal'kander = *elkander*

malle'jan (-s) *m* truck; **malle'moer F** *dat gaat je geen ~ aan* it's none of your business; **'mallemolen, malle'molen** (-s) *m* merry-go-round

'mallen (malde, h. gemald) *vi* fool, dally; **'mallepraat** *m* nonsense; fiddlesticks!; **'malligheid** (-heden) *v* foolishness, folly; *allerlei malligheden* foolish things; **mal'loot** (-loten) *m-v* silly, idiot; **mal'lotig** silly, idiotic

mals tender [meat]; soft, mellow [pears &]; *hij is lang niet ~* he is rather severe; **–heid** *v* tenderness; softness, mellowness

'Malta *o* Malta; **Mal'tezer** *aj* & *m* (-s) Maltese

malver'satie [-'za.(t)si.] (-s) *v* malversation

ma'ma ('s) *v* mamma

'mammoet (-en en -s) *m* mammoth

'mammon *m de ~* mammon

man (-nen) *m* 1 man; 2 (e c h t g e n o o t) husband; *een ~ van zijn woord zijn* be as good as one's word; *een ~ van zaken* a business man; *zes ~ en een korporaal* ✕ six men and a corporal; *duizend ~* ✕ a thousand troops; *1000 ~ infanterie* ✕ a thousand foot; *de kleine ~* the little man, the man in the street; *een stuiver de ~*

a penny a head; *als één ~* to a man, as one man; *hij is er de ~ niet naar om...* he is not the man to..., it is so unlike him...; *~ en paard noemen* give chapter and verse; *~ en vrouw* husband and wife; *als ~ en vrouw leven* cohabit; *zijn ~ staan* be able to hold one's own; *zijn ~ vinden* meet (find) one's match; ● *aan de ~ brengen* sell [goods]; marry off [daughters]; *m e t ~ en macht werken* work all out, with might and main; *met ~ en muis vergaan* ⚓ go down with all hands (on board); *op de ~ af* pointblank; *p e r ~* [so much] a head; *een gevecht van ~ t e g e n ~* a hand-to-hand fight; *t o t op de laatste ~* to the last man; *een ~ een ~, een woord een woord* an honest man's word is as good as his bond; zie ook: *mans*

'manager ['mɛnədʒər] (-s) *m* manager; **–ziekte** *v* manager's disease

manche [mɑnʃ] (-s) *v sp* heat [of a contest, match]; game [at whist, bridge]

'manchester, man'chester ['mɛnʃəstər, mɑn'ʃɛstər] *o* (s t o f) corduroy

man'chet [mɑn'ʃɛt] (-ten) *v* 1 cuff; 2 (v a s t) wristband; **–knoop** (-knopen) *m* cuff-link

'manco ('s) *o* **$** shortage; short delivery

mand (-en) *v* basket, hamper; *hij viel door de ~* he had to own up

man'daat (-daten) *o* 1 mandate; 2 power of attorney, proxy; 3 warrant to pay; *zijn ~ neerleggen* resign one's seat [in Parliament]

'mandag (-dagen) *m* man-day

manda'rijn (-en) *m* mandarin

manda'rijntje (-s) *o* ⚘ tangerine

manda'taris (-sen) *m* mandatary, mandatory

'mandefles (-sen) *v* 1 wicker-bottle; 2 carboy [for acids]; 3 demijohn

mande'ment (-en) *o rk* pastoral letter (from the bishop(s))

'mandenmaken *o* basket-making; **–er** (-s) *m* basket-maker; **'mandewerk** *o* basket-ware, wicker-work; **'mandje** (-s) *o* small basket

mando'line (-s) *v* mandolin(e)

'mandvol *v* basketful, hamperful

ma'nege [ma.'ne.ʒə] (-s) *v* manege, riding-school; **–paard** (-en) *o* riding-school horse

1 'manen (maande, h. gemaand) *vt* dun [a debtor for payment]

2 'manen *mv* mane [of horse]

'maneschijn *m* moonlight; **–straal** (-stralen) *m* & *v* moonbeam

ma'neuver = *manoeuvre*

'manga ['mɑŋɡa.] ('s) *o* mango

man'gaan [mɑn'ɡa.n] *o* manganese; **–erts** *o* manganese ore

'mangat (-gaten) *o* manhole

'mangel (-s) *m* mangling-machine, mangle; **'mangelen** (mangelde, h. gemangeld) *vt* mangle [linen]

'**mangelwortel** (-s) *m* mangel-wurzel

'**mango** ['maŋgo.] ('s) = *manga*

man'haftig I *aj* manful, manly, brave; **II** *ad* manfully; **–heid** *v* manliness, courage

mani'ak (-ken) *m* 1 maniac; 2 (z o n d e r l i n g) faddist, crank; 3 (o p i e t s v e r z o t) F [crossword-puzzle, sex &] fiend; **mania'kaal** maniacal

mani'cure 1 (-n) *m-v* (p e r s o o n) manicure, manicurist; 2 *v* (d e h a n d e l i n g) manicure; (s t e l w e r k t u i g e n) manicure set; **mani'curen** (manicuurde, h. gemanicuurd) *vt* manicure

ma'nie (-nieën) *v* mania, craze, rage, fad

ma'nier (-en) *v* manner, fashion, way; *goede ~en* good manners; *wat zijn dat voor ~en?* where are your manners?; *dat is geen ~ (van doen)* that is not as it should be; *hij kent geen ~en* ook: his manners are bad; ● *bij ~ van spreken* in a manner of speaking; *op deze ~* in this manner (way); after this fashion; *op zijn ~* his way, after his fashion; *op de een of andere ~* (in) one way or another; *op alle (mogelijke) ~en* in every possible way; *o, op die ~* ah, I see what you mean

manië'risme [ma.ni:-] *o* mannerism

mani'fest I (-en) *o* manifesto; ⚓ manifest; **II** *aj* manifest, evident, palpable [error]; **manifes'tant** (-en) *m* demonstrator; **manifes'tatie** [- 'ta.(t)si.] (-s) *v* demonstration; 2 (v. z i e k t e, g e e s t e n) manifestation; **manifes'teren** (manifesteerde, h. gemanifesteerd) **I** *vi* demonstrate; **II** *vr zich ~* (v. g e e s t, z i e k t e) manifest itself

ma'nilla ('s) *v* manilla; **–hennep** *m* Manil(l)a hemp

mani'ok *m* manioc

manipu'latie [- 'la.(t)si.] (-s) *v* manipulation; **manipu'leren** (manipuleerde, h. gemanipuleerd) *vt* manipulate

'**manisch** manic; **~-depres'sief** manic-depressive

mank lame, crippled; *~ gaan* limp; *die vergelijking gaat ~* the comparison is faulty; *aan een euvel ~ gaan* have a defect

manke'ment (-en) *o* defect, trouble; **man'keren** (mankeerde, h. gemankeerd) *vi* fail; *hij mankeert nooit* he never fails to put in an appearance; *er ~ er vijf* 1 five are wanting (missing); 2 five are absent; there are five absentees; *dat mankeert er nog maar aan!* that's all we need!; that's the last straw!; *wat mankeert je?* what's the matter with you?²?; what possesses you?; *er mankeert wat aan* there is something wrong; *ik mankeer niets* I'm all right; *ik zal niet ~ u bericht te zenden* I shall not fail to send you

word; *zonder ~* without fail

'**mankracht** *v* man-power; **–lief** F hubby; **–lijk(heid)** = *mannelijk(heid)*; **man'moedig I** *aj* manful, manly, brave; **II** *ad* manfully; **–heid** *v* manliness, bravery, courage

'**manna** *o* manna

'**mannelijk** 1 male; masculine [ook *gram*]; 2 (m o e d i g) manly; **–heid** *v* manliness, masculinity, manhood; (g e s l a c h t s d e l e n) male genitals; '**mannengek** (-ken) *v* flirt; nymphomaniac; **–klooster** (-s) *o* monastery; **–koor** (-koren) *o* 1 male voice choir; 2 male choir, men's choral society; **–kracht** *v* manly strength; **–moed** *m* manly courage; **–stem** (-men) *v* male voice, man's voice; **–taal** *v* manly (virile) language; **–werk** *o* a man's job

manne'quin [manə'kɛ̃] (-s) 1 *v* (v r o u w) (fashion) model; 2 *m* (m a n) (male) model; (p o p) mannequin

'**mannetje** (-s) *o* 1 little man, manikin, 2 male, ⚥ cock; *~ en wijfje* male and female; *~ aan ~ staan* stand packed together (shoulder to shoulder); '**mannetjesbij** (-en) *m* drone; **–eend** (-en) *m* drake; **–ezel** (-s) *m* jackass; **–gans** (-ganzen) *m* gander; **–olifant** (-en) *m* bull-elephant; **–putter** (-s) *m* he-man; (v r o u w) strapping wench

ma'noeuvre [ma.'nœ.vrə] (-s) *v* & *o* manoeuvre²; **manoeu'vreerbaar** manoeuvrable; **–heid** *v* manoeuvrability; **manoeu'vreren** (manoeuvreerde, h. gemanoeuvreerd) *vi* manoeuvre²

'**manometer** (-s) *m* manometer, pressure gauge

mans *hij is ~ genoeg* he is man enough; *hij is heel wat ~* he is very strong; '**manschappen** *mv* ⚓ (b e m a n n i n g) crew, ratings; ⚔ men, personnel; '**manshoog** to a man's height; **–kleding** *v* male attire, man's dress; '**manslag** (-slagen) *m* homicide; manslaughter [through negligence]; '**manspersoon** (-sonen) *m* male person, male, man

'**mantel** (-s) *m* 1 (in 't alg. en kort of z o n d e r m o u w e n) cloak, mantle; 2 (v a n v r o u w e n e n l a n g) coat; 3 $ (v. e f f e c t) certificate; 4 ✂ jacket; *iets met de ~ der liefde bedekken* cover it with the cloak of charity, draw a veil over it; *iem. de ~ uitvegen* scold sbd.; **–jas** (-sen) *m* & *v* cloak with cape; **–meeuw** (-en) *v* black-backed gull, saddle-back; **–organisatie** [-za.(t)si.] (-s) *v* front (organization); **–pak** (-ken) *o* coat and skirt, suit; **–zak** (-ken) *m* coat pocket

man'tille [man'ti.ljə] (-s) *v* mantilla

manu'aal (-ualen) *o* ♪ manual, keyboard

manufac'turen *mv* drapery, soft goods, (linen-) draper's goods; **–zaak** (-zaken) *v* = *manufactuurzaak*; **manufactu'rier** (-s) *m* (linen-)

draper; **manufac′tuurzaak** (-zaken) *v* drapery business

manus′cript (-en) *o* manuscript

′manusje-van-′alles (manusjes-) *o* handy-man

′manuur (-uren) *o* man-hour; **–volk** *o* menfolk, men; **–wijf** (-wijven) *o* virago; **–ziek** man-crazy, nymphomaniac

map (-pen) *v* 1 (o m s l a g v o o r p a p i e r e n) folder; 2 (t e k e n p o r t e f e u i l l e) portfolio

ma′quette [ma.′kɪtə] (-s) *v* model

′maraboe (-s) *m* marabou

maras′kijn *m* maraschino

′marathon(loop) (-lopen) *m* marathon

marchan′deren [marʃan′de:rə(n)] (marchandeerde, h. gemarchandeerd) *vi* bargain, chaffer, haggle

mar′cheren [mar′ʃe:rə(n)] (marcheerde, h. en is gemarcheerd) *vi* march; *goed* ~ [*fig*] go well

marco′nist (-en) *m* wireless operator

⊙ **′mare** (-n) *v* news, tidings, report

marechaus′see [marəʃo.′se.] 1 *v* constabulary; 2 (-s) *m* member of the constabulary

′maretak(ken) *m(mv)* mistletoe

marga′rine *v* margarine

′marge [′marʒə] (-s) *v* margin; **margi′naal** [marʒi.′na.l] marginal

mar′griet (-en) *v* ⚘ ox-eye (daisy)

Ma′riabeeld (-en) *o* image of the Virgin (Mary); **Maria-′Boodschap** *v* Lady Day, Annunciation Day [March 25th]; **~-′Hemelvaart** *v* Assumption; **~-′Lichtmis** *m* Candlemas; **~-ten-′Hemel-Opneming** *v* Assumption

marihu′ana *v* marijuana, marihuana

mari′nade (-s) *v* marinade

ma′rine *v* navy; *bij de* ~ in the navy; **–blauw** navy blue

mari′neren (marineerde, h. gemarineerd) *vt* marinate; *zie ook: gemarineerd*

ma′rinewerf (-werven) *v* naval dockyard; **mari′nier** (-s) *m* marine

mario′net (-ten) *v* puppet², marionette; **mario′nettenregering** (-en) *v* puppet government; **–spel** (-len) *o* puppet show; **–theater** (-s) *o* puppet theatre

mari′tiem naval

marjo′lein *v* marjoram

mark (-en) *m* (m u n t) mark

mar′kant striking [case], outstanding [example]; **mar′keren** (markeerde, h. gemarkeerd) **I** *vt* mark; *de pas* ~ mark time²; **II** *vi* feather, mark [of a dog]

marke′tentster (-s) *v* sutler, camp-follower

1 mar′kies (-kiezen) *m* marquis, marquess

2 mar′kies (-kiezen) *v* (z o n n e s c h e r m) awning, sunshade

markie′zin (-nen) *v* 1 marchioness; 2 [French]

marquise; **marki′zaat** (-zaten) *o* marquisate

markt (-en) *v* 1 market; 2 (p l a a t s) market (place); *a a n de* ~ *komen* come into the market; *aan de* ~ *zijn* be upon the market; *n a a r de* ~ *gaan* go to market; *o n d e r de* ~ *verkopen* sell below market-price, undersell; *o p de* ~ [*eig*] in the market place; *op de* ~ *brengen* (*gooien*) put (throw) on the market; *t e r* ~ *brengen* put on the market, market; *v a n alle* ~*en thuis zijn* be an all-round man; **–analyse** [-.ana.li.zə] *v* market research; **–bericht** (-en) *o* market report; **–dag** (-dagen) *m* market day; **′markten** (marktte, h. gemarkt) *vi* go to market, go marketing; **′marktgeld** *o* market dues; **–koopman** (-lieden en -lui) *m* market trader; **–kraam** (-kramen) *v* & *o* market stall, booth; **–onderzoek** *o* market research; **–plaats** (-en) *v* 1 market place, market; 2 market town; **–plein** (-en) *o* market square; **–prijs** (-prijzen) *m* market price, ruling price; market quotation [of stocks]; **–vrouw** (-en) *v* market-woman; **–waarde** *v* market (marketable) value

marme′lade (-s en -n) *v* marmalade

′marmer *o* marble; **–achtig** marbly; 1 **′marmeren** *aj* marble² [halls, arms &]; marbly [cheeks]; marble-tiled [floor]; marble-topped [table &]; 2 **′marmeren** (marmerde, h. gemarmerd) *vt* marble; **′marmergroef, –groeve** (-groeven) *v* marble-quarry

mar′mot (-ten) *v* 1 marmot; 2 (c a v i a) guinea-pig

maro′kijn *o* morocco(-leather)

Marok′kaan (-kanen) *m* Moroccan; **–s** Moroccan; **Ma′rokko** *o* Morocco

Mars *m* Mars; **~bewoner** Martian

1 mars (-en) *v* 1 (v. m a r s k r a m e r) (pedlar's) pack; 2 ⚓ top; *grote* ~ ⚓ maintop; *hij heeft heel wat in zijn* ~ he has brains; *hij heeft weinig in zijn* ~ he is not very bright

2 mars (-en) *m* & *v* ⚔ march; ~, *de deur uit!* begone!; *op* ~ on the (their) march

′marsepein *m* & *o* marchpane, marzipan

′marskramer (-s) *m* pedlar, hawker

′marsorde *v* order of march; **–order** (-s) *v* marching orders

′marssteng (-en) *v* topmast

′marstempo *o* 1 ⚔ rate of march; 2 ♪ march-time; **–tenue** [-.tən.y.] (-s) *o* & *v* marching-kit, marching-order; **mars′vaardig** ready to march

′marszeil (-en) *o* topsail

′martelaar (-s en -laren) *m* martyr; **–schap** *o* martyrdom; **martela′res** (-sen) *v* martyr; **′marteldood** *m* & *v* martyrdom; *de* ~ *sterven* die a martyr; **′martelen** (martelde, h. gemarteld) *vt* torment, torture, martyr; **–ling** (-en) *v*

torture, [one long] martyrdom
'marter (-s) *m* marten
marti'aal [mɑrtsi.'a.l] martial
'Marva ('s) *v* Wren
mar'xisme *o* Marxism; **–ist(isch)** *m* (-en) (&
 aj) Marxist
mas'cara *v* mascara
mas'cotte (-s) *v* mascot
'maser ['me.zər] *m* maser
'masker (-s) *o* mask[2]; *iem. het ~ afrukken*
 unmask sbd.; *het ~ afwerpen* throw off (drop)
 the mask; *onder het ~ van vroomheid* under the
 show of piety; **maske'rade** (-s en -n) *v*
 masquerade, pageant; **1 'maskeren**
 (maskerde, h. gemaskerd) *vt* mask; **2
 mas'keren** (maskeerde, h. gemaskeerd) *vt*
 mask
maso'chisme [ma.zo.-] *o* masochism; **–ist** (-en)
 m masochist; **–istisch** masochistic
'massa ('s) *v* **1** mass; crowd; **2** $ bankrupt's
 estate; *de grote ~* the masses, the many; *b ij ~'s*
 in heaps; *i n ~ produceren* mass-produce; *in ~
 verkopen* sell by the lump; **mas'saal** mass
 [attack, unemployment]; wholesale [massacre],
 massive, in mass; **'massa-artikel** (-en en -s) *o*
 mass-produced article; **'massabijeenkomst**
 (-en) *v* mass meeting; **'massacommunicatie**
 [-ka.(t)si.] *v* mass communication; **–middel**
 (-en) *o* mass medium [*mv* mass media]
mas'sage [mɑ'sa.ʒə] (-s) *v* massage, **F** rubdown
'massagraf (-graven) *o* mass grave, common
 grave; **–hysterie** [-hɪstəri.] *v* mass hysteria;
 massali'teit *v* massiveness; **'massamedium**
 (-ia) *o* mass medium [*mv* mass media];
 –produktie [-düksi.] *v* mass production;
 –psychologie [-psi.ɡo.lo.ɡi.] *v* mass psychology; **–psychose** [-psi.ɡo.zə] *v* mass psychosis
mas'seren (masseerde, h. gemasseerd) *vt*
 massage; **mas'seur** (-s) *m* masseur;
 mas'seuse [-zə] (-s) *v* masseuse
mas'sief solid [gold, silver], massive [building]
mast (-en) *m* **1** ⚓, ✗, *RT* mast; **2** ☀ [power]
 pylon; **3** (g y m n a s t i e k) pole; *vóór de ~ varen*
 sail afore the mast; *voor de ~ zitten* have eaten
 one's fill; **–bok** (-ken) *m* sheers, sheer-legs;
 –bos (-sen) *o* fir-wood; **'masten** (mastte, h.
 gemast) *vt* ⚓ mast
mas'tiek *m* & *o* mastic
'mastklimmen *o* pole-climbing; **–koker** (-s) *m*
 mast-hole; **–kraan** (-kranen) *v = mastbok*
masto'dont (-en) *m* mastodon
mastur'beren (masturbeerde, h. gemastur-
 beerd) *vi* masturbate
'mastworp (-en) *m* ⚓ clove-hitch
1 mat (-ten) *v* mat; *zijn ~ten oprollen* **F** pack up
2 mat *aj* tired, faint, weary [patient, voice &];
 dead, dull [tone, colour]; mat [gold], spent

 [cannon-ball]
3 mat *aj* checkmate
4 mat (maten) V.T. v. *meten*
mata'dor (-s) *m* matador; *fig* dab (at *in*)
'mate *v* zie 1 *maat*; **–loos I** *aj* measureless,
 boundless, immense; **II** *ad* immensely
mate'lot [ma.tə'lo.] (-s) *o* sailor-hat, boater
'maten V.T. meerv. v. *meten*
materi'aal (-ialen) *o* material(s); *rollend ~*
 rolling-stock; **materia'lisme** *o* materialism;
 –ist (-en) *m* materialist; **–istisch** material-
 istic(al); **ma'terie** (-iën en -s) *v* matter;
 materi'eel I *aj* material; **II** *ad* materially; **III** *o*
 material(s); *rollend ~* rolling-stock
'matglas *o* frosted glass
'matheid *v* weariness, dul(l)ness, languor
mathe'maticus (-ci) *m* mathematician;
 mathe'matisch mathematical; **ma'thesis**
 [ma.'te.zɪs] *v* mathematics
'matig I *aj* **1** moderate [sum, income &
 smoker]; moderate, temperate, sober, abste-
 mious, frugal [man]; reasonable [prices];
 conservative [estimate]; **2** = *middelmatig*; **II** *ad*
 moderately &; *~ gebruiken* make a moderate
 use of; *maar ~ tevreden* not particularly pleased;
 ik vind het maar ~ I don't think much of it, I'm
 not too pleased; **'matigen** (matigde, h. gematigd) **I** *vt* moderate, temper, modify; zie ook:
 gematigd; **II** *vr kun je je niet wat ~?* can't you
 restrain yourself, keep your temper a bit?;
 'matigheid *v* moderation, temperance,
 soberness, abstemiousness, frugality; **'mati-
 ging** *v* moderation, modification
mati'nee (-s) *v* matinée, afternoon performance; **mati'neus** *~ zijn* be an early riser
'matje (-s) *o iem. op het ~ roepen* have sbd. on the
 carpet, carpet sbd.
ma'tras (-sen) *v* & *o* mattress
matriar'chaat *o* matriarchy
ma'trijs (-trijzen) *v* matrix, mould
'matrix (-trices) *v* matrix
ma'trone [ma.'trɔ:nə] (-s en -n) *v* matron
ma'troos (-trozen) *m* sailor; **ma'trozenlied**
 (-eren) *o* sailor's song, chanty, shanty;
 –pak(je) [-pakken, -pakjes] *o* sailor suit
'matse (-s) *m* matzo(h)
'matteklopper (-s) *m* carpet-beater; **'matten**
 (matte, h. gemat) *vt* mat, rush [chairs];
 'mattenbies (-biezen) *v* bulrush; **–maker** (-s)
 m mat-maker; **mat'teren** (matteerde, h.
 gematteerd) *vt* frost [glass], mat [cigars, gold];
 'matwerk *o* matting
Maure'tanië *o* Mauritania
Mau'ritius [-(t)si.üs] *o* Mauritius
mauso'leum [mɔuzo.'le.üm] (-ea en -s) *o*
 mausoleum
'mauve ['mo.və] mauve

'mauwen (mauwde, h. gemauwd) *vi* mew
'Mavo ('s) *m* ± Secondary School
m.a.w. = *met andere woorden* in other words
maxi'maal, 'maximaal maximum;
  'maximum (-ma) *o* maximum; –prijs (-prijzen) *m*
  maximum price; –snelheid (-heden) *v* 1 speed
  limit [for motor-cars &]; 2 ⚡ top speed
mayo'naise [ma.jo.'nɛ:zə] *v* mayonnaise
'mazelen *mv* measles
'mazen (maasde, h. gemaasd) *vt* darn
ma'zurka ('s) *m* & *v* mazurka
'mazzel *m* F (good) luck
me [mə] (to) me
mecanicien [me.ka.ni.si.'ɛ̃] (-s) *m* mechanic
mece'naat *o* patronage; me'cenas (-sen en
  -'naten) *m* Maecenas
me'chanica *v* mechanics; mecha'niek *v* & *o*
  mechanism; action, works [of a watch];
  me'chanisch mechanical; mechani'seren
  [s = z] (mechaniseerde, h. gemechaniseerd) *vt*
  mechanize; –ring *v* mechanization;
  mecha'nisme (-n) *o* = *mechaniek*
'Mechelen *o* Mechlin, Malines; 'Mechels *aj*
  Mechlin; ~e *kant* Mechlin (lace)
me'daille [mə'da(l)jə] (-s) *v* medal;
  medail'leur [me.da(l)'jø:r] (-s) *m* medallist;
  medail'lon [me.da(l)'jɔ̀n] (-s) *o* 1 △ medal-
  lion; 2 (h a l s s i e r a a d) locket; 3 (i l l u s -
  t r a t i e) inset
1 'mede *v* = 1 *mee*
2 'mede *ad* = 2 *mee*; –aansprakelijk jointly
  liable (responsible); –arbeider (-s) *m* fellow-
  worker, workmate; –beslissingsrecht *o* right
  of co-determination; –brengen[1] = *meebrengen*;
  –burger (-s) *m* fellow-citizen; mede'deelzaam communicative, expansive; –heid *v*
  communicativeness; 'mededelen[1] *vt*
  announce, state, tell; *iem. iets* ~ communicate
  sth. to sbd., impart sth. to sbd., inform sbd. of
  sth.; –ling (-en) *v* communication, information, announcement, statement; *een* ~ *doen*
  make a communication (a statement); 'mede-
  delingenblaadje (-s) *o* newsletter; –bord
  (-en) *o* notice-board; 'mededingen[1] *vi*
  compete; ~ *naàr* compete for; –er (-s) *m* rival,
  competitor; 'mededinging *v* competition,
  rivalry; 'mededirecteur (-en en -s) *m* joint
  manager, joint director, co-director; –dogen *o*
  compassion, pity; –eigenaar (-s en -naren) *m*
  joint owner, part-owner; –erfgenaam
  (-namen) *m* joint heir; –erfgename (-n) *v* joint
  heiress; –firmant (-en) *m* copartner; –gaan[1]
  = *meegaan*; –gevangene (-n) *m-v* fellow-

prisoner; –gevoel *o* sympathy, fellow-feeling;
  –helper (-s) *m*, –helpster (-s) *v* assistant;
  –huurder (-s) *m* co-tenant; –klinker (-s) *m*
  consonant; –leerling (-en) *m* school-fellow,
  fellow-student; –leven[1] = *meeleven*; –lijden *v*
  (-leden) *o* fellow-member; –lijden *o* compassion, pity; ~ *hebben met* have (take) pity on, feel
  pity for, pity; *iems.* ~ *opwekken* rouse sbd.'s
  pity; *uit* ~ 1 out of pity [for him]; 2 in pity [of
  his misery]; mede'lijdend compassionate;
  'medemens (-en) *m* fellow-man; –minnaar
  (-s) *m* rival
1 'Meden *mv. de* ~ the Medes
2 'meden V.T. meerv. v. *mijden*
'medeondertekenaar (-s) *m* co-signatory;
  –passagier [-pasa.ʒi:r] (-s) *m* fellow-
  passenger; mede'plichtig accessory; ~ *aan*
  accessory to; *hij is eraan* ~ he is an accomplice;
  –e (-n) *m-v* accomplice, accessory; –heid *v*
  complicity (in *aan*); 'medereiziger (-s) *m*
  fellow-passenger, fellow-traveller; –schepsel
  (-s en -en) *o* fellow-creature; –schuldeiser
  (-s) *m* fellow-creditor; –schuldige (-n) *m-v*
  accomplice; –slepen[1] = *meeslepen*; –speler (-s)
  m fellow-player, partner; –stander (-s) *m*
  supporter, partisan; –student (-en) *m* fellow-
  student; –vennoot (-noten) *m* copartner;
  'medewerken[1] = *meewerken*; –er (-s) *m* 1
  co-operator, co-worker; 2 [author's] collaborator; contributor [to a periodical]; 'mede-
  werking *v* co-operation; *zijn* ~ *verlenen* co-
  operate, contribute; *met* ~ *van...* with the
  co-operation of; –weten *o* knowledge; *m e t* ~
  van... with the knowledge of...; *z o n d e r z i j n* ~
  without his knowledge, unknown to him;
  –zeggenschap, mede'zeggenschap *v* & *o*
  say; participation [in industrial enterprise],
  (workers') co-management; ~ *hebben* have a say
  [in the matter]
medi'aan (-ianen) *v* median
media'miek mediumistic
medica'ment (-en) *o* medicament, medicine;
  medi'cijn (-en) *v* medicine, physic; ~*en*
  gebruiken take physic; *in de* ~*en studeren* study
  medicine; *student in de* ~*en* medical student;
  –flesje (-s) *o* medicine bottle; –kastje (-s) *o*
  medicine cupboard; –man (-nen) *m* medicine-
  man, witch doctor; medici'naal medicinal;
  'medicus (-ci) *m* 1 medical man, physician,
  doctor; 2 medical student
'medio ~ *mei* (in) mid-May; *tot* ~ *mei* until the
  middle of May
'medisch medical

---

[1] V.T. en V.D. van dit werkwoord volgens het model: 'me(d)edelen, V.T. deelde 'me(d)e, V.D. 'me(d)egedeeld.
Zie voor de vormen onder het grondwoord, in dit voorbeeld: *delen*. Bij sterke en onregelmatige werkwoorden wordt
u verwezen naar de lijst achterin.

medi'tatie [-(t)si.] (-s en -iën) *v* meditation; **medi'teren** (mediteerde, h. gemediteerd) *vi* meditate

'medium (-ia en -s) *o* medium

1 mee *v* 1 (m e e k r a p) madder; 2 (h o n i n g- d r a n k) mead

2 mee also, likewise, as well; ~ *van de partij zijn* make one, too; *hij is* ~ *van de rijksten* he is among the richest; *alles* ~ *hebben* have everything in one's favour; **'meebrengen**[1] *vt* bring along with one; bring[2]; *fig* entail; carry [responsibilities]

meed (meden) V.T. v. *mijden*

'meedelen[1] = *mededelen*; **–dingen**[1] = *mededingen*; **–doen**[1] *vi* join [in the game, in the sport &], take part (in *aan*); *doe je mee?* will you make one?; *ik doe mee* I'm on; *niet* ~ stand out; *daar doe ik niet aan mee* I will be no party to that; **mee'dogend** compassionate; **mee'dogenloos** pitiless, merciless, ruthless, relentless; **'meeëter** (-s) *m* comedo [*mv* comedones], blackhead; **'meegaan**[1] *vi* go (along) with [sbd.], accompany [sbd.]; *ik ga met u mee* I'll accompany you; 2 I concur in what you say, I agree with you; *met zijn tijd* ~ move with the times; *ga je mee?* are you coming? *deze schoenen gaan lang mee* these shoes last long (wear well); **mee'gaand** yielding, accommodating, pliable, compliant; **–heid** *v* compliance, complaisance, pliability; **'meegeven** **I** *vt* give (along with); **II** *vi* yield, give way, give; **–gevoel** = *medegevoel*; **–helpen**[1] *vi* assist, bear a hand; **–komen**[1] *vi* come along [with sbd.]; *hij kan niet* ~ he cannot keep up

'meekrap *v* madder; **–wortel** (-s) *m* madder-root

meekrijgen[1] *vt zij zal veel* ~ she will get a fair dowry; *wij konden hem niet* ~ he could not be persuaded to join us

meel *o* 1 meal; 2 (g e b u i l d) flour

'meelachen *vi* join in the laugh

'meelachtig mealy, farinaceous; **–biet** (-en) *v* bore; **–dauw** *m* mildew; **–draad** (-draden) *m* stamen

'meeleven[1] **I** *va* enter into the feelings & of..., sympathize with... [you]; **II** *o* sympathy

'meelfabriek (-en) *v* flour mill

'meelij = *medelijden*

'meelkost *m* farinaceous food

'meelopen[1] *vi* walk (run) along with; *het loopt hem altijd mee* he is always lucky (in luck); **–er** (-s) *m* hanger-on; fellow-traveller [of a political party]

meelspijs (-spijzen) *v* farinaceous food; **–worm** (-en) *m* meal-worm; **–zak** (-ken) *m* flour-sack, meal-sack

'meemaken *vt veel* ~ go through a great deal; *hij heeft zes veldtochten meegemaakt* he has been through six campaigns; **–nemen**[1] *vt* take away, take (along) with; *dat is altijd meegenomen* that is so much gained; **–praten**[1] *vi* join in the conversation; *hij wil ook* ~ he wants to put in a word; *daar kan ik van* ~ I know something about it

1 meer more; *iets* ~ something more; *iets* ~ *dan...* a little upward of..., a little over...; *niemand* ~ (*dan 100 gulden*)? any advance (on a hundred guilders)?; *niet* ~ no more, no longer; *hij is niet* ~ he is no more; *wie was er nog* ~? who else was there?; *je moet wat* ~ *komen* you should come more often; *ik hoop je* ~ *te zien* I hope to see more of you; *hij kon niet* ~ *lopen* he could not walk any longer (any further); *zij is niet jong* ~ she is not young any longer (any more), she is not so young as she was; *niet* ~ *dan drie* no more than three; *het is niet* ~ *dan natuurlijk* (*billijk*) it is only natural (fair); *niets* ~ *of niets minder dan...* neither more nor less than...; *er is niets* ~ there is nothing left; *te* ~ *daar...* the more so as...; *een reden te* ~ all the more reason, an added (additional) reason; *wat* ~ *is* what is more; ~ *en* ~ more and more; *steeds* ~ more and more, ever more; *zonder* ~ simply, without much ado; zie ook: 1 *dies, geen, onder, 2 woord, zonder* &

2 meer (meren) *o* lake

'meerboei (-en) *v* mooring-buoy

'meerder more, greater, superior; ~*e* (= v e r s c h e i d e n e) several; *mijn* ~*en* my betters, *ix* my superiors; **'meerderen** (meerderde, h. en is gemeerderd) *vi* increase; **'meerderheid** *v* 1 majority; 2 (g e e s t e l i j k) superiority; **meerder'jarig** of age; ~ *worden* come of age, attain one's majority; ~ *zijn* be of age; **–heid** *v* majority; **–verklaring** (-en) *v* emancipation

'meerekenen[1] *vt* count (in); include (in the reckoning); *...niet meegerekend* exclusive of...; **–rijden**[1] *vi* drive (ride) along with; *iem. laten* ~ give sbd. a lift

meer'jarig perennial [plants], long-term [contracts]

meer'keuzetoets (-en) *m* multiple-choice test

'meerkoet (-en) *m* coot

'meermaals, –malen more than once, repeatedly

---

[1] V.T. en V.D. van dit werkwoord volgens het model: **'me(d)edelen**, V.T. deelde **'me(d)e**, V.D. **'me(d)egedeeld**. Zie voor de vormen onder het grondwoord, in dit voorbeeld: *delen*. Bij sterke en onregelmatige werkwoorden wordt 1 verwezen naar de lijst achterin.

'meerman (-nen) *m* merman; **–min** (-nen) *v* mermaid

'meeropbrengst (-en) *v* $ *wet van de afnemende ~* law of diminishing returns

'meerpaal (-palen) *m* mooring-mast

'meerschuim *o*, **–en** *aj* meerschaum

'meerstemmig (to be) sung in parts, polyphonic; ~ *gezang* part-singing; ~ *lied* partsong, gleé; **–trapsraket** (-ten) *v* multi-stage rocket

'meertros (-sen) *m* ⚓ moorings

'meervoud (-en) *o* plural; **–ig, meer'voudig** plural; ~ *onverzadigde vetzuren* poly-unsaturated fatty acids; 'meervoudsuitgang (-en) *m* plural ending; **–vorm** (-en) *m* plural form; **–vorming** *v* formation of the plural

'meerwaarde *v* surplus value

mees (mezen) *v* titmouse, tit

'meeslepen[1] *vt* drag (carry) along (with one); *meegesleept door...* carried away by [his feelings &]; mee'slepend stirring [speech &]

'meesmuilen (meesmuilde, h. gemeesmuild) *vi* smirk, laugh with one's tongue in one's cheek

'meespelen[1] *vi* 1 play too; 2 join in the game; take a part; *deze acteur speelt niet mee* this actor is not in the cast; **–spreken**[1] *vi* = *meepraten*

meest **I** *aj* most; *de ~e vergissingen* most mistakes; **II** *sb de ~en* 1 most of them; 2 most people; *hij heeft het ~* he has got most; *op zijn ~* at (the) most; **III** *aj* 1 mostly; 2 most[-hated man, widely read book]; *hij schrijft het ~* he writes most; *waarvan hij het ~ hield* which he liked best; **–al** mostly, usually;

meestbe'gunstigd most favoured;

meestbe'gunstiging *v* most-favoured-nation treatment; **–sclausule** [-klɔuzy.lə] *v* most-favoured-nation clause; **meest'biedende** (-n) *m-v* highest bidder

'meester (-s) *m* master°; ~ *timmerman* & master carpenter &; *Meester in de rechten* ± doctor juris, (in Eng., zonder proefschrift) LL.B., Bachelor of Laws; *hij is een ~ in dat vak* he is a master (past-master) of his craft (of his trade); *de brand ~ worden* get the fire under control; *de toestand ~ zijn* have the situation (well) in hand; *de bestuurder was de wagen niet meer ~* the driver had lost control of the car; *hij is het Engels (volkomen) ~* he has a thorough command of English; *hij is zich zelf geen ~* he has no control over himself; *zich van iets ~ maken* take possession of a thing; *zijn ~ vinden* meet one's master, meet more than one's match; **meeste'res** (-sen) *v* mistress; **'mees-**

terhand *v* master('s) hand; **–knecht** (-en en -s) *m* foreman; **–lijk I** *aj* masterly; **II** *ad* in a masterly way; **–schap** *o* mastership, mastery;

'meestertitel *m* degree of doctor of law;

'meesterstuk (-ken) *o* masterpiece; **–werk** (-en) *o* masterpiece

meet *v van ~ af* from the beginning

'meetapparatuur *v* measuring apparatus;

'meetbaar measurable, mensurable; **–heid** *v* measurableness, mensurability; 'meetband (-en) *m* = *meetlint*

'meetellen[1] **I** *vt* count (in), include; *...niet meegeteld* exclusive of...; **II** *vi* count; ~ *voor pensioen* count towards pension; *hij telt niet mee* he does not count

'meetinstrument (-en) *o* measuring-instrument; **–kunde** *v* geometry; **meet'kundig** geometrical; **–e** (-n) *m* geometrician; 'meetlat (-ten) *v* rule, measure, measuring-rod; **–lint** (-en) *o* tape-measure, measuring tape; **–lood** (-loden) *o* plummet, plumb

'meetronen[1] *vt* coax along, lure on

'meetstok (-ken) *m* measuring-rod

meeuw (-en) *v* (sea-)gull, sea-mew

'meevallen[1] *vi* turn out (end) better than was expected, exceed expectations; *het valt niet mee* it is rather more difficult & than one expected; *hij valt erg mee* he improves on acquaintance; **–valler** (-s) *m* piece of good luck, windfall; **–vechten**[1] *vi* join in the fight; **–voelen**[1] *vi met iem.* ~ sympathize with sbd., share sbd.'s feelings; **–voeren**[1] *vt* carry along; mee'warig compassionate; **–heid** *v* compassion; 'meewerken[1] *vi* co-operate; contribute [to a paper]; **–zitten**[1] *vi het zat hem niet mee* luck was against him, he was unlucky

mega'foon (-s en -fonen) *m* megaphone, loud-hailer

mei *m* May; **–boom** (-bomen) *m* maypole

meid (-en) *v* 1 (maid-)servant, servant-girl, maid; 2 girl; *...dan ben je een beste* ~ there's a good girl; *een lekkere* ~ S a crumpet

'meidoorn, **–doren** (-s) *m* hawthorn

'meieren (meierde, h. gemeierd) *vi* F bore, nag

'meikers (-en) *v* May cherry; **–kever** (-s) *m* cockchafer, May-bug; **–maand** *v* month of May

mein'edig perjured, forsworn; **–e** (-n) *m-v* perjurer; 'meineed (-eden) *m* perjury; *een ~ doen* perjure (forswear) oneself, commit perjury; *tot ~ aanzetten* suborn

'meisje (-s) *o* 1 girl; **F** missy; 2 (b e d i e n d e) servant-girl, girl; 3 (v e r l o o f d e) fiancée,

---

[1] V.T. en V.D. van dit werkwoord volgens het model: 'me(d)edelen, V.T. deelde 'me(d)e, V.D. 'me(d)egedeeld. Zie voor de vormen onder het grondwoord, in dit voorbeeld: *delen*. Bij sterke en onregelmatige werkwoorden wordt u verwezen naar de lijst achterin.

sweetheart; **'meisjesachtig** girlish; **–gek** (-ken) *m* boy (man) fond of girls; **–naam** (-namen) *m* 1 girl's name; 2 (v. g e t r o u w d e v r o u w) maiden name; **–student** (-en) *v* girl student

'meizoentje (-s) *o* daisy

Mej. = *mejuffrouw*; **me'juffrouw** = *juffrouw*

me'kaar = *elkaar*

meka'niek = *mechaniek*; **meka'nisme** = *mechanisme*

'Mekkaganger (-s) *m* Mecca pilgrim

'mekkeren (mekkerde, h. gemekkerd) *vi* bleat[2]

me'laats leprous; **–e** (-n) *m-v* leper; **–heid** *v* leprosy

melancho'lie *v* melancholy, *ps* melancholia; **–k** melancholy; **melan'cholisch** melancholy

me'lange [me.'lã:ʒə] (-s) *m* & *o* blend

me'lasse *v* molasses

'melden (meldde, h. gemeld) **I** *vt* mention, make mention of; inform of, state, report; **II** *vr* *zich* ~ report (oneself); *zich ziek* ~ report sick; *zich* ~ *bij de politie* report to the police; zie ook: *gemeld*; **–ding** (-en) *v* mention; ~ *maken van* make mention of, mention; report [70 arrests]; **'meldzuil** (-en) *v* = *praatpaal*

mê'leren [mɛ'le:rə(n)] (mêleerde, h. gemêleerd) *vt* 1 mix [goods, ingredients]; blend [coffee, tea &]; 2 ◊ shuffle [cards]

'melig 1 mealy [potatoes]; 2 woolly [pears]; 3 **F** dull, irksome

melk *v* milk; *hij heeft niets in de* ~ *te brokken* he doesn't command any influence; **–achtig** milky; **–bezorger** (-s) *m* milkman, milk roundsman; **–boer** (-en) *m* = *melkbezorger*; **melkboeren'hondehaar** *o* mousy hair; **'melkbrood** (-broden) *o* milk-loaf; **–bus** (-sen) *v* milk-churn, milk-can; **–chocola(de)** [-ʃo.ko.la.(də)] *m* milk chocolate; **–distel** (-s) *m* & *v* sow-thistle; **–emmer** (-s) *m* milk-pail; **'melken*** *vi* & *vt* milk; **melke'rij** (-en) *v* dairy; dairy-farm; **'melkfles** (-sen) *v* milk-bottle; **–gebit** (-ten) *o* milk-dentition; **–inrichting** (-en) *v* dairy; **–kan** (-nen) *v* milk-jug; **–kar** (-ren) *v* milk-float; milk-cart; **–kies** (-kiezen) *v* milk-molar; **–koe** (-koeien) *v* milch-cow[2], [good, bad] milker; **–koker** (-s) *m* milk-boiler; **–machine** [-ma.ʃi.nə] (-s) *v* milking machine; **–man** = *melkbezorger*; **–meid** (-en) *v*, **–meisje** (-s) *o* milk-maid; **–muil** (-en) *m* milksop, greenhorn, sapling; **–poeder** *o* & *m* powdered milk, milk-powder; **–salon** (-s) *m* milk bar, creamery; **–slijter** (-s) *m* = *melkbezorger*; **–spijs** (-spijzen) *v* milk-

food; **–suiker** *m* milk-sugar, lactose; **–tand** (-en) *m* milk-tooth; **–vee** *o* milch cattle, dairy cattle; **–wagen** (-s) *m* 1 milk-cart; 2 ⚊ milk lorry; **'Melkweg** *m* ★ Milky Way, Galaxy; **'melkwegstelsel** (-s) *o* ★ galaxy; **'melkzuur** *o* lactic acid

melo'die (-ieën) *v* melody, tune, ⊙ strain; **melodi'eus, me'lodisch** melodious, tuneful

melo'drama ('s) *o* melodrama; **melodra'matisch** melodramatic(al)

me'loen (-en) *m* & *v* melon

mem'braan (-branen) *o* & *v* membrane; (v a n m i c r o f o o n &) diaphragm

'memo ('s) *o* & *m* memorandum, **F** memo

me'moires [me.'mʋa:rəs] *mv* memoirs; **memo'randum** (-da en -s) *o* memorandum; **memo'reren** (memoreerde, h. gememoreerd) *vt* recall (to mind); **me'morie** *v* 1 (g e - h e u g e n) memory; 2 (-s) (g e s c h r i f t) memorial; ~ *van antwoord* memorandum in reply; ~ *van toelichting* explanatory memorandum, explanatory statement; *pro* ~ pro memoria; **memori'seren** [s = z] (memoriseerde, h. gememoriseerd) *vt* 1 commit to memory; 2 memorize

men one, people, man, a man, they, we, you, **F** a fellow; ~ *hoort* we hear; ~ *zegt* they say, it is said; ~ *zegt dat hij...* he is said to...; ~ *heeft het mij gezegd* I was told so; *wat zal* ~ *ervan zeggen?* what will people (the world) say?; *wat* ~ *er ook van zegge* in spite of anything people may say; ~ *leeft daar zeer goedkoop* it is very cheap living there

menage'rie [me.na.ʒə'ri.] (-ieën en -s) *v* menagerie

me'neer (-neren) *m* = *mijnheer*

'menen (meende, h. gemeend) *vt* 1 (b e d o e - l e n) mean (to say); 2 (d e n k e n) think, feel, suppose; *hoe meent u dat?, wat meent u daarmee?* what do you mean (by that)?; *dat zou ik* ~ *!* I should think so!; *zo heb ik het niet gemeend!* no offence (was) meant!, I didn't mean it thus!; *dat meen je toch niet?* you're not serious (are you?); *hij meent het* he is in earnest, he is quite serious; *hij meent het goed* he means well; *het goed (eerlijk) met iem.* ~ mean well by sbd., be well-intentioned towards sbd.; zie ook: *gemeend*; **'menens** *het is* ~ it is serious

'mengbak (-ken) *m* mixing-basin; **'mengeling** (-en) *v* mixture; **'mengelmoes** *o* & *v* medley, hodge-podge, jumble; **–werk** (-en) *o* miscellany; **'mengen** (mengde, h. gemengd) **I** *vt* mix, blend [tea], alloy [metals], mingle, inter-

---

[1] V.T. en V.D. van dit werkwoord volgens het model: **'me(d)edelen**, V.T. deelde **'me(d)e**, V.D. **'me(d)egedeeld**. Zie voor de vormen onder het grondwoord, in dit voorbeeld: *delen*. Bij sterke en onregelmatige werkwoorden wordt u verwezen naar de lijst achterin.

mingle; **II** *vr zich ~ i n* meddle with, interfere in; *meng u er niet in* don't interfere; *zich in het gesprek ~* join in the conversation; *zich o n d e r de menigte ~* mix with the crowd; zie ook: *gemengd*; **–ging** (-en) *v* mixing, mixture, blending; **'mengkraan** (-kranen) *v* mixer tap; **'mengsel** (-s) *o* mixture; **'mengsmering** *v* [two-stroke] fuel oil

'menie *v* red lead; **'meniën** (meniede, h. gemenied) *vt* paint with red lead

'menig many (a); **–een** many a man, many a one; **–maal** many a time, repeatedly, often; **'menigte** (-n en -s) *v* multitude, crowd; *een ~ feiten* a great number (a host) of facts; **menig'vuldig I** *aj* manifold, frequent, multitudinous; **II** *ad* frequently; **–heid** *v* multiplicity, frequency, abundance

'mening (-en) *v* opinion; *de openbare ~* public opinion; *de openbare ~ in Frankrijk* French opinion; *als zijn ~ te kennen geven dat...* give it as one's opinion that...; *zijn ~ zeggen* 1 give one's opinion; 2 speak one's mind; ● *b ij zijn ~ blijven* stick to one's opinion; *i n de ~ dat...* in the belief that...; *in de ~ verkeren dat...* be under the impression that...; *n a a r mijn ~* in my opinion, to my mind; *naar mijn bescheiden ~* in my humble opinion; *v a n ~ zijn dat...* be of opinion that...; *ik ben van ~ dat...* ook: it is my opinion that..., I feel that...; *van dezelfde ~ zijn* be of the same opinion; *van ~ verschillen* disagree, differ in opinion; *ik ben van een andere ~* I am of a different opinion, I think differently; *zijn ~ niet onder stoelen of banken steken* make no secret of one's opinion, be quite frank [with sbd.]; *zijn ~ voor een betere geven* be open to correction

menin'gitis *v* meningitis

'meningsuiting *v* expression of opinion(s); *vrijheid van ~* freedom of speech (and expression); **–verschil** (-len) *o* difference (of opinion)

me'nist (-en) *m* Mennonite

'mennen (mende, h. gemend) *vt* & *vi* drive

menno'niet (-en) *m* Mennonite

meno'pauze *v* menopause, **F** change of life

mens (-en) *m* 1 man; 2 *o* > woman; *de ~* man; *een ~* a human being; *~ en dier* man and beast; *half ~, half dier* half human, half animal; *geen ~* nobody, no one, not anybody; *ik ben geen half ~ meer* I am dead beat; *de ~en* people, mankind; *er waren maar weinig ~en* there were but few people; *wij ~en* we men (and women); *leraren zijn ook ~en* even teachers are but human; *wij zijn allemaal ~en* we are all human; *de grote ~en* the grown-ups; *als de grote ~en spreken, moeten de kinderen zwijgen* children should be seen and not heard; *dat ~!* that person!, that creature!;

het arme ~ the poor soul; *het oude ~* the old woman; *zo'n goed ~* such a good soul; *de oude ~ afleggen* put off the old man; *wij krijgen ~en* we are going to have company; *de inwendige ~ versterken* refresh one's inner man; *(niet) onder de ~en komen* (not) mix in society, (not) go into company; **–aap** (-apen) *m* anthropoid (ape); **–dom** *o het ~* mankind; **'menselijk** human; **menselijker'wijs ~** *gesproken* humanly speaking; **'menselijkheid** *v* humanity; **'menseneter** (-s) *m* man-eater, cannibal; **–gedaante** (-n en -s) *v* human shape; **–haat** *m* misanthropy; **–hater** (-s) *m* misanthrope; **–heugenis** *v bij (sedert, sinds) ~* within living memory; **–kenner** (-s) *m* judge of men; **–kennis** *v* knowledge of men; **–kind** (-eren) *o* human being; *mensenkinderen!* good heavens; **–leeftijd** (-en) *m* lifetime; **–leven** (-s) *o* span of life; life; *~s redden* save human life; *er zijn geen ~s te betreuren* no lives were lost; **–liefde** *v* philanthropy, love of mankind; **–maatschappij** *v* human society; **–massa** ('s) *v* crowd (of people); **–offer** (-s) *o* human sacrifice; **–paar** (-paren) *o* [the first] human couple; **–ras** (-sen) *o* human race; **–rechten** *mv* human rights; **–schuw** shy, unsociable; **–verstand** *o* human understanding; **–vlees** *o* human flesh; **S** meat; **–vrees** *v* fear of men; **–vriend** (-en) *m* philanthropist; **mens-'erger-je-niet** *sp* ludo; **'mensheid** *v* 1 mankind; 2 human nature; **mens'lievend** philanthropic(al), humane; **–heid** *v* philanthropy, humanity

menson'waardig degrading

menstru'atie [-(t)si.] *v* menstruation, **F** period; **–cyclus** (-sen en -cycli) *m* menstrual cycle; **menstru'eren** (menstrueerde, h. gemenstrueerd) *vi* menstruate, **F** have one's period

mens'waardig fit for a human being; *een ~ loon* a living wage; **'menswording** *v* incarnation

men'taal mental; **mentali'teit** *v* mentality

men'thol *m* menthol

'mentor (-s) *m* mentor

me'nu ('s) *o* & *m* menu, bill of fare

menu'et (-ten) *o* & *m* minuet

mep (-pen) *m* & *v* blow, slap; **'meppen** (mepte, h. gemept) *vt* slap, smack, strike

'merel (-s) *m* & *v* blackbird

'meren (meerde, h. gemeerd) *vt* ⚓ moor [a ship]

'merendeel *o het ~* the greater part, the majority [of countries], the mass [of imports], most of them; **–s** for the greater part, mostly

merg *o* 1 marrow [in bones]; 2 ⚕ pith; 3 *fig* pith; *dat gaat d o o r ~ en been* it pierces you to the very marrow, that sets one's teeth on edge; *een vrijhandelaar i n ~ en been* a free-trader to the backbone (the core)

'**mergel** *m* marl; **–groeve** (-n) *v* marlpit;
–steen (-stenen) *o* & *m* marlstone
'**mergpijp** (-en) *v* marrow-bone
meridi'aan (-ianen) *m* meridian; **–shoogte** (-n) *v* meridian altitude
'**merinos** *o* merino; **–schaap** (-schapen) *o* 🐑 merino
merk (-en) *o* mark; brand [of cigars]; [registered] trade mark; make [of a bicycle, car]; hall-mark [on metals]; *een fijn* ~ a choice brand; *fig* **F** a specimen; **–artikel** (-en) *o* proprietary article; ~*en* ook: branded goods
'**merkbaar** perceptible, noticeable, appreciable, marked [difference]; '**merkelijk** considerable; '**merken** (merkte, h. gemerkt) *vt* 1 (m e t e e n m e r k) mark [goods]; 2 (b e m e r k e n) perceive, notice; *je moet niets laten* ~ don't let on (let it appear) that you know anything
'**merkgaren** *o* marking-thread; **–inkt** *m* marking-ink; **–lap** (-pen) *m* sampler; **–naam** (-namen) *m* brand name; **–teken** (-s en -en) *o* mark, sign, token
merk'waardig remarkable, curious; **–heid** (-heden) *v* remarkableness, curiosity
'**merrie** (-s) *v* mare; **–veulen** (-s) *o* filly
mes (-sen) *o* knife; *het* ~ *snijdt aan twee kanten* it cuts both ways; *het* ~ *erin zetten* [*fig*] take drastic measures, apply the axe; *iem. het* ~ *op de keel zetten* put a knife to sbd.'s throat
mesalli'ance [me.zɑli.'ãsə] (-s) *v* misalliance
'**mesje** (-s) *o* (small) knife; blade [of a safety-razor]
me'sjokke F barmy, daft; crackpot [idea]
'**mespunt** (-en) *o* 1 tip of a knife; 2 pinch [of pepper &]; '**messelegger** (-s) *m* knife-rest; '**messenmaker** (-s) *m* cutler; **–slijper** (-s) *m* knife-grinder
Messi'aans Messianic; **Mes'sias** *m* Messiah
'**messing** 1 *o* brass; 2 *v* ~ *en groef* tongue and groove
'**messteek** (-steken) *m* cut with a knife, knife-thrust
mest *m* dung, manure, dressing, fertilizer; '**mesten** (mestte, h. gemest) *vt* 1 (l a n d) dung, dress, manure; 2 (d i e r e n) fatten; *het gemeste kalf slachten* kill the fatted calf; '**mesthoop** (-hopen) *m* dunghill, muck-heap, manure heap, midden
mes'ties (-tiezen) *m-v* mestizo
'**mestkever** (-s) *m* dung-beetle; **–put** (-ten) *m* dung-pit; **–stof** (-fen) *v* manure, fertilizer; **–vaalt** (-en) *v* dunghill; **–varken** (-s) *o* fattening pig; **–vee** *o* fat cattle; **–vork** (-en) *v* dung-fork; **–wagen** (-s) *m* dung-cart
met I *prep* with; (*u spreekt*) ~ X 🕾 X speaking; (*spreek ik*) ~ X? 🕾 is that you, X?; *hoe is het* ~ *je?* how are you?; *hoe is het* ~ *je vader?* how is

your father?; ~ *dat al* for all that; ~ *de boot, de post, het spoor* by steamer, by post, by rail; ~ *inkt,* ~ *potlood* [written] in ink, in pencil; ~ *de dag* every day; *de man* ~ *de hoge hoed* the man in the top-hat; ~ *de hoed in de hand* hat in hand; *de man* ~ *de lange neus* he of the long nose; ~ *1 januari* on January 1st; ~ *Pasen* at Easter; ~ *10% toenemen* increase by 10%; ~ *hoeveel zijn jullie?* how many are you?; *wij waren* ~ *ons vijven* there were five of us, we were five; ~ *ons allen hadden we één...* between us we had one...; **II** *ad* at the same time, at the same moment
me'taal (-talen) 1 *o* metal; 2 *v* = *metaalindustrie*; **–achtig** metallic; **–bewerker** (-s) *m* metal-worker; **–draad** (-draden) *o* & *m* 1 🔧 metallic wire; 2 💡 metal filament; **metaalgiete'rij** (-en) *v* foundry; **me'taalglans** *m* metallic lustre; **–industrie** *v* metal (metallurgical) industry; **–moeheid** *v* fatigue of metals, metal fatigue; **–slak** (-ken) *v* slag [*mv* slag], scoria [*mv* scoriae]; **–voorraad** (-raden) *m* bullion; **–waren** *mv* metalware
metabo'lisme *o* metabolism
meta'foor (-foren) *v* metaphor, figure of speech; **meta'forisch** metaphorical
meta'fysica [-'fi.zi.ka.] *v* metaphysics; **meta'fysisch** metaphysical
me'talen *aj* metal; **metalli'seren** [s = z] (metalliseerde, h. gemetalliseerd) *vt* metallize; **metallur'gie** *v* metallurgy
metamor'fose [s = z] (-n en -s) *v* metamorphosis [*mv* metamorphoses]
meta'stase [s = z] (-n) *v* metastasis
me'teen 1 at the same time; 2 at once, immediately; presently; *zo* ~ in a minute; *tot* ~*!* so long!
'**meten* I** *vt* measure, gauge; *hij meet 2 meter* he stands 2 metres; *het schip meet 5000 ton* the ship measures (carries) 5000 tons; zie ook: 1 *maat*; **II** *vr zich met iem.* ~ measure one's strength (oneself) against sbd.; *zich niet kunnen* ~ *met...* be no match for
mete'oor (-eoren) *m* meteor; **–steen** (-stenen) *m* meteoric stone; **meteo'riet** (-en) *m* meteorite; **meteorolo'gie** *v* meteorology; **meteoro'logisch** meteorological; **meteoro'loog** (-logen) *m* meteorologist
1 'meter (-s) *m* 1 metre; 2 (g a s) meter; 3 (p e r s o o n) measurer
2 'meter (-s) *v* godmother
'**meteropnemer** (-s) *m* meter-reader; **–opneming** (-en) *v*, **–stand** (-en) *m* meter-reading
'**metgezel** (-len) *m*, **metgezel'lin** (-nen) *v* companion, mate
me'thaangas *o* marsh-gas
me'thode (-n en -s) *v* method; modus

(operandi); **metho'diek** *v* methodology;
me'thodisch methodical
metho'dist (-en) *m* Methodist
methodolo'gie *v* methodology
mé'tier [me.'tje.] (-s) *o* trade, profession
'meting (-en) *v* measuring, measurement
me'triek I *aj* metric; *het* ~*e stelsel* the metric
system; **II** *v* metrics, prosody; **'metrisch**
metrical
'metro ('s) *m* metro; **metro'noom** (-nomen) *m*
metronome; **metro'pool** (-polen) *v* metropolis
'metrum (-s en -tra) *o* metre
'metselaar (-s) *m* bricklayer; **'metselen**
(metselde, h. gemetseld) **I** *vi* lay bricks; **II** *vt* lay
the bricks of, build [a wall &]; **'metselkalk** *m*,
–specie *v* mortar; **–steen** (-stenen) *o* & *m*
brick; **–werk** *o* brickwork, masonry
'metten *mv* matins; *donkere* ~ *rk* tenebrae; *korte*
~ *maken met...* make short work of..., give
[sbd.] short shrift
metter'daad actually; **–'tijd** in course of time;
–'woon *zich* ~ *vestigen* take up (fix) one's
abode, establish oneself, settle
'metworst (-en) *v* German sausage
'meubel (-s en -en) *o* piece (article) of furniture; *onze* ~*en* (~*s*) our furniture (furnishings);
'meubelen (meubelde, h. gemeubeld) *vt*
furnish; **'meubelfabriek** (-en) *v* furniture
factory; **–fabrikant** (-en) *m* furniture manufacturer; **–magazijn** (-en) *o* furniture store;
–maker (-s) *m* cabinet-maker, furniture-
maker, joiner; **meubelmake'rij** (-en) *v*
cabinetmaking, furniture-making (works);
'meubelstuk (-ken) *o* piece (article) of furniture; **meubi'lair** [mø.bi.'lɛ:r] *o* furniture;
meubi'leren (meubileerde, h. gemeubileerd)
vt furnish, fit up; **–ring** *v* 1 furnishing; 2
furniture
meug *m* liking; *elk zijn* ~ everyone to his taste;
zie ook: *heug*
'meute (-n en -s) *v* pack [of hounds]
mevr. = *mevrouw*; **me'vrouw** (-en) *v* 1 lady; 2
(a l s a a n s p r e k i n g z o n d e r n a a m)
madam; ~ *L.* Mrs L.
Mexi'caan(s) Mexican; **'Mexico** *o* Mexico
1 mi ('s) *v* ♪ mi
2 mi *m* (s p ij s) noodles
m.i. = *mijns inziens* zie *inzien*
mi'auw miauw, mew; **mi'auwen** (miauwde, h.
gemiauwd) *vi* miaow, mew, miaul
'mica *o* & *m* mica
mi'crobe (-n) *v* microbe; **'microbiologie** *v*
microbiology; **micro'cosmos** *m* microcosm;
'microfilm (-s) *m* microfilm, **F** mike; *voor de* ~
spreken speak on the radio (on the air);
'micron (-s) *o* & *m* micron; **micro'scoop**

(-copen) *m* microscope; **–'scopisch** micro-
scopic(al)
'middag (-dagen) *m* 1 midday, noon; 2 (n a~)
afternoon; *n a de* ~ in the afternoon; *v o o r de* ~
before noon, in the morning; *'s (des)* ~*s* 1 at
noon; 2 in the afternoon; *om vier uur 's* ~*s*,
ook: at 4 p.m.; **–dutje** (-s) *o* = *middagslaapje*;
–eten *o* midday-meal, dinner; **–hoogte** *v*
meridian altitude; **–maal** (-malen) *o* midday-
meal, dinner; **–pauze** (-n en -s) *v* midday
break (interval), luncheon break; **–slaapje** (-s)
o afternoon nap, siesta; **–voorstelling** (-en) *v*
afternoon performance
'middel (-s) *o* 1 (v. h. l i c h a a m) waist, middle;
2 (-en) (v o o r e e n d o e l) means, expedient;
medium [*mv* media]; 3 (-en) (t o t g e n e -
z i n g) remedy; *eigen* ~*en* private means; *ruime*
~*en* ample funds; ~*en van bestaan* means of
subsistence (of support); *door* ~ *van* 1 by means
of; 2 through [the post &]; *het* ~ *is erger dan de*
kwaal the remedy is worse than the disease;
'middelaar (-s en -laren) *m* mediator;
'middelbaar middle, medium; average;
middelbare grootte middling size; *van middelbare*
grootte medium-sized, middle-sized; *op middel-*
bare leeftijd in middle life, in middle age; *van*
middelbare leeftijd middle-aged; zie ook: *onderwijs*
&; **'middeleeuwen** *mv* Middle Ages;
'middeleeuws medi(a)eval; **middeler'wijl**
meanwhile, in the meantime; **middel-**
even'redige (-n) *v* the mean proportional;
'middelgewicht (-en) *m sp* middle weight;
–groot medium(-sized); **–kleur** *v* intermediate
colour; **'Middellandse Zee** *v* Mediterranean;
'middellang ~*e termijn* medium term;
'middellijk indirect, mediate; **'middellijn**
(-en) *v* 1 central line; 2 diameter;
middel'loodlijn (-en) *v* perpendicular
bisector; **'middelmaat** *v* medium size; *de*
gulden ~ the golden mean; **middel'matig I** *aj*
moderate; middling; mediocre, indifferent; **II**
ad moderately; in a mediocre way; indifferently; **–heid** (-heden) *v* mediocrity; **'middel-**
moot (-moten) *v fig* middle group, centre
group; **–punt** (-en) *o* centre²; **middel-**
punt'vliedend centrifugal; **–'zoekend**
centripetal; **'middelschot** (-ten) *o* partition
[in a room]; **–soort** (-en) *v* & *o* medium
(quality, size &); **'middelste** middle, middle-
most; **'middelvinger** (-s) *m* middle finger
'midden I (-s) *o* middle [of the day, month, of
summer], midst [of dangers], centre [of the
town]; *het* ~ *houden tussen... en...* be midway
between...; be something between... and...; *iets*
i n het ~ *brengen* put sth. forward; *iets in het* ~
laten leave it as it is; give no opinion on sth.,
leave sth. an open question; *hij is niet meer in ons*

~ he is no longer in our midst; *t e* ~ *van* 1 in the midst of [pleasures]; 2 among [friends]; *iemand u i t ons* ~ one from our own number; one of ourselves; *zij kozen iemand uit hun* ~ they selected one from among themselves; **II** *ad* ~ *in* in the middle of [the room, winter, my work]; **Midden-A'merika** *o* Central America; **'middenberm** (-en) *m* centre strip, *Am* median strip; **midden'door** 1 [go] down the middle; 2 in two, [tear it] across; **'midden-en 'kleinbedrijf·***o* shopkeepers and small entrepreneurs; **Midden-Eu'ropa** *o* Central Europe; **'middengewicht** (-en) = *middelgewicht*; **–golf** *v* medium wave; **midden'in** in the middle; **'middenoorontsteking** (-en) *v* inflammation of the middle ear; **Midden-'Oosten** *o* Middle East; **'middenpad** (-paden) *o* (i n b u s &) gangway; (i n k e r k) aisle; (i n t u i n) central path; **–rif** (-fen) *o* midriff, diaphragm **–schip** (-schepen) *o* nave; **–schot** (-ten) = *middelschot*; **–soort** (-en) = *middelsoort*; **–spel** *o* middle game [at chess]; **–speler** (-s) *m* half-back; **–stand** *m* middle class(es); (w i n k e l i e r s) tradespeople, shopkeepers; **–stander** (-s) *m* middle-class man; (w i n k e l i e r) tradesman, shopkeeper; **–standsvereniging** (-en) *v* traders' association; **–voetsbeentje** (-s) *o* metatarsal bone; **midden'voor** (-s) *m sp* centre forward; **'middenweg** *m* middle course, middle way; *de gulden* ~ the golden mean; *de* ~ *bewandelen* tread the middle way, steer a middle course; **–zwaard** (-en) *o* centre-board

midder'nacht *m* midnight; **–elijk** midnight; **–zon** *v* midnight sun

mid'half [mɪt'ha.f] (-s) *m sp* centre half; **–'scheeps** amidships; **–'voor** (-s) = *middenvoor*

mie (-s) *m* **F** effeminate homosexual, sissy

mier (-en) *v* ant; *rode* ~ red ant; *witte* ~ white ant, termite

'mieren (mierde, h. gemierd) *vi* (p i e k e r e n) worry; (z e u r e n) bother

'miereneter (-s) *m* ant-eater; **–hoop** (-hopen) *m* ant-hill, ant-heap; **–leeuw** (-en) *m* ant-lion; **–nest** (-en) *o* ants' nest, ant-hill; **'mierezuur** *o* formic acid

'mierik(s)wortel (-s) *m* horseradish

'mieter (-s) *m* **P** body; *hoge* ~ big shot; *iem. op z'n* ~ *geven* give sbd. a drubbing

'mieteren (mieterde, h. en is gemieterd) *vi* **P** 1 (s m ij t e n) fling, throw [down]; 2 (v a l l e n) pitch down; 3 (z e u r e n) nag, bother

'mieters F smashing, stunning, **S** wizard, corking, super

'Mietje *elkaar geen* ~ *noemen* not beat around the bush, call a spade a spade

'miezerig drizzly [weather]; measly, scanty;

(b e d r u k t) dejected

mi'graine [mi.'grɪː.nə] *v* migraine, sick headache

Mij. = *Maatschappij* Company, Co.

mij (to) me; *dat is van* ~ it is mine

'mijden* *vt* shun, avoid, fight shy of

mijl (-en) *v* mile (1609 metres); ⚓ league; *de* ~ *op zeven* a roundabout way; **–paal** (-palen) *m* milestone[2], milepost; *fig* landmark

'mijmeraar (-s) *m* (day-)dreamer, muser; **'mijmeren** (mijmerde, h. gemijmerd) *vi* dream, muse; brood (on *over*); **–ring** (-en) *v* musing; day-dream

1 mijn my; *de* (*het*) ~*e* mine; *ik en de* ~*en* I and mine; *ik wil er het* ~*e van hebben* I want to know what is what; *het* ~ *en dijn* mine and thine; zie ook: *denken* &

2 mijn (-en) *v* mine; **–ader** (-s) *v* mineral vein; **–bouw** *m* mining; **mijnbouw'kundig** mining; **'mijndetector** (-s) *m* mine detector **'mijnen** (mijnde, h. gemijnd) *vt* buy at a public sale

'mijnenlegger (-s) *m* minelayer

'mijnent *te*(*n*) ~ at my house; *~halve* for my sake; *~wege* as for me; *van ~wege* on my behalf, in my name; *om ~wil*(*le*) for my sake

'mijnenveger (-s) *m* mine sweeper; **–veld** (-en) *o* minefield

'mijnerzijds on my part

'mijngang (-en) *m* gallery of a mine; **–gas** *o* fire-damp

mijn'heer [mə'ne:r] (-heren) *m* 1 gentleman; 2 (a a n s p r e k i n g z o n d e r n a a m) sir; (m e t n a a m) Mr; *is* ~ *thuis?* is Mr... (your master) at home?

'mijnhout *o* pitwood, pit-props; **–ingenieur** [-ɪnʒəni.ø:r, -ɪnʒe.ni.ø:r] (-s) *m* mining-engineer; **–lamp** (-en) *v* safety-lamp, Davy; **–schacht** (-en) *v* shaft [of a mine]; **–werker** (-s) *m* miner, pitman; **–wezen** *o* mining; **–worm** (-en) *m* hookworm

1 mijt (-en) *v* mite [insect]

2 mijt (-en) *v* stack [of hay &]

'mijter (-s) *m* mitre

mik (-ken) *v* (b r o o d) loaf

mi'kado ('s) *m* mikado

'mikken (mikte, h. gemikt) *vi* take aim, aim (at *op*)

'mikmak *m* **F** *de hele* ~ the whole caboodle; *zich het* ~ *schrikken* be frightened out of one's wits

'mikpunt (-en) *o* aim; *fig* butt, target; *het* ~ *van hun aardigheden* their laughing-stock

mild I *aj* 1 (z a c h t) soft, genial [weather &]; 2 (n i e t s t r e n g) lenient [sentence]; 3 (w e l w i l l e n d) charitable [view]; 4 (v r ij-g e v i g) liberal, generous, free-handed, open-handed; 5 (o v e r v l o e d i g) bountiful; *de ~e gever* the generous donor; *~ met* free of, liberal of; *met ~e hand* lavishly; **II** *ad* liberally, generously; **mild'dadig I** *aj* liberal, generous; **II** *ad* liberally, generously; **'mildheid** *v* 1 liberality, generosity; 2 leniency [of a sentence]

mili'eu [mi.l'jø.] (-s) *o* environment, surroundings; **–bescherming** *v* conservation; **–hygiëne** [-.hi.ɡi.e.nə] *v* environmental control; **–verontreiniging** *v* environmental pollution

mili'tair [mi.li.'tɛː r] **I** *ad* military [profession, service &]; *~e dienst* national service; *~e luchtvaart* & service aviation &; **II** (-en) *m* military man, soldier; Serviceman; *de ~en* the military, the troops; **mili'tant** militant; **milita'risme** *o* militarism; **–istisch** militarist; **mi'litie** [-(t)si.] *v* militia

mil'jard (-en) *o* milliard [= thousand million]; *Am* billion; **miljar'dair** [-'dɛː r] (-s) *m* multi-millionaire; *Am* billionaire

mil'joen (-en) *o* a (one) million; **mil'joenen-nota** ('s) *v* budget; **–rede** (-s) *v* budget speech; **mil'joenste** millionth (part); **miljo'nair** [-'nɛː r] (-s) *m* millionaire

mille [mi.l] *o* (a) thousand; **'millibar** *m* millibar; **–gram** (-men) *o* milligramme; **–meter** (-s) *m* millimetre; **–meteren** (millimeterde, h. gemillimeterd) *vt* crop (close)

milt (-en) *v* spleen; **–vuur** *o* anthrax

'Milva ('s) *v* Waac

mi'miek *v* mimicry, mimic art; **'mimisch** mimic

'mimitafeltje (-s) *o* ~*s* nest of (small) tables

mi'mosa [s = z] ('s) *v* mimosa

1 ☉ min *v* (l i e f d e) love

2 min (-nen) *v* (z o o g s t e r) nurse, wet-nurse

3 min I *aj* mean, base; *dat is* (*erg*) *~ van hem* that is very mean (shabby) of him; *het examen was ~* a poor performance; *de zieke is* (*erg*) *~* the patient is very low, **F** very poorly; *dat is mij te ~* that's beneath me; *daar moet je niet zo ~ over denken* don't underestimate it, don't belittle it; *hij is mij te ~* beneath contempt for me; *zo ~ mogelijk* as little as possible; **II** *ad* less; *~ of meer* more or less; somewhat; *7 ~ 5, 7* less 5, 7 minus 5; **'minachten** (minachtte, h. geminacht) *vt* hold in contempt, disdain; **–d** contemptuous, disdainful; **'minachting** *v* contempt, disdain

mina'ret (-ten) *v* minaret

'minder I *aj* less, fewer; inferior [quantity]; *de ~e goden* the lesser gods; *de ~e man* the small man; *dat is ~* that is of less importance; *~ worden* grow less; *de zieke wordt ~* is getting low; *ik heb ze wel voor ~ verkocht* I've sold them for less; *je bent me er niet ~ om* [not with-

standing that] I still like you; **II** *ad* less; *~ worden* decrease, fall off, lessen, decline, diminish, grow less; *~ leuk* (*aardig*) not quite funny (nice), not so funny (nice); *dat doet er ~ toe* that's of less importance; *iets ~ dan een miljoen* just under a million; *~ dan een pond* under a pound; *~ dan een week* within a week; *in ~ dan geen tijd* in less than no time; *niemand ~ dan* no less a person than; *niet ~ dan* no less than; *niets ~ dan* nothing less than, nothing short of; *het zal me er niet ~ om smaken* it will taste none the worse; *hoe ~ je ervan zegt, hoe beter* least said, soonest mended; *kan het niet voor wat ~?* can't you knock off a little from this price?; **–broeder** (-s) *m* Franciscan friar; **–e** (-n) *m* inferior; *hij is de ~ van zijn broer* he is inferior to his brother; *een ~* ✕ a private; *de ~n* ✕ the rank and file; **'minderen** (minderde, h. geminderd) 1 *vi* diminish, decrease; 2 *vt* (b i j b r e i e n) decrease; **'minderheid** (-heden) *v* 1 minority; 2 (g e e s t e l i j k) inferiority; **'mindering** (-en) *v* 1 diminution, diminishing, decrease; 2 (b i j b r e i e n) decrease; *in ~ van de hoofdsom* to be deducted from the principal; *in ~ brengen* deduct; **minder'jarig** under age; **–e** (-n) *m-v* one under age, minor; ⚕ infant; **–heid** *v* minority, nonage; ⚕ infancy; **minder'waardig** 1 inferior; *geestelijk ~* mentally deficient; 2 (v e r a c h t e l i j k) base, mean; **–heid** *v* inferiority; **minder'waardig-heidscomplex** (-en) *o* inferiority complex; **–gevoel** (-ens) *o* sense of inferiority

mine'raal (-ralen) *o* mineral; **–water** *o* mineral water; **mineralo'gie** *v* mineralogy; **minera'loog** (-logen) *m* mineralogist

mi'neur *o* ♪ minor; *in ~* in a minor key

'mini(-auto) & mini(car) &; **minia'tuur** (-turen) *o* miniature; **–schilder** (-s) *m* miniature painter; **mi'niem** small, trifling, negligible; **mini'maal** minimum, minimal; **'minimum** (-ma) *o* minimum; *in een ~ van tijd* in (less than) no time; **–loon** *o* minimum wage

mi'nister (-s) *m* minister, secretary; *eerste ~* Prime Minister, Premier; *~ van Binnenlandse Zaken* Secretary of State for Home Affairs, Home Secretary [in Brit.]; Minister of the Interior; *~ van Buitenlandse Zaken* Secretary of State for Foreign Affairs, Foreign Secretary [in Brit.]; Minister for Foreign Affairs, Foreign Minister; [U.S.] Secretary of State; [Australian, Canadian &] Minister of External Affairs; *~ van Defensie* Secretary of State for Defence [in Brit.]; Minister of Defence; *~ van Financiën* Chancellor of the Exchequer [in Brit.]; Minister of Finance; *~ van (Landbouw, Nijverheid en) Handel* President of the Board of Trade [in Brit.]; Minister of (Agriculture, Industry and) Commerce; ~ *van Justitie* Lord High Chancellor [in Brit.]; Minister of Justice; ~ *van Luchtvaart* Minister of Aviation; ~ *van Marine* First Lord of the Admiralty [in Brit.]; Minister of Marine; ~ *van Onderwijs* Minister of Education; ~ *van Oorlog* Secretary of State for War, War Secretary [in Brit.]; Minister of War; ~ *van Staat* Minister of State; ~ *van Waterstaat* First Commissioner of Works [in Brit.]; Minister of Public Works; **minis'terie** (-s) *o* ministry, department, Office; ~ *van Binnenlandse Zaken* Home Office [in Brit.]; Ministry (Department) of Home Affairs (the Interior); ~ *van Buitenlandse Zaken* Foreign Office [in Brit.], [sinds 1968] Ministry of Foreign Affairs; [U.S.] State Department; ~ *van Defensie* Ministry of Defence; ~ *van Financiën* Treasury [in Brit.]; Finance Department; ~ *van (Landbouw, Nijverheid en) Handel* Board of Trade; ~ *van Justitie* Department of Justice; ~ *van Luchtvaart* Ministry of Aviation; ~ *van Marine* Admiralty [in Brit.]; Ministry (Department) of the Navy; ~ *van Onderwijs* Ministry of Education; ~ *van Oorlog* War Office [in Brit.]; Ministry of War; ~ *van Waterstaat* Board of Works [in Brit.]; Ministry of Public Works; *het ~ Drees* the Drees government; *het Openbaar ~* the Public Prosecutor; **ministeri'eel** ministerial; **mi'nister-presi'dent** (ministerspresidenten) *m* prime minister, premier; **mi'nister-raad** (-raden) *m* cabinet council; **–schap** *o* ministry

'minlijk = *minnelijk*

'minnaar (-s en -naren) *m* lover; **minna'res** (-sen) *v* love, mistress

1 'minne *v* = 1 *min*; *het in der ~ schikken* settle the matter amicably

2 'minne (-n) *v* = 2 *min*

'minnebrief (-brieven) *m* love-letter; **–dicht** (-en) *o* love-poem; **–dichter** (-s) *o* love-poet; **–drank** (-en) *m* love-potion, philtre; **–kozen** (minnekoosde, h. geminnekoosd) *vi* bill and coo; **–lied** (-eren) *o* love-song; **–lijk** amicable, friendly; *bij ~e schikking* amicably; **'minnen** (minde, h. gemind) *vt & vi* love; **'minnenijd** *m* jealousy

'minnetjes poorly

'minnezang (-en) *m* love-song; **–er** (-s) *m* minstrel, troubadour

minst I *aj* least, fewest; smallest; slightest; *niet de ~e moeite* not the least trouble; **II** *ad* least; *de ~ gevaarlijke plaats* the least dangerous place; **III** *sb de ~e zijn* yield; *het ~(e)* (the) least; *waar men ze het ~ verwacht* where you least expect them; *het ~* the least [you can expect &]; *hij eet het ~* he eats least (of all); ● *als u ook maar i n*

het ~ vermoeid bent if you are tired at all; *in het ~ niet, niet in 't ~* not in the least, not at all, by no means; *op zijn ~* 1 at the least; 2 at least [he might have...]; *t e n ~e* at least; **'minstens** at least; at the least; ~ *even... als...* at least as...⁻ as...; ~ *tien* ten at the least; *zij is ~ veertig* she is forty if she is a day; *Moet ik er heen? Minstens!* that's the (very) least (thing) you can do

'minstreel (-strelen) *m* minstrel

'minteken (-s) *o* minus sign

'minus minus

minus'cuul very small, tiny

minuti'eus [mi.ny.(t)si.'ø.s] minute

1 mi'nuut (-nuten) *v* minute; *het is 3 minuten vóór half zeven* it is 27 minutes past six; *het is 3 minuten over half zeven* it is 27 minutes to seven; *op de ~ (af)* to the minute

2 mi'nuut (-nuten) *v* minute [= draft]

mi'nuutwijzer (-s) *m* minute-hand

minver'mogend poor, indigent

'minzaam I *aj* 1 affable, bland, suave; 2 (v a n a a n z i e n l i j k p e r s o o n) gracious; **II** *ad* 1 affably; 2 graciously; **–heid** *v* 1 affability, blandness, suavity; 2 graciousness

miracu'leus miraculous; **mi'rakel** (-s) *o* miracle; *een lelijk ~* **F** a nasty woman; **–spel** (-spelen) *o* miracle play

'mirre *v* myrrh

'mirt(e) (-en), **'mirteboom** (-bomen) *m* myrtle

1 mis (-sen) *v rk* mass; *stille ~* low mass; *de ~ bijwonen* attend mass; *de ~ (be)dienen* serve the mass; *de ~ doen* celebrate mass; *de ~ horen* hear mass; *de ~ lezen (opdragen)* read (say) mass, celebrate mass

2 mis *ad* (& *aj*) amiss, wrong; *het ~ hebben* be wrong, be mistaken; *je hebt het ~ als je denkt dat* you are under a mistake; *je hebt het niet zo ver ~* you are not far out; *dat heb je ~!* that's your mistake!; ~ *poes!* out you are!; *'t is weer ~* things are going wrong again; *dat is ~* that's a miss; *het schot was ~* the shot went wide; *hij schoot ~* he shot wide; *dat was gisteren niet ~* **S** that was some yesterday; *dat was lang niet ~* **S** that was not half bad

mis'baar *o* uproar, clamour, hubbub; *veel ~ maken* raise an outcry

'misbaksel (-s) *o fig* monster

'misboek (-en) *o* missal

'misbruik (-en) *o* abuse, misuse; ~ *maken van* take (an unfair) advantage of, impose (up)on, abuse [kindness &]; trespass on [sbd.'s time]; ~ *maken van sterke drank* indulge too freely in liquor, drink to excess; ~ *van macht* abuse of power; ~ *van vertrouwen* breach of trust; **mis'bruiken** (misbruikte, h. misbruikt) *vt* abuse [sbd.'s kindness &]; misuse, make a bad

use of [time]; **'misdaad** (-daden) *v* crime,
misdeed, misdoing; **mis'dadig** criminal;
wicked, outrageous; **'misdadiger** (-s) *m*
criminal, malefactor; **mis'dadigheid** *v* criminality; **mis'deeld** *niet ~ zijn van...* not be
wanting in...; *~e kinderen* underprivileged
children; *de ~en* the poor, the dispossessed
'misdienaar (-s) *m* server, acolyte, altar-boy
mis'doen (misdeed, h. misdaan) **I** *vi* offend, sin;
II *vt wat heb ik misdaan?* what wrong have I
done?; **mis'dragen** (misdroeg, h. misdragen)
zich ~ misbehave; **'misdrijf** (-drijven) *o* crime,
criminal offence; **mis'drijven** (misdreef, h.
misdreven) *vt* do wrong; **'misdruk** (-ken) *m*
spoilt sheet(s), mackle; **mis'duiden**
(misduidde, h. misduid) *vt* misinterpret,
misconstrue; *misduid het mij niet* don't take it ill
of me
mise-en-'scène [mi.zã'sɛ: nə] *v* setting, staging,
get-up
mise'rabel [s = z] **I** *aj* miserable, wretched,
rotten; **II** *ad* miserably, wretchedly; **mi'sère**
[mi.'zɛ:rə] (-s) *v* misery
'misgaan *vi* go wrong; *het gaat mis met hem* he
is going to the dogs; **'misgeboorte** (-n) *v*
miscarriage, abortion
'misgewaad (-waden) *o* vestments
'misgewas (-sen) *o* bad crop, failure of crops;
'misgooien *vi* miss [in throwing]; **'misgreep**
(-grepen) *m* mistake, error, slip; **'misgrijpen**[1]
vi miss one's hold; **mis'gunnen** (misgunde, h.
misgund) *vt iem. iets ~* grudge (envy,
begrudge) sbd. sth.; **mis'hagen** (mishaagde,
h. mishaagd) **I** *vi* displease; **II** *o* displeasure;
mis'handelen (mishandelde, h. mishandeld)
vt ill-treat, ill-use, maltreat, mishandle, batter;
–ling (-en) *v* ill-treatment, ill-usage, battering
'miskelk (-en) *m* chalice
mis'kennen (miskende, h. miskend) *vt* fail to
appreciate; *een miskend genie* an unrecognized
genius; **–ning** (-en) *v* lack of appreciation;
'miskleun (-en) *m* F blunder, faux pas;
'miskleunen (kleunde 'mis, h. 'misgekleund)
vi F blunder; **'miskleur** *v* discoloured, off-
shade [cigar &]; **–koop** (-kopen) *m* bad
bargain; **–kraam** (-kramen) *v* & *o* miscarriage,
abortion; *een ~ hebben* miscarry; **mis'leiden**
(misleidde, h. misleid) *vt* mislead, deceive,
impose on; **–d** misleading, deceptive;
'mislopen[1] **I** *vi* 1 miss one's way; go wrong;
2 *fig* go wrong, fail, miscarry, turn out badly;
II *vt* miss; *zijn carrière ~* miss one's vocation;
dat ben ik net misgelopen I just missed it; *zij zijn*

elkaar misgelopen they missed each other;
mis'lukkeling (-en) *m* social misfit, failure;
mis'lukken (mislukte, is mislukt) *vi* miscarry,
fail; *het mislukte haar...* she did not succeed... (in
...ing); *doen ~* wreck [a plan &]; zie ook:
mislukt; **–king** (-en) *v* failure, miscarriage;
mis'lukt unsuccessful, abortive [attempt &];
mis'maakt misshapen, deformed, disfigured;
–heid (-heden) *v* deformity; **mis'maken**
(mismaakte, h. mismaakt) *vt* deform, disfigure;
mis'moedig I *aj* discouraged, disheartened,
dejected, despondent, disconsolate; *~ maken*
discourage, dishearten; **II** *ad* dejectedly,
despondently, disconsolately; **–heid** *v* discouragement, despondency, dejection; **mis'noegd**
I *aj* displeased, discontented, dissatisfied; *de*
~en the malcontents; **II** *ad* discontentedly;
–heid *v* discontentedness, dissatisfaction,
discontent, displeasure; **'misnoegen** *o*
displeasure
'misoffer (-s) *o* sacrifice of the Mass
'misoogst (-en) *m* crop failure, failure of crops
'mispel (-s en -en) *v* medlar
mis'plaatst [thing] out of place; misplaced
[faith, confidence], mistaken [zeal];
mis'prijzen (misprees, h. misprezen) *vt*
disapprove (of), condemn; **'mispunt** (-en) *o* 1
♌ miss; 2 (d e u g n i e t) good-for-nothing
fellow, S rotter; (o n a a n g e n a a m m e n s)
beast; **'misraden**[1] *vi* guess wrong; *misgeraden!*
your guess is wrong; **'misrekenen**[1] *vi* miscalculate; **mis'rekenen** (misrekende, h. misre-
kend) *vr zich ~* be out in one's calculations;
'misrekening (-en) *v* miscalculation
mis'saal (-salen) *o* rk missal
mis'schien[1] *vi* maybe
'misschieten[1] *vi* miss, miss the mark, miss
one's aim, shoot wide; **'misschot** (-schoten) *o*
miss
'misselijk I *aj* sick, queasy; *fig* disgusting,
sickening; *je wordt er ~ van* it makes you sick;
II *ad* disgustingly; **–heid** *v* nausea, sickness,
queasiness
'missen (miste, h. gemist) **I** *vi* miss; *dat kan niet*
~ it is bound to happen, you can't fail to see
it, hit it &; **II** *vt* 1 (n i e t h e b b e n) miss; lack
[the courage]; 2 (n i e t n o d i g h e b b e n)
dispense with, do without; *ik mis mijn boek*
(mijn bril &) my book & is missing; *zijn doel ~*
zie *doel*; *wij kunnen dat niet ~* 1 we can't spare
it; 2 we cannot do without it; *zij kunnen hem ~*
als kiespijn they prefer his room to his company; *zij kunnen het best (slecht) ~* they can

---

[1] V.T. en V.D. van dit werkwoord volgens het model: **'mis**gooien, V.T. gooide **'mis**, V.D. **'mis**gegooid. Zie voor
de vormen onder het grondwoord, in dit voorbeeld: *gooien*. Bij sterke en onregelmatige werkwoorden wordt u
verwezen naar de lijst achterin.

well (can't well) afford it; *het kan niet gemist worden* they can't do without it; *de trein (de boot)* ~ miss (lose) the train (the steamer); *de boot* ~ [*fig*] miss the bus; *het mist zijn uitwerking* it is ineffective; *het zal zijn uitwerking niet* ~ it will not fail to produce its effect; **–er** (-s) *m* 1 (m i s s c h o t &) miss; 2 (f i a s c o) **F** flop; 3 (f l a t e r) blunder

'**missie** (-s en -iën) *v* mission; **–huis** (-huizen) *o* mission-house; **–werk** *o* missionary work; **missio'naris** (-sen) *m* missionary; **mis'sive** (-s en -n) *v* missive

'**misslaan**[1] *vt* & *vi* miss; zie ook: 1 *bal*; '**misslag** (-slagen) *m* miss; *fig* error, fault; **mis'staan** (misstond, h. misstaan) *vi* suit ill, be unbecoming; '**misstand** (-en) *m* abuse; '**misstap** (-pen) *m* wrong step, false step; slip; *fig* lapse; *een* ~ *begaan (doen)* make a false step[2]; '**misstappen**[1] *vi* make a false step, miss one's footing; '**misstelling** (-en) *v* (typographical) error; *herplaatsing wegens* ~ amended notice; '**misstoot** (-stoten) *m* miss; ⚇ miss, miscue; '**misstoten**[1] *vi* miss one's thrust; ⚇ give a miss

mist (-en) *m* fog; (n e v e l) mist; [*fig*] *de* ~ *ingaan* come to nothing, fail

'**mistasten** *vi* fail to grasp; *fig* make a mistake

'**mistbank** (-en) *v* fog bank; '**misten** (mistte, h. gemist) *vi* be foggy, be misty; '**misthoorn, –horen** (-s) *m* fog-horn, siren; '**mistig** foggy, misty; **–heid** *v* fogginess, mistiness; '**mistlamp** (-en) *v* 🚗 fog lamp

mis'troostig dejected, sad; **–heid** *v* dejection, sadness

mis'trouwig distrustful

'**misvatting** (-en) *v* misconception, misunderstanding, misapprehension; '**misverstaan** (verstond 'mis, h. 'misverstaan) *vt* misunderstand, misapprehend, misconstrue; '**misverstand** (-en) *o* misunderstanding, misapprehension; **mis'vormd** misshapen, deformed, monstrous, disfigured; **mis'vormen** (misvormde, h. misvormd) *vt* deform, disfigure; **–ming** (-en) *v* deformation, disfigurement; '**miswijzing** (-en) *v* magnetic declination; ⚓ compass variation

mi'taine [mi.'tɛ:nə] (-s) *v* mitten, mitt

mi'tella ('s) *v* sling

mitrail'leren [mi.trɑ(l)'jeː.rə(n)] (mitrailleerde, h. gemitrailleerd) *vt* machine-gun; **mitrail'leur** (-s) *m* machine-gun

mits *cj* provided (that); **mits'dien** therefore, consequently; **mits'gaders** together with

m.i.v. = *met ingang van*

'**mixen** (mixte, h. gemixt) *vt* mix; **–er** (-s) *m* mixer

mm = *millimeter*

m.n. = *met name*

M.O. = *Middelbaar Onderwijs*

mo'**biel** mobile; ~ *maken* mobilize; **mobili'satie** [-'za.(t)si.] (-s) *v* mobilization; **mobili'seren** (mobiliseerde, h. gemobiliseerd) *vt* & *vi* mobilize; **mobilo'foon** (-s) *m* radio-telephone

mocht (mochten) V.T. v. *mogen*

mo'**daal** modal; **modali'teit** *v* modality

'**modder** *m* mud, mire, ooze; **–bad** (-baden) *o* mud-bath; '**modderen** (modderde, h. gemodderd) *vi* dig in the mud; *fig* muddle; '**modderig** muddy, miry, oozy; '**modderpoel** (-en) *m* slough, quagmire, puddle; **–schuit** (-en) *v* mud-scow, mud-boat; **–sloot** (-sloten) *v* muddy ditch

'**mode** (-s) *v* fashion; *de* ~ *aangeven* set the fashion; ~ *worden* become the fashion; ● *in de* ~ *komen* come into fashion, become the vogue; *in de* ~ *zijn* be the fashion, be in fashion, be the wear, be in the wear; *het is erg in de* ~ it is all the fashion, it is quite the go; *n a a r d e laatste* ~ *gekleed* dressed in (after) the latest fashion; *u i t d e* ~ *raken (zijn)* go (be) out of fashion; **–artikel** (-en en -s) *o* 1 fancy-article; 2 fashionable article; **–en** fancy-goods; **–blad** (-bladen) *o* fashion magazine, fashion-paper; **–gek** (-ken) *m* fop, dandy, coxcomb; **–kleur** (-en) *v* fashionable colour; **–koning** (-en) *m* fashionable dress designer, couturier

mo'**del** (-len) **I** *o* 1 model, pattern, cut; (v a n p ij p &) shape; (v. s i g a r e t) size; 2 (v a n k u n s t e n a a r) model [posing for sculpture and painting], sitter [for portrait]; **II** *aj* model...; ✗ regulation...; **–actie** [-'ɑksi.] (-s) *v* *een* ~ a work-to-rule; *een* ~ *voeren* work to rule; **–boerderij** (-en) *v* model farm; **–flat** [-flɛt] (-s) *m* show-flat; **–kamer** (-s) *v* show-room; **model'leren** (modelleerde, h. gemodelleerd) *vt* model, mould; **model'leur** (-s) *m* modeller; mo'**delwoning** (-en) *v* show-house

'**modeontwerper** (-s) *m* fashion designer; **–plaat** (-platen) *v* fashion-plate, fashion-sheet; **–pop** (-pen) *v* (v r o u w) doll; (m a n) fop, dandy

mode'**ramen** (-mina) *o* synodal board, board of moderators; mode'**rator** (-s en -'toren) *m* moderator

mo'**dern** modern; > modernist;

---

[1] V.T. en V.D. van dit werkwoord volgens het model: '**mis**gooien, V.T. gooide '**mis**, V.D. '**mis**gegooid. Zie voor de vormen onder het grondwoord, in dit voorbeeld: *gooien*. Bij sterke en onregelmatige werkwoorden wordt u verwezen naar de lijst achterin.

moderni′seren [s = z] (moderniseerde, h. gemoderniseerd) *vt* modernize; **–ring** *v* modernization

′modeshow [′mo.dǝʃo.] (-s) *m* fashion parade, dress parade, fashion show, dress show; **–vak** *o* millinery; **–winkel** (-s) *m* milliner's shop; **–woord** (-en) *o* vogue-word, fashionable word, catchword; **–zaak** (-zaken) *v* fashion business, fashion house; **modi′eus I** *aj* fashionable; **II** *ad* fashionably; ∼ *gekleed* dressed in the height of fashion

modifi′ceren (modificeerde, h. gemodificeerd) *vt* modify

modi′nette (-s) *v* seamstress

mo′diste (-s en -n) *v* milliner, modiste; dressmaker

modu′latie [-′la.(t)si.] (-s) *v* modulation; **modu′leren** (moduleerde, h. gemoduleerd) *vi* & *vt* modulate

1 moe *aj* tired, fatigued, weary; *ik ben* ∼ I'm tired; *zo* ∼ *als een hond* dog-tired; *ik ben het werken* ∼ I am tired of work; *ik ben* ∼ *van het werken* I am tired with working; ∼ *maken* tire, fatigue

2 moe *v* **F** = *moeder*

moed *m* courage, heart, spirit; *de* ∼ *der wanhoop* the courage of desperation; ∼ *bij elkaar schrapen* muster up courage; *iem.* ∼ *geven* put some heart into sbd.; *goede* ∼ *hebben* be of good heart; *de treurige* ∼ *hebben om...* have the conscience (audacity) to...; ∼ *houden* keep (a good) heart; *de* ∼ *erin houden* keep up one's courage; *de* ∼ *opgeven, verliezen of laten zinken* lose courage, lose heart; ∼ *scheppen (vatten)* take (pluck up) courage, take heart; *je kunt begrijpen, hoe het mij te* ∼*e was* how I felt; *droef te* ∼*e* sad at heart; *wel te* ∼*e* of good cheer, cheerful; *in arren* ∼*e* in despair; ✶ in anger

′moede = 1 *moe*; zie ook: *moed*; **′moedeloos** out of heart, heavy-hearted, with a sunken heart; without courage, despondent, dejected; **moede′loosheid** *v* despondency, dejectedness

′moeder (-s) *v* 1 mother; 2 (v. g e s t i c h t) matron; (v. j e u g d h e r b e r g) warden; ∼ *Natuur* Dame Nature; *de Moeder Gods* Our Lady; ∼ *de vrouw* **F** the wife, **P** the missus, **S** my old Dutch; **–binding** *v* mother fixation; **–dag** (-dagen) *m* Mother's Day; **–huis** (-huizen) *o* parent house, mother institution; **–kerk** (-en) *v* mother church; **–klok** (-ken) *v* master clock; **–koek** (-en) *m* placenta; **–koren** *o* ergot; **–land** (-en) *o* mother country; **–liefde** *v* maternal love; **–lijk I** *aj* motherly, maternal; **II** *ad* maternally; **–loos** motherless; **–maatschappij** (-en) *v* $ parent company; **–melk** *v* breast milk; **–moord** (-en) *m*, **–moordenaar** (-s) *m* matricide; **–naakt** stark naked; **–schap**

o motherhood, maternity; **–schip** (-schepen) *o* mother ship, parent ship; **′moederskant** = *moederszijde*; **–kindje** (-s) *o* mother's darling, molly-coddle; **–zijde** *van* ∼ [related] on the (one's) mother's side; maternal [grandfather]; **′moedertaal** (-talen) *v* mother tongue, native tongue; **′moedertjelief** *daar helpt geen* ∼ *aan* you cannot get away from that; **′moedervlek** (-ken) *v* mother's-mark, mother-spot, birthmark, mole; **–ziel** ∼ *alleen* quite alone

′moedig courageous, brave; spirited

′moedwil *m* wantonness; *uit* ∼ wantonly, wilfully, on purpose; **moed′willig** wanton; **–heid** (-heden) *v* wantonness, wilfulness

′moeheid *v* fatigue, weariness, lassitude

′moeien (moeide, h. gemoeid) *vt* trouble, give trouble; *moei mij er niet in* don't mix me up in it; zie ook: *gemoeid* & *bemoeien*

′moeilijk I *aj* difficult, hard, troublesome; *een* ∼*e taak* a difficult (arduous) task; ∼*e toestand* trying situation; ∼*e tijden* hard (trying) times; **II** *ad* with difficulty, hardly; not easily; *het* ∼ *hebben* have a bad time, **F** go through the hoop; *het zal* ∼ *gaan om...* it will be difficult to...; *ik kan* ∼ *anders* I can hardly do otherwise; **–heid** (-heden) *v* difficulty, trouble, scrape; *in* ∼ (*in moeilijkheden*) *komen* get into trouble; *in moeilijkheden verkeren* be in trouble, be in a scrape, be on the mat; $ be involved; *om moeilijkheden vragen* ask for trouble; **′moeite** (-n) *v* 1 (m o e i l i j k h e i d) trouble; difficulty; 2 (i n s p a n n i n g) trouble, pains, labour; *het is geen* ∼ *!* it's no trouble at all!, don't mention it!; *ik had de grootste* ∼ *om...* it was all I could do to..., I had my work cut out to...; *het was vergeefse* ∼ it was labour lost; *iem. veel* ∼ *bezorgen* cause sbd. a great deal of trouble; ∼ *doen* take pains, exert oneself, try; *alle* ∼ *doen om...* do one's utmost to...; *doet u maar geen (verdere)* ∼ don't give yourself any trouble, please don't trouble; ∼ *geven (veroorzaken)* give trouble; *zich* ∼ *geven* 1 take trouble [to do sth.]; 2 take pains, exert oneself, try; *zich (veel)* ∼ *geven om...* trouble (oneself) to...; ook: be at (great) pains to...; *zich de* ∼ *geven om...* take the trouble to...; *zich niet eens de* ∼ *geven om...* not even trouble (bother) to...; ∼ *hebben met* have difficulty with; ∼ *hebben te* find it difficult to; *de grootste* ∼ *hebben met* make heavy weather of [sth.]; ∼ *hebben om te leren* learn with difficulty; *de* ∼ *nemen* = *zich de* ∼ *geven*; ● *het gaat i n één* ∼ *door, het is één* ∼ it is all in the day's work; *hij deed het in één* ∼ *door* he did it at the same time, he took it in his stride; *m e t (de grootste)* ∼ with (the utmost) difficulty; *z o n d e r veel* ∼ without much difficulty; zie ook: 3 *waard* &; **–loos** effortless; **–vol** hard; **′moeizaam I** *aj* laborious, wearisome, hard;

II *ad* laboriously
'**moeke** (-s) *o* **F** mammy, mummy
moer (-en) *v* 1 mother, dam [of animals]; 2 ✗ nut, female screw; 3 lees, dregs, sediment [of liquids]; *geen* ~ *!* **S** nothing!, not a damn!
moe′ras (-sen) *o* marsh, morass², swamp, bog, fen; **–bever** (-s) *m* coypu; **–gas** *o* marsh gas; **–koorts** (-en) *v* malaria; **moe′rassig** marshy, swampy, boggy; **–heid** *v* marshiness; **moe′rasveen** *o* peat-bog
'**moerbei** (-en) *v* mulberry
'**moerbout** (-en) *m* nut bolt
'**moeren** (moerde, h. gemoerd) *vt* **S** (s t u k m a k e n) spoil, destroy, ruin
'**moerschoef** (-schroeven) *v* nut, female screw; **–sleutel** (-s) *m* monkey-wrench, spanner
1 moes *v* **F** = *moesje* 2
2 moes *o* 1 stewed greens or fruit; 2 mash, mush, pulp; *tot* ~ *maken* squash; *iem. tot* ~ *slaan* beat sbd. to a jelly (a pulp); **–appel** (-s en -en) *m* cooking-apple
'**moesje** (-s) *o* 1 patch, beauty-spot [of woman]; spot [on dress materials], polka dot ; 2 (m o e - d e r) **F** mummy, mammy
'**moeskruid** (-en) *o* greens, pot-herbs, vegetables
'**moesson** (-s) *m* monsoon
moest (moesten) V.T. v. *moeten*
'**moestuin** (-en) *m* kitchen garden
'**moeten*** *vi* & *vt* be compelled, be obliged, be forced; *wat moet je?* what do you want?; *ze* ~ *hem (het) niet* they don't like him (it); *ik moet gaan* I have to go, I must go; *hij moest gaan* 1 he had to go; 2 he should go, he ought to go; *ik zal* ~ *gaan* I shall have to go; *daar moet ik niets van hebben* I'll have none of it; *ze* ~ *het wel zien* they can't fail to see it; *we moesten wel lachen* we could not help laughing; *hij moet erg rijk zijn* he is said to be very rich; *hij moet gezegd hebben, dat...* he is reported to have said that...; *daar moet je... voor zijn* it takes a... to...; *als het moet* if it cannot be helped, if there is no help for it, if it has to be done; under pressure of necessity; *het moet!* it has to be done!; ~ *is dwang* must is for the king; '**moetje** (-s) *o* **F** *een* ~ a shotgun marriage
'**moezen** (moesde, h. gemoesd) *vt* mash
1 mof (-fen) *v* 1 (v o o r d e h a n d e n) muff; 2 ✗ sleeve, socket
2 mof (-fen) *m* (s c h e l d n a a m) **F** Jerry
'**moffelen** (moffelde, h. gemoffeld) *vt* enamel
'**moffeloven** (-s) *m* muffle-furnace
'**mogelijk I** *aj* possible; *alle* ~*e dingen* all sorts of things; *alle* ~*e hulp* all the assistance possible; *op alle* ~*e manieren* in every possible way; *alle* ~*e middelen* all means possible, all possible means; *alle* ~*e moeite* every possible effort; *dat*

is best ~ that's quite possible; *met de grootst* ~*e strengheid* with the utmost possible severity; *zo goed* ~ as best as you can, to the best of your ability; *zo slecht* ~ as bad as bad can be; *het is mij niet* ~ I cannot possibly do it; **II** *sb ik heb al het* ~*e gedaan* all that is possible; all I can do (could do); **III** *ad* possibly; *zo* ~... if possible; *zo spoedig* ~ as soon as possible; ~ *weet hij het* it is possible that he knows it; **mogelijker′wijs** *ad* possibly; '**mogelijkheid** (-heden) *v* possibility; eventuality; *de* ~ *bestaat* there is a possibility; *met geen* ~ *kunnen wij...* we cannot possibly...
'**mogen* I** *hulpww.* be allowed, be permitted; *zij* ~ *komen* they may come; *ze zullen niet* ~ *komen* they will not be allowed to come; *als zij komen mochten* if they should come, should they come; *hij mag wel uitkijken* he had better watch out; *je had je wel eens mogen wassen* you ought have washed yourself; *dat mag niet* that is not allowed; *ik mag niet van mijn moeder* my mother won't let me; *...het mocht wat!* **F** ... not they!, nothing doing!; **II** *vt* like; *zij* ~ *hem niet* they don't like him; *ik mag hem gaarne (wel)* I like him very much, I rather like him
'**mogendheid** (-heden) *v* power; *de grote mogend-heden* the Great Powers
mo′gol (-s) *m* Mogul
mo′hair [mo.′hɛːr] *o* mohair
mohamme′daan(s) (-danen) *m* (& *aj*) Mohammedan
mok (-ken) *v* mug
'**moker** (-s) *m* maul, sledge; '**mokeren** (mokerde, h. gemokerd) *vt* hammer, strike with a maul
Moker′hei *v* Mook heath; **S** *loop naar de* ~ go to blazes!; *ik wou dat hij op de* ~ *zat* I wish he were at (in) Jericho
'**mokka(koffie)** *m* Mocha coffee, mocha
'**mokkel** (-s) *v* & *o* **S** (chubby) girl
'**mokken** (mokte, h. gemokt) *vi* sulk
1 mol (-len) *m* ♦ mole
2 mol (-len) *v* ♪ flat; *b–* ~ B flat
molecu′lair [mo.ləky.′lɛːr] *aj* molecular; **mole′cule** (-n) *v* & *o* molecule
'**molen** (-s) *v* 1 mill; 2 ✗ (v o o r b e t o n &) mixer; (v o o r h a r d e m a t e r i a l e n) masticator, crusher; '**molenaar** (-s) *m* miller; '**molenbeek** (-beken) *v* mill-race; **–rad** (-raderen) *o* mill-wheel; **–steen** (-stenen) *m* millstone; **–tje** (-s) *o* 1 little mill; 2 (k i n d e r - s p e e l g o e d) paper wheel; *hij loopt met* ~*s* he has bats in the belfry; **–wiek** (-en) *v* wing of a mill, sail, vane
mo′lest *o* war risks ‖ ~ *aandoen* molest; **moles′tatie** [-(t)si.] *v* molestation; **moles′teren** (molesteerde, h. gemolesteerd) *vt*

molest; **mo'lestverzekering** *v* war-risk insurance

moli'ère [mo.li.'ɛ:rə] (-s) *m* lace-up shoe

molk (molken) V.T. v. *melken*

'mollen (molde, h. gemold) *vt* S spoil, destroy, ruin

'molleval (-len) *v* mole-trap; **–vel** (-len) *o* moleskin

'mollig 1 plump [arms, legs], chubby [cheeks]; **–heid** *v* plumpness, chubbiness

molm *m* & *o* 1 mould; 2 (v . t u r f) peat dust

'moloch (-s) *m* Moloch

'molotovcocktail [-kɔkte.l] (-s) *m* Molotov cocktail

'molshoop (-hopen) *m* mole-hill; **'molsla** *v* 1 ‰ dandelion; 2 (a l s g e r e c h t) dandelion tops

'molton *o* swanskin

Mo'lukken *mv de* ~ the Moluccas

mom (-men) *o* & *o* mask; *onder de (het)* ~ *van* under the show (mask, cloak) of; **–bakkes** (-en) *o* mask

mo'ment (-en) *o* moment°, instant; **momen'teel I** *aj* momentary; **II** *ad* at the moment; **mo'mentopname** (-n) *v* instantaneous photograph, snapshot

'mommelen (mommelde, h. gemommeld) = *mummelen*

'mompelen (mompelde, h. gemompeld) *vi* & *vt* mutter, mumble

mo'narch (-en) *m* monarch; **monar'chaal** monarchical; **monar'chie** (-ieën) *v* monarchy; **–ist** (-en) *m* monarchist; **–istisch** monarchist [party]

mond (-en) *m* mouth; orifice; muzzle [of a gun]; **F** jaws; *een grote* ~ *hebben* talk big; *de (zijn)* ~ *houden* hold one's tongue; *hij kan zijn* ~ *niet houden [fig]* he can't keep his (own) counsel; *hou je* ~! shut up!; *geen* ~ *opendoen* not open one's lips; *hij durft geen* ~ *open te doen* he cannot say bo to a goose; *een grote* ~ *opzetten tegen iem.* give sbd. lip, talk back to sbd.; *zijn* ~ *roeren* wag one's tongue; *iem. de* ~ *snoeren* stop sbd.'s mouth, silence sbd.; *zijn* ~ *voorbijpraten* shoot off one's mouth, commit oneself, put one's foot in; *zijn* ~ *staat nooit stil* he never stops talking; *iedereen heeft er de* ~ *vol van* they talk of nothing else, it's the talk of the town; ● *bij* ~e *van* by (through) the mouth of; *iem. woorden i n de* ~ *leggen* put words into sbd.'s mouth; *m e t open* ~ *staan kijken* stand open-mouthed, stand gaping (at *naar*); *met de* ~ *vol tanden staan* have nothing to say for oneself, be dumbfounded; *met twee* ~en *spreken* say one thing and mean another; *iem. n a a r de* ~ *praten* toady to sbd.; *u i t zijn eigen* ~ from his own mouth; *als uit één* ~ unanimously; *iem. de woorden uit de* ~ *nemen*

take the words out of sbd.'s mouth; *iets uit zijn* ~ *sparen* save sth. out of one's mouth; *van* ~ *t o t* ~ *gaan* pass from mouth to mouth; *hij zegt alles wat hem v o o r de* ~ *komt* he says whatever comes uppermost

mon'dain [mòn'dɛːn] mundane; fashionable [hotel &]

'mondeling I *aj* oral, verbal; ~*e afspraak* verbal agreement; ~ *bericht* verbal message; ~ *examen* oral examination; ~*e getuigen* verbal references; **II** *o mijn* ~ my viva voce; **III** *ad* orally, verbally, by word of mouth; **mond- en 'klauwzeer** *o* foot-and-mouth disease; **'mondharmonika** (-s) *v* mouth-organ; **–heelkunde** *v* dental surgery; **–hoek** (-en) *m* corner of the mouth; **–holte** (-n en -s) *v* cavity of the mouth; **–hygiëniste** [-hi.gi.e.] (-n) *v* dental hygienist

mondi'aal over the whole world, world-wide

'mondig of age; zie verder: *meerderjarig*; **–heid** *v* majority; **'monding** (-en) *v* mouth; **'mondje** (-s) *o* (little) mouth; ~ *dicht!* mum's the word!; *niet op zijn* ~ *gevallen zijn* have a ready tongue; have plenty to say for oneself; **'mondjesmaat** *v* scanty measure; *het is* ~ we are on short commons; ~ *toebedelen* dole out in driblets; **'mondjevol** *o hij kent een* ~ *Frans* he has a smattering of French; **'mondkost** *m* provisions, victuals; **mond-op-'mondbeademing** *v* mouth-to-mouth resuscitation, mouth-to-mouth method; **'mondorgel** (-s) *o* mouth-organ; **–spoeling** (-en) *v* mouth-wash; **–stuk** (-ken) *o* mouthpiece; chase [of a gun]; tip [of a cigarette]; *met kurken* ~ cork-tipped [cigarette]; *zonder* ~ plain [cigarette]; **–vol** *o* mouthful; **–voorraad** *m* provisions, victuals; **–water** *o* mouth-wash

mone'tair [mo.ne.'tɛːr] monetary

Mon'gool (-golen) *m* Mongol, Mongolian; **–s** Mongolian; **mon'gooltje** (-s) *o* mongol

'monitor (-s) *m* monitor

'monnik (-en) *m* monk, friar; *gelijke* ~*en, gelijke kappen* what is sauce for the goose is sauce for the gander; **'monnikenklooster** (-s) *o* monastery; **–orde** (-n en -s) *v* monastic order; **–werk** *o* monkish work; *dat is* ~ that's labour lost; ~ *doen* flog a dead horse; **'monnikskap** (-pen) *v* 1 cowl, monk's hood; 2 ‰ monk's-hood, aconite; **–pij** (-en) *v* (monk's) frock

mo'nocle [mo.'nɔkəl] (-s) *m* (single) eye-glass, monocle

mono'gaam monogamous; **monoga'mie** *v* monogamy

monogra'fie (-ieën) *v* monograph; **mono'gram** (-men) *o* monogram, cipher

mono'liet (-en) *m* monolith; **mono'lit(h)isch** monolithic[2]

mono'loog (-logen) *m* monologue

mono'maan (-manen) *m* monomaniac; **monoma'nie** *v* monomania

mono'polie (-s en -liën) *o* monopoly; **monopoli'seren** [s = z] (monopoliseerde, h. gemonopoliseerd) *vt* monopolize

monoto'nie *v* monotony; **mono'toon** monotonous

Mon'roeleer [mɔn'ro.-] *v* Monroe Doctrine

monseig'neur [mõsɛ̃'nø:r] (-s) *m* monsignor

'monster (-s) *o* 1 monster; 2 $ sample; pattern; ~ *zonder waarde* $ sample of no value (without value); *als ~ verzenden* $ send by sample post; *volgens ~* $ up to sample, as per sample; **'monsterachtig** monstrous; **–heid** *v* monstrosity

'monsterboek (-en) *o* = *stalenboek*; **–briefje** (-s) *o* sampling order

'monsteren (monsterde, h. gemonsterd) *vt* 1 (i n s p e c t e r e n) muster; 2 = *aanmonsteren*; **–ring** (-en) *v* ⚓ muster, review

'monsterlijk monstrous

'monsterrol (-len) *v* 1 ⚓ & ⚓ muster-roll; 2 ⚓ list of the crew, ship's articles

'monsterzakje (-s) *o* sample-bag

mon'strans (-en) *m* & *v* monstrance

mon'tage [mòn'ta.ʒə] (-s) *v* 1 ⚒ mounting, fitting up, erecting, assembly; (v. a u t o's) assemblage; 2 (v. f i l m) editing, (v. d r u k - w e r k &) montage, (v. f o t o) composing; zie ook: *montering*, **–bouw** *m* prefabrication, prefabricated house construction; **–hal** (-len) *v* assembly shop (hall); **–lijn** (-en) *v* assembly line; **–wagen** (-s) *m* tower wagon; **–werker** (-s) *m* assembler; **–werkplaats** (-en) *v* assembly room

'monter I *aj* brisk, lively, cheerful; **II** *ad* briskly, cheerfully

mon'teren (monteerde, h. gemonteerd) *vt* mount [a picture]; fit up, erect [apparatus], assemble [a motorcar &]; stage [a play]; **–ring** (-en) *v* mounting [of a picture, a play]; staging [of a play]; zie ook: *montage*; **mon'teur** (-s) *m* erector, fitter [of machine]; (i n g a r a g e &) mechanic

mon'tuur (-turen) *o* & *v* frame, mount; setting [of a jewel]; *bril met hoornen ~* horn-rimmed glasses, glasses with horn rims

monu'ment (-en) *o* monument; **monumen'taal** monumental; **monu'mentenlijst** *v* op de ~ *plaatsen* register as a national monument; **–zorg** *v* protection of monuments; *onder ~ staan* be under (a) preservation order

mooi I *aj* handsome, fine, beautiful, pretty; *een ~e hand schrijven* write a fair hand; *een ~e jongen!* a fine fellow!; *mijn ~e pak* my Sunday best; *~*

zo! good!; *dat is niet ~ van u* it is not nice of you; *daar ben je ~ mee!* 1 a lot of good that will do you!; 2 that's a pretty pickle you are in!; *ik ben er al weken ~ mee* I have been troubled with it for weeks; *wat ben je ~!* F what a beauty (swell) you are!; *wel, nu nog ~er!* well I never!; *dat is wat ~s!* a pretty kettle of fish!, fine doings these!, here is a nice go!; *ze hebben wat ~s van je verteld!* fine things they say of you!; **II** 1 *als m* in: *je bent me een ~e!* you are a nice one!; 2 *als o* in: *het ~ste van alles is...* the best of it all is that...; **III** *ad* handsomely, finely, beautifully; < pretty, badly; *hij heeft u ~ beetgehad* he had you there, and no mistake; *ze hebben hem niet ~ behandeld* he has been unhandsomely treated; *zich ~ maken* (smarten) oneself up; *dat staat u niet ~* it does not become you²; **–prater** (-s) *m* coaxer, flatterer; **mooiprate'rij** *v* coaxing, flattery; **moois** *o* fine things; *er het ~ afkijken* look too long at it; zie ook: *mooi*; **'mooizitten** (zat 'mooi, h. 'mooigezeten) *vi* (v. h o n d) beg

Moor (Moren) *m* Moor, blackamoor

moord (-en) *m* & *v* murder (of *op*); *~ en brand schreeuwen* cry blue murder; **–aanslag** (-slagen) *m* attempt upon sbd.'s life, attempted murder; **moord'dadig** murderous; **'moorden** (moordde, h. gemoord) *vi* kill, commit murder(s); **'moordenaar** (-s) *m* murderer; **moordena'res** (-sen) *v* murderess; **'moordend** murderous, deadly; *~e concurrentie* cut-throat competition; **'moordgriet** (-en) *v* S a nice piece of baggage; **–kuil** (-en) *m* cut-throat place; zie *hart*; **–lust** *m* bloodthirstiness; **–partij** (-en) *v* massacre; **–tuig** *o* instrument(s) of murder; **–wapen** (-s) *o* murderous weapon

Moors Moorish, Moresque

moot (moten) *v* slice [of meat &], fillet [of fish]

1 mop (-pen) *m* = *mopshond*

2 mop (-pen) *v* joke; F gag; *een ouwe ~, een ~ met een baard* a stale joke, F a hoary chestnut; *dat is nu juist de ~* that's the joke (the funny part) of it; *voor de ~* for a lark; *~pen tappen* (*vertellen*) gag

3 mop (-pen) *v* 1 blob [of ink]; 2 brick; 3 biscuit

'mopje (-s) *o* ♪ tune

'mopneus (-neuzen) *m* pug-nose

'moppenblaadje (-s) *o* funny paper; **–tapper** (-s) *m* joker

'mopperaar (-s) *m* grumbler, S grouser; **'mopperen** (mopperde, h. gemopperd) *vi* grumble, S grouse; *zonder ~* without grumbling, without a murmur; **'mopperig** grumbling, grumpy

'moppig funny

'mops(hond) (-en) *m* pug(-dog)

mo'raal *v* 1 (z e d e n l e s) moral; 2 (z e d e n-
l e e r) morality, ethics; 3 (z e d e l ij k e
b e g i n s e l e n) morals; **morali'seren** [s = z]
(moraliseerde, h. gemoraliseerd) *vi* moralize,
point a moral; **mora'list** (-en) *m* moralist;
morali'teit *v* morality, principles

mora'torium (-s en -ia) *o* moratorium

mor'bide morbid

mo'reel **I** *aj* moral; **II** *o* ⚹ morale

mo'rel (-len) *v* morello

mo'rene (-s en -n) *v* moraine

'mores *iem.* ~ *leren* teach sbd.

mor'feem (-femen) *o* morpheme

mor'fine *v* morphine, morphia; **morfi'nist**
(-en) *m* morphine addict, morphinomaniac

morfolo'gie *v* morphology

morga'natisch morganatic(al)

1 'morgen (-s) *m* & *o* 2¼ acre [of land]

2 'morgen (-s) *m* morning; *in de vroege* ~ early
in the morning; *op een* ~ one morning; *van de*
~ *tot de avond* from morning till night; *'s (des)*
~*s* in the morning; zie ook: *ochtend*

3 'morgen *ad* to-morrow; ~*avond* to-morrow
evening; ~*ochtend* to-morrow morning; ~ *vroeg*
early to-morrow morning; ~ *komt er weer een
dag* to-morrow is another day; *hij betalen? ~
brengen!* **F** nothing doing!, not likely!; ~ *over
acht dagen* to-morrow week

'morgengebed (-beden) *o* morning prayer;
–land *o* Orient; **–rood** *o* red of dawn; **–schemering** *v* morning twilight; **–ster** *v* morning
star; **–stond** *m* morning time; *de* ~ *heeft goud in
de mond* the early bird catches the worm; **–uur**
(-uren) *o* morning hour; **–wijding** (-en) *v* early
(radio) service

mo'rille [mo: 'ri.ljə] (-s) *v* morel [mushroom]

'mormel (-s) *o* monster

mor'moon(s) (-monen) *m* (& *aj*) Mormon

'morrelen (morrelde, h. gemorreld) *vi* fumble;
~ *aan* monkey with

'morren (morde, h. gemord) *vi* grumble,
murmur

'morsdood stone-dead

'morsebel (-len) *v* slut, slattern, drab; 'morsen
(morste, h. gemorst) **I** *vi* mess, make a mess;
II *vt* spill [tea]; 'morsepot (-ten) = *morspot*

'morseschrift *o* Morse code; **–sleutel** (-s) *m*
Morse key; **–teken** (-s) *o* Morse signal

'morsig dirty, untidy; 'morspot (-ten) *m* dirty
boy (girl &)

'mortel *m* mortar; **–bak** (-ken) *m* hod;
–molen (-s) *m* mortar mixer

mor'tier (-en) *m* & *o* mortar [vessel & ⚹];
–stamper (-s) *m* pestle

mortu'arium (-s en -ia) *o* mortuary

mos (-sen) *o* moss, **–achtig** mossy, moss-like;
–groen moss-green

mos'kee (-keeën) *v* mosque

'Moskou *o* Moscow; **Mosko'viet** (-en) *m*
Muscovite; **Mos'kovisch** Muscovite; ~ *gebak*
sponge-cake

'moslem (-s), 'moslim (-s) *m* Moslem, Muslim

'mosroos (-rozen) *v* moss-rose

'mossel (-s en -en) *v* mussel; **–bank** (-en) *v*
mussel-bank, mussel-bed

'mossig mossy

most *m* must

'mosterd *m* mustard; *dat is* ~ *na de maaltijd* it is
too late to be of any use; *ik zal je tot* ~ *slaan* I'll
beat you to a jelly; zie ook: *weten*; **–pot** (-ten) *m*
mustard pot; **–saus** *v* mustard sauce; **–zaad** *o*
mustard seed; **B** & *fig* grain of mustard seed;
–zuur *o* piccalilli

1 mot (-ten) *v* (clothes-)moth; *de* ~ *zit in die
japon* that dress is moth-eaten

2 mot *v* **F** tiff, squabble; ~ *hebben met iem.* fall
out with sbd.

mo'tel (-s) *o* motel

mo'tet (-ten) *o* motet

'motgaatje (-s) *o* moth-hole; *met* ~*s* moth-eaten

'motie [mo.(t)si] (-s) *v* motion; (a a n g e-
n o m e n ~) resolution; *een* ~ *indienen* bring
forward (move, put in) a motion; *stemmen over
een* ~ vote on a motion; *een* ~ *aannemen* carry a
motion; *een* ~ *ondersteunen* second a motion; *een*
~ *verwerpen* reject a motion; ~ *van afkeuring*
vote of censure; *een* ~ *van vertrouwen aannemen*
pass a vote of confidence; ~ *van wantrouwen*
vote of no-confidence

mo'tief (-tieven) *o* 1 (r e d e n) motive [=
ground]; 2 (i n d e k u n s t) motif;
moti'vatie [– 'va.(t)si.] (-s) *v* motivation;
moti'veren (motiveerde, h. gemotiveerd) *vt*
motivate, motive, state the grounds for,
account for

'motor (-s en -'toren) *m* motor; engine;
(m o t o r f i e t s) motor cycle, **F** motor-bike;
–agent (-en) *m* motor-cycle policeman, police
motor-cyclist; **–barkas** (-sen) *v* motor-launch;
–boot (-boten) *m* & *v* motor-boat, motor-
launch; **–bril** (-len) *m* motoring goggles;
–defect (-en) *o* engine trouble; **–fiets** (-en) *m*
& *v* motor (bi)cycle, **F** motor-bike; **moto'riek**
v 1 motor; 2 (sense of) muscular movement;
mo'torisch motor [nerve &]; **motori'seren**
[s = z] (motoriseerde, h. gemotoriseerd) *vt*
motorize; **–ring** *v* motorization; 'motorjacht
(-en) *o* motor yacht; **–kap** (-pen) *v* 1 🚗
bonnet, *Am* hood; 🚗 cowling, cowl; 2
(h o o f d d e k s e l) motoring helmet; **–pech** *m*
engine trouble; **–rijder** (-s) *m* motor-cyclist;
–rijtuig (-en) *o* motor vehicle

'motregen (-s) *m* drizzling rain, drizzle;
'motregenen (motregende, h. gemotregend)

vi drizzle, mizzle

'**motte(n)bal** (-len) *m* moth-ball; **–zak** (-ken) *m* mothproof storage bag

'**mottig** 1 (p o k d a l i g) pock-marked; 2 (d o o r d e m o t a a n g e t a s t) moth-eaten; 3 (v a n h e t w e e r) drizzly

'**motto** ('s) *o* motto, device

'**mouche** ['mu.ʃə] (-s) *v* beauty-spot

mousse'line [mu.sə'li.nə] *v & o* muslin

mous'seren [mu.'se:rə(n)] (mousseerde, h. gemousseerd) *vi* effervesce; **~de wijn** sparkling (effervescent) wine

mout *o & m* malt

mouw (-en) *v* sleeve; *ze a c h t e r de ~ hebben* be a slyboots; *iem. iets o p de ~ spelden* make sbd. believe sth., gull sbd.; *u i t de ~ schudden* knock off, throw off [verses, articles &]; *ergens een ~ aan passen* arrange matters, find a way out; *de handen uit de ~en steken* put one's shoulder to the wheel; **–loos** sleeveless

moza'ïek (-en) *o* mosaic work, mosaic; **–vloer** (-en) *m* mosaic floor

Mozam'bique [-'bi.k] *o* Mozambique

Mr. = *Meester (in de rechten)*

ms. = *manuscript*

mud (-den) *o & v* hectolitre; **–vol** chock-full

'**muf(fig)** musty, fusty

mug (-gen) *v* mosquito, gnat; midge; *van een ~ een olifant maken* make mountains of molehills; '**muggebeet** (-beten) *m* mosquito-bite, gnat-bite; midge-bite; '**muggeziften** (muggeziftte, h. gemuggezift) *vi* split hairs; **–er** (-s) *m* hair-splitter; **muggezifte'rij** (-en) *v* hair-splitting

muil (-en) *m* mouth, muzzle; ‖ *v* (p a n t o f f e l) slipper; **–band** (-en) *m* muzzle; '**muilbanden** (muilbandde, h. gemuilband) *vt* muzzle[2]

'**muildier** (-en) *o* mule; '**muildierdrijver** (-s) *m* muleteer; '**muilezel** (-s) *m* hinny; '**muilezeldrijver** (-s) *m* muleteer

'**muilkorf** (-korven) *m* muzzle; '**muilkorven** (muilkorfde, h. gemuilkorfd) *vt* muzzle; '**muilpeer** (-peren) *v* box on the ear, cuff, slap

muis (-muizen) *v* mouse [*mv* mice]; ‖ (v a n h a n d) ball of the thumb; ‖ (a a r d a p p e l) kidney potato; **–je** (-s) *o* (little) mouse; *dat ~ zal een staartje hebben* there will be some consequences, the matter will not end there

'**muisstil** noiseless, perfectly silent

'**muiten** (muitte, h. gemuit) *vi* mutiny, rebel; *aan het ~ slaan* mutiny; *de ~de troepen* the mutinous troops; **–er** (-s) *m* mutineer, rebel; **muite'rij** (-en) *v* mutiny, rebellion

'**muizegat** (-gaten), **–hol** (-holen) *o* mousehole; '**muizen** (muisde, h. gemuisd) *vi* 1 mouse; 2 *fig* feed; *katjes die ~ mauwen niet* the silent pig is the best feeder; **muizenest** (-en) *o*

mouse-nest, *fig* worry; '**muizengif(t)** *o* ratpoison; '**muizenissen** *mv* worries; *haal je geen ~ in het hoofd* don't worry

'**muizentarwe** *v* rat-poison; **–vanger** (-s) *m* mouser; '**muizeval** (-len) *v* mousetrap

1 mul *aj* loose; sandy

2 mul *v & o* mould [= loose earth]

3 mul (-len) *m* 🐟 red mullet

mu'lat (-ten) *m,* **mulat'tin** (-nen) *v* mulatto

'**mulder** (-s) *m* miller°

multilate'raal multilateral

'**multimiljonair** [-miljo.nɛ:r] (-s) *m* multimillionaire.

multipli'cator (-s) *m* multiplier

mum *o in een ~* in no time, in a jiffy

'**mummelen** (mummelde, h. gemummeld) *vi* mumble

'**mummie** (-s en -iën) *v* mummy; **mummifi'catie** [-'ka.(t)si.] *v* mummification; **mummifi'ceren** (mummificeerde, h. gemummificeerd) *vt & vi* mummify

'**München** *o* Munich

mundi'aal global

mu'nitie [-(t)si.] *v* (am)munition, munitions; **–wagen** (-s) *m* ammunition wagon

'**munster** (-s) *o,* **–kerk** (-en) *v* minster

munt (-en) *v* 1 (s t u k) coin; (g e l d) money, coinage, coin(s); [foreign] currency; 2 (g e b o u w) mint; ‖ 3 🌿 mint; *iem. met gelijke ~ betalen* pay sbd. (back) in his own coin, repay sbd. in kind, give sbd. tit for tat; *hij neemt alles voor goede ~ aan* he swallows everything; *~ slaan* coin (mint) money; *~ slaan uit* make capital out of, cash in on; zie ook: *kruis*; **–biljet** (-ten) *o* currency note; **–eenheid** (-heden) *v* monetary unit; '**munten** (muntte, h. gemunt) *vt* coin, mint; *het gemunt hebben op* zie *gemunt*; '**muntenkabinet** (-ten) *o* numismatic cabinet; **munt- en 'penningkunde** *v* numismatics; '**muntloon** (-lonen) *o* mintage; **–meester** (-s) *m* mint-master, Master of the Mint; **–meter** (-s) *m* slot-(gas)meter; **–stelsel** (-s) *o* monetary system; **–stempel** (-s) *o* stamp; die; **–stuk** (-ken) *o* coin; **–vervalsing** (-en) *v* debasement of coinage; **–voet** *m* standard; **–wet** (-ten) *v* coinage act; **–wezen** *o* monetary system, coinage

'**murmelen** (murmelde, h. gemurmeld) *vi* murmur, purl, gurgle, burble

murmu'reren (murmureerde, h. gemurmureerd) *vi* grumble

murw [mürf] 1 soft, tender, mellow; 2 *fig* softened up [of enemy, person]; *iem. ~ beuken* beat sbd. to a jelly

mus (-sen) *v* sparrow; zie ook: *blij*

mu'seum [my.'ze.üm] (-ea en -s) *o* museum; **–stuk** (-ken) *o* museum piece

musi′ceren [my.zi.′se: rǝ(n)] (musiceerde, h. gemusiceerd) *vt* make music; **′musici** meerv. van *musicus*; **musicolo′gie** *v* musicology; **musico′logisch** musicological; **–′loog** (-logen) *m* musicologist; **′musicus** [-küs] (-ci) *m* musician

mus′kaat 1 (-katen) *v* 🏵 nutmeg; 2 *m* (w i j n) muscatel; **–noot** (-noten) *v* nutmeg

mus′ket (-ten) *o* musket; **muske′tier** (-s) *m* musketeer

mus′kiet (-en) *m* mosquito; **mus′kietengaas** *o* mosquito-netting; **–net** (-ten) *o* mosquito-net

′muskus *m* musk; **–dier** (-en) *o* musk-deer; **–rat** (-ten) *v* musk-rat, musquash; **–roos** (-rozen) *v* musk-rose

′mussehagel *m* dust-shot

mu′tatie [-(t)si.] (-s) *v* mutation; **~s** (*bij het departement* &) changes; **mu′teren** (muteerde, h. gemuteerd) *vi* mutate

muti′leren (mutileerde, h. gemutileerd) *vt* mutilate

muts (-en) *v* cap; bonnet; *daar staat mij de ~ niet naar* I am not in the vein for it; *er met de ~ naar gooien* have a shot at it

′mutsaard, ′mutserd (-s) *m* faggot; [*fig*] *het riekt naar de ~* it smells of heresy

1 muur (muren) *m* wall; *blinde ~* blank wall; *de muren hebben oren* walls have ears; *tussen vier muren* in prison

2 muur *v* 🏵 = *sterremuur*

′muuranker (-s) *o* cramp-iron, brace; **–bloem** (-en) *v* 🏵 wallflower; **–bloempje** (-s) *o fig* wallflower; **–kast** (-en) *v* wall cupboard; **–krant** (-en) *v* poster; **–schildering** (-en) *v* mural painting, wall-painting; **–tegel** (-s) *m* wall-tile; **–vast** as firm as a rock; **–verf** (-verven) *v* distemper; **–versiering** (-en) *v* mural decoration; **–vlakte** (-n en -s) *v* wall space

′muze (-n) *v* muse

′muzelman (-nen) *m* Muslim, ⚔ Mussulman

mu′ziek *v* music; *~ maken* make music; *op de ~* to the music; *op ~ zetten* set to music;

–avondje (-s) *o* musical evening; **–boek** (-en) *o* music-book; **–criticus** (-ci) *m* music critic; **–doos** (-dozen) *v* musical box, music-box; **–gezelschap** (-pen) *o* musical society; **–handel** (-s) *m* music-house; **–handelaar** (-s en -laren) *m* music-seller; **–instrument** (-en) *o* musical instrument; **–korps** (-en) *o* band (of musicians); **–kritiek** (-en) *v* music criticism; **–leer** *v* theory of music; **–leraar** (-raren en -s) *m* music-master; **–les** (-sen) *v* music-lesson; **–lessenaar** (-s) *v* music-desk; **–liefhebber** (-s) *m* music-lover; **–noot** (-noten) *v* note; **–onderwijs** *o* musical instruction; **–school** (-scholen) *v* school of music; **–sleutel** (-s) *m* ♪ clef; **–standaard** (-s) *m* music-stand; **–stuk** (-ken) *o* piece of music; **–tent** (-en) *v* bandstand; **–uitvoering** (-en) *v* musical performance; **–vereniging** (-en) *v* musical society, musical club; **–wetenschap** *v* musicology; **–winkel** (-s) *m* music-shop; **–zaal** (-zalen) *v* concert-room; **muzi′kaal** musical; *hij is zeer ~* 1 he has a fine ear for music; 2 he is very fond of music; **muzikali′teit** *v* musicality; **muzi′kant** (-en) *m* musician, bandsman

mv. = *meervoud*

my′oom [mi.′o.m] (myomen) *o* myoma

myri′ade [mi.ri.-] (-n) *v* myriad

mys′terie [mis-] (-s en -riën) *o* mystery; **–spel** (-spelen) *o* mystery (play); **mysteri′eus** mysterious

mysti′cisme [misti′sismǝ] *o* mysticism; **′mysticus** (-ci) *m* mystic; **mys′tiek I** *aj* mystical [body, experience, union], mystic [life, rose, vision, way]; **II** *ad* mystically; **III** *v* mysticism; **IV** *mv de ~en* the mystics

mystifi′catie [misti.fi.′ka.(t)si.] (-s) *v* mystification; **mystifi′ceren** (mystificeerde, h. gemystificeerd) *vt* mystify

′mythe [′mi.tǝ] (-n) *v* myth; **′mythisch** mythical; **mytholo′gie** (-ieën) *v* mythology; **mytho′logisch** mythological; **–′loog** (-logen) *m* mythologist

myxoma′tose [mikso.ma.′to.zǝ] *v* myxomatosis

N

n [ɪn] ('s) *v* n
N. = *noord*

na I *prep* after; ~ *elkaar* one after the other, in succession; *twee keer* ~ *elkaar* twice running; ~ *u!* After you!; ~ *u heb ik alles aan hem te danken* next to you; ~ *vijven* after five o'clock; **II** *ad* near, ⊙ nigh; *dat lag hem* ~ *aan het hart* zie *hart*; *je moet hem niet te* ~ *komen* 1 you must not come too near him; 2 *fig* you must not offend him; *dat kwam zijn eer te* ~ *zie eer*; *op mijn broer* ~ except my brother, but for my brother; *op één* ~ one excepted; *de laatste op één* ~ the last but one; *op één* ~ *de grootste ter wereld* the second largest in the world; *neem wat pudding* ~ take some pudding to top up with

naad (naden) *m* 1 seam; 2 (v. w o n d) suture; *nylons met* ~ seamed nylons; **–je** (-s) *o hij wil graag het* ~ *van de kous weten* he wants to know the ins and outs of it; **–loos** seamless

naaf (naven) *v* nave, hub; **–dop** (-pen) *m* hub-cap

'**naaicursus** [-zəs] (-sen) *m* sewing-class; **–doos** (-dozen) *v* sewing-box; '**naaien** (naaide, h. genaaid) **I** *vt* sew; *een knoop aan een...* ~ sew a button on; **P** fuck; **II** *vi* & *va* sew, do needle-work; '**naaigaren** (-s) *o* sewing-thread; **–gerei** *o* sewing-things; **–kistje** (-s) *o* sewing-box; **–krans** (-en) *m* sewing-circle; **–machine** [-maꞏʃiꞏnə] (-s) *v* sewing-machine; **–mand** (-en) *v* work-basket, sewing-basket; **–meisje** (-s) *o* sewing-girl; **–ster** (-s) *v* seamstress, needlewoman; **–werk** *o* needlework

naakt naked[2], bare[2]; nude [figure]; **F** in the altogether; ~*e feiten* hard (dry) facts; *de* ~*e waarheid* the bare (naked, plain) truth; *hij werd* ~ *uitgeschud* he was stripped to the skin; **–figuur** (-guren) *v* nude; **–foto** ('s) *v* nude photograph; **–heid** *v* nakedness, bareness [of the walls &]; nudity; **–loper** (-s) *m* nudist; **–strand** (-en) *o* nudist beach

naald (-en) *v* needle˚; **–boom** (-bomen) *m* conifer; **–bos** (-sen) *o* pine forest, conifer forest; **–koker** (-s) *m* needle-case; '**naaldhak** (-ken) *v* stiletto heel; *schoen met* ~ stiletto-heeled shoe; **–hout** *o* softwood; **–vormig** needle-shaped; **–werk** *o* needlework

naam (namen) *m* name; appellation, designation; *hoe is uw* ~? what's your name?; *zijn* ~ *met ere dragen* not belie one's name; *het mag geen* ~ *hebben* it is not worth mentioning; *een goede* ~ *hebben* have a good name, enjoy a good reputa-

tion; *een slechte* ~ *hebben* have an ill name (a ba reputation); *hij heeft nu eenmaal de* ~ *van...* he has the name of..., he has a name for [honesty &]; ~ *maken* make a name for oneself; *geen namen noemen* mention no names; ● *iem. b i j zijn* ~ *noemen* call sbd. by his name; *i n* ~ *is hij* in name (nominally) he is...; *i n* ~ *der wet* in th name of the law; *noemen m e t* ~ *en toenaam* mention by name; *o n d e r een aangenomen* ~ under an assumed name; *onder een vreemde* ~ ir another name, not in their real names; *bekend staan onder de* ~ *(van)...* go by the name of...; *o een andere* ~ *overschrijven* zie *overschrijven*; *aandele op* ~ zie *aandeel*; *op* ~ *van* in the name of; *hij heeft tien romans op zijn* ~ *(staan)* he has ten novels to his credit (to his name); *t e goeder* ~ *(en faam) bekend staand* enjoying a good reputa-tion, of good standing and repute; *u i t* ~ *van mijn vader* from my father, on behalf of my father; *iem. v a n* ~ *kennen* know sbd. by name; *een ... van* ~ a distinguished...; *z o n d e r* ~ without a name, nameless. Zie ook: **–bordje** (-s) *o* name-plate; **–cijfer** (-s) *o* cipher, monogram, initials; **–dag** (-dagen) *m* saint's day, name-day; **–genoot** (-noten) *m* namesake; **–kaartje** (-s) *o* (visiting-)card; **–lijst** (-en) *v* 1 list of names, roll, register; 2 panel [of jury, doctors &]; **–loos** without a name, nameless, anonymous; zie ook: *vennoot-schap*; **–plaatje** (-s) *o* door-plate, name-plate; **–val** (-len) *m* case; *eerste* ~ nominative; *tweede* ~ genitive; *derde* ~ dative; *vierde* ~ accusative; **–woord** (-en) *o* noun

'**naäpen** (aapte 'na, h. 'nageaapt) *vt* ape, imitate, mimic; **–er** (-s) *m* ape, imitator, mimic; **naäpe'rij** (-en) *v* aping, imitation

1 naar I *prep* to; according to; after; by; ~ *boven* & zie *boven*; *hij heet* ~ *zijn vader* he is called after his father; ~ *huis gaan* go home; *hij kwam* ~ *me toe* he came up to me; ~ *de natuur schilderen* paint from nature; **II** *ad dat is er* ~ that depends; *ja maar het is er ook* ~ but then it is no better than it should be; *hij is er de man niet* ~ *om...* zie *man*; **III** *cj* ~ *men zegt* it is said

2 naar *aj* disagreeable, unpleasant, sad, dismal; *een nare jongen* an unpleasant (nasty) boy; *die nare jongen!* that wretched boy!; *een nare smaak* a nasty taste; *een nare vent* **F** bleeder, cad; ~ *weer* sour weather; *ik voel me zo* ~ I feel so queer (unwell); *hij is er* ~ *aan toe* he is in a bad way; *ik word er* ~ *van* it makes (turns) me sick

naar'dien since, whereas

naar′geestig dismal, gloomy, sombre

naarge′lang zie *gelang*

′naarling (-en) *m* nasty (beastly) fellow

naar′mate according as, as [we grow older]

′naarstig assiduous, diligent, industrious, sedulous; **–heid** *v* assiduity, diligence, industry, sedulity

naast I *aj* nearest, next; *mijn ~e buurman* my next-door neighbour; *mijn ~e bloedverwant* my nearest relation, my next of kin; *de ~e prijs* $ the lowest price; *de ~e toekomst* the near future; *ten ~e bij* approximately, about; *ieder is zichzelf het ~* near is my shirt, but nearer is my skin; **II** *prep* next (to); *~ elkaar* side by side; *het is niet ~ de deur* it is not next door; *~ God heb ik hem alles te danken* next to God; *hij zat ~ haar* beside her, by her side; *~ ons wonen Fransen* next-door to us; *je bent er ~* you are beside the mark (wrong); **naast′bijzijnd** nearest;

′naaste (-n) *m-v* neighbour, fellow-creature; **′naasten** (naastte, h. genaast) *vt* 1 nationalize, take over; 2 confiscate, seize; **′naastenliefde** *v* love of one's neighbour, charity; **′naastgelegen** next-door, adjacent; **′naasting** (-en) *v* 1 nationalization; 2 confiscation, seizure

′nababbelen[1] *= napraten* **II**

′nabauwen[1] *vt* repeat [sth.] parrot-like, echo [what one has heard]

′nabeeld (-en) *o* after-image

′nabehandeling (-en) *v* after-treatment, follow-up

′nabeschouwing (-en) *v* commentary; *een ~ houden* consider in retrospect

′nabestaande (-n) *m* relation, relative; *de ~n* ook: the next of kin

′nabestellen (bestelde ′na, h. ′nabesteld) **I** *vt* give a repeat order for, order a fresh supply of; **II** *vi* repeat an order; **–ling** (-en) *v* repeat order, repeat

′nabetalen (betaalde ′na, h. ′nabetaald) *vi* pay afterwards; **–ling** (-en) *v* subsequent payment

′nabeurs *v* $ (bourse of the) closing hours: the Street

na′bij near, close to; *de dag is ~* the day is near at hand; *van ~* from close by; *van ~ bekeken* seen at close quarters; *iem. van ~ kennen* know sbd. intimately; *het raakt ons van ~* it concerns us nearly, it touches us very closely; *de dood ~* near death; **–gelegen** neighbouring, adjacent; **–heid** *v* neighbourhood, vicinity, proximity; *er was niemand in de ~* there was nobody near; **–komen** (kwam na′bij, is na′bijgekomen) *vt* come near to [sbd.'s ideal], come near [the

mark], run [sbd.] hard; *wie komt hem nabij in...?* who can approach him in...?, who can touch him at...?; **–zijnd** near-by [place]; forthcoming [event]

′nablijven[1] *vi* 1 remain, stay on; 2 ☞ be kept in, be detained (at school)

′nabloeden[1] *vi de wond bleef ~* the wound kept on bleeding

′nabloeien[1] *vi* bloom later; **–er** (-s) *m* ♣ late flowerer; *fig* epigone

′nabob (-s) *m* nabob

′nabootsen (bootste ′na, h. ′nagebootst) *vt* imitate, mimic; **–er** (-s) *m* imitator, mimic; **′nabootsing** (-en) *v* imitation

na′burig neighbouring; **′nabuur** (-buren) *m* neighbour

nacht (-en) *m* night; *'s (des) ~s* [12 o'clock] at night, [work] by night, in the night-time, ✎ of nights; *de ~ van maandag op dinsdag* the night from Monday to Tuesday; *de hele ~* all night (long), the whole night; *het wordt ~* night is falling; ● *b ij ~* by night, in the night-time; *bij ~ en ontij* at unseasonable hours; *i n de ~* at night, during the night; *v a n de ~ een dag maken* turn night into day; **–arbeid** *m* night-work; **–asiel** [s = z] (-en) *o* night-shelter; **–bel** (-len) *v* night-bell; **–blind** night-blind; **–blindheid** *v* night-blindness, ✿ nyctalopia; **–boot** (-boten) *m &* *v* night-boat; **′nachtbraken** (nachtbraakte, h. genachtbraakt) *vi* make a night of it; **–er** (-s) *m* night-reveller; **′nachtclub** (-s) *v* night club, night spot; **–dienst** *m* 1 night-service; 2 night-duty; *~ hebben* be on night-duty

′nachtegaal (-galen) *m* nightingale

′nachtelijk nocturnal [visit], night [attack &], [disorder] by night; *de ~e stilte* the silence of the night; **′nachtevening** (-en) *v* equinox; **–gewaad** (-waden) *o* night-attire; **–goed** *o* night-clothes, night-things, slumber-wear; **–hemd** (-en) *o* night-shirt; **–japon** (-nen) *m* night-dress, night-gown, F nightie; **–kaars** (-en) *v* night-light; *als een ~ uitgaan* fizzle out; **–kastje** (-s) *o* pedestal cupboard; **–kluis** (-kluizen) *v* night-safe; **–lampje** (-s) *o* night-lamp; **–leven** *o* night-life; **–lichtje** (-s) *o* night-light; **–merrie** (-s) *v* nightmare; **–mis** (-sen) *v* midnight mass; **–permissie** (-s) *v* night leave; **–pitje** (-s) *o* rushlight, floating wick; **–ploeg** (-en) *v* night-shift; **–pon** (-nen) *m = nachtjapon*; **–portier** (-s) *m* night-porter; **–rust** *v* night's rest; **–schade** (-n) *v* night-shade; **–schuit** (-en) *v* night-boat; *met de ~*

---

[1] V.T. en V.D. van dit werkwoord volgens het model: ′na**babbelen**, V.T. babbelde ′na, V.D. ′na**ge**babbeld. Zie voor de vormen onder het grondwoord, in dit voorbeeld: *babbelen*. Bij sterke en onregelmatige werkwoorden wordt u verwezen naar de lijst achterin.

komen be late; **–slot** (-sloten) *o* double lock; *op het ~ doen* double-lock; **–spiegel** (-s) *m* chamber pot, **S** jordan; **–stroom** *m* ※ cheap hours; **–tarief** *o* night rate, night tariff; **–trein** (-en) *m* night-train; **–uil** (-en) *m* 🐦 screech-owl; **–uiltje** (-s) *o* 🦋 night-moth; **–vlinder** (-s) *m* (night-)moth; **–vlucht** (-en) *v* night flight; **–vogel** (-s) *m* night-bird²; **–voorstelling** (-en) *v* late-night showing [of a film]; **–vorst** (-en) *m* night-frost; **–wacht** (-en) *m* night-watchman; *v* night-watch; *de Nachtwacht (van Rembrandt) v* the Midnight Round, (Rembrandt's) Night Watch; **–waker** (-s) *m* night-watchman; **–werk** *o* night-work, lucubration; *er ~ van maken* make a night of it, burn the midnight oil; **–zoen** (-en) *m* good-night kiss; **–zuster** (-s) *v* night-nurse; **–zwaluw** (-en) *v* nightjar

'nadagen *mv* the latter days [of sbd.'s life], the declining years; the last stage [of a revolution]
na'dat *cj* after [we had seen it]
'nadeel (-delen) *o* disadvantage; injury, harm, hurt; loss; *dat is het ~ van zo'n betrekking* that is the drawback of such a place; *in uw ~* against you; *ten nadele van* at the cost (expense) of, to the detriment (prejudice) of; *hij kan niets te mijnen nadele zeggen* he can say nothing against me; *tot zijn eigen ~* to his cost; **na'delig** disadvantageous; hurtful, detrimental, prejudicial; *~ zijn voor, ~ werken op* be detrimental to; *~ voor* detrimental to, hurtful to, harmful to, injurious to

'nadenken¹ I *vi* think [about], reflect [(up)on]; *ik moet er eens over ~* I must think about it; *ergens goed over ~* consider sth. carefully, give sth. serious consideration; **II** *o* reflection; *bij ~* on reflection; *tot ~ brengen* make [sbd.] think (reflect), set [sbd.] thinking; *tot ~ stemmen* furnish food for thought; *zonder ~* without thinking, unthinkingly; **na'denkend I** *aj* pensive, meditative, thoughtful; thinking; **II** *ad* pensively, meditatively

'nader I *aj* nearer [road]; further [information]; *hebt u al iets ~s vernomen?* have you got any further information (news)?; **II** *ad* nearer; *je zult er ~ van horen* you will hear of this; *~ aanduiden* indicate more precisely; *er ~ van horen* hear more of it; *~ op iets ingaan* 1 enter into the details of it; 2 make further inquiries; zie ook: *ingaan*; *ik zal u ~ schrijven* I'll write you more fully; *~ verwant (aan)* more nearly allied (to); zie ook: *inzien, kennis, verklaren* &; **nader'bij** nearer; **'naderen** (naderde, is

genaderd) **I** *vi* approach, draw near; *~ tot...* go to [Holy Communion]; **II** *vt* approach, draw near to [of persons, things]; *we ~ het doel* ook: we are nearing the goal; **nader'hand** afterwards, later on; **'nadering** *v* approach
na'dien since
'nadoen¹ *vt* imitate, mimic
'nadorst *m* thirst after drinking to excess
'nadruk (-ken) *m* 1 (k l e m) emphasis, stress, accent; 2 (h e t n a g e d r u k t e o f n a d r u k k e n) reprint; pirated copy; piracy; *de ~ leggen op* stress²; *fig* lay stress on, accentuate emphasize; *~ verboden* all rights reserved; *met ~* emphatically; **na'drukkelijk** emphatic
'nadrukken¹ *vt* reprint; pirate [a book]
'naëten¹ *vt* eat after the others; *wat eten we na?* what are we going to finish with?, what do we have for dessert?
'nafluiten¹ *vt* 1 whistle after; 2 hoot
'nafta *m* naphtha; **nafta'leen** *o* naphthalene
'nagaan (ging 'na, h. en is 'nagegaan) **I** *vt* 1 (v o l g e n) follow; 2 (h e t o o g houden op) keep an eye on, look after; 3 (o n d e r - z o e k e n) trace; *iem.'s gangen ~* keep track of sbd.; *de rekeningen ~* look into (check) the notes; *het verleden ~* retrace the past; *we worden nagegaan* we are watched; *als ik dat naga, dan...* when considering how...; *je kunt ~ hoe...* you can easily imagine how...; *voor zover we kunnen ~* as far as we can ascertain; *dat kan je ~!* you bet!; (a b s o l u u t n i e t) **F** not likely!; **II** *vi* be slow [of a watch]
'nagalm *m* resonance, echo; **'nagalmen¹** *vi* resound, echo
'nageboorte (-n) *v* afterbirth, placenta
'nagedachtenis *v* memory, remembrance; *gewijd aan de ~ van* sacred to the memory of; *ter ~ aan* in commemoration of
'nagekomen *~ berichten* stop-press news; *~ stukken* subsequent correspondence
'nagel (-s en -en) *m* nail°; (k r u i d n a g e l) clove; *dat was een ~ aan zijn doodkist* it was a nail in his coffin
'nagelaten *~ werk* posthumous work
'nagelbed (-den) *o* nail-bed; **'nagelbijten** *o* nail-biting; **–er** (-s) *m* nail-biter; **'nagelborstel** (-s) *m* nail-brush
'nagelen (nagelde, h. genageld) *vt* nail; *aan de grond genageld* rooted to the ground (to the spot)
'nagelkaas (-kazen) *m* clove-cheese
'nagellak *o* & *m* nail-varnish; **–riem** (-en) *m* cuticle; **–schaartje** (-s) *o* nail-scissors; **–vast**

---

¹ V.T. en V.D. van dit werkwoord volgens het model: 'na**babbelen**, V.T. babbelde '**na**, V.D. 'na**gebabbeld**. Zie voor de vormen onder het grondwoord, in dit voorbeeld: *babbelen*. Bij sterke en onregelmatige werkwoorden wordt u verwezen naar de lijst achterin.

fixed with nails; *aard- en* ~ immovable,
clinched and riveted; *alles wat* ~ *is* the fixtures;
–vijltje (-s) *o* nail-file

'**nagemaakt** counterfeit, forged, faked

'**nagenoeg** almost, nearly, all but

'**nagerecht** (-en) *o* dessert

'**nageslacht** *o* posterity, progeny, offspring,
issue

'**nageven**[1] *vt dat moet hem (tot zijn eer) worden
nagegeven* that must be said to his honour
(credit); *dat moet ik hem* ~ I'll say that for him

'**naheffing** (-en) *v* additional income tax assessment

'**naherfst** *m* last days of autumn

'**nahollen**[1] *vt* run (tear) after

'**nahouden**[1] *vt* keep in (at school); *er op* ~ keep
(articles for sale); *fig* hold [theories]; *er geen
bedienden op* ~ not keep (any) servants

na' '**ïef** naive, artless, ingenuous, simple-minded

'**naijlen**[1] *vt* hasten after

'**naijver** *m* 1 envy, jealousy; 2 (w e d ij v e r)
emulation; **na'ijverig** envious, jealous, (of *op*)

naïve'**teit, naïvi'teit** *v* naïvety

'**najaar** (-jaren) *o* autumn; **–sbeurs** (-beurzen) *v*
autumn fair

'**najagen**[1] *vt* chase[2] [chimeras], pursue[2] [game, a
plan, pleasures]; hunt for [a job], hunt (strain)
after [effect]

'**najouwen**[1] *vt* hoot after

'**nakaarten**[1] *vi fig* hold a post-mortem

'**naken** (naakte, is genaakt) *vi* approach, come
near(er), draw near

'**nakie** *o* **F** *in zijn* ~ in the altogether

'**nakijken**[1] *vt = nazien*

'**naklank** *m* resonance, echo[2]; '**naklinken**[1] *vi*
continue sounding, resound

'**nakomeling** (-en) *m* descendant; **–schap** *v*
posterity, progeny, offspring, issue

'**nakomen**[1] **I** *vi* come afterwards, come later
(on), arrive afterwards, follow; **II** *vt*
1 (v o l g e n) come after, follow;
2 (v o l b r e n g e n) fulfil, make good
[a promise], meet, honour [an obligation]

'**nakomertje** (-s) *o* **F** afterthought

'**nakoming** *v* performance, fulfilment

'**nalaten**[1] *vt* 1 (a c h t e r l a t e n, bij o v e r-
l ij d e n) leave (behind); 2 (n i e t m e e r
d o e n) leave off; 3 (n i e t d o e n) omit, fail;
neglect [one's duties]; *ik kan niet* ~ *te...* I
cannot help (forbear, refrain from) ...ing;
na'**latenschap** (-pen) *v* inheritance;
(b o e d e l) estate

na'**latig** negligent, neglectful, remiss, careless;

een ~*e betaler* a bad payer; **–heid** *v* 1 negligence, remissness, carelessness; 2 dereliction
of duty

'**naleven**[1] *vt* live up to [a principle]; observe
[certain rules], fulfil [instructions]

'**naleveren**[1] *vt* deliver subsequently; **–ring** (-en)
v subsequent delivery

'**naleving** *v* living up to [principles &], observance [of rules], fulfilment

'**nalezen**[1] *vt* 1 peruse, read over; 2 glean[2] [a
field &]

'**nalopen**[1] **I** *vt* run after[2], follow[2]; *ik kan niet
alles* ~ I can't attend to everything; **II** *vi* be
slow [of a watch]; *mijn horloge loopt iedere dag een
minuut na* my watch loses one minute a day

nam (namen) V.T. v. *nemen*

'**namaak** *m* imitation, counterfeit, forgery;
wacht U voor ~ beware of imitations; **–sel** (-s) *o*
imitation; '**namaken**[1] *vt* 1 copy, imitate [a
model]; 2 counterfeit, forge [a signature]

'**name** *m e t* ~ especially, notably; *met* ~ *noemen*
name (mention) expressly; *t e n* ~ *van* in the
name of; **–lijk** namely, viz., that is, videlicet,
~ to wit; (w a n t, i m m e r s) for; *ik wist* ~
niet... the fact is that I didn't know...; **–loos**
nameless, unutterable, unspeakable, inexpressible; zie ook: *naamloos*

'**namen** V.T. meerv. v. *nemen*

'**namens** in the name of, on behalf of

'**nameten**[1] *vt* measure again, check

na'**middag** (-dagen) *m* afternoon; *des* ~*s* in the
afternoon; *om 3 uur in de* ~ ook: at 3 p.m.

'**nanacht** (-en) *m* latter part of the night

'**naogen**[1] *vt* follow with one's eyes

'**naoorlogs** post-war

nap (-pen) *m* cup, bowl, basin, porringer

'**napalm** *o* napalm

'**napijn** (-en) *v* after-pain

'**napluizen**[1] *vt* ferret into, investigate

Napole'ontisch Napoleonic

'**nappa(leer)** *o* ± dogskin

'**napraten**[1] **I** *vt* echo [sbd.'s words], repeat
[sbd.'s words]; **II** *vi nog wat* ~ remain talking,
have a talk after the meeting (the session &)

'**napret** *v* fun after the feast, amusement after
the event

nar (-ren) *m* fool, jester

'**narcis** (-sen) *v* narcissus, daffodil; **nar'cisme** *o
ps* narcissism; **nar'cist** (-en) *m* narcissist;
–isch narcissistic

nar'cose [- 'ko.zə] *v* narcosis, anaesthesia; *onder*
~ *brengen* narcotize, anaesthetize; *onder* ~ *zijn*
be under the (an) anaesthetic; **nar'coticum**

---

[1] V.T. en V.D. van dit werkwoord volgens het model: '**na**babbelen, V.T. babbelde '**na**, V.D. '**na**gebabbeld. Zie
voor de vormen onder het grondwoord, in dit voorbeeld: *babbelen*. Bij sterke en onregelmatige werkwoorden wordt
u verwezen naar de lijst achterin.

(-ca) *o* narcotic; *narcotica* narcotics;
nar'cotisch narcotic; ~ *middel* narcotic;
narcoti'seren [s = z] (narcotiseerde, h.
genarcotiseerd) *vt* narcotize, anaesthetize;
narcoti'seur (-s) *m* anaesthetist
'nardus *m* nard, spikenard
'narede (-s) *v* epilogue
narekenen[1] *vt* 1 check; 2 (b e r e k e n e n)
calculate
'narennen[1] *vt* run (gallop) after
'narigheid (-heden) *v* trouble, misery
'naroepen[1] *vt* 1 call after; 2 (u i t s c h e l d e n)
call names
'narrenkap (-pen) *v* fool's cap, cap and bells;
–pak (-ken) *o* fool's dress
'narwal (-s en -len) *m* narwhal
na'saal [s = z] I *aj* nasal; **II** *ad* nasally; **III**
(-salen) *v* nasal
'naschilderen[1] *vt* copy
'nascholing *v* refresher course
'naschreeuwen[1] *vt* cry (bawl) after; *iem.* ~ hoot
at sbd.
'naschrift (-en) *o* postscript; **'naschrijven**[1] *vt*
copy [a model], plagiarize [an author]
'naslaan[1] *vt* look up [a word]; consult [a book];
'nasla(g)werk (-en) *o* book of reference,
reference book, work of reference, reference
work
'nasleep *m* train (of consequences); *de* ~ *van de*
oorlog war's aftermath; **'naslepen**[1] **I** *vt* drag
after; **II** *vi* drag (trail) behind
'nasluipen[1] *vt* steal after
'nasmaak (-smaken) *m* after-taste, tang; *een*
bittere ~ *hebben* leave a bitter taste
'nasnellen[1] *vt* run (hasten) after
'nasnuffelen[1] *vt* pry into [a secret]; ferret in
[one's pockets]
'naspel (-spelen) *o* 1 (v. t o n e e l s t u k) after-
piece; 2 ♪ (concluding) volµntary; 3 *fig* sequel,
aftermath; 4 (s e k s u e e l) afterplay
'naspelen[1] *vt* ♪ replay [by ear]
'naspellen[1] *vt* spell after; spell again
'naspeuren[1] *vt* trace, track, investigate
'nasporen[1] *vt* trace, investigate; **–ring** (-en) *v*
investigation; *zijn* ~*en* ook: his researches
'naspreken[1] *vt* repeat [my words]; > echo
'naspringen[1] *vt* leap (jump) after
'nastaren[1] *vt* gaze (stare) after
'nastreven[1] *vt* strive after, pursue [happiness,
wealth &]; emulate [sbd.]; *het* ~ the pursuit [of
a policy &]
'nasturen[1] *vt* forward [a letter]
'nasynchronisatie [-sɪngro.ni.za.(t)si.] (-s) *v*

dubbing; **'nasynchroniseren**[1] *vt* dub [a film];
'nasynkronisatie [-sɪnkro.ni.za.(t)si.] (-s) =
nasynchronisatie; **'nasynkroniseren** = *nasynchro-*
niseren
nat I *aj* wet; (v o c h t i g) moist, damp; *zo* ~ *als*
een kat as wet as a drowned rat; ~ *van transpi-*
ratie wet with perspiration; ~ *maken* wet; **II** *o*
wet, liquid; *het is een pot* ~ zie *potnat*
'natafelen[1] *vi* remain at table after dinner is
over
'natekenen[1] *vt* copy, draw [from a model]
'natellen[1] *vt* count over, count again, check
'nathals (-halzen) *m* tippler, soaker; **–heid** *v*
wetness, moistness, dampness
'natie [-(t)si.] (-s en natiën) *v* nation; **–vlag**
(-gen) *v* ⚓ ensign; **natio'naal** [-(t)si.o.-]
national; **nationali'satie** [-'za.(t)si.] (-s) *v*
nationalization; **nationali'seren** (nationali-
seerde, h. genationaliseerd) *vt* nationalize;
nationa'lisme *o* nationalism; **nationa'list**
(-en) *m* nationalist; **–isch** nationalistic [state of
mind], [they are very] nationalistic; nationalist
[party, press]; **nationali'teit** (-en) *v* nationality; **nationali'teitsbewijs** (-wijzen) *o* certificate of nationality; **–gevoel** *o* national feeling
'natrekken[1] *vt* 1 go after, march after [the
enemy &]; 2 trace, copy [a drawing]
'natrillen[1] *vi* continue to vibrate
'natrium *o* sodium; **–lamp** (-en) *v* sodium-
vapour lamp
'nattig wet(tish); **–heid** *v* wetness, wet, damp
na'tura *in* ~ in kind
naturali'satie [-'za.(t)si.] (-s) *v* naturalization;
naturali'seren (naturaliseerde, h. genaturali-
seerd) *vt* naturalize; *zich laten* ~ take out letters
of naturalization
natura'listisch naturalistic
na'tuur (-turen) *v* 1 nature; 2 (natural) scenery;
3 disposition, temper; *de* ~ *is er erg mooi* the
scenery is very beautiful there; *er zijn van die*
naturen die... there are natures who...; *dat is bij*
hem een tweede ~ *geworden* it has become a
second nature with him; *de* ~ *is sterker dan de*
leer nature passes nurture; ● *i n de vrije* ~ in
the open air; *n a a r de* ~ from nature; *o v e r -*
e e n k o m s t i g de ~ according to nature; *t e g e n*
de ~ against nature; *v a n nature* by nature,
naturally; **–bad** (-baden) *o* lido; **–behoud** *o*
conservancy (conservation) of nature;
–beschermer (-s) *m* conservationist;
–bescherming *v* preservation (conservation)
of natural beauty; **–boter** *v* natural butter;
–geneeswijze (-n) *v* treatment by natural

---

[1] V.T. en V.D. van dit werkwoord volgens het model: **'na**babbelen, V.T. babbelde **'na**, V.D. **'na**gebabbeld. Zie
voor de vormen onder het grondwoord, in dit voorbeeld: *babbelen*. Bij sterke en onregelmatige werkwoorden wordt
u verwezen naar de lijst achterin.

remedies; **–getrouw** 1 true to nature; 2 true
to life; **natuurhis'torisch** natural-historical,
natural history [society]; **na'tuurkenner** (-s)
m naturalist, natural philosopher; **–kennis** *v*
natural history; zie ook: *natuurkunde*; **–kracht**
(-en) *v* force of nature; **–kunde** *v* physics,
(natural) science; **natuur'kundig** physical; ~
laboratorium physics laboratory; **–e** (-n) *m-v*
natural philosopher, physicist
na'tuurlijk I *aj* natural; ~*e aanleg* natural bent;
~*e historie* natural history; ~ *kind* 1 natural
(artless) child; 2 natural child, child born out
of wedlock; **II** *ad* naturally; ~*!* of course!;
natuurlijker'wijs, –'wijze naturally;
na'tuurlijkheid *v* naturalness, artlessness
na'tuurmens (-en) *m* natural man, child of
nature; **–monument** (-en) *o* place of natural
beauty; **–onderzoeker** (-s) *m* naturalist;
–ramp (-en) *v* natural calamity (catastrophe,
disaster); **–recht** *o* natural right; **–reservaat**
[s = z] (-vaten) *o* nature reserve; **–schoon** *o*
(beautiful) scenery; *ons* ~ our beauty spots;
–staat *m* original state; *i n de* ~ in a state of
nature; *t o t de* ~ *terugkeeren* return to a state of
nature; **–steen** *o &* ~ *m* natural stone; **–tafereel**
(-relen) *o* scene of natural beauty;
–verschijnsel (-en en -s) *o* natural phenomenon [*mv* natural phenomena]; **–vorser** (-s) *m*
naturalist; **–vriend** (-en) *m* lover of nature,
nature lover; **–wet** (-ten) *v* law of nature,
natural law; **–wetenschap(pen)** *v* (*mv*)
(natural) science; **natuurweten'schappelijk**
scientific [research]

nauw I *aj* 1 (e n g) narrow [road &]; tight
[dress]; 2 *fig* close [friendship &]; **II** *ad*
narrowly; tightly; closely [related]; ~ *bij elkaar*
close together; ~ *merkbaar* scarcely perceptible; *hij neemt het (kijkt) zo* ~ *niet* he is not so
very particular; **III** *o* 1 ✠ strait(s); 2 *fig* scrape;
het Nauw van Calais the Straits of Dover; *in het*
~ *zitten* be in a scrape, be in a (tight) corner,
be hard pressed; *iem. in het* ~ *brengen* press sbd.
hard, drive sbd. into a corner; *in het* ~ *gedreven*
with one's back to the wall, cornered
'nauwelijks scarcely, hardly, barely; ~*... of...*
scarcely (hardly)... when...; no sooner... than...
nauwge'zet I *aj* conscientious; painstaking;
punctual; **II** *ad* conscientiously; punctually;
–heid *v* conscientiousness; punctuality
nauw'keurig exact, accurate, close; **–heid** *v*
exactness, accuracy
nauw'lettend close, exact, accurate, strict,
particular; ~*e zorg* anxious care; **–heid** *v*

exactness, accuracy
'nauwsluitend close-fitting, skin-tight
'nauwte (-s en -n) *v* ✠ strait(s), narrows
n.a.v. = *naar aanleiding van* on the occasion of
'navel (-s) *m* navel, § umbilicus; **–breuk** (-en) *v*
umbilical hernia; **–streng** (-en) *v* umbilical
cord, navel-string
nave'nant zie *naar gelang*
'navertellen (vertelde 'na, h. 'naverteld) *vt*
repeat; retell
'naverwant I *aj* closely related; **II** *sb* ~*en*
relations
navi'gatie [-(t)si.] *v* navigation; *Akte van
Navigatie* ⱴ Navigation Act; **navi'gator** (-s) *m*
navigator [ook ⏎]
'navliegen[1] *vt* fly after
NAVO ['na.vo.] *v* = *Noordatlantische Verdrags-
organisatie* NATO
na'volgbaar imitable; **'navolgen**[1] *vt* follow,
imitate; **na'volgend** following; **navol-
gens'waard(ig)** worthy of imitation;
'navolger (-s) *m* follower, imitator; **'navolging** (-en) *v* imitation
'navordering (-en) *v* (v. b e l a s t i n g) additional assessment
'navorsen[1] *vt* investigate, search (into); **–sing**
(-en) *v* investigation; *zijn* ~*en* ook: his researches
'navraag *v* inquiry; $ demand; *er is veel* ~ *naar* $
it is in great demand; ~ *doen naar* inquire after;
bij ~ on inquiry; **'navragen**[1] *vi* inquire
na'vrant harrowing, poignant
'naweeën *mv* afterpains; *fig* after-effects, aftermath
'nawerken[1] *vi* produce after-effects; **–king** *v*
after-effect(s)
'nawijzen[1] *vt* point after (at); zie ook: *vinger*
'nawinter (-s) *m* latter part of the winter
'nawoord (-en) *o* epilogue
'nazaat (-zaten) *m* descendant
'nazeggen[1] *vt* repeat
'nazenden[1] *vt* send (on) after, forward; redirect
'nazetten[1] *vt* pursue, chase
'nazi ['na.zi.] ('s) *m & aj* Nazi
'nazien[1] *vt* 1 (n a o g e n) look after, follow with
one's eyes [a person]; 2 (k r i t i s c h n a g a a n)
examine; ✗ overhaul [a machine, a bicycle &];
go over [one's lessons]; 3 (v e r b e t e r e n)
correct [exercises]; *ik zal het eens* ~ I'll look it
up [in the dictionary]
'naziten[1] *vt* pursue
'nazomer (-s) *m* latter part of the summer; *mooie*
~ Indian summer

---

[1] V.T. en V.D. van dit werkwoord volgens het model: **'na**babbelen, V.T. babbelde **'na**, V.D. **'na**gebabbeld. Zie
voor de vormen onder het grondwoord, in dit voorbeeld: *babbelen*. Bij sterke en onregelmatige werkwoorden wordt
u verwezen naar de lijst achterin.

'nazorg *v* after-care

N.B. = *noorderbreedte; nota bene*

n. Chr. = *na Christus* A.D.

ndl. = *Nederlands*

neces'saire [ne.sɛˈsɪːrɔ] (-s) *m* 1 (m e t
t o i l e t b e n o d i g d h e d e n) dressing-case,
toilet-case; 2 (m e t n a a i g e r e i) housewife

necrolo'gie (-ieën) *v* necrology

'nectar *m* nectar

'neder(-) = *neer*(-)

'Nederduits *o, aj* Low German

'nederig **I** *aj* humble, lowly; **II** *ad* humbly;
−**heid** *v* humility, humbleness, lowliness

'nederlaag (-lagen) *v* defeat, reverse,
overthrow; *de* ∼ *lijden* suffer defeat, be
defeated; *de vijand een zware* ∼ *toebrengen* inflict a
heavy defeat upon the enemy

'Nederland *o* the Netherlands; *de* ∼*en* the
Netherlands; 'Nederlander (-s) *m* Dutchman;
−**schap** *o* Dutch nationality; 'Nederlands **I** *aj*
Dutch, Netherlands; *N*∼*e Antillen* (the)
Netherlands Antilles; **II** *o het* ∼ Dutch; −**talig**
Dutch-speaking [Belgians]

'nederwaarts = *neerwaarts*

'nederzetting (-en) *v* settlement

nee = *neen*

neef (-s en neven) *m* 1 (b r o e d e r s- o f
z u s t e r s z o o n) nephew; 2 (o o m s- o f
t a n t e s z o o n) cousin; *ze zijn* ∼ *en nicht* they
are cousins

neeg (negen) V.T. van *nijgen*

neen no; ∼ *maar!* Well, I never!; ∼ *zeggen* say
no, refuse; *hij zei van* ∼ he said no; *met* ∼
beantwoorden answer in the negative

neep (nepen) V.T.van *nijpen*

neer down

'neerbuigen² **I** *vi* bend (bow) down; **II** *vt* bend
down; **III** *vr zich* ∼ bow (kneel) down;
neer'buigend condescending, patronizing

'neerdalen² *vi* come down, descend; −**ling**
(-en) *v* descent

'neerdoen² *vt* let down; −**draaien**² *vt* turn
down; −**drukken**² *vt* press down, weigh
down, oppress²

'neergaan² *vi* go down; −**d** downward; *in* ∼*e
lijn* on the down grade

'neergooien² *vt* throw (fling) down [sth.];
throw up [one's cards, *fig* one's berth]; *de boel er
bij* ∼ **F** chuck the whole thing

'neerhaal (-halen) *m* downstroke [in writing]

'neerhalen² *vt* pull down, haul down [a flag],
lower; bring down [aircraft]; −**hangen**² *vt*
hang down, droop; −**hurken** (hurkte 'neer, h.
en is 'neergehurkt) *vi* squat (down); −**kijken**²

vi look down [upon]; −**knielen**² *vi* kneel
down; −**komen**² *vi* come down; ∼ *op een tak*
alight on a branch; *daar komt het op neer* it
comes (amounts) to this, it boils down to this;
het komt alles op hetzelfde neer it comes to the
same thing, it works out the same in the end;
alles komt op hem neer all falls on his shoulders
(on him); −**kwakken**² *vt* dump down, slam
down; −**laten**² *vt* 1 let down, lower [a blind];
2 drop [the curtain, a perpendicular, a para-
chutist]; −**leggen**² **I** *vt* lay down, put down;
zijn ambt ∼ resign (one's office); *zijn betrekking*
∼ lay down (vacate) one's office; *het commando*
∼ relinquish the command; *ik moest 25 gulden*
∼ I had to put down 25 guilders; *zijn hoofd* ∼
lay down one's head²; *de praktijk* ∼ retire from
practice; *veel vijanden* ∼ shoot (kill) many
enemies; *de wapens* ∼ lay down one's arms; *het
werk* ∼ 1 (g e w o o n) cease (stop) work; 2
(b i j s t a k i n g) strike work, strike, down
tools; *zoveel stuks wild* ∼ bring down (kill) so
many head of game; *naast zich* ∼ disregard,
ignore, take no notice of; **II** *vr zich bij iets* ∼
acquiesce in it; accept the fact; *men moet er zich
maar bij* ∼ one has to put up with it, one can
only resign oneself to it; *zich* ∼ *bij het vonnis*
defer to the verdict; −**liggen**² *vi* lie down;
−**ploffen**² **I** *vt* dash down; **II** *vi* flop down, fall
down (come down) with a thud; −**sabelen**² *vt*
cut down, put to the sword; −**schieten**² **I** *vt*
shoot down [a bird &]; shoot [a man]; bring
down [aircraft]; **II** *vt* dart down, dash down
[upon...]; ∼ *op* ook: pounce upon, swoop
down; −**schrijven**² *vt* write down; −**slaan**²
I *vt* strike down [a person]; cast down [the
eyes]; let down [a flap &]; lower [a hood];
precipitate [a substance]; *fig* dishearten; beat
down [resistance]; **II** *vi* 1 be struck down; 2
(i n s c h e i k u n d e) precipitate

neer'slachtig dejected, low(-spirited),
depressed; **F** down in the mouth; −**heid** *v*
dejection, low spirits, depression of spirits, **F**
the blues

'neerslag (-slagen) 1 *m* (r e g e n &) precipitation; 2 *m* & *o* (i n d e s c h e i k u n d e) precipitation; precipitate; (b e z i n k s e l) deposit;
sediment; *radioactieve* ∼ fall-out

'neersmijten² *vt* throw down, fling down, slap
down; −**steken**² *vt* stab; −**storten**² **I** *vi* 1 fall
down; 2 ⟨⟩ crash; **II** *vt* dump down; −**strijken**
(streek 'neer, h. en is 'neergestreken) *vi* alight
[on a branch &]; −**stromen**² *vi* stream down;
−**tellen**² *vt* count down; −**trekken**² *vt* pull
down, draw down; −**tuimelen**² *vi* tumble

---

² V.T. en V.D. van dit werkwoord volgens het model: 'neer·dalen, V.T. daalde 'neer, V.D. 'neergedaald. Zie voor
de vormen onder het grondwoord, in dit voorbeeld: *dalen*. Bij sterke en onregelmatige werkwoorden wordt u
verwezen naar de lijst achterin.

down; **–vallen²** *vi* fall down, drop; **–vellen²**
vt fell, strike down; **–vlijen²** **I** *vt* lay down; **II**
vr zich ~ lie down

'neerwaarts **I** *aj* downward; **II** *ad* downward(s)
'neerwerpen² **I** *vt* cast (throw, fling, hurl)
down; ⬇ drop, parachute; **II** *vr zich* ~ throw
oneself down; **–zetten²** **I** *vt* set (put) down; **II**
vr zich ~ 1 sit down; 2 settle [in India &];
–zien² *vi* look down (upon *op*); **–zijgen²**,
–zinken² *vi* sink down; ~ *in* sink into [an
armchair &]; **–zitten** (zat 'neer, is 'neergeze-
ten) *vi* sit down

neet (neten) *v* nit

nega'tief, 'negatief **I** *aj* negative; **II** *ad* negatively; **III** (-tieven) *o* negative

1 'negen nine; *alle* ~ *gooien* throw all nine
2 'negen V.T. meerv. v. *nijgen*

'negende ninth (part); **'negenjarig** of nine
years, nine-year-old; **–oog** (-ogen) *v* 1 🜨
lamprey; 2 🜨 carbuncle; **–tal** (-len) *o* nine;
'negentien nineteen; **–de** nineteenth (part);
'negentig ninety; **–jarig** of ninety years; *een*
~*e* a nonagenarian; **–ste** ninetieth (part);
'negenvoud *o* multiple of nine; **–ig** ninefold
'neger (-s) *m* Negro; **–bevolking** *v* Negro
population

1 'negeren ['ne.gərə(n)] (negerde, h. genegerd)
vt bully, hector

2 ne'geren [nə.'ge:rə(n)] (negeerde, h. gene-
geerd) *vt* ignore [sth., sbd.]; cut [sbd.]

nege'rin (-nen) *v* Negress; **'negertaal** (-talen) *v*
Negro language

negli'gé [ne.gli.'ʒe.] (-s) *o* undress, négligé; *in* ~
in dishabille

nego'rij (-en) *v* hole [of a place]

ne'gotie [-(t)si.] (-s) *v* trade; *zijn* ~ his wares
'neigen (neigde, h. geneigd) **I** *vi* incline, bend;
ter kimme ~ decline; *ten val* ~ totter to its ruin;
geneigd tot... zie *geneigd*; **II** *vt* incline, bend [one's
head]; **–ging** (-en) *v* leaning (towards *to*),
propensity, tendency, bent, inclination; ~
voelen om... feel inclined to...

nek (-ken) *m* back of the neck, nape of the
neck; *hij heeft een stijve* ~ he has got a stiff neck;
~ *aan* ~ *sp* neck and neck; *zij zien hem met de* ~
aan they give him the cold shoulder; *iem. de* ~
breken break sbd.'s neck; *dat zal hem de* ~ *breken*
that will be his undoing; *iem. in de* ~ *zien* **S** do
sbd. in the eye; **–haar** (-haren) *o* hair of the
nape; **'nekken** (nekte, h. genekt) *vt* kill; *een
voorstel* ~ **S** kill (wreck) a proposal; *dat heeft hem
genekt* that has been his undoing; **'nekkramp**
v cerebro-spinal meningitis; **–schot** (-schoten)
o shot in the back of the neck; **–slag** (-slagen)

m stroke in the neck, rabbit-punch; *fig* death-
blow; **–spier** (-en) *v* cervical muscle; **–vel** *o*
scruff of the neck

'nemen* *vt* 1 take [sth.]; 2 (b i j s c h a k e n &)
take, capture [a piece]; 3 🜨 take, carry [a
fortress]; 4 (s p r i n g e n o v e r) take, negotiate [the hurdles]; 5 (b e s p r e k e n) take,
engage, book [seats]; 6 (i e m. v o o r d e
g e k h o u d e n) fool [sbd.], pull sbd.'s leg; 7
(b e d o t t e n) take in, cheat, **F** do [sbd.]; *neem
wat vruchtesap* have some fruit juice; *dat neem ik
niet* I am not having this; *ik zou 't niet* ~ **F** I
wouldn't stand for it; *het* ~ *zoals het valt* take
things just as they come; ● *iem. b ij de a r m* ~
take sbd. by the arm; *iets o p zich* ~ undertake
to do sth.; *het bevel op zich* ~ take command; *een
taak op zich* ~ shoulder a task; *t o t zich* ~ 1 take
[food]; 2 adopt [an orphan]; *een horloge u i t
elkaar* ~ take a watch to pieces; *het er goed v a n*
~ do oneself well; zie ook: *aanvang* &

neolo'gisme (-n) *o* neologism
'neon *o* neon; **–buis** (-buizen) *v* neon tube
nep **S** swindle; fake; **nep-** imitation(-), fake;
'neptent (-en) *v* **S** clip joint

'Nepal *o* Nepal
'nepen V.T. meerv. v. *nijpen*

nepo'tisme *o* nepotism

nerf (nerven) *v* rib, nerve, vein; grain [of wood]
'nergens nowhere; ~ *toe dienen* zie *dienen*; ~ *om
geven* care for nothing; *het is* ~ *goed voor* it is
good for nothing; ~ *zijn* [*fig*] be nowhere

'nering (-en) *v* **$** 1 trade, retail trade; 2 custom,
goodwill; ~ *doen* keep a shop; *drukke* ~ *hebben*
do a roaring trade; **–doende** (-n) *m*
tradesman, shopkeeper

nerts 1 (-en) *m* 🜨 mink; 2 *o* (b o n t) mink
nerva'tuur (-turen) *v* nervation; **ner'veus** **I** *aj*
nervous, **F** nervy; all of a dither; **II** *ad*
nervously; **nervosi'teit** [s = z] *v* nervousness
nest (-en) *o* 1 nest [of birds &]; eyrie [of a bird
of prey]; 2 litter [of pups], set [of kittens]; 3 >
F hole [of a place]; 4 bed; 5 *fig* minx, proud
little thing; **–ei** (-eieren) *o* nest-egg

'nestel (-s) *m* shoulder-knot, tag
'nestelen (nestelde, h. genesteld) **I** *vi* nest, make
its (their) nest; **II** *vr zich* ~ [*fig*] nestle; *de vijand
had zich daar genesteld* 🜨 the enemy had lodged
himself there

'nesthaar *o* first hair, down; **–kastje** (-s) *o*
nest-box, nesting-box; **–kuiken** (-s) *o* 🜨
nestling; **–veren** *mv* first feathers, down
1 net (-ten) *o* 1 net [of a fisherman &]; 2 string
bag [for shopping]; 3 rack [in railway
carriage]; 4 network [of railways], [railway,

---

² V.T. en V.D. van dit werkwoord volgens het model: **'neer**dalen, V.T. daalde **'neer**, V.D. **'neer**gedaald. Zie voor
de vormen onder het grondwoord, in dit voorbeeld: *dalen*. Bij sterke en onregelmatige werkwoorden wordt u
verwezen naar de lijst achterin.

electricity, telephone &] system; *zijn ~ten uitwerpen* cast one's nets²; *a c h t e r het ~ vissen* come a day after the fair, be too late; *zij heeft hem i n haar ~ gelokt* she has netted (trapped) him; *in het ~ vallen* be netted², *fig* fall into the trap

2 net I *aj* 1 (n e t g e m a a k t) neat; 2 (a a r d i g) smart, trim; 3 (p r o p e r) tidy, clean; 4 (f a t s o e n l ij k) decent, nice [girls], respectable [boys, quarters]; **II** *o* fair copy; *in het ~ schrijven* copy fair, make a fair copy of; **III** *ad* 1 neatly, decently; 2 < just; *~ genoeg* just enough; *~ goed!* serves you (him &) right!; *hij is ~ vertrokken* he has just left, he left this minute; *het is ~ zes uur* it is just six o'clock; *zij is ~ een jongen* quite a boy; *dat is ~ wat (iets) voor hem* 1 the very thing for him; 2 that is just like him; *~ zo* in exactly the same manner; *~ zo goed* just as well; *~ zo lang tot...* until (at last)...; *hij is er nog ~ door* he just made it, he has got through by the skin of his teeth; *het kan er ~ in* it just fits in; *ik heb hem ~ nog gezien* I saw him just now

'**netel** (-s en -en) *v* nettle; **–doek** *o* muslin; **–doeks** muslin; **–ig** thorny, knotty, ticklish [situation]; **~e positie** plight; **~e vraag F** floorer; **–roos** *v* nettle rash, hives, ☞ urticaria

'**netheid** *v* 1 neatness, tidiness; 2 cleanness; 3 respectability

'**netje** (-s) *o* net; string-bag

'**netjes I** *ad* neatly; nicely; *ik moest ~ betalen* there was nothing for it but to pay; *~ eten* eat nicely; *een kamer ~ houden* keep a room tidy (clean); *zich ~ kleden* dress neatly; **II** *aj keurig ~* neat as a pin; *dat is (staat) niet ~* that is not becoming, not good form; *dat is niet ~ van hem* it is not nice of him; zie ook: 2 *net* **I**.

'**netmaag** (-magen) *v* reticulum

'**netnummer** (-s) *o* ☎ exchange number, trunk code, *Am* area code

'**netschrift** (-en) *o* fair copy; ⇔ fair-copy book

'**netspanning** (-en) *v* voltage of the network

'**netto** net; *~ à contant* net cash; *~ gewicht* net weight; *~ loon* take-home pay; *~- opbrengst* (*~- provenu*) net proceeds

net'vleugelig net-winged; '**netvlies** (-vliezen) *o* retina; *~ontsteking* retinitis; '**netvormig** reticular; '**netwerk** (-en) *o* network²

'**neuriën** (neuriede, h. geneuried) *vt & vi* hum

'**neurochirur'gie** [-ʃi.rür'ʒi.] *v* neurosurgery; **neurolo'gie** *v* neurology; **neuro'loog** (-logen) *m* neurologist; **neu'rose** [-'ro.zə] (-n en -s) *v* neurosis [*mv* neuroses]; **neu'roticus** (-ci) *m* neurotic; **–tisch** neurotic

'**neus** (neuzen) *m* nose [of man, a ship &]; nozzle [of a spout &]; toe-cap [of boot]; *dat is een wassen ~* that's a blind, it's a mere formality; *een*

fijne ~ hebben have a keen nose; *een fijne ~ hebben voor...* have a nose (a flair) for...; *hij ziet niet verder dan zijn ~ lang is* he does not see beyond his nose; *een lange ~ maken tegen iem.* make a long nose at sbd., cock a snook at sbd.; *zijn ~ achternagaan* follow one's nose; *zijn ~ ophalen* sniff; *dat gaat zijn ~ voorbij* that is not for him; *de ~ voor iets ophalen (optrekken)* turn up one's nose at sth., sneer at sth.; *zijn ~ buiten de deur steken* stick one's nose out of doors; *zijn ~ overal in steken* poke (thrust) one's nose into everything; *de ~ in de wind steken* put on airs; *de neuzen tellen* count noses; ● *iem. b ij de ~ nemen* take sbd. in, pull sbd.'s leg; *d o o r zijn (de) ~ praten* speak through one's nose; *iem. iets door de ~ boren* cheat sbd. of sth., do sbd. out of sth.; *ik zei het zo l a n g s mijn ~ weg* casually; *hij zit altijd m e t zijn ~ in de boeken* he is always poring over his books; *hij moet overal met zijn ~ bij zijn* he wants to be present at everything; *iem. iets o n d e r zijn (de) ~ wrijven* cast sth. in sbd.'s teeth, rub it in; *o p zijn ~ (staan) kijken* look blank (foolish); *iem. iets v o o r zijn ~ wegnemen* take it away from under his (very) nose; *het ligt v o o r je ~* it is under your (very) nose; *iem. de deur voor de ~ dichtdoen* shut the door in sbd.'s face; *wie zijn ~ schendt, schendt zijn aangezicht* it's an ill bird that fouls his own nest; **–been** (-deren) *o* nasal bone; **–bloeding** (-en) *v* nosebleeding, nosebleed; **–druppels** *mv* nosedrops; **–gat** (-gaten) *o* nostril [of man & beast]; **–geluid** (-en) *o* nasal sound, nasal twang; **–holte** (-n en -s) *v* nasal cavity; **–hoorn, –horen** (-s) *m* rhinoceros; **–je** (-s) *o* (little) nose; *het ~ van de zalm* the pick of the bunch; **–klank** (-en) *m* nasal sound; **–ring** (-en) *m* nose-ring; **–vleugel** (-s) *m* wing of the nose, nostril; **–warmer** (-s) *m* nose-warmer, cutty; **–wijs** conceited, pert, cocky

'**neutje** (-s) *o* **F** drop, nip, peg

neu'traal neutral; (n i e t s z e g g e n d) non-committal; *~ blijven* remain neutral, **F** sit on the fence; **neutrali'seren** [s = z] (neutraliseerde, h. geneutraliseerd) *vt* neutralize; **neutrali'teit** *v* neutrality

'**neutron** ['nœy-] *o* neutron

'**neutrum** ['nœy-] (-tra) *o* neuter

'**neuzen** (neusde, h. geneusd) *vi* nose

'**nevel** (-s en -en) *m* 1 mist, haze; 2 ★ nebula [*mv* nebulae]; **–achtig** nebulous², misty², hazy²; '**nevelen** (nevelde, h. geneveld) *vi het nevelt* it is misty; '**nevelig** misty, hazy; '**nevelspuit** (-en) *v* mist spray; **–vlek** (-ken) *v* nebula [*mv* nebulae]

'**nevenbedoeling** (-en) *v* ulterior motive; **–effect** (-en) *o* side effect; **–functie** [-fünksi.] (-s) *v* secondary occupation; side-line;

–geschikt co-ordinate; **–industrie** (-ieën) *v* ancillary industry; **'nevens** zie *naast* & *benevens*; **'nevenschikkend** co-ordinative; **–schikking** *v* co-ordination; **'nevensgaand** accompanying, enclosed

Nica'ragua *o* Nicaragua

nicht (-en) *v* 1 (b r o e d e r s- of z u s t e r s- d o c h t e r) niece; 2 (o o m s- of t a n t e s- d o c h t e r) cousin; 3 *m* (h o m o s e k s u e e l) **F** queer, queen

nico'tine *v* nicotine; **–vergiftiging** *v* nicotine poisoning

'niemand nobody, no one, none; ~ *anders dan*... none other than...; ~ *minder dan*... no less a person than...; ~ *niet?* no one better?; **–sland** *o* no man's land

niemen'dal nothing at all; **–letje** (-s) *o* nothing, trifle

nier (-en) *v* kidney; **–bekkenontsteking** *v* pyelitis; **–lijder** (-s) *m* nephritic patient; **–ontsteking** (-en) *v* nephritis; **–steen** (-stenen) *m* 1 🟦 renal calculus, stone in the kidney; 2 (g e o l o g i e) jade; **–vet** *o* kidneysuet; **–vormig** kidney-shaped; **–ziekte** (-n en -s) *v* nephritic disease, renal disease; kidney complaint

'niesbui (-en) *v* sneezing fit; **'niesen** (nieste, h. geniest) = *niezen*; **'nieskruid** *o* hellebore; **–poeder, –poeier** *o* & *m* sneezing-powder

1 niet I *ad* not; ~ *eens* zie *eens*; ~ *langer* no longer; ~ *te veel* not too much, none too many; ~ *dat ik*... not that I...; *geloof dat maar* ~*!* don't you believe it!; *dat is* ~ *onaardig* that's rather nice; **II** 1 *o* nothingness; 2 *m* blank; ● *in het* ~ *verzinken* (*vallen*) 1 sink into nothingness; 2 pale (sink) into insignificance (beside *bij*); *om* ~ *voor nothing, gratis; om* ~ *spelen* play for love; *te* ~ *doen* nullify, annul, cancel, abolish; dispose of [an argument, a myth]; bring (reduce) to naught [plans, a fortune], dash [sbd.'s hopes], undo [our actions, the good work]; *te* ~ *gaan* be lost, perish; *uit het* ~ *voorschijn roepen* call up from nothingness; *een* ~ *trekken* draw a blank; *als* ~ *komt tot iet kent iet zichzelve* ~ set a beggar on horseback and he'll ride to the devil

2 niet (-en) *v* 🟦 staple [for papers]

niet-'aanvalsverdrag (-dragen) *o* non-aggression pact

'nieten (niette, h. geniet) *vt* 🟦 staple

'niet-gebonden *pol* non-aligned [countries]

'nietig 1 (n i e t s b e t e k e n e n d) insignificant; 2 (o n b e d u i d e n d) miserable, paltry [sums]; 3 (o n g e l d i g) (null and) void; ~ *verklaren* declare null and void, annul, nullify; **–heid** (-heden) *v* 1 (o n b e d u i d e n d h e i d) insignificance; 2 (o n g e l d i g h e i d) nullity;

zulke nietigheden such futilities (nothings, trifles); **–verklaring** (-en) *v* nullification, annulment

'nietje (-s) *o* 🟦 staple

'niet-leden *mv* non-members

'nietmachine [-ma.ʃi.nə] (-s) *v* stapler, stapling machine

niet-'nakoming *v* non-fulfilment

niets I *pron* nothing; ~ *anders dan*... nothing (else) than, nothing (else) but, zie ook: *anders*; ~ *beter dan* no better than; ~ *dan lof* nothing but praise; ~ *minder dan*... nothing less than; ~ *nieuws* nothing new; *het is* ~*!* it is nothing!; ~ *te veel* none too much; *of het zo* ~ *is* without more ado; ...*is er* ~ *bij* ...is nothing to this, ...is not in it; ~ *daarvan!* nothing of the sort!; *het is* ~ *gedaan* it's no good; *om* (*voor*) ~ for nothing; *dat is* ~ *voor jou* that is not in your line; *het is* ~ *voor jou om*... it is not like you to...; *hij had niet voor* ~ *in Duitsland gewerkt* not for nothing had he...; ~ *voor* ~ nothing for nothing; *zij moet* ~ *van hem hebben* she will have none of him; **II** *ad* nothing; ~ *bang* nothing afraid; *het bevalt me* ~ I don't like it at all; *het lijkt er* ~ *op* it's nothing like it; *ik heb er* ~ *geen zin in* I've no mind at all to...; **III** *o* nothingness; **–beduidend, –betekenend** insignificant; **–doen** *o* idleness; **–doend** idle; **–doener** (-s) *m* idler, do-nothing; **–nut** (-ten) *m* good-for-nothing, ne'er-do-well, waster, wastrel; **niets'waardig** worthless; **–'zeggend** meaningless [look], non-committal [words]; inexpressive [features]

niettegen'staande I *prep* in spite of, notwithstanding; **II** *cj* although, though

niette'min nevertheless, for all that

nieuw I *aj* new; fresh [butter, courage, evidence &]; recent [news]; novel [idea]; modern [history, languages &]; ~*ste mode* latest fashion; **II** *ad de* ~ *aangekomene* the new-comer, the new arrival; **'nieuwbakken, nieuw'bakken** new [bread], *fig* newfangled [theories]; **'nieuwbouw** *m* new building, new construction; new buildings; **'nieuweling** (-en) *m* 1 novice, new-comer; beginner, tyro; 2 ☞ new boy; **nieuwer'wets** new-fashioned, novel, > newfangled; **'nieuwigheid** (-heden) *v* novelty, innovation; new way; **nieuwjaar** *o* new year; *een gelukkig* (*zalig*) ~ I wish you a happy New Year; **nieuwjaars'dag** (-dagen) *m* New Year's Day; **nieuw'jaarskaart** (-en) *v* New Year's card; **–wens** (-en) *m* New Year's wish; **'nieuwkomer** (-s) *m* 1 newcomer; 2 novelty; **–lichter** (-s) *m* > modernist, innovator; **nieuw'modisch** new-fashioned, fashionable, stylish

nieuws *o* news, tidings, piece of news; *geen* ~*?* any news?; *dat is geen* ~ that is no news; *dat is* *wat* ~ *!* that's something new (indeed)!; *geen* ~ *goed* ~ no news good news; *iets* ~ something new; *het laatste* ~ the latest intelligence; *laatste* ~ (i n k r a n t) stop-press; *oud* ~ ancient history; *wat voor* ~*?* what's the news?; *het* ~ *van de dag* the news of the day; *niets* ~ *onder de zon* nothing new under the sun; *in het* ~ *komen* hit (make) the headlines; *in het* ~ *zijn* be in the news; **–agentschap** (-pen) *o* news agency; **–bericht** (-en) *o* news item; **–blad** (-bladen) *o* newspaper; **–dienst** (-en) *m* (radio) news service; **nieuws'gierig** inquisitive, curious (about *naar*); *ik ben* ~ *te horen...* I am anxious to know...; **–heid** *v* inquisitiveness, curiosity (about *naar*); **'nieuwslezer** (-s) *m RT* newscaster, newsreader; **–tijding** (-en) *v* news, tidings; **–uitzending** (-en) *v RT* newscast

'nieuwtje (-s) *o* 1 novelty; 2 (b e r i c h t) piece of news; *het* ~ *is eraf* the gilt is off the gingerbread; *als het* ~ *eraf gaat* when the novelty wears off

Nieuw-'Zeeland *o* New Zealand

'niezen (niesde, h. geniesd) *vi* sneeze

'Niger *o* Niger

Ni'geria *o* Nigeria

'nihil nil; **nihi'lisme** *o* nihilism; **nihi'list** (-en) *m* nihilist; **–isch** *aj* nihilist, nihilistic [style, utterance]

nijd *m* envy

'nijdas (-sen) *m* crosspatch

'nijdig I *aj* angry; ~ *worden* get angry, fly into a passion; **II** *ad* angrily; **–heid** *v* anger

'nijdnagel (-s) *m = nijnagel*

'nijgen* *vi* bow, make a bow, drop a curtsy, curtsy; **–ging** (-en) *v* bow, curtsy

Nijl *m* Nile; **–dal** *o* Nile valley

'nijlpaard (-en) *o* hippopotamus

'nijnagel (-s) *m* hang-nail, agnail

'nijpen* *vi* & *vt* pinch; *als het nijpt* when it comes to the pinch; **–d** biting [cold]; dire [poverty]; acute [shortage, crisis]; **'nijptang** (-en) *v* (pair of) pincers

'nijver industrious, diligent; **–heid** *v* industry; **'nijverheidsschool** (-scholen) *v* technical school; **–tentoonstelling** (-en) *v* industrial exhibition

'nikkel *o* nickel; **–en** nickel

'nikken (nikte, h. genikt) *vi* nod

'nikker (-s) *m* (n e g e r) > nigger

niks nothing, nil, **F** = *niets*; ~ *hoor!* **F** nothing doing!

'nimbus (-sen) *m* nimbus

nimf (-en) *v* nymph

'nimmer never; **–meer** nevermore, never again

'Nimrod, 'nimrod (-s) *m* Nimrod²

'nippel (-s) *m* ⚒ nipple

'nippen (nipte, h. genipt) *vi* sip

'nippertje *o op het* ~ in the (very) nick of time, by a narrow margin; *het was net op het* ~ it was touch and go, it was a near thing (a close shave, a narrow squeak); *op het* ~ *komen* cut it fine

nis (-sen) *v* niche; recess [in a wall], embrasure [of a window]

ni'traat (-traten) *o* nitrate

nitroglyce'rine [-gli.sɔ'ri.nə] *v* nitroglycerine

ni'veau [ni.'vo.] (-s) *o* level; *op hetzelfde* ~ *als...* on a level with...; *op universitair* & ~ at university & level; **–verschil** (-len) *o* difference in levels; **nivel'leren** (nivelleerde, h. genivelleerd) *vt* level (up, down); **–ring** (-en) *v* levelling

nl. = *namelijk*

n.m. = (*des*) *namiddag(s)*

N.N. = *Nomen Nescio* anon(ymous)

N.O. = *noordoosten*

n° = *numero, nummer* number

'Noach *m* Noah

'nobel I *aj* noble; **II** *ad* nobly

noch neither... nor

noch'tans nevertheless, yet, still

noc'turne [nɔk'ty:rnə] (-s) *v* ♪ nocturne

'node reluctantly; *van* ~ *hebben* (*zijn*) = *nodig hebben* (*zijn*); **–loos** needless

'noden (noodde, h. genood) *vt* invite; *zij laat zich niet* ~ she does not need much pressing

'nodig I *aj* necessary, requisite, needful; ~ *hebben* be in want of, want, be (stand) in need of, need; *je hebt er niet mee* ~ it is no business of yours; *vandaag niet* ~ not today [thank you]; ~ *maken* necessitate; ~ *zijn* be necessary, be needed; *blijf niet langer dan* ~ *is* than you need, than you can help; *daarvoor is...* ~ there needs... for that; *meer dan* ~ *is* more than is necessary; *er is kracht voor* ~ *om* it requires strength; *er is heel wat voor* ~ *om...* it takes a good deal to...; *zo* ~ if needs be, if necessary; **II** *ad* necessarily, needs; **III** *o het* ~*e* what is necessary; the necessaries of life; *het* ~*e verrichten* **$** do the needful; *het éne* ~*e* the one thing needful

'nodigen (nodigde, h. genodigd) *vt* invite; zie ook: *noden*

'noemen (noemde, h. genoemd) **I** *vt* name: call, style, term, denominate; mention; *zij is naar haar moeder genoemd* she is named after her mother; *hoe noemt u dit?* what do you call this?; *feiten en cijfers* ~ cite facts and figures; *om maar eens iets te* ~ say [fifty guilders]; just to mention one; zie ook: *kind, naam, genoemd*; **II** *vr zich* ~ call oneself; **noemens'waard(ig)** worth mentioning; *niets* ~*s* nothing to speak of; **'noemer** (-s) *m* denominator [of a fraction]

noen *m* noon; **–maal** (-malen) *o* midday-meal, lunch

noest diligent, industrious; *zijn ~e vlijt* his unflagging industry (diligence); **–heid** *v* diligence, industry

nog yet, still, besides, further; *als het A. ~ was* if it was A. now!; *~ een appel* another apple; [*wil je*] *~ koffie?* more coffee?; *is er ~ koffie?* is there any coffee left?; *hoeveel ~?* how many more?; *hoe lang ~* how much longer?; *hoe ver ~?* how much further?; *~ iemand* somebody else, another one; *er is ~ iets* there is something else; *~ enige* a few more; *~ eens* once more, (once) again; *~ eens zoveel* as much (many) again; *dat is ~ eens een hoed* that's something like a hat, there's a hat for you, **S** some hat!; *~ erger* still worse, even worse; *~ iets?* anything else?; *~ geen maand geleden* less than a month ago; *~ geen tien* not (quite) ten, under ten; *~ (maar) vijf* only five (left); *~ vijftig arbeiders te werk stellen* employ an additional fifty workers; *~ vijftig auto's bestellen* order a further fifty cars; *~ meer* [give me] (some) more; *what ~ meer?* what besides?; *een ~ moeilijker taak* a yet more difficult task; *~ niet* not yet; *~ steeds niet* still not; *~ wat* some more; *wacht ~ wat* stay a little longer; *hij zal ~ wel komen* he is sure to turn up yet; *en ~ wel... and... too; en zijn beste vriend ~ wel* and that his best friend; *en dat ~ wel op kerstdag* and that that on Christmas of all days; *neem ~ wat* take some more; *dat weet ik ~ zo net niet* I am not quite sure about that; *gisteren (vorige week) ~* only yesterday (last week); *vandaag (vanmiddag) ~* to-day, this very day (this very afternoon); *~ in de 16e eeuw* as late as the 16th century; *tot ~ toe* up to now, so far, as yet

'noga *m* nougat

nog'al, **'nogal** rather, fairly; *~ gezet* pretty stout; **'nogmaals** once more, once again

nok (-ken) *v* 1 ridge; 2 ⚓ yard-arm; 3 ✘ cam; **–balk** (-en) *m* ridge-pole, rooftree; **'nokkenas** (-sen) *v* ✘ camshaft

'nolens 'volens ['no.lɛns'vo.lɛns] willy-nilly

no'maden *mv* nomads; **–leven** *o* nomadic life; **–stam** (-men) *o* nomadic tribe; **–volk** (-en en -eren) *o* nomad people; **no'madisch** nomadic

nomencla'tuur *v* nomenclature

nomi'naal nominal; **nomi'natie** [-(t)si.] (-s) *v* nomination; **nummer één op de ~** first on the short list; **'nominatief** *m* nominative

non (-nen) *v* nun

'non-acceptatie [nònɑksɛp'ta.(t)si.] *v* non-acceptance

non-ac'tief 1 not in active service; 2 [put] on half-pay; **non-activi'teit** *v* being put on half-pay

non-alco'holisch non-alcoholic, soft [drinks]

noncha'lance [nõʃɑ.'lãsə] *v* nonchalance, carelessness; **noncha'lant** nonchalant, careless

non-combat'tant (-en) *m* non-combatant

non-confor'misme *o* non-conformity; **non-confor'mist** (-en) *m* nonconformist; **–isch** nonconformist

non-'ferrometalen *mv* non-ferrous metals

non-figura'tief non-figurative [painting]

'nonnenklooster (-s) *o* convent, nunnery

'nonnetje (-s) *o* 🦆 smew

non-prolife'ratieverdrag [-(t)si.-] *o* non-proliferation treaty

'nonsens ['nònsɛns] *m* nonsense; **F** rot; *och ~!* fiddlesticks!, rubbish!; **nonsensi'caal** nonsensical, absurd

nood (noden) *m* need, necessity, want, distress; *geen ~!* no fear!; *zijn ~ klagen* disclose one's troubles; complain, lament; *door de ~ gedrongen* compelled by necessity; *in (geval van) ~* 1 at need, in an emergency; 2 in distress [a ship]; *in de ~ leert men zijn vrienden kennen* a friend in need is a friend indeed; *uit ~* compelled by necessity; *iem. uit de ~ helpen* get sbd. out of a scrape, help sbd. out; *van de ~ een deugd maken* make a virtue of necessity; *~ breekt wet* necessity has (knows) no law; *~ leert bidden*, *~ maakt vindingrijk* necessity is the mother of invention; *als de ~ aan de man komt* in case of need; *als de ~ het hoogst is, is de redding nabij* the darkest hour is before the dawn; **–aggregaat** (-gaten) *o* ⚡ stand-by power unit; **–anker** (-s) *o* sheet-anchor; **–brug** (-gen) *v* temporary bridge; **–deur** (-en) *v* emergency door

'nooddruft *m & v* 1 necessaries of life; 2 want; 3 indigence, destitution, poverty; **nood'druftig** *aj* needy, indigent, destitute; *de ~en* the needy, the destitute

'noodgang *m met een ~* like greased lightning, at the double-quick, tearing along; **–gebied** (-en) *o* distress area; **–gebouw** (-en) *o* temporary building; **–gedrongen**, **–gedwongen** compelled by necessity, perforce; **–geval** (-len) *o* (case of) emergency; **–haven** (-s) *v* port of refuge; **–hulp** (-en) *v* 1 (p e r s o o n) emergency worker, temporary help; 2 (z a a k) makeshift, stop-gap; **–klok** (-ken) *v* alarm-bell, tocsin; **–kreet** (-kreten) *m* cry of distress; **–landing** (-en) *v* forced landing, emergency landing; **nood'lijdend** 1 necessitous, distressed [provinces]; 2 indigent, poor, destitute [people]

'noodlot *o* fate, destiny; **nood'lottig** fatal

'noodluik (-en) *o* escape hatch; **–maatregel** (-en en -s) *m* emergency measure; **–mast** (-en) *m* jury-mast; **–oplossing** (-en) *v* temporary (provisional) solution; makeshift; **–rantsoen** (-en) *o* emergency rations; **–rem** (-men) *v* safety-brake; (i n s p o o r r ij t u i g e n) communication cord; **–schot** (-schoten) *o* distress-gun, **–sein** (-en) *o* distress-signal, distress-call, SOS (message); **–sprong** (-en) *m als* ~ as (in) the last resort; **–toestand** *m* (state of) emergency; **–uitgang** (-en) *m* emergency exit; **–vaart** *v* = *noodgang;* **–verband** (-en) *o* first dressing; **–vlag** (-gen) *v* flag of distress; **–vulling** (-en) *v* temporary filling; **1** '**nood-weer** *o* heavy weather; **2** '**noodweer** *v* self-defence; *uit* ~ in self-defence; **–woning** (-en) *v* temporary house, emergency dwelling

'**noodzaak** *v* necessity; **nood**'**zakelijk I** *aj* necessary; **II** *ad* necessarily, of necessity, needs; **–erwijs** of necessity; *daaruit volgt* ~ *dat...* it follows as a matter of course that...; **–heid** (-heden) *v* necessity; *in de* ~ *verkeren om...* be under the necessity of ...ing; '**nood-zaken** (noodzaakte, h. genoodzaakt) *vt* oblige, compel, constrain, force; *zich genoodzaakt zien om...* be (feel) obliged to...

nooit never; ~ *ofte* (*en te*) *nimmer* never in all my born days; at no time; never, never [criticize]; *dat* ~*!* never!; **F** *aan m'n* ~ *niet!* not on my life!; not a bit of it!

Noor (Noren) *m* Norwegian

noord north; '**noordelijk I** *aj* northern, northerly; *de* ~*en* the Northerners; **II** *ad* northerly; '**noorden** *o* north; *o p het* ~ with a northern aspect; *t e n* ~ *van* (to the) north of...; **noorden**'**wind** (-en) *m* north wind; '**noor-derbreedte** *v* North latitude; **noorder**'**licht** *o* northern lights, aurora borealis; '**noorderzon** *v met de* ~ *vertrekken* abscond, **S** shoot the moon; **noord**'**oostelijk I** *aj* north-easterly, north-eastern; **II** *ad* towards the north-east; **noord**'**oosten** *o* north-east; '**noordpool** *v* north pole; **noord**'**poolgebied** (-en) *o* arctic regions; **–reiziger** (-s) *m* arctic explorer; **noords** Nordic [race]; '**noordster** *v* North Star, polar star; **–waarts I** *aj* northward; **II** *ad* northward(s); **noord**'**westelijk I** *aj* north-westerly; **II** *ad* towards the north-west; **noord**'**westen** *o* north-west; **noord**'**wester** (-s) *m* north-wester; '**Noordzee** *v* North Sea '**Noorman** (-nen) *m* Northman, Norseman, Dane; **Noors** *aj* & *o* Norwegian; '**Noor-wegen** *o* Norway

noot (noten) *v* 1 🌰 nut, (w a l n o o t) walnut; ‖ 2 ♪ note; ‖ (a a n t e k e n i n g) note; *achtste* ~ ♪ quaver; *halve* ~ ♪ minim; *hele* ~ ♪ semi-breve; *tweeëndertigste* ~ ♪ demi-semiquaver; *zestiende* ~ ♪ semiquaver; *hij heeft veel noten op zijn zang* he is very exacting; '**nootjeskolen** *mv* nuts; **nootmus**'**kaat** = *notemuskaat*

nop (-pen) *v* burl; pile [of carpet] '**nopen** (noopte, h. genoopt) *vt* induce, urge, compel; *zich genoopt zien* be obliged [to...] '**nopens** concerning, with regard to '**nopjes** *in zijn* ~ *zijn* be in high feather, be as pleased as Punch '**noppen** (nopte, h. genopt) *vt* burl '**noppes S** nothing; *voor* ~ 1 free, for nothing; 2 in vain

nor (-ren) *v* **S** jug; *in de* ~ in quod

norm (-en) *v* norm, rule, standard; **nor**'**maal I** *aj* normal; *hij is niet* ~ 1 he is not his usual self; 2 he is not right in his head; **II** *ad* normally; **–spoor** *o* standard gauge; **normali**'**satie** [- '*za*.(t)si.] *v* standardization, normalization; regulation [of a river]; **normali**'**seren** (normaliseerde, h. genormaliseerd) *vt* standardize, normalize; regulate [a river]; **–ring** (-en) *v* standardization, normalization; regulation [of a river]; **nor**'**maliter** normally

Nor'**mandië** *o* Normandy; **–r** (-s) *m* Norman; **Nor**'**mandisch** Norman; *de* ~*e Eilanden* the Channel Islands; *de* ~*e kust* the Normandy coast

nors I *aj* gruff, surly; **II** *ad* gruffly, surlily; **–heid** *v* gruffness, surliness

nostal'**gie** *v* nostalgia; **nos**'**talgisch** nostalgic '**nota** ('s) *v* 1 [tradesman's] bill, account; 2 [diplomatic] note, [official] memorial; ~ *nemen van* take (due) note of, note

no'**tabel I** *aj* notable; **II** (-en) *m* ~*e* notable; *de* ~*en* ook: the notabilities, **F** the big (great) guns, bigwigs

nota '**bene** nota bene; (i r o n i s c h) if you please

notari'**aat** (-iaten) *o* profession of notary; **notari**'**eel** notarial; **no**'**taris** (-sen) *m* notary (public); **–ambt** *o* profession of notary; **–kantoor** (-toren) *o* notary's office; **–klerk** (-en) *m* notary's clerk

no'**tatie** [-(t)si.] *v* notation '**notawisseling** (-en) *v* exchange of notes (memorandums, memoranda) '**noteboom** (-bomen) *m* walnut-tree; **–dop** (-pen) *m* 1 nutshell; 2 *fig* 🌰 cockleshell; *in een* ~ [*fig*] in a nutshell; **–hout** *o* walnut; **–houten** *aj* walnut; **–kraker** (-s) *m* 1 (pair of) nutcrackers; 2 🦚 nutcracker; **notemus**'**kaat** *v* nutmeg; '**notenbalk** (-en) *m* ♪ staff [*mv* staves], stave

no'**teren** (noteerde, h. genoteerd) *vt* 1 note, jot (note) down, make a note of [a word &]; put [sbd.] down [for...]; 2 **$** quote [prices]; **–ring** (-en) *v* 1 noting &; 2 **$** quotation '**notie** ['no.(t)si.] (-s) *v* notion; *hij heeft er geen* ~ *van* he has not got the faintest notion of it

no'**titie** [no.'ti.(t)si.] (-s) *v* 1 (a a n t e k e n i n g) note, jotting; entry [in a diary]; 2 (a a n-d a c h t) notice; *geen ~ van iets nemen* take no notice of sth., ignore sth.; **–blok** (-ken) *o* notepad; **–boekje** (-s) *o* notebook, memorandum book

no'toir [no.'to:r, -'tva:r] notorious

'notulen *mv* minutes; *de ~ arresteren* confirm the minutes; *de ~ lezen en goedkeuren* read and approve the minutes; *de ~ maken* take the minutes; *het in de ~ opnemen* enter it on the minutes, place on record; **–boek** (-en) *o* minute-book; **notu'leren** (notuleerde, h. genotuleerd) *vt* take down, minute

nou F = *nu*

nouveau'té [nu.vo.'te.] (-s) *v* novelty; *~s* fancy-goods

Nova 'Zembla *o* Novaya Zemlya

no'veen (-venen) *v* novena

no'velle (-n) *v* novella, short novel *v*

no'vember *m* November

no'vene (-n) = *noveen*

no'vice (-n en -s) *m-v* novice; **novici'aat** (-iaten) *o* novitiate; **no'viet** (-en) *m* ☞ freshman

'novum *o* novelty

'nozem (-s) *m* lout

nr. = *nummer*

N.S. = *Nederlandse Spoorwegen* Netherlands Railways

N.T. = *Nieuwe Testament*

nu I *ad* now, at present; by this time, by now [he will be ready]; *tot ~ toe* up to nów, so far; *van ~ af* from this moment, henceforth; *wat ~?* what next?; *~ eens..., dan weer...* now... now...; at one time... at another...; *~ en dan* now and then, occasionally, at times; *~ niet* not now; *~ nog niet* not yet; *~ of nooit* now or never; **II** *ij ~, hoe gaat het?* well, how are you?; *~ ja!* well!; **III** *cj* now that (soms: now)

nu'ance [ny.'ãsə] (-s en -n) *v* nuance, shade; **nuan'ceren** (nuanceerde, h. genuanceerd) *vt* shade[2]

'nuchter sober[2]; *fig* matter-of-fact, hard-headed [man]; down-to-earth; *hij is nog ~* he has not yet breakfasted; *hij is mij te ~* he is too matter-of-fact for me; *~ kalf* newly born calf; *fig* greenhorn; *op de ~e maag* on an empty stomach; **–heid** *v* sobriety; soberness[2]

nucle'air [ny.kle.'ɛ:r] nuclear

nucle'ïnezuur (-zuren) *o* nucleic acid

nu'dist (-en) *m* nudist

nuf (-fen) *v* affected girl; **–fig** prim

nuk (-ken) *v* freak, whim, caprice; **–kig** freakish, whimsical, capricious

nul (-len) *v* nought, naught, cipher, zero; ☞ O;

hij is een ~ (in het cijfer) he is a nonentity, a mere cipher, a nobody; *zijn invloed is gelijk ~* is nil; *twee-~* sp two-nil; *~ komma ~* nil, nothing at all; *~ op het rekest krijgen* meet with a rebuff; *tien graden boven (onder) ~* ten degrees above (below) zero; *op ~* at zero; **nulli'teit** (-en) *v* nullity, nonentity, cipher; **'nulmeridiaan** (-ianen) *m* prime meridian; **–punt** *o* zero; *het absolute ~* the absolute zero; *tot op het ~ dalen* fall to zero[2]

nume'riek numerical; **'numero** ('s) *o* number; **numero'teren** (numeroteerde, h. genumeroteerd) *vt* number; **numero'teur** (-s) *m* numbering stamp; **'numerus** *m* number; *~ clausus, ~ fixus* student stop

'nummer (-s) *o* 1 number; 2 size [in gloves]; 3 item [of programme, catalogue]; turn [of music-hall artist], [circus] act; [sporting] event; 4 lot [at auction]; 5 [Christmas] number, issue [of a newspaper]; *ook een ~!* **F** a fine specimen!; *~ één zijn* ☜ be at the top of one's form; *sp* be first[2]; *~ honderd* **J** the w.c.; *hij moet op zijn ~ gezet worden* he wants to be put in his place; **–bord** (-en) *o* = *nummerplaat*; **'nummeren** (nummerde, h. genummerd) *vt* number; **–ring** (-en) *v* numbering; **'nummerplaat** (-platen) *v* number plate; **–schijf** (-schijven) *v* ☎ dial

nuntia'tuur [nün(t)si.a.'ty:r] *v* nunciature; **nuntius** ['nün(t)si.üs] (-ii en -iussen) *m* nuncio

nurks I *aj* peevish, pettish; **II** (-en) *m* grumbler

nut *o* use, benefit, profit; usefulness [of an inquiry]; *praktisch ~* practical utility; *t e n ~te van* for the use of; *ten algemenen ~te* for the general good; *tot ~ van (het algemeen)* for the benefit of (the community); *het is tot niets ~* it is good for nothing; *v a n ~ zijn* be useful; *van geen (groot) ~ zijn* be of no (great) use

'nutria 1 ('s) *v* ⚥ coypu, nutria; 2 *o* (b o n t) nutria

'nutsbedrijf (-drijven) *o* public utility; **'nutteloos I** *aj* useless; *zijn... waren ~* his... were in vain; **II** *ad* uselessly; in vain; **'nutten** (nutte, h. genut) *vt* be of use, avail; **'nuttig I** *aj* useful [ook ✗ effect &], profitable; **II** *ad* usefully, profitably; **'nuttigen** (nuttigde, h. genuttigd) *vt* take, partake of, eat or drink; **'nuttigheid** (-heden) *v* utility, profitableness

N.V. [ɛn've.] = *Naamloze Vennootschap*

N.W. = *noordwesten*

☺**'nylon** ['nɛilòn, 'na.jlòn] 1 *o & m* nylon; 2 (-s) *v* (k o u s) nylon (stocking)

nymfo'maan [nɪm-] nymphomaniac; **–'mane** (-n en -s) *v* nymphomaniac

O

1 o [o.] ('s) *v* o.
2 o [o.] *ij* oh!, ah!; ~ *God!* my God!; ~ *jee!* good Heavens!, dear me!; ~ *zo!* aha!
O. = *oost*
o. = *onzijdig*
o.a. = *onder andere(n)* among other things, among others
o'ase [o.'a.zə] (-n en -s) *v* oasis [*mv* oases]
ob'ductie [-'düksi.] (-s) *v* post-mortem, autopsy
obe'lisk (-en) *m* obelisk
'o-benen *mv* bandy-legs, bow-legs; *iem. met* ~ a bandy-legged person, a bow-legged person
'ober (-s) *m* head-waiter; ~*!* waiter!
ob'ject (-en) *o* object, thing; (d o e l, o o k ✘) objective; **–glas** (-glazen) *o* slide [of a microscope]; **objec'tief I** *aj* objective, detached; **II** (-tieven) *o* (v. v e r r e k ij k e r, c a m e r a) object-lens, object-glass; **objectivi'teit** *v* objectivity
o'b' ʒ (-s en oblieën) *v* rolled wafer
obli'gaat I *aj* obligatory; ♩ obbligato; **II** (-gaten) *o* ♩ obbligato
obli'gatie [-'ɡa.(t)si.] (-s) *v* bond, debenture; **–houder** (-s) *m* bondholder; **–lening** (-en) *v* debenture loan; **–schuld** (-en) *v* bonded debt
ob'sceen [-'se.n] obscene; **obsceni'teit** (-en) *v* obscenity
ob'scuur I *aj* obscure; *een* ~ *type (zaakje)* a shady character (business); **II** *ad* obscurely
obse'deren (obsedeerde, h. geobsedeerd) *vt* obsess; **–d** obsessive [idea &]
obser'vatie [-'va.(t)si.] (-s) *v* observation; *in* ~ under observation; *ter* ~ *opgenomen* taken in for observation; **–huis** (-huizen) *o* remand home; **–post** (-en) *m* ✘ observation post; **obser'vator** (-s) *m* observer; **observa'torium** (-ia en -s) *o* observatory; **obser'veren** (observeerde, h. geobserveerd) *vt* watch, observe
ob'sessie (-s) *v* obsession
ob'stakel (-s) *o* obstacle, hindrance
obste'trie *v* obstetrics
obsti'naat obstinate
obsti'patie [-'pa.(t)si.] *v* constipation
ob'structie [-'strüksi.] (-s) *v* obstruction; ~ *voeren* practise obstruction, *pol* stonewall
oc'casie (-s) *v* F opportunity, occasion; **occa'sion** [ɔka'ʒɔn] (-s) *v* bargain; **occasio'neel** occasional
oc'cult occult; **occul'tisme** *o* occultism
occu'patie [ɔky'pa(t)si.] (-s) *v* occupation; **occu'peren** (occupeerde, h. geoccupeerd) *vi* & *vt* occupy

oce'aan (-eanen) *m* ocean; *de Grote Oceaan, de Stille Oceaan* the Pacific (Ocean)
och oh!, ah!; ~ *arme* poor woman, poor thing!; ~ *kom!* (b ij t w ij f e l) why, indeed!; 2 (b ij v e r b a z i n g) you don't say so!; ~, *waarom niet?* (well,) why not?; ~ *wat!* come on!, nonsense!
'ochtend (-en) *m* morning; *des* ~*s*, *'s* ~*s* in the morning; **–blad** (-bladen) *o* morning paper; **–gloren** *o* dawn, daybreak; **–humeur** *o* morning crossness; **–jas** (-sen) *m* & *v* housecoat, dressing-gown, *Am* robe; **–ziekte** *v* irritability (ill-temper) in the morning
oc'taaf (-taven) *o* & *v* octave
oc'taan *o* octane; **–getal** *o* octane number; *benzine met een hoog* ~ high-octane petrol
oc'tant (-en) *m* octant
oc'tavo ('s) *o* octavo
oc'tet (-ten) *o* ♩ octet
oc'trooi (-en) *o* 1 patent; 2 $ charter; **–brief** (-brieven) *m* 1 letters patent; 2 $ charter; **octrooi'eren** (octrooieerde, h. geoctrooieerd) *vt* 1 patent; 2 $ charter [a company]; **oc'trooigemachtigde** (-n) *m Br* patent agent, *Am* patent attorney; **–raad** *m* patent office
ocu'latie [-'la.(t)si.] *v* inoculation, grafting; **ocu'leren** (oculeerde, h. geoculeerd) *vt* inoculate, graft
'ode (-n en -s) *v* ode
o'deur (-s) *m*, **–tje** (-s) *o* perfume, scent
'odium *o* odium
oecu'mene [œyky.'me.nə] *v* oecumenical movement; **–nisch** oecumenical [council, movement]
oe'deem [œy'de.m] (-demen) *o* oedema
'oedipuscomplex ['œydi.püskɔmpleks] *o* Oedipus complex
oef ugh!
'oefenen (oefende, h. geoefend) **I** *vt* exercise, practise; train [the ear, soldiers &]; zie ook: *geduld, wraak;* **II** *vr zich* ~ practise, train; *zich* ~ *in* practise, train; **III** *va* practise, train; **–ning** (-en) *v* exercise, practice; *een* ~ an exercise; *vrije* ~*en* free exercises; ~ *baart kunst* practice makes perfect; **'oefenkamp** (-en) *o* training-camp; **–meester** (-s) *m sp* trainer, coach; **–school** (-scholen) *v* training-school; **–terrein** (-en) *o* training-ground; **–vlucht** (-en) *v* practice flight, training-flight; **–wedstrijd** (-en) *m* practice match
Oe'ganda *o* Uganda
oei oh!, ouch!

oe'kaze (-n en -s) *v* ukase

'Oeral *m de* ~ the Ural(s)

'oerge'zond bursting (glowing) with health; **–mens** (-en) *m* primitive man; **–'oud** ancient, age-old; **–'saai** as dull as ditchwater; **–'sterk** strong as a horse; **–tekst** (-en) *m* original text; **–tijd** (-en) *m* primeval age(s); **–vader** (-s en -en) *m* primogenitor; **–vorm** (-en) *m* archetype; **–woud** (-en) *o* primeval forest, virgin forest

'oester (-s) *v* oyster; **–bank** (-en) *v* oyster-bank; **–kweker** (-s) *m* oyster breeder; **–put** (-ten) *m* oyster-pond; **–schelp** (-en) *v* oyster-shell; **–teelt** *v* oyster culture; **–visserij** *v* oyster fishery

'oeuvre ['œːvrə] *o* [Rembrandt's] works, [an author's] writings

'oever (-s) *m* 1 shore [of the sea]; 2 bank [of a river]; *de river is buiten haar ~s getreden* the river has overflowed its banks; **–loos** unlimited, boundless; *fig* endless, aimless [talks]; **–staat** (-staten) *m* riparian state

of 1 (n e v e n s c h i k k e n d) *wit ~ zwart* white or black; ~ *hij ~ zijn broer* either he or his brother; *ja ~ neen* (either) yes or no; *een dag ~ drie* two or three days; *een man ~ twee* a man or two; *een minuut ~ tien* ten minutes or so; *een jaar ~ wat* some years; 2 (o n d e r s c h i k - k e n d) if, whether; (v ó ó r o n d e r w e r p s - z i n n e n) *het duurde niet lang ~ hij...* he was not long in ...ing (v ó ó r v o o r w e r p s z i n n e n) *ik weet niet ~ hij trouweloos is, ~ dom* I don't know whether he is faithless or stupid; (v ó ó r b ij v. bij z i n n e n) *er is niemand ~ hij zal dat toejuichen* there is nobody but (he) will applaud this measure; *hij is niet zo gek ~ hij weet wel wat hij doet* he is not such a fool but (but that, but what) he knows what he is about; (v ó ó r b ij w. bij z i n n e n) *ik kom vanavond ~ ik moet verhinderd zijn* I'll come to-night unless something would prevent me; *ik kan hem niet zien ~ ik moet lachen* I cannot see him without being compelled to laugh; *ik zie hem nooit ~ hij heeft een stok in de hand* I never see him but he has a stick in his hand; (v ó ó r v e r g e l ij k i n g e n) *het is net ~ hij mij voor de gek houdt* it is just as if he is making a fool of me; *Hou je daarvan? Nou, ~ ik! En ~!* Rather!; ~ *ze 't weten* don't they just know it!; ~ *ik 't me herinner?!* Do I remember?

offen'sief I *aj* offensive; II *ad* offensively; ~ *optreden* act on the offensive; III (-sieven) *o* offensive; *tot het ~ overgaan* take the offensive

'offer (-s) *o* 1 offering, sacrifice²; 2 (s l a c h t - o f f e r) victim; *een ~ brengen* make a sacrifice; *hij viel als het ~ van zijn driften* he fell a victim to his passions; *zij zijn gevallen als ~ van...* they have been the victims of [their patriotism]; *ten ~ brengen* sacrifice; **–aar** (-s) *m* offerer, sacrificer; **'offerande** (-n en -s) *v* offering, sacrifice, oblation; *rk* offertory; **'offerblok** (-ken) *o*, **–bus** (-sen) *v* alms-box, poor-box, offertory box; **–dier** (-en) *o* sacrificial animal, victim; **'offeren** (offerde, h. geofferd) *vt* offer as a sacrifice, sacrifice, offer up; **'offergave** (-n) *v* offering, **–lam** (-meren) *o* sacrificial lamb, Lamb of God; **–plechtigheid** (-heden) *v* sacrificial ceremony

of'ferte (-s en -n) *v* $ offer

offer'torium (-s en -ia) *o* offertory;
offer'vaardig willing to make sacrifices; liberal; **–heid** *v* willingness to make sacrifices; liberality

of'ficie [ɔ'fi.si.] (-s) *o* office; **officie'eel** 1 (a m b - t e l ij k) official; 2 (p l e c h t i g) formal

offi'cier (-en en -s) *m* (military) officer; *eerste ~* ⚓ chief officer; ~ *van administratie* paymaster; ~ *van de dag* orderly officer; ~ *van gezondheid* army (military) surgeon, medical officer; ~ *van justitie* Public Prosecutor; ~ *van de wacht* ⚓ officer of the watch; **offi'ciersmess** *m* officer's messroom, ⚓ wardroom; **–rang** (-en) *m* officer's rank

offici'eus semi-official

of'freren (offreerde, h. geoffreerd) *vt* offer

of'schoon although, though

'ogen (oogde, h. geoogd) *vi* 1 look [at]; 2 ~ *op* aim at; 3 look good

'ogenblik (-ken) *o* moment, instant, twinkling of an eye, **F** mo; *een ~!* one moment!; *heldere ~ken* lucid moments; ● *in een ~* in a moment; *in een onbewaakt ~* in an unguarded moment; *op dit ~, op het ~* at the moment, at present, just now; *op het juiste ~* at the right moment; in the very nick of time; *op dit kritieke ~* at this juncture; *een... op het laatste ~* a last-minute...; *voor een ~* for a moment; *voor het ~* for the present, for the time being; *zonder een ~ na te denken* without a moment's thought; zie ook: *ondeelbaar, verloren, zwak;* **ogen'blikkelijk I** *aj* momentary [impression]; immediate [danger]; **II** *ad* immediately, directly, instantly, on (the spur of) the moment

'ogendienst *m* base flattery; **ogen'schijnlijk** apparent; **'ogenschouw** in ~ *nemen* inspect, examine, take stock of, review, survey

o'gief (-gieven) *o* ogive; **ogi'vaal** ogival

o'ho aha!

o.i. = *onzes inziens* in our opinion

o'jief (-jieven) *o* △ ogee

'oker (-s) *m* ochre; **–achtig** ochr(e)ous; **–kleurig** ochr(e)ous

'okkernoot (-noten) *v* walnut

ok'saal (-salen) *o* organ-loft

'oksel (-s) *m* armpit
'okshoofd (-en) *o* hogshead
ok'tober *m* October
ole'ander (-s) *m* oleander
'olie *v* oil; *dat is ~ in het vuur* that is pouring oil on the flames, adding fuel to the fire; **F** *in de ~ zijn* be drunk; *~ op de golven gieten* pour oil on the waters; **–achtig** oily; **–bol** (-len) *m* oil-dumpling; **–bron** (-nen) *v* oil-well; **–carter** (-s) *o* oil-sump; **–dom** very stupid, asinine; **–druk** *m* oil-pressure; *~meter* oil-pressure gauge; **olie-en-a'zijnstel** (-len) *o* cruetstand, set of castors; 'oliefilter (-s) *o* oilfilter; **–goed** *o* oilskins, oils; **–houdend** oily, oil-bearing [seeds]; **–jas** (-sen) *m* & *v* oilskin; **–kachel** (-s) *v* oil-stove; **–lamp** (-en) *v* oil-lamp; **–man** (-nen) *m* 1 ✗ oiler, greaser; 2 (v e r k o p e r) oilman; 'oliën (oliede, h. geolied) *vt* 1 oil; 2 ✗ lubricate; 'olienootje (-s) *o* peanut; **–pak** (-ken) *o* oilskins; **–palm** (-en) *m* oil-palm; **–raffinaderij** (-en) *v* oil refinery; **–reservoir** [-re.zɪrvɑ: r] (-s) *o* oil-tank, sump; **–sel** *o* extreme unction; *het laatste ~ ontvangen (toedienen)* receive (give, administer) extreme unction; **–spuitje** (-s) *o* oil-squirt; **–steen** (-stenen) *m* oilstone; **–stook(inrichting)** *v* oil-heating (apparatus), oil-fired heating (system); **–tanker** [-tɪŋkər] (-s) *m* oil-tanker; **–veld** (-en) *o* oil-field; 'olieverf (-verven) *v* oil-paint, oil-colour; *in ~* in oils; **–portret** (-ten) *o* oil-portrait; **–schilderij** (-en) *o* & *v* oil-painting; **–vlek** (-ken) *v* 1 oil stain [on dress &]; 2 (v e l d v. (s t o o k)o l i e o p (z e e) w a t e r) (oil) slick; **–zaad** (-zaden) *o* oil-seed
'olifant (-en) *m* 🐘 elephant; 'olifantejacht (-en) *v* elephant-hunt(ing); 'olifantshuid *v* elephant's skin; *een ~ hebben* be thick-skinned; **–snuit** (-en) *m* elephant's trunk; **–tand** (-en) *m* elephant's tusk;
oligar'chie *v* oligarchy; oli'garchisch oligarchic
o'lijf (olijven) *v* olive; **–achtig** olivaceous; O'lijfberg *m* Mount of Olives; o'lijfboom (-bomen) *m* olive-tree; **–groen** olive-green; **–kleurig** olive-coloured, olive; **–olie** *v* oil of olives, olive-oil; **–tak** (-ken) *m* olive-branch
'olijk waggish, arch; 'olijkerd (-s) *m* wag
'olim *Lat* formerly; *in de dagen van ~* in the days of yore
olm (-en) *m* elm
O.L.V. = *Onze-Lieve-Vrouw*
olympi'ade [-lɪm-] (-n en -s) *v* ⬚ olympiad;

o'lympisch Olympic [games]
om **I** *prep* 1 (o m... h e e n) round [his shoulders, the table, the world &]; 2 (o m s t r e e k s) about [Easter &]; 3 (t e) at [three o'clock]; 4 (p e r i o d i e k n a) every [fortnight &]; 5 (v o o r, t e g e n) for [money &]; at [sixpence] 6 (w e g e n s) for, because of, on account of [the trouble &]; 7 (w a t b e t r e f t) for [me]; *~ de andere dag* & every other (every second) day; *~ de andere vrijdag* on alternate Fridays; *~ te* in order to, so as to; *hij is bereid ~ u te helpen* he is willing to help you; *het was niet ~ uit te houden* you couldn't stand it; *hij is ~ en bij de vijftig* he is round about fifty; *zij schreeuwden ~ het hardst* they cried their loudest; **II** *ad de hoek ~* round the corner; *wij doen dat ~ en ~* turn and turn about; *het jaar is ~* the year is out; *de tijd is ~* time is up; *mijn tijd is ~* my time has expired; *mijn verlof is ~* my leave is up; *eer de week ~ is* before the week is out; *~ hebben* (v. k l e d i n g s t u k) have on; *'m ~ hebben* be drunk; *dat is wel ~* that is out of the way, a round-about way; *een eindje ~ gaan* take a stroll
o.m. = *onder meer*
'oma ('s) *v* grandmother, **F** grandma, granny
om'armen (omarmde, h. omarmd) *vt* embrace; **–ming** (-en) *v* embrace
'omber *v* umber [pigment]
'ombinden¹ *vt* tie (bind) round; om'boorden (omboordde, h. omboord) *vt* border, hem, edge; om'boordsel (-s) *o* border, edging
'ombouwen¹ *vt* convert, make alterations, modify
'ombrengen¹ *vt* kill, destroy, dispatch, do to death; *zijn tijd ~* kill one's time
'ombudsman (-nen) *m* Ombudsman
'ombuigen¹ **I** *vt* bend; **II** *vi* bend
om'cirkelen (omcirkelde, h. omcirkeld) *vt* encircle, ring
om'dat because, as
'omdoen¹ *vt* put on [clothes]; put [a cord] round...
'omdopen¹ *vt* rename
'omdraai *m* turn, swing (round); 'omdraaien¹ **I** *vt* turn (over); *het hoofd ~* turn (round) one's head; *iem. de nek ~* wring sbd.'s neck; *zijn polsen ~* twist his wrists; **II** *va* (v.d. w i n d) turn; (i n p o l i t i e k &) veer round; *het hart draait mij om in mijn lijf* it makes me sick (to see...); **III** *vr zich ~* 1 (s t a a n d e) turn round; 2 (l i g - g e n d e) turn over [on one's face &] **–iing** (-en) *v* turning, rotation

¹ V.T. en V.D. van dit werkwoord volgens het model: 'ombouwen, V.T. bouwde 'om, V.D. 'omgebouwd. Zie voor de vormen onder het grondwoord, in dit voorbeeld: *bouwen*. Bij sterke en onregelmatige werkwoorden wordt u verwezen naar de lijst achterin.

'ome (-s) *m* = *oom*; *hoge* ~ bigwig, big noise
'omega ('s) *v* omega
ome'let (-ten) *v* omelet(te)
om'floersen (omfloerste, h. omfloerst) *vt*
muffle [a drum]; *fig* veil
'omgaan¹ I *vi* 1 (r o n d g a a n) go about, go
round; 2 (v o o r b ij g a a n) pass; 3 (g e -
b e u r e n) happen, go on; ● *dat gaat b u i t e n*
mij om I have nothing to do with it; *er gaat veel*
om i n die zaak they are doing a roaring business; *er gaat tegenwoordig niet veel om in de handel*
there is not much going on in trade at present; *hij*
kon niet zeggen wat er in hem omging what were his
feelings, what was going on in his mind &; ~
m e t 1 (v. p e r s o n e n) associate with, mix
with; keep company with, **F** rub elbows with;
2 (v. g e r e e d s c h a p &) handle; *ik ga niet veel*
met hen om I don't see much of them; *vertrouwe-*
lijk met iem. ~ be on familiar terms with sbd.;
ik weet (niet) met hem om te gaan I (don't) know
how to manage him; *met leugens* ~ be a liar; *per*
~de by return (of post); **II** *vt een eindje* ~ take a
walk, go for a stroll; *een heel eind* ~ go a long
way about; *een hoek* ~ turn a corner; zie ook:
hoekje; 'omgang (-en) *m* 1 (social, sexual)
intercourse, association [with other people];
company; 2 round; procession; 3 (v. w i e l)
rotation; 4 (v. t o r e n) gallery; ~ *hebben met* zie
omgaan met; 'omgangstaal *v* colloquial
language; *in de* ~ in common parlance, in
everyday speech; –vormen *mv* manners
'omgekeerd I *aj* turned, turned up [card],
turned upside down [box &]; turned over
[leaf]; [coat] inside out; reversed; reverse
[order]; inverted [commas &]; inverse
[proportion]; *precies* ~ the other way round
(on, about), just the reverse; *in het ~e*
geval in the opposite case; **II** *o het ~e* the
reverse; *het ~e van beleefd* the reverse of polite;
het ~e van een stelling the converse of a proposition; **III** *ad* reversely, conversely; *en* ~ ...and
conversely, vice versa; zie ook: *evenredig*
'omgelegen surrounding, neighbouring
'omgespen¹ *vt* buckle on
om'geven (omgaf, h. omgeven) *vt* surround,
encircle, encompass; –ving *v* 1 surroundings,
environs, environment [of a town]; (n a b ij -
h e i d) neighbourhood; 2 surroundings;
entourage [of a person]
'omgooien¹ *vt* 1 knock over, upset, overturn [a
thing]; 2 throw on [a cloak &]; 3 ✕ reverse
om'gorden, 'omgorden (omgordde/gordde
om, h. omgord/omgegord) *vt* gird²; gird on [a

sword]
'omhaal *m* ceremony, fuss; *waartoe al die ~?*
1 why this roundabout?; 2 why all this fuss?;
~ *van woorden* verbiage; *met veel* ~ with much
circumstance; *zonder veel* ~ 1 without much
ado; 2 straight away
'omhakken¹ *vt* cut down, chop down, fell
'omhalen¹ *vt* pull down [walls]; break up
[earth]; pull about [things]
1 'omhangen¹ **I** *vt* 1 put on, wrap round one;
2 hang otherwise; ✄ sling [arms]; **II** *vi* hang
about, loll about
2 om'hangen (omhing, h. omhangen) *vt* hang;
~ *met* hung with
om'heen about, round about
om'heinen (omheinde, h. omheind) *vt* fence in,
fence round, hedge in, enclose; –ning (-en) *v*
fence, enclosure
om'helzen (omhelsde, h. omhelsd) *vt* embrace²;
–zing (-en) *v* embrace; *fig* embracement
om'hoog on high, aloft, up; *de handen* ~! hands
up!; *met zijn voeten* ~ feet up; *naar* ~ up(wards);
van ~ from above; –gaan² *vi* go up²;
–gooien² *vt* throw up; –heffen² *vt* lift (up);
–houden² *vt* hold up; –trekken² *vt* pull up;
–zitten² *vi* ⚓ be aground; *fig* be in a fix
'omhouden¹ *vt* keep on
'omhouwen¹ *vt* = *omhakken*
om'hullen (omhulde, h. omhuld) *vt* envelop,
wrap round, enwrap; om'hulsel (-s) *o* wrapping, wrapper, envelope, cover; *stoffelijk* ~
mortal remains
o'missie (-s) *v* omission
'omkantelen¹ zie *kantelen*
'omkappen¹ *vt* = *omhakken*
'omkeer *m* change, turn; reversal, revolution,
about-face; revulsion [of feeling]; *een hele* ~
teweegbrengen in ook: revolutionize; om'keerbaar reversible [order, motion &]; convertible
[terms]; –heid *v* reversibility; convertibility;
'omkeren **I** *vt* turn [a card, one's coat]; turn
over [hay, a leaf]; turn up [a card]; turn upside
down [a box &]; turn out [one's pockets];
invert [commas &]; reverse [a motion, the
order], convert [a proposition]; zie ook:
omgekeerd; **II** *vi* turn back; **III** *vr zich* ~ turn
(round); –ring (-en) *v* 1 inversion [of order of
words, a ratio]; conversion [of a proposition];
2 reversal, revolution
'omkiepen, –kieperen¹ *vt* tip over, tilt, upset
'omkijken¹ *vi* look back, look round; ~ *naar*
iets 1 turn to look at a thing; 2 look about for a
situation; *hij kijkt er niet meer naar om* he wil

¹,² V.T. en V.D. van dit werkwoord volgens het model: 1 'ombouwen, V.T. bouwde 'om, V.D. 'omgebouwd; 2
om'hooggooien, V.T. gooide om'hoog, V.D. om'hooggegooid. Zie voor de vormen onder het grondwoord, in
deze voorbeelden: *bouwen* en *gooien*. Bij sterke en onregelmatige werkwoorden wordt u verwezen naar de lijst achterin.

not so much as look at it, he doesn't care for it any more; *je hebt er geen ~ naar* it does not need any attention, it needs no looking after

1 'omkleden[1] *zich ~* change (one's dress)

2 om'kleden (omkleedde, h. omkleed) *vt ~ met* clothe with[2], invest with[2] [power]; *met redenen omkleed* motivated

om'klemmen (omklemde, h. omklemd) *vt* clench, clasp in one's arms, hug (in close embrace), grasp tightly

om'knellen (omknelde, h. omkneld) *vt* clench, hold tight (in one's grasp), hold as in a vice

'omkomen[1] **I** *vi* 1 come to an end [of time]; 2 perish [of people]; *van honger* & *~* perish with (from, by) hunger &; **II** *vt een hoek ~* get (come) round a corner

om'koopbaar bribable, corruptible, venal; **'omkopen**[1] *vt* buy, bribe, corrupt [officials]; **S** grease (oil) the palm; **omkope'rij** (-en) *v* bribery, corruption; **S** oil, grease; **'omkoping** (-en) *v = omkoperij*

om'kransen (omkranste, h. omkranst) *vt* wreathe

'omkruipen[1] *vi* creep, drag (on) [of time]

om'laag below, down; *naar ~* down; **–houden** (hield om'laag, h. om'laaggehouden) *vt* keep down

'omleggen[1] *vt* 1 (a n d e r s o m) turn, put about; 2 shift [the helm, railway points]; careen [a ship]; 3 divert [a road, traffic]; 4 apply [a bandage]; **–ging** (-en) *v* diversion [of road, traffic]

'omleiden[1] *vt* divert [traffic, a road]; **–ding** (-en) *v* diversion [of traffic, a road]

'omliggend surrounding

om'lijnen (omlijnde, h. omlijnd) *vt* outline; *duidelijk (scherp) omlijnd* clear-cut; **–ning** (-en) *v* outline

om'lijsten (omlijstte, h. omlijst) *vt* frame; **–ting** (-en) *v* 1 framing; 2 frame, framework[2], mount, *fig* setting

'omloop (-lopen) *m* 1 revolution [of a planet, a satellite]; 2 rotation [of a wheel]; 3 circulation [of the blood; of money]; 4 gallery [round a tower]; 5 ✂ whitlow; *a a n d e ~ onttrekken* withdraw from circulation; *i n ~ brengen* 1 circulate [money], put into circulation; 2 spread [a rumour]; *in ~ zijn* 1 be in circulation [of notes, money]; 2 be abroad, be current [of a story]; **–snelheid** *v* orbital velocity; ✗ running speed; **–(s)tijd** (-en) *m* time (period) of revolution; **'omlopen**[1] *vi* 1 go (run) round, shift [to the North]; 2 walk about [in a

town]; 3 be about [of rumours]; *het hoofd loopt mij om* my head is in a whirl, my head reels; **II** *vt* walk round [the town]; *een straatje ~* go for a stroll

'ommegang (-en) *m* procession; **–keer** = *omkeer*; **–komst** *v* expiration, expiry; **–landen** *mv* environs; **–staand** *zie ~* see overleaf; **–tje** (-s) *o* turn, breather; **–zien** *o in een ~* in a trice, in no time, **F** in a jiffy; **–zij(de)** (-n) *v* back; *aan ~* overleaf; *zie ~* please turn over, P.T.O.; **–zwaai** (-en) *m* volte face

om'muren (ommuurde, h. ommuurd) *vt* wall in

'omnibus (-sen) *m* & *v* omnibus, bus

omni'voor (-voren) *m* omnivorous animal

om'palen (ompaalde, h. ompaald) *vt* fence in, palisade

om'perken (omperkte, h. omperkt) *vt* fence in, enclose

'omploegen[1] *vt* plough (up)

'ompraten[1] *vt* talk round, talk over; *hij wou me ~* he wanted to talk me into doing it (talk me out of it)

om'randen (omrandde, h. omrand) *vt* border, edge

om'ranken (omrankte, h. omrankt) *vt* twine round, encircle

om'rasteren (omrasterde, h. omrasterd) *vt* fence (rail) in; **–ring** (-en) *v* railing

'omrekenen[1] *vt* convert; **–ning** *v* conversion

'omrijden[1] **I** *vt* ride down, knock over; **II** *vi het rijdt om* it is a roundabout way

om'ringen (omringde, h. omringd) *vt* surround, encircle, encompass

'omroep *m* broadcasting; **'omroepen**[1] *vt* cry; *RT* broadcast; **–er** (-s) *m* (town) crier, common crier; *RT* announcer; **–orkest** (-en) *o* broadcasting orchestra; **–ster** (-s) *v* lady announcer; **–vereniging** (-en) *v* broadcasting society

'omroeren[1] *vt* stir [a cup of tea, porridge]

'omrollen[1] **I** *vt* roll over, topple; **II** *vi* roll about; topple (over)

'omruilen[1] *vt* exchange, change, **F** swap

'omrukken[1] *vt* pull down

'omschakelen[1] *vi* & *vt* change over[2]; **–ling** (-en) *v* change-over[2]

'omscholen[1] *vt* retrain; **–ling** *v* transition training

'omschoppen[1] *vt* kick down, kick over

'omschrift (-en) *o* legend [of a coin]

om'schrijven (omschreef, h. omschreven) *vt* 1 (i n t a a l) define; paraphrase; 2 (i n m e e t-k u n d e) circumscribe; 3 (b e s c h r ij v e n)

---

[1] V.T. en V.D. van dit werkwoord volgens het model: **'om**bouwen, V.T. bouwde **'om**, V.D. **'om**gebouwd. Zie voor de vormen onder het grondwoord, in dit voorbeeld: *bouwen*. Bij sterke en onregelmatige werkwoorden wordt u verwezen naar de lijst achterin.

describe; **–ving** (-en) *v* 1 definition; paraphrase; 2 circumscription; 3 description

om'singelen (omsingelde, h. omsingeld) *vt* surround, encircle; invest [a fortress]; round up [criminals]; **–ling** (-en) *v* encircling; investment [of a fortress]; round-up [of criminals]

'omslaan[1] **I** *vt* 1 (o m v e r) knock down; 2 (n é é r) turn down [a collar &]; turn up [one's trousers]; 3 (o m k e r e n) turn over [a leaf], turn [the pages]; 4 (o m l i c h a a m) throw on [a cloak &], wrap [a shawl] round one; 5 (g e l ij k e l ij k v e r d e l e n) apportion, divide (among *over*); *de hoek ~* turn (round) the corner; **II** *vi* 1 (o m v a l l e n) be upset, upset, capsize [of a boat]; be blown inside out [of umbrella]; 2 (v e r a n d e r e n) change, break [of the weather]; *links (rechts) ~* turn to the left (to the right); *het rijtuig sloeg om* the carriage was upset; *het weer is omgeslagen* the weather has broken

om'slachtig cumbersome; long-winded [story]; zie ook: *omstandig;* **–heid** *v* cumbersomeness

'omslag (-slagen) *m & o* 1 (a a n k l e d i n g) cuff [of a sleeve]; turn-up [of trousers]; 2 (v. b o e k) cover, wrapper, (s t o f~) jacket; envelope [of a letter]; 3 ✶ compress; 4 ✗ brace [of a drill]; 5 *m fig* ceremony, fuss, ado; 6 *m* (v.h. w e e r) break (in the weather); 7 *m* (v e r d e l i n g) apportionment; *hoofdelijke ~* poll-tax; *zonder veel ~* without much ado; **–boor** (-boren) *v* brace and bit; **–doek** (-en) *m* shawl, wrap; **–verhaal** (-halen) *o* cover story

om'sluieren (omsluierde, h. omsluierd) *vt* veil

om'sluiten (omsloot, h. omsloten) *vt* enclose, encircle, surround; embosom

'omsmelten[1] *vt* remelt, melt down

'omsmijten[1] *vt* knock down, overturn, upset

om'spannen (omspande, h. omspannen) *vt* span

'omspitten[1] *vt* dig (up)

1 'omspoelen[1] *vt* rinse (out), wash

2 om'spoelen (omspoelde, h. omspoeld) *vt* wash, bathe [the shores]

'omspringen[1] *vi* jump about; *laat mij er mee ~* let me manage it; *...met de jongens ~* manage the boys...; *royaal (zuinig) met iets ~* use something freely (sparingly)

'omstanders *mv* bystanders

om'standig I *aj* circumstantial, detailed; **II** *ad* circumstantially, in detail; **–heid** (-heden) *v* 1 (i n 't a l g.) circumstance; 2 (u i t v o e r i g h e i d) circumstantiality; *zijn omstandigheden his circumstances in life; zijn geldelijke omstan-*

digheden his financial position; *maatschappelijke omstandigheden* ook: social conditions; ● *i n a l l e omstandigheden des levens* in all circumstances of life; *in de gegeven omstandigheden* in (under) the circumstances; *n a a r omstandigheden wel* very well, considering; *o n d e r geen enkele ~* on no account

'omstoten[1] *vt* overturn, upset, push down

om'stralen (omstraalde, h. omstraald) *vt* shine about; *met luister omstraald* in a glorious halo

om'streden controversial [leader; subject]; disputed [territory]

'omstreeks about [fifty, ten o'clock]; in the neighbourhood of [5000]

'omstreken *mv* environs, neighbourhood

om'strengelen (omstrengelde, h. omstrengeld) *vt* entwine, wind (twine) about, wind [a child] in one's arms

om'stuwen (omstuwde, h. omstuwd) *vt* surround, flock (press) round

'omtrappen[1] *vt* = *omschoppen*

'omtrek (-ken) *m* 1 circumference [of a circle]; contour, outline [of a figure]; 2 neighbourhood, environs, vicinity; *in ~* in circumference; *in de ~* in the neighbourhood; *...mijlen in de ~* for... miles around, within... miles; *in ~ schetsen* outline; *in ~ken* in outline

'omtrekken[1] *vt* 1 (o m v e r) pull down [a wall]; 2 (o m m a r c h e r e n) ✗ march about; 3 (o m s i n g e l e n) ✗ turn, outflank [the enemy]; *een ~de beweging* ✗ a turning movement

om'trent, 'omtrent I *prep* 1 (t e n o p z i c h t e v a n) about, concerning, with regard to, as to; 2 (o n g e v e e r) about; 3 (i n d e b u u r t v a n) about; **II** *ad* about, near

'omtuimelen[1] *vi* tumble down, topple over

om'vademen (omvademde, h. omvademd) *vt* put one's arms round; *fig* encompass

'omvallen[1] *vi* fall down, be upset, upset, overturn; *zij vielen haast om van het lachen* they almost split their sides with laughter; *je valt om van de prijzen* the prices are staggering; *~ van verbazing* be knocked over (bowled over) with surprise; *ik val om van de slaap* I can hardly stand for sleep, I am ready to drop with sleep

om'vamen (omvaamde, h. omvaamd) = *omvademen*

'omvang *m* girth [of a tree]; extent, compass, circumference, range [of voice], size [of a book]; latitude [of an idea]; ambit [of meaning]

om'vangen (omving, h. omvangen) *vt* surround, encompass

---

[1] V.T. en V.D. van dit werkwoord volgens het model: **'om**bouwen, V.T. bouwde **'om**, V.D. **'om**gebouwd. Zie voor de vormen onder het grondwoord, in dit voorbeeld: *bouwen*. Bij sterke en onregelmatige werkwoorden wordt u verwezen naar de lijst achterin.

om'vangrijk voluminous, bulky, extensive
1 'omvaren¹ I *vi* sail by a round-about way; II *vt* sail down
2 om'varen (omvoer, h. omvaren) *vt* sail about, circumnavigate; double, round [a cape]
om'vatten (omvatte, h. omvat) *vt* span; embrace²; *fig* comprise, encompass, include; grasp [an idea]; **–d** embracing; ⚔ turning [movement]; *fig* comprehensive
om'ver down, over; **–blazen²** *vt* blow down; **–duwen²** *vt* push over; **–gooien²** *vt* zie *omgooien* 1; **–halen²** *vt* pull down **–lopen²** *vt* run (knock) [sbd.] over (down); **–praten²** *vt* talk down; **–rennen²** *vt* run down; **–schieten²** *vt* shoot down; **–slaan²** I *vt* knock over; II *vi* fall down; **–stoten²** *vt* = *omstoten*; **–trekken²** *vt* pull down; **–tuimelen²** *vi* = *omtuimelen*; **–waaien²** I *vt* blow down; II *vi* be blown down
om'verwerpen² *vt* upset² [a glass, a plan] overturn, overset; overthrow [the government]; **–ping** *v* upsetting; *fig* overthrow
'omvliegen¹ *vi* fly about; *fig* fly, fleet
'omvormen¹ *vt* transform, remodel
'omvouwen¹ *vt* fold down, turn down
'omvraag *v* = *rondvraag*
'omwaaien¹ *vt* & *vi* = *omverwaaien*
om'wallen (omwalde, h. omwald) *vt* wall (round), wall in, circumvallate; **–ling** (-en) *v* circumvallation
'omwandelen¹ *vt* & *vi* walk about
'omwaren¹ *vi* walk, haunt a place (a house &) [of ghosts]
'omwassen¹ *vt* wash (up)
'omweg (-wegen) *m* roundabout way, circuitous route; detour; *een hele* ~ a long way about; *een* ~ *maken* go about (a long way), make a detour (a circuit); *l a n g s een* ~ by a circuitous route, by a roundabout way; *langs* ~*en* by devious ways; *z o n d e r* ~*en* without beating about the bush; point-blank
'omwenden¹ I *vt* turn; II *vr zich* ~ turn
'omwentelen¹ *vi* revolve, rotate, gyrate; **–ling** (-en) *v* revolution, rotation, gyration; *fig* revolution; *een* ~ *teweegbrengen in* revolutionize; 'omwentelingsas (-sen) *v* axis of rotation; **–snelheid** (-heden) *v* velocity of rotation; **–tijd** (-en) *m* time of revolution; **–vlak** (-ken) *o* surface of revolution
'omwerken¹ *vt* remould, remodel, refashion, recast [a book], rewrite [an article &]; **–king** (-en) *v* recast(ing) &
'omwerpen¹ *vt* = *omgooien* 1 & 2
om'wikkelen (omwikkelde, h. omwikkeld) *vt*

wrap round
om'winden (omwond, h. omwonden) *vt* entwine, envelop; wind around
'omwisselen¹ *vt* & *vi* change
'omwoelen¹ 1 *vt* turn up, rout [the earth]; rumple [a bed]; 2 (omwoelde, h. omwoeld) *vt* (o m w i n d e n) muffle [a bell], wind around
'omwonenden, om'wonenden *mv* neighbours
'omwroeten¹ *vt* root up
'omzagen¹ *vt* saw down
1 'omzeilen¹ = 1 *omvaren*
2 om'zeilen (omzeilde, h. omzeild) *vt* = 2 *omvaren*; *een moeilijkheid* ~ evade, get round a difficulty
'omzet (-ten) *m* turnover; sales; *er is weinig* ~ there is little doing; *kleine winst bij vlugge* ~ small profits and quick returns; 'omzetten¹ *vt* 1 (a n d e r s z e t t e n) arrange (place) differently [of things]; shift [furniture]; transpose [letters, numbers &]; 2 ✗ reverse [an engine]; 3 $ turn over, sell; *hij kwam de hoek* ~ he came (driving &) round the corner; ~ *in* convert into; *...in daden* ~ translate... into action; **–ting** (-en) *v* transposition [of a term, a word]; conversion, inversion [of the order of words]; translation [into action]; ✗ reversal [of an engine]
om'zichtig circumspect, cautious; **–heid** *v* circumspection, cautiousness, caution
1 'omzien¹ *vi* look back; ~ *naar* look back at; look out for [another servant]; *niet* ~ *naar* not attend to [one's business], be negligent of [one's affairs], neglect [the children]; *hij ziet er niet naar om* he doesn't care for it
2 'omzien *o* = *ommezien*
1 'omzomen¹ *vt* hem
2 om'zomen (omzoomde, h. omzoomd) *vt fig* border, fringe
'omzwaai *v* = *ommezwaai*; 'omzwaaien¹ I *vt* swing round, swerve; II *vi* (v e r a n d e r e n v. s t u d i e &) switch over, change over
om'zwachtelen (omzwachtelde, h. omzwachteld) *vt* swathe, bandage; swaddle [a baby]
'omzwalken¹ *vi* drift about
'omzwemmen¹ *vi* swim about
'omzwenken¹ *vi* swing (wheel) round
om'zwermen (omzwermde, h. omzwermd) *vt* swarm about
'omzwerven¹ *vi* rove (ramble, wander) about; **–ving** *v* wandering, roving, rambling
om'zweven (omzweefde, h. omzweefd) *vt* hover about, float about
'omzwikken¹ *vi* sprain (wrench) one's ankle

---

¹,² V.T. en V.D. van dit werkwoord volgens het model: 1 'om**bouwen**, V.T. bouw**de 'om**, V.D. 'om**gebouwd**; 2 om'**verduwen**, V.T. duw**de om'ver**, V.D. om'**ver**geduwd. Zie voor de vormen onder het grondwoord, in deze voorbeelden: *bouwen* en *duwen*. Bij sterke en onregelmatige werkwoorden wordt u verwezen naar de lijst achterin.

onaan'doenlijk impassive, apathetic, stolid; **–heid** *v* impassiveness, apathy, stolidity

on'aangebroken unopened, fresh [bottle], unbroached [cask]

on'aangedaan unmoved, untouched

on'aangekondigd unannounced

on'aangemeld unannounced

on'aangenaam disagreeable, offensive [smell], unpleasant[2]; *fig* unwelcome [truths]; **–heid** (-heden) *v* disagreeableness, unpleasantness; *onaangenaamheden krijgen met iem.* fall out with sbd.

on'aangepast maladjusted; **–heid** *v* maladjustment

on'aangeroerd untouched, intact; ~ *laten* leave untouched[2]; *fig* not touch upon

on'aangetast untouched

on'aangevochten unchallenged

onaan'nemelijk 1 unacceptable [conditions]; 2 (weinig geloofwaardig of waarschijnlijk) implausible; **–heid** *v* 1 unacceptableness; 2 implausibility

onaan'tastbaar unassailable[2]; inviolable [rights]; **–heid** *v* unassailableness[2]

onaan'trekkelijk unattractive

onaan'vaardbaar unacceptable

onaan'zienlijk inconsiderable; insignificant; **–heid** *v* inconsiderableness; insignificance

on'aardig unpleasant; unkind; *het is ~ van je* it is not nice of you; **–heid** (-heden) *v* unpleasantness; unkindness

on'achtzaam inattentive, negligent, careless; **–heid** (-heden) *v* inattention, negligence, carelessness

on'afgebroken uninterrupted, continuous

on'afgedaan 1 unfinished [work]; 2 unpaid, outstanding [debts]; 3 $ unsold

on'afgehaald unclaimed [goods, prizes]

on'afgewerkt unfinished

onaf'hankelijk independent; **–heid** *v* independence; **onaf'hankelijkheidsbeweging** (-en) *v* liberation movement; **–verklaring** (-en) *v* declaration of independence

onaf'scheidelijk I *aj* inseparable; **II** *ad* inseparably; **–heid** *v* inseparability

onaf'wendbaar not to be averted, inevitable

onaf'zetbaar irremovable

onaf'zienbaar immense, endless

ona'nie *v* onanism

onappe'tijtelijk unappetizing, unattractive

onat'tent inattentive

onbaat'zuchtig disinterested, unselfish; **–heid** *v* disinterestedness, unselfishness, selflessness

onbarm'hartig merciless, pitiless; **–heid** *v* mercilessness

onbe'antwoord unanswered [letters, questions]; unreturned [love]

'onbebouwd uncultivated, untilled [soil]; unbuilt on [spaces], waste [ground]

onbe'daarlijk uncontrollable, inextinguishable [mirth]

onbe'dacht(zaam) thoughtless, rash, inconsiderate; **onbe'dachtzaamheid** (-heden) *v* thoughtlessness, rashness, inconsiderateness

onbe'dekt uncovered, bare, open

onbe'doeld unintended

onbe'dorven unspoiled, unsophisticated, innocent; sound; undepraved, uncorrupted; **–heid** *v* innocence

onbe'dreigd, 'onbedreigd *sp* unchallenged

onbe'dreven, 'onbedreven unskilled, inexperienced; **–heid** *v* inexperience, unskilfulness

onbe'drieglijk unmistakable [signs]; [instinct, memory] never at fault

onbe'duidend 1 *aj* insignificant [people]; trivial, trifling [sums]; *niet* ~ not inconsiderable; **II** *ad* insignificantly; **–heid** (-heden) *v* insignificance; triviality

onbe'dwingbaar I *aj* uncontrollable, indomitable; **II** *ad* uncontrollably, indomitably

'onbeëdigd unsworn

onbe'gaanbaar impassable, impracticable

'onbegonnen, onbe'gonnen *een* ~ *werk* an endless (hopeless) task

onbe'grensd unlimited, unbounded

onbe'grepen not understood; unappreciated [poet &]; **onbe'grijpelijk I** *aj* inconceivable, incomprehensible, unintelligible; **II** *ad* inconceivably; **'onbegrip** *o* incomprehension

onbe'haaglijk unpleasant, disagreeable; uncomfortable, uneasy; **–heid** *v* unpleasantness &, discomfort

onbe'haard hairless

'onbehagen *o* uneasiness, discomfort

onbe'heerd without an owner, unowned, ownerless; (v. auto, fiets &) unattended

onbe'heerst, 'onbeheerst uncontrolled, unrestrained, wanton, undisciplined

onbe'holpen awkward, clumsy

onbe'hoorlijk I *aj* unseemly, improper, indecent; **II** *ad* improperly; **–heid** (-heden) *v* unseemliness, impropriety, indecency

1 'onbehouwen unhewn [blocks]; **2 onbe'houwen** *fig* ungainly, unwieldy; rugged, unmannerly

onbe'huisd homeless; *de* ~*en* the homeless

onbe'hulpzaam unwilling to help, disobliging

onbe'kend unknown, unfamiliar; *dat is hier* ~ that is not known here; *ik ben hier* ~ I am a stranger here; *hij is nog* ~ he is still unknown; *dat was mij* ~ it was unknown to me, I was not aware of the fact; ~ *met* unacquainted with, unfamiliar with, ignorant of; ~ *maakt onbemind* unknown, unloved; [*fig*] *op ~ terrein* F off (out of) one's beat; **–e** (-n) *m-v* stranger; *de ~ ook:* the unknown; *het ~* the unknown; *twee ~n* 1 two unknown people, two strangers; 2 two unknowns [in algebra]; **–heid** *v* 1 unacquaintedness, unacquaintance; 2 obscurity; *zijn ~ met...* his unacquaintance (unfamiliarity) with, his ignorance of...

onbe'klant without customers

onbe'klimbaar unclimbable, inaccessible

onbe'kommerd, 'onbekommerd unconcerned; *een ~ leven leiden* lead a care-free life; **–heid** *v* unconcern

onbe'kookt inconsiderate, thoughtless, rash

onbe'krompen I *aj* 1 unstinted, unsparing, lavish; 2 liberal, broad-minded; II *ad* 1 unsparingly, lavishly; 2 liberally; *~ leven* be in easy circumstances; **–heid** *v* liberality

onbe'kwaam incapable, unable, incompetent; **–heid** *v* incapacity, inability, incompetence

onbe'langrijk unimportant, insignificant, trifling, inconsequential, immaterial; **–heid** *v* unimportance, insignificance, triflingness

'onbelast 1 unburdened, unencumbered; 2 untaxed; 3 ✕ without load

onbe'leefd I *aj* impolite, uncivil, ill-mannered, rude; II *ad* impolitely, uncivilly, rudely; **–heid** (-heden) *v* impoliteness, incivility, rudeness

onbe'lemmerd, 'onbelemmerd unimpeded, unhampered, free

onbe'loond, 'onbeloond unrewarded [pupils &]; unrequited [toil]; *dat zal niet ~ blijven* that shall not go unrewarded

onbe'mand, 'onbemand unmanned [flight, space-craft]

onbe'merkt, 'onbemerkt I *aj* unperceived, unnoticed, unobserved; II *ad* without being perceived

onbe'middeld without means

onbe'mind unloved, unbeloved, unpopular

onbe'minnelijk unamiable, unlovely

onbe'noemd unnamed; abstract [number]

'onbenul (-len) *o een ~* a mere cipher, a nobody, a nonentity; onbe'nullig I *aj* fatuous, dullheaded; II *ad* fatuously; **–heid** (-heden) *v* fatuousness, fatuity

onbe'paalbaar indeterminable; onbe'paald, 'onbepaald unlimited; indefinite; uncertain; vague; *voor ~e tijd* indefinitely; *~e wijs* infinitive; **–heid** *v* unlimitedness; indefiniteness; uncertainty; vagueness

onbe'perkt I *aj* unlimited, unrestrained, boundless, unbounded; II *ad* unlimitedly

onbe'proefd untried[2]; *niets ~ laten* leave nothing untried, leave no stone unturned

onbe'raden inconsiderate, ill-advised

onberede'neerd I *aj* 1 unreasoned [fear]; 2

inconsiderate [behaviour]; II *ad* inconsiderately

onbe'reikbaar inaccessible; *fig* unattainable, unreachable

onbe'rekenbaar incalculable[2], *fig* unpredictable; onbe'rekend uncalculated; unequal [to a task]

onbe'rijdbaar impassible [roads]

onbe'rispelijk I *aj* irreproachable, blameless, immaculate, faultless, flawless; II *ad* irreproachably, faultlessly

'onberoerd untouched, unmoved

onbe'schaafd 1 ill-bred, unmannerly, uneducated, unrefined, uncultured; 2 uncivilized [nations]; **–heid** (-heden) *v* 1 ill-breeding, unmannerliness; 2 want of civilization

onbe'schaamd I *aj* unabashed, impudent, checky, audacious, impertinent, bold; *~e leugen* barefaced lie; *~e kerel* impudent fellow; II *ad* impudently; **–heid** (-heden) *v* impudence, impertinence; *de ~ hebben om...* have the nerve to..., be cheeky enough to...

onbe'schadigd ondamaged

onbe'scheiden indiscreet, immodest; **–heid** (-heden) *v* indiscretion, immodesty

onbe'schermd unprotected, undefended

onbe'schoft impertinent, insolent, impudent, rude; **–heid** (-heden) *v* impertinence, insolence, impudence, rudeness

onbe'schreven not written upon, blank [paper]; unwritten [laws]; undescribed; onbe'schrijf(e)lijk I *aj* indescribable; II *ad* indescribably, < very

onbe'schroomd undaunted, fearless

onbe'schut unsheltered, unprotected

onbe'slagen unshod; *~ ten ijs komen* be onprepared (for...)

onbe'slapen, 'onbeslapen not slept-in, undisturbed [bed]

onbe'slecht undecided

onbe'slist undecided; *~ spel* drawn game; *het spel bleef ~* the game ended in a tie, in a draw

onbe'smet undefiled

onbe'spied unobserved

'onbesproken, onbe'sproken undiscussed [subjects]; unbooked, free [seat]; *fig* blameless, irreproachable [conduct]

onbe'staanbaar impossible; *~ met* inconsistent (incompatible) with; **–heid** *v* impossibility; inconsistency, incompatibility [with]

onbe'stelbaar, 'onbestelbaar undeliverable; *een onbestelbare brief* ✆ a dead letter

'onbestemd indeterminate, vague

onbe'stendig unsettled, unstable, inconstant; fickle; **–heid** *v* unsettled state, instability, inconstancy; fickleness

'onbestorven too fresh [meat &]; grass
▪ [widow]

onbe′stuurbaar unmanageable, out of control
onbe′suisd I *aj* rash, hot-headed, foolhardy; **II** *ad* rashly; ~ *te werk gaan* go at it boldheaded; **–heid** (-heden) *v* rashness, foolhardiness
onbe′taalbaar 1 unpayable [debts]; 2 *fig* priceless, invaluable; *een onbetaalbare grap* a capital joke; **′onbetaald, onbe′taald** unpaid, unsettled; **~***e rekeningen* outstanding accounts
onbe′tamelijk I *aj* unbecoming, improper, unbefitting, unseemly, indecent; **II** *ad* unbecomingly; **–heid** (-heden) *v* unbecomingness, impropriety, unseemliness, indecency
onbe′tekenend insignificant, unimportant, inconsiderable, trifling
onbe′teugeld unbridled, unrestrained
onbe′treden, ′onbetreden untrodden [paths]
onbe′trouwbaar unreliable; **–heid** *v* unreliability
onbe′tuigd *hij liet zich niet* ~ he rose to the occasion, he was quick to respond; (a a n t a f e l) do justice to a meal
onbe′twist, ′onbetwist undisputed, uncontested; **–baar** indisputable
onbe′vaarbaar innavigable
onbe′vallig ungraceful, inelegant; **–heid** *v* ungracefulness, inelegance
′onbevangen, onbe′vangen 1 unprejudiced, open-minded, unbiassed; 2 unconcerned; **–heid** *v* 1 impartiality; 2 unconcern(edness)
onbe′vattelijk 1 slow [pupil]; 2 incomprehensible [thing]
′onbevestigd unconfirmed [report]
′onbevlekt, onbe′vlekt unstained, undefiled; immaculate; *de Onbevlekte Ontvangenis* the Immaculate Conception
′onbevoegd, onbe′voegd incompetent, unqualified [teacher]; unauthorized [persons, people]; **–e** (-n) *m-v* unauthorized person; **–heid** *v* incompetence
′onbevolkt unpopulated, uninhabited
onbevoor′oordeeld unprejudiced, unbiassed
onbe′vredigd, ′onbevredigd unsatisfied, ungratified
onbe′vredigend unsatisfactory
onbe′vreesd, ′onbevreesd I *aj* undaunted, unafraid, fearless; **II** *ad* undauntedly, fearlessly
onbe′waakt, ′onbewaakt unguarded; zie ook: *ogenblik,* 1 *overweg*
onbe′weegbaar immovable; **onbe′weeglijk I** *aj* motionless, immovable, immobile; **II** *ad* immovably; **–heid** *v* immobility
′onbeweend unwept
onbe′werkt, ′onbewerkt unmanufactured, raw [material]; (n i e t v e r s i e r d) plain
onbe′wezen not proven; **onbe′wijsbaar** unprovable
onbe′wimpeld, ′onbewimpeld I *aj* undis-

guised, frank; **II** *ad* frankly, without mincing matters
onbe′wogen unmoved, untouched, unruffled, impassive, placid
′onbewolkt, onbe′wolkt unclouded, cloudless
onbe′woonbaar uninhabitable [country]; [dwelling] unfit for (human) habitation; ~ *verklaren* condemn; **′onbewoond, onbe′woond** uninhabited [region, place &]; unoccupied, untenanted [house]; ~ *eiland* desert island
′onbewust, onbe′wust unconscious [act]; unwitting [hope]; *mij* ~ *hoe (of, waar* &) not knowing how (if &); ~ *van...* unaware of...; *het* ~*e* the unconscious; **–heid** *v* unconsciousness
′onbezeerd unhurt, uninjured
′onbezet, onbe′zet unoccupied [chair], vacant [post]
′onbezield inanimate, lifeless
onbe′zoedeld undefiled, unsullied
onbe′zoldigd unsalaried, unpaid; *een* ~ *baantje* an honorary job; *een* ~ *politieagent* a special constable
onbe′zonnen inconsiderate, thoughtless, unthinking, rash; **–heid** *v* inconsiderateness, thoughtlessness, rashness
′onbezorgd onbe′zorgd I *aj* free from care, care-free [old age]; unconcerned; ⓣ undelivered; **II** *ad* care-free; unconcernedly; **–heid** *v* freedom from care; unconcern
onbe′zwaard, ′onbezwaard 1 unencumbered [property]; 2 unburdened [mind]; clear [conscience]
on′billijk unjust, unfair, unreasonable; **–heid** (-heden) *v* injustice, unfairness, unreasonableness
′onbloedig bloodless
on′blusbaar inextinguishable, unquenchable
on′brandbaar incombustible, non-flammable [clothing, materials]; **–heid** *v* incombustibility
on′breekbaar unbreakable
′onbruik *o in* ~ *geraken* go out of use [of words], fall into disuse, into desuetude; **on′bruikbaar** unfit for use, useless, unserviceable [things], ineffective [methods]; impracticable [roads]; inefficient [persons]; **–heid** *v* uselessness, unserviceableness; impracticability; inefficiency
on′buigbaar inflexible; **on′buigzaam** inflexible[2]; *fig* unbending, unyielding, rigid, hardset, adamant; **–heid** *v* inflexibility, rigidity
on′christelijk [-′kristələk of -′grɪs-] unchristian
oncollegi′aal disloyal, unlike a colleague
oncontro′leerbaar unverifiable
′ondank *m* thanklessness, ingratitude; *zijns* ~*s* in spite of him; ~ *is ′s werelds loon* the world's wages are ingratitude; **on′dankbaar** un-

grateful, unthankful, thankless; *een ondankbare rol* an unthankful part; **–heid** (-heden) *v* ingratitude, thanklessness, unthankfulness

'ondanks in spite of, notwithstanding

on'deelbaar indivisible; **~** *getal* prime number; *één ~ ogenblik* **F** one split second; **–heid** *v* indivisibility

ondefini'eerbaar indefinable

on'degelijk unsubstantial, flimsy

on'denkbaar unthinkable, inconceivable

'onder I *prep* 1 under², beneath, ⊙ underneath; 2 (t e m i d d e n v a n) among; 3 (g e d u - r e n d e) during; *~ Alexander de Grote* under Alexander the Great; *~ andere(n)* 1 (v. z a k e n) among other things; 2 (v. p e r s o n e n) among others; *~ elkaar* between them [they had a thousand pounds]; [discuss, quarrel, marry] among themselves; *~ meer* zie *~ andere(n)*; *~ ons* between you and me, between ourselves; *'t moet ~ ons blijven* it must not go any further; *~ ons gezegd* between you and me and the bedpost (gate-post); *iets ~ zich hebben* have sth. in one's keeping; *~ een glas wijn* over a glass of wine; *~ het eten* during meals; at dinner; *~ het lezen* while (he was) reading; *~ het lopen* as he went; *~ de preek* during the sermon; *~ de toejuichingen van de menigte* amid the cheers of the crowd; *~ de regering van Koningin Wilhelmina* during (in) the reign of Queen Wilhelmina; *~ vrienden* among friends; *~ vijanden* amid(st) enemies; *~ de modder (het stof &)* zitten be covered with mud (dust &); **II** *ad* below; *de zon is ~* the sun is set (is down); *hoe is hij er ~?* how does he take it?; *er is een kelder ~* underneath there is a cellar; **●** *~ a a n de bladzijde* at the foot (at the bottom) of the page; *~ aan de trap* at the foot of the stairs; *~ i n de fles* at the bottom of the bottle; *n a a r ~(en)* down, below; *t e n ~ brengen* subjugate, overcome; *ten ~ gaan* go to rack and ruin, be ruined; *v a n ~(en)!* below there!; *glad van ~* smooth underneath; *van ~ naar boven* from the bottom upward(s); *van ~ op* from below; *fig* [start] from the bottom (from scratch); *derde regel van ~* 3rd line from the bottom

'onderaan, onder'aan I *prep* at the bottom of; **II** *ad* at the bottom, at (the) foot

'onderaanbesteden (h. onderaanbesteed) *vt* sublet

'onderaandeel (-delen) *o* $ sub-share

'onderaannemer (-s) *m* sub-contractor

onder'aards, 'onderaards subterranean, underground

'onderafdeling (-en) *v* 1 subdivision; 2 subsection

'onderarm (-en) *m* forearm

'onderbaas (-bazen) *m* charge-hand

'onderbelicht, onderbe'licht under-exposed; **–ing** *v* under-exposure

'onderbetalen (h. onderbetaald) *vt* underpay

'onderbevelhebber (-s) *m* second in command

'onderbevolking *v* underpopulation; **onderbe'volkt** underpopulated

'onderbewust subconscious; **onderbe'wuste** *o* subconscious; **'onderbewustzijn** *o* subconscious; subconsciousness

onderbe'zet undermanned, understaffed

'onderbinden[1] *vt* tie on [skates]

'onderbouw *m* substructure, foundation; (v a n l y c e u m) basic years

onder'breken (onderbrak, h. onderbroken) *vt* interrupt, break [a journey, holidays]; **–king** (-en) *v* interruption, break

'onderbrengen[1] *vt* shelter, house, accomodate, place²

'onderbroek (-en) *v* (pair of) pants, drawers; *(dames) ~je* **F** briefs, knickers

'onderbuik (-en) *m* abdomen

'onderdaan (-danen) *m* subject; *onderdanen* nationals [of a country, when abroad]; *mijn onderdanen* **F** my pins [= legs]

'onderdak *o* shelter; *geen ~ hebben* have no shelter (no home, no accommodation); *~ verschaffen* accomodate

onder'danig I *aj* submissive; humble; *Uw ~e dienaar* Yours obediently; **II** *ad* submissively; humbly; **–heid** *v* submissiveness; humility

'onderdeel (-delen) *o* 1 lower part; 2 part; 3 ✕ accessory, part; 4 ✕ unit; *dat is maar een ~* that's only part of it, a fraction; *voor een ~ van een seconde* for a fraction of a second, **F** one split second

'onderdeur (-en) *v* lower half of a door, hatch; *~tje* [*fig*] undersized person, dwarf

'onderdirecteur (-en en -s) *m* submanager; ⊜ second master, vice-principal

'onderdoen[1] **I** *vt* tie on [skates]; **II** *vi niet ~ voor... in...* not yield to... in...; *voor niemand ~ (in)...* be second to none, yield to none in...

'onderdompelen[1] *vt* submerge, immerse; **–ling** (-en) *v* submersion, immersion, **F** ducking

onder'door underneath; *er ~ gaan* [*fig*] succomb, break down; **–gang** (-en) *m* tunnel, subway, underpass

onder'drukken (onderdrukte, h. onderdrukt) *vt*

---

[1] V.T. en V.D. van dit werkwoord volgens het model: **'onder**dompelen, V.T. dompelde **'onder**, V.D. **'onder**ge-dompeld. Zie voor de vormen onder het grondwoord, in dit voorbeeld: *dompelen*. Bij sterke en onregelmatige werkwoorden wordt u verwezen naar de lijst achterin.

keep down [one's anger], oppress [a nation]; suppress [a rebellion, a groan, a yawn &], stifle [a sigh], smother [a laugh, a yawn]; quell [a revolt]; **–er** (-s) *m* oppressor [of people]; **onder'drukking** (-en) *v* 1 oppression [of the people]; 2 suppression [of a revolt]

'**onderduiken**[1] *vi* 1 dive, duck [of birds &]; sink below the horizon [of the sun]; 2 (z i c h v e r b e r g e n) go into hiding; *ondergedoken zijn* be in hiding; **–er** (-s) *m* person in hiding

'**ondereind(e)** (-einden) *o* lower end

'**onderen** *naar* ~, *van* ~ zie *onder* **II**

1 '**ondergaan**[1] *vi* 1 (v. s c h i p) go down, sink; 2 (v. z o n) set, go down; 3 (b e z w ij k e n) go down, perish

2 onder'gaan (onderging, h. ondergaan) *vt* undergo [an operation, a change, punishment], suffer, endure [hardship, misery, pain]; *hij onderging zijn lot* he underwent his fate; *gevangenisstraf* ~ serve a term of imprisonment; *een verandering* ~ undergo (suffer) a change; *wat ik* ~ *heb* what I have undergone (gone through, suffered)

'**ondergang** *m* setting [of the sun]; *fig* (down)fall, ruin, destruction; ☉ doom; *dat was zijn* ~ that was the ruin of him, that was his undoing

onderge'schikt subordinate [person]; inferior [rôle]; *van* ~ *belang* of minor importance; ~ *maken aan* subordinate to; **–e** (-n) *m-v* subordinate, inferior; *zijn* ~*n* those under him, his inferiors; **–heid** *v* subordination, inferiority

'**ondergeschoven** supposititious; ~ *kind* changeling

onderge'tekende (-n) *m-v* undersigned; **J** yours truly; *ik* ~ *verklaar* I the undersigned declare; *wij* ~*n verklaren* we the undersigned declare

'**onder(ge)wicht** *o* short weight

'**ondergoed** *o* underwear, underclothes

onder'graven (ondergroef, h. ondergraven) *vt* undermine, sap

'**ondergrond** (-en) *m* subsoil[2]; *fig* foundation; *op een zwarte* ~ on (against) a black (back)ground

onder'gronds underground[2] [railway; movement]; subterranean; **–e** *v* 1 underground, **F** tube, *Am* subway; 2 resistance movement, underground

onder'hand meanwhile, in the meantime

onder'handelaar (-s en -laren) *m* negotiator; **onder'handelen** (onderhandelde, h. onderhandeld) *vi* negotiate, treat; **–ling** (-en) *v*

negotiation; *in* ~ *treden met...* enter into negotiations with...; *in* ~*met iem. zijn over...* be negotiating with sbd. for...

onder'hands 1 underhand [intrigues]; 2 **$** [sale] by private contract; private [arrangement, contract, sale]

onder'havig *in het* ~*e geval* in the present case

onder'hevig ~ *aan* subject to [fits of...]; liable to [error]; admitting of [doubt]

onder'horig dependent, subordinate, belonging to; **–e** (-n) *m-v* subordinate; **–heid** *v* dependence, subordination; (g e b i e d) dependency

'**onderhoud** *o* 1 (h e t i n s t a n d h o u d e n) maintenance, upkeep [of the roads &], servicing [of a car]; 2 (l e v e n s o n d e r h o u d) maintenance, support, sustenance; 3 (g e s p r e k) conversation, interview, talk; *in zijn* (*eigen*) ~ *voorzien* support oneself, be self-supporting, provide for oneself

1 '**onderhouden**[1] *vt* keep under; *de jongens er* ~ keep the boys in hand

2 onder'houden (onderhield, h. onderhouden) **I** *vt* 1 (i n o r d e h o u d e n) keep in repair [a house &]; 2 (a a n d e g a n g h o u d e n) keep up [the firing, a correspondence, one's French &], maintain [a service]; 3 (i n l e v e n h o u d e n) support, provide for [one's family &]; 4 (b e z i g h o u d e n) amuse; entertain [people]; 5 keep [God's commandments]; *iem. ergens over* ~ call (bring) sbd. to account for sth., take sbd. to task for sth.; *het huis is goed* (*slecht*) ~ the house is in good (bad) repair; *een goed* (*slecht*) ~ *tuin* a well-(badly) kept garden; **II** *vr zich* ~ support (provide for) oneself; *zich* ~ *over...* converse about...; **–d** entertaining, amusing; '**onderhoudskosten** *mv* cost of upkeep, maintenance cost(s)

'**onderhout** *o* underwood, undergrowth, brushwood

'**onderhuid** *v* true skin

'**onderhuids, onder'huids** subcutaneous; hypodermic [injection]

'**onderhuis** (-huizen) *o* lower part of a house; basement

'**onderhuren** *vt* sub-rent; '**onderhuur** *v* subtenancy; **–der** (-s) *m* subtenant

onder'in at the bottom [of the cupboard]

'**onderjurk** (-en) *v* (under)slip

'**onderkaak** (-kaken) *v* lower jaw, mandible

'**onderkant** (-en) *m* bottom

'**onderkast** (-en) *v* lower case

onder'kennen (onderkende, h. onderkend) *vt* discern, perceive; (o n d e r s c h e i d e n)

---

[1] V.T. en V.D. van dit werkwoord volgens het model: '**onder**dompelen, V.T. dompelde '**onder**, V.D. '**onder**gedompeld. Zie voor de vormen onder het grondwoord, in dit voorbeeld: *dompelen*. Bij sterke en onregelmatige werkwoorden wordt u verwezen naar de lijst achterin.

distinguish
'onderkin (-nen) *v* double chin
'onderkleren *mv* = *ondergoed*
onder'koeld supercooled, *fig* cool, unemotional; *~e regen* black ice; **onder'koelen** (onderkoelde, h. onderkoeld) *vi* & *vt* supercool
'onderkomen *o een ~ vinden* find shelter, find accommodation
'onderkoning (-en) *m* viceroy
onder'kruipen (onderkroop, h. onderkropen) *vi* **F** 1 **$** undercut, spoil sbd.'s trade; 2 (b ij s t a k i n g) blackleg; **'onderkruiper** (-s) *m* **F** 1 **$** underseller; 2 (b ij s t a k i n g) blackleg, scab; 3 = *onderkruipsel*; **'onder'kruiping** (-en) *v* **F** 1 **$** undercutting; 2 (b ij s t a k i n g) playing the blackleg; **'onderkruipsel** (-s) *o* dwarf, midget, manikin
'onderlaag (-lagen) *v* substratum [*mv* substrata]
'onderlaken (-s) *o* bottom sheet
onder'langs along the bottom (the foot)
onder'legd *goed ~* well-grounded
'onderlegger (-s) *m* blotting-pad, (writing-)pad
'onderliggen[1] *vi* lie under; *fig* be worsted; *de ~de partij* the underdog
'onderlijf (-lijven) *o* belly, abdomen, lower part of the body
'onderlijfje (-s) *o* (under-)bodice
onder'lijnen (onderlijnde, h. onderlijnd) *vt* underline, underscore
'onderling I *aj* mutual; *~e verzekeringsmaatschappij* mutual insurance company; **II** *ad* 1 mutually; 2 together, between them; *~ verdeeld* divided among themselves
'onderlip (-pen) *v* lower lip
'onderlopen[1] *vi* be flooded, be overflowed, be swamped [of a meadow]; *laten ~* inundate, flood
onder'maans sublunary; *het ~e* the sublunary world; *in dit ~e* here below
onder'mijnen (ondermijnde, h. ondermijnd) *vt* undermine[2], sap[2]; **-ning** *v* undermining[2], sapping[2]
onder'nemen (ondernam, h. ondernomen) *vt* undertake, attempt; **-d** enterprising; **onder'nemer** (-s) *m* 1 undertaker; 2 **$** proprietor, owner, entrepreneur, enterpriser; **onder'neming** (-en) *v* 1 undertaking, enterprise; venture; 2 (business) concern; 3 (p l a n t a g e) estate, plantation; **onder'nemingsgeest** *m* (spirit of) enterprise; **-raad** (-raden) *m* works council
'onderofficier (-en en -s) *m* 1 ✠ non-commissioned officer, N.C.O.; 2 ⚓ petty officer

'onderom round the foot (bottom)
onder onsje (-s) *o* 1 private business; 2 small sociable party, informal gathering
'onderontwikkeld underdeveloped, depressed [areas]; underdeveloped [negative]
'onderpand (-en) *o* pledge, guarantee, security; *op ~* on security; *in ~ geven* pledge
'onderproduktie [-düksi.] *v* underproduction
'onderrand (-en) *m* lower edge [of a page]
'onderregenen (regende 'onder, is 'ondergeregend) *vi* be swamped with rain
'onderricht *o* instruction, tuition; **onder'richten** (onderrichtte, h. onderricht) *vt* 1 instruct, teach; 2 inform (of *van*); **-ting** (-en) *v* 1 instruction; 2 information
'onderrok (-ken) *m* petticoat
onder'schatten (onderschatte, h. onderschat) *vt* undervalue underestimate, underrate; **-ting** *v* underestimation
'onderscheid *o* difference; distinction, discrimination; *de jaren des ~s* the years of discretion [in England: 14]; *~ maken tussen... en...* distinguish (discriminate) between... and...; *dat maakt een groot ~* that makes all the difference; *allen zonder ~* all without exception; zie ook: *oordeel*; **1 onder'scheiden** (onderscheidde, h. onderscheiden) **I** *vt* distinguish, discern; *fig* distinguish, single out; *hij is ~ met de Nobelprijs* he has been awarded the Nobel prize, the Nobel prize has been awarded to him; *~ i n...* distinguish into...; *~ v a n...* distinguish... from, tell... from; **II** *vr zich ~* distinguish oneself; **2 onder'scheiden** *aj* different, various, distinct; **-lijk** respectively [called A, B, C];
onder'scheiding (-en) *v* distinction; *~en* 1 *Br* birthday's honours; 2 [civil, war] decorations; 3 awards [at a show]; **onder'scheidingsteken** (-s en -en) *o* distinguishing mark, badge; **-vermogen** *o* discrimination, discernment
onder'scheppen (onderschepte, h. onderschept) *vt* intercept; **-ping** *v* interception
'onderschikkend *gram* subordinating; **'onderschikking** *v gram* subordination
'onderschrift (-en) *o* 1 subscription, signature [of a letter]; 2 caption, letterpress [under a picture]; **onder'schrijven** (onderschreef, h. onderschreven) *vt het ~* subscribe to that [statement], endorse the statement
'onderschuifbed (-den) *o* fold-away twin bed
onders'hands privately, by private contract
'ondersneeuwen (sneeuwde 'onder, is 'ondergesneeuwd) *vi* be snowed under

'onderspit *o het* ~ *delven* be worsted, have the worse, get the worst of it

'onderstaand subjoined, undermentioned

'onderstand *m* relief, assistance, maintenance

'onderste lowest, lowermost, undermost, bottom; *wie het* ~ *uit de kan wil hebben, valt het lid op de neus* much would have more and lost all; **onderste 'boven** upside down, wrong side up, topsy-turvy; ~ *gooien* overthrow, upset; ~ *halen* turn upside down; *ik was ervan* ~ it bowled me over, I was bowled over (by it)

'ondersteek (-steken) *m* bed-pan

'onderstel (-len) *o* (under-)carriage, underframe; chassis

onder'stellen (onderstelde, h. ondersteld) *vt* suppose; **–ling** (-en) *v* supposition; hypothesis; zie ook: *veronderstelling*

onder'steunen (ondersteunde, h. ondersteund) *vt* support; **onder'steuning** *v* support, relief; **–sfonds** (-en) *o* relief fund

onder'strepen (onderstreepte, h. onderstreept) *vt* underline[2]

'onderstroom (-stromen) *m* undercurrent

'onderstuk (-ken) *o* lower part, bottom piece

'ondertand (-en) *m* lower tooth

onder'tekenaar (-s en -naren) *m* signer, subscriber; signatory [to a convention]; **onder'tekenen** (ondertekende, h. ondertekend) *vt* sign, affix one's signature to; **–ning** (-en) *v* signature, subscription; (d e h a n d e - l i n g) signing; *ter* ~ for signature

'ondertitel (-s) *m* sub-title, sub-heading; **–ing** *v* caption, subscript; subtitling [of a film]

'ondertoon (-tonen) *m* overtone, undertone; *met een duidelijke* ~ *van...* with clear overtones of...

'ondertrouw *m* betrothal; **onder'trouwen** (ondertrouwde, is ondertrouwd) *vi* have their names entered at the registry-office, put up the banns

onder'tussen 1 meanwhile, in the meantime; 2 (t o c h) yet

onder'uit from below; *er niet* ~ *kunnen* be unable to get (wriggle) out of it; ~ *gaan* stumble, tumble down; ~ *zakken* sprawl, slouch [in a chair]

onder'vangen (onderving, h. ondervangen) *vt* obviate [criticism], anticipate, meet [objections]

'onderverdelen (verdeelde 'onder, h. 'onderverdeeld) *vt* subdivide; **–ling** (-en) *v* subdivision

'onderverhuren (h. 'onderverhuurd) *vt* sublet; **'onderverhuurder** (-s) *m* sublessor

'onderverzekerd underinsured

onder'vinden (ondervond, h. ondervonden) *vt* experience, meet with [difficulties]; **–ding**

(-en) *v* experience; ~ *is de beste leermeesteres* experience is the best of all schoolmasters; *bij (door)* ~ [know] by (from) experience

onder'voed underfed, undernourished; **–ing** *v* underfeeding, malnutrition

'ondervoorzitter (-s) *m* vice-chairman

onder'vragen (ondervroeg, ondervraagde, h. ondervraagd) *vt* interrogate, examine, question; **–er** (-s) *m* interrogator, examiner; **onder'vraging** (-en) *v* interrogation, examination

onder'waarderen (h. ondergewaardeerd) *vt* undervalue; **'onderwaardering** (-en) *v* undervaluation

onder'watersport *v* skindiving, underwaterswimming

onder'weg on the way; *hij was* ~ he was on his way

'onderwereld *v* underworld

'onderwerp (-en) *o* 1 subject, topic; theme; 2 *gram* subject

onder'werpen (onderwierp, h. onderworpen) **I** *vt* subject, subdue; ~ *aan* submit to [an examination], subject to [a test]; **II** *vr zich* ~ submit; *zich aan een examen* ~ go in for an examination; *zich aan zijn lot* ~ resign oneself to one's fate; *zich* ~ *aan Gods wil* resign oneself to the will of Heaven; **–ping** *v* subjection, submission

'onderwerpszin (-nen) *m* subjective clause

'onderwicht *o* $ short weight

onder'wijl meanwhile, the while

'onderwijs *o* instruction, tuition, schoolteaching; education, schooling; *bijzonder* ~ denominational education; *hoofdelijk* ~ individual teaching; *hoger* ~ university education, higher education; *lager* ~ primary (elementary) education; *middelbaar* ~ secondary education; *openbaar* ~ public education; *technisch* ~ technical education; *het* ~ *in geschiedenis* history teaching, the teaching of history; ~ *geven (in)* teach; *bij het* ~ *zijn* be a teacher; **'onderwijs-** educational, teaching; **'onderwijsinrichting** (-en) *v* educational establishment, teaching institution; **–kracht** (-en) *v* teacher;

onder'wijzen (onderwees, h. onderwezen) **I** *vt* instruct [persons], teach [persons, a subject]; *het* ~*d personeel* the teaching staff; **II** *va* teach; **–er** (-s) *m* teacher; **onderwijze'res** (-sen) *v* (woman) teacher; **onder'wijzersakte** (-n en -s) *v* teacher's certificate; **onder'wijzing** (-en) *v* instruction

onder'worpen I *aj* 1 submissive; 2 subject [nation, race]; ~ *aan* subject to [stamp-duty &]; **II** *ad* submissively; **–heid** *v* subjection, submissiveness

onder'zeeboot (-boten) *m* & *v*, **onder'zeeër** (-s) *m* submarine; **onder'zees** submarine

'onderzetter (-s) *m* (table) mat, (beer) mat

'**onderzij(de)** (-zijden) *v* bottom

'**onderzoek** *o* inquiry, investigation, examination; [scientific] research; ~ *doen naar iets* inquire into sth.; *een ~ instellen* make inquiries, inquire into the matter, investigate; *bij (nader)* ~ upon (closer) inquiry; *de zaak is in* ~ the matter is under investigation (examination); **onder'zoeken** (onderzocht, h. onderzocht) *vt* inquire (look) into, investigate, examine; make [scientific] researches into; ~ *op* test for, examine for; *een ~de blik* a searching look; **–er** (-s) *m* investigator; researcher, research-worker; **onder'zoeking** (-en) *v* exploration [of unknown regions], zie *onderzoek*; **–stocht** (-en) *m* journey (voyage) of exploration, exploring expedition

ondes'kundig inexpert

'**ondeugd** (-en) *v* 1 (t e g e n o v e r d e u g d) vice; 2 (o n d e u g e n d h e i d) naughtiness, mischief; 3 *m-v* (p e r s o o n) naughty boy (girl); **on'deugdelijk** unsound, faulty, defective; **on'deugend I** *aj* naughty, mischievous [children &]; bad, wicked [people]; vicious [animals]; (g u i t i g) naughty; **II** *ad* naughtily; **–heid** (-heden) *v* naughtiness, mischief

on'dichterlijk unpoetical

'**ondienst** (-en) *m* bad (ill) service, bad (ill) turn; *iem. een* ~ *bewijzen* ook: do sbd. a disservice

on'diep shallow; '**ondiepte** *v* 1 ('t o n d i e p z i j n) shallowness; 2 (-n en -s) (o n d i e p e p l a a t s) shallow, shoal

'**ondier** (-en) *o* brute[2], monster[2]

'**onding** (-en) *o* 1 absurdity; 2 = *prul*

ondoel'matig unsuitable, inexpedient; **–heid** *v* unsuitability, inexpediency

on'doenlijk unfeasible, impracticable

ondoor'dacht inconsiderate, thoughtless, rash

ondoor'dringbaar impenetrable, impervious; ~ *voor...* impervious to...

ondoor'grondelijk inscrutable, unfathomable; **–heid** *v* inscrutability

ondoor'schijnend opaque; **–heid** *v* opacity

ondoor'zichtig untransparent; **–heid** *v* untransparency

on'draaglijk unbearable, not to be borne, intolerable, insupportable, insufferable, beyond bearing

on'drinkbaar undrinkable

ondubbel'zinnig unambiguous, unequivocal

on'duidelijk I *aj* indistinct [utterance, outlines &]; obscure; *het is mij* ~ it is not clear to me; **II** *ad* indistinctly; not clearly; **–heid** (-heden) *v* indistinctness; obscurity

on'duldbaar unbearable, intolerable

ondu'leren (onduleerde, h. geonduleerd) *vt* wave [of the hair]

on'echt, 'onecht not genuine; false, imitation [jewellery]; forged, unauthentic [letters], spurious [coin, MS], improper [fractions]; illegitimate [children]; *fig* sham [feelings], mock [sympathy]

on'edel I *aj* ignoble, base, mean; base [metals]; **II** *ad* basely, meanly; **onedel'moedig** ungenerous

on'eens *zij zijn het* ~ they disagree, they are at variance; *ik ben het met mezelf* ~ I am in two minds about it

'**oneer** *v* dishonour, disgrace; **on'eerbaar** indecent, immodest; **–heid** (-heden) *v* indecency, immodesty

oneer'biedig disrespectful, irreverent; **–heid** (-heden) *v* disrespect, irreverence

on'eerlijk unfair, dishonest; **–heid** (-heden) *v* dishonesty, improbity

on'eervol, 'oneervol dishonourable

on'eetbaar uneatable, inedible

on'effen uneven, rough, rugged; **–heid** (-heden) *v* unevenness, roughness, ruggedness

on'eigenlijk figurative, metaphorical

on'eindig I *aj* infinite, endless; *het* ~*e* the infinite; *tot in het* ~*e* indefinitely; **II** *ad* infinitely; ~ *klein* infinitesimally small; **–heid** *v* infinity

on'enig disagreeing, at variance; **–heid** (-heden) *v* discord, disagreement, dissension; *onenigheden krijgen* fall out

oner'varen inexperienced; **–heid** *v* inexperience

on'even, 'oneven (v. g e t a l) odd; ~ *genummerd* odd numbered

oneven'redig I *aj* disproportionate, out of (all) proportion; **II** *ad* disproportionately, out of (all) proportion; **–heid** (-heden) *v* disproportion

oneven'wichtig unbalanced, unpoised

onfat'soenlijk indecent, improper; **–heid** (-heden) *v* indecency, impropriety

on'feilbaar unfailing, infallible, foolproof [method]; **–heid** *v* infallibility

onfor'tuinlijk unlucky, luckless

on'fris 1 not fresh; 2 *fig* unsavoury, shady [business]; 3 = *onlekker*

ong. = *ongeveer*

on'gaar underdone, not thoroughly cooked

on'gaarne, 'ongaarne unwillingly, reluctantly, with a bad grace

'**ongans** unwell; *zich* ~ *eten* overeat oneself, gorge

ongast'vrij inhospitable

'**ongeacht I** *aj* unesteemed; **II** *prep* irrespective of [race or creed]; in spite of, notwithstanding

'**ongebaand, onge'baand** unbeaten, untrodden

'**ongebleekt, onge'bleekt** unbleached [cotton]

'ongeblust unquenched [of fire]; unslaked [of lime], zie ook: *kalk*

'ongebogen not bent, unbent

onge'bonden I *aj* 1 unbound, in sheets; 2 *fig* dissolute, licentious, loose; ~ *stijl* prose; **II** *ad* dissolutely, licentiously; **–heid** *v* dissoluteness, licentiousness

'ongeboren unborn; ~ *vrucht* foetus, fetus

'ongebreideld unbridled, unchecked, uncurbed

'ongebroken unbroken

onge'bruikelijk, 'ongebruikelijk unusual; unorthodox [methods]; **'ongebruikt** unused, unemployed, idle

'ongebuild, onge'build whole [meal]

'ongecompliceerd uncomplicated, simple

onge'daan undone, unperformed; ~ *maken* 1 undo [it]; 2 $ cancel [a bargain]

'ongedagtekend, 'ongedateerd not dated

'ongedeerd unhurt, uninjured, unscathed, whole

'ongedekt uncovered, bare [head]; un-laid [table]; bad [cheque]

'ongedierte *o* vermin

'ongedrukt unprinted [essays &]

'ongeduld *o* impatience; **onge'duldig** impatient; **–heid** *v* impatience

onge'durig inconstant, restless [person]; *hij is een beetje* ~ he is rather fidgety; *zij is erg* ~ she is a regular fidget; **–heid** *v* inconstancy, restlessness

onge'dwongen unconstrained, unrestrained, unforced; natural, easy [manners]; **–heid** *v* unconstraint, abandon

ongeëve'naard unequalled, matchless, unparalleled [success]

ongeëven'redigd I *aj* disproportionate, out of (all) proportion; **II** *ad* disproportionately, out of (all) proportion

ongefortu'neerd without means

'ongefrankeerd 🐾 not prepaid, unpaid; unstamped [letter]; $ carriage forward

ongege'neerd [-ʒəʒə'ne:rt] unceremonious; ~ *weg* without ceremony, in his free-and-easy way; **–heid** *v* unceremoniousness, free-and-easy way

onge'grond groundless, unfounded, without foundation, baseless; **–heid** *v* groundlessness, unfoundedness, baselessness

'ongehavend undamaged

onge'hinderd, 'ongehinderd unhindered, unhampered

onge'hoord, 'ongehoord unheard (of), unprecedented; *iets* ~*s* a thing unheard-of

onge'hoorzaam disobedient; insubordinate; **–heid** (-heden) *v* disobedience; insubordination

'ongehuwd unmarried; *de* ~*e staat* celibacy,

single life

ongeïnteres'seerd disinterested; **–heid** *v* disinterestedness

'ongekamd uncombed, unkempt

'ongekend, onge'kend unprecedented

'ongekleed, onge'kleed 1 unclothed, undressed; 2 in undress, in dishabille

'ongekleurd, onge'kleurd uncoloured; plain [picture postcard]

onge'kookt, 'ongekookt unboiled [water], raw [egg, milk]

onge'kroond, 'ongekroond uncrowned

'ongekuist 1 coarse [language]; 2 unexpurgated [edition], unbowdlerized

onge'kunsteld I *aj* artless, ingenuous, unaffected, unsophisticated; **II** *ad* artlessly, ingenuously

'ongeladen ⚔ unloaded [gun]; ⚓ unladen [ships]; ⚡ uncharged

on'geldig not valid, invalid; ~ *maken* render null and void, invalidate, nullify; ~ *verklaren* declare null and void, annul; **–heid** *v* invalidity, nullity; **–verklaring** *v* annulment, nullification, invalidation

onge'legen inconvenient, unseasonable, inopportune; *op een* ~ *uur* at an unseasonable hour; *kom ik u* ~? am I intruding?; *het bezoek kwam mij* ~ the visit came at an inopportune moment; **–heid** *v* inconvenience; *geldelijke* ~ pecuniary difficulties; *in* ~ *brengen* inconvenience; *in* ~ *geraken* get into trouble

onge'letterd unlettered, illiterate [savages]

onge'lezen unread

1 **'ongelijk, onge'lijk** uneven, unequal; ~ *van lengte* of unequal lengths

2 **'ongelijk** *o* wrong; ~ *bekennen* acknowledge oneself to be wrong; *iem.* ~ *geven, in het* ~ *stellen* put sbd. in the wrong, give it against sbd.; *ik kan hem geen* ~ *geven* I can't blame him; ~ *hebben* be (in the) wrong; ~ *krijgen* be put in the wrong, be proved wrong

ongelijk'benig scalene [triangle]; **onge'lijkheid** (-heden) *v* unevenness; inequality [of surface, rank &]; dissimilarity, disparity; **ongelijk'matig** unequal [climate]; uneven [temper &]; **–heid** (-heden) *v* inequality; unevenness; **ongelijk'namig** not having the same name; [fractions] not having the same denominator; **ongelijk'soortig** dissimilar, heterogeneous; **–heid** *v* dissimilarity, heterogeneity; **ongelijk'vloers** ~*e (weg)kruising* fly-over; **ongelijk'vormig** dissimilar [triangles]; **–heid** *v* dissimilarity; **ongelijk'zijdig** with unequal sides; ~*e driehoek* scalene triangle

'ongelikt, onge'likt unlicked; *een* ~*e beer* an unlicked cub², ook: quite a bear

'ongelinieerd, ongelini'eerd unruled [paper]

onge'lofelijk not to be believed, unbelievable, incredible, beyond belief, past (all) belief; **–heid** *v* incredibility

'ongelogen *het water was ~ een voet gestegen* the water had risen one foot without exaggeration

'ongeloof *o* unbelief, disbelief; **onge'loof-lijk(heid)** = *ongelofelijk(heid)*; **ongeloof-'waardig** not deserving belief, incredible; **onge'lovig I** *aj* unbelieving, incredulous; **II** *ad* incredulously; **–e** (-n) *m-v* unbeliever, infidel; **–heid** *v* incredulity

'ongeluk (-ken) *o* 1 (d o o r o m s t a n d i g-h e d e n) misfortune; 2 (g e m o e d s t o e-s t a n d) unhappiness; 3 (o n g e l u k k i g e g e b e u r t e n i s) accident, mishap; 4 (t o e-v a l) bad luck; *dat ~ van een...* that wretch of a...; *dat was zijn ~* that was his undoing; *dat zal zijn ~ zijn* that will be his ruin; *een ~ begaan aan iem.* do sbd. a mischief; *zich een ~ eten* eat till one bursts; *een ~ krijgen* meet with an accident; *een ~ komt zelden alleen* it never rains but it pours; *een ~ zit in een klein hoekje* great accidents spring from small causes; ● *bij ~* by accident, accidentally; *z o n d e r ~ken* without accidents; **onge'lukkig I** *aj* unhappy [marriage]; unfortunate, unlucky; ill-starred [attempt]; *diep ~* miserable, wretched; **II** *ad* unfortunately; [married] unhappily; **–erwijs, –erwijze** unfortunately; **'ongeluksbode** (-n) *m* messenger of bad news; **–dag** (-dagen) *m* 1 ill-fated (fatal) day; 2 unpropitious day, off-day, black-letter day; **–kind** (-eren) *o* unlucky person; **–profeet** (-feten) *m* prophet of woe; **–vogel** (-s) *m fig* unlucky person

'ongemak (-ken) *o* 1 inconvenience, discomfort; 2 (k w a a l, g e b r e k) trouble, infirmity; **onge'makkelijk I** *aj* not easy, uneasy, uncomfortable, difficult [man]; **II** *ad* 1 not easily; uncomfortably; 2 < properly; *ik heb hem ~ de waarheid gezegd* I have given him a piece of my mind; *hij heeft er ~ van langs gehad* he has had a sound thrashing

ongema'nierd unmannerly, ill-mannered, ill-bred; **–heid** (-heden) *v* unmannerliness

onge'meen I *aj* uncommon, singular, extraordinary; **II** *ad* < uncommonly, extraordinarily

onge'merkt, 'ongemerkt I *aj* 1 unperceived [approach]; 2 unmarked [linen]; **II** *ad* without being perceived, imperceptibly, inadvertently, unawares

ongemeubi'leerd unfurnished

onge'moeid undisturbed, unmolested; *hem ~ laten* leave him alone

'ongemotiveerd (z o n d e r r e d e n) not motived, unwarranted, uncalled for, gratuitous; (z o n d e r d r ij f v e e r) unmotivated

onge'naakbaar unapproachable, inaccessible [of mountains &, also of persons]; **–heid** *v* unapproachableness, inaccessibility

'ongenade *v* disgrace, disfavour; *in ~ vallen bij iem.* fall out of favour with sbd.; *in ~ zijn* be in disgrace (with *bij*); **onge'nadig I** *aj* merciless, pitiless; **II** *ad* mercilessly; < severely, tremendously; *hij heeft er ~ van langs gehad* he has been mercilessly thrashed

onge'neeslijk incurable [illness], past recovery; *een ~e zieke* an incurable; **–heid** *v* incurableness

onge'negen disinclined, unwilling; **–heid** *v* disinclination

onge'neigd, 'ongeneigd disinclined, unwilling; **–heid** *v* disinclination

onge'neselijk(heid) = *ongeneeslijk(heid)*

onge'nietbaar 1 indigestible; 2 disagreeable

'ongenoegen (-s) *o* 1 displeasure; 2 tiff; *zij hebben ~* they are at variance; *~ krijgen* fall out

onge'noegzaam insufficient; **–heid** *v* insufficiency

'ongenoemd, onge'noemd unnamed, anonymous; *een ~e* a nameless one, an anonymous person

'ongenood, onge'nood unasked, unbidden, uninvited [guest]

onge'oefend untrained, unpractised, inexperienced; **–heid** *v* want of practice, inexperience

onge'oorloofd unallowed, illicit, unlawful

'ongeopend unopened

'ongepaard unpaired; odd [glove &]

onge'past I *aj* unseemly, improper, indecorous; **II** *ad* improperly, indecorously; **–heid** (-heden) *v* unseemliness, impropriety indecorousness

'ongepeld rough [rice]

ongepermit'teerd not permitted

'ongeraden, onge'raden unadvisable

onge'rechtigheid (-heden) *v* iniquity, injustice; *ongerechtigheden* flaws

'ongerede *in het ~ raken* 1 (z o e k) get lost, be mislaid; 2 (o n b r u i k b a a r) get out of order, go wrong

onge'regeld I *aj* irregular, disorderly; **II** *ad* irregularly; *~e goederen* unassorted goods; **–heid** (-heden) *v* irregularity; *ongeregeldheden* disorders, disturbances, riots

'ongerekend uncounted; (*nog*) *~... not including..., apart from...*

onge'remd, 'ongeremd uninhibited

onge'rept untouched; virgin [forests]; *fig* undefiled, pure

'ongerief *o* inconvenience, trouble; *~ veroorzaken* put to inconvenience; **onge'rief(e)lijk** inconvenient; incommodious; **–heid** (-heden) *v* inconvenience; incommodiousness

onge'rijmd *aj* absurd, preposterous, nonsensical; *het ~e van...* the absurdity (preposterousness) of...; *tot het ~e herleiden* reduce to an absurdity; *uit het ~e bewijzen* prove by negative demonstration; **–heid** (-heden) *v* absurdity

'ongeroepen, onge'roepen uncalled, unbidden

'ongeroerd unmoved, impassive

onge'rust uneasy; *~ over iem.* anxious about sbd.; *zich ~ maken, ~ zijn* be worried, worry (about *over*); *zich ~ maken over iets* be uneasy about sth., become anxious about sth.; **–heid** *v* uneasiness, anxiety

onge'schikt unfit, inapt, unsuitable, improper; *~ maken voor...* render unfit for...; **–heid** *v* unfitness, inaptness, inaptitude, unsuitability, impropriety

'ongeschokt, onge'schokt unshaken [faith]

'ongeschonden, onge'schonden undamaged, inviolate, unviolated

'ongeschoold, onge'schoold untrained [new-comers]; unskilled [labourer]

'ongeschoren, onge'schoren unshaved, unshaven [faces]; unshorn [lambs]

'ongeschreven unwritten

'ongeslachtelijk asexual, vegetative [reproduction]

'ongeslagen *sp* unbeaten

onge'stadig I *aj* unsteady, unsettled, inconstant; **II** *ad* unsteadily; **–heid** *v* unsteadiness, inconstancy

onge'steld indisposed, unwell; *~ zijn* have one's period; **–heid** (-heden) *v* indisposition, illness; menstruation

'ongestempeld unstamped

'ongestoffeerd unfurnished

onge'stoord, 'ongestoord undisturbed

onge'straft, 'ongestraft I *aj* unpunished; *~ blijven* go unpunished; **II** *ad* with impunity

'ongetekend, onge'tekend not signed, unsigned

'ongeteld untold, unnumbered, uncounted

'ongetemd untamed; *~e energie* unbridled energy

'ongetrouwd, onge'trouwd unmarried, single

onge'twijfeld, 'ongetwijfeld undoubtedly, doubtless(ly), without doubt, no doubt

onge'vaarlijk, 'ongevaarlijk harmless, without danger

'ongeval (-len) *o* accident, mishap; **'ongevallenverzekering** (-en) *v* accident insurance; **–wet** *v* workmen's compensation act

'ongeveer, onge'veer about, some, approximately, roughly, something like [ten pounds, five years &]; *zo ~* more or less

'ongeveinsd unfeigned, sincere; **onge'veinsdheid** *v* unfeignedness, sincerity

onge'voeglijk improper, unseemly, unbecoming

onge'voelig unfeeling, impassive, insensible (to *voor*); **–heid** *v* unfeelingness, impassiveness, insensibility

'ongevraagd, onge'vraagd unasked, unasked for, unrequested [things], unsolicited [scripts]; uninvited, unbidden [guests]; uncalled for [remarks &]

onge'wapend, 'ongewapend unarmed

onge'wassen, 'ongewassen unwashed, soiled

'ongewenst, onge'wenst undesirable [person], unwanted [children, pregnancy]

'ongewerveld, onge'werveld invertebrate; *~e dieren* invertebrates

'ongewettigd, onge'wettigd 1 unauthorized [proceedings]; **2** unfounded [claims]

'ongewijd unhallowed, unconsecrated

'ongewijzigd, onge'wijzigd unchanged, unaltered

onge'wild, 'ongewild 1 unintentional; **2 $** not in demand

onge'willig unwilling; **–heid** *v* unwillingness

onge'wis 1 uncertain; **2** capricious; **–se** *o in het ~* uncertain, at loose ends

onge'woon, 'ongewoon unusual, uncommon, unfamiliar, unwonted; *fig* **F** off the beaten track; *iets ~s* something uncommon; *niets ~s* nothing out of the common; **'ongewoonte** *v* unwontedness; *dat is maar ~* it comes from my [your &] not being used (accustomed) to it

'ongezegeld unsealed [letters]; unstamped [paper]

onge'zeglijk unruly, unbiddable, intractable, indocile; **–heid** *v* unruly behaviour, intractability, indocility

onge'zellig I *aj* unsociable; cheerless, not cosy [of a room]; **II** *ad* unsociably; **–heid** *v* unsociableness

'ongezien, onge'zien 1 unseen, unobserved, unperceived; **2** *fig* unesteemed, not respected

'ongezocht unsought; unstudied

onge'zond unhealthy [climate]; unwholesome [food]; insalubrious [air]; **–heid** *v* unhealthiness; unwholesomeness, insalubrity

'ongezouten, onge'zouten I *aj* unsalted, fresh; *~ taal* blunt speaking; **II** *ad iem. ~ de waarheid zeggen* zie *waarheid*

'ongezuiverd unpurified, unrefined

'ongezuurd, onge'zuurd unleavened [bread]

ongods'dienstig irreligious; **–heid** *v* irreligiousness

on'grijpbaar elusive; impalpable

ongrond'wettig unconstitutional

'ongunst *v* disfavour; **on'gunstig I** *aj* unfavourable; adverse [balance, effect on prices]; **II** *ad* unfavourably; adversely [affected] on'guur sinister [air, countenance, forest]; unsavoury [business, story]; *een ~ type* a bad character, an ugly customer

on'handelbaar unmanageable, intractable, wanton, unruly

on'handig clumsy, awkward [man]; –heid (-heden) *v* clumsiness, awkwardness

on'handzaam unwieldy

onhar'monisch inharmonious

on'hartelijk I *aj* not cordial, unkind; II *ad* not cordially, unkindly; –heid *v* lack of cordiality, unkindness

on'hebbelijk unmannerly, rude; –heid (-heden) *v* rudeness

'onheil (-en) *o* calamity, disaster, mischief; ~ *stichten* make mischief; onheil'spellend ominous

onher'bergzaam inhospitable; –heid *v* inhospitality

onher'kenbaar unrecognizable; *tot ~ wordens toe* [change] out of recognition, beyond (all) recognition

onher'roepelijk irrevocable [resolution]; –heid *v* irrevocableness

onher'stelbaar I *aj* irreparable, irremediable, past remedy, past redress, irretrievable, irrecoverable [loss]; II *ad* irreparably &, [damaged] beyond repair; –heid *v* irreparableness &, irreparability

on'heuglijk immemorial; *sedert ~e tijden* from time immemorial, time out of mind

on'heus ungracious, discourteous, disobliging; –heid (-heden) *v* ungraciousness, discourtesy, disobligingness

on'hoffelijk = *onheus*; –heid (-heden) *v* = *onheusheid*

on'hoorbaar inaudible

on'houdbaar untenable [position, theory]; unbearable; *het onhoudbare van de toestand* the untenable state of affairs; –heid *v* untenableness

onhygi'ënisch [-hi.gi.'e.ni.s] insanitary

on'inbaar irrecoverable, bad [debts]

on'ingevuld not filled up, blank

on'ingewijd uninitiated; *de ~en* the uninitiated, the outsiders

'oninteressant uninteresting

on'juist inaccurate, inexact, erroneous, incorrect; –heid (-heden) *v* inaccuracy, erroneousness, misstatement, error, incorrectness

on'kenbaar unknowable; zie ook: *onherkenbaar*

on'kerkelijk unchurchly

on'kies indelicate, immodest; –heid (-heden) *v* indelicacy, immodesty

on'klaar, 'onklaar 1 (n i e t h e l d e r) not clear; 2 ✗ out of order; ⚓ fouled [anchor]

on'knap *niet ~* rather pretty (good-looking)

'onkosten *mv* charges, expenses; *algemene ~* overhead charges (expenses), overhead(s); *m e t de ~* charges included; *z o n d e r ~* free of charge; –nota ('s) *v* $ note of charges; –rekening (-en) *v* expense account; –vergoeding *v* expense allowance

on'kreukbaar 1 *fig* unimpeachable; 2 *eig* = *kreukvrij*; –heid *v* integrity

'onkruid *o* weeds; ~ *vergaat niet* ill weeds grow apace; –verdelger (-s) *m* weed-killer

on'kuis unchaste, impure, lewd; –heid (-heden) *v* unchastity, impurity, lewdness

'onkunde *v* ignorance; on'kundig ignorant; ~ *van* ignorant of, not aware of; *iem. ~ laten van* keep sbd. in ignorance of

on'kwetsbaar invulnerable; –heid *v* invulnerability

'onlangs the other day, lately, recently; ~ *op een middag* the other afternoon

on'ledig *zich ~ houden met* busy oneself with

on'leesbaar I *aj* 1 illegible [writing]; 2 unreadable [novels &]; II *ad* illegibly; –heid *v* illegibility

on'lekker out of sorts, off colour

on'lesbaar unquenchable [thirst]

onli'chamelijk incorporeal

on'logisch illogical

on'loochenbaar undeniable

onlos'makelijk indissoluble

'onlust (-en) *m* uneasiness, *ps* displeasure; ~*en* troubles, disturbances, riots

onmaat'schappelijk antisocial

'onmacht *v* 1 impotence, inability; 2 (b e - z w ij m i n g) swoon, fainting fit; *in ~ vallen* faint (away), swoon; on'machtig impotent, unable

on'matig immoderate, intemperate; –heid *v* immoderateness, intemperance, insobriety

onmede'deelzaam taciturn, tight-lipped

onmee'dogend merciless, pitiless, ruthless

on'meetbaar immeasurable; *onmeetbare getallen* irrationals, surds; –heid *v* immeasurableness, incommensurability

'onmens (-en) *m* brute, monster; on'menselijk inhuman, brutal; –heid (-heden) *v* inhumanity, brutality

on'merkbaar imperceptible

on'metelijk immeasurable, immense; –heid *v* immeasurableness, immensity

on'middellijk I *aj* immediate, instant; II *ad* directly, immediately, at once, instantly; –heid *v* immediacy

'onmin *v* discord, dissension; *in ~ geraken* fall out; *in ~ leven* be at variance

on'misbaar indispensable (to *voor*); –heid *v* indispensableness

onmis'kenbaar undeniable, unmistakable

on'mogelijk I *aj* impossible°; *een ~e hoed* (*vent*) an impossible hat (fellow); *het was mij ~ o m...* it was not possible (impossible) for me to...; *het ~e* what is impossible, the impossible; *het ~e vergen* demand an impossibility (impossibilities); II *ad* not... possibly; *die plannen kunnen ~ verwezenlijkt worden* these plans cannot possibly be realized; *niet ~* not impossibly; *een ~ lange naam* an impossibly long name; **–heid** (-heden) *v* impossibility

on'mondig = *minderjarig*; **–heid** *v* = *minderjarigheid*

onna'denkend I *aj* thoughtless, inconsiderate, unthinking; II *ad* thoughtlessly, inconsiderately, unthinkingly; **–heid** *v* want of thought

onna'speurlijk inscrutable, unsearchable, untraceable; **–heid** (-heden) *v* inscrutableness, unsearchableness, inscrutability, untraceableness

onna'tuurlijk not natural, unnatural; **–heid** (-heden) *v* unnaturalness

onnauw'keurig inaccurate, inexact, lax; **–heid** (-heden) *v* inaccuracy, inexactitude, laxity

onna'volgbaar inimitable

on'neembaar impregnable

on'net 1 *eig* untidy, 2 *fig* improper

on'nodig needless, unnecessary; *~ te zeggen* needless to say

on'noem(e)lijk 1 unmentionable, unnameable, unutterable, inexpressible; 2 (v e e l) innumerable, numberless, countless

on'nozel I *aj* 1 (d o m) silly, simple, stupid; 2 (a r g e l o o s) innocent; 3 (l i c h t g e l o v i g) gullible; *een ~e hals* a simpleton, a gander; *een ~e jongen* a silly boy, a simpleton; *een ~e tien gulden* a paltry ten guilders; II *ad* 1 in a silly way, stupidly; 2 innocently; **Onnozele-'kinderen(dag)** *m* Innocents' Day, Childermas (Day); **on'nozelheid** (-heden) *v* 1 silliness, simplicity; 2 innocence

'onnut (-ten) *m-v* cipher

onomato'pee (-eën) *v* onomatopoeia

onom'keerbaar irreversible

onom'koopbaar not to be bribed, incorruptible

onom'stotelijk irrefutable, irrefragable

onom'wonden explicit, plain, without mincing matters, forthright

'ononderbroken = *onafgebroken*

onont'beerlijk indispensable; **–heid** *v* indispensableness, indispensability

onont'bindbaar indissoluble

onont'cijferbaar undecipherable

onont'gonnen uncultivated, unworked [coal], undeveloped [areas]

onont'koombaar ineluctable, inescapable, inevitable

onont'warbaar inextricable

onont'wijkbaar inevitable, unescapable

onont'wikkeld undeveloped; uneducated

on'ooglijk unsightly; **–heid** *v* unsightliness

on'oorbaar improper, indecent

onoordeel'kundig injudicious

on'opgehelderd unexplained, uncleared-up; *de moord bleef ~* the murder remained unsolved

on'opgelost undissolved; *fig* unsolved

on'opgemaakt unmade [bed]; undressed [hair]; *~e drukproef* galley-proof

on'opgemerkt unobserved, unnoticed, unnoted; *dat is niet ~ gebleven* this has not gone unnoted (unremarked)

on'opgesmukt unadorned, uncoloured, unvarnished, plain [tale]; bald [reports &]

on'opgevoed ill-bred

onop'houdelijk incessant

onop'lettend inattentive; **–heid** (-heden) *v* inattention

onop'losbaar insoluble^2 [matter]; unsolvable [problems]; **–heid** *v* insolubility^2; *fig* unsolvableness

onop'merkzaam unobservant

onop'recht insincere; **–heid** (-heden) *v* insincerity

onop'vallend inconspicuous, unobtrusive

onop'zettelijk unintentional, inadverten

on'ordelijk in disorder; **–heid** *v* disorderliness

onover'brugbaar insurmountable; *onoverbrugbare kloof* [*fig*] gulf

onover'dekt uncovered

onover'gankelijk intransitive

onover'komelijk insurmountable, insuperable; **–heid** *v* insuperability

onover'trefbaar unsurpassable; onover'troffen unsurpassed

onover'win(ne)lijk unconquerable, invincible; **–heid** *v* invincibility; onover'wonnen unconquered

onover'zichtelijk badly arranged [matter]; [the position is] difficult to survey

onparlemen'tair [-pɑrləmɛn'tɛr] unparliamentary

onpar'tijdig impartial; **–heid** *v* impartiality

'onpas *te ~* ill-timed; *te pas en te ~* at all times, time after time, at every odd moment

on'passelijk sick; **–heid** *v* sickness

onpeda'gogisch unpedagogical

on'peilbaar unfathomable; **–heid** *v* unfathomableness

onper'soonlijk impersonal

onple'zierig unpleasant, disagreeable

on'praktisch unpractical

'onraad *o* trouble, danger; *daar is ~* there is something wrong, I smell a rat

on'raadzaam unadvisable

'**onrecht** *o* injustice, wrong; *iem.* ~ *aandoen* wrong sbd., do sbd. an injustice (a wrong); *ten* ~*e* unjustly, wrongly; *zij protesteren ten* ~*e* they are wrong to protest (in protesting); **onrecht'matig** unlawful; **–heid** (-heden) *v* unlawfulness; **onrecht'vaardig** unjust; **–heid** (-heden) *v* injustice

on'**redelijk** unreasonable, undue; **–heid** (-heden) *v* unreasonableness

'**onregeerbaar, onre'geerbaar** ungovernable [country]

onregel'matig irregular; **–heid** (-heden) *v* irregularity

on'**rein** unclean, impure; **–heid** (-heden) *v* uncleanness, impurity

onren'dabel non-paying, unremunerative

on'**rijp** unripe, immature[2]; **–heid** *v* unripeness, immaturity[2]

'**onroerend, on'roerend** immovable; zie ook: 2 *goed*

'**onrust** (-en) *m* & *v* 1 restlessness, unrest, disquiet, commotion; 2 restless person, restless child; 3 ✗ fly, balance [of watches]; **onrust'barend** alarming; **on'rustig I** *aj* restless, unquiet, turbulent; troubled [areas, days, sleep, world]; uneasy [night]; **II** *ad* restlessly; **–heid** *v* restlessness, unrest; '**onruststoker** (-s), **–zaaier** (-s) *m* mischief-maker

1 ons I *pers. vnmw.* us; **II** *bez. vnmw.* our; ~ *land* ook: this country; zie ook: *volk*; *de onze* ours; *de onzen* ours

2 ons (-en en onzen) *o* 1 (1 0 0 g r a m) hectogram(me); 2 (E n g e l s g e w i c h t) ounce

on'**samenhangend, onsamen'hangend** incoherent, disconnected, rambling [talk]; disjointed [speech]; scrappy [discourse]; **–heid** *v* incoherence, disjointedness

on'**schadelijk** harmless, innocuous, inoffensive; ~ *maken* render harmless; *hij werd* ~ *gemaakt* he was put out of the way; **–heid** *v* harmlessness

on'**schatbaar** inestimable, invaluable, priceless; *van onschatbare waarde* invaluable

on'**scheidbaar** inseparable, distasteful; **–heid** *v* inseparability

on'**schendbaar** inviolable; **–heid** *v* inviolability

on'**scherp** blurred, vague

'**onschuld** *v* innocence; *ik was mijn handen in* ~ I wash my hands of it; **on'schuldig I** *aj* innocent, guiltless; harmless; *ik ben er* ~ *aan* I am innocent of it; *zo* ~ *als een lam* as innocent as a lamb; **II** *ad* innocently

on'**smakelijk** unsavoury, unpalatable; **–heid** (-heden) *v* unsavouriness &

on'**smeltbaar** not to be melted, infusible

onso'lide, onso'lied I *aj* not strong [furniture &]; unsubstantial [building]; *fig* unsteady [livers]; unsound [business]; **II** *ad* unsubstantially; unsteadily

on'**splinterbaar** unsplinterable

onspor'tief unsporting

onsta'biel unstable, unsteady

onstand'vastig unstable, inconstant; **–heid** *v* instability, inconstancy

onstelsel'matig unsystematic

on'**sterfelijk** immortal; **–heid** *v* immortality

on'**stilbaar** unappeasable, insatiable

on'**stoffelijk** immaterial, insubstantial, spiritual

on'**stuimig** tempestuous; boisterous, turbulent; *fig* impetuous [man]; **–heid** (-heden) *v* tempestuousness; boisterousness, turbulence; *fig* impetuosity

onsympa'thiek [-sɪmpa.'ti.k] uncongenial; soms: unsympathetic [personality]

onsyste'matisch [-sɪste.'ma.ti.s] unsystematic, planless

ont'**aard** degenerate; unnatural [mother]; **ont'aarden** (ontaardde, is ontaard) *vi* degenerate [into], deteriorate; **–ding** *v* degeneration, degeneracy

on'**tactisch** tactless

on'**tastbaar** impalpable, intangible

ont'**beren** (ontbeerde, h. ontbeerd) *vt* be in want of; do without; *wij kunnen het niet* ~ we can't do without it; **–ring** (-en) *v* want, privation; *allerlei* ~*en* all sorts of hardships

ont'**bieden**[1] *vt* summon, send for

ont'**bijt** (-en) *o* breakfast; **ont'bijten**[1] *vi* breakfast (on *met*), have breakfast; **ont'bijtkoek** (-en) *m* ± honey cake; **–spek** *o* streaky bacon

ont'**binden**[1] *vt* untie, undo [a knot, fetters &]; *fig* disband [troops]; decompose [the body, light, a substance]; dissolve [a marriage, Parliament, a partnership]; resolve [forces &]; separate [numbers into factors]; **–ding** (-en) *v* untying &; *fig* dissolution [of a marriage &]; decomposition; resolution [of forces]; disbandment [of troops]; *in staat van* ~ in a state of decomposition; *tot* ~ *overgaan* become decomposed, decay

ont'**bladeren**[1] *vt* strip of the leaves, defoliate;

---

[1] V.T. en V.D. van dit werkwoord volgens het model: **ont'**bladeren, V.T. **ont'**bladerde, V.D. **ont'**bladerd (**ge-** valt dus weg in het V.D.). Zie voor de vormen onder het grondwoord, in dit voorbeeld: *bladeren*. Bij sterke en onregelmatige werkwoorden wordt u verwezen naar de lijst achterin.

ont'bladering *v* defoliation; **–smiddel** (-en) *o* defoliant

ont'bloeien (ontbloeide, is ontbloeid) *vi* effloresce

ont'bloot naked, bare; ~ *van* destitute of, devoid of, without; zie ook: *grond*; **ont'bloten** (ontblootte, h. ontbloot) *vt* bare [the sword]; uncover [the head]; ~ *van* denude of; **–ting** (-en) *v* baring; denudation

ont'boezeming (-en) *v* effusion, outpouring

ont'bolsteren (ontbolsterde, h. ontbolsterd) *vt* shell, husk, hull; *fig* polish [a man]

ont'bossen (ontboste, h. ontbost) *vi* disafforest, deforest; **–sing** *v* disafforestation, deforestation

ont'brandbaar (in)flammable, combustible; **ont'branden** (ontbrandde, is ontbrand) *vi* take fire, ignite; (v. s t r ij d, o o r l o g) break out; *doen* ~ kindle, ignite; **–ding** (-en) *v* ignition, combustion

ont'breken[1] **I** *vi* 1 be absent; 2 be wanting (missing); *er* ~ *er vijf* 1 five are absent; 2 five are wanting (missing); *er ontbreekt nog wel iets aan* something is wanted still; *dat ontbreekt er nog maar aan* that's the last straw; **II** *onpers. ww.* *het ontbreekt hem aan geld* he wants money; *het ontbreekt hem aan moed* he is lacking (wanting) in courage; *laat het hem aan niets* ~ let him want for nothing; *het zou mij daartoe aan tijd* ~ *time* would fail me (to do that); *het* ~*de* the deficiency; the balance; **III** *o* absence

ont'cijferen[1] *vt* decipher [sbd.'s writing]; decode [a telegram]; **–ring** (-en) *v* decipherment; decoding [of a telegram]

ont'daan disconcerted, upset; *geheel* ~ quite taken aback; ~ *van* stripped of [details &]

ont'dooien I (ontdooide, is ontdooid) *vi* thaw[2]; *fig* melt; **II** (ontdooide, h. ontdooid) *vt* thaw[2]; defrost [a refrigerator]; *de waterleiding* ~ thaw out the waterpipe(s)

ont'duiken[1] *vt* elude [a blow]; *fig* get round [the regulations], elude [the laws], evade [a difficulty]; dodge [arguments, conditions, a tax &];

–king (-en) *v* elusion, evasion; 🔁 fraud

ontegen'sprekelijk, –'zeglijk *aj* incontestable undeniable, unquestionable

ont'eigenen (onteigende, h. onteigend) *vt* expropriate; **–ning** (-en) *v* expropriation

on'telbaar I *aj* countless, innumerable, numberless; **II** *ad* innumerably

on'tembaar untamable, indomitable; **–heid** *v* untamableness, indomitableness

ont'eren[1] *vt* dishonour; rape [a woman]; **–d** dishonouring, ignominious; **ont'ering** (-en) *v* dishonouring

ont'erven *vt* disinherit; **–ving** (-en) *v* disinheritance

onte'vreden discontented; ~ *over* discontented (dissatisfied, displeased) with; *de* ~*en* the malcontents; **–heid** *v* discontent(edness); dissatisfaction (with *over*), displeasure (at *over*)

ont'fermen (ontfermde, h. ontfermd) *vr zich* ~ *over* take pity on, have mercy on; **–ming** *v* pity

ont'futselen (ontfutselde, h. ontfutseld) *vt iem. iets* ~ filch (pilfer) sth. from sbd.

ont'gaan[1] *vi* escape, elude; *het is mij* ~ 1 it has slipped my memory; 2 I have failed to notice it; *de humor ontging me* the humour was lost (up)on him; *het kampioenschap ontging hem* he missed the championship

ont'gelden[1] *vt het moeten* ~ have to pay (suffer) for it

ont'ginnen* *vt* reclaim [land], break up [a field]; work exploit [a mine], develop [a region]; **–ning** (-en) *v* reclamation; working, exploitation, development

ont'glippen[1] *vi* slip from one's grasp [of an eel &]; slip from one's tongue [of words]

ont'gon (ontgonnen) V.T. van *ontginnen*

ont'gonnen V.T. meerv. en V.D. van *ontginnen*

ont'goochelen[1] *vt* disillusion, undeceive; **–ling** (-en) *v* disillusionment

ont'graten (ontgraatte, h. ontgraat) *vt* bone [a fish]

ont'grendelen[1] *vt* unbolt

ont'groeien[1] *vi* ~ (*aan*) outgrow, grow out of

ont'groenen (ontgroende, h. ontgroend) *vt* 🔁 rag [a fellow-student]; *fig* **S** put [sbd.] wise

ont'haal *o* treat, entertainment; *fig* reception; *een goed* ~ *vinden* meet with a kind reception; **ont'halen**[1] *vt* treat, entertain, feast, regale; ~ *op* treat [sbd.] to, entertain [sbd.] with

ont'hand inconvenienced

ont'harden[1] *vt* soften; **–er** (-s) *m* softener

ont'haren (onthaarde, h. onthaard) *vt* depilate;

---

[1] V.T. en V.D. van dit werkwoord volgens het model: **ont'**bladeren, V.T. **ont'**bladerde, V.D. **ont'**bladerd (**ge-** valt dus weg in het V.D.). Zie voor de vormen onder het grondwoord, in dit voorbeeld: *bladeren*. Bij sterke en onregelmatige werkwoorden wordt u verwezen naar de lijst achterin.

ont'haring *v* depilation; **–smiddel** (-en) *o* depilatory

ont'heemde (-n) *m-v* displaced person

ont'heffen[1] *vt iem. ~ van zijn ambt* relieve sbd. of his office; *iem. van het commando ~* relieve sbd. of (remove from) his command; *iem. van een verplichting ~* zie *ontslaan;* **–fing** (-en) *v* exemption, dispensation, exoneration; (v a n a m b t, c o m m a n d o) discharge, removal

ont'heiligen[1] *vt* desecrate, profane; **–ging** (-en) *v* desecration, profanation

ont'hoofden (onthoofdde, h. onthoofd) *vt* behead, decapitate; **–ding** (-en) *v* decapitation

ont'houden[1] **I** *vt* 1 (n i e t g e v e n) withhold, keep from; 2 (n i e t v e r g e t e n) remember, bear in mind; *help 't me ~* remind me of it; *onthoud dat wel!* don't forget that!; **II** *vr zich ~ van* abstain from, refrain from; **–ding** (-en) *v* 1 abstinence, abstemiousness; 2 (b ij s t e m - m i n g &) abstention

ont'hullen[1] *vt* unveil [a statue]; *fig* reveal, disclose; **–ling** (-en) *v* unveiling; *fig* revelation, disclosure

ont'hutsen (onthutste, h. onthutst) *vt* disconcert, bewilder; **ont'hutst** disconcerted, dismayed, upset

'ontij *m bij nacht en ~* at unreasonable hours, at all hours of the night

on'tijdig I *aj* untimely, premature; **II** *ad* untimely, prematurely

ont'kalken[1] *vi* decalcify

ont'kennen[1] **I** *vt* deny [that it is so &]; **II** *va* deny the charge; **–d I** *aj* negative; **II** *ad* negatively, [reply] in the negative; **ont'kenning** (-en) *v* denial, negation

ont'kerstening *v* dechristianization

ont'ketenen[1] *vt* unchain; activate; let out, let loose; launch [an attack]

ont'kiemen[1] *vi* germinate; **–ming** *v* germination

ont'kleden[1] *vt & vr* undress

ont'knopen[1] *vt* unbutton; untie; *fig* unravel; **–ping** (-en) *v* dénouement, unravelling

ont'kolen (ontkoolde, h. ontkoold) *vt* ⚒ decarbonize [a cylinder]

ont'komen[1] *vi* escape; *hij wist te ~* he managed to escape; *daaraan kunnen wij niet ~* we cannot escape that, we cannot get away from that; *zij ontkwamen aan de vervolging* they eluded pursuit; **–ming** *v* escape

ont'koppelen[1] **I** *vt* 1 ⚒ uncouple, ungear, throw out of gear, disconnect; 2 unleash [hounds]; **II** *vi* ⚙ declutch; **ont'koppeling** *v*

disconnection; **–spedaal** (-dalen) *o* ⚙ clutch pedal

ont'krachten (ontkrachtte, h. ontkracht) *vt* weaken

ont'kurken (ontkurkte, h. ontkurkt) *vt* uncork

ont'laden[1] *vt* unload; ⚡ discharge; **–ding** (-en) *v* **I** ⚓ unloading; 2 ⚡ discharge

ont'lasten (ontlastte, h. ontlast) **I** *vt* unburden[2]; *iem. van... ~* relieve sbd. of...; **II** *vr zich ~* discharge (itself), disembogue [of a river]; (v a n u i t w e r p s e l e n) relieve oneself; **–ting** (-en) *v* 1 discharge, relief; 2 (u i t w e r p s e l e n) stools; *~ hebben* have a movement, relieve oneself, defecate; *voor goede ~ zorgen* keep the bowels open

ont'leden (ontleedde, h. ontleed) *vt* 1 analyse; 2 (a n a t o m i e) dissect, anatomize; 3 (r e d e - k u n d i g) analyse; 4 (t a a l k u n d i g) parse; **–ding** (-en) *v* 1 analysis [*mv* analyses]; 2 (i n d e a n a t o m i e) dissection; 3 (r e d e k u n - d i g e) analysis; 4 (t a a l k u n d i g e) parsing; **ont'leedkunde** *v* anatomy; **ontleed'kundig** anatomical; **–e** (-n) *m* anatomist; **ont'leedmes** (-sen) *o* dissecting-knife; **–tafel** (-s) *v* dissecting-table

ont'lenen[1] *vt ~ aan* borrow from, adopt from, derive from, take [one's name] from; **–ning** (-en) *v* borrowing, adoption

ont'loken full-blown [flower, talent]

ont'lokken[1] *vt* draw (elicit, coax) from

ont'lopen[1] *vt* run away from, escape, avoid; *ik tracht hem zoveel mogelijk te ~* I always give him a wide berth; *ze ~ elkaar niet veel* there is not much difference between them

ont'luchten[1] *vt* de-aerate, deventilate; **–ting** *v* ventilation, evacuation

ont'luiken (ontlook, is ontloken) *vi* open, expand; *een ~de liefde* a dawning love; *een ~d talent* a budding talent; zie ook: *ontloken*

ont'luisteren (ontluisterde, h. ontluisterd) *vt* 1 tarnish, dim; 2 **F** debunk [heroism, a myth], take the shine out of

ont'luizen (ontluisde, h. ontluisd) *vt* delouse

ont'maagden (ontmaagdde, h. ontmaagd) *vt* deflower; **–ding** *v* defloration

ont'mannen (ontmande, h. ontmand) *vt* castrate, emasculate; *fig* unman

ont'mantelen (ontmantelde, h. ontmanteld) *vt* dismantle; **–ling** *v* dismantling

ont'maskeren (ontmaskerde, h. ontmaskerd) **I** *vt* unmask[2], *fig* show up, expose; **II** *vr zich ~* unmask; **–ring** *v* unmasking, *fig* exposure

ont'moedigd discouraged, disheartened,

---

[1] V.T. en V.D. van dit werkwoord volgens het model: **ont'**bladeren, V.T. **ont'**bladerde, V.D. **ont'**bladerd (**ge-** valt dus weg in het V.D.). Zie voor de vormen onder het grondwoord, in dit voorbeeld: *bladeren.* Bij sterke en onregelmatige werkwoorden wordt u verwezen naar de lijst achterin.

dispirited, down-hearted; **ont′moedigen** (ontmoedigde, h. ontmoedigd) *vt* discourage; **–ging** *v* discouragement

ont′moeten (ontmoette, h. ontmoet) *vt* 1 (t o e v a l l i g) meet with, meet, run into [sbd.]; chance upon [an expression]; 2 (n i e t t o e v a l l i g) meet; *fig* encounter [resistance]; **–ting** (-en) *v* 1 meeting; 2 [hostile] encounter

ont′nemen[1] *vt* take (away) from, deprive of

ont′nuchteren (ontnuchterde, h. ontnuchterd) *vt* sober[2]; *fig* disenchant, disillusion; **–ring** (-en) *v fig* disenchantment, disillusionment

ontoe′gankelijk unapproachable, inaccessible; **–heid** *v* unapproachableness, inaccessibility

ontoe′laatbaar inadmissible [evidence], impermissible

ontoe′passelijk inapplicable; **–heid** *v* inapplicability

ontoe′reikend insufficient, inadequate; **–heid** *v* insufficiency, inadequacy

ontoe′rekenbaar not imputable [crimes]; irresponsible [for one's actions]; **–heid** *v* irresponsibility

ontoe′schietelijk aloof, stand-offish, distant

on′toonbaar not fit to be shown [of things], not fit to be seen [of persons]

ont′pitten (ontpitte, h. ontpit) *vt* stone, take the stone out of [cherries]

ont′plofbaar explosive; *ontploffbare stoffen* explosives; **ont′ploffen**[1] *vi* explode, detonate; **–fing** (-en) *v* explosion, detonation; *tot ~ brengen* explode; *tot ~ komen* explode

ont′plooien (ontplooide, h. ontplooid) *vt & vr* unfurl, unfold[2]; display, show [initiatives, activities]; develop [one's talents]; **ont′plooiing** *v* unfolding, development

ont′poppen (ontpopte, h. ontpopt) *vr zich ~ als...* turn out to be..., show oneself a...

ont′potting *v* $ dishoarding

ont′raadselen (ontraadselde, h. ontraadseld) *vt* unriddle, unravel

ont′raden[1] *vt* dissuade from, advise against

ont′rafelen[1] *vt* unravel[2]

ont′reddered (put) out of joint, disabled; **ont′redderen**[1] *vt* put out of joint, throw out of gear, disable, shatter; **–ring** *v* disorganization, general collapse [of society]

ont′rieven (ontriefde, h. ontriefd) *vt als ik u niet ontrief* if I don't put you to inconvenience

ont′roeren I *vt* move, affect; II *vi* be moved; **–ring** (-en) *v* emotion

ont′rollen *vt & vr* unroll, unfurl, unfold; *iem. iets ~* pilfer sth. from sbd.

ont′romen[1] *vt* skim, cream [milk]

on′troostbaar not to be comforted, disconsolate, inconsolable; **–heid** *v* disconsolateness

′ontrouw I *aj* unfaithful [husband, wife], disloyal, false [to oneself]; II *v* unfaithfulness, disloyalty, [marital] infidelity

ont′roven[1] *vt* rob of, steal from

ont′ruimen[1] *vt* ⚓ evacuate, vacate [the premises, a house], clear [the park &]; **–ming** *v* evacuation, vacation, clearing

ont′rukken[1] *vt* tear from, snatch (away) from, wrest from

ont′schepen (ontscheepte, h. ontscheept) I *vt* unship [cargo], disembark [passengers]; II *vr zich ~* disembark; **–ping** (-en) *v* disembarkation; unshipping [of cargo]

ont′schieten[1] *vi* slip from; *het is mij ontschoten* it has slipped my memory

ont′sieren[1] *vt* disfigure, deface, mar; **–ring** (-en) *v* disfigurement, defacement

ont′slaan[1] *vt* discharge, dismiss, F fire; *~ u i t zijn betrekking* discharge, dismiss; *~ uit de gevangenis* release from gaol; *~ v a n* discharge from, release from, free from; *iem. van een belofte ~* let sbd. off his promise; *iem. van een verplichting ~* relieve sbd. from (absolve sbd. from) an obligation; *we zijn van hem ontslagen* we have got rid of him.; **ont′slag** (-slagen) *o* discharge, dismissal; resignation; release [from gaol]; *iem. zijn ~ geven* discharge (dismiss) sbd., F fire sbd.; *zijn ~ indienen (aanvragen)* tender one's resignation, send in (give in) one's papers; *zijn ~ krijgen* be dismissed, F be fired; *~ nemen* resign; **–briefje** (-s) *o* discharge certificate

ont′slapen (ontsliep, is ontslapen) *vi* pass away; *in de Heer ~ zijn* sleep in the Lord; **–e** (-n) *m-v de ~* the (dear) deceased, the (dear) departed

ont′sluieren[1] *vt* unveil[2]; *fig* disclose, reveal

ont′sluiten[1] I *vt* unlock; open[2]; II *vr zich ~* open; **–ting** (-en) *v* opening up [of new territory]

ont′smetten[1] *vt* disinfect; **ont′smetting** *v* disinfection; **–smiddel** (-en) *o* disinfectant

ont′snappen (ontsnapte, is ontsnapt) *vt* escape, make one's escape; *~ aan* escape from [sbd.]; give [sbd.] the slip; escape [sbd.'s vigilance]; *je kunt er niet aan ~* there is no escape (from it); **–ping** (-en) *v* escape; **ont′snappingsclausule** [-klɔuzy.lə] (-s) *v* let-out clause, contracting-out clause, escape clause; **–luik** (-en) *o* escape hatch

ont′spannen I *vt* unbend [a bow, the mind]; relax [the muscles]; release [a spring]; ease [the

---

[1] V.T. en V.D. van dit werkwoord volgens het model: **ont′bladeren**, V.T. **ont′bladerde**, V.D. **ont′bladerd** (**ge-** valt dus weg in het V.D.). Zie voor de vormen onder het grondwoord, in dit voorbeeld: *bladeren*. Bij sterke en onregelmatige werkwoorden wordt u verwezen naar de lijst achterin.

situation]; **II** *vr zich* ~ unbend, relax; **–er** (-s) *m*
(f o t o g r.) release; **ont'spanning** (-en) *v*
relaxation[2]; *fig* 1 (v e r m i n d e r d e s p a n -
n i n g) relief; [international] détente, easing (of
the political situation); 2 (u i t s p a n n i n g)
diversion, relaxation, recreation; *hij neemt nooit*
~ he never unbends; **ont'spanningslectuur** *v*
light reading, escape literature; **–lokaal**
(-kalen) *o* recreation hall; **–oord** (-en) *o*
[holiday &] resort
ont'sparing *v* $ dissaving, savings outflow
ont'spiegeld ⇦ anti-dazzle [front pane]
ont'spinnen[1] *vi er ontspon zich een belangrijke
discussie* this led to an interesting discussion
ont'sporen[1] *vi* run off the metals (rails), be
derailed, derail; **–ring** (-en) *v* derailment
ont'springen[1] *vi* rise [of a river]; zie ook:
dans
ont'spruiten[1] *vi* spring, sprout; [*fig*] ~ *uit* arise
from, spring from, proceed from
ont'staan I (ontstond, is ontstaan) *vt* come into
existence (into being), originate, start [of a
fire]; develop [of a crisis, fever &]; *doen* ~ give
rise to, cause, create; start [a fire]; ~ *uit* arise
from; **II** *o* origin
ont'steken[1] **I** *vt* kindle, light, ignite, blast off [a
rocket]; *iem. in toorn doen* ~ kindle sbd.'s wrath;
II *vi* become inflamed [of a wound]; *in toorn* ~
fly into a passion (rage); **ont'steking** (-en) *v*
1 kindling [of fire]; 🕯 ignition; blast-off [of a
rocket]; 2 (v. w o n d e n) inflammation;
–sschakelaar (-s) *m* ignition switch
ont'steld alarmed, frightened, dismayed
ont'stelen[1] *vt* steal from; *zij hebben het hem
ontstolen* they have stolen it from him
ont'stellen I (ontstelde, h. ontsteld) *vt* startle,
alarm, frighten, dismay, stun; **II** (ontstelde, is
ontsteld) *vi* be startled, become alarmed; **–d**
I *aj* shocking [news]; **II** *ad* terribly, awfully,
dreadfully, fearfully; **ont'steltenis** *v* consternation, alarm, dismay
ont'stemd ♪ out of tune; *fig* put out,
displeased; **ont'stemmen**[1] *vt* ♪ put out of
tune; *fig* put out, displease; **–ming** *v* displeasure, dissatisfaction, soreness
ont'stentenis *v bij* ~ *van* in default of, in the
absence of, failing...
ont'stichten[1] *vt* offend, give offence
ont'stoken inflamed [of a wound]
ont'stoppen[1] *vt* clear [a choked pipe &]
ont'takelen[1] *vt* ⚓ unrig, dismantle; **–ling** (-en)
v ⚓ unrigging, dismantling
ont'trekken[1] **I** *vt* withdraw (from *aan*); *aan het*

oog ~ hide; **II** *vr zich* ~ *aan* withdraw from;
shirk [a duty]; back out of [an obligation];
–king (-en) *v* withdrawal
ont'tronen[1] *vt* dethrone; **–ning** *v* dethronement
'**ontucht** *v* lewdness, prostitution; **on'tuchtig**
lewd
'**ontuig** *o* riff-raff
ont'vallen[1] *vi* drop (fall) from [one's hands];
zich geen woord laten ~ not drop a single word;
het is mij ~ it escaped me; *zijn kinderen ontvielen
hem* he lost his children
ont'vangbewijs (-wijzen) *o* receipt; **–dag** (-dagen)
m at-home (day); **ont'vangen**[1] **I** *vt* receive°, $ take
delivery of [the goods]; *de vijand werd warm* ~
the enemy was given a warm reception; **II** *va*
receive; *wij* ~ *vandaag niet* we are not at
home to-day
ont'vangenis *v* conception
ont'vanger (-s) *m* 1 recipient, $ consignee; 2
(a m b t e n a a r) tax-collector; 3 (o n t v a n g -
t o e s t e l) receiver; **–skantoor** (-toren) *o*
tax-collector's office; **ont'vangkamer** (-s) *v*
reception room; (s a l o n) drawing room,
parlour, salon; **ont'vangst** (-en) *v* receipt;
reception [of a person & R]; *de ~en van één dag*
$ the takings of one day; *de ~ berichten (beves-
tigen, erkennen) van...* acknowledge receipt of...;
de ~ weigeren van... $ refuse to take delivery
of...; ● *bij de ~ van... on receiving...*; *in ~
nemen* receive, $ take delivery of; *n a ~ van...* on
receipt of...; **ont'vangstation** [-sta.(t)ʃŏn] (-s)
o receiving-station; **ont'vangstbewijs** (-
wijzen) *o* receipt; **ont'vangtoestel** (-len) *o*
receiver, receiving set; **ont'vankelijk** receptive, susceptible; ~ *voor* accessible to, amenable
to; *zijn eis werd* ~ *verklaard* he was entitled to
proceed with his claim, his claim was
admitted; *zijn eis werd niet* ~ *verklaard* it was
decided that the action would not lie, his claim
was dismissed; **–heid** *v* receptivity,
susceptibility
ont'veinzen[1] *vt wij* ~ *het ons niet* we fully realize
it; *wij kunnen ons niet* ~ *dat...* we cannot disguise
from ourselves the fact that (the difficulty &
of...), we are fully alive to the fact that...
ont'vellen (ontvelde, h. ontveld) *vt* graze, **F**
bark [one's knee &]; **–ling** (-en) *v* abrasion,
excoriation
ont'vetten (ontvette, h. ontvet) *vt* remove the
fat (grease) from, degrease [gravy], scour
[wool]
ont'vlambaar inflammable; **–heid** *v* inflam-
mableness; **ont'vlammen**[1] *vi* inflame, kindle[2];

---

[1] V.T. en V.D. van dit werkwoord volgens het model: **ont'**bladeren, V.T. **ont'**bladerde, V.D. **ont'**bladerd (**ge-** valt
dus weg in het V.D.). Zie voor de vormen onder het grondwoord, in dit voorbeeld: *bladeren.* Bij sterke en onregelmatige werkwoorden wordt u verwezen naar de lijst achterin.

–ming *v* inflammation
ont'vlekken[1] *vt* remove stains from
⊙ **ont'vlieden**[1] *vi* fly from, flee from;
ont'vluchten[1] **I** *vi* fly, flee, escape, make
good one's escape; **II** *vt* fly (from), flee (from);
–ting (-en) *v* flight, escape
ont'voerder (-s) *m* abductor, kidnapper;
ont'voeren[1] *vt* carry off, abduct, kidnap;
–ring (-en) *v* abduction, kidnapping
ont'volken (ontvolkte, h. ontvolkt) *vt* depopu-
late; **–king** *v* depopulation
ont'voogden (ontvoogdde, h. ontvoogd) *vt*
emancipate; **–ding** *v* emancipation
ont'vouwen[1] *vt* & *vi* unfold[2]; **–wing** *v* unfolding[2]
ont'vreemden (ontvreemdde, h. ontvreemd) *vt*
steal; **–ding** *v* theft
ont'waarding *v* $ devaluation
ont'waken (ontwaakte, is ontwaakt) *vi* awake[2],
wake up[2], get awake; *uit zijn droom* ~ awake
from a dream; **–king** *v* awakening
ont'wapenen[1] *vt* & *vi* disarm; **–ning** *v*
1 disarming [of a soldier]; 2 disarmament
[movement]
ont'waren (ontwaarde, h. ontwaard) *vt*
perceive, descry
ont'warren (ontwarde, h. ontward) *vt* disentangle, unravel; **–ring** *v* disentanglement,
unravelling
ont'wassen[1] *vi* = *ontgroeien*
ont'wateren[1] *vt* drain, dewater
ont'weien (ontweide, h. ontweid) *vt* disem-
bowel
ont'wellen[1] *vi* spring from
ont'wennen[1] *vt* zie *afwennen*; **ont'wennings-
kuur** (-kuren) *v* treatment for curing alco-
holics [or drug addicts]
ont'werp (-en) *o* project, plan, (rough) draft,
design; (w e t s o n t w e r p) bill; **ont'werpen**[1]
vt draft, draw up, frame, design, style [a car],
project, plan [towns]; **–er** (-s) *m* draftsman [of
a document], [fashion] designer, framer,
planner, projector
ont'wijden *vt* desecrate, profane, defile; **–ding**
v desecration, profanation, defilement
on'twijfelbaar indubitable, unquestionable,
unquestioned, doubtless
ont'wijken[1] *vt* evade, dodge [a blow]; avoid,
shun [a man, a place]; fight shy of [sbd.]; *fig*
blink, evade, elude, fence with [a question],
shirk [the main point], side-step [a problem];
–d evasive; **ont'wijking** (-en) *v* evasion
ont'wikkelaar (-s) *m* (f o t o) developer;

ont'wikkeld (fully) developed; *fig* educated,
well-informed; **ont'wikkelen**[1] **I** *vt* develop;
II *vr zich* ~ develop[2] (into *tot*); **–ling** (-en) *v*
development; *algemene* ~ general education; *tot*
~ *brengen* develop; *tot* ~ *komen* develop;
ont'wikkelingsgebied (-en) *o* development
area; **–hulp** *v* development aid; **–land** (-en) *o*
developing country; **–leer** *v* theory of evolution; **–tijdperk** (-en) *o* period of development
ont'woekeren[1] *vt* ~ *aan* wrest from; *ontwoekerd
aan de baren* reclaimed from the sea, wrested
from the waves
ont'worstelen[1] *vt* wrest from
ont'wortelen (ontwortelde, h. ontworteld) *vt*
uproot
ont'wricht dislocated, out of joint; disrupted;
ont'wrichten (ontwrichtte, h. ontwricht) *vt*
dislocate[2], disjoint; disrupt [society; transport];
–ting (-en) *v* dislocation[2] [also of affairs];
disruption [of society; of postal services]
ont'wringen[1] *vt* wrest from, extort from
ont'zag *o* awe, respect, veneration; ~ *inboezemen*
inspire with awe, (over)awe; ~ *hebben voor*
stand in awe of; **–lijk** awful; enormous,
tremendous [quantity], vast [number]; **–lijkheid** *v* enormousness; **ontzag'wekkend**
awe-inspiring
ont'zegelen[1] *vt* unseal, break the seal of
ont'zeggen[1] **I** *vt* deny; *mijn benen ~ mij de dienst*
my legs fail me; *hij zag zich zijn eis ontzegd* his
suit was dismissed; *iem. zijn huis* ~ forbid sbd.
the house; *ik ontzeg u het recht om...* I deny to
you the right to...; *de toegang werd hem ontzegd* he
was denied admittance; **II** *vr zich iets* ~ deny
oneself sth.; **–ging** *v* denial; ~ *van het rijbewijs*
disqualification from driving, revoking of
sbd.'s driving licence
ont'zeilen[1] *vi* sail away from; *de klip van...* ~
steer clear of the rock of..., steer clear of...
ont'zenuwen (ontzenuwde, h. ontzenuwd) *vt* 1
enervate, unnerve; 2 *fig* refute [grounds,
arguments]; pick holes in [arguments]
1 ont'zet *aj* aghast, appalled; **2 ont'zet** *o* ⚔
relief [of a besieged town]; rescue [of a
person]; **ont'zetten**[1] *vt* 1 ⚔ relieve; rescue [by
the police]; 2 (a f z e t t e n) dismiss; 3 (m e t
o n t z e t t i n g v e r v u l l e n) appal; 4
(o n t w r i c h t e n, v e r b u i g e n) twist,
buckle [metal, a wheel], warp [wood]; *iem. uit
zijn ambt* ~ deprive sbd. of his office; *uit de
ouderlijke macht* ~ deprive of parental rights;
–d I *aj* appalling, dreadful, terrible; *(het is)* ~ *!*
it is awful!; **II** *ad* dreadfully, < awfully,

---

[1] V.T. en V.D. van dit werkwoord volgens het model: **ont'bladeren**, V.T. **ont'bladerde**, V.D. **ont'bladerd** (**ge-** valt
dus weg in het V.D.). Zie voor de vormen onder het grondwoord, in dit voorbeeld: *bladeren*. Bij sterke en onregelmatige werkwoorden wordt u verwezen naar de lijst achterin.

terribly; **ont'zetting** (-en) *v* 1 ✗ relief [of a town]; rescue [of a person]; 2 deprivation [of office], dismissal [of functionary]; 3 horror, dismay; **–sleger** (-s) *o* relieving army

ont'zield inanimate, lifeless

ont'zien[1] **I** *vt* respect, stand in awe of; spare [sbd.], consider (sbd.'s feelings); *hij moet ~ worden* he must be dealt with gently; *geen moeite ~ om...* spare no pains to...; *geen (on)kosten ~d* regardless of expense; **II** *vr zich ~* spare oneself; take care of oneself (of one's health); *zich niet ~ om...* not scruple to...; *hij ontzag zich nota bene niet om...* he had the conscience to [smoke my cigars &]

ont'zilting *v* desalinization

ont'zinken[1] *vi de moed ontzonk mij* my courage gave way

onuit'blusbaar inextinguishable, unquenchable

on'uitgegeven unpublished

on'uitgemaakt unsettled, not settled, open [question]

on'uitgesproken unspoken, unexpressed

onuit'puttelijk inexhaustible, unfailing; **–heid** *v* inexhaustibleness

onuit'roeibaar ineradicable

onuit'spreekbaar unpronounceable; **onuit'sprekelijk I** *aj* unspeakable, inexpressible, unutterable, ineffable [joy]; **II** *ad ~ gelukkig* ook: too happy for words, happy beyond words

onuit'staanbaar insufferable, intolerable, unbearable

onuit'voerbaar impracticable, impossible; **–heid** *v* impracticability

onuit'wisbaar indelible, ineffaceable; **–heid** *v* indelibility

'onvaderlands unpatriotic

on'vast, 'onvast unstable, unsteady [gait, character &]; unsettled, uncertain [state of things]; loose [soil]; light [sleep]; **–heid** *v* instability, unsteadiness &

on'vatbaar *~ voor* immune from [a disease]; insusceptible of [pity]; impervious [to argument], unreceptive [to new ideas]; **–heid** *v* immunity [from disease]; insusceptibility [of pity]

on'veilig unsafe, insecure; *~!* danger!; *~ maken* make unsafe, infest [the roads]; *~ sein* danger signal; *het sein staat op ~* the signal is at danger; **–heid** *v* unsafeness, insecurity

onver'anderbaar unchangeable, immutable; **onver'anderd** unchanged, unaltered; **onver'anderlijk** unchangeable, unalterable,

immutable [decision &]; unvarying, invariable [behaviour &]; immovable [feasts as Christmas &]; **–heid** *v* unchangeableness, immutability, invariableness

'onverantwoord 1 (v. h a n d e l i n g) unjustified, unwarranted; 2 (v. g e l d) not accounted for; **onverant'woordelijk** 1 not responsible, irresponsible; 2 unwarrantable, unjustifiable; **–heid** *v* 1 irresponsibility; 2 unwarrantableness, unjustifiableness

onver'beterlijk 1 incorrigible [child &], confirmed [drunkard]

onver'biddelijk relentless, unyielding, inexorable

'onverbindend, onver'bindend not binding

onver'bloemd, 'onverbloemd I *aj* undisguised, unvarnished, plain, frank; **II** *ad* [tell me] in plain terms, bluntly, point-blank, without mincing matters

'onverbogen *gram* undeclined

onver'brandbaar incombustible

onver'breekbaar, 'onverbreekbaar, onver'brekelijk, 'onverbrekelijk indissoluble, irrefrangible

onver'buigbaar, 'onverbuigbaar *gram* indeclinable

onver'dacht, 'onverdacht above suspicion

onver'dedigbaar, 'onverdedigbaar indefensible; **onver'dedigd** undefended

'onverdeelbaar, onver'deelbaar indivisible; **–heid** *v* indivisibility; **onver'deeld, 'onverdeeld** undivided, whole, entire; unqualified [praise, succes]

onver'diend, 'onverdiend I *aj* unearned [money]; undeserved [reproach], unmerited [praise]; **II** *ad* undeservedly; **onver'dienstelijk** *niet ~* not without merit

onver'draaglijk(heid) = *ondraaglijk(heid)*;

onver'draagzaam intolerant; **–heid** *v* intolerance

onver'droten, 'onverdroten I *aj* indefatigable, unwearying, unflagging [zeal]; sedulous [care]; **II** *ad* indefatigably; sedulously

onver'dund, 'onverdund undiluted, neat [drink]

onver'enigbaar not to be united; *onverenigbare begrippen* irreconcilable ideas; *~ met* incompatible with, inconsistent with; **–heid** *v* incompatibility, inconsistency

onver'flauwd, 'onverflauwd undiminished, unabated [energy], unrelaxing [diligence], unremitting [attention], unflagging [zeal]

onver'gankelijk imperishable, undying; **–heid**

---

[1] V.T. en V.D. van dit werkwoord volgens het model: **ont'**bladeren, V.T. **ont'**bladerde, V.D. **ont'**bladerd (**ge-** valt dus weg in het V.D.). Zie voor de vormen onder het grondwoord, in dit voorbeeld: *bladeren.* Bij sterke en onregelmatige werkwoorden wordt u verwezen naar de lijst achterin.

v imperishableness

onver'geeflijk, onver'gefelijk unpardonable, unforgivable, inexcusable; **–heid** *v* unpardonableness

onverge'lijkelijk I *aj* incomparable, matchless, peerless; **II** *ad* incomparably

onver'getelijk unforgettable

onver'hinderd, 'onverhinderd I *aj* unhindered, unimpeded; **II** *ad* without being hindered

onver'hoeds, 'onverhoeds I *aj* unexpected, sudden; *een ~e aanval* a surprise attack; **II** *ad* unawares, unexpectedly, suddenly; [attack] by surprise

onver'holen, 'onverholen I *aj* unconcealed [disgust], undisguised [contempt]; **II** *ad* frankly, openly, without mincing matters

onver'hoopt, 'onverhoopt unexpected, unlooked-for

'onverhuurd not let, unlet, untenanted

onver'kiesbaar ineligible; **–heid** *v* ineligibility; **onver'kies(e)lijk** undesirable

onver'klaarbaar inexplicable; **–heid** *v* inexplicableness

onver'kocht unsold; *mits ~* $ if unsold; **onver'koopbaar** unsal(e)able, unmarketable

'onverkort unabridged, uncurtailed

onver'kwikkelijk unpleasant, unpalatable, unsavoury [case &]

'onverlaat (-laten) *m* miscreant, vile wretch

onver'let, 'onverlet unhindered, unimpeded

onver'meld unmentioned, unrecorded; *(niet) ~ blijven* (not) go unrecorded

onver'mengd, 'onvermengd unmixed, unalloyed, unqualified, pure

onver'mijdelijk inevitable, unavoidable; *het ~e* the inevitable; **–heid** *v* unavoidableness, inevitability

onver'minderd, 'onverminderd I *aj* undiminished, unabated; **II** *prep* without prejudice to

'onvermoed unsuspected, unthought-of

onver'moeibaar, 'onvermoeibaar indefatigable; unwearying; **–heid** *v* indefatigability; **onver'moeid, 'onvermoeid** unwearied, untired, tireless; **–heid** *v* tirelessness

'onvermogen *o* 1 impotence, inability; 2 impecuniosity; 3 indigence; *~ om te betalen* insolvency; *in staat van ~* insolvent; **–d** 1 (m a c h t e l o o s) unable; 2 (g e l d e l o o s) impecunious; 3 (b e h o e f t i g) indigent

onver'murwbaar unrelenting, inexorable

onver'nielbaar indestructible

onver'poosd, 'onverpoosd I *aj* uninterrupted, unremitting; **II** *ad* uninterruptedly, unceasingly

'onverricht undone, unperformed; *~er zake*

without having attained one's end, [return] without succes

'onversaagd, onver'saagd undaunted, intrepid; **–heid** *v* undauntedness, intrepidity

onver'schillig I *aj* indifferent, careless [person]; [air, tone &] of indifference; *~ door welk middel* no matter by what means; *~ of we... dan wel...* whether... or...; *~ voor...* indifferent to...; *~ wat (wie)* no matter what (who); *het is mij ~* it is all the same (all one) to me; **II** *ad* indifferently, carelessly, insouciantly; **–heid** *v* indifference, insouciance

onver'schrokken(heid) = *onversaagd(heid)*

'onverslapt unflagging; zie ook: *onverflauwd*

onver'slijtbaar, 'onverslijtbaar indestructible, everlasting

'onversneden undiluted, unqualified [wine &]

onver'staanbaar unintelligible; **–heid** *v* unintelligibleness, unintelligibility

'onverstand *o* unwisdom; **onver'standig** unwise; *het ~e ervan* the unwisdom of it

onver'stoorbaar imperturbable; **–heid** *v* imperturbability, phlegm; **onver'stoord, 'onverstoord** undisturbed; *fig* unperturbed

onver'taalbaar untranslatable

onver'teerbaar, 'onverteerbaar indigestible[2]; **'onverteerd** undigested[2]

onver'togen unseemly

onver'vaard, 'onvervaard I *aj* fearless, undaunted; **II** *ad* fearlessly, undauntedly

onver'valst unadulterated, unalloyed, genuine, unsophisticated; *een ~e schurk* an unmitigated blackguard

onver'vangbaar irreplaceable

onver'vreemdbaar inalienable [goods, property], indefeasible [rights]; **–heid** *v* inalienability, indefeasibility

onver'vulbaar unfulfillable; **'onvervuld** unoccupied [place], unaccomplished [wishes], unperformed, unfulfilled [promises]

onver'wacht unexpected, unlooked for; **–s** unexpectedly, unawares

'onverwarmd unheated [room], unwarmed

onver'wijld, 'onverwijld immediate, without delay

onver'woestbaar indestructible; **–heid** *v* indestructibility

onver'zadelijk insatiable; **–heid** *v* insatiability; **onver'zadigbaar** insatiable; **onver'zadigd, 'onverzadigd** 1 unsatiated, unsatisfied; 2 § unsaturated [fatty acid]

'onverzegeld unsealed

onver'zettelijk immovable[2]; *fig* unyielding, inflexible; **–heid** *v* inflexibility

onver'zoenlijk irreconcilable, implacable; **–heid** *v* irreconcilability, implacability

'onverzorgd, onver'zorgd 1 (n i e t o p g e-

p a s t) not attended to; 2 (n i e t g e s o i g-
n e e r d) uncared-for, unkempt [gardens];
untidy [nails]; slovenly [style]; 3 (z o n d e r
m i d d e l e n) unprovided for

'onverzwakt, onver'zwakt not weakened;
unimpaired; zie ook: *onverflauwd*

on'vindbaar not to be found; *het bleek ~* it
could not be found

on'voegzaam indecent, unseemly; –heid *v*
indecency, unseemliness

onvol'daan unsatisfied, dissatisfied [people];
unpaid, unsettled [bills]; –heid *v* dissatisfaction

onvol'doend insufficient; –e (-s en -n) *v* ⌖
insufficient mark; *hij heeft vier ~s, ~n* he is
insufficient in four branches

onvol'dragen immature, unripe

onvol'eind(igd) unfinished, uncompleted

onvol'komen imperfect, incomplete; –heid
(-heden) *v* imperfection, incompleteness

onvol'ledig incomplete, defective; –heid *v*
incompleteness, defectiveness

onvol'maakt imperfect, defective; –heid
(-heden) *v* imperfection, deficiency

onvol'prezen, 'onvolprezen unsurpassed,
beyond praise

onvol'tallig incomplete

onvol'tooid 1 unfinished, incomplete; 2 *gram*
imperfect [tense]

onvol'voerd unperformed, unfulfilled

onvol'waardig [physically] unfit, [mentally]
deficient; *~e arbeidskrachten* partially disabled
workers

onvol'wassen half-grown, not full-grown,
immature [behaviour]

on'voorbereid unprepared, off-hand

onvoor'delig unprofitable; –heid *v* unprofit-
ableness

onvoor'spelbaar unpredictable

onvoor'spoedig unsuccessful

onvoor'stelbaar, 'onvoorstelbaar I *aj* inconceivable, unimaginable [distances]; II *ad*
inconceivably [remote from], incredibly [low
prices]

onvoor'waardelijk unconditional; implicit;
onvoorwaardelijke overgave unconditional
surrender

onvoor'zichtig imprudent; –heid (-heden) *v*
imprudence

onvoor'zien unforeseen, unexpected; –baar
unforeseeable; –s unexpectedly, unawares

'onvrede *m* & *v* (t w i s t) discord, dissension;
(o n b e h a g e n) discontent; *in ~ leven met* be at
variance (on bad terms) with

on'vriendelijk unkind; –heid (-heden) *v*
unkindness; onvriend'schappelijk I *aj*
unfriendly; II *ad* in an unfriendly way

on'vrij not free; *het is hier erg ~* there is no

privacy here; –heid (-heden) *v* want of
freedom, constraint, lack of privacy;
onvrij'willig involuntary, unwilling

on'vruchtbaar infertile [land]; unfruitful[2],
sterile[2], barren[2]; –heid *v* infertility, unfruitful-
ness, sterility, barrenness

on'waar untrue, not true, false;
onwaa'rachtig *v* insincere, untruthfull; –heid
(-heden) *v* insincerity

'onwaarde *v* invalidity, nullity; *van ~ verklaren*
declare null and void; *van ~ zijn* be null and
void; on'waardig I *aj* unworthy; undignified
[spectacle]; II *ad* unworthily; –heid *v* unwor-
thiness

on'waarheid (-heden) *v* untruth, falsehood, lie

onwaar'schijnlijk improbable, unlikely; –heid
(-heden) *v* improbability, unlikeliness

on'wankelbaar unshakable, unwavering
[decision], unswerving [resolution]; –heid *v*
unshakableness

'onwe(d)er (-weren en -weders) *o* thunderstorm, storm; 'onweerachtig thundery

onweer'legbaar irrefutable, unanswerable,
irrefragable; –heid *v* irrefutableness

'onweersbui (-en) *v* thunderstorm; –lucht
(-en) *v* thundery sky

onweer'staanbaar irresistible; –heid *v* irresist-
ibility

'onweerswolk (-en) *v* thunder-cloud, storm-
cloud

on'wel indisposed, unwell, F off-colour

on'welkom unwelcome

onwel'levend discourteous, impolite; –heid
(-heden) *v* discourteousness, impoliteness

onwel'luidend unharmonious; –heid *v* want
of harmony

onwel'riekend unpleasant-smelling, mal-
odorous

onwel'voeglijk indecent, improper; –heid
(-heden) *v* indecency

onwel'willend unkind, uncooperativ; –heid
(-heden) *v* unkindness, uncooperativeness

on'wennig *zich ~ voelen* feel strange, feel
awkward

'onweren (onweerde, h. geonweerd) *vi het zal ~*
there will be a thunderstorm

on'werkelijk unreal; –heid *v* unreality

on'werkzaam inactive; –heid *v* inaction,
inactivity

on'wetend ignorant; *iem. volkomen ~ laten van*
leave sbd. in complete ignorance of; –heid *v*
ignorance

onweten'schappelijk unscientific, unscholarly

on'wettelijk illegal; on'wettig unlawful,
illegal; (v. k i n d) illegitimate; –heid (-heden)
v unlawfulness, illegality, illegitimacy

on'wezenlijk unreal; –heid *v* unreality

on'wijs unwise, foolish; **–heid** (-heden) *v* unwisdom, folly

'onwil *m* unwillingness

onwille'keurig I *aj* involuntary; **II** *ad* involuntarily; *ik moest ~ lachen* I could not help laughing

on'willig I *aj* unwilling, reluctant; *~e manslag* homicide by misadventure; *met ~e honden is het kwaad hazen vangen* one man may lead a horse to water, but fifty cannot make him drink; **II** *ad* unwillingly, with a bad grace; **–heid** *v* unwillingness, reluctance

on'wrikbaar immovable², *fig* unshakable [conviction], unflinching; **–heid** *v* immovability², unshakableness &

'onyx ['o.nɪks] (-en) *o* & *m* onyx

on'zacht, **'onzacht I** *aj* ungentle, rude, rough; **II** *ad* rudely

on'zakelijk unbusinesslike

on'zalig unholy, evil, unhappy

on'zedelijk immoral; **–heid** (-heden) *v* immorality; **on'zedig** immodest; **–heid** *v* immodesty

onzee'waardig ⚓ unseaworthy

on'zegbaar = *onuitsprekelijk*

on'zeker uncertain; insecure [ice, foundation]; unsafe [ice, people]; precarious [income, living]; unsteady [hand, voice, steps]; *het is nog ~* it is still uncertain; *het ~e* what is uncertain; *iem. in het ~e laten* leave sbd. in uncertainty; *in het ~e omtrent iets verkeren (zijn)* be uncertain (in the dark) as to...; **–heid** (-heden) *v* uncertainty; insecurity; *in ~ verkeren* be in uncertainty

onzelf'standig dependent on others; **–heid** *v* dependency on others

onzelf'zuchtig unselfish, self-forgetful; **–heid** *v* unselfishness

Onze-Lieve-'Heer *m* our Lord, the Lord; **onze-lieve-'heersbeestje** (-s) *o* ladybird; **Onze-Lieve-'Vrouw** *v* Our Lady; **onze-lieve-vrouwe'bedstro** *o* woodruff; **Onze-Lieve-'Vrouwekerk** (-en) *v* de ~ Our Lady's Church; **'onzent** *te(n)* ~ at our house, at our place; *~halve* for our sake(s); *~wege* as for us; *van ~wege* on our behalf, in our names; *om ~wil(le)* for our sake(s); **'onzerzijds** on our part, on our behalf; **onze'vader** (-s) *o* Our Father, Lord's Prayer

on'zichtbaar I *aj* invisible; *onzichtbare inkt* sympathetic ink; **II** *ad* invisibly; *~ stoppen* repair by invisible mending; **–heid** *v* invisibility; **on'zienlijk** invisible

on'zijdig 1 neutral; 2 *gram* neuter; *zich ~ houden* remain neutral; **–heid** *v* neutrality

'onzin *m* nonsense, rubbish; *wat een ~!* the very idea!, bosh!, fiddlesticks!, **S** guff!, what rot!; *~*

uitkramen (verkopen) talk (stuff and) nonsense

on'zindelijk uncleanly, dirty; **–heid** (-heden) *v* uncleanliness, dirtiness

on'zinnig nonsensical, absurd, senseless, piffling; **–heid** (-heden) *v* absurdity, nonsense, senselessness

on'zuiver impure; unjust [scales], ♪ out of tune, false; (b r u t o) gross [profit &]; *~ in de leer* unsound in the faith, heterodox; **–heid** (-heden) *v* impurity

ooft *o* fruit; **–boom** (-bomen) *m* fruit-tree

oog (ogen) *o* 1 eye°; 2 (o p d o b b e l s t e e n &) point, spot; *goede (slechte) ogen* [have] good (bad) eyesight; *geheel ~ zijn* be all eyes; *hij kon er zijn ogen niet afhouden* he could not keep his eyes off it; *een ~ dichtdoen zie oogje*; *geen ~ dichtdoen* not sleep a wink [all night]; *het ~ laten gaan over* cast one's eye over; *hij kon zijn ogen niet geloven* he could not believe his eyes; *een ~ op haar hebben* zie *oogje*; *geen ~ voor iets hebben* have no eye for sth.; *een open ~ hebben voor* be (fully) alive to [the requirements of...]; *heb je geen ogen in je hoofd?* have you no eyes (in your head)?; *het ~ wil ook wat hebben* the eye has its claims too; *hij heeft zijn ogen niet in zijn zak* he has all his eyes about him; *het ~ op iets houden* keep an eye on sth.; *ik kan er geen ~ op houden* I can't keep track of them; *een ~ in het zeil houden* keep an eye upon [him, them], keep one's weather-eye open; *zijn ogen de kost geven* look about one; *iem. de ogen openen* open sbd.'s eyes; *grote ogen opzetten* open one's eyes wide, stare; *het ~ slaan op...* cast a look (a glance) at...; *de ogen sluiten voor...* shut one's eyes to...; *een ~ toedoen* zie *oogje*; *geen ~ toedoen* not sleep a wink [all night]; *het ~ treffen* meet the eye; *iem. de ogen uitsteken* zie *uitsteken*; *zijn ~ erop laten vallen* lay eyes on it; cast a glance at it; *mijn ~ viel erop* it caught my eye; ● *d o o r het ~ van een naald kruipen* have a narrow escape; *iets i n het ~ houden* keep an eye upon sth.; *fig* not lose sight of sth.; *iem. in het ~ houden* keep an eye on sbd.'s movements; *iets (iem.) in het ~ krijgen* catch sight of sth. (sbd.), spot sth. (sbd.); *in het ~ lopen (vallen)* strike the eye; *in het ~ lopend (vallend)* conspicuous, striking, obvious; *in het ~ springen* zie *springen*; *in mijn ogen, in mijn ~* in my eyes; *in zijn eigen ogen* in his own conceit; *m e t de ogen volgen* follow with one's eyes; *ik zag het met mijn eigen ogen* I saw it with my own eyes; *met open ogen* with one's eyes open; *een man met een open ~ voor onze noden* a man (fully) alive to our needs; *het met schele (lede) ogen aanzien* view it with a jealous eye, with regret; *met het ~ op...* 1 (i e t s t o e k o m s t i g s) with a view to..., with an eye to...; 2 in view of...; *iem. n a a r d e ogen zien* read sbd.'s wishes; *zij behoeven niemand* *naar de ogen te zien* they are not dependent upon anybody; they can hold up their heads with the best; ~ *o m* ~, *tand om tand* an eye for an eye, a tooth for a tooth; *o n d e r vier ogen* in private, privately; *een gesprek onder vier ogen* a private talk; *iem. iets onder het* ~ *brengen* point out sth. to sbd., remonstrate with sbd. on sth.; *iem. onder de ogen komen* come under sbd.'s eye, under sbd.'s notice, face sbd.; *kom me niet meer onder de ogen* let me never set eyes on you again; *iets onder de ogen krijgen* set eyes upon sth.; *de dood onder de ogen zien* look death in the face; *de feiten (het gevaar) onder de ogen zien* face the facts (the danger); *de mogelijkheid onder het* ~ *zien* envisage the possibility; *o p het* ~ *is het...* when looked at, outwardly, on the face of it; *iets op het* ~ *hebben* have sth. in view (mind); *iem. op het* ~ *hebben* have one's eye on sbd. [as a fit candidate]; have sbd. in mind [when making an allusion]; (*ga*) *u i t mijn ogen!* out of my sight!; *kijk uit je ogen!* look where you are going!; *te lui om uit zijn ogen te kijken* too lazy to open his eyes; (*goed*) *uit zijn ogen kijken (zien)* use one's eyes, have all one's eyes about one; *uit het* ~, *uit het hart* out of sight, out of mind; *iets (iem.) uit het* ~ *verliezen* lose sight of sth. (sbd.); lose track of; *het is alles v o o r het* ~ for show; *God voor ogen houden* keep God in view; *iets voor ogen houden* bear sth. in mind; *met dat doel voor ogen* with that object in view, with this in view; *met de dood voor ogen* in the face of certain death, with death staring [him] in the face; *geen hand voor ogen zien* not see one's hand before one's face; *voor het* ~ *van de wereld* for the world; *het staat mij nog voor ogen* I have a vivid recollection of it; *het* ~ *van de meester maakt het paard vet* the eye of the master makes the cattle thrive; zie ook *naald;* **–appel** (-s) *m* apple of the eye², eyeball; **–arts** (-en) *m* oculist, ophthalmologist, eye specialist; **–badje** (-s) *o* eye-bath; **–bal, –bol** (-len) *m* eye-ball; **–druppelbuisje** (-s) *o* eye-dropper; **–druppels** *mv* eye-drops; **–getuige** (-ɴ) *m-v* eye-witness; **–getuigenverslag** *o* eye-witness's account; *sp* running commentary; **–haar** (-haren) *o* eyelash; **–heelkunde** *v* ophthalmology; **–hoek** (-en) *m* corner of the eye; **–holte** (-ɴ en -s) *v* orbit, socket of the eye, eye-socket; **–hoogte** *v op* ~ at eye-level; **–je** (-s) *o* (little) eye, eyelet; *~s geven* make eyes at; *een* ~ *hebben op* have an eye to [business], have designs on [a girl]; *een* ~ *houden op* keep an eye on; *een* ~ *toedoen (dichtdoen)* turn a blind eye (on *voor*), wink at; **–kas** (-sen) *v* = *oogholte;* **–kleppen** *mv* blinkers; **–lap** (-pen) *m* eye-patch; **–lid** (-leden) *o* eyelid; **–lijder** (-s) *m* eye-patient; **oog'luikend** ~ *toelaten* connive at; **'oogluiking** *v* connivance; **–merk** (-en) *o*

object in view, aim, intention, purpose; *met het* ~ *om...* with a view to ...ing; 🔃 with intent to...; **–ontsteking** (-en) *v* inflammation of the eye, ophthalmia; **–opslag** *m* glance, look; *met één* ~, *bij de eerste* ~ at a glance, at the first glance; **–punt** (-en) *o* point of view, viewpoint; *uit een* ~ *van...* from the point of view of...; *uit dat* ~ *beschouwd* viewed from that angle; **–schaduw** *v* eyeshadow; **–spiegel** (-s) *m* ophthalmoscope, fundoscope; **–spier** (-en) *v* muscle of the eye

oogst (-en) *m* harvest², crop(s); **'oogsten** (oogstte, h. geoogst) *vt* reap², gather, harvest; **'oogstfeest** (-en) *o* harvest home; **–lied** (-eren) *o* harvest-song; **–maand** *v* harvest month = August; **–machine** [-ma.ʃi.nə] (-s) *v* harvester, combine; **–tijd** (-en) *m* reaping-time, harvest time

'oogtand (-en) *m* eye-tooth; **oogver'blindend** dazzling; **'oogvlies** (-vliezen) *o* tunic (coat) of the eye; **–water** (-s) *o* eye-wash; **–wenk** (-en) *m* wink; *in een* ~ in no time, F in a jiffy, before one can say Jack Robinson; **–wit** *o* white of the eye, sclera; **–zalf** (-zalven) *v* eye-salve; **–zenuw** (-en) *v* optic nerve; **–ziekte** (-n en -s) *v* disease of the eyes, eyetrouble

ooi (-en) *v* ewe

'ooievaar (-s en -varen) *m* stork; **–sbek** (-ken) *m* 1 stork's bill; 2 🌿 crane's-bill

'ooilam (-meren) *o* ewe-lamb

ooit ever; *heb je* ~ *(van je leven)* did you ever?, well I never!

ook also, too, likewise, as well; *je bent me* ~ *een groentje!* you are a green one, you are!; *jij bent* ~ *een leukerd (mooie)!* you are a nice one!; *zij is* ~ *zo jong niet meer* she is none so young either; *en het gebeurde (dan)* ~ and so it happened; *het gebeurde (dan)* ~ *niet* nor dit it happen; *hij kon het dan* ~ *niet vinden* nor could he find it, as was to be expected; *ik lees dan* ~ *geen moderne romans* that's why I don't read modern novels; *maar waarom lees je dan* ~ *geen moderne romans?* but then why don't you read modern novels?; *Was het dan* ~ *te verwonderen dat...?* Now was it to be wondered at that...?; *ik houd veel van roeien en hij* ~ I am fond of boating and so is he; *ik houd niet van roken en hij (zijn broer)* ~ *niet* I do not like smoking, neither (no more) does he, nor does his brother either; *wat zei hij* ~ *weer?* what did he say?; *hoe heet hij* ~ *weer?* what's his name again?; *zijn er* ~ *appels?* are there any apples?; *al is het* ~ *nog zo lelijk* though it be ever so ugly; *kunt u mij* ~ *zeggen waar...?* can (could) you tell me where...?; zie ook: *waar, wat, wie* &

oom (-s) *m* uncle; *bij ome Jan* **S** at my uncle's, up the spout; *hoge ome* zie *hoog* **II** (*een hoge*); **–zegger** (-s) *m* nephew; **–zegster** (-s) *v* niece

oor (-oren) *o* ear [ook = handle]; dog's ear [in book]; *het gaat het ene ~ in en het andere uit* it goes in at one ear and out at the other; *geheel ~ zijn* be all ears; *iem. de oren van het hoofd eten* eat sbd. out of house and home; *wel oren naar iets hebben* lend a willing ear to sth.; *ik heb er wel oren naar* I rather like the idea, I don't decline the invitation &; *hij had er geen oren naar* he would not hear of it; *geen ~ hebben voor muziek* have no ear for music; *leen mij het ~* lend me your ears; *het ~ lenen aan* give ear to, lend (an) ear to; *zijn ~ te luisteren leggen* put one's ear to the ground; *zijn oren sluiten voor* turn a deaf ear to; *de oren spitsen* prick (up) one's ears²; *fig* cock one's ears; *een open ~ vinden* find a ready ear; *iem. de oren wassen* rebuke sbd.; • *iem. over iets a a n de oren malen* (*zaniken, zeuren*) din sth. into sbd.'s ears; *hem aan zijn oren trekken* pull his ears; *m e t een half ~ luisteren* listen with half an ear; *iem. o m zijn* (*de*) *oren geven* box sbd.'s ears; *om zijn oren krijgen* have one's ears boxed; *met de hoed o p één ~* his hat cocked on one side; *hij ligt nog op één ~* he is still in bed; *hij is op een ~ na gevild* it is almost finished, *het is mij t e r ore gekomen* it has come to (reached) my ear; *t o t over de oren in de schulden* up to his ears in debt; *tot over de oren blozend* blushing up to the ears; *tot over de oren verliefd* over head and ears in love; *ik zit tot over de oren in het werk* up to the eyes; *wie oren heeft om te horen, die hore* **B** he that hath ears to hear let him hear; **–arts** (-en) *m* ear specialist, aurist, ear-doctor

'oorbaar decent, proper; *het ~ achten om...* see (think) fit to...

'oorbel (-len) *v* earring, ear-drop

oord (-en) *o* place, region, [holiday] resort

'oordeel (-delen) *o* 1 ⚓ judgment, sentence, verdict; 2 (m e n i n g) judgment, opinion; *het laatste ~* the last judgment, the day of judgment; *~ des onderscheids* discernment, discrimination; *een leven als een ~* a clamour (noise) fit to wake the dead, a pandemonium; *zijn ~ opschorten* reserve (suspend) one's judgment; *zijn ~ uitspreken* give one's judgment, pass judgment; *een ~ vellen over* pass judgment on; • *dat laat ik a a n uw ~ over* I leave that to your judgment; *n a a r* (*volgens*) *mijn ~* in my opinion (judgment); *v a n ~ zijn dat...* be of opinion that..., hold that...; *v o l g e n s het ~ der kenners* according to the best opinion;

oordeel'kundig judicious; **'oordeelvelling** (-en) *v* judgment; **'oordelen** (oordeelde, h. geoordeeld) *vi* 1 judge; 2 think, deem [it necessary &]; *te ~ n a a r...* judging from (by); *~ o v e r* judge of; *oordeelt niet, opdat ge niet geoordeeld wordt* **B** judge not that ye be not judged

'oorhanger (-s) *m* ear-pendant, ear-drop; **–heelkunde** *v* otology; **–ijzer** (-s) *o* (gilt, gold, silver) casque, helmet [under a lace cap]; **–klep** (-pen) *v* ear-flap; **–knopje** (-s) *o* ear-drop

'oorkonde (-n) *v* charter, deed, document, instrument [of ratification]; **–nleer** *v* diplomatics

'oorkussen (-s) *o* pillow; zie ook: *ledigheid*

'oorlam (-men) *o* ⚓ allowance of gin, dram

'oorlel (-len) *v* lobe of the ear, earlobe; **–lijder** (-s) *m* ear patient

'oorlog (-logen) *m* war, [naval, aerial, gas &] warfare; *de koude ~* the cold war; *er is ~* there is a war on; *de ~ aandoen* make (declare) war on; *de ~ verklaren* declare war (up)on; *~ voeren* carry on war, make (wage) war; *~ voeren tegen* make (wage) war against (on); • *i n de ~* in war; *in ~ zijn met* be at war with; *t e n ~ trekken* go to war; **'oorlogsbodem** (-s) *m = oorlogsschip*; **–gedenkteken** (-s) *o* war memorial; **–graf** (-graven) *o* war grave; **–haven** (-s) *v* naval port; **–inspanning** (-en) *v* war effort; **–invalide** (-n) *m-v* disabled ex-soldier, war cripple; **–kerkhof** (-hoven) *o* war cemetery; **–kreet** (-kreten) *m* war cry, war whoop; **–lening** (-en) *v* war loan; **–materiaal** *o* war material; **–misdaad** (-daden) *v* war crime; **–misdadiger** (-s) *m* war criminal; **–pad** *o* war path; **–risico** [-ri.zi.ko.] ('s) *o* war risk(s); **–schade** *v* war damage; **–schatting** *v* war contribution; **–schip** (-schepen) *o* man-of-war, war-ship, war-vessel; **–slachtoffer** (-s) *m* war victim; **–sterkte** *v* war strength; **–tijd** *m* time of war, wartime; **–toestand** *m* state of war; **–toneel** (-nelen) *o* theatre (seat) of war; **–tuig** *o = oorlogsmateriaal*; **–verklaring** (-en) *v* declaration of war; **–vloot** (-vloten) *v* navy, (war) fleet; **–wapen** (-s) *o* weapon of war; **–winst** (-en) *v* war profit; *~ maken* profiteer;

oorlogs'zuchtig eager for war, warlike, bellicose; *een ~e geest* a bellicose spirit; **'oorlogvoerend** *aj* belligerent, waging war, at war; *de ~en* the belligerents; **–voering** *v* conduct (prosecution) of the war [against...]; [modern, economic, naval &] warfare

'oormerk (-en) *o* earmark; **'oormerken** (oormerkte, h. geoormerkt) *vt* earmark;

'oorontsteking (-en) *v* inflammation of the ear, otitis; **–pijn** (-en) *v* ear-ache; **–ring** (-en) *m* ear-ring; **–schelp** (-en) *v* auricle; **–sieraad** (-raden) *o* ear-trinket, ear-jewel; **–smeer** *o* earwax, cerumen; **–spiegel** (-s) *m* otoscope

'oorsprong (-en) *m* origin, fountain-head, source; *zijn ~ vinden in...* have its origin in..., originate in...; **oor'spronkelijk I** *aj* original [works, remarks, people]; **II** *o het ~e* the original; *Don Quichotte in het ~e* Don Quixote in the original; **–heid** *v* originality

'oorsuizing (-en) *v* ringing (singing) in the ears

'oortje (-s) *v* ⌷ farthing; *het is geen ~ waard* it is not worth a fig (a button); *hij ziet er uit of hij zijn laatste ~ versnoept heeft* he looks blue (dejected)

'ooruil (-en) *m* eared owl; **–veeg** (-vegen) *v* box on the ear; **oorver'dovend, 'oorverdovend** deafening, ear-splitting; **'oorvijg** (-en) *v* = *oorveeg*; **–worm, –wurm** (-en) *m* earwig; *een gezicht als een ~ zetten* look glum

'oorzaak (-zaken) *v* cause [and effect], origin [of the fire]; *kleine oorzaken hebben grote gevolgen* little strokes fell great oaks; *ter oorzake van* on account of; **oor'zakelijk** causal; *~ verband* causality, causal relation

oost east; *~, west, thuis best* east, west, home's best, home is home be it (n)ever so homely; **Oost** *v de ~* the East; **'oostelijk** eastern, easterly; *~ van Amsterdam* (to the) east of A; **'oosten** *o* east; *het Oosten* the East, the Orient; *het Nabije Oosten* the Near East; *het Verre Oosten* the Far East; *ten ~ van* (to the) east of; **'Oostenrijk** *o* Austria.; **–er** (-s) *m* Austrian; **–s** *aj* Austrian; *een ~e* an Austrian woman; **oosten'wind** (-en) *m* east wind; **ooster'lengte** *v* east longitude; **'oosterling** (-en) *m* Oriental, Eastern, native of the East; *vreemde ~en* ⌷ foreign Asiatics; **'oosters** *aj* Eastern, Oriental; **'Oosterschelde** *v* East Scheldt; **Oost-Eu'ropa** *o* Eastern Europe; **Oosteuro'pees** Eastern European; **Oost-'Friesland** *o* East Friesland; **'Oostgoten** *mv* Ostrogoths; **Oost'gotisch** Ostrogothic; **Oost-'Indië** *o* the East Indies; **Oost'indisch** East-Indian; *de ~e Compagnie* the East India Company; *~e kers* ⚘ nasturtium; zie ook: *doof, inkt;* **'oostkust** (-en) *v* east coast; **–moesson** (-s) *m* north-east monsoon; **'Oostromeins** Eastern; *het ~e rijk* the Eastern (the Lower) Empire; **Oost-'Vlaanderen** *o* East Flanders; **'oostwaarts I** *aj* eastward; **II** *ad* eastward(s); **Oost'zee** *v de ~* the Baltic; **'oostzij(de)** *v* east side

'ootje *iem. in het ~ nemen* make fun of sbd., chaff sbd.

'ootmoed *m* meekness, humility; **oot'moedig** meek, humble; **–heid** *v* meekness, humility

op I *prep* on, upon, at, in; *~ het dak (de tafel &)* on the roof (the table &); *~ het dak klimmen* climb upon the roof; *~ het dak springen* jump on to the roof; *~ een eiland* in an island; *de*

bloemen ~ haar hoed the flowers in her hat; *~ Java* in Java; *~ zijn kamer* in his room; *~ pantoffels* in slippers; *~ school* at school, zie ook: *school;* *~ straat* in the street, zie ook: *straat;* *~ de wereld* in the world; *~ zee* at sea, zie ook: *zee;* *~ zijn Engels* 1 in (after) the English fashion; 2 in English; *~ zijn hoogst* at (the) most; *een antwoord ~ een brief* a reply to a letter; *brief ~ brief* letter after letter; *~ een avond* one evening; *twee keer ~ één avond* twice in one evening; *~ zekere dag* one day; *later ~ de dag* later in the day; *~ dit uur* at this hour; *~ mijn horloge* by my watch [it is 6 o'clock]; *~ de kop af* exactly; *één inwoner ~ de vijf* one inhabitant in every five [owns a bicycle]; *één inwoner ~ de vierkante mijl* one inhabitant to the square mile; **II** *ad* up; *~!* up!; *de trap ~* up the stairs; *mijn geduld is ~* my patience is at an end; *zijn geld is ~* his money is spent (all gone); *die jas is ~* that coat is worn (out); *onze suiker is ~* we are out of sugar; *de wijn is ~* the wine is out; *~ is ~!* gone is gone; *hij heeft twee borrels ~* he has had two drinks; *de zon was ~* the sun had risen (was up); *het is ~* there is nothing left, it has all been eaten; *hij is ~* 1 he is out of bed; he is up; 2 he is quite knocked up, done up, spent, finished; *hij is weer ~ (na zijn ziekte)* he is about again; *zijn de zenuwen zijn* have the jitters; *vraag maar ~!* ask away! *kom ~!* come on!; *~ en af, ~ en neer* up and down

'opa ('s) *m* grandfather, **F** grandad

o'paal (opalen) *m* & *o* opal; **–achtig** opaline

'opbakken[1] *vt* bake again, fry again

'opbaren (baarde 'op, h. 'opgebaard) *vt* place upon a bier; *opgebaard liggen* lie in state

'opbellen[1] *vt* ☎ ring [sbd.] up, **F** give sbd. a ring; (a u t o m a t i s c h) dial

'opbergen[1] *vt* put away, pack up, stow away, store [furniture]; **'opbergmap** (-pen) *v* file, folder

'opbeuren[1] *vt* lift up; *fig* cheer (up), comfort; **–ring** *v* lifting up; *fig* comfort

'opbiechten[1] *vt* confess; *eerlijk ~* make a clean breast of it

'opbieden[1] *vi* make a higher bid; *tegen elkaar ~* try to outbid each other

'opbinden[1] *vt* tie (bind) up

op'blaasbaar inflatable [dinghy]; **'opblazen**[1] *vt* 1 blow up, inflate, insufflate, puff up; 2 blow up [a bridge &]; 3 *fig* magnify, exaggerate [an incident]

'opblijven[1] *vi* sit up, stop up, stay up

'opbloei *m* revival [of interest &]; **'opbloeien**

---

[1] V.T. en V.D. van dit werkwoord volgens het model: 'opbellen, V.T. belde 'op, V.D. 'opgebeld. Zie voor de vormen onder het grondwoord, in dit voorbeeld: *bellen*. Bij sterke en onregelmatige werkwoorden wordt u verwezen naar de lijst achterin.

(bloeide 'op, is 'opgebloeid) *vi* revive
'**opbod** *o bij* ~ *verkopen* sell by auction
'**opbollen I** (bolde op, is opgebold) *vi* bulge; **II** (bolde 'op, h. 'opgebold) *vt* puff up
'**opborrelen**[1] *vi* bubble up; **–ling** *v* bubbling up, ebullition
'**opborstelen**[1] *vt* brush (up), give a brush
'**opbouw** *m* construction, building up;
   '**opbouwen**[1] *vt* build up; *weer* ~ reconstruct; ~*de kritiek* constructive criticism
'**opbranden I** (brandde op, h. opgebrand) *vt* burn, consume; **II** (brandde op, is opgebrand) *vi* be burnt
'**opbreken**[1] **I** *vt* *het beleg* ~ raise the siege; *zijn huishouden* ~ break up one's home; *het kamp (de tenten)* ~ break (strike) camp, strike the tents; *de straat* ~ tear up the pavement; *de straat is opgebroken* the street is up (for repair); **II** *vi* & *va* break camp; break up [of a meeting, of the company]; *dat zal je* ~! you shall smart for it
'**opbrengen**[1] *vt* 1 (o p d o e n) bring in, bring up [dinner]; 2 (i n r e k e n e n) take to the police-station, run in [a thief]; seize [ships]; 3 (a a n b r e n g e n) apply [colours &]; 4 (g r o o t b r e n g e n) bring up, rear; 5 (o p l e v e r e n) bring in [much money], realize, fetch [big sums, high prices], yield [profit]; 6 (b e t a l e n) pay [taxes]; *dat kan ik niet* ~ I cannot afford it; '**opbrengst** (-en) *v* yield, produce, proceeds [from the sale of...]
'**opbruisen** (bruiste 'op, is 'opgebruist) *vt* effervesce, bubble up; **–d** effervescent; *fig* hot-headed
'**opcenten** *mv* additional percentage
'**opdagen**[1] *vi* turn up, come along, appear
op'dat that, in order that; ~ *niet* lest
'**opdelven**[1] *vt* dig up; *fig* unearth [a book &]
'**opdienen**[1] *vt* serve up, dish up
'**opdiepen** (diepte 'op, h. 'opgediept) *vt fig* unearth, fish out
'**opdirken** (dirkte 'op, h. 'opgedirkt) **I** *vt* dress up, prink up, bedizen; **II** *vr zich* ~ prink oneself up
'**opdissen** (diste 'op, h. 'opgedist) *vt* serve up[2], dish up[2]
'**opdoeken** (doekte 'op, h. 'opgedoekt) **I** *vt eig* furl [sails]; **II** *va fig* shut up shop
'**opdoemen** (doemde 'op, is 'opgedoemd) *vi* loom (up)
'**opdoen**[1] **I** *vt* 1 (o p d i s s e n) serve up, bring in [the dinner]; 2 (k r ij g e n) get, gain, acquire, obtain; 3 (i n s l a a n) lay in [provisions]; *kennis* & ~ gather, acquire knowledge; *een nieuwtje* ~

pick up a piece of news; *een ziekte* ~ catch (get, take) a disease; *waar heb je dat opgedaan?* where did you get that (come by that)?, where did you pick it [your English &] up?; **II** *vr zich* ~ arise; *als er zich eens wat opdoet* when (if) something turns up
'**opdoffen** (dofte 'op, h. 'opgedoft) **I** *vt* polish, clean; **II** *vr zich* ~ dress up
'**opdoffer** (-s) *m* thump, punch
'**opdokken**[1] *vi* & *vt* **S** shell out, fork out, pay up
'**opdonder** (-s) *m* sock, clout, blow; *iem. een* ~ *verkopen* clout sbd. on the head, sock it to sbd.; '**opdonderen**[1] *vi* make oneself scarce; *donder op!* get lost!, beat it!, get (the hell) out of here!
'**opdraaien**[1] **I** *vt* turn up [the lamp]; wind up [a gramophone &]; **II** *vi* in: *dan moet ik ervoor* ~ I have to pay the piper (to suffer for it)
'**opdracht** (-en) *v* 1 (t o e w ij d i n g) dedication; 2 (l a s t) charge, mandate, commission, instruction; mission; 3 (a a n k u n s t e n a a r) commission; *wie heeft u die* ~ *gegeven?* who has instructed you?; *een kunstenaar een* ~ *verstrekken* commission an artist [to paint, to write...]; *iets in* ~ *hebben* be instructed to...; *in* ~ *van* by order of; '**opdragen**[1] *vt* 1 (o p d i e n e n) serve up, put on the table; 2 (l e z e n) celebrate [mass]; 3 (t o e w ij d e n) dedicate; *iem. iets* ~ charge sbd. with sth.; instruct him to...; *ik draag u mijn belangen op* I consign my interests to your care
'**opdraven**[1] *vi* run up [the stairs]; **F** *iem. laten* ~ send for sbd., whistle sbd. up; **F** *komen* ~ put in an appearance
'**opdreunen**[1] *vt* rattle off, chant
'**opdrijven**[1] *vt* force up [prices]; start [game]; **–ving** *v* inflation [of prices]
'**opdringen**[1] **I** *vi* press on, press forward; **II** *vt iem. iets* ~ thrust, force [a present, goods &] upon (on) sbd., force [one's views] down sbd.'s throat; **III** *vr zich* ~ obtrude oneself [upon other people], intrude; *die gedachte drong zich aan mij op* the thought forced itself upon me; **op'dringerig** obtrusive, intrusive; **–heid** *v* obtrusiveness, intrusiveness
'**opdrinken**[1] *vt* drink (up), empty, finish, drink off
'**opdrogen**[1] *vt* dry up, desiccate; **–d** ~ *(middel)* desiccative; '**opdroging** *v* desiccation
'**opdruk** (-ken) *m* overprint, surcharge [on postage stamp]; *met* ~ surcharged; '**opdrukken**[1] *vt* (im)print upon
'**opduikelen**[1] *vt* unearth [a book &], pick up
'**opduiken**[1] **I** *vi* 1 emerge, turn up, crop up,

---

[1] V.T. en V.D. van dit werkwoord volgens het model: '**op**bellen, V.T. belde '**op**, V.D. '**op**gebeld. Zie voor de vormen onder het grondwoord, in dit voorbeeld: *bellen*. Bij sterke en onregelmatige werkwoorden wordt u verwezen naar de lijst achterin.

pop up; 2 ⚓ surface; ~ *uit* emerge from; **II** *vt* unearth [a book &]

'**opduvel** (-s) *m* **F** hit, blow, clout; '**opduvelen** (duvelde 'op, is 'opgeduveld) *vi* **F** beat it, hop it

'**opdweilen**[1] *vt* mop up

op'**een** one upon another, together, in a heap

op'**eendringen**[2] *vi* crowd together

op'**eenhopen**[2] **I** *vt* heap up, pile up, accumulate; **II** *vr zich* ~ crowd together; –**ping** (-en) *v* accumulation, congestion

op'**eenjagen**[2] *vt* drive together

op'**eenpakken**[2] *vt* pack together

op'**eens** all at once, suddenly

op'**eenstapelen**[2] **I** *vt* heap up, pile up, accumulate; **II** *vr zich* ~ pile up, accumulate; –**ling** (-en) *v* accumulation

op'**eenvolgen**[2] *vi* succeed (follow) each other; –**d** successive, consecutive; op'**eenvolging** *v* succession, sequence

op'**eisbaar** claimable; '**opeisen**[1] *vt* 1 claim; 2 ✕ summon [a town] to surrender; –**sing** *v* 1 claiming; 2 ✕ summons to surrender

'**open I** *aj* open [door &, credit, letter, knee, question, weather, face, heart, carriage, car, city, tuberculosis], vacant [situation]; sore [leg]; sliding [roof]; *een ~ doekje* applause during the action [in the theatre]; *een ~ plek in een bos* a glade; *is de kruidenier nog ~?* is the grocer's open yet?; *het ligt daar ~ en bloot* open to everybody; **II** *ad* openly; ~ *met iem. spreken* be open with sbd.

op- en '**aanmerkingen** *mv* critical remarks and observations

open'**baar**, '**openbaar I** *aj* public; ~ *maken* make public, publish, disclose, make known; ~ *lichaam* authority; *de openbare mening* public opinion; *openbare school* non-denominational school; ~ *vervoer* public transport; *openbare weg* public road, the (King's) highway; *openbare werken* public works, public utilities; *in het ~* in public, publicly; **II** *ad* publicly, in public; –**heid** *v* publicity; ~ *aan iets geven* make it public; –**making** *v* publication, disclosure; open'**baren** (openbaarde, h. geopenbaard) **I** *vt* 1 reveal, disclose; divulge; 2 (i n h o g e r e z i n) reveal; *geopenbaarde godsdienst* revealed religion; **II** *vr zich* ~ reveal itself, manifest itself; –**ring** (-en) *v* revelation, disclosure; *de Openbaring van Johannes* the Apocalypse, Revelations

'**openbreken**[3] *vt* burst, break (force) open;

–**doen**[3] *vt* open [a door, one's eyes]; answer the door; zie ook *mond*; –**draaien**[3] *vt* open, turn on [the gas, the tap]; '**openen** (opende, h. geopend) **I** *vt* open[*] [a door, the debate, a credit &]; *geopend van... tot...* open from... to...; **II** *vr zich* ~ open; –**er** (-s) *m* [tin-]opener, [bottle-]opener; '**opengaan**[3] *vi* open; '**opengewerkt** open-work [stockings]; '**opengooien**[3] *vt* throw open, fling open; open'**hartig** frank, outspoken, open-hearted; –**heid** *v* frankness, outspokenness, open-heartedness; '**openheid** *v* openness, frankness, candour; '**openhouden**[3] *vt* keep open[2], hold open; '**opening** (-en) *v* opening[*] [also at chess]; gap [in a wall, in a hedge]; aperture; interstice; ~ *van zaken doen (geven)* disclose the state of affairs; '**openingsbod** *o* opening bid; –**koers** (-en) *m* opening price; –**rede** (-s) *v* inaugural address; –**zet** (-ten) *m* opening move; '**openkrabben**[3] *vt* scratch open; –**krijgen**[3] *vt* get open, open; –**laten**[3] *vt* leave [a door, the possibility] open; *ruimte* ~ leave a blank; –**leggen**[3] *vt* lay open; *fig* disclose, reveal; *de kaarten* ~ lay one's cards on the table; –**liggen**[3] *vi* lie open; '**openlijk** open; public; open'**luchtmuseum** [-my.ze.üm] (-ea en -s) *o* (open-air) folk museum; –**spel** *o* 1 (v. k i n d e r e n) outdoor game; 2 (-en) (t o n e e l s p e l) open-air play; –**theater** (-s) *o* open-air theatre; '**openmaken**[3] *vt* open; –**rijten**[3] *vt* rip up[2], tear; –**rukken**[3] *vt* tear open; –**scheuren**[3] *vt* tear open; –**slaan**[3] *vt* open [a book]; ~*d* folding [door], [window] opening outwards; French [window, down to the ground]; –**snijden**[3] *vt* cut open; cut [a book]; –**spalken**[3] *vt* dilate [the eyes]; *met opengespalkte kaken* with distended jaws; –**sperren**[3] *vt* open wide, distend; –**springen**[3] *vi* burst (open); crack [of skin], chap [of hands]; –**staan**[3] *vi* be open, be vacant; *voor allen* ~ be open to all; *er stond mij geen andere weg open* there was no other way open to me, there was no alternative; ~ *voor argumenten* be accessible to argument; ~*de rekening* unpaid account; –**steken**[3] *vt* pick [a lock]; prick [a boil]; –**stellen**[3] *vt* open, throw open [to the public]; –**stelling** *v* opening; –**stoten**[3] *vt* push open

'**op-en-top** ~ *een gentleman* every inch a gentleman, a gentleman all over; ~ *een gek* a downright fool

'**opentrappen**[3] *vt* kick in; –**trekken**[3] *vt* open,

[1,2,3] V.T. en V.D. van dit werkwoord volgens het model: 1 '**op**bellen, V.T. belde '**op**, V.D. '**op**gebeld; 2 op'**een**pakken, V.T. pakte op'**een**, V.D. op'**een**gepakt; 3 '**open**draaien, V.T. draaide '**open**, V.D. '**open**gedraaid. Zie voor de vormen onder het grondwoord, in deze voorbeelden: *bellen, pakken* en *draaien*. Bij sterke en onregelmatige werkwoorden wordt u verwezen naar de lijst achterin.

draw back [the curtains]; uncork, open [a
bottle]; **–vallen**³ *vi* fall open; *fig* fall vacant;
–vouwen³ *vt* unfold; **–waaien**³ *vi* be blown
open, blow open; **–werpen**³ *vt* throw open,
fling open; **–zetten**³ *vt* open [a door]; turn on
[the cock]

'opera ('s) *m* opera; (g e b o u w) opera-house
ope'rabel operable; **opera'teur** (-s) *m* 1
operator; 2 (f i l m~, d i e o p n e e m t) cameraman; (f i l m~, d i e v e r t o o n t) projectionist; **ope'ratie** [-'ra.(t)si.] (-s) *v* operation²; *een*
~ *ondergaan* undergo an operation, be operated
upon; **–basis** [-zɪs] (-sen en -bases)'*v* ⚕ base of
operations; **opera'tief I** *aj* operative [surgery];
II *ad* [remove a tumor] surgically; *slechts* ~
ingrijpen kan... only a surgical operation can...,
only by surgery...; **ope'ratiekamer** (-s) *v*
operating room (theatre); **–tafel** (-s) *v* operating table; **–zaal** (-zalen) *v* operating theatre;
–zuster (-s) *v* surgical nurse; **operatio'neel**
[-ra.(t)si.o.-] operational

'operazanger (-s) *m*, **–es** (-sen) *v* opera(tic)
singer
ope'reren (opereerde, h. geopereerd) **I** *vi* ⚕ &
⚕ operate; **II** *vt* ⚕ operate on
ope'rette (-s) *v* [Viennese] operetta; musical
comedy
'opeten¹ *vt* eat up, eat
'opfleuren (fleurde 'op, *vt* h., *vi is* 'opgefleurd)
vi & vt brighten (up), cheer up
'opflikkeren¹ *vi* flare up, blaze up; **–ring** (-en)
v flare-up, flicker
'opfokken¹ *vt* breed, rear [cattle]
'opfrissen I (friste 'op, is 'opgefrist) *vi* freshen;
daar zal hij van ~ **F** that will make him sit up;
II (friste 'op, h. 'opgefrist) *vt* refresh, revive;
brighten up [colours]; *iems. geheugen eens* ~
refresh (jog, rub up) sbd.'s memory; *zijn kennis
wat* ~ rub up (brush up, touch up) his knowledge; **III** *vr zich* ~ have a wash and brush-up;
–sing (-en) *v* refreshment
'opgaaf (-gaven) = *opgave*
'opgaan¹ **I** *vi* 1 (d e h o o g t e i n) rise [of the
sun, a kite, the curtain]; go up [of a clamour,
cries]; 2 (g e e n r e s t l a t e n) leave no
remainder [of a division sum]; 3 (j u i s t z ij n)
hold (good) [of a comparison]; 4 (v o o r
e x a m e n) go up, go in; 5 (o p r a k e n) run
out, give out; *het eten gaat schoon op* nothing will
be left; *dat gaat niet op hier* that won't do here;
hij gaat dit jaar niet op he is not going to
present himself for the exam this year; 7 *gaat*

niet op 34 7 does (will) not go into 34; ~ *i n* be
merged into [one large organization]; ~ *in rook*
vanish into smoke; ~ *in zijn vrouw* be wrapped
up in one's wife; ~ *in zijn werk* be absorbed in
one's work; **II** *vt* ascend, mount [a hill]; go up
[the stairs]; **'opgang** (-en) *m* 1 rise; 2 entrance
[of house]; ~ *maken* **F** catch on [of a fashion],
become popular; *het maakte (veel)* ~ it achieved
(a great) success, it made a great hit; *het maakte
geen* ~ it fell flat

'opgave (-n) *v* 1 (m e d e d e l i n g) statement [of
reasons], [official] returns; 2 (t a a k) task; ⚖
exercise, problem; *de schriftelijke* ~*n* the written
work, the papers

'opgeblazen blown up; puffed; *fig* bumptious;
puffed up, inflated [with pride]; **–heid** *v fig*
bumptiousness
'opgebruiken¹ *vt* use up
'opgedirkt prinked up
'opgelaten [feel] embarrassed
'opgeld (-en) *o* $ agio; ~ *doen* be in great
demand, **F** be at a premium
'opgelegd 1 laid-up [ship]; 2 veneered [table];
3 marked [faults, changes]; ~ *pandoer* **S** a
(dead) cert
'opgemaakt made-up [dress &]; made [dish];
dressed [hair]
'opgeprikt dressed up [swell, girl]
'opgepropt ~ *met* crammed with
'opgericht raised, erect
'opgeruimd I *aj* in high spirits, cheerful; **II** *ad*
cheerfully; **opge'ruimdheid** *v* high spirits,
cheerfulness
'opgescheept *met iem.* ~ *zijn* have sbd. on one's
back, be saddled with sbd.; *nu zitten we met dat
goed* ~ we have the stuff on our hands now
'opgeschoten half-grown [youths]
'opgeschroefd *fig* stilted [language], unnatural
[enthusiasm]
'opgesmukt ornate, embellished
'opgetogen delighted, elated [with];
opge'togenheid *v* delight, elation
'opgeven¹ **I** *vt* 1 (a f g e v e n) give up [what one
holds]; 2 (t o e r e i k e n) hand up, hand over; 3
(v e r m e l d e n) give, state [one's name &]; 4
(b r a k e n) expectorate, spit [blood]; 5 (a l s
t a a k) set [a task, a sum]; ask [riddles],
propound [a problem]; 6 (l a t e n v a r e n)
give up, abandon [hope]; 7 ⚕ give up [a
patient]; *mijn benen gaven het op* my legs gave
out; *ik geef het op* I give it up; *hij geeft het niet op*
he is not going to yield, he will stick it out;
II *va* expectorate; *hoog (breed)* ~ *van iets* speak

¹,³ V.T. en V.D. van dit werkwoord volgens het model: 1 'opbellen, V.T. belde 'op, V.D. 'opgebeld; 3 'open-
draaien, V.T. draaide 'open, V.D. 'opengedraaid. Zie voor de vormen onder het grondwoord, in deze voorbeelden:
bellen en *draaien*. Bij sterke en onregelmatige werkwoorden wordt u verwezen naar de lijst achterin.

highly of something, make much of a thing;
III *vr zich* ~ enter one's name, apply [for a
situation, for membership]
'**opgewassen** ~ *zijn tegen* be a match for [sbd.],
be equal to [the task], rise to [the occasion]
'**opgewekt I** *aj* 1 (v. p e r s o n e n) cheerful, in
high spirits; 2 (v. g e s p r e k k e n &)
animated; **II** *ad* cheerfully; **opge'wektheid** *v*
cheerfulness, buoyancy, high spirits
'**opgewonden** excited; heated [debate];
opge'wondenheid *v* excitement
'**opgezet** 1 stuffed [birds]; 2 bloated [face]; 3
swollen [vein]
'**opgieten**[1] *vt* pour upon
'**opgooien**[1] *vt* throw up, toss (up); *zullen wij
erom* ~? shall we toss (up) for it?
'**opgraven**[1] *vt* 1 (z a k e n) dig up, unearth; 2
(l ij k e n) disinter, exhume; **–ving** (-en) *v* 1
digging up, excavation [at Pompeii], dig; 2
disinterment, exhumation
'**opgroeien**[1] *vi* grow up
'**ophaal** (-halen) *m* upstroke, hair-line [of a
letter]; snag [in a stocking]; **–brug** (-gen) *v*
drawbridge, lift-bridge; **–dienst** (-en) *m*
collecting service
'**ophakken**[1] *vi* brag; **–er** (-s) *m* braggart,
swaggerer; **ophakke'rij** (-en) *v* brag(ging)
'**ophalen**[1] **I** *vt* 1 (i n d e h o o g t e) draw up [a
bridge], pull up [blinds], raise [the curtain];
hitch up [one's trousers]; weigh [anchor];
shrug [one's shoulders]; turn up [one's nose]
(at); 2 (h e r h a l e n) bring up again [a sermon
&]; revive (old memories); 3 (i n z a m e l e n)
collect [money, rubbish, the books]; 4
(v e r d i e p e n) brush up, rub up [one's
French]; *zijn kous ergens aan* ~ snag one's
stocking; *ladders* ~ mend ladders [in a stock-
ing]; *kan ik het nog* ~? can I make good yet?; *u
moet zo iets (dat) niet weer* ~ let bygones be
bygones; **II** *va* regain health (lost ground &)
op'handen at hand; *het* ~ *zijnde feest* the
approaching (coming) festivity
'**ophangen**[1] **I** *vt* hang [a man, a picture &];
hang out [the washing]; hang up [one's coat
&]; suspend [a lamp &]; *de telefoon* ~ hang up
(replace) the receiver; *een verhaal van iets* ~
paint a picture of sth.; *het schilderij werd opgehangen* the picture was hung (put up); *hij werd
opgehangen* he was hanged (ook: hung); zie ook:
tafereel; **II** *vr zich* ~ hang oneself; **–ging** (-en) *v*
1 hanging; 2 ✕ [frontwheel] suspension
'**ophebben**[1] *vt* have on [one's hat]; have eaten
[one's meal]; ☞ have got to do; *veel* ~ *met* be

taken with [sbd.]; *ik heb niet veel op met...* I can't
say I care for (I fancy)..., I don't hold with...
'**ophef** *m* fuss; *veel* ~ *van (over) iets maken* make a
fuss of (over) sth.
'**opheffen**[1] *vt* 1 (i n d e h o o g t e) lift (up),
raise [something], elevate [the Host]; 2 raise
[one's eyes]; 3 (z e d e l ij k) raise, lift up [the
mind]; 4 (t e n i e t d o e n) abolish [a law], lift
[a ban], do away with [abuses], remove
[doubts], close [a school, a meeting], adjourn [a
meeting], call off [a strike], discontinue [a
branch-office], raise [an embargo, blockade
&], annul [a bankruptcy]; *het ene heft het andere
op* one neutralizes (cancels) the other; '**ophef-
fing** (-en) *v* 1 elevation, raising; 2 (a f s c h a f-
f i n g) abolition [of a law], removal [of doubts],
closing [of a school], discontinuance [of a
branch-office], raising [of an embargo], annulment [of a bankruptcy]; **–suitverkoop** *m*
winding-up sale
'**ophelderen I** (helderde 'op, h. 'opgehelderd)
vt clear up, explain, elucidate; **II** (helderde 'op,
is 'opgehelderd) *vi* = *opklaren* **I**; **–ring** (-en) *v*
explanation, elucidation; clearing up
'**ophelpen**[1] *vt* help up, assist in rising
'**ophemelen** (hemelde 'op, h. 'opgehemeld) *vt*
extol, praise to the skies, cry (write, **F** crack)
up
'**ophijsen**[1] *vt* hoist up, hoist
'**ophitsen** (hitste 'op, h. 'opgehitst) *vt* set on [a
dog]; *fig* set on, stir up, egg on, incite, instigate [people]; **–er** (-s) *m* instigator, inciter;
'**ophitsing** (-en) *v* setting on, incitement,
instigation
'**ophoepelen** (hoepelde 'op, is 'opgehoepeld) *vi*
S beat it, hop it
'**ophoesten**[1] *vt* cough up[2]
'**ophogen** (hoogde 'op, h. 'opgehoogd) *vt*
heighten, raise
'**ophopen** (hoopte 'op, h. 'opgehoopt) **I** *vt* heap
up, pile up, bank up, accumulate; **II** *vr zich* ~
accumulate; **–ping** (-en) *v* accumulation,
piling-up
'**ophoren**[1] *vi er vreemd van* ~ be surprised to
hear it
'**ophouden I** *vt* 1 (i n d e h o o g t e) hold up
[one's head]; 2 hold out [one's hand]; 3
(a f h o u d e n v a n b e z i g h e i d) detain,
keep [sbd.]; 4 (t e g e n h o u d e n) hold up; 5
(n i e t a f z e t t e n) keep on [one's hat]; 6
(n i e t v e r k o p e n) withdraw [a house]; 7 *fig*
(h o o g h o u d e n) keep up [appearances],
uphold [the honour of...]; **II** (hield 'op, is

<hr>

[1] V.T. en V.D. van dit werkwoord volgens het model: '**op**bellen, V.T. belde '**op**, V.D. '**op**gebeld. Zie voor de
vormen onder het grondwoord, in dit voorbeeld: *bellen*. Bij sterke en onregelmatige werkwoorden wordt u verwezen
naar de lijst achterin.

'opgehouden) *vi* cease, stop, come to a stop; *houd op! stop* (it)!, chuck it!; **F** cheese it!; ~ *te bestaan* cease to exist; ~ *lid te zijn* discontinue one's membership; ~ *met* cease (from) ...ing, stop ...ing; ~ *met vuren* ⚓ cease fire; ~ *met werken* stop work; **III** *vr zich* ~ stay, live [somewhere]; *zich onderweg* ~ stop on the road; *houd u daar niet mee op, met hem niet op* have nothing to do with it, with him; **IV** *o zonder* ~ continuously, incessantly; *het heeft drie dagen zonder* ~ *geregend* it has been raining for three days at a stretch

o'pinie (-s) *v* opinion; *naar mijn* ~ in my opinion; **–onderzoek** *o* (public) opinion poll, *Am* Gallup-poll; **–onderzoeker** (-s) *m* pollster

'opium *m* & *o* opium; **–kit** (-ten) *v* opium den; **–pijp** (-en) *v* opium pipe; **–schuiver** (-s) *m* opium smoker

'opjagen[1] *vt* rouse [a stag], start [a hare &], flush [birds], spring [a partridge], dislodge [the enemy]; *fig* force up, send up, run up [prices]; *zich niet laten* ~ refuse to be rushed; **–er** (-s) *m* 1 (o p j a c h t) beater; 2 (b ij v e r k o p i n g) runner-up, puffer

'opjuinen (juinde 'op, h. 'opgejuind) *vi* **F** egg on, stir up

'opjutten (jutte 'op, h. 'opgejut) *vt* 1 (h a a s-t e n) hustle, hurry; 2 (o p z e t t e n) egg on, incite, urge

'opkalefateren[1] *vt* patch up, fix up

'opkammen[1] *vt* comb (up); *iem.* ~ [*fig*] extol sbd., **F** crack sbd. up; **opkamme'rij** (-en) *v* **F** cracking up

'opkijken[1] *vi* look up; *hij zal er* (*vreemd*) *van* ~ he will be surprised, **F** it will make him sit up

'opkikkeren (kikkerde 'op, *vt* h., *vi* is 'opgekik-kerd) *vi* & *vt* buck up; **'opkikkertje** (-s) *o* **F** pick-me-up, bracer

'opklapbed (-den) *o* folding bed; **–tafel** (-s) *v* gate-legged table

'opklaren **I** (klaarde op, is opgeklaard) *vi* clear up, brighten up [of the weather]; *fig* brighten [of the face, prospect]; **II** (klaarde op, h. opgeklaard) *vt* make clear[2] [what we see or what is hidden]; *fig* elucidate [the matter]; **–ring** (-en) *v* *met tijdelijke* ~*en* [rainy weather] with bright intervals

'opklauteren[1] *vt* clamber up

'opklimmen[1] *vi* climb (up), mount, ascend; *fig* rise [to be a captain &, to a high position]

'opkloppen[1] *vt* 1 knock up, call up [a person]; 2 beat up [cream, eggs]

'opknabbelen[1] *vt* munch

'opknappen **I** (knapte 'op, h. 'opgeknapt) *vt* 1 (n e t j e s m a k e n) tidy up [a room]; smarten up [the children]; do up [the garden, an old house]; 2 (b e t e r m a k e n) put right [a patient]; patch up [a thing]; *hij zal het alleen wel* ~ he'll manage it quite well by himself; *hij zal het wel voor je* ~ he will fix it up for you; **II** (knapte op, is opgeknapt) *va* regain strength, recuperate, pick up; *het weer knapt wat op* the weather is looking up; **III** *vr zich* ~ smarten oneself up

'opknopen[1] *vt* tie up; string up, hang [a man]

'opkoken **I** (kookte 'op, is 'opgekookt) *vi* boil up [of milk]; **II** (kookte 'op, h. 'opgekookt) *vt* reboil [syrup]; cook again ‿

'opkomen[1] *vi* 1 (o p s t a a n) get up (again), recover one's legs; 2 ⚓ come up; 3 (u i t-k o m e n) come out [of pox]; 4 (r ij z e n) rise [of dough]; 5 (v e r s c h ij n e n) rise [of the sun]; come on [of actor; of thunderstorm; of fever]; present oneself [of candidates]; ⚓ join the colours; 🎭 appear; 6 *fig* (z i c h v o o r-d o e n) arise, crop up [of questions]; *het getij komt op* the tide is making; *de koning* (*met zijn gevolg*) *komt op* enter king (and attendants); *de leden zijn flink opgekomen* the members turned up in (good) force; *het eten zal wel* ~ they are sure to eat it all up; *laat ze maar* ~ *!* let them come on!; ● *die gedachte kwam b ij mij op* that idea crossed my mind (occurred to me); *het komt niet bij mij op* I don't even dream of it; ~ *t e g e n iets* take exception to sth., protest against sth.; *wij konden tegen de wind niet* ~ we could not make head against the wind; ~ *v o o r zijn rechten* make a stand for one's rights; ~ *voor zijn vrienden* stand up for one's friends; **–d** rising[2] [sun, author &]; **'opkomst** *v* 1 rise; 2 (v. v e r g a d e r i n g &) attendance; turn-out [on election day]

'opkopen[1] *vt* buy up; **–er** (-s) *m* buyer-up; second-hand dealer, junk-dealer

'opkrabbelen (krabbelde 'op, is 'opgekrab-beld) *vi* scramble to one's legs (feet); *fig* pick up

'opkrassen (kraste 'op, is 'opgekrast) *vi* 1 (w e g g a a n) **F** skedaddle; make oneself scarce; 2 (d o o d g a a n) **F** peg out

'op krijgen **I** *vt* get on [the head]; *ik kan het niet* ~ I can't eat all that; *veel werk* ~ be set a great task; **II** *vi met iem.* ~ begin to like sbd.

'opkrikken (krikte 'op, h. 'opgekrikt) *vt* jack up

'opkroppen (kropte 'op, h. 'opgekropt) *vt* bottle up [one's anger]; *opgekropte woede* pent-up wrath

---

[1] V.T. en V.D. van dit werkwoord volgens het model: 'opbellen, V.T. belde 'op, V.D. 'opgebeld. Zie voor de vormen onder het grondwoord, in dit voorbeeld: *bellen*. Bij sterke en onregelmatige werkwoorden wordt u verwezen naar de lijst achterin.

'**opkruipen**[1] *vi* creep up [of insects]
'**opkruisen**[1] *vi* ⚓ beat up
'**op kunnen**[1] **I** *vt ik zou het niet* ~ I could not eat all that; *zijn plezier wel* ~ have a bad (thin) time; **II** *vi niet* ~ *tegen*... be no match for...
'**opkweken**[1] *vt* breed, bring up, rear, nurse
'**opkwikken** (kwikte 'op, h. 'opgekwikt) *vt* refresh
'**oplaag** (-lagen) *v* = *oplage*
'**oplaaien** (laaide 'op, is 'opgelaaid) *vi* blaze up; *hoog* ~ run high [of excitement, passions &]
'**opladen**[1] *vt* load
'**oplage** (-n) *v* impression [of a book]; circulation [of a newspaper]; *de* ~ *is slechts honderd exemplaren* edition limited to 100 copies
'**oplappen**[1] *vt* patch up[2], piece up[2] [old shoes &, a play], cobble [shoes]; *fig* tinker up [a patient]
'**oplaten**[1] *vt* fly [a kite, pigeons], launch [a balloon]
'**oplawaai** (-en) *m* clout, **F** biff, cuff, punch
'**oplazer** (-s) *m* **S** swack, thwack; '**oplazeren**[1] *vi* **P** bugger off
'**opleggen**[1] *vt* 1 (l e g g e n o p) lay on [hands, paint], impose [one's hands]; 2 (b e l a s t e n m e t) charge with [sth.], impose [sth., one's will upon sbd.], set [sbd. a task]; 3 (g e - l a s t e n) lay [an obligation] upon [sbd.], impose [silence], enjoin [secrecy upon sbd.]; 4 ⚓ (v a s t l e g g e n) lay up; 5 ✕ (i n l e g g e n m e t) veneer; *er een gulden* ~ 1 raise the price by one guilder; 2 bid another guilder [at an auction]; *een (grammofoon)plaat* ~ put on a record; *hem werd een zware straf opgelegd* he had a heavy punishment inflicted on him; **–er** (-s) *m* (semi-)trailer [of a tractor]; *truck met* ~ articulated lorry; '**oplegging** *v* laying on, imposition [of hands]; '**oplegsel** (-s) *o* 1 trimming [of a gown]; 2 veneer [of a piece of furniture]
'**opleiden**[1] *vt fig* train, bring up, educate; *iem. voor een examen* ~ prepare (coach) sbd. for an examination; *voor geestelijke opgeleid* bred for the Church; **–er** (-s) *m* teacher, tutor; '**opleiding** (-en) *v* training; '**opleidingsschip** (-schepen) *o* training-ship, school-ship; **–school** (-scholen) *v* training-school
'**oplepelen**[1] *vt* ladle out[2]
'**opletten**[1] *vi* attend, pay attention; **op'lettend** attentive; **–heid** *v* attention, attentiveness
'**opleven** (leefde 'op, is 'opgeleefd) *vi* revive; *doen* ~ revive
'**opleveren**[1] *vt* 1 (o p b r e n g e n) produce, yield, bring in, realize [big sums]; present

[difficulties]; 2 (a f l e v e r e n) deliver (up) [a house]; '**oplevering** (-en) *v* delivery [of a work]; **–stermijn** (-en) *m* completion date ˙
'**opleving** *v* revival, upswing, $ upturn
'**oplezen**[1] *vt* read out
1 '**oplichten**[1] *vt* lift (up); *fig* 1 (w e g v o e r e n) carry off; 2 (b e d r i e g e n) swindle, **S** sharp; *iem.* ~ *voor*... swindle sbd. out of...
2 '**oplichten**[1] *vi* light up [of face, eyes]
'**oplichter** (-s) *m* swindler, sharper; **oplichte'rij** (-en) *v* swindle, swindling, fraud; confidence trick
'**oploeven** (loefde 'op, is 'opgeloefd) *vi* luff up, haul to the wind
'**oploop** *m* 1 tumult, riot, row; 2 (m e n i g t e) crowd; '**oplopen**[1] **I** *vi eig* rise; *fig* 1 (h o g e r w o r d e n) rise, advance [of prices]; mount up [of bills]; add up [nicely]; 2 (o p z w e l l e n) swell (up); *samen (een eindje)* ~ go part of the way together; *even komen* ~ *b ij iem.* drop in, step round; ~ *t e g e n* = *aanlopen tegen*; *een rekening laten* ~ run up a bill; **II** *vt straf* ~ incur punishment; *de trap* ~ go up the stairs; *verwondingen* ~ receive injuries; *een ziekte* ~ catch a disease; **–d** rising[2]
op'losbaar soluble [substance]; solvable [problem]; **–heid** *v* solubility [of a substance]; solvability [of a problem]; '**oploskoffie** *m* instant (soluble) coffee; **–middel** (-en) *o* solvent; '**oplossen I** (loste 'op, h. 'opgelost) *vt* dissolve [in a liquid]; resolve [an equation]; solve [a problem, a riddle]; **II** (loste 'op, is 'opgelost) *vi* dissolve; **–sing** (-en) *v* solution [of a solid or gas, of a problem, an equation]; resolution [of an equation]; *de juiste* ~ *van het vraagstuk* ook: the right answer to the problem
'**opluchten**[1] *vt het zal u* ~ you will be relieved [to hear that...]; **–ting** *v* relief
'**opluisteren** (luisterde 'op, h. 'opgeluisterd) *vt* add lustre to, grace, adorn; **–ring** *v* adornment
'**opmaak** *m* make-up
'**opmaat** (-maten) *v* ♪ upbeat
'**opmaken I** *vt* 1 (v e r t e r e n) use up [one's tea], spend [one's money], < squander [one's money]; 2 (i n o r d e m a k e n &) make [a bed]; trim [hats]; get up[2] [a dress, a programme]; do (up), dress [her hair]; garnish [a dish]; make up [one's face, the type]; make out [a bill], draw up [a report]; *daaruit moeten wij* ~ *dat*... from that we must conclude that..., we gather from this..., we read into this...; **II** *vr zich* ~ 1 set out (for *naar*); 2 make up [of a woman]; *zich* ~ *voor de reis* get ready for the

---

[1] V.T. en V.D. van dit werkwoord volgens het model: '**op**bellen, V.T. belde '**op**, V.D. '**op**gebeld. Zie voor de vormen onder het grondwoord, in dit voorbeeld: *bellen*. Bij sterke en onregelmatige werkwoorden wordt u verwezen naar de lijst achterin.

journey; **–er** (-s) *m* 1 (v. g e l d) spendthrift; 2 (v. z e t s e l &) maker-up

'opmarcheren[1] [-mɑrʃeːrə(n)] *vi* march (on); *dan kun je* ~ **F** you may beat it, **S** you can hop it; **'opmars** (-en) *m* & *v* ⚔ advance, march (on *naar*)

op'merkelijk I *aj* remarkable, noteworthy; **II** *ad* remarkably; **'opmerken**[1] *vt* 1 (w a a r- n e m e n) notice, observe; 2 (c o m m e n t e- r e n d z e g g e n) remark, observe; *mag ik hierbij* ~ *dat...?* may I point out to you that...?; *wat heeft u daarover op te merken?* what have you to remark upon that?; **opmerkens'waard(ig)** remarkable, noteworthy; **'opmerker** (-s) *m* observer; **'opmerking** (-en) *v* remark, obser- vation; **–sgave** *v* power of perceiving [of observation], perception; **op'merkzaam** attentive; observant; ~ *maken op* draw atten- tion to; **–heid** *v* attention, attentiveness

'opmeten[1] *vt* 1 measure [one's garden &]; 2 survey [a country &]; **–ting** (-en) *v* 1 measure- ment; 2 survey

'opmonteren (monterde 'op, h. 'opgemonterd) *vt* cheer up; **–ring** *v* cheering up

'opnaaisel (-s) *o* tuck

'opname (-n) *v* [documentary] record; (h e t o p n e m e n) recording [of music]; shooting [of a film]; *een fotografische* ~ a photo, a view, a picture; (v. f i l m) a shot; zie verder *opneming*; **'opnemen**[1] **I** *vt* 1 (i n h a n d e n n e m e n) take up [a newspaper]; 2 (o p t i l l e n) take up, lift [a weight]; 3 (h o g e r h o u d e n) gather up [one's gown]; 4 (e e n p l a a t s g e v e n) take up, pick up [passengers], insert [an article], include [in a book, in the Govern- ment]; take in [guests, straying travellers], admit [patients]; 5 (t o t z i c h n e m e n) take [food], assimilate[2] [material or mental food]; absorb [heat, a liquid]; 6 $ take up [money at a bank], borrow [money]; 7 (o p h a l e n) collect [the papers, votes]; 8 (w e g n e m e n) take up, take away [the carpet]; 9 (o p d w e i l e n) mop up [a puddle]; 10 (m e t e n) take [sbd.'s tem- perature]; 11 (i n k a a r t b r e n g e n) survey [a property &]; 12 (v o o r g r a m m o f o o n, o p d e b a n d) record; 13 (v o o r b i o s- c o o p) shoot [a film, a scene]; 14 (s t e n o- g r a f i s c h) take down [a letter, in shorthand]; 15 *fig* receive [sth. favourably]; survey [sbd.], take stock of [sbd.], measure [sbd.] with one's eyes; 16 (b e k ij k e n) take in [details]; 17 (b e g i n n e n) take up [a study]; 18 (h e r v a t t e n) *weer* ~ resume one's work;

contact met iem. ~ get in touch with sbd., contact sbd.; *het gemakkelijk* ~ take things easy; *u moet het in de krant laten* ~ you must have it inserted; *het kunnen* ~ *tegen iem.* be able to hold one's own against sbd., be a match for sbd.; *het* ~ *voor iem.* stand up for sbd.; *hoe zullen zij het* ~? how are they going to take it?; *iem.* ~ *van top tot teen* take stock of sbd.; *hij werd in die orde opgenomen* he was received into that order; *iem.* ~ *in een vennootschap* take sbd. into partnership; *iem.* ~ *in een (het) ziekenhuis* admit sbd. to hospital; *iets goed (slecht)* ~ take sth. in good (bad) part; *iets hoog* ~ resent sth.; *iets verkeerd* ~ take sth. ill (amiss); *de gasmeter* ~ read the gas-meter; *een gevallen steek* ~ take up a dropped stitch; *iems. tijd* ~ time sbd.; **II** *vi* catch on, meet with success; **–er** (-s) *m* (l a n d m e t e r) surveyor; **'opneming** (-en) *v* taking &, zie *opnemen*; (o p m e t i n g) survey; (i n k r a n t) insertion; *zijn* ~ *in het ziekenhuis* his admission to (the) hospital

op'nieuw anew, again, a second time

'opnoemen[1] *vt* name, mention, enumerate; *te veel om op te noemen* too numerous to mention; *en noem maar op* **F** or what have you, and what not; **–ming** (-en) *v* naming, mention, enumer- ation

'opoe (-s) *v* **F** granny

'opofferen[1] *vt* sacrifice, offer up; **–ring** (-en) *v* sacrifice; *met* ~ *van* at the sacrifice of; **'opoffe- ringsge'zind** self-sacrificing, selfless

'oponthoud *o* stop(page); (g e d w o n g e n) detention; (v e r t r a g i n g) delay

o'possum (-s) *o* opossum

'oppakken[1] *vt* 1 (o p n e m e n) pick up, take up [a book]; 2 (i n r e k e n e n) run in [a thief], round up [collaborators]

'oppas (-sen) *m-v* baby-sitter; **'oppassen**[1] **I** *vt* (v e r z o r g e n) take care of; nurse, tend [a patient]; **II** *vi* take care, be careful; zie ook: *zich gedragen*; *je moet voor hem* ~ be careful of him, beware of him; **op'passend** well-behaved; **–heid** *v* good behaviour; **'oppasser** (-s) *m* 1 (v. d i e r e n t u i n &) keeper, attendant [of a museum]; 2 ⚔ batman; 3 (l ij f k n e c h t) valet; 4 = *ziekenoppasser*; **'oppassing** *v* attendance, nursing, care

'oppeppen (pepte 'op, h. 'opgepept) *vt* pep up

'opper (-s) *m* 1 (hay)cock; 2 *afk.* van *opperwacht- meester*; *aan* ~*s zetten* cock [hay]

'opperbest excellent; *je weet* ~... you know perfectly well...; **–bestuur** *o* supreme direc- tion; *het* ~ ook: the government; **'opperbevel**

---

o supreme command, [Russian &] High Command, [British] Higher Command; **–hebber** (-s) *m* commander-in-chief; supreme commander [of the Allied Forces]

'opperen (opperde, h. geopperd) *vt* propose, suggest, put forward, advance [a plan]; raise [objections, a question]

'oppergezag *o* supreme authority; **–heer** (-heren) *m* sovereign, overlord; **–heerschappij** *v* sovereignty; **–hoofd** (-en) *o* chief, head; **–huid** *v* epidermis, cuticle, scarfskin; **–jager(meester)** (-s) *m* Master of Hounds; **–kamerheer** (-heren) *m* Lord Chamberlain

'opperlieden, –lui meerv. van *opperman*

'oppermacht *v* supreme power, supremacy; **opper'machtig** supreme; ~ *heersen* (*regeren*) reign supreme

'opperman (-lui, -lieden en -mannen) *m* hodman

'opperofficier (-en) *m* ✕ general officer; **–rabbijn** (-en) *m* chief rabbi(n) **–rechter** (-s) *m* chief justice

'oppersen[1] *vt* press [one's trousers &]

'opperst uppermost, supreme; **'opperstalmeester** (-s) *m* (Lord Grand) Master of the Horse; **–toezicht** *o* supervision, superintendence

'oppervlak (-ken) *o* = *oppervlakte*; **opper'vlakkig I** *aj* superficial[2]; *fig* shallow; **II** *ad* superficially; **–heid** (-heden) *v* superficiality, shallowness; **'oppervlakte** (-n en -s) *v* surface; (g r o o t t e) area, superficies; **–water** *o* surface water

'opperwachtmeester (-s) *m* sergeant-major

'Opperwezen *o* Supreme Being

'oppeuzelen[1] *vt* munch

'oppikken[1] *vt* pick up

'opplakken[1] *vt* paste on; mount [photographs]

'oppoetsen[1] *vt* rub up, clean, polish

'oppoken[1] *vt* poke (up), stir [the fire]

'oppompen[1] *vt* pump up [water]; blow out, inflate [the tyres of a bicycle]

oppo'nent (-en) *m* opponent, objector; **oppo'neren** (opponeerde, h. geopponeerd) *vi* oppose, raise objections

'opporren[1] *vt* stir [the fire]; *fig* shake up, rouse

opportu'nisme *o* opportunism; **opportu'nist** (-en) *m* opportunist; **–isch** opportunist; **opportuni'teit** *v* opportuneness, expediency; **oppor'tuun** opportune, timely, well-timed

oppo'sant [s = z] (-en) *m* opponent; **oppo'sitie** [-'zi.(t)si.] (-s) *v* opposition; **–partij** (-en) *v* opposition party

'oppotten[1] *vt* save, hoard [money]; pot (plants); **–ting** *v* $ hoarding

'opprikken[1] *vt* 1 (v. i n s e k t e n) pin (up); 2 (v. p e r s o n e n) dress up, prink up

'opproppen[1] *vt* cram, fill

'oprakelen[1] *vt* poke (up) [the fire]; *fig* rake up, dig up [old disputes &]; *rakel dat nu niet weer op* don't bring up bygones

'opraken[1] *vi* run low, give out, run out

'oprapen[1] *vt* pick up, take up; *je hebt ze maar voor het* ~ they are as plentiful as blackberries

op'recht I *aj* sincere, straightforward; **II** *ad* sincerely; **–heid** *v* sincerity, straightforwardness

'opredderen[1] *vt* straighten up, tidy up

'oprekken[1] *vt* stretch [gloves]

'oprichten[1] **I** *vt* raise, set up[2]; erect [a statue]; establish [a business], found [a college]; form [a company]; **II** *vr zich* ~ draw oneself up, sit up [in bed], rise; **'oprichter** (-s) *m* erector [of a statue]; founder [of a business]; **–saandelen** *mv* founder's shares; **'oprichting** (-en) *v* erection [of a statue]; establishment, foundation, formation; **'oprichtingskapitaal** (-talen) *o* foundation capital; **–kosten** *mv* formation expenses

'oprijden[1] *vt* ride (drive) up [a hill]; *het trottoir* ~ mount the pavement [of a motor-car]; ~ *tegen* run (crash) into; **'oprijlaan** (-lanen) *v* drive, sweep

'oprijzen *vi* rise, arise

'oprispen (rispte 'op, h. 'opgerispt) *vi* belch, repeat; **–ping** (-en) *v* belch, eructation

'oprit (-ten) *m* 1 ascent, slope; 2 (l a a n) drive, sweep; 3 (n a a r s n e l w e g) slip-road, *Am* access-road

'oproeien[1] *vi* row up [a river]; zie ook: *stroom*

'oproep *m* summons; *fig* call; **'oproepen**[1] *vt* call up [soldiers]; summon, convoke [members]; conjure up, raise [spirits]; excite [criticism]; call up, evoke [the past &]; **–ping** (-en) *v* call, summons; convocation; ✕ call-up [of soldiers]; (b i l j e t) notice (of meeting); ✕ calling-up notice

'oproer (-en) *o* revolt, rebellion, insurrection, mutiny; sedition; (o n g e r e g e l d h e d e n) riot(s); ~ *kraaien* preach sedition; ~ *verwekken* stir up a revolt; **op'roerig** rebellious, mutinous; seditious; **–heid** *v* rebelliousness; seditiousness; **'oproerkraaier** (-s) *m* preacher of revolt, agitator, ringleader; **–ling** (-en) *m* insurgent, rebel; **–politie** [-po.li.(t)si] *v* riot police

---

[1] V.T. en V.D. van dit werkwoord volgens het model: **'op**bellen, V.T. belde **'op**, V.D. **'op**gebeld. Zie voor de vormen onder het grondwoord, in dit voorbeeld: *bellen*. Bij sterke en onregelmatige werkwoorden wordt u verwezen naar de lijst achterin.

'**oproken**[1] *vt* smoke [another man's cigars]; finish [one's cigar]; *een half opgerookte sigaar* a half-smoked cigar

'**oprollen**[1] *vt* roll up[2] [also ⚓]; coil; *fig* break up [a gang, an organization]; *een opgerolde paraplu* a rolled umbrella

'**opruien** (ruide 'op, h. 'opgeruid) *vt* incite, instigate; ~*de artikelen* seditious articles; ~*de woorden* inflammatory (incendiary) words; –**er** (-s) *m* agitator, inciter, instigator; '**opruiing** (-en) *v* incitement, instigation; sedition

'**opruimen**[1] *vt* 1 (w e g r u i m e n) clear away [the tea-things &]; clear [⚓ mines; slum dwellings]; 2 (u i t v e r k o p e n) sell off, clear (off) [stock]; 3 *fig* remove [obstacles]; put [sbd.] out of the way [by poison]; make a clean sweep [of criminals]; *de kamer* ~ tidy up the room; *de tafel* ~ clear the table; **II** *va* put things straight; *dat ruimt op!* (it, he, she is) a good riddance!; –**ming** (-en) *v* 1 clearing away, clean-up; 2 $ selling-off, clearance(-sale), [January] sales; ~ *houden* clear away things; *fig* make a clean sweep (of *onder*)

'**oprukken**[1] *vi* advance; *je kunt* ~ *!* S hop it!; ~ *naar* march upon, advance upon [a town]; ~ *tegen* march against, advance against [the enemy]

'**opscharrelen**[1] *vt* ferret (rout) out, rummage out

'**opschenken**[1] *vt* pour on

'**opschepen** (scheepte 'op, h. 'opgescheept) *vt* saddle with; zie ook: *opgescheept*

'**opscheppen**[1] **I** *vt* ladle out, serve out; *de boel* ~ **F** 1 kick up a dust; 2 paint the town red; *het geld ligt er opgeschept* they are simply rolling in money; *die heb je maar voor het* ~ zie *oprapen*; **II** *vi* boast, brag, **F** swank, shoot a line; –**er** (-s) *m* braggart; **op'schepperig F** swanky; **opscheppe'rij** (-en) *v* bragging, **F** swank

'**opschieten**[1] *vi* shoot up; *fig* make headway, get on; *schiet op!* 1 (h a a s t je) hurry up!, do get a move on!; 2 (g a w e g) S hop it!; (*goed*) *met elkaar* ~ pull together; *je kan niet met hem* ~ you can't get on (along) with him; *schiet het al op?* how is it getting on?; *wat schiet je ermee op?* where does it get you?; *je schiet er niets mee op* it does not get you anywhere, it gets you nowhere

'**opschik** *m* finery, trappings

1 '**opschikken**[1] *vi* move up, close up

2 '**opschikken**[1] **I** *vt* dress up, trick out, prink up; **II** *vr zich* ~ prink oneself up

'**opschilderen**[1] *vt* paint up

'**opschommelen**[1] *vt* dig up, unearth

'**opschorten** (schortte 'op, h. 'opgeschort) *vt*, tuck up [one's sleeves] *fig* reserve [one's judgment]; suspend [hostilities, judgment &]; postpone [a decision]; –**ting** (-en) *v* suspension, postponement

'**opschrift** (-en) *o* heading [of an article &]; inscription [on a coin]; direction [on a letter]; '**opschrijfboekje** (-s) *o* notebook; '**opschrijven**[1] *vt* write down, take down; *wilt u het maar voor mij* ~? will you put that down to me?; *voor hoeveel mogen we u* ~? what may we put you down for?

'**opschrikken**[1] *vi* start, be startled

'**opschroeven**[1] *vt* screw up; *fig* cry (puff) up; zie ook: *opgeschroefd*

'**opschrokken**[1] *vt* bolt, devour, wolf

'**opschudden**[1] *vt* shake, shake up; –**ding** (-en) *v* bustle, commotion, tumult, upheaval, kick-up, **F** to-do; ~ *veroorzaken* create a sensation, cause (make) a stir

'**opschuiven**[1] **I** *vt* 1 push up; 2 (u i t s t e l l e n) postpone, put off; **II** *vi* move up; –**ving** (-en) *v* moving-up

'**opsieren**[1] *vt* embellish, adorn; –**ring** (-en) *v* embellishment, adornment

'**opslaan**[1] **I** *vt* 1 (o m h o o g d o e n) turn up [one's collar &]; put up, raise [the hood of a motor-car]; raise [the eyes]; 2 (o p e n s l a a n) open [a book], turn up [a page]; 3 (o p z e t-t e n) pitch [camp, a tent]; 4 (p r ij z e n) put [a penny] on, raise [the price]; 5 (i n s l a a n) lay in [potatoes &]; 6 (i n e n t r e p o t) store, warehouse [goods]; **II** *vi* go up, advance, rise [in price]; *de suiker is een penny opgeslagen* ook: sugar is up a penny; '**opslag** (-slagen) *m* 1 (p r ij s-, l o o n s v e r h o g i n g) advance, rise; 2 facing [of a uniform], cuff [of a sleeve]; 3 (i n p a k h u i s &) storage; 4 ♪ upbeat; *de* ~ *van de goederen* the storage (storing) of the goods; *het dienstmeisje* ~ *geven* raise the servant's wages; –**plaats** (-en) *v* storage, building, store, depot, [ammunition] dump; –**ruimte** (-n en -s) *v* storage space (accommodation); –**terrein** (-en) *o* storage yard

'**opslokken**[1] *vt* swallow, gulp down

'**opslorpen**[1] *vt* lap up; absorb; –**ping** *v* absorption

'**opsluiten**[1] **I** *vt* lock (shut) up [things, persons]; confine [a thief &]; ⚓ close [the ranks]; *daarin ligt opgesloten...* it implies... (that...); **II** *vr zich* ~ shut oneself up (in one's room); **III** *vi* ⚓ close

---

[1] V.T. en V.D. van dit werkwoord volgens het model: 'opbellen, V.T. belde 'op, V.D. 'opgebeld. Zie voor de vormen onder het grondwoord, in dit voorbeeld: *bellen*. Bij sterke en onregelmatige werkwoorden wordt u verwezen naar de lijst achterin.

the ranks, close up; **–ting** *v* locking up, confinement, incarceration; *eenzame* ~ solitary confinement

'**opslurpen**[1] *vt* = *opslorpen*

'**opsmuk** *m* finery, trappings; '**opsmukken** (smukte 'op, h. 'opgesmukt) *vt* trim, dress up, embellish[2]

'**opsnijden**[1] **I** *vt* cut up, cut open, cut, carve; **II** *vi fig* brag, F swank; **–er** (-s) *m* braggart; **–erig** F swanky; **opsnijde'rij** (-en) *v* bragging, F swank

'**opsnorren**[1] *vt* rout out, ferret out, unearth

'**opsnuiven**[1] *vt* sniff (up), inhale

'**opsodemieteren**[1] *vi* P bugger off

'**opsommen** (somde 'op, h. 'opgesomd) *vt* enumerate, sum up; **–ming** (-en) *v* enumeration

'**opsouperen**[1] [-su.pe:rə(n)] *vt* spend, use up

'**opspannen**[1] stretch, put on [strings], string [a guitar]; mount [a picture]; ✗ fix, clamp

'**opsparen**[1] *vt* save up, lay by, put by

'**opspelen**[1] *vi* 1 play first, lead [at cards]; 2 *fig* kick up a row, cut up rough

'**opsporen**[1] *vt* trace, track (down), find out; '**opsporing** (-en) *v* tracing; exploration [of ore &]; ~ *verzocht* wanted by the police; **–sdienst** *m* 1 tracing and search department; criminal investigation department; 2 (v. m ij n e n) prospecting department

'**opspraak** *v* scandal; *in* ~ *brengen* compromise; *in* ~ *komen* get talked about

'**opspreken**[1] *vi* speak out; *spreek op!* speak!

'**opspringen**[1] *vi* jump (leap, start) up, jump to one's feet; (v. b a l) bounce; *van vreugde* ~ leap for joy

'**opspuiten** **I** *vi* (w a t e r) spout (up), spurt (up), squirt (up); **II** *vt* (v e r f) spray on; (r o o m) squirt on; *fig* (a f r a f f e l e n) spout [Latin verses]; reel of [names]

'**opstaan** (stond 'op, h. en is 'opgestaan) *vi* 1 get up, rise; 2 (u i t b e d) rise; 3 (i n v e r z e t k o m e n) rise, rebel, revolt (against *tegen*); *het eten staat op* dinner is cooking; *het water staat op* the kettle is on; *als je hem te pakken wil nemen, moet je vroeg(er)* ~ you have to be up early to be even with him; zie ook: *dood, tafel*

'**opstal** (-len) *m* buildings

'**opstand** (-en) *m* 1 △ (vertical) elevation; 2 (v. w i n k e l) fixtures; 3 (v e r z e t) rising, insurrection, rebellion, revolt; *in* ~ *komen tegen iets* revolt against (at, from) sth.; *in* ~ *zijn* be in revolt; **–eling** (-en) *m* insurgent, rebel; **op'standig** insurgent, rebel; mutinous; **–heid**

v mutinousness; '**opstanding** *v* resurrection

'**opstapelen**[1] **I** *vt* stack (up), heap up, pile up, accumulate; **II** *vr zich* ~ accumulate [dirt, capital &], pile up; bank up [snow]; **–ling** (-en) *v* piling up, accumulation

'**opstapje** (-s) *o* step; '**opstappen**[1] *vi* go (away); F move on, push off, get along, be off

'**opsteken** **I** (stak 'op, h. 'opgestoken *vt* 1 (i n d e h o o g t e) hold up, lift [one's hand]; put up [one's hair]; prick up [one's ears]; put up [an umbrella]; 2 (o p e n m a k e n) broach [a cask]; 3 (a a n s t e k e n) light [a cigar &]; 4 (i n s t e k e n) pocket [money]; put up [a sword]; *hij zal er niet veel van* ~ he will not profit much by it; *stemmen met het* ~ *der handen* by show of hands; **II** *va* F light up; *wilt u eens* ~*?* F will you light up?; have a smoke;

III (stak 'op, is 'opgestoken) *vi* rise [of a storm]

'**opstel** (-len) *o* composition, theme, paper; *een* ~ *maken over* write (do) a paper on;

'**opstellen**[1] **I** *vt* 1 (o p z e t t e n) set up [a pole]; 2 ✗ (p l a a t s e n) post, draw up [soldiers]; 3 (i n p o s i t i e b r e n g e n) mount [guns]; 4 (i n e l k a a r z e t t e n) mount [machinery]; 5 *fig* (r e d i g e r e n) draft, draw up [a deed]; frame [a treaty]; redact [a paper]; **II** *vr zich* ~ 1 take up a (one's) position; 2 ✗ form up, line up; 3 line up [of a football team]; *zich hard* ~ take a hard line on; **–er** (-s) *m* drafter [of a deed], framer [of a treaty]; '**opstelling** (-en) *v* drawing up &; formation, line-up [of a football team]

'**opstijgen**[1] *vi* ascend, mount, go up, rise; ☞ take off, F hop off; ~*!* to horse!; **–ging** (-en) *v* ascent; ☞ take-off

'**opstijven** **I** (stijfde 'op, is 'opgesteven) *vi* set; **II** (stijfde, steef 'op, h. 'opgesteven, 'opgestijfd) *vt* starch [linen]

'**opstoken**[1] *vt* 1 poke (up), stir (up); 2 *fig* set on, incite, instigate; 3 burn [all the fuel]; **–er** (-s) *m* inciter, instigator; **opstoke'rij** (-en) *v* incitement, instigation

'**opstomen**[1] *vt* steam up [a river]

'**opstommelen**[1] *vt* stumble up [the stairs]

'**opstootje** (-s) *o* disturbance, riot

'**opstoppen**[1] *vt* stop up, fill

'**opstopper** (-s) *m* cuff, slap

'**opstopping** (-en) *v* stoppage, congestion [of traffic]; [traffic] block, jam

'**opstormen**[1] *vt* tear up [the stairs]

'**opstrijken**[1] *vt* 1 (g l a d s t r ij k e n) iron [clothes]; twirl up [one's moustache]; 2 *fig* pocket, rake in [money]

'opstropen[1] *vt* tuck up, roll up [sleeves]
'opstuiven[1] *vi* fly up; *fig* fly out, flare up; **F** fly off the handle
'opsturen[1] *vt* forward, send on
'opstuwen[1] *vt* push up, drive up [water]
'optakelen[1] *vt* ⚓ rig up
'optassen[1] *vt* pile up
'optekenen[1] *vt* note (write, jot) down, note, record; **–ning** (-en) *v* notation
'optellen[1] *vt* cast up, add (up), tot up; **–ling** (-en) *v* casting up, addition; **'optelsom** (-men) *v* addition sum
1 'opteren[1] *vt* eat up, consume
2 op'teren (opteerde, h. geopteerd) *vi* ~ *voor* decide in favour of, choose, opt for
'optica *v* optics; **opticien** [ɔpti.si.'ĩ] (-s) *m* optician
'optie ['ɔpsi.] (-s) *v* option; *in* ~ *geven* (*hebben*) give (have) the refusal of...
op'tiek *v* = *optica*
'optillen[1] *vt* lift up, raise
opti'maal optimum, optimal
opti'misme *o* optimism; **opti'mist** (-en) *m* optimist; **–isch** optimistic(al), sanguine
'optisch optical
'optocht (-en) *m* procession, [historical] pageant
'optomen (toomde 'op, h. 'opgetoomd) *vt* bridle [a horse]
'optooien[1] *vt* deck out, adorn, decorate; **'optooiing** *v* adornment, decoration
'optornen (tornde 'op, h. en is 'opgetornd) *vi* ~ *tegen* struggle against[2]
'optreden[1] **I** *vi* make one's appearance [as an actor], appear (on the stage), enter; appear [on TV], perform [in night clubs &]; *fig* take action, act; ~ *als* act as...; *hij durft niet* ~ he dare not assert himself; ~ *tegen* take action against, deal with; *voor iem.* ~ act on behalf of sbd.; *strenger* ~ adopt a more rigorous action; **II** *o* appearance [on the stage]; *fig* [military, defensive] action; [disgraceful] proceedings; [reckless, aggressive] behaviour; *eerste* ~ first appearance, debut[2]; *gezamenlijk* ~ joint action
'optrekje (-s) *o* cottage; **'optrekken[1] I** *vt* 1 (o m h o o g) draw up [a blind], pull up [a load, ⚙ one's machine &]; raise [the curtain, one's eyebrows; the living standard]; turn up [one's nose]; shrug [one's shoulders]; hitch up [one's trousers]; 2 (b o u w e n) raise [a building]; **II** *vr zich* ~ pull oneself up; **III** *vi* 1 (w e g t r e k-k e n) lift [of a fog]; 2 (m a r c h e r e n) march (against *tegen*); 3 (o m g a a n, z i c h b e z i g

h o u d e n) take care of, be busy with, tag along with; 4 ✕ accelerate [of a motor-car]
'optrommelen[1] *vt* drum up
'optuigen (tuigde 'op, h. 'opgetuigd) **I** *vt* ⚓ rig [a ship]; harness [a horse]; **II** *vr zich* ~ rig oneself up
'optutten (tutte 'op, h. 'opgetut) *vt* **F** doll up, posh up
'opvallen[1] *vi* attract attention; *het zal u* ~ it will strike you; *het valt niet op* it is not conspicuous; **op'vallend** striking
'opvangcentrum (-tra en -s) *o* reception centre; **'opvangen[1]** *vt* catch [a ball, a glance, a sound, a thief, the water]; collect [the water]; snap up [a piece of bread]; R pick up [a station, a transmission]; absorb [shocks]; receive [the sword-point with one's shield]; meet[2] [an attack, the difference, a loss &]; intercept [a telegram]; overhear [what is said]
'opvaren[1] *vt* ⚓ go up, sail up; *de op'varenden* ⚓ those on board
'opvatten[1] *vt* 1 (o p n e m e n) take up[2] [a book, the pen, the thread of the narrative]; 2 (k r ij g e n) conceive [a hatred against, love for, a dislike to]; 3 (v o r m e n) conceive [a plan]; 4 (b e g r ij p e n) understand, interpret, view, take; *de dingen licht* ~ take things easy; *iets somber* ~ take a gloomy view (of things); *u moet het niet verkeerd* ~ 1 you must not take it in bad part; 2 you must not misunderstand me; *het als een belediging* ~ take it as an insult; *zijn taak weer* ~ resume one's task; **–ting** (-en) *v* view, opinion, conception
'opvegen[1] *vt* sweep, sweep up
'opveren[1] *vi* rise buoyantly [from one's seat]; *fig* perk up
'opverven[1] *vt* paint up
'opvijzelen (vijzelde 'op, h. 'opgevijzeld) *vt* jack up, lever up, screw up; *fig* cry up, **F** crack up; send up, force up [prices]
'opvissen[1] *vt* fish up; fish out; *als ik het kan* ~ if I can unearth it
'opvlammen[1] *vi* flame up, flare up
'opvliegen[1] *vi* fly up; *fig* fly out, flare up; *hij kan* ~ *!* he can go to blazes!; **op'vliegend** short-tempered, quick-tempered, irascible, peppery; **–heid** *v* quick temper, irascibility; **'opvlieging** (-en) *v* ⚕ congestion, **F** hot flush
op'voedbaar educable, trainable; *een moeilijk* ~ *kind* a difficult (problem) child; **'opvoeden[1]** *vt* bring up, rear, educate; **–d** educative, pedagogic(al); **'opvoeder** (-s) *m* educator; **'opvoeding** *v* upbringing, bringing-up, education;

[1] V.T. en V.D. van dit werkwoord volgens het model: 'op*bellen*, V.T. belde 'op, V.D. 'opgebeld. Zie voor de vormen onder het grondwoord, in dit voorbeeld: *bellen*. Bij sterke en onregelmatige werkwoorden wordt u verwezen naar de lijst achterin.

(m a n i e r e n) breeding, manners; *lichamelijke* ~ physical training; **–sgesticht** (-en) *o* approved school; borstal institution; **'opvoed-kunde** *v* pedagogy, pedagogics; **opvoed'kundig I** *aj* pedagogic(al) [books]; educative [value]; **II** *ad* pedagogically; **–e** (-n) *m* education(al)ist, pedagogue

'opvoeren¹ *vt* 1 (h o g e r b r e n g e n) carry up; 2 (h o g e r m a k e n) raise, force up [the price, their demands]; (v e r m e e r d e r e n) increase, step up [production]; speed up [an engine]; 3 (t e n t o n e l e v o e r e n) 1 put on the stage; 2 perform, give [a play]; **–ring** (-en) *v* 1 performance [of a play]; 2 raising [of prices], increase, stepping up [of production]

'opvolgen¹ *vt* succeed [one's father, one another]; obey [a command], act upon, follow [advice]; **–er** (-s) *m* successor; *benoemd & als* ~ *van* in succession to; **'opvolging** (-en) *v* succession

op'vorderbaar claimable; *direct* ~ $ on call; **'opvorderen¹** *vt* claim

op'vouwbaar foldable [music stand], collapsible [boat], folding [bicycle]; **'opvouwen¹** *vt* fold (up)

'opvragen¹ *vt* 1 call in, withdraw [money from the bank]; 2 claim [letters]

'opvreten¹ I *vt* devour, eat up; **II** *vr zich* ~ fret away one's life, eat one's heart out

'opvriezen¹ *vi opgevroren wegdek* 1 road surface covered with black ice; 2 road surface damaged by frost

'opvrijen¹ *vt* chat up, play up [to sbd.]

'opvrolijken (vrolijkte 'op, h. 'opgevrolijkt) *vt* brighten, cheer (up), enliven

'opvullen¹ *vt* fill up, fill out; stuff [a cushion], pad; **'opvulsel** (-s) *o* filling, stuffing, padding

'opwaaien¹ I *vt* blow up; **II** *vi* be blown up

'opwaarderen¹ *vt* revalue; **–ring** (-en) *v* revaluation

'opwaarts I *aj* upward; **II** *ad* upward(s)

'opwachten¹ *vt* 1 wait for; 2 waylay; **–ting** *v zijn* ~ *maken bij* pay one's respects to [sbd.], wait upon

'opwarmen¹ *vt* warm up², heat up

'opwegen¹ *vi* ~ *tegen* (counter-)balance

'opwekken¹ *vt* awake², rouse²; stir up; resuscitate, raise [the dead]; *fig* excite [feelings &]; stimulate, provoke [fermentation, indignation &]; generate [electricity]; *iem. tot iets* ~ 1 rouse sbd. to something; 2 invite sbd. to do sth.; **op'wekkend** stimulating; ~ *middel* tonic, cordial, stimulant; **'opwekking** (-en) *v* excite-

ment, stimulation; generation [of electricity]; resuscitation; **B** raising [of Lazarus]; (a a n s p o r i n g) exhortation

'opwellen¹ *vi* well up; *fig* well up (forth); **–ling** (-en) *v* ebullition, outburst; flush [of joy], access [of anger]; *in de eerste* ~ on the first impulse; *in een* ~ on impulse

'opwerken¹ I *vt* work up; touch up; **II** *vr zich* ~ work one's way up; *zich* ~ *tot...* work oneself up to...

'opwerpen¹ I *vt* throw up; put up [barricades]; *een vraag* ~ raise a question; zie ook: 1 *dam*; **II** *vr zich* ~ *tot...* set up for..., constitute oneself the...

'opwinden¹ I *vt eig* wind up; *fig* excite; thrill; **II** *vr zich* ~ get excited; **–ding** *v eig* winding up; *fig* excitement, agitation, thrill

'opwrijven¹ *vt* rub up, polish

'opzadelen¹ *vt* saddle (up)

'opzamelen¹ *vt* collect, gather; **–ling** (-en) *v* collection

op'zegbaar terminable; ~ *kapitaal* capital redeemable at notice; **'opzeggen¹** *vt* 1 (u i t h e t h o o f d) say, repeat, recite [a lesson]; 2 (i n t r e k k e n) terminate [a contract], denounce [a treaty], recall [moneys]; *iem. de dienst* (*de huur*) ~ give sbd. notice; *de krant* ~ withdraw one's subscription; *met drie maanden* ~s at three month's notice; **'opzegging** (-en) *v* termination [of a contract], denunciation [of a treaty]; withdrawal; notice, warning; **–stermijn** (-en) *m* term of notice

'opzeilen¹ *vi* sail up

'opzenden¹ *vt* send, ⚓ forward [a letter]; offer (up) [a prayer]

'opzet *m* design, intention; *boos* ~ malice (prepense), malicious intent; *m e t* ~ on purpose, purposely, intentionally, designedly; *z o n d e r* ~ unintentionally, undesignedly; **op'zettelijk I** *aj* intentional, wilful, premeditated; deliberate [lie]; **II** *ad* zie *met opzet*

'opzetten¹ I *vt* 1 (z e t t e n o p) put on [one's hat &]; 2 (o v e r e i n d) place upright [a plank], put up, set up [skittles], pitch [a tent], turn up [one's collar]; 3 (o p h e t s p e l z e t t e n) stake [money]; 4 (o p s l a a n) erect [booths]; 5 (o p r i c h t e n) set up, establish [a business], start [a shop]; 6 (d o e n s t a a n) spin [a top]; 7 (s p a n n e n) brace [one's biceps]; 8 (o p e n s p a n n e n) put up, open [an umbrella]; 9 (b r e i w e r k) cast on; 10 (p r e p a r e r e n) stuff [birds, a dead lion &]; 11 *fig* (o p h i t s e n) set on [people]; *de*

---

¹ V.T. en V.D. van dit werkwoord volgens het model: **'op**bellen, V.T. belde **'op**, V.D. **'op**gebeld. Zie voor de vormen onder het grondwoord, in dit voorbeeld: *bellen*. Bij sterke en onregelmatige werkwoorden wordt u verwezen naar de lijst achterin.

bajonet(ten) ~ ✕ fix bayonets; *de mensen tegen elkaar* ~ set people against each other, set persons by the ears; *de mensen tegen de regering* ~ set people against the government; **II** (zette *'op, is 'opgezet) vi* swell; *er komt een onweer* ~ a storm is coming on; *toen kwam hij* ~ then he came along; **III** *vr zich* ~ (v. g y m n a s t) heave oneself up; **–ting** *v* swelling [of a limb &]
'opzicht (-en) *o* supervision; *i n ieder* ~, in alle *~en* in every respect, (in) every way; *in dit* ~ in this respect; *in financieel* ~ financially [a disappointing year]; *in zeker* ~ in a way; *t e dien ~e* in this respect; *ten ~e van* with respect (regard) to; **–er** (-s) *m* 1 overseer, superintendent; 2 (b o u w~) clerk of the works; **op'zichtig I** *aj* showy, gaudy, loud [dress]; **II** *ad* showily, gaudily, loudly; **–heid** *v* showiness, gaudiness, loudness
opzich'zelfstaand isolated [case]
'opzien¹ I *vi* look up [to sbd.]; *tegen iets* ~ shrink from the task, the difficulty &; *ik zie er tegen op* I dread having to do it; *tegen geen moeite* ~ not think any trouble too much; *er vreemd van* ~ be surprised; **II** *o* ~ *baren* make (cause, create) a sensation, make a stir; **opzien'barend** sensational; **'opziener** (-s) *m* overseer, inspector
op'zij aside; ~ *gaan* give way, yield; ~ *leggen* put aside (away); ~ *zetten* put aside; *fig* brush away; ~*!* away!
'opzitten¹ *vt* sit up; mount (one's horse); ~*! to horse!; *~, Fidel!* beg!; *er zit niets anders op dan...* there is nothing for it but to...; *er zal een standje voor je* ~ you will be in for a scolding
'opzoeken¹ *vt* 1 (z o e k e n) seek, look for [sth.]; look up [a word]; 2 (b e z o e k e n) call on [sbd.]
'opzouten¹ *vt* salt, pickle; *fig* salt down
'opzuigen¹ *vt* suck (in, up), absorb
'opzwellen¹ *vi* swell, tumefy; *doen* ~ swell, tumefy; **–ling** (-en) *v* swelling, tumefaction, tumescence
'opzwepen¹ *vt* whip up²; *fig* work up
o'raal oral
o'rakel (-s en -en) *o* oracle²; **–achtig** oracular; **o'rakelen** (orakelde, h. georakeld) *vi* talk like an oracle; **o'rakelspreuk** (-en) *v* oracle; **–taal** *v* oracular language
orang-'oetan(g) (-s) *m* orang-utan
o'ranje orange; **–appel** (-s en -en) *m* orange; **–bloesem** *m* ✿ orange blossom; **O'ranjege- zind** loyal to the House of Orange; **–gezind- heid** *v* (i n U l s t e r) Orangeism; **–huis** *o* House of Orange; **o'ranjekleur** (-en) *v* orange colour; **–marmelade** *v* orange marmalade;

oranje'rie (-rieën en -s) *v* orangery, green- house; **o'ranjesnippers** *mv* candied orange- peel; **Oranje-'Vrijstaat** *m* Orange Free State
o'ratie [-(t)si.] (-s) *v* oration; **ora'torisch** oratorical; **ora'torium** (-ia en -s) *o* ♩ oratorio
orchi'dee *v* (-deeën) orchid
'orde (-n en -s) *v* order°; orderliness; *de* ~ *handhaven* maintain order; *de* ~ *herstellen* restore order; ~ *houden* keep order; ~ *scheppen in de chaos* zie chaos; ~ *op zaken stellen* put one's affairs straight, settle one's affairs, set one's house in order; ● *a a n de* ~ *komen* come up for discus- sion; *aan de* ~ *stellen* put on the order-paper; *aan de* ~ *zijn* be under discussion; *aan de* ~ *van de dag zijn* be the order of the day; *dat onderwerp is niet aan de* ~ that question is out of order; *b u i t e n de* ~ out of order; *i n* ~*!* all right!; *in* ~ *brengen* put right, set right; *het zal wel in* ~ *komen* it's sure to come right; *iets in* ~ *maken* zie *in* ~ *brengen*; *het is nu in* ~ it is all right now; *het is niet in* ~ it is out of order; that is not as it should be; *ik ben niet goed in* ~ I don't feel quite well; *in goede* ~ in good order; *we hebben uw brief in goede* ~ *ontvangen* we duly received your letter; *in verspreide* ~ ✕ in extended order; *wij konden niet o p* ~ *komen* we could not get straight; *als jullie (helemaal) op* ~ *zijn* when you are straight; when you are settled in; *gaat over t o t de* ~ *van de dag* passes to the order of the day; *iem. tot de* ~ *roepen* call sbd. to order; *v o o r de goede* ~ for the sake of good order;
–bewaarder (-s) *m* attendant [of a museum]; **–broeder** (-s) *m* brother, friar; **–dienst** (-en) *m* guard (ook: *lid v.e.* ~); **–keten** (-s) *v* chain, collar [of an order]; **–kruis** (-en) *o* cross [of an order]; **orde'lievend** orderly; law-abiding [citizens]; **–heid** *v* love of order; **'ordelijk I** *aj* orderly; **II** *ad* in good order; **–heid** *v* orderli- ness; **'ordelint** (-en) *o* ribbon [of an order]; **–loos** disorderly; **orde'loosheid** *v* disorderli- ness; **'ordenen** (ordende, h. geordend) *vt* 1 (i n o r d e s c h i k k e n) order, arrange, marshal [facts, data &]; regulate [industry], plan [economy]; 2 (w ij d e n) ordain; **'ordener** (-s) *m* file; **'ordening** (-en) *v* 1 arrangement, regulation [of industry], planning [of economy]; 2 (w ij d i n g) ordination; **or'den- telijk** decent [people]; fair [share &]; **–heid** *v* decency; fairness
'order (-s) *v* & *o* order, command; $ order; *gelieve te betalen aan... op* ~ $ or order; *a a n eigen* ~ $ to my own order; *aan de* ~ *van...* $ to the order of...; *o p* ~ *van...* by order of...; *t o t uw* ~*s*

---

at your service; *tot nader* ~ until further orders, until further notice; *wat is er v a n uw* ~*s?* what can I do for you?; **–bevestiging** (-en) *v* $ confirmation of sale; **–biljet** (-ten) *o* = *orderbriefje;* **–boek** (-en) *o* $ order-book; **–briefje** (-s) *o* $ 1 note (of hand); 2 order form; **–portefeuille** [-pɔrtɔfœyjɔ] (-s) *m* $ order-book

'ordeteken (-s en -en) *o* badge, *mv* ook: insignia; **–verstoring** (-en) *v* disturbance of the peace

ordi'nair [ɔrdi.'nɛː r] **I** *aj* 1 low, vulgar, common; 2 inferior [quality]; *een* ~*e vent* a vulgarian; **II** *ad* 1 vulgarly, commonly; 2 inferiorly

'ordner (-s) *m* file

ordon'nans (-en) *m* [officer's] orderly; ~*officier* aide-de-camp

ordon'nantie [-(t)si.] (-s en -iën) *v* order, decree, ordinance; **ordon'neren** (ordonneerde, h. geordonneerd) *vt* order, decree, ordain

o'reren (oreerde, h. georeerd) *vi* declaim, hold forth, **F** orate

or'gaan (-ganen) *o* organ²

organ'die *m* & *o* organdie, organdy

organi'satie [-'za.(t)si.] (-s) *v* organization; **organi'sator** (-'toren en -s) *m* organizer; **organisa'torisch** organizational

or'ganisch I *aj* organic; **II** *ad* organically

organi'seren [s = z] (organiseerde, h. georganiseerd) *vt* organize; arrange [an exhibition &]

orga'nisme (-n en -s) *o* organism

orga'nist (-en) *m* organist

or'gasme (-n en -s) *o* orgasm

'orgel (-s) *o* organ; *een (bet)* ~ *draaien* grind an (the) organ; **–concert** (-en) *o* 1 (u i t v o e - r i n g) organ recital; 2 (m u z i e k s t u k) organ concerto; **–draaier** (-s) *m* organ-grinder; **'orgelen** (orgelde, h. georgeld) *vi fig* warble; **'orgelmuziek** *v* organ music; **–pijp** (-en) *v* organ-pipe; **–register** (-s) *o* organ-stop, stop of an organ; **–spel** *o* organ-playing; **–speler** (-s) *m* organ-player; **–trapper** (-s) *m* organ-blower

or'gie (-gieën) *v* orgy; *fig* riot [of colours]

oriën'taals oriental; **oriën'tatie** [-(t)si.] *v* orientation; **oriën'teren** (oriënteerde, h. georiënteerd) *zich* ~ take one's bearings; *hij kon zich niet meer* ~ he had lost his bearings; *internationaal (links &) georiënteerd* internationally (left- &) minded; **oriën'tering** *v* orientation; *te uwer* ~ for your information; **–svermogen** *o* sense of direction (locality)

originali'teit [o.ri.gi.-, o.ri.ʒi.-] *v* originality; **ori'gine** [-'ʒi.nɔ] *v* origin; **origi'neel I** *aj* original; **II** (-nelen) *o* & *m* original

or'kaan (-kanen) *m* hurricane

or'kest (-en) *o* orchestra, band; *klein* ~ small orchestra; *groot* ~ full orchestra; **–dirigent** (-en), **–leider** (-s) *m* orchestra(l) conductor; **–meester** (-s) *m* leader; **orkes'tratie** [-(t)si.] (-s) *v* orchestration, scoring; **orkes'treren** (orkestreerde, h. georkestreerd) *vt* orchestrate, score

or'naat *o* official robes; (v. g e e s t e l ij k e) pontificals, vestments; *in vol* ~ in full pontificals [of a bishop &]; in state [of a king &]; ⬧ in full academicals

orna'ment (-en) *o* ornament; **ornamen'teel** ornamental, decorative; **ornamen'tiek** *v* ornamental art; **orne'ment** (-en) *o* = *ornament*

ornitholo'gie *v* ornithology; **ornitho'logisch** ornithological; **ornitho'loog** (-logen) *m* ornithologist

orthodon'tie [-'(t)si.] *v* orthodontics

ortho'dox orthodox; **orthodo'xie** *v* orthodoxy

orthope'die *v* orthopaedy; **ortho'pedisch** orthopaedic(al)

os (-sen) *m* ox [*mv* oxen], bullock

oscil'leren (oscilleerde, h. geoscilleerd) *vi* oscilate

os'mose [-'mo.zɔ] *v* osmosis

'ossebloed *o* 1 blood of an ox; 2 (k l e u r) oxblood; **–drijver** (-s) *m* ox-driver, drover; **–haas** (-hazen) *m* fillet of beef; **–huid** (-en) *v* ox-hide; **–kop** (-pen) *m* ox-head; **–staart** (-en) *m* ox-tail; **–stal** (-len) *m* ox-stall; **–tong** (-en) *v* 1 *eig* neat's tongue, ox-tongue; 2 ⅏ bugloss; **–vlees** *o* beef; **–wagen** (-s) *m* bullock-cart, (ZA) ox-wagon

osten'tatie [-(t)si.] *v* ostentation; **ostenta'tief** ostentatious

osteopa'thie *v* osteopathy

O.T. = *Oude Testament*

'otter (-s) *m* otter

Otto'maans Ottoman; **otto'mane** (-n en -s) *v* ottoman

ou'bollig droll, comical

oud I *aj* 1 (b e j a a r d) old, aged; 2 (v. d. o u d e t ij d) antique [furniture], ancient [history, Rome, writers; bridge]; classical [languages]; 3 (v r o e g e r) former, ex-; *hoe* ~ *is hij?* how old is he?, what age is he?; *hij is twintig jaar* ~ he is twenty (years old), twenty years of age; *we zijn net even* ~ we are precisely the same age; *toen ik zo* ~ *was als jij* when I was your age; ~ *maken* age; ~ *worden* grow old, age; *hij zal niet* ~ *worden* he will not live to be old; ~ *brood* stale bread; *een* ~*e firma* an old-established firm; ~ *ijzer* scrap iron; ~*e kaas* ripe cheese; ~ *nummer* back number [of a periodical]; ~ *papier* waste paper; *de* ~*e schrijvers* the ancient writers, the classics; ~*e tijden* olden times; *een* ~*e zondaar* an old sinner, a hardened sinner; *zo* ~ *als de weg naar Rome* as old as Adam (as the hills); **II** *sb* ~ *en jong* old and young; ~ *en nieuw vieren* see the old year out, see the new year in; *alles bij het* ~*e laten* leave things as they are [as they were]; *de* ~*e* **F** 1 the governor [= my father]; 2 the old man [at the office &], the boss; *ik ben weer de* ~*e* I am my usual (old) self again; *de Ouden* the ancients; *(de)* ~*en van dagen* the aged, old people; zie ook: *ouder* & *oudst*; **oud-...** former, late, ex-, retired; **'oudachtig** oldish, elderly; **oud'bakken** stale; **oud-burge'meester** (-s) *m* 1 late burgomaster; 2 (i n E n g e l a n d) ex-mayor; **'oude** (-n) *m* zie **oud II**; **oude'dagsvoorziening** (-en) *v* old-age benefit; **oude'heer** (-heren) *m de* ~ **S** the (my) governor, the old man; **oude'jaar** *o* last day of the year; **oudejaars'avond** (-en) *m* New Year's Eve; **oude'lui** *mv* old folks; **oude'mannenhuis** (-huizen) *o* old men's home

'ouder I *aj* older; elder; *hij is twee jaar* ~ two years older, my elder by two years; *een* ~*e broer* an elder brother; *hoe* ~ *hoe gekker* there's no fool like an old fool; *wij* ~*en* we oldsters; **II** (-s) *m* parent; *van* ~ *op (tot)* ~ from generation to generation; **-avond** (-en) *m* parents' evening; **-commissie** (-s) *v* parent-teacher association **'ouderdom** *m* age, old age; *hoge* ~ great age; *in de gezegende* ~ *van...* at the good old age of; **'ouderdomsklachten** *mv* infirmities of old age, geriatric complaints; **-kwaal** (-kwalen) *v* infirmity of old age; **-pensioen** (-en) *o* old-age pension; **-verschijnsel** (-en en -s) *o* symptom of old age; **-verzekering** (-en) *v* old-age insurance, retirement pension; **-wet** *v* old-age insurance act, retirement pension act **'ouderejaars(student)** (-studenten) *m* senior student

'ouderhuis *o* parental home; **-liefde** *v* parental love; **-lijk** parental **'ouderling** (-en) *m* elder; **-schap** *o* eldership **'ouderloos** parentless; **ouder'loosheid** *v* orphanhood; **'ouderpaar** (-paren) *o* parents; **'ouders** *mv* parents; **'ouderschap** *o* parenthood; **-vereniging** (-en) *v* parent-teacher association; **-vreugde** *v* parental joy (bliss) **ouder'wets I** *aj* old-fashioned, old-fangled; **II** *ad* in an old-fashioned way **oude'wijvenpraatje** (-s) *o* old woman's tale; ~*s* gossip **oudge'diende** (-n) *m* old campaigner **'oudheid** (-heden) *v* antiquity; *de Griekse* ~ Greek antiquity; *Griekse oudheden* Greek antiquities; *koopman in oudheden* antique dealer; **-kenner** (-s) *m* antiquarian, antiquary; **-kunde** *v* archaeology; **oudheid'kundig**

antiquarian, archaeological; **-e** (-n) *m* antiquarian, antiquary, archaeologist; **'oudheid(s)kamer** (-s) *v* local archaeological museum **'oudje** (-s) *o* old man, old woman; *de* ~*s* the old folks **oud-'leerling** (-en) *m* 1 ex-pupil, former pupil; 2 old boy; **-e** (-n) *v* 1 ex-pupil, former pupil; 2 old girl; **'oudoom** (-s) *m* great-uncle; **oud'roest** *o* scrap-iron; **'ouds(her)** *van* ~ of old; **oudst** oldest, eldest; *de* ~*e boeken* the oldest books; *zijn* ~*e broer* his eldest brother; ~*e vennoot* senior partner; **oud-'strijder** (-s) *m* ✠ veteran, ex-Serviceman; **'oudtante** (-s) *v* great-aunt; **oudtesta'mentisch** (of the) Old Testament; **'oudtijds** in olden times **outil'lage** [u.ti.(l)'ja.ʒə] *v* equipment; **outil'leren** [u.ti.'je:rə(n)] (outilleerde, h. geoutilleerd) *vt* equip **ouver'ture** [u.vər'ty:rə] (-s en -en) *v* ♪ overture **ou'vreuse** [u.'vrø.zə] (-s) *v* usherette **ouwe'hoeren** (ouwehoerde, h. geouwehoerd) *vi* **P** tittle-tattle, talk rubbish **'ouwel** (-s) *m* 1 wafer [for letter]; communion wafer; rice-paper; 2 ✞ cachet **'ouwelijk** oldish **o'vaal I** *aj* oval; **II** (ovalen) *o* oval **o'vatie** [-(t)si.] (-s) *v* ovation; *een* ~ *brengen (krijgen)* give (have) an ovation **'oven** (-s) *m* 1 oven, furnace; 2 (k a l k o v e n) kiln; **-want** (-en) *v* oven glove **'over I** *prep* 1 (z i c h b e w e g e n d e o p o f l a n g s e e n o p p e r v l a k t e) along [a good road we sped...]; 2 (b o v e n) over [the meadow]; 3 (o v e r... h e e n) over [the brook, the hedge], across [the river]; on top of [his cassock he wore...]; 4 (a a n d e o v e r z ij d e v a n) beyond [the river]; 5 (m é é r d a n) above, upwards of, over [fifty]; 6 (v i a) by way of, via [Paris]; 7 (n a) in [a week &]; 8 (t e g e n o v e r) opposite [the church &]; *een boek* ~ *Afrika* a book on (about) Africa; ~ *een dag of acht* in a week or ten days; *zondag* ~ *acht dagen* Sunday week; ~ *een maand, een paar jaar* a month, a few years hence; ~ *land* zie *land*; *het is* ~ *vieren* it is past four (o'clock); *hij is* ~ *de zestig* he is turned sixty; *hij heeft iets* ~ *zich* he has certain ways, there is something about him (that...); **II** *ad* over; *ik heb er één* ~ I have one left; *hij is* ~ 1 he has got across; 2 he is staying with us; 3 ⪧ he has been removed; *mijn pijn is* ~ my pain is over (better); ~ *en weer* mutually, reciprocally; *geld (tijd &) te* ~ plenty of money (time &) **over'al, 'overal** everywhere; ~ *waar* wherever **overal(l)** [o.və'rɔl] (-s) *m* overalls, dungarees, boiler-suit

'**overbekend** generally known; notorious
'**overbelasten**[1] *vt* 1 overburden; 2 ✗ over-load[2]; 3 overtax
'**overbeleefd** too polite, (over-)officious
'**overbelicht** over-exposed; –**ing** *v* over-exposure
'**overbesteding** (-en) *v* overexpenditure
'**overbevolking** *v* 1 surplus population; 2 overpopulation [and poverty]; overcrowding [in dwellings &]; **overbe'volkt** 1 overpopulated; 2 overcrowded [hospitals &]
'**overbezet** overcrowded [buses, ⇔ forms]; (d o o r p e r s o n e e l) overstaffed
over'bieden (overbood, h. overboden) *vt* outbid[2], overbid [inz. ◊]
'**overblijfsel** (-s en -en) *o* remainder, remnant, relic, remains [of animals, plants &], rest; '**overblijven**[1] *vi* be left, remain; *X blijft vannacht over* X remains for the night (will stay the night); *er bleef me niets anders over dan...* nothing was left to me (remained for me) but to..., there was nothing for it but to...; **–d** remaining; *~e plant* perennial (plant); *het ~e* the remainder, the rest; *de ~en* the survivors
'**overbloezen** (bloesde 'over, h. 'overgebloesd) *vi* blouse
over'bluffen (overblufte, h. overbluft) *vt* bluff; *overbluft* taken aback, dumbfounded
over'bodig superfluous; –**heid** (-heden) *v* superfluity
'**overboeken**[1] *vt* transfer; –**king** (-en) *v* transfer
over'boord ⚓ overboard; zie ook: *boord*
'**overbrengen**[1] *vt* carry [a thing to another place]; transfer, transport, remove [a piece of furniture &]; transmit a disease, news, heat, electricity &]; take [a message]; convey [a parcel, a letter, sound]; translate [into another language], transpose [algebraic values]; repeat [a piece of news, tales]; *de zetel van de regering ~ naar* transfer the seat of government to; –**er** (-s) *m* carrier, bearer, conveyer; *fig* telltale, informer; –**ging** (-en) *v* carrying, transport, conveyance [of goods]; transfer [of a business, sums]; transmission [of power &]; translation [of a document]; [thought] transference
'**overbrieven** (briefde 'over, h. 'overgebriefd) *vt* tell, repeat [things heard]; –**er** (-s) *m* telltale
over'bruggen (overbrugde, h. overbrugd) *vt* bridge (over), tide over; –**ging** (-en) *v* bridging
'**overbuur** (-buren) *m* opposite neighbour
'**overcompensatie** [-(t)si.] (-s) *v* overcompensation
'**overcompleet** superfluous, surplus

'**overdaad** *v* excess, superabundance; *in ~ leven* live in luxury; *~ schaadt* too much of a thing is good for nothing; **over'dadig I** *aj* superabundant; excessive; **II** *ad* superabundantly &, to excess
over'dag by day, in the day-time; during the day
over'dekken (overdekte, h. overdekt) *vt* cover (up, in); *overdekt* covered, roofed over, indoor [swimming-pool]
over'denken (overdacht, h. overdacht) *vt* consider, meditate (on); –**king** (-en) *v* consideration, reflection
'**overdoen** *vt* 1 (n o g e e n s) do [it] over again; 2 (a f s t a a n) part with, make over, sell, dispose of; *het dunnetjes ~* repeat the thing
over'donderen (overdonderde, h. overdonderd) *vt* = *overbluffen*
'**overdosis** [-zIs] (-doses en -sen) *v* overdose
over'draagbaar transferable; ✗ communicable; '**overdracht** (-en) *v* transfer, conveyance; **over'drachtelijk** metaphorical; '**overdragen**[1] *vt* carry over; *fig* convey, make over, hand over, transfer [property], assign [a right]; delegate [power], depute [a task]; *het bestuur (de leiding, de zaak &) ~* hand over
over'dreven I *aj* exaggerated [statements]; excessive, immoderate [claims]; out of proportion; **II** *ad* exaggeratedly; excessively, immoderately
1 '**overdrijven**[1] *vi* blow over[2]
2 **over'drijven** (overdreef, h. overdreven) **I** *vt* exaggerate, overdo; **II** *vi* exaggerate; –**ving** (-en) *v* exaggeration
1 '**overdruk** (-ken) *m* 1 off-print, separate (reprint) [of an article &]; 2 overprint [on postage stamps]; 3 ✗ overpressure
2 '**over'druk** *aj* too much occupied, over-busy
'**overdrukken**[1] *vt* reprint; overprint [stamps]
'**overduidelijk** very obvious
over'dwars athwart, across
over'eenbrengen[2] *vt dat is niet overeen te brengen met* it cannot be reconciled with, it is not consistent with; zie ook: *geweten*
over'eenkomen[2] **I** *vi* agree [with sbd, on sth.]; be in keeping [with]; *~ met* agree with; correspond with; **II** *vt* agree on [a price &]; **over'eenkomst** (-en) *v* 1 (g e l ij k h e i d) resemblance, similarity, conformity, agreement; *~ vertonen* resemble; 2 (v e r d r a g) agreement; **overeen'komstig I** *aj* conformable; corresponding, similar [period]; *~e hoeken* corresponding angles; *een ~e som* an equivalent sum; **II** *ad* correspondingly; *~ het bepaalde*

[1,2] V.T. en V.D. van dit werkwoord volgens het model: 1 '**overboeken**, V.T. boekte '**over**, V.D. '**over**geboekt; 2 **over'eenstemmen**, V.T. stemde **over'een**, V.D. **over'een**gestemd. Zie voor de vormen onder het grondwoord, in deze voorbeelden: *boeken* en *stemmen*. Bij sterke en onregelmatige werkwoorden wordt u verwezen naar de lijst achterin.

agreeably (conformably) to the provisions; ~ *uw wensen* in accordance with (in compliance with, in conformity with) your wishes; **–heid** (-heden) *v* conformableness, conformity, similarity

over'eenstemmen[2] *vi* agree, concur, harmonize; ~ *met* agree & with, be in accordance (in harmony) with; *dat stemt niet overeen met wat hij zei* that does not tally (is not in keeping) with what he said; **–d** consonant[2], concordant[2], harmonizing[2] [with...]; **over'eenstemming** *v* harmony; consonance; agreement, concurrence; *gram* concord; *in ~ brengen (met)* bring into line (with); *dat is niet in ~ met de feiten* that is not in accordance with the facts; *met iem. tot ~ komen* come to an understanding with sbd.; *in ~ met de omgeving* in harmony with the surroundings; *tot ~ geraken of komen (omtrent)* come to an agreement (about)

over'eind on end, upright, up, erect; *nog ~ staan* be still standing[2]; *hij ging ~ staan* he stood up; ~ *zetten* set up; *hij ging ~ zitten* he sat up; *hij krabbelde ~* to his feet

over'erfelijk hereditary, inheritable; **–heid** *v* heredity; **'overerven**[1] **I** *vt* inherit; **II** *vi* be hereditary [of a disease]; **–ving** *v* heredity, inheritance

over'eten (overat, h. overeten) *zich ~* overeat oneself, overeat

'overgaan[1] **I** *vi* 1 (a a n s l a a n) go, ring [of a bell]; 2 (b e v o r d e r d w o r d e n) be removed, get one's remove [at school]; 3 (o p h o u d e n) pass off, wear off [of suffering &]; ● *i n iets anders ~* change (develop) into something different; *in elkaar ~* become merged, merge [of colours]; *het woord is overgegaan in het Engels* the word has passed into English; *de leiding gaat over van... o p ...* the leadership passes from... to...; *alvorens wij daarto e ~* before passing on to that; ~ *[van...] t o t...* change over [from one system] to [another]; (let oneself) be converted to [Protestantism &]; *tot daden ~, tot handelen ~* proceed to action; *tot liquidatie ~* go into liquidation; *tot stemming ~* proceed to the vote; **II** *vt* go across, cross [the street &]; **'overgang** (-en) *m* transition, change; change-over [to another system]; conversion [to Roman Catholicism &]; **'overgangsbepaling** (-en) *v* temporary provision; **–examen** (-s) *o* qualifying examination; **–jaren** *mv de ~* the change of life, the menopause; **–leeftijd** (-en) *m* climacteric age; **–maatregel** (-en en -s) *m* transitional

measure; **–regeling** (-en) *v* transitional (provisional, temporary) regulation; **–stadium** (-ia en -s) *o* stage (period) of transition, transition(al) stage (phase); **–tijdperk** (-en) *o* transition(al) period; **–toestand** *m* state of transition **over'gankelijk** transitive

'overgave *v* handing over, delivery [of parcels]; giving up; surrender [of fortress, to God's will]

'overgediendig (over-)officious, obsequious

'overgelukkig most happy, overjoyed

'overgeven[1] **I** *vt* 1 (a a n r e i k e n) hand over, hand, pass [sth.]; 2 (a f s t a a n) deliver up, give over (up), yield, surrender [a town]; 3 (b r a k e n) vomit [blood]; **II** *vi* vomit, be sick; *moet je ~?* do you feel sick?; **III** *vr zich ~* surrender; *zich ~ aan...* abandon oneself to..., indulge in...; *zich aan smart, wanhoop ~* surrender (oneself) to grief, to despair

'overgevoelig, overge'voelig over-sensitive [people]; 🎗 allergic [to pollen]; **–heid** *v* oversensitiveness; 🎗 allergy

1 'overgieten[1] *vt* poor (into *in*), transfuse, decant

2 over'gieten (overgoot, h. overgoten) *vt ~ met* pour on, cover with[2], suffuse with[2]

'overgooier (-s) *m* pinafore (dress), *Am* jumper

'overgordijn (-en) *o* curtain

'overgroot vast [majority], major [part]

'overgrootmoeder (-s) *v* great-grandmother; **–vader** (-s) *m* great-grandfather

over'haast I *aj* rash; hurried, hasty, brash; **II** *ad* rashly, hurriedly, in a hurry; **over'haasten** (overhaastte, h. overhaast) *vt & vr* hurry; **–tig** = *overhaast*; **–ting** *v* precipitation, precipitancy

'overhalen[1] *vt* 1 (m e t v e e r p o n t) ferry over; 2 (o m t r e k k e n) pull [a bell, a switch]; cock [a rifle]; 3 (d i s t i l l e r e n) distil [spirits]; 4 *fig* (o v e r r e d e n) talk (bring) round, persuade, win over

'overhand *v de ~ hebben* have the upper hand (of *op*); predominate (over *op*), prevail; *de ~ krijgen* get the upper hand, get the better (of *op*)

over'handigen (overhandigde, h. overhandigd) *vt* hand (over), present, deliver; **–ging** *v* handing over, presentation, delivery

over'hands overhand

'overhangen[1] *vi* hang over, incline, beetle

'overhebben[1] *vt* have left; *daar heeft hij alles voor over* he is willing to give anything for it; *ik heb er een pond voor over* I am willing to pay a pound for it; *wij hebben iem. over* we have sbd. staying with us

over'heen over, across; [she wore a jumper] on

---

top; *daar is hij nog niet* ~ he has not (quite) got over it yet

over'heenstappen (stapte over'heen, is over'heengestapt) *vt* step across; *over de moeilijkheden heenstappen* brush aside the difficulties; *er maar* ~ not mind that, ignore it

'**overheerlijk** delicious, exquisite

over'heersen (overheerste, h. overheerst) **I** *vt* domineer over, dominate; **II** *vi* predominate; **–d** (pre)dominant; **over'heerser** (-s) *m* ruler, tyrant; **over'heersing** *v* rule, domination

'**overheid** (-heden) *v* de ~ the authorities; the Government; '**overheids...** public [authorities, organizations, services &], government [controls]; '**overheidsambt** (-en) *o* public office; ♣ magistracy; **–dienst** (-en) *m in* ~ in the Civil Service; **–instelling** (-en) *v* government authority, administrative body; **–personeel** *o* public servants; **–persoon** (-sonen) *m* public officer; ♣ magistrate; **–wege** *van* ~ by the authorities; *van* ~ *bekendmaken* announce officially

'**overhellen**[1] *vi* hang over, lean over, incline, ⚓ list, ✈ bank; ~ *naar* [*fig*] incline to(wards), have a leaning to, lean towards; **–ling** *v* inclination[2], leaning[2]; ⚓ list

'**overhemd** (-en) *o* shirt

'**overhevelen**[1] *vt* transfer[2]; **–ling** *v* transfer[2]

over'hoeks diagonal

over'hoop in a heap, pell-mell, in a mess, topsyturvy; ~ *halen* turn over, put in disorder; ~ *liggen met* be a variance (at odds) with; ~ *schieten* shoot down; ~ *steken* stab; ~ *werpen* overthrow, upset

over'horen (overhoorde, h. overhoord) *vt* hear [a boy, a lesson]

'**overhouden**[1] *vt* save [money]; *iets overgehouden hebben* have sth. left

'**overig I** *aj* remaining; *het* ~*e Europa* the rest of Europe; **II** *sb het* ~*e* the remainder; *voor het* ~*e* for the rest; *de* ~*en* the others, the rest

'**overigens** apart from that [all is well, he is quite sane], after all, moreover [I don't know...]; by the way, [he] incidentally [looked quite the gentleman]

over'ijld = *overhaast*; **over'ijlen** (overijlde, h. overijld) *zich* ~ hurry; **–ling** *v* precipitation, precipitancy

over'jarig, '**overjarig** last year's, too old, overdue; perennial [plant]

'**overjas** (-sen) *m* & *v* overcoat, greatcoat, top-coat

'**overkalken**[1] *vt fig* copy, crib

'**overkant** *m* opposite side, other side; *aan de* ~ *van* ook: beyond [the river, the Alps], across [the Channel]; *hij woont aan de* ~ he lives over the way (across the road, opposite)

over'kappen (overkapte, h. overkapt) *vt* roof in; **–ping** (-en) *v* roof; zie ook: *luifel*

'**overkijken**[1] *vt* look over, go through

over'klassen (overklaste, h. overklast) *vt sp* outclass

'**overkleed** (-kledaren en -kleren) *o* upper garment [of a priest &]

'**overklimmen**[1] *vt* climb over

over'kluizen (overkluisde, h. overkluisd) *vt* vault, overarch

over'koepelen (overkoepelde, h. overkoepeld) *vt* co-ordinate

'**overkoken** (kookte 'over, is 'overgekookt) *vi* boil over

over'komelijk surmountable

1 '**overkomen**[1] *vi* come over; *goed* ~ [*fig*] **F** come across [of a joke, message, play]; *ik kan maar eens in de week* ~ I can come to see (him, her, them) but once a week

2 over'komen (overkwam, is overkomen) *vt* befall, happen to; *er is hem een ongeluk* ~ he has met with an accident; *dat is mij nog nooit* ~ I never yet had that happen to me

'**overkomst** *v* coming, visit

over'kropt overburdened; *haar overkropt gemoed* her overburdened heart

'**overlaat** (-laten) *m* overflow

1 '**overladen**[1] *vt* 1 tranship [goods]; transfer [from one train into another]; 2 (o p n i e u w) reload

2 over'laden (overlaadde, h. overladen) *vt* overload[2], overburden[2]; *fig* overstock [the market]; overcrowd; *iem. met geschenken* (*verwijten &*) ~ shower presents upon sbd., heap reproaches upon sbd.; *zich de maag* ~ surfeit one's stomach, overeat (oneself)

1 '**overlading** *v* 1 transhipment, transfer; 2 reloading

2 over'lading (-en) *v* surfeit [of the stomach]; *fig* overburdening, overloading

'**overladingskosten** *mv* $ transhipment charges

over'land by land; **–mail** [-me.l] *v* ▓ overland mail

over'langs I *aj* longitudinal; **II** *ad* lengthwise, longitudinally

over'lappen (overlapte, h. overlapt) *vi* & *vt* overlap

'**overlast** *m* annoyance, nuisance; ~ *aandoen* annoy; *tot* ~ *van* to the inconvenience of

---

[1] V.T. en V.D. van dit werkwoord volgens het model: '**over**boeken, V.T. boekte '**over**, V.D. '**over**geboekt. Zie voor de vormen onder het grondwoord, in dit voorbeeld: *boeken*. Bij sterke en onregelmatige werkwoorden wordt u verwezen naar de lijst achterin.

'over'laten[1] *vt* leave; *dat laat ik aan u over* I leave that to you; *laat dat maar aan hem over* let him alone to do it; *aan zich zelf overgelaten* left to himself, left to his own resources; zie ook: *lot*

over'leden deceased, dead; **-e** (-n) *m-v de* ~ the dead (man, woman); *de* ~(*n*) the deceased, the departed, the defunct

'overle(d)er *o* upper leather, vamp

over'leg *o* 1 deliberation, forethought, judg(e)ment, management; 2 (b e r a a d s l a-g i n g) deliberation, consultation; ~ *is het halve werk* a stitch in time saves nine; ~ *plegen* consult together; ~ *plegen met* consult; *i n* ~ *met...* in consultation with...; *m e t* ~ with deliberation; *z o n d e r* ~ without (taking) thought

1 'over'leggen[1] *vt* 1 (a a n b i e d e n) hand over, produce [a document]; 2 (b e s p a r e n) lay by, put by [money]

2 over'leggen (overlegde, h. overlegd) *vt* deliberate, consider; *je moet het maar met hem* ~ you should consult with him about it

1 'overlegging *v* production; *na (onder)* ~ *der stukken* upon (against) presentation and surrender of the documents

2 over'legging (-en) *v* consideration, deliberation; over'legorgaan (-ganen) *o* consultative body

over'leven (overleefde, h. overleefd) *vt* survive, outlive; **-de** (-n) *m-v* survivor, longest liver

'overleveren[1] *vt* transmit, hand down; ~ *aan* give up to, deliver up to; *overgeleverd aan...* at the mercy of [impostors, swindlers &]; **-ring** (-en) *v* tradition

over'levingskans (-en) *v* chance of survival

'overlezen[1] *vt* read over, go through

'overligdag (-dagen) *m* day of demurrage; **-geld** (-en) *o* demurrage; 'overliggen[1] *vi* be on demurrage

over'lijden (overleed, is overleden) **I** *vi* die, ⊙ pass away, depart this life, decease; *aan de bekomen verwondingen* ~ die of injuries; **II** *o* death, ⊙ decease, ⚖ demise; *bij* ~ in the event of death; over'lijdensakte (-s en -n) *v* death certificate; **-bericht** (-en) *o* announcement of sbd.'s death; obituary (notice); **-datum** (-ta en -s) *m* date of death

'overloop (-lopen) *m* 1 (b ij h u i s) corridor; 2 (v a n t r a p) landing; 3 (v a n r i v i e r) overflow

1 'overlopen[1] **I** *vi* 1 run over, overflow; 2 go over, desert, defect [to the West, to the East]; *naar de vijand* ~ go over to the enemy; *hij loopt*

over van vriendelijkheid he is all kindness; **II** *vt* cross [a road]

2 over'lopen (overliep, h. overlopen) *vt* visit too frequently; *je overloopt ons ook niet* we don't see much of you

'overloper (-s) *m* deserter, turncoat, defector [to capitalism, to communism]

over'luid aloud

'overmaat *v* over-measure; *fig* excess; *tot* ~ *van ramp* to make matters (things) worse, on top of all that

'overmacht *v* 1 superior power, superior forces; 2 ⚖ force majeure; 3 ⚓ the Act of God; *voor de* ~ *bezwijken* succumb to superior numbers; over'machtig stronger, superior (in numbers)

'overmaken[1] *vt* 1 (o p n i e u w m a k e n) do over again [one's work]; 2 (o v e r z e n d e n) make over, remit [money]; **-king** (-en) *v* remittance

over'mannen (overmande, h. overmand) *vt* overpower, overcome; *overmand door slaap* overcome by sleep

over'matig excessive

over'meesteren (overmeesterde, h. over-meesterd) *vt* overmaster, overpower, conquer; **-ring** *v* conquest

'overmoed *m* recklessness; (a a n m a t i g i n g) presumption; over'moedig reckless; (a a n m a t i g e n d) presumptuous

'overmorgen *m* the day after to-morrow

over'naads clinker-built [boat]

over'nachten (overnachtte, h. overnacht) *vi* stop (during the night), pass the night, stay overnight [at a hotel]; **-ting** (-en) *v* overnight stay [at a hotel]

'overname *v* taking over; adoption; purchase; *ter* ~ *aangeboden... ...*for sale; 'overnemen[1] *vt* take [something] from; take over [a business, command &], adopt [a word from another language], borrow, copy [something from an author]; take up [the refrain]; buy [books &]; *de dienst (de wacht, de zaak &)* ~ take over; *gewoonten* ~ adopt habits; 'overnemertje (-s) *o* cat's cradle

'overoud very old, ancient

'overpad (-paden) *o* foot-path; *recht van* ~ right of way

'overpakken[1] *vt* 1 pack from one thing into another; 2 repack, pack again

over'peinzen (overpeinsde, h. overpeinsd) *vt* meditate, reflect upon; **-zing** [-en] *v* meditation, reflection

---

[1] V.T. en V.D. van dit werkwoord volgens het model: 'over**boeken**, V.T. boekte 'over, V.D. 'over**geboekt**. Zie voor de vormen onder het grondwoord, in dit voorbeeld: *boeken*. Bij sterke en onregelmatige werkwoorden wordt u verwezen naar de lijst achterin.

'**overpennen**[1] *vt* copy; crib
'**overplaatsen**[1] *vt* remove; *fig* transfer [an officer &]; **–sing** (-en) *v* removal; transfer [of an officer]
'**overplanten**[1] *vt* transplant; **–ting** (-en) *v* transplantation
over'prikkelen (overprikkelde, h. overprikkeld) *vt* overexcite; **–ling** (-en) *v* overexcitement
'**overproduktie** *v* overproduction
over'reden (overreedde, h. overreed) *vt* persuade, prevail upon [sbd.], talk [sbd.] round; *hij wou mij ~ om...* he wanted to persuade met to..., to persuade me into ...ing; *hij was niet te ~* he was not to be persuaded; **–d** persuasive; **over'reding** *v* persuasion; **–skracht** *v* persuasiveness, power of persuasion, persuasive powers
'**overreiken**[1] *vt* hand, reach, pass
over'rijden (overreed, h. overreden) *vt* run over [a person, a dog]
'**overrijp** over-ripe
over'rompelen (overrompelde, h. overrompeld) *vt* surprise, take by surprise, catch off-balance; **–ling** (-en) *v* surprise attack, surprise[2]
over'schaduwen (overschaduwde, h. overschaduwd) *vt* shade, overshadow; *fig* throw into the shade, eclipse
'**overschakelen**[1] *vi* switch over[2], change over[2] [from... to...]; ⚙ change gear; *we schakelen (u) over naar de concertzaal* we are taking you over to the concert hall; *~ op de tweede* ⚙ change into second
over'schatten (overschatte, h. overschat) *vt* overrate, overestimate; **–ting** *v* overestimation, overrating
'**overschenken**[1] *vt* decant, pour over [in a glass]
'**overschepen** (scheepte 'over, h. 'overgescheept) *vt* tranship; **–ping** (-en) *v* transhipment
'**overscheppen**[1] *vt* scoop (ladle) from... into...
'**overschieten**[1] *vi* remain, be left
1 '**overschilderen**[1] *vt* 1 paint over, repaint; 2 **over'schilderen** (overschilderde, h. overschilderd) paint out [to make it invisible]
'**overschoen** (-en) *m* overshoe, galosh, golosh
'**overschot** (-ten) *o* remainder, rest; surplus, overplus; *zie ook: stoffelijk*
over'schreeuwen (overschreeuwde, h. overschreeuwd) **I** *vt* cry down, shout down, roar down; *hij kon ze niet ~ ook:* he could not make himself heard; **II** *vr zich ~* overstrain one's

voice
over'schrijden (overschreed, h. overschreden) *vt* step across, cross; *fig* overstep [the bounds], exceed [one's powers, the speed limit &]
'**overschrijven**[1] *vt* write out (fair), copy (out) [a letter &]; $ transfer; *iets op iemands naam laten ~* have a property transferred; *je hebt dat van mij overgeschreven* you have copied that from me; '**overschrijving** (-en) *v* transcription; $ transfer; **–skosten** *mv*, **–rechten** *mv* transfer duties
'**overseinen**[1] *vt* transmit, telegraph, wire
'**overslaan** **I** *vt* 1 (g e e n b e u r t g e v e n) pass [sbd.] over; 2 (n i e t l e z e n &) omit, skip [a line], jump [some pages], miss [a performance]; 3 ⚓ tranship [goods]; **II** *vi* ...*zei zij, terwijl haar stem oversloeg* with a catch in her voice; *~ op* 1 spread to [of a fire]; 2 infect [of laughter &]; '**overslag** (-slagen) *m* 1 (a a n k l e d i n g s t u k) turn-up; 2 (v. e n v e l o p p e) flap; 3 (r a m i n g) estimate; 4 ⚓ transhipment; **–haven** (-s) *v* ⚓ port of transhipment, transhipment harbour
1 **over'spannen** (overspande, h. overspannen) **I** *vt* span [a river &]; overstrain; **II** *vr zich ~* overexert oneself; 2 **over'spannen** *aj* overstrung, overstrained, overwrought [nerves, imagination]; **–ning** (-en) *v* 1 span [of a bridge]; 2 overstrain, overexertion, overexcitement
'**oversparen**[1] *vt* save, lay aside [money]
'**overspel** *o* adultery
1 '**overspelen**[1] *vt* replay [a match]; *een overgespeelde wedstrijd* a replay
2 **over'spelen** (overspeelde, h. overspeeld) *vt* outclass [a team]
over'spelig adulterous
over'spoelen (overspoelde, h. overspoeld) *vt* flood, overrun
'**overspringen**[1] **I** *vi* 1 leap over, jump over; 2 ⚡ jump over; **II** *vt* jump [ten lines &]
'**overstaan** *ten ~ van* in the presence of, before
'**overstaand** opposite
over'stag *~ gaan* ⚓ tack (about), go about, change one's tack[2]
'**overstapje** (-s), '**overstapkaartje** (-s) *o* correspondence ticket, transfer (ticket); '**overstappen**[1] *vt* 1 cross, step over; 2 change (into another train), transfer [to an open car]
'**overste** (-n) *m* 1 ✠ lieutenant-colonel; 2 *rk* prior, Father Superior; *~ v* prioress, Mother Superior
'**oversteek** (-steken) *m* crossing; **–plaats** (-en) *v*

---

[1] V.T. en V.D. van dit werkwoord volgens het model: '**overboeken**, V.T. boekte '**over**, V.D. '**over**geboekt. Zie voor de vormen onder het grondwoord, in dit voorbeeld: *boeken*. Bij sterke en onregelmatige werkwoorden wordt u verwezen naar de lijst achterin.

pedestrian crossing, crossing; **'oversteken I** (stak 'over, is 'overgestoken) *vi* cross (over); *gelijk* ~ swap at the same time; **II** (stak 'over, h. 'overgestoken) *vt* cross

over'stelpen (overstelpte, h. overstelpt) *vt* overwhelm[2]; *we worden overstelpt met aanvragen* we are swamped (inundated, flooded, overrun) with applications

1 'overstemmen[1] **I** *vt* tune again [a piano]; **II** *vi* vote again

2 over'stemmen (overstemde, h. overstemd) *vt* drown [sbd.'s voice]; outvote [sbd.]

'overstort (-en) *m* overflow

1 'overstromen *vi* overflow

2 over'stromen (overstroomde, h. overstroomd) *vt* inundate[2], flood; *overstroomd door dagjesmensen* overrun by cheap trippers; *de market* ~ *met...* flood, glut (deluge) the market with...; **–ming** (-en) *v* inundation, flood

'oversturen[1] = *overzenden*

over'stuur out of order; upset, in a dither; *zij was helemaal* ~ she was quite upset, she was all of a dither

over'tallig supernumerary

'overtappen[1] *vt* transfer from one cask to another

1 'overtekenen[1] *vt* redraw [a drawing]; (n a t e k e n e n) copy

2 over'tekenen (overtekende, h. overtekend) *vt* oversubscribe [a loan]

'overtellen[1] *vt* count again, recount

'overtikken[1] *vt* type out

'overtocht (-en) *m* passage, crossing

over'tollig superfluous, redundant; surplus [stock]; **–heid** (-heden) *v* superfluity, superfluousness, redundancy

over'treden (overtrad, h. overtreden) *vt* contravene, transgress, infringe [the law]; break (through) [rules]; **–er** (-s) *m* transgressor, breaker [of rules], trespasser; **over'treding** (-en) *v* contravention, transgression, infringement, breach [of the rules], trespass

over'treffen (overtrof, h. overtroffen) *vt* surpass, exceed, excel, outdo, outvie; *iem.* ~ outmatch sbd.; *zich zelf* ~ surpass (excel) oneself; *de vraag overtreft het aanbod* demand exceeds supply

'overtrek (-ken) *o* & *m* case, casing, cover

1 'overtrekken[1] **I** *vt* 1 (t r e k k e n o v e r) pull across; 2 (o v e r h a l e n) pull [the trigger]; 3 (g a a n o v e r) cross [a river &]; 4 (n a - t r e k k e n) trace [a drawing]; **II** *vi* blow over [of a thunderstorm]

2 over'trekken (overtrok, h. overtrokken) *vt* 1 cover, upholster [furniture]; recover [an umbrella]; 2 $ overdraw [one's account]; 3 (v. v l i e g t u i g) stall; 4 (o v e r d r ij v e n) overdraw, overact

'overtrekpapier *o* tracing-paper

over'troeven (overtroefde, h. overtroefd) *vt* overtrump; *fig* go one better than [sbd.], score off [sbd.]

over'tuigd staunch [supporter], true [socialist]; **over'tuigen** (overtuigde, h. overtuigd) **I** *vt* convince; **II** *vr zich* ~ convince oneself, make sure; *zich* ~ *van* ascertain, see for oneself; **III** *va* carry convincing; **–d** convincing;

over'tuiging (-en) *v* conviction; *de* ~ *hebben dat...* be convinced that; *tot de* ~ *komen dat...* come to the conclusion (conviction) that...; *uit* ~ from conviction; *stuk van* ~ 𝕏 exhibit; **–skracht** *v* force of conviction, convincing power, cogency

'overtypen[1] [-ti.pə(n), -tɪpə(n)] *vt* type out.

'overuren *mv* overtime, hours of overtime; ~ *maken* work overtime

'overvaart (-en) *v* passage, crossing

'overval (-len) *m* raid [also by police], hold-up; **over'vallen** (overviel, h. overvallen) *vt* 1 (a a n v a l l e n) raid, assault; 2 (v. o n w e e r &) overtake; 3 (v e r r a s s e n) take by surprise, surprise; *door de regen* ~ caught in the rain; **'overvalwagen** (-s) *m* police van

1 'overvaren[1] **I** *vi* cross (over); **II** *vt* cross [a river]; take [a person] across

2 over'varen (overvoer, h. overvaren) *vt* run down [a vessel]

'oververhitten (oververhitte, h. oververhit) *vt* overheat; superheat [steam]

'oververmoeid over-fatigued, overtired; **over'vermoeidheid** *v* over-fatigue

'oververtellen (vertelde 'over, h. 'oververteld) *vt* repeat, tell

'ververven[1] *vt* 1 redye; 2 = *overschilderen*

'oververzadigen (oververzadigde, h. oververzadigd) *vt* 1 supersaturate [a solution]; 2 *fig* surfeit; **–ging** *v* 1 supersaturation; 2 *fig* surfeit

over'vleugelen (overvleugelde, h. overvleugeld) *vt* 1 surpass, outstrip; 2 𝕏 outflank

'overvliegen[1] *vt* fly over; fly across

'overvloed *m* abundance, plenty, profusion; ~ *hebben van* abound in; *...i n* ~ *hebben* have plenty of...; *t e n* ~*e* moreover, needless to say; **over'vloedig** abundant, plentiful, copious, profuse; lush, rich

'overvloeien[1] *vi* overflow; ~ *van* abound in,

---

[1] V.T. en V.D. van dit werkwoord volgens het model: **'over**boeken, V.T. boekte **'over**, V.D. **'over**geboekt. Zie voor de vormen onder het grondwoord, in dit voorbeeld: *boeken*. Bij sterke en onregelmatige werkwoorden wordt u verwezen naar de lijst achterin.

brim with; swim [with tears]; ~ *van melk en honing* **B** flow with milk and honey
over'voeden (overvoedde, h. overvoed) *vt* overfeed; **–ding** *v* overfeeding
1 **'overvoeren**[1] *vt* carry over, transport
2 **over'voeren** (overvoerde, h. overvoerd) *vt* overfeed; *fig* overstock, glut, flood [the market]
'overvol full to overflowing, chock-full, overcrowded, crowded [house]
'overvracht *v* excess luggage, excess
over'vragen (overvroeg, overvraagde, h. overvraagd) *vt* ask too much, overcharge
'overwaaien[1] *vi* blow over
'overwaarde *v* surplus value
'overwaarderen[1] *vt* overvalue; **–ring** *v* overvaluation
1 **'overweg** (-wegen) *m* level crossing; *onbewaakte* ~ unguarded level crossing
2 **over'weg** *met iets* ~ *kunnen* know how to manage sth.; *ik kan goed met hem* ~ I can get on with him very well; *zij kunnen niet met elkaar* ~ they don't hit it off
1 **'overwegen**[1] *vt* reweigh, weigh again
2 **over'wegen** (overwoog, h. overwogen) *vt* consider, weigh, think over, contemplate
over'wegend preponderant; *van* ~ *belang* of paramount importance; ~ *droog weer* dry on the whole; *de bevolking is* ~ *Duits* predominantly German
over'weging (-en) *v* 1 consideration; 2 (g e d a c h t e) reflection; *iem. iets i n* ~ *geven* suggest sth. to sbd., recommend sth. to sbd.; *in* ~ *nemen* take into consideration; *t e r* ~ for reflection; *u i t* ~ *van* in consideration of
'overwegwachter (-s) *m* gateman, crossing keeper
over'weldigen (overweldigde, h. overweldigd) *vt* overpower [a person]; usurp [a throne]; **–d** overwhelming; **over'weldiger** (-s) *m* usurper; **over'weldiging** *v* usurpation
over'welfsel (-s) *o* vault; **over'welven** (overwelfde, h. overwelfd) *vt* overarch, vault; **–ving** (-en) *v* vault
'overwerk *o* extra work, overwork, overtime;
1 **'overwerken**[1] *vi* work overtime
2 **over'werken** (overwerkte, h. overwerkt) *zich* ~ overwork oneself
'overwerktarief (-rieven) *o* overtime rate; **–uren** zie *overuren*
'overwicht *o* overbalance; *fig* preponderance, ascendancy; *het* ~ *hebben* preponderate
over'winnaar (-s en -naren) *m* conqueror, victor; **over'winnen** (overwon, h. over-

wonnen) **I** *vt* conquer, vanquish, overcome [the enemy]; *fig* conquer, overcome, surmount [difficulties]; *een overwonnen standpunt* an exploded idea; **II** *va* conquer, vanquish, be victorious; **–d** victorious, conquering;
over'winning (-en) *v* victory; *de* ~ *behalen op* gain the victory over; *het heeft mij een* ~ *gekost* it has been an effort to me
'overwinst (-en) *v* surplus profit, excess profit
over'winteren (overwinterde, h. overwinterd) *vi* winter; hibernate; **–ring** (-en) *v* wintering; hibernation
'overwippen[1] **I** *vi* pop over; *kom eens* ~ just slip across, step round; *naar A.* ~ pop over to A.; **II** *vt* pop across [the road]
over'woekeren (overwoekerde, h. overwoekerd) *vt* grow over; *overwoekerd* overgrown (*door,* with)
over'wonnene (-n) *m,* **over'wonneling** (-en) *m* vanquished person; *de overwonnenen* the vanquished
over'zees oversea(s)
'overzeilen[1] **I** *vi* sail over, sail across; **II** *vt* sail across, sail [the seas]
'overzenden[1] *vt* send, forward, dispatch; transmit [a message]; remit [money]; **–ding** *v* dispatch; transmission; remittance
'overzetboot (-boten) *m* & *v* ferry-boat; **'overzetten**[1] *vt* 1 (o v e r v a r e n) ferry over, take across; 2 (v e r t a l e n) translate; **–er** (-s) *m* 1 ♃ ferryman; 2 translator; **'overzetting** (-en) *v* translation
'overzicht (-en) *o* survey, synopsis, [general] view, review [of foreign affairs &]; *beknopt* ~ resumé, summary, abstract; **over'zichtelijk** **I** *aj* clear, neat [arrangement of the matters]; **II** *ad* clearly [arranged]; **–heid** *v* clarity [of the arrangement]
1 **'overzien**[1] *vt* look over, go through
2 **over'zien** (overzag, h. overzien) *vt* overlook, survey; *alles met één blik* ~ take in everything at a glance, sum up a situation; *niet te* ~ immense, vast[2]; incalculable [consequences]
'overzij(de) *v = overkant*
'overzwemmen[1] *vt* swim across, swim [the Channel]
O'vidius *m* Ovid
ovu'latie [-(t)si.] (-s) *v* ovulation
o'weeër (-s) *m* war-profiteer
oxy'datie [ɔksi.'da.(t)si.] (-s) *v* oxidation. **o'xyde** (-n en -s) *o* oxide; **oxy'deren** (oxydeerde, h. geoxydeerd) *vt* & *vi* oxidize
o'zon, 'ozon *o* & *m* ozone

---

[1] V.T. en V.D. van dit werkwoord volgens het model: **'overboeken**, V.T. boekte **'over**, V.D. **'over**geboekt. Zie voor de vormen onder het grondwoord, in dit voorbeeld: *boeken*. Bij sterke en onregelmatige werkwoorden wordt u verwezen naar de lijst achterin.

p [pe.] ('s) *v* p
p.a. = *per adres*
pa ('s) *m* **F** pa(pa), dad(dy)
'**paadje** (-s) *o* footpath, walk
paai (-en) *m* gaffer; *ouwe* ~ ook: old fog(e)y
1 '**paaien** (paaide, h. gepaaid) *vt* appease, soothe
2 '**paaien** (paaide, h. gepaaid) *vi* spawn [of fish]; '**paaiplaats** (-en) *v* spawning grounds; **–tijd** (-en) *m* spawning season
paal (palen) m 1 pile [driven into ground]; pole [rising out of ground], post [strong pole]; stake, ✗ palisade; 2 ∅ pale; ~ *en perk* metes and bounds; ~ *en perk stellen aan* check [a disease], put a stop to, stop [abuses], set bounds to; *dat staat als een* ~ *boven water* that's a fact, that is unquestionable; **–bewoner** (-s) *m* lake-dweller; **–dorp** (-en) *o* lake-village, lacustrine settlement; **–tje** (-s) *o* picket, peg; **–vast** as firm as a rock; **–werk** (-en) *o* pile-work, palisade; **–woning** (-en) *v* pile-dwelling, lake-dwelling
paap (papen) *m* > papist; priest
'**paapje** (-s) *o* ✿ whinchat
paaps > papistic(al), popish
paar (paren) *o* pair [of shoes &]; couple, brace [of partridges &]; *een* ~ *dagen* a day or two; a few days; *een* ~ *dingen* one or two things; *een gelukkig* ~ a happy pair (couple); *verliefde paren* couples of lovers; *zij vormen geen* ~ they don't match; ~ *a a n* ~ two together; *b ij paren, bij het* ~ *verkopen* in pairs
paard (-en) *o* 1 🐴 horse; 2 (s c h a a k s p e l) knight; 3 (g y m n a s t i e k) (vaulting-)horse; ~ *en rijtuig houden* keep a carriage; ~ *rijden* ride (on horseback); *(de)* ~*en die de haver verdienen krijgen ze niet* desert and reward seldom keep company; *het beste* ~ *struikelt wel eens* it is a good horse that never stumbles; *men moet een gegeven* ~ *niet in de bek zien* you must not look a gift horse in the mouth; *het* ~ *achter de wagen spannen* put the cart before the horse; ● *o p het* ~ *helpen* [*fig*] give a leg up; *hij wordt hier o v e r het* ~ *getild* he is made too much of here; *t e* ~ on horseback, mounted; *te* ~ *!* to horse!; zie ook: *stijgen* &; '**paardebloem** (-en) *v* dandelion; **–dek** (-ken) *o*, **–deken** (-s) *v* horse-cloth; **–haar** *o* horsehair; **–haren** *aj* horsehair; **–hoef** (-hoeven) *m* hoof (of a horse); **–hoofdstel** (-len) *o* headstall; **–horzel** (-s) *v* horse-fly, gad-fly; **–knecht** (-en) *m* groom; **–kracht** (-en) *v* horse-power, h.p.; **–middel** (-en) *o*

horse-physic; *fig* kill or cure remedy; **–mop** (-pen) *v* shaggy-dog story; '**paardenfokker** (-s) *m* horse-breeder; **paardenfokke**'**rij** (-en) *v* 1 horse-breeding; 2 stud; stud-farm; '**paardenhandel** *m* horse-trade; **–koper** (-s) *m* horse-dealer, coper; **–markt** (-en) *v* horse-fair; **–rennen** *mv* races; **–slager** (-s) *m* horse-butcher; '**paardenslage**'**rij** (-en) *v* horse-butcher's shop; '**paardenspel** (-len) *o* circus; **paardenstoete**'**rij** (-en) *v* stud; stud-farm; '**paardenvolk** *o* cavalry, horse; '**paarderas** (-sen) *o* breed of horses; **–sport** *v* equestrianism; **–sprong** (-en) *m* knight's move; **–staart** (-en) *m* 1 horse-tail (ook 🌿); 2 (h a a r-d r a c h t) pony tail; **–stal** (-len) *m* stable; **–toom** (-tomen) *m* bridle; **–tram** [-trɪm] (-s), **–trem** (-s) *v* horse-tramway; **–tuig** *o* harness; **–vijg** (-en) *v* ball of horse-dung; ~*en* horse-manure; **–vlees** *o* horseflesh, (a l s g e r e c h t) horse meat; *hij heeft* ~ *gegeten* **J** he has got the fidgets; **–vlieg** (-en) *v* horse-fly; **–voet** (-en) *m* 1 horse's foot; 2 club-foot; '**paardje** (-s) *o* little horse, **F** gee-gee; ~ *spelen* play horses; '**paardmens** (-en) *m* centaur; **–rijden** *o* riding (on horse-back), horse-riding; (a l s k u n s t) horsemanship; *zij gingen* ~ they went out riding; **–rijder** (-s) *m* rider, horseman, equestrian; **–rijdster** (-s) *v* horsewoman, lady equestrian
paarle'**moer** *o* mother-of-pearl, nacre; **–en** *aj* mother-of-pearl [buttons &]
paars *aj* & *o* (~- r o o d) purple, (~- b l a u w) violet
paarsge'**wijs, –ge**'**wijze** in pairs, two and two
'**paartijd** *m* pairing-time, mating-time
'**paartje** (-s) *o* couple [of lovers]
'**paasbest** *o* Easter best, Sunday best; **–brood** (-broden) *o* 1 Easter loaf [of the Christians]; 2 Passover bread [of the Jews]; **–dag** (-dagen) *m* Easter day; **–ei** (-eieren) *o* Easter egg; '**Paaseiland** *o* Easter Island; '**paasfeest** (-en) *o* 1 Feast of Easter; 2 Passover [of the Jews]; **–haas** (-hazen) *m* Easter bunny; **–lam** (-meren) *o* paschal lamb; **Paas**'**maandag** *m* Easter Monday; '**paasplicht** *m* & *v rk* Easter duties; **–tijd** *m* Easter time; **–vakantie** [-(t)si.] (-s) *v* Easter holidays; **–vuur** (-vuren) *o* Easter bonfire; **–week** *v* Easter week; **Paas**'**zondag** *m* Easter Sunday
'**paatje** (-s) *o* **F** daddy
'**pacemaker** ['pe:sme:kər] (-s) *m* pace-maker, *Am* cardiac pacemaker

pacht (-en) *v* 1 ('t p a c h t e n) lease; 2 (g e l d) rent; *in ~ geven* let out, farm out; *in ~ hebben* hold on lease, rent; *in ~ nemen* take on lease, rent; *vrij van ~* rent-free; zie ook *wijsheid*; **–boer** (-en) *m* tenant farmer; **–contract** (-en) *o* lease; **'pachten** (pachtte, h. gepacht) *vt* rent; ✎ farm [a monopoly]; **–er** (-s) *m* tenant, tenant farmer [of a farm]; lessee, leaseholder [of a theatre &]; ✎ farmer [of a monopoly]; **'pachtgeld** (-en) *o* rent; **–hoeve** (-n) *v* farm; **–kamer** (-s) *v* ⅏ court for lend-lease disputes; **–som** (-men) *v* rent; **–termijn** (-en) *m* tenancy; **–vrij** rent-free

pacifi'catie [pa.si.fi.′ka.(t)si.] (-s en -iën) *v* pacification; **pacifi'ceren** (pacificeerde, h. gepacificeerd) *vt* pacify; **paci'fisme** *o* pacifism; **–'fist** (-en) *m* pacifist; **–'fistisch** pacifist

pact (-en) *o* pact

1 pad (paden) *o* path² [of virtue &], walk; (t u s s e n z i t p l a a t s e n) gangway, aisle; *op ~ gaan* set out; *op het ~ zijn* be about

2 pad (-den) *v* ⅏ toad

'paddel (-s) = *peddel*

'paddestoel (-en) *m* 1 toadstool; 2 (e e t b a r e) mushroom; *eetbare ~en* ook: edible fungi; *als ~en verrijzen* spring up like mushrooms; **–wolk** (-en) *v* mushroom cloud

'paden meerv. van 1 *pad*

'padie *m* paddy

'padvinder (-s) *m* 1 (boy) scout; 2 (b a a n - b r e k e r) pathfinder; **padvinde'rij** *v* (boy-) scout movement, scouting; **'padvindster** (-s) *v* girl guide

paf *ij* puff!; bang!; *hij stond er ~ van* he was staggered, **F** he was flabbergasted

'paffen (pafte, h. gepaft) *vi* 1 puff [at a pipe]; 2 pop [with a gun]; **'pafferig** puffy, bloated

pag. = *pagina*

pa'gaai (-en) *m* paddle; **pa'gaaien** (pagaaide, h. gepagaaid) *vi* & *vt* paddle

'page [′pa.ʒə] (-s) *m* page, **F** buttons; **–kop** (-pen) *m* bobbed hair

'pagina ('s) *v* page [of a book]; **pagi'neren** (pagineerde, h. gepagineerd) *vt* page, paginate; **–ring** (-en) *v* paging, pagination

pa'gode (-s) *v* pagoda

pail'let [pai′jɪt] (-ten) *v* spangle, sequin

pair [pɛːr] (-s) *m* peer; **–schap** *o* peerage

pais *v in ~ en vree* amicably, peacefully

pak (-ken) *o* 1 package, parcel, packet [of matches], bundle; [pedlar's] pack; *fig* load; 2 suit [of clothes]; *een ~ slaag* a thrashing, a flogging, a drubbing, **F** a hiding; *een ~ voor de broek* a spanking; *wij kregen een nat ~* we got wet through; *ik ben niet bang voor een nat ~* I don't fear a wetting; *mij viel een ~ van het hart* that was a load off my mind; ● *bij de ~ken*

neerzitten sit down in despair, give it up as a bad job; *m e t ~ en zak* (with) bag and baggage; **–ezel** (-s) *m* pack-mule; **–garen** *o* packthread

'pakhuis (-huizen) *o* warehouse; **–huur** *v* warehouse rent, storage; **–knecht** (-en en -s) *m* warehouseman; **–meester** (-s) *m* warehouse-keeper

'pakijs *o* pack-ice

Paki'staans Pakistani; **'Pakistan** *o* Pakistan; **Paki'stani** ('s) *m* Pakistani

'pakkamer (-s) *v* packing-room; **'pakken** (pakte, h. gepakt) **I** *vt* 1 (g r ij p e n) seize, clutch, grasp, take [sth. up, sbd.'s hands]; 2 (o m h e l z e n) hug, cuddle [a child &]; 3 (i n p a k k e n) pack [one's trunk]; 4 *fig* fetch [one's public], grip [the reader]; *mag ik even mijn zakdoek ~?* may I get my handkerchief?; *pak ze!* sick him!; *het te ~ hebben* have caught a cold; *hij heeft het erg (zwaar) te ~* **F** it's hit him very hard, he has got it badly; *hij zal het gauw te ~ hebben* he will soon get the trick of it; *je hebt de koorts te ~* you have got fever (on you); *als ik hem te ~ krijg* 1 [I'll tell him] if I can get hold of him; 2 [I'll smash him] if he ever falls into my clutches; *ze kunnen hem niet te ~ krijgen* 1 they can't get hold of him; 2 they can't catch him; *iem. te ~ nemen* 1 make a fool of sbd.; pull sbd.'s leg; 2 take sbd. in; **II** *va* ball, bind [of snow]; *ik moet nog ~* 1 must pack (up); *het stuk pakt niet* the play does not catch on; *de zaag pakt niet* the saw doesn't bite; **–d** fetching, taking [manner]; gripping [story]; catchy [melodies, songs]; telling [device]; **'pakker** (-s) *m* packer; **'pakker(d)** (-s) *m* **F** hug, squeeze

pak'ket (-ten) *o* parcel, packet; *fig* package; **–boot** (-boten) *m* & *v* packet-boat; **–post** *v* parcel post; **–vaart** *v* packet service

'pakking (-en en -s) *v* ⚒ packing; gasket; **–ring** (-en) *v* ⚒ gasket-ring

'pakkist (-en) *v* (packing-)case; **–knecht** (-en en -s) *m* packer; **–linnen** (-s) *o* packing-cloth, packing sheet, canvas; **–loon** *o* packing-charges; **–mand** (-en) *v* hamper; **–naald** (-en) *v* packing-needle; **–paard** (-en) *o* pack-horse; **–papier** *o* packing-paper; **–schuit** (-en) *v* barge; **–tafel** (-s) *v* packing table, wrapping table; **–touw** *o* twine; **–zadel** (-s) *m* & *o* pack-saddle; **–zolder** (-s) *m* storage loft

1 pal (-len) *m* click, ratchet, pawl [of a watch]

2 pal I *aj* firm; *~ staan* stand firm; **II** *ad* 1 firmly, [fixed &]; 2 right [in the middle]; *~ noord* due north

pala'dijn (-en) *m* paladin

palan'kijn (-en) *v* palanquin

pala'taal (-talen) *aj* & *v* palatal

pa'laver (-s) *o* palaver

pa′leis (-leizen) *o* palace; *ten paleize* at the palace; at court; **–revolutie** [-(t)si.] (-s) *v* palace revolution; **–wacht** *v* palace guard

′palen (paalde, h. gepaald) *vi* ~ *aan* confine upon

paleogra′fie *v* palaeography; **paleo′grafisch** palaeographic

Pales′tijn (-en) *m* Palestinian; **–s** Palestinian; **Pales′tina** *o* Palestine

pa′let (-ten) *o* palette, pallet; **–mes** (-sen) *o* palette-knife

palfre′nier (-s) *m* groom

′paling (-en) *m* eel; **–fuik** (-en) *v* eel buck

palis′sade (-n en -s) *v* palisade, paling; **palissa′deren** (palissadeerde, h. gepalissadeerd) *vt* palisade; **–ring** (-en) *v* 1 palisading; 2 palisade

palis′sanderhout *o* rosewood

pal′jas (-sen) *m* 1 clown, buffoon; 2 paillasse, pallet [= straw mattress]

palm (-en) *m* 1 palm [of the hand]; decimetre; 2 (b o o m, t a k) palm; **–blad** (-bladeren en -blaren) *o* palm-leaf; **–boom** (-bomen) *m* palm-tree; **–boompje** (-s) *o = palmstruik*; **–bos** (-sen) *o* palm-grove; **–hout** *o* box-wood, box; **–olie** *v* palm-oil; **Palm′paas, Palm′pasen** *m* Palm Sunday; **′palmstruik** (-en) *m* ⚬ box-tree; **–tak** (-ken) *m* palm-branch; (s y m b o l i s c h) palm; **–wijn** *m* palm-wine; **Palm′zondag** *m* Palm Sunday

Palts *v* Palatinate [of the Rhine]; **′paltsgraaf** (-graven) *m* count palatine; **–schap** (-pen) *o* palatinate

pam′flet (-ten) *o* lampoon, broadsheet; (b r o c h u r e) pamphlet; **–schrijver** (-s), **pamflet′tist** (-en) *m* lampoonist, pamphleteer

′Pampus *o voor* ~ *liggen* **F** (m o e d e) be dead-tired (dead-beat); (d r o n k e n) be dead-drunk

pan (-nen) *v* 1 (k e u k e n g e r e i) pan; 2 (v a n d a k) tile; 3 (h e r r i e) **F** row; *wat een* ~ *!* what a go!; *in de* ~ *hakken* cut up, cut to pieces, wipe out

pana′cee (-ceeën en -s) *v* panacea, cure-all

′Panama *o* Panama; **′panamahoed** (-en) *m* Panama hat, panama; **′Panamakanaal** *o* Panama Canal

′pancreas (-sen) *m* & *o* pancreas

pand (-en) 1 *o* pledge, security, pawn, *sp* forfeit; 2 *o* (h u i s e n e r f) premises; 3 *m* & *o* (v. j a s) flap, tail, skirt; ~ *verbeuren* zie *verbeuren*; *in* ~ *geven* offer in pawn, give as (a) security; *t e g e n* ~ on security; **–brief** (-brieven) *m* mortage bond

pan′decten *mv* pandects

′panden (pandde, h. gepand) *vt* seize, distrain upon; **′pandgever** (-s) *m* pawner; **–houder** (-s) *m* pawnee; **–(jes)huis** (-huizen) *o* pawn-shop

′pandjesjas (-sen) *m* & *v* tail-coat

pan′doer *o* & *m* ◊ "pandoer"; *opgelegd* ~ a (dead) cert

′pandrecht *o* lien; **–verbeuren** *o* (game of) forfeits

pa′neel (-nelen) *o* panel

pa′neermeel *o* bread-crumbs; **pa′neren** (paneerde, h. gepaneerd) *vt* (bread-)crumb

′panfluit (-en) = *pansfluit*

pa′niek *v* panic; [war] scare; *in* ~ *geraakt* panic-stricken; *in* ~ *raken* panic; **pa′niekerig** panicky; **pa′niekstemming** *v* panicky atmosphere; **–toestand** *m* state of panic; **–zaaier** (-s) *m* scare-monger; **′panisch** panic; ~*e schrik* panic

′panklaar ready for the frying-pan

′panne (-s) *v* ✗ breakdown

′pannekoek (-en) *m* pancake; **–lap** (-pen) *m* 1 (o m t e r e i n i g e n) (pot) scourer; 2 (o m a a n t e v a t t e n) pot-holder; **–likker** (-s) *m* dough scraper

pannenbakke′rij (-en) *v* tile-works; **′pannendak** (-daken) *o* tiled roof; **–dekker** (-s) *m* tiler

′pannespons (-en en -sponzen) *v* (pot) scourer

pa′nopticum (-ca en -s) *o = wassenbeeldenspel*

pano′rama (′s) *o* panorama

′pansfluit (-en) *v* Pan-pipe, Pandean pipes

panta′lon (-s) *m* [man's] trousers, **F** pants; (s p o r t ~ v o o r d a m e s, h e r e n) slacks; (d a m e s o n d e r k l e d i n g) knickers, panties

′panter (-s) *m* panther

panthe′ïsme *o* pantheism; **panthe′ïst** (-en) *m* pantheist; **–isch** pantheistic(al)

′pantheon (-s) *o* pantheon

pan′toffel (-s) *v* slipper; *onder de* ~ *staan* (*zitten*) be henpecked (by *van*), be under petticoat government; **–held** (-en) *m* henpecked husband; **–parade** (-s) *v* parade; (n a k e r k) church-parade

panto′mime (-s en -n) *v* pantomime, dumb show

′pantry ['pɛntri.] (′s) *m* pantry

′pantser (-s) *o* 1 (h a r n a s) cuirass, (suit of) armour; 2 (b e k l e d i n g) armour-plating; **–auto** [-o.to. of -ɔuto.] (′s) *m* armoured car; **–dek** (-ken) *o* armoured deck; **–divisie** [-zi.] (-s) *v* tank division; **′pantseren** (pantserde, h. gepantserd) *vt* armour-plate, armour; zie ook: *gepantserd*; **′pantserglas** *o* bullet-proof glass; **–kruiser** (-s) *m* armoured cruiser; **–plaat** (-platen) *v* armour-plate; **–schip** (-schepen) *o* armoured ship, armour-clad; **–wagen** (-s) *m* armoured car

′panty ['pɛnti.] (′s) *m* panty-hose

pap (-pen) *v* 1 (o m t e e t e n) porridge [made

of oatmeal or cereals]; pap [soft food for infants or invalids]; 2 🜅 poultice; 3 (i n d e n ij v e r h e i d) dressing [for textiles]; [paper] pulp; 4 (s t ij f s e l) paste; 5 (v. s n e e u w, m o d d e r) slush; *een vinger in de ~ hebben* have a finger in the pie

pa'pa ('s) *m* papa

pa'paver (-s) *v* poppy; **–bol** (-len) *m* poppy-head; **–zaad** *o* poppy-seed

pape'gaai (-en) *m* 1 ☙ parrot²; 2 *sp* popinjay; **–eziekte** *v* psittacosis

'papenvreter (-s) *m* anticlerical

pape'rassen *mv* 1 waste paper; 2 > papers, **P** bumf

'paperback ['pe.pɔrbɪk] (-s) *m* paperback; **–clip** (-s) *m* paper-clip

pa'pier (-en) *o* paper; *~en* papers; *zijn ~en rijzen* his stock is going up²; *goede ~en hebben* have good testimonials; *het ~ is geduldig* anything may be put on paper; ● *het zal i n de ~en lopen* it will run into a lot of money; *o p ~* on paper; *op ~ brengen (zetten)* put on paper; commit to paper; **–binder** (-s) *m* paper-clip; **–en** *aj* paper; *~ geld* paper money, paper currency; **–fabriek** (-en) *v* paper-mill; **–fabrikant** (-en) *m* paper-maker; **–geld** *o* paper money; **–handel** *m* paper-trade; **–handelaar** (-s en -laren) *m* paper-seller; **–industrie** *v* paper-making industry; **–klem** (-men) *v* paper-clip

papier-ma'ché [pa.'pje.ma.'ʃe.] *o* papier mâché

pa'piermand (-en) *v* waste-paper basket; **–molen** (-s) *m* paper-mill; **–tje** *o* bit of paper; **–winkel** *m* stationer's shop; **–wol** *v* paper shavings

pa'pil (-len) *v* papilla [*mv.* papillae]

papil'lot [pa.pɪl'jɔt] *v* curl-paper; *met ~ten in het haar* with her hair in papers

pa'pisme *o* papistry, popery; **–ist** (-en) *m* papist

'papkindje (-s) *o* mollycoddle; **–lepel** (-s) *m* pap-spoon; *het is hem met de ~ ingegeven* he has sucked it in with his mother's milk

'Papoea, Pa'poea ('s) *m,* **'Papoeaas** *aj* Papuan

'pappen (papte, h. gepapt) *vt* 1 poultice [a wound]; 2 ✄ dress

'pappenheimers *mv hij kent zijn ~* he knows his people, his men

'papperig soft, pulpy, pappy, mashy, mushy; **'pappig** pappy; **'pappot** (-ten) *m* pap-pot; *bij moeders ~ blijven* be tied to mother's apron-strings

'paprika ('s) *v* paprika

pa'pyrus (-sen en -pyri) *m* papyrus

'papzak (-ken) *m* fats, fatso

pa'raaf (-rafen) *m* initials [of one's name]

pa'raat ready, prepared, in readiness; *parate kennis* ready knowledge; **–heid** *v* readiness, preparedness

pa'rabel (-s en -en) *v* parable

para'bolisch I *aj* 1 parabolical; 2 parabolic [mirror, reflector]; **II** *ad* parabolically; **para'bool** (-bolen) *v* parabola

parachu'teren (parachuteerde, h. geparachuteerd) *vt* parachute; **para'chutesprong** (-en) *m* parachute jump; **–troepen** *mv* parachute troops, paratroops; **parachu'tist** (-en) *m* parachutist, ✄ paratrooper

pa'rade (-s) *v* 1 ✄ parade, review; 2 parade, parry [in fencing]; 3 *fig* parade, show; *de ~ afnemen* take the salute; *~ houden* hold a review; *~ maken* parade; **–paard** (-en) *o* state-horse; **–pas** (-sen) *m* parade step, [stiff-legged] goose-step; **–plaats** (-en) *v* parade ground; **para'deren** (paradeerde, h. geparadeerd) *vi* 1 ✄ parade; 2 *fig* parade, show off

para'digma (-ta en 's) *o* paradigm

para'dijs (-dijzen) *o* paradise²; **–achtig** paradisiac(al); **–elijk** paradisiac(al); **–vogel** (-s) *m* bird of paradise

para'dox (-en) *m* paradox; **parado'xaal** paradoxical

para'feren (parafeerde, h. geparafeerd) *vt* initial [a document &]; **–ring** *v* initial(l)ing

paraf'fine *v* & *o* 1 (w a s a c h t i g e s t o f) paraffin wax; 2 (b e p a a l d e k o o l w a t e r-s t o f) paraffin

para'frase [s = z] (-s en -n) *v* paraphrase; **parafra'seren** (parafraseerde, h. geparafraseerd) *vt* paraphrase

paragno'sie [s = z] *v* extrasensory perception; **para'gnost** (-en) *m* sensitive; **–isch** extrasensory

para'graaf (-grafen) *m* 1 paragraph, section; 2 (t e k e n) section-mark: §

'Paraguay *o* Paraguay

paral'lel *aj*, (-len) *v* parallel; *~ lopen met* run parallel with; *een ~ trekken* draw a parallel; **parallelle'pipedum** (-da en -s) *o* parallelepiped; **parallello'gram** (-men) *o* parallelogram; **paral'lelschakeling** (-en) *v* shunt; **–weg** (-wegen) *m* parallel road

para'medisch paramedical

para'ment (-en) *o* vestment

'paramilitair [-tɛ:r] para-military

para'noia *v* paranoia; **para'noicus** [-'no:i.küs] (-ci) *m* paranoiac; **parano'ïde** paranoiac

'paranoot (-noten) *v* Brazil nut

'paranormaal paranormal

para'plu ('s) *m* umbrella; **–bak** (-ken), **–standaard** (-s), **–stander** (-s) *m* umbrella-stand

'parapsychologie [-psi.ɣo.lo.ɣi.] *v* parapsychology, [Society for] psychical research; **parapsycho'logisch** parapsychological

para′siet (-en) *m* parasite[2]; **parasi′tair** [- ′tɛːr] parasitic [disease]; **parasi′teren** (parasiteerde, h. geparasiteerd) *vi* be parasitic(al), sponge [on]; **para′sitisch I** *aj* parasitic(al); **II** *ad* parasytically

para′sol (-s) *m* sunshade, parasol; (t u i n~ &) (beach) umbrella

′paratroepen *mv* paratroops

′paratyfus [-ti.füs] *m* paratyphoid

par′cours [- ′kuːr(s)] (-en) *o sp* circuit, course

par′does bang, plump, slap

par′don *o* pardon; ~, *mijnheer!* 1 sorry.!, beg pardon, sir!; 2 excuse me, sir, could you...; *zonder* ~ without mercy, inexorably; *geen* ~ *geven* give no quarter

′parel (-s en -en) *v* pearl[2]; ~*en voor de zwijnen werpen* **B** cast pearls before swine; **–achtig** pearly, pearl-like; **–collier** [-kɔlje.] (-s) *m* pearl-necklace, rope of pearls; **–duiker** (-s) *m* 1 (v i s s e r) pearl-diver, pearl-fisher; 2 ☙ black-throated diver; **′parelen** (parelde, h. gepareld) *vi* pearl, sparkle, bead; *het zweet parelde hem op het voorhoofd* the perspiration stood in beads on his brow; **′parelgerst** *v*, **–gort** *m* pearl-barley; **–grijs** pearl-grey; **–hoen** (-ders) *o* guinea-fowl; **parel′moer(-)** = *paarlemoer*(-); **′pareloester** (-s) *v* pearl-oyster; **–schelp** (-en) *v* pearl-shell; **–snoer** (-en) *o* pearl-necklace, rope of pearls; **–visser** (-s) *m* pearl-fisher; **parelvisse′rij** *v* pearl-fishery, pearling

pare′ment (-en) = *parament*

′paren (paarde, h. gepaard) **I** *vt* pair, couple, match; unite; ...~ *aan* combine... with; **II** *vi* pair, mate, copulate [sexually]; zie ook: *gepaard*

paren′these [-rɛn′te.zə], **pa′renthesis** [-te.zɪs] (-thesen en -theses) *v* parenthesis; *in* ~ within parentheses

pa′reren (pareerde, h. gepareerd) *vt* parry, ward off [a blow]

par′fum (-s) *o* & *m* perfume, scent; **parfu′meren** (parfumeerde, h. geparfumeerd) *vt* perfume, scent; **parfume′rie** (-ieën) *v* 1 perfume, scent; 2 perfumery [shop or trade]

′pari *ad*, (′s) *o* $ par; *a* ~ at par; *b e n e d e n* ~ below par, at a discount; *b o v e n* ~ above par, at a premium; ~ *staan* be at par

′paria (′s) *m-v* pariah

Pa′rijs I *o* Paris; **II** *aj* Parisian, Paris; **Pa′rijze-naar** (-s) *m* Parisian

′paring (-en) *v* mating, pairing, copulation; **′paringsdaad** *v* sexual act, copulation; **–drift** *v* mating instinct, sexual drive

pari′tair [- ′tɛːr] on an equal footing, having equal rights

pari′teit (-en) *v* parity

park (-en) *o* park, (pleasure) grounds; *nationaal* ~ national park

par′keergarage [-ɡa.ra:ʒə] (-s) *v* parking garage; **–geld** (-en) *o* parking fee; **–haven** (-s) *v* lay-by, parking bay; **–licht** (-en) *o* parking light; **–meter** (-s) *m* parking meter; **–plaats** (-en) *v* car park, parking place; **–schijf** (-schijven) *v* parking disc; **–terrein** (-en) *o* car park; **–verbod** (-boden) *o* parking ban; **–wachter** (-s) *m* traffic warden; **par′keren** (parkeerde, h. geparkeerd) *vi* & *vt* park; *dubbel* ~ double-park; *niet* ~ no parking

par′ket (-ten) *o* 1 parquet; 2 ☖ (b u r e a u) Public Prosecutor's Office; (a m b t e n a a r) Public Prosecutor; *iem. in een lastig* ~ *brengen* put (place) sbd. in an awkward predicament (position), embarrass sbd.; *hij zat in een lelijk* ~ **F** he was in an awful scrape (fix); **parket′teren** (parketteerde, h. geparketteerd) *vt* parquet; **par′ketvloer** (-en) *m* parquet floor(ing)

par′kiet (-en) *m* parakeet, paroquet

par′koers (-en) = *parcours*

parle′ment (-en) *o* parliament; **parlemen′tair** [- ′tɛːr] **I** *aj* parliamentary; *de* ~*e vlag* the flag of truce; **II** (-s en -en) *m* bearer of a flag of truce; **parlemen′teren** (parlementeerde, h. geparlementeerd) *vi* (hold a) parley; **parle′mentslid** (-leden) *o* member of parliament, M.P.; **–zitting** (-en) *v* session of parliament

parle′vinken (parlevinkte, h. geparlevinkt) *vi* (k o e t e r e n) jabber, talk gibberish; **–er** (-s) *m* ☖ bumboat trader

par′mantig) *aj* (& *ad*) pert(ly), perky (perkily)

parme′zaan *m* Parmesan cheese

Par′nas, Par′nassus *m de* ~ Parnassus

parochi′aal parochial; **parochi′aan** (-ianen) *m* parishioner; **pa′rochie** (-s en -chiën) *v* parish; **–kerk** (-en) *v* parish church

paro′die (-ieën) *v* parody, travesty, skit; **parodi′ëren** (parodieerde, h. geparodieerd) *vt* parody, travesty, take off; **paro′dist** (-en) *o* parodist

pa′rool (-rolen) *o* 1 (e r e w o o r d) parole; 2 (w a c h t w o o r d) parole, password; 3 *fig* watchword

1 part (-en) *o* part, portion, share; *ik had er* ~ *noch deel aan* I had neither part nor lot in it; *voor mijn* ~ as for me, as far as I am concerned...

2 part *v iem.* ~*en spelen* play a trick on sbd., play sbd. false

par′terre (-s) *o* & *m* 1 pit [in a theatre]; 2 ground floor [of a house]; 3 (b l o e m p e r k) parterre

partici′pant (-en) *m* participant; **partici′patie** [-(t)si.] (-s) *v* participation; **partici′peren** (participeerde, h. geparticipeerd) *vi* participate

particu′lier I *aj* private; ~*e school* private

school; ~*e weg* occupation road; ~*e woning* private house; **II** *ad* privately; **III** (-en) *m* private person

parti'eel [-(t)si.'e.l] partial

par'tij (-en) *v* 1 party°; 2 game [of billiards &]; 3 $ parcel, lot [of goods]; 4 ♪ part; *beide* ~*en* both sides, both parties; *een goede* ~ a good match; *een* ~ *doen* make a good match; *een* ~ *geven* give a party; ~ *kiezen* take sides; (b ij s p e l l e t j e s) pick sides; ~ *kiezen te̱ ɘn* take part against, side against; ~ *kiezen voɔr* ake part with, side with; *de wijste* ~ *kiezen* choose the wisest course; *een* ~ *maken* have a game of billiards [whist &]; *zijn* ~ *meeblazen* keep one's end up; *zijn* ~ *spelen* play one's part; *zich* ~ *stellen* take a side; ~ *trekken van* take advantage of; ~ *trekken voor* take part with, stand up for; ● *b ij* ~*en verkopen* sell in lots; *v a n* ~ *veranderen* change sides; *van de* ~ *zijn* make one, be in on it; **–bons** (-bonzen) *m* party bigwig; **par'tijdig I** *aj* partial, biassed; **II** *ad* in a biassed way; **–heid** *v* partiality, bias; **par'tijganger** (-s) *m* partisan; **–geest** *m* party spirit; **–genoot** (-noten) *m* party member; **–leider** (-s) *m* party leader; **–leus, –leuze** (-leuzen) *v* party cry, slogan; **–lid** (-leden) *o* party member; **–loos** non-party; **–man** (-nen) *m* party man, partisan; **–politiek** *v* party politics, [the] party line; **–programma** ('s) *o* party programme, party platform; **–strijd** *m* party battle, party warfare; **–tje** (-s) *o* 1 party; 2 $ lot; 3 (s p e l l e t j e) game; **–zucht** *v* party spirit

parti'tuur (-turen) *v* score

parti'zaan (-zanen) *m* partisan

'partje (-s) *o* slice, section, small piece, segment [of an orange]

'partner (-s) *m* & *v* partner; **–ruil** *m* partner exchange, mate-swopping

parve'nu ('s) *m* parvenu, upstart; **–achtig I** *aj* parvenu... **II** *ad* like a parvenu

1 pas (-sen) *m* 1 (s t a p) pace, step; 2 (b e r g- w e g) pass; defile; 3 (p a s p o o r t) passport; (v r ij g e l e i d e) pass; *gewone* ~ quick time; *gewone* ~! quick march!; *de* ~ *aangeven* set the pace; *iem. de* ~ *afsnijden* 1 forestall sbd.; 2 cut sbd. short; *daarvoor is mij de* ~ *afgesneden* I find my way barred to that; *iets de* ~ *afsnijden* put a stop to sth. [abuses &]; *er de* ~ *in houden* keep up a smart pace; *er de* ~ *in zetten* step out; ~ *op de plaats maken* mark time²; ● *i n de* ~ step; *in de* ~ *blijven met* keep pace (step) with; *in*, *de* ~ *komen* catch step; *bij iem. in de* ~ *zien te komen* curry favour with sbd.; *in de* ~ *lopen* keep step; *bij iem. in de* ~ *staan* (*zijn*) be in sbd.'s good books; *o p tien* ~ (*afstands*) at ten paces; *u i t de* ~ *raken* get (fall) out of step, break step;

uit de ~ *zijn* be out of step

2 pas *o waar het* ~ *geeft* where proper; *dat geeft geen* ~ that is not becoming; that won't do; ● *een woordje o p zijn* ~ a word in season; *t e* ~ *te onpas* in season and out of season; *iets te* ~ *brengen* work in sth. [a quotation &]; *het zal u nog te* ~ *komen* it will come in handy; *dat komt niet te* ~ that is not becoming; that won't do; *er aan te* ~ *komen* enter into it (the question); *hij moest er aan te* ~ *komen* he had to step in; *je komt net v a n* ~ as if you had been called; *dat kwam mij net van* ~ that came in very handy (opportunely)

3 pas *ad* scarcely, hardly; just (now); new-[born], newly-[married]; ~ *gisteren* not before (not until) yesterday, only yesterday; ~... *of*... zie *nauwelijks*

'pasar (-s) *m* bazaar, market

'pascontrole [-kòntrɔ.lə] (-s) *v* examination of passports, passport check

'Pasen *m* 1 Easter; 2 (b ij d e j o d e n) Passover; *zijn* ~ *houden* rk take the Sacrament at Easter

'pasfoto ('s) *v* passport photo

'pasgeboren newborn

'pasgeld *o* change, small money

'pasja ('s) *m* pasha

'pasje (-s) *o* transfer (ticket)

'paskamer (-s) *v* fitting-room; **–klaar** ready for trying on; *fig* cut and dried [methods]; *het* ~ *maken voor*... [*fig*] adapt it to...

pas'kwil (-len) *o* 1 lampoon; 2 *fig* mockery, farce

'paslood (-loden) *o* plummet

'pasmunt *v* change, small money

'paspoort (-en) *o* passport

'paspop (-pen) *v* tailor's dummy

pas'saatwind (-en) *m* trade wind

pas'sabel I *aj* passable; **II** *ad* passably

pas'sage [-ʒə] (-s) *v* 1 (d o o r g a n g) passage; 2 (g a l e r ij) arcade; 3 (g e d e e l t e) passage [of a book]; 4 ♪ passage; 5 = *passagegeld*; ~ *bespreken* book [by the "Queen Mary" &]; *we hebben hier veel* ~ we've many people passing here; **–biljet** (-ten) *o* ticket; **–bureau** [-by.ro.] (-s) *o* booking-office; **–geld** *o* passage-money, fare

passa'gier [-'ʒi: r] (-s) *m* passenger; **passa'gieren** (passagierde, h. gepassagierd) *vi* ♪ go on shore-leave; **passa'giersaccommodatie** [-(t)si.] *v* passenger accommodation; **–boot** (-boten) *m* & *v* passenger-ship; **–goed** (-eren) *o* passenger's luggage; **–lijst** (-en) *v* list of passengers, passenger-list; **–trein** (-en) *m* passenger-train; **–vliegtuig** (-en) *o* passenger plane

1 pas'sant (-en) *m* 1 (v o o r b ij g a n g e r) passer-by; 2 (d o o r r e i z e n d e) passing

traveller; 3 (s c h o u d e r b e d e k k i n g)
shoulderknot

2 pas'sant *en* ~ [āpɑ'sã] by the way, in passing

passe'ment (-en) *o* passement, passementerie,
galloon

'passen (paste, h. gepast) **I** *vi* 1 (v. k l e r e n) fit;
2 (b ij k a a r t s p e l) pass; *het past me niet* 1 it
[the suit &] does not fit; 2 it [the buying &] is
not convenient, I can't afford it; 3 it is not for
me [to tell him]; *het past u niet om...* it does not
become you to..., it is not (not fit) for you
to...; *deze kleren* ~ *mij precies* these clothes fit
me to a nicety; ● *dat past er niet b ij* it does
not go (well) with it, it doesn't match it; *kunt u
mij zijde geven die bij deze past?* can you match
me this silk?; *ze* ~ *(niet) bij elkaar* they are (not)
well matched; *slecht bij elkaar* ~ be ill-assorted;
de steel past niet i n de opening the handle doesn't
fit the opening; ~ *o p iets* mind sth., take care
of sth.; *op de kinderen* ~ look after the children,
take care of the children; *die kurk past op deze
kruik* that cork [stopper] fits this jar; *op zijn
woorden* ~ be careful of one's words; *ik pas*
I pass; *ik pas er v o o r* that's what I won't put
up with; ~ *en meten* cut and contrive; **II** *vt* fit
on, try on [a coat]; *kunt u het niet* ~? haven't
you got the exact money?; *wanneer kunt u mij*
~? when can you fit me?; zie ook: *gepast*

'passenbureau [-bγ.ro.] (-s) *o* passport office

'passend suitable, fit; appropriate, fitting [coat]

passe-par'tout [pɑspɑr'tu.] (-s) *m & o* passe-
partout

'passer (-s) *m* (pair of) compasses; *kromme* ~
callipers; **–doos** (-dozen) *v* case of mathematical instruments

pas'seren (passeerde, h. en is gepasseerd) **I** *vi*
1 (v o o r b ij g a a n) pass, pass by; 2 (g e b e u -
r e n, o v e r k o m e n) happen, occur; *u mag
dat niet laten* ~ you should not let that pass;
II *vt* pass [a person, the frontier, the time
&]; pass [a dish]; *fig* 1 pass over [sbd. who
ought to be promoted]; 2 execute [a deed]; *hij
is de vijftig gepasseerd* he has turned fifty

'passie (-s) *v* 1 (h a r t s t o c h t) passion; 2
(m a n i e) mania, craze; *de Passie* the Passion [of
Christ]; zie ook: *vos*; **–bloem** (-en) *v* passion-
flower

pas'sief I *aj* passive; *passieve handelsbalans* ook:
$ adverse trade balance; **II** *ad* passively;
III (-siva) *o het* ~ *en actief* $ the liabilities and
assets

'passiespel (-spelen) *o* Passion-play; **–tijd** *m*
Passiontide; **–week** (-weken) *v* Passion Week,
Holy Week

pas'siva *mv* $ liabilities

passivi'teit *v* passiveness, passivity

'passus (-sen) *m* passage

'pasta ('s) *m & o* paste

pas'tei (-en) *v* pie, pasty; **–bakker** (-s) *m*
pastry-cook; **–tje** (-s) *o* patty

pas'tel (-s en -len) 1 *o* (k r ij t; t e k e n i n g)
pastel; 2 *v* ✿ woad; **–schilder** (-s) *m*
pastel(l)ist; **–tekening** (-en) *v* pastel drawing;
–tint (-en) *v* pastel shade

pasteuri'satie [-za.(t)si.] *v* pasteurization;

pasteuri'seren (pasteuriseerde, h. gepasteuri-
seerd) *vt* pasteurize

pas'tille [-'ti.jə] (-s) *v* pastille, lozenge

pas'toor (-s) *m* (parish) priest; *ja,* ~ yes, Father;
'pastor (-s) *m* pastor; **pasto'raal I** *aj* pastoral
[theology, psychology, Epistles, Council;
poetry]; **II** *v rk* pastoral duties

pasto'rale (-s en -n) *v* pastoral; ♪ pastorale

pasto'rie (-ieën) *v* 1 *rk* presbytery; 2 (v a n
d o m i n e e) rectory, vicarage, parsonage;
[Nonconformist] manse

'pasvorm (-en) *m* fit

1 pat stalemate [in chess]; ~ *zetten* stalemate

2 pat (-ten) *v* tab [on uniform]

patates 'frites [patɑt'fri.t] *mv* chips

pâté, patee (-s) *m* pâté, paste

pa'teen (-tenen) *v* paten

1 pa'tent I *aj* capital, first-rate; A 1; *een ~e
jongen* F a brick; *er* ~ *uitzien* look (very) fit; **II**
ad capitally

2 pa'tent (-en) *o* 1 patent [for an invention]; 2
licence [to carry on some business]; ~ *nemen op
iets* take out a patent for sth.; ~ *verlenen* grant a
patent; **paten'teren** (patenteerde, h. gepaten-
teerd) *vt* patent; **pa'tenthouder** (-s) *m*
patentee; **–olie** *v* patent oil; **–recht** (-en) *o*
patent right; **–sluiting** (-en) *v* patent lock,
patent fastening

'pater (-s) *m* father [of a religious order]; *Witte
Pater rk* White Father

pater'noster (-s) *o* 1 *o* (g e b e d) paternoster; 2 *m*
(r o z e n k r a n s) rosary; ~*s* (= h a n d b o e i -
e n) F bracelets

pa'thetisch pathetic(al)

patholo'gie *v* pathology; **patho'logisch** *aj*
pathological; **patho'loog** (-logen) *m* pathologist; ~*-anatoom* pathologist

'pathos *o* pathos

patience [-si.'ãsə] *o* patience

patiënt [-si.'ɛnt] (-en) *m* patient

'patina *o* patina

'patjakker (-s) *m* scamp, rogue, scoundrel

'patjepeeër (-s) *m* F cad, vulgarian

patri'arch (-en) *m* patriarch; **patriar'chaal**
patriarchal; **–'chaat** *o* 1 patriarchate; 2
(g e z i n s v e r b a n d) patriarchy

patrici'aat (-iaten) *o* patriciate; **pa'triciër** (-s) *m* patrician; **–shuis** (-huizen) *o* patrician mansion;
pa'tricisch patrician

pa'**trijs** (-trijzen) *m* & *v* & *o* 🐦 partridge; –**hond** (-en) *m* pointer, setter; –**poort** (-en) *v* port-hole; pa'**trijzejacht** (-en) *v* partridge shooting

patri'**ot** (-ten) *m* patriot; –**tisch** patriotic; patriot'**tisme** *o* patriotism

patro'**naat** (-naten) *o* 1 patronage; 2 (Church) club; patro'**nage** [-ʒə] *m* patronage; patro'**nes** (-sen) *v* 1 (h e i l i g e) patron saint; 2 (b e s c h e r m v r o u w) patroness;
  1 pa'troon (-s) *m* 1 (b a a s) employer, master, principal; 2 (h e i l i g e) patron saint; 3 (b e s c h e r m h e e r) patron

2 pa'troon (-tronen) *v* cartridge; *losse* ~ blank cartridge; *scherpe* ~ ball cartridge

3 pa'troon (-tronen) *o* pattern, design

pa'**troongordel** (-s) *m* cartridge-belt; (o v e r s c h o u d e r) bandoleer; –**houder** (-s) *m* cartridge-clip; –**huls** (-hulzen) *v* cartridge-case; –**tas** (-sen) *v* cartridge-box

pa'**trouille** [- 'tru.(l)jə] (-s) *v* patrol; patrouil'**leren** (patrouilleerde, h. gepatrouil-leerd) *vi* patrol; ~ *door* (*in*) *de straten* patrol the streets; pa'**trouillevaartuig** (-en) *o* patrol vessel (boat)

pats I (-en) *v* smack, slap; **II** *ij* slap!, bang!

'**patser** (-s) *m* **F** cad; –**ig** caddish

pauk (-en) *v* kettledrum; *de* ~*en* the timpani; **pauke'nist** (-en) *m* timpanist, kettledrummer; '**paukeslager** (-s) *m* = *paukenist*

'**pauper** (-s) *m* pauper; paupe'**risme** *o* pauper-ism

paus (-en) *m* pope; –**dom** *o* papacy; –**elijk** papal; –**gezind** *aj* papistic(al); ~*e* papist; –**schap** *o* papacy

pauw (-en) *m* 🐦 peacock[2]; –**achtig** *fig* peacock-ish; '**pauwoog** (-ogen) *m* = *pauwoog*; –**staart** (-en) *m* peacock's tail; –**veer** (-veren) *v* peacock's feather; pau'**win** (-nen) *v* 🐦 pea-hen; '**pauwoog** (-ogen) *m* 🦋 peacock butterfly; –**staart** (-en) *m* 🐦 fantail

'**pauze** (-s en -n) *v* 1 pause; 2 interval, wait [between the acts of a play]; ⌒ break; 3 ♩ rest; pau'**zeren** (pauzeerde, h. gepauzeerd) *vi* make a pause, pause, stop; –**ring** (-en) *v* pause, stop; '**pauzeteken** (-s) *v* interval signal

pavil'**joen** (-en en -s) *o* pavilion

pavoi'**seren** [-vvɑ'ze:rə(n)] (pavoiseerde, h. gepavoiseerd) *vt* dress [with flags]

pct. = *percent, procent*

pech *m* 1 bad luck; 2 ✗ trouble; ~ *hebben* be down on one's luck, have a run of bad luck; –**vogel** *o* unlucky person

pe'**daal** (-dalen) *o* & *m* pedal [of a piano, bicycle &]

pedago'**gie(k)** *v* pedagogics, pedagogy; peda'**gogisch I** *aj* pedagogic(al); ~*e academie* (teacher) training-college; **II** *ad* pedagogically;

peda'**goog** (-gogen) *m* educationalist

pe'**dant I** (-en) *m* pedant; **II** *aj* pedantic; pedante'**rie** (-ieën) *v* pedantry

'**peddel** (-s) *m* paddle; '**peddelen** (peddelde, h. en is gepeddeld) *vi* (f i e t s e n) pedal; ‖ (r o e i e n) paddle

pe'**del** (-len en -s) *m* mace-bearer, beadle

pedi'**ater** (-s) *m* p(a)ediatrician; pedia'**trie** *v* p(a)ediatrics

pedi'**cure** (-s) 1 *m-v* (p e r s o o n) chiropodist, pedicure; 2 *v* (d e h a n d e l i n g) pedicure, chiropody

pedolo'**gie** *v* 1 (b o d e m k u n d e) pedology; 2 (in the Neth.) study of disturbed children

pee *v* **F** *de* ~ (*in*) *hebben* have the hump; *de* ~ *hebben aan* hate [sth.]

peen (penen) *v* 🥕 carrot; *witte* ~ parsnip; –**haar** *o* carroty hair

peep (pepen) V.T. van *pijpen*

peer (-peren) *v* 🥕 1 pear; 2 reservoir [of oil-lamp], [electric] bulb; *iem. met de gebakken peren laten zitten* leave sbd. in the lurch; –**vormig** pear-shaped

pees (pezen) *v* tendon, sinew, string; –**achtig** = *pezig*

peet (peten) *m-v* sponsor, godfather, godmother; –**dochter** (-s) *v* goddaughter; –**oom** (-s) *m* godfather; –**schap** *o* sponsorship; –**tante** (-s) *v* godmother; –**vader** (-s) *m* godfather; –**zoon** (-s en -zonen) *m* godson

'**Pegasus** *m* Pegasus

'**pegel** (-s) *m* (ij s~) icicle; (g u l d e n, **F**) guilder

peig'**noir** [pɪ̃n'va:r] (-s) *m* dressing gown, *Am* robe

peil (-en) *o* gauge, water-mark; *fig* standard, level; *het* ~ *verhogen* raise the level; *b e n e d e n* ~ below the mark, not up to the mark; *beneden (boven) Amsterdams* ~ below (above) Amsterdam water-mark; *o p* ~ *brengen* level up, bring up to the required standard; *op hetzelfde* ~ *brengen* put on the same level; *op* ~ *houden* keep up (to the mark), maintain [exports, stocks &]; *op een laag zedelijk* ~ *staan* stand morally low; *op hem is geen* ~ *te trekken* he can't be relied upon; –**datum** (-ta en -s) *m* set day, date set [for assessment of benefit claims &]; '**peilen** (peilde, h. gepeild) *vt* gauge[2] [the depth of liquid content, the mind]; sound[2] [the sea, a pond, sbd., sbd.'s sentiments on...], fathom[2] [the sea, depth of water, the heart &]; probe [a wound]; plumb[2] [depth, misery]; *fig* search [the hearts]; –**er** (-s) *m* gauger; '**peil-glas** (-glazen) *o* gauge-glass, (water-)gauge; '**peiling** (-en) *v* gauging; ⚓ sounding; '**peil-lood** (-loden) *o* sounding-lead; –**loos** fathom-less, unfathomable; –**schaal** (-schalen) *v* tide-gauge; –**stok** (-ken) *m* 1 gauging-rod; 2

⚫ dip-stick

'**peinzen** (peinsde, h. gepeinsd) *vi* ponder, meditate, muse (upon *over*); **–d** *aj* meditative, pensive; '**peinzer** (-s) *m* muser

peis *v* = *pais*

pejora'tief *aj*, (-tieven) *m* pejorative

pek *o* & *m* 1 pitch; 2 (cobbler's) wax; *wie met ~ omgaat, wordt er mee besmet* they that touch pitch will be defiled; **–draad** (-draden) *o* & *m* = *pikdraad*

'**pekel** *m* pickle, brine; '**pekelen** (pekelde, h. gepekeld) *vt* brine, pickle [a herring], salt [meat]; '**pekelharing** (-en) *m* salt herring; **–nat** *o* brine; *het ~ ook:* **F** the briny [= the sea]; **–vlees** *o* salt(ed) meat; **–zonde** (-n) *v* peccadillo

peki'nees (-nezen) *m* 🐾 pekinese

'**pekken** (pekte, h. gepekt) *vt* pitch

pel (-len) *v* skin [of fruit]; shell [of an egg], pod [of peas, beans]

pele'rine [pɛlə-] (-s) *v* pelerine

'**pelgrim** (-s) *m* pilgrim, 🚶 palmer; **pelgri'mage** [-ʒə] (-s) *v* pilgrimage; '**pelgrimsgewaad** (-waden), **–kleed** (-kleren) *o* pilgrim's garb; **–staf** (-staven), **–stok** (-ken) *m* pilgrim's staff; **–tas** (-sen) *v* pilgrim's scrip; **–tocht** (-en) *m* pilgrimage

peli'kaan (-kanen) *m* 🦤 pelican

'**pellen** (pelde, h. gepeld) *vt* peel [an egg, shrimps, almonds]; shell [nuts, peas]; hull, husk [rice]

pelo'ton (-s) *o* 1 ✗ platoon [= half company]; 2 *sp* (v. w i e l r e n n e r s &) bunch

pels (pelzen) *m* 1 fur, pelt; 2 fur coat, fur; **–dier** (-en) *o* furred animal; **–handelaar** (-s en -laren) *m* furrier; **–jager** (-s) *m* (fur-)trapper; **–jas** (-sen) *m* & *v* fur coat, fur; **–muts** (-en) *v* fur cap; **–werk** *o* furriery; **pelte'rij** (-en) *v* furriery

'**peluw** (-s en -en) *v* bolster

pen (-nen) *v* 1 (i n h e t a l g.) pen; 2 (l o s s e p e n) nib; 3 (v e r e n p e n) feather, quill; 4 (n a a l d o m t e b r e i e n &) needle; 5 = *pin*; *de ~ voeren* wield the pen; *iem. de ~ op de neus zetten* 1 put pressure on sbd.; 2 ook: pull sbd. up a bit; *het is i n de ~ gebleven* it never came off; *in de ~ geven* dictate; *in de ~ klimmen* take up the pen; *het is in de ~* it is in preparation; *het is mij u i t de ~ gevloeid* it was a slip of the pen; *v a n zijn ~ leven* live by one's pen

pe'nant (-en) *o* pier [between two windows]; **–spiegel** (-s) *m* pier-glass; **–tafel** (-s) *v* pier-table

pe'narie *in de ~ zitten* **F** be in a scrape, be in the soup

pe'naten *mv* penates, household gods

pen'dant [pã'dã] (-en) *o* & *m* pendant, companion picture (portrait, piece), counterpart²

'**pendelaar** (-s) *m* commuter; '**pendeldienst** (-en) *m* shuttle service; '**pendelen** (pendelde, h. gependeld) *vi* commute; shuttle

pen'dule (-s) *v* clock, timepiece

pen-en-'gatverbinding (-en) *v* dowel-joint

pene'trant penetrating

'**penhouder** (-s) *m* penholder

pe'nibel painful, embarrassing, awkward

penicil'line [pe.ni.si.'li.nə] *v* penicillin

'**penis** (-sen) *m* penis

peni'tent (-en) *m* penitent; **peni'tentie** [-(t)si.] (-s en -tiën) *v* 1 penance; 2 *fig* vexation, trial

'**pennehouder** (-s) *m* penholder; **–likker** (-s) *m* quill-driver; **–mes** (-sen) *o* penknife; '**pennen** (pende, h. gepend) *vt* pen, write [a letter]; '**pennenbak** (-ken) *m* pen-tray; **–doos** (-dozen) *v* pen-box; **–koker** (-s) *m* pen-case; '**pennestreek** (-streken) *v* stroke (dash) of the pen; *met één ~* with (by) one stroke of the pen; **–strijd** *m* paper war; **–vrucht** (-en) *v* writing

'**penning** (-en) *m* 1 penny; 2 medal; 3 (m e - t a l e n p l a a t j e) badge; *op de ~ zijn* be close-fisted; **–kruid** *o* moneywort; **–kunde** *v* numismatics; **penning'kundige** (-n) *m* numismatist; '**penningmeester** (-s) *m* treasurer; **–schap** *o* treasurership; '**penningske** (-s) *o* *het ~ der weduwe* the widow's mite

pens (-en) *v* paunch; (a l s g e r e c h t) tripe

pen'see [pã'se.] (-s) *v* 🌺 pansy, heart's-ease

pen'seel (-selen) *o* paint-brush, brush, pencil; **–streek** (-streken) *v* stroke of the brush; **pen'selen** (penseelde, h. gepenseeld) *vt* 1 (a a n s t r ij k e n) pencil; 2 (s c h i l d e r e n) paint

pensi'oen [-'ʃu.n] (-en) *o* (retiring, retirement) pension; ✗ retired pay; *~ aanvragen* apply for one's pension; *~ krijgen* be pensioned off; ✗ be placed on the retired list; *~ nemen, met ~ gaan* take one's pension, retire (on (a) pension), ✗ go on retired pay; **–aanspraak** (-spraken) *v* pension claim; **–bijdrage** (-n) *v* = *pensioensbijdrage*; **–fonds** (-en) *o* pension fund; **–gerechtigd** pensionable, entitled to a pension; *de ~e leeftijd bereiken* reach retiring age; **–sbijdrage** (-n) *v* contribution towards pension

pensi'on [pãsi.'òn] (-s) *o* boarding-house; *i n ~ zijn* be living at a boarding-house; *m e t volledig ~* with full board; **pensio'naat** [pɪn-] (-naten) *o* boarding-school; **pensio'nair** [pãsi.ò'nɛ:r] (-s) *m* boarder [at a school]

pensio'naris (-sen) *m* 🖳 pensionary

pensio'neren (pensioneerde, h. gepensioneerd) *vt* pension off; ✗ place on the retired list; *een gepensioneerd generaal* ✗ a retired general; **–ring** (-en) *v* retirement, superannuation

pensi'ongast [pãsi.'òn-] (-en) *m* boarder;

–houd(st)er (-s) *m* (*v*) boarding-house keeper
'pentekening (-en) *v* pen-drawing
pepen V.T. meerv. van *pijpen*
'peper (-s) *m* pepper; *Spaanse* ~ red pepper;
–achtig peppery; –bus (-sen) *v* pepperbox,
pepper-castor; –duur high-priced, stiff
[prices]; 'peperen (peperde, h. gepeperd) *vt*
pepper; zie ook: *gepeperd*; peper-en-'zout-
kleurig pepper-and-salt; 'peperhuisje (-s) *a*
cornet, screw; 'peperig peppery; 'peperkoek
(-en) *m* gingerbread; –korrel (-s) *m* pepper-
corn; –molen (-s) *m* pepper mill;
peper'munt (-en) *v* 1 ⚘ peppermint; 2 =
pepermuntje; –je (-s) *o* peppermint lozenge;
'pepernoot (-noten) *v* gingerbread cube;
–struik (-en) *m* pepper plant; –tuin (-en) *m*
pepper plantation; –vreter (-s) *m* toucan
'pepmiddel (-en) *o* stimulant
'peppel (-s) *m* poplar
'peppil (-len) *v* pep pill
per by [train &, the dozen &]; ~ *dag* a day, per
day; *135 inwoners* ~ *vierkante kilometer* 135
inhabitants to the square kilometre; *er worden
5000 auto's* ~ *week gemaakt* ook: motor-cars are
being manufactured at the rate of 5000 a week
per'ceel (-celen) *o* 1 plot [of ground]; lot [at
auction]; 2 premises; *een lastig* ~ F rather a
handful, a troublesome customer; –sgewijs,
–sgewijze in lots
per'cent (-en) *o* per cent; ~*en* percentage;
percen'tage [-ʒə] (-s) *o* percentage;
per'centsgewijs, –gewijze proportionally;
percentu'eel proportionally
per'ceptie [-'sɛpsi.] (-s en -tiën) *v* perception;
percipi'ëren (percipieerde, h. gepercipiëerd)
vt ps apperceive
perco'lator (-s) *m* percolator
per'cussie *v* percussion; percu'teren (percu-
teerde, h. gepercuteerd) *vt* percuss
'pereboom (-bomen) *m* pear-tree
per'fect *aj* perfect; per'fectie [-si.] (-s) *v*
perfection; *in de* ~ perfectly, to perfection;
perfectio'neren (perfectioneerde, h. geper-
fectioneerd) *vt* perfect; perfectio'nisme *o*
perfectionism
per'fide perfidious
perfo'rator (-s en -'toren) *m* perforator, punch;
perfo'reren (perforeerde, h. geperforeerd) *vt*
perforate
peri'feer peripheral; perife'rie *v* periphery²;
fringe(s), outskirts [of a town &]
pe'rikel (-s en -en) *o* adventure, intricacy,
difficulty
peri'ode (-s en -n) *v* period; spell [of rain,
sunshine &]; *in deze* ~ 1 in this period; 2 at
this stage; perio'diek I *aj* periodical; II (-en) *v*
& *o* periodical

peri'scoop (-copen) *m* periscope
perk (-en) *o* (flower-)bed; *binnen de* ~*en blijven*
remain within the bounds of decency (of the
law); *alle* ~*en te buiten gaan* go beyond all
bounds
perka'ment (-en) *o* parchment, vellum;
–achtig parchmentlike; –en *aj* parchment
perma'nent permanent [wave &], lasting
[peace], standing [committee]; perma'nenten
(permanentte, h. gepermanent) *zich laten* ~
have one's hair permed
per'missie *v* 1 permission; 2 ⚔ leave (of
absence), furlough [of soldiers]; *met* ~ with
your leave; permit'teren [-mi.-] (permit-
teerde, h. gepermitteerd) I *vt* permit; II *vr zich*
~ permit oneself; *dat kan ik mij niet* ~ I cannot
afford it
'peroxyde [-ɔksi.də] (-n en -s) *o* peroxide;
waterstof~ peroxide of hydrogen
per'plex perplexed, taken aback
per'ron (-s) *o* platform; –kaartje (-s) *o* platform
ticket
1 pers (-en) *v* press; *hij is bij de* ~ he is on the
press; *ter* ~*e* at press, in the press; *ter* ~*e gaan*
go to press; *ter* ~*e zijn* be in the press
2 pers (perzen) *m* (t a p ij t) Persian carpet
3 Pers (Perzen) *m* Persian
'persagentschap (-pen) *o* news agency
per 'saldo after all
persattaché ['pɛrsataʃe.] (-s) *m* press attaché;
–auto ('s) *m* press car; –bericht (-en) *o* press
report; –bureau [-by.ro.] (-s) *o* press bureau,
news agency; –campagne [-kampaɲə] (-s) *v*
press campaign; –chef [-ʃɛf] (-s) *m* press and
public relations officer; –communiqué [-ke.]
(-s) *o* press release (handout); –conferentie
[-kònfərɪn(t)si.] (-s) *v* press conference;
–delict (-en) *o* press offence
per 'se [pɛr'se.] by all means, [he must] needs
[go]; *een... is nog niet* ~ *een geleerde* is not per se
(not on that account, not necessarily) a scholar
'persen (perste, h. geperst) *vt* press, squeeze
'persfotograaf (-grafen) *m* press photographer,
cameraman; –gesprek (-ken) *o* interview
persi'aner *o* Persian lamb
persi'enne [pɛrsi.'ɛ:nə] (-s) *v* Persian blind
persi'flage [-'fla.ʒə] (-s) *v* persiflage, banter;
persi'fleren (persifleerde, h. gepersifleerd) *vt*
& *vi* banter
'persijzer (-s) *o* (tailor's) goose
'persing (-en) *v* pressing, pressure
'perskaart (-en) *v* press-ticket, (press) pass;
–klaar ready for (the) press
'persleiding (-en) *v* high-pressure line (pipe);
–lucht *v* compressed air
'persman (-nen) *m* pressman, journalist
perso'nage [-ʒə] (-s) *o* & *v* personage, person,

character; **perso'nalia** *mv* personal notes; *zijn ~ opgeven* give one's name and birth-date [to a policeman]; **personali'teit** (-en) *v* personality

perso'neel I *aj* personal; *personele belasting* duty or tax on houses, property &; **II** *o* personnel, staff, servants; **perso'neelsbezetting** *v* number of persons employed, manpower; **–chef** [-ʃɛf] (-s) *m* personnel manager; **–raad** (-raden) *m* representation of the personnel; **–zaken** *mv* (a f d e l i n g ~) personnel department

per'sonenauto [-o.to. of -ɔuto] ('s) *m* passenger car; **–trein** (-en) *m* passenger train; **–vervoer** *o* passenger traffic

personifi'catie [-ˈka.(t)si.] (-s) *v* personification; **personifi'ëren** (personifeerde, h. gepersonifieerd) *vt* personify

per'soon (-sonen) *m* person; *mijn ~* I, myself; *publieke personen* public characters; ● *i n (hoogst eigen) ~* in (his own) person, personally; *hij is de goedheid in ~* he is kindness personified, he is kindness itself; *...p e r ~ drie gulden* three guilders a head, three guilders each; **per'soonlijk I** *aj* personal; *ik wil niet ~ worden (zijn)* I don't want to be personal; **II** *ad* personally, in person; **–heid** (-heden) *v* personality; *persoonlijkheden* personal remarks; **persoonsbewijs** (-wijzen) *o* identity card; **–verheerlijking** *v* personality cult; **–verwisseling** (-en) *v* [case of] mistaken identity; **per'soontje** (-s) *o* (little) person; *mijn ~* I, my humble self, yours truly

'persorgaan (-ganen) *o* organ of the press

perspec'tief (-tieven) *o* perspective[2]; **perspec'tivisch** perspective

'perspomp (-en) *v* force-pump

'perstribune (-s) *v* reporters' gallery, press gallery; **–verslag** (-slagen) *o* press account; **–vrijheid** *v* liberty (freedom) of the press, press freedom

perti'nent I *aj* categorical, positive; *een ~e leugen* a downright lie; **II** *ad* categorically, positively

'Peru *o* Peru; **Peru'aan** (-ruanen) *m* Peruvian; **'perubalsem** *m* balsam of Peru; **Peruvi'aans** Peruvian

per'vers perverse; **–ie** (-s) *v* 1 (h a n d e l i n g) perversion; 2 (a a r d) perversity; **perversi'teit** (-en) *v* perversity

'Perzië *o* Persia

'perzik (-en) *v* peach; **–(e)boom** (-bomen) *m* peach-tree

'Perzisch I *aj* Persian; **II** *o* Persian

pes'sarium (-ia en -s) *o* pessary, diaphragm

pessi'misme *o* pessimism; **pessi'mist** (-en) *m* pessimist; **–isch** pessimistic

pest *v* plague, pestilence[2]; *fig* pest; *de ~ aan iets hebben* hate and detest sth.; *de ~ in hebben* **S** be in a wax, be mad; *dat is de ~ voor de zenuwen* it plays the devil with (is disastrous for) one's nerves; **–bacil** (-len) *m* plague bacillus; **–bui** (-en) *v*, **–humeur** *o* **F** bad temper, cantankerous mood; **'pesten** (pestte, h. gepest) *vt* tease, nag; **peste'rij** (-en) *v* teasing, nagging; **'pesthaard** (-en) *m* plague spot[2]; **–huis** (-huizen) *o* plague-house

pesti'cide (-n) *o* pesticide, pest killer

pesti'lentie [-(t)si.] (-s en -iën) *v* pestilence, plague; **'pestkop** (-pen) *m* teaser, beast, bully; **–lijder** (-s) *m* plague patient; **–lucht** *v* pestilential air; **–vogel** (-s) *m* waxwing; **–weer** *o* **F** rotten weather; **–ziekte** *v* pestilence, plague

pet (-ten) *v* (v. s t o f, s l a p) (cloth) cap, (m e t k l e p) peaked cap; (d e c o r a t i e f, s t ij f) hat; *zie ook: petje*

'petekind (-eren) *o* godchild; **–moei** (-en) *v* godmother; **'peter** (-s) *m* godfather

peter'selie *v* parsley

pe'tieterig teeny-weeny

petit-'four [pɔti.ˈfu:r] (-s) *m* small cream cake

pe'titie [-(t)si.] (-s en -tiën) *v* petition, memorial; **petitio'neren** [-ʃo'ne:rə(n)] (petitioneerde, h. gepetitioneerd) *vt* petition; **petitionne'ment** (-en) *o* petition

'petje (-s) *o* cap; *dat gaat boven mijn ~* it is beyond me, it beats me, that's streets ahead of me

pe'toet *m* ᚚ **S** clink, jug; *in de ~* in quod

Pe'trarca *m* Petrarch

petro'chemisch petrochemical; **pe'troleum** [-le.üm] *m* petroleum, oil; (g e z u i v e r d) kerosene; **–blik** (-ken) *o* oil-tin; **–boer** (-en) *m* kerosene peddler; **–bron** (-nen) *v* oil-well; **–kachel** (-s) *v* oil-stove, oil-heater; **–lamp** (-en) *v* paraffin-lamp; **–maatschappij** (-en) *v* oil company; **–raffinaderij** (-en) *v* oil refinery; **–stel** (-len) *o* oil-stove; **–veld** (-en) *v* oil-field

'Petrus *m* (St.) Peter

'petto *in ~* in store, in the offing; [have sth.] up one's sleeve

peuk (-en) *m* = *peuter* 2 & *peukje*; **–je** (-s) *o* **F** [candle-, cigarette-, cigar-]end, stub

peul (-en) *v* husk, shell, pod; *~en* = *peultjes*; **–(e)schil** (-len) *v* pea-pod; *dat is maar een ~letje voor hem* that is a mere flea-bite to him; that is nothing to him; **–tjes** *mv* podded peas; **–vrucht** (-en) *v* pulse, leguminous plant; *~en* pulse

peur (-en) *v* bob; **–der** (-s) *m* sniggler, bobber [for eels]; **'peuren** (peurde, h. gepeurd) *vi* sniggle, bob [for eels]

'peuter (-s) *m* 1 pipe-cleaner; 2 (k l e i n p e r s o o n) hop-o'-my-thumb, tiny tot, chit, **S** nipper '**peuteraar** (-s) *m* niggler; '**peuteren** (peuterde, h. gepeuterd) *vi* tinker, fiddle, niggle; *wie heeft daaraan gepeuterd?* who has tampered with it?; *in zijn neus (tanden &)* ~ pick one's nose (teeth); '**peuterig** finical, niggling, **F** pernickety; '**peuterwerk** *o* niggling work

'**peuzelen** (peuzelde, h. gepeuzeld) *vi & vt* munch

'**pezen** (peesde, h. en is gepeesd) *vi* (h a r d rij d e n) tear along, run; (h a r d w e r k e n) toil (and moil), sweat; (z i c h p r o s t i t u- e r e n) walk the streets

'**pezig** 1 tendinous, sinewy, wiry; 2 stringy [meat]

P.G. = *Protestantse Godsdienst; Procureur-Generaal*

pia'nino ('s) *v* pianino, upright piano, cottage piano; **pia'nist** (-en) *m,* **-e** (-s en -n) *v* pianist; **pi'ano** ('s) *v* piano; ~ *spelen* play the piano; **-begeleiding** *v* piano(forte) accompaniment; **-concert** (-en) *o* 1 (u i t v o e r i n g) piano recital; 2 (m u z i e k s t u k) piano(forte) concerto; **-kruk** (-ken) *v* (revolving) piano-stool; **-leraar** (-s en -raren) *m* piano-teacher; **-les** (-sen) *v* piano-lesson; **~-orgel** (-s) *o* piano-organ; **-spel** *o* piano-playing; **-speler** (-s) *m* pianist; **-stemmer** (-s) *m* piano-tuner

pi'as (-sen) *m* > clown, buffoon

pi'aster (-s) *m* piastre

'**piccolo** ['pi.ko.-] ('s) *m* 1 ♪ (f l u i t) piccolo; 2 (b e d i e n d e) page, **F** buttons

'**picknick** (-s) *m* picnic; '**picknicken** (picknickte, h. gepicknickt) *vt* picnic

pick-'up (-s) *m* record player

'**picobello** **F** spick and span, super, **S** ritzy

'**Picten** *mv* Picts

pied-à-'terre [pje.a.'tɛ:r] *o* pied-à-terre

pied de 'poule [pje.də'pu:l] *m* hound's tooth

piëde'stal (-len en -s) *o & m* pedestal

pief ~, *paf, poef!* bang, pop!

piek (-en) *v* 1 pike [weapon]; 2 (t o p) peak; *een* ~ *haar* a wisp of hair; 3 *m* (g u l d e n, **F**) guilder

'**piekeren** (piekerde, h. gepiekerd) *vi* think, brood, reflect; *hij zat er altijd over te* ~ he was worrying it out in his mind

'**piekfijn I** *aj* smart, tip-top, A 1, spick and span; **II** *ad* ~ *gekleed* dressed up to the nines

'**piekuur** (-uren) *o* peak hour

'**piemel** (-s) *m* **F** penis; **-naakt** **F** stark-naked

'**pienter I** *aj* clever, smart, bright; **II** *ad* cleverly &

piep *ij* peep!, chirp, squeak; '**piepen** (piepte, h. gepiept) *vi* peep, chirp, squeak [of birds, mice &]; creak [of a hinge]; '**pieper** (-s) *m* 1 squeaker; 2 **F** spud: potato; **-ig** squeaking, squeaky; '**piepjong** very young; **-klein** tiny,

weeny, minute; **-kuiken** (-s) *o* springchicken; **-stem** (-men) *v* reedy (shrill, piping) voice; **-zak** *in de*(*n*) ~ **F** in a blue funk

1 pier (-en) *m* earthworm; *voor de* ~*en zijn* be done for; *zo dood als een* ~ as dead as mutton (as a doornail)

2 pier (-en) *m* pier, jetty

pierema'chochel (-s) *v* = *straatorgel*

piere'ment (-en) *o* **F** = *straatorgel*

'**pierenbad** (-baden) *o* shallow swimming-bath, paddling pool; **-verschrikker** (-s) *m* **F** wet, dram, drink

'**pierewaaien** (pierewaaide, h. gepierewaaid) *vi* be on the spree; **-er** (-s) *m* rip, rake

pier'rot [pi.ɛ:'ro.] (-s) *m* pierrot

'**piesen** (pieste, h. gepiest) *vi* **P** piss; '**piespot** (-ten) *m* **P** piss-pot

Piet *m* Peter; ~ *de Smeerpoets* Shock-headed Peter

piet (-en) *m een hele* ~ 1 ('n h e l e m e n e e r) **S** a toff; 2 ('n k r a a n) **F** a dab (at *in*); *een hoge (grote)* ~ **F** a bigwig; *een rijke* ~ **F** a rich Johnnie; *een saaie* ~ > a dull dog

pië'teit *v* piety, reverence

piete'peuterig *aj* fussy; **-heid** *v* fussiness

'**Pieter** *m* Peter

'**pieterig** puny

'**pieterman** (-nen) *m* 🐟 weever

pieter'selie *v* = *peterselie*

'**Pieterspenning** (-en) *m de* ~ *rk* Peter's pence

pië'tisme *o* pietism; **-ist** (-en) *m* pietist

'**pietje** (-s) *o* 1 (h o o f d l u i s, **F**) louse; 2 (k a n a r i e, **F**) canary-bird

piet'lut (-ten) *m & v* fuss-pot, niggler; **-tig** niggling, pernickety

'**pietsje** (-s) *o* = *tikkeltje*

pig'ment *o* pigment; **pigmen'tatie** [-(t)si.] *v* pigmentation

pij (-en) *v* frock, habit ·

'**pijjekker** (-s) *m* pea-jacket

pijl (-en) *m* arrow; bolt, dart; *fig* shaft; ~ *en boog* bow and arrow; *hij heeft al zijn* ~*en verschoten* he has shot all his bolts; *als een* ~ *uit de boog* as swift as an arrow, [be off] like a shot; *meer* ~*en op zijn boog hebben* have more strings to one's bow; **-(en)bundel** (-s) *m* bundle of arrows

'**pijler** (-s) *m* pillar, column; (v. e. b r u g) pier

'**pijlkoker** (-s) *m* quiver; **-kruid** *o* arrow-head; **-punt** (-en) *m* arrow-head; **-snel** (as) swift as an arrow; '**pijlstaart** (-en) *m* 1 🐦 pintail duck; 2 🐟 = *pijlstaartrog*; 3 🦋 = *pijlstaartvlinder*; **-rog** (-gen) *m* sting-ray; **-vlinder** (-s) *m* hawk-moth; '**pijlvormig** arrow-shaped; **-wortel** (-s) *m* arrowroot

1 pijn (-en) *m* 🌲 pine, pine-tree

2 pijn (-en) *v* pain, ache; ~ *doen* zie 1 *zeer (doen)*; *ik heb* ~ *aan mijn hand* my hand hurts;

ik heb ~ in mijn borst I have a pain in my chest;
ik heb ~ in mijn keel I have a sore throat
'**pijnappel** (-s) *m* fir-cone, pine-cone; **–klier**
(-en) *v* pineal gland
'**pijnbank** (-en) *v* rack; *iem. op de ~ leggen* put
sbd. to the rack
'**pijnboom** (-bomen) *m* pine-tree, pine
'**pijnigen** (pijnigde, h. gepijnigd) *vt* torture,
rack, torment; **–er** (-s) *m* torturer, tormentor;
'**pijniging** (-en) *v* torture; '**pijnlijk** painful;
het is ~ ook: it hurts; *~e voeten* aching feet,
tender feet; **–heid** (-heden) *v* painfulness;
'**pijnloos** painless; **–stillend** soothing,
anodyne; *~ middel* anodyne, pain-killer
pijp (-en) *v* 1 pipe [for gas, of an organ, for
smoking]; 2 nose, nozzle [of bellows]; 3 socket
[of a candlestick]; 4 leg [of a pair of trousers];
5 (b u i s) pipe, tube, spout; funnel [of a
steamer]; 6 (p l o o i s e l) flute; 7 ♪ fife; *een ~
lak* a stick of sealing-wax; *naar iem.'s ~en dansen*
dance to sbd.'s tune; *een lelijke ~ roken* come in
for something unpleasant; **–aarde** *v* pipe-clay;
'**pijpekop** (-pen) *m* bowl (of a pipe); **–krul**
(-len) *v* ringlet; '**pijpen*** *vi* & *vt* pipe, fife;
'**pijpenla(de)** (-laden) *v* 1 pipe-box; 2 *fig*
long, narrow room; **–rek** (-ken) *o* pipe-rack;
'**pijpepeuter** (-s) *m* pipe cleaner (picker);
'**pijper** (-s) *m* piper, fifer; '**pijpesteel** (-stelen)
m stem (shank) of a tobacco-pipe; *het regent
pijpestelen* it is raining in sheets; '**pijpkaneel** *m*
& *o* cinnamon (in sticks); **–leiding** (-en) *v*
pipe-line; **–orgel** (-s) *o* pipe organ; **–sleutel**
(-s) *m* box-spanner, socket spanner; **–tabak** *m*
pipe tobacco
1 pik *o* & *m* (s t o f n a a m) = *pek*
2 pik *m* peck; || pique, grudge; *hij heeft de ~ op
mij* he owes me a grudge
3 pik (-ken) *v* (h o u w e e l) pick, pickax(e)
4 pik (-ken) *m* (s t e e k) sting, stab; peck
5 pik (-ken) *v* **P** prick, cock
pi'**kant** piquant, seasoned, spicy, pungent;
(g e w a a g d) risqué [story]; *dat gaf het gesprek
iets ~s* that added a zest (that's what gave a
piquancy) to the conversation; **pikante'rie**
(-ieën) *v* piquancy²; *fig* spiciness
'**pikbroek** (-en) *m* **F** (Jack-)tar [sailor]
'**pikdonker I** *aj* pitch-dark; **II** *o* pitch-darkness
'**pikdraad** (-draden) *o* & *m* wax-end, waxed end
pi'**keren** (pikeerde, h. gepikeerd) *vt* nettle; *hij
was erover gepikeerd* he was nettled at it; *zie ook:
gepikeerd*
pi'**ket** 1 *o* (k a a r t s p e l) piquet; 2 (-ten) *m* ⚔
picket; **–paal** (-palen) *m* picket
pi'**keur** (-s) *m* 1 riding-master; 2 (v. c i r c u s)
ringmaster; 3 (j a g e r) huntsman
'**pikhaak** (-haken) *m* ⚓ boat-hook; (b ij
k o r e n o o g s t) reaping-hook; **–houweel**

(-welen) *o* pickaxe
'**pikkedonker** = *pikdonker*
1 'pikken (pikte, h. gepikt) *vt* (b e s m e r e n
m e t p e k) = *pekken*
2 'pikken (pikte, h. gepikt) **I** *vi* pick, peck; **II** *vt*
peck; (p r i k k e n) prick; (s t e l e n, **F**) bag,
filch, pilfer; **F** *dat pik ik niet* I am not having
this
'**pikzwart** coal-black, pitch-black
pil (-len) *v* pill; (d i k k e b o t e r h a m) chunk of
bread; (d i k b o e k) tome; *~len draaien* roll
pills; *een bittere ~ slikken* swallow a bitter pill;
de ~ vergulden gild the pill
pi'**laar** (-laren) *m* pillar, post; **–heilige** (-n) *m*
stylite; **pi'laster** (-s) *m* pilaster
Pi'**latus** *m* Pilate; zie ook: *Pontius*
'**pillendoos** (-dozen) *v* pill-box²; **–draaier** (-s)
m pill-roller
'**pilo** *o* corduroy
pi'**loot** (-loten) *m* pilot; *tweede ~* co-pilot
pils *m* & *o* Pilsen(er); lager; *een ~(je)* a pint (of
light beer)
pi'**ment** *o* pimento, allspice
'**pimpelaar** (-s) *m* boozer, tippler; '**pimpelen**
(pimpelde, h. gepimpeld) *vi* tipple
'**pimpelmees** (-mezen) *v* blue tit(mouse)
'**pimpelpaars** purple
pin (-nen) *v* peg, pin; zie ook: *pen*
pi'**nakel** (-s) *m* pinnacle
pi'**nas** (-sen) *v* pinnace
pince-'**nez** [pɪ̃s'ne.] (-s) *m* pince-nez
pin'**cet** (-ten) *o* & *m* (pair of) tweezers
'**pinda** ('s) *v* peanut; **–kaas** *m* peanut butter;
–man (-nen) *m* peanut vendor
pi'**neut** *m* **S** *de ~ zijn* be for it, be the dupe
ping *m* = *pingping*
'**pingelaar** (-s) *m*, **–ster** (-s) *v* haggler;
'**pingelen** (pingelde, h. gepingeld) *vi* 1
haggle; 2 ⚙ pink, knock [of engine]
ping'**ping** *m* **S** lolly [= money], brass
⊛ '**pingpong** *o* ping-pong
'**pinguïn** ['pɪŋɣʏn] (-s) *m* penguin
1 pink (-en) *m* little finger; zie ook: 1 *pinken*
2 pink (-en) *m* ⚓ pink, fishing-boat
3 pink (-en) *m* ⚓ yearling
1 'pinken *mv bij de ~ zijn* **F** be all there, have
one's wits about one
2 'pinken (pinkte, h. gepinkt) **I** *vi* wink, blink;
II *vt een traan uit de ogen ~* brush away a tear;
'**pinkogen** (pinkoogde, h. pinkoogd) *vi*
blink
'**Pinksterbeweging** *v* Pentecostal movement,
Pentecostalism; '**pinksterbloem** (-en) *v* ⚘
cuckooflower; **–dag** (-dagen) *m* Whit Sunday;
tweede ~ Whit Monday; **Pinkster'dinsdag,
Pinkster'drie** *m* Whit Tuesday; '**Pinksteren**
m Whitsun(tide), Pentecost; '**pinksterfeest**

(-en) *o* 1 Whitsuntide; 2 [Jewish] Pentecost; **Pinkster'maandag** *m* Whit Monday; **'pinkstertijd** *m* Whitsuntide; **–vakantie** [-(t)si.] (-s) *v* Whitsun(tide) holidays; **–week** (-weken) *v* Whit(sun) week; **Pinkster'zondag** *m* Whit Sunday

'pinnen (pinde, h. gepind) *vt* pin, peg, fasten with pins

pint (-en) *v* pint

pi'oen(roos) (-rozen) *v* peony

pi'on (-nen) *m* pawn [at chess]

pio'nier (-s) *m* pioneer[2]; **pio'nieren** (pionierde, h. gepionierd) *vi* pioneer, break new ground; **pio'nierswerk** *o* pioneering; *fig* spadework

pip *v* pip [disease of birds]; *hij kan de ~ krijgen!* **F** he can go to blazes (go climb a tree, go fly a kite)!

pi'pet (-ten) *v* & *o* pipette

pips 1 having the pip; 2 peaked, drawn

pi'qué [pi.'ke.] *o* piqué

pi'raat (-raten) *m* pirate

pirami'daal pyramidal; *het is ~* it is enormous; **pira'mide** (-s en -n) *v* pyramid

pi'ratenzender (-s) *m* pirate (radio station, transmitter); **pirate'rij** *v* piracy

pirou'ette [pi:ru.'ttə] (-s en -n) *v* pirouette; **pirouet'teren** (pirouetteerde, h. gepirouetteerd) *vi* pirouette

pis *m* **P** piss

'pisang (-s) *v* ⚕ banana

'pisbuis (-buizen) *v* urethra; **–nijdig F** furious, in a rage; **–paal** *m* **P** scape-goat; **–pot** (-ten) *m* = *piespot*; **'pissebed** (-den) *v* sow-bug; **'pissen** (piste, h. gepist) *vi* **P** 1 piss; 2 *hij is ~* he is gone; **pis'soir** [pi.s'va.r] (-s) *o* & *m* public urinal, *Am* pissoir

pis'tache [pi.s'taʃ(ə)] (-s) *v* 1 ⚕ pistachio; 2 (k n a l b o n b o n) cracker

'piste (-s en -n) *v* 1 (v. c i r c u s) ring; 2 (v o o r w i e l r e n n e r s) track

pis'ton (-s) *m* ♪ cornet; **pisto'nist** (-en) *m* ♪ cornetist

pis'tool (-tolen) *o* pistol [weapon]; *iem. het ~ op de borst zetten* clap a pistol to sbd.'s breast; **–schot** (-schoten) *o* pistol-shot

pit (-ten) *o* & *v* 1 kernel [of nut]; pip [of an apple, orange], seed [of apple, cotton, grape, orange, raisin, sunflower], stone [of grapes &]; *fig* pith, spirit; body [of wine, a novel]; 2 wick [of a lamp]; burner [of a gas-cooker]; *er zit geen ~ in hem* he has no grit in him; *rozijnen zonder ~(ten)* seedless raisins; **–loos** seedless, pitless; **–riet** *o* ± rattan

'pitten (pitte, h. gepit) *vi* **F** sleep

'pittig I *aj* pithy[2] [style &], lively, stirring [music]; [beer, wine] of a good body; spicy, savoury [dish]; **II** *ad* pithily; **–heid** *v* pithiness[2]

pitto'resk picturesque

'pitvrucht (-en) *v* ⚕ pome

pk [pe.'ka.] = *paardekracht*

plaag (plagen) *v* plague, vexation, nuisance; pest; **–geest** (-en) *m* teaser, tease; **–ziek** fond of teasing, teasing; **–zucht** *v* teasing disposition

plaat (platen) *v* 1 (ij z e r) sheet, plate [also of glass]; 2 (m a r m e r) slab; 3 (w ij z e r p l a a t) dial; 4 (g r a v u r e) picture, engraving, print; 5 (g r a m m o f o o n~) record; 6 (o n d i e p t e) shoal, sands; *de ~ poetsen* bolt, **S** beat it; **–ijzer** *o* sheet-iron; **–je** (-s) *o* 1 (a f b e e l d i n g) picture; 2 (v. ij z e r &) plate; **–koek** (-en) *m* griddle cake

plaats (-en) *v* 1 (in 't a l g.) place; 2 (r u i m t e) room, place; [enclosed] court, yard; 3 (h o f s t e d e) farm; 4 (z i t p l a a t s) seat; 5 (b e t r e k k i n g) place, situation, post, office; [clergyman's] living; 6 (i n b o e k) place; 7 (t o n e e l) scene [of the crime, of the disaster]; *het is hier niet de ~ om...* the present (this) is not a place for ...ing; *~ bieden aan* admit, seat [200 persons]; *de ~ innemen van...* take the place of...; *neemt uw ~ in* take your places; *een eervolle ~ innemen* hold an honoured place; *het neemt te veel ~ in* it takes up too much room; *~ maken* make room; make way [for others]; give place [to doubt], give way [to hesitation]; *~ nemen* sit down, take a seat; ● *in de ~ van de heer H.,* *benoemd tot...* in (the) place of...; *in (op) de allereerste ~* first and foremost; *in (op) de eerste ~* in the first place, first of all, firstly; primarily [intended for pupils, students &]; *in (op) de laatste ~* last of all, lastly; *wat had u in mijn ~ gedaan?* in my place; *in uw ~* if I were (had been) in your place; *ik zou niet graag in zijn ~ zijn* I should not like to stand in his shoes; *in ~ van* instead of; *in ~ daarvan* instead; *in de ~ komen van (voor)* take the place of; *in de ~ stellen van* substitute for; *o p de ~ (dood) blijven* be killed on the spot; *op de ~ rust!* ✕ stand easy!; *op alle ~en* in all places, everywhere; *daar is hij op zijn ~* he is in his element there; *dat woord is hier niet op zijn ~* is out of place, is not in place; *iem. op zijn ~ zetten* put sbd. in his (proper) place; *t e r ~e* on the spot; *daar ter ~e* there, at that place; *wij zijn ter ~e* we have reached our destination; *niet v a n de ~ komen* not move from the spot; *de schoenmaker van de ~* the local shoemaker; **–bekleder** (-s) *m* deputy, substitute; *de P~* the Vicar of Christ; **–bepaling** (-en) *v* location; **–beschrijving** (-en) *v* topography; **–bespreking** *v* (advance) booking; **–bewijs** (-wijzen) *o* ticket

'plaatschade *v* bodywork damage

'plaatscommandant (-en) *m* town major;

'**plaatselijk** *aj* local; '**plaatsen** (plaatste, h. geplaatst) *vt* 1 (z e t t e n) put, place; 2 (e e n p l a a t s g e v e n) seat [guests &]; give employment to [people]; 3 (s t a t i o n e r e n) station, post; 4 (o p s t e l l e n) put up [a machine]; 5 (o p n e m e n) insert [an advertisement]; 6 (a a n d e m a n b r e n g e n) dispose of [articles &]; 7 *sp* place [a horse]; 8 (u i t z e t t e n) invest [money]; *hij heeft zijn zoons goed weten te* ~ he has got his sons into good situations; *geplaatst voor een moeilijkheid (het probleem)* faced with a difficulty (the problem); '**plaatsgebrek** *o* want of space; **–grijpen**[1] *vi* take place; **–hebben**[1] *vi* take place; '**plaatsing** (-en) *v* 1 placing &; 2 insertion [of advertisements]; 3 investment [of capital]; 4 appointment [of servants]; '**plaatsje** (-s) *o* 1 place; 2 yard [of a house]; 3 (z i t p l a a t s) seat; *in die kleine* ~*s* in those small towns; '**plaatskaart** (-en) *v* ticket; **–naam** (-namen) *m* place name; **–opneming** (-en) *v* judicial inspection of the premises; **–ruimte** *v* space, room; ~ *aanbieden* (*hebben*) *voor* have (provide) accommodation for '**plaatstaal** *o* sheet (plate) steel '**plaatsvervangend acting** [manager], deputy [commissioner], temporary; **–vervanger** (-s) *m* 1 (i n h e t a l g.) substitute; 2 (m e t v o l m a c h t) deputy; 3 (d o k t e r) locum tenens, deputy; 4 (a c t e u r) understudy; 5 (b i s s c h o p) surrogate; **–vervanging** *v* substitution; **–vervulling** (-en) *v* 🕎 representation; **–vinden**[1] *vi* take place

'**plaatwerk** (-en) *o* 1 book of pictures (or reproductions); 2 ✂ plating
pla'centa ('s) *v* placenta
placht (plachten) V.T. van *plegen*
pla'fon(d) [- 'fõ] (-s) *o* ceiling; **plafon'neren** (plafonneerde, h. geplafonneerd) *vt* ceil; **plafon'nière** [-fon'jɛrə] (-s) *v* ceiling light
plag (-gen) *v* = *plagge*
'**plagen** (plaagde, h. geplaagd) **I** *vt* 1 tease; 2 (u i t b o o s a a r d i g h e i d) vex; 3 = *kwellen*; *zij* ~ *hem ermee* they chaff him about it; *mag ik u even* ~? excuse my disturbing you; **II** *va* tease; **–er** (-s) *m* teaser, tease; **plage'rij** (-en) *v* teasing; vexation; zie *plagen*
'**plagge** (-n) *v* sod (of turf); '**plaggenhut** (-ten) *v* sod house, turf hut; **–steker** (-s) *m* turf-cutter
plagi'aat (-iaten) *o* plagiarism, plagiary; ~ *plegen* commit plagiarism, plagiarize; **plagi'aris** (-sen), **plagi'ator** (-s) *m* plagiarist
plaid [ple.d] (-s) *m* 1 (S c h o t s e m a n t e l) plaid; 2 (r e i s d e k e n) (travelling-)rug

plak (-ken) *v* 1 slice [of ham &]; slab [of cake, chocolate &]; 2 *sp* [gold &] medal; 3 🞎 [schoolmaster's] ferule; *onder de* ~ *van zijn vrouw zitten* be henpecked [by one's wife]; *flink onder de* ~ *houden* keep a tight hand over '**plakband** *o* 1 (v. c e l l o f a a n) adhesive tape, sellotape; 2 (v. p a p i e r) gummed paper; **–boek** (-en) *o* scrap book; **plak'kaat** (-katen) *o* 1 placard, poster; 2 🞎 edict; **–verf** *v* poster paint (colour); '**plakken** (plakte, h. geplakt) **I** *vt* paste, stick, glue; **II** *vi* stick, be sticky; *blijven* ~ *[fig]* stay on and never know when to go away; '**plakker** (-s) *m* 1 paster, sticker[2]; 2 🦋 gipsymoth; *hij is een echte* ~ **F** he is a sticker; **–ig** sticky[2]; '**plakplaatje** (-s) *o* pasting-in picture; **–pleister** (-s) *v* 1 = *hechtpleister*; 2 *fig* (p l a k k e r) sticker; (l i e f j e) sweetheart; **–sel** (-s) *o* paste; **–zegel** (-s) *m* receipt-stamp
pla'muren (plamuurde, h. geplamuurd) *vt & vi* fill, stop with filler; **pla'muur** *m & o*, **–sel** *o* filler; **–mes** (-sen) *o* stopping-knife
plan (-nen) *o* 1 (v o o r n e m e n) plan, design, project, intention; 2 (v o o r b e r e i d i n g) plan, design, scheme, project; 3 (t e k e n i n g) plan; *dat is zijn* ~ *niet* that is not his intention, that is not part of his plan; ~*nen beramen* make plans, lay schemes; *zijn* ~*nen blootleggen* (*ontvouwen*) unfold one's plans; *een* ~ *ontwerpen* (*opmaken*) draw up a plan; *het* ~ *opvatten om...* conceive the project of ...ing; ~*nen smeden* forge plots; *zijn* ~ *vaststellen* lay down one's plan; *een* ~ *vormen* form a scheme; ● *met het* ~ *om...* with the intention to; *een* ~ *op hoger* ~ *on a higher plane, at a higher level; *v a n* ~ *zijn* (*om*) intend, mean to, think of...; *we zijn niet van* ~ *te werken voor anderen* we are not prepared (are not going) to work for others; **–bureau** [-by.ro.] (-s) *o* planning office; **plan de cam'pagne** [-plɑndəkam'pɑɲə] *o* plan of action (campaign); '**planeconomie** *v* statism
pla'neet (-neten) *v* planet; **–baan** (-banen) *v* orbit of a planet
pla'neren (planeerde, h. geplaneerd) 1 *vt* planish [metals]; size [paper]; 2 *vi* (v l i e g - t u i g, b o o t) glide, plane down
plane'tair [-ne.'tɛːr] planetary; **plane'tarium** (-ia en -s) *o* planetarium, orrery; **pla'neten-stelsel** (-s) *o* planetary system; **planeto'ïde** (-n) *v* planetoid
planime'trie *v* plane geometry
plank (-en) *v* plank [2 to 6 inches thick], board [under 2 $\frac{1}{2}$ in.]; shelf [in book-case &]; *de* ~ *misslaan* be beside (wide of) the mark; ● *hij komt o p de* ~*en* he will appear on the stage;

---

[1] V.T. en V.D. van dit werkwoord volgens het model: '**plaats**grijpen, V.T. greep '**plaats**, V.D. '**plaats**gegrepen. Zie voor de vormen van het grondwoord de lijst van sterke en onregelmatige werkwoorden achterin.

van de bovenste ~ A 1, tophole; *hij is er een van de bovenste* ~ he is a first-rate fellow; **'planken** *aj* made of boards, wooden; *een* ~ *vloer* a boarded floor; **–koorts, –vrees** *v* stage-fright; **'plankgas** *o* ~ *geven* step on it, *Am* step up the gas; **plan'kier** (-en) *o* 1 foot-board; 2 platform

'plankton *o* plankton

plan'matig planned [economy]; **'plannen** [ˈplɪnə(n)] (plande, h. gepland) *vi* & *vt* plan; **'plannenmaker** (-s) *m* planner, schemer, projector; **'planning** [ˈplɪnɪŋ] *v* planning

'plano *in* ~ in sheets

planolo'gie *v* planning; **plano'logisch** planning [problems &]; **plano'loog** (-logen) *m* planner

plant (-en) *v* plant; **plant'aardig** vegetable; ~ *voedsel* a vegetable diet; **plan'tage** [-ʒə] (-s) *v* plantation, estate; **'planteboter** *v* vegetable butter; **–leven** *o* plant life, vegetable life; *een* ~ *leiden* vegetate; **'planten** (plantte, h. geplant) *vt* plant [potatoes &, the flag]; **'plantenetend** plant-eating, herbivorous; **–groei** *m* vegetation; plant-growth; **–kenner** (-s) botanist; **–kweker** (-s) *m* nurseryman; **planten-kweke'rij** (-en) *v* nursery(-garden); **'plantenleer** *v* botany; **–rijk** *o* vegetable kingdom; **–tuin** (-en) *m* botanical garden; **–wereld** *v* vegetable world; **'planter** (-s) *m* planter; **'plantevezel** (-s) *v* vegetable fibre; **'plante-ziekte** (-s en -n) *v* plant disease, blight; **–nkunde** *v* plant pathology; **plante-ziekten'kundig** of plant pathology; **'plant-kunde** *v* botany; **plant'kundig** botanical; **–e** (-n) *m* botanist; **'plantluis** (-luizen) *v* = *bladluis*

plant'soen (-en) *o* public garden, pleasure grounds, park

plas (-sen) *m* puddle, pool; *de Friese* ~*sen* the Frisian "meers" (lakes); *een* ~ *doen* make water, **F** pee, wee-wee

'plasma *o* [blood] plasma

'plasregen (-s) *m* splashing rain, downpour; **'plasregenen** (plasregende, h. geplasregend) *vi* rain cats and dogs

'plassen (plaste, h. geplast) *vi* 1 splash; 2 (u r i n e r e n) make water, **F** pee, wee-wee; **–er** (-s) **F** *m* penis

'plastic [ˈplɪstɪk] **I** (-s) *o* plastic; **II** *aj* plastic; **1 plas'tiek** (-en) *v* (k u n s t) plastic art; **2 plas'tiek** *o* (k u n s t s t o f) plastic; **–en** *aj* plastic; **plastifi'ceren** (plastificeerde, h. geplastificeerd) *vt* plasticize; **'plastisch I** *aj* 1 plastic [art; materials; nature; surgery]; 2

(a a n s c h o u w e l ij k) graphic [description]; **II** *ad* 1 plastically; 2 graphically [told &]

plas'tron (-s) *o* & *m* plastron

plat I *aj* flat [roof &]; *fig* broad [accent], coarse, vulgar [language]; *een* ~*te beurs* an empty purse; ~*te knoop* ⚓ reefknot; ~ *maken* (*worden*) flatten; **II** *ad* flat; *fig* vulgarly, coarsely; **III** (-ten) *o* 1 flat [of a sword &]; 2 flat, leads [of a roof]; 3 cover [of a book]; *continentaal* ~ continental shelf

pla'taan (-tanen) *m* plane(-tree)

'platbodemd, –boomd flat-bottomed; **'platbranden**[1] *vt* burn down; **–drukken**[1] *vt* crush, flatten out, press flat; **'Platduits** *o* Low German

pla'teau [-ˈto.] (-s) *o* plateau, tableland

'platebon (-nen en -s) *m* record token

pla'teel (-telen) *o* Delft ware, faience; **–bakker** (-s) *m* Delft-ware maker; **–bakkerij** (-en) *v* Delft-ware pottery

'platehoes (-hoezen) *v* record sleeve

'platenatlas (-sen) *m* pictorial atlas; **–speler** (-s) *m* record player; **–wisselaar** (-s) *m* record changer

pla'teren (plateerde, h. geplateerd) *vt* plate [metals]

'platform (-s en -en) *o* 1 platform; 2 ✈ apron, tarmac [of airfield]

'platgetreden downtrodden; *fig* beaten [track]; **'platheid** (-heden) *v* flatness; *fig* coarseness, vulgarity

'platina *o* platinum; **–blond** platinum blonde **plati'tude** (-s) *v* platitude, trite (commonplace) remark

'platje (-s) *o* 1 (p l a t d a k j e) flat, leads; 2 (t e r r a s j e) terrace, porch; 3 (p l a t l u i s) crab-louse

'platleggen[1] *vt* (d o o r s t a k i n g) strike; *platgelegd* strikebound; **–liggen**[1] **I** *vi* lie flat; **II** *vt* lie upon, crush; **–lopen**[1] *vt* tread down; zie ook: *deur*; **'platluis** (-luizen) *v* crab-louse

'Plato *m* Plato; **pla'tonisch I** *aj* platonic; **II** *ad* platonically

'platslaan[1] *vt* 1 flatten; 2 beat down

platte'grond (-en) *m* ground-plan [of a building]; plan, map [of the town]; **platte'land** *o* country, countryside; **platte'landsbewoner** (-s) *m* countryman, rural resident; **–vrouw** (-en) *v* countrywoman

'plattrappen[1] *vt* trample (down)

'platvis (-sen) *m* flatfish

plat'vloers banal, low, vulgar; **–heid** (-heden) *v* banality, vulgarity

---

[1] V.T. en V.D. van dit werkwoord volgens het model: **'plat**branden, V.T. brandde **'plat**, V.D. **'plat**gebrand. Zie voor de vormen van het grondwoord, in dit voorbeeld: *branden*. Bij sterke en onregelmatige werkwoorden wordt u verwezen naar de lijst achterin.

'platvoet (-en) *m* flat-foot; flat-footed person
'platweg flatly
'platzak ~ *zijn* have an empty purse, be hard up
plau'sibel [s = z] plausible
pla'veien (plaveide, h. geplaveid) *vt* pave;
pla'veisel (-s) *o* pavement; **pla'veisteen** (-stenen) *m* paving-stone; **pla'vuis** (-vuizen) *m* paving tile, flag (stone)
ple'bejer (-s) *m* plebeian; **ple'bejisch** plebeian;
plebis'ciet [-en en -s] *o* plebiscite; **plebs** *o* rabble, riff-raff
plecht (-en) *v* fore-deck, after-deck; **–anker** (-s) *o* sheet-anchor²
'plechtig I *aj* solemn, ceremonious, stately; formal [opening of Parliament]; ~*e communie rk* solemn communion; **II** *ad* solemnly, ceremoniously, in state; formally [opened]; **–heid** (-heden) *v* ceremony, solemnity; *een* ~ ook: a function; **plecht'statig** solemn, stately, ceremonious; **–heid** *v* solemnity, stateliness, ceremoniousness
'plectrum (-tra en -s) *o* plectrum
plee (-s) **F** *m* privy, **P** bog; **–figuur** *o* **F** *een* ~ *slaan* cut a sorry figure, blunder, make a howler
'pleegbroe(de)r (-s) *m* foster-brother; **–dochter** (-s) *v* foster-daughter; **–gezin** (-nen) *o* foster-family, foster-home; **–kind** (-eren) *o* foster-child; **–moeder** (-s) *v* foster-mother; **–ouders** *mv* foster-parents; **–vader** (-s) *m* foster-father; **–zoon** (zonen en -s) *m* foster-son
'pleegzuster (-s) *v* 1 foster-sister; 2 sick-nurse, nursing sister
pleet *o* electroplate; **–werk** *o* plated articles, plated ware
plegen* *vt* commit, perpetrate; *men pleegt te vergeten dat...* one is apt to forget that...; *hij placht te drinken* he used to drink; *vaak placht hij 's morgens uit te gaan* he often would go out in the morning
plei'dooi (-en) *o* pleading, plea, defence; *een* ~ *houden voor* make a plea for
plein (-en) *o* square; (r o n d) circus; **–vrees** *v* agoraphobia
1 'pleister (-s) *v* plaster; *een* ~ *op de wond* a salve for his wounded feelings
2 'pleister *o* plaster, stucco; **1 'pleisteren** (pleisterde, h. gepleisterd) *vt* plaster, stucco
2 'pleisteren (pleisterde, h. gepleisterd) *vi* fetch up, stop [at an inn]; *de paarden laten* ~ bait the horses
'pleisterkalk *m* parget
'pleisterplaats (-en) *v* halting-place, pull-up; ☐ baiting place, stage
'pleisterwerk *o* plastering, stucco
pleit *o* ⚖ plea, (law)suit; *toen was het* ~ *beslecht*

(*voldongen*) then their fate was decided, then the battle was over; *zij hebben het* ~ *gewonnen* they have gained the day; **–bezorger** (-s) *m* ⚖ solicitor, counsel; *fig* advocate
'pleite S gone
'pleiten (pleitte, h. gepleit) *vi* ⚖ plead; ~ *t e g e n u* tell against you; ~ *v o o r* plead in favour of (for), defend; *fig* advocate; *dat pleit voor je* that speaks well for you, that tells in your favour; **–er** (-s) *m* ⚖ pleader; **'pleitrede** (-s) *v* pleading, plea, defence
Ple'jaden *mv* Pleiades
plek (-ken) *v* 1 (p l a a t s) spot, place; patch; 2 (v l e k) stain, spot; *kale* ~ bald patch
'plekken (plekte, h. geplekt) *vi & vt* stain
'plempen (plempte, h. geplempt) *vt* fill up [with earth, rubbish &]
ple'nair [ple.'nɛ:r] plenary, full
'plengen (plengde, h. geplengd) *vt* shed [tears, blood]; pour out [wine]; **'plengoffer** (-s) *o* libation
plens (plenzen) *m* splash; **–bui** (-en) *v* downpour, cloudburst
'plenum *o* full assembly, plenary session, plenum
'plenzen (plensde, h. geplensd) *vi* splash
pleo'nasme (-n) *o* pleonasm; **–'nastisch** *aj* (& *ad*) pleonastic(ally)
'plethamer (-s) *m* flatt(en)ing-hammer; **–molen** (-s) *m* rolling-mill, flatting-mill; **–rol** (-len) *v* flatt(en)ing-roller; **'pletten** (plette, h. geplet) **I** *vt* flatten, roll [metal]; **II** *vi* (v a n s t o f f e n) crush; **–er** *te* ~ *slaan* smash; ook = *te* ~ *vallen* smash, be smashed, crash; **plette'rij** (-en) *v* rolling-mill, flatting-mill
'pleuris *v* & *o* = *pleuritis*; **pleu'ritis** *v* pleurisy
ple'vier (-en) *m* plover
ple'zant = *plezierig*; **ple'zier** *o* pleasure; *veel* ~*!* enjoy yourself!, have a good time!; *het zal hem* ~ *doen* it will please him, be a pleasure to him; *iem. een* ~ *doen* do sbd. a favour; ~ *hebben* have a good time, enjoy oneself, have fun; ~ *hebben in iets* find, take (a) pleasure in sth.; ~ *hebben van iets* derive pleasure from sth.; *hij had niet veel* ~ *van zijn zoons* his sons never did anything to give him pleasure; ~ *maken* have fun, make merry; *zijn* ~ *wel opkunnen* have a hard time; ~ *vinden in iets* find, take (a) pleasure in sth.; *m e t* ~*!* with pleasure!; *t e n* ~*e van...* to please...; *v o o r (zijn)* ~ for pleasure; **–boot** (-boten) *m* & *v* excursion steamer, pleasure steamer;
ple'zieren (plezierde, h. geplezierd) *vt* please;
ple'zierig pleasant; **ple'zierjacht** (-en) *o* ⚓ (pleasure) yacht; **–reis** (-reizen) *v* pleasure trip; **–reiziger** (-s) *m* excursionist; **–tochtje** (-s) *o* pleasure trip, jaunt; **–trein** (-en) *m* excursion train; **–vaartuig(en)** *o* (*mv*) pleasure craft

plicht (-en) *m* & *v* duty, obligation; *zijn ~ doen* do one's duty; play one's part; *zijn ~ verzaken* neglect (fail in) one's duty; *volgens zijn ~ handelen* act up to one's duty; **–besef** *o* sense of duty; **–betrachting** (-en) *v* devotion to duty; **–enleer** *v* deontology; **–getrouw, plicht'matig** dutiful; **'plichtpleging** (-en) *v* compliment; *geen ~en* no ceremony; **'plichts-besef** = *plichtbesef*; **–betrachting** = *plichtbe-trachting*; **–getrouw** = *plichtgetrouw*; **–gevoel** *o* sense of duty; **plichts'halve** from a sense of duty, dutifully; **'plichtsverzuim** *o* neglect of duty; **'plichtvergeten** forgetful of one's duty, undutiful; **–verzuim** = *plichtsverzuim*

'Plinius *m* Pliny

plint (-en) *v* skirting-board [of a room &]; plinth [of a column]

plis'sé [pli.'se.] (-s) *o* pleating; **plis'seren** (plisseerde, h. geplisseerd) *vt* pleat

1 ploeg (-en) *m* & *v* (w e r k t u i g) plough; *de hand aan de ~ slaan* put one's hand to the plough

2 ploeg (-en) *v* (g r o e p) [day, night] shift, gang [of workmen]; [rescue &] party, **F** batch; team² [of footballers], crew [of rowing-boat]; **–baas** (-bazen) *m* ganger, foreman

'ploegboom (-bomen) *m* plough-beam; **'ploegen** (ploegde, h. geploegd) *vt* 1 plough; 2 ⚒ groove [a board]

'ploegendienst (-en) *m* shift; **–klassement** (-en) *o sp* team holdings; **–stelsel** *o* shift system; *volgens het ~* on the shift system

'ploeger (-s) *m* ploughman, plougher; **'ploeg-ijzer** (-s), **–kouter** (-s) *o* coulter; **–land** *o* land under the plough, ploughland; **–os** (-sen) *m* plough-ox; **–paard** (-en) *o* plough horse; *werken als een ~* work like a horse; **–rister** (-s) *m* mould-board; **–schaar** (-scharen) *v* plough-share; **–staart** (-en) *m* plough-tail; **–voor** (-voren) *v* furrow

ploert (-en) *m* cad; *de koperen ~* **S** the sun; **–achtig** = *ploertig*; **'ploertendoder** (-s) *m* bludgeon, life-preserver; **–streek** (-streken) *m* & *v* dirty (scurvy) trick; **'ploertig** caddish; **ploer'tin** (-nen) *v* ⇒ **S** landlady

'ploeteraar (-s) *m* plodder; **'ploeteren** (ploe-terde, h. geploeterd) *vi* splash, dabble; *fig* toil (and moil), drudge, plod; *~ aan* plod at

plof I *ij* plop!, flop!, plump!; **II** (-fen) *m* thud; **'ploffen** (plofte, is geploft) *vi* plump (down), flop, plop

'plokworst (-en) *v* coarse beef sausage

'plombe (-s) *v* = *plombeerloodje* & *plombeersel*; **plom'beerloodje** (-s) *o* lead seal, lead; **plom'beersel** (-s) *o* stopping, filling, plug; **plom'beren** (plombeerde, h. geplombeerd) *vt* 1 plug, stop, fill [a tooth]; 2 $ lead [goods]

plom'bière [-'bjɛːrə] (-s) *v* icecream with fruit, sundae

1 plomp I *ij* plumb!, flop!; **II** (-en) *m* flop; *in de ~ vallen* fall into the water

2 plomp I *aj* clumsy; 2 (g r o f) rude; **II** *ad* 1 clumsily; 2 rudely

3 plomp (-en) *v* ⚘ (white, yellow) waterlily

'plompen (plompte, is geplompt) *vi* plump, flop, plop

'plompheid (-heden) *v* 1 clumsiness; 2 (g r o f-h e i d) rudeness; rude thing

'plompverloren plump; **–weg** = *botweg*

plons I *ij* plop!; **II** (-en en plonzen) *m* splash; **'plonzen** (plonsde, is geplonsd) *vi* 1 flop, plop; 2 splash

plooi (-en) *v* fold, pleat [in cloth]; crease [of trousers]; wrinkle [in the forehead]; *de ~en gladstrijken* [*fig*] smooth matters over; *zijn gezicht i n de ~ zetten* compose one's counte-nance, put on a straight face; *hij komt nooit u i t de ~* he never unbends; **'plooibaar** pliable, pliant; adaptable; **–heid** *v* pliability, pliancy; **'plooien** (plooide, h. geplooid) *vt* fold, crease; pleat; wrinkle [one's forehead]; *fig* arrange [things]; **'plooiing** (-en) *v* folding; **–sgebergte** (-s en -n) *o* folded mountains; **'plooirok** (-ken) *m* pleated skirt; **'plooisel** (-s) *o* pleating

ploos (plozen) V.T. van *pluizen*

plots *ad* = *plotseling* **II**; **–eling I** *aj* sudden; **II** *ad* suddenly, all of a sudden; **–klaps** all of a sudden

'plozen V.T. meerv v. *pluizen*

pluche [ply.ʃ] *o* & *m* plush; **–n** *aj* plush

plug (-gen) *v* plug

pluim (-en) *v* plume, feather, crest; **plui'mage** [-'ma.ʒə] (-s) *v* plumage, feathers; **'pluimbal** (-len) *m* shuttlecock; **'pluimen** (pluimde, h. gepluimd) *vt* plume; **'pluimpje** (-s) *o* little feather; *fig* compliment; *dat is een ~ voor u* that is a feather in your cap; **'pluimstaart** (-en) *m* bushy tail

'pluimstrijken (pluimstrijkte, h. gepluimstrijkt) *vt* adulate, fawn upon, toady; **–er** (-s) *m* adulator, fawner, toady; **'pluimstrijke'rij** (-en) *v* adulation, fawning, toadyism

'pluimvee *o* poultry; **–houder** (-s) *m* poultry keeper, poultry farmer; **–teelt** *v* poultry farming; **–tentoonstelling** (-en) *v* poultry show

1 pluis (pluizen) *v* & *o* fluff, flue; zie ook: *pluisje*

2 pluis *aj het is er niet ~* it is not as it ought to be, there is sth. wrong; *het is bij hem niet ~* he is not right in his head

'pluisje (-s) *o* bit of fluff; **'pluizen* I** *vi* become fluffy; **II** *vt* pick [oakum]; **'pluizig** fluffy

pluk (-ken) *m* 1 gathering, picking [of fruit];

(b o s j e) tuft, wisp; 2 *fig* handful; **'plukharen**
(plukhaarde, h. geplukhaard) *vi* have a tussle,
tussle; **'plukken** (plukte, h. geplukt) **I** *vt* pick,
gather, cull[2] [flowers &]; pluck [birds]; *fig*
fleece [a player, a customer]; **II** *vi* ~ *aan* pick
at, pull at; **–er** (-s) *m* picker, gatherer, reaper;
'pluksel (-s) *o* lint; **'pluktijd** *m* picking-
season

plu'meau [-'mo.] (-s) *m* feather-duster, feather-
brush

'plunderaar (-s) *m* plunderer, pillager, robber;
'plunderen (plunderde, h. geplunderd) **I** *vt*
plunder, pillage, loot, sack [a town], rifle [a
house], rob [a man]; **II** *vi* plunder, pillage,
loot, rob; **–ring** (-en) *v* plundering, pillage,
looting; sack [of Magdeburg, Rome &]

'plunje (-s) *v* **F** togs; **–zak** (-ken) *m* kit-bag

plu'ralis (-sen en -lia) *m* plural; ~ *majestatis*
royal plural; **plura'lisme** *o* pluralism;
plurali'teit *v* plurality, multiplicity, great
number; **pluri'form** pluriform; **pluri-**
formi'teit *v* multiplicity, great number

plus plus

plus'four [plüs'fɔ:r] (-s) *m* plus-fours

plus'minus about; **'pluspunt** (-en) *o* advantage, asset; **–teken** (-s) *o* plus sign, addition
sign

pluto'craat (-craten) *m* plutocrat; **plutocra'tie**
[-'(t)si.] *v* plutocracy; **pluto'cratisch** pluto-
cratic

plu'tonium *o* plutonium

plu'vier (-en) *m* plover

pneu'matisch pneumatic

pneumo'nie *v* pneumonia

po ('s) *m* chamber (pot), **S** jordan

p.o. = *per omgaande* by return (of post)

'pochen (pochte, h. gepocht) *vi* boast, brag; ~
op boast of; **–er** (-s) *m* boaster, braggart

po'cheren [pò'ʃe:rə(n)] (pocheerde, h. gepo-
cheerd) *vt* poach [eggs]

poche'rij (-en) *v* boasting, boast, brag(ging)

po'chet [pò'ʃɛt] (-ten) *v* fancy handkerchief

'pochhans (-hanzen) *m* = *pocher*

'pocket (-s) = *pocketboek*; **–boek** (-en) *o* paperback; **–editie** [-e.di.(t)si] (-s) *v* paperback
edition

'podagra *o* gout

'podium (-ia en -s) *o* platform, dais,
[conductor's] rostrum

'poedel (-s) *m* 1 🐾 poodle; 2 miss [at ninepins];
'poedelen (poedelde, h. gepoedeld) **I** *vi* miss
[at ninepins]; **II** *vt* 🪣 puddle; **'poedelnaakt**
stark naked; **–prijs** (-prijzen) *m* booby prize,
consolation prize

'poeder (-s) *o & m & v* powder; **–dons**
(-donzen) *m & o* powder-puff; **–doos**
(-dozen) *v* powder-box; **'poederen** (poederde,

h. gepoederd) *vt* powder, strew with powder;
'poederig powdery, powderlike; **'poeder-**
koffie *m* powdered coffee; **–kwast** (-en) *m*
powder-puff; **–sneeuw** *v* powder snow;
–suiker *m* powdered sugar, icing sugar;
–vorm *m in* ~ powdered

po'ëet (poëten) *m* poet

poef (-s en -en) *m* pouffe

poe'ha *o & m* **F** 1 (drukte) fuss; 2 (o p s c h e p -
p e r ij) swank; **–maker** (-s) *m* **F** = *opschepper*

'poeier(-) = *poeder(-)*

poel (-en) *m* puddle, pool, slough

poe'let *o & m* soup meat

poe'lier (-s) *m* poulterer

'poema ('s) *m* puma

poen (-en) **F** *m* 1 vulgarian, > bounder, cad; 2
S *m & o* (g e l d) tin, oof, dust; **–ig** vulgar,
flashy

poep (-en) **F** *m* (o n t l a s t i n g) dirt, excrement;
(w i n d) fart; **'poepen** (poepte, h. gepoept)
vi relieve oneself, relieve nature; **poepe'rij F** *v*
aan de ~ *zijn* have diarrhea

poer (-en) = *peur*

'poeren (poerde, h. gepoerd) = *peuren*

'Poerim = *Purim*

poes (-en en poezen) *v* cat, puss(y); *hij is voor de*
~ **F** it's all up with him, he's finished; *ze is niet*
voor de ~ she is not to be trifled with; *dat is niet*
voor de ~ **!** **S** that's some!; **–je** (-s) *o* pussy-cat;
mijn ~ *!* my kitten; (l i k e u r t j e) = *pousse-café*;
–lief bland, suave, sugary; **–mooi** dressed up
to the nines, dolled-up; **–pas** *m* 1 (r o m m e l)
hotch-potch, hodge-podge; 2 (o m h a a l) fuss

poet S *v* loot, swag

po'ëtisch I *aj* poetic(al); **II** *ad* poetically

poets (-en) *v* trick, prank, practical joke; *iem. een*
~ *bakken* play a trick upon sbd.

'poetsdoek (-en) *m* polishing cloth, cleaning
rag; **'poetsen** (poetste, h. gepoetst) *vt* polish,
clean; *'m* ~, *de plaat* ~ bolt, **S** beat it; **–er** (-s)
m polisher, cleaner; **'poetsgerei, –goed** *o*
cleaning things; **–katoen** *o* cotton waste; **–lap**
(-pen) *m* polishing cloth, cleaning rag;
–pommade *v* polishing paste

'poezelig plump, chubby

poë'zie *v* poetry[2]; [bucolic, Latin &] verse

pof *m* thud; *op de* ~ *kopen* **F** buy (go) on tick

'pofbroek (-en) *v* knickerbockers, plus-fours

'poffen (pofte, h. gepoft) *vt* **F** (o p k r e d i e t
k o p e n) buy on tick; (k r e d i e t g e v e n)
give credit; sell on tick; || roast [chestnuts]

'poffertje (-s) *o* "poffertje" [buttered and
sugared tiny pancake]; **–kraam** (-kramen) *v*
& m & o booth where "poffertjes" are sold

'pofmouw (-en) *v* puff sleeve

'pogen (poogde, h. gepoogd) *vt* endeavour,
attempt, try; **–ging** (-en) *v* endeavour,

attempt, effort; *een ~ doen om... make an
attempt at ...ing; geen ~ doen om... make no
attempt to...; een ~ tot moord (zelfmoord)*
attempted murder (suicide)

'**pogrom** (-s) *m* pogrom

pointe [pwɛ̃t] (-s) *v* point [of a joke]

pok (-ken) *v* pock; *zij kregen de ~ken* they got
smallpox; *van de ~ken geschonden* pock-marked;
pok'dalig pock-marked

'**poken** (pookte, h. gepookt) *vi* poke (stir) the
fire

'**pokeren** (pokerde, h. gepokerd) *vi* play poker

'**pokken** *mv* smallpox, variola; **–briefje** (-s) *o*
vaccination certificate; '**pokstof** *v* vaccine
lymph, vaccine

pol (-len) *m* tuft, tussock [of grass]

po'lair [-'lɛːr] polar; **polari'satie** [-'za.(t)si.] *v*
polarization; **polari'seren** [s = z] (polari-
seerde, h. gepolariseerd) *vt* polarize;
polari'teit *v* polarity

'**polder** (-s) *m* polder **–bestuur** (-sturen) *o*
polder board; **–dijk** (-en) *m* dike of a polder;
–jongen (-s) *m* navvy; **–land** (-s) *v* polder-land

pole'miek (-en) *v* polemic, controversy; polemics; **po'lemisch** polemic(al), controversial; **polemi'seren** [s = z] (polemiseerde,
h. gepolemiseerd) *vi* polemize, carry on a
controversy; be engaged in a paper war; *ik
wil niet met u ~* I'm not going to contest the
point with you; **pole'mist** (-en) *m* polemicist,
controversialist; **polemolo'gie** *v* study of the
causes of war

'**Polen** *o* Poland

polichi'nel [-ʃi.'nɛl] [-s en -len) *m* punchinello,
Punch

po'liep (-en) *v* 1 (d i e r) polyp; 2 (g e z w e l)
polypus [*mv* polypi]

po'lijsten (polijstte, h. gepolijst) *vt* polish,
smooth, sand; (m e t a a l) planish; **–er** (-s) *m*
polisher

polikli'niek (-en) *v* policlinic, outpatients'
department

'**polio** *v* polio; **poliomye'litis** [-mi.e.'li.tɪs] *v*
poliomyelitis

'**polis** (-sen) *v* (insurance) policy

politicolo'gie *v* political science, politics;
po'liticus (-ci) *m* politician

po'litie [-(t)si.] *v* police; **–agent** (-en) *m* policeman, constable, police officer; **–bureau**
[-by.ro.] (-s) *o* 1 police station; 2 (h o o f d b u-
r e a u) police headquarters; **politi'eel**
[-(t)si.'e.l] police [action, operation &];
po'litiehond (-en) *m* police dog

poli'tiek I *aj* 1 political; 2 politic; *de ~e partijen*
the political parties; *dat is niet ~* it is bad
policy, it would not be politic; **II** *v* 1 (s t a a t-
k u n d i g e b e g i n s e l e n) politics; 2 (g e-

d r a g s l ij n) policy, line of policy; 3
(b u r g e r k l e d i n g) plain clothes; *zijn ~* his
policy; *i n ~* in plain clothes, in mufti; *in de ~*
in politics; *u i t ~* from policy, for political
reasons

po'litiekorps (-en) *o* police force; **–macht** *v*
body of police, police force; **–man** (-nen) *m*
police officer, policeman; **–muts** (-en) *v* ☒
forage-cap; **–patrouille** [-tru.jə] (-s) *v* police
patrol; **–post** (-en) *m* police-station, police
post; **–rapport** (-en) *o* police report; **–rechter**
(-s) *m* police magistrate; **–spion** (-nen) *m*
police informer, **S** nark; **–staat** (-staten) *m*
police state; **–toezicht** *o* police supervision;
–verordening (-en) *v* police regulation;
–wezen *o het ~* the police; **politio'neel**
[-(t)si.] police [action, operation &]

politi'seren [s = z] (politiseerde, h. gepoliti-
seerd) *vi* talk politics, politicise

poli'toer *o* & *m* (French) polish; **poli'toeren**
(politoerde, h. gepolitoerd) *vt* (French-)polish

'**polka** ('s) *m* & *v* polka; **–haar** *o* bobbed hair

'**pollepel** (-s) *m* ladle

'**polo** *o sp* polo; **–hemd** (-en) *o* polo shirt

polo'naise [-'nɛːzə] (-s) *v* polonaise

1 pols (-en) *m* pole, leaping-pole

2 pols (-en) *m* 1 (a d e r) pulse; 2 (g e w r i c h t)
wrist; *iem. de ~ voelen* feel sbd.'s pulse[2]; **–ader**
(-s) *v* radial artery, pulse artery; '**polsen**
(polste, h. gepolst) *vt iem. ~* sound sbd. (on
over); '**polsgewricht** (-en) *o* wrist (-joint);
–horloge [-ʒə] (-s) *o* wrist(let) watch; **–mof**
(-fen) *v* wristlet; **–slag** (-slagen) *m* pulsation

'**polsstok** (-ken) *m* leaping-pole, jumping-pole;
–springen *o* pole-jump, pole-vault

poly'ester [y = i.] *o* polyester

poly'ether [y = i.] *m* foam plastic

poly'foon [y = i.] polyphonic

poly'gaam [y = i.] polygamous; **polyga'mie** *v*
polygamy

poly'glot [y = i.] (-ten) *m* polyglot

Poly'nesië [y = i.; s = z] *o* Polynesia; **–r** (-s) *m*,
Poly'nesisch *aj* Polynesian

poly'technisch [y = i.] polytechnic; *~e school*
polytechnic (school)

polyva'lent [y = i.] polyvalent

pome'rans (-en) *v* 1 ⚘ bitter orange; 2 ⚬
(a a n k e u) (cue-)tip; **–bitter** *o* & *m* orange
bitters

pom'made (-s) *v* pomade, pomatum;
pomma'deren (pommadeerde, h. gepomma-
deerd) *vt* pomade

'**Pommeren** *o* Pomerania

pomp (-en) *v* pump; *loop naar de ~!* go to
blazes!; **–bediende** (-s en -n) *m* (petrol) pump
attendant

Pom'peji *o* Pompeii

Pom'pejus *m* Pompey

'pompelmoes (-moezen) *v* pomelo, shaddock; (k l e i n e r) grape-fruit

'pompen (pompte, h. gepompt) *vi* & *vt* pump; ~ *of verzuipen* sink or swim; **–er** (-s) *m* pumper

pomper'nikkel (-s) *m* pumpernickel

pom'peus pompous; **–heid** *v* pompousness, pomposity

pom'poen (-en) *m* pumpkin, gourd

pom'pon (-s) *m* pompon, tuft

'pompstation [-ʃŏn] (-s) *o* 1 pumping station; 2 🛲 filling station; **–water** *o* pump-water

pon (-nen) *m* **F** nighty, night-dress

pond (-en) *o* pound; (het volle ~ eisen exact one's pound of flesh; *in (Engelse)* ~*en betalen* ook: pay in sterling; **'pondenbezit** *o* sterling holdings; **–saldo** (-di en 's) *o* sterling balance; **ponds- pondsge'wijs, –ge'wijze** pro rata, proportionally

po'neren (poneerde, h. geponeerd) *vt* state

'ponjaard (-s en -en) *m* poniard, dagger

1 pons *m* (d r a n k) punch

2 pons (-en) *m* ✂ punch; **–band** (-en) *m* punched tape; **'ponsen** (ponste, h. geponst) *vt* punch; **'ponskaart** (-en) *v* punched card; punch card; **–machine** [-ʃi.nə] (-s) *v* punch(ing) machine, punch(ing) press, puncher

pont (-en) *v* ferry-boat

ponte'neur *o op zijn* ~ *staan* stand on one's dignity

pontifi'caal pontifical; *in* ~ in full pontificals, in full regalia

'Pontius [-(t)si.üs] *m* Pontius; *iem. van* ~ *naar Pilatus zenden* send sbd. from pillar to post

pon'ton (-s) *m* pontoon; **–brug** (-gen) *v* pontoon-bridge; **ponton'nier** (-s) *m* pontonneer, pontonier

'pontveer (-veren) *o* ferry

'pony ['pɔni.] ('s) *m* 1 🐎 (Shetland) pony; 2 = *ponyhaar*; **–haar** *o* bang, fringe

'pooien (pooide, h. gepooid) *vi* **F** booze

'pooier (-s) *m* **S** pimp, ponce, pander, fancyman, procurer

pook (poken) *m* & *v* 1 poker; 2 🛲 gear lever; **–je** (-s) **F** *o* gear lever

1 pool (polen) *v* pole

2 pool (polen) *v* pile [of carpet, velvet]

3 pool [pu.l] (-s) *m* (v. k o l e n, s t a a l, v o e t- b a l &) pool

4 Pool (Polen) *m* Pole

'poolcirkel (-s) *m* polar circle; **–expeditie** [-(t)si.] (-s) *v* polar expedition; **–gebied** (-en) *o* polar region; **–hond** (-en) *m* Eskimo dog, husky; **–ijs** *o* polar ice; **–licht** *o* polar lights; **–onderzoek** *o* exploration of the polar regions

Pools I *aj* Polish; **II** *o het* ~ Polish; **III** *v een* ~*e* a Polish Woman; zie ook: *landdag*

'poolshoogte *v* ★ elevation of the pole, latitude; ~ *nemen* see how the land lies; **'poolster** *v* polar star, pole-star; **–streek** (-streken) *v* polar region; **–tocht** (-en) *m* polar expedition; **–vos** (-sen) *m* arctic fox; **–zee** (-zeeën) *v* polar sea

poon (ponen) *m* 🐟 gurnard

poort (-en) *v* gate, doorway, gateway; **–ader** (-s) *v* portal vein; **–er** (-s) *m* 🏛 citizen, freeman; **–wachter** (-s) *m* gate-keeper

poos (pozen) *v* while, time, interval; **–je** (-s) *o* little while; *een* ~*je for a while

poot (poten) *m* 1 (v. d i e r) paw, foot, leg; 2 (v. m e u b e l) leg; *wat een* ~ *schrijft hij!* **F** what a fist he writes!; *zijn* ~ *stijf houden* refuse to give in, stand firm (fast, one's ground); *iem. een* ~ *uitdraaien* **S** fleece (soak, skin, pluck) sbd.; *geen* ~ *aan de grond krijgen* have no chance of success; *geen* ~ *uitsteken* not stir a finger; *iets op poten zetten* set sth. on foot, set up sth.; *iets weer op poten zetten* set sth. on its feet; *een brief op poten* a sharp (strongly worded) letter; *op hoge poten* up in arms, in high dudgeon; *op zijn* ~ *spelen* = opspelen 2; *op zijn achterste poten gaan staan* 1 *eig* rear [of a horse]; 2 *fig* (z i c h v e r z e t t e n) jib; (o p s t u i v e n) flare up; *op zijn poten terechtkomen* fall (land) on one's legs; *poot'aan* ~ *spelen* work (peg) hard, put one's back into it

'pootaardappel (-s en -en) *m* seed-potato; **–ijzer** (-s) *o* dibble

'pootje (-s) *o* 1 paw; 2 🔥 podagra, gout; *met hangende* ~*s* with one's tail between one's legs, crestfallen; zie ook: *poot*; **–baden** *vi* paddle

'pootvijver (-s) *m* nurse-pond; **–vis** *m* fry

1 pop (-pen) *v* 1 doll; puppet [in a show]; [tailor's] dummy; 2 (v. i n s e k t) pupa [*mv* pupae], chrysalis, nymph; 3 (v. v o g e l s) hen; 4 (i n k a a r t s p e l) picture-card, court-card; 5 (k i n d) darling; 6 **F** (g u l d e n) guilder; *toen had men de* ~*pen aan 't dansen* then there was the devil to pay, the fat was in the fire

2 pop I *m* (= p o p m u z i e k) pop; **II** *aj* pop [art, ♪ group, singer &]

'pope (-s en -n) *m* pope

'popelen (popelde, h. gepopeld) *vt* quiver, throb; *zijn hart popelde* his heart went pit-a-pat; ~ *om te zien* be itching to see

pope'line *o* & *m* poplin

'popgroep (-en) *v* pop group; **–muziek** *v* pop music

'poppegezicht (-en) *o* doll's face; **–goed** *o* doll's clothes; **–jurk** (-en) *v* doll's dress; **'poppenhuis** (-huizen) *o* doll's house; **–kast** (-en) *v* Punch-and-Judy show, puppet-show; *fig* tomfoolery; **–kastpop** (-pen) *v* glove puppet; **–spel** (-len) *o* puppet-show; **–speler**

(-s) *m* puppeteer; **–winkel** (-s) *m* doll-shop; **'popperig** dollish, pretty pretty; **'poppetje** (-s) *o* little doll, dolly; *een teer ~* a delicate child; *~s tekenen* draw figures; **'poppewagen** (-s) *m* doll's carriage, doll's perambulator, doll's pram

popu'lair [-'lɛ.r] popular; **popu'lairweten'schappelijk** popular-science, popularised; **populari'seren** [s = z] (populariseerde, h. gepopulariseerd) *vt* popularize; **populari-'teit** *v* popularity

popu'lier (-en) *m* poplar

'popzanger (-s) *m* pop singer; **–zender** (-s) *m* pop radio-station

por (-ren) *m* thrust, dig [in sbd.'s side], poke, jab

po'reus porous, permeable; **–heid** *v* porosity

por'fier *o* porphyry

'porie (-iën) *v* pore

porno'graaf (-grafen) *m* pornographer; **pornogra'fie** *v* pornography; **porno'grafisch** pornographic

'porren (porde, h. gepord) *vt* 1 poke, stir [the fire]; 2 prod [sbd.]; jab [sbd. in the leg &]; 3 (w e k k e n) knock up, call up; 4 (a a n - s p o r e n) rouse, urge; **F** *daar is hij wel voor te ~* he is always game for that

porse'lein *o* china, china-ware, porcelain; **–aarde** *v* china-clay, kaolin; **–bloempje** (-s) *o* London pride; **–en** *aj* china, porcelain; **–fabriek** (-en) *v* china (porcelain) factory; **–kast** (-en) *v* china-cabinet; *voorzichtigheid is de moeder van de ~* caution is the mother of wisdom; **–winkel** (-s) *m* china shop

1 port (-en) *o* & *m* 🏷 postage

2 port *m* = *portwijn*

por'taal (-talen) *o* 1 landing [of stairs]; 2 porch, hall

porte-bri'see [s = z] (-s) *v* folding doors, double door

por'tee *v* meaning, significance, drift [of an argument]

porte'feuille [-'fœyjə] (-s) *m* 1 (v. m i n i s t e r, s c h i l d e r &) portfolio; 2 (v o o r z a k) wallet, pocket-book, note-case; *de ~ aanvaarden* accept office; *de ~ neerleggen* (*ter beschikking stellen*) resign (office), leave the ministry; *aandelen i n ~* $ unissued shares; *minister z o n d e r ~* minister without portfolio; **portemon'naie** [-'ne.] (-s), **–mon'nee** (-s) *m* purse

'portglas (-glazen) *o* port-wine glass

'portie ['pɔrsi.] (-s) *v* portion, share [of sth.]; helping [at meals]; *fig* dose [of patience]; *een ~ ijs* an ice

por'tiek (-en) *v* 1 (m e t z u i l e n) portico; 2 (u i t g e b o u w d) porch; 3 (o v e r w e l f d e d e u r t o e g a n g) doorway

1 por'tier (-s) *m* 1 door-keeper; 2 hotel-porter, hall-porter, porter

2 por'tier (-en) *o* (carriage-, car-)door; **portière** [-'tjɛ:rə] (-s) *v* portière, door-curtain; **por'tier-raampje** (-s) *o* (v. t r e i n) carriage window; (v. a u t o) car window

por'tierster (-s) *v* portress; **por'tierswoning** (-en) *v* porter's lodge

'porto (-ti en 's) *o* & *m* postage

porto'foon (-s) *m* walkie-talkie

'portokosten *mv* postage

'Porto 'Rico *o* Puerto Rico

por'tret (-ten) *o* portrait, likeness, photo(graph); *ik heb mijn ~ laten maken* I have had my photo taken; **–album** (-s) *o* photograph album; **–lijstje** (-s) *o* photo-frame; **–schilder** (-s) *m* portrait-painter; **–(ten)galerij** (-en) *v* portrait gallery; **portret'teren** (portretteerde, h. geportretteerd) *vt* portray[2], take a photo; **portret'tist** (-en) *m* portraitist

'Portugal *o* Portugal; **Portu'gees** *aj* & *sb* Portuguese; *de Portugezen* the Portuguese

por'tuur (-turen) *v* & *o* match

'portvrij post-paid, free

'portwijn (-en) *m* port(-wine)

'portzegel (-s) *m* postage due stamp

'pose [s = z] (-s en -n) *v* posture, attitude, pose; **po'seren** (poseerde, h. geposeerd) *vi* pose, sit [to a painter]; *fig* pose [as...], attitudinize, strike an attitude; zie ook: *geposeerd*; **po'seur** (-s) *m* poseur

po'sitie [-'zi.(t)si.] (-s) *v* 1 (h o u d i n g &) position; 2 (b e t r e k k i n g) position, situation; 3 (r a n g i n d e m a a t s c h a p p ij) status; *in ~ zijn* be pregnant, **F** be expecting; **–bepaling** *v* position-finding, fixing of position, location

posi'tief [s = z] **I** *aj* positive; **II** *ad* 1 decidedly; 2 positively [charged particles]; *dat weet ik ~* I am quite sure about it; **III** (-tieven) *o* 1 (v a n f o t o) positive; 2 *m gram* positive (degree)

po'sitiekleding [-'zi.(t)si.-] *v* maternity clothes

posi'tieve(n) [s = z] *hij kwam weer bij zijn ~* he came to his senses; *bij zijn ~ zijn* have all one's faculties; *niet wel bij z'n ~* not right in his head, not in his right mind

po'sitieverbetering [-'zi.(t)si.-] *v* improvement in social position

positi'visme [s = z] *o* positivism; (i. d. s o c i o - l o g i e) Comtism

1 post (-en) *m* post [as support]

2 post (-en) *m* 1 (s t a n d p l a a t s) ⚔ post[2] [also place of duty], station; 2 (b e t r e k k i n g) post; office; 3 🏷 postman; 4 $ item, entry [in a book]; 5 (s c h i l d w a c h t) sentry; 6 (b ij s t a k i n g) picket; *~ van vertrouwen* position of confidence; ~ *vatten* take up one's station; *de mening heeft* ~ *gevat, dat...* it is the prevailing opinion that...; *op zijn* ~ *blijven* ✶ remain at one's post; *op* ~ *staan* ✶ stand sentry; *daar op* ~ *staand* posted there; *een* ~ *uitzetten* ✶ post [sentries]; *op zijn* ~ *zijn* be (present) at one's post; *ik moet om 4 uur op mijn* ~ *zijn* I am on at four o'clock

3 post *v* ⚓ 1 post, mail; 2 post office, post; *hij is bij de* ~ he is in the post office; *met deze, de eerste, laatste* ~ by this mail, by first (last) post; *een brief op de* ~ *doen* post a letter, take a letter to the post; *over (met) de* ~ through the post; *per* ~ by post, through the post; *per kerende* ~ by return of post

4 post *o* note-paper, letter-paper

postacademi'aal, –aca'demisch post-graduate, post-doctoral

'postadres (-sen) *o* postal address; **–agent-schap** (-pen) *o* postal agency, sub-post office; **–ambtenaar** (-s en -naren) *m* post-office official; **–auto** [-o.to. of -ɔuto.] ('s) *m* post-office van; **–beambte** (-n) *m-v* post-office servant; **–besteller** (-s) *m* postman; **–bestelling** (-en) *v* postal delivery (round); **–bewijs** (-wijzen) *o* postal order; **–blad** (-bladen) *o* letter-card; **–bode** (-n en -s) *m* postman; **–boot** (-boten) *m* & *v* mail-steamer, mail-boat; **–bus** (-sen) *v* post-office box, box; **–cheque** [-ʃtk] (-s) *m* postal cheque; **–cheque-en-'girodienst** *m* Br National Giro, postal giro service

postda'teren (postdateerde, h. gepostdateerd) *vt* post-date

'postdienst (-en) *m* postal service; **–directeur** (-en en -s) *m* postmaster; **–duif** (-duiven) *v* carrier-pigeon, homing pigeon

poste'lein *m* purslane

'posten (postte, h. gepost) *vt* 1 ⚓ post [a letter]; 2 (b ij s t a k i n g) picket [of workmen]; **'poster** (-s) *m* 1 (b ij s t a k i n g) picketer; ‖ 2 (a f f i c h e) ['po.stər] poster

pos'teren (posteerde, h. geposteerd) *vt* post, station

poste-res'tante to be (left till) called for; **poste'rijen** *mv de* ~ the Post Office; **'postgirodienst** *m* postal giro service, Br National Giro; **–rekening** (-en) *v* (postal) giro account, postal clearing account; **'posthoorn, –horen** (-s) *m* post-horn; **postil'jon** (-s) *m* postilion, post-boy; **'postkantoor** (-toren) *o* post office; **–kwitantie** [-(t)si.] (-s) *v* postal collection order; **–merk** (-en) *o* postmark; *datum* ~ date as per postmark; **–order** (-s) *m* mail-order; **–orderbedrijf** (-drijven) *o* mail-order business; **–pakket** (-ten) *o* parcel, postal parcel; *als* ~ *verzenden* send by parcel post; **–papier** *o* note-paper, letter-paper; **–rekening** (-en) *v* (postal) giro account, postal clearing account

post'scriptum (-ta en -s) *o* postscript

'postspaarbank (-en) *v* post-office savings-bank; **–spaarbankboekje** (-s) *o* P.O. savings-bank book; **–stempel** (-s) *o* & *m* postmark; **–stuk** (-ken) *o* postal article; **–tarief** (-rieven) *o* postal rate(s), postage rates, rates of postage; **–tijd** (-en) *m* post-time, mail-time; **–trein** (-en) *m* mail train

postu'laat (-laten) *o* postulate; **postu'lant** (-en) *m* postulant; **postu'leren** (postuleerde, h. gepostuleerd) *vt* postulate

'postunie *v* postal union

pos'tuum posthumous

pos'tuur (-turen) *o* shape, figure, build; *zich in* ~ *stellen (zetten)* draw oneself up

'postverbinding (-en) *v* ⚓ postal communication; **–verkeer** *o* postal traffic; **–vliegtuig** (-en) *o* mailplane; **–vlucht** (-en) *v* (air-)mail flight; **–wagen** (-s) *m* mail-coach, mail-car, mail-carriage; **–weg** (-wegen) *m* post-road; **–wezen** *o het* ~ the Post Office; **–wissel** (-s) *m* postal order, [foreign, international] money-order; **–wisselformulier** (-en) *o* money-order form; **–zak** (-ken) *m* post-bag, mail-bag

'postzegel (-s) *m* (postage) stamp; **–album** (-s) *o* stamp album; **–automaat** [-o.to.- of ɔuto.-] (-maten) *m* stamp machine; **–veiling** (-en) *v* stamp auction; **–verzamelaar** (-s) *m* stamp collector; **–verzameling** (-en) *v* stamp collection

pot (-ten) *m* 1 (o m i n t e m a k e n &) pot; jar [also for tobacco]; 2 (o m t e d r i n k e n) pot, mug; 3 (p o) chamber (pot); 4 (i n z e t) stakes, pool; ~ *ten en pannen* pots and pans; *een gewone (goede)* ~ plain (good) cooking; *het is één* ~ *nat* it is six of one and half a dozen of the other; *je kan de* ~ *op!* F go fly a kite, go jump into the lake; *de* ~ *verteren* spend the pool; *u moet voor lief nemen wat de* ~ *schaft* you must take pot-luck; *de* ~ *winnen* win the jack-pot; *de* ~ *verwijt de ketel dat hij zwart is* the pot calls the kettle black; **–as** *v* potash; **–deksel** (-s) *o* pot-lid; **–dicht** tightly closed, close(-shut); *fig* very close; **–doof** stone-deaf

'poteling (-en) *m* sturdy (brawny) fellow

'poten (pootte, h. gepoot) *vt* plant [potatoes &], set [fish]

poten'taat (-taten) *m* potentate

potenti'aal [-(t)si.'a.l] (-ialen) *m* potential; **–verschil** (-len) *o* potential difference

po'tentie [-(t)si.] *v* potency; **potenti'eel I** *aj* potential; **II** *o* potential

'poter (-s) *m* 1 planter; 2 seed-potato

'pothoed (-en) *m* cloche (hat)

'potig strong, robust, strapping

'potje (-s) *o* (little) pot; (k i n d e r t a a l) F potty;

een ~ bier a pint of beer; *een ~ biljarten* have a game of billiards; *hij kan een ~ breken* they connive at his doings; *zijn eigen ~ koken* do one's own cooking; *een ~ maken* lay by something against a rainy day; *kleine ~s hebben grote oren* little pitchers have long ears; *op het ~ zetten* F pot [the baby]; **–rol** *o* & *m* & *v* rolypoly; **'potjeslatijn** *o* dog Latin; **'potkachel** (-s) *v* pot-bellied stove; **–kijker** (-s) *= pottekijker*

'potloden (potloodde, h. gepotlood) *vt* blacklead; **'potlood** (-loden) *o* 1 (o m t e s c h r ij v e n) (lead-)pencil; 2 (s m e e r s e l) black lead; **–slijper** (-s) *m* pencil sharpener; **–tekening** (-en) *v* pencil drawing

'potplant (-en) *v* potted plant, pot-plant

'potpourri [-pu.ri.] ('s) *m* & *o* ♪ potpourri, pots (-en) *v = poets* medley[2]

'potscherf (-scherven) *v* potsherd, crock

'potsenmaker (-s) *m* wag, buffoon, clown; **pot'sierlijk I** *aj* ludicrous, comical; **II** *ad* ludicrously, comically

'potspel (-spelen) *o* pool

'pottekijker (-s) *m* (b e m o e i a l) F snooper

'potten (potte, h. gepot) **I** *vt* pot [plants]; *fig* hoard (up) [money]; **II** *va* salt down money

'pottenbakken *vi* make pottery, pot; **–bakker** (-s) *m* potter; **pottenbakke'rij** (-en) *v* pottery, potter's workshop; **'pottenwinkel** (-s) *m* earthenware shop; **'potter** (-s) *m* hoarder; **'potverteren** *o* spending of the pool for a treat to all; **'potvis** (-sen) *m* cachalot

pousse-ca'fé [pu.ska'fe.] (-s) *m* pousse-café, chasse

pous'seren [pu.-] (pousseerde, h. gepousseerd) *vt* promote; (v. w a r e n) boost

'pover poor, shabby; **–heid** *v* poorness; **–tjes** poorly

p.p. = *per persoon; per procuratie*

Praag *o* Prague

'praaien (praaide, h. gepraaid) *vt* hail, speak [ships]

praal *v* pomp, splendour, magnificence; **–bed** (-den) *o* bed of state; *op een ~ liggen* lie in state; **–graf** (-graven) *o* mausoleum; **–hans** (-hanzen) *m* braggart, boaster; **–koets** (-en) *v* coach of state, state carriage; **–vertoon** *o* pomp, ostentation; **–wagen** (-s) *m* float; **–ziek** fond of display, ostentatious; **–zucht** *v* love of display, ostentation

praam (pramen) *v* ⚓ pram [flat-bottomed boat], lighter

praat *m* talk, tattle; *veel ~s hebben* talk big, be boasting; *iem. aan de ~ houden* hold (keep) sbd. in talk; **–avond** (-en) *m* frank discussion on outstanding problems between members and board of a society; **–graag** = *praatziek*; **–je** (-s)

o talk; *het is maar een ~, dat zijn maar ~s (voor de vaak)* it's all idle talk; *een ~ maken (met)* have a chat (with); *och wat, ~s!* fiddlesticks! *het ~ gaat dat...* there is some talk of...; *zoals het ~ gaat* as the talk goes; *er liepen ~s (over haar)* people were talking (about her); *u moet niet alle ~s geloven* you should not believe all that is told; *~s rondstrooien* chat, whisper, spread, set afloat [rumours]; *~s vullen geen gaatjes* fair words butter no parsnips; **–jesmaker** (-s) *m* braggart, swaggerer; **–paal** (-palen) *m* roadside emergency telephone; **–s** zie *praat*; **–ster** (-s) *v* talker, chatterer, gossip; **–stoel** *m op zijn ~ zitten* 1 be in the vein for talking; 2 be talking nineteen to the dozen; **–vaar** (-s) *m* great talker; **–ziek** talkative, loquacious, garrulous; **–zucht** *v* talkativeness, loquacity, garrulity

pracht *v* splendour, magnificence, pomp; *~ en praal* pomp and splendour; **–band** (-en) *m* de luxe binding; **–exemplaar** (-plaren) *o* 1 de luxe copy [of a book]; 2 beautiful specimen [of something], beauty; **–ig** magnificent, splendid, superb, sumptuous; *dat zou ~ zijn* that would be grand (splendid); *~, hoor!* marvellous; **–kerel** (-s) *m* splendid fellow; **pracht'lievend** loving splendour (magnificence); **'prachtstuk** (-ken) *o* beauty; **–uitgave** (-n) *v* de luxe edition

'practicum (-ca en -s) *o* practical training; **–cus** (-ci en -sen) *m* practical person

'praeses ['pre.zəs] (-sides en -sen) *m* chairman, president

pragma'tiek pragmatic [sanction]; **prag-'matisch** pragmatic

'prairie ['prɛ:ri.] (-iën en -s); *v* prairie; **–brand** (-en) *m* prairie fire; **–hond** (-en) *m* prairiedog; **–wolf** (-wolven) *m* prairie-wolf, coyote

prak (-ken) *m* mash; *een auto in de ~ rijden* F wreck (bang up) a car

prakke'zeren, –ki'zeren (prakkezeerde, h. geprakkezeerd) **I** *vi* think; **II** *vt* contrive

prak'tijk (-en) *v* practice; (v. p e r s o n e e l, l e e r k r a c h t e n &) experience; *kwade ~en* evil practices; *die dokter heeft een goede ~* has a large practice; *de ~ uitoefenen* practise [of a doctor]; ● *in de ~* in practice [not in theory]; *in ~ brengen* put in practice; *z o n d e r ~* [doctor] without practice; briefless [barrister]; **'prak-tisch I** *aj* practical; *~e bekwaamheid* practical skill; *~e kennis* working knowledge; *~ plan* practicable (workable) plan; **II** *ad* practically, for all practical purposes, virtually;

prakti'zeren (praktizeerde, h. gepraktizeerd) *vi* practise; be in practice; *~d geneesheer* medical practitioner, general practitioner; *~d katholiek* practising Roman Catholic; **prakti'zijn** (-s) *m* ⚖ legal adviser, *Am* counsel '**pralen** (praalde, h. gepraald) *vi* 1 be resplendent, shine, glitter; 2 boast, flaunt; ~ *met* show off...; –**er** (-s) *m* showy fellow, swaggerer; **prale'rij** (-en) *v* ostentation, showing off, show

pra'line (-s) *v* praline

'**prangen** (prangde, h. geprangd) *vt* press; (b e n a u w e n) oppress

prat ~ *gaan* (*zijn*) *op* pride oneself on

'**praten** (praatte, h. gepraat) *vi* talk, chat; > prate; *u moet hem aan het* ~ *zien te krijgen* 1 make him talk; 2 try to draw him; *hij heeft gepraat* 1 he has talked; 2 he has told tales; *hij kan mooi* ~ he has a smooth tongue; *hij heeft mooi* ~ it is all very well for him to say so; ● *er valt* m e t *hem te* ~ he is a reasonable man; *er valt niet met hem te* ~ there is no reasoning with him; *er* o m h e e n ~ talk round a subject, beat about the bush; *zij waren* o v e r *de kunst aan het* ~ they were talking art; *ze zitten altijd over hun vak te* ~ they are always talking shop; *praat me daar niet over* don't talk to me of that; *u moet hem dat* u i t *het hoofd* ~ talk him out of it; *daar weet ik* v a n *mee te* ~ zie *meepraten*; –**er** (-s) *m* talker

prauw (-en) *v* prau, outrigger-canoe

pré (-s) *m* preference

'**preadvies** (-viezen) *o* preliminary advice, report

pream'bule (-s) *v* preamble

pre'bende (-n) *v* prebend

pre'cair [- 'kε: r] precarious

pre'cario ('s) *o* local tax for installations on public ground

prece'dent (-en) *o* precedent

pre'cies I *aj* precise, exact; **II** *ad* precisely, exactly; *om 5 uur* ~ at five precisely (sharp); *ze passen* ~ zie *passen* **I**

preci'eus affected

preci'osa *mv* valuables

preci'seren [s = z] (preciseerde, h. gepreciseerd) *vt* define, state precisely, specify; **pre'cisie-instrument** (-en) *o* precision instrument, instrument of precision

predesti'natie [-(t)si.] *v* predestination; **predesti'neren** (predestineerde, h. gepredestineerd) *vt* predestine

predi'kaat (-katen) *o* 1 (g e z e g d e) predicate; 2 (t i t e l) title; 3 (b e o o r d e l i n g) rating, marks

predi'kant (-en) *m* 1 = *dominee*; (v. l e g e r, v l o o t, z i e k e n h u i s, g e v a n g e n i s &) chaplain; 2 *rk* = *kanselredenaar*; **predi'kants-plaats** (-en) *v* living; –**woning** (-en) *v* rectory, vicarage, parsonage; **predi'katie** [-(t)si.] (-iën en -s) *v* sermon, homily

predika'tief predicative

'**predikbeurt** (-en) *v* turn to preach; preaching-engagement; '**prediken** (predikte, h. gepredikt) *vt* & *vi* preach; –**er** (-s) *m* preacher; *P*~ **B** Ecclesiastes; '**predikheer** (-heren) *m* Dominican (friar); '**prediking** *v* preaching; '**predikstoel** (-en) = *preekstoel*

predispo'neren (predisponeerde, h. gepredisponeerd) *vt* predispose; **predispo'sitie** [-'zi.(t)si.] *v* predisposition

preek (preken) *v* sermon [ook >]; –**beurt** (-en) *v* = *predikbeurt*; –**heer** *m* (-heren) = *predikheer*; –**stoel** (-en) *m* pulpit; –**toon** *m* preachy tone

prees (prezen) V.T. van *prijzen*

prefabri'catie [-(t)si.] *v* prefabrication; **prefabri'ceren** (prefabriceerde, h. geprefabriceerd) *vt* prefabricate

pre'fatie [-(t)si.] (-s) *v rk* preface

pre'fect (-en) *m* prefect; **prefec'tuur** (-turen) *v* prefecture

prefe'rent preferential; *–e schuldeiser* preferential creditor; *–e schulden* preferred debts; zie ook: *aandeel*; **prefe'rentie** [-(t)si.] (-s) *v* preference; **prefe'reren** (prefereerde, h. geprefereerd) *vt* prefer (to *boven*)

'**prefix** (-en) *o* prefix

preg'nant concise, terse

'**prehistoricus** (-ci) *m* prehistorian; '**prehistorie** *v* prehistory; **prehis'torisch** prehistoric

prei (-en) *v* leek

prejudici'ëren [-si.'e.rə(n)] (prejudicieerde, h. geprejudicieerd) *vi* prejudge; anticipate [on sth.]

'**preken** (preekte, h. gepreekt) *vi* & *vt* preach[2]; '**prekerig** > preachy

pre'laat (-laten) *m* prelate; –**schap** *o* prelacy

prelimi'nair [-'nε: r] preliminary, introductory

pre'lude (-s) *v* prelude; *fig* prelude, introduction; **prelu'deren** (preludeerde, h. gepreludeerd) *vi* prelude; ~ *op* [*fig*] prelude, foreshadow

prema'tuur premature

'**premie** (-s) *v* premium[2]; (b o v e n h e t l o o n) bonus; (v o o r u i t v o e r) bounty; (v a n A O W &) contribution; –**heffing** (-en) *v* social insurance contribution; –**lening** (-en) *v* premium (lottery) loan

pre'mier [-mi.'e.] (-s) *m* prime minister, premier

pre'mière [-mi.'ε: rə] (-s) *v* première, first night [of a play], first run [of a film]; [film, world] première; *in* ~ *gaan* to be premiered

'**premiestelsel** (-s) *o* premium (bounty) system –**vrij** paid-up [policy], non-contributory [pension]

pre'misse (-n) *v* premise, premiss

prena'taal antenatal

prent (-en) *v* print, engraving, picture; –**briefkaart** (-en) *v* picture postcard; '**prenten**

(prentte, h. geprent) *vt* imprint; *het (zich iets) in het geheugen* ~ imprint it on the memory; **'prentenboek** (-en) *o* picture-book; **–kabinet** (-ten) *o* print-room; **'prentje** (-s) *o* picture; **~s kijken** look at the pictures [in a book]; **'prentkunst** *v* copper engraving

preoccu'patie [-(t)si.] (-s) *v* preoccupation

prepa'raat (-raten) *o* preparation; **prepa'reren** (prepareerde, h. geprepareerd) **I** *vt* 1 prepare; 2 dress [skins]; **II** *vr zich* ~ get ready, make ready, prepare oneself

preroga'tief (-tieven) *o* prerogative

presbyteri'aan(s) [-bi.-] (-ianen) *m* (& *aj*) Presbyterian

pre'senning (-s) *v* ♩ tarpaulin

1 pre'sent [s = z] (-en) *o* present; ~ *geven* make a present of; ~ *krijgen* get it as a present; **2 pre'sent** *aj* present; ~*!* here!; **presen'tabel** presentable; **presen'tatie** [-(t)si.] (-s) *v* presentation; **presen'tator** (-s en -'toren) *m*, **presenta'trice** (-s) *v RT* compere; *de* ~ *van dit programma is...* this programme is presented by...; **presen'teerblad** (-bladen) *o* salver, tray; **presen'teren** (presenteerde, h. gepresenteerd) **I** *vt* offer [sth.]; present [a bill &]; *het geweer* ~ present arms; *iets* ~ offer (hand round) some refreshments; **pre'sentexemplaar** (-plaren) *o* presentation copy, complimentary copy, free copy; **pre'sentie** [-(t)si.] *v* presence; **–geld** (-en) *o* attendance money; **–lijst** (-en) *v* list of members present; attendance register

preserva'tief [s = z] (-tieven) *o* contraceptive

presi'dent [s = z] (-en) *m* 1 president [of a meeting, republic, a board], chairman [of a meeting]; 2 foreman [of a jury]; *Mijnheer de* ~ Mr Chairman; **presi'dent-commis'saris** (-sen) *m* chairman of the board [of a company]; **~-direc'teur** (-s en -en) *m* president of the board of directors; **presi'dente** (-n en -s) *v* chairwoman; **presi'dentschap** (-pen) *o* presidency[2], chairmanship; **presi'dentsverkiezing** *v* presidential election; **–zetel** (-s) *m* (presidential) chair; **presi'deren** (presideerde, h. gepresideerd) **I** *vt* preside over, preside at [a meeting]; **II** *va* preside, be in the chair; **pre'sidium** (-ia en -s) *o* 1 presidentship, chairmanship; 2 presidium [of the supreme Soviet of the U.S.S.R.]

'preskop *m* brawn

'pressen (preste, h. geprest) *vt* 1 ꕷ ⚓ & ♩ (im)press (into service); 2 (d w i n g e n) force [to do, into doing sth.]

presse-papier [prɪspa.pi.'e.] (-s) *m* paperweight

pres'seren (presseerde, h. gepresseerd) *vt* press, hurry [sbd.]; **'pressie** *v* pressure; ~ *uitoefenen op* exert pressure on; **–groep** (-en) *v* pressure group

pres'tatie [-(t)si.] (-s) *v* performance [also ꕷ, ⚙], achievement [of our industry], [physical &] feat, accomplishment; **pres'teren** (presteerde, h. gepresteerd) *vt* achieve

pres'tige [-'ti.ʒə] *o* prestige; *zijn* ~ *ophouden* maintain one's prestige; *zijn* ~ *redden* save one's face; **–kwestie** (-s) *v* matter of prestige

pret *v* pleasure, fun; *dat was me een* ~ it was great fun; *ik heb dolle* ~ *gehad* I had great fun, I've had a wonderful time; ~ *hebben over iets* revel in sth.; ~ *maken* enjoy oneself

preten'dent (-en) *m* pretender [to the throne]; suitor [for girl's hand]; **preten'deren** (pretendeerde, h. gepretendeerd) *vt* pretend; **pre'tentie** [-(t)si.] (-s) *v* 1 pretension; 2 pretension, claim [to merit]; *vol* ~*s* pretentious; *zonder* ~ modest, unassuming, unpretentious; **–loos** modest, unassuming, unpretentious; **pretenti'eus** [-si.'ø.s] pretentious

'pretje (-s) *o* bit of fun, frolic, **F** lark; *het is me nogal een* ~*!* a nice job, indeed!; **'pretmaker** (-s) *m* joker

'pretor (-'toren en -s) *m* ꕷ praetor; **pretori'aan** (-ianen) *m* ꕷ praetorian; **–s** ꕷ praetorian [guard]

'pretpark (-en) *o* pleasure ground, amusement park; **'prettig I** *aj* amusing, pleasant, nice, agreeable; likeable [man], comfortable [chair]; *het* ~ *vinden* like it; **II** *aj* pleasantly, agreeably

preuts prudish, prim, demure, squeamish; **–heid** *v* prudishness, prudery, primness, demureness, squeamishness

preva'leren (prevaleerde, h. geprevaleerd) *vi* prevail, predominate

'prevelen (prevelde, h. gepreveld) *vi* & *vt* mutter, mumble

pre'ventie [-(t)si.] (-s) *v* prevention; **preven'tief** preventive; *in preventieve hechtenis houden* keep [him] under remand; ~ *middel* preventive (means)

'prezen V.T. meerv. v. *prijzen*

pri'eel (priëlen) *o* bower, arbour, summerhouse

'priegelen (priegelde, h. gepriegeld) *vi* do detailed (delicate) work

priem (-en) *m* pricker, piercer, awl; **'priemen** (priemde, h. gepriemd) *vt* prick, pierce

'priemgetal (-len) *o* prime number

'priester (-s en -en) *m* priest; **–ambt** *o* priestly office; **~-'arbeider** (-s) *m* worker-priest; **–celibaat** *o rk* clerical celibacy; **prieste'res** (-sen) *v* priestess; **'priestergewaad** (-waden) *o* sacerdotal garments, clerical garb; **–kaste** (-n) *v* priestly caste; **–lijk** priestly; **–schap** *o* priesthood; **–student** (-en) *m rk* clerical student; **–wijding** (-en) *v* ordination '**prietpraat** *m* twaddle, tea-table talk

'**prijken** (prijkte, h. geprijkt) *vi* shine, glitter, blaze; ...*prijkte in al zijn schoonheid* ...was in the pride of its beauty

prijs (prijzen) 1 *m* (w a a r d e) price; (k a a r t j e m e t p r ij s a a n d u i d i n g) price ticket (tag); 2 *m* (b e l o n i n g) prize; award [for the best book of the year]; 3 *v* ♆ (b u i t) prize; *altijd ~!* a sure hit!; *marktprijzen, lopende prijzen* prices current; *speciale prijzen* (i n h o t e l &) special terms [March to May]; *de eerste ~ behalen* win (gain, carry off) the first prize; *~ maken* ♆ make a prize of [a ship], prize, capture, seize [a ship]; *goede prijzen maken* $ command (fetch) good prices [of things]; obtain (make) good prices [of a seller, for his articles]; *~ stellen op* 1 appreciate, value [your friendship]; 2 be anxious to [do sth.]; *een ~ zetten op iems. hoofd* set a price on sbd.'s head; ● *b e n e d e n (o n d e r) de ~ verkopen* $ sell below the market; *o p ~ houden* keep up the price (of...); *o p ~ stellen* appreciate, value; *t e g e n elke ~* at any price²; *tegen lage ~* at a low price, at low prices; *t o t elke ~* at any cost, at all costs, at any price; *v o o r geen ~* not at any price; *voor die ~* at the price; *voor een zacht ~je* cheap; **–afspraak** (-spraken) *v* price agreement; **–beheersing** *v* price control; **–beleid** *o* price policy; **–bepaling** (-en) *v* fixing (fixation) of prices; **prijsbe'wust** price conscious; **'prijsbinding** *v* price maintenance; **–courant** [-ku:rɑnt] (-en) *m* price-list; **–daling** (-en) *v* fall in prices; **–geld** *o* ♆ prize-money; **–gericht** *o* ♆ Prize Court; **–geven** (gaf 'prijs, h. 'prijsgegeven) *vt* abandon [to the waves]; give up [a fortress, hope]; commit [to the flames]; yield [ground, a secret]; *zie ook: vergetelheid* &; **prijs'houdend** firm; **'prijsindex** (-en en -dices) *m* price-index; **–kaartje** (-s) *o* price tag; **–kamp** (-en) *m* competition; **–kartel** [-tɛl] (-s) *o* price cartel; **–klas(se)** (-klassen) *v* price-range; **–lijst** (-en) *v* price-list; **–maatregel** (-en en -s) *m* price control order; **–niveau** [-ni.vo.] (-s) *o* price-level; **–notering** (-en) *v* quotation (of prices); **–opdrijving** *v* upward thrust, *Am* price-hike; **–opgaaf, –opgave** (-gaven) *v* quotation; **–peil** *o* price-level; **–politiek** *v* price-policy; **–recht** *o* prize-law; **–schieten** *o* shooting-match; **–spiraal** (-ralen) *v* price spiral; **–stijging** (-en) *v* rise (in prices); **–stop** *m* price stop (freeze); *een ~ afkondigen* freeze prices; **–uitdeling** *v,* **–uitreiking** (-en) *v* distribution of prizes, prize-giving; **–verbetering** (-en) *v* improvement (in prices); **–verhoging** (-en) *v* increase, rise (in prices); **–verlaging** (-en) *v* reduction, markdown; *grote ~!* sweeping reductions; **–vermindering** (-en) *v* = *prijsver-*

laging; **–verschil** (-len) *o* difference in price; **–vorming** *v,* **–zetting** *v* price formation (setting); **–vraag** (-vragen) *v* competition; *een ~ uitschrijven* offer a prize [for the best...]; **–winnaar** (-s) *m* prize-winner; **'prijzen*** *vt* 1 ★ (l o v e n) praise, commend, extol; 2 (prijsde, h. geprijsd) $ price; *iem. gelukkig ~* call sbd. happy; *zich gelukkig ~* call oneself lucky, thank (bless) one's lucky star; *zijn waren ~* 1 praise one's wares; 2 price one's wares [in guilders &]; *zich uit de markt ~* $ price oneself out of the market; **'prijzenbeschikking** (-en) *v* price control order; **–hof** *o* ♆ prize court; **–oorlog** (-logen) *m* price-war; **prijzens-'waard(ig)** praiseworthy, laudable, commendable; **'prijzig** expensive, F pricey

prik (-ken) *m* 1 prick, stab, sting; 2 (l i m o - n a d e, s p u i t w a t e r) F fizz, pop; ‖ 🐟 lamprey; **–actie** [-aksi.] (-s) *v* brief spell of industrial action; **–bord** (-en) *o* billboard, *Br* notice-board; **–je** (-s) *o* prick; *voor een ~ for a song*

'**prikkel** (-s) *m* 1 (p r i k s t o k) goad; 2 (s t e k e l) sting; 3 *fig* stimulus [*mv* stimuli], spur, incentive, impetus; **'prikkelbaar** irritable, excitable, irascible, prickly; **–heid** *v* irritability, excitability; **'prikkeldraad** *o* & *m* barbed wire; **–versperring** (-en) *v* (barbed) wire entanglement; **'prikkelen** (prikkelde, h. geprikkeld) **I** *vt* 1 *eig* prickle; tickle [the palate]; 2 (o p w e k k e n) stimulate, excite, spur on; 3 (i r r i t e r e n) irritate [the nerves], provoke [a person]; *de nieuwsgierigheid ~* pique (prick) one's curiosity; **II** *va* prickle; *fig* stimulate; irritate; **–d** prickling, prickly; *fig* stimulating; irritating; provoking, piquant, racy; **'prikkeling** (-en) *v* prickling; tickling; *fig* stimulation; irritation; provocation; **'prikkellectuur** *v* trashy literature

'**prikken** (prikte, h. geprikt) *vt* & *vi* prick; (o p f a b r i e k) clock in (out); (o p e e n b o r d) tack; **–er** (-s) *m* pricker; **'prikklok** (-ken) *v* time-clock; **–limonade** (-s) *v* soda(water), F fizz, pop; **–sle(d)e** (-sleden, -sleeën) *v* sledge moved by prickers; **–stok** (-ken) *m* pricker; **–tol** (-len) *m* pegtop

pril *in zijn ~le jeugd* in his early youth

'**prima I** *aj* first-class, first-rate, prime, A 1; **II** ('s) *v* $ first of exchange

1 pri'maat (-maten) *m* primate; **2 pri'maat** *o* primacy [of the pope; of thought]; **–schap** *o* primacy, primateship

prima-'donna ('s) *v* prima donna

pri'mair [-'mɛ:r] primary

pri'meur (-s) *v* (v. k r a n t) scoop; *~s* early fruit, early vegetables; *de ~ van iets hebben* be the first to use sth., to hear sth. &

primi'tief primitive; crude; **primitivi'teit** *v* primitiveness; crudity

'primo in the first place; ~ *januari* on the first of January

'primula ('s) *v* primrose

1 'primus (-sen) *m* first

2 'primus (-sen) *m* (k o o k t o e s t e l) primus

prin'ciep (-en) *o* = *principe*

princi'paal (-palen) *m* master, employer; $ principal

prin'cipe (-s) *o* principle; *i n* ~ in principle; *u i t* ~ on principle; **principi'eel I** *aj* fundamental [differences]; *een* ~ *akkoord* an agreement in principle; *een principiële kwestie* a question of principle; *een* ~ *tegenstander* an opponent on principle; **II** *ad* fundamentally, on principle; ~ *uitmaken* decide the question on principle

prins (-en) *m* prince; *van de* ~ *geen kwaad weten* be as innocent as a newborn babe; *leven als een* ~ lead a princely life; **–dom** (-men) *o* principality; **–elijk** princely; **prin'ses** (-sen) *v* princess; **–senboon** (-bonen) *v* French bean; **prins-ge'maal** *m* Prince Consort; **'prinsgezinde** (-n) *m* Ⓤ one loyal to the Prince of Orange; **–heerlijk** pleased as Punch, happy as a king; **–jesdag** *m* third Tuesday of September when the Queen of the Netherlands opens Parliament; **prins-re'gent** (-en) *m* Prince Regent

'prior (-s) *m* prior; **prio'raat** *o* priorship, priorate; **prio'res** (-sen) *v* prioress

pri'ori *a* ~ apriori, beforehand, previously **prio'rij** (-en) *v* priory

priori'teit *v* priority; **–saandeel** (-delen) *o* preference share

'prisma ('s en -mata) *o* prism; **–kijker** (-s) *m* prism(atic) binoculars; **pris'matisch** prismatic

pri'vaat I *aj* private; **II** (-vaten) *o* privy, w.c.; **–docent** (-en) *m* lecturer; **–les** (-sen) *v* private lesson; **–recht** *o* private law; *internationaal* ~ private international law; ~ *lichaam* private corporation; **priva'tissimum** (-s en -ma) *o* tutorial

pri'vé private, personal; *voor mijn* ~ for my own account; **–adres** (-sen) *o* private (home) address; **–gebruik** *o* personal use; **–kantoor** (-toren) *o* private office; **–leven** *o* private life, privacy; **–secretaresse** (-n) *v* private (confidential, personal) secretary

privi'lege [-le.ʒə] (-s) *o* privilege; **privilegi'ëren** [-ʒi.'e:rə(n)] (privilegieerde, h. geprivilegieerd) *vt* privilege

pro pro; *het* ~ *en contra* the pros and cons **pro'baat** efficacious, approved, sovereign [remedy]

pro'beersel (-s) *o* experiment; **pro'beren** (probeerde, h. geprobeerd) **I** *vt* try [it]; attempt

[to do it]; *je moet het maar eens* ~ just try; *dat moet je niet met mij* ~ you must not try it on with me; *we zullen het eens met u* ~ we shall give you a trial; **II** *va* try; *probeer maar!* (just) try!, have a try!

pro'bleem (-blemen) *o* problem; **–gebied** (-en) *o* depressed (distressed) area; **–loos** unproblematic; **–stelling** (-en) *v* formulation of a problem; **problema'tiek** *v* problems; problematic nature; **proble'matisch** problematic

procé'dé (-s) *o* process, procedure;

proce'deren (procedeerde, h. geprocedeerd) *vi* be at law; go to law [with], proceed against; **proce'dure** (-s) *v* 1 (w e r k w ij z e) procedure; 2 ⚖ (p r o c e s) action, lawsuit, proceedings

pro'cent (-en) *o* per cent; *(voor de volle) honderd* ~ F a hundred per cent; zie ook: *percent*; **procentu'eel I** *aj* proportional; **II** *ad* in terms of percentage

pro'ces (-sen) *o* 1 ⚖ lawsuit, action; [criminal] trial, [divorce] case, proceedings; 2 (b e w e r-k i n g; v e r l o o p) process; *iem. een* ~ *aandoen* bring an action against sbd., take the law of sbd.; *in* ~ *liggen* be engaged in a lawsuit, be at law [with...]; **–kosten** *mv* costs; **–recht** *o* law of procedure

pro'cessie (-s) *v* procession

pro'cesstukken *mv* documents in the case; **proces-ver'baal** (processen-verbaal) *o* 1 (v e r k l a r i n g) (official) report, record (of evidence); minutes [of proceedings]; 2 (b e k e u r i n g) warrant; ~ *opmaken tegen iem.* take sbd.'s name, summons sbd.

procla'matie [-(t)si.] (-s) *v* proclamation; **procla'meren** (proclameerde, h. geproclameerd) *vt* proclaim; *iem. tot...* ~ proclaim sbd.

procu'ratie [-(t)si.] (-s) *v* power of attorney, proxy, procuration; **–houder** (-s) *m* confidential clerk, proxy; **procu'reur** (-s) *m* solicitor, attorney; ~- **generaal** (procureurs-generaal) *m* Attorney General

prode'aan (-deanen) *m* ⚖ Poor Person; **pro-'deozaak** (-zaken) *v* Poor Persons' Procedure

produ'cent (-en) *m* producer; **produ'ceren** (produceerde, h. geproduceerd) *vt* produce, turn out; **pro'dukt** (-en) *o* product* ; *~en* ook: [natural, agricultural] produce; **pro'duktie** [-si.] *v* production, output; **–apparaat** *o* productive machine (machinery); **produk'tief** productive; *iets* ~ *maken* make it pay; **pro'duktiefactoren** *mv* production factors; **–kosten** *mv* cost(s) of production, production costs; **–middelen** *mv* means of production; capital goods; **–vermogen** *o* (productive) capacity; **produktivi'teit** *v* productivity, productive capacity

proef (proeven) *v* proof [of sth. printed or engraved, of photo]; trial, test, experiment [of sth.]; specimen, sample; *de* ~ *op de som* the proof²; *dat is de* ~ *op de som* that settles it; *de* ~ *op de som nemen* put [sth.] to the test; *proeven van bekwaamheid afleggen* give proof of one's ability; *proeven doen* make experiments; *een zware* ~ *doorstaan* stand a severe test; *er eens een* ~ *mee nemen* give it a trial (try); *proeven nemen (met)* make experiments (on), experiment (on); ● *o p* ~ [he is there] on probation; $ on trial; on approval, on approbation, **F** on appro; *op de* ~ *stellen* put to the test, try, tax [one's patience]; *het stelde mijn geduld erg op de* ~ my patience was severely tried; **–balans** (-en) *v* $ trial balance; **–ballon** (-s) *m* 1 pilot-balloon; 2 *fig* kite; *een* ~ *oplaten* throw out a feeler, **F** fly a kite; **–bank** (-en) *v* ✗ test bench; **–bestelling** (-en) *v* trial order; **–boring** (-en) *v* exploratory drilling, trial boring; **–dier** (-en) *o* laboratory animal, experimental animal, subject; **–draaien I** *vi* run on trial; **II** *o* dummy trial, trial run; **–druk** *m* proof; **–flesje** (-s) *o* trial bottle; **–huwelijk** *o* trial marriage; **–jaar** (-jaren) *o* probationary year; **–je** (-s) *o* sample, specimen; **–konijn** (-en) *o* experimental rabbit; *fig* guinea-pig; **–les** (-sen) *v* test lesson; **–lezer** (-s) *m* proof reader; **–lokaal** (-kalen) *o* pub; **–monster** (-s) *o* $ testing sample; **–nemer** (-s) *m* experimenter; **–neming** (-en) *v* 1 (h a n d e l i n g) experimentation; 2 (a f z o n d e r l i j k   g e v a l) experiment; ~*en doen* make experiments, experimentalize; **–nummer** (-s) *o* specimen copy; **proefonder'vindelijk** experimental; **'proeforder** (-s) *v* $ trial order; **–periode** (-n en -s) *v* probationary period; **–persoon** (-sonen) *m* test subject; **–proces** (-sen) *o* test case; **–rit** (-ten) *m* trial run, ⟨o o k:⟩ test drive; **–schrift** (-en) *o* thesis [*mv* theses]; *een* ~ *verdedigen* uphold a thesis; **–station** [-(t)ʃɔn] (-s) *o* experiment(al) station, research-station; **–steen** (-stenen) *m* touchstone; **–stomen** ('proefstoomde, h. 'proefgestoomd) **I** *vi* ↕ make a (her) trial trip; *fig* make a trial; **II** *o* trial trip, trials; **–stuk** (-ken) *o* specimen; **–tijd** *m* period (time) of probation, probation, probationary period, apprenticeship, noviciate; **–tocht** (-en) *m* trial trip (run); **–tuin** (-en) *m* experimental garden (plot), test plot; **–vel** (-len) *o* proof (-sheet); **–veld** (-en) *o* trial field, test (experimental) plot; **–vlucht** (-en) *v* trial flight, test flight; **–werk** (-en) *o* ⟨⟩ (test) paper; **–zending** (-en) *v* trial consignment

'proesten (proestte, h. geproest) *vi* sneeze, splutter; ~ *van het lachen* burst out laughing

'proeve (-n) *v* specimen; **'proeven** (proefde, h. geproefd) **I** *vt* 1 taste [food, drinks &]; 2 $

sample [wine]; *je proeft er niets van* it does not taste; **II** *vi* taste; *proef maar eens* just taste (at) it; **–er** (-s) *m* taster

'prof (-s) *m* **F** 1 professor; 2 *sp* pro (= professional)

pro'faan *aj* profane; **profa'natie** [-(t)si.] (-s) *v* profanation; **profa'neren** (profaneerde, h. geprofaneerd) *vt* profane

'profclub (-s) *v* *sp* professional sports club

pro'feet (-feten) *m* prophet; *hij is een* ~ *die brood eet* his prophecies are of no value; *een* ~ *is niet geëerd in zijn eigen land* a prophet is not without honour save in his own country

pro'fessen (professte, h. geprofest) *vi* profess

pro'fessie (-s) *v* profession; **professio'neel** professional, specialist

pro'fessor (-s en -'soren) *m* professor; ~ *in de...* professor of...; **professo'raal** professorial; **professo'raat** (-raten) *o* professorship

profe'teren (profeteerde, h. geprofeteerd) *vt* prophesy; **profe'tes** (-sen) *v* prophetess; **profe'tie** [-'(t)si.] (-ieën) *v* prophecy; **pro'fetisch** prophetic

pro'ficiat! *ij* congratulations (on *met*)

pro'fiel (-en) *o* profile [esp. of face], half face; side-view, section [of a building]; *in* ~ in profile

pro'fijt (-en) *o* profit, gain; **–elijk** profitable

profi'leren (profileerde, h. geprofileerd) *vt* profile

profi'teren (profiteerde, h. geprofiteerd) *vi van iets* ~ 1 (g u n s t i g) profit by; 2 (o n g u n-s t i g) take advantage of; **profi'teur** (-s) *m* profiteer

pro 'forma for form's sake; ~ *rekening* $ pro forma account

'profspeler (-s) *m* *sp* professional sportsman, **F** pro; **–voetbal** *o* *sp* professional soccer

profy'lactisch [-fi.-] prophylactic, preventive

prog'nose [s = z] (-s) *v* prognosis [*mv* prognoses]

pro'gramma ('s), **pro'gram** (-s) *o* 1 (i n 't a l g.) program(me); 2 (v. s c h o u w b u r g) play-bill, bill; 3 (v. p a r t ij) platform; 4 ⟨⟩ curriculum; syllabus [of a course, of examinations]; *het staat op het* ~ it is on the programme²; **–blad** (-bladen) *o* radio journal; **program'matisch** programmatic; **programma'tuur** *v* software; **program'meren** (programmeerde, h. geprogrammeerd) *vt* programme; **–ring** *v* programming; **program'meur** (-s) *m* programmer

pro'gressie (-s) *v* progression; **progres'sief I** *aj* progressive, graduated [tax]; forward-looking [policy], advanced [intellectuals]; **II** *ad* progressively; **III** *sb de progressieven* the progressives, the progressists

pro'ject (-en) *o* project, scheme, planning;

projec'teren (projecteerde, h. geprojecteerd) *vt* project; *ps* externalize; **pro'jectie** [-si.] (-s) *v* projection; **projec'tiel** (-en) *o* projectile, missile; **pro'jectielamp** (-en) *v* projector; **–lantaarn, –lantaren** (-s) *v*, **–scherm** (-en) *o*, **–toestel** (-len) *o* projector; **pro'jectleider** (-s) *m* divisional head; **–ontwikkelaar** (-s) *m* project developer

prol (-len) *m = proleet*

pro'laps *m* ꬍ prolapse

pro'leet (-leten) *m* cad, vulgarian; **proletari'aat** *o* proletariat; **prole'tariër** (-s) *m* proletarian; **prole'tarisch** proletarian

prolife'ratie [-(t)si.] *v* proliferation

'prollig vulgarian

prolon'gatie [-lòŋ'ga.(t)si.] (-s) *v* continuation; *op ~ $* on security; **–rente** (-n en -s) *v* contango; **prolon'geren** (prolongeerde, h. geprolongeerd) *vt* continue [an engagement, a film]; *$* renew [a bill]

pro'loog (-logen) *m* prologue, proem

prome'nade (-s) *v* promenade, walk; **–dek** (-ken) *o* promenade-deck

pro'messe (-n en -s) *v* promissory note, note of hand

pro'mille [-'mi.l] *o* per thousand, per mil(l)(e), pro mille; **promil'lage** [-ɜə] (-s) *o* pro mille content

promi'nent prominent, outstanding, distinguished

pro'motie [-(t)si.] (-s) *v* promotion, rise, advancement, preferment; ꬍ graduation (ceremony); *$* [sales &] promotion; *~ maken* be promoted; **–diner** [-di.ne.] (-s) *o* ꬍ graduation dinner; **–wedstrijd** (-en) *m sp* match deciding promotion; **pro'motor** (-s en -'toren) *m $* promotor, company promoter; *wie is zijn ~? ꬍ* by whom is he going to be presented [for his degree]?; **promo'vendus** (-di) *m* person taking his doctor's degree; **promo'veren I** (promoveerde, is gepromoveerd) *vi* graduate, take one's degree; **II** (promoveerde, h. gepromoveerd) *vt* confer a doctor's degree on

prompt I *aj* prompt [delivery &], ready [answer]; **II** *ad* promptly [paid]; **–heid** *v* promptitude, promptness, readiness

pronk *m* 1 (a b s t r a c t) show, ostentation, pomp; 2 (c o n c r e e t) finery; *te ~ staan* be exposed to view; **–boon** (-bonen) *v* runner bean; **'pronken** (pronkte, h. gepronkt) *vi* strut (about), show off; (v. p a u w) spread its tail; *~ met* make a show of, show off; **'pronker** (-s) *m* showy fellow; beau; **–ig I** *aj* showy, ostentatious; **II** *ad* showily, ostentatiously; **pronke'rij** (-en) *v* show, parade; **'pronkerwt** [-ɛrt] (-en) *v* sweet pea; **–gewaad** (-waden) *o* dress of state, gala dress; **–juweel** (-welen) *o* jewel, gem;

–kamer (-s) *v* state-room; **–ster** (-s) *v* doll, fine lady; **–stuk** (-ken) *o* show-piece; **–ziek** showy, ostentatious; **–zucht** *v* ostentatiousness, ostentation

pro'nuntius [-(t)si.üs] (-ii) *m* pronuncio

prooi (-en) *v* prey[2]; *ten ~ aan* a prey to; *ten ~ vallen aan* fall a prey to

proos'dij (-en) *v* deanery

1 proost (-en) *m* dean

2 proost *ij* cheers!, your health!, here is to you!, F mud in your eye!

prop (-pen) *v* 1 stopple, stop(per) [of a bottle]; 2 cork [of a bottle]; 3 bung [of a cask]; 4 wad [of a gun, of cotton-wool]; 5 gag [for the mouth]; 6 lump [in the throat]; 7 [antiseptic] plug; 8 pellet [made by schoolboys]; 9 *fig* roly-poly, dumpy person; *op de ~pen komen* turn up; *hij durft er niet mee op de ~pen komen* he dare not come out with it

pro'paangas *o* propane

propae'deuse [pro.pe.'dœyzə], **propae'deutica** *v* propaedeutics; **propae'deutisch** [-ti.s] propaedeutic(al), preliminary [examination]

propa'ganda *v* propaganda; *~ maken* make propaganda, propagandize; *~ maken voor* ook: agitate for [shorter hours &], propagate [ideas]; **–doeleinden** *mv* purposes of propaganda; **–middel** (-en) *o* means of propaganda; **propagan'dist** (-en) *m* propagandist; **–isch** propagandist; **propa'geren** (propageerde, h. gepropageerd) *vt* propagate

pro'peller (-s) *m* propeller

'proper tidy, clean; **–heid** *v* tidiness, cleanness; **–tjes** tidily

'propjes F *o* ꬍ propaedeutic(al) examination, preliminary examination

propo'nent (-en) *m* postulant, probationer

pro'portie [-si.] (-s) *v* proportion; *buiten ~* out of scale; **proportio'neel** proportional

propo'sitie [-'zi.(t)si.] (-s) *v* proposal

'proppen (propte, h. gepropt) *vt* cram; **'propperig** squat, dumpy; **'proppeschieter** (-s) *m* popgun; **'propvol** crammed, chock-full, cram-full

prose'liet [s = z] (-en) *m* proselyte

'prosit [s = z] *ij = 2 proost!*

proso'die [s = z] *v* prosody

pros'pectus (-sen) *o & m* prospectus

pros'taat (-taten) *m* prostate gland, prostate

prostitu'ée (-s) *v* prostitute; **prostitu'eren** (prostitueerde, h. geprostitueerd) **I** *vt* prostitute; **II** *vr zich ~* prostitute oneself; **prosti'tutie** [-(t)si.] *v* prostitution

Prot. *= protestants*

pro'tectie [-si.] *v* protection; *>* patronage, favouritism, interest, influence;

protectio'nisme *o* protectionism;
protectio'nist (-en) *m* protectionist; **–isch**
protectionist; **protecto'raat** (-raten) *o* protec-
torate; **proté'gé** [-te.'ʒe.] (-s) *m* protégé;
proté'gée [-te.'ʒe.] (-s) *v* protégée;
prote'geren [-'ʒe:rə(n)] (protegeerde, h.
geprotegeerd) *vt* protect, patronize
prote'ïne (-n) *v* & *m* & *o* protein
pro'test (-en) *o* protest, protestation; ~ *aantekenen tegen*... protest against; *o n d e r* ~ under
protest; *u i t* ~ in protest; **protes'tant** (-en) *m*
Protestant; **protestan'tisme** *o* Protestantism;
protes'tants Protestant; **pro'testbetoging**
(-en) *v* protest demonstration; **–beweging**
(-en) *v* protest movement; **–demonstratie**
[-(t)si.] (-s) *v* protest demonstration;
protes'teren (protesteerde, h. geprotesteerd)
I *vi* protest, make a protest; ~ *b ij* protest to
[the Government]; ~ *t e g e n* protest against;
II *vt* $ protest [a bill]; **pro'testnota** ('s) *v* note
of protest; **–staking** (-en) *v* strike of protest,
protest strike
'**Proteus** [-tœys] *m* Proteus
pro'these [-te.zə] (-n en -s) *v* prosthesis;
(c o n c r e e t) artificial part (leg, teeth &)
'**prothesis** (-theses en -sen) *v gram* prosthesis
pro'thetisch prosthetic
proto'col (-len) *o* protocol; **protocol'lair**
[-'lɛ: r] formal, according to protocol
'**proton** (-'tonen) *o* proton
proto'plasma *o* protoplasm
'**prototype** [-ti.pə] (-n en -s) *o* prototype
proto'zoën [-'zo.ə(n)] *mv* protozoa
'**protsen** (protste, h. geprotst) *vi* F swank;
'**protser** (-s) *m* F bounder, vulgarian; **–ig** F
swanky, vulgar
prove'nu ('s en -en) *o* proceeds
provi'and *m* & *o* provisions, victuals, stores;
provian'deren (proviandeerde, h. geprovian-
deerd) *vt* provision, cater, victual; **–ring** *v*
provisioning, catering, victualling;
provi'andschip (-schepen) *o* store-ship
provinci'aal I *aj* provincial; **II** (-ialen) *m* 1
provincial; 2 *rk* provincial [of a religious
order]; **provincia'lisme** *o* provincialism;
pro'vincie (-s en -iën) *v* province; **–stad**
(-steden) *v* provincial town
pro'visie [s = z] (-s) *v* 1 (v o o r r a a d) stock,
supply, provisions; 2 $ (l o o n) commission;
(v. m a k e l a a r) brokerage; **–basis** [-zɪs] *v op*
~ $ on a commission basis; **–kamer** (-s) *v*
pantry, larder; **–kast** (-en) *v* pantry, larder
provisio'neel [s = z] provisional
provo'catie [-(t)si.] (-s) *v* provocation;
provo'ceren (provoceerde, h. geprovoceerd)
vt provoke; **–d** provocative
1 pro'voost (-en) *m* provost

2 pro'voost (-en) *v* detention-room
'**proza** *o* prose; **pro'zaïsch** prosaic; **proza''ïst**
(-en) *m*, '**prozaschrijver** (-s) *m* prose-writer
'**prude** prudish, prim; **prude'rie** (-ieën) *v*
prudishness, prudery, primness
pruik (-en) *v* wig, periwig, peruke; (b o s
h a a r) shock (of hair); **–enmaker** (-s) *m*
wig-maker
'**pruilen** (pruilde, h. gepruild) *vi* pout, sulk, be
sulky; **–er** (-s) *m* sulky person
pruim (-en) *v* 1 ⚘ plum; 2 (g e d r o o g d)
prune; 3 (t a b a k) quid, plug; **–eboom**
(-bomen) *m* plum-tree; **pruime'dant** (-en) *v*
prune; '**pruimemondje** (-s) *o een* ~ *zetten*
make a pretty mouth; '**pruimen** (pruimde, h.
gepruimd) **I** *vt* chew [tobacco]; **II** *va* 1 chew
tobacco; 2 munch [= eat]; '**pruimentaart**
(-en) *v* plum-tart; '**pruimepit** (-ten) *v* plum-
stone; '**pruimer** (-s) *m* tobacco-chewer;
'**pruimtabak** *m* chewing-tobacco
Pruis (-en) *m* Prussian; '**Pruisen** *o* Prussia;
'**Pruisisch** Prussian; ~ *blauw* Prussian blue; ~
zuur prussic acid
prul (-len) *o* bauble, rubbishy stuff; *het is een* ~ it
is trash; *wat een* ~ *(van een vent)!* F what a dud!;
allerlei –len all sorts of gewgaws; **–dichter** (-s)
m poetaster, paltry poet; **prul'laria** *mv*
rubbish, gewgaws, knick-knacks; '**prulleboel**
m trashy stuff, trash; '**prullenmand** (-en) *v*
waste-paper basket; '**prullerig** = *prullig*;
'**prullewerk** *o* = *prulwerk*; '**prullig** rubbishy,
trumpery, trashy, cheap; '**prulroman** (-s) *m*
trashy novel, Grub-street novel; **–schrijver**
(-s) *m* hack, Grub-street writer; **–werk** *o* trash,
rubbish
prut *v* (k o f f i e ~) grounds; (s l ij k) slush,
sludge
'**prutsding** (-en) *o* trifle, knick-knack; '**prutsen**
(prutste, h. geprutst) *vi* potter, tinker (at, with
aan), bungle, botch; **–er** (-s) *m* potterer,
tinkerer; **prutse'rij** (-en) *v* pottering (work);
'**prutswerk** *o* bungled work, botch
'**pruttelaar** (-s) *m* grumbler; '**pruttelen** (prut-
telde, h. geprutteld) *vi* simmer; *fig* grumble;
'**pruttelig** grumbling, grumpy
P.S. [pe.'ɛs] = *Postscriptum*
psalm (-en) *m* psalm; **–boek** (-en) *o* psalm-
book, psalter; **–dichter** (-s) *m* psalmist;
–gezang *o* psalm-singing; **psal'mist** (-en) *m*
psalmist; **psalmodi'ëren** (psalmodieerde, h.
gepsalmodieerd) *vi* sing psalms, psalmodize,
intone; '**psalter** (-s) *o* 1 ♩ psaltery; 2 (b o e k)
psalter
'**pseudo...** ['psœydo.] pseudo..., false
pseudo'niem (-en) **I** *o* pseudonym, pen-name;
II *aj* pseudonymous
pst! *ij* (hi)st!

'**psyche** *v* psyche
psy'ché [psi.'ge.] (-s) *m* (s p i e g e l) cheval-glass
psyche'delisch [psi.ge.'de.li.s] psychedelic;
psychi'ater (-s) *m* psychiatrist; **psychia'trie** *v*
psychiatry; **psychi'atrisch** psychiatric; ~
ziekenhuis mental hospital; '**psychisch**
psychic(al); **psychoana'lyse** [- 'li.zə] (-n en -s)
v psychoanalysis; – 'lytisch psychoanalytic;
psycho'geen psychogenic; **psycholo'gie** *v*
psychology; – 'logisch psychological; – 'loog
(-logen) *m* psychologist; – 'paat (-paten) *m*
psychopath; – 'pathisch psychopathic;
–**patholo'gie** *v* psychopathology, abnormal
psychology; **psy'chose** [-zə] (-n en-s) *v*
psychosis [*mv* psychoses]; **psychoso'matisch**
psychosomatic; '**psychotechniek** *v* psycho-
technics; **psycho'technisch** ~ *onderzoek*
testing; '**psychothera'pie** *v* psychotherapy,
psychotherapeutics; **psychothera'peutisch**
[- 'pœyti.s] psychotherapeutic
'**puber** (-s) *m-v* adolescent; **puber'aal** adolescent; **puber'teit** *v* adolescence, puberty;
–**sleeftijd** *m* age of puberty
publi'ceren (publiceerde, h. gepubliceerd) *vt*
publish, bring before the public, make public,
issue; **publi'cist** (-en) *m* publicist;
publici'teit *v* publicity; *er* ~ *aan geven* make it
public; **pu'bliek I** *aj* public; ~ *engagement* open
engagement; *de* –*e opinie* popular verdict
(opinion); *iets* ~ *maken* give publicity to sth.,
publish sth.; ~ *worden* be made public, be
published; **II** *ad* publicly, in public; **III** *o*
public; *in het* ~ in public, publicly; *het grote* ~
the general public; *het stuk trok veel* ~ the play
drew a full house (a large audience); –**elijk**
publicly; **pu'bliekrecht** *o* public law;
publiek'rechtelijk *o* public law; ~ *lichaam*
public corporation; **publi'katie** [-(t)si.] (-s) *v*
publication; –**bord** (-en) *o* notice-board, bill
board
'**puddelen** (puddelde, h. gepuddeld) *vt* ✗
puddle
'**pudding** (-en en -s) *m* pudding; –**poeder,**
–**poeier** (-s) *o* & *m* pudding powder; –**vorm**
(-en) *m* pudding mould
puf *m ik heb er niet veel* ~ *in* I don't feel like it
'**puffen** (pufte, h. gepuft) *vi* puff
pui (-en) *v* lower front of a building, shop front
puik I *aj* excellent, choice, prime, first-rate; **II**
ad beautifully, to perfection; **III** *o* choice, best,
pick (of...); –**je** *o* = *puik* **III**
'**puilen** (puilde, h. gepuild) *vi* protrude, bulge;
zijn ogen puilden uit hun kassen his eyes started
from his head
'**puimen** (puimde, h. gepuimd) *vt* pumice;
'**puimsteen** (-stenen) *m* & *o* pumice (-stone)
puin *o* rubbish, debris, wreckage, [brick] rubble;

~ *storten* shoot rubbish; *in* ~ *gooien* (*leggen*) lay in
ruins, reduce to rubble; *in* ~ *liggen* be (lie) in
ruins; *in* ~ *rijden* wreck [a car]; *in* ~ *vallen* fall
into ruins, crumble to pieces; –**hoop** (-hopen)
m heap of ruins, ruins; heap of rubble, rubble
heap, heap of rubbish; [*fig*] *wat een* ~! what a
mess (muddle)!
puis'sant [pɥi.'sɑnt] exceedingly [rich]
puist (-en) *v* pimple, pustule, tumour; –**achtig,**
–**erig,** –**ig** full of pimples, pimpled, pimply;
–**je** (-s) *o* pimple; ~*s* acne
'**pukkel** (-s) *v* pimple
pul (-len) *v* jug, vase
'**pulken** (pulkte, h. gepulkt) *vi* pick; *in zijn neus*
~ pick one's nose
pull'over [pu.l-] (-s) *m* pullover, jersey
pulp *v* pulp [of beetroots]
puls (-en) *m* ✺ pulse
pul'seren (pulseerde, h. gepulseerd) *vi* pulsate,
throb
✧ '**pulver** *o* 1 powder, dust; 2 gunpowder;
pulveri'seren [s = z] (pulveriseerde, h.
gepulveriseerd) *vt* pulverize, powder
'**pummel** (-s) *m* boor, lout, yokel, bumpkin,
clodhopper; –**ig** boorish
pu'naise [- 'nɛ:zə] (-s) *v* drawing-pin
punch [pʉnʃ] *m* punch
punc'teren (puncteerde, h. gepuncteerd) *vt*
puncture, tap; '**punctie** [-ksi.] (-s) *v* puncture,
tapping; **punctuali'teit** *v* punctuality;
punctu'atie [-(t)si.] *v* punctuation;
punctu'eel punctual
'**Punisch** Punic
1 punt (-en) *m* 1 point [of a pen, pin &]; 2 tip
[of a cravat, the nose &]; corner [of an apron];
3 toe [of shoe]; 4 top [of asparagus]; 5 wedge
[of tart, cake]; 6 ⚓ peak [of anchor]; *daar kan
jij een* ~(*je*) *aan zuigen* that leaves you nowhere
2 punt (-en) *o* point [of intersection]; *fig* point
[of discussion &]; item [on the agenda]; (~
w a a r h e t o m g a a t) nub; ~ *van aanklacht*
count [of an indictment]; *hoeveel* –*en heb je*? 1 ☞
what marks have you got?; 2 *sp* what's your
score?; *10* –*en maken* score ten; ● *o p het* ~
van... in point of...; *op het* ~ *van te...* on the
point of ...ing, about to...; *op dit* ~ *geeft hij niet
toe* on this point he will never yield; *op het dode*
~ at a deadlock; *op het dode* ~ *komen* come to a
deadlock, reach an impasse; *hen o v e r het dode*
~ *heen helpen* lift them from the deadlock;
verslaan (*winnen*) *op* –*en sp* beat (win) on points;
een ~ *zetten achter* call it a day, put a stop to;
~ *v o o r* ~ point by point
3 punt (-en) *v* & *o* (l e e s t e k e n) 1 dot [on i]; 2
full stop, period [after sentence]; *dubbele* ~
colon; ~ *uit!* enough!, that's that!
'**puntbaard** (-en) *m* pointed beard, Vandyke

beard; **–boord** (-en) *o* & *m* butterfly collar, wing collar; **–dak** (-daken) *o* pointed roof; **–dicht** (-en) *o* epigram; **–dichter** (-s) *m* epigrammatist; **'punten** (puntte, h. gepunt) *vt* point, sharpen [a pencil]; trim [the hair]

'puntenlijst (-en) *v* terms' report; list of marks

'punter (-s) *m* punt

'punteslijper (-s) *m* pencil sharpener

'puntgaaf perfect, in mint condition

'puntgevel (-s) *m* gable; **–hoofd** *o* F *ik krijg er een ~ van* it drives me to the wall (up a tree); **'puntig** pointed, sharp; *fig* pointed; **–heid** (-heden) *v* pointedness², sharpness; **'puntje** (-s) *o* point [of a pencil &]; tip [cigar, nose, tongue]; dot [on i]; *de ~s op de i zetten* dot one's i's and cross one's t's; *als ~ bij paaltje komt* when it comes to the point; *alles was in de ~s* everything was shipshape (in apple-pie order); *hij zag er in de ~s uit* he looked very trim (spick and span); zie ook: 1 *punt*

punt'komma ('s) *v* & *o* semicolon

'puntlassen *vi* spot-weld; **–schoen** (-en) *m* pointed shoe; **–zakje** (-s) *o* cornet, screw

pu'pil (-len) 1 *m* & *v* pupil, ward; 2 *v* pupil [of the eye]

pu'ree *v* purée [of tomatoes &]; (v. a a r d a p - p e l e n) mashed potatoes, mash

'puren (puurde, h. gepuurd) *vt ~ uit* suck [honey] from; *fig* draw [wisdom] from

pur'gatie [-(t)si.] (-s) *v* purge; **pur'geermiddel** (-en) *o* laxative, purgative; **pur'geren** (purgeerde, h. gepurgeerd) *vi* purge oneself, take a purgative

'Purim ['pu.rIm] *o* Purim

pu'risme (-n) *o* purism; **pu'rist** (-en) *m* purist; **–isch** puristic

Puri'tein (-en) *m* ⊞ Puritan; **puri'tein** (-en) *m* puritan; **–s** puritanical

purper *o* purple; **–achtig** purplish; 1 **'purperen** (purperde, h. gepurperd) *vt* purple; 2 **'purperen** *aj* purple; **'purperkleurig**

purple; **–rood I** *aj* purple; **II** *o* purple

pus *o* & *m* pus; **'pussen** (puste, h. gepust) *vi* suppurate

put (-ten) *m* 1 (w a t e r p u t) well; 2 (k u i l) pit; *in de ~* [*fig*] in low spirits, under the weather, in the dumps; **–haak** (-haken) *m* bucket-hook; *over de ~ trouwen* marry over the broomstick, jump the besom; **–je** (-s) *o* 1 little hole [in the ground]; 2 dimple [in the chin]; **–jesschepper** (-s) *m* scavenger

putsch [pu.tʃ] (-en) *m* putsch

'puts(e) (putsen) *v* (canvas) bucket

'putten (putte, h. geput) *vt* draw [water, comfort, strength & from...]; *uit zijn eigen ervaringen ~* draw upon one's personal experiences; *waaruit heeft hij dat geput?* what has been his source?; **–er** (-s) *m* 1 water-drawer; ‖ 2 🐦 = *distelvink*; **'putwater** *o* well-water

puur I *aj* pure²; (v. s t e r k e d r a n k) neat, raw, short, straight; *pure chocolade* plain chocolate; *het is pure onzin* it is pure (sheer) nonsense; **II** *ad* purely; *~ uit baldadigheid* out of pure mischief

'puzzel (-s) *m* puzzle; **'puzzelen** (puzzelde, h. gepuzzeld) *vi* solve puzzles; *~ op* (over) puzzle over; **'puzzelrit** (-ten) *m*, **–tocht** (-en) *m* mystery tour; **'puzzle** (-s) = *puzzel*

pyg'mee [pIg-] (-eeën) *m-v* pygmy

py'jama ['pi.-] ('s) *m* pyjamas, pyjama suit; *een ~* a set of pyjamas; **–broek** (-en) *v* pyjama trousers; **–jasje** (-s) *o* pyjama jacket

Pyre'neeën [pi.-] *mv de ~* the Pyrenees; **Pyre'nees** Pyrenean

py'riet [pi.-] *o* pyrites

pyro'maan [pi.-] (-manen) *m* F fire-bug, arsonist, *ps* pyromaniac; **pyroma'nie** *v* pyromania

pyro'meter ['pi.-] (-s) *m* pyrometer

'Pyrrusoverwinning ['pIr-] (-en) *v* Pyrrhic victory

'python ['pi.tɔn] (-s) *m* python

Q

q [ky.] ('s) *v* q
qua qua, in the capacity of
quadril'joen (-en) *o* quadrillion
qua'drille [ka.'dri.(l)jə] (-s) *m* & *v* quadrille
quadrofo'nie *v* quadrophonics
quali'tate qua officially; bij virtue of one's
  office
'quantum (-s en -ta) *o* quantum, amount
quaran'taine [ka.rãn'tɪ:nə] (-s) *v* quarantine;
  –haven (-s) *v* quarantine station; **–vlag** (-gen)
  v quarantine flag, **F** yellow Jack
'quasi ['kʋa.zi.] quasi, seeming [friends],
  miscalled [improvements], pretended [interest]
quater'temperdag (-dagen) *m* Ember day
quatre-'mains [kɑtrə'mĩ] *m* duet (for piano); ∼

spelen play duets
queru'lant [kʋe:ry.-] (-en) *m* querulous person,
  grumbler
queue [kø.] (-s en queueën) *v* queue, line; ∼
  maken stand in a queue, wait in the queue,
  queue up, line up
quitte [ki.t] quits; *we zijn* ∼ we are quits; ∼
  spelen $ break even
qui-'vive [ki.'vi.və] *o op zijn* ∼ *zijn* be on the
  qui vive (on the alert)
quiz (quizzen, quizes) *m* quiz
'quorum (-s) *o* quorum
'quota ('s) *v* quota
quo'tiënt [ko.'ʃɪnt] (-en) *o* quotient
'quotum (-s en -ta) *o* quota, share

R

r [ɛr] ('s) *v* r

ra ('s en raas) *v* ⚓ yard; *grote* ~ ⚓ mainyard

raad (raden) *m* 1 advice, counsel; 2 (r e d - m i d d e l) remedy, means; 3 (r a a d g e - v e n d   l i c h a a m) council; 4 (r a a d g e - v e n d   p e r s o o n) counsellor, counsel; 5 (l i d v. r a a d g e v e n d   l i c h a a m) councillor; *dat is een goede* ~ that is a good piece of advice; *goede* ~ *was duur* we were in a fix; *Hoge Raad* ⚖ Supreme Court; ~ *van beheer* board of directors; ~ *van beroep* board of appeal; ~ *van beroerten* ⏹ council of troubles; ~ *van commissarissen* board of supervisory directors; *de Raad van Europa* the Council of Europe; *Raad van State* Council of State; ~ *van toezicht* supervisory board; *neem mijn* ~ *aan* take my advice; *iem.* ~ *geven* advise sbd.; ~ *inwinnen* ask [sbd.'s] advice; *zij moeten* ~ *schaffen* they must find ways and means; *iems.* ~ *volgen* follow sbd.'s advice; *hij weet altijd* ~ he is sure to find a way (out); *hij wist geen* ~ *meer* he was at his wit's (wits') end; *met zijn... geen* ~ *weten* not know what to do with one's...; *met zijn figuur geen* ~ *weten* be embarrassed; *overal* ~ *voor weten* be never at a loss for an expedient; *daar is wel* ~ *op* I'm sure a way may be found; • *i n d e* ~ *zitten* be on the (town) council; *iem. m e t* ~ *en daad bijstaan* assist sbd. by word and deed; *iem. o m* ~ *vragen* ask sbd.'s advice; *o p zijn* ~ at (on) his advice; *met iem. t e rade gaan* consult sbd.; *iem. v a n* ~ *dienen* advise sbd.; zie ook: *eind*; **–gevend** advisory, consultative [body]; **–gever** (-s) *m* adviser, counsellor; **–geving** (-en) *v* advice, counsel; *een* ~ a piece of advice; **–huis** (-huizen) *o* town hall; **–kamer** (-s) *v* council chamber; **–pensionaris** (-sen) *m* ⏹ Grand Pensionary; **'raadplegen** (raadpleegde, h. geraadpleegd) *vt* consult; **–ging** (-en) *v* consultation; **'raadsbesluit** (-en) *o* 1 decision of the town council; 2 *fig* ordinance, decree [of God] **'raadsel** (-s en -en) *o* riddle, enigma; *...is mij een* ~ *...is* a mystery to me; *in* ~ *en spreken* speak in riddles; *voor een* ~ *staan* be puzzled; **'raadsel-achtig** enigmatic(al), mysterious; **–heid** (-heden) *v* enigmatic character, mysteriousness **'raadsheer** (-heren) *m* 1 (p e r s o o n) councillor; senator; ⚖ justice; 2 (s c h a a k s t u k) bishop; **–lid** (-leden) *o* councillor, town councillor; **–lieden** *mv* advisers, counsellors; **–man** (-lieden) *m* adviser, counsellor; (p r a k - t i z ij n) counsel; **–vergadering** (-en) *v* council meeting; **–verkiezing** (-en) *v* municipal

election; **–verslag** (-slagen) *o* report of the meeting; **–zaal** (-zalen) = *raadzaal*; **–zetel** (-s) *m* seat on the (town) council; **–zitting** (-en) *v* session of the town council; **'raadzaal** (-zalen) *v* council hall; **'raadzaam** advisable; **–heid** *v* advisableness, advisability

raaf (raven) *v* 🐦 raven; *witte* ~ white crow; zie ook: *stelen*

'raagbol (-bollen) *m* = *ragebol*

'raaigras (-sen) *o* darnel; *Engels* ~ rye-grass

raak telling [blow, effect]; *altijd* ~ *!* you can't go wrong there!; *een* ~ *antwoord* a reply that went home; *een rake beschrijving* an effective description; *maar* ~ *kletsen* talk at random; ~ *slaan* hit home; *wat hij zegt, is* ~ what he says gets there; *die was* ~, *zeg!* that shot told!, he had you there!; **–lijn** (-en) *v* tangent; **–punt** (-en) *o* point of contact; **–vlak** (-ken) *o* tangent plane

raam (ramen) *o* 1 (v. h u i s) window; 2 (v a n f i e t s &) frame; *binnen (i n) het* ~ *van* zie *kader*; *u i t het* ~ *kijken* look out of the window; *er hangen gordijnen v o o r het* ~ curtains hang at the window; *het lag voor het* ~ it was in the window; **–antenne** (-s) *v* frame aerial; **–biljet** (-ten) *o* poster, bill; **–kozijn** (-en) *o* window-frame; **–vertelling** (-en) *v* frame story, ,,link and frame" story; **–wet** (-ten) *v* skeleton law

raap (rapen) *v* 🐄 1 turnip; 2 rape [for cattle]; **–koek** (-en) *m* rapeseed cake, rape-cake; **–kool** (-kolen) *v* kohlrabi, turnip-cabbage; **–olie** *v* rapeseed oil, colza oil; **–stelen** *mv* turnip-tops; **–zaad** *o* rapeseed

raar I *aj* strange, queer, odd; *een rare (Chinees, sijs, snoeshaan)* a queer (rum) customer, a queer fish; *ik voel me zo* ~ I feel so faint, funny; *ben je* ~ *?* are you mad?; **II** *ad* strangely

'raaskallen (raaskalde, h. geraaskald) *vt* rave, talk nonsense

raat (raten) *v* honeycomb

ra'barber *v* rhubarb

ra'bat *o* 💲 reduction, discount, rebate

ra'bauw (-en) *m* ugly customer

'rabbelen (rabbelde, h. gerabbeld) *vi* rattle, chatter

'rabbi ('s) *m*, **rab'bijn** (-en) *m* rabbi, rabbin; **rab'bijns, rabbi'naal** rabbinical; **rabbi'naat** (-naten) *o* rabbinate

race [re.s] (-s) *m* race; **–auto** [-o.to. of -ɔuto.] ('s) *m* racing-car, racer; **–baan** (-banen) *v* race-course, race-track; **–boot** (-boten) *m* & *v* speed-boat; **–fiets** (-en) *m* & *v* racing-bicycle, racer; **'racen** ['re.sə(n)] (racete, h. geracet) *vi* race; 'racepaard (-en) *o* race-horse, racer; –terrein (-en) *o* race-track, turf; –wagen (-s) *m* racing-car, racer

'Rachel *v* Rachel

ra'chitis *v* rachitis, rickets; ra'chitisch rickety

ra'cisme *o* racialism, racism; ra'cist (-en) *m* racialist, racist; –isch racialist, racist

'racket ['rɪkət] (-s) *o* racket

1 rad (raderen) *o* wheel; *het* ~ *van avontuur, het* ~ *der fortuin* the wheel of fortune; *iem. een* ~ *voor de ogen draaien* throw dust in sbd.'s eyes; *het vijfde* ~ *aan de wagen* an unwanted, useless person or thing; ~ *slaan* turn cart-wheels

2 rad I *aj* quick, nimble; glib [tongue]; ~ *van tong zijn* have the gift of the gab; II *ad* quickly, nimbly; glibly

'radar *m* radar; –installatie [-(t)si.] (-s) *v* radar installation; –scherm (-en) *o* radar screen

'radbraken (radbraakte, h. geradbraakt) *vt* break upon the wheel [a convict]; *fig* murder [a language]; *ik voel me geradbraakt* I am dead-beat

'raddraaier (-s) *m* ringleader

ra'deergum (-men) *o* eraser, india rubber; –mesje (-s) *o* eraser, erasing-knife; –naald (-en) *v* (etching) needle, point

'radeloos desperate, at one's wit's (wits') end; rade'loosheid *v* desperation

'raden* I *vt* 1 (r a a d g e v e n) counsel, advise; 2 (g o e d g i s s e n) guess; *iem. iets* ~ advise sbd. to do sth.; *te* ~ *geven* leave to guess; *laat je* ~ *!* be advised!; *dat zou ik je* ~, *het is je geraden* you will be well advised to do it; II *vi* & *va* guess; *nou raad eens! (*just) give a guess!; *naar iets* ~ guess at (make a guess at) sth.

'raderboot (-boten) *m* & *v* paddle-boat

1 'raderen *meerv. van* 1 *rad*

2 ra'deren (raderde, h. geradeerd) *vt* (m e t g u m) erase; (m e t m e s) scratch (out); –ring *v* erasure

'raderwerk (-en) *o* wheels[2], gear mechanism; (v. u u r w e r k) watchwork, clockwork

'radheid *v* quickness, nimbleness; ~ *van tong* glibness, volubleness, volubility

radi'aalband (-en) *m* radial (ply) tyre, F radial

radia'teur (-s) *m*, radi'ator (-s en -'toren) *m* radiator; –dop (-pen) *m* radiator cap

radi'caal I *aj* radical; *radicale hervorming* sweeping (root-and-branch, thoroughgoing) reform; II *ad* radically; III (-calen) *m* radical; radi-cali'seren [s = z] (radicaliseerde, h. geradicaliseerd) *vi* radicalize; radica'lisme *o* radicalism

ra'dijs (-dijzen) *v* radish

'radio ('s) *m* radio; (sound) broadcasting; *o v e r de* ~ over the radio, over the air; *v o o r, o p de* ~ on the radio, on the air

radioac'tief radioactive; –activi'teit *v* radioac-tivity

'radioamateur (-s) *m* radio amateur, amateur radio operator, F (radio) ham; –antenne (-s) *v* radio aerial; –baken (-s) *o* radio beacon; –bericht (-en) *o* radio report, radio message; –bode (-s) *m* radio journal; –buis (-buizen) *v* (radio) valve; –centrale (-s) *v* relay exchange, relay company; –distributie [-(t)si.] *v* wire broadcasting, wired transmission; –gids (-en) *m* radio journal; –golf (-golven) *v* radio (broadcast) wave; radiogra'fie *v* radiography; radio'grafisch radiographic; radio'gram (-men) *o* radiogram; radiotelegram; –kast (-en) *v* radio cabinet; –lamp (-en) *v* (radio) valve; –monteur (-s) *m* radio mechanic; radio'nieuwsdienst *m* news-cast, radio news; 'radio-omroep (-en) *m* broadcasting corpora-tion; 'radiopeiling (-en) *v* (radio) direction-finding; –praatje (-s) *o* broadcast talk; –programma ('s) *o* radioprogramme, broad-cast; –rede (-s) *v* broadcast (speech); –repor-tage [-ʒə] (-s) *v* (running) commentary; –reporter (-s) *m* (radio) commentator; –spreker (-s) *m* broadcaster; –station [-sta.-(t)ʃɔn] (-s) *o* radio station; –technicus (-ci) *m* radio engineer; –techniek *v* radio engineer-ing; radio'technisch radio-engineering; radiotelefo'nie *v* radiotelephony; –telegra'fie *v* radiotelegraphy; –telegra'fist (-en) *m* wireless operator; 'radiotelegram (-men) *o* = *radiogram*; –telescoop (-scopen) *m* radiotelescope

radiothera'pie *v* radiotherapeutics, radio-therapy

'radiotoestel (-len) *o* wireless set; –uitzending (-en) *v* broadcast, programme; –zender (-s) *m* radio transmitter

'radium *o* radium

'radius (-sen en -ii) *m* radius [*mv* radii]

'radja ('s) *m* rajah

'radstand (-en) *m* wheel-base; –vormig wheel-shaped

ra'factie [-'faksi.] *v* $ allowance for damage

'rafel (-s) *v* ravel; 'rafelen (rafelde, *vi* is, *vt* h. gerafeld) *vi* & *vt* fray, unravel, ravel out; –lig frayed

'raffia *m* & *o* raffia, bast

raffinade'rij (-en) *v* refinery; raffina'deur (-s) *m* refiner; raffi'neren (raffineerde, h. geraffi-neerd) *vt* refine; *zie ook: geraffineerd*

rag *o* cobweb

'rage ['ra.ʒə] (-s) *v* rage, craze, fad

'ragebol (-len) *m* Turk's head; mop [of hair]; 'ragfijn gossamer, filmy, fine-spun

'raggen F (ragde, h. geragd) *vi* (w o e s t r ij d e n) drive like mad, tear [along]

'raglan ['rɪglən] (-s) *m* raglan [sleeve]

ra'goût [-'ɡu.] (-s) *m* ragout

rail [re.l] (-s) *v* rail; *uit de ~s lopen* leave the metals

rail'leren [rɑ(l)'je:rə(n)] (railleerde, h. gerailleerd) **I** *vt* banter, chaff, poke fun at [sbd.]; **II** *va* banter, chaff, poke fun; **raille'rie** [rɑjə'ri.] (-ieën) *v* raillery, banter, chaff

rai'son [rɛ'zõ] *à ~ van* for the price of; *~ d'être* raison d'être

rak (-ken) *o* (v. r i v i e r) reach

'rakelen (rakelde, h. gerakeld) *vt* rake; **'rakelijzer** (-s) *o* rake

'rakelings *de kogel ging mij ~ voorbij* the bullet brushed past me (grazed my shoulder &); *de auto ging ~ langs het hek* the car just cleared the gate

'raken I (raakte, h. geraakt) *vt* 1 (t r e f f e n) hit; 2 (a a n r a k e n) touch; 3 (a a n g a a n) affect; concern; *deze cirkels ~ elkaar* these circles touch; *dat raakt hem niet* 1 (b e t r e f f e n) that does not concern him; 2 (b e k o m m e r e n) he does not care; **II** (raakte, is geraakt) *vi* get; zie *geraken; gevangen ~* become a prisoner; ● *~ a a n* touch[2]; *aan de drank ~* take to drink(ing), become addicted to drink; *hoe aan mijn geld te ~* how to come by my money; *aan de praat ~* get talking; *i n oorlog ~ met* become involved in a war with; *u i t de mode ~* go out of fashion; **F** *'m flink ~* eat [drink &] one's fill

1 ra'ket (-ten) *o* & *v sp* 1 racket; 2 battledore; **2 ra'ket** (-ten) *v* ✕, ✗ rocket [firework]; **–bal** (-len) *m* shuttlecock; **–basis** [-zɪs] (-sen en -bases) *v* ✕ rocket base; **–bom** (-men) *v* rocket bomb; **–motor** (-s en -toren) *m* rocket engine; **–spel** *o* (game of) battledore and shuttlecock; **ra'ketten** (rakette, h. geraket) *vi* play at battledore and shuttlecock; **ra'ketvliegtuig** (-en) *o* rocket plane

'rakker (-s) *m* rascal, rogue, scapegrace; *ondeugende ~* jackanapes

'rally ['rɛli.] ('s) *m* rally

ram (-men) *m* 1 ♈ ram, tup; 2 ⊞ (battering-) ram; *de Ram* ♈ Aries

'ramen (raamde, h. geraamd) *vt* estimate (at *op*); **–ming** (-en) *v* estimate

ram'mei (-en) *v* ⊞ battering-ram; **ram'meien** (rammeide, h. gerammeid) *vt* ram

'rammel (-s) *m* 1 rattle; 2 *een pak ~* a drubbing, a beating; **–aar** (-s) *m* 1 (s p e e l g o e d & p e r s o o n) rattle; 2 (k o n ij n) buck(-rabbit), (h a a s) buck(-hare); **'rammelen** (rammelde, h. gerammeld) **I** *vi* rattle, clatter, clash, clank; *fig* rattle; *~ m e t...* rattle (clatter, clank) ...; *ik rammel v a n de honger* I am ravenous, I have a terrific hunger; **II** *vt iem. door elkaar ~* give sbd. a good shaking; **–ling** (-en) *v* drubbing; **'rammelkast** (-en) *v* rattletrap; ramshackle

motor-car &; (p i a n o) old piano

'rammen (ramde, h. geramd) *vt* ram

ramme'nas (-sen) *v* black radish

ramp (-en) *v* disaster, calamity; catastrophe; **–enfonds** *o* [national] disaster fund; **–gebied** (-en) *o* disaster area; **–spoed** (-en) *m* adversity; **ramp'spoedig I** *aj* disastrous, calamitous; **II** *ad* disastrously; **ramp'zalig** 1 miserable, wretched; 2 fatal; **–heid** (-heden) *v* misery, wretchedness

ran'cune (-s) *v* rancour, grudge; **rancu'neus** vindictive, spiteful

rand (-en) *m* brim [of a hat]; rim [of a bowl]; margin [of a book]; [black, grass] border; edge [of a table, a bed, a wood]; edging [of a towel]; brink [of a precipice]; fringe [of a wood]; *fig* verge [of ruin]; **'randen** (randde, h. gerand) *vt* border; mill [coins]; **'randgebergte** (-n en -s) *o* border mountains; **–gemeente** (-n en -s) *v* adjoining town; **–schrift** (-en) *o* legend [of a coin]; **–staat** (-staten) *m* border state; **–stad** *v de ~ Holland* the rim-shaped agglomeration of cities in the western part of the Netherlands; **–verschijnsel** (-en en -s) *o* marginal phenomenom; **–versiering** (-en) *v* ornamental border; **–weg** (-wegen) *m* ring road

rang (-en) *m* rank, degree, grade; *~ en stand* rank and station; *i n ~ staan boven* rank above...; *m e t de ~ van kapitein* holding the rank of a captain; *wij zaten o p de eerste ~* we had seats in the first row (in the stalls); *v a n de eerste ~* first-rate [man], first-class [restaurant]

ran'geerder [-'ʒe:rdər] (-s) *m* shunter, yardman; **ran'geerlocomotief** (-tieven) *v* shunting engine, dummy; **–terrein** (-en) *o* marshalling yard, shunting yard; **–wissel** (-s) *m* shunting switch; **ran'geren** (rangeerde, h. gerangeerd) *vt* & *vi* shunt

'ranggetal (-len) *o* ordinal number; **–lijst** (-en) *v* 1 ✕ army list [of officers]; ⚓ navy list; 2 list (of candidates); **–nummer** (-s) *o* number; **–orde** *v* order

'rangschikken (rangschikte, h. gerangschikt) *vt* arrange, range [things]; *fig* marshal [the facts]; *~ onder* class with, subsume under [a category]; **–d** *gram* ordinal; **'rangschikking** (-en) *v* arrangement, classification

'rangtelwoord (-en) *o* ordinal number

'ranja *m* orangeade

1 rank (-en) *v* ✿ tendril

2 rank *aj* slender [of persons]; ⚓ crank(y)

'ranken (rankte, h. gerankt) *vi* ✿ twine, shoot tendrils

'rankheid *v* slenderness; ⚓ crank(i)ness

ra'nonkel (-s) *v* ranunculus

rans rancid

'ransel (-s) *m* 1 ✕ knapsack, pack; 2 (s l a a g)

pak ~ flogging, drubbing

'**ranselen** (ranselde, h. geranseld) *vt* drub, F wallop, whop, thwack

'**ransig** = *ranzig*

rant'soen (-en) *o* ration, allowance; *op* ~ *stellen* put on rations, ration; **rantsoe'neren** (rantsoeneerde, h. gerantsoeneerd) *vt* ration, put on rations; –**ring** (-en) *v* rationing

'**ranzig** rancid; –**heid** *v* rancidness, rancidity

rap I *aj* nimble, agile, quick; **II** *ad* nimbly

ra'paille [-'pɑljə] *o* rabble, riff-raff

'**rapen** (raapte, h. geraapt) *vt* & *vi* pick up, gather; glean [ears of corn]

ra'pier (-en) *o* rapier; foil [to fence with]

rappe'leren (rappeleerde, h. gerappeleerd) *vt* 1 (t e r u g r o e p e n) recall; 2 (h e r i n n e r e n) remind, send a reminder

rap'port (-en) *o* statement, account; report [ook ◡]; ~ *uitbrengen over* report on...; –**cijfer** (-s) *o* report mark; **rappor'teren** (rapporteerde, h. gerapporteerd) *vt* & *vi* report (on *over*); **rappor'teur** (-s) *m* reporter

rapso'die (-ieën) *v* rhapsody

ra'punzel (-s) *o* & *m* rampion

rare'kiek (-en) *m* raree-show, peep-show; '**rarigheid** (-heden) *v* queerness, oddness, oddity, curiosity; **rari'teit** (-en) *v* curiosity, curio; ~*en* curios; '**rariteitenkabinet** (-ten) *o*, –**kamer** (-s) *v* museum of curiosities

1 ras (-sen) *o* race [of men]; breed [of cattle]; *gekruist* ~ cross-breed; *van zuiver* ~ thoroughbred

2 ras I *aj* quick, swift, speedy; **II** *ad* soon, quickly

'**rasartiest** (-en) *m* a natural (true-born) artist; –**discrimi'natie** [-(t)si.] *v* racial discrimination; –**echt** thoroughbred, true-bred; –**hoenders** *mv* pedigree fowls; –**hond** (-en) *m* pedigree dog, true-bred dog; –**kenmerk** (-en) *o* racial characteristic

rasp (-en) *v* grater; [wood] rasp

'**raspaard** (-en) *o* thoroughbred, bloodhorse

'**raspen** (raspte, h. geraspt) *vt* grate [cheese]; rasp [wood]

'**rassehaat** *m* racial hatred, race hatred; '**rassendiscrimi'natie** [-(t)si.] *v* racial discrimination; –**relletjes** *mv* race riots; –**scheiding** *v* racial segregation; apartheid; –**strijd** *m* racial conflict; –**vermenging** *v* mixture of races, racial mixture; –**verschil** (-len) *o* racial difference; '**rassewaan** *m* racism, racialism

'**raster** (-s) *o* & *m* 1 (l a t) lath; 2 (h e k w e r k) = *rastering*; 3 (n e t w e r k v a n l i j n e n) screen; **raster'diepdruk** *m* photogravure; '**rastering** (-en) *v*, '**rasterwerk** (-en) *o* trellis-work, lattice, grill, railing, grating

'**rasverschil** (-len) = *rassenverschil*; –**vooroor-**

deel (-delen) *o* racial prejudice; –**zuiver** thoroughbred, true-bred

rat (-ten) *v* rat; *oude* ~ old hand, old stager; *een oude* ~ *loopt niet zo gemakkelijk in de val* an old bird is not caught with chaff

'**rata** *naar* ~ in proportion (to *van*), pro rata

'**rataplan** 1 *o* sound (rub-a-dub) of drums; 2 *m de hele* ~ F the whole caboodle (show)

'**ratel** (-s) *m* rattle²; clack [= tongue]; *hou je* ~ *!* F shut up!; –**aar** (-s) *m* (p e r s o o n) rattler, rattle; '**ratelen** (ratelde, h. gerateld) *vi* rattle; (v. m o t o r) knock; ~*de donderslagen* rattling peals of thunder; '**ratelslang** (-en) *v* rattlesnake

ratifi'catie [-'ka.(t)si.] (-s) *v* ratification; **ratifi'ceren** (ratificeerde, h. geratificeerd) *vt* ratify

'**ratio** [-(t)si.o.] *v* (r e d e, v e r s t a n d) reason, intellect; (v e r h o u d i n g) ratio

rationali'satie [-'za.(t)si.] (-s) *v* rationalization; **rationali'seren** (rationaliseerde, h. gerationaliseerd) *vt* rationalize; **rationa'lisme** *o* rationalism; **rationa'list** (-en) *m* rationalist; –**isch I** *aj* rationalist, rationalistic; **II** *ad* rationalistically; **ratio'neel** rational

'**ratjetoe** *m* & *o* ⚓ soldiers' hodgepodge; *fig* farrago, hotchpotch

'**rato** *naar* ~ zie *rata*

rats *v in de* ~ *zitten* have the jitters, be in a funk, have the wind up

'**ratteklem** (-men) *v* rat-trap; '**rattengif** *o*, –**kruit** *o* arsenic; –**koning** (-en) *m* tangle of rats; –**plaag** (-plagen) *v* rat plague; –**vanger** (-s) *m* rat-catcher; (h o n d) ratter; *de* ~ *van Hameln* the Pied Piper of Hamelin; –**verdelging** *v* destruction of rats; '**ratteval** (-len) *v* rat-trap

rauw raw, uncooked [food]; raucous, hoarse [voice], harsh [of sounds]; *fig* crude [statements]; –**elijks** ⚓ without previous notice; –**heid** (-heden) *v* rawness; *fig* crudity; –**kost** *m* raw food, uncooked food, raw vegetables, vegetable salads

ra'vage [-ʒə] (-s) *v* 1 (v e r w o e s t i n g) ravage [of the war]; havoc, devastations; 2 (o v e r-b l i j f s e l e n) wreckage [of a motor-car &], debris, shambles [of a building]; *een* ~ *aanrichten* make havoc (of *onder, in*)

'**ravegekras** *o* croaking (of a raven); –**zwart** raven-black; ~*e haren* raven locks

ra'vijn (-en) *o* ravine

ravitail'leren [-tɑ(l)'je: rə(n)] (ravitailleerde, h. geravitailleerd) *vt* supply; –**ring** *v* supply

ra'votten (ravotte, h. geravot) *vi* romp

ray'on [ri'ɔn] (-s) *o* & *m* 1 radius [of a circle]; 2 shelf [of a bookcase]; 3 department [in a shop]; 4 (g e b i e d) area; $ [commercial traveller's] territory; 5 (s t o f n a a m) rayon [artificial silk]; **–garen** *o* rayon yarn; **–vezel** (-s) *v* rayon staple

'razeil·(-en) *o* square sail

'razen (raasde, h. geraasd) *vi* rage, rave; ~ *en tieren* rage and rave, storm and swear; *over de weg* ~ tear along the road; *het water raast in de ketel* the kettle sings; **'razend I** *aj* raving, raging, mad, wild, **F** savage; ~*e honger* ravenous hunger; ~*e vaart* tearing pace; *ben je* ~? are you mad?; *het is om* ~ *te worden* it is enough to drive you mad; *het maakt me* ~ it makes me wild; *je maakt me* ~ *met je...* you drive me mad with your...; *hij is* ~ *op mij* he is furious with me; *hij... als een* ~*e* like mad; **II** *ad hij heeft* ~ *veel geld* he has a mint of money; *wij hebben* ~ *veel plezier gehad* we have enjoyed ourselves immensely; *hij is* ~ *verliefd op haar* he is madly in love with her; **–snel** as quick as lightning; **razer'nij** *v* rage; frenzy, madness

'razzia ['rɑdzi.a.] ('s) *v* razzia, raid, round-up [of suspects]; *een* ~ *houden in een café* raid a café; *een* ~ *houden op verdachten* round up suspects

re *v* ('s) *v* ♪ re

re'aal (realen) *m* real [= silver coin]

re'actie [-si.] (-s) *v* reaction[2] (to *op*); **–motor** (-s en -toren) *m* reaction engine; **–snelheid** (-heden) *v* speed of response; (c h e m i s c h) rate of reaction; **reactio'nair** [-'nɛ:r] *aj* & *m* (-en) reactionary; **re'actor** (-s) *v* reactor

rea'geerbuis (-buizen) *v* test-tube; **–middel** (-en) *o* = *reagens*; **–papier** *o* test-paper; **rea'gens** (-entia) *o* reagent, test; **rea'geren** (reageerde, h. gereageerd) *vi* react (to *op*), *fig* respond (to *op*)

reali'satie [-'za.(t)si.] (-s) *v* realization; **reali'seerbaar** realizable, feasible, practicable; **reali'seren** (realiseerde, h. gerealiseerd) **I** *vt* 1 (i n 't a l g.) realize; 2 **$** realize, cash, convert into money, sell; **II** *vi* **$** realize, sell; **III** *vr zich* ~ realize [that...]; **rea'lisme** *o* realism; **rea'list** (-en) *m* realist; **–isch I** *aj* realistic; **II** *ad* realistically; **reali'teit** (-en) *v* reality

reani'matie [-(t)si.] *v* **𝕿** resuscitation; **reani'meren** (reanimeerde, h. gereanimeerd) *vt* **𝕿** resuscitate

re'bel (-len) *m* rebel, mutineer; **rebel'leren** (rebelleerde, h. gerebelleerd) *vi* rebel, revolt [against...]; **rebel'lie** (-ieën) *v* rebellion, mutiny; **re'bels** rebellious, mutinous

'rebus (-sen) *m* rebus, picture-puzzle

recalci'trant recalcitrant

recapitu'latie [-(t)si.] (-s) *v* recapitulation; **recapitu'leren** (recapituleerde, h. gerecapituleerd) *vi* & *vt* recapitulate

recen'sent (-en) *m* reviewer, critic; **recen'seren** (recenseerde, h. gerecenseerd) **I**

vt review [an author, a book]; **II** *vi* review, write a review; **re'censie** (-s) *v* review, critique, (k o r t) notice; *ter* ~ for review; **–exemplaar** (-plaren) *o* review copy

re'cent recent; **–elijk** recently

rece'pis (-sen) *o* & *v* **$** scrip (certificate)

re'cept (-en) *o* 1 (v o o r k e u k e n &) recipe[2], receipt; 2 **𝕿** prescription; **–enboek** (-en) *o* 1 (household) recipe book; 2 **𝕿** prescription book

re'ceptie [-si.] (-s en -tiën) *v* reception; **recep'tief** receptive; **receptio'nist** [-si.o.'nɪst] (-en) *m* receptionist

receptivi'teit *v* receptivity

recep'tuur *v* dispensing

re'ces (-sen) *o* recess, adjournment; *op* ~ *gaan* (*uiteengaan*) rise, adjourn; *op* ~ *zijn* be in recess

re'cessie *v* **$** recession; **reces'sief** recessive

re'cette (-s) *v* takings, receipts

re'chaud [re.'ʃo.] (-s) *m* & *o* hot plate

re'cherche [rə'ʃɛrʃə] *v* detective force, Criminal Investigation Department, C.I.D.; **recher'cheur** (-s) *m* detective; **re'cherche-vaartuig** (-en) *o* revenue-cutter

1 recht I *aj* right [side, word, angle &]; straight [line]; *wat* ~ *en billijk is* what is just and fair; *zo* ~ *als een kaars* as straight as an arrow; *in de* ~*e lijn* (*afstammend*) (descended) in the direct line, lineal [descendants]; *de* ~*e man op de* ~*e plaats* the right man in the right place; *te* ~*er tijd* zie *tijd*; **II** *sb ik weet er het* ~*e niet van* I do not know the rights of the case; **III** *ad* rightly; < right, quite; straight; ~ *door zee gaand* straight-forward, straight; *hij is niet* ~ *bij zijn verstand* he is not quite right in his head; ~ *op hem af* straight at him; ~ *toe*, ~ *aan* straight on, open and shut

2 recht (-en) *o* 1 (o n g e s c h r e v e n n a t u u r w e t) right; 2 (r e c h t s p r a a k) law, justice; 3 (b e v o e g d h e i d) right, title, claim [to a pension]; 4 (g e h e v e n r e c h t) poundage [on money-orders]; duty, custom [on goods]; [registration] fee; *burgerlijk* ~ civil law; *het gemene* (*gewone*) ~ common law; *het geschreven* ~ statute law; *ongeschreven* ~ unwritten law; *Romeins* ~ Roman law; *verkregen* ~*en* vested rights; ~ *van bestaan* reason for existence; ~ *van eerstgeboorte* (right of) primogeniture; ~ *van gratie* prerogative of pardon; ~ *van initiatief* initiative; ~ *van opstal* building rights; ~ *van opvoering* performing rights; ~ *van spreken hebben* have a right to speak; ~ *van de sterkste* right of the strongest; ~ *van vergadering* right of public meeting; ~*en en plichten* rights and duties; *onze* ~*en en vrijheden* our rights and liberties; ~ *doen* administer justice; *er moet* ~ *geschieden* justice must be done; *iem. het* ~ *geven om...* entitle sbd.

to...; *het ~ hebben om...* have a (the) right to...,
be entitled to...; *het volste ~ hebben om...* have a
perfect right to...; *~ hebben op iets* have a right
to sth.; *op zijn ~ staan* assert oneself; *~en
studeren* read for the bar; *het ~ aan zijn zijde
hebben* have right on one's side; *zich ~ verschaffen*
right oneself; take the law into one's own
hands; *iedereen ~ laten wedervaren* do justice to
everyone; *iem. ~ laten wedervaren* do sbd. right,
give sbd. his due; ● *in zijn ~ zijn* be within
one's rights, be in the right; *iem. in ~en
aanspreken* take legal proceedings against sbd.,
have (take) the law of sbd., sue sbd. [for
damages]; *met ~* rightly, justly; *met welk ~?* by
what right?; *tot zijn ~ komen* show to full
advantage; *beter tot zijn ~ komen* show to better
advantage

recht'**aan** straight on
'**rechtbank** (-en) *v* court of justice, law-court,
tribunal; *fig* bar [of public opinion]; zie ook:
2 *gerecht*
recht'**door**, '**rechtdoor** straight on; '**recht-
draads** with the grain
'**rechte** (-n) **I** *v* straight line; **II** *o het ~* the ins
and outs [of an affair]
'**rechteloos** without rights; (v o g e l v r ij)
outlawed; '**rechtens** by right(s), in justice;
1 '**rechter** (-s) *m* judge, justice; *~ van instructie*
examining magistrate
2 '**rechter** *aj* right [hand &], right-hand [corner
&]; **–achterpoot** (-poten) *m* off hind leg;
–arm (-en) *m* right arm; **–been** (-benen) *o*
right leg
'**rechter-commissaris** (rechters-commis-
sarissen) *m* investigating magistrate; (b ij
f a i l l i s s e m e n t) registrar in bankruptcy
rechter'**hand**, '**rechterhand** (-en) *v* right
hand; *fig* right-hand man, right hand;
'**rechterkant** (-en) *m* right side
'**rechterlijk** judicial; *de ~e macht* the judiciary;
leden van de ~e macht gentlemen of the robe;
'**rechter-plaatsvervanger** (-s) *m* deputy
judge; '**rechtersambt** *o* judgeship; '**rechter-
stoel** (-en) *m* judgment seat², tribunal²
'**rechtervleugel** (-s) *m* right wing; **–voet** (-en)
m right foot; **–voorpoot** (-poten) *m* off fore
leg; **–zij(de)** *v* right side, right; *de ~* the Right
[in Parliament]
'**rechtgeaard** right-minded, upright, honest;
rechtge'lovig orthodox; **–heid** *v* orthodoxy
recht'**hebbende** (-n) *m-v* rightful claimant
'**rechtheid** *v* straightness; **–hoek** (-en) *m*
rectangle; **–hoekig, recht'hoekig** right-
angled, rectangular; *~e driehoek* right-angled
triangle; *~ op* at right angles to; '**rechthoeks-
zijde** (-n) *v* base or perpendicular; **–lijnig**
rectilinear [figure], linear [drawing]; **–maken**

(maakte '*recht*, h. '*rechtgemaakt*) *vt* straighten
(out)
recht'**matig** rightful, lawful, legitimate; **–heid**
v lawfulness, legitimacy
recht'**op** upright, erect; **F** *~ en neer* glass of
Hollands (gin); '**rechtopstaand** vertical,
upright, erect; **recht'over** just opposite
rechts I *aj* 1 right; 2 (r e c h t s h a n d i g)
right-handed; 3 of the Right [in politics];
right-wing [parties]; *de ~en, ~* the Right [in
politics]; *een ~e regering* a right-wing government; **II** *ad* to (on, at) the right; '**rechtsaf** to
the right
'**rechtsbedeling** *v* administration of justice,
judicature; **–begrip** *o* sense of justice;
–bijstand *m* legal assistance
rechts'**binnen** (-s) *m sp* inside right; **–'buiten**
(-s) *m sp* outside right
recht'**schapen** upright, honest; **–heid** *v*
honesty, rectitude
'**rechtscollege** [-kɔle.ʒə] (-s) *o* court; **–dwaling**
(-en) *v* 1 error in law; 2 [case of] miscarriage
of justice; **–dwang** *m* judicial constraint;
–filosofie *v* jurisprudence; **–gebied** (-en) *o*
jurisdiction; **–gebruik** (-en) *o* legal usage,
form of law; **–geding** (-en) *o* lawsuit;
rechts'geldig valid in law, legal; **–heid** *v*
validity, legality; '**rechtsgeleerd** *aj* juridical,
legal; *~e m* jurist, lawyer; **–heid** *v* jurisprudence; **rechtsge'lijkheid** *v* equality (of
rights); '**rechtsgevoel** *o* sense of justice;
–grond (-en) *m* legal ground
'**rechtshandig** right-handed
'**rechtsherstel** *o* rehabilitation; **–ingang** *m ~
verlenen tegen iem.* send sbd. to trial; **–kracht** *v*
legal force, force of law; **rechts'kundig** legal
[adviser, aid &], juridical; '**rechtsmacht** *v*
jurisdiction; **–middel** (-en) *o* legal remedy
'**rechtsom, rechts'om** to the right; *~! ⚔* right
turn!; *... keert! ⚔* about ... turn!; **rechtsom-
'keer(t)** *~ maken ⚔* turn about, cut back; *fig*
turn tail
'**rechtsorde** *v* legal order, legal system;
–persoon (-sonen) *m* corporate body, corporation; **rechtsper'soonlijkheid** *v* incorporation; *~ aanvragen* apply for a charter of incorporation; *~ verkrijgen* be incorporated;
'**rechtspleging** (-en) *v* administration of
justice; **–positie** [-zi.(t)si.] *v* legal status;
'**rechtspraak** *v* jurisdiction, administration of
justice; '**rechtspreken** (sprak '*recht*, h. '*recht-
gesproken*) *vi* administer justice; '**rechtsstaat**
(-staten) *m* constitutional state; **–taal** *v* legal
language
recht'**standig** perpendicular, vertical
'**rechtsterm** (-en) *m* láw-term; **–titel** (-s) *m*
(legal) title

'**rechtstreeks I** *aj* direct; **II** *ad* [send, order, buy] direct, directly
'**rechtsverdraaiing** (-en) *v* chicanery, pettifoggery; **–verkrachting** (-en) *v* violation of right; **–vervolging** (-en) *v* prosecution; *van ~ ontslaan* discharge; **–vordering** (-en) *v* action, (legal) claim; **–vorm** (-en) *m* legal form; **–vraag** (-vragen) *v* question of law; **–wege** *van ~* in justice, by right; **–wetenschap** (-pen) *v* jurisprudence; **–wezen** *o* judicature; **–winkel** (-s) *m* citizen's (legal) advice bureau; **–zaak** (-zaken) *v* lawsuit, cause; **–zaal** (-zalen) *v* court-room; **–zekerheid** *v* legal security; **–zitting** (-en) *v* session (meeting) of the court
recht'toe straight on; ~ *rechtaan* [*fig*] straightforward, outspoken; '**rechttrekken** (trok 'recht, h. 'rechtgetrokken) *vt* straighten; *fig* put right, correct; '**rechtuit, recht'uit** straight on; *fig* frankly
recht'vaardig righteous, just; **recht'vaardigen** (rechtvaardigde, h. gerechtvaardigd) *vt* justify; **recht'vaardigheid** *v* righteousness, justice; **recht'vaardiging** *v* justification, warranty; *ter ~ van...* in justification of...
'**rechtverkrijgende** (-n) *m-v* assign
'**rechtzetten** (zette 'recht, h. 'rechtgezet) *vt* 1 straighten, put straight, adjust [one's hat]; 2 *fig* correct, rectify, put right; **–ting** (-en) *v fig* correction, rectification
recht'zinnig orthodox; **–heid** *v* orthodoxy
reci'dive *v* relapse (into crime), repetition of an offence; **recidi'veren** (recidiveerde, h. gerecidiveerd) *vi* relapse; **recidi'vist** (-en) *m* recidivist, old offender
recipi'ënt (-en) *m* ✕ receiver; **recipi'ëren** (recipieerde, h. gerecipieerd) *vi* entertain, receive
recita'tief (-tieven) *o* recitative; **reci'teren** (reciteerde, h. gereciteerd) **I** *vt* recite, declaim; **II** *vi* recite
re'clame (-s) *v* 1 (in k r a n t &) advertising, publicity, advertisement; [advertisement, illuminated] sign; 2 (p r o t e s t) claim, complaint, protest; *een ~ indienen* put in a claim; *~ maken* advertise; *~ maken voor* advertise, publicize, boost, boom, puff; **–aanbieding** (-en) *v* bargain, special offer; **–artikel** (-en en -s) *o* article that is being sold cheap (as an advertisement); **–biljet** (-ten) *o* (advertising) poster; **–boodschap** (-pen) *v* RT commercial (advertisement); **–bord** (-en) *o* advertisement-board; **–bureau** [-by.ro.] (-s) *o* publicity agency; **–campagne** [-kampaɲə] *v* advertising (promotion) campaign; **–film** (-s) *m* advertising film, publicity film; **–folder** (-s) *m* handbill, throwaway, advertisement leaflet (folder); **–man** (-nen en -lieden) *m*

copywriter, adman; **–plaat** (-platen) *v* (picture) poster; **–plaatje** (-s) *o* advertising picture, show-card; **recla'meren** (reclameerde, h. gereclameerd) **I** *vi* put in a claim; complain (about *over*); **II** *vt* claim;
re'clamespot (-s) *m* RT commercial spot, commercial (advertisement); **–stunt** (-s) *m* publicity stunt; **–tekenaar** (-s) *m* commercial artist, advertising designer; **–tekst** (-en) *m* advertisement text (copy); **–televisie** [s = z] *v* commercial television; **–zuil** (-en) *v* advertising-pillar
reclas'seren (reclasseerde, h. gereclasseerd) *vt* reclaim, assist in finding employment [an offender]; **–ring** *v* after-care of discharged prisoners; *ambtenaar van de ~* probation officer
recomman'datie [-(t)si.] (-s) *v* recommendation; **recomman'deren** (recommandeerde, h. gerecommandeerd) *vt* recommend
recon'structie [-si.] (-s) *v* reconstruction; **reconstru'eren** (reconstrueerde, h. gereconstrueerd) *vt* reconstruct
reconvales'cent (-en) *m* convalescent; **reconvales'centie** [-(t)si.] *v* convalescence
recon'ventie [-(t)si.] *v eis in ~* 🐀 counterclaim
re'cord [rəˈkɔ:r] **I** (-s) *o* record; *het ~ slaan* (*verbeteren*) beat (raise) the record; **II** *aj* record [figure, number, speed], bumper [crop, harvest, season], peak [figure, year]; **–houder** (-s) *m* recordholder
recre'atie [-(t)si.] *v* recreation; **recrea'tief** recreational; **recre'atiegebied** (-en) *o* recreation area; **–zaal** (-zalen) *v* recreation hall
rec'taal rectal
rectifi'catie [-(t)si.] (-s) *v* rectification; **rectifi'ceren** (rectificeerde, h. gerectificeerd) *vt* rectify, put right
'**rector** (-'toren en -s) *m* ⌫ headmaster, principal [of a grammar school]; 2 rector [of a religious institution]; *~ magnificus* Vice-Chancellor; **recto'raat** (-raten) *o* rectorship; zie *rector*
re'çu [rəˈsy.] ('s) *o* 1 (luggage-)ticket; 2 receipt [for something received]; 3 🍂 certificate
redac'teur (-en en -s) *m* editor; **re'dactie** [-si.] (-s) *v* 1 (v. k r a n t) editorship; editorial staff, editors; 2 (v. z i n &) wording; *onder ~ van* edited by; **–bureau** [-by.ro.] (-s) *o* editorial office; **redactio'neel** editorial; **redac'trice** (-s) *v* editress
'**reddeloos I** *aj* not to be saved, past recovery, irrecoverable, irretrievable; **II** *ad* irrecoverably, irretrievably; '**redden** (redde, h. gered) **I** *vt* save, rescue, retrieve; *iem. het leven ~* save sbd.'s life; *we zijn gered!* we are safe!; *de geredde* the rescued person; *de geredden* those saved; *iem. uit de nood ~* help sbd. out of distress; *iem. ~*

van... save (rescue) sbd. from; *er was geen ~ aan* saving was out of the question; **II** *vr zich ~* save oneself; *je moet je zelf maar ~* you ought to manage for yourself; *met 50 gulden kan ik me ~* I can manage with 50 guilders, 50 guilders will do (for me); *hij weet zich wel te ~* leave him alone to shift for himself; *niet weten, hoe zich er uit te ~* how to get out of this; **-er** (-s) *m* saver, rescuer, deliverer, preserver; *de R~* the Saviour

'redderen (redderde, h. geredderd) *vt* put in order, arrange, clear, do [a room]

'redding (-en) *v* saving, rescue, deliverance; salvation²; *fig* retrieval [of situation]

'redding(s)actie [-aksi.] (-s) *v* rescue operation(s); **-boei** (-en) *v* lifebuoy; **-boot** (-boten) *m* & *v* lifeboat, rescue boat; **-brigade** (-s en -n) *v* rescue party; **-gordel** (-s) *m* lifebelt; **-lijn** (-en) *v* life-line; **-maatschappij** (-en) *v* Humane Society; Lifeboat Association; **-medaille** [-mədaljə] (-s) *v* medal for saving (human) life; **-ploeg** (-en) *v* rescue team; **-poging** (-en) *v* attempt at a rescue, rescue attempt; **-toestel** (-len) *o* life-saving apparatus; **-werk** *o* rescue work

1 'rede (-s) *v* 1 (r e d e v o e r i n g) speech, discourse; 2 (d e n k v e r m o g e n) reason, sense; *~ verstaan* listen to reason; *het ligt i n de ~* it stands to reason; *in de ~ vallen* interrupt; *n a a r ~ luisteren* listen to reason; *t o t ~ brengen* bring to reason; *v o o r ~ vatbaar* amenable to reason

2 'rede (-n) *v* ⚓ roads, roadstead; *op de ~ liggen* lie in the roads

'rededeel (-delen) *o gram* part of speech

'redekavelen (redekavelde, h. geredekaveld) *vi* argue, talk, reason; **-ling** (-en) *v* reasoning

'redekunde *v* rhetoric; **rede'kundig** zie *ontleden* en *ontleding*; **'redekunst** *v* rhetoric; **rede'kunstig** rhetorical; *~e figuur* figure of speech, trope

'redelijk *aj* 1 (m e t r e d e b e g a a f d) rational [being]; [be] reasonable; 2 (n i e t o v e r d r e v e n) reasonable, moderate [charges, prices]; 3 (t a m e l i j k) passable, **F** middling; **II** *ad* 1 reasonably, in reason; 2 (a l s g r a a d a a n d u i d i n g) moderately; passably; **-erwijs, -erwijze** reasonably, in reason; **-heid** *v* reasonableness; **'redeloos** irrational, void of reason; *~ dier* brute beast, brute; *de redeloze dieren* the brute creation; **rede'loosheid** *v* irrationality

redempto'rist (-en) *m* Redemptorist

1 'reden *v* 1 (-en en -s) reason, cause, motive, ground; 2 (-s) (v e r h o u d i n g) ratio; *~ van bestaan* reason for existence; *~ hebben om... have reason to...*; *daar had hij ~ voor* he had his

reasons; ● *i n ~ van 1 tot 5* in the ratio of one to five; *in omgekeerde (rechte) ~* in inverse (direct) ratio; *o m ~ dat...* because...; *om ~ van* by reason of, on account of; *om die ~* for that reason; *z o n d e r (enige) ~* without reason

2 'reden V.T. meerv. v. *rijden*

'redenaar (-s) *m* orator; **-stalent** (-en) *o* oratorical talent

rede'natie [-(t)si.] (-s) *v* reasoning; **rede'neertrant** *m* way of reasoning; **rede'neren** (redeneerde, h. geredeneerd) *vt* reason, argue (about *over*); discourse; **-ring** (-en) *v* reasoning

'redengevend *gram* causal

'reder (-s) *m* (ship-)owner; **rede'rij** (-en) *v* ship-owners' society, shipping company; *de ~* the shipping trade

'rederijker (-s) *m* 1 ⊞ rhetorician; 2 member of a dramatic club; **'rederijkerskamer** (-s) *v* 1 ⊞ society of rhetoricians, "rhetorical chamber"; 2 dramatic club; **-kunst** *v* rhetoric

rede'rijvlag (-gen) *v* house-flag

'redetwist (-en) *m* dispute; **'redetwisten** (redetwistte, h. geredetwist) *vi* dispute (about *over*)

'redevoeren (redevoerde, h. geredevoerd) *vi* orate, speak; **-ring** (-en) *v* oration, speech, address, harangue; *een ~ houden* make a speech

redi'geren (redigeerde, h. geredigeerd) *vt* 1 edit, conduct [a paper]; 2 draw up, redact [a note]

'redmiddel (-en) *o* remedy, expedient, resource; *als laatste ~* in the (as the) last resort

redou'bleren [re.du.'ble: rə(n)] (redoubleerde, h. geredoubleerd) *vt* & *vi* ◊ redouble

re'dres *o* redress; **redres'seren** (redresseerde, h. geredresseerd) *vt* redress, right

redu'ceren (reduceerde, h. gereduceerd) *vt* reduce; **re'ductie** [-si.] (-s) *v* reduction; **-bon** (-nen en -s) *m* money-off coupon

'redzaam handy, efficient

1 ree (reeën) *v* & *o* 🦌 roe, hind

2 ree (reeën) *v* ⚓ = 2 *rede*

'reebok (-ken) *m* 🦌 roebuck; **-bout** (-en) *m* haunch of venison; **-bruin** fawn-coloured

reed (reden) V.T. v. *rijden*

reeds already; *~ in...* as early as...; *~ de gedachte...* the mere idea...; zie verder: 2 *al*

re'ëel [re.'e.l] 1 real [value]; 2 $ sound [business]; 3 (n u c h t e r) reasonable

reef (reven) *o* ⚓ reef; *een ~ inbinden* take in a reef²

reeg (regen) V.T. v. *rijgen*

'reegeit (-en) *v* 🦌 roe; **-kalf** (-kalveren) *o* 🦌 fawn

reeks (-en) *v* 1 series, sequence [of things]; train [of consequences &]; 2 progression [in mathematics]

reel (-s) = *rail*

reep (repen) *m* rope, line, string; strip; *een ~ chocolade* a bar of chocolate; **–je** (-s) *o* sliver

'reerug (-gen) *m* saddle (loin) of venison

rees (rezen) V.T. v. *rijzen*

1 reet (reten) *v* cleft, crack, chink, crevice; **P** (a c h t e r w e r k) arse, ass; *het kan me geen ~ schelen* **P** I don't care a damn

2 reet (reten) V.T. v. *rijten*

re'factie [-si.] *v* $ allowance for damage

refec'torium (-s en -ia) *o* refectory

refe'raat (-raten) *o* report

referen'daris (-sen) *m* referendary

refe'rendum (-s en -da) *o* referendum

refe'rent (-en) *m* reviewer, critic; speaker; expert, consultant

refe'rentie [-(t)si.] (-s en -tiën) *v* (i n l i c h t i n g) reference, (p e r s o o n) referee; **–kader** (-s) *o* frame of reference; **refe'reren** (refereerde, h. gerefereerd) *vt* (b e r i c h t e n) report, tell; (v e r w ij z e n) refer; *~de aan uw schrijven* referring to your letter &

re'ferte (-s) *v* reference; *Onder ~ aan mijn schrijven van...* Referring to...

reflec'tant (-en) *m* = *gegadigde*; **reflec'teren** (reflecteerde, h. gereflecteerd) **I** *vt* (w e e r k a a t s e n) reflect; **II** *vi ~ op* consider [an application]; answer [an advertisement]; entertain [an offer, a proposal]; *er zal alleen gereflecteerd worden op...* only... will be considered; **re'flectie** [-si.] (-s) *v* reflection; **re'flector** (-s en -'toren) *m* reflector

re'flex (-en) *m* reflex; *voorwaardelijke ~* conditioned reflex; **–beweging** (-en) *v* reflex action, reflex; **refle'xief** reflexive [verb]

refor'matie [-(t)si.] (-s) *v* reformation; **reforma'torisch** reformatory, reformative

re'formhuis (-huizen) [ri.-] *o* health-food shop

re'frein (-en) *o* burden [of a song], chorus, refrain

'refter (-s) *m* refectory

re'gaal (-galen) *o* 1 rack [for books &]; 2 ♪ vox humana [of organ]; 3 (regalia) royal prerogative

re'gatta ('s) *v* regatta

re'geerakkoord (-en) *o* coalition agreement; **–der** (-s) *m* ruler; **–kunst** *v* art of governing

'regel (-s en -en) *m* 1 (l ij n) line; 2 *fig* rule; *de ~ van drieën* the rule of three; *geen ~ zonder uitzondering* no rule without exception; *nieuwe ~!* new line!; ● *in de ~* as a rule; *tegen alle ~ in, in strijd m e t de ~* against the rule(s), contrary to all rules; *zich t o t ~ stellen* make it a rule; *t u s s e n de ~s* between the lines; *v o l g e n s de ~* according to rule; *volgens de ~en der kunst* in the approved manner; **–aar** (-s) *m* regulator, control; **–afstand** (-en) *m* line space, spacing;

–baar adjustable; **'regelen** (regelde, h. geregeld) **I** *vt* 1 arrange, order, settle [things]; 2 control [the traffic]; **II** *vr zich ~ naar* be regulated (ruled) by, conform to; zie ook: *geregeld*; **–ling** (-en) *v* 1 arrangement, settlement; [pension &] scheme; order; 2 regulation, adjustment; **'regelknop** (-pen) *m* regulator, control

'regelmaat *v* regularity; **regel'matig** regular; **–heid** *v* regularity

'regelrecht straight; **'regeltje** (-s) *o* line; *schrijf me een ~* write (drop) me a line

1 'regen (-s) *m* rain; *n a ~ komt zonneschijn* sunshine follows the rain, every cloud has a silver lining; *v a n de ~ in de drop komen* fall out of the frying pan into the fire

2 'regen V.T. meerv. v. *rijgen*

'regenachtig rainy, wet; **–bak** (-ken) *m* cistern, tank; **–boog** (-bogen) *m* rainbow; **–boogvlies** (-vliezen) *o* iris; **–bui** (-en) *v* shower of rain; **–dag** (-dagen) *m* rainy day; day of rain, rain day; **–droppel** (-s), **–druppel** (-s) *m* drop of rain, raindrop; **–regenen** (regende, h. geregend) *onp. ww.* rain; *het regent dat het giet* (*baksteenen, oude wijven*) it is pouring, it is raining cats and dogs; *het regende klappen op zijn hoofd* blows rained upon his head

'regenjas (-sen) *m* & *v* raincoat, mackintosh; **–kapje** (-s) *o* rain-hood; **–kleding** *v* rainwear; **–mantel** (-s) *m* rain-cloak, waterproof; **–meter** (-s) *m* rain-gauge, pluviometer; **–pijp** (-en) *v* down-pipe; **–put** (-ten) *m* cistern; **–schade** *v* damage done by the rain; **–scherm** (-en) *o* umbrella

re'gent (-en) *m* 1 (v. o o r s t) regent; 2 (v a n i n r i c h t i n g) governor; (v. w e e s h u i s &) trustee; **regen'tes** (-sen) *v* 1 (v. o o r s t) regent; 2 (v. i n r i c h t i n g) lady governor

'regentijd (-en) *m* rainy season; **–ton** (-nen) *v* water-butt

re'gentschap (-pen) *o* regency

'regenval *m* rainfall, fall of rain; **–vlaag** (-vlagen) *v* gust of rain; **–water** *o* rain-water; **–weer** *o* rainy weather; **–wolk** (-en) *v* rain-cloud; **–worm** (-en) *m* earthworm

re'geren (regeerde, h. geregeerd) **I** *vt* reign over, rule, govern; control, manage [a horse &] **II** *vi & va* reign, rule, govern; *~ over* reign over; **re'gering** (-en) *v* reign [of Queen Victoria], rule, [the British, the Kennedy &] government; *a a n de ~ komen* come to the throne [of a king &]; come into power [of a cabinet &]; *o n d e r de ~ van* in (during) the reign of; **–loos** anarchical; **regering'loosheid** *v* anarchy; **re'geringsalmanak** (-ken) *m* Government Year-book; **–beleid** *o* (government) policy; **–besluit** (-en) *o* decree, ordinance; **–commissaris** (-sen) *m* government commissioner; **–crisis** [-zɪs] (-crises en -sen) *v* government(al) crisis; **–kringen** *mv* government circles; **–leider** (-s) *m* prime-minister, premier; **–partij** (-en) *v* party in power, governing party; **–stelsel** (-s) *o* system of government; **–troepen** *mv* government troops; **–verklaring** *v* declaration of intent of a newly formed government; **–vorm** (-en) *m* form of government; **–wege** *van* ~ from the government, officially; **–zaak** (-zaken) *v* affair of the government

re′gie [re.′ʒi.] (-s en -ieën) *v* 1 régie, state monopoly [of tobacco, salt &]; 2 stage-management [in a theatre], staging [of a play]; direction [of a film]

re′gime [re.′ʒi.m] (-s) *o* regime, régime; regimen [= diet]

regi′ment [re.ʒi.-, re.ɡi.-] (-en) *o* regiment; **–svaandel** (-s) *o* regimental colours

′regio (′s en regi′onen) *v* region; **regio′naal** regional; **regi′onen** *mv eig* regions; *in de hogere* ~ *der diplomatie* in the higher reaches of diplomacy

regis′seren [re.ʒi.-] (regisseerde, h. geregisseerd) *vt* stage [a play]; direct [a film]; **regis′seur** (-s) *m* stage-manager; [film] director

re′gister (-s) *o* 1 (b o e k & v. s t e m) register; 2 (i n d e x) index [of a book]; 3 ♪ (organ-)stop; ~ *van de burgerlijke stand* register of births, marriages and deaths; *alle* ~*s uithalen* pull out all the stops[2]; **–accountant** [-əkɔ.untənt] (-s) *m* chartered accountant; **–ton** (-nen) *v* ⚓ register ton; **regi′stratie** [-(t)si.] *v* registration; **–kantoor** (-toren) *o* registry office; **–kosten** *mv* registration fee; **regi′streren** (registreerde, h. geregistreerd) *vt* register, record

regle′ment (-en) *o* regulation(s), rules; ~ *van orde* standing orders; **reglemen′tair** [-′tɛːr] **I** *aj* regulation, prescribed; **II** *ad* according to the regulations; **reglemen′teren** (reglementeerde, h. gereglementeerd) *vt* regulate; **–ring** (-en) *v* regulation

re′gres *o* recourse; **–recht** *o* right of recourse

re′gressie (-s) *v* regression; **regres′sief** regressive

regu′lair [-′lɛːr] regular, usual, ordinary; **regulari′satie** [-′za.(t)si.] (-s) *v* regularization; **regulari′seren** (regulariseerde, h. geregulariseerd) *vt* regularize; **regula′teur** (-s) *m* 1 (u u r w e r k) regulator; 2 ⚒ (r e g e l a a r) governor, regulator; **regu′leren** (reguleerde, h. gereguleerd) *vt* regulate, adjust; **regu′lier I** *aj rk* regular [clergy]; **II** (-en) *m rk* regular [monk &]

rehabili′tatie [-(t)si.] (-s) *v* rehabilitation; **$**

discharge [of bankrupt]; **rehabili′teren** (rehabiliteerde, h. gerehabiliteerd) **I** *vt* rehabilitate; **$** discharge [a bankrupt]; **II** *vr zich* ~ rehabilitate oneself

rei (-en) *m* 1 chorus; 2 (round) dance; **–dans** (-en) *m* round dance

′reiger (-s) *m* heron

′reiken (reikte, h. gereikt) **I** *vi* reach, stretch, extend; *zover het oog reikt* as far as the eye can reach; *zover reikt mijn inkomen niet* I cannot afford it; *ik kan er niet a a n* ~ I can't reach (up to) it, it is beyond my reach; ~ *n a a r* reach (out) for; **II** *vt* reach; *de hand* ~ *aan* extend one's hand to; *iem. de (behulpzame) hand* ~ lend sbd. a helping hand; *elkaar de hand* ~ join hands; **′reikhalzen** (reikhalsde, h. gereikhalsd) *vi* ~ *naar* long for; **′reikwijdte** *v* reach [of the arm]; range [of a gun]; coverage [of a radio station]

′reilen *vi zoals het reilt en zeilt* with everything belonging thereto; lock, stock, and barrel

rein I *aj* pure, clean, chaste; *dat is je* ~*ste onzin* that is unmitigated (rank) nonsense; *in het* ~*e brengen* set right; **II** *ad* purely, cleanly, chastely

′Reinaert *m* ~ *(de Vos)* Reynard the Fox

reïncar′natie [-(t)si.] (-s) *v* reincarnation

reine-′claude [rɛ.nɔ′klo.də] (-s) *v* greengage

′reincultuur (-turen) *v* pure culture

reinheid *v* purity, cleanness, chastity; **′reinigen** (reinigde, h. gereinigd) *vt* clean, cleanse, purify; **′reiniging** *v* cleaning, cleansing, purification; **′reinigingsdienst** *m* sanitary department; **–middel** (-en) *o* detergent, cleanser

′Reintje *o* ~ *(de Vos)* Reynard the Fox

reis (reizen) *v* journey [by land or by sea, by air]; voyage [by sea, by air]; [pleasure] trip, tour [round the world]; *Gullivers reizen* Gulliver's travels; *goede* ~*!* a pleasant journey!; *een* ~ *maken* make a journey; *een* ~ *ondernemen* undertake a journey; *op* ~ on a journey, on a voyage; *op* ~ *gaan* go (away) on a journey, set out on one's journey; *op* ~ *gaan naar* be leaving for; *hij is op* ~ he is (away) on a journey; *als ik op* ~ *ben* when (I am) on a journey; **–agent** (-en) *m* travel agent; **–apotheek** (-theken) *v* portable medicine case; **–avontuur** (-turen) *o* travel adventure; **–benodigdheden** *mv* travel necessaries; **–beschrijving** (-en) *v* book of travel(s), itinerary, account of a journey (voyage); **–beurs** (-beurzen) *v* travel grant; **–biljet** (-ten) *o* ticket; **–bureau** [-by.ro.] (-s) *o* travel agency, tourist agency; **–cheque** [-ʃɛk] (-s) *m* traveller's cheque; **–deken** (-s) *v* travelling rug, *Am* lap robe; **–doel** *o* destination, goal; **reis- en ver′blijfkosten** *mv* hotel and travelling expenses; **′reisexemplaar** (-plaren) *o* dummy copy; **–geld** *o* travelling-money; fare; **–gelegenheid** (-heden) *v* means of conveyance; **–genoot** (-noten) *m* travelling-companion; **–gezelschap** (-pen) *o* party of travellers, travelling party; *mijn* ∼ my fellow-traveller(s), my travelling-companion(s); **–gids** (-en) *m* guide, guide-book; **–goed** *o* luggage, *Am* baggage; **–koffer** (-s) *m* (travelling-)trunk; **–kosten** *mv* travelling-expenses; **reiskre'dietbrief** (-brieven) *m* circular letter of credit; **'reislectuur** *v* reading matter for a journey; **–leider** (-s) *m* tour-conductor, courier; **–lust** *m* love of travel(ling); **reis'lustig** fond of travelling; **'reismakker** (-s) *m* travelling-companion; **–necessaire** [-ne.sɛsːrə] (-s) *m* dressing-case; **–pas** (-sen) *m* passport; **–plan** (-nen) *o* itinerary; travelling-plan; **–route** [-ru.tə] (-s) *v* route (of travel), itinerary; **–seizoen** *o* travelling season; **–tas** (-sen) *v* travelling-bag, holdall; **reis'vaardig** ready to set out; **'reisvereniging** (-en) *v* travel association; **–verhaal** (-halen) *o* = *reisbeschrijving*; **–wekker** (-s) *m* travel alarm; **–wieg** (-en) *v* carry-cot; **'reizen** (reisde, h. en is gereisd) *vi* travel, journey; **'reiziger** (-s) *m* traveller; (i n z i t t e n d e) passenger; **–sver-keer** *o* passenger traffic

1 rek *m* (i n e l a s t i e k) elasticity, spring; *een hele* ∼ a long distance
2 rek (-ken) *o* 1 rack; 2 (v. k l e r e n) clothes-horse; 3 (v. h a n d d o e k) towel-horse; 4 (v. k i p p e n) roost; 5 (i n g y m n a s t i e k) horizontal bar
'rekbaar elastic², extensible; **–heid** *v* elasticity², extensibility
'rekel (-s) *m* dog; *die kleine* ∼*!* the little rascal!
'rekenaar (-s) *m* reckoner, calculator, arithmetician; **–centrum** (-tra en -s) *o* computing centre; **–eenheid** (-heden) *v* unit of account; **'rekenen** (rekende, h. gerekend) **I** *vi* count, cipher, calculate, reckon, ☞ do sums; *reken maar!* you bet!; ● *we* ∼ *hier m e t guldens* we reckon by guilders here; ∼ *o p* depend upon [sbd.]; count upon [good weather]; *je kunt er vast op* ∼ you may rely (depend) on it; **II** *vt* reckon, count; charge; ● *alles b ij elkaar gerekend* all in all, all things considered; *d o o r elkaar gerekend* on an average; *we* ∼ *hen o n d e r onze vrienden* we reckon them among our friends; *wij* ∼ *het aantal o p...* we compute the number at...; *iem.* ∼ *t o t de grote schrijvers* rank sbd. among the great writers; *wat* ∼ *ze er v o o r?* what do they charge for it?; **'rekenfout** (-en) *v* mistake (error) in (the) calculation
'rekening (-en) *v* 1 (c o n c r e e t) bill, account; 2 (a b s t r a c t) calculation, reckoning, compu-

tation; ∼ *en verantwoording* [treasurer's] accounts; ∼ *en verantwoording afleggen* (*doen*) render an account [of one's deeds]; ∼ *houden met* take into account; take into consideration; *geen* ∼ *houden met* take no account of; ● *i n* ∼ *brengen* charge; *o p* ∼ *kopen* buy on credit; *op* ∼ *ontvangen* receive on account; *op nieuwe* ∼ *overbrengen* (*boeken*) carry forward (to new account); *het op* ∼ *stellen van* put it down to the account of; *fig* impute it to, ascribe it to, put it down to [negligence &]; *zet het op mijn* ∼ charge it in the bill, put it down to my account; *v o o r* ∼ *van...* for account of; *voor eigen* ∼ on one's own account; *wanneer zal hij voor eigen* ∼ *beginnen?* when is he going to set up for himself?; *voor gezamenlijke* (*halve*) ∼ on joint account; *dat is voor mijn* ∼ put that down to my account; *dat laat ik voor* ∼ *van de schrijver* I leave the author responsible for that; *dat neem ik voor mijn* ∼ 1 I'll make myself answerable for that; 2 I undertake to negotiate that, I'll account for that; **rekening-cou'rant** [-ku.'rɑnt] (reke-ningen-courant) *v* \$ account current; *in* ∼ *staan met* have a current account with; **'rekening-houder** (-s) *m* current account customer, account holder
'rekenkamer (-s) *v* Government audit office; **–kunde** *v* arithmetic; **reken'kundig** arithmetical; **'rekenlat** (-ten) *v* slide-rule; **–les** (-sen) *v* arithmetic lesson; **–liniaal** (-ialen) *v* & *o* slide-rule; **–machine** [-ma.ʃi.nə] (-s) *v* calculator, [electronic] computer; **–munt** (-en) *v* money of account; **–schap** *v* account; ∼ *geven van* render an account of, account for; *zich* ∼ *geven van* realize..., form an idea of...; *iem.* ∼ *vragen* call sbd. to account; **–schrift** (-en) *o* sum book; **–som** (-men) *v* problem (sum) in arithmetic
re'kest (-en) *o* petition; *een* ∼ *indienen* file (lodge) a petition [with sbd.]; *nul op het* ∼ *krijgen* get a denial (refusal); **rekes'trant** (-en) *m* petitioner; **rekes'treren** (rekestreerde, h. gerekestreerd) *vi* petition, file (lodge) a petition
'rekkelijk elastic, extensible; *fig* pliable, compliant; **'rekken I** (rekte, h. gerekt) *vt* 1 (v. d r a a d) draw out; 2 (v. g o e d) stretch [cloth]; 3 *fig* draw out [one's words]; spin out [a speech]; prolong [a visit]; protract [the proceedings, the time]; **II** (rekte, is gerekt) *vi* stretch [of boots &]; **III** (rekte, h. gerekt) *vr* *zich* ∼ stretch oneself; zie ook: *gerekt*; **–r** (-s) *m* stretcher
rekru'teren (rekruteerde, h. gerekruteerd) *vt* recruit [soldiers, sailors]; *nieuwe leden* ∼ *uit* draw new members from [all classes]; **–ring** *v* recruitment; **re'kruut** (-kruten) *m* recruit
'rekstok (-ken) *m* horizontal bar

'**rekverband** (-en) *o* ✠ extension bandage
re'kwest- = *rekest-*
rekwi'reren (rekwireerde, h. gerekwireerd) *vt* 1 requisition, commandeer; 2 ⚓ demand [a sentence of...]; **rekwi'siet** [s = z] (-en) *o* (stage-)property; **rekwisi'teur** (-s) *m* property-man, property-master, **F** props; **rekwi'sitie** [-(t)si.] (-s) *v* requisition; **rekwisi'toor** (-toren) = *requisitoir*
rel (-len) *m* **F** row
re'laas (-lazen) *o* account, story, tale, narrative
re'lais [rə'lɛ] *o* ✵ relay
re'latie [-(t)si.] (-s) *v* relation, connection; *goede ~s* good connections; *~s aanknopen met* enter into relations with; **rela'tief** relative, comparative; **re'latiegeschenk** (-en) *o* advertising (business) gift, give-away; **relati'veren** (relativeerde, h. gerelativeerd) *vt* moderate, modify; **relativi'teit** (-en) *v* relativity; **–stheorie** *v* theory of relativity, relativity theory
re'laxen [ri.'lɪksə(n)] (relaxte, h. gerelaxt) *vi* relax, take it easy
relay'eren [re.la.'je:rə(n)] (relayeerde, h. gerelayeerd) *vt* R relay
rele'vant relevant (to), pertinent (to), bearing ((up)on); **rele'veren** (releveerde, h. gereleveerd) *vt* call attention to, point out
reli'ëf [rəli.'ɪf] (-s) *o* relief; *en* [ã] *~* in relief, embossed; **–kaart** (-en) *v* relief map
re'liek (-en) *v* & *o* relic; **–schrijn** (-en) *o* & *m* reliquary
re'ligie (-s en -giën) *v* religion; **religi'eus I** *aj* religious; **II** *sb de religieuzen* the religious, the nuns
reli'kwie (-ieën) *v* relic; **–ënkastje** (-s) *o* reliquary
'**reling** (-en en -s) *v* ♪ rail(s)
'**relletje** (-s) *o* disturbance, riot, **F** row; **–smaker** (-s) *m* rioter, rowdy
'**relmuis** (-muizen) *v* dormouse
rem (-men) *v* brake², drag²; *fig* (i n z. p s y c h i s c h) inhibition; **F** *op de ~(men) gaan staan* jam on one's brakes; **–afstand** (-en) *m* stopping distance; **–bekrachtiging** *v* servo-assistance unit; **–blok** (-ken) *o* brake-block, drag, skid, sprag
rem'bours [rɑm'bu:rs] *o* cash on delivery; *onder ~* cash on delivery, C.O.D.
'**remcircuit** [-sɪrkɥi.] (-s) *o* braking unit
re'medie (-s) *v* & *o* remedy
reminis'centie [- 'sɛn(t)si.] (-s) *v* reminiscence, memory
re'mise [s = z] (-s) *v* 1 $ remittance; 2 *sp* draw, drawn game; 3 (k o e t s h u i s) coach-house; [engine] shed; [tramway] depot
remit'tent (-en) *m* remitter; **remit'teren** (remitteerde, h. geremitteerd) *vt* remit

'**remkabel** (-s) *m* brake cable; **–licht** (-en) *o* stop light (signal); '**remmen** (remde, h. geremd) **I** *vt* brake [a train &]; *fig* (i n z. p s y c h i s c h) inhibit; *iem. wat ~* check sbd.; *hij is niet te ~* there is no holding him; *hij is erg geremd* he is very inhibited; *hij wordt geremd door die gedachte* that thought restrains him; *de produktie ~* put a brake on production; *het remt* (= *werkt remmend op*) *de produktie* it acts as a brake on production; **II** *vi* & *va* put on the brake(s); *fig* go slow; zie ook: *geremd*; **–er** (-s) *m* brakesman; **remming** (-en) *v fig* inhibition
remon'toir [-'tʋa:r] (-s) *o* keyless watch
re'mous [-'mu(s)] *m* bumpiness; *er was veel ~* it was bumpy there, there were many air pockets
'**rempaardekracht** *v* brake horse-power, b.h.p.; **–pedaal** (-dalen) *o* & *m* brake (pedal), foot brake
rempla'çant [rɑmpla.'sɑnt] (-en) *m* substitute
'**remraket** (-ten) *v* retro-rocket; **–schijf** (-schijven) *v* brake disc; **–schoen** (-en) *m* brake-shoe, drag, skid; **–spoor** (-sporen) *o* skid mark; **–systeem** [-si.s-] (-stemen) *o* braking system; **–toestel** (-len) *o* brake(s); **–vermogen** *o* stopping power; **–voering** *v* brake lining; **–weg** (-wegen) *m* 1 braking path; 2 (l e n g t e) braking distance
1 **ren** *m* race, run, gallop, trot; *in volle ~* (at) full gallop, (at) full speed
2 **ren** (-nen) *v* chicken-run, fowl-run
renais'sance [rənɛ'sɑsə] *v* Renaissance, renascence, revival
'**renbaan** (-banen) *v* race-course, race-track; **–bode** (-n en -s) *m* courier
ren'dabel profitable, paying, remunerative; **rende'ment** (-en) *o* yield, output; ✗ efficiency, output; **ren'deren** (rendeerde, h. gerendeerd) *vi* pay (its way); **–d** paying, remunerative
rendez-'vous [rãde.'vu.] (rendez-vous) *o* rendezvous; *elkaar ~ geven* make an appointment
'**rendier** (-en) *o* reindeer; **–mos** *o* reindeer-moss
rene'gaat (-gaten) *m* renegade
re'net (-ten) *v* rennet
'**rennen** (rende, h. en is gerend) *vi* race, run, gallop; **–er** (-s) *m* racer
renom'mee *v* reputation, fame
re'nonce [rə'nõsə] *v* revoke; **renon'ceren** (renonceerde, h. gerenonceerd) *vi* revoke
reno'vatie [-(t)si.] (-s) *v* renovation; **reno'veren** (renoveerde, h. gerenoveerd) *vt* renovate
'**renpaard** (-en) *o* race-horse, runner; **–sport** *v* (horse-)racing, the turf; **–stal** (-len) *m* racing-stable
rentabili'teit *v* profitability, remunerativeness;

'**rente** (-n en -s) *v* interest; ~ *op* = at compound interest; *op* ~ *zetten* put out at interest; *van zijn ~n leven* = *rentenieren*; **–berekening** *v* calculation of interest; **–gevend** interest-bearing; **–kaart** (-en) *v* insurance card; **–loos** bearing no interest; idle [capital]; ~ *voorschot* interest-free loan; '**renten** (rentte, h. gerent) *vt* yield interest; *~de 5%* bearing interest at 5%; **rente'nier** (-s) *m* rentier, man of (independent) means, retired tradesman; **rente'nieren** (rentenierde, h. gerentenierd) *vi* live upon the interest of one's money, live on one's means; **rente'spaarbrief** (-brieven) *m* mortgage bond; '**rentestandaard** *m* rate of interest, interest rate; **–trekker** (-s) *m* (v a n o u d e r d o m s r e n t e) (retirement) pensioner; **–vergoeding** *v* interest payment; **–verlaging** *v* lowering of the rate of interest; **–verlies** *o* loss of interest; **–verschil** (-len) *o* difference in the rate of interest, interest difference; **–voet** *m* rate of interest, interest rate; **–zegel** (-s) *m* insurance stamp

'**rentmeester** (-s) *m* steward, (land) agent, bailiff; **–schap** *o* stewardship

'**renwagen** (-s) *m* racing car, racer

reorgani'satie (-'za.(t)si.] (-s) *v* reorganization; **reorgani'seren** (reorganiseerde, h. gereorganiseerd) *vt* reorganize

reo'staat (-staten) *m* rheostat

rep *alles was in ~ en roer* the whole town & was in a commotion; *in ~ en roer brengen* throw into confusion

repara'teur (-s) *m* repairer; **repa'ratie** [-(t)si.] (-s) *v* repair(s), reparation; *in ~ zijn* be under repair; **–kosten** *mv* cost of repair; **repa'reren** (repareerde, h. gerepareerd) *vt* repair, mend

repatri'ëren I (repatrieerde, is gerepatrieerd) *vi* repatriate, go (return) home; **II** (repatrieerde, h. gerepatrieerd) *vt* repatriate; **–ring** *v* repatriation

'**repel** (-s) *m* ripple; '**repelen** (repelde, h. gerepeld) *vt* ripple [flax]

reper'cussie (-s) *v* (v. g e l u i d) repercussion; (t e g e n m a a t r e g e l) retaliation; (r e a c t i e) reaction

reper'toire [-'twa:r] (-s) *o* repertoire, repertory; **–stuk** (-ken) *o* stock-piece, stock-play

reper'torium (-ia) *o* repertory

repe'teergeweer (-weren) *o* repeating rifle, repeater; **repe'tent** (-en) *m* period; **repe'teren** (repeteerde, h. gerepeteerd) *vt* repeat [a word &]; go over [lessons]; coach [sbd. for an exam]; rehearse [a play]; *~de breuk* recurring decimal; **repe'titie** [-(t)si.] (-s) *v* 1 repetition [of a word, a sound &]; 2 ☞ test-paper(s); 3 (v a n e e n s t u k &) rehearsal [of a play]; *algemene ~* full rehearsal; *generale ~*

final rehearsal [of a concert]; dress rehearsal [of a play]; **–horloge** [-ʒə] (-s) *o* repeater; **repe'titor** (-s en -'toren) *m* private tutor, coach

'**replica** ('s) *v* replica, facsimile; **repli'ceren** (repliceerde, h. gerepliceerd) *vt & vi* rejoin, reply, retort

re'pliek (-en) *v* counter-plea, rejoinder; *van ~ dienen* rejoin, retort

repor'tage [-ʒə] (-s) *v* reporting, reportage; *R T* commentary; **–wagen** (-s) *m* recording van; **re'porter** [ri.-] (-s) *m* reporter; *R T* commentator

'**reppen** (repte, h. gerept) **I** *vi* ~ *van* mention, make mention of; *er niet van ~* not breathe a word of it; **II** *vr zich* ~ bestir oneself, hurry, scurry, scutter

repre'saille [-'zajə] (-s) *v* reprisal; *~s nemen* make reprisals, retaliate (upon *tegen*); **–maatregel** (-en) *m* reprisal, retaliatory measure

represen'tant (-en) *m* representative; **represen'tatie** [-(t)si.] (-s) *v* representation, official entertainment; *~kosten* entertainment expenses, expense funds; **representa'tief** representative (of *voor*); *representatieve verplichtingen* social duties; *hij heeft een ~ voorkomen* he has an imposing appearance; **represen'teren** (representeerde, h. gerepresenteerd) **I** *vt* represent; **II** *vi* entertain

re'pressie (-s) *v* repression; **repres'sief** repressive

repri'mande (-s) *v* reprimand, rebuke [sive

re'prise [s = z] (-s) *v* 1 revival [of a play]; 2 ♪ repeat

reprodu'ceerbaar reproducible; **reprodu'ceren** (reproduceerde, h. gereproduceerd) *vt* reproduce; duplicate; **repro'duktie** [-'dʉksi.] (-s) *v* reproduction

reprogra'fie *v* duplication, multiplication, reprography

rep'tiel (-en) *o* reptile

repu'bliek (-en) *v* republic[2]; **republi'kein(s)** (-en) *m* (& *aj*) republican

repu'tatie [-(t)si.] (-s) *v* reputation, name; *een goede ~ genieten* have a good reputation; *hij heeft de ~ van... te zijn* he has a reputation for... [courage &], he is reputed to be... [brave &]

'**requiem** ['re.kʋi.ɛm] (-s) *o* requiem; **–mis** (-sen) *v* requiem mass

requisi'toir [re.kʋi.zi.'to:r] (-s en -en) *o* 🏛 requisitory

res'contre (-s) *v* $ settlement

re'search [ri.'sœ:tʃ] *m* research; **–afdeling** (-en) *v* research department; **–centrum** (-s en -tra) *o* research centre; **–team** [-ti:m] (-s) *o* research team; **–werk** *o* research work

'**reseda** ('s) *v* mignonette

reser'vaat (-vaten) *o* [Indian &] reservation, reserve [for wild animals], [bird] sanctuary

re'serve (-s) *v* $ reserve; ⚔ reserve (troops),

reserves; ~s *hebben* have reservations; *i n* ~ *hebben* (*houden*) hold in reserve, keep in store; *o n d e r* ~ *iets aannemen* accept it with some reserve; **–band** (-en) *m* spare tyre; **–deel** (-delen) *o* spare part, spare; **–fonds** (-en) *o* reserve fund; **–kapitaal** (-talen) *o* reserve capital; **–officier** (-en) *m* reserve officer; **–onderdeel** (-delen) *o* spare part, spare; **–potje** (-s) *o* reserve fund, reserves; **–rekening** (-en) *v* reserve account; **reser'veren** (reserveede, h. gereserveerd) *vt* reserve; **–ring** (-en) *v* [room, table] reservation; **re'servetroepen** *mv* reserve troops, reserves; **–wiel** (-en) *o* spare wheel; **reser'vist** (-en) *m* reservist; **reser'voir** [-'vva:r] (-s) *o* reservoir, tank, container

resi'dent (-en) *m* resident; **resi'dentie** [-(t)si.] (-s) *v* (royal) residence, court-capital; **resi'deren** (resideerde, h. geresideerd) *vi* reside

resi'du ('s en -en) *o* residue, residuum, rest, remainder

reso'lutie [-(t)si.] (-s) *v* resolution

reso'luut resolute, determined

reso'nantie [-(t)si.] (-s) *v* resonance;

reso'neren (resoneerde, h. geresoneerd) *vi* resound

resor'beren (resorbeerde, h. geresorbeerd) *vt* resorb; **re'sorptie** [-si.] *v* resorption

resp. = *respectievelijk*

res'pect *o* respect; **respec'tabel** respectable; **respec'teren** (respecteerde, h. gerespecteerd) *vt* respect

respec'tief respective, several; **respec'tievelijk** respective; or

res'pijt *o* respite, delay; **–dag** (-dagen) *m* day of grace

respon'deren (respondeerde, h. gerespondeerd) *vi* answer; **res'pons** *v* & *o* response; **respon'sorie** (-iën) *v* responsory, response

ressenti'ment *o* resentment

res'sort (-en) *o* jurisdiction, department, province; *i n het hoogste* ~ in the last resort; **ressor'teren** (ressorteerde, h. geressorteerd) *vi* ~ *onder* come within, fall under

rest (-en) *v* rest, remainder; *het laatste* ~*je* the last bit (shred); ~*jes* scraps, left-overs, pickings; **res'tant** (-en) *m* & *o* remainder, remnant

restau'rant [rɪsto:'rã] (-s) *o* restaurant; **restaura'teur** (-s) *m* 1 restaurateur, restaurant keeper; 2 restorer [of monuments &]; **restau'ratie** [-(t)si.] (-s) *v* 1 (h e r s t e l) restoration, renovation; 2 (e e t h u i s) restaurant; refreshment room [of railway station]; **–wagen** (-s) *m* restaurant car, dining-car; **restau'reren** (restaureerde, h. gerestaureerd)

vt restore, renovate

'resten (restte, h. gerest), **res'teren** (resteerde, h. geresteerd) *vi* remain, be left; *mij rest alleen...* it only remains for me to...

restitu'eren (restitueerde, h. gerestitueerd) *vt* repay: return; **resti'tutie** [-(t)si.] (-s) *v* restitution, repayment

res'torno ('s) *m* ⚓ return of premium

re'strictie [-ksi.] (-s) *v* restriction

'restwaarde *v* residual value

resul'taat [s = z] (-taten) *o* result, outcome; *geen* ~ *hebben* fail; *tot een* ~ *komen* arrive at a result; *zonder* ~ without result, to no effect; **resul'tante** (-n) *v* resultant; **resul'teren** (resulteerde, h. geresulteerd) *vi* result

resu'mé [s = z] (-s) *o* résumé, summary, abstract, précis, synopsis; ⚓ summing-up; **resu'meren** (resumeerde, h. geresumeerd) *vt* sum up, summarize

'resusaap [-züs] (-apen) *m* Rhesus monkey; **–factor** *m* Rhesus factor

'reten V.T. meerv. v. *rijten*

reti'cule [-'ky.l] (-s) *m* reticule

reti'rade (-s) *v* w.c., lavatory; **reti'reren** (retireerde, is geretireerd) *vi* retire, retreat

'retor (-s en -'toren) *m* rhetorician; **re'torica** *v* rhetoric; **reto'riek** *v* rhetoric; **re'torisch** rhetorical

re'tort (-en) *v* & *o* retort

retou'cheren [-tu.'ʃe:rə(n)] (retoucheerde, h. geretoucheerd) *vt* retouch, touch up

re'tour [-'tu:r] (-s) *o* return; *op* (*zijn* &) ~ past one's prime; **–biljet** (-ten) *o* return ticket; **–kaartje** (-s) *o* return ticket; **retour'neren** (retourneerde, h. geretourneerd) *vt* return; **re'tourtje** [-'tu:r-] (-s) *o* = *retourbiljet*; **re'tourvlucht** (-en) *v* ✈ return flight; **–vracht** (-en) *v* return freight; **–wissel** (-s) *m* $ redraft; **–zending** (-en) *v* return

re'traite [-'trɛ.tə] (-s) *v* *rk* retreat

retrospec'tief retrospective [exhibition]

reu (-en) *m* ⚲ (male) dog

reuk *m* (z i n t u i g) olfactory sense, sense of smell; (g e u r) smell, odour, scent; *de* ~ *van iets hebben* get wind of sth., smell a rat; *in een goede* (*slechte*) ~ *staan* be in good (bad) odour; *in de* ~ *van heiligheid* in the odour of sanctity; **'reukeloos** odourless; **'reukflesje** (-s) *o* smelling-bottle; **–gras** *o* ⚘ vernal grass; **–loos** = *reukeloos*; **–orgaan** (-ganen) *o* organ of smell, olfactory organ; **–verdrijvend** deodorant, deodorizing; **–water** *o* perfumed water; **–werk** (-en) *o* perfume(s); **–zenuw** (-en) *v* olfactory nerve; **–zin** *m* (sense of) smell

'reuma *o* rheumatism; **reuma'tiek** *v* rheumatism; **reu'matisch** rheumatic

reü'nie *v* reunion, rally; **–diner** [-di.ne.] (-s) *o* reunion dinner

reus (reuzen) *m* giant, colossus; **reus'achtig I** *aj* gigantic, huge, colossal; **II** *ad* gigantically; < hugely, enormously, awfully; zie ook: *reuze* & *reuzen-*; **–heid** *v* gigantic stature (size)

'**reutelen** (reutelde, h. gereuteld) *vi* rattle; *hij reutelde* there was a rattle in his throat; ~*de ademhaling* stertorous breathing; *het ~ van de dood* the death-rattle

'**reutemeteut** *m* F *de hele ~* the whole caboodle (lot)

'**reuze** super, great, smashing, topping; *het was ~!* it was awfully funny!

'**reuzel** (-s) *m* lard

'**reuzen-** ['rø.zə(n)] giant..., monster..., mammoth...; '**reuzenarbeid** *m* gigantic task; **–gestalte** (-n) *v* gigantic stature; **–kracht** *v* gigantic strength; **–letters** *mv* mammoth letters; **–rad** (-raden en -raderen) *o* Ferris wheel, giant wheel; **–schrede** (-n) *v* giant's stride; *met ~n vooruitgaan* advance with giant strides; **–slalom** (-s) *m* giant slalom; **–slang** (-en) *v* python, boa constrictor; **–strijd** *m* battle of giants, gigantomachy; **–taak** (-taken) *v*, **–werk** (-en) *o* gigantic task; **–zwaai** (-en) *m* grand circle; **reu'zin** (-nen) *v* giantess

revali'datie [-(t)si.] *v* rehabilitation; **revali'deren** (revalideerde, h. gerevalideerd) *vt* rehabilitate

revalu'atie [-(t)si.] *v* revaluation; **revalu'eren** (revalueerde, h. gerevalueerd) *vt* revalue

re'vanche [-'vãʃə] *v* revenge; ~ *nemen* have (take) one's revenge; **–partij** (-en) *v sp* return match; **revan'cheren** (revancheerde, h. gerevancheerd) *zich ~ sp* get one's revenge

re'veil [-'vɛij] *o* revival [of religious feeling]

re'veille [-'vɛijə] *v* reveille; *de ~ blazen* sound the reveille

'**reven** (reefde, h. gereefd) *vt* reef [a sail]

rever'beeroven (-s) *m* reverberatory

revé'rence [-'rãsə] (-s) *v* curtsy

re'vers [-'vɛː] *m* revers, facing, lapel

revi'deren (revideerde, h. gerevideerd) *vt* revise

revindi'catie [-(t)si.] [-(t)si.] *v* ⚖ trover; **–proces** (-sen) *o* ⚖ action of trover

revi'seren [s = z] (reviseerde, h. gereviseerd) *vt* ✗ overhaul [engines]; **re'visie** (-s) *v* 1 (in 't alg.) revision; 2 ⚖ review [of a sentence]; 3 (v. d r u k w e r k) revise; 4 ✗ overhaul(ing) [of engines]; **re'visor** (-s en -'soren) *m* reviser

revo'lutie [-(t)si.] (-s) *v* revolution; **–bouw** *m* 1 ('t b o u w e n) jerry-building; 2 ('t g e b o u w - d e) jerry-built houses; **revolutio'nair** [-(t)si.o.'nɛː r] (-en) *m & aj* revolutionary

re'volver (-s) *m* revolver; **–draaibank** (-en) *v* turret lathe, capstan lathe

re'vue [-'vy.] (-s) *v* 1 ✗ review²; 2 (o p t o - n e e l) revue; *de ~ passeren* pass in review; *de ~ laten passeren* pass in review²

'**rezen** V.T. meerv. van *rijzen*

Rho'desië *o* Rhodesia

ri'ant splendid, grand

rib (-ben) *v* 1 rib [in body, of a leaf &]; 2 edge [of a cube]; *de valse (ware)* ~*ben* the false (true) ribs

'**ribbel** (-s) *v* rib; '**ribbelen** (ribbelde, h. geribbeld) *vt* rib

'**ribbenkast** (-en) *v* F body, carcass; '**ribbestuk** (-ken) = *ribstuk*

'**ribfluweel** *o* corduroy

'**ribstuk** (-ken) *o* rib (of beef)

'**richel** (-s) *v* ledge, border, edge

'**richten** (richtte, h. gericht) **I** *vt* direct, aim, point; ✗ dress [ranks]; *zijn schreden ~ n a a r* direct (turn, bend) one's steps towards; *zijn oog ~ o p* fix one's eye upon; *aller ogen waren gericht op hem* all eyes were turned towards him; *het kanon ~ op* aim (point) the gun at; *de motie was gericht t e g e n...* the motion was directed against (aimed at)...; *een brief ~ t o t...* address a letter to...; **II** *vr zich ~ n a a r iem.* take one's cue from sbd.; *zich ~ t o t iem.* address oneself to sbd.

✎ '**richter** (-en) *m* judge; *het boek der Richteren* **B** the book of Judges; '**richtig** right, correct, exact

'**richting** (-en) *v* 1 direction, trend; 2 persuasion, creed, orientation, views, line; *in de goede* ~ in the right direction; *van onze* ~ 1 of our school of thought; 2 of our persuasion; **–aanwijzer** (-s) *m* direction indicator, traffic indicator; **–bord** (-en) *o* 1 (v. v e r k e e r) signpost; 2 (v. a u t o b u s &) destination board (sign), route plate; **–gevend** directive, guiding; **–richtlijn** (-en) *v* directive, line of action; **–prijs** (-prijzen) *m* basic (guiding) price; recommended price; **–snoer** (-en) *o* line of action

ri'cinusolie *v* castor-oil

rico'cheren [-'ʃe.rə(n)] (ricocheerde, h. gericocheerd) *vi* ricochet; **rico'chetschot** [-'ʃɛt-] (-schoten) *o* ricochet (shot); **ricochet'teren** (ricochetteerde, h. gericochetteerd) *vi* ricochet

'**ridder** (-s) *m* knight; *dolende ~* knight errant; ~ *van de droevige figuur* knight of the rueful countenance; ~ *van de Kouseband* knight of the Garter; *tot ~ slaan* dub [sbd.] a knight, knight [sbd.]; '**ridderen** (ridderde, h. geridderd) *vt* knight; (m e t o n d e r s c h e i d i n g) decorate; '**riddergoed** (-eren) *o* manor, manorial estate; **–kruis** (-en) *o* cross of an order of knighthood; '**ridderlijk I** *aj* knightly, chivalrous; **II** *ad* chivalrously; **–heid** *v* chivalrousness, chivalry; '**ridderorde** *v* 1 (-n) order of knighthood; 2 (-s) decoration; **–roman** (-s) *m*

romance (novel) of chivalry; **–schap** *v* & *o*
knighthood; **–slag** (-slagen) *m* accolade; *de ~
ontvangen* be dubbed a knight; be given the
accolade; **–spel** (-spelen) *o* tournament;
–spoor (-sporen) *v* 🌿 larkspur; **–stand** *m*
knighthood; **–tijd** *m* age of chivalry; **–verhaal**
(-halen) *o* tale of chivalry; **–wezen** *o* chivalry;
–zaal (-zalen) *v* hall (of the castle); *de* R~ the
Knights' Hall [of the Binnenhof Palace at the
Hague]
ridi′cuul ridiculous, absurd
ried (rieden) V.T. v. *raden*
riek (-en) *m* three-pronged fork
′rieken* *vi* smell; = *ruiken*
riem (-en) *m* 1 (v. l e e r) strap; 2 (o m ′t l ij f)
belt, girdle; sling [of a rifle]; 3 (v o o r h o n d)
leash, lead; 4 (r o e i r i e m) oar; 5 (p a p i e r)
ream; *de ~en binnenhalen* ⚓ ship the oars; *de ~en
strijken* ⚓ back the oars, back water; **–pje** (-s) *o*
leather thong; **–schijf** (-schijven) *v* belt pulley;
–slag (-slagen) *m* ⚓ stroke of oars
riep (riepen) V.T. van *roepen*
riet *o* 1 🌿 reed, (b a m b o e) cane; 2 🌿 (b i e s)
rush; 3 (v. d a k e n) thatch; 4 🎵 reed; **–dekker**
(-s) *m* thatcher; **–en** *aj* 1 reed [pipe]; 2
thatched [roof]; 3 cane [chair, furniture,
trunk], wicker [basket]; **–fluit** (-en) *v* reed
pipe, reed; **–je** (-s) *o* 1 (s t o k) cane; 2 (o m
t e d r i n k e n) (drinking) straw; **–mat** (-ten) *v*
reed mat, rush mat; **–suiker** (-s) *o* cane-sugar;
–tuin (-en) *m* cane-field; **–veld** (-en) *o* 1
reed-land; 2 (v. s u i k e r r i e t) cane-field;
–voorn, –voren (-s) *m* rudd; **–zanger** (-s) *m*
reed-warbler
1 rif (-fen) *o* 1 (r o t s) reef, skerry; 2
(g e r a a m t e) carcass, skeleton
2 rif (reven) *o* ⚓ (v. z e i l) = *reef*
rigou′reus [-ɡu-] rigorous, severe
rij (-en) *v* row, range, series, file, line, queue [of
shoppers, visitors &]; *a a n ~en* in rows; *i n de
~ staan* queue, be (stand) in the queue; *in de ~
gaan staan* queue up; *m e t éé n ~ (twee ~en) knopen*
single-(double-)breasted [coat]; *o p e e n ~* in a
row
′rijbaan (-banen) *v* 1 (v o o r v o e r t u i g e n)
carriage-way; (a l s s t r o o k v a n d e
r ij b a a n) lane; 2 (v o o r s c h a a t s e n r ij-
d e r s) skating-rink; **–bevoegdheid** *v* driving
licence; **–bewijs** (-wijzen) *o* (driving) licence;
–broek (-en) *v* riding-breeches; **′rijden*** I *vi*
ride [on horseback, on a bicycle]; drive [in a
carriage, in a car]; travel [at 50 miles an hour,
of a car &]; *een ~de auto* a moving car; *een ~de
tentoonstelling* a mobile exhibition; *een ~de trein* a
running train; *St.-Nicolaas heeft goed gereden* St.
Nicholas has brought lots of presents; *(te) hard
~ 🚗 speed; *gaan ~* go (out) for a ride (for a

drive); 2 go by carriage (by car &); *ik zal zelf
wel ~* I'm going to drive myself; ● *d o o r rood
(licht) ~, door het stoplicht ~* jump the lights; *o p
een paard ~* ride a horse, ride on horseback; *hoe
lang rijdt de trein er o v e r?* how long does it take
the train?; **II** *vt* drive [sbd. to a place]; wheel
[sbd. in a chair, a child in a perambulator]; *een
paard kapot ~* override a horse, ride a horse to
death; **III** *va ′m ~* (b a n g zij n) have the wind
up; **–er** (-s) *m* 1 rider, horseman; 2 skater;
′rijdier (-en) *o* riding-animal, mount; **–draad**
(-draden) *m* ⚡ (overhead) contact-wire
′rijen (rijde, h. gerijd) *zich ~* form a row, line
up, follow
′rijexamen (-s) *o* driving-test
′rijgdraad (-draden) *m* tacking-thread, basting-
thread; **′rijgen*** *vt* lace [shoes, stays]; string
[beads], thread [on a string]; tack [with pins];
baste [a garment]; file [papers]; *hem aan de degen
~* run him through with one's sword; **′rijg-
garen** *o* tacking thread; **–laars** (-laarzen) *v*
lace-up boot; **–naald** (-en), **–pen** (-nen) *v*
bodkin; **–schoen** (-en) *m* laced shoe; **–snoer**
(-en) *o* (shoe) lace; **–steek** (-steken) *m* tack
′rijhandschoenen *mv* riding-gloves, **–instruc-
teur** (-s) *m* driving-instructor
1 rijk I *aj* rich², wealthy [people], affluent
[countries], copious [meals]; *hij is geen cent ~* he
is not worth a red cent; *~ aan* rich in [gold &];
~ maken enrich; *de ~en* the rich; **II** *ad* richly
2 rijk (-en) *o* empire², kingdom², realm², *het
Rijk* (d e S t a a t) the State; *het ~ der verbeelding*
the realm of fancy; *zijn ~ is uit* his reign is at
an end; *we hebben nu het ~ alleen* we have it (the
place) all to ourselves now
′rijkaard (-s) *m* rich man; **′rijkdom** (-men) *m* 1
riches, wealth²; 2 *fig* abundance, copiousness,
richness; *natuurlijke ~men* natural resources [of
a country]; **′rijke** (-n) *v* zie 1 *rijk* I; **′rijkelijk**
I *aj* zie 1 *rijk* I; **II** *ad* richly, copiously, amply,
abundantly; *< rather [late &]; ~ voorzien van...*
abundantly provided with...; *rijke′lui* *mv* rich
people, rich folks; **′rijkheid** *v* richness
′rijkleding *v* riding clothes; **–knecht** (-s en
-en) *m* groom; **–kostuum** (-s) *o* riding-suit,
riding-dress
′rijksadel *m* nobility of the Empire; **–adelaar**
(-s) *m* imperial eagle; **–advocaat** (-caten) *m* ±
counsel for the Government; **–ambtenaar,
rijks′ambtenaar** (-s en -naren) *m* government official, civil servant; **′rijksappel** (-s) *m*
orb, globe; **–archief, rijksar′chief** (-chieven)
o Public Record Office, State Archives; **′rijks-
archivaris** (-sen) *m* Master of the Rolls;
–betrekking (-en) *v* government office;
rijks′daalder (-s) *m* "rijksdaalder", two and a
half guilder piece; **′rijksdag** (-dagen) *m* diet;

ⵀ Reichstag [in Germany]; **–deel** (-delen) *o* ±
dominion, [overseas] territory, e.g. the Netherlands Antilles; **–gebied** (-en) *o* territory (of
the empire); **–genoot** (-noten) *m* inhabitant of
Dutch overseas territory; **–gezag** *o* 1 imperial
authority; 2 sovereignty; **–grens** (-grenzen) *v*
frontier (of the empire); **–instelling** (-en) *v*
government institution; **–kanselier** (-s) *m*
Chancellor of the Empire; **–merk** (-en) *o*
government stamp; **–munt, rijks'munt** (-en)
v coin of the realm; *de Rijksmunt* the Mint;
rijks'opvoedingsgesticht (-en) *o* approved
school; **'rijkssubsidie** (-s) *v* & *o* government
grant, state aid; **–wapen** (-s) *o* Ⓩ government
arms; **–weg** (-wegen) *m* national highway;
–wege *van* ~ by the government, govern-
ment(al)

'rijkunst *v* horsemanship; **–laars** (-laarzen) *v*
riding-boot; **–les** (-sen) *v* 1 riding-lesson; 2
(a u t o~) driving-lesson

1 rijm *m* hoar-frost, ⊙ rime

2 rijm (-en) *o* rhyme [in verse]; *slepend (staand)* ~
feminine (masculine) rhyme; *op* ~ in rhyme; *op*
~ *brengen* put into rhyme; **–elaar** (-s) *m* paltry
rhymer, poetaster; **rijmela'rij** (-en) *v*
doggerel; **'rijmelen** (rijmelde, h. gerijmeld) *vt*
write doggerel; **'rijmen** (rijmde, h. gerijmd) *vi*
rhyme; ~ *met (op)* rhyme with, rhyme to; *deze*
woorden ~ *niet met elkaar* these words do not
rhyme; *dat rijmt niet met wat u anders altijd zegt*
that does not tally with what you are always
saying; **II** *vt* rhyme; *hoe is dat te* ~ *met...?* how
can you reconcile that with...?; **–er** (-s) *m*
rhymer, rhymester; zie ook: *rijmelaar*; **'rijm-**
klank (-en) *m* rhyme; **–kunst** *v* art of
rhyming; **–loos** rhymeless, blank; **–pje** (-s) *o*
short rhyme; **–prent** (-en) *v* poster with a
poem on it; **–woord** (-en) *v* rhyme, rhyming
word

Rijn *m* Rhine; **'rijnaak** (-aken) *m* & *v* ⚓ Rhine
barge; **'Rijnland** *o* Rhineland; **–s** Rhineland;
Rijns Rhenish; **'rijnsteen** (-stenen) *m* rhine-
stone; **'Rijnvaart** *v de* ~ navigation on the
Rhine; **'rijnwijn** *m* Rhine-wine, hock

rij-'op-rij-af roll-on roll-off

1 rijp *m* hoar-frost, ⊙ rime

2 rijp *aj* ripe, mature; *na* ~ *beraad (overleg)* after
careful deliberation (reflexion); *de tijd is er nog*
niet ~ *voor* the time is not yet ripe for it; ~
maken, ~ *worden* ripen, mature; *vroeg* ~ *vroeg rot*
soon ripe, soon rotten

'rijpaard (-en) *o* riding-horse, mount

'rijpelijk *iets* ~ *overwegen* consider sth. fully;

1 'rijpen (rijpte, *vt* h., *vi* is gerijpt) *vi* & *vt*
ripen², mature²

2 'rijpen (rijpte, h. gerijpt) *vi het heeft vannacht*
gerijpt there was a hoar-frost last night

'rijpheid *v* ripeness, maturity; **'rijpwording** *v*
ripening, maturation

rijs (rijzen) *o* twig, sprig, osier; **–bezem** (-s) *m*
birch-broom

'rijschool (-scholen) *v* 1 riding-school; 2
(a u t o~) driving-school, school of motoring

'rijshout *o* osiers, twigs, sprigs

'rijsnelheid *v* driving (running) speed

'Rijssel *o* Lille

rijst *m* rice; **–bouw** *m* cultivation of rice,
rice-growing; **'rijstebloem** *v*, **–meel** *o* rice
flour; **rijste'brij** *m*, **'rijstepap** *v* rice-milk;
rijste'brijberg *m zich door een* ~ *heen eten [fig]*
plough one's way through [a mound of
papers]; **'rijstkorrel** (-s) *m* grain of rice,
rice-grain; **–land** (-en) *o* rice-plantation,
rice-field; **–oogst** *m* rice-crop; **–papier** *o*
rice-paper; **rijstpelle'rij** (-en) *v* rice-mill

'rijstrook (-stroken) *v* (traffic) lane, carriage
way

'rijsttafel (-s) *v* Indonesian "rice-table", ± tiffin;
'rijsttafelen (rijsttafelde, h. gerijsttafeld) *vi* ±
take tiffin; **'rijstveld** (-en) *o* rice-field, paddy-
field; **–vogel** (-s) *m* rice-bird; **–water** *o* rice-
water

'rijswerk (-en) *o* banks of osier and earth

'rijten* *vt* tear

'rijtest (-s) *m* driving test; **–tijd** (-en) *m*
(running)time; mileage; **–en** (v. c h a u f f e u r)
drivers' hours; **–toer** (-en) *m* drive, ride; *een* ~
doen take a drive (a ride), go for a drive (a ride)

'rijtuig (-en) *o* carriage; *een* ~ *met vier (zes)*
paarden a coach-and-four (six); *een* ~ *nemen* take
a cab; **–fabriek** (-en) *v* coach-builder's workshop; **–maker** (-s) *m* coach-builder;
–verhuurder (-s) *m* livery-stable keeper

rij'vaardigheid *v* driving ability, efficient
driving; **–sbewijs** (-wijzen) *o* driving license;
'rijverkeer *o* vehicular traffic; **rij'waardig-**
heid *v* roadworthiness; **'rijweg** (-wegen) *m*
carriage-way, road-way

'rijwiel (-en) *o* bicycle, cycle, **F** bike;
–hersteller (-s) *m* cycle repairer; **–pad**
(-paden) *o* cycle-track; **–stalling** (-en) *v* bicycle
shed (shelter), store)

'rijzen* *vi* 1 (v. p e r s o n e n &, d e z o n, h e t
w a t e r &) rise; 2 (v. d e e g, b a r o m e t e r &)
rise; 3 (v. p r ij z e n) rise, go up; 4 (v. m o e i -
l ij k h e d e n &) arise; ~ *en dalen* rise and fall

'rijzig tall

'rijzweep (-zwepen) *v* horsewhip, riding-whip

'rik(ke)kikken (rik(ke)kikte, h. gerik(ke)kikt) *vt*
croak [like a frog]

'rikketik *van* ~ pit-a-pat; *in zijn* ~ *zitten* have
one's heart in one's mouth

riks (-en) *m* **F** = *rijksdaalder*

'riksja ('s) *m* rickshaw, jinricksha

'**rillen** (rilde, h. gerild) *vt* shiver [with], shudder [at]; *ik ril ervan, het doet me ~* it gives me the shudders; '**rillerig** shivery; '**rilling** (-en) *v* shiver, shudder

'**rimboe** (-s) *v* jungle; bush; *we zitten in de ~ hier* [*fig*] we're off the map here

'**rimpel** (-s) *m* wrinkle [of the skin], (d i e p) furrow; ruffle [of water]; '**rimpelen** (rimpelde, *vt* h., *vi* is gerimpeld) *vi* & *vt* wrinkle [the skin]; ruffle [water, the brow]; pucker [a material, the brow, a seam]; *het voorhoofd ~* ook: knit one's brow; –**lig** wrinkled, wrinkly; **+ling** (-en) *v* ripple, ruffle [especially of water]; wrinkling, puckering

'**rimram** *m* balderdash, F rubbish

ring (-en) *m* ring; –**baard** (-en) *m* fringe (of whisker); –**band** (-en) *m* ring binder; –**dijk** (-en) *m* ring-dike, circular embankment; –**(el)duif** (-duiven) *v* ring-dove; –**elmus** (-sen) *v* tree-sparrow

'**ringeloren** (ringeloorde, h. geringeloord) *vt* bully, order about

'**ringelrups** (-en) *v* = *ringrups*; '**ringen** (ringde, h. geringd) *vt* 1 ring [a pig, migratory birds]; 2 girdle [a tree]; '**ringetje** (-s) *o* little ring; *je kan hem wel door een ~ halen* he looks as if he came out of a bandbox; '**ringlijn** (-en) *v* circular railway (line); –**mus** (-sen) *v* tree-sparrow; –**muur** (-muren) *m* ring-wall, circular wall; –**rijden** *vi* tilt at the ring; –**rups** (-en) *v* ring-streaked caterpillar; –**slang** (-en) *v* ring-snake, grass-snake; –**steken** *vi* tilt at the ring; –**vaart** (-en) *v* circular canal; –**vinger** (-s) *m* ring-finger; –**vormig** ring-shaped, annular; –**weg** (-wegen) *m* ringroad; –**werpen** *o* quoits; –**worm** (-en) *m* 1 ringworm; 2 annelid

'**rinkelbel** (-len) *v* 1 (globular) bell; 2 (r a m - m e l a a r) rattle, coral; –**bom** (-men) *v* tambourine; '**rinkelen** (rinkelde, h. gerinkeld) *vi* jingle, tinkle, chink; *~ met* jingle [one's money]; rattle [one's sabre]; **rin'kinken** (rinkinkte, h. gerinkinkt) *vi* tinkle, jingle

ri'noceros (-sen) *m* rhinoceros

rins sourish

ri'olenstelsel (-s) = *rioolstelsel*; **rio'leren** (rioleerde, h. gerioleerd) *vt* sewer; –**ring** (-en) *v* sewerage; **ri'ool** (riolen) *o* & *v* sewer, drain; –**buis** (-buizen) *v* sewer-pipe; –**journalistiek** [-ʒu.r-] *v* gutter press journalism; –**stelsel** (-s) *o* sewerage; –**water** *o* sewage; –**werker** (-s) *m* sewerman

ripos'teren (riposteerde, h. geriposteerd) *vi* riposte[2]

rips *o* rep; –**fluweel** *o* corduroy

ris (-sen) = *rist*

ri'see [s = z] *v* laughing-stock

'**risico** [s = z] ('s) *o* & *m* risk, hazard; *~ lopen* run risks; *eigen ~bedrag* franchise; *op uw ~* at your risk; *op ~ van* at the risk of; **ris'kant** risky, hazardous; **ris'keren** (riskeerde, h. geriskeerd) *vt* risk, hazard

'**rissen** (riste, h. gerist) *vt* = *risten*; **rist** (-en) *v* bunch [of berries]; rope, string [of onions]; *fig* string; '**risten** (ristte, h. gerist) *vt* string [onions]

'**rister** (-s) *o* mouldboard [of a plough]

1 **rit** (-ten) *m* ride, drive; run

2 **rit** *o* (v. k i k k e r s) frog-spawn

'**rite** (-s en -n) *v* rite

'**ritje** (-s) *o* ride, drive; run; *een ~ maken* take a ride (a drive), go for a ride (a drive)

'**ritme** (-n) *o* rhythm

rit'meester (-s) *m* cavalry captain

rit'miek *v* rhythmics; '**ritmisch** rhythmic(al); *~e gymnastiek* callisthenics

rits (-en) *v* = *ritssluiting*

'**ritselen** (ritselde, h. geritseld) **I** *vi* rustle; *~ van de fouten* teem with mistakes; **II** *vt* **S** (v o o r e l k a a r k r ij g e n) fix; –**ling** (-en) *v* rustle, rustling

'**ritsig** ruttish; in (on, at) heat

rits'sluiting (-en) *v* zip (fastening, fastener)

ritu'aal (-ualen) *o* ritual; **ritu'eel I** *aj* (& *ad*) ritual(ly); **II** (-uelen) *o* ritual; '**ritus** (-sen en riten) *m* rites

ri'vaal (-valen) *m* rival; **rivali'seren** [s = z] (rivaliseerde, h. gerivaliseerd) *vi* rival; **rivali'teit** *v* rivalry

ri'vier (-en) *v* river; *aan de ~* on the river; *de ~ op (af) varen* go up (down) the river; –**arm** (-en) *m* branch of a river; –**bedding** (-en) *v* river-bed; –**klei** *v* river-clay; –**kreeft** (-en) *m* & *v* crayfish; –**mond** (-en) *m* river-mouth; *grote ~* estuary; –**oever** (-s) *m* riverside, bank; –**schip** (-schepen) *o* river-vessel; *mv* ook: river-craft; –**vis** (-sen) *m* river-fish; –**water** *o* river-water

r.k., R.K. = *rooms-katholiek*

'**roastbeef** = *rosbief*

rob (-ben) *m* 🦭 seal

'**robbedoes** (-doezen) *m-v* romping boy (girl), (v. m e i s j e) hoyden, tomboy

'**robbejacht** *v* seal-hunting, sealing

'**robber** (-s) *m* rubber [at whist, bridge]

'**robbetraan** *m* seal-oil; –**vel** (-len) *o* sealskin

'**robe** ['rɔ:bə] (-s) *v* robe, gown

'**Robert** *m* Robert, F Bob

ro'bijn (-en) *m* & *o* ruby; –**en** *aj* ruby

'**robot** (-s) *m* robot

ro'buust robust

'**rochel** (-s) *m* phlegm

'**rochelen** (rochelde, h. gerocheld) *vi* 1 expectorate; 2 = *reutelen*

roco'co *o* rococo

'**roddel** (-s) *m* (piece of) gossip; **–aar** (-s) *m* talker, gossip; '**roddelen** (roddelde, h. geroddeld) *vi* talk, gossip

'**rode** (-n) *m* 1 (s c h e l d w o o r d) ginger; 2 red [= socialist]; **rode'hond** *m* 🐕 (E u r o p e s e) German measles; **–'kool** (-kolen) *v* red cabbage; **Rode 'Kruis** *o* [International] Red Cross

'**rodelbaan** (-banen) *v* toboggan slide; '**rodelen** (rodelde, h. gerodeld) *vi* toboggan

rodo'**dendron** (-s) *m* 🌿 rhododendron

roe (-s) *v* = *roede*

'**roebel** (-s) *m* rouble

'**roede** (-n) *v* 1 rod; 2 wand [of a conjurer]; 3 birch [for flogging]; 4 verge [as emblem of office]; 5 (l e n g t e m a a t) decametre; *met de ~ krijgen* be birched; *wie de ~ spaart, bederft zijn kind* spare the rod and spoil the child

'**roedel** (-s) *o* herd [of deer]

'**roedeloper** (-s) *m* dowser, water-diviner

roef (roeven) *v* ⚓ deck-house; cuddy [of a barge]

roef, 'roef helter-skelter, hurry-scurry

'**roeibaan** (-banen) *v* rowing course; **–bank** (-en) *v* thwart, bench; **–boot** (-boten) *m* & *v* rowing-boat, row-boat; **–dol** (-len) *m* thole (-pin); '**roeien** (roeide, h. en is geroeid) *vi* & *vt* 1 ⚓ row, pull; 2 (p e i l e n) gauge; *men moet ~ met de riemen die men heeft* one must cut one's coat according to one's cloth; **–er** (-s) *m* 1 ⚓ oarsman, rower; (g e h u u r d e ~) boatman; 2 (p e i l e r) gauger; '**roeiklamp** (-en) *m* & *v* rowlock; **–pen** (-nen) *v* thole(-pin); **–riem** (-en) *m*, **–spaan** (-spanen) *v* oar, scull; **–sport** *v* rowing, boating; **–stok** (-ken) *m* gauging-rod; **–tochtje** (-s) *o* row; *een ~ gaan maken* go for a row; **–vereniging** (-en) *v* rowing-club; **–wedstrijd** (-en) *m* rowing-match, boat-race

roek (-en) *m* 🐦 rook

'**roekeloos** rash, reckless; **roeke'loosheid** (-heden) *v* rashness, recklessness

roe'**koeën** (roekoede, h. geroekoed) *vi* coo

roem *m* glory, renown, fame; *~ behalen* reap glory; *eigen ~ stinkt* self-praise is no recommendation

Roe'meen (-menen) *m* Rumanian, Roumanian; **–s** *aj* Rumanian, Roumanian

'**roemen** (roemde, h. geroemd) **I** *vt* praise; **II** *vi* boast; *~ op iets* boast of sth.; *onze stad kan ~ op...* our town can boast...

Roe'menië *o* Rumania, Roumania

'**roemer** (-s) *m* (g l a s) rummer

'**roemloos** inglorious; '**roemrijk, roem'rucht(ig),** '**roemvol** illustrious, famous, famed, glorious, renowned; '**roemzucht** *v* vainglory; **roem'zuchtig** vainglorious

roep (-en) *m* call, cry; (n a a m) repute; **–bereik** *o binnen ~* within call, within cooee; '**roepen*** **I** *vi* call, cry; shout; *~ o m* cry (call) for [help, somebody]; *iedereen roept er o v e r* everybody is praising it; *het is nu niet om er (zo) over te ~* it is no better than it should be; **II** *vt* call; *een dokter ~* call in (send for) a doctor; *wie heeft mij laten ~?* who has sent for me?; *u komt als geroepen* you come as if you had been sent for; *ik voel me niet geroepen om...* I don't feel called upon to...; *velen zijn geroepen, maar weinigen uitverkoren* **B** many are called, but few are chosen; **–de** *m de stem des ~n in de woestijn* the voice of one crying in the wilderness; '**roeper** (-s) *m* 1 (p e rs o o n) crier; 2 (v o o r w e r p) speaking-trumpet; megaphone; '**roeping** (-en) *v* call, calling, vocation; *hij heeft zijn ~ gemist* he has mistaken his vocation; *ik voel er geen ~ toe om...* I don't feel called upon to...; *~ voelen voor* feel a vocation for [...teaching &]; *zijn ~ volgen* follow one's vocation; *een toneelspeler uit ~* an actor by vocation; '**roepnaam** (-namen) *m zijn ~ is Jack* they call him Jack; **–stem** (-men) *v* call, voice

roer (-en en -s) *o* 1 ⚓ (b l a d) rudder, (s t o k) helm, (r a d) wheel; 2 (v. p ij p) stem; 3 🔫 (g e w e e r) firelock; *het ~ omleggen* ⚓ shift the helm; *het ~ recht houden* manage things well; *hou je ~ recht* keep straight, steady!; *aan het ~ komen* take the reins (of government); *aan het ~ staan* be at the helm[2]

'**roerdomp** (-en) *m* bittern

'**roereieren** *mv* scrambled eggs; '**roeren** (roerde, h. geroerd) **I** *vi* stir; (r a k e n a a n) touch; **II** *vt* stir [one's tea &], *fig* stir, touch [the heart]; move [sbd. to tears]; *zijn mondje ~* be talking away; *de trom ~* beat the drum; **III** *vr* *zich ~* stir, move; *hij kan zich goed ~* he is well off; **–d** moving, touching [words &]

'**roerganger** (-s) *m* helmsman, man at the helm, man at the wheel

'**roerig** 1 active, stirring, lively; 2 unruly; > turbulent; **–heid** *v* activity, liveliness [of a person]; > unrest [among the population]; '**roering** (-en) *v* (b e w e g i n g) motion, stir; 1 '**roerloos** motionless; *fig* impassive

2 '**roerloos** ⚓ rudderless

'**roerpen** (-nen) *v* tiller, helm

'**roersel** (-en en -s) *o* motive; *de ~en des harten* ☉ the stirrings of the heart

'**roerspaan** (-spanen) *v* stirrer; spatula

'**roervink** (-en) *m* & *v* 1 🐦 decoy-bird; 2 *fig* ringleader

1 **roes** (roezen) *m* drunken fit, intoxication[2]; *fig* ecstasy, frenzy; *~ der vrijheid* intoxication of liberty; *hij is in een ~* he is intoxicated; *in de eerste ~* in a fit [of enthusiasm], in an ecstasy

[of delight]; *zijn ~ uitslapen* sleep oneself sober, sleep it off

2 roes *m in (bij) de ~* in the lump

1 roest (-en) *m & o* perch, roost [of birds]

2 roest *m & o* rust; *~ in het koren* rust, blight, smut; *oud ~* zie *oudroest*; **–bruin** rust-brown, russet

1 'roesten (roestte, h. geroest) *vi* perch, roost [of birds]

2 'roesten (roestte, is geroest) *vi* rust; **'roestig** rusty; **–heid** *v* rustiness; **'roestkleurig** rust-coloured; **–vlek** (-ken) *v* rust-stain; (i n w a s g o e d) iron-mould; **–vorming** (-en) *v* corrosion, rust formation; **–vrij** rust-proof, stainless [steel]; **–werend** rust-resistant, anti-corrosive

roet *o* soot; *~ in het eten gooien* spoil the game; **–achtig** sooty; **–deeltjes** *mv* particles of soot; **–ig** sooty; **–kleur** *v* sooty colour; **–kleurig** of a sooty colour

'roetsjbaan (-banen) *v* slide, chute

'roetvlek (-ken) *v* smut; **–zwart** sooty black

'roezemoezen (roezemoesde, h. geroezemoesd) *vi* bustle, buzz, hum; **'roez(emoez)ig** noisy; *~e stemmen* the hum of many voices

'roffel (-s) *m* ✕ roll [of drums]; **'roffelen** (roffelde, h. geroffeld) *v* roll [the drum]; **'roffelvuur** *o* ✕ drum-fire

rog (-gen) *m* 🐟 ray, thornback

'rogge *v* 🌾 rye; **–brood** (-broden) *o* rye-bread, black bread; **–meel** *o* rye-flour; **–veld** (-en) *o* rye-field

rok (-ken) *m* (o n d e r r o k) underskirt; skirt; petticoat; (h e r e n) tail-coat, dress-coat; *in ~* in (white tie and) tails

ro'kade (-s) *v* castling [in chess]

'rokbroek (-en) *v* divided skirt, culottes

1 'roken (rookte, h. gerookt) **I** *vi* smoke; **II** *vt* 1 smoke [tobacco]; 2 smoke [ham &]

2 'roken V.T. meerv. van *rieken* en *ruiken*

'roker (-s) *m* smoker

ro'keren (rokeerde, h. gerokeerd) *vi* castle [in chess]

'rokerig smoky; **roke'rij** (-en) *v* smoke house; **'rokertje** (-s) *o* F smoke

'rokkostuum (-s) *o* dress-coat, white tie and tails; **–overhemd** (-en) *o* boiled shirt

1 rol (-len) *v* 1 (i n h e t a l g.) roll; 2 ✗ roller, cylinder; 3 (v. d e e g) rolling-pin; 4 (v a n t o n e e l s p e l e r) part, role, rôle, character; 5 ⚖ calendar, (cause-)list; *~ papier of perkament* scroll; *de ~len van de Dode Zee* the Dead Sea Scrolls; *de ~len zijn omgekeerd* the tables are turned; *een ~ spelen* act (play) a part; *een voorname (grote) ~ spelen* play an important part; *de ~len verdelen* assign the parts; ● *i n zijn ~ blijven* follow out the character; *o p de ~ staan* ⚖

appear in the calendar for trial; *u i t de ~ vallen* act out of character

2 rol *m aan de ~ gaan* (*zijn*) be on the spree, be on the loose, go on a pub-crawl

'rolberoerte F *v* fit; *een ~ krijgen* have a fit; **–blind** (-en) *o = rolluik*; **–dak** (-daken) *o* sliding-roof; **–film** (-s) *m* roll film; **–gordijn** (-en) *o* roller-blind; **–handdoek** (-en) *m* roller-towel; **–jaloezie** [-ʒa.lu.zi.] (-ieën) *v* rolling-shutter; **–kraag** (-kragen) *m* roll collar, polo neck, turtle-neck; **rol'lade** (-s en -n) *v* collared beef, rolled roast, collar of brawn &; **–lager** (-s) *o* roller-bearing; **'rollebollen** (rollebolde, h. gerollebold) *vi* roll head over heals, turn summersaults; **'rollen I** (rolde, h. en is gerold) *vi* roll; (v a l l e n) tumble; *~d materieel* rolling stock; *~ m e t de ogen* roll one's eyes; *v a n de trappen ~* tumble down the stairs; **II** (rolde, h. gerold) *vt* roll [paper &]; pick [a man's pockets]; **'rollenspel** *o* sociodrama; **'rolletje** (-s) *o* 1 (l o s) (small) roll [of paper, of sovereigns, tobacco &], wad [of bank-notes]; 2 (o n d e r i e t s) roller [of roller-skate]; castor, caster [of leg of a chair]; *het ging als op ~s* it all went on wheels, without a hitch; **'rolluik** (-en) *o* rolling-shutter; **–mops** *m* collared herring; **–pens** (-en) *v* minced beef in tripe; **–prent** (-en) *v* [cinema] film; **–roer** (-en) *o* ✈ aileron; **–schaats** (-en) *v* roller-skate; **–schaatsbaan** (-banen) *o = rolschaatsenbaan*; **–schaatsen** *o* roller-skating; **–schaatsenbaan** (-banen) *v* (roller-)skating rink; **–split** *o* loose chippings *mv*; **–stoel** (-en) *m* wheelchair, Bath chair; **–tabak** *m* twist (tobacco); **–trap** (-pen) *m* escalator, moving staircase; **–vast** letter-perfect [of an actor]; **–veger** (-s) *m* carpet-sweeper; **–verdeling** (-en) *v* cast [of a play]; casting; **–wagen** (-s) *m* truck

Ro'maans 1 Romance [languages, philology], Romanic; 2 Romanesque [architecture, sculpture]

ro'man (-s) *m* 1 novel; 2 *fig* & 📖 romance [of the Rose]; *een ~netje, o > a* novelette; *~s ook:* fiction; **ro'mance** [-'mɑsə] (-s en -n) *v* romance; **romanci'er** [-mɑsi.'e.] (-s) *m* novelist; **romanci'ère** [-mɑsi.'ɛːrə] (-s) *v* (lady, woman) novelist; **ro'mancyclus** [-si.klʉs] (-cli en -sen) *m* cycle of novels, saga, roman-fleuve; **roma'nesk** *aj* (& *ad*) romantic(ally); **ro'manheld** (-en) *m* book hero, novel hero

romani'seren [s = z] (romaniseerde, h. geromaniseerd) *vt* romanize; **roma'nist** (-en) *m* Romanist, Romanicist; **romanis'tiek** *v* study of Roman languages

ro'mankunst *v* art of fiction; **–lezer** (-s) *m* novel reader, fiction reader; **–lit(t)eratuur** *v* (prose) fiction; **–schrijfster** (-s) *v* (lady, woman) novelist, fiction writer; **–schrijver** (-s) *m* novelist, fiction writer; **–ticus** (-ci) *m* romanticist; **roman′tiek** *v* 1 (k u n s t r i c h - t i n g) romanticism; 2 ('t r o m a n t i s c h e) romance; **ro′mantisch** romantic;

romanti′seren [s = z] (romantiseerde, h. geromantiseerd) *vt* romanticize; **ro′manwereld** *v* fictional world

′**Rome** *o* Rome; **ro′mein** *v* Roman type; **Ro′mein(s)** (-en) *m* (& *aj*) Roman

′**romen I** (roomde, h. geroomd) *vt* cream, skim; **II** (roomde, is geroomd) *vi* cream

′**romer** (-s) *m* = *roemer*

′**romig** creamy

′**rommel** *m* lumber, rubbish, litter, jumble; *de hele ~* the whole lot; *ouwe ~* (old) junk; *koop geen ~* don't buy trash; *maak niet zo'n ~* don't make such a mess; ′**rommelen** (rommelde, h. gerommeld) *vi* 1 rumble [of the thunder]; 2 rummage [among papers &]; ′**rommelhok** (-ken) *o* glory hole; ′**rommelig** untidy, disorderly; ′**rommeling** (-en) *v* rumbling; ′**rommelkamer** (-s) *v* lumber-room; **–markt** (-en) *v* flea market, junk market; **–winkel** (-s) *m* junk shop; **–zo(oi)** (-zooien) *v* = *rommel*

romp (-en) *m* 1 trunk [of the body]; 2 ⚓ hull; 3 ✈ fuselage; **–parlement** *o* 🏛 Rump (parliament)

′**rompslomp** *m* bother

rond I *aj* round; rotund; circular; *een ~ jaar* a full year; *~e som* round sum; *~e vent* straight fellow; *de ~e waarheid* the plain truth; *de zaak is ~* the case is completed, the matter is settled; **II** *ad* = *ronduit* **II**; *zie ook: ongeveer, uitkomen;* **III** *prep* round [the table &]; **IV** *o* round; *in het ~* around, round about; **–achtig** roundish; ′**rondbazuinen¹** *vt* trumpet forth, blazon abroad; ′**rondboog** (-bogen) *m* △ round arch; **rond′borstig I** *aj* candid, frank, open-hearted; **II** *ad* candidly, frankly; **–heid** *v* candour, frankness, open-heartedness; ′**rondbrengen¹** *vt* take round; *de kranten ~* ook: deliver the papers; **–brieven** (briefde ′rond, h. ′rondgebriefd) *vt* rumour about; **–dansen¹** *vi* dance about; **–dartelen¹** *vi* romp around, rollick, scamper; **–delen¹** *vt* distribute, hand round; **–dienen¹** *vt* serve round [tea &], hand round [cakes &]; **–dobberen¹** *vi* drift about; **–dolen¹** *vi* wander about, rove about; **–draaien¹ I** *vi* turn, turn about, turn round, rotate, gyrate; **II** *vt* turn (round); **–draaiend** rotary, rotatory; **–draven¹** *vi* trot about; **–drentelen¹** *vi* lounge ~h~~~; **–drijven¹** *vi* float about, drift about;

–dwalen¹ *vi* wander, roam (about); ′**ronde** (-n en -s) *v* 1 round; 2 ⚔ round; 3 [postman's &] round; beat [of policeman]; 4 *sp* round [in boxing &]; lap [in cycle-racing]; *de ~ doen* 1 make (go) one's rounds; 2 *fig* go round [of rumours]; *het verhaal doet de ~* the story goes the round; *het verhaal deed de ~ door het dorp* the story went the round of the village; **–dans** (-en) *m* round dance

ron′deel (-delen) *o* 1 rondeau, rondel [song]; 2 ⚔ round bastion

′**ronden** (rondde, h. gerond) *vt* round, make round; round off; **ronde-′tafelconferentie** [-(t)si.] (-s) *v* round-table conference; ′**rondfladderen¹** *vi* flutter about; ′**rondgaan¹** *vi* go about (round); *laten ~* hand about, send (pass) [the hat] round, circulate; **–d** *~e brief* circular letter; ′**rondgang** (-en) *m* circuit, tour; *een ~ maken door de fabriek* make a tour of the factory; ′**rondgeven¹** *vt* pass round, hand about; **–hangen¹** *vi* hang (stand, lounge) about; ′**rondheid** *v* roundness, rotundity; *fig* frankness, candour; ′**rondhout¹** (-en) *o* 1 round timber, logs; 2 ⚓ spar; **–ing** (-en) *v* 1 rounding, curve; 2 ⚓ camber; **–je** (-s) *o* round; *hij gaf een ~* he stood drinks (all round); ′**rondkijken¹** *vi* look about; **–komen¹** *vi* make do [with], manage [with], get along [with], make (both) ends meet; ′**rondleiden¹** *vt* lead about; *iem. ~ show* sbd. over the place, take sbd. round; **–leiding** (-en) *v* guided tour; ′**rondlopen¹** *vi* walk about, **F** knock about, gad about; *de dief loopt nog rond* is still at large; *hij loopt weer rond* he is about again [after recovery]; *loop rond!* **F** get along with you; *~ met plannen* go about with plans; **–neuzen¹** *vi* nose (poke) about

′**rondo** ('s) *o* rondeau, rondel

rond′om, ′rondom I *ad* round about, all round; *~ behangen met...* hung round with...; **II** *prep* round about [the house &], around [us]; ′**rondreis** (-reizen) *v* (circular) tour, round trip; **–biljet** (-ten) *o* circular ticket; ′**rondreizen¹** *vi* travel about; *~d* strolling, itinerant [player], touring [company]; ′**rondrijden¹ I** *vi* ride about, drive about; **II** *vt* drive [sbd.] about; tour [the town &]; **–rit** (-ten) *m* tour; **–scharrelen¹** *vi* potter (poke) about; *~ in...* poke about in..., rummage in...; **–schrift** *o* round hand; **–schrijven** *o* circular, circular letter

′**rondsel** (-s) *o* ⚙ pinion

′**rondslenteren¹** *vi* lounge (saunter) about; **–slingeren¹ I** *vt* fling about; **II** *vi* lie about, lie around [of books &]; **–sluipen¹** *vi* steal

---

¹ V.T. en V.D. van het werkwoord volgens het model: ′**rond**bazuinen, V.T. bazuinde ′**rond**, V.D. ′**rond**gebazuind. Zie voor de vormen onder het grondwoord, in dit voorbeeld: *bazuinen*. Bij sterke en onregelmatige werkwoorden wordt u verwezen naar de lijst achterin.

(prowl) about; **–snuffelen**[1] *vi* nose (poke) about; **–spoken**[1] *vi* move about, walk around; **–springen**[1] *vi* jump about; **–strooien**[1] *vt* strew about; *fig* put about; **–tasten**[1] *vi* grope about, grope one's way; *in het duister* ~ grope one's way in the dark; *fig* be in the dark (about *omtrent*); 'rondte (-n en -s) *v* circle, circumference; *in de* ~ *draaien* turn round, zie ook: *rond* **IV** & *ronde*; 'rondtollen[1] *vi* spin around; 'rondtrekken[1] *vi* go about, wander about; **–d** = *rondreizend*; 'ronduit **I** *aj* frank, plain-spoken; **II** *ad* roundly, bluntly, frankly, plainly; *spreek* ~ speak your mind; *hem* ~ *de waarheid zeggen* tell him some home truths; ~ *gezegd...* frankly..., to put it bluntly...; 'rondvaart (-en) *v* = *rondreis*, ook: (circular) cruise; **–vaartboot** (-boten) *m* & *v* [Amsterdam] canal touring boat, tourist motor-boat; 'rondventen[1] *vt* hawk (about); **–er** (-s) *m* hawker; 'rondvertellen** (vertelde 'rond, h. 'rondverteld) *vt* spread [it]; *je moet het niet* ~ ook: you must not tell; **–vliegen**[1] *vi* fly about, fly round; ~ *boven* circle over [a town]; **–vlucht** (-en) *v* sight-seeing flight; circuit flight; **–vraag** *v bij de* ~ when questions are (were) invited; **–wandelen**[1] *vi* walk about; **–waren**[1] *vi* walk (about); *er waren hier spoken rond* ook: the place is haunted; **1** 'rondweg *ad* roundly; zie ook: *ronduit* **II**; **2** 'rondweg (-wegen) *m* by-pass (road), ring-road; 'rondwentelen[1] *vi* revolve; **–zenden**[1] *vt* send round, send out; **–zien**[1] *vi* look around; **–zwalken**[1] *vi* 1 drift about, scour the seas; 2 = *rondzwerven*; **–zwerven**[1] *vi* wander (roam, rove) about

'ronken (ronkte, h. geronkt) *vi* 1 snore; 2 (v a n m a c h i n e) snort, whirr, hum, drone

'ronselaar (-s) *m* crimp; **–sbende** (-n en -s) *v* press-gang; 'ronselen (ronselde, h. geronseld) *vi* & *vt* crimp [sailors &]

'röntgenapparaat ['rœntgən-] (-raten) *o* X-ray apparatus; 'röntgenen (röntgende, h. geröntgend) *vt* X-ray; 'röntgenfoto ('s) *v* X-ray photograph, radiograph; **–laborant** (-en) *m* X-ray assistent; röntgenolo'gie *v* roentgenology; röntgen'loog (-logen) *m* X-ray specialist, radiographer; 'röntgenonderzoek *o* X-ray examination; **–stralen** *mv* X-rays; **–therapie** *v* roentgenotherapy, X-ray therapy

rood **I** *aj* red; ~ *maken* make red, redden; ~ *worden* grow red, redden, blush; *zo* ~ *als een kreeft* as red as a lobster; **II** *o* red; zie ook: *lap*; **–aarde** *v* ruddle; **–achtig** reddish, ruddy; **–bont** red and white; **–borstje** (-s) *o* (robin)

redbreast, robin; **–bruin** reddish brown, russet; bay [horse]; **–gloeiend** red-hot; **–harig** red-haired; **–heid** *v* redness; **–hout** *o* redwood, Brazil wood; **–huid** (-en) *m* redskin, red Indian; **Rood'kapje** *o* Little Red Riding-hood; **rood'koper** *o* copper; **–en** *aj* copper; 'roodrok (-ken) *m* ⚓ redcoat [British soldier]; **–sel** *o* ruddle; **–staartje** (-s) *o* redstart; **–vonk** *v* & *o* scarlet fever, scarlatina; **–wangig** red-cheeked, ruddy; **–wild** *o* red deer

1 roof (roven) *v* scab, slough [on wound]

2 roof *m* robbery, plunder; *op* ~ *uitgaan* 1 go plundering; 2 (v. d i e r) go in search of prey; **–achtig** rapacious; **–bouw** *m* excessive cultivation, exhaustion of the soil; ~ *plegen op iem.'s gezondheid* ruin one's health; **–dier** (-en) *o* beast of prey, predator; **roof'gierig** rapacious; **–heid** *v* rapacity; 'roofhol (-holen) *o*, **–nest** (-en) *o* den of robbers, robbers' den; **–je** (-s) *o* scab, slough, eschar; **–moord** (-en) *m* & *v* murder with robbery; **–overval** (-len) *m* hold-up; **–ridder** (-s) *m* robber baron, robber knight; **–schip** (-schepen) *o* pirate ship; **–tocht** (-en) *m* predatory expedition; **–vis** (-sen) *m* predatory fish, fish of prey; **–vogel** (-s) *m* predatory bird, bird of prey; **–ziek** rapacious; **–zucht** *v* rapacity; roof'zuchtig = *roofziek*

'rooien (rooide, h. gerooid) *vt* lift, dig (up) [potatoes]; pull up [trees]

'rooilijn (-en) *v* building-line, alignment; *op de* ~ *staan* range with the street [of a house]

1 rook (roken) *v* (hay)stack

2 rook (roken) V.T. van *rieken* en *ruiken*

3 rook *m* smoke; *geen* ~ *zonder vuur* no smoke without fire; *onder de* ~ *van...* in the immediate neighbourhood; **–bom** (-men) *v* smoke-bomb; **–coupé** [-ku.pe.] (-s) *m* smoking-compartment, **F** smoker; **–gat** (-gaten) *o* smoke-hole; **–gerei** *o* smoking requisites; **–gordijn** (-en) *o* smoke-screen; **–kamer** (-s) *v* smoking-room; **–kanaal** (-nalen) *o* flue; **–loos** smokeless; **–lucht** *v* smoky smell; **–pluim** (-en) *v* wreath of smoke; **–salon** (-s) *m* & *o* smoking-room; **–scherm** (-en) *o* smoke screen; **–signaal** [-sɪɲa.l] *o* smoke signal; **–spek** *o* smoked bacon; **–tabak** *m* smoking-tobacco; **–tafeltje** (-s) *o* smoker's table; **–vang** (-en) *m* flue [of a chimney]; **–verdrijver** (-s) *m* 1 (g e k) (chimney) cowl; 2 (k a a r s) smoke consumer; 3 (s c h o o r s t e e n v e g e r) chimney-sweep; **rook'vlees** *o* smoked beef; 'rookwolk (-en) *v* cloud of smoke, smoke cloud; **–worst** (-en) *v*

---

[1] V.T. en V.D. van dit werkwoord volgens het model: 'rondbazuinen, V.T. bazuinde 'rond, V.D. 'rondgebazuind. Zie voor de vormen onder het grondwoord, in dit voorbeeld: *bazuinen*. Bij sterke en onregelmatige werkwoorden wordt u verwezen naar de lijst achterin.

smoked sausage

room *m* cream²; **–achtig** creamy; **–boter** *v* (dairy) butter; **–hoorn, –horen** (-s) *m* cream horn; **–ijs** *o* ice-cream; **–kaas** (-kazen) *m* cream cheese; **–kannetje** (-s) *o* cream-jug

rooms Roman, Roman Catholic; *de ~en mv* the Roman Catholics; **roomsge'zind** papistic; **rooms-katho'liek** Roman Catholic; *de ~en mv* the Roman Catholics

'roomsoes (-soezen) *v* cream puff; **–taart** (-en) *v* cream tart; **–vla** *v* cream custard

roos (rozen) *v* 1 ✿ rose; 2 (o p h o o f d) dandruff; 3 (h u i d z i e k t e) erysipelas; 4 ✕ bull's-eye [of a target]; 5 ⚓ (compass-)card; *rozen op de wangen hebben* have a complexion of milk and roses; ● *i n d e ~ treffen* score a bull's-eye; *o n d e r d e ~* under the rose, in secret; *o p rozen zitten* be on a bed of roses; *hij wandelt niet op rozen* his path is not strewn with roses; *geen rozen zonder doornen* no rose without a thorn; **–achtig** rose-like; **–kleur** *v* rose colour; **–kleurig, roos'kleurig** rose-coloured², rosy²; *fig* bright [of prospects, the future &]; zie ook: *bril*

'rooster (-s) *m & o* 1 (o m t e b r a d e n) gridiron, grill; 2 (i n d e k a c h e l) grate; 3 (a f s l u i t i n g) grating; 4 (l ij s t) rota; *~ van werkzaamheden* time-table, time-sheet; *volgens ~ aftreden* go out by rotation; **'roosteren** (roosterde, h. geroosterd) *vt* broil, roast, grill; toast [bread]; *geroosterd brood* toast; **'roosterwerk** *o* grating

'roosvenster (-s) *o* rose-window

root (roten) *v* retting-place [for flax]

1 ros ☉ *ros* (-sen) *o* steed [= horse]

2 ros *aj* reddish [hair], ruddy [glow]; *~se buurt* red-light district

ro'sarium [s = z] (-s) *o* rosary

'rosbief *m & o* roast beef

'rose = *roze*

'rosharig red-haired

'roskam (-men) *m* curry-comb; **'roskammen** (roskamde, h. geroskamd) *vt* 1 curry; 2 *fig* criticize severely

rosma'rijn = *rozemarijn*

'rossig reddish, sandy [hair], ruddy [glow]

1 rot (-ten) *o* ✕ file [consisting of two men], squad [of soldiers]; *een ~ geweren* a stack of arms; *de geweren werden a a n ~ten gezet* ✕ the arms were stacked; *m e t ~ten rechts (links)* ✕ right (left) file

2 rot I *aj* rotten, putrid, putrefied; bad [fruit, tooth &]; *wat ~!* **F** how provoking!; **II** *ad zich ~ vervelen* **F** be bored to death; **III** *o* rot

3 rot (-ten) *v = rat*

'rotan *o & m* rattan

ro'tatiepers [-(t)si.-] (-en) *v* rotary press

'roten (rootte, h. geroot) *vt* ret [flax]

ro'teren (roteerde, h. geroteerd) *vi* rotate

'rotgans (-ganzen) *v* brent-goose

'rothumeur *o* **F** lousy mood

'rotje (-s) *o* (v u u r w e r k) squib; **F** *zich een ~ lachen* laugh one's head off

ro'tonde (-n en -s) *v* 1 △ rotunda; 2 (v e r k e e r s p l e i n) roundabout

'rotor (-s en -'toren) *m* rotor

rots (-en) *v* 1 rock; 2 cliff [= high steep rock]; **–achtig** rocky; **–achtigheid** *v* rockiness; **–blok** (-ken) *o* boulder; **–duif** (-duiven) *v* rock-pigeon; **–eiland** (-en) *o* rocky island; **'Rotsgebergte** *het ~* the Rocky Mountains; **'rotskloof** (-kloven) *v* chasm; **–partij** (-en) *v* rockery; **–plant** (-en) *v* rock-plant; **–schildering** (-en) *v* cave-painting; **–tekening** (-en) *v* cave-drawing; **–tuin** (-en) *m* rock garden, rockery; **–vast** firm as a rock; **–wand** (-en) *m* rock-face; precipice; bluff [of coast]; **–woning** (-en) *v* rock-dwelling

'rotten (rotte, is gerot) *vi* rot, putrefy; **'rottig =** 2 *rot* I; 1 **'rotting** *v* putrefaction

2 'rotting (-en) *m* cane

'rotvent (-en) *m*, **–zak** (-ken) *m* **S** rotter; **P** bastard, stinker; **–zooi** *v* mess

'rouge ['ru.ʒə] *m & o* rouge

rou'lade [ru.-] (-s) *v* roulade

rou'latie [ru.'la.(t)si.] *v in ~ brengen* put into (general) circulation [a film]; **rou'leren** [ru.-] (rouleerde, h. gerouleerd) *vi* 1 circulate, be in circulation; 2 rotate, take turns

rou'lette [ru.-] (-s) *v* roulette; **–tafel** (-s) *v* roulette-table

'route ['ru.-] (-s en -n) *v* route, way

rou'tine [ru.-] *v* 1 (g e w o n e g a n g) routine; 2 (b e d r e v e n h e i d) experience

rouw *m* mourning; *lichte (zware) ~* half (deep) mourning; *de ~ aannemen* go into mourning; *~ dragen (over)* mourn (for); ● *i n d e ~ gaan* go into mourning; *in de ~ zijn* be in mourning; *u i t d e ~ gaan* go out of mourning; **–band** (-en) *m* mourning-band; **–beklag** *o* condolence; *verzoeke van ~ verschoond te blijven* no calls of condolence; **–brief** (-brieven) *m* notification of death; **–dienst** (-en) *m* memorial service; **–drager** (-s) *m* mourner; **'rouwen** (rouwde, h. gerouwd) *vi* go into (be in) mourning, mourn (for *over*); zie ook: *berouwen*; **'rouwfloers** *o* crape; **–gewaad** (-waden) *o* mourning garb; **–ig** sorry; *ik ben er helemaal niet ~ om* I am not at all sorry; **–jaar** (-jaren) *o* year of mourning; **–kamer** (-s) *v* funeral parlour; **–klacht** (-en) *v* lamentation; **–kleed** (-kleden, -kleIeren en -kleren) *o* mourning-dress; *rouwkleren* mourning-clothes; **–koets** (-en) *v* mourning-coach; **–koop** *m* smart-money; *~ hebben* repent one's

bargain; **–rand** (-en) *m* mourning-border,
black edge; **–sluier** (-s) *m* crape veil, weeper;
–stoet (-en) *m* funeral procession; **–tijd** *m*
period of mourning

'**roven** (roofde, h. geroofd) **I** *vi* rob, plunder; **II**
vt steal; '**rover** (-s) *m* robber, brigand; **–bende**
(-n en -s) *v* gang of robbers; **–hoofdman**
(-nen) *m* robber-chief; **rove'rij** (-en) *v* robbery,
brigandage; '**roversbende** (-n en -s) *v* =
roverbende; **–hol** (-holen) *o* den of robbers,
robbers' den; **–hoofdman** (-nen) *m* = *rover-
hoofdman;* '**rovertje** *o* ~ *spelen* play cops and
robbers

ro'**yaal** [rʋɑ-, ro.-] **I** *aj* liberal [man, tip &];
free-handed, open-handed, munificent [man];
handsome, generous [reward &]; *hij is erg* ~
(met zijn geld) he is very free with his money;
II *ad* liberally; **roya'list(isch)** (-en) *m* (& *aj*)
royalist; **royali'teit** (-en) *v* liberality, munifi-
cence, generosity

roye'**ment** [rʋɑjə-, ro.jə] (-en) *o* expulsion [from
a party]; cancellation [of a contract]; ro'**yeren**
(royeerde, h. geroyeerd) *vt* remove from (strike
off) the list; expel [from a party]; cancel [a
contract]

'**roze** ['rɔ:zə] pink

'**rozeblad** (-bladen, -bladeren en -blaren) *o* 1
(v a n   d e   s t r u i k) rose-leaf; 2 (b l o e m-
b l a d) rose-petal; **–boom** (-bomen) *m* rose-
tree; **–bottel** (-s) *v* rose-hip; **–geur** *m* scent of
roses; *het is (was) niet alles* ~ *en maneschijn* life is
not a bed of roses, not all cakes and ale (beer
and skittles); **–hout** *o* rosewood; **–knop** (-pen)
m rose-bud; **–laar** (-s) *m* rose-bush, rose-tree

rozema'**rijn** *m* rosemary

'**rozenbed** (-den) *o* bed of roses; **–hoedje** (-s) *o*
rk chaplet; **–krans** (-en) *m* 1 garland of roses;
2 *rk* rosary; *zijn* ~ *bidden* tell one's beads;
–kruiser (-s) *m* Rosicrucian; **–kweker** (-s) *m*
rose-grower; **–olie** *v* oil (attar) of roses; **–tuin**
(-en) *m* rose-garden, rosary; **–water** *o* rose-
water; '**rozerood** rose-red; **–stek** (-ken) *m*
rose-cutting; **–struik** (-en) *m* rose-bush;
ro'**zet** (-ten) *v* rosette

'**rozig** rosy, roseate

ro'**zijn** (-en) *v* raisin

'**rubber** *m* & *o* rubber; **–boot** (-boten) *m* & *v*
(rubber) dinghy; **–hak** (-ken) *v* rubber heel;
–handschoen (-en) *m* rubber glove; **–laars**
(-laarzen) *v* rubber boot

rubri'**ceren** (rubriceerde, h. gerubriceerd) *vt*
classify, file

ru'**briek** (-en) *v* heading, head; column, section
[of newspaper]

'**ruche** ['ry.ʃə] (-s) *v* ruche, frill(ing), furbelow

'**ruchtbaar** ~ *maken* make public, make known,
spread abroad; ~ *worden* become known, get

abroad, be noised abroad; **–heid** *v* publicity; ~
geven aan make public, disclose, divulge

rudi'**ment** (-en) *o* rudiment; **rudimen'tair**
[-'tɛːr] rudimentary

rug (-gen) *m* 1 back; 2 ridge [of mountains]; 3
back [of a book]; 4 bridge [of the nose]; *ik heb
een brede* ~ I have broad shoulders; *iem. de* ~
toedraaien (toekeren) turn one's back (up)on
sbd.; ● ~ *a a n* ~ back to back; *hij deed het
a c h t e r mijn* ~ behind my back[2]; *de veertig
achter de* ~ *hebben* be turned forty; *dat hebben wij
goddank achter de* ~ thank God it's finished, it's
over now; *de vijand i n de* ~ *(aan)vallen* attack
the enemy in the rear, from behind; *iem. m e t de*
~ *aanzien* give sbd. the cold shoulder; *hij stond
met de* ~ *naar ons toe* he stood with his back to
us; *met de* ~ *tegen de muur staan* have one's back
to the wall; *met de handen op de* ~ one's hands
behind one's back

'**rugby** ['rügbi] *o* Rugby (football), **F** rugger

'**rugcrawl** [-krɔ.l] *m* back-crawl; **–dekking** *v*
backing; '**ruggegraat** (-graten) *v* vertebral
column, backbone[2], spine; **–sverkromming**
(-en) *v* deformity of the spine; '**ruggelings**
backward(s); back to back; '**ruggemerg** *o*
spinal marrow; '**ruggemergsontsteking** *v*
myelitis; **–tering** *v* tabes dorsalis, dorsal tabes;
–zenuw (-en) *v* spinal nerve; '**ruggen** (rugde,
h. gerugd) *vt* back; '**ruggespraak** *v* consultation; ~ *houden met iem.* consult sbd.; **–steun** *m*
backing, support; **–streng** (-en) *v* spine;
–wervel (-s) *m* = *rugwervel;* '**rugleuning** (-en) *v*
back [of a chair]; **–nummer** (-s) *o sp* (player's)
number; **–pand** (-en) *o* back; **–pijn** (-en) *v*
back-ache, pain in the back; **–schild** (-en) *o*
carapace; **–slag** *m* back-stroke [in swimming];
–sluiting *v met* ~ fastened at the back;
'**rugsteunen** (rugsteunde, h. gerugsteund) *vt*
back (up), support; '**rugstuk** (-ken) *o* back,
back-piece; **–titel** (-s) *m* back title; **–vin** (-nen)
v dorsal fin; **–waarts I** *aj* backward; **II** *ad*
backward(s); **–wervel** (-s) *m* dorsal vertebra
[*mv* dorsal vertebrae]; **–zak** (-ken) *m* rucksack;
–zwemmen *vi* swim back-stroke

rui *m* moulting(-time); '**ruien** (ruide, h. geruid) *vi*
moult

ruif (ruiven) *v* rack

ruig 1 hairy, shaggy [beard]; 2 rough [cloth,
sea]; rugged [country]; **–harig** shaggy; wire-
haired [dog]; **–heid** *v* 1 hairiness; shagginess;
2 roughness; ruggedness; **–te** (-n en -s) *v*
roughness, ruggedness; (s t r u i k g e w a s)
brush (-wood)

'**ruiken* I** *vt* smell, scent; *hij ruikt wat, hij ruikt
lont* he smells a rat; *dat kon ik toch niet* ~*?* how
could I know?; **II** *vi* smell; *het ruikt goed* it
smells good; *ze* ~ *lekker* they have a sweet

(nice) smell; ● *ruik er eens a a n* smell (at) it; *hij zal er niet aan* ~ he won't even get a smell of it; *daar kan hij niet aan* ~ he cannot touch it; *het (hij) ruikt n a a r cognac* it (he) smells of brandy; *dat ruikt naar ketterij* that smells of heresy

'**ruiker** (-s) *m* nosegay, bouquet, bunch of flowers

ruil (-en) *m* exchange, barter; *een goede* ~ *doen* make a good exchange; *in* ~ *voor* in exchange for; **–artikel** (-en en -s) *o* article for barter; '**ruilen** (ruilde, h. geruild) **I** *vt* exchange, barter, **F** swop; ~ *tegen* exchange [it] for; ~ *voor* exchange for, barter for, **F** swop for; **II** *va* & *vi* exchange; *ik zou niet met hem willen* ~ I wouldn't be in his shoes; *zullen we van plaats* ~? shall we (ex)change places?; '**ruilhandel** *m* (trade by) barter; '**ruiling** (-en) *v* exchange, barter; '**ruilmiddel** (-en) *o* medium of exchange; **–object** (-en) *o* object in exchange, bartering object; **–verkaveling** *v* re-allotment; **–verkeer** *o* exchange; **–waarde** *v* exchange value

1 ruim I *aj* large, wide, spacious, roomy, capacious; ample; *zijn* ~*e blik* his breadth of outlook; *een* ~ *gebruik van iets maken* use sth. freely; *een* ~ *geweten* easy (lax) conscience; ~*e kamer* spacious room; *in* ~ *kring* in wide circles; *het* ~ *sop* the open sea; ~*e voorraad* ample stores; *het niet* ~ *hebben* be in straitened circumstances, not be well off; **II** *ad* largely, amply, plentifully; ~ *30 jaar geleden* a good thirty years ago; *hij is* ~ *30 jaar* he is past thirty; ~ *30 pagina's* well over thirty pages; ~ *40 pond* upwards of £ 40; *hij sprak* ~ *een uur* he spoke for more than an hour; ~ *meten* measure liberally; ~ *uit elkaar* well apart; ~ *voldoende* amply sufficient; ~ *voorzien van...* amply provided with...

2 ruim (-en) *o* ♨ hold [of a ship]

ruim'denkend broad-minded, liberal, tolerant

'**ruimen I** (ruimde, h. geruimd) *vt* 1 empty, evacuate; 2 clear (away) [the snow, rubble &]; *zie veld* &; **II** (ruimde, is geruimd) *vi* ♨ veer aft, veer [of wind]

'**ruimschoots** *fig* amply, largely, plentifully; ~ *de tijd hebben* have ample (plenty of) time; ~ *zeilen* ♨ sail large

'**ruimte** (-n en -s) *v* room, space, capacity; *de* ~ ♨ the offing; *de oneindige* ~ (infinite) space; ~ *van beweging* elbow-room; ~ *van blik* breadth of outlook; *iem. de* ~ *geven* give sbd. full play; *dat neemt teveel* ~ *in* that takes up too much room; *in de* ~ *kletsen* talk at random; *dit laat geen* ~ *voor twijfel* this leaves no room for doubt; ~ *maken* make room; ~ *openlaten* leave space, leave a blank [for the signature]; **–besparend** space-saving; **–cabine** (-s) *v* space-cabin;

–capsule (-s) *v* space-capsule; **–lijk** spatial; ~*e ordening* area planning; **–gebrek** *o* lack of room (of space); **–maat** (-maten) *v* measure of capacity; **–onderzoek** *o* exploration of space, space research; **–pak** (-ken) *o* spacesuit; **–raket** (-ten) *v* space rocket; **–schip** (-schepen) *o* spaceship; **–sonde** (-s) *v* space probe; **–station** [-sta.(t)ʃɔn] (-s) *o* space station; **–vaarder** (-s) *m* space traveller, spaceman, astronaut, [Soviet] cosmonaut; **–vaart** *v* space travel, astronautics; **–vaartuig(en)** *o* (*mv*) spacecraft; **–vlucht** (-en) *v* space flight; **–vrees** *v* agoraphobia

ruin (-en) *m* gelding

ru'ïne (-s en -n) *v* ruins; *het gebouw is een* ~ the building is a ruin; *hij is een* ~ he is a mere wreck; **ruï'neren** (ruïneerde, h. geruïneerd) **I** *vt* ruin; *hij is geruïneerd* ook: he is a ruined man; **II** *vr zich* ~ 1 (f i n a n c i e e l) ruin oneself, bring ruin on oneself; 2 (f y s i e k) make a wreck of oneself; **ruï'neus** ruinous

ruis *m* (b ij g e l u i d) noise; '**ruisen** (ruiste, h. geruist) *vi* rustle; murmur [of a stream]; **–sing** *v* rustle; murmur [of a stream]

'**ruisvoorn, –voren** (-s) *m* rudd

ruit (-en) *v* 1 diamond; lozenge; rhomb [in mathematics]; 2 pane [of a window]; 3 square [of draught-board]; 4 ⚘ rue; zie ook: *ruitje*

1 'ruiten (ruitte, h. geruit) *vt* chequer; zie ook: *geruit*

2 'ruiten (-s) *v* ♦ diamonds; *ruiten'zes* six of diamonds

'**ruiter** (-s) *m* rider, horseman; *Spaanse (Friese)* ~*s* chevaux-de-frise; **–bende** (-n en -s) *v* troop of horse; **ruite'rij** *v* cavalry, horse; '**ruiterlijk** *aj* frank; '**ruiterpad** (-paden) *o* bridle-path, bridle-way; **–sabel** (-s) *m* sabre, cavalry-sword; **–sport** *v* horse-riding, equestrian sport; **–standbeeld** (-en) *o* equestrian statue; **–stoet** (-en) *m* cavalcade; **–tje** (-s) *o* tag, tab

'**ruitesproeier** (-s) *m* windscreen washer; **–wisser** (-s) *m* (wind)screen wiper

'**ruitijd** (-en) *m* moulting-time, moulting-season

'**ruitje** (-s) *o* 1 (v. r a a m) pane; 2 (o p g o e d) check; '**ruitjesgoed** *o* chequered material, check; **–papier** *o* squared paper; '**ruitvormig** lozenge-shaped, diamond-shaped

ruk (-ken) *m* pull, tug, jerk, wrench; '**rukken** (rukte, h. en is gerukt) **I** *vt* pull, tug, jerk, snatch; *iem. iets uit de handen* ~ snatch sth. out of sbd.'s hands; *een gezegde uit het verband* ~ wrest (tear) a phrase from its context; **II** *vi* pull, tug, jerk; *aan iets* ~ pull at sth., give sth. a tug; '**rukwind** (-en) *m* gust of wind, squall

rul loose [soil], sandy [road]

rum *m* rum; **–boon** (-bonen) *v* rum bonbon

ru'moer (-en) *o* noise, uproar; ~ *maken*

(*verwekken*) make a noise; **ru'moeren**
(rumoerde, h. gerumoerd) *vi* make a noise;
–rig noisy, tumultuous, uproarious
1 run *v* (g e m a l e n   s c h o r s) tan, bark
2 run (-s) *m* run [on the bank; in cricket &]
rund (-eren) *o* cow, ox; [*fig*] *wat ., .n ~!* what a
blockhead; **'runderlapje** (-s) *o* beefsteak;
–pest *v* cattle-plague; **–stal** (-len) *m* stable
(shed) for cattle; **'rundleer** *o* cowhide, neat's
leather; **–vee** *o* (horned) cattle; **–veestam-
boek** (-en) *o* herd-book; **–vet** *o* beef suet;
(g e s m o l t e n) beef dripping; **–vlees** *o* beef
'rune (-n) *v* rune, runic letter; **–nschrift** *o* runic
writing
'runmolen (-s) *m* tan-mill
'runnen (runde, h. gerund) *vt* run [a business];
–er (-s) *m* runner°
rups (-en) *v* caterpillar; **–band** (-en) *m* caterpillar; *met ~en* tracked [vehicles]; **–wiel** (-en) *o*
caterpillar wheel
Rus (-sen) *m* Russian; *r~* **S** (r e c h e r c h e u r)
tec, cop; **–land** *o* Russia; **Rus'sin** (-nen) *v*
Russian lady (woman); **'Russisch I** *aj*
Russian; *~ leer* Russia leather; **II** *o het ~*
Russian; **III** *v een* ~*e* a Russian woman (lady)
rust *v* 1 rest, repose [after exertion], peace,
tranquillity [of mind], calm; 2 *♪* rest; 3 *sp*
half-time, interval; (*op de plaats*) *~!* ⚔ stand
easy!; *~ en vrede* peace and quiet; *~ geven* give a
rest, rest; *zich geen ogenblik ~ gunnen* not give
oneself a moment's rest; *geen ~ hebben vóórdat...*
not be easy till...; *hij is een van die mensen die ~
noch duur hebben* who cannot rest for a moment;
hij moet ~ houden take a rest; *hij is de eeuwige ~
ingegaan* he has entered into his rest; *wat ~
nemen* take a rest, rest oneself; *~ roest* rest
makes rusty; ● *predikant i n ~e = rustend*; *al in
diepe ~ zijn* be fast asleep; *iem. met ~ laten*
leave sbd. in peace, leave (let) sbd. alone; *zich
t e r ~e begeven* go to rest, retire for the night;
t o t ~ brengen set at rest, quiet; *tot ~ komen* quiet
down, settle down, subside; **–altaar** (-taren) *o*
& *m* wayside altar; **–bank** (-en) *v,* **–bed** (-den)
o couch; **–dag** (-dagen) *m* day of rest, holiday;
–eloos *aj* restless; **'rusten** (rustte, h. gerust) *vi*
rest, repose; *hier rust...* here lies...; *hij ruste in
vrede* may he rest in peace; *zijn as(se) ruste in
vrede* peace (be) to his ashes; *wel te ~!* good
night!; *ik moet wat ~* I must take a rest; *laten ~*
let rest²; *de paarden laten ~* rest one's horses; *we*

zullen dat punt (*die zaak*) *maar laten ~* drop the
point, let the matter rest; *er rust geen blaam op
hem* no blame attaches to him; *zijn blik rustte
op...* his gaze rested on...; *op u rust de plicht om...*
on you rests the duty to...; *de verdenking rust op
hem* it is on him that suspicion rests, suspicion
points to him; **–d** retired [official]; *~ predikant*
emeritus minister; **'rustgevend** restful,
soothing; **–huis** (-huizen) *o* home of rest, rest
home
rus'tiek rustic [bridge &]; rural [simplicity &]
'rustig I *aj* quiet, still, tranquil, restful, repose-
ful, placid, calm; **II** *ad* quietly, calmly; **–heid** *v*
quietness, stillnes, restfulness, tranquillity,
placidity, calmness, calm; **–jes** quietly
'rusting (-en) *v* (suit of) armour
'rustkuur (-kuren) *v* rest-cure; **–oord** (-en) *o*
retreat; **–pauze** (-n -en -s) *v* rest, break;
–plaats (-en) *v* resting-place; *iem. naar zijn
laatste ~ brengen* lay sbd. to rest; **–poos**
(-pozen) *v* rest, breathing-space; (r u s t i g e
t ij d) lull, slack; **–punt** (-en) *o* rest, pause;
stopping place; **–stand** *m* position of rest; *sp*
score at half-time; **–stoel** (-en) *m* rest-chair;
–teken (-s) *o ♪* rest; **–tijd** (-en) *m* (time of)
rest, resting-time; **–uur** (-uren) *o* hour of rest;
–verstoorder (-s) *m* disturber of the peace,
peace-breaker; **–verstoring** (-en) *v* disturbance, breach of the peace
rut F broke, cleaned out, penniless
ruw I *aj* 1 raw [materials, silk], rough
[diamonds &], crude [oil]; 2 (g r o f) rough,
coarse², crude², rude²; 3 (o n e f f e n) rugged;
~ ijzer pig-iron; *in het ~e* in the rough,
roughly; **II** *ad* roughly²
'ruwaard (-s) *m* Ⓤ regent, governor
'ruwen (ruwde, h. geruwd) *vt* roughen;
(k a a r d e n) card, tease; **'ruwharig** shaggy,
wire-haired [terrier]; **'ruwheid** (-heden) *v*
roughness, coarseness, rudeness, ruggedness,
crudity; **–weg** roughly
'ruzie (-s) *v* quarrel, brawl, squabble, fray; *~
hebben* be quarrelling, be at odds; *~ hebben over...*
quarrel about...; *~ krijgen* quarrel, fall out
(over *over*); *~ maken* quarrel; *~ stoken* make
mischief, make trouble; *~ zoeken* pick a
quarrel, look for trouble; **–maker** (-s) *m*
brawler, quarrelsome fellow
'Rwanda *o* Rwanda

S

s [ɪs] (s's en s'en) *v* s
1 saai *o* & *m* serge
2 saai I *aj* dull, slow, tedious; **II** *ad* tediously
saaien *aj* serge
saam = *samen*; **saam'horigheid** *v* solidarity, unity
'sabbat (-ten) *m* Sabbath; **–dag** (-dagen) *m* Sabbath-day; **'sabbat(s)schender** (-s) *m* Sabbath-breaker; **–stilte** *v* silence of the Sabbath; **'sabbatviering** *v* observance of the Sabbath
'sabbelen (sabbelde, h. gesabbeld) *vi* suck; ~ *op* suck [a pencil], suck at [one's pipe]
1 'sabel *o* sable
2 'sabel (-s) *m* ⚔ sabre, sword; **–bajonet** (-ten) *v* sword-bayonet
'sabelbont *o* sable (fur); **–dier** (-en) *o* sable
'sabelen (sabelde, h. gesabeld) *vt* hack, cut; **'sabelgekletter** *o* sabre-rattling²; **–houw** (-en) *m* 1 sabre-thrust, cut (stroke) with a• sabre; 2 sabre-cut [wound]; **–kling** (-en) *v* blade of a sword; **–koppel** (-s) *m* & *v* sword-belt; **–kwast** (-en) *m* sword-knot; **–schede** (-n) *v* scabbard; **–schermen** *o* sword exercise; **–tas** (-sen) *v* sabretache
Sa'bijnen *mv* Sabines; **Sa'bijns** Sabine; *de ~e maagdenroof* the rape of the Sabine women
sabo'tage [-ʒə] *v* sabotage; **–daad** (-daden) *v* act of sabotage; **sabo'teren** (saboteerde, h. gesaboteerd) *vt* sabotage; **sabo'teur** (-s) *m* saboteur
sacha'rine *v* saccharin
sache'rijnig cheerless, dismal, glum
sa'chet [-ʃɛt] (-s) *o* sachet
sa'craal sacral, holy
sacra'ment (-en) *o* sacrament; *de laatste ~en toedienen* rk administer the last sacraments; **sacramen'teel** sacramental; **Sacra'mentsdag** *m* Corpus Christi
sacris'tein (-en) *m* sacristan, sexton; **sacris'tie** (-ieën) *v* sacristy, vestry
sa'disme *o* sadism; **sa'dist** (-en) *m* sadist; **–isch** sadistic
sa'fari ('s) *v* safari
'safeloket ['se.f-] (-ten) *o* safe-deposit box
saffi'aan *o* = *marokijn*
'saffie S (-s) *o* fag
saf'fier (-en) *m* & *o*, **–en** *aj* sapphire
saf'fraan *m* saffron; **–geel** saffron
'saga ('s) *v* [Icelandic &] saga

'sage (-en) *v* legend, tradition, myth
'sago *m* sago; **–meel** *o* sago-flour, sago-meal; **–palm** (-en) *m* sago-palm
sai'llant [-'jant] **I** *aj* salient²; **II** (-en) *m* & *o* ⚔ salient
sa'jet *m*, **–ten** *aj* worsted
sakker'loot = *sapperloot*
Saks (-en) *m* Saxon; **'Saksen** *o* Saxony; **'Saksisch** Saxon; ~ *porselein* Dresden china
sa'lade = *sla*
sala'mander (-s) *m* salamander
salari'ëren (salarieerde, h. gesalarieerd) *vt* salary, pay
sa'laris (-sen) *o* salary, pay; **–regeling** (-en) *v* scale of salary (pay); **–verhoging** (-en) *v* (pay) rise, salary increase, pay increase; **–verlaging** (-en) *v* cut, salary reduction
sal'deren (saldeerde, h. gesaldeerd) *vt* $ balance
'saldo ('s en -di) *o* balance; *batig* ~ credit balance, surplus, balance in hand, balance in one's favour; *nadelig* ~ deficit; ~ *in kas* balance in hand; *per* ~ on balance²; *fig* in the end, after all
sa'letjonker (-s) *m* beau, fop, carpet-knight
sali'cylzuur [-'si.l-] *o* salicylic acid
'salie *v* ♣ sage
salmi'ak *m* sal-ammoniac
sa'lon (-s) *m* & *o* 1 drawing-room; 2 [hairdresser's] saloon; **–ameublement** (-en) *o* drawing-room furniture; **–boot** (-boten) *m* & *v* saloon-steamer; **–communist** (-en) *m* drawing-room red, arm-chair communist; **–held** (-en) *m* = *saletjonker*; **–muziek** *v* salon music, drawing-room music; **–tafeltje** (-s) *o* coffee table; **–vleugel** (-s) *m* baby grand; **–wagen** (-s) *m* saloon-car
sal'peter *m* & *o* saltpetre, nitre; **–(acht)ig** nitrous; **–zuur** *o* nitric acid
'salto ('s) *m* somersault
salu'eren (salueerde, h. gesalueerd) *vi* & *vt* salute; **sa'luut** (-luten) *o* ⚔ salute; greeting; ~ *!* goodbye!; *het* ~ *geven* 1 ⚔ give the salute, salute; 2 ⚓ fire a salute; **–schot** (-schoten) *o* salute; *er werden 21 ~en gelost* a salute of 21 guns was fired
'salvo ('s) *o* volley, round, salvo; **–vuur** *o* volley-firing
Samari'taan (-tanen) *m* Samaritan; *de barmhartige* ~ the Good Samaritan; **–s** *aj* Samaritan

'samen together; –ballen[1] *vi* mass together, concentrate, contract; (v. w o l k e n) gather; –binden[1] *vt* bind together; –brengen[1] *vt* bring together; 'samenbundeling *v* gathering, collection; 'samendoen[1] I *vt* put together; II *vi* be partners, act in common, go shares

samen'drukbaar compressible; 'samendrukken[1] *vt* press together, compress

'samenflansen[1] *vt* knock (patch) together, patch up; –gaan[1] *vi* go together[2], *fig* agree; ~ *met* go with[2]; *niet* ~ *met* [*fig*] be incompatible with

'samengesteld compound [leaf, interest &]; complex [sentence]; samenge'steldheid *v* complexity

'samengroeien[1] *vi* grow together; –iing *v* growing together

'samenhang *m* 1 (i n 't a l g.) coherence, cohesion, connection; 2 (v. z i n) context; 'samenhangen[1] *vi* cohere, be connected; *dat hangt samen met* that is connected with; –d coherent [discourse &]; connected [text, whole &]

'samenhokken[1] *vi* herd together; F shack up (with *met*)

'samenhopen[1] *vt* accumulate, heap up, pile up; –ping *v* accumulation

samen'horigheid = *saamhorigheid*; 'samenklank *m* concord

'samenklemmen[1] *vt* squeeze together; –klinken[1] I *vi* ♪ chime together, harmonize; II *vt* ✕ rivet together; –knijpen[1] *vt* press (squeeze) together, squint [one's eyes]; –knopen[1] *vt* tie together

'samenkomen[1] *vi* 1 meet, assemble, get together, gather, ☉ forgather [of persons]; 2 meet [of lines]; 'samenkomst (-en) *v* meeting

'samenkoppelen[1] *vt* couple

'samenleving *v* society

'samenlijmen[1] *vt* glue together

'samenloop *m* concourse [of people], confluence [of rivers], concurrence; ~ *van omstandigheden* coincidence, conjunction of circumstances; 'samenlopen[1] *vi* meet, converge [of lines]; concur [of events]

'samenpakken[1] I *vt* pack up (together); II *vr zich* ~ gather [of a storm]

'samenpersen[1] *vt* press together, compress; –sing *v* compression

'samenplakken I (plakte 'samen, h. 'samengeplakt) *vt* paste together; II (plakte 'samen, is 'samengeplakt) *vi* stick

'samenraapsel (-s) *o* hotchpotch; ~ *van leugens* pack of lies

'samenroepen[1] *vt* call together, convoke, convene [a meeting]; –ping *v* convocation

'samenrollen[1] *vt* roll up

'samenscholen (schoolde 'samen, h. 'samengeschoold) *vi* assemble, gather; –ling (-en) *v* (riotous, unlawful) assembly, gathering

'samenschraapsel (-s) *o* scrapings; 'samenschrapen[1] *vt* scrape together

'samensmeden[1] *vt* forge together

'samensmelten[1] *vt* & *vi* melt together; *fig* amalgamate; –ting (-en) *v* melting together; *fig* amalgamation

'samensnoeren[1] *vt* tie (lace) together; *fig* choke, stifle [with fear]

'samenspannen[1] *vi* conspire, plot; –ning (-en) *v* conspiracy, plot, collusion

'samenspel *o* 1 ♪ ensemble playing; 2 ensemble acting; 3 *sp* team-work

'samenspraak (-spraken) *v* conversation, dialogue

'samenstel *o* structure, system, fabric [logical &], framework, make-up; 'samenstellen[1] *vt* put together, compose, compile, make up; ~*d* component [parts]; –er (-s) *m* compiler, composer; 'samenstelling (-en) *v* composition [of forces]; arrangement *gram* compound word, compound

'samenstemmen[1] *vt* harmonize, chime together

'samenstromen[1] *vi* flow together; *fig* flock together [of people]; –ming (-en) *v* 1 confluence; 2 *fig* concourse [of people]

'samentrekken[1] I *vt* knit [one's brow]; ✕ concentrate [troops]; (s a m e n v o e g e n) gather, draw together, unite; II *vr zich* ~ contract; ✕ concentrate, brew (up), gather [of a storm]; III *vi* contract; –d astringent, constringent; 'samentrekking (-en) *v* contraction; ✕ concentration [of troops]

'samenvallen[1] I *vi* coincide [of events, dates, triangles]; II *o het* ~ the coincidence

'samenvatten[1] *vt* take together; *fig* sum up; –ting (-en) *v* résumé, précis, summing up

'samenvlechten[1] *vt* (h a a r) plaid, braid together; (b l o e m e n &) bind, wreathe together

'samenvloeien[1] *vi* flow together, meet; –iing (-en) *v* confluence

'samenvoegen[1] *vt* join, unite; –ging (-en) *v* junction

'samenvouwen[1] *vt* fold up [a newspaper], fold

---

[1] V.T. en V.D. van dit werkwoord volgens het model: 'samenballen, V.T. balde 'samen, V.D. 'samengebald. Zie voor de vormen onder het grondwoord, in dit voorbeeld: *ballen*. Bij sterke en onregelmatige werkwoorden wordt u verwezen naar de lijst achterin.

[one's hands]

'**samenweefsel** (-s) *o* texture, web, tissue; *fig* tissue [of lies]

'**samenwerken**[1] *vi* act together, work together, co-operate; **–king** *v* 1 co-operation; 2 concerted action; *in* ~ *met* in co-operation with

'**samenwonen**[1] **I** *vi* live together; (o n g e - h u w d) cohabit, **S** shack up [with]; (w e g e n s w o n i n g s c h a a r s t e) share a house; **II** *o* cohabitation; **–ning** *v* living together; (w e g e n s w o n i n g s c h a a r s t e) shared accommodation

'**samenzang** *m* community singing

'**samenzijn** *o* meeting, gathering

'**samenzweerder** (-s) *m* conspirator, plotter; '**samenzweren**[1] *vi* conspire, plot; **–ring** (-en) *v* conspiracy; *een* ~ *smeden* lay a plot

Samo'jeed (-jeden) *m* Samoyed

sam'sam F ~ *doen* go fifty-fifty

sana'torium (-s en -ia) *o* sanatorium [*mv* sanatoria], health-resort

'**sanctie** ['saŋksi.] (-s) *v* sanction; **sanctio'neren** [saŋksi.-] (sanctioneerde, h. gesanctioneerd) *vt* sanction

san'daal (-dalen) *v* sandal

'**sandelhout** *o* sandalwood

'**sandwich** ['sɛntvɪtʃ] (-es) *m* sandwich

sa'neren (saneerde, h. gesaneerd) *vt* reorganize [the finances], reconstruct [a company], redevelop, clean up [a part of the town]; **sa'nering** *v* reorganization, redevelopment; **–splan** (-nen) *o* redevelopment plan

san'guinisch [-'ɣʋi.ni.s] sanguine

'**sanhedrin** *o* sanhedrin, sanhedrin

sani'tair [-'tɛ:r] **I** *aj* sanitary; **II** *o* sanitary fittings, sanitation, plumbing

'**Sanskriet** *o* Sanskrit

san'té [sã'te.], '**santjes!** your health!

'**santenkraam** *v de hele* ~ the whole lot (caboodle)

Sa'oedi-A'rabië *o* Saudi-Arabia

sap (-pen) *o* sap [of plants]; juice [of fruit]

'**sappel F** *zich te* ~ *maken* worry

'**sappelen** (sappelde, h. gesappeld) *vi* drudge, toil, slave

sapper'loot *ij* good gracious, good heavens

'**sappig** sappy; juicy, succulent [fruit]; **–heid** *v* juiciness, succulence; '**saprijk** = *sappig*

sapris'ti *ij* by Jove!, bless my soul!

Sara'ceen (-cenen) *m*, **–s** *aj* Saracen

sar'casme *o* sarcasm, vitriol; **sar'castisch** sarcastic, pungent

sarco'faag (-fagen) *m* sarcophagus [*mv* sarcophagi]

sar'dientje (-s) *o* = *sardine*; **sar'dine** (-s) *v* sardine

sar'donisch sardonic

'**sarong** (-s) *m* sarong

'**sarren** (sarde, h. gesard) *vt* tease, bait

sas *in zijn* ~ *zijn* be in good humour

'**sassen** (saste, h. gesast) *vi* **P** piss

'**satan** (-s) *m* Satan, devil; **sa'tanisch, 'satans** satanic, diabolical; **–kind** (-eren) *o* Satan's brood

satel'liet (-en) *m* satellite[2]; **–staat** (-staten) *m* satellite country; **–stad** (-steden) *v* satellite town

'**sater** (-s) *m* satyr

sa'tijn *o* satin; **~achtig** satiny; **–en** *aj* satin; **–hout** *o* satinwood; **sati'neren** (satineerde, h. gesatineerd) *vt* satin, glaze; *gesatineerd papier* glazed paper; **sati'net** *o* & *m* satinet(te), sateen

sa'tire (-s en -n) *v* satire; *een* ~ *maken op* satirize; **sa'tiricus** (-ci) *m* satirist; **sati'riek, sa'tirisch** satiric(al)

sa'traap (-trapen) *m* satrap

satur'naliën *mv* saturnalia; **Sa'turnus** *m* Saturn

sau'cijs [so.'sɛis] (-cijzen) *v* sausage; **sau'cijzebroodje** (-s) *o* sausage-roll

'**sauna** ('s) *m* sauna

saus (-en en sauzen) *v* 1 sauce[2]; 2 (v o o r t a b a k) flavour, flavouring; 3 (v o o r m u r e n &) (white)wash, distemper; '**sausen** (sauste, h. gesaust) **I** *vt* flavour [tobacco]; (white)wash, distemper [ceilings]; sauce[2] [food &]; **II** *vi* (r e g e n e n) rain; '**sauskom** (-men) *v* sauce-boat; **–lepel** (-s) *m* sauce-ladle

sau'veren [so.-] (sauveerde, h. gesauveerd) *vt* protect, shield, screen

'**sauzen** (sausde, h. gesausd) = *sausen*

sa'vanne (-n en -s) *v* savanna(h)

sa'vooi(e)kool (-kolen) *v* savoy (cabbage)

savou'reren [-vu.-] (savoureerde, h. gesavoureerd) *vt* savour, relish

'**sawa** ('s) *m* paddy-field, rice-field

saxofo'nist (-en) *m* saxophonist; **saxo'foon** (-s en -fonen) *v* saxophone

sca'breus scabrous, indecent; risky [joke]

'**scala** ('s) *v* & *o* scale [ook ♪]; range; variety; *het hele* ~ *van gevoelens* the whole gamut of feelings

scalp (-en) *m* scalp; **scal'peermes** (-sen) *o* scalping knife; **scal'peren** (scalpeerde, h. gescalpeerd) *vt* scalp, cut the scalp off

scan'deren (scandeerde, h. gescandeerd) *vt* scan [verses]

Scandi'navië *o* Scandinavia; **–r** (-s) *m* Scandinavian; **Scandi'navisch** Scandinavian

scapu'lier (-s en -en) *o* & *m rk* scapulary, scapular

sce'nario [se.-] ('s) *o* scenario; (i n z. v. f i l m) script; **–schrijver** (-s) *m* scenarist, scenario writer; (i n z. v. f i l m) script-writer

'scène ['sɛ:nə] (-s) *v* 1 scene; 2 [unpleasant] scene; *in ~ zetten* mount, stage [a play]; undertake, get up

'scepsis ['s(k)ɛp-] *v* scepticism

'scepter ['s(k)ɛp-] (-s) *m* sceptre; *de ~ zwaaien* wield (sway) the sceptre, bear (hold) sway; **F** rule the roost

scepti'cisme [s(k)ɛp-] *o* scepticism; **'scepticus** (-ci) *m* sceptic; **'sceptisch** sceptical

scha = *schade*

schaaf (schaven) *v* 1 plane; 2 [cucumber] slicer; **–bank** (-en) *v* joiner's (carpenter's) bench; **–beitel** (-s) *m*, **–mes** (-sen) *o* plane-iron; **–sel** *o* shavings, scobs; **–wond(e)** (-wonden) *v* graze, gall, chafe, abrasion

schaak *o* check; *~ geven* check; *~ spelen* play (at) chess; *~ staan (zijn)* be in check; **–bord** (-en) *o* chess-board; **–club** (-s) *v* chess-club; **–kampioen** (-en) *m* chess-champion; **–kampioenschap** (-pen) *o* chess-championship; **–klok** (-ken) *v* chess-clock; **schaak'mat** checkmate; *hij werd ~ gezet* 1 *sp* he was mated; 2 *fig* he was checkmated; **'schaakmeester** (-s) *m* chess master, master of chess; **–partij** (-en) *v* game of chess; **–spel** (-len) *o* 1 (game of) chess; 2 chess-board and men; **–speler** (-s) *m* chess-player; **–stuk** (-ken) *o* chess-man, chess-piece; **–toernooi** (-en) *o* chess-tournament; **–wedstrijd** (-en) *m* chess-match

schaal (schalen) *v* 1 (v. s c h a a l d i e r) shell; 2 (d o p) shell [in one piece], valve [as half of a shell]; 3 (s c h o t e l) dish, bowl; 4 (o m r o n d t e g a a n) plate [at church]; 5 (v. w e e g - s c h a a l) scale, pan; 6 (w e e g s c h a a l) (pair of) scales; 7 (v e r h o u d i n g) scale; 8 *fig* scale; *dat doet de ~ overslaan* that's what turns the scale; *met de ~ rondgaan* make a plate-collection; *op ~ tekenen* draw to scale; *op grote (kleine) ~* on a large (small) scale; *op grote ~* ook: large-scale [map, campaign &]; wholesale [arrests, slaughter &]; extensively [used &]; [...] writ large; zie ook: *gewicht*; **–dier** (-en) *o* crustacean; **–model** (-len) *o* scale model; **–tje** (-s) *o* (small) dish; **–verdeling** (-en) *v* graduation-scale; **–vergroting** (-en) *v* scaling-up

'schaamachtig shamefaced, bashful, coy; **–heid** *v* bashfulness, coyness, shame; **'schaambeen** (-deren) *o* pubis, **–delen** *mv* privy (private) parts, privates; **–haar** *o* pubic hair(s); **–heuvel** (-s) *m* mons pubis (veneris);

–luis (-luizen) *v* crab louse; **–rood I** *aj* blushing with shame; *zij werd ~* she blushed with shame; **II** *o* blush of shame; *iem. het ~ op de kaken jagen* put sbd. to the blush; **–streek** *v* pubic (pudendal) region, pubes; **'schaamte** *v* shame; *alle ~ afgelegd hebben* have lost all sense of shame; **–gevoel** *o* sense of shame; *geen ~ hebben* have lost all sense of shame; **–loos** shameless, barefaced, impudent, brazen, unblushing; **schaamte'loosheid** *v* shamelessness, impudence, brazenness

schaap (schapen) *o* sheep²; *verdoold ~* stray(ing) (lost) sheep²; *het zwarte ~* the black sheep; *het arme ~* the poor thing; *de schapen van de bokken scheiden* separate the sheep from the goats; *er gaan veel makke schapen in één hok* heart-room makes house-room; *als er één ~ over de dam is volgen er meer* one sheep follows another; **'schaapachtig** sheepish²; **–heid** *v* sheepishness²; **'schaapherder** (-s) *m* shepherd; **–in** (-nen) *v* shepherdess; **'schaapje** (-s) *o* (little) sheep; *zijn ~s op het droge hebben* have made one's pile; **'schaapskooi** (-en) *v* sheep-fold, (sheep) cote; **–kop** (-pen) *m* sheep's head; *fig* blockhead, mutton-head, mutt; **–le(d)er** = *schapele(d)er*; **–vacht** (-en) = *schapevacht*

1 schaar (scharen) *v* 1 (o m t e k n i p p e n) scissors, pair of scissors; 2 (o m t e s n o e i e n) shears, pair of shears; 3 (v a n p l o e g) share; 4 pincer, nipper, claw [of a lobster]

2 schaar (scharen) *v* (m e n i g t e) = *schare*

3 schaar (scharen) *v* (k e r f) = *schaard(e)*; **'schaard(e)** (schaarden) *v* nick, notch [in a saw, a knife &]

schaars I *aj* scarce, scanty; infrequent [visit]; **II** *ad* 1 scarcely, scantily; 2 seldom; **–heid** *v* scarcity, scantiness, dearth; **–te** *v* scarcity [of teachers &], dearth [of money &], shortage, famine [in glass]

schaats (-en) *v* skate; **'schaatsen** (schaatste, h. geschaatst) *vi* skate; **'schaatsenrijden** (reed 'schaatsen, h. 'schaatsengereden) *vi* skate; **II** *o* skating; **–er** (-s) *m* skater; **'schaatsriem** (-en) *m* skating strap; **–schoen** (-en) *m* skating boot; **scha'blone, scha'bloon** = *sjablone, sjabloon*

schacht (-en) *v* shank [of an anchor]; leg [of a boot]; stem [of an arrow]; quill [of a feather]; shaft [of a mine, an oar]; ⚒ scape; △ well (-hole); **–opening** (-en) *v* pit-head

'schade *v* damage, harm, detriment; *materiële ~* material damage; *~ aanrichten (doen)* cause (do) damage, do harm; *zijn ~ inhalen* make up for sth., compensate for; *~ lijden* sustain damage, be damaged; suffer a loss, lose; *~ toebrengen* do damage to, inflict damage on; zie ook: *verhalen*; *d o o r ~ en schande wordt men wijs* live and learn;

t o t ~ *van zijn gezondheid* to the detriment (to the prejudice) of his health; **–lijk** harmful, hurtful, injurious, detrimental, noxious [fumes, insects, substances]; (o n v o o r d e l i g) unprofitable; **'schadeloos** *iem.* ~ *stellen* indemnify (compensate) sbd.; *zich* ~ *stellen* indemnify (正 recoup) oneself; **–stelling** *v* indemnification, compensation, 正 recoupment; **'schaden** (schaadde, h. geschaad) **I** *vt* damage, hurt, harm; **II** *va* do harm, be harmful; **'schadepost** (-en) *m* unexpected loss; **–regeling** *v* adjustment of claims; settlement of damages; **–vergoeding** (-en) *v* indemnification, compensation; ~ *eisen (van iem.)* claim damages (from sbd.), 正 sue (sbd.) for damages; **–verhaal** (-halen) *o* redress; **–vordering** (-en) *v* claim (for damages)

'schaduw (-en) *v* 1 (z o n d e r b e p a a l d e o m t r e k) shade; 2 (m e t b e p a a l d e o m t r e k) shadow [of a man &]; *een* ~ *van wat hij geweest was* the shadow of his former self; *de* ~ *des doods* the shadow of death; *iem. als zijn* ~ *volgen* follow a man like his shadow; *zijn* ~ *vooruitwerpen* announce itself; *een* ~ *werpen op* cast (throw) a shadow on; *fig* cast a shadow (a gloom) over; *in de* ~ *lopen* walk in the shade; *je kunt niet in zijn* ~ *staan* you are not fit to hold a candle to him; *in de* ~ *stellen* put in (throw into) the shade, eclipse; **–beeld** (-en) *o* silhouette; **'schaduwen** (schaduwde, h. geschaduwd) *vt* shade; *fig* shadow, follow [a criminal]; **'schaduwkabinet** (-ten) *o* shadow cabinet; **–kant** (-en) *m* shady side [of the road]; **–rijk** shady, shadowy; **–zijde** (-n) *v* shady side; *fig* drawback

'schaffen (schafte, h. geschaft) *vt* give, procure; *zij geeft haar moeder heel wat te* ~ she gives her mother a lot of trouble

schaft (-en) *v* = *schacht*; ‖ = *schafttijd*; **'schaften** (schaftte, h. geschaft) *vi* eat; *de werklui zijn gaan* ~ have gone (home) for their meal; *ik wil niets met hem te* ~ *hebben* I will have nothing to do with him; **'schaftje** (-s) *o* diet tin, diet can; **'schaftlokaal** (-kalen) *o* canteen; **–tijd** (-en) *m*, **–uur** (-uren) *o* lunch hour, lunch(time)

'schakel (-s) *m* & *v* link[2]; *de ontbrekende* ~ the missing link; **'schakelaar** (-s) *m* switch; **'schakelarmband** (-en) *m* chain bracelet; **–bord** (-en) *o* switch-board; **'schakelen** (schakelde, h. geschakeld) *vt* link; 🚗 connect, switch; (v. v e r s n e l l i n g) shift gear; **–ling** (-en) *v* linking; 🚗 connection; **'schakelkast** (-en) *v* switch box; **–ketting** (-en) *v* ⚒ link chain; **–meubelen** *mv* unit construction furniture; **–net** (-ten) *o* trammel(-net)

1 'schaken (schaakte, h. geschaakt) *vi sp* play (at) chess

2 'schaken (schaakte, h. geschaakt) *vt* run away with, abduct [a girl]; **–er** (-s) *m* (v r o u w e n - r o v e r) abductor; ‖ (s c h a a k s p e l e r) chess-player

scha'keren (schakeerde, h. geschakeerd) *vt* grade, variegate, chequer; **–ring** (-en) *v* grade, variegation, nuance, shade

'schaking (-en) *v* elopement, abduction

schalk (-en) *m* wag, rogue; **–s** roguish, waggish

'schallen (schalde, h. geschald) *vi* sound, resound; *laten* ~ sound [the horn]

schalm (-en) *m* link

schal'mei (-en) *v* shawm

'schamel poor, humble; **–heid** *v* poverty, humbleness

'schamen (schaamde zich, h. zich geschaamd) *zich* ~ be (feel) ashamed, feel shame; *zich dood* ~, *zich de ogen uit het hoofd* ~ not know where to hide for shame; *schaam u wat!* for shame!; *je moest je* ~ you ought to be ashamed of yourself; ● *zich* ~ *o v e r* be ashamed of; *zich* ~ *v o o r iem.* 1 be ashamed for sbd.; 2 be ashamed in the presence of sbd.

'schampen (schampte, h. en is geschampt) *vt* graze

'schamper scornful, sarcastic; contemptuous; **'schamperen** (schamperde, h. geschamperd) *vi* sneer, say scornfully; **'schamperheid** (-heden) *v* scorn, sarcasm; contempt

'schampschot (-schoten) *o* grazing shot, graze

schan'daal (-dalen) *o* scandal, shame, disgrace; (o p s c h u d d i n g) row; **–pers** *v* scandal (yellow) press, gutter press; **schan'dalig I** *aj* disgraceful, scandalous, shameful; ~, *zeg!* for shame!, shame!; **II** *ad* scandalously; disgracefully, shamefully; < shockingly [bad, dear]; **'schanddaad** (-daden) *v* infamous deed, infamy, outrage, atrocity; **'schande** *v* 1 shame, disgrace, infamy, ignominy; 2 scandal; *het is (bepaald)* ~! it is a (downright) shame!; ~ *aandoen* bring shame upon, disgrace; *er* ~ *over roepen* cry shame upon it; ● *m e t* ~ *overladen* utterly disgraced; *t e* ~ *maken* 1 disgrace [a person]; 2 = *logenstraffen*; *het zal u t o t* ~ *strekken* it will be a disgrace to you; *tot mijn* ~... to my shame [I must confess]; **'schandelijk I** *aj* shameful, disgraceful, infamous, outrageous, ignominious; **II** *ad* shamefully &, < scandalously, disgracefully, infamously, outrageously; **–heid** (-heden) *v* shamefulness, ignominy, infamy; **'schandknaap** (-knapen) *m* catamite; **–merk** (-en) *o* mark of infamy, stigma, brand; **–paal** (-palen) *m* pillory, cucking-stool; **–vlek** (-ken) *v* stain, blemish, stigma; *de* ~ *der familie* the disgrace of the family; **'schandvlekken** (schandvlekte, h. geschandvlekt) *vt* disgrace, dishonour

schans (-en) *v* ⚔ entrenchment, field-work, redoubt; (s k i~) (ski) jump; **–graver** (-s) *m* trencher, entrenchment worker; **–korf** (-korven) *m* gabion

schap (-pen) *o & v* shelf

'schapebout (-en) *m* leg of mutton; **–hok** (-ken) *o* sheep-fold, (sheep-)pen, *Br* (sheep)cote; **–kaas** (-kazen) *m* sheep-cheese; **–kop** (-pen) *m* sheep's head; *fig* blockhead, mutton-head, mutt; **–le(d)er** *o* sheepskin; **–melk** *v* sheep's milk; **'schapenfokker** (-s) *m* sheep-farmer; **schapenfokke'rij** (-en) *v* 1 sheep-farming; 2 sheep-farm; **'schapenscheerder** (-s) *m* sheep-shearer, clipper; **'schaper** (-s) = *scheper*; **'schapestal** (-len) *m* sheep-fold; (sheep-)pen, *Br* (sheep)cote; **–vacht** (-en) *v* fleece; **–vel** (-len) *o* sheepskin; **–vet** *o* mutton fat; **–vlees** *o* mutton; **–wei(de)** (-den) *v* sheep-walk, sheep-run; **–wol** *v* sheep's wool; **–wolkjes** *mv* fleecy clouds

'schappelijk fair, tolerable, moderate, reasonable [prices &]; decent [fellow]

schapu'lier (-s en -en) = *scapulier*

schar (-ren) *v* 🐟 dab, flounder

☉ **'schare** (-n) *v* crowd, multitude; **'scharen** (schaarde, h. geschaard) **I** *vt* range, draw up; **II** *vr zich* ~ range oneself; *zich* ~ *a a n d e zijde van...* range oneself on the side of, range oneself with...; *zich o m d e tafel* ~ draw round the table; *zich om de leider* ~ rally round the chief; *zich o n d e r d e banieren* ~ *van* range oneself under the banners of...

'scharensliep (-en), **–slijper** (-s) *m* knife (scissors) grinder

schar'laken I *aj* scarlet; **II** *o* scarlet; **–rood** scarlet

schar'minkel (-s) *o & m* scrag, skeleton

schar'nier (-en) *o* hinge; **–gewricht** (-en) *o* hinge-joint

'scharrel *m* flirtation; **'scharrelaar** (-s) *m* 1 potterer [on skates &]; bungler; 2 $ petty dealer; **'scharrelen** (scharrelde, h. en is gescharreld) *vi* scrape, rout [among debris &]; potter about [on skates]; bungle; fumble [at a thing]; (v r ij e n) have a flirtation; *b ij elkaar* ~ get together; *er d o o r* ~ muddle through; ~ *i n* rummage in [a drawer &]; *fig* deal in [second-hand books &]

schat (-ten) *m* treasure; (l i e v e l i n g) **F** dream-boat, ducks; *mijn* ~! my darling!; *een* ~ *van kennis* a wealth of information; **–bewaarder** (-s) *m* treasurer, bursar

'schateren (schaterde, h. geschaterd) *vi* ~ *van 't lachen* roar with laughter; **'schaterlach** *m* loud laugh, burst of laughter, peals of laughter; **'schaterlachen** (schaterlachte, h. geschaterlacht) *vt* roar with laughter

'schatgraver (-s) *m* treasure-seeker; **'schatje** (-s) *o* = *liefje*; = *snoes*; **'schatkamer** (-s) *v* treasure-chamber, treasury; *fig* treasure-house, storehouse; **'schatkist** (-en) *v* (public) treasury, exchequer; **–biljet** (-ten) *o* exchequer bill; **–promesse** (-n en -s) *v* treasury bill; **schat'plichtig** tributary; **'schatrijk** very rich, wealthy; **'schattebout** (-en) *m* **F** sweetheart, honey, popsy

'schatten (schatte, h. geschat) *vt* appraise, assess, value [for taxing purposes]; estimate, value; gauge [distances]; *hoe oud schat je hem?* how old do you take him to be?; *op hoeveel schat u het?* what is your valuation?; *ik schat het geheel op een miljoen* I value (estimate) the whole at a million; (*naar waarde*) ~ appreciate; *hij schat het niet naar waarde* he does not estimate it at its true value; *te hoog* ~ overestimate, overvalue; *te laag* ~ underestimate, undervalue; **–er** (-s) *m* appraiser, valuer [of furniture &]; assessor (of taxes)

'schattig sweet

'schatting (-en) *v* 1 valuation, estimate, estimation; 2 (c ij n s) tribute, contribution; *naar* ~ at a rough estimate; an estimated [three million a year]

'schaven (schaafde, h. geschaafd) *vt* plane [a plank]; *zijn knie* ~ graze one's knee; *zijn vel* ~ abrade (graze) one's skin

scha'vot (-ten) *o* scaffold

scha'vuit (-en) *m* rascal, rogue, knave; **–enstuk** (-ken) *o* roguish trick

'schede (-n) *v* sheath, scabbard [of a sword]; ⚓ sheath; (v a g i n a) vagina; *i n de* ~ *steken* sheathe [the sword]; *u i t de* ~ *trekken* unsheathe

'schedel (-s) *m* skull, cranium, brain-pan; *hij heeft een harde* ~ he is thick-skulled; **–basisfractuur** [-zɪs-] *v* fracture of the skull base, fractured skull; **–boor** (-boren) *v* trepan, trephine; **–breuk** (-en) *v* fractured skull, fracture of the skull; **–holte** (-n en -s) *v* brain (cranial) cavity; **–leer** *v* craniology; (~ v a n G a l l) phrenology; **–naad** (-naden) *m* cranial suture

schee (scheeën) = *schede*

scheed 'uit (scheden uit) V.T. v. *uitscheiden*

scheef I *aj* on one side; oblique [angle]; slanting, sloping [mast]; wry [neck, face]; *hij is wat* ~ (*gebouwd*) he is a little on one side; *scheve positie* false position; *de scheve toren van Pisa* the leaning tower of Pisa; *scheve verhouding* false position; *scheve voorstelling* misrepresentation; **II** *ad* obliquely &; awry, askew; *iets* ~ *houden* slant sth.; *zijn hoofd* ~ *houden* hold the head sidewise; *zijn schoenen* ~ *lopen* wear one's boots on one side; *de zaken* ~ *voorstellen* misrepresent things;

–heid *v* obliqueness, wryness; **–hoekig** skew, with oblique angles; **–ogig** slant-eyed; **–te** *v* = *scheefheid*

scheel squinting, squint-eyed, cross-eyed, boss-eyed; *schele hoofdpijn* migraine, bilious headache; ~ [*divergent*] *oog* wall-eye; *iets met schele ogen aanzien* look enviously at sth.; *schele ogen maken* excite envy; *zich* ~ *ergeren* be beside oneself with annoyance; ~ *van de honger* ravenous; ~ *zien* squint; *hij ziet erg* ~ he has a fearful squint; ~ *zien naar* squint at; **–heid** *v* squint(ing); **–ogig** = *scheel*; **–oog** (-ogen) *m-v* squint-eye, squinter; **–zien I** *o* squint(ing); **II** (zag 'scheel, h. 'scheelgezien) *vi* squint

1 scheen (schenen) *v* shin

2 scheen (schenen) V.T. v. *schijnen*

'scheenbeen (-deren) *o* shin-bone, tibia; **–beschermer** (-s) *m* shin guard (pad)

scheep ~ *gaan* go on board, embark, take ship; **'scheepsagent** (-en) *m* shipping agent; **–agentuur** (-turen) *v* shipping agency; **–arts** (-en) *m* ship's doctor (surgeon); **–behoeften** *mv* ship's provisions; **–bemanning** *v* ship's crew; **–berichten** *mv* shipping intelligence; **–beschuit** (-en) *v* ship's biscuit, hard-tack; **–bevrachter** (-s) *m* charterer, freighter; **–bouw** *m* ship-building; **–bouwkunde** *v* naval architecture; **scheepsbouw'kundige** (-n) *m* naval architect; **'scheepsbouw-meester** (-s) *m* ship-builder, naval architect; **–dokter** (-s) *m* ship's doctor (surgeon); **–geschut** *o* naval guns; **–helling** (-en) *v* slip(s), slipway, ship-way; **–jongen** (-s) *m* ship-boy, cabin-boy; **–journaal** [-ʒuː rnaːl] (-nalen) *o* log(-book), ship's journal; **–kapitein** (-s) *m* (ship-)captain; **–kok** (-s) *m* ship's cook; **–kompas** (-sen) *o* ship's compass; **–lading** (-en) *v* shipload, cargo; **–lantaarn, –lantaren** (-s) *v* ship's lantern; **–lengte** (-n en -s) *v* ship's length; **–maat** (-s) *m* shipmate; **–makelaar** (-s en -laren) *m* ship-broker, shipping agent; **–motor** (-s en -toren) *m* marine-engine; **–papieren** *mv* ship's papers; **–raad** (-raden) *m* council of war (on board a ship); **–ramp** (-en) *v* shipping disaster; **–recht** *o* maritime law; *driemaal is* ~ to be allowed to try three times running is but fair; **–roeper** (-s) *m* speaking-trumpet, megaphone; **–rol** (-len) *v* = *monsterrol*: **–ruim** (-en) *o* ship's (cargo) hold; **–ruimte** *v* tonnage, shipping (space); **–tijdingen** *mv* shipping intelligence; **scheeps'timmerman** (-lui en -lieden) *m* 1 shipcarpenter; 2 (b o u-w e r) shipwright, *Am* shipfitter; **–werf** (-werven) *v* 1 ship-building yard; ship-yard; 2 (v. d. m a r i n e) dockyard; **'scheepsvolk** *o* 1 ship's crew; 2 sailors; **–vracht** (-en) *v* ship-load; **–werf** (-werven) *v* = *scheepstimmerwerf*;

'scheepvaart *v* navigation; shipping; **–maat-schappij** (-en) *v* shipping company

'scheerapparaat (-raten) *o elektrisch* ~ electric shaver, electric razor; **–bakje** (-s) *o*, **–bekken** (-s) *o* shaving basin (bowl); **–crème** *v* shaving-cream; **–der** (-s) *m* 1 barber; 2 [sheep] shearer; **–gereedschap, –gerei** *o* shaving-tackle, shaving things; **–kop** (-pen) *m* shaving head; **–kwast** (-en) *m* shaving-brush; **–lijn** (-en) *v* guy-rope [of a tent]

'scheerling (-en) *v* 🌿 hemlock

'scheerlings = *rakelings*; **–mes** (-sen) *o* razor; **–mesje** (-s) *o* blade [of a safety-razor]; **–riem** (-en) *m* (razor-)strop; **–spiegel** (-s) *m* shaving mirror; **–staaf** (-staven) *v* shaving-stick; **–steentje** (-s) *o* shaving-block; **–water** *o* shaving-water; **–winkel** (-s) *m* barber's shop; **–wol** *v* shorn wool; **–zeep** *v* shaving-soap

1 scheet (scheten) **P** *m* fart, wind; *een* ~ *laten* fart

2 scheet (scheten) P V.T. van *schijten*

scheg (-gen) *v* ⚓ cutwater; **–beeld** (-en) *o* figurehead; **'schegge** (-n) = *scheg*

'scheidbaar divisible, separable°; (v a n b e g r i p p e n) differentiable, distinguishable; **–heid** *v* separability°; (v. b e g r i p p e n) distinguishability; **'scheiden* I** *vt* 1 (i n 't a l g.) separate, divide, sever, disconnect, disjoin, disunite, sunder; 2 (h e t h a a r) part; 3 (v. h u w e l ij k) divorce; *het hoofd van de romp* ~ sever the head from the body; *de vechtenden* ~ separate the combatants; *hij liet zich van haar* ~ he divorced her; **II** *vi* part; *als vrienden* ~ part friends; *u i t het leven* ~ depart this life; *zij konden niet* (v a n elkaar) ~ they could not part (from each other); *zij konden niet van het huis* ~ 1 they could not take leave of the house; 2 they could not part with the house; *hier* ~ (zich) *onze wegen* here our roads part; *b ij het* ~ *van de markt* towards the end; **'scheiding** (-en) *v* 1 separation, division, disjunction; 2 partition [between rooms]; 3 parting [of the hair]; 4 divorce [of a married couple]; ~ *van kerk en staat* separation of Church and State, disestablishment; **'scheidingslijn** (-en) *v* dividing line; (g r e n s l ij n) boundary line, demarcation line, line of demarcation; **–wand** (-en) *m* partition(-wall), dividing wall; **'scheidsge-recht** (-en) *o* court of arbitration; *aan een* ~ *onderwerpen* refer to arbitration; **–lijn** (-en) = *scheidingslijn*; **–man** (-lieden) *m* arbiter, arbitrator; **–muur** (-muren) *m* partition(-wall), dividing wall; *fig* barrier; **–rechter** (-s) *m* 1 arbiter, arbitrator; 2 *sp* umpire, referee; **scheids'rechterlijk I** *aj* arbitral; **~e** *uitspraak* arbitral award; **II** *ad* by arbitration

'scheikunde *v* chemistry; **schei'kundig**

chemical; ~ *ingenieur* chemical engineer; ~ *laboratorium* chemistry laboratory; **–e** (-n) *m* & *v* chemist

1 schel (-len) *v* bell; *de ~len vielen hem van de ogen* the scales fell from his eyes

2 schel I *aj* 1 (v. g e l u i d) shrill, strident; 2 (v. l i c h t) glaring; **II** *ad* 1 shrilly, stridently; 2 glaringly

'**Schelde** *v* Scheldt

'**schelden*** *vi* call names, use abusive language; ~ *als een viswijf* scold like a fishwife; ~ *op* abuse, revile; '**scheldkanonnade** (-s) *v* diatribe, torrent of abuse; **–naam** (-namen) *m* nickname, sobriquet; (b ij n a a m) by-name; **–partij** (-en) *v* scolding, exchange of abuse; **–woord** (-en) *o* term of abuse, invective; ~*en* ook: abusive language, abuse

'**schelen** (scheelde, h. gescheeld) *vt* 1 (v e r- s c h i l l e n d zijn) differ; 2 (o n t b r e k e n) want; *zij ~ niets* they don't differ; *dat scheelt veel* that makes a great difference; *zij scheelden veel in leeftijd* there was a great disparity of age between them; *wat scheelt eraan (u)?* what is the matter (with you?), what's wrong?; *hij scheelt wat aan zijn voet* there is something the matter with his foot; *het scheelde maar een haartje* it was a near thing; *het scheelde niet veel of hij was in de afgrond gestort* he had a narrow escape from falling into the abyss, he nearly fell, he almost fell into the abyss; *wat kan dat ~?* what does it matter?; *wat kan hun dat ~?* what do they care?; *wat kan u dat ~?* what's that to you?; *wat kan het je ~?* who cares? *het kan me niet ~* 1 I don't care; 2 I don't mind; *het kan me geen snars ~* I don't care a damn

schelf (schelven) *v* stack, rick [of hay]

'**schelheid** *v* 1 (v. g e l u i d) shrillness; 2 (v a n l i c h t) glare; **–klinkend** shrill, strident

'**schelkoord** (-en) *o* & *v* bell-rope, bell-pull

'**schellak** *o* & *m* shellac

'**schellen** (schelde, h. gescheld) *vi* ring the bell, ring; zie *bellen*

'**schellinkje** (-s) *o het ~* the gallery, **F** the gods; *op het ~* **F** among the gods

schelm (-en) *m* rogue, knave, rascal; **–achtig** roguish, knavish, rascally; **–enroman** (-s) *m* picaresque novel; **schelme'rij** (-en) *v* roguery, knavery; **schelms** roguish[2]; '**schelmstuk** (-ken) *o* piece of knavery, roguish trick

schelp (-en) *v* 1 shell, valve [of a mollusc]; 2 (b ij d i n e r) scallop; **–dier** (-en) *o* shell-fish, testacean; **–envisser** (-s) *m* shell fisher; **–kalk** *m* shell-lime

'**scheluw** (v. h o u t) warped

'**schelvis** (-sen) *m* haddock; **–ogen** *mv* fishy eyes

'**schema** ('s en -mata) *o* diagram, skeleton,

outline(s); pattern, scheme; **sche'matisch** schematic; in diagram, in outline; ~*e voorstelling* diagram; **schemati'seren** [-'ze:-] (schemati- seerde, h. geschematiseerd) *vt* system(at)ize, schematize

'**schemer** *m* twilight; dusk; **–achtig** dim[2], dusky; **–avond** (-en) *m* twilight; **–donker** *o*, **–duister** *o* twilight; '**schemeren** (schemerde, h. geschemerd) *vi* 1 dawn [in the morning]; grow dusk [in the evening]; 2 sit without a light; 3 glisten, gleam [of a light]; *er schemert mij zo iets voor de geest* I have a sort of dim recollection of it; *het schemerde mij voor de ogen* my eyes grew dim, my head was swimming; '**schemerig** dim[2], dusky; '**schemering** (-en) *v* twilight[2], dusk, gloaming; *in de ~* at twilight; '**schemerlamp** (-en) *v* shaded lamp, (k l e i n e, o p t a f e l) table-lamp; (g r o t e, s t a a n d e) standard lamp, *Am* floor-lamp; **–licht** *o* 1 twilight; 2 dim light; **–tijd** *m* twilight; **–toestand** *m ps* twilight state; **–uurtje** (-s) *o* twilight (hour)

'**schendblad** (-bladen) *o* scandal sheet; '**schenden*** *vt* disfigure [one's face &]; damage [a book]; deface [a statue &]; *fig* violate [one's oath, a treaty, a law, a sanc- tuary]; vitiate [a contract]; outrage[2] [law, morality]; break [a promise]; **–er** (-s) *m* violator, transgressor; '**schendig** sacrilegious; '**schending** (-en) *v* disfigurement, deface- ment; *fig* violation, infringement

'**schenen** V.T. meerv. van *schijnen*

'**schenkblaadje** (-s) *o*, **–blad** (-bladen) *o* tray

'**schenkel** (-s) *m* 1 shank, femur; 2 = *schenkel- vlees*; **–vlees** *o* shin of beef

'**schenken* I** *vt* 1 (g i e t e n) pour; 2 (g e v e n) give, grant, present with; donate [to the Red Cross]; *ik schenk u het lesgeld* I let you off the fee; *iem. het leven ~* grant sbd. his life; *een kind het leven ~* give birth to a child; *ik schenk u de rest* never mind the rest, I'll excuse you the rest; *wilt u (de) thee ~?* will you kindly pour out the tea?; *wijn ~* 1 retail wine; 2 serve wine; *ze schonk hem twee zonen* she bore him two sons; **II** *va* serve drinks; **–er** (-s) *m* 1 (d i e i n- s c h e n k t) cupbearer; 2 (d i e g e e f t) donor; '**schenking** (-en) *v* donation, gift; benefac- tion; '**schenkkan** (-nen) *v* flagon, tankard; **–kurk** (-en) *v* cork for pouring out

'**schennis** *v* violation; outrage

schep (-pen) 1 *v* (w e r k t u i g) scoop, shovel; 2 *m* (h o e v e e l h e i d) spoonful, shovelful; *een ~ geld* **F** heaps of money; **–bord** (-en) *o* float- board, float

'**schepel** (-s) *o* & *m* bushel, decalitre

'**schepeling** (-en) *m* member of the crew [of a ship]; sailor; *de ~en* the crew

1 'schepen (-en) *m* sheriff, alderman

2 'schepen *mv.* v. **schip**

'scheper (-s) *m prov* shepherd

'schepnet (-ten) *o* landing-net; **1 'scheppen***
vt scoop, ladle; shovel [coal, snow]; *vol* ~ fill;
leeg ~ empty (out), ladle out; *de auto schepte het
kind* the car hit the child; zie ook: *adem, luchtje*
&

2 'scheppen* *vt* create, make; **–d** creative;
'schepper (-s) *m* 1 (v o o r t b r e n g e r)
creator, maker; || 2 (w e r k t u i g) scoop;
'schepping (-en) *v* creation; **'scheppings-
drang** *m* creative urge; **–geschiedenis** *v*
history of creation; **–kracht** *v* creative power;
–verhaal (-halen) *o* history of creation,
Genesis; **–vermogen** *o* creative power;
–werk *o* (work of) creation

'scheprad (-raderen) *o* paddle-wheel

'schepsel (-s en -en) *o* creature

'schepvat (-vaten) *o* scoop, bail

'scheren* I *vt* shave [men]; shear [sheep &
cloth]; clip [a hedge]; skim [stones over the
water, the waves]; ⚓ reeve [a rope]; ✗ warp
[linen &]; *fig* fleece [customers]; **II** *vr zich* ~
shave; *zich laten* ~ get shaved, have a shave;
scheer je weg! be off!, begone!, get you gone!; **III**
vi ~ *langs* graze (shoot) past; *de zwaluwen* ~ *over
het water* the swallows skim (over) the water

scherf (scherven) *v* potsherd [of a pot]; fragment, splinter [of glass, of a shell]; *scherven*
flinders

'schering (-en) *v* 1 shearing [of sheep]; 2 warp
[of cloth]; ~ *en inslag* warp and woof; *dat is hier
~ en inslag* that is customary, that is quite the
usual thing (practice)

scherm (-en) *o* 1 screen [for the hearth, for
moving or televised pictures]; 2 curtain [on
the stage]; 3 ⚘ umbel [of a flower]; 4 awning
[of a shop &]; *achter de* ~*en* in the wings,
behind the scenes; *fig* behind the scenes; *wie zit
er achter de* ~*en?* who is at the back of it, who is
the wire-puller?; **–bloem** (-en) *v* umbellifer;
scherm'bloemigen *mv* umbellate (umbellif-
erous) plants

'schermdegen (-s) *m* foil; **'schermen**
(schermde, h. geschermd) *vi* fence; *in het wild* ~
talk at random; *met de armen in de lucht* ~
flourish one's arms; *met woorden* ~ fence with
words; **–er** (-s) *m* fencer; **'schermhand-
schoen** (-en) *m* & *v* fencing-glove; **–kunst** *v*
art of fencing, swordsmanship; **–masker** (-s) *o*
fencing-mask; **–meester** (-s) *m* fencing-
master; **–school** (-scholen) *v* fencing-school

scher'mutselen (schermutselde, h. gescher-
mutseld) *vi* skirmish; **–ling** (-en) *v* skirmish

'schermvormig umbellate

'schermzaal (-zalen) *v* fencing-room, fencing-
hall

scherp I *aj* sharp[2] [in de meeste betekenissen];
keen[2] [eyes, smell, intellect &]; trenchant[2]
[sword, language]; acute[2] [angles, judgement];
poignant[2] [taste, hunger]; *gram* hard [conso-
nant]; hot [spices]; *fig* pungent [pen]; keen
[competition]; sharp-cut [features]; acrid
[temper]; caustic [tongue]; tart [reply]; brisk
[trot]; live [cartridge]; strict, close, searching
[examination]; ~ *maken* sharpen; **II** *ad* sharply,
keenly &; [watch them] closely; ~*er kijken* look
closer; **III** *o* edge [of a knife]; *m e t* ~ *schieten* ✗
use ball ammunition; *z o n d e r* ~ *schieten* ✗ run
dry; *een paard o p* ~ *zetten* calk a horse;
'scherpen (scherpte, h. gescherpt) *vt* sharpen[2]
[a pencil, faculties, the appetite &]; **'scherp-
heid** (-heden) *v* sharpness, keenness, acute-
ness, pungency, trenchancy; **–hoekig** acute-
angled; **scherpom'lijnd** sharp-cut, sharp-
edged; **'scherprechter** (-s) *m* executioner;
–schutter (-s) *m* sharpshooter, [good] marksman; (v e r d e k t o p g e s t e l d) sniper;
–slijper (-s) *m* precisian, literalist, bigot;
–snijdend sharp, keen-edged; **–te** (-s en -n)
v sharpness[2], edge; **–ziend** sharp-sighted,
keen-sighted, eagle-eyed, hawk-eyed, penetrating; **scherp'zinnig I** *aj* acute, sharp (-witted);
II *ad* acutely, sharply; **–heid** (-heden)
v acumen, penetration, keen perception

scherts *v* pleasantry, raillery, banter; jest, joke;
in ~ in jest, jokingly; *het is maar* ~ he is only
joking; ~ *terzijde* joking apart; *hij kan geen* ~
verstaan he cannot take a joke; **'schertsen**
(schertste, h. geschertst) *vi* jest, joke; ~*d* in jest,
jokingly; *met hem valt niet te* ~ he is not to be
trifled with; **schertsender'wijs, –'wijze**
jokingly, jestingly, by way of a joke, in jest,
facetiously, jocularly; **'schertsfiguur** (-guren)
v wash-out, nonentity, joke; **–vertoning** (-en)
v wash-out, joke

'schervengericht *o* ostracism

'scheten P V.T. *mv.* v. **schijten**

schets (-en) *v* sketch, draught, (sketchy) outline;
een ruwe ~ *geven van* draw (sketch) in outline;
–boek (-en) *o* sketch-book; **'schetsen**
(schetste, h. geschetst) *vt* sketch, outline; *wie
schetst mijn verbazing* imagine my amazement;
–er (-s) *m* sketcher; **'schetskaart** (-en) *v*
sketch-map; **schets'matig** sketchy; **'schets-
tekening** (-en) *v* sketch

'schetteren (schetterde, h. geschetterd) *vi* 1 (v.
t r o m p e t &) bray, blare; 2 (o p s n ij d e n)
brag, swagger

scheur (-en) *v* tear, rent [in clothes], slit, split,
crack, cleft; **S** (m o n d) trap; *hou je* ~*!* shut
your trap; **–buik** *m* & *o* scurvy; **'scheuren
I** (scheurde, h. gescheurd) *vt* 1 (a a n

s t u k k e n) tear up [a letter]; rend [one's garments]; 2 (e e n s c h e u r m a k e n i n) tear [a dress &]; break up, plough up [grass-land]; *in stukken* ~ tear to pieces; **II** (scheurde, is gescheurd) *va & vi* tear; (v. ijs) crack; (*met een auto*) *door de stad* ~ tear through the town; *het scheurt licht* it tears easily; **–ring** (-en) *v* breaking up [of grass-land]; *fig* rupture, split, disruption, schism; **'scheurkalender** (-s) *m* tear-off calendar; **–maker** (-s) *m* schismatic; **–papier** *o* waste-paper

scheut (-en) *m* 1 ⚘ shoot, sprig; 2 (k l e i n e h o e v e e l h e i d) dash [of vinegar &]; 3 (v a n p ij n) twinge, shooting pain

'scheutig I *aj* open-handed, liberal; (*niet*) ~ *met...* (not) lavish of...; **II** *ad* liberally; **–heid** *v* open-handedness, liberality

'scheutje (-s) *o = scheut*

schibbo'let [ʃibo.'lɪt] (-s) *o = sjibbolet*

schicht (-en) *m* dart, bolt, flash [of lightning]

'schichtig I *aj* shy, skittish; ~ *worden* shy (at *voor*); **II** *ad* shyly

schie'dammer *m* Schiedam, Hollands [gin]

'schielijk quick, rapid, swift, sudden; **–heid** *v* quickness, rapidity, swiftness, suddenness

schiep (schiepen) V.T. v. 2 *scheppen*

schier almost, nearly, all but; **–eiland** (-en) *o* peninsula

'schietbaan (-banen) *v* rifle-range, range; **'schieten* I** *vi* fire [with a gun]; shoot [of persons, pain & ⚘]; (s n e l b e w e g e n) dash, rush; ● *dat schoot mij d o o r het hoofd (i n de gedachte)* it flashed across my mind (upon me); *in de aren* ~ come into ear, ear; *de bomen* ~ *in de hoogte* the trees are shooting up; *hij schoot in de kleren* he slipped (huddled) on his clothes; *de tranen schoten hem in de ogen* the tears started (in)to his eyes; *er n a a s t* ~ miss the mark; *o n d e r een brug door* ~ shoot a bridge; *onder iems. duiven* ~ poach on sbd.'s preserves; ~ *o p* fire at; *u i t de grond* ~ spring up; *iem. laten* ~ **F** drop sbd., give sbd. the go-by; *iets laten* ~ let sth. go; let slip [a chance]; *een touw laten* ~ let go (slip) a rope, pay out a rope; *een kerel om op te* ~ a dreadful (annoying) fellow; *het is om op te* ~ it is hideous (frightful), it is not fit to be seen; **II** *vt* shoot [an animal]; *geld* ~ provide funds; *netten* ~ shoot nets; *een plaatje* ~ take a snapshot; *een schip in de grond* ~ send a ship to the bottom; *vuur* ~ shoot (flash) fire; *de zon* ~ take the sun's altitude; *zich voor de kop* ~ blow out one's brains; **–er** (-s) *m* 1 shooter; 2 ✕ bolt [of a lock]; 3 peel [for the oven]; **'schietgat** (-gaten) *o* ⚔ loop-hole; **–gebed** (-beden) *o* little prayer; **–geweer** (-weren) *o* gun, fire-arm, **F** shooter; **–graag F** trigger-happy, quick on the draw; **–katoen** *o & m* gun-cotton; **–lood** (-loden) *o* plummet, plumb; **–oefeningen** *mv* ✕ target-practice; ⚓ gunnery practice; **–partij** (-en) *v* shooting; **–schijf** (-schijven) *v* target, mark; **–school** (-scholen) *v* 1 ✕ musketry school; 2 ⚓ gunnery school; **–spoel** (-en) *v* shuttle; **–stoel** (-en) *m* ✈ ejector seat; **–tent** (-en) *v* shooting-gallery; **–terrein** (-en) *o* practice-ground, range; **–wedstrijd** (-en) *m* shooting-match, shooting-competition

'schiften I (schiftte, h. geschift) *vt* sort, separate; (z o r g v u l d i g o n d e r z o e k e n) sift; **II** (schiftte, is geschift) *vi* curdle; **–ting** *v* 1 sorting; (z o r g v u l d i g o n d e r z o e k) sifting; 2 curdling [of milk]; zie ook: *geschift*

schijf (schijven) *v* 1 slice [of ham &]; 2 (v a n d a m s p e l) man; 3 (s c h i e t s c h ij f) target; 4 (v. w i e l &) disc, disk; 5 ✕ sheave [of a pulley]; 6 (v. t e l e f o o n &) dial; *dat loopt over veel schijven* there are wheels within wheels; **–je** (-s) *o* thin slice [of meat &]; round [of lemon &]; **–rem** (-men) *v* disc brake; **–schieten I** *o* target-practice; **II** (schijfschoot, h. schijfge-schoten) *vi* fire at a target; **–vormig** disc-shaped, discoid; **–wiel** (-en) *o* disc-wheel

schijn *m* shine, glimmer; *fig* appearance [and reality]; semblance [of truth]; show, pretence, pretext; *het was alles maar* ~ it was all show; *geen* ~ *van kans* not the ghost of a chance; *zonder* ~ *of schaduw van bewijs* without a shred of evidence; ~ *en wezen* the shadow and the substance; ~ *bedriegt* appearances are deceptive; *de* ~ *is tegen hem* appearances are against him; *het heeft de* ~ *alsof...* it looks as if...; *de* ~ *aannemen* pretend, affect; *de* ~ *redden* save appearances; *de* ~ *wekken* create the appearance; ● *i n* ~ in appearance, seemingly; *n a a r alle* ~ to all appearance; *o n d e r de* ~ *van* under the pretence (pretext) of; *v o o r de* ~ for the sake of appearances; **–aanval** (-len) *m* feigned attack, feint; **–baar** seeming, apparent; **–beeld** (-en) *o* phantom; **–beweging** (-en) *v* feint; **–dood I** *aj* apparently dead, in a state of suspended animation; **II** *m & v* apparent death, suspended animation; **'schijnen*** *vi* 1 (l i c h t g e v e n) shine; glimmer; 2 (l ij k e n) seem, look; *naar het schijnt* it would seem, it appears, to all appearance; **'schijngeleerde** (-n) *m* would-be scholar; **–geleerdheid** *v* would-be learning; **–geluk** *o* false happiness; **–gestalte** (-n) *v* phase (of the moon); **–gevecht** (-en) *o* mock (sham) fight, mock (sham) battle; **schijn'heilig** hypocritical; **–e** (-n) *m-v* hypocrite; **–heid** *v* hypocrisy; **'schijnsel** (-s) *o* glimmer; **'schijntje** (-s) *o een* ~ **F** very little, a trifle; **'schijnvertoning** (-en) *v* sham, make-believe; farce, mockery [of a trial]; **–vriend**

(-en) *m* sham friend, fairweather friend;
–vroom sanctimonious; **–vroomheid** *v*
sanctimony; **–vrucht** (-en) *v* accessory
(spurious) fruit, pseudocarp; **–wereld** *v*
make-believe world; **–werper** (-s) *m* searchlight, spotlight, projector

schijt P *m* & *o* shit; *ik heb ~ aan hem* he can go
to hell (blazes, the devil); *daar heb ik ~ aan* I
couldn't care less, I don't care a hoot;
'**schijten* P** *vi* shit, crap; **schijte'rij P** *v*
diarrhoea, **F** the trots; '**schijtlaars** (-laarzen)
m = *schijtlijster*; **–lijster** (-s) **P** *m* scaredy-cat,
funk

'**schijvengeheugen** (-s) *o* disk (disc) storage

schik *m* ~ *hebben* amuse oneself, enjoy oneself;
veel ~ hebben enjoy oneself immensely; have
great fun; *in zijn ~ zijn* be pleased, be in high
spirits; *in zijn ~ zijn met iets* be pleased
(delighted) with sth.; *niet erg in zijn ~ met (over)*
not too pleased with (at)

'**schikgodinnen** *mv de* ~ the Fates, the fatal
Sisters

'**schikkelijk** = *schappelijk*

'**schikken I** (schikte, h. geschikt) *vt* arrange,
order [books &]; *we zullen het wel zien te ~* we'll
try and arrange matters; *de zaak ~* settle the
matter; **II** (schikte, h. geschikt) *onpers. ww.* in:
het schikt nogal! pretty middling; *als het u schikt*
when it is convenient to you; *het schikt me niet*
it is not convenient; *zodra het u schikt* at your
earliest convenience; **III** (schikte, is geschikt)
vi wil je wat deze kant uit ~? move up a little; **IV**
(schikte, h. geschikt) *vr zich ~* come right; *het*
zal zich wel ~ it is sure to come right; ● *zich in*
alles ~ resign oneself to everything; *hoe schikt*
hij zich in zijn nieuwe betrekking? how does he
take to his new berth?; *zich in het onvermijdelijke*
~ resign oneself to the inevitable; *zich naar*
iem. ~ conform to sbd.'s wishes; *zich om de tafel*
~ draw up round the table; zie ook *geschikt*;
–king (-en) *v* arrangement, settlement; *een ~*
treffen come to an arrangement (with *met*); *~en*
treffen make arrangements

schil (-len) *v* peel [of an orange]; skin [of a
banana or potato]; rind [of a melon]; bark [of a
tree]; *~len* (a l s a f v a l) parings [of apples],
peelings [of potatoes]; *aardappelen met de ~*
potatoes in their jackets

schild (-en) *o* 1 shield²; buckler; 2 ⊘ escutcheon; 3 (v. s c h i l d p a d) shell; 4 (v a n
i n s e k t) = *dekschild*; *iets in het ~ voeren* aim at
(drive at) sth.; *ik weet niet wat hij in zijn ~ voert*
I don't know what he's up to; **–drager** (-s) *m*
1 shield-bearer; 2 ⊘ supporter

'**schilder** (-s) *m* 1 (k u n s t e n a a r) painter,
artist; 2 (a m b a c h t s m a n) (house-)painter;
'**schilderachtig** picturesque; *ook ~e figuur, een*

~ *type* a colourful character; **–heid** *v* pictur-
esqueness; 1 '**schilderen** (schilderde, h. geschilderd) **I** *vt* paint²; *fig* ook: picture, portray,
delineate, depict; *naar het leven ~* paint from
life; **II** *va* paint

2 '**schilderen** (schilderde, h. geschilderd) *vt* ⚒
do sentry-go, stand sentry; *ik heb hier al een uur*
staan ~ I've been cooling my heels for an hour

schilde'res (-sen) *v* paintress, woman painter

'**schilderhuisje** (-s) *o* ⚒ sentry-box

schilde'rij (-en) *o* & *v* painting, picture;
schilde'rijenkabinet (-ten) *o* picture-gallery;
–tentoonstelling (-en) *v* art exhibition;
'**schildering** (-en) *v* painting, depiction,
picture, portrayal; '**schilderkunst** *v* (art of)
painting; **–les** (-sen) *v* painting-lesson; ~
krijgen take lessons in painting; **–school**
(-scholen) *v* school of painting; '**schildersezel**
(-s) *m* (painter's) easel; **–kwast** (-en) *m* paint-
brush; **–stok** (-ken) *m* maulstick; '**schilder-
stuk** (-ken) *o* painting, picture; '**schilders-
werkplaats** (-en) *v*, **–winkel** (-s) *m* house-
painter's workshop; '**schilderwerk** (-en) *o*
painting

'**schildklier** (-en) *v* thyroid gland; **–knaap**
(-knapen) *m* 1 ▱ squire, shield-bearer; armour-
bearer; 2 *fig* lieutenant; **–luis** (-luizen) *v* scale
insect; **–pad** 1 (-den) *v* 🐢 tortoise; (z e e d i e r)
turtle; 2 *o* (s t o f n a a m) tortoise-shell; [dark]
turtle-shell; **–padden** *aj* tortoise-shell;
–padsoep *v* turtle soup

schild'vleugeligen *mv* sheath-winged insects,
coleoptera; '**schildvormig** shield-shaped;
–wacht (-en en -s) *m* sentinel, sentry; *op ~*
staan stand sentry; **–wachthuisje** (-s) *o* sentry-
box

'**schilfer** (-s) *m* scale; flake; *~s op het hoofd*
dandruff; '**schilferachtig** scaly; **–heid** *v*
scaliness; '**schilferen** (schilferde, h. en is
geschilferd) *vi* scale (off), peel (off), flake (off);
–rig scaly, scurfy

'**schillen** (schilde, h. geschild) **I** *vt* pare [apples
&]; peel [oranges, potatoes &]; **II** *vi* peel

'**schillerhemd** ['ʃilər-] (-en) *o* open-necked
shirt; **–kraag** (-kragen) *m* Byronic collar

'**schilmesje** (-s) *o* paring-knife, peeling-knife

schim (-men) *v* shadow, shade; ghost; *Chinese*
~men Chinese shades; **–achtig** shadowy,
ghostly

1 '**schimmel** (-s) *m* (p a a r d) grey (horse)

2 '**schimmel** (-s) *m* (u i t s l a g) mould, must;
(o p l e e r, p a p i e r) mildew; **–achtig**
mouldy; '**schimmelen** (schimmelde, is
geschimmeld) *vi* grow mouldy; **–lig** mouldy

'**schimmenrijk** *o het* ~ the land of shadows;
–spel *o* shadow-play (pantomime); '**schim-
metje** (-s) **F** *o* trifle; *hij verdient maar een* ~ he

earns a mere pittance

schimp *m* contumely, taunt, scoff; **–dicht** (-en) *o* satire; **'schimpen** (schimpte, h. geschimpt) *vi* scoff at; ~ *op* scoff at, revile; **'schimpscheut** (-en) *m* gibe, taunt, jeer

'schinkel (-s) = *schenkel*

schip (schepen) *o* 1 ⚓ ship, vessel; [canal] barge, boat; 2 nave [of a church]; *het* ~ *van staat* the ship of state; *schoon* ~ *maken* make a clean sweep (of it); *settle accounts*; *zijn schepen achter zich verbranden* burn one's boats; *een* ~ *op strand een baken in zee* ± one man's fault is another man's lesson; *als het* ~ *met geld komt* when my ship comes home; *een* ~ *met zure appelen* a coming rainshower; a fit of weeping; **–breuk** (-en) *v* shipwreck; ~ *lijden* 1 be shipwrecked; 2 *fig* fail; *zijn plannen hebben* ~ *geleden* his plans have miscarried, his plans were wrecked; **–breukeling** (-en) *m* shipwrecked person, castaway; **–brug** (-gen) *v* bridge of boats, floating-bridge; **–per** (-s) *m* bargeman, boatman; (g e z a g v o e r d e r) master

'schipperen (schipperde, h. geschipperd) *vi* skipper; *fig* compromise, give and take

'schippersbaard (-en) *m* Newgate frill (fringe); **–beurs** *v* shipping-exchange; **–boom** (-bomen) *m* barge-pole; **–haak** (-haken) *m* boat-hook; **–kind** (-eren) *o* bargeman's child; ~*eren* ook: barge children, boat children; **–knecht** (-en en -s) *m* bargeman's mate

'schisma ('s en -mata) *o* schism; **schisma'tiek** schismatic; *de* ~*en* the schismatics

'schitteren (schitterde, h. geschitterd) *vi* shine [of light], glitter [of the eyes], sparkle [of diamonds]; ~ *door afwezigheid* be conspicuous by one's absence; **–d** *fig* brilliant, glorious, splendid; **'schittering** (-en) *v* glittering, sparkling; radiance; lustre; splendour

schizo'freen (-frenen) *aj* & *m-v* schizophrenic; **schizofre'nie** *v* schizophrenia

'schlager ['ʃlaːgər] (-s) *m* hit

schle'miel [ʃlə-] (-en) **F** *m* unlucky devil, *Am* **S** s(c)hlemiel, schlemihl

schmink [ʃmiːŋk] *m* grease-paint; make-up; **'schminken** (schminkte, h. geschminkt) *vt* & *vr* make up

'schnabbel ['ʃnɑ-] (-s) **F** *m* odd job, casual job; **'schnabbelen** (schnabbelde, h. geschnabbeld) *vi* earn on the side

'schnitzel ['ʃnɪtzəl] (-s) *m* schnitzel, scallop

'schobbejak (-ken) *m* scamp, rogue, scallywag

schobberde'bonk *op de* ~ *lopen* sponge on [sbd.], cadge from [sbd.]

'schoeien (schoeide, h. geschoeid) *vt* shoe; zie ook: *leest*; **'schoeisel** (-s) *o* shoes, $ foot-wear

'schoelje (-s) *m* rascal, scamp

schoen (-en) *m* 1 (i n ' t a l g. & l a a g) shoe; 2 (h o o g) boot; *de stoute* ~*en aantrekken* pluck up courage; ● *b u i t e n de* ~*en gaan lopen (van verwaandheid)* get (grow) too big for one's boots; *iem. iets i n de* ~*en schuiven* lay sth. at sbd.'s door, impute sth. to sbd., to pin sth. on sbd., *ik zou niet graag in zijn* ~*en staan* I should not like to be in his shoes; *vast in zijn* ~*en staan* stand firm in one's shoes; *het hart zonk hem in de* ~*en* his spirtis sank, his courage failed him; *m e t loden* ~*en* zie *loden*; *n a a s t zijn* ~*en lopen* suffer from a swelled head; *o p z'n laatste* ~*en lopen* be on one's last legs; *op een* ~ *en een slof* 1 [do sth.] on a shoe-string; 2 (a r m o e d i g) beggarly; *wie de* ~ *past, trekke hem aan* whom the cap fits, let him wear it; *men moet geen oude* ~*en weggooien vóór men nieuwe heeft* one should not throw away old shoes before one has got new ones; *weten waar de* ~ *wringt* know where the shoe pinches; *daar wringt 'm de* ~*!* that's the rub!; **–borstel** (-s) *m* shoe-brush, blacking-brush; **–crème** *v* shoe polish (cream); **'schoenenfabriek** (-en) *v* = *schoenfabriek*; **–winkel** (-s) *m* = *schoenwinkel*

'schoener (-s) *m* schooner; **–brik** (-ken) *v* brigantine

'schoenfabriek (-en) *v* shoe factory; **–gesp** (-en) *m* & *v* shoe-buckle; **–hoorn, –horen** (-s) *m* shoe-horn, shoe-lift; **–lapper** (-s) *m* cobbler; **–le(d)er** *o* shoe-leather; **–leest** (-en) *v* (shoe-) last; **–lepel** (-s) *m* = *schoenhoorn*; **–maker** (-s) *m* shoemaker; ~ *blijf bij je leest* let the cobbler stick to his last; **–makersknecht** *m* shoemaker's mate; **–poets** *m* = *schoensmeer*; **–poetser** (-s) *m* (o p s t r a a t) shoe-black, boot-black; (i n h o t e l) boots; **–riem** (-en) *m* strap of a shoe; *niet waard zijn om iems.* ~*en te ontbinden (los te binden)* not be worthy to (un)tie sbd.'s shoe-strings; **–smeer** *o* & *m* shoe-polish, shoe-black, blacking; **–veter** (-s) *m* shoe-lace, boot-lace; **–winkel** (-s) *m* shoe-shop; **–zool** (-zolen) *v* sole of a shoe

schoep (-en) *v* 1 paddle-board, paddle; 2 blade [of a turbine]

'schoffel (-s) *v* hoe; **'schoffelen** (schoffelde, h. geschoffeld) *vt* hoe

schof'feren (schofferde, h. geschofferd) *vt* dishonour, rape

'schoffie (-s) *o* street arab

1 schoft (-en) *m* scoundrel, rascal, scamp, cad

2 schoft (-en) *v* withers [of a horse]

'schoftachtig = *schofterig*; **'schofterig** scoundrelly, blackguardly, caddish

schok (-ken) *m* 1 (i n ' t a l g.) shock; 2 (v a n r ij t u i g) jolt, jerk; 3 (h e v i g) impact; concussion, convulsion; *het heeft hem een* ~ *gegeven* it has shaken his health; *een* ~ *krijgen* receive a shock²; **–beton** *o* vibrated concrete; **–breker** (-s) *m* shock-absorber; **–buis** (-buizen) *v* percussion-fuse; **–effect** (-en) *o* shock effect; **'schokken** (schokte, h. geschokt) **I** *vt* 1 shake², convulse², jerk; jolt; 2 **S** (b e t a l e n) fork out, shell out; *zijn krediet (vertrouwen) is geschokt* his credit (faith) is shaken; *de zenuwen ~* shatter the nerves; *een ~de gebeurtenis* a startling event; **II** *vi* 1 shake, jolt, jerk; 2 **S** (b e t a l e n) fork out, cough up; **'schokschouderen** (schokschouderde, h. geschokschouderd) *vi* shrug one's shoulders; **schoksge'wijs** by jerks, by fits and starts, intermittently; **'schok-vrij** shock-proof

schol (-len) 1 *m*; 🐟 plaice; ‖ 2 *v* floe [of ice]

scholas'tiek 1 *v* scholastic theology, scholasticism; 2 (-en) *m rk* scholastic

schold (scholden) V.T. van *schelden*

'scholekster (-s) *v* oyster-catcher

1 'scholen (schoolde, h. geschoold) *vi* shoal [of fish]; flock together; ‖ *vt* train; zie ook: *geschoold*

2 'scholen V.T. meerv. van *schuilen*

'scholengemeenschap (-pen) *v* comprehensive school; **scho'lier** (-en) *m* pupil, schoolboy; **'scholing** *v* training

'schollevaar, 'scholver(d) (-s) *m* 🦤 cormorant

'schommel (-s) *m & v* swing; **'schommelen** (schommelde, h. geschommeld) **I** *vi* 1 (o p s c h o m m e l) swing; 2 (v. s l i n g e r) swing, oscillate; 3 (o p s c h o m m e l s t o e l) rock; 4 (v. s c h i p) roll; 5 (m e t h e t l i c h a a m) wobble, waddle; 6 *fig* (v. p r ij z e n) fluctuate; *met de benen ~* swing one's legs; **II** *vt* swing, rock [a child]; **–ling** (-en) *v* swinging, oscillation, fluctuation; **'schommelstoel** (-en) *m* rocking-chair

schond (schonden) V.T. v. *schenden*

'schone (-n) zie 1 *schoon* **II**

schonk (schonken) V.T. v. *schenken*

'schonkig bony, big-boned, large-boned

1 schoof (schoven) *v* sheaf; *aan schoven zetten, in schoven binden* sheave

2 schoof (schoven) V.T. v. *schuiven*

'schooien (schooide, h. geschooid) *vi* beg; **–er** (-s) *m* 1 ragamuffin; 2 beggar, tramp, vagrant; *~!* rascal!

1 school (scholen) *v* 1 school; academy, college; 2 shoal [of herrings]; *de ~* ook: the schoolhouse; *bijzondere ~* 1 private school; 2 denominational school; *lagere ~* primary school; *middelbare ~* secondary school; *militaire ~* military academy (college); *neutrale ~* secular (unsectarian) school; *openbare ~* State primary school; *de Parijse (schilder)~* the school of Paris; *~ met de Bijbel* denominational school for orthodox Protestants; *~ gaan* go to school; *toen ik nog ~ ging* when I was at school; *we hebben*

geen ~ vandaag! no school to-day!; *~ houden* keep in [a pupil]; *een ~ houden* keep a school; *~ maken* find a following, gain followers; ● *n a a r ~ gaan* go to school; *o p ~* at school; *waar ben je op ~?* where are you going to school?; *een jongen op ~ doen* put a boy to school; *daarvoor moet je bij hem t e r ~ gaan* for that you have to go to school to him; *u i t de ~ klappen* let out a secret, blab; *v a n ~ gaan* leave school

2 school (scholen) V.T. van *schuilen*

'schoolagenda ('s) *v* prep book; **–arts** (-en) *m* school doctor, school medical officer; **–atlas** (-sen) *m* school atlas; **–bank** (-en) *v* form [long, without back]; desk [for one or two, with back]; **–behoeften** *mv* school necessaries; **–bestuur** (-sturen) *o* (board of) governors; **–bezoek** *o* 1 (v. d. l e e r l i n g e n) school attendance; 2 (v. d. o v e r h e i d) inspection, visit; **–bibliotheek** (-theken) *v* school library; **'schoolblijven** (bleef 'school, is 'schoolgebleven) *vi* stay in (after hours), be kept in; *het ~* detention; *twee uur ~* two hours' detention; **'schoolboek** (-en) *o* school-book, class-book; **–bord** (-en) *o* blackboard; **–bus** (-sen) *m & v* school-bus; **–dag** (-dagen) *m* school-day; **—engels** *o* schoolboy English; **–examen** (-s) *o* school examination; **–feest** (-en) *o* school festivity (fête); **–frik** (-ken) *m* pedagogue, pedantic schoolteacher; **'schoolgaan** (ging 'school, h. 'schoolgegaan) *vi* go to school, be at school; **'schoolgebouw** (-en) *o* school-building; **–gebruik** *o voor ~* for use in schools; **–geld** (-en) *o* school fee(s), tuition; **–geleerde** (-n) *m* 1 schoolman, scholar; 2 > pedant, schoolmaster; **–geleerdheid** *v* book-learning; **–hoofd** (-en) *o* head of a school, headmaster; **'schoolhouden** (hield 'school, h. 'schoolgehouden) *vt* keep in [a pupil]; **'schooljaar** (-jaren) *o* scholastic year, school-year; *in mijn schooljaren* in my school-days (school-time); **–jeugd** *v* the school-children; **–jongen** (-s) *m* schoolboy; **–juffrouw** (-en) *v* school-mistress, teacher; **–kameraad** (-raden) *m = school-makker*; **–kennis** *v* school (scholastic) knowledge; **–kind** (-eren) *o* school-child; **–klas** (-sen) *v* class, form; **–lokaal** (-kalen) *o* classroom; **–makker** (-s) *m* school-fellow, schoolmate; **–meester** (-s) *m* schoolmaster; *fig* pedant, pedagogue; **–meesterachtig** pedantic; **–meesterachtigheid** *v* pedantry; **–meisje** (-s) *o* schoolgirl; **–onderwijs** *o* school-teaching; **–opziener** (-s) *m* school-inspector; **–plein** (-en) *o* school yard, play ground; **–plicht** *m & v* compulsory school attendance; **school'plichtig** *~e leeftijd* compulsory school age; *verhoging van de ~e* *leeftijd* raising of the school-leaving age; **'schoolradio** *m* school radio programme; **–reisje** (-s) *o* school journey; **–s** scholastic; *~e geleerdheid* book-learning; **–schip** (-schepen) *o* = *opleidingsschip;* **–schrift** (-en) *o* exercise-book; **–slag** *m* breast-stroke [in swimming]; **–tas** (-sen) *v* satchel, schoolbag; **–televisie** [-zi.] *v* school (educational) television; **–tijd** *m* schooltime; *buiten ~* out of school; *n a ~* when school is over; *o n d e r ~* during lessons; *s i n d s mijn ~* since my school-days; **–toezicht** *o* school inspection; **–tucht** *v* school-discipline; **–tuin** (-en) *m* school-garden; **–uur** (-uren) *o* school-hour, lesson, period, class; *buiten de schooluren* &, zie *schooltijd;* **–vak** (-ken) *o* subject; **–vakantie** [-(t)si.] (-s) *v* holidays; **–verlater** (-s) *m* school-leaver; **–verzuim** *o* non-attendance, absenteeism; **–voorbeeld** (-en) *o* classic example, typical example, textbook case; **–werk** *o* task for school, home tasks; **–wezen** *o* public education; **–ziek:** *~ zijn* sham illness; **–ziekte** *v* sham illness, feigned illness

1 schoon I *aj* 1 (z i n d e l ij k) clean; pure; neat; 2 (m o o i) beautiful, handsome, fair, fine; **II** *sb een schone* a belle, a beauty, a fair one, a beautiful woman &; *het schone* the beautiful; **III** *ad* 1 clean(ly); 2 beautifully; *het is ~ op* it is all gone, clean gone; *je hebt ~ gelijk* you are quite right; zie ook: *genoeg*

2 schoon *cj* though, although

'schoonbroeder, –broer (-s) *m* brother-in-law; **–dochter** (-s) *v* daughter-in-law

'schoonheid (-heden) *v* beauty; (m o o i e v r o u w) beauty, belle [of the ball], **S** beaut; **'schoonheidsfoutje** (-s) *o fig* flaw, hitch, snag; **–gevoel** *o* = *schoonheidszin;* **–instituut** (-tuten) *o* beauty parlour; **–koningin** (-nen) *v* beauty queen; **–leer** *v* aesthetics; **–middel** (-en) *o* cosmetic; **–salon** (-s) *m* & *o* beauty parlour; **–specialist(e)** (-en) *m* (*v*) beauty specialist, beautician; **–wedstrijd** (-en) *m* beauty competition, beauty contest; **–zin** *m* aesthetic sense, sense of beauty; **'schoonhouden**[1] *vt* keep clean; **'schoonklinkend** fine-sounding; **'schoonmaak** *m* clean-up, (house-)cleaning; *(de) grote ~ (in het voorjaar)* spring-cleaning; *grote ~ houden* 1 *eig* spring-clean; 2 *fig* make a clean sweep; **–bedrijf** (-drijven) *o* cleaners; **–ster** (-s) *v* cleaning woman; **–tijd** *m* cleaning-time; **'schoonmaken**[1] *vt* clean

'schoonmoeder (-s) *v* mother-in-law; **–ouders** *mv* parents-in-law

'schoonrijden *o* (o p s c h a a t s e n) figure-skating; **–schijnend** specious, plausible; **–schrift** (-en) *o* 1 calligraphic writing; 2 copy-book; **–schrijfkunst** *v* calligraphy; **–schrijver** (-s) *m* calligrapher, penman; **–springen** *o* (v. z w e m m e r s) (fancy) diving **'schoonvader** (-s) *m* father-in-law **'schoonvegen**[1] *vt* sweep clean; clear [the streets, by the police]; **–wassen**[1] *vt* wash; *fig* whitewash

'schoonzoon (-s en -zonen) *m* son-in-law; **–zuster** (-s) *v* sister-in-law

1 schoor (schoren) *m △* buttress, stay, strut, prop, support

2 schoor (schoren) V.T. v. *scheren*

'schoorbalk (-en) *m* summer

'schoorsteen (-stenen) *m* 1 chimney, (chimney-)stack [of a house]; 2 funnel [of a steamer]; *daar kan de ~ niet van roken* that won't keep the pot boiling; **–brand** (-en) *m* chimney-fire; **–kanaal** (-nalen) *o* (chimney) flue; **–kap** (-pen) *v* chimney-cap; **–loper** (-s) *m* (mantel-piece) runner; **–mantel** (-s) *m* mantelpiece; **–plaat** (-platen) *v* hearth-plate; **–veger** (-s) *m* chimney-sweeper, sweep

'schoorvoetend reluctantly, hesitatingly

1 schoot (schoten) *m* 1 lap; *fig* womb; 2 ♨ sheet [of a sail]; 3 ✗ bolt [of a lock]; 4 ♨ shoot, sprig; *de ~ der Kerk* the bosom of the Church; *de handen i n de ~ leggen* give up [a task, as hopeless]; *het hoofd in de ~ leggen* give in, submit; *niet met de handen in de ~ zitten* not be idle; *het wordt hun in de ~ geworpen* it is lavished upon them; *in de ~ der aarde* in the bowels of the earth; *zij had een boek o p haar ~* she sat with a book on her lap; *het kind op moeders ~* the child in its mother's lap

2 schoot (schoten) V.T. v. *schieten*

'schoothondje (-s) *o* lap-dog, toy dog; **–kindje** (-s) *o* 1 baby; 2 favourite child, pet **'schootsafstand** (-en) *m* ✗ range, gunshot **'schootsvel** (-len) *o* leather(n) apron **'schootsveld** (-en) *o* ✗ field of fire; **schoots'verheid** *v* ✗ range; **'schootvrij** shot-proof, bomb-proof; *fig* proof (against *voor*)

1 schop (-pen) *v* 1 shovel, spade; 2 (v. k o r e n &) scoop

2 schop (-pen) *m* kick; *vrije ~ sp* free kick; **1 'schoppen** (schopte, h. geschopt) **I** *vi* kick; *~ naar* kick at; *het ver ~* go far [in the world]; **II** *vt* kick; *herrie (lawaai) ~* kick up a row; *iem. een standje ~* zie *standje*

---

[1] V.T. en V.D. volgens het model: **'schoon**maken, V.T. maakte **'schoon**, V.D. **'schoon**gemaakt. Zie voor de vormen onder het grondwoord, in dit voorbeeld: *maken*. Bij sterke en onregelmatige werkwoorden wordt u verwezen naar de lijst achterin.

2 'schoppen (schoppen en -s) *v* ◊ spades; *~aas* ace of spades

'schopstoel *m op de ~ zitten* be in an insecure position, not be sure of keeping one's job &

schor hoarse, husky

'schorem I *o = schorr(i)emorrie;* **II** *aj* shabby

1 'schoren (schoorde, h. geschoord) *vt* shore (up), buttress, support, prop (up)

2 'schoren V.T. meerv. van *scheren*

'schorheid *v* hoarseness

schorpi'oen (-en) *m* ♏ scorpion; *de Schorpioen* ★ Scorpio

'schorr(i)emorrie *o* rabble, riff-raff, ragtag and bobtail

schors (-en) *v* bark

'schorsen (schorste, h. geschorst) *vt* suspend [the sitting, an official], suspend [a lawyer] from pratice

schorse'neel (-nelen) *v,* **schorse'neer** (-neren) *v* black salsify, scorzonera

'schorsing (-en) *v* suspension [of a meeting, an official

schort (-en) *v* & *o* apron, [child's] pinafore; **–eband** (-en) *m* apron-string

'schorten (schortte, h. geschort) *onp. ww.* in: *wat schort eraan?* what is the matter?

schot *o* 1 (schoten) shot, report [of a gun]; 2 (-ten) partition [in room]; ⚓ bulkhead; *een ~ voor de boeg* a shot across the bows; *fig* a serious warning; *een ~ in de roos* a bull's eye; *er komt ~ in* we are making headway; *een ~ doen* fire a shot; *~ geven* veer [a cable]; *~ en lot betalen* pay scot and lot; ● *binnen ~* within range; *buiten ~* out of range; *trachten buiten ~ te blijven* try to keep out of harm's way; *onder ~ krijgen* get within range; *ze zijn onder ~* they are within range; *geen ~ kruit waard* not worth powder and shot

Schot (-ten) *m* Scotchman, Scotsman, Scot; *de ~ten* the Scotch, the Scots

'schotel (-s) *m* & *v* dish; *vliegende ~* flying saucer; **–tje** (-s) *o* 1 (v o o r k o p) saucer; 2 (e t e n) dish

1 'schoten V.T. mv. v. *schieten*

2 'schoten mv. v. *schot*

'Schotland *o* Scotland, ⊙ Caledonia

1 schots (-en) *v* floe [of ice]

2 schots *~ en scheef door elkaar* higgledy-piggledy

Schots I *aj* Scotch, Scottish; **II** *o het ~* Scotch, Scots; **III** *v een ~e* a Scotchwoman

'schotschrift (-en) *o* libel, lampoon

'schotvrij = *schootvrij;* **–wond(e)** (-en) *v* shot-wound, bullet-wound

'schouder (-s) *m* shoulder; *breed van ~s* broad-shouldered; *de ~s ophalen* shrug one's shoulders, give a shrug; *~ aan ~ staan* stand shoulder to shoulder; *iem. over de ~ aanzien*

give sbd. the cold shoulder; **–band** (-en) *m,* **–bandje** (-s) *o* shoulder-strap; **–bedekking** (-en) *v* ✂ shoulder-strap; **–blad** (-bladen) *o* shoulder-blade, § scapula [*mv* scapulae]; **–breedte** (-n en -s) *v* breadth of shoulders; **'schouderen** (schouderde, h. geschouderd) *vt het geweer ~* shoulder the gun, ✂ shoulder arms; **'schoudergewricht** (-en) *o* shoulder-joint; **–klep** (-pen) *v* ✂ shoulder-strap; **–klopje** (-s) *v* pat on the back; **–mantel** (-s) *m* cape; **–ophalen** *o* shrug (of the shoulders); **–stuk** (-ken) *o* 1 ✂ shoulder-strap; 2 (v a n h e m d &) yoke; 3 (v. v l e e s) shoulder [of lamb &]; **–tas** (-sen) *v* shoulder-bag

schout (-en) *m* ⚖ bailiff, sheriff

schout-bij-'nacht (-s en schouten-bij-nacht) *m* rear-admiral

1 schouw (-en) *v* chimney

2 schouw *m* inspection, survey

3 schouw (-en) *v* ⚓ scow

'schouwburg (-en) *m* theatre, playhouse; **–bezoeker** (-s) *m* theatre-goer; **–publiek** *o* theatre-going public

'schouwen (schouwde, h. geschouwd) *vt* inspect; ⊙ view, behold; *een lijk ~* hold an inquest; **–wing** (-en) *v* inspection

'schouwspel (-spelen) *o* spectacle, scene, sight, view; **–toneel** (-nelen) *o* stage, scene, theatre

1 'schoven (schoofde, h. geschoofd) *vt* sheave

2 'schoven V.T. meerv. van *schuiven*

schraag (schragen) *v* trestle; support; **–pijler** (-s) *m* buttress

schraal I *aj* 1 (p e r s o n e n) thin, gaunt; 2 (i n k o m e n) slender [salary]; lean [purse]; 3 (s p ij s &) meagre [diet], poor, scanty, spare, slender; 4 (g r o n d) poor; 5 (w i n d) bleak; *een schrale troost* cold comfort; **II** *ad* poorly, scantily; **–hans** (-hanzen) *m hier is ~ keukenmeester* we are on short commons here; **–heid** *v* poverty, thinness, scantiness &; **–tjes** poorly, scantily, thinly, slenderly

'schraapachtig scraping, stingy, covetous; **–ijzer** (-s) *o,* **–mes** (-sen) *o* scraper; **–sel** (-s) *o* scrapings; **–zucht** *v* stinginess, covetousness; **schraap'zuchtig** scraping, stingy, covetous

schrab (-ben) *v* scratch; **'schrabben** (schrabde, h. geschrabd) *vt* scratch, scrape [carrots]; **–er** (-s) *m,* **'schrabijzer** (-s) *o,* **–mes** (-sen) *o* scraper

'schragen (schraagde, h. geschraagd) *vt* support, prop (up), stay

schram (-men) *v* scratch, graze; **'schrammen** (schramde, h. geschramd) **I** *vt* scratch, graze; **II** *vr zich ~* scratch oneself, graze one's skin

'schrander I *aj* clever, intelligent, smart, bright, sagacious; **II** *ad* cleverly, intelligently, smartly, sagaciously; **–heid** *v* cleverness, intelligence, sagacity

'**schransen** (schranste, h. geschranst) *vi* gormandize, gorge; *zij waren aan het ~* they were cramming; **–er** (-s) *m* glutton;

'**schranzen** (schransde, h. geschransd) *vi = schransen*; **–er** (-s) *m = schranser*

1 **schrap** (-pen) *v* scratch; *er een ~ door halen* strike it out

2 **schrap** *ad zich ~ zetten* take a firm stand, brace oneself

'**schrapen** (schraapte, h. geschraapt) *vt* scrape; *(zich) de keel ~* clear one's throat; '**schraper** (-s) *m* scraper; **–ig** scraping, stingy, covetous

'**schrapijzer** (-s) *o = schrabijzer*; **–je** (-s) *o* skin test; **–mes** (-sen) *o = schrabmes*; '**schrappen** (schrapte, h. geschrapt) *vt* scrape [carrots &]; scale [fish]; strike out [a name]; cancel [a debt]; delete [a name, a passage]; *iem. van de lijst ~* strike sbd. off the list; **–er** (-s) *m = schrabber*; '**schrapping** (-en) *v* striking out [of a name]; deletion [of a passage, word]; cancellation [of a debt]; '**schrapsel** (-s) *o* scrapings

'**schrede** (-n) *v* pace, step, stride; *de eerste ~ doen* take the first step; *zijn ~n wenden naar...* turn (bend) one's steps to...; *met rasse ~n* with rapid strides, fast; *op zijn ~n terugkeren (terugkomen)* go back on (retrace) one's steps; **schreed** (**schreden**) V.T. van *schrijden*

1 **schreef** (schreven) *v* line, scratch; *buiten (over) de ~ gaan* go over the line, exceed the bounds; *hij heeft een ~je vóór* he is the favourite

2 **schreef** (**schreven**) V.T. van *schrijven*

'**schreefloos** sanserif

schreeuw (-en) *m* cry, shout, screech; *een ~ geven* give a cry; '**schreeuwen** (schreeuwde, h. geschreeuwd) *vi* cry, shout, bawl; *~ als een mager varken* squeal like a (stuck) pig; *(er) om ~* ook: clamour for it; *hij schreeuwt voordat hij geslagen wordt* he cries out before he is hurt; *zich hees ~* cry oneself hoarse; **–d** crying[2] [injustice]; *~e kleuren* loud (glaring) colours; '**schreeuwer** (-s) *m* bawler; *fig* braggart; **–ig** screaming [voice &]; *fig* clamorous [persons]; loud [colours]; vociferous [speeches]; '**schreeuwlelijk** (-en) *m* 1 bawler; 2 (h u i l e-b a l k) cry-baby

'**schreien** (schreide, h. geschreid) *vi* weep, cry; *~ om...* weep for...; *t e n hemel ~* cry (aloud) to Heaven; *t o t ~s toe bewogen* moved to tears; *~ van...* weep for [joy]; **–er** (-s) *m* weeper, crier '**schreven** V.T. meerv. van *schrijven*

schriel I *aj* (g i e r i g) stingy, mean, niggardly; II *ad* stingily, meanly, niggardly; zie ook: *schraal*; **–heid** *v* (g i e r i g h e i d) stinginess, meanness, niggardliness; zie ook: *schraalheid*

schrift (-en) *o* 1 (h e t g e s c h r e v e n e) writing; [Arabic, Latin] script; 2 (s c h r i j f-

b o e k) exercise-book; (v o o r s c h o o n-s c h r i f t) copy-book; *op ~* in writing; *op ~ brengen* put [it] in writing; **Schrift** *v de (Heilige)* ~ Holy Writ, (Holy) Scripture, the Scriptures; '**schriftelijk** I *aj* written, in writing; *~e cursus* correspondence course; II *ad* in writing; by letter; III *o het ~* the written work [of an examination]; '**schriftgeleerde** (-n) *m* scribe; **–kunde** *v* 1 graphology; 2 (o u d e h a n d-s c h r i f t e n) pal(a)eography;

schrift'kundige (-n) *m* 1 graphologist; 2 pal(a)eographer; '**schriftlezing** *v* Bible reading; **–uitleg** *m* exposition of the Scriptures; **schrif'tuur** (-turen) *v & o* writing, document; *de S~* Scripture; **–lijk** scriptural

'**schrijden*** *vi* stride

'**schrijfbehoeften** *mv* writing-materials, stationery; **–blok** (-ken) *o* writing-block, writing-pad; **–boek** (-en) *o = schrift* 2; **–bureau** [-by.ro.] (-s) *o* desk, writing-table; **–fout** (-en) *v* clerical error, slip of the pen; **–gerei** *o* writing-materials; **–inkt** *m* writing-ink; **–kramp** *v* writer's cramp; **–kunst** *v* art of writing, penmanship; **–les** (-sen) *v* writing-lesson; **–lessenaar** (-s) *m* desk, writing-table; **–letter** (-s) *v* written character; *~s* script; **–machine** [-ma.ʃi.nə] (-s) *v* typewriter; **–machinelint** (-en) *o* typewriter ribbon; **–machinepapier** *o* typewriting paper; **–map** (-pen) *v* writing-case; **–papier** *o* writing-paper; **–ster** (-s) *v* (woman) writer, authoress; **–taal** *v* written language; **–tafel** (-s) *v* writing-table; **–trant** *m* manner (style) of writing; **–voorbeeld** *o* copy-book heading; **–werk** *o* clerical work, writing; **–wijs, –wijze** (-wijzen) *v* 1 spelling [of a word]; 2 manner (style) of writing; **–woede** *v* mania for scribbling

'**schrijlings** astride [his father's knee], astraddle (of *op*)

⚲ **schrijn** (-en) *o & m* chest, cabinet; (v a n r e l i k w i e ë n) shrine

'**schrijnen** (schrijnde, h. geschrijnd) *vt* graze, abrade [the skin]; *~d leed* bitter grief; *~de pijn* smarting pain; *~de tegenstelling, ~d verhaal* poignant contrast (story)

'**schrijnwerker** (-s) *m* joiner

'**schrijven*** I *vt* write; *dat kan je op je buik ~* you may whistle for it; II *vi & va* write; ● *~ a a n* write to; *hij schrijft i n de krant* he writes in a paper (for the papers); *~ o p een advertentie* answer an advertisement; *hij schrijft o v e r de oorlog* he writes about the war; *hij heeft over Byron geschreven* he has written on Byron; *niets om over naar huis te ~* nothing to write home about; *er staat geschreven* it is written; III *vr zich ~* sign oneself [John Jones]; IV *o ons laatste ~*

our last letter; *uw ~ van de 20ste* your letter, your favour of the 20th inst.; **–er** (-s) *m* writer [of a letter, books &]; author [of a treatise, books &]; clerk, copyist [in an office]; **schrijve'rij** (-en) *v* writing, scribbling

schrik *m* fright, terror; *met ~ en beven* with fear and terror; *de ~ van het dorp* the terror of the village; *iem. ~ aanjagen, iem. de ~ op het lijf jagen* give sbd. a fright, terrify sbd.; *er met de ~ afkomen* get off with a fright; *er de ~ inbrengen* put the fear of God into them; *een ~ krijgen* get a fright; *de ~ sloeg mij om 't hart* it gave me quite a turn; ● *m e t ~ vervullen* fill with fright (scare), strike terror into; *met ~ wakker worden* start from one's sleep; *met ~ tegemoet zien* dread; *t o t mijn ~* to my dismay (horror); *het v a n ~ besterven* be frightened to death; **–aanjagend** terrifying; **–achtig** easily frightened, **F** jumpy; **–achtigheid** *v* jumpiness; **schrik'barend** frightful, fearful, dreadful, **F** awful; **'schrik-beeld** (-en) *o* dreadful vision, terror, bogy; (g e d r o c h t) incubus; **–bewind** *o* (reign of) terror; **–draad** (-draden) *m* & *o* electric (wire) fence

'schrikkeldag (-dagen) *m* intercalary day; **–dans** *m* ladies' choice (turn); **–jaar** (-jaren) *o* leap-year; **–maand** (-en) *v* leap-month (February)

'schrikken* **I** *vi* be frightened; (o p~) start, give a start; *iem. doen ~* give sbd. a fright, frighten sbd., startle sbd.; *~ van* start at, be startled by [sbd., a noise]; *hij ziet eruit om van te ~* his looks simply frighten you; *~ voor...* take fright at; **II** *vr zich dood (een aap &) ~* be frightened to death (out of one's wits); **schrik'wekkend** terrifying, terrific, appalling

schril I *aj* shrill, strident [sounds]; glaring [light, colours, contrast]; **II** *ad* shrilly, stridently; glaringly

'schrobben (schrobde, h. geschrobd) *vt* scrub, scour [the floor]; **–er** (-s) *m* scrubbing-brush, scrubber

schrob'bering (-en) *v* scolding, **F** dressing-down

'schrobnet (-ten) *o* trawl-net

'schrobzaag (-zagen) *v* compass saw

schroef (schroeven) *v* 1 screw; 2 (b a n k~) vice; 3 ⚓ screw, (screw) propeller; 4 ✈ airscrew, propeller; 5 ♪ peg [of a violin]; *~ van Archimedes* Archimedean screw; *~ zonder eind* endless screw; *~ en moer* male and female screw; *de ~ wat aandraaien* turn the screw²; *alles staat op losse schroeven* everything is unsettled; **–as** (-sen) *v* ⚓ propeller-shaft; **–bank** (-en) *v* vice-bench; **–blad** (-bladen) *o* propeller-blade; **–boor** (-boren) *v* screw-auger; **–bout** (-en) *m* screw-bolt; **–deksel** (-s) *o* screw-cap; **–dop**

(-pen) *m* screw-cap; **–draad** (-draden) *m* screw-thread; **–duik** *m* spin; **–gang** (-en) *m* thread (worm) of a screw; **–lijn** (-en) *v* helix [*mv* helices]; **–moer** (-en) *v* nut, female screw; **–sgewijs, –sgewijze** spirally; **–sleutel** (-s) *m* monkey-wrench, spanner; **–sluiting** (-en) *v* screw-cap; *fles met ~* screw-topped bottle; **–turbine** (-s) *v* propeller turbine; **–vliegtuig** (-en) *o* propeller plane; **–vormig** screw-shaped, spiral

'schroeien I (schroeide, h. geschroeid) *vt* scorch [the grass &]; singe [one's dress, one's hair]; scald [a pig]; cauterize [a wound]; **II** (schroeide, is geschroeid) *vi* get singed

'schroevedraaier (-s) *m* screwdriver; **'schroeven** (schroefde, h. geschroefd) *vt* screw

1 schrok (-ken) *m* glutton

2 schrok (schrokken) V.T. v. *schrikken*

'schrokken (schrokte, h. geschrokt) **I** *vi* eat gluttonously, bolt (wolf down) one's food, guzzle; **II** *vt het naar binnen ~* bolt it down; **–er(d)** (-s) *m* glutton; **'schrokk(er)ig I** *aj* gluttonous, greedy; **II** *ad* gluttonously, greedily; **–heid** *v* gluttony, greediness; **'schrokop** (-pen) *m* glutton, gourmand

'schromelijk I *aj* gross [exaggeration &], < frightful, awful; **II** *ad* grossly [exaggerated &], greatly, grievously, sorely [mistaken], < frightfully, awfully

'schromen (schroomde, h. geschroomd) *vt* fear, dread, hesitate

'schrompelen (schrompelde, is geschrompeld) *vi* shrivel (up); **–lig** shrivelled, wrinkled

schroom *m* diffidence, shyness, scruple; **schroom'vallig** shy, diffident, timorous; **–heid** *v* diffidence, timidity, timorousness

schroot *o* 1 grape-shot; case-shot; 2 ✗ (ij z e r - a f v a l) scrap; **–hoop** (-hopen) *m* scrap-yard, scrap-heap

'schub(be) (schubben) *v* scale [of a fish]; **'schubben** (schubde, h. geschubd) *vt* scale [a fish]; **'schubbig** scaly

'schuchter timid, timorous, shy, bashful; **–heid** *v* timidity, timorousness, shyness, bashfulness

'schuddebollen (schuddebolde, h. geschuddebold) *vi* nod; **'schudden** (schudde, h. geschud) **I** *vt* shake [one's head, a bottle, hands with sbd.]; shuffle [the cards]; *iem. door elkaar ~* shake sbd. up, give sbd. a good shaking; **II** *vi* 1 (in 't a l g.) shake; 2 (v. r ij t u i g) jolt; *~ vóór het gebruik* to be shaken before taking it; *hij schudde met het hoofd (van neen)* he shook his head; *dat deed het hele huis ~* it shook the house; *hij schudde van het lachen* he was convulsed with laughter; *het gebouw schudde op zijn grondvesten* the building shook to its foundations; **–ding** (-en) *v* shaking, concussion

'**schuier** (-s) *m* brush; '**schuieren** (schuierde, h. geschuierd) *vt* brush

schuif (schuiven) *v* slide; sliding-lid [of a box]; bolt [of a door]; slide [of a magic lantern &]; damper [of a stove]; **–blad** (-bladen) *o* extra leaf [of a table]; **–dak** (-daken) *o* sliding-roof; **–deur** (-en) *v* sliding-door

'**schuifelen** (schuifelde, h. en is geschuifeld) *vi* 1 shuffle, shamble; 2 (v. s l a n g) hiss

'**schuifklep** (-pen) *v* slide-(valve); **–knoop** (-knopen) *m* running knot, slipknot; **–ladder** (-s) *v* extending ladder, extension ladder; **–la(de)** (-laden) *v* drawer; **–maat** (-maten) *v* slide-rule, vernier cal(l)ipers; **–potlood** (-loden) *o* sliding-pencil; **–raam** (-ramen) *o* sash-window; **–speldje** (-s) *o* bobby-pin, hair-slide; **–tafel** (-s) = *uittrektafel*; **–trompet** (-ten) *v* trombone

'**schuiladres** (-sen) *o* cover address, accomodation address; '**schuilen*** *vi* 1 take shelter, shelter (from *voor*); 2 hide; *daar schuilt wat a c h t e r* there is something behind it; *de moeilijkheid schuilt in...* the difficulty lies (consists, rests) in...; '**schuilevinkje** (-s) *o* hide-and-seek; ~ *spelen* play at hide-and-seek; '**schuilgaan** (ging 'schuil, is 'schuilgegaan) *vi* hide [of the sun]; '**schuilhoek** (-en) *m* hiding-place; '**schuilhouden** (hield 'schuil, h. 'schuilgehouden) *zich* ~ hide, be in hiding, keep in the shade, lie low; '**schuilkelder** (-s) *m* underground shelter; **–kerk** (-en) *v* clandestine church; **–naam** (-namen) *m* (i n z. v a n s c h r ij v e r) pen-name, pseudonym; (v a n s p i o n &) assumed name; **–plaats** (-en) *v* hiding-place, hide-out; shelter; refuge, asylum; *bomvrije* ~ ⚔ dug-out; bombproof shelter; *een* ~ *zoeken bij...* take shelter (refuge) with, flee for shelter to...

schuim *o* foam [of liquid in fermentation or agitation, of saliva or perspiration]; froth [of liquid, beer &]; lather [of soap]; dross [of metals]; scum² [of impurities rising to the surface in boiling]; *fig* offscourings, scum, dregs [of the people]; *het* ~ *staat hem op de mond* he foams at the mouth; **–achtig** foamy, frothy; **–bad** (-baden) *o* foam bath; '**schuimbekken** (schuimbekte, h. geschuimbekt) *vi* foam at the mouth; ~*d van woede* foaming with rage; '**schuimblusser** (-s) *m* foam extinguisher; '**schuimen** (schuimde, h. geschuimd) **I** *vi* 1 foam [of water, the mouth &]; froth [of beer]; lather [of soap]; 2 (k l a p l o p e n) sponge; *op zee* ~ scour the seas; **II** *vt* skim [soup &]; **–mig** foamy, frothy; '**schuimklopper** (-s) *m* whisk; **–kop** (-pen) *m* crest [of waves]; **–pje** (-s) *o*

meringue; **–plastic** [-plɪsti.k] *o* foam(ed) plastic; **–rubber** *m* & *o* foam rubber; **–spaan** (-spanen) *v* skimmer; **–vlok** (-ken) *v* (foam) flake

schuin I *aj* slanting, sloping [wall &]; oblique [bearing, course, line, winding &]; inclined [plane]; bevel [edge]; *fig* broad, obscene, ribald [stories, songs, jokes], blue [film, joke, talk], dirty [postcard]; ~ *geknipt* cut on the bias; *de* ~*e zijde (van een driehoek)* the hypotenuse; **II** *ad* aslant, slantingly &; awry, askew, on the skew; ~ *aanzien* look askance at²; *het* ~ *houden* tilt it, slant it, slope it; ~ *toelopen* flue; ~ *tegenover* nearly opposite, diagonally opposite; '**schuinen** (schuinde, h. geschuind) *vt* ⚒ bevel, chamfer, splay; '**schuinheid** *v* obliqueness, obliquity; *fig* obscenity; **schuins** = *schuin*; '**schuinschrift** *o* sloping (slanting) writing; '**schuinsmarcheerder** [-ʃeːrdər] (-s) *m* debauchee, rake; '**schuinte** (-n) *v* obliquity, slope; *in de* ~ aslant

schuit (-en) *v* boat, barge; zie ook: *schuitje*; '**schuitehuis** (-huizen) *o* boat-house; **–voerder** (-s) *m* bargeman, bargee; '**schuitje** (-s) *o* 1 ⚓ (little) boat; 2 (v. b a l l o n) car, basket; 3 ⚒ pig, sow [of tin]; *we zitten in het* ~ *en moeten meevaren* in for a penny, in for a pound; *we zitten allemaal in hetzelfde* ~ we are all in the same boat; **–varen** *vi* boat, be boating; '**schuitvormig** boat-shaped

'**schuiven* I** *vt* shove, push [a chair &]; slip [a ring off one's finger]; *opium* ~ smoke opium; *de grendel o p de deur* ~ shoot the bolt; *de schuld op een ander* ~ lay the guilt at another man's door, lay the blame on someone else; *iets v a n zijn hals* ~ shift the responsibility & upon another man's shoulders, rid oneself of something; **II** *vi* slide, slip; *laat hem maar* ~*!* he knows what's what!, he knows his stuff!; '**schuiver** (-s) *m* lurch; *een* ~ *maken* give a lurch; zie ook: *opiumschuiver*, **–tje** (-s) *o* pusher

schuld (-en) *v* 1 (i n g e l d) debt; 2 (f o u t) fault, guilt; *achterstallige* ~ arrears; *kwade* ~*en* bad debts; *lopende* ~ outstanding (running, current) debt; *het is mijn* ~ (*niet*) it is (not) my fault, the fault is (not) mine; *wiens* ~ *is het?* whose fault is it?, who is to blame?; *het weer was* ~ *dat...* it was owing to the weather that...; ~ *bekennen* plead guilty; ~ *belijden* confess one's guilt; *iem. de* ~ *van iets geven* lay (throw) the blame on sbd., blame sbd. for sth.; ~ *hebben* 1 (s c h u l d i g zijn) be guilty; 2 (v e r-s c h u l d i g d zijn) owe (money); *wie heeft* ~*?* who is to blame?; ~ *hebben aan iets* be a party to sth.; *gewoonlijk krijg ik de* ~ usually I am blamed, I get the blame; ~*en maken* contract debts, run into debt; *de* ~ *op zich nemen*

take the blame upon oneself; *vergeef ons onze ~en*
B forgive us our trespasses; ● *b u i t e n mijn ~*
through no fault of mine; *d o o r uw ~* through
your fault; **–bekentenis** (-sen) *v* 1 confession
of guilt; 2 $ I O U, bond; **–belijdenis** *v*
confession of guilt; **–besef** *o* sense of guilt,
consciousness of (his, her) guilt; **–bewijs**
(-wijzen) *o = schuldbekentenis* 2; **schuldbe'wust**
guilty; **'schuldbrief** (-brieven) *m* debenture;
–delging (-en) *v* debt redemption; **–eiser** (-s)
m creditor; **'schuldeloos** guiltless, innocent;
schulde'loosheid *v* guiltlessness, innocence;
'schuldenaar (-s en -naren) *m* debtor;
'schuldenlast *m* burden of debts; encum-
brance(s) [on real estate]; **'schuldgevoel** *o*
guilt feeling, feeling of guilt; **'schuldig I** *aj*
guilty (of *aan*), culpable; *zijn ~e plicht* his
bounden duty; *~ zijn* 1 (s c h u l d h e b b e n)
be guilty; 2 (t e b e t a l e n h e b b e n) owe; *ik
ben u nog wat ~* I owe you a debt; *ik ben niemand
iets ~* I owe no one any money; *ik ben u nog
enige lessen ~* I still owe you for a few lessons;
het antwoord ~ blijven not make an answer; *het
antwoord niet ~ blijven* be ready with an answer;
het bewijs ~ blijven fail to prove that...; *zich ~
maken aan* render oneself guilty of; *hij is des
doods ~* he deserves death; *het ~ uitspreken over*
condemn, find [sbd.] guilty; **II** *sb de ~e* the
guilty party, the culprit; **'schuldvergelijking**
(-en) *v* compensation, set-off; **–vernieuwing**
(-en) *v* renewal of a debt; **–vordering** (-en) *v*
claim; **–vraag** *v de ~ opwerpen* raise the question of guilt
schulp (-en) *v* shell; *in zijn ~ kruipen* draw in
one's horns; **'schulpen** (schulpte, h.
geschulpt) *vt* scallop
'schunnig mean, shabby, shady, scurvy, ribald
'schuren (schuurde, h. geschuurd) **I** *vt* 1 scour
[a kettle &]; (m e t s c h u u r p a p i e r) sand,
sandpaper; 2 chafe [the skin]; **II** *va* scour; **III**
vi ~ langs graze; *over het zand ~* grate over the
sand
schurft *v & o* scabies, itch [of man]; scab [of
sheep]; mange [of cats, dogs, horses]; **S** *de ~
aan iem. (iets) hebben* hate sbd. (sth.) like poison;
S *ergens de ~ over inhebben* be peeved at sth.; **–ig**
scabby, mangy, scurfy; **–mijt** (-en) *v* itch-mite
'schuring *v* friction; **–sgeluid** (-en) *o gram*
fricative
schurk (-en) *m* rascal, rogue, scoundrel, scamp,
knave, villain; **'schurkachtig** rascally, scoundrelly, knavish, villainous; **–heid** (-heden) *v*
rascality, villainy, knavishness
'schurken (schurkte, h. geschurkt) *vi* rub,
scratch
'schurkenstreek (-streken) *m & v*, **schurke'rij**
(-en) *v* roguery, (piece of) villainy, piece of
knavery, knavish trick

schut (-ten) *o* (s c h e r m) screen; (s c h u t t i n g)
fence; (s c h o t) partition; *voor ~ lopen* look a
sight; *voor ~ staan* look a fool; *iem. voor ~ zetten*
make a fool of sbd.; *voor ~ zitten* look a fool;
–blad (-bladen) *o* 1 (v. b o e k) fly-leaf;
endpaper; 2 🌺 bract; **–deur** (-en) *v* lock-gate,
floodgate; **–geld** *o* 1 (v o o r v e e) poundage;
2 (v o o r s c h e p e n) lockage; **–kleur** (-en) *v*
protective coloration, protective colouring;
–kolk (-en) *m & v* lock-chamber; **'schuts-
engel** (-en) *m* guardian angel; **–heer** (-heren)
m patron; **'schutsluis** (-sluizen) *v* lock;
'schutspatroon (-tronen) *m*, **–patrones** (-sen)
v patron saint; **'schutstal** (-len) *m* pound;
'schutsvrouw (-en) *v* patroness; **'schutten**
(schutte, h. geschut) *vt* 1 (v a n v e e) pound; 2
(v. s c h e p e n) lock (through)
'schutter (-s) *m* 1 marksman; ✠ [air-, machine-]
gunner; 2 🏛 soldier of the Civic guard; *de
Schutter* ★ Sagittarius
'schutteren (schutterde, h. geschutterd) *vi* act
awkwardly (clumsily); **–rig** awkward
schutte'rij (-en) *v* 🏛 National guard, Civic
guard
'schutting (-en) *v* fence; hoarding [in the street,
for advertisement]; **–woord** (-en) *o* four-letter
word, dirty word
schuur (schuren) *v* 1 barn [for corn]; 2 shed;
–deur (-en) *v* barn-door, shed-door
'schuurlinnen *o* emery-cloth; **–middel** (-en) *o*
abrasive, scourer; **–papier** *o* emery-paper,
sandpaper; **–poeder** *o & m* scouring powder;
–spons (-en en -sponzen) *v* scourer; **–zand** *o*
scouring-sand
schuw shy, timid, bashful; **F** (e r g) awful;
'schuwen (schuwde, h. geschuwd) *vt* shun [a
man, bad company &]; eschew [action, kind of
food &]; *iets ~ als de pest* shun (avoid) sth. like
the plague; **'schuwheid** *v* shyness, timidity,
bashfulness
schwung [ʃvʊ.ŋ] *m* verve, drive
scle'rose [skle.'ro.zə] *v* sclerosis; *multiple ~*
multiple sclerosis, disseminated sclerosis
'scooter ['sku.-] (-s) *m* (motor) scooter; **–rijder**
(-s) *m* scooterist
'score (-s) *m* score; **–bord** (-en) *o* score-board;
'scoren (scoorde, h. gescoord) *vi & vt* score
'scrabbelen ['skrɪbələ(n)] (scrabbelde, h.
gescrabbeld) *vi* play scrabble
scri'bent (-en) *m* scribbler
'scriptie ['skrɪpsi.] (-s) *v* ⇔ special paper, ±
essay
scrofu'leus scrofulous; **scrofu'lose** [-'lo.zə] *v*
scrofula
scru'pule (-s) *v* scruple; **scrupu'leus** scrupulous

'Scylla ['skɪla.] *tussen* ~ *en Charybdis* between Scylla and Charybdis

se'ance [se.'ãsə] (-s) *v* séance

sec dry °

'secans (-en en -canten) *v* secant

secon'dair [-'dɛːr] secondary

secon'dant (-en) *m* 1 assistant master [in a boarding-school]; 2 second [in a duel]; 3 bottle-holder [at a prize-fight]; **-e** (-s) *v* assistant teacher

se'conde (-n) *v* second

secon'deren (secondeerde, h. gesecondeerd) *vt* second

se'condewijzer (-s) *m* second(s) hand

secre'taire [-tɛːrə] (-s) *m* writing-desk, secretary; **secreta'resse** (-n) *v* (lady) secretary; **secretari'aat** (-iaten) *o* secretaryship, secretariat; **secreta'rie** (-ieën) *v* town clerk's office; **secre'taris** (-sen) *m* 1 (i n 't a l g.) secretary; 2 (v. d. g e m e e n t e) town clerk; **secre'tarisgene'raal** (secretarissen-generaal) *m* 1 permanent under-secretary [of a ministry]; 2 secretary-general [of UNO &]

se'cretie [-(t)si.] (-s en -tiën) *v* secretion

'sectie ['sɪksla.] (-s) *v* 1 section; 2 (v. l ij k) dissection, post-mortem (examination); 3 ⚔ platoon

'sector (-s en -'toren) *m* sector

secu'lair [-'lɛːr] secular; **seculari'satie** [-'za.(t)si.] (-s en -tiën) *v* secularization; **seculari'seren** (seculariseerde, h. geseculariseerd) *vt* secularize; **secu'lier I** *aj* secular; **II** (-en) *m* secular

se'cunda ('s) *v* $ second of exchange

secun'dair [-'dɛːr] secondary

securi'teit *v* security; *voor alle* ~ to be on the safe side, for safety's sake; **se'cuur I** *aj* accurate, precise; **II** *ad* accurately, precisely; *het* ~ *weten* know it positively

se'dan (-s) *m* sedan

se'deren (sedeerde, h. gesedeerd) *vt* calm by means of sedatives; administer a sedative

'sedert = *sinds*; **sedert'dien** = *sindsdien*

sedi'ment (-en) *o* sediment

seg'ment (-en) *o* segment

segre'gatie [-(t)si.] *v* segregation

se'grijn *o* shagreen; **-en** *aj* shagreen; **-le(d)er** *o* shagreen

sein (-en) *o* signal; sign; *het* ~ *geven* give the signal; *dat was het* ~ *tot*... that was the signal for...; ~*en geven* make signals; *iem. een* ~ *geven* sign to sbd., give sbd. a warning look; *hun het* ~ *geven om stil te houden* signal to them to stop; **'seinen** (seinde, h. geseind) *vt & vi* 1 (s e i n e n g e v e n) signal; 2 ↑ telegraph, F wire; **-er** (-s) *m* signaller, signalman; **'seinfluit** (-en) *v* signal-whistle; **-fout** (-en) *v* ↑

telegraphic error; **-huisje** (-s) *o* signal-box; **-paal** (-palen) *m* signal-post, semaphore; **-post** (-en) *m* signal-station; **-station** [-sta.-(t)ʃɔn] (-s) *o* signalling-station; **-tje** (-s) *o* signal; *iem. een* ~ *geven* give sbd. a warning (a hint), tip sbd. off; **-toestel** (-len) *o* 1 signalling-apparatus; 2 ↑ transmitter; **-vlag** (-gen) *v* signal(ling)-flag; **-wachter** (-s) *m* signalman

'seismisch seismic; **seismo'graaf** (-grafen) *m* seismograph

sei'zoen (-en) *o* season; **-arbeider** (-s) *m* seasonal worker; **-kaart** (-en) *v* season ticket; **-opruiming** (-en) *v* clearance sales

se'kreet (-kreten) *o* **P** (w.c.) privy; (s c h e l d-w o o r d) **P** bastard, son of a bitch

seks *m* sex; **-bom** (-men) *v* **F** sexspot; **-e** (-n) *v* sex; *de (schone)* ~ the fair sex; **'seksen** (sekste, h. gesekst) *vt* sex [chickens]; **'seksloos** sexless; **-maniak** (-ken) *m* **F** sex fiend; **seksuali'teit** *v* sexuality, sex; **seksu'eel I** *aj* sexual [organs]; sex [education, factor, life, problem]; **II** *ad* sexually; **seksuolo'gie** *v* sexology; **seksuo'loog** (-logen) *m* sexologist

sek'tariër (-s) *m* sectarian; **sek'tarisch** sectarian; **sekta'risme** *o* sectarianism; **'sekte** (-n) *v* sect; **-geest** *m* sectarianism

se'kwester (-s) 1 *m* sequestrator; 2 *o* sequestration; **sekwes'tratie** [-(t)si.] (-s) *v* sequestration; **sekwes'treren** (sekwestreerde, h. gesekwestreerd) sequester, sequestrate

'selderie, 'selderij *m* celery

se'lect select, choice; **selec'teren** (selecteerde, h. geselecteerd) *vt* select; **se'lectie** [-'lɪksi.] (-s) *v* selection; **selec'tief** selective; **selectivi'teit** *v* selectivity

sema'foor (-foren) *m* semaphore

seman'tiek *v* semantics; **se'mantisch** semantic

se'mester (-s) *o* semester

Se'miet (-en) *m* Semite

semi'narie (-s) *o* 1 seminary; 2 ⚭seminar; *groot (klein)* ~ *rk* major (minor) seminary; **semina'rist** (-en) *m* seminarist

Se'mitisch Semitic

se'naat (-naten) *m* 1 senate; 2 ⚭ committee of senior students

se'nang *zich* ~ *voelen* feel well, comfortable

se'nator (-s en -'toren) *m* senator

'Senegal *o* Senegal

se'niel senile; **~e** *aftakeling* senile decay

'senior senior

sen'satie [-'za.(t)si.] (-s) *v* sensation, stir [among audience &]; [personal] thrill; ~ *maken (veroorzaken)* create a sensation, cause a stir; *op* ~ *belust* sensation-hungry; **-blad** (-bladen) *o* tabloid; **-pers** *v* yellow press, gutter press; **-roman** (-s) *m* sensational novel, shocker,

thriller, penny-dreadful, yellow-back; **–stuk**
(-ken) *o* sensational play, thriller;
sensatio'neel [-'za.(t)si.o.-] sensational;
F front-page [news]
sen'sibel [-'zi.-] (g e v o e l i g) sensitive;
(w a a r n e e m b a a r) perceptible; **sensi-
bili'teit** *v* (g e v o e l i g h e i d) sensibility;
(w a a r n e m i n g) perception
sensu'eel [-zy-] sensual
sentimentali'teit *v* sentimentality;
sentimen'teel sentimental; **~ doen over**
slobber over
sepa'raat *aj* (& *ad*) separate(ly)
'sepia *v* (d i e r & k l e u r) sepia
sep'tember *m* September
sep'tet (-ten) *o* septet(te)
sep'tiem (-en), **sep'time** (-s) *v* ♩ seventh; **~
akkoord** seventh chord
'seraf (-s), **sera'fijn** (-en) *m* seraph [*mv*
seraphim]
se'rail [-'raj] (-s) *o* seraglio
se'reen serene
sere'nade (-s) *v* serenade; **iem. een ~ brengen**
serenade sbd.
'serge [-ʒə] *v* serge
ser'geant [-'ʒant] (-en en -s) *m* sergeant;
'~-ma'joor (-s) *mv* sergeant-major; **–sstrepen**
mv sergeant's stripes
'serie (-s en -iën) *v* 1 (i n h e t a l g.) series; 2
♒ break; 3 *RT* serial; **–bouw** *m* series production; **–nummer** (-s) *o* serial number;
–schakeling (-en) *v* series connection,
sequence circuit
seri'eus *aj* (& *ad*) serious(ly); **serieuze aanvragen**
genuine inquiries; **séri'eux** [se.ri'ø] *au* **~ nemen**
take seriously
se'ring (-en) *v* lilac; **–eboom** (-bomen) *m* ❀
lilac-tree
ser'moen (-en) *o* sermon[2], *fig* lecture
ser'pent (-en) *o* serpent; *fig* shrew
serpen'tine (-s) *v* (paper) streamer
'serre ['sɛːrə] (-s) *v* 1 (l o s s t a a n d o f
u i t g e b o u w d) conservatory; hothouse,
greenhouse; 2 (a l s a c h t e r k a m e r) closed
veranda(h)
'serum (-s en sera) *o* serum
ser'veerboy [-bòj] (-s) *m* serving trolley,
dinner-wagon; **ser'veerster** (-s) *v* waitress;
ser'veren (serveerde, h. geserveerd) *vt* serve
ser'vet (-ten) *o* napkin, table-napkin, [paper]
serviette; **te groot voor ~ en te klein voor tafellaken**
at the awkward age; **–ring** (-en) *m* napkin
ring, serviette ring
ser'veuse [-zə-] (-s) *v* waitress
'servicebeurt ['sœ:rvəs-] (-en) *v* **een ~ laten
geven** have [one's car] serviced
'Serviër (-s) *m* Serbian

ser'vies (-viezen) *o* 1 dinner-set; 2 tea-set
'Servisch *aj* & *o* Serbian
servi'tuut (-tuten) *o* easement, charge
'sessie (-s) *v* session
sex'tant (-en) *m* sextant
sex'tet (-ten) *o* ♩ sextet(te)
Sey'chellen *mv* **de ~** the Seychelles
sfeer (sferen) *v* 1 [celestial, social] sphere; 2
[cordial, cosy, home] atmosphere; **dat ligt
b u i t e n mijn ~** that is out of my domain (my
province); **hij was i n hoger sferen** he was in the
clouds; **'sferisch** spherical; **sfero'ïde** (-n) *v*
spheroid
sfinx (-en) *m* sphinx
shag [ʃɡ] *m* shag, cigarette tobacco
shampo'neren [ʃɑm-] (shamponeerde, h.
geshamponeerd) *vt* shampoo; **'shampoo** *m*
shampoo
'shantoeng ['ʃɑn-] *o* & *m* shantung
'sherry ['ʃɛri] *m* sherry
shock [ʃɔk] (-s) *m* shock; **–behandeling** (-en) *v*
shock treatment; **sho'ckeren** [ʃɔ'ke.-] (shoc-
keerde, h. geshockeerd) *vt* shock; **'shockthe-
rapie** *v* shock therapy
'showen ['ʃo.və(n)] (showde, h. geshowd) *vt*
show [fashion]
sí ('s) *v* ♩ si
Sia'mees I *aj* Siamese; **II** *m* Siamese; **de Siamezen**
the Siamese; **III** *o* **het ~** Siamese; **IV** *v* **een**
Siamese a Siamese woman
Si'berisch Siberian
si'bille (-n) *v* sibyl
sicca'tief (-tieven) *o* siccative
Sicili'aan(s) (-ianen) *sb* & *aj* Sicilian
'sidderaal (-alen) *m* electric eel; **'sidderen**
(sidderde, h. gesidderd) *vi* quake, shake,
tremble, shudder; **~ van...** quake & with; **–ring**
(-en) *v* shudder, trembling; **'sidderrog** (-gen)
m electric ray
'siepelen (siepelde, h. en is gesiepeld) *vi* ooze,
trickle, seep (through)
'siepogen *mv* watery eyes
sier *v* **goede ~ maken** make good cheer; **–aad**
(-raden) *o* ornament[2]; **–bestrating** *v* ornamental paving (pavement); **'sieren** (sierde, h.
gesierd) **I** *vt* adorn, ornament, decorate; **II** *vr*
zich ~ adorn oneself; **'sierheester** (-s) *m*
ornamental shrub; **–kunst** (-en) *v* decorative art;
–lijk graceful, elegant; **–lijkheid** *v* gracefulness, elegance; **–lijst** (-en) *v* (v. a u t o) styling
strip, belt-moulding; **–palm** (-en) *m* ornamental palm; **–plant** (-en) *v* ornamental plant;
–strip (-s en -pen) *m = sierlijst*; **–vis** (-sen) *m*
toy fish
si'ësta ('s) *v* siesta, nap
si'fon (-s) *m* siphon
si'gaar (-garen) *v* cigar; **si'gareaansteker** (-s)

m cigar-lighter; **–as** *v* cigar-ash; **–bandje** (-s) *o* cigar-band; **–knipper** (-s) *m* cigar-cutter; si'**garenfabriek** (-en) *v* cigar-factory, cigar-works; **–handelaar** (-s en -laren) *m* tobacconist, dealer in cigars; **–kistje** (-s) *o* 1 cigar-box; 2 (s c h o e n) **F** beetle-crusher; **–koker** (-s) *m* cigar-case; **–magazijn** (-en) *o* cigar-store; **–maker** (-s) *m* cigar-maker; **–winkel** (-s) *m* tobacconist's shop, cigar-shop; si'**gare-pijpje** (-s) *o* cigar-holder

siga'**ret** (-ten) *v* cigarette; **–teaansteker** (-s) *m* cigarette-lighter; siga'**rettenautomaat** (-maten) *m* cigarette-machine; **–doos** (-dozen) *v* cigarette-box; **–koker** (-s) *m* cigarette-case; **–papier** *o* cigarette-paper; **–tabak** *m* cigarette-tobacco; **–vloei** *o* cigarette-paper; siga'**rettepeukje** (-s) *o* fag-end; **–pijpje** (-s) *o* cigarette-holder

sig'**naal** [si.'pa.l] (-nalen) *o* 1 (i n 't a l g.) signal; 2 ✕ bugle-call, call; 3 ⚓ pipe, call

signale'**ment** [si.pa.-] (-en) *o* description; signa'**leren** (signaleerde, h. gesignaleerd) *vt* call attention to, point out [a fact]; describe, give a description of [sbd. wanted to the police]

signa'**tuur** [si.pa.-] (-turen) *v* signature; sig'**neren** (signeerde, h. gesigneerd) *vt* sign; autograph [copies of one's book, one's photo]; sig'**net** (-ten) *o* signet, seal

'**sijpelen** (sijpelde, h. en is gesijpeld) *vi* ooze, trickle

sijs (sijzen) *v* ✿ siskin; '**sijsjeslijmer** (-s) **F** *m* stick-in-the-mud, milksop

sik (-ken) *v* 1 (d i e r) goat; 2 (b a a r d) goat's beard [of a goat]; goatee, chin-tuft [of a man]

1 '**sikkel** (-s) *v* sickle, reaping-hook

2 '**sikkel** (-s en -en) *m* shekel [Jewish weight & silver coin]

sikke'**neurig** peevish, grumpy

'**sikkepit** *v* **F** bit; *geen* ~ not the least bit

si'**lene** (-n en -s) *v* campion

silhou'**et** [si.lu.'ɪt] (-ten) *v* & *o* silhouette; silhouet'**teren** (silhouetteerde, h. gesilhouet-teerd) *vt* silhouette

sili'**caat** (-caten) *o* silicate; sili'**conen** *mv* silicones; sili'**cose** [-'ko.zə] *v* silicosis

'**silo** ('s) *m* silo; (g r a a n p a k h u i s) elevator

'**simmen** (simde, h. gesimd) **F** *vi* snivel, blubber

simo'**nie** *v* simony

'**simpel** simple, mere; (o n n o z e l) silly; **–heid** *v* simplicity; silliness; **sim'plistisch** (over-) simplified

simu'**lant** (-en) *m* simulator; ✕ malingerer; simu'**latie** [-(t)si.] (-s) *v* simulation; ✕ malingering; simu'**leren** (simuleerde, h. gesimuleerd) **I** *vt* simulate; **II** *va* simulate; ✕ malinger

simul'**taan** simultaneous; **–seance** [-se.ãsə] (-s) *v* simultaneous game

'**sinaasappel** (-s en -en) *m* orange; **–kist** (-en) *v* orange box; **–sap** *o* orange juice

sinds **I** *prep* since; ~ *enige dagen* for some days (past); ~ *mijn komst* since my arrival; **II** *ad* since; **III** *cj* since; sinds'**dien** since

sine'**cure** (-s en -n) *v* sinecure

Singa'**lees** (-lezen) *aj* & *m* Cingalese, Sin(g)halese

'**singel** (-s) *m* 1 (v o o r p a a r d) girth; surcingle; 2 *rk* girdle [of priest's alb]; 3 (o m s t a d) moat; ook: 4 ± boulevard; ~*s* (w e e f s e l) webbing

'**singelen** ['sɪŋgələ(n)] (singelde, h. gesingeld) *vt* girth; **F** (t e n n i s) play a singles match

'**singlet** ['sɪŋlɪt] (-s) *m* vest

si'**nister** sinister, disastrous, calamitous

sin'**jeur** (-s) *m* > fellow

si'**nopel** ⊘ vert

sint (-en) *m* saint; *de goede* ~ St. Nicholas [Dec. 6th]; **sint-'bernardshond** (-en) *m* St. Bernard dog

'**sintel** (-s) *m* cinder; **–baan** (-banen) *v sp* cinder track (path); (v o o r m o t o r f i e t s e n) dirt track

sint-'**elmsvuur** *o* St. Elmo's fire

Sinter'**klaas** St. Nicholas [Dec. 6th]; **sinter-klaas'avond** (-en) *m* St. Nicholas' Eve [Dec. 5th]

Sint-'**Jan** *m* 1 St. John; 2 (f e e s t d a g) Midsummer (day); **sint-'jut(te)mis** *met* ~ (*als de kalveren op het ijs dansen*) tomorrow come never; **Sint-'Maarten** *m* 1 St. Martin; 2 (f e e s t d a g) Martinmas; **Sint-'Nicolaas** *m* St. Nicholas; **sint-'veitsdans, sint-'vitus-dans** *m* St. Vitus's dance

'**sinus** (-sen) *m* sine

sinu'**sitis** [-'zi.-] *v* sinusitis

'**Sion** ~ Zion

sip ~ *kijken* look blue (glum)

'**Sire** sire, your Majesty

si'**rene** *v* 1 (-n) siren, syren; 2 (-s en -n) (f l u i t) siren, [factory] hooter; **–nzang** (-en) *m* siren song

'**sirih** *m* sirih, betel

si'**rocco** ('s) *m* sirocco

si'**roop** (-ropen) *v* = *stroop*

'**sisal** ['si.zɑl] *m* sisal

'**sisklank** (-en) *m* hissing sound, hiss, sibilant; '**sissen** (siste, h. gesist) *vi* hiss; sizzle [in the pan]; **–er** (-s) *m* (v u u r w e r k) squib; *met een* ~ *aflopen* blow over

sits (-en) *o*, '**sitsen** *aj* chintz

situ'**atie** [-(t)si.] (-s) *v* situation; **–tekening** (-en) *v* lay out (plan); **situ'eren** (situeerde, h. gesitueerd) *vt* situate, locate; zie ook: *gesitueerd*

Six'tijns Sixtine

sjaal (-s) *m* 1 shawl; 2 scarf

'sjabbes F (-en) *m* Sabbath

sja'blone, sja'bloon (-blonen) *v* stencil

sja'brak (-ken) *v* & *o* housing, saddle-cloth, caparison

'sjachelaar (-s) *m* = *sjacheraar*; 'sjachelen = *sjacheren*; 'sjacheraar (-s) *m* barterer, huckster; 'sjacheren (sjacherde, h. gesjacherd) *vi* barter

sjah [ʃa.] (-s) *m* shah

'sjakes F *zich* ~ *houden* keep mum

sja'ko ('s) *m* shako

sja'lot (-ten) *v* shallot

sjamber'loek (-s) *m* dressing-gown

'sjanker (-s) *m* chancre

sjans *v* F ~ *hebben* get a (sbd.'s) glad eye; 'sjansen (sjanste, h. gesjanst) *vi* flirt

sjees (sjezen) *v* gig

sjeik (-s) *m* sheik(h)

sjerp (-en) *m* sash

'sjeuïg ['ʃøøx] juicy

'sjezen (sjeesde, h. en is gesjeesd) *vi* F (h a r d l o p e n) race, speed; (z a k k e n) be plucked [in an examination]

sjib'bolet (-s) *o* shibboleth

'sjilpen (sjilpte, h. gesjilpt) *vi* chirp, cheep; 'sjirpen (sjirpte, h. gesjirpt) *vi* chirr

'sjoege F *geen* (*lou*) ~ [*van iets*] *hebben* know nothing about; *geen* ~ *geven* not answer, not react

'sjoelbakspel (-len) *o* shovelboard

'sjoemelen (sjoemelde, h. gesjoemeld) F *vi* cheat, juggle (with)

'sjofel shabby, F seedy, flea-bitten; **-heid** *v* shabbiness, F seediness; **-tjes** shabbily, F seedily

'sjokken (sjokte, h. en is gesjokt) *vi* trudge, jog

'sjorren (sjorde, h. gesjord) *vt* ⚓ lash, seize

sjouw (-en) *m* job, F grind; 'sjouwen (sjouwde, h. gesjouwd) **I** *vt* carry; **II** *vi* (z w a a r w e r k e n) toil and moil; 'sjouwer (-s), **-man** (-lieden en -lui) *m* porter; dock-hand

skald (-en) *m* scald

ske'let (-ten) *o* skeleton

'skelter (-s) *m* (go-)kart; 'skelteren (skelterde, h. geskelterd) *vi* (go-)kart

ski [ski., ʃi.] ('s) *m* ski; **-binding** (-en) *v* ski-binding; 'skiën **I** (skiede, h. en is geskied) *vi* ski; **II** *o* skiing; **-ër** (-s) *m* skier

skiff (-s) *m* single sculler, skiff; skif'feur (-s) *m* sculler

'skileraar ['ski.-, 'ʃi.-] (-s) *m* ski-instructor; **-lift** (-en) *m* ski-lift; **-lopen I** (liep 'ski, h. en is 'skigelopen) *vi* ski; **II** *o* skiing; **-loper** (-s) *m* ski-runner, skier; **-pak** (-ken) *o* ski-suit; **-schoen** (-en) *m* ski-boot; **-sok** (-ken) *v* ski-sock; **-sport** *v* skiing; **-springen** *o* ski-

jumping; **-terrein** (-en) *o* ski-run; **-was** *m* & *o* ski-wax

sla *v* (g e r e c h t) salad; (p l a n t e s o o r t) lettuce

Slaaf (Slaven) *m* Slav

slaaf (slaven) *m* slave, bondman, thrall; **slaafs** *aj* slavish [copy of...], servile; **-heid** *v* slavishness, servility

slaag *m een pak* ~ a beating; ~ *krijgen* get the stick; **-s** ~ *raken* come to blows; ⚔ join battle; ~ *zijn* be fighting; **slaan* I** *vt* 1 (b ij h e r h a - l i n g) beat²; 2 (é é n e n k e l e m a a l) strike; 3 (l e g g e n) put [one's arm round...]; pass [a rope round...]; 4 (v e r s l a a n) beat [the enemy]; 5 (b ij d a m m e n) take, capture; 6 (v. k l o k) strike [the hours, twelve]; *een brug* ~ build a bridge; *een gedenkpenning* ~ strike a medal; *hij heeft mij geslagen* he has struck (hit) me; *u moet mij* (*die schijf*) ~ you ought to take me (to capture that man); *olie* ~ make oil; *touw* ~ lay (make) ropes; *de trommel* ~ beat the drum; *vuur* ~ strike fire (a light); *daar slaat het tien uur!* there goes ten o'clock!, it is striking ten; zie ook: *klok*; ● *hem a a n het kruis* ~ nail him to the cross; *a c h t e r o v e r* ~ whip off [a snorter]; *zich er d o o r heen* ~ fight one's way through²; *fig* pull through, carry it off; *hij sloeg de spijker i n de muur* he drove the nail into the wall; *in elkaar* ~ smash, knock to pieces [sth.]; beat up [sbd.]; *hij sloeg zich o p de borst* he beat his breast; *hij sloeg zich op de dijen* he slapped his thighs; *hij sloeg de armen* (*benen*) *o v e r elkaar* he crossed his arms (legs); zie ook: *acht, alarm, beleg* &; **II** *vi* 1 strike [of a clock]; 2 beat [of the heart]; 3 warble, sing [of a bird], jug [of a nightingale]; 4 kick [of a horse]; 5 flap [of a sail]; ● *a a n het muiten* ~ zie *muiten*; *de bliksem sloeg i n de toren* the steeple was struck by lightning; *m e t de deuren* ~ slam the doors; *hij sloeg met de vuist op tafel* he struck his fist on the table; *hij sloeg n a a r mij* he struck (hit out) at me; *dat slaat o p u* that refers to you, that's meant for you; *dat slaat nergens op* that is neither here nor there; *erop* ~ hit out, lay into them; *de golven sloegen o v e r de zeewering* the waves broke over the sea-wall; *het water sloeg t e g e n de dijk* the water beat against the embankment; *hij sloeg tegen de grond* he fell down with a thud; *de vlammen sloegen u i t het dak* the flames burst from the roof; **-d** *~e ruzie hebben* be at loggerheads, have a blazing row

slaap (slapen) *m* 1 (h e t s l a p e n) sleep; 2 (v a n h e t h o o f d) temple; ~ *hebben* be (feel) sleepy; *zijn* ~ *uit hebben* have had one's fill; ~ *krijgen* get sleepy; *ik heb de* ~ *niet kunnen vatten* I could not get to sleep; *in* ~ *vallen* fall asleep, drop off; *in* ~ *wiegen* rock asleep; *fig* put [doubts] to sleep, lull [suspicions] to sleep; *zich in ~ wiegen* lull oneself to sleep; *uit de ~ houden* keep awake; **–bank** (-en) *v* sofa-bed; **–been** (-deren) *o* temporal bone; **–coupé** [-ku.pe.] (-s) *m* sleeping-compartment; **–drank** (-en) *m* sleeping-draught; **–dronken** hardly able to keep one's eyes open; **–gelegenheid** (-heden) *v* sleeping-accommodation; **–kamer** (-s) *v* bedroom; **–kop** (-pen) *m* sleepy-head, lie-abed; **–liedje** (-s) *o* lullaby; **–middel** (-en) *o* opiate, soporific; **–muts** (-en) *v* 1 night-cap; 2 = *slaapkop*; **–mutsje** (-s) *o* 1 (b o r r e l) night-cap; 2 ⚘ California poppy; **–pil** (-len) *v* sleeping-pill; **–plaats** (-en) *v* sleeping-place, sleeping-accommodation; **–stad** (-steden) *v* dormitory suburb, *Am* bedroom town; **–ste(d)e** (-steden, -steeën) *v* doss-house; **–ster** (-s) *v* sleeper; *de schone ~* the Sleeping Beauty; **–tablet** (-ten) *v* & *o* sleeping-tablet; **–vertrek** (-ken) *o* sleeping-apartment; **–wagen** (-s) *m* sleeping-car, sleeper; **–wandelaar** (-s) *m* sleep-walker; **–wandelen** *o* sleep-walking, walking in one's sleep; **slaap'wekkend** soporific; **'slaapzaal** (-zalen) *v* dormitory; **–zak** (-ken) *m* sleeping-bag; **–ziekte** (-s en -n) *v* 1 sleeping-sickness [of Africa]; 2 [European] sleepy sickness

'slaatje (-s) *o* salad; [*fig*] *ergens een ~ uit slaan* get something out of it

slab (-ben) *v* bib

'slabak (-ken) *m* salad-bowl

sla'bakken (slabakte, h. geslabakt) *vi* slacken (in one's zeal), slack off; idle; dawdle

'slabbetje (-s) *o* bib

'slaboontjes *mv* French beans

'slachtbank (-en) *v* butcher's board, shambles[2]; *ter ~ leiden* lead to the slaughter; **–beest** (-en) *o* beast to be killed; *~en* ook: stock for slaughter, slaughter cattle; **'slachten** (slachtte, h. geslacht) *vt* kill, slaughter; **–er** (-s) *m* butcher[2]; **slachte'rij** (-en) *v* butcher's shop; **'slachthuis** (-huizen) *o* abattoir, slaughterhouse; **'slachting** (-en) *v* slaughter, butchery; massacre; *een ~ aanrichten (houden) onder* slaughter, make a massacre of; **'slachtmaand** *v* November; **–offer** (-s) *o* victim; *het ~ worden van* fall a victim (victims) to; **–plaats** (-en) *v* butchery, shambles; **–vee** *o* slaughter cattle

sla'dood *m een lange ~* a tall lanky individual

1 slag (slagen) *m* 1 (m e t s t o k &) blow, stroke, hit; 2 (m e t h a n d) blow, slap, cuff, box [on the ears]; 3 (m e t z w e e p) stroke, lash, cut; 4 (v. h a r t) beat, beating, pulsation; 5 (v. k l o k) stroke; 6 (v. r o e i e r, z w e m m e r) stroke; 7 (i n h a a r) wave; 8 (v. v o g e l s) warble [of birds], jug [of nightingale]; 9 (v. d o n d e r) clap; 10 (g e l u i d)

bang; crash, thump; thud; 11 ✗ stroke [of piston], turn [of wheel]; 12 (w i n d i n g) turn [of a rope]; 13 ⚓ (b ij l a v e r e n) tack; 14 ◊ trick; 15 (v e l d s l a g) battle; 16 (a a n z w e e p) lash; 17 *fig* blow [of misfortune]; knack [of doing something]; *vrije ~* free style [in swimming]; *het is een ~* it is only a knack; *een zware ~ voor hem* a heavy blow to him; *een ~ in het gezicht* a slap in the face[2]; *de ~ aangeven bij het roeien* stroke the boat; *hij heeft geen ~ gedaan* he has not done a stroke of work; *alle ~en halen* ◊ make all the tricks; *~ van iets hebben* have the knack of sth.; *de ~ van iets beethebben* F have got the hang of it; *een ~ van de molen hebben* F have a tile off; *~ houden* keep stroke; *een ~ om de arm houden* not commit oneself, make reservations; *de ~ (van iets) kwijt zijn* have lost the knack of it; *~ leveren* ⚔ give battle; *zijn ~ slaan* seize the opportunity; make one's coup; *een goede ~ slaan* do a good stroke of business; *hij sloeg er maar een ~ naar* he had (made) a shot at it, he had a wack at it; *iem. een ~ toebrengen (geven)* deal (strike, fetch) sbd. a blow; *de ~ winnen* 1 ◊ make the trick; 2 ⚔ gain the battle[2]; ● *aan de ~ gaan* get going, get busy, set (get) to work, F wire in; *ik kon niet meer aan ~ komen* ◊ [having no hearts] I could not regain the lead; *bij de eerste ~* at the first blow (stroke); *met één ~* at one (a) stroke, at one (a) blow; *met één ~ van zijn zwaard* with one stroke of his sword; *met de Franse ~ iets doen* do sth. perfunctorily, do sth. with a lick and a wash, do sth. in a slap-dash manner; *op ~* at once; *op ~ gedood* killed on the spot, outright, instantly; *op ~ van drieën* on the stroke of three; *ik kon niet op ~ komen* I could not get my hand in; *~ op ~* blow upon blow, at every stroke; *de klok is v a n ~* the clock is off strike; *de roeiers waren van ~* the oarsmen were off their stroke; *iem. een ~ v ó ó r zijn* F be one upon sbd.; *z o n d e r ~ of stoot* without (striking) a blow

2 slag *o* kind, sort, class, description; *het gewone ~ mensen* the common run of people; *iem. van dat ~* sbd. of that kidney; *mensen van allerlei ~* all sorts and conditions of men

'slagader (-s en -en) *v* artery; *grote ~* aorta; **–breuk** (-en) *v* rupture of an artery; **–lijk** arterial

'slagbal *o* rounders; **–boom** (-bomen) *m* barrier[2]

'slagen (slaagde, is geslaagd) *vi* succeed; *ben je goed geslaagd?* have you succeeded in finding what you wanted?; *hij slaagde er in om...* he succeeded in ...ing, he managed to...; *hij slaagde er niet in...* ook: he failed to...; *hij is voor (zijn) Frans geslaagd* he has passed his French examination; zie ook: *geslaagd*

2 'slagen *mv.* v. *slag*

'slager (-s) *m* butcher; **slage'rij** (-en) *v* 1 butcher's shop; 2 butcher's trade; **'slagers-jongen** (-s) *m* butcher's boy; **–knecht** (-s) *m* butcher's man; **–mes** (-sen) *o* butcher's knife; **–winkel** (-s) *m* butcher's shop

'slaghamer (-s) *m* mallet; **–hoedje** (-s) *o* percussion-cap; **–hout** (-en) *o sp* bat; **–instrument** (-en) *o* percussion instrument; **–kruiser** (-s) *m* ⚓ battle-cruiser; **–linie** (-s) *v* line of battle; **–orde** (-n) *v* order of battle, battle-array; *in* ~ *geschaard* drawn up in battle-array; **–pen** (-nen) *v* quill-feather; **–pin** (-nen) *v* 🛠 firing pin; **–regen** (-s) *m* downpour, heavy shower, driving rain; **–roeier** (-s) *m* stroke; **–room** *m* 1 whipping cream; 2 whipped cream; **–schaduw** (-en) *v* cast shadow; **–schip** (-schepen) *o* battleship; **–tand** (-en) *m* 1 (v. o l i f a n t, w a l r u s, w i l d z w ij n) tusk; 2 (v. w o l f &) fang

slag'vaardig ready for battle; *fig* quick at repartee, quick-witted; **–heid** *v* readiness for battle; *fig* quickness at repartee, quick-wittedness

'slagveer (-veren) *v* 1 🛠 main spring; 2 🦅 flight feather, **–veld** (-en) *o* battle-field, field of battle; **–werk** (-en) *o* 1 striking-parts [of a clock], striking-work; 2 ♪ percussion instruments; **–werker** (-s) *m* percussionist, percussion player, (i n z. v. j a z z) drummer; **–zee** (-zeeën) *v* = *stortzee*; **–zij(de)** *v* ⚓ list; 🔄 bank; ~ *maken* ⚓ list; 🔄 bank; **–zin** (-nen) *m* slogan; **–zwaard** (-en) *o* broadsword

slak (-ken) *v* 1 snail [with a shell]; 2 slug [without a shell]; ‖ 3 🛠 slag [*mv* slag], scoria [*mv* scoriae] [of metal]

'slaken (slaakte, h. geslaakt) *vt iems. boeien* ~ loosen sbd.'s fetters; *een kreet* ~ utter a cry; *een zucht* ~ heave (utter) a sigh

'slakkegang *m met een* ~ *gaan* go at a snail's pace, go snail-slow; **–huis** (-huizen) *o* 1 snail-shell; 2 § cochlea [of the ear]; **'slakken-meel** *o* basic slag

'slakom (-men) *v* salad bowl

'slalom (-s) *m* slalom

slam'pampen (slampampte, h. geslampampt) *vi* gad about; **–er** (-s) *m* good-for-nothing

1 slang (-en) *v* 1 (d i e r) snake, serpent; 2 hose [of a fire-engine]; (rubber) tube; worm [of a still]; 3 *fig* serpent, viper

2 slang [slɛŋ] *o* slang, argot

'slangachtig snaky, serpentine, anguine; **'slangebeet** (-beten) *m* snake-bite; **–gif(t)** *o* snake-poison; **–kruid** *o* viper's bugloss; **–leer** *o* snake skin; **–mens** (-en) *m* contortionist; **slangenbezweerder** (-s) *m* snake-charmer; **'slangetong** (-en) *v* 1 serpent's tongue; 2 🌿

adder's-tongue; **–vel** (-len) *o* snake-skin; (a f g e w o r p e n) slough

slank I *aj* slender, slim; ~ *blijven* keep slim; *aan de ~e lijn doen* watch one's figure, slim; **II** *ad* slenderly, slimly; **–heid** *v* slenderness, slimness

'slaolie *v* salad-oil

slap I *aj* soft [nib, collar], supple [limbs], flaccid [flesh]; slack² [rope, tire, season, trade], limp² [binding of a book, cravat, rhymes], flabby² [cheeks, character, language]; thin² [brew, style]; unsubstantial [food]; *fig* lax [discipline]; weak-kneed [attitude]; spineless [fellow]; $ dull [market], weak [market, tea]; **II** *ad* flabbily, limply; ~ *neerhangen* flag, droop

'slapeloos sleepless; **slape'loosheid** *v* sleeplessness, insomnia; **'slapen* I** *vi* sleep, be asleep²; *mijn been slaapt* I've pins and needles in my leg; *gaan* ~ go to bed, go to sleep; *zit je weer te ~?* are you asleep again?; *ik zal er nog eens op* ~ I'll sleep upon (over) it; ~ *als een os* sleep like a log; ~ *als een roos* sleep like a top; **II** *vt* sleep; *de slaap des rechtvaardigen* ~ sleep the sleep of the just; **–d** *fig* unawakened, dormant; **'slaper** (-s) *m* 1 (s l a p e n d p e r s o o n) sleeper; 2 (s l a a p g a s t) lodger; **–ig** sleepy, drowsy

'slapheid *v* slackness, weakness &, zie *slap*

'slapie (-s) 🛠 room-mate

'slapjes I *aj* slack, dull; weak; **II** *ad* slackly; **'slappeling** (-en) *m* weakling, spineless fellow, **F** jellyfish; **'slapte** *v* slackness [of a rope]; $ slack

'slasaus (-en en -sauzen) *v* salad dressing

'slaven (slaafde, h. geslaafd) *vi* drudge, slave, toil; ~ *en zwoegen* toil and moil; **'slavenarbeid** *m* slavery, slave labour; *fig* drudgery; **–armband** (-en) *m* closed-forever bracelet; **–drijver** (-s) *m* slave-driver², overseer; **–handel** *m* slave trade; **–handelaar** (-s en -laren) *m* slave-trader; **–houder** (-s) *m* slave-owner; **–jacht** (-en) *v* slave-hunt; **–juk** *o* yoke of bondage; **–ketenen** *mv* slave's chains; **–leven** *o* slavery, life of toil; **–markt** (-en) *v* slave-market; **–opstand** (-en) *m* slave rebellion; **–schip** (-schepen) *o* ⚓ slave-ship, slaver; **slaver'nij** *v* slavery, bondage, servitude; **sla'vin** (-nen) *v* (female) slave, bondwoman

'Slavisch *aj* o Slav, Slavic, Slavonic; **sla'vist** (-en) *m* Slavicist, Slavist

slecht I *aj* bad; evil [thoughts]; < wicked [person]; poor [quality, stuff &]; *hij is ~ van gezicht* his eye-sight is bad; *de zieke is ~er vandaag* the patient is worse to-day; *op zijn ~st* at one's (its) worst; **II** *ad* badly; ill[-tempered &]; **–aard** (-s) *m* miscreant, villain, scoundrel

'slechten (slechtte, h. geslecht) *vt* level (with the ground, to the ground), raze (to the ground), demolish slechtgema'nierd ill-mannered; 'slechtheid, 'slechtigheid (-heden) v badness; (v a n k a r a k t e r) ook: < wickedness; slecht'horend hard of hearing

'slechting (-en) v levelling, demolition

slechts only, but, merely, nothing but

slecht'ziend weak-sighted, poor-sighted

'slede (-n) v 1 (v o e r t u i g) sledge, sleigh; sled [for dragging loads]; 2 ⚓ (v. s l e e p h e l l i n g) cradle; 'sleden (sleedde, h. en is gesleed) vi & vt sledge; 'sledetocht (-en) m sleigh-ride, sledge-drive; slee (sleeën) = slede; 'n ~ (van een auto) a big car, **F** a swell car

'sleedoorn, –doren (-s) m blackthorn, sloe

'sleeën (sleede, h. en is gesleed) = sleden

1 sleep (slepen) m train; fig train [of followers &]; string [of children]

2 sleep (slepen) V.T. van slijpen

'sleepboot (-boten) m & v tug(-boat); –dienst (-en) m towing-service; –drager (-s) m train-bearer; –helling (-en) v ⚓ slipway; –japon (-nen) m train-gown; –kabel (-s) m towing-line; (v. b a l l o n) drag-rope; –loon (-lonen) o 1 cartage; 2 ⚓ towage; –net (-ten) o drag-net, trailnet; –touw (-en) o 1 ⚓ tow-rope; 2 guide-rope [of a balloon]; op ~ hebben have in tow²; op ~ houden keep [sbd.] on a string; op ~ nemen take in tow²; –tros (-sen) m tow-rope, hawser; –vaart v towing-service; –voeten (sleepvoette, h. gesleepvoet) vi drag one's feet, shuffle

1 sleet v wear and tear

2 sleet (sleten) V.T. van slijten

'sleetje (-s) o 1 small sledge; 2 (v e r s l e t e n p l e k) worn spot, thin spot; 'sleetocht (-en) m = sledetocht

sleets wearing out one's clothes (things) very quickly

'sleg(ge) v (sleggen) v maul

slem o & m ◊ slam; groot (klein) ~ maken make a grand (a little) slam

sle'miel (-en) m = schlemiel

slemp m saffron milk

'slempen (slempte, h. geslempt) vi carouse, feast, banquet; –er (-s) m carouser, feaster; slempe'rij (-en) v carousing, feasting, carousal; 'slempmaal (-malen) o, –partij (-en) v carousal

slenk (-en) v gully; geol fault, trough

'slenteraar (-s) m saunterer, lounger; 'slenteren (slenterde, h. en is geslenterd) vi saunter, lounge; langs de straat ~ knock about the streets; 'slentergang m sauntering gait, saunter

1 'slepen (sleepte, h. gesleept) **I** vi drag; trail; zijn ~de gang his shuffling gait; een ~de ziekte a lingering disease; iets ~de houden keep sth.

dragging; hij sleept met zijn voeten he drags his feet; ~d rijm feminine rhyme; **II** vt 1 drag, haul; 2 ⚓ tow; er b i j ~ [fig] drag in; dat zal lelijke gevolgen n a zich ~ bring... in its train, draw on; **III** vr zij moesten zich naar een hut ~ they had to drag themselves along to a hut

2 'slepen V.T. meerv. v. slijpen

'sleper (-s) m 1 carter; 2 ⚓ tug(-boat); slepe'rij (-en) v carter's business; 'slepenspaard (-en) o dray-horse; –wagen (-s) m dray

slet (-ten) v slut, trollop

'sleten V.T. meerv. v. slijten

sleuf (sleuven) v groove, slot, slit

sleur m routine, rut; de oude ~ the old humdrum way; met de ~ breken get out of the old groove; 'sleuren (sleurde, h. gesleurd) vt & vi trail, drag; 'sleurmens (-en) m slave to routine; –werk o routine work

'sleutel (-s) m 1 key² [of a door, watch &; to success]; 2 regulator, damper, register [of a stove]; 3 ♪ clef; –baard (-en) m key bit; –been (-deren) o collarbone, clavicle; –bloem (-en) v primula, cowslip, primrose; –bos (-sen) m bunch of keys; 'sleutelen (sleutelde, h. gesleuteld) **F** vi tinker (with aan); 'sleutelgat (-gaten) o keyhole; –geld o key money; –industrie (-ieën) v key industry; –kind (-eren) o latch-key kid; –positie [-zi.(t)si.] (-s) v key position; –ring (-en) m key-ring; –roman (-s) m roman à clef

slib o ooze, slime, mud, silt

'slibberen (slibberde, h. en is geslibberd) vi slip, slither; 'slibberig slippery; –heid v slipperiness

sliep ('sliepen) V.T. v. slapen

slier (-en) m = sliert; 'slieren (slierde, h. en is geslierd) vi drag, trail; slide; sliert (-en) m string [of words, children &]

slijk o mud, mire, dirt; ooze; aards ~ filthy lucre; iem. door het ~ sleuren drag sbd.('s name) through the mud (through the mire); zich in het ~ wentelen wallow in the mud; –erig muddy, miry

slijm o & m [nasal] mucus, phlegm; slime [of snail &]; (p l a n t a a r d i g) mucilage; –bal (-len) m, –erd **F** (-s) m creep, bootlicker, toady; –erig slimy; –jurk (-en) m = slijmbal; –klier (-en) v mucous gland; –vlies (-vliezen) o mucous membrane

'slijpen* vt grind, whet, sharpen; cut [glass], polish [diamonds]; een potlood ~ sharpen a pencil; –er (-s) m 1 (m e s s e n &) grinder; 2 (v. g l a s) cutter, (v. d i a m a n t) polisher; slijpe'rij (-en) v grinding-shop; 'slijpma-chine [-ma.ʃi.nə] (-s) v grinding-machine; –middel (-en) o abrasive; –molen (-s) m grinding-mill; –plank (-en) v knife-board;

–sel *o* 1 (s l ij p m i d d e l) abrasive; 2 (a f v a l) grinding grit, abrasive dust; **–steen** (-stenen) *m* grindstone, whetstone; **–zand** *o* abrasive sand

'slijtachtig = *sleets*; **slij'tage** [-'ta.ʒə] *v* wear (and tear), wastage; **'slijten* I** *vi* wear out, wear away²; *dat goed slijt niet gauw* that stuff wears well; *dat leed zal wel ~* it will soon wear off; **II** *vt* 1 wear out [clothes]; 2 sell over the counter, retail [spirits &]; 3 spend [days, time]; *zijn dagen ~* pass one's days; **–er** (-s) *m* 1 retailer, retail dealer; 2 (v. d r a n k e n) licensed victualler; **slijte'rij** (-en) *v* licensed victualler's shop

slik = *slijk*

'slikken (slikte, h. geslikt) **I** *vt* swallow² [food, insults, stories &]; **F** lump [it]; *dat belief ik niet te ~* I'm not having this; *heel wat moeten ~* have to put up with a lot; **II** *vi* swallow

'sliknat soaking (sopping) wet

slim 1 astute; sly; 2 *prov* bad; 3 (p i e n t e r) clever, bright, smart; *hij was mij te ~ af* he was one too many for me, he outmanoeuvred me; **–heid** (-heden) *v* slyness; **'slimmerd** (-s) *m* , **'slimmerik** (-riken) *m* slyboots, sly dog, smart aleck; **'slimmigheid** (-heden) *v* piece of cunning, dodge

'slinger (-s) *m* 1 (v. u u r w e r k) pendulum; 2 (z w e n g e l) handle; 3 (d r a a g b a n d) sling; 4 (w e r p t u i g) sling; 5 (g u i r l a n d e) festoon; **–aap** (-apen) *m* ♋ spider-monkey; **–beweging** (-en) *v* oscillation, oscillating movement; (v. s c h i p) roll; **'slingeren** (slingerde, h. geslingerd) **I** *vi* 1 (v. s l i n g e r) swing, oscillate; 2 (a l s e e n s l i n g e r) swing, dangle, oscillate; 3 (v. s c h i p) roll; 4 (v. r ij t u i g) lurch; 5 (v. d r o n k a a r d) reel; 6 (v. p a d) wind; 7 (o r d e l o o s l i g g e n) lie about; *laten ~* leave about; **II** *vt* fling, hurl; *heen en weer ~* toss to and fro; **III** *vr zich ~* 1 fling oneself [of a person]; 2 wind [of a river &]; **–ring** (-en) *v* swinging, oscillation; **'slingerplant** (-en) *v* ♋ climber, trailer; **–uurwerk** (-en) *o* pendulum-clock

'slinken* *vi* shrink; *in het koken ~* boil down; *tot op... ~* dwindle down to...; **–king** *v* shrinkage; dwindling

slinks I *aj* crooked, artful, cunning; *door ~e middelen* by underhand means; *op ~e wijze* in an underhand way; **II** *ad* crookedly, artfully, cunningly; **–heid** (-heden) *v* crookedness, false dealings

1 slip (-pen) *v* lappet; tail, flap [of a coat]

2 slip (-s) *m* (v o o r m a n n e n) briefs; (v o o r v r o u w e n) panties

3 slip (-s) *m* (h e t s l i p p e n) skid [of a car &]; **–gevaar** *o* danger of skidding; *weg met ~*

slippery road

'slipjacht (-en) *v* drag hunt, drag

'slipjas (-sen) *m* & *v* tailcoat

slip-'over (-s) *m* slip-over

'slippedrager (-s) *m* pall-bearer

'slippen (slipte, h. en is geslipt) *vi* 1 (v a n p e r s o n e n) slip; 2 (v. a u t o) skid; **–ertje** (-s) *o* extramarital escapade; *een ~ maken* have an escapade; **'slipschool** (-scholen) *v* skidding-school; **–spoor** (-sporen) *o* skid marks; **–stroom** *m* ✈ slipstream

'slissen (sliste, h. geslist) *vi* lisp

'slobber *m* 1 (s p o e l s e l) swill, pigwash; 2 (s n e e u w) sludge, slush; **'slobberen** (slobberde, h. geslobberd) *vi* drink (eat) noisily; (v. k l e r e n) bag, hang loosely; **–erig** baggy, loose

'slobkousen *mv* 1 gaiters; 2 spats [= short gaiters]

'slodderen (slodderde, h. geslodderd) *vi* 1 (m o r s e n) slop; 2 (r u i m a f h a n g e n) bag, hang loosely; **'slodderig** slovenly, sloppy; **'slodderkous** (-en) *v*, **–vos** (-sen) *m* sloven, slattern

~~**'sloeber** (-s) *m* arme ~ poor beggar~~

sloeg (sloegen) V.T. v. *slaan*

sloep (-en) *v* (ship's) boat, sloop, shallop; **'sloependek** (-ken) *o* boat-deck; **–rol** *v* ⚓ boat-drill

'sloerie (-s) *v* slut, trollop

slof (-fen) *m* 1 slipper, mule; 2 ♪ nut [of a violin bow]; 3 (v. s i g a r e t t e n) carton; 4 (v a n a a r d b e i e n) basket; *ik kan het o p mijn ~fen (slofjes) af* I have plenty of time for it; *zich het vuur u i t de ~fen lopen* run one's legs off [for sth.]; *uit zijn ~ schieten* bestir oneself, make a sudden display of energy; **'sloffen** (slofte, h. en is gesloft) *vi* shuffle, shamble; (n a l a t i g z ij n) *iets laten ~* neglect sth.; **'sloffig** slack, careless, negligent; **'slof(fig)heid** *v* slackness, carelessness, negligence

slok (-ken) *m* draught, swallow, drink, mouthful; *in één ~* at a draught, at one gulp; **–darm** (-en) *m* gullet, oesophagus

'sloken V.T. meerv. v. *sluiken*

'slokje (-s) *o* 1 (small) draught; 2 (b o r r e l) dram, drop, nip; **'slokken** (slokte, h. geslokt) *vi* guzzle, swallow; **–er** (-s) *m* guzzler, glutton; *arme ~* poor devil; **'slokop** (-pen) *m* gobbler, glutton

slonk (slonken) V.T. v. *slinken*

slons (slonzen) *v* slut, sloven, slattern; **–achtig** slovenly; **'slonzig** slovenly; **–heid** *v* slovenliness

sloof (sloven) 1 (v o o r s c h o o t) apron; 2 (p e r s o o n) drudge

slook (sloken) V.T. van *sluiken*

sloom slow, dull, **F** dim

1 sloop (slopen) *v* & *o* (v. k u s s e n) pillow-slip, pillow-case

2 sloop *m* (v. h u i s) demolition, pulling down; (v. m a c h i n e, s c h i p) breaking down; *een schip voor de ~ verkopen* sell a ship for scrap

3 sloop (slopen) V.T. van *sluipen*

'sloopwerk (-en) *o* demolition (work)

1 sloot (sloten) *v* ditch; *hij loopt in geen zeven sloten tegelijk* he always lands on his feet

2 sloot (sloten) V.T. van *sluiten*

'slootje (-s) *o* 1 (s l o t) snap; || 2 small ditch; **–springen** *vi* leap over ditches; **'slootkant** (-en) *m* side of a ditch, ditch-side; **–water** *o* ditch-water; *fig* bilge-water

slop (-pen) *o* (d o o d l o p e n d) blind alley; 2 (a r m o e d i g) slum; *in het ~ raken* fall into neglect

1 'slopen (sloopte, h. gesloopt) *vt* demolish [a fortification], pull down [a house], break up [a ship]; *fig* sap, undermine [health &]

2 'slopen V.T. meerv. van *sluipen*

'sloper (-s) *m* 1 ship-breaker; 2 house-breaker, demolisher; **slope'rij** (-en) *v* breaking-up yard; **'sloping** (-en) *v* demolition

'sloppenbuurt (-en) *v* slums *pl*

'slordig I *aj* slovenly, sloppy, careless; untidy [hair]; *een ~e duizend pond* a cool thousand pounds; **II** *ad* carelessly

'slorpen (slorpte, h. geslorpt) *vt* sip, gulp, lap; suck [an egg]

slot (sloten) *o* 1 (a a n d e u r &) lock; 2 (a a n b o e k &) clasp; 3 (a a n a r m b a n d &) snap; 4 (k a s t e e l) castle; 5 (b e s l u i t, e i n d) conclusion, end; *batig ~ $* credit balance, surplus; *~ volgt* to be concluded; *iem. een ~ op de mond doen* shut sbd.'s mouth; ● *achter ~ houden* keep under lock and key; *achter ~ en grendel* under lock and key; *de deur o p ~ doen* lock the door; *p e r ~ van rekening* in the end, ultimately; *per ~ van rekening is hij nog zo'n kwaje vent niet* he is not a bad fellow after all; *t e n ~ te* 1 finally, lastly; in the end, eventually; 2 (t o t b e s l u i t) to conclude, in conclusion; *z o n d e r ~ noch zin* without rhyme or reason; **–akkoord** (-en) *o* ♩ final chord; **–alinea** ('s) *v* concluding paragraph; **–bedrijf** (-drijven) *o* final act; **–bewaarder** (-s) *m* governor (of a castle); **–couplet** [-ku.plɛt] (-ten) *o* final stanza

'sloten V.T. meerv. van *sluiten*

'slotenmaker (-s) *m* locksmith

'slotfase [-zə] (-n en -s) *v* end-game; **–gracht** (-en) *v* moat, foss(e); **–klinker** (-s) *m* final vowel; **–koers** (-en) *m $* closing price; **–notering** (-en) *v $* closing price; **–opmerking** (-en) *v* final remark (obsevation); **–poort** (-en) *v* castle-gate; **–rede** (-s) *v* peroration, conclu-

sion; **–regel** (-s) *m* final line; **–som** *v* conclusion, result; *tot de ~ komen dat...* come to the conclusion that...; **–toneel** (-nelen) *o* closing scene, final scene; **–toren** (-s) *m* donjon, keep; **–voogd** (-en) *m* governor (of a castle); **–woord** (-en) *o* last word, concluding words; **–zang** (-en) *m* concluding song, last canto; **–zitting** (-en) *v* final meeting (session)

Slo'veen (-venen) *m* Slovene, Slovenian; **–s** Slovenian

'sloven (sloofde, h. gesloofd) *vi* drudge, toil, slave

Slo'waak(s) (-waken) *m* (& *aj*) Slovak

'sluier (-s) *m* 1 veil²; 2 (o p f o t o) fog; *de ~ aannemen* take the veil; **'sluieren** (sluierde, h. gesluierd) *vt* veil; zie ook: *gesluierd*

sluik lank [hair]

'sluiken* *vi* & *vt* smuggle; **'sluikhandel** *m* smuggling; *~ drijven* smuggle

'sluikharig lank-haired

'sluimeren (sluimerde, h. gesluimerd) *vi* slumber², doze; *fig* lie dormant; **–d** slumbering²; *fig* dormant; **'sluimering** *v* slumber, doze; **'sluimerrol** (-len) *v* bolster, pillow roll

'sluipen* *vi* steal, slink, sneak; slip; **–er** (-s) *m* sneak(er); **'sluipjacht** *v* stalk (hunt), (deer) stalking, still-hunting; **–moord** (-en) *m* & *v* assassination; **–moordenaar** (-s en -naren) *m* assassin; (g e h u u r d e *~*) bravo; **–schutter** (-s) *m* sniper; **–weg** (-wegen) *m* secret path; *fig* secret means, indirection, **F** dodge; **–wesp** (-en) *v* ichneumon(-fly)

sluis (sluizen) *v* sluice, lock; *de sluizen des hemels* the floodgates of heaven; *de sluizen der welsprekendheid* the floodgates of eloquence; **–deur** (-en) *v* lock-gate, floodgate; **–geld** (-en) *o* lock dues, lockage; **–kolk** (-en) *v* lock-chamber; **–wachter** (-s) *m* lock-keeper

'sluitboom (-bomen) *m* 1 (v. d e u r &) bar; 2 (v. e e n s p o o r w e g) gate; **'sluiten* I** *vt* 1 (d i c h t d o e n) shut [the hand, the eyes, a book, a door &]; 2 (o p s l o t d o e n) lock [a door, a drawer &]; 3 (t ij d e l ij k g e s l o t e n v e r k l a r e n) close [a shop, the Exchange]; 4 (v o o r g o e d g e s l o t e n v e r k l a r e n) shut up [a shop], close down [a factory, school]; 5 (b e ë i n d i g e n) conclude [speech]; close [a controversy]; 6 (t o t s t a n d b r e n g e n) close, strike [a bargain], conclude [an alliance], contract [a marriage, a loan]; make [peace]; effect [an insurance]; *de gelederen ~* ✕ close the ranks; *een kind in zijn armen ~* clasp a child in one's arms; **II** *va* shut; lock up (for the night), close [for a week]; *de begroting sluit niet* the budget doesn't balance; *de deur sluit niet* the door does not shut; *de jas sluit goed* is an exact fit; *de redenering sluit niet* the argument halts; *die rekening sluit met een verlies van...* the account shows a loss of...; *wij moeten (tijdelijk of voorgoed)* ~ we must close down; **III** *vr zich* ~ close [of a wound]; 🌸 shut [of flowers]; **–d** tight-fitting [coat &]; balanced [budget]; *niet ~e begroting* unbalanced budget; *de begroting ~ maken* balance the budget; '**sluiter** (-s) *m* (i n f o t o g r a f i e) shutter; '**sluiting** (-en) *v* 1 shutting, closing, locking; 2 lock, fastener, fastening; '**sluitingstijd** (-en) *m* closing time; *na* ~ after hours; *–uur* (-uren) *o* closing hour, closing time; '**sluitmand** (-en) *v* hamper; **–nota** ('s) *v* covering note; **–rede** (-s) *v* syllogism; **–ring** (-en) *m* 🗙 washer; **–spier** (-en) *v* sphincter; **–steen** (-stenen) *m* keystone, coping-stone, capstone; **–stuk** (-ken) *o* 🗙 breech-block [of a gun]; **–zegel** (-s) *m* poster stamp

'**slungel** (-s) *m* lout, hobbledehoy; **–achtig** loutish, gawky; '**slungelen** (slungelde, h. geslungeld) *vi* slouch; *wat loop je hier te ~?* what are you mooning about for?; **–lig** loutish, gawky

slurf (slurven) *v* 1 trunk [of an elephant]; 2 proboscis [of insects]

'**slurpen** (slurpte, h. geslurpt) = *slorpen*

sluw sly, cunning, crafty, astute; **–heid** (-heden) *v* slyness, cunning, craftiness, astuteness

smaad *m* revilement, contumely, obloquy, opprobrium; ⚖ libel; **–rede** (-s) *v* diatribe; **–schrift** (-en) *o* lampoon, libel; **–woord** (-en) *o* opprobrious word

smaak (smaken) *m* 1 taste²; relish; savour, flavour; 2 (z i n) liking; *ieder zijn* ~ everyone to his taste; *er is geen* ~ *aan* it has no taste (no relish); *de* ~ *van iets beethebben* have a liking for sth.; *een fijne* ~ *hebben* 1 (v. s p ij z e n &) taste deliciously; 2 (v. p e r s o n e n) have a fine palate; *fig* have a fine taste; ● *ijs i n zes smaken* six flavours of ice-cream; *dat viel niet in zijn* ~ that was not to his taste (not to his liking); *algemeen in de* ~ *vallen* hit the popular fancy; *erg in de* ~ *vallen bij* be much liked by, appeal strongly to, make a strong appeal to; *m e t* ~ 1 with gusto²; 2 tastefully; *met* ~ *eten* eat with great relish; *met* ~ *uitgevoerd* done in good taste, tastefully executed; *dit is niet n a a r mijn* ~ this is not to my liking; *naar de laatste* ~ after the latest fashion; *o v e r de* ~ *valt niet te twisten* there is no accounting for tastes; *een man v a n* ~ a man of taste; *z o n d e r* ~ tasteless; **–je** (-s) *o er is een* ~ *aan* it has a taste (a tang); **–loos** = *smakeloos*; **–papil** (-len) *v* taste bud; **–stof** (-fen) *v* flavouring; **–vol I** *aj* tasteful, in good taste; **II** *ad* tastefully, in good taste; **–zenuw**

(-en) *v* gustatory nerve

'**smachten** (smachtte, h. gesmacht) *vi* languish; ~ *naar* pine after (for), yearn for; **–d** yearning

'**smadelijk** opprobrious, contumelious, ignominious, scornful; ~ *lachen om* sneer at; **–heid** (-heden) *v* contumeliousness, ignominy, scorn; '**smaden** (smaadde, h. gesmaad) *vt* revile, defame, vilipend

1 smak (-ken) *m* 1 smacking [of the lips]; 2 heavy fall, thud, thump

2 smak (-ken) *v* ⚓ (fishing-)smack

'**smakelijk I** *aj* savoury, tasty, toothsome; **II** *ad* savourily, tastily; ~ *eten* enjoy one's meal; ~ *eten!* good appetite!; ~ *lachen* have a hearty laugh; '**smakeloos I** *aj* 1 tasteless²; 2 *fig* lacking taste, in bad taste; **II** *ad* tastelessly; '**smaken** (smaakte, h. gesmaakt) **I** *vi* taste; *hoe smaakt het?* how does it taste?; *dat smaakt goed* it tastes good, it's delicious; *smaakt het (u)?* do you like it?, is it to your taste?; *het eten smaakt mij niet* I cannot relish my food; *die erwtjes ~ lekker* these peas taste nice; *het ontbijt zal mij ~* I shall enjoy my breakfast; *zich de maaltijd laten ~* enjoy one's meal; *het smaakt als...* it tastes (eats, drinks) like...; ~ *naar* taste of, have a taste of, have a smack of [the cask &], smack of²; *naar de kurk* ~ taste of the cork; *dat smaakt naar meer* it tastes so good as to make one want more (of it); **II** *vt genoegens* ~ enjoy pleasures

'**smakken** (smakte, h. en is gesmakt) **I** *vi* 1 fall with a thud; 2 smack; *met de lippen* ~ smack one's lips; **II** (smakte, h. gesmakt) *vt* dash, fling; '**smakzoen** (-en) *m* buss, smack

smal narrow; (m a g e r) thin; **–bladig** 🌿 narrow-leaved; **–deel** (-delen) *o* ⚓ squadron

'**smalen** (smaalde, h. gesmaald) *vi* rail; ~ *op* rail at; **–d** scornful, contumelious

'**smalfilm** (-s) *m* cine-film, 8 (double-8) film; **–heid** *v* narrowness; **–letjes** smallish; *er* ~ *uitzien* look peaky; **–spoor** (-sporen) *o* narrow-gauge (line)

smalt *v* smalt

'**smalte** *v* narrowness

sma'ragd (-en) *o* & *m* emerald; **–en** *aj* emerald; **–groen** emerald-green

smart (-en) *v* pain, grief, sorrow; *hevige* ~ anguish; *gedeelde* ~ *is halve* ~ a sorrow shared is a sorrow halved; *wij verwachten u met* ~ we have been anxiously waiting for you; **–egeld** (-en) *o* smart-money, compensation; **–(e)kreet** (-kreten) *m* cry of pain (sorrow); '**smartelijk** painful, grievous; **–heid** *v* painfulness; '**smarten** (smartte, h. gesmart) *vt* give (cause) pain, grieve; *het smart mij* it pains me, it is painful to me; '**smartlap** (-pen) *m* sentimental ballad (song), **F** tear-jerker

1 'smeden** (smeedde, h. gesmeed) *vt* forge,

weld; *fig* forge [a lie], coin [new words]; devise, contrive [a plan]; lay [a plot]; zie ook: *ijzer*; 2 '**smeden** meerv. van *smid*; '**smeder** (-s) *m* forger[2], *fig* deviser; **smede'rij** (-en) *v* smithy, forge; '**smeedbaar** malleable; '**smeedijzer** *o* wrought iron; **–werk** *o* wrought iron

'**smeekbede** (-n) *v* supplication, entreaty, appeal, plea; **–schrift** (-en) *o* petition

smeer *o* & *m* grease, fat, tallow; *om der wille van de ~ likt de kat de kandeleer* from love of gain; **–boel** *m* beastly mess; **–der** (-s) *m* greaser; **–geld** (-en) *o* bribe, illicit commission, **F** grease; *~en* ook: payola; **–kaas** *m* cheese spread; **–kuil** (-en) *m* lubrication pit, inspection pit; **–lap** (-pen) *m* 1 (o o r s p r o n k e l i j k) greasing-clout; 2 *fig* dirty fellow; blackguard, skunk, **S** blighter; **smeerlappe'rij** (-en) *v* dirt, filth; '**smeermiddel** (-en) *o* lubricant; **–olie** *v* lubricating oil; **–pijp** (-en) *v* 1 dirty fellow; 2 (l e i'd i n g) waste-water; **–poe(t)s** (-en) *v* dirty person; messy child; **–punt** (-en) *o* lubrication point; **–sel** (-s) *o* 1 ointment, unguent; 2 (v l o e i b a a r) embrocation, liniment; 3 (v. b o t e r h a m) paste

smeet (**smeten**) V.T. van *smijten*

'**smekeling** (-en) *m* suppliant; '**smeken** (smeekte, h. gesmeekt) *vt* entreat, beseech, supplicate, implore; *ik smeek er u om* I beseech you; **–er** (-s) *m* suppliant; '**smeking** (-en) *v* supplication, entreaty

'**smeltbaar** *v* fusible, meltable; **–heid** *v* fusibility, meltability; '**smelten*** I *vi* melt, fuse; *fig* melt [into tears]; *ze ~ in je mond* they melt in your mouth; *~de muziek* mellow music; II *vt* melt, fuse; smelt [ore]; *gesmolten boter* melted butter; *gesmolten lood* molten lead; **smelte'rij** (-en) *v* smelting-works; '**smelting** (-en) *v* melting, fusion; smelting; '**smeltkroes** (-kroezen) *m* melting-pot[2], crucible; **–middel** (-en) *o* flux; **–oven** (-s) *m* smelting-furnace; **–punt** (-en) *o* melting-point; **–stop** (-pen) *m* ☼ fuse; **–water** *o* snow water, melt-water

'**smeren** (smeerde, h. gesmeerd) *vt* grease, oil; lubricate; smear [with paint &]; spread [butter]; *(zich) een boterham ~* butter one's bread; *iem. de handen ~* grease sbd.'s palm; *de keel ~* wet one's whistle; *de ribben ~* thrash; '*m ~* **S** bolt, clear out, cut along; *smeer 'm!* scram!, beat it!, be off!; *het gaat als gesmeerd* it runs on wheels; *als de gesmeerde bliksem* like greased lightning

'**smerig I** *aj* greasy, dirty; messy, squalid; grubby; *fig* dirty, nasty; sordid [trick]; *een ~e jongen* a dirty boy; *~ weer* rotten (dirty, foul) weather; **II** *ad* dirtily; **–heid** (-heden) *v* dirtiness, dirt, filth

'**smering** (-en) *v* greasing, oiling; lubrication

'**smeris** (-sen) *m* **S** cop

smet (-ten) *v* spot, stain[2]; blot[2]; taint[2]; *fig* blemish; slur; *iem. een ~ aanwrijven* cast a slur on sbd.

'**smeten** V.T. meerv. van *smijten*

'**smetstof** (-fen) *v* infectious matter, virus; '**smetteloos** stainless, spotless, immaculate[2]; '**smetten** (smette, *vt* h., *vi* is gesmet) *vt* & *vi* stain, soil

'**smeuïg** smooth; vivid, lively [story]

'**smeulen** (smeulde, h. gesmeuld) *vi* smoulder[2]; *er smeult iets* there is some mischief smouldering

smid (smeden) *m* blacksmith, smith; **–se** (-n) *v* forge, smithy; **–sknecht** (-s en -en) *m* blacksmith's man

smiecht (-en) *m* scamp, rascal, rip

smient (-en) *v* ☙ widgeon

'**smiezen** *mv* **F** *iem. in de ~ hebben* have sbd. taped, twig sbd.; *dat loopt in de ~* that will attract notice, that is conspicuous

'**smijdig** malleable, supple

'**smijten*** I *vt* throw, fling, dash, hurl; II *vi met het (zijn) geld ~* throw (one's) money about; *met de deur ~* slam the door

'**smikkelen** (smikkelde, h. gesmikkeld) *vi* do oneself well, tuck in

'**smis(se)** (smissen) = *smidse*

smoel (-en) *m* **F** (g e z i c h t) phiz, mug; (m o n d) *hou je ~* keep your big mouth (your trap) shut

'**smoesje** (-s) *o* **F** dodge, pretext, poor excuse; *~s, zeg!* **F** all eyewash, it's all dope; *een ~ bedenken* find a pretext; *dat ~ kennen we!* we know that stunt

'**smoezelig** dingy, smudgy, grimy

'**smoezen** (smoesde, h. gesmoesd) *vi* whisper; talk

'**smoken** (smookte, h. gesmookt) *vi* & *vt* smoke; '**smoking** (-s) *m* dinner-jacket, *Am* tuxedo

'**smokkelaar** (-s) *m* smuggler; **smokkela'rij** (-en) *v* smuggling; '**smokkelen** (smokkelde, h. gesmokkeld) I *vi* & *va* smuggle; cheat [at play &]; '**smokkelhandel** *m* smuggling, contraband trade; **–waar** (-waren) *v* contraband (goods)

'**smokken** (smokte, h. gesmokt) *vi* smock; '**smokwerk** *o* smock work, smocking

smolt (**smolten**) V.T. van *smelten*

smook *m* smoke

smoor F *de ~ in hebben* be annoyed, have the hump; **–heet** sweltering, suffocating, broiling; **–hitte** *v* sweltering heat; **–klep** (-pen) *v* throttle(-valve); **–verliefd** over head and ears in love, madly in love; '**smoren I** (smoorde, is gesmoord) *vi* stifle; *om te ~* stifling hot;

II (smoorde, h. gesmoord) *vt* smother, throttle, suffocate; ✖ throttle (down) [the engine]; stew [meat]; *fig* smother up [the discussion]; smother [a curse]; stifle [a sound, the voice of conscience]; choke [the revolution in blood]; *met gesmoorde stem* in a strangled voice

smous (-en en smouzen) *m* (h o n d) schnauzer

smout *o* grease, lard

'smoutwerk *o typ* job printing, jobbing work

smuk *m* finery

'smukken (smukte, h. gesmukt) *vt* trim, adorn, deck out

'smulbaard (-en), **–broer** (-s) *m* free liver, gastronomist, gastronomer, epicure; **'smullen** (smulde, h. gesmuld) *vi* feast (upon *van*), banquet; *zij smulden ervan* (*toen ze 't hoorden*) they simply "ate it"; **–paap** (-papen) *m = smulbaard*; **–partij** (-en) *v* banquet

'smurrie *v* F mess, muck, sludge, slush

'Smyrna ['smɪrna.] *o* Smyrna; **'smyrnatapijt** (-en) *o* Turkey (Turkish) carpet

'snaaien (snaaide, h. gesnaaid) *vt* F snatch away, pilfer

snaak (snaken) *m* wag; *een rare ~* a queer fellow, a queer chap; **snaaks I** *aj* droll, waggish; **II** *ad* drolly, waggishly; **–heid** (-heden) *v* drollery, waggishness

snaar (snaren) *v* string, chord; *een gevoelige ~ aanroeren* touch upon a tender string; *je hebt de verkeerde ~ aangeroerd* you did not sound the right chord; **–instrument** (-en) *o* stringed instrument

'snabbel (-s) *m = schnabbel*

'snackbar ['snɪkbar] (-s) *m & v* snack-bar

'snakerig *= snaaks*; **snake'rij** (-en) *v* drollery, waggishness

'snakken (snakte, h. gesnakt) *vi ~ naar adem* pant for breath, gasp; *~ naar een kop thee* be dying for a cup of tea; *~ naar lucht* gasp for air; *~ naar het uur van de…* yearn (languish) for the hour of…

'snaphaan (-hanen) *m* 🔲 firelock

'snappen (snapte, h. gesnapt) **I** *vt* snap, snatch, catch; *snap je het?* F do you get me?, do you follow me?, see?; *hij snapte er niets van* he did not grasp it, he did not understand it at all, he was baffled; *hij zal er toch niets van ~* 1 F he will never get the hang of it [e.g. mathematics]; 2 F he will never twig [our doings]; *hij snapte het meteen* he tumbled to it at once, he grasped it at once; *men heeft hem gesnapt* he has been caught; *ik snapte dadelijk dat hij geen Hollander was* I spotted him at once as being no Dutchman; **II** *vi* chat, tattle, prattle

'snarenspel *o* string music

snars *geen ~* not a bit; *daar begrijp ik geen ~ van* zie verder: (*geen*) *steek*

'snater (-s) *m hou je ~!* S hold your jaw!; F shut up!; **–aar** (-s) *m* chatterer; **'snateren** (snaterde, h. gesnaterd) *vi* chatter

snauw (-en) *m* snarl; **'snauwen** (snauwde, h. gesnauwd) *vi* snarl; *~ tegen* snarl at, snap at; **–erig** snarling, snappish

'snavel (-s) *m* bill, (k r o m) beak

sneb (-ben) *v* bill, neb, nib, beak

'snede (-n) *v* 1 (s n ij w o n d) cut [with a knife]; 2 (s c h ij f) slice [of bread], rasher [of bacon]; 3 (s c h e r p) edge [of a knife, razor &]; 4 (i n d e p r o s o d i e) caesura, section [of a verse]; 5 *de gulden ~* the golden section; *ter ~* to the point, just to the purpose

'sneden V.T. meerv. van *snijden*

'snedig witty; *een ~ antwoord* a smart reply; *een ~e opmerking* a wisecrack; **–heid** (-heden) *v* smartness [of repartee]

snee (sneeën) *= snede*

sneed (**sneden**) V.T. van *snijden*

sneeuw *v* snow; *als ~ voor de zon verdwijnen* disappear like snow before the sun; **–achtig** snowy; **–bal** (-len) *m* 1 snowball; 2 🌺 snowball, guelder rose; *met ~len gooien* throw snowballs; *iem. met ~len gooien* pelt sbd. with snowballs; **'sneeuwballen** (sneeuwbalde, h. gesneeuwbald) *vi* throw snowballs, snowball; **'sneeuwbank** (-en) *v* snow-bank; **–blind** *v* snow-blind; **–blindheid** *v* snow blindness; **–bril** (-len) *m* snow-goggles; **–bui** (-en) *v* snow-shower, snow-squall; **'sneeuwen** (sneeuwde, h. gesneeuwd) *onpers. ww.* snow; *het sneeuwde bloempjes* flowers were snowing down [from the tree]; *het sneeuwde briefkaarten* there was a shower of postcards; **'sneeuwgrens** *v* snow-line; **–hoen** (-ders) *o* white grouse, ptarmigan; **–jacht** *v* snow-drift, driving snow; **–ketting** (-en) *m & v* non-skid chain; **–klokje** (-s) *o* snowdrop; **–lucht** *v* snowy sky; **–man** (-nen) *m de Verschrikkelijke S~* the Abominable Snowman, yeti; **–ploeg** (-en) *m & v* snow-plough; **–pop** (-pen) *v* snowman; **–ruimer** (-s) *m* snow-plough; **–schoen** (-en) *m* snow-shoe; **–storm** (-en) *m* snowstorm, (h e v i g e ~) blizzard; **–uil** (-en) *m* snow-owl, snowy owl; **–val** *m* 1 snowfall, fall(s) of snow; 2 (l a w i n e) avalanche, snow-slide; **–vlaag** (-vlagen) *v* snow-shower; **–vlok** (-ken) *v* snowflake, flake of snow; **–wit** snow-white, snowy white; **Sneeuw'witje** *o* Little Snow White

snel swift, quick, fast, rapid, speedy; **–binder** (-s) *m* carrier straps; **–blusser** (-s) *m* fire extinguisher; **–buffet** [-byfrt] (-ten) *o* snack-bar; **–dicht** (-en) *o* epigram; **–dienst** (-en) *m* quick service, express service; **–filter** (-s) *m &* *o* (coffee) filter

'snelheid (-heden) *v* swiftness, rapidity, speed, velocity; *met een ~ van* ook: at the rate of… [50 miles an hour]; **'snelheidsbeperking** *v zone met* ~ restricted area; **–maniak** (-ken) *m* roadhog; **–meter** (-s) *m* tachometer, speedometer; **–record** [-rɔkɔːr] (-s) *o* speed record

'snelkoker (-s) *m* quick heater; **–kookpan** (-nen) *v* pressure-cooker

'snellen (snelde, is gesneld) *vi* hasten, rush; zie ook: *koppensnellen*

'snellopend fast [horse, steamer &]; **–schaken** *o* lightning chess; **–schrift** *o* shorthand, stenography; **–tekenaar** (-s) *m* quick-sketch artist, lightning sketcher; **–trein** (-en) *m* fast train, express (train); **–treinvaart** *v in ~* hurry-scurry; *iets er in ~ doorjagen* rush sth. through; **–varend** fast; **–verband** *o* first (aid) dressing; **–verkeer** *o* high-speed traffic, fast traffic; **–voetig** swift-footed, nimble, fleet; **–vuur** *o* rapid fire; **–vuurkanon** (-nen) *o* quick-firing gun; **–wandelen** *o* walking race, walk; **–weg** (-wegen) *m* speedway, motorway; **–weger** (-s) *m* weighing-machine; **–werkend** rapid, speedy [poison]; **–zeilend** fast-sailing, fast; **–zeiler** (-s) *m* fast sailer

snep (-pen) *v* = *snip*

'snerpen (snerpte, h. gesnerpt) *vi* bite, cut; *een ~de koude* a biting cold; *een ~de wind* a cutting wind

snert *v* pea-soup; *fig* trash; **–kerel** (-s), **–vent** *m* good-for-nothing, **S** rotter

sneu disappointing, mortifying; ~ *kijken* look disappointed, look glum

'sneuvelen (sneuvelde, is gesneuveld), **'sneven** (sneefde, is gesneefd) *vi* be killed (in action, in battle), be slain, perish, fall

'snib(be) (snibben) *v* shrew, vixen

'snibbig snappish

'snijbiet (-en) *v* beet greens; **–bloemen** *mv* cut flowers; **–boon** (-bonen) *v* ᴂ French bean, haricot bean; *een rare* ~ a queer fish; **–brander** (-s) *m* ✂ [oxygen, acetylene] cutter, oxy-acetylene torch; **'snijden* I** *vi* 1 cut; 2 ᴂ cut in; 3 ◊ finesse; **II** *vt* 1 cut [one's bread, hair &]; cut ·(up), carve [meat]; carve [figures in wood, stone &]; 2 *fig* (a f z e t t e n) fleece [customers]; *ze ~ je daar lelijk* ook: they make you pay through the nose; *die lijnen ~ elkaar* those lines cut each other, they intersect; *je kon de rook wel ~* the smoke could be cut with a knife; *het snijdt je door de ziel* it cuts you to the heart (to the quick); *aan (in) stukken ~, stuk~* cut to pieces, cut up; **III** *vr zich ~* cut oneself; *ik heb mij in mijn (de) vinger gesneden* I have cut my finger (with a knife); *je zult je (lelijk) in de vingers ~* you'll burn your fingers; **–d** 1 cutting², *fig* sharp, biting, piercing; 2 (i n d e

m e e t k u n d e) secant; **'snijder** (-s) *m* 1 cutter, carver; 2 tailor; **–vogel** (-s) *m* tailorbird; **'snijding** (-en) *v* 1 cutting, section; 2 (i n p r o s o d i e) caesura; 3 (i n d e m e e tk u n d e) intersection; **'snijkamer** (-s) *v* dissecting-room; **–lijn** (-en) *v* secant, intersecting line; **–machine** [-ma.ʃi.nə] (-s) *v* 1 cutting-machine; cutter; [bread, vegetable &] slicer; 2 (v. b o e k b i n d e r) guillotine, plough; **–punt** (-en) *o* (point of) intersection; **–tafel** (-s) *v* dissecting table; **–tand** (-en) *m* incisor, cutting tooth; **–vlak** (-ken) *o* cutting surface (face); **–werk** *o* carved work, carving; **–wond(e)** (-wonden) *v* cut, incised wound; **–zaal** (-zalen) *v* dissecting room

1 snik (-ken) *m* gasp, sob; *laatste* ~ last gasp; *tot de laatste* ~ to one's dying day; *de laatste ~ geven* zie *geest*

2 snik *aj hij is niet goed* ~ he is not quite right in his head, **F** a bit cracked

'snikheet suffocatingly hot, stifling

'snikken (snikte, h. gesnikt) *vi* sob

snip (-pen) *v* ᴂ snipe; **–pejacht** *v* snipe shooting

'snipper (-s) *m* cutting, clipping; scrap, shred, snip, snippet, chip; **–dag** (-dagen) *m* extra day off; **–snipperen** (snipperde, h. gesnipperd) *vt* snip, shred; **'snipperjacht** *v* paper-chase; **–mand** (-en) *v* waste-paper basket; **–tje** (-s) *o* scrap, shred, snippet, chip; **–uurtje** (-s) *o* spare hour, leisure hour; *in mijn ~s* at odd times; **–werk** *o* triffling work

'snipverkouden suffering from a bad cold

snit *m* & *v* cut [of grass, a coat]; *het is naar de laatste* ~ it is after the latest fashion

snob (-s) *m* snob; **sno'bisme** [snɔ-] *o* snobbishness, snobbery; **sno'bistisch** snobbish

'snoeien (snoeide, h. gesnoeid) *vt* lop [trees]; prune [fruit-tree]; 2 clip [money, a hedge]; **–er** (-s) *m* lopper, pruner [of trees]; clipper [of coin, hedges]; **'snoeimes** (-sen) *o* pruning-knife, bill; **–schaar** (-scharen) *v* pruning-shears, secateurs; **–sel** (-s) *o* clippings, loppings, brash; **–tijd** *m* pruning-time

snoek (-en) *m* pike; *een ~ vangen* (b ij r o e i e n) catch a crab; **–baars** (-baarzen) *m* pike-perch; **–sprong** (-en) *m* pike dive, jack-knife dive

snoep *m* = *snoeperij*; **–achtig** fond of eating sweets; **–centje** (-s) *o* tuck-money; **'snoepen** (snoepte, h. gesnoept) *vi* eat sweets; *wilt u eens ~?* have a sweet?; *wie heeft van de suiker gesnoept?* who has eaten of (has been at) the sugar?; **'snoeper** (-s) *m een* ~ *zijn* have a sweet tooth; **–ig I** *aj* lovely, pretty, sweet; **II** *ad* prettily, sweetly; **snoepe'rij** (-en) *v* sweets, sweetmeats, **F** tuck; **'snoepertje** (-s) *o* **F** duck of a child; **'snoepgoed** *o* = *snoeperij*; **'snoepje** (-s

o sweet; **'snoepkraam** (-kramen) *v* & *o*
sweet-stall; **–lust** *m* craving for sweets;
–reisje (-s) *o* pleasure trip, *Am* junketing;
–winkel (-s) *m* sweet-shop, tuck-shop;
–zucht *v* fondness of eating sweets

snoer (-en) *o* 1 string [of beads]; 2 cord; 3 line
[for fishing]; 4 ⚡ flex; **'snoeren** (snoerde, h.
gesnoerd) *vt* string, tie, lace; zie ook: *mond*

snoes (snoezen) *m-v* darling, **F** duck

'snoeshaan (-hanen) *m een vreemde* ~ **F** a queer
customer; zie ook *raar*

snoet (-en) *m* snout, muzzle [of an animal]; *zijn*
~> **S** his mug; **–je** (-s) *o een aardig* ~ a pretty
face

'snoeven (snoefde, h. gesnoefd) *vi* brag, boast,
bluster; ~ *op*... brag (boast) of..., vaunt; **–er**
(-s) *m* boaster, braggart, blusterer; **snoeve'rij**
(-en) *v* boast, brag(ging), braggadocio

'snoezig I *aj* sweet; **II** *ad* sweetly

snol (-len) *v* **F** = *prostituée*

snood I *aj* base [ingratitude]; heinous [crime];
wicked, sinister, nefarious [practices]; **II** *ad*
basely; **–aard** (-s) *m* villain, rascal, miscreant;
–heid (-heden) *v* baseness, wickedness

snoof (snoven) V.T. v. *snuiven*

snoot (snoten) V.T. v. *snuiten*

1 snor (-ren) *v* moustache; [of a cat] whiskers

2 snor *ad* **F** *dat zit wel* ~ that's all right

'snorbaard (-en) *m* moustache; *een oude* ~ an
old soldier

'snorder (-s) *m* crawler [plying for customers],
crawling taxi

'snorkel (-s) *m* s(ch)norkel

'snorken (snorkte, h. gesnorkt) *vi* 1 snore; 2 *fig*
brag, boast; **–er** (-s) *m* 1 snorer; 2 *fig* braggart,
boaster; **snorke'rij** (-en) *v* bragging, brag,
boast

'snorrebaard (-en) *m* = *snorbaard*

'snorren (snorde, h. en is gesnord) *vi* 1 drone,
whir [of engine]; purr [of cat]; roar [of stove];
whiz [of bullet]; 2 (om een vrachtje)
crawl, ply for hire; *het rijtuig snorde langs de weg*
the carriage whirred along the road

snorrepijpe'rij (-en) *v* knick-knack, trifle

snot *o* & *m* mucus, **S** snot; **–aap** (-apen),
–jongen (-s) *m* **F** whipper-snapper; *vervelende*
~! snot-nosed little bastard!

'snoten V.T. meerv. van *snuiten*

'snotje *o* **F** *iets in het* ~ *hebben* be wise to sth.; *iets
in het* ~ *krijgen* twig sth., get wise to sth.;
'snotneus (-neuzen) *m* 1 snivelling nose; 2 *fig*
= *snotaap*; **'snotteren** (snotterde, h. gesnot-
terd) *vi* snivel, blubber; **–rig** snivelling

'snoven V.T. meerv. v. *snuiven*

'snuffelaar (-s) *m* ferreter, Paul Pry; **'snuffelen** (snuffelde, h. gesnuffeld) *vi* nose, ferret,
browse, rummage [in something]

'snufje (-s) *o het nieuwste* ~ the latest thing; *een
nieuw technisch* ~ a new gadget; *een* ~ *zout* a
pinch of salt

'snugger bright, clever, sharp, smart

snuif *m* snuff; **–doos** (-dozen) *v* snuff-box; **–je**
(-s) *o* pinch of snuff; pinch [of salt]; **–tabak** *m*
snuff

snuiste'rij (-en) *v* knick-knack

snuit (-en) *m* snout, muzzle; trunk [of an ele-
phant]; proboscis [of insects]; *zijn* ~ **S** his mug;
'snuiten* I *vt* snuff [a candle]; *zijn neus* ~ blow
one's nose; **II** *va* blow one's nose; **–er** (-s) *m* 1
= *kaarsesnuiter*; 2 **F** *een rare* ~ a queer customer

'snuitje (-s) *o* = *snoetje*

'snuiven* *vi* 1 sniff, snuffle, snort; 2 take snuff;
~ *van woede* snort with rage

'snurken (snurkte, h. gesnurkt) *vi* snore

'sober I *aj* sober, frugal, scanty; austere [life,
building]; **II** *ad* soberly, frugally, scantily; [live]
austerely; **–heid** *v* soberness, sobriety, frugality, scantiness; austerity [of life]; **–tjes** =
sober **II**

soci'aal I *aj* social; *sociale verzekering* social
insurance, *Am* social security; *sociale voorzie-
ningen* social welfare; ~ *werk* social work; *sociale
werkster* social worker; *sociale wetenschappen*
social sciences; **II** *ad* socially; **sociaal-
demo'craat** (-craten) *m* social democrat;
~-demo'cratisch social democratic;
~-eco'nomisch socio-economic; **sociali-
'satie** [–'za.(t)si.] *v* socialization; **sociali'seren**
(socialiseerde, h. gesocialiseerd) *vt* socialize;
socia'lisme *o* socialism; **socia'list** (-en) *m*
socialist; **–isch I** *aj* socialist [party], [be just as]
socialistic; **II** *ad* socialistically

socië'teit [so.si.e.'tɛit] (-en) *v* club-house, club;
de Sociëteit van Jezus rk the Society of Jesus

sociolo'gie *v* sociology; **socio'logisch** socio-
logical; **socio'loog** (-logen) *m* sociologist

'soda *m* & *v* soda; **–water** *o* soda-water

sode'mieter (-s) **P** *m* bugger, bastard; *iem. op
z'n* ~ *geven* give sbd. hell; *als de* ~ like hell
sode'mieteren *vi* **P** 1 (sodemieterde, is gesode-
mieterd) fall; 2 *vt* (sodemieterde, h. gesodemie-
terd) throw; *sodemieter op!* bugger off!

sodo'mie *v* sodomy, p(a)ederasty, **P** buggery; ~
bedrijven **P** bugger; **–t** (-en) *m* sodomite, **P**
bugger

'soebatten (soebatte, h. gesoebat) *vi* & *vt*
implore

'Soedan *m de* ~ the S(o)udan; **Soeda'nees** *sb*
(-nezen) & *aj* S(o)udanese, *mv* S(o)udanese

soe'laas *o* solace, comfort; relief, alleviation

'Soenda *o* Sunda; **~-eilanden** *mv de* ~ the
Sunda Islands; **Soenda'nees I** (-nezen) *m*
Sundanese, *mv* Sundanese; **II** *aj* Sundanese; **III**
o Sundanese

soep (-en) *v* soup; broth; *het is niet veel ~s* it is not up to much; *in de ~ rijden* smash up; *in de ~ zitten* **S** be in the soup; **–balletje** (-s) *o* force-meat ball; **–been** (-benen) *o* soupbone; **–bord** (-en) *o* soup-plate

'soepel supple, flexible; **–heid** *v* suppleness, flexibility

'soeperig soupy²; **'soepgroente** (-n en -s) *v* vegetables for the soup; **–jurk** (-en) *v* loose hanging (baggy) dress; **–ketel** (-s) *m* soup-kettle; **–kip** (-pen) *v* boiler (chicken); **–kom** (-men) *v* soup-bowl; **–kommetje** (-s) *o* porringer; **–lepel** (-s) *m* soup-ladle; **–terrine** (-s) *v* soup-tureen; **–vlees** *o* meat for the soup

1 soes (soezen) *v* (cream) puff

2 soes (soezen) *m* 1 (h a n d e l i n g) doze; 2 (p e r s o o n) dotard

'soesa *m* bother; trouble(s), worry, worries

soeve'rein I *aj* sovereign; *~e minachting* supreme contempt; **II** (-en) *m* 1 sovereign; 2 sovereign [coin]; **soevereini'teit** *v* sovereignty

'soezen (soesde, h. gesoesd) *vi* doze; **'soezerig** dozy, drowsy; **–heid** *v* drowsiness

sof *m* wash-out, **F** flop

'sofa ('s) *m* sofa, settee, *Am* davenport

so'fisme (-n) *o* sophism; **so'fist** (-en) *m* sophist; **sofiste'rij** (-en) *v* sophistry; **so'fistisch I** *aj* sophistic(al); **II** *ad* sophistically

soig'neren [swa'ɲe.-] (soigneerde, h. gesoigneerd) *vt* groom

soi'ree [swa.'re.] (-s) *v* evening party, soirée

soit! [swa] *ij* let it be!, let it pass!, all right!

'soja *m* soy; **–boon** (-bonen) *v* soya bean

sok (-ken) *v* 1 sock; 2 ✕ socket; 3 *fig* (old) fog(e)y; *er de ~ken in zetten* run; *een held op ~ken* a coward; *iem. van de ~ken rijden* knock sbd. down; *van de ~ken gaan* faint

'sokkel (-s) *m* socle

'sokophouder (-s) *m* sock-suspender

sol (-len) *v* ♪ sol

so'laas = *soelaas*

sol'daat (-daten) *m* ⚔ soldier; *gewoon ~* private (soldier); *de Onbekende Soldaat* the Unknown Warrior; *~ eerste klasse* lance-corporal; *een fles ~ maken* crack a bottle; *~ worden* become a soldier, enlist; **–je** (-s) *o* little soldier; sippet; *~ spelen* play (at) soldiers; **sol'datenleven** *o* military life; **solda'tesk** soldier-like

sol'deer *o* & *m* solder; **–bout** (-en) *m* soldering-iron; **–lamp** (-en) *v* soldering-lamp, blowlamp; **–sel** (-s) *o* solder; **–tin** *o* tin-solder; **–water** *o* soldering-water; **sol'deren** (soldeerde, h. gesoldeerd) *vt* solder

sol'dij (-en) *v* ⚔ pay

so'leren (soleerde, h. gesoleerd) *vi* perform a solo

sol'fège [-'fɛːʒə] *m* ♪ solfège, solfeggio

'solfer = *sulfer*

soli'dair [-'dɛːr] solidary; *~ aansprakelijk* jointly and severally liable; *zich ~ verklaren met* solidarize with; **solidari'teit** *v* 1 solidarity; 2 $ joint liability; *uit ~ in* sympathy; **solidari'teitsgevoel** *o* feeling of solidarity; **–staking** (-en) *v* sympathetic strike

so'lide 1 (v. d i n g) solid, strong, substantial; 2 *fig* (v. p e r s o o n) steady; 3 $ respectable [dealers, firms]; sound, safe [investments]; **solidi'teit** *v* 1 solidity; 2 steadiness; 3 $ solvability, solvency, stability; soundness; **so'lied** = *solide*

so'list (-en) *m*, **–e** (-n en -s) *v* soloist

soli'tair [-'tɛːr] **I** *aj* solitary; **II** (-en) *m* 1 solitary; 2 (s p e l & s t e e n) solitaire

'sollen (solde, h. gesold) **I** *vt* toss; **II** *vi ~ met* 1 romp with; 2 *fig* make a fool of; *hij laat niet met zich ~* he doesn't suffer himself to be trifled with

solli'citant (-en) *m* candidate, applicant; **solli'citatie** [-(t)si.] (-s) *v* application; **–brief** (-brieven) *m* (letter of) application;

solli'citeren (solliciteerde, h. gesolliciteerd) *vi* apply (for *naar*)

'solo ('s) *m* & *o* solo; **–vlucht** (-en) *v* solo (flight); **–zanger** (-s) *m* solo vocalist

'solsleutel (-s) *m* ♪ G clef, treble clef

so'lutie [-(t)si.] (-s) *v* solution

sol'vabel solvent; **solvabili'teit** *v* ability to pay, solvency; **sol'vent** solvent; **sol'ventie** [-(t)si.] *v* solvency

som (-men) *v* 1 (t o t a a l b e d r a g) sum, total amount; 2 (v r a a g s t u k) sum, problem; *een ~ geld(s)* a sum of money; *een ~ ineens* a lump sum; *~men maken* do sums

So'malië *o* Somalia

so'matisch somatic

'somber I *aj* gloomy, sombre²; *fig* cheerless, sad, dark, black; **II** *ad* gloomily; **–heid** *v* gloom², sombreness², cheerlessness

'somma *v* sum total, total amount

som'matie [-(t)si.] (-s) *v* summons; **som'meren** (sommeerde, h. gesommeerd) *vt* summon, call upon; ⚖ summon

'sommige some; **~n** some

somnam'bule (-s) *m* & *v* somnambulist

soms sometimes; *~ goed &, ~ slecht &* now..., now..., at times..., at other times...; *kijk eens of hij daar ~ is* if he is there perhaps; *hij mocht ~ denken dat...* he might think that...; *als je hem ~ ziet* if you should happen to see him;

'somtijds, –wijlen sometimes; zie ook: *soms*

so'nate (-s en -n) *v* sonata; **sona'tine** (-s) *v* sonatina

'sonde (-s) *v* probe; **son'deren** (sondeerde, h.

gesondeerd) *vt* sound; probe
'**sonisch** sonic
son'net (-ten) *o* sonnet; –**tenkrans** (-en) *m* sonnet sequence
so'noor sonorous; **sonori'teit** *v* sonority
Sont *v de* ∼ The Sound
soort (-en) *v & o* 1 (i n 't a l g.) sort, kind; 2 (b i o l o g i e) species; *zo'n* ∼ *ding* some such thing, *hij is een goed* ∼ he is a good sort; ∼ *zoekt* ∼ like draws to like, birds of a feather flock together; *zo'n* ∼ *schrijver* he is a kind (a sort) of author, an author of sorts; *enig in zijn* ∼ zie *e n i g; mensen van allerlei* ∼ people of all kinds, all sorts and conditions of men; *van dezelfde* ∼ of the same kind, of a kind, $ of the same description; –**elijk** specific; ∼ *gewicht* specific gravity; **soorte'ment** *o* **F** *een* ∼ *(van)* a sort of, a kind of [dog]; '**soortgelijk** similar, suchlike; –**genoot** (-noten) *m* member of the same species, congener; *zijn soortgenoten* the likes of him; –**naam** (-namen) *m* 1 *gram* common noun; 2 ⚬ generic name
soos *v* **F** club
sop (-pen) *o* 1 broth; 2 (v. z e e p) suds; *het ruime* ∼ the open sea, the offing; *het ruime* ∼ *kiezen* zie *zee (kiezen); laat hem in zijn eigen* ∼ *gaar koken* leave sbd. to his own devices; *met hetzelfde* ∼ *overgoten* tarred with the same brush; *het* ∼ *is de kool niet waard* the game is not worth the candle (not worth powder and shot); '**soppen** (sopte, h. gesopt) *vt* sop, dip, dunk, steep, soak; –**erig** sloppy, soppy
so'praan (-pranen) *v* soprano, treble; –**stem** (-men) *v* soprano voice; –**zangeres** (-sen) *v* soprano singer
'**sorbet** (-s) *m* sorbet, sherbet
sor'dino ('s) *v* = *sourdine*
'**sores** *mv* **F** troubles
sor'teerder (-s) *m* sorter; **sor'teren** (sorteerde, h. gesorteerd) *vt* (as)sort; *onze winkel is goed gesorteerd* our shop is well-stocked; zie ook: *effect;* –**ring** (-en) *v* sorting; assortment
sor'tie (-s) *v* 1 (m a n t e l) opera-cloak; 2 (c o n t r o l e b i l j e t) pass-out check
S.O.S.-bericht [ɛso.'ɛs-] (-en) *o* S.O.S.-message, S.O.S.-call
sou [su.] (-s) *m* **F** *hij heeft geen* ∼ he has not a penny (to his name), he has not a penny to bless himself with
'**souche** ['su.ʃə] (-s) *v* counterfoil
souf'fleren [su.-] (souffleerde, h. gesouffleerd) *vi & vt* prompt; **souf'fleur** (-s) *m* prompter; –**shok** (-ken) *o* prompter's box
sou'per [su.'pe.] (-s) *o* supper; **sou'peren** (soupeerde, h. gesoupeerd) *vi* sup, take supper
sour'dine [su.r-] (-s) *v* ♩ mute

sous'bras [su.'bra] (sousbras) *m* dress shield
sous'pied [su.'pje.] (-s) *m* strap
sou'tache [su.'taʃə] *v* braid
sou'tane [su.-] (-s) *v rk* soutane
soute'neur [su.-] (-s) *m* pimp, pander
'**souterrain** ['su.tɛrɛ̃] (-s) *o* basement(-floor)
souve'nir [su.və'ni:r] (-s) *o* souvenir, keepsake
'**sovjet, 'sowjet** (-s) *m* sovjet; '**Sovjetunie, 'Sowjetunie** *v* (the) Soviet Union
spa ('s) *v* = *spade*
1 spaak (spaken) *v* spoke; *een* ∼ *in het wiel steken* put a spoke in the wheel
2 spaak ∼ *lopen* go wrong
'**spaakbeen** (-deren) *o* radius
spaan (spanen) *v* 1 chip [of wood]; 2 scoop [for butter]; *geen* ∼ *[fig]* not a bit; –**der** (-s) *m* chip; –**plaat** (-platen) *v* chipboard
Spaans I *aj* Spanish; ∼ *riet* rattan; ∼*e vlieg* cantharides, Spanish fly; **II** *o het* ∼ Spanish; **III** *v een* ∼*e* a Spanish woman (lady)
'**spaarbank** (-en) *v* savings-bank; –**bankboekje** (-s) *o* savings-bank book, deposit book; –**brander** (-s) *m* economical burner; –**brief** (-brieven) *m* saving certificate; –**der** (-s) *m* saver; (i n l e g g e r) depositor; –**duitjes** *mv* savings; –**geld** *o* savings; –**kas** (-sen) *v* savings-bank; –**pot** (-ten) *m* money-box; *een* ∼*je maken* lay by (some) money; –**rekening** (-en) *v* savings account; –**tegoed** (-en) *o* savings balance; –**varken** (-s) *o* piggy bank; –**zaam I** *aj* 1 saving, economical, thrifty; 2 = *schaars* **I;** ∼ *zijn met* be economical of; be chary of [praise &]; be sparing of [information, words]; **II** *ad* 1 economically; 2 = *schaars* **II;** –**zaamheid** *v* economy, thrift; –**zegel** (-s) *m* savings-stamp; –**zin** *m* thrift spirit
spaat *o* spar
'**spade** (-n) *v* spade; *de eerste* ∼ *in de grond steken* cut the first sod
spa'gaat *m* splits [in ballet &]
spa'lier (-en) *o* espalier, lattice-work
spalk (-en) *v* 🦴 splint; '**spalken** (spalkte, h. gespalkt) *vt* 🦴 splint, put in splints
span (-nen) 1 *v* (v. h a n d) span; 2 *o* (d i e r e n) yoke [of bullocks]; team [of oxen]; pair, set [of horses]; *een aardig* ∼ a nice couple
'**spanbeton** *o* pre-stressed concrete; –**dienst** *m* ⌷ form of statute labour; –**doek** (-en) *o & m* banner
'**spanen** *aj* chip
spang (-en) *v* clasp, buckle, agraffe
'**spaniël** ['spɛɲəl] (-s) *m* spaniel
'**Spanjaard** (-en) *m* Spaniard; '**Spanje** *o* Spain
spanjo'let (-ten) *v* espagnolette [bolt for French window]
'**spankracht** *v* tensile force; tension, expanding

force [of gases]; *fig* elasticity, resilience

⊙ **'spanne** (-n) *v* span; *een ~ tijds* a brief space of time, a brief while, a (short) spell

'spannen* I *vt* stretch [a cord]; tighten [a rope]; draw, bend [a bow]; strain² [every nerve; the attention]; brace [a drum]; span [a distance]; spread [a net]; lay [snares]; put [a horse] to [a carriage &]; *de haan ~* cock a gun; zie ook: *boog* &; **II** *vr zich ervóór ~* zie *voorspannen*; **III** *vi* be (too) tight [of clothes]; *als het er spant* when it comes to the pinch; *het zal er ~* there will be hot work; *het begint te ~* things are getting lively; *het heeft er om gespannen* it was a near thing; zie ook: *gespannen*; **–d** 1 (n a u w) tight; 2 (b o e i e n d) exciting [scene], thrilling [story], fast-moving [play], tense [moment]; **'span-ning** (-en) *v* stretching; tension², strain²; span [of bridge]; ✗ stress; ⚡ tension, voltage; pressure [of steam]; *fig* tension, strain, suspense; *in angstige ~* in anxious suspense; *iem. in ~ houden* keep sbd. in suspense; **–smeter** (-s) *m* ⚡ voltmeter; ⇔ tyre gauge

'spanraam (-ramen) *o* tenter

'spanrups (-en) *v* looper, geometrid caterpillar

spant (-en) *o* 1 △ rafter; 2 ⚓ frame, timber

'spanwijdte (-n) *v* span

spar (-ren) *m* 1 🌲 spruce-fir; 2 (v. d a k) rafter; **–appel** (-s) *m* fir-cone

'sparen (spaarde, h. gespaard) **I** *vt* 1 save, collect [money]; 2 (o n t z i e n) spare [a friend, no pains]; *spaar mij uw klachten* spare me your complaints; *u kunt u die moeite ~* you may save yourself the trouble; spare yourself the effort; *moeite noch kosten ~* spare neither pains nor expense; *zij zijn gespaard gebleven voor de vernieti-ging* they have been spared from destruction; **II** *vr zich ~* spare oneself, husband one's strength; **III** *vi* save, economize, lay by [money]

'sparreboom (-bomen) *m* spruce-fir; **–hout** *o* fir-wood; **–kegel** (-s) *m* fir-cone; **'sparrenbos** (-sen) *o* fir-wood

Spar'taan(s) (-tanen) *m* (& *aj*) Spartan

'spartelen (spartelde, h. gesparteld) *vi* sprawl, flounder; **–ling** (-en) *v* sprawling, floundering

'spastisch spastic

spat (-ten) *v* 1 (v l e k) spot, speck, stain; 2 (v. p a a r d) (bone-)spavin; **–ader** (-s en -en) *v* varicose vein; **–bord** (-en) *o* splash-board [of vehicle]; mudguard [of motor-car, bicycle], ⇔ wing

'spatel (-s) *v* spatula, slice

'spatie [-(t)si.] (-s) *v* space; **spati'ëren** (spatieerde, h. gespatieerd) *vt* space; **–ring** (-en) *v* spacing

'spatlap (-pen) *m* mud-flap; **'spatten I** (spatte, is gespat) *vi* splash, spatter [of liquid]; spirt [of a pen]; *uit elkaar ~* zie *uiteenspatten*; **II** (spatte,

h. gespat) *vt vonken ~* emit sparks, spark

spe [spe.] *in ~* future, to be, prospective

spece'rij (-en) *v* spice; spices; **–enhandel** *m* spice-trade

specht (-en) *m* woodpecker; *blauwe ~* nuthatch; *bonte ~* pied woodpecker; *groene ~* green woodpecker

speci'aal special, particular; **–zaak** (-zaken) *v* one-line shop, special (specialty) shop; **speciali'satie** [-'za.(t)si.] (-s) *v* specialization; **speciali'seren** (specialiseerde, h. gespeciali-seerd) *vt* specialize; **–ring** *v* specialization; **specia'lisme** (-n) *o* specialism, speciality; **specia'list** (-en) *m* specialist; **speciali'té** (-s) *v* branded product; **speciali'teit** (-en) *v* 1 (i e t s s p e c i a a l s) speciality; 2 (p e r s o o n) specialist: *...is onze ~* we specialize in..., ...a speciality; **'specie** (-s en -iën) *v* 1 $ specie, cash, ready money; 2 △ mortar; **specifi'catie** [-'ka.(t)si.] (-s) *v* specification; **specifi'ceren** (specifi-ceerde, h. gespecificeerd) *vt* specify; **speci'fiek I** *aj* specific; *~ gewicht* specific gravity; **II** *ad* specifically; **'specimen** (-s en -mina) *o* specimen

spectacu'lair [-ky.'lɛ:r] spectacular

spec'traal spectral; **'spectrum** (-s en -tra) *o* spectrum

specu'laas *m* & *o* kind of sweet spicy biscuit

specu'lant (-en) *m* $ speculator, bull [à la hausse], bear [à la baisse]; **specu'latie** [-(t)si.] (-s) *v* $ speculation, stock-jobbing; **specula'tief** *speculative;* **specu'leren** (specu-leerde, h. gespeculeerd) *vi* $ speculate; *~ op* trade upon; hope for...

speech [spi.tʃ] (-es en -en) *m* speech; **'spee-chen** (speechte, h. gespeecht) *vi* speechify

'speeksel *o* spittle, saliva, sputum; **–klier** (-en) *v* salivary gland

'speelautomaat [-o.to.- en ɔuto.-] (-en) *m* fruit machine; **–bal** (-len) *m* playing ball; *fig* play-thing, toy, sport; *een ~ van de golven zijn* be at the mercy of the waves; **–bank** (-en) *v* gam-bling (gaming) house, casino; **–doos** (-dozen) *v* musical box; **–duivel** *m* demon of gambling; **–duur** *m* (v. s p o r t w e d s t r i j d, f i l m &) length, duration; (v. g r a m m. p l a a t) playing time; (v. t o n e e l s t u k) run; **–film** (-s) *m* fiction film, (l a n g) feature film; **–genoot** (-noten) *m* playmate, playfellow; **–goed** *o* toys, playthings; **–goedwinkel** (-s) *m* toyshop; **–hol** (-holen) *o* gambling-den; **–huis** (-huizen) *o* gambling-house; **–kaart** (-en) *v* playing-card; **–kamer** (-s) *v* 1 play-room [for children]; 2 card-room [of a club]; **–kame-raad** (-raden en -s) *m = speelmakker;* **–kwar-tier** (-en) *o* ⇔ break; **–makker** (-s) *m* play-mate, playfellow; **–man** (-lui en -lieden) *m*

musician, fiddler; **–pakje** (-s) *o* playsuit;
–plaats (-en) *v* playground; **–ruimte** *v* ✕
play; *fig* elbowroom, scope, latitude, margin;
speels playful, sportive; **'speelschuld** (-en) *v*
gaming-debt; **–seizoen** (-en) *o* theatrical
season; **–sheid** *v* playfulness, sportiveness;
–tafel (-s) *v* 1 (i n h u i s) card-table; 2 (i n
s p e e l h o l) gaming-table; 3 ♪ (v. o r g e l)
console; **–terrein** (-en) *o* playground, recreation-ground, playing-field; **–tijd** (-en) *m*
playtime; **–tuig** (-en) *o* ♪ (musical) instrument;
–tuin (-en) *m* recreation-ground; **–uur** (-uren)
o play-hour, playtime; **–veld** (-en) *o* playing-
field; **–zaal** (-zalen) *v* gaming-room, gam-
bling-room; **–zucht** *v* passion for gambling
speen (spenen) *v* teat, nipple; (f o p s p e e n)
comforter; **–kruid** (-en) *o* pilewort; **–varken**
(-s) *o* sucking-pig
speer (speren) *v* spear; *sp* javelin; **–drager** (-s)
m spearman; **–punt** (-en) *v* spearhead;
–werpen *o sp* javelin throwing
speet V.T. van *spijten*
spek *o* 1 (g e z o u t e n o f g e r o o k t)
bacon; 2 (v e r s) pork [of swine]; blubber
[of a whale]; *dat is geen ~ voor jouw bek* that
is not for you; *met ~ schieten* draw the long
bow; *voor ~ en bonen meedoen* sit mum;
–bokking (-en) *m* fat bloater; **–glad** slippery;
'spekken (spekte, h. gespekt) *vt* lard [meat];
een welgespekte beurs a well-lined purse; zie ook:
doorspekken; **'spekkig** fat, plump; **'speknek**
(-ken) *m* fat neck; **–pannekoek** (-en) *m* larded
pancake; **–slager** (-s) *m* pork-butcher; **–steen**
o & *m* soap-stone, steatite
spek'takel (-s) *o* racket, hubbub; *~ maken* make
a noise, kick up a row; **–stuk** (-ken) *o* show-
piece
'spekvet *o* bacon dripping; **–zool** (-zolen) *v*
(thick) crepe sole
spel (spelen) *o* 1 (t e g e n o v e r w e r k) play; 2
(v o l g e n s r e g e l s) game; 3 (o m g e l d)
gaming, gambling; 4 (-len) pack [of cards], set
[of dominoes]; 5 (-len) (k a a r t e n v a n é é n
s p e l e r) hand; 6 (-len) (t e n t) booth, show;
het ~ van deze actrice the acting of this actress;
zijn (piano)~ is volmaakt his playing is perfect;
gewonnen ~ hebben have the game in one's own
hands; *vrij ~ hebben* enjoy free play, have free
scope; *iem. vrij ~ laten* allow sbd. full play
[to...], a free hand; *dubbel ~ spelen*
play a double game; *eerlijk ~ spelen* play the
game; *een gewaagd ~ spelen* play a bold game;
● *b u i t e n ~ blijven* remain out of it; *u moet mij
buiten ~ laten* leave me out of it; *er is een dame
i n het ~* there is a lady in it; *als... in het ~ komt*
when... comes into play; *o p het ~ staan* be at
stake; *op het ~ zetten* stake, risk; *alles op het ~*

zetten stake one's all, risk (stake) everything;
–bederver (-s), **–breker** (-s) *m* spoil-sport,
kill-joy, wet blanket
speld (-en) *v* pin; *er was geen ~ tussen te krijgen* 1
you could not get in a word edgeways; 2 there
was not a single weak spot in his reasoning;
men had een ~ kunnen horen vallen you might
have heard a pin drop; **'speldeknop, –kop**
(-pen) *m* pin's head, pin-head; **'spelden**
(speldde, h. gespeld) *vt* pin; zie ook: *mouw*,
'speldendoos (-dozen) *v* pin-box; **–geld** *o*
pin-money; **–kussen** (-s) *o* pin-cushion;
'speldeprik (-ken) *m* pin-prick[2]; **'speld-
jesdag** (-dagen) *m ±* flag-day
1 'spelen (speelde, h. gespeeld) **I** *vi* 1 (i n 't
a l g.) play; 2 (g o k k e n) gamble; *het geschut
laten ~* play the guns; *dat speelt hem d o o r het
hoofd* that is running through his head; *het stuk
speelt i n Parijs* the scene (of the play) is laid in
Paris; *de roman (het verhaal) speelt in..:* the novel
(the story) is set in...; *iem. iets in handen ~* play
sth. in sbd.'s hands; *in de loterij ~* play in the
lottery; *m e t iem. ~* [*fig*] play with sbd.; *hij laat
niet met zich ~* he is not to be trifled with, he
will stand no nonsense; *met de gedachte ~* play
with the idea; *met zijn gezondheid ~* trifle with
one's health; *met vuur ~* play with fire; *zij
speelde met haar waaier* ook: she was trifling
(toying) with her fan; *o m geld ~* play for
money; *een glimlach speelde om haar lippen* a smile
was playing about her lips; *~ t e g e n sp* play [a
team]; *u i t het hoofd ~* play by heart; *v o o r
bediende ~* act the servant; *hij speelt meestal voor
Hamlet* he plays the part of Hamlet; **II** *vt* play;
de baas ~ lord it [over sbd.]; *de beledigde ~* play
the injured one; *biljart & ~* play (at) billiards
&; *krijgertje ~* play tag; *mooi weer ~* do the
grand; *open kaart ~* be frank; *viool ~* play (on)
the violin; *kun je dat allemaal naar binnen ~?* **F**
can you put away all that?, can you polish off
all that?; 2 **'spelen** meerv. v. *spel*; **'spelen-
derwijs, –wijze** 1 in sport; 2 without effort;
~ vechten play at fighting
speleolo'gie *v* speleology, pot-holing;
speleo'logisch speleological; **speleo'loog**
(-logen) *m* speleologist, pot-holer
'speler (-s) *m* player, fiddler, musician,
performer, actor; gamester, gambler; **'spele-
varen I** (spelevaarde, h. gespelevaard) *vi* be
boating; **II** *o* boating
'spelfout (-en) *v* spelling-mistake
'speling (-en) *v* 1 ✕ play; margin; 2 *~ der
natuur* freak (of nature); *~ hebben* have play; zie
ook: *speelruimte*
'spelkunst *v* orthography
'spelleider (-s) *m* 1 *sp* games-master; 2 (v a n
h o o r s p e l) drama producer; (v. q u i z)

quizmaster

'spellen (spelde, h. gespeld) *vt & vi* spell

'spelletje (-s) *o* game; *het is het oude ~* they are still at the old game; *een ~ doen* have a game; *hetzelfde ~ proberen* (*uit te halen*) try the same game

'spelling (-en) *v* spelling, orthography

spe'lonk (-en) *v* cave, cavern, grotto

'spelregel (-s) *m sp* rule of the game²; ‖ *gram* spelling-rule

spen'deren (spendeerde, h. gespendeerd) *vt* spend [on], **F** blow [on]

'spenen (speende, h. gespeend) *vt* wean; zie ook: *gespeend*

'sperma *o* sperm, semen

'sperren (sperde, h. gesperd) *vt* bar, block up; **'spertijd** (-en) *m* curfew; **-vuur** *o* barrage

'sperwer (-s) *m* sparrow-hawk

'sperzieboon (-bonen) *v* French bean

'speten meerv. van *spit*

'spetter (-s) *m* speck, spot; **'spetteren** (spetterde, h. gespetterd) *vi* spatter, splash

'speurder (-s) *m* detective, sleuth, **S** tec; **-sroman** (-s) *m* detective novel, **F** whodunit; **'speuren** (speurde, h. gespeurd) *vt* trace, track; **'speurhond** (-en) *m* tracker dog, sleuth(-hound)²; **-tocht** (-en) *m* search [for rare books, truth]; **-werk** *o* 1 (v a n r e c h e r-c h e u r) detective work; 2 (o p w e t e n-s c h a p p e l i j k g e b i e d) research (work); **-zin** *m* flair

'spichtig lank, weedy; *een ~ meisje* a wisp (a slip) of a girl

spie (spieën) *v* 1 ✂ pin, peg, cotter; 2 **S** [Dutch] cent;

'spieden (spiedde, h. gespied) *vi & vt* spy

'spiegel (-s) *m* 1 mirror, looking-glass, glass; 2 ✝ [doctor's] speculum; 3 ⚓ stern; escutcheon [with name]; 4 surface; *b o v e n d e ~ v a n d e z e e* above the level of the sea; *i n d e ~ kijken* look (at oneself) in the mirror; **-beeld** (-en) *o* (reflected) image, reflection; **-blank** as bright as a mirror; **-ei** (-eren) *o* fried egg, sunny side up; **'spiegelen** (spiegelde, h. gespiegeld) *zich ~* look in a mirror; *zich ~ aan* take warning from, take example by; *die zich aan een ander spiegelt, spiegelt zich zacht* one man's fault is another man's lesson; zie ook: *weerspiegelen*; **'spiegelgevecht** (-en) *o* sham fight; **-glad** as smooth as a mirror, slippery [road]; **-glas** (-glazen) *o* plate-glass; **-hars** *o & m* colophony; **-ing** (-en) *v* reflection; **-kast** (-en) *v* mirror wardrobe; **-ruit** (-en) *v* plate-glass window; **-schrift** *o typ* reflected face (type)

'spieken (spiekte, h. gespiekt) *vi & vt* crib; **'spiekpapiertje** (-s) *o* crib

spier (-en) *v* 1 muscle [of the body]; 2 ⚓ shoot,

blade [of grass]; 3 ⚓ boom, spar; *geen ~* not a bit; zie ook: *vertrekken* **II**; **-ballen** *mv* **F** (k r a c h t) beef; **-bundel** (-s) *m* muscular bundle

'spiering (-en) *m* ⚓ smelt; *een ~ uitwerpen om een kabeljauw te vangen* throw a sprat to catch a whale

'spierkracht *v* muscular strength, muscle, **F** beef; **-kramp** (-en) *v* muscular spasm; **-maag** (-magen) *v* gizzard, muscular stomach; **-naakt** stark naked; **-pijn** (-en) *v* muscular pain(s), muscular ache; **-stelsel** (-s) *o* muscular system, musculature; **-verrekking** (-en) *v* sprain; **-vezel** (-s) *v* muscle fibre; **-weefsel** (-s) *o* muscular tissue; **-wit** as white as a sheet, snow-white

spies (-en), **spiets** (-en) *v* spear, pike, javelin, dart; **'spietsen** (spietste, h. gespietst) *vt* spear [fish]; pierce [a man]; impale [a criminal]

'spijbelaar (-s) *m* truant; **'spijbelen** (spijbelde, h. gespijbeld) *vi* play truant

'spijgat (-gaten) *o = spuigat*

'spijker (-s) *m* nail; *zo hard als een ~* hard as nails; *de ~ op de kop slaan* hit the nail on the head, hit it; *~s met koppen slaan* get down to brass tacks; *~s op laag water zoeken* try to pick holes in sbd.'s coat, split hairs; **F** *een ~ in zijn kop hebben* have a splitting headache; **-bak** (-ken) *m* nail-box; **-broek** (-en) *v* (blue) jeans; **'spijkeren** (spijkerde, h. gespijkerd) *vt* nail; **'spijkergat** (-gaten) *o* nail-hole; **-hard** hard as nails; **-schrift** *o* cuneiform characters (writing); **-tje** (-s) *o* tack; **-vast** = *nagelvast*

spijl (-en) *v* spike [of a fence]; bar [of a grating]; banister, baluster [of stairs]

spijs (spijzen) *v* 1 food; 2 almond paste; *~ en drank* meat and drink; *de spijzen* the viands, the dishes, the food; **-kaart** (-en) *v* menu, bill of fare; **-vertering** *v* digestion; *slechte ~* indigestion, dyspepsia; **'spijsverteringskanaal** (-nalen) *o* alimentary canal, digestive tract; **-stoornis** (-sen) *v* indigestion, digestive trouble

spijt *v* regret; *~ hebben van iets* be sorry for sth., regret sth.; *t e n ~ van* in spite of, notwithstanding; *t o t mijn* (*grote*) *~* (much) to my regret; I am sorry...; **'spijten*** *het spijt me* (*erg*) I am (so) sorry; *het spijt mij, dat...* I am sorry..., I regret...; *he. ; eet me voor de vent* I felt sorry for the fellow; *je ~al hem ~* he will be sorry for it, he will repent it; **-tig** 1 sad, pitiful; 2 (w r o k k i g) spiteful; *het is ~ dat...* it is a pity that...

'spijzen (spijsde, h. gespijsd) **I** *vi* eat; dine; **II** *vt* feed, give to eat; **'spijzigen** (spijzigde, h. gespijzigd) *vt* feed, give to eat; **-ging** *v* feeding

'spikkel (-s) *m* speck, speckle, spot; **'spikkelen** (spikkelde, h. gespikkeld) *vt* speckle;

-lig speckled
'**spiksplinternieuw** = *splinternieuw*
1 spil (-len) *v* 1 ✕ spindle, pivot; (i n u u r-
w e r k) fusee; 2 axis, axle; 3 *sp* (b ij v o e t-
b a l) centre half; *de ~ waarom alles draait*
the pivot on which everything hinges (turns)
2 spil (-len) *o* ⚓ capstan
'**spillebeen** (-benen) *o* spindle-leg
'**spilleleen** (-lenen) *o* apron-string tenure (hold)
'**spillen** (spilde, h. gespild) *vt* spill, waste;
'**spilziek** wasteful, prodigal; **-zucht** *v* prodigality, extravagance
spin (-nen) *v* spider; *zo nijdig als een ~* as cross
as two sticks
spi'nazie *v* spinach
spi'net (-ten) *o* spinet
'**spinhuis** (-huizen) *o* ⬚ spinning-house, house
of correction ·
'**spinklier** (-en) *v* spinneret
'**spinmachine** [-ma.ʃi.nə] (-s) *v* spinning-
machine, spinning-jenny
'**spinnekop** (-pen) *v* spider; (b i t s m e i s j e)
cat
'**spinnen* I** *vi* 1 (o p d e s p i n m a c h i n e)
spin; 2 purr [of cats]; **II** *vt* spin; **-er** (-s) *m*
spinner; **spinne'rij** (-en) *v* spinning-mill
'**spinneweb** (-ben) *o* cobweb
'**spinnewiel** (-en) *o* spinning-wheel
'**spinnig** catty, cattish; '**spinnijdig** irate, cross,
(as) cross as two sticks; **-rag** *o* cobweb
'**spinrokken** (-s) *o* distaff; '**spinsel** (-s) *o* 1 (v.
s p i n n e r ij) spun yarn; 2 (v. z ij d e r u p s)
cocoon
spint *o* ◷ 1 (h o u t l a a g) sap-wood, alburnum;
2 (p l a n t e z i e k t e) red-spider mite
spi'on (-nen) *m* 1 (p e r s o o n) spy; (p o l i t i e-
~) informer; 2 (s p i e g e l t j e) (Dutch) spy-
mirror, window-mirror; **spio'nage** [-ʒə] *v*
spying, espionage; **-net** (-ten) *o* espionage net,
spy (espionage) ring; **spio'neren** (spioneerde,
h. gespioneerd) *vi* spy, play the spy; **spio'nitis**
v spy mania; **spi'onne** (-n) *v* woman spy; **-tje**
o = *spion* 2
spi'raal (-ralen) *v* spiral; **-lijn** (-en) *v* spiral line;
-matras (-sen) *v* & *o* wire mattress; **-gewijs**,
-sgewijze spirally; *zich ~ bewegen* spiral; **-tje**
(-s) *o* **F** coil [intra-uterine device]; **-veer**
(-veren) *v* coil-spring; **-vormig** spiral;
-winding (-en) *v* spire
spi'rant (-en) *m* fricative
spi'rea ('s) *m* spiraea, meadow-sweet
spiri'tisme *o* spiritualism; **spiri'tist** (-en) *m*
spiritualist; **-isch** spiritualistic; **spiritu'aliën**
mv spirits, spirituous liquors; **spirituali'teit** *v*
spirituality; **spiritu'eel** spiritual; **spiritu'osa**
= *spiritualiën*; '**spiritus** *m* methylated spirit;
-lampje (-s) *o* spirit-lamp; **-lichtje** (-s) *o* etna

spit *o* 1 (-ten en speten) (s t a n g) spit; 2 (p ij n)
lumbago; *aan het ~ steken* spit; **-draaier** (-s) *m*
turnspit
1 spits *aj* 1 pointed, sharp, peaky; 2 (s c h e r p-
z i n n i g, p i e n t e r) clever, **F** cute; *~e baard*
pointed beard; *~ gezicht* peaky face; *~e toren*
steeple; *~ maken* point, sharpen; zie ook:
toelopen
2 spits *de (het) ~ afbijten* bear the brunt (of the
battle, of the onset); *de vijanden de (het) ~ bieden*
make head against the enemy
3 spits (-en) *v* point [of a sword]; spire [of a
steeple]; ✕ vanguard [of an army], [armoured]
spear-head; peak, top, summit [of a mountain];
sp striker, forward; *a a n d e ~ van het leger* at the
head of the army; *aan de ~ staan [fig]* hold pride
of place; *het o p d e ~ drijven* push things to
extremes; *op de ~ gedreven* carried to an extreme
4 spits (-en) *m* 🐕 spitz [dog]
'**Spitsbergen** *o* Spitzbergen
'**spitsboef** (-boeven) *m* rascal, rogue; **-boog**
(-bogen) *m* pointed arch; '**spitsen** (spitste, h.
gespitst) **I** *vt* point, sharpen [a pencil &];
prick [2] (up) [one's ears]; **II** *vr zich ~ op* set one's
heart on, look forward to; '**spitsheid** *v*
1 sharpness, pointedness; 2 (p i e n t e r h e i d)
cleverness; **-hond** (-en) *m* = 4 *spits*; **-muis**
(-muizen) *v* shrew-mouse, shrew; **-neus**
(-neuzen) *m* pointed nose; **-roede** (-n) *v door*
de ~n lopen run the gauntlet; **-speler** (-s) *m sp*
striker, forward; **-uur** (-uren) *o* rush hour,
peak hour; **spits'vondig** subtle; **-heid**
(-heden) *v* subtleness, sublety; *spitsvondigheden*
subtleties
'**spitten** (spitte, h. gespit) *vt* & *vi* dig, spade [the
ground]; **-er** (-s) *m* digger
1 spleet (spleten) *v* cleft, chink, crack, fissure,
crevice, slit
2 spleet (spleten)V.T. v. *splijten*
'**spleethoevig** cloven-hoofed, fissiped; **-ogig**
slit-eyed
'**spleten** V.T. meerv. v. *splijten*
'**splijtbaar** 1 cleavable [rock, wood]; 2 (i n d e
k e r n f y s i c a) fissionable, fissile; '**splijten***
I *vi* split; **II** *vt* split, cleave; '**splijting** (-en) *v*
1 cleavage; *fig* scission; 2 (i n d e k e r n f y-
s i c a) fission; **-sprodukt** (-en) *o*, '**splijtpro-
dukt** (-en) *o* fission product; **-stof** (-fen) *v*
fissionable (fissile) material; **-zwam** (-men) *v*
fission fungus; *fig* disintegrating influence
'**splinter** (-s) *m* splinter, shiver; **-s** flinders; *de*
~ zien in het oog van een ander, maar niet de balk in
zijn eigen oog see the mote in one's brother's eye
and not the beam in one's own; '**splinteren**
(splinterde, h. en is gesplinterd) *vi* splinter,
shiver, go to shivers; **-rig** splintery; '**splinter-
groep** (-en) *v* splinter group, faction; **-nieuw**

brand-new; **–partij** (-en) *v* splinter party
split (-ten) *o* 1 (o p e n i n g) slit; 2 (v. j a s) slit; 3
(v. v r o u w e n r o k) placket; **–erwten** [-ɪr-
tə(n)] *mv* split peas; **–pen** (-nen) *v* split pin,
cotter-pin
'splitsen (splitste, h. gesplitst) **I** *vt* 1 split (up) [a
lath, peas &], divide; 2 ⚓ splice [a rope]; **II** *vr
zich* ~ split (up), divide; bifurcate [of a road];
–sing (-en) *v* 1 splitting (up), division, fission
[of atoms]; bifurcation [of a road]; *fig* split,
disintegration; 2 ⚓ splicing [of a rope]
spoed *m* 1 (h a a s t) speed, haste; 2 ✗ pitch [of
screw]; ~! immediate [on letter]; ~ *bijzetten*
hurry up; ~ *maken* make haste; ~ *vereisen* be
urgent; *met (bekwame)* ~ with all (due) speed;
met de meeste ~ with the utmost speed; full
speed; zie ook: *haastig* **I**; **–behandeling** *v* 1
speedy despatch [of a business]; 2 ✗ emergency treatment; **–bestelling** (-en) *v* 1 ⬚
express delivery; 2 $ rush order; **–cursus**
[-züs] (-sen) *m* intensive course, crash course;
–eisend urgent; *~e gevallen* emergency cases;
'spoeden I (spoedde, is gespoed) *vi* speed,
hasten; **II** (spoedde zich, h. zich gespoed) *vr
zich* ~ make haste; speed, hasten (to *naar*);
'spoedgeval (-len) *o* emergency; ✗ emergency
case; **'spoedig I** *aj* speedy, quick; early; **II** *ad*
speedily, quickly, soon, before long; **'spoed-
opdracht** (-en) *v* urgent (rush) order;
–operatie [-(t)si.] (-s) *v* emergency operation;
–order (-s) *v* & *o* $ rush order; **–stuk** (-ken) *o*
urgent document; **–vergadering** (-en) *v*
emergency meeting; **–zending** (-en) *v* express
parcel
spoel (-en) *v* spool, bobbin, shuttle; ✥ coil; reel
[of magnetic tape, for photographic film];
–bak (-ken) *m* washing-tub, rinsing-tub;
1 **'spoelen** (spoelde, h. gespoeld) *vt* spool
[yarn]; 2 **'spoelen** (spoelde, h. gespoeld) *vt*
wash, rinse; *iem. de voeten* ~ ⚓ make sbd. walk
the plank; **–ling** (-en) *v* 1 (v o o r v a r k e n s)
hog-wash, draff; 2 (v o o r h e t h a a r) rinse;
3 (v a n W.C.) flush; **'spoelkom** (-men) *v*
slop-basin; **–tje** (-s) *o* spool, bobbin, shuttle;
–water *o* slops, wash; **–worm** (-en) *m* eelworm
spog *o* spittle
'spogen V.T. meerv. v. *spugen*
'spoken (spookte, h. gespookt) *vi* haunt, walk
[of ghosts]; *het spookt in het huis* the house is
haunted; *je bent al vroeg aan het* ~ you are
stirring early; *het kan geducht* ~ *in de Golf van
Biscaje* the Bay of Biscay is apt to be rough at
times; *het heeft vannacht weer erg gespookt* the
night has been boisterous
1 **spon** (-nen) *v* bung
2 **spon** (sponnen) V.T. van *spinnen*

☉ **'sponde** (-n) *v* couch, bed, bedside
spon'dee (-deeën) = *spondeus*; **spon'deus**
[-'de.üs] (-deeën) *m* spondee
'spongat (-gaten) *o* bung-hole
'sponnen V.T. meerv. van *spinnen*
'sponning (-en) *v* rabbet, groove, slot; (v a n
s c h u i f r a a m) runway
spons (en en sponzen) *v* sponge; *[fig] de* ~ *halen
over* pass the sponge over; **–achtig** spongy;
'sponsen (sponste, h. gesponst) *vt* sponge,
clean with a sponge; **'sponsenvisser** (-s) *m*
sponge-fisher
'sponsor [-zɔr] (-s) *m* sponsor; **'sponsoren**
[-zɔrə(n)] (sponsorde, h. gesponsord) *vt*
sponsor
'sponsrubber *m* & *o* sponge rubber; **–visser**
(-s) *m* sponge-fisher
spon'taan I *aj* spontaneous; **II** *ad* spontane-
ously, on the spur of the moment; **spon-
taneï'teit** *v* spontaneity
'sponzen (sponsde, h. gesponsd) *vt* = *sponsen*;
'sponzenvisser (-s) *m* = *sponsvisser*;
'sponzig spongy, spongelike
spoog (spogen) V.T. van *spugen*
spook (spoken) *o* ghost, phantom, spectre[2];
F spook; *zo'n* ~ *!* the minx!; **–achtig** spooky,
ghostly; **–dier(tje)** (-dieren, -diertjes) *o* tarsier;
–geschiedenis (-sen) *v* ghost-story; **–huis**
(-huizen) *o* haunted house; **–schip** (-schepen) *o*
ghost-ship; **–sel** (-s) *o* spectre, ghost,
phantom; **–verschijning** (-en) *v* apparition,
phantom, ghost, spectre
1 **spoor** (sporen) *v* 1 spur (of a horseman); 2 ⚘
spur [of a flower]; 3 = *spore*; *de sporen geven*
spur, clap (put) spurs to; set spurs to; *hij heeft
zijn sporen verdiend* he has won his spurs
2 **spoor** (sporen) *o* 1 foot-mark, trace, track,
trail; slot [of deer]; spoor [of an elephant];
prick [of a hare]; scent [of a fox]; 2 (v a n
w a g e n) rut; 3 (o v e r b l ij f s e l) trace,
vestige, mark; 4 (t r e i n) track, rails, railway;
5 (s p o o r w ij d t e) gauge; 6 (v. g e l u i d s-
b a n d) track; *dubbel* ~ double track; *enkel* ~
single track; *niet het minste* ~ *van...* not the least
trace (vestige) of...; *het* ~ *kwijtraken* get off the
track; *sporen nalaten* leave traces; *het* ~ *volgen*
follow the track (trail); ● *b ij het* ~ *zijn* be a
railway employee; *als alles weer i n het rechte* ~ *is*
in the old groove again; *o p het* ~ *brengen* put
on the scent; *de dief op het* ~ *zijn* be on the
track of the thief; *het wild op het* ~ *zijn* be on
the track of the game; *het toeval bracht ons op het
·rechte* ~ put us on to the right scent (track); *op
het verkeerde* ~ *zijn* be on the wrong track; *fig*
bark up the wrong tree; *p e r* ~ by rail(way);
u i t het ~ *raken* run (get) off the metals; *iem.
v a n het* ~ *brengen* put sbd. off the track, throw

sbd. off the scent; **–baan** (-banen) *v* railway, track; (b a a n b e d) permanent way; **–boekje** (-s) *o* (railway) time-table, railway guide; **–boom** (-bomen) *m* barrier; **–brug** (-gen) *v* railway bridge; **–dijk** (-en) *m* railway embankment; **–kaartje** (-s) *o* railway ticket; **–lijn** (-en) *v* railway (line); **–loos I** *aj* trackless; **II** *ad* without leaving a trace, without (a) trace; **~** *verdwijnen* vanish into thin air

'**spoorraadje** (-s) *o* rowel [of a spur]; **–slag** *m* spur, incentive, stimulus; **–slags** straight away, immediately, at full speed

'**spoorstaaf** (-staven) *v* rail; **–student** (-en) *m* commuter student; **–trein** (-en) *m* train, railway train; **–verbinding** (-en) *v* railway connection; **–wagon** (-s) *m* railway carriage

'**spoorweg** (-wegen) *m* railway; **–beambte** (-n) *m* railway official, railway employee; **–kaart** (-en) *v* railway map; **–knooppunt** (-en) *o* (railway) junction; **–maatschappij** (-en) *v* railway company; **–net** (-ten) *o* railway system, network of railways; **–ongeluk** (-ken) *o* railway accident; **–overgang** (-en) *m* level crossing; **–personeel** *o* railwaymen; **–station** [-sta.(t)ʃon] (-s) *o* railway-station; **–verkeer** *o* railway traffic

'**spoorwijdte** (-n en -s) *v* gauge; '**spoorzoeken** *vi* track, scent after

spoot (spoten) V.T. v. *spuiten*

spo'**radisch** sporadic(al)

'**spore** (-n) *v* ⚘ spore

1 '**sporen** (spoorde, h. en is gespoord) *vi* go (travel) by rail

2 '**sporen** (spoorde, h. gespoord) *vi* (v a n w i e l e n) track, run in alignment

'**sporenelement** (-en) *o* trace element; '**sporeplant** (-en) *v* cryptogam

1 sport (-en) *v* sport

2 sport (-en) *v* rung [of a chair, ladder &]; *tot de hoogste* **~** *in de maatschappij opklimmen* climb up (go) to the top of the social ladder

'**sportartikelen** *mv* sports goods; **–berichten** *mv* sporting news; **–blad** (-bladen) *o* sporting paper; **–club** (-s) *v* sports club; **–colbert** [-bɛːr] (-s) *o* & *m* sports jacket; '**sporten** (sportte, h. gesport) *vi* go in for sports; '**sporthal** (-len) *v* gymnasium; **–hart** (-en) *o* athlete's heart; **–hemd** (-en) *o* sports shirt; **spor'tief** sporting, sportsmanlike; **sportivi'teit** *v* sportsmanship; '**sportkleding** *v* sportswear; **–kostuum** (-s) *o* sports suit, sporting dress; **–kousen** *mv* knee socks; **–leider** (-s) *m* sports instructor; **–leraar** (-s en -raren) *m* sports instructor, games-master; **–man** (-nen en -lieden) *m* sporting man; **–nieuws** *o* sporting news; **–pak** (-ken) *o* sports suit; **–pantalon** (-s) *m* slacks; **–redacteur** (-s en -en) *m* sports-

editor; **–rubriek** (-en) *v* sports column; **–terrein** (-en) *o* sports ground; **–trui** (-en) *v* sports jersey (vest); **–uitslagen** *mv* sporting results; **–veld** (-en) *o* (sports) grounds; **–vlieger** (-s) *m* amateur pilot; **–vliegtuig** (-en) *o* private plane; **–wagen** (-s) sports car; **–winkel** (-s) *m*, **–zaak** (-zaken) *v* sports shop

1 spot *m* mockery, derision, ridicule; *de* **~** *drijven met* mock at, scoff at, make game of

2 spot (-s) *m* RT spot

'**spotachtig** mocking, scoffing; **–dicht** (-en) *o* satirical poem, satire

'**spoten** V.T. meerv. van *spuiten*

'**spotgoedkoop** dirt-cheap; **–lach** *m* jeering laugh, jeer, sneer; **–lust** *m* love of mockery; **–naam** (-namen) *m* nickname, sobriquet; **–prent** (-en) *v* caricature, [political] cartoon; **–prijs** (-prijzen) *m* nominal price; *voor een* **~** *at a ridiculously low price*, dirt-cheap, **–schrift** (-en) *o* lampoon, satire; '**spotten** (spotte, h. gespot) *vi* mock, scoff; **~** *met* mock at; scoff at, ridicule, deride; make light of; *dat spot met alle beschrijving* it beggars description; **~** *met het heiligste* trifle with what is most sacred; *hij laat niet met zich* **~** he is not to be trifled with; '**spottenderwijs**, **–wijze** mockingly; '**spotter** (-s) *m* mocker, scoffer; **spotter'nij** (-en) *v* mockery, derision, taunt, jeer(ing); '**spotvogel** (-s) *m* 🐦 mocking-bird; *fig* mocker, scoffer; **–ziek** mocking, scoffing; **–zucht** *v* love of scoffing

spouw (-en) *v* space between two cavity walls; **–muur** (-muren) *m* cavity wall

spraak *v* speech, language, tongue; zie ook: *sprake*; **–gebrek** (-breken) *o* speech-defect; **–gebruik** *o* usage; *in het gewone* **~** in common parlance; **–geluid** (-en) *o* speech-sound; **–klank** (-en) *m* speech-sound; **–kunst** *v* grammar; **–leer** *v* grammar; **–leraar** (-s en -raren) *m* speech therapist; **–orgaan** (-ganen) *o* organ of speech; **–vermogen** *o* power of speech; **–verwarring** (-en) *v* confusion of tongues, babel; **–waterval** (-len) *m* torrent (flood) of words; **–zaam** loquacious, talkative; **–zaamheid** *v* loquacity, talkativeness

sprak (spraken) V.T. v. *spreken*

'**sprake** *v er was* **~** *van* there has been some talk of it; *als er* **~** *is van betalen, dan...* when it comes to paying...; *...waarvan in het citaat* **~** *is* ...referred to in the quotation; *geen* **~** *van!* not a bit of it!, that's out of the question; *ter* **~** *brengen* moot, raise [a subject]; *ter* **~** *komen* come up for discussion, be mentioned, be raised; **–loos** speechless, dumb, tongue-tied; **sprake'loosheid** *v* speechlessness

'**spraken** V.T. meerv. v. *spreken*

sprank (-en) *v* spark; **–el** (-s) *v* spark, sparkle;

'**sprankelen** (sprankelde, h. gesprankeld) *vt* sparkle; '**sprankje** (-s) *o* spark[2]

'**spreekbeurt** (-en) *v* lecturing engagement; *een ~ vervullen* deliver a lecture; **–buis** (-buizen) *v* speaking-tube; *fig* mouthpiece; **–cel** (-len) *v* call-box; **–gestoelte** (-s en -n) *o* pulpit, (speaker's) platform, tribune, rostrum; **–hoorn, –horen** (-s) *m* ear-trumpet; **–kamer** (-s) *v* 1 parlour [in a private house]; 2 consulting-room, surgery [of a doctor]; 3 parlour [in a convent]; **–koor** (-koren) *o* chorus, chant; *spreekkoren vormen* shout slogans; **–oefening** (-en) *v* conversational exercise; **–taal** *v* spoken language; **–trant** *m* manner of speaking; **–trompet** (-ten) *v* speaking-trumpet; *fig* mouthpiece; **–uur** (-uren) *o* consulting hour [of a doctor]; office-hour [of a headmaster &]; *~ houden* ⚕ take surgery; *op het ~ komen* ⚕ attend surgery; **spreek'vaardig** elocutionary; '**spreekverbod** (-boden) *o* ban on public pronouncements; **–wijs, –wijze** (-wijzen) *v* phrase, locution, expression, saying; **–woord** (-en) *o* proverb, adage; **spreek'woordelijk** proverbial; *zijn onwetendheid is ~* he is ignorant to a proverb

spreeuw (-en) *m* & *v* starling

sprei (-en) *v* bedspread, counterpane, coverlet

'**spreiden** (spreidde, h. gespreid) *vt* spread˚; disperse [industry]; stagger [holidays]; *een bed ~* make a bed; **–ding** *v* spread [of payments]; dispersal [of industry]; staggering [of holidays]

'**spreidsprong** (-en) *m* split jump; **–stand** *m in ~ staan* straddle, stand with one's legs wide apart

'**spreken*** I *vt* speak, say [a word]; *wij ~ elkaar iedere dag* we see each other every day; *wij ~ niet meer met elkaar* we are no longer on speaking terms; *wij ~ elkaar nog wel, ik zal je nog wel ~!* I'll have it out with you!; *Frans ~* talk (speak) French; *ik moet mijnheer X ~, kan ik mijnheer X ~?* 1 I want to see Mr X, can I see Mr X?; 2 ☏ can I speak to Mr X?; *kan ik u even ~?* can I have a word with you?; *als je nog een woord spreekt, dan...* if you say another word; *een woordje ~* speak a word; say something, make a speech; **II** *vi* & *va* speak, talk; *dat spreekt (vanzelf)* it goes without saying, that is a matter of course, of course; *dat spreekt als een boek* that's a matter of course; *in het algemeen gesproken* generally speaking; *...niet te na gesproken* with all due deference to...; ● *m e t iem. ~* speak to sbd., talk to sbd. (with sbd.); *met wie spreek ik?* 1 (t e g e n o n b e k e n d e) whom have I the honour of addressing?; 2 ☏ is that... [X]?; *spreekt u mee* ☏ speaking; *spreek o p!* speak out!; say away!; *wij ~ o v e r u* we are talking of you (about you); *daar wordt niet meer*

over gesproken there is no more talk about it; *zij spraken over de kunst* they were talking art; *is mijnheer t e ~?* can I see Mr X?; *hij is slecht over u te ~* he has not a good word to say for you; *~ t o t iem.* speak to sbd.; *tot het hart ~* appeal to the heart; *daar u i t sprak de vrouw* that spoke the woman; *v a n... gesproken* talking of..., what about...?; *om nog maar niet te ~ van...* to say nothing of..., not to speak of..., not to mention...; *u moet van u af ~* speak out for yourself; *hij heeft van zich doen ~* he has made a noise in the world; *~ v o o r...* speak for...; *goed voor iem. ~* go bail for sbd.; *voor zich zelf ~* speak for oneself (themselves); **III** *~ is zilver, zwijgen is goud* speech is silvern, silence is golden; *onder het ~* while talking; **–d** speaking; *een ~ bewijs* eloquent evidence; a telling proof; *~e film* talking film; *~e gelijkenis* speaking likeness; *~e ogen* talking eyes; *sterk ~e trekken* (strongly) marked features; *~ voorbeeld* striking example; *het lijkt ~* it is a speaking (striking) likeness; *hij lijkt ~ op zijn vader* he is the very image of his father; '**spreker** (-s) *m* 1 (i n h e t a l g.) speaker; 2 (r e d e n a a r) orator

'**sprenkelen** (sprenkelde, h. gesprenkeld) *vt* sprinkle [with water]; **–ling** (-en) *v* sprinkling

spreuk (-en) *v* saying; apophthegm, aphorism, maxim, (wise) saw; (z i n s p r e u k) motto; *het Boek der Spreuken* **B** the Book of Proverbs

spriet (-en) *m* 1 ⚓ sprit; 2 🌿 blade [of grass]; 3 🦗 feeler [of an insect]; 4 🌾 landrail; **–ig** 1 spiky [hair]; 2 = *spichtig*; **–zeil** (-en) *o* spritsail

'**springader** (-s) *v* spring, fountainhead; **–bak** (-ken) *m* 1 *sp* (jumping) pit; 2 (v. b e d) spring-box; **–bok** (-ken) *m* 1 ⚘, *ZA* springbok; 2 (i n d e g y m n a s t i e k) vaulting-buck; **–bron** (-nen) *v* spring, fountain; **–concours** [-ku: r(s)] (-en) *o* & *m* show jumping; '**springen*** *vi* 1 spring, jump, leap; bound [also of a ball]; skip, gambol; 2 (v. g r a n a a t &) explode, burst; 3 (v. s n a r e n) snap; 4 (v. h u i d) chap; 5 (v a n g l a s) crack; 6 (v. l u c h t b a n d, l e i d i n g-b u i s) burst; 7 (v. f o n t e i n) spout; 8 *fig* 💲 go smash; *het huis (hij) staat op ~* 💲 it (he) is on the verge of bankruptcy; *de bank laten ~* break the bank; *de bruggen laten ~* blow up the bridges; *de fonteinen laten ~* let the fountains play; *een mijn laten ~* spring (explode) a mine; *een rots laten ~* blast a rock; *of je hoog springt of laag* whether you like it or not; ● *het springt i n het oog* it leaps to the eye; *de tranen sprongen hem in de ogen* tears started to his eyes; *hij sprong in het water* he jumped into the water; *o p het paard ~* vault on to his horse, jump (vault) into the saddle; *o v e r een heg ~* leap over a hedge; *over een hek ~* take a fence; *over een sloot ~* clear a ditch; *~ v a n vreugde* jump (leap) for joy; **–er** (-s) *m* jumper,

leaper; 'springerig springy; curly [hair];
'spring-in-'t-veld (-en en -s) *m* harum-
scarum, madcap; 'springkever (-s) *m* spring-
beetle; –lading (-en) *v* explosive charge;
–levend fully alive, alive and kicking;
–matras (-sen) *v* & *o* 1 *sp* mat; 2 (v. b e d)
spring-mattress; –net (-ten) *o* jumping net;
–oefening (-en) *v* jumping-exercise; –paard
(-en) *o* 1 *sp* jumper, fencer; 2 (i n d e
g y m n a s t i e k) vaulting-horse; –plank (-en)
v spring-board; –schans (-en) *v* ski-jump;
–stof (-fen) *v* explosive; –stok (-ken) *m*
jumping-pole, leaping-pole; –tij (-en) *o*
spring-tide; –touw (-en) *o* skipping-rope;
–veer (-veren) *v* spiral metallic spring; –vloed
(-en) *m* = *springtij*; –vorm (-en) *m*
(b a k v o r m) springform; –zeil (-en) *o*
jumping-sheet, life-net
'sprinkhaan (-hanen) *m* grasshopper, locust;
–hanenplaag *v* plague of locusts, locust
plague
sprint (-en en -s) *m* sprint; 'sprinten (sprintte,
h. gesprint) *vi* sprint; –er (-s) *m* sprinter;
'sprintwedstrijd (-en) *m* sprint race
sprits (-en) *v* (butter) shortbread
'sproeien (sproeide, h. gesproeid) *vt* sprinkle,
water; (in l a n d- e n t u i n b o u w) spray;
–er (-s) *m* sprinkler [on the lawn]; rose [of
watering-can]; ✗ jet [of carburettor], nozzle;
'sproeimachine [-ma.ʃi.nə] (-s) *v* spraying
machine; –middel *o* spray; –wagen (-s)
m water(ing)-cart, sprinkler, water-wagon
sproet (-en) *v* freckle; –erig, –ig freckled
'sproke (-n) *v* tale
'sprokkel (-s) *m* dry stick; –aar (-s) *m* gatherer
of dry sticks; 'sprokkelen (sprokkelde, h.
gesprokkeld) *vi* gather dry sticks; 'sprokkel-
hout *o* dead wood, dry sticks; –maand (-en) *v*
February
1 sprong (-en) *m* spring, leap, jump, bound,
caper, gambol; ♪ skip; *een ~ doen* take a leap (a
spring); *een ~ in het duister doen* take a leap
in(to) the dark; *de ~ wagen* [fig] take the plunge;
i n (met) één ~ at a leap; *m e t een ~* with a
bound; *met ~en* by leaps and bounds
2 sprong (sprongen) V.T. v. *springen*
'sprongsgewijs by jumps
'sprookje (-s) *o* fairy-tale[2], nursery tale;
'sprookjesachtig fairy-like; –boek (-en) *o*
book of fairy-tales; –land *o* dreamland;
wonderland, fairyland; –prinses (-sen) *v*
fairy-tale princess; –wereld *v* fairy-tale world,
dreamworld
sproot (sproten) V.T. v. *spruiten*
sprot (-ten) *m* sprat
1 spruit (-en) *v* sprout, sprig, offshoot; scion
2 spruit (-en) *m-v* (a f s t a m m e l i n g(e)) sprig,

offshoot; scion; *een adellijke ~* a sprig of the
nobility; *mijn ~en* my offspring; 'spruiten* *vi*
sprout; *uit een oud geslacht gesproten* sprung from
an ancient race
'spruitjes *v*, 'spruitkool *v* (Brussels) sprouts
'spruitstuk (-ken) *o* ✗ tee, manifold
spruw *v* 𝔗 thrush; *Indische ~* sprue
'spugen* *vi* & *vt* = *spuwen*
spui (-en) *o* sluice; 'spuien (spuide, h. gespuid)
I *vi* sluice[2]; blow off [steam]; *wij moeten eens ~*
ventilate; II *vt* unload [goods, shares &];
'spuigat (-gaten) *o* ⚓ scupper, scupper-hole;
het loopt de ~en uit it goes beyond all bounds
spuit (-en) *v* 1 syringe, squirt; 2 (b r a n d -
s p u i t) fire-engine; 3 (v o o r l a k, v e r f &)
sprayer, gun; 4 (d r u g i n j e c t i e) F shot, S
fix; –bus (-sen) *v* aerosol dispenser; 'spuiten*
vi & *vt* 1 spirt, spurt, spout, squirt; 2 spray [the
paint on a surface]; 3 (v. w a l v i s) blow; 4
(z i c h i n s p u i t e n) F shoot; ~ *met* S fix
[amphetamines]; 'spuitfles (-sen) *v* siphon;
–gast (-en) *m* hoseman; –je (-s) *o* *iem. een ~*
geven give sbd. an injection; –water *o* aerated
water, soda-water
spul (-len) *o* 1 (g o e d j e) stuff; 2 (k e r m i s -
s p e l) booth, show; 3 (e q u i p a g e) turn-out;
4 (l a s t) trouble; *dat is goed ~* good stuff that!;
zijn ~len his things, F his traps; *zondagse ~len* F
Sunday togs; 'spullebaas (-bazen) *m*
showman; 'spulletjes *mv* (m e u b e l t j e s &)
sticks, F traps
'spurrie *v* spurry
spurt (-en en -s) *m* spurt; 'spurten (spurtte, h.
gespurt) *vi* spurt
'sputteren (sputterde, h. gesputterd) *vi* sputter,
splutter [of speakers]
'sputum *o* sputum
'spuug *o* spittle, saliva; –bakje (-s) *o* vomiting
basin (pan); –lelijk ghastly, ugly as sin,
monstrous; –lok (-ken) *v* F cowlick; –misselijk queasy, sick, *fig* disgusted; –zat *iets ~ zijn*
be fed up with sth., be sick of sth.
'spuwbak (-ken) *m* spittoon, 𝔗 sputum cup;
'spuwen (spuwde, h. gespuwd) *vi* & *vt*
1 (u i t s p u w e n) spit; 2 (b r a k e n) vomit;
zie ook: *vuur*
s(s)t! hush!, sh!
St. = *Sint*
staaf (staven) *v* 1 (v a n i j z e r) bar; 2 (v a n
g o u d) ingot; 3 (n i e t v a n m e t a a l) stick;
–antenne (-s) *v* rod (flagpole) aerial;
–batterij (-en) *v* torch battery; –goud *o* gold
in bars, bar-gold; –ijzer *o* bar-iron, iron in
bars; –lantaarn, –lantaren (-s) *v* (electric)
torch; –magneet (-neten) *m* bar-magnet;
–zilver *o* bar-silver, silver in bars
staag = *gestadig*

staak (staken) *m* stake, pole, stick

staakt-het-'vuren *o* cease-fire

1 staal (stalen) *o* (m o d e l) sample, pattern, specimen

2 staal *o* 1 (m e t a a l) steel[2]; 2 ✠ (m e d i c ij n) steel; ~ **innemen** take steel; **–achtig** like steel, steely; **–blauw** steely blue

'**staalboek** (-en) *o* = *stalenboek*

'**staalborstel** (-s) *m* wire brush; **–draad** (-draden) *o* & *m* steel-wire; **–draadtouw** *o* steel wire-rope; **–drank** *m* ✠ tonic; **–fabriek** (-en) *v* steelworks; **–gravure** (-s en -n) *v* steel-engraving; **–grijs** steely grey; **–hard** (as) hard as steel

'**staalkaart** (-en) *v* sample-card, pattern-card

'**staalkabel** (-s) *m* wire rope (cable); **–kleurig** steel-coloured

'**Staalmeesters** *mv de* ~ the Syndics [by Rembrandt]

'**staalpil** (-len) *v* iron pill; **–plaat** (-platen) *v* steel plate; **–smederij** (-en) *v* steelworks

'**staaltje** (-s) *o* sample[2] [of goods &c; of his proceedings]; specimen[2] [of the mass, of his skill]; *fig* piece [of impudence]; *een* ~ *van zijn kunnen* a proof (mark) of his ability; *dat is niet meer dan een* ~ *van uw plicht* it is your duty

'**staalwaren** *mv* steel goods; **–werk** *o* steelwork; **–werker** (-s) *m* steelworker; **–wijn** *m* steel wine; **–wol** *v* steel-wool, wire-wool

staan* I *vi* 1 stand, be [of persons, things]; sleep [of a top]; 2 (p a s s e n) become; 3 (z ij n) be; *staat!* ✕ (eyes) front!; *wat staat daar (te lezen)?* what does it say?; *er stond een zware zee* there was a heavy sea on; *het koren staat dun* is thin; *de hond staat* the dog points; *het staat goed* it is very becoming, it looks well; *zwart staat haar zo goed* black suits her so well; *dat staat niet* it is not becoming; *hiermee staat of valt de zaak* with this the matter will stand or fall; *dat staat te bewijzen (te bezien)* it remains to be proved (to be seen); *wat mij te doen staat* what I have to do; (m e t i n f i n i t i e f) *zij* ~ *daar te praten* they are talking there; *sta daar nu niet te redeneren* don't stand arguing there; (o n p e r s. w.w.) *hoe staat het ermee?* how are things?; *hoe staat het met je geld?* how are you off for money?; *hoe staat het met ons eigen land?* what about our own country?; *als het er zo mee staat* if the matter stands thus; (n a i n f i n i t i e v e n) *blijven* ~ 1 remain standing; 2 stop; *de stoel blijft zo niet* ~ will not stand; *dat moet zo blijven* ~ the passage must stand; *zeg hem dat hij moet gaan* ~ tell him to get (stand) up; *ergens gaan* ~ (go and) stand somewhere, take one's stand somewhere; *komen* ~ come and stand, stand [here]; *te* ~ *komen* run up [against a difficulty]; (n a l a t e n) *alles laten* ~ leave everything on the table &c; *zijn baard laten* ~ grow a beard; *zijn eten laten* ~ not touch one's food; *hij kan niet eens..., laat* ~... let alone...; *laat (dat)* ~ leave it alone!; *weten waar men* ~ *moet* know one's place;● *de zon staat hoog a a n de hemel* the sun is high in the sky; *het staat aan u om...* it lies with you to..., it is for you to...; *ga er maar aan* ~*!* brace yourself!, set your teeth!, pull up your socks!; ~ *a c h t e r* stand (be) behind, support, back; *hij staat b o v e n mij* he is above me in rank, he is my superior; *het staat zo i n de Bijbel* it says so in the Bible; *het staat in de krant* it is in the paper; *iem. n a a r het leven* ~ seek sbd.'s life, seek to kill sbd.; *daar staat mijn hoofd niet naar* I am in no mood for it (to do it); *hij staat o n d e r de kapitein* he is under the captain; *de klok staat o p...* the clock shows..., stands at..., points to...; *de thermometer staat op...* the thermometer stands at..., marks...; *op instorten* & ~ be about to fall down &c; *daar staat boete op* it is liable to a fine; *daar staat de doodstraf op* it is punishable with (by) death; *daar staat drie jaar op* it is liable to three years' imprisonment; *zij* ~ *erop dat je komt* they insist upon your coming; *3 staat t o t 9 als 4 tot 12* 3 is to 9 as 4 is to 12; *de machine tot* ~ *brengen* bring the machine to a stand (to a halt); *de vijand tot* ~ *brengen* check the progress of the enemy, stop the enemy; *het is tot* ~ *gekomen* it has come to a stand; *het staat er goed v o o r* it looks promising; *hij staat er goed voor* all is well with him; *wij* ~ *voor een crisis* we are faced with a crisis; *hij staat voor niets* he sticks (stops) at nothing; **II** *vt hem* ~ stand up to him; **–d** standing [person, army]; stand-up [collar]; upright [writing]; ~*e boord* stand-up collar; ~*e hond* setter, pointer; ~*e klok* 1 mantelpiece clock; 2 grandfather clock; ~*e lamp* standard lamp; ~*e de vergadering* pending the meeting; *op* ~*e voet* on the spot, then and there; *iem.* ~*e houden* stop sbd. [in the street]; ~*e houden* maintain, assert; *zich* ~*e houden* keep on one's feet[2]; *fig* hold one's own; *zich* ~*e houden tegen* bear up against; '**staangeld** *o* 1 (o p m a r k t) stallage; 2 (w a a r b o r g) deposit; **–plaats** (-en) *v* stand; (k a a r t j e v o o r e e n ~) standing ticket; ~*(en)* standing-room

staar *v* cataract; *grauwe* ~ cataract

staart (-en) *m* tail [of an animal, a kite, a comet]; *met de* ~ *tussen de benen weglopen* go off with one's tail between one's legs; **–been** (-deren) *o* coccyx; **–deling** (-en) *v* long division; **–je** (-s) *o* (r e s t j e) rest, left-over; (e i n d) end; *zie ook muisje*; **–mees** (-mezen) *v* long-tailed tit; **–riem** (-en) *m* crupper; **–ster** (-ren) *v* comet; **–stuk** (-ken) *o* 1 rump [of an ox]; 2 ♪ tailpiece [of a violin]; **–vin** (-nen) *v* tail-fin; **–vlak** (-ken) *o* ⟿ tail-plane

staat (staten) *m* 1 (t o e s t a n d) state, condition; 2 (r a n g) rank, status; 3 (g e o r d e n d e g e m e e n s c h a p) state; 4 (l ij s t) statement, list; *burgerlijke ~* civil status; *de gehuwde ~* matrimony, married state; *de ~ van beleg afkondigen, in ~ van beleg verklaren* ✕ proclaim martial law, proclaim a state of siege [in a town]; *~ van dienst* record (of service); *de ~ van zaken* the state of affairs (things); *~ maken op...* rely on..., depend upon...; *een grote ~ voeren* live in state; *iem. tot iets in ~ achten* think sbd. capable of sth.; *iem. in ~ stellen om...* enable sbd. to...; *iem. in ~ van beschuldiging stellen* indict [sbd.]; *in ~ zijn om...* be able to..., be capable of ...ing, be in a position to...; *niet in ~ om...* not able to..., not capable of ...ing, not in a position to...; *hij is tot alles in ~* he is capable of anything; he sticks at nothing; *ik was er niet toe in ~* I was not able to do it; *in goede ~* in (a) good condition; *in treurige ~* in a sad condition; *in ~ van oorlog* in a state of war; *een stad in ~ van verdediging brengen* put a town into a state of defence; *in alle staten zijn* be in a great state
staat'huishoudkunde *v* political economy; **staathuishoud'kundige** (-n) *m* political economist
'**staatkunde** *v* 1 (p o l i t i e k e   l e e r) politics; 2 (b e p a a l d   p o l i t i e k   b e l e i d) policy; *in de ~* in politics; **staat'kundig** political; *~ evenwicht* balance of power; **-e** (-n) *m* politician
'**staatloos** stateless; *staatlozen* stateless persons;
'**staatsalmanak** (-ken) *m* state directory; **-ambt** (-en) *o* public office; **-ambtenaar** (-s en -naren) *m* public servant; **-bankroet** (-en) *o* state bankruptcy, national bankruptcy; **-begrafenis** (-sen) *v* state funeral; **-bedrijf** (-drijven) *o* government undertaking; **-begroting** (-en) *v* budget; **-beheer** *o* state management; **-belang** (-en) *o* interest of the state; **-beleid** *o* policy; **-bemoeiing** (-en) *v* state interference, controls; **-bestel** *o* régime; **-bestuur** (-sturen) *o* government of the state; **-betrekking** (-en) *v* government office; **-bewind** *o = staatsbestuur;* **-bezoek** (-en) *o* state visit; **-blad** (-bladen) *o* official collection of the laws, decrees &; Statute-Book; **staats'bosbeheer** *o* Forestry Commission; '**staatsburger** (-s) *m* subject; citizen; national [of a country, when abroad]; **-burgerschap** *o* citizenship; **-commissie** (-s) *v* government commission; **-courant** [-ku: rɑnt] (-en) *v* Gazette; **-dienaar** (-s en -naren) *m* servant of the state; *hoge staatsdienaren* high officials; **-domein** (-en) *o* state demesne; **-drukkerij** (-en) *v* government printing office, *Br* Her Majesty's Stationary Office; **-eigendom** (-men) 1 *o* state property; 2 *m* state ownership

[of the means of production]; **-examen** (-s) *o* government examination; *het ~* matriculation (for such as have not gone through a grammar-school curriculum); **-exploitatie** [-ɪksplɔɑta.(t)si.] *v* government exploitation; **-geheim** (-en) *o* state secret; **-gelden** *mv* public funds; **staatsge'vaarlijk** subversive [activities]; '**staatsgevangene** (-n) *m* state prisoner; **-gevangenis** (-sen) *v* state prison; **-greep** (-grepen) *m* coup (d'état); **-hoofd** (-en) *o* Chief of a (the) state; **-hulp** *v* state aid, state grant
'**staatsie** *v* state, pomp, ceremony; *met ~ in* (great) state, with great pomp; **-bed** (-den) *o* bed of state; **-kleed** (-kleren en -kleedren) *o* robes of state, court-dress; **-koets** (-en) *v* state coach, state carriage; **-trap** (-pen) *m* grand staircase
'**staatsinkomsten** *mv* public revenue; **-inmenging** *v* government interference; **-inrichting** *v* 1 polity, form of government; 2 *= staatswetenschappen;* **-instelling** (-en) *v* public institution; **-kas** *v* public treasury (exchequer); **-kerk** *v* established church, state church; **-lening** (-en) *v* government loan; **-lichaam** (-chamen) *o* body politic; **-loterij** (-en) *v* state lottery, national lottery; **-man** (-nannen en -lieden) *m* statesman; **-manschap** *v & o* statesmanship; **-manswijsheid** *v* statesmanship, statecraft; **-monopolie** (-s en -iën) *o* state monopoly; **-papieren** *mv* government stocks; **-pensioen** (-en) *o* old-age benefit; **-raad** (-raden) *m* 1 (i n s t e l l i n g) council of state, Privy Council; 2 (p e r s o o n) Councillor of state, Privy Councillor; **-recht** *o* constitutional law; **staats'rechtelijk** constitutional; '**staatsregeling** (-en) *v* constitution; **-schuld** (-en) *v* national debt, public debt; **-secretaris** (-sen) *m* minister of state; **-spoorweg** (-wegen) *m* state railway; **-toezicht** *o* government supervision; **-uitgaven** *mv* government(al) (state, public) expenditure(s), government spending; **-vijand** (-en) *m* public enemy; **-vorm** (-en) *m* form of government; **-wege** *van ~* from the government, by authority, [organized] by the State; **-wet** (-ten) *v* law of the country; **-wetenschappen** *mv* political science; **-zaak** (-zaken) *v* affair of state, state affair; **-zorg** (-en) *v* government care
sta'biel stable; **stabili'satie** [-'za.(t)si.] (-s) *v* stabilization; **-tor** (-s en -'toren) *m* stabilizer; **stabili'seren** (stabiliseerde, h. gestabiliseerd) *vt* stabilize; **stabili'teit** *v* stability, stableness, firmness
stac'cato staccato
stad (steden) *v* 1 (i n 't a l g.) town; 2 (b i s - s c h o p s z e t e l   o f   g r o t e   s t a d) city;

de ~ *Londen* the town of London, London town; *de* ~ *door* through the town; *de hele* ~ *door* it is all over the town; *i n de* ~1 (d o o r o f t o t b e w o n e r g e z e g d) in town; 2 (d o o r v r e e m d e l i n g) in the town; *n a a r* ~ to town; *naar de* ~ to the town; *hij is u i t de* ~ he is out of town; *de* ~ *uit* out of town; **–bewoner** (-s) = *stadsbewoner*

'**stade** *v te* ~ *komen* be serviceable, be useful, come in handy, stand [sbd.] in good stead

'**stadgenoot** (-noten) = *stadsgenoot*

'**stadhouder** (-s) *m* stadtholder; **–lijk** stadt-holder's; **–schap** *o* stadtholdership

stad'huis (-huizen) *o* town hall; **–bode** (-n en -s) *m* town's beadle; **–taal** *v* official language; **–woord** (-en) *o* official term

'**stadion** (-s) *o* stadium

'**stadium** (-s en -ia) *o* stage, phase; *in dit (een later)* ~ at this (a later) stage; *in het eerste* ~ in the first stage

stads- town..., > townish; '**stadsbeeld** *o* townscape; **–bestuur** (-sturen) *o het* ~ the municipality; **–bewoner** (-s) *m* town-dweller, city-dweller; **–bus** (-sen) *v* metropolitan (city) bus; **–genoot** (-noten) *m* fellow-townsman; *is hij een* ~ *van je?* is he a townsman of yours? **–genote** (-n) *v* fellow-townswoman, towns-woman; **–gesprek** (-ken) *o* local call; **–gewest** (-en) *o* conurbation; **–gezicht** (-en) *o* town-view, townscape; **–gracht** (-en) *v* 1 ⊔ city moat; 2 town canal; **–guerilla** [-gɪri.lja.] ('-s) *m* urban guer(r)illa; **–kern** (-en) *v* town-centre, city-centre; **–leven** *o* town-life; **–licht** ⊷ (-en) *o* sidelight, fenderlight; **–mensen** *mv* townsfolk, city dwellers; **–muur** (-muren) *m* town-wall; **–nieuws** *o* town-news; **–omroeper** (-s) *m* town-crier; **–park** (-en) *o* town-park; **–planning** [-plɒnɪŋ] *v* town planning; **–poort** (-en) *v* city gate; **–reiniging** *v* municipal scavenging; **–school** (-scholen) *v* municipal school; **stads'schouwburg** (-en) *m* municipal theatre; '**stadstoren** (-s) *m* steeple (tower) of the town; **–tuin** (-en) *m* town-garden; **–uitbreiding** (-en) *v* town development; **–waag** (-wagen) *v* town weighing-house; **–wal** (-len) *m* rampart; **–wapen** (-s) *o* city-arms, arms of a town; **–wijk** (-en) *v* part of the town, quarter; '**stadwaarts** towards the town, in the direction of the town, town-ward(s)

staf (staven) *m* staff˚; mace [= staff of office]; *de generale* ~ ⚔ the general staff; *de* ~ *breken over* condemn; *bij de* ~ ⚔ on the staff; **–drager** (-s) *m* mace-bearer, verger

'**staffelen** (staffelde, h. gestaffeld) *vt* grade, gradate; '**staffelsgewijs** by graduation (gradation)

'**staffunctionaris** [-fʉŋksi.o.-] (-sen) *m* staff employee; **–kaart** (-en) *v* ordnance map; **–lid** (-leden) *o*, **–medewerker** (-s) *m* staff member, employee; **–muziek** *v* regimental band; **–muzikant** (-en) *m* bandsman; **–officier** (-en) *m* staff-officer; **–rijm** (-en) *o* alliteration; **–vergadering** (-en) *v* staff meeting

stag (stagen) *o* ⚓ stay

stag'natie [-(t)si.] (-s) *v* stagnation; [traffic] hold-up; **stag'neren** (stagneerde, h. gestag-neerd) *vi* stagnate

'**sta-in-de(n)-weg** *m* obstacle, impediment

stak (staken) V.T. van *steken*

1 '**staken** (staakte, h. gestaakt) **I** *vt* suspend, stop [payment]; discontinue [one's visits]; strike [work]; cease [fire]; *een* ~ *van het vuren* ⚔ a cease-fire; *wij zullen het werk* ~ 1 (o m t e r u s t e n) cease work, knock off; 2 (i n e c o n o m i s c h e s t r ij d) we are going to strike, we shall go on strike; **II** *vi & va* 1 cease, leave off, stop; 2 go on strike, strike; be out (on strike); *de stemmen* ~ the votes are equally divided

2 '**staken** V.T. meerv. v. *steken*

'**staker** (-s) *m* striker, man out on strike

sta'ket (-ten) *o*, **–sel** (-s) *o* fence, railing

'**staking** (-en) *v* 1 stoppage, cessation [of work]; suspension [of payment, hostilities]; discontin-uance [of a suit, visits &]; 2 strike; industrial action; *wilde* ~ lightning (wild-cat, unofficial) strike; *b ij* ~ *van stemmen* in case of equality (of votes); *i n* ~ *gaan (zijn)* go (be out) on strike; **–breker** (-s) *m* strike-breaker, **F** blackleg, scab, rat; '**stakingscomité** (-s) *o* strike committee; **–golf** (-gɒlven) *v* wave of strikes; **–kas** (-sen) *v* strike fund; **–leider** (-s) *m* strike-leader; **–recht** (-en) *o* right to strike; **–uitke-ring** (-en) *v* strike pay

'**stakker(d)** (-s) *m* poor wretch; poor thing

1 **stal** (-len) *m* stable [for horses, less usual for cattle]; cowshed, cowhouse [for cattle]; sty [for pigs]; mews [round an open yard]; *de konink-lijke* ~*len* the royal mews; *o p* ~ *zetten* stable [horses]; house [cattle]; *hij werd op* ~ *gezet* he was shelved; *v a n* ~ *halen* trot out again [old arguments]; dig out [retired generals &]; *te hard van* ~ *lopen* rush matters, overdo it

2 **stal (stalen)** V.T. v. *stelen*

stalac'tiet (-en) *o* stalactite

stalag'miet (-en) *m* stalagmite

'**stalbezem** (-s) *m* stable broom, besom; **–deur** (-en) *v* stable door

1 '**stalen** *aj* steel; *fig* iron [constitution, nerves, will]; steely [glance]; ~ *gebouwen* steel-framed buildings; *met een* ~ *gezicht* with a pokerface, dead pan; *een* ~ *voorhoofd* a brazen face

2 '**stalen** (staalde, h. gestaald) *vt* steel²

3 'stalen V.T. meerv. v. *stelen*

'stalenboek (-en) *o* sample book, pattern-book; **–koffer** (-s) *m* sample case

'stalgeld (-en) *o* stabling-money; **–houder** (-s) *m* stablekeeper, jobmaster; **stalhoude'rij** (-en) *v* livery-stable; **'staljongen** (-s) *m* stable-boy; **–knecht** (-s en -en) *m* stableman, groom; **–lantaarn, –lantaren** (-s) *v* stable lantern

'stallen (stalde, h. gestald) *vt* stable [horses &]; house [cattle]; put up [a motor-car]

'stalles *mv* stalls [in theatre]

'stalletje (-s) *o* [market] stall, stand; bookstall

'stalling (-en) *v* 1 (h e t   s t a l l e n) stabling &, zie *stallen*; 2 (d e   p l a a t s) stable, stabling; [motor] garage, [bicycle] shelter

'stalmeester (-s) *m* riding master; (v a n   d e   k o n i n g i n) master of the horse; **–mest** *m* stable dung (manure); **–voe(de)r** *o* fodder

stam (-men) *m* (i n 't a l g.) stem² [of a tree, shrub, verb]; trunk, bole [of a tree]; 2 (a f - s t a m m i n g) stock, race, tribe, *Sc* clan; *de twaalf ~men* the twelve tribes [of Israel]; *wilde ~men* wild tribes; **–boek** (-en) *o* 1 (v a n   p e r s o n e n) book of genealogy, register; 2 (v. p a a r d e n, h o n d e n   &) stud-book; 3 (v. v e e) herd-book; **–boekvee** *o* pedigree cattle; **–boom** (-bomen) *m* family tree, pedigree; **–café** (-s) *o v* favourite pub, habitual haunt, *Am* S hangout

'stamelen (stamelde, h. gestameld) **I** *vi* stammer; **II** *vt* stammer (out); **–ling** *v* stammering [of a child]

'stamgast (-en) *m* regular (customer), habitué; **–genoot** (-noten) *m* congener, tribesman, clansman; **–hoofd** (-en) *o* tribal chief, chieftain; **–houder** (-s) *m* son and heir; **–huis** (-huizen) *o* dynasty; **–kapitaal** (-talen) *o* $ original capital; **–kroeg** (-en) *v* = *stamcafé*; **–land** (-en) *o* country of origin, mother country; **'stammen** (stamde, is gestamd) *vi ~ van* zie *afstammen*; *dit stamt nog uit de tijd toen...* it dates from the time when...; **'stammoeder** (-s) *v* progenitrix, ancestress; **–ouders** *mv* ancestors, progenitors

stamp (-en) *m* stamp [of the foot]

stam'pei *v* **F** *~ maken* kick up a row, kick up dust

'stampen (stampte, h. gestampt) **I** *vi* 1 (m e t   v o e t e n) stamp, stamp one's feet; 2 ⚓ (v a n   s c h i p) pitch, heave and set; 3 (v. m a c h i n e) thud; **II** *vt* pound [chalk &]; crush [ore]; *fijn~* ook: bray; *zich iets in het hoofd ~* drum sth. into one's brains; *gestampte aardappelen* mashed potatoes; *gestampte pot = stamppot*; **–er** (-s) *m* 1 ⚒ stamper; rammer [of a gun]; zie ook: *straatstamper*; pounder, pestle [of a mortar]; [potato] masher; 2 ⚘ pistil; **'stamppot** *m*

mashed food, hotchpotch (of potato, cabbage and meat); **'stampvoeten** (stampvoette, h. gestampvoet) *vi* stamp one's foot (feet); **'stampvol** crowded, chock-full

stamroos (-rozen) *v* standard rose; **–slot** (-sloten) *o* ancestral castle, family seat; **–tafel** (-s) *v* 1 genealogical table; 2 table (in a pub) reserved for regulars; **–vader** (-s) *m* ancestor, progenitor; **–verwant** (-en) **I** *aj* cognate; **II** *m* congener; **–verwantschap** *v* racial or tribal affinity; **–woord** (-en) *o* primitive word, stem

1 stand (-en) *m* 1 (h o u d i n g) attitude, posture; pose [before a sculptor &]; stance [in playing golf, billiards]; 2 (h o o g t e) height [of the barometer]; rate [of the dollar]; 3 (l i g - g i n g) position [of a shop &]; 4 (m a a t - s c h a p p e l ijk) status, social status, standing, position, station [in life]; 5 (t o e s t a n d) situation, position, condition, state [of affairs]; 6 *sp* score; *de betere ~* the better-class people; *(het bureau van) de burgerlijke ~* the registrar's office; *de hogere (lagere) ~en* the higher (lower) classes; *de drie ~en* the (three) estates; *de ~ van zaken* the state of affairs; *zijn ~ ophouden* keep up one's rank, live up to one's station; ● *een meisje b e n e d e n zijn ~* a girl below his social position; *beneden zijn ~ trouwen* marry beneath one; *b o v e n zijn ~ leven* live beyond one's means; *i n ~ blijven* last; *in ~ houden* maintain, keep up [a custom]; keep going [a business]; *een winkel o p goede ~* a shop in a good situation; *t o t ~ brengen* bring about, accomplish, achieve; effect [a sale]; negotiate [a treaty]; *tot ~ komen* be brought about; *een... u i t de gegoede ~* a better-class...; *mensen v a n ~* people of a good social position, people of high rank; *van lage ~* of humble condition; *iemand van zijn ~* a man of his social position

2 stand [stɛnt] (-s) *m* (o p   t e n t o o n s t e l - l i n g) booth, stand

'standaard (-s) *m* standard [= flag; support; model]; **–afwijking** (-en) *v* standard deviation; **standaardi'satie** [-'za.(t)si.] *v* standardization; **standaardi'seren** (standaardiseerde, h. gestandaardiseerd) *vt* standardize; **'standaardloon** (-lonen) *o* standard wage; **–maat** (-maten) *v* standard size; **–uitvoering** (-en) *v* standard type (model, design); **–werk** (-en) *o* standard work

'standbeeld (-en) *o* statue

'stander (-s) *m* stand [for umbrellas &]; clothes-horse; tripod, stand [of a camera &]; △ post, upright [of a roof]

'standhouden (hield 'stand, h. 'standge-houden) *vi* ⚔ 1 make a stand; 2 stand firm, hold one's own, hold out; *zij hielden dapper stand* they made a gallant stand; *het hield geen* *stand* it did not last

'standhouder ['stɛnt-] (-s) *m* exhibitor

'standing ['stɛn-] *v een zaak van ~* a respectable firm

'standje (-s) *o* 1 (b e r i s p i n g) scolding, **F** wigging; 2 (h e r r i e) **F** row, shindy; *een ~ krijgen* get a scolding; *iem. een ~ maken (schoppen)* scold sbd.; *het is een opgewonden ~* he (she) is quick-tempered

'standplaats (-en) *v* 1 standing-place, stand; 2 (v. a m b t e n a a r) station, post; *zij keerden naar hun ~ terug* they returned to their stations; **–punt** (-en) *o* standpoint, point of view, attitude (towards, to *tegenover*); *een duidelijk ~ innemen* take a clear stand [on this issue]; *een nieuw ~ innemen ten opzichte van...* take a new attitude towards...; *zij stellen zich op het ~, dat...* they take the view that...; *van zijn ~ from his point of view; *–recht o* ☟ summary justice

'standsbesef *o* class-consciousness; **–verschil** (-len) *o* class distinction; **–vooroordeel** (-delen) *o* class prejudice

stand'vastig steadfast, firm, constant

'standvogel (-s) *m* non-migratory bird

'standwerker (-s) *m* ± barker

stang (-en) *v* 1 ✗ bar, rod; 2 bit [for horses]; *iem. op ~ jagen* tease, exasperate [sbd.]

stani'ol = *stanniool*

stank (-en) *m* bad smell, stench, stink; *hij kreeg ~ voor dank* he was rewarded with ingratitude; **–afsluiter** (-s) *m* air trap

stanni'ool *o* tinfoil

'stansen (stanste, h. gestanst) *vt* punch

'stante 'pede right away, instantly

stap (-pen) *m* step, pace; *fig* step, move; *dat is een ~ achteruit (vooruit)* that is a step backward (forward); *dat is een gewaagde ~* that is a risky (rash) step (to take); *dat is een hele ~ tot...* that is a long step towards...; *een stoute ~* a bold step; *het is maar een paar ~pen* it is but a step; *de eerste ~ doen (tot)* take the first step (towards); *~pen doen bij de regering* approach the Government; *~pen doen om...* take steps to...; *geen verdere ~pen doen* take no further action; *dat brengt ons geen ~ verder* that does not carry us a step farther; *een ~ verder gaan* go a step further²; *grote ~pen nemen (maken)* take great strides; *[ergens] geen ~ voor verzetten* not lift a hand to..., not stir a finger to...; ● *b ij de eerste ~* at the first step; *bij elke ~* at every step; *i n twee ~pen* in two strides; *m e t één ~* at a (one) stride; *met afgemeten ~pen* with measured steps; *o p ~ gaan* set out; *~ v o o r ~* step by step; *zich hoeden voor de eerste ~* beware of the thin end of the wedge

1 'stapel (-s) *m* 1 pile, stack, heap; 2 ⚓ stocks; 3 ♩ sounding-post [of a violin]; 4 (s t a p e l - p l a a t s) staple; *a a n ~s zetten* pile; *o p ~ staan*

⚓ be on the stocks²; *op ~ zetten* ⚓ put on the stocks²; *v a n ~ lopen* ⚓ leave the stocks, be launched; *goed van ~ lopen* [*fig*] go off well; *te hard van ~ lopen* rush matters, overdo it; *van ~ laten lopen* ⚓ launch [a ship]

2 'stapel *aj ben je ~?* are you crazy?; are you cracked?; zie ook: *stapelgek*

'stapelartikel (-en) *o* staple commodity;

'stapelen (stapelde, h. gestapeld) *vt* pile, heap, stack

'stapelgek **F** stark (raving) mad, loopy, cracked, off one's onion, raving bonkers

'stapelgoederen *mv* staple goods; **–plaats** (-en) *v* staple-town, emporium; **–recht** *o* staple-right; **–stoel** (-en) *m* stacking chair; **–vezel** (-s) *v* staple fibre; **–wolk** (-en) *v* cumulus [*mv* cumuli]

'stappen (stapte, h. en is gestapt) *vi* step, stalk; *deftig ~, trots ~* strut; *i n het vliegtuig & ~* board the plane &; *o p zijn fiets ~* mount one's bike; *~ u i t* zie *uitstappen*; *~ v a n* zie *afstappen*; **–er** (-s) *m* **F** shoe; **'stapvoets** 1 at a foot-pace, at a walk; 2 step by step

1 ☉ **star** (-ren) *v* = *ster*

2 star *aj* stiff; fixed [gaze]; rigid [prejudices, system]

'staren (staarde, h. gestaard) *vi* stare, gaze (at *naar*)

'starheid *v* stiffness; fixedness [of gaze]; rigidity [of a system]

'starogen ['star-] (staroogde, h. gestaroogd) *vi* stare

start (-s) *m* start, ⚐ ook: take-off; *staande (valse, vliegende) ~ sp* standing (false, flying) start; *van ~ gaan* start; *goed van ~ gaan* zie *(goed) starten*; **–baan** (-banen) *v* ⚐ runway; **–blok** (-ken) *o* 1 *sp* starting block; 2 ⚐ chock; **'starten** (startte, h. en is gestart) *vi* start, ⚐ ook: take off; start up [a car]; *goed ~ sp* get away (off) to a good start²; **–er** (-s) *m* ✗ & *sp* starter; **'startklaar** ready to start; *sp* starting; **–knop** (-pen) *m* ✗ starter button; **–lijn** (-en) *v sp* starting line; **–motor** (-toren en -s) *m* starter (starting) motor, starter; **–pistool** (-tolen) *o* starting gun, starting pistol, starter pistol; **–punt** (-en) *o* start(ing place), take-off point; **–schot** (-schoten) *o* starting shot; *het ~ lossen* fire the starting gun; **–teken** (-s) *o* starting signal

'statenbijbel (-s) *m* Authorized Version [of the Bible]; **–bond** (-en) *m* confederation (of States); **Staten-Gene'raal** *mv* States General

'statica *v* statics

'statie ['sta.(t)si.] (-s en -iën) *v rk* Station of the Cross

sta'tief (-tieven) *o* stand, support, tripod

'statiegeld [-(t)si.-] *o* deposit

'statig I *aj* stately, grave; **II** *ad* in a stately

manner, gravely; **–heid** *v* stateliness, gravity

stati'on [sta.'(t)ʃɔn] (-s) *o* (railway) station; ~ *van afzending* forwarding station

statio'nair [sta.ʃɔ'nɛːr] stationary; ~ *draaien* ✘ tick over, idle

'stationcar ['ste:sjɔnkɑr] (-s) *m* estate car, *Am* station-wagon

statio'neren [sta.(t)ʃɔ-] (stationeerde, h. gestationeerd) *vt* station, place

stati'onschef [sta.'(t)ʃɔnʃɛf] (-s) *m* stationmaster; **–hal** (-len) *v* station hall; **–kruier** (-s) *m* railway porter

'statisch static

sta'tist (-en) *m* supernumerary, walker-on, S super; **sta'tisticus** (-ci) *m* statistician, statist; **statis'tiek** (-en) *v* statistics; *de* ~ *ook:* the returns; *de* ~ *opmaken van...* take statistics of...; *Centraal Bureau voor de Statistiek* Central Statistical Office; **sta'tistisch** statistical

'status *m* status; **~-'quo** [-'kwo.] *m* & *o* status quo; **'statussymbool** [sɪm-] (-bolen) *o* status symbol

statu'tair [-'tɛːr] statutory

sta'tuur *v* stature, size

sta'tuut (-tuten) *o* statute; *de statuten van een maatschappij (vereniging)* $ the articles of association of a trading-company; the regulations, the constitution of a society

sta'vast *een man van* ~ a resolute man

1 'staven meerv. v. *staf*

2 'staven (staafde, h. gestaafd) *vt* substantiate [a charge, claim], support, bear out [a statement]; **–ving** *v* substantiation; *tot* ~ *van* in support of

stea'rine *v* stearin, **–kaars** (-en) *v* stearin candle

☉ **'stede** (-n) *v* stead, place, spot; *te dezer* ~ in this town; *in* ~ *van* instead of

'stedebouw(kunde) *m (v)* town (and country) planning; **stedebouw'kundig** town-planning...; **–e** (-n) *m* town-planner, town-planning consultant

'stedehouder (-s) *m* vicegerent, governor, lieutenant; ~ *Christi* Vicar of Christ

'stedelijk municipal, of the town, town...;

'stedeling (-en) *m* townsman, town-dweller; **~e** townswoman; **~en** townspeople; **'stedemaagd** (-en) *v* town-patroness; **'steden** meerv. van *stad*

stee (steeën) *v* stead, place, spot; zie ook: *stede*

1 steeds *ad* always, for ever, ever, continually; *nog* ~ still; ~ *meer* more and more

2 steeds *aj* (s t a d s) town..., > townish

steef (steven) V.T. v. *stijven*

1 steeg (stegen) *v* lane, alley, alleyway, passage

2 steeg (stegen) V.T. v. *stijgen*

steek (steken) *m* 1 stitch [of needlework]; stab [of a dagger]; thrust [of a sword]; sting [of a wasp]; stitch, twinge [of pain]; 2 three-cornered hat, cocked hat; 3 bed-pan; 4 (b ij s p i t t e n) spit; 5 ⚓ hitch; *halve* ~ half-hitch; 6 *fig* (sly) dig; *een* ~ *in de zijde* a stitch in the side; *dat was een* ~ *(onder water) op mij* that was a dig at me; ~ *houden* hold water; *die regel houdt geen* ~ that rule does not hold (good); *een* ~ *laten vallen* drop a stitch; *een* ~ *opnemen* take up a stitch; *hij heeft er geen* ~ *van begrepen* he hasn't understood one iota of it; *het kan me geen* ~ *schelen* I don't care a rap (a fig, a pin); *ze hebben geen* ~ *uitgevoerd* they have not done a stroke of work; *je kan hier geen* ~ *zien* you can't see at all here; *hij kan geen* ~ *meer zien* he is stone-blind; *hij heeft ons in de* ~ *gelaten* he has left us in the lurch, he deserted us; *zijn geheugen & liet hem in de* ~ his memory & failed him; *zij hebben het werk in de* ~ *gelaten* they have abandoned the work; **–beitel** (-s) *m* paring-chisel; **–hevel** (-s) *m* pipette; **–houdend** valid, sound [arguments]; ~ *zijn* hold water; **–partij** (-en) *v* knifing; **–passer** (-s) *m* (pair of) dividers; **–penning** (-en) *m* bribe, illicit commission; **~en** *ook:* payola; **–proef** (-proeven) *v* sample taken at random; *steekproeven nemen* test at random; **–sleutel** (-s) *m* (double-ended) spanner; **–spel** (-spelen) *o* ⛫ tournament, tilt, joust; **–vlam** (-men) *v* 1 ✘ blow-pipe flame; 2 (b ij o n t p l o f f i n g) flash; **–wond(e)** (-wonden) *v* stab-wound; **–zak** (-ken) *m* slit pocket

steel (stelen) *m* stalk [of a flower, fruit]; stem [of a flower, a wine-glass, a pipe]; handle [of a tool]; *de* ~ *naar de bijl werpen* throw the helve after the hatchet; **–pan** (-nen) *v* saucepan

steels stealthy [look]; **–(ge)wijs, –(ge)wijze** stealthily, by stealth

'steelzucht *v* kleptomania

1 steen (stenen) *m* 1 (i n 't a l g.) stone [for building, playing dominoes &, of fruit, hail &]; 2 (b a k s t e e n) brick; *een* ~ *des aanstoots* **B** a stone of stumbling; *fig* a stumbling-block; *de* ~ *der wijzen* the philosopher's stone; *er bleef geen* ~ *op de andere* no stone remained upon another; *iem. stenen voor brood geven* give sbd. a stone for bread; ~ *en been klagen* complain bitterly; *de eerste* ~ *leggen* lay the foundation-stone; *de eerste* ~ *op iem. werpen* cast the first stone at sbd.; *al moet de onderste* ~ *boven* come hell or high water; *met stenen gooien (naar)* throw stones (at); **2 steen** *o* & *m* (s t o f n a a m) 1 (i n 't a l g.) stone; 2 (b a k s t e e n) brick; **–achtig** stony; **–arend** (-en) *m* golden eagle; **–bakker** (-s) *m* brick-maker; **steenbakke'rij** (-en) *v* brick-works, brick-yard; **'steenbok** (-ken) *m* ♑ 1 ibex; 2 *de Steenbok* ★ Capricorn; **–bokskeerkring** *m* tropic of Capricorn; **–boor** (-boren) *v* rock-drill; stone bit; **–breek**

(-breken) *v* saxifrage; **–druk** (-ken) *m* lithography; **–drukker** (-s) *m* lithographer; **steendrukke′rij** (-en) *v* lithographic printing-office; **′steenfabriek** (-en) *v* brickworks; **–goed I** *o* stoneware **II** *aj* super, splendid; **–groef**, **–groeve** (-groeven) *v* quarry, stone-pit; **–grond** (-en) *m* stony ground; **–gruis** *o* stone-dust; **–hard** stone-hard, stony, as hard as (a) stone (as rock), flinty; **–hoop** (-hopen) *m* heap of stones (bricks); **–houwen** *o* stone-cutting; **–houwer** (-s) *m* stone-cutter, stonemason; **steenhouwe′rij** (-en) *v* stone-cutter's yard; **′steenklomp** (-en) *m* lump of stone, rock; **–klopper** (-s) *m* stone breaker; **–kolenengels** *o* ± pidgin English; **–kolenmijn** (-en) & = *kolenmijn* &; **–kool** (-kolen) *v* pit-coal, coal; **–koud** stone-cold; **–marter** (-s) *m* stone-marten; **–oven** (-s) *m* (brick-)kiln; **–puist** (-en) *v* boil, furuncle; **–rijk** immensely rich, rolling in money; **–rood** brick-red; **–rots** (-en) *v* rock; **–slag** *o* broken stones, rubble, (f i j n) (stone-)chippings, road-metal; **–tijd** *m* stone age; **–tijdperk** *o* stone age; **–tje** (-s) *o* (small) stone, pebble; flint [for a lighter]; *ook een ~ bijdragen* contribute one's mite; **–uil** (-en) *m* little owl; **–valk** (-en) *m* & *v* stone-falcon, merlin; **–vrucht** (-en) *v* stone-fruit, drupe; **–weg** (-wegen) *m* paved road, high road; **–wol** *v* rock wool; **–worp** (-en) *m* stone's throw; **–zwaluw** (-en) *v* swift

′steevast I *aj* regular; **II** *ad* regularly; invariably
steg *m over heg en ~* up hill and down dale, across country; *weg (heg) noch ~ weten* zie 1 *weg*
′stegen V.T. meerv. van *stijgen*
′steiger (-s) *m* 1 (a a n h u i s) scaffolding, scaffold, stage; 2 ⚓ pier, jetty, landing-stage; *in de ~s* in scaffolding [of a building]; **–balk** (-en) *m* scaffolding-beam
′steigeren (steigerde, h. gesteigerd) *vi* rear, prance [of a horse]; *fig* boggle at
′steigerpaal (-palen) *m* scaffold(ing)-pole; **–werk** *o* scaffolding
steil 1 (n a a r b o v e n) steep; 2 (n a a r b e-n e d e n) bluff; 3 (l o o d r e c h t) sheer; 4 (l o o d r e c h t e n v l a k) precipitous; 5 *fig* rigid [Calvinist]; **–heid** *v* steepness; **–schrift** *o* upright writing; **–te** (-n) *v* steepness; (s t e i l e k a n t) precipice
stek (-ken) *m* 1 ⚘ slip, cutting; 2 (a a n g e-s t o k e n f r u i t) bruised (specked) fruit
′stekeblind stone-blind[2]
′stekel (-s) *m* prickle, prick, sting [of a thistle; an insect &]; spine, quill [of a hedgehog]; **–achtig** = *stekelig*; **–baars** (-baarzen) *m* stickleback, minnow; **–brem** *m* needle-furze; **′stekelig** prickly, spinous, spiny, thorny; poignant[2]; *fig* stinging, sarcastic, barbed

[discussion, words]; **–heid** (-heden) *v* prickliness, poignancy[2]; *fig* sarcasm; **′stekelrog** (-gen) *m* thornback; **–tje** (-s) *o* = *stekelbaars*; **–varken** (-s) *o* porcupine
′steken* I *vi* 1 sting [of insects], prick [of nettle &]; 2 smart [of a wound]; 3 burn [of the sun]; *blijven ~* stick [in the mud], get stuck; *in zijn rede blijven ~* break down in one's speech; ● *daar steekt iets (wat)* a c h t e r there is something behind it, there is something at the back of it, there is something at the bottom of it; *daar steekt meer achter* more is meant than meets the eye; *i n de schuld ~* be in debt; *de sleutel steekt in het slot* the key is in the lock; *daar steekt geen kwaad in* there is no harm in it; *hij stak n a a r mij* he thrust (stabbed) at me; zie ook: *wal, zee*; **II** *vt* 1 (i e m.) sting, prick [with a pin, sting &]; thrust [with a sword]; stab [with a dagger]; 2 (i e t s e r g e n s i n) put [...in one's pocket]; stick [a pencil behind one's ear]; poke [a finger in water, one's nose into sbd.'s affairs]; 3 (e r g e n s u i t) put, stick [one's head out of the window]; *aal ~* spear eels; *asperges ~* cut asparagus; *gaten ~* prick holes; *monsters ~ uit* sample; *plaggen (zoden) ~* cut sods; *de bij stak mij* the bee stung me; *dat steekt hem* that sticks in his throat, he is nettled at it; ● *hij wilde de ring a a n haar vinger ~* he was going to put the ring on her finger; *steek die brief b ij je* put that letter in your pocket; *steek je arm d o o r de mijne* (slip) put your arm through mine; *geld i n een onderneming ~* put (invest, sink) money in an undertaking; *iem. in de kleren ~* clothe sbd.; **III** *vr zich in gala ~* put on full dress; *zich in schulden ~* run into debt; zie ook: *stokje* &; **–d** stinging
′stekken (stekte, h. gestekt) *vt* ⚘ slip
′stekker (-s) *m* ⚡ plug
′stekkie (-s) *o* **F** spot, place
stel (-len) *o* set [of cups, fire-irons &]; *het is me een ~* **F** a nice lot they are!; *jullie zijn me een ~* you're a nice pair; *op ~ en sprong* immediately, rightaway
′stelen* I *vt* steal[2] [money &, a kiss, sbd.'s heart]; *een kind om te ~* a sweet child; *hij kan me gestolen worden!* he may go to blazes!; *zij ~ wat los en vast is* they steal all they can lay their hands on; **II** *va* steal, pick and steal; *~ als de raven* steal like magpies; **–er** (-s) *m* stealer, thief
′stelkunde *v* algebra; **stel′kundig** algebraic(al)
stel′lage [-ʒə] (-s) *v* scaffolding, scaffold, stage
′stellen (stelde, h. gesteld) **I** *vt* 1 (p l a a t s e n) place, put; 2 ✗ (r e g e l e n) adjust; [a telescope]; 3 (r e d i g e r e n) compose; 4 (v e r o n d e r s t e l l e n) suppose; 5 **$** (v a s t-s t e l l e n) fix [prices]; 6 (b e w e r e n, v e r-k l a r e n) state; *stel eens dat...* put the case

that...; suppose he...; *het goed kunnen* ~ be in easy circumstances; *het goed kunnen* ~ *met* get on with; *een rustig gesteld pleidooi* a calmly worded plea; *strafbaar (verplichtend &)* ~ make punishable (obligatory &); *ik heb heel wat te* ~ *met die jongen* he is rather a handful; ● ...~ *b o v e n rijkdom* place (put)... above riches; *ik kan het b u i t e n (zonder)* u ~ I can do without you; *de prijs* ~ *o p...* fix the price at; *iem. v o o r een voldongen feit* ~ present sbd. with an accomplished fact; *iem. voor de keus* ~ put sbd. to the choice; *voor de keus gesteld...* faced with the choice of... [they...]; **II** *vr zich* ~ put oneself; ● *stel u i n mijn plaats* put yourself in my place; *zich iets t o t plicht* ~ make it one's duty to...; *zich iets tot taak* ~ make it one's task to..., set oneself the task; zie ook: *borg, kandidaat* &; **III** *va* compose; *hij kan goed* ~ he is a good stylist; **–er** (-s) *m* writer, author; ~ *dezes* the present writer

'**stellig I** *aj* positive [answer &]; explicit [declaration]; **II** *ad* 1 (v. v e r k l a r i n g) positively; explicitly; 2 (a l s v e r z e k e r i n g) positively, decidedly; *u kunt er* ~ *op aan* you may be quite sure as to that; *hij zal* ~ *ook komen* he is sure to come too; *kom je?* ~*!* surely!; *je moet* ~ *komen* come by all means; *dat weet ik* ~ I am quite positive as to that; **–heid** (-heden) *v* positiveness

'**stelling** (-en) *v* 1 (s t e l l a g e) scaffolding; 2 (o p s t e l l i n g) ⚔ position; 3 (b e w e r i n g) theorem, thesis [*mv* theses]; 4 × (e n l o g i c a) proposition; *een sterke* ~ *innemen* ⚔ take up a strong position; ~ *nemen* take up a position [regarding a question]; ~ *nemen tegen* make a stand against; *in* ~ *brengen* ⚔ place in position; **–name** *v* position, attitude; view, comment; **–oorlog** (-logen) *m* war of positions

'**stelpen** (stelpte, h. gestelpt) *vt* sta(u)nch [the bleeding], stop [the blood]

'**stelregel** (-s) *m* maxim, precept; **–schroef** (-schroeven) *v* set(ting) screw, adjusting screw

'**stelsel** (-s) *o* system; **–loos** unsystematic, unmethodical; **stelsel'loosheid** *v* want of system (method); **stelsel'matig** systematic; **–heid** *v* systematicalness

stelt (-en) *v* stilt; *op* ~*en lopen* go (walk) upon stilts; *alles op* ~*en zetten* throw everything in (a state of) confusion, throw everything upside down; **–loper** (-s) *m* stilt, stilt-bird

stem (-men) *v* 1 voice; 2 (b ij s t e m m i n g) vote; 3 ♪ part [of a musical composition]; *eerste (tweede)* ~ ♪ first (second) part; *er waren 30* ~*men vóór* there were 30 votes in favour; *de* ~ *eens roependen in de woestijn* **B** a voice crying in the wilderness; *de meeste* ~*men gelden* the majority have it; *iem. zijn* ~ *geven* vote for sbd.; ~ *in*

het kapittel hebben have a voice in the matter; *hij had de meeste* ~*men* he (had) polled most votes; *zij is haar* ~ *kwijt* she has lost her voice; *de* ~*men opnemen* collect the votes; *zijn* ~ *uitbrengen* record one's vote; *zijn* ~ *uitbrengen op...* vote for...; *bijna alle* ~*men op zich verenigen* receive nearly all the votes; *zijn* ~ *verheffen* raise one's voice (against *tegen*); *de tweede* ~ *zingen* ♪ sing a second; ● *b ij* ~ *zijn* ♪ be in (good) voice; *m e t algemene* ~*men* unanimously; *met luider* ~ in a loud voice; *met één* ~ *tegen* with one dissentient vote; *met de* ~*men van... tegen* [rejected] by the adverse votes of...; *met tien* ~*men voor en vier tegen* by ten votes to four; *v o o r drie* ~*men* ♪ [song] in three parts; **–banden** *mv* vocal cords; **–biljet** (-ten) *o*, **–briefje** (-s) *o* voting-paper, ballot-paper; **–buiging** (-en) *v* modulation, intonation; **–bureau** [-by.ro.] (-s) *o* 1 (l o k a a l) polling-booth, polling-station; 2 (p e r s o n e n) polling-committee; **–bus** (-sen) *v* ballot-box; *ter* ~ *gaan* go to the poll; **–geluid** *o* sound of [one's] voice, voice

'**stemgember** *m* stem ginger

stemge'rechtigd entitled to a (the) vote, qualified to vote, enfranchised; '**stemhamer** (-s) *m* tuning-hammer; **–hebbend** [consonant], voiced [consonant]; **–hokje** (-s) *o* cubicle; **–lokaal** (-kalen) *o* polling-booth, polling-station; **–loos** dumb, mute, voiceless; *stemloze medeklinker* voiceless consonant; '**stemmen** (stemde, h. gestemd) **I** *vt* 1 vote [a candidate]; 2 ♪ tune [a violin &], key [the strings], voice [organ-pipes]; (*op*) *links* ~ vote Left; **II** *va* 1 vote, poll; 2 ♪ tune up [of performers]; be in tune; *ze zijn aan het* ~ ♪ they are tuning up; **III** *vi* vote, poll; *er is druk gestemd* voting (polling) was heavy; ● ~ *o p iem.* vote for sbd.; ~ *o v e r* vote upon; divide on... [in Parliament]; *we zullen er over* ~ we'll put it to the vote; ~ *t e g e n* vote against; ~ *t o t dankbaarheid* & inspire one to gratitude; ~ *tot vrolijkheid* dispose the mind to gaiety; ~ *v ó ó r iets* vote for (in favour of) sth.; *ik stem vóór* I'm for it; zie ook: *gestemd*; '**stem-mencijfer** (-s) *o* poll; **–werver** (-s) *m* canvasser; '**stemmer** (-s) *m* 1 voter; 2 ♪ tuner

'**stemmig I** *aj* demure, sedate, grave [person, manner]; sober, quiet [colours, dress]; **II** *ad* demurely, sedately, gravely; soberly, [dressed] quietly; **–heid** *v* demureness, sedateness, gravity; sobriety, quietness

'**stemming** (-en) *v* 1 voting, vote; ballot; division [in Parliament]; 2 ♪ tuning; 3 *fig* (v. é é n p e r s o o n) frame of mind, mood; (v. p u b l i e k) feeling; (v. o m g e v i n g) atmosphere; $ (v. b e u r s &) tone; ~ *houden* ♪ keep in tune; ~ *maken tegen* rouse popular feeling against; ~ *verlangen* challenge a division; ● *het* a a n ~ *onderwerpen* put it to the vote; *b ij* ~ on a division; *bij de eerste* ~ at the first ballot; *iets i n* ~ *brengen* put sth. to the vote; *in de beste* ~ *zijn* be in the very best of spirits; *ik ben niet in een* ~ *om...* I am in no mood for ...ing, not disposed to...; *in* ~ *komen* be put to the vote; *z o n d e r* ~ [motion carried] without a division; **stemmingmake'rij** *v* attempt to manipulate public opinion; **'stemmingsbeeld** (-en) *o* description of a certain atmosphere

'stemomvang *m* vocal register, range of the voice; **–opnemer** (-s) *m* 1 polling-clerk, scrutineer; 2 teller [in House of Commons]; **–opneming** (-en) *v* counting of votes

'stempel (-s) 1 *m* (w e r k t u i g) stamp; die [for striking coins]; 2 *o* & *m* (a f d r u k) stamp[2] [on document]; impress, imprint; hallmark [of gold and silver]; ⏍ postmark; 3 *m* ♺ stigma; *de* ~ *dragen van...* bear the stamp (hallmark) of...; *de* ~ *der waarheid dragen* bear the impress of truth; *zijn* ~ *drukken op* put one's stamp on...; *van de oude* ~ of the old stamp; **–band** (-en) *m* cloth binding; **'stempelen** (stempelde, h. gestempeld) *vt* stamp[2], mark; hallmark [gold and silver]; ⏍ postmark; *hem tot een verrader* ~ stamp him (as) a traitor; **II** *vi* (v a n w e r k l o z e n) sign on (for the dole), be (go) on the dole; **–ling** (-en) *v* stamping; **'stempelinkt** *m* ink for rubber stamps; **–kussen** (-s) *o* stamp pad

'stemplicht *m* & *v* compulsory voting; **–recht** *o* right to vote; suffrage, franchise; $ voting rights [of shareholders]; *het* ~ ook: the vote; *algemeen* ~ universal suffrage; *aandelen zonder* ~ $ non-voting shares; **–sleutel** (-s) *m* tuning-key; **–spleet** (-spleten) *v* glottis; ~... glottal; **–verheffing** *v* raising of the voice; **–vork** (-en) *v* tuning-fork; **–vorming** *v* voice production; **–wisseling** (-en) *v* breaking of the voice

'stencil ['stɛnsəl] (-s) *o* & *m* stencil; **'stencilen** (stencilde, h. gestencild) *vt* stencil, duplicate, mimeograph; **'stencilmachine** [-ma.ʃi.nə] (-s) *v* stencil machine, duplicator, mimeograph; **–papier** *o* stencil paper, **F** flong

1 'stenen (steende, h. gesteend) *vi* (k r e u n e n) moan, groan

2 'stenen *aj* of stone, stone; (b a k s t e n e n) brick; *een* ~ *hart* a heart of stone

'stengel (-s) *m* stalk, stem [of plants]; *zoute* ~ pretzel

'stenig stony; **'stenigen** (stenigde, h. gestenigd) *vt* stone (to death); **–ing** (-en) *v* stoning

'stennis *m* **F** noise, fuss; ~ *maken* kick up a row

'steno *o = stenografie*; **steno'graaf** (-grafen) *m* stenographer, shorthand writer; **stenogra'feren** (stenografeerde, h. gestenografeerd) **I** *vi* write shorthand; **II** *vt* take down

in shorthand; **stenogra'fie** *v* stenography, shorthand; **steno'grafisch** stenographic(al), in shorthand; **steno'gram** (-men) *o* shorthand writer's notes, shorthand report; **stenoty'pist(e)** [-ti.-] (-en, *v* ook -es) *m(-v)* shorthand typist

'stentorstem *v* stentorian voice

step (-pen en -s) *m* step; (a u t o p e d) scooter

step-'in (-s) *m* girdle, roll-on

'steppe (-n) *v* steppe; **–bewoner** (-s) *m* inhabitant of the steppe; **–hoen** (-ders) *o* Pallas's grouse; **–wolf** (-wolven) *m* coyote

ster (-ren) *v* star[2]; *met* ~*ren bezaaid* starry; ☉ star-spangled; *zijn* ~ *rijst* his star is in the ascendant; **–appel** (-s en -en) *m* star apple

'stère ['stɛːrə] (-s en -n) *v* stère, cubic metre

stereofo'nie *v* stereophony; **stereo'fonisch** stereophonic; **stereome'trie** *v* solid geometry; **'stereoplaat** (-platen) *v* stereo record; **stereo'scoop** (-scopen) *m* stereoscope; **stereo'scopisch** stereoscopic; **stereo'tiep** stereotype; *fig* stereotyped, stock [phrase, saying], stereotype [fathers, sons]; **stereoty'peren** [-ti.-] (stereotypeerde, h. gestereotypeerd) *vt* stereotype; **stereoty'pie** (-ieën) *v* stereotype printing

'sterfbed (-den) *o* death-bed; **–dag** (-dagen) *m* day of sbd.'s death, dying day; **–datum** (-s en -data) *m* date of death; **'sterfelijk** mortal; **–heid** *v* mortality; **'sterfgeval** (-len) *o* death; *wegens* ~ owing to a bereavement; **–huis** (-huizen) *o* house of the deceased; **–kamer** (-s) *v* death-room, death-chamber; **–lijk(heid)** = *sterfelijk(heid)*; **'sterfte** *v* mortality; **–cijfer** (-s) *o* (rate of) mortality, death-rate; **'sterfuur** (-uren) *o* dying-hour, hour of death

ste'riel sterile, barren; **sterili'satie** [-'za(t)si.] *v* sterilization; **–tor** (-s en -toren) *m* sterilizer; **sterili'seertrommel** ' s) *v* autoclave; **sterili'seren** (steriliseerde, h. gesteriliseerd) *vt* sterilize; **sterili'teit** *v* sterility, barrenness, infertility

sterk I *aj* 1 strong[2]; powerful [microscope]; $ sharp [rise, fall]; 2 (r a n z i g) strong; *een* ~ *geheugen* a retentive memory; *een* ~ *verhaal* **F** a tall story; ~*e werkwoorden* strong verbs; *dat is* ~, *zeg!* **F** that's what I call steep!; *ik maak me* ~ *dat...* I'm sure that...; *een leger 100.000 man* ~ an army 100.000 strong; *hij is* ~ *in het Frans* he is strong (well up) in French; *daarin is hij* ~ that's his strong point; *daar ben ik niet* ~ *in* I am not good at that; *hij (zijn zaak) staat* ~ he has a strong case; *zo* ~ *als een paard* as strong as a horse; **II** *ad* strongly; *dat is* ~ *gezegd* that is a strong thing to say; ~ *overdreven* wildly exaggerated; ~ *vergroot* much enlarged; **'sterken** (sterkte, h. gesterkt) *vt* strengthen, fortify, invigorate

'**sterkers** *v* = *sterrekers*

'**sterking** *v* strengthening; '**sterkstroom** *m* strong current; '**sterkte** (-n en -s) *v* 1 strength; 2 (f o r t) fortress; **sterk'water** *o* nitric acid, aqua fortis; *op* ~ *zetten* put into spirits

'**sterling** sterling; *pond* ~ pound sterling; **–gebied** (-en) *o* sterling area

'**stermotor** (-s en -'toren) *m* radial (engine)

stern (-s) *v* (common) tern

'**sterrebaan** (-banen) *v* orbit of a star; **–jaar** (-jaren) *o* sideral year; **–kers** *v* garden cress; **–kijker** (-s) *m* telescope; **–muur** *v* chickweed; '**sterrenbeeld** (-en) *o* constellation; **–hemel** *m* starry sky; **–kaart** (-en) *v* star-map; **–kijker** (-s) *m* star-gazer, astrologer; **–kunde** *v* astronomy; **sterren'kundige** (-n) *m* astronomer; '**sterrenlicht** *o* star-light, light of the stars; **–loop** *m* course (motion) of the stars; **–regen** (-s) *m* meteoric shower; **–wacht** (-en) *v* (astronomical) observatory; **–wichelaar** (-s) *m* astrologer; **sterrenwichela'rij** *v* astrology; '**sterretje** (-s) *o* 1 little star; 2 star, asterisk (*); 3 [film] starlet; *een klap dat je de* ~*s voor de ogen dansen* a blow that will make you see stars; '**sterrit** (-ten) *m* [Monte Carlo] rally

'**sterveling** (-en) *m* mortal; *geen* ~ not a (living) soul; *gelukkige* ~*!* happy mortal!; '**sterven* I** *vi* die; *ik mag* ~ *als...* I wish I may die if; ~ *a a n een ziekte* die of a disease; *v a n honger* ~ die of hunger; ~ *van ouderdom* die of old age; ~ *van verdriet* die of a broken heart; *o p* ~ *na dood* all but dead; *op* ~ *liggen* be dying, be at the point of death; **II** *vt* *duizend doden* ~ taste death a thousand times; *een natuurlijke dood* ~ die a natural death; **–d** *aj* dying, moribund; *de* ~*e* the dying person; '**stervensuur** (-uren) *o* dying-hour

'**stervormig** star-shaped

stetho'scoop (-scopen) *m* stethoscope

steun (-en) *m* support[2], prop[2], *fig* stay; *de* ~ *van zijn oude dag* the support of his old age; *hij was ons een grote* ~ he was a great help to us; ~ *en toeverlaat* anchor; *de enige* ~ *van de kandidaat* the only support (backing) of the candidate; (*van de*) ~ *trekken* draw unemployment relief, be on the dole (on the bread-line); ~ *verlenen aan* support; *m e t* ~ *van...* aided by...; *t o t* ~ *van...* in support of...; **–balk** (-en) *m* supporting beam, girder; **–beer** (-beren) *m* buttress; **–comité** (-s) *o* relief committee

1 '**steunen** (steunde, h. gesteund) *vi* moan, groan

2 '**steunen** (steunde, h. gesteund) **I** *vt* support, prop (up); *fig* support [a cause, an institution, a candidate]; back (up); countenance [a move-

ment]; uphold [a practice, a person]; second [a motion]; **II** *vi* lean; ~ *o p* lean on; *fig* lean upon [a person]; *waarop steunt dat?* what is it founded on?, what does it rest upon?; ~ *t e g e n* lean against; '**steunfonds** (-en) *o* relief fund; **–muur** (-muren) *m* supporting wall; **–pilaar** (-laren) *m* pillar[2]; **–punt** (-en) *o* 1 point of support; 2 ✗ fulcrum [of a lever]; 3 ⚓ base; **–sel** (-s) *o* stay, prop, support; **–tje** (-s) *o* rest; **–trekker** (-s) *m* recipient of (unemployment) relief; **–zender** (-s) *m* booster transmitter; **–zool** (-zolen) *v* arch support

steur (-en) *m* sturgeon

1 '**steven** (-s) *m* prow, stem; *de* ~ *wenden* go about; *de* ~ *wenden naar* head for..., make for...

2 '**steven** V.T. meerv. v. *stijven*

'**stevenen** (stevende, is gestevend) *vi* steer, sail; ~ *naar* steer for; make for

'**stevig I** *aj* 1 (v. z a k e n) solid, strong [furniture, ropes &]; substantial [meal &]; firm [post]; 2 (v. p e r s o o n) strong, sturdy; *een* ~*e bries* a stiff breeze; *een* ~*e eter* a hearty eater; *een* ~ *glaasje* a stiff glass; *een* ~*e handdruk* a firm shake of the hand; ~*e kost* substantial food; *een* ~*e meid* a strapping lass; *een* ~ *uur* a stiff hour, one solid hour; **II** *ad* solidly &; ~ *doorstappen* walk at a stiff pace; ~ *geboeid* firmly fettered; ~ *gebouwd* firmly built [houses]; well-knit [lads]; *hem* ~ *vasthouden* hold him tight; **–heid** *v* solidity, substantiality, firmness, sturdiness

stewar'dess [stju.ər'dɛs] (-en) *v* ✈ air hostess, stewardess

sticht (-en) *o* bishopric; *het Sticht* 🕮 (the bishopric of) Utrecht

'**stichtelijk I** *aj* edifying; *een* ~ *boek* a devotional book; **II** *ad* edifyingly; *dank je* ~*!* thank you very much!; **–heid** *v* edification; '**stichten** (stichtte, h. gesticht) **I** *vt* 1 found [a business, colonies, a hospital, a church, a religion, an empire &]; establish [a business]; raise [a fund]; 2 edify [people at church]; *vrede* ~ make peace; *hij is er niet over gesticht* zie 2 *gesticht*; zie ook: *brand, onheil*; **II** *va* edify; **–er** (-s) *m* founder; '**stichting** (-en) *v* 1 (o p r i c h t i n g) foundation; 2 (i n r i c h t i n g) institution, foundation, almshouse; 3 (i n d e k e r k &) edification

'**stiefbroe(de)r** (-s) *m* step-brother; **–dochter** (-s) *v* step-daughter

'**stiefelen** (stiefelde, h. en is gestiefeld) *vi* stride, **F** foot it

'**stiefkind** (-eren) *o* step-child[2]; **–moeder** (-s) *v* step-mother[2]; **stief'moederlijk** step-motherly; *wij zijn altijd* ~ *bedeeld geweest* we have always been the poor cousins; *de natuur heeft hem* ~ *bedeeld* nature has not lavished her gifts upon him; '**stiefvader** (-s) *m* step-father;

–zoon (-s en -zonen) *m* step-son; **–zuster** (-s) *v* step-sister

'**stiekem I** *aj* underhand; **II** *ad* on the sly, on the quiet, secretly; ~ *weglopen* sneak away, steal away; *zich ~ houden* lie low; **–erd** (-s) *m* sneak

stiep (-en) *v* stereotypy

stier (-en) *m* bull; *de Stier* ★ Taurus; '**stieregevecht** (-en) *o* bull-fight; **–nek** (-ken) *m* bull neck; '**stierenvechter** (-s) *m* bull-fighter

stierf (stierven) V.T. v. *sterven*

'**stierkalf** (-kalveren) *o* bull-calf

'**stierlijk** *ad* ~ *het land hebben* have the hump, be terribly annoyed; ~ *vervelend* frightfully boring; *zich ~ vervelen* be bored to death

'**stierven** V.T. v. *sterven*

stiet (stieten) V.T. v. *stoten*

1 stift (-en) *v* pin; (v. v u l p o t l o o d) pencil-lead

2 stift (-en) *o = sticht*

'**stifttand** (-en) *m* pivot tooth

'**stigma** ('s en -ta) *o* stigma; **stigmati'satie** [-'za(t)si.] (-s) *v* stigmatization; **stigmati'seren** (stigmatiseerde, h. gestigmatiseerd) *vt* stigmatize

stijf I *aj* stiff² [collar, leg, neck, breeze; manners, attitude, bow]; rigid [balloon]; *fig* starchy; *zo ~ als een paal* as stiff as a poker; ~ *van de kou* stiff with cold; *u moet het ~ laten worden* leave it to stiffen (to set); **II** *ad* stiffly; *iets ~ en strak volhouden* stoutly maintain it; ~ *dicht* firmly (tightly) closed; '**stijfheid** *o* stiffness², rigidity, starch; **stijf'hoofdig, –'koppig I** *aj* obstinate, headstrong; **II** *ad* obstinately; **stijf'hoofdigheid, –'koppigheid** *v* obstinacy; '**stijfkop** (-pen) *m* obstinate person, *Am* bullet-head

'**stijfsel** *m* & *o* 1 starch [from corn, for stiffening]; 2 paste [of the bill-sticker]; **–achtig** starchy; '**stijfselen** (stijfselde, h. gestijfseld) *vt* starch; '**stijfselkwast** (-en) *m* paste-brush; **–pap** (-pen) *v* paste

'**stijfte** *v* stiffness

'**stijgbeugel** (-s) *m* stirrup; '**stijgen*** *vi* 1 (i n d e h o o g t e) rise, mount [of a road], mount [of blood], *ꞁ* ook: climb; 2 (h o g e r w o r d e n) rise [of a river, prices, of the barometer], go up, advance [of prices]; *n a a r het hoofd ~* go to one's head [of wine &]; mount (rush) to one's head [of the blood]; *t e paard ~* mount one's horse; *v a n het paard ~* alight from one's horse, dismount; *in ~de lijn* on the up-grade; '**stijgijzer** (-s) *o* crampon, climbing iron; '**stijging** (-en) *v* rise², rising,

advance; '**stijgwind** (-en) *m* upwind, updraught

stijl (-en) *m* 1 △ post [of door &]; 2 ⚜ style; 3 (s c h r ij f w ij z e, t r a n t) style; 4 (t ij d r e k e n i n g) style; *oude ~* old style; *in verheven ~* in elevated style; **–bloempje** (-s) *o* flower of speech; **–figuur** (-guren) *v* figure of speech; **–kamer** (-s) *v* period room; **–leer** *v* stylistics; **–loos** devoid of style, styleless; *fig* in bad taste; **–oefening** (-en) *v* stylistic exercise; **–vol** stylish

'**stijven* I** *vt* 1 stiffen [the back of a book &]; 2 starch [linen]; *de kas ~* swell the fund (the treasury); *iem. in het kwaad ~* egg sbd. on, set sbd. on; **II** *vi* stiffen; **–ving** *v* 1 stiffening; 2 starching [of linen]; *tot ~ van de kas* to swell the fund

stik! *ij* F hell!, hang!, blast!; **–donker I** *aj* pitch-dark; **II** *o* pitch-darkness; **–gas** *o* (i n m ij n e n) choke-damp; **–heet** stifling hot; **1 'stikken** (stikte, is gestikt) *vi* stifle, be stifled, choke, be suffocated, suffocate; *ik stik!* I am choking; *ze mogen voor mijn part ~* they may go to hell!; *als ik jou was liet ik de hele boel ~* I should cut the whole concern; *het was om te ~* it was suffocatingly hot; 2 it was screamingly funny; ~ *van het lachen* split one's sides with laughter; *hij stikte van woede* he choked with rage

2 'stikken (stikte, h. gestikt) *vt* stitch [a garment &]; *gestikte deken* quilt; **–er** (-s) *m* stitcher; '**stiknaald** (-en) *v* stitching-needle; '**stiksel** (-s) *o* stitching; '**stiksteek** (-steken) *m* back-stitch

'**stikstof** *v* nitrogen; **–houdend** nitrogenous; **–verbinding** (-en) *v* nitrogen compound

'**stikvol** crammed, chock-full

'**stikwerk** *o* stitching

stil I *aj* still, quiet; silent; ~*!* hush!; ~ *daar!* silence there!; *tabak* ~ $ tobacco quiet; *een ~le drinker* a secret drinker; ~ *spel* stage business, by-play [of actor]; *de Stille Week* Holy Week; *zo* ~ *als een muis(je)* as silent as a mouse; *zo* ~ *als de muisjes* as mum as mice; zie ook: *vennoot* &; **II** *ad* quietly; silently; ~ *leven* have retired from business; ~ *toeluisteren* listen in silence

sti'leren (stileerde, h. gestileerd) *vt* & *vi* 1 compose [a letter &]; 2 stylize [a dress], conventionalize [flowers &]

sti'let (-ten) *o* stiletto

sti'letto ('s) *m* flick-knife

'**stilheid** *v* stillness, quiet, silence; '**stilhouden**¹ **I** *vi* stop, come to a stop; *de wagen hield stil voor*

---

¹ V.T. en V.D. van dit werkwoord volgens het model: '**stil**zetten, V.T. zette '**stil**, V.D. '**stil**gezet. Zie voor de vormen onder het grondwoord, in dit voorbeeld: *zetten*. Bij sterke en onregelmatige werkwoorden wordt u verwezen naar de lijst achterin.

de deur pulled (drew) up at the door; **II** *vt iets* ~ keep sth. quiet (dark), hush sth. up; **III** *vr zich* ~ l keep quiet, be quiet, keep still; 2 keep silent

sti'list (-en) *m* stylist

'stille (-n) *m* **F** plain-clothes man; **'stilleggen**[1] *vt* stop [work]; close down, shut down [a factory]; **'stillen** (stilde, h. gestild) *vt* quiet, hush [a crying child]; still [fears &]; allay, alleviate [pain]; appease [one's hunger]; quench [one's thirst]; **'stilletje** (-s) *o* close-stool, night-stool; **'stilletjes** 1 silently; 2 secretly, on the quiet; **'stilleven** (-s) *o* still life [painting]; **'stilliggen**[1] *vi* lie still [in bed &]; lie idle [a harbour]; have closed down [a factory]; *de handel ligt stil* trade is at a standstill; **'stilling** *v* stilling &, alleviation, appeasement &, zie *stillen*; **'stilstaan**[1] *vi* stand still; stop; *bij blecf* ~ he stopped; *de handel staat stil* trade is at a standstill; *de klok staat stil* the clock has stopped; *de klok laten* ~ stop the clock; *daar heb ik niet bij stilgestaan* I didn't stop at the thought; *er wat langer bij* ~ dwell on it a little longer; zie ook: *mond, verstand;* **–d** standing, stagnant [waters]; standing, stationary [train]; **'stilstand** *m* standstill; cessation; stagnation, stagnancy [of business]; stoppage [in factory, of work]; *tot* ~ *komen* come to a standstill; **'stilte** (-n en -s) *v* stillness, quiet, silence; [*er viel een*] *doodse* ~ deathlike hush, sudden hush; *de* ~ *voor de storm* the lull before the storm; *in* ~ silently; secretly, privately [married]; *in* ~ *lijden* suffer in silence; *de menigte nam twee minuten* ~ *in acht* the crowd stood in silence for two minutes; **'stilzetten**[1] *vt* = *stopzetten;* **–zitten**[1] *vi* sit still; *fig* do nothing [of a minister &]; *we hebben niet stilgezeten* we have not been idle

'stilzwijgen *o* silence; *het* ~ *bewaren* keep (preserve, observe, maintain) silence; be (keep) silent (about *over*); **–d I** *aj* silent, taciturn [person]; tacit [agreement]; implied [condition]; **II** *ad* tacitly [understood]; [pass over] in silence; **stil'zwijgendheid** *v* silence, taciturnity

'stimulans (-'lansen en -'lantia) *m* stimulant; *fig* stimulus [*mv* stimuli], boost; **stimu-.'leren** (stimuleerde, h. gestimuleerd) *vt* stimulate, boost; **'stimulus** (-li) *m* = *stimulans*

'stinkbom (-men) *v* stink-bomb; **–dier** (-en) *o* ~ skunk; **'stinken*** *vi* stink, smell, reek (of *naar*); *erin* ~ **F** get caught, walk into the trap; **–d** stinking, reeking, fetid; ~*e gouwe ** greater celandine; **F** ~ *rijk* stinking rich; **'stinkstok**

(-ken) *m* **F** cheap cigar; **–zwam** (-men) *v* stinkhorn

stip (-pen) *v* point, dot (on the i); (o p s c h e r m) blip

sti'pendium (-s en -ia) *o* stipend, ~ scholar-ship

'stippel (-s) *v* speck, dot; **'stippelen** (stippelde, h. gestippeld) *vt* dot, speckle, stipple; **'stippel-lijn** (-en) *v* dotted line; **'stippen** (stipte, h. gestipt) *vt* point, prick

stipt punctual, precise; ~ *eerlijk* strictly honest; ~ *op tijd* punctually to time; **'stiptheid** *v* punctuality, precision; **–sactie** [-'aksi.] (-s) *v* work-to-rule; *een* ~ *voeren* work to rule

'stobbe (-n) *v* stump [of a tree]

'stoeien (stoeide, h. gestoeid) *vi* romp, have a game of romps; **stoeie'rij** (-en) *v* romp(ing); **'stoeipartij** (-en) *v* romping, romp, game of romps; **–ziek** romping

stoel (-en) *m* 1 (m e u b e l) chair; 2 (v. p l a n t) stool; *de Heilige Stoel* the Holy See; *neem een* ~ take a seat; ● *het niet o n d e r* ~*en of banken steken* make no secret of it, make no bones about it; *t u s s e n twee* ~*en in de as zitten* have come down between two stools; *v o o r* ~*en en banken spelen* (*spreken*) play (lecture) to empty benches; **'stoelen** (stoelde, h. gestoeld) *vi fig* ~ *op* be founded on, be rooted in; **'stoelendans** (-en) *m* "musical chairs"; **–maker** (-s) *m* chair-maker; **–matter** (-s) *m* chair-bottomer; **'stoelgang** *m* movement, stool(s); zie verder: *ontlasting;* **–kussen** (-s) *o* chair-cushion; **–tjeslift** (-en) *m* chair-lift

stoep (-en) *m & v* 1 (flight of) steps; 2 (t r o t-t o i r) pavement, footpath; **stoe'pier** [-'pje.] (-s) *m* ± barker; **'stoeprand** (-en) *m* kerbstone

stoer sturdy, stalwart, stout; **–heid** *v* sturdiness

stoet (-en) *m* cortege, procession; train, retinue

stoete'rij (-en) *v* stud(-farm)

'stoethaspel (-s) *m* clumsy fellow; **'stoethaspelen** (stoethaspelde, h. gestoethaspeld) *vi* fumble, bungle, botch

1 stof *o* dust; ~ *afnemen* dust; ~ *opjagen* make a dust; *dat heeft heel wat* ~ *opgejaagd* that has raised a good deal of dust; *het* ~ *van zijn voeten schudden* shake the dust off one's feet; (*zich*) *i n het* ~ *vernederen* humble (oneself) to the dust (in the dust); *iem. u i t het* ~ *verheffen* raise sbd. from the dust

2 stof (-fen) *v* 1 matter[2]; 2 (z e l f s t a n d i g-h e i d) [radioactive] substance; 3 *fig* subject-matter, theme [of a book, for an essay]; 4 (g o e d) [dress] material, stuff, [silk, woollen]

fabric; ~ *en geest* matter and mind; *dat geeft ~ tot nadenken* that will give food for reflection (thought)

'**stofblik** (-ken) *o* dustpan; **–bril** (-len) *m* goggles; **–dicht** dust-proof; **–doek** (-en) *m* duster

stof′feerder (-s) *m* upholsterer; **stoffeerde′rij** (-en) *v* upholstery (business)

'**stoffel** (-s) *m* blockhead, duffer, ninny

'**stoffelijk** material, concrete; **~***e belangen* material interests; **~***e bijvoeglijke naamwoorden* names of materials used as adjectives; *zijn ~ overschot* his mortal remains; **–heid** *v* materiality, corporality

1 '**stoffen** (stofte, h. gestoft) *vt* (s t o f a f - n e m e n) dust

2 '**stoffen** (stofte, h. gestoft) *vi* (b l u f f e n) boast (of *op*)

3 '**stoffen** *aj* cloth [shoes]; **–winkel** (-s) *m* draper's (shop), drapery store

'**stoffer** (-s) *m* brush; **~** *en blik* (dust)pan and brush

stof′feren (stoffeerde, h. gestoffeerd) *vt* upholster, furnish; **–ring** (-en) *v* upholstering, furnishings; *inclusief ~* with curtains and drapes

'**stoffig** dusty; **~** *worden* gather dust; **–heid** *v* dustiness

'**stofgoud** *o* gold-dust; **–hoek** (-en) *m* dusty corner; **–hoop** (-hopen) *m* heap of dust; **–jas** (-sen) *m & v* dust-coat, overall; **–je** (-s) *o* speck of dust; ‖ = 2 *stof* 4; **–kam** (-men) *m* fine-tooth comb; **–longziekte** *v* silicosis; **–mantel** (-s) *m* dust-cloak

'**stofnaam** (-namen) *m gram* name of a material

'**stofnest** (-en) *o* dust-trap; **–omslag** (-slagen) *m & o* dust jacket; **–regen** *m* drizzling rain, drizzle; '**stofregenen** (stofregende, h. gestofregend) *vi* drizzle; '**stofvrij** free from dust

'**stofwisseling** *v* metabolism

'**stofwolk** (-en) *v* dust cloud, cloud of dust

'**stofzuigen** (stofzuigde, h. gestofzuigd) *vi & vt* vacuum; **–er** (-s) *m* (vacuum) cleaner

stoï′cijn (-en) *m* stoic; **–s I** *aj* stoical [serenity], stoic [doctrines]; **II** *ad* stoically; **stoï′cisme** *o* stoicism; '**stoïsch** = *stoïcijns*

stok (-ken) *m* 1 (i n ′t a l g.) stick; 2 (w a n d e l - s t o k) walking-stick, cane, stick; 3 (z i t s t o k) perch, roost [for birds]; 4 (b ij b a t o n n e r e n) quarterstaff; 5 (v. a g e n t) truncheon, baton; 6 (v. d i r i g e n t; b ij e s t a f e t t e l o o p) baton; 7 (v. v l a g) pole; 8 ⚓ stock [of anchor]; *de ~ achter de deur* the big stick; *het met iem. a a n d e ~ hebben* be at loggerheads with sbd.; *het met iem. aan de ~ krijgen* get into trouble with sbd.; *hij is met geen ~ hierheen te krijgen* wild horses won't drag him here; *o p ~ gaan* go to roost[2]; *op ~ zijn* be at roost; **–brood** (-broden) *o* French

stick; **–doof** stone-deaf

'**stokebrand** (-en) *m* firebrand

'**stoken** (stookte, h. gestookt) **I** *vt* burn [coal, wood]; stoke [a furnace &]; fire [a boiler, an engine &]; distil [spirits]; *fig* stir up [trouble]; brew [mischief]; *het vuur ~* feed the fire; *een vuurtje ~* I make a fire; 2 *fig* blow the coals, stir up trouble; **II** *vi & va* make a fire, have a fire [in a room]; stoke; *fig* blow the coals, stir up trouble; **–er** (-s) *m* 1 stoker, fireman [of steam-engine]; 2 distiller [of spirits]; 3 *fig* firebrand; **stoke′rij** (-en) *v* distillery

'**stokje** (-s) *o* (little) stick; *daar zullen wij een ~ voor steken* we shall stop it; *van zijn ~ vallen* **F** faint, swoon; zie ook: *gekheid*; '**stokken** (stokte, is gestokt) *vi* cease to circulate [of the blood]; break down [in a speech]; flag [of conversation]; *haar adem stokte* her breath failed her; *zijn stem stokte* there was a catch in his voice; '**stokk(er)ig** woody; *fig* stiff, rigid; '**stokoud** very old; **–paardje** (-s) *o* hobby-horse; *fig* fad; *op zijn ~ zitten (zijn)* be on one's hobby-horse, have a pet subject; **–roos** (-rozen) *v* hollyhock; **–slag** (-slagen) *m* stroke with a stick; **–snijboon** (-bonen) *v* runner bean; **–stijf** as stiff as a poker; **~** *volhouden* maintain obstinately; **–stil** stock-still; **–vis** *m* (g e - d r o o g d) stockfish, dried cod; **–voering** *v* ♪ bowing (technique)

'**stola** (′s) *v* stole

'′**stollen** (stolde, is gestold) *vi* (ook: *doen ~*) congeal, coagulate, curdle, clot, fix, set; *het bloed stolde mij in de aderen* my blood froze (ran cold); *het doet het bloed ~* it makes one's blood run cold, it curdles one's blood; '**stolling** *v* congelation, coagulation; **–sgesteente** (-n en -s) *o* extrusive rocks

stolp (-en) *v* cover, glass bell, bell-glass, shade; **–plooi** (-en) *v* box pleat

'**stolsel** (-s) *o* clot

stom I *aj* 1 (n i e t s z e g g e n d) dumb, mute, speechless; silent [film, part]; 2 (d o m) stupid, dull; 3 (n i e t v e r s t a n d i g) foolish; *~ geluk* the devil's luck; *een ~me h* a mute h; *~me idioot!* **F** utter fool!, **S** big stiff!; *~me personen* mutes; *hij sprak (zei) geen ~ woord* he never said a word; *~ van verbazing* speechless with amazement; **II** *ad* 1 mutely; 2 stupidly; zie ook: *stomme*; **–dronken** dead drunk

'**stomen I** (stoomde, h. en is gestoomd) *vi* steam; *de lamp stoomt* the lamp is smoking; **II** (stoomde, h. gestoomd) *vt* 1 steam [rice &]; 2 (c h e m i s c h r e i n i g e n) dry-clean; **stome′rij** (-en) *v* dry-cleaning establishment; *mijn pak is in de ~* my suit is at the (dry-) cleaner's

'**stomheid** *v* 1 dumbness; 2 (-heden) stupidity;

met ~ *geslagen* struck dumb; **–kop** (-pen) *m* = *stommerik*; **'stomme** (-n) *m-v* dumb person; *de* ~*n* the dumb

'stommelen (stommelde, h. gestommeld) *vi* clatter

'stommeling (-en) *m*, **'stommerik** (-riken) *m* blockhead, dullard, duffer; bullhead, numskull; (*jij*) ~*!* **F** you stupid!; **'stommetje** *wij moesten* ~ *spelen* we had to sit mum; **'stommigheid** (-heden), **stommi'teit** (-en) *v* 1 (a b s t r a c t) stupidness, stupidity; 2 (c o n c r e e t) stupidity, blunder, howler

1 stomp (-en) *m* thump, punch, push, dig

2 stomp (-en) *m* stump [of a tree &]

3 stomp *aj* 1 blunt [pencil], dull; 2 *fig* obtuse; ~*e hoek* obtuse angle; ~*e neus* flat nose

'stompen (stompte, h. gestompt) *vt* pummel, thump, punch, push

'stompheid *v* bluntness, dullness; *fig* obtuseness; **–hoekig** obtuse-angled

'stompje (-s) *o* stump [of branch, tree, limb, cigar, pencil], stub [of dog's tail, of a cigarette, of a pencil]; **'stompneus** (-neuzen) *m* 1 snub nose; 2 snub-nosed person

stomp'zinnig obtuse; **–heid** (-heden) *v* obtuseness

'stomtoevallig by sheer chance; **–verbaasd** stupefied; **–vervelend** awfully slow; **–weg** simply, without thinking

1 stond (-en) *m* time, hour, moment; *t e dezer* ~ at this moment (hour); *terzelfder* ~ at the same moment; *v a n* ~*en aan* henceforward, from this very moment

2 stond (stonden) V.T. v. *staan*

stonk (stonken) V.T. v. *stinken*

1 stoof (stoven) *v* foot-warmer, foot-stove

2 stoof (stoven) V.T. v. *stuiven*

'stoofappel (-en en -s) *m* cooking-apple; **–pan** (-nen) *v* stew-pan; **–peer** (-peren) *v* cooking-pear, stewing-pear

'stookgat (-gaten) *o* fire hole; **–gelegenheid** (-heden) *v* fireplace; **–olie** *v* oil fuel, liquid fuel; **–oven** (-s) *m* furnace; **–plaats** (-en) *v* 1 fireplace, hearth; 2 ✗ stoke-hold, stoke-hole

stool (stolen) *v* stole

stoom *m* steam; *we hebben* ~ *op* steam is up; ~ *houden* keep up steam; ~ *maken* get up (raise) steam; *het gaat m e t (volle)* ~ it goes full steam; *o n d e r* ~ ⚓ with steam up; *onder eigen* ~ ⚓ under her own steam; **–bad** (-baden) *o* steam bath; **–barkas** (-sen) *v* steam launch; **–boot** (-boten) *m* & *v* steamboat, steamer, steamship; **–bootmaatschappij** (-en) *v* steam navigation company, steamship company; **–cursus** [-züs] (-sen) *m* intensive course, short course, crash course; **–druk** *m* steam-pressure; **–fluit** (-en) *v* steam-whistle; **–gemaal** (-malen) *o* steam

pumpingstation; **–ketel** (-s) *m* steam-boiler, boiler; **–klep** (-pen) *v* steam-valve; **–kraan** (-kranen) *v* 1 (h e f t o e s t e l) steam-crane; 2 steam-cock; **–kracht** *v* steam-power; **–machine** [-ma.ʃi.nə.] (-s) *v* steam-engine; **–pijp** (-en) *v* steam-pipe; **–schip** (-schepen) *o* steamship, steamer; **–tractie** [-trɑksi.] *v* steam traction; **–tram**, *m* [-trɑm], **–trem** (-s en -men) *m* steam-tram; **–vaart** *v* steam navigation; **–vaartlijn** (-en) *v* steamship line; **–vaartmaatschappij** (-en) *v* steam navigation company, steamship company; **–wals** (-en) *v* steam-roller; **stoomwasse'rij** (-en) *v* steamlaundry

'stoornis (-sen) *v* disturbance, disorder; **'stoorzender** (-s) *m* jamming transmitter, jamming station

stoot (stoten) *m* 1 push [with the elbow &]; punch [in boxing]; thrust [with a sword]; lunge [in fencing]; stab [with a dagger]; shot, stroke [at billiards]; impact [of colliding bodies]; kick [of a rifle]; gust (of wind); 2 blast [on a horn]; *de (eerste)* ~ *tot (aan) iets geven* give the impulse to sth.; *wie heeft er de eerste* ~ *aan (toe) gegeven?* who has been the prime mover?; *dat heeft hem een lelijke* ~ *gegeven* that has dealt him a severe blow; *wie is aan* ~*?* ☍ who is in play?; **–blok** (-ken) *o* buffer; (v. l o c o m o t i e f) fender; ↩ chock; **–je** (-s) *o* push; *hij kan wel een* ~ *hebben* he is not easily hurt, **F** he can take it; **–kant** (-en) *m* protection strip; **–kussen** (-s) *o* buffer, fender; **–plaat** (-platen) *v* guard [of sword]; **–troepen** *mv* shock-troops

stop (-pen) *m* 1 stopper [of a bottle]; darn [in a stocking]; ✺ (s t e k k e r) plug; ✺ (s m e l t s t o p) fuse; (v. b a d k u i p &) plug; 2 (v a n h u u r, l o o n, p r i j z e n) freeze; **–bal** (-len) *m* darning egg (ball); **–bord** (-en) *o* stop sign; **–contact** (-en) *o* (power-)point; (c o n t a c t d o o s) socket; **–fles** (-sen) *v* stoppered bottle, (glass) jar; **–garen** *o* darning cotton, mending cotton; **–horloge** [-ʒə] (-s) *o* stop-watch; **–lap** (-pen) *m* sampler; *fig* stop-gap; **–licht** (-en) *o* traffic light; zie ook *rijden* **I**; **–mes** (-sen) *o* putty-knife; **–naald** (-en) *v* darning-needle; **stop'page** [-ʒə] (-s) *v* invisible mending

'stoppel (-s en -en) *m* stubble; ~*s* stubble; **–baard** (-en) *m* stubbly beard; **–ig** stubbly; **–land** (-en) *o* stubble-field

1 'stoppen (stopte, h. gestopt) **I** *vt* 1 (d i c h t m a k e n) stop [a hole, a leak &]; darn [stockings]; 2 (d i c h t h o u d e n) stop [one's ears]; 3 (v o l s t o p p e n) fill [a pipe &]; 4 (i n b r e n g e n, w e g b e r g e n) put [something in a box, one's fingers in one's ears &]; *een bal* ~ ♟ pocket a ball; *iem. de handen* ~ grease sbd.'s palm, bribe sbd.; *de kinderen i n bed*

~ I put the children to bed; 2 bundle the children off to bed; *iem. iets in de handen* ~ foist sth. off upon sbd.; *hij laat zich alles in de hand(en)* ~ you can foist (palm off) anything upon him; *het in zijn mond (zak)* ~ put it in one's mouth (pocket); *de kleine er lekker o n d e r* ~ tuck the baby up in bed; *iem. onder de grond* ~ put sbd. to bed with a shovel; **II** *va* (v. v o e d s e l) bind the bowels, be binding, cause constipation

2 **'stoppen I** (stopte, is gestopt) *vi* stop, come to a stop, halt; *de trein stopt hier niet* the train does not stop here; *de trein gaat door tot A. zonder* ~ without a stop; **II** (stopte, h. gestopt) *vt* stop

'stopperspil (-len) *m sp* centre half

'stopplaats (-en) *v* stopping-place, stop; **–sein** (-en) *o* stop signal; **–teken** (-s) *o* stop signal; **–trein** (-en) *m* stopping train; **–verbod** *o* [*hier geldt een*] ~ no stopping, no waiting; **–verf** *v* (glazier's) putty; **–wol** *v* darning-wool; **–woord** (-en) *o* expletive

'stopzetten (zette 'stop, h. 'stopgezet) *vt* stop; close down, shut down [a factory]; shut (cut) off [the engine]; **–ting** *v* stoppage; closing down &

'stopzij(de) *v* darning silk

store [stɔ:r] (-s) *v* Venetian blind

'storen (stoorde, h. gestoord) **I** *vt* disturb, derange, interrupt, interfere with; R jam [broadcasts]; *stoor ik (u) soms?* am I intruding?, am I in the way?; **II** *vr hij stoort zich aan alles* he minds everything; *hij stoort zich aan niets* he does not mind (care); *waarom zou ik mij daaraan* ~ *?* why should I mind?; *zonder zich te* ~ *aan wat zij zeiden* heedless (regardless) of what they said; **–d** annoying, irritating; **'storing** (-en) *v* disturbance, interruption, 🗙 trouble, failure, breakdown; R interference; 🌂 disorder; (v a n w e e r) depression; **–sdienst** (-en) *m* fault-clearing service

storm (-en) *m* storm[2] [also of applause, cheers, indignation]; tempest, gale; *een* ~ *in een glas water* a storm in a tea-cup; **–aanval** (-len) *m* ✕ assault; **–achtig** stormy, tempestuous, tumultuous, boisterous; **–bal** (-len) *m* storm-ball, storm-cone; **–band** (-en) *m* ✕ chin-strap; **–dek** (-ken) *o* hurricane deck; **'stormen** (stormde, h. en is gestormd) *vi* storm; *het stormt* it is blowing a gale; *het zal er* ~ [*fig*] **F** there will be ructions; *hij kwam uit het huis* ~ he came tearing (dashing, rushing) out of the house; **stormender'hand** ✕ by storm; ~ *innemen* take by storm[2]; **'stormklok** (-ken) *v* alarm-bell, tocsin; **–ladder** (-s) *v* ✕ scaling-ladder; **–lamp** (-en) *v* hurricane lamp; **–loop** (-lopen) *m* rush[2]; ✕ assault; **'stormlopen** (liep 'storm, h. 'stormgelopen) *vi* ~ *op (tegen)* storm,

rush, assault [a fortified town]; [*fig*] *het loopt storm* there's a run [on]; **'stormpas** (-sen) *m* ✕ double-quick step; *in de* ~ at the double-quick; **–ram** (-men) *m* battering-ram; **–schade** *v* damage caused by storm; **–sein** (-en) *o* storm-signal; **–troepen** *mv* ✕ storm-troops; **–vogel** (-s) *m* stormy petrel; **–we(d)er** *o* stormy (tempestuous) weather; **–wind** (-en) *m* storm-wind, gale

'stortbad (-baden) *o* shower-bath; **–bak** (-ken) *m* 1 ✕ shoot; 2 (v. W.C.) cistern; **–bui** (-en) *v* heavy shower, downpour; **–buisteren** (stortte, h. gestort) **I** *vt* spill [milk]; shed [tears, blood]; shoot, dump [rubbish]; pour [concrete]; pay in [money]; contribute [towards one's pension]; *elk 10 gulden* ~ deposit 10 guilders each; *het geld moet gestort worden bij een bank (op een rekening)* the money must be paid into a bank (into an account); **II** *vr zich* ~ *in de armen van...* throw oneself into the arms of...; *de rivier stort zich in zee bij...* falls (pours itself) into the sea near...; *zich in een oorlog* ~ plunge into a war; *zich* ~ *op* fall upon, throw oneself upon, swoop down on [the enemy]; **III** *vi & va het stort* it is pouring; **'stortgoederen** *mv* bulk cargo, bulk goods; **'storting** (-en) *v* 1 spilling, shedding, pouring [of a liquid]; 2 payment, deposit, contribution [of money]; **'stortingsbewijs** (-wijzen) *o* paying-in slip, deposit slip; **–termijn** (-en) *m* term for paying in; **'stortkar** (-ren) *v* tip-cart; **–koker** (-s) *m* chute, shoot; **–plaats** (-en) *v* dumping-ground, (rubbish) shoot, (rubbish) tip; **–regen** (-s) *m* heavy shower (of rain), pouring rain, downpour; **'stortregenen** (stortregende, h. gestortregend) *vi* pour (with rain), rain cats and dogs; **'stortvloed** (-en) *m* flood, torrent, deluge; *fig* shower; **–zee** (-zeeën) *v* sea, surge, roller; *wij kregen een flinke* ~ we shipped a heavy sea

'stoten* I *vi* 1 (i n 't a l g.) push; 2 (m e t h o r e n s) butt; 3 (v. g e w e e r) recoil, kick; 4 (v. s c h i p) touch the ground; 5 (v. s p o o r-t r e i n) bump; 6 ♂₀ play; *a a n iets* ~ push sth., give sth. a push; ~ *n a a r* thrust at; *o p iets* ~ stumble upon sth., come across sth.; meet with [difficulties]; *het schip stootte op een ijsberg* struck an iceberg; *t e g e n iets* ~ bump against sth. [a wall &]; push [the table]; *tegen elkaar* ~ bump (knock) against each other; **II** *vt* 1 (a a n-k o m e n t e g e n) stub [one's toes]; bump [one's head against a wall]; nudge [sbd. with one's elbow]; 2 (d u w e n) push [me &]; poke [a hole in a thing]; thrust [sbd. from his rights]; 3 (f ij n s t a m p e n) pound; 4 *fig* shock, scandalize [people]; *iem. v a n zich* ~ repudiate sbd.; *iem. v o o r het hoofd* ~ offend sbd.; zie ook: *bezit*

&; **III** *vr zich ~* bump against sth.; *zich aan iems. gedrag ~* be shocked at sbd.'s conduct; **–d** pushing, thrusting; *fig* shocking, offensive 'stotteraar (-s) *m* stammerer, stutterer; 'stotteren (stotterde, h. gestotterd) *vt* stammer, stutter

1 stout *m* & *o* (b i e r) stout

2 stout I *aj* 1 (m o e d i g) bold, daring, audacious [behaviour]; sanguine [expectations]; 2 (o n d e u g e n d) naughty; **II** *ad* 1 boldly; 2 naughtily; 'stouterd (-s) *m* naughty child (boy, girl); 'stoutheid *v* 1 (m o e d) boldness, audacity; 2 (-heden) (o n d e u g e n d h e i d) naughtiness; stout'moedig bold, daring, undaunted; **–heid** *v* courage, daring, boldness stou'wage [-ʒə] *v* = *stuwage*; 'stouwen (stouwde, h. gestouwd) *vt* ⚓ stow [goods]

1 'stoven (stoofde, h. gestoofd) **I** *vt* stew; **II** *vr zich ~* bask [in the sun]

2 'stoven V.T. meerv. v. *stuiven*

1 straal (stralen) *m* & *v* 1 ray, beam [of light], gleam, ray [of hope]; flash [of lightning]; 2 spout, jet [of water &]; 3 radius [*mv* radii] [of a circle]

2 straal *ad* **F** (v o l k o m e n) completely, through and through

'straalaandrijving *v* jet propulsion; *met ~* jet-propelled; **–bommenwerper** (-s) *m* jet bomber; **–breking** (-en) *v* refraction; **–dier** (-en) *o* radiolarian; **–jager** (-s) *m* jet fighter; **–kachel** (-s) *v* electric (reflector) heater; **–motor** (-s en -'toren) *m* jet engine; **–pijp** (-en) *v* jet nozzle, ⚡ jet exhaust; **–sgewijs**, **–sgewijze** radially; **–turbine** (-s) *v* turbojet (engine); **–vliegtuig** (-en) *o* jet(-propelled) plane, jet; *~(en)* ook: jet aircraft; **–zender** (-s) *m* ray (beam) transmitter

straat (straten) *v* 1 (v. s t a d) street; 2 (z e e - s t r a a t) straits; *l a n g s de ~ slingeren* knock (gad) about the streets; *o p ~* in the street(s); *op ~ lopen* walk (run) about the streets; *op ~ staan* be on the streets; *iem. op ~ zetten* turn sbd. into the street; *hij is niet v a n de ~ opgeraapt* he was not picked out of the gutter; **–arm** very poor, as poor as a churchmouse; **–beeld** (-en) *o* streetscape; **–collecte** (-s en -n) *v* street collection; **–deun** (-en) *m* street-song, street-ballad; **–deur** (-en) *v* street-door, front door; **–fotograaf** (-grafen) *m* street photographer; **–gevecht** (-en) *o* street fight; *~en* street fighting; **–handel** *m* street sale, street vending (hawking); **–handelaar** (-s en -laren) *m* street trader; **–hond** (-en) *m* mongrel, cur; **–jongen** (-s) *m* street-boy; **–kei** (-en) *m* cobble(-stone); **–lantaarn, –lantaren** (-s) *v* street-lamp; **–lied(je)** (-liederen en -liedjes) *o* street-song, street-ballad; **–maker**

(-s) *m* road-maker, paviour; **–muzikant** (-en) *m* street-musician; **–naam** (-namen) *m* streetname; **–naambordje** (-s) *o* street-sign; **–orgel** (-s) *o* street-organ, barrel-organ; **–roof** *m* street-robbery; **–rover** (-s) *m* street-robber; straatrove'rij (-en) *v* street-robbery

'Straatsburg *o* Strasbourg

'straatschender (-s) *m* street rough, hooligan; straatschende'rij (-en) *v* disorderliness in the street(s), hooliganism; 'straatslijpen *va* loaf about the streets; **–er** (-s) *m* street-lounger, loafer; 'straatstamper (-s) *m* paviour's beetle, rammer; **–steen** (-stenen) *m* paving-stone; *iets aan de straatstenen niet kwijt kunnen* not be able to sell sth. for love or money; 'straattaal *v* language of the street; **–veger** (-s) *m* (m a n; m a c h i n e) road-sweeper, street-sweeper; **–venter** (-s) *m* street-vendor, hawker; **–verlichting** *v* streetlighting; **–vuil** *o* street-refuse; **–weg** (-wegen) *m* high road; **–werker** (-s) *m* road-maker, paviour; **–zanger** (-s) *m* street-singer, busker

1 straf (-fen) *v* punishment, penalty; *~ krijgen* be (get) punished; *het brengt zijn eigen ~ mee* it carries its own punishment; *voor (zijn) ~* as a punishment, for punishment, by way of punishment; *de ~ volgt op de zonde* punishment follows sin

2 straf I *aj* severe, stern [looks]; stiff [drink]; strong [tea]; **II** *ad* [look] severely, sternly 'strafbaar punishable; penal [offences]; *als ~ beschouwen* criminate; **–bankje** (-s) *o* dock; **–bepaling** (-en) *v* penal provision; penalty clause [in contract]; **–blad** (-bladen) *o* = *strafregister*; **–exerceren** *o* ⚔ pack drill; **–expeditie** [-(t)si.] (-s) *v* ⚔ punitive expedition; 'straffe *op ~ van* on penalty of; *op ~ des doods* upon pain of death; **–loos** unpunished, with impunity; straffe'loosheid *v* impunity; 'straffen (strafte, h. gestraft) *vt* punish; *met boete ~* punish by a fine; *met de dood ~* punish with death; 'strafgericht *o* punishment, judgement [of God]; **–gevangenis** (-sen) *v* (convict) prison; **–inrichting** (-en) *v* penal establishment; **–kolonie** (-s en -iën) *v* penal (convict) settlement, penal (convict) colony; **–maat** *v* sentence, degree of penalty (punishment); **–maatregel** (-s en -en) *m* punitive measure; **–middel** (-en) *o* means of punishment; **–oefening** (-en) *v* execution; **–port** *o* & *m* additional postage, extra postage, surcharge; **–preek** (-preken) *v* lecture, **F** talking-to; **–proces** (-sen) *o* criminal procedure (proceedings); **–punt** (-en) *o* *een mededinger 10 ~en geven* penalize a competitor 10 points; **–recht** *o* criminal law; straf'rechtelijk of criminal law, criminal; 'strafrechter (-s) *m* criminal judge; **–regels** *mv* ✎ lines; **–register** (-s) *o* 🚓 police record, criminal record; *een schoon ~ hebben* have a clean record; **–schop** (-pen) *m* penalty kick; **–schopgebied** (-en) *o* penalty area; **–tijd** *m* term of imprisonment; **–vervolging** *v* prosecution, criminal action; **–vordering** (-en) *v* criminal procedure (proceedings); **–werk** *o* ☞ imposition, detention work; **–wet** (-ten) *v* penal law; **–wetboek** (-en) *o* penal code; **–wetgeving** *v* penal legislation; **–zaak** (-zaken) *v* criminal case

strak I *aj* tight, taut, stiff; *fig* fixed [looks], set [face]; *een ~ touw* a taut (tight) rope; **II** *ad ~ aanhalen* tighten, tauten [a rope]; *~ aankijken* look fixedly at; **–heid** *v* tightness, stiffness; fixedness [of his gaze]

'strak(je)s 1 presently, by and by; 2 just now, a little while ago; *tot ~!* so long!

'stralen (straalde, h. gestraald) *vi* beam, shine, radiate[2]; **'stralenbundel** (-s) *m* pencil of rays, beam; **'stralend** radiant; **'stralenkrans** (-en) *m* aureole, nimbus, halo; **'straling** (-en) *v* radiation; **'stralingsgevaar** *o* radiation danger; **–gordel** (-s) *m* radiation belt; **–ziekte** *v* radiation illness

stram stiff, rigid; **–heid** *v* stiffness, rigidity

stra'miën *o* canvas

strand (-en) *o* beach; (k u s t) shore; *spelende kinderen op het ~* children playing on the sand(s); *op het ~ lopen* run aground; *op het ~ zetten* run ashore, beach; **–boulevard** [-bu.lə-va:r] (-s) *m* marine parade, (beach) promenade, sea-front; **–dief** (-dieven) *m = strandjut(ter)*; **'stranden** (strandde, is gestrand) *vi* strand, run aground; *fig* come to grief (upon *op*); **'strandgoed** (-eren) *o* wrecked goods, wreck, jetsam, flotsam; **–hotel** (-s) *o* sea-front hotel; **–ing** (-en) *v* ⚓ stranding, grounding; **–jut(ter)** (-jutten en -jutters) *m* wrecker, beachcomber; **–kleding** *v* beach wear; **–loper** (-s) *m* 🐦 sanderling; **–piama, –pyjama** ('s) *m* beach pyjamas; **–schoenen** *mv* sand-shoes; **–stoel** (-en) *m* beach chair; (g e v l o c h t e n) beehive chair; **–vond** *m = strandgoed*; **–vonder** (-s) *v* receiver of wreck, wreck-master

stra'patsen *mv* antics; *~ maken* [*fig*] be extravagant

stra'teeg (-tegen) *m* strategist; **strate'gie** [-'ʒi., -'ɡi.] (-ieën) *v* strategy, strategics; **stra'tegisch** strategic(al)

'stratemaker (-s) *m* roadman, pavier, paviour

stratifi'catie [-'ka.(t)si.] *v* stratification

strato'sfeer *v* stratosphere

'streber (-s) *m* careerist, go-getter

streed (streden) V.T. v. *strijden*

'streefcijfer (-s) *o* target figure, target; **–datum** (-s en -data) *m* target date

1 streek (streken) 1 *v* stroke [with the pen, of

the bow on a stringed instrument &]; tract; district, region, part of the country; point [of the compass]; 2 *m* & *v* (l i s t, p o e t s) trick; *dat is net een ~ voor hem* it is just like him; *gekke streken* foolish pranks, tomfoolery; *een gemene* (*smerige*) *~* a dirty trick; *een stomme ~* a stupid move; *we zullen hem die streken wel afleren* we shall teach him; *lange streken maken* (*bij het schaatsen*) skate with long strokes; *een ~ uithalen* play a trick; ● *i n deze ~* in this region, in these parts; *in de ~ van de lever* in the region of the liver; *weer o p ~ komen* get into one's stride again; *goed op ~ zijn* be in splendid form; *morgen zijn we weer op ~* to-morrow we shall be in the old groove again; *hij was helemaal v a n ~* he was quite upset; *mijn maag is van ~* my stomach is out of order; *dat heeft hem van ~ gebracht* that's what has upset him

2 streek (streken) V.T. v. *strijken*

'streekplan (-nen) *o* regional plan; **–roman** (-s) *m* regional novel; **–taal** (-talen) *v* dialect

streep (strepen) *v* stripe, streak, stroke, dash, line; *A—* [g e l e z e n: A ~] A— A dash; *dat was voor hem een ~ door de rekening* there he was out in his calculations; *er loopt bij hem een ~ door* he has a tile loose; *er maar een ~ door halen* strike it out, cancel it[2]; *ergens een ~ onder zetten* let bygones be bygones, have done with sth.; *op zijn strepen staan* pull rank on sbd.; **–je** (-s) *o* dash; *een ~ vóór hebben* be the favourite; **'streepjesbroek** (-en) *v* striped trousers; **–goed** *o* striped material

'strekdam (-men) *m* breakwater

'streken V.T. meerv. v. *strijken*

'strekken (strekte, h. gestrekt) **I** *vi* stretch, reach, extend; *per ~de meter* per running meter; *~ om...* serve to...; *~de tot het welslagen van de onderneming* tending (conducive) to the succes of the enterprise; zie ook: *eer, schande* &; **II** *vt* stretch, extend; **III** *vr zich ~* stretch oneself [in the grass &]; **–king** *v* tendency, purport, drift; *de ~ hebbend om...* purporting to...; *van dezelfde ~* of the same tenor; in the same vein

streks *aj ~e steen* stretcher

'strekspier (-en) *v* (ex)tensor

'strelen (streelde, h. gestreeld) *vt* stroke, caress; *fig* flatter; *dat streelt zijn ijdelheid* it tickles his vanity; *de zinnen ~* gratify the senses; **–d** *fig* flattering; **'streling** (-en) *v* stroking, caress

'stremmen I (stremde, is gestremd) *vi* congeal, coagulate [of blood]; curdle [milk]; **II** (stremde, h. gestremd) *vt* 1 congeal, coagulate; curdle; 2 stop, obstruct, block [the traffic]; **–ming** (-en) *v* 1 congelation, coagulation; curdling; 2 obstruction, stoppage; **'stremsel** *o* (v. k a a s) rennet

1 streng (-en) *v* strand [of rope], skein [of yarn];

trace [for horse]
2 streng I *aj* 1 (i n 't a l g.) severe [look, discipline, sentence, master, winter &]; 2 (v a n u i t e r l ij k) severe, stern [countenance], austere [mien]; 3 (o p v a t t i n g) stern [ruler, treatment, rebuke, virtue, father]; rigid [justice, Catholics]; strict [parents, masters, discipline]; stringent [rules]; austere [morals]; rigorous [winter, execution of the law, definition]; close [examination]; **II** *ad* severely &; strictly [scientific]; closely [guarded]
'**strengel** (-s) *m* strand [of hair]
'**strengelen** (strengelde, h. gestrengeld) *vt* & *vr* twine, twist [about, round]; **–ling** (-en) *v* twining, twisting
'**strengheid** *v* severity, rigour, sternness
'**strepen** (streepte, h. gestreept) *vt* stripe, streak
'**streven** (streefde, h. gestreefd) **I** *vi* strive; ~ *naar* strive after (for), strain after, aim at, aspire after (to); *er naar* ~ *om...* strive to..., endeavour to...; *opzij* ~ emulate; **II** *o zijn* ~ his ambition, his study, his endeavours; *het zal mijn* ~ *zijn om...* it will be my study (my endeavour) to...
'**stribbeling** (-en) *v* = *strubbeling*
striem (-en) *v* stripe, wale, weal; '**striemen** (striemde, h. gestriemd) *vt* lash²
strijd (-en) *m* fight, combat, battle, conflict, contest, struggle; contention, strife; *inwendige* ~ inward struggle; *de* ~ *om het bestaan* the struggle for life; *de* ~ *aanbinden met* join issue with; *de* ~ *aanvaarden* (*met*) accept battle, join issue (with); *dat heeft een zware* ~ *gekost* it has been a hard fight; *de* ~ *opgeven* abandon the contest, throw up the sponge; ~ *voeren* (*tegen*) wage war (against); ● *i n* ~ *met de afspraak* (*met de regels*) contrary to our agreement (the rules); *in* ~ *met de waarheid* at variance with the truth; *die verklaringen zijn met elkaar in* ~ these statements clash; *o m* ~ *boden zij hun diensten aan* they vied with each other as to who should be the first to...; *t e n* ~*e trekken* go to war; *op, ten* ~*e!* on!; *z o n d e r* ~ without a fight, without a struggle; **–baar** capable of bearing arms, warlike; *fig* fighting, militant [spirit]; **–baarheid** *v* fighting spirit, militancy; **–bijl** (-en) *v* battle-axe, broad-axe; *de* ~ *begraven* bury the hatchet; '**strijden*** *vi* fight, combat, battle, struggle, contend; ~ *m e t* fight against (with); *fig* clash with, be contrary to...; ~ *t e g e n* fight against; ~ *v o o r* fight for; **II** *vt de goede strijd* ~ fight the good fight; **–d** fighting, contending; *de* ~*e kerk* the church militant; '**strijder** (-s) *m* fighter, combatant, warrior; '**strijdgenoot** (-noten) *m* brother in arms; **–gewoel** *o* turmoil of battle; **–ig** conflicting², *fig* discrepant, contradictory, contrary; ~ *met* contrary to,

incompatible with; **–igheid** (-heden) *v* contrariety; **–krachten** *mv* armed forces; **–kreet** (-kreten) *m* war-cry, war-whoop, slogan; **–leus, –leuze** (-leuzen) *v* battle-cry; zie ook: *strijdkreet*; **–lied** (-eren) *o* battle song, battle hymn; **–lust** *m* combativeness, pugnacity; **strijd'lustig** combative, pugnacious, militant; '**strijdmakker** (-s) *m* comrade in arms; **–middel** (-en) *o* weapon; **–perk** (-en) *o* lists, arena; *in het* ~ *treden* enter the lists; **–ros** (-sen) *o* war-horse, battle-horse; **–schrift** (-en) *o* controversial (polemic) pamphlet; **strijd'vaardig** ready to fight; **–heid** *v* readiness to fight; '**strijdvraag** (-vragen) *v* question at issue, issue; **–wagen** (-s) *m* chariot
strijk ~ *en zet* every moment, again and again; invariably [at 7 o'clock]; **strij'kage** (-[zə] (-s) *v* bow; ~*s maken* bow and scrape (to *voor*); '**strijkbout** (-en) *m* heater; **–concert** (-en) *o* concert for strings; **–deken** (-s) *v* ironing-cloth, ironing-blanket; **–elings** = *rakelings*; '**strijken*** **I** *vi* ~ *l a n g s...* brush past...; skim [the water]; *hij is m e t alle koopjes* (*prijzen*) *gaan* ~ he has snapped up all the bargains, the prizes were all scooped up by him; *hij is met de winst gaan* ~ he has scooped up the profits; *wij hebben gekaart, hij is alweer met de winst gaan* ~ he has swept the board; *de wind streek o v e r de velden* the wind swept the fields; *hij streek met de hand over het voorhoofd* he passed his hand across his brow; **II** *va* iron; **III** *vt* smooth [cloth]; iron [linen]; stroke [with the hand]; *een boot* ~ lower (get out) a boat; *de vlag* ~ strike (lower) the flag (one's colours); zie ook: *riem & vlag*; *een zeil* ~ lower a sail; *de zeilen* ~ strike sail; *het haar n a a r achteren* ~ smooth back one's hair; *hij streek haar o n d e r de kin* he chucked her under the chin; *kalk o p een muur* ~ spread plaster on a wall; *kreukels u i t het papier* ~ smooth out creases; **–er** (-s) *m de* ~*s ♩* the strings; '**strijkgeld** (-en) *o* lot money, premium; **–goed** *o* linen (clothes) to be ironed, [a pile of] ironing; **–ijzer** (-s) *o* flat-iron, iron; *elektrisch* ~ electric iron; **–instrument** (-en) *o* stringed instrument; *voor* ~ ook: for strings; **–je** (-s) *o* string band; **–kwartet** (-ten) *o* string(ed) quartet(te); **–licht** *o* floodlight; **–muziek** *v* string-music; **–orkest** (-en) *o* string orchestra, string band; **–plank** (-en) *v* ironing-board; **–stok** (-ken) *m* 1 ♩ bow, fiddlestick; 2 (b ij m a t e n) strickle, strike; *er blijft heel wat aan maat- en* ~ *hangen* much sticks to the fingers [of the officials]
strik (-ken) *m* 1 (o m t e v a n g e n) snare², noose, gin [to catch birds]; 2 (o p j a p o n & v a n l i n t) knot, bow; (i n s i g n e) favour; 3 (d a s j e) bow(-tie); *een* ~ *maken* make a knot;

~ken spannen lay snares²; *iem. een ~ spannen* lay a
snare for sbd.; *in zijn eigen ~ gevangen raken* be
caught in one's own trap; *hij haalde bijtijds zijn
hoofd uit de ~* he got his head out of the noose
in time; **–das** (-sen) *v* bow(-tie); **–je** (-s) *o*
bow; *(allerlei) ~s en kwikjes* gewgaws, fal-lals;
'strikken (strikte, h. gestrikt) *vt* 1 tie; 2
(v a n g e n) snare² [birds, gullible people]
strikt I *aj* strict, precise, rigorous; **II** *ad* strictly;
~ genomen strictly speaking; **–heid** *v* strictness,
precision
'strikvraag (-vragen) *v* catch
strip (-pen en -s) *m* strip; 〜 strip, tract;
(b e e l d v e r h a a l) comic strip; **–boek** (-en) *o*
comic (strip), picture-book; **'strippen** (stripte,
h. gestript) *vt* strip, stem [tobacco]; **F** strip, do
a striptease act; **'stripverhaal** (-halen) *o*
picture strip, comic strip
stro *o* straw; **–achtig** strawy; **–bed** (-den) *o*
straw-bed; **–bloem** (-en) *v* immortelle;
–blond flaxen; **–bos** (-sen) *m* bundle of
straw
strobo'scoop (-scopen) *m* stroboscope;
strobo'scopisch stroboscopic
'strobreed *iem. geen ~ in de weg leggen* not put the
slightest obstacle in sbd.'s way; **–dak** (-daken)
o thatched roof; **–dekker** (-s) *m* thatcher
stroef I *aj* stiff² [hinge, piston & translation];
harsh [features]; stern [countenance]; jerky
[verse]; **II** *ad* stiffly²; **–heid** *v* stiffness, harshness &
'strofe (-n) *v* strophe; **'strofisch** strophic
'strogeel straw-yellow, straw-coloured; **–halm**
(-en) *m* straw; *zich aan een ~ vasthouden* catch at
a straw; **–hoed** (-en) *m* straw hat, straw;
–huls (-hulzen) *v* straw case; **–karton** *o*
straw-board
'stroken (strookte, h. gestrookt) *vi ~ met* be in
keeping with
'strokenproef (-proeven) *v* galley-sheet, galley-
proof
'strokleurig straw-coloured; **–leger** (-s) *o* bed
of straw; **–man** (-nen) *m* man of straw,
dummy; **–mat** (-ten) *v* straw mat; **–matras**
(-sen) *v & o* straw mattress
'stromen (stroomde, h. en is gestroomd) *vi*
stream, flow; *~ van de regen* teem with rain; *~
naar [fig]* flock to; *het stroomt er naar toe* they are
flocking to the place; *de tranen stroomden haar
over de wangen* the tears streamed down her
cheeks; **–d** (-stroming [rain], running [water];
'stroming (-en) *v* current², *fig* trend
'strompelen (strompelde, h. en is gestrompeld)
vi stumble, hobble, totter
stronk (-en) *m* 1 (v. b o o m) stump, stub; 2 (v.
k o o l) stalk; 3 (v. a n d ij v i e) head
stront *m* **P** 1 excrement, muck; shit; 2 (r u z i e)

quarrel, squabble
'strontium ['stròntsi.üm] *o* strontium
'strontje (-s) *o* sty, stye
'strooibiljet (-ten) *o* handbill, leaflet, throw-
away; **–bus** (-sen) *v* dredger, sprinkler, castor
1 'strooien *aj* straw; *een ~ hoed* a straw hat
2 'strooien (strooide, h. gestrooid) **I** *vt* strew,
scatter [things], sprinkle [salt], dredge [sugar
&]; **II** *va* throw [nuts, apples &] to be scrambled for [on St. Nicholas' Eve]; **–er** (-s) *m*
(v o o r w e r p) dredger, sprinkler, castor;
'strooisel *o* litter; **'strooisuiker** *m* castor
sugar
strook (stroken) *v* strip [of cloth, paper, terri-
tory]; slip [of paper]; band, flounce [of a
dress]; counterfoil [of receipt &]; label [indicat-
ing address]; ⊢ tape [of recording telegraph]
stroom (stromen) *m* 1 (h e t s t r o m e n)
stream², current [of a river]; 2 ⚡ current; 3
(r i v i e r) stream, river; 4 *fig* flow [of words];
een ~ van mensen (tranen) a stream of people
(tears); *de ~ van zijn welsprekendheid* the tide of
his eloquence; ● *b ij stromen* in streams, in
torrents; *m e t de ~ meegaan* go with the stream;
o n d e r ~ ⚡ live [wire], charged; *niet onder ~* ⚡
dead; *o p ~ liggen* ⚓ be in mid-stream; *t e g e n de
~ inroeien* row against the stream; *vele gezinnen
zaten z o n d e r ~* many homes were without
power; **stroom'af(waarts)** down the river,
downstream; **'stroombed** (-den) *o* river-bed;
–draad (-draden) *m* electric wire; **–gebied**
(-en) *o* (river-)basin, water shed; **–kabel** (-s) *m*
electric (power) cable; **–kring** (-en) *m* circuit;
–levering *v* current supply; **–lijn** (-en) *v*
streamline; **'stroomlijnen** (stroomlijnde, h.
gestroomlijnd) *vt* streamline;
stroom'op(waarts) up the river, upstream;
'stroomsterkte (-n en -s) *v* ⚡ strength of
current; **–verbruik** *o* consumption of current,
current consumption; **–versnelling** (-en) *v*
rapid; **–wisselaar** (-s) *m* commutator
stroop (stropen) *v* 1 (d o n k e r) treacle; 2
(l i c h t) syrup; *iem. ~ om de mond smeren* butter
sbd. up; **–achtig** 1 treacly; 2 syrupy; **–je** (-s) *o*
syrup; **–kwast** (-en) *m met de ~ lopen* butter up
people; **'strooplikken** *va* toady; **–er** (-s) *m*
lickspittle, toady; **strooplikke'rij** *v* toadyism
'stroopnagel (-s) *m* hang nail, agnail
'strooppot (-ten) *m* treacle-pot; *met de ~ lopen*
butter up people
'strooptocht (-en) *m* predatory incursion, raid
'stroopwafel (-s) *v* treacle waffle
'strootje (-s) *o* 1 straw; 2 straw cigarette [in the
East]; *~ trekken* draw straws; *over een ~ vallen*
stumble at a straw
strop (-pen) *m & v* 1 (o m i e m a n d o p t e
h a n g e n) halter, rope; 2 (v o o r w i l d)

snare; 3 (a a n l a a r s) strap; 4 ⚓ strop; grummet; *dat is een* ~ (g e l d e l ij k n a d e e l) it is a bad loss, a bad bargain; ('n t e g e n-v a l l e r) bad luck!; *iem. de* ~ *om de hals doen* put the halter round sbd.'s neck; *hij werd veroordeeld tot de* ~ he was condemned to be hanged, he was sentenced to death by hanging

'**stropapier** *o* straw-paper

'**stropdas** (-sen) *v* 1 (o u d e r w e t s) stock; 2 (z e l f b i n d e r) knotted tie

'**stropen** (stroopte, h. gestroopt) **I** *vi* (v. w i l d-d i e v e n) poach; 2 (v. a n d e r e d i e v e n) maraud, pillage; **II** *vt* 1 strip [a branch of its leaves, a tree of its bark]; skin [an eel, a hare]; 2 poach [game]; **–er** (-s) *m* 1 poacher [of game]; 2 marauder

'**stroperig** treacly[2], syrupy[2]

strope'rij (-en) *v* 1 poaching [of game]; 2 marauding

'**stropop** (-pen) *v = stroman*

'**stroppen** (stropte, h. gestropt) *vt* snare

'**strosnijder** (-s) *m* straw-cutter

strot (-ten) *m* & *v* throat; *hij heeft zich de* ~ *afgesneden* he has cut his throat; **–klepje** (-s) *o* epiglottis; **–tehoofd** (-en) *o* larynx

'**strovuur** *o* 1 straw fire; 2 *fig* flash in the pan; **–wis** (-sen) *v* wisp of straw; **–zak** (-ken) *m* straw mattress, pallet

'**strubbeling** (-en) *v* difficulty, trouble; *dat zal* ~*en geven* there will be trouble

structu'reel structural; **structu'reren** (structureerde, h. gestructureerd) *vt* structure; **–ring** (-en) *v* structuring; **struc'tuur** (-turen) *v* structure [of organism]; texture[2] [of skin, a rock, a literary work]; **–formule** (-s) *v chem* structural formula

struif (struiven) *v* 1 contents of an egg; 2 omelet(te)

struik (-en) *m* bush, shrub

'**struikelblok** (-ken) *o* stumbling-block, obstacle; '**struikelen** (struikelde, h. en is gestruikeld) *vi* stumble, trip[2]; *wij* ~ *allen wel eens* we are all apt to trip; ~ *over een steen* be tripped up by a stone; ~ *over zijn eigen woorden* stumble over one's own words; *iem. doen* ~ trip sbd. up[2]; **–ling** (-en) *v* stumbling, stumble

'**struikgewas** (-sen) *o* shrubs, bushes, brushwood, scrub; **–hei(de)** *v* ⚘ ling; **–rover** (-s) *m* highwayman; **struikrove'rij** (-en) *v* highway robbery

1 struis *aj* robust, sturdy

2 struis (-en) *m* ⚘ = *struisvogel*; **–veer** (-veren) *v* ostrich feather, ostrich plume; **–vogel** (-s) *m* ostrich; **–vogelpolitiek** *v* ostrich policy

'**struma** *o* & *m* goitre

⊙ **stru'weel** (-welen) *o* shrubs

strych'nine [strix-] *v* en *o* strychnine

stuc [sty.k] *o* stucco

stu'deerkamer (-s) *v* study; **–lamp** (-en) *v* reading-lamp; **–vertrek** (-ken) *o = studeerkamer*; **stu'dent** (-en) *m* student, undergraduate; **stu'dentenbond** (-en) *m* student's association; **–corps** [-ko:r] (-corpora) *o* ± students' society, fraternity; **–grap** (-pen) *v* students' prank; **–haver** *v* nuts and raisins; **–jaren** *mv* college years; **–korps** (-en) *= studentencorps*; **–leven** *o* college life; **–lied** (-eren) *o* students' song; **–pastor** (-s) *m* college chaplain, student pastor; **–sociëteit** [-so.si.e.tεit] (-en) *v* students' club; **–tijd** *m* student days, college days; **studenti'koos** student-like; **stu'deren** (studeerde, h. gestudeerd) *vi* 1 study; read [for an examination, a degree]; be at college; 2 ♪ practise; *heeft hij aan de universiteit gestudeerd?* is he a University man?; *hij heeft in Winchester en Oxford gestudeerd* he was educated at W. and O.; *wij kunnen hem niet laten* ~ we cannot send him to college; *(in) talen* ~ study languages; *(in de) rechten (wiskunde &)* ~ study law (mathematics &); *erop* ~ *om...* study to...; *op de piano* ~ practise the piano; '**studie** (-s en -iën) *v* 1 (i n 't a l g.) study [also in painting & ♪]; 2 ☞ preparation [of lessons]; ~ *maken van* make a study of...; *i n* ~ *nemen* study [a proposal]; put [a play] in rehearsal; *o p* ~ *zijn* ☞ be at college (at school); *een man v a n* ~ a man of studious habits, a student; **–beurs** (-beurzen) *v* scholarship, bursary, exhibition, grant; **–boek** (-en) *o* text-book; **–cel** (-len) *v* carrel; **–commissie** (-s) *v* research committee, study group; **–fonds** (-en) *o* foundation; **–groep** (-en) *v* study group; working party; **–jaar** (-jaren) *o* year of study; *ik ben in het eerste* ~ I am in the first standard (form); **–kop** (-pen) *m* 1 [painter's] study of a head; 2 head for learning; **–kosten** *mv* college expenses; **–reis** (-reizen) *v* study tour; **–richting** (-en) *v* subject, branch of science; **–tijd** *m* years of study, college days; **–toelage** (-n) *v = studiebeurs*; **–vak** (-ken) *o* subject [of study]; **–verlof** *o* leave; **–vriend** (-en) *m* student (college) friend

'**studio** ('s) *m* studio

stuf *o* (india-)rubber, [ink-]eraser; '**stuffen** (stufte, h. gestuft) *vt* erase, rub out

stug I *aj* 1 stiff; 2 surly; **II** *ad* 1 stiffly; 2 surlily; **–heid** *v* 1 stiffness; 2 surliness

'**stuifmeel** *o* pollen; **–sneeuw** *v* flurry of snow; **–zand** *o* drift sand; **–zwam** (-men) *v* puff-ball

stuip (-en) *v* convulsion, fit; *fig* whim; ~*en* fits of infants; *zich een* ~ *lachen* be convulsed with laughter; *iem. de* ~*en op het lijf jagen* give sbd. a fit; **–achtig** convulsive; '**stuiptrekken** (stuiptrekte, h. gestuiptrekt) *vi* be (lie) in

convulsions; **–d** convulsive; **'stuiptrekking**
(-en) *v* convulsion, twitching

'stuit(been) (stuiten, -beenderen) *v* (*o*) coccyx

'stuiten I (stuitte, h. gestuit) *vt* 1 stop, check,
arrest, stem; 2 *fig* shock, offend; *het stuit me*
(*tegen de borst*) it goes against the grain with me;
II (stuitte, is gestuit) *vi* bounce [of a ball]; **~ o p**
moeilijkheden meet with difficulties; **~ t e g e n e e n**
muur strike a wall; **–d** offensive, shocking

'stuiter (-s) *m* big marble, taw

'stuiven* *vi* fly about; dash, rush; *het stuift* there
is a dust; *hij stoof de kamer in* he dashed into the
room; *hij stoof de kamer uit* he ran out of the
room

'stuiver (-s) *m* five cent piece, ✎ penny; ✎
stiver; *ik heb geen* **~** I have not got a stiver; *hij*
heeft een aardige (*mooie*) **~** *verdiend* he has earned
a pretty penny; **–sroman** (-s) *m* yellowback,
penny-dreadful, *Am* dime novel; **–stuk** (-ken)
o five cent piece; **–tje** (-s) *o* five cent piece; **~**
wisselen (play) puss in the corner

stuk I (-ken en -s) *o* 1 (v. g e h e e l) piece, part,
fragment; 2 (l a p) piece; 3 (v u u r m o n d)
gun, piece (of ordnance); 4 (s c h a a k s t u k)
piece, (chess-)man; 5 (d a m s c h ij f)
(draughts)man; 6 (s c h r i f t s t u k) paper,
document; article [in a periodical]; **$** security;
7 (t o n e e l s t u k) play, piece; 8 (s c h i l d e r-
s t u k) piece, picture; 9 (a a n t a l) head [of
cattle]; 10 **S** (m e i s j e) bint, crumpet; *inge-*
zonden **~** zie *ingezonden*; *een stout* **~** a bold feat;
een **~** *artiest* a bit of an artist; *een* **~** *neef van me* a
sort of cousin of mine; *een mooi* **~** *werk* a fine
piece of work; *een* **~** *wijn* a piece of wine; *een* **~**
zeep a piece (a cake) of soap; *een* **~** *of vijf* (*tien*)
four or five; nine or ten; *een* (*heel*) **~** *ouder*,
~ken *ouder* a good deal older; *een* **~** *verder* well
ahead; *een* **~** *beter* much better; **~**ken *en brokken*
odds and ends; *vijf gulden het* **~** five guilders
apiece; *vijftig* **~***s* fifty; *vijftig*
~*s vee* fifty head of cattle; *een* **~** *in zijn kraag*
hebben be in one's cups; *zijn* **~**ken *inzenden* send
in one's papers; ● *a a n é é n* **~** of one piece; *uren*
aan één **~** (*door*) for hours at a stretch, on end;
aan het **~** in the piece; *aan* **~**ken *breken* (*scheuren*
&) break (tear) to pieces; *b ij* **~**ken *en brokken*
piecemeal, bit by bit, piece by piece; *i n één* **~**
dóór at a stretch; *het schip sloeg in* **~**ken was
dashed to pieces; *o p* **~** *werken* work by the
piece; *op geen* **~**ken *na* not by a long way; *het is*
op geen **~**ken *na genoeg om te...* it is nothing like
enough to...; *op het* **~** *van politiek* in point of (in
the matter of) politics; *op* **~** *van zaken* after all;

when it came to the point; *op zijn* **~** *blijven*
staan keep (stick) to one's point; *zoveel p e r* **~** so
much apiece, each; *per* **~** *verkopen* sell by the
piece (singly, in ones); *u i t één* **~** of one piece;
hij is een man uit één **~** he is a plain, downright
fellow; *iem. v a n zijn* **~** *brengen* upset sbd.; *van*
zijn **~** *raken* be upset; *hij is klein van* **~** he is of
a small stature, short of stature; **~** *v o o r* **~** one
by one; **II** *aj* broken; out of order, in pieces,
gone to pieces

stuka'door (-s) *m* plasterer, stucco-worker;
–swerk *o* plastering, stucco(-work);

stuka'doren (stukadoorde, h. gestukadoord)
I *vt* plaster, stucco; **II** *vi* & *va* work in plaster

'stukbreken¹ *vt* break [it] to pieces; **–gaan¹** *vi*
break, go to pieces

'stukgoederen *mv* 1 **$** [textile] piece-goods;
2 ⚓ (l a d i n g) general cargo

'stukgooien¹ *vt* smash

'stukje (-s) *o* bit; *een kranig* **~** a fine feat; *van* **~**
tot beetje vertellen tell in detail

'stuklezen¹ *vt* read to pieces (to shreds)

'stukloon (-lonen) *o* piece-wage, task-wage

'stukmaken¹ *vt* break, smash; **–scheuren¹** *vt*
tear to pieces, tear up

'stuksgewijs, –gewijze piecemeal

'stukslaan¹ *vt* smash, knock to pieces; *veel geld*
~ make the money fly; **–smijten¹** *vt* smash;
–trappen¹ *vt* kick to pieces; **–vallen¹** *vi* fall to
pieces

'stukwerk *o* piece-work; **–er** (-s) *m* piece-
worker

stulp (-en) *v* hut, hovel; zie ook: *stolp*

'stulpen (stulpte, h. gestulpt) *vt* turn inside out

'stumper (-s) = *stumperd*; **–achtig** = *stumperig*;
'stumperd (-s) *m arme* **~**! poor wretch; poor
thing; **'stumperig** 1 bungling; 2 wretched

'stuntelen (stuntelde, h. gestunteld) *vi* fumble,
muff, bungle; **'stuntelig I** *aj* clumsy; **II** *ad*
clumsily

'stuntvliegen *o* stunt-flying, aerobatics; **–er** (-s)
m stunt man

stu'pide stupid; **stupidi'teit** (-en) *v* stupidity

'sturen (stuurde, h. gestuurd) **I** *vt* 1 (z e n d e n)
send; 2 (b e s t u r e n) steer [a ship, a motor-
car], drive [a car]; *iem. o m iets* **~** send sbd. for
sth.; *een kind de kamer u i t* **~** order a child out
of the room; *een speler uit het veld* **~** *sp* send
(order) a player off the field; **II** *vi* & *va* ⚓ steer;
drive; *wij stuurden n a a r Engeland* we steered
(our course) for England; *o m de dokter* **~** send
for the doctor; *ik zal er om* **~** I'll send for him

stut (-ten) *m* prop, support², stay²; **'stuthout** *o*

---

sprag; **'stutten** (stutte, h. gestut) *vt* prop, prop up, shore (up), support, buttress up, underpin[2]

stuur (sturen) *o* 1 helm, rudder [of a ship]; 2 handle-bar [of a bicycle]; 3 wheel [of a motor-car]; *links (rechts)* ~ ⚓ left-hand (right-hand) drive; **–as** (-sen) *v* ✗ steering shaft; **–bekrachtiging** *v* power steering; **–boord** *o* starboard; zie ook: *bakboord*; **–groep** (-en) *v* steering committee; **–huis** (-huizen) *o* ⚓ wheel-house; (v. a u t o) steering box; **–hut** (-ten) *v* ⚓ cockpit; **–inrichting** (-en) *v* steer-ing-gear; **–knuppel** (-s) *m* control stick, control column; **–kolom** (-men) *v* steering column; **–kunde** *v* cybernetics; **–loos** out of control; **–man** (-lui en -lieden) *m* ⚓ 1 steers-man, mate [chief, second]; man at the helm; 2 coxswain [of a boat], *sp* cox [of a racing boat]; *de beste stuurlui staan aan wal* bachelors' wives and maidens' children are well taught; **–manskunst** *v* (art of) navigation; **–mecha-nisme** (-n) *o* homing device; **–rad** (-raderen) *o* steering-wheel; **–reep** (-repen) *m* tiller-rope

stuurs surly, sour; **–heid** *v* surliness, sourness **'stuurslot** (-sloten) *o* steering (column) lock; **–stang** (-en) *v* 1 (v. f i e t s) handlebar; 2 ⚓ drag link; 3 ✈ **S** joy-stick; **–stoel** (-en) *m* ✈ pilot's seat; **–wiel** (-en) *o* steering wheel

stuw (-en) *m* weir, dam, barrage **stuwa'door** (-s) *m* ⚓ stevedore **stu'wage** [-ʒə] *v* ⚓ stowage **'stuwbekken** (-s), **–meer** (-meren) *o* storage lake; **–dam** (-men) *m* = *stuw*; **'stuwen** (stuwde, h. gestuwd) *vt* 1 ⚓ stow [the cargo]; 2 (v o o r t b e w e g e n) propel; 3 (t e g e n - h o u d e n) dam up [the water]; **–er** (-s) *m* ⚓ stower, stevedore; **'stuwing** (-en) *v* conges-tion; **'stuwkracht** (-en) *v* propulsive (impul-sive) force; *fig* driving power

'subagent ['süpa.ɣɛnt] (-en) *m* sub-agent **subal'tern** subaltern **'subcommissie** (-s) *v* subcommittee **'subcontinent** (-en) *o* subcontinent **'subdiaken** (-s) *m* subdeacon **su'biet I** *aj* sudden; **II** *ad* suddenly; at once **'subject** (-en) *o* subject; **subjec'tief** subjective; **subjectivi'teit** *v* subjectivity **su'bliem** sublime **subli'maat** (-maten) *o* 1 sublimate; 2 mercury chloride; **subli'meren** (sublimeerde, h. gesublimeerd) *vt* sublimate **subsidi'air** [-'ɪː r] in the alternative, with the alternative of **sub'sidie** (-s) *v* & *o* subsidy, subvention, grant; **subsidi'ëren** (subsidieerde, h. gesubsidieerd) *vt* subsidize; **–ring** *v* subsidization **sub'sonisch** subsonic **sub'stantie** [-(t)si.] (-s) *v* substance;

substanti'eel [-si.'e:l] substantial; **'substan-tief** (-tieven) *o* substantive, noun **substitu'eren** (substitueerde, h. gesubstitueerd) *vt* substitute; **substi'tutie** [-(t)si.] (-s) *v* substi-tution; **substi'tuut** (-tuten) *o* substitute; ✗ *m* Deputy Prosecutor; **~-griffier** ✗ Deputy Clerk **sub'straat** (-straten) *o* substrate, substratum **sub'tiel** subtle; **subtili'teit** (-en) *v* subtlety **'subtropen** *mv* subtropics; **sub'tropisch** subtropical **subver'sief** subversive **suc'ces** [sük'sɛs] (-sen) *o* success; *veel ~!* good luck!; ~ *hebben* score a success, be successful; *geen ~ hebben* meet with no success, be unsuc-cessful, fail, fall flat; *veel ~ hebben* score a great success, be a great success; *met ~* with good success, successfully; **–nummer** (-s) *o* hit **suc'cessie** (-s) *v* succession; **–belasting** (-en) *v* = *successierechten*; **succes'sief** successive; **suc'cessieoorlog** (-logen) *m* war of succes-sion; **–rechten**, *mv* death duties, *Am* inher-itance tax; **succes'sievelijk** successively **suc'cesstuk** (-ken) *o* hit; **–vol** successful **succu'lent** (-en) *m* succulent **'sudderen** (sudderde, h. gesudderd) *vi* simmer; *laten* ~ simmer **su'ède** [sy.'ɛ.də] *o* & *v* suède **suf** dazed [in the head]; muzzy [look]; dull, sleepy [boys]; **'suffen** (sufte, h. gesuft) *vi* doze; *zit je daar te* ~? are your wits wool-gathering?; **'suffer(d)** (-s) *m* duffer, muff, dullard; **'sufferig** doting; **'sufheid** *v* dullness **sugge'reren** (suggereerde, h. gesuggereerd) *vt* suggest [something]; **sug'gestie** (-s) *v* sugges-tion; **sugges'tief** suggestive **'suiker** *m* sugar; *gesponnen* ~ candy floss, spun sugar; ~ *doen in* sugar, sweeten; **–achtig** sugary; **–bakker** (-s) *m* confectioner; **–biet** (-en) *v* sugar-beet; **–boon** (-bonen) *v* 1 ⚜ French bean; 2 (s n o e p) sugar-plum; **–brood** (-broden) *o* (sugar-)loaf; **–cultuur** *v* sugar-culture; **'suikeren** (suikerde, h. gesuikerd) *vt* sugar, sweeten; **'suikererwt** (-en) *v* ⚜ sugar-pea; **–fabriek** (-en) *v* sugar factory; **–gehalte** *o* sugar content; **–glazuur** *o* icing [of cakes &]; **–goed** *o* confectionery, sweet-meats; **–houdend** containing sugar; **–ig** sugary; **–klontje** (-s) *o* sugar cube, lump of sugar; **–lepeltje** (-s) *o* sugar-spoon; **–meloen** (-en) *m* & *v* sweet melon; **–oogst** *m* sugar-crop; **–oom** (-s) *m* rich uncle, sugar daddy; **–patiënt** [-si.ɛnt] (-en) *m* diabetic; **–plantage** [-ʒə] (-s) *v* sugar-plantation, sugar-estate; **–pot** (-ten) *m* sugar-basin, sugar-bowl; **–produktie** [-si.] *v* sugar output; **–raffinaderij** (-en) *v* sugar-refinery; **–raffinadeur** (-s) *m* sugar-refiner; **–riet** *o* sugar-cane; **–schepje** (-s) *o* sugar-spoon; **–spin** (-nen) *v* candy floss, spun sugar; **–strooier** (-s) *m* sugar-caster; **–stroop** *v* molasses; **–tang** (-en) *v* sugar-tongs; **–tante** (-s) *v* rich aunt; **–tje** (-s) *o* sugar-plum; **–water** *o* sugar and water; **–werk** (-en) *o* sweetmeats, sweets, confectionery; **–zakje** (-s) *o* sugar-bag; **–ziek** diabetic; **–zieke** (-n) *m-v* diabetic; **–ziekte** *v* diabetes; *lijder aan* ~ diabetic; **–zoet** as sweet as sugar; sugary²

'suite ['sɥi.tə] (-s) *v* 1 suite (of rooms); 2 ◊ sequence [of cards]; 3 ♩ suite

'suizebollen (suizebolde, h. gesuizebold) *vi de klap deed hem* ~ the blow made his head reel

'suizelen (suizelde, h. gesuizeld) *vi* 1 rustle [of trees]; 2 (d u i z e l e n) = *suizebollen*; **–ling** (-en) *v* rustling; (d u i z e l i n g) fit of giddiness

'suizen (suisde, h. gesuisd) *vi* buzz, sough; sing, ring, tingle [of ears]; whisk (along, past &) [of motor-cars]; **–zing** (-en) *v* buzzing, tingling; ~ *in de oren* singing (ringing) in the ears

su'jet [sy.'ʒɛt] (-ten) *o* individual, person, fellow; *een gemeen* ~ a scallywag, a mean fellow

su'kade *v* candied peel

'sukkel (-s) 1 *m* simpleton; crock; 2 *v* poor soul; *aan de* ~ *zijn* be ailing; *arme* ~! poor wretch!; **–aar** (-s) *m* 1 (t.o.v. g e z o n d h e i d) valetudinarian; 2 = *sukkel*; **–draf** *m op een* ~*je* at a jog-trot; **'sukkelen** (sukkelde, h. en is gesukkeld) *vi* 1 be ailing; 2 (l o p e n) jog (along); *hij was al lang aan het* ~ he had been in indifferent health for a long time; *hij sukkelde a c h t e r zijn vader aan* he pottered in his father's wake; ~ *m e t zijn been* suffer from his leg; *die jongen sukkelt met rekenen* that boy is weak in arithmetic; **–d** ailing; **'sukkelgangetje** *o* jog-trot; *het gaat zo'n* ~ we are jogging along

sul (-len) *m* noodle, muff, simpleton, dunce, dolt, ninny, F softy, soft Johnny, juggins, flat

sul'faat (-faten) *o* sulphate

'sulfer *o* & *m* sulphur, brimstone

'sullen (sulde, h. gesuld) *vi* slide; **'sullig** soft, goody-goody; **–heid** *v* softness

'sultan (-s) *m* sultan; **sulta'naat** (-naten) *o* sultanate; **sul'tane** (-s) *v* sultana, sultaness

sum'mier summary, brief

'summum *o dat is het* ~ zie *toppunt*

'superbenzine *v* high-grade petrol; *Am* high-octane petrol (gasoline); **superi'eur I** *aj* superior; **II** (-en) *m* superior; ~*e v* Mother Superior [of a convent]; *zijn* ~*en* his superiors; **superiori'teit** *v* superiority; **'superlatief** (-tieven) *m* superlative; **'supermarkt** (-en) *v* supermarket; **super'sonisch** supersonic; **super'visie** [-zi.] *v* supervision, superintendence

supple'ment (-en) *o* supplement; **sup'pleren** (suppleerde, h. gesuppleerd) *vt* supplement,

make up the deficiency; **sup'pletie** [-(t)si.] *v* supplementary payment; completion; **supple'toir** [-'to:.r, -'tʋɑ.r], **supple'toor** ~*toire begroting* supplementary estimates

sup'poost (-en) *m* usher; attendant [of a museum]

sup'porter (-s) *m sp* supporter

supranatio'naal [-(t)si.] supra-national

suprema'tie [-'(t)si.] *v* supremacy

surnume'rair [sy:.rny.mə'rɛ:r] (-s) *m* supernumerary

Suri'name *o* Surinam

sur'plus [sy:r'ply.s] *o* surplus, excess; **$** margin, cover

sur'prise [-zə] (-s) *v* 1 surprise; 2 surprise present, surprise packet

surrea'lisme [sy:r-] *o* surrealism; **surrea'list** (-en) *m* surrealist; **–isch** surrealist

surro'gaat [sy:r-] (-gaten) *o* substitute

sursé'ance [sy:rse.'ãnsə] (-s) *v* delay, postponement; ~ *van betaling* **$** letter of licence, moratorium

surveil'lance [sy:rvɛi'ãnsə] *v* surveillance, supervision; (b ij e x a m e n) invigilation; **–wagen** (-s) *m* patrol car, *Am* prowl car, squad car; **surveil'lant** (-en) *m* 1 overseer; 2 ⊷ master on duty; (b ij e x a m e n) invigilator; **surveil'leren** (surveilleerde, h. gesurveilleerd) **I** *vt* keep an eye on, watch (over) [boys, students]; **II** *va* be on duty; (b ij e x a m e n) invigilate; (d o o r p o l i t i e) patrol (the roads)

sus'pect suspect(ed), suspicious

suspen'deren (suspendeerde, h. gesuspendeerd) *vt* suspend [clergymen, priests];

sus'pensie (-s) *v* suspension; **suspen'soir** [-'sʋa:r] (-s) *o* suspensory bandage, suspensor

'sussen (suste, h. gesust) *vt* hush [a child], soothe [a person]; *fig* hush up [an affair], pacify [one's conscience]

suze'rein (-en) *m* suzerain; **suzereini'teit** *v* suzerainty

'swastika ('s) *v* swastika, fylfot

'Swaziland *o* Swaziland

'syfilis ['si.-] *v* syphilis

syl'labe [sɪl-] (-n) *v* syllable

'syllabus ['sɪl-] (-sen en -bi) *m* syllabus

symbi'ose [sɪmbi.'o.zə] *v* symbiosis

symbo'liek [sɪm-] (-en) *v* symbolism; **sym'bolisch I** *aj* symbolic(al); ~*e betaling* token payment; **II** *ad* symbolically; **symboli'seren** [-'ze.-] (symboliseerde, h. gesymboliseerd) *vt* symbolize; **symbo'lisme** *o* symbolism; **sym'bool** (-bolen) *o* symbol, emblem

symfo'nie [sɪm-] (-ieën) *v* symphony; **–concert** (-en) *o* symphony concert; **–orkest** (-en) *o* symphony orchestra; **sym'fonisch** symphonic

symme′trie [sɪm-] *v* symmetry; **sym′metrisch** symmetric(al)

sympa′thetisch [sɪm] sympathetic [ink]; **sympa′thie** (-ieën) *v* fellow-feeling; sympathy (with *voor*); ~**ën en antipathieën** ook: likes and dislikes; **sympa′thiek I** *aj* congenial [surroundings]; likable [fellow], nice [man], attractive [woman]; engaging [trait]; soms: sympathetic; *hij was mij dadelijk* ~ I took to him at once; *hij werd mij* ~ I came to like him; **II** *aj* sympathetically; **sympathi′sant** [-′zɑnt] (-en) *m* sympathizer; **sym′pathisch** sympathetic [nervous system]; **sympathi′seren** [-′ze.-] (sympathiseerde, h. gesympathiseerd) *vi* sympathize; ~ *met* sympathize with, be in sympathy with

sympto′matisch [sɪm-] symptomatic (of *voor*); **symp′toom** (-tomen) *o* symptom

syna′goge, syna′goog [si.-] (-gogen) *v* synagogue

synchroni′satie [sɪŋgro.ni′za.(t)si.] (-s) *v* synchronization; **synchroni′seren** (synchroniseerde, h. gesynchroniseerd) *vt* synchronize; **syn′chroon** synchronous; **–klok** (-ken) *v* synchronous electric clock

synco′peren [sɪn-] (syncopeerde, h. gesyncopeerd) *vt* ♪ syncopate; **syn′copisch** ♪ syncopated

syndi′caat [sɪn-] (-caten) *o* syndicate, pool

syn′droom [sɪn-] (-dromen) *o* syndrome

synkroni′satie (-s) = *synchronisatie*; **synkroni′seren** ⇌ *synchroniseren*; **syn′kroon(-)** = *synchroon(-)*

sy′node [si.-] (-n en -s) *v* synod

syno′niem I *aj* synonymous; **II** (-en) *o* synonym

sy′nopsis [si.-] (-sen) *v* synopsis [*mv* synopses]

syn′tactisch [sɪn-] syntactic; **syn′taxis** *v* syntax

syn′these [sɪn′te.zə] (-s) *v* synthesis [*mv* syntheses]; **syn′thetisch I** *aj* synthetic [rubber, food &]; **II** *ad* synthetically

′Syrië *o* Syria; **′Syrisch I** *aj* Syrian; **II** *o* Syriac

sys′teem [si.s-] (-temen) *o* systeem; **–analist** (-en) *m* system analist; **–bouw** *m* system-building, prefabrication; **–kaart** (-en) *v* index card, filing card; **systema′tiek** *v* systematics; **syste′matisch** systematic; **systemati′seren** [-′ze.r seerd) *vt* systematize, codify

T

t [te.] (ʼs) *v* t

Taag *m* Tagus

taai tough [beefsteak, steel, clay &]; (v a n
v l o e i s t o f f e n) viscous, sticky, gluey; *fig*
tough [fellow], tenacious [memory], dogged
[determination]; (s a a i) dull; *het is een* ~ *boek* it
is dull reading; *hij is* ~ 1 he is a wiry fellow; 2
he is a tough customer; *hou je* ~! 1 keep
hearty!; 2 bear up!, never say die!; *een* ~ *gestel* a
tough constitution; *het is een* ~ *werkje* it is a dull
job; *zo* ~ *als leer* as tough as leather; **–heid** *v*
toughness; wiriness; *fig* tenacity

taaiˈtaai *m* & *o* ± gingerbread

taak (taken) *v* task; *een* ~ *opleggen* (*opgeven*) set
[sbd.] a task; *zich iets tot* ~ *stellen* zie *stellen* II;
–omschrijving (-en) *v* terms of reference;
–verdeling *v* assignment (allotment) of duties

taal (talen) *v* language, speech, tongue; ~ *noch*
teken neither word nor sign; *hij gaf* ~ *noch teken*
he neither spoke nor moved; *zonder* ~ *of teken*
te geven without (either) word or sign; *wel ter*
tale zijn be a fluent speaker; **–barrière** [-bɑr-
jɛːrə] (-s) *v* language barrier; **–beheersing** *v*
command (mastery) of language; **–boek** (-en)
o language-book, grammar; **–eigen** *o* idiom;
–fout (-en) *v* grammatical error; **–gebied**
(-en) *o* speech (linguistic) area; **–gebruik** *o*
[English &] usage; **–geleerde** (-n) *m* philologist, linguist; **–gevoel** *o* feeling (flair) for
language, linguistic instinct; **–grens**
(-grenzen) *v* language boundary; **–groep** (-en)
v language group (family); **–kaart** (-en) *v*
language (linguistic, dialect) map; **–kenner**
(-s) *m* linguist; **–kunde** *v* philology, linguistics; **taalˈkundig I** *aj* grammatical, philological; ~*e ontleding* parsing; **II** *ad* ~ *juist* gram-
matically correct; ~ *ontleden* parse; **–e** (-n) *m*
linguist, philologist; **ˈtaaloefening** (-en) *v*
grammatical exercise; **–onderwijs** *o* language
teaching; **–regel** (-s) *m* grammatical rule;
–schat *m* vocabulary; **–strijd** *m* language
conflict; **–studie** (-s en -diën) *v* study of
language(s); **–tje** (-s) *o* lingo, jargon, gibberish;
–wet (-ten) *v* linguistic law; **–wetenschap** *v*
science of language, linguistics, philology;
–zuiveraar (-s) *m* purist; **–zuivering** *v* purism

taan *v* tan; **–kleur** *v* tan-colour, tawny colour;
–kleurig tan-coloured, tawny

taart (-en) *v* fancy cake, tart; **–enbakker** (-s) *m*
confectioner; **–(e)schaal** (-schalen) *v* tart-
dish; **–(e)schep** (-pen) *v* tart-server; **–je** (-s) *o*
pastry, tartlet; ~s ook: fancy pastry

taˈbak (-ken) *m* tobacco; [*fig*] *ergens* ~ *van hebben*
F be fed up with sth.; **taˈbaksblad** (-bladen,
-bladeren en -blaren) *o* tobacco-leaf; **–bouw**
m, **–cultuur** *v* tobacco-culture, tobacco-
growing; **–doos** (-dozen) *v* tobacco-box;
–fabriek (-en) *v* tobacco-factory; **–handel** *m*
tobacco-trade; **–handelaar** (-s en -laren) *m*,
–koper (-s) *m* tobacco-dealer, tobacconist;
–onderneming (-en) *v* tobacco-plantation;
–pijp (-en) *v* tobacco-pipe; **–plant** (-en) *v*
tobacco-plant; **–plantage** [-ʒə] (-s) *v* tobacco-
plantation; **–planter** (-s) *m* tobacco-planter;
–pot (-ten) *m* tobacco-jar; **–pruim** (-en) *v*
quid; **–regie** [-re.ʒi.] *v* (tobacco) régie, tobacco
monopoly; **–veiling** (-en) *v* sale of tobacco;
–verkoper (-s) *m* tobacconist; **–zak** (-ken) *m*
tobacco-pouch

ˈtabbaard, ˈtabberd (-en en -s) *m* tabard,
gown, robe

taˈbel (-len) *v* table, schedule, index, list;
tabelˈlarisch I *aj* tabular, tabulated; **II** *ad* in
tabular form

taberˈnakel (-s en -en) *o* & *m* tabernacle; *het*
feest der ~*en* the Feast of Tabernacles; *ik zal je*
op je ~ *komen, je krijgt op je* ~ **F** I'll dust your
jacket

taˈbleau [-ˈblo.] (-s) *o* 1 scene; 2 (g e s c h o t e n
w i l d) bag; ~! *tableau!*, curtain!; ~ *vivant* [-ˈvã]
living picture

taˈblet (-ten) *v* & *o* 1 (p l a k) tablet; 2 (k o e k j e)
lozenge, square

taˈboe *aj, o* & *m* (-s) taboo; ~ *verklaren* taboo

taboeˈret (-ten) *m* tabouret, stool; (v o o r d e
v o e t e n) footstool

ˈtachtig eighty; ook: four score [years]; **–er** (-s)
m octogenarian, man of eighty; *de Tachtigers* the
writers of the eighties; **–jarig** of eighty years;
de Tachtigjarige Oorlog the Eighty Years' War;
–ste eightieth (part)

tact *m* tact; **ˈtacticus** (-ci) *m* tactician; **tacˈtiek**
v tactics

tacˈtiel tactile, tactual

ˈtactisch I *aj* tactical; **II** *ad* tactically; **ˈtactloos**
tactless, gauche; **–vol** tactful

taf (-fen) *m* & *o* taffeta

ˈtafel (-s en -en) *v* table [ook = index]; ⊙
board; *de groene* ~ 1 *sp* the green table, the
gaming-table; 2 (b e s t u u r s t a f e l) the
board-table; *hij deed de hele* ~ *lachen* he set the
table in a roar; *de Ronde T*~ the Round Table;
de T~ *des Heren* the Lord's Table; *de* ~*s* (*van*
vermenigvuldiging) the multiplication tables; *de*

~*en der wet* the tables of the law; *de ~ afnemen* (*afruimen*) clear the table, remove the cloth; *de ~ dekken* lay the cloth, set the table; *een goede ~ houden* keep a good table; *van een goede ~ houden* like a good dinner; *open ~ houden* keep open table; ● *a a n ~ gaan* go to table; *aan ~ zijn* (*zitten*) be at table; *aan de ~ gaan zitten* sit down at the table; *n a ~* after dinner; *o n d e r ~* during dinner; *iem. onder de ~ drinken* drink sbd. under the table; *iets t e r ~ brengen* bring sth. on the carpet (on the tapis), introduce sth.; *ter ~ liggen* lie on the table; *t o t de ~ des Heren naderen rk* go to Communion; *v a n ~ opstaan* rise from table; *gescheiden* (*scheiding*) *van ~ en bed* separated (separation) from bed and board; *v ó ó r ~* before dinner; **–appel** (-s en -en) *m* dessert apple; **–bel** (-len) *v* table-bell, hand-bell; **–berg** (-en) *m* table mountain; **–blad** (-bladen) *o* 1 table-leaf; 2 (o p p e r v l a k) table-top; **–buur** (-buren) *m* neighbour at table; **–dame** (-s) *v* partner (at table); **–dans** *m* table-tipping, table-turning; **–dekken** *o het ~* laying the table; **–dienen** *o* waiting at table; **–drank** (-en) *m* table-drink; **'tafelen** (tafelde, h. getafeld) *vi* sit (be) at table; **'tafelgast** (-en) *m* dinner guest; **–geld** (-en) *o* table-money, messing-allowance; **–gerei** *o* tableware, dinner-things; **–gesprek(ken)** *o* (*mv*) table-talk; **–goed** *o* table-linen, ✎ napery; **–heer** (-heren) *m* partner (at table); **–kleed** (-kleden) *o* table-cover; **–la(de)** (-laden, -laas, -la's) *v* table-drawer; **–laken** (-s) *o* table-cloth; **–land** (-en) *o* table-land, plateau; **–linnen** *o* (table) linen; **–loper** (-s) *m* (table-)runner; **–matje** (-s) *o* table-mat; **–poot** (-poten) *m* table-leg; **'Tafelronde** *v de ~* the Round Table; **–schel** (-len) *v* table-bell; **–schikking** (-en) *v* seating order (at table); **–schuier** (-s) *m* table-brush, crumb-brush; **–schuimer** (-s) *m* sponger; **–tennis** (-en) *o* table-tennis; **–toestel** (-len) *o* ☏ desk telephone; **–water** *o* table-water; **–wijn** (-en) *m* table-wine; **–zilver** *o* plate, silverware; **–zout** *o* table-salt; **–zuur** *o* pickles

tafe'reel (-relen) *o* picture, scene; *een... ~ van iets ophangen* give a... picture of it, paint in... colours

'taffen *aj* taffeta; **'tafzij(de)** *v* taffeta silk

tai'foen (-s) *m = tyfoon*

'taille ['tɑ(l)jə] (-s) *v* waist; **–band** (-en) *m* waistband; **tail'leren** (tailleerde, h. getailleerd) *vt* fit [a coat] at the waist (to the figure); *getailleerd ook*: well-cut, waisted; **tail'leur** (-s) *m* 1 (p e r s o o n) tailor; 2 (k o s t u u m) tailored dress; **'taillewijdte** (-n en -s) *v* waist (measurement)

tak (-ken) *m* 1 (v. b o o m) bough; branch[2] [of a

tree springing from bough; also of a river, of science &]; 2 (v. g e w e i) tine; ~ *van dienst* branch of (the) service; ~ *van sport* sport

'takel (-s) *m* & *o* pulley, tackle; **take'lage** [-ʒə] *v* tackle, rigging; **'takelblok** (-ken) *o* tackle; **'takelen** (takelde, h. getakeld) *vt* 1 ⚓ rig; 2 (o p h ij s e n) hoist (up); **'takelwagen** (-s) *m* breakdown lorry; **–werk** *o* tackling, rigging

'takje (-s) *o* twig, sprig; **'takkenbos** (-sen) *m* faggot; **'takkig** branchy

1 taks (-en) *m* 🐕 (German) badger-dog, dachshund

2 taks (-en) *m* & *v* share, portion

tal *o* number; *zonder ~* numberless, countless, without number; ~ *van* a great number of, numerous

'talen (taalde, h. getaald) *vi bij haalt er niet naar* he does not show the slightest wish for it

'talenkenner (-s) *m* linguist, polyglot; **–kennis** *v* knowledge of languages; **–knobbel** *m* bump of languages; **–practicum** (-s en -ca) *o* language laboratory

ta'lent (-en) *o* talent [= gift & weight, money]; **–enjacht** (-en) *v* talent scouting; **–loos** talentless; **–vol** talented, gifted

talg *m* sebum; **–klier** (-en) *v* sebaceous gland

'talhout (-en) *o* firewood; *zo mager als een ~* all skin and bones

'talie (-s) *v* tackle

'taling (-en) *m* teal

'talisman (-s) *m* talisman

talk *m* 1 (d e l f s t o f) talc; 2 (s m e e r) tallow; **–achtig** 1 talcous; 2 tallowy, tallowish; **–poeder, –poeier** *o* & *m* talcum powder; **–steen** *o* talc

'talloos numberless, countless, without number

'talmen (talmde, h. getalmd) *vi* loiter, linger, dawdle, delay; **–er** (-s) *m* loiterer, dawdler; **talme'rij** (-en) *v* lingering, loitering, dawdling, delay

'talmoed, 'talmud [-mu.t] *m* Talmud

ta'lon (-s) *m* talon; counterfoil [of cheque]

'talrijk numerous, multitudinous; **–heid** *v* numerousness

'talstelsel (-s) *o* notation

ta'lud [-'lyt] (-s) *o* slope

tam I *aj* tame, tamed, domesticated, domestic; *fig* tame; ~ *maken* domesticate [wild beast], tame[2] [a wild beast, a person]; **II** *ad* tamely[2]

tama'rinde (-n en -s) *v* tamarind

tama'risk (-en) *m* tamarisk

tam'boer (-s) *m* 🥁 drummer; **tam'boeren** (tamboerde, h. getamboerd) *vi ~ op iets* insist on sth. being done; lay stress on a fact; **tamboe'rijn** (-en) *m* ♪ tambourine, timbrel; **tam'boer-ma'joor** (-s) *m* drum-major

'tamelijk I *aj* fair, tolerable, passable; **II** *ad*

fairly, tolerably, passably; ~ *wel* pretty well

'tamheid *v* tameness²

tam'pon (-s) *m* tampon, plug; **tampon'neren** (tamponneerde, h. getamponneerd) *vt* tampon, plug

tam'tam (-s) *m* tomtom; *met veel* ~ with a great fuss, with a lot of noise

tand (-en) *m* tooth [of the mouth, a wheel, saw, comb, rake]; cog [of a wheel]; prong [of a fork]; *de* ~ *des tijds* the ravages of time; *~en krijgen* cut (its) teeth, be teething; *de ~en laten zien* show one's teeth; ● *iem. a a n de* ~ *voelen* put sbd. through his paces; interrogate sbd. [a prisoner, a suspect]; *m e t lange ~en eten* trifle with one's food; *t o t de ~en gewapend zijn* be armed to (up to) the teeth; zie ook: *hand, mond* &; **–arts** (-en) *m* dentist, dental surgeon; **–artsassistente** (-n) *v* dental surgery assistant; **–bederf** *o* dental decay, caries; **–been** *o* dentine; **–eloos** toothless [old woman]

'tandem ['tɛndəm] (-s) *m* tandem

'tanden (tandde, h. getand) *vt* ✗ tooth, indent, cog; **'tandenborstel** (-s) *m* tooth-brush; **–geknars** *o* gnashing of teeth; **'tanden-knarsen** (tandenknarste, h. getandenknarst) *vi* gnash one's teeth; **'tandenkrijgen** *o* dentition, teething; **–stoker** (-s) *m* toothpick; **'tandfor-mule** (-s) *v* dental formula; **–heelkunde** *v* dental surgery, dentistry; **tandheel'kundig** dental; **-e** (-n) *m* dentist, dental surgeon; **'tanding** *v* perforation [in philately]; **'tandkas** (-sen) *v* socket (of a tooth); **–pasta** ('s) *m* & *o* tooth-paste; **–pijn** (-en) *v* toothache; **–prothese** [-te.zə] (-n) *v* 1 (v e r v a n g i n g v. e c h t e t a n d e n d o o r k u n s t-t a n d e n) dental prosthesis; 2 (-n en -s) (k u n s t t a n d) denture; **–rad** (-raderen) *o* cog-wheel, toothed wheel; **–radbaan** (-banen) *v* rack-railway, cog-railway; **–steen** *o* & *m* scale, tartar; **–stelsel** (-s) *o* dentition; **–tech-nicus** (-ci) *m* dental technician; **–verzorging** *v* dental care; **–vlees** *o* gums; **–vulling** (-en) *v* filling, stopping, plug; **–wiel** (-en) *o* cog-wheel, toothed wheel; **–wortel** (-s) *m* root of a tooth; **–zenuw** (-en) *v* dental nerve

'tanen I (taande, is getaand) *vi* tan; *fig* fade, pale, tarnish, wane; *aan het* ~ *zijn* be fading, [renown] on the wane; *doen* ~ tarnish;
II (taande, h. getaand) *vt* tan

tang (-en) *v* 1 (pair of) tongs; 2 (k n ij p t a n g) pincers; nippers; 3 ⚕ forceps; *wat een* ~! what a shrew!; *dat slaat als een* ~ *op een varken* there's neither rhyme nor reason in it, that's neither here nor there; *ze ziet eruit om met geen* ~ *aan te pakken* you wouldn't touch her with a barge-pole; **–beweging** *v* ✗ pincer movement

'tangens ['taŋɡıns] (-en en -genten) *v* tangent

'tango ['taŋɡo.] ('s) *m* tango

'tangverlossing (-en) *v* ⚕ forceps delivery

'tanig tawny

tank [tɛŋk] (-s) *m* tank°; **–auto** [-o.to. en ɔuto.] ('s) *m* tank-car, tanker; **'tanken** (tankte, h. getankt) *vi* fill up; **'tanker** (-s) *m* ⚓ tanker; **'tankgracht** (-en) *v* antitank ditch; **–schip** (-schepen) tank-steamer, tanker; **–station** [-sta.(t)ʃɒn] (-s) *o* filling station; **–val** (-len) *v* tank trap; **–wagen** (-s) *m* 🚋 tanker, tanker lorry

tan'nine *v* & *o* tannin

'tantalusbeker (-s) *m* Tantalus cup; **–kwelling** (-en) *v* torment of Tantalus; tantalization

'tante (-s) *v* aunt; *een oude* ~ > an old woman; *och wat, je* ~ *!* **S** rats!

tanti'ème [-ti.'ɛ.mə] (-s) *o* bonus, royalty, percentage

Tanza'nia *o* Tanzania; **Tanzani'aan(s)** (-ianen) *m* (& *aj*) Tanzanian

tap (-pen) *m* 1 (k r a a n) tap; 2 (s p o n) bung; 3 ✗ tenon; 4 ⚙ & ✗ trunnion [of a gun, in steam-engine]; 5 = *tapkast*

'tapdans ['tɛp-] *m* tap-dance; **–er** (-s) *m* tap-dancer

'tapgat (-gaten) *o* 1 ✗ tap-hole; mortise; 2 bung-hole

ta'pijt (-en) *o* carpet; *op het* ~ *brengen* bring on the tapis (carpet); **–werker** (-s) *m* carpet-maker

tapi'oca *m* tapioca

tapir ['ta.pi:r] (-s) *m* tapir

tapisse'rie [-pi.sə-] (-ieën) *v* tapestry

tapissi'ère [-pi.si.'ɛ:rə] (-s) *v* furniture-van, pantechnicon

'tapkast (-en) *v* buffet, bar

'tappelings ~ *lopen langs* trickle down

'tappen (tapte, h. getapt) **I** *vt* tap [beer, rubber]; draw [beer]; *aardigheden (moppen)* ~ crack jokes; **II** *va* keep a public house; **–er** (-s) *m* publican; **tappe'rij** (-en) *v* public house, ale-house

taps tapering, conical; ~ *toelopen* taper

'taptemelk *v* skim-milk

'taptoe (-s) *v* ⚔ tattoo; *de* ~ *slaan* beat the tattoo

ta'puit (-en) *m* wheatear, chat

'tapverbod (-boden) *o* prohibition

ta'rantula ('s) *v* tarantula

'tarbot (-ten) *m* turbot

ta'rief (-rieven) *o* tariff; rate; (legal) fare [for cabs]; **–muur** (-muren) *m* tariff wall; **–werk** *o* piece-work; **ta'rievenoorlog** *m* tariff war, war of tariffs

'tarra *v* **$** tare

tar'taar, tar'tare *m* (b i e f s t u k) chopped raw beef

Tar'taar(s) (-taren) *m* (& *aj*) Tartar

'**tarten** (tartte, h. getart) *vt* challenge, defy; *het tart alle beschrijving* it beggars description; **–d** defiant
'**tarwe** *v* wheat; **–bloem** *v* flour of wheat; **–brood** (-broden) *o* wheaten bread; *een ~* a wheaten loaf; **–meel** *o* wheaten flour
1 tas (-sen) *m* (s t a p e l) heap, pile
2 tas (-sen) *v* bag, pouch, satchel
'**tassen** (taste, h. getast) *vt* heap (up), pile (up)
tast *m op de ~ zijn weg zoeken* grope one's way; '**tastbaar** tangible, palpable [lie]; **–heid** *v* palpableness, palpability, tangibleness, tangibility; '**tasten** (tastte, h. getast) **I** *vi* feel, grope, fumble (for *naar*); *in het duister ~* be in the dark; *in de zak ~* put one's hand into one's pocket, dive into one's pocket; *fig* dip into one's purse; **II** *vt* touch; *iem. in zijn eer ~* 1 cast a slur on sbd.'s honour; 2 appeal to sbd.'s sense of honour; *iem. in zijn gemoed ~* work on sbd.'s feelings; *iem. in zijn zwak ~* zie *zwak* **III**; **–er** (-s) *m* feeler; '**tastorgaan** (-ganen) *o* tentacle; **–zin** *m* (sense of) touch
Ta'taar(s) (-taren) = *Tartaar(s)*
'**tater** (-s) *m* **F** *hou je ~* stop chattering
tatoe'ëerder (-s) *m* tattooer, tattooist; **tatoe'ëren** (tatoeëerde, h. getatoeëerd) *vt* tattoo; **–ring** (-en) *v* 1 (h a n d e l i n g) tattooing; 2 (h e t g e t a t o e ë e r d e) tattoo
tautolo'gie (-ieën) *v* tautology; **tauto'logisch** tautological
taxa'meter (-s) *m* taximeter
taxa'teur (-s) *m* (official) appraiser, valuer; **ta'xatie** [-(t)si.] (-s en -tiën) *v* appraisement, appraisal, valuation; **–prijs** (-prijzen) *m* valuation price; *tegen ~* at a valuation; **–waarde** *v* appraised value; **ta'xeren** (taxeerde, h. getaxeerd) *vt* appraise, assess, value (at *op*)
'**taxi** ('s) *m* taxi-cab, taxi; **–chauffeur** [-ʃo.fø:r] (-s) *m* taxi-driver
'**taxiën** (taxiede, h. en is getaxied) *vi* taxi
'**taxistandplaats** (-en) *v* cab-stand
'**taxus(boom)** (taxussen, -bomen) *m* yew-tree
t.b.c. [te.be.'se.] = *tuberculose*
T.B.R. [te.be.'ɛr] = *terbeschikkingstelling van de regering* preventive detention
te [tə] 1 (v ó ó r p l a a t s n a a m) at, in; 2 (v ó ó r b i j v. n a a m w.) too; 3 (v ó ó r i n f i n i t i e f) to; *~ A.* at A.; *~ Londen* in London; *~ middernacht* at midnight; zie verder *bed, des* &
'**teakhout** ['ti.k-] *o* teak(-wood)
team [ti.m] (-s) *o* team; **–geest** *m* team spirit; **–work** *o* team-work
te'boekstellen (stelde te'boek, h. te'boekgesteld) *vt* record
'**technicus** (-ci) *m* 1 technician; 2 (v o o r b e p a a l d v a k) engineer; **tech'niek** (-en) *v*

1 (w e t e n s c h a p) technology, technics; 2 (b e d r e v e n h e i d) technique [of an artist, of piano-playing &]; 3 (m a n i e r, w e r k w ij z e) technique, method [of illustrating, printing]; 4 (a l s t a k v a n n ij v e r h e i d) [heat, illuminating, refrigerating &] engineering; '**technisch I** *aj* technical; technological [achievement, advance, know-how]; *een prachtige ~e prestatie* ook: a magnificent engineering achievement; *~e hogeschool* college (institute) of technology; *hogere ~e school* technical college; *lagere ~e school* technical school; *middelbaar ~e school* senior technical school, polytechnic; **II** *ad* technically; technologically [advanced]; **techno'craat** (-craten) *m* technocrat; **technocra'tie** [-'(t)si.] *v* technocracy; **technolo'gie** *v* technology; **techno'logisch** technological; **techno'loog** (-logen) *m* technologist
'**teckel** (-s) *m* ᵈᵉ dachshund
'**teddybeer** [-di.-] (-beren) *m* teddy bear
'**teder** = 1 *teer*; **–heid** *v* tenderness; delicacy
Te-'Deum [te.'de.üm] (-s) *o* Te Deum
teef (teven) *v* (v. h o n d) bitch
teek (teken) *v* tick
'**teelaarde** *v* (vegetable) mould; **–bal** (-len) *m* testis, testicle
teelt *v* cultivation, culture; breeding [of stock]; **–keus** *v* ♉ selective breeding; ᵈᵉ selective growing (cultivation)
1 teen (tenen) *v* osier, twig, withe
2 teen (tenen) *m* toe; *grote (kleine) ~* big (little) toe; *op de tenen lopen* walk on tiptoe; tiptoe; *iem. op de tenen trappen* tread on sbd.'s toes² (*fig* corns); *hij is gauw op zijn tenen getrapt* he is quick to take offence, he is touchy; *hij was erg op zijn tenen getrapt* he was very much huffed; **–ganger** (-s) *m* digitigrade; **–tje** (-s) *o een ~ knoflook* a clove of garlic
1 teer I *aj* tender [heart, subject], delicate [child, question]; **II** tenderly; *~ bemind* dearly loved
2 teer *m* & *o* tar; **–achtig** tarry
teerge'voelig I *aj* tender, delicate, sensitive; **II** *ad* tenderly; **–heid** *v* tenderness, delicacy, sensitiveness; **teer'hartig** tender-hearted; **–heid** *v* tender-heartedness; '**teerheid** *v* = *tederheid*
'**teerkwast** (-en) *m* tar-brush
'**teerling** (-en) *m* die; *de ~ is geworpen* the die is cast
'**teerpot** (-ten) *m* tar-pot; **–ton** (-nen) *v* tarbarrel; **–water** *o* tar-water; **–zeep** (-zepen) *v* tar-soap
'**tegel** (-s) *m* tile; **–bakker** (-s) *m* tile-maker; **–bakkerij** (-en) *v* tile-works
tege'lijk at the same time, at a time, at once; together; *niet allemaal ~* not all together; *hij is*

~ *de ...ste en de ...ste* ook: he is both the ...st and the ...st; **tegelijker'tijd** at the same time, zie ook: *tegelijk*

'**tegeltje** (-s) *o* (small) tile; *blauwe* ~*s* Dutch tiles; '**tegelvloer** (-en) *m* tiled pavement, tiled floor; **–werk** *o* tiles

tege'moetgaan[1] *vt* go to meet; *zijn ondergang (ongeluk)* ~ be heading for ruin (disaster)

tege'moetkomen[1] *vt* come to meet; *fig* meet (half-way); ~ *aan* cater for [a certain taste]; **–d** accommodating; **tege'moetkoming** (-en) *v* 1 accommodating spirit; 2 concession; 3 compensation, allowance

tege'moetlopen[1] *vt* go to meet; **–treden**[1] *vt* 1 go to meet; 2 meet [difficulties &]; **–zien**[1] *vt* look forward to [the future with confidence], await [your reply]

'**tegen I** *prep* 1 *eig & fig* against [the door &, the law &]; 2 (o m s t r e e k s) towards [the close of the week, evening &]; by [nine o'clock]; 3 (v o o r) at [the price]; 4 (i n r u i l v o o r) for; 5 (t e g e n o v e r) to, against; 6 (c o n t r a) & *sp* versus; *het is goed* ~ *brandwonden* it is good for burns; *er is* ~ *dat...* there is this against it that...; *wie is er* ~*?* who is against it?; *zijn ouders waren er* ~ his parents were opposed (were hostile) to it; *hij spreekt niet* ~ *mij* he does not speak to me; *tien* ~ *één* ten to one; *5000* ~ *verleden jaar 500* 5000 as against 500 last year; ~*... in* against...; zie ook: *hebben*; **II** *aj* in: (*ik ben*) ~ I'm against it; *de wind is* ~ the wind is against us; *ze zijn erg* ~ *bescherming* they are strongly opposed to protection; **III** *ad de wind* ~ *hebben* have the wind against one; **IV** *o het vóór en* ~ the pros and cons; **tegen'aan** against; '**tegenaanval** (-len) *m* counter-attack; *een* ~ *doen* counter-attack; **–beeld** (-en) *o* 1 antitype; 2 counterpart, pendant; **–bericht** (-en) *o* message to the contrary, $ advice to the contrary; *als wij geen* ~ *krijgen* unless we hear to the contrary, $ if you don't advise us to the contrary; **–beschuldiging** (-en) *v* counter-charge, recrimination; **–bevel** (-velen) *o* counter-order; **–bewijs** (-wijzen) *o* counter-proof, counter-evidence; **–bezoek** (-en) *o* return visit, return call; *een* ~ *brengen* return a visit (a call); **–bod** *o* counter-bid; **–deel** *o* contrary; **tegen'draads** against the grain; '**tegendruk** *m* counter-pressure; reaction; **–eis** (-en) *m* counter-claim

'**tegeneten**[2] *zich iets* ~ begin to loathe some food by eating too much of it; **–gaan**[2] *vt* go to meet; *fig* oppose, check

'**tegengesteld** *aj* opposite, contrary; *het* ~*e* the opposite, the contrary, the reverse; **–gewicht** (-en) *o* counter-weight; **–gif(t)** (-giffen, -giften) *o* antidote[2]; **–hanger** (-s) *m* counterpart[2]

'**tegenhouden**[2] *vt* stop, hold up [a horse &], arrest, retard, check [the progress of]; **–kammen**[2] *vt* backcomb, tease [hair]

'**tegenkandidaat** (-daten) *m* rival candidate, candidate of the opposition; *zonder* ~ unopposed; **–kanting** (-en) *v* opposition; ~ *vinden* meet with opposition; **–klacht** (-en) *v* counter-charge

'**tegenkomen**[2] *vt* meet [a person]; come across [a word &], encounter [a difficulty &]; **–lachen**[2] *vt* smile upon, smile at

'**tegenlichtopname** (-n) *v* against-the-light photograph, exposure against the sun, contre-jour picture; **–ligger** (-s) *m* ⚓ meeting ship; ⇔ oncoming car, approaching vehicle

'**tegenlopen**[2] *vt* go to meet; *alles loopt hem tegen* everything goes against him

'**tegenmaatregel** (-en) *m* countermeasure
'**tegenmaken**[2] *vt iem. iets* ~ put sbd. off sth.
'**tegenmijn** (-en) *v* ✕ countermine; **tegenna'tuurlijk** against nature, contrary to nature; unnatural; '**tegenoffensief** (-sieven) *o* counter-offensive; **–offerte** (-s en -n) *v* counter-offer; **tegen'op** *ergens* ~ *rijden* drive against sth.; *er niet* ~ *kunnen* not be able to cope; *daar kan niemand* ~ nobody can match that; (*ergens*) ~ *zien* dread, fear, shrink from, be reluctant; '**tegenorder** (-s) *v & o* counter-order

tegen'over opposite (to), over against, facing [each other, page 5]; vis-à-vis; *onze plichten* ~ *elkander* our duties towards each other; ~ *mij* [*gedraagt hij zich fatsoenlijk*] with me; *hier* ~ opposite, over the way; *schuin* ~, zie *schuin* **II**; *vlak* (*recht, dwars*) ~*... right opposite...*; **–gelegen** opposite, [house] facing [ours]; **–gesteld** *aj* opposed [characters]; opposite [directions]; *zij is het* ~*e* she is the opposite; *precies het* ~*e* quite the contrary; **–liggend** = *tegenovergelegen*; **tegen'overstaan** (stond tegen'over, h. tegen'overgestaan) *vi daar staat tegenover, dat...* on the other hand..., but then...; **–d** opposite; **tegen'overstellen** (stelde tegen'over, h. tegen'overgesteld) *vt* set [advantages] against [disadvantages]

'**tegenpartij** (-en) *v* antagonist, adversary, opponent, other party, other side; **–paus** (-en) *m* antipope; **–pool** (-polen) *v* antipole, opposite pole

---

[1],[2] V.T. en V.D. van dit werkwoord volgens het model: 1 **tege'moet**gaan, V.T. ging **tege'moet**, V.D. **tege'moet**gegaan. 2 '**tegen**kammen, V.T. kamde '**tegen**, V.D. '**tegen**gekamd. Zie voor de vormen onder het grondwoord, in dit voorbeeld: *gaan* en *kammen*. Bij sterke en onregelmatige werkwoorden wordt u verwezen naar de lijst achterin.

'tegenpraten[2] *vi* contradict, answer back

'tegenprestatie [-(t)si.] (-s) *v* (service in) return

'tegenpruttelen[2] *vi* grumble

'tegenrekening (-en) *v* contra account; **–slag** (-slagen) *m* reverse, set-back

'tegenspartelen[2] *vi* struggle, kick; *fig* jib; **–ling** (-en) *v* resistance

'tegenspeler (-s) *m* opponent; *fig* opposite number; **–spoed** *m* adversity; bad luck; **–spraak** *v* contradiction; *b ij de minste* ~ at the least contradiction; *i n* ~ *met...* in contradiction with; *in* ~ *komen met zichzelf* contradict oneself; *in* ~ *zijn met* collide (with); *z o n d e r* ~ 1 without (any) contradiction; 2 incontestably, indisputably

'tegenspreken[2] **I** *vt* 1 contradict; 2 answer back; *het bericht wordt tegengesproken* the report is contradicted; *elkaar* ~ contradict each other, be contradictory; **II** *vr zich* ~ contradict oneself; **–sputteren[2]** *vi* protest; **–staan[2]** *vt het staat mij tegen* I dislike it, I have an aversion to it; *fig* it is repugnant to me

'tegenstand *m* resistance, opposition; ~ *bieden* offer resistance, resist; *geen* ~ *bieden* make (offer) no resistance; **–er** (-s) *m* opponent, antagonist, adversary

'tegenstelling (-en) *v* contrast, antithesis, contradistinction, opposition; *in* ~ *met* as opposed to, as distinct from, in contrast with, contrary to [his habit, received ideas]

'tegenstem (-men) *v* 1 dissentient vote, adverse vote; 2 ♪ counterpart; 'tegenstemmen[2] *vi* vote against; **–er** (-s) *m* voter against [a motion &]

'tegenstreven[2] **I** *vt* resist, oppose; **II** *vi* resist; **–stribbelen[2]** *vi* struggle, kick; *fig* jib

tegen'strijdig contradictory [reports, feelings]; conflicting [emotions, opinions]; clashing [interests]; **–heid** (-heden) *v* contrariety, contradiction, discrepancy

'tegenstroom (-stromen) *m* 1 counter-current; 2 ✺ reverse current

'tegenvallen *vi* not come up to expectations; *het zal u* ~ you will be disappointed; you may find yourself mistaken; *je valt me lelijk tegen* I am sorely disappointed in you; **–er** (-s) *m* disappointment, come-down

'tegenvergif(t) (-giffen, -giften) *o* = *tegengif(t)*; **–voeter** (-s) *m* antipode[2]; **–voorstel** (-len) *o* counter-proposal; **–vordering** (-en) *v* counter-claim; **–vraag** (-vragen) *v* counter-question; **–waarde** *v* equivalent, counter-value; **–weer** *v* defence, resistance

'tegenwerken[2] *vt* work against, counteract, oppose, cross, thwart; **–king** (-en) *v* opposition

'tegenwerpen[2] *vt* object; **–ping** (-en) *v* objection

'tegenwicht (-en) *o* counterpoise[2], counterweight[2], counterbalance[2]; *een* ~ *vormen tegen...* counterbalance...; **–wind** *m* adverse wind, head wind

tegen'woordig **I** *aj* present; present-day [readers &], [the girls] of to-day; ~ *zijn bij...* be present at...; *onder de* ~*e omstandigheden* under existing circumstances; **II** *ad* at present, nowadays, these days; **–heid** *v* presence; ~ *van geest* presence of mind; *in* ~ *van...* in the presence of...

'tegenzang (-en) *m* antiphony; **–zet** (-ten) *m* counter-move; **–zin** *m* antipathy, aversion, dislike (of, for *in*); *een* ~ *hebben in...* dislike...; *een* ~ *krijgen in* take a dislike to; *met* ~ with a bad grace, reluctantly

'tegenzitten[2] *vi het zat me tegen* luck was against me, I was unlucky

te'goed (-en) **I** *o* $ [bank] balance; **II** *ad* ~ *hebben* have an outstanding claim [against sbd.]; *ik heb nog geld* ~ money is owing me; *ik heb nog geld van hem* ~ he owes me money

te'huis (-huizen) *o* home

teil (-en) *v* basin, pan, tub

teint (.nt] *v* & *o* complexion

'teisteren (teisterde, h. geteisterd) *vt* harass, ravage, visit

te'keergaan (ging te'keer, is te'keergegaan) *vi* **F** go on, take on, raise the roof; storm (at sbd. *tegen iem.*)

'teken (-s en -en) *o* 1 sign, token, mark; symptom [of a disease]; 2 (s i g n a a l) signal; *het* ~ *des kruises* the sign of the cross; *een* ~ *des tijds* a sign of the times; *een* ~ *aan de wand* the writing on the wall; *een slecht* ~ a bad omen; *iem. een* ~ *geven om...* make sbd. a sign to...; *motion sbd. to...*; ~ *van leven geven* give a sign of life; ● *i n het* ~ *van...* ★ in the sign of [Gemini]; *alles komt in het* ~ *van de bezuiniging te staan* retrenchment is the order of the day; *de organisatie staat in het* ~ *van de vrede* the keynote of the organization is peace; *o p een* ~ *van...* at (on) a sign from...; *t e n* ~ *van...* in token of..., as a token of... [mourning, respect &]

'tekenaap (-apen) *m* pantograph; 'tekenaar (-s) *m* drawer, designer, draughtsman; (v a n s p o t p r e n t e n) cartoonist; 'tekenacademie (-s en -iën) *v* drawing-academy;

---

[2] V.T. en V.D. van dit werkwoord volgens het model: 'tegenkammen, V.T. kamde 'tegen, V.D. 'tegengekamd. Zie voor de vormen onder het grondwoord, in dit voorbeeld: *kammen*. Bij sterke en onregelmatige werkwoorden wordt u verwezen naar de lijst achterin.

–achtig graphic, picturesque; **–behoeften** *mv* drawing-materials; **–boek** (-en) *o* drawing-book, sketch-book; **–bord** (-en) *o* drawing-board; **–doos** (-dozen) *v* box of drawing-materials; **'tekenen** (tekende, h. getekend) **I** *vt* 1 (n a t e k e n e n) draw², delineate²; 2 (o n d e r-t e k e n e n) sign; 3 (i n t e k e n e n) subscribe; 4 (m e r k e n) mark; *dat tekent hem* that's characteristic of him, that's just like him; *fijn getekende wenkbrauwen* delicately pencilled eyebrows; **II** *vi* & *va* 1 draw; 2 sign; *n a a r het leven ~* draw from (the) life; *v o o r gezien ~* visé, visa; *voor zes jaar ~* ⚔ sign for six years; *voor de ontvangst ~* sign for the receipt (of it); *voor hoeveel heb je getekend?* how much have you subscribed?; **III** *vr zich ~* sign oneself [X]; *ik heb de eer mij te ~* I remain, yours respectfully, X; **–d** characteristic (of *voor*); **'tekenfilm** (-s) *m* cartoon (picture, film); **–gereedschap** (-pen) *o* drawing-instruments; **–haak** (-haken) *m* (T-)square; **–ing** (-en) *v* 1 (v o o r l o p i g e s c h e t s) design [for a picture, of a building]; 2 (e i g e n a a r d i g e s t r e p i n g &) marking(s) [of a dog], pattern; 3 (g e t e k e n d b e e l d, l a n d s c h a p &) drawing; 4 (h e t o n d e r t e k e n e n) signing [of a letter &]; 5 (o n d e r t e k e n i n g) signature; *het hem ter ~ voorleggen* submit it to him for signature; *er begint ~ in te komen* things are taking shape; **–inkt** (-en) *m* drawing-ink; **–kamer** (-s) *v* drawing-office; **–krijt** *o* crayon, drawing-chalk; **–kunst** *v* art of drawing; **–leraar** (-s en -raren) *m* drawing-master; **–les** (-sen) *v* drawing-lesson; **–papier** *o* drawing-paper; **–pen** (-nen) *v* 1 (h o u d e r) crayon-holder, ✎ portcrayon; 2 (p e n) drawing-nib; **–plank** (-en) *v* drawing-board; **–portefeuille** [-fœyjə] (-s) *m* drawing-portfolio; **–potlood** (-loden) *o* drawing-pencil; **–school** (-scholen) *v* drawing-school; **–tafel** (-s) *v* drawing-table; **–voorbeeld** (-en) *o* drawing-copy; **–werk** *o* drawing

'tekkel (-s) *m* ⚔ dachshund

te'kort (-en) *o* shortage (of *aan*), [budget] deficit, deficiency, [budget, dollar &] gap; *een ~ aan werklieden* a shortage of hands; *een ~ aan werklieden hebben* ook: be short of hands; *het ~ op de handelsbalans* the trade gap; *een maandelijks ~ van £... blijft* a monthly gap of £... remains; **–koming** (-en) *v* shortcoming, failing, deficiency, imperfection

tekst (-en) *m* 1 text; (s a m e n h a n g) context; 2 letterpress [to a print, an engraving]; 3 ♪ words; 4 *RT* script; 5 (v. r e c l a m e) copy; 6 wording [on a packet of cigarettes]; *~ en uitleg geven* give chapter and verse (for *van*); *b ij de ~ blijven* stick to one's text; *v a n de ~ raken* lose

the thread of one's speech &; **–boekje** (-s) *ι* libretto, book (of words); **–kritiek** (-en) *v* textual criticism; **–schrijver** (-s) *m* 1 (v a n r e c l a m e) copy writer; 2 *RT* script writer; **–uitgave** (-n) *v* original text edition; **–verdraaiing** (-en) *v* false construction (put) upon a text; **–verklaring** (-en) *v* textual explanation; **–vervalsing** (-en) *v* falsification of a text

tel (-len) *m* count; *de ~ kwijt zijn* have lost count; *niet i n ~ zijn* be of no account; *hij is niet meer in ~* he is out of the running now; *in twee ~len* in two ticks, **F** in a jiffy; *o p zijn ~len passen* mind one's p's and q's; *als hij niet op zijn ~len past* if he is not careful

te'laatkomen (kwam te'laat, is te'laatgekomen) *vi* be late (for); **–er** (-s) *m* late-comer

te'lastlegging (-en) *v = tenlastelegging*

'telbaar numerable, countable

'telecamera ('s) *v* telecamera

'telecommunicatie [-(t)si.] *v* telecommunication

telefo'nade (-s) *v* (lengthy) phone call; **telefo'neren** (telefoneerde, h. getelefoneerd) *vt* & *vi* telephone, **F** phone; make a call, ring [sbd.], speak (be) on the telephone, call; **telefo'nie** *v* telephony; **tele'fonisch I** *aj* telephonic; telephone [bookings, calls &]; **II** *ad* telephonically, by (over the) telephone; **telefo'nist** (-en) *m* telephonist, telephone operator; **–e** (-n en -s) *v* telephone operator, telephone girl, switchboard girl, (female) telephonist; **tele'foon** (-s en -fonen) *m* telephone, **F** phone; *wij hebben ~* we are on the telephone; *de ~ aannemen* answer the telephone; *de ~ aan de haak hangen* hang up the receiver; *de ~ neerleggen* lay down the receiver; *de ~ van de haak nemen, de ~ opnemen* take off (unhook) the receiver; ● *a a n de ~* [she is] on the telephone; *aan de ~ blijven* hold the line, hold on; *p e r ~* by telephone, over the telephone; **–aansluiting** (-en) *v* telephonic connection; **–beantwoorder** (-s) *m* answer-phone machine; **–boek** (-en) *o* telephone directory, telephone book; **–cel** (-len) *v* call-box, telephone kiosk; **–centrale** (-s) *v* (telephone) exchange; **–dienst** *m* telephone service; **–district** (-en) *o* local exchange area; **–draad** (-draden) *m* telephone wire; **–gesprek** (-ken) *o* telephone call; conversation over the telephone, telephone conversation; **–gids** (-en) *m* = *telefoonboek*; **–juffrouw** (-en) *v* = *telefoniste*; **–net** (-ten) *o* telephone system (network); **–nummer** (-s) *o* telephone number; **–paal** (-palen) *m* telephone pole; **–tje** (-s) *o* (telephone) call; **–toestel** (-len) *o* telephone set; **–verbinding** (-en) *v* telephone connection;

(v e r k e e r t u s s e n l a n d e n &) telephone communication; **–verkeer** *o* telephone communication

'**telefoto** ('s) *v* telephotograph; **telefotogra'fie** *v* telephotography

telege'niek [-ʒe.'ni.k] telegenic

tele'**graaf** (-grafen) *m* telegraph; *per* ~ by wire; **–draad** (-draden) *m* telegraph wire; **–kabel** (-s) *m* telegraph cable; **–kantoor** (-toren) *o* telegraph office; **–net** (-ten) *o* telegraph system; **–paal** (-palen) *m* telegraph pole; **–toestel** (-len) *o* telegraphic apparatus; **telegra'feren** (telegrafeerde, h. getelegrafeerd) *vt* & *vi* telegraph, wire, cable; **telegra'fie** *v* telegraphy; **tele'grafisch I** *aj* telegraphic; **II** *ad* telegraphically, by wire; **telegra'fist(e)** (-fisten) *m(-v)* telegraphist, (telegraph) operator

tele'**gram** (-men) *o* telegram, wire, cablegram; ~ *met betaald antwoord* reply-paid telegram; **–adres** (-sen) *o* telegraphic address; **–besteller** (-s) *m* telegraph messenger, telegraph boy; **–formulier** (-en) *o* telegram form, telegraph form; **–stijl** *m* telegraphese

teleki'nese [s = z] *v* telekinese

'**telelens** (-lenzen) *v* telelens

'**telen** (teelde, h. geteeld) *vt* 1 breed, rear, raise [animals]; 2 grow, cultivate [plants]

tele'**paat** (-paten) *m* telepathist; **telepa'thie** *v* telepathy; **tele'pathisch** telepathic

'**teler** (-s) *m* 1 (v. v e e) breeder; 2 (v. p l a n -t e n) grower

tele'**scoop** (-scopen) *m* telescope; **tele'scopisch** telescopic

te'**leurstellen** (stelde te'leur, h. te'leurgesteld) *vt* disappoint [a person, hope &]; *teleurgesteld over* disappointed at (with); **–ling** (-en) *v* disappointment (at, with *over*)

tele'**visie** [s = z] *v* television, **F** telly; *op de* ~, *per* ~, *voor de* ~ on television; *per* ~ *overbrengen* (*uitzenden*) televise; **–antenne** (-s) *v* television aerial (antenna); **–beeld** (-en) *o* television picture; **–camera** ('s) *v* television camera; **–kanaal** (-nalen) *o* television channel; **–kijker** (-s) *m* television viewer, televiewer; **–mast** (-en) *m* television mast; **–omroeper** (-s) *m* television announcer; **–programma** ('s) *o* television programme, *Am* telecast; **–scherm** *o* television screen; **–spel** (-spelen) *o*, **–stuk** (-ken) *o* television play; **–toestel** (-len) *o* television set; **–uitzending** (-en) *v* television broadcast, telecast; **–zender** (-s) *m* television transmitter; television broadcasting station

'**telex** (-en) *m* 1 (t o e s t e l) teleprinter; 2 (d i e n s t, n e t) telex

telg (-en) *m-v* descendant, scion, shoot; *zijn* ~ *en ook*: his offspring

'**telgang** *m* ambling gait, amble; **–er** (-s) *m* ambling horse

'**teling** *v* 1 breeding [of animals]; 2 growing, cultivation [of plants]

'**telkenmale** = *telkens*; '**telkens** 1 (v o o r t -d u r e n d) again and again, at every turn; 2 (i e d e r e k e e r) every time, each time; ~ *als*, ~ *wanneer* whenever, every time

'**tellen** (telde, h. geteld) **I** *vt* 1 count; 2 (t e n g e t a l e z i j n v a n) number; *dat telt hij niet* he makes no account of it; *iets licht* ~ make little account of sth., make light of sth.; *hij kijkt of hij geen tien kan* ~ he looks as if he could not say bo to a goose; *wij* ~ *hem onder onze vrienden* we count (number, reckon) him among our friends; *hij wordt niet geteld* he doesn't count; *zijn dagen zijn geteld* his days are numbered; **II** *vi* & *va* count; *dat telt niet* that does not count; that goes for nothing; *dat telt b ij mij niet* that does not count (weigh) with me; *t o t 100* ~ count up to a hundred; *v o o r twee* ~ count as two; **–er** (-s) *m* 1 (p e r s o o n) counter, teller; 2 (v. b r e u k) numerator; '**telling** (-en) *v* count(ing); '**telmachine** [-ʃi.nə] (-s) *v* adding machine

te'**loorgaan** (ging te'loor, is te'loorgegaan) *vi* be lost, get lost

'**telpas** *m* amble

'**telraam** (-ramen) *o* counting-frame, abacus; **–woord** (-en) *o* numeral

'**tembaar** tamable; **–heid** *v* tamability

te'**meer** *ad* all the more

'**temen** (teemde, h. geteemd) *vi* drawl, whine; '**temerig** drawling, whining, **teme'rij** *v* drawling, whining

'**temmen** (temde, h. getemd) *vt* tame[2]; **–ming** *v* taming

'**tempel** (-s en -en) *m* temple, ☉ fane; **–bouw** *m* building of a (the) temple; **–dienst** (-en) *m* temple service; **tempe'lier** (-s en -en) *m* Knight Templar, templar; *hij drinkt als een* ~ he drinks like a fish; '**tempelridder** (-s) *m* Knight Templar

'**tempera** *v* tempera, distemper

tempera'**ment** (-en) *o* temperament, temper; **–vol** temperamental

tempera'**tuur** (-turen) *v* temperature; *zijn* ~ *opnemen* take his temperature; **–verhoging** (-en) *v* rise of temperature; **–verschil** (-len) *o* difference in temperature

'**temperen** (temperde, h. getemperd) *vt* 1 (m a t i g e n) temper[2] [the heat, one's austerity &]; deaden[2] [the sound, brightness]; damp[2] [fire, zeal]; soften [light, colours]; tone down[2] [the colouring, an expression]; 2 (d e b r o s -h e i d o n t n e m e n) temper [steel]; **–ring** (-en) *v* tempering, softening; '**tempermes**

(-sen) *o* palette-knife; **–oven** (-s) *m* tempering-furnace

'**tempo** ('s) *o* 1 (ook: tempi) ♩ time; 2 pace, tempo; *in een snel* ~ at a quick rate; *in zes* ~ '*s* ♩ in six movements; *het* ~ *aangeven* set the pace, mark the running; **tempo'reel** temporal; (t ij d e l ij k) temporary; **tempori'seren** [s = z] (temporiseerde, h. getemporiseerd) *vt* temporize

temp'tatie [-(t)si.] (-s en -tiën) *v* 1 (v e r z o e-k i n g) temptation; 2 (k w e l l i n g) vexation; **temp'teren** (tempteerde, h. getempteerd) *vt* 1 (i n v e r z o e k i n g b r e n g e n) tempt; 2 (p l a g e n) vex

ten at, to &; ~ *zesde*, ~ *zevende* & sixthly, in the sixth place, seventhly, in the seventh place &; zie verder *aanzien, bate* &

ten'dens (-en) *v* tendency, trend; **–roman** (-s) *m* novel with a purpose; **ten'dentie** [-(t)si.] (-s) *v* tendency; **tendenti'eus** [-si.'ø.s] tendentious

'**tender** (-s) *m* tender

ten'deren (tendeerde, h. getendeerd) *vi* tend, incline; show a tendency (to, toward)

'**tenderlocomotief** (-tieven) *v* tank-engine

ten'einde *cj* in order to

'**tenen** *aj* osier, wicker [basket]

te'neur *v* drift, tenor

'**tengel** (-s) *m* 1 lath; 2 **S** (h a n d) paw

'**tenger** slight, slender; ~ *gebouwd* slightly built; **–heid** *v* slenderness

te'nietdoen (deed te'niet, h. te'nietgedaan) *vt* nullify, annul, cancel, abolish; undo; bring (reduce) to naught, dash [sbd.'s hopes]; **–ing** (-en) *v* nullification, annulment; **te'nietgaan** (ging te'niet, is te'nietgegaan) *vi* come to nothing, perish

ten'lastelegging (-en) *v* charge, indictment

ten'minste at least

'**tennis** *o* (lawn-)tennis; *een partijtje* ~ a tennis game; **–arm** (-en) *m* tennis elbow (arm); **–baan** (-banen) *v* tennis-court; **–bal** (-len) *m* tennis-ball; **–racket** [-rkɔt] (-s) *o* & *v* tennis racket; **–schoen** (-en) *m* tennis shoe; '**tennissen** (tenniste, h. getennist) *vi* play (lawn-)tennis; '**tennisspeler** (-s) *m* tennis player; **–veld** (-en) *o* tennis-court(s); **–wedstrijd** (-en) *m* tennis match

te'nor [tɔ'no:r] (-s en -noren) *m* ♩ tenor; **–stem** (-men) *v* tenor voice, tenor; **–zanger** (-s) *m* tenor(-singer)

tent (-en) *v* 1 (⚓ & v a n I n d i a n e n &) tent; 2 (o p k e r m i s) booth; 3 ⚓ awning [on a ship]; 4 (v. r ij t u i g) tilt; 5 **F** (c a f é, d a n c i n g &) joint; *de* ~*en opslaan* pitch tents; *ergens zijn* ~*en opslaan* pitch one's tent somewhere; *in* ~*en (ondergebracht)* ook: under canvas; *hem uit zijn* ~ *lokken* draw him

ten'takel (-s) *m* tentacle

ten'tamen (-s en -mina) *o* preliminary examination; **F** prelim; **tentami'neren** (tentamineerde, h. getentamineerd) *vt* examine, give an examination

'**tentbewoner** (-s) *m* tent dweller; **–dak** (-daken) *o* pavilion roof; **–doek** (-en) *o* & *m* canvas, tent-cloth; **–enkamp** (-en) *o* camp of tents, tented camp

ten'teren (tenteerde, h. getenteerd) = *tentamineren*

'**tentharing** (-en) *m* tent-peg; **–luifel** (-s) *v* tent-fly

ten'toonspreiden (spreidde ten'toon, h. ten'toongespreid) *vt* display; **–ding** *v* display; **ten'toonstellen** (stelde ten'toon, h. ten'toongesteld) *vt* exhibit, show; **ten'toonstelling** (-en) *v* exhibition, show; **–sterrein** (-en) *o* exhibition ground(s)

'**tentpaal** (-palen) *m*, **–stok** (-ken) *m* tent-pole; **–wagen** (-s) *m* tilt-cart; **–zeil** *o* canvas

te'nue [tə'ny.] (-s en -uën) *o* & *v* dress, uniform; *in groot* ~ in full dress, in full uniform; *in klein* ~ in undress

ten'uitvoerbrenging, –legging (-en) *v* execution

'**tenzij** unless

'**tepel** (-s) *m* nipple; (v. z o o g d i e r) dug; teat [of udder]

ter at (in, to) the; zie ook: *aarde* &

ter'aardebestelling (-en) *v* burial, interment

terbe'schikkingstelling (-en) *v* ⚖ preventive detention (under the Mental Health Act, in *Br*)

ter'dege, ter'deeg properly, thoroughly, vigorously; well [aware of the fact]

ter'doodbrenging *v* execution

te'recht rightly, justly, with justice; *zij protesteren* ~ they are right (they are correct) to protest (in protesting); ~ *of ten onrechte* rightly or wrongly; ~ *zijn* be found; *het is weer* ~ it has been found; *ben ik hier* ~? am I right here?; *ben ik hier* ~ *bij X*? does X live here?; **te'rechtbrengen**[1] *vt het* ~ arrange matters; *ik kan hem niet* ~ I cannot 'place' him; *een zondaar* ~ reclaim a sinner; *er niets van* ~ make a mess of it; *er (heel) wat van* ~ make a success of it; **–helpen**[1] *vi* help on, set right; **–komen**[1] *vi* be found (again); *het zal wel* ~ it is sure to come

---

[1] V.T. en V.D. van dit werkwoord volgens het model: **te'recht**stellen, V.T. stelde **te'recht**, V.D. **te'recht**gesteld. Zie voor de vormen onder het grondwoord, in dit voorbeeld: *stellen*. Bij sterke en onregelmatige werkwoorden wordt u verwezen naar de lijst achterin.

right; *het zal van zelf wel* ~ it is sure to right itself; *het boek zal wel weer* ~ the book is sure to turn up some day; *de brief is niet terechtgekomen* the letter has not come to hand; *wat de betaling betreft, dat zal wel* ~ never mind about the payment, that will be all right; *hij zal wel* ~ he will make his way (in the world); he is sure to 'make good' after all; *in een moeras* ~ land in a bog; ~ *in de zakken van...* go to the pockets of...; *er komt niets van hem terecht* he will come to no good; *daar komt niets van terecht* it will come to nothing; **–staan**[1] *vi* be committed for trial, stand (one's) trial, be on (one's) trial

te'rechtstellen[1] *vt* execute; **–ling** (-en) *v* execution

te'rechtwijzen[1] *vt* 1 set right [sbd. who has lost his way]; 2 reprimand, reprove [a naughty child &]; **–zing** (-en) *v* reprimand, reproof

te'rechtzitting (-en) *v* session, sitting

1 'teren (teerde, h. geteerd) *vt* tar

2 'teren (teerde, h. geteerd) *vi achteruit* ~ be eating into one's capital; ~ *op* live on; *op eigen kosten* ~ pay one's way

'tergen (tergde, h. getergd) *vt* provoke, irritate, aggravate, tease, torment; **–d** provocative, provoking &; exasperating

ter'handstelling *v* handing over, delivery

'tering *v* 1 (u i t g a v e n) expense; 2 (z i e k t e) (pulmonary) consumption, phthisis; *de* ~ *hebbend* in consumption, consumptive; *de* ~ *krijgen* go into consumption; *de* ~ *naar de nering zetten* cut one's coat according to one's cloth; zie ook: *vliegend*; **–achtig** consumptive; **–lijder** (-s) *m* consumptive

ter'loops in passing, incidentally; ~ *gemaakte opmerkingen* incidental (off-hand) remarks

term (-en) *m* term [= limit & word]; *er zijn geen* ~*en voor* there are no grounds for it; *i n d e* ~*en vallen om* be liable to...; *in bedekte* ~*en* in veiled terms; *v o l g e n s d e* ~*en van de wet* within the meaning of the law

ter'miet (-en) *m* & *v* termite, white ant; **–enheuvel** (-s) *m* termite hill

ter'mijn (-en) *m* 1 (t ij d r u i m t e) term; 2 (a f b e t a l i n g s s o m) instalment; *de uiterste* ~ $ the latest time, the latest date (for delivery, for payment); *een* ~ *vaststellen* fix a time; • *b i n n e n d e vastgestelde* ~ within the time fixed; *i n* ~*en betalen* pay by (ook: in) instalments; *o p* ~ $ [securities] for the account; [goods] for future delivery; *op korte* ~ $ at short notice; *krediet op korte (lange)* ~ short (long)-term credit; **–affaires** [-fɛ:rəs] *mv* $

futures; **–betaling** (-en) *v = afbetaling*; **–handel** *m* $ (dealing in) futures; **–markt** (-en) *v* $ futures market

terminolo'gie (-ieën) *v* terminology, nomenclature; **termino'logisch** terminological

ter'nauwernood scarcely, barely, hardly, [escape] narrowly

ter'ne(d)er *ad* down; **ter'neerdrukken** (drukte ter'neer, h. ter'neergedrukt) *vt* depress, sadden; **ter'neergeslagen** cast down, dejected, low-spirited; **ter'neerslaan** (sloeg ter'neer, h. ter'neergeslagen) *vt* cast down, dishearten, depress

terp (-en) *m* mound, hill

terpen'tijn *m* 1 (h a r s) turpentine; 2 (o l i e) oil of turpentine, turpentine, **F** turps

'terra terra-cotta; **terra'cotta I** *v* & *o* terra cotta; **II** *aj* terra-cotta

ter'rarium (-s en -ia) *o* terrarium

ter'ras (-sen) *o* 1 terrace; 2 (v. c a f é) pavement; **–bouw** *m* terrace cultivation; **–vormig** terraced

ter'rein (-en) *o* ground, plot [of land]; (building-)site; ✠ terrain; *fig* domain, province, field; *open* ~ open ground; *het* ~ *verkennen* ✠ reconnoitre; *fig* see how the land lies; ~ *verliezen* lose ground; ~ *winnen* gain ground[2]; *op bekend* ~ *zijn* be on familiar ground; *daar was je op gevaarlijk* ~ you were on dangerous ground; *op internationaal* ~ in the international field; **–gesteldheid** *v* state, condition of the ground; **–rit** (-ten) *m* cross country; **–verkenning** *v* reconnoitring, preliminary survey; **–wedstrijd** (-en) *m* (v o o r m o t o r e n) motocross; **–winst** (-en) *v* gain of ground

ter'reur *v* (reign of) terror; *de T*~ the (Reign of) Terror; *daden van* ~ acts of terrorism, terrorist acts

'terriër (-s) *m* ᵅ terrier

ter'rine (-s) *v* tureen

terri'toir [-'tʋa:r] (-s) *o*, **–'toor** (-toren) *o = territorium*; **territori'aal** territorial; **terri'torium** (-s en -ia) *o* territory

terrori'satie [-'za.(t)si.] (-s) *v* terrorization; **terrori'seren** (terroriseerde, h. geterroriseerd) *vt* terrorize; **terro'risme** *o* terrorism; **–ist(isch)** (-en) *m* (& *aj*) terrorist

ter'sluik(s) stealthily, by stealth, on the sly

ter'stond directly, immediately, at once, forthwith

'tertia [-tsi.a.] ('s) *v* $ third of exchange

terti'air [tɛrtsi.'ɛ:r] tertiary

---

[1] V.T. en V.D. van dit werkwoord volgens het model: **te'recht**stellen, V.T. stelde **te'recht**, V.D. **te'recht**gesteld. Zie voor de vormen onder het grondwoord, in dit voorbeeld: *stellen*. Bij sterke en onregelmatige werkwoorden wordt u verwezen naar de lijst achterin.

terts (-en) *v* ♩ third; *grote* (*kleine*) ~ ♩ major (minor) third

te'rug back, backward; ~*!* stand back!, back there!; *30 jaar* ~ thirty years back, thirty years ago; *ik heb het* (*boek*) ~ I've got it (the book) back; *heb je van een gulden* ~? can you change a guilder?; *ik heb niet* ~ (*van een gulden*) I've no change (out of a guilder); *daar had hij niet van* ~ [*fig*] he did not know what to say to that; *hij kan niet meer* ~ he can't go back on it; *ik moet het* (*boek*) ~ I want it (the book) back; *ze zijn* ~ they have returned, they are back (again); **–begeven** (begaf te'rug, h. te'rugbegeven) *zich* ~ return; **–bekomen**[1] *vt* get back; **–bellen**[1] *vt* ☏ ring back

te'rugbetaalbaar repayable; **te'rugbetalen**[1] *vt* pay back, repay, refund; **–ling** (-en) *v* repayment [to a person]; withdrawal [from a bank]

te'rugblik *m* look(ing) backward, retrospective view, retrospection; retrospect; *een* ~ *werpen op* look back on; **te'rugblikken**[1] *vi* look back (on, to *op*)

te'rugbrengen[1] *vt* bring (take) back; *tot op...* ~ reduce to...; **–deinzen**[1] *vi* shrink back; (*niet*) ~ *voor...* (not) shrink from...; *voor niets* ~ ook: stick (stop) at nothing; **–denken**[1] I *vi* ~ *aan* recall (to mind); II *vr zich* ~ *in die toestand* think oneself back into that state; **–doen**[1] *vt iets* ~ do sth. in return; **–draaien**[1] *vt* turn back, put back; **–drijven**[1] *vt* drive back, repulse, repel; **–dringen**[1] *vt* drive back, push back, repel; force back [tears]; **–eisen**[1] *vt* reclaim, demand back

te'ruggaaf = *teruggave*

te'ruggaan[1] *vi* 1 go back, return; 2 recede, go down [prices]; *enige jaren* ~ go back a few years; **te'ruggang** *m* 1 going back; 2 (v e r v a l) decay; 3 $ fall [in prices]

te'ruggave *v* return, restitution

te'ruggetrokken retiring, keeping oneself to oneself, retired [life]; **–heid** *v* retirement

te'ruggeven[1] I *vt* give back, return, restore; II *va kunt u van een gulden* ~? can you let me have my change out of a guilder?; **–grijpen**[1] *vi* ~ *op* revert to, hark back to; **–groeten**[1] *vt* & *vi* return a salute (salutation, greeting); acknowledge sbd.'s bow; ※ acknowledge (return) a salute; **–halen**[1] *vt* fetch back

te'rughouden[1] *vt* retain, hold back [wages]; *iem. van iets* ~ restrain sbd. (hold sbd. back) from doing sth.; **terug'houdend** reserved, restrained; **–heid** *v* reserve, restraint; **te'rughouding** *v* reserve

te'rugjagen[1] *vt* drive back [a person &]

te'rugkaatsen[1] I *vt* strike back [a ball &]; throw back, reflect [sound, light, heat]; reverberate [sound, light]; (re-)echo [sound]; II *vi* rebound [of a ball]; be thrown back, be reflected; reverberate; (re-)echo; **–sing** (-en) *v* reflection, reverberation

te'rugkeer *m* coming back, return; **te'rugkeren** *vi* return, turn back; *op zijn schreden* ~ retrace one's steps

te'rugkomen *vi* return, come back; ~ *o p iets* return to the subject; ~ *v a n een besluit* go back on a decision; *ik ben ervan teruggekomen* I don't hold with it any longer; **te'rugkomst** *v* coming back, return

te'rugkoop *m* 1 buying back, repurchase; 2 (i n l o s s i n g) redemption; **te'rugkopen**[1] *vt* 1 buy back, repurchase; 2 (i n l o s s e n) redeem

te'rugkoppeling *v* ⚙ feed-back

te'rugkrabbelen (krabbelde te'rug, is te'ruggekrabbeld) *vi* go back on it (on the bargain), back out of it, cry off, back-pedal, draw in one's horns; **–krijgen**[1] *vt* get back; **–lopen**[1] *vi* 1 (i n 't a l g.) run (walk) back; 2 (v. w a t e r) run (flow) back; 3 $ (v. p r ij z e n &) recede, fall; 4 ※ (v. k a n o n) recoil

te'rugmarcheren[1] [-mɑrʃə: rə(n)] *vi* march back; **te'rugmars** *m* & *v* march back, march home

te'rugnemen[1] *vt* take back; *fig* withdraw, retract; *zijn woorden* ~ ook: eat one's words

te'rugreis (-reizen) *v* return-journey, journey back, ⚓ return-voyage, ⚓ voyage back; **te'rugreizen**[1] *vi* travel back, return

te'rugrijden[1] *vi* ride (drive) back

te'rugroepen[1] *vt* call back, recall; *teruggeroepen worden* 1 (i n 't a l g.) be called back; 2 (v a n a c t e u r) get a 'recall'; *in het geheugen* ~ recall (to mind), recapture [the past]; **–ping** *v* recall

te'rugschakelen *vi* ⚙ change down [from fourth to third]; **–schrijven**[1] *vi* & *vt* write in reply, write back; **–schrikken**[1] *vi* start back, recoil; (*niet*) ~ *voor* (not) shrink from

te'rugslaan[1] I *vt* 1 strike (hit) back; 2 ✕ back-fire [of an engine]; II *vt* strike back, return [the ball &]; beat back, repulse [the enemy]; **te'rugslag** *m* 1 repercussion [after impact]; 2 back-fire [of an engine]; back-stroke [of a piston]; 3 *fig* reaction, revulsion, repercussion, set-back

te'rugsnellen[1] *vi* hasten (hurry) back; **–spoelen**[1] *vt* rewind; **–springen**[1] *vi* start back, leap back [of person]; recoil, rebound

---

[1] V.T. en V.D. van dit werkwoord volgens het model: **te'rug**blikken, V.T. blikte **te'rug**, V.D. **te'rug**geblikt. Zie voor de vormen onder het grondwoord, in dit voorbeeld: *blikken*. Bij sterke en onregelmatige werkwoorden wordt u verwezen naar de lijst achterin.

[after impact]; recede [of chin, forehead &]

te'rugstoot (-stoten) *m* rebound, recoil; ⚔ recoil [of a gun], kick [of a rifle]

te'rugstorten[1] *vt* (g e l d) refund

te'rugstorten[1] **I** *vt* push back; *fig* repel; **II** *vi* ⚔ recoil [of a gun], kick [of a rifle]; –d repellent, repulsive, forbidding

te'rugstromen[1] *vi* flow back; –stuiten[1] *vi* rebound, recoil

te'rugtocht *m* 1 retreat; 2 = *terugreis*

te'rugtrappen[1] **I** *vi* 1 kick [him] back; 2 backpedal [on bike]; **II** *vt* kick back;
te'rugtraprem (-men) *v* back-pedalling brake [of a bicycle]

te'rugtreden[1] *vi* step back

te'rugtrekken[1] **I** *vt* pull back, draw back, withdraw[2] [one's hand, troops, a candidature, a remark]; retract[2] [its claws, a promise]; **II** *va* ⚔ retire, retreat, withdraw; ~ *op* ⚔ fall back on; **III** *vr zich* ~ retire [also: from business], withdraw; –king *v* retirement [from business], withdrawal [of troops]; retraction [of claws]; *fig* retractation [of a promise]

te'rugvallen[1] *vi* fall back[2]; –varen[1] *vi* sail back, return; –verlangen[1] **I** *vi* long to go back [to India &]; **II** *vt* want back; –vinden[1] *vt* find again, find; –vliegen[1] *vi* fly back; –vloeien[1] *vi* flow back; –voeren[1] *vt* carry back

te'rugvorderen[1] *vt* claim back, ask back; –ring (-en) *v* reclamation

te'rugvragen[1] *vt* ask back, ask for the return of

te'rugweg *m* way back

te'rugwerken[1] *vi* react; –d retroactive, reacting; ~*e kracht* retrospective (retroactive) effect; *een bepaling* ~*e kracht verlenen* make a provision retroactive; *salarisverhogingen* ~*e kracht verlenen* back-date salary increases; te'rugwerking (-en) *v* reaction, retroaction

te'rugwerpen[1] *vt* throw back[2]; –wijken[1] *vi* 1 (i n 't a l g.) recede; 2 ⚔ retreat, fall back; –wijzen[1] *vt* refer back [the reader to page...]; zie ook: *afwijzen*; –winnen[1] *vt* win back, regain; –zenden[1] *vt* send back [a person, thing], return [a book &]; –zetten[1] *vt* put back; –zien[1] **I** *vi* look back [to the past, on my youth]; **II** *vt* see again [a lost friend &]; –zwemmen[1] *vi* swim back

ter'wijl **I** *cj* 1 (v. t ij d) while, whilst; as; 2 (t e g e n s t e l l e n d) whereas; **II** *ad* meanwhile

ter'zake zie *zaak*

ter'zet [tɛr'tsɛt] (-ten) *o* ♪ terzetto

ter'zijde (-s) *o* aside; –stelling *v* putting aside, neglect, disregard; *met* ~ *van* putting aside; in disregard of

test (-en) *v* 1 chafing-dish; 2 (h o o f d) **S** nob, nut, **F** noddle; ‖ (-s) *m* (p r o e f) test, trial

testa'ment (-en) *o* 1 will, last will (and testament); 2 Testament; *het Oude en Nieuwe T*~ the Old and New Testament; *zijn* ~ *maken* make one's will; ● *b ij* ~ *vermaken aan* bequeath to, will away to; *iem. i n zijn* ~ *zetten* remember sbd. in one's will; *z o n d e r* ~ *na te laten* intestate; testamen'tair [-'tɛːr] testamentary; testa'teur (-s) *m* testator; testa'trice (-s) *v* testatrix

'testbeeld (-en) *o* (t e l e v i s i e) test pattern; 'testen (testte, h. getest) *vt* test (for *op*)

tes'teren (testeerde, h. getesteerd) *vt* 1 (g e - t u i g e n) state; 2 (v e r m a k e n) bequeath

tes'tikel (-s) *m* testicle

testi'monium (-s en -ia) *o* testimonial, ⟿ testamur; 'testpiloot (-loten) *m* test pilot

'tetanus *m* tetanus, **F** lockjaw

tête-à-'tête [tɛːta.'tɛːt] (-s) *o* tête-à-tête

'tetteren (tetterde, h. getetterd) *vi* 1 blare; 2 (l u i d s p r e k e n) **F** yap, cackle

teug (-en) *m* & *v* draught; pull; *in één* ~ at a draught; *m e t volle* ~*en* taking deep draughts

'teugel (-s) *m* rein, bridle; *de* ~*s van het bewind in handen hebben (nemen)* hold (assume, seize, take over) the reins of government; *de* ~ *strak houden* hold the rein tight, keep him (them) on a tight rein; *de vrije* ~ *geven (laten)* give [a horse] the reins; give free rein, give rein (the reins) to [one's imagination]; *de* ~*s aanhalen* tighten the reins; *de* ~ *vieren* give full rein to; *met losse* ~ with a loose rein; *met strakke* ~ with tightened rein(s); 'teugelen (teugelde, h. geteugeld) *vt* bridle [a horse]; 'teugelloos unbridled, unrestrained; teugel'loosheid *v* unrestrainedness, unbridled passion

'teugje (-s) *o* sip; *met* ~*s drinken* sip

'teunisbloem (-en) *v* evening primrose

1 teut (-en) *m-v* slow-coach, dawdler

2 teut **F** *aj* (d r o n k e n) tight

'teutachtig dawdling; 'teuten (teutte, h. geteut) *vi* dawdle; 'teutkous (-en) *v* dawdler, slow-coach

Teu'toon (-tonen) *m* Teuton; –s Teutonic

te'veel *o* surplus

'tevens at the same time; *de ...ste en* ~ *de ...ste* both the ...st and the ...st

tever'geefs in vain, vainly, for nothing

te'voren zie 2 *voren*

te'vreden **I** *aj* 1 (p r e d i k a t i e f) content; 2 (a t t r i b u t i e f) contented; ~ *m e t* content

---

[1] V.T. en V.D. van dit werkwoord volgens het model: te'rug*blikken*, V.T. blikte te'rug, V.D. te'rug*geblikt*. Zie voor de vormen onder het grondwoord, in dit voorbeeld: *blikken*. Bij sterke en onregelmatige werkwoorden wordt u verwezen naar de lijst achterin.

with; ~ *zijn over* be satisfied with; **II** *ad* contentedly; **–heid** *v* contentedness, contentment, content, satisfaction; *tot zijn (volle)* ~ to his (entire) satisfaction; *een boterham met* ~ bread and scrape; **te'vredenstellen** (stelde te'vreden, h. te'vredengesteld) **I** *vt* content, satisfy; **II** *vr zich* ~ *met* content oneself with
te'waterlating (-en) *v* launch, launching
te'weegbrengen (bracht te'weeg, h. te'weeggebracht) *vt* bring about, cause
te'werkstellen (stelde te'werk, h. te'werkgesteld) *vt* engage, employ; **–ling** (-en) *v* employment
tex'tiel I *aj* textile; **II** *m* & *o* textiles; **–industrie** (-ieën) *v* textile industry
te'zamen together
'Thailand *o* Thailand
thans at present, now; by this time
the'ater (-s) *o* theatre; **thea'traal I** *aj* theatrical, stag(e)y, histrionic; **II** *ad* theatrically, stagily, histrionically
The'baan(s) (-banen) *m* (& *aj*) Theban; **'Thebe** *o* Thebes
thee *m* tea; ~ *drinken* have (take) tea, tea; *ze zijn aan het* ~ *drinken* they are at tea; *komt u op de* ~? will you come to tea (with us)?; *kunnen we op de* ~ *komen?* can you have us to tea?; **–blad** 1 (-bladeren en -blaren) *o* ⚘ tea-leaf; 2 (-bladen) *o* tea-tray; **–builtje** (-s) *o* tea-bag; **–busje** (-s) *o* tea-caddy, tea-canister; **–cultuur** *v* tea-culture, tea-growing; **–doek** (-en) *m* tea-towel, tea-cloth; **–ëi** (-eren) *o* tea infuser, tea-egg (-ball); **–fabriek** (-en) *v* tea-works, tea-factory; **–gerei, –goed** *o* tea-things; **–handel** *m* tea-trade; **–handelaar** (-s en -laren) *m* tea-merchant, tea-dealer; **–huis** (-huizen) *o* tea-house; **–ketel** (-s) *m* tea-kettle; **–kist** (-en) *v* tea-chest; **–kistje** (-s) *o* tea-caddy; **–kopje** (-s) *o* teacup; **–land** (-en) *o* tea-plantation, tea-estate; **–lepeltje** (-s) *o* 1 teaspoon; 2 teaspoonful; **–lichtje** (-s) *o* spirit-stove; **–lood** *o* tea-lead
Theems *v* Thames
'theemuts (-en) *v* tea-cosy; **–oogst** (-en) *m* tea-crop; **–pauze** (-s en -n) *v* tea break; **–plantage** [-ta.ʒə] (-s) *v* tea-plantation, tea-garden; **–pot** (-ten) *m* teapot; **–roos** (-rozen) *v* tea-rose; **–salon** (-s) *m* & *o* tea-room(s), tea-shop; **–schoteltje** (-s) *o* saucer; **–servies** (-viezen) *o* tea-service, tea-set; **–stoof** (-stoven) *v* tea-kettle stand; **–tafel** (-s) *v* tea-table; **–tante** (-s) *v* gossip; **–tuin** (-en) *m* (uitspanning & plantage) tea-garden; **–visite** [s = z] (-s) *v* five o'clock visit; tea-party; **–wagen** (-s) *m* tea-trolley; **–water** *o* water for tea; *hij is boven zijn* ~ he is in his cups; **–zakje** (-s) *o* tea-bag; **–zeefje** (-s) *o* tea-strainer
the'ïsme *o* theism; **the'ïst** (-en) *m* theist; **–isch I** *aj* theistic(al); **II** *ad* theistically
'thema ('s) 1 *v* & *o* ✎ exercise; 2 *o* theme; **the'matisch** thematic
theo'craat (-craten) *m* theocrat; **theocra'tie** [-'(t)si.] *v* theocracy; **theo'cratisch I** *aj* theocratic; **II** *ad* theocratically
theolo'gie *v* theology; **theo'logisch** theological; **theo'loog** (-logen) *m* 1 theologian; 2 student of theology, divinity student
theo'rema ('s) *o* theorem
theo'reticus (-ci) *m* theorist; theoretician; **theo'retisch I** *aj* theoretical; **II** *ad* theoretically, in theory; **theoreti'seren** [s = z] (theoretiseerde, h. getheoretiseerd) *vi* theorize; **theo'rie** (-ieën) *v* theory; ⚔ theoretical instruction
theoso'fie *v* theosophy; **theo'sofisch** theosophical; **theo'soof** (-sofen) *m* theosophist
thera'peut [-'pœyt] (-en) *m* therapeutist; **–isch** therapeutic(al); **thera'pie** (-ieën) *v* 1 (onderdeel der geneeskunde) therapeutics; 2 (behandeling) therapy
ther'maal thermal; **'thermen** *mv* thermal springs, baths; **ther'miek** *v* thermal current, updraught of warm air; **'thermisch** thermal, thermic; **thermody'namica** [-di.'na.-] *v* thermodynamics; **thermo'geen** thermogenic, thermogenetic; **'thermometer** (-s) *m* thermometer; **thermo'metrisch** thermometric(al); **thermonucle'air** [-kle.'ɛ:r] thermonuclear
Ⓜ **'thermosfles** (-sen) *v* thermos (flask); **thermo'staat** (-staten) *m* thermostat
thesau'rie [te.zo:'ri.] (-ieën) *v* treasury; **thesau'rier** (-s) *m* treasurer
'these [te.z
'thesis (-sissen en -ses) *v* thesis [*mv* theses]
'Thomas *m* Thomas; *ongelovige* ~ doubting Thomas; ~ *van Aquino* St. Thomas Aquinas
thuis I *ad* at home; (naar huis) home; ~ *blijven* (*zijn*) stay (be) at home; *is...* ~? ook: is... in?; *ergens goed* ~ *in zijn* be at home with (on) a subject; *doe of je* ~ *bent* make yourself at home; *handen* ~! hands off!; *niemand* ~ nobody at home, nobody in; *niet* ~ *geven* not be at home [to visitors]; **II** *o* home; **–bezorgen** (bezorgde 'thuis, h. 'thuisbezorgd) *vt* send to sbd.'s house; **–blijven**[1] *vi* stay at home, stay in;

[1] V.T. en V.D. van dit werkwoord volgens het model: **'thuis**horen, V.T. hoorde **'thuis**, V.D. **'thuis**gehoord. Zie voor de vormen onder het grondwoord, in dit voorbeeld: *horen*. Bij sterke en onregelmatige werkwoorden wordt u verwezen naar de lijst achterin.

–brengen[1] *vt* 1 see home [a friend]; 2 *fig* place [a man]

'thuisclub (-s) *v* home team, home side; **–front** *o* home front; **–haven** (-s) *v* home port

'thuishoren[1] *vi daar* ~ belong there; *die opmerkingen horen hier niet thuis* are out of place; *ik geloof dat ze in Haarlem* ~ I think they belong to H; **–houden**[1] *vt* keep [sbd.] at home, keep [sbd.] in(doors); **–komen**[1] *vi* come (get) home

'thuiskomst *v* home-coming, return (home)

'thuiskrijgen[1] *vt* get home, get delivered; zie ook *trek*

'thuislading *v* return (homeward) cargo; **–reis** (-reizen) *v* homeward journey, journey home; ♃ homeward passage, voyage home; *op de* ~ homeward bound; **–vlucht** *v* ✈ flight home

'thuisvoelen[1] *zich* ~ feel at home

'thuiswedstrijd (-en) *m* at home game, home match; **–werker** (-s) *m* home-worker, outworker

ti'ara ('s) *v* tiara

'Tiber *m* Tiber

Tibe'taan(s) *m* (& *aj*) Tibetan

tic [ti. k] (-s) *m* tic

'tichel (-s) *v* tile, brick; **–bakker** (-s) *m* tilemaker, brick-maker; **tichelbakke'rij** (-en) *v* brick-works; **'ticheloven** (-s) *m* tile-kiln; **–steen** (-stenen) *m* tile, brick

tien ten

tiend (-en) *m* & *o* tithe

'tiendaags of ten days, ten-days'; **'tiende I** *aj* tenth; **II** (-n) 1 *o* tenth part, tenth; 2 *m* & *o* tithe; *de ~n heffen* levy tithes; **'tiendelig** consisting of ten parts; decimal [fraction]

'tiendheffer (-s) *m* tithe-gatherer, tither; **–heffing** (-en) *v* tithing; **–pachter** (-s) *m* farmer of tithes; **tiend'plichtig** tithable; **'tiendrecht** *o* right to levy tithes

'tiendubbel tenfold; **–duizend** ten thousand; **~en** tens of thousands

'tiendverpachting (-en) *v* farming out of tithes

'tiener (-s) *m* teen-ager; **'tienhoek** (-en) *m* decagon; **–jarig** 1 decennial; 2 of ten years, ten-year-old; **–kamp** *m* decathlon; **–tal** (-len) *o* (number of) ten, decade; *het* ~ the ten (of them); *twee ~len* two tens; **–tallig** decimal; **–tje** (-s) *o* 1 (b e d r a g) ten guilders; (g o u d e n) gold ten-guilder piece; (p a p i e r e n) ten-guilder note; 2 *rk* decade (of the rosary); 3 tenth of a lottery-ticket; **–voud** (-en) *o* decuple; **–voudig** tenfold; **–werf** ten times

tierelan'tijntje (-s) *o* flourish; **~s** scrolls and flourishes

tiere'lieren (tierelierde, h. getierelierd) *vi* warble, sing

1 'tieren (tierde, h. getierd) *vi* (w e l i g g r o e i e n) thrive [of a plant, a tree]; *fig* flourish; *de ondeugd tiert daar* vice is rampant (rife) there

2 'tieren (tierde, h. getierd) *vi* (r a z e n) rage, rave, storm bluster, zie ook: *razen*

'tierig thriving, lively, lush

tierlan'tijntje (-s) = *tierelantijntje*

tiet (-en) *v* **P** tit

tij (-en) *o* tide; zie ook: *getij*

tijd (-en) *m* 1 (i n 't a l g.) time; 2 (p e r i o d i e k) period; season; 3 *gram* tense [of a verb]; *de goede oude* ~ the good old times, the good old days *de hele* ~ all the time; *een hele (lange)* ~ (*was hij ziek*) for a long time, for ages; *dat is een hele* ~ that's quite a long time; *wel, lieve* ~! dear me!; *middelbare* ~ mean time; *plaatselijke* ~ local time; *vrije* ~ leisure (time), spare time; *het zal mijn* ~ *wel duren* it will last my time; *het is* ~ time is up; *het is hoog* ~ it is high time; *er was een* ~ *dat...* time was when...; *het wordt* ~ *om...* it is getting time to...; *(geen)* ~ *hebben* have (no) time; *alles heeft zijn* ~ there is a time for everything; *het heeft de* ~ there is no hurry; *ik heb de* ~ *aan mijzelf* my time is my own; *hij heeft zijn* ~ *gehad* he has had his day; *als men maar* ~ *van leven heeft* if only one lives long enough; *de* ~ *niet klein weten te krijgen* have time on one's hands; ~ *maken* make time; *er de* ~ *voor nemen* take one's time (over it); ~ *winnen* gain time; ~ *trachten te winnen* ook: play for time; ● *wij zijn a a n geen* ~ *gebonden* we are not tied down to time; *b ij* ~ *en wijle* 1 in due time; 2 now and then; *bij* ~*en* at times, sometimes; occasionally; *bij de* ~ *brengen* update [the Church &]; *g e d u r e n d e de* ~ *dat...* during the time that..., while, whilst; *i n* ~ *van nood* in time of need; *in* ~ *van oorlog* in times of war; *in de* ~ *van een maand* in a month's time, within a month; *in de* ~ *toen (dat)...* at the time when; *in een* ~ *dat...* at a time when...; *in mijn* ~ in my time (day); *in mijn jonge* ~ in my young days; *in geen* ~ *heb ik...* I have not... for ever so long; *in de laatste* ~ of late; *in lange* ~ for a long time past; *in minder dan geen* ~ in (less than) no time; *in onze* ~ in our days; *in de goede oude* ~ in the good old times (days); *in vroeger* ~ in former times; *m e t de* ~ as time goes (went) on, with time; *met zijn* ~ *meegaan* zie *meegaan*; *n a die* ~ after that time; *na korter of langer* ~ sooner or later;

---

[1] V.T. en V.D. van dit werkwoord volgens het model: **'thuis**horen, V.T. hoorde **'thuis**, V.D. **'thuis**gehoord. Zie voor de vormen onder het grondwoord, in dit voorbeeld: *horen*. Bij sterke en onregelmatige werkwoorden wordt u verwezen naar de lijst achterin.

morgen o m deze ~ this time to-morrow; *o m t r e n t deze* ~ about this time; *o p* ~ in time [for breakfast, for the train]; [the train is] on time; *hij kwam net op* ~ in the nick of time; *de trein kwam precies op* ~ punctually to (schedule) time; *op* ~ *kopen* $ buy for forward delivery; *een woord op* ~ a word in season; *op de bepaalde* ~ at the appointed time, at the time fixed; *op gezette ~en* at set times; *alles op zijn* ~ all in good time; *op welke* ~ *ook* (at) any time; *hij is o v e r zijn* ~ he is behind (his) time; *het schip (de trein, de baby) is over (zijn)* ~ the ship (the train, the baby) is overdue; *s e d e r t die* ~ from that time, ever since; *t e allen* ~*e* at all times; *te bekwamer* ~ in due time; *te dien* ~*e* at the time; *te eniger* ~ at some time (or other); *zo hij te eniger* ~*...* if at any time he...; *te gelegener (rechter)* ~ in due time; *te zijner* ~ in due time; *ten* ~*e dat...* at the time when...; *ten* ~*e van* at (in) the time of...; *terzelfder* ~ at the same time; *t e g e n die* ~ by that time; *t o t* ~ *en wijle dat... till...; dat is u i t de* ~ it is out of date, it has had its day; *hij is uit de* ~ he has had his day; *dichters v a n deze (van onze)* ~ contemporary poets; *van de laatste (nieuwere)* ~ recent; *van die* ~ *af* from that time forward; *van* ~ *tot* ~ from time to time; *v o o r de* ~ *van 6 maanden* for a period of six months; *voor de* ~ *van het jaar* for the time of year; *dat was heel mooi voor die* ~ as times went; *voor enige* ~ 1 for some time; for a time; 2 some time ago; *voor korte (lange)* ~ for a short (long) time; *vóór de* ~ [repay a loan] ahead of time; *vóór zijn* ~ *(werd hij oud)* prematurely, before his time; ~ *is geld* time is money; *de* ~ *zal het leren* time will show (tell); *de* ~ *is de beste heelmeester* time heals all; *andere* ~*en, andere zeden* other times other manners; *komt* ~, *komt raad* with time comes counsel; *er is een* ~ *van komen en een* ~ *van gaan* to everything there is a season and a time to every purpose; **–aanwijzing** (-en) *v* indication of time; **–affaire**[-fɛ:rə] (-s) *v* time bargain; **–bal** (-len) *m* ⚓ time-ball; **–bepaling** (-en) *v gram* 1 determination of time; 2 adjunct of time; **tijdbe'sparend** time-saving [measures]; **'tijdbesparing** *v* saving of time; **–bom** (-men) *v* delayed-action bomb, time bomb; **'tijdelijk I** *aj* temporary; (w e r e l d - l ij k) temporal; *het* ~*e met het eeuwige verwisselen* depart this life; **II** *ad* temporarily; **'tijdeloos** timeless

'tijdens *prep* during

'tijdgebrek *o* lack of time; **–geest** *m* spirit of the age (of the time); **–genoot** (-noten) *m* contemporary; **'tijdig I** *aj* timely [help &], early, seasonable; **II** *ad* in good time, betimes; **–heid** *v* timeliness, seasonableness

'tijding(en) *v (mv)* tidings, news, intelligence

'tijdje (-s) *o* (little) while; **'tijdlang** *m een* ~ for some time, for a while; **–maat** (-maten) *v* time; **–melding** (-en) *v* ☎ speaking clock; (v i a d e r a d i o) time-check; **–meter** (-s) *m* chronometer, time-keeper; **–nood** *m* time shortage, time trouble [of a chess-player]; *in* ~ *verkeren* be short of (rushed for) time, be hard-pressed, be under time pressure; **–opname** (-n) *v* 1 *sp* timing; 2 (f o t o) time exposure; **–opnemer** (-s) *m sp* timekeeper, timer; **–passering** (-en) *v = tijdverdrijf;* **–perk** (-en) *o* period; [stone &] age; [a new] era; **–rekening** (-en) *v* chronology; [Christian] era; [Julian &] calendar; **–rit** (-ten) *m sp* race against time; **–rovend** time-consuming, taking up much time; **–ruimte** (-n) *v* space of time, period

'tijdsbeeld (-en) *o* image of the time; **–bepaling** (-en) *= tijdbepaling;* **–bestek** *o* space of time, period

'tijdschakelaar (-s) *m* time switch; **–schema** ('s) *o* time-table; **–schrift** (-en) *o* periodical, magazine, review; **–schriftenzaal** (-zalen) *v* periodicals room; **–schrijver** (-s) *m* time-keeper [of workmen]; **'tijdsduur** *m* length of time, period, duration, term; **'tijdsein** (-en) *o* time-signal; **'tijdsgewricht** *o* period; **'tijdsignaal** [-sŋa.l] (-nalen) *o* time-signal; **'tijdslimiet** (-en) *v* time-limit, deadline; **'tijdsluiter** (-s) *m* delayed-action shutter; **'tijdsorde** *v* chronological order; **–ruimte** (-n) *= tijdruimte;* **'tijdstip** (-pen) *o* moment; date; **'tijdsverloop** *o* course of time; *na een* ~ *van...* after a lapse of...; **–verschil** (-len) *o* time difference, difference in time; **'tijdtafel** (-s) *v* chronological table; **–vak** (-ken) *o* period; **–verdrijf** *o* pastime; *tot (uit)* ~ *as a pastime;* **–verlies** *o* loss of time; **–verspilling** *v* waste of time; **–winst** *v* gain (saving) of time; *dat is een* ~ *van 2 uur* that saves two hours

⊙ **'tijgen*** *vi* go; *aan het werk* ~ set to work; *ten oorlog* ~ go to war

'tijger (-s) *m* tiger; **–achtig** tig(e)rish; **tijge'rin** (-nen) *v* tigress; **'tijgerjacht** (-en) *v* tiger-hunt(ing); **–kat** (-ten) *v* tiger-cat; **–lelie** (-s en -liën) *v* tiger-lily; **–vel** (-len) *o* tiger's skin

'tijhaven (-s) *v* tidal harbour

tijk 1 (-en) *m* tick; 2 *o* (d e s t o f) ticking

'tijloos (-lozen) *v = herfsttijloos*

tijm *m* thyme

tik (-ken) *m* touch, pat, rap, flick; *een* ~ *om de oren* a box on the ears; **–fout** (-en) *v* typist's error, slip of the typewriter; **–je** (-s) *o* 1 (k l a p j e) pat, tap; 2 (b e e t j e) bit; *fig* dash, tinge, touch [of malice &]; *een* ~ *arrogantie* a touch of arrogance; *een* ~ *beter* a shade better; *een* ~ *korter* a thought shorter; **'tikkeltje** (-s) *o*

touch; zie verder *tikje*; **'tikken** (tikte, h. getikt)
I *vi* tick [of a clock], click; *a a n de deur* ~ tap at
the door; *aan zijn pet* ~ touch one's cap; *iem. o p
de schouder* ~ tap sbd. on the shoulder; *iem. op de
vingers* ~ rap sbd. over the knuckles; **II** *va*
type(write); **III** *vt* 1 touch [a person]; 2
type(write) [a letter &]; **'tikker** (-s) *m* ticker
[ook: = watch]; **–tje** (-s) *o* 1 ticker [= watch];
2 **F** (h a r t) ticker; 3 (s p e l) tag; **'tiktak** 1 *m*
(g e l u i d) tick-tack; 2 *o* (s p e l) backgammon

til 1 *m* lift; 2 (-len) *v = duiventil*; *op ~ zijn* be
drawing near, be at hand; *er is iets op* ~ ook:
there is something in the wind
'tilbaar movable
'tilbury [-büri.] ('s) *m* tilbury, gig
'tilde (-s) *v* tilde, swung dash
'tillen (tilde, h. getild) *vt* lift, heave, raise; *zwaar
~ aan* [*fig*] make heavy weather of
'timbre ['tɛ̃brə] (-s) *o* timbre
'timen ['taimə(n)] (timede, h. getimed) *vt* time
ti'mide timid, shy, bashful
'timmeren (timmerde, h. getimmerd) **I** *vi*
carpenter; *hij timmert niet hoog* he will not set
the Thames on fire; *er op* ~ pitch into him
(into them), lay about one; *men moet er op blijven
~* one ought to keep harping on the subject;
II *vt* construct, build, carpenter; *in elkaar* ~
(s t u k s l a a n) smash, knock to pieces; *iets vlug
in elkaar* ~ knock sth. together; zie ook: *weg*;
'timmergereedschap (-pen) *o* carpenter's
tools; **–hout** *o* timber; **–man** (-lieden en -lui)
m carpenter; **–mansbaas** (-bazen) *m* master
carpenter; **–werf** (-werven) *v* (carpenter's)
yard; **–werk** *o* carpentry, carpenter's work;
carpentering
tim'paan (-panen) *o* tympanum
tin *o* tin, (l e g e r i n g v a n t i n e n l o o d)
pewter; (t i n n e n a r t i k e l e n) tinware
tinc'tuur (-turen) *v* tincture
'tinerts *o* tin-ore; **–foelie** *v* (tin-)foil
'tingelen (tingelde, h. getingeld) *vi* tinkle,
jingle; **tinge'ling(e'ling)** ting-a-ling(-a-ling);
'tingeltangel (-s) *m* café-chantant
'tinkelen (tinkelde, h. getinkeld) *vi* tinkle
'tinmijn (-en) *v* tin-mine
'tinne (-n) *v* battlements, crenel
'tinnegieter (-s) *m* tinsmith, pewterer; *politieke
~* pot-house politician, political upholsterer;
'tinnen *aj* pewter; **'tinpest** *v* tin disease, tin
pest; **–schuitje** (-s) *o* pig of tin
tint (-en) *v* tint, tinge, hue, shade, tone
'tintel *m* tingling [of the fingers]; **'tintelen**
(tintelde, h. getinteld) *vi* twinkle; ~ *van*
1 sparkle with [wit]; 2 tingle with [cold]; **–ling**
(-en) *v* 1 twinkling; sparkling; 2 tingling
'tinten (tintte, h. getint) *vi* tinge, tint; *getint
papier* toned paper; *blauw getint* tinged with

blue; **'tintje** (-s) *o* tinge[2]
'tinwerk *o* tinware; **–winning** *v* tin-mining
1 tip (-pen) *m* tip [of finger]; corner [of a
handkerchief &]; *een ~ van de sluier oplichten* lift
a corner of the veil
2 tip (-s) *m* tip [information]; **–gever** (-s) *m*
(a a n p o l i t i e) informer
'tippel *m* tramp; *een hele* ~ quite a walk; *op de* ~
on the trot; **–aarster** (-s) *v* **F** street-walker;
'tippelen (tippelde, h. getippeld) *vi* trot,
tramp; **F** (v. p r o s t i t u é e s) walk the streets;
ergens in ~ take the bait, walk into the trap
'tippen (tipte, h. getipt) **I** *vt* clip, trim; **II** *vi*
...*kan er niet aan* ~ ...cannot touch it, **F** ...is not
a patch on it
'tiptop first-rate, A1, **F** tiptop
ti'rade (-s) *v* tirade
tirail'leren [ti.rɑ(l)'je:rə(n)] (tirailleerde, h.
getirailleerd) *vi* ⚔ skirmish; **tirail'leur** (-s) *m* ⚔
skirmisher
ti'ran (-nen) *m* tyrant, *fig* bully; **tiran'nie** (-ieën)
v tyranny; **–k** tyrannical; **tiranni'seren** [s = z]
(tiranniseerde, h. getiranniseerd) *vt* tyrannize
over, *fig* bully
ti'taan *o* titanium
'titan (-s en -'tanen) *m* Titan; **ti'tanisch** titanic
'titel (-s) *m* title [of a poem, book &, of a
person]; heading [of a column, chapter];
–blad (-bladen) *o* title-page; **–gevecht** (-en) *o*
title-fight; **–houder** (-s) *m sp* holder of the
title; **–plaat** (-platen) *v* frontispiece; **–rol** (-len)
v title-role, title-part, name-part; **–woord**
(-en) *o* headword
'titer *m* titre; **ti'treren** (titreerde, h. getitreerd)
vt titrate
'tittel (-s) *m* tittle, dot; *geen ~ of jota* not one jot
or tittle
titu'lair [-'lɛ:r] titular; *majoor* ~ brevet major;
titu'laris (-sen) *m* holder (of an office, of a
title); office-bearer; incumbent [of a parish];
titula'tuur (-turen) *v* style, titles; forms of
address; **titu'leren** (tituleerde, h. getituleerd)
vt style, title; *hoe moet ik u ~?* what is your style
(and title)?
tja! *gj* well!
tjalk (-en) *m* & *v* (sailing) barge
tjee *gj* oh dear!
'tjiftjaf (-fen en -s) *m* chiff-chaff
'tjilpen (tjilpte, h. getjilpt) *vi* chirp, cheep,
twitter
'tjokvol chock-full, cram-full, crammed
'tjonge *gj* well!, have you ever!
T.L.-buis [te.'tl-] (-buizen) *v = fluorescentielamp*
'tobbe (-s en -n) *v* tub
'tobben (tobde, h. getobd) *vi* toil, drudge; *m e t
iem.* ~ have a lot of trouble with sbd.; *o v e r iets
~* worry about sth., brood over sth.; **'tobber**

(-s) *m* 1 toiler, drudge; 2 worrier; **–ig** worried, broody; **tobbe'rij** (-en) *v* 1 trouble, difficulty; 2 worrying

toch 1 (n i e t t e g e n s t a a n d e d a t) yet, still, for all that, in spite of (all) that, nevertheless; 2 (w e r k e l ij k) really; 3 (z e k e r) surely, to be sure; 4 (o n g e d u l d u i t d r u k k e n d) ever; 5 (v e r z o e k e n d, g e b i e d e n d) do..., pray...; 6 (i m m e r s) *je bent ∼ ziek?* you are ill, aren't you?; *hij doet ∼ zijn best* he is doing what he can, doesn't he?; *je hebt er ∼ nog een* you have another, haven't you?; 7 (n i e t v e r t a a l d) in: *wat is het ∼ jammer!* what a pity it is!; *je moest nu ∼ klaar zijn* you should be ready by this time; *het is ∼ te erg* it really is too bad; *je komt ∼?* you are coming, to be sure?; *een ...is ∼ een mens* a ... is a man for all that; *wat wil hij ∼?* what ever does he want?; what does he want?; *wie kan het ∼ zijn?* who ever can it be?; *welke Jan bedoel je ∼?* which ever John do you mean?; *maar Jan ∼!* I say, John!, John! Really, you know!; *wat mankeert hij ∼?* what is the matter with him, anyhow?; *hoe (waar, waarom, wanneer) ∼?* how (where, why, when) ever...?; *wij gaan morgen – Neen ∼?* Not really?, you don't say!; *waar zou hij ∼ zijn?* 1 (n i e u w s g i e r i g) where may he be?; 2 (v e r b a a s d) where can he be?; 3 (o n g e d u l d i g) where ever is he?; *wees ∼ stil!* do be quiet, please!; *ja ∼, nu herinner ik het me* yes indeed, now I remember; *het is ∼ al moeilijk* it is difficult as it is (anyhow); *hij komt ∼ niet* he surely won't come, he will not turn up for sure; *antwoord ∼ niet* (pray) don't answer; *hij is ∼ wel knap* he is a clever fellow though

tocht (-en) *m* 1 (r e i s) journey, march, expedition, voyage [by sea]; 2 (t r e k w i n d) draught; *op de ∼ zitten* sit in a draught; **–band** (-en) *o* & *m* weather-strip; **–deken** (-s) *v* draught-rug; **–deur** (-en) *v* swing-door; **'tochten** (tochtte, h. getocht) *vi het tocht hier* there is a draught here; **'tochtgat** (-gaten) *o* vent-hole, air-hole; **–genoot** (-noten) *m* fellow-traveller, companion; **'tochtig** (w a a r h e t t o c h t) draughty; **–heid** *v* draughtiness; **'tochtje** (-s) *o* excursion, trip; **'tochtlat** (-ten) *v* weatherstrip; **F** (b a k k e b a a r d) mutton-chop, whisker; **–raam** (-ramen) *o* double window; **–scherm** (-en), **–schut** (-ten) *o* (draughtscreen; **–strip** (-s en -pen) *m* weather-strip

tod (-den) *v* rag, tatter

toe to; *∼, jongens, nu stil!* I say, boys, do be quiet

now!; *∼ dan!* come on!; *∼ dan maar* well, all right; *∼, kom nou toch!* Oh, do come!; *∼ maar!* 1 (a a n m o e d i g e n d t o t d a a d) go it!; 2 (a a n m. t o t s p r e k e n) fire away!; 3 (u i t i n g v. v e r w o n d e r i n g) never!, good gracious!; *deur ∼!* shut the door!; *de deur is ∼* the door is shut; *∼ nou!* do, now!; *ik ben er nog niet aan ∼* I've not got so far yet; *hij is aan vakantie ∼* he (badly) needs a holiday; *nu weet ik waar ik aan ∼ ben* now I know where I am (where I stand); *hij is er slecht aan ∼* 1 he is badly off; 2 he [the patient] is in a bad way; *dat is tot daar aan ∼* ... for one thing [for another ...]; *naar de stad ∼* 1 in the direction of the town; 2 to (the) town; *wat hebben we ∼?* what's for sweet? (for afters?); **–bedelen** [-bə.də.lə(n)] (bedeelde 'toe,h. 'toebedeeld) *vt* allot, assign, apportion, deal out, dole (parcel, mete) out; **–behoren** (behoorde 'toe, h. 'toebehoord) **I** *vi* belong to; **II** *o met ∼* with appurtenances, with accessories

'toebereiden[1] *vt* prepare; **–ding** (-en) *v* (k l a a r m a k e n) preparation [of food]; **'toebereidselen** *mv* preparations; *∼ maken voor...* make preparations for, get ready for

'toebijten[1] **I** *vi* bite[2]; *hij zal niet ∼* he won't take the bait; **II** *vt ,,weg", beet hij mij toe* he snarled (snapped) at me; **–binden**[1] *vt* bind (tie) up; **–blijven**[1] *vi* remain shut; **–brengen**[1] *vt* inflict [a wound, a loss, a defeat upon]; deal, strike [sbd. a blow], do [harm]; **–bulderen**[1] *vt* shout (roar) at; **–dekken**[1] *vt* cover (up) [something], tuck in [a child in bed]; **–delen**[1] *vt = toebedelen*; **–denken**[1] *vt iem. iets ∼* destine sth. for sbd., intend sth. for sbd.; **–dichten**[1] *vt* ascribe, impute [sth. to sbd.]

'toedienen *vt* administer [remedies, the sacraments]; give, deal [a blow]; **–ning** *v* administration [of remedies, sacraments]

1 'toedoen[1] *vt* shut; zie ook: *oog(je)*

2 'toedoen *o het geschiedde b u i t e n mijn ∼* I had no part in it; *d o o r zijn ∼* through him; *z o n d e r uw ∼ zou ik niet...* but for you

'toedraaien[1] *vt* close (by turning), turn off [a tap]; zie ook: *rug*

'toedracht *v de ∼* the way it happened; *de (ware) ∼ der zaak* how it all came to pass, the ins and outs of the affair; **'toedragen I** *vt achting ∼* esteem, hold in esteem; *iem. een goed hart ∼* be kindly disposed towards sbd., wish sbd. well; *iem. geen goed hart ∼* be ill-affected towards sbd.; *ze dragen elkaar geen goed hart toe* there is no love

---

[1] V.T. en V.D. van dit werkwoord volgens het model: 'toe**dekken**, V.T. dekte 'toe, V.D. 'toe**gedekt**. Zie voor de vormen onder het grondwoord, in dit voorbeeld: *dekken*. Bij sterke en onregelmatige werkwoorden wordt u verwezen naar de lijst achterin.

lost between them; **II** *vr zich* ~ happen; *hoe heeft het zich toegedragen?* how did it come to pass?

'toedrinken[1] *vt iem.* ~ drink sbd.'s health; **–drukken**[1] *vt* close, shut; **–duwen**[1] *vt* push [a door] to; *iem. iets* ~ slip sth. into sbd.'s hands

'toeëigenen (eigende 'toe, h. 'toegeëigend) *vt zich iets* ~ appropriate sth.; **–ning** *v* appropriation

'toefje (-s) *o* 1 (d o t, p l u k) tuft; 2 (k l e i n b o s j e b l o e m e n) posy, nosegay

'toefluisteren[1] *vt iem. iets* ~ whisper sth. in sbd.'s ear, whisper sth. to sbd.

'toegaan *vi* 1 (d i c h t g a a n) close, shut; 2 (z i c h t o e d r a g e n) happen, come to pass; *het gaat er raar toe* there are strange happenings there; *zo is het toegegaan* thus the matter went

'toegang (-en) *m* 1 entrance, way in; ingress; approach [to a town]; 2 access, entrance; 3 admission, admittance; *verboden* ~ private, no admittance; trespassers will be prosecuted; *vrije* ~ admission free; *vrije* ~ *hebben tot* ook: have the run of [a library &]; be free of [the house]; ~ *geven tot* give access to [another room]; *iem.* ~ *verlenen* admit sbd.; *zich* ~ *verschaffen tot* get into, force an entrance into [a house]; *de* ~ *weigeren* deny [sbd.] admittance;

'toegangsbewijs (-wijzen) *o*, **–biljet** (-ten) *o*, **–kaart** (-en) *v* admission ticket; **–poort** (-en) *v* entrance gate; *fig* gateway; **–prijs** (-prijzen) *m* (charge for) admission; **–weg** (-wegen) *m* approach, access road, access route;

toe'gankelijk accessible, approachable, get-at-able; *moeilijk* ~ [sources] difficult of access; *hij is voor iedereen* ~ he is a very approachable man; *niet* ~ *voor het publiek* not open to the public; **–heid** *v* accessibility

'toegedaan *ik ben hem zeer* ~ I am very much attached to him; *ik ben die mening* ~ I hold that opinion; *de vrede oprecht* ~ *zijn* be sincerely devoted to peace

toe'geeflijk indulgent; **–heid** *v* indulgence; **toe'gefelijk(-)** = *toegeeflijk(-)*

'toegenegen affectionate, devoted to; *Uw* ~ *X* Yours affectionately X; **–heid** *v* affectionateness, affection

'toegepast applied

'toegeven[1] **I** *vt* give into the bargain; *fig* concede, admit, grant; *dat geef ik u toe* I grant you that; *toegegeven dat u gelijk hebt* granting you

are right; *de zangeres gaf nog wat toe* gave an extra; *ze geven elkaar niets toe* they are well matched; *men moet kinderen wat* ~ children should be humoured (indulged) a little; *zij geeft hem te veel toe* she is too indulgent; **II** *vi* give in [to a person], give way [to grief, one's emotions &], yield; *hij wou maar niet* ~ he could not be made to yield the point; *zoals iedereen* ~ *zal* as everybody will readily admit; ~ *a a n zijn hartstochten* indulge one's passions; *je moet maar niet i n alles* ~ not give way in everything; **toe'gevend** indulgent; *gram* concessive; **–heid** *v* indulgence

'toegewijd devoted [friend], dedicated [fighter]

'toegift (-en) *v* make-weight; extra; *als* ~ into the bargain

'toegooien[1] *vt* throw to, slam [a door]; fill up [a hole]; throw [me that book]; **–grijpen**[1] *vi* make a grab [at a thing]; **–halen**[1] *vt* draw closer, draw tighter; **–happen**[1] *vi* snap at it; swallow the bait[2]; *gretig* ~ jump at a proposal (an offer)

'toehoorder (-s) *m* auditor, hearer, listener; **'toehoren**[1] *vi* 1 listen to; 2 = *toebehoren*

'toehouden[1] *vt* 1 (t o e r e i k e n) hand to; 2 (d i c h t h o u d e n) keep shut

'toejuichen[1] *vt* applaud, cheer; *fig* welcome [a measure &]; **–ching** (-en) *v* applause, shout, cheer

'toekan (-s) *m* toucan

'toekennen[1] *vt* adjudge, award [a prize, punishment]; give [marks in examination &]; *een grote waarde* ~ *aan...* attach great value to...; **–ning** (-en) *v* granting, award

'toekeren[1] *vt* turn to; zie ook: *rug*

'toekijken[1] *vi* look on; *wij mochten* ~ we were left out in the cold; **–er** (-s) *m* looker-on, onlooker, spectator

'toeknikken[1] *vt* nod to [a person]; **–knopen**[1] *vt* button up

'toekomen[1] *vi zij kunnen niet* ~ they can't make (both) ends meet; *dat komt ons toe* that is our due, it is due to us, we have a right to it; *iem. iets doen* ~ send sbd. sth.; *zult u er mee* ~? will that be sufficient?; *ik kan er lang mee* ~ it goes a long way with me; ~ *op* zie *afkomen op*; **–d** future, next; ~*e tijd gram* future tense, future; *het hem* ~*e* his due

'toekomst *v* future; *in de* ~ in (the) future; *in de* ~ *lezen* look into the future; **–droom** (-dromen) *m* dream of the future; **toe'komstig** future; **'toekomstmuziek** *v fig*

[1] V.T. en V.D. van dit werkwoord volgens het model: 'toedekken, V.T. dekte 'toe, V.D. 'toegedekt. Zie voor de vormen onder het grondwoord, in dit voorbeeld: *dekken*. Bij sterke en onregelmatige werkwoorden wordt u verwezen naar de lijst achterin.

dreams of the future; **–plan** (-nen) *o* plan for the future

'toekrijgen[1] *vt* 1 get shut, succeed in shutting; 2 get into the bargain

'toekruid (-en) *o* seasoning, condiment

'toekunnen[1] *vt het kan niet toe* you can't shut it; *zult u er mee ~?* will that be sufficient?; *ik kan er lang mee toe* it goes a long way with me

toe'laatbaar admissible; **–heid** *v* admissibility

'toelachen[1] *vt* smile at; *fig* smile on; *het lacht me niet toe* it doesn't appeal to me, it doesn't commend itself to me

'toelage (-n) *v* allowance, gratification; grant [for students]; bonus; extra pay (salary, wages)

'toelaten[1] *vt* 1 (d u l d e n) permit, allow, suffer, tolerate; 2 (t o e g a n g v e r l e n e n) admit; 3 (d ó ó r l a t e n) pass [a candidate]; *...kunnen niet toegelaten worden* no... admitted; *het laat geen twijfel (geen andere verklaring) toe* it admits of no doubt (of no other interpretation); **'toelating** *v* 1 permission, leave; 2 admission, admittance; **–sexamen** (-s) *o* 1 entrance examination; eleven-plus [for secondary education]; 2 matriculation [at the university]

'toeleg *m* attempt, design, purpose, intention, plan; **'toeleggen**[1] I *vt* cover up; *er geld op ~* be a loser by it; *er 10 gulden op ~* be ten guilders out of pocket; *het erop ~ om...* be bent upon ...ing; *het op iems. ondergang ~* be out to ruin sbd.; II *vr zich ~ op de studie van...* apply oneself to [mathematics &]

'toeleveren[1] *vt* supply, effect ancillary supplies for; **'toeleveringsbedrijven** *mv* service industries, ancillary suppliers

'toelichten[1] *vt* clear up, elucidate, explain; *het met voorbeelden ~* illustrate it; **–ting** (-en) *v* explanation, elucidation

'toelonken[1] *vt* ogle [a girl]

'toeloop *m* concourse; **'toelopen**[1] *vi* come running on; *u moet maar ~* you just walk on; *op iem. ~* go up to sbd.; *hij kwam op mij ~* 1 he came up to me; 2 he came running towards me; *spits ~* taper, end in a point

'toeluisteren[1] *vi* listen; **–maken**[1] *vt* close, shut [a door &]; fold up [a letter]; button up [one's coat]; **–meten**[1] *vt* measure out, mete out

toen I *ad* then, at that time; *van ~ af* from that time, from then; II *cj* when, as

'toenaam (-namen) *m* 1 surname, nickname; 2 family name, surname

'toenadering *v* rapprochement; *~ zoeken* try to get closer [to sbd.]; **–sproging** (-en) *v ~en* advances

'toename *v* increase, rise

'toendra ('s) *v* tundra

'toenemen[1] *vi* increase, grow; **–ming** *v* increase, rise

'toenmaals then, at the (that) time; **toen'malig** then, of the (that) time; *de ~e voorzitter* the then president; **toenter'tijd** at the (that) time

toe'passelijk apposite, appropriate, suitable, bearing upon the matter; *~ op* applicable to, pertinent to, relevant to; **–heid** *v* applicability; appropriateness, relevancy

'toepassen[1] *vt* apply [rules & to]; **–sing** (-en) *v* application; *i n ~ brengen* put into practice; *dat is ook van ~ op...* it is also applicable to..., it also applies to...

toer (-en) *m* 1 (o m d r a a i i n g) turn [of a wheel &], revolution [of an engine, of a long-play record]; 2 (t o c h t) tour, trip; 3 (w a n d e - l i n g, r i t j e) turn [= stroll, drive, run, ride]; 4 (k u n s t s t u k) feat, trick; 5 (v a n k a p s e l) front [of false hair]; 6 (v. h a l s s n o e r) string [of pearls]; 7 (b i j h e t b r e i e n) round; 8 *op de Russische & ~ F* on the Russian & tack; *~en doen* perform tricks; do stunts; *het is een hele ~* it is quite a job; *het is zo'n ~ niet* there is nothing very difficult about it; *de fabriek draait o p volle ~en zie draaien* I; *op (volle) ~en (laten) komen* ✗ run up, rev up [of an engine]; *o v e r zijn ~en zijn* be overwrought (overstrung); **–auto** [-o.to. of -ɔuto.] ('s) *m* touring-car; **–beurt** (-en) *v* turn; *bij ~* by (in) rotation; by turns

'toereiken[1] I *vt* reach, hand [sth. to sbd.]; II *vi* suffice, be sufficient; **toe'reikend** sufficient, enough; *~ zijn* ook: suffice

toe'rekenbaar accountable, responsible [for one's actions]; **–heid** *v* accountability, responsibility; **toerekenings'vatbaar** responsible, compos mentis; *niet ~* of unsound mind, not responsible for one's actions

'toeren (toerde, h. getoerd) *vi* take a drive (a ride &)

'toerental *o* number of revolutions; **–teller** (-s) *m* revolution-counter, speed indicator

toe'risme *o* tourism; tourist industry; **toe'rist** (-en) *m* tourist; **toe'ristenindustrie** *v* tourist industry; **–klas(se)** *v* tourist class; **–seizoen** *o* tourist season; **toe'ristisch** tourist [traffic &]

toer'nooi (-en) *o* tournament, tourney, joust; **toer'nooien**[1] (toernooide, h. getoernooid) *vi* tilt, joust; **toer'nooiveld** (-en) *o* tilt-yard, tilting-ground

'toeroepen[1] *vt* call to, cry to

---

[1] V.T. en V.D. van dit werkwoord volgens het model: **'toe**dekken, V.T. dekte **'toe**, V.D. **'toe**gedekt. Zie voor de vormen onder het grondwoord, in dit voorbeeld: *dekken*. Bij sterke en onregelmatige werkwoorden wordt u verwezen naar de lijst achterin.

'**toertje** (-s) *o* turn [in the garden]; drive, run [in motor-car], spin [on bicycle]; ride [on horseback]; *een ~ gaan maken* go for a walk (a drive, a spin; a ride)

'**toerusten** (rustte 'toe, h. 'toegerust) **I** *vt* equip, fit out; **II** *vr zich ~ voor* equip oneself for, prepare for; **–ting** (-en) *v* equipment, fitting out, preparation

toe'**schietelijk** 1 friendly; 2 (i n s c h i k k e l ij k) obliging; **–heid** *v* 1 friendliness; 2 obligingness

'**toeschieten**[1] *vi* (t o e s n e l l e n) dash forward; *~ op* rush at [sbd.]; pounce upon [its prey]; **–schijnen**[1] *vi* seem to, appear to

'**toeschouwer** (-s) *m* spectator, looker-on, onlooker, observer

'**toeschreeuwen**[1] *vt* cry to; **–schrijven**[1] *vt* ascribe, attribute, impute [it] to, put [it] down to; **–schuiven**[1] *vt* close (by pushing), draw [the curtains]; *iem. iets ~* push sth. over to sbd.; *iem. stiekem iets ~* give sbd. sth. secretly; **–slaan**[1] **I** *vi* 1 (d i c h t s l a a n) slam (to) [of a door]; 2 (e r o p s l a a n) lay about one, hit out; 3 (e e n s l a g t o e b r e n g e n) strike; *sla toe!* 1 pitch into them!, go it!; 2 (b ij k o o p) shake (hands on it)!; **II** *vt* 1 (d i c h t s l a a n) slam, bang [a door]; shut [a book]; 2 (b ij v e i l i n g) knock down to

'**toeslag** (-slagen) *m* 1 (i n g e l d) extra allowance (pay); [war] bonus; (p r ij s v e r m e e r d e r i n g) extra charge; extra fare, excess fare [on railways &]; 2 (b ij v e i l i n g) knocking down; **–biljet** (-ten) *o* extra ticket

'**toesmijten**[1] *vt = toegooien*; **–snauwen**[1] *vt* snarl at; **–snellen**[1] *vi* rush forward; *~ op* rush to; **–spelden**[1] *vt* pin up

'**toespelen**[1] *vt elkaar de bal ~* play into each other's hands; **–ling** (-en) *v* allusion, insinuation, hint; *een ~ maken op* allude to, hint at

'**toespijs** (-spijzen) *v* 1 side-dish; 2 dessert

'**toespitsen**[1] **I** *vt* drive to extremes, exacerbate [the position, relations &]; **II** *vr zich ~* grow worse [of a situation]

'**toespraak** (-spraken) *v* speech, talk, address, harangue, allocution; *een ~ houden* give an address, make a speech; '**toespreken**[1] *vt* speak to [a person]; address [a meeting]

'**toespringen**[1] *vi* spring forward; *komen ~* come bounding on; *~ op* spring at

'**toestaan**[1] *vt* 1 (t o e l a t e n) permit, allow; 2 (v e r l e n e n) grant, accord, concede

'**toestand** (-en) *m* 1 state of affairs, position, situation, condition, state; 2 (o p s c h u d-

d i n g) commotion; 3 (z a a k, g e v a l) affair; *wat een ~!* what a muddle!; *in hachelijke ~* in a precarious situation; in a sorry plight

'**toesteken**[1] *vt iem. de hand ~* put (hold) out one's hand to sbd.; *de toegestoken hand* the proffered hand

'**toestel** (-len) *o* appliance, contrivance, apparatus; *⌁ machine*; [wireless, TV] set; (f o t o~, f i l m~) camera; *~ 13* ☏ extension 13

'**toestemmen**[1] **I** *vt dat wil ik u gaarne ~* I readily grant you that; **II** *vi* consent; *~ in* consent to, agree to; grant; accede to; **–d I** *aj* affirmative; **II** *ad* [reply] in the affirmative, affirmatively; *hij knikte ~* he nodded assent; '**toestemming** (-en) *v* consent, assent; *met (zonder) ~ van* with (without) the permission of

'**toestoppen**[1] *vt* stop up [a conduit]; stop [one's ears]; tuck in [a child]; *iem. iets ~* slip sth. into sbd.'s hand; **–stromen**[1] *vi* flow (stream, rush) towards, flock in, come flocking to [a place]; **–sturen**[1] *vt* send, forward; remit [money]

toet (-en) *m* 1 **F** (g e z i c h t) face; 2 (h a a r) bun, knot of hair

'**toetakelen**[1] **I** *vt* 1 (u i t d o s s e n) dress up, rig out; 2 (m i s h a n d e l e n) **F** knock about [a person]; damage [a thing]; *hij werd lelijk toegetakeld* **F** he was awfully knocked about; **II** *vr zich (gek) ~* dress up, rig oneself out; *wat heb jij je toegetakeld!* what a sight you are!; **–tasten**[1] *vt* help oneself, fall to [at dinner]

'**toeten** (toette, h. getoet) *vi* toot(le), hoot; *hij weet van ~ noch blazen* he doesn't know the first thing about it; **–er** (-s) *m* ⌁ horn, hooter; (a n d e r s) tooter; '**toeteren** (toeterde, h. getoeterd) *vi* toot, hoot; sound the (one's) horn

'**toetje** (-s) *o* 1 sweet, dessert; **F** afters; 2 bun, knot [of hair]; 3 pretty face

'**toetreden**[1] *vi o p iem. ~* walk up to sbd.; *~ t o t* join [a club, union &], accede to [a treaty]; **–ding** (-en) *v* accession, joining; *~ tot de E.E.C.* entry into the E.E.C.

toets (-en) *m* 1 (p e n s e e l s t r e e k) touch; 2 (p r o e f) test[2], assay; 3 key [of a piano; of a typewriter]; also: note [of a piano]; fingerboard [of guitar, violoncello &]; *de ~ (der kritiek) kunnen doorstaan* stand the test, pass muster; '**toetsen** (toetste, h. getoetst) *vt* try, test, put to the test [a person, thing, quality]; assay [metals]; *~ a a n* test by [the original]; *~ o p* test for [reliability]; '**toetsenbord** (-en) *o* keyboard; '**toetsinstrument** (-en) *o* ♪ keyboard instrument; **–naald** (-en) *v* touch-needle; **–steen** (-stenen) *m* touchstone[2];

[1] V.T. en V.D. van dit werkwoord volgens het model: 'toe**dekken**, V.T. dekte 'toe, V.D. 'toegedekt. Zie voor de vormen onder het grondwoord, in dit voorbeeld: *dekken*. Bij sterke en onregelmatige werkwoorden wordt u verwezen naar de lijst achterin.

–wedstrijd (-en) *m* test-match
'**toeval** (-len) 1 *o* accident, chance; 2 *m* & *o* ⚡ fit of epilepsy; *het ~ wilde dat*... it so happened that..., it chanced that...; *a a n ~len lijden* be epileptic; *b ij ~* by chance, by accident, accidentally; *bij louter ~* by sheer chance; *bij ~ ontmoette ik hem* ook: I happened to meet him; *d o o r een gelukkig ~* by some lucky chance
'**toevallen**[1] *vi* fall to; *hem ~* fall to his share; accrue to him [of interest]
toe'**vallig I** *aj* accidental, casual, fortuitous; *een ~e ontmoeting* ook: a chance meeting; **II** *ad* by chance, by accident, accidentally; *~ zag ik het* ook: I happened to see it; *wat ~!* what a coincidence!; **–erwijs, –erwijze** = *toevallig* **II**; **–heid** (-heden) *v* 1 (a b s t r a c t) casualness, fortuitousness, fortuity; 2 (c o n c r e e t) fortuity, coincidence, accident; '**toevalstreffer** (-s) *m* lucky shot
'**toeven** (toefde, h. getoefd) *vi* stay, ⊙ tarry
'**toeverlaat** *m* refuge, shield
'**toevertrouwen** (vertrouwde'toe, h. 'toevertrouwd) *vt iem. iets ~* entrust sbd. with sth., entrust sth. to sbd.; confide sth. [a secret] to sbd.; commit (consign) sth. to sbd.'s charge; *dat is hun wel toevertrouwd* trust them for that
'**toevliegen**[1] *vi ~ op* fly at
'**toevloed** *m* influx, inflow, flow
'**toevloeien**[1] *vi* flow to; accrue to; **–iing** *v* = *toevloed*
'**toevlucht** *v* refuge; recourse; *zijn ~ nemen tot* have recourse to, resort to; **–soord** (-en) *o* (haven of) refuge
'**toevoegen**[1] *vt* 1 add, join [something] to, subjoin [a subscript]; 2 address [words] to; *„zwijg!" voegde hij mij toe* 'silence!' he said to me; *wat heeft u daaraan toe te voegen?* what have you to add to that?; **–ging** *v* addition; '**toevoegsel** (-s) *o* supplement, additive
'**toevoer** (-en) *m* supply; **–buis** (-buizen) *v* supply-pipe; '**toevoeren**[1] *vt* supply; '**toevoerlijn** (-en) *v* supply line
'**toevouwen**[1] *vt* fold up; **–vriezen**[1] *vi* freeze over (up); **–wenden**[1] *vt = toekeren*; **–wenken**[1] *vt* beckon to; **–wensen**[1] *vt* wish; **–werpen**[1] *vt* cast [a glance &] at, throw, fling [it] to; *de deur ~* slam the door
'**toewijden**[1] **I** *vt* consecrate, dedicate [a church & to God]; dedicate [a book to a friend]; devote [one's time & to]; **II** *vr zich ~ aan* devote oneself to; **–ding** *v* devotion [to duty]
'**toewijzen**[1] *vt* allot, assign, award [a prize to...], allocate [sugar, fats &]; knock down [to the highest bidder]; **–zing** (-en) *v* allotment, assignment, award, allocation [for sugar, fats &]
'**toewuiven**[1] *vt* wave to; *zich koelte ~ met zijn strooien hoed* fan oneself with one's straw hat
'**toezeggen**[1] *vt* promise; **–ging** (-en) *v* promise
'**toezenden**[1] *vt* send, forward; remit [money]; **–ding** *v* sending, forwarding; remittance [of money]
'**toezicht** *o* surveillance, supervision, superintendence, inspection; *~ houden op de jongens* keep an eye on (look after) the boys; *wie moet ~ houden?* who is charged with the surveillance?; *het ~ uitoefenen over*... be charged with the supervision over..., supervise..., superintend...; *onder ~ van*... under the supervision of...;
'**toezien** *vi* 1 (t o e k ij k e n) look on; 2 (o p p a s s e n) take care, be careful; *ergens op ~* be careful; see to it that...; *~ op zie toezicht houden op, het toezicht uitoefenen over*; **–d voogd** co-guardian
'**toezingen**[1] *vt* sing to; *iem. een welkom ~* welcome sbd. with a song; **–zwaaien**[1] *vt* wave to; *lof ~* praise
tof S fine, swell
'**toffee** [-fe-, -fi.] (-s) *m* toffee
'**toga** ('s) *v* gown, robe, toga; *~ en bef* bands and gown
'**togen** V.T. meerv. v. *tijgen*
'**Togo** *o* Togo
toi'**let** [tʋɑ'lɛt] (-ten) *o* 1 toilet; dress; 2 toilettable, dressing-table; 3 (W.C.) lavatory, **F** loo; *Am* washroom; (d a m e s~) ladies' room, (h e r e n~) men's room; *~ maken* make one's toilet, dress; *een beetje ~ maken* smarten oneself up a bit; *in groot ~* in full dress; **–artikelen** *mv* toilet articles, toiletries; **–benodigdheden** *mv* toilet requisites; **–doos** (-dozen) *v* dressingcase; **–emmer** (-s) *m* slop-pail; **–juffrouw** (-en) *v* lavatory (cloakroom) attendant; **–papier** *o* toilet-paper; **–poeder** *o* & *m* toilet powder; **–spiegel** (-s) *m* toilet-mirror; chevalglass; **–tafel** (-s) *v* toilet-table, dressing-table; **–tas** (-sen) *v* dressing-case, sponge bag; **–zeep** *v* toilet soap
'**tokkelen** (tokkelde, h. getokkeld) **I** *vt* pluck, touch [the strings], touch [the harp &], twang [a guitar], thrum [a banjo]; **II** *va* thrum; '**tokkelinstrument** (-en) *o* plucked (string) instrument
'**tok-tok** (v a n h e n) cluck-cluck!
tol (-len) *m* 1 (s p e e l g o e d) top; ‖ 2 (s c h a t t i n g) toll[2], tribute; (b ij i n- e n u i t v o e r)

---

[1] V.T. en V.D. van dit werkwoord volgens het model: 'toe**dekken**, V.T. dekte 'toe, V.D. 'toe**ge**dekt. Zie voor de vormen onder het grondwoord, in dit voorbeeld: *dekken*. Bij sterke en onregelmatige werkwoorden wordt u verwezen naar de lijst achterin.

customs, duties; (b ij d o o r t o c h t) toll;
3 (t o l b o o m) turnpike; 4 (t o l h u i s) toll-
house; ~ *betalen* pay toll; *hij betaalde de* ~ *aan de
natuur* he paid the debt of (to) nature; ~ *heffen
van*... levy toll on; **–baas** (-bazen), **–beambte**
(-n en -s) *m* toll-collector, tollman; **–boom**
(-bomen) *m* turnpike, toll-bar; **–brug** (-gen) *v*
toll-bridge

tole'rant 1 tolerant; 2 (m o d e r n) permissive
[age,society]; **tole'rantie** [-(t)si.] 1 (v e r-
d r a a g z a a m h e i d) tolerance; 2 (g o d s-
d i e n s t i g) toleration; 3 (g e r i n g e a f-
w ij k i n g) allowance; **tole'reren** (tolereerde,
h. getolereerd) *vt* tolerate

'**tolgaarder** (-s) *m* toll-gatherer; **–geld** (-en) *o*
toll; **–hek** (-ken) *o* toll-gate; **–huis** (-huizen) *o*
toll-house

tolk (-en) *m* interpreter; *fig* mouthpiece

'**tolkantoor** (-toren) *o = tolhuis*

'**tollen** (tolde, h. getold) *vi* 1 (m e t t o l) spin a
top, play with a top; 2 (r o n d d r a a i e n)
whirl, go round and round; *in bed* ~ tumble
into bed; ~ *van de slaap* reel (stagger) with
sleep; *in het rond* ~ tumble about; *iem. in het
rond doen* ~ send sbd. spinning

'**tollenaar** (-s en -naren) *m* **B** publican;

'**tolmuur** (-muren) *m* tariff wall; **tol'plichtig**
subject to toll; **tolunie** (-s) *v*, **–verbond** *o*
customs union

'**tolvlucht** *v* ⁀ spin

'**tolvrij** toll-free, free of duty, duty-free; **–weg**
(-wegen) *m* toll-road, *Am* turnpike (road)

to'maat (-maten) *v* tomato; **to'matenpuree** *v*
tomato purée (pulp); **–soep** *v* tomato-soup;
to'matesap *o* tomato juice

'**tombe** (-s en -n) *v* tomb

'**tombola** ('s) *m* tombola

'**tomeloos** unbridled, unrestrained, ungovernable; **tome'loosheid** *v* licentiousness

'**tomen** (toomde, h. getoomd) *vt* bridle[2], *fig*
curb, check

ton (-nen) *v* 1 (v a t) cask, barrel; 2 (m a a t) ton;
3 ⚓ buoy; 4 a hundred thousand guilders

to'naal tonal; **tonali'teit** *v* tonality

'**tondel** *o* tinder; **–doos** (-dozen) *v* tinder-box

ton'deuse [s = z] (-s) *v* (pair of) clippers

to'neel (-nelen) *o* 1 stage; 2 scene [of an act]; 3
drama [as branch of literature of a country or
period], theatre [= plays and acting]; 4 *fig*
theatre, scene; *het* ~ *van de oorlog* the theatre
(seat) of war; ~ *spelen* act[2]; ● *b ij het* ~ on the
stage; *bij het* ~ *gaan* go on the stage; *o p het* ~
verschijnen appear on the stage, come on; *fig*
appear on the scene[2]; *t e n tonele voeren* put upon
the stage; *v a n het* ~ *verdwijnen* make one's
exit[2], disappear from the stage[2], make one's
bow[2]; **–aanwijzing** (-en) *v* stage-direction;

–achtig theatrical, stagy; **–benodigdheden**
mv stage-properties; **–bewerking** (-en) *v* stage
version; **–criticus** (ci) *m* dramatic critic;
–effect (-en) *o* stage-effect; **–gezelschap**
(-pen) *o* theatrical company; **–held** (-en) *m*
stage-hero; **–kapper** (-s) *m* theatre hairdresser;
–kijker (-s) *m* opera-glass, binoculars;
–knecht (-s) *m* stage-hand, flyman; **–kritiek**
(-en) *v* dramatic criticism; **–kunst** *v* dramatic
art, stage-craft; **–laars** (-laarzen) *v* buskin;
toneel'matig theatrical; **to'neelmeester** (-s)
m property master, stage manager; **–opvoering** (-en) *v* (theatrical) performance;
–scherm (-en) *o* 1 (g o r d ij n) (stage-)curtain,
(act-)drop; 2 (c o u l i s s e) side-scene; **–schikking** (-en) *v* setting of a (the) play; **–school**
(-scholen) *v* school of acting, academy of
dramatic art; **–schrijver** (-s) *m* playwright,
dramatist; **–speelster** (-s) *v* (stage-)actress;
–spel *o* 1 acting; 2 (-spelen) = *toneelstuk*;
–speler (-s) *m* (stage-)actor, player; **–stuk**
(-ken) *o* (stage-)play; **–voorstelling** (-en) *v*
theatrical performance; **–zolder** (-s) *m* flies;
tone'list (-en) *m* actor

'**tonen** (toonde, h. getoond) **I** *vt* show; **II** *vr zich*
~ show oneself; **III** *va* make a show; *zó* ~ *ze
meer* they make a better show

tong (-en) *v* 1 tongue; 2 ⚠ sole [a fish]; *hij heeft
een gladde* ~ he has got a glib tongue; *een kwade*
~ *hebben* have an evil tongue; *hij heeft een lange
(scherpe)* ~ he has a long (a sharp) tongue; *zijn*
~ *laten gaan (roeren)* be talking away; *zijn* ~
uitsteken put out (stick out) one's tongue (at
tegen); *steek uw* ~ *uit* put out your tongue, show
me your tongue; *zijn* ~ *slaat dubbel* he speaks
thickly; *o p de* ~ *rijden*, *o v e r de* ~ *gaan* be the
talk of the town; **–been** (-deren) *o* tongue-
bone

'**tongewelf** (-welven) *o* barrel vault

'**tongklank** (-en) *m* lingual; **–klier** (-en) *v*
lingual gland; **–riem** *m* string of the tongue;
goed van de ~ *gesneden zijn* have a ready tongue;
–spier (-en) *v* lingual muscle; **–val** (-len) *m*
1 accent; 2 dialect; **–vormig** tongue-shaped;
–wortel (-s) *m* root of the tongue; **–zenuw**
(-en) *v* lingual nerve

'**tonic** ['tònık] *m* tonic, tonic water

'**tonicum** (-s en -ca) *o* tonic [medicine]

to'nijn (-en) *m* tunny

ton'nage [-'na.ʒə] *v* tonnage; '**tonnegeld** (-en)
o tonnage; '**tonneninhoud** *m*, **–maat** *v*
tonnage; '**tonrond** tubby

ton'sil (-len) *v* tonsil

ton'suur [s = z] (-suren) *v* tonsure

1 toog (togen) *m* cassock [of a priest]

2 toog (togen) V.T. van *tijgen*

'**toogdag** (-dagen) *m* rally

tooi *m* attire, array, trimmings; **'tooien** (tooide, h. getooid) **I** *vt* adorn, decorate, array, (be)deck; **II** *vr zich* ~ adorn & oneself; **'tooisel** (-s) *o* finery, ornament

toom (tomen) *m* bridle, reins; *een* ~ *kippen* a brood of hens; *in* ~ *houden* keep in check, check², *fig* bridle, curb [one's tongue &]

toon (tonen) *m* 1 tone; 2 (t o o n h o o g t e) pitch; 3 (k l a n k) sound; 4 (k l e m t o o n) accent, stress; 5 *fig* tone [of a letter, debate &, also of a picture &]; *de goede* ~ good form; *de* ~ *aangeven* give the tone²; *fig* ook: set the tone; set the fashion; *een* ~ *aanslaan* strike a note; *fig* take a high tone; *u hoeft tegen mij niet zo'n* ~ *aan te slaan* you need not take this tone with me; *een andere* ~ *aanslaan* change one's tone; *in zijn brieven slaat hij een andere* ~ *aan* his letters are in a different strain; *een hoge* ~ *aanslaan* take a high tone; (*goed*) ~ *houden* keep in tune [of singer]; keep in tune [of instrument]; *de juiste* ~ *treffen* strike the right note; ● *o p bevelende* (*gebiedende*) ~ in a tone of command; *op hoge* (*zachte*) ~ in a high (low) tone; *op de tonen van de muziek* to the strains of the music; *het is t e g e n de goede* ~ it is bad form; **–aangevend** leading; **–aard** (-en) *m ♪* key [major or minor]; **–afstand** *m ♪* interval; **–baar** presentable, fit to be shown, fit to be seen; **–bank** (-en) *v* counter; **–beeld** (-en) *o* model, pattern, paragon; *een* ~ *van...* the very picture of...; **–demper** (-s) *m ♪* mute; **–der** (-s) *m* $ bearer; *betaalbaar aan* ~ (*dezes*) $ payable to bearer; **–dichter** (-s) *m ♪* (musical) composer; **–gevend** leading; **–hoogte** (-n en -s) *v ♪* pitch; **–kamer** (-s) *v* show-room; **–kunst** *v ♪* music; **–kunstenaar** (-s) *m,* **–kunstenares** (-sen) *v ♪* musician; **–ladder** (-s) *v ♪* gamut, scale; ~*s spelen* practise scales; **–loos** 1 toneless [voice]; 2 unaccented, unstressed [syllable]; **–schaal** (-schalen) *v* scale, gamut; **–soort** (-en) *v ♪* key; mode; **–teken** (-s) *o gram* accent, stressmark; **–tje** (-s) *o een* ~ *lager zingen* climb down, F sing small; *iem. een* ~ *lager doen zingen* make sbd. sing another tune, take sbd. down a peg or two, knock sbd. off his perch; **–vast** *♪* keeping tune; **–zaal** (-zalen) *v* show-room; **–zetter** (-s) *m ♪* (musical) composer; **–zetting** (-en) *v ♪* (musical) composition

toorn *m* anger, wrath, choler, ☉ ire; **'toornen** (toornde, h. getoornd) *vi* be angry (wrathful); **'toornig I** *aj* angry, wrathful, irate; **II** *ad* angrily, wrathfully

toorts (-en) *v* 1 torch, link; 2 ♫ mullein; **–drager** (-s) *m* torch-bearer; **–licht** (-en) *o* torch-light

toost (-en) *m* toast [to the health of...]; *een* ~ *instellen* (*uitbrengen*) give (propose) a toast;

'toosten (toostte, h. getoost) *vi* give (propose) a toast

1 top (-pen) *m* 1 top, summit [of a mountain]; 2 tip [of the finger]; 3 apex [of a triangle]; *de* ~ *van de mast* the mast-head; *met de vlag in* ~ the flag flying at the mast-head; *t e n* ~ to extremes; *ten* ~ *stijgen* rise to a climax; *v a n* ~ *tot teen* from top to toe, from head to foot

2 top *ij* 1 done!, it's a go!, I'm on!; 2 (b ij w e d-d e n s c h a p) taken!

to'paas (-pazen) *m & o* topaz

'topartiest (-en) *m* (all) star, top-liner; **–conditie** [-(t)si.] *v = topvorm*; **–conferentie** [-(t)si.] (-s) *v* summit meeting, summit conference; **–functie** [-ksi.] (-s) *v* leading (top) function; **–functionaris** (-sen) *m* leading (senior) executive; **–hoek** (-en) *m* vertical angle

topi'namboer (-s) *m* Jerusalem artichoke

'topjaar (-jaren) *o* peak year; **–licht** (-en) *o* mast-head light

topo'graaf (-grafen) *m* topographer; **topogra'fie** (-ieën) *v* topography; **topo'grafisch** topographic(al)

'toppen (topte, h. getopt) *vt* top [a tree]

'topprestatie [-(t)si.] (-s) *v* record; ✗ maximum performance; maximum output [of a factory]; **–punt** (-en) *o* 1 (i n 't a l g.) top², summit²; 2 (i n m e e t k u n d e) vertex, apex; 3 (i n s t e r r e n k u n d e) culminating point; 4 *fig* top, culminating point, acme, pinnacle, zenith, climax; *dat is het* ~ *!* F that's the limit!, that puts the lid on!, that beats all!; *het* ~ *van mijn eerzucht* the top of my ambition; *het* ~ *van onbeschaamdheid* the height of insolence; *het* ~ *van volmaaktheid* the summit (the acme) of perfection; *het* ~ *bereiken* reach its acme, reach a climax; *op het* ~ *van zijn* (*haar*) *roem* at the height of his (her) fame; **–salaris** (-sen) *o* top salary; **–snelheid** *v* top speed; **–speler** (-s) *m* top player, first-rate player; **–vorm** *m in* ~ *zijn* be at the top of one's form, be in top form; **–zwaar** top-heavy²

'toque [tɔ.k] (-s) *v* toque

tor (-ren) *v* beetle

'toren (-s) *m* tower [not tapering]; steeple [with a spire]; turret [for guns]; *hoog van de* ~ *blazen* boast, bag; **–flat** [-flit] (-s) *m* tower-block of flats, multi-storey flat; **–garage** [-ʒə] (-s) *v* multi-storey car park; **–hoog** as high as a steeple, towering; **–klok** (-ken) *v* 1 tower-clock, church-clock; 2 church-bell; **–kraan** (-kranen) *v* tower-crane; **–spits** (-en) *v* spire; **–springen** *o* (v. z w e m m e r s) high diving; **–tje** (-s) *o* turret; *van* ~*s voorzien* turreted; **–uil** (-en) *m = kerkuil*; **–valk** (-en) *m & v* kestrel, windhover; **–wachter** (-s) *m* watchman on a tower; **-zwaluw** (-en) *v* = *gierzwaluw*

torn (-en) *v* seam come undone (unstitched)

tor'nado ('s) *v* tornado

'**tornen I** (tornde, h. getornd) *vt* rip (up); **II** (tornen, is getornd) *vi* come unsewed; *daar valt niet aan te ~* that is irrevocable, unshakable; *niet ~ aan* not meddle with, not tamper with [rights]; '**tornmesje** (-s) *o* ripper

torpe'deren (torpedeerde, h. getorpedeerd) *vt* torpedo[2]; **tor'pedo** ('s) *v* torpedo; **-boot** (-boten) *m* & *v* torpedo-boat; **-jager** (-s) *m* (torpedo-boat) destroyer; **-lanceerbuis** (-buizen) *v* torpedo-tube

tors (-en) *m* = *torso*

'**torsen** (torste, h. getorst) *vt* carry [a bag, on the back], bear [a heavy burden]

'**torsie** [s = z] *v* torsion

'**torso** ('s) *m* torso

'**tortel** (-s) *m* & *v* turtle-dove; **-duif** (-duiven) *v* turtle-dove; '**tortelen** (tortelde, h. getorteld) *vi* bill and coo

Tos'caan(s) (-canen) *m* (& *aj*) Tuscan; **Tos'cane** *o* Tuscany

'**tossen** (toste, h. getost) *vi* toss (up) for

tot I *prep* 1 (v. a f s t a n d) to, as far as; 2 (v a n t ij d) till, until, to; 3 (b ij b e p a l i n g v a n g e s t e l d h e i d) as, for & o n v e r t a a l d; *benoemd ~ gouverneur* appointed governor; *~ vriend kiezen* choose [sbd.] for (as) a friend; *die woorden ~ de zijne maken* make those words his own; *~ 1848* till (up to) 1848; [go] as far back as 1848; *van 8 ~ 12* from 8 to (till) twelve o'clock; *~ de laatste cent* to the last farthing; *~ dan toe* until then, up to then; *~ hier(toe)* thus far; *~ nu toe (nog toe)* till now, up to now; so far; *~ en met...* up to and including [May 15], as far as [page 50] inclusive; ● *~ a a n de armen* up to their arms; *~ aan de borst (de knieën)* breast-high, knee-deep; *~ aan de top* as high as the top; up to the top; *~ b o v e n 3 2°* to above 32°; *~ i n de dood (getrouw)* (faithful) (un)to death; *~ in zijn laatste regeringsjaar* down to the last year of his reign; *~ o p de bodem* down to the bottom; as low down as the bottom; *~ op een stuiver* to within a penny; *~ v o o r enkele jaren* up to a few years ago; **II** *cj* till,until

to'taal I *aj* total, all over; **II** (-talen) *o* total (amount), sum total; *in ~* in all, altogether, totalling [1500 persons]; **-bedrag** *o* sum total, total amount; **-beeld** *o* overall picture; **-indruk** *m* general impression

totali'sator [s = z] (-s) *m* totalizator, **F** tote

totali'tair [- 'tɛ: r] totalitarian; **totalita'risme** *o* totalitarianism

totali'teit *v* entirety, totality

tot'dat till, until

'**totebel** (-len) *v* 1 *eig* square net; 2 *fig* slattern; *ouwe ~* old frump

'**totem** (-s) *m* totem; **-paal** (-palen) *m* totem pole

'**toto** *m* 1 (s p o r t~, v o e t b a l~) pool; 2 (b ij w e d r e n) = *totalisator*

tot'standkoming *v* realization, completion

tou'cheren [tu: 'ʃe.rə(n)] (toucheerde, h. getoucheerd) *vt* 1 touch°; 2 ☛ examine [rectally, vaginally]

tou'peren [tu:-] (toupeerde, h. getoupeerd) *vt* tease, backcomb; **tou'pet** (-s en -ten) *m* toupet, toupee

'**touringcar** ['tu:rɪŋka:r] (-s) *m* & *v* (motor-) coach

tour'nee [tu:r'ne.] (-s) *v* tour (of inspection); *een ~ maken (in)* tour; *op ~ gaan* go on tour

tourni'quet [tu:rni.'kɛt] (-s) *o* & *m* turnstile

touw (-en) *o* 1 (v o o r w e r p) rope [over one inch thick]; cord [= thin rope]; string [= thin cord]; 2 (s t o f) rope; *~ pluizen* pick oakum; *er is geen ~ aan vast te knopen* you can make neither head nor tail of it; *ik ben de hele dag i n ~ geweest* I have been in harness all day; *o p ~ zetten* undertake [something]; get up [a show]; engineer [a war]; launch [a scheme]; **-klimmen** *o* rope-climbing; **-ladder** (-s) *v* rope-ladder; **-slager** (-s) *m* rope-maker; **-slagerij** (-en) *v* rope-walk; **-tje** (-s) *o* (bit of) string; *de ~s in handen hebben, aan de ~s trekken* pull the strings; **-tjespringen I** *vi* skip; **II** *o* skipping; **-trekken** *o* tug-of-war[2]; **-werk** *o* 1 cordage, ropes; 2 ⚓ rigging

t.o.v. = *ten opzichte van* zie *opzicht*

'**tovenaar** (-s en -naren) *m* sorcerer, magician, wizard, enchanter; **tovena'res** (-sen) *v* sorceress, witch; **tovena'rij** (-en) *v* = *toverij*; '**toverachtig I** *aj* fairy-like, magic(al); charming, enchanting; **II** *ad* magically; **-beker** (-s) *m* magic cup; **-boek** (-en) *o* conjuring-book; **-cirkel** (-s) *m* magic circle; **-drank** (-en) *m* magic potion; '**toveren** (toverde, h. getoverd) **I** *vi* 1 practise sorcery; 2 (g o o c h e l e n) conjure; *ik kan niet ~* I am no wizard; **II** *vt* conjure (up)[2]; *een ei uit een hoed ~* conjure an egg out of a hat; '**toverfluit** (-en) *v* magic flute; **-formule** (-s) *v*, **-formulier** (-en) *o* magic formula, spell, charm, incantation; **-godin** (-nen) *v* fairy; **-hazelaar** (-s) *m* wych-hazel, witch-hazel; **-heks** (-en) *v* witch; **tove'rij** (-en) *v* sorcery, witchcraft, magic; '**toverkol** (-len) *v* witch, hag; **-kracht** *v* witchcraft, spell; **-kunst** (-en) *v* sorcery, magic (art); **~en** magic tricks, tricks of magic, witchcraft; **-lantaarn, -lantaren** (-s) *v* magic lantern; **-middel** (-en) *o* charm, spell, magic means; **-paleis** (-leizen) *o* enchanted palace;

–ring (-en) *m* magic ring; **–roede** (-n) *v* magic wand; **–slag** *m als bij* ~ as if (as) by magic; **–spiegel** (-s) *m* 1 (i n s p r o o k j e) magic mirror; 2 (o p k e r m i s) distorting mirror; **–spreuk** (-en) *v* incantation, spell, charm, abracadabra; **–staf** (-staven) *m* magic wand; **–woord** (-en) *o* magic word, spell, charm

'toxisch toxic

traag I *aj* slow, tardy, indolent, sluggish, slothful, inert; ~ *van begrip* slow-witted; **II** *ad* slowly, tardily &; **–heid** *v* 1 (i n 't a l g.) slowness, indolence, inertness, sluggishness, slothfulness; 2 (i n n a t u u r k u n d e) inertia

1 traan (tranen) *m* & *v* tear, tear-drop; *de tranen stonden hem in de ogen* tears were in his eyes, his eyes brimmed with tears; *hij zal er geen* ~ *om laten* he will not shed a tear over it; *tranen met tuiten schreien, hete tranen schreien* cry one's heart out, cry bitterly, shed hot tears; *tot tranen geroerd zijn* be moved to tears

2 traan *m* train-oil; **–achtig** = *tranig*

'traanbuis (-buizen) *v* tear-duct; **–gas** *o* tear-gas; **–gasbom** (-men) *v* tear-gas bomb; **–klier** (-en) *v* lachrymal gland

'traankoker (-s) *m* train-oil boiler; **traan-koke'rij** (-en) *v* try-house; *drijvende* ~ ⚓ factory-ship

'traanogen (traanoogde, h. getraanoogd) *vi* have watery eyes; **–vocht** *o* lachrymal fluid; **–zak** (-ken) *m* lachrymal sac

tra'cé (-s) *o* (ground-)plan, trace; **tra'ceren** (traceerde, h. getraceerd) *vt* trace, trace out [a plan]

'trachten (trachtte, h. getracht) *vt* try, attempt, endeavour; ~ *naar* = *streven naar*

'tractie ['traksi.] *v* traction, haulage; **'tractor** ['trak-, 'trɪk-] (-s en - 'toren) *m* tractor

trad (traden) V.T. van *treden*

tra'ditie [- 'di.(t)si.] (-s) *v* tradition; **–getrouw** true to tradition (custom); **traditiona'listisch** traditionalist; **traditio'neel** traditional; time-honoured; customary

tra'gedie (-s en -iën) *v* tragedy; **tra'giek** *v* tragedy [of life]; **tragi'medie** (-s) *v* tragi-comedy; **tragi'komisch** tragi-comic; **'tragisch I** *aj* tragic(al); **II** *ad* tragically

'trainen ['tre.nə(n)] (trainde, h. getraind) **I** *vt* train, coach; **II** *vr zich* ~ train; **–er** (-s) *m* trainer, coach

trai'neren [trɪ'ne:rə(n)] (traineerde, h. getraineerd) **I** *vi* hang fire, drag (on); ~ *met* delay; **II** *vt* drag one's feet over [a matter]

'training ['tre.-] *v* training; **'trainingsbroek** (-en) *v* track-suit trousers; **–pak** (-ken) *o* track suit

trait d'union [trɪdy.ni.'õ] (-s) *o* & *m* hyphen

traite [trɪ.t] (-s) *v* $ draft

tra'ject (-en) *o* way, distance, stretch; section [of railway line]; stage [of bus &]

trak'taat (-taten) *o* treaty; **–je** (-s) *o* tract

trak'tatie [-(t)si.] (-s) *v* treat

trakte'ment (-en) *o* salary, pay; **trakte'mentsdag** (-en) *m* pay-day; **–verhoging** (-en) *v* rise, increase (of salary)

trak'teren (trakteerde, h. getrakteerd) **I** *vt* (o n t h a l e n) treat, regale [one's friends]; *hen op een fles* ~ stand them a bottle, treat them to a bottle, regale them with a bottle; **II** *va* & *vi* stand treat, stand drinks; *ik trakteer!* my treat!, this is on me!

'tralie (-s en -iën) *v* bar; ~*s* ook: lattice, trellis, grille; *achter de* ~*s* behind (prison) bars, under lock and key, **F** inside; **–deur** (-en) *v* grated door; **'traliën** (traliede, h. getralied) *vt* grate, lattice, trellis; **'tralievenster** (-s) *o* 1 (m e t t r a l i e s, v. g e v a n g e n i s &) barred window; 2 (v a n l a t w e r k) lattice-window; **–werk** *o* lattice-work, trellis-work

tram [trɪm] (-s en -men) *v* tram, tram-car; **–bestuurder** (-s) *m* motorman; **–conducteur** (-s) *m* tramconductor; **–halte** (-s) *v* stopping-place, (tram-)stop; **–huisje** (-s) *o* (tram) shelter; **–kaartje** (-s) *o* tramway ticket, tram ticket; **–lijn** (-en) *v* tramline

tramme'lant *o* & *m* row, to-do, rumpus

'trammen ['trɪmə(n)] (tramde, h. en is getramd) *vi* go by tram

trampo'line (-s) *v* trampoline

'tramwagen (-s) *m* tram-car; **–weg** (-wegen) *m* tramway

trance [trãs] (-s) *v* trance

tranche [trɑɲʃ] (-s) *v* $ instalment [of a loan]; **tran'cheren** [- 'ʃe.rə(n)] (trancheerde, h. getrancheerd) *vt* carve

'tranen (traande, h. getraand) *vi* water; ~*de ogen* watering eyes; **'tranendal** *o* vale of tears; **–vloed** *m* flood of tears

'tranig like train-oil, train-oil...

'trans (-en) *m* 1 (o m g a n g v. t o r e n) gallery; 2 (r a n d) battlements

trans'actie [- 'aksi.] (-s) *v* transaction, deal

transat'lantisch transatlantic

transcenden'taal transcendental

transcri'beren (transcribeerde, h. getranscribeerd) *vt* transcribe [in z. ♪]; transliterate [Russian names &]

tran'scriptie [-skrɪpsi-] (-s) *v* transcription [in z. ♪]; transliteration [of Russian names &]

tran'sept (-en) *o* transept

transfor'matie [-(t)si.] (-s) *v* transformation; **transfor'mator** (-s en - 'toren) *m* ⚡ transformer; **transfor'meren** (transformeerde, h. getransformeerd) *vt* transform

trans'fusie [-zi.] (-s) *v* transfusion

tran'sistor [-'zɪs-] (-s) *m* transistor; **transis-**
tori'seren [-'ze.rɔ(n)] (transistoriseerde, h.
getransistoriseerd) *vt* transistorize; **tran-**
'sistorradio ('s) *m* transistor radio; **–toestel**
(-len) *o* transistor set

'transitief [s = z] transitive

tran'sito [s = z] *m* transit; **–handel** *m* transit-
trade; **–magazijn** (-en) *o* transit store,
entrepot

transi'toir [-zi.'tʋa:r] transitory

transla'teur (-s) *m* translator

trans'missie (-s) *v* transmission

transpa'rant I *aj* transparent; **II** (-en) *o*
1 transparency [picture]; 2 black lines
[for writing]

transpi'ratie [-(t)si.] *v* perspiration;
transpi'reren (transpireerde, h. getranspi-
reerd) *vi* perspire

transplan'taat (-taten) *o* 🏵 transplant, graft;
transplan'tatie [-(t)si.] (-s) *v* 🏵 trans-
plant(ation), graft(ing); **transplan'teren**
(transplanteerde, h. getransplanteerd) *vt* 🏵
transplant, graft

transpo'neren (transponeerde, h. getranspo-
neerd) *vt* transpose

trans'port (-en) *o* 1 (v e r v o e r) transport,
conveyance, carriage; 2 (i n r e k e n i n g e n)
amount carried forward; *per* ~ **$** carried
forward (over); **–band** (-en) *m* 🪓 conveyor
belt; **transpor'teren** (transporteerde, h.
getransporteerd) *vt* 1 transport, convey;
2 **$** carry forward [in book-keeping];
transpor'teur (-s) *m* 1 (p e r s o o n) transporter; 2 (i n s t r u m e n t) protractor;
trans'portfiets (-en) *m* & *v* carrier cycle;
–kabel (-s) *m* telpher; **–kosten** *mv* cost'of
transport, carriage; **–middelen** *mv* means of
transport (conveyance); **–schip** (-schepen) *o*
transport(-ship); 🪝 troop-ship; **–vliegtuig**
(-en) *o* transport plane; ~*(en)* ook: transport
aircraft; **–wezen** *o* transport

transsubstanti'atie [-stɑnsi.'a.(t)si.] *v* transub-
stantiation

trant *m* manner, way, fashion, style; *i n d e* ~ *van*
after the manner of; *n a a r d e oude* ~ in the old
style

1 **trap** (-pen) *m* 1 (s c h o p) kick; 2 (t r e d e)
step; 3 (g r a a d) degree, step; 4 (v. r a k e t)
stage; *de* ~*pen van vergelijking* the degrees of
comparison; *stellende* ~ positive (degree);
vergrotende ~ comparative (degree); *overtreffende*
~ superlative (degree); *iem. een* ~ *geven* give
sbd. a kick; *op een hoge* ~ *van beschaving* at a high
degree of civilization; *op de laagste* ~ *van*
beschaving on the lowest plane of civilization

2 **trap** (-pen) *m* 1 (h e t g e h e e l v a n
t r e d e n) stairs, staircase, flight of stairs;

2 (t r a p l a d d e r) step-ladder, (pair of) steps;
de ~ *af* down the stairs, downstairs; *de* ~ *op* up
the stairs, upstairs; ~ *op,* ~ *af* up and down the
stairs, upstairs and downstairs; *iem. van de* ~*pen*
gooien kick sbd. downstairs

tra'peze (-s) *v* trapeze; **tra'pezium** (-s en -zia)
o 1 (m e e t k u n d e) trapezium; 2 (g y m n a s -
t i e k) trapeze

'trapgans (-ganzen) *v* bustard

'trapgat (-gaten) *o* (stair)well; **–gevel** (-s) *m*
stepped gable; **–ladder** (-s), **–leer** (-leren) *v*
step-ladder, (pair of) steps; **–leuning** (-en) *v*
banisters, handrail; **–loper** (-s) *m* stair-carpet

'trap(naai)machine [-ʃi.nə] (-s) *v* treadle
sewing-machine

'trappehuis (-huizen) *o* staircase, well

'trappelen (trappelde, h. getrappeld) *vi*
trample, stamp [with impatience]

'trappen (trapte, h. getrapt) I *vi* 1 kick (at *naar*);
2 (o p f i e t s) pedal; *erin* ~ [*fig*] fall for it,
swallow (take) the bait; ~ *op* step (tread) on;
II *vt* tread; kick; *het orgel* ~ blow the organ; *ik*
laat me niet ~ I won't suffer myself to be
kicked; *ze moeten zulke... eruit* ~ they ought to
kick them out of the service; *hij werd eruit*
getrapt he got the boot, **F** he was fired [from
his billet]; ⊗ **F** he was chucked out; zie ook: 2
teen; **–er** (-s) *m* treadle [of organ, lathe, bicycle
&]; pedal [of bicycle]

trap'pist (-en) *m* Trappist; **–enklooster** (-s) *o*
Trappist monastery

'trapportaal (-talen) *o* landing; **–roe(de)** (-roes,
-roeden) *v* stair-rod; **–sgewijs, –sgewijze I** *aj*
gradual; **II** gradually, by degrees; **–tre(d)e**
(-treden en -treeën) *v* stairstep

tras'saat (-saten) *m* **$** drawee; **tras'sant** (-en) *m*
$ drawer; **tras'seren** (trasseerde, h. getras-
seerd) *vi* **$** draw

'trauma ('s en -ta) *v* & *o* trauma; **trau'matisch**
traumatic; **traumati'seren** [s = z] (traumati-
seerde, h. getraumatiseerd) *vt* traumatize,
shock

tra'vee (-veeën) *v* trave

tra'verse [s = z] (-n) *v* (d w a r s b a l k) cross-
beam; (d w a r s v e r b i n d i n g) traverse

traves'teren (travesteerde, h. getravesteerd) *vt*
travesty; **traves'tie** (-ieën) *v* 1 (l a c h w e k -
k e n d e v o o r s t e l l i n g) travesty; 2 (v e r -
k l e d i n g a l s h e t a n d e r e g e -
s l a c h t) transvestism; **traves'tiet** (-en) *m*
& *v* transvestite

tra'want (-en) *m* satellite², *fig* > henchman

'trechter (-s) *m* 1 funnel; 2 (v. m o l e n)
hopper; 3 (v. g r a n a a t) crater; **–vormig**
funnel-shaped

tred (treden) *m* tread, step, pace; *gelijke* ~ *houden*
met keep step (pace) with; *met vaste* ~ with a

firm step; **'trede** (-n) *v* 1 (b ij 't l o p e n) step, pace; 2 (v. t r a p, rijt u i g) step; 3 (v a n l a d d e r) rung; 4 (t r a p p e r) treadle [of a sewing-machine]; **'treden* I** *vi* tread, step, walk; *daarin kan ik niet ~* I cannot accede to that; I can't fall in with the proposal; *in bijzonderheden ~* enter into detail(s); *in dienst ~ & zie dienst &; nader ~* approach; *naar voren ~* come to the front; *~ uit* withdraw from [a club], leave [the Church, a party &]; **II** *vt* tread; **'tredmolen** (-s) *m* treadmill[2]; *fig* jogtrot; **tree** (treeën en -s) = *trede*

treeft (-en) *v* trivet

'treeplank (-en) *v* foot-board [of railway carriage]

tref *m* chance; *wát een ~!* how lucky!; *het is een ~ als je...* it is a mere chance if...; **'treffen* I** *vt* 1 (r a k e n) hit, strike[2]; *fig* touch, move; (s t e r k ~) shock; 2 (a a n t r e f f e n) meet (with); *het doel ~* hit the mark[2]; *hij is door een ongeluk getroffen* he met with an accident; *hem treft geen schuld* no blame attaches to him; *regelingen ~* make arrangements; *personen die door dit verbod getroffen worden* persons affected by this prohibition; *u heeft de gelijkenis goed getroffen* you have hit off the likeness; *je treft het, dat...* lucky for you that...; *je treft het niet* bad luck for you; *we hebben het goed getroffen* we have been lucky; *dat treft u ongelukkig* bad luck for you; *ik heb het die dag slecht getroffen* I was very unlucky that day; *iem. thuis ~* find sbd. at home; *waar kan ik je ~?* where can I find you?; *we troffen hem toevallig te S.* we came across him (chanced upon him) at S.; **II** *vi dat treft goed* nothing could have happened better, that's lucky; **III** *o* encounter, engagement, fight; *-d* striking [resemblance]; touching [scene]; well-chosen [words]; **'treffer** (-s) *m* ⚔ hit[2]; *fig* lucky hit; **'trefkans** (-en) *v* hit probability; **–punt** (-en) *o* 1 ⚔ point of impact; 2 (v. p e r s o n e n) meeting place; **–woord** (-en) *o* entry, headword; **tref'zeker** sure [hit]; precise; sound [player]; **–heid** *v* sureness; precision; soundness

treil (-en) *m* 1 tow-line; 2 trawl(-net); **'treilen** (treilde, h. getreild) *vt* 1 tow; 2 trawl [with a net]; **–er** (-s) *m* ⚓ trawler

trein (-en) *m* 1 (railway) train; 2 retinue, suite; 3 ⚔ train; **–beambte** (-n) *m* railway official; **–botsing** (-en) *v* train collision, train crash; **–conducteur** (-s) *m* (railway) guard; **–enloop** *m* train-service; **–personeel** *o* train staff; **–ramp** (-en) *v* train disaster; **–reis** (-reizen) *v* train journey; **–stel** (-len) *o* train unit, coach

'treiteraar (-s) *m* tease, teaser, pesterer; **'treiteren** (treiterde, h. getreiterd) *vt* vex, nag, tease, pester

trek (-ken) *m* 1 (r u k) pull, tug, haul; 2 (a a n

p ij p) pull; 3 (v. s c h o o r s t e e n) draught; 4 (t o c h t) draught; 5 (h e t t r e k k e n) migration [of birds]; (*ZA*) trek [journey by ox-wagon]; 6 (h a a l m e t d e p e n &) stroke; dash; 7 ◊ trick; 8 (i n g e w e e r l o o p) groove; 9 (g e l a a t s t r e k) feature, lineament; 10 (k a r a k t e r t r e k) trait; 11 (l u s t) mind, inclination; 12 (e e t l u s t) appetite; *een paar ~ken (aan zijn pijp) doen* have a few whiffs; *alle ~ken halen* ◊ make all the tricks; *(geen) ~ hebben* have an (no) appetite; *~ hebben in iets* have a mind for sth.; *ik zou wel ~ hebben in een kop thee* I should not mind a cup of tea; *(geen) ~ hebben om te...* have a (no) mind to..., (not) feel like ...ing; *zijn ~ken thuis krijgen* have the tables turned on one, have one's chickens come home to roost; *er is geen ~ in de kachel* the stove doesn't draw; ● *aan zijn ~(ken) komen* [*fig*] come into one's own; *i n ~ zijn* be in demand (request); *ze zijn erg in ~ bij* they are in great request with, very popular with; *in brede ~ken* in broad outline; *in korte ~ken* in brief outline, briefly; *in vluchtige ~ken* in broad outline; *in grote ~ken aangeven* outline [a plan]; *m e t één ~ (van de pen)* with one stroke; *o p d e ~ zitten* sit in a draught; **–automaat** [-o.to. of -ɔuto-] (-maten) *m* slot-machine; **–bal** (-len) *m* ♋ twister; **–bank** (-en) *v* ⚔ draw-bench; **–beest, –dier** (-en) *o* draught-animal; **–haak** (-haken) *m* towing-hook; **–hond** (-en) *m* draught-dog

'trekje (-s) *o* (a a n e e n s i g a r e t &) puff, drag

'trekkebekken (trekkebekte, h. getrekkebekt) *vi* bill and coo

'trekken* I *vi* 1 (r u k k e n) draw, pull, tug; 2 (v. s c h e e r m e s) pull; 3 (g a a n, r e i z e n) go, march; *sp* hike; *ZA* trek [of people]; migrate [of birds]; 4 (k r o m t r e k k e n) warp, become warped; 5 (v a n t h e e &) draw; 6 (v a n s c h o o r s t e e n &) draw; 7 *fig* draw [customers &]; *het trekt hier* there is a draught here; *er op uit ~* set out, ☉ set forth; *zij ~ heen en weer* they go up and down the country; *de thee laten ~* let the tea draw; *de thee staat te ~* the tea draws; ● *a a n* pull (tug, tear) at; pull, tug; *aan de bel ~* pull the bell; *aan zijn haar ~* pull one's hair; *hij trok aan zijn pijp, maar zijn pijp trok niet* he pulled at his pipe, but his pipe didn't draw; *aan zijn sigaret ~* draw on one's cigarette; *m e t zijn linkerbeen trekt hij* he has a limp in his left leg; *met de mond trekt hij* his mouth twitches; *zij trokken n a a r het westen* they moved (marched) west; *o p iem. ~* \$ draw on sbd.; *u i t dit huis ~* move out of this house; *zij ~ v a n d e ene plaats naar de andere* they move from place to place; *als dat niet trekt, trekt niemendal* if that doesn't fetch them, I don't know what will; **II** *vt* 1 draw² [a load, a line, a revolver, his sword, many people, customers &]; rule [lines]; take out [a gun]; pull [something]; tow [a ship, motorcar]; 2 force [plants]; *een bal* ~ ∞ twist a ball; *draad* ~ draw wire; *een prijs* ~ $ draw a prize; *een mooi salaris* & ~ draw a handsome salary &; *een tand* ~ draw a tooth; *een tand laten* ~ have a tooth drawn; *een wissel* ~ *(op)* $ draw a bill (on); ● *hij trok mij a a n mijn haar* he pulled my hair; *hij trok mij aan mijn mouw* he pulled (at) my sleeve; *iem. aan de (zijn) oren* ~ pull sbd.'s ears; *hij trok zijn hoed i n de ogen* he pulled his hat over his eyes; *hem o p zij* ~ draw him aside; *zich de haren u i t het hoofd* ~ tear one's hair; *iem. uit het water* ~ draw (pull, haul) sbd. out of the water; *een les* ~ *uit* draw a lesson from; *we moesten hen v a n elkaar* ~ we had to pull them apart; *zij trokken hem de kleren van het lijf* they tore the clothes from his back; **–er** (-s) *m* 1 drawer [of a bill]; 2 *sp* hiker; 3 trigger [of fire-arms]; 4 tab, tag [of a boot]; 5 (v a n W.C.) (pull) chain; 6 (t r a c t o r) tractor; **'trekking** (-en) *v* 1 (in 't a l g.) drawing; 2 (v. l o t e r ij) drawing, draw; 3 (in s c h o o r-s t e e n) draught; 4 (v. z e n u w e n) twitch, convulsion; **'trekkingslijst** (-en) *v* list of prizes; **–rechten** *mv* $ drawing rights; **'trek-kracht** (-en) *v* tractive power; **–net** (-ten) *o* drag-net, seine; **–paard** (-en) *o* draught-horse; **–pen** (-nen) *v* drawing-pen; **–pleister** (-s) *v* vesicatory; *fig* attraction, draw; **–pot** (-ten) *m* tea-pot; **–proef** *v* ✗ tension test, pull test; **–schakelaar** (-s) *m* pull switch; **–schroef** (-schroeven) *v* tractor screw; **–schuit** (-en) *v* tow-boat; **–sel** (-s) *o* infusion, brew [of coffee]; **–sluiting** (-en) *v* zip-fastener, zip(per); **–tijd** (-en) *m* migration time; **–tocht** (-en) *m sp* hike; *een* ~ *maken* hike; **–vaart** (-en) *v* ship-canal; **–vast** *aj* ✗ tension-proof; **trek'vastheid** *v* tensile strength; **'trekvogel** (-s) *m* migratory bird, migrant, bird of passage²; **–zaag** (-zagen) *v* ✗ crosscut saw; whip-saw

trem (-s en -men) *m = tram*

'trema ('s) *o* diaeresis [*mv* diaereses]

'tremel (-s) *m* (mill-)hopper

'tremmen (tremde, h. getremd) *vt* trim [coals]; **–er** (-s) *m* trimmer

trend (-s) *m* trend

trens (-trenzen) *v* 1 (a a n b i t) snaffle; 2 (l u s) loop

trepa'natie [-(t)si.] (-s) *v* trepanning; **trepa'neerboor** (-boren) *v* trepan; **trepa'neren** (trepaneerde, h. getrepaneerd) *vt* & *vi* trepan

tres (-sen) *v* braid

'treurboom (-bomen) *m* weeping tree [weeping beech &]; **–dicht** (-en) *o* elegy; **'treuren**

(treurde, h. getreurd) *vi* be sad, grieve; *fig* languish [of plants &]; ~ *o m* mourn for, mourn over [a loss²]; ~ *o v e r* grieve over, mourn for; **'treurig** sad, sorrowful, mournful, pitiful; **–heid** (-heden) *v* sadness; **'treurjaar** (-jaren) *o* year of mourning; **–kleed** (-kleden) *o* mourning-dress; **–lied** (-eren) *o* elegy, dirge; **–mare** (-n) *v* sad news (tidings); **–mars** (-en) *m* & *v* funeral march, dead march; **–muziek** *v* funeral music; **–spel** (-spelen) *o* tragedy; **–speldichter** (-s) *m* tragic poet; **–spelspeler** (-s) *m* tragedian; **–wilg** (-en) *m* weeping willow; **–zang** (-en) *m* elegy, dirge

'treuzel, –aar (-s) *m* slow-coach, dawdler, loiterer, slacker; **–achtig** dawdling; **'treu-zelen** (treuzelde, h. getreuzeld) *vi* dawdle, loiter, linger

tri'angel (-s) *m* ♪ triangle

'trias *v* triad

tribu'naal (-nalen) *o* tribunal, court of justice

tri'bune (-s) *v* tribune, rostrum, [speaker's] platform; [reporters' &] gallery; *sp* (grand)stand; *publieke* ~ public gallery, [in House of Parliament] strangers' gallery

tri'buun (-bunen) *m* tribune

tri'chine (-n) *v* trichina; **trichi'neus** trichinous; **trichi'nose** [s = z] *v* trichinosis

'tricot ['tri.ko.] 1 *o* tricot [woollen fabric], stockinet; 2 (-s) *m* & *o* jersey [for children &]; tights [for acrobats &]; **trico'tage** [-ʒə] (-s) *v* knitwear

trien (-en) *v* loutish girl, woman

Trier *o* Treves

'triest(ig) dreary, dismal, melancholy, sad

trigonome'trie *v* trigonometry; **trigono'metrisch** trigonometric(al)

'trijntje *van wijntje en* ~ *houden* love wine, women and song

trijp *o* mock-velvet; **–en** *aj* mock-velvet

trijs (-en) *m* ✗ whip

'triktrak *o* backgammon; **–bord** (-en) *o* backgammon board; **'triktrakken** (triktrakte, h. getriktrakt) *vi* play at backgammon

'trilbeton *o* vibrated concrete; **–gras** *o* quaking-grass; **–haar** (-haren) *o* cilium, *mv* cilia

tril'joen (-en) *o* trillion [1000.000³]

'trillen (trilde, h. getrild) *vi* 1 (v. p e r s o n e n, s t e m &) tremble; 2 (v. s t e m) vibrate, quaver, quiver; 3 (v. g r a s) quake, dither; 4 (in d e n a t u u r k u n d e) vibrate; ~ *van* tremble with [anger]; **–er** (-s) *m* ♪ trill, shake; **'trilling** (-en) *v* vibration, quivering, quiver; **–sgetal** (-len) *o* ♪ frequency (of oscillations)

trilo'gie (-ieën) *v* trilogy

tri'mester (-s) *o* term, three months

'trimmen (trimde, h. getrimd) **I** *vt* trim [a dog];

II *vi* jog, do keep-fit exercises; **III** *o* jogging

'trio ('s) *o* trio[2]

trio'let (-ten) *v* & *o* triolet

tri'omf (-en) *m* triumph; **~en vieren** achieve great triumphs; **in ~** in triumph; **triom'fante-lijk I** *aj* triumphant; triumphal [entry]; **II** *ad* triumphantly; **triom'fator** (-s en -toren) *m* triumpher; **tri'omfboog** (-bogen) *m* triumphal arch; **triom'feren** (triomfeerde, h. getriom-feerd) *vi* triumph (over *over*); **tri'omflied** (-eren) *o* triumphal song, paean; **–poort** (-en) *v* triumphal arch; **–tocht** (-en) *m* triumphal procession; **–wagen** (-s) *m* triumphal car (chariot); **–zuil** (-en) *v* triumphal column

tri'ool (triolen) *v* ♪ triplet

trip (-s) *m* [hallucinogenic] trip

'triplexhout *o* three-ply wood, plywood

'triplo *in ~* in triplicate

'trippelen (trippelde, h. en is getrippeld) *vi* trip (along); **'trippelpas** (-sen) *m* tripping-step, trip

'trippen (tripte, h. en is getript) *vi* 1 (m e t k l e i n e p a s j e s l o p e n) trip; 2 (h a l l u-c i n o g e n e m i d d e l e n g e b r u i k e n) trip

trip'tiek (-en) *v* 1 triptych; 2 triptyque [for international travel]

'tritonshoorn, –horen (-s) *m* triton

trits (-en) *v* set of three, triad, trio, triplet

triumvi'raat (-raten) *o* triumvirate

trivi'aal trivial, trite, banal; **triviali'teit** (-en) *v* triviality, triteness, banality

tro'chee (-cheeën) *m*, **tro'cheus** [-'ge.üs] (-cheeën) *m* trochee

'troebel troubled, turbid, thick, cloudy; **–en** *mv* disturbances; **–heid** *v* troubled condition, turbidity, turbidness, thickness, cloudiness; **troe'bleren** (troebleerde, h. getroebleerd) *vt* disturb; zie ook: *getroebleerd*

troef (troeven) *v* trump, trumps; *harten is ~* hearts are trumps; **~ bekennen** follow suit; **~ maken** declare trumps; **~ uitspelen** play a trump, play trumps; *zijn ~ uitspelen* play one's trump card; *zijn laatste ~ uitspelen* play one's last trump; **~ verzaken** fail to follow suit; zie ook: *armoe(de)*; **troef'aas** (-azen) *m* & *o* ace of trumps; **'troefkaart** (-en) *v* trump-card[2]; **–kleur** (-en) *v* trumps

troel (-en) *v* 1 (s c h e l d w o o r d) bitch, broad; 2 (l i e f k o z e n d) sweetie (pie)

troep (-en) *m* troupe [of actors], (theatrical) company; band, gang [of robbers]; flock [of cattle]; herd [of sheep, geese]; drove [of cattle]; pack [of dogs, wolves]; troop [of people]; > pack [of kids: children]; ⚔ body of soldiers; **~en** ⚔ troops, forces; *bij ~en* in troops; *een ~* (= e e n r o m m e l, j a n b o e l, r o t z o o i) a mess, a muddle, a clutter; *de hele ~* the whole crowd, the whole lot, the whole caboodle; **'troepenconcentratie** [-(t)si.] (-s) *v* concentration of troops, troop concentration; **–macht** (-en) *v* force; **–vervoer** *o* transport of troops; **'troepsgewijs, –gewijze** in troops

'troetelen (troetelde, h. getroeteld) *vt* pet, coddle; **'troetelkind** (-eren) *o* darling, pet; **–naam** (-namen) *m* pet name

'troeven (troefde, h. getroefd) **I** *vt* trump, overtrump; **II** *vi* play trumps

trof (troffen) V.T. van *treffen*

tro'fee (-feeën) *v* trophy

'troffel (-s) *m* trowel

'troffen V.T. meerv. van *treffen*

trog (-gen) *m* trough

troglo'diet (-en) *m* troglodyte, cave-dweller

trois-'pièces [trva'pjɛs] (-pièces) *v* & *o* three-piece (suit)

Tro'jaan (-janen) *m* Trojan; **–s** Trojan; *het ~e paard binnenhalen* drag the Trojan horse within the walls; **'Troje** *o* Troy

'trojka ('s) *v* troika

trok (trokken) V.T. van *trekken*

'trolleybus [-li.-] (-sen) *m* & *v* trolley-bus

trom (-men) *v* drum; *de grote ~ roeren* beat the big drum[2]; *kleine ~* ⚔ snare-drum; *de Turkse ~* the big drum; *met slaande ~ en vliegende vaandels* ⚔ with drums beating and colours flying; *met stille ~* ⚔ with silent drums; *met stille ~ vertrekken* slip away

trom'bone [-'bɔːnə] (-s) *v* trombone; **trombo'nist** (-en) *m* trombonist

trom'bose [s = z] *v* thrombosis

'tromgeroffel *o* roll of drums; **'trommel** (-s) *v* 1 ♪ drum; 2 ⚔ drum; barrel; 3 box, case, tin; **–aar** (-s) *m* drummer; **'trommelen** (trom-melde, h. getrommeld) *vi* 1 drum [on a drum, table &]; 2 strum, drum [on a piano]; **'trom-melholte** (-n en -s) *v* tympanic cavity; **–rem** (-men) *v* drum brake; **–slag** (-slagen) *m* drum-beat, beat of drum; *bij ~* by beat of drum; **–slager** (-s) *m* drummer; **–stok** (-ken) *m* drumstick; **–vel** (-len) *o* drumhead; **–vlies** (-vliezen) *o* tympanum, ear-drum, tympanic membrane; **–vliesontsteking** *v* tympanitis; **–vuur** *o* ⚔ drum fire

tromp (-en) *v* 1 mouth, muzzle [of a fire-arm]; 2 trunk [of an elephant]

trom'pet (-ten) *v* trumpet; (*op*) *de ~ blazen* blow (sound) the trumpet; **–blazer** (-s) *m* trum-peter; **–geschal** *o* sound (flourish, blast) of trumpets; **–signaal** [-si.ɲa.l] (-nalen) *o* trumpet-call; **trom'petten** (trompette, h. getrompet) *vi* trumpet; **–er** (-s) *m* trumpeter; **trompet'tist** (-en) *m* trumpet-player, trum-peter; **trom'petvogel** (-s) *m* trumpeter; **–vormig** trumpet-shaped

1 'tronen (troonde, h. getroond) *vi* sit enthroned, throne

2 'tronen (troonde, h. getroond) *vt* allure, entice

'tronie (-s) *v* face, **F** phiz, **P** mug

tronk (-en) *m* stump [of a tree]

troon (tronen) *m* throne; *de ~ beklimmen* mount (ascend) the throne; *o p de ~ plaatsen* enthrone, place on the throne; *v a n de ~ stoten* dethrone; **–hemel** (-s) *m* canopy, baldachin; **–opvolger** (-s) *m* heir to the throne; **–opvolging** *v* succession to the throne; **–pretendent** (-en) *m* pretender to the throne; **–rede** (-s) *v* speech from the throne, King's (Queen's) speech, royal speech; **'troonsafstand** *m* abdication; **–bestijging** *v* accession to the throne; **'troonstoel** (-en) *m* chair of state; **–zaal** (-zalen) *v* throne-room

troop (tropen) *m* trope

troost *m* comfort [= consolation & person who consoles], consolation, solace; *een kommetje ~* **J** a cup of coffee; *dat is tenminste één ~* that's a (one, some) comfort; *een schrale ~* cold comfort; *dat zal een ~ voor u zijn* it will afford you some consolation; *~ vinden in...* find comfort in...; *zijn ~ zoeken bij...* seek comfort with...; **–brief** (-brieven) *m* consolatory letter; **–eloos** disconsolate, cheerless, desolate; **–eloosheid** *v* disconsolateness; **'troosten** (troostte, h. getroost) **I** *vt* comfort, console; **II** *vr zich ~* console oneself; *zich ~ met de gedachte dat...* take comfort in the thought that...; **–er** (-s) *m* comforter; **trooste'res** (-sen) *v* comforter; **'troostprijs** (-prijzen) *m* consolation prize; **–rijk, –vol** comforting, consoling, consolatory; **–woord** (-en) *o* word of comfort

'tropen *mv* tropics; **–helm** (-en) *m* sun-helmet, topee; **–kleding** *v* tropical clothes (wear); **–kolder** *m* tropical frenzy; **–uitrusting** (-en) *v* tropical outfit; **'tropisch** tropical

tropo'sfeer *v* troposphere

tros (-sen) *m* 1 bunch [of grapes]; cluster [of fruits]; string [of currants]; (b l o e i w) raceme; 2 ⚓ train; 3 ⚓ hawser; *aan ~sen* in bunches, in clusters; **–vormig** *aj* ⚘ racemed, racemose

trots I *m* pride; *ten ~ van* = **II** *prep* in spite (defiance) of, notwithstanding; *~ de beste* with the best; **III** *aj* proud, haughty; *~ zijn op* be proud of; *zo ~ als een pauw* as proud as a peacock (as Lucifer); **IV** *ad* proudly, haughtily; **–aard** (-s) *m* proud person

trot'seren (trotseerde, h. getrotseerd) *vt* defy, set at defiance, dare, face, brave [death]; **–ring** *v* defiance

'trotsheid *v* pride, haughtiness

trot'toir [trɔ'tva:r] (-s) *o* pavement, footpath,

Am sidewalk; **–band** (-en) *m* kerb(stone), curb(stone); **–tegel** (-s) *m* paving stone

trouba'dour [tru.ba.'du:r] (-s) *m* troubadour

trou'vaille [tru.'vajə] (-s) *v* 1 happy find; 2 *fig* bright idea

trouw I *aj* 1 (v. m e n s & d i e r) faithful; 2 (v. o n d e r d a n e n) loyal; 3 (v. v r i e n d e n) true, trusty; *een ~ afschrift* a true copy; *~ bezoeker* regular attendant; *~ aan* loyal to, ook: true to; **II** *ad* faithfully, loyally; **III** *v* (g é t r o u w h e i d) loyalty, fidelity, faithfulness, faith; *beproefde ~* tried faithfulness, staunch loyalty; *goede (kwade) ~* good (bad) faith; *te goeder ~* bona fide, in good faith; *~ zweren* swear fidelity (allegiance) to; ● *i n ~e* in faith, honestly; *t e goeder (kwader) ~* in good (bad) faith; *te goeder (kwader) ~ zijn* be quite sincere (insincere); **IV** *m* (h u w e l i j k) marriage

'trouwakte (-n en -s) *v* marriage certificate; **–belofte** (-n) *v* promise of marriage; **–boekje** (-s) *o* marriage certificate annex family record [issued to newly married couples]; **–breuk** *v* breach of faith; **–dag** (-dagen) *m* 1 wedding-day; 2 (v. h u w e l i j k) wedding-anniversary

'trouweloos faithless, disloyal, perfidious; **trouwe'loosheid** (-heden) *v* faithlessness, disloyalty, perfidy, perfidiousness

'trouwen I (trouwde, is getrouwd) *vi* marry, wed; *~ met* marry; *getrouwd met een Duitser* married to a German; **II** (trouwde h. getrouwd) *vt* marry; *hij heeft veel geld getrouwd* he has married a fortune; *je bent er niet aan getrouwd* you are not wedded to it; *zo zijn we niet getrouwd* **J** that was not in the bargain; *wanneer zijn ze getrouwd?* when were they married?, when did they get married?

'trouwens for that matter, apart from that, by the way

trouwe'rij (-en) *v* wedding, marriage; **'trouwfeest** (-en) *o* wedding, wedding-feast; **–gewaad** (-waden) *o* wedding-dress

trouw'hartig true-hearted, candid, frank; **–heid** *v* true-heartedness, candour

'trouwjapon (-nen) *m*, **–jurk** (-en) *v* wedding-dress; **–kamer** (-s) *v* wedding-room; **–pak** (-ken) *o* wedding-suit; **–partij** (-en) *v* wedding-party; **–plannen** *mv* marriage plans; **–plechtigheid** (-heden) *v* wedding-ceremony; **–ring** (-en) *m* wedding-ring; **–zaal** (-zalen) *v* wedding-room

truc [try.k] (-s) *m* trick, stunt, **F** dodge

truck (-s) *m* truck

'truffel (-s) *v* truffle

truf'feren (truffeerde, h. getruffeerd) *vt* stuff with truffles; *getruffeerd* truffled

trui (-en) *v* jersey, sweater

trust (-s) *m* $ trust; **–vorming** *v* $ trustification, formation of trusts

'trut (-ten) *v* P (v r o u w) square, drag

tsaar (tsaren) *m* Czar, Tsar; **tsa'rina** ('s) *v* Czarina, Tsarina; **tsa'ristisch** Tsarist

'tseetseevlieg (-en) *v* tsetse fly

Tsjaad *o* Chad

Tsjech (-en) *m* Czech; **–isch I** *aj* Czech; **II** *o* Czech; **Tsjechoslo'waak(s)** (-waken) *m* (& *aj*) Czechoslovak; **Tsjechoslowa'kije** *o* Czechoslovakia

'tsjilpen (tsjilpte, h. getsjilpt), **'tsjirpen** (tsjirpte, h. getsjirpt) cheep, twitter, chirp, chirrup

'tuba ('s) *m* ♪ tuba

'tube (-n en -s) *v* (collapsible) tube

tubercu'leus tuberculous, tubercular, consumptive; **tubercu'lose** [s = z] *v* tuberculosis, T.B.; **–bestrijding** *v* fight against tuberculosis; **–lijder** (-s) *m* tubercular patient; **tu'berkel** (-s) *m* tubercle; **–bacil** (-len) *m* tubercle bacillus

'tuberoos (-rozen) *v* ❀ tuberose

'tubifex (-en) *m* live food for aquarium fishes

tucht *v* discipline; *onder ~ staan* be under discipline; **–college** [-ʒə] (-s) *o* disciplinary board (committee); **–eloos** 1 undisciplined, indisciplinable, insubordinate; 2 dissolute; **tuchte'loosheid** *v* 1 insubordination; indiscipline; 2 dissoluteness; **'tuchthuis** (-huizen) *o* house of correction; **–boef** (-boeven) *m* convict, jail-bird; **–straf** (-fen) *v* imprisonment; **'tuchtigen** (tuchtigde, h. getuchtigd) *vt* chastise, punish; **–ging** (-en) *v* chastisement, punishment; **'tuchtmiddel** (-en) *o* means of correction; **–recht** *o* disciplinary law; **–roede** (-n) *v* rod, birch; **–school** (-scholen) *v* ± reformatory; (i n E n g e l a n d) approved school

tuf *o* tuff

'tuffen (tufte, h. en is getuft) *vi* motor, chug

'tufsteen (-stenen) *o* & *m* tuff

'tuier (-s) *m* tether

tuig (-en) *o* 1 (g e r e e d s c h a p) tools; 2 fishing-tackle; 3 ⚓ rigging [of a ship]; 4 harness [of a horse]; 5 ~ (*van goed*) stuff, trash, rubbish; ~ (*van volk*) riff-raff, rabble, vermin; **tui'gage** [-ʒə] *v* ⚓ rigging; **'tuigen** (tuigde, h. getuigd) 1 ⚓ rig; 2 harness [a horse]; **'tuighuis** (-huizen) *o* arsenal

tuil (-en) *m* 1 bunch [of flowers], nosegay; 2 posy [of verse]

'tuimelaar (-s) *m* 1 (p e r s o o n) tumbler; 2 ❦ (d u i f) tumbler; 3 (b r u i n v i s) porpoise; 4 ✗ tumbler [of a lock]; 5 (g l a s) tumbler; **'tuimelen** (tuimelde, h. en is getuimeld) *vi* tumble, topple, topple over; **–ling** (-en) *v* tumble; *een ~ maken* have a spill [from one's bicycle, horse]; **'tuimelraam** (-ramen) *o* tilting window, balance window

tuin (-en) *m* garden; *hangende ~en* hanging gardens [of Babylon]; *iem. om de ~ leiden* hoodwink (deceive, mislead) sbd.; F lead sbd. up the garden-path; **–aarde** *v* vegetable mould; **–ameublement** *o* set of garden-furniture; **–architect** [-αrgi.-, -αrʃi.-] (-en) *m* landscape gardener; **–architectuur** *v* landscape gardening; **–baas** (-bazen) *m* gardener, head-gardener; **–bank** (-en) *v* garden-seat, garden-bench; **–bed** (-den) *o* garden-bed; **–bloem** (-en) *v* garden-flower; **–boon** (-bonen) *v* broad bean

'tuinbouw *m* horticulture; **–leraar** (-s en -raren) *m* horticultural teacher; **–school** (-scholen) *v* horticultural school; **–tentoonstelling** (-en) *v* horticultural show

'tuincentrum (-centra en -s) *o* garden centre

'tuinder (-s) *m* horticulturist, market-gardener; **tuinde'rij** (-en) *v* market-garden

'tuindeur (-en) *v* garden-door; (d u b b e l e ~) French windows; **–dorp** (-en) *o* garden suburb, garden city; **–feest** (-en) *o* garden-party, garden-fête; **–fluiter** (-s) *m* 🐦 garden-warbler; **–gereedschap** (-pen) *o* garden(ing) tools; **–gewassen** *mv* garden-plants; **–hek** (-ken) *o* (o m h e i n i n g) garden fence; (t o e g a n g) garden gate; **–huis** (-huizen) *o* summer-house

tui'nier (-s) *m* gardener; **tui'nieren** (tuinierde, h. getuinierd) *vi* garden; **tui'niersvak** *o* gardening

'tuinkabouter (-s) *m* pixy, gnome; **–kamer** (-s) *v* room that looks on a garden; **–kers** *v* garden-cress; **–kruiden** *mv* pot-herbs; **–man** (-lieden, -lui) *m* gardener; **–manswoning** (-en) *v* gardener's lodge; **–meubelen** *mv* garden furniture; **–muur** (-muren) *m* garden wall; **–pad** (-paden) *o* garden path; **–parasol** (-s) *m* (garden) umbrella; **–plant** (-en) *v* garden plant; **–schaar** (-scharen) *v* garden shears, secateurs; **–schuurtje** (-s) *o* garden-shed, potting-shed; **–slak** (-ken) *v* garden-slug; **–slang** (-en) *v* garden-hose; **–sproeier** (-s) *m* garden syringe; **–stad** (-steden) *v* garden-city; **–stoel** (-en) *m* garden-chair; **–tje** (-s) *o* garden-plot; **–vrucht** (-en) *v* garden-fruit; **–werk** *o* garden-work, gardening

tuit (-en) *v* spout, nozzle

'tuitelen (tuitelde, h. getuiteld) *vi* totter; **'tuitelig** tottering, shaky, rickety

'tuiten (tuitte, h. getuit) *vi* tingle

'tuithoed (-en) *m* poke-bonnet

tuk *aj* ~ *op* keen on, eager for

'**tukje** (-s) *o* nap; *een* ~ *doen* take a nap

'**tulband** (-en) *m* 1 turban; 2 sponge-cake

'**tule** *v* tulle; **–n** *aj* tulle

tulp (-en) *v* tulip; **–ebol** (-len) *m* tulip-bulb; '**tulpenbed** (-den) *o* bed of tulips; **–kweker** (-s) *m* tulip-grower

'**tumbler** (-s) *m* tumbler

'**tumor** (-s en -'moren) *m* tumour

tu'mult (-en) *o* tumult; **tumultu'eus** tumultuous, uproarious

Tu'nesië [s = z] *o* Tunisia; **Tu'nesiër** (-s) *m*, **Tu'nesisch** *aj* Tunisian

'**tunica** ('s) *v* tunic; *rk* tunicle; **tu'niek** (-en) *v* tunic

'**tunnel** (-s) *m* 1 (in 't alg.) tunnel; 2 (van station, onder straat) subway

tur'bine (-s) *v* turbine; **–straalmotor** (-s en -toren) *m* turbojet engine; **–straalvliegtuig(en)** *o* (*mv*) turbojet aircraft

'**tureluur** (-s en -luren) *m* 🐦 redshank

ture'luurs wild, mad; *het is om* ~ *te worden* it's enough to drive you mad

'**turen** (tuurde, h. getuurd) *vi* peer; ~ *naar* peer at

turf (turven) *m* peat; ook: (dry) turf; *een* ~ a block (a square, a lump) of peat; (van een boek) a tome; **–achtig** peaty; **–graver** (-s) *m* peat-digger; **–molm** *m* en *o* peat dust; **–schip** (-schepen) *o*, **–schuit** (-en) *v* peat-boat; **–steker** (-s) *m* peat-cutter; **–strooisel** *o* [peat-litter

Tu'rijn *o* Turin

Turk (-en) *m* Turk²; **Tur'kije** *o* Turkey

tur'koois (-kooizen) *m* & *o* turquoise; **tur'kooizen** *aj* turquoise

Turks I *aj* Turkish; **II** *o het* ~ Turkish; **III** *v een* ~*e* a Turkish woman

'**turnen** (turnde, h. geturnd) *vi* do gymnastics; **–er** (-s) *m* gymnast; '**turnvereniging** (-en) *v* gym(nastic) club

'**turven** (turfde, h. geturfd) *vi* score, mark in fives

'**tussen** 1 between; 2 (temidden van) among [of more than two]; *dat blijft* ~ *ons* that is between you and me, between ourselves; *er is iets* ~ *gekomen* something has come between; *iem. er* ~ *nemen* pull sbd.'s leg; *ze hebben je er* ~ *genomen* they had you there, you have been had; **tussen'beide** between-whiles; ~ *komen* intervene, interpose, step in, **F** put one's oar in; *er is iets* ~ *gekomen* something has come between

'**tussendek** (-ken) *o* between-decks, 'tween-decks; (voor passagiers) steerage; **tussen'deks** *ad* between-decks, 'tween-decks; *de reis* ~ *maken* go (travel) steerage; '**tussendekspassagier** [-ʒi.r] (-s) *m* steerage passenger

'**tussendeur** (-en) *v* communicating door; **–ding** (-en) *o* [not a..., and not a..., but] something between the two; **–gas** *o* ~ *geven* **F** blip the throttle; **–gelegen** intermediate; **–gerecht** (-en) *o* entremets, side-dish; **–gevoegd** interpolated, inserted; **–handel** *m* intermediate trade, commission business; **–handelaar** (-s) *m* commission-agent, intermediary, middleman; **–haven** (-s) *v* intermediate port; **tussen'in** (*er* ~) in between; '**tussenkleur** (-en) *v* intermediate colour, middle tint; **–komst** *v* intervention, interposition, intercession, intermediary, agency; *door* ~ *van* through; **–laag** (-lagen) *v* intermediate layer, interlayer; **–landing** (-en) *v* ✈ stop, intermediate landing; *zonder* ~(*en*) non-stop [flight]; **–landingsplaats** (-en) *v* staging-post; **–liggend** intermediate, in-between; **–maat** (-maten) *v* medium size, intermediate size; **–muur** (-muren) *m* partition-wall; **–persoon** (-sonen) *m* agent, intermediary, middleman; go-between; *tussenpersonen komen niet in aanmerking* $ only principals dealt with; **–poos** (-pozen) *v* interval, intermission; *bij tussenpozen* at intervals, now and then; *met vaste tussenpozen* at regular intervals; **–regering** (-en) *v* interregnum; **–ruimte** (-n en -s) *v* interspace, spacing, interstice, interval, intervening space; **–schakel** (-s) *m* & *v* intermediate (connecting) link, interlink; **–schakeling** *v* 🕸 interconnection, interconnexion, insertion; **–schot** (-ten) *o* 1 partition; 2 🐟 & 🐦 septum [of the nose &]; **–soort** (-en) *v* medium sort; **–spel** (-spelen) *o* interlude; **–stand** (-en) *m* *sp* intermediate score; **–station** [-sta.(t)ʃɔn] (-s) intermediate station; –stuk (-ken) *o* ✕ adapter, -tor; **–tijd** (-en) *m* interim, interval; *in die* ~ in the meantime, meanwhile; **–tijds, tussen'tijds I** *aj* interim [dividend]; ~*e verkiezing* by-election; **II** *ad* between times; **tussen'uit** *er* ~ *gaan* zie *uitknijpen* II; '**tussenuur** (-uren) *o* intermediate hour, odd hour; **–verdieping** (-en) *v* mezzanine

'**tussenvoegen** (voegde 'tussen, h. 'tussengevoegd) *vt* intercalate, insert, interpolate; **–ging** (-en) *v* intercalation, insertion, interpolation; '**tussenvoegsel** (-s en -en) *o* insertion, interpolation

'**tussenvorm** (-en) *m* intermediate form; **–wand** (-en) *m* partition; **–weg** (-wegen) *m fig* middle course; **–wervelschijf** (-schijven) *v* intervertebral disc; **–werpsel** (-s) *o gram* interjection); **–zin** (-nen) *m* parenthetic clause, parenthesis [*mv* parentheses]

tut (-ten) *v* **P** dull and awkward woman, girl

tutoy'eren [ty.tʋɑ'je:rə(n)] (tutoyeerde, h. getutoyeerd) *vt* be on familiar terms with, use

the more intimate form
tu'tu ('s) *m* tutu
t.w. = *te weten* zie *weten* **IV**
twaalf twelve; **–de** twelfth (part); **–delig** of twelve parts; × duodecimal; **–hoek** (-en) *m* dodecagon; **–tal** (-len) *o* twelve, dozen; **–tallig** duodecimal; **twaalf'toonmuziek** *v* twelve-note (twelve-tone, serial, dodecaphonic) music; **twaalf'uurtje** (-s) *o* lunch; **'twaalfvingerig** ~*e darm* duodenum; *van de ~e darm* duodenal [ulcer]; **–vlak** (-ken) *o* dodecahedron; **–voud** (-en) *o* multiple of twelve; **–voudig** twelvefold
twee (tweeën) *v* two; *sp* deuce; ~ *a's* two a's; *met* ~ *a's* [to be written] with double a; ~ *aan* ~ two and two, by (in) twos; *met z'n* ~*ën* the two of us [you, them]; ~ *naast elkaar* two abreast; ~ *weten meer dan één* two heads are better than one; *in* ~*iën snijden* cut in halves, in half, in two; **–armig** two-armed; **–baansweg** (-wegen) *m* two-lane(d) road; **–benig** two-legged; **–daags** of two days, two-days'...; **–de** second; *maar ... dat is een* ~ that is another matter; *ten* ~ secondly; zie ook: *eerst* **I**; **tweede'hands** second-hand; **'tweedejaars** *m* second-year student; *Am* sophomore; **'tweedekker** (-s) *m* ✈ biplane; **–delig** 1 bipartite; 2 (v. k l e d i n g) two-piece [(bathing-)suit]; **tweede'rangs** second-rate; **'tweedraads** two-ply; **–dracht** *v* discord; ~ *zaaien* sow dissension; **–ërhande, –ërlei** of two kinds; **–gesprek** (-ken) *o* duologue; **–gevecht** (-en) *o* duel, single combat; **–handig** two-handed; **–honderdjarig** two hundred years old; ~*e gedenkdag* bicentenary; **–hoofdig** two-headed; **–hoog** of two flights up; **–huizig** ⚥ dioecious, unisexual; **–jarig** two-year, biennial; two-year-old [child]; **–kamp** (-en) *m* duel; **–klank** (-en) *m* diphthong; **–ledig** double, binary, binomial; twofold [purpose]; **–lettergrepig** dissyllabic; ~ *woord* dissyllable; **–ling** (-en) *m* twin, pair of twins; *de Tweelingen* ★ Gemini; **–lingbroe(de)r** (-s) *m,* **–zuster** (-s) *v* twin-brother, twin-sister; **–maal** twice; **–maandelijks** bimonthly; *een* ~ *tijdschrift* a bimonthly; **–master** (-s) *m* two-masted ship; **–motorig** twin-engined; **–ogig** two-eyed; **–persoons** for two; double [bed, room]; ~*auto* two-seater; **–pitsstel** (-len) *o* two-burner stove; **–regelig** of two lines; ~ *vers* distich, couplet; **–rijig** double-breasted [coat]
tweern *m* twine; **'tweernen** (tweernde, h. getweernd) *vt* twine
'tweeslachtig 1 amphibious; 2 bisexual; **–snarig** two-stringed; **–snijdend** two-edged, double-edged; **–spalt** *v* discord, dissension, split; **–span** (-nen) *o* two-horse team, two-

some; **–spraak** (-spraken) *v* duologue; **–sprong** (-en) *m* cross-road(s); *fig* watershed; *op de* ~ at the cross-roads; **–stemmig** for two voices; **–strijd** *m* inward struggle; *in* ~ *staan* be in two minds; **–taktmotor** (-s en -toren) *m* two-stroke engine; **–tal** (-len) *o* two, pair; **–talig** bilingual; **–tallig** binary; **–term** (-en) *m* binomial; **–tongig** two-tongued; *fig* double-tongued; **–vleugelig** two-winged; dipterous [insects]; **–voetig** two-footed; ~ *dier* biped; **–voud** (-en) *o* double; *in* ~ in duplicate (twofold); **–voudig** twofold, double; **–waardig** bivalent; **–wegskraan** (-kranen) *v* two-way cock; **–werf** twice; **–zijdig** two-sided, bilateral
'twijfel (-s) *m* doubt; *zijn bange* ~ his misgivings; ~ *koesteren* have one's doubts [about...], entertain doubts [as to...]; *het lijdt geen* ~ (*of...*) there is no doubt (that...); *iems.* ~ *wegnemen* remove sbd.'s doubts; ~ *wekken* create doubts (a doubt); *daar is geen* ~ *aan* there is no doubt of it; *er is geen* ~ *aan of hij...* there is no doubt that he...; ● *het is a a n geen* ~ *onderhevig* that admits of no doubt, it is beyond doubt; *het is b o v e n a l l e* ~ *verheven* it is beyond all doubt; *hij is b u i t e n* ~... he is without doubt (doubtless, undoubtedly) the...; *i n* ~ *staan* (*zijn*) doubt, be in doubt [whether...]; be in two minds about the matter; *in* ~ *trekken* call in question, question; *z o n d e r* ~*!* without (any) doubt; *hij is zonder* ~... he is undoubtedly (doubtless)...; **–aar** (-s) *m* doubter, sceptic; **–achtig, twijfel'achtig I** *aj* doubtful, dubious, questionable; **II** *ad* doubtfully, dubiously, questionably; **–heid** *v* doubtfulness, dubiousness, questionableness; **'twijfelen** (twijfelde, h. getwijfeld) *vi* doubt; ~ *aan* doubt (of); *ik twijfel er niet aan* I have no doubt about it, I make no doubt of it; *wij* ~ *of...* we doubt whether (if)...; *wij* ~ *niet of...* we do not doubt (but) that...; **'twijfelgeval** (-len) *o* dubious case; moot question; **'twijfeling** (-en) *v* 1 hesitation; 2 (t w ij f e l) doubt; **twijfel'moedig** vacillating, wavering, irresolute; **–heid** *v* irresolution; **'twijfelzucht** *v* doubting disposition; **twijfel'zuchtig** of a doubting disposition
twijg (-en) *v* twig
twijn *m* twine, twist; **–der** (-s) *m* twiner, twister; **twijnde'rij** (-en) *v* twining-mill; **'twijnen** (twijnde, h. getwijnd) *vt* twine, twist
'twintig twenty; **–er** (-s) *m* person of twenty (years); **–jarig** of twenty years, twenty-year-old [girl]; **–ste** twentieth (part); **–tal** (-len) *o* twenty, score; **–voud** (-en) *o* multiple of twenty; **–voudig** twentyfold
1 twist (-en) *m* 1 (c o n c r e e t) quarrel, dispute,

altercation, brawl; 2 (a b s t r a c t) dispute, discord, ☉ strife; *binnenlandse* ~*en* internal strife; *een* ~ *beslechten (bijleggen)* settle a dispute; ~ *krijgen* fall out; ~ *stoken (tussen)* stir up strife, make mischief (between); ~ *zaaien* sow discord, sow (stir up) dissension; ~ *zoeken* pick a quarrel

2 twist *o* twist [kind of yarn]

3 twist *m* twist [dance]

'**twistappel** (-s) *m* apple of discord, bone of contention; **1** '**twisten** (twistte, h. getwist) *vi* quarrel, dispute; *m e t iem.* ~ quarrel (wrangle) with sbd., dispute with sbd.; ~ *o m iets* quarrel about sth.; *daar kunnen we nog lang o v e r* ~ that is a debatable point; *ik wil niet met u daarover* ~ I'm not going to contest the point with you

2 '**twisten** (twistte, h. getwist) *vi* (d a n s e n) twist

'**twistgeding** (-en) *o* lawsuit; **–geschrijf** *o* controversy, polemics; **–gesprek** (-ken) *o* dispute, disputation; **–punt** (-en) *o* (point at) issue, disputed point, controversial question; **–stoker** (-s) *m* firebrand, mischief-maker; **–vraag** (-vragen) *v* (question at) issue, controversial question; **–ziek** quarrelsome, cantankerous, contentious, disputatious; **–zoeker** (-s) *m* quarrelsome fellow; **–zucht** *v* quarrelsomeness, cantankerousness, contentiousness

ty'**feus** [y = i.] typhoid, typhous; *tyfeuze koorts* = *tyfus* 1

ty'**foon** [y = i.] (-s) *m* typhoon

'**tyfus** [y = i.] *m* 1 (b u i k) typhoid (fever), enteric fever; 2 (v l e k) typhus (fever); **–lijder** (-s) *m* typhoid patient

'**type** [y = i.] (-n en -s) *o* type [also in printing]; character [in novels of Dickens]; *zij is 'n* ~ **F** she is quite a character; *wat een* ~*!* **F** what a specimen!

'**typekamer** [y = i.] (-s) *v* typing pool; '**typen** (typte, h. getypt) *vt* type(write); *het document beslaat wel 300 getypte pagina's* the document runs to 300 pages of typescript

ty'**peren** [y = i.] (typeerde, h. getypeerd) *vt* characterize, typify; ~*d voor* typical of..., characteristic of...; **–ring** (-en) *v* characterization, typification

'**typeschrift** [y = i.] *o* typescript; **–werk** *o* typing

'**typisch** [y = i.] typical

ty'**pist(e)** [y = i.] (-pisten) *m(-v)* typist

typo'**graaf** [y = i.] (-grafen) *m* typographer; **typogra**'**fie** *v* typography; **typo**'**grafisch** typographical

typolo'**gie** [y = i.] *v* typology

Ty'**roler** [y = i.] (-s) *m* Tyrolean, Tyrolese; **Ty**'**rools** *aj* Tyrolean, Tyrolese

Tyr'**rheens** [y = 1] Thyrrhenian; *de* ~*e Zee* the Tyrrhenian Sea

t.z.t. = *te zijner tijd* in due time (course)

U

1 u [y] ('s) *v* u

2 U, u *pron* you

über'haupt *ad* at all

'uchtend = *ochtend*

ui (-en) *m* 1 🌰 onion; 2 *fig* (g r a p) joke; **'uien-saus** (-en) *v* onion-sauce; **–soep** *v* onion soup

'uier (-s) *m* udder

'uiig I *aj* funny, facetious; **II** *ad* funnily, facetiously

uil (-en) *m* 1 🦉 owl; 2 🦋 moth; 3 *fig* = *uilskuiken; ~en naar Athene dragen* carry owls to Athens; *elk meent zijn ~ een valk te zijn* everyone thinks his own geese swans; **–achtig** owlish; **'uilebal** (-len) *m* pellet; **–bril** (-len) *m* F horn-rimmed glasses, horn-rims; **'Uilenspiegel** *m* Owlglass; **'uilig** owlish; **'uilskuiken** (-s) *o* goose, dolt, ninny; **'uiltje** (-s) *o* 1 🦉 owlet; 2 🦋 moth; *een ~ knappen (vangen)* F take forty winks

uit I *prep* 1 (p l a a t s e l ij k) out of, from; 2 (e m o t i o n e e l) from, out of, for [joy &]; 3 (o o r z a k e l ij k) from; ~ *achteloosheid* ook: through carelessness; *mensen ~ Amsterdam* people from Amsterdam; ~ *ervaring* by (from) experience; *de goedheid sprak ~ haar gelaat* goodness spoke in her face; zie ook: *armoede, ervaring* &; **II** *ad* out; *het is ~ met zijn meisje* his engagement is off; *het boek is ~* 1 the book is out (has appeared); 2 I have finished the book; *als de kerk ~ is* when church is over; *Mijnheer X is ~* Mr X is out, has gone out; *hier is het verhaal ~* here the story ends; *het vuur is ~* the fire is out; *daarmee is het ~* there's an end of the matter; *en daar was het mee ~!* and that was all; *en daarmee ~!* so there!; *het moet nu ~ zijn met die ruzies* these quarrels must stop; *er ~!* out with him (with you)!, get out!; *ik ben er een beetje ~* I'm rather out of it, my hand is out; *er eens helemaal ~ willen zijn* want to get away from it all; *hij is er op ~ om...* he is bent (intent) upon ...ing; *zij is op mijn geld ~* she is after my money; ~ *en thuis* out and home; ~ *en terna* zie *uit-en-te(r)-na*

'uitademen[1] **I** *vi* & *va* expire; **II** *vt* expire, breathe out[2], exhale[2]; **–ming** (-en) *v* expiration, breathing out, exhalation

'uitbaggeren[1] *vt* dredge; **'uitbakenen**[1] *vt* peg out, mark out; **'uitbakken**[1] *vt* fry (render) the fat out of; **'uitbalanceren**[1] *vt* balance

uitbannen[1] *vt* 1 banish[2] [fear &], expel [people]; 2 exorcise [spirits]; **–ning** *v* 1 banishment; 2 exorcism

'uitbarsten[1] *vi* burst out, break out, explode; erupt [of volcano]; *in lachen ~* burst out laughing; *in tranen ~* burst into tears; **–ting** (-en) *v* eruption [of volcano], outburst[2] [of feeling], outbreak[2] [of anger]; explosion[2], burst[2] [of flame, anger &]; *het zal wel tot een ~ komen* there will be an explosion

'uitbazuinen[1] *vt* trumpet forth

'uitbeelden (beeldde 'uit, h. 'uitgebeeld) *vt* personate, represent; **–ding** (-en) *v* personation, representation

'uitbeitelen[1] *vt* 1 (i n s t e e n &) chisel (out); 2 (i n h o u t) carve; **'uitbenen** (beende 'uit, h. 'uitgebeend) *vt* bone; *fig* exploit; **'uitbesteden**[1] *vt* 1 put out to nurse [a child], put out to board, board out, farm out; 2 (v. w e r k) put out to contract

'uitbetalen[1] *vt* pay (down), pay out; **–ling** (-en) *v* payment

'uitbijten I (beet 'uit, h. 'uitgebeten) *vt* bite out; corrode; **II** (beet 'uit, is 'uitgebeten) *vi* corrode; **'uitblazen**[1] **I** *vt* blow out [a candle]; puff out [smoke]; *de laatste adem ~* breathe one's last, expire; **II** *va even ~* breathe, have a breathing-spell; *laten ~* breathe [a horse], give a breathing-spell; **'uitblijven**[1] *vi* stay away; stop out [all night]; hold off [for rain &]; *een verklaring bleef uit* a statement was not forthcoming; *het kan niet ~* it is bound to come (happen, occur &)

'uitblinken[1] *vi* shine, excel; ~ *boven zijn mededingers* outshine (eclipse) one's rivals; **–er** (-s) *m* one who excels, F ace

'uitbloeden I (bloedde 'uit, is 'uitgebloed) *vi* cease bleeding; *een wond laten ~* allow a wound to bleed; **II** (bloedde uit, h. uitgebloed) *vt* bleed [cattle]; **'uitbloeien** (bloeide 'uit, is 'uitgebloeid) *vi* cease blossoming; *uitgebloeid zijn* 🌰 be out of flower; **'uitblussen**[1] *vt* extinguish, put out; *uitgeblust* [*fig*] dead [look], spent [man]; **'uitboenen**[1] *vt* scrub (scour) out; **'uitbombarderen**[1] *vt* bomb out; **uitboren**[1] *vt* bore out, drill; **'uitborstelen**[1] *vt* brush; **'uitbotten** (botte 'uit, 'is uitgebot) *vi* bud

---

[1] V.T. en V.D. van dit werkwoord volgens het model: **'uit**ademen, V.T. ademde **'uit**, V.D. **'uit**geademd. Zie voor de vormen onder het grondwoord, in dit voorbeeld: *ademen*. Bij sterke en onregelmatige werkwoorden wordt u verwezen naar de lijst achterin.

(forth), put forth buds

'**uitbouw** (-en) *m* 1 annex(e) [to a building]; 2 extension[2]; '**uitbouwen**[1] *vt* enlarge, extend

'**uitbraak** *v* escape, break-out; **–poging** (-en) *v* attempted escape

'**uitbraaksel** (-s) *o* vomit

'**uitbraden**[1] fry (render) the fat out of; '**uitbraken**[1] *vt* vomit[2] [one's food, fire, smoke]; *fig* belch forth [smoke &, blasphemous or foul talk]; disgorge [waters, people]; '**uitbranden I** (brandde 'uit, h. 'uitgebrand) *vt* 1 burn out; 2 cauterize [a wound]; **II** (brandde 'uit, is 'uitgebrand) *vi* be burnt out; *het huis was geheel uitgebrand* the house was completely gutted; *een uitgebrande vulkaan* an extinct volcano

'**uitbrander** (-s) *m* scolding, **F** wigging; *ik kreeg een ~ van hem* **F** he gave it me hot

'**uitbreiden** (breidde 'uit, h. 'uitgebreid) **I** *vt* 1 spread [one's arms]; 2 enlarge [the number of..., a business, a work &], increase [the staff]; extend [a domain]; **II** *vr zich ~* 1 (v. o p p e r-v l a k t e) extend, expand; 2 (v. z i e k t e n o f b r a n d) spread; zie ook *uitgebreid;* '**uitbrei-ding** (-en) *v* 1 spreading[2], *fig* spread; 2 enlarge-ment, extension, expansion; **–splan** (-nen) *o* plan for the extension

'**uitbreken I** *vi* 1 break out [of disease, a fire, war &]; 2 break out (of prison); *het koude zweet brak hem uit* a cold sweat came over him; the cold sweat started on his brow; *er een dagje ~* manage to have a holiday (a day off); **II** *vt* break out [a tooth &]; **II** *o het ~* the outbreak; **–er** (-s) *m* prison-breaker

'**uitbrengen**[1] *vt* bring out [words], emit [a sound]; disclose, divulge, reveal [a secret]; ⚓ run out [a cable], get out [a boat]; *advies ~ over...* report on...; *...bracht hij stamelend uit* ook: ...he faltered; *wie heeft het uitgebracht?* who has told about it?; zie ook: *rapport, stem, toost* &;

'**uitbroeden**[1] *vt* hatch [birds, a plot];

'**uitbrullen**[1] *vt* roar (out); *het ~ (van lachen, pijn)* roar (with laughter, with pain);

'**uitbuigen**[1] *vt* bend out(wards)

'**uitbuiten** (buitte 'uit, h. 'uitgebuit) *vt* exploit, take advantage of; **–ting** (-en) *v* exploitation

'**uitbulderen I** (bulderde 'uit, h. 'uitgebulderd) *vt* bellow (out), roar (out); **II** (bulderde 'uit, is 'uitgebulderd) *vi* cease blustering

uit'bundig I *aj* exuberant; **II** *ad* exuberantly; **–heid** (-heden) *v* exuberance, excess

'**uitcijferen**[1] *vt* calculate, compute

'**uitclub** (-s) *v sp* visiting team

'**uitdagen**[1] *vt* challenge[2], *fig* defy; *~ tot een duel* challenge (to a duel); **uit'dagend I** *aj* defiant; **II** *ad* defiantly; '**uitdager** (-s) *m* challenger; '**uitdaging** (-en) *v* challenge

'**uitdampen I** (dampte 'uit, is 'uitgedampt) *vi* evaporate; **II** (dampte 'uit, h. 'uitgedampt) *vt* evaporate [water], exhale [fumes]; air [linen]; **–ping** *v* evaporation, exhalation

'**uitdelen**[1] *vt* distribute, dispense, dole (deal) out [money &]; measure out, mete out [punishment]; deal [blows]; give out, hand out, share out; **–er** (-s) *m* distributor; dispenser; '**uitdeling** (-en) *v* 1 distribution; 2 (b ij f a i l l i s s e m e n t) dividend; **–slijst** (-en) *v* notice of dividend

'**uitdelven**[1] *vt* dig out, dig up; '**uitdenken**[1] *vt* devise, contrive, invent; '**uitdeuken**[1] *vt* flatten, bump out; '**uitdienen**[1] **I** *vt* serve [one's time]; **II** *vi dat heeft uitgediend* that has had its day; '**uitdiepen** (diepte 'uit, h. 'uitgediept) *vt* deepen

'**uitdijen** (dijde 'uit, is 'uitgedijd) *vi* expand, swell (to *tot*); '**uitdijing** *v* expansion, swelling

'**uitdoen**[1] *vt* 1 (u i t d o v e n) put out, extinguish [a light]; 2 (w e g m a k e n) take out [a stain]; 3 (d o o r h a l e n) cross out [a word]; 4 (a f-l e g g e n) put (take) off [a coat]; '**uitdok-teren**[1] *vt* **F** devise, work out, invent, excogi-tate; '**uitdossen** (doste 'uit, h. 'uitgedost) **I** *vt* attire, array, dress up; **II** *vr zich ~* attire oneself

'**uitdoven I** (doofde 'uit, h. 'uitgedoofd) *vt* extinguish[2] [fire, faculty]; quench, put out [a fire, light]; **II** (doofde 'uit, is 'uitgedoofd) *vi* go out; *een uitgedoofde vulkaan* an extinct volcano; **–ving** *v* extinction

'**uitdraaien I** *vt* turn out [the gas], switch off [the electric light]; *er zich netjes ~* wriggle (shuffle) out of it; **II** *vi op niets ~* come to nothing; *waar zal dat op ~?* what is it to end in?

'**uitdragen**[1] *vt* carry out; *fig* propagate; **–er** (-s) *m* second-hand dealer, old-clothes man; **uitdrage'rij** (-en) *v*, '**uitdragerswinkel** (-s) *m* second-hand shop, junk shop

'**uitdrijven**[1] *vt* drive out, expel [people]; cast out [of devils]; **–ving** (-en) *v* expulsion [of people]; casting out [of devils]

'**uitdringen**[1] *vt* push out, crowd out; '**uitdrinken**[1] *vt* drink off, empty, finish [one's glass]

'**uitdrogen I** *vi* dry up, become dry; **II** *vt* dry up, desiccate; **–ging** *v* desiccation

'**uitdruipen**[1] *vi* drain, drip [dry]

---

[1] V.T. en V.D. van dit werkwoord volgens het model: 'uit**ademen**, V.T. ademde 'uit, V.D. 'uit**ge**ademd. Zie voor de vormen onder het grondwoord, in dit voorbeeld: *ademen.* Bij sterke en onregelmatige werkwoorden wordt u verwezen naar de lijst achterin.

uit'drukkelijk I *aj* express, explicit, formal; **II** *ad* expressly, explicitly; **–heid** *v* explicitness; **'uitdrukken**[1] *vt* squeeze out, press out, express [juice &]; *fig* express [feelings]; **II** *vr* zich ~ express oneself; **–king** (-en) *v* 1 expression, term, locution, phrase; 2 expression, feeling; *tot ~ komen* find expression; *vol ~* expressive; *zonder ~* expressionless

'uitduiden[1] *vt* point out, show; **–ding** (-en) *v* explanation

'uitdunnen[1] *vt* thin (out)

'uitduwen[1] *vt* push out, shove out

uit'een asunder, apart; **–drijven**[2] *vt* disperse; **–gaan**[2] *vi* part, separate, disperse; *de vergadering ging om 5 uur uiteen* the meeting rose at five, broke up at five; **–nouden**[2] *vt* 1 (o n d e r s c h e i d e n) tell apart, distinguish (between); 2 (g e s c h e i d e n h o u d e n) keep apart (separately); **–jagen**[2] *vt* disperse

uit'eenlopen[2] *vi* diverge[2], *fig* differ; **–d** divergent[2]

uit'eenrukken[2] *vt* tear asunder; **–slaan**[2] *vt* disperse [the crowd &]; **–spatten**[2] *vi* burst (asunder); *fig* break up; **–stuiven**[2] *vi* scatter, fly apart; **–vallen**[2] *vi* fall apart, fall to pieces; *fig* break up; **–vliegen**[2] *vi* fly apart, scatter

uit'eenzetten[2] *vt* explain, expound, set out; **–ting** (-en) *v* explanation, exposition

'uiteinde (-n) *o* end[2], extremity

uit'eindelijk I *aj* ultimate, final [aim &], eventual [ruin]; **II** *ad* ultimately, in the end, finally, eventually, in the event

'uiten (uitte, h. geuit) **I** *vt* utter, give utterance to, express; **II** *vr* zich ~ express oneself

'uit-en-te(r)-na *ad* 1 (g r o n d i g) thoroughly; 2 (d i k w ij l s) over and over again

uiten'treuren continually, for ever, endlessly [debated]

uiter'aard naturally

'uiterlijk I *aj* outward, external; **II** *ad* 1 outwardly, externally; looked at from the outside; 2 at the utmost, at the latest; **III** *o* (outward) appearance, aspect, exterior, looks; *hij doet alles voor het ~* for the sake of appearance; **–heid** (-heden) *v* exterior; *uiterlijkheden* externals

uiter'mate extremely, excessively

'uiterst I *aj* utmost, utter, extreme; *uw ~e prijzen* $ your lowest prices, your outside prices; zie ook: *wil* &; **II** *ad* in the extreme, extremely, highly; *een ~ rechtse partij* an extreme right-wing party; **–e** (-n) *o* extremity,

extreme; *de vier ~n* the four last things; *de ~n raken elkaar* extremes meet; ● *i n ~ vervallen* rush to extremes; *o p het ~ liggen* be in the last extremity; *t e n ~* in the extreme, exceedingly; *t o t het ~* to the utmost (of one's power); [go &] to the limit; *tot het ~ brengen* drive to distraction; *tot het ~ gaan* go to the limit, carry matters to an extreme, go (to) all lengths; *zich tot het ~ verdedigen* defend oneself to the last; *v a n het ene ~ in het andere vervallen* rush from one extreme to the other, rush (in)to extremes; zie ook: *drijven*

'uiterwaard (-en) *v* foreland

'uiteten I (at 'uit, is 'uitgegeten) *vi* finish eating; **II** (at 'uit, h. 'uitgegeten) *vt iem. ~* give sbd. a farewell dinner; **'uitflappen**[1] *vt* blurt out [everything, the truth], blab [a secret]; **'uitfluiten**[1] *vt* hiss, catcall [an actor]; **'uitfoeteren**[1] *vt iem. ~* fly out at sbd., storm at sbd., scold sbd.

'uitgaaf (-gaven) *v* 1 (g e l d) expenditure, expense; 2 (v. b o e k &) publication; [first &] edition

'uitgaan *vi* go out [of persons, light, fire]; *het gebouw ~* leave (go out of) the building; *de kerk gaat uit* church is over; *die schoenen gaan makkelijk uit* these shoes come of easily; *de vlekken gaan er niet uit* the spots won't come out; *wij gaan niet veel uit* we don't go out (go into society) much; *vrij ~* be free from blame; ● *er o p ~ om...* set out to...; *~ op een klinker* end in a vowel; *het gaat uit v a n...* it originates with..., it emanates from...; *hij gaat uit van het idee dat...* his starting point is that...; *~de van...* starting from... [this principle &]; *er gaat niet veel van hem uit* he is not a man of light and leading; **–d** theatre-going, concert-attending, café-frequenting [public]; outward [cargo], outward-bound [ships]; *~e rechten* export duties; *~e stukken* outgoing letters (correspondence); **'uitgaansdag** (-dagen) *m* day out, off-day, outing; **–verbod** (-boden) *o* curfew

'uitgalmen[1] *vt* sing out, bawl out

'uitgang (-en) *m* 1 (v. h u i s &) exit, way out, issue, outlet, egress; 2 (v. w o o r d) ending, termination; **–spunt** (-en) *o* starting point

'uitgave (-n) = *uitgaaf*

'uitgebreid I *aj* extensive, comprehensive, wide [knowledge, powers, choice]; *~e voorzorgsmaatregelen* elaborate precautions; **II** *ad* extensively, comprehensively; **uitge'breidheid** (-heden) *v* extensiveness, extent

---

[1],[2] V.T. en V.D. van dit werkwoord volgens het model: 1 'uit**ademen**, V.T. ademde 'uit, V.D. 'uitgeademd; 2 uit'een**rukken**, V.T. rukte uit'een, V.D. uit'eengerukt. Zie voor de vormen onder het grondwoord, in deze voorbeelden: *ademen* en *rukken*. Bij sterke en onregelmatige werkwoorden wordt u verwezen naar de lijst achterin.

'**uitgediend** ✗ time-expired; (n u t t e l o o s
g e w o r d e n) past use, having done its time
'**uitgedroogd** dried up², shrivelled
'**uitgehongerd** famished, starving, ravenous
'**uitgekookt** *fig* shrewd, crafty, thorough-paced
'**uitgelaten** elated; exuberant; rollicking [fun];
~ *van vreugde* elated with joy; **uitge'latenheid**
v elation; exuberance
'**uitgeleefd** decrepit, worn out
'**uitgeleerd** ~ *zijn* 1 (v. l e e r j o n g e n) have
served one's apprenticeship; 2 (v. s c h o l i e r)
have done learning; *men is nooit* ~ live and
learn
'**uitgeleide** *o* ~ *doen* show [sbd.] out; see [sbd.]
off [the premises, by the Mauretania]; give
[sbd.] a send-off
'**uitgelezen** 1 (g e l e z e n) read, finished
[books]; 2 (u i t g e z o c h t) select [party of
friends]; choice [cigars]; picked [troops];
uitge'lezenheid *v* choiceness, excellence
'**uitgeloot** drawn
'**uitgemaakt** *dat is een ~e zaak* that's a settled
thing; that's an established truth; ook: that's a
foregone conclusion
'**uitgerammeld** ~ *van de honger* ravenous
'**uitgerekend** calculating [man, woman]; ~
vandaag today of all days [it rained]; ~ *jij* you
of all people
'**uitgescheiden** V.D. van *uitscheiden*
'**uitgeslapen** *fig* wide-awake, long-headed,
knowing
'**uitgesloten** *dat is* ~ it is out of the question, it
is quite impossible
'**uitgesproken** I *aj fig* downright, avowed
[purpose, fascist &]; obvious [success]; II *ad fig*
avowedly [democratic]; frankly [schizoid]
'**uitgestorven** extinct [animals]; deserted [of a
place]
'**uitgestreken** smug, demure; *met een* ~ *gezicht*
smooth-faced
'**uitgestrekt** extensive, vast; **uitge'strektheid**
(-heden) *v* extensiveness, extent; expanse,
stretch, reach [of water &]
'**uitgestudeerd** 1 having finished one's studies;
2 *fig* cunning, sly
'**uitgeteerd** emaciated, wasted
'**uitgeven**[1] I *vt* 1 (a f g e v e n) give out, distribute [provisions]; 2 (v e r t e r e n) spend [money
on...]; 3 (u i t v a a r d i g e n) issue [a proclama-
tion]; 4 (p u b l i c e r e n) publish [a book &]; 5
$ issue [bank-notes &]; 6 (v o o r d e d r u k
b e z o r g e n) edit [memoirs &]; *een boek* ~ *bij*
Harpers publish a book with H.; II *vr zich*

~ *voor...* give oneself out as [a medium &];
pass oneself off as (for) [a...], set up for a...;
–er (-s) *m* publisher; **uitge've'rij** (-en) *v*
publishing business; '**uitgeversfirma** ('s) *v*
publishing firm; **–maatschappij** (-en) *v*
publishing business
'**uitgewekene** (-n) *m-v* refugee
'**uitgewerkt** 1 elaborate [plan]; 2 worked
[example]; 3 extinct [volcano]
'**uitgewoond** pauperized, decaying [dwellings],
[house] in disrepair
'**uitgezocht** excellent; zie ook: *uitgelezen* 2
'**uitgezonderd** except, excepted, barring, save;
dat ~ barring this; *niemand* ~ not excepting
anybody, nobody excepted
'**uitgieren** *vt het* ~ scream with laughter;
'**uitgieten**[1] *vt* pour out
'**uitgifte** (-n) *v* issue
'**uitgillen**[1] *vt* scream out; *het* ~ *van pijn* scream
with pain; '**uitglijden**[1] *vi* slip; lose one's
footing; ~ *over* slip on; '**uitgommen**[1] *vt* erase,
rub out; '**uitgooien**[1] *vt* throw out; throw off
[clothes]
'**uitgraven**[1] *vt* dig out, dig up, disinter; exhume
[a corpse]; excavate [a buried city &]; deepen
[a ditch]; **–ving** (-en) *v* excavation
'**uitgroeien**[1] *vi* grow, develop (into *tot*); *hij is er*
uitgegroeid he has outgrown it; '**uitgummen**[1]
= *uitgommen*; '**uithakken**[1] *vt* cut out, hew out;
'**uithalen** I *vt* 1 pull out, draw out [sth.]; root
out [weeds]; ♪ draw out [a tone]; 2 (s c h o o n –
m a k e n) clean [a pipe]; gut [fish]; turn out [a
room]; 3 (u i t v o e r e n) do [some devilry],
play [pranks]; be up [to something]; *nestjes* ~
go bird('s)-nesting; *het zal niet veel* ~ it will not
be of much use; *dat haalt niets uit* that will be
no use (no good); *er* ~ *zoveel als men kan* use it
for all it is worth; get as much as possible out
of it; *fig* make the most of it; II *vi*
(u i t w ij k e n) pull out (swerve) [to the left]
'**uithangbord** (-en) *o* sign-board, (shop) sign;
'**uithangen**[1] I *vt* hang out [the wash, a flag
&]; *de grote heer* ~ show off; *de brave Hendrik* ~,
de vrome ~ play the saint; II *vi waar zou hij* ~?
where can he hang out?
'**uithebben**[1] *vt* have finished
uit'**heems** foreign [produce]; exotic [plants]
'**uithelpen**[1] *vt* help out
'**uithoek** (-en) *m* remote corner, out-of-the-way
corner
'**uithoesten** I (hoestte '*uit*, h. '*uitgehoest*) *vt*
expectorate, cough up; II (hoestte '*uit*, is
'*uitgehoest*) *vi ben je uitgehoest?* have you

---

[1] V.T. en V.D. van dit werkwoord volgens het model: '**uit**ademen, V.T. ademde '**uit**, V.D. '**uit**geademd. Zie voor
de vormen onder het grondwoord, in dit voorbeeld: *ademen*. Bij sterke en onregelmatige werkwoorden wordt u
verwezen naar de lijst achterin.

finished coughing?; *eens goed* ~ have a good cough

'**uithollen** (holde 'uit, h. 'uitgehold) *vt* 1 hollow (out), scoop out, excavate; 2 *fig* erode [a policy]; **–ling** (-en) *v* 1 hollowing (out), excavation; 2 (h o l t e) hollow, excavation; 3 *fig* erosion

'**uithongeren**¹ *vt* famish, starve (out); **–ring** *v* starvation

'**uithoren**¹ *vt* draw, pump [sbd.]

'**uithouden**¹ *vt* hold out; *fig* bear, suffer, stand; *het* ~ hold out; stand it, stick it (out); *je hebt het uitgehouden!* what a time you have been!; '**uithoudingsvermogen** *o* staying-power(s), (power of) endurance, stamina

'**uithouwen**¹ *vt* carve, hew (from *uit*); '**uithozen**¹ *vt* bail out, bale out; '**uithuilen**¹ *vi* weep oneself out; *eens* ~ ook: have a good cry

uit'**huizig** *bij is erg* ~ he is never at home

'**uithuwelijken** (huwelijkte 'uit, h. 'uitgehuwelijkt), '**uithuwen**¹ *vt* give in marriage, marry off [daughters]

'**uiting** (-en) *v* utterance, expression; ~ *geven aan* give expression to, give utterance to, give voice to; *tot* ~ *komen* find expression

'**uitje** (-s) *o* (small) onion; ‖ **F** outing

'**uitjouwen**¹ *vt* hoot (at), boo; '**uitkafferen** (kafferde 'uit, h. 'uitgekafferd) *vt* fly out at, rage at [sbd.]; '**uitkammen**¹ *vt* comb out; (d o o r z o e k e n) go over (through) sth. with a fine-tooth comb

'**uitkeren**¹ *vt* pay; **–ring** (-en) *v* 1 payment; 2 (v. f a i l l i s s e m e n t) dividend; 3 (b ij z i e k t e &) benefit; 4 (v. s t a k i n g) strike-pay; 5 (v a n w e r k l o z e n) unemployment benefit, dole

'**uitkermen**¹ *vt het* ~ *van pijn* groan with pain; '**uitketteren**¹ = *uitkafferen*; '**uitkienen**¹ *vt* **F** devise, work out, invent [sth.]; '**uitkiezen**¹ *vt* choose, select, single out, pick out

'**uitkijk** (-en) *m* 1 look-out; 2 (p e r s o o n) look-out (man); *op de* ~ on the look-out; '**uitkijken**¹ **I** *vi* look out, be on the look-out; *goed* ~ keep a good look-out; ~ *naar* look out for; *ik kijk wel uit!* I know better (than that); **II** *vt zich de ogen* ~ stare one's eyes out; '**uitkijkpost** (-en) *m* observation post; **–toren** (-s) *m* watch-tower

'**uitklaren**¹ *vt* **$** clear; **–ring** *v* **$** clearance

'**uitkleden**¹ **I** *vt* undress, strip; *naakt* ~ strip to the skin; (b e r o v e n) strip [sbd.] of his possessions; **II** *vr zich* ~ undress, strip; '**uitkloppen**¹ *vt* knock out [the ashes, a pipe]; beat [carpets]

'**uitknijpen I** (kneep 'uit, h. 'uitgeknepen) *vt*

press (squeeze) out, squeeze; *een uitgeknepen citroen* [*fig*] a squeezed orange; **II** (kneep 'uit, is 'uitgeknepen) *vi* 1 (s t i l l e t j e s w e g g a a n) decamp, abscond; 2 **F** (d o o d g a a n) pop off

'**uitknippen**¹ *vt* 1 cut out; 2 ✲ switch off; '**uitknipsel** (-s) *o* cutting, scrap

'**uitknob(b)elen** (kno(b)belde 'uit, h. 'uitgekno(b)beld) *vt* think out, puzzle out; '**uitkoken**¹ *vt* boil

'**uitkomen**¹ *vi* 1 (e r g e n s u i t k o m e n) come out; 2 ⚘ (u i t l o p e n) come out, bud; 3 ⚘ hatch, come out of the shell [of chickens]; 4 (e e r s t u i t s p e l e n) ◊ lead; (o p k o m e n) *sp* turn out, compete [in a tournament &]; 5 (g e l e g e n k o m e n) suit; 6 (a f s t e k e n) stand out; 7 (i n h e t o o g v a l l e n) show; *fig* 1 (a a n h e t l i c h t k o m e n) come out, be brought to light [of crimes]; 2 (b e k e n d w o r d e n) become known [of secrets, plots &]; 3 (u i t v a l l e n) turn out; 4 (b e w a a r h e i d w o r d e n) come true; 5 (v e r s c h ij n e n) come out, appear, be published [of books &]; 6 (g o e d k o m e n) work out [of sums]; 7 (t o e k o m e n, r o n d k o m e n) make (both) ends meet; *dat komt uit* that's correct; *wat komt er uit (die som)?* what is the result?; *de krant kwam niet meer uit* the paper has ceased to appear; *ik kom er wel uit* [don't trouble] I can find my way out; *je komt er niet uit* you shan't leave the house; *het kwam anders uit* things turned out differently; *zo komt het béter uit* 1 that's a better arrangement; 2 (in) this way it will be brought out to better advantage, it shows better; *dat kwam duidelijk uit* that was very evident; *dat komt goed uit* that is very opportune; how lucky!; *die kleur doet het borduursel goed* ~ brings out (sets off) the embroidery to advantage; *u moet dat eens goed doen* ~ do bring it out very clearly, underline it properly; *het komt mij niet goed uit* it doesn't suit me; *het kwam net zo uit* things turned out exactly that way; *dat komt goedkoper uit* it comes cheaper, it is cheaper in the end; *dat zal wel* ~ that goes without saying; *wie moet* ~? ◊ whose turn is it to play?; *u moet* ~ ◊ your lead!; ● ~ *m e t goede spelers sp* turn out good players; *ik kan met die som (gelds) niet* ~ this sum is not enough for me; ~ *o p* open on (on to, into) [a garden &]; *ik kwam op de weg uit* I emerged into the road; ~ *t e g e n* stand our against [the sky]; *sp* play (against); *dat beeldje komt goed uit tegen die achtergrond* the statuette stands out well against that background; *hij kwam er v o o r uit* he admitted it; (b e k e n d e s c h u l d) he owned up; *hij kwam er rond voor uit* he made no secret of it; *(rond) ~ voor zijn mening* speak one's mind; **'uitkomst** (-en) *v* 1 (u i t s l a g) result, issue; (v a n s o m) result; 2 (r e d d i n g) relief, deliverance, help; *een ~ voor iedere huisvrouw* a boon and a blessing (a godsend) to every housewife

'uitkoop (-kopen) *m* buying out, buying off; **'uitkopen**[1] *vt* buy out, buy off

'uitkraaien[1] *vt het ~* crow; **'uitkrabben**[1] *vt* scratch out; **'uitkramen** (kraamde 'uit, h. 'uitgekraamd) *vt zijn geleerdheid ~* show off one's learning; *onzin ~* talk nonsense, say silly things; **'uitkrijgen**[1] *vt* get off [his boots &]; *ik kan het boek niet ~* I can't get through the book; **'uitkrijten**[1] *vt iem. ~ voor* decry sbd. as a..., denounce sbd. as a...; **'uitkruipen**[1] *vi* creep out; **'uitkunnen**[1] *vi je zult er niet ~* you won't be able to get out; *mijn schoenen kunnen niet uit* my shoes won't come off; *ermee ~* manage (make do) with; *ergens niet over ~* be dumbfounded about sth., be flabbergasted about sth.

'uitlaat (-laten) *m* exhaust; **–gassen** *mv* exhaust gases (fumes); **–klep** (-pen) *v* exhaust-valve

'uitlachen I (lachte 'uit, h. 'uitgelachen) *vt* laugh at; **II** (lachte 'uit, is 'uitgelachen) *vi* laugh one's fill

'uitladen[1] *vt* unload, discharge; **–ding** *v* unloading, discharge

'uitlaten[1] **I** *vt* 1 let out [a dog, a hidden person &]; see out [a visitor]; let off [fumes]; 2 (w e g l a t e n) leave out, omit [a word &]; 3 (w ij d e r m a k e n) let out [a garment]; 4 (n i e t m e e r d r a g e n) leave off [one's coat]; leave off wearing [Jaeger &]; **II** *vr zich ~ over iets* speak about it; **–ting** (-en) *v* 1 (w e g l a t i n g) letting out, omission; 2 (g e z e g d e) utterance, statement

'uitleenbibliotheek (-theken) *v* lending-library

'uitleg *m* 1 (a a n b o u w) extension [of a town]; 2 (v e r k l a r i n g) explanation, interpretation [of sbd.'s words]; **'uitleggen**[1] *vt eig* 1 (g e - r e e d l e g g e n) lay out [articles of dress, books &]; 2 (g r o t e r m a k e n) let out [a garment]; extend [a town]; 3 *fig* explain, interpret; **–er** (-s) *m* explainer, interpreter; **'uitlegging** (-en) *v* explanation, interpretation [of words, a text]; exegesis [of Scripture]

'uitleiden[1] *vt* expel [an alien], conduct [him] across the frontier; **'uitlekken**[1] *vi* leak out[2], strain; *fig* trickle out, filter through, ooze out; transpire; **'uitlenen**[1] *vt* lend (out)

'uitleveren[1] *vt* extradite [a person]; **'uitleve-**

ring (-en) *v* extradition [of a person]; **–sver-drag** (-dragen) *o* extradition treaty

'uitlezen[1] *vt* 1 read through (to the end), finish [a book], finish reading [the morning paper]; 2 pick out, select; **'uitlichten**[1] *vt* lift out [sth. from]; **'uitlikken**[1] *vt* lick out; **'uitlogen**[1] *vt =* 1 *logen*; **'uitlokken**[1] *vt* provoke [action, war &]; elicit [an answer]; invite [criticism]; evoke [a smile]; call forth [protests]; ask for [trouble]; court [comparison, disaster]; **'uitloodsen**[1] *vt* ⚓ pilot out

'uitloop (-lopen) *m* (v. w a t e r) outlet

uit'lootbaar redeemable

'uitlopen[1] *vi* 1 (v. p e r s o n e n) run out; go out; (v. b e v o l k i n g) turn out; 2 (v a n s c h e p e n) put out to sea, sail; 3 (u i t - b o t t e n) bud, shoot; sprout [of potatoes]; 4 (v. k l e u r e n) run, bleed; 5 (v o o r s p r o n g krij g e n) get ahead, gain; 6 *de vergadering is uitgelopen* the meeting was drawn out (prolonged); *heel Parijs liep uit om hem toe te juichen* all Paris turned out to cheer him; ● *~ i n een baai* run into a bay; *het is o p niets uitgelopen* it has come to nothing; *waar moet dat op ~?* what is it to end in?; **–er** (-s) *m* 1 (p e r s o o n) gadabout; 2 (v. p l a n t e n) runner, offshoot, sucker; 3 (v. b e r g) spur; 4 *fig* offshoot

'uitloten[1] *vt* draw out, draw; **–ting** (-en) *v* drawing [for the prizes &]

'uitloven[1] *vt* offer [a reward, a prize], promise

'uitlozen[1] *vi* discharge (itself); **–zing** (-en) *v* discharge

'uitluchten[1] *vt* air, ventilate; **'uitluiden**[1] *vt* ring out

'uitmaken[1] *vt* 1 finish [a book, a game]; break off [an engagement]; 2 (u i t d o v e n) put out [fire]; 3 (w e g m a k e n) take out [stains]; 4 (b e s l i s s e n) decide, settle [a dispute]; 5 (v o r m e n) form, constitute [the board, the government], make up [the greater part of]; 6 (u i t s c h e l d e n) call [sbd.] names; *dat moeten zij samen maar ~* they should settle that between themselves; *dat maakt niet(s) uit* it does not matter, it is immaterial; *wat maakt dat uit?* what does it matter?; *dat is een uitgemaakte zaak* zie *uitgemaakt*; *dat is nu uitgemaakt* that is settled now; *iem. voor leugenaar ~* call sbd. a liar; *iem. ~ voor al wat lelijk is* call sbd. all sorts of names; **'uitmalen**[1] *vt* 1 (w a t e r) drain; 2 (m e e l) extract; **'uitmelken**[1] *vt* strip [a cow]; *fig* exhaust [a subject]; milk, bleed [sbd.]

'uitmergelen[1] *vt* exhaust; **–ling** *v* exhaustion

---

[1] V.T. en V.D. van dit werkwoord volgens het model: 'uitademen, V.T. ademde 'uit, V.D. 'uitgeademd. Zie voor de vormen onder het grondwoord, in dit voorbeeld: *ademen*. Bij sterke en onregelmatige werkwoorden wordt u verwezen naar de lijst achterin.

'uitmesten¹ *vt* muck out, clean out;
  'uitmeten¹ *vt* measure (out); *breed ~* exaggerate [one's grievances]
uitmiddel'puntig eccentric; –heid *v* eccen-
'uitmikken¹ *vt* time; hit (upon)   [tricity
'uitmonden (mondde 'uit, h. en is 'uitgemond)
  vi (v. r i v i e r) flow (empty) into; (v. s t r a a t)
  lead (open) in(to); *fig* end in, result in; –ding
  (-en) *v* mouth
'uitmonsteren¹ *vt* fit out, rig out;
  'uitmoorden¹ *vt* massacre
'uitmunten¹ *vi ~ b o v e n* excel, surpass; *~ i n*
  excel in (at); **II** *aj* excellent; **II** *ad*
  excellently; –heid *v* excellence
'uitnemen¹ *vt* take out; uit'nemend = *uitmun-*
  tend; –heid *v* excellence; *bij ~* pre-eminently,
  par excellence
'uitnoden¹, 'uitnodigen¹ *vt* invite; 'uitnodiging (-en) *v* invitation; *op ~ van* at (on) the
  invitation of; –skaart (-en) *v* invitation card
'uitoefenen¹ *vt* exercise [a profession, a right
  &]; bring to bear [pressure]; practise, carry on
  [a trade]; –ning *v* exercise [of a right],
  discharge [of a function], practice [of an art];
  prosecution [of a trade]
'uitpakkamer (-s) *v* commercial room;
  'uitpakken (pakte uit, h. en is uitgepakt) **I** *vt*
  unpack; unwrap, undo [birthday presents]; **II**
  vi [a f l o p e n, u i t k o m e n] work out; *als hij*
  aan het ~ gaat [*fig*] when he begins to pour out
  his heart; *~ o v e r een onderwerp* let out on a
  subject; *~ t e g e n* inveigh against
'uitpellen¹ *vt* peel off; enucleate; 'uitpersen¹ *vt*
  express, press out, squeeze; 'uitpeuteren¹ *vt*
  pick (out); 'uitpiekeren¹ *vt* puzzle out, figure
  out; 'uitpikken¹ *vt* 1 *eig* peck out; 2 (u i t -
  k i e z e n) pick out, select, single out;
  'uitplanten¹ *vt* plant out, bed out;
  'uitpluizen¹ *vt* pick; *fig* sift out, sift;
  'uitplukken¹ *vt* pluck out
'uitplunderen¹ *vt* plunder, pillage, ransack,
  sack; –ring (-en) *v* plundering, pillage, sack
'uitplussen (pluste 'uit, h. 'uitgeplust) *vt* puzzle
  out, work out; 'uitpompen¹ *vt* pump (out);
  'uitpoten¹ *vt* = *poten*; 'uitpraten (praatte 'uit,
  is 'uitgepraat) *vi* finish talking; *laat mij ~* let
  me have my say; *daarover raakt hij nooit uitge-*
  praat that is a theme of which he never tires;
  dan zijn we uitgepraat then there is nothing
  more to say; 'uitproesten¹ *vt het ~* burst out
  laughing
'uitpuilen (puilde 'uit, h. en is 'uitgepuild) *vi*
  protrude, bulge; –d protuberant; *~e ogen*

bulging eyes; *met ~e ogen* 1 goggle-eyed; 2 with
  eyes starting from their sockets
'uitputten¹ **I** *vt* exhaust; **II** *vr zich ~* exhaust
  oneself; 'uitputting *v* exhaustion; –soorlog
  (-logen) *m* war of attrition
'uitpuzzelen¹ *vt* puzzle out
'uitrafelen¹ *vt* ravel out, fray; 'uitraken (raakte
  'uit, is 'uitgeraakt) *vi* (v. v r i e n d s c h a p) be
  off, be broken; come to an end; *er helemaal ~*
  be out of it, get out of practice (out of the
  habit); 'uitrangeren¹ [-rɑnʒeːrə(n)] *vt* [*fig*]
  shunt, shelve [sbd.]; 'uitrazen (raasde 'uit, h.
  en is 'uitgeraasd) *vi* 1 (v. s t o r m) rage itself
  out, spend itself; 2 (v. p e r s o n e n) vent one's
  fury; *de jeugd moet ~* youth will have its fling;
  hij is nu uitgeraasd he has sown his wild oats
'uitredden¹ **I** *vt er ~* help out, deliver; **II** *vr zich*
  er ~ get out of it; –ding *v* deliverance, (means
  of) escape
'uitreiken¹ *vt* distribute, deliver, give, issue
  [tickets], present [prizes]; –king (-en) *v* distribution, delivery, issue [of tickets], presentation
  [of prizes]
'uitreis (-reizen) *v* outward journey; ⚓ voyage
  out; *op de ~* ⚓ outward bound; –vergunning
  (-en) *v* exit permit; –visum [-züm] (-s en
  -visa) *o* exit visa
'uitrekenen¹ *vt* calculate, compute, figure out,
  reckon up; *een som ~* work out a sum; zie ook:
  uitgerekend & *vinger*; –ning *v* calculation,
  computation
'uitrekken¹ **I** *vt* stretch (out); **II** *vr zich ~*
  stretch oneself; 'uitrichten¹ *vt* do; *wat heb jij*
  uitgericht? what have you done?, what have you
  been at?; *er is niet veel mee uit te richten* it is not
  much good
'uitrijden¹ *vi* ride out, drive out; *de stad ~* ride
  (drive) out of the town; *de trein reed het station*
  uit the train was moving (pulling) out of the
  station; 'uitrijstrook (-stroken) *v* exit lane,
  deceleration lane
'uitrijzen¹ *~ b o v e n* rise above, overtop [neigh-
  bouring buildings]
'uitrit (-ten) *m* way out, exit
'uitroeien¹ *vt* root out² [trees]; weed out²,
  extirpate², eradicate² [weed, an error]; exterminate [a tribe, a nation, vice]; –iing *v* extirpa-
  tion, extermination, eradication
'uitroep (-en) *m* exclamation, shout, cry;
  'uitroepen¹ *vt* cry (out), exclaim; declare [a
  strike &]; *~ tot* (*koning* &) proclaim [sbd.] king;
  'uitroep(ings)teken (-s) *o* exclamation mark
'uitroken¹ *vt* 1 (t e n e i n d e r o k e n) smoke

---

¹ V.T. en V.D. van dit werkwoord volgens het model: 'uitademen, V.T. ademde 'uit, V.D. 'uitgeademd. Zie voor
de vormen onder het grondwoord, in dit voorbeeld: *ademen*. Bij sterke en onregelmatige werkwoorden wordt u
verwezen naar de lijst achterin.

out [pipe]; finish [a pipe, cigar]; 2 (o m t e
o n t s m e t t e n &) smoke, fumigate; 3 (d o o r
r o o k v e r d r i j v e n) smoke out [animals];
'uitrollen[1] *vt* unroll [carpet]; roll out [pastry];
'uitrukken[1] **I** *vt* pull out, pluck out [sth.]; tear
[one's own hair]; tear out [weeds]; **II** *vi* 1 ⚔
march (out); 2 (v. b r a n d w e e r) turn out; *de
stad* ~ ⚔ march out of the town; *je kunt* ~ *!, ruk
uit!* clear out!; **S** hop it!, beat it!; *de politie moest*
~ the police were called out
1 'uitrusten (rustte 'uit, h. en is 'uitgerust) *vi*
rest, take rest; *bent u nu helemaal uitgerust?* are
you quite rested?; *ik heb de mannen laten* ~ I
have given the men a rest, I have rested them;
~ *van* rest from [one's labours]
2 'uitrusten (rustte 'uit, h. 'uitgerust) *vt* equip
[an army, a ship, a person]; fit out [a fleet]; rig
[cabin as operating-room]; **–ting** (-en) *v*
equipment, outfit; **'uitrustingsstukken** *mv*
equipment
'uitschakelen[1] *vt* ✲ cut out, switch off; *fig*
eliminate, leave out, rule out; **–ling** *v* ✲
putting out of circuit; *fig* elimination
'uitschateren[1] *vt het* ~ burst out laughing
'uitscheiden* I *vi* stop, leave off; *er* ~
1 (t ij d e l ij k) stop working; 2 (v o o r g o e d)
shut up shop; *schei uit!* stop (it)!; *schei uit met dat
geklets!* stop that jawing!; **II** *vt* excrete;
'uitschelden[1] *vt* abuse, call [sbd.] names; ~
voor call; zie ook: *uitmaken*; **'uitschenken**[1] *vt*
pour out; **'uitscheppen**[1] *vt* bail out, bale out,
scoop out; **'uitscheuren**[1] **I** *vt* tear out; **II** *vi*
tear; **'uitschieten**[1] **I** *vt* 1 shoot out, throw out
[a cable]; shoot [rays]; 2 whip off [one's coat];
er werd hem een oog uitgeschoten he had one of his
eyes shot out; **II** *vi* slip; *de boot kwam de kreek* ~
the boat shot out from the creek; zie ook:
uitlopen 3 en voorschieten; **'uitschiften**[1] *vt* sift
(out); **'uitschilderen**[1] *vt* paint, portray;
'uitschoppen[1] *vt* kick out[2]; kick off [one's
shoes]
'uitschot (-ten) *o* refuse, offal, trash; offscourings, riff-raff, dregs [of the people]
'uitschrabben[1], **–schrapen**[1] *vt* scrape out;
'uitschreeuwen[1] *vt* cry out; *het* ~ cry out;
'uitschreien[1] *vi* = *uithuilen*; **'uitschrijven**[1] *vt*
write out, make out [an invoice &]; zie ook:
lening, prijsvraag, vergadering &; **'uitschudden**[1]
vt shake (out) [a carpet]; strip [a person] to the
skin
uit'schuifbaar sliding, extensible; telescopic
[antenna]; **'uitschuifblad** (-bladen) *o* pull-out
leaf, (draw-)leaf; **–tafel** (-s) *v* extension table,

pull-out table; **'uitschuiven**[1] *vt* push out;
draw out [a table]
'uitschulpen[1] *vt* scallop; **'uitschuren**[1] *vt* scour
(out); (u i t h o l l e n) wear out
'uitslaan[1] **I** *vt* beat out, strike out; drive out [a
nail]; knock out [a tooth &]; hammer, beat
(out) [metals]; shake out [carpets], unfold [a
map]; throw out [one's legs]; put forth [one's
claws]; stretch, spread [one's wings]; *mallepraat*
~ talk nonsense; *de taal die zij* ~*!* the language
they use!; **II** *vi* break out [of flames, measles];
sweat [of a wall]; grow mouldy [of bread];
deflect [of indicator]; **–d** ~*e brand* blaze; ~*e
plaat* folding picture (plate)
'uitslag *m* 1 (-slagen) outcome, result, issue,
event, success; 2 (s c h i m m e l) mouldiness; 3
(p u i s t j e s) eruption, rash; 4 (v. w ij z e r)
deflection; *stille* ~ **$** draft; *de* ~ *van de verkiezing*
the result of the poll; *de bekendmaking van de* ~
van de verkiezing the declaration of the poll; *wat
is de* ~ *van uw examen?* what is the result of
your examination?; *met goede* ~ with good
success, successfully
'uitslapen (sliep 'uit, h. en is 'uitgeslapen) *vt* &
vi lie in, sleep late, have one's sleep out; *zijn
roes* ~ sleep off one's debauch, sleep it off;
'uitslepen[1] *ergens iets* ~ get sth. out of it;
'uitsliepen (sliepte 'uit, h. 'uitgesliept) *vt iem.*
~ ± jeer at sbd.; *sliep uit!* ± sold again;
'uitslijpen[1] *vt* grind out, hollow-grind; wear
out; **'uitslijten**[1] *vi* wear out, wear away; wear
off; **'uitsloven**[1] *zich* ~ do one's best, drudge,
toil, work oneself to the bone [for one's
livelihood, for others]; lay oneself out [to
please]
'uitsluiten[1] *vt* shut (lock) out; *fig* exclude; lock
out [workmen]; **uit'sluitend** exclusive;
'uitsluiting (-en) *v* 1 exclusion; 2 lock-out
[workmen]; *met* ~ *van* exclusive of; **'uitsluitsel**
o decisive answer
'uitsmeren[1] *vt* spread [over a longer period]
'uitsmijten[1] *vt* chuck out, throw out; **–er** (-s) *m*
1 chucker-out, bouncer; 2 slice of bread with
veal & and a fried egg on top, ± ham and
eggs
'uitsnellen[1] *vi de deur* ~ rush out
'uitsnijden[1] *vt* cut out, carve out, excise; **–ding**
(-en) *v* cutting out, excision
'uitsnikken[1] **I** *vt* sob out; **II** *vi* sob till one is
calmed down
'uitspannen[1] *vt* 1 (u i t s t r e k k e n) stretch out,
extend [one's fingers &]; spread [a net]; 2 (u i t
h e t t u i g h a l e n) take out, unharness [the

[1] V.T. en V.D. van dit werkwoord volgens het model: **'uit**ademen, V.T. ademde **'uit**, V.D. **'uit**geademd. Zie voor
de vormen onder het grondwoord, in dit voorbeeld: *ademen*. Bij sterke en onregelmatige werkwoorden wordt u
verwezen naar de lijst achterin.

horses], unyoke [oxen]; **–ning** (-en) *v* tea-garden; **'uitspansel** *o* firmament, heavens, sky

'uitsparen[1] *vt* save, economize, (o p e n l a t e n) leave blank, leave free; **–ring** (-en) *v* saving, economy; blank space, free space

'uitspatting (-en) *v* dissipation, debauchery; excess; *zich aan ~en overgeven* indulge in dissipation (in excesses)

'uitspelen[1] *vt* play; *ze tegen elkaar ~* play them off against each other; **'uitspinnen**[1] *vt* spin out[2]; **'uitspoelen**[1] *vt* rinse (out); wash away; **'uitspoken**[1] *wat spookt hij daar uit?* what is he up to?, what is he doing there?

'uitspraak (-spraken) *v* 1 pronunciation; 2 (o o r d e e l) pronouncement, utterance, statement; 3 (a r b i t r a a l) award; 丸 finding, verdict; *~ doen* pass judg(e)ment, pass (pronounce) sentence

'uitspreiden[1] *vt* spread (out); **'uitspreken I** (sprak 'uit, h. 'uitgesproken) *vt* pronounce [a word, judg(e)ment, a sentence]; deliver [a message]; express [thanks, the hope]; **II** (sprak 'uit, is 'uitgesproken) *vi* finish

'uitspringen[1] *vi* project, jut out; *ergens ~* jump out, leap out; *[fig] dat springt eruit* that stands out; **–d** jutting out, projecting [part]; salient [angle]

'uitspruiten[1] *vi* sprout, shoot; **'uitspruitsel** (-s) *o* sprout, shoot

'uitspugen[1], **'uitspuwen**[1] *vt* spit out; **'uitstaan I** *vt* endure, suffer, bear; *ik kan hem niet ~* I cannot stand the fellow, I have no patience with him; *wat ik moest ~* what I had to suffer (bear, endure); *ik heb niets met hem uit te staan* I have nothing to do with them; *dat heeft er niets mee uit te staan* that has nothing to do with it; **II** *vi* 1 stand out; 2 be put out at interest; *mijn geld staat uit tegen 4%* my money is put out at 4%; *~de schulden* outstanding debts

'uitstalkast (-en) *v* show-case; **'uitstallen**[1] *vt* expose for sale, display; **–ling** (-en) *v* display (in the shop-window), (shop-)window display; **'uitstalraam** (-ramen) *o* show-window

[7]**'uitstamelen**[1] *vt* stammer (out)

'uitstapje (-s) *o* excursion, tour, trip, outing, jaunt; *een ~ doen (maken)* make an excursion, make (take) a trip; **'uitstappen**[1] *vi* get out [of tram-car &]; step out, alight [from a carriage]; *allen ~!* all get out here

uit'stedig absent from town, out of town; **–heid** *v* absence from town

'uitsteeksel (-s) *o* projection; protuberance

'uitstek (-ken) *o* projection; *bij ~* pre-eminently

'uitsteken[1] **I** *vt* stretch out, hold out [one's hand], put out [the tongue, the flag]; *iem. de ogen ~* 1 put out sbd.'s eyes; 2 *fig* make sbd. jealous; zie ook: *hand &*; **II** *vi* 1 (i n e l k e r i c h t i n g) stick out; 2 (h o r i z o n t a a l) jut out, project, protrude; *hoog ~ boven...* rise far above..., tower above...; *hoog boven de anderen ~* rise (head and shoulders) above the others, tower above one's contemporaries; *boven anderen ~ in...* excel others in...; **1 –d** *aj* protruding &, prominent

2 uit'stekend I *aj* excellent, first-rate, eminent, admirable; **II** *ad* excellently, extremely well, splendidly, admirably; very well!; **–heid** *v* excellence

'uitstel *o* postponement, delay, respite; *~ van betaling* extension of time for payment; *het kan geen ~ lijden* it admits of no delay; *~ van executie* stay of execution; *~ geven (verlenen)* grant a delay; *~ vragen* ask for a delay; *van ~ komt dikwijls afstel* delays are often dangerous, ± procrastination is the thief of time; *~ is geen afstel* all is not lost that is delayed; *zonder ~* without delay; **'uitstellen**[1] *vt* delay, defer, postpone, put off; *stel niet uit tot morgen, wat ge heden doen kunt* don't put off till to-morrow what you can do to-day

'uitsterven[1] *vi* die out[2], become extinct; **–ving** *v* extinction

'uitstijgen[1] *vi* get out; *~ boven* rise above; **'uitstippelen**[1] *vt* dot [a line]; *fig* outline [a policy], lay down [lines, a programme]; **'uitstoelen** (stoelde 'uit, is 'uitgestoeld) *vi* 🌿 stool; **'uitstomen**[1] **I** *vt* 1 clean by steam; 2 = stomen **II** 2; **II** *vi* steam away; *het schip stoomde uit* the ship steamed out to sea

'uitstorten[1] **I** *vt* pour out, pour forth; *zijn gemoed, zijn hart ~* pour out one's heart, unbosom oneself; **II** *vr zich ~* discharge itself [of a river, into the sea]; **–ting** (-en) *v* effusion; *de ~ van de Heilige Geest* the outpouring of the Holy Ghost

'uitstoten[1] *vt* thrust out; *fig* expel [a person]; *kreten ~* utter cries; **–ting** *v* expulsion

'uitstralen[1] *vt* radiate, beam forth; **–ling** (-en) *v* radiation, emanation; **'uitstralingsvermogen** *o* radiating power; **–warmte** *v* radiant heat

'uitstrekken[1] **I** *vt* stretch, stretch forth, extend; stretch out, reach out [one's hand]; **II** *vr zich ~* 1 (v. l e v e n d e w e z e n s) stretch oneself; 2 (v. d i n g e n) stretch, extend, reach; (v. t ij d) cover [a period of 10 years]; *zich ~ naar het oosten* stretch away to the east

---

[1] V.T. en V.D. van dit werkwoord volgens het model: 'uit**ademen**, V.T. ademde 'uit, V.D. 'uit**geademd**. Zie voor de vormen onder het grondwoord, in dit voorbeeld: *ademen*. Bij sterke en onregelmatige werkwoorden wordt u verwezen naar de lijst achterin.

'**uitstrijken**[1] *vt* spread; smooth; cross out; 🖝 take a swab

'**uitstrijkje** (-s) *o* 🖝 smear, swab

'**uitstromen**[1] *vi* flow out, stream forth, gush out; (v. g a s) escape, pass out; ~ *in* flow into

'**uitstrooien**[1] *vt* strew, spread[2], disseminate[2]; *fig* spread [rumours], put about [lies &];
'**uitstrooisel** (-s) *o* rumour, false report

'**uitstuffen**[1] *vt* erase, rub out

'**uitstulpen I** (stulpte 'uit, is 'uitgestulpt) *vi* bulge, protrude, budge; **II** (stulpte 'uit, h. 'uitgestulpt) *vt* turn out [the inside of sth.];
–ping (-en) *v* bulge, protrusion

'**uitsturen**[1] *vt* send out; '**uittanden**[1] *vt* indent, tooth, jag

'**uittarten**[1] *vt* defy, challenge, provoke; **–ting** (-en) *v* defiance, challenge, provocation

'**uittekenen**[1] *vt* draw, delineate, portray, picture; '**uittellen**[1] *vt* count out

'**uitteren** (teerde 'uit, is 'uitgeteerd) *vi* pine (waste) away, waste; **–ring** *v* emaciation

'**uittikken**[1] *vt* type out

'**uittocht** (-en) *m* exodus[2]

'**uittorenen** (torende 'uit, h. 'uitgetorend) *vi* ~ *boven* tower above; '**uittrappen**[1] *vt* stamp out [a fire]; kick off [one's shoes]; kick [you] out [of the job]; '**uittreden**[1] *vi* step out; (*uit de firma*) ~ retire (from partnership); *rk* (h e t a m b t v e r l a t e n) give up (forsake) the priesthood (one's ministry); zie ook: *treden uit* & *aftreden*

'**uittrekblad** (-bladen) *o* pull-out leaf, (draw-) leaf; '**uittrekken**[1] **I** *vt* draw out [a nail &]; pull off [boots]; take off [one's coat]; pull out, extract [a tooth, herbs &]; *een som* ~ *voor* earmark (set aside) £... for...; **II** *vi* 1 ⚔ march out; set out, set forth; 2 move out [of a house]; '**uittreksel** (-s) *o* 1 (a f k o o k s e l) extract; 2 (k o r t e i n h o u d) abstract; (v. d. b u r g e r l. s t a n d) [birth, marriage &] certificate; $ (v a n r e k e n i n g) statement; 3 (h e t o n t l e e n d e) extract; '**uittrektafel** (-s) *v* pull-out table, extending table, telescope-table

'**uittrompetten**[1] *vt* trumpet forth

'**uitvaagsel** *o* scum, dregs, offscourings [of society]

'**uitvaardigen** (vaardigde 'uit, h. 'uitgevaardigd) *vt* issue [an order]; promulgate [a law]; **–ging** (-en) *v* issue; promulgation

'**uitvaart** (-en) *v* funeral, obsequies, **–dienst** (-en) *m* funeral ceremonies, obsequies; **–stoet** (-en) *m* funeral procession

'**uitval** (-len) *m* 1 ⚔ sally[2], sortie; 2 (b ij h e t s c h e r m e n) thrust, lunge, pass; 3 *fig* outburst, sudden fit of passion; *een* ~ *doen* 1 ⚔ make a sally (a sortie); 2 (b ij h e t s c h e r m e n) make a pass, lunge, lash out;

'**uitvallen**[1] *vi* 1 fall out, come off [hair]; 2 ⚔ fall out [while on the march]; 4 (b ij s c h e r m e n) make a pass, lunge, lash out; 5 (b ij s p e l) drop out; 6 (v. e l e k t r. l i c h t, s t r o o m &) fail; 7 *fig* fly out (at *tegen*), cut up rough; *goed* (*slecht*) ~ turn out well (badly); *tegen iem.* ~ fly out at sbd.; *hij kan lelijk tegen je* ~ he is apt to cut up rough; *die trein is uitgevallen* that train has been cancelled; *het* ~ *van de stroom* (*een transformator*) a power (a transformer) failure; **–er** (-s) *m* ⚔ straggler; *er waren twee* ~*s sp* two competitors dropped out; '**uitval(s)poort** (-en) *v* sally port; **–weg** (-wegen) *m* arterial road

'**uitvaren**[1] *vi* 1 ⚓ sail (out); put to sea; 2 *fig* storm, fly out; ~ *tegen* fly out at, inveigh against, declaim against; '**uitvechten**[1] *vt het onder elkaar maar* ~ fight (have) it out among themselves; '**uitvegen**[1] *vt* 1 sweep out; 2 (m e t g u m &) wipe out, rub out, efface; *iem. de mantel* ~ haul sbd. over the coals, give sbd. a bit of one's mind; '**uitventen**[1] *vt* hawk about; '**uitvergroten**[1] *vt* enlarge; **F** blow up

'**uitverkiezing** *v* predestination

'**uitverkocht** out of print [book]; sold out, out of stock [goods]; *de druk was gauw* ~ the edition was exhausted in a very short time; ~*e zaal* full house; '**uitverkoop** (-kopen) *m* $ selling-off, clearance sale, sale(s); **–prijs** (-prijzen) *m* sale price; '**uitverkopen** (verkocht 'uit, h. 'uitverkocht) *vt* & *va* sell off, clear

'**uitverkoren** *aj* chosen, elect; *het* ~ *volk* the Chosen People (Race); ~*e* favourite; *zijn* ~*e* his sweetheart; *de* ~*en* the chosen

'**uitvertellen** (vertelde 'uit, h. 'uitverteld) *vt* tell to the end; *ik ben uitverteld* I am at the end of my story; '**uitveteren** (veterde 'uit, h. 'uitgeveterd) *vt* scold, rate, fly out at; '**uitvieren**[1] *vt* veer out, pay out [a cable]; *een kou* ~ nurse one's cold

'**uitvinden**[1] *vt* invent [a machine &]; find out [the secret &]; **–er** (-s) *m* inventor; '**uitvinding** (-en) *v* invention; '**uitvindsel** (-s) *o* invention

'**uitvissen**[1] *vt* fish out[2], *fig* ferret out; '**uitvlakken**[1] *vt* blot out, wipe out; (m e t g u m) rub out; *dat moet je niet* ~! bear that in mind!, that is not to be scorned!, it is not to be sneezed at; '**uitvliegen**[1] *vi* fly out

---

[1] V.T. en V.D. van dit werkwoord volgens het model: '**uit**ademen, V.T. ademde 'uit, V.D. 'uitgeademd. Zie voor de vormen onder het grondwoord, in dit voorbeeld: *ademen*. Bij sterke en onregelmatige werkwoorden wordt u verwezen naar de lijst achterin.

'uitvloeien[1] *vi* flow out; **'uitvloeisel** (-s en -en) *o* consequence, outcome, result

'uitvloeken[1] *vt* swear at, curse

'uitvlucht (-en) *v* evasion, pretext, subterfuge, excuse, shift; ~*en zoeken* prevaricate, shuffle

'uitvoer (-en) *m* export, exportation; (d e g o e d e r e n) exports; *de ~ verhogen en de invoer verlagen* increase exports and reduce imports; *ten ~ brengen* (*leggen*) carry (put) into effect, execute, carry out [a threat]; **–artikel** (-en en -s) *o* article of export; ~*en* ook: exports; **uit'voerbaar** practicable, feasible; **–heid** *v* practicability, practicableness, feasibility; **'uitvoerder** (-s) *m* (v. c o n c e r t) performer; (v. p l a n) executor; (v. b o u w w e r k) building supervisor; **'uitvoeren**[1] *vt* 1 carry out [harbour-works &]; execute [an order, a plan, a sentence &]; perform [an operation, a task, music, a play, tricks &]; carry (put) into effect, carry out [a resolution]; 2 **$** fill [an order]; export [goods]; *hij heeft weer niets uitgevoerd* he has not done a stroke of work; *wat voer jij daar uit?* what are you doing?, what are you up to?, what are you at?; *wat heb jij toch uitgevoerd, dat je...?* what ever have you been doing? (been up to?); *wat heb je vandaag uitgevoerd?* what have you done to-day?; *wat moet ik daarmee ~?* what am I to do with it?; *de ~de macht* the Executive; *de ~de Raad* the Executive Council; **'uitvoerhandel** *m* export trade; **–haven** (-s) *v* harbour of exportation

uit'voerig I *aj* ample, lengthy [discussion]; full [particulars], copious [notes], detailed, circumstantial, minute [account]; **II** *ad* amply &, in detail; *enigszins ~ citeren* quote at some length; *ik zal ~er schrijven* ook: I'll write more fully; **–heid** *v* ampleness, copiousness

'uitvoering (-en) *v* 1 execution [of an order &]; get-up [of a book]; 2 (v o o r s t e l l i n g) performance; ~ *geven aan* carry (put) into effect, carry out; *werk in ~* road works ahead; **'uitvoerpremie** (-s) *v* export bounty, bounty on exportation; **–rechten** *mv* export duties; **–verbod** (-boden) *o* export prohibition; **–vergunning** (-en) *v* export licence

'uitvorsen[1] *vt* find out, ferret out; **'uitvouwen**[1] *vt* fold out, open out; **'uitvragen**[1] *vt* question, catechize, **F** pump; *ik ben uitgevraagd* 1 I have been asked out [to dinner &]; 2 I have no more questions to ask

'uitvreten[1] *vt* eat out, corrode; *fig* sponge on [sbd.]; **–er** (-s) *m* sponger, parasite

'uitvullen[1] *vt* space [evenly]; **'uitwaaien**

I (waaide, woei 'uit, h. 'uitgewaaid) *vt* blow out; **II** (waaide, woei 'uit, is 'uitgewaaid) *vi* be blown out [of a candle]; *het is nu uitgewaaid* the wind (gale) has spent itself; **'uitwaaieren** (waaierde 'uit, h. en is 'uitgewaaierd) *vi* fan (out), spread, unfold

'uitwaarts I *aj* outward; **II** *ad* outward(s)

'uitwas (-sen) *m* & *o* outgrowth, excrescense, protuberance

'uitwasemen[1] **I** *vi* evaporate; **II** *vt* exhale; **–ming** (-en) *v* evaporation, exhalation

'uitwassen[1] *vt* wash (out)

'uitwateren[1] *vi* ~ *in* discharge itself into..., flow into...; **–ring** (-en) *v* discharge [of a stream]

'uitwedstrijd (-en) *m* away game (match)

'uitweg (-wegen) *m* way out[2], outlet; *fig* escape; loophole

'uitwegen[1] *vt* weigh out

'uitweiden[1] *vi* ~ *over* enlarge upon, expatiate on, dwell upon, digress upon; **–ding** (-en) *v* expatiation, digression

uit'wendig I *aj* external, exterior; *voor ~ gebruik* for outward application; *zijn ~ voorkomen* his outward appearance; **II** *ad* externally, outwardly; **–heid** (-heden) *v* exterior; *uitwendigheden* externals

'uitwerken I (werkte 'uit, h. 'uitgewerkt) *vt* 1 work out [a plan &]; elaborate [a scheme]; work [a sum]; labour [a point]; 2 (t o t s t a n d b r e n g e n) effect, bring about; *niets ~* be ineffective; **II** (werkte 'uit, is 'uitgewerkt) *vi* work; *dit geneesmiddel is uitgewerkt* this medicine has lost its efficacy; zie ook: *uitgewerkt*; **–king** (-en) *v* 1 working-out; 2 (g e v o l g) effect; ~ *hebben* be effective, work; *geen ~ hebben* produce no effect, be ineffective

'uitwerpen[1] *vt* throw out [ballast], cast (out); eject; ⚓ drop [bombs, arms], parachute [a man, troops]; (s p u w e n) vomit; *duivelen ~* cast out devils; **'uitwerpsel** (-en en -s) *o* excrement

'uitwieden[1] *vt* weed out

'uitwijken[1] *vi* 1 (o p z ij) turn aside, step aside, make way, make room; pull out [of a motor-car]; 2 (u i t h e t l a n d) go into exile, leave one's country; ~ *n a a r* emigrate to, take refuge in [a country]; ~ *v o o r* make way for, get out of the way of, avoid [a dog on the road]; **–king** (-en) *v* 1 turning aside; 2 emigration

'uitwijzen[1] *vt* 1 show; 2 (b e s l i s s e n) decide; 3 expel [persons]; **–zing** (-en) *v* expulsion

---

[1] V.T. en V.D. van dit werkwoord volgens het model: **'uit**ademen, V.T. ademde **'uit**, V.D. **'uit**geademd. Zie voor de vormen onder het grondwoord, in dit voorbeeld: *ademen*. Bij sterke en onregelmatige werkwoorden wordt u verwezen naar de lijst achterin.

'uitwinnen¹ *vt* save; 'uitwippen¹ *vi* nip out

'uitwisselen¹ *vt* exchange; –ling (-en) *v* exchange

'uitwissen¹ *vt* wipe out, blot out, efface; 'uitwoeden (woedde 'uit, h. en is 'uitgewoed) *vi* spend itself [of a storm]

'uitwonend non-resident [masters &]; ⊗ non-collegiate [students]

'uitwrijven¹ *vt* rub out; *zich de ogen* ~ rub one's eyes²; 'uitwringen¹ *vt* wring out

'uitzaaien¹ *vt* sow², disseminate²; –iing (-en) *v* 𝔗 metastasis

'uitzagen¹ *vt* saw out; 'uitzakken¹ *vi* sag; 'uitzeilen¹ *vi* sail out, sail

'uitzendbureau [-by.ro.] (-s) *o* temporary employment agency; 'uitzenden¹ *vt* send out; *RT* broadcast; transmit; *T* ook: televise; –ding (-en) *v* sending out; *RT* broadcast, broadcasting; transmission; 'uitzendkracht (-en) *v-m* temporary employee, F temp

'uitzet (-ten) *m* & *o* [bride's] trousseau; ~ *voor de tropen* = *tropenuitrusting*; zie ook: *babyuitzet*

uit'zetbaar expansible, dilatable; –heid *v* expansibility, dilatability; 'uitzetten I (zette 'uit, is 'uitgezet) *vi* 1 (i n 't a l g.) expand, dilate, swell; 2 (i n d e n a t u u r k u n d e) expand; II (zette 'uit, h. 'uitgezet) *vr zich* ~ expand [of metals &]; III (zette 'uit, h. 'uitgezet) *vt* 1 (v e r g r o t e n) expand; 2 (d o e n z w e l l e n) distend, inflate; 3 set out [a rectangle]; mark out [distances]; ⚓ put out, get out [a boat]; ✕ post [a sentinel]; put out [a post]; throw out [a line of sentinels]; 🏛 evict, eject [a tenant]; turn [sbd.] out [of the room]; $ invest [money], put out [at 4 % interest]; *iem.* · *het land* ~ expel, banish sbd. from the country; –ting (-en) *v* expansion; dilat(at)ion; inflation; expulsion, 🏛 eviction, ejection; 'uitzettings-coëfficiënt [-ko.ffi.si.ɛnt] (-en) *m* coefficient of expansion; –vermogen *o* power of expansion, expansive power, dilatability

'uitzicht (-en) *o* view, prospect, outlook; *het* ~ *hebben op...* command a (fine) view of..., overlook [the Thames], give (up)on...; *...in* ~ *stellen* hold out a prospect that...; –loos *fig* hopeless [situation]; –toren (-s) *m* belvedere

'uitzieken (ziekte 'uit, is 'uitgeziekt) *vi* nurse one's illness; 'uitzien¹ I *vi* look out; *er* ~ look; *je ziet er goed uit* you look well; *zij ziet er goed uit* (= *knap*) *uit* she is good-looking; *zij ziet er niet goed uit* she doesn't look well; *dat ziet er mooi uit!* a fine prospect!, a pretty state of affairs!; *dat ziet er slecht uit* things look black; *hoe ziet hij (het)*

eruit? what does he (it) look like?, what is he (it) like?; *wat zie jij eruit!* what a state you are in!; you look a sight!; *ziet het er zó uit?* 1 does it look like this?; 2 is it thus that matters stand?; *het ziet eruit alsof het gaat regenen* it looks like rain; ● *n a a r een betrekking* ~ look out for a situation; *naar iem.* ~ look out for sbd.; ~ *naar zijn komst* look forward to his coming; ~ *o p een plein* look out (up)on a square; ~ *op de Theems* overlook the Thames; ~ *op het zuiden* look (face) south; ~ *op iemands ogen* stare one's eyes out; 'uitziften¹ *vi* sift (out)²; *fig* thrash out; 'uitzingen¹ *vt* sing out, sing [the chorus &] to the finish; *als we het maar kunnen* ~ if we can hold out, F stick it [until...]

uit'zinnig beside oneself, distracted, demented, mad, frantic; –heid (-heden) *v* distraction, madness

'uitzitten¹ *vt* sit out; *zijn tijd* ~ serve one's time [in prison], do time; 'uitzoeken¹ *vt* select [an article, seeds &], choose [an article]; look out [the wash], sort out²

'uitzonderen (zonderde 'uit, h. 'uitgezonderd) *vt* except; –ring (-en) *v* exception; *een* ~ *op de regel* an exception to the rule; ~*en bevestigen de regel* the exception proves the rule; *b ij* ~ by way of exception; *bij hoge* ~ very rarely; *bij* ~ *voorkomend* exceptional; *m e t* ~ *van...* with the exception of...; *z o n d e r* ~ without exception; *allen zonder* ~ *hadden handschoenen aan* they one and all wore gloves; 'uitzonderingsbepaling (-en) *v* exceptional disposition; saving clause; –geval (-len) *o* exceptional case; –positie [-zi.(t)si.] (-s) *v* special position, privileged position; –toestand (-en) *m* state of emergency; –verlof (-loven) *o* ⚔ compassionate leave; 'uitzonderlijk I *aj* exceptional [ability], outstanding [merit]; II *ad* exceptionally [large], outstandingly [important]

'uitzuigen¹ *vt* 1 *eig* suck (out); 2 *fig* extort money from [a person]; sweat [labour]; –er (-s) *m* extortioner; sweater [of labour]

'uitzuinigen (zuinigde 'uit, h. 'uitgezuinigd) *vt* economize, save (on *op*); 'uitzwavelen¹ *vt* fumigate, sulphur; 'uitzwermen (zwermde 'uit, is 'uitgezwermd) *vi* 1 swarm off [of bees]; 2 ⚔ disperse; 'uitzweten¹ *vt* exude, ooze out, sweat out

'ukkepuk (-ken) *m*, 'ukkie (-s) *o* tiny tot

'ulevel (-len) *v* kind of sweet in a papèr wrapper

'ulster (-s) *m* ulster

ult. = *ultimo*; ultima'tief *ultimatieve nota* note in

(of) the nature of an ultimatum; **ulti'matum** (-s) *o* ultimatum; *een ~ stellen* issue an ultimatum (to *aan*); **'ultimo ~ *mei*** at the end of May

'ultra I ('s) *m* extremist; **II** *ad* extremely, ultra [short wave]; **–kort** ultrashort [wave]; **ultrama'rijn** *o* ultramarine; **ultramon'taan(s)** *m* (-tanen) (& *aj*) ultramontane; **ultra'soon** ultrasonic; **ultravio'let** ultra-violet

'umlaut ['u.mlɔut] (-en) *m* Umlaut, (vowel) mutation; *a-~* modified a

una'niem I *aj* unanimous; **II** *ad* unanimously, with one assent (accord); **unanimi'teit** *v* unanimity, consensus [of opinion]

'unicum (-s en -ca) *o* 1 single copy; 2 unique phenomenon, thing unique of its kind

'unie (-s) *v* union

u'niek unique

unifi'catie [-(t)si.] (-s) *v* unification

uni'form I *aj* uniform; **II** (-en) *o* & *v* (i n 't a l g.) uniform; ✄ (o o k:) regimentals; **uniformi'teit** *v* uniformity; **uni'formjas** (-sen) *m* & *v* ✄ tunic; **–pet** (-ten) *v* uniform cap

uni'tariër (-s) *m* Unitarian

universali'teit [s = z] *v* universality; **univer'seel** universal, sole; *~ erfgenaam* sole heir, residuary legatee

universi'tair [-zi'tɛ:r] **I** *aj* university...; **II** *ad ~ opgeleid* college-taught; **universi'teit** (-en) *v* university, zie *hogeschool*; **universi'teitsbibliotheek** (-theken) *v* university library; **–gebouw** (-en) *o* university building; **–stad** (-steden) *v* university town

uni'versum [s = z] *o* universe

'unster (-s) *v* steelyard, weigh-beam

u'ranium *o* uranium

ur'baan urbane; **urbani'satie** [-'za.(t)si.] *v* urbanization; **urbani'teit** *v* urbanity

Ur'banus *m* Urban

'ure (-n) *v = uur*; **'urenlang** for hours, for hours on end

ur'gent urgent; **ur'gentie** [-(t)si.] *v* urgency; **–programma** ('s) *o* crash programme; **–verklaring** (-en) *v* declaration of urgency

uri'naal (-nalen) *o* urinal; **u'rine** *v* urine; **–blaas** (-blazen) *v* urinary bladder; **–leider** (-s) *m* ureter, urinary duct; **uri'neren** (urineerde, h. geürineerd) *vi* urinate, make (pass) water; **uri'noir** [-'nʋa:r] (-s) *o* public lavatory, public convenience, public urinal

'urmen (urmde, h. geürmd) *vi* complain, grumble

'urn(e) (urnen) *v* urn; **'urnenveld** (-en) *o* cinerarium

'Ursula *v* Ursula; **ursu'line** (-n) *v* Ursuline (nun); **ursu'linenklooster** (-s) *o* Ursuline convent; **–school** (-scholen) *v* Ursuline school

'Uruguay *o* Uruguay

u'sance [y.'zãsə] (-s), **u'santie** [-(t)si.] (-s en -iën) *v* custom, usage; **'uso** *o* $ usance

usur'patie [y.zurpa.(t)si.] (-s en -toren) *v* usurpation; **usur'pator** (-s) *m* usurper; **usur'peren** (usurpeerde, h. geüsurpeerd) *vt*

ut *v* ♪ ut, do   [usurp

utili'teit *v* utility; **utili'teitsbeginsel** *o* utilitarian principle; **–bouw** *m* functional architecture

U'topia *o* Utopia; **uto'pie** (-ieën) *v* utopian scheme, Utopia; **u'topisch** utopian; **uto'pist** (-en) *m* Utopian

uur (uren) *o* hour; *een half ~* half an hour; *driekwart ~* three quarters of an hour; *een ~ gaans* an hour's walk; *alle uren* every hour; *uren lang* for hours (together, on end); ● *a a n geen ~ gebonden* not tied down to time; *b i n n e n het ~* within an hour; *i n het ~ van het gevaar* in the hour of danger; *in een verloren ~* zie *uurtje*; *o m drie ~* at three (o'clock); *om het ~* every hour; *om de twee ~* every two hours; *o p elk ~* every hour; at any hour; *op elk ~ van de dag* at all hours of the day, at any hour; *op een vast ~* at a fixed hour; *o v e r een ~* in an hour; *zoveel p e r ~* so much per hour (an hour); *een rijtuig per ~ nemen* by the hour; *t e goeder (kwader) ure* in a happy (an evil) hour; *t e r elfder ure* at the eleventh hour; *t e g e n drie ~* by three o'clock; *v a n ~ tot ~* from hour to hour, hourly; **–dienst** *m* hourly service; **–glas** (-glazen) *o* hour-glass; **–loner** (-s) *m* hourly-paid worker; **–loon** *o* hourly wage; **–tje** (-s) *o* hour; *in een verloren ~* in a spare hour; *de kleine ~s* the small hours; **–werk** (-en) *o* 1 clock, timepiece; 2 (r a d e r w e r k) works, clockwork; **–werkmaker** (-s) *m* clock-maker, watchmaker; **–wijzer** (-s) *m* hour-hand, short hand

uw your, ☉ thy; *de, het ~e* yours, ☉ thine; *geheel de ~e...* Yours truly...; **'uwent** *te(n) ~* at your house; **~halve** for your sake; **~wege** as for you; *van ~wege* on your behalf, in your name; *om ~wil(le)* for your sake; **'uwerzijds** on your part, on your behalf

V

v [ve.] ('s) *v·v*

v. = *van; vrouwelijk; voor; vers*

vaag I *aj* vague, hazy; indefinite; **II** *ad* vaguely; **–heid** (-heden) *v* vagueness

1 vaak *m* sleepiness; ~ *hebben* be sleepy; zie ook: *praatje*

2 vaak *ad* often, frequently

vaal sallow; *fig* drab; **–bleek** sallow; **–bruin** dun, drab; **–grijs** greyish; **–heid** *v* sallowness

vaalt (-en) *v* dunghill

vaam (vamen) *m* = *vadem*

vaan (vanen) *v* flag, banner, standard; *de* ~ *des oproers opheffen* raise the standard of revolt

'vaandel (-s) *o* flag, standard, ensign, colours; *met vliegende* ~*s* with colours flying; *onder het* ~ *van...* [fight] under the banner of...; **–drager** (-s) *m* standard-bearer[2]; **–wacht** *v* colour guard, colour party

'vaandrig (-s) *m* 1 standard-bearer; 2 🔲 (v o e t v o l k) ensign; (r u i t e r ij) cornet; (m a r i n e) midshipman; (l e g e r) cadet-sergeant; (l u c h t m a c h t) acting pilot officer

'vaantje (-s) *o* 1 vane; 2 weathercock

'vaarboom (-bomen) *m* punting-pole

'vaardig I *aj* 1 skilled, skilful, adroit, clever, proficient; 2 fluent [speech]; 3 ready; *hij is* ~ *met de pen* he has a ready pen; *de geest werd* ~ *over hem* the spirit moved him; ~ *in... zijn* be clever at...; **II** *ad* adroitly, cleverly &; **'vaardigheid** (-heden) *v* 1 skill, cleverness, proficiency; 2 fluency [of speech]; 3 readiness; *zijn* ~ *in...* his proficiency in...; **–sproef** (-proeven) *v* trial of skill

'vaargeul (-en) *v* channel; fairway, lane

vaars (vaarzen) *v* heifer

vaart *v* 1 (d e s c h e e p v a a r t) navigation; 2 (-en) (r e i s t e w a t e r) = *reis*; 3 (s n e l - h e i d) speed [of a vessel &]; 4 (v o o r t g a n g) career [of a horse &]; 5 (-en) (k a n a a l) canal; *de grote* ~ foreign(-going) trade, ocean-going trade; *de kleine* ~ home trade; *wilde* ~ tramp shipping; ~ *hebben* have speed; *een* ~ *hebben van ...knopen* run ...knots; ~ *krijgen* gather way, ⚓ gain headway; *het zal zo'n* ~ *niet lopen* (*niet nemen*) things won't take that turn, it won't come to that; ~ (*ver*)*minderen* slacken speed, slow down; ~ *achter iets zetten* put on steam, speed up the thing; ● *i n d e* ~ *brengen* put into service [ships]; *in dolle* ~ at breakneck speed, in mad career; *in volle* ~ (at) full speed; *m e t e e n* ~ *van...* at the rate of...; *u i t d e* ~ *nemen* withdraw from service

'vaartje (-s) *o* zie *aardje*

'vaartuig (-en) *o* vessel; ~(*en*) ook: craft

'vaarwater (-s en -en) *o* fairway, channel; *iem. i n het* ~ *zitten* thwart sbd.; *ze zitten elkaar altijd in het* ~ they are always at cross-purposes; *je moet maar u i t zijn* ~ *blijven* you had better give him a wide berth

vaar'wel I *ij* farewell, adieu, goodbye!; **II** *o* farewell, valediction; *hun een laatst* ~ *toewuiven* wave them a last adieu (good-bye); ~ *zeggen* say good-bye, bid farewell (to), take leave (of), leave; *de studie* ~ *zeggen* give up studying; *de wereld* ~ *zeggen* retire from the world

vaas (vazen) *v* vase

vaat *v de* ~ *wassen* wash up

'vaatbundel (-s) *m* vascular bundle

'vaatdoek (-en) *m* dish-cloth

'vaatje (-s) *o* small barrel, cask, keg; *uit een ander* ~ *tappen* change one's tune

'vaatkramp (-en) *v* 🜊 angiospasm, vasospasm

'vaatkwast (-en) = *vatenkwast*

'vaatstelsel (-s) *o* vascular system; **–vernauwend** vaso-constricting; **–verwijdend** vaso-dilating

'vaatwasmachine [-ma.ʃi.nə] (-s) *v* (automatic) dishwasher; **–water** *o* dish-water; **–werk** *o* 1 casks; 2 plates and dishes; 3 vessels [in dairy-factory]

'vaatziekte (-n en -s) *v* vascular disease

va'cant vacant

va'catie [-(t)si.] (-s en -iën) *v* 🜊 sitting; **–geld** (-en) *o* fee

vaca'ture (-s) *v* vacancy; *bij de eerste* ~ on the occurence of the next vacancy; **vaca'tuur** (-tures) *v* = *vacature*

vac'cin [vak'sɛ̃] (-s) *o* vaccine; **vaccina'teur** (-s) *m* vaccinator; **vacci'natie** [-(t)si.] (-s) *v* vaccination; **–bewijs** (-wijzen) *o* vaccination certificate; **vac'cine** (-s) *v* (s t o f) vaccine; **vacci'neren** (vaccineerde, h. gevaccineerd) *vt* vaccinate

va'ceren (vaceerde, h. gevaceerd) *vi* 1 be vacant; 2 sit; *komen te* ~ fall vacant

vacht (-en) *v* fleece, pelt, fur

'vacuüm [-ky.üm] (-cua) *o* vacuum; **–ver-pakking** (-en) *v* vacuum package; vacuum packaging; **–verpakt** vacuum-packed

'vadem (-en en -s) *m* fathom; *een* ~ *hout* a cord of wood

vade'mecum (-s) *o* vade-mecum

'vader (-s en -en) *m* 1 father; 2 (v. w e e s h u i s e. d.) master; (v. j e u g d h e r b e r g) warden;

(de) Heilige V~ (the) Holy Father; Onze Hemelse V~ Our Heavenly Father; de V~ des Vaderlands the father of his country; van ~ op zoon from father to son; zo ~, zo zoon like father like son; tot zijn ~en verzameld worden be gathered to one's fathers; –dag m Father's Day; –figuur v father figure; –hart o father's heart; –huis o paternal home

'vaderland (-en) o (native) country, ⊙ fatherland; home; –er (-s) m patriot; vaderland'lievend = vaderlandslievend; 'vaderlands patriotic [feelings]; national [history, songs]; native [soil]; –liefde v love of (one's) country, patriotism; vaderlands'lievend patriotic

'vaderliefde v a father's love, paternal love; –lijk I aj fatherly, paternal; II ad in a fatherly way; –loos fatherless; –moord (-en) m & v parricide; –moordenaar (-s) m parricide; –plicht (-en) m & v paternal duty, duty as a father; –schap o paternity, fatherhood; –skant m = vaderszijde; –stad v native town; 'vaderszijde v van ~ [related] on the (one's) father's side; paternal [grandfather]

'vadsig I aj lazy, indolent, slothful; II ad lazily, indolently, slothfully; –heid v laziness, indolence, sloth

va'gant (-en) m travelling scholar, itinerant priest

'vagebond (-en) m vagabond, tramp; vagebon'deren (vagebondeerde, h. gevagebondeerd) vi vagabond, tramp

'vagelijk vaguely

'vagevuur o purgatory[2]; in het ~ in purgatory

'vagina ('s) v vagina

vak (-ken) o 1 (v. k a s t &) compartment, partition, pigeon-hole; 2 (v. g e r u i t v e l d) square, pane; 3 (v. m u u r) bay; 4 (v. d e u r &) panel; 5 (v. s p o o r)w e g &) section, stretch; 6 (v. s t u d i e) subject; 7 (b e r o e p) line [of business]; trade [of a carpenter &]; profession [of a teacher &]; zijn ~ verstaan understand (know) one's job; dat is mijn ~ niet that is not my line of business (not in my line); ik ben in een ander ~ I am in another line of business; een man van het ~ a professional; hij praat altijd over zijn ~ he is always talking shop

va'kantie [-'kansi.] (-s) v holiday(s), vacation; grote ~ summer holidays; [of University] long vacation; een dag ~ a holiday, a day off; een maand ~ a month's holiday; ~ nemen take a holiday; ● in de ~ during the holidays; met ~ gaan go (away) on holiday; met ~ naar huis gaan go home for the holidays; waar ga je met de ~ naar toe? where are you going for your holidays?; met ~ zijn be (away) on holiday; –adres (-sen) o holiday address; –cursus [züs] (-sen) m holiday course, summer school; –dag (-dagen)

m holiday; –ganger (-s) m holiday-maker; –geld (-en) o holiday pay, leave pay; –kaart (-en) v holiday ticket; –kolonie (-s) v holiday camp; –oord (-en) o holiday resort; –plan (-nen) o holiday plan; –reis (-reizen) v holiday trip; –spreiding v staggering of holidays, staggered holidays; –tijd m holidays, holiday season; –werk o holiday task

'vakarbeider (-s) m skilled worker; –bekwaam skilled; –bekwaamheid v professional skill; –beurs (-beurzen) v trade fair; –beweging (-en) v trade-unionism, trade-union movement; –blad (-bladen) o professional journal, trade journal, technical paper; –bond (-en) m trade-union; –bondsleider (-s) m trade-union leader; –centrale (-s) v federation of trade unions; –geleerde (-n) m specialist, expert; –genoot (-noten) m colleague; –groep (-en) v trade association; –jargon o lingo, technical jargon; –je (-s) o compartment, partition; (v. b u r e a u) pigeonhole; (o p p a p i e r) square, box; –kennis v professional (specialized, expert) knowledge; –kringen mv professional (expert) circles; in ~ among experts; vak'kundig expert, skilled, competent; –heid v (professional) skill; 'vakliteratuur v technical (specialized) literature; –man (-nen, -lui, -lieden en -mensen) m professional man, professional, craftsman, expert, specialist; geschoolde ~ skilled tradesman; –manschap o craftsmanship; skill; –onderwijs o technical (specialized) instruction; –opleiding v professional training; –organisatie [-za.(t)si.] (-s) v trade union, professional organization; –school (-scholen) v technical school; –studie v professional studies; –taal v technical (professional) language; in ~ in technical terms; –term (-en) m technical term; –terminologie (-ieën) v technical (professional) terminology; –tijdschrift (-en) o = vakblad; –verbond (-en) o federation of trade unions; –vereniging (-en) v trade-union; –werk o 1 expert work, skilled work; professional job; 2 (b o u w w ij z e) half-timber; (b ij s k e l e t b o u w) skeleton structure

1 val m 1 fall[2]; fig ook: overthrow [of a minister]; vrije ~ free fall; een ~ doen have a fall; ten ~ brengen ruin [a man]; overthrow [the ministry], bring down [the government]

2 val (-len) v 1 (o m t e v a n g e n) trap; 2 (s t r o o k) valance [round a chimney]; een ~ opzetten set a trap; in de ~ lopen walk (fall) into the trap[2]

3 val (-len) o ⚓ halyard

'valbijl (-en) v guillotine; –blok (-ken) o 1 = hijsblok; 2 = heiblok; –brug (-gen) v drawbridge; **–deur** (-en) *v* 1 trapdoor, trap; 2 (v. s l u i s) penstock

va'lentie [-(t)si.] (-s) *v* valence

valeri'aan 1 *v* ♚ valerian; 2 *v* & *o* (s t o f - n a a m) valerian

'valgordijn (-en) *o* & *v* blind; **–hek** (-ken) *o* portcullis; **–helm** (-en) *m* crash-helmet; **–hoogte** (-n en -s) *v* fall

va'lide 1 valid; 2 able-bodied [men]; **vali'deren** (valideerde, h. gevalideerd) *vt* validate, make valid; **validi'teit** *v* validity

va'lies (-liezen) *o* portmanteau

valk (-en) *m* & *v* falcon, hawk; **–ejacht** (-en) *v* falconry, hawking; **valke'nier** (-s) *m* falconer

'valkuil (-en) *m* trap, pit(fall)

val'lei (-en) *v* valley, ☉ vale; (k l e i n e r) dale [cultivated or cultivable], dell [with tree-clad sides]; *Sc* glen

'vallen* I *vi* fall² [ook = be killed]; drop, go down, come down; *de avond valt* night is falling; *het gordijn valt* the curtain drops; *de minister is gevallen* the minister fell; *de motie (het voorstel) is gevallen* the motion (the proposal) was defeated; *velen zijn in die slag gevallen* many fell; *het kleed valt goed* sits (hangs) well; *het zal hem hard* ~ he'll find it a great wrench; zie ook: *hardvallen; de tijd valt mij lang* time hangs heavy on my hands; *dat valt mu moeilijk (zwaar)* it is difficult for me; I find it difficult; *het valt zo het valt* come what may; *er zullen klappen (slagen)* ~ there will be blows; *er vielen woorden* there were high words; *er valt wel met hem te praten* zie *praten; daar valt niet mee te spotten* that is not to be trifled with; *wat valt daarvan te zeggen?* what can be said about it?; *doen* ~ trip up [sbd.]; bring about the fall of [the ministry]; *laten* ~ drop [sth.]; let [it] fall; *wij kunnen niets van onze eisen laten* ~ we cannot bate a jot of our claims; *wij kunnen niets van de prijs laten* ~ we cannot knock off anything; *zich laten* ~ drop [into a chair]; ● *aan stukken* ~ fall to pieces; *het huis viel aan mijn broeder* the house fell to my brother; *al ma a r het valt* as the case may be; *dat valt hier niet o n d e r* it does not fall (come) under this head; *de klem valt o p de eerste lettergreep* falls on the first syllable; *het valt op een maandag* it falls on Monday; *de keuze is op u gevallen* the choice has fallen on you; *hij valt o v e r elke kleinigheid* he stumbles at every trifle; *ik ken hem niet, al viel ik over hem* I don't know him from Adam; *v a n zijn paard* ~ fall from one's horse; **II** *o met de avond* nightfall; *bij het* ~ *van de avond* at nightfall; **'vallend** *~e ster* falling star; *~e ziekte* epilepsy; *lijdend (lijder) aan ~e ziekte* epileptic

'valletje (-s) *o* valance

'vallicht (-en) *o* skylight; **'valling** (-en) *v* 1

slope; 2 ⚓ rake [of mast]; **'valluik** (-en) *o* trapdoor

valori'satie [-'za(t)si.] (-s) *v* valorization

'valpoort (-en) *v* portcullis; **–reep** (-repen) *m* ⚓ gangway; *een glaasje op de* ~ a stirrup-cup, a final glass, **F** one for the road

vals I *aj* 1 (n i e t e c h t) false [coin, hair, teeth &, ideas, gods, pride, shame; ♩ note], forged [writings, cheque, Rembrandt], fake [picture, Vermeer], **F** dud [cheques]; 2 (n i e t o p - r e c h t) false, guileful, perfidious, treacherous; 3 (b o o s a a r d i g) vicious; *~ geld* base ⌣ coin, counterfeit money; *een ~e handtekening* a forged signature; *een ~e hond* a vicious dog; *~e juwelen* imitation jewels; *~ spel* foul play; *~e speler* (card-)sharper; *~ spoor [fig]* red herring; *~e start [sp]* breakaway; **II** *ad* falsely; *iem.* ~ *aankijken* look viciously at sbd.; *~ klinken* have a false ring; *~ spelen* 1 ♩ play out of tune; 2 *sp* cheat [at cards]; *~ zingen* sing false (out of tune); *~ zweren* swear falsely, forswear oneself, perjure oneself; **–aard** (-s) *m* false (perfidious) person

'valscherm (-en) *o* parachute

'valselijk falsely; **valse'munter** (-s) *m* coiner; **'valserik** (-riken) *m* false person; **'valsheid** (-heden) *v* falseness, falsity, treachery, perfidy; *~ in geschrifte* forgery; **'valsmunter** (-s) = *valsemunter*

'valstrik (-ken) *m* gin; snare², trap²

va'luta ('s) *v* 1 value; 2 (k o e r s) rate of exchange; 3 (m u n t) [foreign, hard, soft] currency

'valwind (-en) *m* fall wind, down wind, föhn

'vampier (-s) *m* vampire-bat, vampire²

van I *prep* 1 (b e z i t a a n d u i d e n d) of [ook uitgedrukt door 's]; 2 (o o r z a k e l ij k) from, with, for; 3 (s c h e i d i n g a a n d u i d e n d) from; 4 (a f k o m s t) of [noble blood]; 5 (v o o r s t o f n a m e n) of [gold]; 6 (v o o r t ij d s a a n d u i d i n g) zie beneden; 1 *het boek* ~ *mijn vader* my father's book; *dat boek is* ~ *mij* that book is mine; *een vriend* ~ *mij* a friend of mine; *zij was een eigen nicht* ~ *de Koningin* ook: she was own niece to the Queen; *de E* ~ *Eduard* ☜ E for Edward; *de stijging* ~ *prijzen en lonen* the rise in prices and wages; 2 ~ *kou omkomen* perish with cold; ~ *vreugde schreien* weep with (for) joy; 3 ~ *A tot B* from A to B.; ~ *de morgen tot de avond* from morning till night; *het is een uur* ~ *A.* it is an hour's walk from A.; *eten* ~ *een bord* eat off a plate; *hij viel* ~ *de ladder (* ~ *de trappen)* he fell off the ladder (down the stairs); *negen* ~ *de tien* 1 nine out of (every) ten [have a...]; 2 × nine from ten [leaves one]; 4 *dat heeft hij niet* ~ *mij* it is not me he takes it from; *een roman* ~ *Dickens* a novel by Dickens; *een schilderij* ~ *Rembrandt* a picture of Rembrandt's; *het was dom* ~ *hem* it was stupid of him; 5 *een kam* ~ *zilver* a comb of silver, a silver comb; 6 ~ *de week* this week; ● *de schurk* ~ *een kruidenier* that rascal of a grocer; *de sneltrein* ~ *3 uur 16* the 3.16 express; *hij zegt* ~ *ja* he says yes; *ik vind* ~ *wel* I think so; **II** (-nen en -s) *m & o zijn* ~ his family name

van'af from

van'avond this evening, to-night; **van'daag** to-day; ~ *de dag* 1 (o p d e z e d a g) to-day; 2 (t e g e n w o o r d i g) these days; ~ *of morgen* [*fig*] sooner or later

van'daal (-dalen) *m* vandal

van'daan *ergens* ~ *gaan* go away, leave; *ik kom daar* ~ from that place; *waar kom jij* ~? where do you come from?

van'daar hence, that's why; *ik kom* ~ I come from that place

vanda'lisme *o* vandalism

'vandehands *het* ~*e paard* the off horse

van'doen *ergens mee* ~ *hebben* have to do with sth.

van'door away; *er* ~ *gaan* run away, make (run) off; (v l u c h t e n) bolt, turn tail; *er stilletjes* ~ *gaan* take French leave; *kom, ik ga er eens* ~ well, I'm off now

van'een apart, asunder

vang (-en) *v* stay [of a mill]; **-arm** (-en) *m* tentacle; **'vangen*** *vt* catch, capture; *zich niet laten* ~ not walk into the trap; **-er** (-s) *m* catcher; **'vanglijn** (-en) *v* ⚓ painter; **-net** (-ten) *o* safety net; **-rail** [-re.l], **-reel** (-s) *v* guard-rail, crash barrier; **vangst** (-en) *v* catch, capture; bag, taking; *een goede* ~ a fine bag, a large take, a big haul; **'vangzeil** (-en) *o* jumping sheet

van'hier from here

va'nille [-'ni.(l)jə] *v* vanilla; **-ijs** *o* vanilla ice; **-stokje** (-s) *o* stick of vanilla

van'middag this afternoon; **van'morgen** this morning; **van'nacht** 1 (t o e k o m s t i g) to-night; 2 (v e r l e d e n) last night; **van'ochtend** this morning

van'ouds of old

van'waar from what place, from where, whence; (o m w e l k e r e d e n) why

van'wege 1 on account of, because of, due to; 2 on behalf of, in the name of

van'zelf [fall, happen] of itself, [come] of its own accord; ~! of course!; zie ook: *spreken* **II**; **vanzelf'sprekend I** *aj* self-evident; *het is* ~ it goes without saying; *als* ~ *aannemen* take it for granted; **II** *ad* naturally, as a matter of course; **-heid** *v een* ~ a matter of course

vapori'sator [s = z] (-s en -'toren) *m* vaporizer, spray

1 **'varen** (-s) *v* ⚘ fern, bracken, brake

2 **'varen* I** *vi* sail, navigate; *hoe vaart u?* how are you?, how do you do?; *om hoe laat vaart de boot?* what time does the steamer leave (sail)?; *gaan* ~ go to sea; *zullen we wat gaan* ~? shall we go for a sail?; *zij hebben dat plan laten* ~ they have abandoned (relinquished, given up, dropped) the plan; ● *wel b ij iets* ~ do well by sth.; *u zult er niet slecht bij* ~ you will be none the worse for it; *de duivel is i n hem gevaren* the devil has taken possession of him; *wij voeren o m de Kaap* we went via the Cape, sailed round the Cape; *zij* ~ *o p New York* they trade to New York; *t e n hemel* ~ ascend to Heaven; *ter helle* ~ go to hell; **II** *vt* row, take [a person across &]

'varensgezel (-len), **-man** (-lieden en -lui) *m* sailor

'varia *mv* miscellanies, miscellanea; **vari'abel** variable; ~*e werktijden* flexible hours, **F** flexitime; **vari'ant** (-en) *v* variant; **vari'atie** [-(t)si.] (-s) *v* variation; *voor de* ~ for a change; **vari'ëren** (varieerde, h. gevarieerd) **I** *vi* vary; ~*d tussen de 10 en 20 gulden* ranging from 10 to 20 guilders (between 10 and 20 g.); **II** *vt* vary

varié'té (-s) *v* variety theatre, music-hall; **-artiest** (-en) *m* variety artist, music-hall entertainer; **-nummer** (-s) *o* variety act; **varié'teit** (-en) *v* variety

'varken (-s) *o* ♈ pig², hog², swine²; *wild* ~ (wild) boar; *we zullen dat* ~ *wel wassen!* we'll deal with it!; *het* ~ *is op één oor na gevild* everything is almost over; **'varkensblaas** (-blazen) *v* hog's bladder; **-draf** *m* swill, swillings; **-fokker** (-s) *m* pig-breeder, pig-farmer; **varkensfokke'rij** (-en) *v* 1 pig-breeding; 2 pig-farm; **'varkenshaar** *o* hog's bristles; **-hok** (-ken) *o* pigsty², piggery²; **-karbonade** (-s en -n) *v* pork-chop; **-kost** *m* food for swine, hog's meat; **-kot** (-ten) *o* pigsty², piggery²; **-kotelet** (-ten) *v* pork-cutlet; **-lapjes** *mv* pork-collops; **-le(d)er** *o* pigskin; **-markt** (-en) *v* pig-market; **-poot** (-poten) *m* 1 (v. l e v e n d d i e r) pig's leg; 2 (v. g e s l a c h t) pig's trotter; ~*jes* pettitoes; **-slachterij** (-en) *v* pork-butcher's shop; **-slager** (-s) *m* pork-butcher; **-staart** (-en) *m* pig's tail; **-stal** (-len) *m* pigsty², piggery²; **-trog** (-gen) *m* pig-trough, pig-tub; **-vet** *o* fat of pigs, pork dripping; **-vlees** *o* pork; **-voer** *o* = *varkenskost*; **'varkentje** (-s) *o* piglet, pigling, **F** piggy

Ⓦ **vase'line** [s = z] *v* vaseline

vasomo'torisch [va.zo.-] vaso-motor

vast I *aj* fast, firm, fixed, steady; *oliewaarden* ~ $ oil shares were a firm market; ~*e aanstelling* permanent appointment; ~*e aardigheden* stock jokes; ~*e arbeider* regular workman; ~*e avondjes* set evenings; *zijn* ~*e benoeming* his permanent appointment; ~*e betrekking* permanent situation; ~*e bezoeker* regular visitor, patron; ~*e brandstoffen* solid fuel; ~*e brug* fixed bridge; ~*e goederen* fixed property, immovables; ~*e halte* compulsory stop; ~*e hand* firm (steady) hand; *een* ~ *inkomen* a fixed income; ~*e inwoners* resident inhabitants; ~*e klanten* regular customers; ~ *kleed* fitted carpet; ~*e kleuren* fast colours; ~*e kost* solid food; ~*e lasten* overhead expenses, overheads; ~*e lichamen* solid bodies, solids; *een* ~*e massa* a solid mass; *een* ~ *nummer* a fixture; ~*e offerte* $ firm offer; ~*e overtuiging* firm conviction; ~*e planten* perennials; ~*e positie* stable position; ~*e prijzen* fixed prices; no discount given!; ~ *salaris* fixed salary; *onze* ~*e schotel op zondag* our standing Sunday-dish; ~*e slaap* sound sleep; ~*e spijzen* solid food; ~*e ster* fixed star; ~*e tussenpozen* [at] regular intervals; ~*e uitdrukking* stock phrase; ~*e vloerbedekking* fitted floor-covering; ~ *voornemen* firm (fixed, set) intention; ~*e wal* shore; ~*e wastafel* fitted wash-basin; ~ *weer* settled weather; ~ *werk* regular work (employment); ~*e woonplaats* fixed abode; *het is* ~ *en zeker* it is quite certain; ~ *worden* congeal [of liquids], solidify [of cheese &], set [of custard]; settle [of the weather]; ~*er worden* $ firm up, stiffen [of prices]; **II** *ad* 1 (f e r m) fast, firmly, $ [offer] firm; 2 (a l v a s t) as well, in the meantime; 3 (z e k e r) certainly, surely, for certain; ~ *en zeker* quite certain; ~ *niet* certainly not; *wij zullen maar* ~ *beginnen* we'll begin meanwhile; ~ *slapen* be sound asleep, sleep soundly

'**vastbakken** (bakte vast, is vastgebakken) *vi* stick to the pan

vastbe'raden resolute, firm, determined; **–heid** *v* resoluteness, resolution, firmness, determination; '**vastbesloten** determined, resolute, firm, of set purpose

'**vastbijten**[1] *zich* ~ *in iets* get one's teeth into sth.; **–binden**[1] *vt* bind fast, fasten, tie up; **–draaien**[1] *vt* turn on, screw down

vaste'landen (-en) *o* continent, mainland; **–sklimaat** *o* continental climate

1 '**vasten** *m* Lent; *in de* ~ in Lent; 2 '**vasten** (vastte, h. gevast) *vi* fast; *het* ~ fasting, the fast; **vasten'avond** (-en) *m* Shrove Tuesday, Pancake Day, Shrovetide; **–gek** (-ken) *m* carnival reveller; **–grap** (-pen) *v* carnival joke; **–pret** *v* carnival fun; **–zot** (-ten) *m* = *vastenavondgek*; '**vastenbrief** (-brieven) *m rk* Lenten pastoral; **–dag** (-dagen) *m* fast-day, fasting-

day; **–preek** (-preken) *v* Lenten sermon; **–tijd** *m* time of fasting; *de* ~ Lent; **–wet** (-ten) *v* 1 law of fasting; 2 *rk* Lenten regulations; '**vaster** (-s) *m* faster

'**vastgeroest** rusted; *fig* stuck in a groove

'**vastgespen**[1] *vt* buckle; **–grijpen**[1] *vt* seize, catch hold of, grip; **–groeien**[1] *vi* grow together; **–haken**[1] *vt* hook (on to *aan*); **–hebben**[1] have got hold [of sth.]; **–hechten**[1] **I** *vt* attach, fasten, fix, affix [sth. to...]; **II** *vr zich* ~ (*aan*) attach itself (themselves) to...[2]; *fig* become (get) attached to...

'**vastheid** *v* firmness, fixedness, solidity

'**vasthouden** **I** *vt* hold fast, hold [sth.]; retain [facts]; detain [the accused]; **II** *va* ~ *aan* be tenacious of [one's rights &]; stick to [one's opinion, old fashions &]; **III** *vr zich* ~ hold fast, hold on; *zich* ~ *aan de leuning* hold on to the banisters; **vast'houdend** 1 tenacious; 2 (g i e r i g) stingy, tight-fisted; **–heid** *v* 1 tenacity; 2 (g i e r i g h e i d) stinginess

'**vastigheid** *v* 1 fixedness, fixity, stability; 2 fixed property, real property; 3 certainty

'**vastketenen**[1] *vt* chain up; **–klampen** (klampte 'vast, h. 'vastgeklampt) *zich* ~ *aan* cling to[2]; clutch at [a straw]; **–klemmen**[1] *zich* ~ *aan* hold on to [the banisters]; zie ook: *vastklampen*; **–kleven**[1] *vi* & *vt* stick (to *aan*); **–klinken**[1] *vt* rivet; **–kluisteren**[1] *vt* fetter[2], shackle[2]; **–knopen**[1] *vt* (k n o o p) button (up); (t o u w) tie, tie up, fasten; **–koppelen**[1] *vt* couple[2]; **–leggen**[1] *vt* fasten, tie up, chain up [a dog]; ⚓ moor [a ship]; *fig* tie up, lock up [capital]; record [by photography &]; lay down [in a contract]; *het geleerde* ~ fix what one has learned; *het resultaat van het onderzoek* ~ *in...* embody (record) the result of the investigation in...; **–liggen**[1] *vi* lie firm [of things]; be chained up [of a dog]; be tied (locked) up [of a capital]; ⚓ be moored [of a ship]; **–lijmen**[1] *vt* glue; **–lopen**[1] 1 get stuck[2]; ⚒ jam [of a machine]; 2 ⚓ run aground; 3 *fig* come to a deadlock [of conference &]; **–maken**[1] *vt* fasten, make fast, tie, bind, secure [sth.]; ⚓ furl [sails]; *die blouse kan je van achteren* ~ this blouse fastens at the back; **–meren**[1] *vt* ⚓ moor [a ship]; **–naaien**[1] *vt* sew together, sew (on to *aan*); **–nagelen**[1] *vt* nail (down)

'**vastomlijnd** clearly defined; *een* ~ *idee* a clear (definite) idea

'**vastpakken**[1] *vt* seize, take hold of, grip; *het goed* ~ take fast hold of it; **–pinnen**[1] *vt* pin, fasten with pins; *iem op iets* ~ pin sbd. down to

---

[1] V.T. en V.D. van dit werkwoord volgens het model: '**vastgroeien**, V.T. groeide '**vast**, V.D. '**vastgegroeid**. Zie voor de vormen onder het grondwoord, in dit voorbeeld: *groeien*. Bij sterke en onregelmatige werkwoorden wordt u verwezen naar de lijst achterin.

sth.; **–plakken**[1] I *vi* stick; ~ *aan* stick to; **II** *vt* stick; *het* ~ *aan... paste it on to...;* **–praten**[1] I *vt* corner [sbd.]; **II** *vr zich* ~ be caught in one's own words; **–prikken**[1] *vt* pin (up); **–raken**[1] *vi* get stuck[2]; ♒ run aground

vast'recht *o* fixed charge, flat rate

'vastrijgen[1] *vt* lace (up); **–roesten**[1] *vi* rust (on to *aan*); **–schroeven**[1] *vt* 1 screw tight, screw home; 2 screw down, screw up; **–sjorren**[1] *vt* 1 (v. t o u w e n) lash, belay; 2 secure [sth.]; **–slaan**[1] *vt* fasten, nail down; **–spelden**[1] *vt* pin (on to *aan*); **–spijkeren**[1] *vt* nail (down); **–staan**[1] *vi* stand firm; *dat staat vast!* that's a fact!; *zijn besluit stond vast* his resolution was fixed; **–stampen**[1] *vt* ram down; **–steken**[1] *vt* fasten [with pins or pegs]

'vaststellen[1] *vt* establish, ascertain [a fact]; determine [the amount &]; ⚕ diagnose [ulceration]; lay down [rules], draw up [a programme]; assess [the damages]; appoint [a time, place]; settle, fix [a day &]; state [that...]; *vastgesteld op 1 mei* fixed for May 1st; **–ling** (-en) *v* establishment; determination, fixation; settlement, appointment

'vaststrikken[1] *vt* tie; **–trappen**[1] *vt* stamp (tread) down; **–vriezen**[1] *vi* be frozen in (up); ~ *aan* freeze on to; **–wortelen**[1] *vi* root; *fig* establish firmly; *vastgeworteld* firmly rooted; **–zetten**[1] *vt* fasten [sth.]; secure [a cask &]; *fig* check [sbd. at draughts]; tie up [money]; commit [sbd.] to prison; *geld* ~ *op iem.* settle a sum of money upon sbd.; *iem.* ~ 1 pose (nonplus, corner) sbd.; 2 commit sbd. to prison; **–zitten**[1] *vi* 1 (v. d i n g e n) stick fast, stick; ♒ be aground; 2 (v. p e r s o n e n) be in prison; *fig* be stuck; be at a nonplus; *wij zitten hier vast* we are marooned here; *daar zit meer a a n vast* 1 more belongs to that; 2 more is meant than meets the ear (the eye); *nu zit hij eraan vast* he can't back out of it now; *ik zit er niet aan vast* I am not wedded to it; ~ *i n het ijs* be ice-bound

1 vat *m* hold, grip; *ik heb geen* ~ *op hem* I have no hold on (over) him; *...heeft geen* ~ *op hem ...has* no hold upon him, he is proof against...; *niets had* ~ *op hem* it was all lost upon him; *ik kon geen* ~ *op hem krijgen* I could not get at him

2 vat (vaten) *o* 1 cask, barrel, tun, butt, vat; 2 🜾 & 🜾 vessel; *de heilige* ~*en* the holy vessels; *een uitverkoren* ~ **B** a chosen vessel; *het zwakke* ~ **B** the weaker vessel; *de* ~*en wassen* wash up (the plates and dishes); *wat in het* ~ *is verzuurt niet* it will keep; *nog wat in het* ~ *hebben* have a

rod in pickle [for]; *holle* ~*en klinken het hardst* the empty vessel makes the greatest sound; *bier van het* ~ beer on draught, draught ale; *wijn van het* ~ wine from the wood

'vatbaar ~ *voor* capable of [improvement], open to, accessible to, amenable to, susceptible to [reason &]; susceptible to [cold]; susceptible of [impressions]; ~ *voor indrukken* impressionable; **–heid** *v* capacity, accessibility, susceptibility; ~ *voor indrukken* impressionability

'vatbier *o* beer on draught, draught ale

'vaten meervoud van 2 *vat*

'vatenkwast (-en) *m* dish-mop

Vati'caan *o* Vatican; **–s** Vatican [Council, library]; **–stad** *v* Vatican City

'vatten (vatte, h. gevat) **I** *vt* catch[2], seize[2], grasp[2] [sth.]; *fig* understand [sth., the meaning], see [a joke]; zie ook: *kou, moed*, 2 *post* &; *in goud* ~ mount in gold; *in lood* ~ set in lead, frame with lead, lead; **II** *va vat je?* (you) see?

va'zal (-len) *m* vassal; **–staat** (-staten) *m* vassal state

'vechten* *vi* fight; **F** have a scrap; ~ *m e t de stadsjongens* fight (with) the townboys; ~ *o m iets* fight for sth.; ~ *t e g e n* fight against, fight; *ik heb er altijd v o o r gevochten* I've always fought in behalf of it, stood up for it; **–er** (-s) *m* fighter, combatant; **vechte'rij** (-en) *v* fighting; **'vechtersbaas** (-bazen) *m* fighter; **'vechthaan** (-hanen) *m* 🐓 game-cock; **–jas** (-sen) *m* fighter, tough; **–lust** *m* pugnacity; combativeness; **vecht'lustig** pugnacious, combative; **'vechtpartij** (-en) *v* fight, scuffle; **F** scrap; **–pet** (-ten) *v* battle-cap, forage-cap; **–wagen** (-s) *m* 🜾 tank

'vedel (-s en -en) *v* fiddle; **–aar** (-s) *m* fiddler; **'vedelen** (vedelde, h. gevedeld) *vi* fiddle

'veder (-s en -en) = 1 *veer*; **–achtig** feathery; **–bal** (-len) *m* shuttlecock; **–bos** (-sen) *m* tuft, crest, plume; panache; **–gewicht** *o sp* featherweight; **–licht** light as a feather, feathery; **–loos** 1 featherless; 2 unfledged; **–vormig** feather-shaped; **–wolk** (-en) *v* cirrus [*mv* cirri]

ve'dette (-s en -n) *v* vedette, star

vee *o* cattle[2]; **–arts** (-en) *m* veterinary surgeon, **F** vet; **veeartse'nijkunde** *v* veterinary science, veterinary surgery; **–school** (-scholen) *v* veterinary college; **'veeboer** (-en) *m* cattle-breeder, stock-famer; **–boot** (-boten) *m* & *v* cattle-boat; **–dief** (-dieven) *m* cattlestealer, cattle-lifter; **veédieve'rij** (-en) *v* cattle-lifting; **'veedrijver** (-s) *m* cattle-drover, drover; **–fokker** (-s) *m* cattle-breeder, stock-

---

[1] V.T. en V.D. van dit werkwoord volgens het model: **'vast**groeien, V.T. groeide **'vast**, V.D. **'vast**gegroeid. Zie voor de vormen onder het grondwoord, in dit voorbeeld: *groeien*. Bij sterke en onregelmatige werkwoorden wordt u verwezen naar de lijst achterin.

breeder; **veefokke'rij** (-en) *v* 1 cattle-breeding, cattle-raising; 2 stock-farm

1 veeg *aj het vege lijf redden* get off with one's life; *een ~ teken* an ominous sign

2 veeg (vegen) *m & v* wipe [with a cloth]; whisk [with a broom]; slap [in the face], box [on the ear]; (*vette*) ~ smear; *iem. een ~ uit de pan geven* have a smack (a fling) at sbd.; *hij kreeg ook een ~ uit de pan* he got a smack as well; **–sel** *o* sweepings

'veehandel *m* cattle-trade; **–handelaar** (-s) *m* cattle-dealer; **–hoeder** (-s) *m* herdsman; **–houder** (-s) *m* stock farmer; **–koek** (-en) *m* oil-cake

1 veel I *aj* 1 (v o o r e n k e l v o u d) much; a great deal, **F** a lot; lots of [money]; 2 (v o o r m e e r v o u d) many; *vele* many; *de velen die...* the many that...; *heel ~* zie *zeer ~*; *te ~* 1 too much; 2 too many; *ben ik hier te ~?* am I one too many?; *niets is hem te ~* he thinks nothing too much trouble; *te ~ om op te noemen* too numerous to mention; *~ te ~* 1 far too much; 2 far too many; *zeer ~* 1 very much, a great deal; 2 very many, a great many; *zo ~* 1 so much; 2 so many; *zo ~ je wilt* as much (as many) as you like; *~ hebben van...* be much like; **II** *ad* much [better &]; *~ te mooi* much too fine, a good (great) deal too fine; *hij komt er ~* he often goes there; *hij heeft ~ in Europa en Afrika gereisd* ook: he travelled widely in Europe and Africa; *een ~ gelezen roman* a widely read novel

2 veel (velen) *v = vedel*

'veelal often, mostly; **–begeerd** much sought after, much in demand; **–belovend** promising; **–besproken** much-discussed; **–betekenend I** *aj* significant, meaning; **II** *ad* significantly, meaningly; **–bewogen** very agitated, eventful [life, times], chequered [life]; **–eer** rather, sooner; **veel'eisend** exacting, exigent; **–heid** *v* exactingness; **'veelgelezen** widely read; **–geprezen** much-belauded; **veel'godendom** *o*, **veelgode'rij** *v* polytheism; **'veelheid** (-heden) *v* multiplicity, multitude; **–hoek** (-en) *m* polygon; **–hoekig** polygonal; **–hoofdig, veel'hoofdig** many-headed; **'veeljarig, veel'jarig** of many years; **'veelkleurig, veel'kleurig** multi-coloured, variegated, varicoloured; **veelletter'grepig** polysyllabic; **veelmanne'rij** *v* polyandry; **'veelmeer, veel'meer** rather; **'veelomstreden** much disputed, vexed [question]; **–omvattend** comprehensive, wide [programme]; **–prater** (-s) *m*, **–praatster** (-s) *v* voluble person; **–schrijver** (-s) *m* scribbler, voluminous writer; **veel'soortig** manifold, multifarious; **veel'stemmig** 1 many-voiced; 2 ♩ = *meerstemmig*; **'veeltalig** polyglot; **–term**

(-en) *m* multinomial; **–vermogend** powerful, influential; **–vlak** (-ken) *o* polyhedron; **–vlakkig** polyhedral; **–vormig** multiform; **–voud** (-en) *o* multiple; *kleinste gemene ~* least common multiple; **–voudig, veel'voudig** manifold, multifarious; **'veelvraat** (-vraten) *m* 1 ⌖ wolverene; 2 *fig* glutton, greedy-guts; **veel'vuldig** frequent; zie ook: *veelvoudig*; **–heid** *v* frequency; **veelwijve'rij** *v* polygamy; **veel'zeggend** significant; **veel'zijdig** multilateral²; *fig* many-sided, versatile [mind]; wide [knowledge]; all-round [sportsman]; **–heid** *v* many-sidedness, versatility

veem (vemen) *o* $ dock company; warehouse company; (g e b o u w) warehouse
'veemarkt (-en) *v* cattle-market
'veemgericht (-en) *o* Ⓥ vehmic court
veen (venen) *o* peat-moor, peat-bog, peat; **–achtig** boggy, peaty; **–bes** (-sen) *v* cranberry; **–brand** (-en) *m* peat-moor fire; **veende'rij** (-en) *v* 1 peat-digging; 2 peatery; **'veengrond** (-en) *m* peat-moor, peat; **–kolonie** (-iën en -s) *v* fen-colony, peat-colony; **–land** (-en) *o* peat-moor, peat-bog; **–mol** (-len) *m* mole-cricket
'veepest *v* cattle-plague, rinderpest

1 veer (veren) *v* 1 feather [of a bird]; 2 spring [of a watch &]; 3 side-piece [of spectacles]; *hij is nog niet uit de veren* he is still between the sheets; *elkaar in de veren zitten* be at loggerheads; *met andermans veren pronken* strut in borrowed feathers; *iem. een ~ op de hoed zetten* put a feather in sbd.'s cap

2 veer (veren) *o* ferry; ferry-boat
'veerbalans (-en) *v* spring-balance
'veerboot (-boten) *m & v* ferry(-boat), ferrysteamer; **–dienst** (-en) *m* ferry-service; **–geld** (-en) *o* passage-money, ferriage; **–huis** (-huizen) *o* ferryman's house, ferry-station
'veerkracht *v* elasticity², resilience², spring²; **veer'krachtig** elastic², resilient², springy
'veerman (-lieden en -lui) *m* ferryman; **–pont** (-en) *v* ferry-boat
'veertien fourteen; *~ dagen* a fortnight; **–daags** fortnightly; **–de** fourteenth (part)
'veertig forty; **–er** (-s) *m* person of forty (years); **–jarig** of forty years, forty-year-old; **–ste** fortieth (part)
'veestal (-len) *m* cow-house, cow-shed, byre; **–stapel** (-s) *m* live-stock, stock of cattle; **–teelt** *v* cattle-breeding, stock-breeding; **–tentoonstelling** (-en) *v* cattle-show; **–verzekering** (-en) *v* live-stock insurance; **–voe(de)r** *o* cattle-fodder, forage; **–wagen** (-s) *m* cattle-truck; **–ziekte** (-n en -s) *v* cattle-plague
'vegen (veegde, h. geveegd) *vt* sweep [a floor, a room, a chimney]; wipe [one's feet, one's

hands]; **–er** (-s) *m* 1 (p e r s o o n) sweeper; 2
(b o r s t e l) brush
vege'tariër (-s) *m* vegetarian; **vege'tarisch**
vegetarian; **vegeta'risme** *o* vegetarianism;
vege'tatie [-(t)si.] (-s) *v* vegetation;
vegeta'tief vegetative; vegetating [existence];
vege'teren (vegeteerde, h. gevegeteerd) *vi*
vegetate
ve'hikel (-s) *o* vehicle
veil venal, corruptible; *een ~e vrouw* a prostitute;
zijn leven ~ hebben be ready to sacrifice one's life
'veilcondities [-(t)si.s] *mv* conditions of sale;
–dag (-dagen) *m* auction-day; **'veilen** (veilde,
h. geveild) *vt* sell by auction, auction; **–er** (-s)
m auctioneer
'veilheid *v* venality, corruptibility
'veilig I *aj* safe, secure; *~ !* all clear!; *een ~e
plaats* ook: a place of safety; *de (spoor)lijn is ~*
the line is clear; *~ voor* safe from, secure from;
II *ad* safely; **'veiligheid** (-heden) *v* 1 safety,
security; 2 ✯ fuse; *collectieve ~* collective
security; *openbare ~* public safety; *i n ~ brengen*
put (place) in safety; *v o o r de ~* for safety('s
sake); **'veiligheidsdienst** *m* security service;
–glas *o* safety glass; **–gordel** (-s) *m* seat belt,
safety belt; **–grendel** (-s) *m* safety bolt; **veilig-
heids'halve** for safety's sake, for reasons of
safety; **'veiligheidsklep** (-pen) *v* safety valve;
–lamp (-en) *v* safety lamp; (v. m ij n w e r-
k e r s) Davy [lamp]; **–maatregel** (-en en -s) *m*
precautionary measure, safety measure;
–marge [-mɑrʒə] (-s) *v* margin of safety,
safety margin; **–overwegingen** *mv uit ~* for
safety (security) reasons; **–pal** (-len) *m* safety
catch; **'Veiligheidsraad** *m* Security Council;
'veiligheidsriem (-en) *m* safety belt, seat belt;
–scheermes (-sen) *o* safety-razor; **–speld**
(-en) *v* safety-pin; **–voorschrift** (-en) *o* safety
regulation; **'veiligstellen** (stelde 'veilig, h.
'veiliggesteld) make safe [the currency],
safeguard [our interests]
'veiling (-en) *v* public sale, auction; *in ~ brengen*
put up for auction (for sale), sell by auction;
–condities [-(t)si.s] *mv* conditions of sale;
–kosten *mv* sale expenses; **–meester** (-s) *m*
auctioneer; **–prijs** (-prijzen) *m* sale price;
'veilingzaal (-zalen) *v* auction-room, sale-
room
'veine ['vɛːnə] *v* luck, run of luck; *hij heeft altijd
~* he is always in luck
'veinzaard (-s) *m* dissembler, hypocrite;
'veinzen (veinsde, h. geveinsd) **I** *vi* dissemble,
feign; **II** *vt* feign, simulate; *~ doof te zijn* feign
that one is deaf, feign (sham) deafness; **–er** (-s)
m dissembler, hypocrite; **veinze'rij** (-en) *v*
dissimulation, hypocrisy
vel (-len) *o* 1 skin [of the body], (v. d i e r e n)

ook: hide; skin [on milk]; 2 sheet [of paper];
niet meer dan ~ over been zijn be only skin and
bone; *iem. het ~ over de oren halen* fleece sbd.; *hij
steekt i n een slecht ~* he is delicate; *ik zou niet
graag in zijn ~ steken* I should not like to be in
his skin; *u i t zijn ~ springen* be beside oneself;
het is om uit je ~ te springen it is enough to drive
you wild
veld (-en) *o* field; *het ~ van eer* the field of
honour; *een ruim ~ van werkzaamheid* a wide
field (sphere) of activity; *het ~ behouden* hold
the field²; *het ~ ruimen* retire from the field,
abandon (leave) the field²; *~ winnen* gain
ground; ● *i n het open (vrije) ~* in the open
field; *in geen ~en of wegen* nowhere at all; *hoeveel
mannen kunnen zij in het ~ brengen?* can they put
into the field?; *o p het ~ werken* work in the
fields; *de t e ~e staande gewassen* the standing
crops; *de te ~e staande legers* the armies in the
field; *te ~e trekken* take the field; *te ~e trekken
tegen* [*fig*] fight; *u i t het ~ geslagen zijn* be
discomfited, be put out (of countenance);
–arbeid *m* work in the fields, field-work;
–artillerie [-ɑrtɪləri.] *v* field artillery; **–bed**
(-den) *o* field-bed, camp-bed; **–bloem** (-en) *v*
field-flower, wild flower; **–boeket** (-ten) *o* &
m bunch (bouquet) of wild flowers; **–dienst**
(-en) *m* ✖ field service, field duty; **–fles** (-sen)
v case-bottle, ✖ water-bottle, canteen; **–gewas**
(-sen) *o* ✖ field crop; **–heer** (-heren) *m*
general; **–heerschap** *o* generalship; **–heers-
staf** (-staven) *m* baton; **–hospitaal** (-talen) *o*
field hospital, ambulance; **–keuken** (-s) *v*
field-kitchen; **–kijker** (-s) *m* field-glass(es);
–krekel (-s) *m* field-cricket; **–loop** *m sp*
cross-country; **–maarschalk** (-en) *m* field-
marshal; **–muis** (-muizen) *v* field-mouse, vole;
–post *v* field-post, field-post office; **–prediker**
(-s) *m* army chaplain; **–rit** *m* cross-country
race; **–sla** (-en) *v* corn-salad; **–slag** (-slagen) *m*
battle; **–spaat** *o* feldspar; **–telefoon** (-s) *m*
field telephone; **–tent** (-en) *v* army tent;
–tenue [-tɔny.] (-s) *o* & *v* field-service
uniform, battle-dress; **–tocht** (-en) *m*
campaign; **–uitrusting** *v* field-kit; **–vruchten**
mv produce of the fields; **–wacht** (-en) *v* ✖
picket; **✎ –wachter** (-s) *m* village policeman;
–werk *o* 1 farm-work; 2 field-work
1 'velen *vt* *hij kan het niet ~* he cannot stand it;
ik kan hem niet ~ I can't stand him, I can't bear
the sight of him; *hij kan niets ~* he is very
touchy
2 'velen many; zie ook: *veel* **I**
'velerhande, –lei of many kinds, of many
sorts, various, sundry, many
velg (-en) *v* rim, felly, felloe; **–band** (-en) *m*
tubeless tyre; **–rem** (-men) *v* rim-brake

ve'lijn *o* 1 vellum; 2 vellum-paper
'vellen (velde, h. geveld) *vt* 1 fell, cut down [trees]; 2 lay in rest [a lance], couch [arms]; 3 *fig* pass [judgment, a sentence]; zie ook: *bajonet*
'velletje (-s) *o* skin, film, membrane; *een ~ postpapier* a sheet of note-paper; **'vellig** skinny
'velling (-en) *v* = *velg*
ve'lours [və'lu:r] *o* & *m* velours
ven (-nen) *o* fen
'vendel (-s en -en) *o* 1 ⊞ company; 2 = *vaandel*; **–zwaaien** *o* flag throwing
ven'detta *v* vendetta
ven'duhouder (-s) *m* auctioneer; **–huis** (-huizen), **–lokaal** (-kalen) *o* auction-room, sale-room; **–meester** (-s) *m* auctioneer; **ven'dutie** [-(t)si.] (-s) *v* auction, public sale; *op ~ doen* put up for auction
ve'nerisch venereal [disease]
Veneti'aan(s) [-(t)si.'a.n(s)] (-ianen) *m* (& *aj*) Venetian; **Ve'netië** [-(t)si.ə] *o* Venice
ve'neus venous [blood]
Venezu'ela *o* Venezuela
ve'nijn *o* venom[2]; **ve'nijnig** virulent, vicious; **–heid** (-heden) *v* virulence, viciousness
'venkel *v* ❀ fennel; **–olie** *v* fennel-oil
'vennoot, ven'noot (-noten) *m* $ partner; *beherend ~* managing partner; *commanditaire ~* limited partner; *stille ~* silent (sleeping) partner; *werkend ~* active partner; **'vennootschap, ven'nootschap** (-pen) *v* $ partnership, company; *besloten ~* private company with limited liability; *commanditaire ~* limited partnership; *naamloze ~* limited liability company; *een ~ aangaan* enter into partnership; **'vennootschapsbelasting** *v* company tax; *Am* corporate tax; **–recht** *o* company law
'venster (-s) *o* window; **–bank** (-en) *v* window-sill, window-ledge; (b r e d e z i t p l a a t s) window-seat; **–blind** (-en) *o* shutter; **–envelop(pe)** [-ã̃və-] (-loppen) *v* window envelope; **–glas** (-glazen) *o* 1 window-pane; 2 (g l a s v o o r v e n s t e r s) window-glass; **–gordijn** (-en) *o* window-curtain; **–luik** (-en) *o* shutter; **–raam** (-ramen) *o* window-frame; **–ruit** (-en) *v* window-pane
vent (-en) *m* F fellow, chap; (a a n s p r e k i n g) sonny, little man [to a boy]; *een beste ~* F a good fellow; *een goeie ~* F a good sort; *geen kwaaie ~* F not a bad sort; *een rare ~* F a queer fellow (customer)
'venten (ventte, h. gevent) *vt* hawk, peddle; **–er** (-s) *m* hawker, pedlar; (v. f r u i t, v i s &) costermonger

ven'tiel (-en) *o* valve; **–dop** (-pen) *m* valve-cap; **–slang** *v* valve rubber tube
venti'latie [-(t)si.] *v* ventilation; **venti'lator** (-s en -'toren) *m* ventilator, fan; **–riem** (-en) *m* fan-belt; **venti'leren** (ventileerde, h. geventileerd) *vt* ventilate[2], air[2]
'ventje (-s) *o* little fellow, little man
'ventweg (-wegen) *m* service road
'Venus *v* Venus; **'venushaar** *o* ❀ maidenhair; **–heuvel** (-s) *m* mons veneris
ver I *aj* 1 far [way &]; distant [ages, past, connection, likeness]; remote [ages]; 2 (v e r-w a n t s c h a p) distant [relation, relatives], remote [kinsman &]; **II** *ad* far; *het is ~ it is far*, a long way (off); *het is mijlen ~ it is miles and miles away* (off); *nu ben ik nog even ~ I'm no further forward than before*; *dat is nog heel ~ that is very far off yet*; *het ~ brengen zie brengen*; *~ gaan go far*; *te ~ gaan go too far[2]*; *zo ~ gaan wij niet we shall not go so far[2]*; *het te ~ laten komen let things go too far*; *~ beneden mij far beneath me*; *~ van hier far away*; *~ van rijk far from being rich*; zie ook: *verder, verre & verst*
ver'aangenamen (veraangenaamde, h. veraangenaamd) *vt* make agreeable, make pleasant
veraan'schouwelijken (veraanschouwelijkte, h. veraanschouwelijkt) *vt* illustrate
verabsolu'teren (verabsoluteerde, h. verabsoluteerd) *vt* absolutize [sth.]
verac'cijnzen (veraccijnsde, h. veraccijnsd) *vt* 1 (b e t a l e n) pay the excise; 2 (o p l e g g e n) excise
ver'achtelijk 1 despicable, contemptible; 2 contemptuous; *~e blik contemptuous look*; *~e kerel contemptible fellow*; **–heid** *v* contemptibleness; **ver'achten**[1] *vt* despise, have a contempt for, hold in contempt, scorn; *de dood ~ scorn death*; **–er** (-s) *m* despiser; **ver'achting** *v* contempt; scorn; *iem. aan de ~ prijsgeven hold sbd. up to scorn*
ver'ademen[1] *vt* breathe again; **–ming** *v* 1 (o p l u c h t i n g) relief; 2 (t ij d) breathing-time, breathing-spell
'veraf at a great distance, far (away); **–gelegen** remote, distant
ver'afgoden (verafgoodde, h. verafgood) *vt* idolize; **–ding** *v* idolization
ver'afschuwen (verafschuwde, h. verafschuwd) *vt* abhor, loathe
veralge'menen (veralgemeende, h. veralgemeend) *vt* generalize
verameri'kaansen (veramerikaanste, is veramerikaanst) *vi* americanize

---

[1] V.T. en V.D. van dit werkwoord volgens het model: **ver'**achten, V.T. **ver'**achtte, V.D. **ver'**acht (**ge-** valt dus weg in het V.D.). Zie voor de vormen onder het grondwoord, in dit voorbeeld: *achten*. Bij sterke en onregelmatige werkwoorden wordt u verwezen naar de lijst achterin.

ve′randa (′s) *v* veranda(h)

ver′anderen I (veranderde, is veranderd) *vi* change, alter; *het weer verandert* the weather changes; ~ *i n* change into; ~ *v a n gedachte* zie *gedachte*; *van godsdienst (mening, toon)* ~ change one's religion (one's opinion, one's tone); *ik kon haar niet van mening doen* ~ I could not get her to change her mind; **II** (veranderde, h. veranderd) *vt* 1 (i n ′t a l g.) change; 2 (w ij z i g e n) alter; convert [a motor-car &]; 3 (t o t i e t s g e h e e l a n d e r s m a k e n) transform; *dat verandert de zaak* that alters the case; *dat verandert niets a a n de waarheid* that does not alter the truth; *...i n...* ~ change (alter, convert, turn, transform) *...into...*; ⚡ commute [death-sentence] to [imprisonment]; *hij is erg veranderd* he has altered a good deal, a great change has come over him; **–ring** (-en) *v* change, alteration, transformation, conversion, ⚡ commutation; ~ *ten goede (ten kwade)* change for the better (for the worse); ~ *van weer* a change in the weather (of weather); ~ *van woonplaats* change of residence; *–en aanbrengen* make alterations, alter things; ~ *in iets brengen* change sth.; ~ *ondergaan* undergo a change; *voor de* ~ for a change; *alle* ~ *is geen verbetering* let well alone; ~ *van spijs doet eten* a change of food whets the appetite; **ver′anderlijk** changeable, variable; (w i s p e l t u r i g) inconstant, fickle; **–heid** *v* changeableness, variability; (w i s p e l t u r i g h e i d) inconstancy, fickleness

ver′ankeren[1] *vt* 1 ⚓ anchor, moor [a ship]; 2 △ brace, tie, stay [a wall]; 3 *fig* root

verant′woordelijk responsible, answerable, accountable; ~ *stellen voor* hold responsible for; *zich* ~ *stellen voor* accept responsibility for; ~ *zijn voor...* be (held) responsible for..., have to answer for...; **verant′woordelijkheid** *v* responsibility; *de* ~ *van zich afschuiven* shift the responsibility upon another; *de* ~ *op zich nemen* take the responsibility [of...], accept responsibility [for...]; *b u i t e n* ~ *van de redactie* the editor not being responsible; *o p eigen* ~ on his (her) own responsibility; **–sgevoel** *o* sense of responsibility; **ver′antwoorden**[1] **I** *vt* answer for, account for; justify; *hij zegt niet meer dan hij* ~ *kan* he doesn't like to say more than he can stand to; *het hard te* ~ *hebben* be hard put to it; *heel wat te* ~ *hebben* have a lot to answer for; *ik ben niet verantwoord* I am not justified; **II** *vr zich* ~ justify oneself; **–ding** (-en) *v* 1 justification; 2 responsibility; *o p eigen* ~ on one's own

responsibility; *t e r* ~ *roepen* call to account

ver′armen I (verarmde, h. verarmd) *vt* impoverish, reduce to poverty, pauperize; **II** (verarmde, is verarmd) *vi* become poor; *verarmd* in reduced circumstances; **–ming** *v* impoverishment, pauperization, pauperism

ver′assen (veraste, h. verast) *vt* cremate, incinerate; **–sing** *v* cremation, incineration

ver′baal verbal

ver′baasd I *aj* surprised, astonished, amazed; ~ *staan (over)* be surprised (at), be astonished (at), be amazed (at); **II** *ad* wonderingly, in wonder, in surprise; ~ *kijken* look puzzled; **–heid** *v* surprise, astonishment, amazement

ver′babbelen[1] **I** *vt* waste [one's time] chattering; **II** *vr zich* ~ let one's tongue run away with one

verbali′seren [s = z] (verbaliseerde, h. geverbaliseerd) *vt iem.* ~ take sbd.'s name, summons sbd....

ver′band (-en) *o* 1 🗲 bandage, dressing; 2 (v a n a d e r) ligature; 3 (s a m e n h a n g) connection; 4 (b e t r e k k i n g) relation [between smoking and cancer]; 5 (z i n s v e r b a n d) context; 6 (v e r p l i c h t i n g) charge, obligation; *hypothecair* ~ mortgage; ~ *houden met...* be connected with...; *een* ~ *leggen* apply a dressing; *een* ~ *leggen op een wond* dress a wound; *in* ~ *brengen met* connect with; *iets met iets anders in* ~ *brengen* put two and two together; *zijn arm in een* ~ *dragen* carry one's arm in a sling; *dat staat in* ~ *met...* it is connected with...; *dat staat in geen* ~ *met...* it is in no way connected with...; it does not bear upon...; *in* ~ *hiermee...* in this connection; *in* ~ *met uw vraag* in connection with your question; **–cursus** [-züs] (-sen) *m* ambulance class(es); **–gaas** *o* sterilized gauze; **–kamer** (-s) *v* dressing-room; **–kist** (-en) *v* first-aid kit; **–leer** *v* wound-dressing; **–linnen** *o* rolls of bandage; **–middelen** *mv* dressings; **–plaats** (-en) *v* ✝ dressing-station; **–stoffen** *mv* dressings; **–watten** *mv* medicated cottonwool

ver′bannen *vt* exile, banish, expel; ~ *n a a r* exile & to; relegate to [the past]; ~ *u i t het land* banish from the country; **ver′banning** (-en) *v* exile, banishment, expulsion; **–soord** (-en) *o* place of exile

ver′basteren (verbasterde, is verbasterd) *vi* 1 degenerate; 2 be corrupted [of words]; **–ring** (-en) *v* 1 degeneration; 2 corruption [of words]

ver′bazen (verbaasde, h. verbaasd) **I** *vt* surprise, astonish; amaze; *het verbaast me dat...* it surprises me that..., what astonishes me is that...; *dat*

---

[1] V.T. en V.D. van dit werkwoord volgens het model: **ver′**achten, V.T. **ver′**achtte, V.D. **ver′**acht (**ge-** valt dus weg in het V.D.). Zie voor de vormen onder het grondwoord, in dit voorbeeld: *achten.* Bij sterke en onregelmatige werkwoorden wordt u verwezen naar de lijst achterin.

verbaast me niet I am not surprised (astonished) at it; *dat verbaast mij van je* I am surprised at you; **II** *vr zich* ~ be astonished & (at *over*); **–d** surprising; prodigious; marvellous; *wel* ~! **F** by Jove!; good gracious!; ~ *veel...* ook: no end of...; ~ *weinig* 1 precious little; 2 surprisingly & few; **ver'bazing** *v* surprise, astonishment, amazement; ⊙ amaze; *één en al* ~ *zijn* look all wonder; *vol* ~ all astonishment; *i n* ~ *brengen* astonish, amaze; *m e t* ~ zie *verbaasd* **II**; *t o t mijn* ~ to my astonishment; *tot niet geringe* ~ *van...* to the no small astonishment of...; **verbazing'wekkend** astounding, stupendous

ver'bedden (verbedde, h. verbed) *vt een patient* ~ make (change the sheets of) a patient's bed

ver'beelden (verbeeldde, h. verbeeld) **I** *vt* represent; *dat moet...* ~ that's meant for...; **II** *vr zich* ~ imagine, fancy; *verbeeld je!* Fancy!; *wat verbeeld je je wel?* who do you think you are?; *verbeeld je maar niet dat...* don't fancy that...; *verbeeld je maar niets!* don't you presume!; *hij verbeeldt zich heel wat* he fancies himself; *hij verbeeldt zich een dichter te zijn* he fancies himself a poet; **ver'beelding** (-en) *v* 1 imagination; fancy; 2 (e i g e n w a a n) conceit, conceitedness; *dat is maar* ~ *van je* that is only your fancy; *hij heeft veel* ~ *van zich zelf* he is very conceited; **–skracht** *v* imagination

⊙ **ver'beiden**[1] *vt* wait for, await

ver'bena *v* verbena

ver'benen (verbeende, is verbeend) *vi* ossify; **–ning** *v* ossification

ver'bergen[1] **I** *vt* hide, conceal; *iets* ~ *voor* hide (conceal) sth. from; *je verbergt toch niets voor mij?* you are not keeping anything from me?; **II** *vr zich* ~ hide, conceal oneself; *zich* ~ *achter...* [*fig*] screen oneself behind...; **–ging** *v* hiding, concealment

ver'beten grim, dogged [struggle]; ~ *woede* pent-up rage; **–heid** *v* grimness

ver'beterblad (-bladen) *o* leaf with errata; **ver'beteren**[1] **I** *vt* 1 make better [things & men], better [the condition of..., men], improve [land, one's style &]; ameliorate [the soil, the condition of...]; mend [the state of...]; amend [a law]; 2 (c o r r i g e r e n) correct [work, mistakes &]; rectify [errors]; 3 (z e d e - l ij k b e t e r m a k e n) reform, reclaim [people]; *dat kunt u niet* ~ you cannot improve upon that; **II** *va* correct; **III** *vr zich* ~ 1 (v a n g e d r a g) reform, mend one's ways; 2 (v a n c o n d i t i e) better one's condition; **ver'beter-**

huis (-huizen) *o* house of correction; **ver'betering** (-en) *v* 1 change for the better, improvement, amelioration; amendment; betterment; 2 correction, rectification; 3 reformation, reclamation; ~*en aanbrengen* make corrections; effect improvements; *voor* ~ *vatbaar* corrigible; zie *verbeteren*; **–sgesticht** (-en) *o* approved school

ver'beurbaar confiscable; **ver'beurdverklaren** (verklaarde ver'beurd, h. ver'beurdverklaard) *vt* confiscate, seize, declare forfeit; **–ring** (-en) *v* confiscation, seizure, forfeiture; **ver'beuren**[1] *vt* 1 (v e r l i e z e n) forfeit; 2 (v e r b e u r d v e r k l a r e n) confiscate; *die...*, *verbeurt een pand* must pay a forfeit; *pand* ~ play (at) forfeits; *er is niets aan verbeurd* it is no great loss; **ver'beurte** *v op* (*onder*) ~ *van* on (under) penalty of

ver'beuzelen[1] *vt* trifle away, fritter away, dawdle away; fiddle away [one's time]

ver'bidden[1] *zich niet laten* ~ be inexorable

ver'bieden[1] *vt* forbid, prohibit [by law], interdict, veto; *een boek (film, partij* &) ~ ban 'a book (a film, a party &); *ten strengste verboden* strictly forbidden; *verboden in te rijden* no thoroughfare, no entry; *verboden te roken* no smoking (allowed); *verboden hier vuilnis neer te werpen* no rubbish (to be) shot here; *verboden (toegang) voor militairen* ✠ out of bounds [to British troops], *Am* off limits; *verboden toegang* zie *toegang*

ver'bijsterd bewildered, perplexed, dazed, aghast, h. thunderstruck; **ver'bijsteren** (verbijsterde, h. verbijsterd) *vt* bewilder, perplex, daze; **–ring** *v* bewilderment, perplexity

ver'bijten[1] *zich* ~ bite one's lip(s), set one's teeth; *zich* ~ *van woede* chafe; zie ook: *verbeten*

verbij'zonderen [vərbi.-] (verbijzonderde, h. verbijzonderd) *vt* peculiarize; **–ring** (-en) *v* peculiarization

ver'binden I *vt* 1 join [two things, persons]; connect [two things, points, places]; link, link up [two places], tie [two rafters]; combine [elements]; 2 ⚕ bind up, bandage, tie up, dress [a wound]; 3 ⚕ connect, put through; *er is wel enig gevaar aan verbonden* it involves some danger; *de moeilijkheden verbonden aan...* the difficulties with which... is attended; *er is een salaris van £ 500 aan verbonden* it carries a salary of £ 500; *het daaraan verbonden salaris* the salary that goes with it; *welke voordelen zijn daaraan verbonden?* what advantages does it offer?; *er is een voorwaarde aan verbonden* there is a condition attached to it; *hen in de echt* ~ join (unite) them

---

[1] V.T. en V.D. van dit werkwoord volgens het model: **ver'achten**, V.T. **ver'achtte**, V.D. **ver'acht** (ge- valt dus w :g in het V.D.). Zie voor de vormen onder het grondwoord, in dit voorbeeld: *achten*. Bij sterke en onregelmatige werkwoorden wordt u verwezen naar de lijst achterin.

in marriage; *wilt u mij ~ met nummer...?* ☏ put me through to number...; *na een uur was ik verbonden met onze firma* ☏ I was through to our firm; **II** *vr zich ~* 1 (v. p e r s o n e n) enter into an alliance; 2 (v. s t o f f e n, e l e m e n t e n) combine; *zich ~ om...* pledge oneself to...; *hij had zich verbonden om...* he was under an engagement to...; *zich ~ tot iets* bind oneself (commit oneself, undertake, pledge oneself) to do it; *zich tot niets ~* not commit oneself to anything; zie ook: *verbonden*; **–ding** (-en) *v* 1 (g e m e e n - s c h a p) communication; 2 connection [of two points]; junction [of railways]; union [of persons]; ☏ dressing, bandaging [of a wound]; *deze scheikundige ~* 1 (a b - s t r a c t) this combination; 2 (c o n c r e e t) this compound; *de ~ tot stand brengen (verbreken)* ☏ make (break) the connection; *i n ~ staan met...* be in communication with..., have connection with...; *zich in ~ stellen met...* communicate with [the police &], get into touch with...; *kunt u mij in ~ stellen met...?* can you put me in communication with...?; *in ~ treden met...* zie: *zich in ~ stellen met...*; *z o n d e r ~ $* without engagement; **ver'bindings- dienst** (-en) *m* ✕ Signals; **–lijn** (-en), **–linie** (-s) *v* line of communication; **–officier** (-en) *m* ✕ 1 liaison officer; 2 (t e c h n i s c h) Signals officer; **–spoor** (-sporen) *o* junction railway; **–stuk** (-ken) *o* connecting piece, link, adapter, adaptor; **–teken** (-s) *o* hyphen; **–troepen** *mv* ✕ (Corps of) Signals; **–weg** (-wegen) *m* connecting road; zie ook: *verbindingslijn*; **–woord** (-en) *o gram* copulative; **ver'bintenis** (-sen) *v* engagement, undertaking; alliance [ook = marriage], bond; contract; *bestaande ~sen* existing commitments; *een ~ aangaan* 1 enter into an engagement; 2 enter into an alliance

ver'bitterd 1 embittered, exasperated; 2 fierce, furious [battle]; *~ o p...* embittered against...; *~ o v e r...* exasperated at...; **–heid** *v* bitterness, embitterment, exasperation; **ver'bitteren** (verbitterde, h. verbitterd) *vt* embitter, exasperate; **–ring** *v* = *verbitterdheid*

ver'bleken (verbleekte, is verbleekt) *vi* 1 (v a n p e r s o n e n) grow (turn) pale; 2 (v a n p e r s o n e n & k l e u r e n) pale[2]; 3 (v a n k l e u r e n) fade; *doen ~ pale*[2]

ver'blijd = *verheugd*; **ver'blijden** (verblijdde, h. verblijd) **I** *vt* rejoice, gladden; **II** *vr zich ~* (*over*) rejoice (at); **–d** gladdening, joyful, cheerful

ver'blijf (-blijven) *o* 1 (p l a a t s) abode, resi-

dence; 2 (r u i m t e o m i n t e v e r b l ij - v e n) [crew's, emigrants'] quarters; 3 (h e t v e r b l ij v e n) residence, stay, sojourn; *~ houden* reside; **–kosten** *mv* hotel expenses, lodging expenses; **–plaats** (-en) *v* (place of) abode; *zijn tegenwoordige ~ is onbekend* his present whereabouts are unknown; **–sver- gunning** (-en) *v* residence permit; **ver'blijven**[1] *vi* stay, remain; *hiermee verblijf ik...* I remain yours truly...

verblikken[1] *vi zonder te ~* without batting an eyelid

ver'blind blinded[2], dazzled[2]; **ver'blinden** (verblindde, h. verblind) *vt* blind[2], dazzle[2]; *~ voor...* blind to...; **ver'blindheid** *v* blindness, infatuation; **ver'blinding** *v* 1 blinding, dazzle; 2 = *verblindheid*

ver'bloeden (verbloedde, is verbloed) *vi* bleed to death; **–ding** (-en) *v* bleeding to death

ver'bloemd disguised, veiled; **ver'bloemen** (verbloemde, h. verbloemd) *vt* disguise [the fact that...]; palliate, veil, gloze over [unpleasant facts]; **–ming** (-en) *v* disguise, palliation

ver'bluffen[1] *vt* put out of countenance, dumbfound, baffle, bewilder; *~d* startling; **ver'bluft** put out of countenance, dumbfounded

ver'bod (-boden) *o* prohibition, interdiction; ban [on a book &]; *een ~ uitvaardigen* issue a prohibition; **ver'boden** forbidden; zie ook: *verbieden*; **ver'bodsbepaling** (-en) *v* prohibitive regulation; **–bord** (-en) *o* prohibition sign

ver'bolgen angry, incensed, wrathful; **–heid** (-heden) *v* anger, wrath

ver'bond (-en) *o* alliance; league; union; (v e r d r a g) pact; covenant; *drievoudig ~* triple alliance; *het Nieuwe (Oude) ~* the New (Old) Testament; **ver'bonden** allied; *de ~ mogendheden* the allied powers; zie ook *verbinden*

ver'borgen concealed, hidden [things, treasure &]; obscure [view, corner]; secret [sin, place, influence, life]; occult [qualities]; *in het ~(e)* in secret, secretly; zie ook: *verbergen*; **–heid** (-heden) *v* secrecy; *de verborgenheden van Parijs* the mysteries of Paris

ver'bouw *m* = *verbouwing*; **ver'bouwen**[1] *vt* 1 △ rebuild [a house], convert [a bank building into...]; 2 (t e l e n) cultivate, raise, grow [potatoes]

verbouwe'reerd perplexed, dumbfounded; **–heid** *v* perplexity

ver'bouwing (-en) *v* 1 △ rebuilding [of a house]; structural alterations; 2 (t e e l t) cultivation, culture, growing

---

[1] V.T. en V.D. van dit werkwoord volgens het model: **ver'**achten, V.T. **ver'**achtte, V.D. **ver'**acht (**ge-** valt dus weg in het V.D.). Zie voor de vormen onder het grondwoord, in dit voorbeeld: *achten*. Bij sterke en onregelmatige werkwoorden wordt u verwezen naar de lijst achterin.

ver′brandbaar burnable, combustible;
ver′branden I (verbrandde, h. verbrand) *vt* 1
burn [papers &]; burn to death [martyrs]; 2
(v e r a s s e n) cremate [a body], incinerate; *zijn
door de zon verbrand gezicht* his sunburnt (tanned)
face; **II** (verbrandde, is verbrand) *vi* 1 be burnt
(to death); 2 (d o o r d e z o n) get sunburnt,
tan; **–ding** *v* 1 burning, combustion; 2 (v a n
l ij k e n) cremation; **ver′brandingsmotor** (-s
en -toren) *m* internal combustion engine;
–proces (-sen) *o* process of combustion;
–produkt (-en) *o* product of combustion
ver′brassen[1] *vt* squander
ver′breden (verbreedde, h. verbreed) **I** *vt*
widen, broaden; **II** *vr zich* ~ widen, broaden
(out); **–ding** *v* widening, broadening
ver′breiden (verbreidde, h. verbreid) **I** *vt*
spread [malicious reports]; propagate [a
doctrine]; **II** *vr zich* ~ spread [of rumours &];
–ding *v* spread(ing), propagation
ver′breken[1] *vt* break [a contract, a promise &];
break off [an engagement]; sever [diplomatic
relations]; cut [communications]; burst [one's
chains]; violate [vows]; **–king** *v* breaking;
severance; violation
ver′brijzelen (verbrijzelde, h. verbrijzeld) *vt*
break (smash) to pieces, smash, shatter[2]; **–ling**
v smashing, shattering[2]
ver′broddelen[1] *vt* bungle, spoil
ver′broederen (verbroederde, h. verbroederd)
zich ~ fraternize; **–ring** *v* fraternization
ver′brokkelen[1] *vi* & *vt* crumble
ver′bruid *aj* deuced, wretched; *wel* ~ *!* the
deuce!; **ver′bruien** (verbruide, h. verbruid) *vt
het bij iem.* ~ incur sbd.'s displeasure; *zie ook:
vertikken*
ver′bruik *o* 1 consumption [of foodstuffs,
petrol &]; expenditure [of energy, time]; 2
(v e r s p i l l i n g) wastage, waste; **ver′bruiken**
(verbruikte, h. verbruikt) *vt* consume [food,
time], use up [coal, wood &; one's strength],
spend [money, time &]; **–er** (-s) *m* consumer;
ver′bruiksartikel (-en en -s) *o* article of
consumption; **–belasting** (-en) *v* consumer
tax, consumption tax; **–goederen** *mv*
consumer goods, consumption goods
ver′buigbaar *gram* declinable; **ver′buigen**[1] *vt* 1
bend (out of shape); ✗ buckle; 2 *gram* decline;
–ging (-en) *v gram* declension
ver′burgerlijken (verburgerlijkte, is verburger-
lijkt) *vi* become (turn) bourgeois
ver′chroomd chromium-plated
ver′dacht I *aj* suspected [persons]; suspicious

[circumstances]; (a l l é é n p r e d i k a t i e f)
suspect; ~ *e personen* suspicious characters;
suspected persons, suspects; *iem.* ~ *maken*
make sbd. suspected; *er* ~ *uitzien* have a
suspicious look; *er* ~ *uitziend* suspicious-
looking; *dat komt me* ~ *voor* I think it suspicious; *op iets* ~ *zijn* be prepared for it; *eer ik
erop* ~ *was* before I was prepared for it, before
I knew where I was; *hij wordt* ~ *van...* he is
suspected of...; **II** *sb de* ~*e* 1 the suspected
party, the person suspected; 2 ⚖ the accused;
the prisoner; *één* ~*e* one suspect [arrested]; ~*en*
suspected persons, suspects; **III** *ad* suspiciously; **–making** (-en) *v* insinuation
ver′dagen[1] *vt* adjourn, (v. p a r l e m e n t s-
z i t t i n g) prorogue; **–ging** (-en) *v* adjournment, (v. p a r l e m e n t s z i t t i n g) prorota-
tion
ver′dampen (verdampte, *trs* h., *intr* is
verdampt) *vi* & *vt* evaporate, vaporize; **–er** (-s)
m evaporator; **ver′damping** *v* evaporation,
vaporization
ver′dedigbaar defensible; **–heid** *v* defensibil-
ity; **ver′dedigen** (verdedigde, h. verdedigd) **I**
vt defend [a town]; stand up for [one's rights];
wie zal u ~? ⚖ who will defend you?; *een* ~*de
houding aannemen* stand (act) on the defensive;
een ~*d verbond* a defensive alliance; **II** *vr zich* ~
defend oneself; **–er** (-s) *m* 1 defender [of
liberty &]; 2 ⚖ defending counsel, counsel for
the defendant (for the defence); **ver′dediging**
(-en) *v* defence′; *ter* ~ *van* in defence of;
ver′dedigingslinie (-s) *v* ✗ line of defence,
defence line; **–middel** (-en) *o* means of
defence; **–oorlog** (-logen) *m* war of defence;
–wapen (-s) *o* defensive weapon; **–werken**
mv ✗ defences, defensive works
ver′deeld divided; **–heid** *v* dissension, discord
[between...], division, disunity; **ver′deel-
sleutel** (-s) *m* distribution (distributive) code
verdee′moedigen[1] *vt* humble, humiliate;
–ging *v* humbling, humiliation
ver′dek (-ken) *o* ⚓ deck
ver′dekt ✗ under cover; ~ *opgesteld zijn* ✗ be
under cover
ver′delen[1] **I** *vt* divide, share out, distribute; **II**
va divide [and rule]; ~ *in* divide into [...parts];
~ *o n d e r* divide (distribute) among; ~ *o v e r*
spread over [a period of...]; **III** *vr zich* ~
divide; **–er** (-s) *m* distributor
ver′delgen[1] *vt* destroy, exterminate;
ver′delging *v* destruction, extermination;
–soorlog (-logen) *m* war of extermination

---

[1] V.T. en V.D. van dit werkwoord volgens het model: **ver′achten**, V.T. **ver′achtte**, V.D. **ver′acht** (**ge-** valt dus weg
in het V.D.). Zie voor de vormen onder het grondwoord, in dit voorbeeld: *achten*. Bij sterke en onregelmatige
werkwoorden wordt u verwezen naar de lijst achterin.

ver'deling (-en) *v* division [of labour], distribution [of food], partition [of Palestine]

ver'denken[1] *vt* suspect; *iem. van iets* ~ suspect sbd. of sth.; zie ook: *verdacht*; **–king** (-en) *v* suspicion; *een aantal personen op wie de* ~ *rustte* to whom suspicion pointed; *de* ~ *viel op hem* suspicion fell on him; *b o v e n* ~ above suspicion; *i n* ~ *brengen* cast suspicion on; *in* ~ *komen* incur suspicion; *in* ~ *staan* be under suspicion, be suspected; *o n d e r* ~ *van...* on suspicion of...

'verder I *aj* 1 (m e e r v e r w ij d e r d) farther, further; 2 (b ij k o m e n d, l a t e r) further; **II** *o het* ~*e* the rest; **III** *ad* farther, further; ~ *op* further on; ~ *gaan* 1 go farther; 2 proceed; 3 go on; *hij schrijft* ~*...* he goes on to write...; *we zouden al veel* ~ *zijn als...* we should be much further[2] if...

ver'derf *o* ruin, destruction, undoing, perdition; *in zijn* ~ *lopen* go to meet one's doom; *in het* ~ *storten* bring ruin upon; *ten verderve voeren* lead to perdition; **ver'derfelijk** pernicious, baneful, noxious, ruinous; **–heid** *v* perniciousness

verder'op further on

ver'derven* *vt* ruin, pervert, corrupt; **–er** (-s) *m* perverter, corrupter

ver'dicht 1 assumed [names]; fictitious [names &]; 2 condensed [vapour]; **ver'dichten**[1] **I** *vt* 1 condense [steam]; || 2 invent [a name, a story]; **II** *vr zich* ~ condense; **–ting** (-en) *v* 1 (v a n g a s s e n) condensation || 2 (v e r z i n n e n) invention, fiction; **ver'dichtsel** (-s en -en) *o* fabrication, fable, fiction, story, figment, invention

ver'dienen[1] *vt* earn [money, one's bread]; deserve [praise &]; merit [a reward, punishment]; *hoeveel verdien je?* how much do you earn?; *veel geld* ~ make heaps of money; *een vermogen* ~ make a fortune; *er wat bij* ~ make some money on the side; *zij* ~ *niet beter* they don't deserve any better; *het verdient de voorkeur* it is preferable; *dat heb ik niet aan u verdiend* that I have not deserved at your hands; *dat is zijn verdiende loon* that serves him right, he richly deserves that; *een verdiende overwinning* a deserved victory; *er is niets aan (mee) te* ~ there is no money in it; *daar zul je niet veel aan (op)* ~ you will not make much out of it; *daar verdient hij goed aan* he makes a good profit on that; **ver'dienste** (-n) *v* 1 (l o o n) earnings, wages; 2 (w i n s t) profit, gain; 3 (v e r d i e n s t e- l ij k h e i d) merit, desert; *n a a r* ~ according to merit, [punish] condignly; *zich iets t o t een* ~

(aan)rekenen take merit to oneself for sth.; *een man v a n* ~ a man of merit; **ver'dienstelijk** deserving, meritorious; creditable [attempt], useful [contribution]; *hij heeft zich jegens zijn land* ~ *gemaakt* he has deserved well of his country; **–heid** *v* deservingness, meritoriousness, merit

ver'diepen (verdiepte, h. verdiept **I** *vt* deepen[2]; **II** *vr zich* ~ *in* lose oneself in; *verdiept in gedachten* deep (absorbed) in thought, in a brown study; *zich in allerlei gissingen* ~ lose oneself in conjectures [as to...]; *in zijn krant verdiept* engrossed in his newspaper; **–ping** (-en) *v* 1 deepening[2]; 2 storey, story, floor; *eerste &* ~ first floor, second stor(e)y; *op de eerste &* ~ on (in) the first floor; *op de bovenste* ~ on the top floor; **ver'dieping(s)huis** (-huizen) *o* multi-storey house

ver'dierf (verdierven) V.T. v. *verderven*

ver'dierlijken I (verdierlijkte, h. verdierlijkt) *vt* brutalize; **II** (verdierlijkte, is verdierlijkt) *vi* become a brute; **–king** *v* brutalization; **ver'dierlijkt** brutalized, brutish

ver'dierven V.T. meerv. v. *verderven*

ver'dietsen (verdietste, h. verdietst) *vt* = *verhollandsen*

ver'dikken (verdikte, *vt* h., *vi* is verdikt) *vt & vi* thicken; **–king** (-en) *v* thickening

verdiscon'teerbaar $ negotiable; **verdiscon'teren**[1] *vt* $ negotiate [bills]; **–ring** *v* $ negotiation

ver'dobbelen[1] *vt* dice away, gamble away

ver'doeken (verdoekte, h. verdoekt) *vt* re- canvas for [a painting]

ver'doemd = *verdomd*; **ver'doemelijk** damnable; **ver'doemeling** (-en) *m* reprobate; **ver'doemen**[1] *vt* damn; **ver'doemenis** *v* damnation; **verdoemens'waard(ig)** damnable; **ver'doeming** *v* damnation

ver'doen[1] I *vt* dissipate, squander, waste; **II** *vr zich* ~ make away with oneself

ver'doezelen[1] *vt* blur, obscure [a fact], disguise [the truth]

ver'dokteren[1] *vt* pay out in doctor's fees

ver'dolen (verdoolde, is verdoold) *vi* lose one's way, go astray

ver'domboekje *o bij iem. in het* ~ *staan* be in sbd.'s bad (black) books; **ver'domd I** *aj* damned; **P** damn; *die* ~*e...!; II ad < damn; ver'domhoekje o hij zit in het ~ he cannot do any good; ver'domme! P goddamn!, goddamned!; –lijk = verdoemelijk; 1 ver'dommen (verdomde, h. verdomd) vt (d o m m a k e n) dull the mind(s) of, render*

---

[1] V.T. en V.D. van dit werkwoord volgens het model: **ver'**achten, V.T. **ver'**achtte, V.D. **ver'**acht (**ge-** valt dus weg in het V.D.). Zie voor de vormen onder het grondwoord, in dit voorbeeld: *achten*. Bij sterke en onregelmatige werkwoorden wordt u verwezen naar de lijst achterin.

stupid; **2 ver'dommen** (ve'rdomde, h. verdomd) *vt* = *vertikken*; **ver'dommenis** = *verdoemenis*

verdonkere'manen (verdonkeremaande, h. verdonkeremaand) *vt* spirit away, embezzle [money]; purloin [letters]

ver'donkeren (verdonkerde, *vt* h., *vi* is verdonkerd) *vt* & *vi* darken[2]; **–ring** (-en) *v* darkening, obscuration

ver'doofd benumbed, numb; torpid; (d o o r s l a g) stunned

ver'doold strayed, stray, wandering, having gone astray[2]

ver'dord withered; **–heid** *v* withered state; **ver'dorren** (verdorde, is verdord) *vi* wither; **–ring** *v* withering

1 ver'dorven depraved, corrupt, wicked, perverse; **2 ver'dorven** V.D. van *verderven*; **–heid** (-heden) *v* depravity, depravation, corruption, perverseness, perversity

ver'doven[1] *vt* 1 deafen, make deaf; 2 (g e l u i d) deafen, deaden, dull [sound]; 3 (l e d e m a t e n, g e v o e l) benumb [with cold], numb; 4 (p e r s o n e n) stupefy, stun; 5 (p ij n) *Ŧ* anaesthetize; **–d** 1 deafening; 2 stupefying; *Ŧ* anaesthetic; ~ *middel* *Ŧ* anaesthetic, narcotic, (i n z. a l s g e n o t m i d d e l) drug; **ver'doving** (-en) *v* stupefaction, stupor, torpor; numbness; *Ŧ* anaesthesia; **–smiddel** (-en) *o* = *verdovend middel*

ver'draaglijk bearable, endurable, tolerable; **ver'draagzaam** tolerant, forbearing; **–heid** *v* tolerance, forbearance, toleration

ver'draaid I *aj* distorted, disfigured, deformed [features]; *met een ~e hand geschreven* written in a disguised hand; **II** *ad* < damned; ~ *knap* jolly clever; *wel ~!* dash it!, damn!; **ver'draaien**[1] *vt* spoil [a lock]; distort[2], contort[2], twist[2] [features, facts, motives, statements, the truth &]; *fig* pervert [words, facts, a law]; *de ogen ~* roll one's eyes; *iems. woorden ~* ook: twist sbd.'s words; *ik verdraai het om...* I refuse to..., I just won't...; zie ook: *verdraaid*; **–iing** (-en) *v* distortion, contortion, twist, perversion [of fact]

ver'drag (-dragen) *o* treaty, pact; *een ~ aangaan (sluiten)* conclude (make, enter into) a treaty **ver'dragen**[1] *vt* 1 (d u l d e n) suffer, bear, endure, stand; 2 (w e g d r a g e n) remove; *ik kan geen bier ~* beer does not agree with me; *men moet elkander leren ~* you must try to put up with each other; *zo iets kan ik niet ~* I can't stand it; *ik heb heel wat van hem te ~* I have to

suffer (to put up with) a good deal at his hands **'verdragend** *♩* carrying; *⚔* long-range [guns] **ver'dragshaven** (-s) *v* treaty port **verdrie'dubbelen** (verdriedubbelde, h. verdriedubbeld) *vt* treble, triple

ver'driet *o* grief, sorrow; ~ *aandoen* cause sorrow, give pain; ~ *hebben* grieve, sorrow; **ver'drietelijk** vexatious, irksome; **–heid** (-heden) *v* vexatiousness, irksomeness, vexation; *verdrietelijkheden* vexations; **ver'drieten*** *vt* vex, grieve; *het verdriet mij dat te horen* I'm grieved to hear this; **ver'drietig** sad, sorrowful

verdrie'voudigen (verdrievoudigde, h. verdrievoudigd) *vt* treble, triple

ver'drijven[1] *vt* drive away, drive out, chase away; dissipate, dispel [clouds, fears, suspicion]; oust, expel [from a place]; dislodge [the enemy from his position]; pass (while) away [the time]; **–ving** *v* expulsion, ousting

ver'dringen[1] **I** *vt* push away, crowd out[2], *fig* oust, supplant, supersede, cut out; *ps* repress [desires, impulses]; *elkaar ~* (d r i n g e n) jostle (each other); ~ *van de markt* oust from the market; **II** *vt zich ~* crowd (round *om*); **–ging** *v* ousting, supplanting [of a rival]; *ps* repression [of desires, impulses]

ver'drinken I (verdronk, h. verdronken) *vt* 1 drown [a young animal]; 2 spend on drink [one's money], drink [one's wages], drink away [one's fortune]; 3 drink down [one's sorrow], drown [one's sorrow in drink]; 4 inundate [a field]; **II** (verdronk, is verdronken) *vi be* drowned, drown; **III** *vr zich ~* drown oneself; **–king** (-en) *v* drowning; *dood door ~* death from drowning

ver'drogen[1] *vi* dry up; wither [of plants &] **ver'dromen**[1] *vt* dream away

ver'dronken 1 drowned [person]; 2 submerged [fields]

ver'droot (verdroten) V.T. v. *verdrieten*

ver'droten V.T. meerv. en V.D. v. *verdrieten*

ver'drukken[1] *vt* oppress; **–er** (-s) *m* oppressor; **ver'drukking** (-en) *v* oppression; *in de ~ komen* zie *gedrang*; *tegen de ~ in groeien* prosper in spite of opposition

ver'dubbelen (verdubbelde, h. verdubbeld) **I** *vt* double [a letter &]; *fig* redouble [one's efforts]; *zijn schreden ~* quicken one's pace; **II** *vr zich ~* double; **–ling** (-en) *v* 1 doubling, duplication; *fig* redoubling; 2 *gram* reduplication

ver'duidelijken (verduidelijkte, h. verduidelijkt) *vt* elucidate, explain; **–king** (-en) *v*

---

[1] V.T. en V.D. van dit werkwoord volgens het model: **ver'achten**, V.T. **ver'achtte**, V.D. **ver'acht** (**ge-** valt dus weg n het V.D.). Zie voor de vormen onder het grondwoord, in dit voorbeeld: *achten*. Bij sterke en onregelmatige verkwoorden wordt u verwezen naar de lijst achterin.

elucidation, explanation

ver'duisteren I (verduisterde, h. verduisterd) *vt* 1 (d o n k e r m a k e n) darken[2], obscure[2]; cloud[2] [the sky, the mind, eyes with tears]; ★ eclipse [the sun, the moon]; (t e g e n l u c h t- a a n v a l) black out; 2 (o n t v r e e m d e n) embezzle [money], misappropriate [funds]; **II** (verduisterde, is verduisterd) *vi* darken, grow dark; **–ring** (-en) *v* 1 obscuration[2]; ★ eclipse [of sun and moon]; (t e g e n l u c h t a a n v a l) black-out; 2 embezzlement [of money], misappropriation [of funds]

ver'duitsen (verduitste, h. verduitst) *vt* 1 Germanize; 2 translate into German

ver'duiveld = *verdomd*

verduizend'voudigen (verduizendvoudigde, h. verduizendvoudigd) *vt* multiply by a thousand

ver'dunnen[1] *vt* 1 thin; 2 (v l o e i s t o f) dilute; 3 (l u c h t) rarefy; **–ning** (-en) *v* 1 thinning; 2 dilution; 3 rarefaction

ver'duren[1] *vt* bear, endure; *het hard te ~ hebben* zie *verantwoorden*; *heel wat te ~ hebben* zie *verdragen*

ver'duurzamen (verduurzaamde, h. verduurzaamd) *vt* preserve; *verduurzaamde levensmiddelen* tinned food, canned food; **–ming** *v* preservation

ver'duiveld = *verdomd*

ver'duwen[1] *vt* push away; *fig* digest [foods]; swallow [an insult]

ver'dwaald lost [child, traveller, sheep], stray [bullet]; *~ raken* lose one's way; *~ zijn* have lost one's way

ver'dwaasd foolish; **–heid** *v* folly

ver'dwalen (verdwaalde, is verdwaald) *vi* lose one's way, go astray?

ver'dwazen (verdwaasde, h. verdwaasd) *vt* make foolish, misguide; **–zing** *v* foolishness

ver'dween (verdwenen) V.T. v. *verdwijnen*

ver'dwenen V.T. meerv. en V.D. v. *verdwijnen*

ver'dwijnen* *vi* disappear, vanish [suddenly or gradually]; fade away; *verdwijn (uit mijn ogen)!* out of my sight!, be off!; *deze regering (minister &) moet ~* must go; **–ning** *v* disappearance, vanishing; **ver'dwijnpunt** (-en) *o* vanishing point

ver'edelen (veredelde, h. veredeld) *vt* improve [fruit], grade (up) [cattle]; *fig* ennoble, elevate [the feelings], refine [manners, morals, the taste]; **–ling** *v* improvement; up-grading; *fig* ennoblement, elevation [of the feelings], refinement

ver'eelt callous[2], horny [hands]; **ver'eelten I** (vereeltte, h. vereelt) *vt* make callous, make horny; **II** (vereeltte, is vereelt) *vi* become callous, become horny; **ver'eeltheid, ver'eelting** *v* callosity

vereen'voudigen (vereenvoudigde, h. vereenvoudigd) *vt* simplify; × reduce [a fraction]; **–ging** (-en) *v* simplification; × reduction [of a fraction]

ver'eenzamen (vereenzaamde, is vereenzaamd) *vi* grow lonely; **–ming** *v* isolation

vereen'zelvigen (vereenzelvigde, h. vereenzelvigd) *vt* identify; **–ging** *v* identification

ver'eerder (-s) *m* worshipper, admirer, [her] adorer

ver'eeuwigen (vereeuwigde, h. vereeuwigd) *v* perpetuate, immortalize; **–ging** *v* perpetuation, immortalization

ver'effenen[1] *vt* balance, settle [an account]; square [a debt]; adjust, settle [a difference, a dispute]; **–ning** (-en) *v* settlement, adjustment; *ter ~ van* in settlement of

ver'eisen[1] *vt* require, demand; **ver'eist** required; **–e** (-n) *o & v* requirement, requisite; *...is een eerste ~* ...is a prerequisite

1 'veren (veerde, h. geveerd) *vi* be elastic, be springy, spring; *~d* elastic, springy, resilient; *~d zadel* spring-mounted saddle; *ze ~ niet* they have no spring in them

2 'veren *aj* feather; *~ bed* feather-bed

ver'enen (vereende, h. vereend) *vt* = *verenigen*; *met vereende krachten* with united efforts, unitedly

ver'engelsen I (verengelste, h. verengelst) *vt* Anglicize; **II** (verengelste, is verengelst) *vi* become Anglicized

ver'engen (verengde, h. verengd) *vt & vr* narrow

ver'enigbaar (*niet*) *~ met* (not) compatible (consistent, consonant) with...; **ver'enigd** united; *de V~e Naties* the United Nations [Organization]; *~ optreden* united action; *de V~e Staten* the United States; *~e vergadering* joint meeting; **ver'enigen** (verenigde, h. verenigd) **I** *vt* 1 unite, join [their efforts, two nations]; combine [data]; 2 (v e r z a m e l e n) collect; ● *hen i n de echt ~* join (unite) them in marriage, join A to B in marriage; *die belangen zijn niet m e t elkaar te ~* these interests are not consistent with each other; *voor zover het te ~ is met...* in so far as is consistent (compatible, reconcilable) with...; *~ t o t...* unite into...; **II** *vr zich ~* 1 unite; 2 (z i c h v e r z a m e l e n) assemble; ~ *met* join [also of rivers]; join hands (forces) with [sbd. in doing sth.]; *ik kan mij met die mening niet* ~ I cannot agree with (concur in) that opinion; *ik kan mij met het voorstel niet* ~ I cannot agree to the proposal; **–ging** (-en) *v* 1 (h a n d e l i n g o f r e s u l-t a a t) joining, junction, combination, union; 2 (g e n o o t s c h a p) union, society, association, club; *recht van* ~ *en vergadering* right of association and of assembly; **ver'enigingsleven** *o* corporate life; **–lokaal** (-kalen) *o* club-room; **–punt** (-en) *o* junction; rallying-point

ver'eren[1] *vt* honour, revere, worship, venerate; *iem. iets* ~ present sbd. with sth.; ~ *met* honour with; grace with [one's presence, a title &]; **–d** *in* ~*e bewoordingen* in flattering terms

ver'ergeren I (verergerde, is verergerd) *vi* grow worse, change for the worse, worsen, deteriorate; **II** (verergerde, h. verergerd) *vt* make worse, worsen, aggravate; **–ring** *v* worsening, growing worse, change for the worse, aggravation, deterioration

ver'ering (-en) *v* veneration, worship, reverence

ver'erven I (vererfde, h. vererfd) *vt* descend, pass (to); **II** (vererfde, is vererfd) *vi* be transmitted to

ver'etteren (veretterde, is veretterd) *vi* fester, suppurate; **–ring** (-en) *v* suppuration

vereuro'pesen I (vereuropeeste, h. vereuropeest) *vt* Europeanize; **II** (vereuropeeste, is vereuropeest) *vi* become Europeanized

ver'evenen (verevende, h. verevend) *vt* = *vereffenen*

verf (verven) *v* 1 paint; 2 (v. k u n s t-s c h i l d e r) colour, paint; 3 (v o o r s t o f f e n &) dye; **–doos** (-dozen) *v* box of colours, paintbox; **–handel** *m* 1 colour-trade; 2 (-s) colourman's business; **–handelaar** (-s) *m* colourman; **–hout** *o* dye-wood

ver'fijnen (verfijnde, h. verfijnd) *vt* refine; **–ning** (-en) *v* refinement

ver'filmen[1] *vt* film; **–ming** (-en) *v* 1 (h a n d e-l i n g) filming; 2 (r e s u l t a a t) film version, screen version

'verfkuip (-en) *v* dyeing-tub; **–kwast** (-en) *m* paintbrush; **–laag** (-lagen) *v* coat of paint

ver'flauwen (verflauwde, is verflauwd) *vi* 1 (v. k l e u r e n &) fade; 2 (v. w i n d) abate; 3 (v. ij v e r &) flag, slacken; 4 **$** flag; **–wing** *v* fading; abatement; flagging

ver'flensen (verflenste, is verflenst) *vi* fade, wither

'verflucht *v* smell of paint, painty smell

ver'foeien (verfoeide, h. verfoeid) *vt* detest, abhor, abominate; **–iing** *v* detestation, abomination; **ver'foeilijk** detestable, abominable; **–heid** (-heden) *v* detestableness, abominableness, abomination

ver'fomfaaien (verfomfaaide, h. verfomfaaid) *vt* crumple, rumple

'verfpot (-ten) *m* paint-pot

ver'fraaien (verfraaide, h. verfraaid) *vt* embellish, beautify; **–iing** (-en) *v* embellishment, beautifying

ver'fransen I (verfranste, h. verfranst) *vt* Frenchify; **II** (verfranste, is verfranst) *vi* become French

ver'frissen (verfriste, h. verfrist) **I** *vt* refresh; **II** *vr zich* ~ 1 refresh oneself; 2 (i e t s g e b r u i-k e n) take some refreshment; **–sing** (-en) *v* refreshment

'verfroller (-s) *m* paint roller

ver'frommelen[1] *vt* crumple (up), rumple, crush

'verfspuit (-en) *v* paint spray, spray gun; **–stoffen** *mv* dye-stuffs, dyes, colours; **–waren** *mv* oils and colours; **–winkel** (-s) *m* paint shop, colour shop

ver'gaan *vi* 1 (v. h e t a a r d s e) perish, pass away; decay; rot; 2 ⚓ founder, be wrecked, be lost [a vessel]; *het verging hun slecht* they fared badly; *het zal je er n a a r* ~ you will meet with your deserts; ~ *v a n afgunst* be consumed (eaten up) with envy; ~ *van kou* be perishing with cold; *vergane glorie* departed glory

'vergaand = *verregaand*

ver'gaarbak (-ken) *m* reservoir, receptacle

ver'gaderen (vergaderde, h. is vergaderd) *vi* meet, hold a meeting, assemble; **–ring** (-en) *v* assembly, meeting; *geachte* ~ *!* (ladies and) gentlemen!; ~ *met debat* discussion meeting; *een* ~ *bijeenroepen (houden)* call (hold) a meeting; *de* ~ *openen* open the meeting; *de* ~ *opheffen (sluiten)* close the meeting; *een* ~ *uitschrijven* convene a meeting; **ver'gaderplaats** (-en) *v* meeting-place, place of meeting; **–zaal** (-zalen) *v* meeting-room, meeting-hall

ver'gallen[1] *vt* break the gall-bladder of [a fish]; *iem. het leven* ~ embitter sbd.'s life; *iems. vreugde* ~ spoil (mar) sbd.'s pleasure

vergalop'peren[1] *zich* ~ commit oneself, put one's foot in it

ver'gankelijk perishable, transitory, transient, fleeting; **–heid** *v* perishableness, transitoriness, instability

---

[1] V.T. en V.D. van dit werkwoord volgens het model: **ver'**achten, V.T. **ver'**achtte, V.D. **ver'**acht (**ge-** valt dus weg in het V.D.). Zie voor de vormen onder het grondwoord, in dit voorbeeld: *achten*. Bij sterke en onregelmatige werkwoorden wordt u verwezen naar de lijst achterin.

ver'gapen[1] *zich* ~ *aan* gape at; *zich aan de schijn* ~ take the shadow for the substance

ver'garen[1] *vt* gather, collect, hoard

ver'gassen[1] 1 gasify [solids]; 2 gas [people]; **–er** (-s) *m* paraffin stove; primus; **ver'gassing** (-en) *v* 1 gasification [of solids]; 2 gassing [of people]

ver'gasten (vergastte, h. vergast) **I** *vt* treat (to *op*), regale (with *op*); **II** *vr zich* ~ *aan* feast upon, take delight in

ver'gat (vergaten) V.T. v. *vergeten*

ver'geeflijk pardonable, forgivable, excusable [fault]; venial [sin]; **–heid** *v* pardonableness &, veniality

ver'geefs I *aj* vain, useless, fruitless; **II** *ad* in vain, vainly, to no purpose

ver'geestelijken (vergeestelijkte, h. vergeestelijkt) *vt* spiritualize; **–king** *v* spiritualization

ver'geetachtig apt to forget, forgetful; **–heid** *v* aptness to forget, forgetfulness; **ver'geetal** (-len) *m* forgetful person; **–boek** *o het raakte in het* ~ it was forgotten, it fell into oblivion; **ver'geet-mij-niet** (-en) *v* ⚘ forget-me-not

ver'gefelijk(heid) = *vergeeflijk(heid)*

ver'gelden[1] *vt* repay, requite; *goed met kwaad* ~ return evil for good; *God vergelde het u!* God reward you for it!; **–er** (-s) *m* rewarder; avenger [of evil]; **ver'gelding** (-en) *v* requital, retribution; *de dag der* ~ the day of reckoning; *ter* ~ *van...* in return for...; **–smaatregel** (-en en -s) *m* retaliatory measure; reprisal

ver'gelen[1] *vi* yellow

verge'lijk (-en) *o* agreement, accommodation, compromise; *een* ~ *treffen, tot een* ~ *komen* come to an agreement; **–baar** comparable; **verge'lijken**[1] *vt* compare; ~ *b ij...* compare to, liken to; ~ *m e t* compare with; *u kunt u niet met hem* ~ you can't compare with him; *vergeleken met...* in comparison with..., as compared with...; **–d** comparative; ~ *examen* competitive examination; **verge'lijkenderwijs, –wijze** by comparison; **verge'lijking** (-en) *v* 1 comparison; 2 equation [in mathematics]; 3 simile [in stylistics]; ~ *van de eerste graad met een onbekende* simple equation with one unknown quantity; ~ *van de tweede (derde) graad* quadratic (cubic) equation; *de* ~ *doorstaan kunnen met...* bear (stand) comparison with...; *een* ~ *maken (trekken)* make a comparison, draw a parallel; ● *in* ~ *met...* in comparison with..., as compared with...; *dat is niets in* ~ *met wat ik heb gezien* that is nothing to what I have seen; *t e r* ~ for (purposes of) comparison; **–smateriaal** *o*

comparative material

verge'makkelijken (vergemakkelijkte, h. vergemakkelijkt) *vt* make easy (easier), facilitate

'vergen (vergde, h. gevergd) *vt* require, demand, ask; *te veel* ~ *van* ook: overtax [one's strength]

verge'noegd contented, satisfied; **–heid** *v* contentment, satisfaction; **verge'noegen** (vergenoegde, h. vergenoegd) **I** *vt* content, satisfy; **II** *vr zich* ~ *met te...* content oneself with ...ing

ver'getelheid *v* oblivion; *aan de* ~ *ontrukken* save (rescue) from oblivion; *aan de* ~ *prijsgeven* consign (relegate) to oblivion; *in* ~ *raken* fall (sink) into oblivion; **ver'geten* I** *vt* forget; *ik ben* ~ *hoe het moet* I forget (I've forgotten) how to do it; *...niet te* ~ not forgetting...; *ik ben zijn adres* ~ I forget his address; *ik heb de krant* ~ I have forgotten the newspaper; *hebt u niets* ~? haven't you forgotten something?; *vergeet het maar!* forget it!; *(het)* ~ *en vergeven* forget and forgive; **II** *vr zich* ~ forget oneself; **III** *aj* forgotten

1 ver'geven[1] *vt* 1 (w e g g e v e n) give away [a situation]; 2 (v e r g i f f e n i s g e v e n) forgive, pardon; 3 (v e r k e e r d g e v e n) misdeal [cards]; 4 (v e r g i f t i g e n) poison; *vergeef (het) mij!* forgive me!; *vergeef me dat ik u niet gezien heb* forgive me for not having seen you; *dat zal ik u nooit* ~ I'll never forgive you for it; *(alles)* ~ *en vergeten* forgive and forget; *wie heeft die betrekking te* ~? in whose gift is the place?

2 ver'geven *[het is er]* ~ *van de muizen* infested with mice

vergevensge'zind forgiving; **–heid** *v* forgivingness; **ver'geving** *v* 1 pardon, remission [of sins]; 2 collation [of a living]

'vergevorderd (far) advanced[2]

verge'wissen (vergewiste, h. vergewist) *zich* ~ *van* make sure of [sth.]; ascertain [the facts]

verge'zellen (vergezelde, h. vergezeld) *vt* accompany [equals]; attend [superiors]; *vergezeld gaan van* be attended with; *vergezeld doen gaan van* accompany with [a threat]

'vergezicht (-en) *o* view, prospect, perspective, vista

'vergezocht far-fetched

ver'giet (-en) *o* & *v* strainer, colander; **ver'gieten**[1] *vt* shed [blood, tears]

ver'gif *o* poison[2], venom [of animals]

ver'giffenis *v* pardon, forgiveness; remission [of sins]; *iem.* ~ *schenken* forgive sbd.; ~ *vragen*

---

[1] V.T. en V.D. van dit werkwoord volgens het model: **ver'**achten, V.T. **ver'**achtte, V.D. **ver'**acht (**ge-** valt dus weg in het V.D.). Zie voor de vormen onder het grondwoord, in dit voorbeeld: *achten*. Bij sterke en onregelmatige werkwoorden wordt u verwezen naar de lijst achterin.

beg sbd.'s pardon, ⊙ ask (sbd.'s) forgiveness

ver′gift (-en) = *vergif*; **–enleer** *v* toxicology; **ver′giftig** poisonous², venomous²; **ver′giftigen** (vergiftigde, h. vergiftigd) *vt* poison², envenom²; *ze wilden hem ~* they wanted to poison him; **ver′giftigheid** *v* poisonousness, venomousness; **ver′giftiging** (-en) *v* poisoning²

Vergili′aans Virgillian; **Ver′gilius** *m* Virgil; *van ~* Virgilian

ver′gissen (vergiste, h. vergist) in: *zich ~* mistake, be mistaken, be wrong; make a mistake; *vergis u niet!* make no mistake; *als ik me niet vergis* if I am not mistaken; *of ik zou me zeer moeten ~* unless I am greatly mistaken; *u vergist u als u...* you are under a mistake if...; *zich ~ in...* be mistaken in; *ik had mij in het huis vergist* I had mistaken the house; *u hebt u lelijk in hem vergist!* you have mistaken your man!; *~ is menselijk* we all make mistakes, to err is human; **–sing** (-en) *v* mistake, error; *bij ~* by mistake, in mistake; unintentionally

ver′glaassel *o* glaze, enamel; **ver′glazen** (verglaasde, h. verglaasd) *vt* 1 (v. b u i t e n) glaze, enamel; 2 (d o o r e n d o o r) vitrify; **–zing** *v* 1 glazing, enamelling; 2 vitrification

ver′goddelijken (vergoddelijkte, h. vergoddelijkt) *vt* deify; **–king** *v* deification; apotheosis [of Roman emperors]; **ver′goden** (vergoodde, h. vergood) *vt* 1 deify; 2 *fig* idolize; **–ding** *v* 1 deification; 2 *fig* idolization

ver′goeden (vergoedde, h. vergoed) *vt* make good [cost, damages, losses], compensate; reimburse [expenses]; pay [interest]; *iem. iets ~* indemnify sbd. for a loss (expenses); *dat vergoedt veel* that goes to make up for a lot; **–ding** (-en) *v* 1 compensation, indemnification; 2 (t e g e m o e t k o m i n g) allowance; 3 (l o o n) remuneration; 4 (b e l o n i n g) recompense, reward; *tegen een (kleine) ~* for a consideration

ver′goelijken (vergoelijkte, h. vergoelijkt) *vt* gloze over, smooth over [faults], palliate, extenuate [an offence], excuse [weakness], explain away [wrong done &]; **–king** (-en) *v* glozing over, palliation, extenuation, excuse

ver′gokken *vt* gamble away

ver′gooien¹ I *vt* throw away; *een kans ~* throw (chuck) away a chance; **II** *vr zich ~* throw oneself away (on *aan*)

ver′gramd angry, wrathful; **–heid** *v* anger, wrath; **ver′grammen** (vergramde, h. vergramd) *vt* make angry, kindle the wrath of

ver′grijp (-en) *o* transgression; offence [against decency and morals]; outrage [on virtue]; **ver′grijpen¹** *zich ~ aan* lay hands upon

ver′grijsd grown grey [in the service], grizzled; **ver′grijzen¹** *vi* grow (go, turn) grey

ver′groeien¹ *vi* 1 grow together; 2 grow out of shape; become crooked [of persons]; 3 disappear [of cicatrices]

ver′grootglas (-glazen) *o* magnifying-glass; **ver′groten** (vergrootte, h. vergroot) *vt* enlarge [a building, a portrait &]; increase [one's stock, their number]; add to [his wealth]; magnify [the size with a lens &]; **–ting** (-en) *v* enlargement; increase; magnifying

ver′groven (vergroofde, *vt* h., *vi* is vergroofd, vergrofd) *vt* & *vi* coarsen

ver′gruizen I *vt* (vergruisde, h. vergruisd) pulverize, pound; **II** *vi* (vergruisde, is vergruisd) crumble

ver′guizen (verguisde, h. verguisd) *vt* revile, abuse; **–zing** *v* revilement, abuse

ver′guld gilt; *~ op snee* gilt-edged; *er ~ mee zijn* feel very flattered (be highly pleased) with it; **ver′gulden** (verguldde, h. verguld) *vt* gild; zie ook: *pil*; **–er** (-s) *m* gilder; **ver′guldsel** (-s) *o* gilding, gilt

ver′gunnen¹ *vt* permit, allow; grant [privileges]; **ver′gunning** (-en) *v* 1 permission, allowance, leave; permit; 2 licence [for the sale of drinks]; 3 concession; *herberg m e t ~* licensed public house; *met ~ van...* by permission of...; *z o n d e r ~* 1 without permission; 2 without a licence, unlicensed; **–houder** (-s) *m* licensee; (v. h e r b e r g) licensed victualler; **–srecht** *o* licence

ver′haal (-halen) *o* 1 story, tale, narrative, account, recital, relation, narration; 2 ⅛ (legal) remedy, redress; *het korte ~* the short story; *een ~ doen* tell a story; *allerlei verhalen doen (opdissen) over...* pitch yarns about; *er is geen ~ op* there is no redress; *hij kwam weer op zijn ~* he collected himself, he picked himself up again; **–baar** ⅛ recoverable (from *op*); **–trant** *m* narrative style

ver′haasten¹ *vt* hasten, accelerate, quicken [one's steps &]; expedite [the process]; **–ting** *v* hastening, acceleration, expedition

ver′halen¹ *vt* 1 (v e r t e l l e n) tell, relate, narrate; 2 ⚓ (w e g t r e k k e n) shift [a ship]; 3 (v e r g o e d i n g v e r k r i j g e n) *men heeft hem bedrogen en nu wil hij het op mij ~* he wants to recoup the loss on me; *hij wil het op mij ~* he wants to take it out of me; *de schade ~ op een ander* recoup oneself out of another man's

---

¹ V.T. en V.D. van dit werkwoord volgens het model: **ver′**achten, V.T. **ver′**achtte, V.D. **ver′**acht (**ge-** valt dus weg in het V.D.). Zie voor de vormen onder het grondwoord, in dit voorbeeld: *achten*. Bij sterke en onregelmatige werkwoorden wordt u verwezen naar de lijst achterin.

pocket; **–d** narrative; **ver'haler** (-s) *m* relater, narrator, story-teller

ver'handelbaar negotiable; **–heid** *v* negotiability; **ver'handelen**[1] *vt* 1 deal in [goods]; negotiate [a bill]; 2 (b e s p r e k e n) discuss; **–ling** (-en) *v* treatise, essay, discourse, dissertation, paper [read to learned society]

ver'hangen[1] **I** *vt* rehang, hang otherwise; **II** *vr zich ~* hang oneself; **–ging** (-en) *v* hanging

ver'hapstukken (verhapstukte, h. verhapstukt) **F** *vt* discuss, deliberate

ver'hard hardened[2]; metalled [road]; *fig* (case-) hardened, indurated, obdurate, hard-hearted; **ver'harden I** (verhardde, h. verhard) *vt* harden[2], indurate[2]; *een weg ~* metal a road; **II** (verhardde, is verhard) *vi* become hard [mortar &]; harden[2], indurate[2]; **ver'hardheid** *v* hardness, obduracy; **ver'harding** (-en) *v* hardening[2]; metalling [of a road]; (v e r e e l t i n g) callosity

ver'haren (verhaarde, is verhaard) *vi* lose (shed) one's hair; (v. d i e r e n o o k:) moult

ver'haspelen[1] *vt* spoil, botch; mangle [a word, a quotation]

ver'heerlijken (verheerlijkte, h. verheerlijkt) *vt* glorify; **–king** *v* glorification

ver'heffen[1] **I** *vt* lift [one's head], raise [one's eyes, one's voice], lift up [the soul], elevate [the mind, a person above the mass]; exalt, extol [a person]; *een getal tot de 2de macht (in het kwadraat) ~* raise a number to the sècond power (square it); zie ook: *stem* &; **II** *vr zich ~* rise (above *boven*); *zich ~ op* [fig] pride oneself on, glory in; **–d** elevating, uplifting; **ver'heffing** (-en) *v* raising; elevation, exaltation; *~ in (tot) de adelstand* ennoblement, [in England] raising to the peerage; *met ~ van stem* raising his voice

ver'heimelijken (verheimelijkte, h. verheimelijkt) *vt* secrete [goods], zie verder: *verbergen* **I**

ver'helderen I (verhelderde, is verhelderd) *vi* brighten[2] [of sky, face, eyes &]; clear up [of weather]; **II** (verhelderde, h. verhelderd) *vt* clarify [liquids, a question]; brighten, light up, lighten [sbd.'s face]; *fig* enlighten [the mind]; **–ring** *v* clearing, clarification; brightening; *fig* enlightenment

ver'helen[1] *vt* conceal, hide, keep secret; *iets voor iem. ~* conceal (hide, keep back) sth. from sbd.; *hij verheelt 't niet* he makes no secret of it; *wij ~ het ons niet* we fully realize this; *wij kunnen ons niet ~, dat...* we cannot disguise from ourselves the fact that... (the difficulty & of...); **–ling** *v*

concealment

ver'helpen[1] *vt* remedy, redress, correct; **–ping** *v* remedy, redress, correction

ver'hemelte (-n en -s) *o* palate [of the mouth]; *het ~ ook:* the roof (of the mouth); *zacht ~* soft palate, velum

ver'heugd I *aj* glad, pleased; *~ over* glad of, pleased at; **II** *ad* gladly; **ver'heugen**[1] *vt* gladden, rejoice, delight; *dat verheugt mij* I am glad of that; *het verheugt ons te horen, dat...* we are glad to hear that...; **II** *vr zich ~* rejoice, be glad; *zich ~ i n* rejoice in; *zich in een goede gezondheid (mogen) ~* enjoy good health; *daar verheug ik mij (nu reeds) op* I am looking forward to it; *zich ~ o v e r iets* rejoice at sth., be rejoiced at sth.; **–d I** *aj* welcome [sign, example, announcement &]; *het is ~ te weten, dat...* it is gratifying to know that...; **II** *ad* gratifyingly [high numbers]; **ver'heugenis** (-sen) *v* joy

ver'heven I *aj* 1 *fig* elevated, exalted, lofty, sublime, august; 2 (v. b e e l d w e r k) raised, embossed, in relief; *~ zijn boven* be above; **II** *ad* loftily, sublimely; **–heid** (-heden) *v* elevation[2], *fig* loftiness, sublimity; *een kleine ~* a slight elevation (eminence, height)

ver'hevigen (verhevigde, h. verhevigd) *vt* intensify; **–ging** *v* intensification

ver'hinderen[1] *vt* prevent, hinder; *dat zal mij niet ~ om te...* that will not prevent me from ...ing; *dat zal hem misschien ~ te schrijven* this may prevent him from writing; *hij zal verhinderd zijn* he will have been prevented (from coming); *iem. ~ in de uitoefening van zijn beroep* obstruct sbd. in the execution of his duty; **–ring** (-en) *v* 1 ('t v e r h i n d e r e n) prevention; 2 (b e l e t s e l) hindrance, obstacle, impediment; *bij ~* in case of prevention

ver'hip F ~! bother!; **ver'hippen** *vt* & *vi* (verhipte, h. en is verhipt) **F** *het kan me niks ~* I don't care [a damn]; *hij verhipte het* he wouldn't do it; **ver'hipt F** *ad ~ vervelend* an awful nuisance; *~ koud* damned cold

ver'hit heated[2], overheated, flushed[2]; **ver'hitten** (verhitte, h. verhit) **I** *vt* heat[2] [iron, the blood]; *fig* heat, fire [the imagination]; **II** *vr zich ~* (over)heat oneself; **–ting** *v* heating[2]

ver'hoeden[1] *vt* prevent, avert; *dat verhoede God!* God forbid!; **–ding** *v* prevention

ver'hogen (verhoogde, h. verhoogd) **I** *vt* 1 heighten[2] [a wall &, the illusion]; raise[2] [a platform, a man, prices, salary &]; ♪ raise [a tone]; *fig* advance, put up [the charges]; enhance [their prestige]; increase, add to [the

---

[1] V.T. en V.D. van dit werkwoord volgens het model: **ver'**achten, V.T. **ver'**achtte, V.D. **ver'**acht (**ge-** valt dus weg in het V.D.). Zie voor de vormen onder het grondwoord, in dit voorbeeld: *achten*. Bij sterke en onregelmatige werkwoorden wordt verwezen naar de lijst achterin.

beauty of...]; 2 (b e v o r d e r e n) promote [in rank]; ⇨ move up to a higher form; ~ *met* raise (increase) by; **II** *vr zich* ~ exalt oneself; **ver′hoging** (-en) *v eig* 1 dais, (raised) platform; 2 elevation, eminence, height [of ground]; *fig* 1 rise, increase, advance [of salary, of prices]; 2 heightening², raising², enhancement; promotion [in rank]; ⇨ remove [of pupils]; *jaarlijkse* ~ 1 annual increment [of salary]; 2 ⇨ yearly promotion; *hij heeft wat* ~ he has a rise of temperature; **–steken** (-s) *o* ♪ sharp

ver′holen concealed, hidden, secret; **–heid** *v* concealment, secrecy

ver′hollandsen I (verhollandste, h. verhollandst) *vt* 1 Dutchify, make Dutch; 2 turn into Dutch; **II** (verhollandste, is verhollandst) *vi* become Dutch

verhonderd′voudigen (verhonderdvoudigde, h. verhonderdvoudigd) *vt* increase a hundredfold, centuple

ver′hongeren (verhongerde, is verhongerd) *vi* be starved to death, starve (to death), die of hunger; *doen* (*laten*) ~ starve (to death); **–ring** *v* starvation

ver′hoor (-horen) *o* hearing, examination [before the magistrate], interrogation; *wie zal het* ~ *afnemen?* who is going to examine?; *een* ~ *ondergaan* be under examination; *in* ~ *nemen* hear, interrogate; *in* ~ *zijn* be under examination; **ver′horen¹** *vt* hear, answer [a prayer]; hear [a lesson]; hear, examine [a witness]; **–ring** (-en) *v* hearing

ver′houden¹ *zij* ~ *zich als... en...* they are in the proportion of... to...; *2 verhoudt zich tot 4 als 3 tot 6* 2 is to 4 as 3 is to 6; **ver′houding** (-en) *v* 1 (t u s s e n g e t a l l e n) proportion; ratio; 2 (t u s s e n p e r s o n e n) relation(s); relationship [of master and servant, with God]; 3 (m i n n a r ij) (love-)affair; *een gespannen* ~ strained relations; ● *b u i t e n* ~ *tot...* out of proportion to...; *i n* ~ *tot* in proportion to; *in de juiste* ~ [see the story] in (the right) perspective; *in geen* ~ *staan tot...* be out of (all) proportion to..., be totally disproportionate to...; *n a a r* ~ proportionally, proportionately; comparatively, relatively; *naar* ~ *van hun...* in proportion to their; **–sgetal** (-len) *o* ratio

verho′vaardigen (verhovaardigde, h. verhovaardigd) *zich* ~ (*op*) pride oneself (on), be proud (of); **–ging** *v* pride

ver′huisboel *m* furniture in course of removal; **–dag** (-en) *m* moving-day; **–drukte** *v* worry

and trouble of (re)moving; **–kosten** *mv* expenses of (re)moving; **–wagen** (-s) *m* furniture van, pantechnicon (van); **ver′huizen I** (verhuisde, is verhuisd) *vi* remove, move (into another house), move house; **II** (verhuisde, h. verhuisd) *vt* remove; **–er** (-s) *m* (furniture) remover, removal contractor; **ver′huizing** (-en) *v* removal, move

ver′hullen¹ *vt* conceal

ver′huren¹ I *vt* let [apartments]; let out (on hire) [things]; hire (out) [motor-cars, bicycles]; **II** *vr zich* ~ go into service; **–ring** (-en) *v* letting (out), hiring (out); **ver′huur** *m* [car, dress] hire; zie verder: *verhuring*; **–der** (-s) *m* letter, lessor, landlord; hirer out [of bicycles]

verhypothe′keren [vərhi.-] (verhypothekeerde, h. verhypothekeerd) *vt* mortgage

verifica′teur (-s) *m* verifier; **verifi′catie** [-(t)si.] (-s) *v* verification; **–vergadering** (-en) *v* $ first meeting of creditors; **verifi′ëren** (verifieerde, h. geverifieerd) *vt* verify, check [figures, a reference &]; audit [accounts]

ver′ijdelen (verijdelde, h. verijdeld) *vt* frustrate, foil, baffle, baulk, defeat [attempts &]; upset [a scheme]; *dat verijdelde hun verwachtingen* that shattered their hopes; **–ling** *v* frustration

′vering (-en) *v* 1 (h e t v e r e n) spring action; 2 (d e v e r e n) springs

ver′innigen (verinnigde, is verinnigd) *vi* grow closer

ver′int(e)resten (verint(e)restte, h. verint(e)-rest) **I** *vt* put out at interest; **II** *vi* bear no interest

ver′jaard superannuated, statute-barred [debts]; prescriptive [rights]; **ver′jaardag** (-dagen) *m* anniversary [of a victory, marriage &]; birthday [of a person]; **ver′jaar(s)feest** (-en) *o* birthday party; **–geschenk** (-en) *o* birthday present; **–partij** (-en) *v* birthday party

ver′jagen¹ *vt* drive (chase, frighten, shoo) away [birds &]; expel [a person]; drive out [the enemy]; dispel [fear]; **–ging** *v* chasing away, expulsion

ver′jaren (verjaarde, h. en is verjaard) *vi* 1 celebrate one's birthday; 2 become superannuated, become statute-barred; *ik verjaar vandaag* it is my birthday to-day; **–ring** (-en) *v* 1 ⚖ superannuation; 2 = *verjaardag*; **ver′jaringsrecht** *o* statute of limitations; **–termijn** (-en) *m* term of limitation

ver′jongen I (verjongde, is verjongd) *vi* grow young again, rejuvenate; **II** (verjongde, h. verjongd) *vt* make young again, rejuvenate;

---

¹ V.T. en V.D. van dit werkwoord volgens het model: **ver′achten**, V.T. **ver′achtte**, V.D. **ver′acht** (**ge-** valt dus weg in het V.D.). Zie voor de vormen onder het grondwoord, in dit voorbeeld: *achten*. Bij sterke en onregelmatige werkwoorden wordt u verwezen naar de lijst achterin.

ver'jonging *v* rejuvenescense, rejuvenation; **–skuur** (-kuren) *v* rejuvenation cure

ver'kalken[1] *vi* & *vt* calcine, calcify; **–king** *v* calcination, calcification; ~ *van de bloedvaten* arteriosclerosis

ver'kankeren (verkankerde, is verkankerd) *vi* canker

ver'kapt disguised; veiled [threat]

ver'kassen (verkaste, is verkast) **F** *vi* shift, move (house)

ver'kavelen[1] *vt* lot (out), parcel out; **–ling** (-en) *v* lotting (out), parcelling out.

ver'kazen (verkaasde, is verkaasd) *vi* caseate, become caseous (cheesy)

ver'keer *o* 1 traffic; 2 (o m g a n g) intercourse; *geslachtelijk* ~ sexual intercourse; *gezellig* (*huiselijk*) ~ social (family) intercourse; *veilig* ~ road safety

ver'keerd I *aj* wrong, bad; *de* ~*e kant* the wrong side; zie ook: *been, kantoor, wereld* &; **II** *m de* ~*e voorhebben* mistake one's man; *dan heb je de* ~*e voor, mannetje!* then you have come to the wrong shop!; **III** *ad* wrong(ly), ill, amiss; *zijn kousen* ~ *aantrekken* put on one's stockings the wrong way; (*iets*) ~ *doen* do (sth.) wrong; *iets* ~ *uitleggen* misinterpret sth.; *iets* ~ *verstaan* misunderstand sth.; **–elijk** wrong(ly), mistakenly; **–heid** (-heden) *v* fault

ver'keersader (-s) *v* (traffic) artery, arterial road, thoroughfare; **–agent** (-en) *m* policeman on point-duty, pointsman, traffic policeman, **S** traffic cop; **–bord** (-en) *o* road sign, traffic sign; **–brigadiertje** (-s) *o* = *jeugdverkeersbrigadiertje*; **–brug** (-gen) *v* road-bridge; **–chaos** *m* traffic chaos; **verkeers'dichtheid** *v* traffic density; **ver'keersheuvel** (-s) *m* island, refuge; **–leider** (-s) *m* air-traffic controller; **–licht** (-en) *o* traffic light; **–middel(en)** *o* (*mv*) means of communication, means of transport; **–ongeval** (-len) *o* road accident; **–opstopping** (-en) *v* traffic congestion, traffic jam, traffic block, traffic tie-up; **–overtreding** (-en) *v* road offence, traffic offence; **–plein** (-en) *o* traffic circus, roundabout; **–politie** [-(t)si.] *v* traffic police; **–regel** (-s) *m* traffic rule; **–regeling** *v* traffic regulation; **–reglement** (-en) *o* highway code, traffic regulations; **–stroom** (-stromen) *m* traffic flow; **–teken** (-s) *o* traffic sign; **–toren** (-s) *m* ✈ control tower; **–tunnel** (-s) *m* road tunnel; underpass, subway; **–veiligheid** *v* road safety; **–vliegtuig** (-en) *o* ✈ airliner, passenger aircraft; **–voorschriften** *mv* traffic regulations; **–weg** (-wegen) *m* thoroughfare; (h a n d e l s w e g) trade route; **–wezen** *o* traffic; *minister van het* ~ minister of transport; **–zondaar** (-s) *m* road offender; **–zuil** (-en) *v* bollard

ver'kennen[1] *vt* reconnoitre; **–er** (-s) *m* scout; **ver'kenning** (-en) *v* reconnoitring, scouting; *een* ~ a reconnaissance; *op* ~ *uitgaan* go reconnoitring, make a reconnaissance; **ver'kenningspatrouille** [-tru.(l)jə] (-s) *v* reconnoitring patrol; **–tocht** (-en) *m* reconnoitring expedition; **–vliegtuig** (-en) *o* scoutingplane, scout; ~(*en*) ook: reconnaissance aircraft; **–vlucht** (-en) *v* reconnaissance flight; **–wagen** (-s) *m* ✕ scout car

ver'keren[1] *vi* (v e r a n d e r e n) change; *het kan* ~ (*zei Breeroo*) things may change; *a a n het hof* ~ move in court-circles; *vreugd kan i n droefheid* ~ joy may turn to sadness; *in twijfel* ~ be in doubt; ~ *m e t iem.* associate with sbd.; *hij verkeert met ons dienstmeisje* he keeps company with our servant; **–ring** *v* courtship; *hij heeft* ~ *met ons dienstmeisje* he keeps company with our servant; *zij heeft* ~ she is walking out with a fellow; *zij hebben* ~ they are walking out; *vaste* ~ *hebben* **F** go steady

ver'kerven[1] *vt* *het bij iem.* ~ incur sbd.'s displeasure

ver'ketteren[1] *vt* charge with heresy; *fig* decry, denounce

ver'kiesbaar eligible; *zich* ~ *stellen* accept to stand for an election (an office &), stand as a candidate; **–heid** *v* eligibility; **ver'kies(e)lijk** preferable (to *boven*); **ver'kiezen**[1] *vt* 1 choose; elect; return [a member of Parliament]; 2 (d e v o o r k e u r g e v e n) prefer; *wij* ~ *naar de schouwburg te gaan* 1 we choose to go to the theatre; 2 we prefer to go to the theatre; *hij verkoos niet te spreken* he did not choose to speak; *ik verkies niet dat je...* you must not...; *zoals u verkiest* just as you like, please yourself;
● ~ *b o v e n* prefer to; *iem.* ~ *t o t president* choose him for a president, elect him president; **–zing** (-en) *v* 1 (k e u s) choice; 2 (p o l i t i e k) election; *een* ~ *uitschrijven* order elections, go (appeal) to the country; *b ij* ~ for choice; for (by, in) preference; *n a a r* ~ at choice, at pleasure, at will; *u kunt naar* ~ .., *òf...* the choice lies with you whether... or...; *meen je dat naar eigen* ~ *te kunnen doen?* at your own sweet will?; *handel naar eigen* ~ use your own discretion; please yourself; *u i t eigen* ~ of one's own free will; **ver'kiezingsagent** (-en) *m* election(eering) agent, electioneer, *Am*

---

[1] V.T. en V.D. van dit werkwoord volgens het model: **ver'**achten, V.T. **ver'**achtte, V.D. **ver'**acht (**ge-** valt dus weg in het V.D.). Zie voor de vormen onder het grondwoord, in dit voorbeeld: *achten*. Bij sterke en onregelmatige werkwoorden wordt u verwezen naar de lijst achterin.

canvasser; **–belofte** (-n) *v* election promise; **–campagne** [-kɑmpɑɲə] (-s) *v* election(eering) campaign; **–dag** (-dagen) *m* election day, polling-day; **–leus** (-leuzen) *v* election cry, slogan; **–manifest** (-en) *o* election manifesto; **–program** (-s) *o* election programme; **–rede** (-s) *v* election speech; **–uitslag** (-slagen) *m* election result, election returns

ver′kijken[1] **I** *vt hij heeft zijn kans verkeken* he has lost his chance, **F** he missed the bus; **II** *vr zich* ~ (*op*) be mistaken, misjudge

ver′kikkerd ~ *op iets* keen on sth.; ~ *op een meisje* **F** gone on a girl

ver′killen I (verkilde, h. verkild) *vt* chill; **II** (verkilde, is verkild) *vi* chill, cool

ver′kitten[1] *vt* lute

ver′klaarbaar explicable, explainable; *om verklaarbare redenen* for obvious reasons; **ver′klaard** declared, avowed [enemy]

ver′klappen[1] **I** *vt* blab; *de boel* ~ give the game (the show) away; *iem.* ~ **S** peach on sbd.; **II** *vr zich* ~ let one's tongue run away with one, give oneself away; **–er** (-s) *m* telltale

ver′klaren[1] **I** *vt* 1 explain, elucidate, interpret [a text]; 2 (z e g g e n) declare [that..., sbd. to be a...], (o f f i c i e e l) certify; ⚥ depose, testify [that...]; 3 (a a n z e g g e n) declare [war]; *hoe kunt u het gebruik van dit woord hier* ~? can you account for the use of this word?; *het onder ede* ~ declare it upon oath; **II** *vr zich* ~ declare oneself; *verklaar u nader!* explain yourself; *zich* ~ *tegen* (*vóór*)... declare against (in favour of)...; **–d** explanatory [notes]; **ver′klaring** (-en) *v* 1 explanation; 2 declaration, statement; [doctor's] certificate; ⚥ deposition, evidence; *beëdigde* ~ sworn statement; (s c h r i f t e l ij k) affidavit

ver′kleden[1] **I** *vt* (v e r m o m m e n) disguise; *een kind* ~ (= a n d e r s k l e d e n) change a child's clothes; **II** *vr zich* ~ 1 change (one's clothes, [of woman] one's dress); 2 dress up, disguise oneself; **–ding** (-en) *v* 1 change of clothes; 2 (v e r m o m m i n g) disguise

ver′kleinbaar reducible; **ver′kleinen** (verkleinde, h. verkleind) *vt* make smaller, reduce [a design &], diminish [weight, pressure]; lessen [the number, the value &]; minimize [an incident]; belittle, disparage [merits]; *een breuk* ~ reduce a fraction; **ver′kleining** (-en) *v* reduction, diminution; disparagement, belittlement [of merits &]; reduction [of fractions]; **–suitgang** (-en) *m* diminutive

ending; **ver′kleinwoord** (-en) *o* diminutive

ver′kleumd benumbed, numb; **–heid** *v* numbness; **ver′kleumen** (verkleumde, is verkleumd) *vi* grow numb, be benumbed (with cold)

ver′kleuren (verkleurde, is verkleurd) *vi* lose (its) colour, discolour, fade; **–ring** (-en) *v* discoloration, fading

ver′klikken[1] *vt* 1 (i e t s) tell, disclose; 2 (i e m.) **S** tell on [sbd.], give [sbd.] away, peach on; **–er** (-s) *m*, **ver′klikster** (-s) *v* 1 (p e r s o o n) telltale; 2 ⚔ (i n s t r u m e n t) telltale [of an air-pump], indicator; *stille* ~ police spy

ver′klungelen[1] *vt* trifle, fritter away

ver′knallen[1] **F** *vt* bungle, botch, make a hash (mess, botch) of, **S** muck up

ver′kneukelen (verkneukelde, h. verkneukeld), **ver′kneuteren** (verkneuterde, h. verkneuterd) *zich* ~ chuckle, hug oneself (rub one's hands) with joy; *zich* ~ *in* revel in

ver′kniezen[1] *zich* ~ fret (mope) oneself to death

ver′knippen[1] *vt* 1 cut up; 2 spoil in cutting; *verknipt* [*fig*] mixed-up, ill-adjusted

ver′knocht attached, devoted (to *aan*); **–heid** *v* attachment, devotion

ver′knoeien[1] *vt* 1 spoil, bungle [some work]; 2 (s l e c h t b e s t e d e n) waste [food, paper &]; *de boel* ~ make a mess of it

ver′koelen I *vt* cool[2], refrigerate, chill; **II** *vi* cool[2]; **–ling** (-en) *v* cooling[2], *fig* chill [between two persons]

ver′koken (verkookte, is verkookt) *vi* boil away

ver′kolen I (verkoolde, h. verkoold) *vt* carbonize, char; *een verkoold lijk* a charred body; **II** (verkoolde, is verkoold) *vt* become carbonized, char [wood]; **–ling** *v* 1 carbonization; 2 charring

ver′kommeren (verkommerde, is verkommerd) *vi* pine, (s t e r k e r) starve, (v a n p l a n t e n) wither

ver′kond(ig)en (verkond(ig)de, h. verkond(igd)) *vt* proclaim [the name of the Lord]; preach [the Gospel]; enunciate [a theory]; **–er** (-s) *m* proclaimer; preacher; **ver′kondiging** (-en) *v* proclamation; preaching [of the Gospel]

′verkoop, ver′koop (-kopen) *m* sale; *ten* ~ *aanbieden* offer for sale; ~ *bij afslag* Dutch auction; ~ *bij opbod* sale by auction, auction-sale; **′verkoopafdeling** (-en) *v* sales department; **–akte** (-n en -s) *v* deed of sale; **–automaat** [-o.to.- of-ɔuto.-] (-maten) *m* vending

---

[1] V.T. en V.D. van dit werkwoord volgens het model: **ver′**achten, V.T. **ver′**achtte, V.D. **ver′**acht (**ge-** valt dus weg in het V.D.). Zie voor de vormen onder het grondwoord, in dit voorbeeld: *achten*. Bij sterke en onregelmatige werkwoorden wordt u verwezen naar de lijst achterin.

machine; ver'koopbaar sal(e)able, marketable, vendible; **–heid** *v* sal(e)ability, vendility; 'verkoopboek (-en) *o* sales-book; **–briefje** (-s) *o* sold note; **–campagne** [-kɑm-pɑɲə] (-s) *v* sales (selling) campaign, sales drive; **–dag** (-dagen) *m* day of sale; **–huis** (-huizen) *o* auction-room, sale-room; **–kunde** *v* salesmanship; **–leider** (-s) *m* sales manager, sales executive; **–lokaal** (-kalen) *o* auction-room, sale-room; **–prijs** (-prijzen) *m* selling price; **–punt** (-en) *o* $ outlet; **–rekening** (-en) *v* $ account sales; **–koopster** (-s) *v* saleswoman, sales-lady, shop-assistant; *eerste (tweede)* ~ first (second) saleswoman; 'verkoopwaarde *v* selling value, market value; ver'kopen[1] **I** *vt* sell [goods]; dispose of [a house, horses]; *grappen* ~ crack jokes; *leugens* ~ tell lies; *in het groot (klein)* ~ sell wholesale (by retail); *in het openbaar of onderhands* ~ sell by public auction or by private contract; **II** *vr zich* ~ sell oneself; **–er** (-s) *m* seller, vendor; $ salesman [of a firm]; (shop-)assistant

ver'koperen[1] *vt* copper [iron &]; sheathe (with copper) [a ship]

ver'koping (-en) *v* sale, auction, public sale; *op de* ~ *doen* put up for auction

⚒ ver'koren chosen, elect

ver'korten[1] *vt* shorten[2]; abridge[2] [a novel &]; abbreviate [a word]; *iem. in zijn rechten* ~ abridge sbd. of his rights; **–ting** (-en) *v* shortening[2]; abridg(e)ment[2]; abbreviation

ver'korven V.D. v. *verkerven*

ver'kouden having a cold, with a cold; *je zult* ~ *worden* you'll catch cold; *als... dan ben je* ~ [*fig*] you are in for it; ver'koudheid (-heden) *v* cold (in the head); *een* ~ *opdoen (oplopen)* catch (a) cold; *ik kan niet van mijn* ~ *afkomen* I cannot get rid of my cold

ver'krachten (verkrachtte, h. verkracht) *vt* violate [a law]; rape [a woman]; **–er** (-s) *m* rapist; ver'krachting (-en) *v* violation [of the law]; rape [of a woman]

ver'kreuk(el)en[1] *vt* rumple, crumple (up)

ver'krijgbaar obtainable, available, to be had; *niet meer* ~ sold out, out of stock, no longer to be had; ver'krijgen[1] *vt* obtain, acquire, gain, get, come by; *hij kon het niet van (over) zich* ~ he could not find it in his heart, he could not bring himself to; **–ging** *v ter* ~ *van* [in order] to acquire, to obtain; *verkregen rechten* vested rights

ver'kromming (-en) *v* ⚕ curvature [of the spine]

ver'kroppen[1] *vt* swallow[2] [one's anger]; *hij kan het niet* ~ it sticks in his throat; *verkropte gramschap* pent-up anger

ver'kruimelen[1] *vt* & *vi* crumble

ver'kwanselen (verkwanselde, h. verkwanseld) *vt* barter (bargain) away; fritter away [one's time, money]

ver'kwijnen (verkwijnde, is verkwijnd) *vi* pine away, languish

ver'kwikkelijk refreshing; comforting; ver'kwikken (verkwikte, h. verkwikt) *vt* refresh; comfort; **–king** (-en) *v* refreshment; comfort

ver'kwisten (verkwistte, h. verkwist) *vt* waste, dissipate, squander; *...*~ *aan* waste... on; **–d** wasteful, extravagant, prodigal; ~ *met* lavish of; ver'kwister (-s) *m* spendthrift, prodigal; ver'kwisting (-en) *v* waste, wastefulness, dissipation, prodigality

1 ver'laat (-laten) *o* lock, weir

2 ver'laat *aj* belated

ver'laden[1] *vt* ⚓ ship; **–ding** (-en) *v* ⚓ shipment

ver'lagen (verlaagde, h. verlaagd) **I** *vt* lower[2]; reduce [prices]; cut [prices, wages]; ♩ flatten [a note]; ⚐ put [a boy] in a lower form; *fig* debase, degrade; ~ *met* reduce (cut, lower) by; **II** *vr zich* ~ lower (degrade, debase) oneself; *ik wil me tot zo iets niet* ~ I refuse to stoop to such a thing; ver'laging (-en) *v* lowering[2]; reduction [of prices]; cut [in wages]; *fig* debasement, degradation; **–steken** (-s) *o* ♩ flat

ver'lak *o* lacquer, varnish; ver'lakken[1] *vt eig* lacquer, varnish, japan; *iem.* ~ [*fig*] bamboozle sbd.; **–er** (-s) *m* [*fig*] bamboozler; verlakke'rij (-en) *v* [*fig*] bamboozlement, spoof; *het was maar* ~ **F** it was all a do, all gammon; ver'lakt lacquered, japanned [boxes]; patent-leather [shoes]

ver'lamd paralyzed[2], palsied; *een* ~*e* a paralytic; ver'lammen[1] (verlamde, h. verlamd) *vt* paralyze[2]; *fig* cripple; **II** (verlamde, is verlamd) *vi* become paralyzed[2]; **–ming** (-en) *v* paralysis[2], palsy

ver'langen (verlangde, h. verlangd) **I** *vt* desire, want; *ik verlang dat niet te horen* I don't want to hear it; *ik verlang (niet), dat je...* I (do not) want you to...; *verlangt u, dat ik...?* do you want (wish) me to...?; *ik verlang niets liever* I'd ask nothing better, I shall be delighted (to...); *dat is alles wat men* ~ *kan* it is all that can be desired; *wat zou men meer kunnen* ~*?* what more could one ask for?; *verlangd salaris* salary required; **II** *vi* long, be longing; ~ *naar* long for [his

---

[1] V.T. en V.D. van dit werkwoord volgens het model: ver'achten, V.T. ver'achtte, V.D. ver'acht (**ge-** valt dus weg in het V.D.). Zie voor de vormen onder het grondwoord, in dit voorbeeld: *achten*. Bij sterke en onregelmatige werkwoorden wordt u verwezen naar de lijst achterin.

arrival]; *er naar ~ om...* long to..., be anxious to...; *wij ~ er niet naar om...* ook: we have no desire to...; **III** (-s) *o* desire; longing; *zijn ~ naar* his longing for; *op ~* [to be shown] on demand; *op ~ van...* at (by) the desire of...; *op speciaal ~ van...* at the special desire of...; **–d** longing (for *naar*); *~ n a a r* desirous of, eager for; *~ o m...* desirous of ...ing, eager (anxious) to...; **ver′langlijst** (-en) *v* list of the presents one would like to get [at Christmas &]; *u moet maar eens een ~ opmaken* draw up a list of the things you would like to have

ver′langzamen (verlangzaamde, h. verlangzaamd) *vt* slow down

ver′lanterfanten[1] *vt* idle away

1 ver′laten[1] **I** *vt* leave, quit, abandon, forsake, desert; *de dienst ~* quit the service; *iem. ~* 1 (b ij b e z o e k) leave sbd.; 2 (i n d e s t e e k l a t e n) abandon (desert) sbd.; *het ambt ~ rk =* *uittreden*; *zijn post ~* desert one's post; *de stad ~* leave the town; *de wereld ~* 1 give up the world; 2 depart this life; **II** *vr zich ~ op* trust to [Providence], rely (depend) upon; *daar kunt u zich op ~* depend upon it, you may rely upon it

2 ver′laten (verlaatte, h. verlaat) *ik heb mij verlaat* I am late

3 ver′laten *aj* 1 (n i e t b e w o o n d) abandoned, deserted [islands, villages &]; 2 (a f g e l e g e n) lonely; **–heid** *v* abandonment, desertion, forlornness, loneliness

ver′lating *v* 1 abandonment, desertion; || 2 retardation, delay

ver′leden I *aj* past, last; *~ tijd* [*gram*] past tense; *dat is ~ tijd* [*fig*] zie *dat behoort tot het ~*; *~ vrijdag* last Friday; **II** *ad* the other day, lately, recently; **III** *o* past; *zijn ~* his past, his record, his antecedents; *dat behoort tot het ~* that's a thing of the past

ver′legen I *aj* 1 (b e d o r v e n) shop-worn, shop-soiled [articles]; stale [wine]; 2 (b e s c h r o o m d) shy, timid, bashful; self-conscious [through inability to forget oneself]; 3 (b e s c h a a m d) confused, embarrassed; *u maakt me ~* you make me blush; *dat maakte hem ~* that put him out of countenance, embarrassed him; ● *~ m e t iets zijn* not know what to do with sth.; *hij was met zijn figuur ~* he was self-conscious, embarrassed; *~ zijn o m* stand in need of [it], want [it] badly; be at a loss for [a reply]; *om geld ~ zijn* ook: be hard up; **II** *ad* shyly &; **–heid** *v* 1 shyness, timidity, bashfulness; self-consciousness [in speech &]; 2 confusion, embarrassment, perplexity; *i n ~*

brengen 1 embarrass; 2 get into trouble; *in ~ geraken* get into difficulties; *u i t de ~ redden* help out of a difficulty

ver′leggen[1] *vt* remove, shift, lay otherwise [things]; divert [a road, a river]; **–ging** *v* removal; shifting [of things]; diversion [of a road, a river]

ver′leidelijk I *aj* alluring, tempting, seductive; **II** *ad* alluringly &; **–heid** (-heden) *v* allurement, seductiveness; **ver′leiden**[1] *vt* 1 (t o t h e t s l e c h t e) seduce [inexperienced youths, girls]; 2 (t o t i e t s l o k k e n) allure, tempt; *kan het mooie weer u niet ~?* can't the fine weather tempt you?; *hij liet zich door zijn... ~ tot een daad van...* by his... he was betrayed into an act of...; *tot zonde ~* tempt (entice) to sin; **–er** (-s) *m* seducer; tempter; **ver′leiding** (-en) *v* seduction; temptation; *de ~ weerstaan om...* resist the temptation to...; *in de ~ komen om...* be tempted to...; **ver′leidster** (-s) *v* seducer; temptress

ver′lekkerd ~ op keen on

ver′lenen[1] *vt* grant [a pension, credit &]; give [permission, support, help]; confer [an order, full powers &] upon [him]; *hulp ~* render (lend, give) assistance

ver′lengbaar extensible; renewable [contract, passport]; **ver′lengen**[1] *vt* make longer, lengthen, prolong [in space, in time]; produce [a line: in geometry]; renew [bills, passports, a subscription]; extend [a contract, ticket &]; *de pas ~* step out; **–ging** (-en) *v* lengthening, prolongation; production [of a line: in geometry]; renewal [of a bill, a passport, a subscription]; extension [of leave]; **ver′lengsnoer** (-en) *o* ⚡ extension cord; **–stuk** (-ken) *o* lengthening-piece; extension[2]

ver′lening *v* granting; conferment

ver′leppen (verlepte, is verlept) *vi* wither, fade; *een verlepte schoonheid* a faded beauty

ver′leren (verleerde, h. en is verleerd) *vt* unlearn; zie ook: *afleren*

ver′let *o* 1 delay; 2 loss of time; *zonder ~* without delay; **–sel** (-s) *o* hindrance, obstacle, impediment; **ver′letten**[1] *vt* 1 prevent; 2 neglect; 3 lose time; *niets te ~ hebben* be in no hurry

ver′leuteren[1] *vt* trifle (idle, fritter) away

ver′levendigen (verlevendigde, h. verlevendigd) *vt* revive [trade], quicken, enliven [the conversation]; **–ging** *v* revival [of trade], quickening, enlivening [of a conversation]

ver′licht 1 (m i n d e r d o n k e r) lighted (up),

---

[1] V.T. en V.D. van dit werkwoord volgens het model: **ver′**achten, V.T. **ver′**achtte, V.D. **ver′**acht (**ge**- valt dus weg in het V.D.). Zie voor de vormen onder het grondwoord, in dit voorbeeld: *achten*. Bij sterke en onregelmatige werkwoorden wordt u verwezen naar de lijst achterin.

illuminated; *fig* enlightened; 2 (m i n d e r
z w a a r) lightened; 3 (o p g e l u c h t) relieved;
4 (v r ij v. v o o r o o r d e l e n) enlightened;
zich ~ voelen feel relieved; *onze,~e eeuw* our
enlightened age; *een ~e geest* a luminary;
ver'lichten[1] *vt eig* 1 light, light up, illuminate
[a building]; 2 (m i n d e r z w a a r m a k e n)
lighten [a ship]; *fig* 1 enlighten [the mind]; 2
lighten [a burden]; relieve, ease, alleviate
[pain]; zie ook: *verlicht*; **-ting** *v eig* 1 lighting,
illumination [of a town]; 2 lightening; *fig* 1
enlightenment [of the mind]; 2 alleviation [of
pain]; relief [of pain, from anxiety]

ver'liederlijken (verliederlijkte, is verlieder-
lijkt) *vi* become a debauchee, go to the bad

ver'liefd enamoured, in love; amorous [look];
~ *op* in love with, sweet on; ~ *worden op* fall in
love with; *een ~ paar* a couple of lovers; **-heid**
(-heden) *v* (state of) being in love, amorous-
ness; *dwaze ~* infatuation

ver'lies (-liezen) *o* loss; bereavement; *ons ~ op de
tarwe* our loss(es) on the wheat; *het was een groot
~* it was a great loss; *hun groot ~ door zijn dood*
their sad bereavement; *iem. een ~ berokkenen*
inflict a loss upon sbd.; *een ~ goedmaken* make
good (make up for, recoup) a loss; ● *m e t ~
verkopen (werken)* sell (work) at a loss; *niet t e g e n
zijn ~ kunnen* be a bad loser; **-cijfer** (-s) *o*
number of casualties; **-lijst** (-en) *v* casualty
list, list of casualties

☉ **ver'lieven** (verliefde, is verliefd) *vi ~ op* fall
in love with

ver'liezen* I *vt* lose [a thing, a battle, one's life
&]; *u zult er (niet) bij ~* you will (not) lose by it,
you will (not) be a loser by it (by the bargain);
zie ook: *verloren*; II *vr zich ~* lose oneself
(itself); **-er** (-s) *m* loser

ver'liggen (verlag, is verlegen) *vi* (b e d e r -
v e n) spoil, get spoiled; (a n d e r s l i g g e n)
shift, move [one's lying position]

ver'lijden[1] *vt* draw up [a deed]; *verleden voor een
notaris* notarially executed

ver'linken (verlinkte, h. verlinkt) **S** *vt* betray, **S**
peach

ver'loederen (verloederde, is verloederd) *vi*
become debase (degenerate, demoralised); run
to seed, go to the bad

ver'lof (-loven) *o* 1 (v e r g u n n i n g) leave,
permission; 2 (v a k a n t i e) leave (of absence);
⚓ ook: furlough; 3 (t a p v e r g u n n i n g)
licence for the sale of beer; *groot ~* ⚓ long
furlough; *klein ~* ⚓ short leave; *onbepaald ~* ⚓
unlimited furlough; *~ aanvragen* apply for

leave; *~ geven* grant leave; *~ geven om...* give
(grant) permission to...; *alle ~ intrekken* ⚓
cancel all leave; *~ nemen* go on leave; ● *m e t
~* on leave; *met ~ gaan* go on leave; *met ~ zijn*
be on leave; *met uw ~* excuse me; *z o n d e r ~*
without permission; **-aanvrage** (-n) *v* application for leave; **-centrum** (-tra en -s) *o* ⚓ leave
centre; **-ganger** (-s) *m* ⚓ soldier on leave;
-pas (-sen) *m* leave pass; **ver'lof(s)trakte-
ment** (-en) *o* leave pay; **ver'lofsverlenging** *v*
extension of leave; **ver'loftijd** (-en) *m* (time
of) leave

ver'lokkelijk alluring, tempting, seductive;
-heid (-heden) *v* allurement, seductiveness;
ver'lokken[1] *vt* allure, tempt, entice, seduce;
zij heeft mij er toe verlokt ook: she wiled me into
doing it; **-king** (-en) *v* temptation, allurement,
enticement

ver'loochenen[1] I *vt* deny [God], disown [a
friend, an opinion], disavow [an action],
repudiate [an opinion, a promise], renounce
[one's faith, the world], belie [one's words]; II
vr zich ~ 1 belie one's nature; 2 deny oneself,
practise self-denial; *zijn... verloochende zich niet*
his... did not belie itself; **-ning** *v* denial,
repudiation, disavowal, renunciation

ver'loofd engaged (to *met*); **-e** (-n) *m-v*
fiancé(e), betrothed, affianced; *de ~n* the
engaged couple

ver'loop *o* 1 course, progress [of an illness];
course, lapse, expiration [of time]; 2
(a c h t e r u i t g a n g) decline; wastage [among
married women in industry]; 3 (w i s s e l i n g
v a n p e r s o n e e l) turnover; *het moet zijn ~
hebben* it must take its normal course; *het gewone
~ hebben* take the accustomed course; *een
noodlottig ~ hebben* end fatally; *de vergadering had
een rustig ~* the meeting passed off quietly; *de
besprekingen hebben een vlot ~* the conversations
are proceeding smoothly; *een gunstig ~ nemen*
take a favourable turn; *na ~ van drie dagen* after
a lapse of three days; *na ~ van tijd* in course (in
process) of time; **-stuk** (-ken) *o* ⚔ reducer

ver'loor (verloren) V.T. v. *verliezen*

1 ver'lopen[1] *vi* 1 ♻ run into the pocket; 2 (v a n
t ij d) pass, pass away, elapse, go by; 3 (v a n
b i l j e t, p a s p o o r t &) expire; 4 (v. z a a k)
go down, run to seed; 5 (n a u w e r w o r-
d e n) ⚔ reduce, narrow; *het getij verliep* the
tide was ebbing; *de staking verliep* the strike
collapsed; *de demonstratie verliep zonder incidenten*
the demonstration passed off without incident;
zie ook: *verloop*

---

[1] V.T. en V.D. van dit werkwoord volgens het model: **ver'achten**, V.T. **ver'achtte**, V.D. **ver'acht** (*ge-* valt dus weg
in het V.D.). Zie voor de vormen onder het grondwoord, in dit voorbeeld: *achten*. Bij sterke en onregelmatige
werkwoorden wordt u verwezen naar de lijst achterin.

2 ver'lopen *aj* seedy-looking, seedy [man]; run-down [business]

ver'loren I *aj* lost; *een ~ man* a lost man, a dead man; *~ moeite* labour lost; *het V~ Paradijs van Milton* Milton's Paradise Lost; *~ ogenblikken* spare moments, odd moments; *de ~ zoon* the prodigal son; *~ gaan (raken)* be (get) lost; *er zou niet veel aan ~ zijn* it would not be much (of a) loss; **II** V.T. meerv. van *verliezen*; **III** V.D. van *verliezen*

ver'loskamer (-s) *v* 🜊 delivery room; **–kunde** *v* obstetrics, midwifery; **verlos'kundig** obstetric(al); **–e** (-n) *m-v* obstetrician; *v* (v r o e d v r o u w) midwife; **ver'lossen**[1] *vt* 1 deliver, rescue, release [a prisoner], free [from...]; (v. C h r i s t u s) redeem [mankind]; 2 (b ij b e v a l l i n g) deliver; **–er** (-s) *m* liberator, deliverer; *de Verlosser* the Redeemer, the Saviour; **ver'lossing** (-en) *v* 1 deliverance, rescue; redemption [of mankind]; 2 (b e v a l l i n g) delivery; **ver'lostang** (-en) *v* forceps

ver'loten[1] *vt* dispose of [sth.] by lottery, raffle; **–ting** (-en) *v* raffle, lottery

1 ver'loven *zich ~* become engaged

2 ver'loven meerv. van *verlof*

ver'loving (-en) *v* betrothal, engagement (to *met*); **ver'lovingsfeest** (-en) *o* engagement party; **–kaart** (-en) *v* engagement card; **–ring** (-en) *m* engagement ring

ver'luchten[1] *vt* illuminate [a manuscript]; **–er** (-s) *m* illuminator; **ver'luchting** *v* illumination

ver'luiden (verluidde, is verluid) *vi naar verluidt* it is understood that..., it is rumoured that...; *wat men hoort ~* what one hears; *niets laten ~* not breathe a word about it

ver'luieren[1] *vt* idle away

ver'lummelen[1] *vt* laze away, fritter away [one's time]

ver'lustigen (verlustigde, h. verlustigd) **I** *vt* divert; **II** *vr zich ~ in* take delight in, delight in, take (a) pleasure in; **–ging** (-en) *v* diversion

ver'maagschappen (vermaagschapte, h. vermaagschapt) *zich ~ aan* become related to, marry into the family of...

ver'maak (-maken) *o* pleasure, diversion, amusement; *~ scheppen in* take (a) pleasure in, find pleasure in, take delight in; *tot ~ van...* to the amusement of...; *tot groot ~ van...* much to the amusement of...; **–scentrum** (-tra en -s) *o* night-life district

ver'maan *o* admonition, warning

ver'maard famous, renowned, celebrated, illustrious; **–heid** (-heden) *v* fame, renown,

celebrity; *een van de vermaardheden van de stad* one of the celebrities of the town

ver'mageren I (vermagerde, is vermagerd) *vi* grow lean (thin); (d o o r d i e e t) reduce, slim; **II** (vermagerde, h. vermagerd) *vt* make lean (thin), emaciate; **ver'magering** *v* emaciation; (s l a n k m a k e n) slimming; **–skuur** (-kuren) *v* reducing cure, slimming course

ver'makelijk I *aj* amusing, entertaining; **II** *ad* amusingly; **ver'makelijkheid** (-heden) *v* amusingness; *publieke vermakelijkheden* public amusements; **–sbelasting** *v* entertainment tax

ver'maken[1] **I** *vt* 1 (v e r a n d e r e n) alter [a coat &]; 2 (a m u s e r e n) amuse, divert; 3 (n a l a t e n) bequeath [it]; will away [money]; **II** *vr zich ~* enjoy (amuse) oneself; *zich ~ met...* amuse oneself with [sth.], amuse oneself (by) [doing sth.]; **–king** (-en) *v* ('t n a l a t e n) bequest

vermale'dij(d)en (vermaledij(d)de, h. vermaledijd) *vt* curse, damn

ver'malen[1] *vt* grind [corn &]; crush [sugarcane]

ver'manen[1] *vt* admonish, exhort, warn; **–er** (-s) *m* admonisher, exhorter; **ver'maning** (-en) *v* admonition, exhortation, warning, **F** talking-to

ver'mannen (vermande, h. vermand) *zich ~* take heart, nerve oneself, pull oneself together

ver'meend fancied, pretended; supposed [culprit, thief], reputed [father]

ver'meerderen I (vermeerderde, h. vermeerderd) *vt* increase, augment, enlarge; *(het getal) ~ met 10* add 10 (to the number); *het aantal inwoners is vermeerderd met...* has increased by...; *vermeerderde uitgave* enlarged edition; **II** (vermeerderde, is vermeerderd) *vi* grow, increase (by *met*); **III** *vr zich ~* 1 (v. d i n g e n, g e t a l l e n &) increase; 2 (v. m e n s e n d i e r) multiply; **–ring** (-en) *v* increase, augmentation

ver'meesteren (vermeesterde, h. vermeesterd) *vt* master [one's passions]; capture [a town], conquer [a province], seize [a fortress &]

ver'meien (vermeide, h. vermeid) *zich ~* amuse oneself, disport oneself, enjoy oneself; *zich ~ in...* revel in...

ver'melden[1] *vt* mention, state; (b o e k - s t a v e n) record; **vermeldens'waard(ig)** worth mentioning, worthy of mention; **ver'melding** (-en) *v* mention; *eervolle ~* 1 (o p t e n t o o n s t e l l i n g) honourable mention; 2 ⚔ being mentioned in dispatches; *met ~*

---

[1] V.T. en V.D. van dit werkwoord volgens het model: **ver'**achten, V.T. **ver'**achtte, V.D. **ver'**acht (**ge-** valt dus weg in het V.D.). Zie voor de vormen onder het grondwoord, in dit voorbeeld: *achten*. Bij sterke en onregelmatige werkwoorden wordt u verwezen naar de lijst achterin.

van... mentioning..., stating...

ver'menen[1] *vt* be of opinion, opine

ver'mengen[1] **I** *vt* mix, mingle [substances or groups]; blend [tea, coffee]; alloy [metals]; **II** *vr zich ~* mix, mingle, blend; **–ging** (-en) *v* mixing, mixture, blending

vermenig'vuldigbaar multipliable; **vermenig'vuldigen** (vermenigvuldigde, h. vermenigvuldigd) *vt* multiply; *~ met...* multiply by...; **II** *vr zich ~* multiply; **–er** (-s) *m* multiplier; **vermenig'vuldiging** (-en) *v* multiplication; *~en maken* do sums in multiplication; **vermenig'vuldigtal** (-len) *o* multiplicand

ver'menselijken (vermenselijkte, *vt* h., *vi* is vermenselijkt) *vt* & *vi* humanize

ver'metel I *aj* audacious, bold, daring; **II** *ad* audaciously, boldly, daringly; **–heid** *v* audacity, boldness, daring

ver'meten[1] *zich ~* 1 (d u r v e n) dare, presume, make bold; 2 (v e r k e e r d m e t e n) measure wrong

vermi'celli *m* vermicelli; **–soep** *v* vermicelli soup

ver'mijdbaar avoidable; **ver'mijden**[1] *vt* avoid; (s c h u w e n) shun; **–ding** *v* avoidance, avoiding

vermil'joen *o* vermilion, cinnabar; **–kleurig** vermilion, cinnabar

ver'minderen[1] **I** *vi* lessen, diminish, decrease [of strength &]; abate [of pain &]; fall off [of numbers]; **II** *vt* lessen, diminish, decrease, reduce; *verminder a met b* from *a* take *b*; *ik zal zijn verdienste niet ~* I am not going to detract from his merit; **–ring** (-en) *v* diminution, decrease, falling-off [of the receipts &]; abatement [of pain &]; reduction [of price], cut [in wages]

ver'minken (verminkte, h. verminkt) *vt* maim, mutilate[2], disfeature; **–king** (-en) *v* mutilation[2]; **ver'minkt** maimed, mutilated[2]; crippled, disabled [soldier]; *de in de oorlog ~en* ook: the war cripples

ver'missen[1] *vt* miss; *hij wordt vermist* he is missing; *de vermisten* the (number of) missing

ver'mits whereas, since

ver'moedelijk I *aj* presumable, probable; supposed [thief]; [heir] presumptive; **II** *ad* presumably, probably; *~ wel* ook: most likely; **ver'moeden** (vermoedde, h. vermoed) **I** *vt* suspect; suppose, presume, surmise, conjecture; guess; *je hebt..., vermoed ik* I suppose, I guess; *geen kwaad ~d* unsuspecting(ly); **II** (-s) *o*

suspicion; surmise, supposition, presumption; *~s hebben* have one's suspicions; *~s hebben dat...* suspect that...; *~ hebben tegen iem.* suspect sbd.; *~ krijgen tegen iem.* begin to suspect sbd.; *het ~ wekken dat...* suggest that...; *kwade ~s wekken* arouse suspicion

ver'moeid tired, weary, fatigued; *~ van* tired with; **–heid** *v* tiredness, weariness, fatigue; **ver'moeien** (vermoeide, h. vermoeid) **I** *vt* tire, weary, fatigue; **II** *vr zich ~* tire oneself; get tired; **–d** tiring, fatiguing; trying [journey, light]; **ver'moeienis** (-sen) *v* weariness, fatigue, lassitude

ver'moet = *vermout*

ver'mogen[1] **I** *vt* be able; *dat zal niets ~* it wil be to no purpose; *veel b ij iem.* ~ have great influence with sbd.; *niets ~ t e g e n* be of no avail against; **II** (-s) *o* 1 (m a c h t) power; 2 (g e s c h i k t h e i d) ability; 3 (f o r t u i n) fortune, means, wealth, riches; 4 (w e r k v e r-m o g e n) capacity; *zijn ~s* his (intellectual) faculties; *geen ~ hebben* have no fortune, have no means; *goede ~s hebben* be naturally gifted; *ik zal doen al wat i n mijn ~ is* all in my power; *n a a r mijn beste ~* to the best of my ability; **–d** 1 (m a c h t i g) influential [friends]; 2 (r ij k) wealthy, rich, well-to-do, well-off

ver'mogensaanwas *m* capital gains; increment of assets (of property); **–belasting** *v* capital gains tax; **–deling** *v* excess-profit sharing

ver'mogensbelasting (-en) *v* property tax; **–heffing** (-en) *v* capital levy

ver'molmen[1] *vi* moulder

ver'mommen (vermomde, h. vermomd) **I** *vt* disguise; **II** *vr zich ~* disguise oneself; **–ming** (-en) *v* disguise

ver'moorden[1] *vt* murder, kill, **S** do in

ver'morsen[1] *vt* waste, squander [money]

ver'morzelen (vermorzelde, h. vermorzeld) *vt* crush, pulverize; **–ling** *v* crushing, pulverization

'vermout, ver'mout [-mu.t] *m* vermouth

ver'murwen (vermurwde, h. vermurwd) *vt* soften, mollify

ver'nachelen (vernachelde, h. vernacheld), **ver'naggelen** (vernaggelde, h. vernaggeld) **S** *vt* spoof, fool, hoax

ver'nagelen[1] *vt* ✂ spike [a gun]; **–ling** *v* ✂ spiking [of a gun]

ver'nauwen (vernauwde, h. vernauwd) **I** *vt* narrow; **II** *vr zich ~* narrow; **–wing** (-en) *v* 1 narrowing; 2 ✆ stricture

ver'nederen (vernederde, h. vernederd) **I** *vt*

---

[1] V.T. en V.D. van dit werkwoord volgens het model: **ver'**achten, V.T. **ver'**achtte, V.D. **ver'**acht (**ge-** valt dus weg in het V.D.). Zie voor de vormen onder het grondwoord, in dit voorbeeld: *achten*. Bij sterke en onregelmatige werkwoorden wordt u verwezen naar de lijst achterin.

humble, humiliate, mortify, abase; *vernederd worden* be brought low; **II** *vr zich* ~ humble (humiliate) oneself, **F** eat humble pie; *zich voor zijn God* ~ humble oneself before one's Maker; **–d** humiliating, degrading; **ver′nedering** (-en) *v* humiliation, mortification, abasement

ver′nemen[1] **I** *vt* hear, understand, learn; **II** *vi naar wij* ~ we learn [that...]

ver′neuken[1] **P** *vt* cheat, spoof, diddle, dupe, gull; **verneukera′tief P** cunning, artful, sly

ver′nevelen (vernevelde, h. verneveld) *vt* spray

ver′nielal (-len) *m* destroyer, smasher; **ver′nielen** (vernielde, h. vernield) *vt* 1 wreck [a car, machinery]; 2 (v e r w o e s t e n) destroy; *die jongen vernielt alles* that boy smashes everything; **–d** destructive; **ver′nieler** (-s) *m* destroyer, smasher; **ver′nieling** (-en) *v* destruction; **–swerk** *o* work of destruction; **ver′nielziek** destructive, ruinous; **–zucht** *v* love of destruction, destructiveness, vandalism; **verniel′zuchtig** destructive

ver′nietigen (vernietigde, h. vernietigd) *vt* 1 (s t u k m a k e n) destroy, annihilate, wreck; 2 (n i e t i g v e r k l a r e n) nullify, annul, quash, reverse [a verdict]; *het leger werd totaal vernietigd* the whole army was annihilated (wiped out); **–d** destructive [fire, acids]; *fig* smashing [victory], crushing [review], withering [phrases, look], slashing [criticism]; **ver′nietiging** *v* destruction, annihilation [of matter, credit &]; ⚖ annulment, nullification, quashing [of a verdict]

ver′nieuwen (vernieuwde, h. vernieuwd) *vt* renew, renovate; **–er** (-s) *m* renewer, renovator; **ver′nieuwing** (-en) *v* renewal, renovation

ver′nikkelen (vernikkelde, h. vernikkeld) *vt* (plate with) nickel, nickel-plate

ver′nis (-sen) *o* & *m* varnish²; *fig* veneer; **–je** (–s) *o* = *vernis*; **ver′nissen** (verniste, h. gevernist) *vt* varnish²; *fig* veneer; **–er** (-s) *m* varnisher

ver′noemen[1] *vt* name after

ver′nuft (-en) *o* 1 ingenuity, genius; 2 wit; *vals* ~ would-be wit; **ver′nuftig I** *aj* ingenious; **II** *ad* ingeniously; **–heid** *v* ingenuity

ver′nummeren[1] *vt* renumber

veron′aangenamen (veronaangenaamde, h. veronaangenaamd) *vt* make unpleasant

veron′achtzamen (veronachtzaamde, h. veronachtzaamd) *vt* disregard [warning &], neglect [one's duty &]; slight [one's wife]; **–ming** *v* neglect, negligence, disregard; *met* ~

van... neglecting

veronder′stellen[1] *vt* suppose; *veronderstel dat...* suppose, supposing (that)...; **–ling** (-en) *v* supposition; *in de* ~ *dat...* in (on) the supposition that...; *wij schrijven in de* ~ *(van de* ~ *uitgaand) dat...* we are writing on the assumption that...

ver′ongelijken (verongelijkte, h. verongelijkt) *vt* wrong, do [sbd.] wrong; **–king** (-en) *v* wrong, injury

ver′ongelukken (verongelukte, is verongelukt) *vi* 1 (v. p e r s o n e n) meet with an accident; perish, come to grief; 2 (v. s c h e p e n &) be wrecked, be lost

ve′ronica ('s) *v* 🌿 speedwell

veront′heiligen (verontheiligde, h. verontheiligd) *vt* 1 desecrate [a tomb]; 2 profane [the name of God]; **–ging** (-en) *v* 1 desecration; 2 profanation

veront′reinigen (verontreinigde, h. verontreinigd) *vt* defile, pollute; **–ging** (-en) *v* defilement, pollution

veront′rusten (verontrustte, h. verontrust) **I** *vt* alarm, disturb, perturb; **II** *vr zich* ~ *(over)* be alarmed (at), be agitated, be disturbed; **–d** alarming, disquieting, disturbing; **veront–′rusting** *v* alarm, perturbation, disturbance

veront′schuldigen (verontschuldigde, h. verontschuldigd) **I** *vt* excuse; *dat is niet te* ~ that is inexcusable; **II** *vr zich* ~ apologize (to *by*; for *wegens*); excuse oneself [on the ground that...]; **–ging** (-en) *v* excuse, apology; *zijn* ~*en aanbieden* apologize; *vermoeidheid als* ~ *aanvoeren* plead fatigue; *ter* ~ by way of excuse [he said that...]; *ter* ~ *van zijn...* in excuse of his... [bad temper &]

veront′waardigd indignant; ~ *over* indignant at [sth.]; indignant with [sbd.]; **veront′waardigen** (verontwaardigde, h. verontwaardigd) **I** *vt* make indignant; *het verontwaardigde hem* it roused his indignation; **II** *vr zich* ~ be (become) indignant, be filled with indignation; **–ging** *v* indignation

ver′oordeelde (-n) *m-v* condemned man (woman), convicted person; **ver′oordelen**[1] *vt* 1 ⚖ give judgment against, condemn, sentence, convict, pass sentence on; 2 (i n ′t a l g.) condemn; 3 (a f k e u r e n) condemn; *iem. in de kosten* ~ order sbd. to pay costs; *ter dood* ~ condemn to death; *de ter dood veroordeelden* those under sentence of death; *tot 3 maanden gevangenisstraf* ~ sentence to three months(′ imprisonment); ~ *w e g e n s* convict of

---

[1] V.T. en V.D. van dit werkwoord volgens het model: **ver′achten**, V.T. **ver′achtte**, V.D. **ver′acht** (**ge-** valt dus weg in het V.D.). Zie voor de vormen onder het grondwoord, in dit voorbeeld: *achten*. Bij sterke en onregelmatige werkwoorden wordt u verwezen naar de lijst achterin.

[drunkenness &]; **–ling** (-en) *v* 1 condemnation°; 2 🕮 conviction (for *wegens*)

ver'oorloofd allowed, allowable; permitted; **ver'oorloven** (veroorloofde, h. veroorloofd) **I** *vt* permit, allow, give leave; **II** *vr zich ~ om...* take the liberty to..., make bold to...; *zij ~ zich heel wat* they take great liberties; *zij kunnen zich dat ~* they can afford it; **–ving** (-en) *v* leave, permission

ver'oorzaken (veroorzaakte, h. veroorzaakt) *vt* cause, bring about, occasion; **–er** (-s) *m* cause, author

veroot'moedigen (verootmoedigde, h. verootmoedigd) *vt* humble, humiliate; **–ging** (-en) *vt* humiliation

ver'orberen (verorberde, h. verorberd) *vt* consume, **F** dispose of, polish off

ver'ordenen[1] *vt* order, ordain, decree; **–ning** (-en) *v* regulation; (g e m e e n t e l ij k e) by-law; *volgens ~* by order; (**verordi'neren** (verordineerde, h. verordineerd) *vt* order, ordain, prescribe

ver'ouderd out of date, antiquated, archaic, obsolete [word]; aged [man]; **ver'ouderen** **I** (verouderde, is verouderd) *vi* 1 (v a n p e r-s o n e n) grow old, age; 2 (v. w o o r d e n &) become obsolete; *hij is erg verouderd* he has aged very much; **II** (verouderde, h. verouderd) *vt* make older, age; **ver'oudering** *v* growing old, ageing [of people]; obsolescence [of a word]; **–sproces** (-sen) *o* ageing process

ver'overaar (-s) *m* conqueror; **ver'overen** (veroverde, h. veroverd) *vt* conquer, capture[2], take (from *op*); **ver'overing** (-en) *v* conquest[2], capture[2]; **–soorlog** (-logen) *m* war of conquest

ver'pachten[1] *vt* lease [land]; farm out [taxes]; **–er** (-s) *m* lessor; **ver'pachting** (-en) *v* leasing [of land]; farming out [of taxes]

ver'pakken[1] *vt* pack, put up [... in tins], (k a n t e n k l a a r v o o r v e r k o o p) package; **–er** (-s) *m* packer; **ver'pakking** (-en) *v* packing; [modern, plastic] packaging

ver'panden[1] *vt* pawn [at a pawnbroker's shop]; pledge [one's word]; mortgage [one's house]; **–ding** (-en) *v* pawning; pledging; mortgaging

ver'patsen (verpatste, h. verpatst) **S** *vt* flog

ver'pauperen (verpauperde, is verpauperd) *vi* pauperize, be reduced to pauperism

verper'soonlijken (verpersoonlijkte, h. verpersoonlijkt) *vt* personify, impersonate; **–king** *v* personification, impersonation

ver'pesten[1] *vt* infect[2] [the air &]; *fig* poison [the mind]; **–d** pestilential, pestiferous;

ver'pesting *v* infection[2]; *fig* poisoning

ver'pieteren (verpieterde, is verpieterd) *vi* wither, dwindle, (v. p l a n t e n) wilt

ver'plaatsbaar movable, removable; portable [radio]; **ver'plaatsen**[1] **I** *vt* move, remove, transpose, displace [things, persons]; transfer [persons]; **II** *vr zich ~* move; *zich in iems. toestand ~* put oneself in sbd.'s place; *zich ~ in de toestand van iem. die...* put (place) oneself in the position of sbd. who...; **–sing** (-en) *v* 1 movement; removal [of furniture]; displacement [of water]; transposition [of words]; 2 (o v e r p l a a t s i n g) transfer [of officials]

ver'planten[1] *vt* transplant, plant out; **–ting** (-en) *v* transplantation

ver'pleegde (-n) *m-v* patient; inmate [of an asylum]; **ver'pleeginrichting** (-en) *v* nursing-home; **–kunde** *v* nursing; **verpleeg'kundig** nursing; **–e** (-n) *m-v* nurse; **ver'pleegster** (-s) *v* nurse; **ver'pleegtehuis** (-huizen) *o* nursing-home; **ver'plegen**[1] *vt* nurse, tend; **–er** (-s) *m* male nurse, (hospital) attendant; **ver'pleging** *v* 1 (v. z i e k e n, g e w o n d e n) nursing; **–skosten** *mv* hospital charges, nursing fees

ver'pletteren (verpletterde, h. verpletterd) *vt* crush, smash, shatter, dash to pieces; *~de meerderheid* overwhelming (crushing) majority; *een ~de tijding* crushing news; **–ring** *v* crushing, smashing, shattering

ver'plicht due (to *aan*); compulsory [subject, branch, insurance], obligatory; *ik ben u zeer ~* I am much obliged to you; *iets ~ zijn aan iem.* be indebted to sbd. for sth.; owe sth. to sbd.; *~ zijn om...* be obliged to, have to; zie ook: *verplichten*; **ver'plichten** (verplichtte, h. verplicht) **I** *vt* oblige, compel, force; *daardoor hebt u mij (aan u) verplicht* by this you have (greatly) obliged me, you have put me under an obligation; **II** *vr zich ~ tot* bind oneself to; zie ook: *verplicht*; **–ting** (-en) *v* obligation; commitment; *mijn ~en* ook: my engagements; *~en aangaan* enter into obligations; *grote ~en aan iem. hebben* be under great obligations to sbd.; *zijn ~en nakomen* 1 (i n t a l g.) meet one's obligations, meet one's engagements; 2 (g e l d e l ij k) meet one's liabilities; *de ~ op zich nemen om...* undertake to...

ver'poppen (verpopte, h. verpopt) *zich ~* pupate; **–ping** (-en) *v* pupation

ver'poten[1] *vt* transplant, plant out

ver'potten[1] *vt* repot

ver'pozen[1] *zich ~* take a rest, rest; **–zing** (-en) *v* rest

---

[1] V.T. en V.D. van dit werkwoord volgens het model: **ver'**achten, V.T. **ver'**achtte, V.D. **ver'**acht (**ge**- valt dus weg in het V.D.). Zie voor de vormen onder het grondwoord, in dit voorbeeld: *achten*. Bij sterke en onregelmatige werkwoorden wordt u verwezen naar de lijst achterin.

ver′praten[1] **I** *vt* waste [one's time] talking, talk away [one's time]; **II** *vr* ~ let one's tongue run away with one, give oneself away

ver′prutsen[1] = *verknoeien*

ver′pulveren (verpulverde, *vt* h., *vi* is verpulverd) *vt* & *vi* pulverize; **–ring** *v* pulverization

ver′raad *o* treason, treachery, betrayal; ~ *plegen* commit treason; ~ *plegen jegens* betray; **S** blow the gaff; **–ster** (-s) *v* traitress; **ver′raden**[1] **I** *vt* betray[2], give away; *fig* show, bespeak; *dat verraadt zijn gebrek aan beschaving* that betrays his want of good-breeding; **II** *vr zich* ~ betray oneself, give oneself away; **–er** (-s) *m* betrayer, traitor [to his country]; **verrade′rij** (-en) *v* treachery, treason; **ver′raderlijk I** *aj* treacherous, traitorous, perfidious; insidious [disease]; *een* ~ *blosje* a telltale blush; **II** *ad* treacherously, perfidiously; **–heid** *v* treacherousness

ver′rassen (verraste, h. verrast) *vt* surprise, take by surprise; *uw bezoek verraste ons* ook: your visit was a (pleasant) surprise, came as a surprise, took us unawares; *zij willen u eens* ~ they intend to give you a surprise; *door de regen verrast worden* be caught in the rain; **–d** surprising, startling [news]; *een* ~*e aanval* ✗ a surprise attack; **ver′rassing** (-en) *v* surprise; *iem. een* ~ *bereiden* prepare a surprise for sbd., give sbd. a surprise; *b ij* ~ ✗ by surprise; *t o t mijn grote* ~ to my great surprise; **–saanval** (-len) *m* ✗ surprise attack

′verre far, distant, remote; *het zij* ~ *van mij dat...* far be it from me to...; ~ *van...* (so) far from..., nowhere near...; ~ *van gemakkelijk* far from easy; *o p* ~ *na niet* not nearly, not by far; *v a n* ~ from afar; **–gaand I** *aj* extreme, excessive [cruelty &]; **II** *ad* < extremely, excessively

ver′regenen (verregende, is verregend) *vi* be spoiled by the rain(s)

′verreikend far-reaching [proposals], sweeping [changes]

ver′reisd travel-worn, travel-stained; **ver′reizen**[1] *vt* spend in travelling

ver′rek *ij* **F** Hell!, **P** damn (it), damn you!

ver′rekenen[1] **I** *vt* settle; clear [cheques]; **II** *vr zich* ~ miscalculate, make a mistake in one's calculation; **–ning** (-en) *v* 1 settlement; clearance; 2 miscalculation; **ver′rekenkantoor** *o* clearing-house; **–pakket** (-ten) *o* 🏷 C.O.D. parcel

′verrekijker (-s) *m* = *kijker* 2

1 ver′rekken[1] **I** *vt* strain, rick [a muscle], wrench, dislocate [one's arm], sprain [one's ankle], crick [one's neck]; **II** *vr zich* ~ strain

oneself

2 ver′rekken[1] **P** *vi* (d o o d g a a n) die, perish [from starvation, from cold]; starve [for hunger]; zie ook: *verrek, verrekt*

ver′rekking (-en) *v* strain(ing), sprain(ing) [of ankle, wrist]; crick [of neck]

ver′rekt *aj* & *ad* **F** damned, **P** damn

′verreweg by far, far and away; ~ *te verkiezen boven* much to be preferred to, infinitely preferable to

ver′richten[1] *vt* do, perform, execute, make [arrests].; **–ting** (-en) *v* action, performance, operation, transaction

ver′rijken (verrijkte, h. verrijkt) **I** *vt* enrich; **II** *vr zich* ~ enrich oneself; **–king** *v* enrichment

ver′rijzen[1] *vi* rise [from the dead]; arise [of difficulties &]; *doen* ~ raise; zie ook: *paddestoel*; **ver′rijzenis** *v* resurrection

ver′roeren *vt* & *vr* stir, move, budge; *zich niet* ~ stay put

ver′roest 1 rusty; 2 **F** = *verrekt*; **ver′roesten**[1] *vi* rust

ver′roken *vt* spend on cigars, tobacco &

ver′rollen *vi* & *vt* roll away

ver′rot rotten, putrid, putrefied; **–heid** *v* rottenness; **ver′rotten**[1] *vi* rot, putrefy; **ver′rotting** *v* rotting, putrefaction; *tot* ~ *overgaan* rot, putrefy; **–sproces** (-sen) *o* process of putrefaction

ver′ruilen[1] *vt* exchange, barter (for *tegen, voor*); **–ling** (-en) *v* exchange, barter

ver′ruimen[1] *vt* enlarge, widen[2]; *fig* enlarge, broaden [one's outlook]; **–ming** *v* enlargement[2], widening[2], broadening[2]

ver′rukkelijk I *aj* delightful, enchanting, charming, ravishing; delicious [food]; **II** *ad* delightfully &; ook: < wonderfully; **–heid** (-heden) *v* delightfulness, charm; **ver′rukken** (verrukte, h. verrukt) *vt* delight, ravish, enchant, enrapture; zie ook: *verrukt*; **–king** (-en) *v* delight, ravishment, transport, rapture, ecstasy; **ver′rukt I** *aj* delighted &, zie *verrukken*; ook: rapturous [smile]; *zij waren er* ~ *over* they were in raptures about it; *zij zullen er* ~ *over zijn* they will be delighted at (with) it; **II** *ad* rapturously, in raptures

ver′ruwen (verruwde, *vt* h., *vi* is verruwd) *vt* & *vi* coarsen; **–wing** *v* coarsening

1 vers (verzen) *o* 1 (r e g e l) verse; 2 (c o u p l e t) stanza; 3 (t w e e r e g e l i g) couplet; 4 (v. B ij b e l) verse; 5 (g e d i c h t) poem

2 vers I *aj* fresh, new, new-laid [eggs], green

---

[1] V.T. en V.D. van dit werkwoord volgens het model: **ver′achten**, V.T. **ver′achtte**, V.D. **ver′acht** (ge- valt dus weg in het V.D.). Zie voor de vormen onder het grondwoord, in dit voorbeeld: *achten*. Bij sterke en onregelmatige werkwoorden wordt u verwezen naar de lijst achterin.

[vegetables]; *het ligt nog ~ in het geheugen* it is fresh in men's minds; **II** *ad* fresh(ly)

ver'saagd faint-hearted; **–heid** *v* faint-heartedness; **ver'sagen** (versaagde, h. en is versaagd) *vi* grow faint-hearted, quail, despair, despond

'versbouw *m* metrical construction

ver'schaffen[1] **I** *vt* procure [sbd. sth., sth. for sbd.], provide, furnish, supply [sbd. with sth.]; *wat verschaft mij het genoegen om...?* what gives me the pleasure of ...ing?; **II** *vr zich ~* procure; zie ook: 2 *recht, toegang*; **–fing** *v* furnishing, procurement, provision [of food and clothing]

ver'schalen (verschaalde, is verschaald) *vi* grow (go) flat (stale, vapid)

ver'schalken (verschalkte, h. verschalkt) *vt* outwit; *er eentje ~, een glaasje & ~* **F** have one; *een vogel ~* catch a bird; **–king** *v* deception

ver'schansen (verschanste, h. verschanst) **I** *vt* entrench [a town &]; **II** *vr zich ~* ⚓ entrench oneself[2]; **–sing** (-en) *v* 1 ⚓ entrenchment [of a fortress]; 2 ⚓ bulwarks, (r e l i n g) rails [of a ship]

1 ver'scheiden[1] **I** *vi* depart this life, pass away; **II** *o* passing (away), death, decease

2 ver'scheiden 1 several; 2 (v e r s c h i l l e n d) various, diverse, different, sundry; **–heid** (-heden) *v* diversity, variety; difference; range [of colours, patterns &]

ver'schelen[1] 1 **F** = *verschillen*; 2 **F** *dat kan me niet ~* I don't care a damn

ver'schenken[1] *vt* pour out.

ver'schepen (verscheepte, h. verscheept) *vt* ship; **–er** (-s) *m* shipper; **ver'scheping** (-en) *v* shipment; **ver'schepingsdocumenten** *mv* shipping documents

ver'scherpen[1] *vt* sharpen[2]; *de wet ~* stiffen (tighten up) the law; **–ping** *v* sharpening[2]; *fig* stiffening, tightening up [of the law]

ver'scheurdheid *v* disunity [of a nation]; distraction [with grief]; **ver'scheuren**[1] *vt* 1 tear, tear up [a letter], tear to pieces; 2 (s t u k s c h e u r e n) ⊙ rend [one's garments]; 3 (v e r s l i n d e n) lacerate, mangle [its prey]; *~de dieren* ferocious animals; *verscheurd door verdriet* distracted with grief

ver'schiet (-en) *o* distance; perspective[2]; *fig* prospect; *in het ~* in the distance; *fig* ahead

ver'schieten[1] **I** *vt* 1 (a f s c h i e t e n) shoot; use up, consume [ammunition]; 2 (v o o r-s c h i e t e n) advance [money]; 3 (o m z e t t e n) stir [grain]; zie ook: *kruit & pijl*; **II** *vi* 1 (v. s t e r r e n) shoot; 2 (v. k l e u r e n) fade; 3 (v. s t o f f e n) lose colour; *ik zag hem (van kleur) ~*

I saw him change colour; *niet ~d* unfading, sunproof [dress-materials]

ver'schijnen (verscheen, is verschenen) *vi* 1 (v. h e m e l l i c h a m e n, p e r s o n e n &) appear; 2 (v. z a k e n, p e r s o n e n) make one's appearance; put in an appearance; 3 (v a n t e r m ij n) fall (become) due; *de verdachte was niet verschenen* **t̶t̶** had not entered an appearance; *het boek zal morgen ~* is to come out to-morrow; *bij wie laat je het boek ~?* through whom are you going to publish the book?; *voor de commissie ~* attend before the Board.; **–ning** (-en) *v* 1 (h e t v e r s c h ij n e n) appearance; publication [of a book]; 2 (g e e s t) apparition, phantom, ghost; 3 (p e r s o o n) figure; *het is een mooie ~* she has a fine presence (a magnificent figure); **ver'schijnsel** (-s en -en) *o* 1 phenomenon [of nature], *mv* phenomena; 2 symptom

ver'schikken[1] **I** *vt* arrange differently, re-arrange, shift; **II** *vi* move (higher) up; **–king** (-en) *v* different arrangement, shifting

ver'schil (-len) *o* difference [ook = remainder after subtraction & disagreement in opinion], disparity; distinction; *~ van mening* difference of opinion; *~ in leeftijd* difference in age, disparity in years; *het ~ delen* split the difference; *dat maakt een groot ~* that makes a big difference (all the difference); *het maakt geen groot (niet veel) ~ of ...* it is not much odds whether...; *~ maken tussen...* make a difference between, differentiate (distinguish) between...; *met dit ~ dat...* with the (this) difference that...; zie ook: *geschil & hemelsbreed*; **ver'schillen** (verschilde, h. verschild) *vi* differ, be different, vary; *~ van* differ from; *~ van mening* differ (in opinion); **–d I** *aj* different, various; differing; *~ van...* different from...; *~e personen* various persons, several persons; *ik heb het van ~e personen gehoord* ook: I've heard the story from several different people; **II** *ad* differently; **ver'schilpunt** (-en) *o* point of difference, point of controversy

ver'schimmelen[1] *vi* grow mouldy

ver'scholen hidden

ver'schonen (verschoonde, h. verschoond) **I** *vi* *eig* put clean sheets on [a bed]; change [the baby's clothes, sheets]; *fig* excuse [misconduct &]; *verschoon mij van die praatjes* spare me your talk!; *van iets verschoond blijven* be spared sth.; *ik wens van uw bezoeken verschoond te blijven* spare me your visits; **II** *vr zich ~* 1 change one's linen; 2 *fig* excuse oneself; **–ning** (-en) *v* 1 *eig* clean

---

[1] V.T. en V.D. van dit werkwoord volgens het model: ver'achten, V.T. ver'achtte, V.D. ver'acht (ge- valt dus weg in het V.D.). Zie voor de vormen onder het grondwoord, in dit voorbeeld: *achten*. Bij sterke en onregelmatige werkwoorden wordt u verwezen naar de lijst achterin.

linen, change (of linen); 2 *fig* excuse; *waar is mijn ~?* where are my clean things?; *~ vragen* apologize; **ver'schoonbaar** excusable

ver'schoppeling (-en) *m* outcast, pariah

ver'schot (-ten) *o* 1 assortment, choice; 2 *~ten* out-of-pocket expenses, disbursements

ver'schoten faded [dresses &]

ver'schraald scanty, poor, meagre; **ver'schralen** (verschraalde, *vt* h., *vi* is verschraald) *vi* (& *vt*) become (make) scanty, meagre, poor

ver'schrijven[1] *zich ~* make a mistake in writing; **-ving** (-en) *v* slip of the pen

ver'schrikkelijk I *aj* frightful, dreadful, terrible; **II** *ad* frightfully &, < awfully; **-heid** (-heden) *v* frightfulness, dreadfulness, terribleness; **ver'schrikken**[1] **I** *vt* frighten, terrify [persons &]; scare [birds]; **II** *vi = schrikken*; **-king** (-en) *v* 1 (h e t s c h r i k k e n) fright, terror; 2 (h e t v e r s c h r i k k e n d e) horror

ver'schroeien[1] **I** *vt* scorch, singe; **II** *vi* be scorched, be singed; *de tactiek der verschroeide aarde* scorched earth tactics; **-iing** *v* scorching, singeing

ver'schrompeld shrivelled, wizened; **ver'schrompelen**[1] *vi* shrivel (up), shrink, wrinkle

ver'schuilen[1] *zich ~* hide (from *voor*), conceal oneself; *zich ~ achter het ambtsgeheim* shelter oneself behind professional secrecy

ver'schuiven[1] **I** *vt* 1 *eig* move, shift; 2 (u i t s t e l l e n) put off; **II** *vi* shift; **-ving** (-en) *v* 1 shifting; 2 putting off

ver'schuldigd indebted, due; *met ~e eerbied* with due respect; *wij zijn hem alles ~* we are indebted to him for everything we have; we owe everything to him; *het ~e* the money due; *het hem ~e* his dues

ver'schutting *v* disgrace, humiliation

'versgebakken freshly-baked [bread]; **'versheid** *v* freshness

'versie [s = z] (-s) *v* version, rendering [of a story]

ver'sierder (-s) *m* decorator; **F** (v e r l e i d e r) seducer, Don Juan, Lothario; **ver'sieren**[1] *vt* adorn [with jewels], beautify, embellish [with flowers], ornament, decorate, deck [with flags, flowers &]; *ik kon het niet ~* [*fig*] **F** I couldn't fix it; *een meisje ~* chat up [a girl]; **ver'siering** (-en) *v* adornment, decoration, ornament; *~en* ♩ grace notes; **-skunst** *v* decorative art; **ver'siersel** (-s en -en) *o* ornament

ver'sjacheren[1] *vt* barter away

ver'sjouwen[1] *vt* lug away

ver'sjteren (versjteerde, h. versjteerd) **F** *vt* spoil [maliciously]

ver'slaafd ~ *aan...* a slave to...; addicted to [drink], **S** hooked on [amphetamines]; *hij is ~ aan verdovende middelen (cocaïne, morfine &)* he is a drug (cocaine, morphine &) addict; **-heid** *v* addiction

ver'slaan[1] *vt* 1 beat, defeat [an army, a man &]; 2 (l e s s e n) quench [thirst]; 3 (v e r s l a g u i t b r e n g e n o v e r) report [a match], cover [a meeting], review [a book]; **II** *vi* 1 (v. w a r m e d r a n k e n) cool; 2 (v. k o u d e d r a n k e n) have the chill taken off; **ver'slag** (-slagen) *o* account, report; *officieel statistisch ~* returns; *schriftelijk ~* written account; *woordelijk ~* verbatim report; *~ doen van...* give an account of...; *een ~ opmaken van* draw up a report on; *~ uitbrengen* deliver a report, report (on *over*); **ver'slagen** *aj* beaten, defeated; *fig* dejected, dismayed; *de ~e* the person killed; **-heid** *v* consternation, dismay, dejection; **ver'slaggever** (-s) *m* reporter; **-geving** (-en) *v* reporting; **-jaar** (-jaren) *o* year under review

ver'slapen[1] **I** *vt* sleep away; **II** *vr zich ~* oversleep oneself

ver'slappen I (verslapte, is verslapt) *vi* slacken[2] [of a rope, one's zeal], relax[2] [of muscles, discipline]; *fig* flag [of zeal, interest]; **II** (verslapte, h. verslapt) *vt* slacken[2], relax[2]; enervate [of climate]; **-ping** (-en) *v* slackening, relaxation; flagging; enervation

ver'slavend addictive, habit-forming; **ver'slaving** *v* addiction; **-svergif(t)** (-giften) *o* addictive drug; habit-forming drug

ver'slecht(er)en I (verslechterde, verslechtte, h. verslechterd, verslecht) *vt* make worse, worsen, deteriorate; **II** (verslechterde, verslechtte, is verslechterd, verslecht) *vi* grow worse, worsen, deteriorate; **ver'slechtering** (-en) *v* worsening, deterioration

'versleer *v* metrics, prosody

ver'slepen[1] *vt* drag away, tow away, haul away

ver'sleten the worse for wear, worn (out)[2]; threadbare[2]; **ver'slijten I** *vi* wear out, wear off, wear away; **II** *vt* wear out [a coat &]; *iem. ~ voor...* take sbd. for...

ver'slikken[1] *zich ~* choke [on sth.], swallow sth. the wrong way

ver'slinden* *vt* devour[2]; *fig* swallow up [much money &]; *een boek ~* devour a book; *zijn eten ~,bolt (wolf down) one's food; *iets met de ogen ~* devour sth. with one's eyes

---

[1] V.T. en V.D. van dit werkwoord volgens het model: **ver'achten**, V.T. **ver'achtte**, V.D. **ver'acht** (**ge-** valt dus weg in het V.D.). Zie voor de vormen onder het grondwoord, in dit voorbeeld: *achten*. Bij sterke en onregelmatige werkwoorden wordt u verwezen naar de lijst achterin.

ver'slingerd ~ *aan* stuck on, crazy about;
  ver'slingeren¹ *zich* ~ *aan* throw oneself away
  on
ver'sloffen¹ *vt* neglect
ver'slond (verslonden) V.T. van *verslinden*
ver'slond (verslonden) V.T. v. *verslinden*
ver'slonden V.T. v. *verslinden*
  (through carelessness), neglect
ver'sluieren¹ *vt* veil, blur, fog
'versmaat (-maten) *v* metre
ver'smachten (versmachtte, is versmacht) *vi fig*
  languish, pine away; ~ *van dorst* be parched
  with thirst
ver'smaden¹ *vt* disdain, despise, scorn; *dat is
  niet te* ~ that is not to be despised; **-ding** *v*
  disdain, scorn
ver'smallen (versmalde, *vt* h., *vi* is versmald) *vt*
  & *vr* narrow
ver'smelten¹ **I** *vt* melt [butter, metals], smelt
  [ore], fuse [metals]; *zijn zilverwerk* ~ melt down
  one's plate; **II** *vi* melt², melt away; **-ting** (-en)
  v melting, smelting, fusion; melting down
ver'snapering (-en) *v* titbit, dainty, refreshment
ver'snellen¹ *vi* & *vt* accelerate; *de pas* ~ mend
  (quicken) one's pace; *met versnelde pas* ⚓ at the
  double-quick; **-er** (-s) *m* accelerator; **ver'snel-
  ling** (-en) *v* 1 acceleration [of movement]; 2 ✗
  gear, speed; *eerste* ~ first (bottom) gear; *hoogste*
  ~ top gear; **ver'snellingsbak** (-ken) *m*
  gear-box, gear-case; **-handel** [-hɛndəl] (-s) *o*
  & *m* gear-lever, gear-shift; **-hendel** (-s) =
  versnellingshandel
ver'snijden¹ *vt* 1 (a a n s t u k k e n) cut up [a
  loaf]; cut [sth.] to pieces; 2 (d o o r s n ij d e n
  b e d e r v e n) spoil in cutting; 3 (m e n g e n)
  dilute [wine]; **-ding** (-en) *v* 1 cutting up &; 2
  dilution [of wine]
ver'snipperen¹ *vt* 1 cut into bits; cut up; 2 *fig*
  fritter away [one's time]; **-ring** (-en) *v* cutting
  up &
ver'snoepen¹ *vt* spend on sweets
ver'soberen (versoberde, h. versoberd) *vi*
  economize, cut down expenses; **-ring** (-en) *v*
  economization, austerity
ver'somberen (versomberde, is versomberd) *vi*
  grow gloomy (dismal)
ver'spelen¹ *vt* 1 play away, lose in playing; 2
  lose [sbd.'s esteem, ⚓ her rudder]
ver'spenen (verspeende, h. verspeend) *vt* prick
  out [seedlings]
ver'sperren¹ *vt* obstruct [the way], barricade [a
  street], block up [a road], block² [a passage,
  the way]; bar [the entrance]; **ver'sperring**

(-en) *v* blocking up, obstruction [of the way
&]; ⚓ barricade; [barbed wire] entanglement;
[balloon &] barrage; **-sballon** (-s) *m* barrage
balloon
ver'spieden¹ *vt* spy out, scout; **-er** (-s) *m* spy,
  scout; **ver'spieding** (-en) *v* spying (out)
ver'spillen¹ *vt* waste [one's time], dissipate
  [one's strength]; squander [one's money]; *er
  geen woord meer aan* ~ not waste another word
  upon it; **-er** (-s) *m* spendthrift; **ver'spilling**
  (-en) *v* waste, dissipation
ver'splinteren **I** (versplinterde, h. versplinterd)
  vt splinter, shiver; **II** (versplinterde, is
  versplinterd) *vi* splinter, break up into splinters
ver'spreid scattered² [houses, showers,
  writings]; sparse [population]; ⚓ extended
  [order]; **ver'spreiden¹ I** *vt* disperse [a crowd];
  spread² [a smell, a report, a rumour]; scatter²
  [seed, people]; distribute [pamphlets]; *fig*
  disseminate [doctrines]; diffuse [happiness];
  propagate [the Christian religion]; **II** *vr zich* ~
  spread² [of odour, disease, fame, rumour,
  people]; disperse [of a crowd]; **-er** (-s) *m*
  spreader, propagator; distributor [of pam-
  phlets]; **ver'spreiding** *v* spreading [of reports
  &]; dispersion [of a crowd]; spread [of knowl-
  edge]; distribution [of animals on earth, of
  pamphlets]; dissemination [of doctrines &];
  propagation [of a creed]
ver'spreken¹ *zich* ~ make a mistake in speaking, make a slip of the tongue; zie ook: *zich
  vergalopperen*; **-king** (-en) *v* slip of the tongue
1 ver'springen¹ *vi* shift; *een dag* ~ move up one
  day
2 'verspringen *o sp* long jump
'versregel (-s) *m* verse, line of poetry; **-snede**
  (-n) *v* caesura
verst **I** *aj* furthest, farthest, furthermost; *in de* ~*e
  verte niet* zie *verte*; **II** *ad het* ~ furthest, ook:
  farthest
ver'staald steeled²
ver'staan¹ **I** *vt* understand, know; *ik heb het niet*
  ~ I did not understand, I did not catch what
  you (he) said; *versta je?* you understand?; *men
  versta mij wel* be it (distinctly) understood; *wel te*
  ~ that is to say; *iem. te* ~ *geven* give sbd. to
  understand that...; *iem. verkeerd* ~ misunderstand sbd.; *onder pasteurisatie* ~ *wij...* by p. is
  meant...; *wat verstaat u daaronder?* what do you
  understand by that?; *zijn vak* ~ know (understand) one's job; *de kunst* ~ know how [to];
  II *vr zich* ~ *met...* come to an understanding
  with...; **ver'staanbaar I** *aj* understandable,

¹ V.T. en V.D. van dit werkwoord volgens het model: **ver**'achten, V.T. **ver**'achtte, V.D. **ver**'acht (**ge-** valt dus weg
in het V.D.). Zie voor de vormen onder het grondwoord, in dit voorbeeld: *achten*. Bij sterke en onregelmatige
werkwoorden wordt u verwezen naar de lijst achterin.

intelligible; *zich ~ maken* make oneself understood; **II** *ad* intelligibly; **–heid** *v* intelligibility; **ver'staander** (-s) *m een goed ~ heeft maar een half woord nodig* a word to the wise is enough, a nod is as good as a wink

ver'stalen[1] *vt* steel[2], harden[2]

ver'stand *o* understanding, mind, intellect, reason; *gezond ~* common sense; *zijn ~ gebruiken* 1 use one's brains; 2 listen to reason; *~ genoeg hebben om...* have sense enough (the wits) to...; *hij spreekt naar hij ~ heeft* according to his lights; *~ van iets hebben* understand about a thing, be good at sth., be at home in sth., be a good judge of sth.; *daar heb ik geen ~ van* I don't know the first thing about it, I'm no judge of that; *heeft u ~ van schilderijen?* do you know about pictures?; *het (zijn) ~ verliezen* lose one's reason (one's wits); *heb je je ~ verloren?* have you taken leave of your senses?; *daar staat mijn ~ bij stil* it is beyond my comprehension how...; ● *dat zal ik hem wel a a n zijn ~ brengen* I'll bring it home to him, I'll give him to understand it; *je kunt hun dat maar niet aan het ~ brengen* you can't make them understand it; *hij is niet b ij zijn ~* he is not in his right mind; *hij is nog altijd bij zijn volle ~* he is still in full possession of his faculties; he is still quite sane; *dat gaat b o v e n mijn ~ (mijn ~ te boven)* it is beyond (above) my comprehension, it passes my comprehension, it is beyond me; *m e t ~ lezen* understandingly, intelligently; *met dien ~e dat...* on the understanding that...; **ver'standelijk** intellectual; *~e leeftijd* mental age; **ver'standeloos** senseless, stupid; **ver'stand-houding** (-en) *v* understanding; *geheime ~* secret understanding, ⚓ collusion; *in ~ staan met* have an understanding with, ⚓ be in collusion with; have dealings with, be in league with [the enemy]; *in goede ~ staan met* be on good terms with [one's neighbours]; **ver'standig I** *aj* intelligent, sensible, wise; *wees nu ~!* do be sensible! (reasonable!); *hij is zo ~ om...* he has the good sense to...; *het ~ste zal zijn, dat je...* the wisest thing you can (could) do will be to...; **II** *ad* sensibly, wisely; *je zult ~ doen met...* you will be wise to...; *hij zou ~ gedaan hebben, als...* he would have been well-advised if...; *~ praten* talk reason; *het ~ vinden om...* judge it wise to...; **–heid** *v* good sense, wisdom; **ver'standshuwelijk** (-en) *o* marriage of convenience; **–kies** (-kiezen) *v* wisdom-tooth; *hij heeft zijn ~ nog niet* he has not cut his wisdom-teeth yet; **–verbijstering** *v*

mental derangement, insanity

ver'starren I (verstarde, h. verstard) *vt* 1 stiffen [limbs, the body]; 2 *fig* petrify, fossilize; **II** (verstarde, is verstard) *vi* 1 stiffen; 2 *fig* become petrified, become fossilized; **–ring** *v* 1 stiffening [of limbs, the body]; 2 *fig* petrifaction, fossilization

ver'stedelijken (verstedelijkte, is verstedelijkt) *vi* urbanize, citify; **–king** *v* urbanization

ver'steend petrified[2]; fossilized[2]; *als ~* petrified [with terror]; *een ~ hart* a heart of stone

1 ver'stek *o* ⚖ default; *~ laten gaan* make default; *hij werd bij ~ veroordeeld* he was sentenced by default (in his absence)

2 ver'stek (-ken) *o* (s c h u i n e n a a d v a n p l a n k) mitre(-joint); **–bak** (-ken) *m* mitre-box, mitre-block

ver'stekeling (-en) *m* stowaway

ver'stekvonnis (-sen) *o* ⚖ judgement by default

ver'stekzaag (-zagen) *v* nitre-saw

ver'stelbaar adjustable [instrument]

ver'steld 1 mended, repaired, patched; ‖ 2 *~ staan* be taken aback, be dumbfounded; *ik stond er ~ van* I was quite taken aback, it staggered me; *hem ~ doen staan* take him aback, stagger him; *de wereld ~ doen staan* stagger humanity; **–heid** *v* perplexity

ver'stelgoed *o* mending; **ver'stellen** *vt* 1 (h e r s t e l l e n) mend, repair [clothes], patch [a coat]; 2 (a n d e r s s t e l l e n) adjust [apparatus]; **–ling** (-en) *v* 1 mending; 2 ✕ adjustment; **ver'stelnaaister** (-s) *v* seamstress; **–ster** (-s) *v* mender; **–werk** *o* mending

ver'stenen (versteende, *vt* h., *vi* is versteend) *vi* & *vt* petrify; fossilize; **–ning** (-en) *v* petrifaction; *~en* ook: fossils

ver'sterf *o* 1 (d o o d) death; 2 (e r f e n i s) inheritance; *bij ~* in case of death; **–recht** *o* right of succession

ver'sterken[1] *vt* strengthen [the body, memory, the evidence &]; invigorate [the energy, the body, mind &]; fortify [the body, a town, a statement]; corroborate [a statement]; reinforce [sbd. with food, and army, a party, the orchestra]; consolidate [a position, power]; intensify [light]; R amplify; *~de middelen* restorative food, restoratives; *met versterkt orkest* ♪ with an increased orchestra; zie ook: *mens*; **–er** (-s) *m* amplifier; **ver'sterking** (-en) *v* strengthening, reinforcement, consolidation; intensification; R amplification; ⚔ 1 (t r o e p e n) reinforcement(s); 2 (w e r k) fortification; **–swerken** *mv* fortifications

---

[1] V.T. en V.D. van dit werkwoord volgens het model: **ver'achten**, V.T. **ver'achtte**, V.D. **ver'acht** (**ge-** valt dus weg in het V.D.). Zie voor de vormen onder het grondwoord, in dit voorbeeld: *achten*. Bij sterke en onregelmatige werkwoorden wordt u verwezen naar de lijst achterin.

ver'sterven I (verstierf, is verstorven) *vi* 1
(s t e r v e n) die; 2 (b ij e r f e n i s o v e r-
g a a n) devolve upon; **II** (verstierf, h.
verstorven) *vr zich ~ rk* mortify the flesh;
–ving (-en) *v* 1 death; 2 *rk* mortification
ver'stevigen (verstevigde, h. verstevigd) *vt*
strengthen; **–er** (-s) *m* (h a a r ~) setting lotion
ver'stijfd 1 stiff; 2 (v. k o u d e o o k)
benumbed, numb; **–heid** *v* stiffness; numbness; **ver'stijven I** (verstijfde, is verstijfd) *vi*
stiffen; grow numb [with cold]; **II** (verstijfde,
h. verstijfd) *vt* 1 stiffen; 2 benumb; **–ving** (-en)
v stiffening; numbness
ver'stikken¹ I *vt* suffocate, stifle, choke,
smother, asphyxiate; **II** *vi* = 1 *stikken*; **–d**
suffocating, stifling, choking; **ver'stikking**
(-en) *v* suffocation, asphyxiation, asphyxia;
ver'stikt suffocated; *met ~e stem* in a strangled
voice
ver'stild ⊙ stilly; **ver'stillen** (verstilde, is
verstild) *vi* still
ver'stoffelijken (verstoffelijkte, h. verstoffelijkt)
vt materialize
1 ver'stoken ~ *van* destitute of, deprived of,
devoid of
2 ver'stoken¹ *vt* burn, consume
ver'stokken (verstokte, *vt* h., *vi* is verstokt) *vi* &
vt harden; **ver'stokt** obdurate [heart],
hardened [sinner], confirmed [bachelors &],
seasoned [gamblers], case-hardened [malefac-
tors]; **–heid** *v* obduracy, hardness of heart
ver'stolen stealthy, furtive
ver'stomd struck dumb, speechless; ~ *staan* zie
versteld 2; **ver'stommen I** (verstomde, h.
verstomd) *vt* strike dumb, silence; **II** (verstomde, is verstomd) *vi* be struck dumb,
become speechless (silent); *alle geluid verstomde*
every sound was hushed
ver'stompen I (verstompte, h. verstompt) *vt*
blunt, dull; *fig* blunt, dull, stupefy [the mind];
II (verstompte, is verstompt) *vi* become dull²;
–ping *v* blunting², dulling², *fig* stupefaction
ver'stoord disturbed; *fig* annoyed, cross, angry;
–er (-s) *m* disturber; **–heid** *v* annoyance,
crossness, anger
ver'stoppen *vt* 1 (d i c h t s t o p p e n) clog [the
nose, the pipes]; choke (up), stop up [a drain-
pipe]; 2 (v e r b e r g e n) put away, conceal,
hide; **ver'stoppertje** *o* ~ *spelen* play at hide-
and-seek; **ver'stopping** (-en) *v* 1 stoppage; 2
ƒ constipation, obstruction; **ver'stopt**
stopped up [pipes, drains]; clogged [nose]; ~
raken become clogged, be choked up (stopped

up); ~ *(in het hoofd) zijn* have (got) the snuffles
(a clogged nose)
ver'storen *vt* 1 disturb [sbd.'s rest, the peace];
interfere with [sbd.'s plans]; 2 annoy, make
angry; **–ring** (-en) *v* disturbance, interference
ver'stoteling (-en) *m* outcast, pariah;
ver'stoten¹ *vt* repudiate [one's wife]; disown
[a child]; **–ting** *v* repudiation
ver'stouten (verstoutte, h. verstout) *zich ~*
pluck up courage; *zij zullen zich niet ~ om...*
they won't make bold to...
ver'stouwen *vt* stow away
ver'strakken (verstrakte, is verstrakt) *vi* set [of
the face]
ver'strekken¹ *vt* furnish, procure; *hun al het
nodige ~* furnish (provide) them with the
necessaries of life; *gelden ~* supply moneys;
inlichtingen ~ give information; *levensmiddelen ~*
serve out provisions
'verstrekkend far-reaching
ver'strijken (verstreek, is verstreken) *vi* expire,
elapse, go by; *de termijn is verstreken* has
expired; **–king** *v* expiration, expiry, passage
[of time]
ver'strikken¹ I *vt* ensnare, trap, entrap,
enmesh, entangle; **II** *vr zich ~* get entangled²
[in a net, in a dispute], be caught [in one's own
words]; **–king** *v* ensnaring, entanglement
ver'strooid 1 scattered, dispersed; 2 (v. g e e s t)
absent-minded, distrait; **–heid** (-heden) *v*
absent-mindedness, absence of mind;
ver'strooien I *vt* scatter, disperse, rout [an
army]; **II** *vr zich ~* 1 disperse; 2 seek amusement, unbend; **–iing** (-en) *v* 1 dispersion; 2
diversion
ver'stuiken (verstuikte, h. verstuikt) **I** *vt* sprain
[one's ankle]; **II** *vr zich ~* sprain one's ankle;
–king (-en) *v* sprain(ing)
ver'stuiven¹ I *vi* be blown away [of dust]; be
dispersed (scattered); *doen ~* scatter, disperse;
II *vt* (v. p o e d e r) pulverize, (v. v l o e i s t o f)
spray; **–er** (-s) *m* (v. p o e d e r) pulverizer, (v.
v l o e i s t o f) atomizer, spray, nebuliser;
ver'stuiving (-en) *v* 1 dispersion; 2 pulverization; 3 = *zandverstuiving*
ver'sturen¹ = *verzenden*
ver'stuwen¹ = *verstouwen*
ver'suffen I (versufte, is versuft) *vi* grow dull,
grow stupid; **II** (versufte, h. versuft) *vt* dream
away [one's time]; **ver'suft** stunned, dazed,
dull; ~ *van schrik* dazed with fright; **–heid** *v*
stupor; (v. o u d e r d o m) dotage
ver'suikeren (versuikerde, h. versuikerd) *vt*

---

¹ V.T. en V.D. van dit werkwoord volgens het model: **ver'**achten, V.T. **ver'**achtte, V.D. **ver'**acht (**ge-** valt dus weg
in het V.D.). Zie voor de vormen onder het grondwoord, in dit voorbeeld: *achten*. Bij sterke en onregelmatige
werkwoorden wordt u verwezen naar de lijst achterin.

candy, crystallize

ver'sukkeling *v in de* ~ *raken* run to seed

'versvoet (-en) *m* (metrical) foot

ver'taalbaar translatable; **–kunde** *v* (art of) translation; **–machine** [-ma.ʃi.nə] (-s) *v* translating machine; **–oefening** (-en) *v* translation exercise; **–recht** *o* right of translation, translation rights; **–ster** (-s) *v* translator; **–werk** *o* translations, translation work

ver'takken (vertakte, h. vertakt) *zich* ~ branch, ramify; **–king** (-en) *v* branching, ramification

ver'talen (vertaalde, h. vertaald) **I** *vt* translate; ~ *in* translate (render, turn) into [English &]; ~ *uit het... in het...* translate from [Persian] into [Turkish]; **II** *vi* translate; **–er** (-s) *m* translator; **ver'taling** (-en) *v* translation; ~ *uit het... in het...* translation from... into...; **–srecht** *o* right of translation, translation rights

'verte (-n en -s) *v* distance; *in de* ~ in the distance; *heel in de* ~ far away (in the distance); *het leek er in de* ~ *op* it remotely resembled it; *nog in de* ~ *familie van...* a distant relation of..., distantly related to...; *in de verste* ~ *niet* not in the least; *ik heb er in de verste* ~ *niet aan gedacht om...* I have not had the remotest idea of ...ing, nothing could be further from my thoughts; *uit de* ~ from afar, from a distance

ver'tederen (vertederde, h. vertederd) *vt* soften, mollify; **–ring** (-en) *v* softening, mollification

ver'teerbaar digestible; *licht* ~ easily digested, easy to digest; **–heid** *v* digestibility

vertegen'woordigen (vertegenwoordigde, h. vertegenwoordigd) *vt* represent, ook: be representative of; ~*d* representative; representative of, representing; **–er** (-s) *m* representative; $ ook: agent, salesman; **vertegen-'woordiging** *v* representation; $ ook: agency

ver'tekend 1 out of drawing; 2 *fig* distorted

ver'tellen[1] **I** *vt* tell, relate, narrate; *men vertelt van hem dat...* he is said to...; *vertel me (er) eens... just tell me...*; *ik heb horen* ~ *dat...* I was told that...; *vertel het niet verder* don't let it get about; **II** *va* tell a story; *hij kan aardig* ~ he can tell a story well; **III** *vr zich* ~ miscount, make a mistake in adding up; **–er** (-s) *m* narrator, relater, story-teller; **ver'telling** (-en) *v* tale, story, narrative; **ver'telsel** (-s) *o* tale, story; **–boek** (-en) *o* story-book

ver'teren I (verteerde, h. verteerd) *vt* 1 (v o e d s e l) digest; 2 (g e l d) spend; 3 *fig* (v. v u u r &) consume; (v. h a r t s t o c h t) eat up, devour [a man]; *de afgunst verteert hem* he is consumed (eaten up) with envy; *de roest verteert*

het ijzer rust corrodes iron; **II** (verteerde, is verteerd) *vi* digest; *het verteert gemakkelijk* it is easy of digestion; *dat verteert niet goed* it does not digest well; *het hout verteert* the wood wastes away; **–ring** (-en) *v* 1 (v. v o e d s e l) digestion; 2 (v e r b r u i k) consumption; 3 (g e l a g) expenses; *wat is mijn* ~? how much am I to pay for what I have had?; *grote* ~*en maken* spend largely

ver'teuten[1] *vt* fritter (dawdle, idle) away

verti'caal vertical; (bij k r u i s w o o r d - r a a d s e l) down

vertien'voudigen (vertienvoudigde, h. vertienvoudigd) *vt* decuple

ver'tier *o* 1 (v e r k e e r) traffic; 2 (d r u k t e) bustle; 3 (v e r m a a k) amusement

ver'tikken[1] *vt het* ~ refuse; *hij vertikte het* he just wouldn't do it

ver'tillen[1] **I** *vt* lift, move; **II** *vr zich* ~ strain oneself in lifting

ver'timmeren[1] *vt* make alterations in; **–ring** *v* alterations

ver'tinnen (vertinde, h. vertind) *vt* tin, coat with tin; **ver'tinsel** (-s) *o* tinning, tin coating

ver'toeven[1] *vi* sojourn, stay, abide

ver'tolken (vertolkte, h. vertolkt) *vt* interpret; *fig* voice [the feelings of...]; *J* interpret, render; **–er** (-s) *m* interpreter[2]; *fig* exponent; **ver'tolking** (-en) *v* interpretation[2]

ver'tonen[1] **I** *vt* 1 show [one's card]; exhibit [signs of..., a work of art]; display [the beauty of...]; 2 (o p v o e r e n) produce, present [said of the theatrical manager]; perform [a play]; show, present [a film]; **II** *vr zich* ~ show, appear [of buds, flowers &]; show oneself [in public]; *hij vertoonde zich niet* ook: he did not put in an appearance, he did not show up (turn up); **–er** (-s) *m* shower; producer; performer; **ver'toning** (-en) *v* 1 show, exhibition; 2 (o p v o e r i n g) performance, representation; *stichtelijke* ~ edifying spectacle

ver'toog (-togen) *o* remonstrance, representation; expostulation; *vertogen richten tot* make representations to

ver'toon *o* 1 show; 2 (p r a a l) show, ostentation, > parade; ~ *van geleerdheid* parade of learning; (*veel*) ~ *maken* 1 (v. m e n s e n) make a show; 2 (v. d i n g e n) make a fine show; ~ *maken met* show off, parade; ● *op* ~ on presentation; *z o n d e r* ~ *van geleerdheid* without showing off one's learning; **–baar** = *toonbaar*

ver'toornd incensed, wrathful, angry; ~ *op* angry with; **ver'toornen** (vertoornde, h.

---

[1] V.T. en V.D. van dit werkwoord volgens het model: **ver'achten**, V.T. **ver'achtte**, V.D. **ver'acht** (**ge**- valt dus weg in het V.D.). Zie voor de vormen onder het grondwoord, in dit voorbeeld: *achten*. Bij sterke en onregelmatige werkwoorden wordt u verwezen naar de lijst achterin.

vertoornd) **I** *vt* make angry, anger, incense; **II** *vr zich* ~ become angry

ver'tragen (vertraagde, h. vertraagd) *vt* retard, delay, slacken, slow down [the pace, movement]; *vertraagde film* slow-motion picture, slow-motion film; *vertraagd telegram* belated telegram; **–ging** (-en) *v* slackening, slowing down [of the pace, a movement]; delay [in replying to a letter]; *de trein heeft 20 minuten* ~ the train is 20 minutes behind schedule (behind time), is running 20 minutes late

ver'trappen[1] *vt* trample (tread) upon[2]; **ver'trapt** trampled down, *fig* downtrodden

ver'treden[1] **I** *vt* tread upon; *in het stof* ~ trample under foot; **II** *vr ik moet mij eens* ~ I want to stretch my legs

ver'trek *o* 1 departure, ⚓ sailing; 2 (-ken) room, apartment; *bij zijn* ~ at his departure, when he left; **–hal** (-len) *v* departure hall; **ver'trekken I** *vi* depart, start, leave, set out; go away (off); ⚓ sail; *je kunt* ~*!* you may go now!; ~ *van Parijs naar Londen* leave Paris for London; **II** *vt* distort [one's face]; *hij vertrok geen spier* he did not move a muscle, he did not turn a hair; **–king** (-en) *v* distortion; **ver'trekpunt** (-en) *o* point of departure; place of departure; **–sein** (-en) *o* starting signal; **–tijd** (-en) *m* time of departure, departure time; (v. b o o t) sailing time

ver'treuzelen[1] *vt* trifle away, loiter away

ver'troebelen (vertroebelde, h. vertroebeld) *vt* make cloudy (thick, muddy); *fig* cloud [the issue]; trouble [relations, the atmosphere]

ver'troetelen[1] *vt* coddle, pamper, pet

ver'troosten[1] *vt* comfort, console, solace; **–er** (-s) *m* comforter; **ver'troosting** (-en) *v* consolation, comfort, solace

ver'trouwd reliable, trusted, trustworthy, trusty; safe; ~ *vriend* 1 intimate friend; 2 trusted friend; ~ *met* conversant (familiar) with; *zich* ~ *maken met* make oneself familiar with [a subject]; ~ *raken met* become conversant with; **–e** (-n) *m-v = vertrouweling, vertrouwelinge*; **–heid** *v* familiarity [with the subject]; **ver'trouwelijk I** *aj* confidential; ~*e vriend* intimate friend; *streng* ~*!* strictly private!; **II** *ad* confidentially, in confidence; ~ *omgaan met* zie *omgaan*; **–heid** (-heden) *v* confidentialness; familiarity; **ver'trouweling(e)** (-lingen) *m(-v)* confidant(e); **ver'trouwen**[1] **I** *vt* trust; *iem. iets* ~ zie *toevertrouwen*; *wij* ~ *dat...* we trust that...; *zij* ~ *hem niet* they don't trust him; *hij vertrouwde het zaakje niet* he did not trust the business; *hij*

is niet te ~ he is not to be trusted; **II** *vi* ~ *op God* trust in God; *ik vertrouw erop* I rely upon it; *kunnen wij op u* ~*?* can we rely on you?; *op de toekomst (het toeval &)* ~ trust to the future (to luck); **III** *o* confidence, trust, faith; *zijn* ~ *op...* his reliance on..., his faith in...; *het* ~ *beschamen* betray sbd.'s confidence; *het volste* ~ *genieten* enjoy sbd.'s entire confidence; ~ *hebben* have confidence, be confident; *geen* ~ *meer hebben in...* have lost confidence in...; ~ *hebben op* = ~ *stellen in*; *iem. zijn* ~ *schenken* admit (take) sbd. into one's confidence; ~ *stellen in* put trust in, repose (place, have) confidence in, put one's faith in; *zijn* ~ *verliezen* lose faith [in]; *zijn* ~ *is geschokt* his confidence has been shaken; ~ *wekken* inspire confidence; ● *i n* ~ in (strict) confidence; *iem. in* ~ *nemen* take sbd. into one's confidence; *in* ~ *op* relying upon; *m e t* ~ with confidence, confidently; *met het volste* ~ with the utmost confidence, with every confidence; *o p goed* ~ on trust; *goed van* ~ *zijn* be of a trustful nature; **ver'trouwenscrisis** [-zɪs] (-sen en -crises) *v* crisis of confidence, confidence crisis; **–kwestie** *v = kabinetskwestie*; **–man** (-nen en -lieden) *m* confidential agent; trusted representative; **–positie** [-zi.(t)si.] (-s) *v*, **–post** (-en) *m* position of trust; **–votum** *o* vote of confidence, confidence vote; **vertrouwen'wekkend** inspiring confidence (trust)

ver'vaard alarmed, frightened; *voor geen kleintje* ~ not easily frightened, nothing daunted; **–heid** *v* alarm, fear

ver'vaardigen (vervaardigde, h. vervaardigd) *vt* make, manufacture; **–er** (-s) *m* maker, manufacturer; **ver'vaardiging** *v* making, manufacture

ver'vaarlijk I *aj* frightful, awful; huge, tremendous; **II** *ad* frightfully, awfully; **–heid** *v* frightfulness, awfulness

ver'vagen (vervaagde, is vervaagd) *vi* fade, blur, grow blurred, become indistinct

ver'val *o* fall [difference in the levels of a river]; *fig* 1 (a c h t e r u i t g a n g) decay, decline, deterioration; 2 (o m m e k o m s t) maturity [of a bill of exchange]; 3 (f o o i e n) perquisites; ~ *van krachten* senile decay; *in* ~ *geraken* fall into decay; **–dag** (-dagen) *m* day of payment, due date; *op de* ~ at maturity, when due; **1 ver'vallen**[1] *vi* 1 decay, fall into decay, go to ruin; fall into disrepair [of a house]; 2 (n i e t l a n g e r l o p e n) expire [of a term]; fall (become) due, mature [of bills];

---

[1] V.T. en V.D. van dit werkwoord volgens het model: **ver**'achten, V.T. **ver**'achtte, V.D. **ver**'acht (**ge-** valt dus weg in het V.D.). Zie voor de vormen onder het grondwoord, in dit voorbeeld: *achten*. Bij sterke en onregelmatige werkwoorden wordt u verwezen naar de lijst achterin.

3 (w e g v a l l e n) be taken off [of a train]; be cancelled [of a service]; 4 (n i e t l a n g e r g e l d e n) lapse [of a right], be abrogated [of a law]; ● ~ *aan de Kroon* fall to the Crown; *in boete* ~ incur a fine; *in zijn oude fout* ~ fall into the old mistake; *in herhalingen* ~ repeat oneself; *in onkosten* ~ incur expenses; *tot zonde* ~ lapse into sin; zie ook: *armoede, uiterste* &; 2 ver'vallen *aj* 1 (v. g e b o u w e n &) ruinous, out of repair, dilapidated, ramshackle [house &]; worn (out), broken down [person]; 2 (v. r e c h t) lapsed; 4 (v a n t e r m ij n, p o l i s) expired; *van de troon* ~ *verklaard* deposed

ver'valsen (vervalste, h. vervalst) *vt* falsify [a text], forge [a document], cook [the accounts]; adulterate [food], debase [coin &], counterfeit [banknotes], load [dice], doctor [wine], fake [a painting]; –er (-s) *m* falsifier, adulterator, forger, faker: ver'valsing (-en) *v* falsification [of a document], adulteration [of food]; forgery [= forged document], [art] fake

ver'vangbaar replaceable, commutable; ver'vangen[1] *vt* 1 take (fill, supply) the place of, replace, be used instead of; 2 (a f l o s s e n) relieve; *wie zal u* ~? who is going to take your place?, who is going to stand in for you?; *het* ~ *door iets anders* replace it by something else, substitute something else for it; –er (-s) *m* = *plaatsvervanger*; ver'vanging *v* replacement, substitution; *ter* ~ *van* in (the) place of, in substitution for; ver'vangingsmiddel (-en) *o* substitute; –waarde *v* replacement value

ver'vat ~ *in* implied in [this statement &]; couched in [energetic terms]; *daarin is alles* ~ everything is contained therein

'verve *v* verve, enthusiasm, vigour

ver'veeld bored

verveel'voudigen (verveelvoudigde, h. verveelvoudigd) *vt* multiply, duplicate

ver'velen (verveelde, h. verveeld) I *vt* bore, tire, weary; (e r g e r e n) annoy; *hij zal je dood* ~ he will bore you stiff; *het zal je dood* ~ you will be bored to death; *het begint me te* ~ I am beginning to get tired of it (bored with it); II *va* tire, bore, become a bore; *tot* ~s *toe* over and over again, ad nauseam; III *vr zich* ~ be bored, feel bored; –d I *aj* tiresome, boring [fellow &]; dull [book, play, town &], tedious [speech &]; irksome [task]; (e r g e r l ijk) annoying; *hè, wat* ~ *is dat nou!* how provoking!, how annoying!; Oh bother!; *wat is dat* ~ what a bore it is!; *wat is die vent* ~! what a bore!; *het wordt* ~ it

becomes wearisome; II *ad* boringly, tediously; ver'veling *v* tiresomeness, tedium, boredom, weariness, ennui

ver'vellen (vervelde, is verveld) *vi* cast its skin [of a snake], slough; *mijn neus begint te* ~ begins to peel; –ling (-en) *v* sloughing [of a snake]; peeling

'verveloos paintless, badly in need of (a coat of) paint; discoloured; verve'loosheid *v* paintlessness, colourlessness; 'verven (verfde, h. geverfd) *vt* 1 paint [a door, one's face &]; 2 dye [clothes, one's hair]

ver'venen (verveende, is verveend) *vi* become peaty (boggy)

'verver (-s) *m* 1 (house-)painter; 2 dyer [of clothes]; verve'rij (-en) *v* dye-house, dyeworks

ver'versen (ververste, h. ververst) *vt* refresh, renew; *olie* ~ change oil; –sing (-en) *v* refreshment

ver'vetten (vervette, is vervet) *vi* turn to fat; ♂ become fatty; –ting *v* ♂ fatty degeneration

vervier'voudigen (verviervoudigde, h. verviervoudigd) *vt* quadruple

ver'vilten (verviltte, is vervilt) *vi* felt

ver'vlakken (vervlakte, is vervlakt) *vi* (v a n k l e u r e n) fade; *fig* become trivial (shallow), peter out

ver'vlechten[1] *vt* interweave, interlace, intertwine

ver'vliegen[1] *vi* 1 (w e g v l i e g e n) fly [of time]; 2 (v e r v l u c h t i g e n) evaporate, volatilize [of liquids, salt &]; 3 *fig* evaporate; zie ook: *vervlogen*

ver'vloeien *vi* flow away; run [of ink], melt [of colours]

ver'vloeken[1] *vt* 1 curse, damn, execrate; 2 (m e t b a n v l o e k) anathematize; –king (-en) *v* 1 curse, imprecation, malediction; 2 anathema; ver'vloekt I *aj* cursed, damned, execrable; *die* ~*e...!* damn the...!; *een* ~*e last a* damned nuisance; (*wel*) ~*!* damn it!; II *ad* < damned, deuced, confoundedly [difficult &]

ver'vlogen gone; *in* ~ *dagen* in days gone by; ~ *hoop* hope gone; ~ *roem* departed glory

ver'vluchtigen (vervluchtigde, *vt* h., *vt* is vervluchtigd) *vi* & *vt* volatilize, evaporate[2]; –ging *v* volatilization, evaporation[2]

ver'voegbaar *gram* that can be conjugated; ver'voegen[1] I *vt* conjugate [verbs]; II *vr zich* ~ *bij* apply to; –ging (-en) *v gram* conjugation

ver'voer *o* transport, conveyance, carriage; transit; *openbaar* ~ public transport; ~ *te water*

---

[1] V.T. en V.D. van dit werkwoord volgens het model: ver'achten, V.T. ver'achtte, V.D. ver'acht (ge- valt dus weg in het V.D.). Zie voor de vormen onder het grondwoord, in dit voorbeeld: *achten*. Bij sterke en onregelmatige werkwoorden wordt u verwezen naar de lijst achterin.

water-carriage; **–adres** (-sen) *o* way-bill; **–baar** transportable; **–biljet** (-ten) *o* $ permit; **–der** (-s) *m* transporter, conveyer, carrier; **ver'voeren**[1] *vt* transport, convey, carry; **–ring** (-en) *o* transport, conveyance; *in* ~ *raken* go into raptures [over it], be carried away [by these words]; **ver'voerkosten** *mv* transport charges, cost of carriage; **–middel** (-en) *o* (means of) conveyance, means of transport; **–verbod** (-boden) *o* prohibition of transport; **–wezen** *o* transport

ver'volg (-en) *o* continuation, sequel; (t o e k o m s t) future; ~ *op bl. 12* continued on page 12; *i n het* ~ in future, henceforth; *t e n* ~*e op (van) mijn brief van...* $ further to my letter of..., following up my letter of...; *ten* ~*e van...* in continuation of...; **–baar** ⚖ actionable, indictable [offence]; (c i v i e l) suable, (c r i m i n e e l) prosecutable [persons]; **–deel** (-delen) *o* supplementary volume; **ver'volgen**[1] *vt* 1 continue [a story, a course &]; proceed on [one's way]; 2 (a c h t e r n a z e t t e n) pursue [the enemy]; 3 persecute [for political or religious reasons]; 4 ⚖ prosecute [sbd.]; sue [a debtor]; proceed against, have the law of [sbd.]; *...vervolgde hij* ...he went on, ...he continued, ...he went on to say; *wordt vervolgd* to be continued (in our next); *die gedachte (herinnering) vervolgt mij* the thought (memory) haunts me; *door pech vervolgd* dogged by ill-luck, pursued by misfortune

ver'volgens then, further, next; afterwards; *hij vroeg* ~... ook: he went on (he proceeded) to ask...

ver'volger (-s) *m* 1 pursuer; 2 persecutor; **ver'volging** (-en) *v* 1 pursuit; 2 persecution; 3 ⚖ prosecution; *een* ~ *instellen tegen iem.* bring an action against sbd.; *aan* ~ *blootstaan* be exposed to persecution; **–swaanzin** *m* persecution mania; **ver'volgverhaal** (-halen) *o* serial (story); **–werk** (-en) *o* serial publication, work in instalments

vervol'maken (vervolmaakte, h. vervolmaakt) *vt* perfect, complete; **–king** *v* perfection, completion

ver'vormen[1] *vt* 1 transform, refashion; 2 deform; **–ming** (-en) *v* 1 transformation, refashioning; 2 deformation

ver'vrachten (vervrachtte, h. vervracht) *vt* zie *bevrachten*

ver'vreemd alienated, estranged (from *van*); **ver'vreemdbaar** alienable; **–heid** *v* alienability; **ver'vreemden I** (vervreemdde, h.

vervreemd) *vt* alienate [property]; ~ *van* alienate (estrange) from; *zijn familie van zich* ~ alienate one's relations; **II** (vervreemdde, h. zich & is vervreemd) (*vr* &) *vi* (*zich*) ~ *van* become estranged from, become a stranger to; **–ding** (-en) *v* alienation, estrangement

ver'vroegen (vervroegde, h. vervroegd) *vt* fix at an earlier time (hour), advance, bring (move) forward [the date by a week], put [dinner] forward; *vervroegde betaling* accelerated payment; **–ging** (-en) *v* anticipation

ver'vrouwelijken (vervrouwelijkte, *vt* h., *vi* is vervrouwelijkt) *vi* & *vt* feminize

ver'vuild 1 filthy; 2 polluted [river]; **ver'vuilen I** (vervuilde, is vervuild) *vi* grow filthy; **II** (vervuilde, h. vervuild) *vt* 1 make filthy; 2 pollute [air, water, the environment]; **–ling** *v* 1 filthiness; 2 [environmental] pollution [by industry]

ver'vullen[1] *vt* fill[2] [a room with..., a part, a place, a rôle]; fulfil [a prophecy, a promise]; occupy, fill [a place]; perform, carry out [a duty], accomplish [a task]; comply with [a formality]; *hij zag zijn hoop (zijn wensen) vervuld* his hopes (his wishes) were realized, his desires were fulfilled; *iems. plaats* ~ take sbd.'s place; ~ *m e t* fill with; *v a n angst vervuld* full of anxiety; **–ling** *v* fulfilment, performance; realization; *in* ~ *gaan* be realized, be fulfilled; (v. d r o o m) come true

ver'waaid blown about; *er* ~ *uitzien* look tousled (ruffled); **ver'waaien**[1] *vi* be blown away (about)

ver'waand conceited, bumptious, cocky, **F** stuck-up, uppish; ~ *zijn* give oneself airs; **–heid** (-heden) *v* conceitedness, conceit, bumptiousness, cockiness

ver'waardigen (verwaardigde, h. verwaardigd) **I** *vt iem. met geen blik* ~ not deign to look at sbd.; **II** *vr zich* ~ *om...* condescend to..., deign to...

ver'waarloosd neglected [health, studies, garden], uncared for [children, garden], untended, unkempt [hair]; **ver'waarlozen** (verwaarloosde, h. verwaarloosd) *vt* neglect, take no care of; (b u i t e n b e s c h o u w i n g l a t e n) disregard, ignore [third decimal]; *te* ~ negligible; **–zing** *v* neglect; *met* ~ *van...* to the neglect of...

ver'wachten[1] *vt* expect [people, events]; look forward to, anticipate [an event]; *wij* ~ *dat ze komen zullen* we expect them to come; *dat had ik niet van hem verwacht* I had not expected it of

---

[1] V.T. en V.D. van dit werkwoord volgens het model: **ver**'achten, V.T. **ver**'achtte, V.D. **ver**'acht (**ge-** valt dus weg in het V.D.). Zie voor de vormen onder het grondwoord, in dit voorbeeld: *achten*. Bij sterke en onregelmatige werkwoorden wordt u verwezen naar de lijst achterin.

him (at his hands); *zoals te ~ was* as was to be expected; **–ting** (-en) *v* expectation; *blijde ~* joyful anticipation; *grote ~en hebben van...* entertain great hopes of...; *de ~ koesteren dat...* cherish a hope that..., expect that...; *zonder de minste ~(en) te koesteren dienaangaande* without entertaining any expectation on that score; *zijn ~ hoog spannen* pitch one's expectations high; *de ~en waren hoog gespannen* expectation ran high; *vol ~* in expectation, expectantly; ● *het beantwoordde niet a a n de ~en* it did not come up to my (their &) expectations, it fell short of my (his &) expectations; *b o v e n ~* beyond expectation; *b u i t e n ~* contrary to expectation; *zij is i n (blijde) ~* she is pregnant, **F** she is expecting (a baby), she is in the family way; *t e g e n alle ~* against all expectations, contrary to expectation

ver'want allied, related, affined, connected, kindred, congenial [spirits]; cognate [words]; (a l l é é n   p r e d i k a t i e f) akin; *~ aan* allied (related, akin) to; *het naast ~ aan* most closely allied to; *die hem het naast ~ zijn* his next of kin; **ver'want(e)** (-wanten) *m(-v)* relative, relation; *zijn ~en* his relations, his relatives; **ver'wantschap** *v* relationship, kinship, consanguinity, affinity [of blood]; congeniality [of character &]; relation

ver'ward I *aj* 1 entangled, tangled [threads, hair, mass &]; tousled [hair]; confused [mass], disordered [things]; *fig* confused [thoughts, talk], woolly [mind, ideas]; 2 (i n g e w i k - k e l d) entangled, intricate [affair]; *~ raken in* get entangled in; **II** *ad* confusedly[2]; **–heid** *v* confusion[2]

ver'warmen[1] *vt* warm, heat; **–ming** *v* warming, heating; *centrale ~* central heating; **ver'warmingsbuis** (-buizen) *v* (central-) heating pipe; **–kachel** (-s) *v* heater; **–ketel** (-s) *m* heater; **–toestel** (-len) *o* heating-apparatus

ver'warren I *vt eig* entangle, tangle [threads &]; *fig* confuse [names &]; confound, mix up [facts]; muddle up [things]; **II** *vr zich ~* get entangled; **–ring** (-en) *v* entanglement; confusion[2], muddle; *~ stichten* create confusion; *in ~ brengen* throw into disorder [things]; confuse, confound [sbd.]; *in ~ raken* get confused[2]

ver'waten I *aj* arrogant, overbearing, overweening, presumptuous; **II** *ad* arrogantly; **–heid** *v* arrogance, presumption

ver'waterd spoiled by the addition of too much water; *fig* watered (down); **ver'wateren**[1] *vt*

dilute too much, water [the milk]; *fig* water [the capital], water down [the truth &]

ver'wedden[1] *vt* 1 bet, wager; 2 (d o o r   w e d d e n   v e r l i e z e n) lose in betting; *ik verwed er 10 gulden onder* I bet you ten guilders; *ik verwed er mijn hoofd onder* I'll stake my life on it

ver'weer (-weren) *o* 1 resistance; 2 defence

ver'weerd weathered [stone &]; weather-beaten [pane, face]

ver'weerder (-s) *m tt* defendant; **ver'weermiddel** (-en) *o* means of defence; **–schrift** (-en) *o* (written) defence, apology

ver'weesd orphaned, orphan...

ver'wekelijking *v* enervation, effeminacy

ver'weken[1] *vt* soften; **–king** *v* softening

ver'wekken[1] *vt* procreate, beget [children]; *fig* raise, cause [discontent]; rouse [feelings of...]; stir up [dissatisfaction, a riot]; breed [disease, strife]; *rk* make [an act of contrition]; **–er** (-s) *m* procreator, begetter, author, cause [of a disease]; **ver'wekking** *v* procreation, begetting; raising

ver'welf(sel) (-welven, -welfselen) *o* vault

ver'welken[1] *vi* fade, wither[2]; *doen ~* fade, wither[2]; **–king** *v* fading, withering[2]

ver'welkomen (verwelkomde, h. verwelkomd) *vt* welcome, bid [sbd.] welcome; *hartelijk ~* extend a hearty welcome to...; **–ming** (-en) *v* welcome

ver'welkt faded, withered

ver'welven[1] *vt* vault

ver'wend spoilt [children]; *op het punt van... zijn wij niet ~* they don't spoil us with..., as for... we only get what is just better than nothing; **ver'wennen**[1] **I** *vt* spoil, pamper, indulge (too much) [a child]; **II** *vr zich ~* coddle oneself; **verwenne'rij** (-en) *v* spoiling, pampering, over-indulgence

ver'wensen[1] *vt* curse; **–sing** (-en) *v* curse; **ver'wenst** confounded, damned

ver'wereldlijken I (verwereldlijkte, h. verwereldlijkt) *vt* secularize; **II** (verwereldlijkte, is verwereldlijkt) *vi* grow (more) worldly

1 ver'weren[1] *vr zich ~* defend oneself

2 ver'weren (verweerde, is verweerd) *vi* weather, become weather-beaten

1 ver'wering *v* 1 defence; 2 zie ook: *verweerschrift*

2 ver'wering *v* weathering

ver'werkelijken (verwerkelijkte, h. verwerkelijkt) *vt* realize; **–king** *v* realization

ver'werken[1] *vt* work up [materials], process

---

[1] V.T. en V.D. van dit werkwoord volgens het model: **ver'**achten, V.T. **ver'**achtte, V.D. **ver'**acht (**ge-** valt dus weg in het V.D.). Zie voor de vormen onder het grondwoord, in dit voorbeeld: *achten*. Bij sterke en onregelmatige werkwoorden wordt u verwezen naar de lijst achterin.

[information, gases into ammonia]; digest[2], assimilate[2] [food, what is taught]; *fig* cope with [the demand, the rush, a record number of passengers], deal with, handle [large orders, normal traffic]; ~ *tot* make into; **–king** *v* working up, processing [of information]; handling [of traffic]; assimilation[2], digestion[2] [of food, of what is taught]

ver'werpelijk objectionable; **–heid** *v* objectionableness; **ver'werpen**[1] *vt* reject [an offer]; reject, negative, defeat [a bill &]; repudiate the authority of...]; *het amendement werd verworpen* the amendment was lost (defeated); *het beroep werd verworpen* ☂ the appeal was dismissed; **–ping** *v* rejection, repudiation; ☂ dismissal [of an appeal]

ver'werven[1] *vt* obtain, acquire, win, gain; **–ving** *v* obtaining, acquiring, acquisition

ver'wester(s)en (verwesterste, verwesterde, *vt* h., *vi* is verwesterst, verwesterd) *vt* & *vi* westernize

ver'weven[1] *vt* interweave

ver'wezen dazed, dumbfounded; *hij stond als* ~, *als een* ~*e* he seemed to be in a daze

ver'wezenlijken (verwezenlijkte, h. verwezenlijkt) *vt* realize; **–king** (-en) *v* realization

ver'wijden (verwijdde, h. verwijd) **I** *vt* widen; **II** *vr zich* ~ widen; dilate [of eyes]

ver'wijderd remote, distant; *van elkaar* ~ *raken* drift apart[2]; **ver'wijderen** (verwijderde, h. verwijderd) **I** *vt* remove [things, a stain, a tumour, an official from office &]; get [sbd., sth.] out of the way; expel [a boy from school]; *de mensen van elkaar* ~ estrange people; **II** *vr zich* ~ withdraw, retire, go away [of persons]; move away, move off [of ships &]; grow fainter [of sounds]; *mag ik mij even* ~*?* excuse me one moment?; ☞ may I leave the room?; **–ring** (-en) *v* 1 removal; expulsion [of a boy from school]; 2 (t u s s e n p e r s o n e n) estrangement

ver'wijding (-en) *v* widening, dila(ta)tion

ver'wijfd effeminate; **–heid** (-heden) *v* effeminacy, effeminateness

ver'wijl *o* delay; *zonder* ~ without delay

ver'wijlen (verwijlde, h. verwijld) *vi* stay, sojourn; ~ *bij* dwell on [a subject]

ver'wijskaart (-en) *v* referral card [to medical specialist]

ver'wijt (-en) *o* reproach, blame, reproof; *iem. een* ~ *van iets maken* reproach sbd. with sth.; *ons treft geen* ~ no blame attaches to us, we are not to blame; **ver'wijten**[1] *vt* reproach, upbraid;

iem. iets ~ reproach sbd. with sth.; *zij hebben elkaar niets te* ~ they are tarred with the same brush; *ik heb mij niets te* ~ I have nothing to reproach myself with; **–d** reproachful

ver'wijven I (verwijfde, h. verwijfd) *vt* render effeminate; **II** (verwijfde, is verwijfd) *vi* become effeminate

ver'wijzen[1] *vt* refer; *hij werd in de kosten verwezen* ☂ he was cast in costs; **ver'wijzing** (-en) *v* reference; (cross-)reference [in a book]; *onder* ~ *naar...* referring to..., with reference to...; **–steken** (-s) *o* reference mark

ver'wikkelen intricate, complicated; ~ *zijn in* be mixed up in; **ver'wikkelen**[1] *vt* make intricate; *iem.* ~ *in* implicate sbd. in [a plot], mix sbd. up in [it]; **–ling** (-en) *v* 1 entanglement, complication; 2 (v. r o m a n, t o n e e l s t u k) plot; ~*en* complications

ver'wilderd *eig* 1 (v. d i e r, k i n d, p l a n t) run wild; 2 (t u i n) overgrown, neglected; *fig* wild [looks]; *hij keek* ~ he looked bewildered, perplexed; *wat zien die kinderen er* ~ *uit!* how unkempt these children look!; *de* ~*e jeugd* lawless youth; **ver'wilderen** (verwilderde, is verwilderd) *vi* run wild[2] [also of children]; *fig* sink back into savagery; **–ring** *v* running wild; *fig* sinking back into savagery; lawlessness [of youth, morals]

ver'wisselbaar interchangeable; **ver'wisselen I** (verwisselde, h. verwisseld) *vt* (inter)change; exchange [things]; *u moet ze niet met elkaar* ~ you should not mistake one for the other; you should not confound them; ~ *tegen* exchange for; **II** (verwisselde, is verwisseld) *vi van kleren* ~ change clothes; ~ *van kleur* change colour; *van paarden* ~ change horses; *van plaats* ~ change places; **–d** ~*e hoeken* alternate angles; **ver'wisseling** (-en) *v* (inter)change; exchange; mistake; ~ *van plaats* change of place

ver'wittigen (verwittigde, h. verwittigd) *vt* inform, tell; *iem. van iets* ~ inform sbd. of sth.; **–ging** *v* notice, information

ver'woed I *aj* furious, fierce, grim; keen [sportsman]; **II** *ad* furiously, fiercely, grimly; **–heid** *v* rage, fierceness, grimness

ver'woest destroyed, laid waste, devastated, ruined; ~ *gebied* devastated area; **ver'woesten** (verwoestte, h. verwoest) *vt* destroy, lay waste, devastate, ruin; **–d** destructive, devastating; **ver'woester** (-s) *m* destroyer, devastator; **ver'woesting** (-en) *v* destruction, devastation, ravage, havoc; ~*en* ravages; *(grote)* ~*en aanrichten (onder)* work (great) havoc, make

---

[1] V.T. en V.D. van dit werkwoord volgens het model: **ver'**achten, V.T. **ver'**achtte, V.D. **ver'**acht (**ge-** valt dus weg in het V.D.). Zie voor de vormen onder het grondwoord, in dit voorbeeld: *achten*. Bij sterke en onregelmatige werkwoorden wordt u verwezen naar de lijst achterin.

havoc (among, of)

ver′wonden[1] *vt* wound, injure, hurt

ver′wonderd I *aj* surprised, astonished (at *over*); **II** *ad* wonderingly, in wonder, in surprise;

ver′wonderen (verwonderde, h. verwonderd) **I** *vt* surprise, astonish; *wat mij verwondert is dat...* what surprises me is that...; *het verwondert me alleen dat...* the only thing that astonishes me is...; *dat verwondert mij niet* I am not surprised at that; *het zou me niets ~ als...* I should not wonder, I should not be at all surprised if...; *het is niet te ~ dat...* no wonder that...; *is het te ~ dat...?* is it any wonder that...?; **II** *vr zich ~* (*over*) be surprised (at), be astonished (at), marvel (at), wonder (at); *~ing* astonishment, wonder, surprise; *~ baren* cause a surprise; *tot mijn grote ~* to my great surprise; **ver′wonderlijk** astonishing, surprising; *het ~ste is dat...* the queer thing about it is that...

ver′wonding (-en) *v* wound, injury

ver′wonen[1] *vt* pay for rent

ver′woorden (verwoordde, h. verwoord) *vt* put into words, verbalize

ver′worden[1] *vi* degenerate (into *tot*); **–ding** *v* degeneration

ver′worgen[1] *vt* strangle, throttle; **–ging** *v* strangulation

ver′worpeling (-en) *m* outcast, reprobate; **ver′worpen** *fig* reprobate; **–heid** *v* reprobation

ver′worvenheid (-heden) *v* achievement

ver′wrikken[1] *vt* move (with jerks)

ver′wringen[1] *vt* twist, distort[2]; **–ging** *v* twisting, distortion[2]; **ver′wrongen** twisted, distorted[2]

ver′wulf(sel) (-wulven, -wulfsels) = *verwelf(sel)*

ver′wurgen[1] = *verworgen*; **–ging** = *verworging*

ver′zachten (verzachtte, h. verzacht) *vt* soften[2] [the skin, colours, light, voice]; *fig* soothe; mitigate, palliate, alleviate, allay, assuage, relieve [pain]; relax [the law]; **–d** softening, mitigating; *~ middel* emollient, palliative; *~e omstandigheden* mitigating (extenuating) circumstances; **ver′zachting** *v* softening [of the skin &]; mitigation, alleviation [of pain]; relaxation [of a law]

ver′zadigbaar 1 satiable [person]; 2 § saturable [substance, vapour &]; **ver′zadigd** 1 (v. e t e n) satisfied, satiated; 2 § saturated; **–heid** *v* 1 satiety; 2 § saturation; **ver′zadigen** (verzadigde, h. verzadigd) **I** *vt* 1 satisfy, satiate; 2 § saturate; *niet te ~* insatiable; **II** *vr zich ~* eat one's fill, satisfy oneself; **ver′zadiging** *v*

1 satiation; 2 § saturation; **–spunt** *o* § saturation point

ver′zaken (verzaakte, h. verzaakt) *vt* renounce, forsake; *kleur ~* ◊ revoke; zie ook: *plicht*; **–king** *v* 1 renunciation, forsaking; neglect [of duty]; 2 ◊ revoke

ver′zakken *vi* sag, sink, subside, settle; **–king** (-en) *v* sagging, sag [of a door], sinking, subsidence; ✝ prolapse

ver′zamelaar (-s) *m*, **–ster** (-s) *v* collector, gatherer, compiler; **ver′zamelband** (-en) *m* omnibus book (volume); **–bundel** (-s) *m* miscellany; **ver′zamelen I** *vt* gather [honey &]; collect [things]; store up [energy, power &]; assemble [one's adherents]; rally [troops]; compile [stories]; *zijn gedachten ~* collect one's thoughts; *zijn krachten ~* gather one's strength; *zijn moed ~* muster one's courage; *~ blazen* ⚔ sound the assembly; *fig* sound the rally; **II** *vr zich ~* 1 (v. p e r s o n e n, d i e r e n) come together, gather, meet, assemble, rally, congregate; 2 (v. s t o f &) collect; *zich ~ om...* gather (rally) round...; **–ling** (-en) *v* 1 collection; 2 gathering; 3 compilation; **ver′zamelnaam** (-namen) *m* collective noun; **–plaats** (-en) *v* 1 meeting-place, trysting-place, meet; 2 ⚔ rallying-place; **–werk** (-en) *o* compilation; **–woede** *v* collector's mania, craze for collecting

ver′zanden (verzandde, is verzand) *vi* choke up with sand, silt up; *fig* come to a dead end; **–ding** *v* choking up with sand, silting up

ver′zegelen[1] *vt* seal (up); ⚖ put under seal, put seals upon; **–ling** (-en) *v* sealing (up); ⚖ putting under seal

ver′zeilen *vi* hoe *kom jij hier verzeild?* what brings you here?; *ik weet niet waar hij verzeild is* I don't know where he has got to

ver′zekeraar (-s) *m* 1 assurer; 2 insurer; ⚓ underwriter; **ver′zekerd** 1 (z e k e r) assured, sure; 2 (g e a s s u r e e r d) insured; *u kunt ~ zijn van..., houd u ~ van...* you may rest assured of...; *de ~e* the insurant, the insured; *verplicht ~* obligatorily insured; zie ook: *bewaring*;

ver′zekeren (verzekerde, h. verzekerd) **I** *vt* 1 assure [sbd. of a fact]; 2 (w a a r b o r g e n) assure, ensure [success]; 3 (a s s u r e r e n) insure [property], assure, insure [one's life]; 4 (v a s t m a k e n) secure [windows &]; *dat ~ wij u* we assure you; *niets was verzekerd* there was no insurance; **II** *vr zich tegen... ~* insure against..., take out an insurance against...; *zich van iems. hulp ~* secure sbd.'s help; *ik zal er mij*

---

[1] V.T. en V.D. van dit werkwoord volgens het model: **ver′**achten, V.T. **ver′**achtte, V.D. **ver′**acht (**ge-** valt dus weg in het V.D.). Zie voor de vormen onder het grondwoord, in dit voorbeeld: *achten*. Bij sterke en onregelmatige werkwoorden wordt u verwezen naar de lijst achterin.

van ~ I am going to make sure of it; **–ring** (-en) *v* 1 assurance; 2 assurance, insurance; ~ *tegen glasschade* plate-glass insurance; ~ *tegen inbraak* burglary insurance; ~ *tegen ongelukken* accident insurance; ~ *tegen ziekte en invaliditeit* health insurance; *sociale* ~ social security; *ik geef je de* ~ *dat...* I assure you that...; *een* ~ *sluiten* effect an insurance; **ver'zekeringsagent** (-en) *m* insurance agent; **–bank** (-en) *v* insurance bank; **–kantoor** (-toren) *o* insurance office; **–maatschappij** (-en) *v* insurance company; **verzekerings'plichtig** obliged to insurance; **ver'zekeringspolis** (-sen) *v* insurance policy; **–premie** (-s en -miën) *v* insurance premium; **–wet** (-ten) *v* insurance act; **–wiskundige** (-n) *m* actuary

'**verzenboek** (-en) *o* book of poetry; **–bundel** (-s) *m* volume of verse

ver'zenden *vt* send (off), dispatch, forward, ship; **–er** (-s) *m* sender; shipper; **ver'zendhuis** (-huizen) *o* mail-order house, mail-order business; **ver'zending** (-en) *v* sending, forwarding, dispatch; shipment [of goods]; **–skosten** *mv* forwarding-charges; **ver'zendlijst** (-en) *v* mailing list

'**verzenen** *mv de* ~ *tegen de prikkels slaan* **B** kick against the pricks

ver'zengd scorched [grass]; torrid [zone]; **ver'zengen**[1] *vt* singe, scorch, parch; **–ging** *v* singeing &

'**verzenmaker** (-s) *m* > poetaster

ver'zepen (verzeepte, *vt* h., *vi* is verzeept) *vt* & *vi* (v. v e t t e n) saponify

ver'zet *o* 1 (t e g e n s t a n d) opposition, resistance; 2 (o n t s p a n n i n g) diversion, recreation; *gewapend* (*lijdelijk*) ~ armed (passive) resistance; ~ *aantekenen* enter a protest, protest (against *tegen*); *in* ~ *komen* offer resistance; *fig* protest; *in* ~ *komen tegen* offer resistance to, resist, oppose; *fig* oppose; protest against [a measure &]; stand up against [tyranny &]; *in* ~ *komen tegen een vonnis* 🕱 appeal against a sentence; **–je** (-s) *o* diversion, recreation; **ver'zetsbeweging** (-en) *v* resistance movement; **–man** (-nen en -lieden) *m* member of a resistance movement; **–organisatie** [-za.(t)si.] (-s) *v* resistance movement; **ver'zetten**[1] **I** *vt* 1 move, shift; 2 (a f l e i d i n g g e v e n) divert; *bergen* ~ **B** remove mountains; *de klok* ~ put the clock forward (back); *een vergadering* ~ put off a meeting; *heel wat werk* ~ get through (put in, do) a lot of work; *zij kan het niet* ~ she cannot get over it, it sticks in her throat; **II** *vr*

zich ~ 1 (z i c h s c h r a p z e t t e n) recalcitrate, kick against the pricks, kick; 2 (w e e r s t a n d b i e d e n) resist, offer resistance; 3 (z i c h o n t s p a n n e n) take some recreation, unbend; *zich krachtig* ~ offer (make) a vigorous resistance; *zich niet* ~ make (offer) no resistance; *zich* ~ *tegen* resist; oppose[2] [a measure &]; stand up against [tyranny &]; stand out against [a demand]

ver'zieken I (verziekte, is verziekt) *vi* waste (away); **II** (verziekte, h. verziekt) **F** *vt* spoil, frustrate

ver'zien[1] *vt hij heeft het op mij* ~ **F** he has a down on me; *het niet op iem.* (*iets*) ~ *hebben* not like (hold with) sbd. (sth.)

'**verziend** far-sighted, long-sighted, presbyopic; **–heid** *v* far-sightedness, long-sightedness, presbyopia

ver'zilten (verziltte, *vt* h., *vi* is verzilt) *vi* & *vt* salt up

ver'zilveren (verzilverde, h. verzilverd) *vt eig* silver; *fig* $ convert into cash, cash [a banknote]; *verzilverd* ook: silver-plated [wares]; **–ring** *v eig* silvering; *fig* $ cashing

ver'zinken (verzonk, *vt* h., *vi* is verzonken) *vt* sink (down, away); (v. s c h r o e v e n) countersink; *verzonken in gedachten* absorbed (lost) in thought; *in dromen verzonken* lost in dreams; *in slaap verzonken* deep in sleep

ver'zinnen[1] *vt* invent, devise, contrive; *dat verzin je maar* you are making it up; *ik wist niemand te* ~ *die...* I could not think of anybody who...; **–er** (-s) *m* inventor, contriver; **ver'zinsel** (-s en -en) *o* invention

ver'zitten[1] *vi gaan* ~ move to another seat; shift one's position [in a chair]

ver'zoek (-en) *o* request; petition; *een* ~ *doen* make a request; *op* ~ [cars stop] by request, [samples sent] on request; *op dringend* ~ *van* at the urgent request of...; *op speciaal* ~ by special request; *op* ~ *van..., ten* ~*e van...* at the request of...; *op zijn* ~ at his request; **ver'zoeken**[1] *vt* 1 beg, request; 2 (u i t n o d i g e n) ask, invite; 3 (i n v e r z o e k i n g b r e n g e n) tempt; *verzoeke antwoord, antwoord verzocht* an answer will oblige; *verzoeke niet te roken* please do not smoke; *mag ik u* ~ *de deur te sluiten?* may I trouble you to close the door?, will you kindly close the door?; ~ *o m* ask for; *mogen wij u om de klandizie* ~? may we solicit your custom?; *hem op de bruiloft* ~ invite him to the wedding; **–er** (-s) *m* 1 petitioner; 2 (v e r l e i d e r) tempter; **ver'zoeking** (-en) *v* temptation; *in* ~ *brengen*

---

[1] V.T. en V.D. van dit werkwoord volgens het model: **ver'**achten, V.T. **ver'**achtte, V.D. **ver'**acht (**ge**- valt dus weg in het V.D.). Zie voor de vormen onder het grondwoord, in dit voorbeeld: *achten*. Bij sterke en onregelmatige werkwoorden wordt u verwezen naar de lijst achterin.

tempt; *in de ~ komen om*... be tempted to...;
ver'zoekprogramma ('s) *o* (musical) request
programme; **–schrift** (-en) *o* petition; *een ~
indienen* present a petition
ver'zoendag (-dagen) *m*
day of reconciliation; *Grote Verzoendag* Day of
Atonement; **ver'zoenen[1]** *vt* 1 reconcile,
conciliate; 2 placate, propitiate; *~ met* reconcile with (to); *ik kan daar niet mee verzoend raken*
I cannot reconcile myself to it; **II** *vr zich ~*
become reconciled; *ik kan me daar niet mee ~* I
cannot reconcile myself to it; **–d** conciliatory,
propitiatory; **ver'zoener** (-s) *m* conciliator;
ver'zoening (-en) *v* reconciliation, reconcile-
ment; atonement; **verzoeningsge'zind**
conciliatory
ver'zoeten[1] *vt* sweeten[2]; **–ting** *v* sweetening
ver'zolen (verzoolde, h. verzoold) *vt* resole
ver'zorgd 1 (b e z o r g d) provided for; 2
(g e s o i g n e e r d) well-groomed [men &];
well-trimmed [nails]; well cared-for [baby];
well got-up [book]; 3 *geheel ~e reis* package
tour, all-in tour; **ver'zorgen[1]** *vt* take care of,
attend to, look after, provide for; edit [sbd.'s
writings]; **II** *vr zich ~* take care of oneself; **–er**
(-s) *m* 1 provider; 2 fosterer [of a child];
ver'zorging *v* care; provision; **ver'zorgings-
flat** [-flɛt] (-s) *m* service flat; **–huis** (-huizen) *o*
home for the aged, old people's home; **–staat**
m welfare state
ver'zot *~ op* very fond of, infatuated with, mad
on
ver'zuchten[1] *vt* sigh; **–ting** (-en) *v* sigh; lamentation; *een ~ slaken* heave a sigh
ver'zuiling *v* ± compartmentalization [of
society]
ver'zuim (-en) *o* 1 neglect, oversight, omission;
2 non-attendance [at school], absenteeism
[from work]; 🕱 default; **–d** neglected &; *het ~e
inhalen* make up for time lost; **ver'zuimen**
(verzuimde, h. verzuimd) **I** *vt* 1 (n a l a t e n)
neglect [one's duty]; 2 (n i e t d o e n) omit, fail
[to...]; 3 (n i e t w a a r n e m e n) lose, miss [an
opportunity]; *de school ~* stop away from
school; *niet ~ er heen te gaan* not omit going;
II *va* stop away from school (from church &)
ver'zuipen F I (verzoop, h. verzopen) *vt* 1
drown; 2 spend on drink; **II** (verzoop, is
verzopen) *vi* be drowned, drown
ver'zuren[1] I *vi* grow sour, sour[2]; turn [of milk];
II *vt* make sour, sour[2]; **ver'zuurd** soured[2]
ver'zwageren (verzwagerde, is verzwagerd) *vi*
become related by marriage (to *met*)

ver'zwakken I (verzwakte, h. verzwakt) *vt*
weaken [the body, the mind, a solution, the
force of argument]; enfeeble [the mind, a
country &]; debilitate [the constitution];
enervate [sbd. physically]; **II** (verzwakte, is
verzwakt) *vi* weaken, grow weak; **–king** (-en)
v weakening, enfeeblement, debilitation
ver'zwaren (verzwaarde, h. verzwaard) *vt* make
heavier; strengthen [a dike]; *fig* aggravate [a
crime]; stiffen [an examination]; increase,
augment [a penalty]; *~de omstandigheden* aggravating circumstances
ver'zwelgen[1] *vt* swallow (up); **–ging** *v*
swallowing (up)
ver'zweren (verzwoor, is verzworen) *vi* fester,
ulcerate; **–ring** (-en) *v* festering, ulceration
ver'zwijgen[1] *vt iets ~* not tell sth., keep sth. a
secret, conceal sth., suppress sth.; *je moet het
voor hem ~* keep it from him; **–ging** *v* suppression [of the truth], concealment
ver'zwikken[1] I *vt* sprain, wrench [one's ankle];
II *vr zich ~* sprain one's ankle; **–king** (-en) *v*
sprain
'vesper (-s) *v* vespers, evensong; **–dienst** (-en)
m vespers; **–klokje** (-s) *o* vesper-bell, evening-
bell; **–tijd** *m* vesper-hour, evening-time
1 vest (-en) *o* 1 (v. m a n) waistcoat; 2 (i n
w i n k e l t a a l) vest; 3 (g e b r e i d) cardigan
2 vest (-en) *v = veste*
Ves'taals Vestal; **ves'tale** (-n) *v* vestal virgin,
vestal
⚓ **'veste** (-n) *v* 1 fortress, stronghold; 2
rampart, wall; 3 moat
vesti'aire [-'tːrə] (-s) *m* cloakroom
vesti'bule (-s) *m* hall, vestibule
'vestigen (vestigde, h. gevestigd) **I** *vt* establish,
set up; *de blik, de ogen ~ op* fix one's eyes upon;
zijn geloof ~ op place one's faith in; *zijn hoop ~
op* set one's hopes on; *waar is hij gevestigd?*
where is he living?; *waar is die maatschappij
gevestigd?* where is the seat of that company?;
II *vr zich ~* settle, settle down, establish oneself,
take up one's residence; *zich ~ als dokter* set up
as a doctor; **'vestiging** (-en) *v* establishment,
settlement; **–svergunning** (-en) *v* permit to
establish a business; permit to take up residence
'vesting (-en) *v* fortress; **–artillerie** *v* garrison
artillery; **–gracht** (-en) *v* moat; **–stelsel** (-s) *o*
fortifications; **–straf** (-fen) *v* imprisonment
(detention, confinement) in a fortress;
–werken *mv* fortifications
'vestzak (-ken) *m* waistcoat pocket
Ve'suvius [-'zy-] *m de ~* Vesuvius

---

[1] V.T. en V.D. van dit werkwoord volgens het model: **ver'**achten, V.T. **ver'**achtte, V.D. **ver'**acht (**ge-** valt dus weg
in het V.D.). Zie voor de vormen onder het grondwoord, in dit voorbeeld: *achten*. Bij sterke en onregelmatige
werkwoorden wordt u verwezen naar de lijst achterin.

1 vet (-ten) *o* 1 (in 't alg.) fat; 2 grease [of game, or dead animals when melted and soft]; *dierlijke en plantaardige ~ten* animal and vegetable fats; *iem. zijn ~ geven* **F** give sbd. a piece of one's mind, give it to sbd.; *zijn ~ krijgen* get a beating, get what for; *we hebben nog wat in het ~* there is something in store for us; *ik heb voor jou nog wat in het ~* I have a rod in pickle for you; *laat hem in zijn eigen ~ gaar koken* let him stew in his own juice; *iets in het ~ zetten* grease sth.; *op zijn ~ teren (leven)* live on one's own fat; **2 vet** *aj* fat [people, coal, clay, lands, type, benefices &]; greasy [fingers, skin &, wool]; *een ~ baantje* a fat job; *~te druk* ook: heavy (bold) type; *~ gedrukt* printed in heavy (bold) type; *daar ben je ~ mee* a lot of good that will do you!; *daar zal hij niet ~ van soppen* he won't make a pile out of that; *het ~te der aarde genieten* **B** live upon the fat of the land; **–achtig** fatty, greasy

'vete (-n en -s) *v* feud, enmity

'veter (-s) *m* 1 boot-lace, shoe-lace; 2 (van korset) stay-lace

vete'raan (-ranen) *m* veteran, war-horse

'veterband (-en) *o* & *m* tape; **–beslag** *o* tag; **–gat** (-gaten) *o* eyelet

veteri'nair [- 'nɛːr] **I** *aj* veterinary; **II** (-s) *m* veterinary surgeon, **F** vet

'vetgedrukt bold-faced, in bold type; **–gehalte** *o* fat-content, percentage of fat; **–gezwel** (-len) *o* fatty tumour; **–heid** *v* fatness; greasiness; **–kaars** (-en) *v* tallow candle, dip; **–klier** (-en) *v* sebaceous gland; **–laag** (-lagen) *v* layer of fat; **–le(d)er** *o* greased leather; **–leren** (of) greased leather; **vetmesten** (mestte 'vet, h. 'vetgemest) **I** *vt* fatten²; **II** *vr zich ~ met* [fig] batten on

'veto ('s) *o* veto; *zijn ~ uitspreken* interpose one's veto; *zijn ~ uitspreken over...* put one's (a) veto on, veto; **–recht** *o* right of veto

'vetpan (-nen) *v* dripping-pan; **–plant** (-en) *v* succulent; **–pot** (-ten) *m* grease-pot; *het is er ~* they do themselves well there; **–potje** (-s) *o* lampion, fairy-lamp; **–puistje** (-s) *o* pimple; **~s** acne; **'vettig** fatty, greasy; **–heid** (-heden) *v* fatness, greasiness; **'vetvlek** (-ken) *v* grease-spot, greasy spot; **–vorming** *v* formation of fat; **–vrij** greaseproof [paper]; **–weefsel** (-s) *o* adipose (fatty) tissue; **'vetweiden** (vetweidde, h. gevetweid) *vt* fatten [cattle]; **–er** (-s) *m* grazier; **'vetzucht** *v* fatty degeneration; **–zuur** (-zuren) *o* fatty acid

'veulen (-s) *o* 1 (in 't alg.) colt; 2 (mannetje) foal; 3 (wijfje) filly; **'veulenen** (veulende, h. geveulend) *vi* foal

'vezel (-s) *v* fibre, filament, thread; **–achtig** = *vezelig*; **'vezelig** fibrous, filamentous; stringy

[beans]; **–heid** *v* fibrousness &; **'vezelplaat** (-platen) *v* fibre-board; **–plant** (-en) *v* fibrous plant; **–stof** (-fen) *v* fibre

v.g.g.v. = *van goede getuigen voorzien* with good references

vgl. = *vergelijk* confer, cf

v.h.t.h. = *van huis tot huis* zie *huis*

'via 1 via, by way of; 2 through [a newspaper advertisement]

via'duct (-en) *m* & *o* viaduct; 🚋 fly-over

vi'aticum (-s) *o* viaticum

vibra'foon (-s en -fonen) *m* vibraphone; **vi'bratie** [-(t)si.] (-s) *v* vibration; **vi'breren** (vibreerde, h. gevibreerd) *vi* vibrate, quaver, undulate

vicari'aat (-iaten) *o* vicariate; **vi'caris** (-sen) *m* vicar; *apostolisch ~* vicar apostolic; **vi'caris-generaal** (vicarissen-generaal) *m* vicar general

'vice-admiraal (-s) *m* vice-admiral, **~-consul**, **~-konsul** (-s) *m* vice-consul; **~-presi'dent** [s = z] (-en) *m* vice-president

vice 'versa vice versa

'vice-voorzitter (-s) *m* vice-president, deputy chairman

vici'eus vicious [circle]

vic'torie (-s) *v* victory; *~ kraaien* shout victory, triumph

victu'aliën *mv* provisions, victuals

'videoband (-en) *m* video tape; **–recorder** [-ri.kɔrdər] (-s) *m* video recorder

vief lively, smart

viel (vielen) V.T. v. *vallen*

vier four; *met ~en!* 🚣 form fours!; **–armig** four-armed; **–baansweg** (-wegen) *m* dual carriageway, *Am.* divided highway; **–benig** four-legged; **–bladig** 1 four-leaved; 2 🔩 four-bladed [screw]; **–daags** of four days, four days'; **–de** fourth (part); *~ man zijn* sp make a fourth; *ten ~* fourthly, in the fourth place; **–delig** divided into (consisting of) four parts, quadripartite; four-section [screen]; **–dendaags** quintan [fever]; **–derhande**, **–derlei** of four sorts; **–draads** four-ply

'vieren (vierde, h. gevierd) *vt* 1 celebrate, keep [Christmas]; observe (keep holy) [the Sabbath]; 2 (laten schieten) veer out, pay out, ease off [a rope]; zie ook: *teugel*; *hij wordt daar erg gevierd* he is made much of there

'vierendeel (-delen) *o* quarter [of weights and measures, of a year]; **'vierendelen** (vierendeelde, h. gevierendeeld) *vt* quarter [sth., ⊘ a shield, ⬜ a traitor's body]; **'vierhandig** four-handed [pieces of music]; § quadrumanous; **–hoek** (-en) *m* quadrangle; **–hoekig** quadrangular ,

'viering (-en) *v* celebration [of a feast]; observance [of the Sunday] 'vierjaarlijks quadrennial; vier'jarenplan (-nen) *o* four-year plan; 'vierjarig of four years, four-year-old; 'vierkant I *aj* 1 (v a n f i g u r e n) square; 2 (v. g e t a l l e n) square; *een ~e kerel* 1 a square-built fellow; 2 *fig* a blunt fellow; *drie ~e meter* three square metres; ~ *maken* square; II (-en) *o* 1 (f i g u u r) square; 2 (g e t a l) square; *3 meter in het* ~ 3 metres square; III *ad* squarely; *iem.* ~ *de deur uitgooien* bundle sbd. out without ceremony; *het* ~ *tegenspreken* contradict it flatly; *het* ~ *weigeren* refuse flatly; ~ *tegen iets zijn* be dead against sth.; 'vierkantsvergelijking (-en) *v* quadratic equation; –wortel (-s) *m* square root; –worteltrekking (-en) *v* extraction of the square root; vier'kleurendruk (-ken) *m* four-colour printing; 'vierkleurig four-coloured; –kwartsmaat *v* quadruple time; –ledig consisting of four parts, quadripartite; –lettergrepig quadrisyllabic; ~ *woord* quadri-syllable; –ling (-en) *m* quadruplets; –motorig four-engined; –persoonsauto [-o.to. of -ɔuto.] ('s) *m* four-seater; –potig four-legged; –regelig of four lines; ~ *gedicht* quatrain; –schaar (-scharen) *v* tribunal, court of justice; *de* ~ *spannen* sit in judgment (upon *over*); –snarig four-stringed; –span (-nen) *o* four-in-hand; –sprong (-en) *m* cross-road(s); *op de* ~ [*fig*] at the cross-roads (at the parting of the ways); –stemmig for four voices, fourpart; –taktmotor (-s en -toren) *m* four-stroke engine; –tal (-len) *o* (number of) four; *het* ~ the four (of them); *ons* ~ the four of us, our quartet(te); –talig quadrilingual; –tallig quaternary; –vlak (-ken) *o* tetrahedron; –vlakkig tetrahedral; –voeter (-s) quadruped; –voetig four-footed, quadruped; –voud (-en) *o* quadruple; *in* ~ in quadruplicate; –voudig fourfold, quadruple; –wielig four-wheeled; –zijdig four-sided, quadrilateral

vies I *aj* 1 dirty, grubby [hands]; nasty[2] [smell, weather &] filthy [stories]; 2 (k i e s k e u r i g) particular, fastidious, dainty, nice; *hij valt niet* ~ he is not over-particular; *ik ben er* ~ *v a n* it disgusts me; *daar ben ik niet* ~ *van* F I shouldn't mind that; II *ad* ~ *kijken* make a wry face; ~ *ruiken* have a nasty smell; *dat valt* ~ *tegen* F that's very disappointing; *hij is* ~ *bij* F he is very clever; *je bent er* ~ *bij* F you are in for it, you are done for; –heid (-heden) *v* dirtiness, nastiness, filthiness; –p(e)uk (-peuken, -pukken) *m* F dirty pig, mucky pup

Viët'nam *o* Vietnam, Viet(-)Nam; Viëtna'mees I *aj* Vietnamese; II (-mezen) *m* Vietnamese; *de Viëtnamezen* the Vietnamese; III *o het* ~ Vietnamese

'viezerik (-riken) *m* F dirty Dick, dirty pig,

nasty fellow; 'viezigheid (-heden) *v* 1 (a b-s t r a c t) dirtiness, nastiness; 2 (c o n c r e e t) dirt, filth

vi'geren (vigeerde, h. gevigeerd) *vi* be in force
vigi'lante [vi.ʒi.-] (-s) *v* cab
vi'gilie (-iën en -s) *v* vigil [= eve of a festival]
vig'net [vi.'ɲɪt] (-ten) *o* vignette, (k o p~) head-piece, (s l u i t~) tail-piece

'vijand (-en) *m* enemy, ⊙ foe; vij'andelijk 1 ⚔ (v a n e e n v ij a n d) enemy('s) [fleet], hostile; 2 (a l s v a n e e n v ij a n d) hostile [to...]; –heid (-heden) *v* hostility; vij'andig hostile, inimical; *hun* ~ *gezind* unfriendly disposed towards them; *hun niet* ~ *gezind zijn* bear them no enmity; –heid (-heden) *v* enmity, hostility; vijan'din (-nen) *v* enemy, ⊙ foe; 'vijandschap (-pen) *v* enmity; *in* ~ at enmity

vijf five; *geef mij de* ~ F shake, shake hands; *een van de* ~ *is op de loop bij hem* F he has a screw loose; –daags of five days, five days'; ~*e werkweek* five-day working week; –de fifth (part); *ten* ~ fifthly, in the fifth place; vijfen-zestig'plusser (-s) *m* senior citizen; 'vijfhoek (-en) *m* pentagon; –hoekig pentagonal; –jaarlijks quinquennial; vijf'jarenplan (-nen) *o* five-year plan; 'vijfjarig of five years, five-year-old; quinquennial; –kamp *m* pentathlon; –lettergrepig of five syllables; –ling (-en) *m* quintuplets; –snarig five-stringed; –stemmig for five voices; –tal (-len) *o* (number of) five; quintet(te); *het* ~ the five (of them); –tallig quinary

'vijftien fifteen; –de fifteenth (part)
'vijftig fifty; –er (-s) *m* person of fifty (years); –jarig of fifty years; *de* ~*e* the quinquagenar-ian; –ste fiftieth (part)

'vijfvoetig five-footed; ~ *vers* pentameter; –voud (-en) *o* quintuple; –voudig fivefold, quintuple

vijg (-en) *v* fig; 'vijgeblad (-bladeren, -bladen en -blaren) *o* fig-leaf[2]; –boom (-bomen) *m* fig-tree

vijl (-en) *v* file; *er de* ~ *over laten gaan* [*fig*] polish it; 'vijlen (vijlde, h. gevijld) *vt* file; *fig* polish; 'vijlsel (-s) *o* filings

'vijver (-s) *m* pond, (g r o o t) (ornamental) lake
1 'vijzel (-s) *m* (s t a m p v a t) mortar
2 'vijzel (-s) *v* (h e f s c h r o e f) jack; 'vijzelen (vijzelde, h. gevijzeld) *vt* screw up, jack (up)
'viking (-s en -en) *m* viking
'vilder (-s) *m* flayer, (horse-)knacker
vi'lein vile, bad
'villa ['vi.la.] ('s) *v* villa, country-house, (k l e i n) cottage; –park (-en) *o* villa park; –wijk (-en) *v* residential area

'villen (vilde, h. gevild) *vt* flay[2], fleece[2], skin[2];

ik laat me ~ als... I'll be hanged if...
vilt *o* felt; **–achtig** felty, felt-like; **1** '**vilten** *aj* felt; **2** '**vilten** (viltte, h. gevilt) *vt* felt; '**vilthoed** (-en) *m* felt hat; **–stift** (-en) *v* felt(-tipped) pen

vin (-nen) *v* 1 fin [of a fish]; 2 acne [on the human body]; *hij verroerde geen ~* he did not stir (move) a finger; he didn't move hand or foot

'**vinden* I** *vt* 1 find, *soms:* meet with, come across; 2 think [it fair &]; feel [that they should be abolished, it churlish to say nothing]; *hoe ~ ze het?* how do they like it?; *hoe vind je onze stad?* what do you think of our town?; *ik vind het niets aardig* I don't think it nice; *ik vind het niet erg* I don't mind; *ik vind niet dat het zo koud is als gisteren* I don't find it so cold as yesterday; *vind je het goed?* do you approve, do you mind [if]; *ik vind het niet goed* I don't approve of that; *wij kunnen het goed met elkaar ~* we get on very well together; *zij kunnen het niet goed met elkaar ~* somehow they don't hit it off; *het niets ~ om...* think nothing of ...ing; *ik zal hem wel ~ he shall smart for this!; he shall not go unpunished; *dat zullen wij wel ~* we'll make it all right, get it settled; ● *wat ~ ze daar nu a a n?* what can they see in it (in him)?; *er iets o p ~ om...* find (a) means to; *daar is hij altijd v o o r te ~* he is always game for it; *daar is hij niet voor te ~* he will not be found willing to do it, he does not lend himself to that sort of thing; **II** *vr hij vond zich door iedereen verlaten* he found himself left by everybody; *dat zal zich wel ~* it is sure to come all right; **–er** (-s) *m* finder; (u i t v i n d e r) inventor; '**vinding** (-en) *v* invention, discovery; **–rijk** inventive [mind], ingenious, resourceful [person]; **vinding'rijkheid** *v* ingeniousness, ingenuity, inventiveness, resourcefulness; '**vindloon** *o* finder's reward; **–plaats** (-en) *v* place where something has been found, place of finding (discovery); deposit [of ore]; habitat [of animal, plant]

ving (vingen) V.T. v. *vangen*

'**vinger** (-s) *m* finger; *middelste ~* middle finger; *voorste ~* forefinger, index; *vieze ~s* **F** fingermarks; *de ~ Gods* the finger of God; *als men hem een ~ geeft, neemt hij de hele hand* give him an inch, and he will take an ell; *het in de ~s hebben* be gifted; *een ~ in de pap hebben* have a finger in the pie; *lange ~s hebben, zijn ~s niet thuis kunnen houden* be light-fingered; *de ~ aan de pols houden* keep a finger on the pulse; *de ~s jeuken mij om...* my fingers itch to...; *iem. in de ~s krijgen* get hold of sbd., lay one's hands on sbd.; *de ~ op de wond leggen* put one's finger on the spot, touch the sore; *zijn ~ opsteken* show (put up) one's finger; *hij zal geen ~ uitsteken om...* he will not lift (raise, stir) a finger to...; *als je een ~ naar hem uitsteekt* if you wag a finger at him; ● *iets d o o r de ~s zien* shut one's eyes to sth., turn a blind eye to sth., overlook sth.; *m e t zijn ~s ergens aan komen (zitten)* finger it, meddle with it; *als je hem maar met de ~ aanraakt* if you lay a finger on him; *iem. met de ~ nawijzen* point (one's finger) at sbd.; *iem. o m de ~ winden* twist (turn) sbd. round one's (little) finger; *iem. o p de ~s kijken* keep a close eye on sbd.; *dat kun je op je ~s natellen (narekenen, uitrekenen)* you can count it on your fingers, that's as clear as daylight; *zie ook: snijden* **III**, *tikken* **II** &; **–afdruk** (-ken) *m* finger-print; **–alfabet** *o* finger-alphabet; **–breed I** *aj* of a finger's breadth; **II** *o* finger's breadth; **–dik** as thick as a finger; **–doekje** (-s) *o* small napkin; **–gewricht** (-en) *o* finger-joint; **–hoed** (-en) *m* 1 thimble; 2 centilitre; **–hoedskruid** *o* foxglove; **–kommetje** (-s) *o* finger-bowl; **–lid** (-leden) *o* finger-joint; **–ling** (-en) *m* fingerstall; **–oefening** (-en) *v* ♩ (five-)finger exercise; **–ring** (-en) *m* finger ring; **–spraak** *v* finger-and-sign language; **–top** (-pen) *m* finger-tip; **–vlug** deft, dext(e)rous, **vinger'vlugheid** *v* dexterity, deftness; '**vingervormig** finger-shaped; **–wijzing** (-en) *v* hint, indication; **–zetting** (-en) *v* ♩ fingering; *met ~ van...* ♩ fingered by

vink (-en) *m* & *v* ♒ finch; *blinde ~en* (meat) olives; **–entouw** *o op het ~ zitten* [fig] eagerly bide one's time

'**vinnig I** *aj* sharp, fierce; biting [cold, wind]; smart [blow]; keen [fight]; cutting [remarks]; **II** *ad* sharply &; **–heid** (-heden) *v* sharpness, fierceness &

'**vinvis** (-sen) *m* rorqual

vio'let *aj* & *o* violet

vio'lier (-en) *v* stock-gillyflower

vio'list (-en) *m* violinist, violin-player; *eerste ~* first violin; violon'cel (-len) *v* violoncello, **F** 'cello; violoncel'list (-en) *m* violoncellist; vi'ool (violen) *v* 1 ♩ violin, **F** fiddle; 2 ♒ violet; *hij speelt de eerste ~* he plays first fiddle; *op de ~ spelen* play (on) the violin; **–bouwer** (-s) *m* violin maker; **–concert** (-en) *o* 1 (u i t v o e r i n g) violon recital; 2 (m u z i e k - s t u k) violin concerto; **–hars** *o* & *m* colophony; **–kam** (-men) *m* bridge; **–kist** (-en) *v* violin-case; **–les** (-sen) *v* violin lesson; **–muziek** *v* violin music; **–partij** (-en) *v* violin part; **–sleutel** (-s) *m* treble clef; **–snaar** (-snaren) *v* violin-string; **–sonate** (-s en -n) *v* violin sonata; **–spel** *o* violin-playing; **–speler** (-s) *m* violinist, violin-player

vi'ooltje (-s) *o* ♒ violet; *driekleurig ~* pansy; *Kaaps ~* African violet

vi'riel virile; virili'teit *v* virility

virolo'gie *v* virology; viro'loog (-logen) *m* virologist

virtu'oos **I** (-uozen) *m* virtuoso [*mv* virtuosi]; *een piano* ~ a virtuoso pianist; **II** *aj* masterly; **III** *ad* in a masterly way; virtuosi'teit [s = z] *v* virtuosity

'virus (-sen) *o* virus; –ziekte (-n en -s) *v* virus disease

vis (-sen) *m* fish; *de Vissen* ★ Pisces; ~ *noch vlees* neither fish nor flesh; *als een* ~ *op het droge* like a fish out of water; –aas *o* fish-bait; –achtig fish-like, fishy; –afslag (-slagen) *m* fish auction; –akte (-n en -s) *v* fishing-licence; –angel (-s) *m* fish-hook; –arend (-en) *m* osprey

vis-à-'vis [vi.za.'vi.] *ad* & *v* & *m* vis-à-vis

'visboer (-en) *m* fish-monger, fish-hawker

vis'cose [-'ko.zə] *v* viscose; viscosi'teit *v* viscosity

'viscouvert [-ku.vɛ:r] (-s) *o* (set of) fish eaters, fish knife and fork; –diefje (-s) *o* tern

vi'seren [s = z] (viseerde, h. geviseerd) *vt* visa

'visfuik (-en) *v* fish trap; –graat (-graten) *v* fish-bone; –gronden *mv* fishing grounds, fisheries; –haak (-haken) *m* fish-hook; –hal (-len) *v* fish market (hall); –handelaar (-s) *m* fishmonger; –hengel (-s) *m* fishing rod

'visie [s = z] (-s) *v* 1 [prophetic] vision; 2 (k ij k) outlook [on art], view [of the problem]; *ter* ~ *liggen* = (*ter*) *inzage* (*liggen*)

visi'oen [s = z] (-en) *o* vision; visio'nair [-'nɛ:r] *aj* & (-s en -en) *m* visionary

visi'tatie [vi.zi.'ta.(t)si.] (-s) *v* 1 visit [of a ship], search; customs examination, [customs] inspection; 2 *rk* Visitation; –recht *o* right of visit

vi'site [s = z] (-s) *v* 1 (h a n d e l i n g) visit, call; 2 (v. p e r s o n e n) visitor(s); *er is* ~, *wij hebben* ~ we have visitors; *een* ~ *maken* pay a visit (call), make a call; *een* ~ *maken bij* pay a visit to, call on, give a call to visit; –kaartje (-s) *o* (visiting-)card

visi'teren [s = z] (visiteerde, h. gevisiteerd) *vt* examine, search, inspect, **F** frisk

'viskaar (-karen) *v* fish-basket, corf; –kom (-men) *v* fish bowl; –koper (-s) *m* fishmonger; viskweke'rij (-en) *v* 1 fish-farm; 2 (h e t k w e k e n) fish-farming, pisciculture; 'vislijm *m* fish-glue, isinglass; –lucht *v* fishy smell; –markt (-en) *v* fish-market; –meel *o* fish meal; –mes (-sen) *o* fish-knife; –mijn (-en) *v* = *visafslag*; –net (-ten) *o* fishing net; –ooglens (-lenzen) *v* fish-eye lens; –otter (-s) *m* common otter; –pan (-nen) *v* fish-kettle; –recht *o* fishing-right; –rijk abounding in fish; –rijkheid *v* abundance of fish; –schotel (-s) *m* & *v* 1 fish-strainer; 2 (g e r e c h t) fish-dish;

–schub (-ben) *v* scale [of fish]; –sebloed *o* fish blood; *hij heeft* ~ he is as cold(-blooded) as a fish; –seizoen *o* fishing-season; 'vissen **I** (viste, h. gevist) *vi* fish; *naar een complimentje* ~ fish (angle) for a compliment; **II** *va* fish; *uit* ~ *gaan* go out fishing; **III** *o* fishing; –er (-s) *m* 1 (h e n g e l a a r) angler; 2 (v a n b e r o e p) fisherman; visse'rij *v* fishery, fishing-industry; –grens (-grenzen) *v* fishery limit; 'vissersboot (-boten) *m* & *v* fishing-boat; –dorp (-en) *o* fishing-village; –haven (-s) *v* fishing-port; –ring (-en) *m* Fisherman's ring; –schuit (-en) *v* fishing-boat; –vloot *v* fishing-fleet; –volk *o* nation of fishermen; –vrouw (-en) *v* fisherman's wife; 'vissmaak *m* fishy taste; –stand *m* fish stock; –sterfte *v* fish mortality, death of fish; –stick (-s) *m* fish finger

'vista ['vi:sta.] *a* ~ **$** on presentation

'visteelt *v* fish-culture, pisciculture; –tijd *m* fishing-season; –tuig (-en) *o* fishing-tackle

visu'eel [s = z] visual

'visum [s = z] (visa en -s) *o* visa

'visvangst *v* fishing; *de wonderdadige* ~ **B** the miraculous draught of fishes; –vijver (-s) *m* fish-pond; –vrouw (-en) *v* fish-woman, fishwife; –water (-s en -en) *o* fishing-water, fishing-ground; *goed* ~ good fishing; –wijf (-wijven) *o* fish-woman, fishwife; –wijventaal *v* Billingsgate (language); –winkel (-s) *m* fish-shop

vi'taal vital

'vitachtig = *vitterig*

vitali'teit *v* vitality

vita'mine (-n en -s) *v* vitamin; ~ *C* ascorbic acid; vitami'neren (vitamineerde, h. gevitamineerd) *vt* vitaminize; vita'minetablet (-ten) *v* & *o* vitamin tablet; vitamini'seren [s = z] (vitaminiseerde, h. gevitaminiseerd) *vt* vitaminize

vi'trage [-'tra.ʒə] (-s) 1 *v* (g o r d ij n) lace curtain, net curtain, glass curtain; 2 *v* & *o* (s t o f) lace, net

vi'trine [-s] *v* (glass) show-case, show-window

vitri'ool *o* & *m* vitriol

'vitten (vitte, h. gevit) *vi* find fault, cavil, carp; ~ *op* find fault with, carp at; –er (-s) *m* fault-finder, caviller; 'vitterig fault-finding, cavilling, censorious, captious; –heid *v*, vitte'rij (-en) *v* fault-finding, cavilling, censoriousness; carping criticism

'vitusdans *m* St. Vitus's dance

'vitzucht *v* censoriousness

'vivat (-s) *o* long live [the King!], three cheers [for the King]

vivi'sectie [-'sɛksi.] *v* vivisection; ~ *toepassen op* vivisect [animals]

1 vi'zier (-s en -en) *m* vizi(e)r

2 vi′zier (-en) *o* 1 visor [of a helmet]; 2 ⚔ (back-)sight [of a gun]; *in het ~ krijgen* catch sight of; *met open ~* with visor raised; *fig* openly; **–klep** (-pen) *v* ⚔ leaf; **–korrel** (-s) *m* ⚔ bead, foresight; **–lijn** (-en) *v* ⚔ line of sight

vla (′s en vlaas) *v* 1 (cr è m e) custard; 2 (b a k s e l) flan, tart

vlaag (vlagen) *v* shower [of rain], gust [of wind]; *fig* fit [of anger, insanity &]; access [of generosity]; *bij vlagen* by fits and starts

vlaai (-en) *v* flan, tart

Vlaams I *aj* Flemish; *~e gaai* 🦜 jay; **II** *o het ~* Flemish; **III** *v een ~e* a Flemish woman; **′Vlaanderen** *o* Flanders

vlag (-gen) *v* 1 flag, ⚔ (v. r e g i m e n t) colours; *fig* standard; 2 vane, web [of a feather]; *de witte ~* the white flag, the flag of truce; *dat staat als een ~ op een modderschuit* it suits you as a saddle suits a sow; *de ~ hijsen* hoist the flag; *de ~ neerhalen* lower the flag; *de ~ strijken voor…* lower one's flag to…; *de ~ uitsteken* put out the flag; *de Engelse ~ voeren* fly the English flag; *m e t ~ en wimpel* with flying colours; *o n d e r Franse ~ varen* fly the French flag; *onder valse ~ varen* sail under false colours, *fig* wear false colours; *de ~ dekt de lading* the flag covers the cargo; free flag makes free bottom; **–gekoord** (-en) *o* & *v* flag-line; **′vlaggen** (vlagde, h. gevlagd) *vi* put out (fly, hoist, display) the flag (flags); *de stad vlagde* the town was beflagged; **′vlaggendoek** *o* & *m* bunting; **′vlaggeschip** (-schepen) *o* flagship; **–stok** (-ken) *m* flagstaff, flag-pole; **–touw** (-en) *o* flag-line; **′vlagofficier** (-en) *m* flag-officer; **–vertoon** *o* showing the flag

1 vlak I *aj* flat, level; plane; *~ land* flat (level) country; *~ke meetkunde* plane geometry; *~ke tint* flat tint; *~ke zee* smooth sea; **II** *ad* flatly[2]; right [in the centre &]; *~ oost* due east; ● *~ a c h t e r elkaar* close after one another, in close succession; *~ achter hem* close behind him, close upon his heels; *~ b ij* close by; *het huis is ~ bij de kerk* the house is close to the church; *ik sloeg hem ~ i n zijn gezicht* I hit him full in the face; *ik zei het hem ~ in zijn gezicht* I told him so to his face; *~ v ó ó r je* right in front of you; *~ voor de start* just before the start; **III** (-ken) *o* 1 plane, level; 2 area, space; 3 face [of a cube]; 4 surface; 5 flat [of the hand, sword]; 6 sheet [of ice, water &]; *hellend ~* inclined plane; *wij zijn op een hellend ~* we are on a slippery slope

2 vlak (-ken) *v* = 2 *vlek*

′vlakdruk *m* planographic printing, plano-graphy

′vlakgom *m* & *o* india-rubber, [ink-]eraser

′vlakheid *v* flatness

1 ′vlakken (vlakte, h. gevlakt) *vt* flatten, level

2 ′vlakken (vlakte, *vt* h., *vi* is gevlakt) *vt* & *vi* = *vlekken*

′vlakte (-n en -s) *v* plain, level; *zich op de ~ houden* not commit oneself, give a non-committal answer; *hem tegen de ~ slaan* knock him down; *jongens van de ~* riff-raff; *meisje van de ~* streetwalker, hussy; **–maat** (-maten) *v* superficial (square) measure

vlam (-men) *v* flame[2], blaze; *een oude ~ van hem* F an old flame of his; *~men schieten* flash fire; *~ vatten* catch fire[2]; *fig* fire up; *in ~men opgaan* go up in flames; *in (volle) ~ staan* be ablaze (in a blaze)

′Vlaming (-en) *m* Fleming

′vlammen (vlamde, is gevlamd) *vi* flame, blaze, be ablaze; **–d** flaming, ablaze; **′vlammenwerper** (-s) *m* ⚔ flame-thrower; **′vlammetje** (-s) *o* 1 little flame; 2 light [for pipe]

vlas *o* flax; **–achtig** flaxy [plants]; flaxen [hair]; **–akker** (-s) *m* flax-field; **–baard** (-en) *m* 1 flaxen (downy) beard; 2 beardless boy, milksop; **–blond** flaxen [hair]; flaxen-haired [person]; **–bouw** *m* flax-growing; **–braak** (-braken) *v* flax-brake; **–haar** (-haren) *o* flaxen hair; *met ~* flaxen-haired; **–kleur** *v* flaxen colour; **–kleurig** flaxen; **–leeuwebek** *m* toadflax; **1 ′vlassen** *aj* flaxen

2 ′vlassen (vlaste, h. gevlast) *vi ~ op* look forward to, be keen on

′vlassig = *vlasachtig*; **′vlasspinne′rij** (-en) *v* flax-mill; **′vlasstengel** (-s) *m* flax stalk; **–vink** (-en) *m* & *v* linnet; **–zaad** (-zaden) *o* flax-seed, linseed

vlecht (-en) *v* braid, plait, tress; *valse ~* false plait; *haar ~* her [i. e. the girl's] pigtail; *in een (neerhangende) ~* in a pigtail; **′vlechten*** *vt* twist [thread, rope]; twine [strands of hemp &]; plait [hair, ribbon, straw, mats]; braid [the hair]; wreathe [a garland]; make [baskets]; *een opmerking in zijn rede ~* weave a remark into one's speech; **′vlechtwerk** *o* wicker-work, basket-work

′vleermuis (-muizen) *v* bat; **–brander** (-s) *m* batwing burner

vlees (vlezen) *o* 1 flesh; 2 meat [when cooked]; 3 pulp [of fruit]; *~ in blik* tinned beef; *het levende ~* the quick; *wild ~* proud flesh; *zijn eigen ~ en bloed* his own flesh and blood; *ik weet wat voor ~ ik in de kuip heb* I know with whom I have to deal; ● *i n het ~ snijden* cut to the quick; *goed in zijn ~ zitten* be in flesh; *het gaat hem n a a r den vleze* he is doing well; *hij bijt zijn nagels af tot o p het ~* he bites his nails to the quick; **–bal** (-len) *m* meat-ball; **–blok** (-ken) *o* butcher's block; **–boom** (-bomen) *m* uterine myoma; **–dag** (-dagen) *m* meat-day; **–etend** flesh-eating, carnivorous; *~e dieren* carnivores, carnivora; ~*e planten* carnivore, insectivore plants; **–extract** (-en) *o* meat extract; **–gerecht** (-en) *o* meat-course; **–hal(le)** (-hallen) *v* meat-market, shambles; **–houwer** (-s) *m* butcher; **vleeshouwe′rij** (-en) *v* butcher's shop; **′vleeskleur** *v* flesh colour; **–kleurig** flesh-coloured; **–klomp** (-en) *m* hunk of meat; *fig.* **F** lump of a man (woman); **–loos** meatless; **–made** (-n) *v* maggot; **–mes** (-sen) *o* carving-knife; butcher's knife; **–molen** (-s) *m* mincing-machine, meat-mincer; **–nat** *o* broth; **–pastei** (-en) *v* meat-pie; **–pasteitje** (-s) *o* meat-patty; **–pin** (-nen) *v* skewer; **–plank** (-en) *v* carving board; (i n k e u k e n) chopping board; **–pot** (-ten) *m* flesh-pot; *verlangen naar de ~ten van Egypte* be sick for the flesh-pots of Egypt; **–schotel** (-s) *m* & *v* meat-dish; meat-course; **–soep** (-en) *v* meat-soup; **–spijs** *v,* **–spijzen** *mv* meat; **–vork** (-en) *v* carving fork; **–waren** *mv* meats and sausages; **–wond(e)** (-wonden) *v* flesh-wound; **–wording** *v* incarnation

vleet (vleten) *v* herring-net; *bij de ~* lots of..., plenty of..., ...galore

′vlegel (-s) *m* 1 flail; 2 *fig* lout, cur, boor, tyke; **–achtig** loutish, currish, boorish; **–achtigheid** (-heden) *v* loutishness, currishness, boorishness; *een ~* a piece of impudence; *zijn vlegelachtigheden* his impudence; **–jaren** *mv* years of indiscretion, awkward age

′vleien (vleide, h. gevleid) **I** *vt* flatter, coax, cajole, wheedle; **II** *vr zich ~ dat...* flatter oneself that...; *zich ~ met de hoop dat...* indulge a hope that..., flatter oneself with the belief that...; *zich ~ met ijdele hoop* delude oneself with vain hopes; *zich gevleid voelen door...* feel flattered by...; **–er** (-s) *m* flatterer, coaxer; **vleie′rij** (-en) *v* flattery, **S** grease, oil; **′vleinaam** (-namen) *m* pet name, endearing name; **–ster** (-s) *v* flatterer, coaxer; **–taal** *v* flattering words, flattery

1 vlek (-ken) *o* small market-town

2 vlek (-ken) *v* 1 spot[2], stain[2], blot[2], blemish[2]; 2 speck [in fruit]; *een ~ op zijn naam* a blot on his reputation; **′vlekkeloos** spotless, stainless, speckless; **vlekke′loosheid** *v* spotlessness; **′vlekken I** (vlekte, h. gevlekt) *vt* blot, soil, stain, spot; **II** (vlekte, is gevlekt) *vi* soil; get spotted; *het vlekt gemakkelijk* it soils easily; **′vlekkenwater** *o* stain (spot) remover; **′vlekkig** spotted, full of spots; **′vlektyfus** [-ti.füs] *m* typhus (fever); **–vrij** spotless, stainless

1 vlerk (-ken) *v* wing; *fig* **F** paw [= hand]

2 vlerk (-en) *m* (l o m p e r d) churl, boor

′vlerkprauw (-en) *v* outrigger canoe (prau, proa)

′vleselijk carnal; *mijn ~e broeder* my own brother; *~e lusten* carnal desires

vlet (-ten) *v* ⚓ flat, flat-bottomed boat

vleug (-en) *v* (v. v i l t &) nap, hair, grain; *tegen de ~* against the hair (grain); *fig* unruly; zie ook: *vleugje*

′vleugel (-s) *m* 1 wing[2] [of a bird, the nose, a building, an army]; ☉ pinion; 2 leaf [of a door]; 3 (v. mo l e n) wing, vane; 4 ♪ grand piano; *kleine ~* ♪ baby grand; *de ~s laten hangen* droop one's wings; *de ~s uitslaan* spread one's wings; *iem. de ~s korten* clip sbd's wings; *m e t de ~s slaan* beat its wings [of a bird]; *iem. o n d e r zijn ~en nemen* take sbd. under one's wing; **–adjudant** (-en) *m* ✕ aide-de-camp; **–boot** (-boten) *m* & *v* hydrofoil; **–deur** (-en) *v* folding-door(s); **–lam** winged; **–man** (-nen) *m* ✕ guide, leader of the file; **–moer** (-en) *v* butterfly-nut, wing-nut; **–piano** ('s) *v* grand piano; *kleine ~* baby grand; **–schroef** (-schroeven) *v* thumb-screw, wing-screw; **–slag** (-slagen) *m* wing-beat; **–speler** (-s) *m* wing

′vleugje (-s) *o* (l i c h t e v l a a g) breath [of wind], waft [of scent], whiff [of fresh air]; *fig* hint [of mockery], touch [of bitterness], flicker [of hope]

′vleze zie *vlees;* **′vlezig** 1 fleshy [arms &, women, tumours, ✍ leaves]; meaty [cattle]; 2 pulpy [fruits]; **–heid** *v* fleshiness &

vlg. = *volgende* following

′vlieden* **I** *vi* flee, fly [from...]; **II** *vt* flee, fly, shun, eschew [dangers &]

vlieg (-en) *v* fly; *iem. een ~ afvangen* steal a march upon sbd; *geen ~ kwaad doen* not hurt a fly; *twee ~en in één klap slaan* kill two birds with one stone; *je bent niet hier gekomen om ~en te vangen* you are not here to sit idle

′vliegbasis [-zɪs] (-sen en -bases) *v* air base; **–bereik** *o* radius of action; **–biljet** (-ten) *o* air ticket; **–boot** (-boten) *m* & *v* flying-boat; **–brevet** (-ten) *o* flying certificate; **–dek** (-ken) *o* flight-deck; **–dekschip** (-schepen) *o* (aircraft) carrier; **–dienst** *m* flying-service, air service

′vliegeklap (-pen) *m* fly-flap(per), (fly)swatter

′vliegen* **I** *vi* fly[2] [of birds, aviators, time]; *erin ~* be taken in, fall into a trap; *hij ziet ze ~* **F** he is cracked (potty); ● *i n brand ~* catch (take) fire; *zij vloog n a a r de deur* she flew to the door; *iem. naar de keel ~* fly at sbd.'s throat; *de kogels vlogen ons o m de oren* the bullets were flying about our ears; *wij vlogen o v e r het ijs* we were simply flying over the ice; *hij vloog de kamer u i t* he flew (tore) out of the room; *hij vliegt v o o r haar* he is at her beck and call; *ze ~ voor je* they will fly to serve you; **II** *vt* ⬲ fly; **–d** flying; *~ blaadje* pamphlet; *~e bom* ✕ fly(ing)-

bomb; *in* ~*e haast* in a great hurry; ~*e jicht* wandering gout; ~*e schotel* flying saucer; ~*e start* running start; ~*e tering* galloping consumption; ~*e vis* 🐟 flying fish; ~*e winkel* travelling shop; zie ook: *geest, Hollander* &;
'vliege'nier (-s) *m* ⚙ = *vlieger* 2
'vliegenkast (-en) *v* meat-safe; **–net** (-ten) *o* fly-net; **–papier** *o* fly-paper
'vliegensvlug as quick as lightning
'vliegenvanger (-s) *m* 1 fly-catcher; fly-paper; 2 🐟 fly-trap; 3 🐦 fly-catcher; **–vergif(t)** *o* fly-poison
'vlieger (-s) *m* 1 kite; 2 ⚙ airman, flyer, flier, flying-man, aviator; *een* ~ *oplaten* fly a kite; *die* ~ *gaat niet op* that cock won't fight, that cat won't jump; **'vliegeren** (vliegerde, h. gevliegerd) *vi* fly kites
vliege'rij *v de* ~ flying, aviation
'vliegertijd *m* kite-season; **–touw** (-en) *o* kite-line
'vlieggewicht *o* (v. b o k s e r s) fly weight; (v. v l i e g t u i g) all-up; **–haven** (-s) *v* airport; **–kunst** *v* aviation; **–machine** [-ma.ʃi.nə] (-s) *v* = *vliegtuig*; **–ongeluk** (-ken) *o* flying-accident, air crash; **–plan** *o* 1 flight plan; 2 (air service) time-table; **–post** *v* air mail; **–ramp** (-en) *v* air crash, aircraft disaster; **–reis** (-reizen) *v* air journey; **–terrein** (-en) *o* flying-ground, aerodrome
'vliegtuig (-en) *o* plane, airplane, aeroplane, ✈ flying-machine; ~*(en)* ook: aircraft; *per* ~ ook: by air; **–bemanning** *v* air crew; **–benzine** *v* aviation petrol, aviation spirit; **–bouw** *m* aircraft construction; **–fabriek** (-en) *v* aircraft factory; **–industrie** *v* aircraft industry; **–kaper** (-s) *m*, **–kaapster** (-s) *v* hijacker; **–kaping** (-en) *v* hijacking; **vliegtuig'moederschip** (-schepen) *o* carrier; **'vliegtuigmonteur** (-s) *m* air mechanic; **–motor** (-s en -toren) *m* aircraft engine, aero-engine; **–ongeluk** (-ken) *o* air(craft) crash
'vlieguren *mv* flying hours; **–veld** (-en) *o* airport, *mil* airfield; **–wedstrijd** (-en) *m* air race; **–weer** *o* ⚙ flying weather; **–werk** *o met kunst en* ~ zie *kunst*; **–wezen** *o* flying, aviation; **–wiel** (-en) *o* ⚒ fly-wheel
vliem (-en) *v* = *vlijm*
vlier (-en) *m* 🌿 elder; **–bes** (-sen) *v* elder-berry; **–boom** (-bomen) *m* elder-tree; **–bosje** (-s) *o* elder-grove
'vliering (-en) *v* loft, garret, attic; *op de* ~ under the leads
'vlierstruik (-en) *m* elder-bush; **–thee** *m* elder-tea
vlies (vliezen) *o* film [of any material]; 🐑 & 🐟 1 membrane [in body]; 2 🐑 cuticle; pellicle [= film & membrane]; 3 fleece [= woolly cover-

ing of sheep &]; *het Gulden Vlies* the Golden Fleece; **–achtig** filmy, membranous;
vlies'vleugeligen membrane-winged, hymenoptera
vliet (-en) *m* brook, rill
'vlieten* *vi* flow, run
'vliezig membranous, filmy
'vlijen (vlijde, h. gevlijd) **I** *vt* lay down; **II** *vr zich* ~ *in het gras* nestle down in the grass; *zich tegen iem. aan* ~ nestle up to sbd.
vlijm (-en) *v* lancet; **'vlijmen** (vlijmde, h. gevlijmd) *vt* open with a lancet; **–d** sharp², biting²; **'vlijmscherp** (as) sharp as a razor, razor-sharp
vlijt *v* industry, diligence, assiduity, application; **–ig** industrious, diligent, assiduous
'vlinder (-s) *m* butterfly²; **–achtig** like a butterfly, butterfly-like; *fig* fickle;
vlinder'bloemigen *mv* 🌿 papilionaceous flowers; **'vlinderdas** (-sen) *v* bow(-tie); **–net** (-ten) *o* butterfly-net; **–slag** *m* butterfly stroke [in swimming]
'Vlissingen *o* Flushing
vlo (vlooien) *v* flea
'vlocht (vlochten) V.T. v. *vlechten*
'vloden V.T. meerv. v. *vlieden*
vloed (-en) *m* 1 (g e t ij) flood-tide, flux, flood, tide; 2 (r i v i e r) stream, river; 3 (o v e r- s t r o m i n g) flood; 4 *fig* flood [of tears, of words], flow [of words]; *een* ~ *van scheldwoorden* a torrent of abuse; **–deur** (-en) *v* floodgate; **–golf** (-golven) *v* tidal wave², bore
vloei *o* = *vloeipapier* & *vloeitje*
'vloeibaar liquid, fluid; ~ *maken (worden)* ook: liquefy; **–heid** *v* liquidity, fluidity; **–making, –wording** *v* liquefaction
'vloeiblad (-bladen) *o* blotter; **–blok** (-ken) *o* blotting-pad, blotter; **–boek** (-en) *o* blotting-book, blotter; **'vloeien** (vloeide, h. en is gevloeid) **I** *vi* 1 flow; 2 (in 't p a p i e r t r e k k e n) run; blot [of blotting-paper]; 3 🐟 bleed; *die verzen* ~ *(goed)* those lines flow well; *er vloeide bloed* 1 there was bloodshed; 2 (b ij d u e l) blood was drawn; **II** *vt* (m e t v l o e i- p a p i e r) blot; **–d I** *aj* flowing, fluent²; *een* ~*e stijl* a smooth style; ~*e verzen* flowing verse; **II** *ad* [speak] fluently, [run] smoothly; **'vloeiing** (-en) *v* 🐟 bleeding, menorrhagia; **'vloeipapier** (-en) *v* 1 blotting-paper; 2 (z ij d e p a p i e r) tissue-paper; **–stof** (-fen) *v* liquid; **–tje** (-s) *o* cigarette paper
vloek (-en) *m* 1 oath, **F** swear-word; 2 (v e r- v l o e k i n g) curse, malediction, imprecation; *er rust een* ~ *op* a curse rests upon it; *in een* ~ *en een zucht* in two shakes, in the twinkling of an eye; **'vloeken** (vloekte, h. gevloekt) **I** *vi* swear, curse (and swear); ~ *als een ketter*

swear like a trooper; ~ *op* swear at; *die kleuren*
~ *(tegen elkaar)* these colours clash (with each
other); **II** *vt* curse [a person &]; **–er** (-s) *m*
swearer; **'vloekwoord** (-en) *o* oath, **F** swear-
word

vloer (-en) *m* floor; *altijd over de* ~ *zijn* be always
about the house; **–bedekking** *v* floor-covering, fitted carpet; **'vloeren** (vloerde, h.
gevloerd) *vt* floor; **'vloerkleed** (-kleden) *o*
carpet; **–kleedje** (-s) *o* rug; **–mat** (-ten) *v*
floor-mat; **–steen** (-stenen) *m* paving-tile,
flag(-stone); **–tegel** (-s) *m* floor-tile, paving-
tile; **–verwarming** *v* floor heating; **–was** *m* &
o floor-polish; **–wrijver** (-s) *m* floor-polisher;
–zeil (-en) *o* floor-cloth, linoleum

'vlogen V.T. meerv. v. *vliegen*

vlok (-ken) *v* 1 flock [of wool]; 2 flake [of snow,
soap &]; 3 tuft [of hair]; **'vlokken** (vlokte, is
gevlokt) *vi* flake; **'vlokkenzeep** *v* soap flakes;
'vlokkig flocky, flaky

'vlonder (-s) *m* plank-bridge

vlood (vloden) V.T. v. *vlieden*

vloog (vlogen) V.T. v. *vliegen*

'vlooiebeet (-beten) *m* flea-bite; **1 'vlooien**
(vlooide, h. gevlooid) *vt* clean of fleas [a dog
&]; **2 'vlooien** *mv.* v. *vlo*; **'vlooiendres-**
seur (-s) *m* flea trainer; **–kruid** *o* fleabane;
–markt (-en) *v* flea market; **–spel** (-len) *o*
tiddly-winks; **–theater** (-s) *o* flea circus,
performing fleas; **'vlooiepik** (-ken) *m* flea-bite

1 vloot (vloten) *v* fleet, navy

2 vloot (vloten) V.T. v. *vlieten*

'vlootaalmoezenier (-s) *m rk* naval chaplain,
F padre; **–basis** [-zıs] (-sen en -bases) *v* naval
base

'vlootje (-s) *o* butter-dish

'vlootpredikant (-en) *m* naval chaplain,
F padre; **–schouw** *m* naval review; **–voogd**
(-en) *m* commander of the fleet, admiral

'vlossen *aj* floss; **'vlossig** flossy

1 vlot (-ten) *o* raft

2 vlot I *aj* 1 (d r ij v e n d) ⚓ afloat; 2 (v l u g)
fluent [speaker]; prompt [payment]; ready
[answer]; smooth [journey, landing &]; 3
(n i e t s t r o e f) easy [manner, style, to live
with], flowing [style]; *een* ~ *hoedje* a smart little
hat; *zijn* ~*te pen* his facile pen; *een schip* ~
krijgen ⚓ get a ship afloat, float her; ~ *worden*
⚓ get afloat; **II** *ad* fluently; *het gaat* ~ it goes
smoothly; *de... gaan* ~ *weg* $ there is a brisk sale
of..., ...are a brisk sale,... sell like hot cakes; ~
opzeggen get off pat [a lesson]

'vlotbrug (-gen) *v* floating bridge

'vloten V.T. meerv. van *vlieten*

'vlotheid *v* fluency; smoothness

'vlothout *o* drift-wood

'vlotten (vlotte, h. gevlot) **I** *vi* float; *fig* go

smoothly; *het gesprek vlotte niet* the conversation
dragged; *het werk wil maar niet* ~ I can't make
headway, I'm not getting anywhere; *het werk*
vlot goed we are making headway; ~*de bevolking*
floating population; ~*d kapitaal* circulating
capital; ~*de middelen* liquid resources; ~*de*
schuld floating debt; **II** *vt* raft [wood, timber];
–er (-s) *m* 1 (p e r s o o n) raftsman, rafter; 2 ⚒
float

vlucht (-en) *v* 1 (h e t v l u c h t e n) flight,
escape; 2 (h e t v l i e g e n) flight; 3 (a f s t a n d
v a n v l e u g e l u i t e i n d e n) wing-spread;
4 flight, flock [of birds]; bevy [of larks,
quails]; covey [of partridges]; *de* ~ *nemen*
flee, take to flight, take to one's heels; *zijn* ~
nemen take wing [of birds]; *een hoge* ~ *nemen* fly
high, soar; *fig* soar high, take a high (lofty)
flight; *een te hoge* ~ *nemen* fly too high; ● *een*
vogel i n de ~ *schieten* shoot a bird on the wing;
o p de ~ *drijven (jagen)* put to flight, put to rout,
rout; *op de* ~ *gaan (slaan)* = *de* ~ *nemen*; *op de* ~
zijn be on the run; **'vluchteling** (-en) *m* 1
fugitive; 2 refugee; **–enkamp** (-en) *o* refugee
camp; **'vluchten I** (vluchtte, is gevlucht) *vi*
fly, flee; ~ *n a a r* flee (fly) to; *u i t het land* ~
flee (from) the country; ~ *v o o r* flee from, fly
from, fly before; **II** (vluchtte, h. gevlucht) *vt*
fly, flee, shun [dangers &]; **'vluchtgat**
(-gaten) *o* bolt-hole; **–haven** (-s) *v* port
(harbour) of refuge; **–heuvel** (-s) *m* island,
refuge

'vluchtig I *aj* volatile [oils, persons]; cursory
[reading], hasty [glance, sketch]; flecting
[glimpse, impression, visit], transient [plea-
sure]; **II** *ad* cursorily; **–heid** *v* volatility;
cursoriness; hastiness

'vluchtleiding *v* flight control; **–plan** (-nen) *o*
1 flight plan; 2 (air service) time-table

'vluchtstrook (-stroken) *v* refuge lane, slip
road; **–weg** (-wegen) *m* escape-route

vlug I *aj* 1 quick² [trot & walk; to act, perceive,
learn, think, or invent]; nimble² [in movement, of mind]; agile² [frame, arm, movements &]; 2 (k u n n e n d e v l i e g e n) fledged
[birds]; ~ *i n het rekenen* quick at figures; ~ *m e t*
de pen zijn have a ready pen; ~ *v a n begrip*
quick(-witted); *hij behoort niet tot de* ~*gen* he is
none of the quickest; **II** *ad* quickly, quick; ~
(wat)! (be) quick!, make it snappy!, look sharp!;
hij kan ~ *leren* he is a quick learner; **–gerd** (-s)
m-v quick child, sharp child; **–gertje** (-s) *o*
quickie; **–heid** *v* quickness, nimbleness,
rapidity, promptness; **–schrift** (-en) *o*
pamphlet; **–zout** *o* sal volatile

V.N. = *Verenigde Naties* United Nations

vnl. = *voornamelijk*

1 vo'caal *aj* (& *ad*) vocal(ly)

2 vo'caal (-calen) *v* vowel
vocabu'laire [-'lɪ:rə] (-s) *o* vocabulary
voca'list (-en) vocalist, singer
voca'tief (-tieven) *m* vocative
1 vocht 1 (-en) *o* (v l o e i s t o f) fluid, liquid; 2 *o* & *v* (c o n d e n s a t i e) moisture, damp, wet
2 vocht (vochten) V.T. v. *vechten*
1 'vochten (vochtte, h. gevocht) *vt* moisten, wet, damp
2 'vochten V.T. meerv. v. *vechten*
'vochtgehalte *o* percentage of moisture, moisture content; **'vochtig** moist, damp, dank, humid; ~ *maken* moisten, wet, damp; ~ *worden* become moist &, moisten; **–heid** *v* moistness, dampness, humidity; (h e t v o c h t) moisture, damp; **'vochtigheidsgraad** *m* humidity; **–meter** (-s) *m* hygrometer; **'vochtmaat** (-maten) *v* liquid measure; **–vlek** (-ken) *v* damp-stain
vod (-den) *o* & *v* rag, tatter; *een* ~ *van een boek* some rubbishy book, some trashy novel; *iem. a c h t e r de ~den zitten* keep sbd. hard at it; *iem. b ij de ~den krijgen* catch hold of sbd.; **'vodde** (-n) *v* rag, tatter; **–boel** *m*, **–goed** *o* trash, rubbish, trumpery things; **'voddenboer** (-en) *m = voddenman;* **–koper** (-s) *m* dealer in rags, ragman; **–kraam** (-kramen) *v* & *o* trash, rubbish; **–man** (-nen) *m* ragman, rag-and-bone man; **–markt** (-en) *v* rag-market; **–raper** (-s) *m,* **–raapster** (-s) *v* rag-picker; **'voddig** ragged; *fig* trashy; **'vodje** (-s) *o* rag; *fig* scrap [of paper]
'vodka = *wodka*
'voeden (voedde, h. gevoed) **I** *vt* feed [a man, a pump &]; nurse [her baby]; nourish[2] [one's family, a hope &] *fig* foster, nurse, cherish [a hope]; **II** *va* be nourishing [of food]; **III** *vr zich* ~ feed; *zich* ~ *met...* feed on...; **1 'voeder** *m* feeder; **2 'voeder** (-s) *o* fodder, forage, provender; **–artikelen** *mv* feeding stuffs; **–bak** (-ken) *m* manger; **–biet** (-en) *v* mangel (-wurzel); **'voederen** (voederde, h. gevoederd); **I** *vt* feed; **II** *o* feeding; **'voedergewas** (-sen) *o* fodder plant, fodder crop; **–graan** (-granen) *o* feeding grain; **–tijd** (-en) *m* feeding time; **–zak** (-ken) *m* nose-bag, feed bag
'voeding *v* 1 (h a n d e l i n g) feeding, nourishment, alimentation; 2 (v o e d s e l) food, nourishment; 3 (v o e d i n g s w ij z e) diet; *een gebalanceerde* ~ a balanced diet; **'voedingsbodem** (-s) *m* 1 *eig* (culture) medium [of bacteria]; matrix [of fungus]; 2 *fig* breeding ground; **–deskundige** (-n) *m-v* dietician; **–gewas** (-sen) *o* food plant, food crop; **–leer** *v* dietetics, science of nutrition; **–middel** (-en) *o* article of food, food; **~en** foodstuffs; **–stoffen** *mv* nutritious matter, nutrients; **–stoornis**

(-sen) *v* nutritional problem (difficulty); **–waarde** *v* food value, nutritional value
'voedsel *o* food, nourishment; ~ *geven aan* encourage; **–schaarste** *v* food shortage;. **–vergiftiging** *v* food poisoning; **–voorraad** (-raden) *m* food supply; **–voorziening** *v* food supply
'voedster (-s) *v* nurse, foster-mother
'voedzaam nourishing, nutritious, nutritive; **–heid** *v* nutritiousness, nutritiveness
voeg (-en) *v* joint, seam; *uit zijn ~en rukken* put out of joint, disrupt; *[fig] dat geeft geen* ~ that is not seemly, it is not the proper thing (to do)
'voege *v in dier* ~ in this manner; *in dier* ~ *dat...* so as to..., so that...
1 'voegen (voegde, h. gevoegd) **I** *vi* (& *onpers. ww.*) (b e t a m e n) become; (g e l e g e n k o m e n) suit; **II** *vr zich* ~ *naar...* conform to..., comply with...
2 'voegen (voegde, h. gevoegd) **I** *vt* 1 (b ij d o e n) add; 2 (d i c h t v u l l e n) △ point, joint, flush; ~ *bij* add to; zie ook: *daad;* **II** *vr zich* ~ *bij iem.* join sbd.
'voegijzer (-s) *o* pointing-trowel; **–werk** *o* pointing
'voegwoord (-en) *o* conjunction
'voegzaam suitable, becoming, (be)fitting, seemly, fit, proper; **–heid** *v* suitableness, becomingness, seemliness, propriety
'voelbaar to be felt; palpable; perceptible;
'voeldraad (-draden) *m* antenna, palp;
'voelen (voelde, h. gevoeld) **I** *vt* feel, ook: be sensible of [shame]; sense [danger, deceit]; be alive to [an insult]; *ik vòel mijn benen* my legs are aching; *ik zal het hem laten* ~ he shall be made to feel it; *ik voel daar niet veel voor* I don't sympathize with the idea, I don't care for it, it does not appeal to me; I don't care to... [be kept waiting &]; **II** *va het voelt zacht* it is soft to the touch; **III** *vr zich...* ~ feel [ill], feel oneself...; *hij begint zich te* ~ he is getting above himself; *hij voelt zich nogal* he rather fancies himself; *zich thuis* ~ feel at home[2]; **–er** (-s) *m* feeler; **'voelhoorn, –horen** (-s) *m* feeler, antenna; *zijn ~s uitsteken [fig]* put out feelers, feel one's ground; **'voeling** *v* feeling; touch; ~ *hebben met* be in touch with; ~ *houden met* keep (in) touch with; ~ *krijgen met* come into touch with; **'voelspriet** (-en) *m* antenna, palp, feeler
1 'voer *o* 1 fodder, forage, provender; feed, food; 2 (-en) cartload [of hay]
2 voer (voeren) V.T. v. *varen*
'voerbak (-ken) *m* manger
1 'voeren (voerde, h. gevoerd) *vt = voederen*
2 'voeren (voerde, h. gevoerd) *vt* 1 carry, convey, take, bring, lead; 2 (h a n t e r e n) wield [the sword &]; 3 (d r a g e n) bear [a

name, a title]; 4 conduct [negotiations], carry on [propaganda]; *dat zou ons te ver ~* that would carry us too far; *wat voert u hierheen?* what brings you here?; *een adelaar in zijn wapen ~* have an eagle in one's coat of arms; zie ook: *gesprek, woord &*

3 **'voeren** (voerde, h. gevoerd) *vt* line [a coat]

4 **'voeren** V.T. meerv. van *varen*

'voering (-en) *v* lining; **–stof** (-fen) *v* lining

'voerloon *o* cartage; **–man** (-lieden en -lui) *m* 1 (k o e t s i e r) driver, coachman; 2 (v r a c h t-r ij d e r) wag(g)oner, carrier; *de Voerman* ★ the Wag(g)oner; **–taal** *v* official language, vehicle; **–tuig** (-en) *o* carriage, vehicle²

voet (-en) *m* foot [of man, hill, ladder, page &]; *fig* foot, footing; *zes ~ lang* six feet long; *je moet hem daarin geen ~ geven* you should not indulge him too much, you should not encourage him; *de ~ in de stijgbeugel hebben* [*fig*] be in the saddle; *het heeft heel wat ~en in de aarde* it takes (will take) some doing; *~ bij stuk houden* 1 keep to the point; 2 stick to one's guns, stand one's ground; *vaste ~ krijgen* obtain a foothold, obtain a firm footing; *geen ~ verzetten* not move hand or foot; *geen ~ kunnen verzetten* not be able to stir; *ik zet daar geen ~ meer* I'll never set foot there again; *iem. de ~ dwars zetten* thwart sbd.'s plans; *iem. de ~ op de nek zetten* put one's foot upon sbd.'s neck; *~ aan wal zetten* set foot on shore; *geen ~ buiten de deur zetten* not stir out of the house; ● *a a n de ~ van de bladzijde, van de brief* at the foot of the page, at foot; *met het geweer b ij de ~* ⚔ with arms at the order; *met de ~en bij elkaar* with joined feet; *met één ~ in het graf staan* have one foot in the grave; *met ~en treden* trample under foot, tread under foot²; *fig* set at naught, override [laws]; *o n d e r de ~ geraken* be trampled on; *een land onder de ~ lopen* overrun a country; *onder de ~ vertrappen* tread (trample) under foot; *o p de ~ van 5 ten honderd* at the rate of five per cent.; *iem. op de ~ volgen* 1 follow close at sbd.'s heels; 2 follow sbd.'s example; *(iets) op de ~ volgen* closely follow [a text]; *op die ~ at that rate; op bescheiden ~ on a* modest footing *op blote ~en* barefoot; *op dezelfde ~* on the old footing; in the old way; on the same lines; *op gelijke ~* on an equal footing, on a footing of equality, on the same footing; *zij staan op gespannen ~* relations are strained between them; *op goede ~ staan met* be on good terms with, stand well with; *op grote ~ leven* live in (grand) style; *op de oude ~* on the old footing; *op staande ~* off-hand, at once, on the spot, then and there; *op vertrouwelijke ~* on familiar terms; *op vrije ~en* at liberty, at large; *op ~ van gelijkheid* on a footing of equality, on equal terms; *op ~ van oorlog* on a war footing;

op ~ van vrede on a peace footing; *t e ~* on foot; *te ~ bereikbaar* within walking distance; *te ~ gaan* go on foot, walk; *iem. te ~ vallen* throw oneself at sbd.'s feet;... *t e n ~en uit...* all over; *ten ~en uit geschilderd* full-length [portrait]; *u i t de ~en kunnen* [*fig*] get on, get by; *zich uit de ~en maken* take to one's heels, make off; *~ v o o r ~* foot by foot, step by step; *iem. iets voor de ~en gooien* cast (fling, throw) it in sbd.'s teeth; *iem. voor de ~en lopen* be in sbd.'s way; **–afdruk** (-ken) *m* footprint; **–angel** (-s) *m* mantrap; *hier liggen ~s en klemmen* beware of mantraps; *fig* it is full of pitfalls, there are snakes in the grass; **–bad** (-baden) *o* foot-bath

'voetbal 1 (-len) *m* (b a l) football; 2 *o* (s p e l) (Association) football, **F** soccer; **~ spelen** play football, **F** play soccer; **–competitie** [-(t)si.] *v* ± Association football season; **–knie** (-ieën) *v* football knee; **'voetballen** (voetbalde, h. gevoetbald) *vi* play football, **F** play soccer; **–er**, **'voetbalspeler** (-s) *m* football-player, **F** soccer-player; **–pool** [-pu.l] (-s) *m* football pools; **–schoen** (-en) *m* football boot; **–stadion** (-s) *o* football stadium; **–toto** ('s) *m* football pools; **–trainer** [-tre.nər] (-s) *m* football coach; **–veld** (-en) *o* football ground, football field

'voetboeien *mv* fetters; **–boog** (-bogen) *m* cross-bow; **–breed** *o geen ~ wijken* not budge an inch; **–brug** (-gen) *v* foot-bridge; **–eind(e)** (-einden) = *voeteneind(e)*; **'voet(en)bank** (-en) *v* footstool; **'voeteneind(e)** (-einden) *o* foot-end, foot [of a bed]; **'voet(en)kussen** (-s) *o* hassock; **–schrapper** (-s) *m* scraper; **–werk** *o* footwork; **–zak** (-ken) *m* foot-muff

'voetganger (-s) *m*, **–ster** (-s) *v* pedestrian; **'voetgangersgebied** (-en) *o* pedestrian area (precinct); **–oversteekplaats** (-en) *v* pedestrian crossing, zebra (crossing); **–tunnel** (-s) *m* pedestrian subway (tunnel)

'voetje (-s) *o* small foot; *een wit ~ bij iem. hebben* be in sbd.'s good graces (in sbd.'s good books); *een wit ~ bij iem. zien te krijgen* insinuate oneself into sbd.'s good graces; *~ voor ~* step by step; **'voetkleedje** (-s) *o* rug; **–knecht** (-en) *m* 🛢 foot-soldier; **–kus** (-sen) *m* 1 foot-kissing; 2 kissing the Pope's toe; **–licht** *o* footlights; *voor het ~ brengen* put on the stage; *voor het ~ komen* appear before the footlights; **–mat** (-ten) *v* doormat; **–noot** (-noten) *v* foot-note; **–pad** (-paden) *o* footpath; **–pomp** (-en) *v* foot-pump, inflator; **–punt** (-en) *o* ★ nadir; (v a n l o o d l ij n) foot; **–reis** (-reizen) *v* journey (excursion) on foot, walking-tour, *sp* hike; **–reiziger** (-s) *m* foot-traveller, wayfarer; **–rem** (-men) *v* foot-brake; **–rempedaal** (-dalen) *o &* *m* foot-brake pedal; **–spoor** (-sporen) *o* foot-mark, footprint, track; *iems.* ~ *volgen* follow in sbd.'s track; **–stap** (-pen) *m* step, footstep; *iems.* ~*pen drukken, in iems.* ~*pen treden* follow (tread, walk) in sbd.'s (foot)steps; **–stoots** 1 $ [buy, sell] outright, as it is (as they are); 2 out of hand; **–stuk** (-ken) *o* pedestal; **–titel** (-s) *m* sub-title; **–tocht** (-en) *m = voetreis;* **–val** (-len) *m* prostration; *een ~ doen voor...* prostrate oneself before...; **–veeg** (-vegen) *m* & *v* door-mat²; **–volk** *o* ⚔ foot-soldiers; *het* ~ the foot, the infantry; **–vrij** ankle-length [dress]; **–wassing** (-en) *v* washing of the feet; **–wortel** (-s) *m* tarsus; **–wortelbeentje** (-s) *o* tarsal bone; **–zak** (-ken) *m* foot-muff; **–zoeker** (-s) *m* squib, cracker; **–zool** (-zolen) *m* sole of the foot

'**vogel** (-s) *m* bird, ☉ fowl; *de* ~*en des hemels* the fowls of the air; *een slimme* ~ a sly dog, a wily old bird; *beter één* ~ *in de hand dan tien in de lucht* a bird in the hand is worth two in the bush; *de* ~ *is gevlogen* the bird is flown; **–aar** (-s) *m* fowler, bird-catcher; **–bekdier** (-en) *o* duckbill, platypus; **–ei** (-eren) *o* bird's egg; **–gekweel** *o* warbling of birds; **–handelaar** (-s) *m* bird-seller, bird-fancier; **–huis** (-huizen) *o* aviary; **–huisje** (-s) *o* nest box; **–jacht** (-en) *v* fowling; **–kers** *v* bird-cherry; **–knip** (-pen) *v* bird-trap; **–kooi** (-en) *v* bird-cage; **–koopman** (-lieden en -lui) *m = vogelhandelaar;* **–kunde** *v* ornithology; **–leven** *o* bird-life; **–liefhebber** (-s) *m* bird-lover; **–lijm** *m* 1 bird-lime; 2 ♣ mistletoe; **–markt** (-en) *v* bird-market; **–melk** *v* ♣ star of Bethlehem; **–nest** (-en) *o* 1 bird's nest; 2 (e e t b a a r) edible bird's nest; **–net** (-ten) *o* bird-net; **–pest** *v* fowl plague; **–pik** *m sp* darts; **–poot** (-poten) *m* bird's foot; **–roer** (-en en -s) *o* fowling-piece; **–slag** (-slagen) *o* & *m* bird-trap

'**vogeltje** (-s) *o* little bird, **F** dicky-bird, dicky; ~*s die zo vroeg zingen krijgt 's avonds de poes* sing before breakfast (and you'll) cry before night; *ieder* ~ *zingt zoals het gebekt is* if better were within, better would come out; every one talks after his own fashion

'**vogeltrek** *m* bird migration; **–vanger** (-s) *m* bird-catcher, fowler; **–verschrikker** (-s) *m* scarecrow²; *er uitzien als een* ~ look a perfect fright; **–vlucht** *v* bird's-eye view; *...in* ~ bird's-eye view of...;

'**vogelvrij, vogel'vrij** outlawed; ~ *verklaren* outlaw; **–verklaarde** (-n) *m-v* outlaw; **–verklaring** (-en) *v* outlawry

'**vogelzaad** *o* bird-seed; **–zang** *m* singing

(warbling) of bird, birds' song, bird song

Vo'gezen *mv de* ~ the Vosges

'**voile** ['vva.lə] 1 (-s) *m* (v o o r w e r p s n a a m) veil; 2 *o & m* (s t o f n a a m) voile

vol full, filled; *de autobus, tram & is* ~ ook: is full up; *hij was er* ~ *van* he was full of it; ~ *(van) tranen* full of tears; *hij was* ~ *verontwaardiging* he was filled with indignation; *een boek* ~ *wetenswaardigheden* ook: packed with interesting facts; ~*le broeder* full brother; *een* ~*le dag* a full day; *in* ~*le ernst* in all seriousness, in dead earnest; *in de* ~*le grond* outside, outdoors; ~*le leerkracht* full-time (whole-time) teacher; ~ *matroos* able seaman; ~*le melk* full-cream milk, whole milk; ~*le neef (nicht)* first cousin, cousin german; ~*le stem* rich (full) voice; *een* ~ *uur* a full hour, a solid hour; *een* ~*le winkel (met mensen)* a crowded shop; *zij willen hem niet voor* ~ *aanzien* they don't take him seriously; ~ *doen* fill, fill up; *de tafel lag* ~ *papieren* the table was covered with papers; *ten* ~*le* to the full, fully, [pay] in full

'**volaarde** *v* fuller's earth

vo'lant [-'lã] (-s) *m* 1 *sp* shuttlecock; 2 flounce [of dress]

volauto'matisch [-o.to.- of -ɔuto.-] fully automatic

'**volbloed** thoroughbred, full-blooded [horses &]; *fig* out-and-out [radical]; **vol'bloedig** full-blooded

'**volbrassen**[1] *vt* ♣ brace full

vol'brengen (volbracht, h. volbracht) *vt* fulfil, execute, accomplish, perform, achieve; *het is volbracht* **B** it is finished; **–ging** *v* fulfilment, performance, accomplishment

vol'daan 1 satisfied, content; 2 $ (b e t a a l d) paid, received; *voor* ~ *tekenen* $ receipt [a bill]; **–heid** *v* satisfaction, contentment

'**volder** *= voller*

'**vol doen**[1] *vt* fill (up)

vol'doen (voldeed, h. voldaan) **I** *vt* 1 satisfy, give satisfaction to, content, please [people]; 2 (b e t a l e n) pay [a bill]; **II** *va (& vi)* satisfy, give satisfaction; *wij kunnen niet aan alle aanvragen* ~ we cannot cope with the demand; *aan een belofte* ~ fulfil a promise; *aan een bevel* ~ obey a command; *aan het examen* ~ satisfy the examiners; *aan zijn plicht* ~ do (carry out) one's duty; *aan zijn verplichtingen* ~ meet one's obligations ($ one's liabilities); *(niet) aan de verwachting* ~ (not) answer expectations; *aan een verzoek* ~ comply with a request; *aan een voorwaarde* ~ satisfy (fulfil) a condition; *aan iems. wens* ~

---

[1] V.T. en V.D. van dit werkwoord volgens het model: '**vol**gooien, V.T. gooide '**vol**, V.D. '**vol**gegooid. Zie voor de vormen onder het grondwoord, in dit voorbeeld: *gooien*. Bij sterke en onregelmatige werkwoorden wordt u verwezen naar de lijst achterin.

satisfy sbd.'s wish; zie ook: *eis*; **–d(e) I** *aj*
satisfactory [proof]; sufficient [amount,
number, provisions &]; ... enough; ample
[room]; *dat is ~e* ook: that will do; *meer dan ~e*
more than enough, plenty; **II** *ad* satisfactorily;
sufficiently; **–de** (-s en -n) *v & o* ⮂ sufficient
mark; *ik heb ~* I have got sufficient (marks);
vol'doening *v* 1 satisfaction; 2 **$** settlement,
payment; 3 atonement [by Christ]; *zijn ~ over...*
his satisfaction at or with [the results &]; *~
geven (schenken)* give satisfaction; *ter ~ aan...* in
compliance with [regulations]; *ter ~ van...* in
settlement of [a debt]

vol'dongen *~ feit* accomplished fact
vol'dragen mature, full-term [child]
vol'eind(ig)en (voleind(ig)de, h. voleind(igd))
vt finish, complete; **–d(ig)ing** *v* completion
Volen'dammer (-s) *aj* (& *m*) Volendam (man)
'volgaarne right willingly
'volgauto [-o.to. of -ɔuto.] ('s) *m* car in funeral
(or marriage) procession; **–briefje** (-s) *o* **$**
delivery order
'volgeboekt booked up (to capacity), fully
booked [aircraft &]; **'volgefourneerd** [-fu:r-]
= *volgestort*
'volgeling(e) (-lingen) *m(-v)* follower, adherent, votary [of a sect]; **'volgen** (volgde, h. en
is gevolgd) **I** *vt* follow [a person, a path, a
speaker, an argument, the fashion, an admonition, a command &]; follow up [a clue];
pursue [a policy]; watch [the course of events,
a football match &]; track [spacecraft]; attend
[a series of concerts, lectures]; take [a course of
training]; *zijn eigen hoofd ~* go one's own way;
een verdachte ~ shadow (dog) a suspect; *ik heb
het (verhaal) niet gevolgd* I have not followed it
up; *hij is niet te ~* I cannot follow him; *hij liet
deze verklaring ~ door...* he followed up this
explanation by...; **II** *va* follow; *hij kan niet ~ (in
de klas)* he can't keep up with his form; *je hebt
weer niet gevolgd* you have not attended [to your
book &]; **II** *vi* follow, ensue; *ik volg* I am next;
Nederland en België ~ met 11% the Netherlands
and Belgium come next with 11 percent.; *slot
volgt* zie *slot*; *wie (die) volgt?* next, please; *hij
schrijft als volgt* as follows; ● *~ o p* follow (on);
op de p volgt de q p is followed by q; *de ene ramp
volgde op de andere* disaster followed disaster; *de
op haar ~de zuster* the sister next to her [in
years]; *hieru i t volgt dat...* it follows that...; *wat
volgt daaruit?* what follows?; **–d** *aj* following,
ensuing, next; *de ~e week* 1 next week; 2 the
next (the ensuing) week; *het ~e* the following;

'volgenderwijs, –wijze in the following way,
as follows; **'volgens** according to; *~ paragraaf
zoveel* under such and such a paragraph; *~ de
directe methode* by the direct method; *~ factuur* **$**
as per invoice; *~ hemzelf* by his own account;
'volger (-s) *m* follower
'volgestort **$** paid-up (in full), fully-paid
[shares]
'volgieten[1] *vt* fill (up)
'volgkoets (-en) *v* mourning-coach; **–nummer**
(-s) *o* serial number
'volgooien[1] *vt* fill (up)
'volgorde (-n en -s) *v* order (of succession),
sequence; **'volgreeks** (-en) *v* series, sequence;
–rijtuig (-en) *o* mourning-coach
vol'groeid full-grown
'volgstation [-sta(t).ʃǒn] (-s) *o* tracking station;
–trein (-en) *m* relief train; **–wagen** (-s) *m* 1
(r o u w k o e t s) mourning-coach; 2 = *aanhangwagen*
'volgzaam docile, tractable; **–heid** *v* docility,
tractability
vol'harden (volhardde, h. volhard) *vi* persevere, persist; *~ b ij zijn besluit* stick to one's
resolution; *~ bij zijn weigering* persist in one's
refusal; *~ i n de boosheid* persevere in one's evil
courses; **–d** persevering, persistent;
vol'harding *v* perseverance, persistency;
tenacity (of purpose); **–svermogen** *o*
perseverance, persistency
vol'heid *v* ful(l)ness; *uit de ~ van haar gemoed* out
of the fulness of her heart
vol'houden[1] **I** *vt* maintain [a war, statement &];
keep up [the fight]; sustain [a character, rôle];
zelfs een... kan dat niet lang ~ even a... won't last
long at that; *het ~* hold on, hold out, stick it
(out); *iets tot het eind toe ~* see sth. through (to
the end); *hij bleef maar ~ dat...* he (stoutly)
maintained that..., he insisted that..., he was
not to be talked out of his conviction that...; **II**
va persevere, persist, hold on, hold out, stick it
out (to the end); *~ maar!* never say die!
voli'ère (-s) *v* aviary
'volijverig zealous, full of zeal, assiduous
volk (-en en -eren) *o* people, nation; (*er is) ~!*
Shop!; *het ~* 1 the people; 2 ⚓ the crew; *ons ~*
our nation, this nation, the people of this
country; *er was veel ~* there were many people;
zulk ~ such people; *de ~en van Europa* the
nations (peoples) of Europe; *het gemene ~* the
mob, the vulgar; *wij krijgen ~* we expect
people [to-night]; *een man u i t het ~* a man of
the people; *v o o r het ~* for the many, for the

---

[1] V.T. en V.D. van dit werkwoord volgens het model: **'volgooien**, V.T. gooide **'vol**, V.D. **'volgegooid**. Zie voor de
vormen onder het grondwoord, in dit voorbeeld: *gooien*. Bij sterke en onregelmatige werkwoorden wordt u
verwezen naar de lijst achterin.

people; **'Volkenbond** *m* League of Nations; **'volkenkunde** *v* ethnology; **–recht** *o* law of nations, international law, public law; **'Volkerenbond** = *Volkenbond;* **'Volkerenslag** *m* ⬜ Battle of the Nations; **'volkje** (-s) *o* people; *het jonge* ~ the young folks; *dat jonge* ~ *!* those youngsters

vol'komen I *aj* perfect [circle, ⬚ flower]; complete [victory &]; **II** *ad* perfectly [happy &]; completely [satisfied]; **–heid** *v* perfection, completeness

vol'korenbrood (-broden) *o* wholemeal bread **'volkrijk** populous; **–heid** *v* populousness **'volksaard** *m* national character; **–begrip** (-pen) *o* popular notion; **–belang** (-en) *o* matter of national concern; *het* ~ the interest of the nation; **–beschaving** *v* national culture; **–bestaan** *o* existence as a nation; **–bestuur** *o* popular government; **–beweging** (-en) *v* popular movement; **–bibliotheek** (-theken) *v* free (circulating) library; **–blad** (-bladen) *o* popular paper; **–boek** (-en) *o* 1 popular book; 2 ⬜ chap-book; **–buurt** (-en) *v* popular neighbourhood, working-class quarter; **–concert** (-en) *o* popular concert; **–dans** (-en) *m* folk-dance; **–democratie** [-(t)si.] (-ieën) *v* people's democracy; **–dichter** (-s) *m* popular poet; *onze* ~ our national poet; **–dracht** (-en) *v* national dress, national costume; **–drank** (-en) *m* national drink; **–duitser** (-s) *m* ethnic German; **–etymologie** [-e.ti.-] (-ieën) *v* folk (popular) etymology, ghost-word; **–feest** (-en) *o* 1 national feast; 2 public amusement; ~*en* public rejoicings; **–front** *o* popular front; **–gebruik** (-en) *o* popular custom, national custom; ~*en* ook: folk-customs; **–geest** *m* national spirit; **–geloof** *o* popular belief; **–gemeenschap** (-pen) *v* national community, nation; **–gericht** (-en) *o* ± kangaroo court; **–gewoonte** (-n en -s) *v* popular (national) habit; **–gezondheid** *v* public health; **–gunst** *v* public favour, popularity; *de* ~ *trachten te winnen* make a bid for popularity; **–hogeschool** (-scholen) *v* people's college; **–huishouding** *v* national (political) economy; **–huishoudkunde** *v* economics; **–huisvesting** *v* housing; **–karakter** (-s) *o* national character; **–kind** (-eren) *o* child of the people; **–klas(se)** (-klassen) *v* lower classes; **–kunde** *v* folklore; **–kunst** *v* folk art, popular art; **–leger** (-s) *o* popular army; **–leider** (-s) *m* leader of the people; > demagogue; **–leven** *o* life of the people; **–lied** (-eren) *o* national song, national

anthem; ~*eren* popular songs, folk-songs; **–menigte** (-n en -s) *v* crowd, multitude; **–menner** (-s) *m* demagogue; **–mond** *m in de* ~ in the language of the people; *zoals het in de* ~ *heet* as it is popularly called; **–muziek** *v* folk music; **–naam** (-namen) *m* 1 name of a people; 2 popular name; **–onderwijs** *o* national (popular) education; **–oploop** (-lopen) *m* street-crowd; **–oproer** (-en) *o* popular rising; **–opruier** (-s) *m* agitator; **–opstand** (-en) *m* insurrection, riot; **–overlevering** (-en) *v* popular tradition; **–partij** (-en) *v* people's party; **–planting** (-en) *v* colony, settlement; **–raadpleging** (-en) *v* = *volksstemming;* **–redenaar** (-s) *m* popular orator; **–regering** (-en) *v* government by the people, popular government; **–republiek** (-en) *v* people's republic [of China]; **–school** (-scholen) *v* public elementary school; **–soevereiniteit** *v* sovereignty of the people; **–spel** (-spelen) *o* popular game; **–stam** (-men) *m* tribe, race; **–stem** (-men) *v* voice of the people; **–stemming** (-en) *v* 1 plebiscite; 2 popular feeling; **–taal** *v* 1 language of the people, popular language, vulgar tongue; 2 national idiom, vernacular; **–telling** (-en) *v* census (of population); *een* ~ *houden* take a census; **–tribuun** (-bunen) *m* tribune of the people; **–tuintje** (-s) *o* allotment (garden); **–uitdrukking** (-en) *v* popular expression; **–uitgave** (-n) *v* cheap (popular) edition; **–verdrukker** (-s) *m* oppressor of the people; **–vergadering** (-en) *v* national assembly; **–verhuizing** (-en) *v* migration (wandering) of the nations; **–vermaak** (-maken) *o* public (popular) amusement; **–vertegenwoordiger** (-s) *m* representative of the people, member of Parliament; **–vertegenwoordiging** (-en) *v* representation of the people; *de* ~ Parliament; **–verzekering** (-en) *v* national insurance; **–vijand** (-en) *m* enemy of the people; **–vooroordeel** (-delen) *o* popular prejudice; **–vriend** (-en) *m* friend of the people; **–wil** *m* will of the people (of the nation), popular will; **–woede** *v* anger (fury) of the people; **–zang** *m* community singing; **–ziekte** (-n en -s) *v* endemic **'volle** *ten* ~ zie *vol*

vol'ledig I *aj* complete [set, work &]; full [confession, details, report]; plenary [session]; **II** *ad* completely, fully; **vol'ledigheid** *v* completeness, full(l)ness; **–shalve** for the sake of completeness

vol'leerd finished, proficient, full(y)-fledged; ~

---

[1] V.T. en V.D. van dit werkwoord volgens het model: **'volgooien**, V.T. gooide **'vol**, V.D. **'volgegooid**. Zie voor de vormen onder het grondwoord, in dit voorbeeld: *gooien*. Bij sterke en onregelmatige werkwoorden wordt u verwezen naar de lijst achterin.

zijn have done learning, have left school; *een ~e schurk* a consummate scoundrel

volle'maan *v* full moon; **–sgezicht** (-en) *o* full-moon face

'vollen (volde, h. gevold) *vt* full; **–er** (-s) *m* fuller; **volle'rij** (-en) *v* 1 fulling; 2 fulling-mill; **'vollersaarde** *v* fuller's earth; **–kuip** (-en) *v* fuller's tub

'volleybal ['vòli.-] 1 (-len) *m* (b a l) volleyball; 2 *o* (s p e l) volleyball

'vollopen[1] *vi* fill[2]

vol'maakt I *aj* perfect; **II** *ad* perfectly, to perfection; **–heid** (-heden) *v* perfection

'volmacht (-en) *v* full powers, power of attorney; procuration, proxy; *iem. ~ verlenen* confer full powers upon sbd.; *iem. ~ verlenen om...* authorize, empower sbd. to... [do sth.]; *bij ~* by proxy

1 'volmaken[1] *vt* fill

2 vol'maken (volmaakte, h. volmaakt) *vt* perfect; **–king** *v* perfection

vol'mondig I *aj* frank, unqualified [yes &]; **II** *ad* frankly

volon'tair [-'tɛːr] (-s) *m* 1 ✠ volunteer; 2 improver, (practical) trainee; unsalaried clerk

'volop plenty of..., ...in plenty; *we hebben ~ genoten van ons uitstapje* we thoroughly enjoyed our trip

'volproppen[1] *vt* stuff, cram [with food, knowledge]; *volgepropt ook:* **F** chock-a-block [with]; **–schenken**[1] *vt* fill (to the brim); **–schrijven**[1] *vt* cover (with writing)

vol'slagen *aj* (& *ad*) complete(ly), total(ly), utter(ly)

'volslank rather plump, with a full figure

vol'staan (volstond, h. volstaan) *vi* suffice; *daar kunt u mee ~* that will do; *daar kan ik niet mee ~* it's not enough; *wij kunnen ~ met te zeggen dat...* suffice it to say that...

'volstoppen[1] *vt* zie *volproppen*

'volstorten[1] *vt* $ pay up (in full); **–ting** *v* $ payment in full

vol'strekt I *aj* absolute; **II** *ad* absolutely, wholly; *~ niet* not at all, by no means, nothing of the kind; **–heid** *v* absoluteness

volt (-s) *m* ✠ volt; **vol'tage** [-'ta.ʒǝ] *v* & *o* ✠ voltage

vol'tallig complete [set of...]; full [meeting]; plenary [assembly]; *zijn we ~?* all present?; *~ maken* make up the number, complete; **–heid** *v* completeness

1 'volte *v* 1 (v o l h e i d) ful(l)ness; 2 (g e d r a n g) crowd

2 'volte (-s) *v* (z w e n k i n g) volt

volte 'face [vòltǝ'fa.s] *v* volte-face; *~ maken* make (execute) a volte-face

1 'voltekenen[1] *vt* fill (cover) with drawings

2 vol'tekenen *vt de lening is voltekend* the loan is fully subscribed

volti'geren [-'ʒe:rǝ(n)] (voltigeerde, h. gevoltigeerd) *vi* vault; **volti'geur** (-s) *m* vaulter

'voltmeter (-s) *m* voltmeter

vol'tooid ~ *tegenwoordige tijd* present perfect; *~ toekomende tijd* future perfect; *~ verleden tijd* past perfect; zie ook: *deelwoord*; **vol'tooien (voltooide, h. voltooid) *vt* complete, finish; **–iing** (-en) *v* completion; *zijn ~ naderen* be nearing completion

'voltreffer (-s) *m* direct hit

vol'trekken (voltrok, h. voltrokken) *vt* execute [a sentence]; solemnize [a marriage]; **–king** (-en) *v* execution [of a sentence]; solemnization [of a marriage]

'voluit in full

vo'lume (-n en -s) *o* volume, size, bulk; **volumi'neus** voluminous, bulky

'volvet ~*te kaas* full fat cheese

vol'voeren (volvoerde, h. volvoerd) *vt* perform, fulfil, accomplish; **–ring** *v* performance, fulfilment, accomplishment

vol'waardig full, adequate [worker, employee]; highly nutritious [food]; (mentally, physically) fit; *fig* full(y)-fledged [partner]

vol'wassen full-grown, grown-up, adult; *half ~* half-grown; **–e** (-n) *m-v* adult, grown-up [man, woman]; *fig* mature; *~n* grown people, **F** grown-ups; *school voor ~n* adult school; **–heid** *v* adulthood, (v. m a n n e n o o k) manhood, (v. v r o u w e n o o k) womanhood

vol'wichtig of full weight

'volzin (-nen) *m gram* sentence, period

vo'meren (vomeerde, h. gevomeerd) *vi* vomit

vond (vonden) V.T. v. *vinden*

'vondel (-s) = *vonder*

'vondeling (-en) *m* foundling; *een kind te ~ leggen* expose a child; **–enhuis** (-huizen) *o* foundling-hospital

'vonden V.T. meerv. v. *vinden*

'vonder (-s) *m* plank-bridge, foot-bridge

vondst (-en) *v* find, discovery, invention; *een ~ doen* make a find

vonk (-en) *v* spark; **'vonkelen** (vonkelde, h. gevonkeld) *vi* 1 (v o n k e n) spark; 2 (f o n k e l e n) sparkle; **'vonken** (vonkte, h. gevonkt) *vi* spark, sparkle; **'vonkje** (-s) *o* sparklet, scintilla[2]; **'vonkvrij** non-sparking

---

[1] V.T. en V.D. van dit werkwoord volgens het model: **'volgooien**, V.T. gooide **'vol**, V.D. **'volgegooid**. Zie voor de vormen onder het grondwoord, in dit voorbeeld: *gooien*. Bij sterke en onregelmatige werkwoorden wordt u verwezen naar de lijst achterin.

'vonnis (-sen) *o* sentence, judg(e)ment; ~ *bij verstek* judg(e)ment by default; *een ~ uitspreken* pronounce (give) a verdict; *een ~ vellen* pass (pronounce) sentence; *toen was zijn ~ geveld* then his doom was sealed; **'vonnissen** (vonniste, h. gevonnist) *vt* sentence, condemn

vont (-en) *v* font

voogd (-en) *m,* **voog'des** (-sen) *v* guardian; **voog'dij** (-en) *v* 1 guardianship, tutelage; 2 trusteeship [of the United Nations]; *onder ~* [child] in tutelage (to *van*); **–kind** (-eren) *o* ward of court; ward in chancery; **–raad** (-raden) *v* 1 ± Guardians' Supervisory Board; 2 Trusteeship Council [of the United Nations]; **–schap** (-pen) *o* guardianship, tutelage

1 voor (voren) *v* furrow

2 voor I *prep* 1 (t e n b e h o e v e v a n) for [soms: to]; 2 (i n p l a a t s v a n) for; 3 (v o o r d e d u u r v a n) for; 4 (n i e t a c h t e r) before, in front of [the house]; at [the gate]; off [the coast]; 5 (t e g e n o v e r na) before, prior to; 6 (e e r d e r d a n) before; 7 (g e l e d e n) [weeks &] ago; 8 (t e r o n t k o m i n g, o n t h o u d i n g) [hide, keep, shelter] from; 9 *fig* for, in favour of [a measure &]; *ik ~ mij* I for one, I for my part; *dat is niets ~ hem* 1 it's not in his line; 2 it's not like him to...; *het doet mij genoegen ~ hem* for him I am glad; *hij is een goed vader ~ hem geweest* he has been a good father to him; *hij werkte ~ de vooruitgang* he worked in the cause of progress; *vijf minuten ~ vijf* five minutes to five; *kom ~ vijven* come before five o'clock; *gisteren ~ een week* yesterday week; *hij had een kamer ~ zich alleen* he had a room all to himself; *mijn cijfers ~ algebra* my marks in algebra; *~ en achter mij* in front of me and behind me; **II** *ad* in front; *~ in de tuin* in the front of the garden; *het is pas 1 uur, u bent (uw horloge is)* ~ your watch is fast; *er is iemand ~* there is somebody in the hall; *de auto staat ~* the car is at the door, is waiting; *er is veel ~* there is much to be said in favour of it; *ik ben er ~* I am for it (in favour of it); *wij waren hun ~* 1 we were ahead² of them; 2 we had got beforehand with them, we had got the start of them, we had forestalled them; *wij wonen ~* we live in the front of the house; *de een ~ de ander na* one after another; *~ en achter* in front and at the back; *~ en na* again and again; *het was „beste vriend" ~ en na* it was "dear friend" here, there, and everywhere; *van ~ tot achter* from front to rear; ⚓ from stem to stern; **III** *o het ~ en tegen* the pros and cons; **IV** *cj* before, ⊙ ere

'vooraan, voor'aan in front; *~ in het boek* at the beginning of the book; *~ in de strijd* in the forefront of the battle; *hij is ~ in de dertig* he is in the (his) early thirties; *~ onder de ... stond X* [*fig*] pre-eminent among the... was X; **–staand** standing in front; *fig* prominent, leading

'vooraanzicht *o* front view

voor'af beforehand, previously; **voor'afgaan** (ging voor'af, is voor'afgegaan) *vt & vi* go before, precede; *...laten ~ door...* precede... by...; **–d** foregoing, preceding [word]; prefatory [remarks]; previous [knowledge]; *het ~e* what precedes; **voor'afschaduwing** (-en) *v* adumbration, foreshadowing

voor'al especially, above all things; *ga er ~ heen* do go by all means

'vooraleer *cj* before

voorals'nog for the present, for the time being, as yet

'voorarm (-en) *m* forearm; **–arrest** *o* detention under remand; *in ~* under remand; **–as** (-sen) *v* front-axle; **–avond** (-en) *m* 1 first part of the evening; 2 eve; *aan de ~ van de slag* on the eve of the battle; *wij staan aan de ~ van grote gebeurtenissen* we are on the eve (on the threshold) of important events; **–baat** *bij ~* in advance, in anticipation; *bij ~ dank* thanking you in anticipation, thanking you in advance; **–balkon** (-s) *o* 1 front-balcony [of a house]; 2 driver's platform [of a tram-car]; **–band** (-en) *m* front-tyre

voor'barig I *aj* premature, rash, (over-)hasty; *je moet niet zo ~ zijn* you should not anticipate, don't rush to conclusions; *dat is nog wel wat ~* it is early days yet to...; **II** *ad* prematurely, rashly; **–heid** (-heden) *v* prematureness, rashness, (over-)hastiness

'voorbedacht premeditated; *met ~en rade* of malice prepense, of (with) malice aforethought, zie ook: *voorbedachtelijk*; **voorbe'dachtelijk** premeditatedly, with premeditation, on purpose

'voorbede (-n) *v* intercession

'voorbeding (-en) *o* condition, stipulation, proviso; *onder ~ dat...* on condition that...; **'voorbedingen** (bedong 'voor, h. 'voorbedongen) *vt* stipulate (beforehand)

'voorbeeld (-en) *o* 1 example, model; 2 (g e v a l) example, instance; 3 ✎ (i n s c h r i j f b o e k) copy-book heading; *~en aanhalen van...* cite instances of...; *een ~ geven* set an example; *kunt u een ~ geven?* can you give an instance?; *een goed ~ geven* set a good example; *het ~ geven* give the example, set the example; *een ~ nemen aan* take example by, follow the example of...; *een ~ stellen* make an example of sbd.; *iems. ~ volgen* follow sbd.'s example; take a leaf out of (from) sbd.'s book; follow suit; ● *b ij ~* for instance, for example; e.g.; *t o t ~ dienen* serve as a model; *z o n d e r ~* without

example, unexampled; **voor'beeldeloos**
unexampled, matchless; **voor'beeldig** exemplary; **–heid** *v* exemplariness

'voorbehoedmiddel (-en) *o* contraceptive; preservative

'voorbehoud *o* reserve, reservation; proviso; *geestelijk* ~ mental reservation; *o n d e r* ~ *dat...* with a (the) proviso that; *het onder* ~ *aannemen* accept it [the statement] with reservations, with al proper reserve; *onder alle* ~ with all reserve; *onder gewoon* ~ $ under usual reserve; *onder het nodige* ~ with due reserve; *onder zeker* ~ with reservations, with some reserve; *z o n d e r* ~ [state] without reserve; [agree] unreservedly; **'voorbehouden** (behield 'voor, h. 'voorbehouden) *vt* reserve; *zich het recht* ~ reserve to oneself the right [of...]

'voorbereiden[1] **I** *vt* prepare; *iem.* ~ *op* prepare sbd. for [sth., some news, the worst]; **II** *vr zich* ~ prepare (oneself); *zich* ~ *voor een examen* read for an examination; **–d** preparatory [school &]; **'voorbereiding** (-en) *v* preparation; **'voorbereidsel** (-en en -s) *o* preparation

'voorbericht (-en) *o* preface; foreword [esp. by another than the author]

'voorbeschikken (beschikte 'voor, h. 'voorbeschikt) *vt* preordain [of God]; predestinate, predestine [to greatness &]; **–king** (-en) *v* predestination

'voorbespreking (-en) *v* 1 preliminary talk; 2 (v. p l a a t s e n) advance booking

'voorbestaan *o* pre-existence

'voorbestemmen (bestemde 'voor, h. 'voorbestemd) *vt* predestine, predestinate; foreordain [to any fate]; **–ming** *v* predestination

'voorbidden[1] *vi* lead in prayer, say the prayers; **–er** (-s) *m* intercessor; **'voorbidding** (-en) *v* intercession

voor'bij I *prep* beyond, past; **II** *ad* past; *het huis* ~ past the house; *het is* ~ it is over now, it is at an end; **III** *aj* past; **–drijven**[2] **I** *vi* float past (by); **II** *vt* drive past; **–gaan**[2] **I** *vi* 1 (v a n p e r s o n e n) go by, pass by, pass; 2 (v. t ij d &) go by, pass; *het zal wel* ~ it is sure to pass off; *hemel en aarde zullen* ~ heaven and earth shall pass away; **II** *vt* pass (by) [a house, person &]; *iem.* ~ pass sbd.; *fig* pass sbd. over; *een kans laten* ~ miss a chance, miss the bus; *met stilzwijgen* ~ pass over in silence; **III** *o in het* ~ in passing[2]; *fig* by the way; **–gaand** passing, transitory, transient; *...is slechts van ~e aard* ...is but temporary; **–gang** *m met* ~ *van...* over the

head(s) of..., ...being passed over; **–ganger** (-s) *m* passer-by; **–komen**[2] **I** *vi* pass (by); **II** *vt* pass (by); **–laten**[2] *vt* let [sbd.] pass; **–lopen**[2] *vt* & *vi* pass; **–marcheren**[2] [-ʃe:rə(n)] *vi* & *vt* march past; **–praten**[2] *vt zijn mond* ~ let one's tongue run away with one; **–rijden**[2] *vi* & *vt* ride (drive) past, pass; **–schieten**[2] **I** *vi* dash past; **II** *vt* shoot past, *fig* overshoot [the mark]; **–snellen**[2] *vi* & *vt* pass by in a hurry; **–snorren**[2] *vi* & *vt* whir past, whizz by; **–streven** (streefde voor'bij, is voor'bijgestreefd) *vt* outstrip; zie ook: *doel;* **–trekken**[2] *vi* march past [of an army]; pass over [of a thunderstorm]; **–varen**[2] **I** *vt* outsail; **II** *vi* pass; **–vliegen**[2] **I** *vi* fly past; **II** *vt* fly past, rush past; **–wandelen**[2] *vi* & *vt* walk past, pass; **–zien**[2] *vt* overlook; *wij moeten niet* ~ *dat...* not overlook the fact that...

'voorbinden[1] *vt* tie on, put on; **–blijven**[1] *vi* keep ahead of, lead, remain in front

'voorbode (-n en -s) *m* foretoken, forerunner[2], precursor[2], ☉ harbinger

'voorbrengen[1] *vt* 1 bring on the carpet, put forward [a proposal]; 2 ⚖ bring up [the accused]; produce [witnesses]

voor'christelijk [-grɪs- of -krɪs-] pre-Christian era

'voorcijferen[1] *vt* = *voorrekenen*

voord (-en) *v* ford

'voordacht *v met* ~ with premeditation, deliberately

'voordansen[1] **I** *vi* lead the dance; **II** *vt* show how to dance

'voordat before; ☉ ere

'voorde (-n) = *voord*

'voordeel (-delen) *o* 1 advantage, benefit; 2 (w i n s t) profit, gain; *zijn* ~ *doen met* take advantage of, profit by, turn to (good) account; *dat heeft zijn* ~ there is an advantage in that; ~ *bij iets hebben* derive advantage from sth., profit by sth.; *wat voor* ~ *zal hij daarbij hebben?* what will it profit him?; ~ *opleveren* yield profit; ~ *trekken van* turn to (good) account, profit by, take advantage of; *zijn* ~ *zoeken* seek one's own advantage; ● *i n het* ~ *zijn van* be an advantage to; *is het in uw* ~? is it in your favour?, to your advantage?; *in zijn* ~ *veranderd* changed for the better; *m e t* ~ with advantage; $ at a profit; *t e n (tot)* ~ *strekken* be to sbd.'s advantage, benefit, be beneficial to [trade]; be all to the good; *ten voordele van* for the benefit of; *z o n d e r* ~ without profit;

[1,2] V.T. en V.D. van dat werkwoord volgens het model: 1 **'voor**cijferen, V.T. cijferde **'voor**, V.D. **'voor**gecijferd; 2 **voor'bij**praten, V.T. praatte **voor'bij**, V.D. **voor'bij**gepraat. Zie voor de vormen onder het grondwoord, in deze voorbeelden: *cijferen* en *praten*. Bij sterke en onregelmatige werkwoorden wordt u verwezen naar de lijst achterin.

–regel *m sp* advantage rule; **–tje** (-s) *o* windfall

voordegekhoude'rij *v* fooling

'**voordek** (-ken) *o* ⚓ foredeck

voor'delig I *aj* 1 profitable, advantageous; 2 (i n h e t g e b r u i k) economical, cheap; 3 (g o e d k o o p) low-budget [prices]; *dat is ~er in het gebruik* ook: that goes farther; **II** *ad* profitably, advantageously, to advantage; *zij kwamen niet op hun ~st uit* ook: they did not show at their best; **–heid** *v* profitableness, advantageousness

'**voordeur** (-en) *v* front door, street-door

voor'dezen, **–'dien** before this, previously, before

'**voordienen** *vt* serve

'**voordoen**[1] **I** *vt* 1 show [sbd.] (how to...); 2 put on [an apron]; **II** *vr zich ~* present itself, offer [of an opportunity]; arise, crop up, occur [of a difficulty]; *zich ~ als...* set up for a..., pass oneself off as a...; *hij weet zich goed voor te doen* he has a good address; *ik wil me niet beter ~ dan ik ben* I don't want to make myself out better than I am

'**voordracht** (-en) *v* 1 (w ij z e v a n v o o r-d r a g e n) utterance, diction, delivery; elocution; ♪ execution, rendering, playing; 2 (h e t v o o r g e d r a g e n e) recitation, recital [of a poem]; discourse, lecture, address; 3 (k a n d i-d a t e n l ij s t) short list; nomination; 4 (d o-m i n e e s a a n b e v e l i n g) presentation; *een ~ houden* give a lecture, read a paper; *een ~ indienen* submit (present) a list of names; *een ~ opmaken* make out a short list; *nummer één op de ~* first in the short list; *op ~ van* on the recommendation of; **–skunstenaar** (-s) *m* elocutionist, reciter; '**voordragen**[1] *vt* 1 (i e m.) propose, nominate [a candidate]; present [a clergyman]; 2 (e e n g e d i c h t &) recite; *ik zal voor die betrekking voorgedragen worden* I shall be recommended for that post; **–er** (-s) *m* reciter

'**voorechtelijk** pre-marital

voor'eerst (v o o r l o p i g) for the present, for the time being; *~ niet* not just yet

'**vooreind(e)** (-einden) *o* fore-part, fore-end

voor- en 'nadelen *mv* advantages and disadvantages

'**voorgaan**[1] *vi* 1 go before, precede; *fig* set an example; 2 (v o o r b i d d e n) lead in prayer, say the prayers; 3 (v. u u r w e r k) be fast, gain [5 minutes a day]; 4 (d e v o o r r a n g h e b b e n) take precedence; *gaat u voor!* after you!; *dames gaan voor!* ladies first!; *iem. laten ~*

let sbd. go first; *zal ik maar ~?* shall I lead the way?; *dat gaat voor* that comes first; *de generaal gaat voor* the general takes precedence; *de majoor liet de generaal ~* the major yielded the *pas* to the general; **–d** preceding [century &]; antecedent [term]; *het ~e* the foregoing; *in het ~e* in the preceding pages

'**voorgalerij** (-en) *v* front veranda(h)

'**voorganger** (-s) *m* 1 (i n a m b t) predecessor; 2 (p r e d i k a n t) pastor; **–gangster** (-s) *v* predecessor

'**voorgebergte** (-n en -s) *o* promontory, headland; **–geborchte** *o het ~ der hel* limbo; **–gebouw** (-en) *o* front part of a building

'**voorgekrompen** pre-shrunk

'**voorgeleiden**[1] *vt* bring up [the accused]; **–ding** *v* (enforced) appearance in court

'**voorgemeld** = *voormeld*; **–genoemd** = *voornoemd*; **–genomen** intended, proposed, contemplated

'**voorgerecht** (-en) *o* entrée

'**voorgeschiedenis** *v* 1 (v. z a a k, z i e k t e &) (previous) history, case history; 2 (v a n p e r s o o n) antecedents; 3 (p r e h i s t o r i e) prehistory

'**voorgeschreven** prescribed, regulation...

'**voorgeslacht** (-en) *o ons ~* our ancestors

'**voorgespannen** *~ beton* = *spanbeton*

'**voorgevallene** *o het ~* what has happened

'**voorgevel** (-s) *m* front, forefront, façade

'**voorgeven**[1] **I** *vt* 1 pretend, profess [to be a lawyer &]; 2 *sp* give odds; **II** *o volgens zijn ~* according to what he pretends (to what he says)

'**voorgevoel** (-ens) *o* presentiment; *mijn angstig ~* ook: my misgiving(s)

'**voorgift** (-en) *v* odds (given); handicap

voor'goed for good (and all), forever, permanently

'**voorgoochelen**[1] *vt iem. iets ~* delude sbd. with sth.

'**voorgrond** (-en) *m* foreground; (v. t o n e e l) downstage; *zich op de ~ plaatsen* put oneself forward; *op de ~ staan* be in the foreground; *fig* be to the fore; be the centre [of the discussion]; be the main theme [of the conference]; *dat staat op de ~* that is a conditio sine qua non; *dat moeten wij op de ~ stellen* that's what we should emphasize; *op de ~ treden* come to the front, come (be) to the fore

'**voorhamer** (-s) *m* sledge-hammer

'**voorhand** (-en) *v* 1 front part of the hand; 2

---

[1] V.T. en V.D. van dit werkwoord volgens het model: '**voor**cijferen, V.T. cijferde '**voor**, V.D. '**voor**gecijferd. Zie voor de vormen onder het grondwoord, in dit voorbeeld: *cijferen*. Bij sterke en onregelmatige wérkwoorden wordt u verwezen naar de lijst achterin.

forehand [of a horse]; *aan de ~ zitten* have the lead, play first

voor'handen 1 on hand, in stock, in store, to be had, available; 2 existing, extant; *de ~ gegevens* the data on hand; *niet ~* sold out, exhausted

'voorhang (-en) *m* **B** veil [of the temple]; **'voorhangen**[1] **I** *vt* 1 (i e t s) hang in front; 2 (i e m. a l s l i d) put up, propose for membership; **II** *va* be put up, be proposed for membership; **'voorhangsel** (-s en -en) *o* curtain; **B** veil [of the temple]

'voorhaven (-s) *v* outport

'voorhebben[1] *vt* have before one; *fig* intend, be up to, drive at, purpose; *een schort ~* wear an apron; *weet je wie je voorhebt?* do you know whom you are talking to?; ● *het goed m e t iem. ~* mean well by sbd.; *wat zouden ze met hem ~?* what do they intend to do with him?; *wat ~ o p* have an advantage (the pull) over [sbd.]

voor'heen formerly, before, in the past; *Smith & Co. ~ Jones* $ Smith & Co., late Jones; *~ en thans* past and present

'voorheffing *v* advance levy

'voorhistorisch prehistoric

'voorhoede (-n en -s) *v* ⚔ advance(d) guard[2], van[2], vanguard[2]; *fig* forefront; *de ~ sp* the forwards; **–speler** (-s) *m sp* forward

'voorhof (-hoven) *o* & *m* forecourt

'voorhoofd (-en) *o* forehead, brow, ⊙ front; **'voorhoofdsbeen** (-deren) *o* frontal bone; **'voorhoofdsholte** (-n en -s) *v* sinus; **–ontsteking** *v* sinusitis

'voorhouden[1] *vt* 1 (i e t s) keep on [an apron]; 2 (i e m. i e t s) hold [a book &] before; hold up [a mirror] to...; *fig* point sth. out [to sbd.], remonstrate with [sbd.] on [sth.], expostulate with [sbd.] about [sth.]

'voorhuid (-en) *v* foreskin, prepuce

'voorhuis (-huizen) *o* hall, front part of the house

'voorin, voor'in in (the) front; at the beginning [of the book]

'Voor-Indië *o* India (proper)

voor'ingenomen prepossessed, prejudiced, bias(s)ed; **–heid** *v* prepossession, prejudice, bias

'voorjaar (-jaren) *o* spring; **'voorjaarsbeurs** *v* spring fair; **–bloem** (-en) *v* spring-flower; **–moeheid** *v* spring fatigue, *Am* spring fever; **–nachtevening** (-en) *v* vernal equinox;

–opruiming (-en) *v* $ spring sale(s); **–schoonmaak** *m* spring-cleaning

'voorkamer (-s) *v* front room; **–kant** (-en) *m* = *voorzij(de)*

'voorkauwen[1] *vt 40 jaar heb ik het hun voorge-kauwd* for 40 years I have repeated it over and over again to them (I have spoonfed it to them)

'voorkennis *v* (v. d. t o e k o m s t) prescience, (m e d e w e t e n) (fore)knowledge; *m e t ~ van...* with the (full) knowledge of; *z o n d e r ~ van* without the knowledge of, unknown to

'voorkeur *v* preference; *de ~ genieten* 1 be preferred [of applicants, goods &]; 2 $ have the preference [for a certain amount]; *de ~ geven aan* give preference to, prefer; *de ~ geven aan... boven* prefer... to; *de ~ hebben* 1 enjoy (have) the preference, be preferred; 2 $ have the (first) refusal [of a house &]; *bij ~* for preference, preferably; **–sbehandeling** *v* preferential treatment; **'voorkeurspelling** *v* preferred spelling [of Dutch]; **–stem** (-men) *v pol* preferential vote; **–tarief** (-rieven) *o* preferential tariff

'voorkind (-eren) *o* 1 child by a previous marriage; 2 child born before marriage

1 'voorkomen[1] **I** *vi* 1 (b ij h a r d l o p e n &) get ahead[2]; 2 (v. a u t o) come round; 3 ⚖ (v. z a a k) come on, come up for trial; (v a n p e r s o o n) appear; 4 (g e v o n d e n w o r d e n, b e s t a a n) occur, be found, be met with [of instances &]; appear, figure [on a list]; 5 (g e b e u r e n) happen, occur; 6 (l ij k e n) appear to, seem to; *het komt vaak voor* it frequently occurs, ook: it is of frequent occurrence; *het komt mij voor dat...* it appears (seems) to me that...; *laat de auto ~* order the car round; *het laten ~ alsof...* make it appear as if...; **II** *vt* get ahead of [sbd.], outstrip, outdistance [sbd.]; **III** *o* appearance, mien, aspect, look(s), air; *het ~ van dit dier* 1 the appearance of this animal; 2 the occurrence of this animal

2 voor'komen (voorkwam, h. voorkomen) *vt* 1 anticipate, forestall [sbd.'s wishes]; 2 (v e r h i n d e r e n) prevent, preclude; *~ is beter dan genezen* prevention is better than cure

1 'voorkomend *aj* occurring; zie ook: *gelegenheid*

2 voor'komend obliging, polite, courteous; **–heid** *v* obligingness, courtesy

voor'koming *v* prevention [of crime]; anticipation [of wishes]; *ter ~ van...* in order to

[1] V.T. en V.D. van dit werkwoord volgens het model: **'voor**cijferen, V.T. cijferde **'voor**, V.D. **'voor**gecijferd. Zie voor de vormen onder het grondwoord, in dit voorbeeld: *cijferen*. Bij sterke en onregelmatige werkwoorden wordt u verwezen naar de lijst achterin.

prevent..., for the prevention of...

'voorkoop (-kopen) *m* pre-emption

'voorkrijgen[1] *vt sp* receive [fifty points]

'voorlaatst last [page &] but one; penultimate [syllable]

'voorlader (-s) *m* muzzle-loader

'voorland (-en) *o* foreland

'voorlaten[1] *vt iem.* ~ let sbd. go first

'voorleggen[1] *vt* put before, place before, lay before, submit [the papers to him]; propound [a question to sbd.]; *iemand de feiten* ~ lay the facts before one; *hem die vraag* ~ put the question to him

'voorleiden[1] *vt* bring up [the accused]

'voorletter (-s) *v* initial

'voorlezen[1] *vt* read to [a person]; read out [a message]; **–er** (-s) *m* reader [also in church]; **'voorlezing** (-en) *v* reading; lecture

'voorlicht (-en) *o* headlight

'voorlichten[1] *vt* enlighten [public opinion], advise [the government on...]; inform [a person of..., on...]; give [sbd.] information [about sth.]; *iem. seksueel* ~ explain the facts of life to sbd.; **'voorlichting** *v* enlightenment, [vocational, marriage] guidance, [marital] advice; [sex] education (instruction); information [on...]; **–sdienst** (-en) *m* information service, ± Public Relations (Department)

'voorliefde *v* liking, predilection, partiality; *(een zekere)* ~ *hebben voor* be partial to...

'voorliegen[1] *vt iem. (wat)* ~ lie to sbd.

'voorlijk precocious, forward [plant, child]; **–heid** *v* precocity, forwardness

'voorlopen[1] *vi* 1 (v. p e r s o o n) lead the way; 2 (v. u u r w e r k) be fast, gain [5 minutes a day]; **–er** (-s) *m* forerunner, precursor, ⊙ harbinger

voor'lopig I *aj* provisional; ~*e cijfers (conclusie* &) ook: tentative figures (conclusion &); ~ *dividend* $ interim dividend; ~*e hechtenis* = *voorarrest*; **II** *ad* provisionally; for the present, for the time being

voor'malig former, late, sometime, one-time, ex-[enemy]

'voorman (-nen en -lieden) *m* 1 (o n d e r b a a s) foreman; 2 ✗ front-rank man; 3 $ preceding holder; *de* ~*nen der beweging* the leaders, the leading men; **–mast** (-en) *m* foremast

voor'meld above-mentioned, afore-said; ~*e...* ook: the above...

voor'menselijk pre-human

'voormiddag (-dagen) *m* morning, forenoon; *om 10 uur des* ~*s* at 10 o'clock in the morning,

at 10 a.m.

voorn (-s) *m* roach

1 **'voornaam** (-namen) *m* forename, first name, Christian name

2 **voor'naam** *aj* 1 distinguished [appearance]; prominent [place]; 2 (b e l a n g r ij k) important; **–heid** *v* distinction; **–ste** chief, principal, leading; *het* ~ the principal (main) thing

'voornaamwoord (-en) *o* pronoun; **voor-naam'woordelijk** pronominal

'voornacht (-en) *m* first part of the night

voor'namelijk chiefly, principally, mainly, primarily

'voornemen[1] **I** *vr zich* ~ resolve, make up one's mind [to do sth.]; zie ook: *voorgenomen;* **II** (-s) *o* 1 (b e d o e l i n g) intention; 2 (b e s l u i t) resolution; *het* ~ *hebben om* intend to; *het* ~ *opvatten om...* make up one's mind to..., resolve to...; ~*s zijn (om)* intend (to), propose (to); *het ligt in het* ~ *van de directie om...* it is the intention of the management to...

voor'noemd = *voormeld*

voor'onder (-s) *o* ⚓ forecastle

vooronder'stellen (vooronderstelde, h. voor-ondersteld) *vt* presuppose; **–ling** (-en) *v* presupposition, hypothesis

'vooronderzoek *o* preliminary examination; **–ontsteking** *v* ✗ advanced ignition; **–ontwerp** (-en) *o* preliminary draft; **voor'oordeel** (-delen) *o* prejudice, bias (against *tegen*)

voor'oorlogs pre-war

voor'op in front; **–gezet** preconceived [opinion]

'vooropleiding *v* (a l g e m e e n) preliminary training, pre-school education; (s p e c i a a l) preparatory training

voor'oplopen[2] *vi* go first, walk in front, lead the way; *fig* lead

voor'opstellen[2] *vt* premise; *vooropgesteld dat het verhaal waar is* assuming the truth of the story; *ik stel voorop dat..., het zij vooropgesteld dat...* I wish to point out that...; **–zetten**[2] *vt* premise; zie ook: *vooropgezet*

voor'ouderlijk ancestral; **'voorouders** *mv* ancestors, forefathers; **'voorouderverering** *v* ancestor worship, veneration of ancestors

voor'over forward, bending forward, prone, face down; **–buigen**[3] **I** *vt* bend (lean) forward, stoop; **II** *vt* bend [sth.]; **–hangen**[3] *vi* hang forward; **–hellen**[3] *vi* incline forward

'vooroverleg *o* preliminary consultation

[1,2,3] V.T. en V.D. van dit werkwoord volgens het model: 1 **'voor**cijferen, V.T. cijferde **'voor**, V.D. **'voor**gecijferd; 2 **voor'op**stellen, V.T. stelde **voor'op**, V.D. **voor'op**gesteld; 3 **voor'over**leunen, V.T. leunde **voor'over**, V.D. **voor'over**geleund. Zie voor de vormen onder het grondwoord, in deze voorbeelden: *cijferen, leunen* en *stellen*. Bij sterke en onregelmatige werkwoorden wordt u verwezen naar de lijst achterin.

voor'overleunen[3] *vi* lean forward; **–liggen**[3] *vi* lie prostrate; **–liggend** prostrate, prone

'**vooroverlijden** *o* predecease

voor'overlopen[3] *vi* stoop, walk with a stoop; **–vallen**[3] *vi* fall forward (headlong), fall head foremost; **–zitten**[3] *vi* bend forward

'**voorpaard** (-en) *o* leader; **–pagina** ('s) *v* front page; **–pand** (-en) *o* front; **–plecht** (-en) *v* forecastle; **–plein** (-en) *o* forecourt, castle-yard; **–poort** (-en) *v* front gate, outer gate; **–poot** (-poten) *m* foreleg, front paw; **–portaal** (-talen) *o* porch, hall

'**voorpost** (-en) *m* ✖ outpost; '**voorpostengevecht** (-en) *o* ✖ outpost skirmish; **–linie** (-s) *v* ✖ line of outposts

'**voorpraten**[1] *vt* prompt; *hij zegt maar na wat ze hem ~* he parrots everything

'**voorpreken**[1] *vt* preach to

'**voorproefje** (-s) *o* foretaste, taste; '**voorproeven**[1] *vt* taste (beforehand)

'**voorprogram(ma)** (-grams, -gramma's) *o* supporting programme

'**voorraad** (-raden) *m* store, stock, supply [of books, wares &]; *zolang de ~ strekt* subject to stock being available (being unsold); *nieuwe ~ opdoen* (*in ~ opslaan*) lay in a fresh supply; *in ~* on hand, in stock, in store; *uit ~ leveren* supply from stock; **–kamer** (-s) *v* store-room; **–kelder** (-s) *m* store-cellar; **–schuur** (-schuren) *v* storehouse, granary; **–vorming** *v* stocking of supplies; (*strategische*) *~* stockpiling; **voor'radig** in stock, on hand, available; *niet meer ~* out of stock, sold out

'**voorrang** *m* precedence, priority; (v. a u t o &) right of way; *de ~ hebben* (*boven*) take precedence (of), have priority (over); *om de ~ strijden* contend for the mastery; (*dè*) *~ verlenen* give (right of) way to [another car]; give precedence [to pedestrians on a zebra crossing]; yield precedence to [sbd.]; give priority to [a good cause]; '**voorrangskruising** (-en) *v* priority crossroad; **–weg** (-wegen) *m* major road

'**voorrecht** (-en) *o* privilege, prerogative

'**voorrede** (-s) *v* preface; foreword [esp. by another than the author]

'**voorrekenen**[1] *vt iem. iets ~* show sbd. how sth. works out

'**voorrijden**[1] *vi* ride in front [of horseman], drive in front [of motor-car]; come round [of car]; **–er** (-s) *m* outrider; postilion

'**voorronde** (-n en -s) *v* qualifying round

'**voorruit** (-en) *v* 🚗 windscreen

'**voorschieten**[1] *vt* advance [money]; **–er** (-s) *m* money-lender

'**voorschijn** *te ~ brengen* produce, bring out, bring to light; *te ~ halen* produce [a key, revolver &]; take out [one's purse]; *te ~ komen* appear, make one's appearance, come out; *te ~ roepen* call up

'**voorschip** *o* fore-part of the ship; **–schoot** (-schoten) *m* & *o* apron

'**voorschot** (-ten) *o* advanced money, advance, loan; *~ten* out-of-pocket expenses; (*geen*) *~ geven op...* advance (no) money upon...; *~ nemen* obtain an advance; **–bank** (-en) *v* loan-bank

'**voorschotelen** (schotelde 'voor, h. 'voorgeschoteld) *vt* dish up, serve up

'**voorschrift** (-en) *o* prescription [of a doctor]; precept [respecting conduct]; instruction, direction [what or how to do]; [traffic, safety] regulation; *op ~ van de dokter* by medical orders; '**voorschrijven**[1] *vt eig* write for, show how to write; *fig* prescribe [a medicine, a line of conduct]; dictate [conditions]; *de dokter zal het u ~* the doctor will prescribe it for you; *hij zal u wat* (*een recept*) *~* he will write you out a prescription; *de dokter schreef me volkomen rust voor* the doctor ordered me a complete rest

'**voorschuiven**[1] *vt* push, shoot [a bolt]

voors'hands for the time being, for the present

'**voorslaan**[1] *vt* propose, suggest

'**voorslag** (-slagen) *m* first stroke; warning [of clock]; ♪ appoggiatura

'**voorsmaak** *m* foretaste, taste

'**voorsnijden**[1] *vt* carve; '**voorsnijmes** (-sen) *o* carving-knife, carver; **–vork** (-en) *v* carving-fork

'**voorsorteren**[1] *vi* (i n h e t v e r k e e r) move into the correct (traffic) lane; *~!* get in lane

'**voorspan** (-nen) *o* leader(s)

'**voorspannen**[1] **I** *vt* put [the horses] to; **II** *vr zich ergens ~* take sth. in hand

'**voorspel** (-spelen) *o* 1 ♪ prelude; overture; 2 prologue, introductory part [of a play]; *dat was het ~ van* [*fig*] it was the prelude to...

voor'spelbaar predictable

'**voorspelden**[1] *vt* pin on

'**voorspelen**[1] *vt* 1 show how to play, play [it to you]; audition; 2 play first, have the lead [at cards]

1 '**voorspellen**[1] *vt* spell [a word] to

2 **voor'spellen** (voorspelde, h. voorspeld) *vt* predict, foretell, prophesy, presage, prognosti-

[1,3] V.T. en V.D. van dit werkwoord volgens het model: 1 '**voor**cijferen, V.T. cijferde '**voor**, V.D. '**voor**gecijferd; 3 **voor'over**leunen, V.T. leunde **voor'over**, V.D. **voor'over**geleund. Zie voor de vormen onder het grondwoord, in deze voorbeelden: *cijferen* en *leunen*. Bij sterke en onregelmatige werkwoorden wordt u verwezen naar de lijst achterin.

cate; forebode, portend, bode [evil], spell [rain]; *dat heb ik je wel voorspeld* I told you so!; *het voorspelt niet veel goeds* it bodes us no good; *het voorspelt niet veel goeds voor de toekomst* it bodes ill for the future; **–er** (-s) *m* predictor, prophet; **voor'spelling** (-en) *v* prediction, prophecy, prognostication, [weather] forecast

'**voorspiegelen**[1] *vt iem. iets ~* hold out hope, promises & to sbd., hold out to sbd. the prospect that...; *zich iets ~* delude oneself with the belief that...; *hij had zich van alles daarvan voorgespiegeld* he had deluded himself with all manner of vain hopes about it; **–ling** (-en) *v* false hope, delusion

'**voorspijs** (-spijzen) *v* hors d'œuvres, entrée

'**voorspoed** *m* prosperity; *~ hebben* be prosperous; *~ en tegenspoed* ups and downs; *in ~ en tegenspoed* in storm or shine; for better for worse; **voor'spoedig I** *aj* prosperous [in affairs], successful; **II** *ad* prosperously, successfully

'**voorspraak** *v* 1 intercession, mediation; 2 (-spraken) (p e r s o o n) intercessor, advocate; '**voorspreken**[1] *vt* speak in favour of; **–er** (-s) *m* intercessor, advocate

'**voorsprong** (-en) *m* start, lead; *hem een ~ geven sp* give him a start; *een ~ hebben van 5 km* have a lead of 5 km; *een ~ hebben op* have a lead over; *een ~ krijgen op* gain a lead over; *met een 2-0 ~* leading 2-0

'**voorstaan**[1] **I** *vt* advocate [pacifism &]; champion [a cause]; *hij laat zich daarop (heel wat) ~* he prides himself on it; **II** *vi* be present to one's mind; stand in front; *sp met 2-0 ~* lead with 2-0; *het staat mij voor* I think I remember; *het staat mij nog duidelijk voor* it still stands out clearly before me; *er staat mij nog zo iets van voor* I have a hazy recollection of it

'**voorstad** (-steden) *v* suburb

'**voorstander** (-s) *m* advocate, champion, supporter

'**voorste** foremost, first; *~ rij* ook: front row

'**voorstel** (-len) *o* 1 proposal; (w e t s v o o r-s t e l) bill; (m o t i e) motion; 2 (v. w a g e n) fore-carriage; *een ~ aannemen* accept (agree to) a proposal; *een ~ doen* make a proposal [to sbd.]; *een ~ indienen* move (put, hand in) a motion [in an assembly]; *op ~ van...* 1 on the proposal of..., on a (the) motion of...; 2 on (at) the suggestion of...; '**voorstellen**[1] **I** *vt* 1 represent; 2 (o p t o n e e l) represent [a forest, a king], (im)personate [Hamlet &]; 3 (e e n

v o o r s t e l d o e n) propose, move, suggest [a scheme]; 4 (t e r k e n n i s m a k i n g) present, introduce; *mag ik u mijnheer X ~?* allow me to introduce to you Mr X; *ik heb ze aan elkaar voorgesteld* I introduced them; *hij werd aan de koning voorgesteld* he was presented to the King; *een amendement ~* move an amendment; *ik stel voor dat wij heengaan* I move we go, **F** I vote we go; *de feiten verkeerd ~* misrepresent the facts; **II** *vr zich ~* introduce oneself; *zich iets ~* 1 (z i c h v e r b e e l d e n) figure (picture) to oneself, imagine, fancy, conceive (of); 2 (z i c h v o o r-n e m e n) intend, propose, purpose; *stel je voor!* (just) fancy!; **–er** (-s) *m* 1 proposer; 2 (i n v e r g a d e r i n g) mover; '**voorstelling** (-en) *v* 1 idea, notion, image; 2 representation; 3 performance [of a play]; 4 introduction [of people], presentation [at court]; *een verkeerde ~ van de feiten* a mis-representation of the facts; *zich een verkeerde ~ maken van...* form a mistaken notion of...; *u kunt u er geen ~ van maken hoe...* you can't imagine how...; **–svermogen** *o* imaginative faculty, imagination

'**voorstemmen**[1] *vi* vote for it; **–ers** *mv* ayes

'**voorsteven** (-s) *m* stem; **–studie** (-s en diën) *v* preliminary study; (s c h e t s t e k e n i n g) preliminary sketch; **–stuk** (-ken) *o* 1 front-piece; front [of a shoe]; 2 (t o n e e l) curtain-raiser

voort 1 (v e r d e r) forward, onwards, on, along; 2 (w e g) away; 3 (t e r s t o n d) at once, directly

'**voortaan** henceforward, henceforth, in future, from this time on

'**voortand** (-en) *m* front tooth, incisor

'**voortbestaan I** (bestond '**voort**, h. '**voortbe-staan**) *vi* continue to exist, survive; **II** *o* survival, continued existence; **–bewegen** (bewoog '**voort**, h. '**voortbewogen**) **I** *vt* move (forward), propel; **II** *vr zich ~* move, move on; **–beweging** *v* propulsion; ('t z i c h v e r p l a a t s e n) locomotion; **–bomen**[2] *vt* punt, pole [a boat]; **–borduren**[2] *vi ~ op* elaborate on, develop [a plan]; return to, harp on [a remark]; **–bouwen**[2] *vi* go on building; *~ op* build (up)on[2]

'**voortbrengen**[2] *vt* produce, bring forth, generate, breed; **–er** (-s) *m* producer, generator; '**voortbrenging** *v* production, generation; '**voortbrengsel** (-s en -en) *o* product, production; *~(en)* (v. d. n a t u u r) ook: produce

'**voortdrijven**[2] **I** *vt* drive on, drive forward,

spur on, urge on; **II** *vi* float along

'**voortduren**[2] *vi* continue, last, go on; **voort'durend I** *aj* (h e r h a a l d e l ij k) continual; (o n a f g e b r o k e n) continuous, constant, lasting; **II** *ad* continually; continuously; '**voortduring** *v* continuance, continuation, persistence, persistency; *bij* ~ continuously, persistently

'**voortduwen**[2] *vt* push on [forward]

'**voorteken** (-s en -en) *o* sign, indication, omen, portent, presage; *de ~en van een ziekte* the precursory symptoms

'**voortellen**[1] *vt* count down

'**voortentamen** (-s en -mina) *o* prelim(inary examination); **–terrein** (-en) *o* front court, front yard

'**voortgaan**[2] *vi* go on, continue, proceed; '**voortgang** (-en) *m* progress; ~ *hebben* proceed; *het had geen* ~ it didn't come off

'**voortgezet** prolonged [investigations]; secondary [education]

'**voortglijden**[2] *vi* glide on; **–helpen**[2] *vt* help on, give a hand

'**voortijd** (-en) *m* prehistoric times

'**voortijdig** premature

'**voortijds** in former times, formerly

'**voortijlen**[2] *vi* hurry (hasten) on; **–jagen**[2] *vt* & *vi* hurry on; **–kankeren**[2] *vi* ulcerate[2], putrefy[2], rankle[2]; **–komen**[2] *vi* get on, get along; ~ *uit* proceed from, originate from, arise from, spring from, result from, emanate from; **–kruipen**[2] *vi* creep on (along); **–kunnen**[2] *vi* be able to go on[2] (get on); **–leven**[2] *vi* live on; **–maken**[2] *vi* make haste; *maak wat voort!* hurry up!, get a move on!; ~ *met het werk* press on with the work, speed up the work; **–moeten**[2] *vi* have to go on

'**voortoneel** *o* proscenium

'**voortoveren**[1] *vt* call up, conjure up

'**voortplanten**[2] **I** *vt* carry on [the race]; propagate, spread [the gospel, faith]; transmit [sound]; **II** *vr zich* ~ breed, propagate; ℀ & ♒ propagate itself; travel [of sound & light]; '**voortplanting** *v* propagation [of the race, a plant, vibrations &; *fig* of the faith]; [human] reproduction, procreation; transmission [of sound]; **–sorganen** *mv* reproductive organs

'**voortreden**[1] *vi* come forward; *fig* come to the fore

voor'**treffelijk I** *aj* excellent, admirable; **II** *ad* excellently, admirably; **–heid** *v* excellence

'**voortrein** (-en) *m* relief train

'**voortrekken**[1] *vt iem.* ~ treat sbd. with marked preference, favour sbd....

'**voortrekker** (-s) 1 *ZA* voortrekker; 2 *fig* pioneer; 3 rover [boy scout]

'**voortrennen**[2] *vi* gallop (run) on; **–rijden**[2] *vi* ride (drive) on; **–roeien**[2] *vi* row on; **–rollen**[2] *vi* (& *vt*) roll on, bowl along; **–rukken**[2] **I** *vi* march on; **II** *vt* pull along

voorts further, moreover, besides; then; *en zo* ~ and so on, et cetera

'**voortschoppen**[2] *vi* kick forward; **–schrijden**[2] *vi* proceed; (v. t ij d) move on, pass; *een gestadig ~de techniek* a constantly advancing technology; *een ~de vermindering* a progressive diminution; **–schuiven**[2] *vt* push (shove) on; **–sjokken**[2] *vi* trudge along, jog along; **–slepen**[2] *vt* drag along [sth.]; drag out [a miserable life]; **–sleuren**[2] *vt* drag along [sth.]; **–sluipen**[2] *vi* steal along, sneak along; **–snellen**[2] *vi* hurry on, hurry along; **–spoeden** *zich* ~ hurry on, hasten away; **–spruiten**[2] *vi* ~ *uit* proceed (spring, arise, result) from; **–stappen**[2] *vi* step on; **–stormen**[2] *vi* dash on; **–strompelen**[2] *vi* hobble (stumble) along

'**voortstuwen**[2] *vt* propel, drive; **–wing** *v* propulsion

'**voortsukkelen**[2] *vi* 1 trudge on; 2 potter along; **–telen**[2] *vt* procreate, multiply; **–trekken**[2] **I** *vt* draw (on), drag (along); **II** *vi* march on

'**voortuin** (-en) *m* front garden

voort'**varend I** *aj* energetic, **F** go-ahead; **II** *ad* energetically; **–heid** *v* energy, drive

'**voortvliegen**[2] *vi* fly on; **–vloeien**[2] *vi* flow on; ~ *uit* result (follow) from

voort'**vluchtig** fugitive; *de ~e* the fugitive

'**voortwoekeren** (woekerde '**voort**, h. en is '**voortgewoekerd**) *vi* spread; **–zeggen**[2] *vt* make known; *zegt het voort!* tell your friends!

'**voortzetten**[2] *vt* continue [a business, story &], proceed [one's journey], go on with [one's studies], carry on; **–ting** *v* continuation

'**voortzeulen**[2] *vt* drag along; **–zwoegen**[2] *vi* toil on

voor'**uit** 1 (v. p l a a t s) forward; 2 (v. t ij d) before, beforehand, in advance; ~! come along!, come on!; ~ *dan maar* well, all right; ~ *maar,* ~ *met de geit!* go it!; **F** fire away! [= say it!]; *borst* ~! chest out!; *zijn tijd* ~ *zijn* be ahead of his time(s); **voor'uitbepalen** (bepaalde voor'uit, h. voor'uitbepaald) *vt* determine beforehand; **voor'uitbestellen** (bestelde voor'uit, h. voor'uitbesteld) *vt* order in advance; **–ling** (-en) *v* advance order;

[1,2] V.T. en V.D. van dit werkwoord volgens het model: 1 '**voor**cijferen, V.T. cijferde '**voor**, V.D. '**voor**gecijferd; 2 '**voort**bomen, V.T. boomde '**voort**, V.D. '**voort**geboomd. Zie voor de vormen onder het grondwoord, in deze voorbeelden *cijferen* en *bomen*. Bij sterke en onregelmatige werkwoorden wordt u verwezen naar de lijst achterin.

voor'uitbetalen[3] *vt* prepay, pay in advance; **–ling** (-en) *v* prepayment, payment in advance; *bij ~ te voldoen* payable in advance; **$** cash with order; **voor'uitboeren** (boerde voor'uit, is voor'uitgeboerd) **F** *vi* get on in the world, make one's way in life; go ahead; **–brengen**[3] *vt* bring forward [sth.]; advance [a cause, the line]; help forward; **–drijven**[3] *vt* drive forward; **–gaan**[3] *vi* go first, walk on before; *fig* make progress, improve; rise [of barometer]; *de zieke gaat goed vooruit* the patient is getting on well; **voor'uitgang** *m* progress, improvement; **voor'uithelpen**[3] *vt* help on; **–komen**[3] *vi* get on[2], go ahead[2], make headway[2]; ~ (*in de wereld*) get on (in the world); **–lopen**[3] *vi* go first, walk on ahead; ~ *op...* anticipate [events]; **–rijden**[3] *vi* ride (drive) on before [you &]; sit with one's face to the engine (to the driver); **–schieten**[3] *vi* shoot forward; **–schoppen**[3] *vt* kick on; **–schuiven**[3] **I** *vt* shove (push) forward; **II** *vi* shove along; **–snellen**[3] *vi* hurry on ahead; **–springend** jutting out, projecting; **voor'uitsteken**[3] **I** *vt* put forward, advance; **II** *vi* jut out, project; **–d** projecting, jutting out; **vooruit'strevend** progressive, go-ahead; **–heid** *v* progressiveness; **voor'uitwerpen**[3] *vt fig zijn schaduw* ~ foreshadow; **–zenden**[3] *vt* send in advance (ahead); **–zetten**[3] *vt* advance, put [the clock] forward (ahead); **voor'uitzicht** (-en) *o* prospect, outlook; *de ~en van de oogst* the crop prospects; *geen prettig* ~ not a cheerful outlook; *geen ~en hebben* have no prospects in life; *goede ~en hebben* have good prospects; ● *iets i n het* ~ *hebben* have something in prospect; *iem. iets in het* ~ *stellen* promise sbd. sth.; *m e t dit* ~ with this prospect in view; **voor'uitzien**[3] **I** *vt* foresee; **II** *va* look ahead; **–d** far-seeing; *zijn ~e blik* his foresight; *mensen met ~e blik* far-sighted people; *hij had een ~e blik* he was far-sighted

'**voorvader** (-s en -en) *m* forefather, ancestor; *onze ~en* ook: our forbears; **–lijk** ancestral

'**voorval** (-len) *o* incident, event, occurrence; '**voorvallen**[1] *vi* occur, happen, pass

'**voorvechter** (-s) *m* champion, advocate [of women's rights &]; **–vergadering** (-en) *v* preliminary meeting; **–verkoop** *m* (i n t h e a t e r &) advance booking; (i n w i n k e l) advance sale; **–verpakt** prepacked; **–vertoning** (-en) *v* preview [of films]; **–vertrek** (-ken) *o* front-room

'**voorverwarmen** (verwarmde 'voor, h. 'voorverwarmd) *vt* (b o r d e n &) warm (up) before-

hand; ⚓ preheat

'**voorvlak** (-ken) *o* front face

'**voorvoegen**[1] *vt* prefix; '**voorvoegsel** (-s) *o gram* prefix

voor'voelen (voorvoelde, h. voorvoeld) *vt iets* ~ have a presentiment

'**voorvoet** (-en) *m* forefoot

'**voorvorig** [year &] before last

voor'waar indeed, truly, in truth

'**voorwaarde** (-n) *v* condition, stipulation; *~n* ook: terms; *~n stellen* make (one's) conditions; *o n d e r* ~ *dat...* on (the) condition that...; *onder de bestaande ~n* under existing conditions; *onder geen enkele* ~ not on any account; *onder zekere ~n* on conditions; *o p deze* ~ on this condition; **voor'waardelijk** conditional; *~e veroordeling* suspended sentence

'**voorwaarts** forward, onward; ~ *mars!* ⚓ quick march

'**voorwenden**[1] *vt* pretend, feign, affect, simulate, sham; *voorgewend* ook: put on; '**voorwendsel** (-s en -en) *o* pretext, pretence, blind; *onder* ~ *van...* on (under) the pretext of..., on (under) pretence of...

'**voorwereld** *v* prehistoric world; **voor'wereldlijk** 1 prehistoric; 2 *fig* antediluvian

'**voorwerk** (-en) *o typ* preliminary pages, front matter, **F** prelims; (v. v e s t i n g) outwork

'**voorwerp** (-en) *o* 1 (d i n g) object, thing, article; 2 *gram* object; *gevonden ~en* lost property; *lijdend* ~ [*gram*] direct object; *medewerkend* ~ [*gram*] indirect object; ~ *van spot* object of ridicule, laughing-stock; **–glaasje** (-s) *o* slide [of a microscope]; '**voorwerpsnaam** (-namen) *m gram* name of a thing; **–zin** (-nen) *m gram* object(ive) clause

'**voorweten** *o* = *voorkennis*; **–schap** *v* foreknowledge, prescience

'**voorwiel** (-en) *o* front-wheel; **–aandrijving** *v* front(wheel) drive; **–ophanging** *v* front suspension

'**voorwinter** (-s) *m* beginning of the winter; **–woord** (-en) *o* preface; foreword [esp. by another than the author]; **–zaal** (-zalen) *v* 1 front room; 2 ante-chamber, ante-room; **–zaat** (-zaten) *m* ancestor, forefather; *onze voorzaten* ook: our forbears

'**voorzang** (-en) *m* 1 introductory song; 2 proem [to poem &]; 3 hymn before the sermon; **–er** (-s) *m* precentor, cantor, clerk

1 '**voorzeggen**[1] *vt* prompt

2 voor'zeggen (voorzegde, voorzei, h. voorzegd) *vt* predict, presage, prophesy; **–ging**

[1,3] V.T. en V.D. van dit werkwoord volgens het model: 1 '**voor**cijferen, V.T. cijferde '**voor**, V.D. '**voor**gecijferd; 3 **voor'uit**schoppen, V.T. schopte **voor'uit**, V.D. **voor'uit**geschopt. Zie voor de vormen onder het grondwoord, in deze voorbeelden: *bomen* en *schoppen*. Bij sterke en onregelmatige werkwoorden wordt u verwezen naar de lijst achterin.

(-en) *v* prediction, prophecy

voor'zeker certainly, surely, assuredly, to be
sure

'voorzet (-ten) *m sp* centre

'voorzetlens (-lenzen) *v* close-up lens, supplementary lens

'voorzetsel (-s) *o* preposition

'voorzetten[1] *vt* 1 (i e t s) put [sth.] before [sbd.];
2 (d e k l o k) put [the clock] forward, put [the
clock an hour] ahead; 3 *sp* centre [the ball]

voor'zichtig I *aj* prudent, careful, cautious;
conservative [estimate]; ~! 1 be careful!; look
out!; mind the paint (the steps &); 2 (o p k i s t
&) with care!; *naar ~e schatting* at a conservative estimate; **II** *ad* prudently, carefully,
cautiously; conservatively [valued at...]; **–heid**
v prudence, care, caution; ~ *is de moeder van de
porseleinkast* safety first!; **voorzichtigheids-
'halve** by way of precaution; **voor'zichtig-
heidsmaatregel** (-en en -s) *m* = *voorzorgsmaat-
regel*

voor'zien (voorzag, h. voorzien) **I** *vt* foresee
[evil &]; *het was te ~* it was to be expected; *wij
zijn al ~* we are suited; ~ *van* (*met*) provide
with, supply with, furnish with; fit with
[shelves &]; *van etiketten ~* labelled; **II** *vi* ~ *i n*
supply, meet, fill [a deficiency]; *in een* (*lang
gevoelde*) *behoefte ~* supply a (long-felt) want; ~
in de behoeften van... supply (provide for) the
wants of...; *de wet heeft daarin* (*in een dergelijk
geval*) *niet ~* the law makes no provision for a
case of the kind; *daarin moet worden ~* that
should be seen to; *in de vacature is ~* the
vacancy has been filled; *het o p iem. ~ hebben*
F have a down on sbd.; *het niet op iem. ~ hebben*
zie *begrijpen* (*begrepen*); **III** *vr zich ~* suit oneself;
zich ~ van provide oneself with; **voor'zien-
baar** forseeable; **voor'zienigheid** *v* providence; *de Voorzienigheid* Providence;
voor'ziening (-en) *v* provision, supply

'voorzij(de) (-zijden) *v* front [of a house &],
face

'voorzingen[1] **I** *vt* sing to [a person]; **II** *vi* lead
the song

'voorzitten[1] **I** *vi* preside, be in the chair; *dat
heeft bij hem voorgezeten* that has been his main
consideration (his motive); **II** *vt* preside over,
at [a meeting]; **'voorzitter** (-s) *m* 1 chairman,
president; 2 Speaker [of the House of
Commons]; *Mijnheer de ~* Mr Chairman;
–schap *o* chairmanship, presidency; *onder ~
van...* presided over by..., under the chairmanship of...; **'voorzittershamer** (-s) *m*

chairman's hammer; **–plaats** (-en) *v* chair;
'voorzitting = *voorzitterschap*

'voorzomer (-s) *m* beginning of the summer

'voorzorg (-en) *v* precaution, provision; *uit ~*
by way of precaution; **–smaatregel** (-s en
-en) *m* precautionary measure, precaution

voorzo'ver zie 2 *zover*

voos spongy, woolly [radish]; *fig* sham [piety],
hollow [phrases]; **–heid** *v* sponginess, woolli-
ness

1 'vorderen (vorderde, is gevorderd) *vi*
advance, make headway, make progress,
progress; **2 'vorderen** (vorderde, h. gevorderd) *vt* 1 demand, claim; 2 requisition [for
war purposes]; **–ring** (-en) *v* 1 (v o o r t g a n g)
advance, progress, improvement; ‖ 2 (e i s)
demand, claim; 3 requisitioning [of buildings
for war purposes]; *~en maken* make progress

'vore (-n) = 1 *voor*

1 'voren (-s) *m* ᛒ roach

2 'voren *ad n a a r ~* to the front; *naar ~ brengen*
put forward, advance [a claim &]; *naar ~
komen* 1 be put forward, be advanced [of plans
&]; 2 emerge [from the discussion]; *t e ~* 1
(e e r d e r) before, previously; 2 (v o o r a f)
beforehand, [pay, book] in advance; *nooit te ~*
never before; *drie dagen te ~* three days earlier;
v a n ~ in front; *van ~ af* (*aan*) from the beginning; *van de ~* zie *tevoren*; **–staand** mentioned
before, above-mentioned, above-said; *het ~e*
ook: the above

'vorig former, previous; *in ~e dagen* in former
days; *de ~e maand* last month; *de ~e oorlog*
(*regering*) the late war (government)

vork (-en) *v* fork; *hij weet hoe de ~ aan* (*in*) *de steel
zit* he knows the ins and outs of it; **–been**
(-deren en -benen) *o* wish(ing)-bone;
–heftruck (-s) *m* fork-lift (truck)

vorm (-en) *m* 1 (g e s t a l t e) form, shape; 2 ⚒
(g i e t m a l) mould, matrix; 3 *gram* [strong,
weak] form; [active, passive] voice; 4
(p l i c h t p l e g i n g) form, formality, ceremony; *vaste ~ aannemen* take definite form, take
shape; *de ~en in acht nemen* observe the forms;
hij heeft (*kent*) *geen ~en* he has no manners; ●
i n de ~ van in the shape (form) of; *in welke ~
ook* in any shape or form; *in ~ zijn sp* be in
(good) form; *n a a r de ~* in form; *v o o r de ~*
for form's sake, as a matter of form; formal
[invitation]; *z o n d e r ~ van proces* without trial;
fig without ceremony, without more ado;
'vormelijk *aj* (& *ad*) formal(ly), ceremo-
nious(ly); **–heid** (-heden) *v* formality, ceremo-

---

[1] V.T. en V.D. van dit werkwoord volgens het model: **'voor**cijferen, V.T. cijferde **'voor**, V.D. **'voor**gecijferd. Zie
voor de vormen onder het grondwoord, in dit voorbeeld: *cijferen*. Bij sterke en onregelmatige werkwoorden wordt u
verwezen naar de lijst achterin.

niousness; **'vormeling** (-en) *m rk* confirmee;
'vormeloos = *vormloos*; **vorme'loosheid** =
vormloosheid; **'vormen** (vormde, h. gevormd)
I *vt* 1 form, fashion, frame, shape, model,
mould [sth.]; 2 form, constitute, make up [the
committee &], build up [stocks, reserves]; 3 *rk*
confirm; **II** *vr zich* ~ form; **–d** forming &,
formative [influences]; *fig* educative [methods],
informing [books]; **'vormendienst** *m* formal-
ism; **'vormer** (-s) *m* framer, moulder,
modeller; **'vormgever** (-s) *m* designer;
–geving *v* design; **–gieter** (-s) *m* moulder;
'vorming (-en) *v* formation, forming, shaping,
moulding; *fig* education, cultivation, culture;
'vormleer *v* 1 morphology [of words; ⅔ &
♋]; 2 *gram* accidence; **–loos** shapeless, form-
less; **vorm'loosheid** *v* shapelessness, formless-
ness; **'vormraam** (-ramen) *o* 1 moulding-
frame; 2 [printer's] chase; **–school** (-scholen) *v*
training-school; **–sel** *o rk* confirmation; *het ~
toedienen* confirm, administer confirmation;
–vast that keeps its shape, that keeps in shape;
–verandering (-en) *v* transformation, metamorphosis [*mv* metamorphoses]
'vorsen (vorste, h. gevorst) *vi* investigate; ~
naar inquire into; **–d** searching [look], inquiring [mind]; **'vorser** (-s) *m* investigator; researcher
1 vorst (-en) *v* △ ridge [of a roof]
2 vorst *m* (h e t v r i e z e n) frost
3 vorst (-en) *m* sovereign, monarch, king,
emperor; prince; *de ~ der duisternis* the prince
of darkness; **'vorstelijk I** *aj* princely [salary],
royal, lordly; **II** *ad* in a princely way, royally;
–heid *v* royalty; **'vorstendom** (-men) *o*
principality; **–gunst** *v* royal favour; **–huis**
(-huizen) *o* dynasty
'vorstgrens (-grenzen) *v* frost limit (range);
'vorstig frosty
vor'stin (-nen) *v* sovereign, monarch, queen,
empress; princess
'vorstperiode (-s en -n) *v* spell (period) of
frost, freeze; **–schade** *v* frost damage; **–verlet**
o loss of working hours due to frost; **–vrij**
frost-proof [cellar]
vort off with you!, **S** hop it!
vos (-sen) *m* 1 fox²; 2 (h a l s b o n t) fox fur; 3
(p a a r d) sorrel (horse); 4 ※ tortoise-shell
(butterfly); *zo'n slimme ~!* the slyboots!; *een ~
verliest wel zijn haren maar niet zijn streken*
Reynard is still Reynard though he put on a
cowl; what is bred in the bone will not come
out of the flesh; *als de ~ de passie preekt, boer pas
op je ganzen* when the fox preaches beware of
your geese; **'vossebont** *o* fox (fur); **–hol** (-en)
o fox-hole; **–jacht** (-en) *v* fox-hunt(ing);
–klem (-men) *v* fox trap

'vossen (voste, h. gevost) *vi* & *vt* swot, mug;
'vossestaart (-en) *m* foxtail; ⅔ foxtail-grass;
–val (-len) *v* fox-trap; **–vel** (-len) *o* fox-skin
vo'teren (voteerde, h. gevoteerd) *vt* vote
vo'tief votive; **–kerk** (-en) *v* votive church
'votum (vota en -s) *o* vote; *een ~ van vertrouwen*
(*wantrouwen*) a vote of (want of) confidence
vouw (-en) *v* fold [in paper &]; crease, pleat [in
cloth &]; **–baar** foldable, pliable; **–been**
(-benen) *o* paper-knife; **–blad** (-bladen) *o*
folder; **–deur** (-en) *v* folding-door(s);
'vouwen* *vt* fold; *de handen ~* fold one's
hands; *in vieren ~* fold in four; **'vouwfiets**
(-en) *m* & *v* folding bicycle; **–scherm** (-en) *o*
folding-screen; **–stoel** (-en) *m* folding-chair,
camp-stool
voy'eur [vʋa'jør] (-s) *m* voyeur, **F** Peeping
Tom; **voyeu'risme** *o* voyeurism
vraag (vragen) *v* 1 question; query; 2 **$** request,
demand; ~ *en aanbod* supply and demand; ~ *en
antwoord* question and answer; *een ~ doen* ask
[sbd.] a question; put a question to [sbd.];
vragen stellen ask questions; *de ~ stellen is haar
beantwoorden* the question is answered by being
asked; *een ~ uitlokken* invite a question; *er is veel
~ naar...* **$** ...is much in demand, it is in great
request, there is a great demand for...; *dat is nog
de ~* that's a question; *het is de ~ of...* it is a
question whether...; *de ~ doet zich voor of...* the
question arises whether...; **–achtig** inquisitive;
–al (-len) *m* inquisitive person; **–baak**
(-baken) *v* (b o e k) vade-mecum; (p e r s o o n)
oracle; **–gesprek** (-ken) *o* interview; **–prijs**
(-prijzen) *m* asking price; **–punt** (-en) *o* point
in question; **–steller** (-s) *m* questioner; **–stuk**
(-ken) *o* problem; **–teken** (-s) *o* question-mark,
note (point) of interrogation, query; *daar zullen
we een ~ achter moeten zetten* we shall have to put
a note of interrogation to it²; **–woord** (-en) *o*
interrogative word; **–ziek** inquisitive
vraat (vraten) *m* glutton; **–zucht** *v* gluttony,
greed, voracity; **vraat'zuchtig** gluttonous,
greedy, voracious
vracht (-en) *v* 1 load; ⚓ cargo; 2 (p r ij s) fare
[for passengers]; carriage; ⚓ freight
'vrachtauto [-o.to. of -ʋuto.] ('s) *m* (motor-)
lorry, (motor-)truck, (motor-)van;
–bestuurder (-s), **–chauffeur** [-ʃo.fø:r] (-s) *m*
lorry driver
'vrachtboot (-boten) *m* & *v* cargo-boat,
freighter; **–brief** (-brieven) *m* **$** 1 [railway]
consignment note; 2 ⚓ bill of lading; **–dienst**
m cargo service; **–enmarkt** *v* freight market;
–goed (-eren) *o* goods; *als ~ zenden* send by
goods-train; **–je** (-s) *o* small load, burden; (v.
t a x i) fare; **–lijst** (-en) *v* **$** manifest; **–loon**
(-lonen) *o*, **–prijs** (-prijzen) *m* = *vracht* 2;

–overeenkomst (-en) *v* contract of carriage, *Am* freight contract; **–rijder** (-s) *m* carrier; **–schip** (-schepen) *o* ⚓ cargo-boat, freighter; **–tarief** (-rieven) *o* 1 railway rates, tariff; 2 ⚓ freight rates; **–vaarder** (-s) *m* 1 = *vrachtschip*; 2 (s c h i p p e r) carrier; **–vaart** *v* carrying-trade; **–verkeer** *o* goods traffic (transport); *Am* freight transport; **–vervoer** *o* carrying trade; **–vliegtuig** (-en) *o* freight plane, freighter; **~**(*en*) ook: cargo aircraft; **–vrij** carriage paid; ⚓ freight paid; ⚓ post-paid; **–wagen** (-s) *m* truck, van; zie ook: *vrachtauto*; **–zoeker** (-s) *m* ⚓ tramp (steamer)

'vragen* I *vt* ask; *gevraagd: een 2de bediende* & Wanted; *wij ~ een tekenaar* we require a draughtsman; *mij werd gevraagd of...* I was asked if...; *zij is al tweemaal gevraagd* she has had two proposals; *zult u haar ~?* 1 are you going to propose to her (to ask her hand in marriage)?; 2 shall you invite her?; 3 are you going to question her (to hear her lesson)?; *iem. iets ~* ask 'sth. of sbd.; *je moet het hem maar ~* (you had better) ask him; *vraag het maar aan hem* 1 ask him (about it); 2 ask him for it; *dat moet je mij niet ~!* don't ask me!; *hoeveel vraagt hij ervoor?* 1 how much does he ask for it?; 2 what does he [the tailor &] charge for it?; *waarom vraagt u dat?* what makes you ask that?; *hoe kunt u dat ~?* how can you ask (the question)?; ● *iem. op een feestje ~* invite sbd. to a party; *iem. t e n eten ~* ask sbd. to dinner; II *vi* & *va* ask; *nu vraag ik je!* I ask you!; *...als ik ~ mag* if I may ask (the question); ● *~ n a a r iem.* ask after (inquire for) sbd.; *~ naar iets* inquire after sth.; *vraag er uw broer maar eens naar* ask your brother (about it); *~ naar die waren* inquire for these commodities; *er wordt veel naar gevraagd* there is a great demand for it (them); *naar uw mening wordt niet gevraagd* your opinion is not asked; *(iem.) naar de weg ~* ask one's way (of sbd.), ask (sbd.) the way; *daar ~ ze niet naar* they never care about that; *~ o m iets* ask for sth.; *je hebt ze maar v o o r het ~* they may be had for the asking; III *o ~ kost niets* there's no harm in asking; **'vragen-boek** (-en) *o* 1 questionbook; 2 catechism; **'vragend** I *aj* inquiring, questioning [eyes]; [look] of inquiry, of interrogation; interrogatory [tone]; *gram* interrogative; II *ad* inquiringly; *gram* interrogatively; **vragender'wijs**, **–'wijze** interrogatively; **'vragenlijst** (-en) *v* questionnaire; **–uurtje** (-s) *o* question-time [in Parliament]; **'vrager** (-s) *m* interrogator, questioner, inquirer

vrat (vraten) V.T. v. *vreten*

'vrede *m* & *v* peace; *de Vrede van Munster* 🕮 the Peace of Westphalia; *de Vrede van Utrecht* 🕮 the Treaty of Utrecht, the Utrecht Treaty; *ik heb er*

~ mee I don't object, all right!; *wij kunnen daar geen ~ mee hebben* we can't accept (agree with, put up with) that; ● *ga i n ~* go in peace; *in ~ leven met iedereen* live at peace with all men; *laat mij m e t ~* let me alone; *o m de lieve ~* for the sake of peace; **–breuk** (-en) *v* breach of the peace; **–kus** (-sen) = *vredeskus*; **vrede'lievend** I *aj* peace-loving, peaceable, peaceful; II *ad* peaceably, peacefully; **–heid** 1 love of peace, peaceableness, peacefulness

'vredesaanbod *o* peace offer; **–apostel** (-s en -en) *m* apostle of peace; **–bespreking** (-en) *v* **~en** preliminary peace talks; **–beweging** *v* peace movement; **–conferentie** [-(t)si.] (-s) *v* peace conference; **–congres** (-sen) *o* peace congress; **–duif** (-duiven) *v* dove of peace, peace dove; **–korps** *o* Peace Corps [of the U.S.A.]; **–kus** (-sen) *m* kiss of peace; **–macht** *v* peace-keeping force [of the U.N.O.]; **–naam** *in ~* zie *godsnaam*; **–onderhandelingen** *mv* peace negotiations; **'Vredespaleis** *o* Palace of Peace, Peace-Palace; **'vredespijp** (-en) *v* pipe of peace; **–prijs** (-prijzen) *m* (Nobel) peace prize; **–sterkte** *v* ⚔ peace establishment; **~** *25.000 man* ook: 25,000 men on a peace footing

'vredestichter (-s) *m* peacemaker; **'vredestijd** *m* time of peace, peace-time; **–verdrag** (-dragen) *o* treaty of peace, peace treaty; **–voorstel** (-len) *o* peace proposal; **–voorwaarden** *mv* conditions of peace, peace terms

'Vredevorst *m* B Prince of Peace; **'vredig** *aj* (& *ad*) peaceful(ly), quiet(ly)

1 vree = *vrede*

2 vree (vreeën) F V.T. van *vrijen*

'vreedzaam I *aj* peaceable; peaceful [citizen, coexistence]; II *ad* peaceably; peacefully; **–heid** *v* peaceableness; peacefulness

'vreeën V.T. meerv. van *vrijen*

vreemd I *aj* 1 (n i e t b e k e n d) strange, unfamiliar; 2 (b u i t e n l a n d s) foreign [persons, interference, tyranny]; alien [enemy]; 3 exotic [plants]; 4 (r a a r) strange, queer, odd; *~ geld* foreign money; *~e goden* strange gods; *~e hulp* hired assistance; *~ lichaam* ✖ foreign body; *een ~e taal* 1 a foreign language; 2 a strange (queer) language; *ik ben hier ~* I am a stranger here; *dat is toch ~* that is strange, it is a strange thing; *het is (valt) mij ~* it is strange to me; *hij is me ~* he is a stranger to me; *afgunst is mij ~* envy is foreign to my nature; *niets menselijks is mij ~* nothing human is alien to me; *alle vrees is hem ~* he is an utter stranger to fear; *het werk is mij ~* I am strange to the work; *~ zijn aan iets* have nothing to do with it; *hoe ~!* how strange (it is); *ik voel me hier zo ~* I feel so strange here; *het ~e van de zaak is, dat...* the strange thing about the matter is; **II** *ad* strangely; *~ gaan* **F** be unfaithful, commit adultery; *er ~ uitziend* strange-looking; **1** '**vreemde** (-n) *m-v* (o n b e k e n d e) stranger; *dat heeft hij van geen ~* it runs in the family; **2** '**vreemde** *in den ~* in foreign parts, abroad

'**vreemdeling** (-en) *m* **1** (o n b e k e n d e) stranger; **2** (b u i t e n l a n d e r) foreigner; (n i e t g e n a t u r a l i s e e r d e) alien; *een ~ in Jeruzalem* a stranger in Jerusalem (in the place, to the place); '**vreemdelingenboek** (-en) *o* arrival book, (hotel) register, visitor's book; **–bureau** [-by.ro.] (-s) *o* tourist office; **–dienst** *m* Aliens Branch (of the Home Office); **–legioen** *o* Foreign Legion; **–verkeer** *o* tourist traffic, tourism; *Vereniging voor ~* ± Travel Association

'**vreemdheid** (-heden) *v* strangeness, queerness, oddness, oddity; **vreemd**'**soortig** strange, odd; quaint; **–heid** *v* strangeness, oddity; quaintness

vrees (vrezen) *v* fear, fears, dread [= great fear], apprehension; *ps* phobia; *zijn ~ voor...* his fear of...; *~ aanjagen* intimidate; *heb daar geen ~ voor!* no fear!; *~ koesteren voor* be afraid of, stand in fear of, fear; ● *u i t ~ dat...* for fear (that)..., for fear lest [he should...], lest...; *uit ~ voor...* for fear of...; *ridder z o n d e r ~ of blaam* knight without fear and without reproach; zie ook: *vreze*; **–aanjaging** *v* intimidation; '**vreesachtig** timid, timorous; **–heid** *v* timidity, timorousness; '**vreeslijk** = *vreselijk*; **–heid** = *vreselijkheid*; **vrees**'**wekkend** fear-inspiring, frightful

'**vreetzak** (-ken) **F** *m* glutton, hog, pig, greedyguts

vrek (-ken) *m* miser, niggard, skinflint; **–achtig**, '**vrekkig** miserly, stingy; **–heid** *v* miserliness, stinginess

'**vreselijk I** *aj* dreadful, frightful, terrible; **II** *ad* fearfully &c; ook: < awfully; **–heid** (-heden) *v* dreadfulness, terribleness

'**vreten*** **I** *vt* (v. d i e r) eat, feed on; **II** *va* **1** (v. d i e r) feed; **2** (v. m e n s) feed, gorge, **F** stuff; **–er** (-s) *m* glutton; **vrete**'**rij** **P** *v* grub

'**vreugd(e)** (-den) *v* joy, gladness; *Vreugde der Wet* Rejoicing of the Law; *~ scheppen in het leven* enjoy life; **–bedrijf** (-drijven), **–betoon** *o* rejoicings; **–dag** (-dagen) *m* day of rejoicing; **–dronken** drunk with joy, elated with joy, **–kreet** (-kreten) *m* shout (cry) of joy; *vreugdekreten* cheerings; **–loos** joyless, cheerless; **–traan** (-tranen) *m* & *v* tear of joy; **–vol** full of joy, joyful, joyous; **–vuur** (-vuren) *o* bonfire; **–zang** (-en) *m* song of joy

☉ '**vreze** (-n) *v* fear; *in duizend ~n* in constant fear; *de ~ des Heren* the fear of the Lord; '**vrezen** (vreesde, h. gevreesd) **I** *vt* fear, dread; *God ~* fear God; *iem. ~* fear (be afraid of) sbd.; *iets ~* dread sth.; *niets te ~ hebben* have nothing to fear; *het is te ~* it is to be feared; **II** *vi* be afraid; *~ voor zijn leven* fear for his life

vriend (-en) *m* friend; *een ~ van de natuur* a lover of nature, a nature lover; *een ~ zijn van...* be a friend of..., be fond of...; *een ~ der armen* a friend of the poor; *zeg eens, beste ~* I say, dear fellow; *even goede ~en, hoor!* we'll not quarrel for that; *goede ~en zijn met* be friends with; *kwade ~en worden* fall out; *kwade ~en zijn* be on bad terms; *een trouwe ~* a loyal friend; *een ware ~* a true friend; *iem. te ~ hebben* be friends with sbd.; have sbd. for a friend; *iem. te ~ houden* keep friends with sbd., keep on good terms with sbd.; *~en en verwanten* friends and relations, kith and kin; *~ en vijand* friend and foe; *~en in de nood, honderd in een lood* ± a friend in need is a friend indeed; *God bewaar me voor mijn ~en* God save me from my friends; '**vriendelijk I** *aj*.1 kind, friendly, affable; **2** (v. h u i s, s t a d j e) pleasant; **II** *ad* kindly, affably, in a friendly way; **–heid** (-heden) *v* kindness, friendliness, affability; *vriendelijkheden* kindnesses; '**vriendendienst** (-en) *m* kind turn, good office; **–feest** (-en) *o* friendly feast (gathering); **–groet** (-en) *m* friendly greeting; **–kring** (-en) *m* circle of friends; **–paar** (-paren) *o* **1** two friends; **2** homosexual couple; **vrien**'**din** (-nen) *v* (lady, woman) friend; **–netje** (-s) *o* girl friend; '**vriendje** (-s) *o* (little) friend, *Am* buddy; boy friend; **–spolitiek** *v* favouritism, nepotism; '**vriendschap** (-pen) *v* friendship; *~ sluiten met* contract (form, strike up) a friendship with, make friends with, befriend; *uit ~* out of friendship, for the sake of friendship; **vriend**'**schappelijk I** *aj* friendly, amicable; **II** *ad* in a friendly way, amicably; **–heid** *v* friendliness, amicableness; '**vriendschapsband** (-en) *m* tie (bond) of friendship; **–betuiging** (-en) *v* profession (protestation) of friendship; **–verdrag** (-dragen) *o* treaty of friendship

'**vrieskamer** (-s) *v* freezing-chamber; **–kast** (-en) *v* upright freezer; **–kist** (-en) *v* freezer; **–mengsel** (-s) *o*, **–middel** (-en) *o* cryogen; **–punt** *o* freezing-point; *boven (onder, op) het ~* above (below, at) freezing-point; **–vak** (-ken) *o* freezing'(ice) compartment; **–we(d)er** *o* frosty weather; '**vriezen*** *vi* freeze; *het vriest hard (dat het kraakt)* it is freezing hard; **–d** freezing, frosty

vrij I *aj* **1** (n i e t s l a a f, o n b e l e m m e r d) free; **2** (z o n d e r b e l e t o f w e r k) free, at liberty, at leisure, disengaged; **3** (n i e t bezet of besproken) not engaged, vacant [seats]; [taxi] for hire; ~e arbeid free labour; ~e avond evening (night) out, night off; ~ beroep profession; ~ bovenhuis self-contained flat; een ~e dag a free day, a day off; ~ kwartier ⤳ break; een ~e middag a free afternoon, a half-holiday; ~e ogenblikken leisure (spare) moments; ~e tijd spare time; ~ uitzicht free view; een ~ uur a spare (leisure, idle) hour, an off-hour; het ~e woord free speech; mijn ~e zondag my Sunday out; zo ~ als een vogeltje in de lucht as free as air (as a bird); 60 gld. per maand en alles ~ and everything found; goed loon en veel ~ and liberal outings; ~ hebben be off duty, have a holiday, a day off; ~ krijgen get a holiday, be free [3 times a week]; ~ vragen ask for a (half-) holiday; ~ zijn be free; mag ik zo ~ zijn? may I take the liberty?, may I be so bold [as to]; zij is nog ~ she is still free; de lijn is ~ the line is clear; ~ van accijns free (exempt) from excise; ~ van dienst 1 off duty, free, disengaged; 2 exempt from duty; ~ van port ⚓ post-free; II ad 1 (v r ij e l ij k) freely; 2 (g r a t i s) free (of charge); 3 (t a m e l ij k) rather, fairly [sunny weather], pretty; ~ goed pretty good; ~ veel rather much (many); ~ wat... a good deal of...; ~ wat meer much more; vrij'af a holiday, a day (evening) off; ~ nemen take a holiday

vrij'age [-'a.ʒə] (-s) v courtship, wooing
'**vrijbiljet** (-ten) o = vrijkaart
'**vrijblijven**[1] vi remain free; **vrij'blijvend $** without engagement, not binding
'**vrijbrief** (-brieven) m passport; charter, licence, permit
'**vrijbuiten** (vrijbuitte, h. gevrijbuit) vi practise piracy; **-er** (-s) m freebooter; **vrijbuite'rij** (-en) v freebooting
'**vrijdag** (-dagen) m Friday; Goede Vrijdag Good Friday; **-s I** aj Friday; **II** ad on Fridays
'**vrijdenker** (-s) m free-thinker; **vrijdenke'rij** v free-thinking, free thought
'**vrijdom** (-men) m freedom, exemption; '**vrije** (-n) m freeman; '**vrijelijk** freely
'**vrijen*** I vi 1 court; 2 make love, F pet, neck, S spoon; uit ~ gaan go courting; ~ met een meisje court a girl, make love to her; ~ om (naar) een meisje court a girl, ☉ woo her; II vt court, ☉ woo; **-er** (-s) m suitor, lover, sweetheart, ☉ wooer; oude ~ bachelor; haar ~ F ook: her young man, her chap; **vrije'rij** (-en) v love-making, courtship; '**vrijersvoeten** mv op ~ gaan go (a-)courting
vrije'tijdsbesteding v use (employment) of

leisure, leisure activity; **–kleding** v leisure-wear, ± casual wear
'**vrijgeboren** free-born
'**vrijgeest** (-en) m free-thinker; **vrijgeeste'rij** v free-thinking, free thought
'**vrijgelatene** (-n) m-v freedman, freed woman
'**vrijgeleide** (-n en -s) o safe-conduct; onder ~ under a safe-conduct
'**vrijgestelde** (-n) m paid (full-time) trade-union official
'**vrijgeven**[1] vt release, free, decontrol [government butter &]; manumit, emancipate [a slave]; set at liberty [sbd.]; give a holiday [to boys &]
vrij'gevig I aj liberal, open-handed; **II** ad liberally; **–heid** v liberality, open-handedness
'**vrijgevochten** het is een ~ land it is Liberty Hall there; **vrije'zel** (-len) m bachelor
'**vrijhandel** m free trade; **–aar** (-s en -laren) m free-trader; '**vrijhandelsassociatie** [-si.a.(t)si.] v Europese V~ European Free Trade Association, EFTA
'**vrijhaven** (-s) v free port
'**vrijheid** (-heden) v liberty, freedom; dichterlijke ~ poetic licence; persoonlijke ~ personal freedom; ~ van drukpers (van gedachte, van geweten) liberty (freedom) of the press (of thought, of conscience); ~ van vergadering freedom of association; ~ van het woord freedom of speech; geen ~ hebben om... not be at liberty to...; de ~ nemen om... take the liberty to..., make bold to..., make free to...; zich vrijheden veroorloven take liberties; ik vind geen ~ om... I don't see my way to...; in ~ free, at liberty; in ~ stellen release, set at liberty, set free; **vrijheid'lievend** fond of liberty, liberty-loving, freedom-loving [people]; '**Vrijheidsbeeld** o [the New York] Statue of Liberty; '**vrijheidsberoving** v deprivation of liberty; **–beweging** (-en) v liberation movement; **–boom** (-bomen) m tree of liberty; **–geest** m spirit of liberty; **–liefde** v love of liberty; **–muts** (-en) v cap of liberty, Phrygian cap; **–oorlog** (-logen) m war of independence; **–straf** (-fen) v ⚖ imprisonment; **–strijder** (-s) m freedom fighter; **–vaan** (-vanen) v flag (standard) of liberty; **–zin** m spirit of liberty; **–zucht** v love of liberty
'**vrijhouden**[1] vt 1 (l e t t e r l ij k) keep free; 2 defray sbd.'s expenses; ik zal je ~ I'll stand treat
'**vrijkaart** (-en) v free ticket, complimentary

---

[1] V.T. en V.D. van dit werkwoord volgens het model: '**vrijloten**, V.T. lootte '**vrij**, V.D. '**vrijgeloot**. Zie voor de vormen onder het grondwoord, in dit voorbeeld: loten. Bij sterke en onregelmatige werkwoorden wordt u verwezen naar de lijst achterin.

ticket; (v. s c h o u w b u r g, s p o o r &) free
pass

'**vrijkomen**[1] *vi* get off; come out [of prison]; be
released [of forces]; be liberated [in chemistry];
~ *met de schrik* get off with a fright

'**vrijkopen**[1] *vt* buy off, ransom, redeem; **–ping**
(-en) *v* buying off, redemption

'**vrijkorps** (-en) *o* volunteer corps

'**vrijlaten**[1] *vt* set at liberty, release [a prisoner],
let off [their victim]; emancipate, manumit [a
slave]; release, free, decontrol [government
butter &]; leave [a country] free [to determine
its own future]; *iem. de handen* ~ leave (allow)
sbd. a free hand; **–ting** (-en) *v* release; emancipation, manumission [of a slave]

'**vrijloop** *m* free wheel; (v. m o t o r) idling

'**vrijlopen**[1] *vi* go free, get off, escape; (v a n
m o t o r) idle

'**vrijmaken**[1] **I** *vt* emancipate [a slave]; free [a
person]; liberate [a nation]; free [the mind];
disengage, free [one's arm]; clear [the way];
II *vr zich* ~ disengage (extricate, free) oneself;
zich ~ *van* get rid of; **–king** (-en) *v* liberation,
emancipation

vrij'**metselaar** (-s en -laren) *m* freemason,
mason; **–sloge** [-lɔ:ʒə] (-s) *v* 1 masonic lodge;
2 (g e b o u w) masonic hall; **vrijmetsela'rij** *v*
freemasonry

vrij'**moedig** outspoken, frank, free, bold;
–heid *v* frankness, outspokenness, boldness

'**vrijpartij** (-en) **F** *v* petting, necking

'**vrijplaats** (-en) *v* sanctuary, refuge, asylum

'**vrijpleiten**[1] **I** *vt* exculpate, exonerate, clear
[from blame]; **II** *vr zich* ~ exculpate oneself,
clear oneself

vrij'**postig I** *aj* bold, free, forward, pert; **II** *ad*
boldly; **–heid** (-heden) *v* boldness, forwardness, pertness; *vrijpostigheden* liberties

'**vrijspraak** *v* acquittal; '**vrijspreken**[1] *vt* acquit

'**vrijstaan**[1] *vi* be permitted; *het staat u vrij om...*
you are free to...

'**vrijstaand** ~ *huis* detached house; ~ *beeld*
free-standing statue; ~*e muur* self-supporting
wall; *sp* ~*e speler* unguarded player

'**vrijstaat** (-staten) *m* free state; **–stad** (-steden)
v free city, free town

'**vrijstellen**[1] *vt* exempt (from *van*); **–ling** (-en) *v*
exemption, freedom (from *van*)

'**vrijster** (-s) *v* sweetheart; *oude* ~ old maid,
spinster

vrij'**uit** freely, frankly; *hij spreekt altijd* ~ he is
very free-spoken; *spreek* ~*!* ook: speak out!

'**vrijverklaren** (verklaarde 'vrij, h. 'vrijver-

klaard) *vt* declare free

'**vrijwaren** (vrijwaarde, h. gevrijwaard) *vt* ~ *voor*
(*tegen*) guarantee from, safeguard against,
protect from, secure from, guard from
(against); **–ring** (-en) *v* safeguarding, protection

'**vrijwel** *hij is* ~ *genezen* practically cured; ~ *alles
wat men kan wensen* pretty well everything that
could be wanted; ~ *hetzelfde* much the same
(thing); ~ *iedereen* almost everybody; ~ *niets*
next to nothing; ~ *nooit* hardly ever; ~ *onmogelijk* well-nigh impossible; *ik ben er* ~ *zeker van*
I am all but certain of it

'**vrijwiel** (-en) *o* free wheel

vrij'**willig I** *aj* voluntary, free; ~*e brandweer*
volunteer fire-brigade; **II** *ad* voluntarily, freely,
of one's own free will; **–er** (-s) *m* volunteer;
–heid *v* voluntariness

vrij'**zinnig I** *aj* liberal; *een* ~*e* a liberal; **II** *ad*
liberally; **–heid** *v* liberalism, liberality

'**vrille** ['vri.jə] (-s) *v* ⚙ spin

vrind (-en) *m* = *vriend*

vroed wise, prudent; *de* ~*e vaderen* the City
Fathers; **–schap** (-pen) *v* town-council; *de* ~
ook: the City Fathers; **–vrouw** (-en) *v* midwife

1 vroeg I *aj* early; *zijn* ~*e dood* his untimely
(premature) death; **II** *ad* early; at an early
hour; *het is nog* ~ it is still early; *niets te* ~ none
too early, none too soon; *een uur te* ~ an hour
early (before one's time); *al* ~ *in maart* early in
March; *'s morgens* ~ early in the morning; *te* ~
komen come too early, be early; ~ *opstaan* rise
early; zie ook: *opstaan*; ~ *en laat* early and late;
~ *of laat* sooner or later; *van* ~ *tot laat* from
early in the morning till late at night; zie ook:
vroeger & *vroegst*

2 vroeg (vroegen) V.T. v. *vragen*

'**vroegdienst** (-en) *m* early service

'**vroegen** V.T. meerv. v. *vragen*

'**vroeger I** *aj* former [friends, years &]; earlier
[documents]; previous [statements]; past [sins];
late, ex- [president &]; **II** *ad* [come] earlier; [an
hour] sooner; of old, in former days (times), in
times gone by, on former occasions,
previously, before now; *daar stond* ~ *een molen*
there used to be a mill there

'**vroegkerk** *v* early service; **–mis** (-sen) *v rk*
early mass; **–preek** (-preken) *v* early service

'**vroegrijp** early-ripe, precocious [child];
vroeg'rijpheid *v* precocity

vroegst earliest; *op zijn* ~ at the earliest

'**vroegte** *v in de* ~ early in the morning

vroeg'**tijdig I** *aj* early, untimely, premature

[1] V.T. en V.D. van dit werkwoord volgens het model:. '**vrijloten**, V.T. lootte '**vrij**, V.D. '**vrijgeloot**. Zie voor de
vormen onder het grondwoord, in dit voorbeeld: *loten*. Bij sterke en onregelmatige werkwoorden wordt u verwezen
naar de lijst achterin.

[death]; **II** *ad* 1 early, betimes, at an early hour; 2 prematurely, before one's time

'**vrolijk I** *aj* merry, gay, cheerful; *een ~e Frans* a gay dog, a jolly fellow; *zich ~ maken over* make merry over; **II** *ad* merrily, gaily, cheerfully; **–heid** *v* mirth, merriment, gaiety, cheerfulness; *grote ~ onder het publiek* great hilarity

'**vrome** (-n) *m-v* pious man or woman; **vroom** *aj* (& *ad*) devout(ly), pious(ly); *vrome wens* pious wish; **–heid** *v* devoutness, devotion, piety

vroor (vroren) V.T. v. *vriezen*

vrouw (-en) *v* 1 woman; 2 (e c h t g e n o t e) wife, ⊙ spouse; 3 ◊ queen; *de ~ des huizes* the lady (mistress) of the house; *~ van de wereld* woman of the world; *~ Hendriks* Mrs H.; *hoe is het me je ~?* how is Mrs H.?; *Maar ~!* 1 But woman!; 2 I say, wife!; *haar tot ~ nemen* take her to wife; **–achtig** effeminate, womanish; '**vrouwelijk I** *aj* 1 female [animal, plant, sex &]; feminine [virtues, rhyme &]; womanly [conduct, modesty &], womanlike; *2 gram* feminine; *~e kandidaat (kandidaten)* woman candidate, women candidates; **II** *o het ~e in haar* the woman in her; **–heid** *v* womanliness, feminity; '**vrouwenaard** *m* woman's nature, female character; **–arbeid** *m* women's labour; **–arts** (-en) *m* gynaecologist; **–beeld** (-en) *o* image (statue) of a woman; **–beul** (-en) *m* wife beater; **–beweging** *v* woman's rights movement; **–blad** (-bladen) *o* woman's magazine, woman's weekly (monthly); **–bond** (-en) *m* woman's league; **–gek** (-ken) *m* ladies' man, philanderer; **–haar** (-haren) *o* 1 woman's hair; 2 ♣ maidenhair; **–hater** (-s) *m* woman-hater, misogynist; **–jager** (-s) *m* womanizer; **–kiesrecht** *o* woman suffrage, votes for women; **–kleding** *v* woman's (women's) dress; **–klooster** (-s) *o* nunnery, convent for women; **–koor** (-koren) *o* choir for female voices; **–kwaal** (-kwalen) *v* female (woman's) complaint, women's disease; **–liefde** *v* woman's love; **–list** (-en) *v* woman's ruse, female cunning; **–rechten** *mv* women's rights; **–regering** *v* woman's rule; **–rok** (-ken) *m* woman's skirt; **–stem** (-men) *v* woman's voice; **–vereniging** (-en) *v* women's association; **–verering** *v* woman-worship; **–werk** *o* women's work; **–zadel** (-s) = *dameszadel*; **–ziekte** (-n en -s) *v* women's disease; '**vrouwlief** my dear, my dear wife; **–mens** (-en en -lui), **–spersoon** (-sonen) *o* woman, **F** female; **–tje** (-s) *o* 1 little woman; 2 wif(e)y; **–volk** *o* women, womenfolk

vrucht (-en) *v* fruit²; *deze ~en* these fruit; *de ~en der aarde (van zijn vlijt)* the fruits of the earth (of his industry); *~en op sap (in blik)* tinned fruit; *verboden ~ is zoet* forbidden fruit is sweet; *~en*

afwerpen, ~ dragen (opleveren) bear fruit; *de ~(en) plukken van...* reap the fruits of...; *aan hun ~en zult gij ze kennen* **B** by their fruits ye shall know them; *aan de ~ kent men de boom* a tree is known by its fruit; ● *met ~* with success, successfully; profitably, with profit, usefully; *z o n d e r ~* without avail, fruitless(ly); **–afdrijvend ~ middel** abortifacient; **–afdrijving** *v* abortion; '**vruchtbaar** fruitful² [fields, minds, collaboration, discussion &]; fertile² [soil, inventions]; < prolific² [females, brain, writer &]; *~ in* fruitful in [great events &]; fertile in, fertile of [great men]; prolific in; prolific of [offspring, honey &]; **–heid** *v* fruitfulness², fertility²; '**vruchtbeginsel** (-s) *o* ♣ ovary; **–bodem** (-s) *m* ♣ receptacle; **–boom** (-bomen) *m* fruit-tree; **–dragend** fruit-bearing, *fig* fruitful; '**vruchteloos I** *aj* fruitless, vain, futile, unavailing; **II** *ad* fruitlessly, vainly, in vain, to no purpose, without avail; **vruchte'loosheid** *v* fruitlessness, futility; '**vruchtemesje** (-s) *o* fruit-knife; '**vruchtengelei** [-ʒəlɛi] *m* & *v* fruit jelly; **–ijs** *o* fruit ice; **–koopman** (-lieden en -lui) *m* fruit-seller, dealer in fruit, fruiterer; **–kweker** (-s) *m* fruit-grower; **vruchtenkweke'rij** (-en) *v* fruit farm; '**vruchtenlimonade** *v* fruit lemonade; **–mand** (-en) *v* fruit basket; **–schaal** (-schalen) *v* fruit-dish; **–slaatje** (-s) *o* fruit salad; **–taart** (-en) *v* fruit tart, fruit pie; **–wijn** *m* fruit wine

'**vruchtepers** (-en) *v* fruit-squeezer; **–sap** (-pen) *o* fruit juice; **–suiker** *m* fruit sugar, fructose

'**vruchtgebruik** *o* usufruct; **–gebruiker** (-s) *m* usufructuary; **–genot** *o* usufruct; **–vlees** *o* ♣ pulp; **–vlies** (-vliezen) *o* amnion; **–vorming** *v* fructification; **–water** *o* amniotic fluid, **F** the waters; **–wisseling** *v* rotation of crops, crop rotation; **–zetting** *v* ♣ setting

V.U. = *Vrije Universiteit* Free (Calvinist) University of Amsterdam

vue [vy.] *~s hebben op* have an eye on; *a ~* at first sight

vuig *aj* (& *ad*) vile(ly), sordid(ly), base(ly); **–heid** *v* vileness, sordidness, baseness

vuil I *aj* dirty², filthy², grimy, grubby [hands]; *fig* nasty, smutty, obscene; (*er*) *~ (uitziend)* dingy; *~e borden* used plates; *~e ~ ei* an addled egg; *~e taal* obscene language; *het ~e wasgoed* the soiled linen; **II** *ad* dirtily²; **III** *o* dirt²; zie ook: *vuilnis*; **–bek** (-ken) *m* foul-mouthed fellow; '**vuilbekken** (vuilbekte, h. gevuilbekt) *vi* talk smut; **vuilbekke'rij** *v* smutty talk, smut; '**vuilheid** *v* dirtiness², filthiness²; *fig* obscenity; '**vuiligheid** (-heden) *v* filth, filthiness, dirt, dirtiness; *fig* obscenity; '**vuilik** (-liken) *m* dirty fellow; *fig* dirty pig; '**vuilmaken** (maakte 'vuil, h. 'vuilgemaakt) **I** *vt* make dirty, dirty, soil; *ik zal mijn handen niet ~ aan die vent* I am not going to mess my hands with such a fellow; *ik wil er geen woorden over ~* I will waste no words over the affair; **II** *vr zich ~* dirty oneself

'vuilnis *v* & *o* [household] refuse, dirt, rubbish; *Am* garbage; **–auto** [-o.to. of -ɔuto.] ('s) *m* refuse collector; **–bak** (-ken) *m* dustbin, ash-bin, *Am* ash-can, garbage-box; **–belt** (-en) *m* & *v* refuse dump; **–blik** (-ken) *o* dustpan; **–emmer** (-s) *m* dustbin, refuse bin; **–hoop** (-hopen) *m* refuse heap, rubbish heap, midden; **–kar** (-ren) *v* dust-cart, refuse cart; **–koker** (-s) *m* refuse chute; **–man** (-nen) *m* dustman, refuse collector, *Am* garbage man (collector); **–vat** (-vaten) *o* refuse bin; **–wagen** (-s) *m* dust-cart, refuse lorry

'vuilpoes (-en en -poezen) *v* dirty woman (girl &)

'vuilstortplaats (-en) *v* refuse dump

'vuiltje (-s) *o* speck of dirt

'vuilverbranding *v* refuse incineration; **–verwerking** *v* refuse dressing, waste-treatment

vuist (-en) *v* fist; *met de ~ op tafel slaan* bang one's fist on the table; *op de ~ gaan* take off the gloves, resort to fisticuffs; *voor de ~* offhand, extempore, without notes; *RT* unscripted [programme]; *een ~ maken* make a fist; *fig* get tough; **–gevecht** (-en) *o* fist-fight, **F** set-to; **–je** (-s) *o* (little) fist; *in zijn ~ lachen* laugh in one's sleeve; **–recht** *o* fist-law, club-law; **–regel** (-s) *m* rule of thumb; **–slag** (-slagen) *m* blow with the fist; **–vechter** (-s) *m* boxer, prize-fighter

vulcani'satie [-'za.(t)si.] *v* vulcanization; **vulcani'seren** (vulcaniseerde, h. gevulcaniseerd) *vt* vulcanize

'vuldop (-pen) *m* ⚬ filler cap

vul'gair [-'gɛ:r]*aj* (& *ad*) vulgar(ly); **vulgari'satie** [-'za.(t)si.] (-s) *v* vulgarization; **vulgari'sator** (-s en -'toren) *m* vulgarizer; **vulgari'seren** (vulgariseerde, h. gevulgariseerd) *vt* vulgarize; **vulgari'teit** (-en) *v* vulgarity; **'vulgus** *o het ~* the vulgar herd, the hoi-polloi, the rabble

'vulhaard (-en) *m = vulkachel*

vul'kaan (-kanen) *m* volcano

'vulkachel (-s) *v* base-burner

vul'kanisch volcanic, igneous [rock]

'vullen (vulde, h. gevuld) **I** *vt* fill [a glass, the stomach &]; stuff [chairs, birds]; pad [sofas]; fill, stop [a hollow tooth]; inflate [a balloon]; ⚡ charge [an accumulator]; **II** *vr zich ~* fill

'vulles, 'vullis *o* **F** = *vuilnis*

'vulling (-en) *v* 1 (in 't alg.) filling; 2 (van opgezette dieren & in de keuken)

stuffing; 3 (v. s o f a) padding; 4 (v. b o n b o n) centre; 5 (v. b a l l o n) inflation; *nieuwe ~* refill [for ball-point pen &]

'vulpen (-nen) *v* fountain-pen; **–houder** (-s) *m* fountain-pen; **–inkt** *m* fountain-pen ink

'vulpotlood (-loden) *o* propelling pencil

'vulsel (-s) *o* stuffing; filling, stopping [of a tooth]

'vultrechter (-s) *m* (filling) funnel; ✗ hopper

'vulva *v* vulva

vuns dirty, smutty, wasty; **–heid** *v* dirtiness, smuttiness; **'vunzig(heid)** = *vuns(heid)*

'vurehout *o* deal; **–en** deal

1 'vuren (vuurde, h. gevuurd) **I** *vi* ✗ fire; *~ op* fire at, fire on; **II** *o* firing

2 'vuren *aj* deal

'vurig **I** *aj* 1 fiery[2] [coals, eyes, horses &]; ardent[2] [rays, love, zeal]; *fig* fervent [hatred, prayers]; fervid [wishes]; 2 red, inflamed [of the skin]; **II** *ad* fierily, ardently, fervently, fervidly; **–heid** *v* 1 fieriness[2]; *fig* fervency [of prayer]; ardour [to do sth.]; spirit [of a horse]; 2 redness, inflammation [of the skin]

vuur (vuren) *o* 1 fire; *fig* ardour; 2 (in hout) dry rot; *het ~ was niet van de lucht* the lightning was continuous; *~ commanderen* ✗ command fire; *~ geven* ✗ fire; *geef me eens wat ~* just give me a light; *heeft u wat ~ voor me?* have you got a light for me?; *iem. het ~ na aan de schenen leggen* make it hot for sbd., press sbd. hard; *~ maken* light a fire; *een goed onderhouden ~* ✗ [keep up] a well-sustained fire; *~ spuwen* spit fire; *~ en vlam spuwen* boil over with rage; *~ vatten* catch fire[2]; *fig* flare up; ● *bij het ~ zitten* sit near (close to) the fire; *voor iem. door het ~ gaan* go through fire (and water) for sbd.; *in ~ (ge)raken* catch fire[2]; *fig* warm (up) [to one's subject]; *de troepen zijn nog nooit in het ~ geweest* ✗ the troops have never been under fire; *in het ~ van het gesprek* in the heat of the conversation; *in ~ en vlam zetten* set [Europe] ablaze; *met ~ spelen* play with fire; *iem. met ~ verdedigen* defend sbd. spiritedly; *onder ~* ✗ under fire; *onder ~ nemen* ✗ subject to fire; *te ~ en te zwaard verwoesten* destroy by fire and sword; *tussen twee vuren* ✗ [enclose the enemy] between two fires; *fig* between the devil and the deep blue sea; *ik heb wel voor heter vuren gestaan* I have been up against a stiffer proposition; **–aanbidder** (-s) *m* fire-worshipper; **–aanbidding** *v* fire-worship; **–baak** (-baken) *v* beacon-light; **vuurbe'stendig** fireproof, heat resistant; **'vuurbol** (-len) *m* fire-ball; **–dood** *m* & *v* death by fire; **–doop** *m* baptism of fire; **–doorn** (-s) *m* ⚘ fire thorn, pyracantha; **–eter** (-s) *m* fire-eater; **–gevecht** (-en) *o* exchange of shots (fire); **–gloed** *m* glare, blaze; **–haard**

(-en) *m* hearth, fireplace; **–kast** (-en) *v* ✕ fire-box; **–kolom** (-men) *v* pillar of fire; **–lak** *o* & *m* black japan; **'Vuurland** *o* Tierra del Fuego; **'vuurlijn** (-en) *v* ⚓ firing-line, line of fire; **–linie** (-s) *v* ⚓ = *vuurlijn*; **–mond** (-en) *m* (muzzle of a) gun; *tien ~en* ten guns; **–peloton** (-s) *o* firing-party, firing-squad; **–pijl** (-en) *m* rocket; **–plaat** (-platen) *v* hearth-plate; **–poel** (-en) *m* sea of fire, blaze; **–proef** (-proeven) *v* fire-ordeal; *fig* crucial (acid) test; *het heeft de ~ doorstaan* it has stood the test; **–rad** (-raderen) *o* Catherine wheel; **–regen** (-s) *m* 1 rain of fire; 2 golden rain [pyrotechnics]; **–rood** as red as fire, fiery red; scarlet [blush, cheeks]; **–scherm** (-en) *o* fire-screen; **–schip** (-schepen) *o* ⬚ fire-ship; ⚓ lightship; **–slag** (-slagen) *o* (flint and) steel; **–spuwend** fire-spitting, spitting fire; *~e berg* volcano; **–staal** (-stalen) *o* fire-steel; **–steen** (-stenen) *o* & *m* flint; **–tje** (-s) *o* small fire; (v o o r s i g a r e t &) light; *een ~ stoken* make a fire; *als een lopend ~* like wild-fire; **–toren** (-s) *m* lighthouse; **–torenwachter** (-s) *m* lighthouse keeper; **–vast** fire-proof [dish], incombustible; *~e klei* fire-clay; *~e steen* fire-brick, refractory brick; **–vlieg** (-en) *v* fire-fly; **–ᵪreter** (-s) *m* fire-eater[2]; **–wapen** (-s en -en) *o* fire-arm; **–water** *o* fire-water; **–werk** (-en) *o* fireworks; pyrotechnic display, display of fireworks; *~ afsteken* let off fireworks; **–zee** (-zeeën) *v* sea of fire; *het was één ~* it was one sheet of fire, one blaze; **–zuil** (-en) *v* pillar of fire

v.v. = *vice versa*

V.V.V. = *Vereniging voor Vreemdelingenverkeer* ± Travel Association

W

w [ve.] ('s) *v* w
W. = *west*
W.A. = *wettelijke aansprakelijkheid*
'**waadbaar** fordable; *waadbare plaats* ford;
–poot (-poten) *m* wading-foot; **–vogel** (-s) *m*
wading-bird, wader
1 waag (wagen) *v* 1 balance; 2 weighing-house
2 waag *m dat is een hele* ~ that is a risky thing;
–hals (-halzen) *m* dare-devil, reckless fellow;
–halzerig venturesome, reckless; **waag-**
halze'rij (-en) *v* recklessness
'**waagmeester** (-s) *m* weigh-master; **–schaal** *v*
zijn leven in de ~ *stellen* risk (venture, stake)
one's life
'**waagstuk** (-ken) *o* risky undertaking, venture,
piece of daring
'**waaien* I** *vi* 1 (v. w i n d) blow; 2 (v. v l a g &)
flutter in the wind; *laten* ~ hang out [a flag];
hij laat de boel maar ~ he lets things slide; *laat*
hem maar ~*!* give him the go-by; *laat maar* ~*!*
blow the letter (the thing &)!; *de appels* ~ *van de*
bomen the apples are blown from the trees; *het*
waait it is blowing; *het waait hard* it is blowing
hard, there is a high wind, it is blowing great
guns; **II** *vt* in: *iem. met een waaier* ~ fan sbd.;
III *vr zich* ~ fan oneself
'**waaier** (-s) *m* fan; **–boom** (-bomen) *m* fan-
tree; '**waaieren** (waaierde, h. gewaaierd) *vi*
fan; '**waaierpalm** (-en) *m* ☙ fan-palm;
–vormig I *aj* fan-shaped; **II** *ad* fan-wise
waak (waken) *v* = *wake*; '**waakhond** (-en) *m*
watch-dog, house-dog; **waaks** = *waakzaam*;
'**waakster** (-s) *v* watcher; '**waakvlam** (-men)
v pilot-light; '**waakzaam** vigilant, watchful,
wakeful; **–heid** *v* vigilance, watchfulness,
wakefulness
1 Waal *v* Waal [river]
2 Waal (Walen) *m* Walloon; **–s I** *aj* Walloon; *de*
~*e Kerk* the French Reformed Church [in the
Netherlands]; **II** *o* Walloon
waan *m* erroneous idea, delusion; *i n d e* ~
brengen lead to believe; *hem in de* ~ *laten dat...*
leave him under the impression that...; *in de* ~
verkeren dat... be under a delusion that...; *u i t de*
~ *helpen* undeceive; **–denkbeeld** (-en) *o*
. fallacy; **–voorstelling** (-en) *v* delusion
'**waanwijs** self-conceited, opinionated; **–heid** *v*
self-conceit
'**waanzin** *m* madness, insanity, dementia;
waan'zinnig mad, insane, demented,
distracted, deranged; *als* ~ like mad; **–e** (-n)
m-v madman, mad woman, maniac, lunatic;

waan'zinnigheid *v* madness; lunacy
1 waar (waren) *v* ware(s), commodity, stuff; *alle*
~ *is naar zijn geld* you only get value for what
you spend; ~ *voor zijn geld krijgen* get (good)
value for one's money, get one's money's
worth; *goede* ~ *prijst zichzelf* good wine needs
no bush
2 waar *aj* true°; *een ware weldaad* ook: a veritable
boon; ~ *maken* prove, make good [an asser-
tion]; live up to [the expectations, one's name
&]; *dat zal je mij* ~ *maken* you'll have to prove
that to me; *het is* ~, *het zou meer kosten* (it is)
true, it would cost more; *het is* ~ *ook, heb je...?*
that reminds me, have you...?; well, now I
come to think of it, have you...?; *dat zal wel* ~
zijn! I should think so!; *daar is niets van* ~ there
is not a word of truth in it; *niet* ~? isn't it?; *jij*
hebt het gezegd, niet ~? didn't you?; *jij hebt het,*
niet ~? haven't you?; *wij zijn er, niet* ~? aren't
we? &; *zo* ~ *ik leef (ik hier voor je sta)* as I live
(as I stand here); *daar is iets* ~*s in* there is some
truth in that; *hij is daarvoor de ware niet* he is not
the right man for it; *dat is je ware* that is the
real thing, the real McCoy, that is it!
3 waar I *ad* where; ~ *ga je naar toe?* where are
you going?; ~ *het ook zij* wherever it be; ~ *ook*
maar wherever; ~ *vandaan* zie *vandaan*; **II** *cj*
1 where; 2 (a a n g e z i e n) since, as
waar'aan, '**waaraan** on which, to which &; *de*
persoon, ~ *ik gedacht heb* of whom I have been
thinking (whom I have been thinking of); ~
denk je? what are you thinking of?;
waar'achter, '**waarachter** 1 (v. z a k e n)
behind which; 2 (v. p e r s o n e n) behind
whom
waa'rachtig I *aj* true, veritable; **II** *ad* truly,
really; ~*!* surely, certainly!; ~*?* is it true?; ~
niet! 1 certainly not; 2 indeed I won't!; *ik weet*
het ~ *niet!* (I am) sure I don't know!; *en daar*
ging hij me ~ *weg!* and he actually went away;
daar is hij ~*!* sure enough, there he is; **–heid** *v*
truth, veracity
waar'bij, '**waarbij** by which, by what,
whereby, whereat &; on which occasion,
[accident] in which [people were killed]
'**waarborg** (-en) *m* guarantee, warrant, security;
'**waarborgen** (waarborgde, h. gewaarborgd)
vt guarantee, warrant; ~ *tegen* secure against;
'**waarborgfonds** (-en) *o* guarantee fund;
–kapitaal (-talen) *o* guarantee capital; **–maat-**
schappij (-en) *v* insurance company; **–som**
(-men) *v* security; deposit

waar'boven, 'waarboven above (over) which, above (over) what, above (over) whom

1 waard (-en) *m* 1 innkeeper, landlord, host; 2 🐝 = *woerd*; *zoals de ~ is, vertrouwt hij zijn gasten* you (they) measure other people's cloth by your (their) own yard; *buiten de ~ rekenen* reckon without one's host

2 waard (-en) *v* 1 holm; 2 polder

3 waard I *aj* worth; *het is geen antwoord ~* it is not worthy of a reply; *het aanzien niet ~* not worth looking at; *het is de moeite niet ~* it is not worth (your, our) while, it is not worth it (the trouble); *dank u! – het is de moeite niet ~!* it is no trouble (at all), don't mention it!; *het is niet veel ~* it is not worth much; *het is niets ~* it is worth nothing; *dat is al heel wat ~* that's worth a good deal; *ik geef die verklaring voor wat ze ~ is* for what it may be worth; *hij was haar niet ~* he was not worthy of her; *~e vriend* dear friend; *W~e heer* Dear Sir; **II** *m mijn ~e!* (my) dear friend

'waarde (-n) *v* 1 worth, value; 2 (b e d r a g v. o n d e r d e e l) denomination [of coins, of stamps]; *~n* $ stocks and shares, securities; *aangegeven ~* declared value; *belastbare ~* ratable value; *~ in rekening* $ value in account; *~ genoten* $ value received; *belasting over de toegevoegde ~* zie *BTW*; *~ hebben* be of value; *veel (weinig) ~ hebben* have much (little) value; *~ hechten aan* set value on, attach (great) value to; *zijn ~ ontlenen aan…* owe its value to…; ● *in ~ houden* value; *in ~ stijgen* increase in value, go up; *in ~ verminderen* 1 fall in value; 2 (v. g e l d) depreciate; *n a a r ~ schatten* judge [sth.] by its true merits; *o n d e r d e ~ verkopen* sell for less than its value; *t e r ~ van, t o t e e n ~ van* to the value of; *v a n ~* of value, valuable; *dingen van ~* things of value, valuables; *van geen ~* of no value, valueless, worthless; *van gelijke ~* of the same value; *van grote ~* of great value, valuable; *van nul en gener ~* null and void; *van weinig ~* of little value; **–bepaling** (-en) *v* valuation; **–bon** (-nen en -s) *m* (a l s g e s c h e n k) gift token; (v o o r g r a t i s m o n s t e r) gift voucher; **waar'deerbaar** valuable, appreciable; **'waardeleer** *v filos* axiology; **–loos** worthless; **waarde'loosheid** *v* worthlessness; **'waardemeter** (-s) *m* standard of value; **–oordeel** (-delen) *o* value judg(e)ment; **–papieren** *mv* securities

waar'deren (waardeerde, h. gewaardeerd) *vt* value (at its true worth), appreciate (at its proper value), esteem; value, estimate, appraise [by valuer]; **–d** *aj* (& *ad*) appreciative(ly); **waar'dering** (-en) *v* valuation, estimation, appraisal [by valuer]; appreciation [of sbd.'s worth &]; esteem; (*geen, weinig*) ~ vinden meet with (no, little) appreciation; *met ~ spreken van* speak appreciatingly of; **–scijfer** (-s) *o* rating

'waardeschaal (-schalen) *v* scale of values; **–vast** stable [currency]; **–vermeerdering** (-en) *v* 1 increase in value; 2 [tax on] increment; **–vermindering** (-en) *v* depreciation, fall in value; **–vol** valuable, of (great) value

'waardig I *aj* worthy, dignified; *een ~ zwijgen* a dignified silence; *~ zijn* be worthy of; **II** *ad* [conduct oneself] with dignity; **–heid** (-heden) *v* 1 (h e t w a a r d z ij n) worthiness; 2 (v a n h o u d i n g &) dignity; 3 (a m b t) dignity; *de menselijke ~* human dignity; *het is b e n e d e n zijn ~* it is beneath his dignity, it is beneath him; *i n a l zijn ~* in all his dignity; *m e t ~* with dignity; **–heidsbekleder** (-s) *m* dignitary

waar'dij *v* worth, value

waar'din (-nen) *v* landlady, hostess

waar'door, 'waardoor 1 through which; 2 by which, by which means, whereby; **waar'heen, 'waarheen** where, where… to, to what place, ↖ whither

'waarheid (-heden) *v* truth; *de zuivere ~* the truth and nothing but the truth; *een ~ als een koe* a truism; *de ~ spreken* speak the truth; *de ~ zeggen* tell the truth, be truthful; *iem. (ongezouten, vierkant) de ~ zeggen* tell sbd. some home truths, give sbd. a piece of one's mind; *om de ~ te zeggen* to tell the truth; ● *dat is dichter b ij de ~* that is nearer the truth; *n a a r ~* truthfully; truly; **waarheid'lievend, –'minnend** truthloving, truthful, veracious; **'waarheidsgetrouw** truthful, faithful, true, factual; **–liefde** *v* love of truth, truthfulness, veracity; **–serum** *o* truth serum; **–zin** *m* sense of truth

waa'rin, 'waarin in which, ☉ wherein; **waar'langs, 'waarlangs** past which, along which

'waarlijk truly, indeed, sure enough, upon my word, ☉ in truth, of a truth

'waarmaken (maakte 'waar, h. 'waargemaakt) *vt zich ~* prove oneself; prove to come up to expectations

waar'me(d)e, 'waarme(d)e with which; with whom

'waarmerk (-en) *o* stamp; hallmark [on metal objects]; **'waarmerken** (waarmerkte, h. gewaarmerkt) *vt* stamp, authenticate, attest, certify, validate; hallmark [metal objects]; **–king** *v* stamping, authentication

waar'na after which, whereupon; **waar'naar, 'waarnaar** to which; **waar'naast, 'waarnaast** beside which, by the side of which, next to which &

waar'neembaar perceptible; **–heid** *v* percepti-

bility; **'waarnemen** (nam 'waar, h. 'waarge-
nomen) **I** *vt* 1 (m e t h e t o o g &) observe,
perceive; 2 (g e b r u i k m a k e n v a n) avail
oneself of, take [the opportunity]; 3
(u i t v o e r e n) perform [one's duties]; *hij neemt
de betrekking waar* he fills the place temporarily;
II *va* 1 observe; 2 fill a place temporarily; act
(as a deputy, as a substitute) for, deputize for;
act as a locum tenens, stand in [for a doctor or
clergyman]; **–d** acting, deputy, temporary;
'waarnemer (-s) *m* 1 (d i e w a a r n e e m t)
observer; 2 (p l a a t s v e r v a n g e r) deputy,
locum tenens [of doctor or clergyman], substitute; **'waarneming** (-en) *v* 1 observation;
perception; 2 performance [of duties]; **'waar-
nemingsfout** (-en) *v* observational error;
–post (-en) *m* observation post; **–vermogen** *o*
1 perceptive faculty; 2 power(s) of observation
waar'nevens next to which; **waa'rom,
'waarom I** *cj* why, ⊙ wherefore; **II** *o het* ∼ the
why (and wherefore); **'waaromtrent,
waarom'trent** about which; **waa'ronder,
'waaronder** 1 under which; 2 among whom;
including...; **waar'op, 'waarop** 1 on which; 2
upon which, after which, whereupon;
waar'over, 'waarover across which; *fig* about
which
waar'schijnlijk I *aj* probable, likely; **II** *ad*
probably; *hij zal* ∼ *niet komen* ook: he is not
likely to come; **waar'schijnlijkheid** (-heden)
v probability, likelihood; *naar alle* ∼ *zal hij...* in
all probability (likelihood) he will...; **–sreke-
ning** *v* theory (calculus) of probabilities
'waarschuwen (waarschuwde, h. gewaarschuwd) **I** *vt* warn, admonish, caution; (e e n
s e i n g e v e n) let [sbd.] know, tell;
(r o e p e n) call [a doctor], alarm [the police];
∼ *voor (tegen)* caution against, warn of [a
danger], warn against [person or thing]; *wees
gewaarschuwd!* take my warning!, let this be a
warning to you!; **II** *va* warn; **–d I** *aj* warning;
II *ad* warningly; **'waarschuwing** (-en) *v* 1
warning, admonition, caution; 2 [tax-
collector's] summons for payment; **'waar-
schuwingsbord** (-en) *o* notice-board, danger-
board; **–commando** ('s) *o* cautionary word of
command; **–schot** (-schoten) *o* warning shot
waar'tegen, 'waartegen against which;
waar'toe, 'waartoe for which; ∼ *dient dat?*
● what's the good?; **waar'tussen, 'waartussen**
between which, between whom; **waar'uit,
'waaruit** from which, whence; **waar'van,
'waarvan** of which, ⊙ whereof; **waar'voor,
'waarvoor** for what; ∼? what for?, for what
purpose?
'waarzeggen (waarzegde, h. gewaarzegd,
waargezegd) *vi* tell fortunes; *iem.* ∼ tell sbd.'s

fortune; *zich laten* ∼ have one's fortune told;
–er (-s) *m* fortune-teller, soothsayer; **waar-
zegge'rij** (-en), **'waarzegging** (-en) *v*
fortune-telling, soothsaying; **–zegster** (-s) *v*
fortune-teller, soothsayer
waas *o* 1 haze [in the air]; 2 bloom [of fruit]; 3
mist [before one's eyes]; 4 *fig* air [of secrecy]
wacht (-en en -s) *m & v* 1 watch, guard; 2 clue
[of an actor]; *de* ∼ *aflossen* ✠ relieve guard; ⚓
relieve the watch; *de* ∼ *betrekken* ✠ mount
guard; *de* ∼ *gaan op* watch; *de* ∼ *hebben* ✠ be on
guard; ⚓ be on watch; *de* ∼ *houden* keep watch;
de ∼ *overnemen* ✠ take over guard; ⚓ take over
the watch; *de* ∼ *in het geweer roepen* ✠ turn out
the guard; ● *in de* ∼ *slepen* walk away with,
spirit away; *in de* ∼ *zijn* be on night-duty [of
nurses]; *op* ∼ *staan* ✠ be on duty, stand guard;
–dienst *m* ✠ guard-duty; ⚓ watch
'wachten (wachtte, h. gewacht) **I** *vi* wait; *wacht
even!* just a moment!; *wacht (even), je vergeet dat...*
wait a bit! you forget that...; *wacht (jij) maar!*
just wait!, you wait!; *dat kan* ∼ it can wait; *iem.
laten* ∼ keep sbd. waiting; > leave sbd. to cool
his heels; *give sbd. a long wait; *staan* ∼ be
waiting; *wat u te* ∼ *staat* what awaits you, what
is in store for you; ∼ *met iets tot...* wait to...
till..., delay ...ing till...; ∼ *met het eten op vader*
wait dinner for father; ∼ *met schieten* wait to
fire; ∼ *o p* wait for; *hij laat altijd op zich* ∼ he
always has to be waited for; *u hebt lang op u
laten* ∼ you have given us a long wait; **II** *vt*
wait for [letter, visitors &]; *zij heeft geld te* ∼ *van
een oom* she has expectations from an uncle of
hers; *wat u wacht* what awaits you, what is in
store for you; **III** *vr zich* ∼ be on one's guard;
zich wel ∼ *o m... * know better than to...; *zich* ∼
v o o r iets be on one's guard against sth.; *wacht u
voor zakkenrollers!* beware of pickpockets!; **–er**
(-s) *m* 1 watchman, keeper; 2 satellite [of a
planet]
'wachtgeld (-en) *o* half-pay; **–gelder** (-s) *m*
official on half-pay; **–hebbend** on duty;
–huisje (-s) *o* 1 ✠ sentry-box; 2 [tram, bus]
shelter; **–kamer** (-s) *v* 1 waiting-room; ook: [a
doctor's] ante-room; 2 ✠ guard-room [for
soldiers]; **–lijst** (-en) *v* waiting-list; **–lokaal**
(-kalen) *o* ✠ guard-room; **–meester** (-s) *m*
sergeant; **–parade** (-s) *v* guard-mounting,
parade for guard; **–post** (-en) *m* guard-post;
–schip (-schepen) *o* ⚓ guard-ship; **–tijd** *m*
waiting time, waiting period; **–toren** (-s) *m*
watch-tower; **–verbod** *o* waiting prohibition;
–vuur (-vuren) *o* watch fire; **–woord** (-en) *o* 1
✠ password, word, countersign, parole; 2
watchword[2]; 3 cue [of an actor]; *het* ∼ *uitgeven*
✠ give the word
wad (-den) *o* shoal, mud-flat; *de Wadden* the

Dutch Wadden shallows

⊙ 'wade (-n) v shroud

'waden (waadde, h. en is gewaad) vi wade

'wadjan (-s) m wok

'wadlopen o wading in the mud-flats

waf (waf)! bow-wow!

'wafel (-s en -en) v waffle; (d u n) wafer; hou je ~ F shut your head!, shut up!; –bakker (-s) m waffle-baker; –doek 1 o & m (s t o f n a a m) honeycomb cloth; 2 (-en) m (v o o r w e r p s-n a a m) honeycomb towel; –ijzer (-s) o waffle-iron; –kraam (-kramen) v & o waffle-baker's booth; –stof v honeycomb cloth

1 'wagen (waagde, h. gewaagd) I vt risk, hazard, venture, dare; het ~ venture [to go &]; er alles aan ~ risk one's all; er een gulden aan ~ venture a guilder on it; hij durft alles ~ he is ready for any venture; daar waag ik het op I'll risk it, I'll take my chance of it; waag het niet! don't you dare!; hij zal het niet ~ he won't venture (up)on doing it (to do it); hoe durft u 't ~? how dare you (do it)?; wie het waagt hem tegen te spreken who should venture upon contradicting him; ze zijn aan elkaar gewaagd they are well matched, it is diamond cut diamond; zijn leven ~ risk (venture) one's life; II vr zich ~ aan iets venture on sth., take the risk; zich aan een voorspelling ~ venture on a prophecy; zich op het ijs ~ venture upon the ice, zie ook: ijs; III va die niet waagt, die niet wint nothing venture, nothing have

2 'wagen (-s) m (v o e r t u i g) vehicle; (r ij t u i g) [railway] carriage, [state] coach; (v r a c h t w a g e n) waggon, wagon, [delivery, goods] van, [flat, open] truck; (k a r) [milk-, hand-] cart; [tram-, motor-] car; ✎ & ⌨ chariot; (v. s c h r ij f m a c h i n e) carriage; de Wagen ★ Charles's Wain; krakende ~s duren (lopen) het langst creaking doors hang (the) longest, cracked pots last longest; –as (-sen) v axle-tree; –bestuurder (-s) m driver; –huis (-huizen) o cart-shed, coach-house; –maker (-s) m 1 cartwright, wheelwright; 2 coach-builder; wagenmaker'rij (-en) v 1 cartwright's (wheelwright's) shop; 2 coach-builder's shop; 'wagenmenner (-s) m driver, ⊙ charioteer; –park (-en) o 1 = autopark; 2 (r o l l e n d m a t e r i a a l) rolling-stock, (p l a a t s d a a r-v o o r) rolling-stock depot; 3 ⚔ artillery park, wagon park; –rad (-raderen) o carriage-wheel, cartwheel; –schot o wainscot; –smeer o & m cart-grease; –spoor (-sporen) o rut, track; –vol v, –vracht (-en) v cart-load, wagon-load; –wijd (very) wide; –ziek carsick, trainsick

'waggelen (waggelde, h. en is gewaggeld) vi stagger, totter, reel, waddle [like a duck]; een ~de tafel a rickety table

wa'gon (-s) m carriage [for passengers]; van [for luggage, goods], wag(g)on, truck [for cattle, open or flat]; –lading (-en) v wagon-load, truck-load

'wajang (-s) m wayang [Javanese shadow-play]

wak (-ken) o blow-hole in the ice

'wake (-n) v watch, vigil; 'waken (waakte, h. gewaakt) vi wake, watch; ~ b ij watch by, watch over, sit up with, watch with [the sick]; ~ o v e r watch over, look after; ~ t e g e n (be on one's guard against; ~ v o o r watch over, look after [sbd.'s interests]; ervoor ~ dat... take care that..., see to it that...; –d 1 wakeful, watchful, vigilant; 2 waking; een ~ oog houden op... keep a wakeful (watchful) eye on...; 'waker (-s) m watchman, watcher

'wakker I aj 1 (w a k e n d) awake, waking; 2 (w a a k z a a m) awake, vigilant; 3 (f l i n k) smart, spry; brisk; ~ liggen lie awake; ~ maken wake2, awake2, waken2, wake up2; ~ roepen wake (up), call up2 [a person, an image, memories]; fig evoke [feelings &]; ~ schrikken start from one's sleep; rouse2; hem ~ schudden uit zijn droom rouse him from his dream2; ~ worden wake up2, awake2; II ad smartly; briskly; –heid v spryness; briskness

wal (-len) m 1 ⚓ bank, coast, shore; quay, embankment; 2 ⚔ rampart; ~len onder de ogen bags under the eyes; a a n (de) ~ ashore, on shore; aan ~ brengen land; aan ~ gaan go ashore; aan lager ~ geraken ⚓ get on a lee-shore; fig go downhill, come down in the world, be thrown on one's beam-ends; aan lager ~ zijn [fig] be in low water; v a n de ~ $ ex quay; van de ~ in de sloot out of the frying-pan into the fire; van ~ steken ⚓ push off, shove off; fig start, go ahead; steek maar eens van ~! F fire away!; van twee ~len eten play a double game and take advantage of both sides; –baas (-bazen) m wharfinger, superintendent

'waldhoorn, –horen (-s) m ♪ French horn

'Walenland o Walloon country

Wales [ve.ls] o Wales; van ~ Welsh

walg m loathing, disgust, aversion; een ~ hebben van loathe; 'walgelijk = walglijk; –heid = walglijkheid; 'walgen (walgde, h. gewalgd) vi ik walg ervan I loathe it, I am disgusted at (with) it, it makes me sick; tot je ervan walgt till you become nauseated (disgusted) with it; ik walg van mezelf I loathe myself; iem. doen ~ fill sbd. with disgust, turn sbd.'s stomach; tot ~s toe to loathing; –ging v loathing, disgust, nausea; 'walglijk I aj loathsome, revolting, nauseating, sickening, nauseous, disgusting; II ad disgustingly &; ~ braaf disgustingly good;

~ **zoet** revoltingly sweet; **–heid** *v* loathsome-ness &
wal'halla *o* Valhalla
'walkapitein (-s) *m* landing captain; **–kraan** (-kranen) *v* (lifting) crane
Wal'lonië *o* Wallonia
walm (-en) *m* smoke; **'walmen** (walmde, h. gewalmd) *vi* smoke; **–d, 'walmig** smoky [lamp]
'walnoot (-noten) *v* walnut
'walrus (-sen) *m* walrus
wals (-en) 1 *m* & *v* (d a n s) waltz; ‖ 2 *v* ✕ roller, cylinder; **1 'walsen** (walste, h. gewalst) *vi* ♩ waltz; **2 'walsen** (walste, h. gewalst) *vt* ✕ roll; **walse'rij** (-en) *v* ✕ rolling-mill; **'walsma-chine** [-ma.ʃi.nə] (-s) *v* ✕ rolling-machine; **–tempo** *o* ♩ waltz-time
'walstro *o* ⚘ bedstraw
'walvis (-sen) *m* whale; **–achtig** cetacean; **–baard** (-en) *m* whalebone; **–spek** *o* (whale-) blubber; **–traan** *m* whale-oil, train-oil; **–vaarder** (-s) *m* whaler; **–vangst** *v* whale-fishery, whaling
'wambuis (-buizen) *o* jacket, ⌂ doublet
wan (-nen) *v* winnower, fan
'wanbegrip (-pen) *o* false notion; **–beheer** *o* mismanagement; **–beleid** *o* mismanagement; **–bestuur** *o* misgovernment; **–betaler** (-s) *m* defaulter; **–betaling** (-en) *v* non-payment; *bij* ~ in default of payment; **–bof** *m* bad luck; **'wanboffen** (wanbofte, h. gewanboft) *vi* be down on one's luck
wand (-en) *m* 1 wall; 2 (v. b e r g, s c h i p) side; (v. r o t s, s t e i l) face
'wandaad (-daden) *v* crime, outrage, misdoing
'wandbekleding (-en) *v* wall-lining
'wandel *m fig* conduct, behaviour; *aan (op) de* ~ *zijn* be out for a walk; **–aar** (-s) *m,* **–aarster** (-s) *v* walker; **–dek** (-ken) *o* ⚓ promenade deck; **'wandelen** (wandelde, h. en is gewan-deld) *vi* walk, take a walk; **~d blad** leaf-insect; *de Wandelende Jood* the Wandering Jew; **~de nier** wandering kidney; **~de tak** stick-insect; **'wandelgang** (-en) *m* lobby; **'wandeling** (-en) *v* walk, stroll; *een* ~ *doen* take a walk; *een* ~ *gaan doen (maken)* go for a walk; *in de* ~ *... genoemd* popularly called...; **'wandelkaart** (-en) *v* tourist's map; **–kostuum** (-s) *o* walking-dress [of a lady]; lounge-suit [of a gentleman]; **–pad** (-paden) *o* footpath; **–pier** (-en) *m* promenade pier; **–plaats** (-en) *v* promenade; **–sport** *v* hiking; **–stok** (-ken) *m* walking-stick; **–tocht** (-en) *m* walking tour, hike; **–wagen** (-s) *m* push chair; **–weg** (-wegen) *m* walk
'wandgedierte *o* bugs; **–kaart** (-en) *v* wall-map; **–kalender** (-s) *m* wall-calendar; **–kleed**

(-kleden) *o* (wall) tapestry, arras; **–luis** (-luizen) *v* (bed-)bug; **–plaat** (-platen) *v* ⚐ wall-picture; **–rek** (-ken) *o* rib stalls, wall bars; **–schildering** (-en) *v* mural painting, mural, wall-painting; **–tapijt** (-en) *o* tapestry; **–versiering** (-en) *v* mural decoration
'wanen (waande, h. gewaand) *vt* fancy, think
wang (-en) *v* cheek; **–been** (-deren) *o* cheek-bone
'wangedrag *o* bad conduct, misconduct, misbehaviour; **–gedrocht** (-en) *o* monster; **–geluid** (-en) *o* dissonance, cacophony
'wangunst *v* envy; **wan'gunstig** envious
'wangzak (-ken) *m* cheek-pouch
'wanhoop *v* despair; *uit* ~ in despair; **'wanhoopsdaad** (-daden) *v* act of despair, desperate act; **–kreet** (-kreten) *m* cry of despair; **'wanhopen** (wanhoopte, h. gewan-hoopt) *vi* despair (of *aan*); **wan'hopig** desper-ate, despairing; *iem.* ~ *maken* drive sbd. to despair, drive sbd. mad; ~ *worden* give way to despair; ~ *zijn* be in despair
'wankel unstable, unsteady; rickety [chairs &]; shaky[1]; delicate [health]; **–baar** unstable, unsteady, changeable; ~ *evenwicht* unstable equilibrium; **–baarheid** *v* instability, unsteadi-ness, changeableness; **'wankelen** (wankelde, h. en is gewankeld) *vi* totter[2], stagger[2], shake[2]; *fig* waver, vacillate; *een slag die hem deed* ~ a staggering blow; *aan het* ~ *brengen* stagger[2], shake[2] [the world, his resolution]; *fig* make [him] waver; *aan het* ~ *raken* (begin to) waver[2]; **–ling** (-en) *v* tottering; *fig* wavering, vacila-tion; **wankel'moedig** wavering, vacillating, irresolute; **–heid** *v* wavering, vacillation, irresolution
'wankelmotor (-s en -toren) *m* Wankel engine
'wanklank (-en) *m* discordant sound, disso-nance; *fig* jarring note
wan'luidend dissonant, jarring; **–heid** *v* dissonance
'wanmolen (-s) *m* winnower
wan'neer I *ad* when; **II** *cj* when; (i n d i e n) if; ~ *...ook* whenever
'wannen (wande, h. gewand) *vt* winnow, fan
'wanorde *v* disorder, confusion; *in* ~ *brengen* throw into disorder, confuse, disarrange; **wan'ordelijk** disorderly, in disorder; **–heid** *v* disorderliness; *wanordelijkheden* disturbances
'wanprestatie [-(t)si.] (-s) *v* non-fulfilment, non-performance, default
'wanschapen misshapen, deformed, monstrous; **–heid** *v* deformity, monstrosity
'wanschepsel (-s) *o* monster; **–smaak** (-smaken) *m* bad taste
wan'staltig misshapen, deformed; **–heid** *v* deformity

1 want (-en) *v* (v u i s t h a n d s c h o e n) mitten

2 want *o* 1 ⚓ rigging; 2 (v i s~) nets; *lopend ~* running rigging; *staand ~* standing rigging

3 want *cj* for

'**wanten** *hij weet van ~* he knows the ropes

'**wantoestand** (-en) *m* abuse

'**wantrouwen** (wantrouwde, h. gewantrouwd) **I** *vt* distrust; suspect; **II** *o* distrust (of *in*); suspicion; zie ook: *motie*; **wan'trouwend** = *wantrouwig*; **wan'trouwig I** *aj* distrustful; suspicious; **II** *ad* distrustfully; suspiciously; **–heid** *v* distrustfulness; suspiciousness

wants (-en) *v* 🐛 bug

'**wanverhouding** (-en) *v* disproportion; *~en* abuses

'**wapen** (-s) *o* 1 (ook: -en) weapon, arm; 2 arm of service, arm; 3 ⊘ arms, coat of arms; *het ~ der infanterie, artillerie* ook: the infantry, artillery arm; *de ~s dragen* bear arms; *de ~s (~en) opnemen of opvatten* take up arms; • *b ij welk ~ dient hij?* in what arm is he?; *hoog i n zijn ~ zijn* be very proud; *o n d e r de ~s komen* ✕ join the army; *onder de ~s roepen* ✕ call up; *onder de ~s staan (zijn)* ✕ be under arms; *t e ~!* to arms!; *te ~ snellen* spring to arms; **–boek** (-en) *o* ⊘ armorial; **–broeder** (-s) *m* brother in arms, companion in arms, comrade in arms, fellow-soldier; **–drager** (-s) *m* ▯ armour-bearer, squire; '**wapenen** (wapende, h. gewapend) **I** *vt* arm; **II** *vr zich ~* arm oneself, arm; *zich ~ tegen* arm against²; '**wapenfabriek** (-en) *v* arms factory; **–fabrikant** (-en) *m* arms manufacturer; **–feit** (-en) *o* feat of arms; **–gekletter** *o* clash (clang, din) of arms; **–geweld** *o* force of arms; **–handel** *m* 1 ✕ use of arms; 2 $ trade in arms, > arms traffic; **–handelaar** (-s) *m* arms dealer; **–industrie** *v* armaments industry; '**wapening** *v* ✕ arming, armament, equipment; '**wapenkamer** (-s) *v* armoury; **–koning** (-en) *m* king-of-arms; **–kreet** (-kreten) *m* war-cry; **–kunde** *v* ⊘ heraldry; **wapen'kundig** ⊘ 1 heraldic; 2 versed in heraldry; **–e** (-n) *m* ⊘ heraldist; '**wapenmagazijn** (-en) *o* arsenal; **–rek** (-ken) *o* arm-rack; **–rok** (-ken) *m* 1 ✕ tunic; 2 ▯ coat of mail; **–rusting** (-en) *v* ▯ (suit of) armour; **–schild** (-en) *o* ⊘ escutcheon, scutcheon, armorial bearings, coat of arms; **–schouwing** (-en) *v* review; **–smid** (-smeden) *m* armourer; **–smokkelarij** *v* gun-running; **–spreuk** (-en) *v* device; **–stilstand** *m* armistice; **–stok** (-ken) *m* truncheon, baton; **–tuig** *o* weapons, arms; **–zaal** (-zalen) *v* armoury

'**wapperen** (wapperde, h. gewapperd) *vi* wave, float, fly, flutter, stream

war *v i n de ~* tangled, in a tangle, in confusion, confused; *iem. in de ~ brengen* put sbd. out,

confuse sbd.; *in de ~ gooien* zie *in de ~ sturen*; *in de ~ maken* 1 (p e r s o n e n) confuse, disconcert; 2 (d i n g e n) disarrange, muddle up [things]; tangle [threads, hair]; tumble, rumple [clothes, hair]; *in de ~ raken* 1 (v. p e r s o n e n) be put out; 2 (v. d i n g e n) get entangled [of thread &], get mixed up, be thrown into confusion [of things]; *in de ~ sturen* derange [plans]; upset, spoil [everything]; *de boel in de ~ sturen* ook: make a mess of it; *een openbare bijeenkomst in de ~ sturen* break up a public meeting; *in de ~ zijn* 1 (v. p e r s o o n) be confused, be at sea; be (mentally) deranged; 2 (v. d i n g e n) be in confusion, be in a tangle, be at sixes and sevens; *mijn maag is in de ~* my stomach is out of order, is upset; *het weer is in de ~* the weather is unsettled; *u i t de ~ halen* disentangle

wa'rande (-n) *v* park, pleasure-grounds

wa'ratje = *waarachtig* **II**

'**warboel** (-en) *m* confusion, muddle, mess, tangle, mix-up

ware zie *waar*

wa'rempel = *waarachtig* **II**

1 'waren *mv* wares, goods, commodities

2 'waren (waarde, h. gewaard) *vi* = *rondwaren*

3 'waren V.T. meerv. v. *wezen, zijn*

'**warenhuis** (-huizen) *o* department store(s), stores; **–wet** *v* food and drugs act

'**warhoofd** (-en) *o* & *m-v* scatter-brain, muddle-head; **war'hoofdig** scatter-brained, muddle-headed

'**warhoop** (-hopen) *m* confused heap

wa'ringin (-s) *m* 🌿 1 banyan (tree) [Ficus Benjamina]; 2 pagoda tree [Ficus religiosa]

'**warkruid** *o* dodder

warm I *aj* warm² [food &, friend, partisan, thanks, welcome], hot² [water &]; *~e baden* 1 hot baths; 2 thermal baths; *~e bron* thermal spring; *je bent ~! sp* you are warm (hot)!; *het wordt ~* 1 it is getting warm; 2 the room is warming up; *het ~ hebben* be warm; *het eten ~ houden* keep dinner warm; *iem. ~ maken voor iets* rouse sbd.'s interest in sth., make sbd. enthusiastic for sth.; **II** *ad* warmly², hotly²; *~ aanbevelen* recommend warmly; *het zal er ~ toegaan* it will be hot work; **warm'bloedig** warm-blooded; '**warmen** (warmde, h. gewarmd) **I** *vt* warm, heat; **II** *vr zich ~ (aan)* warm oneself (at); *warm je eerst eens* have a warm first; '**warmlopen** (liep 'warm, is 'warmgelopen) *vi* ✕ run hot, heat; *fig* warm up, warm [to one's work]; kindle to

warmoeze'rij (-en) *v* market-garden

'**warmpjes** = *warm* **II**; zie ook: *inzitten*;

'**warmte** *v* warmth², heat, ardour²; *b ij zulk een ~* in such hot weather, in such a heat; *m e t ~ (verdedigen &)* warmly; **–besparend** heat

saving; **–bron** (-nen) *v* source of heat;
–ëenheid (-heden) *v* heat unit, thermal unit,
calorie; **–geleider** (-s) *m* conductor of heat;
–geleiding (-en) *v* conduction of heat;
–graad (-graden) *m* degree of heat; **–ïsolatie**
[-ï.zo.la.(t)si.] *v* heat insulation; **–leer** *v* theory
of heat, thermodynamics; **–meter** (-s) *m*
thermometer; calorimeter; **–ontwikkeling** *v*
development of heat; **–techniek** *v* heat
engineering; **~-uitslag** *m* heat rash, prickly
heat; **warm'waterkraan** (-kranen) *v* hotwater
tap (cock); **–kruik** (-en) *v* hot-water bottle;
–reservoir [-re.zɪrvʋaː r] (-s) *o* (water-)heater;
–zak (-ken) *m* hot-water bag
'warnet (-ten) *o* maze, labyrinth
'warrelen (warrelde, h. gewarreld) *vi* whirl;
–ling (-en) *v* whirl(ing); **'warrelwind** (-en) *m*
whirlwind
'warren (warde, h. geward) *vt door elkaar ~*
entangle
wars *~ van* averse to (from)
'Warschau ['ʋarʃɔu] *o* Warsaw
'wartaal *v* incoherent talk, gibberish
'wartel (-s) *m* swivel
'warwinkel (-s) *m = warboel*
1 was *m* rise [of a river]
2 was *m* & *o* wax; *slappe ~* dubbin(g); *goed in de
slappe ~ zitten* **F** be well-heeled
3 was *m* wash, laundry; *bonte (witte) ~* coloured
(white) washing; *schone ~* clean linen; *vuile ~*
soiled linen; *zij doet zelf de ~* she does the
washing herself; *het blijft goed in de ~* it will
wash; it doesn't shrink in the wash; *in de ~
doen (geven)* put in the wash, send to the
laundry; *de ~ uit huis doen* send the washing out
4 was (waren) V.T. v. *wezen, zijn*
'wasachtig waxy, cereous; **–afdruk** (-ken) *m*
impression in wax
'wasautomaat [-o.to.- of -ɔuto.-] (-maten) *m*
(automatic) washing-machine; **–baar** =
wasecht; **–baas** (-bazen) *m* washerman, laun-
dryman; **–bak** (-ken) *m* (wash-)basin; **–beer**
(-beren) *m* raccoon
'wasbleek waxen
'wasbord (-en) *o* washboard, scrubbing board;
–dag (-dagen) *m* washing-day, wash-day
'wasdoek (-en) *o* & *m* oilcloth
'wasdom *m* growth
'wasecht washable, fast-dyed, fast [colours],
washing [silk, frock]; *is het ~?* does it wash?
'wasem (-s) *m* vapour, steam; **'wasemen**
(wasemde, h. gewasemd) *vi* steam
'wasgeel as yellow as wax
'wasgeld (-en) *o* 1 laundry charges, washing-
money; 2 laundry allowance; **–goed** *o*
washing, laundry; **–handje** (-s) *o* washing-
glove, flannel; **–hok** (-ken), **–huis** (-huizen) *o*

wash-house; **–inrichting** (-en) *v* laundry
'waskaars (-en) *v* wax candle, taper
'waskan (-nen) *v* ewer, jug; **–ketel** (-s) *m*
wash-boiler; **–klem** (-men) *v = wasknijper*
'waskleur *v* wax colour; **–ig** wax-coloured
'wasknijper (-s) *m* clothes-peg, clothes-pin;
–kom (-men) *v* wash-basin, wash-hand basin;
–kuip (-en) *v* washing-tub, wash-tub; **–lapje**
(-s) *o* face-cloth, flannel
'waslicht (-en) *o* wax-light
'waslijn (-en) *v* clothes-line; **–lijst** (-en) *v*
wash-list, laundry list; **–lokaal** (-kalen) *o*
wash-room
'waslucifer (-s) *m* wax-match, (wax-)vesta
'wasmachine [-ma.ʃi.nə] (-s) *v* washing-
machine; **–man** (-nen) *m* washerman, laun-
dryman; **–mand** (-en) *v* laundry-basket;
–merk (-en) *o* laundry mark; **–middel** (-en) *o*
detergent
'waspitje (-s) *o* night-light
'waspoeder, –poeier (-s) *o* & *m* washing-
powder
1 'wassen* *vi* 1 (g r o e i e n) grow; 2 rise [of a
river]; *de maan is aan het ~* the moon is on the
increase (is waxing)
2 'wassen* *vt* wax
3 'wassen* I *vt* 1 wash [one's hands, dirty linen
&]; 2 wash up [plates]; 3 shuffle [cards, dom-
inoes]; **II** *va* wash [for a living], take in
washing; **III** *vr zich ~* wash oneself; wash
[before dinner &]
4 'wassen *aj* wax(en); **wassen'beeld** (-en) *o*
wax figure, dummy; **–enspel** (-len) *o* waxwork
show, waxworks
'wasser (-s) *m* washer; **wasse'rij** (-en) *v* laun-
dry(-works); *automatische ~* launderette;
'wasstel (-len) *o* toilet-service, toilet-set;
–tafel (-s) *v* wash-hand basin, wash-hand
stand; *vaste ~* fitted wash-basin; **–tobbe** (-n en
-s) *v* washing-tub, wash-tub; **–verzachter** (-s)
m (fabric) softener, softening agent; **–voorschrift** (-en) *o* washing instructions; **–vrouw**
(-en) *v* washerwoman, laundress; **–water** *o*
wash-water, washing-water
wat I *vragend vnmw* 1 (i n v r a g e n d e
z i n n e n) what; *~ is er?* what is the matter?; *~
zegt hij?* what does he say?; *mooi, ~?* fine, what?
~ nieuws? what news?; *~ voor een man is hij?*
what man (what sort of man) is he?; *ik weet ~
voor moeilijkheden er zijn* I know what difficulties
there are; *~, meent u het?* what, do you really
mean it?; *wel, ~ zou dat?* well, what of it?,
what's the odds?; *en al zijn we arm, ~ zou dat?*
what though we are poor?; *en ~ al niet* and
what not; 2 (i n u i t r o e p e n d e z i n n e n)
what; *~ een mooie bomen!* what fine trees!; *~ een
idee!* what an idea!; *~ was ik blij!* how glad

I was!; ~ *liepen ze!* how they did run!; ~ *mooi* & *!* how fine!; ~ *dan nog!* so what!; *weet je ~?, we gaan...* you know what (I'll tell you what), let's...; **II** *onbep. vnmw.* something; *het is me ~!* it is something awful!; *ja, jij weet ~!* **F** fat lot you know!; ~ *je zegt!* as you say!, indeed!; *hij zei ~* he said something; ~ *hij ook zei, ik...* whatever he said I...; *voor ~ hoort ~* nothing for nothing; ~ *nieuws* something new; ~ *papier* some paper; **III** *betr. vnmw.* what; which; that; *alles ~ ik heb* all (that) I have; *doe ~ ik zeg* do as I say; *hij zei dat hij het gezien had,* ~ *een leugen was* he said he had seen it, which was a lie; **IV** *ad* 1 (e e n b e e t j e) a little, somewhat, slightly, rather; 2 (h e e l e r g) very, quite; *hij was ~ beter* a little better; *hij was ~ blij* he was very glad, **F** that pleased; *het is ~ leuk* awfully funny; *heel ~ last* a good deal (a lot) of trouble; *heel ~ mensen* a good many (quite a few) people; *dat is heel ~* that is quite a lot, that is saying a good deal; *het scheelt heel ~* it makes quite a difference; *hij kent vrij ~* he knows a pretty lot of things
wat'blief? 1 (b ij n i e t v e r s t a a n) beg pardon?; 2 (b ij v e r b a z i n g) what did you say?, what?
'water (-s en -en) *o* water; (w a t e r z u c h t) dropsy; *de ~en van Nederland* the waters of Holland; *stille ~s hebben diepe gronden* still waters run deep; *het ~ komt je ervan in je mond* it makes your mouth water; *Gods ~ over Gods akker laten lopen* let things drift, let things take their course; *er zal nog heel wat ~ door de Rijn lopen, eer het zover is* much water will have to flow under the bridge; *er valt ~* it is raining; ~ *en melk [fig]* milk and water; *ze zijn als ~ en vuur* they are at daggers drawn; ~ *in zijn wijn doen* water one's wine; *fig* climb down; ~ *naar (de) zee dragen* carry coals to Newcastle; *het ~ hebben* suffer from dropsy; *het ~ in de knieën hebben* have water on the knees; ~ *inkrijgen* 1 (d r e n k e - l i n g) swallow water; 2 *↨* (s c h i p) make water; ~ *maken ↨* make water; ~ *treden* tread water; ● *bij laag* ~ at low water, at low tide; *het hoofd (zich) b o v e n* ~ *houden* keep one's head above water; *hij is weer boven* ~ he is above water again; *weer boven ~ komen* turn up again; *i n het ~ vallen* fall into the water; *fig* fall to the ground, fall through; *in troebel ~ vissen* fish in troubled waters; *o n d e r ~ lopen* be flooded; *onder ~ staan* be under water, be flooded; *onder* ~ *zetten* inundate, flood; *o p ~ en brood zetten (zitten)* put (be) on bread and water; *t e ~ gaan, zich te ~ begeven* take the water; *een schip te ~ laten* launch a vessel; *het verkeer te ~* by water; *te ~ en te land* by sea and land; *een diamant (een schurk) v a n het zuiverste* ~ a diamond (a rascal) of the first water

'**waterachtig** watery[2]; –**afstotend** water-repellent; –**afvoer** (-en) *m* water-drainage; –**bak** (-ken) *m* 1 cistern, tank; watertrough [for horses]; 2 urinal; –**ballet** *o* water ballet, *fig* inundation, flood; –**bestendig** waterproof, water-resistant; –**bewoner** (-s) *m* aquatic animal; –**bloem** (-en) *v* aquatic flower; –**bouwkunde** *v* hydraulics, hydraulic engineering; **waterbouw'kundig** hydraulic; –**e** (-n) *m* hydraulic engineer; '**watercloset** [s = z] (-s) *o* water-closet; –**cultuur** (-turen) *v* hydroponics, tankfarming; –**damp** (-en) *m* (water-)vapour; –**deeltje** (-s) *o* water-particle, particle of water; –**dicht** 1 impermeable to water; 2 (v. k l e r e n) waterproof; 3 (v a n b e s c h o t t e n &) watertight; 4 *fig* watertight; ~ *(be)schot* watertight bulkhead; –**dier** *o* aquatic animal; –**drager** (-s) *m* water-carrier; –**droppel** (-s) = *waterdruppel*; –**druk** *m* waterpressure; –**druppel** (-s) *m* drop of water, waterdrop; –**emmer** (-s) *m* water-pail; '**wateren** (waterde, h. gewaterd) **I** *vt* water; **II** *vi* make water, urinate; '**waterfiets** (-en) *m* & *v* pedal boat; –**geest** (-en) *m* water-sprite; –**gehalte** *o* percentage of water; –**gekoeld** water-cooled; –**geneeswijze** *v* hydropathy; –**geus** (-geuzen) *m* ⌂ Water-Beggar; *de watergeuzen* ook: the Beggars of the Sea; –**glas** (-glazen) *o* 1 (o m u i t t e d r i n k e n) drinking-glass, tumbler; (v o o r u r i n e) urinal; 2 (s t o f) water-glass, soluble glass; –**god** (-goden) *m* water-god; –**godin** (-nen) *v* naiad, nereid; –**golf** (-golven) *v* set, waterwave; '**watergolven** (watergolfde, h. gewatergolfd) *vt* set, water-wave; *wassen en* ~ wash and set; '**waterhoen** (-ders) *o ⚥* water-hen; –**hoofd** (-en) *o* hydrocephalus; *hij heeft een* ~ he has water on the brain; –**hoos** (-hozen) *v* water-spout; –**houdend** aqueous; –**huishouding** *v* water-balance; –**ig** watery[2]; –**igheid** *v* wateriness[2]; –**juffer** (-s) *v* dragon-fly; –**kan** (-nen) *v* ewer, jug; –**kanon** (-nen) *o* water-cannon; –**kant** (-en) *m* water's edge, waterside; –**karaf** (-fen) *v* water-bottle; –**kering** (-en) *v* weir, dam; –**kers** (-en) *v* watercress; –**ketel** (-s) *m* water-kettle; –**koeling** *v* watercooling; *motor met* ~ water-cooled engine; –**kolom** (-men) *v* column of water; –**kom** (-men) *v* bowl, water-basin; –**koud** damp cold; –**kraan** (-kranen) *v* water-tap, watercock; –**kracht** *v* water-power; –**krachtcentrale** (-s) *v* hydro-electric power-station; –**kruik** (-en) *v* pitcher; –**kuur** (-kuren) *v* water-cure, hydropathic cure; –**laarzen** *mv* waders; –**landers** *mv* tears; *de ~ kwamen voor de dag* he turned on the waterworks; –**leiding** (-en) *v* waterworks; aqueduct; *er is geen ~ (in* *huis*) there is no piped water, no water-supply; **–leidingbuis** (-buizen) *v* conduit-pipe, water-pipe; **–lelie** (-s en -liën) *v* water-lily; **–lijn** (-en) *v* water-line; **–linie** (-s) *v* ♃ & ✕ water-line; **–loop** (-lopen) *m* watercourse; **–loos** waterless; **–lozing** *v* 1 drain(age); 2 urination

'Waterman *m de* ~ ★ Aquarius
'watermassa ('s) *v* mass of water; **–meloen** (-en) *m* &.*v* water-melon; **–merk** (-en) *o* watermark; **–meter** (-s) *m* water-meter; **–molen** (-s) *m* 1 water-mill [worked by water-wheel]; 2 draining-mill; **–nimf** (-en) *v* water-nymph, naiad; **–nood** *m* want of water, water-famine; **–ontharder** (-s) *m* water softener; **–pas I** (-sen) *o* water-level; **II** *aj* level; **–passen** (waterpaste, h. gewaterpast) **I** *vt* level, grade; **II** *va* take the level; **III** *o het* ~ levelling; **–peil** (-en) *o* 1 watermark; 2 (w e r k t u i g) water-gauge; **–pest** *v* water-weed; **–pijp** (-en) *v* water-pipe; **–pistool** (-tolen) *o* water pistol, squirt gun; **–plaats** (-en) *v* 1 urinal; 2 horse-pond; 3 watering-place [for ships]; **–plant** (-en) *v* aquatic plant, water-plant; **–plas** (-sen) *m* puddle; **–pokken** *mv* chicken-pox; **–polo** *o* water-polo; **–pomp** (-en) *v* water pump; **–proef, –proof** ['vòtə-pru.f] **I** *aj* waterproof; **II** (-s) *o* waterproof; **–put** (-ten) *m* draw-well; **–rad** (-raderen) *o* water-wheel; **–rat** (-ten) *v* 1 ⅏ water-vole, water-rat; 2 *fig* water-dog; **–reservoir** [-re.zɪr-vva:r] (-s) *o* water-tank, cistern; **–rijk** watery, abounding with water; **–rot** (-ten) *v* = *waterrat*; **–salamander** (-s) *m* newt; **–schade** *v* damage caused by water; **–schap** (-pen) *o* 1 body of surveyors of the dikes; 2 jurisdiction of the water-board; **–scheiding** (-en) *v* watershed, waterparting; **–schouw** *m* inspection of canals; **–schuw** afraid of water; **–schuwheid** *v* hydrophobia; **–ski** 1 ('s) *m* (e e n s k i) water ski; 2 *o* (d e s p o r t) water-skiing; **–skiën** *vi* water-ski; **–skiër** (-s) *m* water-skier; **–slang** (-en) *v* water-snake; **–snip** (-pen) *v* ⚋ snipe; **'watersnood** *m* inundation, flood(s); **'water-spiegel** *m* water-level; **–spin** (-nen) *v* water-spider; **–sport** *v* aquatic sports; **–spuwer** (-s) *m* gargoyle; **–staat** *m* ± Department of Buildings and Roads; **–stand** (-en) *m* height of the water, level of the water, water-level; *bij hoge (lage)* ~ at high (low) water; **–stof** *v* hydrogen; **–stofbom** (-men) *v* hydrogen bomb; **–stofgas** *o* hydrogen gas; **waterstof'peroxyde** [-ɔksi.-də] *o* hydrogen peroxide; **'waterstraal** (-stralen) *m* & *v* jet of water
'watertanden (watertandde, h. gewatertand) *vi het doet mij* ~, *ik watertand ervan* it makes my mouth water; **'watertank** [-tɑŋk] (-s) *m* water-tank, cistern; **–tje** (-s) *o* 1 streamlet; 2

[eye-, hair-]wash; **–tocht** (-en) *m* trip by water, water-excursion; **–toevoer** *m* water supply; **–ton** (-nen) *v* water-cask; **–toren** (-s) *m* water-tower; **–trappen** *vi* tread water; **–val** (-len) *m* (water)fall; cataract; (k l e i n) cascade; *de Niagara* ~ the Niagara Falls; **–vat** (-vaten) *o* water-cask; **–verband** (-en) *o* wet compress; **–verbruik** *o* water consumption; **–verf** (-verven) *v* water-colour(s); **–verontreiniging** *v* water pollution; **–verplaatsing** *v* displacement [of a ship]; **–vlak** *o* sheet of water; **–vlek** (-ken) *v* water-stain; **–vliegtuig** (-en) *o* sea-plane, hydroplane; **–vlo** (-vlooien) *v* water-flea; water-louse; **–vloed** (-en) *m* great flood, inundation; **–vogel** (-s) *m* water-bird, aquatic bird; **–voorziening** *v* water supply; **–vrees** *v* hydrophobia; **–vrij** free from water; **–weg** (-wegen) *m* waterway, water-route; *de Nieuwe Waterweg* the New Waterway; **–werend** water-repellent; **–werken** *mv* 1 bridges, canals, sluices &; 2 fountains, ornamental waters; **–wilg** (-en) *m* water-willow; **–winning** *v* procurement of water; **–zak** (-ken) *m* water-bag; **–zucht** *v* dropsy; **water'zuchtig** dropsical
'watje (-s) *o* wad of cotton-wool
'watjekouw (-en) *m* **F** box on the ear, cuff
1 'watten *mv* 1 wadding [for padding]; 2 cotton-wool [for medical purposes]; *in de* ~ *leggen [fig]* feather-bed, coddle; *met* ~ *voeren* wad, quilt; **2 'watten** *aj* cotton-wool [beard]; **–prop** (-pen) *v* cotton-wool plug
wat'teren (watteerde, h. gewatteerd) *vt* wad, quilt
'wauwelaar (-s) *m,* **–ster** (-s) *v* twaddler, driveller; chatterbox; **'wauwelen** (wauwelde, h. gewauweld) *vi* twaddle, drivel; chatter; **'wauwelpraat** *m* twaddle, drivel, **F** rot
⑨ **wa'xinelichtje** (-s) *o* wax light
'wazig hazy; **–heid** *v* haziness
W.C. [*ve*.'se.] ('s) *v* lavatory, w.c., **F** loo; **W.'C.-papier** *o* toilet-paper
we [və] = *wij*
web (-ben) *o* web
weck *m* 1 preservation; 2 (h e t g e w e c k t e) preserves; **'wecken** (weckte, h. geweckt) *vt* preserve; **'weckfles** (-sen) *v* preserving-bottle; **–glas** (-glazen) *o* preserving-jar
wed (-den) *o* 1 (w a a d p l a a t s) ford; 2 (d r i n k p l a a t s) (horse-)pond, watering-place
wed. = *weduwe*
'wedde (-n) *v* salary, pay
'wedden (wedde, h. gewed) *vi* bet, wager, lay a wager; *durf je m e t me* ~? will you wager anything?; *ik wed met je o m tien tegen één* I'll bet you ten to one; *ik wed met je om 100 pop dat...* I bet (go) you a hundred guilders; *ik wed om wat*

je wil, dat... I'll bet you anything that...; ~ *o p* bet on [a horse &]; *ik zou er niet op durven* ~ I should not like to bet on it; *op het verkeerde paard* ~ put one's money on the wrong horse[2]; *ik wed v a n ja* I bet you it is; *ik wed dat de hele straat het weet* I bet the whole street knows it; **'weddenschap** (-pen) *v* wager, bet; *een* ~ *aangaan* lay a wager, make a bet; *de* ~ *aannemen* take the bet, take the odds; **'wedder** (-s) *m* better, bettor, betting-man

'wede (-n) *v* ⚘ (& v e r f s t o f) woad
1 'weder *o* = 2 *weer*
2 'weder *ad* = 3 *weer*
'wederantwoord (-en) *o* reply
'wederdienst (-en) *m* service in return; *iem. een* ~ *bewijzen* do sbd. a service in return; *(gaarne) tot* ~ *bereid* ready to reciprocate
'wederdoper (-s) *m* anabaptist
'wederga(de) *v* = *weerga*
'wedergeboorte (-n) *v* re-birth, regeneration; **–geboren** born again, reborn, regenerate
'wedergeven[1] = *weergeven*
'wederhelft (-en) *v* **J** better half [= wife]
'wederhoor *o het hoor en* ~ *toepassen* hear both sides
'wederik (-riken) *m* loosestrife
'wederkeren[1] = *weerkeren*
weder'kerend *gram* reflexive; **weder'kerig** *aj* (& *ad*) mutual(ly), reciprocal(ly)[2]; ~ *voornaamwoord gram* reciprocal pronoun; **–heid** *v* reciprocity
'wederkomen[1] = *weerkomen*; **'wederkomst** *v* 1 return; 2 second coming [of Christ]
'wederkrijgen[1] = *weerkrijgen*
'wederliefde *v* love in return; ~ *vinden* be loved in return
wede'rom 1 (n o g e e n s, o p n i e u w) again, once again, anew, once more, a second time; 2 (t e r u g) back
weder'opbloei *m* revival, reflourish
weder'opbouw *m* rebuilding[2], reconstruction[2]
weder'opleving *v* renaissance
weder'opstanding *v* resurrection
weder'opzeggens *tot* ~ until further notice
'wederpartij (-en) *v* = *tegenpartij*
weder'rechtelijk illegal, unlawful; **–heid** *v* illegality, unlawfulness
weder'spannig ⚖ contumacious; **–heid** *v* ⚖ contumacy
1 weder'varen (wedervoer, h. en is wedervaren) *vi* befall; *wat mij is* ~ what has befallen me, my experiences; zie ook: 2 *recht*
2 'wedervaren *o* adventure(s), experience(s); *zijn* ~ ook: what has (had) befallen him
'wedervergelden (vergold 'weder, h. 'wedervergolden) *vt iem. iets* ~ 1 retaliate upon sbd.; 2 recompense (reward) sbd. for sth.; **–ding** *v*

1 retaliation; 2 recompense, reward
'wederverkoper (-s) *m* retailer, retail dealer
'wedervinden[1] = *weervinden*
'wedervraag (-vragen) *v* counter-question
weder'waardigheid (-heden) *v wederwaardigheden* vicissitudes
'wederwoord (-en) *o* answer, reply
'wederwraak = *weerwraak*
'wederzien[1] = *weerzien*
'wederzijds mutual
'wedijver *m* emulation, competition, rivalry; **'wedijveren** (wedijverde, h. gewedijverd) *vi* vie, compete; ~ *m e t* vie with, compete with, emulate, rival; ~ *o m* vie for, compete for; **'wedkamp** (-en) *m* = *wedstrijd*; **–loop** (-lopen) *m* running-match, race[2]; **–ren** (-nen) *m* race; **–strijd** (-en) *m* match, [athletic, beauty] contest, competition; [tennis] tournament; [sailing, ski, sprint] race; **–strijdsport** (-en) *v* competitive sport(s)
'weduwe (-n) *v* widow; *onbestorven* ~ grass widow; **'weduwenfonds** (-en) *o*, **–kas** (-sen) *v* widows' fund; **'weduwnaar** (-s) *m* widower; *onbestorven* ~ grass widower; **–schap** *o* widowerhood; **–vrouw** (-en) *v* widow(-woman)
wee I (weeën) *o* & *v* woe; zie ook: *barensweeën*; **II** *aj* sickly [smell]; ~ *zijn* feel bad, feel sick; faint [with hunger]; **III** *ij* ~ *mij!* woe is me!; ~ *u!* woe be to you!; ~ *je gebeente als...!* unhappy you, if...!; *o* ~*!* o dear!
'weeffout (-en) *v* flaw; **–getouw** (-en) *o* weaving-loom, loom; **–kunst** *v* textile art; **'weefsel** (-s en -en) *o* tissue[2], texture, fabric, weave; **–leer** *v* histology; **'weefspoel** (-en) *v* shuttle; **–ster** (-s) *v* weaver; **–stoel** (-en) *m* loom
'weegbree (-s en -breeën) *v* ⚘ plantain
'weegbrug (-gen) *v* weigh-bridge, weighing-machine; **–haak** (-haken) *m* weigh-beam, steelyard; **–loon** (-lonen) *o* weighage; **–machine** [-ma.ʃi.nə] (-s) *v* weighing-machine
weegs *hij ging zijns* ~ he went his way; *elk ging zijns* ~ they went their separate ways; *een eind* ~ *vergezellen* accompany part of the way
'weegschaal (-schalen) *v* (pair of) scales, balance; *de Weegschaal* ★ Libra
'weeïg sickly
1 week (weken) *v* week; *de volgende* ~ next week; *de vorige* ~ last week; *witte* ~ $ white sale; *de* ~ *hebben* be on duty for the week; ● *d o o r de* ~, *i n de* ~ during the week, on weekdays; *o m de* ~ every week; *om de andere* ~ every other week; *o v e r een* ~ a week hence, in a week; *vandaag (vrijdag &) over een* ~ to-day (Friday) week; *v o o r een* ~ 1 for a week; 2 a week ago

2 week *aj* soft, *fig* soft, tender, weak; *~ maken* soften[2]; *~ worden* soften[2]

3 week *v in de ~ staan* lie in soak; *in de ~ zetten* put in soak

4 week (weken) V.T. v. *wijken*

'**weekbericht** (-en) *o* weekly report; **–beurt** (-en) *v* weekly turn; *de ~ hebben* be on duty for the week; **–blad** (-bladen) *o* weekly (paper); **–dag** (-dagen) *m* week-day

'**weekdier** (-en) *o* mollusc

'**weekend** ['ʋi.kɪnt] (-s en -en) *o* week end; '**weekenden** (weekendde, h. geweekend) *vi* week-end; '**weekendhuisje** (-s) *o* week-end cabin

'**weekgeld** (-en) *o* 1 weekly allowance; 2 weekly pay, weekly wages

week'**hartig** soft-hearted, tender-hearted; **–heid** *v* soft-heartedness, tender-heartedness; '**weekheid** *v* softness

'**weekhuur** (-huren) *v* weekly rent; **–kaart** (-en) *v* weekly ticket

'**weeklacht** (-en) *v* lamentation, lament, wailing; '**weeklagen** (weeklaagde, h. geweeklaagd) *vi* lament, wail; *~ over* lament, bewail

'**weekloon** (-lonen) *o* weekly wages

'**weekmaker** (-s) *m* plasticizer; softener

'**weekmarkt** (-en) *v* weekly market; **–overzicht** (-en) *o* weekly review; **–staat** (-staten) *m* weekly report, weekly return

'**weelde** *v* 1 (l u x e) luxury; 2 (o v e r v l o e d) abundance, opulence, wealth; 3 luxuriance [of vegetation]; 4 (d a r t e l h e i d) wantonness; *een ~ van bloemen* a wealth of flowers; *...is een ~ voor een moeder* ...is the highest bliss to a mother; *ik kan mij die ~ (niet) veroorloven* I can(not) afford it; **–artikel** (-en en -s) *o* article of luxury; *~en* ook: luxuries; **–belasting** *v* luxury tax; '**weelderig** 1 (l u x u e u s) luxurious; 2 (w e l i g t i e r e n d) luxuriant; lush [meadows]; 3 (v o l v a n v o r m) opulent [bosom, nudes]; 4 (d a r t e l) wanton; **–heid** *v* 1 luxuriousness, luxury; 2 luxuriance [of vegetation]; lushness; 3 opulence; 4 wantonness

'**weemoed** *m* sadness, melancholy; wee'**moedig I** *aj* sad, melancholy; **II** *ad* sadly; **–heid** *v* sadness, melancholy

Weens Viennese, Vienna [Congress &], [the Congress] of Vienna

1 weer *v* defence, resistance; *i n de ~ zijn* be busy; be on the go [the whole day]; *zich t e ~ stellen* defend oneself

2 weer *o* weather; *mooi ~* fine weather; *mooi ~ spelen van iems. geld* live in style at sbd.'s expense; *a a n ~ en wind blootgesteld* exposed to wind and weather; *b ij gunstig ~* weather permitting; *i n ~ en wind, ~ of geen ~* in all weathers, rain or shine

3 weer *ad* (o p n i e u w) again; *heen en ~* there and back, to and fro; *over en ~* mutually

'**weerbaar** defensible [stronghold]; [men] capable of bearing arms, able-bodied

weer'**barstig** unmanageable, unruly, refractory

'**weerbericht** (-en) *o* weather-report

'**weerga** *v* equal, match, peer; *hun ~ is niet te vinden* they can't be matched; *a l s de ~!* like blazes!, (as) quick as lightning!; *o m de ~ niet!* Hell, no!; *z o n d e r ~* matchless, unequalled, unrivalled, unparalleled, without precedence

'**weergaaf** = *weergave*

'**weergaas** devilish, deuced

'**weergalm** *m* echo; **weer'galmen**[1] *vi* resound, re-echo, reverberate; *~ van* resound (ring, echo) with

'**weergaloos** matchless, peerless, unequalled, unrivalled, unparalleled

'**weergave** (-n) *v* reproduction; rendering; '**weergeven** (gaf 'weer, h. 'weergegeven) *vt* return, restore; *fig* render [the expression, poetry in other words &]; reproduce [in one's own words, a sound &]; voice [feelings]

'**weerglas** (-glazen) *o* weather-glass, barometer

'**weerhaak** (-haken) *m* barb, barbed hook

'**weerhaan** (-hanen) *m* weather-vane, weathercock[2], *fig* time-server

weer'**houden**[1] **I** *vt* keep back, restrain, check, stop; *dat zal mij niet ~ om* that will not keep me from ...ing; **II** *vr zich ~* restrain oneself; *zich van lachen ~* forbear laughing; *ik kon mij niet ~ het te zeggen* I could not refrain from saying it

'**weerhuisje** (-s) *o* weather-box; **–kaart** (-en) *v* weather chart, weather map

weer'**kaatsen**[1] **I** *vt* reflect [light, sound, heat]; reverberate [sound, light]; (re-)echo [sound]; **II** *vi* be reflected; reverberate; (re-)echo; **–sing** (-en) *v* reflection

'**weerkeren** (keerde 'weer, is 'weergekeerd) *vi* return, come back

'**weerklank** *m* echo[2]; *~ vinden* meet with a wide response; **weer'klinken**[1] *vi* ring again, resound, re-echo, reverberate; *schoten weerklonken* shots rang out

'**weerkomen** (kwam 'weer, is 'weergekomen) *vi* come back, return

'**weerkrijgen** (kreeg 'weer, h. 'weergekregen) *vt* get back, recover

'**weerkunde** *v* meteorology; **weer'kundig**

---

[1] V.T. en V.D. van dit werkwoord volgens het model: **weer'**galmen, V.T. **weer'**galmde, V.D. **weer'**galmd (**ge-** valt dus weg in het V.D.). Zie voor de vormen onder het grondwoord, in dit voorbeeld: *galmen*. Bij sterke en onregelmatige werkwoorden wordt u verwezen naar de lijst achterin.

meteorological; **–e** (-n) *m* weather-man, meteorologist

weer′legbaar refutable; **weer′leggen**[1] *vt* refute; **–ging** (-en) *v* refutation

′**weerlicht** *o* & *m* sheet lightning, heat lightning, summer lightning; *als de* ~ zie *weerga*; ′**weerlichten** (weerlichtte, h. geweerlicht) *vi* lighten [on the horizon]

′**weerloos** defenceless; **–heid** *v* defencelessness

′**weermacht** *v* armed forces; **–middelen** *mv* means of defence

weer′om back; zie ook: *wederom*

weer′omstuit *m* rebound; *van de* ~ *lachen* laugh again

′**weerpijn** (-en) *v* sympathetic pain

weer′plichtig liable to military service

′**weerprofeet** (-feten) *m* weather-prophet; **–satelliet** (-en) *m* weather satellite

′**weerschijn** *m* reflex, reflection; lustre; **weer-** ′**schijnen**[1] *vi* reflect

′**weerschip** (-schepen) *o* weather ship; ′**weers- gesteldheid** (-heden) *v* state of the weather; *de* ~ *(van dit land)* the weather conditions; *bij elke* ~ in all weathers

′**weerskanten** *a a n* ~ on both sides, on either side; *aan* ~ *van* on either side of...; *v a n* ~ from both sides, on both sides

′**weerslag** (-slagen) *m* reaction, revulsion, repercussion

′**weersomstandigheden** *mv* weather conditions

weer′spannig recalcitrant, rebellious, refractory; **–heid** *v* recalcitrance, rebelliousness, refractoriness

weer′spiegelen[1] **I** *vt* reflect, mirror; **II** *vr zich* ~ be reflected, be mirrored; **–ling** (-en) *v* reflection, reflex

weer′spreken[1] *vt* = *tegenspreken*

weer′staan[1] *vt* resist, withstand

′**weerstand** (-en) *m* resistance [of steel, air &, of a person to...]; ☼ resistor; ~ *bieden* offer resistance; ~ *bieden aan* resist; *krachtig* ~ *bieden* make′ (put up) a stout resistance; ′**weer- standskas** (-sen) *v* fighting-fund; **–vermogen** *o* (power of) resistance, endurance, staying power, stamina [of body, a horse], resistibility

′**weerstation** [-(t)ʃon] (-s) *o* weather-station

weer′streven[1] *vt* oppose, resist, struggle against, strive against

′**weersverandering** (-en) *v* change of weather, break in the weather; **–verwachting** (-en) *v* weather-forecast

′**weerszij(den)** = *weerskanten*

′**weertype** [-ti.pə] (-n en -s) *o* weather type

′**weervinden** (vond ′weer, h. ′weergevonden) *vt* find again

′**weervoorspeller** (-s) *m* weather-prophet; **–voorspelling** (-en) *v* weather-forecast

′**weervraag** (-vragen) = *wedervraag*

′**weerwerk** *o* reaction; opposition

′**weerwil** *m in* ~ *van* in spite of, notwithstanding, despite, despite of

′**weerwolf** (-wolven) *m* wer(e)wolf

′**weerwoord** (-en) = *wederwoord*

′**weerwraak** *v* retaliation, revenge

′**weerzien I** (zag ′weer, h. ′weergezien) *vt* see again; **II** *o* meeting again; *tot* ~*s* till we meet again, **F** so long

′**weerzin** *m* aversion, reluctance, repugnance; ~ *tegen* aversion to; **weerzin′wekkend** revolting, repugnant, repulsive

1 wees (wezen) *m-v* orphan

2 wees (wezen) V.T. v. *wijzen*

weesge′groet(je) (-groeten, -groetjes) *o rk* Hail Mary

′**weeshuis** (-huizen) *o* orphans′ home, orphanage; **–jongen** (-s) *m* orphan-boy; **–kamer** (-s) *v* 1 orphans′ court; 2 (i n E n g e l a n d) Court of Chancery; **–kind** (-eren) *o* orphan (child); **–meisje** (-s) *o* orphan-girl; **–moeder** (-s) *v* matron of an orphanage; **–vader** (-s) *m* master of an orphanage

1 weet *v* ~ *van iets hebben* be in the know; *het kind heeft al* ~ *van een en ander* the child takes notice already; *geen* ~ *van iets hebben* not be aware of sth.; *het aan de* ~ *komen* find out

2 weet (weten) V.T. v. *wijten*

′**weetal** (-len) *m* know-all, wiseacre; **weet′gierig** eager for knowledge, inquiring; **–heid** *v* thirst for knowledge; ′**weetje** *o zijn* ~ *weten* know what's what, know one's stuff; ′**weetlust** *m* = *weetgierigheid*; **–niet** (-en) *m* know-nothing, ignoramus

′**weeuwtje** (-s) *o* 1 widow; 2 **✿** = *nonnetje*

1 weg (wegen) *m* way, road, path, route; *fig* way, road, course, channel, path, avenue; *de* ~ *afleggen* cover the distance; *zich een* ~ *banen* hew one's way; *de juiste* ~ *bewandelen* take the right course; *de* ~ *van alle vlees gaan* go the way of all flesh; *zijn eigen* ~ *gaan* go one's own way; *deze* ~ *inslaan* take this road; *een andere* ~ *inslaan* take another road; *fig* take another course; *de slechte* ~ *opgaan* go [morally] wrong; ook: go to the bad; *dezelfde* ~ *opgaan* go the same way[2]; *fig* follow the rest; *het zal zijn* ~ *wel vinden* it is sure to find its way; *hij zal zijn* ~ *wel vinden* he is

[1] V.T. en V.D. van dit werkwoord volgens het model: **weer**′galmen, V.T. **weer**′galmde, V.D. **weer**′galmd (gevalt dus weg in het V.D.). Zie voor de vormen onder het grondwoord, in dit voorbeeld: *galmen*. Bij sterke en onregelmatige werkwoorden wordt u verwezen naar de lijst achterin.

sure to make his way (in the world); *u kunt de ~ wel vinden, niet?* 1 you know your way, don't you?; 2 you know your way out, don't you?; *~ noch steg weten* not know one's way at all; *hij weet ~ met zijn eten, hoor!* he can shift his food!; *geen ~ weten met zijn geld* not know what to do with one's money; *de ~ wijzen* show the way; *fig* point the way; *de ~ naar de hel is geplaveid met goede voornemens* the road to hell is paved with good intentions; *alle ~en leiden naar Rome* all roads lead to Rome; ● *a a n de ~ gelegen* skirting the road, by the roadside; *aan de ~ timmeren* make oneself conspicuous; *altijd b ij de ~ zijn* be always gadding about; be always on the road [of commercial travellers]; *iem. iets i n de ~ leggen* thwart sbd.; *ik heb hem niets (geen strobreed) in de ~ gelegd* I have never given him cause for resentment; *een zaak moeilijkheden in de ~ leggen* put obstacles in the way; *in de ~ lopen* be in the way; *in de ~ staan* be in sbd.'s way; *fig* stand in sbd.'s light; stand in the way of a scheme &; *in de ~ zitten* be in the way, hinder; *fig* bother; *l a n g s de ~* along the road; by the roadside; *langs dezelfde ~* by the same way; *langs deze ~* 1 *[fig]* in this way; 2 through the medium of this paper; *langs diplomatieke ~* through diplomatic channels; *langs gerechtelijke ~* legally, by legal steps; *n a a r de bekende ~ vragen* ask what one knows already; *o p ~* on his (her) way; *op ~ naar* on the way to, destined for; *zich op ~ begeven, op ~ gaan* set out (for *naar*); *iem. op ~ helpen* give sbd. a start; help sbd. on; *het ligt niet op mijn ~* it is out of my way; *fig* it is not my business; *het ligt niet op mijn ~ om...* it is not for me to...; *op de goede (verkeerde) ~ zijn* be on the right (wrong) road; *mooi op ~ zijn om...* be in a fair way to...; *well on the road to...; *u i t de ~!* out of the way there!, away!; *je moet hem uit de ~ blijven* keep out of his way, avoid him, give him a wide berth; *uit de ~ gaan* 1 make way; 2 side-step [an issue, a problem]; *voor iem. uit de ~ gaan* get out of sbd.'s way, make way for sbd.; *daarin ga ik voor niemand uit de ~* in this I don't yield to anybody; *iem. uit de ~ ruimen* make away with sbd., put sbd. out of the way [by poison &]; *moeilijkheden uit de ~ ruimen* remove obstacles, smooth over (away) difficulties; *v a n de goede ~ afgaan* stray from the right path

2 weg I *ad* 1 (niet meer aanwezig) away; 2 (verloren) gone, lost; 3 (vertrokken) gone; *ik ben ~* I'm off; *hij was helemaal ~* 1 he was quite at sea; 2 he was

unconscious; *hij was ~ van haar* he was crazy about her (smitten with her); *dan ben je ~* then you are done for; *mijn horloge is ~* my watch is gone; *~ van iets zijn* be crazy about sth.; **II** *ij ~ wezen!* **S** beat it!, scram!; *~ jullie!* be off!, get out!; *~ daar!* make way there!, get away!; *~ ermee!* away with it!; *~ met die verraders!* down with those traitors!; *~ van hier!* get away!, get out!

'**wegbereider** (-s) *m fig* pioneer
'**wegbergen**[2] *vt* put away, lock up; **–blazen**[2] *vt* blow away; **–blijven**[2] *vi* stay away; **–branden**[2] *vt* burn away; cauterize [a wart]; *[fig] hij is er niet weg te branden* he never leaves the spot; **–breken**[2] *vt* pull down [a wall &]; **–brengen**[2] *vt* take (carry) away [sth.]; see off [sbd.]; remove, march off [a prisoner]; **–cijferen**[2] **I** *vt* eliminate, set aside; leave out of account; **II** *vr zich (zelf) ~* put oneself aside, efface oneself
'**wegdek** (-ken) *o* road surface
'**wegdenken**[2] *vt* think away, eliminate; **–doen**[2] *vt* 1 (wegleggen) put away; 2 (van de hand doen) dispose of, part with; **–dragen**[2] *vt* carry away; *de goedkeuring ~ van* meet with the approval of..., be approved by...; *de prijs ~* bear away the prize; **–drijven**[2] **I** *vt* drive away; **II** *vi* float away; **–dringen**[2] *vt* push away, push aside; **–duiken**[2] *vi* dive, duck (away); *weggedoken in zijn fauteuil* ensconced in his arm-chair; **–duwen**[2] *vt* push aside, push away; **–ebben** (ebde 'weg, is 'weggeëbd) *vi* ebb away
1 'wegen*** **I** *vt* weigh[2] [luggage, 6 tons, one's words]; scale [100 pounds]; poise [on the hand]; **II** *vi* weigh; *hij weegt niet zwaar* he doesn't weigh much; *fig* he is a light-weight; *dat weegt niet zwaar bij hem* that point does not weigh (heavy) with him; *wat het zwaarst is moet het zwaarst ~* first things come first
2 'wegen** *mv v. weg*; **–aanleg** *m* = *weg-bouw*; **–belasting** *v* road-tax; **–bouw** *m* road-making, road-building, road-construction; **–kaart** (-en) *v* road-map; **–net** (-ten) *o* road-system, network of roads; **–plan** *o* road-construction plan
'**wegens** on account of, because of; for [lack of evidence, the murder of]
'**wegverkeersreglement** *o* highway code; **–wacht** 1 *v ±* road patrol, (Automobile Association) scouts; 2 (en) *m* (persoon) *±* (Automobile Association) scout
'**weger** (-s) *m* weigher

'**wegfladderen**² *vi* flutter away, flit away;
–gaan² *vi* go away, leave; *ga weg!* go away!, **F**
buzz off!; *fig ach, ga weg!* (= *ik geloof het niet*) oh,
get along with you!
'**weggebruiker** (-s) *m* road-user; **–geld** (-en) *o*
road-tax, toll
'**weggeven**² *vt* give away; **–glippen**² *vi* slip
away, slip out; **–goochelen**² *vt* spirit away
'**weggooien**² **I** *vt* throw away, chuck away
[sth.]; throw away, waste [money on...];
discard [the eight of clubs &]; *fig* pooh-pooh
[an idea]; **II** *vr zich* ~ throw oneself away
'**weggraaien**², **–grissen**² *vt* snatch, grab
(away); **–graven**² *vt* dig away; **–haasten**² *zich*
~ hasten away, hurry away; **–hakken**² *vt* cut
away, chop away; **–halen**² *vt* take (fetch)
away, remove; **–hebben**² *vt veel van iem.* ~
look much like sbd.; *het heeft er veel van weg,
alsof...* it looks like... [rain &]; **–hollen**² *vi* run
away, scamper away; **–ijlen**² *vi* hurry (hasten)
away
'**weging** *v* weighing
'**wegjagen**² *vt* drive away [beggars, beasts, a
visitor &]; turn [people] out [of doors]; expel
[from office]; send about one's business [of
people]; shoo away [birds]
'**wegkampioen** (-en) *m* cycling champion (on
the road); **–kant** (-en) *m* roadside, wayside
'**wegkapen**² *vt* snatch away, pilfer, filch;
–kappen² *vt* chop away, cut off; **–kijken**² *vt
iem.* ~ freeze sbd. out; **–knippen**² *vt* 1 (m e t
s c h a a r) cut off; 2 (d o o r v i n g e r-
b e w e g i n g) flick away [the ash of a cigar &];
–komen² *vi* get away; *ik maak dat ik wegkom*
I'm off; *ik maakte dat ik wegkwam* I made
myself scarce; *maak dat je wegkomt!* take yourself off!, clear out!; **–krijgen**² *vt* get away; *ik
kon hem niet* ~ I couldn't get him away; *de
vlekken* ~ get out the spots; **–kruipen**² *vi*
creep away, hide away
'**wegkruising** (-en) *v* intersection, cross-roads
'**wegkunnen**² *vi het kan weg* it may be left out, it
may go; *niet* ~ not be able to get away;
–kussen² *vt* kiss away; **–kwijnen** (kwijnde
'weg, is 'weggekwijnd) *vi* languish, pine away;
–lachen² *vt* laugh away, laugh off
'**weglaten**² *vt* leave out, omit; '**weglating** (-en)
v leaving out, omission; *met* ~ *van...* leaving
out..., omitting...; **–steken** (-s) *o* apostrophe
'**wegleggen**² *vt* lay by, lay aside; *dat was niet voor
hem weggelegd* that was not reserved for him;
–leiden² *vt* lead away, march off
'**wegligging** *v* road-holding qualities

'**weglokken**² *vt* entice away, decoy; **–lopen**² *vi*
run away (off); make off; *hij loopt niet zo hoog
weg met dat idee* he is not in favour of the idea;
ze lopen erg met die man weg they are greatly
taken with him, he is a great favourite; *met iem.*
(*hoog*) ~ make much of sbd., think much of
sbd.; *het loopt niet weg, hoor!* there is no hurry!, it
can wait; *het werk loopt niet weg* the work can
wait; **–maaien**² *vt* mow down²; zie ook: *gras*;
–maken² **I** *vt* 1 (i e t s) make away with,
mislay [sth.]; remove, take out [grease-spots]; 2
(i e m.) anaesthetize [a patient]; **II** *vr zich* ~
make off
'**wegmarkering** (-en) *v* road marking
'**wegmoffelen** (moffelde 'weg, h. 'weggemof-
feld) *vt* spirit away
'**wegnemen**² *vt* 1 take away, remove [sth.,
apprehension, doubt]; *fig* do away with [a
nuisance &]; obviate [a difficulty]; 2 steal,
pilfer; *dat neemt niet weg, dat...* that does not
alter the fact that...; **–ming** *v* taking away &,
removal
'**wegomlegging** (-en) *v* diversion; **–opzichter**
(-s) *m* road-surveyor
'**wegpakken**² **I** *vt* snatch away; **II** *vi pak weg 20,
30 jaar geleden* say 20, 30 years ago; **III** *vr zich*
~ take oneself off; *pak je weg!* be off!; **–pesten**²
vt get rid of sbd. by annoying him, **S** freeze
sbd. out; **–pikken**² *vt* peck away; *fig* snatch
away; **–pinken**² *vt een traan* ~ brush away a
tear
'**wegpiraat** (-raten) *m* road-hog
'**wegpromoveren**² *vt* kick sbd. upstairs;
–raken² *vi* be (get) lost; **–redeneren**² *vt*
reason (explain) away
'**wegrenner** (-s) *m sp* road-racer; **–restaurant**
[-rısto:rã] (-s) *o* road-house
'**wegrijden**² *vi* ride away, drive away, drive off;
–roepen² *vt* call away; **–roesten**² *vi* rust away;
–rollen² *vt* & *vi* roll away; **–rotten**² *vi* rot, rot
off
'**wegruimen**² *vt* remove, clear away; **–ming** *v*
removal
'**wegrukken**² *vt* snatch away²; **–schenken**² *vt*
give away; ~ *aan* make [sbd.] a present of;
–scheren² **I** *vt* shave (shear) off; **II** *vr zich* ~
make oneself scarce, decamp; **–scheuren**² **I** *vt*
tear off; **II** *vi* (s n e l w e g r i j d e n) tear away;
–schieten² **I** *vt* shoot away; **II** *vi* dart off;
–schoppen² *vt* kick away; **–schuilen**² *vi* hide
(from *voor*); **–schuiven**² *vt* push away (aside),
shove away; **–slaan**² *vt* beat (strike) away; *de
brug werd weggeslagen* the bridge was swept

---

² V.T. en V.D. van dit werkwoord volgens het model: '**weg**cijferen, V.T. cijferde '**weg**, V.D. '**weg**gecijferd. Zie
voor de vormen onder het grondwoord, in dit voorbeeld: *cijferen*. Bij sterke en onregelmatige werkwoorden wordt u
verwezen naar de lijst achterin.

away; **–slepen**[2] *vt* drag away; ⚓ tow away;
–slikken[2] *vt* swallow[2]; **–slingeren**[2] *vt* fling
(hurl) away; **–sluipen**[2] *vi* steal (sneak) away;
–sluiten[2] *vt* lock up; **–smelten**[2] *vi* melt away,
melt [into tears]; **–smijten**[2] *vt* fling (throw)
away; **–snellen**[2] *vi* hasten away, hurry away;
–snijden[2] *vt* cut away; **–snoeien**[2] *vt* prune
away, lop off; **–spoelen**[2] **I** *vt* wash away; **II** *vi*
be washed away; **–steken**[2] *vt* put away;
–stelen[2] *vt* steal, pilfer; **–stemmen**[2] *vt* vote
[sth. or sbd.] down; **–sterven**[2] *vi* die away, die
down; **–stevenen**[2] *vi* sail away; **–stompen**[2] *vt*
strike (punch, shove) away; **–stoppen**[2] *vt* put
away, tuck away, hide; **–stormen**[2] *vi* gallop
off, tear away; **–stoten**[2] *vt* push away;
–stuiven[2] *vi* fly away [of dust &]; dash away,
rush off [persons]; **–sturen**[2] *vt* send away
[sth.]; dismiss [a servant]; send [sbd.] away;
turn [people] away; ⇔ expel [a boy from
school]; **–teren** (teerde 'weg, is 'weggeteerd)
vi waste away; **–toveren**[2] *vt* spirit away,
conjure away; **–trappen**[2] *vt* kick away;
–trekken[2] **I** *vt* pull (draw) away; **II** *vi* 1 march
away, march off, pull out [of troops]; leave
[here]; 2 blow over [of clouds]; lift [of a fog];
disappear [of a headache]; (b l e e k w o r d e n)
grow pale, lose colour; **–vagen** (vaagde 'weg,
h. 'weggevaagd) *vt* sweep away[2]; wipe out,
blot out [memories &]
'wegvak (-vakken) *o* section of a (the) road
'wegvallen[2] *vi* fall off; *fig* be left out (omitted);
tegen elkaar ~ cancel one another; **–varen**[2] *vi*
sail away; **–vegen**[2] *vt* sweep away [dirt]; wipe
away [tears]; rub out, erase [a written word]
'wegverkeer *o* road traffic; **–vernauwing** (-en)
v road narrowing; **–versmalling** (-en) *v* road
narrowing; **–versperring** (-en) *v* road-block;
–vervoer *o* (road) haulage; **–vervoerder** (-s)
m (road) haulier
'wegvliegen[2] *vi* fly away; *ze vliegen weg* they [the
goods, the tickets] are going (are being
snapped up) like hot cakes; **–vloeien**[2] **I** *vi* flow
away; **II** *o het* ~ the outflow; **–vluchten**[2] *vi*
flee
'wegvoeren[2] *vt* carry off, lead away [a
prisoner]; **–ring** *v* carrying off
'wegvreten[2] *vt* eat away, corrode; **–waaien**[2] **I**
vi be blown away, blow away; **II** *vt* blow away
'wegwals (-en) *v* ⚒ road-roller; **–wedstrijd**
(-en) *m* road-race
'wegwerken[2] *vt* 1 (i n d e a l g e b r a) eliminate; 2 (v. p e r s o n e n) get rid of [a minister
&]; manoeuvre [an employee] away; 3 (v a n

w e r k) clear off [arrears of work]
'wegwerker (-s) *m* road-man; (b ij h e t
s p o o r) surface-man
'wegwerp... disposable [containers, nappies &],
non-returnable [bottles], throw-away [pack-
aging]; **'wegwerpen**[2] *vt* throw away
'wegwijs *iem.* ~ *maken* show sbd. the ropes; ~
zijn know one's way; *fig* know the ropes;
–wijzer (-s) *m* 1 (p e r s o o n) guide; 2 signpost, finger-post; 3 handbook, guide
'wegwippen[2] *vi* whip away, pop away (off);
–wissen[2] *vt* wipe away, wipe off; **–wuiven**[2] *vt*
fig wave aside; **–zakken**[2] *vi* 1 (v. p e r s o n e n,
g r o n d &) sink away; 2 (v. b o d e m) give
way; **–zenden**[2] *vt* = *wegsturen*; **–zetten**[2] *vt* put
away
'wegzijde (-n) *v* roadside, wayside
'wegzinken[2] *vi* sink away; **–zuigen**[2] *vt* suck up
(away); *fig* drain
1 wei *v* 1 whey [of milk]; 2 serum [of blood]
2 wei (-den) = *weide*
'Weichsel *m* Vistula
'weide (-n) *v* meadow; *koeien in de* ~ *doen* (*sturen*)
put (send, turn out) cows to grass; *in de* ~ *lopen*
be at grass; **–grond** (-en) *m* = *weigrond;*
'weiden (weidde, h. geweid) **I** *vi* graze, feed;
zijn ogen (de blik) laten ~ *over* pass one's eyes
over; **II** *vt* tend [flocks]; *zijn ogen* ~ *aan* feast
one's eyes on; **'weiderecht** *o* grazing-rights,
common of pasture
weids stately, grandiose [name]; **–heid** *v*
stateliness, grandiosity
'weifelaar (-s) *m* waverer; **'weifelachtig** =
weifelend; **'weifelen** (weifelde, h. geweifeld) *vi*
hesitate, waver, vacillate; **–d** hesitating,
wavering, vacillating; **'weifeling** (-en) *v*
hesitation, wavering, vacillation;
weifel'moedig wavering, vacillating, irresolute; **–heid** *v* wavering, vacillation, irresolution
'weigeraar (-s) *m* refuser; **'weigerachtig**
unwilling to grant a request; *een* ~ *antwoord
ontvangen* meet with a refusal; ~ *blijven* persist
in one's refusal; ~ *zijn te...* refuse to...;
'weigeren (weigerde, h. geweigerd) **I** *vt* 1
(n i e t w i l l e n) refuse [to do sth., duty]; 2
(n i e t a a n n e m e n) refuse, reject [an offer],
decline [an invitation]; 3 (n i e t t o e s t a a n)
refuse [a request], deny [sb. sth., sth. to sbd.];
II *vi* refuse [of persons]; refuse to act [of
things], fail [of brakes], misfire [of fire-arms, of
an engine]; **–ring** (-en) *v* 1 refusal, denial; <
rebuff; 2 failure [of brakes], misfire [of fire-

---

[2] V.T. en V.D. van dit werkwoord volgens het model: **'weg**cijferen, V.T. cijferde **'weg**, V.D. **'weg**gecijferd. Zie
voor de vormen onder het grondwoord, in dit voorbeeld: *cijferen*. Bij sterke en onregelmatige werkwoorden wordt u
verwezen naar de lijst achterin.

arms]; *ik wil van geen* ~ *horen* I will take no denial

'**weigrond** (-en) *m*, **–land** (-en) *o* meadow-land, grass-land, pasture

'**weinig** 1 (e n k e l v.) little; 2 (m e e r v.) few; ~ *goeds* little good (that is good); ~ *of niets* little or nothing; ~ *maar uit een goed hart* little but from a kind heart; *een* ~ a little; *het* ~ *e dat ik heb* what little (money) I have; *maar* ~ but little; *niet* ~ not a little; *6 stuiver te* ~ six pence short; *al te* ~ too little; *veel te* ~ 1 much too little; 2 far too few; ~*en* few; *maar* ~*en* only a few

weit *v* wheat

'**weitas** (-sen) *v* game-bag

'**wekamine** (-n) *v* amphetamine

'**wekelijk** *aj* (& *ad*) soft(ly), tender(ly), weak(ly), effeminate(ly); **–heid** *v* weakness, effeminacy

'**wekelijks I** *aj* weekly; **II** *ad* weekly, every week

'**wekeling** (-en) *m* weakling

1 '**weken I** (weekte, h. geweekt) *vt* soak [bread in coffee &], put in soak, steep, soften, macerate; **II** (weekte, is geweekt) *vi* be soaking, soak, soften

2 '**weken** V.T. meerv. v. *wijken*

'**wekken** (wekte, h. gewekt) *vt* (a)wake², awaken², (a)rouse²; *fig* ook: evoke, call up [memories]; create [an impression]; raise [expectations]; cause [surprise]; provoke [indignation]; *wek me om 7 uur* call me (knock me up) at seven o'clock; **–er** (-s) *m* 1 (p e r s o o n) caller-up; 2 (w e k k e r k l o k) alarm(-clock)

1 **wel** (-len) *v* spring, well

2 **wel I** *ad* 1 (g o e d) well; rightly; *zij danst* (*heel*) ~ she dances (very) well; *als ik het mij* ~ *herinner* if I remember rightly; 2 (z e e r) very (much); *dank u* ~ thank you very much; *u is* ~ *vriendelijk* it is very kind of you, indeed; 3 (v e r s t e r k e n d) indeed, truly; ~ *een bewijs dat...* a proof, indeed, that...; ~ *ja!* yes, indeed! ~ *neen!* Oh no!, certainly not!; ~ *zeker* yes, certainly, to be sure (I do, I have &); *hij moet* ~ *rijk zijn om...* he must needs be rich to...; *hij zal* ~ *moeten* he will jolly well have to; 4 (n i e t m i n d e r d a n) no less (no fewer) than, as many as; *er zijn er* ~ *50* no fewer (no less) than 50, as many as 50; 5 (v e r m o e d e n u i t d r u k k e n d of g e r u s t s t e l l e n d) surely; *hij zal* ~ *komen* he is sure to come, I daresay he will come; *ik behoef* ~ *niet te zeggen...* I need hardly say...; 6 (t o e g e v e n d) (indeed); *zij is* ~ *mooi, maar niet...* handsome she is (indeed), but not...; 7 (t e g e n o v e r o n t k e n n i n g) ...is, ...has, &; *Jan kan het niet, Piet* ~ but Peter can; *ik heb mijn les* ~ *geleerd* I did learn my lesson; *vandaag niet, morgen* ~ not

to-day, but to-morrow; 8 (a l s b e l e e f d - h e i d s w o o r d) kindly; *zoudt u me dat boek* ~ *willen aangeven?* would you kindly hand me that book?; would you mind handing me that book?; 9 (v r a g e n d) are you, have you? &; *je gaat niet uit,* ~*?* you aren't going out, are you?; 10 (u i t r o e p e n d) why, well; ~, *heb ik je dat niet gezegd?* why, didn't I tell you?; ~ *van me leven!,* ~ *nu nog mooier!* well, I never!; ~, *wat is er?* why, what is the matter?; ~, *waarom niet?* well, why not?; ~ *!* ~ *!* well, well!, well, to be sure!; ~ *zo!* well!; *er is nog wat mooiers, en* ~... and it is this...; *zijn beste vriend nog* ~ and that his best friend, his best friend of all people; *wat denk je* ~*?* what do you take me for!, certainly not!; *ik heb het* ~ *gedacht!* I thought so (as much); *ik moest* ~ I had to, I could do no other, it couldn't be helped; *je moet... of* ~... you must either... or...; ~ *eens* now and again; *hebt u* ~ *eens...?* have you ever...?; **II** *aj* *alles* ~ *aan boord* all well on board; *hij is niet* ~ he does not feel well, he is unwell; *het is mij* ~ *!* all right!, I have no objection; *hij is niet* ~ *bij het hoofd* zie *hoofd*; *laten we* ~ *wezen* to be quite honest; *als ik het* ~ *heb* if I am not mistaken; **III** *o* well-being; ~ *hem die...* happy he who...; *het* ~ *en wee* the weal and woe [of his subjects]; **wel'aan** well then

'**welbedacht** well-considered, well thought-out; **–begrepen** well-understood

'**welbehagen** *o* pleasure, complacency

'**welbekend** well-known; **–bemind** well-beloved, beloved; **–beraamd** well thought-out, well-planned; **–bereid** well-prepared; **–beschouwd** after all, all things considered

welbe'spraakt fluent, well-spoken; **–heid** *v* eloquence, fluency

'**welbesteed** well-used, well-spent; **–bewust** deliberate

'**weldaad** (-daden) *v* benefit, benefaction; *een* ~ *voor iedereen* a boon to everybody; *een* ~ *bewijzen* confer a benefit [upon sbd.]; **wel'dadig** 1 beneficent, benevolent, (l i e f d a d i g) charitable; 2 (h e i l z a a m) beneficial; **wel'dadig-heid** *v* beneficence, benevolence, (l i e f d a - d i g h e i d) charity; **–sbazaar** (-s) *m* (charity) bazaar

'**weldenkend** right-thinking, right-minded

'**weldoen** (deed 'wel, h. 'welgedaan) *vi* 1 (g o e d d o e n) do good; 2 (l i e f d a d i g z ij n) give alms; be charitable [to the poor]; *doe wel en zie niet om* zie *doen* **II**; '**weldoener** (-s) *m* benefactor; '**weldoenster** (-s) *v* benefactress

'**weldoordacht** well thought-out, well-considered

'**weldra** soon, before long, shortly

wel'edel, –geboren, –gestreng *W* ~*e heer*

Dear Sir; *de W~e heer J. Botha* J. Botha Esq.;
–zeergeleerd *de W~e heer Dr. V.* Dr. V.

wel'eer formerly, in olden times, of old

weleer'waard reverend; *zeker, ~e!* certainly,
your Reverence; *de W~e heer A. B.* (the)
Reverend A. B., the Rev. A. B.

'welfboog (-bogen) *m* vaulted arch; **'welfsel**
(-s en -en) *o* vault

'welgeaard well-natured; genuine [Dutchman]

'welgedaan well-fed, portly; **welge'daanheid**
v portliness

'welgekozen well-chosen; **–gelegen** well-
situated; **–gelijkend** *een ~ portret* a good
likeness

'welgemaakt well-made [person, thing];
well-built [man], shapely [figure];
welge'maaktheid *v* handsomeness

'welgemanierd well-bred, well-mannered,
mannerly; **welgema'nierdheid** *v* good breeding, good manners

'welgemeend well-meant [advice &]; heartfelt
[thanks]; **–gemoed** cheerful; **–geordend**
well-regulated; **–geschapen** well-made

welge'steld well-to-do, in easy circumstances,
well of, substantial [man]; **–heid** *v* easy
circumstances

'welgeteld exactly; ...in all

'welgevallen I *zich iets laten ~* put up with
sth.; **II** *o* pleasure; *met ~* with pleasure, with
satisfaction; *naar ~* at will, at (your) pleasure;
welge'vallig pleasing [to God], agreeable [to
the Government]

'welgevormd well-made, well-shaped, shapely;
–gezind well-disposed [man]; well-affected,
friendly [tribes]

wel'haast 1 (w e l d r a) soon; 2 (b ij n a) almost,
nearly; *~ niets (niemand)* hardly anything
(anybody)

'welig luxuriant, < rank; *~ groeien* thrive[2]; zie
ook *tieren*; **–heid** *v* luxuriance

'welingelicht well-informed

welis'waar it is true, true

welk I *vragend vnmw* which, what; *~e jongen (van
de zes)?* which boy?; *~e jongen zal zo iets doen?*
what boy?; **II** *uitroepend* what; *~ een schande!*
what a shame!; **III** *betr. vnmw* 1 (v. p e r s o -
n e n) who, that; 2 (n i e t v a n p e r s o n e n)
which, that; *het Polyolbion, ~ boek ik niet had*
which book I hadn't got; *~(e) ook* which-
(so)ever, what(so)ever; any

'welken (welkte, is gewelkt) *vi* wither, fade

'welkom I *aj* welcome; *wees ~!* welcome!; *~ in
Amsterdam* Welcome to A.!; *~ thuis* welcome
home; *iem. ~ heten* bid sbd. welcome, welcome
sbd.; *iem. hartelijk ~ heten* extend a hearty
welcome to sbd., give sbd. a hearty welcome;
iets ~ heten welcome sth.; **II** *o* welcome;

'welkomst *v* welcome; **–geschenk** (-en) *o*
welcoming-gift; **–groet** (-en) *m* welcome

1 'wellen (welde, is geweld) *vi* well

2 'wellen (welde, h. geweld) *vt* ✖ weld

3 'wellen (welde, h. geweld) *vt* draw [butter]

'welletjes *het is zo ~* 1 that will do; 2 we have
had enough of it

wel'levend polite, well-bred; **–heid** *v* politeness, good breeding

wel'licht perhaps

wel'luidend melodious, harmonious; **–heid** *v*
melodiousness, harmony

'wellust (-en) *m* 1 (g u n s t i g) delight; 2
(o n g u n s t i g) voluptuousness, lust, sensuality; **wel'lusteling** (-en) *m* voluptuary, sensualist, sybarite; **wel'lustig I** *aj* sensual, voluptuous, lustful, lascivious; **II** *ad* sensually &;
–heid (-heden) *v* voluptuousness, sensuality,
lasciviousness

'welmenend well-meaning, well-intentioned;
wel'menendheid *v* good intention

'welnemen *o met uw ~* by your leave

wel'nu well then

wel'opgevoed well-bred

'weloverwogen well-considered, deliberate

welp (-en) 1 *m* & *o* cub, whelp; 2 *m* (b ij d e
p a d v i n d e r ij (wolf-)cub

wel'riekend sweet-smelling, sweet-scented,
fragrant, odoriferous; **–heid** *v* fragrance,
odoriferousness

'welslagen *o* success

wel'sprekend eloquent; **–heid** *v* eloquence

'welstand *m* 1 welfare, well-being; 2 health; 3
(w e l g e s t e l d h e i d) prosperity; *in ~ leven* be
well off [in easy circumstances]; *naar iems. ~
informeren* inquire after sbd.'s health

'welste *van je ~* with a vengeance, with a will,
like anything; *een klap van je ~* **F** a spanking
blow; *een lawaai van je ~* a terrible din, a
deafening uproar; *een ruzie van je ~* **F** a regular
row

'weltergewicht *o* welter-weight

'welvaart *v* 1 (m a a t s c h a p p e l ij k, e c o n o -
m i s c h) prosperity; 2 (w e l z ij n) well-being;
'welvaartsstaat (-staten) *m* 1 affluent society;
2 (v e r z o r g i n g s s t a a t) welfare state

'welvaren I (voer 'wel, h. en is 'welgevaren) *vi*
1 prosper, thrive, be prosperous; 2 be in good
health; **II** *o* 1 prosperity; 2 health; *er uitzien als
Hollands ~* be the picture of health, glow with
health; **wel'varend** 1 (v o o r s p o e d i g)
prosperous, thriving; 2 (g e z o n d) healthy;
–heid *v* 1 prosperity; 2 good health

'welven (welfde, h. gewelfd) **I** *vt* vault, arch;
II *vr zich ~* vault, arch

'welverdiend well-deserved

'welversneden *een ~ pen hebben* write well

'**welving** (-en) *v* vaulting, vault

wel'voeglijk becoming, seemly, decent, proper; **–heid** *v* seemliness, decency, propriety; **welvoeglijkheids'halve** for decency's sake

'**welvoorzien** well-provided [table]; well-loaded [table]; well-stocked [shop &]; well-lined [purse]

'**welwater** *o* spring water

wel'willend benevolent, kind; sympathetic; **–heid** *v* kindness; sympathy; benevolence

'**welzijn** *o* welfare, well-being; *n a a r* iems. ~ *informeren* inquire after sbd.'s health; *o p* iems. ~ *drinken* drink sbd.'s health; *v o o r uw* ~ for your good; **–swerk** *o* welfare work

'**wemelen** (wemelde, h. gewemeld) *vi* ~ *van* swarm (teem) with [flies, people, spies &]; crawl with, be infested with [vermin]; bristle with [mistakes]

'**wendbaar** manoeuvrable; **–heid** *v* manoeuvrability; '**wenden** (wendde, h. gewend) **I** *vi* turn; ⚓ go about, put about; **II** *vt* turn; ⚓ put about [ship]; **III** *vr zich* ~ turn; *je kunt je daar niet* ~ *of keren* there is hardly room enough to swing a cat; *ik weet niet hoe ik mij* ~ *of keren moet* which way to turn; *zich* ~ *tot* apply to, turn to, approach [the minister]; **–ding** (-en) *v* turn; *het gesprek een andere* ~ *geven* give another turn to the conversation, turn the conversation; *een gunstige* ~ *nemen* take a favourable turn

1 '**wenen** (weende, h. geweend) *vi* weep, cry; ~ *over iets* weep for sth., weep over sth.

2 '**Wenen** *o* Vienna; **–er I** *aj* Viennese, Vienna [Congress &], [the Congress] of Vienna; ~ *meubelen* Austrian bentwood furniture; **II** (-s) *m* Viennese

wenk (-en) *m* wink, nod, hint; *de* ~ *begrijpen* (*opvolgen*) take the hint; *iem. een* ~ *geven* I beckon to sbd.; 2 *fig* give sbd. a hint; *iem. op zijn* ~*en bedienen* be at sbd.'s beck and call; **–brauw** (-en) *v* eyebrow; '**wenken** (wenkte, h. gewenkt) *vt* beckon

'**wennen I** (wende, h. gewend) *vt* accustom, habituate [a person to something]; **II** (wende, is gewend) *vi* ~ *aan iets* accustom oneself to sth.; *men went aan alles* one gets used to everything; *het zal wel* ~, *u zult er wel aan* ~ you will get used to it; *hij begint al goed te* ~ *bij hen* he begins to feel quite at home with them; zie ook: *gewend*

wens (-en) *m* wish, desire; *mijn* ~ *is vervuld* I have my wish; *n a a r* ~ according to our wishes; *t e g e n de* ~ *van*... against the wishes of [his parents]; *de* ~ *is de vader van de gedachte* the wish is father to the thought; **–dromen** *mv* wishful dreams; *fig* wishful thinking; '**wense-lijk** desirable; *al wat* ~ *is!* my best wishes!; *het*

~ *achten* think it desirable; **–heid** *v* desirableness, desirability; '**wensen** (wenste, h. gewenst) *vt* 1 wish; 2 desire, want; *wij* ~ *te gaan* we wish to go; *ik wenste u te spreken* I should (would) wish to have a word with you; *ik wens dat hij dadelijk komt* I wish (want) him to come at once; *ik wens u alle geluk* I wish you every joy; *wat wenst u?* 1 (i n 't a l g.) what do you wish?; 2 (i n w i n k e l) what can I do for you?; *het is te* ~ *dat*... it is to be wished that...; *niets (veel) te* ~ *overlaten* leave nothing (much) to be desired; *iem. naar de maan* ~ wish sbd. at the devil; *ja, als men 't maar voor het* ~ *had* if wishes were horses, beggars might ride

'**wentelen I** (wentelde, h. gewenteld) *vt* turn over, roll; **II** (wentelde, is gewenteld) *vi* revolve; **III** *vr zich* ~ welter, roll, wallow [in mud], revolve; *de planeten* ~ *zich om de zon* the planets revolve round the sun; **–ling** (-en) *v* revolution, rotation; '**wentelteefjes** *mv* French toast, fried sop; **–trap** (-pen) *m* winding (spiral) staircase

werd (**werden**) V.T. van *worden*

'**wereld** (-en) *v* world, universe; *de* ~ *is een schouwtoneel* all the world is a stage; *wat zal de* ~ *ervan zeggen?* what will the world (what will Mrs. Grundy) say?; *de andere* ~ the other world, the next world; *de boze* ~ the wicked world; *de Derde Wereld* the Third World; *de geleerde* ~ the learned (the scientific) world; *de grote* ~ society, the upper ten; *de hele* ~ the whole world, all the world [knows]; *de Nieuwe (Oude) Wereld* the New (Old) World; *de verkeerde* ~ the world turned upside down; *de vrije* ~ the free world; *de wijde* ~ the wide world; *iets de* ~ *in sturen* launch [a manifesto], give it to the world; *zijn* ~ *kennen (verstaan)* have manners; *de* ~ *verzaken* renounce the world; ● *zich d o o r de* ~ *slaan* fight one's way through the world; *i n de* ~ in the world; *zo gaat het in de* ~ so the world wags, such is the way of the world; *n a a r de andere* ~ *helpen* dispatch; *naar de andere* ~ *verhuizen* go to kingdom come; *reis o m de* ~ voyage round the world; *o p de* ~, *t e r* ~ in the world; *ter* ~ *brengen* bring into the world, give birth to [a child &]; *ter* ~ *komen* come into the world, see the light; *voor alles ter* ~ [I would not do it] for the world; *hij zou alles ter* ~ *willen geven om*... he would give the world to...; *niets ter* ~ nothing on earth, no earthly thing; *voor niets ter* ~ not for the world; *wat ter* ~ *moest hij*... what in the world should he...; *hoe is 't Gods ter* ~ *mogelijk!* how in the world is it possible; *een zaak u i t de* ~ *helpen* settle a business; *die zaak is uit de* ~ that business is done with; *een leven v a n de andere* ~ a noise fit to raise the dead; *een man* *van de* ~ a man of the world; *wat van de* ~ *zien* see the world; *alleen v o o r de* ~ *leven* live for the world only, be worldy-minded; **–beeld** *o* weltanschauung, world-view, philosophy of life; **–beheerser** (-s) *m* world-ruler, master of the world; **–beroemd** world-famous, world-famed; **–beschouwing** (-en) *v* view (conception) of the world; philosophy; **–bevolking** *v* world population; **–bewoner** (-s) *m* inhabitant of the world; **–bol** (-len) *m* globe; **–bouw** *m* cosmos; **–brand** *m* world conflagration; **–burger** (-s) *m* citizen of the world, cosmopolitan, cosmopolite; *de nieuwe* ~ **J** the little stranger, the new arrival; **–deel** (-delen) *o* part of the world, continent; **–gebeuren** *o* world events, world affairs; **–gebeurtenis** (-sen) *v* world event; **–geschiedenis** *v* world history; **–handel** *m* world (international) trade; **–heer** (-heren) *m rk* secular priest; **–heerschappij** *v* world dominion; **–hervormer** (-s) *m* world reformer; **–kaart** (-en) *v* map of the world; **–kampioen** (-en) *m* world champion; **–kampioenschap** *o* world championship; **–kennis** *v* knowledge of the world; **wereld′kundig** universally known; *iets* ~ *maken* spread it abroad, make it public; **′wereldlijk** worldly; secular [clergy], temporal [power]; ~ *maken* secularize; **′wereldlit(t)eratuur** *v* world literature; **–macht** (-en) *v* world power; **–markt** *v* world market; **–naam** *m* world reputation; **wereldom′vattend** world-wide; global [warfare]; **′wereldoorlog** (-logen) *m* world war; *de Eerste Wereldoorlog* the Great War [of 1914–'18]; *de jaren tussen de twee* ~*en* the inter-war years, the interbellum; **–opinie** *v* world opinion; **–orde** *v* world order; **–première** (-s) *v* world première; **–record** [-rəkɔ:r, -rəkɔrt] (-s) *o* world record; **–recordhouder** (-s) *m* world-record holder; **–reis** (-reizen) *v* world tour; **–reiziger** (-s) *m* world traveller, globe-trotter; **–rond** *o* world, globe; **–ruim** *o het* ~ space; **–s** 1 (v o o r d e w e r e l d l e v e n d, v a n d e w e r e l d) worldly, worldly-minded; 2 (t ij d e l ij k) secular, temporal [power]; **wereld′schokkend** world-shaking; **′wereldsgezind** worldly-minded, worldly; **wereldsge′zindheid** *v* worldly-mindedness, worldliness; **′wereldstad** (-steden) *v* metropolis; **–stelsel** (-s) *o* cosmic system, cosmos; **–streek** (-streken) *v* region of the world, zone; **–taal** (-talen) *v* world language; **–tentoonstelling** (-en) *v* world('s) fair, international exhibition; **–titel** *m sp* world title; **–toneel** *o* stage of the world; **–verkeer** *o* world traffic, international traffic; **–vermaard** world-famous; **–vrede** *m* & *v* world peace; **–vreemd**

unworldly; **–wijs** worldly-wise, sophisticated; **–wonder** (-en) *o* wonder of the world; **–zee** (-zeeën) *v* ocean

′weren I (weerde, h. geweerd) *vt* prevent, avert [mischief]; keep out [a person]; *we kunnen hem niet* ~ we cannot keep him out; **II** *vr zich* ~ 1 (zij n b e s t d o e n) exert oneself; 2 (z i c h v e r d e d i g e n) defend oneself

werf (werven) *v* 1 ship-yard, ship-building yard; (v. d. m a r i n e) dockyard; 3 (h o u t w e r f) timber-yard

′werfbureau [-by.ro.] (-s), **–kantoor** (-toren) *o* recruiting-office

′wering *v* prevention; *tot* ~ *van* for the prevention of

1 werk *o* tow; (g e p l o z e n) oakum; ~ *pluizen* pick oakum

2 werk (-en) *o* work [= task; employment; piece of literary or musical composition &]; labour; *de* ~*en van Vondel* the works of Vondel, Vondel's works; *het* ~ *van een horloge* the works of a watch; *een* ~ *van Gods handen* (of) God's workmanship; *het* ~ *van een ogenblik* the work (the business) of an instant; *dat is uw* ~ that is your work (your doing); *het is mooi* ~ it is a fine piece of work, a fine achievement: *er is* ~ *aan de winkel* there's much work to be done, he (you) will find his (your) work cut out for him (you); *een goed* ~ *doen* do a work of mercy; *geen half* ~ *doen* not do things by halves; *honderd mensen* ~ *geven* employ a hundred people; *dat geeft veel* ~ it gives you a lot of work; ~ *hebben* have a job, be in work; *geen* ~ *hebben* 1 ⌣ have no work; 2 be out of work (out of employment); *lang* ~ *hebben om* be long about ...ing; *zijn* ~ *maken* do one's work; *er dadelijk* ~ *van maken* see to it at once; *er veel* ~ *van maken* take great pains over it; *hij maakt (veel)* ~ *van haar* he is making up to her; *ik maak er geen* ~ *van (van die zaak)* I'll not take the matter up; ~ *verschaffen* give employment; ~ *vinden* find work (employment); ~ *zoeken* be looking for work; ● *a a n het* ~*!* to work!; *aan het* ~ *gaan, zich aan het* ~ *begeven* set to work; *weer aan het* ~ *gaan* resume work; *iem. aan het* ~ *zetten* set sbd. to work; *aan het* ~ *zijn* be at work, be working, be engaged; *aan het* ~ *zijn aan* be engaged (at work) on [a dictionary &]; *hoe gaat dat i n zijn* ~*?* how is it done?; *hoe is dat in zijn* ~ *gegaan?* how did it come about?; *alles in het* ~ *stellen om...* leave no stone unturned (do one's utmost) in order to...; *pogingen in het* ~ *stellen* make efforts (attempts); *n a a r zijn* ~ *gaan* go to one's work; *o n d e r het* ~ *gaan* while at work, while working; *goed (verkeerd) t e* ~ *gaan* set about it the right (wrong) way; *voorzichtig te* ~ *gaan* proceed cautiously; *te* ~ *stellen* employ, set

to work; *z o n d e r* ~ out of work; **–baas**
(-bazen) *m* foreman; **–bank** (-en) *v* (work-)
bench; **–bezoek** (-en) *o* working visit; **–bij**
(-en) *v* worker (bee); **–broek** (-en) *v* overalls;
–college [-le.ʒə] (-s) *o* ≈ seminar; **–comité**
(-s) *o* working committee; **werk′dadig** efficacious, active, operative; **–heid** *v* efficacy,
activity; **′werkdag** (-dagen) *m* work-day,
week-day; [eight-hours'] working day
′werkelijk I *aj* real, actual; ~*e dienst* active
service; *ik heb het niet gedaan,* ~ *!* really!, fact!;
II *ad* really; **′werkelijkheid** *v* reality; *in* ~ in
reality, in point of fact, in fact, really; **–szin** *m*
realism
′werkeloos = *werkloos*; **werke′loosheid** =
werkloosheid; **′werkeloze(-), werke′loze(-)** =
werkloze(-)
′werken (werkte, h. gewerkt) **I** *vi* 1 (w e r k
d o e n) work, act, operate, take effect, be effective [of
medicine &]; ✗ work, function [of an engine];
3 (s t a m p e n e n s l i n g e r e n) labour [of a
ship]; 4 (v e r s c h u i v e n) shift [of cargo]; 5
(t r e k k e n) get warped [of wood]; *de rem werkt
niet* the brake doesn't act; *het schip werkte
vreselijk* the ship laboured heavily; *hij heeft nooit
van* ~ *gehouden* he never liked work; *hij laat hen
te hard* ~ he works them too hard, he over-
works them; *hij moet hard* ~ he has to work
hard; ● *a a n e e n b o e k* & ~ be at work (engaged)
on a book; *nadelig* ~ *o p* have a bad effect
upon; *op iems. gemoed* ~ work on sbd.'s feelings;
het werkt op de zenuwen it affects the nerves;
v o o r Engels ~ be reading for English; **II** *vt iets
naar binnen* ~ get [food] down; *hij kan heel wat
naar binnen* ~ he can negotiate a lot of food; *ze*
~ *elkaar eronder* they are cutting each other's
throats; **–d** 1 working; active; 2 efficacious; ~
lid active member; *de* ~*e stand* the working
classes; **′werker** (-s) *m* worker; **′werkezel** (-s)
m drudge; *hij is een echte* ~ he is a glutton for
work; **–gelegenheid** *v* employment; *volledige*
~ full employment; **–gever** (-s) *m* employer;
~*s en werknemers* employers and employed;
–groep (-en) *v* working party; **–handen** *mv*
callous hands; **–huis** (-huizen) *o* (v. w e r k-
s t e r) place; **–hypothese** [-hi.po.te.zə] (-n en
-s) *v* working hypothesis [*mv* working hypoth-
eses]; **′werking** (-en) *v* working, action,
operation; (u i t w e r k i n g) effect; *die bepaling
is b u i t e n* ~ has ceased to be operative; *buiten*
~ *stellen* suspend; *i n* ~ in action; *in* ~ *stellen*
put in operation, set going, work; *in* ~ *treden*
come into operation (into force); *in* ~ *zijn* be
working; be operative; *in volle* ~ in full operation, in full swing; **′werkinrichting** (-en) *v*
labour colony; **–je** (-s) *o* piece of work, (little)

work, job; **–kamer** (-s) *v* study; **–kamp** (-en)
o (v. v r ij w i l l i g e r s) work-camp; (s t r a f-
k a m p) labour camp; **–kiel** (-en) *m* overalls;
–kleding *v* working clothes; **–kracht** *v* 1
energy; 2 (-en) hand, workman; *de Europese*
~*en* European labour; **–kring** (-en) *m* sphere
of activity (of action); **–lieden** *mv* work-
people, workers, operatives; **–loon** (-lonen) *o*
wage(s), pay
′werkloos 1 inactive, idle; 2 out of work, out
of employment, unemployed, jobless; ~ *maken*
throw out of work; **werk′loosheid** *v* 1 inactivity, idleness, inaction; 2 unemployment;
werk′loosheidsuitkering (-en) *v* unemployment benefit, (unemployment) dole; **–verzekering** *v* unemployment insurance; **′werk-
loze** (-n) *m* out-of-work; *de* ~*n* the unemployed; **werk′lozencijfer** (-s) *o* unemployment index; **–kas** (-sen) *v* unemployment fund
′werklust *m* zest for work; **–maatschappij**
(-en) *v* subsidiary company; **–man** (-lieden en
-lui) *m* workman, labourer, operative,
mechanic; **–mandje** (-s) *o* work-basket;
–meid (-en) *v* work-maid, housemaid;
–methode (-n en -s) *v* (working) method;
–mier (-en) *v* worker (ant); **–nemer** (-s) *m*
employee, employed man; zie ook: *werkgever*;
–paard (-en) *o* work-horse; **–pak** (-ken) *o*
working clothes, overalls; **–plaats** (-en) *v*
workshop, shop, workroom; **–plan** (-nen) *o*
working plan, plan of work; **–program(ma)**
(-grams, -gramma's) *o* working-programme;
–rooster (-s) *m* & *o* time-table; **–schoen** (-en)
m working-boot; **–schuw** work-shy; **–staker**
(-s) *m* striker; **–staking** (-en) *v* strike; **–ster**
(-s) *v* 1 (female) worker; 2 charwoman, daily
woman; **–student** (-en) *m* working student;
–stuk (-ken) *o* 1 (piece of) work, workpiece;
2 (i n d e m e e t k.) proposition, problem;
–tafel (-s) *v* desk; ✗ work-bench; **–tekening**
(-en) *v* working drawing; ✗ **–terrein** *o* area
(sphere, field) of work; **–tijd** (-en) *m* working-
hours; (v. e. p l o e g) shift; *lange* ~*en hebben*
work long hours; *variabele* ~*en* flexible hours,
F flexitime; **–tijdverkorting** (-en) *v* short-
time working
′werktuig (-en) *o* 1 tool², instrument², implement; 2 organ [of sight]; ~*en* (v o o r
g y m n a s t i e k) apparatus; **–bouwkunde** *v*
mechanical engineering; **werktuig-
bouw′kundige** (-n) *m* mechanical engineer,
mechanician; **′werktuigkunde** *v* mechanics;
werktuig′kundig I *aj* mechanical [action,
drawing, engineer &]; **II** *ad* mechanically;
–e (-n) *m* mechanician, instrument-maker;
werk′tuiglijk *aj* (& *ad*) mechanical(ly)²,
automatic(ally)²; **–heid** *v* mechanicalness

'**werkuur** (-uren) *o* working-hour; **–verdeling** *v* division of labour; **–vergunning** (-en) *v* work permit; **–verschaffing** *v* the procuring (creation, provision) of employment (work); relief work(s); **–volk** *o* work-people, workmen, labourers; **–vrouw** (-en) *v* charwoman; **–week** (-weken) *v* working week; **–wijze** (-n) *v* (working) method; **werk'willige** (-n) *m* willing worker, nonstriker; '**werkwinkel** (-s) *m* workshop; **–woord** (-en) *o gram* verb; **werk'woordelijk** verbal; '**werkzaam** I *aj* active, laborious, industrious; *hij is ~ op een fabriek* he is employed at a factory, he works in a factory; *een ~ aandeel hebben in* have an active part in; II *ad* actively, laboriously, industriously; **–heid** (-heden) *v* activity, industry; *mijn talrijke werkzaamheden* my numerous activities; *de verschillende werkzaamheden* the various proceedings; '**werkzoekende, werk'zoekende** (-n) *m-v* person looking for a job (for work, for employment)

'**werpen*** I *vt* throw, cast, fling, hurl, toss; *jongen ~* zie 2 *jongen; iem. met stenen ~* zie *gooien;* II *vr zich ~* throw oneself; *zich in de armen ~ van...* fling oneself into the arms of...; *zich o p iem. ~* fall on sbd., set upon sbd.; *zich op de knieën ~* go down on one's knees, prostrate oneself [before sbd.]; *zich op de studie van... ~* apply oneself to the study of... with a will; *zich t e paard ~* fling oneself into the saddle; '**werpnet** (-ten) *o* casting-net; **–pijl** (-en), **–schicht** (-en) *m* dart; **–speer** (-speren), **–spies** (-sen), **–spiets** (-en) *v* javelin; **–tros** (-sen) *m ⚓* warp; **–tuig** (-en) *o* missile, projectile

'**wervel** (-s) *m* vertebra [*mv* vertebrae]; '**wervelen** (wervelde, h. gewerveld) *vi* whirl; '**wervelkolom** (-men) *v* spinal column, spine; **–storm** (-en) *m* tornado; **–wind** (-en) *m* whirlwind

'**werven*** *vt* recruit, enlist, enrol; canvass for [customers]; **–er** (-s) *m* ⚒ recruiter, recruiting-officer; '**werving** (-en) *v* recruitment, enlistment, enrolment; canvassing [for customers]

'**weshalve** wherefore, for which reason

wesp (-en) *v* wasp; '**wespendief** (-dieven) *m* honey-buzzard; **–nest** (-en) *o* wasps' nest, vespiary; *fig* hornets' nest[2]; *zich in een ~ steken* bring a hornets' nest about one's ears; '**wespesteek** (-steken) *m* wasp-sting; **–taille** [-tɑ(l)jə] (-s) *v* wasp-waist

west west; **West** *v de ~* the West Indies; **–duits** West German; **–duitser** (-s) *m* West German; **West-'Duitsland** *o* West Germany; '**westelijk** western, westerly; '**westen** *o* west; *het Westen* the West, the Occident; *buiten ~*

unconscious; *t e n ~ van* (to the) west of; **–wind** (-en) *m* westwind; '**wester** western; **–kim(me)** *v* western horizon; **–lengte** *v* West longitude; **–ling** (-en) *m* Westerner; **–s** western, occidental; '**Westerschelde** *v de ~* the West Scheldt; '**West-Europa** *o* Western Europe; **Westeuro'pees** West(ern) European; **West-'Indië** *o* the West Indies; **West'indisch** West-Indian; '**westkant** *m* west side; **–kust** (-en) *v* west coast, western coast; **–moesson** (-s) *m* south-west monsoon; '**Westromeins** *het ~e Rijk* the Western Empire, the Empire of the West; '**westwaarts** I *aj* westward; II *ad* westward(s)

wet (-ten) *v* 1 (in 't a l g.) law; 2 (in 't b i j z o n d e r) act; *de Mozaïsche ~* the Mosaic Law; *~ op het Lager Onderwijs* Primary Education Act; *de ~ van Archimedes* Archimedes' principle, the Archimedian principle; *de ~ van Boyle (Grimm, Parkinson &)* Boyle's (Grimm's, Parkinson's &) law; *de ~ van vraag en aanbod (der zwaartekracht &)* the law of supply and demand (of gravitation &); *een ~ van Meden en Perzen* a law of the Medes and Persians; *korte ~ten maken met* make short work of; *iem. de ~ stellen (voorschrijven)* lay down the law for sbd.; *~ worden* become law; ● *b o v e n d e ~ staan* be above the law; *b u i t e n de ~ stellen* outlaw; *d o o r de ~ bepaald* fixed by law, statutory; *t e g e n de ~* against the law; *t o t ~ verheffen* put [a bill] on the Statute Book; *v o l g e n s de ~* by law; *volgens de Franse ~* 1 according to French law [you are right]; 2 [married &] under French law; *v o o r de ~* in the eye of the law; [equality] before the law; zie ook: *volgens de ~; voor de ~ niet bestaan* not exist in law; *voor de ~ getrouwd* married at the registrar's office; **–boek** (-en) *o* code; *~ van koophandel* commercial code; *~ van privaatrecht, burgerlijk ~* civil code; *~ van strafrecht* penal code, criminal code

1 '**weten*** I *vt* 1 (in 't a l g.) know; 2 (k e n n i s d r a g e n v a n) be aware of; *doen (laten) ~* let [one] know, send [one] word, inform [sbd.] of; *wie weet of hij niet zal...* who knows but he may...; *God weet het!* God knows!; *dat weet ik niet* I don't know; *hij is mijn vriend moet je ~ (weet je)* he is my friend, you know; *wel te ~ ...* that is to say...; *het te ~ komen* get to know it; find out, learn; *hij wist te ontkomen* he managed to escape; *hij weet zich te verdedigen* he knows how to defend himself; *er iets op ~* know a way out; *het uit de krant ~* know it from the paper(s); *van wie weet je het?* whom did you hear it from?, who told you?; *eer je het weet* before you know where you are; *zij ~ het samen* they are as thick as thieves; they are hand and glove; *hij weet er alles van* he knows all about it; *hij weet er niets*

van he doesn't know anything about it; *dat moeten zij zelf maar ~* that's their look-out; *zij willen er niet(s) van ~* they will have none of it; *zij wil niets van hem ~* she will not have anything to say to him; *dat moet je zelf ~* that's your look-out; *wat niet weet, wat niet deert* what one does not know causes no woe; *weet je wat?, we gaan naar ...* I'll tell you what, we'll go to...; *zij weet wat zij wil* she knows what she wants, she knows her own mind; *hij weet zelf niet wat hij wil* he doesn't know his own mind; *daar weet jij wat van!* F fat lot you know about it!; *ik weet wat van je* I know something about you; *dat schoonmaken dat weet wat!* what a nuisance!; *hij wil het wel ~ (dat hij knap is* &) he needn't be told that he is clever; *hij wil het niet ~* he never lets it appear; *zonder het zelf te ~* unwittingly; *~ waar Abraham de mosterd haalt* know what's what; II *va* know; *wie weet?* who knows?; *men kan nooit ~* you never can tell; *hij weet niet beter* he doesn't know any better; *hij weet wel beter* he knows better (than that); *niet dat ik weet* not that I know of; III *o* knowledge; ● *niet bij mijn ~* not to my knowledge; *buiten mijn ~* without my knowledge, unknown to me; *met mijn ~* with my knowledge; *naar mijn beste ~* to the best of my knowledge; *tegen beter ~ in* against one's better judgment; *zonder mijn ~* without my knowledge; IV *ad te ~ appels, peren...* viz., namely, to wit...

2 'weten V.T. meerv. van *wijten*
'wetens zie *willens*
'wetenschap (-pen) *v* 1 science; learning; 2 (k e n n i s) knowledge; *er geen ~ van hebben* know nothing about it, not be aware of it; weten'schappelijk I *aj* scientific; learned; II *ad* scientifically; **–heid** *v* scientific character; 'wetenschapsmensen, 'wetenschappers *mv* scientists
wetens'waardig worth knowing; **–heid** (-heden) *v* thing worth knowing
'wetering (-en) *v* watercourse
'wetgeleerde (-n) *m* one learned in the law, jurist; **–gevend** law-making, legislative; *de ~e macht* the legislature; *~e vergadering* Legislative Assembly; **–gever** (-s) *m* law-giver, legislator; **–geving** (-en) *v* legislation, **–houder** (-s) *m* alderman; wet'matig regular; 'wetsartikel (-en en -s) *o* article of a (the) law; **–bepaling** (-en) *v* provision of a (the) law; **–herziening** (-en) *v* revision of the (a) law; **–ontduiking** *v* evasion of the law; **–ontwerp** (-en) *o* bill; **–overtreding** (-en) *v* breach of the law; **–rol** (-len) *v* scroll of the (Mosaic) law
1 'wetstaal (-stalen) *o* (sharpening) steel
2 'wetstaal *v* legal language
'wetsteen (-stenen) *m* whetstone, hone

'wetsverkrachting (-en) *v* violation of the law; **–voorstel** (-len) *o* bill; **–wijziging** (-en) *v* amendment (modification, alteration) of the law; *een ~ invoeren* amend the law; **–winkel** (-s) *m* (neighbourhood) law-centre; 'wettelijk I *aj* legal; statutory; *~e aansprakelijkheid* ❧ liability; II *ad* legally; **–heid** *v* legality; 'wetteloos lawless; wette'loosheid *v* lawlessness
'wetten (wette, h. gewet) *vt* whet, sharpen
'wettig I *aj* legitimate, legal, lawful; *een ~ kind* a legitimate child; II *ad* legitimately, legally, lawfully; 'wettigen (wettigde, h. gewettigd) *vt* legitimate, legalize; *fig* justify; sanction [by usage]; 'wettigheid *v* legitimacy; 'wettiging (-en) *v* legitimation, legalization
'weven* I *vt* & *vi* weave; **–er** (-s) *m* 1 weaver; 2 ❧ weaver-bird; weve'rij (-en) *v* 1 weaving; 2 weaving-mill
'wezel (-s) *v* weasel
1 'wezen* I *vi* be; *ik ben hem ~ opzoeken* I have been to see him; *hij mag er ~* F he is all there; *dat mag er ~* S that is not half bad, that is some; II (-s) *o* 1 (p e r s o o n) being, creature, [human, social] animal; 2 (b e s t a a n) being, existence; 3 (a a r d) nature; 4 (w e z e n l i j k- h e i d) essence, substance; 5 (v o o r k o m e n) countenance, aspect; *geen levend ~* not a living being (soul)
2 'wezen V.T. meerv. van *wijzen*
'wezenfonds (-en) *o* orphans' fund
'wezenlijk I *aj* real, essential; substantial; *het ~e* the essence; II *ad* 1 essentially; substantially; 2 < really; **–heid** *v* reality
'wezenloos vacant, vacuous, blank [stare]; **–heid** *v* vacancy, vacuity
wezens'vreemd foreign to one's nature
w.g. = *was getekend* (signed)
'whisky ['vɪski.] *m* whisky, whiskey; whisky'soda *v* whisk(e)y and soda
whist *o* whist; 'whisten (whistte, h. gewhist) *vi* play (at) whist
w.i. = *werktuigkundig ingenieur*
'wichelaar (-s) *m*, **–ster** (-s) *v* augur, soothsayer; wichela'rij (-en) *v* augury, soothsaying; 'wichelen (wichelde, h. gewicheld) *vt* augur, soothsay; 'wichelroede (-n) *v* divining-rod, dowsing-rod; **–loper** (-s) *m* diviner, douser, rhabdomancer
1 wicht (-en) *o* (k i n d) baby, child, babe, mite; *arm ~!* poor thing!; *een of ander mal ~* some foolish creature; *mal ~!* you fool!
2 wicht (-en) *o* (g e w i c h t) weight; 'wichtig weighty²; **–heid** *v* weight²
wie I *betr. vnmw.* he who; *~ ook* who(so)ever; II *vragend vnmw.* who?; *~ van hen?* which of them?; *~ daar?* ⚔ who goes there
'wiebelen (wiebelde, h. gewiebeld) *vi* wobble,

wiggle; **–d** wobbly

'wieden (wiedde, h. gewied) *vt* & *va* weed; **–er** (-s) *m* weeder

'wiedes F *dat is nogal* ~ it goes without saying

'wiedijzer (-s) *o* weeding-hook, spud; **'wiedster** (-s) *v* weeder

wieg (-en) *v* cradle; *voor dichter i n de* ~ *gelegd* a born poet; *hij was voor soldaat in de* ~ *gelegd* he was cut out for a soldier; *hij is niet voor soldaat in de* ~ *gelegd* he will never make a soldier; *voor dat werk was hij niet in de* ~ *gelegd* he was not fitted for that sort of work; *v a n de* ~ *af* from the cradle; **–edruk** (-ken) *m* incunabulum, incunable

'wiegelen (wiegelde, h. gewiegeld) *vi* rock

'wiegelied (-eren) *o* cradle-song, lullaby; **'wiegen** (wiegde, h. gewiegd) *vt* rock; zie ook: *slaap*

wiek (-en) *v* (v l e u g e l) wing; (l a m p e k a-t o e n) wick; (v. m o l e n) sail, wing, vane; *hij was in zijn* ~ *geschoten* he was affronted (affended); he was stung to the quick; *op eigen* ~*en drijven* stand on one's own legs, shift for oneself

wiel (-en) *o* wheel; ‖ (p l a s) pool; *het vijfde* ~ zie 1 *rad*; *iem. in de* ~*en rijden* put a spoke in sbd.'s wheel; **–basis** [-zɪs] *v* wheel-base; **–dop** (-pen) *m* ⬤ hub-cap, wheel-disc

'wielerbaan (-banen) *v* cycle race-track; **–sport** *v* cycling; **–wedstrijd** (-en) *m* bicycle race

'wielewaal (-walen) *m* golden oriole

'wielrennen *o* cycle-racing; **–er** (-s) *m* racing cyclist

'wielrijden *vi* cycle, wheel; **'wielrijder** (-s) *m* cyclist; **–sbond** *m* cyclists' union

wier (-en) *o* seaweed, alga [*mv* algae]

wierf (wierven) V.T. van *werven*

'wierook *m* incense[2], frankincense; **–geur** (-en) *m*, **–lucht** *v* smell of incense; **–scheepje** (-s) *o* incense-boat; **–vat** (-vaten) *o* censer, thurible, incensory

wierp (wierpen) V.T. van *werpen*

'wierven V.T. meerv. van *werven*

wies (wiesen) V.T. van *1, 3 wassen*

wig (-gen), **–ge** (-n) *v* wedge; *een* ~ *drijven tussen* drive a wedge between; **–vormig** wedge-shaped [thing]; cuneiform [inscription]

wij we

'wijbisschop (-pen) *m* suffragan (bishop)

wijd I *aj* wide, ample, large, broad, spacious; **II** *ad* wide(ly); *de ramen* ~ *openzetten* open the windows wide; ~ *en zijd* far and wide; ~ *en zijd bekend* widely known; **–beens** with (one's) legs apart

'wijdeling (-en) *m* ordinand

'wijden (wijdde, h. gewijd) **I** *vt* ordain [a priest]; consecrate [a church, churchyard, a bishop &];

~ *a a n* dedicate to [God, some person &]; *fig* consecrate to [some purpose]; *zijn tijd* & ~ *aan...* devote one's time & to...; *hem t o t priester* ~ ordain him priest; **II** *vr zich* ~ *aan iets* devote oneself to sth.

'wijders further, besides, moreover

'wijding (-en) *v* 1 ordination, consecration; 2 devotion; *hogere* (*lagere*) ~*en rk* major (minor) orders

wijd'lopig prolix, diffuse, verbose; **–heid** *v* prolixity, diffuseness, verbosity; **wijd'mazig** wide (coarse-)mashed; **'wijdte** (-n en -s) *v* 1 width, breadth, space; 2 gauge [of a railway]; **'wijdverbreid** widespread, extensive; **–vermaard** widely known, far-famed; **–verspreid** widespread, extensive; **–vertakt** wide-spread [plot]

wijf (wijven) *o* woman, female; > mean woman, virago, vixen, shrew; *een oud* ~ an old woman[2]; **–je** (-s) *o* 1 female [of animals]; 2 (a l s a a n s p r e k i n g) wifey, little wife

'wijgeschenk (-en) *o* votive offering

wijk (-en) *v* quarter, district, ward; beat [of policeman]; round [of milkman], walk [of postman]; *de* ~ *nemen naar Amerika* fly (flee) to America, take refuge in America

'wijken* *vi* give way, give ground, yield; *geen voet* ~ not budge an inch; ⚔ not yield an inch of ground; *niet van iem.* ~ not budge from sbd.'s side; ~ *voor niemand* not yield to anybody; *moet ik voor hem* ~*?* should I make way for him?; ~ *voor de overmacht* yield to superior numbers; *het gevaar is geweken* the danger is over; *de pijn is geweken* the pain has gone

'wijkgebouw (-en) *o* church hall, community centre; **–hoofd** (-en) *o* chief (air-raid) warden

'wijkplaats (-en) *v* asylum, refuge

'wijkverpleegster (-s) *v* district nurse; **–verpleging** *v* district nursing; **–zuster** (-s) *v* district nurse

1 wijl *cj* since, because, as

2 'wijl(e) (wijlen) *v* while, time

1 'wijlen *aj* ~ *Willem I* the late William I; ~ *mijn vader* my late father

2 'wijlen (wijlde, h. gewijld) *vi* zie *verwijlen*

wijn (-en) *m* wine; *rode* ~ red wine, claret; *witte* ~ white wine; *klare* ~ *schenken* speak frankly, be frank; *er moet klare* ~ *geschonken worden!* plain language wanted!; *goede* ~ *behoeft geen krans* good wine needs no bush; **–achtig** vinous; **–appel** (-s en -en) *m* wine-apple; **–azijn** *m* wine-vinegar; **–berg** (-en) *m* vineyard; **–boer** (-en) *m* wine-grower; **–bouw** *m* viniculture, wine-growing; **–bouwer** (-s) *m* wine-grower; **–druif** (-druiven) *v* grape; **–fles** (-sen) *v* wine-bottle; **–gaard** (-en) *m* vineyard; **wijn-**

gaarde′nier (-s) *m* vine-dresser; **′wijngaard-slak** (-ken) *v* edible-snail; **–geest** *m* spirit of wine, alcohol; **–glas** (-glazen) *o* wine-glass; **–handel** (-s) *m* 1 wine-trade; 2 wine-business; wine-shop; **–handelaar** (-s en -laren) *m* wine-merchant; **–huis** (-huizen) *o* wine-house; **–jaar** (-jaren) *o* vintage [of 1910], vintage year; **–kaart** (-en) *v* wine-list; **–kan** (-nen) *v* wine-jug; **–karaf** (-fen) *v* wine-decanter; **–kelder** (-s) *m* wine-cellar, wine-vault; **–kenner** (-s) *m* judge of wine, wine connoisseur; **–kleur** *v* wine colour; **–kleurig** wine-coloured; **–koeler** (-s) *m* wine cooler; **–koper** (-s) *m* wine-merchant; **–kuip** (-en) *v* wine-vat; **–lezer** (-s) *m* vintager; **–maand** *v* October; **–merk** (-en) *o* brand of wine; **–oogst** *m* vintage; **–oogster** (-s) *m* vintager; **–pers** (-en) *v* winepress; **–rank** (-en) *v* vine-tendril; **–rijk** abounding in wine, viny; **–rood** wine-red; **–saus** (-en en -sauzen) *v* wine-sauce; **–smaak** *m* vinous (winy) taste; **–soort** (-en) *v* kind of wine; **–steen** *m* wine-stone, tartar; **–steen-zuur** *o* tartaric acid; **–stok** (-ken) *m* vine; **–vat** (-vaten) *o* wine-cask; **–vlek** (-ken) *v* 1 wine-stain [in napkin &]; 2 strawberry mark [on the skin]

1 wijs (wijzen) *v* 1 (m a n i e r) manner, way; 2 *gram* mood; 3 ♪ tune, melody; zie ook: **2** *wijze*; *de* ~ *niet kunnen houden* ♪ not be able to keep tune; *o p de* ~ *van...* ♪ to the tune of...; *op die* ~ in this manner, in this way; *v a n de* ~ ♪ out of tune; *iem. van de* ~ *brengen* [*fig*] put sbd. out; *zich niet van de* ~ *laten brengen* 1 not suffer oneself to be put out; 2 not suffer oneself to be misled [by idle gossip]; *van de* ~ *raken* ♪ get out of tune; *fig* get flurried; *ik ben geheel van de* ~ [*fig*] I am quite at sea; *'s lands* ~, *'s lands eer* when in Rome, do as Rome does

2 wijs I *aj* wise; *ben je* (*wel*) ~? are you out of your senses?, are you in your right senses?, where are your senses?; *nu ben ik nog even* ~ I am just as wise as (I was) before, I am not any the wiser; *hij is niet goed* (*niet recht*) ~ he is not in his right mind, not his right senses (not quite in his senses); *ze zijn niet wijzer* they know no better; *hij zal wel wijzer zijn* he will know better (than to do that); ~ *worden* learn wisdom; *ik kan er niet uit* ~ *worden* I can make neither head nor tail of it; I cannot make it out; *ik kan niet* ~ *uit hem worden* I don't know what to make of him; **II** *ad* wisely; *die hoed staat het kind te* ~ makes the child look older; **–begeerte** *v* philosophy; **–elijk** wisely; **–geer** (-geren) *m* philosopher; **wijs′gerig** philosophical; **′wijsheid** (-heden) *v* wisdom; *alsof zij de* ~ *in pacht hebben* as if they had a monopoly of wisdom, as if they were the only

wise people in the world; **′wijsmaken** (maakte wijs, h. wijsgemaakt) *vt iem. iets* ~ make sbd. believe sth.; *zich* (*zelf*) ~ *dat...* delude oneself into the belief that...; *maak dat anderen wijs* tell that story somewhere else; *dat maak je mij niet wijs* I know better, tell me another; *maak dat de kat wijs* tell that to the (horse-) marines; *ik laat me niets* ~ I don't suffer myself to be imposed upon; *hij laat zich alles* ~ he will swallow anything; **′wijsneus** (-neuzen) *m* know-all, wiseacre, smart-aleck; **wijs′neuzig** conceited, smart-alecky

′wijsvinger (-s) *m* forefinger, index finger

′wijten* *vt iets* ~ *aan* impute sth. to; blame [sbd.] for sth.; *het was te* ~ *aan...* it was owing to...; *dat heeft hij zichzelf te* ~ he has no one to thank for it but himself, he has only himself to blame for it

′wijting (-en) *m* 🐟 whiting

′wijwater *o* holy water; **–bakje** (-s) *o* holy-water font (basin); **–kwast** (-en) *m* holy-water sprinkler

1 ′wijze (-n) *m* sage, wise man; *de Wijzen uit het Oosten* the Wise Men from the East, the Magi

2 ′wijze (-n) *v* manner, way; zie **1** *wijs*; *b ij* ~ *van proef* by way of trial; *bij* ~ *van spreken* in a manner of speaking, so to speak, so to say; *n a a r mijn* ~ *van zien* in my opinion; *o p die* ~ in this manner, in this way; *op die een of andere* ~ somehow or other; *op generlei* ~ by no manner of means, in no way

′wijzen* I *vt* 1 show, point out [sth.]; 2 🖃 pronounce [sentence]; *dat zal ik u eens* ~ I'll show you; *dat wijst* (*ons*) *op...* this points to...; *iem. op zijn ongelijk* ~ point out to sbd. where he is wrong; **II** *vi* point; *ik zou erop willen* ~ *dat...* I should like to point out the fact that...; *alles wijst erop dat...* everything points to the fact that...; **′wijzer** (-s) *m* 1 🖈 indicator; 2 hand [of a watch]; 3 (h a n d w ij z e r) finger-post; *grote* ~ minute-hand; *kleine* ~ hour-hand; **–plaat** (-platen) *v* dial(-plate), face [of a clock], clock face; **–tje** (-s) *o* hand [of a watch]; *het* ~ *rond slapen* sleep the clock round

′wijzigen (wijzigde, h. gewijzigd) *vt* modify, alter, change; **–ging** (-en) *v* modification, alteration, change; *een* ~ *aanbrengen* (*in*) make a change (in); *een* ~ *ondergaan* undergo a change, be altered

′wijzing *v* 🖃 pronouncing [of a sentence]

′wikke (-n) *v* 🌿 vetch

′wikkel (-s) *m* wrapper; (v. s i g a a r) filler; **′wikkelen** (wikkelde, h. gewikkeld) **I** *vt* wrap (up) [in brown paper &]; envelop [person, thing in]; swathe [in bandages]; wind [on a reel]; involve² [sbd. in difficulties &]; *gewikkeld in een strijd op leven en dood* engaged in a life-

and-death struggle; **II** *vr zich ~ in...* wrap [a shawl] about [her]; **–ling** (-en) *v* ✺ winding
'**wikken** (wikte, h. gewikt) *vt* weigh² [goods, one's words]; poise [on the hand]; *~ en wegen* weigh the pros and cons; weigh one's words; *de mens wikt, maar God beschikt* man proposes, (but) God disposes

wil *m* will, desire; *zijn uiterste ~* his last will (and testament); *de vrije ~* free will; *het is zijn eigen ~* he has willed it himself, it's his own wish; *~ van iets hebben* derive satisfaction from sth.; *u zult er veel ~ van hebben* it will prove very serviceable; *voor elk wat ~s* something for everyone, all tastes are catered for; *de ~ voor de daad nemen* take the will for the deed; *zijn goede ~ tonen* show one's willingness; *waar een ~ is, is een weg* where there's a will there's a way; ● *b u i t e n mijn ~* without my will and consent; *m e t de beste ~ van de wereld* with the best will in the world; *met mijn ~ gebeurt het niet* not with my consent, not if I can help it; *o m 's hemels ~* for Heaven's sake; goodness gracious!; *om harent (mijnent, uwent) ~* for her (my, your) sake; *t e g e n mijn ~* against my will; *tegen ~ en dank* against his will, in spite of himself, willy-nilly; *iem. t e r ~le zijn* oblige sbd.; *ter ~le van mijn gezin* for the sake of my family; *ter ~le van de vrede* for peace's sake; *(niet) u i t vrije ~* (not) of my own free will

wild I *aj* 1 (i n ' t w i l d g r o e i e n d) wild [flowers]; 2 (i n ' t w i l d l e v e n d) wild [animals], savage [tribes]; 3 (n i e t k a l m) wild, unruly; 4 (w o e s t k ij k e n d) fierce [looks]; *~e boot* ⚓ tramp (steamer); *in het ~(e weg)* at random, wildly; *in het ~ groeien* grow wild; *de in het ~ levende dieren* wild life; *in het ~ opgroeien* run wild; *in het ~(e weg) redeneren* reason at random; *in het ~(e weg) schieten* shoot at random; fire random shots; **II** *ad* wildly; **III** *o* 1 game, quarry; 2 (g e b r a d e n) game; *grof (klein) ~* big (small) game; zie *wilde*; **–baan** (-banen) *v* hunting ground (preserve); **–braad** *o* game; **–dief** (-dieven) *m* poacher; **wild-dieve'rij** (-en) *v* poaching; '**wilde** (-n) *m* savage; wild man; *de ~n* the savages; **–bras** (-sen) *m-v* 1 (j o n g e n) wild monkey; 2 (m e i s j e) tomboy, romp; **–man** (-nen) *m* wild man; '**wildernis** (-sen) *v* wilderness, waste; '**wildheid** (-heden) *v* wildness, savageness; **–le(d)er** *o* doeskin, buckskin; suède; **–park** (-en) *o* game preserve; deer park; **–pastei** (-en) *v* game-pie; **–reservaat** [s = z] (-vaten) *o* game reserve, game sanctuary; **–rijk** gamy, abounding in game; **–smaak** *m* gamy taste, taste of venison; **–stand** *m* game population, stock of game; **–stroper** (-s) *m* poacher; **–vreemd** *ik ben hier ~* I am a perfect stranger

here; **wild-'westfilm** (-s) *m* western; **–verhaal** (-halen) *o* western; '**wildzang** (-en) *m* 1 wild notes, untaught song; 2 *m-v = wildebras*

wilg (-en) *m* willow; '**wilgeboom** (-bomen) *m* willow-tree; **–roos** (-rozen) *v* willow herb

Wil'helmus *o het ~* the Dutch national anthem

'**willekeur** *v* arbitrariness; *naar ~* at will; **wille'keurig I** *aj* arbitrary [actions &]; voluntary [movements]; *een ~ getal* any (given) number; **II** *ad* arbitrarily; **–heid** (-heden) *v* arbitrariness

'**willen* I** *vi* & *va* will; be willing; *ik wil* I will; *ik wil niet* I will not, I won't; *hij kan wel, maar hij wil niet* but he will not; *hij wil wel* he is willing; *of hij wil of niet* willy-nilly; *hij moge zijn wie hij wil* whoever he may be; *zij ~ er niet aan* they won't hear of it; *dat wil er bij mij niet in* that won't go down with me; **II** *vt* will; v ó ó r inf. 1 (z i c h n i e t v e χ z e t t e n) be willing [to go &]; 2 (w e n s e n) wish, want [to go, write &]; 3 (n a d r u k k e l ij k w e n s e n) insist [on being obeyed &]; 4 (b e w e r e n) say [sth. to have occurred]; *wilt u het zout aangeven?* would you pass the salt?; *ik wil je wel vertellen...* I don't mind telling you...; *hij was zieker dan hij wel wilde bekennen* than he was willing to own; *zij ~ hebben dat wij...* they want us to...; *hij zal hard moeten werken, wil hij slagen* if he wants to succeed; *wil je wel eens zwijgen!* keep quiet, will you?; *als ik iets wilde* 1 if I willed a thing; 2 whenever I wanted anything; *zij ~ het zo* it is their pleasure; *dat zou je wel ~, he?* wouldn't you like it?; *ik zou wel een glaasje bier ~* I should not mind a glass of beer; *ik zou hem wel om de oren ~ slaan* I should like to box his ears; *ik wilde liever sterven dan...* I would rather die than...; *zij ~ het niet (hebben)* 1 they don't want it, they will have none of it; 2 they don't allow it; *zij ~ dat u...* they want (wish) you to...; *ik wou dat ik het kon* I wish I could; *hij kan niet ~ dat wij...* he cannot want us to...; *als God wil dat ik...* if God wills me to...; *het gerucht wil dat...* rumour has it that...; *het toeval wilde dat...* zie *toeval*; *wat wil je?* what do you want?; what is your desire?; *wat ze maar ~* anything they like; *men kan niet alles doen wat men maar wil* a man cannot do all he pleases; *hij mag (ervan) zeggen wat hij wil, maar...* he may say what he will, but...; *wat wil hij er voor?* what does he ask for it?; **III** *o* volition; *~ is kunnen* where there's a will there's a way; *het is maar een kwestie van ~* is but a question of willing; '**willens** on purpose; *~ of onwillens* willy-nilly; *~ en wetens* (willingly and) knowingly; *~ zijn* intend [to...]; '**willig** 1 willing; 2 $ firm; **–heid** *v* 1 willingness; 2 $ firmness [of the market]; '**willoos**

will-less; **–heid, wil'loosheid** *v* will-lessness;
'wilsbeschikking *v* last will (and testament),
will; **–kracht** *v* will-power, energy; **–zwakte**
v infirmity of purpose

'wimpel (-s) *m* pennant, streamer; *de blauwe ~*
the blue ribbon

'wimper (-s) *v* (eye)lash

wind (-en) *m* 1 wind; 2 (b u i k w i n d) flatus, **P**
fart; *~ van voren* head wind; *dat is maar ~* that
is mere gas; *~ en weder dienende* weather permitting; *zien uit welke hoek de ~ waait* find out how
the wind lies (blows); *waait de ~ uit die hoek?*
sits the wind in that quarter?; *de ~ waait uit een
andere hoek* the wind blows from another
quarter; *ga & als de ~!* like the wind!; *iem. de ~
van voren geven* take sbd. up roundly; *de ~ van
achteren hebben* go down the wind; *toen wij de ~
mee hadden* when the wind was with us; *er de ~
onder hebben* have them well in hand; *de ~ tegen
hebben* sail against the wind; *de ~ van iets krijgen*
zie *lucht*; *de ~ van voren krijgen* catch it; *een ~
laten* break wind, **F** let one go, **P** fart; *~ maken*
cut a dash; ● *a a n de ~ zeilen, b ij de ~ zeilen* ⚓
sail close to (near) the wind; *scherp bij de ~
zeilen* ⚓ sail close-hauled; *de Eilanden b o v e n de
~* the Windward Islands; *d o o r de ~ gaan* ⚓
tack; *i n de ~ praten* be talking to the wind; *zijn
raad in de ~ slaan* fling his advice to the winds;
een waarschuwing in de ~ slaan disregard a
warning; *m e t alle ~en draaien (waaien)* trim
one's sails to every wind; *met de ~ mee* down
the wind; *de Eilanden o n d e r de ~* the Leeward
Islands; *t e g e n de ~ in* against the wind; *vlak
tegen de ~ in* in the teeth of the wind; *iem. de ~
u i t de zeilen nemen* take the wind out of sbd.'s
sails; *v a n de ~ kan men niet leven* you cannot
live on air; *v o o r de ~ downwind*; *het gaat hem
vóór de ~* he is sailing before the wind, he is
thriving; *vóór de ~ zeilen* ⚓ sail before the
wind; *wie ~ zaait, zal storm oogsten* sow the wind
and reap the whirlwind; *zoals de ~ waait, waait
zijn jasje* he hangs his cloak to the wind; **–as**
(-sen) *o* windlass, winch; **–buil** (-en) *v*
windbag, gas-bag, braggart; **–buks** (-en) *v*
air-gun, air-rifle; **–dicht** wind-proof; **–druk**
m wind-pressure

'winde (-n en -s) *v* 🌿 bindweed, convolvulus

'windei (-eren) *o* wind-egg; *het zal hem geen
~eren leggen* he will do well out of it

'winden* I *vt* 1 wind, twist [yarn &]; 2
(o p h ij s e n) hoist (up); ⚓ heave [an anchor
&]; *het op een klos ~* wind it on a reel, reel it;
II *vr zich ~* wind, wind itself [round a pole &]

'winderig windy²; **–heid** *v* windiness²;
'windgat (-gaten) *o* vent-hole; **–handel** *m*
speculation, stock-jobbery, gambling; **–hoek**
(-en) *m* 1 quarter from which the wind blows;

2 windy spot; **–hond** (-en) *m* greyhound;
–hondenrennen *mv* greyhound races; **–hoos**
(-hozen) *v* wind-spout, tornado

'winding (-en) *v* winding, coil [of a rope];
convolution [of the brain]

'windjak (-ken) *o* wind-cheater, *Am* wind-
breaker; **'windje** (-s) *o* breath of wind; **'wind-
kant** *m = windzij(de)*; **–kracht** *v* 1 (s t e r k t e)
wind-force; 2 (e n e r g i e) wind power; *storm
met ~ 10* force 10 gale; **–kussen** (-s) *o* air-
cushion; **–meter** (-s) *m* wind-gauge, anemom-
eter; **–molen** (-s) *m* windmill; *tegen ~s vechten*
tilt at (fight) windmills; **–richting** (-en) *v*
direction of the wind, wind direction; **–roos**
(-rozen) *v* ⚓ compass-card; **–scherm** (-en) *o*
windscreen; wind-break

'windsel (-s en -en) *o* bandage, swathe; *~s*
swaddling clothes;

'windsingel (-s) *m* shelterbelt, wind-break;
–snelheid (-heden) *v* wind speed, wind velocity;
–stil calm, windless; **–stilte** (-s en -n) *v* calm;
–stoot (-stoten) *m* gust of wind; **–streek** (-streken
v point of the compass; **–surfing** *v* sail-surf; **–tun
nel** (-s) *m* wind-tunnel; **–vaan** (-vanen) *v* weather
vane; **–vlaag** (-vlagen) *v* gust of wind, squall;
–waarts to windward; **–wijzer** (-s) *m* weathercock, weather-vane; **–zak** (-ken) *m* 🪁
wind-sock, wind-sleeve, drogue; **–zij(de)** *v*
wind-side, windward side, weather-side

'wingerd (-s en -en) *m* 1 (w ij n g a a r d) vineyard; 2 🍇 (w ij n s t o k) vine; *wilde ~* 🍇
Virginia(n) creeper

'wingewest (-en) *o* conquered country,
province

'winkel (-s) *m* 1 shop; 2 (v. a m b a c h t s m a n)
workshop, shop; *een ~ doen (houden)* keep a
shop; *de ~ sluiten* close the shop, shut up shop;
–bediende (-n en -s) *m-v* shop-assistant;
–centrum (-s en -tra) *o* shopping-centre;
–chef [-ʃɛf] (-s) *m* shopwalker; **–dief** (-dieven)
m shoplifter; **–diefstal** (-len) *m* shoplifting;
–dievegge (-n) *v* shoplifter; **'winkelen**
(winkelde, h. gewinkeld) *vi* go (be) shopping,
shop; **'winkelgalerij** (-en) *v* arcade

'winkelhaak (-haken) *m* 1 (v. t i m m e r m a n)
square; 2 (s c h e u r) tear

winke'lier (-s) *m* shopkeeper, shopman;
'winkeljuffrouw (-en) *v* shop-girl, salesgirl;
–kast (-en) *v* show-window; **–la(de)** (-laden,
-la's en -laas) *v* till; **–nering** *v* custom, goodwill; *gedwongen ~* truck(-system); **–opstand** *m*
shop-fittings, fixtures; **–prijs** (-prijzen) *m* retail
price; **–pui** (-en) *v* shop-front; **–raam**
(-ramen) *o* shop-window; **–sluiting** *v* closing
of shops; **–stand** (-en) *m* 1 shopping quarter;
2 community of shop-keepers; **–straat** (-stra-
ten) *v* shopping street; **–vereniging** (-en) *v*

co-operative store(s); **–waar** (-waren) *v* shop-wares; **–wijk** (-en) *v* shopping quarter; **–zaak** (-zaken) *v* shop

'**winnaar** (-s) *m* winner; '**winnen* I** *vt* 1 win [money, time, a prize, a battle &], gain [a battle, a lawsuit &]; 2 (v e r k r ij g e n) make [hay &]; ook: win [hay, ore &]; *het* ~ win, be victorious, carry the day; *het van iem.* ~ get the better of sbd.; *het in zeker opzicht* ~ *van...* have the pull over...; *u hebt 10 pond (de weddenschap) van me gewonnen* you have won £ 10 of me, you have won the bet from me; *(het) gemakkelijk* ~ win hands down; *het glansrijk van iem.* ~ beat sbd. hollow; *iem. voor de goede zaak* ~ win sbd. over to the (good) cause; *iem. voor zich* ~ win sbd. over (to one's side); **II** *va* win, gain; *a a n (in) duidelijkheid* ~ gain in clearness; *b ij iets* ~ gain by sth.; *bij nadere kennismaking* ~ improve upon acquaintance; *o p iem.* ~ gain (up)on sbd.; *Oxford wint v a n Cambridge* O. wins from C., O. beats C.; *zo gewonnen, zo geronnen* zie *gewonnen*; **–er** (-s) *m* winner

winst (-en) *v* gain, profit, winnings, return(s); ~ *behalen (maken) op* make a profit on; *grote ~en behalen* make big profits; ~ *geven (opleveren)* yield profit; *met* ~ *verkopen* sell at a profit; ~ *en verlies* $ profits and losses; **–aandeel** (-delen) *o* share in the profit(s); **–bejag** *o* pursuit (love) of gain, profiteering; **–belasting** *v* profits tax; **–cijfer** (-s) *o* profit; **–deling** (-en) *v* profit-sharing; **–derving** (-en) *v* loss of profit; **winst-en-ver'liesrekening** (-en) *v* profit and loss account; **winst'gevend** profitable, lucrative; '**winstje** (-s) *o* (little) profit; *met een zoet* ~ with a fair profit; '**winstmarge** [-mɑr-zə] (-s) *v* profit margin, margin of profit; **–punt** (-en) *o* plus, advantage; **–saldo** ('s en -saldi) *o* balance of profit(s); **–uitkering** (-en) *v* distribution of profits

'**winter** (-s) *m* 1 winter; 2 (z w e l l i n g) chilblain(s); *des ~s, in de* ~ in winter; *van de* ~ 1 this winter [present]; 2 next winter [future]; 3 last winter [past]; **–achtig** wintry; **winter'avond** (-en) *m* winter evening; '**winterdag** (-dagen) *m* winter-day; **–dienst** *m* 1 winter-service; 2 winter time-table; '**winteren** (winterde, h. gewinterd) *het wintert* it is freezing, it is wintering; '**wintergezicht** (-en) *o* wintry scene; **–goed** *o* winter-clothes; **–groen** *o* ℀ wintergreen; **–handen** *mv* chilblained hands; **–hard** ℀ hardy; **–hiel** (-en) *m* chilblained heel; **–jas** (-sen) *m &* *v* winter overcoat; **–kleed** (-klederen en -kleren) *o* winter-dress; *& v* winter-plumage; **–kleren** *mv* winter-clothes; **–koninkje** (-s) *o* wren; **–koren** *o* winter-corn; **–kost** *m* winter-fare; **–kwartier** (-en) *o* winter quarters; **–land-**

schap (-pen) *o* wintry landscape; **–maand** (-en) *v* December; *de ~en* the winter-months; **–mantel** (-s) *m* winter-coat; **–nacht** (-en) *m* winter-night; **–provisie** [s = z] (-s) *v* winter-store; **–s** *aj* wintry; **–seizoen** *o* winter-season; **–slaap** *m* winter sleep, hibernation; *een* ~ *houden* hibernate; '**Winterspelen** *mv Olympische* ~ Winter Olympic Games; '**wintersport** *v* winter sport(s); **–tenen** *mv* chilblained toes; **–tijd** *m* winter-time; **–tuin** (-en) *m* winter garden; **–verblijf** (-blijven) *o* winter-resort; winter-residence; **–vermaak** (-maken) *o* winter-amusement; **–voe(de)r** *o* winter-fodder; **–voeten** *mv* chilblained feet; **–voorraad** (-raden) *m* winter-store; **–we(d)er** *o* winter-weather, wintry weather; **–zonnestilstand** *m* winter solstice

'**winzucht** *v* love of gain, covetousness; **win'zuchtig** greedy of gain

1 wip (-pen) *v* 1 (p l a n k) seesaw; 2 (w i p-g a l g) Ⓤ strappado; 3 (v. b r u g) bascule; *op de* ~ *zitten* [*fig*] hold the balance [in politics]; *hij zit op de* ~ [*fig*] his position is shaky

2 wip *m* skip; *in een* ~ in no time, **F** in a jiffy; *en* ~ *was hij weg!* pop! he was gone

'**wipbrug** (-gen) *v* drawbridge, bascule-bridge; **–galg** (-en) *v* Ⓤ strappado; **–kar** (-ren) *v* tip-cart; **–neus** (-neuzen) *m* turned-up nose, nez retroussé; '**wippen** (wipte, h. en is gewipt) **I** *vi* 1 seesaw, move up and down; 2 skip, whip, nip; *even binnen* ~ pop in; *naar binnen* ~ skip into the house; *de hoek om* ~ whip round the corner; *de straat over* ~ nip across the street; **II** *vt* turn out [an official, a Liberal &]; '**wippertje** (-s) *o* 1 jack [in a piano]; 2 nip [of gin], dram; '**wippertoestel** (-len) *o* breeches buoy; '**wipplank** (-en) *v* seesaw; **–staart** (-en) *m* wagtail; **–stoel** (-en) *m* rocking-chair

'**wirwar** *m* tangle; maze [of narrow alleys]

1 wis *aj* certain, sure; *van een ~se dood redden* save from certain death; ~ *en zeker* yes, to be sure!

2 wis *v* wisp

wi'sent (-en) *m* wisent

'**wiskunde** *v* mathematics; **–leraar** (-s en -raren) *m* mathematics master; **wis'kundig** *aj* (& *ad*) mathematical(ly); **–e** (-n) *m* mathematician

wispel'turig inconstant, fickle, flighty, fly-away; **–heid** (-heden) *v* inconstancy, fickle-ness, flightiness

'**wissel** (-s) 1 *m &* *o* (v. s p o o r) switch, points [of a railway]; 2 *m* $ bill (of exchange), draft; *de* ~ *omzetten* shift the points; **–aar** (-s en -laren) *v* money-changer; **–agent** (-en) *m* exchange-broker; **–arbitrage** [-trɑ.zə] *v* arbitration of exchange; **–baden** *mv* alternating hot and cold baths; **–bank** (-en) *v* discount-bank; **–beker** (-s) *m* challenge cup; **–boek** (-en) *o* bill-book; **–bouw** *m* rotation of crops, crop rotation; **–brief** (-brieven) *m* bill of exchange; **'wisselen** (wisselde, h. gewisseld) **I** *vt* 1 change, give change for [a guilder &]; 2 (t a n d e n) shed [one's teeth], get one's second teeth; 3 exchange [glances, words &]; bandy [jests]; *zij hebben een paar schoten met elkaar gewisseld* they have exchanged a few shots; **II** *va* change, give [sbd.] change; *ik kan niet ~* I have no change; *dat kind is aan het ~* it is shedding its teeth; *zijn stem is aan het ~* his voice is turning; *die trein moet nog ~* must shunt; **III** *vi* change; *de a wisselt met de o a* varies with *o*; *van gedachten ~ over...* exchange views about...; *van paarden ~* change horses; *met ~d succes* with varying success; *~d bewolkt* cloudy with bright intervals; **'wisselgeld** *o* (small) change; **–handel** *m* exchange business; **–ing** (-en) *v* 1 (v e r a n d e r i n g, a f w i s s e l i n g) change; 2 turn [of the century, of the year]; 3 (r u i l) exchange; **–kantoor** (-toren) *o* exchange-office; **–kind** (-eren) *o* changeling; **–koers** (-en) *m* rate of exchange, exchange rate; **–loon** *o* bill-brokerage; **–loper** (-s) *m* collector; **–makelaar** (-s) *m* bill-broker; **–paard** (-en) *o* fresh horse; **–personeel** *o* parties to a bill; **–plaats** (-en) *v* stage [of a coach]; **–portefeuille** [-pɔrtəfœjə] *v* bill-case; **–provisie** [s = z] *v* bill-commission; **–rekening** *v* bill-account; **–ruiterij** *v* **F** kite-flying; **–slag** *m sp* medley relay; **–spoor** (-sporen) *o* siding; **–stand** *o* position of the points; **–stroom** (-stromen) *m* alternating current; **–stroomdynamo** [-di.na.mo.] ('s) *m* alternator; **–tand** (-en) *m* permanent tooth; **wissel'vallig** precarious [living], uncertain [weather]; **–heid** (-heden) *v* precariousness, uncertainty; *de wisselvalligheden des levens* the vicissitudes of life; **'wisselvervalser** (-s) *m* bill-forger; **–wachter** (-s) *m* pointsman; **–werking** (-en) *v* interaction; **–zegel** (-s) *m* & *o* bill-stamp

'wissen (wiste, h. gewist) *vt* wipe [plates &]; **–er** (-s) *m* wiper, mop

'wissewasje (-s) *o* trifle; *~s* fiddle-faddle

wist (wisten) V.T. van *weten*

wit I *aj* white; *Witte Donderdag* Maundy Thursday; *~ maken* whiten, blanch; *~ worden* 1 (v. d i n g e n) whiten, go (turn) white; 2 (v. p e r s o n e n) turn pale; *zo ~ als een doek* as white as a sheet; **II** *o* white; *het ~ van een ei* the white of an egg; *het ~ van de ogen* the white(s) of the eye(s); *het ~ van de schijf* the white; **–achtig** whitish; **–boek** (-en) *o* white paper; **–bont** black with white spots; **–geel** whitish yellow; **–gekuifd** white-crested; **–gloeiend**

white-hot; **–harig** white-haired; **–heid** *v* whiteness; **–hout** *o* whitewood; **–je** (-s) *o* ⚘ white [cabbage butterfly]; **–jes** *ad* palely; *~ lachen* smile wanly; **–kalk** *m* whitewash; **–kiel** (-en) *m* railway-porter; **–kwast** (-en) *m* whitewash brush; **–lo(o)f** *o* chicory; **–sel** *o* whitewash; **–staart** (-en) *m* 1 ✿ wheatear; 2 🐟 white-tailed horse; **'wittebrood** (-broden) *o* white bread; *een ~* a white loaf; **–sweken** *mv* honeymoon; **'wittekool** *v* white cabbage; **'witten** (witte, h. gewit) *vt* whitewash; **–er** (-s) *m* whitewasher; **'witvis** (-sen) *m* 🐟 whiting, whitebait

W.L. = *westerlengte*

wnd. = *waarnemend*

w.o. = *waaronder*

'Wodan *m* Wotan

'wodka *m* vodka

'woede *v* rage, fury; *machteloze ~* impotent rage; *zijn ~ koelen op* wreak one's fury on, vent one's rage on; **–aanval** (-len) *m* fit of rage, flare-up, **S** wax; *een ~ krijgen,* fly off the handle, fly into a tantrum, **S** get into a wax; **'woeden** (woedde, h. gewoed) **I** *vi* rage² [of the sea, wind, passion, battle, disease]; **II** *o* raging; *het ~ der elementen* ook: the fury of the elements; **–d I** *aj* furious; *iem. ~ maken* put sbd. in a passion, infuriate sbd.; *zich ~ maken* fly into a passion, fly into a rage; *~ zijn* be in a rage, be furious, be in a white heat; *~ zijn op* be furious with; *~ zijn o v e r* be furious at (about), be in a rage at (about); **II** *ad* furiously; **'woedeuitbarsting** (-en) *v* outburst of fury (rage)

woef! woof!

woei (woeien) V.T. van *waaien*

'woeker *m* usury; *~ drijven* practise usury; **–aar** (-s) *m* usurer; **–dier** (-en) *o* parasite; **'woekeren** (woekerde, h. gewoekerd) *vi* 1 practise usury; 2 (v. o n k r u i d &) be rampant; *~ m e t zijn tijd* make the most of one's time; *~ o p* be parasitic on; **'woekergeld** *o* money got by usury; **–handel** *m* usurious trade; **–huur** (-huren) *v* rack rent; **–ing** (-en) *v* excrescence²; (*v.* p l a n t e n) rampancy, rankness; (g e z w e l) growth, tumour; **–plant** (-en) *v* parasitic plant, parasite; **–prijs** (-prijzen) *m* usurious price, exorbitant price; **–rente** (-n) *v* usurious interest, usury; **–winst** (-en) *v* exorbitant profit; *~ maken* profiteer

'woelen (woelde, h. gewoeld) **I** *vi* 1 (in d e s l a a p) toss (about), toss in bed; 2 (in d e g r o n d) burrow, grub; *zit niet in mijn papieren te ~* stop rummaging in my papers; **II** *vt* 1 (in d e bloot ~) kick the bed-clothes off; *gaten in de grond ~* burrow holes in the ground; *iets uit de grond ~* grub sth. up; **'woelgeest** (-en) *m* turbulent spirit, agitator; **'woelig** turbulent; *de kleine is erg ~ geweest* has been very restless; *het is erg ~ op straat* the street is in a tumult; *in ~e tijden* in turbulent times; **–heid** (-heden) *v* turbulence, unrest; **'woeling** (-en) *v* turbulence, agitation; *~en* disturbances; **'woelmuis** (-muizen) *v* field-vole; **–rat** (-ten) *v* water-vole; **–water** (-s) *m-v* fidget; **–ziek** turbulent; **–zucht** *v* turbulence

'woensdag (-dagen) *m* Wednesday; **–s I** *aj* Wednesday; **II** *ad* on Wednesdays

woerd (-en) *m* ☘ drake

woest I *aj* 1 (o n b e b o u w d) waste [grounds]; 2 (o n b e w o o n d) desolate [island]; 3 (w i l d) savage [scenery]; wild [waves]; fierce [struggle]; furious [speed]; reckless [driver, driving]; 4 **F** (n ij d i g) savage, wild, mad; *hij werd ~* **F** he got wild, mad; *hij was ~ op ons* **F** he was wild with us, mad with us; *~e gronden* waste lands; **II** *ad* wildly &; **–aard** (-s), **–eling** (-en) *m* brute

woeste'nij (-en) *v* waste (land), wilderness

'woestheid (-heden) *v* wildness, savagery, fierceness

woes'tijn (-en) *v* desert

'wogen V.T. meerv. van *wegen*

wol *v* wool; *een i n de ~ geverfde schurk* a double-dyed villain; *ik ging vroeg o n d e r d e ~* **F** I turned in early; *onder de ~ zijn* be between the sheets; **–achtig** woolly; **–baal** (-balen) *v* bale of wool, woolsack; **–bereider** (-s) *m* wool-dresser; **–bereiding** *v* wool-dressing

wolf (wolven) *m* 1 ☘ wolf; 2 caries [in the teeth]; *een ~ in schaapskleren* **B** a wolf in sheep's clothing; *~ en schapen sp* fox and geese; *wee de ~ die in een kwaad gerucht staat* give a dog a bad name and hang him; *eten als een ~* eat ravenously; *een honger hebben als een ~* be as hungry as a hunter

'wolfabriek (-en) *v* wool mill; **–fabrikant** (-en) *m* woollen manufacturer

'wolfachtig wolfish

'wolfra(a)m *o* wolfram, tungsten; **–lamp** (-en) *v* tungsten filament lamp

'wolfsangel (-s) *m* trap (for wolves); **–hond** (-en) *m* wolf-dog, wolf-hound; **–kers** (-en) *v* belladonna; **–klauw** (-en) *m & v* 1 wolf's claw; 2 ☘ club-moss; **–melk** *v* ☘ spurge; **–vel** (-len) *o* wolfskin

'Wolga *v* Volga

'wolgras *o* cotton-grass; **–haar** *o* woolly hair; **–handel** *m* wool-trade; **–handelaar** (-s en -laren) *m* wool-merchant; **–harig** woolly-haired

wolk (-en) *v* cloud; *een ~ van insekten* a cloud of insects; *een ~ van een jongen* the baby (boy) is a picture of health; *een ~ van een meid* she is all

peaches and cream; *er lag een ~ op zijn voorhoofd* there was a cloud on his brow; *hij is in de ~en* he is beside himself with joy, he walks on air, he is on cloud seven; *iem. tot in de ~en verheffen* extol sbd. to the skies

'wolkaarder (-s) *m* wool-carder

'wolkbreuk (-en) *v* cloud-burst, torrential rain; **'wolkeloos** cloudless, clear [sky]; **'wolkenbank** (-en) *v* cloud bank; **–dek** *o* cloud cover, blanket of clouds; **–krabber** (-s) *m* skyscraper; **'wolkig** cloudy, clouded; **'wolkje** (-s) *o* cloudlet [in the sky]; *een ~ melk* a drop of milk; *er is geen ~ aan de lucht* there is not a cloud in the sky[2]

'wolkoper (-s) *m* wool-merchant; **'wollegras** = *wolgras*; **'wollen** *aj* woollen; *~ goederen* woollens; **–goed** *o* 1 (k l e r e n) woollen things; 2 (g o e d e r e n) $ woollens; **'wolletje** (-s) *o* woolly; **'wollig** woolly; **–heid** *v* woolliness; **wolspinne'rij** (-en) *v* wool mill

'wolveaard *m* wolfish nature

'wolvee *o* wool-producing cattle

'wolvejacht *v* wolf-hunting

'wolverver (-s) *m* wool-dyer; **wolverve'rij** (-en) *v* 1 wool-dyeing; 2 dye-works

'wolvevel (-len) = *wolfsvel*; **wol'vin** (-nen) *v* ☘ she-wolf

'wolwever (-s) *m* wool-weaver; **–zak** (-ken) *m* woolsack

won (wonnen) V.T. v. *winnen*

1 wond *aj* sore; *de ~e plek* the sore spot

2 wond (-en) *v* wound; *oude ~en openrijten* rip up (reopen) old sores; *diepe ~en slaan* inflict deep wounds

3 wond (winden) V.T. van *winden*

'wonde (-n) = 2 *wond*; **'wonden** (wondde, h. gewond) *vt* wound, injure, hurt

'wonder (-en) *o* wonder, miracle, marvel, prodigy; *de ~en in de Bijbel* the miracles in the Bible; *~en van dapperheid* prodigies of valour; *een ~ van geleerdheid* a prodigy of learning; *de zeven ~en van de wereld* the seven wonders of the world; *de ~en zijn de wereld nog niet uit* wonders will never cease; live and learn; *(het is) geen ~ dat...* (it is) no wonder that..., small wonder that...; *~en doen* work wonders, perform miracles; *en ~ boven ~, hij...* miracle of miracles, he..., and for a wonder, he...; **–baar** 1 miraculous; 2 strange; **wonder'baarlijk I** *aj* miraculous, marvellous; **II** *ad* miraculously, marvellously; **–heid** (-heden) *v* marvellousness; **'wonderbeeld** (-en) *o* miraculous image; **–daad** (-daden) *v* miracle; **wonder'dadig** miraculous; **'wonderdier** (-en) *o* prodigy, monster; **–doend** wonder-working; **–doener** (-s) *m* wonder-worker; **–dokter** (-s) *m* quack (doctor); **–kind** (-eren) *o* wonder-child, child prodigy, infant prodigy; **–kracht** *v* miraculous power; **–lijk** strange; **–lijkheid** (-heden) *v* strangeness; **–macht** *v* miraculous power; **–mens** (-en) *o* human wonder, prodigy; **–middel** (-en) *o* wonderful remedy; **–olie** *v* castor-oil; **–schoon** most beautiful, absolutely beautiful; **–teken** (-s en -en) *o* miraculous sign; **–wel** to a miracle; **–werk** (-en) *o* miracle

'**wondkoorts** (-en) *v* wound-fever, traumatic fever; **–roos** *v* 🜊 erysipelas

'**wonen** (woonde, h. gewoond) *vi* live, reside, dwell; *hij woont b ij ons* he lives in our house (with us); *i n de stad* ~ live in town; *o p kamers* ~ zie *kamer*; *op het land* ~ live in the country; *vrij* ~ *hebben* live rent-free, have free housing;

'**woning** (-en) *v* house, dwelling, residence, ☉ mansion; **–bouw** *m* house-building, house construction, housing; **–bureau** [-by.ro.] (-s) *o* house-agent's office; **–gids** (-en) *m* directory; **–inrichting** *v* furnishings, appointments; **–nood** *m* housing shortage; **–ruil** *m* exchange of houses; **–tekort** *o* housing shortage; **–textiel** *m* & **–toestanden** *mv* housing conditions; **–vraagstuk** *o* housing problem; **–wet** *v* housing act; **–wetwoning** (-en) *v* ± council house; **woning'zoekende** (-n) *m* & *v* house-hunter, home-seeker, person looking for accomodation

'**wonnen** V.T. meerv. van *winnen*

woof (**woven**) **F** V.T. van *wuiven*

woog (**wogen**) V.T. van *wegen*

woon'achtig resident, living; '**woonark** (-en) *v* houseboat; **–huis** (-huizen) *o* dwelling-house; **–kamer** (-s) *v* sitting-room, living-room; **–kazerne** (-s) *v* tenement-house; **–keuken** (-s) *v* kitchen-cum-livingrooom; **–laag** (-lagen) *v* storey; **–plaats** (-en) *v* dwelling-place, home, residence, domicile; 🜚 & 🜚 habitat; **–ruimte** (-n) *v* housing accommodation, living accommodation, living space; **–schip** (-schepen) *o*, **–schuit** (-en) *v* houseboat; **–ste(d)e** (-steden) *v* home; **–vertrek** (-ken) *o* = *woonkamer*; **–wagen** (-s) *m* caravan; **–wagenkamp** (-en) *o* caravan camp; (v a n z i g e u n e r s) gipsy camp; **–wijk** (-en) *v* housing estate; (d e f t i g) residential quarter (district)

1 woord (-en) *m* 🜚 = *woerd*

2 woord (-en) *o* word, term; *grote* ~*en* big words; *hoge* ~*en* high words; *het hoge* ~ *is er uit* at last the truth is out; *het hoge* ~ *kwam er uit* he owned up; *een vies* ~ a dirty word²; *het Woord* (*Gods*) God's Word, the Word (of God); *het Woord is vlees geworden* **B** the Word was made flesh; *hier past een* ~ *van dank aan...* thanks are due to...; ~*en en daden* words and deeds; *geen* ~ *meer!* not another word!; *er is geen* ~ *van waar*

there is not a word of truth in it; *zijn* ~ *breken* break one's word; *een* ~ *van lof brengen aan...* pay a tribute to...; *het* ~ *doen* act as spokesman; *hij kan heel goed zijn* ~ *doen* he is never at a loss what to say, he has the gift of the gab; *een goed* ~ *voor iem. doen bij...* put in a word for sbd. with...; *iem. het* ~ *geven* call upon sbd. to speak (to say a few words); *(iem.) zijn* ~ *geven* give (sbd.) one's word; *het éne* ~ *haalt* (*lokt*) *het andere uit, van het éne* ~ *komt het andere* one word leads to another; *het* ~ *hebben* be speaking; be on one's feet, have the floor; *het* ~ *alléén hebben* have all the talk to oneself; *ik zou graag het* ~ *hebben* I should like to say a word; ~*en met iem. hebben* have words with sbd.; *het hoogste* ~ *hebben* do most of the talking; *hij wil het laatste* ~ *hebben* he wants to have the last word; *(zijn)* ~ *houden* keep one's word, be as good as one's word; *het* ~ *vrees & kent hij niet* fear & is a word that has no place in his vocabulary; *het* ~ *krijgen* zie *aan het* ~ *komen; men kan er geen* ~ *tussen krijgen* you could not get in a word; *ik kan geen* ~ *uit hem krijgen* I cannot get a word out of him; ~*en krijgen met iem.* come to words with sbd.; *het* ~ *nemen* begin to speak, rise, take the floor; *hem het* ~ *ontnemen* ask the speaker to sit down; *het* ~ *richten tot iem.* address sbd.; *hij kon geen* ~ *uitbrengen* he could not bring out a word; *men kon zijn eigen* ~*en niet verstaan* you couldn't hear your own words; *ik kan geen* ~*en vinden om...* I have no words to..., words fail me to...; *het* ~ *bij de daad voegen* suit the action to the word; *het* ~ *voeren* act as spokesman; *de heer A. zal het* ~ *voeren* Mr A. will speak; *een hoog* ~ *voeren* talk big; *het* ~ *vragen* 1 ask leave to speak; 2 try to catch the Speaker's eye; *wenst iem. het* ~? does any one desire to address the meeting?; *geen* ~ *zeggen* not say a word; *ik heb er geen* ~ *in te zeggen* I have no say in the matter; *het* ~ *is aan u* the word is with you; *het* ~ *is nu aan onze tegenstander* it is for our antagonist to speak now; ● *wie is a a n het* ~? who is speaking?; *iem. aan zijn* ~ *houden* take sbd. at his word; *ik kon niet aan het* ~ *komen* 1 I could not get in a word; 2 I could not catch the Speaker's eye; *b ij het* ~ *des meesters zweren* zie *zweren* **I**; *i n één* ~ in a word, in one word; *de oorlog in* ~ *en beeld* the war in words and pictures; *met andere* ~*en* in other words; *hetzelfde met andere* ~*en* the same thing though differently worded; *met deze* ~*en* with these words; *met een paar* ~*en* in a few words; *met zoveel* ~*en* in so many words; *iets o n d e r* ~*en brengen* put sth. into words; *o p één* ~ *van u* on a word from you; *op dat* ~ on the word, with the word; *iem. op zijn* ~ *geloven* take sbd.'s word for it; *op mijn* ~ 1 at this word of mine; 2 upon my word; *op mijn ~ van eer* upon my word (of honour); *iem. t e ~ staan* give sbd. a hearing, listen to sbd.; *~ v o o r ~* [repeat] word by (for) word, verbatim; *een goed ~ vindt een goede plaats* a good word is never out of season; *~en wekken, voorbeelden trekken* example is better than precept; **–accent** (-en) *o* word stress, word accent; **–afleiding** (-en) *v* etymology; **–blind** word-blind, dyslexic; **–breker** (-s) *m* promise-breaker; **–breuk** *v* breach of promise (faith); **–elijk I** *aj* verbal, literal; verbatim [report]; **II** *ad* verbally, literally, word for word, verbatim

'**woordenboek** (-en) *o* dictionary, lexicon; **–kraam** *v* verbiage, verbosity; **–lijst** (-en) *v* word-list, vocabulary; **–praal** *v* pomp of words, bombast; **–rijk** 1 rich in words; 2 wordy, verbose, voluble [speaker]; **–rijkheid** *v* 1 wealth of words; 2 flow of words, wordiness, verbosity, volubility; **–schat** *m* stock of words, vocabulary; **–spel** *o* play upon words, pun; **–strijd** *m*, **–twist** *m* verbal dispute, altercation; **–vloed** (-en) *m* flow (torrent) of words; **–wisseling** (-en) *v* altercation, dispute; **–zifter** (-s) *m* word-catcher, verbalist; **woordenzifter'rij** (-en) *v* word-catching, verbalism; '**woordje** (-s) *o* (little) word; *een ~, alstublieft!* just a word, please!; *doe een goed ~ voor me* put in a good word for me; *een ~ meespreken* put in a word

'**woordkeus** *v* choice of words; **–kunst** *v* (art of) word-painting; **–kunstenaar** (-s) *m* artist in words; **–merk** (-en) *o* brand name; **–ontleding** (-en) *v* parsing; **–orde** *v*, **–schikking** *v* order of words, word-order; **–soorten** *mv* parts of speech; **–speling** (-en) *v* play (up)on words; pun; *~en maken* pun; **–verdraaier** (-s) *m* perverter of words; **–verdraaiing** (-en) *v* perversion of words; **–voerder** (-s) *m* spokesman, mouthpiece; **–vorming** *v* formation of words, word formation

'**worden*** *vi* become, get, go, grow, turn, fall; ✎ wax; *arm ~* become poor; *bleek ~* turn pale; *blind ~* go blind; *dronken ~* get drunk; *gek ~* go mad; *hij is gisteren (vandaag) 80 geworden* he was eighty yesterday (he is eighty to day); *hij is bijna honderd jaar geworden* he lived to be nearly a hundred; *nijdig ~* get angry; *oud ~* grow old; *soldaat ~* become a soldier; *hij zal een goed soldaat ~* he will make a good soldier; *wat wil je later ~?* what do you want to be when you grow up?; *ijs wordt water* ice turns into water; *ziek ~* be taken ill, fall ill; *wanneer het lente wordt* when spring comes; *het wordt morgen een week* tomorrow it will be a week; *wat is er van hem geworden?* what has become of him?; *er zal gedanst ~* there is to be dancing; '**wording** *v*

origin, genesis; *in ~ zijn* be in process of formation; **–geschiedenis** *v* genesis

'**worgband** (-en) *m* choke chain; '**worgen** (worgde, h. geworgd) *vt* strangle, throttle; *~de greep* stranglehold; **–er** (-s) *m* strangler; '**worggreep** (-grepen) *m* stranglehold; '**worging** *v* strangulation

worm (-en) *m* 1 worm; 2 (m a d e) grub, maggot; **–achtig** wormy, vermicular; **–ig** wormy, worm-eaten; **–middel** (-en) *o* vermifuge; **–pje** (-s) *o* small worm, vermicule; **worm'stekig** worm-eaten, wormy; **–heid** *v* worm-eaten condition; '**wormverdrijvend** vermifuge; **–vormig** vermiform [appendix]

worp (-en) *m* throw [of dice &]; litter [of pigs]

worst (-en) *v* sausage; **–ebroodje** (-s) *o* sausage-roll

'**worstelaar** (-s en -laren) *m* wrestler; '**worstelen** (worstelde, h. geworsteld) **I** *vi* wrestle; *~ m e t* wrestle with[2], *fig* struggle with, grapple with; *t e g e n d e wind ~* struggle with the wind; **II** *o vrij ~* catch-as-catch-can, all-in wrestling; **–ling** (-en) *v* wrestling[2], wrestle; *fig* struggle; '**worstelperk** (-en) *o* ring, arena; **–strijd** *m* struggle; **–wedstrijd** (-en) *m* wrestling-match

'**worstmachine** [-ma.ʃi.nə] (-s) *v* sausage-machine

'**wortel** (-s en -en) *m* 1 root[2]; 2 (p e e n) carrot; 3 (v. g e t a l) root; *gele ~ 🅰 carrot; witte ~ 🅰 parsnip; *~ schieten* take (strike) root[2]; *~ trekken* extract the root of a number; *met ~ en tak uitroeien* root out, cut up root and branch; **–boom** (-bomen) *m* mangrove; '**wortelen** (wortelde, h. en is geworteld) *vi* take root; *~ in* [*fig*] be rooted in; '**wortelgetal** (-len) *o* root (number); **–gewas** (-sen) *o* root crop; **–grootheid** (-heden) *v* radical quantity; **–haren** *mv* 🅰 fibrils; **–hout** *o* root-wood; **–kiem** (-en) *v* radicle; **–knol** (-len) *m* tuber; **–notehout** *o* figured walnut; **–noten** walnut [table]; **–stelsel** (-s) *o* root-system, rootage; **–stok** (-ken) *m* root-stock, rhizome; **–teken** (-s) *o* radical sign; **–tje** (-s) *o* 🅰 1 rootlet, radicle; 2 *~s* carrots; **–trekking** (-en) *v* extraction of roots; **–vezel** (-s) *v* 🅰 root-fibre, fibril; **–woord** (-en) *o* root-word, radical (word)

wou (**wouwen**) F V.T. v. *willen*

woud (-en) *o* forest; **–duif** (-duiven) *v* wood-pigeon; **–ezel** (-s) *m* 🐾 wild ass, onager; **–loper** (-s) *m* 🄌 coureur de(s) bois [French trapper in Canada]; **–reus** (-reuzen) *m* giant of the forest

'**Wouter** *m* Walter

1 wouw (-en) *m* 🪶 kite

2 wouw (-en) *v* 🅰 weld

'**wouwen** F V.T. meerv. v. *willen*

'**woven** F V.T. meerv. van *wuiven*

'**wraak** *v* revenge, vengeance; *de ~ is zoet* sweet is revenge; *zijn ~ koelen* wreak one's vengeance; *~ nemen op* take revenge on, revenge oneself on, be revenged on; *~ nemen over iets* take revenge [on sbd.] for sth.; *~ oefenen* take revenge; *~ zweren* swear vengeance; *om ~ roepen* cry for vengeance; *u i t ~* in revenge; **–baar** 1 ♃ challengeable [witness]; 2 (l a a k-b a a r) blamable; **–gevoelens** *mv* vindictive feelings; **wraak'gierig** vindictive, revengeful; **–heid** *v* vindictiveness, revengefulness, thirst for revenge; '**wraakgodin** (-nen) *v* avenging goddess; *de ~nen* the Furies; **–lust** *m = wraak-gierigheid;* **–neming** (-en), **–oefening** (-en) *v* retaliation, (act of) revenge; **–zucht** *v = wraakgierigheid;* **wraak'zuchtig** *= wraakgierig*

1 **wrak** *aj* crazy, unsound, rickety; ♃ cranky

2 **wrak** (-ken) *o* wreck

⊙ '**wrake** *= wraak; mij is de ~! B* vengeance is mine!

'**wraken** (wraakte, h. gewraakt) *vt* 1 challenge, rule out of court [a witness]; 2 denounce [abuses &]

'**wrakgoederen** *mv* wreck, wreckage, flotsam and jetsam; **–heid** *v* craziness, unsound condition, ricketiness; ♃ crankiness; **–hout** *o* ♃ wreckage

'**wraking** (-en) *v* ♃ challenge

wrang sour, acid, tart, harsh [in the mouth]; *de ~e vruchten van zijn luiheid* the bitter fruit of his idleness; **–heid** *v* sourness, acidity, tartness, harshness

wrat (-ten) *v* wart; **–achtig** warty

weed I *aj* cruel, ferocious; grim [scenes]; II *ad* cruelly; **–aard** (-s) *m* cruel man; **weed'aardig** *aj* (& *ad*) cruel(ly); '**weedheid** (-heden) *v* cruelty, ferocity

1 **wreef** (wreven) *v* instep

2 **wreef** (wreven) V.T. v. *wrijven*

'**wreekster** (-s) *v* avenger, revenger; '**wreken*** I *vt* revenge [an offence, a person]; avenge [a person, an offence]; II *vr zich ~* revenge oneself, avenge oneself, be avenged; *het zal zich wel ~* it is sure to avenge itself; *zich ~ op* revenge oneself (up)on; *zich ~ over... op...* revenge oneself for... (up)on...; **–er** (-s) *m* avenger, revenger

'**wrevel** I *m* resentment, spite; (k n o r r i g-h e i d) peevishness; II *aj* & *ad = wrevelig;* '**wrevelig** I *aj* resentful; (k n o r r i g) peevish, crusty, testy; II *ad* resentfully; (k n o r r i g) peevishly, crustily, testily; **–heid** *v* resentment, spite; (k n o r r i g h e i d) peevishness, crustiness, testiness

'**wreven** V.T. meerv. v. *wrijven*

'**wriemelen** (wriemelde, h. gewriemeld) *vi*

wriggle; (f r i e m e l e n) fiddle; *~ van* crawl with

'**wrijfdoek** (-en), **–lap** (-pen) *m* rubbing cloth, polishing cloth; **–hout** (-en) *o* ♃ fender; **–paal** (-palen) *m eig* rubbing-post; *fig* butt; **–steen** (-stenen) *m* rubbing-stone; **–was** *m* & *o* beeswax; '**wrijven*** I *vt* 1 rub [chairs &, things against each other]; 2 bray [colours]; *het ~ over...* rub it over; *ze t e g e n elkaar ~* rub them together; *het t o t poeder ~* rub it to powder; *zich de handen (de ogen) ~* rub one's hands (one's eyes); II *vi* rub; *~ tegen iets* rub (up) against something; **–er** (-s) *m* rubber; '**wrijving** (-en) *v* rubbing, friction[2]; *de ~ tussen hen* the friction between them; '**wrijvings-elektriciteit** *v* frictional electricity; **–hoek** (-en) *m* angle of friction

'**wrikken** (wrikte, h. gewrikt) I *vi* jerk [at sth.]; II *vt* ♃ scull [a boat]; '**wrikriem** (-en) *m* scull

'**wringen*** I *vt* wring [one's hands]; wring out, wring [wet clothes]; *iem. iets uit de handen ~* wrest sth. from sbd.; *daar wringt hem de schoen* that's where the shoe pinches; II *vr zich ~* twist oneself; *zich ~ als een worm* writhe like a worm; *zich door een opening ~* worm oneself through a gap; *zich in allerlei bochten ~* wriggle, twist and turn; *zich in allerlei bochten ~ van pijn* writhe with pain; **–ging** *v* wringing; twisting, twist; '**wringmachine** [ma.ʃinə] (-s) *v* wringing-machine, wringer

'**wroeging** (-en) *v* remorse, compunction, contrition

'**wroeten** (wroette, h. gewroet) I *vi* root, rout [= turn up the earth], grub[2] [in the earth, *fig* for a livelihood]; *in de grond ~* root (rout) up the earth; II *vt een gat in de grond ~* burrow a hole

wrok *m* grudge, rancour, resentment; *een ~ tegen iem. hebben (jegens iem. koesteren)* bear (owe) sbd. a grudge, have a spite against sbd., bear sbd. ill-will; *geen ~ koesteren* bear no malice; '**wrokken** (wrokte, h. gewrokt) *vi* chafe, sulk; *~ o v e r* chafe at; *~ t e g e n* have a spite against [him]; '**wrokkig** rancorous

1 **wrong** (-en) *m* 1 (r u k) wrench, twist; 2 (v. k r a n s) wreath; 3 (v. h a a r) coil; 4 (t u l b a n d) turban; 5 ⊘ wreath; *een ~ sajet* a skein of worsted

2 **wrong** (wrongen) V.T. v. *wringen*

'**wrongel** *v* curdled milk, curds

'**wrongen** V.T. meerv. v. *wringen*

wsch. *= waarschijnlijk*

wuft I *aj* fickle, frivolous; II *ad* frivolously; **–heid** (-heden) *v* fickleness, frivolity

'**wuiven*** *vi* wave; *~ met de hand* wave one's hand

wulp (-en) *m* ♋ curlew

wulps *aj* wanton, lascivious, lewd, voluptuous [nude]; **–heid** (-heden) *v* wantonness, lasciviousness, lewdness, voluptuousness

'**wurgen** (wurgde, h. gewurgd) = *worgen*; **–er** (-s) = *worger*; '**wurging** = *worging*

wurm (-en) 1 *m* worm; 2 *o* het ~ the poor mite

'**wurmen** (wurmde, h. gewurmd) **I** *vi* worm, wriggle; *fig* drudge, toil; **II** *vr* zich er uit ~ wriggle out of it

W.v.K. = *Wetboek van Koophandel*

W.v.Str. = *Wetboek van Strafrecht*

X

x [ɪks] ('en) *v* x
Xan'tippe, xan'tippe (-s) *v* Xanthippe[2]
'x-as (-sen) *v* x-axis

'x-benen *mv* turned-in (knock-kneed) legs; *iem.*
met ~ a knock-kneed person
xylo'foon [ksi.lo.-] (-s en -fonen) *m* xylophone

y [i.'gr
ya(c)k [jɑk] = 2 *jak*
'yamswortel ['jɑms-] (-s) *m* yam
'yankee ['jɛŋki.] (-s) *m* Yankee, **F** Yank
'y-as ['ɛi-ɑs] (-sen) *v* y-axis

yen [jɛn] (-s) *m* yen
'yoga ['jo.ga.] *v* yoga
'yoghurt ['jɔɡərt] *m* yogurt
'yogi ['jo.gi.] ('s) *m* yogi

Z

z [ztt] ('s) *v* z

Z. = *zuid*

z.a. = *zie aldaar* which see

zaad (zaden) *o* seed² [of plants &, of strife, vice]; sperm [of mammalia]; *het ~ van Abraham* **B** the seed of Abraham; *het ~ der tweedracht* the seed(s) of dissension (of discord); *i n het ~ schieten* run (go) to seed; *o p zwart ~ zitten* be hard up; **–bakje** (-s) *o* seed-box [of a bird-cage]; **–bal** (-len) *m* testicle; **–bed** (-den) *o* seed-bed; **–doos** (-dozen) *v* capsule; **–handel** *m* seed-trade; **–handelaar** (-s en -laren) *m* seedsman; **–huid** (-en) *v* seed-coat; **–huisje** (-s) *o* seed-vessel; **–kiem** (-en) *v* germ; **–korrel** (-s) *m* grain of seed; **–lob** (-ben) *v* seed-lobe, cotyledon; **–loos** seedless; **–lozing** (-en) *v* ejaculation (of semen); **–monster** (-s) *o* seed-sample; **–rok** (-ken) *m* tunic; **–streng** (-en) *v* spermatic cord, funiculus; **–teelt** *v* seed-growing; **–veredeling** *v* seed-improvement; **–vlies** (-vliezen) *o* tunic; **–winkel** (-s) *m* seed-shop

zaag (zagen) *v* 1 ✂ saw; 2 (m e n s) bore; **–blad** (-bladen) *o* saw-blade; **–bok** (-ken) *m* trestle, saw-horse; **–machine** [-ma.ʃi.nə] (-s) *v* sawing-machine; **–meel** *o* sawdust; **–molen** (-s) *m* saw-mill; **–sel** *o* sawdust; '**zaagsnede** (-n) *v* kerf; *mes met ~* serrated knife; **–tand** (-en) *m* tooth of a saw; **–vijl** (-en) *v* saw-file; **–vis** (-sen) *m* sawfish; **–vormig** saw-shaped, serrate(d)

'**zaaibed** (-den) *o* seed-bed; '**zaaien** (zaaide, h. gezaaid) *vt* sow²; *wat gij zaait zult gij oogsten* you must reap what you have sown; **–er** (-s) *m* sower; '**zaaigoed** *o* seeds for sowing; **–graan** *o* seed-corn; **–ing** *v* sowing; **–koren** *o* seed-corn; **–land** (-en) *o* sowing-land; **–ling** (-en) *m* seedling; **–machine** [-ma.ʃi.nə] (-s) *v* sowing-machine; **–sel** (-s) *o* seed (sown); **–tijd** (-en) *m* sowing-time, sowing-season; **–zaad** (-zaden) *o* seed for sowing

zaak (zaken) *v* 1 (d i n g) thing; 2 (a a n g e l e-g e n h e i d) business, affair, matter, concern, cause; 3 ⚖ case, (law)suit; 4 (b e d r ij f) business, concern, trade; *zaken* $ 1 business; 2 *zijn twee zaken te A.* his two businesses at A.; *zaken zijn zaken* business is business; *gedane zaken nemen geen keer* what is done cannot be undone, it's no use crying over spilt milk; *de goede ~* the good cause; *de ~ is dat ik de ~ niet vertrouw* the fact is that I don't trust the whole thing; *dat is de hele ~* that is the whole matter; *het is ~ dat te*

bedenken it is essential for us to consider that; *dat is uw ~* that's your look-out; that's your affair; *het is mijn ~ niet* it is not my business, it is no concern of mine; *niet veel ~s* not much of a thing, not up to much, not worth much; *eens zien hoe de zaken staan* how things stand; *zoals de ~ nu staat* as matters (things) stand at present; *een ~ beginnen* start a business, set up in business, open a shop; *zaken doen* do (carry on) business; *zaken doen met iem.* do business (have dealings) with sbd.; *goede zaken doen* do good business; do a good trade [in ice-creams &]; *zijn advocaat de ~ in handen geven* place the matter in the hands of one's solicitor; *gemene ~ maken met...* make common cause with; *er een ~ van maken* ⚖ take proceedings; ● *hoe staat het m e t de zaken? t e r zake!* 1 to the point!; 2 (p a r l e m e n t a i r) Question!; *dat doet niets ter zake* 1 (that is) no matter; 2 it is not to the purpose, it is neither here nor there; *laat ons ter zake komen* let us come (get) to business (to the point); *het is niet ter zake dienende* it is not to the point; *ter zake van...* on account of...; zie ook: *inzake*; *hij is u i t de ~* he has retired from business; *v o o r een goede ~* in a good cause; *voor zaken op reis* away on business; *suiker & z o n d e r zaken* $ without any transactions; **–bezorger** (-s) *m* man of business, solicitor, agent, proxy; **–gelastigde** (-n) *m* agent, proxy; [diplomatic] chargé d'affaires; **–kennis** *v* (expert) knowledge of a subject, practical knowledge; **zaak'kundig** expert; *een ~e* an expert; '**zaakregister** (-s) *o* subject-index; **–waarnemer** (-s) *m* solicitor

1 zaal (zalen) *v* hall, room; ward [in hospital]; auditorium [of a theatre]; *een volle ~* a full house [of theatre &] .

2 zaal (zalen) *o* = *zadel*

'**zaalsport** (-en) *v* indoor-sport(s), indoor game(s); **–wachter** (-s) *m* attendant, custodian [in a museum]

'**zabbelen** (zabbelde, h. gezabbeld) = *sabbelen*

Zacha'rias *m* Zachariah, Zachary

zacht I *aj* 1 (n i e t h a r d) *eig* soft [bed, cushion, bread, butter, fruit, palate, steel]; *fig* gentle [rebuke, treatment]; mild [punishment]; 2 (n i e t r u w) *eig* soft, smooth [skin]; *fig* soft, mild [weather]; mild [climate]; 3 (n i e t l u i d) soft [whispers, music, murmurs]; low [voice]; gentle [knock]; mellow [tones]; 4 (n i e t h e v i g) soft [rain]; gentle [breeze]; slow [fire]; 5 (n i e t s t r e n g) soft, mild [winter]; 6 (n i e t

s c h e l) soft [hues]; 7 (n i e t s c h e r p)
soft [air, letters, water, wine]; 8 (n i e t
g e p r o n o n c e e r d) gentle [slope]; 9 (n i e t
d r a s t i s c h) mild, gentle [medicine]; 10
(n i e t p ij n l ij k) easy [death]; ~ *van aard* of a
gentle disposition, gentle; *zo ~ als een lammetje*
as gentle (meek) as a lamb; **II** *ad* softly &; ~
wat! gently!; ~ *spreken* speak below (under)
one's breath, whisper; *~er spreken* lower (drop)
one's voice; *ze hadden de radio ~ aanstaan* they
had the radio turned on low; *de radio ~er zetten*
turn down the radio; *op zijn ~st gezegd* to put it
mildly, to say the least (of it); **zacht'aardig**
gentle, mild; 𝕱 benign; **–heid** *v* gentleness,
mildness; 𝕱 benignity; **'zachtgekookt** soft-
boiled; **'zachtheid** *v* softness, smoothness &;
'zachtjes softly, gently; in a low voice; ~!
hush!; **zachtjes'aan** slowly, zie ook: *zoetjesaan*;
zacht'moedig I *aj* gentle, meek; **II** *ad* gently,
meekly; **–heid** *v* gentleness, meekness; **'zacht-
werkend** mild; **zacht'zinnig I** *aj* gentle,
meek; **II** *ad* gently, meekly; **–heid** *v* gentleness, meekness

'zadel *o* & *m* (-s) saddle; *iem. i n het ~ helpen* help
sbd. into the saddle, give sbd. a leg up²; *in het
~ springen* vault into the saddle; *in het ~ zitten*
be in the saddle; *vast in het ~ zitten* have a firm
seat; *u i t het ~ lichten (werpen)* unseat (un-
horse); *fig* oust; **–boog** (-bogen) *m* saddle-
bow; **–boom** (-bomen) *m* saddle-tree; **–dak**
(-daken) *o* saddle(back) roof; **–dek** (-ken) *o*
saddle-cloth; **'zadelen** (zadelde, h. gezadeld) *vt*
saddle; **'zadelkleed** (-kleden) *o* saddle-cloth;
–knop (-pen) *m* pommel; **–kussen** (-s) *o*
saddle-cushion, pillion; **–maker** (-s) *m*
saddler; **zadelmake'rij** (-en) *v* 1 saddler's
shop; 2 saddlery; **'zadelpaard** (-en) *o* saddle-
horse; **–pijn** *v* saddle-soreness; ~ *hebben* be
saddle-sore; **–riem** (-en) *m* (saddle-)girth;
–rug (-gen) *m* saddle-back; *met een ~* saddle-
backed; **–tas** (-sen) *v* 1 saddle-bag; 2 (a a n
f i e t s) tool-bag; **–tuig** *o* tack; saddle and
harness; saddle saddlefast, firmly seated (in the
saddle); ~ *zijn* have a firm seat²; **–vormig**
saddle-shaped; **–zak** (-ken) *m* saddle-bag

zag (zagen) V.T. van *zien*

1 'zagen (zaagde, h. gezaagd) **I** *vt* saw; **II** *vi* >
scrape [on a violin]; zie ook: *zaniken*

2 'zagen V.T. meerv. van *zien*

'zager (-s) *m* 1 sawyer; 2 > scraper [on a
violin]; 3 (v e r v e l e n d m e n s) bore;
zage'rij (-en) *v* 1 sawing; 2 saw-mill

Za'ïre *o* Zaire

zak (-ken) *m* 1 bag [for money &]; sack [for
corn, coal, potatoes, wool &]; 2 (a a n
k l e d i n g s t u k) pocket; 3 (k l e i n e r of
l o s t e m a k e n) pouch [for tobacco]; 4 (v.

p a p i e r) bag; 5 ♂ pocket; 6 (s n e r t v e n t) **F**
= *klootzak*; 7 ♂ & ♟ sac; *geen ~* **P** nothing; *hij
weet er geen ~ van* **P** he knows nothing about it,
he hasn't a clue; *het kan hem geen ~ schelen* **P** he
doesn't care a rap (a fig); *de ~ geven (krijgen)* **F**
give (get) the sack; ● *i n ~ken doen* bag, sack;
in eigen ~ steken pocket [the profit]; *steek het in je
~* put it in your pocket; *steek die in je ~* put
that in your pipe and smoke it; *iem. in zijn ~
kunnen steken* be more than a match for sbd.,
run rings around sbd.; *in ~ en as zitten* **B** be in
sackcloth and ashes; *ik heb niets o p ~* I have no
money with me (about me); *met geen (zonder een)
cent op ~* penniless; *u i t eigen ~ betalen* pay out
of one's own pocket; **–agenda** ('s) *v* pocket-
diary; **–almanak** (-ken) *m* pocket-almanac;
–bijbeltje (-s) *o* pocket-bible; **–boekje** (-s) *o*
1 notebook; 2 ♅ paybook; **–centje** (-s) *o*
pocket money; **–doek** (-en) *m* (pocket-)hand-
kerchief; *~je leggen* drop the handkerchief

'zake *ter ~* zie *zaak*; **'zakelijk I** *aj* 1 essential
[differences]; real [tax]; matter-of-fact [state-
ment &]; objective [judgment]; business-like
[management]; 2 (z a a k r ij k) full of matter,
matterful [paper, study &]; *een ~e aangelegenheid*
a matter of business; *~e belangen* business
interests; *~e inhoud* sum and substance, gist; ~
onderpand collateral security; ~ *blijven (zijn)*
keep to the point, not indulge in personalities;
II *ad* in a matter-of-fact way, without indulg-
ing in personalities, objectively; in a business-
like way; **–heid** *v* 1 business-like character;
objectivity; 2 (z a a k r ij k h e i d) matterfulness;
'zakenbrief (-brieven) *m* business letter;
–kabinet (-ten) *o* caretaker government;
–man (-lieden en -lui) *m* business man; **–reis**
(-reizen) *v* business tour, business trip;
–relatie [-(t)si.] *v* business relation;
–vriend (-en) *m* business friend; **–vrouw** (-en)
v business woman; **–wereld** *v* business world;
–wijk (-en) *v* business quarter

'zakformaat *o* pocket-size; *een... in ~* a
pocket...; **–geld** *o* pocket-money; **–je** (-s) *o* 1
small pocket (bag, &); 2 paper bag; *met het ~
rondgaan* take up the collection [in church];
–kammetje (-s) *o* pocket-comb

1 'zakken (zakte, is gezakt) *vi* 1 (b a r o m e t e r)
fall; 2 (m u u r &) sag; 3 (w a t e r) fall; *fig* 1
(a a n d e l e n) fall; 2 (w o e d e) subside; 3 (b ij
e x a m e n s) fail, **F** be ploughed; 4 (b ij
z i n g e n) go flat; *d o o r het ijs ~* go (fall)
through the ice; *i n de modder ~* sink in the
mud; *in elkaar ~* collapse; *~ v o o r* fail [one's
driving test &]; *het gordijn laten ~* let down the
curtain; *het hoofd laten ~* hang one's head; *een
leerling laten ~* fail [a pupil], **F** plough a pupil;
de moed laten ~ lose courage, lose heart; *de stem*

laten ~ lower one's voice; *zich laten* ~ *l*et oneself down

2 'zakken (zakte, h. gezakt) *vt* bag, sack; **'zakkendrager** (-s) *m* porter; **-goed** *o* bagging; **-linnen** *o* sackcloth, sacking; **-roller** (-s) *m* pickpocket

'zaklantaarn (-s), **-lantaren** (-s) *v* electric torch; **-lopen** *o* sack-race; **-mes** (-sen) *o* pocket-knife, penknife; **-pistool** (-stolen) *o* pocket-pistol; **-potloodje** (-s) *o* pocket-pencil; **-radio** ('s) *m* pocket radio (set); **-spiegel** (-s) *m* pocket-mirror; **-uitgave** (-n) *v* pocket-edition; **-vol** *v* pocketful, bagful, sackful; **-vormig** sack-shaped, bag-shaped; **-woordenboek** (-en) *o* pocket dictionary

zalf (zalven) *v* ointment, unguent, salve; **-je** (-s) *o* zie *zalf*; *een* ~ *op de wond* a salve for his wounded feelings; **-olie** (-liën) *v* anointing-oil; **-pot** (-ten) *m* gallipot

'zalig 1 (i n d e h e m e l) blessed, blissful; **2** (h e e r l ij k) lovely, heavenly, divine, delicious; ~ *maken* save [a sinner]; ~ *verklaren rk* beatify [a dead person], declare [him] blessed; *wat moet ik doen om* ~ *te worden?* what am I to do to be saved?; ~ *zijn de bezitters* **B** possession is nine points of the law; *het is* ~*er te geven dan te ontvangen* **B** it is more blessed to give than to receive; *de* ~*en* the blessed; **'zaligen** (zaligde, h. gezaligd) *vt rk* beatify; **'zaliger** late, deceased; ~ *gedachtenis* of blessed memory; *mijn vader* ~ my late father, **F** my poor father, my sainted father; **'zaligheid** (-heden) *v* salvation, bliss, beatitude; *wat een* ~*!* how delightful!; **'zaligmakend** beatific, (soul-)saving; **'Zaligmaker** *m* Saviour; **'zaligmaking** *v* salvation; **-sprekingen** *mv* **B** beatitudes; **-verklaring** *v* *rk* beatification

zalm (-en) *m* salmon; **-forel** (-len) *v* salmon-trout; **-kleurig** salmon(-coloured), salmon-pink; **-teelt** *v* salmon-breeding; **zalmvisse'rij** *v* salmon-fishing

'zalven (zalfde, h. gezalfd) *vt* 1 🗡 rub with ointment; 2 (c e r e m o n i e e l) anoint; **-d I** *aj* *fig* unctuous, oily, soapy [words &]; **II** *ad* unctuously; **'zalving** (-en) *v* anointing; *fig* unction, unctuousness

'zamelen (zamelde, h. gezameld) *vt* collect, gather

'Zambia *o* Zambia; **Zambi'aan(s)** (-anen) *m* (& *aj*) Zambian

'zamen *te* ~ together

zand *o* sand; *iem.* ~ *in de ogen strooien* throw dust in sbd.'s eyes; *op* ~ *bouwen* build on sand; ~ *erover!* let's forget it!, let bygones be bygones!; **-achtig** sandy; **-bak** (-ken) *m* sand-pit; **-bank** (-en) *v* sandbank [ook: the sands], sand-bar; flat(s); shallow, shoal [showing at

low water]; **-berg** (-en) *m* sand-hill; **-blad** (-bladen) *o* sand-leaf [of tobacco]; **-duin** (-en) *v* & *o* sand-dune; **'zanden** (zandde, h. gezand) *vt* sand

'zander (-s) *m* 🐟 = *snoekbaars*

'zanderig sandy; gritty; **-heid** *v* sandiness; grittiness; **zande'rij** (-en), **'zandgroef** (-groeven), **-groeve** (-n) *v* sand-pit; **-grond** (-en) *m* sandy soil, sandy ground; **-haas** (-hazen) *m* **F** infantryman; **-heuvel** (-s) *m* sand-hill; **-hoop** (-hopen) *m* heap of sand; **-hoos** (-hozen) *v* sand-spout; **-ig** = *zanderig*; **-kever** (-s) *m* tiger-beetle; **-koekje** (-s) *o* (kind of) shortbread; **-korrel** (-s) *m* grain of sand; ~*s* ook: sands; **-kuil** (-en) *m* sand-pit; **-laag** (-lagen) *v* layer of sand; **-lichaam** *o* sandy body [of a road]; **-loper** (-s) *m* hour-glass, sand-glass; zie ook: *strandloper* & *zandkever*; **-mannetje** *o* sandman; **-plaat** (-platen) *v* sand-bar, flat(s), shoal; **-ruiter** (-s) *m* **J** unseated horseman; **-schuit** (-en) *v* sand-barge; **-steen** *o* & *m* sandstone; **-steengroef** (-groeven), **-steengroeve** (-n) *v* sandstone quarry; **-storm** (-en) *m* sand-storm; **-straal** (-stralen) *m* & *v* sandblast; **zandstralen** (zandstraalde, h. gezandstraald) *vt* & *va* sand-blast; **'zandstrand** (-en) *o* sandy beach; **-strooier** (-s) *m* sand-box; **-taart** (-en) *v* sand-cake; **-verstuiving** (-en) *v* sand-drift, shifting sand; **-vlakte** (-n en -s) *v* sandy plain; **-weg** (-wegen) *m* sandy road; **-woestijn** (-en) *v* sandy desert; **-zak** (-ken) *m* sandbag; **-zee** (-zeeën) *v* sea of sand; **-zuiger** (-s) *m* suction-dredger

zang (-en) *m* 1 (h e t z i n g e n) singing, song; 2 (g e z a n g, l i e d) song; 3 (i n d e p o ë z i e) stave [of a poem]; canto [of a long poem]; **'Zangberg** *m de* ~ Parnassus; **'zangboek** (-en) *o* book of songs, song-book; **-cursus** [-züs] (-sen) *m* singing-class; **'zanger** (-s) *m* 1 *eig* singer, vocalist; 2 (d i c h t e r) singer, songster, bard, poet; **zange'res** (-sen) *v* (female) singer, vocalist; **'zangerig** melodious; **-heid** *v* melodiousness; **'zangkoor** (-koren) *o* choir; **-kunst** *v* art of singing; **-leraar** (-s en -raren) *m* singing-master; **-lerares** (-sen) *v* singing-mistress; **-les** (-sen) *v* singing-lesson; **-lijster** (-s) *v* song-thrush; **-muziek** *v* vocal music; **-noot** (-noten) *v* musical note; **-nummer** (-s) *o* vocal number; **-oefening** (-en) *v* singing-exercise; **-onderwijs** *o* singing-lessons; *het* ~ the teaching of singing; **-parkiet** (-en) *m* budgerigar, **F** budgie; **-partij** (-en) *v* voice part; **-school** (-scholen) *v* singing-school; **-stem** (-men) *v* 1 singing-voice; 2 = *zangpartij*; **-stuk** (-ken) *o* song; **-uitvoering** (-en) *v* vocal concert; **-vereni-**

ging (-en) *v* choral society; **–vogel** (-s) *m* singing-bird, song-bird; **–wedstrijd** (-en) *m* singing-contest; **–wijs** (-wijzen), **–wijze** (-n) *v* tune, melody; **–zaad** *o* mixed bird-seed

'**zanik** (-niken) *m-v* bore; '**zaniken** (zanikte, h. gezanikt) *vi* nag, bother; *lig toch niet te* ~ don't keep nagging (bothering); **–er** (-s) *m* bore

1 zat 1 satiated; 2 drunk; (*oud en*) *der dagen* ~ **B** full of days; *hij heeft geld* ~ he has plenty of money; *ik ben het* ~ **F** I am fed up with it, I'm sick of it; *zich* ~ *eten* eat one's fill

2 zat (zaten) V.T. v. *zitten*

'**zaterdag** (-dagen) *m* Saturday; **–s I** *aj* Saturday; **II** *ad* on Saturdays

'**zatheid** *v* satiety; weariness; '**zatladder** (-s), **–lap** (-pen) *m* = *zuiplap*

Z.B., Z.Br. = *zuiderbreedte*

Z.E. 1 = *Zijne Edelheid*; 2 = *Zijn Eerwaarde*

ze 1 she, her; 2 they, them; ~ *zeggen, dat hij...* they say he..., he is said to..., people say he...

Zebe'deus [-'de.üs] *m* Zebedee

'**zeboe** (-s) *m* zebu

'**zebra** ('s) *m* 1 ♒ zebra; 2 (o v e r s t e e k - p l a a t s) zebra crossing; **–pad** (-paden) *o* = *zebra* 2

'**zede** (-n) *v* custom, usage, zie ook: *zeden;* '**zedelijk** *aj* (& *ad*) moral(ly); *een* ~ *lichaam* a corporate body, a body corporate; '**zedelijk- heid** *v* morality; '**zedelijkheidsapostel** (-en en -s) *m* sermonizer; **–gevoel** *o* moral sense; '**zedeloos** *aj* (& *ad*) immoral(ly), profligate(ly); **zede'loosheid** *v* immorality, profligacy; '**zeden** *mv* 1 morals; 2 manners; *hun* ~ *en gewoonten* their manners and customs; **–bederf** *o* demoralization, corruption (of morals), depravity; **–delict** (-en) *o* sexual offence; **–kunde** *v* ethics, moral philosophy; **zeden'kundig** moral, ethical; '**zedenkwet- send** shocking, immoral; **–leer** *v* morality, ethics; **–les** (-sen) *v* moral, moral lesson; **–meester** (-s) *m* moralist, moralizer; **–misdrijf** (-drijven) *o* sexual offence; **–politie** [-(t)si.] *v* ± **F** vice squad; **–preek** (-preken) *v* moralizing sermon; **–preker** (-s) *m* moralizer, moralist, moral censor; **–spreuk** (-en) *v* maxim; **–verwildering** *v* moral corruption, demoralization, depravity; **–wet** (-ten) *v* moral law; '**zedig** *aj* (& *ad*) modest(ly), demure(ly); **–heid** *v* modesty, demureness

zee (zeeën) *v* sea², ocean², ☉ main; *een* ~ *van bloed* (*licht, rampen*) a sea of blood (light, troubles); *een* ~ *van tijd* plenty of time; ~ *kiezen* put to sea; ~ *winnen* get sea-room; ● *a a n* ~ at the seaside; *aan* ~ *gelegen* on the sea, situated by the sea; *recht d o o r* ~ *gaan* zie 1 *recht* **III**; *i n* ~ *steken* 1 ⚓ put to sea; 2 *fig* launch forth, go ahead; *in open* ~, *in volle* ~ on the high seas, in

the open sea; [a ship seen] in the offing; *n a a r* ~ *gaan* 1 (a l s m a t r o o s) go to sea; 2 (v o o r g e n o e g e n) go to the seaside; *o p* ~ at sea; *hij is* (*vaart*) *op* ~ he is a seafaring man (a sailor), he follows the sea; *o v e r* ~ *gaan* go by sea; *in de landen van over* ~ in the countries beyond the seas, overseas, in oversea coun- tries; *hij kan niet t e g e n de* ~ he is a bad sailor; *t e r* ~ *varen* follow the sea; *de oorlog ter* ~ the war at sea; **–aal** (-alen) *m* sea-eel, conger; **–ajuin** *m* squill; **–anemoon** (-monen) *v* sea-anemone; **–arend** (-en) *m* white-tailed eagle; **–arm** (-en) *m* arm of the sea, estuary, firth; **–assurantie** [-(t)si.] (-s) *v* marine insur- ance; **–baak** (-baken) *v* sea-mark; **–baars** (-baarzen) *m* sea-perch; **–bad** (-bladen) *o* sea-bath; **–badplaats** (-en) *v* seaside resort; **–baken** (-s) *o* sea-mark; **–banket F** *o* herring; **–benen** *mv* sea-legs; **–beving** (-en) *v* sea- quake; **–bewoner** (-s) *m* inhabitant of the sea; **–bodem** (-s) *m* bottom of the sea, sea-bottom; **–boezem** (-s) *m* gulf, bay; **–bonk** (-en) *m* (Jack-)tar; *een oude* ~ an old salt; **–breker** (-s) *m* breakwater; **–brief** (-brieven) *m* certificate of registry; **–cadet** (-ten) *m* naval cadet; **–den** (-nen) *m* cluster pine; **–dienst** *m* naval service; **–dier** (-en) *o* marine animal; **–dijk** (-en) *m* sea-bank, sea-dike; **–drift** *v* flotsam; **–duivel** (-s) *m* 🐟 sea-devil; **–ëgel** (-s) *m* sea-urchin; **–ëngte** (-n en -s) *v* strait(s), narrows

zeef (zeven) *v* sieve, strainer; riddle, screen [for gravel &]

'**zeefauna** *v* marine fauna

'**zeefdoek** (-en) *m* & *o* strainer; **–druk** (-ken) *m* silk-screen (printing); **–je** (-s) *o* sieve

1 zeeg (zegen) *v* ⚓ sheer

2 zeeg (zegen) V.T. v. *zijgen*

'**zeegat** (-gaten) *o* mouth of a harbour or river, outlet to the sea; *het* ~ *uitgaan* put to sea; **–gevecht** (-en) *o* sea-fight, naval combat; **–gezicht** (-en) *o* seascape, sea-piece; **–god** (-goden) *m* sea-god; **–godin** (-nen) *v* sea- goddess; **–gras** *o* seaweed; **–groen** sea-green; **–handel** *m* oversea(s) trade; **–haven** (-s) *v* seaport; **–held** (-en) *m* naval hero; **–hond** (-en) *m* seal; **–hondevel** (-len) *o* sealskin; **–hoofd** (-en) *o* pier, jetty

zeek (zeken) P V.T. v. *zeiken*

'**zeekaart** (-en) *v* (sea-)chart; **–kanaal** (-nalen) *o* ship-canal; **–kant** *m* seaside; **–kapitein** (-s) *m* sea-captain; (b i j d e m a r i n e) captain in the navy; **–kasteel** (-telen) *o* sea-castle; **–klaar** ready for sea; **–klimaat** *o* marine (maritime) climate; **–koe** (-koeien) *v* sea-cow, manatee; **–koet** (-en) *m* guillemot; **–komkommer** (-s) *m* sea-cucumber; **–kompas** (-sen) *o* mariner's compass; **–krab** (-ben) *v* sea-crab; **–kreeft**

(-en) *m* & *v* lobster; **–kust** (-en) *v* sea-coast, sea-shore

zeel (zelen) *o* strap, trace

'**Zeeland** *o* Zeeland, Zeeland; '**zeeleeuw** (-en) *m* sea-lion; **–lieden** *mv* seamen, sailors, mariners

zeelt (-en) *v* tench

'**zeelucht** *v* sea-air

1 zeem *o* = *zeemle(d)er*; **2 zeem** (zemen) *m* & *o* = *zeemlap*

'**zeemacht** (-en) *v* naval forces, navy

'**zeeman** (-lieden en -lui) *m* seaman, sailor, mariner; **–schap** *o* seamanship; **~** *gebruiken* steer cautiously; '**zeemansgraf** *o een ~ krijgen* be buried at sea, **F** go to Davy Jones's locker; **–huis** (-huizen) *o* sailors' home; **–kunst** *v* art of navigation, seamanship; **–leven** *o* seafaring life, sailor's life

'**zeemeermin** (-nen) *v* mermaid; **–meeuw** (-en) *v* (sea-)gull, seamew; *drietenige ~* kittiwake; **–mijl** (-en) *v* sea-mile, nautical mile; **–mijn** (-en) *v* sea-mine

'**zeemlap** (-pen) *m* wash-leather; **–le(d)er** *o* chamois-leather, shammy; **–leren** *aj* shammy; *een ~ lap* a (wash-)leather

'**zeemogendheid** (-heden) *v* maritime (naval, sea) power; **–monster** (-s) *o* 1 sea-monster; 2 $ shipping-sample; **–mos** *o* sea-moss, seaweed

zeen (zenen) *v* tendon, sinew

'**zeenatie** [-(t)si.] (-s en -tiën) *v* seafaring nation; **–nimf** (-en) *v* sea-nymph; **–officier** (-en) *m* naval officer; **–oorlog** (-logen) *m* naval war

zeep (zepen) *v* soap; *groene ~* soft soap; *om ~ brengen* kill; *hij ging om ~* he went west

'**zeepaard** (-en) *o* sea-horse [of Neptune]; **–je** (-s) *o* 𝕊 sea-horse

'**zeepachtig** soapy, saponaceous

'**zeepaling** (-en) *m* sea-eel, conger; **–pas** (-sen) *m* passport

'**zeepbakje** (-s) *o* soap-dish; **–bekken** (-s) *o* shaving-basin; **–bel** (-len) *v* soap-bubble, bubble; **–fabriek** (-en) *v* soap-works; **–fabrikant** (-en) *m* soap-maker, soap-boiler; **–kist** (-en) *v* soap-box

'**zeeplaats** (-en) *v* seaside town; **–polis** (-sen) *v* marine policy; **–post** *v* oversea(s) mail

'**zeeppoeder, –poeier** *o* & *m* soap-powder

'**zeeprik** (-ken) sea-lamprey

'**zeepsop** *o* soap-suds; **–water** *o* soap and water, soapy water; **–zieden** *o* soap-boiling; **–zieder** (-s) *m* soap-boiler; **zeepziede'rij** (-en) *v* soap-works

1 zeer *o* sore, ache; *~ doen* ache, hurt[2]; *fig* pain; *heb je je erg ~ gedaan?* were you much hurt?; *het doet geen ~* it doesn't hurt; *zich ~ doen* hurt oneself; *iem. in zijn ~ tasten* touch sbd. on the

raw, touch the tender spot

2 zeer *aj* sore [arm &]; *ik heb een zere voet* my foot is sore

3 zeer *ad* 1 very; 2 (v ó ó r d e e l w o o r d) much, greatly [astonished &]; **~** sorely [needed &]; *al te ~* overmuch

'**zeeraad** (-raden) *m* maritime court; **–ramp** (-en) *v* catastrophe at sea; **–recht** *o* maritime law

'**zeereerwaard** *de ~e heer A. B.* the Reverend A. B., Rev. A. B.

'**zeereis** (-reizen) *v* (sea-)voyage; *ook:* sea-journey

'**zeergeleerd** very learned; *een ~e* a doctor

'**zeerob** (-ben) *m* 1 🦭 seal; 2 *fig* (Jack-)tar, sea-dog; *een oude ~* an old salt; **–roof** *m* piracy; **–rover** (-s) *m* pirate, corsair; **zeerove'rij** (-en) *v* piracy

zeerst *om het ~* as much as possible; *ten ~e* very much, highly, greatly

'**zeeschade** *v* sea-damage; **–schelp** (-en) *v* sea-shell; **–schilder** (-s) *m* marine painter; **–schildpad** (-den) *v* turtle; **–schip** (-schepen) *o* sea-going vessel; **–schuimen** *vi* practise piracy; **–schuimer** (-s) *m* pirate, corsair; **–slag** (-slagen) *m* sea-battle, naval battle; **–slak** (-ken) *v* sea-snail; **–slang** (-en) *v* sea-serpent; **–sleper** (-s) *m* seagoing tug(boat); **–spiegel** *m* sea-level, level of the sea; *beneden (boven) de ~* below (above) sea-level; **–stad** (-steden) *v* seaside town; **–ster** (-ren) *v* starfish; **–straat** (-straten) *v* strait(s); **–strand** (-en) *o* beach; *het ~ ook:* the sands; **–stroming** (-en) *v* ocean current; **–stuk** (-ken) *o* sea-piece, seascape; **–term** (-en) *m* nautical term; **–tijdingen** *mv* shipping intelligence; **–tje** (-s) *o* sea; *een ~ overkrijgen* ship a sea; **–tocht** (-en) *m* voyage; **–transport** *o* sea-carriage, sea-transport

Zeeuw (-en) *m* inhabitant of Zealand (Zeeland); **–s I** *aj* Zealand; **II** *v* Zealand dialect; **Zeeuws-'Vlaanderen** *o* Dutch Flanders

'**zeevaarder** (-s) *m* seafarer; **zee'vaardig** ready to sail; '**zeevaart** *v* navigation; **–kunde** *v* art of navigation; **zeevaart'kundig** nautical; '**zeevaartschool** (-scholen) *v* school of navigation; **–varend** seafaring [nation]; **–verkenner** (-s) *m* sea-scout; **–verzekering** (-en) *v* marine insurance; **–vis** (-sen) *m* sea-fish; **–vogel** (-s) *m* sea-bird; **–volk** *o* seamen, sailors; **–vracht** *v* freight; **zee'waardig** seaworthy; **–heid** *v* seaworthiness;

'**zeewaarts** seaward; **–water** *o* sea-water; **–weg** (-wegen) *m* sea-route; **–wering** (-en) *v* sea-wall; **–wezen** *o* maritime (nautical) affairs; **–wier** (-en) *o* seaweed; **–wind** (-en) *m* sea-wind, sea-breeze; **–wolf** (-wolven) *m* sea-wolf;

–ziek seasick; **–ziekte** *v* seasickness; **–zout** *o* sea-salt; **–zwaluw** (-en) *v* sea-swallow

'zefier (-en en -s) *m* zephyr

'zege *v* victory, triumph; **–boog** (-bogen) *m* triumphal arch

'zegel (-s) 1 *o* (v. d o c u m e n t) seal; 2 (p a p i e r) stamped paper; 3 (i n s t r u m e n t) seal, stamp; 4 *m* (v. b e l a s t i n g, p o s t &) stamp; (v. w i n k e l) trading stamp; *zijn ~ drukken op een document* affix one's seal to a document; *zijn ~ aan iets hechten* set one's seal to sth.; *a a n ~ onderhevig* liable to stamp-duty; *alles is o n d e r ~* everything is under seal; *onder het ~ van geheimhouding* under the seal of secrecy; *alle stukken moeten o p ~* all documents must be written on stamped paper; *vrij v a n ~* exempt from stamp-duty; **–belasting** *v* stamp-duty; **–bewaarder** (-s) *m* Keeper of the Seal; **–doosje** (-s) *o* seal-box; **'zegelen** (zegelde, h. gezegeld) *vt* 1 seal; 𝌆 place under seal; 2 (s t e m p e l e n) stamp; *gezegeld papier* stamped paper; **'zegelkantoor** (-toren) *o* stamp-office; **–kosten** *mv* stamp-duties; **–lak** *o* & *m* sealing-wax; **–merk** (-en) *o* impression of a seal; **–recht** *o* stamp-duty; **–ring** (-en) *m* seal-ring, signet-ring; **–was** *m* & *o* sealing-wax; **–wet** (-ten) *v* stamp-act

1 'zegen *m* blessing, benediction; *welk een ~!* what a mercy!; what a blessing!, what a godsend!

2 'zegen (-s) *v* seine, drag-net

3 'zegen V.T. meerv. v. *zijgen*

'zegenen (zegende, h. gezegend) *vt* bless; **–ning** (-en) *v* blessing [of civilization], benediction; **'zegenrijk** 1 salutary, beneficial; 2 most blessed; **–wens** (-en) *m* blessing

'zegepalm (-en) *m* palm (of victory); **–poort** (-en) *v* triumphal arch; **–praal** (-pralen) *v* triumph; **'zegepralen** (zegepraalde, h. gezegepraald) *vi* triumph (*over* over); **'zegeteken** (-en en -s) *o* trophy; **–tocht** (-en) *m* triumphal march; **–vaan** (-vanen) *v* victorious banner; **'zegevieren** (zegevierde, h. gezegevierd) *vi* triumph (*over* over); **–d** victorious, triumphant; **'zegewagen** (-s) *m* triumphal chariot, triumphal car; **–zang** (-en) *m* song of triumph, paean

'zegge (-n) *v* 🦆 sedge

'zeggen* I *vt* say [to him]; tell [him]; *wat een prachtstuk, zeg!* I say, what a beauty!; *zegge vijftig gulden $* say fifty guilders; *u zei...?* you were saying ...?; *doe dat, zeg ik je* I tell you; *nu u het zegt* now you mention it; *zeg eens!* I say!; *al zeg ik het zelf* though I say it who shouldn't, though I do say myself; *goede nacht ~* say (bid) good night; *dat zegt (meer dan) boekdelen* that speaks volumes; *en dat zegt wat!, dat wil wat ~!*

which is saying a good deal, and that is saying a lot; *hij zegt maar wat* he is just talking; (s t e r k e r) he is talking through his hat; *ik heb gezegd!* I have had my say; *hij zegt niets maar denkt des te meer* he says nothing but thinks a lot; *de mensen ~ zóveel* people will say anything; *ik heb het wel gezegd* I told you so; *heb ik het niet gezegd?* didn't I tell you?; *daarmee is alles gezegd* that's all you can say of him (them &); (b a s t a!) and there's an end of it; *anders gezegd* to put it differently, in other words; *dat is gauw (gemakkelijk) gezegd* it is easy (for you) to say so; *dat is gauwer gezegd dan gedaan* that is sooner said than done; *zo gezegd, zo gedaan* no sooner said than done; *dat behoef ik u niet te ~* I need not tell you; *dat hoef je hem geen twee maal te ~* he need no be told twice; *wat heeft u te ~?* what have you got to say?; *wat zou je ervan ~ als...* what about..., suppose...; *wat zeg je van...?* how about...?; *alle leden hebben evenveel te ~* all the members have an equal say; *ik heb er ook iets in te ~* I have some say in the matter; *ga het hem ~* go and tell him; *dat kan ik u niet ~* I cannot tell you; *dat zou ik u niet kunnen ~* I could not say; *ze hebben het laten ~* they have sent word; *laten we ~ tien* (let us) say ten; *dat laat ik mij niet ~!* I don't have to take that!; *dat mag ik niet ~* I must not tell (you), that would be telling; *hij is..., dat moet ik ~* I cannot but say that; *wij hadden het eerder moeten ~* we should have spoken sooner; *dat wil ~* that is (to say); *rechts..., ik wil ~, links* right, I mean, left; *dat wil nog niet ~ dat...* that is not to say that..., that does not mean (imply) that...; *hij zegt het* he says so, so he says; *zeg dat niet* don't say so; *zegt u dat wel!* you may well say so!; *dat zeg je nu wel, maar...* you are pleased to say so, but...; *wat zegt dat dan nog?* well, what of it?; *mag ik ook eens iets ~?* may I say something?; *hij zeit wat!* listen to him!; *niets ~, hoor!* keep quiet (keep mum) about it!; *hij zegt niet veel* he is a man of few words; *deze titel zegt al genoeg* this title speaks for itself; *dat zegt niet veel* that doesn't mean much; *die naam zegt mij niets* this name means nothing to me; *wat zegt u?* 1 what did you say?; 2 (b ij v e r b a z i n g) you don't say so!; *wat u zegt!* you don't say so!; *hij weet niet wat hij zegt* he doesn't know what he's talking about; *...wat ik je zeg* I tell you; *doe wat ik je zeg* do as I tell you; *het is wat te ~* it is awful; *als ik wat te ~ had* if I could work my will; *wat ik ~ wil (wou)...* à propos, by the way, that reminds me...; *wat wou ik ook weer ~?* what was I going to say?; *daar zeg je zo iets* that's not a bad idea; *iem. ~ waar het op staat* give sbd. a piece of one's mind; *wat is er op hem te ~?* what is there to be said against him?; *wat heb je daarop te ~?* what have you got to say to that?; *je hebt niets over mij te* ~ you have no authority over me; *om ook iets te* ~ by way of saying something; *om zo te* ~ so to say, so to speak; *daar is alles (veel) voor te* ~ there is everything (much) to be said for it; *het voor het* ~ *hebben* be in charge; *zonder iets te* ~ without a word; *zonder er iets van te* ~ without saying anything about it; **II** *o* saying; ~ *en doen zijn twee* to promise is one thing to perform another; *naar zijn* ~, *volgens zijn* ~ according to what he says; *als ik het voor het* ~ *had* if I had my say in the matter; *je hebt het maar voor het* ~ you need only say the word; **'zeggenschap** *v* & *o* right of say; control; ~ *hebben* have a say (in the matter); **'zeggingskracht** *v* expressiveness, eloquence; **'zegje** *o zijn* ~ *doen (zeggen)* say one's piece; **'zegsman** (-lieden en -lui) *m* informant, authority; *wie is uw* ~? who is your informant?, who told (it) you?; **–wijs** (-wijzen), **–wijze** (-n) *v* saying, expression, phrase

zei (zeiden) V.T. v. *zeggen*

'zeiken* P = *urineren*; = *zaniken*

zeil (-en) *o* 1 ⚓ sail; 2 (v. w i n k e l &) awning; 3 (t o t d e k k i n g) tarpaulin; tilt [of cart]; 4 (v. v l o e r) floor-cloth; 5 = *zeildoek*; ~ *bijzetten* set more sail; *alle* ~*en bijzetten* crowd on all sail; *fig* leave no stone unturned, do one's utmost; ~*(en) minderen* take in sail, shorten sail; *m e t een opgestreken (opgestoken)* ~ in high dudgeon; *met volle* ~*en* (in) full sail, all sails set; *o n d e r* ~ *gaan* ⚓ get under sail, set sail; *fig* drop off (to sleep), doze off; *onder* ~ *zijn* 1 ⚓ be under sail; 2 *fig* be sound asleep; *een vloot v a n 20* ~*en* a fleet of twenty sail; zie ook *oog*; **–boot** (-boten) *m* & *v* sailing-boat; **–doek** *o* & *m* sailcloth, canvas; (w a s d o e k) oilcloth; **'zeilen** (zeilde, h. en is gezeild) *vi* sail; *gaan* ~ go for a sail, go sailing; ~*d(e)* $ sailing, floating [goods]; ~*de verkopen* $ sell on sailing terms, sell to arrive; *een uur* ~*s* an hour's sail; **–er** (-s) *m* 1 (p e r s o o n) yachtsman; 2 (s c h i p) sailing-ship; **'zeiljacht** (-en) *o* sailing-yacht; **–jopper** (-s) *m* (sailing) jacket; **–kamp** (-en) *o* sailing camp; **–klaar** ready to sail, ready for sea; *zich* ~ *maken* get under sail; **–maker** (-s) *m* sail-maker; **zeilmake'rij** (-en) *v* sail-loft; **'zeilpet** (-ten) *v* yachting cap; **–ree** ready to sail, ready for sea; **–schip** (-schepen) *o* sailing-vessel, sailing-ship; **–sport** (-en) *v* sailing; **–tocht** (-en) *m* sailing-trip, sail; **zeil'vaardig** = *zeilklaar*; **'zeilvaartuig** (-en) *o* sailing-vessel; **–vereniging** (-en) *v* yacht-club; **–wagen** (-s) *m* sailing-car; **–wedstrijd** (-en) *m* sailing-match, sailing-race, regatta

zeis (-en) *v* scythe

'zeken P V.T. meerv. v. *zeiken*

'zeker I *aj attributief* 1 (v a s t s t a a n d) certain [event &]; 2 (b e t r o u w b a a r) sure [proof]; 3 (n i e t n a d e r a a n t e d u i d e n) certain [gentleman, lady of a certain age]; 4 (e n i g e) a certain, some [reluctance &]; *predikatief* 1 (m e t p e r s o o n s-o n d e r w e r p) certain, sure, assured, positive, confident; 2 (m e t d i n g-o n d e r w e r p) sure, certain; *(een)* ~*e dinges* F a certain Mr Thingumbob, a Mr Th., one Th.; *een* ~*e wrijving tussen hen* a certain friction (a certain amount of friction, some friction) between them; *ik ben* ~ *van hen* I can depend on them; ~ *van zijn zaak zijn* be sure of one's ground; *ben je er* ~ *van?* are you (quite) sure?, are you quite positive?; *ik ben er* ~ *van dat...* I am sure (that)..., I am sure of his (her, their...); *je kunt er* ~ *van zijn dat...* ook: you may feel (rest) assured that...; *men is er niet* ~ *van zijn leven* a man's life is not safe there; *iets* ~*s* something positive; *niets* ~*s* nothing certain; *zo* ~ *als 2 × 2 (4 is)* as sure as two and two make four, as sure as eggs is eggs; **II** *o het* ~*e* what is certain; *het* ~*e voor het onzekere nemen* take a certainty for an uncertainty; prefer the one bird in the hand to the two in the bush; **III** *ad* 1 (w o o r d b e p a l i n g) for certain; for a certainty, positively; 2 (z i n s b e p a l i n g) certainly, surely &; *(wel)* ~! 1 (b e v e s t i-g e n d) certainly; 2 (a f w ij z e n d) why not!; *ik weet het* ~ I know it for certain (for a certainty, for a fact); ~ *weet jij dat ook wel* surely you know it too; *jij weet dat* ~ *ook, hè?* I daresay (I suppose) you know it too; *hij komt* ~ *als hij het weet* he is sure to come if he knows; *we kunnen* ~ *op hem rekenen* we can safely count on him; *Kunnen wij op hem rekenen? Zeker!* Certainly! To be sure you can!; **–heid** (-heden) *v* 1 certainty; 2 (v e i l i g h e i d) safety; 3 (b o r g) security; ~ *bieden dat...* hold out every certainty that...; *voldoende* ~ *geven dat...* guarantee that...; ~ *hebben* be certain; ~ *stellen* give security; *niet met* ~ *bekend* not certainly known; *we kunnen niet met* ~ *zeggen of...* we cannot say with certainty (for certain); *voor de* ~, *voor alle* ~ to be on the safe side, to make sure; **zeker-heids'halve** for safety('s sake); **'zekerheid-stelling** (-en) *v* security

'zekering (-en) *v* ⚡ fuse

'zelden seldom, rarely; *niet* ~ not unfrequently

'zeldzaam I *aj* rare [= seldom found & of uncommon excellence]; scarce [books, moths]; **II** *ad* uncommonly, exceptionally [beautiful]; **–heid** (-heden) *v* rarity, scarceness; *zeldzaam-heden* rarities, curiosities; *een van de grootste zeldzaamheden* one of the rarest things; *het is een grote* ~ *als...* it is a rare thing for him to...; *het is geen* ~ *dat...* it is no rare thing to [find them &]

zelf self; *ik* ~ I myself; *u, jij* ~ you yourself; *de man* ~ the man himself; *de vrouw* ~ the woman herself; *het kind* ~ the child itself; *zij hebben* ~... they have... themselves; *zij kunnen niet* ~ *denken* they cannot think for themselves; *wees u* ~ be thyself; *hij is de beleefdheid* ~ he is politeness itself; zie ook: *zich, zichzelf* &
'zelfbediening *v* self-service; **'zelfbedieningswasserij** (-en) *v* launderette; **-winkel** (-s), **-zaak** (-zaken) *v* self-service shop, self-service store
'zelfbedrog *o* self-deceit, self-deception; **-begoocheling** *v* self-delusion; **-behagen** *o* self-complacency; **-beheersing** *v* self-control, self-command, self-possession, restraint; *zijn* ~ *herkrijgen* regain one's self-control, collect oneself; **-behoud** *o* self-preservation; **-beklag** *o* self-pity; **-beschikkingsrecht** *o* right of self-determination; **-beschuldiging** (-en) *v* self-accusation; **-bestuiving** *v* ⚛ self-pollination; **-bestuur** *o* self-government; **-bevlekking** *v* self-abuse, masturbation; **-bevrediging** *v* masturbation; **-bevruchting** *v* ⚛ self-fertilization, autogamy; **zelfbe'wust** self-assured; **-be'wustheid** *v,* **-be'wustzijn** *o* self-assuredness; **'zelfbinder** (-s) *m* 1 (l a n d - b o u w m a c h i n e) self-binder; 2 (d a s) knotted tie; **'zelfde** same; **'zelfgebreid** home-knitted; **-gemaakt** home-made [jam]; **zelfge'noegzaam** complacent, smug, self-satisfied; **-ge'noegzaamheid** *v* complacency, smugness, self-satisfiedness; **'zelfgevoel** *o* self-esteem; **zelf'ingenomen** self-opinionated, self-satisfied; **'zelfkant** (-en) *m* selvage, selvedge, list; *aan de* ~ *der maatschappij* [live] on the fringe of society; **-kastijding** (-en) *v* self-chastisement; **-kennis** *v* self-knowledge; **-klevend** self-adhesive; **-kritiek** *v* self-criticism; **-kwelling** (-en) *v* self-tormenting, self-torture; **-moord** (-en) *m* & *v* suicide, self-murder; ~ *plegen* commit suicide; **-moordenaar** (-s) *m,* **-moordenares** (-sen) *v* suicide, self-murderer; **-onderricht** *o* self-tuition; **-onderzoek** *o* self-examination, heart-searching; **-ontbranding** *v* spontaneous combustion; **-ontplooiing** *v* self-realization; **-ontspanner** (-s) *m phot* automatic release, self-timer; **-ontsteking** *v* 🔆 self-ignition; **-opoffering** (-en) *v* self-sacrifice; **-overschatting** *v* exaggerated opinion of oneself, presumption; **-overwinning** (-en) *v* self-conquest; **-plakkend** (self-)adhesive; **-portret** (-ten) *o* self-portrait; **-registrerend** self-registering, self-recording; **-respect** *o* self-respect; **-rijzend** self-raising [flour]
zelfs even; ~ *zijn vrienden* ook: his very friends; *zij klommen* ~ *tot op de daken* ook: on to the very roofs
'zelfspot *m* self-derision, self-mockery; **zelf'standig I** *aj* independent; ~ *naamwoord* substantive, noun; *de kleine* ~*en* the self-employed; **II** *ad* 1 [act] independently; 2 [used] substantively; **-heid** (-heden) *v* 1 independence; 2 (s t o f) substance; **'zelfstrijd** *m* inward struggle; **-strijkend** non-iron; **-studie** *v* self-tuition; **-tucht** *v* self-discipline; **-verblinding** *v* infatuation; **-verbranding** *v* (v. m e n s) self-burning; **-verdediging** *v* self-defence; *uit* (*ter*) ~ in self-defence; **-vergoding** *v* self-idolization; **-verheerlijking** *v* self-glorification; **-verheffing** *v* self-exaltation; **-verloochening** *v* self-denial; **-verminking** *v* self-mutilation; **-vernedering** *v* self-abasement; **-vernietiging** *v* self-destruction; **-vertrouwen** *o* self-confidence, self-reliance; **-verwijt** *o* self-reproach; **-verzekerd** self-assured, self-confident, self-possessed; **zelfver'zekerdheid** *v* self-assurance, self-confidence, self-possession; **'zelfvoldaan** self-complacent; **zelfvol'daanheid** *v* self-complacency; **'zelfvoldoening** *v* self-satisfaction, self-content; **-werkend** self-acting, automatic; **-zucht** *v* egotism, egoism, selfishness; **zelf'zuchtig I** *aj* selfish, egoistic, egotistic, self-seeking; *een* ~*e* an egoist, an egotist; **II** *ad* selfishly, egoistically, egotistically
ze'loot (-loten) *m* zealot
1 'zemelen *mv* bran
2 'zemelen (zemelde, h. gezemeld) *vi* = *zaniken*
1 'zemen *aj* shammy; *een* ~ *lap* a leather, (wash-)leather; **2 'zemen** (zeemde, h. gezeemd) *vt* clean [windows] with a (wash-) leather
'zendapparatuur *v* transmitting set, transmitter; **-bereik** *o RT* service area, transmission range; **-bode** (-n) *m* messenger; **-brief** (-brieven) *m* pastoral letter; **B** epistle; **'zendeling** (-en) *m* missionary; **'zenden*** *vt* send [sth., sbd.], forward, dispatch [a parcel &], ship, consign [goods &]; ~ *om* send for; **'zendenergie** [-e.ntrʒi. en -gi.] *v R* emissive power; **'zender** (-s) *m* sender; *R* transmitter; *over de Moskouse* ~ over Moscow radio; *over een Nederlandse* ~ on a Dutch transmitter; *over alle* ~*s* over all radio stations; **'zending** (-en) *v* 1 (h e t z e n d e n) sending, forwarding, dispatch; 2 (h e t g e z o n d e n) shipment, consignment; parcel; 3 (r o e p i n g, o p d r a c h t) mission; 4 (z e n d i n g s w e r k) mission (to Jews *onder de joden*); **'zendingsgenootschap** (-pen) *o* missionary society; **-post** (-en) *m* mission, missionary post; **-school** (-scholen) *v* missionary school; **-station**

[-sta.ʃòn] (-s) *o* mission station; **–werk** *o* missionary work; **'zendinstallatie** [-(t)si.] (-s) *v* R transmitting set, radio transmitter; **–lamp** (-en) *v* R transmitting valve; **–mast** (-en) *m* R transmitter mast; **–station** [-sta.ʃòn] (-s) *o* R transmitting station; **–tijd** (-en) *m* R air time, transmission time, broadcast(ing) time; **–toestel** (-len) *o* R transmitting set, transmitter; **–uur** (-uren) *o* R broadcasting hour; **–vergunning** (-en) *v* R transmitting licence

'zengen (zengde, h. gezengd) *vt* & *vi* singe [hair], scorch [grass &]; **–ging** *v* singeing, scorching

'zenig stringy, sinewy [meat]

'zenit *o* zenith

'zenuw (-en) *v* nerve; *de ~ van de oorlog* the sinews of war; *stalen ~en* iron nerves; *hij was één en al ~en* he was a bundle of nerves; *het op de ~en hebben* be in a fit of nerves, **F** have the jitters; *het op de ~en krijgen* go into hysterics, throw a fit, **F** get the jitters; *dat werkt op mijn ~en* that gets (grates) on my nerves; *in de ~en zitten* be very nervous, **F** be in a flap; **–aandoening** (-en) *v* affection of the nerves, nervous disease; **–achtig I** *aj* nervous, agitated, nervy, jumpy; *iem. ~ maken* ook: get on sbd.'s nerves; **II** *ad* nervously; **–achtigheid** *v* nervousness; **–arts** (-en) *m* neurologist; **–cel** (-len) *v* nerve-cell; **–crisis** [-zɪs] (-sen en -crises) *v* nervous attack, nervous breakdown; **–enoorlog** *m* war of nerves; **–gas** (-sen) *o* nerve gas; **–gestel** *o* nervous system; **–inrichting** (-en) *v* mental home (hospital); **–inzinking** (-en) *v* nervous breakdown; **–knoop** (-knopen) *m* ganglion; **–kwaal** (-kwalen) *v*, **–lijden** *o* nervous disease; **–lijder** (-s) *m* nervous sufferer; **–ontsteking** (-en) *v* neuritis; **–oorlog** = *zenuwenoorlog*; **–patiënt** [-sjɛnt] (-en) *m* neuropath; **–pees** (-pezen) *v* **F** fuss-pot; **–pijn** (-en) *v* neuralgia, nerve pains; **–schok** (-ken) *m* nervous shock; **zenuw'slopend** nerve-racking; **'zenuwstelsel** *o* nervous system; *het centrale ~* the central nervous system; **–toeval** (-len) *m* nervous attack; **–trekking** (-en) *v* nervous twitch; **–ziek** suffering from nerves; **–ziekte** (-n en -s) *v* nervous disease; **–zwakte** *v* neurasthenia, nervous debility

'zepen (zeepte, h. gezeept) *vt* soap; lather [before shaving]

zerk (-en) *v* slab, tombstone

zes (-sen) *v*; *dubbele ~* double six; *met ons ~sen* the six of us; *tegen ~sen* by six o'clock; *hij is v a n ~sen klaar* he is an all-round man; *ze hadden pret v o o r ~* they were having no end of fun; **zes'achtste** six eights; *~ maat* six-eight time; **'zesdaags** of six days, six days'; *de Zesdaagse*

oorlog the Six-Day War; **zes'daagse** (-n) *v sp* six-day bicycle-race; **'zesde** sixth (part); **'zeshoek** (-en) *m* hexagon; **–hoekig** hexagonal; **–jarig** of six years, six-year-old; **–kantig** hexagonal; **–regelig** of six lines; *~ versje* sextain; **–tal** (-len) *o* six, half a dozen; *het ~ the* six of them

'zestien sixteen; **–de** sixteenth (part)

'zestig sixty; *ben je ~!* are you mad?; *–er* (-s) *m* person of sixty (years); **–jarig** of sixty years; *de ~e* the sexagenarian; **–ste** sixtieth (part)

'zesvlak (-ken) *o* hexahedron; **–voud** (-en) *o* multiple of six; **–voudig** sixfold, sextuple

zet (-ten) *m* 1 (d u w) push, shove; 2 (s p r o n g) leap, bound; 3 *sp* move[2] [at draughts, chess &]; *een domme ~* a stupid move[2]; *een geestige ~* a stroke of wit; *een gelukkige ~* a happy move; *een handige ~* a clever move (stroke); *een verkeerde ~* a wrong move; *een ~ doen sp* make a move; *aan ~ zijn sp* be playing, be at play; *wit is aan ~ sp* it's white's move; *iem. een ~ geven* give sbd. a shove; **–baas** (-bazen) *m* manager; *fig* agent, hired man; **–boer** (-en) *m* tenant-farmer

'zetel (-s) *m* 1 seat, chair; 2 (v e r b l ij f) see [of a bishop]; 3 seat [in parliament, on a committee, of government, of a company]; **'zetelen** (zetelde, h. gezeteld) *vi* sit, reside; *~ te Amsterdam* have its seat at A; **'zetelverdeling** *v* distribution of seats [in parliament]; **–winst** *v ~ behalen* gain seats [in parliament]

'zetfout (-en) *v* typographical error, misprint; **–haak** (-haken) *m* (v. l e t t e r z e t t e r s) composing-stick; **–je** (-s) *o* shove; **–lijn** (-en) *v* 1 set-line, night-line [for fishing]; 2 ✂ [compositor's] setting-rule; **–loon** (-lonen) *o* compositor's wages; **–machine** [-ma.ʃi.nə] (-s) *v* type-setting machine

'zetmeel *o* starch, farina; **–achtig** starchy, farinaceous

'zetpil (-len) *v* suppository

'zetsel (-s) *o* 1 brew [of tea]; 2 ✂ matter [of compositors]; **'zetspiegel** (-s) *m* type area; **'zetten** (zette, h. gezet) **I** *vt* 1 set, put; 2 (o p d e d r u k k e r ij) set up, compose; 3 (l a t e n t r e k k e n) make [tea, coffee]; 4 *een diamant in goud ~* enchase a diamond in gold; *een arm & ~* set an arm [a bone, a fracture]; *een ernstig gezicht ~* put on a serious face; *zijn handtekening (naam) ~ (onder)* sign (one's name), put one's name to [a document], set one's hand to [a deed &]; *ze kunnen elkaar niet ~* they can't get on (get along) together; *ik kan hem niet ~* **F** I can't stick the fellow; *ik kon het niet ~* I could not stomach it; ● *het glas a a n de mond ~* put the glass to one's mouth; *iets i n elkaar ~* put sth. together; *een stukje in de krant ~* put a notice (a paragraph) in; *o p muziek ~* zic *muziek*; *de wekker op 5 uur* ~ set the alarm for five o'clock; *waar zal jij op* ~*?* what are you going on?; *hij schijnt het erop gezet te hebben om mij te plagen* he seems to be bent upon teasing me; *zet 'm op!* go at it!; *een ladder t e g e n de muur* ~ put a ladder against the wall; *iem. u i t het land* ~ expel sbd. from the country; *een ambtenaar eruit* ~ turn out (**F** fire) an official; *ik kan de gedachte niet v a n mij* ~ I can't dismiss the idea; *gezet v o o r piano en viool* arranged for the piano and the violin; **II** *vr zich* ~ 1 (v a n p e r s o n e n) sit down; 2 (v. v r u c h t e n) set; *zich iets i n het hoofd* ~ take (get) sth. into one's head; *zich o v e r iets heen* ~ get over sth.; *als hij er zich t o e zet* when he sets himself to do it; *zet u dat maar u i t het hoofd* put (get) it out of your head; **–er** (-s) *m* (d r u k k e r ij) compositor, type-setter; **zette'rij** (-en) *v* composing room; **'zetting** (-en) *v* 1 setting [of a bone &]; 2 (v a n j u w e e l) setting; 3 *♪* arrangement; **'zetwerk** *o* type-setting

zeug (-en) *v* 🐗 sow

'zeulen (zeulde, h. gezeuld) *vt* drag

zeur (-en) *m-v* bore; **'zeuren** (zeurde, h. gezeurd) *vi* worry; tease; *hij zeurde o m het boek* he was teasing me to get the book (for the book); *hij zit daar altijd o v e r te* ~ he keeps on at it; he goes on and on about it; he is always harping on the subject; *ergens over door* ~ **F** chew the rag (the fat); **'zeurig** 1 (v a n p e r s o o n) worrying; 2 (v. s p r e k e n) whining, drawling; **'zeurkous** (-en) *v*, **–piet** (-en) *m* bore

1 'zeven 7, seven

2 'zeven (zeefde, h. gezeefd) *vt* sieve, sift; riddle, screen [coal, gravel &]

'zevende seventh (part); *in de* ~ *hemel zijn* tread on air, be on cloud seven (six); **'Zevengesternte** *o* Pleiades; **'zevenhoek** (-en) *m* heptagon; **–hoekig** heptagonal; **–jarig** of seven years, seven-year-old; **–klapper** (-s) *m* squib, cracker; **zevenmijls'laarzen** *mv* seven-league boots; **'zevenslaper** (-s) *m* 1 🐗 dormouse [*mv* dormice]; 2 *fig* lie-abed; **'Zevenster** *v* Pleiades; **'zevental** (-len) *o* seven

'zeventien seventeen; **–de** seventeenth (part)

'zeventig seventy; **–er** (-s) *m* person of seventy (years); **–jarig** of seventy years; *de* ~ *e* the septuagenarian; **–ste** seventieth (part)

'zevenvoud (-en) *o* multiple of seven; **–ig** sevenfold, septuple

'zever *m* slaver, slobber, drivel; **'zeveren** (zeverde, h. gezeverd) *vi* 1 drivel, slaver; 2 = *zaniken*

z.g. = *zogenaamd*

z.i. = *zijns inziens*

zich oneself, himself, themselves; *hij heeft het niet bij* ~ he has not got it with him; *op* ~ in itself

1 zicht (-en) *v* reaping-hook, sickle

2 zicht *o* 1 sight; 2 [good, poor] visibility; *i n* ~ in sight, within sight; *drie dagen n a* ~ at three days' sight, three days after sight; *betaalbaar o p* ~ payable at sight; *boeken op* ~ *zenden* send books on approval (for inspection); **'zichtbaar I** *aj* visible, perceptible; **II** *ad* visibly; **–heid** *v* visibility, perceptibility

'zichten (zichtte, h. gezicht) *vt* cut, reap [corn]

'zichtkoers (-en) *m* sight-rate; **–papier** *o* sight-bills; **–wissel** (-s) *m* sight-bill; **–zending** (-en) *v* consignment on approval, goods on approval

zich'zelf oneself, himself; *hij was* ~ *niet* he was not himself; *b ij* ~ to himself [he said...]; *b u i t e n* ~ beside himself; *i n* ~ [talk] to oneself; *o p* ~ in itself [it is...]; [a class] by itself; [look at it] on its own merits; *op* ~ *staand* isolated [event, instance &]; self-contained [book, volume, school &]; *u i t* ~ of his own accord; *v a n* ~ *Jansen* her maiden name is J.; *zij is van* ~ *chic* she is smart in her own right; *v o o r* ~ for himself (themselves)

zie'daar there; ~ *wat ik u te zeggen had* that's what I had to tell you

'zieden* *I vi* seethe, boil; ~ *van toorn* seethe with rage; **II** *vt* boil

zie'hier 1 look here; 2 (o v e r r e i k e n d) here you are!; here is... [the key &]; ~ *wat hij schrijft* this is what he writes

ziek 1 (p r e d i k a t i e f) ill, diseased; 2 (a t t r i b u t i e f) sick, diseased; ~ *worden* fall ill, be taken ill; *hij is zo* ~ *als een hond* he is as sick as a dog; zie ook: *zieke*; **–bed** (-den) *o* sick-bed; **'zieke** (-n) *m-v* sick person, patient, invalid; ~*n* sick people; *de* ~*n* the sick; **'ziekelijk** sickly, ailing; morbid[2] [fancy]; **–heid** *v* sickliness; morbidity[2]; **'ziekenauto** [-o.to. of -outo.] ('s) *m* motor ambulance, ambulance; **–bezoek** (-en) *o* sick-call, visit to a sick person; **–boeg** (-en) *m* ⚓ sick-bay; **–broeder** (-s) *m* male nurse; **–drager** (-s) *m* stretcher-bearer; **–fonds** (-en) *o* sick-fund; **–geld** *o* sick-pay, sickness-benefit; **–huis** (-huizen) *o* hospital, infirmary; *particulier* ~ nursery home; **–huisbed** (-den) *o* hospital bed; *particulier* ~ pay-bed; **–kamer** (-s) *v* sick-room; **–kost** *m* invalid's food, sick-diet; **–oppasser** (-s) *m* hospital attendant, male nurse; ⚔ hospital orderly; **–rapport** (-en) *o* ⚔ sick parade; **–stoel** (-en) *m* invalid chair; **–troost** *m* comfort of the sick; **–verpleegster** (-s) *v* nurse; **–verpleger** (-s) *m* male nurse; **–verpleging** (-en) *v* 1 nursing; 2 nursing-home; **–wagen** (-s) *m* ambulance (wagon);

–zaal (-zalen) *v* (hospital) ward, infirmary; **–zuster** (-s) *v* nurse

'**ziekte** (-n en -s) *v* illness; [contagious, tropical] disease, [bowel, liver, heart] complaint, ailment; *lichte* ~ indisposition; ~ *van de maag, lever, nieren* & disorder of the stomach, liver, kidneys &; *wegens* ~ on account of ill-health; **–beeld** *o* clinical picture; **–geschiedenis** *v* anamnesis, medical history, case history; **–geval** (-len) *o* case; **–kiem** (-en) *v* disease germ; **–(kosten)verzekering** *v* health-insurance; '**ziektenleer** *v* pathology; '**ziekteverlof** (-loven) *o* sick-leave; *met* ~ absent on sick-leave; **–verloop** *o* course of the disease; **–verschijnsel** (-en en -s) *o* symptom; **–verwekker** (-s) *m* agent (of a disease), pathogen; **–verzekering** (-en) *v* health insurance; **–verzuim** *o* absence due to illness, **–wet** *v* health insurance act

ziel (-en) *v* 1 soul², spirit; 2 ✗ (v. f l e s) kick; 3 ⋈ (v. k a n o n) bore; *arme* ~! poor soul!; *die eenvoudige* ~*en* these simple souls; *een goeie* ~ F a good sort; *geen levende* ~ not a (living) soul; *de ouwe* ~! poor old soul!; *hij is de* ~ *van de onderneming* he is the soul of the undertaking; *een stad van...* ~*en* of... souls; *God hebbe zijn* ~! God rest his soul!; *hoe meer* ~*en hoe meer vreugd* the more the merrier; ● *b ij mijn* ~! upon my soul!; *het ging* (*sneed*) *me door de* ~ it cut me to the quick; *i n het binnenste van zijn* ~ in his heart of hearts; *m e t zijn* ~ *onder zijn arm lopen* be at a loose end; *iem. o p zijn* ~ *geven* S sock sbd. (on the jaw), sock it to sbd.; *op zijn* ~ *krijgen* get a sound thrashing; *t e r* ~*e zijn* be dead and gone; *t o t in de* ~ [moved] to the heart

'**zieleadel** *m* nobility of soul, nobleness of mind; **–grootheid** *v* magnanimity; **–heil** *o* salvation; **–leed** *o* mental suffering, agony of the soul; **–leven** *o* inner life; **–mis** (-sen) = *zielmis*, '**zielenherder** (-s) *m* pastor; '**zielenood** *m* mental distress; '**zielental** *o* number of inhabitants; **–zorg** = *zielzorg*; '**zielepijn** *v* mental anguish; **–piet** (-en), **–poot** (-poten) *m* poor thing, wretch; **–rust** = *zielsrust*; **–smart** *v* mental anguish; **–strijd** *m* struggle of the soul, inward struggle; **–vrede** *m* & *v* peace of mind; **–vreugde** (-n) = *zielsvreugde*

'**zielig** pitiful, pitiable, piteous, pathetic; *hoe* ~! how sad!, what a pity!

'**zielkunde** *v* psychology; ziel'**kundig** *aj* (& *ad*) psychological(ly); '**zielloos** 1 (z o n d e r z i e l) soulless; 2 (d o o d) inanimate, lifeless; **–mis** (-sen) *v* rk mass for the dead; **–roerend** soul-moving, pathetic; '**zielsangst** (-en) *m* (mental) agony, anguish; **–bedroefd** deeply afflicted; **–beminde** (-n) *m-v* dearly beloved; **–blij(de)** very glad, overjoyed; **–gelukkig** radiant, blissful, perfectly happy; **–genot** *o* heart's delight; **–kracht** *v* strength of mind, fortitude; **–kwelling** (-en) *v* = *zielsangst*; **–lief** *iem.* ~ *hebben* love sbd. dearly, love sbd. with all one's soul; **–rust** *v* peace of mind, tranquillity of mind; repose of the soul [after death]; **–veel** ~ *houden van* be very, very fond of; love dearly; **–verdriet** *o* deep-felt grief; **–vergenoegd** pleased as Punch, very content; **–verhuizing** (-en) *v* (trans)migration of souls, metempsychosis; **–verrukking, –vervoering** *v* trance, rapture, ecstasy; **–verwanten** *mv* congenial spirits; **–verwantschap** *v* congeniality, psychic affinity; **–vreugde** (-n) *v* soul's delight; **–vriend** (-en) *m*, **–vriendin** (-nen) *v* bosom friend; **–ziek** mentally deranged; **–ziekte** (-n en -s) *v* mental derangement, disorder of the mind; **–zorg** = *zielzorg*; '**zieltje** (-s) *o* soul; *een* ~ *zonder zorg* a carefree (light-hearted) soul, a happy-go-lucky fellow; ~*s winnen* make proselytes; '**zieltogen** (zieltoogde, h. gezieltoogd) *vi* be dying; **–d** dying, moribund; '**zielverheffend** elevating, soulful; **–zorg** *v* cure of souls, pastoral care; **–zorger** (-s) *m* pastor

zien* I *vt* 1 (i n h e t a l g.) see, perceive; *hij is..., dat zie ik* ...I see; *de directie ziet dat niet gaarne* the management does not like it; (*geen*) *mensen* ~ see (no) people, see (no) company; (not) entertain; *mij niet gezien!* F nothing doing!; 2 (v ó ó r i n f i n i t i e f) *ik heb het* ~ *doen* I've seen it done; *ik heb het hem* ~ *doen* I have seen him do(ing) it; *ik zie hem komen* I see him come (coming); zie ook: *aankomen; men zag hem vallen* he was seen falling (seen to fall); *ik zal het* ~ *te krijgen* I'll try to get it for you; *je moet hem* ~ *over te halen* you must try to persuade him; 3 (n a i n f i n i t i e f) *doen* ~ make [us] see; *iem. niet kunnen* ~ not be able to bear the sight of sbd.; *laten* ~ show; *laat eens* ~... let me see; *laat me ook eens* ~ let me have a look; *hij heeft het mij laten* ~ he has shown it to me; *zich laten* ~ show oneself; *laat je hier niet weer* ~ don't show yourself again, let me never set eyes on you again; *dat zou ik wel eens willen* ~ I will see if...; *wat ze hier te* ~ *geven* what they let you see; ● *ik zie het a a n je dat...* I can see it by your looks that...; *n a a r iets* ~ look at sth., have a look at sth.; *ze moest naar de kinderen* ~ she had to look after the children; *naar het spel* ~ look on at the game; *zie eens o p je horloge* look at your watch; *hij ziet op geen rijksdaalder* he is not particular to a few guilders; *de kamer ziet op de tuin* the room looks out upon the garden, overlooks the garden, commands a view of the garden; *op eigen voordeel* ~ seek one's own advantage; *u i t uw brief zie ik dat...* from (by) your letter I see that...; *uit eigen ogen* ~ look through one's own eyes; *hij kon van de slaap niet uit zijn ogen* ~ he could not see for sleep; *zijn... ziet hem de ogen uit* his... looks through his eyes; *ik zie hem nog v o o r mij* I can see him now; *geen ... te* ~ not a... to be seen; *het is goed te* ~ 1 it can easily be seen, it shows; 2 it is distinctly visible; *er is niets te* ~ there is nothing to be seen; *er is niets van te* ~ there is nothing that shows; *iedere dag te* ~ on view every day; **II** *vi* & *va* see; look; *bleek* ~ look pale; *donker* ~ look black[2]; *dubbel* ~ see double; *ik zie niet goed* my eye-sight is none of the best, my sight is poor; *hij ziet bijna niet meer* his sight is almost gone; *hij ziet slecht* his eye-sight is bad; *het ziet zwart van de mensen* the place is black with people; *we zullen* ~ well, we shall see; *zie beneden* see below; *zie boven* see above; *zie je?* you see?, **F** see?; *zie je wel?* (do you) see that, now?, I told you so!; *zie eens hier!* look here!; *En zie, daar kwam...* and behold!; *~de blind zijn* see and not perceive; **III** *o* seeing, sight, vision; *bij (op) het* ~ *van* on seeing; *tot* ~*s!* see you again!, **F** see you soon!, be seeing you!, so long!; zie ook: *gezien;* **'zienderogen** visibly; **'ziener** (-s) *m* seer, prophet; **'zienersblik** (-ken) *m* prophetic eye; **'zienlijk** visible; **'zienswijs** (-wijzen), **–wijze** (-n) *v* opinion, view; *iems.* ~ *delen* share sbd.'s views

zier *v* whit, atom; *het is geen* ~ *waard* it is not worth a pin (straw, bit); **–tje** *o* = *zier;* *geen* ~ *beter* not a whit better

zie'zo well, so; ~*!* that's it!, there (it is done)!

'ziften (ziftte, h. gezift) *vt* sift; **–er** (-s) *m* sifter; *fig* fault-finder, hair-splitter; **zifte'rij** (-en) *v* fault-finding, hair-splitting; **'ziftsel** (-s) *o* siftings

zi'geuner (-s) *m* gipsy; **zigeune'rin** (-nen) *v* gipsy (woman); **zi'geunertaal** *v* gipsy language, Romany

'zigzag *m* zigzag; ~ *lopen* zigzag; **–lijn** (-en) *v* zigzag line; **zigzagsge'wijs, –ge'wijze** zigzag

1 'zij (e n k e l v.) she; (m e e r v.) they

2 zij (-den) *v* side; ~ *aan* ~ side by side; zie verder: 1 *zijde*

3 zij *v* = 2 *zijde*

'zijaanzicht *o* side-view

'zijachtig = *zijdeachtig*

'zijaltaar (-taren) *o* & *m* side-altar; **–beuk** (-en) *m* & *v* (side-)aisle

zijd *wijd en* ~ far and wide

1 'zijde (-n) *v* 1 side [of a cube, a house, a table, the body &]; 2 flank [of an army]; *een* ~ *spek* a side of bacon; 3 *wiskunde is (niet) zijn sterkste* ~ mathematics is his strong (weak) point; *zijn goede* ~ *hebben* have its good side; *iems.* ~ *kiezen* take sbd.'s side, side with sbd.; ● *a a n beide* ~*n*

on both sides, on either side; *aan deze* ~ on this side of, (on) this side [the Alps &]; *aan de ene* ~ *heeft u gelijk* on one side you are right; *aan zijn* ~ at his side; *hij staat aan onze* ~ he is on our side; *de handen i n de* ~ *zetten* set one's arms akimbo; *iem. in zijn zwakke* ~ *aantasten* attack sbd. where he is weakest; *n a a r alle* ~*n* in every direction; *o p* ~*!* stand clear!, out of the way there!; *op zij van het huis* at the side of the house; *met een degen op zij* sword by side; *op zij duwen* push aside; *op zij gaan* make way (for *voor*); *niet voor... op zij gaan* not give way to...; *fig* not yield to...; *op zij leggen* lay by [money]; save [money]; *op zij schuiven* shove on one side; set aside[2]; *iem. op zij zetten* shove sbd. on one side; *t e r* ~ aside; *ter* ~ *gezegd* in an aside; *ter* ~ *laten* leave on one side; *ter* ~ *leggen* lay on one side; *iem. ter* ~ *nemen* draw sbd. aside; *ter* ~ *staan* stand by [a friend]; support [an actor on the stage]; *ter* ~ *stellen* put on one side, waive [considerations of...]; *v a n alle* ~*n* from all quarters [they flock in]; [you must look at it] from all sides; *van bevriende* ~ from a friendly quarter; *van de* ~ *van de regering* on the part of the Government; *van die* ~ *geen hulp te verwachten* no help to be looked for in that quarter; *van militaire* ~ *vernemen wij* from military quarters we hear; *van mijn* ~ on my part; *van ter* ~ *vernemen wij* from other sources we hear...; *van verschillende* ~*n* from various quarters

2 'zijde *v* (s t o f) silk; *daar spint hij geen* ~ *bij* he doesn't profit by it; **–achtig** silky; **–cultuur** *v* sericulture; **–fabriek** (-en) *v* silk factory; **–fabrikant** (-en) *m* silk manufacturer; **–glans** *m* silk lustre (gloss); **–handelaar** (-s en -laren) *m* silk merchant

'zijdelings I *aj een* ~*e blik* a sidelong look; *een* ~ *verwijt* an indirect reproach; **II** *ad* sideways, sidelong; indirectly

'zijdelinnen *o* rayon; **'zijden** *aj* silk; *fig* silken [hair]; **'zijdepapier** *o* tissue paper; **–rups** (-en) *v* silkworm; **zijdespinne'rij** (-en) *v* 1 silk spinning; 2 silkmill, silk spinnery, filature; **'zijdeteelt** *v* sericulture

'zijdeur (-en) *v* side-door

'zijdewever (-s) *m* silk weaver; **zijdeweve'rij** (-en) *v* silk weaving; **'zijdeworm** (-en) *m* = *zijderups*

'zijgang (-en) *m* 1 side-passage [in a house]; 2 lateral gallery [in a mine]; 3 corridor [in a train]

'zijgen* *vt* strain

'zijgevel (-s) *m* side-façade

'zijig silky; *fig* **F** soft, effeminate

'zijingang (-en) *m* side-entrance; **–kamer** (-s) *v* side-room; **–kanaal** (-nalen) *o* branch-canal;

–kant (-en) *m* side; **–kapel** (-len) *v* side-chapel; **–laan** (-lanen) *v* side-avenue; **–laantje** (-s) *o* side-alley, by-walk; **–leuning** (-en) *v* handrail, railing; armrest [of a chair]; **–licht** (-en) *o* sidelight; **–lijn** (-en) *v* 1 side-line, branch line, loop-line [of railway]; 2 *sp* touch-line [of football field]; 3 = *zijlinie*; **–linie** (-s) *v* collateral line [of a dynasty]; **–lings** = *zijdelings*; **–loge** [-lɔ: ʒə] (-s) *v* side-box; **–muur** (-muren) *m* side-wall

1 zijn *pron* his; *de* (*het*) *~e* his; *elk het ~e* every one his due; *Hitler en de ~en* Hitler and company

2 zijn* I *vi* 1 (z e l f s t a n d i g) be; *2 × 2 is 4* twice two is four; *hij is er* 1 he is there; 2 *fig* he is a made man; *daarvoor is de politie er* that is what the police is there for; *hij* (*zij*) *mag er ~* zie *wezen* **I**; *wij ~ er nog niet* we have not got there yet; *hoe is het?* how are you?, how do you do?; *hoe is het met de zieke?* how is the patient?; *wat is er?* what is the matter?; **II** (k o p p e l - w e r k w.) be; *God is goed* God is good; *dat ben ik!* that's me; *hij is soldaat* he is a soldier; *ze ~ officier* they are officers; *jongens ~* (*nu eenmaal*) *jongens* boys will be boys; *het is te hopen, dat... it* is to be hoped that...; *het is makkelijk* & *te doen* it is easy to do; **III** (h u l p w e r k w.) have, be; *hij is geslaagd* he has succeeded; *hij is gewond* 1 he has been wounded; 2 he is wounded; *ik ben naar A. geweest* I have been to A., [yesterday] I went to A.; **IV** *o* being

'zijnent *te*(*n*) *~* at his house, at his place; *~halve* for his sake; *~wege* as for him; *van ~wege* on his behalf, in his name; *om ~wil*(*le*) for his sake; **'zijnerzijds** on his part, from him

'zijnsleer *v filos* ontology

'zijpad (-paden) *o* by-path

'zijpelen (zijpelde, h. en is gezijpeld) = *sijpelen*

'zijraam (-ramen) *o* side-window; **–rivier** (-en) *v* tributary (river), affluent, confluent; **–schip** (-schepen) *o* (side-)aisle; **–span** (-nen) *o* & *m*, **–spanwagen** (-s) *m* side-car; **–spoor** (-sporen) *o* side-track, siding, shunt; *de trein werd op een ~ gebracht* the train was shunted on to a siding; **–sprong** (-en) *m* side-leap; **–straat** (-straten) *v* side-street, off-street, by-street; **–stuk** (-ken) *o* side-piece; **–tak** (-ken) *m* 1 side-branch; 2 branch [of a river]; 3 spur [of a mountain]; 4 *fig* collateral branch [of a family]; **–venster** (-s) *o* side-window; **–vlak** (-ken) *o* side, lateral face; **–waarts I** *aj* sideward, lateral; **II** *ad* sideways, sideward(s); **–wand** (-en) *m* side-wall; **–weg** (-wegen) *m* side-way, by-way; **–wind** (-en) *m* side-wind; **–zwaard** (-en) *o* ⚓ leeboard

zilt, –ig saltish; briny; *het ~e nat* the salty sea, the briny waves, the brine; **–heid, –igheid** *v*

saltishness, brininess

'zilver *o* 1 (i n 't a l g.) silver; 2 (h u i s r a a d) plate, silver, silverware; *~ in staven* bar-silver, bullion; **–achtig** silvery; **–blank** as bright as silver; **–bon** (-s en -nen) *m* currency note; **–draad** (-draden) *o* & *m* 1 (m e t z i l v e r o m w o n d e n) silver thread; 2 (v a n zilver) silver wire; **–en** *aj* silver; **–erts** (-en) *o* silver-ore; **–fazant** (-en) *m* silver pheasant; **–gehalte** *o* silver content; **–geld** *o* silver money, silver; **–glans** *m* silvery lustre; **–goed** *o* (silver) plate, silver; **–grijs** silver-grey, silvery grey; **–houdend** containing silver; **–kast** (-en) *v* 1 silver-cabinet; 2 silversmith's show-case; **–kleur** *v* silvery colour; **–kleurig** silver-coloured; **–ling** (-en) *m* **B** piece of silver; **–meeuw** (-en) *v* herring gull; **–mijn** (-en) *v* silver mine; **–munt** (-en) *v* silver coin; **–nitraat** *o* silver nitrate; **–papier** *o* silver-paper; tinfoil; **–poeder, –poeier** *o* & *m* 1 powder to clean silver; 2 silver-dust; **–populier** (-en) *m* white poplar, abele; **–reiger** (-s) *m* *grote ~* great white heron; *kleine ~* little egret; **–schoon** *v* silverweed; **–smid** (-smeden) *m* silversmith; **–spar** (-ren) *m* ⚶ silver fir; **–staaf** (-staven) *v* bar of silver; **–stuk** (-ken) *o* silver coin; **–uitje** (-s) *o* shallot; **–visje** (-s) *o* ⚘ silver-fish; **–vloot** (-vloten) *v* silver-fleet; **–vos** (-sen) *m* silver-fox; **–werk** (-en) *o* silverware; plate; **–wit** silvery white

zin (-nen) *m* 1 (b e t e k e n i s) sense, meaning; 2 (z i e l s v e r m o g e n) sense; 3 (l u s t) mind; 4 (v o l z i n) sentence; *~ voor humor* a sense of humour; (*geen*) *~ voor het schone* a (no) sense of beauty; *waar zijn uw ~nen?* have you taken leave of your senses?; *zijn eigen ~ doen* do as one pleases; *iems. ~ doen* do what sbd. likes; *hij wil altijd zijn eigen ~* he always wants to have his own way; *als ik mijn ~ kon doen* if I could work my will; *iem. zijn ~ geven* let sbd. have his way, indulge sbd.; *wat voor ~ heeft het om...?* what's the sense (the point) of ...ing?; *dat heeft geen ~* 1 that [sentence] makes no sense; 2 that is nonsense, **F** that's no go; *het heeft geen ~... there* is no sense (no point) in ...ing; *nu heb je je* now you have it all your own way; *zij heeft ~ in hem* she fancies him; *ik heb ~ om I* have a mind to...; *als je ~ hebt om...* if you feel like ...ing, if you care to...; *ik heb er geen ~ in* I have no mind to, I don't feel like it; *ik heb er wel ~ in om* I have half a mind to; *zijn ~nen bij elkaar houden* keep one's head; *zijn ~ krijgen* get (have) one's own way, get (have) one's will; *zijn ~ niet krijgen* not carry one's point; *zijn ~nen op iets gezet hebben* have set one's heart upon sth.; ● *niet goed b ij zijn ~nen zijn* not be in one's right senses, be out of one's senses; *i n* *dezelfde (die)* ~ [speak] to the same (to that) effect; *in eigenlijke* ~ in its literal sense, in the proper sense; *in engere* ~ in the strict (the limited) sense of the word; *in figuurlijke* ~ in a figurative sense, figuratively; *in ruimere* ~ in a wider sense; *opvoeding in de ruimste* ~ education in its widest sense; *in de ruimste (volste)* ~ *des woords* in the full sense of the world; *in zekere* ~ in a certain sense; in a sense, in a way; *iets in de* ~ *hebben* be up to sth.; *hij heeft niets goeds in de* ~ he is up to no good; *dat zou mij nooit in de* ~ *komen* I should not even dream of it, it would never occur to me; *is het n a a r u w* ~*?* is it to your liking?; *men kan het niet iedereen naar de* ~ *maken* it is impossible to please everybody; *t e g e n mijn* ~ against my will; *v a n zijn* ~*nen beroofd zijn* be out of one's senses; *wat is hij van* ~*s?* what does he intend?; *hij is niets goeds van* ~*s* he is up to no good; *ik ben niet van* ~*s om* I have no thought of ...ing; *één van* ~ *handelen* act in harmony; *één van* ~ *zijn* be of one mind; **–deel** (-delen) = *zinsdeel*

'**zindelijk** clean, cleanly, tidy; (v. e. k i n d) trained; (v. e. h o n d) house-trained; **–heid** *v* cleanness, cleanliness, tidiness

'**zingen* I** *vi* (& *va*) sing [of people, birds, the wind, a kettle]; ☉ chant; ☙ sing, carol, warble; *dat lied zingt gemakkelijk* sings easily; *zuiver* ~ sing true, sing in tune; *vals* ~ sing out of tune; *er naast* ~ sing off-key; **II** *vt* sing; *iem. in slaap* ~ sing sbd. to sleep; *kom, zing eens wat* give us a song

'**zingenot** *o* sensual pleasure(s)

zink *o* zinc; $ spelter

1 '**zinken*** *vi* sink; *goederen laten* ~ sink goods; *tot* ~ *brengen* sink; (z e l f o p z e t t e l i j k) scuttle [to prevent capture]

2 '**zinken** *aj* zinc

'**zinker** (-s) *m* underwater main

'**zinklaag** (-lagen) *v* layer of zinc

'**zinklood** (-loden) *o* 1 (a a n h e n g e l &) sinker; 2 = *dieplood*

'**zinkplaat** (-platen) *v* zinc plate

'**zinkput** (-ten) *m* cesspool, sink; **–stuk** (-ken) *o* mattress

'**zinkwit** *o* zinc-white; **–zalf** *v* zinc ointment

zin'ledig meaningless, nonsensical; **–heid** *v* meaninglessness

'**zinlijk(heid)** = *zinnelijk(heid)*

'**zinloos** senseless, meaningless, inane, pointless; **zin'loosheid** (-heden) *v* senselessness, meaninglessness, inanity, pointlessness

'**zinnebeeld** (-en) *o* emblem, symbol; **zinne'beeldig I** *aj* emblematic(al), symbolic(al); **II** *ad* emblematically, symbolically

'**zinnelijk I** *aj* 1 (v a n d e, d o o r m i d d e l

d e r z i n t u i g e n) of the senses; 2 (v. h e t z i n g e n o t) sensual; **II** *ad* 1 by the senses; 2 sensually; **–heid** *v* sensuality, sensualism

'**zinneloos** insane, mad; **zinne'loosheid** *v* insanity, madness

1 '**zinnen*** *vi* meditate, ponder, muse, reflect; ~ *op* meditate on; *op wraak* ~ brood on revenge

2 '**zinnen*** *vi het zint mij niet* I do not like it, it is not to my liking

'**zinnenprikkelend, zinnen'prikkelend** sensual; '**zinnenstrelend, zinnen'strelend** sensuous

'**zinnia** ('s) *v* zinnia

'**zinnig** sensible; *geen* ~ *mens zal...* no man in his senses (no sane man) will...

'**zinrijk** full of sense, significant, meaningful, pregnant; **–heid** *v* significance, meaningfulness, pregnancy

'**zinsbedrog** *o*, **–begoocheling** (-en) *v* illusion, delusion

'**zinsbouw** *m*, **–constructie** [-strüksi.] *v* construction (of a sentence), sentence structure; **–deel** (-delen) *o* part of a sentence; '**zinsnede** (-n) *v* passage, clause; '**zinsontleding** (-en) *v* analysis

'**zinspelen** (zinspeelde, h. gezinspeeld) *vi* ~ *op* allude to, hint at; **–ling** (-en) *v* allusion (to *op*), hint (at *op*); *een* ~ *maken op* allude to, hint at

'**zinspreuk** (-en) *v* motto, device; **–storend** confusing

'**zinsverband** *o* context

'**zinsverbijstering** *v* mental derangement; **–verrukking, –vervoering** *v* exaltation

'**zinswending** (-en) *v* turn (of phrase)

'**zintuig** (-en) *o* organ of sense, sense-organ; *een zesde* ~ a sixth sense; **zin'tuiglijk** sensorial

'**zinverwant** synonymous; '**zinvol** meaningful; **–heid** *v* meaningfulness

zio'nisme *o* Zionism; **zio'nist** (-en) *m*, **–isch** *aj* Zionist

zit *m het is een hele* ~ it is quite a long journey [from A.]; it is quite a long stretch [from 9 to 4]; *hij heeft geen* ~ *in 't lijf* **F** he is fidgety; **–bad** (-baden) *o* hip-bath, sitz-bath; **–bank** (-en) *v* 1 bench, seat; 2 (i n k e r k) pew; **–dag** (-dagen) *m* ☵ court-day; **–kamer** (-s) *v* sitting-room, parlour; **–plaats** (-en) *v* seat; *er zijn* ~*en voor 5000 mensen* the hall (church &) can seat 5000 people, the seating accommodation is 5000; **zit'slaapkamer** (-s) *v* bed-sittingroom, **F** bed-sitter, bedsit; '**zitstaking** (-en) *v* stay-in strike; **–stok** (-ken) *m* perch; '**zitten*** *vi* sit; *die zit!* that is one in the eye for you; *sp* goal!; *ze* ~ *al* they are seated; *hij heeft gezeten* he has done time, he has been in prison; *die stoelen* ~ *gemakkelijk* these chairs are very comfortable;

zit je daar goed? are you comfortable there?; *de jas zit goed (slecht)* is a good (bad) fit; *dat zit wel goed* it's (it'll be) all right; *de boom zit vol vruchten* is full of fruit; *daar zit je nou!* there you are!; *waar ~ ze toch?* where can they be?; *zit daar geld?* are they well off?; *hoe zit dat toch?* how is that?; *daar zit het hem* there's the rub; *dat zit nog!* that's a question!; *dat zit zo* it is like this; *het zit hem als aangegoten, als (aan het lijf) gegoten (geschilderd)* it fits him like a glove; (v ó ó r i n f i n i t i e f) *de kip zit te broeden* the hen is sitting; *ze zaten te eten* they were having dinner; they were eating [apples]; *hij zit weer te liegen* he is telling lies again; *hij zit de hele dag te spelen* he does nothing but sit and play all day long; (m e t i n f i n i t i e f) *blijven ~* remain seated; *blijft u ~* keep your seat, don't get up; *~ blijven!* keep your seats!; *die jongen is blijven ~* he has missed his remove; *zij is blijven ~* she has been left on the shelf; *hij is met die goederen blijven ~* he was left with his wares (on his hands); *ze is met vier kinderen blijven ~* she was left with four children; *je boed blijft zo niet ~* your hat won't stay on; *gaan ~* 1 sit down; 2 (v. v o g e l s) perch; *gaat u ~* sit down; be seated, take a seat; *kom bij mij ~* come and sit by me; *iem. laten ~* make sbd. sit down; *hij heeft haar laten ~* he has deserted her; *er veel geld bij laten ~* lose a lot of money over it; *dat kan ik niet op mij laten ~* I won't take it lying down, I cannot sit down under this charge; *laat (het) maar ~* keep the change [waiter], it is all right; *iets wel zien ~* see one's way to do sth.; *het niet zo zien ~* think sth. unworkable (unrealizable); *het niet meer zien ~* be despondent, see no way out; ● *a a n t a f e l ~* be at table; *het zit er aan, hoor* you seem to have plenty of money; *het zit er niet aan* I can't afford it; *hij zit a c h t e r mij* he sits behind me; *hij zit er achter* he is at the bottom of it; *er zit iets achter* there is something behind; *ze ~ altijd b ij elkaar* they are always (sitting) together; *ze ~ er goed bij* they are well off; *er zit niet veel bij die man* he is a man with nothing in him; *i n angst ~* be in fear; *hij zit in de commissie* he is on the committee; *hoe zit dat in elkaar?* how is that?; *het zit in de familie* it runs in the family; *dat zit er wel in* that's quite on the cards; *het zit niet in hem* it is not in him, he hasn't got it in him; *er zit wel wat in hem* he has (jolly) good stuff in him; zie ook: *inzitten; wij ~ er m e e (te houden, te kijken &)* we don't know what to do (with it), what to make of it; *dat zit ik niet mee* that doesn't worry me; *o m het vuur ~* sit (be seated) round the fire; *daar zit een jaar o p, als je...* it will be a year (in prison) if you...; *dat zit er weer op* that job is jobbed; zie ook: *opzitten; hij zit nu al een uur o v e r dat opstel* he has been at work on it

for an hour; *het zit me t o t hier* **F** I am fed up with it; *hij zit v o o r het kiesdistrict A.* he represents the constituency of A., he sits for A.; *zij zit voor een schilder* she sits to a painter; **II** *o stemmen bij ~ en opstaan* vote by rising or remaining seated; **'zittenblijver** (-s) *m* non-promoted pupil; **'zittend** 1 seated, sitting; 2 sedentary [life]; **'zittijd** *m* 1 (time of) session; 2 ↟ term [= period during which a court holds sessions]; **'zitting** (-en) *v* 1 session, sitting [of a committee &]; 2 seat, bottom [of a chair]; *geheime ~* secret session; *een stoel met een rieten ~* a cane-bottomed chair; *~ hebben* sit, be in session [of a court]; *~ hebben in* sit on [a committee]; be on [the board]; serve on [a jury]; *~ hebben voor...* sit [in Parliament] for...; *~ houden* sit; *~ nemen in een commissie* serve on a committee; *~ nemen in het ministerie* accept office; **'zittingsdag** (-dagen) *m* day of session; (v. r e c h t b a n k) court-day; **–zaal** (-zalen) *v* (v. r e c h t b a n k) court-room; **'zitvlak** (-ken) *o* seat, bottom; **–vlees** *o hij heeft geen ~* **F** he is fidgety

Z.K.H. = *Zijne Koninklijke Hoogheid*
Z.M. = *Zijne Majesteit*
Z.O. = *zuidoosten*

1 zo I *ad* 1 (z o d a n i g) so, like that, such; zie ook: *zo'n*; *het is ~* 1 so it is; 2 that is true, it's a fact!; 3 you are right; *~ is het* quite so!, that's it!; *~ is het niet* it is not like that (like this); *het is niet ~* it is not true; *als dat ~ is* if that is the case; if that is true; *~ was het* that's how it was; *~ zij het!* so be it; *~ is hij (niet)* he is (not) like that; *~ is hij nu eenmaal* he is built that way; *het is nu eenmaal ~* things are so; *~ is het leven* such is life; *~ zijn soldaten (nu eenmaal)* it is the way with soldiers; *het voorstel kan zó niet worden aangenomen* the proposal cannot be accepted as it stands; 2 (o p d i e o f z o'n m a n i e r) thus, like this, like that, in this way, in this manner, so; *alleen ~ kan je het doen* so and only so; *~ moet je het doen* ook: that's how you should do it; *zó bang dat...* so much (so) afraid that...; *zó hoog dat...* so high that...; 3 (z o a l s i k h i e r b ij a a n g e e f) as ... as; *het was zó dik* it was as big as this; *~ groot dat...* of such a size that...; *hij sprong zó hoog* he jumped as high as this, he jumped that high; *~ (e v e n) b e v e s t i g e n d:* as... as; o n t k e n n e n d: not so (ook: not as)... as; *~ groot als zijn broer* as tall as his brother; *~ wit als sneeuw* (as) white as snow, snow-white; *hij is lang niet ~...als...* he is not nearly so... as...; 5 (i n d i e m a t e) so; *zijn ze zó slecht?* are they so bad (as bad as that, all that bad)?; *ik betaalde hem dubbel, zó tevreden was ik* I paid him double, I was so pleased; *wees ~ vriendelijk mij mede te delen...* be so kind as to inform me, be kind enough to inform me, kindly inform me...; 6 (i n h o g e m a t e) so; *ik ben ~ blij!* I am so glad!; *ik ben zó blij!* I am so very glad!; *ik verlang ~ hen weer te zien* I so long to see them again; 7 (d a d e l ij k) directly; in no time; 8 (a a n s t o n d s) presently; 9 (s t o p w o o r d) I say, well; *~, ben jij daar!* I say, that you!; *~, en waar is Marie?* well, and where is Mary?; 10 (u i t r o e p v. t e v r e- d e n h e i d) that's it, well; *~, dat is in orde! Well,* that's all right!; *~, nu kunnen we gaan* that's it, now we can be off; 11 (v r a g e n d) Really?, did he?, has he? &; *~ dat* so... that, in such a way that, so as not to...; *~ een* zie *zo'n*; *net ~ een* just such another; *~ eentje* such a one; *om ~ en ~ laat* at something something o'clock; *~ en zoveel gulden* umpty guilders; *in het jaar ~ en zoveel* zie *zóveel*; *~ iem.* such a man, such a one; *~ iets* such a thing, such things; *...of ~ iets* or some such thing; *~ iets als £ 5000* about £ 5000; *zó maar* without further ado; *waarom? och, zó maar!* I just thought I would!; just like that; *en ~ meer* and so on; *~ dadelijk, ~ meteen* in a moment, presently; *~ mogelijk* if possible; *~ net* just now; *~ niet!* not so!; *~ pas = zoëven; ~ zeer* so much that, zie ook: *zozeer*; *~ ~!* so so!; *hij was niet ~ doof of hij hoorde mij binnenkomen* he was not so deaf but he heard me enter; *al is hij nog ~* zie 3 *al*; *net ~* zie 2 *net* **III**; *o ~!* Aha!; *het was o ~ koud* ever so cold; **II** *cj* 1 (v e r g e l ij k e n d) as; 2 (v e r o n d e r- s t e l l e n d) if; 3 (v o o r w a a r d e l ij k) if; *hij is, ~ men zegt, rijk* he is said to be rich; *je bent weer hersteld, ~ ik zie* I see; *~ ja...* if so; *~ neen (niet)...* if not...; *~ hij nu eens binnenkwam* if he were to come into the room now; *~ hij al moeite gedaan heeft om...* (even) if he has been at pains to... **2 zo** (zooien) *v = zooi*

zo'als as, like; *zij stemmen ~ men hun zegt* they vote the way one tells them; *in landen ~ België, Frankrijk...* in countries such as Belgium, France...

zocht (zochten) V.T. van *zoeken*

zo'danig, 'zodanig I *aj* such (as this, as these); *~e mensen* such people, people such as these; *op ~e wijze* in such a manner; *als ~* as such; **II** *ad* so (much), in such a manner

zo'dat so that

'zode (-n) *v* turf, sod [of grass]; *onder de groene ~n liggen* **F** push up the daisies; *dat zet geen ~n aan de dijk* that cuts no ice; **'zodenrand** (-en) *m* turf-border

zodi'ak *m* zodiac; **zodia'kaallicht** *o* zodiacal light

'zodoende thus, in this way; so

zo'dra as soon as; *niet ~..., of...* no sooner [had he, did he &]... than..., scarcely (hardly)...

when...

zoe'aaf (zoeaven) *m* zouave

zoek *het is ~* it has been mislaid, it is not to be found; *~ maken* mislay [sth.]; *~ raken* be (get) lost; *op ~ naar...* in search of...; **'zoekbrengen** (bracht 'zoek, h. 'zoekgebracht) *vt* kill [time]; **'zoeken* I** *vt* look for [something, a person &]; seek [assistance, the Lord]; *ja, maar hij zoekt het ook altijd* he is always asking for trouble; *hij zoekt mij ook altijd* he is always down on me; *hij zocht mij te overreden* he sought to persuade me; *zoek me eens een krant* go and find a newspaper for me; *ruzie ~* look for trouble; *wij ~ het in...* we go in for [quality]; *de waarheid ~* seek truth; ook: search after truth; *arbeiders die werk ~* in search of work; zie ook: *ruzie* &; *hij wordt gezocht* they are looking for him; (d o o r p o l i t i e) he is wanted; *dat had ik niet achter hem gezocht* 1 (o n g u n s t i g) I never thought him capable of such a thing; 2 (g u n s t i g) I never thought he had it in him; *er wat achter ~* suspect something behind it; *hij zoekt overal wat achter* he always tries to find hidden meanings; *dat is nog ver te ~* far to seek; *hij wist niet waar hij het ~ moest* he didn't know where to turn; *hij heeft hier niets te ~* he has no business here; *ik heb daar niets (meer) te ~* there's no point going there; **II** *vi* & *va* seek, search, make a search; *zoek, Castor!* seek!; *ik zal wel eens ~* I'll have a look [in the cupboard &]; *wie zoekt, die vindt, zoekt en gij zult vinden* **B** seek, and ye shall find; *naar iets ~* look for (search for, seek) something; *naar zijn woorden ~* grope for words; **III** *o* search, quest; *aan het ~ zijn* be looking for it; **–er** (-s) *m* 1 seeker; 2 ✕ view-finder; **'zoeklicht** (-en) *o* searchlight; **–plaatje** (-s) *o* puzzle picture

zoel mild, balmy [weather]; **–heid** *v* mildness, balminess

'Zoeloe (-s) *m* Zulu; **–kaffer** (-s) *m* Zulu-Kaffir

'zoelte *v* 1 mildness, balminess; 2 soft breeze

'zoemen (zoemde, h. gezoemd) *vi* buzz, hum; **'zoemer** (-s) *m* 1 ✻ buzzer; 2 ↩ = *zoemvlucht*; **–toon, 'zoemtoon** *m* buzzing tone, ☎ dialling tone; **'zoemvlucht** (-en) *v* ↩ zoom

zoen (-en) *m* 1 (k u s) kiss; 2 (v e r z o e n i n g) expiation, atonement; **–dood** *m* & *v* redeeming death; **'zoenen** (zoende, h. gezoend) *vt* & *va* kiss; **'zoenoffer** (-s) *o* expiatory sacrifice, sin-offering, peace-offering, piacular offer

zoet 1 sweet²; 2 (g e h o o r z a a m) good; *een ~ kind* a good child; *~ water* fresh water, sweet water; *het kind ~ houden* keep (the) baby quiet; *~ maken* sweeten; **–achtig** sweetish; **'zoete-kauw** (-en) *m-v een ~ zijn* have a sweet tooth; **–lijk** sugary; **–melks** *~e kaas* cream cheese; **'zoeten** (zoette, h. gezoet) *vt* sweeten;

'zoeterd (-s) *m* darling, dear; 'zoetgevooisd mellifluous, melodious; 'zoetheid (-heden) *v* sweetness; –houdertje (-s) *o* sop; –hout *o* liquorice; 'zoetig sweetish; 'zoetigheid (-heden) *v* sweetness; (*allerlei*) ~ sweet stuff, sweets, dainties; 'zoetje (-s) *o* (v. z o e t s t o f) sweetener, saccharin; 'zoetjes 1 softly, gently; 2 sweetly; zoetjes'aan 1 softly; 2 gradually; ~ *dan breekt het lijntje niet* easy does it; 'zoetluidend melodious; –middel (-en) *o* sweetening; zoet'sappig *fig* sugary, saccharine; –heid *v* sugariness; 'zoetschaaf (-schaven) *v* smoothing plane; –stof (-fen) *v* sweetening; –vijl (-en) *v* smoothing file; zoet'vloeiend mellifluous, melodious; –heid *v* mellifluence, melodiousness; zoet'watervis (-sen) *m* freshwater fish; 'zoetzuur I *aj* sweet-and-sour; II *o* sweet pickles
'zoeven (zoefde, h. gezoefd) *vi* whiz
zo'éven just now, a minute ago
zog *o* 1 (mother's) milk; 2 ⚓ wake [of a ship]; *in iems.* ~ *varen* follow in sbd.'s wake
1 'zogen (zoogde, h. gezoogd) *vt* suckle, give suck, nurse
2 'zogen V.T. meerv. van *zuigen*
zoge'naamd I *aj* so-called; self-styled, would-be; II *ad* ~ *om te* ostensibly to; zoge'noemd so-called; zoge'zegd so to say; zoge'zien so to see, on the face of it
zo'lang I *cj* so (as) long as; II *ad* meanwhile
'zolder (-s) *m* 1 garret, loft; 2 (z o l d e r i n g) ceiling; 'zolderen (zolderde, h. gezolderd) *vt* 1 warehouse, lay up, store; 2 △ ceil; 'zoldering (-en) *v* ceiling; 'zolderkamertje (-s) *o* attic, attic room, garret; –ladder (-s) *v* loft ladder; –licht (-en) *o* skylight, garret window; –luik (-en) *o* trapdoor; –raam (-ramen) *o* dormer-window; –schuit (-en) *v* ⚓ barge; –trap (-pen) *m* garret stairs; –venster (-s) *o* garret-window; –verdieping (-en) *v* attic-floor
'zolen (zoolde, h. gezoold) *vt* sole [boots]
'zomen (zoomde, h. gezoomd) *vt* hem
'zomer (-s) *m* summer; *des ~s, in de* ~ in summer; *van de* ~ 1 this summer [present]; 2 next summer [future]; 3 last summer [past]; –achtig = *zomers*; zomer'avond (-en) *m* summer-evening; –dag (-dagen) *m* summer's day, summer day; –dienst (-en) *m* 1 summer-service; 2 summer time-table; –goed *o* = *zomerkleren*; –hitte *v* summer-heat; –hoed (-en) *m* summer hat; –huis(je) (-huizen, huisjes) *o* summer-cottage; –japon (-nen) *m*, –jurk (-en) *v* summer-frock, summer-dress; –kleed *o* 𝔁 summer-plumage; –kleren *mv* summer-clothes; –maand (-en) *v* June; *de ~en* the summer-months; –mantel (-s) *m* summer-coat; zomer'morgen (-s) *m* summer-

morning; 'zomerpak (-ken) *o* summer-suit; 'zomers *aj* summery; 'zomersproeten *mv* freckles; –tarwe *v* summer-wheat, spring-wheat; –tijd *m* 1 summer-time; 2 daylight-saving time; –vakantie [-kɑnsi.] (-s) *v* summer-holidays; –verblijf (-blijven) *o* summer-residence; –we(d)er *o* summer-weather; –zonnestilstand *m* summer solstice
zo'min ~ *als* no more than
zo'n [zo.n] such a; ~ *leugenaar!* the liar!; ~ *twintig* & about twenty &, zie verder *ongeveer*
1 zon (-nen) *v* sun; *in de* ~ *staan* stand in the sun; *hij kan de* ~ *niet in het water zien schijnen* he is a dog in the manger; zie ook: *schieten* II & *zonnetje*
2 zon (zonnen) V.T. v. *zinnen*
'zonnaal zonal
'zonaanbidder (-s) *m* sun-worshipper
zond (zonden) V.T. v. *zenden*
'zondaar (-s en -daren) *m* sinner; –sbankje (-s) *o* penitent form
'zondag (-dagen) *m* Sunday; 'zondags I *aj* Sunday; *mijn ~e pak* my Sunday suit, my Sunday best; II *ad* on Sundays; –blad (-bladen) *o* Sunday paper; –dienst (-en) *m* Sunday service [at church]; Sunday duty [of employees]; –gezicht (-en) *o* 1 sanctimonious mien; 2 soms: best mien; *een ~ zetten* look as if butter wouldn't melt in one's mouth; –heiliging *v* Sunday observance; –kind (-eren) *o* Sunday child; *fig* one born with a silver spoon in his mouth; –rijder (-s) *m* weekend driver; –ruiter (-s) *m* would-be horseman, Sunday rider; –rust *v* Sunday rest; –school (-scholen) *v* Sunday school; –sluiting *v* Sunday closing; –viering *v* Sunday observance
zonda'res (-sen) *v* sinner; 'zonde (-n) *v* sin; *dagelijkse* ~ *rk* venial sin; ~ *tegen de H. Geest rk* sin against the Holy Ghost; *een kleine* ~ a peccadillo; *het is* ~ 1 it is a sin; 2 it is a pity; *het is* ~ *en jammer* it is a pity; *het is* ~ *en schande* it is a sin and a shame; *het is* ~ *van het meisje* it is a pity of the girl; ~ *doen* commit a sin, sin; –besef *o* sense of sinfulness; –bok (-ken) *m* scapegoat[2]; –last *m* burden of sins; –loos sinless
'zonden V.T. meerv. v. *zenden*
'zondenregister (-s) *o* register of sins
'zonder without; ~ *zijn hulp* 1 without his help [you can't do it]; 2 but for his help [I should have been drowned]; ~ *hem zou ik verdronken zijn* but for him I should have been drowned; ~ *het te weten* without knowing it; ~ *meer* just, simply, frankly; in its own right [a work of art]
'zonderling I *aj* singular, queer, odd, eccentric; II *ad* singularly &; III (-en) *m* eccentric (person); –heid (-heden) *v* singularity, queer-

ness, oddity, eccentricity

'**zondeval** *m de* ~ (*van Adam*) the Fall (of man); '**zondig** sinful; '**zondigen** (zondigde, h. gezondigd) *vi* sin²; ~ *tegen* sin against; '**zondigheid** *v* sinfulness

'**zondvloed** *m* deluge², flood²; *van vóór de* ~ antediluvian

'**zone** ['zɔːnə, 'zo.nə] (-n en -s) *v* zone [of earth] '**zoneclips** (-en) *v* solar eclipse

zong (**zongen**) V.T. v. *zingen*

zonhoed (-en) = *zonnehoed*

zonk (**zonken**) V.T. v. *zinken*

'**zonkant** (-en) *m* sunny side; –**licht** *o* sunlight; '**zonnebaan** (-banen) *v* ecliptic; –**bad** (-baden) *o* sun-bath; '**zonnebaden I** (zonne-baadde, h. gezonnebaad) *vi* sun-bathe; **II** *o* sun-bathing; '**zonneblind** (-en) *o* Persian blind; –**bloem** (-en) *v* sunflower; –**brand** *m* sunburn; –**brandolie** *v* tanning oil; –**bril** (-len) *m* sun-glasses; –**dauw** *m* sundew; –**gloed** *m* heat (glow) of the sun; –**gloren** *o* daybreak, dawn; –**god** *m* sun-god; –**hoed** (-en) *m* sun-hat; –**jaar** (-jaren) *o* solar year; –**klaar** as clear as daylight; *het* ~ *bewijzen* prove it up to the hilt; –**klep** (-pen) *v* 🔊 (sun) visor; –**licht** = *zonlicht*; **1** '**zonnen** (zonde, h. gezond) **I** *vt* sun; **II** *vr zich* ~ sun oneself **2** '**zonnen** V.T. meerv. v. *zinnen*

'**zonnepitten** *mv* sunflower seeds; –**scherm** (-en) *o* **1** (v o o r p e r s o n e n) sunshade, parasol; **2** (a a n h u i s) sun-blind, awning [over a shop-window]; –**schijf** *v* disc of the sun; –**schijn** *m* sunshine; –**spectrum** *o* solar spectrum; –**stand** *m* sun's altitude; –**steek** (-steken) *m* sunstroke; *een* ~ *krijgen* be sunstruck; –**stelsel** (-s) *o* solar system; **zonne'stilstand** (-en) *m* solstice; **zonne'straal** (-stralen) *m* & *v* sunbeam, ray of the sun; –**tent** (-en) *v* awning; –**tje** (-s) *o* sun; *het* ~ *van binnen* the sunshine in our heart(s); *zij is ons* ~ *in huis* she is the sunshine of our home; *iem. in het* ~ *z e t t e n* praise sbd.; –**vis** (-sen) *m* John Dory; –**vlek** (-ken) *v* sun-spot, solar spot; –**wagen** *m* chariot of the sun, Phoebus' car; –**wende** *v* [summer, winter] solstice; –**wijzer** (-s) *v* sun-dial; '**zonnig** sunny; '**zonshoogte** *v* sun's altitude; **zons'onder-gang** (-en) *m* sunset, sundown; –'**opgang** (-en) *m* sunrise; '**zonsverduistering** (-en) *v* eclipse of the sun, solar eclipse; '**zonwering** (-en) *v* = *zonnescherm*; –**zij(de)** *v* sunny side

zoog ('zogen) V.T. van *zuigen*

'**zoogbroe(de)r** (-s) *m* foster-brother; –**dier** (-en) *o* mammal [*mv* mammalia]; –**kind** (-eren) *o* **1** (z u i g e l i n g) suckling; **2** (v o e d s t e r-k i n d) nurse-child; –**zuster** (-s) *v* foster-sister **zooi** (-en) *v* F lot, heap; *het is (me) een* ~! they are

a nice lot!; *de hele* ~ the whole lot, the whole caboodle

zool (zolen) *v* sole; –**beslag** *o* sole protectors; –**ganger** (-s) *m* plantigrade; –**le(d)er** *o* sole-leather

zoölo'gie *v* zoology; **zoö'logisch** zoological; **zoö'loog** (-logen) *m* zoologist

zoom (zomen) *m* hem [of a dress, handkerchief]; edge, border; fringe [of a forest, a town]; bank [of a river]

'**zoomlens** ['zu.mlɛns] (-lenzen) *v* zoom lens

zoon (zonen en -s) *m* son²; *de verloren* ~ zie *verloren*; *de Zoon Gods* the Son of God; *de Zoon des Mensen* the Son of Man; *Neerlands zonen* the sons of Holland; *hij is de* ~ *van zijn vader* he is his father's son

zoop (**zopen**) F V.T. van *zuipen*

'**zootje** (-s) *o* F lot; *het hele* ~ the whole lot, the whole caboodle

'**zopen** F V.T. meerv. van *zuipen*

zorg (-en) *v* **1** (z o r g z a a m h e i d) care; **2** (b e z o r g d h e i d) solicitude, anxiety, concern; **3** (m o e i l i j k h e i d, l a s t) care, trouble, worry; **4** (s t o e l) easy chair; *het zal mij een* ~ *zijn* that is the last thing I am concerned about, F I couldn't care less, fat lot I care!; *zij is een trouwe* ~ she is a faithful soul; ~ *dragen voor* take care of, see to; *geen* ~ *over de tijd* sufficient unto the day is the evil thereof; *heb daar geen* ~ *over* don't worry about that; *vol* ~ *over...* ook: solicitous concerning...; *ik neem de* ~ *daarvoor op mij* that shall be my care; *zich* ~*en maken* worry; *geen* ~*en voor morgen* care killed the cat; ● *i n* ~ *zijn over...* be anxious about...; *in de* ~ *zitten* sit in the easy chair; *fig* be in trouble; *m e t* ~ *gedaan* carefully done; *z o n d e r* ~ *gedaan* carelessly done; –**barend** alarming, critical; –**dragend** careful, solicitous; '**zorgelijk(heid)** = *zorglijk(heid)*; –**loos I** *aj* **1** (a c h t e l o o s) careless, improvident, unconcerned; **2** (z o n d e r z o r g e n) care-free; **II** *ad* carelessly; **zorge'loosheid** (-heden) *v* carelessness, improvidence, unconcern;

'**zorgen** (zorgde, h. gezorgd) *vi* care; ~ *voor...* **1** take care of...; **2** (v e r s c h a f f e n) provide [entertainment &]; *voor de oude dag* ~ make provision for one's old age, lay by something for the future; *er was voor. eten gezorgd* provision had been made for food; *de vrouw zorgt voor de-keuken (de kinderen)* looks after the kitchen (the children); *u moet zelf voor uw kleren* ~ **1** you have to take care of your clothes yourself; **2** you have to find your own clothing; *voor de lunch* ~ see to lunch; *hij kan wel voor zich zelf* ~ **1** (f i n a n c i e e l) he can support himself, he can fend (shift) for himself; **2** (o p p a s s e n) he is able to look after himself; *zorg er voor dat het* *gedaan wordt* see to it that it is done; *daar zal ik wel voor* ~ I shall see to that, that shall be my care; *zorg (er voor) dat je om 9 uur thuis bent* mind (that) you are (at) home at nine; **'zorgenkind** (-eren) *o* problem child; **'zorglijk** precarious, critical; **–heid** *v* precariousness; **zorg'vuldig** careful; **–heid** *v* carefulness; **zorg'wekkend** alarming, critical; **'zorgzaam** careful, tender; **–heid** *v* carefulness, tender care

zot I *aj* foolish; **II** (-ten) *m* fool; **–heid** (-heden) *v* folly; **–skap** (-pen) *v* 1 fool's cap; 2 (p e r s o o n) fool; **'zottenklap, –praat** *m* foolish talk, stuff and nonsense; **zotter'nij** (-en) *v* folly; **zot'tin** (-nen) *v* fool

zou zie *zouden*

'zou(den) V.T. v. *zullen;* 1 (v a n v o o r- w a a r d e) [I, we] should, [he, they, you] would; 2 (v a n a f s p r a a k) was to..., were to...; *wij ~ gaan, als...* we should go if...; *wij ~ er allemaal heengaan* we were to go all of us; *ik zou je danken!* thank you very much!; *wat zou dat?* zie *wat* **I**

zout (-en) **I** *o* salt; *Attisch* ~ Attic wit (salt); *het* ~ *der aarde* **B** the salt of the earth; [adventure is] the salt of life [to some men]; *hij verdient het* ~ *in de pap niet* he earns a mere pittance; **II** *aj* salt, salty, saltish, briny; salted [almonds, peanuts]; ~ *water* salt water; **–achtig** saltish; **–arm** salt-poor, low-salt [diet], with little salt; **–eloos** saltless, *fig* insipid; **zoute'loosheid** (-heden) *v fig* insipidity; **'zouten*** *vt* salt down, salt [meat]; corn [meat]; **–er** (-s) *m* salter; **'zoutevis** *m* salt fish, salt cod; **'zoutgehalte** *o* salt content, percentage of salt, salinity; **–heid** *v* saltness, salinity; **–houdend** saline; **–ig** saltish; **–je** (-s) *o* salted biscuit; **–korrel** (-s) *m* grain of salt; **–laag** (-lagen) *v* salt deposit; **–loos** salt-free [diet]; **–meer** (-meren) *o* salt-lake; **–mijn** (-en) *v* salt-mine; **–pan** (-nen) *v* salt-pan, saline; **–pilaar** (-laren) *m* pillar of salt; **–raffinaderij** (-en) *v* salt-refinery; **–raffinadeur** (-s) *m* salt-refiner; **–smaak** *m* salty taste; **–strooier** (-s) *m* salt-sprinkler; **–te** *v* saltiness; (v. z e e w a t e r) salinity; **'zoutvaatje** (-s), **–vat** *o* salt cellar; **zout'watervis** (-sen) *m* salt-water fish; **'zoutwinning** *v* salt-making; **–zak** (-ken) *m* salt-bag; *fig* lump (of a fellow); **–zieden** *o* salt-making; **–zieder** (-s) *m* salt-maker; **zoutziede'rij** (-en) *v* salt-works; **'zoutzuur** *o* hydrochloric acid

1 'zoveel so much, thus (that) much; ~ *is zeker* that much is certain; *dat is* ~ *gewonnen* that much gained; *in 1800* ~ in 1800 odd, in 1800 and something; *in het jaar* ~ in such and such a year; *om drie uur* ~ at three something; *de trein van 5 uur* ~ the five something train; *ik geef er niet* ~ *om!* I don't care that about it!; *voor nog* ~

niet not for anything, not for the world

2 zo'veel so much; ~ *als* as much as; *hij is daar* ~ *als opziener* he is by way of being an overseer there; ~ *mogelijk* as much as possible

'zoveelste n'th, **S** umpteenth; *dat is de* ~ *keer* the n'th time, the hundredth time; *bij het* ~ *regiment* in the -th (**S** the umpteenth) regiment

1 'zover so far, thus far; *ga je* ~*?* will you go that far²?; ~ *zal hij niet gaan* he will never go as far as that, he will never go that length; *hij heeft het* ~ *gebracht dat...* he has succeeded so well that...; *hij zal het* ~ *niet laten komen* he won't let things go so far; *het is* ~ *gekomen dat...* things have come to such a pass that...; ● *in* ~ *ben ik het met u eens* so far I am with you; *t o t* ~ as far as this, so far, thus far

2 zo'ver so far; ~ *ik weet* as far as I know, for aught (for all, for anything) I know; ● *in (voor)* ~ *(als)...* (in) so far as..., as far as...; *v o o r* ~ *men weet* (in) so far as is known, as far as is known

zo'waar actually; sure enough

zo'wat about; *dat is* ~ *alles* that's about all; ~ *hetzelfde* pretty much the same (thing); ~ *even groot* about the same size, much of a size; ~ *niets* next to nothing

zo'wel ~ *als* as well as; *hij is* ~...*als...* he is... as well as..., he is both... and...; *hij* ~ *als zijn broer* both he and his brother

z.o.z. = *zie ommezijde* please turn over, P.T.O.

zo'zeer so much, to such an extent; *niet* ~..., *als wel...* not so much... as...

1 zucht (-en) *m* (v e r z u c h t i n g) sigh

2 zucht *v* (b e g e e r t e) desire; ~ *n a a r* desire for, desire of, love of [liberty, adventure]; ~ *o m te zien en te weten* desire to see and know; ~ *t o t navolging (tot tegenspraak)* spirit of imitation (contradiction)

'zuchten (zuchtte, h. gezucht) **I** *vi* sigh; ~ *n a a r (om) iets* sigh for sth.; ~ *o n d e r het juk* groan under the yoke; ~ *o v e r zijn werk* sigh over one's task (work); **II** *o het* ~ *van de wind* the sighing of the wind; **'zuchtje** (-s) *o* 1 sigh; 2 sigh, sough, zephyr; *geen* ~ not a breath of wind

zuid south; **Zuid-'Afrika** *o* South Africa; **Zuidafri'kaans** South African; **–afri'kaner** (-s) *m ZA* Afrikaner; **Zuid-A'merika** *o* South America; **Zuidameri'kaan** (-kanen) *m*, **–s** *aj* South American; **'zuidelijk I** *aj* southern, southerly; **II** *ad* southerly; **'zuiden** *o* south; *o p het* ~ *gelegen* having a southern aspect; *t e n* ~ *van...* (to the) south of...; **–wind** *m* south wind; **'zuiderbreedte** *v* South latitude; **'Zuiderkruis** *o* Southern Cross; **'zuiderlicht** *o* southern lights, aurora australis; **–ling** (-en) *m* 1 somebody from the south; 2 somebody from a South-European country; **Zuider'zee** *v* Zuider

Zee; **'zuidkust** (-en) *v* south-coast;
zuid'oostelijk south-easterly; **–'oosten** *o*
south-east

zuid'pool *v* south pole, antarctic pole; **–cirkel**
m Antarctic Circle; **–expeditie** [-(t)si.] (-s) *v*
antarctic expedition; **–gebied** *o het* ~ the
Antarctic; **–landen** *mv* antarctic regions;
–tocht (-en) *m* antarctic expedition
'zuidvruchten *mv* tropical and subtropical
fruit; **–waarts I** *aj* southward; **II** *ad* south-
ward(s); **zuid'westelijk** south-westerly;
–'westen *o* south-west; **–'wester** (-s) *m* 1
(w i n d) southwester; 2 (h o o f d d e k s e l)
southwester; **'Zuidzee** *v Stille* ~ Pacific
(Ocean)

'zuigbuis (-buizen) *v* suction-pipe, sucker;
'zuigeling (-en) *m* baby, infant, babe; **'zuige-
lingensterfte** *v* infant mortality; **–zorg** *v*
infant care; **'zuigen* I** *vi* suck; *a a n zijn pijp* &
~ suck at one's pipe &; *ergens even aan* ~ take
(have) a suck at it; *o p zijn duim* & ~ suck one's
thumb &; **II** *vt* suck; *iets uit zijn duim* ~ invent
a story; **'zuiger** (-s) *m* 1 (p e r s o o n) sucker; 2
✕ piston, plunger [of a pump]; **–klep** (-pen) *v*
piston-valve; **–slag** (-slagen) *m* piston-stroke;
–stang (-en) *v* piston-rod; **–veer** (-veren) *v*
piston-ring; **'zuigfles** (-sen) *v* feeding-bottle,
baby's bottle; **'zuiging** *v* sucking; suction;
'zuigklep (-pen) *v* suction-valve; **–kracht** *v* 1
suction; 2 absorptiveness, absorptivity; **–leer**
(-leren) *o* sucker; **–napje** (-s) *o* sucker; **–pijp**
(-en) *v* suction-pipe, sucker; **–pomp** (-en) *v*
suction-pump

zuil (-en) *v* pillar², column; *Dorische* ~ Doric
column; *de* ~*en van Hercules* the Pillars of
Hercules; ~ *van Volta* Voltaic pile; **'zuilenga-
lerij** (-en) *v*, **–gang** (-en) *m* colonnade, arcade,
portico; **–rij** (-en) *v* colonnade

'zuinig I *aj* 1 economical, thrifty, frugal,
sparing, saving [woman, housekeeper &]; 2
demure [look, mien]; ~ *zijn* be economical &;
~ *zijn met...* use... sparingly, economize [one's
strength &], husband [provisions &]; be chary
of [favours]; **II** *ad* 1 economically &; 2 [look]
demurely; *(ik heb ervan gelust) en niet* ~ *ook* **S** not
half!; **–heid** *v* economy, thrift, thriftiness;
verkeerde ~ *betrachten* be penny-wise and
pound-foolish; *uit (voor de)* ~ from motives of
economy, for reasons of economy, for
economy's sake; **–heidsmaatregel** (-en en -s)
m measure of economy; **–jes** economically

'zuipen* I *vi* tipple, **F** booze, soak; **II** *vt* swig;
–er (-s), **'zuiplap** (-pen) *m* boozer, soaker,
tippler

'zuivel *m* & *o* butter and cheese, dairy-produce,
dairy-products; **–bereiding** *v* dairy industry;
–boer (-en) *m* dairy-farmer; **–fabriek** (-en) *v*

dairy-factory; **–produkten** *mv* dairy-produce,
dairy-products

'zuiver I *aj* 1 (s c h o o n, z i n d e l ij k) clean
[hands]; 2 (z o n d e r o n r e i n h e d e n) pure
[air, water &]; 3 (o n v e r m e n g d) pure,
unadulterated [alcohol &]; 4 (z o n d e r
s c h u l d) pure, clear [conscience]; 5 (k u i s,
r e i n) pure, chaste [thoughts &]; 6 (l o u t e r)
pure, sheer, mere [nonsense &]; 7 **$** clear, net
[profit]; 8 **♪** pure [sounds]; *dat (die zaak) is niet*
~ **F** that is a bit fishy; *dat is* ~*e taal* that is
plain speaking; *het is daar niet* ~ things are not
as they ought to be; *hij is niet* ~ *in de leer* he is
not sound in the faith, he is unsound in
doctrine; **II** *ad* purely [accidental]; ~ *schrijven*
write pure English (Dutch &), write grammat-
ically correct English; ~ *zingen* **♪** sing in tune;
niet ~ *zingen* **♪** sing out of tune; *het is* ~ *(en
alléén) daarom* simply and solely (purely and
simply) for that reason; **–aar** (-s) *m* purifier;
purist [in language]; **'zuiveren** (zuiverde, h.
gezuiverd) **I** *vt* clean [of dirt]; cleanse [of sin];
purify [the air, blood, language, liquor, metal
&]; refine [oil, sugar, metals]; clear [the air²];
purge² [the belly, our moral life &]; wash [a
wound]; ~ *van* clean of [dirt]; purge of [impu-
rities, sin &]; clean of [foreign elements,
suspicion &]; cleanse of [sin]; **II** *vr zich* ~ [*fig*]
clear oneself; *zich* ~ *van het ten laste gelegde*
purge (clear) oneself of the charge; **–d** puri-
fying; **𝕋** purgative; **'zuiverheid** *v* cleanness²,
purity²; **'zuivering** (-en) *v* cleaning, cleansing,
purification, purgation, [political] purge;
refining [of oil, sugar, metals]; **'zuiverings-
actie** [-aksi.] (-s) *v* 🗡 mopping-up operation,
[political] purge; **–zout** *o* bicarbonate of soda

zulk such; **zulks** such a thing, such, this, it, the
same

'zullen* 1 (g e w o n e t o e k o m s t) [I, we]
shall; [you, he, they] will; *we* ~ *gaan* we shall
go; *zij* ~ *gaan* they will go, they'll go; *ze* ~
morgen gaan ook: they are going tomorrow; *ik
hoop dat hij komen zal* I hope he may come; 2
(v e r m o e d e l ij k o f w a a r s c h ij n l ij k)
will (probably); *dat zal Jan zijn* that will be
John; *dat zal Waterloo zijn* this would be
Waterloo, I suppose; *ze* ~ *ziek zijn* they are ill
maybe; 3 (a f s p r a a k) are to; *hij zal om 5 uur
komen* he is to call here at five o'clock; 4 (w i l
v. s p r e k e r t e g e n o v e r e e n a n d e r)
shall; *hij wil niet? hij zal* he shall [go &]; *gehoorzamen* ~ *ze!* they shall obey!; 5 (b e l o f t e)
shall; *u zult ze morgen krijgen* you shall have
them to-morrow; 6 (v o o r s p e l l i n g) shall;
de aarde zal vergaan the earth shall pass away; 7
(b e d r e i g i n g) shall; *dat zal je berouwen* you
shall smart for it; *ik zal je!* you shall catch it; 8

(g e b o d) shall; *gij zult niet stelen* thou shalt not steal; 9 (n a *te*) *hij beloofde te* ~ *komen* he promised to come; *hij zei te* ~ *komen* he said he would come; 10 (a n d e r e g e v a l l e n) *ja, dat zal wel* I daresay you have (he is &); *voetbal? ik zal hem voetballen* I'll give him football

zult *m* pork pickled in vinegar; **'zulten** (zultte, h. gezult) *vt* pickle, salt

'zundgat (-gaten) *o* touch-hole, vent

'zuren I (zuurde, h. gezuurd) *vt* sour, make sour; **II** (zuurde, is gezuurd) *vi* sour, turn sour; **'zurig** sourish; **–heid** *v* sourishness

'zuring *v* 🌱 sorrel; *eetbare* ~ dock; **–zout** *o* salt of sorrel; **–zuur** *o* oxalic acid

1 zus (-sen) *v* sister

2 zus so, thus; ~ *of zo handelen* act one way or the other; *juffrouw* ~ *en juffrouw zo* Miss Blank and Miss Dash

'zusje (-s) *o* (little) sister, baby sister; **'zuster** (-s) *v* sister; (v e r p l e e g s t e r) nurse, sister; *ja, je* ~ *!* F your grandmother!; **–huis** (-huizen) *o* 1 (k l o o s t e r) nunnery; 2 (v. g e e s t e l ij k e o r d e) affiliated house; 3 (v. v e r p l e e g s t e r s) nurses' home; **–liefde** *v* sisterly love; **–lijk** sisterly; **–maatschappij** (-en) *v* affiliated (associated) firm; **–paar** (-paren) *o* pair of sisters; *het* ~ the two sisters; **–schap** *o* & *v* sisterhood; **–schip** (-schepen) *o* sister ship; **–school** (-scholen) *v* convent school; **–vereniging** (-en) *v* sister association

zuur I *aj* sour² [apples, grapes &, bread &, temper]; acid² [taste, expression & in chemistry]; acetous [fermentation]; tart [apple]; *fig* ook: soured [spinsters]; crabbed [expression]; *een* ~ *stukje brood* a hard-earned livelihood; ~ *werk* disagreeable work; *nu ben je* ~ *!* your number is up!; *dan zijn we allemaal* ~ we are all in for it; *iem. het leven* ~ *maken* make life a burden to sbd.; ~ *worden* turn sour, sour²; **II** *ad* sourly &; ~ *kijken* look sour; ~ *verdiend* hard-earned; **III** (zuren) *o* 1 (i n g e m a a k t) pickles; 2 (i n d e s c h e i k.) acid; *het* ~ *in de maag* heartburn; *gemengd* ~ mixed pickles; *uitjes in 't* ~ pickled onions; **–achtig** sourish, acidulous, subacid; **–bestendig** acid resistant, acid-proof, non-corrosive; **–deeg** *o,* **–desem** *m* leaven²; **–graad** *m* (degree of) acidity; **–heid** *v* sourness, acidity; tartness; **–kool** *v* sauerkraut; **–pruim** (-en) *v* F sourpuss, crab-apple; **–stel** (-len) *o* pickle-stand

'zuurstof *v* oxygen; **–apparaat** (-raten) *o* oxygen apparatus; resuscitator; **–cilinder** (-s) *m* oxygen cylinder; (v. d u i k e r) aqualung; **–tent** (-en) *v* oxygen tent; **–verbinding** (-en) *v* oxide

'zuurtje (-s) *o* acid drop; **'zuurvast** acid resistant, acid proof; **–verdiend** hard-earned

[money]; **–zoet** sour-sweet, sweet-and-sour

Z.W. = *zuidwesten*

zwaai *m* swing, sweep, flourish; **'zwaaien I** (zwaaide, h. gezwaaid) *vt* sway [a sceptre]; flourish [a flag]; swing, wield [a hammer]; brandish [the lance]; zie ook: *scepter; wij zwaaiden de hoek om* we swung round the corner; **II** (zwaaide, h. en is gezwaaid) *vi* 1 (v. t a k k e n &) sway, swing; 2 (v. d r o n k e m a n) reel; 3 ⚓ (v. s c h i p) swing; *met de hoed (een vlag &)* ~ wave one's hat (a flag &); **'zwaailicht** (-en) *o* flashing light

zwaan (zwanen) *m* & *v* swan; *een jonge* ~ a cygnet

'zwaar I *aj* 1 heavy [of persons, things &], ponderous, weighty [bodies]; 2 (z w a a r g e b o u w d) heavily built, stout [man], hefty [Hollander]; 3 (d i k) heavy [materials]; 4 🌾 (g r o f) heavy [ordnance, guns]; 5 (s t e r k) heavy [wine], strong [cigars, beer &]; *fig* 1 (g r o o t) heavy [costs, losses]; 2 (e r n s t i g) severe [illness], grievous [crime]; 3 (m o e i l ij k) heavy, hard, difficult [task]; stiff [examination]; hard [times]; 4 (h a r d, s t r e n g) severe [punishment]; *een zware slag* 1 a heavy report [of gun &]; 2 a heavy thud [of falling body]; 3 a heavy blow² [with the hand, of fortune]; *dat is 5 kg* ~ it weighs 5 kg; *het is tweemaal zo* ~ *als...* ook: it is twice the weight of...; *ik ben* ~ *in mijn hoofd* I feel a heaviness in the head; *hij is* ~ *op de hand* he is heavy on hand; **II** *ad* heavily &, soms: heavy [e.g. heavy-laden]; ~ *getroffen* hard hit, badly hit (by *door*); ~ *gewond* badly wounded; ~ *verkouden* having a bad cold; ~ *ziek* seriously ill; **–beladen** heavily laden, heavy-laden

zwaard (-en) *o* 1 🌾 sword; 2 ⚓ (= z ij~) leeboard [of a ship], (m i d d e n~) centre-board; *met het* ~ *in de vuist* sword in hand; **–leen** (-lenen) *o* male fief; **–lelie** (-s en -iën) *v* sword-lily, gladiolus [*mv* gladioli]; **–slag** (-slagen) *m* stroke with the sword, sword-stroke; **–vechter** (-s) *m* gladiator; **–vis** (-sen) *m* sword-fish; **–vormig** sword-shaped

'zwaargebouwd heavy, hefty, big-boned; **–gewapend** heavily armed; **–gewicht** *o* heavyweight; **–gewond** critically wounded; **–heid** *v* heaviness, weight; **zwaar'hoofdig** pessimistic; **zwaar'lijvig** corpulent, stout, obese; **–heid** *v* corpulence, stoutness, obesity; **zwaar'moedig** melancholy, melancholic, hypochondriac; **–heid** *v* melancholy, hypochondria; **'zwaarte** *v* weight, heaviness; **–kracht** *v* gravitation, gravity; *middelpunt van* ~ centre of gravity; *de wet der* ~ the law of gravitation; **–lijn** (-en) *v* median line; **–punt** *o* centre of gravity; *fig* main point, emphasis;

zwaar′tillend pessimistic, gloomy;
zwaar′wichtig weighty, ponderous; **–heid**
(-heden) *v* weightiness, ponderousness
′zwabber (-s) *m* 1 (b o r s t e l) swab, mop; 2
(b o e m e l a a r) rake; *aan de ~ zijn* be on the
loose (on the spree); **′zwabberen** (zwabberde,
h. gezwabberd) **I** *vt* swab, mop; **II** *vi fig = aan
de zwabber zijn*
′zwachtel (-s) *m* bandage, swathe; **′zwach-
telen** (zwachtelde, h. gezwachteld) *vt* swathe,
bandage
zwad (zwaden) *o,* **′zwade** (-n) *v* swath
′zwager (-s) *m* brother-in-law
zwak I *aj* 1 *eig* weak [barrier, enemy, eyes,
stomach &]; *gram* weak [conjugation, verb]; *fig*
weak [argument, character, mind, team]; >
feeble; 2 (n i e t k r a c h t i g) weak, mild
[attempt]; weak [resistance]; weak, low [pulse];
frail [old man]; 3 (n i e t h a r d) faint [sound];
4 (n i e t h e l d e r) faint [light]; 5 (z e d e l ij k
o n s t e r k) weak [man], frail [woman]; *stemming ~* $ market weak; *het ~ke geslacht* zie 1
geslacht; in een ~ ogenblik in a moment of weakness; *~ in Frans* weak (shaky) in French; *~ van
karakter* of a weak character; *~ staan* be shaky;
II *ad* weakly &; **III** (-ken) *o* weakness; *de
Engelsen hebben een ~ voor traditionele vormen* the
British have a weakness for traditional forms;
een ~ hebben voor iem. have a weak spot for sbd.;
iem. in zijn ~ tasten touch sbd. in his weakest
(tenderest) spot; **–begaafd** (mentally) retarded
[child]; **–heid** (-heden) *v* 1 (v. l i c h a a m s -
k r a c h t) weakness, feebleness, 2 (g e b r e k
a a n k r a c h t o f e n e r g i e) feebleness; 3
(t e g r o t e t o e g e e f l ij k h e i d) weakness;
4 (m o r e e l) frailty; *zwakheden* weaknesses,
failings, foibles; **–hoofd** (-en) *m-v* feeble-
minded person; **zwak′hoofdig** feeble-
minded, weak-minded; **′zwakjes I** *aj hij is ~*
weakly, weakish; **II** *ad* weakly; **′zwakkelijk** a
little weak, weakish; **–ling** (-en) *m* weakling[2];
′zwakstroom *m* weak current; **′zwakte** *v*
weakness, feebleness; **zwak′zinnig** feeble-
minded, (mentally) deficient, defective; **–heid**
v feeble-mindedness, mental deficiency
′zwalken (zwalkte, h. gezwalkt) *vi* ⚓ drift
about; wander about; *op zee ~* rove the seas
′zwaluw (-en) *v* 🐦 swallow; *één ~ maakt nog geen
zomer* one swallow does not make a summer;
–staart (-en) *m* 1 *eig* swallow's tail; 2 ⚒
dovetail; 3 swallow-tail [butterfly]; 4 swallow-
tail(ed coat)
1 zwam (-men) *v* fungus [*mv* fungi]
2 zwam *o* tinder, touchwood
′zwamachtig fungous
′zwammen (zwamde, h. gezwamd) *vi* **S** talk
tosh, jaw; **′zwamneus** (-neuzen) *m* twaddler,

F gas-bag
′zwanedons *o* swan'sdown; **–hals** (-halzen) *m*
swan-neck; **–zang** *m* swan-song
zwang *m in ~ brengen* bring into vogue; *in ~
komen* become the fashion, come into vogue; *in
~ zijn* be fashionable, be the vogue
′zwanger pregnant[2], with child; **–schap** (-pen)
v pregnancy; **–schapsonderbreking** (-en) *v*
termination of pregnancy, induced abortion
′zwarigheid (-heden) *v* difficulty, scruple; *heb
daar geen ~ over* don't bother about that; *~
maken* make (raise) objections
zwart I *aj* black[2] [colour, bear, bread, list,
hands, ingratitude, sable ⊘ &]; *~ maken*
blacken[2] [things, character]; *het was er ~ van de
mensen* the place was black with people; *~e
handel* black market, black-market traffic
(dealings, transactions); *~ kopen* buy on the
black market; *~e winst* & black-market profit
&; *het in de ~ste kleuren afschilderen* paint it in
the darkest colours; **II** *ad alles ~ inzien* look at
the gloomy (black) side of things; *~ kijker*
look black; **III** *o* black; *de ~en* the blacks; *het ~
op wit hebben* have it in black and white;
–achtig blackish; **–bont** mottled; **′zwarte**
(-n) *m* & *v* black; **zwarte′handelaar** (-s) *m*
black marketeer; **–′piet** (-en) *m* ◇ knave of
spades; *iem. de ~ toespelen* pass the buck to sbd.;
zwarte′pieten (zwartepiette, h. gezwartepiet)
vi play the game of Old Maid; **Zwarte ′Woud**
o het ~ the Black Forest; **Zwarte ′Zee** *v de ~*
the Black Sea; **zwart′gallig** melancholy,
ill-tempered, atrabilious; **–heid** *v* melancholy;
′zwartgestreept 1 (a a n d e o p p e r -
v l a k t e) black-striped; 2 (d o o r a d e r d)
black-streaked; **–handelaar** (-s en -laren) =
zwartehandelaar; **–harig** black-haired; **–heid** *v*
blackness; **–hemd** (-en) *m* Blackshirt, Fascist;
–je (-s) *o* **F** darky; **–kijker** (-s) *m* 1 pessimist,
melancholic; 2 **F** non-paying television
viewer; **–kop** (-pen) *m* black-haired boy (girl
&); **′zwartmaken** (maakte ′zwart, h. ′zwart-
gemaakt) *vt* blacken[2]; **′zwartogig** black-eyed;
′zwartsel *o* black; **zwart-′wit** black and white
′zwavel *m* sulphur; **–achtig** sulphurous; **–bad**
(-baden) *o* sulphur-bath; **–bloem** *v* flowers of
sulphur; **–bron** (-nen) *v* sulphur-spring;
–damp (-en) *m* sulphur-fume, sulphurous
vapour; **′zwavelen** (zwavelde, h. gezwaveld)
vt treat with sulphur, sulphurize, sulphurate;
′zwavelerts (-en) *o* sulphur-ore; **–geel**
sulphur-yellow; **–houdend** sulphurous; **–ig**
sulphurous; **–ijzer** *o* ferric sulphide; **–lucht** *v*
sulphurous smell; ⚒ **–stok** (-ken) *m* (sulphur-)
match; **zwavel′waterstof** *v,* **–gas** *o* sulphur-
etted hydrogen; **′zwavelzuur** *o* sulphuric
acid

'**Zweden** *o* Sweden; **Zweed** (Zweden) *m*
Swede; **–s I** *aj* Swedish; **II** *o het* ~ Swedish;
III *v een* ~*e* a Swedish woman

'**zweefbaan** (-banen) *v* overhead railway;
telpher way; **–molen** (-s) *m* giant('s)-stride;
–rek (-ken) *o* trapeze; '**zweefvliegen** (zweef-
vliegde, h. gezweefvliegd) **I** *vi* ~ glide; **II** *o* ~
gliding; **–er** (-s) *m* ~ glider-pilot; '**zweef-
vliegtuig** (-en) *o* ~ glider; **–vlucht** (-en) *v* ~
volplane, glide; (v. z w e e f v l i e g e r) glide

zweeg (zwegen) V.T. v. *zwijgen*

zweem *m* 1 semblance, trace [of fear &]; 2
touch [of mockery], shade [of difference], tinge
[of sadness]; *geen* ~ *van hoop* not the least flicker
of hope

zweep (zwepen) *v* whip; *er de* ~ *over leggen* whip
up the horses; *fig* lay one's whip across their
(her, his) shoulders; **–diertje** (-s) *o* flagellate;
–draad (-draden) *m* flagellum; **–slag** (-slagen)
m lash; **–tol** (-len) *m* whipping-top

zweer (zweren) *v* ulcer, sore, boil

zweet *o* perspiration, sweat; *het klamme* ~ the
cold perspiration; *het koude* ~ *brak hem uit* zie
uitbreken **I**; *in het* ~ *uws aanschijns* **B** in the sweat
of thy brow (face); *zich in het* ~ *werken* work
oneself into a sweat; **–bad** (-baden) *o* sweat-
ing-bath, sudatory; **–doek** (-en) *m* sweat-
cloth; [Veronica's] sudarium; **–druppel** (-s) *m*
drop of perspiration, drop of sweat; **–handen**
mv perspiring (sweaty) hands; **–kamer** (-s) *v*
sweating-room; **–klier** (-en) *v* sweat-gland;
–kuur (-kuren) *v* sweating-cure; **–lucht** *v*
sweaty smell; **–middel** (-en) *o* sudorific;
–voeten *mv* perspiring feet

'**zwegen** V.T. meerv. van *zwijgen*

zwei (-en) *v* bevel

zwelg (-en) *m* gulp, draught

'**zwelgen*** **I** *vt* swill, quaff; guzzle; **II** *vi* carouse;
~ *in...* luxuriate in..., revel in...; **–er** (-s) *m*
guzzler, carouser; **zwelge'rij** (-en) *v* guzzling,
revelling; '**zwelgpartij** (-en) *v* carousal,
revelry, orgy

'**zwellen*** *vi* swell [= grow bigger or louder],
fill out; *de* ~*de zeilen* the swelling (bellying)
sails; *doen* ~ swell; **–ling** (-en) *v* swelling

'**zwembad** (-baden) *o* swimming-bath; **–band**
(-en) *m* swimming-belt; **–bassin** [-bas!] (-s) *o*
swimming-pool; **–blaas** (-blazen) *v* swim-
ming-bladder, sound; **–broek** (-en) *v* swim-
ming-trunks, bathing-trunks

'**zwemen** (zweemde, h. gezweemd) *vi* ~ *naar* be
(look) like; ~ *naar het blauw* have a bluish cast

'**zwemgordel** (-s) *m* swimming-belt; **–inrichting** (-en) *v* swimming-baths; **–kunst** *v* art of
swimming, natation; **–les** (-sen) *v* (a l g.)
swimming instruction; swimming-lessons;
'**zwemmen*** *vi* swim; *de aardappels* ~ *i n de*

boter are swimming in butter; *in het geld* ~ roll
in money; *haar ogen zwommen in tranen* her eyes
were swimming with tears; *o p de buik (rug)* ~
swim on one's chest (back); *zullen we gaan* ~?
shall we have (take) a swim?; *zijn paard o v e r
de rivier laten* ~ ook: swim one's horse across
the river; **–er** (-s) *m* swimmer; '**zwempak**
(-ken) *o* swim-suit, bathing suit; **–poot**
(-poten) *m* flipper; zie ook: *zwemvoet*; **–school**
(-scholen) *v* swimming-school; **–sport** *v*
swimming; **–vest** (-en) *o* life-jacket, air-jacket;
–vlies (-vliezen) *o* 1 web; 2 *sp* flipper [for
frogman]; *met zwemvliezen* web-footed
[animals], webbed [feet]; **–voet** (-en) *m* web-
foot [of birds]; **–vogel** (-s) *m* web-footed bird,
swimming-bird; **–wedstrijd** (-en) *m* swim-
ming-match

'**zwendel** *m* = *zwendelarij*; **–aar** (-s) *m* swindler,
F sharper; **zwendela'rij** (-en) *v* swindling;
swindle; '**zwendelen** (zwendelde, h. gezwen-
deld) *vi* swindle

'**zwengel** (-s) *m* 1 wing [of a mill]; 2 pump-
handle; 3 crank [of an engine]; 4 splinter-bar,
swingle-tree [of a carriage]; '**zwengelen**
(zwengelde, h. gezwengeld) *vi* swing, turn,
pump

zwenk (-en) *m* turn; '**zwenken** (zwenkte, h. en
is gezwenkt) *vi* turn to the right (left), swing
round; ✕ wheel; swerve [of motorcar]; *fig*
change front; *links (rechts)* ~! ✕ left (right),
wheel!; **–king** (-en) *v* turn, swerve; ✕ wheel;
fig change of front

'**zwepen** (zweepte, h. gezweept) *vt* whip, lash
'**zweren*** **I** *vi* 1 ulcerate, fester; ‖ 2 swear; *b ij
hoog en laag (bij kris en kras)* ~ swear by all that
is holy; *ze* ~ *bij die pillen* they swear by these
pills; *bij het woord des meesters* ~ swear by the
word of a (one's) master; *o p de bijbel* ~ swear
upon the bible; *men zou erop* ~ one could swear
to it; **II** *vt* swear [an oath]; *dat zweer ik (u)!* I
swear it!; *iem. geheimhouding laten* ~ swear sbd.
to secrecy

'**zwerfdier** (-en) *o* stray animal; **–kei** (-en),
–steen (-stenen) *m* erratic block, erratic
boulder; **–tocht** (-en) *m* wandering, ramble;
–vogel (-s) *m* nomadic bird; **–ziek** of a roving
disposition

⊙ **zwerk** *o* 1 welkin, firmament, sky; 2 rack,
drifting clouds

zwerm (-en) *m* swarm [of bees, birds, horsemen
&]; '**zwermen** (zwermde, h. gezwermd) *vi*
swarm

'**zwerveling** (-en) *m* wanderer, vagabond;
'**zwerven*** *vi* wander, roam, ramble, rove;
~*de kat* stray cat; ~*de stammen* wandering
tribes, nomadic tribes; **–er** (-s) *m* wanderer,
vagabond, rambler, rover, tramp

'**zweten** (zweette, h. gezweet) **I** *vi* perspire, sweat [also of new hay, bricks &]; **II** *vt* sweat [blood]; '**zweterig** sweaty; **–heid** *v* sweatiness; '**zwetsen** (zwetste, h. gezwetst) *vi* boast, brag, **F** talk big air; **–er** (-s) *m* boaster, braggart; **zwetse'rij** *v* boasting, boast, bragging, brag

'**zweven** (zweefde, h. en is gezweefd) *vi* be in suspension, be suspended [in a liquid]; float [$, in the air]; hover [over sth.]; ↝ glide [ook: over the ice]; ● *het zweeft mij o p de tong* I have it on the tip of my tongue: ~ *t u s s e n leven en dood* be hovering between life and death; *v o o r de geest* ~ be present to the mind [of an image]; have [a thought] in mind; '**zweverig** (v a a g) dreamy, vague, in the clouds; (d u i z e l i g) dizzy

'**zwezerik** (-riken) *m* sweetbread

'**zwichten** (zwichtte, h. en is gezwicht) *vi* yield, give way; ~ *voor* yield to [him, his arguments, persuasion]; yield to, succumb to [superior numbers]; give in to [threats]

'**zwiepen** (zwiepte, h. gezwiept) *vi* swish, switch

zwier *m* 1 (d r a a i) flourish; 2 (p o m p e u z e g r a t i e) dash; jauntiness, smartness; *a a n de ~ zijn* be on the spree (on the randan); *m e t edele ~* with a noble grace; '**zwieren** (zwierde, h. gezwierd) *vi* 1 reel [when drunk]; glide [over the ice &]; whirl [round the ball-room]; 2 (p r e t m a k e n) go the pace

zwierf (zwierven) V.T. van *zwerven*

'**zwierig I** *aj* dashing, jaunty, stylish, smart; **II** *ad* smartly; **–heid** *v* dash, jauntiness, stylishness, smartness

'**zwierven** V.T. meerv. van *zwerven*

'**zwijgen* I** *vi & va* 1 be silent; 2 fall silent; *zwijg!, zwijg stil!* hold your tongue!, silence!, be silent!; *wie zwijgt, stemt toe* silence gives consent; *hij kan niet ~* he cannot keep a secret, he cannot keep his (own) counsel; *iem. doen ~* put sbd. to silence, silence sbd.; *wie zwijgt stemt toe* silence gives consent; *daarop moest ik ~* to this I could make no reply; *maar je moet er o v e r ~* hold your tongue about it; *de geschiedenis zwijgt daarover* history is silent about this; *een batterij t o t ~ brengen* ⚔ silence a battery; *iem. tot ~ brengen* reduce (put) sbd. to silence, silence sbd.; *daarva n zullen wij maar ~* let it pass; *zwijg mij daarvan!* don't talk to me about that!; *om nog maar te ~ van...* to say nothing of..., not to mention..., let alone...; **II** *vt iets ~* be silent

about sth.; **III** *o* silence; *het ~ bewaren* keep silence; *hij moest er het ~ toe doen* he could make no reply; *iem. het ~ opleggen* impose silence (up)on sbd.; *het ~ verbreken* break silence; **–d I** *aj* silent; **II** *ad* silently, in silence; '**zwijger** (-s) *m* silent person; *Willem de Zwijger* William the Silent; '**zwijggeld** (-en) *o* hush-money; '**zwijgzaam** silent, taciturn; **–heid** *v* silence, taciturnity

zwijm *in* ~ *liggen* lie in a swoon; *in* ~ *vallen* faint, swoon

'**zwijmel'm** 1 giddiness, dizziness; 2 intoxication; '**zwijmelen** (zwijmelde, h. gezwijmeld) *vi* become dizzy

zwijn (-en) *o* 1 🐖 pig[2], hog[2], (*mv & fig*) swine[2]; 2 **S** fluke; *wild ~* (wild) boar; **–achtig** hoggish, swinish; '**zwijneboel** *m* piggery, mess; *in een ~ leven* hog it; **–jacht** (-en) *v* boar-hunting; '**zwijnen** (zwijnde, h. gezwijnd) *vi* (b o f f e n) be lucky, be in luck; '**zwijnenhoeder** (-s) *m* swineherd; '**zwijnepan** *v* (pig) sty, dirty mess; **zwijne'rij** (-en) *v* filth, dirt, muck, beastliness; '**zwijnestal** (-len) *m* 1 piggery, pigsty; 2 = *zwijnepan*; '**zwijnjak** (-ken) *m* pig, hog, swine, dirty tike; '**zwijntje** (-s) *o* 1 piggy; 2 **F** (f i e t s) bike; **–sjager** (-s) *m* **F** bicycle-thief

zwik (-ken) *m* 1 vent-peg, spigot, spile; 2 ⚒ kit; *de hele ~* the whole lot, the whole caboodle; **–boor** (-boren) *v* auger; **–gat** (-gaten) *o* vent-hole; '**zwikken** (zwikte, is gezwikt) *vi* sprain one's ankle

'**zwingel** (-s) *m* swingle(-staff); **–aar** (-s) *m* flax-dresser; '**zwingelen** (zwingelde, h. gezwingeld) *vt* swingle [flax]

'**Zwitser** (-s) *m* Swiss; *de ~s* the Swiss; **–land** *o* Switzerland; **–s** *aj* Swiss

'**zwoegen** (zwoegde, h. gezwoegd) *vi* toil, toil and moil, drudge; **–er** (-s) *m* toiler, drudge

zwoel sultry; **–heid** *v*, **–te** *v* sultriness

zwoer (zwoeren) V.T. van *zweren* **II**

zwoerd (-en) *o* rind [of bacon], pork-rind

'**zwoeren** V.T. meerv. van *zweren* **II**

zwol (zwollen) V.T. van *zwellen*

zwolg (zwolgen) V.T. van *zwelgen*

'**zwollen** V.T. meerv. v. *zwellen*

zwom (zwommen) V.T. van *zwemmen*

zwoor (zworen) V.T. van *zweren* **I**

zwoord (-en) *o* = *zwoerd*

'**zworen** V.T. meerv. van *zweren* **I**

Z.Z.O. = *zuidzuidoost*

Z.Z.W. = *zuidzuidwest*

Nederlandse sterke en onregelmatige werkwoorden

ONBEPAALDE WIJS	VERLEDEN TIJD	VERLEDEN DEELWOORD[1]
bakken	bakte (bakten)	h. gebakken
bannen	bande (banden)	h. gebannen
barsten	barstte (barstten)	is gebarsten
bederven	bedierf (bedierven)	vt h., vi is bedorven
bedriegen	bedroog (bedrogen)	h. bedrogen
beginnen	begon (begonnen)	is begonnen
bergen	borg (borgen)	h. geborgen
bersten	borst, berstte (borsten, berstten)	is geborsten
bevelen	beval (bevalen)	h. bevolen
bevriezen	bevroor, bevroos (bevroren, bevrozen)	vt h., vi is bevroren, bevrozen
bezwijken	bezweek (bezweken)	is bezweken
bidden	bad (baden)	h. gebeden
bieden	bood (boden)	h. geboden
bijten	beet (beten)	h. gebeten
binden	bond (bonden)	h. gebonden
blazen	blies (bliezen)	h. geblazen
blijken	(het) bleek	is gebleken
blijven	bleef (bleven)	is gebleven
blinken	blonk (blonken)	h. geblonken
braden	braadde (braadden)	h. gebraden
breken	brak (braken)	h. en is gebroken
brengen	bracht (brachten)	h. gebracht
brouwen	brouwde (brouwden)	h. gebrouwen
buigen	boog (bogen)	vt h., vi is gebogen
delven	dolf, delfde (dolven, delfden)	h. gedolven
denken	dacht (dachten)	h. gedacht
dingen	dong (dongen)	h. gedongen
doen	deed (deden)	h. gedaan
dragen	droeg (droegen)	h. gedragen
drijven	dreef (dreven)	vt h., vi is gedreven
dringen	drong (drongen)	h. en is gedrongen
drinken	dronk (dronken)	h. gedronken
druipen	droop (dropen)	h. en is gedropen
duiken	dook (doken)	h. en is gedoken
dunken	(mij) docht, dacht	h. gedocht, gedunkt
durven	durfde, dorst (durfden, dorsten)	h. gedurfd
dwingen	dwong (dwongen)	h. gedwongen
ervaren	ervaarde, ervoer (ervaarden, ervoeren)	h. ervaren
eten	at (aten)	h. gegeten
fluiten	floot (floten)	h. gefloten
gaan	ging (gingen)	is gegaan
gelden	gold (golden)	h. gegolden
genezen	genas (genazen)	vt h., vi is genezen
genieten	genoot (genoten)	h. genoten
geven	gaf (gaven)	h. gegeven
gieten	goot (goten)	h. gegoten
glijden	gleed (gleden)	h. en is gegleden
glimmen	glom (glommen)	h. geglommen

[1]) h. = hulpwerkwoord *hebben*; is = hulpwerkwoord *zijn*.

ONBEPAALDE WIJS	VERLEDEN TIJD	VERLEDEN DEELWOORD[1])
graven	groef (groeven)	h. gegraven
grijpen	greep (grepen)	h. gegrepen
hangen	hing (hingen)	h. gehangen
hebben	had (hadden)	h. gehad
heffen	hief (hieven)	h. geheven
helpen	hielp (hielpen)	h. geholpen
heten	heette (heetten)	h. geheten
hijsen	hees (hesen)	h. gehesen
hoeven	hoefde (hoefden)	h. gehoefd, gehoeven
houden	hield (hielden)	h. gehouden
houwen	hieuw (hieuwen)	h. gehouwen
jagen	joeg, jaagde (joegen, jaagden)	h. gejaagd
kerven	korf, kerfde (korven, kerfden)	vt h., vi is gekorven, gekerfd
kiezen	koos (kozen)	h. gekozen
kijken	keek (keken)	h. gekeken
kijven	keef (keven)	h. gekeven
klieven	kliefde, ZN kloof (kliefden, kloven)	h. gekliefd, ZN gekloven
klimmen	klom (klommen)	h. en is geklommen
klinken	klonk (klonken)	h. geklonken
kluiven	kloof (kloven)	h. gekloven
knijpen	kneep (knepen)	h. geknepen
komen	kwam (kwamen)	is gekomen
kopen	kocht (kochten)	h. gekocht
krijgen	kreeg (kregen)	h. gekregen
krijten (schreeuwen)	kreet (kreten)	h. gekreten
„ (met krijt)	krijtte (krijtten)	h. gekrijt
krimpen	kromp (krompen)	vt h., vi is gekrompen
kruipen	kroop (kropen)	h. en is gekropen
kunnen	kon (konden)	h. gekund
kwijten	kweet (kweten)	h. gekweten
lachen	lachte (lachten)	h. gelachen
laden	laadde (laadden)	h. geladen
laten	liet (lieten)	h. gelaten
leggen	legde, lei (legden, leien)	h. gelegd
lezen	las (lazen)	h. gelezen
liegen	loog (logen)	h. gelogen
liggen	lag (lagen)	h. gelegen
lijden	leed (leden)	h. geleden
lijken	leek (leken)	h. geleken
lopen	liep (liepen)	h. en is gelopen
luiken	look (loken)	h. geloken
malen (met molens)	maalde (maalden)	h. gemalen
„ (bezorgd zijn, schilderen)	maalde (maalden)	h. gemaald
melken	molk, melkte (molken, melkten)	h. gemolken
meten	mat (maten)	h. gemeten
mijden	meed (meden)	h. gemeden
moeten	moest (moesten)	h. gemoeten
mogen	mocht (mochten)	h. gemoogd, gemogen, gemocht
nemen	nam (namen)	h. genomen
nijgen	neeg (negen)	h. genegen

[1]) h. = hulpwerkwoord *hebben*; is = hulpwerkwoord *zijn*.

ONBEPAALDE WIJS	VERLEDEN TIJD	VERLEDEN DEELWOORD[1])
nijpen	neep (nepen)	h. genepen
ontginnen	ontgon (ontgonnen)	h. ontgonnen
pijpen	peep (pepen)	h. gepepen
plegen (gewoon zijn)	placht (plachten)	—
„ (begaan)	pleegde (pleegden)	h. gepleegd
pluizen	ploos (plozen)	h. geplozen
prijzen (loven)	prees (prezen)	h. geprezen
„ (een prijs aangeven)	prijsde (prijsden)	h. geprijsd
raden	ried, raadde (rieden, raadden)	h. geraden
rieken	rook (roken)	h. geroken
rijden	reed (reden)	h. en is gereden
rijgen	reeg (regen)	h. geregen
rijten	reet (reten)	vt h., vi is gereten
rijzen	rees (rezen)	is gerezen
roepen	riep (riepen)	h. geroepen
ruiken	rook (roken)	h. geroken
scheiden	scheidde (scheidden)	vt h., vi is gescheiden
schelden	schold (scholden)	h. gescholden
schenden	schond (schonden)	h. geschonden
schenken	schonk (schonken)	h. geschonken
scheppen (creëren)	schiep (schiepen)	h. geschapen
„ (met een schep)	schepte (schepten)	h. geschept
scheren	schoor, scheerde (schoren, scheerden)	h. en is geschoren, gescheerd
schieten	schoot (schoten)	h. en is geschoten
schijnen	scheen (schenen)	h. geschenen
schijten P	scheet (scheten)	h. gescheten
schrijden	schreed (schreden)	h. en is geschreden
schrijven	schreef (schreven)	h. geschreven
schrikken	schrikte, schrok (schrikten, schrokken)	h. en is geschrokken, geschrikt
schuilen	school, schuilde (scholen, schuilden)	h. gescholen, geschuild
schuiven	schoof (schoven)	h. en is geschoven
slaan	sloeg (sloegen)	h. en is geslagen
slapen	sliep (sliepen)	h. geslapen
slijpen	sleep (slepen)	h. geslepen
slijten	sleet (sleten)	vt h., vi is gesleten
slinken	slonk (slonken)	is geslonken
sluiken	slook (sloken)	h. gesloken
sluipen	sloop (slopen)	h. en is geslopen
sluiten	sloot (sloten)	h. gesloten
smelten	smolt (smolten)	vt h., vi is gesmolten
smijten	smeet (smeten)	h. gesmeten
snijden	sneed (sneden)	h. gesneden
snuiten	snoot (snoten)	h. gesnoten
snuiven (krachtig in-, „ uitademen)	snoof (snoven)	h. gesnoven
(van snuif)	snuifde, snoof (snuifden, snoven)	h. gesnuifd
spannen	spande (spanden)	h. gespannen
spijten	(het speet)	h. gespeten
spinnen	spon (sponnen)	h. gesponnen
splijten	spleet (spleten)	vt h., vi is gespleten
spouwen	spouwde (spouwden)	h. gespouwd, gespouwen

[1]) h. = hulpwerkwoord *hebben*; is = hulpwerkwoord *zijn*.

ONBEPAALDE WIJS	VERLEDEN TIJD	VERLEDEN DEELWOORD¹)
spreken	sprak (spraken)	h. gesproken
springen	sprong (sprongen)	h. en is gesprongen
spruiten	sproot (sproten)	is gesproten
spugen	spuugde, spoog (spuugden, spogen)	h. gespuugd, gespogen
spuiten	spoot (spoten)	h. en is gespoten
staan	stond (stonden)	h. gestaan
steken	stak (staken)	h. gestoken
stelen	stal (stalen)	h. gestolen
sterven	stierf (stierven)	is gestorven
stijgen	steeg (stegen)	is gestegen
stijven (met stijfsel)	steef (steven)	h. gesteven
„ (versterken)	stijfde (stijfden)	h. gestijfd
stinken	stonk (stonken)	h. gestonken
stoten	stootte, stiet (stootten, stieten)	h. gestoten
strijden	streed (streden)	h. gestreden
strijken	streek (streken)	h. gestreken
stuiven	stoof (stoven)	h. en is gestoven
tijgen	toog (togen)	is getogen
treden	trad (traden)	h. en is getreden
treffen	trof (troffen)	h. getroffen
trekken	trok (trokken)	h. en is getrokken
uitscheiden (ophouden)	scheidde, scheed uit (scheidden, scheden uit)	is uitgescheiden, uitgescheden
„ (afscheiden)	scheidde uit (scheidden uit)	h. uitgescheiden
vallen	viel (vielen)	is gevallen
vangen	ving (vingen)	h. gevangen
varen	voer (voeren)	h. en is gevaren
vechten	vocht (vochten)	h. gevochten
verderven	verdierf (verdierven)	h. en is verdorven
verdrieten	verdroot (verdroten)	h. verdroten
verdwijnen	verdween (verdwenen)	is verdwenen
vergeten	vergat (vergaten)	h. en is vergeten
verliezen	verloor (verloren)	h. en is verloren
verslinden	verslond (verslonden)	h. verslonden
vinden	vond (vonden)	h. gevonden
vlechten	vlocht (vlochten)	h. gevlochten
vlieden	vlood (vloden)	is gevloden
vlieten	vloot (vloten)	is gevloten
vliegen	vloog (vlogen)	h. en is gevlogen
vouwen	vouwde (vouwden)	h. gevouwen
vragen	vroeg, vraagde (vroegen, vraagden)	h. gevraagd
vreten	vrat (vraten)	h. gevreten
vriezen	vroor (vroren)	h. en is gevroren
vrijen	vrijde, F vree (vrijden, vreeën)	h. gevrijd, F gevreeën
waaien	waaide, woei (waaiden, woeien)	h. en is gewaaid
wassen (groeien)	wies (wiesen)	is gewassen
„ (schoonmaken)	waste, wies (wasten, wiesen)	h. gewassen
„ (met was bewerken)	waste (wasten)	h. gewast

¹) h. = hulpwerkwoord *hebben*; is = hulpwerkwoord *zijn*.

ONBEPAALDE WIJS	VERLEDEN TIJD	VERLEDEN DEELWOORD[1])
wegen	woog (wogen)	h. gewogen
werpen	wierp (wierpen)	h. geworpen
werven	wierf (wierven)	h. geworven
weten	wist (wisten)	h. geweten
weven	weefde (weefden)	h. geweven
wezen	was (waren)	is geweest
wijken	week (weken)	is geweken
wijten	weet (weten)	h. geweten
wijzen	wees (wezen)	h. gewezen
willen	wou, wilde (wouwen, wilden)	h. gewild
winden	wond (wonden)	h. gewonden
winnen	won (wonnen)	h. gewonnen
worden	werd (werden)	is geworden
wreken	wreekte (wreekten)	h. gewroken
wrijven	wreef (wreven)	h. gewreven
wringen	wrong (wrongen)	h. gewrongen
wuiven	wuifde, F woof (wuifden, woven)	h. gewuifd, F gewoven
zeggen	zegde, zei(de) (zegden, zeiden)	h. gezegd
zeiken P	zeikte, zeek (zeikten, zeken)	h. gezeikt, gezeken
zenden	zond (zonden)	h. gezonden
zieden	ziedde (ziedden)	h. gezoden
zien	zag (zagen)	h. gezien
zijgen	zeeg (zegen)	vt h., vi is gezegen
zijn (ik ben, wij zijn)	was (waren)	is geweest
zingen	zong (zongen)	h. gezongen
zinken	zonk (zonken)	is gezonken
zinnen (peinzen)	zon (zonnen)	h. gezonnen
„ (aanstaan)	zinde (zinden)	h. gezind
zitten	zat (zaten)	h. gezeten
zoeken	zocht	h. gezocht
zouten	zoutte (zoutten)	h. gezouten
zuigen	zoog (zogen)	h. gezogen
zuipen F	zoop (zopen)	h. gezopen
zullen (zal)	zou (zouden)	—
zwelgen	zwolg, zwelgde (zwolgen, zwelgden)	h. gezwolgen
zwellen	zwol (zwollen)	is gezwollen
zwemmen	zwom (zwommen)	h. en is gezwommen
zweren (een eed)	zwoer (zwoeren)	h. gezworen
„ (van een wond)	zweerde, zwoor (zweerden, zworen)	h. gezweerd, gezworen
zwerven	zwierf (zwierven)	h. gezworven
zwijgen	zweeg	h. gezwegen

[1]) h. = hulpwerkwoord *hebben*; is = hulpwerkwoord *zijn*.

NOTES/AANTEKENINGEN

NOTES/AANTEKENINGEN

NOTES/AANTEKENINGEN

NOTES/AANTEKENINGEN

NOTES/AANTEKENINGEN

NOTES/AANTEKENINGEN